The New
Royal Horticultural Society

# DICTIONARY OF GARDENING

The New

Royal Horticultural Society

# DICTIONARY OF GARDENING

3

L TO Q


Editor-in-Chief ANTHONY HUXLEY

Editor MARK GRIFFITHS

Managing Editor MARGOT LEVY



M

THE MACMILLAN PRESS LIMITED, LONDON
THE STOCKTON PRESS, NEW YORK



*The New Royal Horticultural Society Dictionary of Gardening*
Editor-in-Chief Anthony Huxley, Editor Mark Griffiths,
Managing Editor Margot Levy
in four volumes, 1992

Published in the United Kingdom by
THE MACMILLAN PRESS LIMITED, 1992
London and Basingstoke
Associated companies in Auckland, Delhi, Dublin, Gaborone,
Hamburg, Harare, Hong Kong, Johannesburg, Kuala Lumpur, Lagos,
Manzini, Melbourne, Mexico City, Nairobi, New York, Singapore,
Tokyo.

Published in the United States of America and Canada by
THE STOCKTON PRESS, 1992
257 Park Avenue South, New York, NY 10010, USA

Library of Congress Cataloging-in-Publication Data
Dictionary of Gardening / editor in chief, Anthony Huxley,
editor, Mark Griffiths, managing editor, Margot Levy,
3353p. 27.2×21.2cm.
At head of title: The new Royal Horticultural Society.
Includes bibliographical references and index.
ISBN 1-56159-001-0 (set); $795.00 (U.S.)
1. Gardening—Dictionaries. 2. Horticulture—Dictionaries.
I. Huxley, Anthony Julian, 1920- .
II. Griffiths, Mark, 1963- . III. Levy, Margot, 1939- .
IV. Royal Horticultural Society (Great Britain)
V. Title: New Royal Horticultural Society dictionary of gardening.
SB450,95,D53 1992 92-3261
635'.03—dc20 CIP

British Library Cataloguing in Publication Data
New Royal Horticultural Society
Dictionary of Gardening
I. Huxley, Anthony Julian, 1920- .
II. Griffiths, Mark, 1963- . III. Levy, Margot, 1939- .
ISBN 0–333–47494–5

Database management and typesetting by
Morton Word Processing Ltd, Scarborough, Yorkshire

Printed and bound in MEXICO

# CONTENTS

# BIOGRAPHIES

Addison, Joseph
Aiton, William
Aiton, William Townsend
Alberti, Leon Battista
Bacon, Francis
Bailey, Liberty Hyde
Balfour, Sir Isaac Bayley
Balls, Edward Kent
Banks, Sir Joseph
Barragán, Luis
Bartram, John
Bartram, William
Bateson, William
Bauer, Franz Andreas
Bauhin, Jean
Bean, William Jackson
Bentham, George
Bobart [Bobert], Jacob
Bonpland, Aimé Jacques Alexandre Goujaud
Bridgeman, Charles
Bridges, Thomas
Brown, Lancelot 'Capability'
Brown, Nicholas Edward
Brown, Robert
Buffon, George-Louis Leclerc
Bull, William
Burbank, Luther
Burle Marx, Roberto
Burton, Decimus
Candolle, Augustin-Pyramus de
Catesby, Mark
Cesalpino, Andrea
Church, Thomas Dolliver
Clusius, Carolus
Collinson, Peter
Commelin, Jan and Caspar
Crowe, Dame Sylvia
Culpeper, Nicholas
Cunningham, Allan
Curtis, William
Darwin, Erasmus
Delavay, Jean Marie
Dillenius, Johann Jacob
Dioscorides
Don, George
Douglas, David
Du Pont, Pierre Samuel
Duchêne, Henri
Eckbo, Garrett
Ehret, Georg Dionysius
Evelyn, John
Everett, Thomas Henry
Fairchild, David
Fairchild, Thomas
Farrand, Beatrix Cadwalader Jones
Farrer, Reginald
Fitch, Walter Hood
Forrest, George
Forster, Johann Reinhold
Forsyth, William
Fortune, Robert
Gerard [Gerarde], John
Goethe, Johann Wolfgang von
Gray, Asa
Hanbury, Daniel
Hartweg, Carl Theodor
Hellyer, Arthur George Lee
Henry, Augustine
Hillier family
Hooker, Sir Joseph Dalton
Hooker, Sir William Jackson
Ingram, Collingwood
Ingwersen, Walter Edward Theodore
Innes, John
Jefferson, Thomas
Jekyll, Gertrude
Jellicoe, Sir Geoffrey Alan
Jensen, Jens
Jones, Inigo
Justice, James
Kaempfer, Engelbert
Kalm, Pehr
Kent, William
Kingdon-Ward, Francis
Lavallée, Pierre Alphonse Martin
Lawrence, Sir Trevor
Lemoine, Pierre Louis Victor
Le Nôtre, André
Linden, Jean Jules
Lindley, John
Linnaeus, Carolus
Lobb, William
Loddiges, Conrad
Loder, Gerald Walter Erskine
London, George
Loudon, Jane Wells
Loudon, John Claudius
Ludlow, Frank
Lutyens, Sir Edwin Landseer
Masson, Francis
Maximowicz, Carl Johann
McMahon, Bernard
Mee, Margaret Ursula
Menzies, Archibald
Meyer, Frank Nicholas
Michaux, André
Miller, Philip
Mollet family
Morin family
Morren, Charles Jacques Edouard
Mueller, Ferdinand von
North, Marianne
Nuttall, Thomas
Olmsted, Frederick Law
Page, Russell
Palladio, Andrea
Parkinson, John
Parkinson, Sydney
Paxton, Sir Joseph
Perry, Frances
Pope, Alexander
Pückler-Muskau, Hermann
Purdom, William
Ray, Rev. John
Redouté, Pierre-Joseph
Regel, Eduard August von
Rehder, Alfred
Reichenbach, Heinrich Gustav
Repton, Humphry
Robin, Jean
Robinson, William
Rochford family
Rock, Josef Franz Karl
Roezl, Benedict
Roper, Lanning
Roscoe, William
Rothschild family
Rousseau, Jean-Jacques
Royle, John Forbes
Sackville-West, Vita
Sander, Henry Frederick Conrad
Sargent, Charles Sprague
Savill, Sir Eric Humphrey
Shaw, Henry
Siebold, Philipp Franz von
Sloane, Sir Hans
Snelling, Lilian
Solander, Daniel Carl
Southcote, Philip
Sowerby, James
Spruce, Richard
Stearn, William Thomas
Steele, Fletcher
Stern, Sir Frederick Claude
Sutton family
Temple, Sir William
Theophrastus
Thomas, Graham Stuart
Thunberg, Carl Peter
Torrey, John
Tradescant, John
Tradescant, John the Younger
Tunnard, Christopher
Turner, Richard
Van Houtte, Louis Benoît
Vanbrugh, John
Veitch family
Vilmorin family
Virgil, Publius Virgilius Maro
Wallace, Alfred Russel
Wallich, Nathaniel
Ward, Nathaniel Bagshaw
Wilson, Ernest Henry

# GENERAL ENTRIES

*All other entries in the Dictionary are plant names*

# L

**LABIATAE** Juss. (*Lamiaceae* Lindl.). MINT FAMILY. Dicot. 221 genera and 5600 species of shrubs (rarely trees, *Hyptis*) or herbs, usually with epidermal glands containing volatile fragrant oils; young stems usually 4-angled. Leaves simple, rarely pinnate, opposite, sometimes whorled or spirally arranged, estipulate. Flowers bisexual, usually bracteolate, on compact axillary cymes (verticillasters) or single in axils; calyx 5-toothed or -lobed or bilabiate, persistent; corolla of 5 fused petals, bilabiate, less often almost regular with 4 lobes as in *Mentha*; stamens typically 4, 2 fertile and 2 staminodes in *Salvia*; style gynobasic, bifid; ovary superior, of 2 united carpels on a nectary disc or sometimes on a gynophore; each carpel divided in 2. Fruit (1-) 4 nutlets, each 1-seeded, rarely a drupe; seed with a straight embryo and little or no oily endosperm. Cosmopolitan, with chief centres in the Mediterranean to Central Asia. Some are pot herbs and others yield essential oils used in perfumery and pharmaceutical preparations. *Acinos, Adenandra, Agastache, Ajuga, Amethysteya, Ballota, Calamintha, Cedronella, Clinopodium, Colebrookea, Collinsonia, Colquhounia, Conradina, Cunila, Dracocephalum, Elsholtzia, Eremostachys, Galeopsis, Glechoma, Horminum, Hyssopus, Lallemantia, Lamium, Lavandula, Leonotis, Leonurus, Lepechinia, Lycopus, Macbridea, Marrubium, Meehania, Melissa, Melittis, Mentha, Micromeria, Moluccella, Monarda, Monardella, Nepeta, Ocimum, Origanum, Perilla, Perovskia, Phlomis, Physostegia, Plectranthus, Prostanthera, Prunella, Pycnanthemum, Pycnostachys, Rosmarinus, Salazaria, Salvia, Satureja, Scutellaria, Sideritis, Solenostemon, Stachys, Tetradenia, Teucrium, Thymbra, Thymus, Tinnea, Trichostema, Westringia.*

**Lablab** Adans. (From a Hindu plant name.) Leguminosae (Papilionoideae). 1 species, a perennial herb, to 6m. Stems usually twining. Leaves alternate, trifoliolate; petiole slender, narrow-ridged above, base pulvinate; stipules lanceolate to triangular; leaflets to 15×15cm, ovate to triangular or rhombic, downy to glabrous, acute or acuminate; petiolules also pulvinate. Inflorescences to 40cm, axillary, erect; flowers in clusters of 5, white or purple; calyx 4-lobed, upper 2 sepals joined; standard to 15mm, reflexed, notched, wings obovate; stamens 10. Fruit to 15×5cm, oblique-oblong, margin warty; seeds 3–6, rounded, slightly flattened. Tropical Africa, widely cultivated in India, SE Asia, Egypt, Sudan. Z9.

CULTIVATION The pods and seeds of *L. purpureus* are a popular vegetable on the Indian subcontinent. This fast-growing, short-lived climber has ornamental values too, chiefly its fragrant, pea-like flowers and maroon pods. In temperate zones it is suitable for the cool glasshouse or conservatory, where it is trained on wires and up pillars; is also grown as an annual outdoors, on trellis, fence or cane supports.

Grow outdoors in well-drained soils in full sun, planting out only when danger of frost is passed. Under glass, use a freely draining soilless mix and maintain a minimum winter temperature of 7–10°C/45–50°F; water plentifully when in growth, but avoid waterlogged and stagnant conditions in the pot. Apply liquid feed weekly when growing strongly.

In warm zones, with a temperature range of 18–30°C/65–85°F and moderate rainfall (up to about 900mm/36in. per annum), *Lablab* is grown for its edible cultivars. Short-day, long-day and daylength-neutral cultivars are available; some are drought-resistant. Well-drained soils with a high organic content and pH 5.5–6.0 are preferred. Sow seed on ridges, 6–8 seeds per station, later thinning to four, or at 30–45cm/12–18in. intervals in rows 75–90cm/30–36in. apart. Vigorously climbing forms, which may reach 6m/20ft, require stakes or other support. Apply fertilizers high in P and K, and top-dress regularly. Young pods are harvested 70–120 days after sowing, and may be stored at a relative humidity of 90% at 1–2°C/34–36°F; they can also be preserved by salting. Yields of 250–450g/$m^2$ (8–14oz/$yd^2$) can be obtained.

In cool temperate zones, use daylength-neutral or long-day cvs. Sow seed in early spring in a soilless propagating mix at 18–22°C/65–72°F, and transfer to growing bags or 25cm/10in. pots when plants are 10–12cm/4–5in. high. Regular watering, and applications of a balanced NPK fertilizer such as that used for tomatoes, will be suitable.

***L. purpureus*** (L.) Sweet. DOLICHOS BEAN; HYACINTH BEAN; BONAVIST; LUBIA BEAN; SEIM BEAN; INDIAN BEAN; EGYPTIAN BEAN. As for the genus. 'Giganteus': fls large, white.

***L. niger*** hort. See *L. purpureus*.
For further synonymy see *Dolichos*.

**+Laburnocytisus** C. Schneid. Leguminosae (Papilionoideae). A graft hybrid between *Laburnum anagyroides* and *Chamaecytisus purpureus*. Tree to 7.5m. As for *L. anagyroides* in overall habit, but young shoots subglabrous; leaflets smaller, to 6.5cm, subglabrous; inflorescence racemes smaller, to 18cm, flowers smaller, yellow tinged purple, appearing fleshy pink or pale bronze. The chimaera frequently breaks down, leading to sporadic 'true' growths and inflorescences of *Laburnum anagyroides* and distinct brooms of *Chamaecytisus purpureus* on the same plant. Spring. Garden origin (France, 1826). Z5.

CULTIVATION +*L. adamii* forms a small tree suitable as a lawn or border specimen. Its ornamental interest lies not in exceptional beauty (although when it remains true to type its flowers are attractive), but in its curious habit of exhibiting the floral and vegetative characteristics of both its parents together with blooms intermediate between the two, so that golden yellow, purple and coppery pink blooms appear on the same plant. Cultivate as for *Laburnum*. Propagate by grafting carefully chosen scions of intermediate form on to *Laburnum anagyroides*.

+***L. adamii*** (Poit.) C. Schneid. As for the genus.

For synonymy see *Cytisus* and *Laburnum*.

**Laburnum** Medik. (Classical Lat. name.) BEAN TREE. Leguminosae (Papilionoideae). 2 species and 1 nothospecies, deciduous shrubs or trees; bark smooth, tinged green, later grey. Leaves alternate, trifoliolate; leaflets subsessile; stipules absent. Inflorescence pendent, simple, axillary or pseudoterminal; calyx campanulate, 5-toothed, slightly bilabiate; petals free, standard rounded to obovate, keel convex, wings obovate; stamens 10, joined. Fruit a flat, linear legume, slightly torulose between seeds; seeds flattened. SC & SE Europe, W Asia.

CULTIVATION *L. anagyroides* is commonly found on limestone, in hedgerows, scrub and woodland, often in association with *Quercus pubescens, Prunus mahaleb* and *Sorbus aria*. In the wild, *L. alpinum* is found in stony hillside habitats, reaching higher altitudes than *L. anagyroides*, and is naturalized in parts of Scotland. *Laburnum* spp. are used as lawn and border specimens, may be fan-trained as screens and living fences, and are perhaps at their most beautiful when grown in the classic manner over arches and pergolas. None is better suited for this purpose than *L.* × *watereri*, whose fragrant racemes of golden yellow flowers may reach a half metre in length on well-grown specimens. *Laburnum* is also amenable to cultivation in large tubs, to be forced into early flower. *L. alpinum* characteristically develops a more shrubby habit, branching from low down on its short and stubby trunk; the smooth green stems are decorative in winter. All are useful in cold and exposed sites, and are tolerant of industrial pollution and a range of soil types.

Plant in any moderately fertile, well-drained soil in sun. *L. alpinum* will achieve greater stature in a deep, fertile, moist loam and shows greater tolerance of shade than other species. *L.* × *watereri* is tolerant of very alkaline soils. They will withstand transplanting, even as quite large specimens. When container-grown, use a well-drained, high-fertility, loam-based mix. Bring indoors for forcing in late winter, growing in full light with a night temperature of 7–10°C/45–50°F. Raise the temperature by about 5°C/9°F as growth commences, and spray frequently with fresh water until the leaf buds are fully open. Give cooler temperatures when the flowers begin to open, moving out of doors into a sheltered sunny spot when danger of frost is passed. Pruning of free-standing specimens is rarely necessary, but may best be done in late summer, to reduce bleeding. To make a laburnum arch, support young plants with wooden stakes which will eventually rot, by which time trunks will be self-supporting. Space at about 2m/6½ft, and train side branches along wires between the pillars and over the top. As branches meet at the top of the structure, they can be grafted together. Spur-prune these branches in early winter to within one or two buds of the old wood.

Propagate species from seed sown ripe under glass or in the frame. Take hardwood cuttings of the past season's growth in late winter; treat with rooting hormone and insert into open ground, with sharp sand around the base. Propagate hybrids by budding onto seedling stock of *L. anagyroides* in summer.

*Pleiochaeta setosa* causes leaf spots; damage is usually cosmetic, but many cause premature leaf fall on young plants. Control with a copper-based fungicide. *Laburnum* is also susceptible to *Armillaria* root rot, and silver leaf, *Chondostereum purpureum*. *Leucoptera laburnella*, a leaf miner, makes spiral mines within the leaves; although rarely fatal, heavy infestations disfigure small plants. Leafcutter bees, *Megachile* spp., remove semi-circular or oblong sections of leaves, causing little lasting damage. In warmer climates, *Laburnum* may be infested by mealybugs.

***L. alpinum*** (Mill.) Bercht. & Presl. SCOTCH LABURNUM; ALPINE GOLDEN CHAIN. Shrub or tree, to 5m+. Twigs glabrous, green. Leaflets to 8cm, elliptic, pale green beneath. Infl. to 35cm+, denser than in *L. anagyroides*; pedicels equalling fls; fls 1.5cm+; cor. bright yellow. Fr. to 5cm, oblong, glabrous, one margin thickened; seeds brown. Early summer. SC Europe. 'Macrostachys': racemes very long. 'Pendulum': slow-growing, crown low-domed, branches weeping. 'Pyramidale': branches erect. Z5.

***L. anagyroides*** Medik. COMMON LABURNUM; GOLDEN CHAIN. Shrub or small tree, to 7m. Twigs grey-green, thinly and weakly pubesc. Leaflets to 8cm, elliptic to elliptic obovate, obtuse, abruptly acute or mucronulate, adpressed short-pubesc. beneath when young. Raceme to 20cm, pubesc.; pedicels shorter than fls; cor. 2cm, lemon to golden yellow. Fr. to 6cm+, subglabrous when mature, one margin thickened; seeds black. Late spring. C & S Europe. 'Pendulum': branches pendent. 'Aureum': lvs pale yellow to lime green. 'Erect': branches stiffly erect. 'Quercifolium': leaflets deeply lobed. Z5.

***L.* × *watereri*** (Kirchn.) Dipp. (*L. alpinum* × *L. anagyroides*.) Typically closer to *L. anagyroides*, but only shoot apices pubesc. Leaflets to 7cm, elliptic, glabrous, veins pubesc. beneath. Racemes to 50cm, fragrant. Fr. rarely produced, narrow-winged. Tyrol, S Switzerland. 'Parkesii': habit as for *L. alpinum*; shoots glabrous; leaflets to 6×3cm, oblong to obovate, dark green, shiny above, paler green, sparsely pubesc. beneath; racemes to 30cm, pubesc.; fl. pedicel glabrous, to 2cm; cal. margin pubesc.; cor. bright yellow, standard ovate, notched, base with brown lines. 'Alford's Weeping': small tree, crown widely spreading, weeping. 'Vossii': exceptionally floriferous with long racemes. Z6.

***L. adamii*** Kirchn. See +*Laburnocytisus adamii*.
***L. alschingeri*** K. Koch. See *L. anagyroides*.
***L. anagyroides*** var. ***pendulum*** (Bosse) Rehd. See *L. anagyroides* 'Pendulum'.
***L. caramanicum*** Benth. & Hook. f. See *Podocytisus caramanicus*.
***L. purpurascens*** hort. ex Vilm. See +*Laburnocytisus adamii*.
***L.* × *vossii*** hort. See *L.* × *watereri* 'Vossii'.
***L. vulgare*** Presl. See *L. anagyroides*.

**Laccopetalum** Ulbr. (From Gk *lakkos*, pond, and *petalon*, leaf.) Ranunculaceae. 1 species, a large perennial herb formerly included in *Ranunculus*. Stems to 0.75m, thick, pachycaul, forming after some years, plants initially stemless, rosette-forming. Leaves in a close spiral, appearing rosulate, to 0.75m, fleshy, dark green, long-petioled, the blade semi-rigid, obovate, coarsely toothed or lobed with a silvered epidermis. Scape to 1.75m; inflorescence loosely paniculate; flowers few, to 10cm diam.; sepals thickly fleshy, petaloid, orbicular, in a rosette, slate grey to yellow-green; staminodes small, petaloid, yellow-orange. Peru. Z8.

CULTIVATION A spectacular native of wet montane grasslands. Cultivate on a gritty, acid substrate in a cool, buoyant, humid position in alpine house or conservatory. In milder areas it may be suited to a well-drained area of the bog garden or a damp corner of the scree (min. temp. −10°C/15−F). Avoid wetting crowns and flowers. Propagate by seed sown by division of established plants.

***L. giganteum*** (Wedd.) Ulbr. GIANT BUTTERCUP. As for the genus.

**Laccospadix** Drude & H.A. Wendl. (From Gk *lakkos*, fovea, and *spadix*, spadix; the flowers are bedded in pits on the inflorescence.) ATHERTON PALM. Palmae. 1 species, an unarmed, pleonanthic, monoecious palm to 6m. Stems erect, solitary or clustered, conspicuously ringed. Crownshaft absent. Crown sparse; leaves pinnate, arching to 2m, marcescent, sheaths sparsely scaly, margins fibrous; petiole to 1m, channelled above, convex beneath, sparsely scaly; pinnae single-fold, acute, acuminate, sparsely scaly, midrib covered with ramenta beneath. Flowers arranged in triads (2 male, 1 female), bedded in pits on simple interfoliar spikes, exceeding 1m, enclosed in 2 thin papery bracts: male flowers yellow, falling before female flowers open, sepals 3, imbricate, petals 3, stamens 6–12, pistillode small; female flowers green, sepals and petals 3, overlapping; pistil 1-celled. Fruit ellipsoid, yellow, red when ripe, smooth with apical stigmatic scar and persistent perianth, to 1.5cm; mesocarp thin, fleshy. NE Queensland. Z10.

CULTIVATION Native to montane rainforest, *Laccospadix* is a slender, elegant feather palm suitable for outdoor cultivation in humid warm temperate and subtropical zones, or for the shaded intermediate glasshouse, in similar conditions to those that suit *Howea*. Propagate by seed; germination may take 12 months or more and growth is slow when young. See also PALMS.

***L. australasica*** H.A. Wendl. & Drude. As for the genus.

**Lachenalia** Jacq. f. ex Murray. (For Werner von Lachenal, late 18th-century Swiss botanist, frequently mentioned in Haller.) Liliaceae (Hyacinthaceae). Some 90 species of bulbous perennial herbs. Bulbs fleshy, usually pearly white; tunics thin, fragile. Leaves synanthous, paired, numerous or solitary, erect to arching or lying flat on soil surface, highly varied in shape: lorate-lanceolate, linear and grass-like, or broadly ovate-acute, glossy glabrous, pubescent or glaucous, sometimes tuberculate, often spotted or banded darker green, red or purple-brown. Inflorescence scapose, erect and terminal, spicate, subspicate or racemose; peduncle stout or slender, usually solid, glaucescent, sometimes spotted, banded or strongly tinted; flowers zygomorphic, tubular or campanulate, pendulous to erect; perianth segments free, 6, in 2 whorls, the outer whorl shorter, forming a fleshy tube or cup, often with a marked apical swelling, the inner whorl protruding, usually broader and more showy, with lips coloured and recurved; stamens 6, arising from base of perianth, usually declinate, exserted or inserted; ovary superior, trilocular; style simple, stigma capitate. Fruit a capsule, dehiscing lengthways; seeds numerous, black, shiny. S Africa (Namaqualand to SE Cape), Namibia; all species described are from the SE Cape Province unless otherwise specified. Z9.

CULTIVATION A large and ornamental genus of frost-tender South African bulbs. Some species bear tubular blooms in many flowered racemes in vibrant yellows, orange or red; these are usually bird-pollinated. Others, with sweetly scented bell-shaped flowers, often in pink or blues, are bee-pollinated. In general terms, species from the Cape flower in winter and very early spring, those from more northerly, summer rainfall areas flower in early summer. *L. aloides* and its variants have long been cultivated, often for early blooming at Christmas or New Year; *Lachenalia* spp. sometimes flower for 6–8 weeks.

In zones where temperatures seldom fall below freezing and bulbs will remain dry when dormant, *Lachenalia* spp. are grown in sunny sheltered positions, with a dry mulch, out of doors but will require some protection from sun at the hottest parts of the day. Otherwise grow in the cool glasshouse or conservatory in a medium fertility loam based mix, in direct sunlight. Plant in late autumn and water sparingly as growth commences and plentifully when in full growth. Dry off as leaves wither and keep almost completely dry when dormant. Propagate by ripe seed when available; seedlings may flower in the season following first dormancy. Offsets and bulbils are also produced.

***L. aloides*** (L.f.) Engl. A highly variable species. Lvs 2, lorate-lanceolate, glabrous, glossy or glaucous, often heavily blotched green or purple above. Infl. seldom exceeding 28cm, racemose, peduncle often mottled and tinted red-brown; fls pendulous, tubular to funnelform, outer seg. half length of inner, fleshy, lemon yellow to apricot or white, sometimes flushed orange, scarlet or blue-green from the base, apical swellings bright green, inner seg. 2–3.5cm, protruding, reflexed, tipped cinnabar red, magenta, scarlet or green or self-coloured; stamens included or inserted to 2mm. Winter-early summer. var. ***aloides.*** Lvs to 18cm, rather glaucous, plain green or mottled red-brown. Flowering stem 15–26cm; outer seg. yellow-orange, apical swelling bright green, inner seg. deep yellow, tips wide, stains red. 'Pearsonii': Lvs to 15cm, glossy green spotted red-brown above. Flowering stem to 18cm, stout, strongly mottled red-brown; outer seg. to 1.5cm, apricot, apical swelling lime green, inner seg. to 3cm, apricot to gold, the tips broad, reflexed, stained red to maroon; stamens inserted. A popular garden plant developed in New Zealand and possibly of hybrid origin. The true *L. pearsonii* is a narrow-lvd plant with small, campanulate white fls tipped brown or opal; it hails from the Great Karasberg and is not cultivated. var. ***aurea*** (Lindl.) Engl. Lvs sometimes blotched or spotted maroon. Flowering stem 6–25cm, dark maroon; fls golden yellow, apical swelling on outer seg. lemon yellow to lime green. var. ***luteola*** (Jacq.). Lvs glaucous, densely marked purple-brown above. Outer perianth seg. pale yellow shading to green with lime green apical swellings, inner perianth seg. yellow-green, uppermost fls often sterile, unopened and tinted vivid red. var. ***quadricolor*** (Jacq.) Engl. Stoloniferous, increasing from bulbils. Lvs glaucous, usually blotched maroon. Flowering stem 9–20cm; outer perianth seg. scarlet or orange-red at base, fading to yellow or apricot with large lime green apical swellings, inner perianth seg. golden or sulphur yellow with broad magenta or crimson tips. var. ***vanzyliae*** W. Barker. Lvs ovate-lanceolate to lorate, usually marked maroon above. Flowering stem 8–26cm; fls subtended by conspicuous pale bracts, outer perianth seg. grey-blue at base fading to white, with grey-green apical swellings, inner perianth seg. olive green, tipped and edged grey-white.

***L. arbuthnotiae*** W. Barker. Lvs 1–2, lanceolate, coriaceous, green or maroon, sometimes densely spotted maroon above. Infl. 18–40cm, dense, spicate, fragrant; fls oblong, bright yellow fading to dull red subtended by narrow white bracts, apical swelling on outer perianth seg. pale green, inner seg. protruding; stamens included or exserted to 2mm. Late winter-spring.

***L. bachmanii*** Bak. Resembles *L. contaminata* but lvs 2, linear, conduplicate, unmarked, infl. 15–30cm, inner perianth seg. only slightly protruding with dark red mark near tip.

***L. bulbifera*** (Cyr.) Engl. Robust, variable. Bulb large, fleshy. Lvs to 30×4cm, 1–2, narrowly to broadly ovate, lanceolate or lorate, often heavily spotted on upper surface, sometimes producing bulbils on basal margins. Infl. 8–30cm, racemose; pedicels 2mm+; fls cylindrical, pendulous, orange to red, apical swelling on outer perianth seg. dark red or brown, inner seg. slightly longer, tips green, flanked by purple shading; stamens included or exserted to 2mm. Winter-spring.

***L. carnosa*** Bak. Robust. Lvs 2, ovate to broadly ovate, lanceolate, with depressed longitudinal veins on upper surface, sometimes green or brown pustules above. Infl. 8–25cm, spicate; fls sessile, urceolate-oblong, white, swelling on outer perianth seg. green or maroon, inner seg. protruding, tips white or magenta; stamens inserted or exserted to 2mm. Spring.

***L. contaminata*** Ait. WILD HYACINTH. Variable. Lvs to 20×0.3cm, numerous, grass-like, linear, channelled above, semi-terete, erect to horizontal; peduncle usually marked maroon. Infl. 6–25cm, dense, subspicate; pedicel to 2mm; fls campanulate, white, apical swelling on outer perianth seg. maroon-brown, inner seg. protruding, striped maroon near tips; stamens sometimes exserted. Spring.

***L. elegans*** W. Barker. var. ***elegans.*** Lvs 1–2, lanceolate, sometimes spotted or with thickened brown margins. Infl. 18–24cm, spicate; fls sessile, oblong-urceolate, outer perianth seg. bright blue at base shading to rose, apical swelling brown, inner seg. protruding, white with pink spot near tips; stamens included or exserted to 2mm. var. ***flava*** W. Barker. Lf usually solitary, lanceolate to ovate-lanceolate, glaucous, blotched dark green above, margins maroon, crispate. Infl. 15–25cm, spicate; fls spreading, urceolate, bright yellow tipped maroon, apical swelling on outer perianth seg. pale green, margin of inner seg. narrow, white, membranous. Winter. var. ***membranacea*** W. Barker. As for var. *flava* but lvs 1–2, infl. 15–20cm, inner perianth seg. protruding, pale green stained brown near tips, margin broad, white, membranous. Early spring. var. ***suaveolens*** W Barker. As for var. *elegans* except infl. 10–27cm, fragrant, fls spreading, outer perianth seg. pale blue or green at base shading to pink to dark maroon, apical swelling dark maroon, upper half of inner perianth seg. dark maroon, margins white, membranous. Early spring.

***L. juncifolia*** Bak. var. ***juncifolia.*** Lvs 2, filiform to linear, sometimes terete, base usually banded or marked maroon. Infl. 7–23cm, racemose; fls oblong-campanulate, outer perianth seg.. usually white tinged pink, apical swelling purple, deep pink or green, inner perianth seg. protruding with pink keels; stamens exserted 2mm+. Late winter-spring. var. ***campanulata*** W. Barker. Infl. 8–30mm; fls white, campanulate, apical swelling on outer perianth seg. deep rose, inner seg. with deep rose keels; stamens less exserted than var. *juncifolia*.

***L. liliiflora*** Jacq. Lvs to 23×1cm, 2, lanceolate, densely tuberculate above. Infl. 10–20cm, subspicate to racemose; pedicels *c*2mm; fls oblong-campanulate, white, apical swelling on outer perianth seg. brown, inner seg. slightly protruding, tips dark magenta; stamens included or exserted to 2mm. Spring.

***L. mathewsii*** W. Barker. Lvs 2, glaucous, narrow-lanceolate, tapering, apex terete. Infl. 10–20cm, subspicate; fls yellow, oblong-campanulate, apical swelling on outer perianth seg. bright green, inner seg. protruding with central green spot near tip; stamens exserted 2mm+. Spring.

***L. mediana*** Jacq. Variable, close to *L. pallida* and *L. orchioides*. var. ***mediana.*** Lvs 2, lanceolate. Infl. 20–40cm, subspicate, pedicels about 2mm; fls oblong or oblong-campanulate, pale, opalescent; outer perianth seg. pale blue at base shading to dull white, swelling green or purple, inner perianth seg. dull white, marked green or purple near tip; stamens included or exserted to 2mm. Spring. var. ***rogersii*** (Bak.) W. Barker. Lf solitary, broader than var. *mediana*, undulate to crispate, base clasping, banded dark maroon or magenta. Fls blue to pink.

***L. mutabilis*** Sweet. Lf to 20×2cm, solitary, sometimes glaucous, occasionally spotted or banded maroon on clasping base, often crispate; peduncle swollen below infl. Infl. 10–45cm, spicate; fls sessile, outer perianth seg. pale blue shading to white, apical swelling dark brown, inner seg. dark yellow with brown markings near tips; apex of rachis bright blue; stamens included or exserted to 2mm. Winter.

***L. namaquensis*** Schltr. ex W. Barker. Stoloniferous, producing bulbils at ground level. Lvs 1–2, linear-lanceolate, plicate. Infl. 8–23cm, spicate, floriferous; fls sessile, urceolate-oblong, outer tepals palest blue at base, shading to magenta, apical swellings green-purple or maroon, the upper pair of inner perianth seg. protruding, white, tipped magenta, the lower pair magenta; stamens included or exserted to 2mm. Winter-spring. Namaqualand.

***L. orchioides*** (L.) Ait. var. ***orchioides.*** Lvs to 28×2cm, 1–2, lanceolate or lorate, coriaceous, sometimes spotted brown above. Infl. 8–40cm, spicate, fragrant; fls sessile, oblong-cylindrical, fading to dull red, outer perianth seg. pale blue at base shading to green-yellow or cream, apical swellings green, inner perianth seg. protruding, tips often recurved; stamens included or exserted to 2mm. Winter-spring. var. ***glaucina*** (Jacq.) W. Barker. As for var. *orchioides* but less strongly scented, outer perianth seg. blue at base, shading to purple, with apical swelling dark purple, sometimes entirely blue with dark blue swelling.

***L. orthopetala*** Jacq. Lvs 10–15×0.6cm, 4–5, linear, grass-like, deeply channelled above, sometimes spotted green or brown above; petiole slender, dark maroon. Infl. 9–27cm, subspicate, dense, pedicels about 2mm; fls oblong-campanulate, upward-facing, white, sometimes with a pale maroon central stripe, outer perianth seg. with dark maroon apical swelling, inner marked dark maroon at tips; stamens included or exserted to 2mm; style projecting. Spring.

***L. pallida*** Ait. Lvs 15–23×2–3cm, 1–2, upper surface sometimes tuberculate. Infl. 12–30cm, subspicate, pedicels about 2mm; fls numerous, oblong-campanulate, cream to yellow, fading to dull red, outer perianth seg. with brown or green apical swelling, inner seg. protruding; stamens included or exserted to 2mm. Late winter–spring.

***L. peersii*** Marloth ex W. Barker. Lvs 1–2, lorate, green to maroon. Infl. 15–30cm, racemose; fls white fading to dull pink, swelling on outer perianth seg. green or green-brown, inner seg. protruding, tips recurved; stamens included or exserted to 2mm. Early summer.

***L. purpureo-caerula*** Jacq. Lvs 15–20×1cm, 2, lanceolate or lorate, densely tuberculate above. Infl. 10–28cm, subspicate; pedicels to 2mm; fls widely campanulate, fragrant, outer perianth seg. blue to white at base shading to magenta or purple, apical swelling green-brown, inner seg. broader, slightly longer, magenta, tips darker; stamens exserted 2mm+. Early summer.

***L. pustulata*** Jacq. Lvs to 28×2.5cm, 1–2, lanceolate or lorate, often tuberculate above. Infl. 15–35cm, racemose; fls oblong-campanulate, usually cream or straw-yellow, apical swelling on outer perianth seg. green, inner seg. with dark pink or pale green central mark at tips; stamens exserted 2mm+. Later winter–early summer.

***L. reflexa*** Thunb. Lvs to 15×3cm, 1–2, bright green, glaucous, lanceolate to lorate, usually reflexed, sometimes heavily spotted above, margins sometimes thickened, usually undulate; peduncle short, clasped by leaf bases. Infl. to 20cm, subspicate, pedicels to 2mm; fls cylindrical, erect, green-yellow fading to dull red, outer perianth seg. with green or yellow-green apical swelling, inner seg. protruding; stamens included or exserted to 2mm. Winter.

***L. rosea*** Andrews. Lf usually solitary, sometimes marked maroon or brown above. Infl. 8–30cm, racemose, pedicels 2mm+; fls oblong-campanulate, outer perianth seg. blue to rose pink, often variegated, apical swelling brown or deep pink, inner seg. rose pink; stamens included or exserted to 2mm. Winter–mid summer.

***L. rubida*** Jacq. Lvs 1–2, lanceolate or lorate, often spotted green or dark purple above. Buds appearing before lvs are fully mature. Infl. 6–25cm, subspicate, pedicels about 2mm; fls pendulous, cylindrical, outer perianth seg. bright pink to ruby red, or pale yellow, heavily spotted ruby-red, apical swelling yellow-green or pink-red, inner perianth seg. exceeding outer, tips purple, marked white; stamens included or exserted to 2mm. Autumn–winter (the earliest flowering species).

***L. salteri*** W. Barker. Lvs 2, lanceolate, coriaceous, upper surface sometimes blotched brown. Infl. 15–35cm, subspicate; fls oblong-campanulate, cream to red-purple, outer perianth seg. often pale blue at base, apical swelling brown-purple, inner perianth seg. protruding, pink; stamens exserted 2mm+. Early summer.

***L. splendida*** Diels. Lvs 2, lanceolate. Infl. 6–25cm, spicate; fls oblong-campanulate, sessile, outer perianth seg. pale blue at base shading to white or pale lilac, apical swelling green-brown, inner perianth seg. protruding, dark lilac with central purple stripe; stamens exserted 2mm+. Winter.

***L. trichophylla*** Bak. Lf solitary, cordate, stellate-hairy. Infl. 8–20cm, spicate; fls oblong-cylindric, pale yellow, outer perianth seg. sometimes flushed pink, apical swellings green, inner seg. protruding; stamens included or exserted to 2mm. Spring.

***L. unicolor*** Jacq. Lvs to 15×1.5cm, 2, lanceolate or lorate, usually densely tuberculate above, dark green to maroon. Infl. 8–30cm, racemose; fls oblong-campanulate, cream with green apical swelling on outer perianth seg. to pink, lilac, magenta, blue or purple with darker swellings; stamens conspicuously exserted. Spring. Closely related to *L. pustulata*.

***L. unifolia*** Jacq. Lf 15–20×0.5–1cm, solitary, linear, widening at base and loosely clasping peduncle, base banded maroon and magenta. Infl. 10–35cm, racemose; pedicels 2mm+; fls oblong-campanulate, outer perianth seg. blue at base, shading to white, pale yellow or pink, apical swellings brown, green-brown or deep pink, inner perianth seg. protruding, white. Winter–early summer.

***L. violacea*** Jacq. Robust, variable. var. ***violacea***. Lvs 1–2, lanceolate, sometimes spotted maroon, undulate to crispate. Infl. 10–35cm, racemose, peduncle often swollen below infl., pedicels 2mm+; fls numerous, campanulate, outer perianth seg. pale blue-green shading to pale magenta or purple, swellings brown, inner seg. purple to violet; stamens purple, exserted 2mm+. Winter–spring. var. ***glauca*** W. Barker. Lf solitary, lanceolate, undulate. Infl. 10–23cm, coconut-scented, as for var. *violacea* but outer perianth seg. grey-blue shading to pale magenta, swelling slightly darker, inner tepals pale magenta.

***L. viridiflora*** W. Barker. Lvs 2, lanceolate, pale green, longitudinally veined above, sometimes spotted dark green, occasionally tuberculate. Infl. 8–20cm, subspicate, pedicels about 2mm; fls cylindrical-ventricose, outer perianth seg. viridian to turquoise with viridian central stripe and apical swelling, inner perianth seg. protruding, tips white, with viridian central stripe; stamens included or exserted to 2mm. Winter.

***L. glaucina*** Jacq. See *L. orchioides* var. *glaucina*.
***L. glaucina*** var. ***pallida*** Lindl. See *L. orchioides* var. *orchioides*.
***L. massonii*** Bak. See *L. trichophylla*.
***L. ovatifolia*** L. Guthrie. See *L. carnosa*.
***L. pearsonii*** hort. non (Glover) W. Barker. See *L. aloides* 'Pearsonii'.
***L. pendula*** Ait. See *L. bulbifera*.
***L. roodeae*** Phillips. See *L. splendida*.
***L. tricolor*** Jacq. f. See *L. aloides*.
***L. tricolor*** var. ***luteola*** Jacq. See *L. aloides* var. *luteola*.
***L. unifolia*** var. ***rogersii*** Bak. See *L. mediana* var. *rogersii*.

**Lachnosiphonium** Hochst.
***L. niloticum*** (Stapf) Dandy. See *Catunaregam nilotica*.
***L. obovatum*** Hochst. See *Catunaregam spinosa*.

**Laciniaria** Hill.
***L. ligustylis*** A. Nels. See *Liatris ligustylis*.
***L. scariosa*** var. ***novae-angliae*** Lunell. See *Liatris novae-angliae*.

**Lactuca** L. (From Lat. *lac*, milk, for the milky sap.) LETTUCE. Compositae. About 100 species of annual to perennial herbs with milky sap. Stem usually solitary, erect, branched. Leaves alternate, sometimes rosulate, entire to pinnatifid, often prickly. Capitula few to many, ligulate; receptacle, naked; involucre cylindrical; phyllaries few, imbricate, in 3–4 series; ligules yellow or blue, rarely almost white. Fruit a flattened, beaked, usually ribbed cypsela; pappus of 2 equal rows of simple, soft, white or straw-coloured hairs. Cosmopolitan, especially N Temperate.

CULTIVATION Found in dry, sandy or rocky habitats, with the possible exception of *L. perennis*, most *Lactuca* spp. are too weedy to be considered ornamental. *L. serriola* is a compass plant: the vertical blades of its upper leaves are aligned north–south. See also LETTUCE.

***L. perennis*** L. BLUE LETTUCE. Perenn. to 80cm, glabrous. Stems branched above. Lvs deeply dissected, grey-green, seg. lanceolate, entire or dentate, lower lvs shortly petiolate, upper sessile or subsessile. Capitula few, 3–4cm diam. in a loose corymbose panicle; peduncles to 8cm; ligules blue to lilac. Fr. 10–14mm, narrowly elliptic, slightly warty, 1-ribbed, black; pappus white, persistent. Spring–summer. C and S Europe. Z6.

***L. sativa*** L. GARDEN LETTUCE; COMMON LETTUCE. Annual or bienn., to 1m, glabrous. Rosulate lvs to 25cm, undivided or runcinate-pinnatifid, shortly petiolate; stem lvs ovate to orbicular, simple, sessile, cordate, clasping. Capitula many, to 1.5cm diam., in a dense, corymbose panicle; involucre erect in fruit; ligules pale yellow, frequently streaked with violet. Fr. 6–8mm, obovate 5–9-ribbed, grey or black. Summer. Probably originated in Near East, Mediterranean or Siberia from *L. serriola*. Z6.

***L. serriola*** L. PRICKLY LETTUCE. Annual or bienn., to 1.8m. Stem glabrous or setose. Lvs stiff, grey-green, dorsal midrib spinulose; basal lvs to 20cm, narrowly obovate-oblong, usually pinnatifid, petiolate, stem lvs less divided, erect. Capitula many, *c*12mm diam., in a much-branched pyramidal or spike-like panicle; ligules pale yellow. Fr. 6–8mm, elliptic, setose at apex, 5–9-ribbed, rough, green-grey. Spring–summer. Eurasia and N Africa. Z7.

***L. tenerrima*** Pourr. Perenn., to 50cm. Stems setose below. Lvs deeply pinnatisect, often glabrous or spinulose, especially on veins, seg. narrow, linear, lower lvs shortly petiolate, middle and upper lvs clasping. Capitula usually solitary; ligules lilac. Fr. 8–12mm, obovate, 1–3-ribbed, dark brown; pappus persistent, straw-yellow. Summer. SW Europe, Morocco. Z8.

***L. virosa*** L. Annual or bienn., to 2m; roots foetid. Stem glabrous or setose below. Lvs obovate-oblong, dentate or shallowly pinnatifid, spinulose on midrib below, stem lvs horizontal. Capitula 1cm diam., many, in a long, pyramidal panicle; ligules pale yellow. Fr. 6–10mm, elliptic, narrowly winged, rugose, 5-ribbed, black. Summer. S, W & C Europe. Z6.

***L. albana*** C.A. Mey. See *Cicerbita racemosa*.
***L. alpina*** (L.) A. Gray. See *Cicerbita alpina*.
***L. macrantha*** C.B. Clarke. See *Cicerbita macrantha*.
***L. macrophylla*** (Willd.) A. Gray. See *Cicerbita macrophylla*.
***L. macrorhiza*** (Royle) Hook. See *Cephalorrhynchus macrorhizus*.
***L. plumieri*** (L.) Gren. & Godron. See *Cicerbita plumieri*.
***L. racemosa*** Willd. See *Cicerbita racemosa*.
***L. scariola*** L. See *L. serriola*.

**Laelia** Lindl. (For Laelia, one of the Vestal Virgins.) Orchidaceae. About 70 species of epiphytic or lithophytic, rarely terrestrial orchids, allied to *Cattleya* and *Encyclia*. Rhizome creeping, short or long; pseudobulbs elliptic, ovoid, conical, subglobose or cylindrical, with papery bracts at base. Leaves 1 to several, borne at apex of pseudobulb, leathery or fleshy, ovate to linear-lanceolate or ligulate, midrib often carinate below. Inflorescence on pseudobulb, emerging from a sheath, subsessile or pedunculate, usually racemose but sometimes paniculate or single-flowered; flowers showy, white, mauve, pink, scarlet, orange or yellow; sepals more or less equal, free, spreading; petals similar to sepals but usually longer or shorter and often wider; lip free or slightly joined to column, trilobed, lateral lobes folded up and enveloping column, usually larger than midlobe, disc smooth or lamellate; column usually long, sometimes winged, usually toothed at apex, anther terminal, operculate, pollinia 8, 4 in each anther cell, waxy, ovoid. C & S America, from W Indies south to Brazil. Z10.

CULTIVATION A spectacular genus of orchids allied to *Cattleya* and involved in many hybrids with that genus. Suitable for the intermediate house, growing cases or sunny humid positions in the home. Very broadly, *Laelia* falls into three groups on the basis of vegetative characters; cultural requirements vary accordingly. In the first group, large and showy species such as *L. crispa*, *L. purpurata* and *L. tenebrosa* should be grown as for the unifoliate *Cattleya* spp. they superficially resemble. *Laelia anceps*, *L. autumnalis* and *L. gouldiana* are somewhat squatter plants with slender racemes of beautiful magenta flowers. Again, pot in a very open medium or mount on rafts, as for *Cattleya*; water, syringe and feed copiously when in growth; impose a dry rest from mid-autumn and cooler, drier atmosphere to encourage the development of flowers in winter. This group will tolerate lower temperatures than most (winter min. 7°C/45°F) and will succeed in most situations provided they have maximum sunlight at all times. In the third group, typified by *L. harpophylla*, habit tends to be rather willowy, with narrow leaves and slender, cane-like pseudobulbs: several of these species produce short racemes of flowers in vivid tones of flame, orange and yellow. They require a somewhat dense potting medium, high humidity and partial shade when in growth, and misting or infrequent watering when at rest to prevent shrivelling.

Semi-dwarf plants with rounded pseudobulbs and broader leaves, for example the orange-flowered *L. milleri* or the exceptionally showy magenta *L. speciosa*, again favour a denser medium, perhaps with additional rockwool or sphagnum and very small pots or baskets. Grow in full sunlight in intermediate conditions; water and feed freely when in growth and impose a cool dry rest otherwise, watering only to prevent shrivelling and root death. *L. pumila*, a dwarf species with disproportionately large and extravagant blooms, is most closely allied to species in Group 1. Because of its size, however, it requires very careful cultivation in pans or half-pots of fern or coconut fibre, charcoal and sphagnum. Water and feed sparingly when in growth, maintaining high temperatures and humidity in a well-ventilated position shaded from full sunlight; at other times, reduce temperatures and atmospheric humidity; admit full sunlight; maintain turgor by misting on warmer days (except when in flower). This species may grow continuously and is an excellent plant for growing cases.

Propagate by divisions of leaders with 2–3 backbulbs when repotting. For pests and diseases see ORCHIDS.

***L. albida*** Lindl. Resembling *L. autumnalis* but with smaller, paler fls. Pseudobulbs *c*5cm, ovoid, oblong or conical, 2-lvd. Lvs *c*15cm, linear to ligulate, leathery, dark green. Scape to 35cm, raceme 3–8-fld; fls scented, *c*5cm diam., white tinged pink, lip lined yellow; sep. 30×8mm, lanceolate, acute; pet. 25×12mm, narrowly elliptic, margins undulate; lip 20×16mm, oblong, lateral lobes obtuse, enclosing column, midlobe broadly ovate, reflexed, edge undulate. Winter. Mexico.

***L. anceps*** Lindl. Pseudobulbs 5–7cm, ovoid, obscurely 4-angled or laterally compressed, 1–2-lvd. Lvs to 15cm, fleshy, lanceolate, glossy green. Raceme erect, 50–70cm, 3–6-fld; fls fragrant, 8–10cm diam., rose-lilac or magenta, lip deep purple tinged with pink and yellow in the throat, something wholly or largely white; sep. 50–60×15mm, lanceolate, acute; pet. 50–60×30mm, elliptic, acute; lip 45–50mm, funnel-shaped toward base, midlobe tongue-like, undulate. Winter. Mexico, Honduras. Many variants of this sp. have been described.

***L. angereri*** Pabst. Lithophytic, to 55cm with short rhiz.; pseudobulbs *c*20cm, cylindrical, somewhat thickened basally, 1-lvd. Lvs about 18×2cm, lanceolate. Peduncle erect, 20–25cm, rachis 10cm; raceme densely about 10-fld; fls brick-red, erect; ovary and pedicel 23mm; dorsal sep. 20×6mm, linear-elliptic, lateral sep. similar but slightly shorter and oblique; pet. 23×5.5mm, linear-elliptic; lip broadly elliptic in outline, lateral lobes semi-elliptic, apex rounded and slightly undulate, midlobe broadly elliptic with a short claw, disc 4-ridged, the 2 inner ridges extending to the centre of the midlobe; column narrowly winged. Brazil.

***L. autumnalis*** Lindl. Pseudobulbs 6–15cm, flask- or pear-shaped, ribbed, 2–3-lvd. Lvs 10–15cm, fleshy, lanceolate, bright green. Raceme to 60cm, laxly 3–6-fld; fls scented, to 10cm diam., tepals rose-purple, lip rose-white with purple apex and yellow in centre; sep. to 50mm, lanceolate, acute; pet. rhomboid-elliptic, all with edges undulate; lip deeply trilobed with 2 crests in centre, lateral lobes ovate, obtuse, enclosing column, midlobe narrowly elliptic, deeply emarginate with an apiculus in the sinus. Autumn. Mexico. The name *L. gouldiana* is usually applied to variants with broader, solid magenta blooms and a stouter habit. It has been suggested that *L. gouldiana* may be a cross between *L. anceps* and *L. autumnalis*.

***L. bahiensis*** Schltr. To 45cm; rhiz. short; pseudobulbs 4–7cm×5–6mm, cylindrical, 1-lvd. Lvs 6–9×1.5–2cm, suberect, narrowly oblong, subacute, slightly fleshy. Raceme slender, erect, laxly 4–8-fld; peduncle to 30cm, rachis about 9cm; fls golden-yellow; pedicel and ovary 17–20mm; sep. 17mm, ligulate-oblong, obtuse, lateral sep. oblique; pet. similar to lateral sep. but slightly narrower; lip 15×10mm, ovate in outline, slightly clawed at base, the edges adnate to column, with 2 parallel ridges, trilobed in apical third, lateral lobes ovate-oblong, obtuse, midlobe obovate, apiculate, the edges slightly undulate; column 8mm, slightly curved. Brazil.

***L. bradei*** Pabst. Small lithophyte; pseudobulbs 4×1cm, cylindrical. Lvs 3×1.5cm, elliptic, fleshy, the margins incurved. Infl. short; scape 5–6cm, raceme laxly few-fld; fls pale yellow; dorsal sep. 16×4mm, oblong, acute, lateral sep. slightly shorter and wider; pet. 16×4mm, falcate, acute; lip 11×9.5mm, lateral lobes 8×4mm, obtuse, midlobe 6–7×5mm, spathulate, with 2 ridges, the margins somewhat crisped; column 5mm. Brazil.

***L. briegeri*** Blum. Lithophytic; pseudobulbs pear-shaped. Racemes much taller than lvs; fls yellow; sep. lanceolate, acute, dorsal sep. 25×9mm, lateral sep. slightly shorter and broader; pet. similar to dorsal sep.; lip 17×16mm with 3–5 keels running from the base, the middle keel reaching the apex, deeply trilobed in apical half, midlobe 16×17mm, almost orbicular, lateral lobes erect. Brazil.

***L. cinnabarina*** Lindl. Lithophytic; pseudobulb 10–20cm, cylindrical, dark green, 1- rarely 2-lvd. Lvs 15–25cm, erect, linear-lanceolate, acute, rigid, fleshy. Raceme 25–50cm, 5–15-fld; fls about 5cm diam., deep orange-red, slender; tepals 22–28×4–5mm, linear, somewhat falcate, spreading; lip about 15mm, recurved, trilobed at about halfway, lateral lobes acute, midlobe very undulate on margin. Spring–early summer. Brazil. Fls easily mistaken for those of *L. harpophylla* or *L. milleri*: the former is a much more reedy plant with narrow lvs and short infl., the latter a squat, diminutive plant with obtuse – not acute – lateral lobes to lip.

***L. crispa*** (Lindl.) Rchb. f. Habit *Cattleya*-like. Pseudobulbs remotely spaced on rhiz., ovate-elliptic, laterally compressed, to 25cm, somewhat stalked at base. Lvs to 30cm, 1–2 per bulb, oblong-ligulate, obtuse, pale green. Raceme 4–7-fld, emerging from a tough sheath; fls very showy, 12cm diam., white, lip usually mainly purple with some yellow marks; sep. 7cm, lanceolate-spathulate; pet. wider, narrowly elliptic, undulate; lip lateral lobes enfolding column, midlobe oblong, acute, edge undulate. Autumn. Brazil.

***L. crispata*** (Thunb.) Garay. Lithophyte; pseudobulbs 4–10cm, oblong-cylindrical, 1-lvd. Lvs to 16×3cm, narrowly oblong, leathery, keeled below. Raceme to 26cm, 2–10-fld; fls to 4.5cm diam., pale pink, lip white in throat, midlobe purple; tepals 20–22×8mm, broadly lanceolate, acute, the edges slightly undulate; lip 16×12mm, clawed at base, trilobed, lateral lobes erect, rounded, undulate, midlobe orbicular or ovate, reflexed, margin crisped. Brazil.

***L. endsfeldzii*** Pabst. Lithophyte; pseudobulbs 12×1.5cm, conical, 1-lvd. Lvs oblong-lanceolate, transversely wrinkled on upper surface, midvein prominent below. Scape 30cm; raceme laxly several-fld; fls pale yellow, opening in succession; dorsal sep. 16×4mm, linear-oblong, obtuse, lateral sep. slightly shorter and wider; pet. 16×5mm, lanceolate, slightly curved; lip elliptic in outline, trilobed in upper third, lateral lobes semi-elliptic, rounded, midlobe orbicular, crisped, with 4 lamellae reaching the apex; column obscurely winged. Brazil.

***L. esalqueana*** Blum. Lithophytic; pseudobulbs pyriform. Infl. barely exceeding lvs; fls yellow to orange; dorsal sep. 11×3.5mm, lateral sep. similar but slightly wider; pet. 12×4mm; lip 8×8mm, deeply trilobed in apical third, lateral lobes erect, midlobe 2.5×2.5mm, almost orbicular, with 3 longitudinal keels. Brazil.

***L. ×esperito-santensis*** Pabst. (*L. pumila* × *L. xanthina*.) Fl. colour showing influence of both parents – golden and mauve; dorsal sep. 40×12mm, oblanceolate, lateral sep. similar but wider; pet. 40×22mm, ovate; lip 40×38mm, obscurely trilobed in apical quarter, all lobes rounded. Brazil.

***L. fidelensis*** Pabst. Epiphyte to 30cm; pseudobulbs about 4×3cm, ovoid, laterally compressed, 1-lvd. Lvs 10–12×3.5–4cm, oblong, obtuse, midvein impressed above and prominent below. Raceme 2-fld; fls rose-pink, disc usually pale yellow or white; sep. 45–55×8.5–12mm, lanceolate, dorsal sep. slightly wider than lateral sep.; pet. 40–55×15–30mm, ovate or oblong, abruptly apiculate; lip 35–45×25–40mm, ovate, trilobed, lateral lobes minute, midlobe with apex rounded, slightly emarginate. Brazil.

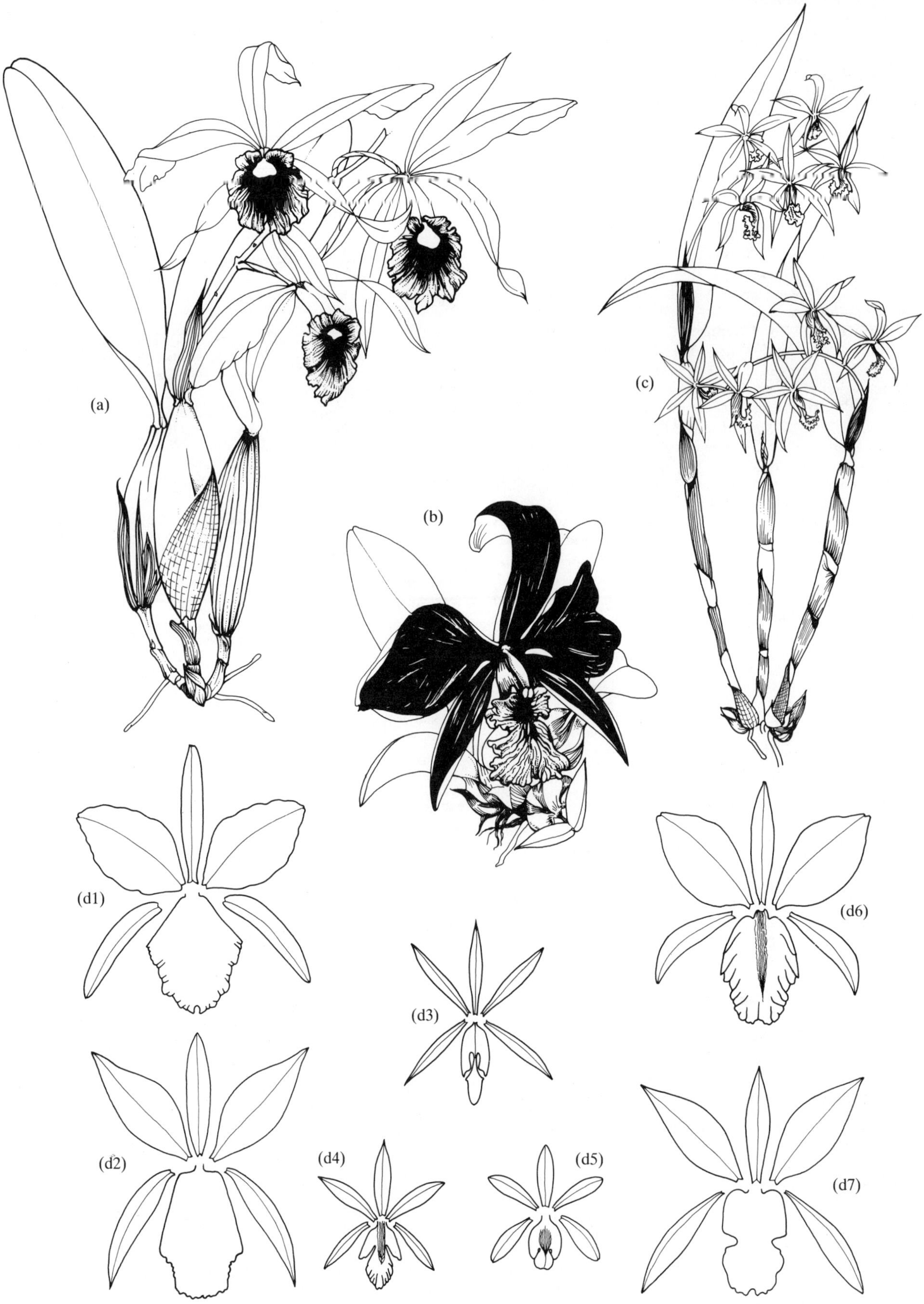


**Laelia** (a) *L. purpurata* (×0.3) (b) *L. speciosa* (×0.5) (c) *L. harpophylla* (×0.3) (d) Exploded flower outlines (×0.3) (i) *L. purpurata* (ii) *L. tenebrosa* (iii) *L. cinnabarina* (iv) *L. milleri* (v) *L. flava* (vi) *L. pumila* (vii) *L. autumnalis*

***L.*×*finckeniana*** O'Brien. (*L. anceps* var. *sanderiana* × *L. albida.*) Believed to be a natural hybrid of the above species and intermediate in character between them. Pseudobulbs ovoid, 1-lvd. Fls white, the lip striped purple towards base, with a purple crescent-shaped mark on the midlobe and 3 yellow ridges at junction of lobes.

***L. flava*** Lindl. Lithophytic; pseudobulbs 3–4cm, narrowly ovoid, 1-lvd. Lvs 7–8cm, elliptic. Racemes 30–50cm, 3–10-fld; fls canary yellow, about 6cm diam.; tepals 20–30mm, lanceolate, falcate; lip narrow, recurved, trilobed, with 4–6 keels, lateral lobes obtuse, midlobe quadrate, edge undulate. Late spring. Brazil.

***L. furfuracea*** Lindl. Closely allied to *L. autumnalis*. Pseudobulbs to 4cm, ovoid, slightly ribbed, 1-lvd. Lvs erect, to 10cm, lanceolate, acute, fleshy. Racemes to 35cm, 1–3-fld, fls to 12cm diam., sep. and pet. light purple, lip deep purple; sep. 50–60mm, lanceolate; pet. similar but wider, undulate; lip deeply trilobed, lateral lobes rounded, midlobe oblong or elliptic; ovary scurfy-glandular. Mexico.

***L. ghillanyi*** Pabst. Dwarf, lithophytic, about 15cm; pseudobulbs about 3×1cm, narrowly ovoid, 1–2-lvd. Lvs 4×2–2.5cm, elliptic, somewhat folded, obtuse, purple-green. Infl. 10cm; scape short, 5–6cm; raceme laxly 3-fld; fls pale to deep rose-violet or violet and white; sep. oblong, obtuse, dorsal sep. 18×7mm, lateral sep. slightly shorter and wider; pet. 18×9mm, elliptic; lip 12×14–15mm, trilobed, lateral lobes 10×6mm, midlobe 5mm wide, more or less orbicular, edge crisped, slightly emarginate, disc verrucose with 2 crests; column winged, 10mm. Brazil.

***L. gloedeniana*** Hoehne. Lithophytic with short, creeping rhiz.; pseudobulbs clustered, 7–10×2–3cm, almost cylindrical but tapered to apex, 1-lvd. Lvs 7–10×2.5–3.5cm, more or less erect, elliptic, fleshy. Infl. 20–40cm; raceme rather laxly about 8-fld; pedicel and ovary 25mm; fls yellow, lip veined red; tepals spreading, sep. oblong-lanceolate, dorsal sep. 24×6mm, obtuse, lateral sep. 22×5mm, slightly falcate, apex acute and reflexed, pet. 22×4mm, narrowly oblong; lip 15–16mm with 3 longitudinal ridges, ovate in outline, base truncate, trilobed at about halfway, lateral lobes acute, erect, midlobe reflexed, obovate, margin crisped; column 7mm. Brazil.

***L. grandis*** Lindl. & Paxt. Pseudobulbs to 30cm, conical, 1–2-lvd. Lvs to 25cm, oblong. Raceme to 18cm, 2–5-fld; fls 10–18cm diam., sep. and pet. yellow-brown, lip white or off-white veined rose-purple; sep. to 8cm, lanceolate, acute; pet. wider and undulate; lip long-tubed, midlobe with serrate, wavy margin. Late spring–summer. Brazil.

***L. harpophylla*** Rchb. f. Epiphytic; pseudobulbs 15–30cm, clustered, slender, semi-terete, 1–2-lvd, dark green flushed maroon. Lvs 15–20×3cm, linear-lanceolate, acute, thick-textured. Raceme shorter than lvs, 3–7-fld; fls 5–8cm diam., vermilion, lip with a paler margin and yellow in centre; tepals spreading, subequal, 40–45mm, narrowly lanceolate, acute; lip deeply trilobed, lateral lobes acute, midlobe linear-lanceolate, acute with 2 ridges in throat, margins crisped. Winter–spring. Brazil. cf. *L. cinnabarina*, *L. milleri*.

***L. itambana*** Pabst. Dwarf lithophyte; pseudobulbs 2.5–3.5cm×6–8mm, narrowly cylindrical. Lvs 4.5×2.5cm, ovate, somewhat folded, fleshy. Raceme slightly exceeding lvs, 2-fld; fls erect, deep yellow; pedicel and ovary 4cm; dorsal sep. 25×10mm, narrowly elliptic, lateral sep. 20×12mm, narrowly ovate, slightly oblique; pet. 23×12mm, narrowly ovate, somewhat falcate, lip 15×15mm, orbicular, lateral lobes semicircular, midlobe round, edge crisped, disc with 2 smooth lamellae. Brazil.

***L. jongheana*** Rchb. f. Pseudobulbs 5cm, oblong, slightly compressed, 1-lvd. Lvs erect, 10–15cm, elliptic, obtuse. Infl. about 10cm, 1–2-fld; fls 12cm diam., rose-purple, sometimes pure white, lip yellow and white in throat; tepals spreading, sep. 50–60×14mm, lanceolate, pet. 60–70×28mm, obovate, very slightly undulate; lip 55×30mm with about 7 ridges in throat, trilobed, lateral lobes triangular, forming a short tube, midlobe rounded, edge crisped; column about 3cm. Spring. Brazil.

***L. liliputana*** Pabst. Dwarf lithophyte to 6cm; pseudobulbs 8–15×8–10mm, tightly clustered, globose or oblong, dark purple. Lvs 10–15×8–12mm, stiff, ovate, fleshy, somewhat folded, purple. Scape 1cm; infl. single-fld, fls rose-pink; ovary rose-violet, 2cm; dorsal sep. 14×4mm, linear-oblong, subacute, lateral sep. 12.5×4mm, narrowly falcate-triangular; pet. 15×3.5mm, falcate-lanceolate; lip almost orbicular, trilobed, lateral lobes oblong, almost equalling midlobe, midlobe 5×3.5mm, oblong, undulate, with 2 lamellae reaching apex, disc yellow with 4 lamellae. Brazil.

***L. lobata*** (Lindl.) Veitch. Pseudobulbs to 20cm, conical or fusiform, 1-lvd. Lvs to 20cm, lanceolate, coriaceous. Raceme to 40cm, 2–5-fld; fls about 13cm diam., rose-purple with darker veins, rarely pure white, lip with carmine-red markings; sep. 70mm, linear-lanceolate, acute, margins reflexed; pet. lanceolate, somewhat twisted and undulate; lip ovate, obscurely trilobed, lateral lobes erect forming a fairly long tube, midlobe with crisped edge and emarginate apex. Spring. Brazil.

***L. longipes*** Rchb. f. Pseudobulbs 6–8×2cm, narrowly oblong or conical, covered with white or pink membranous sheaths, 1-lvd. Lvs 7–15×2–3cm, elliptic-oblong, obtuse, fleshy, keeled below. Raceme far exceeds lvs, usually 2–4-fld but sometimes with more; fls to 5cm diam., sep. and pet. pale mauve-purple, rarely pure white, lip golden yellow or white with yellow throat; sep. 16–20×5mm, linear-oblong, obtuse; pet. similar but very slightly shorter; lip 12×10mm, trilobed, lateral lobes oblong, erect, margins recurved and undulate, midlobe ovate or oblong, obtuse, margin crisped-undulate; column very short. Brazil.

***L. lucasiana*** Rolfe. Lithophyte; pseudobulbs squat, pyriform, 1-lvd. Raceme few-fld, slightly longer than lvs; fls lilac to purple; dorsal sep. 20×7.5mm, oblong, apiculate, lateral sep. slightly wider; pet. 18×7.5mm; lip 15×15mm, deeply trilobed in apical half, lateral lobes erect, acute, midlobe orbicular, undulate. Brazil.

***L. lundii*** Rchb. f. & Warm. Small, epiphytic; pseudobulbs 3–4×1–1.5cm, oblong, slightly compressed. Lvs 8–9×0.5cm, erect or spreading, fleshy, channelled above. Raceme arched, 2-fld, much shorter than lvs; fls white with rose-purple veins on lip; sep. 20–22×4–5mm, ligulate, acute, rather fleshy; pet. similar but slightly narrower; lip 20–23×11–12mm, narrowly elliptic-ovate, fleshy, deeply trilobed, lateral lobes erect, acute, midlobe reflexed, margin crisped and undulate, disc fleshy with 4 ridges; column 7–8mm. Brazil.

***L. milleri*** Bl. Diminutive lithophyte; pseudobulbs to 4cm, squat, flask-shaped, clustered, basally sheathed. Lvs to 6×3cm, rarely 2 per bulb, ovate-oblong, acute, keeled below, rigid, erect, dark green colouring purple in full sunlight. Raceme to 1m, few-fld; fls 6cm diam., orange-red, tinged with yellow in throat; tepals spreading, elliptic, sep. 26–30×10–20mm, lateral sep. narrower than dorsal sep., pet. 30×18mm; lip 24×13mm, trilobed at about halfway, lateral lobes erect so that basal half is tubular, midlobe oblong, margin very undulate. Summer. Brazil. cf. *L. cinnabarina, L. harpophylla.*

***L. perrinii*** Batem. Epiphytic; pseudobulbs 15–25cm, ovoid, laterally compressed, 1-lvd. Lvs 15–25cm, dark green. Raceme 2–6-fld; fls showy, 12–14cm diam., flat, rose-pink or pure white, lip magenta with a yellow blotch in the throat; sep. to 70mm, lanceolate, acute; pet. wider, elliptic, acute; lip shorter than sep., lateral lobes small, midlobe reflexed, acute. Winter. Brazil.

***L. pfisteri*** Pabst & Sengh. Lithophytic; pseudobulbs 5–6cm, pear-shaped, 1-lvd. Lvs about 7×2.5cm, narrowly elliptic, somewhat conduplicate, leathery. Scape with several triangular sheaths; raceme densely 3–5-fld; fls purple, lip white in centre, edged dark purple; ovary 15–20mm; bracts 4–5mm; sep. 15–17×5mm, lanceolate, acute, dorsal sep. exceeds lateral sep.; pet. 17×4.5mm, narrowly lanceolate, slightly curved; lip 14×10–11mm, almost oblong with 4 longitudinal ridges, trilobed in apical third, lateral lobes rounded, midlobe 5.5mm diam., rounded, margin undulate. Brazil.

***L. pumila*** (Hook.) Rchb. f. Diminutive epiphyte; pseudobulbs 3–10cm, 1-lvd, slender, laterally compressed. Lvs to 10cm, oblong, obtuse. Infl. short, 1-fld; fls to 10cm diam., flat, slightly drooping, showy, spreading across lvs and pseudobulbs, rose-purple, rarely white, lip deep purple with yellow throat, sometimes edged and veined amethyst (*L. dayana* Rchb. f.); sep. 40–50×15–18mm, lanceolate, somewhat recurved; pet. similar but ovate, about 25mm wide; lip about 50×25mm, trilobed, lateral lobes erect, midlobe emarginate, margin undulate. Spring or autumn. Brazil.

***L. purpurata*** Lindl. Epiphytic, habit *Cattleya*-like: cf *L. crispa*, *L. tenebrosa*. Pseudobulbs to 50cm, spindle-shaped, somewhat laterally compressed, 1-lvd. Lvs 30–40×4–5cm, narrowly elliptic, leathery. Raceme to 30cm tall, 3–7-fld; fls fleshy, 15–20cm diam., tepals white tinged with pink, sometimes pure white, lip white at apex, purple towards base, yellow with purple veins in throat, rarely deep violet; tepals spreading, undulate with margins strongly revolute, particularly in basal portions, sep. 75–90×15mm, oblong-lanceolate, pet. similar but broader; lip 60–70mm, trilobed at about halfway, lateral lobes enfolding column so that base funnel-shaped, midlobe ovate to orbicular, 40mm diam., margin undulate. Spring–summer. Brazil.

***L. rubescens*** Lindl. Epiphytic; pseudobulbs 3–6.5×2.5–3.5cm, orbicular, ovoid or oblong, compressed, glossy, 1–2-lvd. Lvs 5–20×2–4.5cm, oblong-elliptic, obtuse, rather fleshy. Scape to 75cm; raceme few- to several-fld; fls scented, very pale mauve to rose-purple, rarely white, lip with central purple or carmine blotch; pedicel and ovary 25–35mm; sep. 28–42×6–9mm, linear-lanceolate to oblanceolate, acute or obtuse; pet. 30–45×8–18mm, elliptic, acute, obtuse or apiculate; lip 22–35×20–22mm, trilobed at about halfway, lateral lobes short, midlobe more or less oblong, margins undulate, apex truncate or acute, disc with 2–3 central ridges; column 8–10mm. From Mexico through C America to Panama.

***L. sincorana*** Schltr. Pseudobulbs 2–2.5cm, subglobose, somewhat laterally compressed, 1-lvd. Lvs 3.5–4.5×3–3.5cm, ovate or elliptic, apex rounded or slightly emarginate with a short apiculus, stiff, fleshy. Infl. about 6cm, 1–2-fld; fls showy, purple; sep. 45×15mm, oblong-ligulate, obtuse; pet. 45×30–35mm with 5 parallel ridges running from base to apex, lip trilobed in apical third, lateral lobes oblong, obtuse, midlobe subquadrate, deeply emarginate, margin undulate; column 20mm, apex slightly enlarged. Brazil.

***L. speciosa*** (HBK) Schltr. Diminutive epiphyte; pseudobulbs to 6cm, ovoid-squat-pyriform, 1-lvd. Lvs to 15cm, oblong, subacute. Infl. to 15cm, usually 1-fld, occasionally 2-fld; fls 12–18cm diam., tepals rose-lilac, rarely white, lip white spotted with deep lilac, margin pale lilac; sep. lanceolate, acute; pet. elliptic, undulate; lip lateral lobes small, obtuse, midlobe orbicular with 2 yellow ridges. Mexico.

***L. tenebrosa*** Rolfe. Epiphytic, resembling *L. purpurata* in habit. Pseudobulbs conical to fusiform, to 30cm, 1-lvd. Lvs 20–30×6cm, oblong. Raceme to 30cm, about 4-fld; fls about 16cm diam.; tepals copper-bronze, lip purple, darker in throat; tepals lanceolate, acute, undulate, sep. 75–80×14–16mm, pet. 75×20–25mm; lip 65–70×40–50mm with a short claw, trilobed in apical third, lateral lobes small, rounded, midlobe more or less truncate, edge crisped. Summer. Brazil.

***L. thomsoniana*** (Rchb. f.) L.O. Williams. Pseudobulbs 15–20cm, spindle-shaped, yellow-green. Panicle 1m or more, many-fld, the fls opening over a long period; fls to 7cm diam., creamy-white to yellow, lip dark purple; pet. linear-lanceolate, crisped in apical third; lip with undulate margin. Spring. Cuba, Cayman Is.

***L. xanthina*** Lindl. Pseudobulbs to 25×3cm, club-shaped, slightly ribbed, 1–lvd. Lvs to 30×6cm, ligulate, fleshy, blue-green. Raceme to 25cm, laxly 2–6-fld; fls to 8cm diam., sep. and pet. rich yellow, lip white, yellow in throat, streaked with crimson-purple; sep. 40×10–20mm, oblong, obtuse; pet. similar but slightly wider and more undulate, with margins rolled back; lip 30–35×25–30mm, fan-shaped, obscurely trilobed in basal half and forming a short tube, midlobe short, rounded, margin undulate; column 22mm. Spring–summer. Brazil.

***L.* grexes and cultivars** (see also under × Laeliocattleya, × Brassolaelia, × Brassolaeliocattleya, × Sophrolaeliocattleya and ×*Potinara,* intergeneric hybrids in which *Laelia* has been bred).

*L.* Amoena: compact plants with one leaf per pseudobulb; few purple fls on long infl.

*L.* Brazilian Gold: compact plants with one fleshy leaf per pseudobulb; clusters of golden yellow fls on tall infl.

*L.* Coronet: tall plants with one leaf per pseudobulb; clusters of small, bright orange fls on tall stems.

*L.* Gold Star: compact plants with one leaf per pseudobulb; fls in small clusters, deep gold.

*L.* Seagull: small plants with clusters of bright red fls on long infl.

*L.* Sparkling Ruby: small plants with brilliant red fls.

***L. acuminata*** Lindl. See *L. rubescens*.
***L. autumnalis*** var. ***furfuracea*** (Lindl.) Rolfe. See *L. furfuracea*.
***L. boothiana*** Rchb. f. See *L. lobata*.
***L. discolor*** A. Rich. See *L. albida*.
***L. fulva*** Lindl. See *L. flava*.
***L. gloriosa*** (Rchb. f.) L.O. Williams. See *Schomburgkia gloriosa*.
***L. gouldiana*** Rchb. f. See *L. autumnalis*.
***L. grandiflora*** Lindl. See *L. speciosa*.
***L. humboldtii*** (Rchb. f.) L.O. Williams. See *Schomburgkia humboldtii*.
***L. lyonsii*** (Lindl.) L.O. Williams. See *Schomburgkia lyonsii*.
***L. majalis*** Lindl. See *L. speciosa*.
***L. monophylla*** (Griseb.) Hook. f. See *Neocogniauxia monophylla*.
***L. ostermayeri*** Hoehne. See *L. lucasiana*.
***L. peduncularis*** Lindl. See *L. rubescens*.
***L. reguellii*** Barb. Rodr. See *L. lundii*.
***L. rupestris*** Lindl. See *L. crispata*.
***L. superbiens*** Lindl. See *Schomburgkia superbiens*.
***L. tereticaulis*** Hoehne. See *L. crispata*.
***L. undulata*** (Lindl.) L.O. Williams. See *Schomburgkia undulata*.
***L. virens*** Lindl. See *L. xanthina*.
***L. weberbaueriana*** (Kränzl.) Schweinf. See *Schomburgkia weberbaueriana*.

**×Laeliocattleya**. *(Laelia × Cattleya.)* Orchidaceae. A wide range of colourful hybrids between various members of these two genera and their hybrids. The plants are usually robust, upright, with one or two leaves at the apex of the pseudobulb. The inflorescence is terminal, with few to many flowers of various size. Always brightly coloured and conspicuous. Easily grown in bright light in intermediate conditions. A selection of some of the best grexes and cultivars is given below.

× *L.* Ann Follis 'Lime Drop': small, strong plants; lovely pale green, starry fls, with spade shaped purple lip.

×*L.* Autumn Symphony: strong plants; fls wonderful iridescent hues of red and copper with wine red lip and white column.

×*L.* Belle of Celle: well known hybrid with large, deep purple fls with full burgundy red lip and white column; several awarded clones.

×*L.* Blue Kahili: strong slender plants; fls in upright clusters, clear pale blue-lavender.

×*L.* Bonanza: large, strong plants; fls few but large and of excellent shape, deep lavender, with two golden eyes in the darker lip; many awarded clones.

×*L.* Cecile Simmons: strong plants; fls large, plum red with glistening texture.

×*L.* Chine 'Bouton d'Or': strong erect plants; large clusters of fls which are a vivid buttercup yellow with a broad red band across the apical part of the lip.

×*L.* Chit Chat: primary hybrid of great charm, very floriferous and quickly making large plants; small bright orange fls.

×*L.* Culminant 'La Tuilerie': strong large plants; beautiful pale lavender fls with dark lip; vigorous grower.

×*L.* Dorset Gold 'Orchidhurst': strong plants; fls large, bright golden yellow with dominant crimson lip and contrasting white column; many awards.

×*L.* Drumbeat 'Triumph': strong plants which are very floriferous; splendid deep lavender fls, lip velvety purple with 2 yellow patches near the base.

×*L.* Dusky Maid 'Christina': vigorous plants; fls outstanding, rich deep purple sep. and pet. with crimson velvet lip.

×*L.* Ecstasy: strong plants; fls stunning, pure white sep. and pet. contrast with brilliant purple lip; fragrant.

×*L.* Edgard Van Belle: early hybrid which is still in demand, vigorous plants with large infl; fls rich chinese yellow with brilliant deep red lip.

×*L.* Elegans: a primary hybrid, tall plants of slender habit; fls with creamy white sep. and pet., lip lavender or blue depending on the parental clones used; some clones are a beautiful pale 'blue'.

×*L.* Elizabeth Off 'Sparkling Burgundy': strong plants; fls in large clusters, rich sparkling burgundy.

×*L.* Fire Dance: compact plants; tall infl. bearing clusters of small, bright orange-red fls; several awarded clones.

×*L.* Gila Wilderness: strong growing compact plants; fls basically white but heavily coloured splash pet. types; 'Red Flare' has most purple-red colour on pet. and lip, 'Sunrise' is most peloric and 'Grandeur' is probably the finest.

×*L.* Gold Digger: strong plants of medium size; very floriferous, the fls yellow-orange, shiny, lip bright gold with a deep red flash in the throat.

×*L.* Golden Girl: tall plants with 2 lvs per pseudobulb; medium size, golden yellow fls in large clusters, long-lasting.

×*L.* Janice Matthews 'Ceylon': large plants with upright infl; fls rich chestnut coppery shade of reddish brown, very glossy, with fuchsia coloured lip.

×*L.* Jay Markell: strong plants, one of the finest semi-alba cattleyas; sep. and pet. clear crystal white, lip deep purple with two yellow eyes in the throat; several awarded clones.

×*L.* Lisa Ann: vigorous plants; strong dark reddish bronze fls in clusters, sep. orange, pet. magenta flushed with orange at the tip, lip deep magenta; several awarded clones.

×*L.* Mildred Rives: strong plants; very large fls, white sep. and pet., lip with deep magenta-purple mid lobe margined with a white frill; several awarded clones.

×*L.* Mini-Purple: one of the true mini-catts, a primary hybrid; lovely lavender-purple fls with darker lip.

×*L.* Mollie Tyler: large bifoliate plants with large clustered infl.; fls medium sized, brilliant lavender with dark magenta lip.

×*L.* Nippon: strong plants; large full fls with ruffled pet. and lip, white sep. and pet. faintly flushed pink, bright red purple lip with yellow throat; many awarded clones.

×*L.* Orange Sherbet 'Ripe Orange': tall plants with upright spikes; fls medium sized, frosty orange; other awarded clones.

×*L.* Orglade's Cheer: strong plants; large clusters of dark red shiny fls, beautiful cerise to purple lip.

×*L.* Prism Palette 'Mischief': strong compact plants; fls extraordinary splash pet. types, almost peloric, sep. cream, pet, basically pale pink with pink-purple tips, yellow centrally and a purple stripe on either side of the centre, lip frilly, purple in apical half, yellow at the base.

×*L.* Quadroon: tall plants; excellent flowers of medium lavender, lip brilliant red-purple.

×*L.* Roan Mountain: vigorous plants; fls 4–6 per pseudobulb, medium to large size, rich green sep. and pet., lip blood red with creamy white side lobes.

×*L.* Rojo: primary hybrid forming small upright plants; fls in dense clusters on tall infl., small, bright red, deep pink or scarlet; several awarded clones.

×*L.* Royal Emperor: medium sized plants; fls large, dark orange red with a yellow flash in the throat of the lip; several awarded clones.

×*L.* S.J. Bracey: one of the famous early yellows with red lip.

×*L.* Summerland Girl: tall plants with 2–3 leaves per pseudobulb; fls in large clusters, deep maroon red, very glossy, lip with white side lobes over the column, rich magenta mid lobe; several awarded clones.

×*L.* Teruko: primary hybrid which forms strong plants; fls rose lavender with darker centre on tall infl.

×*L.* Trick or Treat 'Orange Magic': tall plants with many clusters of fls soon making a specimen size; fls bright orange, glossy, with red dots on the narrow lip.

×*L.* Wine Festival: tall plants with 2–3 leaves per pseudobulb; large clusters of small fls, deep maroon red, very shiny, with magenta lip, spectacular; several awarded clones.

**Laeliopsis** Lindl. (From *Laelia* and Gk *opsis*, appearance, owing to its affinity to the genus *Laelia*.) Orchidaceae. 2 species of epiphytic orchids closely allied to *Broughtonia*. Rhizome short, creeping or ascending. Pseudobulbs clustered, ovoid to fusiform, unifoliate to trifoliate. Leaves fleshy, tips erose. Inflorescence terminal, a raceme or a panicle, few- to many-flowered; flowers showy; sepals and petals similar, free, spreading; lip entire or obscurely trilobed, narrowly obovate, tubular, enclosing column; column elongate, clavate, narrowly winged at apex, anther terminal, incumbent, operculate, pollinia 4. W Indies. Z10.

CULTIVATION As for the smaller *Laelia* spp.

***L. domingensis*** (Lindl.) Lindl. Pseudobulbs to 6×5cm, clustered, somewhat laterally compressed, bifoliate or trifoliate. Lvs to 18×3cm, oblong, obtuse. Infl. to 104cm, slender, erect, usually a panicle; fls to 6cm diam., pink to lavender veined purple, short-lived; sep. to 33×6mm, linear-oblong; pet. to 30×12mm, broadly oblanceolate to obovate, acute; lip to 40×25mm, narrowly obovate, obscurely trilobed, lateral lobes forming tube, interior yellow, midlobe fringed, undulate, disc banded purple; column to 1.5cm, pink, slender, anth. pink. Mostly spring–summer. Hispaniola.

For synonymy see *Broughtonia*.

**Lagarosiphon** Harv. (Gk *lagaros*, narrow, and *siphon*, tube, alluding to the female perianth.) CURLY WATER THYME. Hydrocharitaceae. 9 species of dioecious, perennial, aquatic herbs. Stems terete, branded. Leaves alternate, opposite or whorled, usually closely spiralling, sessile, linear-lanceolate, with 2 minute nodal scales, on elongated stems. Male inflorescence axillary, many-flowered; spathe of 2 united bracts, ovate or obovate, denticulate; receptacle bearing numerous flower buds which detach and rise to surface; sepals 3, broader than petals; petals 3; stamens 3; staminodes 2–3, papillose, acting as a sail. Female inflorescence sessile in leaf axil; spathe narrowly ovate to oblong or cylindric, entire or dentate; sepals broader than petals; perianth tube exserted, 6-segmented, lengthening to surface at maturity to accept floating pollen; staminodes 3, minute; ovary unilocular, styles 3, each with 2 papillose stigmas. Fruit a capsule, ovate, pericarp honeycombed, becoming mucilaginous; seed ellipsoid, ribbed or honeycombed, buoyant, later sinking. Africa, introduced to Europe and New Zealand. Z4.

CULTIVATION A good aquarium oxygenator (for which purpose *L. major* is the most commonly available plant in commerce) with the same habits as *Elodea*, although easier to control and remaining attractive throughout the year. Cultivate as for *Egeria*.

***L. major*** (Ridl.) Moss. Stem to 3mm diam. Lvs 6.5–25×2–4.5mm, thick, opaque, usually alternate, spreading or recurved, linear, margins with 2–3 rows of sclerenchyma fibres, denticulate. Male spathe to 5×3mm, subtending to 50 fls; pet. to 1×0.5mm, tinged pink; female fls similar to males, stigmas tinged purple. Capsule to 5×1mm, ovoid. S Africa, introduced to Europe and New Zealand.

***L. muscoides*** Harv. Stems 0.5–1.5 diam. Lvs 5–20×0.5–1.5mm, thin, transparent, linear; apex attenuate to acute, margin with 5–6 rows of sclerenchyma fibres, serrate, teeth long, ascending, sharp. Spathe of male fls to 4×3cm subtending to 40 buds; pet. white to pink, 1×0.5mm. Capsule to 8mm, ovoid. C & S Africa.

***L. dregeana*** Presl. See *L. muscoides*.
***L. muscoides*** var. ***major*** Ridl. See *L. major*.
***L. schweinfurthii*** Caspary. See *L. muscoides*.
For further synonymy see *Hydrilla*.

**Lagarostrobus** Quinn. (From Gk *lagaros*, lax, and *strobilos*, cone, referring to the lax nature of the female cones.) Podocarpaceae. 2 species of dioecious evergreen trees, similar to *Dacrydium* in habit but seed cones lax. Juvenile leaves narrow-linear, subulate, spiral, but twisted to distichous arrangement, decurrent, grading gradually into adult leaves, adult leaves scale-like, adpressed, imbricate. Male cones solitary, terminal, sessile. Seed cones terminal, borne on decurved twigs, lax; scales to 10, distant, spreading, concave; ovules oblique, becoming erect at maturity, ripening in 6–8 months. Receptacle asymetric, slightly swollen, sheathing seed base. New Zealand, Tasmania.

CULTIVATION Both species are hardy in the mild, damp maritime climates in zone 8 and over. *L. franklinii* is the most commonly seen, a highly attractive weeping evergreen to 9m/30ft, but very slow growing. High rainfall and humidity is essential for both species, and warm summers for good growth. Sheltered sites with protection from dry east winds essential; both will tolerate shade, which may be essential for their survival in drier situations.

***L. colensoi*** (Hook.) Quinn. WESTLAND PINE. Resembles *L. franklinii* but mature lvs longer, to 3mm. Tree to 12m, small bush in cult. Crown conic; bark exfoliating in large plates. Juvenile lvs acicular, persistent, to 3cm; adult lvs scale-like, 1.5–2.5mm, obtuse. Seeds in groups to 3, to 3mm, smooth. Receptacle swollen, white. New Zealand. Z8.

***L. franklinii*** (Hook. f.) Quinn. HUON PINE. Tree to 15m, rarely to 30m. Crown conic to spreading; bark smooth, silver-grey to brown; branches arching to pendulous. Lvs spirally arranged, small, scale-shaped, to 1mm, keeled, apex incurved, stomata white on inner face, not easily visible. Seed cone to 15mm. Seeds globose, to 2mm diam., inconspicuous. Male cones 3mm. W Tasmania. 'Pendulum': branches slender, weeping. Z8.

For synonymy see *Dacrydium*.

**Lagenandra** Dalz. (From Gk *lagenos*, flask, and *aner*, man, stamen.) Araceae. 12 species of aquatic evergreen perennials, close to *Cryptocoryne*. Rhizomes creeping or erect, cataphylls present. Leaves to 60cm, with involute vernation, simple, narrow-elliptic to ovate, main veins running to lamina apex; petioles shortly sheathed below, long, to 50cm, much exceeding peduncle. Spathe to 12cm, margins united below, forming floral compartment, limb with opening narrow or broad, often long-caudate-acuminate, smooth to wrinkled or verrucose, purple; spadix shorter than spathe; flowers unisexual, male and female zones separated by slender sterile portion; short appendix present; perianth absent; stamen one, dehiscent through two horns; female flowers in spiral rows, ovules many. Fruit a spherical mass of berries, detached individually; seeds large, longitudinally ridged, inviable if dried. Sri Lanka, India. Z10.

CULTIVATION Tropical marginals and semi-aquatics, all are tolerant of long periods of complete submergence, and are suitable for cultivation in large aquaria or pools in the tropical glasshouse and for pot cultivation, if partially submerged in water. Grow in full light with a minimum depth of 10cm/4in. of soft water, in a fertile and lime-free mix of sharp sand, turfy loam with additional leafmould. Maintain a minimum temperature of 23°C/75°F. Propagate by division of the rhizome and by seed sown fresh and not allowed to dry out.

***L. koenigii*** (Schott) Thwaites. Lvs 30–60×0.8×2cm, narrowly linear-lanceolate, acuminate, subsessile, spotted white beneath; petiole sheathed. Peduncle to 20cm; spathe to 9cm, with limb much longer than tube, smooth within, subulate. Sri Lanka.

***L. lancifolia*** (Schott) Thwaites. Lvs to 10×2cm, elliptic to lanceolate, base rounded or acute, coriaceous, dark green above, spotted white beneath; petiole to 10cm, shortly sheathed. Spathe to 5cm, oblong, acuminate, rugose within, dark purple, spadix appendix short. Sri Lanka.

***L. ovata*** (L.) Thwaites. Lvs 30–45×7.5–10cm, ovate-lanceolate to elliptic, acuminate, coriaceous, dark green above, spotted beneath; petioles to 50cm, subtended by long cataphylls. Spathe to 30cm, limb expanded, to 15cm across, caudate, undulate, verrucose, purple with white veins. Sri Lanka, S. India.

***L. praetermissa*** De Wit. Close to *L. ovata*. Lvs 20–50×4–12cm, narrow-ovate, fleshy, bright glossy green. Spathe to 12cm+, rough, green to brown externally, red within. Sri Lanka.

***L. thwaitesii*** Engl. Lvs to 15–20×3.5–4cm, oblong- to linear-lanceolate, base acute to obtuse, dark green, margin undulate, silver-white; petiole 5–15cm, slender. Peduncle very short, to 2.5cm; spathe to 5cm, slender, convolute, open above, finely wrinkled. Sri Lanka.

***L. insignis*** Trimen. See *L. ovata*.
***L. ovata*** misapplied. See *L. praetermissa*.
For further synonymy see *Cryptocoryne*.

**Lagenaria** Ser. (From Gk *lagenos*, bottle, referring to the shape of the fruit.) WHITE-FLOWERED GOURD; CALABASH GOURD; BOTTLE GOURD. Cucurbitaceae. 6 species of annual or perennial herbs, climbing or scandent, robust, monoecious. Tendrils simple or bifid. Leaves simple, ovate, cordate, 3–5-lobed; petiole bearing pair of glands below lamina. Male flowers solitary or in racemes, large, white; calyx tubular, lobes 5, small, narrow; petals 5, free, obovate, entire; stamens 3; anthers often coherent, thecae triplicate, contorted; female flowers solitary, campanulate, large, white; staminodes 3; ovary pubescent; stigmas 3, bilobed. Fruit to 1m, cylindric, bent, shaped like a club, skittle or a crooknecked flask, indehiscent, epicarp hard, mesocarp fleshy; seeds many, oblong, compressed. Pantropical, widely naturalized. Z10.

CULTIVATION Strong-growing annual climbers grown for their calabash gourds. The fruit of *L. siceraria* is edible when young and its hard epicarp is used to make various receptacles. Cultivate as *Trichosanthes* except that multiple planting and cross-pollination are not required. The large flowers open in the evenings and are attractive, but some find the softly hairy leaves malodorous when bruised. Sometimes troubled by whitefly. See also GOURDS.

***L. siceraria*** (Molina) Standl. To 10m, monoecious, viscid-pubesc. annual. Lvs ovate-cordate, rarely lobed, sinuate-toothed, pubesc., 3–23×4–23cm; petiole 3–13cm. Fls solitary; male peduncle to 12cm, female shorter; pet. obovate, 3–4.5×2–4cm, male larger than female; ovary villous. Fr. smooth, green to green-yellow, pubesc., subglobose to lageniform; seeds white, slightly 2-horned, to 2cm. Pantropical, domesticated separately in the Old and New Worlds. The many cultivated variants of *L. siceraria* are named according to their appearance and the use to which they are put, e.g. sugar trough gourd; Hercules' club; bottle gourd; dipper; knobkerry; trumpet gourd.

***L. leucantha*** Duchesne. See *L. siceraria*.
***L. longissima*** hort. See *L. siceraria*.
***L. vulgaris*** Ser. See *L. siceraria*.
For further synonymy see *Cucurbita*.

For illustration see GOURDS.

**Lagenophora** Cass. (From Gk *lagenos*, bottle, and *phoros*, bearing; involucre is flask-shaped.) Compositae. About 15 species of perennial herbs, to 40cm. Leaves mostly basal, obovate to oblanceolate, dentate or lobed, petiolate, stem leaves few. Capitula radiate, usually solitary; receptacle flat to hemispheric, naked; involucre campanulate to hemispherical; phyllaries in 3–4 series, oblong-lanceolate, acute to obtuse, herbaceous, margins narrow, scarious, subglabrous or hispid beneath, becoming reflexed; ray florets female, white to purple; disc florets male or hermaphrodite. Fruit a compressed cypsela, obovate to oblanceolate, shortly beaked, glandular, straw-coloured to dark brown; pappus absent. Australasia, C & S America.

CULTIVATION Found in diverse habitats from lowland to subalpine, in scrub grassland and at forest margin, *Lagenophora* is suited to cultivation on the rock garden and on open, sunny slopes on freely draining soils where they will spread by means of their slender rhizomes to form low cover with *Bellis*-like flowers. Tolerant of cold to about −10°C/14°F, with good drainage and a position in full sun. Sometimes short lived, they are but are easily propagated by division or from seed sown in spring.

***L. pinnatifida*** Hook. f. Lvs crowded at base, to 6×3cm, obovate-spathulate, obtuse, cuneate, usually deeply crenate to pinnatifid, lobes in 4–6 pairs, apiculate, soft, densely long-hairy, petioles to 2cm. Capitula 10–15mm diam.; phyllaries narrowly oblong to lanceolate, acute, ciliate above, glabrous beneath; ray florets numerous, white to purple. Summer. New Zealand. Z7.

***L. pumila*** (Forst. f.) Cheesem. Lvs rosulate at nodes on rootstocks, to 2cm, suborbicular to ovate-oblong or broadly elliptic, obtuse, cuneate, crenate-dentate to very shallowly lobed or subentire, thinly coriaceous, roughly hairy, with slender petioles, stem lvs to 3cm, occasionally absent. Capitula 10–12mm diam.; about 3×5–6mm; phyllaries linear, acute; ray florets numerous, white to pink. Spring–autumn. New Zealand. Z7.

***L. stipitata*** (Labill.) Druce. Lvs subrosulate, to 5×1.5cm, oblanceolate to elliptic, serrate to crenate or sublobate, densely hairy, petiole short, stem lvs occasionally absent. Capitula 4–10mm diam.; phyllaries lanceolate, acute, hairy beneath; ray florets many, white, pink or tinged blue. Spring–summer. E & S Australia, Tasmania, Papua New Guinea. Z9.

For synonymy see *Lagenifera*.

**Lagerstroemia** L. (For the Swedish merchant, Magnus von Lagerstrom (1691–1759) of Göteborg, friend of Linnaeus.) Lythraceae. 53 species of shrubs or trees to 42m. Leaves often opposite, distichous, obovate to ovate-oblong, elliptic, rounded or oblong-lanceolate, to 19.5×8.5cm, glabrous or veins pubescent, apex acuminate, acute or obtuse, base rounded, margins entire, often undulate, venation reticulate, subsessile or petioles to 9mm. Panicles axillary and terminal, erect or pyramidal to cylindric, to 40×20cm, initially with pale grey, brown or rust-coloured hairs; pedicels to 1.5cm; calyx tube funnel-shaped or campanulate, glabrous or hairy, grooved, angular or awl-shaped, lobes 6 or 7–9, ovate, subacute or valvate; petals 6 or more, clawed, crumpled, rose, purple or white, to 3×2cm, margins undulate, crispate; stamens many, filaments long and slender, exserted; ovary subglobose or ellipsoid, sessile, 3–6-celled; style long, bent; stigmas capitate, ascending, ovules many. Fruit a capsule, adnate to calyx, globose to oblong, to 22×22mm, glabrous, stalk to 12mm, 4–6-valved, seeds 300+, flat-winged. Tropical Asia to Australia.

CULTIVATION Shrubs for warm subtropical climates or continental regions with hot summers, bearing loose panicles of crinkled, clawed flowers in pink, mauve and white. They are frequently used in Mediterranean areas and in southern California and Florida for specimen, hedge, screen and avenue plantings. They have the additional interest of muted autumn colours and a smooth, fluted, and shredding bark. In colder areas (down to winter temperatures of about −12°C/10°F), *L. indica* will succeed given the shelter of a warm south-facing wall. It will tolerate still harsher winters provided hot, humid summers promote rapid growth and flowering from bases stooled by hard frosts. Other spp. are less frequently cultivated and then only locally in the tropics and subtropics. Responding well to pruning, *Lagerstroemia* makes an excellent container shrub, with flowering occurring on the current year's shoots. In the US, hybridization between *L. indica*, *L. fauriei* and *L. subcostata* has produced dwarf (1.2m/4ft) and medium-sized (1.8–3m/6–10ft) forms, as well as cold- and mildew-resistant cvs.

Grow in any well-drained soil in a sheltered, sunny spot; soil low in nutrients will suffice, since given excessive nitrogen, foliage and shoot growth will increase at the expense of flowering. Unless pollarding or coppicing is to be carried out, prune annually in late winter only to remove congested older wood and to open up the plant centre: tip back long shoots as required.

*Lagerstroemia* spp. do not transplant well and must be moved with a large root-ball in late spring. Overwinter container-grown specimens at a minimum temperature of 13°C/55°F and water very sparingly. Cut back to a 7–10cm/2½–4in. basal framework in late winter or early spring and top-dress annually; apply dilute liquid feed fortnightly from spring to autumn. Repot every 3–4 years in a high-fertility loam-based medium. Propagate by semi-ripe cuttings rooted under mist or with bottom heat in summer; alternatively, by hardwood cuttings in winter or from seed sown in spring, although the flower colour of seedlings is often inferior.

***L. indica*** L. CRAPE MYRTLE; CREPE FLOWER. Deciduous small tree or shrub to 6m. Lvs obovate to oblong, to 10×4cm, dark green, glossy, glabrous, veins sometimes pubesc., subsessile; petiole 1mm. Panicle subpyramidal to 20×20cm, briefly pubesc. with angled branchlets; cal. tube rounded in bud, glabrous, to 4×6mm; pet. sub-orbicular, to 11×12mm, pink, purple or white, margins crispate, undulate; stamens 36–42, lobes 4–6, erect, triangular, to 4mm; ovary subglobose, glabrous; style long, slender. Fruiting cal. cup-shaped, capsule to 10×8mm, 4–6-valved. Spring–autumn. China, Indochina, Himalaya, Japan. *Tall growing shrubs or trees*: 'Basham's Party Pink' (to 10.5m, spreading; lvs pale green, yellow to orange-red in autumn; fls lavender in large clusters), 'Country Red' (upright; fls blood red; late-flowering) 'Natchez' (vigorous, fast growth, very tolerant; bark dark brown; fls white), 'Tuskegee' (hardy, broad habit; bark mottled, exfoliating; lvs orange-red in autumn; fls dark pink), 'Wichita' (upright, vase-shaped; bark russet; fls lavender, recurrent), 'Wonderful White' (fls white). *Medium growing shrubs or trees*: 'Catawba' (lvs bright orange-red; fls purple), 'Comanche' (habit upright, spreading; bark pale; lvs orange to purple red in autumn; fls dark pink), 'Near East' (habit semi-weeping; fls pink in large clusters), 'Sioux' (to 2.5m, densely upright; fls very large, pink), 'William Toovey' (to 3.5m, broad, spreading habit; fls pale red). *Small shrubs or trees*: 'Acoma' (habit spreading; lvs red in autumn; fls white, pendulous), 'Hopi' (very tolerant of cold, compact, spreading habit; lvs orange-red in autumn; fls clear pink), 'Okmulgee' (fls dark red), 'Zuni' (habit globose; lvs orange-red in autumn; fls lavender). *Dwarf shrubs*: 'Lavender Dwarf' (low, spreading habit; fls lavender), 'Pink Ruffles' (to 150cm; fls pink), 'Victor' (compact; fls bright red, abundant), 'White Dwarf' (rounded habit; fls white, abundant). Z7.

***L. speciosa*** (L.) Pers. QUEEN'S CRAPE MYRTLE; PRIDE OF INDIA; PYINMA. Tree, to 24m. Lvs oblong or elliptic-oblong, to 19.5×8.5cm, glabrous, leathery, apex acute or obtuse, base rounded, grey-green above, brown below, 10–15-nerved; petiole to 9mm. Panicle erect, to 40cm, deciduously pale grey- or rust-pubesc.; pedicels to 1.5cm; cal. tube campanulate, rounded in bud, lightly 12–14-ribbed, to 12×10mm; pet. 6, suborbicular, to 3×2cm, slender-clawed, purple or white, lobes 6, spreading or reflexed; stamens 130–200, subequal; ovary glabrous or scaly, globose; style filiform. Capsule to 22×22mm, woody, glabrous, globose, apiculate. Spring–autumn. Tropical Asia. var. ***intermedia*** (Koehne). Flower buds to 9×8mm. Z9.

***L. elegans*** Wallich ex Paxt. See *L. indica*.
***L. flos-reginae*** Retz. See *L. speciosa*.

**Lagotis** Gaertn. (Probably from Gk *lagos*, hare, and *ous*, ear.) Scrophulariaceae. 20 species of glabrous perennial herbs. Leaves mostly basal, simple, almost entire, alternate or opposite. Inflorescence a raceme, dense, terminal, spike-like, bracteate; calyx membranous, spathe-like, obscurely dentate, 2-lobed, usually split to base below; flowers zygomorphic; corolla tube cylindrical, sharply curved near middle, limb bilabiate, upper lip erect, entire or bifid, lower lip spreading, 2 or 3-lobed; stamens slightly exserted, anthers unilocular, glabrous, lacking a mucro; stigma capitate. Fruit usually hard, indehiscent; seeds 1 or 2. N & C Asia to Caucasus, Himalaya, W China.

CULTIVATION A creeping perennial, spreading by means of stolons and forming low groundcover covered throughout summer with small spikes of violet flowers. Suitable for the rock garden or sunny banks and wall tops in any moderately fertile, moisture retentive and well-drained loamy soil in sun. Propagate by seed or division.

***L. stolonifera*** (K. Koch) Maxim. Stoloniferous; rootstock 2–14cm diam., with fibrous roots and collar of fibrous petiolar debris. Lvs 1.5–13×5–1.5cm, revolute, narrow, oblong-elliptic, entire or subcrenate, glabrous, sessile or with short, flattened petiole; lvs on stolon small, alternate. Infl. an ovate or oblong spike elongating in fr., fls numerous; bracts 10–14mm, enclosing cal.; pedicels 1–2mm; cal. lobes 3–4×2mm; cor. 8–12mm, blue or purple to mauve-pink, tube 5–7mm, upper lip entire or emarginate, lower lip 2.5–4mm equalling upper lip, 2 lobes oblong, obtuse. Fr. 7.5×6mm, ovate-oblong, obtuse, exocarp almost woody. C Asia (Georgia, Armenia, NW, W Iran, E Turkey). Z6.

***L. armena*** Boiss. See *L. stolonifera*.
For further synonymy see *Gymnandra*.

**Lagunaria** G. Don. (For Andres de Laguna (*d*1560), Spanish botanist.) Malvaceae. 1 species, a columnar-pyramidal evergreen tree to 15m; young growth scurfy. Leaves 5–10cm, alternate, ovate to broadly lanceolate, entire, base cuneate, apex obtuse, white-scurfy beneath, subcoriaceous. Flowers 4–6cm diam., hibiscus-like, solitary in upper leaf axils; epicalyx 3–5-parted, caducous; calyx cup-shaped, shallowly 5-lobed; petals pale pink to magenta; stamens united into a tubular included column; styles with 5 free radiating stigmas. Fruit to 2.5cm, a 5-celled, obovoid-ellipsoid, pubescent capsule; seeds glossy, red, somewhat fleshy. Australasia (Queensland, Norfolk Is., Lord Howe Is.). Z9.

CULTIVATION A handsome evergreen ornamental for garden, park and landscape plantings in essentially frost-free, warm-temperate climates. It is grown for its distinctive form, its attractive leathery foliage, grey-white beneath, and its beautiful magenta blooms, carried in late summer. Also suited to pot cultivation in the cool glasshouse or conservatory. The seed pods contain needle-like spicules that can be extremely irritating to the skin and mucous membranes, causing violent sneezing. In continental climates, *L. patersonii* has been known to tolerate short-lived frosts to about −5°C/23°F, and in regions at the limits of its hardiness may be attempted at the base of a warm sunny wall. In containers, use a porous, loamless potting mix; water plentifully when in growth, keeping just moist in winter. Maintain a well-ventilated and buoyant atmosphere with a minimum temperature of 3–5°C/37–40°F. Prune after flowering to shape or to restrict size.

***L. patersonii*** (Anderss.) G. Don. NORFOLK ISLAND HIBISCUS; QUEENSLAND PYRAMID TREE; COW ITCH TREE. As for the genus.

**Lagurus** L. (From Gk *lagos*, hare, and *oura*, tail, referring to the fluffy panicles.) HARE'S TAIL. Gramineae. 1 species, an annual grass to 60cm. Stems tufted, erect, flexible, branching at base, hairy. Leaf blades arching, flat, linear to narrowly lanceolate, to 20×1cm, downy; sheaths loose, hairy; ligules papery, translucent. Panicle spike-like, ovoid to oblong-cylindric, dense, softly hairy, light green or tinged mauve, to 6×2cm; spikelets densely overlapping, 1-flowered, to 1cm; glumes to 1cm, unequal, 1-ribbed, aristate, hairy; lemma shorter than glumes, bifid at apex, glabrous, awned from dorsal surface; awn exserted, bent, to 2cm; palea with 2 keels extending into short awns. Summer. Mediterranean. Z9.

CULTIVATION Grown for the very soft, hare's-tail flowerheads, used fresh or air dried in floral arrangements. Grow in light, sandy, freely draining soils in sun; cut or pull flowerheads for drying before maturity. Seed may be sown *in situ* in spring, or in pots in autumn and overwintered in well-ventilated frost-free conditions for planting out in spring.

***L. ovatus*** L. As for the genus. 'Nanus': very dwarf, to 15cm.
For illustration see ORNAMENTAL GRASSES.

**Lallemantia** Fisch. & Mey. (For J.L. Avé-Lallemant (1803–1867), German botanist.) Labiatae. 5 small annual or biennial, grey-pubescent herbs to 50cm. Stems tetragonal, simple or branching. Leaves opposite, toothed, petiolate, sessile toward apex. Inflorescence a spike of axillary whorls, 6 flowers per whorl on short erect pedicels; bracteoles large, dentate and ciliate; calyx tubular, 15-veined, teeth 5, the uppermost broadest; corolla tube slender broadening at throat, bilabiate, upper lip erect, 2-lobed with 2 longitudinal folds within, lower lip 3-lobed, the middle broadest; petals blue or violet, rarely yellow or white. Nuts ovoid and smooth. SW Asia, C Asia, Himalaya. Very close to *Dracocephalum* and *Nepeta*: distinguished by minor characteristics such as the broad uppermost calyx tooth, and the longitudinal folds inside the upper corolla lip. Z7.

CULTIVATION Attractive narrow-leaved plants for flower beds and borders and rock gardens, bearing spikes of (usually) bright blue flowers in summer, *Lallemantia* spp. need light, well-drained soil and a sunny location. Propagate by root division or softwood cuttings in spring, or alternatively by seed sown *in situ* in spring and thinned to 15cm/6in. Otherwise, cultivation as for *Dracocephalum*.

***L. canescens*** (L.) Fisch. & Mey. Bienn. or short-lived perenn., pubesc., to 50cm. Lower lvs to 1.5cm, obovate to lanceolate, petiolate, to 1.5cm, upper lvs smaller and narrower, subsessile. Infl. racemose to 25cm, whorls to 5-fld; floral lvs 3×4cm, sessile, equal to cor.; bracteoles 9×2.5mm; cal. to 20mm with upper tooth to 5mm, all teeth mucronate; cor. to 30mm, upper lip with rounded lobes, lower lip with wide middle lobe, blue or lavender, rarely white. Late summer. Iran, Anatolia, Transcaucasia.

***L. iberica*** (Bieb.) Fisch. & Mey. Annual to 40cm, slightly pubesc. to near glabrous. Stems erect and simple or with few branches. Lower lvs petiolate, generally ovate, crenate. Infl. a spike, floral lvs linear-lanceolate nearly entire with awned teeth; cal. 15mm; cor. blue. Late spring. Caucasia, naturalized elsewhere.

***L. peltata*** (L.) Fisch. & Mey. Annual, glabrous or puberulent, to 50cm. Lower lvs to 4.5×2cm, with petioles twice as long. Infl. lax; whorls to 10-fld; floral lvs lanceolate to linear, subsessile; bracteoles 10×9mm, ovate to round, denticulate, pale green; cal. to 13mm, teeth lanceolate-ovate; cor. to 18mm, upper lip 3mm wide, lower lip, violet rarely white. Anatolia, Iraq, Iran, C Asia.

***L. royleana*** (Benth. in Wallich) Benth. Stems to 20cm, simple or branched, pubesc. Lower lvs 3×2cm, crenate, base truncate, petioles to 2cm, upper lvs obovate, subsessile. Infl. dense axillary whorls; bracteoles 14×45mm, cuneate; cal. tubular, veins prominent, teeth short; cor. to 8.5mm, easily exceeding cal.; exterior of whole fl. glandular-pubesc., blue. Nutlets triquetrous, brown or black. Iran, Afghanistan, S Russian, S China.

For synonymy see *Dracocephalum* and *Nepeta*.

**Lamarckia** Moench. (For the French naturalist J.B.A.P. Monet de Lamarck (1744–1829).) GOLDEN TOP. Gramineae. 1 species, an annual grass to 30cm. Stems tufted, smooth. Leaf blades flat, linear, acute, twisted, to 12.5×1cm; sheaths inflated; ligules papery, translucent. Panicle oblong, branched, secund, dense, golden-yellow, often tinged purple, to 7.5×2.5cm; branches short, erect; spikelets dimorphic, in groups of 5, laterally compressed, one of group fertile, 2–13-flowered, to 5mm; upper floret asexual, vestigial; glumes equal, acute; lemmas obtuse, 5-ribbed, membranous, aristate; other spikelets sterile, many-flowered, enclosing fertile spikelets, to 8mm; lemmas obtuse, papery, without awns; palea 2-keeled. Summer. Mediterranean. Z7.

CULTIVATION A beautiful grass with downswept silky plumose inflorescences in shining golden yellow, sometimes flushed purple when mature; these are excellent for drying. Sow seed *in situ* in spring in a light sandy, well-drained soil in full sun. For earlier flowers, sow in autumn and overwinter in frost-free conditions under glass.

***L. aurea*** (L.) Moench. As for the genus.

**Lambertia** Sm. (For Aylmer Bourke Lambert (1761–1842), author the *The Genus Pinus*, 1803–14.) Proteaceae. Some 10 species of shrubs. Leaves often in whorls of 3, sometimes opposite. Flowers solitary or in terminal clusters of 2–7, subtended by an involucre of sessile, coloured bracts; perianth usually red or yellow, tube elongate, slightly incurved, lobes 4, spirally revolute; anthers borne on perianth lobes; nectary scales 4, sometimes absent; ovary pubescent, with 2 pendent ovules, style filiform, stigma small. Fruit a hard follicle, truncate, sessile, abaxial margin corniculate; seeds 2, compressed, narrowly alate. Australia. Z9.

CULTIVATION As for *Banksia*.

***L. ericifolia*** R. Br. Shrub, 2–3m. Lvs 1–1.5cm, linear to lanceolate, margins revolute. Fls cream, orange or pink in clusters of to 7; floral bracts deciduous, 12mm. Throughout the year. W Australia.

***L. formosa*** Sm. MOUNTAIN DEVIL. Erect, bushy shrub, 2m high, 1.5m wide. Lvs 5cm, linear, with a pungent point. Fls red in terminal clusters of 7; perianth 5cm, densely hairy within. Throughout the year. E Australia.

***L. multiflora*** Lindl. MANY-FLOWERED HONEYSUCKLE. Glabrous shrub to 1.5m. Lvs to 5cm in whorls of 3, broad-linear, with a network of veins. Fls yellow in terminal clusters of 7; perianth 4cm. Late winter–early summer. W Australia.

**Lamiastrum** Heist. ex Fabr.
***L. galeobdolon*** (L.) Ehrend. & Polats. See *Lamium galeobdolon*.

**Lamium** L. (Lat. name used by Pliny.) DEAD NETTLE. Labiatae. Some 50 species of perennial or annual herbs. Stems often stoloniferous and creeping at base, glabrous to pubescent. Leaves petiolate, opposite, ovate to kidney-shaped, base usually cordate, rugose. Flowers in to 12-flowered verticillasters; calyx tubular or turbinate to bell-shaped, 5–10-veined, teeth 5, usually equal; corolla 2-lipped, upper lip hooded, arched, ovate to oblong, lower lip spreading, 3-lobed, cordate to obovate, lateral lobes reduced, occasionally appendaged, middle lobe short-petiolate, obovate; stamens 4, upper pair reduced, style bifid. Fruit of 4 nutlets. Mediterranean.

CULTIVATION Useful groundcovering plants, particularly the silver-leaved forms of *L. maculatum* (the silver coloration is due to air-filled blisters below the leaf surface) and *L. garganicum*, useful for fairly dry shaded areas. *L. galeobdolon* is one of the most commonly encountered groundcover plants in cool temperate gardens. The cv. Florentinum, with leaves zoned in silver and tinted purple, provides colour throughout the year. Like other members of this genus it is invasive, and should be used with care. *L. orvala* is a herbaceous perennial which forms clumps of handsome leaves and attractive flowers in late spring. These plants are tolerant of a wide range of soil types, climates and light conditions. Propagate by removal of rooted running stems of most species, division of herbaceous clumps (*L. orvala*) or seed of non-variegated plants.

***L. album*** L. WHITE DEAD NETTLE. Perenn. to 1m. Stems erect to ascending, stoloniferous, 4-angled, pubesc. Lvs to 6×5cm, ovate to oblong, apex acute or obtuse, base truncate or cordate, margin toothed to notched, glandular, glabrous to pubesc.; petioles to 45mm. Verticillasters 2–8, 8–10-fld, distant; bracts to 7mm, ovate or lanceolate to linear; cal. to 15mm, bell-shaped, teeth to 8mm, lanceolate apex subulate, ciliate to bristly; cor. white, tube to 16mm, plane, interior annular-pubesc., upper lip to 18mm, lower lip to 1cm, obcordate, lateral lobes minutely toothed. Fr. to 3×2mm, ovoid, grey to brown. Europe to W Asia. 'Friday': lvs two shades of green, with central area gold. 'Goldflake': lvs striped gold. 'Pale Peril': shoots tinted gold when young. Z4.

***L. galeobdolon*** (L.) L. YELLOW ARCHANGEL. Perenn. to 60cm. Stems erect, occasionally stoloniferous, 4-angled, white-pubesc. on angles. Lvs to 5.5×5cm, ovate or rhomboid to orbicular, apex acute, base cordate or truncate, margin toothed to notched. Verticillasters 6, 2–10-fld, approximate; bracts foliaceous, to 5×2cm; cal. to 12mm; cor. to 2cm, yellow, flecked brown, tube plane, interior annular-pubesc. Fr. to 3×2mm, obovoid, apex truncate. Summer. Europe to W Asia. 'Florentinum': tall; lvs large, splashed silver, and, in winter, purple; stems upright. 'Hermann's Pride': mat-forming; lvs narrow, toothed, streaked and spotted silver. 'Silberteppich' ('Silver Carpet'): slow growing, clump-forming; lvs silver. 'Silver Angel': prostrate, fast-growing; lvs marked silver; stems upright. 'Silver Spangled': spreading; lvs jagged-edged, hairy, heavily spotted silver. 'Variegatum': lvs smaller, rounded, mottled, a less vigorous selection. 'Type Ronsdorf': similar to 'Variegatum'. Z6.

***L. garganicum*** L. Perenn., to 45cm. Stems ascending, occasionally mat-forming, simple or sparsely branched. Lvs to 7×5cm, ovate or deltoid to reniform, base cordate, margin notched. Verticillasters to 5, 2–12-fld, approximate or distant; bracts to 1cm, apex subulate; cal. to 2cm, glabrous to pubesc., teeth to 1cm, lanceolate; cor. pink or red to purple or, rarely, white, tube to 3cm, usually plane, distended above, interior glabrous, upper lip to 16mm, entire to bifid, lower lip to 2cm, obcordate, lateral lobes occasionally appendaged, deltoid, minutely toothed. Fr. to 4×2mm, mottled to verrucose, green to brown or black. Europe and N Africa to W Asia. 'Golden Carpet': to 45cm high; lvs variegated gold; fls pink and white striped.

***L. maculatum*** L. Perenn. to 80cm. Stems ascending to trailing, stoloniferous, pubesc. Lvs to 9×7cm, ovate or deltoid to suborbicular, base cordate or truncate, margin notched, pubesc., white-striped; petioles to 5.5cm. Verticillasters 4–5, 4–8-fld, distant; bracts to 3×3mm, orbicular to ovate; cal. to 16mm, pubesc., teeth to 1cm; cor. red to purple, rarely white, tube to 2cm, curved, interior annular-pubesc., upper lip to 13mm, lower lip to 6mm, obcordate, lateral lobes to 2mm, apex subulate. Summer. Europe and N Africa to W Asia. Over 20 cvs: height from 20–45cm; lvs with range of variegation in silver or gold; fls white to pink or purple. Notable cvs include 'Aureum' (lvs gold with white centre; fls pink), 'Beacon's Silver' (habit low; lvs silver, thin green edge; fls pink), 'Cannon's Gold' (lvs gold; fls purple), 'Chequers' (lvs broad, thin silver stripe), 'Immaculate' (lvs green; fls purple), 'Pink Pewter' (lvs tinted silver; fls rich pink), 'Red Nancy' (lvs silver, thin green edge; fls red), 'Shell Pink' (lvs blotched white; fls large, pink, abundant), 'Sterling Silver' (lvs pure silver; fls purple), 'White Nancy' (lvs silver, thin green edge; fls white). Z4.

***L. orvala*** L. Perenn. to 1m. Lvs to 15×10cm, ovate to deltoid, margin toothed. Cal. to 2cm; cor. red to purple, occasionally white, tube to 2cm, plane, exterior pubesc., lips to 2cm, toothed, lateral lobes of lower lip deltoid. Summer. SC Europe (Austria to Yugoslavia). 'Album': lvs large, hair-less; fls large, off-white, abundant. Z6.

***L. brachyodon*** (Bordz.) Kuprian. See *L. album*.
***L. luteum*** (Huds.) Krocker. See *L. galeobdolon*.
***L. vulgatum*** var. ***album*** (L.) Benth. See *L. album*.
For further synonymy see *Galeobdolon, Galeopsis, Lamiastrum* and *Leonurus*.

**Lampranthus** N.E. Br. (From Gk *lampros*, bright, brilliant, and *anthos*, flower, referring to the brilliant flowers.) Aizoaceae. 200 species of branched subshrubs to 60cm; stems erect, spreading or prostrate, compressed, glabrous. Leaves shortly connate at base, numerous, terete or 3-angled, blunt or tapering, more or less curved. Flowers solitary or several together, terminal or axillary, medium or large, white, pink, red, purple-rose, orange or yellow. Summer. S Africa (Cape Province). Z9.

CULTIVATION Shrubby succulent plants with large, brightly coloured flowers produced over long periods during the summer. Most make excellent summer bedding or container plants in temperate regions and a few are frost hardy to −1°C/30°F or −2°C/28°F and thus can be grown outside the year round in sheltered favourable sites in temperate regions. They require a position in full sun and a low-fertility, well-drained soil. Plant as soon as frosts are over and leave outside until the first frosts of autumn; the plants should then be dug up and potted or cuttings taken and kept frost-free for the winter.

Cuttings can be taken and rooted at any time of the year but normally either in late summer or early autumn from plants growing outside or in early spring from plants overwintered in the greenhouse. Remove young growths 5–10cm/2–4in. long with 3–4 pairs of leaves from just below a node. Leave to dry for 1–2 days and insert into a sandy/gritty rooting mix. Place in a warm position in the greenhouse or in an open propagating frame with bottom heat (around 15–20°C)/60–68°F and keep just moist. Rooting normally takes place within 2–3 weeks. Once rooted, the cuttings can be potted into any well-drained, low-fertility potting mix and grown on until planted outside in late spring/early summer. Keep in a sunny position and only water when dry. Pests and diseases as for *Conophytum*.

***L. aurantiacus*** (DC.) Schwantes. Erect shrub to 30–45cm, becoming prostrate, sparsely branched. Lvs 20–30×4mm, more or less tapered, apiculate, green, grey-pruinose, minutely rough, spotted. Fls 4–5cm diam., orange. Cape: Cape District.

***L. aureus*** (L.) N.E. Br. To 30–40cm; stems erect. Lvs 5cm+, mucronate, fresh green, slightly grey-pruinose, minutely spotted. Fls 6cm diam., glossy, deep orange. Cape: Cape Town District.

***L. bicolor*** (L.) N.E. Br. To 30cm, stiff-stemmed. Lvs semicylindric, 12–25×2mm, tapered, triquetrous above, green with translucent spots. Fls 3.5cm diam., inside yellow, deep red below. Cape: Cape Town District.

***L. blandus*** (Haw.) Schwantes. Stems erect, 30–50cm; bark deep red. Lvs 3–4cm, triquetrous, short-tapered, light grey-green with minute translucent spots. Fls 6cm diam., pale pink-red. Cape: Bathurst District.

***L. comptonii*** (L. Bol.) N.E. Br. Loosely branched subshrub; stems 25–35cm. Lvs 40×6×1mm, falcate, swollen, triquetrous, apically truncate, red-apiculate. Fls 2.7cm diam., inside white, outside tinged pink. Cape: Van Rhynsdorp District.

***L. conspicuus*** (Haw.) N.E. Br. Stems to 45cm, 2cm thick, branches curved. Lvs 60–70×4–5mm, inward-curving, tapered, semicylindric, green edged red, often spotted. Fls 5cm diam., purple-red. Cape: Albany District.

***L. copiosus*** (L. Bol.) L. Bol. Spreading subshrub with prostrate stems. Lvs 15–20×3×6mm, laterally compressed, more or less falcate. Fls 2.6cm diam., pink, opening day and night. Cape Province: Albany District.

***L. deltoides*** (L.) Glen. Small subshrub; stems erect or spreading. Lvs 10–20×8–11mm, more or less united at base, triquetrous, short, expanded toward apex with a short point, entire or with margins and keel denticulate, grey-green. Fls 3 together, short-pedicellate, 12–18mm diam., pink to red, sometimes fragrant. W Cape.

***L. emarginatus*** (L.) N.E. Br. Stems erect, 30–40cm, compressed, brown. Lvs semicylindric, 12–16mm, 1–2mm thick, mucronate, curved, grey-green, rough with raised dots. Fls numerous, 3cm diam., violet to pink. W Cape.

***L. falcatus*** (L.) N.E. Br. Mat-forming with many tangled filiform stems. Lvs 4–6mm, triquetrous, compressed, falcate, grey-green, spotted. Fls 12–16mm diam., pink, fragrant. Cape. var. ***galpinii*** (L. Bol.) L. Bol. More erect, to 25cm, rarely mat-forming. Lvs 5–7×1.5×2mm. Fls 17mm diam., pink. Cape: Bredasdorp District.

***L. haworthii*** (Donn) N.E. Br. To 60cm, freely branched. Lvs 24–40×4–6mm, semicylindric, tapered, light green, densely light grey-pruinose. Fls to 7cm diam., light purple. Cape.

***L. primavernus*** (L. Bol.) L. Bol. Erect shrub with stiff stems to 30cm. Lvs 24×2×3mm, falcate, laterally compressed, tip short-tapered. Fls many together on an infl. 18mm diam., pink to salmon pink. Cape Province: Piquetberg District.

***L. promontorii*** (L. Bol.) N.E. Br. Erect shrub with spreading slender branches, 15–20cm. Lvs 10–33×3×3mm, compressed triquetrous, apiculate, falcate. Fls 14–23mm diam., yellow. SW Cape.

***L. roseus*** (Willd.) Schwantes. Erect to spreading shrub to 60cm. Lvs 25–30×4×4mm, compressed triquetrous, apiculate, decussate, with more or less prominent translucent dots, green to grey-green. Fls 4cm diam., pale pink. Cape Province: Cape District.

***L. spectabilis*** (Haw.) N.E. Br. Stems prostrate. Lvs clustered, 50–80×6mm, upcurved, triquetrous, carinate, with an apiculus and reddened awn. Fls 5–7cm, diam., purple-red. Cape. 'Tresco Apricot': fls apricot. 'Tresco Brilliant': fls magenta. 'Tresco Red': fls fiery red.

***L. bicolorus*** (L.) Jacobsen. See *L. bicolor*.
***L. glaucoides*** (Haw.) N.E. Br. See *L. aurantiacus*.
***L. vereculatus*** (L.) L. Bol. See *Scopelogena vereculata*.
For further synonymy see *Erepsia, Mesembryanthemum, Mesembryanthus* and *Oscularia*.

For illustration see AIZOACEAE.

**Lancisia** Fabr. See *Cotula*.

**Langloisia** E. Greene (For Fr. Langlois, a French priest in Louisiana.) Polemoniaceae. 5 species of rigid, sparsely branching, annual herbs, to 20cm. Leaves alternate, linear to cuneate, pinnate, lower segments reduced to bristles, upper bristle-tipped. Inflorescence a few-flowered bracteate head; bracts foliaceous, with bristly teeth; calyx with 5 equal spine-tipped lobes, sinuses scarious and splitting to base; corolla actinomorphic to 2-lipped, tubular-funnelform; stamens 5. Fruit a 3-sided capsule; seeds 2–9, mucilaginous when wet. SW US (deserts). Z9.

CULTIVATION As for *Gilia*.

***L. punctata*** (Cov.) Goodd. LILAC-SUNBONNET. 3–5cm, branched or simple, sparsely tomentulose to subglabrous. Lvs 2.5–3cm, linear, bristle-teeth fine, upper lvs wider, with 3–5 toothed, deltoid apices. Cal. 8–9mm; cor. 1.5–2cm, subactinomorphic, lilac, lobes purple-spotted, entire; stamens exserted. Fr. 7–8mm, narrowly oblong; seeds *c*1mm. Spring–early summer.

For synonymy see *Gilia*.

**Languas** J.G. Koenig. See *Alpinia*.

**Lanium** (Lindl.) Benth. (From Lat. *lana*, wool, referring to the pilose appearance of the flowers.) Orchidaceae. Some 6 species of epiphytic orchids. Rhizome short or long-creeping, often branched. Secondary stems either pseudobulbous and apically bifoliate or narrowly cylindrical and multifoliate. Leaves rigid to fleshy, oblong to elliptic-ovate. Inflorescence a terminal raceme or a panicle, loosely few- to many-fld; flowers small, spreading; sepals linear-lanceolate to ovate-lanceolate, lateral sepals oblique, adnate to column base; petals similar to dorsal sepals, shorter; lip adnate to column to apex forming a short tube, lamina simple, concave, ovate or rhombic, acuminate; column dilated above, apex bidentate or biauriculate, anther terminal, operculate, incumbent, bilocular, pollinia 4, ovoid. Colombia, Venezuela, Guianas, Brazil, Peru. Z10.

CULTIVATION As for *Epidendrum*.

***L. avicula*** (Lindl.) Benth. Rhiz. stout, creeping. Secondary stems to 3cm, pseudobulbous. Lvs to 3×1.5cm, spreading, sessile, broadly elliptic to suborbicular, rounded or acute. Raceme to 16cm, several- to many-fld; peduncle densely tomentose; fls cream to yellow-brown or yellow-green, sometimes spotted red; sep. to 7mm, densely tomentose, lanceolate to oblong-lanceolate, acute or acuminate, lateral sep. oblique; pet. to 5mm, oblique, linear; lip lamina to 5×4mm, suborbicular to ovate-rhombic, acute to apiculate, base cuneate; column to 5mm, apex bidentate, dilated above. Brazil, Peru.

***L. microphyllum*** (Lindl.) Benth. Rhiz. elongate, creeping, branched; branches (stems) to 4cm, erect to ascending, multifoliate. Lvs to 3cm, distichous, linear-oblong, spreading, fleshy, acute. Raceme to 7cm, few- to several-fld; peduncle pilose, erect or suberect; fls yellow-brown flushed pink; sep. to 8×2mm, pilose, lanceolate or linear-lanceolate, carinate; pet. oblique, linear, shorter than sep., glabrous; lip lamina to 5×4mm, ovate, acuminate, glabrous, base rounded; column to 4mm, dilated above, obliquely bidentate below. Venezuela, Colombia, Ecuador, Peru, Surinam, Guianas.

For synonymy see *Epidendrum*.

**Lankesteria** Lindl. (From Dr E. Lankester, (mid-19th century) British botanist.) Acanthaceae. Some 7 species of erect, shrubby herbs and small shrubs. Leaves entire. Flowers in dense terminal spikes, clusters or panicles; bracts slender, conspicuous; calyx lobes 5, narrow, subequal; corolla tube slender, limb spreading, lobes 5, usually obovate; stamens 2, staminodes 2. Fruit a capsule, ellipsoid; seeds 2. Tropical Africa, Madagascar. Z10.

CULTIVATION As for *Eranthemum*.

***L. barteri*** Hook. f. Evergreen. Stems erect, to 1.25m. Lvs to 20cm, ovate-oblong, opposite. Infl. a spike; fls emerging from closely overlapping, bright green bracts; cor. slaverform, primrose yellow, tube minutely downy, limb with a vivid orange central blotch extending into throat. Tropical W Africa.

***L. elegans*** (P. Beauv.) Anderson. Lvs to 22cm, elliptic, acuminate, short-stalked. Infl. a cone-like spike to 15cm; bracts to 2.5cm, glabrous, lustrous, loosely overlapping; cor. to 4cm, pale orange darkening with age, tube slender, lobes ovate, to one-third length of tube. Tropical N Africa.

For synonymy see *Eranthemum*.

**Lantana** L. (From the superficial similarity to *Viburnum lantana*.) SHRUB VERBENA. Verbenaceae. Some 150 species of shrubs or perennial herbs, sometimes decumbent or scandent. Leaves opposite or whorled, often rugose, dentate. Inflorescence of axillary or terminal spikes or heads; flowers often red, yellow, blue or white, sessile; calyx small, membranous; corolla salverform, tube subcylindrical, exterior pubescent, limb spreading, 4 or 5-lobed, lobes obtuse or retuse; stamens 4, included, didynamous, inserted near middle of corolla tube; ovary bilocular, each locule with 1 ovule, style short, terminal. Fruit a drupe, bilocular or separating into 2 unilocular pyrenes. Tropical Americas and Africa, a widespread weed elsewhere in the tropics and subtropics.. Z10.

CULTIVATION Grown for the dense heads of bloom, carried from spring until autumn, *Lantana* spp. are suited to hedging and specimen plantings in frost-free zones and for bedding out or for the glasshouse or conservatory in cool temperate climates. Selections of *L. camara* are available with a colour range from pure whites to lilac; some of the most attractive emerge yellow and colour through bronze and red with maturity. *L. camara* is easily trained as a standard. The trailing *L. montevidensis*, suited to groundcover in the conservatory border or to hanging baskets, bears smaller flowers intermittently throughout the year.

Grow in full sun in a freely draining, loam-based mix with additional leafmould or screened well-rotted manure. Water plentifully when in full growth, reducing as light levels and temperatures fall to keep just moist in winter with a minimum temperature of 10–13°C/50–55°F. Propagate by seed in spring or by semi-ripe cuttings in summer; tip back young plants to ensure bushy growth, or train up as single-stemmed standards.

***L. camara*** L. Shrub to 2m, much-branched, puberulent to subglabrous. Lvs to 12×7cm, usually opposite, ovate to ovate-oblong, acute or acuminate, base rounded to cordate, pubesc. above and beneath, scabrous above, somewhat crenate-dentate; petiole to 2cm, glandular-pubesc. Infl. axillary, many-fld; peduncle to 14cm, adpressed-pubesc.; cal. to 3mm, truncate to dentate, glabrous to puberulent; cor. yellow to orange or red, tube to 12mm, curved, exterior puberulent, limb to 9mm diam. Fr. to 4mm diam., shiny, violet or black. Tropical America. Over 20 cvs: habit dwarf to standard; fls mostly bicolours, often changing colour, white and mauve forms also occur. 'Arlequin': fls dark pink and yellow; 'Brazier': fls bright red; 'Fabiola': fls salmon pink and yellow; 'Hybrida': low-growing; fls orange. 'Mr. Bessieres': strong growth; fls pink and yellow; 'Miss Tibbs': fls yellow turning pink; 'Naide': white, with yellow eye; 'Professor Raoux': fls scarlet and orange; 'Schloss Ortenburg': fls brick red and salmon yellow; 'Varia': fls yellow, exterior turning purple, interior orange.

***L. montevidensis*** (Spreng.) Briq. Herb or shrub to 1m, usually much-branched, trailing or scandent, branches often woody, strigose or hirsute. Lvs opposite or whorled, to 3.5×1.5cm, ovate to oblong or lanceolate, obtuse or subacute, coarsely dentate, pubesc.; petiole to 2mm. Fls to 12mm, sessile; cal. to 2mm, minutely dentate, pubesc.; cor. rose-lilac to violet, infundibular, tube to 10mm, pubesc., limb to 6mm diam., spreading. Fr. to 4×4mm, deep violet, globose, fleshy. S America.

***L. rugulosa*** HBK. Shrub. Lvs to 6cm, ovate, scabrous above, pubesc. beneath. Heads hemispherical, long-pedunculate; fls lilac. Fr. red. Ecuador.

***L. tiliifolia*** Cham. Shrub to 1.5m, coarsely spreading-hirsute. Lvs to 10×7cm, opposite, broadly ovate to elliptic or suborbicular, acuminate to obtuse, base truncate to subcordate, crenate-dentate; petiole to 1.5cm. Heads to 5cm diam., hemispherical; peduncle subequal to lvs; cal. to 2mm; cor. to 10mm, yellow or orange becoming brick red with age, tube white-pubesc. Drupe to 5mm diam., globose. S America.

***L. trifolia*** L. Erect shrub to 2m, unarmed, villous. Lvs to 12×6cm, usually whorled, oblong-lanceolate to elliptic-lanceolate, base cuneate, villous, crenate-serrate; petiole to 2cm. Infl. a dense spike; peduncle to 10cm, villous; cor. pink, lavender or violet, sometimes white, tube to 7mm, interior glabrous, limb to 6mm diam. Fr. red-violet or lavender. W Indies, Mexico, C & S America.

***L. camara*** var. ***aculeata*** (L.) Mold. See *L. camara*.
***L. delicatissima*** hort. See *L. montevidensis*.
***L. hispida*** HBK. See *L. camara*.
***L. horrida*** HBK. See *L. camara*.
***L. sellowiana*** Link & Otto. See *L. montevidensis*.
***L. urticifolia*** Mill. See *L. camara*.
For further synonymy see *Lippia*.

**Lapageria** Ruiz & Pav. (For Joséphine Tascher de la Pagérie, wife of Napoleon Bonaparte and an enthusiastic patron of gardening.) CHILEAN BELLFLOWER; CHILE BELLS; COPIHUE. Liliaceae (Philesiaceae). 1 species, an evergreen climbing monocot, spreading strongly by subterranean stolons. Stems to 10m, thickly wiry, becoming woody at base, twining, branching toward summit, clothed with sharp scale-like bracts. Leaves 6–12×2.5cm, alternate, ovate or ovate-lanceolate to subcordate, acute, glossy dark green, leathery, with 3–5 prominent parallel veins; petioles to 1cm. Flowers 1–3, oblong-campanulate, pendulous, short-stalked, solitary or a few clustered in the axils of upper leaves; tepals 6.5–9.5cm, 6 in 2 whorls, each with a basal pouched nectary, outer tepals flesh pink to magenta, crimson or white, broader than inner and rather heavily textured, inner tepals brighter, often faintly spotted or streaked crimson; stamens 6, free or slightly joined at base; style longer than stamens, clavate, apex slightly lobed. Fruit a many-seeded, oblong-ovoid, edible berry; seeds pale yellow or yellow-brown. Summer–winter. Chile. The national flower of Chile. Z9.

CULTIVATION One of the most handsome climbers, *L. rosea* is grown for the nodding, waxy rose flowers, carried from summer into autumn. Given the protection of a partially shaded and sheltered wall, it will grow outside where temperatures seldom fall below −5°C/23°F, but otherwise makes a fine specimen for the borders of the cold glasshouse or conservatory. Grow in cool, well-drained but moisture-retentive, humus-rich, lime-free soils in light shade or where direct sunlight reaches the leaves for short periods only. Under glass grow in bright filtered light, ensuring protection from bright sunlight especially during high summer. Propagate by layering in spring or autumn or by seed, pre-soaked for about 48 hours before sowing.

***L. rosea*** Ruiz & Pav. As for the genus. 'Beatrice Anderson': fls deep red. 'Flesh Pink': fls flesh coloured. 'Nash Court Pink': fls pink, marbled darker. 'Nash Court Red': fls red. 'Penheale': fls dark red. 'Superba': fls brilliant crimson. var. ***albiflora*** Hook. Fls white.

**Lapeirousia** Pourr. (For Philippe Picot de Lapeirouse, botanist at the University of Toulouse, late 18th century.) Iridaceae. About 38 species of perennial herbs. Corms bell-shaped with flat base and hard, woody tunics. Leaves 2 to several, iris-like, deciduous in dry season. Stem 2–3-angled, sometimes winged, usually branched. Inflorescence a simple or usually branched spike or panicle. Flowers regular or zygomorphic, usually brightly coloured; perianth forming a long or short tube, tepals 6, subequal or unequal; stamens 3; style with 3 usually forked branches. Tropical & S Africa. Z9.

CULTIVATION As for *Ixia*.

***L. anceps*** (L. f.) Ker-Gawl. Stem erect, 10–30cm, usually much-branched; branches flattened, 2–3-winged, the wings somewhat serrate. Basal lvs 1 to few, the lowest linear, ribbed, upper ones sword-shaped. Spike about 6-fld, distichous; bracts small, 5–7mm; fls irregular, white or pink, the lower 3 seg. marked with red; tube 25–80mm, very slender; tepals 10–30mm, narrowly lanceolate, the upper 3 larger, erect or reflexed, the lower 3 each with a small tooth at the base. Late winter–spring. S Africa (Cape Province).

***L. corymbosa*** (L. f.) Ker-Gawl. 5–45cm. Basal lvs 1 or more, 8–30cm, linear, often ribbed, the edge sometimes undulate or crisped. Stem branched, flattened, 2-winged. Panicle several-fld, each branch 2-fld; fls regular or slightly irregular, white, yellow, blue or violet, the seg. often with a dark mark at base; tube 4–15mm, tepals usually also 4–15mm, lanceolate or narrowly ovate, obtuse or acuminate. Late spring–summer. S Africa (Cape Province). ssp. ***corymbosa***. To 20cm high with 1 basal lf. Fls blue, marked with white in throat, rarely cream, less than 20cm; tepals 7–10mm, tube 4–10mm. ssp. ***alta*** Goldbl. Over 30cm tall, usually with more than 1 basal lf. Tepals shorter than perianth tube. ssp. ***fastigiata*** (Lam.) Goldbl. To 20cm high, basal lf 1, the edge usually crisped. Fls over 20mm, violet not marked with white, or cream or yellow with purple marks.

***L. divaricata*** Bak. Plants 7–25cm tall. Basal lf 1, 10–35cm, linear to awl-shaped, ribbed. Stem branched near base or unbranched; spike 5–12-fld. Fls irregular, somewhat 2-lipped, white or cream, often pink-tinged; perianth tube to 15mm long, slender at base then curving and becoming wider; tepals lanceolate, acute, the top one longest, to 16mm, erect; upper laterals reflexed, lowest 3 tepals 12mm. Late winter–spring. S Africa (W Cape).

***L. erythrantha*** (Klotzsch ex Klatt) Bak. A variable species; plants 15–45cm high, corms to 1.5cm wide at base. Lvs 3–4, linear or lanceolate, about half length of stem. Stem flattened, 2–3-angled, branched. Infl. paniculate, many-fld; fls slightly irregular, violet-blue with white, arrow-shaped mark outlined in purple on lower tepals, or crimson; tube 6–14mm, slender, slightly curved; tepals subequal, 6–11×2–4mm, lanceolate-spathulate; anth. white, red, blue or purple. Summer. Southern tropical Africa.

***L. fabricii*** (Delaroche) Ker-Gawl. 15–25cm, rarely more. Basal lf 1, of variable length, linear or sword-shaped, ribbed. Stem branched, flattened and 2-winged, the wings serrate. Spike to 8-fld; fls large, irregular, cream or yellow with red marks, often pink-tinged on outside. Tube 30–50mm long, slender, constricted near apex, then wider; tepals subequal, 13–20mm long, the topmost erect or reflexed, the others spreading, the 3 lowest often narrower and forming a lip. Spring–early summer. S Africa (Cape Province).

***L. jacquinii*** N.E. Br. Dwarf, 8–12(–20)cm. Basal lf 1; stem flattened, 3-angled. Infl. laxly to 10-fld, bracts large, to 20mm long. Fls irregular, violet with cream marks, the tube paler; tube 30–40mm, erect, slender, somewhat curved and wider near apex; tepals subequal, oblong, acute, the topmost slightly larger and hooded, the others spreading. Late winter–spring. S Africa (Cape Province).

***L. pyramidalis*** (Lam.) Goldbl. Dwarf 5–12cm, sometimes branched. Basal lvs usually 1, linear or lanceolate, ribbed. Infl. many-fld, at first distichous, later spirally arranged; fls white, pale to deep blue or carmine red, the lower seg. marked with white or cream; tube 20–40mm, slender, curved; topmost tepal erect, hooded, ovate; upper laterals spreading; lower 3 forming platform at right angles to tube, often with small calli near base. Winter–spring. S Africa (Cape Province).

***L. silenoides*** (Jacq.) Ker-Gawl. 5–12(–20)cm, often branched at base. Basal lf 1, to 10cm long, linear to lanceolate, ribbed. Spike fairly densely several to many-fld; fls irregular, magenta or cerise with cream-yellow markings on lower seg.;

tube 30–50mm long, slender, curved; tepals subequal, broadly ovate; upper 3 erect, lower 3 geniculate and forming a lip, each with red spot in centre. Winter–spring. S Africa (Cape Province).

***L. compressa*** Pourr. See *L. fabricii*.
***L. denticulata*** (Lam.) Lawrence. See *L. fabricii*.
***L. fissifolia*** (Jacq.) Ker-Gawl. See *L. pyramidalis*.
***L. laxa*** (Thunb.) N.E. Br. See *Anomatheca laxa*.
***L. purpureo-lutea*** (Klatt) Bak. See *L. corymbosa* ssp. *fastigiata*.
***L. rhodesiana*** N.E. Br. See *L. erythrantha*.
***L. sandersonii*** Bak. See *L. erythrantha*.

**Lapidaria** (Dinter & Schwantes) Schwantes ex N.E. Br. (From Lat. *lapis*, a stone, referring to the clustered, stone-like appearance of the plants.) Aizoaceae. 1 species, a highly succulent perennial related to *Schwantesia* and *Dinteranthus*, differing from the former by having 7 stigmas instead of 5, and from the latter by the cells being protected by lids, which are not present in *Dinteranthus*. It also shows developmental similarities to *Lithops*: the seedlings are identical to *Lithops*, and each succeeding leaf pair becomes less and less united until its reaches the flowering stage. Stems very short, branching with age, forming open mats. Leaves 6–8 per shoot, united below, divaricate, much thickened, 10–15×10×10mm, upper surface flat, lower surface more or less hemispherically convex and acutely carinate, obtusely triquetrous toward the tip, surface smooth, white or red-white, margins reddened. Pedicels 5–6cm, broadly compressed; flowers 3–5cm diam., golden-yellow above, white-yellow below, turning yellow-red when fading. Namibia: Great Namaqualand. Z9.

CULTIVATION As for *Lithops*.

***L. margaretae*** (Schwantes) Schwantes ex N.E. Br. As for the genus.

For synonymy see *Argyroderma, Dinteranthus* and *Mesembryanthemum*.

**Lapiedra** Lagasca. Amaryllidaceae. 2 species of bulbous perennial herbs. Leaves few, basal. Flowers erect, in a 4–9-flowered umbel; spathe of 2 bracts; tepals 6, free, equal, spreading; filaments as long as the basifixed anthers. Fruit a flattened, spherical, 3-lobed capsule, surrounded by the persistent, withered perianth; seeds few. W Mediterranean. Z8.

CULTIVATION Occurring in rocky habitats in the western Mediterranean, *Lapiedra* bears its short-lived, small white flowers in succession in late summer, before the emergence of the leaves which persist until the following spring. A warm dry period during summer dormancy is essential. *Lapiedra* spp. are suitable for cultivation in pans in the alpine house or frame, flowering more reliably when restricted at the root, and for hot, dry positions on the rock garden. Plant 7.5cm/3in. deep in spring. Otherwise cultivate as for *Ixiolirion*.

***L. martinezii*** Lagasca. Bulb to 5cm diam. Lvs to 25×1cm, appearing after fls, with a pale band on upper surface. Tepals 8–12mm, white with a green stripe on the outside. Late summer. S Spain, N Africa.

**Lappula** Gilib.
***L. micrantha*** Eastw. See *Hackelia micrantha*.

**Lapsana** L.
***L. capillaris*** L. See *Crepis capillaris*.
***L. zacintha*** L. See *Crepis zacintha*.

**Lardizabala** Ruiz & Pav. (For Miguel de Lardizabel y Uribe, 18th-century Spanish naturalist.) Lardizabalaceae. 2 species of evergreen, monoecious climbers. Leaves alternate. Flowers unisexual, sepals 6, petaloid, nectaries 6, petaloid, male flowers in drooping to ascending raceme; with 6 united stamens; female flowers solitary, with 6 staminodes and 3 to 6 carpels. Fruit developing from 1 carpel, a many-seeded berry. Chile.

CULTIVATION A handsome twining climber with dark green compound leaves and slender spikes of dark male flowers. Where pollination is successful (flowers are unisexual and the plants themselves sometimes dioecious) dark mauve-blue fruit follow the solitary female flowers. Hardy to −10°C/14°F, this vine nevertheless prefers a shady protected site in well-drained soils rich in decayed matter. A pleasing, if rather subdued choice for city gardens and sheltered groves. Propagate by seed in spring or stem cuttings in spring and autumn.

***L. biternata*** Ruiz & Pav. Twining to 4m. Lvs ternate, biternate or triternate, dark glossy green above, paler with distinct reticulate venation beneath, coriaceous, leaflets 5–10cm, 3–9, ovate, the central leaflet largest, lateral leaflets often sessile, margins entire or shallowly crenate, with 1–2 thorny teeth. Male fls in axillary, pendulous to ascending spikes, 7.5–10cm long, sep. 6, fleshy arranged in 2 whorls, broadly ovate, green edged dark brown-purple, pet. small, lanceolate, white, farinose, stamens 6, connate, carpels rudimentary; female fls solitary, axillary, 1.5–1.8cm long, pedicel 2.5cm, slender, carpels 3 (rarely 6), stamens 6, free, sterile. Fr. 6cm, ovoid-oblong, dark purple, edible. Winter. Chile. Z9.

**LARDIZABALACEAE** Decne. LARDIZABALA FAMILY. Dicot. 8 genera and 21 species of pachycaul shrubs and lianes. Leaves alternate, palmate, pinnate in *Decaisnea*; stipules usually absent. Flowers small, 3-merous, regular, in usually drooping racemes from scaly axillary buds; calyx 6-numerous, 3 in *Akebia*, usually petaloid, imbricate, or outer valvate; corolla 6 petals, smaller, nectariferous or absent; stamens 6 opposite corolla lobes, filaments ± basally connate; ovary superior, 3 (or 6–15) free carpels, in 1 (–5) whorls of 3 in each; staminodes about 6; pistillodes sometimes in male flowers; stigma terminal, more or less sessile; ovules few – numerous. Fruit a berry or fleshy follicle, often edible, the pericarp in *Decaisnea* with latex system; seeds with short embryo; endosperm copious, oily, sometimes with carbohydrate. Some are cultivated as ornamentals. Some have edible fruits, e.g. *Akebia, Lardizabala* and *Stauntonia*. Himalaya to S E Asia and Taiwan, Central Chile. *Akebia, Decaisnea, Holboellia, Lardizabala, Sinofranchetia, Stauntonia*. See illustration overleaf.

**Larix** Mill. LARCH. (Classical Lat. name.) Pinaceae. Some 12–14 species of deciduous, monoecious, coniferous trees to 50m, though *L. occidentalis* once known to 80m. Bark furrowed, scaly, exfoliating. Crown usually conic in young trees, becoming domed or irregular in some species with age; branches horizontal or somewhat drooping; shoots dimorphic: long and short. Buds ovoid; scales overlapping. Leaves acicular, 2–5(–7)cm, in loose spirals on long shoots, in dense spirals on short shoots, forming pseudowhorls, flexible, apex acute to obtuse, keeled beneath, often also above, occasionally quadrangular in section, with stomata beneath, occasionally also above. Cones terminal on short shoots; male cones composed of many pollen sacs in spirals, spherical to ovoid, pink or yellow; female cones erect, ripening in 4–7 months, with a basal pseudowhorl of leaves, cylindric or ovoid to spherical, 1–8cm, green, red or purple, then brown, scales tough, leathery; bracts shorter or longer than scales; seeds 2 per scale, 4–6mm, off-white, without resin vesicles, deltoid, wing adnate, mid-brown, 6–9mm, angled at 45° to seed. N Hemisphere. Three species cover almost the entire circumpolar plains with three relatives in mountains a little further south; the others form two groups of relict populations in small areas on scattered mountain ranges far to the south.

CULTIVATION In cool temperate maritime climates, only two species, *L. decidua* and *L. kaempferi* (and the hybrid between them), are wholly successful, making healthy 25–40m/80–130ft trees in most areas. Most of the others are adapted to longer, colder winters than occur here and are tempted into premature spring growth by mild spells in January/February, only to be damaged by later frost; notably *L. lyallii* and *L. russica* are impossible to grow in lowland Britain, though they should succeed above 300m/975ft in the E Scottish Highlands. The poor growth of the Sino-Himalayan larches is unexplained; they do best in the South-west, but are poor in Scotland, where most Sino-Himalayan species grow best. Rainfall is adequate for all species throughout GB; all tolerate acid and infertile soils, *L. decidua* also chalk. Only *L. laricina* and *L. gmelinii* tolerate waterlogged soils; best growth of all spp. is on freely drained stony hillside soils. Almost all will hybridize freely in cultivation.

Always use 1+1 plants (1-year seedlings lined out for one year more), which should be 25–70cm/10–28in. tall, and do not plant

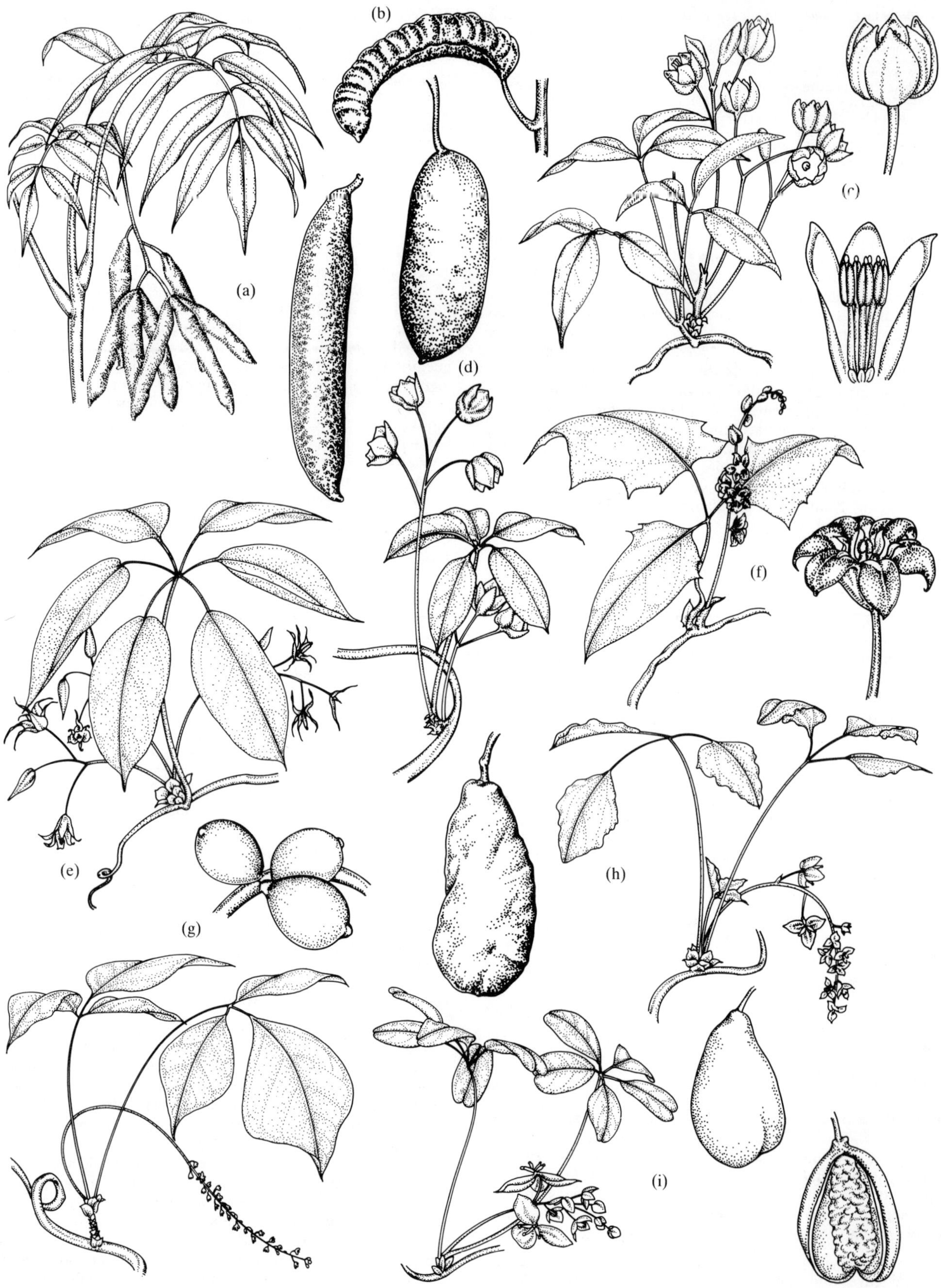


**Lardizabalaceae** (a) *Decaisnea fargesii* (×0.17) and (right) fruit (×0.6) (b) *D. insignis* fruit (×0.6) (c) *Holboellia coriacea* (×0.25), pistillate flower (×1), staminate flower LS (×3) (d) *H. latifolia* and (above) fruit (×0.3) (e) *Stauntonia hexaphylla* (×0.3) (f) *Lardizabala biternata* (×0.6), pistillate flower (×1) (g) *Sinofranchetia chinensis* (×0.3), fruit (×1) (h) *Akebia trifoliata* (×0.5) and (left) fruit (×0.3) (i) *A. quinata* (×0.5) and fruit (×0.3)

from pots or containers with spiralled roots. Pruning is limited to singling forks and early cleaning up 2m/6½ft of trunk, preferably followed to 3–6m/10–20ft later; dead branches should also be removed as they are very brittle and can be dangerous. *L. decidua* is best for single specimens, although *L.* ×*marschlinsii* may be preferred on less fertile sites for more rapid growth. They and *L. kaempferi* make fine shelterbelts, summer screening and copse groups, attractive to small finches, tits and treecreepers, covered in small pink flowers in early spring, leafing out bright green, then gold or old gold to russet in late autumn.

Pests common to Europe and North America include the larch sawfly (*Pristophora erichsonii*) with defoliating olive-green larvae up to 25mm/1in. long, the only pest likely to necessitate control measures (treat with a contact insecticide) and larch adelgids (*Adelges* spp.) made conspicuous by a covering of white woolly wax. The larch casebearer (*Coleophora laricella*) has small caterpillars which make holes and mines in the foliage and cover themselves with a cigar-shaped case made from pieces of needles.

A needlecast disease caused by the fungus *Meria laricis* can cause serious damage to young larch trees in the nursery. The needles turn brown from the tips and fall off prematurely. High volume sprays of a sulphur fungicide can control the disease. Canker and dieback caused by the fungus *Trichoscyphella willkommii* is mainly a problem of plantations and unlikely to affect garden trees; Japanese larch is less susceptible than European larch. Larches are an alternate host for the birch rust, *Melampsoridium betulinum*, which produces rows of cluster cups containing orange aeciospores on the needles. This is one of several similar rust fungi which affect larches but they do not cause sufficient damage to warrant control measures. Larches can also be affected by armillaria root rot (*Armillaria* spp.) and root and butt rot caused by the bracket fungus *Heterobasidion annosum* (*Fomes annosus*).

1 Bract scales shorter than seed scales and not or rarely visible on closed cone. Leaves flat.
*Ll. decidua, gmelinii, kaempferi, laricina, principis rupprechtii, russica.*

2 Bract scales longer than seed scales, readily visible on closed cone. Leaves usually keeled.

2.1 Seed scales reflexing over 90° on opening.
*Ll. lyallii, occidentalis.*

2.2 Seed scales opening to 60° or less.
*Ll. griffithiana, himalaica, mastersiana, potaninii, speciosa.*

***L. decidua*** Mill. EUROPEAN LARCH. To 50m. Bark grey-brown, fissured, flaking. Crown slender, conic, broader with age; branches horizontal, upswept at tips; branchlets and shoots drooping to fully pendulous; shoots yellow-brown to buff, glabrous. Buds elliptic, to 3mm, yellow-brown, resinous. Lvs 2–4(–6.5)cm, soft, flat or slightly keeled beneath pale green. Female fls red-purple. Cones 1.5–4cm, rarely to 6cm, conic to cylindric, brown; scales 40–50, straight or incurved, sometimes short-hairy on outer surface; bracts shorter than scales, not, or very rarely slightly exserted. Alps, Carpathians. About 20 cvs described, nearly all varying in habit, from dwarf ('Compacta', 'Corley', 'Repens'), erect ('Fastigiata'), pendulous ('Pendula', 'Viminalis') to twisted ('Cervicornis', 'Tortuosa') and sparsely branched ('Virgata'). In 'Alba', the immature cones are pale green, almost white. ssp. ***polonica*** (Racib.) Domin. POLISH LARCH. To 30m, crown very slender. Branchlets pale straw to white, slender, drooping. Cones smaller, 1–2.8cm, more obtuse than species type; scales concave. W Poland, Ukraine. Z4.

***L. gmelinii*** (Rupr.) Rupr. ex Kuzn. DAHURIAN LARCH. To 35m or shrubby. Bark rust-brown. Crown broad conic, open; branches and branchlets horizontal; shoots yellow or red, usually glabrous. Buds spherical, without resin. Lvs to 3cm, obtuse, light green, with two stomatal bands beneath and a diffuse band above. Cones 1.5–3, rarely 4×1–2cm, ovoid, lustrous pale brown; scales with truncate, undulate apices, to 1cm; bracts to 5mm, often slightly exserted. E Asia. var. ***japonica*** (Reg.) Pilger. KURILE LARCH. Shoots rust-brown to purple, pruinose. Lvs to 2.5cm, outspread, rigid, subulate. Cones ovoid, 1–2cm, rarely to 3cm; seed scales more pointed than species type. USSR (Sakhalin, Kurile Is.) var. ***olgensis*** (Henry) Ostenf. & Larsen. OLGA BAY LARCH. Shoots beige, densely brown-pubesc. Lvs subulate, to 2.5cm. Cones ovoid-oblong, to 3×1–2cm; scales truncate to obtuse, faintly emarginate. E Siberia (Olga Bay). Z1.

***L. griffithiana*** (Lindl. & Gordon) Carr. SIKKIM LARCH. To 40m, to 20m in cult. Bark grey-brown, grooved, forming rough ridges. Crown conic; shoots buff, short-hairy. Buds conic, downy, without resin. Lvs obtuse, 25–50×2mm, keeled beneath, light green, with stomata in 2 bands beneath and scattered above. Female fls with red scales. Cones narrow conic-cylindric, 4–8×1.5cm closed, opening to 3cm wide near base, 2cm wide near apex, purple-brown; seed scales to 1.5cm broad, base pubesc.; bracts exserted by 1cm, reflexed at apex, longer than seed scales. Himalaya (E Nepal, Bhutan, Sikkim to Tsangpo river, Tiber/Assam border). Z7.

***L. himalaica*** Cheng & L.K. Fu. To 40m; crown similar to *L. potaninii*. Shoots yellow-grey, pendulous on level branches; buds 3mm brown. Lvs 10–25×1.5–2mm, pale green with two indistinct stomatal bands beneath. Cones 4–6.5×2cm, pale buff (not purple-brown as *L. potaninii*); scales slightly truncate rounded, bracts exserted 5–6mm, erect, extending only 1–2mm beyond the scale tip, cuspidate. SC Tibet, C Nepal (Langtang Khola to N side of Everest). Z7.

***L. kaempferi*** (Lamb.) Carr. JAPANESE LARCH. To 45m. Bark rust-brown to grey-er, fissured and scaly. Crown broad conic; branches and shoots horizontal or slightly ascending, shoots grooved or glabrous, red brown, bloomed grey at first. Lvs 2–3.5cm, slightly keeled beneath, grey-green, with stomatal bands above and beneath. Cones 2–3, rarely 4cm; ovoid; scales flexible, truncate to apically emarginate, apex reflexed, to 5mm; bract scales shorter than seed scales; seeds to 5mm; peduncle orange-red. Japan (Honshu). About 20 cvs described, mainly varying in habit, and mostly dwarf ('Blue Dwarf', 'Nana', 'Varley', 'Wehlen') or with pendulous branchlets ('Georgengarten', 'Inversa', 'Pendula'), or both ('Hanan'). In 'Blue Haze' the lvs are very bright glaucous, as also in the semi-fastigiate 'Pyramidalis Argentea'. Z4.

***L. laricina*** (Du Roi) K. Koch. TAMARACK; AMERICAN LARCH. To 20(–30)m. Bark grey, becoming brown and scaly. Crown conic; branches horizontal, branchlets drooping, thin, often curved, glabrous, glossy red-brown; short shoots dark black. Buds maroon, resinous. Lvs 2–3cm, keeled beneath, pale green with 2 stomatal bands beneath. Cones ovoid, 12–24mm, green or purple, becoming straw-brown; scales 15–20, nearly circular, margins slightly incurved; bracts much smaller than scales; seeds 3mm with 5mm wing. Northern N America. 'Arethusa Bog': dwarf; shoots short, narrow, branches over-arching. 'Aurea': young lvs gold, later light green. 'Glauca': lvs metallic blue. var. ***alaskensis*** (Wight) Raup. Differs little, but tends to have smaller 1–1.5cm cones with paler, more spreading scales. C Alaska. Z2.

***L. lyallii*** Parl. SUBALPINE LARCH. Closely related to *L. occidentalis*, but shoots pubesc.; to 25m, bark thin, flaking, grey-brown. Shoots densely woolly-pubesc., orange-red but obscured by the buff hairs; becoming glabrous by second year. Lvs 2–4cm, slender, quadrangular in section (not flattened); glaucous green above, two pale glaucous stomatal bands beneath. Cones 2.5–4.5cm, pubesc. at first, maturing glabrous, buff, with broad, long exserted purple bracts; scales to 1cm broad, opening widely at maturity to reveal dense long pubescence on rachis. N America (Rocky Mts). Zone 3.

***L.* ×*marschlinsii*** Coaz. (*L. decidua* × *L. kaempferi.*) DUNKELD LARCH; HYBRID LARCH. Vigorous. Similar to *L. decidua* but shoots and lvs faintly glaucous, brown or pale orange; buds red-brown; bracts of young cones reflexed; peduncle yellow; cones conic, scale tips slightly reflexed. Garden origin (Dunkeld, Scotland, *c*1897).

***L.* ×*marschlinsii*** hort. non Coaz. (*L. kaempferi* × *L. russica.*) Cultivated hybrid intermediate between the two spp. It has no currently valid name.

***L. mastersiana*** Rehd. & Wils. To 25m. Bark dull brown, furrowed. Branches outspread, horizontal; long shoots drooping, straw-brown, near-glabrous. Lvs 1–3.5cm, keeled above and beneath, acuminate, light green, with 2 stomatal bands beneath. Cones 3–4cm, subsessile, cylindric, finely downy; seed scales reniform to broadly rounded; bracts strongly exserted, reflexed, purple-brown; seeds 3mm with a 7mm wing. W China (Sichuan). Z7.

***L. occidentalis*** Nutt. WESTERN LARCH. To 50m, previously reported to 80m. Bole to 1.8m diam. Bark grey-brown, flaking in thin scales, becoming maroon-brown and deeply furrowed. Branches horizontal; shoots grooved, glabrous to sparsely pubesc. at first, yellow-brown to orange-brown, becoming brown. Buds spherical, brown, resinous, bud scales hairy. Lvs 2.5–5cm, outspread, keeled beneath, slightly convex above, acute, sharp, blue-green to grey-green, with 2 stomatal bands beneath. Cones 2.5–4.5×1cm closed, ovoid, scales rounded, to 12mm broad, scales reflexing widely on opening, to 2.5cm broad; bracts exserted; seeds with wings 8mm long. Western N America. Z4.

***L.* ×*pendula*** (Sol.) Salisb. WEEPING LARCH. To 30m. Branchlets pendent; young shoots glabrous, pink, maturing to brown. Lvs similar to *L. decidua*, apex blunter. Cones 2–3.2cm, ovoid; scales 20–30, exterior base downy; bracts hidden. Origin obscure, possibly Newfoundland but not found in the wild and now known to be of hybrid origin. 'Contorta': young shoots twisted. 'Repens': branches creeping horizontally. Z4.

***L. potaninii*** Batal. CHINESE LARCH. To 40m, to 20m in cult. Bark becoming deeply grooved, brown. Crown columnar; shoots rust-brown, lustrous, slightly hairy, eventually glabrous. Buds rust-brown, resinous. Lvs 1.5–3cm, keeled above and beneath, acute, light green bloomed glaucous on some plants. Cones 3–5cm, short-pedunculate oblong-ovate, purple becoming brown; scales rounded, often emarginate, bracts exserted, erect; seeds 5mm with 7mm wing. W China (NW Sichuan, S Gansu, S Shaanxi). var. ***macrocarpa*** Law. Shoots lustrous red-brown. Cones stout, cylindric-conic, 5–8.5×2cm opening to 4cm wide; bract scales long, broad based, erect. China (SW Sichuan, SW Xizang, NW Yunnan). Z5.

***L. principis-rupprechtii*** Mayr. PRINCE RUPPRECHT LARCH. To 40m, crown broad conic, branches level; shoots stout, orange-brown with a waxy bloom. Lvs similar to *L. gmelinii*, but to 35mm long. Cones 2.5–4×2cm, with numerous scales; scales shorter than in *L. gmelinii*, smoothly rounded and not or only slightly wavy or emarginate at apex. N China (Hebei, N Shanxi). Z4.

***L. russica*** (Endl.) Sab. ex Trautv. SIBERIAN LARCH. To 30m. Bark rust-brown, scaly, becoming deeply grooved. Crown narrowly conic; branches horizontal to upswept; shoots lustrous yellow, minutely pubesc., becoming glabrous; short shoots very closely spaced. Buds conic, resinous, surrounded by hairs. Lvs 2.5–4cm, clustered, very narrow, soft, bright green above, with 2 stomatal bands beneath and scattered stomata above. Cones 2.5–3.5cm, rarely 4cm, subsessile; seed scales thick, tough, densely pubesc., margins incurved, bracts obscured; seeds 5mm with wings to 12mm. Russia (near Finnish border), E to C Siberia (Yenisei). 'Fastigiata': columnar and compact. 'Glauca': needles glaucous. 'Longifolia': needles longer than species type. 'Pendula': branches weeping. 'Robusta': more vigorous than species type. Z1.

***L. speciosa*** Cheng & Law. To 30m; crown as *L. potaninii*. Shoots orange-brown, glabrous; lvs 25–55×1.5–2mm, green with 2 white-green stomatal bands beneath. Cones with reflexed bracts as in *L. griffithiana*, but cylindric and stouter, more like *L. potaninii* var. *macrocarpa*, in shape, 7–9×2–3cm opening to ×4cm. SW China (SW Yunnan), NE Burma. *L. griffithiana*). Z8.

***L. chinensis*** Beissn. See *L. potaninii*.
***L. dahurica*** Turcz. ex Trautv. See *L. gmelinii*.
***L. ×eurolepis*** Henry. See *L. ×marschlinsii* Coaz non hort.
***L. europaea*** DC. See *L. decidua*.
***L. gmelinii*** var. ***principis-rupprechtii*** (Mayr) Pilger. See *L. principis-rupprechtii*.
***L. griffithiana*** var. ***speciosa*** (Cheng & Law). See *L. speciosa*.
***L. griffithii*** Hook. f. See *L. griffithiana*.
***L. leptolepis*** (Sieb. & Zucc.) Gordon. See *L. kaempferi*.
***L. olgensis*** Henry. See *L. gmelinii* var. *olgensis*.
***L. sibirica*** Ledeb.. See *L. russica*.
***L. wulingschanensis*** Liou & Wang. See *L. principis-rupprechtii*.

**Larrea** Cav. (For John Antony Larrea, Spanish benefactor of the Sciences.) CREOSOTE BUSH. Zygophyllaceae. 5 species of xerophytic shrubs, resinous, evergreen, often suckering; stems jointed, swollen at base. Leaves 2-lobed or -pinnate, stipulate; leaflets 1–7 pairs, sessile, asymmetric. Flowers solitary, bisexual, axillary or terminal on short lateral twigs; sepals 5, unequal, imbricate; petals 5, oblong-spathulate, clawed; stamens 10 borne on a lobed disc; ovary 5-loculate, superior; style 1, slender, bearing 5 lobed stigma; ovules 1–6 per locule. Fruit globose, pubescent, 5-seeded, separating at dehiscence to 5 nutlets; seeds 3-angled. S America to SW US.

CULTIVATION As for *Guaiacum*.

***L. divaricata*** Cav. JARRILLA. 1–4m, much-branched, glutinous; shoots angled, grooved; bark ashen. Stipules small, tuberculate; leaflets 6–12×2–3mm, ovate-oblong, acuminate, olive green, sessile, 3–5-nerved; sep. obtuse, concave, downy, outer 2 shorter than inner 3; pet. to 6mm, bright yellow; ovary pubesc., becoming shaggier in fruit. Fr. globose, white pubesc. Argentina. Z9.

***L. nitida*** Cav. Shrub, 1–3m; shoots angular, downy, terete. Lvs to 1cm, imparipinnate, sessile, glutinous, shining; stipules 2, lanceolate; leaflets 11–15, linear-oblong, obtuse. Fls axillary on short pedicels that lengthen in fr.; cal. seg. oblong-lanceolate, mucronate; pet. bright yellow. Fr. about 4mm, 5-cleft. Chile, Argentina. Z9.

***L. tridentata*** (DC.) Cov. CREOSOTE BUSH; COVILLE. To 4m, aromatic; bark dark grey to black. Lvs trifoliate; leaflets 5–10mm, 2, oblong-lanceolate, opposite, divaricate, falcate, united at base, mucronate, dark green to yellow-green. Fls axillary; pet. to 1cm, yellow; sep. silky, tinged yellow; fil. winged. Fr. densely white downy. SW US to N Mexico. Z8.

**Lasiagrostis** Link.
***L. calamagrostis*** (L.) Link. See *Stipa calamagrostis*.
***L. splendens*** (Trin.) Kunth. See *Stipa splendens*.

**Lasianthaea** DC. (From Gk *lasios*, woolly, and *anthos*, flower.) Compositae. About 12 species of perennial herbs or shrubs. Leaves usually opposite, ovate to lanceolate, serrate, shortly petiolate or sessile. Capitula radiate, solitary, or terminal, few in umbelliform clusters; involucre campanulate or hemispheric; phyllaries in 2–3 series, outer herbaceous, inner scarious; receptacle convex, scaly; florets yellow, orange or purple-red, ray florets female, disc florets hermaphrodite. Fruit a black or purple-black, dimorphic cypsela, ray fruit often shorter than disc fruit sharply 3-angled, -awned or -toothed, disc fruit laterally compressed, oblanceolate to obovate, 2–3-awned; pappus of scales or hairs, sometimes from a corona. Arizona to Venezuela, especially Mexico. Z9.

CULTIVATION As for *Tithonia*.

***L. aurea*** (D. Don) K. Becker. Perenn. herb, to 60cm; stems simple or sparingly branched. Lvs usually opposite in 3–5 pairs, lanceolate or elliptic, upper lvs to 7×2cm, acute or obtuse, base subauriculate, sessile, margins serrulate or denticulate, often revolute. Capitula 2–2.5cm diam., solitary or few in clusters; phyllaries 15–25, outer elliptic to ovate or suborbicular, acute to rounded, hispid, inner lanceolate-ovate to lanceolate, acute, stiffly scarious, usually purple-tipped; ray florets to 10×5mm, 8–11, bright yellow; disc florets yellow. Summer–autumn. Mexico.

***L. helianthoides*** DC. Shrub or subshrub to 4m; stems branched. Lvs to 12×6cm, ovate or lanceolate, apex acute or shortly acuminate, base rounded or subcordate, margin crenate-denticulate or serrate, somewhat revolute; petioles to 1cm. Capitula 2–4cm diam., 3–12, in dense clusters; phyllaries 30–40, rigid, outer broadly ovate, obtuse, adpressed, inner elliptic-obovate or elliptic-ovate to almost linear, with broad fragile tips; ray florets to 15×7mm, 9–21, bright yellow or orange, disc florets yellow or orange. Summer–autumn. Mexico.

For synonymy see *Tithonia* and *Wedelia*.

**Lasiostelma** Benth.
***L. sandersonii*** Oliv. See *Brachystelma sandersonii*.

**Lasthenia** Cass. (For Lasthenia, a Gk girl who attended Plato's lectures in male attire.) Compositae. About 16 species of annual to perennial herbs. Leaves opposite, simple, entire or pinnatifid. Capitula radiate, terminal, often showy, pedunculate; receptacle hemispherical to conical or pointed; involucre cylindrical to hemispherical; phyllaries few to many, free to partially or wholly connate, often deciduous; ray florets white to green or golden-yellow, female; disc florets hermaphrodite. Fruit a terete to compressed, linear, glabrous or pubescent cypsela; pappus of awns or scales or both, or absent. Pacific N America, C Chile.

CULTIVATION Most cultivated species are treated as annuals in flower borders and as edging and are easily grown in any well-drained soil, including nutritionally poor soils, in full sun. Sow seed *in situ* in spring or, in zones that are essentially frost free, in autumn. Shear over after flowering to encourage a second flush of bloom.

***L. chrysostoma*** (Fisch. & Mey.) Greene. Erect to decumbent, white-pubesc. annual, to 40cm. Lvs linear, occasionally shortly dentate, hirsute or strigose. Capitula sometimes nodding at first; receptacle conical; involucre hemispherical; phyllaries to 1cm, to 13, ovate-lanceolate to oblong, free; ray florets to 1cm, bright yellow, apex sometimes lighter. Fr. to 3mm, glabrous or white to yellow pubesc.; pappus of 1–7 white to brown, pointed awns, or ovate-lanceolate, awned scales, or absent. Oregon to NW Mexico and Arizona.

***L. coronaria*** (Nutt.) Ornd. Erect, pubesc. annual, to 40cm. Lvs to 6cm, linear and entire, or pinnate, or laciniate with seg. to 3cm. Receptacle more or less conical; involucre hemispherical to top-shaped, densely pubesc.; phyllaries to 7mm, to 14, lanceolate to ovate, free; ray florets to 1cm, yellow. Fr. to 2.5mm; pappus variable, of truncate, fimbriate, white scales, or of long awned, lanceolate scales, or both, or absent. SW California to NW Mexico.

***L. glabrata*** Lindl. Erect, glabrous or pubesc. annual, to 60cm. Lvs to 15cm, linear or subulate, entire or obscurely dentate, fleshy, glabrous, connate at base. Receptacle narrowly to broadly conical; involucre to 1cm high, depressed-hemispherical; phyllaries to 14, connate; ray florets to 14mm, golden- or lemon-yellow. Fr. to 3.5mm, glabrous, grey, shining; pappus absent. CW California.

***L. macrantha*** (A. Gray) Greene. Erect or decumbent, more or less caespitose, short-lived perenn., rarely annual or bienn., often flowering in first year, pubesc. Lvs to 21×1.5cm, linear to oblong, entire or few-dentate, glabrous to densely hirsute, margins ciliate. Capitula large, showy; receptacle broadly conical; involucre campanulate to depressed-hemispherical; phyllaries to 14mm, 13–16, ovate to elliptic, free; ray florets to 16mm, bright yellow. Fr. to 4mm, silver-grey at maturity, warty or short yellow pubesc., or glabrous; pappus of 1–4, yellow, pointed awns, or absent. SW Oregon to CW California. Z8.

***L. californica*** Lindl. See *L. glabrata*.
***L. gracilis*** (DC.) Greene. See *L. chrysostoma*.
***L. hirsutula*** Greene. See *L. chrysostoma*.
For further synonymy see *Baeria, Burrielia, Hymenoxys* and *Ptilomeris*.

**Lastrea** Bory.
***L. acuminata*** Houlst. See *Lastreopsis acuminata*.
***L. articulata*** Brackenr. See *Arthropteris articulata*.
***L. decomposita*** (R. Br.) J. Sm. See *Lastreopsis decomposita*.
***L. gracilescens*** Bedd. See *Parathelypteris beddomei*.
***L. hispida*** (Sw.) Moore & Houlst. See *Lastreopsis hispida*.
***L. maximowiczii*** (Bak.) Moore. See *Arachniodes maximowiczii*.
***L. microsora*** (Endl.) Presl. See *Lastreopsis microsora*.

***L. oreopteris*** (Ehrh.) Bory. See *Oreopteris limbosperma.*
***L. quinquangulare*** (Kunze) J. Sm. See *Lastreopsis microsora.*
***L. standishii*** Moore. See *Arachniodes standishii.*
***L. thelypteris*** (L.) Bory. See *Thelypteris palustris.*

**Lastreopsis** Ching. (From and *Lastrea*, Gk *opsis*, appearance.) Dryopteridaceae. Some 30–35 species of terrestrial or, rarely, epilithic or epiphytic ferns. Rhizomes short to long-creeping, or tufted, or, rarely, erect, covered with roots as well as scales; scales not clathrate, ovate to lanceolate, apex acute to narrowly acute, margin entire to slightly toothed, fimbriate, or glandular, chestnut to brown or black. Fronds stipitate, uniform, anadromous to catadromous, 2–5-pinnate or -pinnatifid, more or less deltoid, glandular-pubescent (hairs yellow to orange or red), lowest pair of primary pinnae unequal and basiscopically produced at base, segments decurrent; veins free, simple or forked; rachis with 2 more or less prominent ridges, and usually veined and pubescent between these, as well as generally pubescent or glandular-pubescent; stipes often ridged and glandular-pubescent. Sori on or terminating veins, more or less superficial, circular; indusia usually present, globose to kidney-shaped or peltate, margin entire to glandular-fimbriate or notched, glabrous or pubescent, brown to black; paraphyses absent; sporangia stalked, glabrous; annulus 12–18-celled; spores globose to ellipsoid, bilateral, monolete, echinate to rugose. Tropics. Z10.

CULTIVATION As for *Dryopteris*, but requiring frost protection.

***L. acuminata*** (Houlst.) Morton. SHINY SHIELD FERN. Rhiz. tufted; scales brown. Fronds to 90cm, 2-pinnate-pinnatifid, deltoid, apex narrowly acute, lustrous, seg. oblong, margin toothed; rachis pubesc.; stipes to 80cm. Sori medial; indusia kidney-shaped, brown. Australia.

***L. calantha*** (Endl.) Tind. Fronds to 80cm, 3–4-pinnate, glaucous; stipes approximate and clustered. Norfolk Is.

***L. decomposita*** (R. Br.) Tind. TRIM SHIELD FERN. Rhiz. to 12mm, short-creeping, branched; scales to 5×1mm, dense, lanceolate, margin entire to subentire, lustrous, brown. Fronds to 50×40cm, catadromous, 2–4-pinnate, ovate to deltoid or pentagonal, apex acute or narrowly acute, leathery to membranous and thin-textured, stiff, initially pubesc., pinnae to 35×25cm, petiolate, opposite or subopposite, erect to spreading, approximate to imbricate, ovate to deltoid, apex acute to narrowly acute, secondary pinnae to 12×5cm, sessile to short-petiolate, alternate, oblique, distant, ovate to lanceolate, apex acute to narrowly acute, pinnules to 5×1cm, alternate, oblique, distant, lanceolate to oblong, apex acute, seg. to 10×3mm, ovate to lanceolate, apex narrowly acute to mucronate, margin entire or notched; veins oblique; rachis rough and glandular-pubesc. below, costa scaly and white-pubesc.; stipes to 50cm, approximate and clustered, rough and scaly at base, pale brown. Australia.

***L. effusa*** (Sw.) Tind. Rhiz. to 2cm, short-creeping, woody; scales ovate to lanceolate, margin subentire to toothed, red-brown. Fronds to 1×1m, 2–5-pinnate or -pinnatifid, deltoid, apex narrowly acute, lustrous above, more or less glabrous to glandular-pubesc. on lower surface of seg., pinnae to 45×30cm, uppermost reduced, petiolate, deltoid, pinnules petiolate, approximate, lanceolate, seg. ovate or lanceolate to oblong, apex narrowly acute, margin notched to lobed, lobes falcate to oblique, apex acute; stipes to 1m, approximate, scaly at base, straw-coloured. Tropical America (Mexico to northern S America).

***L. glabella*** (A. Cunn.) Tind. SMOOTH SHIELD FERN. Rhiz. short-creeping or erect; scales to 5×1mm, linear, brown. Fronds to 35×25cm, 2–3-pinnate, ovate to deltoid, apex narrowly acute, membranous, pinnae to 12×8cm, uppermost reduced, oblique, ovate to deltoid, apex narrowly acute, pinnules to 6×2cm, lanceolate, oblong, seg. approximate or distant, ovate to deltoid, apex acute, margin toothed and spiny; rachis glabrous to pubesc. above; stipes to 30cm, approximate and clustered, glabrous or sparsely pubesc. at base. Australia, New Zealand, Polynesia.

***L. grayii*** D. Jones. Rhiz. tufted; scales brown. Fronds to 90cm, 2-pinnate or -pinnatifid, deltoid, lustrous, seg. distant; stipes flexible, sparsely scaly, brown. Sori marginal, dispersed, to 4 per seg.; indusia brown. Australia.

***L. hispida*** (Sw.) Tind. BRISTLY SHIELD FERN. Rhiz. to 8mm, long-creeping; scales to 10×1mm, dense, linear to lanceolate, apex hair-tipped, margin glandular and toothed, lustrous, red-brown. Fronds to 40×25cm, 3–4-pinnate or -pinnatifid, deltoid, apex acute to narrowly acute, leathery to membranous, pinnae to 13×10cm, petiolate, opposite or alternate, erect to spreading, oblique, occasionally falcate, ovate or lanceolate to deltoid, apex narrowly acute, secondary pinnae to 10×6cm, petiolate, ovate or lanceolate to rhomboid, apex narrowly acute, pinnules opposite, seg. to 12×2mm, falcate, ovate or lanceolate to deltoid, or oblong, apex acute to mucronate, margin thickened and toothed; veins simple; rachis and costa scaly, lustrous; stipes to 50cm, approximate and clustered, grooved, scaly at base, pubesc. to bristly, lustrous, grey to brown. Australia, New Zealand.

***L. marginans*** (F. Muell.) D.A. Sm. & Tind. Rhiz. to 7mm, short-creeping; scales to 4×1mm, sparse, linear to lanceolate, margin entire or toothed, brown. Fronds to 70×60cm, 3–4-pinnate, pentagonal, apex acute, leathery and lustrous, glabrous, pinnae to 38×20cm, 13–18 pairs, sessile to petiolate, opposite, erect to spreading, approximate to distant, oblique, often falcate, ovate, apex narrowly acute, pinnules to 16×4cm, 14–20 pairs, sessile to short-petiolate, lanceolate to rhomboid or oblong, apex acute to mucronate, seg. sessile, approximate, oblique, ovate to deltoid, apex acute to mucronate, margin thickened and entire or toothed; rachis more or less smooth, pubesc. and sparsely scaly; stipes to 50cm, approximate and clustered, smooth to rough, scaly at base and sparsely pubesc., red-brown. Australia.

***L. microsora*** (Endl.) Tind. CREEPING SHIELD FERN. Rhiz. to 7mm, long-creeping, branched; scales to 4×1mm, ovate to lanceolate, margin glandular-fimbriate, brown. Fronds to 50×45cm, 3–4-pinnate or -pinnatifid, deltoid to pentagonal, apex narrowly acute, glabrous or pubesc. beneath, pinnae to 40×20cm, petiolate, opposite, erect to spreading, approximate to overlapping, oblique, ovate to lanceolate, apex narrowly acute, secondary pinnae to 20×5cm, ovate or lanceolate to oblong, pinnules petiolate, alternate, erect to spreading, approximate, ovate or lanceolate to oblong, apex obtuse, seg. sessile, opposite or alternate, erect to spreading, approximate, oblique, apex obtuse, margin thickened and toothed; rachis and costa smooth, scaly, brown, stipes to 50cm, to 3cm distant, rough, brown. Australia, New Zealand.

***L. munita*** (Mett.) Tind. Rhiz. to 6mm, long-creeping; scales to 3×1mm, sparse, ovate to lanceolate, margin entire or glandular-fimbriate, lustrous, brown to black. Fronds to 50×45cm, catadromous, 2–3-pinnate, pentagonal, apex narrowly acute, leathery, lustrous above, pinnae to 25×19cm, petiolate, opposite or subopposite to alternate, erect to spreading, approximate or distant, falcate, ovate to lanceolate, apex narrowly acute, pinnules to 15×6cm, sessile or petiolate, alternate, erect to spreading, distant, lanceolate or elliptic to oblong, apex truncate or obtuse, base unequal and acroscopically auriculate, seg. sessile, alternate, erect to spreading, approximate, elliptic to oblong, apex truncate, margin thickened and toothed; rachis smooth to rough, pubesc., straw-coloured to brown; stipes to 50cm, distant, rough, scaly at base, pubesc., brown. Australia.

***L. nephrodioides*** (Bak.) Tind. Rhiz. long-creeping. Fronds to 90cm, 2–3-pinnate, deltoid, firm-textured, lustrous, pinnae to 10cm, pinnules to 25mm, uppermost reduced, approximate to imbricate, margin toothed to lobed. Australia.

***L. rufescens*** (Bl.) Ching. Rhiz. short-creeping; scales brown to black. Fronds to 45×30cm, initially involute, 2–3-pinnate or -pinnatifid, deltoid, lustrous, glabrous, initially dark green to purple, pinnae to 20×10cm, uppermost reduced, deltoid, pinnules lanceolate, margin toothed to lobed; rachis sparsely pubesc.; stipes to 45cm, stiff, glabrous or sparsely pubesc. Tropical Asia (Sri Lanka to Java, New Caledonia, Bali), Australia.

***L. smithiana*** Tind. Rhiz. to 4cm, tufted to erect; scales linear to lanceolate, margin glandular-fimbriate, brown. Fronds to 45×45cm, more or less anadromous, 2–4-pinnate or -pinnatifid, deltoid, apex narrowly acute, stiff, sublustrous, pinnae to 28×22cm, 10–25 pairs, petiolate, distant, oblique, falcate, ovate to lanceolate, apex narrowly acute, secondary pinnae to 18×5cm, 12–15 pairs, distant, seg. alternate, approximate, falcate, rhomboid to oblong, apex obtuse, margin thickened, toothed and spiny; veins forked; rachis glabrous below, straw-coloured; stipes to 55cm, approximate and clustered, scaly at base, pubesc. above, lustrous above. Australia.

***L. velutina*** (A. Rich.) Tind. Rhiz. erect; scales to 15mm, linear, brown. Fronds to 45×40cm, 2–4-pinnate, deltoid, membranous, pubesc., pinnae to 25×15cm, uppermost reduced, oblique, ovate to deltoid, secondary pinnae to 10×4cm, lanceolate, pinnules to 2×1cm, uppermost reduced, oblong, seg. deltoid to oblong, apex acute to obtuse; rachis and costa pubesc.; stipes to 50cm, approximate and clustered, scaly at base, pubesc. above, brown. New Zealand.

***L. shepherdii*** (Kunze ex Mett.) Tind. See *L. acuminata.*
For further synonymy see *Aspidium, Ctenitis, Deparia, Dryopteris, Lastrea, Phegopteris, Polystichum* and *Rumohra.*

**Latace** Philippi. Liliaceae (Alliaceae). 1 species, a perennial herb, allied to *Leucocoryne* but with a more tubular perianth and style included. Bulb tunicated. Leaves 2, basal, narrow. Scape to 25cm; flowers small, in a terminal umbel; spathe valves 2, lanceolate; perianth segments 6, white, lower half united into a tube, white; stamens 3, staminodes 3. Summer. Chile. Z9.

CULTIVATION As for *Leucocoryne.*

***L. volckmanni*** Philippi. As for the genus.

**Latania** Comm. (From the vernacular Mauritian name.) Palmae. 3 species of pleonanthic, dioecious palms to *c*16m. Stem solitary, erect, with elliptic scars, roughened, sometimes swollen at base.

Crown dense; leaves costapalmate, marcescent or neatly abscising, to 3m, tinged red, blue or yellow; sheath angled, base split, glabrous or tomentose; petiole to 1m, channelled above near base, distally flattened, convex and floccose beneath, sometimes armed with shallow marginal teeth; adaxial hastula conspicuous, abaxial hastula absent; blade divided to half its length into segments, segments single-fold, rigid, sometimes divided again at apex, acute or acuminate, pale-grey floccose or waxy beneath. Male inflorescences interfoliar, shorter than leaves with short branches arising from tubular bracts, branched again at apex into 1–14 radiating and rigid rachillae; flowers borne in pits formed by overlapping bracteoles; sepals 3; petals 3, free or basally connate; stamens 15–30; pistillode columnar. Female inflorescences less branched than male, with only 1–2 rachillae sheathed in fewer bracts; flowers subtended and exceeded by bracteoles; sepals 3, overlapping, rigid; petals resembling sepals; staminodes 6–9, united to form cup; pistil 3-celled, globose. Fruit to 5×2.5cm, oblong or obovoid, with apical stigmatic remains, 3-seeded, smooth, yellow-green to brown; endocarp of obovoid pyrenes, variously sculptured. Mascarene Is.; almost extinct in the wild. Z10.

CULTIVATION *Latania* spp. are usually found in exposed coastal habitats and experience marked seasonal rainfall, with cooler, drier, conditions in winter. They are extremely handsome fan palms, with beautifully formed and well-coloured foliage and are well suited to cultivation in the coastal tropics. In temperate zones they need the protection of the warm glasshouse with good light and deep pots of rich and well-drained growing media. Propagate by fresh seed.

***L. loddigesii*** Mart. BLUE LATAN. To 15m. Lf blades to 1.5m, blue-green. Infl. to 1.5m, with 5–12 branches; male rachillae lanate, to 25cm. Fr. to 6cm; seeds irregularly and coarsely ribbed at apex with a central longitudinal ridge. Mauritius Is.

***L. lontaroides*** (Gaertn.) H.E. Moore. RED LATAN. 10–16m. Stem to 20cm. Lf blades to 1.5m, grey-green; petiole and base of blade tinged red-purple; hastula broad and rounded. Infl. to 1.5m; male rachillae to 30cm, glabrous. Fr. to 4.5cm; seeds with low, curved ribs on one side. Réunion.

***L. verschaffeltii*** Lem. YELLOW LATAN. 12–16m. Stem to 20cm diam. Lf blades to 1.35m, tinged pale green and edged yellow; hastula small. Male infl. to 3m, male rachillae to 30cm, glabrous; female infl. to 1.8m. Fr. to 5cm; seeds parallel-sided with one strong central rib and pointed apex. Rodrigues Is.

***L. aurea*** Duncan. See *L. verschaffeltii*.
***L. borbonica*** Lam. See *L. lontaroides*.
***L. commersonii*** J.F. Gmel. See *L. lontaroides*.
***L. rubra*** Jacq. See *L. lontaroides*.

**Lathraea** L. (From Gk *lathraios*, hidden: most of the plant is subterranean.) Scrophulariaceae. Some 7 species of parasitic, rarely saprophytic herbs, lacking chlorophyll. Leaves borne in 4 rows on largely subterranean rhizomes, ivory to mauve, fleshy, scale-like, closely involute, adaxial surface forming a permeable cavity. Inflorescence a racemose extension of stems; flowers axillary, among scales; corolla 2-lipped; calyx erect, campanulate, 4-lobed; corolla 2-lipped, upper lip hooded, lower lip entire or 3-lobed; stamens 4, concealed or protruding from upper lip; style apically decurved. Fruit a bivalved capsule. Summer. Temperate Europe, Asia. Z6.

CULTIVATION *L. squamaria*, the species most commonly grown, is usually encountered in company with hazel, alder, beech and elm on rich, calcareous woodland soils; *L. clandestina*, also seen in gardens, usually with willow or poplar. Both possess a curious beauty, the latter especially, its amethyst flowers breaking the soil surface and leaf litter in early spring and set among dull, fleshy bracts. *L. squamaria* is best naturalized in damp, dark woodland gardens. *L. clandestina* will flourish in more open sites provided they are never dry. Seed of both should be mixed with the tilth surrounding fibrous roots of host plants in summer or autumn.

***L. clandestina*** L. Stems partly or completely subterranean, freely branching to form pale yellow clumps. Scale lvs reniform, alternate or opposite. Raceme 4–8-fld, subterranean except tip and fls; pedicels to 3cm; cal. 16–20mm, glabrous, pale lilac; cor. to 5cm, amethyst, lower lip shorter than upper. Fr. ovoid, to 5mm, reticulate to rugose. Parasitic on Salicaceae. SW Europe, naturalized in GB.

***L. squamaria*** L. TOOTHWORT. Perenn., white or pale yellow below ground, pale lilac above. Stems to 30cm, erect, appearing above ground to flower. Scale lvs alternate, dense, scattered above. Raceme spike-like, secund; pedicels short; bracts broadly ovate; cal. glabrous to glandular-pubesc., to 1cm; cor. 15–20mm, white, tinted rose or lilac. Fr. subglobose to ovoid. Parasitic on many species, especially *Alnus*, *Corylus* and *Fagus*. Europe.

**Lathyrus** L. (Name used by Theophrastus, from the Ancient Gk name for the pea or pulse, combining *la-*, very, and *thoures*, a stimulant: the seeds were said to have excitant or irritant properties.) Leguminosae (Papilionoideae). VETCHLING; WILD PEA. 110+ species of annual or perennial herbs, often climbing by means of tendrils on the leaves. Stems usually winged. Leaves usually paripinnate, occasionally reduced to grass-like phyllodes; stipules often leaf-like; leaflets usually distinctly parallel-veined. Flowers in axillary racemes, or single, axillary; calyx actinomorphic to 2-lipped; keel usually obtuse; stamens 10, 1 free; style pubescent below. Fruit a narrow-oblong, flat, dehiscent legume, 2+-seeded. Eurasia, N America, mts of E Africa and temperate S America.

CULTIVATION Grown primarily for their decorative qualities; those described have handsome flowers, are often fragrant and most will tolerate temperatures below −15°C/5°F. Some are useful as green manure and in erosion control, for example *L. hirsutus*, *L. sativus* and *L. sylvestris*. Most climb by means of tendrils, and are useful for clothing trellis and pergola or for trailing unsupported over walls, slopes and embankments etc. *L. japonicus* ssp. *maritimus*, a sprawling native of sand and shingle beaches, is especially useful for hot, sunny banks, and is sometimes grown on the rock garden with due consideration for its vigour. *L. splendens*, with rich red-crimson blooms, *L. nervosus*, with periwinkle blue flowers, and *L. pubescens* are suitable for similar uses where winter temperatures do not fall much below zero for prolonged periods; *L. nervosus* thrives best in zones with cool moist summers.

The perennial clump-forming species are suited to the flower border (in particular those without tendrils formerly included in *Orobus*) some of these are suitable in scale for the rock garden, among them *L. gmelinii* (*L. aureus* hort.) with rich, deep orange yellow flowers, *L. hirsutus*, *L. niger* and *L. vernus*. The last is especially delightful in late winter when its light bunches of emerging stems packed with rose and mauve blooms bring relief to the woodland garden and the foreground of herbaceous borders.

*L. palustris* is well adapted to the bog garden and, with *L. venosus*, to other damp situations that approximate to their natural habitat; similarly, *L. sylvestris* is eminently suited to wild gardens and native plant collections. *L. latifolius*, the everlasting sweetpea, is a favourite plant for cottage gardens.

Grow *Lathyrus* spp. in any moderately fertile, well-drained soil in sun, or in light dappled shade for *L. rotundifolius*, *L. grandiflorus*, *L. venosus* and *L. sylvestris*. *L. latifolius*, *L. vernus*, *L. niger* and *L. luteus* are tolerant of part day shade. Provide appropriate support (i.e. canes, trellis or host-shrubs for climbers, for semi-scandent or erect perennials, a few birch twigs pushed into the ground around their crowns should suffice), dead head throughout the season and cut back in autumn to ground level. An annual application of a general fertilizer may be given on very poor soils.

Propagate from pre-soaked seed under glass in early spring or *in situ* in spring, also by division in early spring. This last method is most successful other *L. vernus* and the non-climbing species; many of the climbing perennials do not transplant well and even seed-grown specimens are best planted out when young and left undisturbed.

*L. odoratus* (sweetpea) has been subjected to much horticultural improvement on both sides of the Atlantic, giving rise to a range of types of classes suited to a variety of horticultural purposes. The tall types, 2–3m/6½–10ft or more in height, with long-stemmed blooms, are grown for cutting and exhibition; they are judged on trueness of colour, freshness, placement, size and form of bloom, and its proportion to stem length, and on presentation. Tall sweetpeas include the Grandiflora types, commonly known as 'old-fashioned' sweetpeas, raised mostly before 1900 by Henry Eckford; some named varieties are still available. Old-fashioned types are valued for their dainty and beautifully scented flowers in a range of intense colours, but they have been largely superseded by the Spencer types, originating in the early years of the 20th century primarily from 'Countess Spencer' and 'Gladys Unwin', and differing from earlier types in the much enlarged, frilled or waved standards. The multitude of modern Spencer sweetpeas show almost infinite variation in size and degree of waviness or frilling, length of stem, number and spacing of flowers in the raceme, some with doubling of the standard, and with a colour range including selfs, bicolours, picotees and those with flecks and ripples of contrasting colour. Other talls include the Early Multiflora Giganteas, earlier-flowering than Spencer types, the Cuthbertson Floribundas, also earlier, with a reputation for tolerance of hot weather, and the Galaxy and Mammoth series; all show an increased number of blooms per stem.

Dwarf types are plants of bushy habit reaching heights of 15–30cm/6–12in., with large but short-stemmed flowers, less useful for cutting but well suited to tubs, pots and boxes, and as edging and bedding plants; they require little or no support other than perhaps a layer of pea sticks to keep the foliage off the soil in wet seasons. These include the Little Sweetheart series. The Cupid and Patio series are classified as dwarf prostrate forms, usually achieving heights of above 10cm/4in. The Snoopea series are prostrate but slightly taller, 30cm/12in. Semi-dwarfs or intermediates, to 100cm/39in. in height, include the Jet Set, Knee High and Continental series. They have the advantage of being largely self-supporting, with longer-stemmed flowers than dwarf types.

Sweetpeas are grown using the natural system where a supply of cut flowers is required, on the cordon system for larger blooms for cutting and exhibition, and under glass for early blooms. Under the natural system, plants are grown in rows, into soil prepared in autumn by the incorporation of well-rooted manure or compost, with pea sticks or netting for support for tall types. Sow seed in autumn, and overwinter in the cold frame, or sow in spring under glass or *in situ*. In mild winter areas, seed may be sown *in situ* in autumn. All side shoots are left on, faded blooms are removed, and feeding and watering as necessary will prolong the flowering season.

For cordon culture, ground preparation is more thorough. In autumn prepare a bed, two spits (45cm/18in.) deep, and a metre wide (for a double row), incorporating well-rotted animal manure by double digging. The addition of bonemeal in new beds is beneficial and where necessary apply lime to achieve pH 6.5–7. The site should be sunny and open and rows ideally run north to south; shelter to north and east is desirable. Sow pre-soaked or chipped seed in autumn or early winter, into well-crocked pots or boxes of loam-based propagating mix, or into a 4:1:1 mix of loam, leafmould and sharp sand. Overwinter in a well-ventilated cold frame, giving protection of frame lights only when temperatures drop below zero; where temperatures drop below −2°C/28°F, protect with additional hessian sacks or similar material. In late winter/early spring, stop plants to encourage grown of side shoots, harden off for planting out in mid-spring or late spring (depending on sowing date).

The cordon consists of a framework of wires between stout posts with a cane for each plant tied into the framework. Plant firmly at the base of the cane, and when plants are established and have reached 25–30cm/10–12in., select the strongest leader and tie in to the cane; exceptionally vigorous varieties are grown on with two leaders. All subsequent side-shoots and tendrils are removed, either at the base or by removing the growing tip beyond the first pair of leaves. Tie in at each leaf joint, with wire rings or raffia, and remove the first few flower stems.

Plants in full bloom may be given a fortnightly application of high phosphate fertilizer, (e.g. 5:15:5 NPK), but all additional feeding must be done judiciously to avoid oversoft, pest- and disease-prone growth. An organic mulch of spent hops, straw or very well rotted manure retains moisture and keeps the plants weed free. It is common practice to 'drop' plants which may reach the top of their canes well before the end of the flowering season, to obtain improved quality blooms at a convenient height for cutting. Remove ties, lay plants carefully along the row, and gently bend the top 30–40cm/12–16in. of growth upwards, re-attaching to a conveniently placed cane. Plants resume flowering in about 14–16 days.

For early blooms in the cold glasshouse, autumn-sown plants are brought under glass in winter and planted out into a prepared site in the glasshouse border, or into large pots of a medium-fertility loam-based mix. Provide a minimum temperature of 5–10°C/40–50°F, good ventilation, and bright indirect light; reduce water when temperatures are low to avoid bud drop. Early-flowering varieties are most suitable for glasshouse cultivation; those in the peach/salmon pink colour range retain their colour particularly well, when grown under these conditions.

The foliage of *Lathyris* spp. may become infested by thrips, especially onion thrips (*Thrips tabaci*), polyphagous aphids particularly the peach potato aphid (*Myzus persicae*) and gall midge, the pea midge *Continaria pisi*. The flowers may be damaged by bumble bees or become infested with pollen beetles (*Meligethes* spp.). Seedlings are vulnerable to slugs and snails and roots may be injured by symphylids and the larvae of fungus ghats. Mice may remove and/or resow seed at sowing time. Birds, especially sparrows take seedlings on emergence.

A foot and root rot, in which roots and stem bases are discoloured and eventually decay, can be caused by the fungi *Aphanomyces euteiches, Rhizoctonia solani* or *Thielaviopsis basicola*. Seedlings should be raised in a sterile medium but if the disease does occur a systemic fungicide drench may give some control. White mould, which resembles powdery mildew, is caused by the fungus *Ramularia deusta*; a white, powdery growth occurs on the stems and on both leaf surfaces. The disease is favoured by damp conditions and sulphur or dithiocarbamate fungicides have been recommended for its control. Sweetpeas can also be affected by crown gall (*Agrobacterium tumefaciens*), damping-off (*Phytophthora* and *Pythium* spp.), downy mildew (*Peronospora viciae*), fasciation (*Corynebacterium fascians*), grey mould (*Botrytis cinerea*), powdery mildew (*Erysiphe polygoni*), sclerotinia rot (*Sclerotinia sclerotiorum*) and wilt (*Fusarium* spp.). Several aphid-transmitted viruses including bean yellow mosaic, pea venation mosaic and pea mosaic affect sweetpeas causing such symptoms as leaf vein-clearing, mottling and yellowing as well as flower colour breaks. Aphid control is unlikely to give fully effective control and any obviously affected plants should be rogued. White clover mosaic virus, which causes leaf mottling and flower distortion is easily transmitted by contact if healthy plants are handled after touching affected ones. Bud drop sometimes occurs as a result if overwatering, sudden temperature drops or from too little sun.

***L. aphaca*** L. YELLOW VETCHLING. Annual to 1m; stem angled. Mature lvs terminate in a tendril; stipules to 5×4cm, paired, leaf-like, hastate, grey-green; leaflets 1 pair on juvenile lvs, absent on mature lvs. Fls to 18mm, usually single, yellow; peduncles to 5cm. Fr. to 3.5cm×0.8cm, brown, glabrous, 6–8-seeded. Late spring–summer. W & C Europe.

***L. aureus*** (Steven) Brañdza. Sparsely pubesc. Leaflets 2.5–5cm across, in 3–6 pairs, oval to ovate, with brown glands beneath. Fls in racemes; cor. 1.7–2.2cm, brown to yellow-orange. Fr. glandular at first. Balkans. Z6.

***L. cyaneus*** (Steven) K. Koch. Perenn., some 30.5cm. Stem ascending or sub-erect, angular. Stipules to 1.5cm×0.5cm, lanceolate-linear, sagittate; leaflets to 8cm×1.2cm, in 1–3 pairs, linear-lanceolate. Racemes 1–15-fld; cor. to 2.5cm, blue-lilac, white at base; ovules 5–7. Fr. to 4.5cm, linear, acuminate at apex, brown, slightly inflated. Summer. Caucasus. Z6.

***L. davidii*** Hance. Perenn. to 120cm; stems erect or ascending, glabrous. Lvs terminate in a 2- or 3-branched tendril; stipules to 6×2.5cm, semi-sagittate or -cordate; leaflets to 8×4cm, 3–4 pairs, rhomboid-oval, or oval-oblong. Racemes many-fld; peduncles to 10cm; cor. yellow-white, later ochre. Fr. 10×0.6cm, to glabrous, many-seeded. Summer. Manchuria, N China, Korea, Japan. Z6.

***L. gmelinii*** (Fisch. ex DC.) Fritsch non Rouy. To 1.5m; stems erect, glabrous or somewhat pubesc. Stipules to 3×1.5cm, semi-sagittate, ovate or ovate-lanceolate, acuminate, dentate at base; leaflets to 10×5cm, 3–6 pairs, broad-lanceolate, gradually tapering above, acuminate, to 10×5cm, slightly glaucous beneath. Racemes 4–15-fld; cal. campanulate, subglabrous; cor. to 3cm, light- to orange-yellow, brown-striped. Fr. to 8×0.9cm, slightly curved, glabrous, 12–15-seeded. Summer. C & S Urals, mts of C Asia. The name *L. luteus*, a synonym of this species, is misapplied to *L. aureus*. Z4.

***L. grandiflorus*** Sibth. & Sm. TWO-FLOWERED PEA; EVERLASTING PEA. Perenn. to 2m; stems angled, not winged, scabrous to pubesc. Lvs terminating in a 3-branched tendril; stipules linear, occasionally sagittate, to 10×1.5mm; leaflets to 5×3.5cm, 1 pair, occasionally 3 pairs, ovate, weakly parallel-veined. Racemes 1–4-fld; cor. to 3cm, standard violet, growing paler towards the margin, keel pink, wings purple. Fr. to 9×0.7cm, brown, glabrous, 15–20-seeded. Summer. S Italy, Sicily, S Balkans. Z6.

***L. heterophyllus*** L. Resembles *L. latifolius*, but with 2–3 pairs of leaflets, and fls smaller, to 2.5mm. Summer. C & W Europe. Z6.

***L. hirsutus*** L. SINGLETARY PEA; CALEY PEA; ROUGH PEA; WINTER PEA; AUSTRIAN PEA. Perenn. to 50cm; stems angular, not winged. Lvs not terminating in a tendril; stipules to 3×1.5cm, lanceolate to ovate-orbicular, sagittate or semi-sagittate; leaflets to 4×2cm, 1 pair, lanceolate to suborbicular, acute. Racemes 2–6-fld; cor. to 2cm, blue-violet. Fr. 4×0.5cm, linear, pubesc., usually 6-seeded. compressed-globose, brown. SE Europe. Z7.

***L. japonicus*** Willd. CIRCUMPOLAR PEA; BEACH PEA; SEA PEA. Perenn. to 90cm; stems angled, not winged. Lvs occasionally not terminating in a tendril; stipules to 2.5×2cm, triangular-hastate; leaflets to 4×2cm, 2–5 pairs, elliptic, pinnately-veined. Racemes 2–7-fld; cor. to 2.5cm, purple, becoming blue. Fr. to 5×1cm, brown, glabrescent, 4–11-seeded. Summer. Coasts of W & N Europe, China, N America; inland in NW Russia and N Norway. Seeds viable 4–5 years in sea-water. ssp. ***maritimus*** (L.) P.W. Ball. Racemes 5–12-fld; cor. to 18mm. Coasts of W Europe & Baltic, N America. Z3.

***L. laetiflorus*** Greene. Perenn. to 2m; stems not winged. Lvs terminate in a tendril; stipules ovate-lanceolate to lanceolate; leaflets to 5×4.5cm, 4–6 pairs, narrow-linear to ovate. Racemes 5–12-fld; cal. to 1.5cm; cor. to 2.5cm, white or pink-flushed, to blue or crimson. Fr. to 8×0.8cm. Summer. W US (California). Z8.

***L. laevigatus*** (Waldst. & Kit.) Gren. To 70cm. Stem erect, angular, occasionally few-branched, glabrous or soft-hairy. Stipules to 2.5×0.8cm, lanceolate or ovate-lanceolate; leaflets to 7×3cm, 2–6 pairs, elliptic to ovate, usually short-acuminate, blue-green beneath. Racemes 3–17-fld; cal. tubular-campanulate; cor. 2.5cm, yellow. Fr. to 7×0.8cm, black, glabrous, 11–14-seeded. Summer. C Europe to N Spain, N Balkans and N Ukraine. Z5.

***L. latifolius*** L. PERENNIAL PEA; BROAD-LEAVED EVERLASTING PEA. Perenn. to 3m; stems prostrate or climbing, broad-winged, coarsely pubesc., downy or glabrous. Lvs terminate in a 3-branched tendril; stipules to 6×1cm, lanceolate to ovate, semi-hastate, conspicuously nerved, nerves longitudinal; leaflets to 15×5cm, 1 pair, linear to elliptic, acute, thin-mucronate at apex, blue-green, reticulate-veined. Racemes long-stalked, 5–15-fld; cal. broad-campanulate; cor. to 3cm diam., magenta-purple, pink, or white. Fr. to 11×1cm, brown, glabrous, 10–15-seeded. Summer. C & S Europe, naturalized N America. 'Albus' ('Snow Queen'): fls white. 'Pink Beauty': fls dark-purple and red. 'Splendens': fls deep-pink. 'White Pearl' ('Weisse Perle'): fls white. There have been white, pink and red forms, including the following examples: 'Blushing Bride': fls white flushed pink. 'Red Pearl': fls carmine red. 'Rosa Perle' ('Pink Pearl'): vigorous; fls pink, long-lasting. 'Weisse Perle' ('White Pearl'): fls white. Z5.

***L. laxiflorus*** (Desf.) Kuntze. Glabrous or pubesc. perenn. Stem to 50cm, not winged. Leaflets 2–4×1–2cm, each lf with one pair, lanceolate to suborbicular. Racemes with 2–6 fls; cor. 1.5–2cm, violet. Fr. 3–4×0.5cm, pubesc. SE Europe. Z7.

***L. linifolius*** (Reichard) Bässler. var. ***montanus*** (Bernh.) Bässler. Stem to 50cm, winged. Leaflets 1–5(–10)×0.1–1.2(–1.6)cm, in 1–4 pairs, oval or linear. Racemes with 2–6 fls; cor. 1–1.6cm, deep pink to blue. Fr. 2.5–4.5×0.5cm, russet, glabrous. W & C Europe. Z6.

***L. nervosus*** Lam. LORD ANSON'S BLUE PEA. Vigorous perenn. to 60cm. Stem not winged. Lvs terminate in a 3-branched tendril; stipules to 2.5cm×1.8cm, sagittate, oval or suborbicular; leaflets to 4cm, 1 pair, ovate to ovate-oblong. Racemes long-stalked, 3–7-fld; cal. glabrous; cor. to 2.2cm, indigo. Fr. to 6cm×5mm, black, glossy. Summer. S America. Z9.

***L. neurolobus*** Boiss. & Heldr. Perenn. to 50cm. Lower lvs lacing tendrils, upper lvs with simple tendril; stipules to 3mm, linear; leaflets to 12×0.4cm, 1 pair, oblong. Racemes 1–2-fld; cor. to 1cm, blue. Fr. to 3×0.4cm, brown, glabrous, with prominent longitudinal veins, 3–6-seeded. Crete. Z8.

***L. niger*** (L.) Bernh. BLACK PEA. Perenn. to 80cm. Stem erect, angular. Stipules to 10×0.2cm, semi-sagittate, linear-lanceolate; leaflets to 3.5×1.2cm, 3–6 pairs, elliptic or oblong-oval, mucronate at apex, grey-green below, obscurely-nerved. Racemes 3–6-fld; cal. broad-campanulate, short-ciliate at margin; cor. to 1.5cm, lilac-violet. Fr. to 5×0.5cm, sessile, somewhat inflated, 10–12-seeded. Summer. Europe, Caucasus, Syria, N Africa. Z6.

***L. nissolia*** L. GRASS VETCHLING. Annual to 90cm; stems erect or ascending, not winged, glabrous. Lvs simple, reduced to a blade-like midrib, without a tendril, acuminate; stipules to 2mm, filiform. Racemes 1–2-fld; cal. tubular-campanulate; cor. to 18mm, crimson. Fr. sessile, to 6×0.4cm, pale-brown, glabrous or pubesc., 12–20-seeded. Late spring–early summer. W, C & S Europe.

***L. odoratus*** L. SWEETPEA. Annual to 2m; stems somewhat downy. Stipules to 2.5×0.4cm, lanceolate, semi-sagittate; leaflets to 6×3cm, 1 pair, oval to ovate-oblong, to 6×3cm. Racemes 1–3-fld; cal. campanulate; cor. to 3.5cm, typically purple but, of course, now lightly developed and much varied. Fr. to 7cm×12mm, brown, downy, 8-seeded; seeds smooth, black-brown. Summer. Crete, Italy, Sicily. For cultivars and seed races see cultivation note above. var. ***nanellus*** L.H. Bail. Plants compact, not climbing.

***L. ornatus*** Nutt. ex Torr. & A. Gray. Erect perenn. to 30cm or more. Leaflets in 4–7 pairs, linear. Racemes 3–5-fld; fls 2.5cm, purple. US (South Dakota to Wyoming and Oklahoma). Z3.

***L. palustris*** L. MARSH PEA. Perenn. to 120cm; stems ascending or climbing, narrow-winged. Lvs terminate in branched tendrils; stipules to 2×0.8cm, lanceolate or ovate, semi-sagittate; leaflets to 8×1.6cm, in 2–5 pairs, linear to lanceolate. Racemes long-stalked, 2–8-fld; cal. to 1.2cm, campanulate; cor. to 2.2cm, purple-blue. Fr. to 7×1cm, brown, glabrous, 8–10-seeded. Summer. Europe to E Asia, Japan and E North America. Z5.

***L. pratensis*** L. COMMON VETCHLING; MEADOW VETCHLING; YELLOW VETCHLING. Perenn. to 120cm. Lvs terminate in a tendril; stipules to 3×1.2cm, linear to lanceolate, rarely ovate; leaflets 4×1cm, 1 pair, linear-lanceolate to elliptic. Racemes long-stalked, 2–12-fld; cal. 0.8cm, tubular-campanulate, sparsely white-pubesc.; cor. to 1.6cm, yellow. Fr. to 3.5×0.6cm, sessile, black, occasionally pubesc., 8–10-seeded. Late spring–summer. Europe, N Africa to Asia, Siberia and Himalaya. Z4.

***L. pubescens*** Hook. & Arn. Vigorous climber to 3m+; stems pubesc., glandular. Lvs terminate in a 3-branched tendril; stipules to 3×1.5cm, semi-sagittate, ovoid-lanceolate; leaflets to 7.5×2.5cm, 1 pair, occasionally 2 pairs, elliptic-lanceolate. Racemes 6–16-fld; peduncles to 18cm; cal. villous; cor. 2.5cm diam., lilac or indigo. Fr. to 7.5×0.6cm, 8–10-seeded. Summer. Chile, Argentina. Z9.

***L. roseus*** Steven. Perenn. to 1.5m; stems erect, angular, not winged, glabrous. Lvs not usually terminating in a tendril; stipules to 1.5cm, semi-sagittate, lanceolate or subulate; leaflets to 5×3.5cm, 1 pair, ovate-orbicular, pinnately-veined. Racemes 1–5-fld; cal. short-campanulate; cor. to 2cm, rose-pink. Fr. to 5.5×1cm, pale-brown, glabrous, 5–11-seeded. Summer. Turkey, Caucasus. Z6.

***L. rotundifolius*** Willd. PERSIAN EVERLASTING PEA. Perenn. to 1m; stems angular, glabrous. Lvs terminate in a 3-branched tendril; stipules to 2.5×0.6cm, hastate, oblong-lanceolate, acuminate; leaflets to 6×4.5cm, 1 pair, ovate-orbicular. Racemes 3–8-fld; cal. to 1cm, broad-campanulate; cor. to 2cm, deep-pink. Fr. to 7×1cm, sessile, brown, glabrous, 8–10-seeded. Summer. E Europe, W Asia. Z6.

***L. sativus*** L. INDIAN PEA; RIGA PEA; DOGTOOTH PEA; KHESARI. Annual to 1m; stems angular. Stipules to 2.5×0.5cm, lanceolate, semi-sagittate; leaflets to 15×1cm, 1–2 pairs, linear to lanceolate, acuminate. Fls solitary on stalks to 3cm long; cal. short-campanulate; cor. to 2.5cm, white, pink or blue. Fr. to 4×1.8cm, brown, glabrous, 2–6-seeded. Europe.

***L. splendens*** Kellogg. PRIDE OF CALIFORNIA. Shrubby perenn. to 3m; stems angled, not winged. Lvs terminate in a branched tendril; stipules narrow-lanceolate; leaflets to 7×5cm, 3–5 pairs, narrow-linear to ovate-oblong. Racemes 4–12-fld; cal. to 1.2cm, pubesc.; cor. to 4cm, rose, violet, or magenta-red. Fr. to 8×1cm, beaked. US (California), Baja California. Z8.

***L. sylvestris*** L. FLAT PEA; NARROW-LEAVED EVERLASTING PEA. Perenn. to 2m; stems prostrate or climbing, angular, winged. Lvs with a branched tendril; stipules to 3×0.5cm, linear to lanceolate, semi-sagittate; leaflets to 15×4cm, 1 pair, linear to lanceolate. Racemes long-stalked, 3–12-fld; cal. to 0.7cm, broad-campanulate, to 7mm; cor. to 2cm, purple-pink mottled purple and green. Fr. to 7×1cm, brown, glabrous, 10–15-seeded. Summer. Europe (except extreme N and extreme S, Middle East.) 'Wagneri': fls deep red. Z6.

***L. tingitanus*** L. TANGIER PEA. Annual to 120cm; stems winged, glabrous. Stipules to 2.5×1.2cm, lanceolate to ovate, semi-sagittate or -hastate; leaflets to 8×1.8cm, 1 pair, linear-lanceolate to ovate. Racemes 1–3-fld; cal. 1cm; cor. to 3cm, rose-pink. Fr. to 10×1cm, brown, glabrous, somewhat coriaceous, 6–8-seeded. S & E Iberian Peninsula, Sardinia, Azores.

***L. tuberosus*** L. EARTH CHESTNUT; TUBEROUS PEA; FYFIELD PEA; EARTH-NUT PEA; DUTCH-MICE; TUBEROUS VETCH. Perenn. to 120cm; stems ascending or prostrate, 4-angled, not winged, glabrous, from a creeping rootstock which produces small, fleshy and edible tubers. Lvs terminate in a 3-branched tendril; stipules to 2×0.4cm, linear to lanceolate, semi-sagittate; leaflets to 4.5×1.5cm, 1 pair, oblong-ovate weakly parallel-veined. Racemes long-stalked, 2–7-fld; cal. to 0.7cm, broadly campanulate; cor. to 2cm, rose-pink. Fr. 4×0.7cm, brown, glabrous, 3–6-seeded. Summer. Europe (except N and extreme S). Z6.

***L. venetus*** (Mill.) Wohlf. Resembles *L. vernus*, but stipules ovate-orbicular, leaflets ovate-orbicular, acute, very short-acuminate; fls more numerous, 6–30 on racemes, cor. smaller, to 1.5cm; fr. dotted with brown glands. SE & EC Europe. Z6.

***L. venosus*** Muhlenb. ex Willd. Perenn. to 1m; stems stout, erect or climbing, strongly 4-angled, not winged, pubesc. Lvs terminate in a well-developed, usually simple tendril; stipules linear-lanceolate to lanceolate; leaflets to 6×3cm, 4–7 pairs, oblong-ovate, glabrous to dense short-pubesc. Racemes 5–25-fld; cal. to 1.4mm, usually dense pubesc.; cor. to 2cm, purple. Fr. to 6×0.8cm, glabrous or pubesc. Late summer. N America. Z4.

***L. vernus*** (L.) Bernh. SPRING VETCH. Bushy herbaceous perenn. to 60cm, usually shorter; stems several erect, angular, not winged. Lvs terminate in a point, not a tendril; stipules to 2.5×0.8cm, ovate-lanceolate, rarely linear, semi-sagittate; leaflets to 10×3cm, 2–4, oval to lanceolate, acuminate, weakly parallel-veined. Racemes terminal and axillary, 3–15-fld, to 25.5cm; cal. to 1cm, gibbous; cor. to 2cm, initially red-violet, becoming green-blue. Fr. to 6×0.8cm, brown, glabrous, 8–14-seeded. Winter–spring. Europe (except extreme N). 'Albiflorus': fls blue-white. 'Albo-roseus': fls rose-white. 'Roseus': fls rose-blue. Z4.

***L. vestitus*** Nutt. ex Torr. & A. Gray. Perenn. to 40cm. Leaflets 3.5cm, in 5 pairs. Fls white veined pink or purple, pink to violet blue or purple-red, fading yellow. Fr. 5cm, pubesc. US (Oregon, California). ssp. ***puberulus*** (Wight ex Greene) Hitchc. Taller, usually twining, pubesc. Fls pink to pale purple US (California). Z8.

***L. angustifolius*** Martrin-Donos. See *L. latifolius*.
***L. angustifolius*** Medik. See *L. sylvestris*.
***L. acutifolius*** Vogel. See *L. pubescens*.
***L. affinis*** Guss. See *L. aphaca*.
***L. americanus*** (Mill.) Kupicha. See *L. nervosus*.
***L. andicolus*** Gand. See *L. pubescens*.
***L. armitageanus*** Westc. ex Loud. See *L. nervosus*.
***L. asiaticus*** (Zalk.) Kudrj. See *L. sativus*.
***L. aureus*** hort. non (Steven) Brañdza. See *L. gmelinii*.
***L. azureus*** hort. See *L. sativus*.
***L. californicus*** Douglas. See *L. japonicus* ssp. *maritimus*.
***L. drummondii*** hort. See *L. rotundifolius*.
***L. dumetorum*** Philippi. See *L. pubescens*.
***L. ewaldii*** (Meinsh.) Meinsh. See *L. laevigatus*.
***L. gmelinii*** (Fisch. ex DC.) Rouy non Fritsch. See *L. laevigatus*.
***L. gramineus*** A. Gray. See *L. nissolia*.
***L. incurvus*** Rchb. See *L. palustris*.
***L. inermis*** Rochel ex Friv. See *L. laxiflorus*.
***L. japonicus*** var. ***glaber*** (Ser.) Fern. See *L. japonicus* ssp. *maritimus*.
***L. luteus*** (L.) Peterm. non Moench. See *L. gmelinii*.
***L. magellanicus*** Lam. See *L. nervosus*.
***L. megalanthus*** Steud. See *L. latifolius*.
***L. membranaceus*** C. Presl. See *L. latifolius*.
***L. montanus*** Bernh. See *L. linifolius* var. *montanus*.
***L. myrtifolius*** Muhlenb. See *L. palustris*.
***L. occidentalis*** Nutt. ex Torr. & A. Gray. See *L. palustris*.
***L. petiolaris*** Vogel. See *L. pubescens*.
***L. pilosus*** Cham. See *L. palustris*.
***L. polyanthus*** Boiss. & Bl. See *L. aphaca*.
***L. pseudoaphaca*** Boiss. See *L. aphaca*.
***L. strictus*** Torr. & A. Gray. See *L. laetiflorus*.
***L. variegatus*** (Ten.) Gren. & Godron. See *L. venetus*.
***L. violaceus*** auct. See *L. laetiflorus* and *L. vestitus*.
For further synonymy see *Orobus* and *Pisum*.

**LAURACEAE** Juss. LAUREL FAMILY. Dicot. 45 genera and 2200 species of aromatic evergreen trees and shrub. (*Cassytha*, a parasitic twiner). Leaves alternate, rarely whorled or opposite, simple, lobed (*Sassafras*) or scale-like (*Cassytha*), venation usually pinnate; stipules absent. Flowers bisexual, or plants polygamous to dioecious, with a well-developed hypanthium like a corolla-tube, regular, small, in axillary inflorescence, rarely solitary; perianth 6 (4), usually in 2 whorls, sepaloid; stamens (3–) 9 (–12) or more, filaments often with 2 basal nectariferous appendages, the innermost stamen often staminodal; ovary superior (inferior in *Hypodaphnis*), of 1 carpel, 1-loculed, with 1 large ovule. Fruit a 1-seeded berry or drupe, rarely dry and indehiscent, often enclosed in persistent accrescent hypanthium; seeds with large oily embryo, endosperm absent. Some are grown as ornamentals, especially *Laurus* and *Lindera*. Several provide products of economic importance, such as avocado pear, *Persea americana*, camphor and cinnamon *Cinnamomum* spp., oil of *Sassafras* and timber *Beilschmiedia*, *Litsea*, *Ocotea* (greenheart) and others. Tropical and warm, especially S E Asia and Brazil. *Cinnamomum, Laurus, Lindera, Neolitsea, Persea, Phoebe, Sassafras, Umbellularia.*

**Laurelia** Juss. (From Spanish *laurel*, local name for the type species *L. sempervirens*.) Monimaceae. 2 species of evergreen trees, polygamous or dioecious, aromatic. Leaves opposite, coriaceous, dark green, usually glabrous, entire or toothed, petiolate. Inflorescence a panicle or raceme, axillary, bracteate; male flowers with perianth 5–12-parted in 2–3 series, stamens 6–12, filaments short; anthers 2-thecous, staminodes sometimes present, receptacle slightly concave; female or hermaphrodite flowers with perianth similar to male, elongating in fruit, stamens (when present) similar to male, staminodes always present, ovary superior, carpels several to many, fusiform, pilose, styles persistent, ovule solitary, receptacle concave. Fruit an achene, pilose, enclosed by pseudocarp formed by elongated perianth. New Zealand, Chile, Peru. Z9.

CULTIVATION Strongly aromatic, sometimes buttressed forest trees in habitat, found in moist and wet soils in forest, deep gullies and creek beds to altitudes of 660m/2145ft., *Laurelia* spp. make handsome foliage shrubs or small trees for cultivation in mild climates. They are hardy to about −5°C/23°F but are susceptible to cold winds, and need a warm sheltered position in zones at the limits of hardiness; wall-grown plants may need tying in to give additional support. Grow in sun or part shade in any moderately fertile soil, including limy soils, that do not dry out in summer. Propagate by seed or by semi-ripe cuttings in a closed case; also by layering.

***L. novae-zealandiae*** (Hook. f.) A. Cunn. PUKATEA. To 30m, sometimes taller in habitat; trunk becoming buttressed; bark pale grey. Lvs 3–7cm, elliptic oblong to obovate, obtuse, cuneate, entire or coarsely serrate, glaucescent above, paler below. Raceme to 2.5cm; peduncle silky-pubesc., 5–6-parted, spreading and shorter in female; fil. bearing 2 fleshy appendages; staminodes scale-like; styles silky-pubesc. Pseudocarp 2–5cm, 3–5 valvate; achenes 6–12 per fruit. New Zealand.

***L. sempervirens*** (Ruiz & Pav.) Tul. To 30cm. Lvs 6–9×1–4cm, elliptic to ovate, entire and subrevolute towards base, otherwise serrate, cuneate, glossy green; petiole downy. Infl. a panicle 5–17 fld, peduncle 1–3cm; perianth 8- or more times parted, ciliate; pseudocarp to 3cm. Chile, Peru.

***L. aromatica*** Juss. See *L. sempervirens*.
***L. philippiana*** Looser. See *Laureliopsis philippiana*
***L. serrata*** Bertero non Philippi. See *L. sempervirens*.
***L. serrata*** Philippi non Bertero. See *Laureliopsis philippiana*.
For further synonymy see *Atherosperma*.

**Laureliopsis** Schodde. (From *Laurelia*, and Gk *opsis*, appearance, alluding to the similarity with the related genus *Laurelia*.) Monimaceae. 1 species, an aromatic tree. Leaves 10–45×5–25mm, elliptic, or ovate to obovate, serrate except at base. Inflorescence a thyrse, bracteate; buds partially enclosed by bracteoles; flowers 3–11, staminate or bisexual; perianth segments 8, in 2 whorls, oblong, obtuse, coarsely pubesc., persisting into fruiting; stamens and staminodes in 2–3 tetramerous whorls, more numerous in bisexual flowers, persisting into fruiting; stamens with ovate to ovoid, stipitate staminal glands, anthers cylindric, valvate, staminodes sometimes reduced to glands; ovary superior, absent in male flowers; carpels about 10; style connate. Fruit 10×6mm, a cylindric pseudocarp, 8-ribbed, dehiscing in 3–4 valves; seed a silky nutlet. S Chile, Patagonia. Z9.

CULTIVATION As for *Laurelia*.

***L. philippiana*** (Looser) Schodde. As for the genus.

For synonymy see *Laurelia*.

**Laurocerasus** Duhamel.
***L. caroliniana*** (Mill.) M. Roem. See *Prunus caroliniana*.
***L. lusitanica*** (L.) Roem. See *Prunus lusitanica*.
***L. maackii*** Schneid. See *Prunus maackii*.
***L. officinalis*** Roem. See *Prunus laurocerasus*.

**Laurus** L. (Lat. name for these plants.) Lauraceae. 2 species of evergreen trees or shrubs. Leaves alternate, simple, semi-rigid, aromatic when crushed. Inflorescence an axillary cluster, flowers unisexual or, rarely, hermaphrodite; perianth 4-parted, male flowers with at least 12 stamens; anther opening by valves; female flowers with 2–4 staminodes. Fruit a berry, subglobose, black. S Europe, Canary Is., Azores.

CULTIVATION Occurring in moist rocky valleys around the Mediterranean, and widely naturalized in similar climates, *L. nobilis* is widely grown for its foliage both as an ornamental and culinary herb. Tolerant of clipping, it is grown as screening and hedging in essentially frost-free zones, and is well suited to its traditional use as a tub or large pot specimen trained as a standard or pyramid. *L. nobilis* is reliably hardy to −5°C/23°F; given perfect drainage, warm wall placement and protection from cold drying winds, it will withstand occasional lows to −15°C/5°F and although it may then defoliate, it will recover in spring and early summer. Formally trained specimens may be more safely overwintered under glass.

Grow in a moisture-retentive but well-drained fertile soil in full sun. In containers use a high-fertility loam-based mix and liquid feed fortnightly when in full growth. Overwinter in cool, well-lit and well-ventilated conditions with a maximum temperature of 10°C/50°F. Trim formal shapes in summer using secateurs rather than shears to avoid unsightly damage to the foliage. Propagate named varieties by semi-ripe cuttings in summer or by basal hardwood cuttings of the previous season's growth in mid to late winter; root in a closed case with bottom heat. Increase species by seed sown in autumn.

***L. azorica*** (Seub.) Franco. CANARY LAUREL. Tree to 10m (more in habitat), branches robust. Young branchlets flushed purple, soft-pubesc., aromatic when crushed. Lvs 5–12×3–8cm, lanceolate-elliptic to suborbicular, apex acute, base rounded to cuneate, dark green, glabrous, shining above, paler and pubesc., especially on midrib beneath, with conspicuous venation; petiole to 1.2cm. Fls unisexual, to 9mm across, green-yellow, peduncles pubesc. Fr. 1.2cm, black, ovoid; peduncle 6mm. Canary Islands, Azores. Z9.

***L. nobilis*** L. TRUE LAUREL; BAY LAUREL; SWEET BAY; BAY TREE. Small tree or shrub 3–15m, sometimes more, densely branched. Young branchlets glabrous. Lvs 5–10×2–4cm, alternate, narrowly elliptic to ovate, apex tapered, acute, base tapered, margin often undulate, dark green, glabrous and shining above, glabrous beneath; petiole to 8mm. Fls unisexual, green-yellow, small, peduncle short. Fr. 1–1.5cm, ovoid, black, shiny; peduncle 3–4mm. Mediterranean. 'Aurea': lvs tinged yellow. 'Angustifolia': lvs 3–7×0.6–2cm, narrowly oblong-elliptic. 'Crispa' ('Undulata'): lf margin conspicuously undulate. Z8.

***L. benzoin*** L. See *Lindera benzoin*.
***L. camphora*** L. See *Cinnamomum camphora*.
***L. canariensis*** Webb & Berth. See *L. azorica*.
***L. glandulifera*** Wall. See *Cinnamomum glanduliferum*.

**Lavallée, Pierre Alphonse Martin** (1836–1884). Botanist. Alphonse Lavallée was born in Paris. He established one of the most impressive private collections in the world at his arboretum and fruticetum at Segrez, near Paris, begun in 1857 with the help of his father. He also undertook a critical study and illustration of hardy trees and shrubs. A catalogue of his collections published in 1874 attempted to systematize the nomenclature of forms and varieties of tree genera. He spent much of his later life working on a massive history of the rarer plants in his collection, *Icones selectae ... in hortis Segrezianus collectorum* (1880–85), of which only five parts were published. This was to have been followed by a monograph on the genus *Crataegus*, of which he had a unique collection.

Lavallée was president of the Central Horticultural Society of France, perpetual treasurer of the National Agricultural Society and was offered the post of professor of botany at the Muséum National d'Histoire Naturelle, which he declined shortly before his death. His publications include *Les clématites à grandes fleurs* (1884) and *Arboretum Segrezianum* (1877), as well as articles on horticultural subjects, notably vines. The genus *Lavallea* was named in his honour.

**Lavandula** L. (From Lat. *lavo*, I wash; lavender water, made from oil of lavender, has long been used as a fragrant wash.) LAVENDER. Labiatae. 28 species of aromatic shrubs and subshrubby perennials. Stems branched, erect or spreading. Leaves linear-oblong, simple and entire or dentate to pinnate or bipinnate margins usually revolute. Inflorescence a terminal, long-stalked, verticillate spike, simple or branched at base; bracts differing distinctly from leaves; calyx (8)–13-(15)-veined, cylindrical or urceolate, 5-toothed, subequal, uppermost tooth often appendiculate; corolla 2-lipped, usually purple or blue, sometimes white or pink, upper lip 2-lobed, lower lip 3-lobed, lobes equal. Nutlets 4, elliptic or oblong, smooth or roughened. Atlantic Is., Mediterranean, N Tropical Africa, W Asia, Arabia, India.

CULTIVATION Aromatic shrubs grown for ornament and perfume. A few are frost tolerant to −10°C/14°F, e.g. *L. angustifolia, L. latifolia, L.* ×*intermedia* and their cultivars. Others are frost tolerant to at least −5°C/23°F, e.g. *L. stoechas, L. dentata*, and *L. lanata*. These slightly tender species are worth attempting in Zone 7, however, in sheltered, sunny sites on perfectly drained soils. Oil of lavender has been extracted from several species for its scent and antiseptic properties. Several spp. are grown as bee plants for their high nectar content.

All are found in exposed, usually parched, hot, rocky situations. Although often found on calcareous soils, lavenders are not affected by different soil types but prefer well-drained positions to damp waterlogged ones during winter. The English Lavender complex, *L. angustifolia, L. latifolia* and *L.* ×*intermedia*, are not very long lived, becoming untidy in less than 10 years. They may be trimmed back after 3–4 years to prolong their shape, but in time will need to be replaced by young plants.

*L. canariensis* and *L. pinnata* are attractive shrubs in pots for the cool greenhouse or conservatory. They flower under glass in late spring or early summer but have attractive aromatic foliage all year round. Grow in a loam-based compost, potted on finally into an 18cm/7in. clay pot where they may remain for a number of years. They prefer direct sunlight and frost-free conditions in winter with sparing watering. In summer they may be placed outside in full sun. Plants of the *L. stoechas* complex, and *L. dentata* and *L. viridis*, may be similarly treated. *L. multifida* and *L. viridis* are best treated as annuals, sowing the seed under glass in spring, pricking the seedlings out into a tray or pan and planting these out in a sunny position in early summer. Propagate from seed sown under glass in spring, from cuttings of new growth in early summer or from semi-ripe cuttings put into a cold frame in late summer.

***L. angustifolia*** Mill. ENGLISH LAVENDER. Shrub, 1–2m. Stems tomentose. Lvs 2–6×0.6cm, entire, lanceolate, oblong or linear, tomentose, grey when young, greening with age. Spike 2–8cm, lowest verticil distant from the rest; bracts ovate to broadly obovate, acuminate or apiculate, membranous, glabrous or hispid; bracteoles very small, linear or absent; verticillasters 6–10-fld; cal. 4–7mm, 13-veined, the upper tooth with an obcordate appendage, teeth often purple, lanuginous; cor. 10–12mm, dark purple or blue, lobes large. Nutlets narrowly oblong. Mediterranean. ssp. ***angustifolia.*** Bracts usually shorter than cal.; cal. 4–6mm, appendage on upper tooth obscure. 'Alba': fls white. 'Rosea': fls pink; this cultivar is used in Eau de Cologne. 'Atropurpurea': fls very dark purple. 'Dutch White': tall; lvs to 7cm long; fls white, in small heads, profuse. 'Hidcote': to 30cm, dense; lvs lanceolate, grey; fls lilac, cal. deep lilac, spikes dense. 'Hidcote Giant': tall; fls to 115cm, deep purple. 'Hidcote Pink': as 'Hidcote' but lvs linear; cal. grey, in loose spikes, fls pale lilac-pink. 'Imperial Gem': similar to 'Hidcote', but prolific; lvs grey; fls dark purple. 'Jean Davis': lvs grey-green; fls pale pink, in compact heads. 'Loddon Pink': to 45cm; fls soft pink. 'Munstead' ('Compacta Nana'): to 45cm; lvs small; fls large, blue-lilac, spikes loose, cal. purple. 'Nana Alba' ('Alba Nana'): dwarf and compact, to 15cm; lvs linear, silver-grey; fls white. 'Old English': large, to 50cm; lvs to 7cm; flowering spikes branching, to 115cm; fls pale lavender to violet, spikes dense, cal. lilac. 'Royal Purple': fls lavender, in long heads. 'Seal': tall; stems strong; fls pale lavender. 'Twickel Purple': broad, bushy and compact; lvs sometimes flushed purple in winter; fls purple, spikes long, dense. var. ***delphinensis*** Rouy & Foucaud. Robust. Lvs lanceolate to oblong, scarcely revolute at margins. Spikes tall, more interrupted than in type. Switzerland, France, Italy. ssp. ***pyrenaica*** (DC.) Guinea. Bracts usually exceeding cal.; cal. 6–7mm, appendage on upper tooth distant, hairs on cal. confined to ribs. Pyrennees, N Spain. Z5.

***L. canariensis*** Mill. Shrub to 1.5m. Stems glabrous, much-branched. Lvs to 3cm, green, pubescent, bipinnatisect. Spikes to 10cm, much branched at base; bracts ovate-lanceolate, acuminate, tinged blue towards apex, glabrous; cal. 15-nerved, 3–4mm, scarcely hirsute, upper tooth without an appendage cor. 10–12mm, pubesc. on outer surface. Nutlets oblong. Canary Is. (Tenerife, La Palma). Z9.

***L. dentata*** L. Shrub to 1m. Stems branched, grey-tomentose. Lvs 1.5–3.5cm, oblong, linear or lanceolate, margins crenate-dentate to pectinate-pinnatifid, surfaces grey-tomentose beneath, scarcely tomentose above. Spike 2.5–5cm; bracts 5–8mm, ovate-rhombic to obovate, apiculate, usually lilac or tinged purple; sterile bracts sometimes forming a coma to 1.5cm; cal. 5–6mm, 13-veined, upper tooth with an obcordate appendage; cor. 8mm, dark purple. Nutlets oblong. Spain, N Africa. var. ***balearica*** Ging. Habit smaller. Lvs smaller, more revolute, sparsely tomentose. Spikes shorter, coma often prominent.

Balearic Is. var. ***candicans*** Battand. Lvs, young stems and peduncles white-tomentose; lvs larger margins revolute. N Africa, Madeira, Cape Verde Islands. 'Silver Form': lvs soft, silver; fls large, blue. Z9.

***L. ×intermedia*** Lois. Encompasses various hybrids between *L. angustifolia* and *L. latifolia*. There are many described wild variants which vary in plant size, bract shape, density of pubescence, length of peduncle, etc.; there are also many cultivated hybrids which might collectively come under this name. Many plants previously called *L. spica* L. are of hybrid origin. Z5.

***L. lanata*** Boiss. Shrub to 1m. Stem and lvs persistently white-lanate, tomentose. Lvs 3–5×1.2cm, linear, spathulate or oblong-lanceolate, margins scarcely revolute. Spike 4–10cm; bracts 4–8mm, linear or lanceolate, equal to or exceeding cal.; bracteoles 2–5mm, setaceous; cal. lanate, 8-veined, upper tooth with an elliptic, cucculate appendage; cor. 8–10mm, lilac. Nutlets narrowly oblong. S Spain (mts). 'Richard Gray': habit upright, to 60cm; stems short; lvs grey tinted silver; fls large, rich purple. Z8.

***L. latifolia*** Medik. Shrub, 1–2m. Stems grey-tomentose. Lvs 6×1.2cm, elliptic, spathulate, lanceolate to oblong lanceolate, margins entire, scarcely revolute, densely or scarcely grey-tomentose, glandular, especially on lower surface. Peduncles branching, to 20cm; bracts linear to lanceolate, tomentose, acute, equal to cal. or longer; bracteoles 2–3mm, linear-subulate, green or grey-green; cal. 3–5mm, 13-nerved, grey-tomentose, sometimes tinged purple, teeth obtuse or rounded, upper tooth with an elliptic or ovate appendage; cor. dark purple, 8–10mm, lobes small. Nutlets broadly oblong. Mediterranean. Z7.

***L. multifida*** L. Subshrub to 1m. Stems erect and branched, grey-tomentose and often with large straight hairs. Lvs to 3.5cm, green, sparsely puberulent, bipinnatisect, petiole to 6mm. Spike 2–7cm, branching at base; bracts 5mm, pubesc., cordate-ovate, acuminate; verticillasters 2-fld; cal. 5mm, 15-veined, white-tomentose, upper tooth without an appendage; cor. 12mm, blue-violet, lobes large. Nutlets obovate-elliptic verruculose. S, C & SW Europe, N Africa. 'French Laçe': lvs lacy green-grey. Z7.

***L. pinnata*** L. f. Shrub to 1m; whole plant covered in very short white hairs. Stems branched. Lvs to 8.5cm, pinnate, canescent, lobes broad, petiole rounded, to 3cm. Spikes to 9cm, branched at base; bracts lanceolate, shorter than cal., tinged blue-purple; cal. 4–5mm, 15-nerved, canescent, sometimes tinged purple, upper tooth without an appendage; cor. 10mm. Nutlets oblong. Canary Is. (Tenerife, Lanzarote, Gomera). var. ***buchii*** Benth. Bracts shorter than in type, ovate. Lvs smaller, lf seg. narrower. In cult., often confused with *L. canariensis* Mill. Z9.

***L. stoechas*** L. FRENCH LAVENDER. A polymorphic species. Shrubs 30–100cm. Lvs 1–4cm, linear to oblong-lanceolate, entire, usually grey-tomentose. Spike 2–3cm, peduncles of ranging length; fertile bracts 4–8mm, rhombic-cordate, tomentose, sterile bracts 10–50mm, oblong-obovate, erect, petal-like, red-purple, rarely white; verticillasters 6–10 fld; cal. 4–6mm, 13-veined, upper tooth with an obcordate appendage; cor. 6–8mm, usually dark purple rarely white or pale pink. Mediterranean region. ssp. ***stoechas.*** Peduncle shorter than spike, usually 1–2cm long. Spain to Greece. 'Alba': fls white. ssp. ***cariensis*** (Boiss.) Rozeira. Peduncle longer than spike, usually 20cm long, cal. appendage lobed. Turkey. ssp. ***pedunculata*** (Mill.) Samp. Peduncle longer than spike, usually 20–30cm long; cal. appendage entire, lower bracts exceeding cal.; sterile bracts tinged red, forming a coma, rarely white. 'James Compton': habit upright, to 1m; lvs tinted grey, fragrant; fls deep purple, bracts large, pale purple. 'Papillon': sterile bracts very long, narrow, bright purple. Z8.

***L. viridis*** L'Hérit. Shrub to 1m. Stem and lvs shortly hirsute, usually glandular. Peduncle equal to or longer than spike; upper bracts 8–20mm, green; cal. 5–6mm, tubular, upper tooth appendage to 3.5mm wide; cor. green-white or white, to 8mm. Nutlets rotund-oblong. Spain, Portugal, Madeira. Z9.

***L. abrotanoides*** Lam. See *L. canariensis*.
***L. officinalis*** Chaix. See *L. angustifolia*.
***L. pedunculata*** Cav. See *L. stoechas* ssp. *pedunculata*.
***L. spica*** L. See *L. angustifolia*.
***L. vera*** DC. See *L. angustifolia*.

For illustration see HERBS.

**Lavatera** L. (For J.R. Lavater, 16th-century physician and naturalist in Zürich.) TREE MALLOW. Malvaceae. 25 species of annual, biennial and perennial herbs or soft-wooded shrubs, usually stellate-pubescent. Leaves usually long-petiolate, palmately angled or lobed. Flowers showy, axillary or in terminal clusters or racemes; epicalyx segments 3–9, connate at the base to form a deep or shallow cup; petals 5, obcordate, emarginate, white or rose-purple; styles filiform, stigmatic on the inner edge, as many as the mericarps. Fruit a schizocarp; mericarps 5 or more, uniseriate, each 1-seeded, usually indehiscent. Macronesia, Mediterranean to NW Himalaya, C Asia, E Siberia, Australia, California and Baja California.

CULTIVATION Grown for their showy flowers, usually with beautifully textured petals, the blooms of *Lavatera* are individually short-lived but are produced in generous profusion throughout summer and late summer. *Lavatera* spp. are suitable for a range of garden situations and are usually tolerant of maritime conditions. Annuals such as *L. trimestris* and its cultivars, forming lush mounds of foliage studded with lustrous blooms, are particularly useful as seasonal fillers in the flowers border or for summer bedding; the blooms also last well when cut. *L. trimestris* is occasionally grown as a pot plant under glass, flowering in spring from late autumn sowings. Overwinter in the well-ventilated greenhouse, in full sun with a minimum temperature of 10°C/50°F. *L. arborea*, a biennial which will flower in its first year from seed, is suitable for the mixed border and for more naturalistic plantings in the wild garden, where it will self-seed freely where conditions suit. The elegant *L. cachemiriana*, a perennial with silken blooms carried on slender stems above the downy foliage, and *L. thuringiaca* and its cultivars are suitable for the herbaceous and mixed borders, the last requiring a warm, sheltered position in zones at the limits of hardiness. In zones that are frost-free or almost so, *L. assurgentiflora*, with its richly coloured blooms, proves drought-tolerant and in its native regions is widely planted in coastal gardens and as a windbreak.

Grow all species in full sun in a light, well-drained, moderately fertile soil; too rich soils generate excessive foliar growth at the expense of flowering. Give shrubby perennials such as *L. thuringiaca* protection from cold drying winds and a protective mulch at the root in autumn. Propagate annuals and biennials by seed; sow *in situ* in spring or late summer respectively. Increase perennials by cuttings of basal shoots in spring, shrubs and perennials also by softwood cuttings in spring/early summer.

***L. arborea*** L. TREE MALLOW. Tree-like bienn. or perenn. to 3m, often flowering the first year; stems woody at base, young parts stellate-tomentose. Lvs 8–18cm, orbicular-cordate, 5-, 7- or 9-lobed, the upper more deeply lobed, stellate-pilose, crenate. Fls axillary, in clusters of 2–7 in lf axils; pedicels 1–2.5cm; epicalyx seg. 3, 0.8–1cm, elliptic to suborbicular, accrescent and spreading in fruit; cal. 3.5–4.5mm, triangular, acute, white-pilose, connivent in fruit; pet. 1.5–2.5cm, lilac or purple-red, with darker veins at the base. Mericarps 6–9, glabrous or tomentose, transversely rugose, with sharp edges. Europe, Mediterranean, Macronesia; naturalized in some temperate regions including California and Baja California. 'Ile d'Hyéres': to 3.5m; lvs large, palmate; fls small, magenta, in leaf axils, early summer. 'Variegata': habit vigorous; lvs large, marbled white. Z8.

***L. assurgentiflora*** Kellogg. MALVA ROSA. Deciduous shrub to 6m; trunk grey, twisted; branches glabrous to sparingly stellate-pubesc. Lvs 8–15cm, 5- or 7-lobed, lobes triangular, coarsely toothed, base deeply cordate, white-pubesc. beneath. Fls axillary, solitary or in clusters of 2–4; pedicels recurved; epicalyx seg. 3, 5mm, ovate, connate at the base, persistent; cal. 1cm, campanulate, deeply 5–7-toothed, densely pubesc.; pet. 4cm, red-purple, with darker veins, obovate, emarginate, with long narrow claw; staminal column exserted, glabrous. Mericarps 6–8, 6mm, woody. SW US (Channel Is. off California), naturalized in California and Baja California. Z9.

***L. cachemiriana*** Cambess. Annual or short-lived perenn. herb to 2.5m, soft-pubesc. Lvs subglabrous above, downy beneath, long-petiolate, lower lvs cordate-orbicular, 5-lobed, crenate, upper lvs more distinctly 3- or 5-lobed, the middle lobe acute and longest. Fls solitary in the upper lf axils; pedicels as long as lvs; epicalyx seg. 3, ovate, united to about the middle; cal. longer than the epicalyx; pet. to 4cm, pink, deeply bifid; staminal column villous. Mericarps reniform, smooth. Kashmir. Z8.

***L. cretica*** L. Annual or bienn. herb to 2m, stellate-pubesc.; stems erect. Lvs to 20cm, lower lvs cordate-orbicular, upper lvs truncate, shallowly and broadly 5- or 7-lobed, denticulate. Fls 2–8 in loose axillary clusters; pedicels unequal, shorter than the subtending petiole; epicalyx seg. 3, to 6mm, free nearly to the base, ovate; cal. to 8mm, triangular-ovate, acuminate, slightly accrescent; pet. 1–2cm, lilac to purple. Mericarps 7–11, smooth or slightly ridged, angles rounded. S Europe.

***L. maritima*** Gouan. Shrub to 1.2m, new growth densely grey stellate-pubesc. Lvs to 6cm, suborbicular, 5–7-angled, lobes broadly triangular, acute, crenate-serrate; petioles 2–7cm. Fls solitary or rarely in pairs; pedicels 2–3cm; epicalyx seg. 3, 0.8–1.3cm, almost free to the base, elliptic-ovate, acute; cal. 1.3–1.5cm, campanulate, lobed to the middle, lobes ovate, apiculate; pet. 1.8–3cm, white, rose or pink, with long purple veins at the base, cordate with long slender claws; staminal column dark purple, with white spreading hairs. Mericarps 9–13, prominently ridged, with sharp denticulate edges. W Mediterranean. Z9.

***L. mauritanica*** Durieu. Annual herb to 80cm, stellate-tomentose; stems erect. Lvs suborbicular to cordate, shallowly 5- or 7- lobed, lobes acute, dentate. Fls in clusters; pedicels shorter than the subtending petioles; epicalyx seg. 6–7mm, ovate to oblong, free nearly to the base; sep. 8–9mm, broadly triangular-ovate, accrescent; pet. 0.8–1.5cm, purple. Fr. completely included in the cal. at maturity; mericarps about 14, reticulate, ridged, angles sharp, denticulate. Algeria and Morocco. ssp. ***davaei*** (Cout.) Cout. Differs by its smaller mericarps and more accrescent sep. Portugal and Spain. Z9.

***L. occidentalis*** S. Wats. Small shrub to 1.2m; foliage grey-green, sparsely puberulent. Lvs 5- or 7-lobed, lobes acute, coarsely dentate; petioles equalling or longer than blades. Fls solitary, axillary; pedicels 2.5–3.5cm; cal. densely stellate-puberulent, accrescent in fruit to 3–4cm; pet. 4–6cm, spreading, cream or pale green with purple veins, narrowly spathulate; staminal column 2–3cm, included; styles 6–10, pale purple. Fr. 1.2cm diam.; mericarps 6–10, smooth. Guadelupe and Coronado Is., off Baja California coast. Z9.

***L. olbia*** L. TREE LAVATERA. Shrub to 2m; stems hispid, young parts stellate-tomentose. Lvs tomentose, lower lvs to 15cm, 3- or 5-lobed, middle lobe longest, upper lvs smaller, oblong-ovate to lanceolate, often slightly 3-lobed. Fls solitary, in lf axils or in elongate leafless racemes; pedicels 2–7mm; epicalyx seg. 3, 0.7–1.3cm, united to the middle, ovate-acuminate; pet. 1.5–3cm, red-purple. Mericarps 15–18, tomentose or hispid, not ridged, edges rounded. W Mediterranean. The true *L. olbia* is scarcely cultivated; the plant widely grown under that name is *L. thuringiaca*.

***L. thuringiaca*** L. TREE LAVATERA. Perenn. herb to 1.8m, all parts shortly grey-tomentose; stems erect. Lvs to 9×9cm, cordate-orbicular, 3- or 5-lobed. Fls solitary in the axils of upper lvs or in loose terminal racemes; pedicels to 1.2cm at anthesis, longer in fruit; epicalyx seg. 3, to 1cm, united to about half its length; cal. to 1.2cm, sep. triangular, acuminate, accrescent; pet. 1.5–4.5cm, purple-pink. Mericarps about 20, slightly ridged, edges rounded. C & SE Europe. 'Barnsley': shrub, to 2m; lvs lobed; fls opening white with red eye, fading to pink. 'Barnsley Perry's Dwarf': habit low, to 1.2m; stems slender; from a cutting of 'Barnsley'. 'Bredon Springs': shrub, to 2m; lvs softly pubesc.; fls dusky pink flushed mauve, packed on spikes to 90cm long. 'Bressingham Pink': to 1.8m; fls pale pink. 'Burgundy Wine': habit sprawling, to 1.2m high; fls vivid light peony-purple. 'Candy Floss': lvs softly tinted grey; fls bright pink, stamens white. 'Ice Cool' ('Peppermint Ice'): to 1.8m; lvs pale green; fls pure white, occasionally fading to pink. 'Kew Rose': habit robust, to 4m; fls dark pink. 'Rosea': to 2m; lvs downy, tinted grey; fls pinky mauve, in leaf axil, free-flowering, long-lasting. 'Shorty': habit semi-prostrate, to 1m high; a sport of 'Rosea'. 'Wembdon Variegated' ('Variegata'): to 2m; lvs marbled yellow and white; fls dark pink. Z8.

***L. trimestris*** L. Annual herb to 1.2m, sparsely covered with strigose simple or few-rayed deflexed hairs; stems erect or ascending. Lvs 3–6×3–7cm, suborbicular to cordate, upper lvs slightly 3-, 5- or 7-lobed. Fls solitary in axils of upper lvs; pedicels usually exceeding the subtending petioles; epicalyx seg. 3, united for most of their length, broadly ovate, accrescent; sep. 1–1.4cm, connivent in fruit; pet. 2.5–4.5cm, white, rose, pink or red. Mericarps 10–15, ridged, covered by a discoid expansion of the central axis, dorsally rounded. Mediterranean. 'Loveliness': to 1.2m; fls large, trumpet-shaped, striking deep rose. 'Mont Blanc': habit dwarf and compact, to 50cm; lvs dark green; fls pure white. 'Pink Beauty': habit dwarf and bushy, to 60cm; fls large, delicate pale pink with violet veins and eye area. 'Silver Cup': habit dwarf and bushy, to 60cm; fls large, to 12cm diam., glowing pink. 'Splendens': fls large, white or red.

***L. alba*** Medik. See *L. trimestris*.
***L. bicolor*** Rouy. See *L. maritima*.
***L. davaei*** Cout. See *L. mauritanica* ssp. *davaei*.
***L. insularis*** S. Wats. See *L. occidentalis*.
***L. olbia*** hort. non L. See *L. thuringiaca*.
***L. rosea*** Medik. See *L. trimestris*.

**Lavauxia** Spach. See *Oenothera*.
***L. taraxacoides*** Wooton & Standl. See *Oenothera flava* ssp. *taraxacoides*.

**Lawns**. A lawn is an area covered with grass or other plants, usually closely mown, to produce a dense low cover. Apart from a reference by Pliny the Younger (61–113AD) to a small lawn on the upper terraces of his Tuscan villa, the widespread use of the lawn is first known from medieval Europe. The medieval standard, as described by Boccaccio and illustrated by sundry painters (especially of 'Mary' or 'Paradise' gardens, like the famous painting in Frankfurt by an unknown artist around 1410), was a meadow spangled with flowers. Similar 'flowery medes' were favoured by the Persians and Mughals; Persian lawns were described by the French Chevalier Chardin in 1688 as 'sown with a mixture of flowers in natural confusion'. Such medes were favoured by the Mughal Emperor Babur.

The word 'lawn' is not recorded before 1674, and its modern meaning as a closely mown cover not until 1733. In the 14th century lawns were used as decorative features, almost always hemmed in with vertical wooden plants, for tournaments, and games such as bowls. The lawn today serves to set off plants in a garden, as a viewing platform for planted areas, or as a surface for games and other recreations.

Most early lawns were made by laying turf cut from wild grassland and then beating it down with a wooden mallet or 'beetle'. The growing of lawns from seed did not start till around 1700. Medieval lawns were only cut two or three times a year, but by the 17th century regular cutting was practised. By 1625, Francis Bacon was able to praise 'closely mown lawns ... because nothing is more pleasant to the Eye than Greene Grasse, kept finely shorn'. This cutting was of course done with a scythe; the lawnmower was not invented until 1830.

Although usually composed of grasses, other broad-leaved species of other families are sometimes used but are seldom successful when subjected to heavy wear. Such species include fragrant chamomile (*Anthemis nobilis*), used since medieval times, dichondra (*Dichondra repens* and *D. micrantha*), hydrocotyle (*Hydrocotyle novae-zealandiae*) and even various species of moss, as in some Japanese gardens. Cotula (*Cotula dioica, C. pulchella* and *C. maniototo*) makes a fine, feathery, close-knit surface of some durability. It will tolerate drought and damp and has been used for bowling greens. once established, it has become quite widely used on bowling greens in New Zealand. In the past, clover, medick and sainfoin were used for lawns in Europe, as well as chamomile, which is still grown in a limited way.

In most instances where any amount of wear is anticipated, grasses are almost always used. Turfgrasses are commonly divided into two main groups depending on their temperature tolerance. Those which grow predominantly in a temperate climate and have a temperature optimum of 15–24°C/60–75°F are known as cool-season grasses, while those which grow best in subtropical or tropical climates and have a higher optimum temperature requirement, 26.5–35°C/80–95°F, are known as warm-season grasses.

COOL-SEASON TURFGRASSES. The cool-season or temperate grass species are used for lawns in Britain, Northern Europe, North America and other temperate regions. The most commonly used species are fescues (*Festuca rubra* ssp. *rubra* and *F. rubra* ssp. *commutata*), bents (*Agrostis tenuis, A. castellana* and *A. stolonifera*), meadowgrasses, which are also known as bluegrasses (*Poa pratensis, P. trivialis, P. nemoralis*), and perennial ryegrass (*Lolium perenne*). *Poa annua* (annual meadowgrass) is a widely found invasive weed-grass of temperate lawns and may often make up the greatest proportion of a lawn, but it is never intentionally sown.

Cool-season grasses are usually sown as mixtures of more than one species, although in many areas of the temperate US smooth-stalked meadowgrass (*Poa pratensis*), also known as Kentucky bluegrass, is sown on its own. In cases of single-species lawns it is usual to blend several cultivars together to give some resistance to disease or improve year-round colour. Although seedsmen sell many different grass-seed mixtures they fall mainly into three types: those which will produce a fine-textured, high-quality turf similar to a bowling green or golf green; those which are able to withstand wear and general use by the family; and those mixed to cope with problem areas such as shady or wet sites.

For the finest lawns a grass species mixture of bents and fescues is used. Browntop and Highland bent (*Agrostis tenuis* and *A. castellana*) are mixed with Chewings and slender creeping red fescue (*Festuca rubra* ssp. *commutata* and *F. rubra* sensu stricto) in a ratio of 20–30% bent to 70–80% fescue by weight. This weighting allows for the much greater number of bent seeds per unit weight than fescues (bents 10–15,000 seeds per gram, fescues 1000–1200 seeds per gram). Such mixtures help give the turf protection against disease, as turfgrass diseases tend to attack individual species. Fescues tend to be susceptible to red thread disease while the bents are more prone to fusarium patch disease. A mixture of both species means that the unaffected species can fill the gaps caused by the death of diseased grasses.

Lawns likely to receive hard wear from the family will need to include appropriate species. In Britain, the major wear-resistant species is perennial ryegrass (*Lolium perenne*); it is usually mixed with red fescue (*Festuca rubra*), smooth-stalked meadowgrass/Kentucky bluegrass (*Poa pratensis*), and browntop or Highland bent (*Agrostis tenuis* and *A. castellana*). Pure swards of smooth-stalked meadowgrass/Kentucky bluegrass (*Poa pratensis*) are extensively used in the northeast, midwest and other temperate regions of the US.

For lawns subjected to less than ideal growing conditions such as shade, grasses which are naturally adapted to such problems will be included in the mixture. Wood meadowgrass (*Poa nemoralis*) is often sown on moist shady sites along with rough-stalked meadowgrass (*Poa trivialis*), although neither species will survive close mowing. Other species included in such mixtures are the fescues, which will grow reasonably well in such areas and take a lower height of cut. Turf timothy (*Phleum bertolonii*) may also be used in place of perennial ryegrass (*Lolium perenne*) on moist areas.

WARM-SEASON TURFGRASSES. While the cool-season grasses have a European origin, the warm-season species come from a number of tropical and subtropical areas including Asia, South America, Africa and southern China. Due to these diverse origins they are adapted to a wide range of tropical climatic zones. The major warm-season species used for lawns and areas of intensive use are the various species of bermuda grass, zoysia grass, and St Augustine grass. These species originated in East Africa, Asia and the West Indies respectively, although all three are now widely distributed throughout the warm, humid regions of the world.

The bermuda grasses include common bermuda grass (*Cynodon dactylon*), Africa bermuda grass (*C. transvaalensis*), Megennis bermuda grass (*C.* ×*magennisii*), and Bradley bermuda grass (*C. incompletus* var. *hirsutus*). Bermuda grass forms a dense, uniform, high-quality turf which tolerates heavy wear.

Three of the zoysia grasses are used for lawns: Japanese lawn grass (*Zoysia japonica*), Manila grass (*Z. matrella*) and Mascarene grass (*Z. tenuifolia*). This species is often used in warm humid regions and areas where the climate is subtropical only in the summer months. It forms a fine if rather slow-growing turf. St Augustine grass (*Stenotaphrum secundatum*) is by nature a coarse-textured, invasive species. Despite this it forms an acceptable species for general-purpose lawns which do not receive heavy wear.

Other grass species for low-maintenance lawns include centipede grass (*Eremochloa ophiuroides*), carpet grass (*Axonopus* spp.), and Bahia grass (*Paspalum notatum*). Their coarse-textured leaves restrict their use to low-quality lawns.

Unlike the cool-season turfgrass species, warm-season grasses are not usually mixed but make a single-species turf. This is because they have a strong creeping habit and do not integrate well, tending to form distinct individual groups which give a patchy appearance. In addition, warm-season species also become dormant and lose their colour at temperatures below 10°C/50°F. In areas where the temperature falls below 10°C/50°F, cool-season species including ryegrass and fescue may be oversown in the autumn to maintain colour during the winter. The cool-season species gradually die out as the temperature rises and the warm-season species start to regrow the following year.

SOIL PREPARATION. The requirements for weed control, drainage, soil cultivation, and irrigation will depend on climatic conditions. Conditions in northwest England, where annual rainfall will vary from 1125mm/43in. to 2500mm/96in. and drought conditions rarely occur, contrast dramatically with areas of Europe and North America where annual summer drought is a regular occurrence. Allowing that exact requirements will vary from site to site, the following basic preparation will be needed for most areas.

Prior to soil cultivation, the site of the lawn should be cleared of all other herbage. If perennial weeds are present they should be removed by cultivation or, if absolutely necessary, sprayed with a suitable systemic herbicide and allowed to die back fully before starting soil cultivation. In addition, the area can be prepared ready for sowing or turfing and left for a period of time for the weed seeds to germinate. The weed seedlings can then be killed off either by further light soil cultivation or by a herbicide spray before sowing or turfing. This technique is known as fallowing and significantly reduces the weed competition experienced by the young grass plants during subsequent establishment.

With the exception of those in arid regions, most lawns require drainage if they are to be fully used. Drain spacing and depth will vary depending on the rate at which water will move through the soil and how much water must be removed from the lawn surface. For a lawn with a deep sandy loam soil and receiving 1000–2000mm/39–78in. of rainwater each year, drains spaced 5–8m apart are probably adequate. On the other hand, a lawn with a clay soil will require more drains while a lawn receiving less rainfall will need fewer.

Once the drains have been installed, with a fall of between 1:200 and 1:300, they should be backfilled to the surface with permeable gravel and sand. Usually 100mm/4in. depth of 10–12mm/3/8–½in.-gauge clean river gravel is placed immediately above the drain; this is blinded with 50mm/2in. of coarse sand and then finally the drainage trench is filled to the surface with a sandy soil.

After all perennial weeds have been controlled and the drains installed, the site intended for the lawn can be cultivated to form the final surface. This may involve ploughing, rotary cultivation or hand-digging, depending on the size of the lawn. For most medium-sized lawns it would be common to rotary-cultivate the area in two or three directions before finishing with hand tools. On soils containing a large percentage of clay, rotary cultivation or ploughing may produce a compacted layer or pan which could affect drainage. In such cases the compacted layer should be broken by subsoiling machines or double digging. At this stage all large stones and rubble should be removed. Additional sand, as described below, may also be added to improve the soil texture.

The ideal topsoil for a lawn is a well-drained sandy loam between 200mm/8in. and 300mm/12in. in depth. This will provide a free-draining yet nutrient-retentive root zone, enabling the grasses to be deep rooted and extract the maximum amount of water and nutrients. Other well-structured soils are also suitable, provided that the lawn is not intended for heavy wear or use during wet conditions. If the lawn is to be used heavily, even in wet conditions, and the soil in the garden is not naturally free draining, then additional sand can be added to improve the drainage rate of the soil. Generally speaking, soil which contains 70% or more of its particles in the medium to fine sand range (0.6–0.106mm) will drain freely even after the compaction caused by people walking or playing games on the lawn.

How much sand is needed depends on the proportion of medium to fine sand already in the soil. For the average garden soil, at least twice as much sand as soil would be required to provide a suitable mixture. Soils with an extremely high sand content may benefit from the addition of fine organic matter to help retain nutrients and water.

If the area requires levelling, the topsoil should be removed prior to levelling the subsoil and then replaced in an even layer. On areas where there is a deep topsoil this would not be necessary provided that there was a minimum of 200–300mm/8–12in. of topsoil over the entire site after levelling. Low areas which need to have soil added should be thoroughly consolidated after every 100mm/4in. layer to prevent sinkage later. In such cases it is also advisable to allow enough time elapse between the filling and final surface preparations to accommodate possible ground settling. Levelling operations should take place before drainage is installed.

Once the site has been levelled and drained, the soil must be firmed to prevent further settling. This is usually done on small areas by treading the area by foot. Failure to do so may leave soft spots which could sink later on, thereby causing the mower to scalp the turf. After the soil has been firmed, the surface should be raked to produce a fine tilth and to remove stones. The final surface should be level without humps or hollows and should have a fine crumb structure without any stones larger than 25mm/1in. in diameter.

After preparing the surface to receive the seed or turf, a pre-seed or base dressing of fertilizer should be applied. This should contain nitrogen (N), phosphorus (P), and potassium (K) to ensure that the major nutrients are available for grass growth. Sites that have not been fertilized for many years are often deficient in all three (especially phosphorus, which is particularly needed at the seedling stage). It is possible to use straight fertilizers such as superphosphate as a base dressing, but it is now easier and more common to apply a compound granular or mini-granular fertilizer which contains all three nutrients. A compound fertilizer containing 10% N, 15% $P_2O_5$, and 10% $K_2O$, applied at 100–150g/m$^2$ and lightly raked into the soil surface, will be suitable for most soils.

The soil pH may also be adjusted at this stage. For most grasses, satisfactory growth can be achieved at pH levels of between 5.5 and 7.0. Fine fescues and bents have an optimum range of 5.5–6.5 while perennial ryegrass, the meadowgrasses and many of the warm-season grasses grow better at pH levels between 6.0 and 7.0.

LAWN ESTABLISHMENT. Lawns can be established from seed, from turf (sod), or by vegetative propagation. Most cool-season lawns are produced from seed or turf, while those using warm-season species are generally produced by vegetative means. Which method is chosen depends on a number of factors including the cost and the desired speed of establishment.

*Seed.* Establishing a lawn from seed is by far the cheapest method, it enables the gardener to sow specific grass species and cultivars; however, seed takes much longer to establish than turf. It is also only possible to sow seed during warm moist periods unless irrigation is available: then it can also be sown during the warm summer months. Mulches of straw, wood chips and bark are used in some countries during hot periods to reduce water loss and encourage conditions conducive to germination. Ideally, cool-season species are best sown in late summer or early autumn, with spring the second-best option. Grass seed should be sown at a rate of 25–30g/m$^2$ for most seed mixtures, although the rate for single-species swards will vary with number of seeds per gram. Pure bent lawns should be sown at a rate of between 8g–10g/m$^2$, while pure perennial ryegrass and smooth-stalked meadowgrass will require higher seed rates. The exact rate of sowing will vary with the seed quality, seed-bed preparation and the estimated losses to birds, other animals and adverse weather conditions. Sowing too much seed may cause conditions which encourage seedling diseases such as damping-off. Fungicides should be applied if disease becomes apparent at this time, especially under warm humid conditions.

Once a seed bed has been prepared as previously described and the amount of seed needed for the area concerned calculated, the seed can be sown. The total seed lot should be divided into at least two halves, one half sown in one direction and the other at right angles to the first. This helps make sure that an even coverage is obtained and that the seed does not run out before all the area is sown. The seed can be either broadcast by hand (marking out the area in metric squares with string and pegs to ensure the correct sowing rate) or sown more accurately by machine. After sowing, the seed should be lightly raked into the surface. On sandy soils the surface can be rolled with a light (50–100kg) roller to consolidate the surface. Heavy clay soils may, however, form a compacted surface which could affect seedling emergence if rolled at this stage, and rolling on such soils should be left until after germination. The grass seedlings will take 7–14 days to emerge from the soil depending on species, temperature, and water availability. Once emerged, a medium roller (250–500kg) can be used (prior to mowing the lawn) to firm the surface and press back into the soil, small stones that may have come to the surface. The lawn should be regularly irrigated in dry weather. When the seedlings are 25–38mm/1–1½in high they should be mown using a rotary mower. Any excess clippings should be raked up and removed. If sown in the late summer or autumn, the lawn should be mown when necessary through the late autumn period, before gradually lowering the height of cut the following spring to that required for use during the summer. Young lawns should be subjected to as little wear as possible during their first season.

TURF. Turf (US: sod), an already established grass sward which is lifted intact and transplanted to a new site, gives an immediate visual effect and can usually be walked on within a short period of time. It is, however, much more expensive than seed and has in the past been found to carry pests, diseases and turf weeds. Nowadays, purpose-grown turf provides a very high-quality lawn and its only disadvantage is its high cost compared with seed.

A number of different qualities of turf are available including meadow turf, treated meadow turf, sea-marsh turf, purpose-grown turf, custom-grown turf and seedling turf. When buying turf, care must be taken to inspect it for desired grass species, soil type, presence of weeds, and the amount of compacted surface organic matter (thatch).

Meadow turf, grown initially for agricultural purposes, tends to contain coarse grasses, including annual meadowgrass and broad-leaved weed species such as the daisy. Treated meadowgrass has been treated with selective herbicide to eliminate broad-leaved weed species. The quality of meadow turf is very variable and this is reflected in its low price. It does, however, have a place for low-quality lawns.

Sea-marsh turf was once considered the finest turf available in the UK because it contains fine fescues and bents. However, it often grows in river estuaries where silt and clay are deposited and care must be taken not to cover a free-draining soil with a silty impermeable barrier. With the advent of purpose-grown turf, fine fescue and bent swards grown on better soils have become available.

Seedling turf, 6–15 weeks old, grown on a shallow soilless medium, is also available. This turf can be quickly grown to order and, because it is grown on a soilless medium, is light and easy to transport. It does not, however, have the maturity of older turf and will need to be protected from heavy use until it has established itself.

Turf is available in a range of sizes. High-quality turf was traditionally sold in the UK in 300mm/12in. squares (originally one foot square), with lesser-quality turf sold in 900×300m/36×12ft strips. Most turf sold by the larger producers is now lifted using tractor-mounted machines which cut turf in units of one square metre (or square yard).

The soil should be prepared as if for seeding, although the final surface need not be finely finished. The turf should be laid with an alternate bond (brick fashion) so that each turf tightly meets the one next to it. Turf should be laid on moist soil so that rapid rooting is encouraged. After the turf has been laid it should be rolled with a light roller to ensure that there are no air pockets between the turf and the soil. In wet conditions, the rolling should be left until after the turf has rooted and knitted together. A light topdressing of sand or sandy loam is then applied over the top of the turf and luted or brushed into any gaps that may be present between the turf. Regular irrigation which penetrates the turf and soil beneath to a depth of 100–150mm/4–6in. will be needed in dry conditions.

Turf can be laid almost year round in Britain, although in the more extreme climates of continental Europe and North America turfing will be restricted by very hot or very cold conditions.

VEGETATIVE PROPAGATION. The three common vegetative means of producing lawns – stolonizing, sprigging and plugging – are only suitable for propagating those species which produce vigorous stolons and rhizomes. The strong, creeping, warm-season grasses such as Bermuda grass, zoysia grass and St Augustine grass are commonly propagated this way, along with the cool-season creeping bent grass in North America. The vegetative propagation of lawn grasses is not commonly practised in Britain. Sprigs, stolons and plugs are best planted in late spring or early summer. The advantage of using vegetative propagation is that less material is required than turf for a given area. It does not, however, give an instant cover like turf and about two months is required for the material to root and spread over the soil.

For stolonizing, the soil is prepared as for seeding and the stolons are spread over the soil at a rate of around 2.25–5 litres/$m^2$. The stolons are then pressed into the surface of the soil and topdressed with a light sandy soil before being rolled with a light roller and irrigated.

Sprigging involves the planting of stolons and rhizomes in holes or furrows 25–50mm/1–2in. deep and 75mm–150mm/3–6in. apart. The sprigs, planted at a rate of 0.5–1.5 litres/$m^2$/¾–2¼ UK pt/sq yd/1–2¾ US pt/sq yd, are then firmed in and irrigated.

Plugs are small pieces of turf, 50–100mm/2–4in. in diameter and deep, which are planted at 250mm–450mm/10–18in. centres. Once planted and irrigated, the plugs produce stolons and rhizomes which fill in the empty ground between.

MOWING. Once the lawn has established, regular maintenance is essential if it is to be kept in good order. The most frequent lawn maintenance operation is mowing. Mowing provides the finished surface necessary for both aesthetic and practical reasons. The height at which a lawn should be cut and how often it needs cutting are both important factors to consider. The height of cut will depend on the type of grasses being grown, the use of the lawn, and the time of year. How often it needs to be cut will be determined by the height of cut and the rate of growth. As a rule, no more than one third of the leaf growth should be removed at any one time if growth is not to be adversely affected.

Fine fescues and bents used in high-quality lawns can take very low heights of cut. Such lawns can be cut as low as 6mm/¼in. in the summer and 12mm/½in. in the winter without causing damage to the grasses. In this instance, the lawn will need to be cut every other day in the summer so as not to remove more than one-third of the growth.

Ryegrasses and other species used in utility lawns grow better at heights between 12–25mm/½–1in. in the summer and 25–37mm/1–1½in. in the winter. In addition, the greater amount of grass will protect the surface against wear by children or animals. Lawns cut at these heights will only need to be cut once or twice a week in summer if no more than a third of the grass is to be removed.

Grass mowing will be at its most frequent in the warm, moist conditions of early and late summer and least frequent in the cold of winter and the drought conditions of summer. For all lawns, infrequent heavy mowing will cause the greatest damage to the grasses and will lead to a deterioration in the quality and density of the lawn.

Four types of mower are available for mowing lawns: the two most commonly used are the cylinder or reel mower, and the rotary (including the hover-type) mower. The cylinder mower gives the best finish, although the rotary type gives perfectly acceptable finishes for utility lawns.

On high-quality lawns, grass clippings should be removed ('boxed off'), especially if the earthworm population has been killed. Boxing off clippings tends to discourage earthworms from returning, lessens the spread of annual meadowgrass seed and other weeds such as speedwells, may reduce organic matter accumulation (thatch), and leaves a better surface finish.

Utility lawns may benefit from allowing the clippings to return, as the clippings will be rapidly recycled by earthworms (which are often not killed on organic lawns), thereby returning valuable matter to the soil. Excessive amounts of clippings should be raked up, as large clumps of cut grass may prevent the turf underneath from photosynthesizing and will provide suitable conditions for the germination and spread of fungal diseases.

FERTILIZERS. How much fertilizer is needed depends on whether or not the clippings are removed, how rapidly water is lost from the soil, how much rainfall or irrigation the lawn receives, and on the species of grass in question.

On heavy clay soils, where clippings are returned and rainfall or irrigation rates are low, only small amounts of fertilizer will be required. It is likely that 30kg of nitrogen per hectare per annum (3g/$m^2$) will keep the lawn in good condition. For a fertilizer containing 10% nitrogen this will mean applying 300kg of fertilizer per hectare (30g/$m^2$). This could be applied as one application at the start of the growing season (mid- to late spring) or split into two and applied in early summer and early autumn after autumn renovations. On lawns such as these nitrogen is probably the only nutrient required each year. Phosphorus and potassium may be needed every 3–5 years.

On light sandy soils, which receive a high rainfall or plentiful irrigation and where the clippings are removed, as much as 150kg of nitrogen per hectare per annum (15g/$m^2$) may be needed. For a fertilizer containing 10% nitrogen this will mean applying 1500kg of fertilizer per hectare (150g/$m^2$). Such a large amount of fertilizer should be applied in at least three applications throughout the growing season. One application in late spring, one application in summer and one after autumn renovation work are the usual times. Unless heavy rain is expected, fertilizers, especially those containing ammonium sulphate, should be watered in after application to prevent scorch. In addition to nitrogen, phosphorus and potassium will also be required at a quarter of the rate of nitrogen for phosphorus and three-quarters of the rate of nitrogen for potassium.

Most lawns will fall somewhere between the two extremes mentioned above and fertilizer requirements will need to be adjusted accordingly. Two types of fertilizer are commonly sold for the amateur market. A spring/summer fertilizer which contains N, P and K, with a high N and low K content, and an autumn/winter fertilizer which also contains N, P and K but has a low N and high K content. This is because large nitrogen applications can encourage diseases such as fusarium patch if applied too late in the year.

Iron (Fe) is not usually applied on its own but is widely applied as a constituent of lawn sand. Lawn sand, which contains ammonium sulphate and sand as a carrier in addition to iron, is used to control moss and encourage grass growth. Some complete fertilizers also contain iron.

Fertilizer must be applied evenly over the entire surface of the lawn. Any variation in the rate of application will usually be more than obvious within a week and excessive doses may cause the grass to be killed off, leaving a bare patch. For best results, the fertilizer should be applied with a properly calibrated machine.

IRRIGATION. It is essential that grass has sufficient water to grow at times of drought. Enough water should be applied to ensure that the soil is moistened to a depth of 100–150mm/4–6in. Shallow watering will encourage surface rooting which will make the lawn more susceptible to drought and in need of more frequent fertilizing. A deep and well-rooted lawn will be able to exploit the nutrient and water reserves in the soil. Heavy infrequent irrigation is in general better than light frequent applications. Water may be applied lightly at times of heat stress to cool the surface of the lawn. This may also help to prevent or reduce the incidence of certain diseases which require very high temperatures to spread. These are not usually found in the temperate climate of Britain but occur quite frequently in continental Europe and North America.

Exactly how much water will be needed to fully moisten the soil will depend on a number of factors, including the soil type and the amount of water already in the soil. A small hole can be dug to see just how deeply the water has penetrated after watering the lawn.

Overwatering, especially on poorly drained heavy soils, can reduce the amount of air in the soil which in turn may lead to the build-up of surface organic matter (thatch), cause restricted root growth and lead to an overall reduction in lawn quality.

SURFACE AND SUBSURFACE CULTIVATIONS. To keep the lawn in good condition it should be thoroughly renovated each autumn. There are two common problems which occur on well-used lawns that lack an earthworm population: soil compaction and thatch accumulation.

On well-trodden areas the soil becomes very compact, this restricts grass root growth and prevents rapid drainage. In addition, on lawns which have become very acidic and from which earthworms have been removed, organic debris (thatch) can build up at the soil surface, a particular problem where clippings are not carefully removed. On lawns which contain earthworms and which have a pH between 6.0 and 7.0, thatch is unlikely to be found unless a very vigorous grass species such as *Agrostis stolonifera* or *Poa pratensis* is used or excessive amounts of fertilizer are applied. To find out whether the lawn needs to be treated for thatch, dig out a small area with a trowel and look for an organic layer between the grass and the soil. If the organic layer is greater than 12mm/½in. deep, then regular treatment is required each year.

To remove thatch and relieve soil compaction, a number of cultivation techniques have been developed which penetrate the lawn. These include scarification, hollow tining (coring), spiking and slitting.

A lawn scarifier has vertical blades which rotate at a high speed and penetrate the lawn up to 12mm/½in. in depth. Scarification removes surface thatch, cuts stolons and rhizomes, and allows air to enter the surface of the lawn. Allowing air into the thatch layer is important as the soil organisms which naturally break down thatch require air in addition to a suitable soil pH. To remove the maximum amount of thatch, the lawn can be scarified to two directions, one at 30° to the other. Light scarification can be undertaken using a wire rake, although this is much harder work than using a powered machine.

Hollow tining or coring, as it is also known, removes cores of grass, thatch, and soil 6–18mm/¼–¾in. in diameter and 75–100mm/3–4in. in depth. The resulting holes can be left open, or more often filled with a suitable sandy topdressing which prevents the hole from closing and, with time, improves the soil. Hollow tining both removes thatch, aerates the soil, and relieves soil compaction. It can be undertaken with a special hand tool or by machine.

Spiking, which can be undertaken with a purpose-made tool or with a hand fork, relieves soil compaction and allows air and more water into the soil, which encourages root growth. The greatest effect of spiking is found if the spikes are angled back after entering the soil, thereby lifting the turf. This creates cracks and fissures in the soil which are very beneficial to root growth, but also causes more surface disruption than straight spiking.

Slitting involves the penetration of the soil with flat, knife-like blades to a depth of 75–100mm/3–4in., which also allows air into the soil and cuts grass stolons, rhizomes and roots.

Heavy scarification and hollow tining are usually only undertaken in early autumn when the warm, moist conditions permit rapid recovery. Light scarification, spiking and slitting can be undertaken throughout the season except in dry conditions when such operations may increase susceptibility to drought.

Bulky topdressing is also beneficial after autumn work as it can aid thatch breakdown, fill core holes, and correct surface irregularities. For most lawns sandy topdressings containing medium/fine sand, sieved soil and peat are best. A 6:3:1 ratio of sand, soil and peat would be suitable for most lawns. The topdressing should be applied at a rate of 1–3kg/$m^2$ on a dry day and luted or brushed well into the surface and core holes. The topdressing should not be allowed to remain on the surface completely covering the grass leaves as this will affect growth.

Rolling the lawn in spring will resettle the surface. Over-use of the roller can, however, cause soil compaction.

Brushing can be undertaken either first thing in the morning to remove dew or to lift the grass prior to mowing. Brushing the dew off the grass, especially in the autumn, helps prevent fungal disease spread by reducing the length of time when conditions are suitable for spore germination and growth.

WEEDS, PESTS AND DISEASES. Broad-leaved weeds should be treated, using a hormonal herbicide or a weed-and-feed fertilizer which contains herbicide. For small amounts of weed, individual plants such as daisy, dandelion and plantain can easily be cut out by hand using a knife or killed by a herbicide applied with a 'spot-weeder'. On the finest lawns, broad-leaved weeds may not be tolerated at all, but on the average home lawn the occasional daisy and other flowering species may add an additional feature to the lawn. Moss is usually found in lawns with poor drainage, low fertility and low pH, but it can be a problem even in the best-kept lawns. Where moss is known to build up it should be treated for each year with a chemical moss killer or lawn sand.

Fungi are the main cause of diseases of lawns and sports turf. It is often difficult to identify the diseases because symptoms vary according to the grass species and environmental conditions. The fact that turf may contain several plant species and that more than one disease may be present at the same time also complicates the diagnosis. Furthermore, dead patches of grass can be the result of causes other than disease, e.g. damage by leatherjackets (*Tipula* spp.), drought stress, fertilizer scorch, nutrient deficiency, spillage of agricultural or household chemicals and animal urine.

Pre- or post-emergence damping-off is caused by fungi such as *Fusarium, Drechslera, Pythium* and *Rhizoctonia.* Prevention depends on good seed-bed preparation, proper drainage and on sowing at the correct seed rate during good growing conditions. Cold moist conditions conducive to damping-off may occur if sowing takes place too early in the spring or too late in the autumn. Fungicidal seed dressings can be used to control pre-emergence damping-off and broad-spectrum fungicides may give some control of post-emergence problems.

Fusarium patch disease caused by *Microdochium nivale* (more familiar as *Fusarium nivale*) is the most common and damaging disease of both lawns and sports turf in the UK. It causes patches of dead grass which are dark brown or orange at their margins and paler in the centre. The diseased grass is usually wet and slimy, and white or pink fungal mycelium, matting the dead leaves together, may be present around the edges of the patches. The disease is favoured by wet conditions, excessive nitrogen and a dense thatch, so good turf management practice is the first line of defence. If conditions are especially favourable to the disease it may be necessary to apply fungicidal sprays; when growth is slow, protectant fungicides can be used but during active growth systemics are more effective. The disease is particularly troublesome on *Poa* spp. (meadowgrass, blue grass). A similar disease usually called fusarium blight caused by *Fusarium* spp. is important in North America.

Pink snow mould or snow mould are names given to another disease also caused by *Microdochium nivale*, when the damage occurs under snow. The dead bleached patches of grass are covered with white mycelium and may have an orange-brown border. Prevention involves controlling fusarium patch disease and not allowing long grass to persist into winter. Fungicides applied after the snow melts will have little effect because the damage is already done. A grey snow mould, caused by *Typhula* spp., is a similar but less uncommon disease whose effects may be reduced by the application of phosphate fertilizer.

Dollar spot is caused by *Sclerotinia homoeocarpa.* In the UK this disease is common in some locations on creeping red fescue (*Festuca rubra*) especially that of sea-marsh origin, but otherwise is not often seen; in the US it occurs more commonly and a wider range of grasses, including *Agrostis, Poa* and *Stenotaphrum* are affected. Infected leaves are white or straw-coloured and the disease occurs in spots of up to 5cm diameter ('silver dollar' size), although in severe attacks these may merge to form larger patches. Poor fertility, especially low nitrogen, favours the disease which tends to occur during wet weather at the end of the growing season. Control can be achieved by providing adequate nitrogen and by fungicide applications, but it is best to grow resistant species or varieties.

Take-all patch, also known as Ophiobolus patch, is caused by *Gaeumannomyces graminis* (syn. *Ophiobolus graminis*). This disease is uncommon in the UK but is very prevalent in the northwest US. It affects many different grasses but especially creeping bent (*Agrostis stolonifera*). Dark brown 'runner' hyphae are visible on the surface of infected roots. Above ground, rings of yellow or orange grass can be up to 1m in diameter although the centre of the patch may be green with weeds and resistant grasses. Wet conditions and surface alkalinity favour the disease. Fungicides are not particularly effective, so management must aim at improving drainage and reducing pH; ammonium sulphate or sulphur can be applied to increase soil acidity and liming should be avoided.

Red thread or pink patch caused by *Laetisaria fuciformis* (syn. *Corticium fuciforme*) is a common and widespread disease especially under conditions of low fertility combined with hot weather. Red fescue (*Festuca rubra*) and perennial rye-grass (*Lolium perenne*) are most often affected but many other grasses are also susceptible. Patches of diseased grass, up to 35cm in diameter, are pink or red due to needle-like threads of fungus sticking out from the leaves. The application of systemic or contact fungicides and nitrogenous fertilizer can control the disease; too much nitrogen, however, will favour other diseases such as Fusarium patch.

Fairy rings, more or less circular rings of mushrooms or toadstools, can be caused by many different fungi but the most common and most damaging of them is *Marasmius oreades*. A fairy ring may be many, even hundreds, of years old and can grow radially at a rate of 30cm or more per year. The ring of dead grass around the outside of the circle is surrounded by an inner and an outer zone where growth is stimulated and the grass is dark green. In the dead area the grass has been killed by the fungus, which breaks down organic matter and releases nutrients, especially nitrogen; the dark green areas are benefiting from this. To be certain of eradicating the fairy ring fungus it is necessary to dig out the soil from the infected area and sterilize the site with formaldehyde. Some fungicides with specific action against basidiomycetes can be effective if mixed with a wetting agent and watered onto the spiked and de-thatched infected area and may be worth trying before the more laborious alternative is attempted.

Other fungi may cause unsightly darker rings without killing the grass: the rings are more conspicuous if lawns are unfertilized and lacking nitrogen.

There are many other, usually less important, fungus diseases of grasses including anthracnose (*Colletotrichum graminicola*), copper spot (*Gloeocercospora sorghi*), grey leaf spot (*Pyricularia grisea*), melting out (*Drechslera poae*), powdery mildew (*Erysiphe graminis*), pink patch (*Limonomyces* spp.), rusts (*Puccinia* and *Uromyces* spp.) and smuts (*Ustilago* spp.).

Turf grasses can be affected by a wide range of pests, most of which feed underground or at soil level. The roots can be eaten by leatherjackets (the larvae of crane flies) and chafer grubs (larvae of various beetles such as the garden chafer and May bugs). The latter group also includes Japanese beetle, which is a serious pest in the US, where other root-feeding pests such as nematodes and mole crickets may also cause problems. In North America lawns may also be damaged by caterpillars of sod webworms (e.g. *Crambus teterrellus*), cutworms and army worms (larvae of various moths) feeding on stems and leaves at soil level, and by sap-feeding insects such as chinch bugs (*Blissus leucopterus*) and various leafhoppers. Several pests such as moles, ants, burrowing bees and earthworms spoil a lawn's appearance by depositing soil on the surface. This can interfere with mowing and create muddy patches on the lawn. Ant nests may also cause grass roots to dry out. Confirmation of a pest attack can easily be made if the infected part of the lawn is dug up. The pest can usually be seen in the soil as it feeds on the grass plants. Some pests such as nematodes are, however, very small and may need to be identified in a laboratory. Most of the insect pests can be controlled by treating the lawn with an appropriate pesticide, usually when the newly hatched larvae or nymphs are present rather than when obvious signs of damage caused by the older stages are seen.

Some grass species are resistant to pest and disease attack: a degree of resistance to sod webworm and leaf spot has been found on *Poa pratensis*.

AMENITY GRASSLAND. Grassland which is used primarily for recreational and aesthetic purpose is generally referred to as amenity grassland. A distinction can be made between the intensive amenity areas such as lawns and sports areas and extensive amenity areas such as road verges and country parks. In some instances, the distinction between agricultural and amenity grassland may become blurred. Animals may be grazed on extensive amenity areas such as golf courses and country parks which are designated primarily for recreational purposes. Indeed, in country parks the animals, which may be rare breeds of sheep and cattle, may themselves form part of the amenity feature.

SPECIES-RICH GRASSLAND. The management and/or establishment of a grass area may encourage a floristically rich sward. Such a sward will be composed of a number of broad-leaved species grown among the grasses for their attractive flowers. It is the flowery mede *in extenso*. They are found naturally on sites which are regularly grazed by animals such as sheep and rabbits and are nutritionally poor, thus restricting the vigour of the associated grass species. Many people appreciate the diverse and attractive nature of such areas not only for the plant species which grow in them but also for the insect and other animal life associated with them. This has led many groups and individuals to establish species-rich grassland on roadside verges, waste areas, and in areas of the garden where regular close mowing is not essential.

Floristically rich swards can be established by allowing the natural flora to develop unaided or by introducing species which would normally survive under the environmental conditions present on site. To encourage the natural seeding of species already present in the sward, the herbage should not be cut until it has set seed. This usually means not cutting the area until at least the first week of July in Britain. To develop a floristically rich area in an already established area of grassland which contains few broad-leaved species requires the seed of desired species to be scattered or slot-seeded into the turf. Some success has been gained with this method, although it is likely that a high proportion of the seed sown may not develop into established plants. To overcome the competition of the established sward with the wild-flower seedlings, the seeds can be first germinated in pots and, once established, transplanted in plugs into the grassland area. Several seed merchants now offer wild-flower seed, although care should be taken to make sure that the species are of the type native to the country and area in which they are sown. Most seed merchants will offer several seed mixtures suitable for different locations, including wet, dry, acid and alkaline soils, and shady places.

Areas can also be established from bare soil by a number of methods, including spreading topsoil containing seed, using turf transplants and by sowing grass-herb mixtures. Most topsoils contain a large number of viable seeds, although, many of them are likely to be from heavy-seeding 'weed' species such as daisy and dandelion. Clearly, establishment from the importation of topsoil is risky and may lead to the establishment of a less than desirable sward. If turf from an area of species-rich grassland is available it can be used to establish such a sward elsewhere. If the soil or environmental conditions are different from those on the original site, it is likely that the species will change with time to form a new community adapted to the conditions on the new site. Sowing a particular grass/herb mixture compiled for a specific soil type or environment can overcome the problems of moving an established turf to a new site. The mixture is usually composed of 85% grasses and 15% dicotyledons, with the grass species being those which do not produce a large amount of leaf growth such as red fescue, fine-leaved sheep's fescue, creeping bent and crested dogstail. By sowing a mixture of species known to survive on a particular soil type, maximum survival is ensured. Even if all the species do not succeed, a mature, balanced plant community is likely to be established.

Once established, the species-rich sward must be managed correctly to ensure its survival. This entails enabling the species present to flower and set seed before the seed heads are cut and removed. A low level of soil fertility will ensure that the grasses do not out-compete the broad-leaved species for light and water. This will involve mowing the site after seed-set has occurred in July, removing the herbage after it has been allowed to dry out so that seeds can fall on to the site, and keeping the area mown at 100–150mm/4–6in. until growth ceases in the autumn. On rougher areas mowing may be limited to two cuts, one in early summer and one prior to the onset of winter.

SPORTS TURF. Mown grass areas used for sport are generally referred to as sports turf. Unlike most lawns, sports turf areas must not only have a good appearance but must also provide an ideal surface for play and take a great deal of wear. Wear is the major problem encountered on natural grass playing-surfaces because extensive use, especially when by heavy players wearing studded footwear, not only damages the grass plant but also destroys the surface soil structure. Soil structure is essential for drainage and, once lost, water is prevented from moving through the soil to the drains. Water retained at the surface can easily lead to mud formation once the grass cover has been worn away. While drainage is perhaps more obviously needed in cool-temperate climates such as Britain, where rainfall is a regular occurrence throughout the year, drainage is needed in almost all situations where significant rainfall is likely during the playing season.

Choosing the correct mixture is important if the grass is to withstand wear and close mowing. Perhaps the most important grass species on areas of very high wear in temperate regions is perennial ryegrass (*Lolium perenne*). Perennial ryegrass is widely used in Britain and other climatically similar areas for sports pitches where heavy wear caused by studded boots is sustained (football and rugby pitches). It is generally mixed with species such as red fescue (*Festuca rubra*) and browntop or highland bent (*Agrostis tenuis* and *A. castellana*). Pure swards of the finer perennial ryegrass cultivars have been used on top-class cricket squares with some success. In the eastern and midwest US pure swards of smooth-stalked meadowgrass/Kentucky bluegrass (*Poa pratensis*) are used for such areas, while in the warmer southern states warm-season grasses such as Bermuda grass (*Cynodon* spp.) are common.

Perhaps the greatest advance in the selection and breeding of grasses has been the development of much more wear-tolerant cultivars of perennial ryegrass (*Lolium perenne*) and Kentucky bluegrass (*Poa pratensis*). However, all the major turfgrass species have been much improved over recent years and are now more wear-resistant, disease-resistant, compact, finer-leaved and tolerant of mowing than before. For this reason, named sports-turf cultivars should always be used in preference to unnamed or agricultural-type cultivars, even though they will cost slightly more. Details of turfgrass cultivars can be obtained from turfgrass research establishments such as the Sports Turf Research Institute in the UK which publishes an annual cultivar assessment called 'Turfgrass Seed'.

The soil in which grass grows is extremely important when it comes to how often and under what conditions the surface can be used. On heavy loam soils, poor drainage can quickly render the surface unusable in wet weather and can lead to the ingress of moss and other weeds. For areas which are only to be used on warm dry days in summer by a family group perhaps only basic drainage is required. However, if any considerable amount of use is expected throughout the season a correctly constructed and drained area is essential. Such areas must be able to support a healthy, wear-tolerant turf; they must have good drainage and must provide a suitable playing surface.

Agricultural drainage systems consisting of a pipe drain backfilled with soil will, over time, allow water to drain from the soil. However, such a system does not usually work fast enough for sports areas, as the speed at which the water can get to the drain is restricted by the soil backfill. In addition, drainage on its own does not necessarily improve the quality of the soil at all and if soil structure is damaged by play, water infiltration will be reduced, possibly leading to mud formation during play. For these reasons, modern drainage systems have been developed to speed up the infiltration of water into the soil surface and enable it to move quickly to the drain pipe.

Although drainage designs will vary depending on the site and the type of sport, they are usually laid in either a herringbone or grid pattern. In a herringbone system, the lateral drains join a central main drain alternatively from either side in a similar way to the rib bones of a fish joining the backbone. The laterals join the main at a 30° angle every 10–15 metres or so depending on requirements and soil type. Drains laid out in a grid usually join the main every 10–15 metres or so from one side only and at an angle nearer to 90°. Herringbone systems tend to be used to drain very extensive areas or circular constructions where the laterals can reach most of the site. Grid systems are usually used on square or rectangular pitches and courts.

To enable rainwater to reach the drainage pipe rapidly, the pipe must be backfilled to the surface with permeable fill. A suitable backfill will consist of 10mm washed gravel directly over the drain to within 200mm of the surface. This should be blended with 50mm of coarse sand before being topped up to the surface with either a pure medium/fine sand or a sand/soil mixture containing at least 70% medium/fine sand. For tennis courts or cricket squares, the top 100mm should consist of a medium loam (20–24% clay) and heavy loam (24–30%) respectively. Drainage trenches should be kept as narrow as possible and where the trench is more than 150mm wide it should be sown or turved. The turf used should have a sandy soil otherwise the permeable fill will be covered with a less permeable layer. If this is not possible then the trench can be turved, leaving a gap of 100mm at one side of the trench which can be topped up with sandy backfill and sown.

Once a free-draining system has been installed it can be improved even further by installing slits of sand or gravel at right angles to the drains. This is often done on football pitches and enables rainwater to reach the drains even more quickly. Such 'sand slit' systems are installed using specialist equipment and must be topdressed with medium/fine sand to stop the slit being capped with soil from alongside. (See also DRAINAGE.)

While draining sports areas will enable them to dry out quicker after rain, it will not change the soil on site. Where soils are unsuitable or where very freely drained areas are needed, the entire area is often reconstructed using ideal materials. There are three basic types of construction system: (a) *Sand/Soil Amelioration* – a sand/soil mixture either over drains alone or over a gravel drainage layer, which directs the water to the drains; (b) *Sand Carpet System* – a sand layer, in which the grass grows, placed over a drainage system; (c) *All Sand System* – sand root-zone placed in a sealed area over a drainage system. By adding large quantities of sand to the soil or by having sand alone and doing away with soil altogether, the root-zone mixture will drain freely on its own and will not need to rely on the soil structure, which can break down under heavy wear. Systems such as these would be used when building bowling greens, tennis courts and putting greens. The design and construction of such systems are, however, expensive and complex. It is advisable for professional expertise to be sought as to the suitability of a particular system for a particular site and sport prior to installation. It is unlikely that 'all sand' systems would be suitable for areas which are not maintained by full-time trained groundstaff.

*Tennis courts.* Ideally, tennis courts should be laid out in a north–south direction. This means that the sun will not set or rise in the face of players, thereby causing difficulty in seeing the ball. The court should have a surface gradient of between 1:100 and 1:150, ideally running across the court. Clearly there can be exceptions to these rules as to stick strictly to them may be impossible on some sites due to cost or restrictions in size or shape. For recreational play a minimum of 144×56 feet (34.75×17.07m) is needed for a single enclosure. This will give sufficient area around the court markings – 78×36 feet (23.77×10.97m) – to play the ball. Each court is usually enclosed with netting to enable easy retrieval of the ball.

Tennis courts should be sown with a mixture which will quickly recover after wear. For temperate regions such as Britain a mixture containing 60% creeping red fescue, 20% Chewing's fescue, 10% smooth-stalked meadowgrass/Kentucky bluegrass and 10% browntop bent would be suitable. However, a mixture containing 40% perennial ryegrass, 50% Chewing's fescue and 10% browntop bent may be better where heavy wear is anticipated. A sward of pure smooth-stalked meadowgrass/Kentucky bluegrass or Bermuda grass would be suitable for their respective climatic zones.

Provided the soil is relatively free draining, almost any soil would be suitable for a home court. Ideally, the soil should contain 20–24% clay, as this will help prevent the surface from breaking up during play if the grass is worn away. If the soil tends to hold water at the surface then a gradient can be created to encourage the rainwater to run off the surface. In addition, drains can be installed every five metres across the gradient.

Maintenance will be as the other lawn areas and will include the following practices in summer: mowing 2–3 times per week at 8–12mm height; brushing to remove the dew in the morning, thereby discouraging disease germination and spread; applying fertilizer 2–3 times through the season; scarifying or slitting to keep the surface open (not in dry weather); treating for pests, diseases and weeds; rolling to firm the surface prior to marking out the court and erecting the net; irrigation in dry weather; and a full renovation programme after the playing season to relieve soil compaction and remove thatch.

*Croquet.* Croquet is easily played on any reasonably level lawn area although a full croquet lawn will require a minimum area of 105×84 feet (32×25.6m). Construction and maintenance can be as for an average lawn or as mentioned above for tennis, although there is no requirement for netting or a north – south orientation. The croquet lawn may in addition require to be mown slightly lower, at 6mm, and must be constructed flat for top-level games.

*Flat bowling greens.* Rink bowling is played throughout the world and is becoming more popular. A full-sized flat bowling green is 126 feet square ($38.4m^2$); however, unlike crown green bowling, rink bowling can be played on one rink 126×19 feet (38.4×5.8m), or 14 feet wide and perhaps shorter for recreational play. To play correctly a ditch at either end is required, as under certain circumstances bowls which go into the ditch are still in play. Crown green bowling, a game played in the North and Midlands of England, requires a green 120 feet square ($36.6m^2$) with a raised crown (usually 10 inches/254mm) in the centre. The crown green game, which is played all over the green and not in straight rinks, requires a good-sized area.

Bowling greens are usually sown with a fescue and bent mixture consisting of 70–80% Chewing's fescue and 20–30% browntop and highland bent. Bermuda grass is often used in subtropical and tropical climates, while non-grass species such as *Cotula* are quite widely used on bowling greens in New Zealand.

A common construction for a flat green involves installing a main drain under the peripheral ditch. This main has lateral drains running to it diagonally across the green at every 6–10 metres depending on the likely rainfall in the area. The drains are backfilled with 10–12mm gravel, covered or blinded with 50mm of coarse sand and topped with up to 200mm of sandy soil. The soil is then sown or turved. The ditches should be 200–375mm wide and 50mm–200mm below the green. The bank on the outside of the ditch should be not less than 225mm above the green and upright or at an angle of no more than 35° from the upright.

Maintenance will be as the other lawn areas and should include the following practices in summer: mowing 3 times per week at 5–6mm; brushing to remove the dew in the morning, thereby discouraging disease germination and spread; applying fertilizer 2–3 times through the season; scarifying or slitting to keep the surface open (not in dry weather); treating for pests, diseases and weeds; rolling to firm the surface prior play in the spring; irrigation in dry weather; and a full renovation programme after the playing season to relieve soil compaction and remove thatch.

ARTIFICIAL TURF SURFACES. Artificial turf surfaces are used on areas of high wear or to give the visual effect of a turf area without the associated maintenance. There are several types of artificial turf surface, from a range of materials including nylon, polypropylene and other plastics. They are available as either a pile or needle-punch carpet, the former giving a grass-like appearance. If they are to be used for sport, associated base material and shock pads are also necessary. Artificial surfaces are widely used for sports, including American football, soccer (mainly at amateur level), field hockey and cricket (for practice and low-level competition). They are not widely used in Britain for other purposes, although they have been used in the US to replace home lawns or for visual effects in front of commercial premises. Most people, it would seem, prefer natural turf for their home lawns.

**Lawrence,** Sir (James John) **Trevor** (1831–1913). Horticulturist. Born in London, Lawrence was educated at Winchester and studied medicine at St Bartholomew's Hospital, London. He was the son of the distinguished surgeon, Sir William Lawrence, and the eminent botanist and orchid-grower, Louisa Lawrence. He served on the Army Medical Staff in India for ten years from 1854, during the period of the Mutiny. In 1867 he succeeded to the baronetcy, and from 1875 to 1892 served as an MP for mid-Surrey, after which he became treasurer and principal administrator to St Bartholomew's Hospital.

He inherited his great love of gardening from his mother and continued in her footsteps to build up his famous collection of orchids at Burford Lodge, Surrey, probably the finest private collection in the country at that time. Like his mother, he was a frequent and well-known exhibitor at Royal Horticultural Society shows, gaining numerous successes.

He was appointed President of the Royal Horticultural Society in 1885, remaining in the post for 28 years. During his presidency the Society was transformed into a strong and thriving organization, the New Hall was built at Vincent Square and the membership increased rapidly. His work was recognized by the award of the Society's Victoria Medal of Honour in 1900, the establishment of the Lawrence Medal, and by the presentation to him of the Veitch Memorial Medal in 1913.

The genus *Trevoria* was named in his honour.

**Lawsonia** L. (For Dr. Isaac Lawson (*d.* *c*1747), Scottish army doctor who helped pay for the publication of Linnaeus' *Systema Naturae* in 1735.) HENNA; MIGNONETTE TREE. Lythraceae. 1 species, a shrub to 6m. Leaves decussate, narrowly obovate to oblong to broadly lanceolate, entire, apex acuminate, mucronate, base attenuate, nervation pinnate, venation reticulate; stipules 2, minute, white, conical. Inflorescence a pyramidal terminal panicle, to 40cm; flowers 4-merous, to 0.5cm across, fragrant; calyx turbinate, to 0.5cm, fruiting calyx petallate, slightly leathery, calyx lobes about one quarter length of tube, broadly ovate-triangular; petals small, clawed, reniform, crumpled, white, pink or scarlet; stamens 8; ovary sessile, subglobose, 2–4-locular; style longer than stamens. Fruit a spherical, indehiscent capsule to 6×8mm; seeds thick, trigonal, pyramidal, to 2.6mm. N Africa, SW Asia, Australia, naturalized tropical America. Z9.

CULTIVATION Cultivated for centuries for henna, *Lawsonia* is used in ornamental plantings in the tropics and subtropics as a small tree or open shrub with fragrant flowers. Grow in any well-drained soil in a sunny position: plants respond well to pruning in late spring. In temperate areas, grow in an intermediate to hot glasshouse in a light, loam-based compost. Propagate from seed or by softwood cuttings in spring and hardwood cuttings in winter.

***L. inerma*** L. As for the genus.

**Laxmannia** R. Br. (For Erik Laxmann (1737–96), pastor in Kolywan, Siberia and traveller.) Liliaceae (Asphodelaceae). 8 species of fibrous-rooted perennial herbs. Stems short and tufted or long, branched and diffuse. Leaves crowded narrow-linear or subulate, trigonous or channelled, tough, in radical or terminal tufts, dilated at base, where sheathing and scarious, often produced into bristles. Inflorescence axillary, several- to many-flowered heads, subtended by bracts that are often divided into woolly hairs; tepals 6, in 2 whorls, outer 3 free, inner 3 fused below. Fruit a capsule; seeds few, black. Australia. Z10.

CULTIVATION As for *Thysanotus*. Propagate by division.

***L. gracilis*** R. Br. Stems slender, branched, in loose tufts to 30cm+. Lvs 1.25–2.5cm, crowded at base and ends of branches, filiform, erect or spreading, bases short, broad, sheathing, overlapping, margins sparsely woolly-hairy. Fls pink; peduncles long. W Australia.

***L. grandiflora*** Lindl. Stems to 4cm, erect, forming a compact tuft, covered with lf remains. Lvs 2.5–5cm, crowded in dense terminal tufts, sheaths usually with 3 awn-like apical appendages. Infl. 2–30cm, erect, pedunculate, several from each lf tuft, exceeding lvs; tepals white, the outer 6.5–9mm, the inner half as long; peduncles 15–25cm. W Australia.

**Layering**. See VEGETATIVE PROPAGATION.

**Layia** Hook. & Arn. (For George Tradescant Lay (*d.* *c*1845), botanist to Captain Beechey's voyage in the *Blossom*, which visited California in 1827.) Compositae. About 15 species of annual herbs. Leaves usually alternate, narrow, subentire or dentate to pinnatifid. Capitula usually radiate, solitary, terminal; involucre campanulate to broadly hemispheric; phyllaries in 1 series, margins thin, dilated, infolded; receptacle scaly; ray florets white, yellow or yellow with white tip; disc florets yellow. Fruit an obcompressed cypsela, outer usually glabrous, inner usually pubescent; pappus of many bristles or scales. W US.

CULTIVATION Frost-tender annuals for dry sunny banks, *Layia* spp. bear a profusion of flowers throughout summer. They do not thrive where summers are hot and humid. Sow seed *in situ* is spring (or earlier under glass), in any well-drained soil in sun.

***L. chrysanthemoides*** (DC.) A. Gray. Stem erect, branched, to 40cm. Lower lvs pinnate, seg. linear or oblong, obtuse, glabrous, scabrous. Ray florets yellow with white lobes. Spring. US (California).

***L. glandulosa*** (Hook.) Hook. & Arn. Stem usually branched, to 40cm, hispid, often red. Lower lvs dentate or lobed, hispid, often densely strigose above, upper lvs mostly entire. Ray florets white, becoming rose-purple, anth. yellow. Spring–summer. Washington to New Mexico.

***L. platyglossa*** (Fisch. & G. Mey.) A. Gray. TIDY TIPS. Stems decumbent to erect, stout, glandular, hirsute, to 30cm. Lvs linear to narrowly oblong, dentate to pinnatifid, seg. rounded, shortly hirsute or pilose, upper lvs entire. Ray florets yellow with white tips, anth. black. Spring–summer. California.

***L. calliglossa*** A. Gray. See *L. chrysanthemoides*.
***L. douglasii*** Hook. & Arn. See *L. glandulosa*.
***L. elegans*** Torr. & A. Gray. See *L. platyglossa*.
***L. emarginata*** Hook. & Arn. See *Ormosia emarginata*.

**Lecanopteris** (Reinw.) Bl. (From Gk *lekane*, basin, and *pteris*, fern.) Polypodiaceae. Some 15 species of epiphytic ferns. Rhizomes slender, creeping to swollen and forming irregularly shaped masses, branched, interior hollow, in habitat often ant-inhabited; scales persistent or deciduous, peltate, circular. Fronds stipitate, simple or pinnate, glabrous, somewhat fleshy, main veins indistinct, veins forked, anastomosing, areolae with free, included veinlet; stipes jointed to swollen, conical phyllopodia. Sori uniserial each side of costa; paraphyses absent; annulus 13-celled; spores ellipsoid, smooth, glassy. SE Asia to New Guinea. Z10.

CULTIVATION See MYRMECOPHILOUS PLANTS.

***L. crustacea*** Copel. Rhiz. to 5cm across, wide-creeping, gouty, crustaceous; scales adpressed, persistent, clathrate. Fronds to 35×15cm, somewhat dimorphous, oblong, deeply lobed, leathery dark green above, paler beneath, sterile lobes to 17 pairs, to 8×2cm, horizontal, oblong, obtuse at apex, fertile lobes to 30 pairs, to 10×0.5cm, linear, obtuse at apex; costa winged; stipes to 20cm, erect, phyllopodia scaly. Malaysia to Indonesia.

***L. sinuosa*** (Wallich) Copel. Rhiz. to 2cm across, scandent or long-creeping, fleshy to woody; scales adpressed, persistent, clathrate, to 3×2mm. Fronds somewhat dimorphous, simple, leathery to membranous, glabrous: sterile fronds to 20×3cm, elliptic to oblong, obtuse at apex, cuneate at base, entire at margin; fertile fronds to 40×2cm, linear to oblong, obtuse at apex, attenuate at base, sinuous at margin; stipes to 7cm, to 2cm apart, phyllopodia to 1cm, scaly. Malaysia to Solomon Is.

For synonymy see *Onychium* and *Phymatodes*.

For illustration see MYRMECOPHILOUS PLANTS.

**LECYTHIDACEAE** Poit. LECYTHIS FAMILY. Dicot. 20 genera and 280 species of trees and shrubs, often pachycaul. Leaves alternate, usually at branch-tips, simple, entire or toothed; stipules small and caducous or absent. Flowers bisexual, regular or not, epigynous, with hypanthium sometimes extended beyond the ovary, often large and conspicuous, insect- or bat-pollinated, with much nectar, axillary, solitary or in terminal or axillary panicles, fascicles or racemes, sometimes from old wood; calyx (2–) 4–6 (–12) free sepals, rarely connate and forming calyptra; corolla 4–6 free petals, or absent; stamens (10–) numerous, sometimes up to 1200, symmetrical, in several centrifugal series, basally connate on a basal ring; in flowers with no corolla outer stamens sterile and connate forming a corona; ovary inferior, of 2–6 fused carpels, with a terminal style and as many locules as ovary; placentation axile, basal in *Eschweilera*; ovules 1-numerous per locule. Fruit a capsule with a distal operculum, often very large (monkey-pots) or a drupe or berry; seeds often nut-like, winged or with funicular aril; endosperm usually absent. Brazil nut from *Bertholletia excelsa* and paradise nuts from *Lecythis* species. The woody capsules of *Lecythis* are used to trap monkeys, which try to obtain baits placed inside the 'monkey pots' and cannot then withdraw their hands. Many provide timber such as *Bertholletia, Careya, Cariniana, Couratari, Couroupita* and *Lecythis*. Tropical, especially S American rain forests. *Barringtonia, Bertholletia, Couroupita, Grias, Gustavia, Lecythis, Napoleonaea*.

**Lecythis** Loefl. (From Gk *lekythos*, an oil jar, in reference to the pot-like fruit.) Lecythidaceae. 26 species of small to large trees, deciduous or evergreen, with smooth or deeply fissured bark. Leaves to 25×15cm, alternate, simple, usually glabrous, leathery, dentate or entire. Inflorescence a raceme, spike or corymb; flowers zygomorphic, to 8cm diam.; sepals 6; petals 6, subequal; androecium extended into a flat hood, its appendages sometimes bearing anthers; staminal ring with 70–1000 stamens; ovary usually 4-celled; style to 11mm, straight or bent. Fruit a large woody capsule, to 25×30cm, the so-called monkey pot (used as a monkey trap), opening by means of a lid; seeds often with a basal aril projecting beyond the micropylar end. Nicaragua to São Paolo, Brazil. Z9.

CULTIVATION The nuts, which mature 18 months after flowering, are ivory-white and of a sweet and creamy texture, more digestible than that of the related Brazil nut, *Bertholletia*. Outside their native habitats, they are cultivated on a small scale in Guyana, Brazil, and the West Indies. *L. ollaria* is also grown in Sri Lanka and Malaya, although the seeds are highly toxic, as are those of *L. minor*.

*L. zabucaya*, the sapucaia nut, takes its specific name from the native word for chicken, having been commonly used as chicken food. The fruits, suspended from the branch ends, develop a perfectly fitting 'lid', which drops off as the nuts ripen, thus scattering them to the predations of monkeys and wild pigs. The dried empty fruits are used domestically, and also as monkey traps; when baited, the aperture at the top is of sufficient size to allow insertion of a monkey paw, but when clenched around the bait the fist is too big to remove.

When cultivated in temperate climates, they require hot glasshouse conditions, and a sandy loam based medium. Propagate from seed, or by semi-ripe cuttings under mist, or with bottom heat in a closed case.

***L. lurida*** (Miers) Mori. To 35m, with grey, deeply fissured bark. Lvs to 18×9cm, deciduous, ovate, elliptic or oblong, glabrous, chartaceous to coriaceous, apex acuminate, margins crenate to nearly entire; petiole to 13mm. Infl. a terminal raceme; rachis to 10cm; fls 1–20; pedicels to 5mm; fls to 4cm diam.; sep. to 13×11mm, green, sometimes with red markings; pet. to 33mm, the upper part curled under, red or pink outside, white inside; androecial hood to 2×2cm, yellow, with inwardly curved anther-less appendages; staminal ring with to 260 stamens, fil. to 0.7mm; style to 6mm. Fr. indehiscent, depressed-globose, to 9×11cm, pericarp leathery, to 4mm thick; seeds 2–7, to 6×5mm. E coastal Brazil and E Amazonia.

***L. minor*** Jacq. Tree, branched from the base in open habitat, to 25m; bark grey, becoming fissured. Lvs to 24.5×10cm, ovate to oblong, mucronate to acuminate, glabrous, leathery, margins crenulate to serrate; petiole to 2cm. Infl. a terminal or axillary raceme, the main rachis to 35cm; fls to 7cm diam.; sep. to 11×9mm, green; pet. to 42×25mm, white; androecial hood with inwardly curving anthersless appendages, white or pale yellow; staminal ring with to 410 stamens, fil. to 2mm; style to 4.5mm. Fr. globose or turbinate, to 7×9cm, pericarp to 11m thick; seeds to 3×2cm, red-brown, smooth. Venezuela, Colombia, Panama, Cuba.

***L. pisonis*** Cambess. PARADISE NUT; CREAM NUT; BRAZILIAN MONKEY POT. Deciduous tree, to 50m; bark grey to dark brown, fissured. Lvs flushed before flowering, to 15×8cm, ovate to elliptic, dark green, glabrous, becoming leathery, acuminate, margins crenate; petiole to 12mm. Infl. of racemes; rachis to 15cm; pedicels to 12mm subtended by a lf or caducous bract; fls 3–7 cm diam.; sep. to 8mm, purple; pet. to 35mm, purple or white; androecial hood flat, purple or white, its appendages bearing anthers; staminal ring with 350 stamens, fil. 2mm; style 2mm. Fr. globose, to 15×30cm, pericarp to 3cm thick; seeds 10–30, to 6×3cm, fusiform. Caribbean, Peru, Brazil.

***L. tuyrana*** Pittier. PANAMA MONKEY POT. To 60m, with a straight unbuttressed bole. Lvs to 37×16cm, oblong, glabrous, leathery, acuminate, entire to crenulate. Infl. spicate, terminal or axillary, rachis with rusty pubesc. when young; fls to 6cm diam., each subtended by a bract and 2 bracteoles; sep. to 15×12mm, green; pet. sulphur yellow, to 40×22mm; androecial hood yellow, with vestigial anth. or none; staminal ring with to 360 stamens; style to 2mm. Fr. to 14.5×17.5cm, subglobose, dark brown; seeds to 7×3cm, oblong, red-brown, smooth. Panama, Ecuador, Colombia.

***L. zabucaya*** Aubl. SAPUCAIA NUT; PARADISE NUT; MONKEY NUT. Deciduous tree to 55m, with deeply fissured bark. Lvs to 11.5×5.5cm, elliptic, acuminate, glabrous, papery, margins crenate; petiole to 10mm. Infl. of racemes with 5–30 fls; rachis to 10.5cm; pedicels to 5mm, subtended by a leaf or bract; fls to 5cm diam.; sep. to 10×9mm, green; pet. to 25×19mm, yellow or rarely white, often with purple on the margins and apex; androecial hood flat, yellow or sometimes white; style to 2mm. Fr. to 16.5×17.5cm, globose to turbinate, lid convex; seeds fusiform, to 4×1.5cm. Guianas, E Venezuela, Amazonia.

***L. elliptica*** HBK. See *L. minor*.
***L. urnigera*** Mart. ex Berg. See *L. pisonis*.
***L. usitata*** Miers. See *L. pisonis*.

**Ledebouria** Roth. (For Carl Friedrich von Ledebour (1785–1851), German botanist.) Liliaceae (Hyacinthaceae). Some 16 species of bulbous, perennial herbs. Leaves basal, frequently stripped or spotted red or green. Inflorescence an axillary raceme, simple, slender often flexuous; bracts inconspicuous; flowers small or minute, green or purple; perianth segments recurved; filaments free; ovary superior, expanding to a wide base below, conical or broadly conical, stipitate, ovules basal, 2 per locule. S Africa. Z9.

CULTIVATION Grown for their leaf coloration and green-mauve flowers in sunny positions in the cool greenhouse or conservatory in a moderately fertile potting mix, with good ventilation and a minimum temperature of 5–7°C/40–45°F. They often do well grown in association with succulents and cacti.

***L. apertiflora*** (Bak.) Jessop. Bulbs to 6cm, frequently tinged pink towards apex. Lvs 4 to 7, to 35×2.5cm, erect, sublinear, base attenuate. Fls numerous, in an erect or flexuous raceme; perianth seg. green, grey or marked pink. S Africa.

***L. concolor*** (Bak.) Jessop. Bulbs to 5cm, epigeal. Lvs 2 to 6, to 15×5cm, erect or erect-spreading, oblong-lanceolate to ovate, often undulate. Fls numerous, mostly green, in a suberect raceme; perianth seg. green, grey or marked pink. S Africa.

***L. cooperi*** (Hook. f.) Jessop. Bulbs to 4cm, usually absent. Lvs 1–3, to 25×2cm, erect, somewhat fleshy, oblong to ovate-oblong or linear, base slightly narrowed, sometimes with brown longitudinal stripes. Infl. suberect; perianth seg. pale purple or with a green keel. S Africa.

***L. floribunda*** (Bak.) Jessop. Bulbs to 15cm. Lvs 4 or 5, to 35×15cm, suberect, lanceolate to oblong-linear. Infl. suberect; perianth seg. grey or green with pink. S Africa.

***L. hypoxidioides*** (Schönl.) Jessop. Bulbs to 4cm, sometimes pink towards apex. Lvs 2–4, to 15×3.5cm, firm, suberect, oblong-lanceolate to oblong-ovate, densely covered with silky hairs above and beneath. Infl. suberect, 75–150-fld; perianth seg. green, grey or marked pink. S Africa.

***L. inquinata*** (C.A. Sm.) Jessop Bulbs to 6.5cm, with glossy, dark outer scales, sometimes tinged pink. Lvs to 15×3.5cm, erect, ovate-lanceolate, glaucous, mostly without spots, narrowed near base. Infl. suberect to flexuous, 50–150-fld; perianth seg. green, grey or marked pink. S Africa.

***L. luteola*** Jessop. Bulbs to 5cm, scales producing abundant threads, inner scales yellow. Lvs 4–10, to 8cm, erect or arcuate, narrowly lanceolate to linear-lanceolate, firm, spotted or with indistinct transverse markings. Infl. suberect, 30–60-fld; perianth seg. to 4mm, green, grey or marked pink. S Africa.

***L. marginata*** (Bak.) Jessop. Bulbs to 8cm, exterior scales glossy, dark, often speckled pink. Lvs 4–10, to 16×3cm, firm, erect, with prominent venation. Infl. mostly flexuous, 50–150-fld; perianth seg. green, grey or marked pink. S Africa.

***L. ovalifolia*** (Schräd.) Jessop. Bulbs to 2.5cm. Lvs 3–5, to 3.5×1cm, erect-spreading or spreading, base narrowed, margins involute near base. Infl. to 9cm, to 20-fld; pedicels spreading; fls striped pink. S Africa.

***L. ovatifolia*** (Bak.) Jessop. Bulbs to 4cm, scales truncate, imbricate, producing abundant threads, exterior scales inconspicuous or absent. Lvs 2–5, to 25cm, ovate, with a wide base. Infl. mostly flexuous, densely 50–150-fld; perianth seg. green, grey or marked pink. S Africa.

***L. revoluta*** (L. f.) Jessop Bulbs to 7.5cm, spherical, exterior scales glossy, dark often speckled pink. Lvs 4–8, to 15×3cm, suberect or spreading, lanceolate to narrowly ovate, usually attenuate, often with dark spots above. Infl. suberect, to 100-fld; perianth seg. green. S Africa.

***L. socialis*** (Bak.) Jessop. Bulbs to 2cm, ovoid, often purple, produced into a neck. Lvs few to several, to 10×2cm, erect-spreading or spreading, slightly fleshy, lanceolate, narrowed into a petiole-like base, with a silver sheen and some dark green blotches above, green or deep pink-purple beneath. Infl. suberect, to 25-fld; perianth seg. pale purple with green keels. S Africa.

***L. undulata*** (Jacq.) Jessop. Bulbs to 5cm, with several dry outer scales which often form a neck; roots often forming fusiform tubers. Lvs 2 to 6, to 15×2cm, suberect to spreading, firm, lanceolate or linear-lanceolate. Infl. erect, lax; perianth seg. green, sometimes striped pink. S Africa.

***L. viscosa*** Jessop. Bulbs to 10×2cm, sometimes marked pink. Lvs 1 to 3, to 23×3cm, erect, spathulate-oblanceolate, viscid. Infl. erect, lax, 20–30-fld; perianth seg. grey, green or marked pink. S Africa.

For synonymy see *Drimia, Hyacinthus* and *Scilla*.

**Ledum** L. (From Gk *ledon*, mastic, name used for *Cistus ledon*.) Ericaceae. 3–4 species of erect or diffuse evergreen shrubs. Leaves alternate, scented, entire. linear or oblong, revolute, coriaceous, ferruginous-lanate or, more rarely, glandular-scaly beneath; petioles short. Flowers small, in terminal, umbellate corymbs; pedicels slender; bracts dry and shrivelled, bracteoles absent; calyx small, lobes 5; corolla rotate, white, petals 5, diffuse, conspicuous, oblong to inversely ovate; stamens 5–10, anthers dehiscing through 2 apical slits, filaments thread-like; ovary, oblong or inversely ovoid, 5-locular. Fruit a subglobose or oblong capsule; seeds numerous, winged. N Temperate.

CULTIVATION Natives of peat bogs, swamps or coniferous woodlands. *L. groenlandicum*, Labrador tea, was an important beverage during the American War of Independence. All are grown in the bog or damp woodland garden for their aromatic evergreen foliage and terminal clusters of fragrant white flowers in spring or early summer. The more compact species are suitable for damp, semi-shaded pockets on the rock garden. *L. glandulosum* ssp. *columbianum*, the most tender, is hardy to −15°C/5°F. Grow in shade or semi-shade in moist, humus-rich, acid soils. Deadheading and maintenance of an organic mulch are beneficial and, where possible, the incorporation of soil from established specimens to provide fungal associations. Propagate by semi-ripe cuttings in a closed case with bottom heat, by simple layering or by seed.

***L. glandulosum*** Nutt. TRAPPER'S TEA; GLANDULAR LABRADOR TEA. Erect, evergreen shrub, 50–150cm. Branchlets glandular, downy. Lvs 1.5–6×0.5–2cm, oblong to broadly elliptic-oval, base and apex acuminate, sometimes revolute, dark green and channelled above, glaucous and glandular-scaly beneath; petioles 4–10mm. Fls in terminal clusters to 5cm diam.; pedicels 2.5–4cm, downy, often glandular, recurved during fruiting; calyx lobes rounded, ciliolate, margins ciliate; petals 5–8mm, oblong, white; stamens 10, fil. usually glabrous, occasionally downy at base. Fr. 3–5mm, subspherical. Summer. Western N America. var. ***columbianum*** (Piper) C. Hitchc. Lvs 3–5×1cm, strongly revolute. Fr. 4–5.5mm, ovoid.

***L. groenlandicum*** Oeder. LABRADOR TEA. Erect, evergreen shrub 50–200cm. Young branches ferruginous-lanate. Lvs 20–60×3–15mm, linear-oblong, margins conspicuously revolute, coriaceous, apex blunt, dark green and somewhat hirsute above, thickly ferruginous-lanate beneath; petiole 1–5mm. Fls many in corymbs, grouped in terminal clusters to 5cm diam.; pedicels 6–25mm, short- and white-stiff hirsute, glandular; bracts hirsute. Cal. to 1mm, dentate, white-ciliate; pet. 5–8mm, oblong, apex rounded, base narrowed, white; stamens 5–10, fil. glabrous or, more rarely, base downy; style 4–6mm. Fr. 4–7mm, oblong, downy. Late spring–summer. Northern N America, Greenland. 'Compactus': habit dwarf.

***L. palustre*** L. CRYSTAL TEA; WILD ROSEMARY. Erect or decumbent evergreen shrub, 30–120cm. Young shoots ferruginous-lanate. Lvs 12–50×1.5–12mm, linear to elliptic-oblong, strongly revolute, dark and dull green above, ferruginous-hirsute beneath. Fls many in densely packed, terminal clusters; pedicels 5–25mm, glandular, often ferruginous-hairy when young; cal. dentate; pet. 4–8mm, white, obovate, spreading; ovary glandular-warty; stamens 7–10. Fr. c5mm, ovoid. Late spring–summer. N & C Europe, N US. 'Minus': dwarf variant; lvs narrow. f. ***dilatatum*** (Wahlenb.) O. Fedtsch. Lvs somewhat broader. Japan, Korea, E Siberia. Z2.

***L. buxifolium*** Berg. See *Leiophyllum buxifolium*.
***L. hypoleucum*** Komar. See *L. palustre*.
***L. latifolium*** Jacq. See *L. groenlandicum*.
***L. nipponicum*** (Nak.) Tolm. See *L. palustre*.

**Leea** Royen ex L. (For James Lee (1715–1795), the renowned London nurseryman.) Leeaceae. 34 species of shrubs and small trees. Stems erect, glabrous, glossy, sometimes ridged and lenticellate. Leaves opposite or alternate, simple or unequally 1–3 pinnate, usually held horizontally and outspreading, often flushed bronze or red, especially when young; petiole slender, usually basally clasping, lacking tendrils (cf. vitaceae in which this genus was once included). Inflorescence a crowded axillary corymb or terminal cyme; flowers small, perianth segments purple-red, yellow or green united at base, filaments united at base into a tube arising from perianth, anthers introrse; ovary 4–8 celled. Fruit a berry. Old World tropics. Z10.

CULTIVATION Valued primarily for their beautiful, often velvet-textured foliage, especially well-coloured when young, and for their stately habit; some, notably *L. coccinea*, are also attractive in flower and fruit, and begin to bloom when relatively small (*c*30cm/12in. tall). They are suitable for outdoor cultivation only in the humid tropics and subtropics, where they require a position in part shade in any moderately fertile and freely draining but retentive soil. In cooler climates they are handsome specimens for the warm glasshouse or conservatory, or (with sufficient atmospheric humidity) in the home. Under glass, provide bright filtered light or shade from direct sun in high summer, and grow in well-crocked pots with a high-fertility loam-based medium. Maintain high humidity, water plentifully, and feed fortnightly with a dilute liquid feed when in full growth, reducing water in winter when a minimum temperature of 16°C/60°F is appropriate. In drier conditions, slightly lower temperatures may be maintained, although in these conditions plants may defoliate. Prune to shape and confine to bounds in late winter or early spring. Propagate by stem cuttings, air-layering, or by seed.

***L. amabilis*** hort. Shrub to 2m. Stem slender, erect, sparsely branched, glossy. Lvs to 1m, 1–3 pinnate, leaflets to 6cm, lanceolate, acute or acuminate, sparsely toothed, deep lustrous bronze-green above with a broad white central stripe, claret beneath with a translucent, central, green stripe. Borneo. 'Splendens': whole plant flushed dark claret to bronze.

***L. coccinea*** Planch. non Bojer. WEST INDIAN HOLLY. Glabrous shrub to 2.25m. Lvs 2–3 pinnate, leaflets 5–10cm, elliptic to obovate, acuminate to cuspidate, margins revolute, sometimes toothed. Cymes 8–12.5cm diam., crowded, flat-topped; fls to 1cm diam., cor. lobes pink (scarlet in bud), stamens yellow. Burma.

***L. guineensis*** G. Don. Shrub, 2.2–7.5m. Lvs 1–2 pinnate, leaflets 10–20cm, elliptic, obscurely serrate towards apex, glabrous. Cyme densely branched, cor. lobes vermilion above, yellow to orange beneath. Tropical Africa.

***L. manillensis*** Walp. Glabrous shrub or tortuously branched tree to 6m. Lvs 3–4 pinnate, leaflets 3–22cm, elliptic to ovate-oblong, acuminate, serrulate. Cymes 25–50cm diam., axis and pedicels flushed red; cor. lobes pink beneath, yellow above edged pink. Fr. 3mm diam., deep red. Philippines.

***L. sambucina*** (L.) Willd. non Blanco. Shrub to 4m. Lvs 1–1.75cm, 1–3 pinnate, broadly elliptic, acute or acuminate, obscurely to coarsely crenately toothed, flushed bronze, veins sometimes tinted rosy-purple. Fls green-white. Tropical Asia, Polynesia, New Guinea, N Australia.

***L. coccinea*** Bojer non Planch. See *L. guineensis*.
***L. sambucina*** Blanco non (L.) Willd. See *L. manillensis*.

**LEEACEAE** Dumort. See *Leea*.

**Leeks**. *Allium ampeloprasum* var. *porrum*. Liliaceae (Alliaceae). A monocotyledenous biennial plant with long green leaves with white bases which form a tight cylinder. It is similar to the onion but leaves are flat and the plant does not normally form a distinct bulb. Wild relatives of leek occur in the eastern Mediterranean region and into western and southern Russia. Leek is adapted to a temperate climate and is able to withstand cold weather to a much greater extent than the onion. However, like the onion it is vernalized by cold temperature and subsequently bolts, making it unusable. Leeks are a hardy winter vegetable with a harvesting season extending from late summer until late spring the following year. They have a milder flavour than onion and are used as a cooked vegetable and in soups.

Germination is optimum at soil temperatures between 11–23°C/52–73°F but is drastically reduced at soil temperatures below 7°C/45°F and above 27°C/80°F. Cool conditions favour optimum growth and day temperatures greater than 24°C/75°F may reduce yields. Under these temperature conditions leek does not develop a conspicuous bulb but under extreme long-day conditions (greater than 19 hours) at high latitudes bulbing may occur, particularly at a temperature of 15–18°C/60–65°F.

Leeks grow best in a deep, well-cultivated soil into which well-rotted organic manure has been worked. Optimum soil pH is 6.5–7.5 and should be raised by liming if too acid. Soil temperatures should be at least 7°C/45°F before sowing; the earliest crops should be raised from sowings in gentle heat under protection during early spring. These should be pricked out and hardened off before planting out. Early outdoor sowings can also be made under cloches in drills approximately 2cm/¾in. deep. Spring sowings should be planted out during the summer when the seedlings are between 10–15 weeks old and are about 20cm/8in. tall. Longer leaves can be trimmed back slightly to facilitate planting and the seedbed should be watered well before lifting the seedlings.

A number of cultivars should be used to provide a succession of croppings. Recommended spacing for optimum yield of average-sized leeks is in rows 30cm/12in. apart with 15cm/6in. between plants within rows. Higher-density plantings will give similar yields of small, more slender leeks.

The length of the blanched portion of leaf bases depends in part on the cultivar but can also be affected by the planting method. Several methods are aimed at increasing the proportion of blanched leaf. The simplest is to make 15cm/6in.-deep holes with a dibber into which individual plants are dropped. The holes should then be filled with water. The holes will gradually fill up as the season progresses, increasing the proportion of leaf excluded from light. An alternative approach is to plant into V-shaped drills 7.5cm/3in. deep which are later closed in around the plants to blanch the lower portion of the leaves. Plants can also be established on the flat and earthed up in a similar way several times during growth. Seeds can be sown direct into their final position but this makes weed control more difficult and the leeks are likely to have a reduced portion of blanched stem. Plants should be kept well watered and free from weed competition during growth.

Leeks can be lifted as required and later cultivars can remain outside during the winter until late spring when plants will commence flowering and are no longer suitable for consumption. The early cultivars for harvesting during the later summer and autumn period tend to be taller, with longer white shafts and paler foliage then the later ones, which tend to be thicker with a shorter region of blanched stem and have darker leaves.

Recommended cultivars include: (early) 'Autumn Mammoth', 'Gennevilliers Splendid', 'King Richard'; (very long) 'Swiss Giant-Pancho'; (mid-season) 'Argenta', 'Lyon', 'Lyon Prizetaker'; (late) 'Blauwgroen Winter-Alaska (short and bulbous), 'Catalina', 'Giant Winter', 'Giant Winter Royal Favourite', 'Goliath', 'Musselburgh', 'Snowstar', 'Wintra', ('Winterreuzen'). 'Broad London' or 'Large American Flag', and 'Unique' are recommended in the US for overwintering. Leek fanciers grow 'pot leeks' for exhibition and competition for maximum weight, using specialized cultural methods and home-saved seed strains.

Leeks have many disease problems in common with onions; leaf blotch (*Cladosporium allii*), rust (*Puccinia allii*) and white tip (*Phytophthora porri*) are especially important. Symptoms of leaf blotch are as described for onion. The rust causes long leaf lesions containing red-brown urediospores. In white tip the leaves at first turn yellow at the tips and eventually become bleached and die; they may also rot at ground level. Plant debris should be destroyed to prevent the fungus oospores from contaminating the soil. Rust and white tip can be controlled with fungicide sprays.

**Legousia** Durande. (Possibly from the French popular name for *L. arvensis*, 'legonz des champs'.) Campanulaceae. Some 15 species of small annual herbs, stems simple or branched at base. Leaves ovate to lanceolate, sinuate, lower ones shortly petiolate. Flowers in panicles, compact corymbs or solitary near end of branches; calyx 5-lobed; corolla 5-lobed, rotate to campanulate; stamens 5, filaments short, anthers free. Fruit a capsule, dehiscing by 3 valves near apex. Mediterranean

CULTIVATION *L. speculum-veneris* is found as a wild flower on arable land and on bare and stony ground, and *L. hybrida* on sandy and calcareous soils, frequently as a weed of turnip and corn fields. They are charming additions to the wild flower garden and other informal or naturalistic plantings. All are easily cultivated in any well-drained soil in sun, from seed sown *in situ* in spring.

***L. hybrida*** (L.) Delarb. VENUS' LOOKING GLASS. To 35cm, shortly hispid or subglabrous. Lvs oblanceolate to oblong, sinuate, generally sessile. Fls few, in small terminal clusters, sessile; cal. lobes subulate; cor. broadly campanulate, maroon to lilac. Europe, N Africa.

***L. pentagonia*** (L.) Druce. To 30cm, often hispid, occasionally glabrous. Lvs to 5cm, obovate to oblong. Fls solitary or in panicles; cal. lobes mostly a quarter to half the size of the ovary at flowering time; cor. campanulate, white at base, blue to violet further up. Fr. a capsule, cylindric. E Mediterranean, Balkans.

***L. speculum-veneris*** (L.) Chaix. VENUS' LOOKING GLASS. Stems to 30cm, glabrous or occasionally shortly hispid, erect, usually branched, ascending. Lvs oblanceolate to oblong, sinuate. Fls solitary or numerous, forming a panicle; cal. lobes linear-lanceolate, shorter than or about as long as ovary at flowering; cor. rotate, violet, rarely white or mauve. C & S Europe. 'Alba': fls white. 'Grandiflora': fls larger.

For synonymy see *Campanula* and *Specularia*.

**LEGUMINOSAE** Juss. (*Fabaceae* Lindl.). PEA FAMILY. (Including Caesalpiniaceae, Papilionaceae and Mimosaceae.) Dicot. 657 genera and 16,400 species of trees, shrubs, lianes and herbs, sometimes spiny, often with root nodules containing nitrogen-fixing bacteria, frequently with alkaloids. Leaves pinnate, bipinnate (rarely palmate), unifoliolate, trifoliate or simple, sometimes phyllodic or reduced to a tendril, usually alternate, petiole and leaflets with basal pulvini often controlling orientation and 'sleep movements'; stipules present, sometimes large or represented by spines (in some *Acacia* species ant-inhabited) or prickles; leaflets sometimes with stipullules. Flowers usually bisexual, regular or irregular, hypogynous to perigynous, usually in racemes, spikes or heads; calyx 5 free sepals or (3–) 5 (6) fused forming a tube with valvate lobes, or often more or less bilabiate; corolla (0–) 5 free petals, irregular, in Caesalpinioideae adaxial small and lying within its laterals, in Papilionoideae large (standard) and outside them, in Mimosoideae (3–) 5 (6) sometimes basally connate, regular and usually valvate; stamens usually twice the petals (to numerous in Mimosoideae and rarely so in Caesalpinioideae), free or ± connate, alike or not, sometimes some staminodal, often coloured and long-exserted in Caelsalpinioideae, nectary often a ring on receptacle around ovary; ovary superior, of 1 carpel (2–16 in some Mimosoideae), with equal number of locules and 1-numerous ovules per locule. Fruit typically a legume, sometimes a loment, samara or drupe; seeds hard, endosperm absent or little, copious in *Prosopis*. Important food crops such as kidney beans, *Phaseolus vulgaris*; broad bean, *Vicia faba*; chick pea, *Cicer arietinum*; garden pea, *Pisum sativum*; groundnut or peanut, *Arachis hypogaea*; lentil, *Lens culinaris*; mung bean, *Phaseolus aureus*; pigeon pea, *Cajanus cajan*; scarlet runner beam, *Phaseolus coccineus*, soya bean *Glycine max*, and many others. Some provide edible oils, while the cowpea, *Vigna unguiculata, Trifolium* species and lucerne or alfalfa, *Medicago sativa* are grown as forage crops. Some trees are used for timber and some *Acacia* species yield bark for tanning as well as gum Arabic. Some species of *Caesalpinia, Genista* and *Indigofera* are sources of dyes. Some are of medicinal uses such as the leaves of some *Cassia* species, which provide the purgative senna. Cosmopolitan. Subfamilies (sometimes treated as separate families): Caesalpinioideae: 162 genera and 2000 species, usually trees and shrubs, tropical; Mimosoideae: 58 genera and 3100 species, trees, some shrubs, including aquatics, mainly tropical and warm; papilionoideae: 437 genera and 11,300 species, from rainforests to deserts, with great diversity of form especially in Brazilian planalto, Mexico, E Africa, Madagascar and Sin-Himalaya; some spectacular stocks in Mediterranean, Cape and Australia.

*Acacia, Acrocarpus, Adenanthera, Adenocarpus, Afzelia, Albizia, Amicia, Amorpha, Amphicarpaea, Anadenanthera, Anagyris, Andira, Anthyllis, Apios, Argyrocytisus, Aspalathus, Astragalus, Baphia, Baptisia, Bauhinia, Bolusanthus, Bossiaea, Brachysema, Brachystegia, Brownea, Burtonia, Butea, Caesalpinia, Cajanus, Calicotome, Calliandra, Calophaca, Calpurnia, Camoensia, Camptosema, Campylotropis, Canavalia, Caragana, Carmichaelia,* × *Carmispartium, Cassia, Castanospermum, Centrosema, Ceratonia, Cercis, Chamaecrista, Chamaecytisus, Chesneya, Chordospartium, Chorizema, Christia, Cicer, Cladrastis, Clianthus, Clitoria, Codariocalyx, Colutea, Colvillea, Corallospartium, Coronilla, Crotalaria, Cyamopsis, Cytisophyllum, Cytisus, Dalbergia, Dalea, Daviesia, Delonix, Derris, Desmanthus, Desmodium, Dichrostachys, Dillwynia, Dipogon, Dorycnium, Ebenus, Enterolobium, Erinacea, Erythrina, Eutaxia, Galega, Gastrolobium, Genista, Geoffroea, Gleditsia, Gliricidia, Glycine, Glycyrrhiza, Gymnocladus, Haematoxylum, Halimodendron, Hardenbergia, Hedysarum, Hippocrepis, Hovea, Hypocalyptus, Indigofera, Inga, Jacksonia, Kennedia, Lablab, +Laburnocytisus, Laburnum, Lathyrus, Lens, Lespedeza, Leucaena, Lonchocarpus, Lotus, Lupinus, Lysidice, Lysiloma, Maackia, Macrotyloma, Medicago, Millettia, Mimosa, Mucuna, Mundulea, Myroxylon, Neptunia, Notospartium, Onobrychis, Ononis, Ormocarpum, Ormosia, Oxylobium, Oxytropis, Pachyrhizus, Paramacrolobium, Parkia, Parkinsonia, Parochetus, Peltophorum, Petteria, Phaseolus, Phyllocarpus, Phyllota, Pickeringia, Piptanthus, Piscidia, Pisum, Pithecellobium, Platylobium, Platymiscium, Podalyria, Podocytisus, Pongamia, Prosopis, Psophocarpus, Psoralea, Pterocarpus, Pterolobium, Pueraria, Pultenaea, Retama, Robinia, Sabinea, Saraca, Schizolobium, Schotia, Senna, Sesbania, Sophora, Spartium, Strongylodon, Sutherlandia, Swainsona, Tamarindus, Templetonia, Tephrosia, Thermopsis, Tipuana, Trifolium, Trigonella, Ulex, Vicia, Vigna, Viminaria, Virgilia, Wagatea, Wiborgia, Willardia, Wisteria.*

**Leibnitzia** Cass. Compositae. About 4 species of scapose perennial herbs, with spring and autumn flowering forms. Leaves in a basal rosette, lyrate, pinnatifid-lyrate, pinnatifid or sinuate, petiolate. Capitula solitary, dimorphic, radiate; peduncles 1–11, bracteate; receptacle flat, naked; phyllaries imbricate, in a few series, linear to elliptic or ovate-oblong; ray florets female' or neuter; disc florets tubular, hermaphrodite. Fruit a hairy cypsela, more or less compressed; pappus of persistent hairs. Spring state: leaves often few or absent, arachnoid to tomentose; capitula small; florets all fertile, ray florets 12. Autumn state: leaves large; capitula large, ray florets inconspicuous; fruit larger than in spring forms. Himalaya, S & E Asia.

CULTIVATION Occasionally grown for botanical interest, in well-drained soil in sun or part shade on the rock garden.

***L. anandria*** (L.) Turcz. Spring state: lvs to 13×6cm, lanceolate, sinuate, subglabrous above, arachnoid to tomentose beneath, petiole to 7.5cm. Capitula to 2cm diam.; peduncles to 26cm; ray florets white above and rose-pink beneath or white-pink to rose above and beneath. Fr. sometimes tinged red, 4–6mm; pappus pale golden. Autumn state: lvs to 23×7cm, elliptic-oblong, ovate, lyrate or pinnatifid-lyrate or sinuate, apical seg. usually large, rounded, cordate or more or less triangular, base margin crenate various. Capitula to 2×4cm; peduncles to 60cm; ray florets white. Spring–autumn. S Siberia to Nepal and Japan. Z3.

***L. nepalensis*** (Kunze) Kitam. Spring state: lvs to 8×2cm, markedly underdeveloped, tomentose beneath, petiole to 4cm. Capitula peduncles c1cm diam., to 5cm; ray florets like *L. anandria*. Fr. tinged purple; pappus violet-purple. Autumn state: lvs to 21×4cm, lyrate with a cordate terminal apical seg. and rounded lateral seg., or sinuate, slightly undulate and remotely crenate, petiole to 13cm. Capitula to 2×2cm; peduncles to 35cm; ray florets red, or white with red tips. Spring–autumn. Himalaya. Z8.

***L. kunzeana*** (R. Br. & Asch.) Pobed. See *L. nepalensis*.
For further synonymy see *Gerbera*.

**Leiophyllum** (Pers.) Hedw. f. (From Gk *leios*, smooth, and *phyllon*, a leaf.) Ericaceae. 1 species, an evergreen shrub, erect or, more commonly, low or prostrate, usually 5–30cm, exceptionally to 1m tall. Leaves 6–12×2–6mm, simple, entire, alternate or opposite, oblong, ovate or obovate, apex blunt or acuminate, glabrous, glossy, coriaceous, dark green above, paler beneath; petioles short. Flowers *c*6mm diam., in dense, terminal, umbellate corymbs 18–25mm diam.; pedicels glabrous or short-downy, covered with stalked glands; calyx lobes 5, narrowly lanceolate, about half petal length; petals 5, separate, white to pale pink, oval, spreading; stamens 10, diffuse, filaments narrow, anthers ferruginous, dehiscing through a split; style threadlike. Fruit a glabrous capsule, 3mm, 2–5 valved; seeds many. Late spring–early summer. E US.

CULTIVATION Grown for their freely produced, white, star-shaped flowers which open from pink buds in spring and early summer, and for the glossy evergreen foliage with bronze tones in winter. They are suitable for the rock garden or peat terrace, with care in placement, since the root system is extensive. Grow in good light or semi-shade, leafy, acidic soils, with protection from cold drying winds. Maintain an acidic organic mulch. Propagate by semi-ripe heel cuttings, treat with rooting hormone and root in a closed case with bottom heat; also by layers.

***L. buxifolium*** (Berg) Elliott. SAND MYRTLE. As for the genus. New Jersey to Florida. 'Nanum': habit dwarf; branches abundant; fls pink. var. ***hugeri*** (Small) Schneid. Shrub to 20cm, habit more cushion-like. Lvs generally alternate, longer. Fls pink; pedicels glandular. Fr. rough-textured. var. ***prostratum*** (Loud.) A. Gray. ALLEGHENY SAND MYRTLE. Lvs 7–12×4–6mm, generally opposite, orbicular to elliptic, downy. Pedicels glandular. Z5.

***L. lyonii*** (Sweet) Sweet. See *L. buxifolium* var. *prostratum*.

**Leiostemon** Raf.

***L. thurberi*** Greene. See *Penstemon thurberi*.

**Leipoldtia** L. Bol. (For Christian L. Leipoldt, collector and friend of L. Bolus.) Aizoaceae. 21 species of glabrous, erect or prostrate shrublets to 50cm. Leaves 4–40mm, frequently laterally compressed, obtuse to truncate at tip, usually thicker than wide, glabrous, smooth. Flowers 1–5, 2–3cm diam., purple-pink, rarely pale pink or yellow, bracteate; pedicels to 6.5cm; sepals 5; stigmas to 10. Capsule with winged valves. S Africa (Cape Province), Namibia. Closely related to *Cephalophyllum*. Z9.

CULTIVATION As for *Cephalophyllum*.

***L. amplexicaulis*** (L. Bol.) L. Bol. Prostrate, branches 14–19mm, stiff. Leaves 12–30×4–6.5×4–5mm, sabre-shaped, swollen, rounded triquetrous, tip rounded. Fls 2.5–3cm diam., purple-pink, paler below. Cape Province: Clanwilliam, Calvinia and Sutherland Districts.

***L. frutescens*** (L. Bol.) Hartmann. Erect or prostrate, extent to 60×90cm; stems 5–6mm diam., internodes 2–5cm. Lvs 50–80×6–9×6–9mm, 4 together on short shoots, cylindric, apiculate, sheath 2–8mm. Fls 6cm diam., yellow to lemon-yellow. Cape Province: Little Namaqualand.

***L. weigangiana*** (Dinter) Dinter & Schwantes. Erect shrub to 50cm with 3–20 stems 2–3mm thick, bark yellow-white. Lvs 15×4mm, patent, navicular, triquetrous, blue-green, densely spotted. Fls solitary, 2cm diam., violet-pink. Namibia: Great Namaqualand.

For synonymy see *Mesembryanthemum* and *Rhopalocyclus*.

**Leitneria** Chapm. (For E.F. Leitner (1812–1838) German naturalist.) Leitneriaceae. 1 species, a deciduous, dioecious small tree or, more commonly, freely suckering shrub seldom exceeding 5m. Crown spreading; branches downy at first, becoming grey and thick-barked with very light wood. Leaves 6.5–16cm, narrowly ovate-lanceolate or elliptic, acuminate, entire, initially downy throughout, ultimately grey-sericeous below only. Catkins erect, borne before leaves at axils, males to 3.5cm, longer and stouter than females; perianth absent; stamens 8–12; ovary 1-celled. Fruit to 1.5cm, a deep brown drupe. E US. Z5.

CULTIVATION Of interest because of its extremely lightweight wood, *Leitneria* occurs in damp habitats. Grow in a moist, lime-free, humus-rich soil. Propagate by seed or removal of suckers.

***L. floridana*** Chapm. CORKWOOD. As for the genus.

**LEITNERIACEAE** Benth. See *Leitneria*.

**Leleba** Nak.

***L. multiplex*** (Lour.) Nak. See *Bambusa multiplex*.
***L. oldhamii*** (Munro) Nak. See *Bambusa oldhamii*.
***L. vulgaris*** (Schräd. ex Wendl.) Nak. See *Bambusa vulgaris*.

**Lemaireocereus** Britt. & Rose.

***L. beneckei*** (Ehrenb.) Britt. & Rose. See *Stenocereus beneckei*.
***L. cartwrightianus*** Britt. & Rose. See *Armatocereus cartwrightianus*.
***L. chende*** (Roland-Goss.) Britt. & Rose. See *Polaskia chende*.
***L. chichipe*** (Roland-Goss.) Britt. & Rose. See *Polaskia chichipe*.
***L. deficiens*** Otto & A. Dietr. See *Stenocereus griseus*.
***L. dumortieri*** (Scheidw.) Britt. & Rose. See *Stenocereus dumortieri*.
***L. eruca*** (Brandg.) Britt. & Rose. See *Stenocereus eruca*.
***L. euphorbioides*** (Haw.) Werderm. See *Neobuxbaumia euphorbioides*.
***L. gladiger*** (Lem.) Backeb. See *Stenocereus griseus*.
***L. godingianus*** Britt. & Rose. See *Armatocereus godingianus*.
***L. griseus*** (Haw.) Britt. & Rose. See *Stenocereus griseus*.
***L. gummosus*** (Engelm. ex Brandg.) Britt. & Rose. See *Stenocereus gummosus*.
***L. hollianus*** (F.A.C. Weber ex J. Coult.) Britt. & Rose. See *Pachycereus hollianus*.
***L. laetus*** (Kunth) Britt. & Rose. See *Armatocereus laetus*.
***L. littoralis*** (Brandg.) Gates. See *Stenocereus thurberi*.
***L. marginatus*** (DC.) A. Berger. See *Pachycereus marginatus*.
***L. martinezii*** Gonz. Ortega. See *Stenocereus martinezii*.
***L. pruinosus*** (Pfeiff.) Britt. & Rose. See *Stenocereus pruinosus*.
***L. queretaroensis*** (F.A.C. Weber) Safford. See *Stenocereus queretaroensis*.
***L. stellatus*** (Pfeiff.) Britt. & Rose. See *Stenocereus stellatus*.
***L. thurberi*** (Engelm.) Britt. & Rose. See *Stenocereus thurberi*.
***L. treleasei*** Britt. & Rose. See *Stenocereus treleasei*.
***L. weberi*** (J. Coult.) Britt. & Rose. See *Pachycereus weberi*.

**Lemboglossum** Halbinger. (From Gk *lembos*, boat or canoe, and *glossa*, tongue, referring to the boat-shaped lip.) Orchidaceae. Some 14 species of epiphytic orchids formerly included in *Odontoglossum*. Rhizome short, creeping. Pseudobulbs clustered, rounded, laterally compressed, unifoliate to trifoliate at apex, subtended by 1–3 distichous, leaflike sheaths. Inflorescence a raceme or panicle, erect to pendent, few- to many-flowered; flowers large, showy; sepals subequal; petals subequal to sepals or wider; lip short-clawed, fused to column, lamina showy, variously shaped, callus fleshy, somewhat curved, lateral margins raised, central portion usually bidentate; column long, broad or slender, sometimes auriculate; pollinia 2, with laminar stipe. C America, Mexico. Z10.

CULTIVATION Cool to intermediate conditions in light shade with humid, buoyant air and frequent watering when in growth, somewhat less so at other times. See also *Odontoglossum*.

***L. bictoniense*** (Batem.) Halbinger. Pseudobulbs to 18×3.5cm. Lvs to 45×5.5cm, elliptic-oblong to lanceolate or linear, acute to acuminate, bright green or yellow-green, prominently nerved, conduplicate at base. Raceme or panicle to 80cm, erect, many-fld; fls to 5cm diam., often fragrant; tepals usually pale green or yellow-green banded or spotted red-brown, sep. to 2.5×1cm, elliptic-lanceolate to elliptic-oblanceolate, acute or acuminate, apex recurved, pet. smaller than sep., oblanceolate to linear-elliptic, oblique, obtuse to acute; lip to 2×2.5cm, subcordate, acute to rounded, crisped or crenulate, white to rose or magenta-tinted. Mexico, Guatemala, El Salvador. White, golden and lime-green self-coloured forms occur.

***L. cervantesii*** (La Ll. & Lex.) Halbinger. Pseudobulbs to 6×3cm, ovoid, ancipitous. Lvs to 15×3cm, ovate-lanceolate to elliptic-oblong, acute to acuminate, slightly chartaceous. Raceme to 32cm, usually shorter, to 6-fld, covered with brown sheaths; fls fragrant; tepals white to rose irregularly banded brown-red in basal half, sep. to 3.5×1cm, narrowly ovate-oblong, pet. to 3×2cm, ovate-elliptic to suborbicular, abruptly acute or rounded; lip white to rose, striped purple at base, to 2.5×3cm, 3-lobed, lateral lobes erect, midlobe broadly cordate, irregularly dentate, callus yellow, 2-lobed; column white, to 1cm. Mexico, Guatemala.

***L. cordatum*** (Lindl.) Halbinger. Pseudobulbs to 7.5×3.5cm. Lvs to 30×5cm, elliptic to lanceolate or oblong-ligulate, subacute, dark green, coriaceous. Raceme or panicle to 60cm, erect, many-fld; tepals yellow blotched and barred deep red-brown, sep. to 5×1cm, elliptic-lanceolate, acuminate, concave, keeled below, pet. to 3.5×1cm, ovate-lanceolate to elliptic-lanceolate, oblique, long-acuminate; lip to 2.5×2cm, usually white spotted red-brown, cordate, acuminate, margins involute at apex, slightly erose, callus 3-keeled. Mexico, Guatemala, Honduras, Costa Rica, Venezuela.

***L. maculatum*** (La Ll. & Lex.) Halbinger. Pseudobulbs to 9.5×3cm, ovoid. Lvs to 32×5.5cm, elliptic-lanceolate to elliptic-ligulate, acute to obtuse, fleshy. Infl. to 40cm, arcuate to pendent, sometimes branched, few- to many-fld; sep. chestnut-brown or pale yellow marked red-brown, sometimes barred green at base, to 4×1cm, lanceolate, acute or acuminate, keeled below; pet. yellow heavily spotted red-brown at base, to 3×1.5cm, elliptic-lanceolate, acute or acuminate; lip similar in colour to sep., to 2×2.5cm, cordate-reniform or cordate-triangular, subacute, dentate, crisped, callus yellow marked red, fleshy; column white. Mexico, Guatemala.

***L. majale*** (Rchb. f.) Halbinger. Pseudobulbs to 7×2.5cm, ovoid, almost concealed by pale brown sheaths. Lvs to 30×3cm, linear-ligulate, subacute or obtuse, subcoriaceous, conduplicate at base. Raceme erect, to 14cm, 2–4-fld; tepals purple or rose, sep. to 3×1cm, narrowly oblong to lanceolate, acute, concave, keeled below, pet. smaller than sep., narrowly oblanceolate to elliptic-oblong, acute to subobtuse; lip rose blotched deep purple or carmine, to 3×3cm, ovate-subquadrate, retuse, recurved, callus bilobulate, dentate; column white, to 1.5cm, clavate. Guatemala.

***L. rossii*** (Lindl.) Halbinger. Pseudobulbs to 6×3.5cm, ovoid to ovoid-elliptic, wrinkled with age. Lvs to 14×2.75cm, elliptic to elliptic-lanceolate, acute or acuminate, subcoriaceous. Raceme to 20cm, usually far shorter, erect or arcuate, 1–4-fld; tepals white, pale yellow or pale pink, the sep. and lower portions of pet. mottled and spotted chocolate to rust, sep. to 4.5×1cm, oblong-elliptic to linear-lanceolate, acute or acuminate, slightly reflexed, pet. to 4×2cm, short-clawed, broadly elliptic to oblong-elliptic, acute or obtuse, crisped to undulate; lip to 3×3cm, broadly orbicular-subcordate, apex rounded or emarginate, undulate, callus deep yellow spotted red-brown; column rose-purple, to 2cm. Mexico, Guatemala, Honduras, Nicaragua.

***L. stellatum*** (Lindl.) Halbinger. Pseudobulbs ovoid-ellipsoid to cylindrical, to 6×1.5cm. Lvs to 15×2.5cm, narrowly elliptic to oblanceolate or linear-ligulate, subobtuse to acuminate, narrowed and conduplicate at base. Raceme to 8.5cm, slender, 1–2-fld; tepals subsimilar, yellow-bronze barred brown, to 30×5mm, lanceolate to linear-lanceolate, acute to acuminate, sep. concave, keeled below, pet. sometimes yellow-white; lip white or pink marked mauve, to 2×2cm, ovate-triangular to suborbicular, obtuse to rounded, lacerate-dentate, callus extending onto base of blade as a short bifid plate; column to 12mm. Mexico, Guatemala, El Salvador.

***L. uro-skinneri*** (Lindl.) Halbinger. Resembles *L. bictoniense* except lvs lanceolate; tepals deep red to green, barred and mottled brown, to 3×1.5cm, pet. obliquely ovate-elliptic, lip to 3×3.5cm, pink, veined or spotted white. Guatemala, Honduras.

For synonymy see *Odontoglossum*.

## Lembrotropis L.

***L. nigricans*** (L.) Griseb. See *Cytisus nigricans*.

## Lemmaphyllum Presl.

**Lemmaphyllum** Presl. (From Gk *lemma*, husk, and *phyllon*, leaf.) Polypodiaceae. Perhaps 4 species of epiphytic ferns. Rhizomes long-creeping, filiform, occasionally branching, roots matted, hairy; scales ovate to lanceolate, entire or ciliate at margin, clathrate. Stipes remote where present. Fronds short-stipitate or sessile and jointed to rhizome, usually dimorphous: sterile fronds simple, ovate to obovate or elliptic, entire at margin, fleshy, more or less glabrous or, rarely, scaly; fertile fronds simple, linear to oblanceolate, long-attenuate at apex, entire at margin; veins indistinct, reticulate, with free, included veinlets. Coenosori continuously uniserial, medial on each side of costa, not confluent at apex, usually linear; paraphyses initially peltate, clathrate, dentate; annulus approximately 14-celled; spores glassy. Asia (India, China, Japan, to Malaysia, Indonesia, Polynesia). Z10.

CULTIVATION As for *Pyrrosia*.

***L. accedens*** (Bl.) Donk. Rhiz. long-creeping, to 1mm wide; scales to 2mm, sparse, narrow, dentate, clathrate. Fronds short-stipitate, dimorphous: sterile fronds to 3×2cm, elliptic or oblong to ovate, apex obtuse or acute, base cuneate, entire, membranous to somewhat leathery, glabrous; fertile fronds (usually so only in upper half) elliptic to ovate, apex narrowed, base broadly cuneate, occasionally entirely fertile and narrowed to 15×1cm, entire, leathery; veins indistinct, areolae many, irregular, with free, included veinlets; stipes to 5mm. Malaysia, New Guinea, Polynesia.

***L. carnosum*** Presl. Rhiz. long-creeping, wiry; scales peltate. Fronds stipitate, simple, dimorphous: sterile fronds to 7cm, elliptic, lanceolate, obovate, or spathulate or, rarely, rounded to heart-shaped, entire, apex narrowly acute, fleshy, leathery; fertile fronds to 6cm long, spathulate to linear, apex obtuse, veins anastomosing, with free, included, usually simple veinlets; stipes remote. India to China.

***L. microphyllum*** Presl. Rhiz. long-creeping, to 1mm wide; scales to 1.5mm, sparse, spreading, filiform to linear or acicular, clathrate. Fronds stipitate, simple, dimorphous: sterile fronds to 5×1.5cm, often sessile, rounded to ovate or obovate, or elliptic or spathulate, apex obtuse, base cuneate, entire, leathery, glabrous; fertile fronds to 3×0.5cm, stipitate, simple, narrowly linear to oblanceolate, apex obtuse, 3×0.5cm, base narrowed, entire. E Asia (China, Taiwan, Korea, Japan).

For synonymy see *Drymoglossum, Pleopeltis* and *Polypodium*.

## Lemna L.

**Lemna** L. (Gk name for a water plant.) DUCKWEED; DUCKMEAT; FROG'S BUTTONS. Lemnaceae. 13 species of minute, aquatic herbs, floating on or below the water surface, consisting of a leaflike frond or plant body and single root, fronds sometimes cohering. Frond lanceolate to ovate, with or without distinct papules, usually not more than 8mm across, with 1–5 (rarely 7) veins, lacking pigment cells, and crystal cells containing needle-shaped raphides. Root with a tubular sheath at tip. Flowering fronds sometimes similar to vegetative fronds. Flowers rarely produced, 1–2 per frond, in marginal pouches; stamens 2, pistil 1; ovary with 1–7 ovules. Fruit winged or not; seeds ribbed. Cosmopolitan.

CULTIVATION The duckweeds may be invasive in cultivation, spreading rapidly across the water to form a thick green carpet; they are also, however, good food plants for fish, ducks and other birds. The so-called rootcap (really only an apical swelling) has a higher specific gravity than any other part of the plant, righting capsized individuals. In nature, *Lemna* produces winter resting buds which sink to pond bottoms; under aquarium conditions, they remain in growth throughout the year. *L. triscula*, forming a spongy mass below the water's surface, is possibly the best for cold-water aquarium cultivation, giving some cover to young fish (although all *Lemna* spp. may harbour fish parasites); *L. minor* tolerates tropical and cold-water aquaria. Introduce all spp. by throwing small colonies on to the water's surface and give full light in still water rich in nitrates and lime: control by skimming.

***L. aequinoctialis*** Welw. Fronds 1–6.5×0.8–4.5mm, floating on the water surface, margins entire, 3-veined, usually with one papule above the node, anthocyanins absent. Root to 3.5cm, root sheath wing 1–2.5 times longer than wide, rootcap pointed. Fls and fr. often produced, flowering fronds similar to vegetative fronds; style 0.05–0.20mm. Fr. not winged, dehiscent, 0.5–0.8×0.4–0.7mm; seed 0.45–0.8mm long, 0.3–0.7mm thick, tinged brown, with 8–26 longitudinal ribs and 30–80 lateral ribs. Widely distributed in tropics and subtropics. 10.

***L. gibba*** L. Fronds 1–8×0.8–6mm, often to 4mm thick, rather shiny and sometimes spotted red above, sometimes red below, usually without distinct papules (except sometimes the smaller fronds), 4–5-veined (rarely 7-, small fronds sometimes 3-veined). Rootcap usually rounded in fresh material, 0.6–1.8mm. Fls often present; style 0.05–0.1mm; ovary with 1–7 ovules. Fr. winged, dehiscent, 0.6–1.0×0.8–1.2mm; seeds 1–5, 0.7–0.9mm long, 0.4–0.6mm thick, pale, with 8–16 ribs. Temperate regions, especially in America, Europe, Africa, SW Asia. Z4.

***L. miniscula*** Herter. Fronds 0.8–4.0×0.5–2.5mm, floating on the water surface, usually pale green, often with a pale line above, solitary or 2–3 cohering, margins entire, veins absent or, more usually, 1 short vein not extending beyond the larger-celled air spaces. Root to 1.5cm, root sheath not winged, rootcap often rounded to rather pointed. Fls and fr. occasional, flowering fronds similar to vegetative fronds; style 0.2–0.4mm. Fr. 0.6–1.0×0.4–0.7mm; seed 0.4–0.55mm long, 0.3mm thick, 12–15-ribbed. America, Europe, E Asia. Z4.

***L. minor*** L. COMMON DUCKWEED; LESSER DUCKWEED. Fronds 1–8×0.6–5.0mm, not more than about 1mm thick, shiny and occasionally diffusely tinged red above, rarely tinged slightly red below, some indistinct papules in the median line, 3-veined (rarely 4–5). Rootcap usually rounded. Fls occasionally produced; style 0.10–0.15mm; ovary with 1 ovule. Fr. rare, indehiscent, winged, 0.8–1.0×0.8–1.1mm; seed 0.7–1.0mm long, 0.4–0.6mm thick, pale, with 10–16 ribs. Temperate regions with mild winters, except E Asia, Australia. Z4.

***L. perpusilla*** Torr. Fronds 1–4×0.8–3.0mm, floating on the water surface, margins entire, 3-veined, often with 2–3 papules above the node, anthocyanins absent. Root sheath wing 2–3 times longer than wide, rootcap jointed. Fls and fr. often produced, flowering fronds similar to vegetative fronds; style 0.2–0.4mm. Fr. winged, indehiscent, 0.7–1.0×0.5–0.7mm; seed 0.6–0.8mm long, 0.4–0.6mm thick, pale, indistinctly 35–70-ribbed. N America. Z5.

***L. trisulca*** L. STAR DUCKWEED. Fronds 3–15×1–5mm, submerged except when flowering, narrowing at the base to form a 2–20mm stalk, cohering and often forming branched chains, margins toothed at the base, 3-veined, anthocyanins present. Root to 2.5cm (sometimes not developed), root sheath not winged, rootcap pointed. Fls occasional; style 0.15mm. Fr. rare, winged, 0.6–0.9×0.7–1.2mm;

seed 0.6–1.1mm long, 0.5–0.8mm thick, 12–18-ribbed. Cosmopolitan in temperate climates, except N America.

***L.paucicostata*** Hegelm. See *L.aequinoctialis*.

**LEMNACEAE** Gray. DUCKWEED FAMILY. Monocot. 6 genera and 30 species of small or minute fee-floating thalloid plants, glabrous, with several unbranched roots or rootless, xylem absent but tracheids present in *Spirodela* roots. Thallus more or less fleshy, globular to flat and linear, sometimes with visible veins (without xylem), reproductive pouches 2, 1 marginal, the other on upper surface or marginal, with vegetative budding of new plants within. Inflorescences (rare, reproduction mainly vegetative) in 1 marginal pouch, with 2 (3) male and 1 female flowers with small membranous spathe; males with 1 stamen, perianth absent; females with pseudomonomerous gynoecium, 1-loculed; style 1, terminal, short; ovules 1–7. Fruit a utricle; seeds 1–4, embryo large, straight, sometimes radicle absent; endosperm absent or starchy. Important source of food for fish and waterfowl but can also become serious weeds. *Wolffia* species are the smallest-known flowering plants, sometimes used to test levels of herbicide in water. Cosmopolitan. *Lemna, Spirodela, Wolffia, Wolffiella*.

**Lemoine, Pierre Louis Victor** (1823–1911). Nurseryman. The son of a gardener, Lemoine was born in Delme, Moselle, and after studying at the college at Vic-sur-Seille left home to work in Bollweiller. For several years he worked under Louis van Houtte in Ghent, then continued training with Miellez, a company in Lille. At the age of 27 he founded a nursery in Nancy, and devoted himself to the introduction of new specimens. He also developed an interest in hybridization. His reputation was founded on his work with tropical and subtropical plants, hardy herbaceous perennials, trees and shrubs. He received plants from all over the world at a time when there was an unprecedented number of collectors abroad. He became very interested in Japanese flora, and introduced *Anemone hupehensis,* as well as valuable plants from South Africa, including the predecessors of the garden pelargoniums and gladioli. He introduced nearly 100 species into cultivation and more than 600 cultigens.

His work on hybridization was also highly profitable since the hybrids Lemoine created were sold to other gardeners to breed on a large scale. In 1854 his nursery produced the first *Potentilla* cultivar under the name 'Gloire de Nancy'; his most successful creations include 450 cultivars of *Fuchsia*, of which 'Heron' and 'Dollar Princess' are still popular, and his crossing of *Begonia socotrana* with *B.dregei* to produce *Begonia* 'Gloire de Lorraine'. He was the first to notice the value of *Streptocarpus biflorus* and *S.polyanthus* and produced many *Streptocarpus* hybrids.

He was elected an officer of the Legion of Honour in 1894. He was Honorary Vice-President of the Central Horticultural Society of Nancy, an Honorary Member of the National Horticultural Society of France, the Royal Society of Agriculture and Botany and the Royal Bavarian Horticultural Society, and was a committee member of the Massachusetts Horticultural Society in Boston. He was also the first foreigner to be awarded the Veitch Memorial Medal by the Royal Horticultural Society.

**Lenophyllum** Rose. Crassulaceae. 6 species of succulent perennial herbs. Stem branching at base. Leaves opposite, paired or clustered near base of stem, thick, concave above. Flowering stem sparsely leafy. Inflorescence a branching raceme or single terminal flower; flowers small; sepals 5, fused below; petals 5, erect, tips spreading, tapering to the base, just exceeding sepals; stamens 10, in 2 whorls, 5 fused to petals, 5 free; carpels 5, free, narrow. SW US, New Mexico. Z9.

CULTIVATION As for *Echeveria*.

***L.acutifolium*** Rose. Similar to *L.pusillum* except infl. a spike or raceme; fls sessile or nearly so; pet. green-yellow, spreading beyond sep. Mexico.

***L.guttatum*** Rose. To 30cm. Stem much-branched near base. Lvs ovate-elliptic, blunt, 2–3cm, grey-green, spotted dark purple. Infl. 3–4-branched; fls sessile or nearly so; sep. 3–4mm, nearly free; pet. 5mm, yellow turning red, blunt; stamens exceeded by pet.; styles as long as carpels. Autumn. Mexico.

***L.pusillum*** Rose. To 7cm. Lvs 8–16mm, pointed, concave above, convex below. Flowering stems 4–5cm with numerous, small, very thick lvs. Fls terminal, solitary; sep. fleshy, pointed, green; pet. 6–7mm, lemon yellow, oblong, blunt, spreading beyond sep.; stamens of 2 lengths, at least the longest exceeding pet. Texas, Mexico.

***L.texanum*** (J.G. Sm.) Rose. 10–20cm. Lvs 15–30mm, lanceolate to ovate, pointed. Infl. a spike or thyrse. Fls subsessile; sep. ovate to lanceolate, acute, 3mm; pet. 4–5mm, oblong, pointed, suffused red. Late summer–winter. Texas.

***L.weinbergii*** Britt. Lvs 15×10–15mm, obovate-ovate, grooved above, apex blunt. Infl. few-fld; sep. 3–4mm, blunt, tapering below; pet. yellow, tips erect or deflexed, blunt, just exceeding sep.; stamens exceeded by pet. Mexico.

For synonymy see *Sedum* and *Villadia*.

**Le Nôtre, André** (1613–1700). Architect and landscape designer. He was born in Paris in a house near the Tuileries, where his father, Jean Le Nôtre (*d*1655) was a head gardener; his grandfather, Pierre (*c*1570–*c*1610) had also been a gardener. As a young man Le Nôtre took to painting and studied in the studio of Simon Vouet, where he met the artist Charles Le Brun (1619–1690), another pupil. He also studied architecture under either Jacques Lemercier (1583–1654) or François Mansart (1598–1666). Le Nôtre began to work as a gardener and in 1635 was stated to be in the service of Gaston d'Orléans at the Luxembourg as 'jardinier de Monsieur frère du roi'. His father wished André to succeed him as 'premier jardinier du Roi au grand jardin des Tuileries' and in 1637 Louis XIII granted this request. Le Nôtre was then provided with his own apartment at the Tuileries, taking over the post in 1649.

In 1640 he married Françoise Langlois, a member of the minor nobility, by whom he had three children, none of whom survived infancy. While still working for Gaston, Le Nôtre had already worked for Louis XIII and was in 1643 'Dessinateur des Plants et Parterres de tous les Jardins de Sa Majesté'. The same year Louis died, but Le Nôtre continued his rise to fame and in 1657 was appointed 'contrôleur général des bâtiments, jardins, tapisseries et manufactures de France'. By 1666 he was 'conseiller du Roi aux conseils et contrôleur général des bâtiments de sa majesté', a post requiring him to advise on and inspect all new public buildings. This important post came with an accordingly large salary and, together with that from other posts and private commissions, enabled Le Nôtre to indulge his passion for collecting. He was particularly fond of paintings and possessed works by Nicolas Poussin and Claude Lorrain among others.

Le Nôtre's first great work was at Vaux-le-Vicomte, near Melun, 50km/30miles from Paris, the estate of the Finance Minister Nicolas Fouquet. He started work there in 1656 with the architect Louis Le Vau (1612–1670) and Charles Le Brun, he himself being responsible for the layout of the garden. The whole project was hurried along by Fouquet and completed in five years at considerable cost. In complexity and grandeur it was unlike anything previously created in France, involving drastic alterations to the surrounding area. Three villages were levelled and the River Anqueil was enlarged to form a canal 1km long. The entire garden was arranged along the axis of an immense vista, one of its most spectacular features being the Grille d'Eau, a cascade of water running down a vast triple-flighted staircase.

The garden at Vaux-le-Vicomte marked the beginning of Le Nôtre's fame and the end of Fouquet's career. It was visited by Louis XIV in 1661, just before he ordered Fouquet's arrest for treason, and the king was so impressed that he resolved to create yet greater gardens for himself. Soon Le Nôtre was set to work on redesigning Fontainebleau, having already modified the Jardin de la Reine there in 1645. Between 1661 and 1664, he laid out the Grand Parterre, four areas arranged around a central pool. Measuring 310×395m, it was one of the largest he ever made.

The most famous of Le Nôtre's designs was however at Versailles. As at Vaux-le-Vicomte he was jointed by Le Vau and Le Brun, this time under the direction of Jean-Baptiste Colbert. Work seems to have begun at the end of 1661. The king wished to revitalize Versailles, making it the new centre of France, and so planned to build a town around the château.

The château was expanded by Le Vau between 1662 and 1668 and, as at Vaux, Le Nôtre accordingly cleared the surrounding area to generate the best architectural effects. By 1665 the plan of the Petit Parc was in place and the Allée Royale, the axial vista of the design, was set out in 1667 and expanded over succeeding years. Traversing the Allée Royale was the Grand Canal, begun in 1668 and finished in 1671, 1.5km in length. Throughout the garden, so as to reduce the overwhelming sense size, bosquets or wooded thickets were placed into which the visitor could walk. The first important bosquet was the Marais, begun in 1670, followed by the Théâtre d'Eau, one of the most spectacular hydraulic features at Versailles, with others coming later. Further changes to the palace were carried out by Le Vau from 1669 to 1678 and more radical ones by Jules Hardouin-Mansart from 1678 onwards, including the construction of the Orangerie. The gardens underwent similar changes and expansion throughout this period, and the last phase included the creation of the Lac des Suisses and the Basin de Neptune. In all, Versailles occupied Le Nôtre from 30 years, its grandeur serving to symbolize the power of its creator, the Sun King. The extensive vistas emanating from the palace like tentacles into the surrounding town, perfectly express absolutism at its height.

As well as this vast commission Le Nôtre was involved with a whole host of other projects. With the royal gardens under his control, from 1665 to 1672 he reworked the parterres, bosquets and other aspects of the Tuileries gardens, as well as laying out what was to become the Champs Elysées. At the Trianon, near Versailles, Le Nôtre laid out the formal gardens in 1671–2.

For 20 years following his start at Versailles, Le Nôtre was also employed by the Grand Condé at Chantilly redesigning the grounds there, assisted by his nephew Claude Desgots and his pupil Gottard. Parterres were planted around the chateau and from this level a huge staircase leads down to the great water parterre below, which extends into the Manche and Grand Canal. At the west of the chateau were the gardens known as Le Canadière, one of Le Nôtre's finest achievements, now destroyed. Other commissions include Saint Cloud for Philippe d'Orléans and Saint Germain-en-Laye where, beginning in 1669, he created the Grand Terrasse, a vast 2.5km avenue parallel to the River Seine.

Throughout his lifetime Le Nôtre enjoyed royal favour and considerable wealth. He was awarded the Order of Saint Michel by Louis XIV in 1693 and died in his house near the Tuileries seven years later. Possibly he visited England in 1662 at Charles II's request, though the evidence is inconclusive. Nevertheless gardens in his style were created in England, notably at Chatsworth. Throughout Europe, Le Nôtre's ideas were enormously influential and remained so well into the 20th century.

**Lens** Mill. (Classical Lat. name.) Leguminosae (Papilionoideae). Some 6 species of annual herbs, close to *Vicia* but with calyx teeth equal, to twice length of calyx tube. Fruit flattened; seeds flat, orbicular. Mediterranean, W Asia, Africa. Z8.

CULTIVATION Lentils are a valuable source of fibre, protein, iron and B group vitamins and, with other pulses, have the lowest fat content of any protein-rich foods. *L. culinaris* grown for seeds, cotyledons split when sold, used especially in soups, rendered as a thick broth or *dhal*, or as flour. Also used as a forage species for animals. Lentils have a long history in cultivation; they have been discovered in Egyptian tombs dating to 2000 BC and are referred to in the Bible as the 'mess of pottage' for which Esau traded his birthright.

*L. culinaris* is widely cultivated in southern Europe, North Africa, India, parts of the US and other warm regions of the world for its edible seeds, and in these regions is often found naturalized on grassy hillsides and in sandy places. One genotype, W H 2040, withstands temperatures to −23°C/−10°F at seedling stage. *Lens* can be grown for interest in temperate vegetable gardens, but since the fruits contain only two seeds per pod and are cheap to buy, yields may not be considered sufficient to warrant the space. In the US, in commercial cultivation, yields of 1500–1600 pounds per acre are not uncommon.

Grow in moist but well-drained, sandy soils in a sunny, warm and sheltered position. Sow seed in spring into a firm, fine seedbed, 2.5cm/1in. deep, 20–30cm/8–12in. apart, with 45cm/18in. between the rows. Irrigate in dry periods. They normally take about 90 days to reach maturity; harvest as the foliage begins to yellow and air-dry, preferably in sun. Store in their pods, in a cool dry place, and remove seed from pods as required.

***L. culinaris*** Medik. LENTIL; MASUR; SPLIT PEA. Erect annual, to 45cm. Lvs pinnate, bearing a terminal tendril; leaflets to 2×0.8cm, in 4–7, usually 6 pairs, narrowly oblong-lanceolate; stipules entire. Infl. racemose, long-stipitate, few-fld (fls sometimes solitary); cal. teeth to 6× as long as tube; cor. pale blue; stamens 10, 1 free. Fr. pods to 16mm, usually 1- or 2-seeded; seeds lens-shaped. SW Asia, occasionally naturalized Europe. A cleistogamous-fld cultigen, possibly derived from *L. orientalis* (Boiss.) Hand.-Mazz.

***L. esculenta*** Moench. See *L. culinaris*.
For further synonymy see *Ervum*.

**LENTIBULARIACEAE** Rich. BLADDERWORT FAMILY. Dicot. 4 genera and 245 species of carnivorous plants of wet places, sometimes rootless and free-floating, with stalked and/or sessile glands. Leaves simple, very diverse, alternate or in basal rosette in *Pinguicula* and *Genlisea* (also with tubular trap-leaves); stipules absent; stems in *Polypompholyx* and *Utricularia* with alternate or whorled simple or dissected photosynthetic appendages bearing bladders with a trap-mechanism capturing small animals. Flowers bisexual, in bracteate racemes, or solitary and terminal without bracts (*Pinguicula*); calyx 4 or 5 fused sepals, lobed or 2-cleft; corolla 5 fused petals, 2-lipped, lower lip basally spurred; stamens 2 (anterior pair), borne on corolla tube; ovary superior, of 2 fused carpels, 1-loculed; placentation free-central; stigma sessile or subsessile, unequally 2-lobed; ovules 2-numerous. Fruit usually a capsule, dehiscence with 2–4 valves, or irregular, or indehiscent and 1-seeded; seeds with scarcely differentiated embryo; endosperm absent. Some *Utricularia* species are weedy in ricefields. Cosmopolitan. *Genlisea, Pinguicula, Utricularia.*

**Leocereus** Britt. & Rose (For A. Pacheco Leão (1872–1931), Director of the Botanical Garden, Rio de Janeiro.) Cactaceae. 1 species, a shrubby cactus, few-branched; rootstock woody; stems to 2(–3)m×1–2.5cm, slender, erect, clambering or decumbent, ribbed; ribs (10–)12–20, low, rounded; areoles 4–7mm apart; spines slender acicular, yellow to dark brown; central spines 1–3 or more, 6–20mm, more or less erect, radial spines 7–17, 3–5mm, adpressed. Fertile zone undifferentiated; flower subapical, tubular, nocturnal, 4–7.3×2–3.4cm; pericarpel and tube *c*1cm diam., green; scales numerous, small, acute, tinged brown; areoles of pericarpel with spines to 4mm; areoles of pericarpel with dark hairs and bristles to 12mm; tepals short, the outer spreading to reflexed, green to dull red-brown, the inner suberect, pure white. Fruit 2–3.6cm, globose to ovoid, red indehiscent, with deciduous spine-clusters; pulp purple; seeds broadly oval, 1.6×1.1mm, black-brown, shiny, smooth. E Brazil. Z9.

CULTIVATION Grow in a heated greenhouse (min. 10–15°C/50–60°F), use 'acid standard' cactus compost: moderate to high inorganic content (more than 50% grit), below pH 6; grow in full sun; maintain low humidity; water very sparingly in winter (to avoid shrivelling).

***L. bahiensis*** Britt. & Rose. As for the genus. Z9.

***L. melanurus*** (Schum.) Britt. & Rose. See *Arthrocereus melanurus*.

**Leochilus** Knowles & Westc. (From Gk *leios*, smooth, and *cheilos*, lip, referring to the smooth lip of most species.) Orchidaceae. Some 15 species of epiphytic orchids allied to *Oncidium*. Rhizome short. Pseudobulbs clustered, ovoid to ellipsoid, laterally compressed, enveloped by several leaf sheaths, apically unifoliate or bifoliate. Leaves ligulate to elliptic-lanceolate, coriaceous, short-petiolate. Inflorescence a raceme or a panicle, basal, base of pseudobulb, erect or arching, loosely few- to many-flowered; flowers small, resupinate; sepals subequal, spreading, lateral sepals free or shortly connate; petals free, similar to sepals, slightly wider; lip adnate to column base, spreading, simple or obscurely trilobed, exceeding sepals, disc fleshy, callose; column short, erect, foot absent, biauriculate below stigma, apex truncate, rostellum elongate, anther terminal, incumbent, operculate, 1-celled, pollinia 2, waxy, globose. Mexico to Argentina, W Indies. Z10.

CULTIVATION As for the cool-growing, markedly pseudobulbous *Oncidium* spp.

***L. carinatus*** (Lindl.) Knowles & Westc. Pseudobulbs to 2.5×2cm, ovate to sub-orbicular, compressed, usually bifoliate. Lvs to 12×1.5cm, elliptic-lanceolate. Infl. to 15cm, erect to pendent, few- to many-fld; fls fragrant; sep. to 12×6mm, free, yellow-green flushed brown; pet. cream-yellow striped chestnut-brown; lip to 12×9mm, cream-yellow spotted brown near callus, ovate, concave, obtuse to retuse, disc with tuberculate callus, glabrous; column to 6mm, cream, anth. cream to yellow. Mostly summer. Mexico.

***L. labiatus*** (Sw.) Kuntze. Pseudobulbs to 1.5×1.5cm, suborbicular, bright green, usually unifoliate. Lvs to 6.5×2cm, elliptic-lanceolate, tinged red-purple, sharply carinate below. Infl. to 23cm, erect to arching; fls fragrant; sep. to 8×5mm, yellow-green marked dark red-brown, lateral sep. connate to middle; pet. similar to sep., elliptic-oblong; lip yellow streaked red-brown, elliptic-oblong, base concave, disc with fleshy callus; column to 2mm, cream to pale brown, anth. cream to yellow. Mostly spring–summer. W Indies, Guatemala, Honduras, Panama, Trinidad, Costa Rica, Venezuela.

***L. oncidioides*** Knowles & Westc. Pseudobulbs to 5×2.5cm, ovate to elliptic, compressed, unifoliate or bifoliate. Lvs to 17×3cm, oblong-lanceolate or elliptic-lanceolate, acute. Infl. to 16cm, arching to pendent, few- to many-fld; fls fragrant; sep. to 11×5mm, grey-green spotted and tinged dull red, lateral sep. connate to middle; pet. to 11×7mm, similar to sep.; lip to 12×9mm, grey-green with large red central blotch, obovate to elliptic, obtuse to retuse, disc with cup-shaped callus, pilose to shortly pubesc.; column to 5mm, pale green, anth. cream. Autumn–winter. Mexico to Guatemala, Honduras.

***L. scriptus*** (Scheidw.) Rchb. f. Pseudobulbs to 5×2.5cm, ovoid to suborbicular, compressed, unifoliate. Lvs to 15×3cm, elliptic-ligulate to elliptic-lanceolate, obtuse. Infl. to 25cm, erect to arching, 1- to several-fld; fls fragrant, pale yellow-green, marked or striped red-brown; sep. to 12×6mm, elliptic to lanceolate, lateral sep. free or shortly connate; pet. obovate to elliptic-lanceolate, subequal to sep.; lip to 14×9mm, obovate to obcordate, obtuse to retuse, callus cup-shaped, pilose to shortly pubesc.; column to 4mm, cream-green, anth. cream. Mostly autumn–winter. Mexico, Brazil, Guatemala to Panama, Cuba.

***L. lieboldii*** Rchb. f. See *Papperitzia lieboldii*.
***L. major*** Schltr. See *L. scriptus*.
***L. mattogrossensis*** Cogn. See *Solenidium lunatum*.
***L. pulchellus*** (Reg.) Cogn. See *Oncidium waluewa*.
For further synonymy see *Oncidium, Rodriguezia* and *Cryptosaccus*.

**Leonotis** (Pers.) R. Br. (From Gk *leon*, lion, and *ous*, ear, alluding to the appearance of the hair-fringed corolla lip.) LION'S EAR. Labiatae. 30 species of aromatic, annual or perennial herbs and subshrubs to 1m or more. Stems tetragonal. Leaves opposite, toothed, simple, ovate to lanceolate. Inflorescence dense, distant, axillary whorls; bracteoles many, linear, subulate; calyx tubular, 10-veined, 8–10-toothed, acuminate; corolla tube longer than calyx, ciliate within, bilabiate, upper lip much longer than lower, fringed with long orange hairs; stamens 4, fertile, lower pair shorter than upper; petals showy, white, yellow, orange or scarlet. Fruit 4 nutlets. 1 species pantropical, the others Southern Africa.

CULTIVATION A frost-tender genus, grown for its whorls of striking lipped flowers. The annual *L. nepetifolia*, a widely naturalized weed in many subtropical regions, is too tender to become a nuisance in climates that experience frost; in cool-temperate climates it makes a large and handsome addition to the annual flower border. In zones that are frost-free or almost so, the grassland native *L. ocymifolia* and its varieties make subshrubby herbaceous perennials of considerable stature, growing 2–3m/6½–10ft in a season given full sun, abundant water and a rich soil. 'E.M. Rix', an albino variant of *L. ocymifolia* var. *raineriana*, shows a curious rusty-brown lower lip on its otherwise white flowers.

*L. leonurus* tolerates temperatures down to freezing. It makes a handsome semi-evergreen shrub, grown for its large whorls of vivid orange flowers, carried in autumn and early winter. In cool climates, it is cultivated as a conservatory specimen or treated as a tender biennial; plants in their second year make striking specimens for the summer border.

Grow frost-tender species under glass, in full sun, in a high-fertility loam-based mix. Water pot-grown plants plentifully when in full growth, sparingly and infrequently at other times. Overwinter in good light and frost-free conditions; avoid high winter temperatures, which produces soft, leggy and disease-prone growth. Cut back perennials, subshrubs and shrubs to within 15cm/6in. of the ground in early spring. Propagate by seed sown in early spring under glass, or from greenwood cuttings in late spring. Often infested by red spider mite and whitefly, especially under glass. When glasshouse plants are shaded, overwatered or underventilated they are likely to succumb to botrytis.

***L. leonurus*** (L.) R. Br. Pubesc., tender shrub to 2m. Lvs lanceolate to oblanceolate, to 11cm, entire or crenate, short-petioled. Cal. campanulate; cor. 3× length of cal., to 6cm, orange-red to scarlet; stamens hooded by upper lip. Late autumn. S Africa. 'Harrismith White': fls white. Z9.

***L. nepetifolia*** (L.) R. Br. Erect annual to 120cm. Stems pubesc. Lvs opposite, ovate, to 13cm, coarsely serrate. Cal. campanulate, spiny, teeth to 2.5cm; cor. to 4cm with 3 distinct rings of hairs inside tube, bilabiate, upper lip much longer than lower, orange. Winter. India, pantropical, naturalized US. Z8.

***L. ocymifolia*** (Burm. f.) Iwarsson. Subshrub to 70cm. Stems hirsute, woody at base, grooved. Lvs ovate, to 80×60mm, base cordate to cuneate, dentate, villous beneath. Infl. 2–5 dense whorls; cor. to 4cm, orange-hairy, upper lip 2× lower. S Africa. var. ***ocymifolia.*** Lvs grey-green, densely pubesc. beneath, crenate. var. ***raineriana*** (Vis.) Iwarsson. Lvs silver-pubesc. to yellow-pubesc. beneath. Cor. hairs rarely cream. S Africa. Z9.

For synonymy see *Phlomis*.

**Leontice** L. (From Gk *leon*, lion, alluding to the apparent lion's footprint pattern on the leaves.) Berberidaceae. 3–5 species of rhizomatous, perennial herbs, close to *Bongardia* and *Gymnospermium*. Rhizome tuberous. Leaves alternate, 2–3 times pinnately divided or cut; flowering stem leaves few. Inflorescence a raceme, bracteate, somewhat paniculate; flowers yellow; sepals 6–9, petaloid; petals 6, smaller than sepals, blunt at tip; stamens 6. Fruit a dry, inflated capsule, 1–4-seeded. SE Europe to E Asia.

CULTIVATION *Leontice* occurs in steppes and semi-deserts from the Balkans to Central Asia, in exposed rocky places, sometimes on limestone and often as a weed of cultivated ground. Long-stalked yellow flowers in dense clusters appear in early spring over the fleshy blue-grey leaves. Hardy to at least −5°C/23°F, *Leontice* will grow outside in warm dry areas in perfectly drained soil, given a dry period for dormancy in late summer, but is best grown in a bulb frame or alpine house as it dislikes damp conditions. Plant tubers at least 20cm/8in. deep. Propagate from seed. Seed-grown specimens may take several years to reach flowering size. In the wild, the large seeds germinate in autumn and pull themselves down to depths of 21–36cm/8½–15in. before the cotyledons emerge. In addition to the species described below, *L. armeniaca* Boiv., *L. ewersmannii* Bunge and *L. incerra* Pall. are sometimes grown. The first seldom exceeds 7cm; the second differs from *L. leontopetalum* in its elliptic-lanceolate leaflets; the third attains 16cm, has bi- to triternate leaves and slightly fleshy, broad leaflets to 5cm long.

***L. leontopetalum*** L. 20–80cm. Rhiz. large, knobbly. Lvs to 20cm wide, 2–3× ternately divided, somewhat fleshy, seg. ovate-obovate, rarely cordate, 25–40cm. Infl. many-fld, terminal or lateral, dense, becoming lax; pedicel spreading; sep. round to obovate, early deciduous, around 8mm; pet. one-third length of sep.; stamens two-thirds length of sep. Fr. ovoid, 2–4cm, papery. Spring. E Mediterranean, Aegean. Z6.

***L. albertii*** Reg. See *Gymnospermium albertii*.
***L. altaica*** Pall. See *Gymnospermium altaicum*.
***L. chrysogonum*** L. See *Bongardia chrysogonum*.

**Leontodon** L. (From Gk *leon*, lion, and *odos*, tooth, alluding to the toothed leaves.) HAWKBIT. Compositae. About 40 species of scapose, annual to perennial herbs, with milky sap. Leaves in basal rosettes, entire to pinnatifid. Capitula 1 to many, ligulate; phyllaries imbricate, in several series; receptacle naked; florets yellow, rarely orange, the outer often with a red or grey dorsal stripe. Fruit a more or less cylindric, somewhat compressed, strongly longitudinally ribbed cypsela; pappus of hairs, scales or absent. Temperate Eurasia to Mediterranean and Iran. Z6.

CULTIVATION A common wildflower found in grassy habitats on well-drained calcareous soils *L. hispidus* is occasionally offered as a nectar plant for butterflies. Treat as for *Pilosella*.

***L. hispidus*** L. ROUGH HAWKBIT. Perenn. to 70cm. Lvs to 35×4cm, oblanceolate, sinuate-dentate to runcinately pinnatifid, narrowed to winged petiole, usually hispid. Capitula usually solitary, to 2.5–4cm; peduncles 1 to few with 1–2 small bracts beneath head; phyllaries linear-lanceolate, outermost lax, dark to black-green; florets bright yellow, outermost orange or tinged red, rarely grey-violet beneath. Fr. 5–8mm; pappus of grey-white hairs. Summer. Europe to N Iran.

***L. apenninum*** Ten. See *Taraxacum apenninum*.
***L. aureum*** L. See *Crepis aurea*.
***L. glaucanthum*** Ledeb. See *Taraxacum glaucanthum*.
***L. megalorhizon*** Forssk. See *Taraxacum megalorhizon*.
***L. terglouensis*** Jacq. See *Crepis terglouensis*.

**Leontopodium** R. Br. ex Cass. (From Gk *leon*, lion, and *pous*, foot, in reference to the shape of the flowerheads.) EDELWEISS. Compositae. About 35 species of perennial herbs. Stems erect or ascending. Leaves alternate, mostly crowded at base, simple and entire. Capitula discoid, several in compact terminal cymes, surrounded by a star-shaped arrangement of conspicuous, ray-like, lanceolate, usually white-woolly hairy leaves; receptacle convex, naked; phyllaries in several series; florets hermaphrodite, tubular. Fruit a glabrous or hairy, cylindric cypsela; pappus of minutely toothed hairs. Eurasia especially mts, possibly also Andes.

CULTIVATION Given good drainage and protection from excessive winter wet, *Leontopodium* spp. are generally amongst the more vigorous and least demanding of alpines. (The more downy species and subspecies such as *L. alpinum* ssp. *nivale* and tight cushion or mound-forming types like *L. souliei* may be more safely grown in the alpine house.) Suitable for the rock garden, trough and raised bed, *Leontopodium* spp. are grown for their clusters of small flowers held amongst the star of glistening or densely felted bracts; they are occasionally used for drying, picked before the flowers begin to open and air dried, face up on a muslin screen. Taller species such as the lemon-scented *L. haplophylloides* may be grown in the herbaceous border, given the same attention to drainage.

Grow in full sun in any gritty, perfectly drained, not too fertile, circumneutral or alkaline soil; in areas with damp winters provide shelter from prevailing (rain-bearing) winds and a collar of grit or gravel to avoid excessive moisture at the crown. Under glass, use a mix of equal parts loam leafmould and sharp sand; water plentifully when in growth, avoiding water on the foliage and keep almost dry in winter. Propagate by seed sown fresh or by division.

**1** Lowest leaves spathulate, spathulate-lanceolate or oblanceolate, generally broadest above middle; plants to 20cm, very rarely to 30cm **2**
Lowest leaves narrowly linear to linear-lanceolate or ovate-lanceolate, generally broadest at middle or below, or opposite sides parallel; plants of variable height **7**

**2** Leaves subtending inflorescence forming a star to 10cm diam., white-woolly *L. alpinum*
Leaves subtending inflorescence forming a star to *c*4cm diam., grey- or yellow-woolly **3**

**3** Phyllaries long white or yellow woolly, margin light brown scarious; capitula to 10, to 6mm diam. **4**
Phyllaries villous, margin and apex dark black-brown; capitula to 15, to 8mm diam. *L. ochroleucum*

**4** Leaves to 2×0.5cm, rarely larger; capitula usually fewer than 4, rarely to 7 **5**
At least some leaves 3–7×0.5–1cm; capitula usually 4–10 **6**

**5** Indumentum grey; leaves subtending inflorescence 1–3.5mm wide; fruit glabrous *L. shinanense*
Indumentum white to yellow; at least some of leaves subtending inflorescence 4–5mm wide; fruit hairy *L. monocephalum*

**6** Leaves to 5mm wide, acute, silver-downy beneath; involucre *c*3mm; pappus white *L. fauriei*
Leaves to 10mm wide, obtuse, grey-downy beneath; involucre to 6mm; pappus pale yellow *L. kurilense*

**7** Capitula to 4–7, rarely to 11mm diam.; inflorescence. leaves narrowly lanceolate to ovate or oblong **8**
Capitula to *c*12mm diameter; inflorescence leaves triangular; lowest leaves withering before anthesis *L. calocephalum*

**8** Inflorescence leaves few, not forming an obvious star; capitula to *c*1cm diam. *L. leontopodioides*
Inflorescence leaves few to many, forming a tight star beneath heads; capitula to 7mm diam. **9**

**9** Inflorescence leaves forming star to 1cm diameter, rarely larger, brown-downy beneath; phyllaries and fruit glabrous *L. wilsonii*
Inflorescence leaves forming star to at least 3cm diam., white, green, grey, yellow or silvery beneath; phyllaries and/or fruit hairy **10**

**10** Leaves black glandular-punctate beneath, strongly lemon scented *L. haplophylloides*
Leaves not as above. **11**

**11** Flowering stems to 50cm; leaves to 12mm wide **12**
Flowering stems to *c*30cm, often much shorter, leaves to 3–6mm wide **14**

**12** Subshrub to 70cm, much branched; lvs obtuse, inflorescence lvs few; pappus white *L. stoechas*
Herb to 55cm, leaves acute, inflorescence leaves many; pappus white or tinged yellow or pink **13**

**13** Leaves to 9cm, inflorescence leaves producing star to 4cm diam., or in several irregular stars forming a corymb to 10cm; fruit glabrous to densely hairy; pappus white, often tinged pink *L. japonicum*
Leaves to 4cm, inflorescence leaves producing star to 6.5cm diam., or rarely 2 smaller star; fruit hairy; pappus white and yellow *L. stracheyi*

**14** Stems tufted; indumentum of leaves often sulphur-yellow *L. ochroleucum*
Stems usually solitary; indumentum of leaves usually white to grey or silver **15**

**15** Leaves with opposite margins parallel (long-linear to lingulate-linear) *L. souliei*
Leaves tapering equally at each end, broadest towards middle (lanceolate order) **16**

**16** Leaves to 8cm, at least some amplexicaul *L. hayachinense*
Leaves to 5.5cm, rarely amplexicaul. **17**

**17** Capitula *c*7mm diam.; leaves to 4–5.5cm **18**
Capitula *c*4mm diam.; leaves to 3cm, often smaller *L. jacotianum*

**18** Leaves lanceolate, silver-woolly on both sides; fruit glabrous or hairy *L. himalayanum*
Leaves linear-lanceolate to lanceolate, often glabrous above, white-downy beneath; fruit glabrous *L. discolor*

***L. alpinum*** Cass. EDELWEISS. To 20cm. Stems erect, simple. Basal lvs spathulate; stem lvs to 4cm, linear-lanceolate, green above; infl. lvs linear-oblong, densely white-woolly, star to 10cm diam. Capitula to 12mm diam.; phyllaries acute, woolly, margin and apex scarious. Fr. glabrous or hairy. Mts of Europe. Z4. 'Mignon' ('Silberstern'): compact, to 10cm; florets white. ssp. ***nivale*** (Ten.) Tutin. To 5cm. Lvs spathulate, white-woolly, infl. lvs spathulate, only equalling capitula. Mts of SE & SC Europe. Z5.

***L. calocephalum*** (Franch.) Beauverd. To 50cm. Stems erect. Lower lvs to 17cm, lanceolate to linear-lanceolate, acute, withering before anthesis, upper lvs shorter, ovate-lanceolate, glabrous to grey-hairy above, white- or grey-hairy beneath, infl. lvs triangular, acute, white-hairy above, green beneath, star to 11cm diam. Capitula to 12mm diam.; phyllaries more or less woolly. Fr. hairy. Himalayas of W China and Tibet. Z5.

***L. discolor*** Beauverd. To 25cm. Lvs to 6cm, lanceolate or linear-lanceolate, arachnoid or glabrous above, white-downy beneath, infl. lvs densely white-downy above, more sparsely so beneath, star to 7cm diam. Capitula to 7mm diam.; phyllaries downy. Fr. glabrous. Japan, SE China to Korea. Z6.

***L. fauriei*** (Beauverd) Hand.-Mazz. To 20cm. Lvs to 7cm, spathulate-lanceolate, acute, grey-downy above, silver-downy beneath; lvs long-petiolate, basal, upper stem lvs sessile, infl. lvs many, crowded, densely silvery grey-villous, star to 5cm diam. Capitula to 5mm diam.; phyllaries woolly. Fr. papillose. Japan (Hondo). Z6.

***L. haplophylloides*** Hand.-Mazz. To 36cm. Stems erect. Lvs to *c*40m, narrowly linear-lanceolate, hairy, with black glandular spots beneath, strongly lemon-scented, margin revolute, infl. lvs many, white-hairy, star to 5cm diam. Capitula to 5mm, diam.; phyllaries linear to oblong, more or less woolly. Fr. hairy. S China. Z6.

***L. hayachinense*** (Tak.) Hara & Kitam. To 20cm. Lvs to 8cm, lanceolate, green, woolly above, grey-woolly beneath, amplexicaul, infl. lvs 5–15, narrowly lanceolate, acute, star to 7cm diam. Capitula to 10mm diam.; phyllaries obtuse, woolly. Fr. papillose. Japan (Mt Hayachine). Z6.

***L. himalayanum*** DC. To 25cm. Stems erect. Lvs to 5cm, lanceolate, acute, silver-hairy, infl. lvs silver-woolly, star to 7cm diam. Capitula to 7mm diam.; phyllaries generally narrow, woolly. Fr. glabrous or hairy. Himalayas of China, Tibet and Kashmir. Z5.

***L. jacotianum*** Beauverd. To 27cm. Stems erect. Lvs to 3cm, lanceolate or linear-lanceolate, acute, white-hairy, especially beneath, upper largest, infl. lvs many, larger than stem lvs, white-hairy, star to 6cm diam. Capitula to 4mm diam.; phyllaries woolly, mostly obtuse. Fr. glabrous or hairy. N India, SW China, Burma. Z7.

***L. japonicum*** Miq. To 50cm. Stems erect. Lvs to 7cm, narrowly or ovate-lanceolate, acute; infl. lvs many, ovate or oblong, pale grey-hairy, star to 4cm, or in several irregular stars forming a corymb to 10cm diam. Capitula to 5mm diam.; phyllaries pale grey-hairy, obtuse. Fr. glabrous to densely hairy. E China, Korea, Japan. Z5.

***L. kurilense*** Tak. To 20cm. Stems erect. Lvs to 5cm, obovate-lanceolate or spathulate, obtuse, grey-downy, infl. lvs many, woolly, star to 4cm. Capitula to 6mm diam.; phyllaries woolly. Fr. glabrous or hairy. E Siberia. Z4.

***L. leontopodioides*** (Willd.) Beauverd. To 46cm. Stems simple or branched above. Lvs to 5cm, linear to linear-lanceolate, acute, grey-villous, infl. lvs few, oblong or linear, to 2.5× length of infl., not forming a conspicuous star. Capitula to 10mm diam.; phyllaries white-woolly. Fr. hairy. S Siberia, Mongolia, NE China. Z5.

***L. monocephalum*** Edgew. To 12cm. Stems purple, white-woolly. Lvs to 1.5cm, spathulate, obtuse, densely white- or sulphur yellow-woolly, infl. lvs to 5mm wide, yellow-woolly, star to 3.5cm diam. Capitula to 5mm; phyllaries white- or yellow-woolly. Fr. hairy. Himalaya. Z6.

***L. ochroleucum*** Beauverd. To 30cm. Stems tufted. Lvs to 5.5cm, spathulate or linear-lanceolate, infl. lvs pale yellow-hairy star to 3.5cm diam., regular. Capitula to 7mm diam.; phyllaries villous, apex dark brown to black. Fr. glabrous or hairy. C Tibet and Sikkim Himalaya to Altai Mts. var. ***campestre*** (Ledeb.) Grubov. To 17cm. Infl. lvs, pale yellow or white, star to 2.5cm, irregular. Z4.

***L. shinanense*** Kitam. To 7cm. Stem woolly. Lvs to 2cm, oblanceolate or spathulate, grey-woolly, infl. lvs to 14mm, 6–9, lanceolate. Capitula to 1cm diam.; phyllaries woolly acute. Fr. 2mm, glabrous. Japan. Z6.

***L. souliei*** Beauverd. To 25cm. Stems often geniculate at base. Lvs to 4cm, long-linear or lingulate-linear, acute, silvery silky-hairy, margins reflexed, infl. lvs many, silver-hairy, star to 5cm diam., compact. Capitula to 6mm diam.; phyllaries brown-tipped. Fr. glabrous or hairy. S China. Z5.

***L. stoechas*** Hand.-Mazz. To 70cm. Stem much-branched. Lvs to 3.5cm, narrow-oblong, obtuse, margin undulate, sparsely downy above, white- or glaucous-hairy beneath, infl. lvs few, star to 4cm diam. Capitula to 4mm diam.; phyllaries off-white to pale brown at apex. Fr. sparsely hairy. China (NW Sichuan). Z6.

***L. stracheyi*** (Hook. f.) C.B. Clarke. To 50cm. Stems erect. Lvs to 4.5cm, ovate-lanceolate to linear, acute, margins sometimes undulate, sparsely grey-hairy above, pale grey-downy beneath, infl. lvs many, grey-hairy, or green and glandular at tips and beneath, star to 6.5cm diam., or rarely 2 small stars. Capitula to 5mm diam.; phyllaries villous. Fr. hairy. Himalaya. Z5.

***L. wilsonii*** Beauverd. To 25cm. Stems erect or ascending, simple. Lvs to 6cm, narrow-lanceolate, acute, pale green above, brown-downy beneath, margins narrowly reflexed, infl. lvs many, compact, white-hairy above, brown-downy beneath, star, to 2cm diam. Capitula *c*5mm diam.; phyllaries glabrous, apex hyaline or pale brown. Fr. glabrous. China (Sichuan), Tibet. Z6.

***L. aloysiodorum*** hort. See *L. haplophylloides*.
***L. alpinum*** var. ***campestre*** Beauv. non Ledeb. See *L. leontopodioides*.
***L. alpinum*** var. ***sibiricum*** (Cass.) O. Fedtsch. See *L. sibiricum*.
***L. alpinum*** var. ***stracheyi*** Hook. f. See *L. stracheyi*.
***L. campestre*** (Ledeb.) Hand.-Mazz. See *L. ochroleucum* var. *campestre*.
***L. crasense*** hort. See *L. alpinum* ssp. *nivale*.
***L. kamtschaticum*** Komar. See *L. kurilense*.
***L. leontopodinum*** (DC.) Hand.-Mazz. See *L. ochroleucum*.
***L. nivale*** (Ten.) Huet ex Hand.-Mazz. See *L. alpinum* ssp. *nivale*.
***L. palibinianum*** auctt. See *L. ochroleucum* var. *campestre*.
***L. sibiricum*** Cass. See *L. leontopodioides*.
***L. tataricum*** Komar. See *L. discolor*.
For further synonymy see *Antennaria* and *Gnaphalium*.

**Leonurus** L. Labiatae. About 9 species of perennial herbs. Leaves opposite, lobed or toothed, sometimes palmatipartite. Inflorescence of dense, well-spaced axillary whorls; calyx bell-shaped with 5 almost equal, spine-tipped teeth; corolla tube shorter than calyx, not enlarged at throat; flower 2-lipped. Europe, temperate Asia, tropics.

CULTIVATION Occurring in hedgebanks and at woodland margins, frequently on gravelly and calcareous soils, *L. cardiaca* has been cultivated since medieval times for medicinal uses, one of which was to ease the after-effects of childbirth. Culpepper claimed that 'There is no better herb to take melancholy vapours from the heart.' Suitable for the herb garden or in the wild flower garden in conditions approximating to those in habitat, it undemanding as to soil and situation and may self-seed where conditions suit. Propagate by seed or division.

***L. cardiaca*** L. MOTHERWORT. 60–200cm; stem branched, leafy, usually pubesc. Lvs petiolate, lower lvs palmate, 5–7-lobed, lobes dentate, upper lvs shallowly trilobed, lanceolate, grading into leafy bracts. Fls white or pale pink, usually with purple dots, *c*12mm, upper lip densely covered with long hairs on upper surface. Europe from Scandinavia to N Spain, Italy and Greece, naturalized S Britain. Z3.

***L. galeobdolon*** (L.) Scop. See *Lamium galeobdolon*.

For illustration see HERBS.

**Leopoldia** Parl. See *Muscari*.
***L. tenuiflora*** Heldr. See *Muscari tenuiflorum*.

**Lepachys** Raf..
***L. columnaris*** (Sims) Torr. & A. Gray. See *Ratibida columnifera*.
***L. pinnata*** (Vent.) Torr. & A. Gray. See *Ratibida pinnata*.

**Lepanthes** Sw. (From Gk *lepos*, scale, bark, and *anthos* flower, as the plant grows on the bark of trees.) Orchidaceae. Some 60 species of usually dwarf epiphytic or lithophytic orchids. Rhizome short. Secondary stems tufted, erect or ascending, slender, generally bearing a single terminal leaf, enveloped by tubular sheaths. Leaves sessile or subsessile, coriaceous, sometimes papillose, appearing velvety and colourfully marked, ovate to suborbicular, apex tridentate. Inflorescence a raceme, axillary, small, solitary or fasciculate, 1- to many-flowered, usually lying flat on leaf surface; flowers small; sepals subequal, spreading, carinate, ovate to elliptic-lanceolate, lateral sepals variously connate; petals shorter than sepals, short-clawed, generally adnate to column; lip minute, 2- or 3-lobed, lateral lobes erect, acute, midlobe inconspicuous, adnate to column, column short, fleshy, footless, anther terminal, incumbent, operculate, 1-celled, pollinia 2, waxy, pyriform. Tropical America, W Indies. Z10.

CULTIVATION As for *Pleurothallis*, but in somewhat warmer, shadier conditions. These plants, small and fragile, are often best grown in closed cases.

***L. calodictyon*** Hook. 2.5–5.25cm. Lvs sessile, lime to emerald-green, densely veined or patterned chocolate-brown to rusty red. Fls minute, yellow and red; sep. and pet. ciliate; lip red, spathulate. Peru.

***L. lindleyana*** Ørst. & Rchb. f. Secondary stems to 1cm, erect. Lvs 2.5–4.5×0.75–1.5cm, ovate to linear-lanceolate, acuminate. Infl. 1 to several, shorter than lvs, few-fld; fls to 1.5cm diam., produced in succession; sep. 2.5×1mm, yellow to tan, veins tinged red-brown, ovate-oblong to ovate-lanceolate, acute, minutely ciliate; pet. to 1×1.5mm, orange-yellow and scarlet, transversely elliptic or lanceolate, ciliate; lip to 1×2mm, maroon or dull red, papillate, transversely oblong-bilobed; column pink, to 1mm. Costa Rica, Panama, Colombia, Venezuela, Nicaragua.

***L. pulchella*** (Sw.) Sw. Secondary stems 0.5–1cm. Lvs 8–15×3–6mm, ovate, acute. Infl. to 2cm, 1 to several, few- to several-fld; fls minute; sep. 6–8×2–3mm, yellow with a median crimson line, ovate, long-acuminate, ciliate; pet. crimson, margins yellow, lobed, lobes subtriangular, ciliate; lip crimson, obscurely lobed, minutely ciliate; column to 1mm, crimson. Jamaica.

***L. rotundifolia*** L.O. Williams. Secondary stems short. Lvs 16–25×18–28mm, suborbicular to ovate-suborbicular. Infl. shorter than lvs, many-fld; fls minute, yellow and red; sep. to 3×2mm, suborbicular, acute or acuminate; pet. bilobed, lobes to 3.5×1mm, obliquely lanceolate, acute; lip to 1.5×2mm, bilobed. Panama.

***L. chiriquensis*** Schltr. See *L. lindleyana*.
***L. micrantha*** Ames. See *L. lindleyana*.
***L. secunda*** Barb.Rodr. See *Lepanthopsis floripectin*.

**Lepanthopsis** Ames. (From the generic name *Lepanthes* and the Gk *opsis*, appearance, referring to the similarity of the genus of *Lepanthes*.) Orchidaceae. Some 6 species of diminutive epiphytic orchids allied to *Lepanthes*. Rhizome slender, minute, creeping. Secondary stems tufted, slender, erect, enveloped by tubular sheaths, apically unifoliate. Leaves suborbicular to elliptic-oblong, acute to rounded, short-petiolate. Inflorescence raceme, axillary, solitary or clustered, few to many-flowered, often secund, flowers minute sepals subequal, lateral sepals deeply connate; petals thin, elliptic-oblong to orbicular; lip adnate to column base, sessile, simple; column minute, foot absent; anther terminal, opercular, incumbent, pollinia 2, waxy, pyriform. Tropical Americas. Z10.

CULTIVATION As for *Pleurothallis*.

***L. astrophora*** (Rchb. f. ex Kränzl.) Garay. Secondary stems to 7×1cm, erect, terete. Lvs to 2.5×1cm, erect, coriaceous, elliptic to oblong-elliptic, obtuse. Infl. to 12cm, many-fld; peduncle filiform; fls bright rose-purple; sep. to 3×1.5mm, papillose, ovate, acute to obtuse, lateral sep. oblique; pet. to 2×1mm, papillose, obovate, acuminate to obtuse; lip to 2×1mm, fleshy, subquadrate, base obovate, subacuminate, papillose; column short, with a stigmatic wings, pale pink, anth. cream. Venezuela.

***L. floripectin*** (Rchb. f.) Ames. Secondary stems to 7cm. Lvs to 3.5×1.2cm, fleshy, suborbicular to elliptic-oblong, rounded. Infl. to 10cm, 1 to several, densely many-fld; peduncle filiform, erect, pink-green; fls thin-textured, white to yellow-green, slightly tinged pink; sep. to 3mm, spreading, ovate, acute or obtuse; pet. minute, suborbicular-ovate, subacute; lip to 1×1mm, suborbicular to ovate, rounded at apex; column minute, dilated above, stigmas widely divergent, anth. white. Spring. Honduras, Costa Rica, Colombia, Venezuela, Brazil, Panama, Peru.

***L. vinacea*** Schweinf. Secondary stems to 5.5cm, erect-ascending, slender. Lvs fleshy, to 2×1cm, ovate to elliptic-oblong, obtuse. Infl. to 5cm, 1 to several, suberect, few to many-fld; peduncle filiform, pale green; fls bright purple, smooth-glandular; sep. to 3×1.5mm, ovate-lanceolate, subacute to obtuse, lateral sep. oblique; pet. to 1mm, ovate-elliptic to lanceolate, acute; lip to 1×1mm, fleshy suborbicular or orbicular, retuse; column minute, cream, anth. white. Venezuela.

For synonymy see *Pleurothallis* and *Lepanthes*.

**Lepechinia** Willd. (For Frau Lepechin (1737–1802).) Labiatae. 35 species of much-branched shrubs or procumbent perennial herbs. Upper stems glabrous to villous or tomentose, usually tinged purple. Leaves petiolate or sessile, blades ovate, elliptic, linear-lanceolate or oblong, margins crenate to serrate, dentate, or entire, upper surfaces bullate. Inflorescences spicate, paniculate or racemose, flowers in cymes, either verticils, glomerules or solitary in leaf axils; calyx 5-toothed, 2-lipped to nearly regular, usually accrescent, tube campanulate, interior glabrous, teeth subequal, upper teeth somewhat longer; corolla blue, purple, red, yellow or white, weakly bilabiate, upper lip bilobed, lower lip trilobed, lobes broadly rotund or erect and spreading, middle lower lobe longest, tube inside with ring of hairs; stamens 4, paired, usually shortly exserted. Nutlets ovoid, usually smooth. Americas. Z8.

CULTIVATION The shrubby species are occasionally cultivated for their attractive flowers. Most are hardy to −5°C/23°F and will survive undisturbed in all but the coldest winters if planted in a favoured, sunny, sheltered place. *Lepechinia* spp. prefer a well-drained sandy soil to heavy clay soils. They may be overwintered under cool glasshouse conditions in direct sunlight, potted into a loamless compost with extra sand added. Low humidity and sparing watering are beneficial. Propagate from semi-ripe cuttings taken in early autumn or from seed sown under glass in spring. In addition to those described below, other species occasionally cultivated are *L. speciosa* (St.-Hil.) Epling, flowers red, and *L. floribunda* (Benth.) Epling, flowers blue.

***L. calycina*** (Benth.) Epling. PITCHER SAGE. Shrub, 1–3m, much-branched. Lvs 4–11×2–5cm, narrowly to broadly ovate, upper surfaces bullate to smooth, margins dentate to nearly entire. Infl. racemose, fls single in leaf axils; cal. 1.5–3cm, scarcely bilabiate villous, tube inflated at base, teeth more or less equal, deltoid, 1cm; cor. lavender or pink, rarely white, tube 2.5–3.8cm, broadly campanulate with a ring of hairs within. Nutlets puberulent. California.

***L. chamaedryoides*** (Balb.) Epling. Including *Sphacele chamaedryoides* hort. Shrub to 3m. Leaves 10–45×3–8mm, linear-oblong to linear, upper lf surfaces bullate. Infl. spicate, paniculate or racemose; fls solitary in leaf axils; cal. to 2cm, weakly 2-lipped, tube campanulate, teeth acuminate, lower teeth longer than upper; cor. 1.5–2cm, blue, broadly campanulate, tube with a ring of hairs inside. Chile.

***L. salviae*** (Lindl.) Epling. Shrub to 2m. Lvs 5–8×2.5–3.5cm, ovate to deltoid, upper surfaces bullate and tomentose. Infl. spicate, floral lvs large, verticils of 1–3 fld cymes; cal. to 2.5cm, weakly 2-lipped, tubes long, campanulate, teeth 4–8mm, cuspidate to acuminate, lower teeth usually longest; cor. 2–3cm, red, somewhat decurved, long, tube with a ring of hairs within. Chile.

***L. subhastata*** (Benth.) Epling. See *L. salviae*.
For further synonymy see *Dracocephalum* and *Sphacele*.

**Lepechiniella** Popov.
***L. microcarpa*** (Boiss.) Riedl. See *Paracaryum microcarpum*.

**Lepidium** L. (From Gk *lepis*, scale, alluding to the shape of the fruits; name used by Dioscorides.) Cruciferae. Around 150 species of annual, biennial and perennial herbs. Leaves pinnatifid to simple, hairy or glabrous. Inflorescence small, racemose; sepals 4; petals 4, sometimes absent; stamens 6, 4 or 2. Fruit a silicle, dehiscent, compressed, winged or wingless; seeds 2, mucilaginous when wet. Cosmopolitan.

CULTIVATION For a salad garnish, press seed thickly and evenly or to the surface of shallow trays of a friable propagating medium, or on to thoroughly moistened kitchen paper or flannel in a shallow dish (the latter method makes cutting easier). Maintain a temperature of about 10°C/50°F, germinate without light, and keep moist until harvest in 10–14 days. The companion mustard should be sown 3–4 days later, as it germinates more quickly.

As a salad green, sow in early spring, as soon as the soil is workable, in shallow drills 30cm/12in. apart, with successional sowings at 2–3-weekly intervals. Soil must be fertile and moisture-retentive and the site sunny to ensure rapid growth, which yields the best harvest if the first cut is not too hard. Summer sowings may rapidly run to seed, but sowings may be made from early autumn onwards for winter salads, with cloche protection in regions where temperatures drop below −5°C/23°F. Seeding cress is extremely susceptible to damping off, and provides a convenient demonstration of the disease. The disease quickly develops on seed sown thickly on unsterilized soil, watered plentifully and covered with glass to maintain high humidity.

***L. sativum*** L. COMMON GARDEN CRESS; PEPPER GRASS; PEPPERWORT. Annual, 20–60cm. Stem erect, branching. Basal lvs 1–3× pinnatifid, soon withering; stem lvs bipinnate to entire higher up stem. Pet. 2–3mm white-lilac. Fr. 6×5mm, broadly elliptic-ovate or nearly round, bluntly winged; pedicel 2–3mm. Most N temperate regions. 'Broad Leaved' ('Mega', 'Broad Leaved French'): slender-stalked, recommended for soups; 'Curled': ornamental, lvs finely divided; 'Greek': fast growing, for cutting young; 'Moss Curled': dwarf, very fast growing, lvs finely cut.

***L. alpina*** L. See *Pritzelago alpina*.
***L. oppositifolium*** Labill. See *Aethionema oppositifolium*.

**Lepidochiton** Sealy. Amaryllidaceae. 2–3 bulbous perennial herbs closely related to *Hymenocallis*. Leaves usually 5–9, synanthous, linear, keeled, weakly sheathing at base. Scape with solitary flower subtended by 3 linear-lanceolate bracts; flower large, sessile, somewhat declinate, fragrant; perianth crateriform, white or yellow; perianth tube long, cylindric, green; segments lanceolate, recurved, subequal; staminal cup large, widely spreading, rotate or campanulate, margin laciniate or coarsely lobed, striped green or yellow along filamental traces, free part of filaments short, incurved; style exceeding stamens, stigma capitate; ovary 3-locular, ovules 16–20 per locule. Capsule oblong, dehiscent; seeds 1–5, fleshy. S America.

CULTIVATION As for *Hymenocallis*.

***L. quitoensis*** (Herb.) Sealy. Bulb globose, 3–5cm diam., neck 3–7cm, grey-brown. Lvs deciduous, 5–7, 30–60×1.5–3cm, keeled along midrib, glossy bright green above, dull green beneath. Scape 8–35cm, ancipitous, emerging after lvs; spathe valves linear 3–5cm; fls 15–20×13–20cm wide; perianth tube erect, curved at throat, green, seg. white, keeled at base, outer whorl 9–13×1.2cm, apiculate, inner whorl to 15×1.8cm; staminal cup 4.5–6.5×7–9cm, irregularly 2-lobed or bifid between fil., margin laciniate to coarsely dentate, striped green along filamental traces, yellow in throat; free filaments to 2.5cm, style to 23.5cm. Ecuador.

***L. andreana*** (Bak.) Nichols. See *L. quitoensis*.
For further synonymy see *Hymenocallis*.

**Lepidothamnus** Philippi. (From Gk *lepis*, scale and *thamnos*, shrub.) Podocarpaceae. 3 species of evergreen, dioecious, occasionally monoecious, shrubs or trees. Leaves dimorphic, narrow-linear, spreading, becoming keeled, subulate, decurrent, adpressed. Male cones sessile, terminal, solitary. Seed cones solitary, terminal; bracts rose, to 5, 2 fertile; ovules erect; receptacle surrounding base of seed unequal; seeds dark brown to black, basally sheathed. S Chile, New Zealand.

CULTIVATION *L. fonkii* is among the hardiest species in the Podocarpaceae, adapted to a climate with 350 or more rainy days per year and seven stormy days per week, where it grows on exposed mountain-sides. It is sensitive to desiccation, and elsewhere in Britain should be given a cool, damp shady site protected from dry east winds. *L. laxifolius* is similar in requirements, while *L. intermedius* comes from lower altitudes and requires more warmth. *L. laxifolius* is the smaller conifer; specimens only 7cm/2½in. tall and wide bearing fertile seed have been found.

***L. fonkii*** Philippi. CHILEAN RIMU. Shrub to 30cm tall; prostrate, spreading, with short erect branchlets rising from level branches. Juvenile lvs narrow triangular, grading into adult scale lvs, 1–1.5mm long. Fr. similar to *L. laxifolius*. S Chile (mts). Z7.

***L. intermedius*** (T. Kirk) Quinn. YELLOW SILVER PINE. Dioecious shrub or small resinous tree, to 10m+. Bark grey. Juvenile lvs linear-spathulate, 10–15mm; grading into shorter, more densely crowded, adult scale-shaped, triangular, 1.5–3mm lvs, densely imbricate, keeled, apex obtuse. Receptacle orange. Seeds to 5mm, striated, blunt. New Zealand. Z8.

***L. laxifolius*** (Hook. f.) Quinn. MOUNTAIN RIMU. Low-growing to prostrate, usually dioecious shrub. Stems spreading, to 1m+, with erect branchlets rising to 10–15cm. Lvs subulate, spreading, to 12mm on young plants, later linear-oblong, to 2mm. Receptacle crimson; fr. to 3mm, apex curved. New Zealand (mts). Z7.

For synonymy see *Dacrydium*.

**Lepidozamia** Reg. (From Gk *lepis*, scale, plus *Zamia*, referring to the scale-like petiole bases which clothe the caudex.) Zamiaceae. 2 species of cycads, evergreen, perennial, dioecious, bearing cones and palm-like fronds atop columnar trunks, to 20m. Leaves pinnate, to 3m, borne at crown in whorls, semi-erect, later arching, reflexed, felty at first, then glabrous; pinnae to 200, opposite, somewhat reflexed at tips, drooping in appearance, entire, lanceolate, recurved to falcate, acute, attenuate at base, glossy, light green above, conspicuously veined beneath, to 35cm×30mm. Caudex usually unbranched, columnar, 2–20m high, clothed with persistent leaf bases. Female strobilus ovoid, to 60×25cm, female sporophylls to 8×6cm, tomentose, deflexed terminally and upturned again bearing 2 ovules, rarely 3. Male strobilus borne quasi-terminally, oblong-cylindric, to 80×15cm, male sporophylls lozenge-shaped, to 4cm wide. Seeds to 6×3cm with fleshy, scarlet outer coat. Australia. Z10.

CULTIVATION As for *Macrozamia*. *L. hopei* requires higher humidity than *L. peroffskyana* and semi-shade.

***L. hopei*** Reg. As for the genus. NE Queensland.

***L. peroffskyana*** Reg. Differs from *L. hopei* in having pinnae linear-lanceolate, to 35cm×12mm, dark green, glossy, narrowed basally to join rachis in green-yellow, waxy gland. Suptropical Queensland & northern coast NSW.

**Lepisanthes** Bl. (From Gk *lepis*, scale and *anthos*, flower, probably referring to the well-developed scale of the petals.) Sapindaceae. 24 species of trees or shrubs, sometimes climbing. Leaves spirally arranged, sometimes paripinnate, pinnae in 1–40 pairs, hairy or glabrous. Inflorescences terminal, axillary or cauliflorous; flowers unisexual; sepals 4–5, free, overlapping, entire or, if petaloid, denticulate; petals 4–5, distinctly clawed; disc crescent-shaped, slightly lobed, hairy or glabrous; stamens 8, anther basally attached; ovary sessile to short-stipitate, 2–3-chambered, style apical, globose or dome-shaped. Fruit subsessile with smooth or slightly warty skin, hairy to glabrous, seeds black to brown, shining, hairy or glabrous. Old World Tropics, W Africa, New Guinea. Often labelled *Aphania* or *Erioglossum* in commerce. Z9.

CULTIVATION As for *Sapindus*

***L. rubiginosa*** (Roxb.) Leenh. Shrub or tree to 9m. Lvs to 60cm, pinnae 4–16, to 18×8cm, oblong-lanceolate to elliptic. Infl. 10–35cm; sep. 5, oval to orbicular, outer 3 smaller; pet. 4, longer than sep., disc interrupted, glabrous; stamens 8, fil. longer than anth.; ovary 3-chambered, sparsely to densely hairy. Fr. glabrous red becoming black when mature, 1–3-lobed. Tropical Asia to N Australia.

***L. senegalensis*** (Poir.) Leenh. Small tree. Lvs to 60cm, pinnae 6–12, to 25cm, ovate-lanceolate to elliptic, or oblong-acuminate, to 25cm, rarely unifoliate. Infl. to 50cm, fls red; sep., pet. 4–5, imbricate; stamens 6–8, included; ovary glabrous, bilobed. Fr. red to dark purple, ellipsoid, with edible aril. Himalaya.

For synonymy see *Aphania, Erioglossum, Euphoria, Nephelium, Sapindus, Scytala*.

**Lepismium** Pfeiff. (From Gk *lepisma*, scale, peel, referring to the persistent scale-like leaf rudiments of the type species.) Cactaceae. A genus of about 14 species of shrubby cacti, usually epiphytic or saxicolous; stems cylindric, ribbed, angled, winged or flat, usually segmented, the younger segments arising singly from the sides or apices of older segments; rudimentary scale-leaves often clearly visible; spines present or absent. Flowers mostly small, rotate, campanulate or rarely tubular-campanulate (*L. micranthum*); pericarpel often tuberculate and spiny or angled and with or without spines, rarely almost terete; tube very short or none, rarely well-developed. Fruit berry-like, spiny or naked; seed *c*1.5–2×0.7–1mm, narrowly oval or oval, black-brown or brown, shiny; relief flat or low-domed; hilum medium, oblique, superficial; mucilage-sheath present, covering entire seed or restricted to hilum area. Brazil, Bolivia and Argentina. Closely related to *Rhipsalis*, but lacking the characteristic branching pattern of that genus, and often more or less spiny.

CULTIVATION Grow in an intermediate heated greenhouse (min. 10–15°C/50–60°F), 'epiphyte' compost: equal parts organic/inorganic matter, below pH 6 (essential); shade (11:00–15:00 hrs) all summer; maintain high humidity; reduce watering in winter and rest winter-flowering species in late summer.

***L. cruciforme*** (Vell. Conc.) Miq. Stem-seg. variable, to 50×2cm, 3–5-angled or winged, or flat, usually suffused purple, margins more or less deeply crenate; areoles in the crenations, tufted with white hairs, subtended by a scale-like leaf-rudiment. Fl. lateral 1–5 per areole, 10–13mm, almost white; outermost tepals tinged red or brown; pericarpel somewhat sunken in stem. Fr. *c*6mm diam., subglobose, purple-red. Summer–autumn. SE Brazil to N Argentina. Z9.

***L. houlletianum*** (Lem.) Barthlott. Stems 1–2m, slender and terete below, 2–4mm diam., flat above and then 10–20×1–5cm, margins deeply serrate-dentate; areoles without bristles or hairs. Fl. 1.5–2cm, lateral, numerous (but 1 per areole), campanulate; pericarpel 4–5-angled; tepals almost white. Fr. 5–6mm diam., globose, red. Autumn–winter. E Brazil. Z9.

***L. ianthothele*** (Monv.) Barthlott. Stems to 60cm, spreading or pendent, stem seg. 8–12×1–2cm, ribbed; ribs 3–5, somewhat crenate-tuberculate; areoles *c*1cm apart; spines 6–7, 5–7mm. Fl. 15mm; pericarpel tuberculate, tinged purple; floral areoles with bristly spines; tepals pale yellow. Fr. 12–16mm, globose, red, spiny. Spring. NW Argentina. Z9.

***L. lumbricoides*** (Lem.) Barthlott. Stems slender, to 3–4m×6mm, terete when turgid, slightly angled when dormant, creeping or clinging with numerous aerial roots; areoles of juvenile stems with 5–8 bristle-spines, 3–5mm, those of mature growth spineless. Fl. *c*2×2.5(–3.5)cm, rotate, said to be orange-scented; pericarpel naked. Fr. globose, ripening deep purple, with purple pulp. Spring. Uruguay, N Argentina. Z9.

***L. micranthum*** (Vaupel) Barthlott. Stems to 1m×1.5–2cm, erect at first, then sprawling or pendent, flat or 3-winged, crenate; areoles between the crenations, 6–10mm apart, subtended by a leaf-rudiment *c*2×1mm; spines 3–10, 5–10mm, brown or nearly black. Fl. 27×24mm, lateral, solitary, tubular-campanulate; pericarpel 4×6mm, turbinate with small scales and woolly areoles; tube *c*12mm, with recurving tepaloid scales, purple-red; tepals suberect, purple-red, the tips spreading; stigmas pale yellow-green. Fr. 1cm, globose to short-cylindric, slightly angled; areoles with wool and an occasional spine to 2mm. SE Peru. Not to be confused with *Rhipsalis micrantha*, which is a very different species. Z9.

***L. monacantha*** (Griseb.) Barthlott. Stems to 45×2–3cm, erect at first, then pendent, flattened or 3-angled, crenate-serrate, cuneate at base; areoles 10–12mm apart, white-felted; spines 0–6, to 1cm, yellow or white. Fl. *c*15×12mm, lateral, solitary; pericarpel 7×6mm, strongly 4–5-angled, with 2–5 scales and felted areoles; tepals bright waxy orange; stigmas exserted, white. Fr.

to 12mm diam., globose, orange-red, fading to pale pink, obscurely ribbed; floral remnant persistent. Spring–summer. NW Argentina. Z9.

***L. warmingianum*** (Schum.) Barthlott. Stems slender, elongate, 3–4-angled or flat; seg. to 30×1cm, margins crenate, areoles glabrous. Fl. *c*2cm, lateral, solitary, campanulate, white scented; pericarpel angled. Fr. 5–6mm diam., globose, dark purple or nearly black. E Brazil. Z9.

***L. commune*** Pfeiff. See *L. cruciforme*.
***L. dissimile*** G.A. Lindb. See *Rhipsalis dissimilis*.
***L. floccosum*** (Salm-Dyck) Backeb. See *Rhipsalis floccosa*.
***L. gibberulum*** (F.A.C. Weber) Backeb. See *Rhipsalis floccosa*.
***L. grandiflorum*** (Haw.) Backeb. See *Rhipsalis hadrosoma*.
***L. megalanthum*** (Loefgr.) Backeb. See *Rhipsalis megalantha*.
***L. paradoxum*** Salm-Dyck ex Pfeiff. See *Rhipsalis paradoxa*.
***L. pulvinigerum*** (G.A. Lindb.) Backeb. See *Rhipsalis pulvinigera*.
***L. puniceo-discus*** (G.A. Lindb.) Backeb. See *Rhipsalis puniceodiscus*.
***L. trigonum*** (Pfeiff.) Backeb. See *Rhipsalis trigona*.
For further synonymy see *Acanthorhipsalis*, *Pfeiffera* and *Rhipsalis*.

**Lepisorus** J. Sm. Ching. (From Gk *lepos*, husk, and *sorus*.) Polypodiaceae. Some 25 species of epiphytic ferns. Rhizomes creeping, dictyostelic; scales clathrate. Fronds in 2 rows on rhizome, uniform, short-stipitate, simple, linear to lanceolate or elliptic, entire at margin, fleshy or leathery, occasionally herbaceous; veins usually concealed, reticulate, anastomosing into irregular areolae with free, included, forking veinlets; stipes approximate, jointed. Sori uniserial each side of costa, circular to oval; paraphyses many, shield- or umbrella-shaped, clathrate, deciduous. Asia.

CULTIVATION As for *Pyrrosia*.

***L. clathratus*** (Clarke) Ching. Rhiz. to 5mm wide; scales to 5×2mm, dense, ovate or ovate-lanceolate, apex narrowly acute to apex, base shield-like and obtuse, dentate, membranous, dark brown to black but iridescent. Fronds to 15cm×18mm, lanceolate to elliptic, apex acute or obtuse, base narrowed; stipes to 4cm, glabrous, straw-coloured. N India, Nepal and Afghanistan north to Siberia, east to China, Taiwan and Japan. Z6.

***L. thunbergianus*** (Kaulf.) Ching. Rhiz. long-creeping, to 3mm wide; scales to 4mm, dense, lanceolate or linear to awl-shaped, apex narrowly acute, base shield-like, margin dentate, dark brown to black. Fronds 25×1cm, narrowly linear to elliptic, apex narrowly acute, base narrowed, 1cm apart, margin entire and more or less falcate, leathery, dark green above and paler beneath, veins immersed and obscure, but costa prominent, clothed with ovate, adpressed scales; stipes to 3cm. Asia (China, Taiwan, Korea, Japan, Philippines). Z9.

**Leptarrhena** R. Br. (From Gk *leptos*, fine or slender, and *arren*, male, referring to the filaments.) Saxifragaceae. 1 species, a rhizomatous perennial herb, to 40cm. Leaves mostly basal, 3–15cm, ovate to obovate, glabrous, bright green above pale green beneath; margin crenate; petiole less than half length of blade; stipule membranous, fused with petioles. Flowering stems with 1–3 sessile, oblong leaves, much smaller than basal leaves; inflorescence cymose, crowded, becoming lax; flowers minute; sepals 5, 1mm, fused at base to form a saucer; petals 5, white, spathulate, twice sepal length; stamens 10, 1.5× petal length; carpels 2, fused only at base. Fruit a red, many-seeded, dehiscent follicle, 5–6mm; seeds light brown. Summer. NW US. Z5.

CULTIVATION A plant of high mountain streamsides and wet meadows, grown for its glossy leathery foliage and red fruits; good groundcover for cool places. Cultivate as for *Heuchera* but plant in a gritty soil (pH 5.5–6.0) and ensure some shade against midday sun.

***L. pyrolifolia*** (D. Don) R. Br. ex Ser. As for the genus.

***L. amplexifolia*** (Sternb.) R. Br. See *L. pyrolifolia*.
For further synonymy see *Saxifraga*.

**Leptasea** Haw.
***L. flagellaris*** (Willd.) Small. See *Saxifraga flagellaris*.

**Leptinella** Cass. Compositae. About 30 species of tufted or, annual to perennial creeping herbs, usually aromatic. Stems prostrate or rarely suberect. Leaves alternate or clustered, simple, entire to 2-pinnatifid, rarely toothed. Capitula discoid, monoecious or subdioecious; involucre hemispherical, phyllaries sometimes extending after anthesis to enclose fruit; inner florets male, marginal florets female, white or yellow, rarely black. Fruit a small, ribbed, often hairy, cypsela. Australasia, temperate S America. Z8 unless specified.

CULTIVATION Valued for their neat, low carpets of fine, soft, often fern-like foliage, which makes good cover for early spring bulbs and is well suited to colonizing paving crevice and gravel paths where most species will tolerate at least light treading; *L. squalida* and *L. dioica* are sometimes used as a low traffic herb lawn. *Leptinella* spp. are occasionally grown on the rock garden, but may perhaps best be confined to the foot of rockwork where their invasive tendencies will not threaten less robust alpines. Most of the commonly grown species will tolerate temperatures down to −15°C/5°F, with *L. squalida* and *L. dioica*, hardy where winter temperatures fall as low as −20°C/−4°F, although where prolonged low temperatures are not accompanied by snow cover, they should be protected with a layer of evergreen branches. Grow in sun or part shade in moist gritty freely draining humus rich soils that are not too fertile. Propagate by fresh seed or by division.

***L. albida*** (D. Lloyd) D. Lloyd & C. Webb. Creeping perenn., forming compact mats, to 1m diam., densely silver-hairy. Lvs to 10×3mm, pinnatifid, lobes in 4–8 pairs, entire, leathery, dark green, densely hairy. Capitula to 1cm diam., on peduncles, to 2cm, naked; phyllaries *c*20; female florets to *c*50, pale yellow or yellow-red. Fr. to 2mm, compressed, golden brown. New Zealand.

***L. atrata*** (Hook. f.) D. Lloyd & C. Webb. Tufted, monoecious perenn., to 40cm. Lvs to 8×1.3cm, broadly elliptic, 2-pinnatifid, lobes in 5–15 pairs, grey-green, leathery, fringed red. Capitula to 1.3cm diam., on peduncles, to 12cm, 4–10 bracteate; phyllaries 10–30; female florets numerous, pale yellow or dark red, almost black. Fr. to 3×1mm, brown, wrinkled. New Zealand. ssp. ***luteola*** (D. Lloyd) D. Lloyd & C. Webb. Lvs less divided, lobes 5–10. Capitula conic, not convex; florets yellow, with a red-brown apex.

***L. dendyi*** (Ckn.) D. Lloyd & C. Webb. Tufted, often subdioecious perenn., to 40cm. Lvs to 5×0.8cm, 2-pinnatifid, grey-green, tinged red, lobes in 8–10 pairs, leathery. Capitula to 2cm diam., on peduncles to 8cm, 6–15 bracteate; phyllaries many, grey-green tinged red; female florets numerous, yellow, apex brown. Fr. to 3mm, golden brown, wrinkled. New Zealand.

***L. dioica*** Hook. f. Creeping, fleshy, usually subdioecious perenn., to 15cm . Lvs to 12×1.5cm, obovate or elliptic, entire to pinnatifid, often dentate, lobes or teeth in 4–12 pairs, green, glabrous. Capitula to 7mm diam., on peduncles to 6cm, phyllaries to 30; female florets 10–80, yellow-green. Fr. to 2mm, becoming brown and smooth. New Zealand. Z5.

***L. goyenii*** (Petrie) D. Lloyd & C. Webb. Creeping, monoecious perenn., forming compact mats to 1m diam., long silver-hairy. Lvs to 10×3mm, pinnatifid, lobes in 4–8 pairs, entire, leathery, dark green, densely tomentose. Capitula to 1cm diam., on peduncles to 2cm; phyllaries 20; female florets 20–50, pale yellow or yellow-red, sometimes with 1–2 dark stripes. Fr. to 2mm, convex on both sides. New Zealand.

***L. lanata*** Hook. f. Diffuse, creeping, monoecious perenn., to 20cm, lanate becoming glabrous. Lvs to 2.5×1cm, elliptic, pinnatifid, lobes in 3–5 pairs, toothed, light green, thick. Capitula to 1cm diam., on peduncles to 3cm; phyllaries around 30; female florets 50–100, yellow-green. Fr. to 2mm, golden brown, shiny. New Zealand.

***L. pectinata*** (Hook. f.) D. Lloyd & C. Webb. Tufted or creeping, monoecious perenn., to 15cm. Lvs to 4×1cm, pinnatifid, occasionally entire, lobes in 1–10 pairs, sometimes toothed, villous or glabrous. Capitula to 8mm diam., on peduncles to 10cm; phyllaries 12–24; female florets numerous, white or pale yellow-red, often with 1–2 dark stripes. Fr. to 2mm, convex on both sides, golden brown. New Zealand.

***L. plumosa*** Hook. f. Creeping, monoecious perenn., to 20cm. Lvs to 20×6cm, elliptic, 1–2-pinnatifid, lobes in 5–20 pairs, green, glabrous or villous. Capitula to 1cm diam., on peduncles to 12cm; phyllaries 15–20; female florets numerous, yellow-green. Fr. to 2mm, golden brown, sparsely wrinkled. New Zealand.

***L. potentillina*** F. Muell. Creeping, monoecious perenn., to 20cm. Lvs to 12×2.5cm, pinnate, lobes in 6–15 pairs, toothed, yellow-green, glabrous. Capitula to 8mm diam., on peduncles to 7cm; phyllaries 15–30; female florets yellow-green. Fr. to 2mm, brown, smooth. New Zealand.

***L. pyrethrifolia*** (Hook. f.) D. Lloyd & C. Webb. Creeping, often subdioecious perenn., spreading in patches, to 1m diam. Lvs to 4×1cm, elliptic to ovate, pinnatifid, occasionally entire and narrow, lobes in 1–5 pairs, fleshy, dark green, glabrous. Capitula to 1.5cm diam., on peduncles to 12cm, 1–8 bracteate; phyllaries 20–110; female florets numerous, white. Fr. to 2mm, convex on both surfaces, golden brown. New Zealand.

***L. reptans*** (Benth.) D. Lloyd & C. Webb. Creeping, monoecious, perenn., to 25cm, glabrous or pubesc. Lvs to 10×2.5cm, ovate, pinnatifid, lobes ovate, toothed or divided into short linear segs. Capitula to 5mm diam., on peduncles to 11cm; phyllaries 15–numerous; female florets, many, yellow. Fr. to 2mm, flattened. S and SE Australia, Tasmania.

***L. rotundata*** (Cheesem.) D. Lloyd & C. Webb. Creeping, monoecious perenn., to 10cm, forming a loose turf. Lvs elliptic to oblong, to 5×1.5cm, toothed in distal half, obtuse, yellow-green, with scattered long hairs, margin toothed in distal half. Peduncles on rhiz., to 6cm; capitula to 7mm diam., convex; involucre hemispheric, phyllaries 6–12, green, villous; female florets absent or to 12, to 2mm, yellow-green; male florets 40–90. Fr. to 2×1mm, smooth, brown. New Zealand (North Is.).

***L. scariosa*** Cass. Creeping, subdioecious perenn., to 15cm. Lvs to 5×1cm, elliptic or obovate, 1 pinnatifid, lobes in 6 12 pairs, toothed, leathery, green. Capitula to 6mm diam., on peduncles, to 6cm; phyllaries several; female florets *c*20, yellow-green. Fr. to 2mm, smooth, brown. Temperate S America.

***L. squalida*** Hook. f. Creeping, subdioecious perenn., to 15cm. Lvs to 10×2cm, elliptic or obovate, pinnatifid, lobes in 6–20 pairs, bright green, glabrous to pilose. Capitula to 5mm diam., on peduncles, to 6cm; phyllaries to 40 female florets to 70, yellow-green. Fr. to 2mm, slightly compressed, brown, smooth. New Zealand. Z5.

***L. traillii*** (T. Kirk) D. Lloyd & C. Webb. Creeping, subdioecious, perenn., to 10cm, forming a loosely matted turf. Lvs to 5×1cm, obovate, pinnatifid, lobes in 4–10 pairs, toothed, dark green, leathery. Capitula to 5mm diam., or peduncles, to 4cm; phyllaries to 20 female florets to 70, yellow-green. Fr. to 2mm, slightly compressed, becoming brown, smooth. New Zealand.

***L. dioica*** var. ***rotundata*** Cheesem. See *L. rotundata*.
For further synonymy see *Cotula*.

**Leptocereus** (Berger) Britt. & Rose. (From Gk *leptos*, slender, and *Cereus*, referring to the thin ribs.) Cactaceae. To 12 species of trees and shrubs, sometimes prostrate or scandent, to 8–10m, much branched; stems usually segmented, ribbed; ribs 3–8. Flowers 2–5×1.5–3cm, tubular-campanulate, diurnal or nocturnal, in one species clustered at the felted apex of terminal segments, almost white or pale green, yellow or pink; floral areoles spiny to nearly naked; epigynal tube short; perianth-limb short, spreading or rotate. Fr. 1.5–10×1.5–6cm, globose to oblong, fleshy, spiny to nearly naked; seeds *c*2.5×1.6–1.7mm, oval or broadly oval, black-brown or brown, dull, rugose or ruminate, periphery undifferentiated or crested with larger cells; relief flat or low-domed; hilum medium, oblique, impressed. Cuba, Hispaniola and Puerto Rico.

CULTIVATION Grow in an intermediate greenhouse (min. 10–15°C/50–60°F), use 'standard' cactus compost: moderate to high inorganic content (more than 50% grit), pH 6–7.5; shade in hot weather; maintain low humidity; keep dry from mid-autumn until early spring, except for light misting on warm days in late winter.

***L. weingartianus*** (Hartmann ex Dams) Britt. & Rose. Decumbent or climbing shrub, sometimes to 10m, eventually with a woody trunk; rootstock tuberous; distal branches 1–2cm thick; ribs 4–7; areoles 15mm apart; central spines 6, to 1.5cm, radial spines 10–12, shorter, yellow to red-brown. Fl. *c*4cm. Summer. Hispaniola. Z9.

For synonymy see *Neoabbottia*.

**Leptochilus** Kaulf. (From Gk *leptos*, slender, and *cheilos*, lip.) Polypodiaceae. Some 12 species of epiphytic ferns. Rhizomes creeping or climbing, branched, dictyostelic; scales lanceolate, narrowly acute, clathrate, dark brown. Fronds distinctly dimorphous: sterile fronds subsessile or short-stipitate, simple and entire, or lobed, or pinnatifid, broadly lanceolate to ovate, glabrous, herbaceous; fertile fronds long-stipitate, narrowly linear, revolute at margin, main veins prominent, pinnate, veinlets anastomosing into areoles, with many included, simple and branched veinlets; stipes remote, articulate. Sporangia acrostichoid below, or, occasionally, sori uniserial, linear, confluent; annulus 14-celled; spores elliptic to kidney-shaped, glabrous, glassy. Tropical Asia. Z10.

CULTIVATION As for *Polypodium*.

***L. decurrens*** Bl. Rhiz. to 4mm wide; scales to 3mm, dense at apex, deciduous. Fronds to 3cm apart; sterile fronds to 35×10cm, ovate, apex narrowly acute, base cuneately narrowed and long-decurrent, margin entire or pinnatifid, membranous; fertile to 25×1cm; stipes to 30cm, ridged, without scales. Tropical Asia to Polynesia.

***L. cladorrhizans*** (Spreng.) Maxon. See *Bolbitis portoricensis*.
***L. cuspidatus*** C. Chr. See *Bolbitis quoyana*.
***L. harlandii*** (Hook.) C. Chr. See *Hemigramma decurrens*.
***L. kanashirai*** Hayata. See *Hemigramma decurrens*.
***L. nicotianifolius*** (Sw.) C. Chr. See *Bolbitis nicotianifolia*.
***L. zeylanicus*** C. Chr. See *Quercifilix zeylanica*.
For further synonymy see *Acrostichum* and *Gymnopteris*.

**Leptodactylon** Hook. & Arn. (From Gk *leptus*, narrow, and *dactylon*, finger, due to the palmate or subpinnately lobed leaves.) Polemoniaceae. 12 species of perennial shrubs, subshrubs or herbs, habit compact of straggly, to 1m. Leaves alternate or opposite, glandular, subpinnately to palmately divided into linear lobes, apices pungent. Inflorescence usually a dense terminal glomerule or cyme, occasionally solitary and axillary; flowers often subsessile; calyx lobes entire, pungent, two-thirds of sinus filled by membrane; corolla hypocrateriform or narrowly funnelform, cream or white to pink or lilac; stamens and style included. Western N America. Z8.

CULTIVATION As for *Gilia*.

***L. californicum*** Hook. & Arn. PRICKLY PHLOX. Erect, branching shrub, to 1m; stems hairy but not glandular. Lvs palmately 5–9-lobed, lobes 3–12mm, linear, unequal, acerose, glabrous or subglabrous, with bundles of prickly young lvs in axils. Infl. with subvillous, foliaceous bracts; fls sessile; cal. *c*1cm, deeply and subequally divided into linear, acerose lobes; cor. 2–2.5cm, hypocrateriform, tube 1–1.5cm, lobes 1–1.5cm, rounded to elliptic-ovate, lavender-pink to bright rose-pink. Fr. elongate. Late winter–summer. California.

***L. pungens*** (Torr.) Rydb. GRANITE GILIA. Erect to low and branching shrub to 1m, glandular-villous, densely leafy. Lvs mostly alternate, palmately 3–7-lobed, central lobe 8–15mm, rigidly acerose or pungent. Infl. a glomerule, terminal, subterminal or in apical axils; fls (sub)sessile; cal. 8–10mm, lobes deep, linear, unequal, acerose; cor. 1.5–2.5cm, narrowly funnelform, white to cream-yellow or pink-purple-hued, tube narrow, lobes 7–10mm, narrowly obovate. Fr. cylindric; seeds *c*1.2cm, many brown. Late spring–summer. British Columbia to California and Baja California.

For synonymy see *Gilia*.

**Leptodermis** Wallich. (From Gk *leptos*, slender, delicate, and *derma*, skin.) Rubiaceae. Some 30 species of deciduous shrubs. Leaves opposite, entire; stipules persistent, acute. Flowers subsessile, in terminal or axillary clusters or panicles, white or purple, bracteate and bracteolate; bracteoles united, 2 into a tube; calyx lobes 5, leathery, persistent; corolla funnelform to tubular, interior hairy, glabrous at throat, lobes 5, valvate; stamens 5, inserted in corolla throat, anthers exserted or included; ovary 5-celled, ovules solitary in each cell; style filiform, 5-armed, arms linear. Fruit a 5-valved capsule, cylindric or ovoid; seeds erect, surrounded by a loose or adpressed, simple or reticulate, fibrous coat. India and China (Himalaya), Japan.

CULTIVATION Low-growing, much-branched, deciduous shrubs, grown for their clusters of tubular flowers in late summer; the foliage of some spp. is malodorous when bruised. Given hot dry summers to ripen the wood, they will tolerate temperatures to about −10°C/14°F. Grow in a warm dry situation in full sun, on perfectly drained soils. Propagate from softwood cuttings in early summer, or from seed sown under glass in spring.

***L. kumaonensis*** Parker. Stems to 1.5m, grey or brown; branchlets glabrous. Lvs entire, 6–7-veined, ovate-lanceolate to narrow-oval or narrow-elliptic, to 8×3cm, cuneate, dark green, downy above and especially on midrib and veins beneath. Fls sessile, 3–5 in axillary clusters, white or pink to purple when mature; cor. to 1cm, lobes spreading, acuminate, pubesc. Fr. to 5mm, glossy, malodorous when crushed or bruised; seeds ovoid. Summer. C to NW Himalaya. Z8.

***L. lanceolata*** Wallich. Stems stiff, erect, to 2m; bark grey; branchlets scabrous, bristly or glabrous. Lvs lanceolate to ovate- or elliptic-lanceolate, narrowly acute, 8–10-veined, to 10×4cm, pubesc., especially beneath and on veins; petiole to 8mm. Fls in loose terminal panicles, white to purple; bracteoles to 4mm, glabrous; cor. to 1cm, glabrous or pubesc., 4–6-lobed. Fr. to 8mm, cylindric or subcylindric, truncate, black, glossy; seed fusiform. Summer–autumn. N India. Z9.

***L. oblonga*** Bunge. Stems to 1m; branchlets purple, minutely pubesc. Lvs ovate to oblong, acute or obtuse, attenuate at base, to 18×8mm, scabrous above, sparsely pubesc. beneath, 3–5-veined; petiole to 3mm. Fls few, clustered in axils, violet-purple; cor. to 18mm, exterior and throat pubesc., lobes oblong-lanceolate. Summer–autumn. N China. Z6.

***L. pilosa*** Diels. Stems to 3m; branchlets pubesc. Lvs ovate, acute at apex, cuneate at base, to 2.5×1.5cm, glaucous, pilose; petiole to 6mm. Fls in dense terminal and axillary clusters, lilac; cal. lobes subtruncate; cor. to 1cm, funnel form exterior densely pubesc., lobes 5, suberect or spreading, ovate. Summer–autumn. C to SW China (Yunnan). Z8.

***L. purdomii*** Hutch. Stems to 3m; branchlets at first minutely pubesc. Lvs clustered at nodes, linear-oblanceolate, falcate, margins revolute, to 10×3mm, glabrous. Fls in sessile, axillary clusters, pink; bracts connate at base; cal. lobes oblong ovate; cor. to 1cm, tubular, lobes erect. Summer autumn. N China. Z6.

For synonymy see *Hamiltonia*.

**Leptolepia** Mett. (From Gk *leptos*, thin, and *lepis*, scale, alluding to the indusia.) Dennstaedtiaceae. 1 species, a terrestrial fern. Rhizomes slender, wiry, creeping and interlacing, branching slowly, siphonostelic, covered with fine brown or russet scales. Fronds to 60×3cm, deltoid, 3-pinnatifid to 3-pinnate, narrowly acute at apex, glabrous, pale green; primary pinnae obliquely paired, ovate to lanceolate-oblong, narrowly acute, to 15×5cm, secondary pinnae obliquely paired, oblong to ovate, narrowly acute, to 6×1cm, tertiary pinnules lanceolate to ovate, pinnatifid to pinnatisect, to 1cm, ultimate segments to 7, narrowly oblanceolate to deltoid, acute at apex; rachis flexible, grooved in upper part, somewhat pubescent; stipes to 45cm, rough and setose or scaly to lustrous and smooth, russet. Sori solitary on final segments, to 1mm wide, indusia broadly circular to ovate, delicately membranous. New Zealand. Z9.

CULTIVATION As for *Hypolepis*.

***L. novae-zelandiae*** (Colenso) Kuhn. As for the genus.

For synonymy see *Davallia*.

**Leptomeria** R. Br. (From Gk *leptos*, slender, and *meros*, part.) Santalaceae. 17 species of small deciduous shrubs. Branches terminating in pseudospines. Leaves reduced, scale-like, caducous, giving the plant a leafless appearance. Inflorescence racemose; flowers small, bisexual; sepals 5; stamens 5. Fruit fleshy, drupaceous. Australia. Z10.

CULTIVATION As for *Santalum*.

***L. billardieri*** R. Br. Upright shrub. Fls white. Fr. red. NSW, Queensland.

**Leptopteris** Presl. (From Gk *leptos*, slender, and *pteris*, fern, referring to the slender fronds.) Osmundaceae. 6 or 7 species of terrestrial ferns. Rhizomes erect, forming a woody trunk between 45 and 100cm. Stipes smooth, or sometimes rusty-lanate at first, often winged at base. Fronds in to 14 crowns, arching in a tussock, tripinnate to tripinnatifid, pale to dark green, membranous or softly herbaceous. Sori in patches on lower part of frond, globular, splitting at maturity, spores green, splitting when mature. Polynesia, Australasia, New Guinea. Z10.

CULTIVATION Terrestrial ferns growing in wet forest understorey in deep shade and high atmospheric humidity. Not easily grown, they require conditions in cultivation as for *Hymenophyllum*, but ideally in a house designed specifically for filmy ferns as they are of large stature: broadly spreading, diaphanous fronds arise in a whorl round a stout vertical rhizome which forms a trunk with age. A protected environment is essential as plants are sensitive to high light levels and low humidity, and the fronds too delicate to withstand high winds. Frost-free conditions should be provided and the temperature should not be allowed to rise above 25°C/80°F. Copious moisture at all times is important – frequent misting of the foliage, even during dull weather, is highly beneficial; free ventilation will prevent the growth of algae on leaf surfaces. Use only rain or deionized water. Grow young plants in pots of acid terrestrial fern mix, older plants in beds where they should be left undisturbed. Feeding with artificial fertilizers is not recommended, but an annual mulch with organic matter (especially leafmould) satisfies nutritional needs.

Plants are unbranching, spores being the only means of propagation. They are green and should be sown as soon as possible after harvest.

***L. fraseri*** (Hook. & Grev.) Presl. CREPE FERN. Stipes erect, firm, 15–22cm, glabrous, not winged. Fronds 30–60×20–30cm, arching, bipinnate to tripinnatifid, light or dark green, filmy and membranous, pinnae 10–15×2–2.5cm, close-set, lanceolate, terminal seg. bifid or trifid, rachis narrowly winged; pinnules linear-oblong, sharply dentate, 12×3–6mm, rachis naked. Australia.

***L. hymenophylloides*** (A. Rich.) Presl. Stipes 15–30cm, tufted, erect, firm, naked. Fronds 30–60×20–30cm, tripinnatifid; pinnae 10–15×2–3cm, close-set, lanceolate, lowest not reduced in size, rachis winged near apex only: pinnules 12–20×6mm, close-set, linear-oblong, dissected almost to rachis into linear, simple or forked, erecto-patent seg., rachis glabrous or somewhat tomentose. New Zealand.

***L. ×intermedia*** hort. A garden hybrid, intermediate between *L. hymenophylloides* and *L. superba*. Stipes 15–30cm, tufted, erect, firm, densely closely lanate. Fronds 30–60×20–30cm, tripinnatifid; pinnae 10–15×2–3cm, close-set, lanceolate, lowest progressively reduced, rachis winged near apex only; pinnules 12–20×6mm, close-set, linear-oblong, dissected almost to rachis into linear, simple or forked, erecto-patent seg., rachis glabrous or somewhat tomentose. Garden origin.

***L. moorei*** (Bak.) Christ. Fronds to 45×60×30cm including stipes, broadly oblong, thicker and more substantial than in other species; pinnae overlapping, 4–5cm wide, lanceolate, sessile: pinnules close-set, lanceolate, sessile, cut almost to rachis into rather obtuse ligulate lobes dentate on outer margin. Lord Howe Is.

***L. superba*** (Colenso) Presl. PRINCE-OF-WALES'S FERN; PRINCE-OF-WALES'S PLUME. Stipes 5–7.5cm, erect, firm. glabrous. Fronds 60–120×15–25cm, tripinnatifid; pinnae 10–12×1.5cm, close-set, narrowly lanceolate, lower progressively reduced; pinnules close-set, 6–20mm, linear-oblong, dissected almost to rachis into linear, simple or forked, erecto-patent seg.; rachis densely tomentose. New Zealand.

For synonymy see *Todea*.

**Leptospermum** Forst. & Forst. f. TI-TREE; TEA TREE. Myrtaceae. 79 species of shrubs or trees with smooth and flaking, fibrous or papery bark. Leaves alternate, usually no more than 1cm long, often variable in shape (within the species) but mostly elongate-subelliptic to rhombic, often thick or firm, often aromatic, occasionally lemon-scented (most notably in *L. petersonii*). Flowers 2-bracteolate, often pedicellate, axillary in bract-axils on condensed shoots or, rarely monads in leaf axils; sepals 5, imbricate; petals 5, spreading, conspicuous, deciduous, white, pink or red; stamens usually shorter than petals, appearing free. Fruit a rigid or woody capsule with valves opening at the top; seeds somewhat ovoid, with the testa reticulate, occasionally ridged or winged; or irregularly linear and striate. Mostly S Australia; 1 species common in Tasmania is widespread in New Zealand, 2 found in southeast Asia. Z9 unless specified.

CULTIVATION Grown for their glossy, usually pleasantly aromatic evergreen foliage, and for the small but abundant flowers, *Leptospermum* spp. are useful shrubs for mild coastal gardens, provided they are not too exposed, as border specimens or as informal hedging. In cooler inland gardens they can be grown against a warm, sheltered south- or southwest-facing wall; in areas experiencing prolonged winter frosts, many are amenable to tub cultivation in the cool glasshouse or conservatory. The flowering stems last well in water when cut.

*Leptospermum* spp. are generally considered rather tender, although *L. lanigerum* and *L.* 'Silver Sheen' will tolerate temperatures down to −15°C/5°F; *L. scoparium* is hardy to about −10°C/14°F, with *L. liversidgei*, the mound-forming *L. rupestre* and the gracefully arching *L. polygalifolium* showing similar tolerances. Under natural conditions *L. scoparium* is found in a range of coastal to montane habitats on wet and dry soils, varying in form from a small tree to prostrate ground hugging types; as with other species, hardiness will vary according to provenance, and where many plants are grown from seed, the genus lends itself to experimentation with cold tolerances.

Plant young plants directly from their pots to minimize root disturbance into a position in full sun with shelter from both hot and cold drying winds. Grow in a freely draining, humus-rich, neutral or acid soil. Pinch shoot tips or trim back lightly after flowering every year to maintain a neat bushy habit; plants otherwise tend to become leggy and untidy with age and will not regenerate from old wood. Under glass grow in a fertile, well drained but moisture-retentive ericaceous medium, water moderately when in growth reducing as temperatures and light levels fall to keep just moist in winter with a minimum temperature of 5–10°C/40–50°F. Maintain good ventilation and plunge pot-grown specimens outdoors in a sunny spot for the summer months. Propagate cultivars by semi-ripe or softwood cuttings in summer, species by seed as described for *Callistemon*.

***L. arachnoides*** Gaertn. Much-branched shrub, prostrate or erect, occasionally attaining 2m or more. Bark rough and peeling in flaky layers. Younger stems stout, with long, spreading hairs over a persistent pubescence of usually very short, irregular, crisped hairs. Lvs 10–20×1–3mm, elliptical to lanceolate or oblanceolate, glabrous or variously partially pubesc., thick, especially near the apex. Fls white, *c*10mm diam., single on modified shoots at the ends of crowded, short, leafy, axillary branches; bracts pale yellow or red-brown; sep. persistent, *c*2mm; pet. *c*4mm; stamens *c*2mm. SE Queensland to NSW.

***L. epacridoideum*** Cheel. Erect rather rigid bushy shrub, usually more than 2m. Bark close, firm, corrugated towards the base of the plant. Younger stems very stout. Lvs 2–3×2mm, somewhat aromatic, dense and erect or narrowly divergent, broadly elliptic to almost orbicular, incurved in cross-section, thick, glossy. Fls white or pink, *c*10mm diam., single on modified shoots on leafy side branches; bracts golden to red-brown; sep. persistent, *c*3.5mm; pet. *c*5mm; stamens 2.5mm. NSW.

***L. grandiflorum*** Lodd. Much-branched shrub 1.5 to 5m or more. Bark rough and close. Younger stems with a rather stiff white, shining, mostly adpressed, indumentum with a few curled hairs. Lvs (5–)10–15(–18)×(2–)4–8mm, narrowly to broadly ovate or elliptic, thick, grey-green, often with a dense adpressed pubescence. Fls white (may be pink), *c*20mm diam., singly on modified shoots at the ends of leafy branches; bracts red-brown and scarious; sep. deciduous, 2.5–3.5mm; pet. *c*8mm; stamens 4–5mm. Tasmania.

***L. javanicum*** Bl. Shrub or tree, often gnarled, to 8m+. Bark persistent and rather flaky. Younger stems with a silky pubescence. Lvs divergent, usually 15–35×3–7mm, broadly oblanceolate to obovate. Fls white, rarely flushed pink, *c*10–12mm diam., single or 2 or more together on modified shoots, terminal, in upper lf axils and on very short axillary branches; bracts red-brown; sep. deciduous, sometimes tardily, *c*1.5–2mm; pet. *c*4–6mm; stamens 2–3mm. Burma and southern Thailand to the Philippines, Moluccas and the Lesser Sunda Is.

***L. juniperinum*** Sm. Erect, compact, broom-like shrub, often 2–3m. Bark close. Younger stems slender, often adpressed-pilose. Lvs *c*5–15×to 2mm, dense, the youngest silvery sericeous but soon becoming glabrous, usually narrowly elliptic or narrowly lanceolate, thick, apex almost terete. Fls white, 6–10mm diam., solitary or, rarely, paired, on modified shoots at the ends of very short usually several-leaved branches; bracts red-brown and scarious; sep. deciduous, usually 1.5mm; pet. *c*3.5mm; stamens 1–1.5mm. Queensland to NSW.

***L. laevigatum*** (Gaertn.) F. Muell. Shrub or small tree, often reaching more than 4m. Bark close, tends to be shed in strips from the older trunks. Younger stems usually rather stout, sericeous pilose. Lvs 15–30×5–8mm, usually narrowly obovate, rather thin-textured. Fls white, usually 15–20mm diam., usually 2 together on short modified shoots that are terminal and close in the leaf axils; sep. persistent, 2mm; pet. 5–8mm; stamens 1.5–2.5mm. S Australia, Victoria, NSW, Tasmania. 'Compactum': habit neat, to 1m.

***L. lanigerum*** (Sol. ex Ait.) Sm. Shrub or tree to 5m+. Bark close, firm. Younger stems rather stout and densely pubesc. Lvs mostly divergent to spreading, 2–15×2–4mm, oblong to narrowly oblanceolate, usually grey-pubesc. at least on the lower surface. Fls white, *c*15mm diam., occurring singly on modified shoots at the ends of short densely leafy side-branches, the subtending lvs often longer-petiolate or otherwise modified; bracts pale or red-brown; sep. persistent, 2–4mm; pet. *c*6mm; stamens 2–3mm. Tasmania, S Australia, NSW, Victoria. 'Silver Sheen' (*L. cunninghamii* of gardens): lvs silver-grey on red-tinted stems; fls produced later than in *L. lanigerum* (i.e. summer, not spring); very cold-hardy. Z8.

***L. liversidgei*** R. Bak. & H.G. Sm. Compact shrub to 4m, but often 0.5m or less. Bark close. Younger stems slender, with a short, often crisped pubescence. Lvs usually 5–7×1–2mm, lemon-scented, dense and erect to spreading, narrowly obovate, thick. Fls white or pink, *c*10–12mm diam., occurring singly on modified shoots at the ends of short few-leaved branches in adjacent axils; bracts rather pale and scarious; sep. persistent or tardily deciduous, *c*2mm; pet. *c*5mm; stamens 1.5–2.5mm. NSW, Queensland. Z8.

***L. minutifolium*** C.T. White. Shrub from less than 1m to 2m+. Bark close or smooth flaking. Younger stems usually adpressed-hirsute. Lvs usually 2–4×2mm, usually dense and diverging widely or spreading, narrowly to broadly obovate, thick, concave, glossy. Fls white, usually *c*8mm diam., single on modified shoots at the ends of short or long leafy axillary branches; bracts red-brown and scarious; sep. deciduous, 1.5–2mm; pet. 2.5–3mm; stamens 3–3.5mm. Queensland, NSW.

***L. myrtifolium*** Sieber ex DC. Slender shrub 1–2(–3)m. Bark close forming flaky layers on old plants. Younger stems densely pubesc. Lvs 5–10×2–5mm, broadly obovate to oblanceolate or elliptic, usually sericeous-pilose, grey-green, rarely sparsely so or glabrous, thick-textured. Fls white, 7–11mm diam., occurring singly or occasionally 2 together in modified shoots usually at the ends of short few-leaved branches in adjacent lf-axils; bracts scarious, red-brown; sep. deciduous, *c*1.5mm; pet. 3.5–4.5mm; stamens *c*2mm. NSW, Victoria. Z8.

***L. nitidum*** Hook. f. Compact shrub often 2m tall. Bark scaly, layered. Stems stout, pubesc. Lvs usually 8–20×3–6mm, aromatic, dense, erect or narrowly divergent, elliptic, often with pubesc. margins, usually glossy, thick. Fls white, usually *c*15mm diam., solitary on modified shoots at the ends of dense leafy side-branches whose upper lvs are reduced in size; bracts golden-brown; sep. persistent, often 5–6mm; pet. *c*6mm; stamens in bundles of *c*7, 2.5–3mm. Tasmania.

***L. obovatum*** Sweet. Dense erect shrub often 2m or more. Bark close and firm. Younger stems with close adpressed pubescence. Lvs 5–20×2–8mm, aromatic, erect to spreading, narrowly oblanceolate to very broadly obovate, usually rather thick. Fls white, 8–12mm diam., solitary or paired on modified shoots on very short few-leaved or leafless branchlets; bracts red-brown and scarious; sep. deciduous, 2–2.5mm; pet. 3–4mm; stamens 2–2.5mm. NSW, Victoria.

***L. parviflorum*** Val. Multi-stemmed shrub or small tree to more than 6m. Bark seasonally exfoliating in strips to expose a smooth shining and often purple-red surface below. Younger stems very slender, pendulous, glabrescent or pubesc. Lvs diverging, 20–70×2–10mm, linear-lanceolate, rather thin. Fls white or cream, 2–7mm diam., usually several (to 6) together, each subtended by a bract, at the ends of branches; sep. persistent, 1mm or less; pet. 1–2.5mm; stamens to 1.25mm. New Guinea, W Australia, Northern Territory, Queensland.

***L. petersonii*** Bail. Dense shrub or diffuse small tree to 5m+. Bark rather flaky, persistent fibrous. Younger stems slender, only briefly somewhat hirsute. Lvs usually 20–40×2–5mm, strongly lemon-scented, elliptic to narrowly lanceolate. Fls white, 10–15mm diam., solitary or, rarely, paired, on modified shoots in adjacent lf axils or at the ends of very short axillary branches; bracts pale red-brown, scarious; sep. deciduous, 1.5–2.5mm; pet. 5–6mm; stamens 2.5–3.5mm. Queensland, NSW.

***L. polygalifolium*** Salisb. Shrub, often from 0.5 to 3m, or slender to stout-trunked tree to 7m or more. Bark usually close and firm but soft, thick and rather flaky in some arborescent forms. Younger stems pubesc. Lvs sometimes aromatic, but not strongly so, usually somewhat divergent to spreading or occasionally deflexed, 5–20×1–5mm, oblanceolate-elliptic to narrowly linear-elliptic. Fls white, often green or creamy-white, occasionally pink, usually 10–15mm diam., solitary on modified shoots at the ends of very short or long leafy axillary branches; bracts dark red-brown, scarious; sep. deciduous, 1.5–2.5mm; petals 4–6mm; stamens (2–)2.5–4(–4.5)mm. E Australia, Lord Howe Is. Z8.

***L. roei*** Benth. Spreading shrub to 2m or more, with erect rather slender branches. Bark close but shedding fibres. Younger stems with dense or sparse, long, silky hairs. Lvs diverging, usually 7–13×2–3mm, elongate-obovate to narrowly cuneate, often sericeous throughout but when older sometimes glabrous. Fls white or pink, usually 10–13mm diam., solitary or paired on short modified shoots in adjacent lf axils or on the ends of adjacent short few-leaved side-branches; bracts pale red-brown scarious; sep. persistent, 1–1.5mm; pet. *c*5mm; stamens *c*2mm. W Australia.

***L. rotundifolium*** (Maid. & Betche) F. Rodway ex Cheel. Shrub from less than 1m to 2m+. Bark close and ultimately gnarled. Younger stems stout, with a dense pubescence of short ascending to recurved hairs. Lvs mostly 4–7mm long and wide, in general orbicular but variable, thick. Fls white to purple-pink, to 3cm diam.+, solitary on modified shoots at the ends of many-leaved adjacent axillary branchlets; bracts light to dark red-brown; sep. deciduous, *c*3–4mm; pet. *c*8–12mm; stamens 4–6mm. NSW.

***L. rupestre*** Hook. f. Shrub rarely more than 1.5m, usually low-growing. Bark flaky. Younger stems with a long, later short, silky pubescence. Lvs (2–)5–7(–9)mm×2–3mm, aromatic, divergent, generally broadly to narrowly obovate to elliptic, rather glossy, thick. Fls white, 7–10mm diam., solitary or paired on modified shoots on very short usually few-leaved axillary branches; bracts red-brown, scarious; sep. deciduous, *c*2mm; pet. 3–3.5mm; stamens 1.5–2mm. Tasmania.

***L. scoparium*** Forst. & Forst. f. MANUKA; TEA TREE. Shrub usually *c*2m but occasionally reaching 4m+. Bark usually close and firm, rarely layered. Younger stems with a long fine silky pubescence. Lvs mostly widely divergent, spreading or even deflexed, variable in size and shape, *c*7–20×2–6mm, narrowly to broadly elliptic, or broadly lanceolate or oblanceolate, often silvery pubesc. on new shoots, thick. Fls white or, rarely, pink or red, usually 8–12mm diam., occasionally larger, singly on very short leafless or few-leaved branches in adjacent axils and on adjacent branches; bracts scarious and red-brown; sep. deciduous, *c*2mm; pet. 4–7mm; stamens *c*2.5–3.5mm. NSW, Victoria, Tasmania, New Zealand. 'Album Flore Pleno': habit compact, erect; fls white, double. 'Boscawenii': compact; fls to 2.5cm diam, white with a rose centre. 'Burgundy Queen': fls deep red. 'Chapmanii': lvs maroon to red-green; fls cerise. 'Cherry Brandy': lvs deep red-bronze; fls cerise. 'Decumbens': semi-prostrate; fls pale rose. 'Gaiety Girl': fls double, salmon pink. 'Jubilee': habit densely bushy. 'Keatleyi': young growth red-tinted, silky; fls large, waxy, pink. 'Kiwi': dwarf; foliage bronze; fls deep pink. 'Nanum': dwarf form to 30cm; fls rose, profuse. 'Nanum Tui': dwarf; lvs bronze. 'Nichollsii': lvs purple-red to bronze; fls carmine. 'Pink Cascade': habit weeping. 'Red Damask': fls double, deep red, long-lasting. 'Roseum Multipetalum': fls double, rose pink, profuse. 'Ruby Glow': fls semi-double, crimson with a darker centre. Z8.

***L. sphaerocarpum*** Cheel. Shrub to 2m, usually erect, rarely spreading. Bark close and firm. Younger stems rather stout, usually with a dense short pubescence and often with a few to numerous long, ascending hairs. Lvs mostly 5–20×2–5mm, broadly to narrowly elliptic, rather thick. Fls green-white or pink, (10–)15–20mm diam., solitary on modified shoots at the ends of leafy side-branches; bracts pale or red-brown; sep. persistent, 3.5–5mm; pet. *c*5–7mm; stamens 4–6mm. NSW.

***L. spinescens*** Endl. Spinescent shrub, usually less than 1.5m. Bark corrugated, firm but soft, corky. Younger stems stout and tapering, glabrous or pubesc. Lvs divergent, variable in size, usually 5–15×2–5mm, obovate, elliptic, thick. Fls white or green-cream, 10–15mm diam., solitary, each subtended by a series of bracts, or in leaf-axils subtended only by bracteoles; bracts red-brown, scarious; sep. persistent, *c*2mm; pet. 3–6mm; stamens 2.5–4mm. W Australia.

***L. squarrosum*** Gaertn. Rather open woody shrub of variable habit, from less than 1 to more than 4m. Bark close, firm. Younger stems often stout, sericeous-pilose. Lvs usually widely divergent, spreading or deflexed, mostly 5–15×2–5mm, usually broadly elliptic to broadly ovate-lanceolate, occasionally narrower, usually thick. Fls white or pink, to 10–20mm diam., solitary on modified shoots on very short, leafless or few-leaved axillary branches in adjacent axils on adjacent branches; bracts thinly scarious, dark red-brown; sep. deciduous, 2–3mm+; pet. 3–7mm+; stamens usually *c*3–4mm. NSW.

***L. trinervium*** (Sm.) J. Thomps. WEEPING TI-TREE. Rigid shrub or small tree 2–5m with a stout trunk in proportion to the rather short side-branches. Bark in many thin layers. Younger stems rather stout and pubesc. Lvs erect to spreading, usually 10–20×1–6mm, broadly ovate to very narrowly elliptic and somewhat falcate, usually sericeous when young. Fls white, 7–15mm diam., singly or together on condensed shoots at the ends of short few-leaved side-branches; sep. persistent, 1.5–2.5mm; pet. 5–7mm; stamens 1.5–2mm. Queensland, Victoria, NSW.

***L. attenuatum*** Sm. See *L. trinervium*.
***L. baccatum*** Sm. See *L. arachnoides*.
***L. bullatum*** hort. ex Loud. See *L. scoparium*.
***L. citratum*** Chall. See *L. petersonii*.
***L. citriodorum*** auct. See *L. liversidgei*.
***L. cunninghamii*** S. Schauer. See *L. myrtifolium* and *L. lanigerum*.
***L. flavescens*** Sm. See *L. polygalifolium*.
***L. floribundum*** Jungh. See *L. javanicum*.
***L. floribundum*** Salisb. See *L. scoparium*.
***L. humifusum*** Cunn. ex Schauer, nom. nud. See *L. rupestre*.
***L. persiciflorum*** Rchb. f. See *L. squarrosum*.
***L. pubescens*** Lam. See *L. lanigerum*.
***L. rodwayanum*** Summerh. & Comber. See *L. grandiflorum*.
***L. scoparium*** var. ***prostratum*** hort. non Hook. f. See *L. rupestre*.
***L. stellatum*** Cav. See *L. trinervium*.
For further synonymy see *Melaleuca*.

**Leptosyne** DC.
***L. bigelovii*** A. Gray. See *Coreopsis bigelovii*.
***L. californica*** Nutt. See *Coreopsis californica*.
***L. douglasii*** DC. See *Coreopsis douglasii*.
***L. gigantea*** Kellogg. See *Coreopsis gigantea*.
***L. stillmanii*** A. Gray. See *Coreopsis stillmanii*.

**Leptotes** Lindl. (From Gk *leptotes*, delicacy, referring to the delicate leaves of many of the species.) Orchidaceae. Some 4 species of diminutive epiphytic orchids. Rhizome creeping. Pseudobulbs stem-like small, thickened, cylindrical, apically unifoliate. Leaves fleshy, terete or subterete, erect. Inflorescence a terminal raceme, loosely 1- to few-flowered; peduncle short, slender, erect or arched; bracts inconspicuous; flowers spreading; sepals and petals subequal, subsimilar, free; lip adnate to column base, trilobed, lateral lobes distinctly short-unguiculate, clasping column, small, auriculate, midlobe larger than lateral lobes, reflexed, entire, disc smooth or with prominent midrib; column fleshy, short, erect, apex sometimes winged, anther terminal, pollinia 6, waxy. Brazil, Paraguay, Argentina. Z10.

CULTIVATION Tufted orchids for the cool or intermediate house with small white and rose flowers. Cultivate as for small *Laelia pygmaea*.

***L. bicolor*** Lindl. Pseudobulbs to 30×8mm, fusiform-cylindrical, fleshy, erect or suberect. Lvs to 10×1cm, usually shorter, terete, acute, recurved to suberect, with a central groove above, lustrous dark green. Infl. shorter than lvs, 1- to several-fld; fls opening in succession, to 5cm diam., fragrant, sparkling white, the lip with a rose to purple, white-tipped midlobe; sep. to 22×5mm, linear-oblong to linear-lanceolate, acute; pet. to 22×3mm, linear-ligulate to linear-oblong, acute; lip to 20×7mm, fleshy, lateral lobes orbicular to subquadrate, midlobe narrowly ovate or oblong, acute; column to 5mm, purple or green, obscurely triquetrous. E Brazil, Paraguay.

***L. tenuis*** Rchb. f. Resembles *L. unicolor* except tepals yellow, lip white with a central violet blotch, midlobe transversely oblong or elliptic, obtuse or emarginate. Brazil.

***L. unicolor*** Barb. Rodr. Pseudobulbs to 1.5cm. Lvs to 55×8mm, erect to slightly curved, fleshy, subterete, acute, deeply grooved above. Infl. 1–2-fld, pendent; fls to 6cm diam., nodding, fragrant, white-pink to pale rose-lilac; sep. to 25×3mm, narrowly ligulate or linear-ligulate, acute; pet. to 25×2mm, subspathulate to linear-subspathulate, acute, somewhat fleshy, darker than sep.; lip to 2.5×1cm, fleshy, erect or recurved, lateral lobes minute, triangular, midlobe ovate to lanceolate, acuminate; column to 5mm, white-green, stout. Winter. Brazil.

For synonymy see *Tetramicra*.

**Leschenaultia** R. Br. (Named in honour of Leschenault de la Tour, botanist of the voyage of discovery under Captain Nicolas Baudin in 1802.) Goodeniaceae. Some 24 species of glabrous herbs, subshrubs or shrubs. Habit heath-like. Leaves usually linear, entire, sessile. Flowers solitary and terminal or several in terminal, leafy corymbs; calyx tube entirely adnate to ovary, narrow, glabrous, lobes linear, lanceolate or subulate; corolla white, yellow, blue or red, tube split to base, exterior glabrous, interior lanate, lobes 5, erect or spreading, narrowly or broadly alate, the apex usually 2-lobed and often bearing a mucro in the sinus; anthers usually cohering round style, linear; ovary inferior, bilocular, ovules numerous, in 2 ascending rows; indusium broadly labiate. Fruit a capsule, brown, linear-cylindrical, 4-valved, glabrous. Australia. Z9.

CULTIVATION Grow in full light, but with some protection from the strongest summer sun, in a light and freely draining mix of equal parts fibrous peat and silver sand or another soilless mix low in phosphates and nitrates. A topdressing of grit or gravel is beneficial in pots or in the open garden. Water carefully and moderately in growth and sparingly at other times; maintain good ventilation and a winter minimum of 7–10°C/45–50°F. Tip back immediately after flowering to maintain the neat and compact habit. Repot carefully, ensuring that the stem remains at the original soil level; reestablish in a closed frame for a short period before restoring to the preferred well-ventilated conditions. Propagate by seed or by greenwood or semi-ripe cuttings in sand in a closed case with gentle bottom heat.

***L. acutiloba*** Benth. Shrubby annual to 30cm. Stems erect, numerous, much-branched. Lvs to 3mm, crowded, sometimes overlapping, light green, narrow, acute or obtuse. Fls solitary, terminal, sessile; cal. lobes acute, lanceolate; cor. to 12mm, cream, lobes short, erect to spreading, acute or acuminate. W Australia.

***L. biloba*** Lindl. Evergreen shrub to 60cm, erect or straggling. Lvs to 10×1mm, linear, obtuse or mucronate. Fls in terminal leafy corymbs; bracts linear to subulate; cal. to 25mm, lobes to 8mm, linear to subulate, mucronate; cor. bright blue, sometimes white, lobes to 1.25cm wide, broadly alate, 2-lobed at apex, mucronate, style glabrous. W Australia.

***L. expansa*** R. Br. Shrubby annual to 60cm. Stems weak, diffuse. Lvs to 10×1mm, linear, mucronate. Fls in dense leafy corymbs, sessile, blue, mauve or white; cal. to 13mm, lobes to 6mm, linear to subulate, mucronate; cor. to 8mm, interior densely villous, lobes narrowly winged, wings undulate, white-ciliate; style white-pubesc. at apex. W Australia.

***L. floribunda*** Benth. Shrubby annual to 1m. Stems erect; branches spreading. Lvs to 8×1mm, narrowly oblong to linear, obtuse to mucronate. Fls sessile in loose leafy corymbs; cal. to 16mm, lobes to 5mm, linear to subulate, mucronate; cor. to 16mm, blue or white, interior pubesc., lobes narrowly alate, mucronate, wings flat or undulate, slightly ciliate; style glabrous. W Australia.

***L. formosa*** R. Br. Short-lived shrub to 60cm. Stem much-branched, suckering. Lvs to 12mm, linear, light green or grey-green, acute or obtuse. Fls solitary in axils toward tips of branches; cal. lobes linear or linear-lanceolate; cor. to 2m diam., red, scarlet or orange, lobes large, spreading, erect, rounded. W Australia.

***L. hirsuta*** F. Muell. Short-lived subshrub to 60cm. Stems vigorous, erect or decumbent, slightly branched. Lvs to 3cm, narrowly linear, acute. Fls large, sessile in upper axils; cal. lobes linear to subulate; cor. to 3cm, bright scarlet, exterior slightly glandular-pubesc., lobes shorter than tube; style elongate. Fr. elongate. W Australia.

***L. laricina*** Lindl. Short-lived shrub to 60cm. Stems erect, much-branched. Lvs to 12mm, slender, crowded. Fls in upper lf axils, sessile; cal. lobes shorter than cor. tube; cor. usually vivid red (white and lilac forms reported), tube to 13mm, lobes broadly alate, 2-lobed at apex with a mucro in the sinus. W Australia.

***L. linarioides*** DC. Short-lived shrub to 10cm. Stems erect or procumbent, branches sometimes sprawling. Lvs to 20×1mm, linear, acute to mucronate. Fls terminal, solitary, sessile; cal. to 28mm, lobes to 8mm, narrowly oblong, acute; cor. tube to 10mm, limb to 3.25cm diam., 2-lipped, upper 3 lobes broadly alate, deep yellow, lower 2 lobes vivid red; style glabrous, subulate. W Australia.

***L. longiloba*** F. Muell. Shrub to 15cm. Stems several, prostrate, branching above. Lvs small, linear, acute-mucronate. Fls in upper lf axils, sessile; cal. lobes long, acute; cor. to 2.5cm, cream and red, lobes spreading, equalling tube, acuminate-mucronate. W Australia.

***L. superba*** F. Muell. Annual shrub to 60cm. Stems erect, branches straight, rod-like. Lvs to 2.5cm, crowded, finely linear. Fls in terminal clusters; cal. lobes linear to subulate; cor. to 2.5cm, yellow, orange or red, tube cylindric, lobes short, broadly alate, subequal. Fr. to 2.5cm. W Australia.

***L. tubiflora*** R. Br. Shrub to 15cm. Stems prostrate, densely branched, branches divaricate or short, virgate. Lvs crowded, linear. Fls solitary, sessile, at tips of short branches; cor. cream, orange, pink or red, tube cylindric, lobes shorter than tube, wings short. Fr. narrow. W Australia.

***L. arcuata*** Vriese. See *L. linarioides*.
***L. drummondii*** Vriese. See *L. biloba*.
***L. grandiflora*** DC. See *L. biloba*.
***L. multiflora*** Lodd. See *L. formosa*.
***L. splendens*** Hook. See *L. laricina*.

**Lespedeza** Michx. (For Vincente Manuel de Cespedes, the Spanish governor of Eastern Florida during the late 18th century at the time of Michaux's travels in that region; the name of the governor was rendered Lespedez in Michaux's Flora.) BUSH CLOVER. Leguminosae (Papilionoideae). Some 40 species of prostrate or trailing, perennial or annual shrubs or herbs, often downy. Leaves trifoliolate, petiolate; leaflets entire, terminal leaflet frequently somewhat longer than lateral ones; stipules small, persistent, shorter stipules subulate, the longer stipules bristle-like or linear; stipels reduced or absent. Flowers small, rarely solitary, usually few to numerous and arranged in racemes, axillary fascicles or, more rarely, terminal panicles, chasmogamous i.e. with showy petals, calyx campanulate, lobes 5, subequal, sharp-tipped, the upper 2 somewhat connate, stamens 10, filaments united forming 2 bundles, anthers equal, style long, thread-like, or cleistogamous i.e. some *c*90% smaller, and located in separate racemes, petals substantially reduced, calyx as for chasmogamous flowers, style short, strongly recurved; bracts persistent, bracteoles 2, located near to, or at, pedicel apex. Fruit rounded or elliptic, compressed, reticulate, not dehiscent; stalk short or absent; seed 1, oval, somewhat compressed laterally, ochre to black-brown. E US, E & Tropical Asia, Australia.

CULTIVATION As for *Indigofera*.

***L. bicolor*** Turcz. EZO-YAMA-HAGI. Bush to 3m, usually woody-based, somewhat scandent. Leaflets 1–7.5×0.8–3.5cm, ovate or elliptic, apex minute, blunt to broadly rounded, base blunt to rounded, vivid green above, paler beneath, thinly downy above while young, pilose to glabrous beneath. Fls loosely packed in numerous axillary racemes, or in terminal, paniculate clusters composed of several racemes; peduncles 10–50mm, downy; pedicels 1.5–5mm, hirsute; bracts ovate, rusty-pubesc.; bracteoles to 1.2mm; cor. 10–12mm, purple-rose or rose-violet; cal. 5–6.5mm, thickly to sparsely stiff-hirsute, tube 1.5–2.5mm, cylindrical, lobes 2.5–4.5mm, acute, linear-lanceolate. Fr. 5–8×*c*5–8mm, sub-spherical, loosely white-downy. Late summer. Japan, China, Manchuria, Korea, Taiwan; naturalized SE US. 'Summer Beauty': habit spreading, to 1.6m tall; fls long-lasting. 'Yakushima': habit dwarf, to 30cm tall; lvs and fls small. Z5.

***L. buergeri*** Miq. KI-HAGI. Shrub, 40–80cm; branches narrow and delicate, horizontally spreading, downy. Leaflets 2–4×1–3cm, elliptic-ovate, apex generally sharp-tipped, deep green, usually glabrous or virtually so above, adpressed-downy beneath. Fls 10–12mm, in ascending racemes; pedicels very short or absent; bracts blunt, ovate; bracteoles broadly ovate, generally ciliolate, usually exceeding cal. tube, multi-nerved, cal. teeth equal, blunt to sharp-tipped, ovate, upper 2 united; cor. white to purple. Fr. 12×4mm, oblong, loosely soft-hirsute. Late summer. Japan (Honshu, Kyushu, Shikoku), China. Z6.

***L. capitata*** Michx. Perenn., 50cm–1.5m. Leaflets 1.5–4.5×0.5–1.5cm, oblong to narrowly elliptic, apex minute and blunt to broadly rounded or, more rarely, acute, base blunt to rounded or, acute, glabrous to adpressed sericeous above, velutinous to sericeous beneath. Fls 7–9mm, 14–30 overlapping in densely packed axillary racemes; peduncles 5–25mm, velutinous; pedicels 1–3mm; bracts and bracteoles 2–3.5mm, linear, downy; cal. 7–13mm, thickly downy, tube 1–1.5mm, lobes subulate, narrowly lanceolate, equalling cor.; cor. yellow-white or plain white, standard 0.8–1.2mm, blotched purple at base, exceeding wings and keel. Fr. 4–7mm, narrowly elliptic, inconspicuously veined, often irregular. Late summer–early autumn. US (Maine, Kansas, N Minnesota, SE Texas, W Florida). Z4.

***L. cyrtobotrya*** Miq. MARABU-HAGI; MIYAMA-HAGI. Scandent or erect woody-based herb, 70cm–1.2m. Leaflets 2–4.4×1.5–2cm, obovate or elliptic, apex rounded, bunt or somewhat notched, base tapering, midrib terminating in a short bristle, glabrous above, downy beneath. Fls 1–1.5cm, crowded in axillary clusters or racemes; pedicels absent or nearly so; bracts sharp-tipped, narrowly ovate, 1-nerved; bracteoles narrower than bracts, cal. teeth, spine-tipped; cor. rose-purple. Fr. 6–7×5mm, suborbicular, beaked, soft- and white-hirsute. Late summer–early autumn. Japan (Shikoku, Kyushu, Honshu), China, Korea. Z6.

***L. juncea*** (L. f.) Pers. KARA-MEDO-HAGI; INU-MEDO-HAGI. Stiffly erect, rather woody perenn., 60cm–1.2m. Leaflets 0.8–2×0.2–0.6cm, narrowly obovate to oblanceolate, apex rounded to retuse, tapering towards base, canescent beneath, glabrous above. Fls 7–8mm, 2–6 in axillary, umbellate racemes; cal. 4–5mm, lobes lanceolate, bristle-tipped; cor. yellow-white, the standard blotched purple. Fr. 3mm, broad-ovate, downy, sessile. Autumn. Japan (Honshu), Manchuria, N China, Korea, India (Kunawar & Kashmir), E Siberia, Australia (SE Queensland). Z5.

***L. maximowiczii*** C. Schneid. CHOSEN-KI-HAGI. Closely allied to *L. buergeri*. Shrub to 4m; shoots cylindric, initially downy. Leaflets 2.5–5cm, oval-elliptic to ovate, apex sharp-tipped, base rounded to broadly cuneate, sericeous beneath. Fls purple, in ascending racemes 30–80mm long; cal. teeth broadly lanceolate, bustle-tipped, exceeding tube length. Fr. 10–15mm. Summer. Japan (Kyushu), Korea. Z5.

***L. thunbergii*** (DC.) Nak. MIYAGINO-HAGI. Perenn. herb or subshrub, 1–2m. Leaflets 3–5×1–2.5cm, narrowly oblong or, more rarely, ovate or elliptic, apex sharp-tipped, glabrous above, adpressed grey-hirsute beneath. Fls 15–18mm, in numerous pendulous racemes to 15cm, these grouped in pendulous, terminal panicles 60–80cm long; bracts and bracteoles narrow-ovate or broad-lanceolate, small, sharp-tipped; cal. 6mm, grey-hirsute, teeth 5, subulate; cor. rose-purple. Fr. 10–13×4–5mm, narrowly obovate to oblong, flat, adpressed sericeous. Late summer. Japan (Honshu), China. 'Alba': fls white. Z6.

***L. macrocarpa*** Bunge. See *Campylotropis macrocarpa*.
For further synonymy see *Hedysarum*.

**Lesquerella** S. Wats. (For Leo Lesquereux, late 19th-century American paleobotanist.) BLADDER POD. Cruciferae. 40 species of annual or perennial herbs, densely hairy throughout. Leaves linear-oblanceolate, entire to pinnatifid, usually borne in rosettes; flowering stem leaves oblanceolate or oblong-ovate, short-petioled or sessile. Inflorescence a raceme, usually elongating in fruit; flowers small, numerous; sepals 4, erect to spreading; petals 4, broad-obovate to narrow-spathulate; stamens 6. Fruit a silicle, usually globose, sometimes compressed. N America, Greenland. Z5.

CULTIVATION Grown for their tufted grey or silvery foliage and their (usually) yellow and moderately showy flowers, sometimes followed by ornamental seed pods. The genus includes neat rosette-forming species for the rock garden, such as *L. alpina*, and the variable *L. ludoviciana*, both native of the Rockies; these and other mountain species do not thrive where summers are hot and humid. The Texan native, *L. grandiflora*, bears a fine loose raceme of large flowers, for the flower border. Grow in well-drained soils, in sun. Propagate from seed.

***L. alpina*** (Nutt.) S. Wats. Tufted perenn., to 25cm. Base woody, branched. Stems erect, simple. Lvs to 7cm, oblanceolate-spathulate to linear, tapering to petiole; flowering stem lvs to 5cm, linear to oblanceolate. Raceme dense, sometimes elongating in fruit; sep. 3.5–7mm, spathulate; pet. 4–10mm, yellow, oblong-elliptic. Fr. 2.5–8mm, compressed toward apex, style 1.5–6mm. Rocky Mts. Z5.

***L. arctica*** (Wormsk. ex Hornem.) S. Wats. Perenn., 30cm. Base woody. Stems few. Lvs to 15cm, oblanceolate or linear-spathulate, silver-hairy, 2–6, tapering to a slender petiole; flowering stem lvs oblanceolate, ligulate, sessile or short-petioled. Raceme arching; sep. elliptic to ovate, 4–6mm; pet. obovate, yellow, not distinctly clawed. Fr. 4–9mm, subglobose, style 1–3mm. Summer. Northern N America, Greenland. Z3.

***L. globosa*** (Desv.) S. Wats. Perenn., to 50cm. Base woody. Lvs to 5×1.5cm, white-pubesc., oblanceolate to obovate, entire to sinuate, sometimes pinnatifid; flowering stem lvs to 4×1cm, obovate to elliptic. Racemes dense; sep. 2.5–4mm; pet. 3.5–7mm, bright yellow. Fr. globose, to 3mm, sparsely hairy, often compressed toward apex, style 2–4mm. Indiana to Tennessee. Z6.

***L. gracilis*** (Hook.) S. Wats. Annual or bienn., to 70cm. Stems numerous, scabrid, thin. Lvs 1–11cm, oblanceolate to lyrate, subglabrous, mostly entire; flowering stem lvs to 7cm, obovate, upper lvs sessile, lower lvs short-petioled. Racemes long; sep. 3–8mm; pet. 6–11mm, spreading, ovate, tapering to claw, 6–11mm, yellow-orange. Fr. 3–10mm, globose, glabrous, style 2–5mm; seed wingless. Summer. Texas, Oklahoma, Kansas.

***L. grandiflora*** (Hook.) S. Wats. Annual, to 75cm. Stem densely hairy, branched. Lvs hairy, oblong, pinnatifid, petiolate, flowering stem lvs oblong-lanceolate, auriculate. Pet. 8–12mm, broad-ovate to nearly round, yellow, short-clawed, 8–12mm; pedicels 10–20mm. Fr. subglobose, glabrous, 4–6mm; seeds narrow-winged. Summer. Texas.

***L. ludoviciana*** (Nutt.) S. Wats. Perenn. to 50cm. Stems few, lvs rosulate, outermost 2–9cm, oblanceolate and obtuse, innermost linear-elliptic, erect; flowering stem lvs smaller, elliptic-oblanceolate. Raceme dense, elongating in fruit; sep. 4–8mm; pet. 5–11mm, oblanceolate, indistinctly clawed. Fr. obovoid to subglobose, slightly compressed, densely hairy, style 3–5mm; seed wingless. Spring–summer. Colorado to Montana and Minnesota. Z3.

***L. montana*** (Gray) S. Wats. Perenn., to 35cm. Base woody. Stem erect or prostrate. Lvs 2–7cm, nearly round to obovate-elliptic, entire or sinuate; flowering stem lvs 1–3cm, obovate to linear, shallow-toothed to entire. Raceme elongating in fruit; sep. 5–8mm; pet. 7–12mm, indistinctly clawed, yellow-orange fading to purple. Fr. 7–12mm, ovoid, densely hairy, slightly compressed; seed wingless. New Mexico, Colorado, Wyoming. Z3.

***L. spatulata*** Rydb. See *L. alpina*.
For further synonymy see *Alyssum* and *Vesicaria*.

**Lessingia** Cham. (For the Lessing family, German scientists and authors.) Compositae. About 7 species of glandular, white-woolly or glabrous annuals; stems simple or branched. Leaves alternate, entire, toothed or pinnatifid. Capitula discoid; involucre cylindric to campanulate; phyllaries in several series; florets mauve, pink, yellow or rarely white, outermost enlarged, reflexed. Fruit a silky-haired cypsela; pappus of bristles. W US (California).

CULTIVATION As for *Layia*.

***L. hololeuca*** Greene. To 30cm; stems erect or ascending, branching from base. Basal lvs to 12cm, obovate to oblanceolate, entire or toothed, sessile or attenuate at base. Capitula solitary, terminal, rarely axillary; involucre to 12mm; phyllaries in 5–6 rows; florets 13–18, pink or mauve.

***L. leptoclada*** A. Gray. To 80cm, glabrescent; stems erect, branching above, rarely at base. Basal lvs to 5cm, oblanceolate or spathulate, attenuate at base, entire or toothed. Capitula terminal, solitary, rarely 2 or more; involucre to 10mm high; phyllaries in to 8 rows; florets to 22, mauve to purple.

**Lettuce**. *Lactuca sativa*. Compositae. Lettuce is an annual salad vegetable. A cultigen possibly derived from the wild lettuce *Lactuca serriola*, it originated east of the Mediterranean, in the region encompassing Asia Minor, Transcaucasia, Iran and Turkestan. First used as a medicinal plant it was treated as a food plant as early as 4500 BC. By the 1st century AD it was in general use by the Greeks and Romans. Original forms of the plant were non-head-forming loose-leaf types and the headed types did not appear until the 16th century. It is now widely cultivated in both temperate and tropical regions and is also important as a glasshouse crop in cooler regions.

Lettuce is usually grown where mean temperatures are in the range 10°–20°C/50–68°F. Higher temperatures prevent head formation and cause bolting and also produce a bitter flavour in the leaves. Cool temperatures and adequate soil moisture are required during heading. The range of cultivars enables lettuce to be produced in the open throughout most of the year. Some are hardy enough to overwinter in milder areas but cloches or cool glass are needed in regions experiencing frost. The ideal site for lettuce is an open area where the soil is light, well-drained and fertile, with an optimum pH around 6.0. Well-rotted organic manure should be incorporated to increase the moisture retention of the soil. The crop is fairly tolerant of high salinity.

Lettuce may either be sown direct, or in seed trays or peat blocks for subsequent transplanting. They do not transplant well in hot weather, so later sowings are best direct-sown or established by using peat blocks or modular-raised plants. Seeds should be sown in drills 2cm/¾in. deep and at intervals of about two weeks for continuity of supply. Mosaic-tested seed is preferable as it reduces the risk of virus infection. Sowing can be made from early spring until autumn but germination, particularly of the butterhead types, is often erratic when soil temperatures are greater than 25°C/77°F. Watering will help to reduce soil temperature and improve the germination of sowings made during the summer. Except during midsummer, when lettuce does not readily recover from transplanting, thinnings from direct sowings can be used to provide a successive crop maturing approximately 10 days later. Plants should be kept well watered, particularly during the later stages of growth.

The earliest sowings for outdoor production should be made in trays or blocks under protection or direct-seeded in frames or under cloches, where they can be harvested *in situ* or provide transplants for establishing later in open ground.

The main period of outdoor sowings should commence as soon as soil temperatures begin to rise in the spring. A succession of sowings with appropriate cultivars will provide harvests through the summer months until autumn. The later crops will benefit from protection from cloches during the autumn. Autumn sowings for a protected winter crop can either be sown in the open or under glass for transplanting to frames or cool glass during the later autumn.

Cold-hardy cultivars can be overwintered outdoors to provide an early crop during late spring the following year. These should be sown direct during late summer and thinned to approximately 8cm/3in. apart during the autumn. Final thinning should be carried out during the following spring when growth recommences to allow 30cm/12in. between plants. Overwintered crops benefit from a topdressing of a nitrogen fertilizer during early spring.

The choice of cultivar will to a large extent determine the final plant spacing. However, it is possible to modify the growth habit of lettuce by planting at high density to encourage the formation of leaves and inhibit head formation. The leaves can then be cut off 2-3cm/1in. above soil level and the remaining stumps will produce a second crop that will be ready to harvest 4–7 weeks later. For maximum leaf growth, plants should be sown in a fertile weed-free soil in rows 12cm/5in. apart and a final within-row spacing of approximately 2.5cm/1in. between plants. Cos lettuce are more suited for leaf production than other types.

For heading lettuce, the time from planting to maturity varies from 60 to 80 days during the summer to 90–145 days during the cooler period of the year. The harvested crop is highly perishable, particularly at high temperatures and low humidity. Shelf life can be extended to two weeks at 1°C/34°F and 95% relative humidity.

The large number of lettuce cultivars available can be broadly divided into two groups – the cabbage and cos types. Cabbage lettuce are further divided into the soft-leaved butterheads (looseheads in US) and the crisp-leaved 'crispheads'. The butterheads are earlier maturing than the crispheads but have a greater tendency to bolt. The cos lettuce are upright in shape with thicker, long leaves. They normally take longer to mature than the cabbage type. In addition to the heading lettuces there are a number of non-heading or 'salad bowl' types which are less prone to bolting and from which leaves can be harvested as required throughout the summer months. Leaf shape can range from entire to deeply indented and colours extend from green to red. Forms with a thick main stem that can be cooked are called celtuce.

The following cultivars cover a range of types and maturity periods. *For early sowing under protection*: 'Little Gem', 'Tom Thumb', 'Winter Density', and 'Salad Bowl' types. Main summer sowings in the open: (Butterheads): 'All the Year Round', 'Avondefiance', 'Buttercrunch', 'Continuity', 'Red Sails', 'Reskia', 'Royal Oak Leaf', 'Ruby', 'Sabine', 'Unrivalled'. (Cos): 'Little Gem', 'Valmaire', 'Winter Density'; (Crispheads): 'Avoncrisp', 'Great Lakes', 'Iceberg', 'Malika', 'Minetto', 'Musette'. 'Salad Bowl' types, 'Black Seeded Simpson': 'Early Curled Simpson', 'Grand Rapids', 'Lollo Biondo', 'Lollo Rosso',

'Oakleaf', 'Red Oakleaf', 'Red Salad Bowl', 'Saladini', 'Slobolt', 'Wallopo'. *Protected winter crop*: (Butterheads): 'Columbus', 'Cynthia', 'Dandie', 'Kwiek', 'Magnet', 'Pascal', 'Ravel'; (Crisp-head): 'Kelly's'. *Outdoor overwintering crop*: (Butterhead): 'Imperial Winter'; (Cos): 'Little Gem', 'Lobjoits Green'.

Lettuce ring spot is caused by the fungus *Microdochium panattonianum*. Small, round, brown-yellow spots occur on the underneath surfaces of the leaves and elongated, sunken areas resembling slug damage develop on the midribs. Other, usually less important, leaf spots are caused by the fungi *Pleospora herbarum* and *Septoria lactucae*. These diseases can be controlled by fungicide sprays and infected crop debris should be destroyed. Marginal leaf spot, in which the leaf edges shrivel, is caused by infection with the soil-borne bacterium *Pseudomonas marginalis*. The bacteria enter the leaves through the stomata and measures which reduce humidity and prevent the leaves being wetted will help control the disease. Lettuce can also be affected by bacterial soft rot (*Erwinia carotovora*), damping-off and foot rot (*Rhizoctonia solani*), downy mildew (*Bremia lactucae*), grey mould (*Botrytis cinerea*) and sclerotinia rot (*Sclerotinia sclerotiorum*). The aecidial stage of the rust *Puccinia opizii* occasionally occurs on lettuce; uredio- and teliospores are produced on *Carex* species, the alternate hosts.

The aphid-transmitted beet western yellows virus causes intense inter-veinal yellowing of the outer, maturing leaves. Good weed control should reduce the incidence of this disease, which is present in weeds such as cleavers (*Galium aparine*), groundsel (*Senecio vulgaris*), hairy bittercress (*Cardamine hirsutum*), shepherd's purse (*Capsella bursa-pastoris*) and wild radish (*Raphanus raphanistrum*); in North America the virus infects beetroot and sugar beet. Lettuce big-vein virus causes pale yellow vein-banding, especially near the bases of the outer leaves. It is transmitted by the zoospores of a soil-borne, phycomycete fungus, *Olpidium brassicae*, which enter the plant roots. Lettuce should be grown in uncontaminated soil otherwise soil sterilization will be necessary. Plants affected by the seed-borne lettuce mosaic virus are likely to be stunted, yellowed, and have crinkly leaves or poorly developed hearts. Certified seed, with less than 0.1% or 0.01% infection, can be obtained. Cucumber mosaic virus sometimes produces symptoms similar to those of lettuce mosaic.

Lettuces may become infested with several species of polyphagous foliar aphids and also by the lettuce root aphid (*Pemphigus bursarius*). This root-feeding species which migrates from poplars is difficult to control unless a soil drench of suitable contact or systemic insecticide is applied early at the first sign of attack; in areas where attacks persist resistant cultivars should be planted instead of susceptible ones. The foliage may also be attacked by slugs and snails, caterpillars of cabbage moth (*Mamestra brassicae*), the stem eelworm (*Ditylenchus dipsaci*) springtails and the chrysanthemum leaf miner (*Phytomyza syngenesiae*). In North America caterpillars of the omnivorous leaf roller (*Platynota stultana*) may also infest lettuces. Cutworms attack plants at soil level and can cause extensive damage especially on light soils during dry summers. The roots of lettuces may be damaged by the caterpillars of swift moths (*Hepialus* spp), the grubs of chafer beetles (various species), wireworms (*Agriotes* spp.), symphylids (*Scutigerella* spp.) and the root knot eelworm (*Meloidogyne* spp.).

INDIAN LETTUCE. *Lactuca indica* (Compositae). An erect perennial up to 1.3m/4.3ft; both leaves and stems contain latex. The centre of origin is China, but the vegetable is now grown in India, Malaysia, Indonesia, the Philippines and Japan. In warm climates, seeds are sown in nursery beds or containers and transplanted to well prepared beds at a spacing of approximately 30×30cm/12×12in. Propagation by root cuttings is also possible and axillary buds from the base may develop to produce a ratoon crop. In temperate areas, seeds may be sown early in the year under greenhouse conditions, in temperatures ranging from 20–25°C/68–77°F and seedlings transferred to 25–30cm/10–12in. pots when 10–15cm/4–6in. high. The first leaves may be harvested about 60 days from sowing or planting.

STEM LETTUCE (asparagus lettuce, Chinese lettuce, celtuce). *Lactuca sativa* var. *asparagina* (Compositae). The centre of origin is China, where it is widely grown, although it is also cultivated in many parts of tropical Southeast Asia. This is a non-heading form of lettuce: the mature leaves are large, coarse and inedible but the basal leaves are narrow and lanceolate. The thickened stems may grow to 1m/3ft; both immature stems and young leaves and stems are used as a cooked vegetable. Propagation and planting are similar to the method described for Indian lettuce (*L. indica*). In temperate climates, this crop can be grown under greenhouse conditions, with a temperature range of 20–25°C/68–77°F. Seeds may be sown early in the year and seedlings transferred to 25–30cm/10–12in. pots when about 15cm/6in. high.

**Leucadendron** R. Br. (From Gk *leukos*, white, and *dendron*, tree, alluding to the best-known species, *L. argenteum*, the silver tree.) Proteaceae. Some 80 species of dioecious shrubs or trees to 10m, occasionally with lignotubers. Leaves entire, toughened, downy when young. Inflorescences terminal, solitary, surrounded by conspicuous involucral leaves which are larger than stem leaves and coloured when the flowers open; male flowers with 4 sessile anthers, 4 hypogynous scales (occasionally absent), style slender, pubescent or glabrous, with terminal pollen-presenter, stigma abortive; female flowers with 4 rudimentary sessile staminodes at base of perianth, 4 hypogynous scales (occasionally absent), style slender, glabrous. Fruiting structure cone-like, with thick woody bracts concealing fruit; fruit a nut or samara, released at maturity or after a few years have passed. S Africa. Many species grown commercially to produce spectacular cut flowers. Z9.

CULTIVATION Grown for the beautiful silver foliage and for the flowers, which although themselves insignificant are surrounded by conspicuous silvery bracts; both flower and foliage are valued by flower arrangers. *Leucadendron* spp. are frost-tender, needing a winter minimum temperature of 5–7°/40–45°F and similar conditions in cultivation to those for *Protea*. Propagate by seed in spring.

***L. argenteum*** Meissn. SILVER TREE. Tree to 10m. Branchlets stout, terete, 8mm diam., densely pubesc. and frequently also pilose. Lvs to 15×2cm, lanceolate, acute and mucronate at apex, sessile, with adpressed silvery hairs. Male infl. spherical, to 4×5cm with oblong, obtuse, villous involucral lvs to 7mm; female infl. spheric, to 5×4cm, involucral lvs very broadly ovate to suborbicular, rigidly coriaceous, minutely velvety-tomentose without, glabrous and slightly shining within. Fruiting cones to 9×6cm, silvery, with bracts in 3 ascending spirals; fruit retained for several years. Summer. S Africa (Cape Province, Cape Peninsula).

***L. daphnoides*** Meissn. in DC. Branches terete, densely softly pubesc. Lvs 4.5–5.5×1–1.5cm, lanceolate, obtusely mucronate at apex, coriaceous, densely softly tomentose above and beneath, or subglabrous, lateral veins distinct, 2–3 each side. Male infl. 4cm diam., depressed-globose, involucral lvs 12×2mm, in about 2 series, imbricate, oblanceolate-spathulate, tawny villous and ciliate in lower part without, otherwise glabrous; female infl. 2.5–3cm diam., subglobose, involucral lvs to 1.5cm, ovate, acute, coloured, densely pilose beneath. S Africa (Cape Province).

***L. discolor*** Buek. Branches grooved, purple, glabrous. Lvs 2.5–4×1–1.5cm, oblanceolate, subobtuse, rigidly coriaceous, margins somewhat cartilaginous and minutely tomentose particularly when young, lvs surrounding female head to 5cm, very broad and overlapping. Female infl. to 3cm diam., subglobose to somewhat ellipsoid-globose; involucral bracts about 10-seriate, oblong, rounded at apex, spreading in lower part, ascending in upper, 8–10×4mm, hirsute-tomentose on upper part without, otherwise glabrous. Seeds 6mm, flattened, slightly 3-sided, winged, black, glabrous. S Africa (Cape Province).

***L. gandogeri*** Schinz ex Gand. Robust shrub to 160cm. Lvs 8cm+, elliptic, softly hairy when young, smooth and shiny when mature, young lvs turning red in late summer or autumn. Involucre formed from huge top lvs, bright yellow, flushed orange and red, retaining colour after all male infl. have dropped. Fruiting cones 4–6×3–4.5cm, globose; bract very broad, subglabrous; fr. 9–12mm, winged, sometimes retained in cones for years. S Africa.

***L. laureolum*** (Lam.) Fourc. Shrub to 2m, male plants forming conspicuous, bushy plants, female plants smaller and sparser. Lvs oblong, obtuse, recurved at apex, to 7.5×1.5cm (male plants), or to 9.5cm (female plants), green, tinged red at tip, glabrescent. Male infl. spherical, to 23×20mm, surrounded by yellow involucral lvs, the innermost of which are broader than are the stem lvs; female infl. elongate, to 27×14mm, concealed by lime-green involucral lvs. Fruiting cone to 4.5×3.5cm, distinctly 8-sided, fr. retained for several years. Summer. S Africa (Cape Province).

***L.* 'Safari Sunset'.** (*L. salignum* × *L. laureolum.*) Horticultural hybrid, developed in New Zealand; a female plant. Vigorous shrub to 2.5m, reaching 120cm within 18 months, bushy, densely branched. Lvs 9×1.5cm, deep green, flushed with wine red particularly towards branch apices. Involucre 10–20cm diam. on flowering stems to 1m; bracts light red becoming deep wine red at peak, paling from centre to golden yellow toward end of season. Autumn–winter. Garden origin.

***L. salignum*** Bergius. Shrub to about 1m, with lignotuber. Lvs linear-lanceolate, acute, twisted below, 2–5×0.5cm (male plants), or to 6cm (female plants), glabrous. Male infl. spherical, to 1.5cm diam., surrounded by yellow involucral lvs which are longer than stem lvs; female infl. to 15×12mm, ovoid, surrounded by or often concealed by ivory involucral lvs, often broader than stem lvs, in which case concealing infl. Fruiting cone spherical, to 2cm diam. Summer. S Africa (Cape Province).

***L. tinctum*** Williams. Shrub to 130cm at most, low and bushy; branches stout, bent towards base. Lvs oblong, rounded at apex, increasing in size and becoming more crowded upwards, sessile. Involucre large, yellow during flowering season. Fruiting cones with spicy aroma, releasing seeds after 4 months; bracts recurved, shiny, glabrous; seeds biconvex nutlets. S Africa (Cape Province).

***L. ascendens*** R. Br. See *L. salignum*.

**Leucaena** Benth. (From Gk *leukos*, white, referring to flower colour.) Leguminosae (Mimosoideae). Some 40 species of evergreen shrubs or trees. Leaves bipinnate; leaflets few to many; stipules inconspicuous, deciduous. Inflorescence mimosoid in solitary leaf axils or fascicled; calyx small, tubular to campanulate, 5-lobed, short-toothed; stamens 10, free, eglandular; ovary stipitate. Fruit short-stipitate, dehiscent, linear, flattened, not septate. Subtropical tropical America, Polynesia. Z9.

CULTIVATION *Leucaena* spp. grow in a range of soils including limestone, wet and dry soils, and soils of volcanic origin. *L. leucocephala* is naturalized in Hong Kong, forming dense thickets on surrounding hillsides, and is a vigorous and fast-growing tree with feathery *Acacia*-like foliage, producing close heads of fluffy, off-white, ball-shaped flowers throughout the year. The young stems are an attractive deep copper colour with noticeably paler lenticels. It responds well to coppicing, quickly producing dense regrowth, and is sometimes used in reafforestation, land reclamation, in controlling soil erosion and as a shade plant for coffee crops. In tropical, subtropical and frost-free warm temperate zones, grow as border specimens or shade trees. In cool temperate regions grow under glass as for *Acacia*. Propagate from seed pre-soaked for 24 hours in warm water, or from semi-ripe cuttings.

***L. leucocephala*** (Lam.) De Wit. LEAD TREE; WHITE POPINAC. Unarmed shrub or tree. Pinnae 8–16, paired; leaflets to 1.4cm, 26–42, oblong, asymmetric, glabrous. Fl. heads 2cm diam., white tinged yellow. Fr. to 20×2cm, cuneate-stipitate, oblong, flattened, coriaceous, green, later red, hardening. S Florida, S Texas, S California.

***L. pulverulenta*** (Schldl.) Benth. Tree to 8m, frequently more bush-like in habit; young shoots white-pubesc. Pinnae 8–30; leaflets to 0.5cm, 40 or more. Infl. heads to 2cm diam. Fr. to 20×1.7cm, flat. Mexico.

***L. retusa*** Benth. Glabrous shrub or tree, to 7.5m. Shoots velutinous, yellow. Pinnae 4–8; leaflets 8–16, obovate to elliptic-lanceolate. Fl. heads to 2.5cm diam., golden yellow. Fr. to 25×1.5cm, linear, base cuneate. US (Texas), N Mexico.

***L. glauca*** auct. See *L. leucocephala*.
***L. latisiliqua*** (L.) Gillis. See *L. leucocephala*.
For further synonymy see *Caudoleucaena*.

**Leucanthemella** Tzvelev. (Diminutive of Gk *leukos*, white, and *anthemon*, flower.) Compositae. 2 species of perennial herbs. Stems pilose, usually branched. Leaves alternate, simple, lanceolate to broadly elliptic, glandular punctate. Capitula radiate, solitary or few in a loose corymb; receptacle strongly convex, naked; phyllaries in 2–3 more or less imbricate series; ray florets sterile; disc florets hermaphrodite, tubular or tubular-campanulate, yellow. Fruit a small, ribbed cypsela; pappus minute, or absent. SE Europe, E Asia. Z7.

CULTIVATION As for *Tanacetum*.

***L. serotina*** (L.) Tzvelev. To 1.5m. Stems branched above. Lvs to 12cm, lanceolate to oblong, base 2–4-lobed, sessile middle stem lvs, with forward pointing teeth. Ray florets white or red. Fr. c3mm, thick, white rib bed. SE Europe. 'Herbstern': fls clear white, centres tinted yellow.

For synonymy see *Chrysanthemum* and *Pyrethrum*.

**Leucanthemopsis** (Giroux) Heyw. (From *Leucanthemum*, and Gk *opsis*, appearance.) Compositae. 6 species of dwarf, tufted perennials. Leaves pinnately lobed or dissected, glabrous or hairy. Capitula radiate, solitary; receptacle convex; ray florets yellow or white; disc florets tubular-campanulate, usually yellow. Fruit a cypsela with 3–10 inconspicuous ribs entire or crenate; pappus a short corona. European mts and N Africa.

CULTIVATION As for the alpine species of *Leucanthemum*.

***L. alpina*** (L.) Heyw. Tufted or matting; stems to 15cm, ascending. Lvs to 4cm, usually basal, ovate to spathulate, crenate to pinnatifid or palmatifid, grey-hairy or glabrous. Capitula to 4cm diam.; ray florets 8–12, white, sometimes becoming pink; disc florets orange-yellow. European mts. ssp. ***tomentosa*** (Lois.) Heyw. Extreme dwarf. Lvs ovate, palmatifid, with 5–7, closely proximate lobes. Z6.

***L. pallida*** (Mill.) Heyw. Often white-pubesc. Stems to 20cm, simple, ascending, with few lvs. Lower lvs spathulate, dissected. Capitula to 5cm diam.; outer phyllaries lanceolate, acute, dark margin; ray florets yellow, or white with a yellow or purple base. Fr. 5–7-ribbed; pappus a short corona. Mts of C & E Spain. ssp. ***spathulifolia*** (Gay) Heyw. Lvs cuneate- to orbicular-spathulate, incised-toothed; phyllaries long-pubesc., ray florets yellow. SE Spain. Z8.

***L. radicans*** (Cav.) Heyw. Densely tufted, with stolons. Stems ascending. Lvs basal and toward base of stem, pinnate, lobes oblong, 5–9. Capitula to 2cm diam.; outer phyllaries ovate, ciliate, margin broad, red-brown; ray florets yellow, becoming orange-red. Fr. 3–6-ribbed. S Spain. Z8.

***L. hosmariense*** hort. See *Pyrethropsis hosmariensis*.
For further synonymy see *Chrysanthemum* and *Pyrethrum*.

**Leucanthemum** Mill. (From Gk *leukos*, white, and *anthemon*, flower.) Compositae. About 25 species of annual or perennial herbs. Leaves alternate, entire to pinnate. Capitula usually radiate, terminal, solitary or occasionally in small clusters; receptacle usually convex, naked; phyllaries in 2–3-series; ray florets white or tinged pink, female, rarely absent; disc florets tubular-campanulate, usually yellow. Fruit an obconic-cylindric cypsela, usually prominently 10-ribbed; pappus a corona or auricle, sometimes vestigial or absent. Europe, N Asia.

CULTIVATION *Leucanthemum* includes low-growing alpine species of scree and rocky slopes such as *L. atratum* and *L. burnatii*, suited to the rock garden, raised bed or dry stone walls, and taller species such as *L. lacustre, L. maximum* and *L. vulgare* for naturalizing in rough grass and meadow; most occur naturally on calcareous soils, *L. vulgare* is found on both slightly acid and alkaline soils. The range of border perennials grouped under *L.* ×*superbum* is greatly valued for the profusion of blooms carried over long periods in summer, providing generous quantities of flower for cutting.

Grow in full sun, with gritty well drained soils for alpine species. *L.* ×*superbum* performs best in moderately fertile, well-drained and moisture-retentive soils; division of clumps every second or third year will maintain flower quality although a number of the named cultivars are easily raised and flower abundantly in their first year from seed. *L. vulgare* and other species for naturalizing are best raised in cellular trays or small pots to be introduced as plugs. Propagate by seed or division.

***L. atratum*** (Jacq.) DC. Perenn. Stems 10–50cm, simple or branched, sometimes hairy. Basal lvs spathulate, margins crenate or lobed, apex often 3–5-toothed, petioles long, stem lvs oblong to linear, deeply toothed to pinnatifid. Capitula 2–5cm diam., solitary; phyllaries lanceolate to oblong, outermost with scarious apical appendages; ray florets white. Pappus usually present on fr. Summer. SE European mts. ssp. ***ceratophylloides*** (All.) Horvatić. Stems usually 20–30cm. Basal lvs spathulate-cuneate; mid-stem lvs pinnatifid to bipinnatifid. Alps, Apennines. ssp. ***coronopifolium*** (Vill.) Horvatić. Stems usually 20–30cm. Basal lvs spathulate-cuneate, incised-dentate. Alps. Z6.

***L. burnatii*** Briq. & Cavillier. Perenn. Stems erect or ascending. Basal lvs linear-oblong, cuneiform, entire, apex sometimes 2–3-toothed; stem lvs linear to filiform, entire to remotely toothed, amplexicaul base persistent, white and scarious. Capitula 2–4cm diam., radiate, solitary; phyllaries oblong-ovate, apex obtuse, margins dark brown or black, scarious, fimbriate. Pappus of outer fr. a fimbriate auricle. SE France. Z7.

***L. graminifolium*** (L.) Lam. Perenn. Stems 15–30cm, simple, often woody toward base, rufescent and pubesc. below. Basal lvs oblong-lanceolate or obovate-spathulate, apex with 3–5 teeth, on long, red-hairy petioles, stem lvs oblong to linear, lower lvs bristly toothed at base, other lvs sparsely toothed to entire. Capitula 3–3.5cm diam., solitary; phyllaries oblong to lanceolate, margins broad, dark brown. Pappus of outer fr. a corona. France. Z7.

***L. lacustre*** (Brot.) Samp. Similar to *L. vulgare* but basal lvs toothed; capitula 4.5–6cm diam.; pappus of outer fr. auriculate. Summer. W Portugal. Z8.

***L. maximum*** (Ramond) DC. Similar to *L. vulgare* but basal lvs entire to toothed and capitula to 9cm diam. Pyrenees. Z6.

***L. pallens*** (Gay) DC. Similar to *L. vulgare* but basal lvs crenate-dentate; petioles with basal wings; capitula 1.5–5cm diam. S Europe mts (Spain to Albania). Z7.

***L. paludosum*** (Poir.) Bonnet & Barratte. Glabrous annual. Stems to 15cm, branched. Lvs toothed to pinnatifid, basal lvs obovate-spathulate, lower lvs oblong-cuneate, petiole basally auriculate, upper lvs oblong to lanceolate. Capitula 2–3cm diam., radiate; ray florets pale yellow or white tinged yellow near base; disc florets more or less zygomorphic. Fr. narrowly 7–10-ribbed; pappus of outer fr. a corona. S Spain, S Portugal, Balearic Is.

***L. ×superbum*** (J. Ingram) Bergmans ex Kent. *(L. maximum × L. lacustre.)* SHASTA DAISY. Perenn. Stems erect, glabrous to 1m+. Lvs dentate, lower lvs to 30cm, oblanceolate, petiolate, upper lvs lanceolate, sessile. Capitula to 10cm diam., solitary; ray florets pure white; disc florets yellow. Garden origin. Over 50 cvs, mostly white, some clones, others (such as the Princess Group) seed raised; the original single fls now mostly superseded by fringed, semi-double and double cvs; notable single-fld cvs include the old 'Phyllis Smith' and the feathery 'Bishopstone'; notable semi-doubles include 'Aglaia' and the 90cm 'Esther Read'; anenome-centred doubles include 'Wirral Supreme' and 'T.E. Killin'; fully double fls include 'Cobham Gold' with yellow central florets and the tall (to 100cm) 'Fiona Coghill' and 'Starburst'; dwarf cvs include 'Powis Castle' and the 45cm 'Little Silver Princess'. Z5.

***L. vulgare*** Lam. OX-EYE DAISY; MOON DAISY; MARGUERITE. Perenn. herb. Stems to 1m, simple or branched. Basal lvs 1.5–10cm, obovate-spathulate to oblong, usually crenate, on long petioles; stem lvs oblong to lanceolate, entire to pinnatifid, green or glaucous, uppermost sessile. Capitula 2.5–9cm diam., usually radiate, solitary or clustered; phyllaries lanceolate to ovate-oblong, margins usually dark and scarious; ray florets white, occasionally short or absent. Pappus absent or of outer fr. a corona or auricle only. Summer. Temperate Eurasia. 'Hofenkrone': erect to 60cm; fls fully double, white. 'Hullavington': stems and lvs blotched yellow. 'Maikönigin' ('May Queen'): to 70cm; fls white; early. 'Maistern': to 60cm; fls profuse, white. 'Rheinblick': to 60cm; fls single, profuse. Z3.

***L. waldsteinii*** (Schultz-Bip.) Pouzar. Perenn. Stems 20–70cm, simple or sparingly branched, densely leafy. Basal and lower stem lvs broadly ovate to suborbicular, cordate, evenly crenate-toothed upper petiolate lvs cuneiform to ovate-oblong. Capitula 4–6cm diam., radiate, solitary or clustered in a loose corymb; phyllaries with dark margins. Carpathians. Z6.

***L. atlanticum*** (Ball) Maire. See *Pyrethropsis atlantica*.
***L. catananche*** (Ball) Maire. See *Pyrethropsis catananche*.
***L. depressum*** (Ball) Maire. See *Pyrethropsis depressa*.
***L. gayanum*** (Coss. & Dur.) Maire. See *Pyrethropsis gayana*.
***L. hosmariense*** (Ball) Font Quer. See *Pyrethropsis hosmariensis*.
***L. maresii*** (Coss.) Maire. See *Pyrethropsis maresii*.
***L. mawii*** hort. See *Pyrethropsis gayana*.
***L. maximum*** (hort.) non (Ramond) DC. See *L. ×superbum*.
***L. nipponicum*** Franch. ex Maxim. See *Nipponanthemum nipponicum*.
For further synonymy see *Chrysanthemum*.

**Leuchtenbergia** Hook. (The name under which Hooker received the plant, later said to honour Prince Eugéne de Bauharnais, Duke of Leuchtenberg (1781–1824).) Cactaceae. 1 species, a terrestrial cactus allied to *Ferocactus*; low-growing, rarely to 70cm high, simple or occasionally clustering; rootstock fleshy; stem globose to short-cylindric, tuberculate; tubercles 10–12cm, glaucous, triangular; areoles apical; spines to 15cm, papery, flattened and flexuous. Flowers borne at the ventral edge of areoles of young tubercles, otherwise like those of *Ferocactus*, to 8×5–6cm, yellow. Fruit as in *Ferocactus* (sect. *Ferocactus*), *c*3cm, ovoid-oblong, excluding perianth, grey-green; seed broadly oval, 2.4×2.0mm, black-brown, matt, periphery keeled; relief low-domed; hilum small, basal, deeply impressed. N Mexico. Z9.

CULTIVATION Grow in a cool frost-free greenhouse (min. 2–7°C/36–46°F), use 'standard' cactus compost: moderate to high inorganic content (more than 50% grit), pH 6–7.5; full sun; low air-humidity; keep dry from mid-autumn until early spring, except for light misting on warm days in late winter.

***L. principis*** Hook. As for the genus. Summer–autumn.

**Leucocarpus** D. Don (From Gk *leukos*, white, and *karpos*, fruit.) Scrophulariaceae. 1 species, a perennial herb, to 80cm. Stems 4-angled, winged. Leaves to 25cm, opposite, lanceolate, basally cordate and clasping, serrate. Flowers borne in axillary, branching, long-stalked cymes; calyx 5-lobed; corolla yellow, to 2cm, 2-lipped, upper lip 2-lobed, lower lip 3-lobed, midlobe with 2 pubescent calli in throat; stamens 4. Fruit a white berry. Summer. Mexico. Z9.

CULTIVATION *Leucocarpus*, grown primarily for its decorative white fruits, is suitable for cultivation in the open in warm temperate areas or under glass in colder gardens, as for *Mimulus*.

***L. perfoliatus*** (Kunth) Benth. As for the genus.

**Leucocoryne** Lindl. (From Gk *leukos*, white, and *koryne*, club, referring to the sterile anthers.) Liliaceae (Alliaceae). 12 species of herbaceous perennials, to 50×10cm, many with characteristic smell of garlic. Bulbs to 2cm wide, with dark brown tunics. Leaves 2–5, to 35cm×5mm, basal, linear, often channelled, senescent before flowering. Flowers 2–12, funnel-shaped, in umbels with 2 spathes; perianth segments 6, similar, white, blue or violet, lower parts fused into a basal tube, upper parts free, spreading; stamens 6, 3 joined to perianth within basal tube, staminodes 3, club-shaped, joined to perianth at mouth of basal tube. Chile. Z9.

CULTIVATION Grown for their loose heads of scented, soft blue flowers carried over long periods in spring and early summer, *Leucocoryne* spp. start into growth early in the year; the grass-like foliage dies down at or slightly before flowering, and bulbs enter dormancy during summer and autumn. They are suitable for outdoor cultivation only in areas that are essentially frost-free. They require a position in full sun and in well-drained soil. Otherwise, grow in a frost-free glasshouse; a minimum winter temperature of 5–7°C/40–45°F is suitable. Grow in direct sun, in well-crocked pots with a medium-fertility loam-based mix with additional sharp sand. Water sparingly in spring when growth resumes, and reduce after flowering for a dry rest period. Top dress annually and repot every second or third year if necessary. Propagate from seed sown when ripe, or under glass in spring. Also by offsets, although these are not produced in quantity.

***L. alliacea*** Lindl. 15–30cm. Lvs several, grass-like, 15–20cm×2mm. Fls to 18mm, basal tube to 8mm; tepals narrow, acute, white, tinged green. Spring.

***L. ixioides*** (Hook.) Lindl. GLORY OF THE SUN. To 45cm. Lvs to 45cm, slender, grass-like. Fls 6–9 in a loose fragrant umbel; pedicels 2–6.5cm; tepals 12–15mm, free portions white or, more usually, deeply edged lilac to violet-blue, basal tube white; stamens and staminodes yellow-white, slender. Spring.

***L. odorata*** Lindl. Distinguished from *L. ixioides* only by pedicels to 2cm, tepals smaller, pale blue.

***L. purpurea*** Gay. To 50cm. Lvs to 30cm, grass-like. Fls 2–6 per umbel; bracts channelled, 5–6cm; pedicels 2.5–4cm; tepals obovate, 2.5–3×1cm, white tinted purple, ageing mauve-indigo; staminodes yellow tipped purple. Spring.

***L. ixioides*** var. ***purpurea*** (Gay) Bak. See *L. purpurea*.
For further synonymy see *Brodiaea*.

**Leucocrinum** Nutt. ex A. Gray. (From Gk *leukos*, white, and *krinon*, a type of lily.) SAND LILY; STAR LILY; MOUNTAIN LILY. Liliaceae (Funkiaceae). 1 species, a perennial herb. Rhizomes subterranean; roots fleshy. Leaves 10–20×0.2–0.6cm, narrowly linear, radical, forming tufts, the bases sheathed by membranous bracts. Flowers white, fragrant, in clusters on 0.5–3cm subterranean stems barely breaking soil surface; perianth salverform, tube 2.5–12cm, slender, 6-lobed, lobes 1.4–2cm, narrowly oblong; stamens 6, near mouth of perianth tube, anthers yellow; style 1, slender; stigma shallowly 3-lobed. Fruit a capsule; seeds black, angled. Spring–early summer. W US (Oregon to New Mexico).

CULTIVATION Grown for the fragrant white flowers carried at ground level in spring and early summer, *Leucocrinum* is cold tolerant to between −20°C/−4°F. Grow in sun in a well-drained but moisture-retentive alkaline soil. Propagate by seed.

*L. montanum* Nutt. ex A. Gray. As for the genus.

**Leucogenes** Beauv. (From Gk *leukos*, white, and *genea*, race.) Compositae. 2–3 species of tomentose perennial herbs, woody at base. Leaves dense, imbricate. Capitula discoid in a dense cluster, subtended by a collar of leaves; involucre campanulate; phyllaries imbricate, in many series; receptacle slightly convex, naked florets tubular, outer female, inner hermaphrodite. Fruit a sericeous cypsela; pappus of hairs. Summer. New Zealand. Z8.

CULTIVATION *L. leontopodium* occurs naturally in herbfields and fell fields and in other rocky habitats, often in intimate natural association with *Euphrasia revoluta* and *Celmisia spectabilis* on a dense carpet of moss and lichen; more vigorous and competitive in habitat than *L. grandiceps*, which is found on exposed rock ledges, scree and moraine, it requires a longer growing season and shows less cold tolerance in cultivation in northern temperate gardens. Both species are extremely desirable for the alpine house and rock garden, with their densely silver-white woolly foliage, each flower-head surrounded by a ray of white felted bracts.

Grow *L. grandiceps* in crevices on the rock garden in a lean, gritty and moisture-retentive medium, in good bright light but with shade from hot sun. In the alpine house, grow in well-crocked pots in a mix of equal parts loam, leafmould and coarse sand. Keep in cool and well-ventilated conditions avoiding hot sun, water plentifully and carefully when in growth and keep only just moist in winter. Repot as growth recommences in spring. Propagate by softwood cuttings in moist sand in early summer, or from fresh seed sown ripe.

***L. grandiceps*** (Hook. f.) Beauv. SOUTH ISLAND EDELWEISS. Lvs to 10×4cm, obovate-cuneate, apex obtuse, tomentose. Capitula 5–15, subtended by a collar of some 15 tomentose lvs; phyllaries linear, acute. South Is.

***L. leontopodium*** (Hook. f.) Beauv. NORTH ISLAND EDELWEISS. Lvs to 2×0.5cm, linear to lanceolate-oblong, apex, acute to subacute, silver-white- to yellow-tomentose. Capitula to 2.5cm diam., subtended by a conspicuous collar of some 20 white lvs; phyllaries linear-lanceolate, ciliate toward apex. North & South Is.

For synonymy see *Helichrysum* and *Raoulia*.

**Leucohyle** Klotzsch. (From Gk *leukos*, white, and *hyle*, wool, referring to the white pilose covering on the floral axis.) Orchidaceae. Some 4 species of epiphytic orchids allied to *Trichopilia*. Rhizome short, creeping. Pseudobulbs small or minute, erect, apically unifoliate. Leaves fleshy to subcoriaceous, suberect or arching, usually linear or narrow-lanceolate, basally sheathed. Racemes basal, from axils of sheaths, several-flowered; flowers mostly white, spotted crimson or purple on lip; sepals and petals similar, free, spreading, sometimes twisted; lip parallel to column, porrect, simple to trilobed, concave, base cuneate, enveloping column, callus 2-ridged; column erect, hooded over anther at apex, pollinia 2, pyriform, stipe oblong-linear. Tropical America from Panama to Peru. Z10.

CULTIVATION As for *Trichopilia*.

***L. subulata*** (Sw.) Schltr. Pseudobulbs to 3×0.5cm, narrowly cylindrical or subcylindrical, clustered. Lvs to 25×1cm. Infl. to 15cm, pendent; fls to 4cm diam., slightly fragrant; sep. and pet. translucent white to pale yellow, lanceolate to linear-lanceolate, acute, slightly twisted; lip to 15×15mm, white spotted rose-purple, obscurely trilobed, suborbicular to obovate, emarginate to apiculate, deeply erose-lacerate; column to 9mm, erect, white, terete, anth. white. Panama, Trinidad, Peru, Venezuela, Colombia.

For synonymy see *Trichopilia*.

**Leucojum** L. (From Greek *leukos*, white, and *ion*, violet, a reference to the delicate fragrance, name first applied by Theophrastus to *Matthiola* and a white-flowered bulbous plant; other miscellaneous applications until Fuchs's *De Historia Stirpium*, when attached to *L. vernum*, but later again variously applied.) SNOWFLAKE. Amaryllidaceae. About 10 slender to stout, bulbous perennials, resembling and related to *Galanthus*. Morphology diverse and 4 subgenera have been described. Bulbs globose to ovoid, with brown, membranous, outer scales. Leaves at first enclosed by a membranous sheath, filiform to linear or broadly ligulate, emerging with or before flowers. Scape slender and solid or stout and hollow; terminal spathe with 1–2 bracteoles, united by membranes; flowers emerging from spathe on pendulous pedicels, 1–5+ per scape; perianth segments free, equal, oblanceolate or oblanceolate-oblong, acute or apiculate, white, sometimes spotted green or yellow at apex, or tinged pink; anthers yellow, conic, opening by apical pores; filaments white, short; style filiform to clavate, exceeding anthers; ovary inferior, globose, 3-locular, green. Seeds black or brown, smooth or carunculate or with air pockets. W Europe to Middle East, N Africa.

CULTIVATION Grown for their pendent white flowers which bear a superficial resemblance to those of *Galanthus* but generally have a firmer, more waxen texture. The common name snowdrop, which usually refers to *Galanthus* spp., is applied to *Leucojum* in the southern US. *Leucojum* spp. occur in a variety of habitats; *L. vernum* grows in moist woodland and on shaded hillsides, blooming there at snow-melt; *L. aestivum* in wet fields and woods and in swamps, especially near rivers. The remaining species are more typically found in drier habitats such as on the Mediterranean dunes under pines (*L. trichophyllum*) or on dry rocky grassland (*L. nicaeense*, *L. roseum*). *L. autumnale* grows in the wild in open woodland, or scrub and in dry rocky grassland.

*L. vernum* and *L. aestivum* are suited to naturalizing in damp rough grass, or for growing in damp pockets in the rock garden; the latter thrives in moist, rich, heavy soils, especially by pond or streamside, and is tolerant of waterlogged conditions. Grow in partial shade, or in sun where soils remain permanently moist. *L. autumnale*, for the sunny border front, path edging and for warm sunny locations on the rock garden, is one of the least demanding of the smaller species for growing in the open, given a well-drained sandy soil. *L. nicaeense, L. trichophyllum* and *L. roseum*, although sometimes grown in the open in similar warm and perfectly drained situations, are eminently suited to cultivation in the alpine house or bulb frame, where their delicate beauty can be appreciated at close quarters, and where their requirement for hot dry dormancy in summer and protection from winter wet is more easily accommodated. Propagate by division in spring or autumn, after flowering, or by seed sown when ripe.

***L. aestivum*** L. SUMMER SNOWFLAKE; LODDON LILY. Bulb ovoid, to 4cm diam. Lvs ligulate, obtuse at apex, to 50×2cm, glossy deep green. Scape stout, hollow, somewhat flattened with 2 membranous wings, to 60cm; spathe solitary, lanceolate, green-membranous, to 5cm; fls 2–7, faintly chocolate-scented; pedicels to 6cm; seg. broad-oblong, to 2cm, white, marked green just below apiculate apex; style clavate; ovary oblong-oval, green, to 8mm diam. Seeds black, testa loose, forming air pockets. Spring. Europe including GB to Iran. 'Gravetye' ('Gravetye Giant'): robust, vigorous, to 75cm; fls 5–7; seg. to 2.5cm (GB, early 20th century). var. ***pulchellum*** (Salisb.) Fiori. Smaller in all parts than type of species. Scape lacking transparent wings; fls 2–4; seg. to 14mm. Flowering earlier than type. Balearic Is., Sardinia. Z4.

***L. autumnale*** L. Bulb globose to ovoid, about 1cm diam., forming many offsets. Lvs filiform, to 16cm at maturity, pale green, appearing after fls. Scape slender, green- to red-brown, usually about 15cm; spathe solitary, linear to lanceolate; fls 1–4, on slender pedicels; seg. oblong, apiculate or toothed, 1cm, crystalline white flushed pink at base; style filiform; ovary globose, green, 3mm in diam. Seeds soon ripening, black. Summer–autumn. W Europe (Portugal, Spain, Sardinia, Sicily, Crete), N Africa. 'Cobb's Variety': to 20cm; fls white flushed pink. var. ***oporanthum*** (Jordan & Fourr.) Maire. Lvs absent at flowering. Scape to 25cm; all seg. 3-toothed. Morocco. Plants in commerce under this name are var. *pulchellum*. var. ***pulchellum*** (Jordan & Fourr.) Dur. & Schinz. Lvs present at flowering. Outer seg. 3-toothed; inner seg. entire, acute. Morocco, Gibraltar. Z5.

***L. longifolium*** (M. Roem.) Gren. & Godron. Bulb ovoid, to 1cm diam. Lvs 2–3, slender, to 25cm, green. Scape slender, to 20cm; spathes 2, linear, 2.5cm; fls 1–3; seg. oblanceolate, 9mm, white; style slender; ovary globose, green, 3mm diam. Spring. Corsica. Z7.

***L. nicaeense*** Ardoino. Bulb globose, to 2cm diam. Lvs 2–4, narrow-linear, to 30cm, often curled, deep green, slightly glaucous, appearing in autumn. Scape to 15cm, usually less; spathes 2, linear, to 2cm; fls 1–3, on short pedicels; seg. oblanceolate, 3 outer seg. apiculate, to 12mm, white, spreading; style slender, just exceeding stamens; ovary subglobose, 3mm diam., green, with 6-lobed disc. Seeds black, carunculate. Spring. S France, Monaco. Z7.

***L. roseum*** Martin. Bulb globose, to 1.5cm diam. Lvs narrow-linear, to 10cm, deep glossy green, appearing with or after fls. Scape to 15cm; spathes 2, linear;

fls usually solitary; seg. oblanceolate, to 9mm, pale pink, deepest along median line; style filiform; ovary globose, deep green, 3mm in diam. Seeds deep brown. Summer–autumn. Corsica, Sardinia. Z7.

***L. trichophyllum*** Schousb. Bulb ovoid, to 1.5cm diam. Lvs filiform, to 20cm, green, in the wild often withered before flowering. Scape slender, to 25cm; spathes 2, lanceolate; fls 2–4 on slender pedicels to 4cm; seg. oblanceolate-oblong, 3 outer seg. apiculate, to 2.5cm, white or flushed pink to purple, especially at base; style filiform, exceeding anth.; ovary turbinate, green, to 5mm diam. Winter–spring. S Portugal, SW Spain, Morocco. Z7.

***L. valentinum*** Pau. Bulb globose, about 2cm diam. Lvs narrow-linear, to 25cm, grey-green, appearing after fls. Scape to 15cm; spathes 2, linear; fls 1–3; seg. broad obovate, apiculate, to 1.5cm, milk white; style filiform; ovary turbinate, with 6-lobed disc. Autumn. C Spain, Greece. Z7.

***L. vernum*** L. SPRING SNOWFLAKE. Bulb ovoid, to 3cm+ diam. Lvs stout, ligulate, to 20×2cm, deep green, extending after flowering. Scape stout, hollow, to 20cm, deep green; spathe membranous; fls solitary, occasionally 2; seg. broad-oblong, acute, 2×1cm, white, marked green or yellow just below apex; style clavate; ovary subglobose, green, 6mm diam. Winter. France to EC Europe, naturalized England. var. ***vagneri*** Stapf. Robust. Scape to 25cm; fls paired. Hungary. ssp. ***carpathicum*** (Loud.) E. Murray. Fls solitary; seg. marked yellow at tips. Poland, Romania. Yellow markings usually constant in ssp. *carpathicum*, but sometimes occur in other vars, especially in newly opened fls. Z5.

***L. hernandezii*** Cambess. See *L. aestivum* var. *pulchellum*.
***L. hiemale*** DC. See *L. nicaeense*.

**Leucophyllum** Humb. & Bonpl. (From Gk *leukos*, white, and *phyllon*, leaf.) Scrophulariaceae. Some 12 species of low, spreading shrubs. Leaves simple, entire, obovate to round, hoary tomentose to glabrous. Flowers axillary, solitary; calyx and corolla 5-lobed; corolla lavender to violet, campanulate to funnel-shaped, 2-lipped; stamens 4. Fruit a capsule. Summer. SW US. Z9.

CULTIVATION These slow-growing evergreens are found on sandy, sometimes impoverished soils in warm dry climates. They make excellent and undemanding specimen foliage shrubs for lawns or may be planted in association with other plants where their soft, grey foliage and stems provide contrast for darker greens. A warm, sheltered, sunny spot and winter temperatures which rarely fall below freezing are essential. In the southern US and the Middle East, woolly-grey foliaged *L. frutescens* is used as hedging plant, valued for its ability to withstand hard pruning and shearing; it is particularly valuable in maritime areas for its tolerance to salt spray. In colder regions, grow under glass for foliage effect. Plant out in spring into any light soil. Under glass grow in a low- to medium-fertility, light, sandy, loam-based mix; water moderately throughout the year. Propagate from seed in spring or by greenwood cuttings in a cold frame in late summer.

***L. frutescens*** (Berl.) I.M. Johnst. BAROMETER BUSH; ASH PLANT. Compact, lax-stemmed, white-tomentose shrub, to 2.50m. Lvs to 2.5cm, woolly with stellate-pubescence, subsessile, elliptic to obovate. Cal. lobes oblong-lanceolate; cor. pink to mauve, campanulate, interior pubesc., limb to 25mm diam. Fr. 2-valved. Spring–summer. Texas, Mexico. 'Compactum': habit compact shrub, loosely branched; lvs silver-grey; fls orchid-pink, bell-like. 'Green Cloud': habit small shrub, compactly branched; lvs dark green; fls purple-violet.

***L. minus*** A. Gray. Stellate-pubesc. shrub, to 1m. Lvs to 1.3cm, spathulate-obovate, tapering basally. Cal. lobes linear; cor. purple, funnel-shaped, slender, interior pubesc. Spring–summer. SW US.

***L. texanum*** Benth. See *L. frutescens*.

**Leucopogon** R. Br. (From Gk *leukos*, white and *pogon*, beard, alluding to the white-bearded corolla lobes.) Epacridaceae. Some 150 species of robust, evergreen, open-branched shrubs or small trees, of erect or spreading habit. Leaves aristate or with a callused tip, sessile to shortly petiolate, erect to reflexed, glabrous, margins entire, sometimes ciliolate. Flowers subtended by a pair of bracteoles and bracts, solitary or clustered in spikes, usually white; calyx 5-lobed; corolla tubular at base, spreading to reflexed above, lobes valvate in bud, becoming bearded with white woolly hairs inside; staminal filaments slender, terete, inserted on throat, anthers partly concealed in corolla tube; ovary 2–5 celled. Fruit a drupe. Australia, New Zealand, Malaysia, New Caledonia, Pacific Is. Z9.

CULTIVATION *L. virgatus* and *L. ericoides* grow on sandy soils on old dune systems, on heath and open forest, *L. australis* and *L. verticillatus* occur on moister soils, often in forest. *Leucopogon* spp. associate well with other heathland natives in naturalistic plantings or in more intimate plantings on the rock garden, where their small, bearded flowers can be appreciated at close quarters; those of *L. australis* are sweetly scented. Although several spp. tolerate frost in their native regions, in cool temperate climates they are more safely regarded as frost tender and grown in the cool glasshouse. Grow in a shaded position in moist, humus-rich, acid soil and provide a cool root run, mulching if necessary with organic matter, as for *Epacris*. Propagation, as with other members of this family, is not straightforward; seed has a short viability, is difficult to germinate and cuttings may be slow to root. Division of vigorous plants is possible.

***L. amplexicaulis*** R. Br.. Small shrub of lax habit to 1m; branchlets slender, pubesc. Lvs to 2.5×1.5cm, apex acuminate, base broadly cordate, sheathing stem, margins ciliolate. Fls white, held 6–10 in axillary racemes; cor. lobes recurved, pubesc. Summer. Australia. Easily identified by its broadly cordate lvs and downy branchlets.

***L. australis*** R. Br. Tall glabrous shrub with erect branches, to 2.5m. Lvs to 5cm, lanceolate to narrowly elliptic, pale green, apex blunt or mucronate, upper surface convex, veins numerous, conspicuous. Fls white, in dense axillary or terminal spikes 3.25–5cm long; sep. ovate, margins ciliate; cor. to 5mm, lobes equalling tube, densely bearded. Fr. ovoid-globose, white to pale yellow. Autumn. Australia, Tasmania.

***L. collinus*** (Labill.) R. Br. Low-growing shrub to 70cm, glabrous or downy. Lvs 0.5–1cm, linear to obovate, highly variable in width with a short point, often ciliate, crowded. Fls white, usually crowded in terminal spikelets, white; sep. and cor. tube to 5mm, interior of cor. lobes villous. Fr. small, usually 1-seeded. Summer. Australia, Tasmania.

***L. ericoides*** (Sm.) R. Br. Small, heath-like shrub to 90×90cm; branches pubesc. Lvs to 0.5cm, linear in upper reach of plant, broader (oblong to ovate) below, shortly aristate, glabrous, margin recurved to revolute. Fls crowded in numerous very short axillary spikes or clusters, giving the overall impression of a long leafy panicle; cor. tube 2–4mm, cylindric, interior minutely tomentose. Fr. pubesc., obovoid, ridged. Summer. S & W Australia, Tasmania.

***L. interruptus*** R. Br. Small glabrous shrub to 70cm. Lvs to 3cm, ovate to oblong, acuminate or blunt, crowded toward the end of each season's growth. Fls small, white, borne in short interrupted spikes; cor. tube to 0.5cm, lobes bearded at tips. Summer. W Australia.

***L. lanceolatus*** (Sm.) R. Br. Upright, glabrescent or glabrous shrub to 3m. Lvs 2–5cm, elliptic to narrow-lanceolate, erect to spreading scattered, apex acute to pungent, base cuneate, margin entire to serrulate, shortly petiolate, rigid, glaucous. Fls white in terminal and upper axillary spikes 2.5–5cm long; cor. tube to 2mm, campanulate, interior densely pubesc. Fr. elliptic-ovoid, glabrous, red. Spring. S Australia, Tasmania.

***L. verticillatus*** R. Br. Erect glabrous shrub to 2m; branchlets slender, bronze-brown. Lvs 5–10×0.25–5cm, whorled at ends of shoots, narrowly elliptic to lanceolate, margins pale green with close, visible, longitudinal veins. Fls in slender terminal or axillary whorled spikes to 3.25cm long, rose to crimson; cor. to 5mm, lobes bearded at base only. Fr. ellipsoid. Autumn. Australia. Easily identified by the large lvs and brightly coloured fls.

***L. virgatus*** (Labill.) R. Br. Decumbent diffuse shrub or subshrub to 60cm; branchlets wiry, lax, glabrous. Lvs to 1.5cm, linear-lanceolate to ovate, scattered or crowded at shoot tips, apex acuminate, base truncate, margin with minute hooked hairs. Fls in congested or axillary, rather flattened clusters; cor. tube 2–4mm, cylindric or campanulate, white, densely long-pubesc. Fr. globose to obovoid. Summer. S Australia, Tasmania.

***L. colensoi*** Hook. f. See *Cyathodes colensoi*.
***L. ericoides*** Schldl. See *Brachyloma ericoides*.
***L. forsteri*** A. Rich. See *Cyathodes juniperina*.
***L. parviflorus*** Andrews. See *Cyathodes parviflora*.
***L. richei*** (Labill.) R. Br. See *Cyathodes parviflora*.
For further synonymy see *Styphelia*.

**Leucospermum** R. Br. (From Gk *Leukos*, white, and *sperma*, seed.) Proteaceae. 46 species of small trees or shrubs, or erect or sometimes prostrate habit. Leaves alternate, toughened. Inflorescences axillary; perianth tubular in bud, bilaterally symmetric in flower, the claws of the 3 upper segments remaining fused after flowering; anthers all fertile, sessile or nearly so; hypogynous scales 4; style straight or curved, with terminal pollen presenter and stigmatic groove. Fruit a 1-seeded nut. S Africa, Zimbabwe. Z9.

CULTIVATION As for *Protea*.

***L. catherinae*** Compton. CATHERINE'S PINCUSHION; CATHERINE-WHEEL LEUCOSPERMUM. Shrub to 2.5×2.5m, densely bushy, with short thick trunk at base. Lvs 10–12×2–2.5cm, oblong, deeply 3–4-dentate at apex, narrowed to base, petiolate, green tinged grey or yellow, often flushed red at teeth apices and along margins, glabrous. Flowerheads to 15cm diam. on stems to 40cm, pale orange, deepening to red-gold with age; style slender, bent, bright mauve-pink at apex. Late spring–early summer. S Africa.

***L. conocarpodendron*** L. Shrub or small tree, 2–2.5m; branches stout, softly hirsute and minutely tomentose. Lvs crowded around infl., obscuring stem, 5–10×1–3.5cm, obovate to oblanceolate, generally 4–9-dentate at apex, margins and base hirsute, otherwise glabrescent; veins prominent. Infl. generally solitary, terminal, 5–7cm, golden yellow; peduncle short, very stout; involucral bracts ovate, caudate-acuminate, 1cm, fulvous-villous; receptacle conic-cylindric, to 2.5cm; perianth to 4cm in bud, tube 8–10mm, sometimes finely pubesc. above, fused claws forming flexuosus sheath 2.5cm, all claws loosely softly hirsute; style 5cm. S Africa (Cape Province).

***L. cordifolium*** (Knight) Fourc. Shrub to 2m. Lvs 2–8×2–4.5cm, ovate, entire or apically 3–6-dentate, cordate at base, pubesc., glabrescent. Infl. spherical, to 12cm diam., borne at right-angles to the spreading flowering stems; perianth yellow, orange or crimson, tube glabrous, claws slightly hairy; pollen-presenter obliquely top-shaped. Summer. S Africa (Cape Province).

***L. cuneiforme*** (Burm.) Rourke. Shrub to 3m, with lignotuber. Lvs 4.5–11×0.5–3cm, linear to lanceolate, tapered to base, apically 3–11-dentate, glabrous. Infl. ovoid, 9cm diam.; flowering stems erect; perianth yellow, becoming orange with age, tube hairless, claws slightly hairy; pollen presenter conical; style slightly curved, yellow, becoming orange. Summer. S Africa (Cape Province).

***L. lineare*** R. Br. Slender bush, decumbent or erect; branches glabrous. Lvs scattered, on decumbent branches twisted to point vertically, exposing stem, linear, subobtuse, margins flat or recurved, 6–8mm broad, glabrous, veins indistinct. Infl. 4–5×4–5cm, usually solitary, generally exserted from uppermost lvs, orange-yellow; peduncle 1–2cm, covered by spreading bracts to 6mm; involucral bracts to 12×6mm, closely imbricate, elliptic to obovate, acute to acuminate, hirsute-tomentose; receptacle cylindric, 25×3mm; perianth 3cm in bud, tube 7–8mm, rather wide from narrow base, pubesc. in upper part, fused claws forming an upwardly flattened revolute sheath to 2cm, softly hirsute; style 5cm. S Africa (Cape Province).

***L. reflexum*** Buek ex Meissn. in DC. Small erect shrub to 2m; branches minutely grey-tomentose. Lvs 2–4×0.5–1cm, rather crowded towards base of long flowering branches, more distant above, oblong to oblanceolate, obtuse, entire or 3-dentate, minutely grey-tomentose, veins obscure. Infl. 4.5–6×4.5–6cm, usually solitary, far-exserted from uppermost lvs; peduncle 5–10cm, stout, grey-villous; bracts to 1cm, ovate, acuminate, densely villous particularly toward base; receptacle oblong-cylindric, to 25×4mm; perianth crimson, to 5cm in bud, flowers reflexed, tube 8–10mm, curved, gibbous, finely villous above, glabrous at base, fused claws forming a flattened sheath revolute in upper part, softly villous; style to 8cm. S Africa (Cape Province).

***L. tottum*** R. Br. Slender shrub. Branches horizontally spreading, grey-hirsute to glabrous. Lvs 2.5–4×0.5–1cm, rather scattered, more or less spreading, exposing stem, oblong, obtuse to subacute, callous-pointed, occasionally 3-dentate, more or less hairy particularly when young, or glabrous, veins distinct. Infl. 4–5×4–5cm, solitary, exserted from upper lvs; peduncles to 2.5cm, clad with ciliate bracts; involucral bracts to 1.5cm, imbricate, sometimes spreading, broadly ovate acuminate, rufescent; receptacle cylindric, 2.5cm; perianth 4.5–5cm in bud, tube 6–8mm, pubesc. above, fused claws forming a concave or upwardly flattened and revolute sheath, 3cm, all claws hirsute all over; style 5cm. S Africa (Cape Province).

***L. vestitum*** (Lam.) Rourke. Erect bush to 2.5m, often lower. Lvs overlapping, oblong, entire or distinctly notched or dentate at apex, deep green, slightly pubesc. when young, glabrous when mature. Flowerheads large, slightly flattened globose, to 9cm diam. on flowering stems to 40cm; perianth seg. rolled back, purple or dark red, darkening with age; styles dark yellow or light orange. Winter–summer. S Africa.

***L. attenuatum*** R. Br. See *L. cuneiforme*.
***L. conocarpum*** R. Br. See *L. conocarpodendron*.
***L. ellipticum*** (Thunb.) R. Br. See *L. cuneiforme*.
***L. nutans*** R. Br. See *L. cordifolium*.

**Leucostegia** Presl. (From Gk *leukos*, white, and *stege*, covering.) Davalliaceae. 2 species of epiphytic or terrestrial ferns. Rhizomes creeping, meristelic, fleshy, covered with hairs and roots as well as scales; scales dense, lanceolate to ovate, attenuate to narrowly acute. Fronds stipitate, uniform, 3 or 4× finely pinnate, deltoid, firm, glabrous, pinnae deltoid, all segments oblique, veins free, forked, midrib and rachis sulcate above; stipes remote, jointed with phyllopodia, glabrous or initially pubescent or scaly. Sori sunken and protuberant above, submarginal, dorsal, at vein tips; indusia basally and/or laterally attached, circular or cup-shaped; annulus 16-celled; spores reniform to oblong, tuberculate, glassy. Tropical Asia to Polynesia. Z10.

CULTIVATION As for *Davallia*.

***L. immersa*** (Wallich) Presl. Rhiz. long-creeping, to 6mm wide; scales to 4×1mm, russet. Fronds arching, 60×40cm or, occasionally, more, 3–4-pinnate, pinnae to 8×3cm, final seg. rhomboid, acute or obtuse at apex, truncate at base, irregularly dentate at margin, to 15mm, veins prominent, pinnate; stipes to 10cm apart, erect, to 25cm, red. Indochina, Taiwan, to Malaysia, Philippines.

***L. pallida*** (Mett.) Copel. Rhiz. wide-creeping; scales to 4×1mm, minutely dentate, pale brown. Fronds to 60×60cm, 1-pinnate, pinnae remote, to 7×1mm, alternate, final seg. rhomboid to obovate, obtuse at apex, cuneate at base, notched at margin, veins indistinct, few, forked, with terminal hydathodes; stipes to 40cm, subterete, light green to straw-coloured. Malaysia and Indonesia to Polynesia.

***L. falcinella*** (Presl) J. Sm. See *Trogostolon falcinellus*.
***L. hirsuta*** J. Sm., nom. nud. See *Davallodes hirsutum*.
***L. membranulosa*** Wallich. See *Davallodes membranulosum*.
For further synonymy see *Davallia* and *Humata*.

**Leucothoë** D. Don. (For the daughter of Orchamur, king of Babylon and beloved of Apollo.) Ericaceae. Some 44 species of deciduous and evergreen shrubs. Leaves alternate, oblong-lanceolate, leathery, usually dentate, petiolate. Flowers in terminal or axillary racemes or panicles; bracts and bracteoles small, dry and shrivelled or somewhat white; calyx lobes 5, overlapping; corolla white to pink, ovoid, tubular or urceolate, lobes 5, small; stamens 10, anthers narrowing toward apex, usually terminating in 2–4 awns or, more rarely, awns absent; ovary 5 locular, ovules numerous. Fruit depressed-globose, dehiscent, membranous, 5-valved; seeds small, numerous. US, S America, Himalaya, E Asia, Madagascar.

CULTIVATION A shade-tolerant genus grown for its beautiful white flowers and handsome glossy foliage. They are found predominantly in damp and often shaded conditions, such as moist woodland (*L. axillaris* and *L. fontanesiana*), swamps and bogs (*L. davisiae*) or the wet, shaded cliff faces of Japan, the natural habitat of *L. keiskei*. The summer flowers of *L. davisiae* are held upright above the foliage; those of *L. fontanesiana* appear in spring, hanging in pendent racemes along the length of the gracefully arching stems. *L. keiskei*, whose pure white flowers are the largest of the hardy species, has red-flushed young foliage which, with that of *L. fontanesiana* and *L. axillaris*, also colours deep bronze-red or purple in autumn and winter. *L. fontanesiana* 'Rainbow' has become one of the most successful variegated evergreen introductions. Some of the deciduous species, notably *L. grayana* also colour well in autumn.

*Leucothoë* is suitable for the peat terrace, for open situations in the woodland garden and other naturalistic areas, and for moist sites on the rock garden. *L. keiskei* makes attractive groundcover, and is also amenable to pot cultivation in the alpine house. The genus includes some extremely hardy species. *L. fontanesiana* and *L. davisiae* both tolerate temperatures to −20°C/−4°F; given the sheltered and stable environment of the woodland garden many species will grow in zones where temperatures drop almost as low, the exceptions being *L. griffithiana* and *L. populifolia*, which are both subject to damage where temperatures drop much below −5°C/23°F.

Grow in dappled shade in moist, humus-rich, lime-free soils, and mulch annually with leafmould. Deciduous species, especially *L. racemosa*, tolerate sunnier and slightly drier conditions. They are tolerant of transplanting, best done in autumn. In the alpine house, use a well-drained, leafy and lime-free mix; keep moist throughout the year and water plentifully when in growth. Top-dress in early spring, and repot when necessary after flowering. Move into the shaded plunge frame after flowering, spraying in the evenings in very hot weather with rainwater. Prune when necessary to restrict growth after flowering, cutting out old and weak growth at ground level to preserve the graceful and arching habit, especially important in species like, *L. fontanesia*. Propagate by semi-ripe cuttings in late summer in a closed case with bottom heat, or by lightly covered seed in early spring; also by division of suckering species, and from layer.

***L. axillaris*** (Lam.) D. Don. Evergreen shrub *c*1.5m. Shoots long, diffuse, finely downy when young. Lvs 5–11×2–3.8cm, ovate to ovate-oblong, coriaceous, apex abruptly acute, dentate mainly in apical half, dark lustrous green and glabrous above, paler and sparsely hirsute beneath; petiole to *c*6mm. Fls crowded in axillary racemes 2–7cm long; pedicels short, pubesc.; cal. lobes ovate; cor. 6–8mm, white, urceolate or cylindric, lobes ovate. Spring–early summer. SE US. 'Compacta': habit compact. Z6.

***L. catesbaei*** (Walter) A. Gray. Evergreen shrub to 1.8m. Branches diffuse, somewhat procumbent; young shoots red, downy. Lvs 7.5–15×2–3.8cm, lanceolate or ovate, apex tapering to an acute point, margins setose-dentate, sparsely setose beneath. Fls crowded in terminal racemes; cal. lobes narrow ovate, somewhat overlapping, apex obtuse; cor. *c*6mm, white, cylindric, lobes somewhat reflexed. Spring. SE US. Z5.

***L. davisiae*** Torr. SIERRA LAUREL. Evergreen shrub, 30–180cm. Branches stiff, erect, glabrous. Lvs 2–7×0.6–3cm, ovate-oblong, apex shortly acute or obtuse, base rounded or somewhat cordate, texture firm, glossy green above, margins sparsely and evenly toothed; petioles 3–6mm. Fls in erect, sparsely short-setose, terminal racemes 5–15cm long; cal. lobes ovate, short, sparsely fringed with glandular teeth; cor. *c*6mm, white, pitcher-shaped. Fr. depressed-globose. Summer. California. Z5.

***L. fontanesiana*** (Steud.) Sleumer. DOG-HOBBLE; DROOPING LAUREL; SWITCH IVY. Fast-growing, evergreen shrub to 2m. Branches diffuse, arching, tinged red, downy when young. Lvs 6–16cm, oblong-lanceolate to ovate-lanceolate, tapering to a long point at apex, glabrous, margins spiny-ciliate dentate, lustrous green above, paler beneath. Fls in axillary racemes 4–6cm long; bracts lanceolate-acuminate; cal. lobes deltoid-ovate; cor. *c*8mm, white, almost cylindric. Spring. SE US. 'Lovita': vigorous, compact, mound-forming; lvs deep-bronze in winter. 'Naña': compact, low-growing. 'Rainbow' ('Girard's Rainbow'): young growth crimson; leaf variegation pink and cream, later white and green. 'Rollissonii': lvs small, narrow. 'Scarletta': lvs rich scarlet turning green shaded burgundy in winter. 'Trivar': strong grower; lvs red with cream and green variegation. Z5.

***L. grayana*** Maxim. Deciduous or almost evergreen, slow-growing or erect shrub, 50–120cm. Shoots tinged red, glabrous. Lvs 3.8–8.8cm, oval, oblong, ovate or somewhat inversely ovate, apex acute, tapering to or somewhat rounded at base, coriaceous, setose and conspicuously veined beneath, margins setose; petiole very short. Fls in erect, terminal, drooping racemes 7–10cm long, the fls borne at intervals of 3–12mm; bracts awl-shaped or linear; cal. lobes membranous, ovate to ovate-lanceolate; cor. 4–6mm, pure white to somewhat pink, campanulate, hirsute inside. Late spring–early autumn. Japan. Z6.

***L. griffithiana*** Clarke. Evergreen shrub, *c*1m. Twigs pendulous. Lvs 7–12cm, lanceolate, apex a tail-like appendage, base tapered to almost round, margins finely crenate to subentire. Fls in elongate axillary racemes; cor. white; anth. awned. Summer. Bhutan, W China (Yunnan, Kweichow). Z8.

***L. keiskei*** Miq. Evergreen shrub. Branches erect or somewhat prostrate, slender. Young shoots red, hairless. Lvs 3.8–8.8×1.2–3.8cm, narrow-ovate to broadly lanceolate, apex long and slender, base rounded, leathery, margins shallowly dentate, glossy deep green, sparsely adpressed-setose beneath; petioles 4–8mm. Fls few in drooping, axillary and terminal racemes 3–5cm long; pedicels 10–15mm, curved upwards in fruit; cal. lobes *c*2.5mm, broadly ovate, ciliolate; cor. 12–20mm, white, cylindric; lobes small, deltoid, erect. Summer. Japan (Honshu). Z5.

***L. populifolia*** (Lam.) Dipp. Evergreen shrubs to 1m. Stems glabrous; twigs arching broadly. Lvs 3–10cm, lanceolate to ovate-lanceolate, apex tapering slenderly to an acute tip, coriaceous, margins entire or inconspicuously serrate, reticulate-veined above and beneath. Fls few, in axillary racemes; pedicels slender, 6–9mm, cal. lobes deltoid, fringed with hairs; cor. *c*15mm, white cylindric, lobes short; fil. twisted near apex, anth. unawned. Spring–summer. SE US (S Carolina to Florida). Z8.

***L. racemosa*** (L.) A. Gray. SWEET BELLS. Bushy deciduous shrub, 1–2.5m. Young shoots finely pubesc. Lvs 2.5–6.2×1.2–3.2cm, oblong to ovate or elliptic, apex and base acute, firm-textured, shallowly round-dentate, margins finely serrate, pubesc. on midrib beneath; petiole *c*3mm. Fls in secund, terminal racemes 2.5–10cm long; pedicels short, hairless; bracteoles 2; cal. lobes deltoid-ovate, finely hirsute on margins; cor. *c*8mm, white, long, cylindric to cylindric-ovate; anth. 4-awned. Spring–late summer. E US. var. ***elongata*** (Small) Fern. Shoots soft-hirsute. Cal. lobes ciliate. Z5.

***L. recurva*** (Buckl.) A. Gray. RED TWIG. Diffuse, deciduous, shrub, 90cm–3.6m. Shoots somewhat pubesc. or glabrous. Lvs 3.8–10×1.2–3cm, elliptic-lanceolate to obovate, apex tapering to a sharp tip, tapering toward base, margins serrate, pubesc. on venation and midrib beneath; petiole very short. Fls in secund, terminal, decurved racemes 2–10cm long; pedicel very short and stocky; cal. lobes ovate, acute at apex; cor. *c*6mm, white, cylindric; anth. 2-awned. Spring–summer. SE US. Z6.

***L. acuminata*** (Ait.) G. Don. See *L. populifolia*.
***L. editorum*** Fern. & Schubert. See *L. fontanesiana*.
For further synonymy see *Andromeda* and *Lyonia*.

**Leuzea** DC. (For J.P.F. Deleuze (1753–1835) of Avignon and Paris, friend of de Candolle.) Compositae. 3 species of biennial or perennial herbs. Stem simple or sparingly branched. Leaves entire to lyrate or pinnatifid. Capitula discoid, solitary, ovoid-globose, terminal; phyllaries imbricate with membranous appendages; florets hermaphrodite. Fruit an ovoid or turbinate, glabrous cypsela; pappus of hairs. Mediterranean.

CULTIVATION *L. conifera*, occurring in dry and freely draining habitats, is suited to hot dry situations on the rock garden. The larger perennials, found in alpine pasture and meadows are useful for naturalizing in the wild garden and other informal situations; *L. rhapontica* which may reach 1–1.8m in height under favourable conditions is handsome enough to be given placement at the back of the herbaceous border. Grow in sun, in any deep, well-drained moderately fertile soil. Propagate by seed or division.

***L. centauroides*** (L.) Holub. Perenn. to 1m; stem arachnoid-tomentose, to 100cm. Basal lvs to 30×20cm, petiolate, pinnatisect, seg. lanceolate, white-tomentose beneath, serrate-dentate, stem lvs smaller, sessile. Involucre 5cm diam., globose; phyllaries lanceolate, acuminate, without appendages, margins brown; florets purple. Pyrenees.

***L. conifera*** (L.) DC. Perenn. to 30cm; stem white-lanate. Lower lvs ovate-lanceolate, entire or lyrate-pinnatifid, petiolate, white-tomentose beneath. Involucre to 4cm diam., ovoid-globose; middle phyllaries puberulent, with brown-red appendages; florets purple to white. Pappus to 6cm. Summer. W Mediterranean, Portugal. Z8.

***L. rhapontica*** (L.) Holub. Perenn.; stem white-lanate. Lvs glabrous above, tomentose beneath, basal lvs 60×15cm, base, subcordate, petiolate, stem lvs entire to lyrate, sessile. Involucre to 11cm diam., globose; phyllaries oblong to ovate, appendages 1cm wide, orbicular, brown; florets red or purple. Pappus to 2cm. Late summer–autumn. Alps. Z6.

For synonymy see *Centaurea* and *Cnicus*.

**Levisticum** Hill. Umbelliferae. 1 species, a glabrous perennial herb to 2m, strongly scented of celery; stems hollow, finely striate, flushed purple-pink at base. Leaves to 70cm, outline triangular-rhombic, 2–3-pinnate, emerging bronze, ultimately dark green, segments rhombic, base cuneate, to 11cm, margins irregularly toothed and lobed above middle; petiole hollow. Umbels with 12–20 rays; involucre of linear-lanceolate bracts, deflexed, margin scarious; involucel of similar bracteoles, connate at base; flowers bisexual, green-yellow. Fruit 5–7mm. Summer. E Mediterranean, naturalized over much of Europe and US. Z4.

CULTIVATION *L. officinale*, lovage, is widely naturalized in meadow land throughout Britain and much of Europe, having long been cultivated in herb and vegetable gardens for its sharp but pleasantly yeasty-flavoured leaves, roots and stems. *Levisticum* has a number of culinary uses; the dried root was once ground for use as a condiment, having a pleasant nutty flavour. The grated fresh root is eaten as a cooked vegetable or raw in salads, and the leaves and shoots are used as savory herbs. A sweetly scented herbal tea can be made from the dried leaves, and the seed adds a distinctive flavour to savoury biscuits.

A tall and undemanding perennial, reaching 1.8m/6ft in good conditions, *Levisticum* often has a long and useful life in cultivation and is hardy to at least −15°C/5°F. Grow in sun or part shade in any deep, fertile, reasonably moist and well-drained soil; apply a mulch of well-rotted manure annually to conserve moisture. Cut some stems back almost to ground level throughout the season to maintain a supply of fresh young leaves. Stems may be blanched by earthing-up in the manner of trench celery. Divide and replant the fleshy rootstocks in early spring every third or fourth year to maintain vigour, or propagate from ripe seed. Sometimes attacked by leaf-mining flies and celery fly; cut out and burn affected shoots.

***L. officinale*** Koch. LOVAGE. As for the genus.

For illustration see HERBS.

**Levya** Bur. ex Baill.
***L. nicaraguensis*** Bur. ex Baill. See *Cydista aequinoctialis* var. *hirtella*.

**Lewisia** Pursh. (For Capt. Meriwether Lewis (1774–1809) of the Lewis and Clark expedition across America.) Portulacaceae. 19 species glabrous, succulent, low-growing, perennial herbs with fleshy rootstocks. Basal leaves (if present) clustered at the apex of caudex, evergreen or dying away after flowering, usually numerous, arranged in a well-defined rosette or in a half irregular tuft; stem lvs usually reduced but sometimes well developed and similar to the basal lvs. Inflorescence usually cymes or panicles, sometimes racemose or reduced to a single flower; bracts subtending the flowers and the branches of the inflorescence, alternate, opposite or whorled, entire or glandular-toothed; flowers hermaphrodite, large and showy; sepals 2, persistent, small and green or purple-green, or 2–9, rather large, petaloid and white or pale pink; petals (4–)5–19, thin-textured, often unequal, especially in width, white, pink, magenta or yellow, often veined darker, sometimes striped; stamens 5–50; ovary subglobose to ovoid. Fruit a thin-walled capsule, circumsessile near base, allowing the whole upper portion to fall off like a cap; seeds several to many. Western N America.

CULTIVATION *Lewisia* spp. are grown for their beautifully coloured and textured flowers carried above the basal rosettes of more or less fleshy foliage in spring and early summer or, as with *L. columbiana, L. cotyledon* and its hybrids, intermittently through the summer. They occur naturally in a range of habitats in the mountains of north western America. The deciduous species are characteristically found in meadow and stony grassland which are moist in spring and early summer, later drying off so that after flowering the plants experience warm, dry conditions when they become dormant. The evergreen species occur more commonly in niches where moisture remains available to the deeply penetrating roots throughout the summer, frequently on steep, semi-shaded slopes, or on mossy, shaded canyon walls as with *L. serrata*. *Lewisia* spp. are suitable in cultivation for the rock garden, scree, crevice and dry stone walls and for the alpine house and frame; they seldom thrive on the flat, demanding the enhanced drainage that planting on slopes or vertical crevice confers. Most are cold-tolerant but susceptible to rotting at the neck in wet conditions; where low temperatures are prolonged protect with evergreen branches. The majority can be grown to perfection in the alpine house; a number of species are more safely grown there, where they can be guaranteed protection from excessive moisture (either in winter or summer). These include *L. congdonii, L. disepala, L. kelloggii, L. rediviva* and *L. tweedyi*.

Grow deciduous species in perfectly draining, gritty and humus-rich soils on sloping sites in sun; site evergreen species in a north- or northeast-facing niche ensuring shade from the hottest sun, in a circumneutral or slightly acid medium and provide a collar of grit at their neck, or grow in a vertical crevice where excess moisture will not accumulate in the rosette. Despite their alpine origins, *Lewisia* spp. need a fairly fertile soil to perform well and the addition of bonemeal or finely graded, well-rotted manure to the medium is recommended. In the alpine house use well-crocked pots with an open mix of equal parts loam, leafmould and sharp sand; top dress with a collar of grit. Water moderately and carefully when in growth allowing the medium to become almost dry between waterings; withold water from deciduous species as they enter dormancy and keep warm and dry. Continue watering evergreens until late summer, then reduce water to keep almost dry in winter. Repot after flowering, removing dead leaves at the same time to avoid rots. Propagate by fresh seed sown in a mix 1:2:2 fibrous loam, leafmould and sharp sand in the shaded cold frame; species hybridize readily and may not come true. Increase evergreen species also by offsets in summer, and establish in a shaded frame in a gritty propagating mix before potting on. Increase by leaf cuttings detached with a tiny portion of stem is also possible.

***L. brachycalyx*** Engelm. ex A. Gray. Low, near-stemless, deciduous perenn. less than 10cm when in flower, with a tuft of many basal lvs. Basal lvs 3–8×(0.2–)0.5–1.5(–2.2)cm, oblanceolate, dull, slightly glaucous green. Infl. of several semi-prostrate to suberect, 1-fld scape, 1–6cm long; fls sessile, 3–6cm diam.; sep. 2, 4–9mm, ovate; pet. 5–9, 12–26mm, obovate, white or occasionally veined with pink, or wholly white-pink; stamens 10–15. S California, Arizona, possibly also S Utah and New Mexico. 'Phyllellia' *(L. brachycalyx × L. cotyledon)*: fls pale pink striped rose, on low stalks. Z5.

***L. cantelovii*** J.T. Howell. Evergreen perenn. to 30 (rarely 40)cm in flower, with a flattened rosette of basal lvs. Basal lvs 2–5.5×0.5–1.7cm, spathulate, thick and fleshy, stem lvs much reduced, 3–5(–10)mm. Dull green suffused with pink-purple beneath. Infl. of several loose, many-fld panicles 15–30(–40)cm long; fls 1–1.5cm diam.; sep. 2, 2–3×c2mm, broadly elliptic; pet. 5 or 6, 6–9×3–5mm, elliptic-ovate or elliptic obovate, white or pale pink veined darker pink; stamens 5–6. NE California. Z7.

***L. columbiana*** (Howell ex A. Gray) Robinson. Subsessile, evergreen perenn. to 30cm in flower, with the lvs forming either loose, rather irregular rosettes or compact symmetrical rosettes. Basal lvs many, 2–10×0.3–0.8cm, narrowly oblanceolate or nearly linear, deep rather dull green, not glaucous, fleshy, flat or slightly channelled above; stem lvs 5–18mm, alternate, reduced and bract-like. Infl. loose, many-fld panicles 10–12(–30)cm long; fls 1–2.5cm diam.; sep. 2, 1.5–3cm, suborbicular; pet. 4–9(–11), 5–13mm, oblong or obovate, varying from off-white veined pink to pink or deep pink-magenta; stamens 5–6. Western N America. A widespread and variable species. 'Rosea': stems long; lvs narrow; fls brilliant magenta. ssp. ***rupicola*** (English) Ferris. Pet. 10–13mm, mid- to deep purple magenta or rose. ssp. ***wallowensis*** (Hitchc.) J.E. Hohn ex B. Mathew. 5–15cm in flower. Lvs to 4cm. Pet. 5–11mm, white veined pink. Z5.

***L. congdonii*** (Rydb.) S. Clay. Deciduous perenn. to 60cm in flower, with a loose tuft of somewhat erect lvs. Basal lvs 5–20×1–5cm, oblanceolate, rather pale green, fleshy but fairly soft and flaccid, flat; stem lvs much reduced, 5–10mm, lanceolate or linear-lanceolate, becoming smaller toward apex. Infl. of widely branching, lax panicles 20–60cm long; fls 1.5–2cm diam.; sep. 2, 2–4mm, suborbicular or broadly obovate; pet. 6–7, 7.5–10×c5mm, obovate, pale pink, veined darker purple-red with a yellow-green base; stamens 4–5. California. Z7.

***L. cotyledon*** (S. Wats.) Robinson. Evergreen perenn. to 30cm in flower, with the lvs forming tight, flat, symmetrical rosettes to 30cm diam., but usually much less; sometimes multiple rosettes are formed. Basal lvs 3–14×1–4cm, spathulate, oblanceolate or obovate, deep green and slightly glaucous, sometimes tinged pink, thick fleshy, narrowed at base into a winged, keeled petiole; stem lvs 5–10mm, alternate, oblong to ovate, 5–10mm long, bract-like. Infl. fairly dense compact panicles, 10–30cm long; fls 2–4cm diam.; sep. 2, 4–6×3.5–7mm, suborbicular or broadly ovate; pet. 7–10, 10–20×3–6mm, oblanceolate, obovate or spathulate, pink-purple with pale and dark stripes, sometimes white, cream with pink-orange stripes, apricot or yellow; stamens 5–12mm. var. ***cotyledon.*** Lf margins smooth. Pet. (8–)12–14mm. NW California, SW Oregon. var. ***heckneri*** (C. Morton) Munz. Lf margins with fleshy teeth. Pet. 16–20mm. N California. var. ***howellii*** (S. Wats.) Jeps. Lf margins strongly crisped-undulate. Pet. 12–15mm. NW California, SW Oregon. Ashwood Strain: lvs usually darker veined; fls pink, red, apricot, yellows seed race. 'Carroll Watson': fls pure yellow. 'John's Special': lvs sinuate; fls rose-purple. 'Kathy Kline': fls white. 'Pinkie': dwarf; lvs narrow, fleshy; fls in shade of pink, abundant. 'Rose Splendour': fls pale pink. Sunset Strain: lvs sinuate; fls in range of oranges; seed race. 'Trevosia' *(L. cotyledon* var. *howelli × L. columbiana)*: lvs fleshy, dark green; fls salmon pink. Z6.

***L. disepala*** Rydb. Low, subsessile, deciduous perenn. to 5cm with a tuft of basal lvs. Basal lvs 8–20mm, fleshy, terete, linear or slightly clavate, dying away at flowering time. Infl. several 1-fld scapes 5–30mm long; fls 2.5–3(–3.5)cm diam.; sep. 2, 7–8mm, broadly obovate or broadly ovate, white or pink-white; pet. 5–7, 13–18mm, oblanceolate or obovate, pale rose pink; stamens 10–15. California (Sierra Nevada): known only from exposed mountain summits around Yosemite valley. Z5.

***L. kelloggii*** K. Brandg. Near-stemless, deciduous perenn. to 3cm in flower, with rosettes of basal lvs. Basal lvs many, 1–6.5cm, spathulate, fleshy, the lower narrow portion petiole-like. Infl. 1-fld scapes 0.5–5cm long; fls sessile, 2–3cm diam.; sep. 2, tinged-pink, 5–12mm, ovate-lanceolate or oblanceolate, pet. 5–12, 10–15×2–5mm, obovate or oblanceolate, white; stamens 8–15(–26). California, C Idaho. Z5.

***L. leana*** (T. Porter) Robinson. Near-stemless, evergreen perenn., 10–20cm in flower, with the lvs forming loose tufts of ill-defined rosettes. Basal lvs many, 1.5–6×0.2–0.4cm, linear and somewhat terete, glaucous, fleshy; stem lvs c5mm, alternate, narrowly lanceolate, bract-like. Infl. loose, many-fld panicles 8–20cm long; fls 1–1.4cm diam.; sep. 2, 1–4mm, suborbicular; pet. 5–8, 5–7mm, obovate, magenta, pale purple-pink, white with magenta veining or occasionally white; stamens 4–8. California, Oregon. Z6.

***L. nevadensis*** (A. Gray) Robinson. Near-stemless, deciduous perenn. to 15cm in flower, with loose tufts of suberect lvs. Basal lvs 4–15×0.2–0.6cm, narrowly linear or linear-oblanceolate, fleshy. Infl. of several stout 1-fld scapes, suberect at first but usually becoming horizontal or deflexed with age; fls 2–3.5cm diam.; sep. 2, 5–13mm, broadly ovate; pet. 5–10, 10–15(–20)×4mm, elliptic or oblanceolate, white or rarely pink-white; stamens 6–15. Washington to New Mexico, W Colorado; possibly also in Idaho, Wyoming, Utah, and Arizona. Z4.

***L. oppositifolia*** (S. Wats.) Robinson. Caulescent deciduous perenn., 10–20(–25)cm with basal lvs and erect stems bearing opposite stem lvs. Basal lvs few, 4–10×0.5–1cm, green and shiny above, linear-spathulate or linear-oblanceolate; stem lvs similar but smaller, in 1–3 pairs low down on the stem. Infl. 1 to several, bearing loose 1–6-fld corymbs or subumbels; fls 2–3cm diam.; sep. 2, 4–8(–10)mm, suborbicular, coarsely dentate with red or pink teeth; pet. 8–11, 9–15×4–8mm, oblanceolate or obovate, pink in bud, opening to white or sometimes faintly pink; stamens 8–18. SW Oregon, NW California. Z6.

***L. pygmaea*** (A. Gray) Robinson. Low, deciduous, stemless, perenn., less than 10cm when in flower with a tuft of mostly suberect, but sometimes spreading lvs. Basal lvs several to many, 3–9×0.1–0.4(–0.45)cm, dark green, linear or linear-oblanceolate, widening at base into a winged petiole with scarious margins. Infl. of several scapes 1–6cm long, each carrying 1–7 fls, somewhat prostrate, or suberect but if so becoming deflexed in the fruiting stage; fls 1.5–2cm diam.; sep. 2, 2–6mm, suborbicular, broadly ovate or obovate; long. Pet. 5–9, 6–10mm, narrowly oblong, elliptic or oblanceolate, white or pink to magenta-purple, sometimes green at base; stamens (4–)5–8. Alaska south to New Mexico, east to Wyoming. Z3.

***L. rediviva*** Pursh. BITTERROOT. Stemless, deciduous perenn. to 5cm in flower, the lvs forming compact tufts early in the year and then dying away at or before flowering time. Lvs many, 1.5–5×0.2–0.3cm, linear or clavate, subterete. Infl. 1-fld scapes; peduncles 1–3cm; fls 5–6(–7.5)cm diam.; sepals (4–)6–9, unequal, white or pink, with a green or purple midvein; broadly elliptic or ovate, 10–25mm; pet. 12–19, 15–35mm, elliptic, oblong or narrowly oblanceolate, rose-pink, purple-pink or white; stamens 20–50. N America. A diminutive variant of *L. rediviva*, which occurs in a somewhat restricted area in Utah, Nevada and southern California, may be recognized as ssp. *minor* (Rydb.) A.H. Holmgren. Z4.

***L. triphylla*** (S. Wats.) Robinson. Deciduous perenn., 2–25cm in flower, with no basal lvs at flowering time. Basal lvs to 5cm, narrowly linear; stem lvs 2–3(–5), subtending the infl., 1–5×0.1–0.2mm, linear. Stems 1–5 per plant, 3–11cm. Infl. subumbellate or paniculate, with up to 25-fls, rarely only 1 or 2; fls 8–14mm diam.; sep. 2, 2–4mm, ovate; pet. 5–9, 4–7×2–2.5mm, elliptic, elliptic-obovate or elliptic-ovate, white or pink, with darker veins; stamens (3–)4(–5). N America. Z5.

***L. tweedyi*** (A. Gray) Robinson. Low, near-stemless, evergreen perenn., 10–20cm at flowering time with loose tufts of basal lvs. Basal lvs 4–8×2.5–5cm, green, often with a purple suffusion, broadly oblanceolate or obovate, fleshy, narrowed to a winged petiole 2–5cm long. Infl. of several scapes, 10–20cm long, each with 1–4(–8) fls; fls 4–5.5(–7)cm diam.; sep. 2, 9–10mm, broadly ovate; pet. (7–)8–9(–12), 2.5–4cm, obovate, pink-peach to yellow or rarely white; stamens 10–23. Washington State, Canada. 'Alba': fls white. 'Elliot's Variety': fls tinged pink, abundant. Z5.

***L. ×whiteae*** Purdy. A natural hybrid between *L. cotyledon* and *L. leana*. Lvs narrow. Fls salmon-rose. Z6.

***L. cultivars***. 'Ben Chace': fls large, pink. 'George Henley': fls brick red, abundant. 'Joyce Halley': fls pink to red. 'Karen': fls salmon-pink, red-veined. 'L.W. Browne': fls mauve, flushed salmon-pink. 'Paula': fls pale purple. Z5.

***L. eastwoodiana*** Purdy. See *L. leana*.
***L. finchae*** Purdy. See *L. cotyledon* var. *cotyledon*.
***L. heckneri*** (C. Morton) Gabr. See *L. cotyledon* var. *heckneri*.
***L. howellii*** (S. Wats.) Robinson. See *L. cotyledon* var. *howellii*.
***L. longifolia*** S. Clay. See *L. cotyledon* var. *cotyledon*.
***L. millardii*** S. Clay. See *L. cotyledon* var. *heckneri*.
***L. minima*** (A. Nels.) A. Nels. See *L. pygmaea*.
***L. purdyi*** (Jeps.) Gabr. See *L. cotyledon* var. *cotyledon*.
***L. rupicola*** English. See *L. columbiana* ssp. *rupicola*.

**Leycesteria** Wallich. (For William Leycester, Chief Justice of Bengal *c*1820.) Caprifoliaceae. 6 species of deciduous or semi-evergreen suckering shrubs. Stems cane-like, arising basally, green, branching and becoming lignified in second year, seldom surviving into fifth year. Leaves opposite, petioled. Racemes terminal and axillary, pendent, conspicuously bracteate; calyx persistent; sepals 5, small, 1–2 often more prominent; corolla tube funnelform, gibbous, usually 5-lobed; stamens 5; ovary inferior, 4–5-locular. Fruit a many-seeded berry. W Himalaya to SW China.

CULTIVATION *L. formosa*, the Himalaya honeysuckle, occurring in shady forests on its native mountains, is grown for its sea-green stems and its pendulous spikes of flowers, with persistent claret-coloured bracts. The shining purple berries are attractive to gamebirds, especially pheasants, and *L. formosa* has been commonly planted as pheasant covert, to the extent that is has become naturalized in parts of Britain and France. It makes a handsome understorey plant in the woodland garden although, despite its natural habitat, the bracts and fruit colour better in sun. *L. formosa* tolerates urban and maritime conditions, limey soils and windswept locations, and is hardy to about −15°C/60°F.

*L. crocothyrsos* is native to steep and sheltered Gneiss rock faces, at 2000m/6500ft in the mountains of Assam, and is grown outdoors only in the mildest districts; it will tolerate temperatures to −5°C/23°F if given protection from east and north winds. Nevertheless, its pendent racemes of fleshy, rich yellow flowers are unusual and attractive, and it can be grown in the cool greenhouse in areas with cold winters, given direct light, low humidity, and a medium-fertility loam-based mix.

Plant *L. formosa* when dormant, in rich moisture-retentive soil, in sun or part shade. *L. crocothyrsos* should be planted outdoors only when danger of frost is past. Sow fresh seed in autumn in loamless propagating medium in the cold frame, or store in damp peat and sand for sowing in early spring. Alternatively, divide established clumps in autumn. Propagate *L. crocothyrsos* by semi-ripe cuttings of lateral shoots with a heel, in summer, in the cold frame. The hollow stems of *L. formosa* are liable to be cut back by frost, but since best stem colour is seen in young growth, cut to the ground in spring and apply a general fertilizer and an organic mulch.

***L. crocothyrsos*** Airy Shaw. To 2.5m. Lvs 5–16×3.75–7cm, ovate, acuminate, rounded at base, margins sparsely serrate and somewhat pubesc., rich dull green above, somewhat glaucous, lanuginose, reticulate-veined beneath; petiole 3mm; interpetiolar stipules reniform, to 2cm diam. Fls rich yellow in whorls of 6 on arching, terminal racemes to 18cm; cal. green, 9.5mm diam.; cor. 2×2cm, tubular at base, pubesc. outside. Fr. to 16mm diam., globose, translucent yellow-green; cal. persistent. Himalaya (Assam), N Burma. Z9.

***L. formosa*** Wallich. HIMALAYA HONEYSUCKLE. Stems erect, to 1.5m, glaucous-pruinose at first, later shiny, glabrous. Lvs 7–18×4–9cm, ovate, long-acuminate, cordate at base, entire or serrulate, deep green above, paler and downy beneath when young; petiole to 2.5cm. Fls purple, sessile, in verticillasters on pendulous racemes to 10cm, subtended by claret, ovate, persistent bracts to 4cm; cal. 6.5mm; sep. erect, subulate, pubesc.; cor. funnelform, to 2×2cm, somewhat pubesc. Fr. bead-like, glossy sea-green becoming maroon then soft, purple-black, ripening at different speeds giving a multicoloured effect. Summer–autumn. Himalaya, W China, E Tibet. 'Rosea': fls pink. Z7.

**Leymus** Hochst. (From Gk *elymos*, a kind of millet.) Gramineae. Some 40 species of rhizomatous, perennial grasses. Leaves stiff, flat or rolled, glaucous, scabrous, pungent. Inflorescence racemose, linear; spikelets borne singly or in pairs, subsessile, adpressed to the rachis axis, to 7-flowered; rachis tough; glumes opposite or overlapping, linear to narrow-lanceolate, coriaceous, to 5-ribbed, acute to short-awned; palea equal to lemma, 2-keeled; lemmas lanceolate, acute to short-awned. N Temperate, 1 species Argentina.

CULTIVATION *L. arenarius* is often used as a sand binder with marram grass, *Ammophila arenaria*, but is valuable in gardens as (invasive) ground cover especially in association with other coastal natives; shear over before flowering for a flush of fresh blue green growth in summer. Cultivate as for *Elymus*.

***L. angustus*** (Trin.) Pilger. Rhizomatous stems to 1m, clustered. Lvs to 1cm diam. inrolled, scabrous above. Spike to 25cm; spikelets paired, with 2–3 fls; glumes to 2cm, lanceolate; lemmas to 1.5cm, 5–7-nerved; awn pointed. USSR. Z3.

***L. arenarius*** (L.) Hochst. LYME GRASS; SEA LYME GRASS; EUROPEAN DUNE GRASS. Stems robust, to 1.5m, upright, glabrous. Lvs flat, to 60cm×15mm, margins convolute; ligule truncate. Infl. spikes to 35×25cm; spikelets paired, oblong to deltoid, to 3.5cm, 4-fld; glumes narrow-lanceolate, to 2.5cm×3mm, apex attenuate, acuminate, keeled, glabrous to short-pubesc.; lemmas oblong-lanceolate, to 2.5cm, to 7-ribbed, densely pubesc., awns absent. Summer–autumn. N & W Europe, Eurasia. Z6.

***L. chinensis*** (Trin.) Tzvelev. Rhiz. to 3.6m. Stems to 45cm, coarse; spike to 20cm; rachilla joint smooth; lemma acuminate or awned; callus glabrous. China.

***L. condensatus*** (Presl & C. Presl). GIANT WILD RYE. To 2.7m. Rhiz. short, thick. Stems robust. Lvs to 75×2cm, ribs conspicuous above, scabrous. Infl. spikes upright, compact, to 30cm; spikelets in fascicles to 5, to 4-fld, to 2cm; glumes subulate or awl-shaped, to 1.5cm; lemmas lanceolate, to 13mm, awns absent, or apex mucronate, smooth or slightly scabrous. US (California). Z7.

***L. mollis*** (Trin.) Hara. Perenn. to 1.3m. Lvs to 1.5cm, broad, as with inrolled margins, rigid, smooth beneath, scabrous above. Spikes to 26cm, dense, with 3–5 fls ; glumes to 4mm, lanceolate, long-acuminate, thin, membranous, 3–5-nerved; lemma to 2.5cm, broadly lanceolate, 5–7-nerved, pointed, awnless, soft-pubesc. USSR. Z4.

***L. multicaulie*** (Karel. & Kir.) Tzvelev. ARAL WILD RYE. Close to *L. arenarius*, but differing in its shorter rhiz. and more erect lvs. USSR. Z4.

***L. racemosus*** (Lam.) Tzvelev. To 120cm, to 1cm diam. Lvs to 30×1.5cm, glabrous below, scabrous above. Infl. spikes to 35×2cm; apex attenuate; spikelets flattened, in clusters to 6, to 6-fld; glumes linear-lanceolate, to 2.5cm; lemma to 1.5cm, 7-ribbed, softly pubesc.; apex acute, glabrous. Summer–autumn. Eurasia. 'Glaucus': upright to arching, to 75cm; lvs clear light blue. Z5.

***L. secalinus*** (Georgi) Tzvelev. To 120cm. Stems upright, clumped, bent at base. Lvs narrow, to 20×1.5cm, convolute, scabrous. Infl. spicate, graceful; spikelets to 6-fld, adpressed to infl. axis; glumes to 1.5cm, to 5-ribbed, apex acute to awned; lemma awned, erect to spreading. US. Z5.

For synonymy see *Elymus* and *Agropyron*.

**Liabum** Adans.
***L. maronii*** (André) Nichols. See *Munnozia maronii*.
***L. ovatum*** (Wedd.) J. Ball. See *Paranephelius ovatus*.
***L. uniflorum*** (Poepp. & Endl.) Schultz-Bip. See *Paranephelius uniflorus*.

**Liatris** Gaertn. ex Schreb. BUTTON SNAKE ROOT; GAY FEATHER; BLAZING STAR; SNAKE ROOT. Compositae. About 35 species of perennial herbs arising from corms or much-flattened rootstocks. Leaves alternate, linear to ovate-lanceolate, simple, glandular-punctate, radical leaves elongate, stem leaves numerous, reduced above. Capitula discoid, clustered in corymbose spikes or racemes; phyllaries imbricate in several series, lanceolate to orbicular, herbaceous, margins ciliate or deeply erose; receptacle flat; florets hermaphrodite, tubular, purple to rose-purple, rarely white. Fruit a somewhat cylindric, basally attenuate, *c*10-ribbed cypsela; pappus or plumose or barbellate bristles. Eastern N America.

CULTIVATION With the exception of *L. spicata*, which occurs on streambanks and ditchsides, most *Liatris* spp. are found in prairie or open forest glades on dry stony soils. Valued for their late summer and autumn flowers, which are unusual in opening from the top of the spike downwards, *Liatris* is suited to the herbaceous and cut flower border and to native plant collections and other more informal situations. Flowering is prolonged by removing spent blooms at the tip of the spike, and when cutting for indoor display, care must be taken not to remove too much foliage to ensure good development of the tubers. Most species are tolerant of poor dry soils in cultivation but perform best on fertile, well-drained and moderately retentive soils, with emphasis on good moisture retention for *L. spicata*. Tubers are prone to rot in soils that are excessively wet in winter and also make a desirable food source for various rodents. Propagate by division or seed sown ripe in autumn.

***L. acidota*** Engelm. & A. Gray. To 80cm. Stems 1–4, stiffly erect, glabrous or puberulent. Lvs to 40×0.5cm, linear-lanceolate, shorter above. Capitula numerous, loosely clustered in a spike, sessile; phyllaries few, glabrous, adpressed, ovate to oblong-lanceolate, sometimes purple-tinged; florets red-purple. Fr. to 5mm; pappus *c*7mm. Coastal Louisiana and Texas. Z9.

***L. aspera*** Michx. To 1.1m. Stems usually 1, sometimes several, glabrous below with scattered hairs above, often rough throughout. Lvs to 15×2cm, rhombic-lanceolate to linear-lanceolate or almost linear, especially above, long-petiolate, glabrous and often rough, upper becoming sessile. Capitula at least 20, in a long open spike, sessile or pedunculate; phyllaries glabrous, with broad scarious margins, slightly wrinkled, inner oblong-spathulate, rounded, sometimes strongly wrinkled; florets usually purple, rarely white. Fr. to 6mm; pappus to 8mm. Z5.

***L. ×creditonensis*** Gaiser. *(L. ligulistylis × L. squarrosa.)* To *c*50cm. Stems 12 or more, glabrous below, sparsely pubesc. above. Lvs to 20×1cm, linear-lanceolate, glabrous, uppermost grading into the phyllaries. Capitula few to many in a racemose infl.; phyllaries laxly erect, oblong, apex subarcuate, acute, most herbaceous, with scarious, slightly revolute margins; florets pale purple. Fr. to 5mm; pappus *c*6mm. Garden origin. Z4.

***L. cylindracea*** Michx. To 60cm. Stems 1 to several, mostly glabrous, sometimes hirsutulous. Lvs to 20×0.5cm, linear, rigid, glandular-punctate, mostly glossy, glabrous, glabrous, mostly radical. Capitula few to several in a lax corymbose infl., often only the terminal developing; phyllaries mostly glossy, rigid, ovate and rounded, apex abruptly pointed, outer sometimes spreading; florets purple or rarely white. Fr. to 6mm; pappus *c*10mm. Late summer–early autumn. S Ontario and W New York State to Missouri. Z4.

***L. elegans*** (Walter) Michx. To 1.2m. Stems 1–2, finely pubesc. and leafy. Lvs to 10×0.5cm, linear to linear-lanceolate, glabrous, reduced upwards, upper soon deflexed. Capitula few to many, subsessile, in cylindrical or pyramidal racemose infl.; phyllaries lanceolate, outer short, herbaceous, inner red-pink, elongated and petaloid; florets white or purple. Fr. to 6mm; pappus to 11mm. Autumn. S & SE US. Z7.

***L. gracilis*** Pursh. To 1m. Stems slender to stiff, often thick, usually purple. Fr. to 4mm; pappus to 6mm. Autumn. CE & SE US. Z6.

***L. helleri*** Porter. To 20cm. Stems 1–2. Lvs to 30×1cm, radical, linear-lanceolate, attenuate to long, winged petioles, stem lvs gradually reducing upwards. Capitula few to many, in dense clusters to 7cm; phyllaries oblong-ovate, with a narrow scarious rim and finely ciliolate margin; florets purple. Fr. to 3.5mm; pappus to 4mm. N Carolina. Z7.

***L. ligulistylis*** (Nels.) C.B. Lehm. To 60cm. Stems 1 or several glabrous below and adpressed white-pubesc. above, or mostly pubesc., red-tinged. Lvs to 15×1.5cm, lanceolate-oblong or oblanceolate, usually long-petiolate, glabrous to sparingly hispidulous on midvein beneath, or densely pubesc. on both surfaces, more ciliate, reduced abruptly upwards. Capitula few, in a racemose cluster, shortly pedunculate; phyllaries glabrous, erect, with irregular, spathulate, broadly lacerate, scarious, often coloured tips, outer oblong to orbicular, shortest; florets purple. Fr. to 6mm; pappus to 10mm. Autumn. S Manitoba and Wisconsin to N New Mexico. Z3.

***L. novae-angliae*** (Lunell) Shinn. To 60cm. Stem glabrous or sparingly pubesc., somewhat striate. Lvs to 15×1cm, numerous, often twisted, glabrous or sparsely hairy along lower midrib, or hairy beneath and margin ciliate, lower amplexicaul, upper linear-lanceolate, sessile, gradually reduced. Capitula few to many in a simple raceme; phyllaries rounded to ovate or linear, outer herbaceous, slightly pubesc., margins ciliate, sometimes coloured, inner narrower, often coloured; florets purple, rarely white. Fr. to 7mm; pappus *c*8mm. SW Maine to Pennsylvania. Z4.

***L. punctata*** Hook. SNAKEROOT. To 80cm. Stems numerous, glabrous, striate. Lvs to 15×0.6mm, numerous, glabrous, rigid, linear, glandular-punctate, gradually reduced above. Capitula numerous, crowded in a usually dense spike, to 30×3cm; phyllaries herbaceous, thick, glandular-punctate, closely adpressed except for apices, outer short, rigid, ovate-acuminate or cuspidate, inner oblong, apices acute to mucronate or lanceolate-acuminate, margins ciliate; florets purple, rarely white. Fr. to 7mm; pappus to 11mm. Autumn. E Canada to SE US and New Mexico. Z3.

***L. pycnostachya*** Michx. BUTTON SNAKEROOT. To 1.5m. Stems 1 to many, stiff, striate, generally hirsute. Lvs to 10×0.5cm, linear, hirsute or glabrous, gradually reducing up stem. Capitula crowded in very dense spikes to 30×3cm, sessile; phyllaries green or purple-tinged, lanceolate-acuminate or oblong, usually laxly spreading; florets red-purple, sometimes white. Fr. to 7mm; pappus to 7mm. Autumn. SE US. Z3.

***L. scariosa*** (L.) Willd. To 80cm. Stems 1 to several, usually densely pubesc. Lvs few to many, to 15×5cm, broadly oblanceolate, oblong to ovoid, base attenuate, amplexicaul, gradually reducing up stem. Capitula few to many, in particular infl.; phyllaries leathery, mostly recurved, outer ovate, mostly herbaceous, sometimes coloured; florets purple. Fr. to 5mm; pappus to *c*9mm. SE US. 'Alba': fls white. 'Gracious': to 1.5m; fls snow-white. 'Magnifica' ('Alba Magnifica'): fl. heads very large, white. 'September Glory': to 125cm; fls deep purple. 'White Spire': fls in long white spikes. Z3.

***L. spicata*** (L.) Willd. BUTTON SNAKEWORT. To 1.5m. Stems stiff, glabrous, rarely hirsute. Lvs to 40×2cm, linear-lanceolate or linear. Capitula clustered in a dense spike, to 70cm, sessile or pedunculate, to 1.5cm; phyllaries adpressed elliptic-oblong, glabrous, margin scarious, purple-tinged at anthesis; florets red-purple. Fr. to 6mm; pappus to 7mm. Late summer. E US. 'Alba': fls white. 'Blue Bird': fls vivid blue. 'Floristan': to 90cm; fls white ('Floristan Weiss') and deep violet ('Floristan Violet'); seed race. 'Kobold' ('Goblin'): dwarf to 40cm; fls bright violet. 'Picador': fls ranging from white to violet; seed race. 'Snow Queen': to 75cm; fls snow-white. T & M Border Mixed: to 1.5m, fls from white to dark purple-blue; seed race from named selections of *L. scariosa* and *L. spicata*. Z3.

***L. squarrosa*** (L.) Michx. To 60cm. Stems several to numerous, glabrous, softly pubesc. or hairy. Lvs to 25×0.7mm, linear, rigid, glandular-punctate, glabrous or hirsute, gradually reduced upwards. Capitula 1 to few in a raceme, or many in a branched panicle; phyllaries leaf-like, glabrous or hirsute, inner narrowly linear, outer elongate triangular-lanceolate, apex more or less squarrose; florets red-purple. Fr. to 6mm; pappus to 12mm. Summer–early autumn. CE & SE US. Z4.

***L. ×weaveri*** Shinn. *(L. aspera × L. punctata.)* To 50cm. Stems slender, 12–24, glabrous below, white-pubesc. above. Lvs to 15×1cm, linear to narrowly linear-lanceolate, glandular-punctate, reduced gradually upwards. Capitula numerous, in a dense spike-like infl., to 30cm long; phyllaries linear-lanceolate, erect and moderately loose, outer herbaceous, oblong-triangular, inner oblong, with a narrow scarious, erose, pale margin; florets purple. Fr. *c*5mm; pappus 8mm. Ontario, probably elsewhere. Z2.

***L. callilepis*** hort. See *L. spicata*.
***L. glabrata*** Rydb. See *L. squarrosa*.
***L. montana*** hort. See *L. spicata*.
***L. pumila*** Lodd. See *L. spicata*.
For further synonymy see *Anonymos, Laciniaria, Serratula* and *Staehelina*.

**Libanothamnus** Ernst. (From the Gk *libanos*, incense, and *thamnos*, shrub.) Compositae. 1 species, a shrub, to 4m. Stems stout, terete, densely white-lanate. Leaves in congested whorls, 10–20×2–5cm, lanceolate, entire, sessile, leathery, glabrous above, densely white-lanate with black gland-like marginal spots beneath, midrib more or less conspicuous. Capitula radiate, 15–22mm diam., shortly pedunculate, in a terminal branched corymb; receptacle convex, scaly; involucre subhemispherical; outer phyllaries 5–6, imbricate, widely triangular, prominently 5-nerved, inner 10–12, imbricate, concave, enfolding outer fruit; ray florets 15–18, white, elliptic; disc florets 40–50, green-yellow. Fruit a 3-sided cypsela, outer face somewhat rough, inner faces smooth; pappus of densely villous hairs. Venezuela. Z10.

CULTIVATION As for *Bartlettina*.

***L. neriifolius*** (Bonpl. ex Humb.) Ernst. As for the genus.

For synonymy see *Espeletia* and *Trixis*.

**Libertia** Spreng. (For Marie A. Libert (1782–1865), Belgian student of liverworts.) Iridaceae. 20 species of rhizomatous perennial herbs. Rhizomes short, creeping, bearing fibrous roots. Leaves tufted, basal, or a few on stem, equitant, flattened long-linear, overlapping at base, stiff or pliable (in *L. pulchella*). Flowering stems erect, clothed with a few reduced leaves, bearing a terminal cluster or panicle; flowers radially symmetric, on slender pedicels emerging from sheathing bracts; perianth segments free, spreading, inner segments usually exceeding outer segments; stamens free, filaments briefly united at base; style branches 3, entire, slender, spreading. Fruit a trilocular, many-seeded capsule. Australia, temperate S America. Z8.

CULTIVATION Elegant evergreen perennials grown for the small, symmetrical, saucer-shaped flowers carried in loose clusters on erect stems; the seeds are brightly coloured. With the exception of the frost-tender *L. caerulescens*, most spp. are suitable for borders or informal plantings in regions where winter temperatures drop to about −10°C/14°F; *L. formosa* will survive short exposure to temperatures of −15°C/5°F. *L. pulchella*, with slender spikes of white flowers, is suitable for the rock garden or pans in the alpine house. Grow in sun or dappled shade in a moist but well-drained, slightly acid soil. In regions at the limits of their hardiness, mulch in winter with bracken litter or other organic matter. Leave established plants undisturbed, and when they begin to deteriorate, lift, divide and replant into well-cultivated and fertilized soil. Propagate by careful division in spring or by seed.

***L. caerulescens*** Kunth. Basal lvs 30–45cm, rigid, green; stems lvs to 12cm, usually shorter, 2–4. Flowering stem to 60cm; infl. 8–15cm, composed of numerous, sessile, many-fld umbels; outer bracts ovate to lanceolate, semi-rigid, inner bracts ovate, thin-textured; pedicels short; outer seg. far smaller than inner seg., olive to bronze, inner perianth seg. to 0.6cm, sky-blue, oblong; stamens equalling perianth. Spring. Chile.

***L. formosa*** Graham. Basal lvs 12–40×0.6–1.25cm, linear-ensiform, dark green, persisting; stem lvs to 3.5cm, 1–2, sheathing stem and subtending infl. Infl. composed of numerous, crowded, sessile umbels toward summit of simple stem or terminal on branches; outer bracts thin-textured, obovate, larger than oblong inner bracts; pedicels 0.6–1.2cm; outer perianth seg. olive to bronze, oblong, 0.5–0.8cm, inner seg. 1.2–1.8cm, obovate to cuneate, white or pale yellow. Spring. Chile.

***L. grandiflora*** (R. Br.) Sweet. Differs from *L. ixioides* in its lvs 30–70×0.5–1.25cm, 3–6-fld stalked umbels, outer perianth seg. to 0.6cm with an olive to bronze keel, inner seg. to 1.5cm; capsule 1–1.5cm. Summer. New Zealand.

***L. ixioides*** (Forst.) Spreng. Basal lvs 20–40×0.4–0.6cm, numerous, tufted, linear, rigid, subcoriaceous, striate, margins thickened, dark green, midrib paler. Flowering stem 30–60cm, branched in apical half, bearing a broad panicle composed of numerous umbellate clusters with membranous sheathing bracts; fls long-stalked, 2–10 per cluster; outer perianth seg. 0.4–0.8cm, oblong, white tinted brown or green, inner seg. 0.6–0.9cm, rounded to oblong, white; stamens to 0.4cm. Capsule 0.5–0.7cm, conical to oblong. Summer. New Zealand, Chatham Is.

***L. paniculata*** (R. Br.) Spreng. Basal lvs 25–60cm, linear, spreading, flaccid; stem lvs 1. Flowering stem to 60cm, branched; infl. composed of numerous pedunculate many-fld umbels; fls 1–2cm diam., white or cream; seg. spreading, outer 0.5–0.8mm, green-tinged externally, inner ovate, 0.8–1.2cm; stamens equalling outer seg. Capsule ovoid-globose. Australia (Queensland, NSW, Victoria).

***L. peregrinans*** Ckn. & Allan. Basal lvs to 70cm, green, with conspicuous veins. Flowering stem shorter than lvs, branched, upper bracts brown; fls to 2cm, pedicellate; outer seg. obtuse, narrow; inner seg. orbicular, unguiculate, twice size outer seg., anth. dark orange-brown. New Zealand.

***L. pulchella*** Spreng. Rhiz. sometimes rather elongate. Basal lvs 5–15×0.2–0.5cm, linear, grassy, pliable, mid-green. Flowering stem 6–28cm bearing a single reduced lf in basal half; fls 3–8 in a terminal umbellate cluster, occasionally with 1–2 lateral clusters; bracts 0.6–1.5cm, lanceolate, green; pedicels slender, downy; outer perianth seg. 0.3–0.5cm, oblong to ovate, white, inner perianth seg. 0.4–0.6cm, oblong-ovate, white. Capsule 0.3–0.4cm diam., subglobose.

***L.* cultivars**. 'Gold Leaf': lvs golden orange; fls white.

***L. chilensis*** Klotzsch. See *L. formosa*.
***L. ixioides*** Klatt. See *L. formosa*.

**Libidibia** Schltr.
***L. coriaria*** (Jacq.) Schltr. See *Caesalpinia coriaria*.
***L. punctata*** (Willd.) Britt. See *Caesalpinia punctata*.

**Libocedrus** Endl. (From Gk *libanos*, incense, and *kedros*, cedar, referring to the scented wood of this genus and of *Cedrus*.) Cupressaceae. 6 species (8 if the barely different genus *Papuacedrus* included) of coniferous, evergreen, monoecious trees to 25m. Crown ovoid to conic, bark brown, exfoliating in vertical stringy strips. Branchlets in 2 planes but often 1 predominating, somewhat flattened. Juvenile leaves flat linear, to 1cm, in decussate whorls of 4, borne in first few months. Immature leaves, found on most cult. trees, in decussate pairs on flattened fan-like sprays; facial leaves scale-like, 1–4mm; side leaves larger, falcate, scale-like, 3–6mm. Adult leaves on fertile shoots in more or less equal decussate pairs, scale-like, 2–4mm, on shoots not or slightly flattened and branching tetragonally to a greater or lesser extent. Male cones small, oblong, apical. Female cones apical, 7–16mm, ovoid, with 2 pairs of enlarged bract-like leaves at base and 4, rarely 6 valvate scales, with a 3–10mm acuminate bract placed centrally or toward the tip of each scale; lower pair(s) of scales smaller and sterile, upper pair fertile, equal in length to whole cone, with 2 seeds on each scale. Seeds 3–6mm, oval, flattened, with 2 very unequal wings (1mm and 4–6mm) at sides, ripening in 6–8 months. SW of S America, New Zealand, New Caledonia.

CULTIVATION Attractive cypress-like trees with glossy bright green foliage and exquisite small cones, slow growing to 10m/33ft and suitable for the smaller garden. High humidity and protection from dry east winds are more important than frost protection, and all New Zealand species should succeed in zone 8 given good shelter, some shade and reliably moist soil; *L. uvifera* is the most cold-tolerant, to −20°C/−4°F, but also demands very constant high rainfall except in the slightly drier Argentinian part of the range. The species from New Caledonia are not hardy and require glasshouse cultivation; they have much larger leaves, white beneath, and open, lax growth, very similar to *Papuacedrus*. Semi-fixed immature states are sometimes found under glass lacking the natural stimulation of weather variation and UV light to promote adult growth. Propagation as for *Chamaecyparis*; no significant diseases or pests.

***L. austrocaledonica*** Brongn. & Griseb. Small tree to 8m. Immature lvs broad triangular, to 8×6mm at sides, facial lvs 3×2mm, green with white stomatal patches beneath. Adult lvs scales-like, falcate-subulate at sides to 7mm, facial lvs 2mm, shoots remaining flattened. Cones 8–10mm, sterile scales very small, 2mm; bracts long and straight, 10mm. New Caledonia. Z10.

***L. bidwillii*** Hook. f. PAHAUTEA. Tree to 20m, 10m in cult., crown avoid-conic. Immature shoots flattened, largely in one plane, with 3mm lateral lvs and 1mm facial lvs; adult shoots tetragonal with shoots in two planes, all lvs equal, 2mm; all lvs glossy yellow-green with inconspicuous stomatal patches. Cones 8–10mm, matt brown, sterile pair of scales 5mm; bracts 3–4mm, outcurved or S-shaped. New Zealand (mts). Z8.

***L. chevalieri*** Buchholz. To 5m, similar to *L. austrocaledonica* but adult shoots narrower, and less difference between lateral and facial lvs, to 3–4mm and 2–4mm respectively. Cone larger, 15mm, sterile scales 10mm; bracts curved, 6mm. New Caledonia. Z10.

***L. plumosa*** (D. Don) Sarg. KAWAKA. Tree to 25m, 10m in cult., crown ovoid-conic. Immature shoots very flattened, with 5mm falcate lateral lvs and 1–2mm facial lvs; adult shoots slightly flattened with many but not all shoots in one plane, lvs nearly equal in size, lateral lvs 2–3mm, facial lvs 1.5–2mm; all lvs glossy bright green with inconspicuous stomatal patches. Cones 14–16mm, glossy brown, sterile pair of scales 10mm with often an extra pair of 2mm sterile scales below the fertile pair; bracts 4–6mm, s-shaped or spreading. New Zealand (mts). Z8.

***L. uvifera*** (D. Don) Pilger. Tree to 20m; 8m with crown slender conic with erect branches in cult. Immature shoots little flattened, largely in two planes, with all lvs 3–4mm, outcurved-falcate with white patches of stomata on inner surfaces; adult shoots tetragonal with shoots in two planes, all lvs scale-like, equal, 2mm; glossy dark green with stomatal patches on inner faces less obvious. Cones 7–8mm, matt brown, sterile pair of scales 5mm; bracts 3–4mm, adpressed to scales and incurved at tips. S Chile and SW Argentina, to Tierra del Fuego. Z7.

***L. yateensis*** Guillaum. To 8m, similar, to *L. austrocaledonica* but adult shoots narrower, and less difference between lateral and facial lvs, to 3–4mm and 2–3mm respectively. Cone similar size, 10mm, but sterile scales 6mm; bracts straight, 9mm. New Caledonia. Z9.

***L. arfakensis*** Gibbs. See *Papuacedrus arfakensis*.
***L. chilensis*** (D. Don Endl. See *Austrocedrus chilensis*.
***L. decurrens*** Torr. See *Calocedros decurrens*.
***L. doniana*** (Hook.) Endl. See *L. plumosa*.
***L. papuana*** F. Muell. See *Papuacedrus papuana*.
***L. tetragona*** (Hook.) Endl. See *L. uvifera*.
***L. torricellensis*** Schltr. ex Laut. See *Papuacedrus papuana*.
For further synonymy see *Pilgerodendron*.

**Libonia** K. Koch.
***L. floribunda*** K. Koch. See *Justicia rizzinii*.

**Licania** Aubl. (Anagram of local French Guianan name.) Chrysobalanaceae. 171 species of trees to 35m, shrubs or, rarely, shrubs with subterranean stems. Leaves simple, often glandular below, lower surface of lamina glabrous, lanate or strigose; stipules present, persistent. Inflorescence a simple or branched raceme of sessile, subsessile or pedicellate clusters of small flowers; flowers hermaphrodite, actinomorphic or weakly zygomorphic; receptacle tube 1–6mm, variable in shape, hairy within; sepals 5, subequal, acute; petals 5, equalling sepals, or absent; stamens 3–40, included or exserted, united at base; ovary monocarpellary, unilocular; style filiform, 3-lobed. Fruit a dry or fleshy drupe, to 10×5cm, dispersed by many types of animal. Americas, Africa, Asia.

CULTIVATION As for *Chrysobalanus*.

***L. michauxii*** Prance. Shrub or small tree. Stems mostly subterranean, glabrous, not lenticellate, 8cm thick, spreading 30m; above ground shoots to 30cm. Lvs lanceolate to oblong-lanceolate, 4–11×1–3.5cm, serrulate, apex acute to rounded, mucronate, leathery, glabrous, sometimes pubesc. beneath. Infl. lax terminal and subterminal panicles; fls minute, 3mm, in small groups; receptacle tube campanulate, tomentose; cal. lobes acute; pet. 5, densely pubesc.; stamens 14–17, united, exceeding cal. lobes. Fr. ovoid, to 3cm, smooth. Spring. SE US (Louisiana to S Carolina).

For synonymy see *Chrysobalanus* and *Geobalanus*.

**Licuala** Thunb. (From the native Moluccan name for these palms, *leko wala*.) PALAS. Palmae. Some 108 species of acaulescent or shrubby, pleonanthic and usually hermaphrodite palms, 1–6m. Stems underground, creeping or erect, one to many, partially clothed with leaf bases and fibres, becoming closely ringed. Leaves palmate, marcescent, fibrous; petiole to 1.5m, channelled above, convex beneath, margins unarmed or armed with sharp teeth; adaxial hastula triangular, abaxial hastula absent, blade to 1.5m, entire or divided to base into multiple-fold, cuneate segments, apices truncate, regularly notched, ribs often tomentose. Flowers borne on simple or 1–3-branched spikes amid sheathing bracts and with bracts subtending rachillae; calyx tubular, truncate or 3-lobed; corolla exceeding calyx with 3 valvate lobes; stamens 6, distinct or united in tube; pistil 3-carpellate, glabrous or hairy. Fruit to 1.2cm, globose to ovoid, red, with basal stigmatic remains and persistent perianth. SE Asia through Malaysia to Australia and New Hebrides. Z10.

CULTIVATION Attractive fan palms with their distinctive, almost circular leaves and wedge-shaped leaflets, *Licuala* spp. are suitable for outdoor cultivation in the humid tropics or in cooler zones for the warm glasshouse with consistent high humidity. Propagate by seed in a sandy propagating mix with strong bottom heat. See also PALMS.

***L. grandis*** H.A. Wendl. Stem solitary, to 3m×6cm, clothed with persistent lf bases. Petioles to 1m, margins serrate proximally; blades usually entire, sometimes divided into 3 broad, orbicular, undulate seg. to 90cm across. Infl. exceeding lvs, pendent. Fr. to 12mm, spherical, glossy, crimson. New Hebrides.

***L. pumila*** Bl. Stems to 1.5m. Lvs to 45cm across, divided into 7–8 several-folded seg. or 20–24 2-folded seg. Infl. shorter than lvs, branches rigid; fls single, to 0.5cm, stamens united in ring, fil. awl-shaped. Fr. *c*1cm, globose to oblong, red, orange or purple. Java, Sumatra.

***L. ramsayi*** Domin. Stem to 12m×10cm, clothed with lf bases and fibres above. Petioles to 1.5m, margins armed with spines proximally; lvs to 1m across, divided into seg., seg. cuneate, or of varying width, sometimes fused at apex, juvenile blades entire. Infl. equalling or exceeding lvs; fls cream. Fr. to 1cm diam., spherical, orange-red. NE Queensland.

***L. spinosa*** Thunb. Stems clustered, to 5m×8cm, clothed with lf bases and fibres above. Petioles to 1.5m, margins armed with robust, curved spines; lvs to 1m across, divided into many seg., seg. cuneate, apices truncate, praemorse. Infl. to 2.5m, branches spreading. Fr. to 10×8mm, spherical to ovoid, red. W Indonesia, Philippines, Malay Peninsula, Thailand.

***L. elegans*** Bl. See *L. pumila*.
***L. gracilis*** Bl. See *L. pumila*.
***L. horrida*** Bl. See *L. spinosa*.
***L. muelleri*** H.A. Wendl. & Drude. See *L. ramsayi*.
For further synonymy see *Dammera* and *Pericycla*.

For illustration see PALMS.

**Ligularia** Cass. (From Lat. *ligula*, a little tongue, referring to the tongue-shaped ray florets.) LEOPARD PLANT. Compositae. About 180 species of perennial herbs. Basal leaves radical, broad, ovate-oblong to reniform, usually cordate, petioles long, broadly sheathing, stem leaves alternate, bract-like above. Capitula usually radiate, few to many, in corymbs or racemes; involucre cylindrical or campanulate; phyllaries in 1 series, imbricate, sometimes more or less connate; ray florets yellow to orange, female; disc florets yellow, hermaphrodite. Fruit a terete, striate, usually glabrous cypsela; pappus of hairs. Temperate Eurasia.

CULTIVATION Grown for flower and foliage, ranging from the large, deeply lobed, groundcovering clumps of species such as *L. wilsoniana* and *L. veitchiana* to the more finely cut leaves in *L. przewalskii*, with dark wand-like flowering stems which are handsome even before the yellow flowers emerge. A number have attractively coloured leaves, notably the dark leaves of *L. dentata* 'Othello', 'Moor's Blood' and 'Desdemona', the last with mahogany undersides and rich orange blooms.

Grown as specimens by lake and stream side or in massed plantings in the dappled shade of the woodland garden, they demand deep, moist, fertile and humus-rich soils and benefit from a mulch of organic matter; on bright windy days they may wilt very quickly, even where soil moisture may appear adequate. Large-leaved species like *L. veitchiana* and *L. wilsonii* need a cool moist situation to perform well, and dark-leaved forms need some shade to prevent foliage scorch. Propagate by division or (species) by seed.

***L. achyrotricha*** (Diels) Ling. Erect, to *c*1m. Stems densely and minutely fulvous-pubesc. Basal lvs to 33×41cm, broadly orbicular, base strongly cordate, undulate, dentate, glabrous above, minutely fulvous-pubesc. beneath, palmately veined. Capitula discoid, to 1cm diam., in a panicle; involucre obconical, to 17×9mm; phyllaries oblong-linear, acute, free, glabrous above, minutely fulvous-pubesc. beneath, margins membranous; florets to 1.5cm. Fr. *c*5mm; pappus 6mm, white. NW China. Z5.

***L. altaica*** DC. Erect, to 1m. Basal lvs elliptic, obtuse, cuneate, more or less entire. Capitula in a dense, bracteate raceme; involucre ovoid; phyllaries 7, oblong, margins scarious, barbellate at apex; ray florets 3–5, yellow. Pappus white, exceeding involucre. Altai Mts of C Asia. Z5.

***L. dentata*** (A. Gray) Hara. To 1m, glabrous to hairy above. Basal lvs to 30×40cm, reniform-orbicular, deeply cordate, dentate, thinly chartaceous, pubesc. beneath and on veins above, stem lvs shortly petiolate. Capitula to 12cm diam., few to many, in lax corymbs; involucre cylindric-campanulate, to 2×3cm, densely pubesc.; phyllaries oblong, shortly cuspidate, free or slightly connate at base; ray florets *c*10, to 5cm, bright orange. Fr. *c*9mm; pappus to 12mm, tinged red. China, Japan. 'Dark Beauty': lvs very dark; fls vivid light orange. 'Desdemona': to 120cm; lvs purple; fls deep orange. 'Dunkellaubig': to 100cm; fls bright orange. 'Golden Queen': fls bright gold. 'Gregynog Gold' (*L. dentata* × *L. veitchiana)*: to 120cm; lvs green; rounded, saw-edged; fls orange, in pyramidal spikes. 'Moorblut' ('Moor's Blood'): lvs very dark purple; fls orange. 'Orange Princess': to 120cm; lvs green; fls light orange. 'Orange Queen': lvs green; heads large, fls deep orange. 'Othello': to 120cm; lvs rounded, long-stemmed, dark purple; fls deep orange. 'Sommergold': fls rich gold. Z4.

***L. fischeri*** (Ledeb.) Turcz. To 2m. Stem arachnoid below, pubesc. above. Basal lvs to 32×40cm, reniform-cordate, dentate, chartaceous, glabrous except at margins, stem lvs shortly petiolate. Capitula to 5cm diam., many, in a raceme to 75cm; involucre cylindric-campanulate, to 12×10mm; phyllaries 8–9, oblong; ray florets to 25×4mm, 5–9. Pappus to 10mm, tinged brown or purple. E Siberia, China, Korea, Japan.

***L. ×hessei*** (Hesse) Bergmans. *(*Probably derived from a cross between *L. dentata* and *L. wilsoniana.)* Intermediate between the putative parents. To 2m. Lvs cordate-reniform. Capitula to 9cm diam., in a panicle; florets orange-yellow. Garden origin. Z5.

***L. hodgsonii*** Hook. To 80cm. Stem succulent, striate, tinged purple below, green and pubesc. above. Basal lvs to 13×27cm, cordate to suborbicular, serrate-dentate, chartaceous, glabrous, petiole very long. Capitula to 5cm diam., in capitate corymbs; involucre campanulate, to 12×10mm; phyllaries linear-lanceolate, arachnoid, subtended by few, subulate bracts; ray florets to 27×8mm, orange or bright yellow. Fr. to 7mm, pappus white to dark tawny. Japan. Z5.

***L. intermedia*** Nak. To 1m. Lvs to 23×33cm, reniform or broadly cordate, coarsely dentate, glabrous, amplexicaul. Capitula to 4cm diam., in cylindrical racemes to 35×7cm; peduncles subtended by narrowly lanceolate bracts; involucre narrowly campanulate, to 10×5mm; phyllaries *c*6, linear-oblong, obtuse, connate, fleshy, margins scarious, minutely pubesc. toward apex; ray florets 1–5, spreading, bright yellow, 8–20mm; disc florets few. Fr. 4mm, glabrous; pappus to 5mm, tinged purple. N China, Japan.

***L. japonica*** (Thunb.) DC. To 1m. Stems glabrous, purple-spotted. Basal lvs to 30×30cm, cordate-orbicular, palmately-parted, seg. coarsely lobed and incised, strongly revolute, densely pubesc. beneath at first, chartaceous, petiole-winged, stem lvs *c*3, broadly amplexicaul. Capitula 2–8, *c*10cm diam., in a corymb; involucre campanulate-cylindric, to 24×24mm; phyllaries 9–12, elliptic, acuminate, densely and minutely pubesc.; ray florets *c*10, orange-yellow, to 6.5×1cm. Fr. *c*9mm, glabrous; pappus to 7.5mm, rusty brown. China, Korea, Japan. Z5.

***L. macrophylla*** (Ledeb.) DC. To 1.8m. Basal lvs to 60×30cm, elliptic to ovate-oblong, dentate, petiole winged, decurrent, glaucous, stem lvs amplexicaul. Capitula 2.5–5cm diam., in dense panicles to 30cm; ray florets 3–5, bright yellow; disc florets few. Fr. glabrous. Altai Mts of C Asia. Z4.

***L. ×palmatiloba*** hort. *(L. dentata × japonica.)* Intermediate between parents. To 1m. Lvs orbicular, cordate, lobed, serrate. Capitula several, in a corymb; florets yellow. Garden origin. Z5.

***L. przewalskii*** (Maxim.) Diels. To 2m. Stems dark purple. Basal lvs deeply palmately lobed, seg. lobed or toothed. Capitula many, small, in a long, narrow raceme; ray florets *c*2, yellow; disc florets *c*3. N China. Z4.

***L. sibirica*** (L.) Cass. To 1.5m, often purple-tinged. Stems glabrous or hairy. Basal lvs to 25×20cm, triangular-reniform to subsagittate, dentate, subglabrous to densely hairy beneath, stem lvs smaller, few, upper narrower, subsessile. Capitula numerous, *c*3cm diam., in lax, bracteate racemes, the bracts linear to lanceolate; involucre to 20mm, subtended by 2 linear bracts equalling the involucre; phyllaries 8–10, lanceolate; ray florets 7–11, yellow, to 20×5mm; disc florets many. Fr. 4–6mm; pappus grey-white, exceeding fr. body. Temperate Eurasia. Z3.

***L. stenocephala*** (Maxim.) Matsum. & Koidz. To 1.5m. Stems dark purple. Basal lvs to 35×30cm, spreading or ascending, hastate-cordate to triangular, acuminate, basal seg. acute, dentate, thinly chartaceous, shortly pilose on veins beneath. Capitula radiate or discoid, to 3cm diam., many, in long slender racemes; involucre narrowly cylindrical, to 12×3mm, subtended by linear-lanceolate bracts; phyllaries 5; ray florets 1–3, to 25×4mm or absent; disc florets 6–12. Fr. to 7mm, oblanceolate, slightly compressed; pappus white or pale brown. China, Japan, Taiwan. 'The Rocket': to 180cm; stems black; fls in long yellow trusses. 'Weihenstephan': to 180cm; fls large, gold. Z5.

***L. veitchiana*** (Hemsl.) Greenman To 1.8m, subglabrous. Basal lvs to 30×35cm, triangular-cordate, dentate, bright green, petioles semiterete, solid. Capitula to *c*6.5cm diam., many; peduncles bracteate, outer bracts leafy, covering capitula before flowering, inner bracts 2, linear, shorter than involucre; ray florets 8–12, to 2.5cm, bright yellow; disc florets many. Fr. cylindrical, glabrous; pappus hairs shorter than disc florets, sordid to purple-tinged. China. Z5.

***L. wilsoniana*** (Hemsl.) Greenman GIANT GROUNDSEL. To 2m. Basal lvs to 50×25cm, reniform-cordate, sharply dentate, deep green, petiole terete, hollow. Capitula *c*2.5cm diam., many, in an elongated raceme; peduncles bracteate, bracts all small, linear; ray florets 6–8, yellow. Fr. cylindric; pappus sordid, scarcely exceeding fr. body. China. Z5.

***L. clivorum*** (Maxim.) Maxim. See *L. dentata.*
***L. kaempferi*** Sieb. & Zucc. See *Farfugium japonicum.*
***L. smithii*** hort. See *Senecio smithii.*
***L. tangutica*** (Maxim.) Bergmans. See *Sinacalia tangutica.*
***L. tussilaginea*** (Burm. f.) Mak. See *Farfugium japonicum.*
For further synonymy see *Arnica, Cineraria* and *Senecio.*

**Ligusticum** L. (From Gk *ligystikos*, referring to the abundance of this plant in the province of Liguria.) ALPINE LOVAGE. Umbelliferae. 25 species of erect perennials. Leaves 2–5-pinnate, or ternate. Lateral umbels sterile or male, smaller; involucral bracts deciduous; involucel bracteoles several, persisting; calyx teeth small or absent; flowers white to white-green, occasionally tinged purple; petals obcordate. Fruit oblong, not compressed; mericarps prominently ridged, with narrow wings; vittae numerous. Circumboreal.

CULTIVATION *L. scoticum*, the Scots lovage, which occurs in rocky coastal habitats, is not of great ornamental merit but is occasionally grown for use as pot herb and in green salads. Grow this and other species in any well-drained soils in sun. Propagate by seed in autumn or by division. The small alpine lovage, *L. mutellinoides*, which occurs on stabilized scree and on rock ridges to altitudes of 3000–3400m/9750–11050ft, is not noticeably decorative, but is of interest since no other umbellifer occurs at such high altitudes in Europe.

***L. lucidum*** Mill. Stems to 1.5m, subglabrous, arising from a coarse, fibrous rootstock; branches subopposite or whorled. Lvs *c*30cm, 3–5-pinnate, seg. linear, to 1.5cm. Umbels 20–50-rayed; involucre often absent; involucel of 5–8 bracteoles. Fr. 5–6mm; mericarps with narrowly winged ridges. Summer. Mts S Europe. Z6.

***L. mutellina*** (L.) Crantz. ALPINE LOVAGE. Stems to 50cm; branches subtended by reduced lvs; rootstock densely and coarsely fibrous. Lvs to 10cm, 2–3-pinnate, seg. linear-lanceolate, *c*5mm. Umbels 7–15-rayed; involucral bracts few or absent; involucel of few bracteoles, lanceolate; fls red or purple. Fr. 4–6mm; mericarps with smooth ridges. Summer. C & SE Europe. Z6.

***L. mutellinoides*** (Crantz) Vill. SMALL ALPINE LOVAGE. Stem simple, nearly leafless, to 30cm; rootstock scarcely fibrous, or lacking fibres. Lvs to 10cm, 2–3-pinnate, seg. linear-lanceolate, 2–5mm. Umbels with 8–20 rays; involucral bracts 5–20, often 2–3-parted; involucel similar; fls white to pink. Fr. ellipsoid, 3–5mm; mericarps with smooth ridges. Summer. Mts C Europe (Carpathians, Urals to Arctic USSR). Z3.

***L. scoticum*** L. SCOTS LOVAGE; SCOT LOVAGE. Stems leafy, celery-scented, to 90cm. Lvs 8–25cm, 2-ternate, seg. ovate-cuneate, 2–5cm, bright green, margin dentate to lobed. Umbels 4–6cm diam.; rays 8–20; involucral bracts 3–6, linear; involucel similar; fls green-white or tinged pink. Fr. 6–8mm; mericarps with narrowly winged ridges. Summer. N Europe, Greenland and eastern N US. Z4.

***L. acutiloba*** Sieb. & Zucc. See *Angelica acutiloba.*
***L. aromaticum*** Hook. f. See *Anisotome aromatica.*
***L. capillifolia*** Cheesem. See *Anisotome capillifolia.*
***L. haastii*** F. Muell. ex Hook. f. See *Anisotome haastii.*
***L. imbricata*** Hook. f. See *Anisotome imbricata.*
***L. latifolium*** Hook. f. See *Anisotome latifolia.*
***L. piliferum*** Hook. f. See *Anisotome pilifera.*
***L. pyrenaeum*** Gouan. See *L. lucidum.*
***L. seguieri*** Vill. See *L. lucidum.*

**Ligustrum** L. (Lat. name for privet.) PRIVET. Oleaceae. Some 50 species of shrubs and small trees, deciduous or evergreen. Leaves opposite, entire, thick, glabrous, oblong or ovate. Flowers small, white, in terminal panicles, hermaphrodite; corolla tubular, 4-lobed; stamens 2. Fruit a black, fleshy drupe, 1–4-seeded. Europe, N Africa, E & SE Asia, Australia.

CULTIVATION Tough shrubs or small trees for hedging or informal screens, even in part shade and on city sites. *L. ovalifolium* and its cv. Aureum have largely replaced *L. vulgare* as a popular hedging plant since they are more likely to remain evergreen, although very severe winters may kill hedges back to ground level. More choice spp. like *L. lucidum, L. quihoui, L. confusum* and *L. sinense* are grown as specimen shrubs or trees in sunny, sheltered sites for their foliage, soft, plume-like spires of cream or white, late summer flowers and attractive fruits.

Plant in any soil in spring and keep well supplied with moisture, mulching on dry ground if necessary. Although drought- and shade-tolerant, hedges of *L. ovalifolium* and *L. vulgare* will make a healthier backdrop given sufficient moisture, sun and an annual application of fertilizer. Prune hedge plants 2–3 times annually. Old, straggly hedging may be rejuvenated by pruning hard back and watering and feeding thoroughly. Propagate evergreens from greenwood cuttings in spring or summer in a closed case or under mist; deciduous plants from hardwood cuttings in winter. Alternatively, increase from seed sown in spring.

Susceptible to privet thrips (*Dendrothrips ornatus*); privet aphid (*Myzus ligustri*); willow scale (*Chionaspis salicis*); crown gall (*Agrobacterium radiobacter* var. *tumefaciens*); white root rot (*Rosellinia necatrix*); wilt (*Verticillium* sp.); leaf spot (*Mycophaerella ligustri*); lilac leaf miner (*Caloptilia syringella*) and anthracnose twig blight.

***L. chenaultii*** Hickel. Sp. probably not distinct from *L. compactum*, differs only in having acute dormant buds and lvs to 25cm. China (Yunnan). Z8.

***L. compactum*** (Wallich ex G. Don) Hook. f. & Thom. ex Brandis. Small tree to 8m high. Young growth and petioles downy; lvs to 17cm, lanceolate, narrow-acuminate, glabrous dark green. Fls off-white, malodorous, profusely borne in terminal panicles to 15×15cm at base; anth. pink. Fr. to 1cm, purple-black, pruinose. Summer. NW Himalaya, SW China. Z8.

***L. confusum*** Decne. Medium-sized, semi-evergreen tree in warm locations, elsewhere smaller (to 8m), deciduous. Growth emerging downy. Lvs to 9×3cm, lanceolate, pale green, glossy, glabrous; petiole sulcate. Fls on 1-year-old growth, in pubesc. panicles, white, each to 4mm wide, short-stalked; cal. cupped, divisions cuneate, glabrous, anth. pink, fil. white. Fr. blue-black, pruinose, 1cm. Summer. E Nepal, Bhutan, India (Khasi Hills). Z8.

***L. delavayanum*** Hariot. Evergreen shrub, to 2m, divaricate; new growth downy. Lvs to 3cm, elliptic to ovate, acute glabrous, glossy above, paler beneath, midrib pubesc. Fls in panicles, leafy and downy at base, to 5cm; cor. tube to 5mm, twice as long as lobes; anth. mauve, not exserted. Fr. globose, black, clustered. Late spring. W China, Burma. Z7. Z8.

***L. gracile*** Rehd. Deciduous shrub to 3m, branches arching gracefully. Lvs to 4cm, glabrous. Fls in panicles to 7×7cm; cor. tube as long as lobes. Late spring. China Z8.

***L. henryi*** Hemsl. Evergreen shrub to 3m. New growth densely pubesc. Lvs to 3cm, oval, acuminate, dark metallic green above. Fls in terminal panicles to 15cm, white, fragrant; cor. 6mm; cal., pedicel glabrous. Fr. oblong, black, to 8mm. Summer. C China. Z7.

***L. ×ibolium*** Coe (*L. obtusifolium* × *L. ovalifolium.*) Semi-evergreen, close to *L. ovalifolium* except young branches, infl. axis and lf undersides pubesc. Anth. equal cor. lobes. Garden origin, US 1910. 'Variegatum': fast-growing, erect and tightly branched; lvs edged with soft cream. Z4.

***L. ibota*** Sieb. & Zucc. Deciduous shrub to 2m, bushy. Shorter growth pubesc., extensions glabrous. Lvs to 5cm, ovate or lozenge-shaped, minutely ciliate, olive green above, paler beneath with downy midrib. Fls white, to 8, to 8mm, terminally in heads to 1.5cm. Summer. Japan. Z5.

***L. indicum*** (Lour.) Merrill. Evergreen shrub to 8m. New growth pale grey-green, muricate, woolly. Lvs to 8cm, oblong, acuminate, glossy green above, yellow to pale green beneath. Fls in panicles to 18cm, terminal and axillary, small, fragrant. Early summer. Himalayas, Indochina. Z8.

***L. japonicum*** Thunb. Related to *L. lucidum*, differs in having darker, smaller, obovate lvs with prominent rather than sunken veins below and cor. tube twice length of cal., as are lobes (cf. *L. lucidum*, where cor. and cal. are equal in length and panicles are denser). Evergreen shrub to 4m, bushy. New growth minutely dark-pubesc., later glabrous. Lvs to 10cm, glabrous, lustrous dark green, ovate, blunt-acuminate, with red-green margins and midrib; venation paired ×5, distinct. Fls in pyramidal panicles to 15cm. Late summer. Japan, Korea. 'Revolutum': narrow, erect, to 1m, shoots densely foliate; lvs small to 3cm, narrow. 'Rotundifolium': rigidly erect evergreen shrub to 2m; shoots appearing stunted; lvs crowded, to 4cm, round or broadly ovate, obtuse or emarginate, dark green coriaceous; not found in wild. 'Silver Star': slow-growing, compact, erect; lvs dark green edged with cream, tinged silver. 'Texanum': vigorous; lvs large, to 5cm, thick and lustrous, paler when young, later very dark green; fls in clusters, white, fragrant. 'Variegatum': lvs stippled and edged white. Z7.

***L. lucidum*** Ait. f. CHINESE PRIVET; WHITE WAX TREE. Resembles *L. japonicum*. Evergreen to 10m. New growth glabrous with lenticels. Lvs to 10cm, long-acuminate. Fls white, in panicles 10–20cm. Fr. blue-black, oblong, to 1cm. Late summer. China, Korea, Japan. 'Alivonii': young lvs yellow-variegated, otherwise dull green. 'Aureovariegatum': lvs yellow-variegated, tough. 'Ciliatum': lvs small. 'Compactum': dense in growth; lvs waxy, dark green. 'Excelsum Superbum': vigorous, lvs deep yellow, flecked and edged off-white. 'Gracile' and 'Nobile': upright, branches fastigiate. 'Latifolium': lvs very large, glossy dark green. 'Macrophyllum': lvs large. 'Microphyllum' lvs small. 'Pyramidale': narrow and conic in growth. 'Recurvifolium': leaf margins recurved. 'Repandum': lvs narrow, curling upwards. 'Tricolor': vigorous, lvs smaller than species type, marked white and yellow, flushed pink when young. Z7.

***L. massalongianum*** Vis. Evergreen shrub, erect to 1m. Growth papillose, slender, densely pubesc. Lvs 4–8×1cm, linear, narrow-acuminate, glabrous, often falling with cold conditions. Fls pedicellate, crowded in branching panicles to 8cm. Fr. subglobose, blue. Summer. Himalayas. Z8.

***L. obtusifolium*** Sieb. & Zucc. Related to *L. ovalifolium*, differs in luxuriant, graceful habit and lvs with pubesc. midribs. Deciduous shrub to 3m. Smaller branches pubesc., arching. Lvs to 9cm, oblong to obovate, abruptly acuminate, dark green above, paler beneath, midrib pubesc. Fls in semi-pendent panicles to 5cm, cor to 10mm. Fr. to 5mm diam., dark grey. Summer. Japan. var. ***regelianum*** (Koehne) Rehd. To 2×1.5m. Growth spreading, short, bristly. Lvs in 2 ranks, obovate, 5–7cm, pubesc. below. Fls crowded in short axillary panicles. Fr. globose, blue black, to 5mm diam. Summer. Japan. Z3.

***L. ovalifolium*** Hassk. CALIFORNIA PRIVET. Semi-evergreen shrub to 4m, branching densely, upright. Lvs to 7cm, elliptic-ovate, shining deep green above, yellow-green beneath. Fls malodorous, many, in panicles to 10cm, near-sessile; cor. off-white, 8mm, with lobes and anth. of equal length. Summer. Japan. 'Albomarginatum': lvs edged white. 'Argenteum': lvs margined silver. 'Aureum': lvs yellow, margins broad and golden. 'Compactum': dense and slow-growing. 'Globosum' and 'Nanum': dwarf, dense and slow-growing. 'Lemon and Lime': similar to 'Aureum' with lvs variegated pale green and yellow. 'Multiflorum': particularly floriferous. 'Tricolor': new growth flushed pink, lvs ultimately variegated yellow-white. 'Variegatum': lvs stippled pale yellow. Z5.

***L. pricei*** Hayata. Evergreen shrub to 3m. New growth minutely downy, purple-green. Lvs 3×2cm, coriaceous, oval, acuminate, dark green, glabrous; petiole purple-green. Fls insignificant, in terminal panicles to 5cm, slightly pubesc., loose, nodding. Summer. Taiwan. Z8.

***L. quihoui*** Carr. Deciduous shrub to 2m. Shorter branches bearing spine-like reduced shoots, rusty-pubesc. Lvs to 5cm, oblong-lanceolate, persisting into late autumn, glossy, glabrous above; petiole downy. Fls fragrant, white, widely spaced in lax, narrow-cylindric panicles to 20cm. Late summer. China. Z6.

***L. sempervirens*** (Franch.) Lingl. Evergreen shrub to 2m. Lvs to 4cm, ovate, glabrous, tough, shiny, dark-punctuate beneath. Fls sessile, many, in panicles to 10cm; cor. to 1cm, tube twice length of lobes; stamens slightly exserted. Fr. fleshy at first, later drying as hard capsule. Summer. W China. Z7.

***L. sinense*** Lour. Deciduous shrub to 4m, erect, densely branching. Smaller branches felty-pubesc., yellow-grey. Lvs to 7cm, elliptic-oblong, olive green above, paler beneath, midrib downy. Fls off-white, fragrant, in panicles to 10cm, pedicels pubesc. Fr. globose, claret-coloured, to 4mm diam., persistent. Summer. China. 'Multiflorum': particularly floriferous, anth. tinted red. 'Pendulum': branches pendulous. 'Variegatum': lvs variegated soft grey-green and white. 'Wimbei': dwarf to 50cm after 5 years, upright and columnar in growth; lvs small, to 6mm, very dark green. var. ***stauntonii*** (DC.) Rehd. Shorter and more spreading than species type, to 3×2m. Smaller branches flushed purple. Lvs to 4cm, ovate, obtuse, deep green above, paler, sparsely pubesc. below. Late summer. C China. Z7.

***L. strongylophyllum*** Hemsl. Evergreen, erect shrub. Branches slender, grey pubesc. Lvs to 2.5cm, small, broadly ovate, coriaceous, glossy, deep green above, paler beneath. Fls to 7mm, white, borne loosely in pyramidal panicles to 10cm. Summer. C China. Z9.

***L. 'Suwannee River'***. Slow-growing and compact. Branches ascending. Lvs lustrous, dark green, dense and adpressed to stems.

***L. tschonoskii*** Decne. Deciduous shrub, erect, to 2m. Branches arching. Lvs to 8cm, rhombic or ovate, acuminate, margins ciliate, adaxial surface pubesc. near margins. Fls in short-stalked panicles, 4–6cm, densely pubesc. Summer. Japan. Z6.

***L. ×vicaryi*** Rehd. (*L. ovalifolium* × *L. vulgare.*) Deciduous, spreading. Branches densely divaricate. Lvs golden. Garden origin. Z5.

***L. vulgare*** L. COMMON PRIVET. Deciduous shrub to 5m, upright, habit dense. New growth downy. Lvs oblong-ovate to lanceolate, glabrous, dark green. Fls off-white on dense, erect, terminal panicles to 5cm, malodorous. Fr. small, ovoid to globose, black-blue, glossy. Summer. N Europe, Mediterranean, N Africa, Asia Minor; distribution enlarged and confused by cultivation. Numerous cvs include: 'Argenteovariegatum': lvs speckled white. 'Aureovariegatum': lvs marked golden yellow. 'Aureum': lvs golden. 'Buxifolium': lvs persistent, small, ovate. 'Chlorocarpum': fls green-yellow. 'Glaucum': lvs appearing grey-green due to thick cuticle. 'Laurifolium': vigorous, erect, dense habit; lvs ovate, tough, dark green, suffused purple in winter. 'Leucocarpum': fr. white-green. 'Lodense': semi-prostrate, matted habit; lvs narrow elliptic, dark green, to 5cm, bronze, persistent in winter. 'Pyramidale': fastigiate; side shoots dense, appearing whorled. 'Xanthocarpum': fr. bright yellow. Z4.

***L. acuminatum*** Koehne. See *L. tschonoskii*.
***L. angustifolium*** hort. See *L. massalongianum*.
***L. brachystachyum*** Decne. See *L. quihoui*.
***L. californicum*** hort. See *L. ovalifolium*.
***L. ciliatum*** Rehd. non Sieb. ex Bl. See *L. tschonoskii*.
***L. ciliatum*** Sieb. ex Bl. See *L. ibota*.
***L. coriaceum*** Carr. See *L. japonicum* 'Rotundifolium'.

***L. formosanum*** Rehd. See *L. pricei*.
***L. ibota*** Sieb. (1830) non Sieb. & Zucc. (1846). See *L. obtusifolium*.
***L. ionandrum*** Diels. See *L. delavayanum*.
***L. longifolium*** Carr. non hort. See *L. compactum*.
***L. longifolium*** hort. non Carr. See *L. massalongianum*.
***L. magnoliifolium*** hort. See *L. lucidum*.
***L. medium*** Franch. & Savat. non hort. See *L. ovalifolium*.
***L. medium*** hort. non Franch. & Savat. See *L. tschonoskii*.
***L. nepalense*** Wallich. See *L. indicum*.
***L. prattii*** Koehne. See *L. delavayanum*.
***L. rosmarinifolium*** hort. See *L. massalongianum*.
***L. simonii*** Carr. See *L. compactum*.
***L. spicatum*** Hamilt. See *L. indicum*.
***L. stauntonii*** (A. DC.) See *L. sinense* var. *stauntonii*.
***L. villosum*** May. See *L. sinense*.
***L. yunnanense*** L. Henry. See *L. compactum*.
For further synonymy see *Parasyringa*.

**LILIACEAE** Juss. LILY FAMILY. Monocot (including Alliaceae, Aloeaceae, Alstroemeriaceae, Aphyllanthaceae, Ruscaceae, Smilacaceae, Tecophilaeaceae, Trilliaceae, Xanthorrhoeaceae). 240 genera and 4640 species of herbs with rhizomes or bulbs and few shrubs or trees often with unusual mode of growth in thickness, many are xerophytes, some are succulents (*Aloe*, *Gasteria*), others have tuberous stems and narrow leaves (*Dasylirion*), or climbing plants (*Smilax, Gloriosa*), *Smilax* with peculiar tendrils, *Ruscus* exhibiting phyllocladodes. Inflorescence usually racemose, sometimes cymose. Flowers usually with no bracteoles, when present, the further branching from their axils usually cymose (e.g. the heads of *Allium* and *Agapanthus*); solitary terminal flowers occur, e.g. *Tulipa*; flowers bisexual, regular; perianth 3+3, free or united, petaloid or sometimes sepaloid; stamens 3+3, or fewer, rarely more; ovary of 3 fused carpels, superior, rarely inferior or half-inferior, 3-loculed with axil *placentation*, rarely 1-loculed with parietal placentation; ovules usually numerous, in 2 rows in each locule. Fruit usually loculicidal or septicidal capsule, sometimes a berry; seeds with straight or curved embryo; endosperm copious, fleshy or cartilaginous, never mealy. Some are edible, such as onion, garlic, leek, asparagus, etc. Some are medicinal plants e.g. *Urginea* and *Colchicum*; colchicine from the latter is used to induced polyploidy in plants.

The correct classification of the monocots, especially within the Liliaceae, is at present a contentious issue. Opinion is divided between those who wish to maintain a broad view of the family, such as Cronquist, who, to maintain consistency, incorporate into an all-encompassing Liliaceae many families that others would separate, most notably perhaps Alliaceae, Amaryllidaceae and Trilliaceae. The other extreme is that of Dahlgren, Clifford and Yeo, who distinguish many small families, amongst which is a very reduced Liliaceae. Both systems have their merits and dismerits, although the second is probably a more accurate representation of affinities. As it has not been widely accepted, the system of Dahlgren *et al.* has not been followed here. Instead, the broad groupings of the petaloid monocots familiar to generations of horticulturists as the Liliaceae (distinguished by the superior ovary) and the Amaryllidaceae (with an inferior ovary) has been maintained. Agavaceae, a family of heterogeneous origins, has also been retained on the strength of its distinct morphological unity. The families into which Dahlgren *et al.* would place each genus are indicated in parenthesis at the start of each genus description, together with the traditional family as accepted here, e.g. *Colchicum* Liliaceae (Colchicaceae); *Trillium* Liliaceae (Trilliaceae).

Cosmopolitan, the smaller group often confined to restricted regions. *Agapanthus, Agrostocrinum, Albuca, Alectorurus, Aletris, Allium, Aloe, Alstroemeria,* × *Alworthia, Amianthum, Androcymbium, Androstephium, Anemarrhena, Anthericum, Aphyllanthes, Arthropodium, Asparagus, Asphodeline, Asphodelus, Aspidistra, Astelia, Astroloba,* × *Astroworthia, Baeometra, Behnia, Bellevalia, Bessera, Blandfordia, Bloomeria, Bomarea, Bowiea, Brimeura, Brodiaea, Bulbine, Bulbinella, Bulbinopsis, Bulbocodium, Burchardia, Calochortus, Caloscordum, Camassia, Camptorrhiza, Cardiocrinum, Chamaelirion, Chionodoxa, Chionographis,* × *Chionoscilla, Chlorogalum, Chlorophytum, Clintonia, Colchicum, Conanthera, Convallaria, Daiswa, Danaë, Daubenya, Dianella, Dichelostemma, Dipcadi, Disporum, Drimia, Drimiopsis, Eremurus, Erythronium, Eucomis, Fritillaria, Gagea, Galtonia,* × *Gasteraloe,* × *Gasterhaworthia, Gasteria,* × *Gastroloba, Gilliesia, Gloriosa, Haworthia, Helonias, Heloniopsis, Hemerocallis, Herpolirion, Hesperocallis, Hosta, Hyacinthella, Hyacinthoides, Hyacinthus, Ipheion, Kinugasa, Kniphofia, Lachenalia, Lapageria, Latace, Laxmannia, Ledebouria, Leucocoryne, Leucocrinum, Lilium, Liriope, Littonia, Lloydia, Lomatophyllum, Luzuriaga, Maianthemum, Massonia, Medeola, Melanthium, Merendera, Milla, Milligania, Muilla, Muscari, Narthecium, Nectaroscordum, Nomocharis, Notholirion, Nothoscordum, Ophiopogon, Ornithogalum, Paradisea, Paris, Pasithea, Peliosanthes, Periboea, Petronymphe,* × *Philageria, Philesia, Poellnitzia, Polygonatum, Polyxena, Pseudogaltonia, Puschkinia, Reineckea, Ripogonum, Rohdea, Ruscus, Sandersonia, Scilla, Scoliopus, Semele, Simethis, Smilacina, Smilax, Sowerbaea, Speirantha, Stenanthium, Streptopus, Stypandra, Tecophilaea, Theropogon, Thysanotus, Tofieldia, Trichopetalum, Tricyrtis, Trillium, Tristagma, Triteleia, Tulbaghia, Tulipa, Urginea, Uvularia, Veltheimia, Veratrum, Whiteheadia, Wurmbea, Xanthorrhoea, Xeronema, Xerophyllum, Zigadenus.*

**Lilium** L. (Lat. form of Gk *leirion*, used by Theophrastus for the Madonna Lily.) LILY. Liliaceae (Liliaceae). About 100 species of perennial monocots, to 3m. Stems subterranean forming bulbs, with white or yellow fleshy scales, sometimes purple when exposed to light. Bulbs of 5 types: concentric, central growing point with overlapping scales (e.g. *L. medeloides*); subrhizomatous, growing horizontally in only one direction with declining basal plate (e.g. *L. washingtonianum*); rhizomatous scales forming extensive mats (e.g. *L. pardalinum*); stoloniferous, developing new bulbs at apices of one or more horizontal stolons (e.g. *L. canadense*); stoloniform, developing horizontal stems before shoots appear above ground (e.g. *L. wardii*). Some species stem-rooting, roots developing on underground stems above bulbs. Stems unbranched above ground; bulbils develop in leaf axils or on lower leafless portion. Leaves linear or lanceolate, whorled, horizontal or with recurved tips; veins parallel; petioles very short or absent. Flowers in a terminal raceme or umbel, occasionally solitary, erect (cup-shaped), horizontal (funnel-shaped or bowl-shaped), pendulous (bell-shaped or turk's-cap with recurved tips), to 10–30cm wide; tepals 6, free, inner usually broader, white, yellow, orange, red or maroon, interior surface often spotted, nectary and filament of stamen at base of each tepal; anthers versatile; stigma 3-lobed, style 1, ovary superior. Fruit a 3-celled capsule, seeds numerous, flat, in 2 rows per cell. Temperate northern hemisphere.

CULTIVATION All lilies have a bulbous rootstock comprised of a base upon which are few to numerous scales, always without any outer protective sheath. There are several types of bulb: concentric, with the scales firmly clustered around a central growing point, as in *L. dauricum*; rhizomatous, where the base elongates in one direction and the new growing point is set away from the old, as in *L. pardalinum*; and stoloniferous, where during the growing season a stolon or horizontal stem is thrust out by the current bulb at the end of which a new concentric bulb is formed, as in *L. canadense*. Another term, stoloniform, depicts a type of growth where the stem wanders some distance underground before emerging; new bulbs often arise at intervals on the section below ground: *L. nepalense* is typical of this type. Most hybrid lilies have concentric bulbs, except those derived from western American species, which are generally rhizomatous. Some Asiatic Hybrids have stoloniform stems.

Most lilies grow in acidic soils, but some grow in alkaline soils (or even on both alkaline and acid) and on limestone formations. The following are considered as lime-loving or lime-tolerant: *Ll. amabile, bolanderi, brownii* (?), *bulbiferum, callosum, canadense var. editorum, candidum, cernuum, chalcedonicum, concolor, dauricum, davidii, duchartrei, hansonii, henryi, humboldtii, lankongense, leucanthum, longiflorum, martagon, monadelphum, pardalinum*, *parryi*, *pomponium*, *primulinum*, *pyrenaicum*, *regale*, *sulphureum*. Hybrid lilies based on these species may be considered lime tolerant and often accept a wider range of soil types than their parents. A few lime-loving species, such as *L. henryi* and *L. candidum*, appear to do less well when grown in acid soils.

*Lilium* spp. grow in a variety of conditions, but most enjoy an open free-draining loamy soil, with a high humus content. Some demand drier conditions at times other than in spring when in full growth. A few are native to bogs, ditches or streamsides, but still require free-draining sites in spring, tolerating wetter conditions at other seasons.

As nearly all lilies like deep planting – *L. candidum* being a notable exception – the soil should be well worked to the necessary depth. The subsoil should be broken up, but not brought to the surface, to improve drainage and to allow free run for basal roots. Coarse grits and gravels (free of sticky sand) may be added to the subsoil, and bulbs may be planted on a layer of sharp sand, if the subsoil is heavy. Topsoils may be improved with leafmould, coir and other well-decomposed vegetable matter with the addition of grits and sharp sand, so that the surface will always absorb light rains and artificial watering without lateral run-off when dry. If the quality of drainage is in doubt, the whole bed should be improved rather than creating good conditions immediately below the bulbs, producing pockets which will fill with water in winter with disastrous results. If drainage cannot easily be improved, raised beds may be the only answer, but in such conditions the bulbs must be provided with regular and adequate moisture when necessary. Soil moisture should be plentiful in late winter and spring, easing gradually in summer so that, following flowering, the soil is moist enough for the bulb to replenish itself.

Because lily bulbs have their outer scales exposed, they are easily damaged and can quickly lose moisture by evaporation, rendering them more susceptible to pathogens. The aim should be to obtain high-quality bulbs in firm fresh condition with sound fleshy basal roots at the correct time for planting outdoors. In cool-temperate areas planting time is early to mid-autumn, or into later autumn in warmer regions. If this is not possible, planting should be delayed until late winter or early spring. Bulbs received in winter months should be potted up, and nurtured and protected until spring. On receipt bulbs should be examined and any damaged badly marked outer scales removed. If flaccid, the bulbs should be placed in cool moist sawdust for 10–14 days to absorb water and plump up. If the bulbs have obviously been out of the ground for some time or shows signs of rot or other moulds, particularly near the base, they should be washed clean and then immersed in a fungicide solution for 20 minutes. If the bulbs are uncommon or expensive, it is a wise precaution to take off two or three scales to propagate some new bulblets (see below).

Many lilies produce roots from the subterranean portion of the stem allowing them to take up extra moisture and nutrients at the height of their activity; even so, those not normally stem-rooting still require deep planting to gain stability for the stems. However, planting should not be deeper than soil conditions and cultivation allow and usually 8cm/3in. of soil above the bulb is adequate. Many lilies have the ability, when established, to adjust their depth in the soil by contractile roots, stolons, rhizomatous bulbs or stoloniform stems.

Sprinkle a balanced fertilizer over the planting area at 140g/m$^2$ (4½oz/yd$^2$) and also the extracted portion, mixing it into the soil. Thin sandy soils often need a more complete fertilizer including trace elements. Fresh organic manure should be kept away from the bulbs and young root growth. If there is a fear of soil-borne pests, a dressing of insecticidal dust may be mixed with the soil, and for subterranean slugs, a drench of metaldehyde liquid should be given in advance. When planting, spread the basal roots carefully. Mark the outline of the area with short sticks and fill in with the loam. Should conditions seem over-dry, controlled watering is helpful to compact the soil around the bulbs and give them a good start.

The often-quoted advice to keep the roots in the shade while allowing the heads in the sun is generally sound. Many of the Asiatic species, like *L. pumilum* and *L. dauricum*, will accept full sun. Most of the Oriental species and hybrids will appreciate dappled shade for some of the day; this applies also to forms of *L. martagon* and Western American species. The Caucasian lilies will take full sun as in the wild but must have adequate moisture, and as will *L. candidum* and other southern European species used to the heat of sun at lower latitudes. Lilies are best not grown in one bed together but in small groups interspersed with shrubs, dwarf conifers and strong-growing perennials. These plants will help in producing a barrier between the groups and restrict the movement of aphids, the main vector in carrying lily virus diseases. Lilies will also look more natural in these surroundings, continuing the floral sequence into late summer and, if *L. speciosum* and *L. formosanum* can be flowered successfully, in early autumn.

In early spring, as growing shoots emerge, slugs must be carefully controlled. The succulent stems are very vulnerable and if the top is eaten out or the stem eaten through, all is lost for the year and the bulb loses its vigour. Extra feeding with a high-potash fertilizer to promote flower quality, and a mulch of decayed leafmould over moist soil to promote stem roots, are desirable. The plants should be watered if soil moisture declines, without waiting for the soil to dry out. Water plants at ground level rather than over the foliage, as wetting the leaves may encourage botrytis, even in cool dry conditions.

Most lilies, other than those which are stoloniferous or stoloniform, may be grown in containers, the Asiatic and Oriental and hybrid trumpet lilies are particularly suitable. Bulbs must not be crammed into pots: as a guide, three *L. concolor* fit into a 15cm/6in. pot, one large *L. auratum* hybrid or three *L. chalcedonicum* will go into a 23cm/9in. pot, while three or four medium-sized *L. auratum* hybrids could go into a 30cm/12in. pot. Space the bulbs at equal distance, allowing 2cm/1in. between them or at least to avoid their touching, and keep the bulbs at least 1cm/½in. from the sides of the pot. If deeper than average pots are available, so much the better. To maintain very good drainage throughout the season, cover the base of the pot with a layer of dust-free sherds and grit with 2–3cm/1in. of potting medium above. When the stem starts to emerge fill the remainder of the container with rich open compost in two stages. This ensures good new basal root growth while providing fresh nourishment for the stem roots. This method may be used to start plants to be transferred to urns and large tubs. It is also helpful in bringing soft, poorly rooted bulbs back into prime condition, although wherever possible high-quality bulbs should be used for container cultivation. Loam-based mediums with good aeration, drainage and a high humus level are best, but soilless mediums can be used if compaction is avoided, adequate moisture is always provided, and the appropriate liquid feeding carried out.

In frost-prone areas in zones lower than 8, certain lilies should be grown under glass, among them *Ll. alexandrae*, *bakerianum**, *brownii* var. *australe*, *catesbaei*, *iridollae*, *longiflorum*, *neilgherrense**, *nepalense**, *nobilissimum*, *primulinum**, *sulphureum*, *wallichianum**. (Those marked * are stoloniform and are not considered suitable for normal pot culture.) In colder areas the following species may be added to the list: *Ll. candidum*, *formosanum*, *leucanthum*, *maritimum*, *occidentale*, *parryi*, *philippinense*, *pomponium*, *sargentiae*, *speciosum*.

The more tender lilies with stoloniform stems (marked * above) are not suitable for pot culture and may be grown in greenhouse borders in specially prepared soil with a high humus level. If this is not practical, then they may be planted in broad boxes with plentiful drainage provided. Depth of soil is not so much the criterion as lateral spread. It should be recognized that some lilies, like *L. speciosum*, require a long growth season and so do not perform satisfactorily where this is not available. Others, for instance *L. pomponium*, need a hot flowering and ripening season to grow well in subsequent years.

PROPAGATION. Lilies may be increased by seed, from above-ground stem bulbils and below-ground stem bulblets, by division of the main bulb and by scaling the bulb.

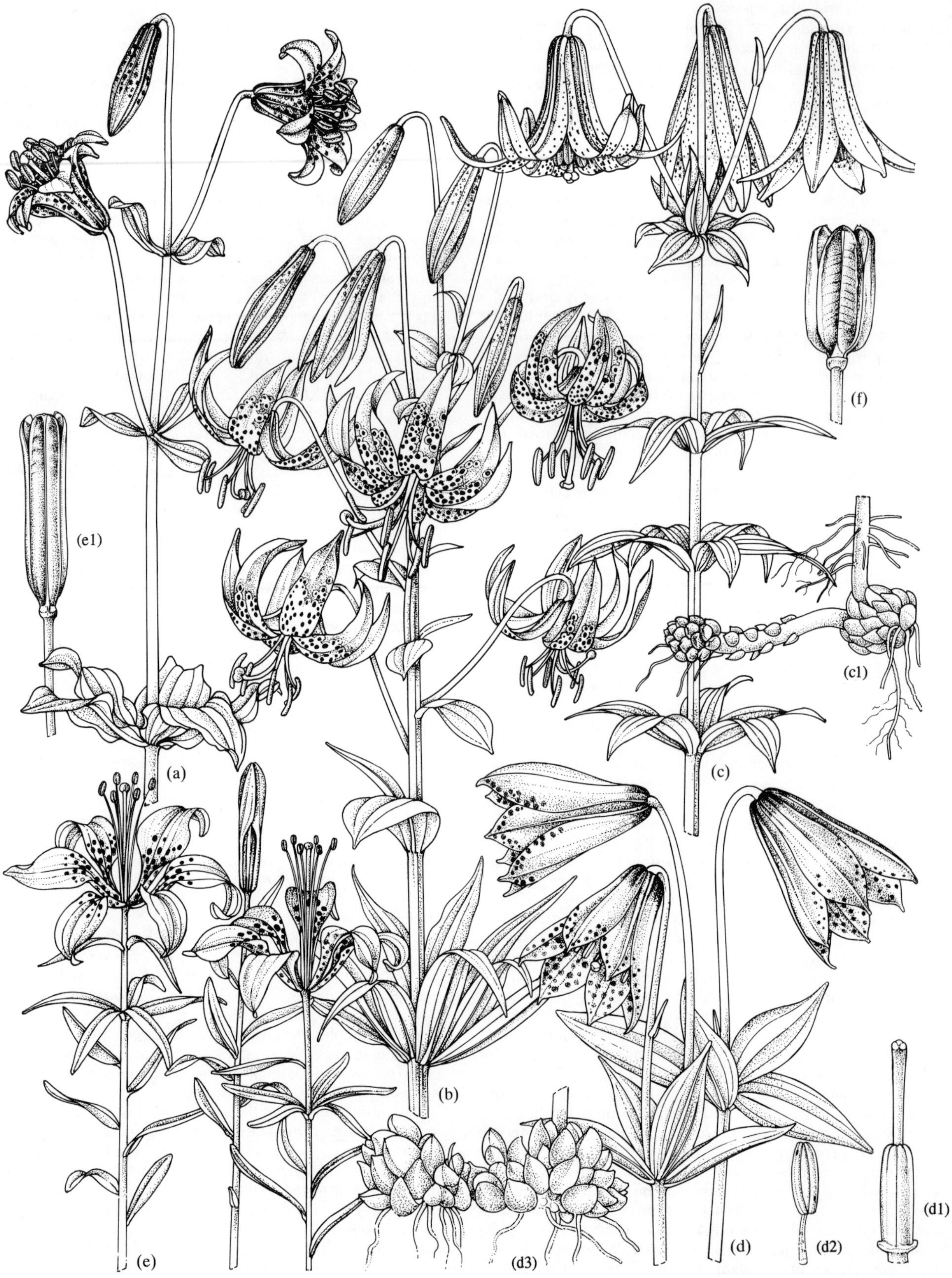


**Lilium American species** (a) *L. parvum* f. *crocatum* (×0.6) (b) *L. superbum* (×0.6) (c) *L. canadense* (×6) (c1) rhizomatous bulb (×0.6) (d) *L. grayi* (×0.6) (d1) stigma and style (d2) stamen (d3) bulb (×0.6) (e) *L. philadelphicum* (×0.5) (e1) *L. philadelphicum* var. *andinum*, capsule (×0.6) (f) *L. pardalinium* capsule (×0.6)

*Division.* Following maturity, most lilies will produce two or possibly three stems in the subsequent year. In remaking the beds in autumn or late winter, advantage can be taken of this and the bulbs carefully split up by prising apart or by cracking the basal plate with firm hold and deft motion before replanting. (If gross proliferation has occurred, then inherent disease – possibly virus – should be suspected and the bulbs discarded.)

*Bulblets.* Many lilies will produce these on the underground portion of the stem. When the stem has died down or begun to wither, wrench the stem from the bulb, holding the bulb firm. Most of the bulblets will also come away and can be picked out from among the stem roots; others may need to be eased out from the top soil. Those of sufficient size may be replanted around the main bulbs or grown on elsewhere. The smaller bulblets should be treated as for bulbils.

*Bulbils.* These occur most commonly on *L. lancifolium* and many Asiatic Hybrids, also *L. bulbiferum* in the typical form, *L. sargentiae*, *L. sulphureum*, and casually on other lilies, particularly when flowering is frustrated. When bulbils are few in number, planting may be in a pot of suitable size, potting on as soon as necessary or planting outdoors according to suitability of the season. Larger numbers of hardy kinds may be planted outside immediately into drills 2.5cm/1in. deep made in friable humus-rich soil. Once covered over, water well and keep free of weeds, avoiding damage to the single leaves arising from the bulbils which often have brittle petioles. Oriental Hybrids may often have a few stem bulbils arising in leaf axils near the base of the stem, frequently with a leaflet and extending root while still on the stem. These are best grown on in pots under glass for a season.

*Scales* (scaling). This is the most important method of propagation for producing large numbers of a particular cultivar. The method is very simple. The required number of firm clean scales is snapped off the base of the bulb. The scales are kept in conditions that prevent any dehydration, as in trays of moist sharp sand, or sealed in polythene bags. A callus grows on the base of the scale and in a few weeks one or more small bulbs will develop on the callus. When large enough, the bulblets are carefully prised from the scales and grown on in a sterilized medium. Scales of some lilies may produce bulblets freely, others are slow, difficult and the bulblets small in size and number. Numbers may usually be increased, especially with broad scales, if the base is cut to a depth of, say, 5mm/¼in. every 5mm/¼in. of its length. A similar effect is often produced when the scale is dipped in rooting hormone. The more bulblets produced per scale the smaller each individual will be and the more aftercare it will need in the early stages of growing on. Likewise, whereas the outer scales of a bulb may respond strongly, the innermost scales, being softer and smaller, are more likely to rot off, so if these are used they should first be treated with a fungicide solution. Small numbers of scales may be placed in thin polythene bags to which a small amount of moist sterilized sharp sand or sawdust has already been added. With most air excluded, the bags should be tightly folded over at the top two or three times, pleated in and tied firmly to prevent escape of moisture. Each bag should be clearly named and dated.

Asiatic, Oriental, Caucasian, Martagon, European and Eastern North American lilies benefit from being kept in a dark moderately warm (18–23°C/65–73°F) cupboard. Most Asiatic species and hybrids will usually grow away freely, according to season and conditions, but the other kinds should be given a cool period, equivalent to a winter season, as advocated for seeds below. These lilies should be scaled in the relatively dormant period from after flowering until early spring. Western American lilies should be scaled in autumn and late autumn/early winter. The small, numerous scales of these bulbs make cutting unnecessary; the often jointed scales may easily be snapped into separate portions and usually each section will provide a new bulblet. These should be kept in cool conditions (3–10°C/37–50°F) in dark or reasonably dark conditions, allowing them to initiate bulblets, and as the winter progresses into early spring, produce young leaves without recourse to refrigeration. At this stage they are easy to pot up (leaving the scales attached), 1cm/½in. apart in 15cm/6in. half-pots in sterilized medium, preferably with additional sharp sand. Watered in, they will grow in this medium for the season, requiring occasional liquid feeds, the stronger kinds being transferred as a whole into deep pots when necessary and practical to maintain their active growth. Asiatic spp. and hybrid lily bulbs may be treated likewise, teasing them gently from the scales with, or preferably without, top growth yet showing. Bulblets from their dormancy period in the refrigerator should be potted up in similar manner.

It is essential to take the greatest care of all bulblets and to avoid handling the roots, exerting minimal pressure. If leaflets must be handled, hold only the tip. After spending a season in pots, the new small bulbs should be suitable for planting outside in nursery beds, the tender kinds for planting in large pots. Other containers which may be used for scales are half-pots, deep seed trays and propagating trays, using an open medium of equal parts peat/sharp sand or similar material; if refrigeration is to be given, convenience and ease of storage are key factors – the quantities of compost required at this stage are minimal.

*Seed* is often the best and easiest means of propagating the species. Seed from hybrid lilies, produce either seed parent accurately, but produce a variable new race of hybrids. Seed will produce virus-free seedlings.

Seed germination may be epigeal or hypogeal. If epigeal, the cotyledon rises above ground, similar in action to the germination of an onion seedling, with the first true leaf, normally broader, appearing soon after. If hypogeal, the cotyledon remains below ground at germination, feeding a tiny growing bulb from the endosperm; usually a genetic delay mechanism inhibits growth above ground until a cold period, representing winter, has passed. Thus the first sign of the seedling is a true leaf in spring. The species in each group are listed below. It will be noted that a few members of the epigeal group exhibit delay characteristics, whereas it is very rare for hypogeal seed to be witnessed above ground without previous delay, except in respect of the Western American species which, despite their differing native climatic conditions, germinate in a cool (winter) period, emerging in the spring with a true leaf following in a seemingly continuous process.

EPIGEAL GERMINATION. (a) Immediate: *Ll. amabile*, *arboricola*, *bakerianum*, *brownii*, *callosum*, *candidum*, *catesbaei* (?), *cernuum*, *concolor*, *dauricum*, *davidii*, *duchartrei*, *formosanum*, *henrici*, *henryi*, *lankongense*, *leichtlinii*, *leucanthum*, *longiflorum*, *mackliniae*, *maculatum*, *nanum*, *neilgherrense*, *nepalense*, *oxypetalum*, *papilliferum*, *philadelphicum*, *philippinense*, *primulinum*, *pumilum*, *pyrenaicum*, *regale*, *sargentiae*, *sherriffiae*, *sulphureum*, *taliense*, *tigrinum*, *wallichianum*, *wardii*. (b) Delayed: *Ll. carniolicum*, *chalcedonicum*, *ponticum*. (c) Autumnal/winter: *L. pomponium*.

HYPOGEAL GERMINATION. (a) Immediate: *Ll. iridollae* (?), *medeoloides* (?), *parryi*. (b) Delayed: *Ll. auratum*, *bulbiferum*, *canadense*, *ciliatum*, *distichum*, *grayi*, *hansonii*, *japonicum*, *kesselringianum*, *ledebourii*, *martagon*, *michauxii*, *michiganense*, *monadelphum*, *polyphyllum*, *rubellum*, *speciosum*, *superbum*, *tsingtauense*. (c) Autumnal/winter: *Ll. alexandrae**, *bolanderi*, *columbianum*, *humboldtii*, *kelleyanum*, *kelloggii*, *maritimum*, *nobilissimum**, *occidentale*, *pardalinum*, *parvum*, *pitkinense*, *rubescens*, *vollmeri*, *washingtonianum*, *wigginsii*. (*Oriental species germinating in similar manner to those on the American Pacific coast.)

'Epigeal' seeds should be sown according to conventional methods. Ordinary seed trays are too shallow, whereas half-pots and other plastic containers of similar depth are very suitable. Adequate drainage may be ensured by covering the base of the container with potting grit to 1cm/½in. depth before adding a medium-fertility loam-based mix, or one with slow-release fertilizers, with sharp sand added to approximately 20% of the whole. This allows the seedlings to be retained in the original container for a full season, or even for two seasons if necessary, should *en bloc* potting-on to deeper containers be feasible. The consistency of the compost should allow the roots of the seedlings to be freed one from another with relative ease and so produce the least damage when transplanted. Peat-based mediums are not usually so suitable even with extra sand added and will require more frequent liquid feeding.

This method is also suitable for 'hypogeal' seeds, but then conventional germination would require two growing seasons. 'Hypogeal' seeds may be treated in far less space and time by germinating them in thin polythene bags, each containing a small quantity of a moist sterilised perlite mixture. Seed may be freed of superficial fungus spores by immersion in household bleach. Whereas good quality fresh seed should conventionally be thinly sown, many seeds may go into one bag with relatively little compost, sufficient only for ensuring moist seed, but the resulting seedlings must be pricked out individually, with great care, with their initial leaf and fragile root. The bags should be tightly sealed, labelled with name and date and, except for western American kinds which need cool conditions, kept in a warm cupboard (18–23°C/65–73°F). Germination varies, but will take at least three weeks, possibly as much as six or more, and then the bulbs will increase in size over about a further three weeks. Older seed would take longer than indicated. When the tiny bulbs look plump and white, the polythene bags – after indicating the date on the label – may be transferred to a refrigerator. The precise time required in these cool (not freezing) conditions varies. Two months may be sufficient for many species, but a period closer to three months ensures regular growth once the seedlings have been pricked out. (Keeping the bags in the refrigerator over-long will not necessarily inhibit or delay growth of the seedlings. When ready they will send forth their first leaves and, with lack of light, these will be soft and etiolated; losses following pricking out could be considerable.) Using sterile compost, half-pots are large enough for first growth.

When roots fill the pot, seedlings may be transferred *en bloc* to a pot of full depth and, if the seedlings are particularly vigorous, a wider one, with fresh sterile compost in the base and around the sides. Further growth in these conditions will produce seedlings large enough to handle easily to place in nursery beds, or even in their final position depending on species and garden conditions. The best time to do this is spring when the young bulbs will grow fast. Choose moist mild conditions, when night frosts are not imminent. An outdoor site for seedlings should be in semi-shade with fair protection from harsher winds. The free-draining friable loam should have a high humus content, preferably with a pH 5.5–6.5, suitably free of pests and weeds.

MICROPROPAGATION. *Tissue culture* has a number of advantages for the lily grower: it can produce a continuing supply of bulblets; it can take reproductive tissue from many parts of the plant; it can (but not necessarily) produce virus-free material from a virus-infected plant; it can aid the production of difficult hybridization; cultures can be put on 'ice' and so stored in a 'bank', thus helping conservation and the storage of genetic material.

Various kinds of material may be used for tissue culture. (a) The seed embryos, best taken from green seed pods, being at this stage virtually sterile and easily removed. (b) Basal pieces of bulb scale up to 5mm/¼in. cube from clean outer scales; contamination is generally high from this source as soil-borne pathogens are often growing *inside* the tissue. (c) Flower buds, either using tepal sections or ovary sections. The process takes longer than with other material – small buds are quicker – but the material is generally less contaminated and yields a fair proportion of virus-free stock, when this is the aim. (d) Basal portions of young leaves taken well before flowering time. (e) Shoot tips – traditional meristem cultures – though these are not normal nor best with lilies.

The tissue, once it has been cleaned properly, needs to be grown on agar-nutrient mediums containing, as necessary, growth regulators or 'hormones', auxins for cell division and cytokinins for cell division and shoot initiation. The dry mediums are available as proprietary products. The aim is to produce a reasonable amount of callus on which bulblets will grow, and for those bulblets to grow leaves in due course. Variations in the growing medium are necessary at particular stages to achieve this, aided by variations in light and temperature. Careful weaning from cultures to outdoor life is required, maintaining sterile conditions as carefully and closely as possible in the early days. Bulblet cultures will normally need a cool period of up to eight weeks before active growth recommences.

*All-Year-Round Cultivation*. The production of lilies for sale as cut flowers and pot-grown plants at all seasons is based on micropropagation at specific intervals from the desired time of maturity. The interval varies according to the variety involved. This AYR cultivation is widely practised, especially in the Netherlands and California.

PESTS AND DISEASES. Attacks by aphids must be dealt with promptly, they lurk behind partly exposed young flower-buds and under fresh unfolding foliage. Botrytis may normally be controlled, if dealt with promptly with appropriate fungicide, preferably systemic, on a regular basis. Spray when the foliage is dry, thoroughly wetting the undersurface of the leaves, as this is where infection originates. *L. candidum* is particularly vulnerable and can carry the disease on its overwintering basal foliage, so it should be sprayed before stem growth begins and, if signs are visible, in autumn.

Basal rot (*Fusarium oxysporum*) may attack and destroy bulbs, especially where another pathogen is present, so it is best to plant high-quality bulbs fresh and clean, giving them good cultivation, never too wet or too dry, nor allowing them to be exposed or out of the ground for any longer than absolutely necessary. New bulbs should not be planted in soil where others may have died. Remedial action with affected bulbs is to cut away and burn all dead and rotting parts, sterilizing the remainder in 2% formalin or immersing in a suitable fungicide solution. Fortunately, many newer hybrids are more resistant, and with better commercial practice and the use of virus-free stocks this disease is less formidable than heretofore.

I. ERECT LILIES. Flowers erect, open.

**1** Tepals narrowed (clawed) at base.

1.1 Leaves in whorls of 6–8 along stem.
*L. philadelphicum*.

1.2 Leaves scattered along stem (a single whorl may be present near the inflorescence).

1.2.1 Tepals recurved throughout.
*Ll. concolor, dauricum, wilsonii*.

1.2.2 Tepals recurved at tips.
*Ll. catesbaei, philadelphicum* var. *andinum*.

1.2.3 Tepals not recurved at tips.
*Ll. bulbiferum, ×hollandicum, maculatum*.

**2** Tepals not narrowed (clawed) at base.

2.1 Leaves partly in a single conspicuous whorl of to 16 units, otherwise smaller and scattered. Flowers yellow, orange-yellow, vermilion or red.
*L. tsingtauense*.

2.2 Leaves scattered throughout. Flowers white.
*L. nobilissimum*.

II. HORIZONTAL OR PENDULOUS-FLOWERED LILIES. Flowers horizontal or pendulous, but not 'martagon' or 'turk's cap' in form.

**3** At least some leaves in 1 or more whorls.

3.1 Whorls 1–4, leaves otherwise scattered.

3.1.1 Flowers white (ageing purple).
*L. rubescens*.

3.1.2 Flowers yellow or lemon-yellow.
*Ll. oxypetalum* (whorl only just under inflorescence), *parryi*.

3.1.3 Flowers crimson or orange.
*L. maritimum*.

3.2 Leaves all or mostly in whorls.

3.2.1 Flowers yellow, orange or red.
*Ll. canadense, grayi, parvum*.

3.2.2 Flowers maroon, pink or white.
*Ll. bolanderi, kelloggii* (almost of martagon form), *washingtonianum*.

**4** Leaves all scattered, not forming any whorls.

4.1 Tepals at least 10cm. Flowers bowl- or funnel-shaped.

4.1.1 Flowers bowl-shaped; tepals basically white, at least inside.
*Ll. alexandrae, auratum*.

4.1.2 Flowers funnel-shaped; tepals pink inside and out.
*L. japonicum*.

**Lilium Asiatic species** (a) *L. speciosum* var. *rubrum* (×0.5) (a1) flower (×0.5) (a2) bulb (×0.25) (b) *L. leucanthum* var. *centifolium* (b1) flower (×0.5) (b2) capsule (×0.5) (b3) bulb (×0.5) (c) *L. maculatum* (×0.5) (d) *L. pumilum* (×0.5) (e) *L. nepalense* (×0.5) (f) *L. bakerianum* (×0.5) (g) *L. lancifolium* (×0.5)

4.1.3 Flowers funnel-shaped; tepals green-white to green-yellow, sometimes red inside towards base.
*L. nepalense* (uniformly coloured in var. *concolor*).

4.1.4 Flowers funnel-shaped; tepals white inside and out, forming a basal tube.
*L. longiflorum*.

4.1.5 Flowers funnel-shaped; tepals basically cream or white inside, at least partly green or pink or (most often) purple outside.

a Tepals reaching over 20cm.
*Ll. sulphureum, wallichianum*.

b Tepals not more than 20cm.
*Ll. brownii, formosanum,* ×*imperiale, leucanthum* var. *centifolium, longiflorum* var. *takeshima, philippinense, regale, sargentiae*.

4.2 Tepals 6–15cm; flowers funnel-shaped, basically yellow.
*Ll. primulinum, rhodopaeum*.

4.3 Tepals 1–10cm. Flowers funnel-, bell-, or cup-shaped (the last only in *L. oxypetalum*), occasionally almost martagon (turk's cap) in form (*L. monadelphum*).

4.3.1 Flowers basically yellow or yellow-green, at least inside.
*Ll. kesselringianum, monadelphum, nanum* var. *flavidum, oxypetalum, sherriffiae*.

4.3.2 Flowers basically white inside.
*Ll. bakerianum, candidum* (overwintering basal rosette of leaves produced in autumn), *henrici* (segments suffused with purple).

4.3.3 Flowers basically purple to pink inside.
*Ll. henrici, mackliniae, nanum, oxypetalum* var. *insigne, rubellum*.

III. MARTAGON OR TURK'S CAP LILIES. Flowers usually pendulous, of 'martagon' or 'turk's cap' form

**5** At least some leaves in 1 or more whorls.

5.1 Whorls 1–3, leaves otherwise scattered.

5.1.1 Tepals white or pink; tube elongate, yellow-green. Leaves lanceolate to narrowly elliptic.
*L. polyphyllum* (see also lead 6.2.1: tube somewhat elongate).

5.1.2 Tepals scarlet, yellow towards base. Leaves linear.
*L. pitkinense*.

5.1.3 Tepals green to yellow to apricot to orange to orange-red. Leaves lanceolate to oblanceolate to narrowly elliptic.
*Ll. columbianum, distichum, iridollae* (with a late-developing, overwintering basal rosette of leaves), *kelleyanum, medeoloides, vollmeri, wigginsii*.

5.2 Whorls more than 3, sometimes including nearly all leaves on the stem.

5.2.1 Tepals remaining white throughout flowering.
*L. martagon* vars *albiflorum, album*.

5.2.2 Tepals initially white, later becoming suffused with pink. (Not quite a true martagon; see lead 3.2.2.)
*L. kelloggii*.

5.2.3 Tepals dull pink. Whorls many.
*Ll. martagon, martagon* var. *caucasicum, hirsutum*.

5.2.4 Tepals in some way orange.
*Ll. hansonii, humboldtii, michauxii, michiganense, occidentale, pardalinum,* ×*pardaboldtii, superbum*.

5.2.5 Tepals in some way crimson.
*Ll. pardalinum, pardalinum* var. *giganteum*.

5.2.6 Tepals maroon or deep red.
*L. martagon* vars *cattaniae, pilosiusculum* and *sanguineo-purpureum*.

**6** Leaves all scattered (alternate or spirally arranged).

6.1 Leaves linear to linear-lanceolate, sometimes very crowded.

6.1.1 Tepals marble white.
*L. taliense*.

6.1.2 Tepals basically yellow.
*Ll. ledebourii, leichtlinii* (flowers rather widely spreading), *pyrenaicum, pyrenaicum* ssp. *carniolicum,* ssp. *carniolicum* var. *albanicum* and var. *jankae, pyrenaicum* ssp. *ponticum,* ×*testaceum* (variable).

6.1.3 Tepals orange to red.
*Ll. callosum, davidii,* ×*davimottiae, leichtlinii* var. *maximowiczii, pyrenaicum* ssp. *carniolicum, pyrenaicum* ssp. *ponticum,* ssp. *ponticum* var. *artvinense* and f. *rubrum*.

6.1.4 Tepals scarlet.
*Ll. pomponium, pumilum*.

6.1.5 Tepals maroon to purple to lilac to pink
*Ll. cernuum, papilliferum*.

6.2 Leaves lanceolate to elliptic to obovate or ovate.

6.2.1 Tepals basically white or cream.
*Ll. ciliatum, duchartrei, polyphyllum* (see also lead 5.1.1; tube somewhat elongate), *speciosum, speciosum* var. *album*.

6.2.2 Tepals basically yellow.
*Ll. amabile* var. *luteum, ciliatum, henryi* var. *citrinum, iridollae* (see also lead 5.1.3), *monadelphum* (not quite a true martagon; see also lead 4.3.1), *lancifolium* var. *flaviflorum*.

6.2.3 Tepals orange to red.
*Ll. amabile, chalcedonicum, henryi, lancifolium* (tepals later more widely spreading), *lancifolium* var. *fortunei* and var. *splendens, speciosum*.

6.2.4 Tepals rose or carmine.
*L. speciosum* var. *magnificum,* var. *roseum* and var. *rubrum*.

6.2.5 Tepals mauve to pink or pink-purple.
*Ll. lankongense, wardii*.

***L. alexandrae*** (Wallace) Coutts. UKE-YURI. Stems to 1m; bulbils above and below ground; stem-rooting; bulbs concentric, to 15cm wide, scales white, lanceolate, acute. Lvs 20×4cm, lanceolate to ovate, 3–5-veined, petiolate. Fls 1–5, fragrant, 16×10cm, bowl-shaped, horizontal or erect; tepals to 18×3–4cm, white with green bases and tips, exterior occasionally striped pink; stamens shorter than pistil; anth. and pollen brown; style pale green, stigma brown. Fr. 5cm; seeds brown, 7×5mm. Summer. Japan, Ryukyu Is. Z5.

***L. amabile*** Palib. Stems to 90cm, pubesc., stem-rooting; bulbs concentric, 4×3cm, scales white, broad. Lvs to 9cm, scattered, lanceolate, 3-veined, absent on lower part of stem, numerous towards top. Fls 1–5, turk's-cap, in a raceme, malodorous; pedicels 2.5–5cm, pubesc.; tepals 5.5cm, red with dark purple spots, 2–3 fleshy papillae on upper surface; anth. dark brown; pollen red; stigma red-brown. Fr. 3×2cm. Summer. Korea. var. ***luteum*** anon. Fls yellow. Z5.

***L. auratum*** Lindl. GOLDED-RAYED LILY OF JAPAN; MOUNTAIN LILY; YAMA-YURI. Stems 60–150cm, sometimes to 225cm, purple-green, stem-rooting; bulbs concentric, 10cm diam., scales pale yellow, lanceolate. Lvs to 22×4cm, numerous, scattered, lanceolate, dark green, 5–7-veined, petiolate. Fls 6–30, 30cm wide, bowl-shaped, horizontal or slightly pendulous, in a raceme, very fragrant; tepals 12–18×4–5cm, white with yellow or crimson central streaks and crimson-spotted, fleshy papillae on basal part, tips recurved; pollen chocolate to red. Fr. 8cm; seeds 11×9mm. Short-lived, requiring lime-free soil in full sun with shade provided by low-growing plants. Summer–autumn. Japan (Honshu Is.). 'Apollo': central band and spots ruby-red. 'Crimson Beauty': cherry red, margin white. 'Praecox': heavily spotted; early flowering. 'Rubrum': pet. band crimson. 'Tom Thumb': dwarf. Crossed with *L. speciosum, L. japonicum* and *L. rubellum* to give rise to a wide range of cvs. var. ***platyphyllum*** Bak. Stems to 2.3m. Lvs broadly lanceolate. Fls larger, fewer spots on tepals. var. ***rubro-vittatum*** Duchartre. Band on tepals yellow at base, deep crimson at apex. var. ***virginale*** Duchartre. Stems to 2m. Albino form, tepals white, streaked yellow, spotted pale yellow or pink. 'Album': fls white. Z6.

***L.*** ×***aurelianense*** Debras. (*L. henryi* × *L. sargentiae.*) Stems to 2.5m, stem-rooting. Lvs 12×3.5cm, lanceolate, 3-veined, bulbils in axils. Fls to 12, scented, 12.5cm wide, horizontal or slightly pendulous. Autumn. Garden origin. Many cvs, white to apricot and pink fls, some not lime-tolerant.

***L. bakerianum*** Collett & Hemsl. Stems 60–90cm, usually hairy, stem-rooting; bulbs stoloniform, 3.5×5cm, scales white, 2×1cm, lanceolate. Lvs 10×1.5cm, scattered on upper part of stem, linear to lanceolate, 1–3-veined. Fls 1–6, bell-shaped, pendulous; tepals white, interior spotted red-brown, exterior tinged green, 7×1.5cm; anth. orange. Fr. 3.5cm. Summer. N Burma, SW China (Sichuan, Yunnan). Z8.

***L. bolanderi*** S. Wats. Stems to 140cm, glaucous green, marked brown; bulbs concentric, 5cm wide, scales to 5×9cm, yellow, lanceolate. Lvs to 5×1.5cm, in whorls, sessile, oblanceolate, 1–3-nerved. Fls 1–18, 6.5cm wide, funnel-shaped, pendulous; tepals 3–4.5×1cm, maroon, interior spotted dark red or purple, exterior green at base, tube yellow, spotted chocolate; anth. purple; pollen deep yellow; stigma purple. Fr. 4cm. Summer. W US (S Oregon, N California). Z5.

***L. brownii*** Miellez. Stems to 1m, green tinged dark brown, stem-rooting; bulbs concentric, 7cm wide, scales ovate, cream. Lvs to 25×2cm, scattered, lanceolate, 5–7-veined. Fls fragrant, 1–4, funnel-shaped; tepals 12–15×2.5–6.5cm, interior white, exterior purple, tinged green; anth. brown; pollen red-brown. Fr. 5cm. Summer. China, Burma. var. ***australe*** (Stapf) Stearn. Stems to 3m. Interior of tepals white, exterior flushed green. SE China, Hong Kong. var. ***viridulum*** Bak. Stem green. Fls strongly scented, exterior of tepals tinged yellow-green and pale purple, tube interior yellow, fading to white. China. Z6.

***L. bulbiferum*** L. FIRE LILY. Stems 40–150cm, ribbed, green, occasionally spotted purple, woolly toward top, stem-rooting, green bulbils in lf axils; bulbs concentric, 9cm wide, scales lanceolate, white. Lvs 10×2cm, lanceolate, scattered, 3–7-veined. Fls usually to 5, occasionally to 50, erect, cup-shaped, tepals 6–8.5×2–3cm, bright orange, bases and tips deeper in colour, interior spotted maroon; anth. brown; pollen orange. Grows in well-drained soil in summer shade. Summer. S Europe. var. ***croceum*** (Chaix) Pers. Tepals orange, bulbils absent. Z7.

***L.*** ×***burbankii*** anon. (*L. pardalinum* × *L. parryi.*) Stems 1–2m. Lvs in whorls. Fls horizontal, fragrant; tepals reflexed, 8cm, yellow, spotted chocolate-brown, tips red. Summer. Garden origin. Z5.

***L. callosum*** Sieb. & Zucc. SLIMSTEM LILY. Stems to 90cm, green, stem-rooting; bulbs concentric, 2.5cm wide, scales oval, white. Lvs 8–13×0.3–0.8cm, scattered, linear, 3–5-veined, apices thickened. Fls to 10, pendulous turk's-cap, 4cm wide, in a raceme; pedicels 7cm; tepals 3–4cm, orange-red, spotted black toward base; pollen orange. Fr. 4×2cm. Late summer. China, Japan, Korea, Taiwan, USSR (Amur region). Z6.

**Lilium European species** (a) *L. candidum* (×0.5) (b) *L. chalcedonicum* (×6), (b1) single leaf (×2) (c) *L. martagon* flower spike (×0.5), (c1) seed (×3), (c2) capsule (×2), (c3) bulb (×0.5) (d) *L. monadelphum* (×0.5) (e) *L. pyrennaicum* (×0.5) (f) *L. bulbiferum*, bulbils in leaf axils (×0.5)

***L. canadense*** L. MEADOW LILY; WILD MEADOW LILY. Stems to 1.5m, green, stem-rooting; bulbs stoloniferous, scales white or pale yellow. Lvs 15×2cm, lanceolate to oblanceolate, mostly in whorls, veins 5–7. Fls 10–12, bell-shaped, pendulous, in an umbel; pedicels to 20cm; tepals 5–7.5×1–2.5cm, yellow, basally spotted maroon, apices recurved; pollen yellow to red-brown. Fr. 3cm. Plant in moist but well-drained soil. Summer. Eastern N America (Quebec to Alabama). 'Chocolate Chips': tepal exterior and tips crimson, fading to orange then yellow toward the interior base, spots large. 'Fire Engine': tepals slightly recurved, exterior and interior tips crimson, fading to orange then yellow near the base; pollen burnt-orange. 'Melted Spots': lvs whorled; fls yellow-orange, spots dense on the basal two-thirds. 'Peaches and Pepper': fls peach-orange; tepals recurved, finely spotted. var. ***coccineum*** Pursh. Fls red, throat yellow. var. ***editorum*** Fern. Lvs broader than var. *L. canadense*. Fls red, tepals 8–13mm wide. Appalachian Mts. Z5.

***L. candidum*** L. MADONNA LILY; WHITE LILY. Stems 1–2m, dark maroon; bulbs concentric, 9cm wide, scales white or pale yellow, ovate. Basal lvs 22×5cm, 3–5-veined, produced in autumn, retained in winter, stem lvs scattered, 7.5×1cm, lanceolate. Fls 5–20, funnel-shaped, fragrant, in a raceme; tepals 5–8×1–4cm, white, interior base yellow, tips recurved; pollen bright yellow. Fr. not usually formed in cult. Summer. Balkans, E Mediterranean. var. ***plenum*** West. Fls double. Very rare. var. ***salonikae*** Stoker. Stems dark green. Fls fertile; tepals widely spreading; pollen pale yellow. W Greece. Z6.

***L. catesbaei*** Walter. LEOPARD LILY; PINE LILY; TIGER LILY. Stems 30–60cm; bulbs concentric, 2.5cm wide, scales lanceolate, white. Lvs to 10cm, alternate, lanceolate, acute. Fls 1–2, erect, cup-shaped; tepals 5–12×1–2.5cm, bottom half of tepals narrowed into a claw, interior deep yellow, tips recurved, scarlet, exterior pale yellow to green; pollen orange-red; stigma dark red. Late summer. SE US. Z5.

***L. cernuum*** Komar. NODDING LILY. Stems to 60cm, green, sometimes spotted brown, ribbed, stem-rooting; bulbs 3×3cm, scales imbricate, lanceolate to ovate, thick, white, smooth. Lvs 8–15×0.1–0.5cm, scattered, mostly crowded on centre third of stem, 1–3-veined, sessile. Fls 1–14, turk's-cap, 3.5cm wide, fragrant, in a pendent raceme; pedicels spreading, 6–10cm; tepals lilac, purple, pink or occasionally white, spotted purple; pollen lilac. Fr. 2cm; seeds 6–7×4.5mm. Summer. Korea, NE Manchuria, USSR (Ussuri region). Z3.

***L. chalcedonicum*** L. SCARLET TURK'S-CAP LILY; RED MARTAGON OF CONSTANTINOPLE. Stems 45–150cm, stem-rooting; bulbs concentric, 7.5×10cm, scales pale yellow, lanceolate. Lvs to 11.5×1.5cm, edged silver, spirally arranged, sessile, 3–5-veined. Fls to 12, pendulous turk's-cap, 7.5cm wide, slightly scented; tepals scarlet, recurved, without spots; pollen scarlet. Fr. 3×2cm. Summer. Greece, S Albania. 'Maculatum': scarlet, spotted black. *L. chalcedonicum* × *L.* ×*testaceum* has produced a number of cvs including 'Apollo', 'Hephaistos' and 'Zeus'. Z5.

***L. ciliatum*** P.H. Davis. Stems 60–150cm, white-hairy on upper part until fls drop, stem-rooting; bulbs 10–12cm wide, scales yellow, narrow. Lvs 7–12.5×1.5cm, spirally arranged, glabrous, margins hairy. Fls 5–8, sometimes to 21, turk's-cap, 5cm wide, scented; tepals ivory, cream or pale yellow, interior purple-brown toward base, upper portion finely spotted; pollen orange-red. Fr. 2.5cm. Summer. NE Turkey. Z5.

***L. columbianum*** Bak. COLUMBIA TIGER LILY; OREGON LILY. Stems to 2.5m; bulbs concentric, 4×4cm, scales white, lanceolate. Lvs 5–14×1–4cm, oblanceolate, 3–5-veined, upper lvs scattered, lower lvs in whorls. Fls 6–10, occasionally to 40, pendulous turk's-cap, 7.5cm wide, in a long-pedicellate raceme; tepals 3.5–6.5×0.8–1.2cm, recurved, yellow to orange-red, base spotted maroon; anthers 6–11mm, pollen deep yellow to brown. Summer. Western N America. 'Ingramii': fls large, many deep orange. Z5.

***L. concolor*** Salisb. MORNING STAR LILY. Stems 30–90cm, green flushed purple, lightly pubesc., stem-rooting; bulbs concentric, 2×2cm, scales ovate-lanceolate, white, closely overlapping. Lvs 8.5×1.5cm, scattered, linear or linear-lanceolate, 3–7-veined, ciliate on margins and below. Fls 1–10, erect, star-shaped, 8.5cm wide; pedicels erect, 5cm, 2 basal leafy bracts; tepals 3–4×1cm, recurved, scarlet, glossy, unspotted; pollen red. Fr. 2cm. Summer. China (Hupei, Yunnan). 'Racemosum': stems taller than type of species; more vigorous. var. ***partheneion*** (Sieb. & De Vries) Bak. Fls red, streaked green and yellow, black spots few. var. ***pulchellum*** (Fisch.) Reg. Stems green, not pubesc. Fls spotted, buds woolly. Summer. NE Asia. Z4.

***L. ×dalhansonii*** Baden-Powell. *(L. hansonii × L. martagon* var. *cattaniae.)* Stems 1.5–2m, stem-rooting. Fls turk's-cap, 3cm, malodorous; tepals recurved, dark maroon, to pink, white or yellow, spotted darker; style purple. Summer. 'Backhouse hybrids': fls cream, yellow, pink to maroon with darker spots. Damson': fls plum-purple. 'Destiny': fls yellow, spotted brown; tepal tips reflexed. 'Discovery': fls turk's-cap, rose-lilac, base white, tinged pink, spotted deep crimson, tips darker, exterior pink with a silvery sheen.

***L. dauricum*** Ker-Gawl. Stems to 75cm, ribbed, green, spotted red-brown, woolly, stem-rooting; bulbs 1.5×2cm, stoloniferous, scales 1×0.6cm, white, lanceolate. Lvs 5–15×0.5–0.3cm, scattered, linear to lanceolate, 3–5-veined, margins hairy, whorl of small lvs below fls. Fls 1–6, erect, cup-shaped, to 10cm wide, in an umbel; pedicels hairy, to 9cm, spreading; tepals 5–10×1.5–3.5cm, recurved, oblanceolate, vermilion to scarlet, spotted brown-red, base yellow, narrow; pollen red. Fr. 5cm. Summer. NE Asia. Z5.

***L. davidii*** Elwes. Stems 1–1.4m, green, spotted brown, stem-rooting; bulbs concentric or stoloniferous, 4×4cm, scales white, pink when exposed to light, ovate or ovate-lanceolate. Lvs 6–10×0.2–0.4cm, numerous, linear, acute, dark green, 1-veined, margins finely toothed and inrolled, basally white-hairy. Fls 5–20, turk's-cap, unscented, pendulous, in a raceme, buds hairy; pedicels to 15cm, horizontal, stiff; tepals to 8cm, vermilion spotted purple; pollen orange or scarlet. Fr. 3.5×2cm. Summer. W China (Sichuan, Yunnan). var. ***unicolor*** (Hoog) Cotton. Stems shorter, to 1m; bulbs not stoloniferous. Lvs more numerous and longer, very crowded. Fls paler, spots red, mauve or absent. Summer. N China. var. ***willmottiae*** (Wils.) Raffill. Stems to 2m, arching; bulbs stoloniferous. Lvs to 6mm wide. Fls to 40. Summer. China (Shensi, Hupei, Sichuan, NW Yunnan). Preston Hybrids, Patterson Hybrids, Fiesta Strain and North Hybrids developed from *L. davidii*; see LILIES. Z5.

***L. davimottiae***. Name given to hybrid between *L. davidii* var. *davidii* and *L. davidii* var. *willmottiae*.

***L. distichum*** Nak. in Kamib. KOCHANG LILY. Resembles *L. tsingtauense* but tepals recurved and bulb scales jointed. Stems 60–120cm, hollow, lower part ribbed, stem-rooting; bulbs to 3×4cm, concentric, scales 1.5–2×0.4–0.6cm, white, lanceolate, jointed. Lvs 8–15×2–4cm, obovate-elliptical, in 1–2 whorls in middle of stem, none below, sparsely scattered above. Fls 3–8, turk's-cap, horizontal or slightly pendulous, in a raceme; pedicels 6–8cm; tepals 3.5–4.5×0.6–1.3cm, recurved, pale orange usually with darker spots. Fr. 2×1.5cm. Summer. E USSR, N Korea, NE China. Z5.

***L. duchartrei*** Franch. MARBLE MARTAGON. Stems 60–100cm, green flushed brown, ribbed, white-hairy in lf axils, stem-rooting; bulbs stoloniferous, 2.5–4cm wide, scales white, ovate, acute. Lvs 10.5×1.5cm, dark green above, pale green beneath, lanceolate, scattered, sessile, margin rough, veins 3–5. Fls to 12, turk's-cap, pendulous, fragrant, in an umbel; pedicels 7–15cm; tepals recurved, interior white, spotted deep purple, tubes green at base, exterior white flushed purple, ageing red; pollen orange. Fr. purple, 2.5×1.5cm; seeds 1.8cm. Summer. W China (NW Yunnan, W Sichuan, SW Kansu). Z5.

***L. formosanum*** Wallace. Stems 30–150cm, purple-brown toward base, 1–3 per bulb, stem-rooting; bulbs 3×4cm, stoloniferous, white tinged purple, scales oblong-ovate, acute. Lvs 7.5–20×1cm, scattered, dark green, oblong-lanceolate, spreading, margins recurved, 3–7-veined, scattered, crowded near base. Fls 1–2, sometimes to 10, in umbels, fragrant, funnel-shaped, horizontal; pedicels 5–15cm, erect; tepals 12–20×2.5–5cm, interior white, exterior white flushed purple, tips recurved, nectary furrows green; anth. yellow to purple; pollen brown or yellow. Fr. 7–9×2cm; seeds 0.5cm. Often grown as bienn. Summer–autumn. Taiwan. var. ***pricei*** Stoker. Stems 30–60cm. Fls 1–2, more deeply coloured than species type. Summer. Taiwan. Z5.

***L. grayi*** S. Wats. Stems to 1.75m; bulbs stoloniferous, scales white, fleshy, to 1cm. Lvs to 5–12×1.5–3cm, lanceolate or oblong-lanceolate, sessile, in whorls. Fls 1–8, unscented, bell-shaped; pedicels to 20cm; tepals 6.25×0.5cm, interior light red with yellow base, spotted purple, exterior crimson, darker towards base, upper part spreading, lower part forming a tube 3×0.5cm; anth. yellow; pollen orange-brown; style red, stigma green. Fr. 4cm; seeds 9×7mm. Summer. E US (Alleghany Mts). 'Gulliver's Thimble': fls bright crimson. Z5.

***L. hansonii*** Moore. Stems to 120cm, green, stem-rooting; bulbs 7×6cm, stoloniferous, scales yellow-white, purple when exposed, triangular to ovate. Lvs 18×4cm, dark green, oblanceolate to elliptic, 3–5-veined. Fls 3–12, turk's-cap, fragrant, pendulous; tepals 3–4×1.5cm, thick, recurved, oblanceolate, deep orange-yellow, spotted purple-brown toward base; anth. purple; pollen yellow; style green. Fr. 3.5×3.5cm, rarely produced. Summer. E USSR, Korea, Japan. Z5.

***L. henrici*** Franch. Stems to 90cm, smooth, green flushed brown; bulbs concentric, 5×4.5cm, scales 1.5–3.5×1.0–1.5cm, lanceolate, purple. Lvs 10–12×0.7–1.2cm, numerous, lanceolate, margins rough. Fls 1–7, in a raceme, bell-shaped, pendulous; pedicels 3.5–6cm; tepals 3.5–5×1–2cm, apically recurved forming a short basal tube, white suffused purple, tube dark purple within, anth. and pollen yellow. Summer. China (NW Yunnan, W Sichuan). Z5.

***L. henryi*** Bak. Stems 1–3m, green marked purple, stem-rooting; bulbs 8–18×7–15cm, concentric, scales 3.5–4.5×1.5cm, thick, white, red when exposed, acute, lanceolate, imbricate. Lvs 8–15×2–3cm, shiny, scattered, upper lvs ovate, sessile, basal lvs lanceolate, petiolate, 3–5-veined, crowded below fls, some axils bulbiliferous. Fls 4–20, turk's-cap, pendulous, in a raceme; pedicels 5–9cm, horizontal, 1–2 leafy bracts below fls; tepals 6–8×1–2cm, orange, spotted black, lanceolate, recurved; anth. deep red. Fr. 4×2cm, seeds golden brown, 9×6mm. Summer. China (Hubei, Jiangxi, Gouzhou). 'Citrinum': fls pale lemon-yellow, spotted brown. Z5.

***L. ×hollandicum*** Bergmans. *(L. maculatum × L. bulbiferum.)* UMBEL LILY. Stems 70–130cm, stem-rooting. Lvs crowded, veins 3. Fls erect, cup-shaped, to 7.5cm wide, in umbels; tepals yellow, orange or red. Summer. Garden origin. Z5.

***L. humboldtii*** Duchartre. Stems to 2.25m, green flushed purple, non-rooting; bulbs subrhizomatous, scales white, purple when exposed, lanceolate-ovate, unjointed, 7cm. Lvs to 12.5×3cm, oblanceolate, in whorls of 10–20. Fls 10–15, occasionally 80, pendulous, turk's-cap, in a raceme; pedicels horizontal; tepals 6.5–10×1.5–2.5cm, recurved, yellow to orange, spotted maroon and purple;

pollen brown. Fr. to 5cm. Summer. US (California: Sierra Nevada). var. ***ocellatum*** (Kellogg) Elwes. Tepals tinged red, the spots ringed red, eye-like. Z5.

***L.×imperiale*** Wils. *(L.regale × L.sargentiae.)* SARGALE LILY. Stems to 120cm, grey-green. Lvs alternate, linear, 1–5-veined, axils of upper lvs bulbiliferous. Fls bowl-shaped; tepals recurved, interior white, basal tube yellow, exterior purple; anth. orange-brown. Summer. Z5.

***L.iridollae*** M.G. Henry. POT-OF-GOLD LILY. Stems to 175cm; bulbs stoloniferous, 2cm wide. Lvs 9.0×2.3cm, usually whorled, obovate, basal rosettes of lvs persisting through winter. Fls 1–8, pendulous, turk's-cap; tepals 10×2.5cm, yellow, spotted brown, apex speckled red; anth. red-brown. Late summer. SE US (S Alabama, N Florida). Z4.

***L.japonicum*** Houtt. BAMBOO LILY; SASA-YURI. Stems 40–90cm; bulbs 4cm wide, scales white, pink when exposed, ovate, imbricate. Lvs 15×2.5cm, scattered, lanceolate, 3–5-veined, margins rough; petiole to 1cm. Fls 1–5, fragrant, funnel-shaped, horizontal; tepals 10–15×2–3.5cm, oblanceolate to oblong, pink, occasionally white; anth. brown; pollen red or brown. Fr. 4cm, seeds brown, 8.5×7mm. Summer. Japan. 'Albomarginatum': lf margins white. 'Album': fls white. var. ***platyfolium*** anon. More vigorous, with broader lvs. Z5.

***L.kelleyanum*** Lemmon. Stems to 1m, occasionally to 2m; bulbs stoloniferous, scales white. Lvs 5–15×1.5–3.5cm, lanceolate to elliptic, scattered, sometimes in 2 whorls of 7–16. Fls pendulous, turk's-cap, fragrant; tepals 2.5–5×1cm, yellow or orange, maroon or basally spotted brown, apex sometimes red; anth. brown. Summer. W US (California, S Oregon). Z5.

***L.kelloggii*** Purdy. Stems 30–125cm; bulbs 5×4cm, concentric, scales 5×1cm, white, lanceolate. Lvs to 10×2cm, in whorls of 12 or more, sessile, lanceolate or oblanceolate, acute, 1–3-veined. Fls to 20, pendulous, turk's-cap, fragrant, in a raceme; pedicels slender with leafy bracts, 3.5cm; tepals 5.5×1cm, reflexed, mauve-pink or white with dark purple spots and central yellow stripe toward base; anth. and pollen orange, stigma green. Fr. 5×2cm; seeds 5mm. Summer. W US (S Oregon, NW California). Z5.

***L.kesselringianum*** Misch. Stems to 1m; bulbs 5×5cm, concentric, scales yellow. Lvs lanceolate, 9–13×1–1.5cm. Fls 1–3, 9–14cm wide, bell-shaped; tepals 9cm, recurved, pale cream to yellow, spotted purple; anth. brown; pollen orange. Summer. S USSR (Georgia), NE Turkey. Z5.

***L.lancifolium*** Thunb. DEVIL LILY; KENTAN; TIGER LILY. Stems 60–150cm, dark purple with white hairs, stem-rooting; bulbs to 7×8cm, scales ovate, white, overlapping; black bulbils in lf axils. Lvs 12–20×1–2cm, numerous, lanceolate, scattered, 5–7-veined, margins rough. Fls to 40, in a raceme, pendulous, turk's-cap, to 12.5cm wide, unscented; pedicels to 10cm, stiff; tepals 7–10×1–2.5cm, lanceolate, recurved when first open, gradually spreading, interior orange, spotted deep purple; anth. orange-red to purple; pollen brown. Summer–early autumn. E China, Japan, Korea. 'Flore Pleno': fls double; tepals 24–36, narrow; stamens absent. 'Yellow Tiger': fls lemon-yellow, spotted dark purple. var. ***flaviflorum*** Mak. Fls yellow. Japan. var. ***fortunei*** (Standish) V. Matthews. Stems to 2m, densely woolly. Fls 30–50, tepals orange-red. Korea (Dagelet Is.), China (Lushan Mts). var. ***splendens*** (Van Houtte) V. Matthews. Stems black with shiny bulbils. Fls to 25, larger; tepals bright orange-red, spotted black. Japan. Z4.

***L.lankongense*** Franch. Stems to 120cm, rough, ribbed, green, stem-rooting; bulbs 4cm wide, stoloniferous, scales white, pink on exposure, ovate, acute. Lvs 10×0.8cm, numerous, sessile, scattered, crowded near base, oblong-lanceolate, acute, 3–7-veined, margins rough. Fls to 15, 5cm wide, in a raceme, pendulous, turk's-cap, fragrant; pedicels recurved, green, 12.5cm; tepals 4–6.5×1–2.5cm, rose-pink, spotted purple, green central stripe, recurved, acute; anth. purple; pollen brown. Fr. to 4×2cm, seeds to 8mm. Summer. W China (SE Xizang). Z5.

***L.ledebourii*** (Bak.) Boiss. Stems slender to 1.25m, green, smooth, stem-rooting; bulbs concentric, 11×7–9cm, scales white turning yellow when exposed. Lvs scattered, spirally arranged, lower 11–12×2cm, upper narrower, 5-veined. Fls 1–5, fragrant, turk's-cap; tepals 6–7×1.3cm, creamy white to yellow, centrally spotted dark purple or red; anth. and pollen red. Fr. 4×2cm; seeds to 250. Summer. NW Iran, USSR (Azerbaijan). Z5.

***L.leichtlinii*** Hook. f. Stems to 120cm, green with a few white hairs in lf axils, stem-rooting; bulbs stoloniferous, 4×4cm, scales white, ovate, imbricate, 1.5cm. Lvs to 15×1cm, numerous, scattered, linear-lanceolate, 1–3-veined, margins rough. Fls 1–6, in a raceme, unscented, pendulous turk's-cap, buds white-hairy; tepals to 8×2cm, lemon yellow spotted maroon, lanceolate, tips recurved; anth. and pollen red-brown. Summer. Japan. var. ***maximowiczii*** (Reg.) Bak. Stems to 2.5cm; bulbs stoloniferous, 4×4cm, scales white. Lvs numerous, linear-lanceolate, 3–7-veined. Fls 1–12; tepals bright orange-red, spotted purple-brown; anth. and pollen red. Japan, C Korea. Z5.

***L.leucanthum*** (Bak.) Bak. Not in cultivation. var. ***centifolium*** (Stapf) Stearn. Stems 2–3m, glaucous; bulbs concentric, to 8×6.5cm, scales 5×2cm, dark yellow to red-brown, imbricate, ovate. Lvs 15–20cm, dark green, ascending, recurved, scattered, linear to lanceolate, 1-veined, non-flowering lvs shorter and 3-veined. Fls to 18, scented, funnel-shaped, horizontal or slightly pendulous; pedicels horizontal, 6–12cm; tepals 14–18×3–6cm, interior white with yellow basal tube, exterior flushed purple-red, green toward base, recurved toward tip; anth. red-brown; pollen brown. Fr. 6×2.5cm; seeds 1cm. Summer. W China (W Kansu). Z5.

***L.longiflorum*** Thunb. EASTER LILY. Stems to 1m, green, stem-rooting; bulbs 4×6cm, scales creamy yellow, oblong-lanceolate, imbricate. Lvs to 18×1.5cm, numerous, scattered, lanceolate or oblong-lanceolate. Fls to 6, funnel-shaped, scented, in an umbel; pedicels horizontal, to 12cm; tepals to 18cm, white, forming a basal tube, tips slightly recurved; pollen yellow; stigma green. Fr. 7cm. Summer. S Japan, Taiwan. 'Albomarginatum': lvs blue-green, margins white. 'Gelria': fls white; tepals slightly recurved at apex; pollen yellow. 'Holland's Glory': fls white, to 20cm. 'White America': fls white, tips and nectary green, pollen deep yellow. 'White Europe' ('Georgia', 'Avai No. 5'): fls white, tepals strongly recurved, throat venation lettuce-green, exterior green-white below, venation cream above, pollen lemon-yellow. var. ***eximium*** (Courtois) Bak. Tepals more recurved, basal tube narrower. Japan. 'Howardii' ('Romanii'): fls pure white, firm-textured. var. ***takeshima*** Duchartre. Stems taller, purple-brown. Fls flushed purple outside; pollen orange. Japan (Takeshima Is.). 'Erabu No Hikari' ('Erabu'): taller, more floriferous. Z5.

***L.mackliniae*** Sealy. Stems to 40cm, green, sometimes tinged purple, stem-rooting; bulbs 4.5×4–6cm, concentric, scales brown, ovate-lanceolate, 3×2cm. Lvs 3–6×0.4–1cm, spiral, horizontal, linear-lanceolate or elliptic-lanceolate. Fls 1–6, in a raceme, pendulous, bell-shaped; pedicels 3–6cm; tepals 5×2cm, interior rose-pink, exterior purple-pink; anth. purple; pollen yellow-orange or brown. Fr. 3×2cm; seeds brown, 8×7mm. Late spring–summer. NE India (Manipur). Z5.

***L.maculatum*** Thunb. Considered by some to be *L.dauricum × L.concolor*. Stems to 60cm, ribbed, stem-rooting; bulbs concentric, 4cm wide, scales white, unjointed. Lvs 5–15×1.5cm, lanceolate to elliptic, scattered, 3–7-veined. Fls cup-shaped, erect; tepals 8–10cm, yellow, orange or red, variably spotted. Summer. Japan. 'Alutaceum': fls deep apricot, spotted purple-black. 'Aureum': fls orange-yellow, spotted black. 'Bicolor': fls brilliant orange, margins bright red, spots few, faint. 'Biligulatum': fls deep chestnut-red. 'Sanguineum': stems to 40cm; fls solitary, orange-red. 'Wallacei': fls apricot with raised maroon spots. Many selections have been made; see *International Lily Register*, 3rd edition (1982) and Supplements. Z4.

***L.×marhan*** Bak. *(L.hansonii × L.martagon* var. *album.)* Stems to 1.5m. Fls pendulous, turk's-cap, 5–6cm wide; tepals thick, orange-yellow, spotted red-brown. Summer. Garden origin. Z5.

***L.maritimum*** Kellogg. COAST LILY. Stems 30–70cm, occasionally 2m, dark green; bulbs 5×3.5cm, rhizomatous, scales white, 3.5cm wide. Lvs 12.5×1.5cm, linear to oblanceolate, scattered, with a central whorl. Fls 1–12, pendulous, wide bell-shaped, in a raceme; pedicels arching; tepals 4.5cm, apically recurved, deep crimson or orange, spotted maroon inside; pollen brown. Fr. to 4cm. Summer. W US (N California coast). Z4.

***L.martagon*** L. MARTAGON; TURK'S-CAP. Stems to 2m, purple-green, stem-rooting; bulbs concentric, ovoid, 7.5cm wide, scales yellow, oblong or lanceolate, acute. Lvs to 16×6.5cm, oblanceolate, 7–9-veined, in whorls of 8–14. Fls to 50, in raceme, pendulous, recurved, turk's-cap, 5cm wide, fragrant; pedicels short; tepals 3–4.5×0.6–1cm, dull pink, spotted maroon; pollen yellow; stigma purple. Fr. 3.5×2.5cm. Summer. NW Europe, NW Asia. var. ***albiflorum*** Vukot. Fls white, pink spotting, rare in cultivation. Yugoslavia. var. ***album*** Weston. Stem green. Fls white, not spotted. var. ***cattaniae*** Vis. Stems and buds hairy. Fls maroon, unspotted. Balkans. var. ***caucasicum*** Misch. Stems to 2.5m. Fls lilac-pink. var. ***hirsutum*** Weston. Stem hairy, purple. Lvs downy beneath, Fls purple-pink, spotted. var. ***pilosiusculum*** Freyn. Stems purple, hairy. Lvs narrow, margins hairy. Fls deep red, sparsely spotted; bracts and buds hairy. Mongolia, Siberia. var. ***sanguineo-purpureum*** G. Beck. Fls dark maroon, spotted. Balkans. Z4.

***L.medeoloides*** A. Gray. WHEEL LILY. Stems to 75cm, hollow, stem-rooting; bulbs 2.5×2.5cm, concentric, scales 2cm, white, jointed, acute, easily detached. Lvs to 12×3.5cm, lanceolate, sessile or short-petioled, 1–2-whorled, a few scattered. Fls 1–10, turk's-cap, 5cm wide, unscented, in a raceme or umbel; pedicels erect, arched; tepals lanceolate, 4.5×1cm, recurved, apricot to orange-red, usually with darker spots; anth. purple; pollen orange-red. Fr. 1.5×1.5cm. Summer. China, Japan, S Korea, USSR. Z5.

***L.michauxii*** Poir. CAROLINA LILY. Stems to 1m, green, sometimes spotted, stem-rooting; bulbs stoloniferous, scales white, lanceolate to ovate. Lvs to 11.5×2.5cm, fleshy, glaucous, oblanceolate to obovate, in whorls of 3–7. Fls 1–5, pendulous, turk's-cap, to 10cm wide, scented; tepals to 10cm, lanceolate, recurved, orange-red to pale crimson, yellow toward base, inner surface spotted purple or black; anth. brown; pollen red. Fr. 4×2cm. Early autumn. SE US. Z6.

***L.michiganense*** Farw. Stems to 1.5m; bulbs stoloniferous, 3×3cm, each flowering once only, scales thick, yellow, flushed pink or brown. Lvs 9–12cm, lanceolate or elliptic-lanceolate, in up to 4 whorls of 4–8. Fls 3–6, occasionally to 25, pendulous turk's-cap, 7.5cm wide; pedicels to 24cm, curved; tepals 7×2cm, recurved, orange-red, spotted deep crimson, basal tube green; pollen orange-brown. Summer. Central N America. Z4.

***L.monadelphum*** Bieb. CAUCASIAN LILY. Stems 100–150cm, stem-rooting; bulbs 4–8cm wide, scales yellow-white, lanceolate. Lvs 12.5×2.5cm, lanceolate or oblanceolate, spirally arranged, 9–13-veined. Fls 1–5, occasionally to 30, fragrant, pendulous, turk's-cap; tepals 6–10×1–2cm, recurved, yellow, interior spotted purple or maroon, exterior flushed purple-brown; pollen orange-yellow. Summer. NE Turkey, USSR (Caucasus). var. ***armenum*** (Misch.) P.H. Davis &

D.M. Henderson. Inner tepals acute, 1–1.6cm wide. NE Turkey, USSR (Armenia). Z5.

***L. nanum*** Klotzsch. Stems 6–45cm; bulbs concentric, 4×2cm, scales white, imbricate, lanceolate. Lvs to 12×0.5cm, linear, scattered, 3–5-veined. Fls solitary, pendulous, bell-shaped, scented; tepals to 1–4×0.3–1.6cm, pale pink to purple with fine dark purple or brown mottling; anth. yellow-brown. Summer. Himalaya, W China. var. ***flavidum*** (Rendle) Sealy. Fls pale yellow. Z5.

***L. nepalense*** D. Don. Stems to 1m, smooth, green; bulbs to 9cm wide, stoloniferous, scales white, pink on exposure, ovate-lanceolate. Lvs to 14×3cm, oblong-lanceolate, 5–7-veined. Fls 1–3, slightly pendulous, funnel-shaped, with a musky nocturnal scent; pedicels ascending, to 10cm; tepals to 15cm, recurved, ribbed, green-white to green-yellow, base red-purple; anth. purple; pollen orange-brown. Summer. Bhutan, Nepal, N India. var. ***concolor*** Cotton. Fls green-yellow, throat not red. Bhutan. Z5.

***L. nobilissimum*** (Mak.) Mak. Stems purple-green, to 1.7m, stem-rooting; bulbs concentric, to 15cm wide, scales creamy white. Lvs to 12×5cm, scattered, dark green, short-petioled, lf axils bulbiliferous. Fls 1–3, vertical, 15×13cm, funnel-shaped, fragrant; tepals white; anth. green; pollen yellow. Summer. S Japan. Z6.

***L. occidentale*** Purdy. EUREKA LILY. Stems 70–200cm, smooth, green tinged purple; bulbs rhizomatous, scales jointed. Lvs to 13×1.5cm, in whorls, linear-lanceolate to lanceolate, 7-veined. Fls 1–5, occasionally 20, in a raceme, pendulous, turk's-cap, to 7cm wide; pedicels arching, to 15cm; tepals 3.5–6×1.5cm, reflexed, crimson with green-yellow throat, or vermilion with orange throat and brown spots; anth. purple; pollen orange-red. Fr. 2.5×1cm; seeds 6–7mm wide. Summer. W US (Coast of S Oregon and N California). Z5.

***L. oxypetalum*** (Royle) Bak. Stems to 25cm, bright green; bulbs concentric, to 5cm high, scales lanceolate, 1cm wide. Lvs to 7.5×1.25cm, scattered, sessile, elliptic, whorl immediately below fl. Fls 1–2, cup-shaped, pendulous; pedicels very short; tepals to 5.5cm, ovate, lemon-yellow, often spotted purple; pollen orange. Fr. 3×2cm; seeds pale brown, 9×7mm. Summer. NW Himalaya. var. ***insigne*** Sealy. Fls purple. Z4.

***L. papilliferum*** Franch. LIKIANG LILY. Stems to 90cm, green mottled purple, stem-rooting; bulbs 3×2.5cm, stoloniferous, scales white, lanceolate-ovate to ovate. Lvs to 10×0.8cm, scattered, linear or linear-oblong. Fls 1–3, 7.5cm wide, in a raceme, fragrant, pendulous, turk's-cap; pedicels stiff; tepals 4×1.5cm, reflexed, apex acute, deep purple or maroon with lighter central stripe, exterior green; anth. brown; pollen orange-yellow. Fr. 4×2cm. Late spring–late summer. SW China. Z5.

***L. ×pardaboldtii*** Woodcock & Coutts. (*L. humboldtii* × *L. pardalinum*.) Stems to 150cm. Lvs whorled. Fls pendulous, turk's-cap; tepals orange-red, spotted dark crimson. Summer. Bellingham Hybrids: rhizomatous, orange-fld (US).

***L. pardalinum*** Kellogg. LEOPARD LILY; PANTHER LILY. Stems 2–3m; bulbs rhizomatous, 4cm wide, forming large clumps, scales to 2cm, numerous, brittle, yellow-white, pink on exposure, jointed. Lvs to 18×5cm, in whorls of to 16, elliptic or oblanceolate, glabrous, to 3-veined. Fls to 10 in a raceme, unscented, pendulous, turk's-cap, to 9×9cm; pedicels arching; tepals reflexed, lanceolate, acute, orange-red to crimson, spotted deep maroon toward base, some spots outlined yellow; anth. red-brown; pollen orange. Summer. W US (S Oregon, N California). 'Californicum': fls deep orange, spotted maroon, tips scarlet. 'Johnsonii': stems tall; fls finely spotted. var. ***angustifolium*** Kellogg. Lvs narrow. US (California around San Francisco). var. ***giganteum*** Woodcock & Coutts. Stems to 2.5m. Fls to 30; tepals crimson and yellow, densely spotted. *L. pardalinum* 'Red Sunset' is a synonym of *L. pardalinum* var. *giganteum*. Z5.

***L. ×parkmanii*** T. Moore. (*L. auratum* × *L. speciosum*.) Lvs broad. Fls fragrant, bowl-shaped, to 20cm wide; tepals recurved, crimson, margins white. Summer. 'Allegra': fls white with sparse pink papillae. 'Empress of China': fls white, spotted pink. 'Empress of India': fls deep red, margin white. 'Empress of Japan': fls white with a golden band, spotted deep maroon. 'Excelsior': fls china-rose, pet. tips and narrow margins white. 'Imperial Crimson': fls deep crimson, margin white. 'Imperial Silver': fls white with small maroon spots. 'Jillian Wallace': fls rose, margin white, interior spotted deep crimson. 'Pink Glory': fls shell-pink to salmon-pink, golden spots few. Many selections have been made; see *International Lily Register*, 3rd edition (1982) and Supplements.

***L. parryi*** S. Wats. LEMON LILY. Stems to 2m, glabrous; bulbs to 4×4cm, rhizomatous, scales numerous, 3-pointed, brittle, yellow-white. Lvs to 15cm, oblanceolate, 3-veined, margins slightly rough. Fls to 15, occasionally many more, fragrant, horizontal, funnel-shaped; pedicels long, sharply angled; tepals to 7–10×0.8–1.2cm, oblanceolate, apically recurved, lemon-yellow, base sparsely spotted maroon; anth. orange-brown; pollen red. Fr. to 5cm. Summer. SW US (S California, S Arizona). Z5.

***L. parvum*** Kellogg. SIERRA LILY. Stems to 2m; bulbs 3.5×3.5cm, rhizomatous, scales thick, white, lanceolate, acute. Lvs 12.5×3cm, mostly in whorls, lanceolate or linear, 1–3-veined. Fls to 30, bell-shaped, borne horizontally in a raceme; pedicels to 6cm; tepals to 4cm, oblanceolate, recurved, red, interior spotted deep maroon. Fr. to 1.2mm. Summer. W US (Oregon to C California). f. ***crocatum*** Stearn. Fls yellow or orange. Z4.

***L. philadelphicum*** L. WOOD LILY. Stems to 1.25m; bulbs 2.5cm wide, stoloniferous, scales 1.35cm, white, ovate. Lvs 5–10×1.5cm, mostly in whorls of 6–8, oblanceolate, margins sometimes rough, 3–5-veined. Fls 1–5, cup-shaped, erect, in an umbel; tepals to 7.5cm, oblanceolate, orange to vivid orange-red, spotted purple, edges revolute; pollen deep red. Fr. 2.5cm; seeds brown, 8×7mm. Summer. Eastern N America. var. ***andinum*** (Nutt.) Ker-Gawl. Lvs to 5mm wide, scattered. US and S Canada (Rocky Mts). Z4.

***L. philippinense*** Bak. Stems 30–40cm, occasionally to 1m, green, purple towards base; bulbs 3.5×4cm, stoloniferous, scales white, acute, lanceolate. Lvs to 15×0.6cm, scattered, linear. Fls 1–6, scented, to 25cm, funnel-shaped; tepals to 5cm wide, oblanceolate to spathulate, apices spreading, interior white, exterior flushed green and purple; anth. yellow; pollen yellow. Summer. Philippine Is. (N Luzon). Z9.

***L. pitkinense*** Beane & Vollmer. Stems 1–2m, glabrous; bulbs rhizomatous, occasionally stoloniferous, scales unjointed. Lvs scattered and in 2–3 whorls, linear or lanceolate, 3-veined. Fls 1–3, occasionally to 8 in cult., unscented, in an umbel or raceme; pedicels long, arched; tepals scarlet, yellow toward base, spotted dark purple; anth. purple; pollen brown. Summer. W US (California). Z5.

***L. polyphyllum*** D. Don. Stems 1–2m; bulbs 7.5×2.5cm; scales sharply acute, pink. Lvs to 12×2cm, scattered, linear to oblong-lanceolate. Fls 1–6, sometimes to 30, fragrant, turk's-cap, 11cm wide, in an umbel or raceme; tepals recurved, white or pink, sometimes spotted red, base yellow-green; pollen orange. Fr. 4cm; seeds 7mm wide. Summer. Afghanistan, W Himalaya. Z7.

***L. pomponium*** L. Stems to 1m, base spotted purple; bulbs concentric, 6.5cm wide, scales white, yellow on exposure, ovate lanceolate, acute. Lvs to 12.5×2cm, numerous, crowded, linear, margin silver-ciliate. Fls to 6, pendulous, turk's-cap, 5cm wide, in a raceme, malodorous; pedicels long; tepals recurved, bright scarlet, base spotted black inside, outside purple-green toward base; pollen orange-red. Fr. 4×2.5cm. Summer. Europe (Maritime Alps). Z4.

***L. primulinum*** Bak. OCHRE LILY. Stems to 2.4m, green spotted brown, or brown, stem-rooting; bulbs 3–4×3.5cm, stoloniform, scales to 5×1.5cm, cream, purple on exposure, ovate-lanceolate, acute. Lvs to 15×4cm, scattered, lanceolate, 1–3-veined. Fls 2–8, occasionally 18, fragrant, funnel-shaped, pendulous; pedicels to 15cm, decurved below fls; tepals 6–15×1–5cm, oblong-lanceolate, recurved, yellow, sometimes with purple-red markings; pollen brown. Fr. 2.5–3.4cm; seeds winged. Summer–autumn. W China (Yunnan), N Burma, Thailand. var. ***primulinum.*** Tepals entirely yellow, upper half recurved. N Burma. var. ***burmanicum*** (W.W. Sm.) Stearn. Stems 120–240cm. Lvs to 4cm wide. Tepals 6.5–15cm, upper third recurved, base purple-red. N Burma, Thailand. var. ***ochraceum*** (Franch.) Stearn. Stems to 120cm. Lvs 2cm wide. Tepals 6cm, red-purple toward base, upper two-thirds recurved. Z4.

***L. pumilum*** DC. CORAL LILY. Stems 15–45cm, occasionally 90cm, green, stem-rooting; bulbs concentric, 4×2.5cm, scales white, imbricate, ovate-lanceolate. Lvs to 10×0.3cm, scattered, sessile, linear, 1-veined. Fls to 7–20, scented, pendulous, turk's-cap, in a raceme; buds woolly; tepals 5×5cm, oblong-lanceolate, reflexed, scarlet, base sometimes dotted black; pollen scarlet. Fr. 3×1.5cm. Summer. N China, N Korea, Mongolia, USSR (Siberia). 'Golden Gleam': fls apricot yellow. Z5.

***L. pyrenaicum*** Gouan. Stems 15–135cm, green, sometimes spotted purple, often stem-rooting; bulbs 7×7cm, scales oblong-lanceolate, yellow-white, pink on exposure. Lvs to 12.5×2cm, linear-lanceolate, acute, margins sometimes silver or ciliate. Fls to 12, pendulous, turk's-cap, 5cm wide, in a raceme; pedicels to 12.5cm; tepals recurved, green-yellow, streaked and spotted dark maroon; pollen orange-red. Fr. 3.5×2.5cm. Summer. Europe (SE Alps, Pyrenees, Balkans, NE Turkey), USSR (Georgia). 'Aureum': fls deep yellow. ssp. ***pyrenaicum.*** Stems 30–135cm, green, sparsely spotted purple. Lvs 7–15×0.3–2cm, 3–15-veined. Fls to 12; tepals 4–6.5cm, yellow, interior lined and spotted dark purple. SW France, N Spain. ssp. ***pyrenaicum*** f. ***rubrum*** Stoker. Fls orange-red. ssp. ***carniolicum*** (Koch) V. Matthews. Stems to 120cm, green, stem-rooting; bulbs 7.5×6.5cm, scales ovate-lanceolate, yellow-white. Lvs 3–11×0.4–1.7cm, 3–9-veined, pubesc. beneath. Fls 6–12; tepals 3–7cm, yellow, orange or red, sometimes spotted purple. SE Europe. var. ***albanicum*** (Griseb.) V. Matthews. Stem to 40cm. Fls yellow. Lf veins not pubesc. Albania, NW Greece, SW Yugoslavia. var. ***jankae*** (Kerner) Matthews. Stems to 80cm. Lf veins pubesc. below. Fls yellow. W Bulgaria, NW Italy, C Romania, NW Yugoslavia. ssp. ***ponticum*** (K. Koch) V. Matthews. Stems 15–90cm. Lvs 3–8×0.8–2cm, 7–15-veined, pubesc. beneath. Fls 5–12, tepals 7–10mm wide, deep yellow or deep orange, interior red-brown, spotted purple toward base. NE Turkey, USSR (Georgia). var. ***artvinense*** (Misch.) V. Matthews. Fls deep orange; tepals 5–6mm wide. NE Turkey, USSR (Georgia). Z3.

***L. regale*** Wils. Stems 50–200cm, grey-green flushed purple, stem-rooting; bulbs 6.5–15.5cm wide, concentric, scales thick, imbricate, lanceolate to ovate-lanceolate, acute, deep red. Lvs 5–13×0.4–0.6cm, scattered, sessile, linear, 1-veined. Fls 1–25, fragrant, horizontal, funnel-shaped, in an umbel; pedicels 2–12cm, spreading; tepals 12–15×2–4cm, apically recurved, white, interior of basal tube yellow, exterior purple; anth. and pollen golden; style and stigma green. Fr. purple, 5–7×2.5cm; seeds to 7mm. Summer. W China (W Sichuan). 'Album': fls almost pure white; anth. orange. 'Royal Gold': fls yellow. Z5.

***L. rhodopaeum*** Delip. Stems to 80–100cm; bulbs concentric, 2–8–4cm wide, scales white or pale yellow, linear-lanceolate. Lvs numerous, alternate, linear, acute, hairy on margins and on veins beneath. Fls 1–5, funnel-shaped, pendulous, strongly scented; tepals 8–12cm, lemon yellow, recurved; anth. and pollen scarlet. Summer. Bulgaria, Greece. Z6.

***L. rubellum*** Bak. Stems 30–80cm, stem-rooting; bulbs concentric, 3cm wide, scales white, lanceolate. Lvs 10×3.5cm, scattered, petiolate, ovate-lanceolate to oblong-elliptic, 5–7-veined. Fls 1–9, very fragrant, horizontal, funnel-shaped; tepals 7.5cm, oblanceolate to oblong, apically recurved, rose-pink, base sometimes spotted maroon; pollen orange-yellow, style green. Fr. 2.5cm. Summer. Japan (N Honshu). Z6.

***L. rubescens*** S. Wats. CHAPARRAL LILY. Stems to 3m, green flushed purple; bulbs 6×5.5cm, rhizomatous or subrhizomatous, scales 5×2cm, white flushed purple. Lvs to 12×3.5cm, lanceolate to oblanceolate, scattered and in 1–4 whorls. Fls 1–30, occasionally 100 or more, fragrant, broadly funnel-shaped, 10cm wide, in an umbellate raceme; tepals 3.5–6.5cm, apically recurved, white, finely spotted purple, ageing to purple; pollen and stigma yellow. Summer. W US (NW California, S Oregon). Z6.

***L. sargentiae*** Wils. Stems to 1.5m, purple, stem-rooting; bulbs concentric, 4×15cm, scales thick, lanceolate to ovate-lanceolate, acute, imbricate, yellow-white with wine-red apices. Lvs 10–20×0.5–2cm, fleshy, scattered, sessile, linear-oblong to oblong-lanceolate, basally adpressed, 3–7-veined, axils bulbiliferous. Fls 2–5, fragrant, funnel-shaped, 13–18cm wide, horizontal or pendulous, in a corymb or umbel; pedicels horizontal or ascending, 3–10cm; tepals 12–15cm, interior white with yellow basal tube, exterior suffused green or purple; anth. purple; pollen brown. Fr. 5–6cm. Summer. W China (Sichuan). Z6.

***L. sherriffiae*** Stearn. Stems 35–90cm, green flushed purple, stem-rooting; bulbs 2.5×2cm, concentric, scales 2.5×0.8cm, lanceolate or ovate-lanceolate, acute. Lvs 3–13×0.3–0.6cm, scattered, linear-lanceolate or linear. Fls 1–2, narrow funnel-shaped; tepals recurved, acute, dark purple outside, inside tessellated golden yellow–green toward apex; pollen yellow. Summer. Bhutan, Nepal. Z6.

***L. speciosum*** Thunb. Stems 120–170cm, green tinged purple, stem-rooting; bulbs 10×10cm, concentric, scales white, yellow or brown, imbricate, lanceolate, acute. Lvs to 18×6cm, scattered, lanceolate, petiolate, 7–9-veined. Fls to 12, fragrant, pendulous, turk's-cap, 15cm wide, in a raceme; pedicels to 10cm; tepals to 10×4.5cm, white, base flushed carmine, spotted pink or crimson, recurved, lanceolate or ovate-lanceolate, margins wavy; pollen dark red. Late summer. China, Japan, Taiwan. 'Grand Commander': fls deep pink tinted lilac, edged white, spotted red. 'Krätzeri': fls white, exterior with central green stripe. 'Melpomene': fls deep carmine, segments edged white. 'Uchida': fls brilliant crimson, spotted green, tips white. var. ***album*** Mast. ex Bak. Stems purple-brown. Fls white. var. ***gloriosoides*** Bak. Tepals spotted scarlet. China (Kiangsi, Anwhei), Taiwan. var. ***magnificum*** Wallace. Fls rose, spotted deep crimson, margins paler; pollen red. var. ***roseum*** Mast. ex Bak. Fls rose. var. ***rubrum*** Mast. ex Bak. Stems purple-brown. Fls carmine. Z6.

***L. sulphureum*** Bak. Stems 150–200cm, ribbed, green, mottled with purple, stem-rooting; bulbs 10×10cm, concentric, scales dark purple, lanceolate-ovate. Lvs to 20×2cm, scattered, linear-lanceolate, 3–7-veined, axillary brown bulbils. Fls 1–15, fragrant, pendulous or horizontal, funnel-shaped; tepals to 25×6cm, apically recurved, interior surface creamy white with yellow basal tube, exterior flushed pink; anth. brown; pollen orange-brown. Fr. 10×2.5cm; seeds golden brown, winged. Late summer. Burma, W China (Yunnan). *L. sulphureum* × *L. regale* is known as *L.* ×*sulphurgale*. Z6.

***L. superbum*** L. TURK'S-CAP LILY. Stems 1.5–3m high, green, mottled purple, stem-rooting; bulbs concentric, stoloniferous, scales white, ovate, imbricate. Lvs 3.5–11×0.8–2.8cm, lanceolate or elliptic, 3–7-veined, in whorls of 4–20 and scattered. Fls to 40, pendulous, turk's-cap in a raceme; pedicels ascending, bracteolate; tepals recurved, orange flushed red, spotted maroon toward green base; anth. red, 1.6–2cm; pollen orange-brown. Summer. E US. Z3.

***L. taliense*** Franch. Stems to 140cm, dark purple or green, mottled purple, stem-rooting; bulbs 4.5cm wide, stoloniferous, scales ovate, acute, cream with purple markings. Lvs to 12.7×0.6cm, scattered, sessile, linear-lanceolate, 3-veined. Fls to 12, scented, pendulous turk's-cap, in a raceme; pedicels horizontal, stiff, tepals 5.7×1.2cm, recurved, lanceolate, white, interior spotted purple; anth. mauve-white; pollen yellow. Fr. 2.5×2cm; seeds brown, winged, 8×6mm. Summer. W China (NE Yunnan). Z5.

***L.*** ×***testaceum*** Lindl. (*L. candidum* × *L. chalcedonicum.*) NANKEEN LILY. Stems to 100–150cm, purple with grey bloom. Lvs 5–10cm, scattered, linear, margins ciliate, veins pubesc. beneath. Fls 6–12, scented, pendulous, turk's-cap; tepals to 8cm, yellow to pale orange, interior spotted red; anth. red; pollen orange. Summer. Garden origin. Z6.

***L. tsingtauense*** Gilg. Stems to 120cm, glabrous, hollow, stem-rooting; bulbs to 4×4cm, scales 2–2.5×0.6–0.8cm, white, lanceolate, imbricate. Lvs to 15×4cm, glabrous, oblanceolate, petiolate, often in 2 whorls. Fls 2–7, in a raceme, unscented, erect, bowl-shaped; pedicels to 8.5cm, tepals to 5×1.5cm, orange or vermilion with purple spotting; anth. and pollen orange. Fr. ribbed; seeds brown, 8×7mm. Summer. NE China, Korea. var. ***carneum*** Nak. Fls red, unspotted. var. ***flavum*** Wils. Fls yellow, spotted red. Z6.

***L. vollmeri*** Eastw. Stems to 1m; bulbs rhizomatous, scales white, ageing to yellow. Lvs to 15cm, scattered or in 1–2 whorls, elliptic-linear. Fls 1–10, turk's-cap, in a raceme; pedicels long, arching; tepals to 8×1cm, reflexed, red-orange with dark margins, dark purple or black spots ringed with yellow on inner surface; pollen orange-red. Summer. W US (S Oregon, N California). Z5.

***L. wallichianum*** Schult. & Schult. f. Stems to 2m, green, tinged purple, stem-rooting; bulbs stoloniferous, 9cm wide, scales lanceolate, white. Lvs 25×1.2cm, scattered, linear or lanceolate. Fls 1–4, scented, horizontal, funnel-shaped, 20cm wide with basal tube to 10cm; tepals 15–30cm, apically recurved, interior creamy white, exterior tinged green; pollen yellow. Fr. to 4cm. Summer–autumn. Himalaya. var. ***neilgherrense*** (Wight) Hara. Stems to 90cm. Lvs to 12×3cm, lanceolate. S India. Z5.

***L. wardii*** F. Stern. Stems to 1.5m, dark green flushed purple, stem-rooting; bulbs 5cm wide, stoloniform, scales ovate, imbricate, light brown speckled red, becoming purple on exposure. Lvs 3–8×0.6–2cm, scattered, sessile, glabrous, 3-veined, oblong to linear-lanceolate, apex acute. Fls to 35, fragrant, pendulous, turk's-cap, in a raceme; pedicels stiff, horizontal; tepals 5–6.5×1.5cm, pink with purple basal median line and spotting, recurved; anth. mauve; pollen yellow. Fr. 4×1.5cm; seeds brown, 8×6mm. Summer. W China. Z5.

***L. washingtonianum*** Kellogg. Stems 2.5cm; bulbs subrhizomatous, scales lanceolate, acute, white, to 5cm. Lvs to 15×3.5cm, in whorls, oblanceolate, margins wavy. Fls to 20, scented, to 11cm wide, bowl-shaped, horizontal, in a raceme; pedicels bracteate, erect; tepals 8×2.5cm, oblanceolate, white, spotted purple at base, apex acute, recurved; pollen yellow. Fr. cylindrical, furrowed. Summer. W US (NW California, S Oregon). var. ***purpurascens*** Stearn. Fls opening white, becoming pink then purple. Z4.

***L. wigginsii*** Beane & Vollmer. Stems to 90cm, stem-rooting; bulbs rhizomatous, scales entire or jointed, producing bulbils. Lvs to 22×2cm, linear-lanceolate. Fls solitary or in a raceme, pendulous, turk's-cap; pedicels arching; tepals to 7cm, reflexed, yellow with variable purple spotting; pollen yellow. Summer. W US (N California, S Oregon). Z4.

***L. wilsonii*** Leichtlin. Stems to 1m; bulbs 5.5×3.5cm, concentric, scales white. Lvs 10×2.5cm, lanceolate, 5–7-veined. Fls cup-shaped, erect, 12.5cm wide, tepals recurved, to 10cm, orange-red with basal central yellow stripe, dark spotting. Summer. Japan. Z5.

### HYBRIDS AND THEIR CLASSIFICATION

The vast majority of the hybrids slot easily into the various divisions, such as Orientals, Asiatics, Martagons, etc. In 1963 the Royal Horticultural Society Lily Committee drew up a Horticultural Classification for show, exhibition, catalogue and registration purposes. This classification has stood the test of time, although in recent years the barriers between the various divisions, which at one time seemed almost inviolable, have been broken, as hybridizers with particular skills have created 'bridge-builders' between one division and another. Notable within these has been *L. henryi*, which was originally crossed with the trumpet lily, *L. leucanthum* ssp. *chloraster* to produce *L.* ×*kewense* (flowered 1900). This was followed by Debras's cross in 1925 with *L. sargentiae* and named *L.* ×*aurelianense*. In the 1950s Woodriff crossed *L. henryi* with *L. speciosum* ssp. *rubrum* to achieve *L.* 'Black Beauty', and in the 1970s North eventually obtained a successful cross with an Asiatic hybrid which he named *L.* 'Eureka'. Another link between different divisions has been *L. longiflorum* and various Asiatic hybrids. These few instances may show a trend which will continue and flourish with genetic engineering.

This classification follows the *International Lily Register*. Each category is followed by a list of examples.

Division 1: Hybrids derived from such species or hybrid groups as *Ll. cernuum, davidii, lancifolium, leichtlinii, maculatum,* ×*hollandicum, amabile, pumilum, concolor* and *bulbiferum*.

1(a): Early-flowering with upright flowers, single or an umbel. 'Apeldoorn': 80cm; flowers bright orange-red. 'Connecticut King': to 1m; flowers golden-yellow. 'Connecticut Star': flowers yellow, with yellow-orange throat, sparsely flecked purple. 'Cote d'Azur': flowers deep pink with paler centre. 'Enchantment': 75cm; flowers bright nasturtium red, to 15 per stem. 'Joan Evans': flowers orange, with basal spots inside petals. 'Marilyn Monroe': to 1.2m; flowers yellow. 'Ming Yellow': to 1.2m; leaves glossy; flowers broad, somewhat recurved, bright golden yellow. 'Mont Blanc': flowers broad, open, cream-white, spotted brown. 'Peach Blush': to 90cm; flowers rose-pink, darker at the base, sparsely spotted maroon. 'Sterling Star': to 1.2m; flowers white with a cream tinge and brown spots.

1(b): Flowers outward-facing. 'Brandywine': to 1m; flowers deep orange with red spots. 'Corsage': to 1.2m; flowers pale pink with an ivory-white centre, spotted burgundy, tinged yellow and cream outside. 'Fireking': to 90cm; flowers bright orange-red with purple spots. 'Prosperity': flowers lemon-yellow. 'Tamara': flowers red with yellow-orange centre and grey-purple flecks.

1(c): Flowers pendent. 'Black Butterfly': 90cm; flowers deep burgundy-red. 'Citronella': to 1.5m; lemon-yellow, with small, feint, black spots, to 30 per stem. 'Connecticut Yankee': stems 1.2m; flowers vivid orange-red, unspotted. Fiesta Hybrids: flowers golden-yellow to bright red. Harlequin Hybrids: to 1.5m; flowers salmon-pink, with shades of cream, lilac, rose, and purple. 'Lady Bowes Lyon': flowers rich red with black spots. Tiger Hybrids: flowers dark red.

Division 2: Hybrids of Martagon type of which one parent has been a form of *L. martagon* or *L. hansonii*. Backhouse hybrids: flowers ivory, yellow, cream, pink, and burgundy, occasionally flecked pink. 'Marhan': to 1.3m; flowers orange with red-tinged spots, or bright yellow with dark purple-brown spots.

Division 3: Hybrids derived from *L. candidum*, *L. chalcedonicum*, and other related European species (but excluding *L. martagon*). 'Apollo': to 75cm; flowers dwarf, pure white. 'Ares': flowers bright orange-red. 'Artemis': flowers pale pink to rich yellow-orange. 'Prelude': flowers orange-red, darker red at tips.

Division 4: Hybrids of America species. Bellingham Hybrids: flowers bicoloured orange-yellow and red, with deep brown spots. 'Bellmaid Hybrids': flowers golden-yellow, tinged orange, eventually turning red, with median spots.

Division 5: Hybrids derived from *L. longiflorum* and *L. formosanum*. 'Formobel': flowers very large, white, flushed green on the throat. 'Formolongi': flowers snow-white.

Division 6: Hybrid Trumpet Lilies and Aurelian Hybrids derived from Asiatic species including *L. henryi*, but excluding those derived from *Ll. auratum, speciosum, japonicum*, and *rubellum*.

6(a): Flowers trumpet-shaped. 'African Queen': 1.5m; flowers large, rich apricot orange. 'Black Dragon': flowers white inside, very dark rich purple-red outside. 'Black Magic': flowers snow-white inside, purple-black outside. 'Golden Clarion': flowers golden-yellow. 'Golden Splendour': flowers deep golden-yellow; petals with one dark burgundy stripe outside. 'Green Dragon': flowers snow-white inside with yellow flush at base, striped brown and green outside. 'Limelight': flowers lime-yellow. Olympic Hybrids: flower white outside, shade cream or fuchsia-pink inside, occasionally tinged green. 'Pink Perfection': 1.5m; flowers very large, deep purple-pink, fragrant.

6(b): Flowers bowl-shaped. 'First Love': flowers golden-yellow, edged pink, with pale-green throat. 'Heart's Desire': flowers flushed yellow through cream to white, occasionally with orange throat. 'New Era': flowers large, white, tinged green.

6(c): Flowers flat, or only petal tips recurved. 'Christmas Day': flowers cream, with bright orange and clear green centre. 'Golden Showers': flowers golden-yellow inside, brown outside. 'Summer Song': flowers yellow.

6(d): Flowers distinctly recurved 'Bright Star': flowers ivory-white, with light orange star in centre. 'Golden Sunburst': flowers vivid golden-yellow, veined green outside. 'Magic Fire': flowers deep apricot. 'Mimosa Star': flowers yellow, fragrant. 'T.A. Havemeyer': flowers deep orange with dark ivory tips and green throat. 'White Henryi': flowers white, flushed deep orange on throat.

Division 7: Hybrids of Far Eastern species, such as *Ll. auratum, speciosum, japonicum* and *rubellum*, including any of their hybrids with *L. henryi*. 'Dominique': flowers red-purple, with red spotted throat and somewhat crinkled petals. 'Empress of Mars': flowers blood-red, tipped white. 'Omega': flowers white, with a median band of salmon-pink on each petal. 'Suzanne Sumerville': flowers white, blotched pale pink and lavender.

7(a): Flowers trumpet-shaped.

7(b): Flowers bowl-shaped. 'Bonfire': flowers carmine inside with a silver edge, silver-white outside with a very pale pink flush. 'Casablanca': flowers very large, pure white, very fragrant. 'Empress of China': flowers pure white, with heavy dark red or burgundy spots inside. 'Empress of India': flowers carmine, edged white. 'Empress of Japan': flowers pure white, banded gold, spotted deep burgundy. 'Imperial Jewel': flowers white with red throat.

7(c): Flowers flat. 'Imperial Red Band': flowers very large, with a deep red stripe on each petal. 'Imperial Pink': flowers large, pink. 'Imperial Salmon': flowers large, salmon-pink. 'Imperial Silver': flowers large, pure white, spotted burgundy. 'Spectre': flowers pale to deep pink. 'Stargazer': flowers very wide, rich carmine, spotted crimson. 'Troubador': flowers very large, heavily spotted, rich carmine at centre, edged pink and white.

7(d): Flowers recurved. 'Jamboree': flowers carmine with darker spots, edged white. 'Journey's End': flowers very large, carmine, tipped and margined white, spotted red. 'Pink Solace': fls off-white, turning red, with yellow-green throat. Rangotito hybrids: flowers white through pink to deep rich red, occasionally with burgundy spots or white margin.

***L. albanicum*** Griseb. See *L. pyrenaicum* ssp. *carniolicum* var. *albanicum*.
***L. artvinense*** Misch. See *L. pyrenaicum* ssp. *ponticum* var. *artvinense*.
***L. atrosanguineum*** anon. See *L. maculatum*.
***L. australe*** Stapf. See *L. brownii*.
***L. avenaceum*** Fisch. See *L. medeloides*.
***L. batemanniae*** Wallace. See *L. maculatum*.
***L. biondii*** Baroni. See *L. davidii* var. *unicolor*.
***L. bloomerianum*** Kellogg. See *L. humboldtii*.
***L. camschatcensis*** L. See *Fritillaria camschatcensis*.
***L. carniolicum*** Koch. See *L. pyrenaicum* ssp. *carniolicum*.
***L. carniolicum*** ssp. ***ponticum*** P.H. Davis & D.M. Henderson. See *L. pyrenaicum* ssp. *ponticum* var. *ponticum*.
***L. cathayanum*** Wils. See *Cardiocrinum cathayanum*.
***L. centifolium*** Stapf. See *L. leucanthum* var. *centifolium*.
***L. chaixii*** Maw. See *L. bulbiferum*.
***L. chinense*** Baroni. See *L. davidii* var. *willmottiae*.
***L. colchicum*** Steven. See *L. monadelphum*.
***L. cordatum*** (Thunb.) Koidz. See *Cardiocrinum cordatum*.
***L. ×creelmannii*** hort. See *L. ×imperiale*.
***L. croceum*** Chaix. See *L. bulbiferum* var. *croceum*.
***L. dahuricum*** Elwes. See *L. dauricum*.
***L. davuricum*** Wils. See *L. dauricum*.
***L. elegans*** Thunb. See *L. maculatum*.
***L. excelsum*** Endl. & Hartinger. See *L. ×testaceum*.
***L. farreri*** Turrill. See *L. duchartrei*.
***L. fauriei*** Lév. & Vaniot. See *L. amabile*.
***L. formosum*** Lem. See *L. dauricum*.
***L. forrestii*** W.W. Sm. See *L. lankongense*.
***L. fortunei*** Lindl. See *L. maculatum*.
***L. giganteum*** Wallich non hort. See *Cardiocrinum giganteum*.
***L. glehnii*** F. Schmidt. See *Cardiocrinum cordatum*.
***L. harrisii*** Carr. See *L. longiflorum* var. *eximium*.
***L. heldreichii*** Freyn. See *L. chalcedonicum*.
***L. howellii*** I.M. Johnst. See *L. bolanderi*.
***L. isabellinum*** Kunze. See *L. ×testaceum*.
***L. jankae*** Kerner. See *L. pyrenaicum* ssp. *carniolicum* var. *jankae*.
***L. krameri*** Hook. f. See *L. japonicum*.
***L. linifolium*** Hornem. See *L. pumilum*.
***L. lowii*** anon. See *L. bakerianum*.
***L. makinoi*** Koidz. See *L. japonicum*.
***L. martagon*** var. ***dalmaticum*** Elwes. See *L. martagon* var. *cattaniae*.
***L. maximowiczii*** Reg. See *L. leichtlinii* var. *maximowiczii*.
***L. montanum*** Nels. See *L. philadelphicum*.
***L. myriophyllum*** Franch. See *L. sulphureum*.
***L. neilgherrense*** Wight. See *L. wallichianum* var. *neilgherrense*.
***L. nevadense*** Eastw. See *L. kelleyanum*.
***L. nitidum*** Bull. See *L. columbianum*.
***L. parviflorum*** Hook. See *L. columbianum*.
***L. pennsylvanicum*** Ker-Gawl. See *L. dauricum*.
***L. ponticum*** K. Koch. See *L. pyrenaicum* ssp. *ponticum* var. *ponticum*.
***L. ponticum*** var. ***artvinense*** P.H. Davis & D.M. Henderson. See *L. pyrenaicum* ssp. *ponticum* var. *artvinense*.
***L. ×princeps*** Wils. See *L. ×imperiale*.
***L. pseudotigrinum*** Carr. See *L. leichtlinii* var. *maximowiczii*.
***L. pulchellum*** Fisch. See *L. concolor* var. *pulchellum*.
***L. roezlii*** Reg. non Purdy. See *L. pardalinum* var. *angustifolium*.
***L. roezlii*** Purdy non Reg. See *L. vollmeri*.
***L. ×sargale*** Crow. See *L. ×imperiale*.
***L. shastense*** Eastw. See *L. kelleyanum*.
***L. sutchuenense*** Franch. See *L. davidii* var. *willmottiae*.
***L. szovitsianum*** Fisch. & Avé-Lall. See *L. monadelphum*.
***L. tenuifolium*** Schrank. See *L. pumilum*.
***L. thayerae*** Wils. See *L. davidii*.
***L. thunbergianum*** Schult. & Schult. f. See *L. maculatum*.
***L. tigrinum*** Ker-Gawl. See *L. lancifolium*.
***L. tigrinum*** var. ***fortunei*** Standish. See *L. lancifolium* var. *fortunei*.
***L. tigrinum*** var. ***flaviflorum*** Mak. See *L. lancifolium* var. *flaviflorum*.
***L. tigrinum*** var. ***splendens*** Van Houtte. See *L. lancifolium* var. *splendens*.
***L. umbellatum*** hort. See *L. ×hollandicum*.
***L. washingtonianum*** var. ***purpureum*** hort. See *L. rubescens*.
***L. washingtonianum*** var. ***rubescens*** S. Wats. See *L. rubescens*.
For further synonymy see *Nomocharis*.

**Lime**. The word lime covers several substances containing calcium. The most common is calcium carbonate which can be bought as crushed chalk or limestone. Calcium oxide or quicklime is made by heating limestone: it is caustic and dangerous to handle. Slaked or hydrated lime, calcium hydroxide, is less harmful and acts more quickly, although it will scorch plant foliage. One kilogram of calcium oxide is as effective as 1.5kg/3⅓lb of calcium hydroxide and 2kg/4½lb of calcium carbonate, although the efficiency of the latter is also influenced by the degree of crushing. In most gardens the cheapness and ease of handling crushed limestone or chalk makes up for its relative bulk.

Lime is most important for its effect on the acid/alkaline balance in the soil, measured on the pH scale. A reading of 7.0 is neutral: anything below that is acidic and anything above is alkaline. The soil pH influences nutrient availability. The calcium that is added is rarely directly needed as a nutrient, but magnesian or dolomitic limestone contains a percentage of magnesium carbonate ($MgCO_3$) which can be important for overcoming magnesium deficiency. Most crops do best at pH 6.5 on mineral soils and at pH 5.8 on peats, and yield can fall if the pH moves below this optimum. Although the effect is gradual at first, a point is often reached where there is a sharp decline and for many crops this point lies around pH 5–5.5.

Many gardeners have a habit of regularly liming vegetable plots, although it is always preferable to assess the pH beforehand with a soil test to avoid over-liming. Many vegetables actually do better in relatively acid soils, and overliming can lead to nutrient deficiencies especially with phosphorus, iron, manganese and other trace elements, especially if the pH rises above 7.5. The same is generally true of ornamentals, although some lime-loving, or calcicolous, plants such as alpines do have a requirement for a higher pH. Lime-hating plants, or calcifuges, such as *Rhododendron* and almost all the related Ericaceae, need a low pH and should never be limed; they have no requirement for calcium.

Adding lime to a clay soil can also improve its structure by the chemical process known as flocculation which helps to aggregate the soil particles into larger, stable blocks with good-sized air spaces in between. Liming can also encourage the beneficial activities of earthworms and of nitrogen-fixing bacteria, both of which dislike acid conditions. And because acidic soil hinders the action of the soil bacteria which convert ammonium salts into nitrates, lime can make more readily available important plant nutrients.

Liming can discourage certain diseases such as club root, and also pests including leatherjackets, slugs and wireworms. However, too much calcium can encourage other pathogens such as potato scab. It can 'lock up' iron, magnesium and other soil elements, leading to plant deficiency problems like chlorosis. 'Sequestered' or chelated compounds called sequestrols can help control such deficiency-related problems.

The lime requirement of a soil, that is, the amount of lime needed to change the pH by one unit, can be determined by a home or laboratory soil test. (It depends on the soil texture, type of clay, type and quantity of organic matter, and the starting and required pH.) Clay soils have a high buffering capacity and large amounts of lime need to be added to affect its pH. The alkalinity of sands can be easily raised with lime, but the effect may be short-lived.

The liming factor is the degree by which the amount of lime needed as a surface application to raise the pH in the field is actually greater than that suggested by the test sample. For some soils there can be a two- or threefold increase. This discrepancy is due to variables such as the buffering capacity of soils, rate of rainfall and leaching in the field, the soil structure, the evenness of incorporation of the lime and so on.

In gardens it is common to follow a rule-of-thumb approach. The table here shows the *approximate* amounts of hydrated lime needed to raise the pH level to 6.5 on different soils, in kilograms per square metre and pounds per square yard. If crushed chalk or limestone is used, amounts are increased by about one third (see Table).

*Approximate quantities of hydrated lime in g/m² (oz/yd²) required as a surface application to raise the pH level of different soil types to 6.5*

| Original pH | Sandy or gravelly | Medium loams | Peat or clay |
|---|---|---|---|
| 4.5 | 270 (8) | 410 (12) | 545–610 (16–18) |
| 5.0 | 410 (12) | 340 (10) | 475–510 (14–15) |
| 5.5 | 185 (5.5) | 270 (8) | 375–445 (11–13) |
| 6.0 | 170 (5) | 220 (6.5) | 300–340 (9–10) |
| 6.5 | 0 | 0 | 0 |

Although, as the table indicates, the lime requirement to bring very acid soils to near neutral are extremely high, in practice it is seldom wise to make surface applications of more than 0.5–0.6kg/m²(¾–1lb/sq yd) of hydrated lime at any one time; even lower limits – about 0.3kg/m²(½lb/sq yd) – may be applicable on sandy soils. Not only are such heavy applications wasteful because of leaching, they are also dangerous because of potential burning, and because of the inevitable risk of inducing nutrient deficiencies. Such ambitious modifications of soil pH should be undertaken over several seasons, with lime applications planned to occur at least several months before the onset of the growing season, and preferably made in split applications, with one being deeply incorporated into the soil; pH testing between subsequent applications is strongly recommended.

Lime can be applied to bare ground at any time of the year but the safest and most convenient period in cold climates is usually autumn or winter. It can be spread as a top-dressing or worked in with a fork or rake. It should not be applied at the same time as animal manures because the chemical reaction between manure and lime causes much of the nitrogen in the manure to be converted into ammonia gas which is released into the atmosphere. Lime and animal manures are often applied in alternate years or at least with a gap of several weeks. The lime being applied after the manure.

Lime dressings can work through to an acidic subsoil but the process may take a decade or more to show an effect. On acid plots any opportunity for deep liming when cultivating the soil should not be overlooked. Deep liming is recommended where an orchard is planned on acid soil.

Although some gardeners sprinkle lime between layers on their compost heaps, this is no longer recognized as necessary practice and it is just as easy to apply it directly on the garden bed. Moreover, doing so prevents the possibility of a loss of nitrogen through ammonia volatilization.

Standard seed and potting mediums, even when peat-based, contain one form of lime or another, but there are special mediums available for acid-loving plants. Several fertilizers have an alkaline reaction on the soil because they contain free lime (available calcium); these include basic slag, calcium cyanamide, nitrate of lime and nitro-chalk.

**LIMNANTHACEAE** R. Br. POACHED EGG FLOWER FAMILY. Dicot. 2 genera and 8 species of small delicate sub-succulent annuals of moist places, often with mustard oils. Leaves alternate, pinnatisect to pinnate; stipules absent. Flowers regular, bisexual, solitary, on long axillary pedicels, (4) 5-merous (*Limnanthes*) or 3-merous (*Floerkea*); calyx more or less distinct, valvate; corolla distinct, convolute; stamens twice petals, in 2 whorls or as many as and alternate with them; filaments opposite calyx with basal nectary gland; ovary superior, of 2 or 3 carpels (*Floerkea*), (4) 5 (*Limnanthes*), united by gynobasic style, deeply lobed into globular segments, style cleft or with lobed stigma, each locule with 1 basal ovule. Fruit separating into indehiscent 1-seeded mericarps; embryo with unusual fats; endosperm absent. N America. *Limnanthes* .

**Limnanthemum** S.G. Gmel.
***L. aquaticum*** (Walter) Britt. See *Nymphoides aquatica*.
***L. indicum*** Thwaites. See *Nymphoides indica*.
***L. nymphoides*** (L.) Hoffsgg. & Link. See *Nymphoides peltata*.
***L. peltatum*** S.G. Gmel. See *Nymphoides peltata*.

**Limnanthes** R. Br. (From Gk *limne*, marsh, and *anthos*, flower, referring to the habitat.) MEADOW FOAM. Limnanthaceae. 7 species of annual herbs. Leaves alternate, pinnately divided. Sepals and petals 5, petals with a U-shaped band of hairs on the claw, stigmas 5, capitate. Fruit 3–5 nutlets. W US. Z8.

CULTIVATION Native to marshland in coastal western US, *Limnanthes* spp. are annuals that will self-sow in profusion where conditions suit. They are suitable as path and border edging, for the interstices of paving, at the base of walls and in other situations offering a cool, moist root run. The lightly scented flowers, carried over long periods in summer, are a good nectar source for bees. Easily grown in sun in any moderately fertile and reliably moisture-retentive soil, from seed sown *in situ* in spring or, in mild winter areas, in autumn.

***L. douglasii*** R. Br. POACHED EGG FLOWER. To 30cm. Lvs 2-pinnatifid, glabrous, succulent, yellow-green, leaflets dentate. Fls fragrant, to 2.5cm diam., peduncle 5–10cm, pet. yellow with white tips, or entirely white. Nutlets smooth or nearly so. California, S Oregon. var. ***sulphurea*** C. Mason. Pet. yellow. Point Reyes (California).

**Limnobium** Rich. (From Gk *limne*, marsh, and *bios*, life, alluding to the habitat.) Hydrocharitaceae. 2 species of perennial herbs, forming floating mats or sometimes rooting from base of leaves; stems contracted, bearing leaves or runner-like. Leaves 5–90×3–80mm, rosulate, elliptic to ovate to circular or cordate, sometimes aerenchymatous below; venation longitudinal; also 2 scale leaves at base of rosette. Inflorescence unisexual, cymose; male sessile or pedunculate; flowers to 25, subtended by spathe of 1–2 free bracts, held above water; petals white, 3, free, linear to lanceolate; stamens 2–5, anthers 4-celled; female inflorescence sessile or subsessile; flowers 1–6, held above water; sepals 3, free, elliptic, spreading at anthesis; petals 0–3, free, lanceolate, green-white; staminodes 2–6; ovary inferior, 3–9 carpellate, stigmas filamentous. Fruit a capsule, beaked, ellipsoid; seeds beaked. Americas.

CULTIVATION Floating aquatics or wet-soil herbaceous perennials, *Limnobium* spp. are found rooted in the muddy bottoms of lakes, ponds and ditches: in cultivation, plants may be grown as free-floating specimens, but the best results are had from rooted individuals. Grow *L. spongia* in cold aquaria and outdoor pools, *L. laevigatum* in tropical aquaria: both respond best to high light levels and *L. laevigatum* demands an extremely humid atmosphere, usually best achieved in a covered tank. Propagate from runners and offsets, rooted into aquaria/pond bottoms or grown in aquatic baskets of a still loam, topped off with pea gravel.

***L. laevigatum*** (Humb. & Bonpl. ex Willd.) Heine. Lvs 2–5×1–4cm, spathulate, elliptic, rarely obovate, apex rounded, rarely acute or mucronate; stipules to 22cm. Stamens in 2–3 whorls; female pet. poorly developed or absent; ovary 3–6-carpellate. Fr. 2.5mm diam., ellipsoid to obovoid. C & S America. Z10.

***L. spongia*** (Bosc) Steud. AMERICAN FROGBIT. Lvs 1–10×1–8cm, ovate to depressed-ovate or cordate, acute; stipules to 8cm. Stamens 9–12 in 5–6 whorls; female pet. well-developed; ovary 6–9 carpellate. Fr. 4–12mm, diam., ellipsoid to oblong; seeds 200+, 1–2mm. US. Z5.

For synonymy see *Hydrocharis* and *Hydromystria*.

**Limnocharis** Humb. & Bonpl. (From Gk *limne*, a marsh, and *charis*, delight.) Limnocharitaceae. 2 species of annual or perennial herbs without stolons. Leaves in rosettes, lanceolate to ovate, petiolate, variable in size and shape. Peduncle erect, triangular in cross-section; flowers yellow, 2–15 borne in umbels; sepals 3, persistent; petals 3, fugacious, hermaphrodite; stamens numerous surrounded by staminodes; carpels numerous and laterally flattened, stigma sessile. SE Asia, Malesia.

CULTIVATION As for *Hydrocleys* in neutral to slightly acidic water: a tendency to become invasive in indoor ponds is easily curbed by cutting back.

***L. flava*** (L.) Buchenau. Perenn., with erect, evergreen, aquatic growth, to 60cm. Lvs 20cm, ovate, base cordate; petiole long. Fls 2–12 in an umbel, velvety green, scape triangular in cross-section, fls hermaphrodite, 2.5cm diam.; pet. yellow with off-white border. Fr. a capsule, scape bends to water, germinates *in situ*. Summer. W Indies, tropical America. 'Minor': dwarf. Z10.

***L. commersonii*** Spreng. See *Hydrocleys nymphoides*.
***L. emarginata*** Humb. & Bonpl. See *L. flava*.
***L. humboldtii*** Rich. See *Hydrocleys nymphoides*.
***L. nymphoides*** Michx. See *Hydrocleys nymphoides*.
***L. plumieri*** Rich. See *L. flava*.

**LIMNOCHARITACEAE** Tacht. ex Cronq. WATER POPPY FAMILY. Monocot. 3 genera and 12 species of perennial aquatic herbs, more or less glabrous, aerenchymatous, sometimes free floating; laticifers present; vessels only in roots. Leaves alternate, petiolate, lamina often expanded; intravaginal scales at nodes. Flowers bisexual, regular, 3-merous, solitary or in an involucre cymose umbel on a scape; calyx 3 free sepals, persistent; corolla 3 petals, larger, deciduous; stamens 3-numerous, in trunk bundles when numerous, outer ones often sterile; ovary superior, of 3, 5–9 or 12–20 free carpels in one whorl, sometimes weakly connate basally, nectariferous towards the base; ovules numerous. Fruit a head of follicles; embryo horse-shoe-shaped; endosperm absent. Tropical and warm. *Hydrocleys, Limnocharis*.

**Limnophila** R. Br. (From Gk *limne*, marsh and *-philos*, loving; referring to its habitat.) Scrophulariaceae. Some 36 species of annual or perennial aquatic or marsh herbs. Stems creeping, ascending or erect, rooting at nodes. Aerial leaves whorled or opposite, sessile or petiolate, entire to serrate; aquatic leaves pinnatifid to pinnate. Flowers in spikes or racemes or solitary and axillary; calyx and petals 5-lobed; corolla tube campanulate, throat rarely pilose, 2-lipped, lower lip 3-lobed; stamens 4. Fruit a capsule. Summer. Old World Tropics. Z9.

CULTIVATION Marsh and swamp plants or shallow water aquatics in the humid tropics and subtropics; *L. indica* is a common plant of paddy fields and irrigation ditches in sugar cane plantations. Most are polymorphic depending on degree of immersion, from the slender plants of firm mud-banks to luxuriant, much-branched aquatics when growing fully submerged.

They are most frequently cultivated in tropical aquaria, where they make erect festoons of largely submerged, light green foliage, occasionally over 50cm/20in. in length. Flowering seldom occurs except where growth extends well above water level, indicating a need for strong filtered light in cultivation, boosted artificially during the winter. High temperatures (20–25°C/68–77°F), soft neutral water and a growing medium of sandy loam are essential elements for luxuriant growth. When damaged, *L. indica* may be poisonous to fish or herbivores and therefore should only be grown in a spacious tank.

Propagate by cuttings or from seed in spring; seeds should be kept dry at temperatures of 15–18°C/60–65°F, sown in spring on to moist sand at 25°C/77°F, and covered with a pane of glass. Give seedlings maximum light, prick out into a 1:1 mix of loam/sand and, when rooted, gradually raise the water level around the seedlings.

***L. heterophylla*** Benth. Perenn. Stems to 60cm. Aquatic lvs whorled, 6–12, filiform. Aerial lvs whorled, sometimes opposite, 4–6, crenate to entire. Fls solitary, sessile. Summer. Indonesia, Malaya.

***L. indica*** (L.) Druce. Aromatic perenn. Stems glabrous, many-branched, slender, to 90cm. Upper lvs whorled, variously dissected, glandular; aquatic lvs finely dissected, to 3cm, whorled, 6–12. Fls axillary, solitary; pedicels pubesc; cal. 3–7mm; cor. tube pink to purple, or white to pale yellow, 8–12mm, upper lip entire or 2-lobed, lower lip 3-lobed. Fr. elliptic to globose. Summer. Tropical Africa, Asia, N Australia.

***L. sessiliflora*** Bl. Stem to 20cm. Aquatic lvs whorled, pinnatisect; aerial lvs lanceolate to pinnatifid, entire or dentate. Fls solitary, sessile to subsessile. Summer. Indonesia, Japan.

**Limonia** L. (From Dioscoridean plant-name *leimonion*.) Rutaceae. 1 species, a deciduous small tree to 9m, often evergreen in tropical climates; bark smooth, white; armed with spines in leaf axils, ascending, straight, sharp, 1.5–3.5cm. Leaves 7.5–10cm, pinnate, very minutely pubescent when young, later glabrous, with aniseed scent; leaflets 2.5–4cm, opposite, in 2–3 pairs generally with a terminal leaflet, ovate to obovate, obtuse, entire to slightly minutely crenate, subsessile, basal largest; petiole and rachis narrowly winged. Inflorescence in leaf axils, of lax panicles, small; flowers numerous, small, white to pale green stained maroon to deep red; pedicels slender, pubescent; calyx 5-dentate, very small, deciduous; petals usually 5, spreading, acutely ovate, smooth, imbricate in bud; stamens 10–12, filaments very short, united at base by woolly pubescence, anthers very large, dark red; ovary incompletely 4–6-locular, becoming 1-locular, ovules many per locule, style very short. Fruit 5–6cm, globose, 1-celled; pericarp hard and woody, rough, pale grey; pulp gum-like, aromatic, bitter-sweet; seeds embedded in pulp, compressed-oblong, pilose. India, Sri Lanka. Citrus can be grafted onto this genus, often resulting in premature flowering, perhaps useful in accelerating breeding programmes. Z10.

CULTIVATION As for *Citrus*.

***L. acidissima*** L. WOOD APPLE; INDIAN WOOD APPLE; KAITHA; ELEPHANT APPLE. As for the genus.

For synonymy see *Feronia*.

**Limoniastrum** Heist. ex Fabr. (From Gk plant name *Leimonion*, and suffix *-aster*, related to.) Plumbaginaceae. About 10 species of small, evergreen shrubs and subshrubs. Leaves in basal rosettes, simple, entire or pinnatifid. Inflorescence a corymbose panicle of terminal spikelets, spikelets subtended by 3 bracts, flowering stem often bearing a scale; sterile stems often present; calyx gamosepalous, infundibular, tubular or obconical, straight or curved below, occasionally dentate between lobes, often coloured, persisting to fruiting, limb sometimes hyaline, 10-ribbed; corolla tubular, 5-lobed, somewhat longer than calyx, lobes equalling tube; stamens 5, inserted at base of petals; ovary superior, unilocular, subovoid; styles 5, connate in basal half, cylindric, filiform. Fruit a capsule, compressed-ellipsoid, in calyx, dehiscent, 1-seeded. Mediterranean.

CULTIVATION Occurring on salt marsh and dune habitats, *Limoniastrum* is a slightly frost-tender shrublet grown for its fleshy glaucous foliage and for the loose, airy panicles of pink flowers which turn violet when dried. In cooler climates, plants sown in later winter/early spring will flower in their first season, and may be grown in the annual border, for cutting and drying. Grow in sun in any well-drained, light sandy soil. Propagate by seed.

***L. monopetalum*** (L.) Boiss. To 1.2m, much-branched. Lvs about to 5×2cm, occasionally much more, many, oblanceolate to narrowly spathulate, somewhat fleshy, glaucous, sheathing; sheath amplexicaul. Panicle large, loosely branched; spikes 5–10cm; spikelets to 1cm, 1- or sometimes 2-fld; outer bract 4mm, truncate, inner bract 8mm, ellipsoid, enveloping fls; cal. about 1cm; cor. limb 1–2cm, diam., pink to purple. S Portugal and N Mediterranean. Z8.

For synonymy see *Statice*.

**Limonium** Mill. (From Gk *leimon*, a meadow, salt meadows are a common habitat of these plants.) SEA LAVENDER; MARSH ROSEMARY; STATICE. Plumbaginaceae. About 150 species of perennial herbs or shrubs, rarely annuals. Leaves simple, entire or pinnatifid, in basal rosettes or, sometimes, clustered at axils. Inflorescence a corymbose panicle of terminal spikelets on a scaly, bracteate stem; spikelets subtended by 3 floral bracts; calyx gamosepalous, infundibular, tubular or obconical, straight or curved below, occasionally dentate between lobes, often coloured, limb sometimes hyaline, 10-ribbed, persisting to fruiting; corolla 5-lobed, slightly exceeding calyx, connate only at base or short-tubular; stamens 5, inserted at base of petals; ovary superior, unilocular, subovoid; styles 5, free at base, cylindric, filiform, usually dimorphic. Fruit a capsule, ellipsoid, compressed, enclosed in calyx, dehiscent, 1-seeded. Cosmopolitan.

CULTIVATION Occurring in a wide range of coastal, plains, desert and semi-desert habitats, frequently on saline soils, *Limonium* spp. exhibit a range of size and hardiness. The tender, mostly shrubby species, notably those native to the Canary Islands, are suitable for cultivation outdoors only in zones that are frost-free or almost so. In favoured temperate gardens, species such as *L. macrophyllum* may thrive with the protection of a south- or southwest-facing wall, otherwise these tender subjects are better suited to the cool glasshouse or conservatory (min. 7°C/45°F). Grow in a well-drained sandy, loam-based mix, water moderately when in growth and keep almost dry in winter. Pot-grown specimens may be plunged in the open garden during the summer months.

Perennials of scale suitable for the rock garden include *L. caesium*, *L. cosyrense*, *L. gougetianum*, the calcicole *L. minutum*, *L. ramossisimum* and *L. thouinii*. Most of these species originate in Mediterranean- type climates and show a degree of susceptibility to winter wet in combination with cold. They need well-drained, sandy or gritty soils in full sun. Where winter temperatures fall below –5°C/23°F for long periods, they are perhaps more safely grown in the alpine house; alternatively, overwinter replacement stock in a well-ventilated, frost-free frame or glasshouse. *L. bellidifolium*, *L. binervosum* and the smaller subspecies of *L. vulgare* will tolerate lower temperatures in similar situations and conditions.

More robust perennials, such as *L. latifolium* and *L. gmelinii*, from the steppes of Central Europe and Russia, with *L. vulgare*, *L. nashii* and *L. carolinianum* from coastal salt flats, are hardy to −20°C/−4°F; *L. ferulaceum* is almost as tolerant, given the protection of a winter mulch until established. As with many of the genus they are well adapted to coastal gardens and dry soils. Valued for their long flowering period and often grown in the herbaceous border, their horticulturally unrefined forms are particularly suited to more informal and naturalistic paintings. Good textural contrasts may be achieved by naturalizing in gravel or shingle. Grow in any deep, well-drained soil in full sun.

The flowers of most species of *Limonium* can be air-dried for winter decoration; they range in form and colour from the most subtle and delicate sprays on fine sinuous stems as in *L. latifolium* and *L. ornatum* to the more extravagant and densely flowered panicles of the improved cultivars of *L. sinuatum*, frequently seen as a florist's flower. *L. sinuatum*, usually grown as an annual, is particularly valued for the strong bright colours it retains when drying, provided the flowers are kept away from bright light. Single colours are available in a spectrum ranging from the pure white 'Iceberg' through the aptly named 'Sunset' mixtures to deep blues and violets. Cut stems when most flowers in the spray are fully open and hang to dry in small bunches; the wings may first be stripped from the fleshy stems to reduce risk of rotting. In areas with cool summers, those treated as annuals are best started early under glass, since they need a long growing season to produce satisfactory quantities of open flowers. They can also be grown under glass with full sun; autumn sowings overwintered in well-ventilated conditions with a minimum temperature of 8–10°C/46–50°F will flower in late winter early spring.

All species are most easily raised from seed; many spp. are apomitic. Division is possible but difficult and re-establishment may be slow. *L. latifolium* and other large perennials may be increased by root cuttings in a sandy propagating mix in late winter/early spring.

***L. angustatum*** (A. Gray) Small. Perenn. herb, slender. Lvs 5–9×0.5–2cm, linear to lanceolate, stemless, few, 1-nerved, tapering to slightly shorter petiole. Flowering stems to 30cm, erect; panicle 12–24cm diam., loose; spikelets 1-fld; floral bracts broadly oblong, margins hyaline, outer bracts to 2.5mm, middle bracts to 3mm, inner to 4.5mm; cal. to 5mm; tube glabrous, lobes to 1mm, 5. S & E US. Z6.

***L. arborescens*** (Brouss.) Kuntze. Shrub, 0.5–2m; stems terete, glabrous, branching above. Lvs 15–30×5–10cm, oblong-obovate, obtuse, mucronate, coriaceous, tapering to stout petiole. Flowering stem branching above to form panicle; branches recurved, 3-winged, wings becoming triangular-falcate below spike; spikelets 2-fld; cal. blue, tube glabrous; cor. about 6mm wide, white. Late spring. Tenerife. Z9.

***L. aureum*** (L.) Hill ex Kuntze. Perenn. herb to 30cm. Lvs 1–5×0.2–1cm, oblong-spathulate to lanceolate, grey-green, tapering to petiole. Flowering stems to 20cm, verruculose, forming a panicle; sterile branches present; spikes to 1cm; spikelets 3–5-fld, about 5 per spike; outer bract ovate, broadly scarious at margin, inner bracts much longer, concave; cal. about 5mm, funnelform, tube to 3mm, partially pubesc., limb bright yellow; cor. orange-yellow. Siberia, Mongolia. 'Sahin's Gold': to 75cm; fls yellow, profuse. 'Supernova': to 1m; fls vibrant yellow, papery. Z3.

***L. auriculaeursifolium*** (Pourr.) Druce. To 40cm, glabrous. Lvs 25–100×9×20mm, spathulate-oblanceolate, acute, mucronate, glaucous. Infl. pyramidal; spikes dense, to 2.5cm; spikelets 2–3-fld; outer bract to 1.5mm, inner bract to 4.5mm; cal. to 5.5.mm; cor. to 8mm, blue-violet. France, Iberian peninsula, Balearic Is. Z8.

***L. australe*** (Spreng.) Kuntze. Perenn. herb, about 30cm, glabrous. Lvs 3–7cm, oblong-obovate to oblong-spathulate, entire, tapering to petiole. Flowering stem to 50cm, dichotomously branching forming a corymb; spikes straight, terminal; spikelets 4–5-fld; cal. white to pale pink, ribs pubesc. at base, tube smooth, limb 5-lobed, mucronate; cor. yellow. Spring. Australia. Z9.

***L. bellidifolium*** (Gouan) Dumort. Perenn. herb, 10–30cm, partially woody at base. Lvs 2–5×1.5–2cm, obtuse to broadly rounded or spathulate, acute, tapering into long petiole, withering at anthesis. Flowering stems branching from base, tuberculate, bearing spikes on upper branches; spikes dense, compact, spikelets 4–5mm, 1–4-fld; outer bract broadly ovate, hyaline, inner bract 1.5–4mm, partially hyaline; cal. obconical, pilose on veins and base, white, limb longer than tube; cor. about 5mm, blue-violet. Mediterranean and Black Sea to E England. 'Caspica': to 85cm; fls in large fluffy sprays. 'Filigree': fls purple-blue. 'Spangle': to 1m; fls small, pale blue, in loose sprays. Z8.

***L. binervosum*** (G.E. Sm.) Salmon. Perenn. herb to 30cm; rhiz. woody. Lvs about 5×1cm, in many rosettes, obovate to spathulate, acute or obtuse, 1–3-veined. Infl. to 30cm, pyramidal; sterile stems absent; spikelets 1–3-fld, borne in 2 rows; inner bract to 5mm, twice length of overlapping outer bract; cal. about 5mm, pubesc. on veins beneath, teeth blunt; cor. about 8mm, pet. overlapping, blue-violet. W Europe.

***L. bourgaei*** (Webb) Kuntze. Perenn. herb to 40cm, woody-based. Lvs broadly ovate-rhombic, often sinuately lobed at base, otherwise entire. Flowering stem and branches pubesc., not winged; cal. deep violet, funnel-shaped; cor. white. Lanzarote. Z7.

***L. brassicifolium*** (Webb & Berth.) Kuntze. Perenn. herb 20–40cm; rhiz. woody, thick; stems winged. Lvs 10–30cm, broadly ovate, terminal lobe to 5–15×4–11cm, base tapering; petiole winged. Infl. paniculate; spikelets single-fld; inner bract about 5mm, cylindric-truncate; cal. tubular to funnelform, purple, glabrous, limb crenate; cor. white, exceeding cal. Canary Is., naturalized Iberia. Z9.

***L. caesium*** (Girard) Kuntze. Perenn. herb branching from base. Lvs to 3cm, obovate, spathulate, deciduous, 1–3-veined. Infl. 20–60cm, paniculate with many white, farinose sterile stems; spikes about 1cm; spikelets single-fld; inner bract about 3mm, outer bract about 0.5mm; cal. to 5mm, exceeding inner bract and cor.; cor. about 8mm, deep pink, limb about 6mm diam. Spain.

***L. carolinianum*** (Walter) Britt. Perenn. herb. Lvs to 15cm, spathulate to elliptic or obovate-elliptic. Infl. paniculate; flowering stems to 60cm; cal. to 6mm, usually glabrous, teeth about half length of lobes; cor. lilac. E US. Z5.

***L. caspium*** (Willd.) Gams. Perenn. herb, 10–35cm. Lvs 2–6×0.5–1.5cm, mostly basal, obovate to oblong-spathulate, obtuse, glaucescent, dying at anthesis, tapering into narrow petiole. Flowering stems many, paniculate from near base; sterile branches many; infl. dense, corymbose-paniculate; spikes small, dense, terminal; inner bract 4–6mm, concave, partially enclosing fls; cal. about 4mm, obconical, densely pubesc. at base and on nerves, limb white; cor. pale violet to blue-violet. C Europe, Balkans to Asia Minor. Often confused with *L. bellidifolium*. Z6.

***L. commune*** var. ***californicum*** (A. Gray) Greene. To 45cm. Lvs obovate to oblong spathulate, obtuse or retuse, tapering into petiole to 23cm. Cor. violet-purple; pet. oblong, narrowed toward base. California. Z8.

***L. confusum*** (Gren. & Godron) Fourr. Perenn., glabrous herb 10–50cm. Lvs rosulate, obovate-spathulate, mucronate, 1–3-nerved. Flowering stem erect, short, forming a panicle; sterile branches few to absent; spikes unilateral, narrow, lax; involucral bracts subacute, keeled, inner far exceeding outer; spikelets 2–3-fld, remote; cal. tube pilose on nerves; lobes short, obtuse; cor. violet. S France, Iberia, Sardinia. Z8.

***L. cordatum*** (L.) Mill. Herb to 30cm, grey-pubesc. Lvs 1.5–3×0.2–0.6cm, linear to linear-spathulate. Infl. an acutely branching corymb; sterile stems numerous; spikes to 1cm, compact; spikelets clustered, 1-fld; bracts hyaline, inner bract about 4mm, pubesc., outer bract slightly overlapping inner; cal. about 5mm; lobes acute; cor. violet. Italy, SE France. Z8.

***L. cosyrense*** (Guss.) Kuntze. Perenn., glabrous, woody-based herb 15–50cm. Lvs 2–2.5×2.5–3cm, linear-spathulate, in basal rosettes. Flowering stems to 15cm, slender, terete; infl. dichotomously branching; sterile branches many; spikes 2–5cm, loose; spikelets usually 1-fld; inner bract to 4mm, slightly overlapped by outer; cal. about 4mm, limb campanulate; cor. about 8mm. SE Europe, Malta. Z9.

***L. delicatulum*** (Girard) Kuntze. Perenn. herb, 40–70cm, glabrous. Lvs 3.5–5×2–3cm, oblanceolate to spathulate. Infl. a corymb, dichotomously branching; sterile branches absent or few at base; scales 6–15mm; spikes 1–3cm; spikelets 2–3 fld; inner bract to 3mm, outer to 1mm; cal. about 4mm, tubular; cor. about 6mm, pale pink. Mediterranean Spain, Balearic Islands. ssp. ***tournefortii*** Pign. Lvs spathulate, rounded, truncate or emarginate, 3–7-veined. Scales 2–3mm; spikelets 2–3-fld. E Spain, Balearic Is. ssp. ***valentinum*** Pign. Lvs oblanceolate-spathulate, 5–9-veined. Scales 10–15mm; spikelets 2-fld. E Spain. Z8.

***L. dregeanum*** (Presl) Kuntze. Perenn. herb, tufted, becoming somewhat woody. Lvs to 4cm, linear-spathulate, base tapering and clasping; peduncle to 25cm, erect, scabrid, pitted; bases often persisting. Spikelets 3–9-fld; fls short-stalked; cal. 3mm, tubular, partially pubesc.; cor. pink, exceeding cal. S Africa (Natal). Z9.

***L. echioides*** (L.) Mill. Annual herb, 15–25cm. Lvs 2–3.5×0.5–1.2cm, obovate to spathulate, obtuse, tapering into petiole, pinnately veined, glandular. Peduncle branching from near base, slender; spikes 2–10cm, lax; spikelets about 1cm, 1-occasionally 2-fld; inner bract concave, tuberculate, narrowly hyaline, outer bracts much smaller and slightly overlapping inner; cal. about 5mm, tube curved, hirtellous, lobes becoming barbed; cor. pink or pale violet. Mediterranean. Z8.

***L. emarginatum*** (Willd.) Kuntze. To 50cm, glabrous. Lvs 4–6×1–1.5cm, linear, somewhat spathulate, 1–5-veined, truncate to emarginate. Infl. cylindric, lacking sterile branches; scales 7mm or more; spikes 2–3cm, loose; spikelets 1–2-fld; inner bract about 6mm, outer bract about 2mm, partially overlapping inner; cal. about 7mm, limb 2–3mm; cor. to 12mm, purple. S Spain. Z8.

***L. ferulaceum*** (L.) Kuntze. Stems to 40cm, flexuous with persistent brown scales at base. Lvs ovate, caducous, absent at anthesis. Spikes borne towards apex of flowering stems, clavate; scales about 3mm, tinged red, awned; spikelets 1-fld; bracts many, inner bract 4–5mm, truncate, enclosing cal., other bracts much smaller; cal. about 3mm, cylindric; cor. about 6mm, pink. Iberia to C Mediterranean. Z7.

***L. fruticans*** (Webb) Kuntze. Shrub; stems short glabrous, terete. Lvs 4–5cm, ovate, obtuse, mucronate, tapering into petiole, borne at base of flowering stems; flowering stem 10–15cm, forming a panicle, puberulent; upper branches 2-winged, forming round auricles below spike; cal. bright blue, tube glabrous, limb dentate; cor. yellow. Tenerife. Z9.

***L. gmelinii*** (Willd.) Kuntze. Perenn. herb to 60cm. Lvs 10–30×2–8cm, broadly elliptic to oblong-ovate, in basal rosettes, tapering into short petiole. Flowering stem to 70cm, paniculate; spikes compact; spikelets 2–3-fld; outer bract 1–1.5mm, ovate, broadly hyaline margined, inner bract to 4.5mm; cal. 3–5mm, tube with pubesc. veins, lobes subacute; cor. blue. E Europe, Siberia. Z4.

***L. gougetianum*** (Girard) Kuntze. Perenn., to 20cm. Lvs 1.5–3×0.3–1cm, in basal rosettes, obovate to spathulate, tapering into petiole, 1-veined. Infl. paniculate; flowering stem to 25cm; sterile branches usually absent; scales 3–5mm; spikelets 2–3 fld, tightly packed; inner bract to 4mm; cal. tubular, red below, white above; cor. lavender. Algeria, Balearic Is. Z9.

***L. imbricatum*** (Webb ex Girard) Hubb. Perenn. herb. Lvs caespitose, pinnatifid, lobes broadly lanceolate to ovate, pubesc., terminal lobe to 5cm. Flowering stem and branches winged; cal. mauve, funnelform; cor. white. Tenerife. Z9.

***L. insigne*** (Coss.) Kuntze. Perenn. herb to 60cm, robust, rigid. Lvs 4–5×1–1.5cm, obovate, emarginate, tapering into long petiole, usually single-veined. Flowering stems dichotomously branching, paniculate, scales brown; sterile stems many; spikes to 3cm, linear; spikelets usually 1–2-fld; cor. to 1.5cm, dark rose, exceeding cal. SE Spain. ssp. ***carthaginense*** Pign. 20–60cm; branches tinged white. Spikelets usually 1-fld; cal. to 6mm. Z8.

***L. latifolium*** (Sm.) Kuntze. Stellate-pubesc., woody-based perenn. to 80cm. Lvs 20–60×8–15cm, basal, few, spathulate to elliptic, sparsely pubesc., pinnately veined, tapering into petiole; petiole equalling blade. Flowering stems to 60cm, much-branched, subspherical; sterile branches few or absent, scales about 5mm; spikes to 2cm, dense; spikelets 1–2 fld; inner bract about 2mm, hyaline, slightly overlapped by outer bract; cal. about 3mm, lobes 5, rounded, half length of tube, white; cor. about 6mm, pale violet. SE & C Europe. 'Violetta': fls violet blue. Z5.

***L. macrophyllum*** (Brouss.) Kuntze. Subshrub to 70cm. Lvs obovate-spathulate, obtuse, attenuate, sessile, sinuate. Flowering stem to 70cm, much branching to form a corymbose panicle; upper branches 3-winged, wings widest below spikes, often forming auricles, minutely pubesc.; spikelets 2-fld, erect, terminal; cal. blue; tube minutely pubesc.; cor. yellow to yellow-white. Late spring. Tenerife. Z9.

***L. macropterum*** (Webb & Berth.) Kuntze. Perenn. herb. Lvs to 35×12cm, obovate, lobed. Flowering stem to 30cm, branching towards apex; spikelets about 2cm, 2–4 fld, naked on 1 side, borne on winged rachis; cal. 1cm diam., deep blue to purple. Canary Is. Z9.

***L. minutum*** (L.) Fourr. 1–15cm, branches short, somewhat woody. Lvs *c*1×0.3cm, in tight cushion-like rosettes, spathulate, revolute, 1-veined, margins revolute. Infl. 2–12cm; branches segmented, smooth; sterile branches few to many; spikes subglobose, the apical one to 3cm, others smaller; spikelets 1–4-fld; bracts narrowly hyaline, the inner to 4mm, acute, overlapped by apex of smaller outer bract; cal. about 0.5cm, limb exceeding tube; cor. purple. SE France. Z8.

***L. mouretii*** (Pitard) Maire. Woody-based perenn.; branches winged. Lvs 7–15×1–3cm, basal, oblanceolate, mucronate, glabrous, tapering into slender petiole, lobes irregular. Flowering stems to 80cm, thinly branched, branches slightly winged; spike 2–5cm, unilateral; cal. tube green with purple-tinged lobes; cor. bright white. Summer–early autumn. Morocco. Z9.

***L. nashii*** Small. Perenn. Lvs 4–10cm, basal, oblong or elliptic to narrowly obovate, apex rounded or notched, occasionally mucronate, tapering into slender petiole. Flowering stem 30–70cm, erect; branches recurved at tips, spreading, forming a panicle; bracts 4mm, oval, obtuse; cal. 6–7mm, tube sparsely and softly pubesc. at base, seg. 5, triangular, acuminate; cor. deep blue. SE US. Z6.

***L. ornatum*** (Ball) Kuntze. To 1m; stems numerous, glabrous or puberulous. Lvs radical, lanceolate-spathulate, obtuse, glabrous, tapering into petiole. Infl. a lax panicle; spikes lax, arching; involucral bracts crimson, the outer 1–1.5mm, acute, obtuse, the inner 2–3mm, abruptly truncate; cal. 4–5mm, 5-lobed, awns about 0.5mm; cor. about 1cm, rose-purple. Morocco. Z9.

***L. otolepis*** (Schrenk) Kuntze. Perenn., 40–80cm occasionally more. Heterophyllous: basal lvs to 7cm, few, obovate-spathulate, narrowing towards base, dying at anthesis, short-stalked; stem lvs 1–3cm, sessile, sometimes clasping, rounded-reniform to suborbicular. Infl. a panicle composed of many spikes, sterile branches many; spikes short, terminal; spikelets 1–2-fld in tight clusters; inner bract about 2mm, concave, enclosing fl.; cal. about 3mm, narrow, funnelform, white; sparsely pubesc.; cor. blue. Summer. Asia Minor, Soviet C Asia. Z6.

***L. pectinatum*** (Ait.) Kuntze. Subshrub, glabrous. Lvs to 4×1cm, obovate-spathulate, rounded, emarginate, tapering to petiole, in basal rosettes. Flowering stem to 70cm, erect or decumbent; branches 3-angled or -winged; spikelets 3-fld; cal. lavender or pale violet, ribs partially pilose, limb 5-angled; cor. pale pink to rose. Late summer. Canaries. Z9.

***L.peregrinum*** (Bergius) R.A. Dyer. Shrub to 1m; branches with persistent lf bases towards base. Lvs to 10cm, obovate, enveloping stem at base, scabrid-glandular. Flowering stem scabrid; infl. dichotomously branching; spikes dense; spikelets 1-fld; cal. to 2cm, funnelform, 5-ribbed, bright pink; cor. bright pink, exceeding cal. S Africa. Z9.

***L.perezii*** (Stapf) Hubb. Subshrub to 70cm, more in cult.; stem woody, to 1cm diam. Lvs 12–15×6–10cm, broadly triangular-ovate, acuminate, glabrous, truncate, decurrent on long petiole. Panicle pubesc.; branches not winged, scales sulcate-caudate, ciliate; floral bracts undivided, downy; cal. purple to blue, downy, limb blue, truncate; cor. yellow. Canary Is. Z9.

***L.preauxii*** (Webb) Kuntze. To 70cm, somewhat woody. Lvs to 20cm, orbicular-triangular; petiole longer than blade. Peduncle bearing many flattened branches; spike naked on one side; cal. funnelform, lavender; cor. white, exceeding cal. Canary Is. Z9.

***L.×profusum*** Hubb. (*L.macrophyllum* × *L.puberulum.*) Subshrub, 30–70cm, rarely more. Lvs 15–20×4–5cm, oblong-obovate, coriaceous, glossy dark green, ciliate, sparsely downy; petiole winged. Infl. paniculate; branches winged; cal. 1cm wide, blue-purple; cor. white, shorter than cal. Autumn. Garden origin. Z9.

***L.puberulum*** (Webb) Kuntze. Small shrub or subshrub, puberulous to white-pilose. Lvs to 3cm, basal, obovate, stellate-pubesc., tapering at base; petiole winged. Peduncle to 25cm; infl. a panicle; spikelets 2-fld; cal. narrowly tubular to funnelform, purple; cor. white, exceeding cal. Canary Is. Z9.

***L.ramosissimum*** (Poir.) Maire. To 50cm. Lvs 3–10×1–2cm, usually oblanceolate-spathulate, occasionally obovate or spathulate, 1–5-veined. Infl. 20–50cm, sometimes with sterile branches; scales occasionally leaf-like; spikes 1–4cm, compact; spikelets 2–5-fld; inner bract about 5mm, rust-brown and occasionally partially hyaline, partially overlapped by outer bract; cal. about 5mm, subcylindric, usually incurved; cor. about 6mm, pale pink or violet. Mediterranean. ssp. ***confusum*** (Gren. & Godron) Pign. Lvs to 5×1cm, oblanceolate-spathulate, rounded at apex; scales 11–20mm, leaf-like; sterile branches absent. W Mediterranean. ssp. ***doerfleri*** (Hal.) Pign. Lvs to 5×1.5cm, obovate-spathulate to spathulate, acute or obtuse. Sterile branches absent; scales to 12mm. Cyclades. ssp. ***provinciaie*** (Pign.) Pign. Lvs to 10×2cm, obtuse or acute, base tapering to petiole. Scales to 12mm; sterile branches absent; spikes to 4cm. SE France, Sardinia and Corsica. ssp. ***siculum*** Pign. Lvs to 6×1.5cm, base tapering to petiole. Infl. with numerous sterile branches at base; inner bract and cal. to 6mm. Sicily. ssp. ***tommasinii*** (Pign.) Pign. Lvs to 4×1.2cm, acute or obtuse; base tapering into petiole. Sterile branches few; spikes to 2cm; scales to 12mm; inner bract and cal. to 4.5mm. NE Italy. Z8.

***L.reniforme*** (Girard) Lincz. Perenn., 60–80cm occasionally taller. Heterophyllous: basal lvs 3–8×1–2cm, obovate-spathulate, glaucescent, dying off at anthesis; stem lvs 4–6×3cm, ovate or oblong-elliptic, sessile, clasping. Flowering stems few, erect, paniculate; sterile branches absent or few; spikes loose, spreading; inner bract 2–5mm, broadly ovate, partially enclosing fls; cal. 3–4mm, narrowly funnelform, densely pubesc., limb white, lobes tinged red, cor. red-violet. Late spring–early autumn. Iran. Z8.

***L.sieberi*** (Boiss.) Kuntze. Suffruticose perenn.; stems branching from base. Lvs 2–5×0.5–1cm, obovate-spathulate, rounded or acute, tapering into petiole; petiole at least equalling blade. Flowering stems branching from base to form a panicle; sterile branches many; spikes loose; spikelets to 1cm, 1–2-fld, erect, unilateral on branchlets; bracts rust brown, hyaline, the outer about 1mm, inner about 4mm; cal. to 7mm, tubular, adpressed-pilose below; cor. exceeding cal., pale violet. S Greece, N Syria. Z8.

***L.sinuatum*** (L.) Mill. Perenn. to 40cm, densely pubesc. Lvs 3–10×1–3cm, oblong-lanceolate, pinnatifid or pinnatisect, sinuate. Flowering stem winged; infl. dense; branches winged; spikelets compact; outer bract to 9mm, narrowly triangular, inner bract slightly longer, with 2 ciliate keels; cal. infundibular, pubesc., limb truncate, white or pale violet; cor. white or pink, becoming purple. Mediterranean. *L.bonduellii* (Lestib.) Kuntze is probably conspecific with this plant. Art Shades: fls in range of pastel colours including cream, rose, lilac and gold, uniform flowering time. California series: fls in range of colours including 'American Beauty' (deep rose), 'Apricot' (salmon), 'Blue Bonnet' (sky blue), 'Gold Coast' (fls deep yellow), 'Iceberg' (white), 'Midnight' (deep violet), 'Pacific Twilight' (clear pink), 'Purple Monarch' (deep purple) and 'Roselight' (carmine rose). Fortress hybrids: fls white, yellow, apricot, rose, dark blue, sky blue, purple. Soirée hybrids: to 80cm, stems strong; fls richly coloured, from yellow, through to deep blue. Sunburst Mixed: fls large, uniform colour, in white, yellow, rose, light blue, dark blue. Z9.

***L.spathulatum*** (Desf.) Kuntze. Perenn. Lvs to 4cm, basal, spathulate, glaucous, tapering to short petiole. Flowering stem to 25cm; infl. a dichotomously branching panicle; fls distichous, borne on upper side of stem; cal. to 1cm, tubular, white, lobes obtuse; cor. purple, exceeding cal. Mediterranean. Z7.

***L.tetragonum*** (Thunb.) Bullock. Bienn., glabrous. Lvs 8–15×1.5–3cm, oblong-spathulate, radical, firm, muricate, entire. Flowering stems 20–50cm, few, erect; bracts 2–3mm, deltoid; bracteoles to 4mm, scarious-margined, rounded, cuspidate; cal. 5–6mm, pink, adpressed white-pilose, 5-ribbed; cor. yellow, slightly exceeding cal. Autumn. Japan, Korea, China, New Caledonia. Z6.

***L.thouinii*** (Viv.) Kuntze. Annual to 20cm, glabrous, glaucous. Lvs 3–6×1–2cm, basal, oblong-lanceolate in outline, coarsely pinnatifid, lobes 5–7 pairs, base tapering into short petiole. Infl. a panicle of spikes, compact, branches winged; spikelets 2-fld; inner bract about 6mm; cal. tube about 5mm, limb 5mm, pale blue or white, lobes somewhat acute, exceeding cor.; cor. yellow. Mediterranean.

***L.tomentellum*** (Boiss.) Kuntze. Perenn., 30–80cm. Lvs 5–15×3–7cm, radical, ovate to broadly elliptic, obtuse, round-tipped or mucronate, pale green or glaucescent, pubesc., base gradually tapering to broad petiole. Flowering stems few, terete, forming a compound panicle; sterile branches usually absent; scales 3–5cm, brown; spikes compact; spikelets about 5mm, 2–3-fld; outer bract to 2mm, concave, usually pubesc.; cal. 3–5mm, pale violet; cor. blue-violet. Summer. USSR (Russia, Crimea). Z6.

***L.virgatum*** (Willd.) Fourr. Suffruticose subshrub; stem branching from base. Lvs to 3cm, oblong to lanceolate-spathulate, obtuse, rounded or acute, tapering to petiole. Flowering stems to 30cm, dichotomously branching from base to form a panicle; sterile branches many; spikes compact; spikelets 3–4 fld; outer bract 1–1.5mm, ovate-triangular, inner bract 4–6mm, concave, enclosing fls; cal. tubular, veins pilose; cor. pale violet. Mediterranean & W Europe. Z7.

***L.vulgare*** Mill. Perenn., 15–70cm, glabrous. Lvs 10–15×1–4cm, in basal rosettes, oblong-lanceolate, mucronate, strongly pinnately veined, tapering to petiole; petiole 5–8cm, winged. Flowering stems to 30cm, occasionally longer, terete, corymbose, typically branching above middle; sterile branches few or absent; scales 6–18mm; spikes 1–2cm, spreading; spikelets usually 2-fld; inner bract 3–5mm, outer bract 1–3mm, slightly overlapping inner; cal. 3–6mm, pale purple, pubesc. at bases, lobes acute; cor. 6–8mm deep blue. NW Europe to N Africa. ssp. ***serotina*** (Rchb.) Gams. To 70cm. Flowering stems often branching below middle; cal. 3–5mm, 5-lobed with intermediate teeth. S Europe, N Africa. Z6.

***L.brasiliense*** (A. Gray non Boiss.) Small. See *L.carolinianum*.
***L.californicum*** A. Gray. See *L.commune* var. *californicum*.
***L.callicomum*** (C.A. Mey.) Kuntze. See *Goniolimon callicomum*.
***L.dubium*** Gamaun. See *L.tomentellum*.
***L.elatum*** Fisch. & Spreng. See *Goniolimon elatum*.
***L.eximium*** (Schrenk) Kuntze. See *Goniolimon eximium*.
***L.globulariifolium*** (Desf.) Kuntze. See *L.ramosissimum*.
***L.globulariifolium*** ssp. ***provinciale*** Pign. See *L.ramosissimum* ssp. *provinciale*.
***L.globulariifolium*** ssp. ***tommasinii*** Pign. See *L.ramosissimum* ssp. *tommasinii*.
***L.gmelinii*** var. ***tomentellum*** ((Boiss.) Trautv. See *L.tomentellum*.
***L.halfordii*** hort. See *L.macrophyllum*.
***L.hirsuticalyx*** Pign. See *L.gmelinii*.
***L.japonicum*** (Sieb. & Zucc.) Kuntze. See *L.tetragonum*.
***L.lychnidifolium*** (Girard) Kuntze. See *L.auriculaeursifolium*.
***L.oleifolium*** Pign. non Mill. See *L.virgatum*.
***L.perfoliatum*** (Karel.) Kuntze. See *L.reniforme*.
***L.reticulatum*** Mill. See *L.bellidiflorum*.
***L.roseum*** (Sm.) Kuntze. See *L.peregrinum*.
***L.sinense*** (Girard) Kuntze. See *L.tetragonum*.
***L.speciosum*** (L.) Kuntze. See *Goniolimon incanum*.
***L.spicatum*** (Willd.) Kuntze. See *Psylliostachys spicata*.
***L.suworowii*** (Reg.) Kuntze. See *Psylliostachys suworowii*.
***L.tataricum*** (L.) Mill. See *Goniolimon tataricum*.
***L.tetragonum*** hort. See *L.dregeanum*.
***L.transwallianum*** (Pugsley) Pugsley. See *L.binervosum*.
For further synonymy see *Statice*.

**LINACEAE** Gray. FLAX FAMILY. Dicot. 15 genera and 300 species of trees, lianes, shrubs and herbs, sometimes cyanogenic. Leaves spirally arranged to opposite, simple, entire; stipules deciduous, often small, sometimes glands or absent. Flowers bisexual, usually regular, in cymose or racemose inflorescences; calyx of 5 free sepals, sometimes united at the base; petals 5, free, convolute, often clawed; stamens 5, alternate with petals (opposite in *Anisadenia*), or 10 or 15, staminodes often present, filament bases united at the base into a ring or a tube; ovary superior, 2–5 fused carpels, many-locular, sometimes 1-loculed; placentation axile or apical-axile; styles distinct or 1 deeply cleft; each locule 1–2-ovuled. Fruit septicidal capsule, drupe, nut or pair of 1-seeded mericarps; seeds with oily embryo, little or no endosperm. *Linum usitatissimum* provides flax and linseed oil. Cosmopolitan. *Linum, Reinwardtia.*

**Linanthus** Benth. (From Gk *linon*, flax, and *anthos*, flower, due to the similarity between the flowers of plants in this genus and *Linum.*) Polemoniaceae. About 35 species of annual or perennial herbs of erect or branching habit, to 60cm. Leaves alternate or opposite, simple or usually subpinnately or palmately lobed, seg. 3–11, linear. Inflorescence a lax cyme or dense head; flowers sessile or almost so, or on long pedicels; calyx deeply lobed, sometimes with hyaline membrane in sinuses; corolla hypocrateriform or campanulate to funnelform, blue, white or yellow; stamens 5, included or exserted; stigma 3–4-lobed; style included or exserted. Fruit a capsule, cylindrical to ellipsoid, sometimes mucilaginous or forming spiracles when wet. W US, Chile. Z7.

CULTIVATION As for *Gilia*.

***L. androsaceus*** (Benth.) Greene. Pubesc. annual, 5–30cm, usually erect. Lvs 1–3cm, few, with stiff hairs or cilia, 5–9-lobed, lobes oblanceolate or narrowly so. Infl. terminal, a dense, bracteate head; cal. 6–8mm, lobes subulate, sinuses slightly membranaceous; cor. 0.9–2.4(–3.6)cm, hypocrateriform, white or cream to pink or lilac, tube *c*1mm diam., usually yellow at apex, lobes 5–8mm, obovate; stamens subexserted; style subexserted. Fr. 4–5mm, ellipsoid; seeds *c*1.3mm. Spring–early summer. S California. ssp. ***lutea*** (Benth.) H.L. Mason. Cor. pink or yellow to lilac, limb 6–10mm diam., style subexserted. Spring. ssp. ***micranthus*** (Steud.) H.L. Mason. Cor. lilac or pink to yellow, style long-exserted. Spring.

***L. aureus*** (Nutt.) E. Greene. Slender annual, 5–16cm, erect or ascending, hairy or glandular to subglabrous. Lvs 3–7-lobed, few, lobes 3–6mm, linear-oblong. Infl. a lax cyme; pedicels to 1.5cm; cal. 4–6mm, narrowly campanulate, sinuses two-thirds filled by hyaline membrane; cor. 6–13mm, funnelform, dark to pale yellow, throat brown-purple to orange, tube surrounded by cal., style exserted. Spring–early summer. Nevada to Baja California.

***L. dianthiflorus*** (Benth.) E. Greene. GROUND-PINK. Very slender, erect, branching, puberulent annual, 5–12cm. Lvs 1–2cm, usually opposite, entire, filiform. Infl. a few-fld, leafy cyme or fls solitary; pedicels short or fls subsessile; cal. 1–1.6cm, lobes linear, sinuses half-filled by hyaline membrane; cor. 1–2.5cm, short-funnelform, white or pink to lilac, dark-spotted at base, throat yellow, lobes long, toothed. Fr. short-oblong; seeds *c*0.5mm, red-brown. Spring–summer. S California to Baja California.

***L. dichotomus*** Benth. EVENING SNOW. Slender, erect annual, 5–20cm, often dichotomously branched, usually glabrous. Lvs 3–7-lobed, opposite, lobes 1–2.2cm, linear-filiform. Infl. a cyme; fls opening in the evening; pedicels short; cal. 8–14mm, cylindric, glabrous, lobe apices linear, subulate, sinuses with subtruncate hyaline membrane; cor. 1.5–3cm, funnelform, wholly white or with some purple markings in throat, tube surrounded by cal., lobes broadly obovate, convolute in bud; stamens included. Seeds *c*0.7mm, testa loose, minutely alveolate. Spring–summer. California, Nevada, Arizona.

***L. grandiflorus*** (Benth.) E. Greene. Erect annual, puberulent to subglabrous, 10–50cm. Lvs 5–11-lobed, lobes 1–3cm, linear. Infl. a dense head, few to several-fld; cal. 1–1.4cm, densely white-hairy, lobes linear, sinuses two-thirds filled by hyaline membrane; cor. 1.5–3cm, funnelform, pale lilac to white, tube 1–2.8cm, with a pubesc. ring inside, lobes spreading, obtuse, toothed. Fr. ellipsoid; seeds *c*1.5–2mm, pale brown. Spring–summer. S California.

***L. liniflorus*** (Benth.) E. Greene. Erect annual, 10–50cm, glabrous to puberulent, nodes often with paired branches. Lvs 3–9-lobed, lobes 1–3cm. Infl. a cymose panicle; pedicels 1–2.5cm; cal. 3–4mm, top-shaped, lobes linear, subglabrous to pilose-ciliate, sinuses two-thirds filled by hyaline membrane; cor. 1–3cm, white, blue or pink to lilac, lobes obovate. Spring–summer. California.

***L. nuttallii*** (A. Gray) E. Greene ex Milliken. Bushy, densely branched, villous-hispid perenn., 10–20cm, base woody. Lvs 3–9-lobed, opposite, lobes 1–1.5cm. Infl. cymose or subcapitate; fls (sub)sessile; cal. 8–9mm, narrowly campanulate, lobes lanceolate-subulate, sinuses with traces of hyaline membrane only; cor. 1.2–1.5cm, subhypocrateriform to funnelform, tube *c*8mm, yellow, lobes 4–5mm, oblanceolate, white; stamens subexserted. Fr. *c*5mm, oblong; seeds *c*2mm, oblong, yellow-brown. California to Washington. ssp. ***nuttallii.*** 10–20cm. Lvs often with bundles of small lvs in axils, 5–9-lobed, lobes linear-oblanceolate. Infl. subcapitate, dense. Spring–summer. ssp. ***floribundus*** (A. Gray) Munz. 10–40cm. Lvs 3–5-lobed, lobes subfiliform. Infl. fairly lax, cymose. Late spring–summer. Colorado to Baja California.

For synonymy see *Gilia*.

**Linaria** Mill. (From Lat. *linum*, flax, referring to the flax-like leaves of some species, particularly *L. vulgaris.)* TOADFLAX; SPURRED SNAPDRAGON. Scrophulariaceae. About 100 species of annual to perennial herbs. Leaves generally verticillate below, alternate above, simple, entire, usually narrow, sessile. Inflorescence terminal, bracteate, racemose or spike-like, or flowers solitary in leaf axils; calyx deeply 5-lobed, lobes often unequal, lowest usually longest; corolla tube cylindric, with conic to cylindric basal spur, limb bilabiate, upper lip 2-lobed, lower 3-lobed with palate at base closing tube, glabrous except for palate; stamens 4, included, didynamous. Fruit a capsule, globose, loculi numerous, each rupturing near apex of capsule; seeds numerous. N temperate regions, especially Europe.

CULTIVATION Usually found in the wild on dry, stony land or on scree, they range in habit from the tall, slender border perennials, such as *L. purpurea*, which carry long-lived and graceful spires of delicate flowers, to small tufted or prostrate spp., like *L. alpina* and *L. supina*, suitable for scree, rock gardens, raised beds and wall crevices. The taller species, such as *L. maroccana* and *L. reticulata*, make good cut flowers; the tiny flowers, closely observed, are often richly toned in dark purples and chocolate-browns with contrasting markings, especially attractive in *L. reticulata* and *L. bipartita*. Annuals are sometimes grown as flowering pot plants.

Most will tolerate temperatures to −15°C/5°F. Mediterranean species such as *L. triornithophora* and *L. tristis* are slightly more tender, to −5°C/23°F, but may be treated as annuals, or protected in winter with a mulch of bracken or evergreen prunings; the latter, with other small perennials, is sometimes grown in the alpine house. They are remarkably drought-tolerant, thriving in poor, gravelly soils; nitrogen-rich soils give rise to excessive foliar growth at the expense of flowers. Perennial species tend to be short-lived, but will self-seed, proving most persistent in perfectly drained sunny sites. Plant when dormant in sunny well-drained situations; on heavy soils dig in sharp grit before planting to improve drainage. Stake tall plants in exposed positions. To flower *L. maroccana* in pots, overwinter autumn-sown plants in a low-fertility loam-based medium, in well-ventilated, frost-free conditions, in full sun, and allow medium to dry out between waterings. Commence feeding in spring with a weekly application of dilute liquid fertilizer.

Propagate annuals and *L. alpina* from seed sown *in situ* in spring or, in mild climates, in autumn. Sow perennials in early spring, under glass or in the cold frame. Some cultivars, notably *L. purpurea* 'Canon Went', come true from seed. Alternatively, increase perennials by division, or from 2.5–5cm/1–2in., basal of softwood cuttings in spring, in the cold frame. Susceptible to downy and powdery mildews, and to root and stem rots. Sometimes attacked by aphids, flea beetle, and nematodes.

***L. aeruginea*** (Gouan) Cav. Perenn., rarely annual, glaucous, glabrous or minutely glandular-pubesc. beneath; stems 3–40cm, decumbent to ascending, generally simple. Lvs verticillate below, alternate above, 4–18×0.5–1.5mm, linear, margins revolute. Infl. racemose, dense, 2–35-fld, glandular-pubesc.; pedicels 0.5–3mm; cal. 3–6mm, lobes unequal, linear-lanceolate, subacute; cor. 15–27mm, yellow tinged purple-brown, rarely completely purple-brown, violet, yellow or creamy white, lobes of lower lip very short, spur 5–11mm. Fr. globose, 4–6mm; seeds 1.5–2.5mm, broadly grey- to pale brown-winged, disc brown to black. Portugal, S & E Spain, Balearic Islands. var. ***nevadensis*** (Boiss.) Valdés. Smaller in all parts; cor. always yellow. Spain & Portugal, in mts. Z6.

***L. alpina*** (L.) Mill. Annual, bienn. or perenn., glaucous, generally glabrous; stems 5–25cm, decumbent or ascending, simple or branched. Lvs mostly verticillate, linear-lanceolate to oblong-lanceolate. Infl. racemose, 3–15-fld, generally dense, rarely glandular-pubesc.; pedicels 2–5mm in fl., to 13mm in fr.; cal. 3–5mm, lobes unequal, oblong-oblanceolate to linear-oblanceolate, subobtuse, unequal; cor. 13–22mm, violet with yellow palate, rarely wholly yellow, white or pink, spur 8–10mm. Fr. 3–5mm; seeds suborbicular, flat, broadly winged, 2–2.5mm, black. Summer–autumn. C & S Europe (mts). 'Alba': fls white. 'Rosea': fls rose-pink, palate orange-yellow. Z4.

***L. amethystea*** (Lam.) Hoffm. & Link. Annual, glabrous to minutely glandular-pubesc. below; stems ascending, usually simple. Lvs verticillate below, 5–35cm, alternate above, 4–20×0.5–2.5mm, linear to oblanceolate. Infl. racemose, often interrupted, 2–5-fld, generally lax, often violet-pubesc.; pedicels to 3mm; cal. 3–4mm, lobes rather unequal, linear-oblong; cor. 10–22mm, blue-violet, rarely white or yellow, with purple spots, spur slender, 4–11mm, violet. Fr. 3–4.5mm; seeds suborbicular, flat, 1–1.5mm, dark brown, wing finely papillose. Spain and Portugal. ssp. ***multipunctata*** (Brot.) Chater & D.A. Webb. Cor. 19–27mm, yellow, spur 10–15mm, often violet; racemes dense in fr. C Portugal, SW Spain.

***L. angustissima*** (Lois.) Borb. Similar to *L. vulgaris* but glabrous throughout; lvs 1–2mm wide; sep. linear-lanceolate, acuminate; cor. 15–20mm, pale yellow, spur narrower than and at least as long as lower lip, 7–10mm; fr. ovoid, 4–6mm. Summer. S & EC Europe, absent from much of Mediterranean region. Z6.

***L. anticaria*** Boiss. & Reut. Perenn., glaucous, glabrous below infl.; stems to 45cm, procumbent to ascending, much-branched. Lvs in verticels of 4–6 or upper alternate, 10–30×2–10mm, elliptic-lanceolate to linear, obtuse. Infl. racemose, dense in fl., lax in fr.; pedicels 1–2mm; cal. 4–7mm, lobes unequal, oblong-obovate; cor. 2cm, white with blue stripes, very rarely entirely yellow, palate purple tinged blue, sometimes with yellow spot, spur about half total length of cor., lilac. Fr. 4–7mm; seeds 2–3mm, suborbicular, flat, brown to black, with broad paler wing. Spring. S Spain. Z8.

***L. bipartita*** (Vent.) Willd. CLOVEN-LIP TOADFLAX. Annual, glabrous; stems to 40cm, slender. Lvs in whorls of 4 or opposite below, alternate above,

40–50×2–5mm, linear. Infl. racemose, lax; pedicels 4–7mm; cal. 4mm, lobes oblong-lanceolate, margins scarious; cor. 20–24mm, violet, lips widely diverging, palate orange, spur straight, slender, conic, 10–12mm; stigma irregularly bifid. Fr. suborbicular, 3–4mm; seeds 0.5mm, bluntly angled, transversely rugose. Summer–early autumn. NW Africa, Portugal. 'Alba': fls white. 'Queen of Roses': fls pink. 'Splendida': fls deep purple.

***L. caesia*** (Pers.) DC. ex Chav. Annual, bienn. or perenn., glaucous, glabrous below; stems 10–40cm, procumbent to erect, generally simple. Lvs alternate or lower verticillate, 5–30×0.5–2mm, linear-subulate to linear-oblong. Infl. racemose, dense in fl., lax in fr., to 15-fld, sparsely glandular-pubesc.; pedicels 1–2mm; cal. 3–7mm, lobes generally unequal, oblanceolate to linear-oblong, subacute to obtuse; cor. 19–25mm, yellow with red-brown stripes, spur 9–12mm. Fr. 5mm, globose; seeds 2–2.5mm, flattened suborbicular, broadly pale brown- to grey-winged, disc metallic, grey to black. Portugal, W Spain. Z9.

***L. canadensis*** (L.) Dum.-Cours. OLD-FIELD TOADFLAX. Annual or bienn., glabrous, somewhat glaucous; stems 25–80cm, erect, generally simple. Lvs verticillate below, alternate above, 15–30×1–2.5mm, linear to linear-oblanceolate, obtuse. Infl. racemose, dense at anthesis, lax in fr.; pedicels to 3mm at anthesis, to 6mm in fr.; cal. 3mm, lobes equal, linear-lanceolate, acute; cor. 10–15mm, lilac to off-white, palate rudimentary, lower lip very large, spur curved, very slender, 4–6mm. Fr. 3mm; seeds 0.5mm, irregularly tetrahedral, faces concave, smooth. Americas; naturalized C Russia. Z4.

***L. cavanillesii*** Chav. Perenn., glandular-pubesc.; stems 15–40cm, decumbent or ascending, simple or branched above. Lvs verticillate or opposite, sometimes alternate above, 1.5–2×1–1.5cm, ovate to ovate-elliptic, acute. Infl. racemose, dense; pedicels 1–4mm; cal. 6–9mm, lobes very irregular, linear-spathulate, obtuse; cor. 25–30mm, yellow, spur 10–12mm. Fr. 5mm; seeds angular, compressed, 1–1.5mm, very dark brown tinged black, densely minutely rugose-tuberculate. S & E Spain. Z7.

***L. ×dominii*** Druce. 'Yuppie Surprise': to 1m; lvs glaucous; fls pink-lilac.

***L. elegans*** Cav. Annual, glandular-pubesc. above, glabrous below; stems 20–70cm, erect, simple or branched. Lvs alternate, 7–35×0.5–4mm, filiform to linear-lanceolate, obtuse. Infl. racemose, long, lax; pedicels 4–8mm, more or less erect, greatly exceeding bracts; cal. 3–5mm, lobes equal, lanceolate-acuminate, margins scarious, white or violet; cor. 17–25mm, violet to lilac, palate pale to white, mouth of tube more or less open, spur 10–14mm; distinctly curved; stigma entire to emarginate, clavate. Fr. 3–4mm; seeds 0.5mm, tetrahedral, dark grey, finely tuberculate. N & C Spain, N Portugal. Z7.

***L. faucicola*** Leresche & Levier. Annual or short-lived perenn., glabrous; stems 10–25cm, ascending, branched, slender. Lvs mostly in whorls of 4, 7–20×1.5–5mm, linear-oblong to oblanceolate. Infl. racemose, rather lax, 2–4-fld; pedicels 1.5–5mm; cal. 4.5–6mm, seg. oblong, adaxial longest; cor. 22–27mm, violet, throat paler, palate blue-violet, densely hairy, spur 10–13mm, straight or slightly curved. Fr. 5mm; seeds 2–2.5mm, suborbicular, flat, narrowly winged, black. Summer. NW Spain. Z7.

***L. filicaulis*** Boiss. ex Leresche & Levier. Very similar to *L. alpina*, except infl. lax, few-fld; pedicels not elongating in fr. Spring. NW Spain. Probably a ssp. of *L. alpina*. Z7.

***L. genistifolia*** (L.) Mill. Perenn., glabrous; stems 30–100cm, erect, branched particularly above, leafy to infl. Lvs alternate, to 1.5cm wide, 6–12× as long as wide, suberect, linear to ovate, acute, more or less amplexicaul, rigid. Infl. racemose, lax to dense, 10–20cm; pedicels to 12mm; cal. 2–12mm, lobes subequal, linear-lanceolate to triangular-ovate, acute to acuminate; cor. 13–22mm, lemon-yellow to orange, palate orange-bearded, spur 0.5–2.5cm. Fr. 3–7mm; seeds 1–1.5mm, compressed-tetrahedral, black, often with pale narrow flange on angles, minutely rugose. SE & C Europe (Italy to Russia), Asia Minor. ssp. ***dalmatica*** (L.) Maire & Petitmengin. Lvs suberect, ovate to lanceolate, to 4cm wide, 2–4× as long as wide, rigid; cor. 2–5cm. Summer. Balkan peninsula, Rumania, S Italy; naturalized locally in C Europe. 'Nymph': fls cream. Z5.

***L. glacialis*** Boiss. Annual to perenn., glaucous, mostly glabrous; stems ascending, generally simple, 5–15cm, leafless below, above densely leafy to infl. Lvs generally in whorls of 4, 10–15×2–6mm, elliptic to linear-oblanceolate. Infl. racemose, capitate, 3–8-fld, glandular-pubesc.; bracts 12–20mm; pedicels 3–4mm; cal. 8–16mm, seg. linear to linear-oblanceolate; cor. 20–27mm, dull violet tinged yellow, spur 8–15mm, yellow with violet veining. Fr. 7–10mm; seeds 2.5–3mm, suborbicular, flat, grey-brown, wing pale brown. Spring. S Spain (Sierra Nevada). Z6.

***L. heterophylla*** Desf. Annual; stems 15–60cm, erect, robust, stems sometimes hairy near base. Lvs mostly alternate, lowest opposite or verticillate in whorls of 6, rather crowded particularly below, 7–40×0.5–1mm, linear, obtuse, glabrous. Infl. racemose, short, rather dense, densely glandular-pubesc.; pedicels to 8mm, erect, shorter than cal. in fr.; cal. to 6mm, lobes subequal, oblong-lanceolate, often acuminate, with broad scarious margins; cor. 18–30mm, bright yellow or very occasionally violet, lips approximately closed, spur 9–18mm; stigma deeply bifid. Fr. 4mm; seeds 0.5–1mm, tetrahedral, black, coarsely rugose. Summer. Italy & Sicily, NW Africa. 'Aureo-purpurea': fls purple and orange. 'Purpurea': fls purple. Splendens': fls crimson, palate conspicuous, golden.

***L. hirta*** (L.) Moench. Annual, more or less densely glandular-pubesc. particularly above; stems 15–80cm, erect, generally simple, rather stout. Lvs mostly alternate, lowest opposite, 2.5–5×0.5–1.5cm, oblong-lanceolate, acute to rather obtuse, semiamplexicaul. Infl. racemose, rather dense, elongating in fr.; fls subsessile; cal. 7–8mm, lobes very unequal, elliptic, obtuse; cor. 2–3cm, yellow, spur 10–16mm. Fr. 5–6mm; seeds 1–1.5mm, tetrahedral, acutely angled, narrowly winged on angles, brown tinged grey, distinctly ruminate-alveolate. Spring–early autumn. Spain & Portugal.

***L. japonica*** Miq. Perenn., glaucous and glabrous; stems 15–40cm, erect, branched. Lvs opposite or in whorls of 3–4, upper alternate, 1.5–3×0.5–1.5cm, elliptic to elliptic-lanceolate, obtuse to subacute, sessile. Infl. racemose, short; pedicels short; cor. 15–18mm, pale yellow, spur 5–10mm. Fr. 6–8mm; seeds 3mm, winged. Summer. Japan. Z8.

***L. maroccana*** Hook. f. Annual, glabrous below, viscid-pubesc. above; stems to 45cm, erect, branched, slender. Lvs rather remote, verticillate below, to 4cm, narrowly linear. Infl. racemose, terminal, short or long, becoming lax; cor. 1.5cm, brilliant violet-purple, palate orange to yellow with smaller paler patch, spur 1–2cm, vertical, conic, almost straight, slender, pointed. Summer. Morocco; naturalized NE US. var. ***hybrida*** hort. Fls red to rose, lilac and violet. 'Carminea': 22–30cm; fls bright rosy carmine. 'Diadem': to 15cm; fls very large, rich violet with white eye. Excelsior hybrids: 22–30cm; fls in many shades, from white to yellow and beige, to salmon, rose-carmine and crimson, to purple and blue. 'Fairy Bouquet': to 20cm; fls large, copiously produced, colour range similar to Excelsior hybrids. 'Fairy Bride': to 20cm; fls white. 'Fairy Bridesmaid': 22–30cm; fls rich lemon yellow. 'Ruby King': 22–30cm; fls deep blood red. 'White Pearl': to 22cm; fls large, glistening white. 'Yellow Prince': to 30cm; fls pure yellow.

***L. nigricans*** Lange in Willk. & Lange. Annual, glabrous throughout or sometimes very minutely glandular-pubesc. in infl.; stems to 17cm, simple or branched, flexuous-ascending. Lvs mostly alternate, lowest verticillate, 5–12×1–2mm, linear-oblong to broadly elliptic, obtuse. Infl. racemose, lax, 3–8-fld; pedicels patent to ascending, 4–10mm; cal. 3–4mm, lobes equal, oblong, subacute; cor. 16–20mm, lilac or violet, spur straight, 9–12mm. Fr. 3.5–4mm; seeds crescentic-trigonous to 0.5mm, black, very minutely rugose-tuberculate. SE Spain.

***L. purpurea*** (L.) Mill. Perenn., glabrous and glaucous; stems 20–60cm, ascending to erect, often branched in upper part. Lvs verticillate below, alternate above, 20–60×1–4mm, linear, subacute. Infl. racemose, slender, elongate, rather dense; pedicels 1.5–4mm; cal. 3mm, lobes equal, linear-lanceolate, acute; cor. 9–12mm, violet tinged purple, spur curved, 5mm. Fr. 3mm; seeds trigonous, 1–1.5mm, blackened, rugose-ruminate. Summer. C Italy to Sicily; locally naturalized elsewhere in Europe, including GB. 'Canon J. Went': tall; fls tiny, pale pink. 'Springside White': lvs grey-green; fls white. Z6.

***L. repens*** (L.) Mill. STRIPED TOADFLAX. Perenn. with creeping rhiz., glabrous; stems 30–120cm, erect, generally branched above. Lvs verticillate, rarely alternate above, 15–40×1–2.5cm, linear to linear-oblanceolate, acute. Infl. racemose, long, dense at anthesis, lax in fr.; pedicels 2–3mm at anthesis, to 4.5mm in fr.; cal. 2–3mm, lobes subequal, narrowly lanceolate, acute; cor. 8–15mm, white to pale lilac with violet veining, palate orange, spur straight, conic, 3–5mm; stigma capitate. Fr. 3–4mm; seeds 1.5mm, ovoid-trigonous, angles acute, almost winged, dark grey, rugose. W Europe (N Italy & N Spain to NW Germany, Britain); naturalized C Europe. 'Alba': to 30cm; fls white. Z6.

***L. reticulata*** (Sm.) Desf. PURPLE-NET TOADFLAX. Annual, glaucous; stems 60–120cm. Lvs verticillate below, alternate and remote above, linear, channelled. Infl. racemose, short, tapering, dense, downy; cor. deep purple, reticulate-veined, palate coppery orange or yellow with purple striations, spur less than half length of cor., straight, slender. Late spring to summer. Portugal, N Africa. 'Aureo-purpurea': fls deep rich purple with orange or yellow palate. 'Crown Jewels': clouds of small bright fls, bicolour, in maroon, red, gold and orange.

***L. sagittata*** Poir. Perenn., glabrous throughout; stems 2–3m or 20–60cm, ascending, slender, twining. Lvs opposite, scattered, 2.5–4cm, lanceolate-oblong, hastate at base, entire, petiolate, stem lvs narrowly linear, much smaller than basal. Fls solitary, axillary; pedicels 3.5cm, slender; cor. to 4cm, broad, yellow. Summer. N Africa. Z9.

***L. saxatilis*** (L.) Chaz. Perenn., rarely annual, subglabrous to densely glandular-pubesc.; stems 7–50cm, ascending to erect, simple or branched above. Lvs mostly alternate, lowest verticillate, 4–20×1–5mm, linear to oblong-elliptic. Infl. racemose, to 10-fld; pedicels to 3mm; cal. 3–4.5mm, lobes somewhat unequal, linear-oblong; cor. 9–17mm, yellow with pair of brown marks on palate, spur slender, 5–8mm. Fr. 3–4mm; seeds suborbicular with narrow thin wing, dark brown. Summer. N & C Spain, Portugal. Z8.

***L. spartea*** (L.) Willd. Annual; stems erect, branched, 15–60cm, flowering stems glabrous, non-flowering stems hairy. Lvs mostly alternate, lowest opposite or verticillate, rather remote, 7–40×0.5–1mm, linear, obtuse, glabrous. Infl. racemose, short and lax in fl., very lax in fr., glandular-pubesc.; pedicels 3–15mm, erecto-patent, greatly exceeding bracts; cal. 4mm, lobes subequal, oblong-lanceolate, obtuse to subacute, with broad scarious margins; cor. 18–30mm, bright yellow or very occasionally violet, lips approximately closed, spur 9–18mm, straight; stigma deeply bifid. Fr. 4mm; seeds 0.5–1mm, tetrahedral, black, coarsely rugose. Summer–autumn. SW Europe. Z7.

***L. supina*** (L.) Chaz. Annual, bienn. or perenn., glaucous, glabrous below; stems 5–30cm, procumbent to erect, simple. Lvs verticillate at least below, often alternate above, 5–20×0.5–1mm, linear to linear-oblanceolate. Infl. racemose, 2–5-fld, or occasionally to 20-fld, lax or dense, sparsely glandular-pubesc.; pedicels 1–2mm in fl., to 6mm in fr.; cal. 3–7mm, lobes generally unequal, oblanceolate to linear-oblong, subacute to obtuse; cor. 13–20mm, pale yellow sometimes tinged violet, spur 10–15mm. Fr. globose, 3–7mm; seeds 2–2.5mm, flattened suborbicular, broadly black- to grey-winged, disc black. Spring–autumn. SW Europe.

***L. triornithophora*** (L.) Willd. THREE-BIRDS-FLYING. Perenn., glabrous and somewhat glaucous; stems 50–130cm, erect or diffuse, simple or branched above. Lvs in remote whorls of 3, rarely to 5, 2.5–7.5×0.5–3cm, lanceolate to ovate-lanceolate, acute. Infl. lax, 3–15-fld, mostly in whorls, to 10cm; pedicels erect, 1–3cm; cal. 6–9mm, lobes equal, ovate-lanceolate, long acuminate; cor. 3.5–5.5cm, pale lavender striped with lavender-purple with yellow palate, tube inflated, spur 16–25mm, inflated. Fr. 3–6mm; seeds 2–2.5mm, suborbicular, narrowly winged, dark brown. Summer. W Spain, N & C Portugal. 'Rosea': fls pink. Z7.

***L. triphylla*** (L.) Mill. Annual or perenn., glabrous and rather glaucous; stems 10–45cm, usually single, erect, simple or branched above, stout. Lvs mostly verticillate, a few alternate or opposite, 1.5–3.5×1–2.5cm, elliptic to obovate, truncate to semiamplexicaul at base, rather fleshy. Infl. racemose, rather dense, greatly elongating in fr.; fls subsessile; cal. 9–12mm, lobes unequal, ovate to lanceolate; cor. 2–3cm, white, occasionally faintly tinged violet or yellow, palate orange or yellow, spur 8–11mm, curved, violet. Fr. 8mm; seeds tetrahedral, acutely angled, distinctly ruminate-alveolate, brown tinged grey. Spring–summer. Mediterranean Europe. Z8.

***L. tristis*** (L.) Mill. DULL-COLOURED LINARIA; SAD-COLOURED LINARIA. Perenn., glaucous, glabrous or minutely glandular-pubesc. below; stems 10–90cm, decumbent to ascending, generally simple, last 1–8cm below infl. leafless. Lvs mostly alternate, often irregularly verticillate near base, 0.5–4.5cm, linear to oblong-lanceolate, obtuse to subacute, flat. Infl. racemose, lax or dense, 2–15-fld, more or less densely glandular-pubesc.; pedicels 0.5–5mm; cal. 7–9mm, lobes unequal, linear-oblanceolate, subobtuse; cor. 21–28mm, yellow tinged purple-brown, lobes of lower lip very short, spur stout, striped, arched, 11–13mm. Fr. 4–8mm, globose; seeds 2–3mm, broadly grey-winged, disc black. Summer. S Spain & S Portugal, NW Africa, Canary Is. Z9.

***L. ventricosa*** Coss. & Bal. Perenn., glaucous and glabrous; stems to 1m, erect. Lvs alternate, to 5cm, attenuate-lanceolate, acute. Infl. racemose, terminal and axillary, dense, many-fld; cor. 3cm, pale yellow with yellow-brown or red veining, palate very hairy, tube swollen, spur 1cm, almost straight, slender. Summer. SW Morocco. Z9.

***L. verticillata*** Boiss. Perenn., glandular-pubesc. at least below; stems to 30cm, numerous, ascending to erect, simple or sparingly branched above. Lvs in whorls of 3–5 below, alternate above, remote, oblong to elliptic, acute. Infl. racemose, dense, few-fld; bracts 3–10mm; pedicels 0–4mm; cal. 3–6mm, lobes unequal, oblong to oblanceolate, obtuse; cor. 15–35mm, yellow, sometimes with violet or green tinged stripes, palate orange, striate, lobes obtuse, spur curved, 9–17mm. Fr. 3.5–4.5mm; seeds 1.5–3mm, suborbicular, wing pale brown, disc dark brown to black. Spring–early summer. S Spain. Z8.

***L. viscida*** Moench. (Perhaps a synonym of *Chaenorrhinum minus* (L.) Lange.) Annual, glandular-pubesc.; stems erect, freely branched, 8–25cm. Lvs opposite below, alternate above, oblong to linear-lanceolate, obtuse at apex, tapered to base, petiolate. Infl. short, obtusely conic; pedicels short; cal. lobes linear-spathulate, recurved; cor. 8–10mm, pale violet, throat yellow, spur conic. Fr. obliquely ovoid, slightly shorter than cal.; seeds ovoid. Summer–autumn. Mediterranean Europe. Z8.

***L. vulgaris*** Mill. COMMON TOADFLAX; BUTTER-AND-EGGS; WILD SNAPDRAGON. Perenn.; stems 15–90cm, erect, simple or branched at base and in infl. only, glabrous or glandular-pubesc. above. Lvs mostly alternate, crowded, 20–60×1–5mm, linear to linear-oblanceolate, veins 1, rarely 3. Infl. racemose, dense in fl., lax in fr., 5–30-fld; pedicels 2–8mm, often minutely glandular-pubesc.; cal. 3–6mm, often minutely glandular-pubesc., lobes subequal, ovate to oblanceolate, subacute; cor. 25–33mm, pale to bright yellow, palate coppery, spur 10–13mm, curved, stout, broader and shorter than lower lip. Fr. ovoid to oblong-globose, 5–11×5–7mm; seeds 2–3mm. Spring–autumn. Europe including GB, except extreme north and much of Mediterranean region. The peloric form has cor. regular, 5-spurred. Z4.

***L. aequitriloba*** (Viv.) A. Spreng. See *Cymbalaria aequitriloba*.
***L. angustifolia*** Rchb. See *L. angustissima*.
***L. antirrhinifolia*** hort. See *L. cavanillesii*.
***L. antirrhioides*** Coss. ex Boiss. See *L. cavanillesii*.
***L. aparinoides*** Dietr. See *L. heterophylla*.
***L. blanca*** Pau. See *L. repens*.
***L. broussonetii*** (Poir.) Chav. See *L. amethystea*.
***L. cymbalaria*** (L.) Mill. See *Cymbalaria muralis*.
***L. dalmatica*** (L.) Mill. See *L. genistifolia* ssp. *dalmatica*.
***L. delphinioides*** Gay ex Knowles & Westc. See *L. elegans*.
***L. elatine*** (L.) Mill. See *Kickxia elatine*.
***L. fragrans*** Porta & Rigo. See *L. nigricans*.
***L. geminiflora*** F. Schmidt. See *L. japonica*.
***L. hepaticifolia*** (Poir.) Steud. See *Cymbalaria hepaticifolia*.
***L. italica*** Trev. See *L. angustissima*.
***L. japonica*** var. ***geminiflora*** (F. Schmidt) Nak. See *L. japonica*.
***L. jattae*** Palanza. See *L. genistifolia* ssp. *dalmatica*.
***L. macedonia*** Griseb. See *L. genistifolia* ssp. *dalmatica*.
***L. melantha*** Boiss. & Reut. See *L. aeruginea*.
***L. minor*** (L.) Desf. See *Chaenorrhinum minus*.
***L. monspessulana*** (L.) Mill. See *L. repens*.
***L. multipunctata*** (Brot.) Hoffm. & Link. See *L. amethystea* ssp. *multipunctata*.
***L. nevadensis*** (Boiss.) Boiss. & Reut. See *L. aeruginea* var. *nevadensis*.
***L. origanifolia*** (L.) Cav. See *Chaenorrhinum origanifolium*..
***L. petraea*** Jordan See *L. alpina*.
***L. petraea*** Steven non Jordan See *L. genistifolia*.
***L. pilosa*** (Jacq.) Lam. & DC. See *Cymbalaria pilosa*.
***L. sapphirina*** Hoffm. See *L. nigricans*.
***L. spuria*** (L.) Mill. See *Kickxia spuria*.
***L. striata*** L. See *L. repens*.
***L. stricta*** (Sibth. & Sm.) Guss. See *L. heterophylla*.
***L. supina*** ssp. ***nevadensis*** (Boiss.) Nyman. See *L. aeruginea* var. *nevadensis*.
For further synonymy see *Antirrhinum*.

**Lindelofia** Lehm. (Named in honour of Friedrich von Lindelof of Dormstadt, 19th-century botanist.) Boraginaceae. Some 12 species of perennial herbs, pubescent. Basal leaves mostly petiolate; cauline leaves alternate, ovate to linear-lanceolate. Inflorescence terminal or axillary; bracts absent; calyx deeply lobed, spreading in fruit; corolla blue to dark purple, infundibular to cylindrical or cylindrical-campanulate, lobes spreading; faucal appendages mostly conspicuous, oblong to trapeziform; stamens 5, filaments short, anthers linear to oblong, often sagittate; ovary 4-lobed, style slender, elongate, stigma small. Nutlets depressed, ovoid to globose, dorsally deeply concave, margins appendiculate. C Asia to Himalaya.

CULTIVATION Suitable for the large rock garden or the foregrounds of borders, they bear intensely blue flowers over long periods from spring into autumn above clumps of foliage that is markedly less coarse than that of most members of the family. Grow in sharply drained but moisture-retentive soils in sun, with shelter from drying winds and with a dry mulch against prolonged winter frosts. Propagate from seed in early spring, to flower in their second year, or by division.

***L. anchusoides*** (Lindl.) Lehm. Stems to 100cm, erect or sometimes decumbent, fistulose, simple or branched above. Basal lvs to 25×7cm, lanceolate, acute, base attenuate, with adpressed bristly hairs above and sometimes beneath; petiole to 18cm; cauline lvs to 13×2cm, lanceolate to linear-lanceolate, sessile or short-stalked. Infl. terminal and axillary, few-fld; peduncle elongate; pedicel to 20mm in fruit, densely pubesc.; cal. lobes to 6×2mm in fruit, ovate-oblong or oblong, obtuse, densely pubesc.; cor. to 10mm, blue, pink or purple, campanulate, lobes suborbicular, faucal appendages puberulent, usually ciliate; anth. sagittate; style to 9mm, filiform, stigma capitate. Nutlets to 5×4mm, ovate to orbicular, marginal appendages to 2mm, triangular, puberulent. Afghanistan to W Himalaya. Z7.

***L. longiflora*** (Benth.) Baill. Stems to 60cm, usually solitary, simple, covered with white bristle-hairs. Basal lvs to 18×8cm, lanceolate, acute, covered with bristle-hairs throughout, base attenuate, petiolate; cauline lvs ovate to oblong-lanceolate, acute, base rounded or subcordate, sessile. Infl. ultimately to 15cm, usually terminal; pedicels to 12mm in fruit, pubesc.; cal. lobes to 10mm in fruit, ovate to oblong, obtuse to subacute, dorsal surface densely hoary, margins densely pubesc.; cor. dark blue, infundibular, tube to 13mm; lobes to 6mm, ovate, spreading, faucal appendages to 4mm, ciliate; filaments to 2mm, anth. to 2mm; style to 15mm, filiform, stigma capitate. Nutlets to 4×2.5mm, ovate, marginal appendages to 2mm, glochidiate at apex. W Himalaya. Z7.

***L. spectabilis*** Lehm. See *L. longiflora*.
For further synonymy see *Cynoglossum*.

**Linden, Jean Jules** (1817–1898). Botanist, nurseryman and publisher. Born in Luxembourg, he was one of the first students at the Science Faculty in the new University of Brussels. Gaining his degree at the age of 19, he was sent by the Belgian government to explore in Brazil. He left Europe at the end of 1835, accompanied by the illustrator M.M. Funck and the zoologist Ghiesbrecht. This first trip lasted only some 18 months, but was successful enough to warrant a further government commission in the year of their return, 1837, this time to Central America. From Havana, the expedition made its way to war-torn Mexico. At this point the group had to leave Linden, who was suffering from yellow fever, and it was not until 1841 that he found his way back to Belgium.

Later that year he journeyed to Venezuela with Louis Schlim, touring widely throughout the region, from Caracas north to Barquisameto, then south done the Eastern Cordilleras to Bogotá, on to the Pacific via Mt Tolima and finally to Cuba and North America. Linden introduced many plants as a result of this expedition, notably the orchids *Masdevallia coccinea*, *Odontoglossum hastilabium* and *O. lindenii*. He returned to Europe in 1845, much worn by ten years of exploration, but with another half century to publish his plant discoveries and to institute his successful orchid business. In 1853 he moved his nursery from Luxembourg to Brussels after being appointed Director of the Zoological and Botanic Gardens there, a post he held until 1861.

On his return to Europe, Linden gave his orchid collection to John Lindley, who documented its content in *Orchidaceae Lindenianae* (1846), subtitled *Notes on a Collection Formed in Colombia and Cuba*. This work detailed 143 species, 76 of which were new to science. Linden's notes were also to provide invaluable information for the cultivation of orchids; he noted the importance of altitude and climate, factors to which European growers had hitherto paid scant regard. His nursery, Horticultre Internationale, employed a number of collectors, notably Schlim and Wallis, and was responsible for the introduction of more than 2000 species of plants.

Linden also worked on a variety of publications, including *Pescatorea* and *Lindenia*, illustrated magazines devoted to orchids, and *L'Illustration Horticole*, one of the most beautiful and methodical horticultural journals in which he documented the proliferation of exotics and hybrids in European cultivation and created a fusion of botany and plantsmanship. He remained its director for 25 years. Through his nursery in Brussels, with its authoritative catalogues and the collectors it employed, and through his own work in the field, Linden was responsible for introducing many orchids and other tropical plants into cultivation. The genus *Lindenia* was named in his honour as were many orchids, bromeliads and other exotic species.

**Lindenbergia** Lehm. (For Johann B.W. Lindenberg (1781–1851).) Scrophulariaceae. Some 15 species of annuals, herbaceous perennials or subshrubs. Stems decumbent or erect. Leaves simple, opposite, toward apex sometimes alternate. Flowers in spikes, racemes or axillary; calyx 5-lobed; corolla red, yellow or purple, 2-lipped, upper lip bilobed or notched, lower lip trilobed, throat with 2 pouches; stamens 4. Fruit a capsule. Summer. Old World Tropics. Z9.

CULTIVATION *L. grandiflora* is found at altitudes of 700–2400m/2275–7800ft in coastal areas, the damp undergrowth of mountainous terrain and on the banks of paddy fields, its supple stems show a tendency to ramble upwards into the branches of companion plants. Rarely cultivated, it may be tried under intermediate to hot glasshouse conditions in a well-drained, medium-fertility loam-based mix.

***L. grandiflora*** Benth. Villous perenn. to 60cm. Stems flexuous. Lvs 5–20cm, ovate, dentate, petiolate. Racemes lax, foliose; cor. yellow, to 2.5cm, throat and palate spotted red.

**Lindenia** Benth. (For J.J. Linden (1817–98), Belgian botanist.) Rubiaceae. 4 species of shrubs often found growing marginally on waterways; branches terete. Leaves short-petiolate, entire, opposite; stipules interpetiolar, united. Flowers short-peduncled, terminal, solitary to few in clusters, bracteate; calyx top-shaped, 5-ribbed or -angled, lobes 5, sometimes irregular, lanceolate or awl-shaped, persistent; corolla salverform, pubescent, lobes 5, spreading; stamens 5, inserted at top of corolla, anthers sessile, oblong, rounded, exserted from mouth of corolla; ovary 2-celled; style filiform, 2-fid, hairy; ovules many and dense in each cell. Fruit a club- or pear-shaped capsule, 2-celled; seeds many, angled. C America, SW Pacific Is. (Fiji, New Caledonia). Z10.

CULTIVATION Beautiful evergreen shrubs grown for their large, long-tubed white flowers produced at the ends of the shoots in summer. Grow in the hot glasshouse with direct sunlight, in a rich loam-based mix, with additional organic matter to retain moisture. Water plentifully when in growth and maintain high humidity. Propagate from softwood cuttings in summer or from semi-ripe cuttings in autumn in a closed case with bottom heat or under mist. Sometimes infested with mealybug; treat with appropriate insecticide.

***L. rivalis*** Benth. Shrub, evergreen, to 1m; branches pubesc. to glabrous, red brown. Lvs to 15×2cm, fascicled terminally on branches, lanceolate to narrow-elliptic, acute to narrowed at apex, narrowed at base, glabrous above, pubesc. beneath, 6–12-veined. Fls to 5, often 3, in clusters, or solitary, white; cal. to 1cm, hairy, lobes erect, to 2cm, hairy, green; cor. to 15cm, pubesc., lobes 3cm; anth. 1cm, yellow. Fr. to 2cm, ribbed, hairy, woody. Spring–summer. Mexico to Guatemala.

***L. acutiflora*** Hook. See *L. rivalis*.

**Lindera** Thunb. (For Johann Linder (1678–1723), Swedish botanist.) Lauraceae. 80 species of aromatic, evergreen or deciduous, dioecious shrubs or trees. Leaves alternate, margin entire or 3-lobed, venation pinnate or with only 3 veins at base. Flowers yellow, in dense, false umbels, subtended by 4 involucral, persistent bracts which enclose the umbel in bud; perianth segments 6; male flowers with stamens 9(–12), anthers 2-celled; female flowers with staminodes 9; style short or elongate, stigma peltate. Fruit a 1-seeded drupe, globose or ovoid, fleshy or dry, subtended by a shallow cup. Temperate and tropical E Asia, (Himalayas to Malaysia, China, Japan), N America.

CULTIVATION Grown for their early spring flowers and aromatic foliage which in the deciduous species often gives clear rich yellow autumn colour *Lindera* spp. have a slender and open habit and are well suited to the open woodland garden and other informal plantings. Grow in part shade or dappled sunlight in a moisture retentive, fertile, lime-free soil enriched with leafmould. *L. benzoin* tolerates temperatures as low as −25°C/−13°C, *L. umbellata* and *L. obtusiloba* to −15°C/5°F, but should be given a position where they have some protection from late spring frosts. *L. praecox* is slightly more tender and needs wall protection in zones at the limits of hardiness. Prune if necessary to remove deadwood in spring; old leggy specimens may be rejuvenated by cutting hard back to the base if necessary although this is best carried out over several seasons.

Propagate by fresh seed sown ripe, seed has short viability and should not be allowed to dry out before sowing. Also by semi-ripe cuttings in a closed case or by layering.

***L. benzoin*** (L.) Bl. SPICE BUSH; BENJAMIN BUSH. Deciduous, highly aromatic shrub to 4×3m. Habit rounded. Branches glabrous or initially puberulent. Lvs 6–15×2–8cm, obovate, acuminate, gradually so towards petiole, thin-textured, pinnately veined, glabrous above, glabrous or puberulent beneath, margins entire, ciliate; petiole 0.5–1.5cm. Fls unisexual, to 0.5cm diam., pale yellow-green, sessile, in small clusters on 1-year-old wood, cal. lobes 6, cor. absent. Fr. to 0.75cm, ellipsoid, bright red. E US. 'Xanthocarpa': fr. yellow. Z5.

***L. megaphylla*** Hemsl. Evergreen shrub or tree to 20m, usually far shorter in cult. Branches initially dark purple-brown, with sparse, pale lenticels. Lvs 10–20×2–6cm, lanceolate-elliptic, apex acuminate, coriaceous, dark green and lustrous above, glaucous beneath, venation pinnate, midrib yellow; petiole 1–2cm. Fls clustered in umbels 3cm across, yellow-green. Fr. 1.5cm, ovoid-globose, fleshy, black. Spring. China. Z8.

***L. obtusiloba*** Bl. Deciduous shrub or small tree to 10m. Branches grey-yellow sometimes flushed purple, sparsely lenticellate. Lvs 6–12×3–10cm, ovate, apex acute or obtuse, often 3-lobed, with 3 veins at base, green above, glaucous beneath, venation pubesc., colouring pale gold in autumn; petiole 1–2cm. Fls to 4mm diam., precocious, yellow-green, borne in crowded clusters to 1.5cm diam. on 1 year-old wood; pedicels to 0.4cm, densely sericeous. Fr. to 0.75cm diam., globose, glossy black. Korea, China, Japan. Z6.

***L. praecox*** (Sieb. & Zucc.) Bl. Deciduous shrub or small tree to 7m. Young branches glossy dark brown, glabrous, covered in prominent, pale lenticels. Lvs 2.5–8.75×1.25–3.5cm, ovate, oval or near orbicular, apex acuminate or blunt, thin-textured, glabrous, deep green above, paler, glaucous beneath, pinnately veined; petiole 0.75–2.5cm. Fls to 6mm diam., yellow-green, borne in short-stalked clusters to 1.5cm diam., formed in pairs or threes in leaf axils the summer prior to anthesis. Fr. to 2cm diam., globose, olive to red-brown, with many, pale sports. Japan, Korea.

***L. strychnifolia*** (Sieb. & Zucc.) Vilm. Evergreen tree or shrub to 10m. Branches brown, initially downy. Lvs to 6×3cm, ovate to ovate-oblong, acuminate coriaceous, conspicuously 3-nerved; petiole to 1cm. Fls clustered 3–8; pedicels to

0.2cm, thickly tomentose. Fr. ovoid-globose, pubesc. China, Taiwan, Philippines, SE Asia.

***L. umbellata*** Thunb. Deciduous shrub to 4m. Branches deep red-brown, lacking lenticels. Lvs 0.6–1.25cm, obovate-elliptic, acute or acuminate, with pinnate venation; petioles 1–1.8cm. Fls yellow, opening with emergence of lvs, in clusters to 2.5cm across. Fr. to 1cm, subglobose, black. Japan.

For synonymy see *Benzoin, Laurus* and *Parabenzoin*.

**Lindheimera** A. Gray & Engelm. (For Ferdinand Jacob Lindheim (1801–1879), German botanist.) Compositae. 1 species, an annual herb to 65cm. Lower leaves alternate, oblanceolate, coarsely pinnatifid, petiolate, upper leaves opposite, ovate-lanceolate, entire, bract-like, uppermost sessile. Capitula radiate, to 4cm diam., clustered in a corymb; phyllaries in 2 series; ray florets female, white; disc florets hermaphrodite, yellow. Fruit a compressed cypsela; pappus of 2 awns. Late spring. S US.

CULTIVATION Occurring predominantly on the limestone soils of central Texas, *L. texana* is an undemanding annual for the cut-flower border and for native plant collections. Grow in sun in any well-drained soil. Sow *in situ* in spring or earlier under glass.

***L. texana*** A. Gray. TEXAS STAR. As for the genus.

**Lindley, John** (1799–1865). Botanist, horticulturist and administrator. Born at Catton near Norwich, the son of George Lindley, a nurseryman and author of *The Guide to Orchard and Kitchen Garden* (1831), Lindley was educated at the grammar school in Norwich and showed an interest in horticulture at an early age. In 1815 he went to Belgium to collect plants and seeds for Wrench the nurseryman, and for a seed merchant at Camberwell. On his return he devoted much of his time to the study of horticulture and entomology and corresponded with Hooker, who visited Lindley to procure plants and insects.

In 1818 Lindley moved to Halesworth, Suffolk, and translated (at one sitting) Richard's *Analyse du Fruit*. The translation was published in 1819. He prepared to travel to Sumatra and Malaysia on a plant-collecting expedition, but the trip did not take place. In 1818–19 he was introduced to Sir Joseph Banks and was invited to London to serve as Banks's library assistant. In 1820 Lindley published his *Rosarum monographia* and (with Bauer) a monograph on *Flora Scotica*. In the following year Banks recommended Lindley to Cattley, who needed an editor for his *Collectanea botanica* (1821–25). Lindley was a skilled illustrator and in 1820 was commissioned to draw roses and larches sent to the Horticultural Society by the Duke of Atholl.

In 1822 he was appointed assistant secretary at the Horticultural Society's new garden at Chiswick. Four years later he was made assistant secretary to the Horticultural Society and when the Society was in difficulties in the 1830s Lindley was instrumental in promoting and supporting its works. From 1826 he was editor of the *Botanical Register*, one of several tasks he undertook in an attempt to alleviate the financial burden he had inherited from his father. He encouraged and aided many of the Society's collectors, including Robert Fortune and David Douglas, and through the provision of a library and reading room he actively promoted botanical study. He was also responsible for arranging the first flower shows in the 1830s. From 1829 to 1860 he was Professor of Botany at University College, London, where he promoted the natural system of classification developed by Jussieu and de Candolle as opposed to Linnaeus's sexual system. He produced several important works for his students such as *A Synopsis of the British Flora* (1829), *Introduction to the Natural System of Botany* (1830), *A Natural System of Botany* (1836) and *The Vegetable Kingdom* (1846). Lindley was a celebrated horticulturist (he believed his *Theory of Horticulture* (1840) to be his finest work) specializing in orchids. In 1836 he was appointed superintendent of the Chelsea Physic Garden. In 1841 he helped to found the *Gardener's Chronicle*, which he edited until 1863. From 1841 he was vice secretary and from 1858 he held the post of secretary of the Horticultural Society, resigning in 1863 due to ruined health brought about by his massive workload.

Lindley was an outstandingly energetic and productive figure; one of his notable achievements was the 1838 report on Kew which led to its establishment as a national institution.

He was elected a Fellow of the Linnean Society in 1820, a Fellow of the Royal Society in 1828 and gained an honorary PhD from Munich in 1832. His published works include *Genera and Species of Orchidaceous Plants* (1830–40), *Introduction to Botany* (1832), *Folia Orchidacea* (1852–59), *Fossil Flora of Great Britain* (1831–37), with Hutton, and (with Sir Joseph Paxton) *Paxton's Flower Garden* (1850–53). The genus *Lindleya* was named in his honour.

**Lindsaea** Dryand. (For Dr John Lindsay (*fl.* 1785–1803), botanist in Jamaica.) Dennstaedtiaceae. Some 200 species of terrestrial or epiphytic ferns. Rhizomes short- to long-creeping, very short and caespitose or, occasionally, scandent; scales narrow, often hair-like. Fronds stipitate, erect or ascending, pinnate, or 2–3-pinnate to- pinnatifid, glabrous, final segments generally flabellate, semi-ovate, crescent-shaped, trapezoid or parallelogram-shaped, lower margin thickened and decurrent on rachis; rachis sulcate above, 4-angled in cross-section; veins dichotomous, free or anastomosing into serial areolae lacking free, included veinlets; stipes crowded or remote, 2-ranked, not jointed, usually sulcate, occasionally 4-angled. Sori marginal or submarginal, terminating 1 to several veins on outer and upper margin, elongate-linear or oblong to circular; indusia basally or laterally attached, running to or short of margin, linear or circular or 2-valved and opening outwards; sporangia stalked; paraphyses absent; annulus 7–15-celled, vertical, oblique, incomplete; spores globose, oblong, or tetrahedral, monolete or trilete, smooth or finely granulate. Tropics and subtropics. Z10.

CULTIVATION Tropical ferns occasionally introduced into cultivation, but usually only surviving for short periods. *L. odorata* has been successfully maintained in conditions suitable for warm-growing filmy ferns: it originates in inundated sandy soils on banks of rivers and streams where it may be periodically submerged. Plants appear to adapt better to cultivation raised from spores.

***L. adiantoides*** J. Sm. Rhiz. short. Fronds to 15×3cm, tufted, pinnate, lanceolate, pinnae deciduous, crowded, upwardly overlapping, horizontal, semi-ovate, obtuse, plane and entire at lower margin, curved and lobed at upper margin, to 12×6mm, lobes somewhat erose, membranous; stipes to 5cm, lustrous black. Malaysia to Philippines, Polynesia.

***L. concinna*** J. Sm. Rhiz. short-creeping. Fronds to 30×2cm, tufted, simply pinnate, narrowly acute at apex, herbaceous, pinnae crowded toward apex, remote at base, spreading, flabellate, obtuse at apex, somewhat notched at upper margin, to 8×4mm, membranous; stripes erect, wiry, to 8cm. Malaysia.

***L. cultrata*** (Willd.) Sw. Rhiz. short-creeping, to 2mm wide; scales to 3mm, hair-like, linear to lanceolate, entire, lustrous brown. Fronds to 30×3cm, pinnate, lanceolate to linear, acute to narrowly acute at apex, glabrous, pinnae to 18×7mm, short-petiolate, remote, horizontal, crescent- or kidney-shaped, obtuse, curved and entire at lower margin, plane and usually lobed at upper margin, upper pinnae reduced, lobes to 4, obtuse or truncate; veins obscure; stipes to 15cm, crowded, wiry, scaly at base, lustrous and pale green or brown to black. Madagascar, Tropical Asia, Australia (Queensland).

***L. davallioides*** Bl. Rhiz. short-creeping. Fronds 1–2-pinnatifid, deltoid to ovate, pinnae sessile, falcate, lanceolate, narrowly acute at apex, plane to upcurved at lower margin, lobed at upper margin, to 12×4mm, thin-textured, lobes 4–6, close, oblique, obtuse; stipes crowded, 10cm+. Malaysia to Philippines.

***L. decomposita*** Willd. Rhiz. short-creeping; scales to 2mm. Fronds to 20×4cm, 1–2-pinnatifid, pinnae 13, to 20×8mm, subsessile, ascending to spreading, lanceolate, falcate at lower margin, lobed at upper margin, lobes 3–4; veins obscure above; stipes erect, to 20cm, pale purple to brown. Sri Lanka, Malaysia, to Polynesia.

***L. dubia*** Spreng. Rhiz. short-creeping. Fronds to 20×5cm, pinnate, oblong to ovate, pinnae to 25×3mm, spreading, lanceolate to linear, narrowly acute, cuneate and oblique at lower margin, notched at upper margin; costa centre at apex; stipes to 15cm, close, wiry, dark brown. Tropical America.

***L. guianensis*** Dryand. Rhiz. short-creeping. Fronds to 60cm, 2-pinnatifid, pinnae 13, to 12×6mm, erect to spreading, falcate, strap-shaped to linear, narrowly acute, pinnules close or overlapping, horizontal, obtuse at apex, entire and plane to arched at lower margin, rounded at upper margin; stipes terete, erect, rigid, to 30cm. Tropical America.

***L. lancea*** (L.) Bedd. Rhiz. short- to -long-creeping, to 3mm wide; scales to 2mm, lanceolate, narrowly acute at apex, lustrous brown. Fronds to 50cm, 1–2-pinnatifid, pinnae to 30cm, erect to spreading, pinnules to 33×11mm, approximate, falcate, trapeziform, entire and plane or somewhat curved at lower margin, rounded at upper margin; stipes approximate, erect, to 30cm, purple or brown. Tropical America.

***L. linearis*** Sw. Rhiz. creeping, to 1mm wide; scales linear, pale brown. Fronds to 20×1cm, simply pinnate, linear, narrow-acute, membranous, pinnae to 6×4mm or, rarely, more, sessile or subsessile, remote spreading, flabellate to deltoid, oblong, or crescent-shaped, entire at lower margin, shallowly to deeply lobed or toothed at upper margin; stipes remote, erect, wiry, to 30cm, glabrous, lustrous russet to dark brown or black. Australia, New Zealand.

***L. media*** R. Br. Rhiz. long-creeping, to 2mm wide; scales to 1mm, deciduous, ovate to deltoid. Fronds to 30×17cm, 2-pinnate, oblong or deltoid, papery or grass-like in texture, pinnae 5cm×6mm or more, subopposite, ascending to spreading, rhomboid to ovate or flabellate, lobed or notched and plane at lower margin, entire and rounded at upper margin, leathery, seg. flabellate or trapezoid, to 10×6mm; veins sunken and obscure, forked; stipes 5mm apart, terete or flattened, wiry, to 30cm, straw-coloured to brown. Australia.

***L. microphylla*** Sw. Rhiz. short-creeping; scales brown. Fronds to 45×10cm, 2–3-pinnate or -pinnatifid, lanceolate to oblong, narrowly acute, pinnae remote, to 5cm, sterile pinnules lanceolate to ovate, lobed or toothed, fertile pinnules obovate, wedge-shaped or flabellate, entire, notched or lobed, lobes deltoid, to 2mm wide; stipes close, wiry, to 15cm, scaly at base, lustrous brown. Australia, New Zealand.

***L. odorata*** Roxb. Rhiz. short- to long-creeping, to 2mm wide; scales lanceolate to 2mm, lustrous red-brown. Fronds to 30×3cm, erect, pinnate, oblong to lanceolate or elliptic, acute to narrowly acute, grass-like in texture, pinnae to 20×8mm, petiolate, ascending to spreading, alternate, approximate, rhomboid or elliptic, acute or obtuse, convex and entire at lower margin, lobed and plane at upper margin, basal pinnae reduced and distant, lobes to 6, oblique; veins sunken, free; stipes to 1cm apart, terete, to 20cm, scaly at base, straw-coloured to brown. Tropical Africa, Madagascar, to Tropical Asia (Indo-China to Japan).

***L. orbiculata*** (Lam.) Mett. ex Kuhn. Rhiz. short-creeping, to 2mm wide; scales to 2mm, deltoid or lanceolate to linear, lustrous brown. Fronds to 20×3cm, 1–2-pinnate or pinnatifid, deltoid or lanceolate to linear, pinnae flabellate, dentate or incised at margin (basal pinnae only), pinnules petiolate, ovate, elliptic or flabellate, dentate or lobed and plane or decurved at lower margin, rounded at upper margin, to 12×6mm; stipes erect, wiry, to 20cm, scaly at base, lustrous red-brown. China, Taiwan, Japan.

***L. parvula*** Fée. Rhiz. creeping. Fronds to 35cm, 2-pinnate, grass-like in texture or papery to leathery, pinnae 9 lateral and 1 terminal, sessile or petiolate, remote, ascending to spreading, subopposite, linear, apex attenuate to narrowly acute, to 12×1cm, pinnules to 6×4mm, close, ascending to spreading, alternate or subopposite, ovate, falcate at upper margin; stipes to 60cm, grooved and glabrous, straw-coloured to red-brown. W Indies, S America.

***L. pectinata*** Bl. Rhiz. scandent to creeping, to 3mm wide; scales to 3mm, brown. Fronds to 40×4cm, pinnate, membranous, pinnae to 16×8mm, sessile or subsessile, close, ascending to spreading, oblong, obtuse, plane to decurved at lower margin, curved and subentire to notched or somewhat lobed at upper margin, apical and basal pinnae reduced; veins distinct; stipes erect, to 3cm. Malaysia to Philippines.

***L. rigida*** J. Sm., nom. nud.; Hook. Rhiz. long-creeping, to 2mm wide; scales to 2mm, sparse, deltoid, lustrous dark brown. Fronds to 35cm, rigid, bipinnatifid, oblong, pinnae 9–13, ascending, remote, alternate, linear, attenuate, to 25×2cm, pinnules close, oblique, flabellate to rhomboid, oblong, or ovate, plane to somewhat falcate at lower margin, convex at upper margin, notched or dentate in sterile fronds, lobed in fertile fronds, lobes 3–4; veins distinct; stipes to 3cm apart, erect and rigid, to 30cm, prickly and scaly at base, purple to brown. Malaysia to Polynesia.

***L. stricta*** (Sw.) Dryand. Rhiz. short-creeping, to 3mm wide; scales to 2mm, lanceolate, narrowly acute. Fronds 60cm+, erect, 1–2-pinnatifid, rigid, pinnae to 8×4mm, erect to spreading, opposite, linear, pinnules subsessile, close, trapezoid to flabellate, lunate or cuneate, lower margin decurved, upper margin rounded and falcate, subentire to notched, apical pinna reduced; veins sunken; stipes erect and rigid, approximate, terete to flattened, straw-coloured to brown. W Indies, C to S America.

***L. trichomanoides*** Dryand. Rhiz. creeping, to 2mm wide; scales dense, linear, brown. Fronds to 25×10cm, 2–3-pinnate or -pinnatifid, lanceolate to ovate or oblong, leathery, pinnae to 8cm, erect to spreading, subopposite, deeply incised, pinnules obovate or oblong to cuneate, apex obtuse, upper margin entire to dentate or lobed, lobes deltoid; stipes erect, wiry, to 15cm, lustrous dark brown, base scaly. Australia, New Zealand.

***L. clavata*** (L.) Mett. See *Sphenomeris clavata*.
***L. cuneata*** (Forst. f.) C. Chr. See *L. trichomanoides*.
***L. falcata*** var. ***lancea*** (L.) Jenman. See *L. lancea*.
***L. lobata*** Poir. See *L. decomposita*.
***L. recurvata*** Wallich. See *L. decomposita*.
***L. stricta*** var. ***parvula*** (Fée) Kramer. See *L. parvula*.
***L. taiwaniana*** Ching. See *L. orbiculata*.
***L. trapezoidea*** Copel. See *L. decomposita*.
***L. trilobata*** Colenso. See *L. linearis*.
For further synonymy see *Odontoloma*.

**Linnaea** Gronov. (Named for Carl Linnaeus (1707–1778), by Gronovius at Linnaeus' request.) TWIN-FLOWER. Caprifoliaceae. 1 species, a creeping, dwarf, evergreen shrub. Branches to 35cm, slender, forming a loose carpet, trailing, rooting sporadically when in contact with the soil, pubescent at first, later woody. Leaves alternate or paired along branches, 0.25–1×0.25–0.75cm, oval, rounded, entire, somtimes crenate or serrulate in apical half, subcoriaceous, glossy dark green and sparsely pubescent above, buff to pale green, downy on veins beneath. Inflorescence a slender pink-flushed stalk, erect to 8cm; flowers campanulate, to 2cm, fragrant, paired and nodding atop stalk; pedicel to 2cm, thread-like, arching; sepals 5, narrow; corolla to 12.5mm, light candy-pink with deeper markings, lobes 5, rounded. Fruit to 3mm diam., coriaceous, ochre, 1-seeded, indehiscent. Summer. Circumpolar regions. Z2.

CULTIVATION The smallest member of the Caprifoliaceae, the flowers of *Linnaea* are delicate and fragrant tubular bells, borne above slender, trailing, evergreen stems. Named for Linnaeus at his own request, it was his favourite flower and commonly appears in his portraits. Native to cool moist woodland, heathland and mossy tundra of northern temperate zones, *Linnaea* grows as an extensive and twiggy mat, so that it is useful groundcover for the peat bed, rock garden and shaded woodland garden. It requires an acid soil and may be difficult to establish in gardens. Plant between autumn and early spring in a cool, moist but well-drained soil, in shade. Propagate by rooted runners in spring.

***L. borealis*** L. As for the genus. var. ***americana*** (Forbes) Rehd. Lvs glabrous, ciliate only at base. Fls deep rose; cor. tube to 16mm. N America.

***L. americana*** Forbes. See *L. borealis* var. *americana*.

**Linnaeus, Carolus** (Carl von Linné) (1707–1778). Botanist. Born at Røshult, Smøland, in southern Sweden, the son of a clergyman, the rectory garden cultivated by his father was the scene of Linnaeus's first encounter with native and exotic plants and their nomenclature. In 1714 he was sent to school in Växjö, where he was influenced and encouraged in his interest in the reproduction of plants by a local doctor. In 1727 he entered the University of Lund, where Stobaeus (1690–1742) befriended him and, while living in the latter's house, Linnaeus began to collect plants for a herbarium. In 1729 he went to Uppsala University, where his work on plant and animal reproduction was noted by Rudbeck, who soon asked Linnaeus, still a student, to give botanical lectures to his peers. Linnaeus lived in Rudbeck's house, and began work on his attempt to define comprehensive new systems for plant, animal and mineral nomenclature. It was at this time that he also began a close friendship and collaboration with Petrus Artedi, who unfortunately drowned in 1735 by falling into an unlit canal in Amsterdam.

In 1732 Linnaeus visited Lapland, observing and collecting plants for his *Flora Lapponica* (1737) and writing a journal, which was published in English in 1811 as *Lachesis Lapponica, or a Tour in Lapland*. After three years in the Netherlands, where he gained a degree in medicine at the University of Hardewijk and served as physician and garden superintendent to George Clifford, a Haarlem merchant and owner of a renowned botanical garden, Linnaeus returned to Sweden in 1738. At this time Linnaeus produced two decisive early works, *Systema naturae* (1735), a seminal treatise on his theory of nomenclature, and *Genera plantarum* (1737), which contains brief descriptions of all 935 genera then known. He also published *Bibliotheca botanica* (1736), an inventory of botanical literature; *Fundamenta botanica* (1736); *Critica botanica* (1737), containing rules for botanical nomenclature and *Classes plantarum* (1738), a critique of previous plant systems. Linnaeus established a medical practice in Stockholm and was appointed physician to the Admiralty. In 1741 he was appointed professor of medicine and (a year later) botany at Uppsala and began work on the reconstruction of the Uppsala botanic garden. He made three journeys of which he wrote significant botanical accounts, travelling to the Baltic islands of Oland and Götland in 1741, to Västergötland in 1746 and to Skane in 1749.

Linnaeus's work, and particularly his *Species Plantarum* (1753), established the use of the binomial nomenclature which remains the basis of all plant classification. He established the so-called sexual system: plants are identified by the visual aspects of their flower parts and named diagnostically. In this way, a purely mechanical and logical ordering procedure, Linnaeus standardized botanical taxonomic procedure and terminology, which he clarified in *Philosophia botanica* (1751). The advance of Linnaeus's research into natural history is reflected in his continual revisions of his *Systema naturae*, culminating in a definitive tenth edition of 1758–9. An analysis of his role as the father of modern taxonomy will be found at the end of this work.

He was made a Knight of the Polar Star in 1758 and was ennobled in 1761. He was in correspondence with naturalists throughout Europe and some 23 of his students became professors. In addition to the works mentioned, Linnaeus's botanical publications include *Hortus Cliffortianus* (1737); *Flora Suecica* (1745) and *Hortus Upsaliensis* (1748). He also produced a number of medical works (notably on the classification of diseases) including *Materia Medica* (1749–63), and several on the theme of order in nature, such as *Oeconomia naturae* (1749) and *Politia naturae* (1760).

**Linoma** Cook.
***L. alba*** (Bory) Cook. See *Dictyosperma album*.

**Linospadix** H.A. Wendl. (From Gk *linon*, a fishing-line, and *spadix*, spike, referring to the slender inflorescence.) Palmae. Some 11 species of unarmed, pleonanthic, monoecious palms to *c*3m. Stems solitary or clustered, to 3cm diam., conspicuously ringed. Crownshaft not well developed. Leaves 20cm–1.5m, pinnately divided or simple and deeply emarginate, marcescent or neatly abscising; sheaths scaly, with fibrous margins; petiole channelled above, sparsely scaly beneath; pinnae 1- to several-fold, acute, acuminate, emarginate or praemorse, minutely scaly. Flowers borne on simple, erect spikes to *c*1m.; bud enclosed in 2 papery bracts, lower bract hidden among the leaves, the upper bract conspicuous, deciduous; flowers arranged in triads (2 male, 1 female) in shallow pits on spike, with solitary or paired male flowers apically: male flowers sessile, cream, falling before female flowers open, sepals 3, imbricate, petals exceeding sepals, ovate, stamens 6–15, pistillode minute or absent; female flowers green; petals overlapping, staminodes minute teeth, pistil 1-celled. Fruit *c*1cm, ellipsoid, smooth, scarlet, with apical stigmatic remains and persistent perianth; mesocarp thin, fleshy. New Guinea, Australia. Z10.

CULTIVATION Small and slender feather palms occurring in moist, acid, humus-rich soils in the deep shade of rainforest understorey, requiring similar conditions in cultivation. Propagate by seed; germination may take up to 12 months. See also PALMS.

***L. monostachya*** (Mart.) H.A. Wendl. WALKING STICK PALM. Stem solitary, to *c*3m. Lvs to 1m; petiole slender; pinnae of variable width. Infl. to 1m, erect, becoming pendulous. Fr. globose to obovate, *c*1cm. Australia.

For synonymy see *Bacularia*.

For illustration see PALMS.

**Linum** L. (Lat. for flax.) FLAX. Linaceae. Some 200 species of annual, biennial or perennial herbs or shrubs, usually glabrous. Leaves simple, alternate or rarely opposite, narrow, entire, 1- or many-veined. Flowers blue, yellow, rarely rosy, blood-red or white, very fugitive, in terminal or axillary racemes, sometimes in close clusters or spike-like heads; sepals 5; petals 5, falling early; stamens 5, basally united, sometimes with a whorl of staminodes; styles 5. Fruit an 8–10-valved capsule, often beaked. Temperate N hemisphere.

CULTIVATION A beautiful and generally undemanding genus grown for the long succession of fugacious flowers of remarkable satin texture and soft clear colours, *Linum* includes species suited in scale to the rock garden and herbaceous border, where taller species such as *L. narbonense* and *L. perenne* are much valued for their slender graceful habit. The smaller spp such as *L. hirsutum* and *L. campanulatum* are suited to the alpine house. The annual *L. usitatissimum* (flax) replaces its blooms every morning, dropping the silky, clear blue petals by mid afternoon. The seed heads are particularly attractive when dried, offering a range of golden yellow and chestnut browns for winter arrangements. *L. grandiflorum* 'Rubrum' bears clear, deep red flowers on slender but sturdy stems throughout summer into autumn.

Grow in a sheltered position in sun, in any light, well-drained, moderately fertile and humus-rich soil, with greater emphasis on good drainage for the alpine and hirsute species. *L. viscosum* will tolerate light shade. Sow seed of annual species *in situ* in early spring, or in autumn for early flowers in pots under glass; overwinter at 10°C/50°F, watering carefully and sparingly until light levels and temperatures rise in spring, thereafter water moderately and liquid feed as roots fill pots until flower buds form. Propagate perennials by seed, named varieties by cuttings of basal shoots in spring; perennials are frequently short-lived and should be propagated frequently. Increase shrubby species by semi-ripe cuttings in a shaded cold frame.

***L. africanum*** L. Shrubby perenn. to 90cm. Lvs to 1.5cm, opposite, narrow-lanceolate, acute, sessile. Fls in forked corymbs, yellow. S Africa. Z9.

***L. album*** Kotschy ex Boiss. Glabrous, glaucous perenn. herb to 30cm. Lvs to 2cm, elliptic-oblanceolate, sessile, narrower at infl. Fls in few-fld, lax cymes, white. Iran. Z9.

***L. altaicum*** Ledeb. ex Juz. Glabrous, caespitose perenn. to 60cm. Lvs to 3cm, oblong, becoming linear-lanceolate or lanceolate above. Fls violet blue; sep. 6mm, margins scarious; pet. 2.2cm. C Asia. Z7.

***L. arboreum*** L. Glabrous shrub to 1m. Lvs to 2cm, spathulate, thick, persistent, 1-veined, margins cartilaginous, with a pair of glands at base, often crowded in rosettes. Fls yellow, in a compact, few-fld cyme; sep. 8mm, lanceolate, acuminate, as long as fr. S Aegean. Z8.

***L. austriacum*** L. Glabrous, erect perenn. to 60cm; branches racemose. Lvs to 1.5cm, linear, 1–3-veined, with many pellucid dots. Fls blue, to 2cm diam., in a many-fld cyme; sep. elliptic, obtuse, rarely mucronate; pet. retuse; pedicels deflexed in fruit. Fr. to 5mm. S Europe. 'Loreyi': semi-prostrate; fls lilac with darker lines. ssp. ***collinum*** Nyman. Smaller than species type; lvs shorter; fr. to 8mm. Z3.

***L. bienne*** Mill. PALE FLAX. Glabrous annual or perenn. to 60cm, with several stems from base. Lvs to 2.5cm, linear, 1–3-veined. Fls to 1.75cm diam., pale blue, in loose cymes; sep. ovate, acuminate, unequal, the inner sometimes glandular-pubesc. W Europe, Mediterranean. Z7.

***L. campanulatum*** L. Glabrous perenn. to 30cm, base woody. Lower lvs spathulate, apex rounded, upper lvs lanceolate, apex mucronate to slender-pointed, margins narrow-hyaline, minutely glandular at base. Fls yellow, veined orange, to 3cm diam., in 3–5-fld corymbs; sep. lanceolate, narrowly acuminate, much exceeding fr., margins white; pet. 3.5cm, with a long claw. S Europe. Z7.

***L. capitatum*** Kit. ex Schult. Robust perenn. to 45cm. Lvs acute to obtuse with marginal glands toward base, basal lvs obovate-lanceolate, apex obtuse, upper stem lvs lanceolate, apex acute. Fls yellow, to 2.5cm diam., in a subcapitate cyme; sep. lanceolate, acuminate. S Europe. In cult., often confused with *L. flavum*, which has yellow fls in a looser head. Z7.

***L. compactum*** A. Nels. Pubesc. perenn. to 10cm. Lvs to 1cm, linear, 1-veined. Fls yellow; sep. glandular ciliate; pet. twice length of sep. C US (E Wyoming). Possibly not distinct from *L. rigidum*. Z3.

***L. dolomiticum*** Borb. Tufted perenn., 15–20cm. Basal lvs to 4.5cm, linear-oblanceolate, stem lvs to 1.25cm, oblong-lanceolate. Fls yellow; pet. 2–2.5cm. Hungary. Z6.

***L. elegans*** Sprun. ex Boiss. Dwarf, to 15cm, tufted from a woody base. Basal lvs in compact rosettes, obovate to spathulate, 3-veined, margin hyaline, upper lvs linear, acute. Fls yellow with distinct veins, 3cm diam., in 2–7-fld cymes; sep. narrow-lanceolate, acuminate, much longer than fr.; pet. short-clawed. Balkan Peninsula. Z6.

***L. flavum*** L. GOLDEN FLAX. Erect, glabrous perenn., 30–40cm, base somewhat woody. Lvs 2–3.5cm, alternate, lower lvs spathulate, upper lvs narrow-lanceolate, acute, 3–5-veined, with marginal glands at base. Fls golden yellow, 2.5cm diam., in dense, much-branched cymes; sep. lanceolate-acuminate, glandular-ciliate, keeled, scarcely longer than fr. C & S Europe. 'Compactum': dwarf form; fls cool yellow. Z5.

***L.* 'Gemmels Hybrid'** (*L. campanulatum* × *L. elegans.)* To 15cm. Lvs tinted grey. Fls rich yellow. Z6.

***L. grandiflorum*** Desf. FLOWERING FLAX. Erect glabrous annual to 75cm, branched at base. Lvs to 3cm, linear-lanceolate, acute, sparsely hairy. Fls rose with a dark centre, to 4cm diam., in loose panicles; sep. lanceolate, acute, ciliate-toothed; sep. 12mm, margins membranous and ciliate. N Africa. 'Bright Eyes': to 45cm; fls ivory with deep brown centre. 'Caeruleum': fls blue-purple. 'Coccineum': fls scarlet. 'Roseum': fls rose pink. 'Rubrum': fls bright red.

***L. hirsutum*** L. Erect perenn. to 45cm, more or less downy. Lvs to 1.5cm, broad-lanceolate, 3–5-veined. Fls lavender with white or pale yellow eye, to 1.25cm diam.; sep. broad-lanceolate, densely hairy. C Europe, Mediterranean. Z6.

***L. hologynum*** Rchb. Glabrous perenn., to 60cm. Lvs linear to lanceolate, 1-veined. Fls blue, to 2.5cm diam.; pet. 2–3× length of cal. C Europe (mts). Z6.

***L. maritimum*** L. Perenn., to 60cm. Lvs oblanceolate or elliptic to linear-lanceolate, 1–3-nerved. Fls yellow, 2cm diam., in loose panicles; sep. elliptic to ovate, glandular-ciliate; pet. 4× length of cal. Sardinia. Z8.

***L. monogynum*** Forst. f. Glabrous perenn., to 60cm; stem shrubby, erect, branching. Lvs to 2.5cm, linear to lanceolate, acute to acuminate. Fls white, to 2.5cm diam., in corymbs; sep. ovate to lanceolate-ovate, margins white. New Zealand. Z8.

***L. narbonense*** L. Glabrous, glaucous perenn. to 60cm. Lvs to 2cm, linear-lanceolate, margins of upper lvs and bracts scarious. Fls azure with white eye, to 4.5cm diam., in few-fld cymes; sep. lanceolate-acuminate, margins white. Mediterranean. Close to *L. perenne*, distinguished by more robust habit, scarious-margined bracts and longer sep. and pet. 'Heavenly Blue': fls clear vivid blue. 'Six Hills': fls bright blue. Z5.

***L. nervosum*** Waldst. & Kit. Perenn., 30–40cm; stem hairy at base. Lvs lanceolate, acute. Fls blue, in loose panicles; pet. crenate at apex. E Europe. Z6.

***L. perenne*** L. PERENNIAL FLAX. Glabrous, erect perenn., to 60cm; lower stem usually leafless. Lvs to 2.5cm, linear to lanceolate, acute, mostly 1-veined, margins scarious except on upper lvs and bracts. Fls pale blue, to 2.5cm diam., in much-branched panicles; outer sep. scarcely mucronate, inner sep. blunt, longer and broader than outer. Europe. 'Alba': fls white. 'Caerulea': fls sky blue. ssp. ***alpinum*** (Jacq.) Ockend. To 30cm. Lvs to 2cm, linear-lanceolate, usually close together on lower stem. Fls to 2cm diam., inner and outer sep. equal. ssp. ***lewisii*** (Pursh) Hult. PRAIRIE FLAX. Stouter with lvs longer (to 3cm) and sep. larger. Western N America. Z7.

***L. rhodopeum*** Velen. Close to *L. flavum*, differs in its fewer stems and smaller pet. S Bulgaria, N Greece. Z7.

***L. rigidum*** Pursh. Glabrous perenn. to 50cm; branches rigid, angled, fastigiate. Lvs few, erect, linear, with stipular glands. Fls yellow, to 3cm diam.; sep. with marginal glands, outer longer than inner. N America (Manitoba south to New Mexico).

***L. strictum*** L. Annual, to 40cm. Lvs to 2.5cm, linear-lanceolate, strongly revolute. Fls yellow, to 6mm diam., in tight clusters. C Europe and Mediterranean east to Iran and Afghanistan. Z6.

***L. suffruticosum*** L. Perenn., 25–40cm with many short sterile shoots, base woody, flowering stems procumbent. Lvs linear, involute. Fls white, veined purple with a violet or pink centre, 4–5cm diam.; sep. ovate-acuminate, glandular-ciliate. Spain. ssp. ***salsoloides*** Rouy. Stems to 25cm, less woody at base. Lvs narrower, filiform or subulate. Fls to 3cm diam., pale pearly-white. Spain to N Italy. 'Nanum': prostrate, forming clumps 8–10cm high and to 45cm across. Z5.

***L. sulcatum*** Riddell. Erect annual to 75cm; stems angled. Lvs to 2.5cm, linear, with minute glands at base. Fls yellow, to 1.25cm diam.; sep. lanceolate, glandular-serrate. Eastern N America (Manitoba to Georgia and Texas). Z3.

***L. tauricum*** Willd. Perenn. to 40cm with many sterile lf rosettes. Basal and lower stem lvs narrow-spathulate, 3-veined, upper lvs lanceolate, narrower, usually 1-veined. Fls pale yellow, sep. linear-lanceolate, acuminate. SE Europe. Z6.

***L. tenuifolium*** L. Glabrous, shrubby perenn. to 40cm, with erect flowering shoots and short non-flowering shoots. Lvs to 2.5cm, linear, 1-veined, margins scarious, sometimes inrolled. Fls lilac to pale pink, with purple veins or centre, to 2.5cm diam.; sep. ovate-lanceolate, acuminate, margins glandular-ciliate, much longer than fr. C Europe, Mediterranean. Z6.

***L. usitatissimum*** L. FLAX. Erect annual, to 120cm. Lvs linear to lanceolate, to 3mm wide, acute. Fls blue, to 1.25cm diam., in terminal, leafy, corymbose panicles; sep. ovate, acute, the inner scarious-margined; pet. somewhat crenate. Europe. An ancient cultigen, probably originating in Asia, an escape in N America. Cvs have been selected for their fibre content (linen) and the oil content of their seeds (linseed). Z4.

***L. viscosum*** L. Glandular-hairy perenn. to 60cm. Lvs to 1.5cm, few, distant, oblong-lanceolate, 3–5-veined, densely glandular-ciliate. Fls to 3cm diam., lilac-rose or rarely blue, with violet lines in erect terminal corymbs; sep. lanceolate, glandular-pubesc. S Europe. Z6.

***L. alpinum*** Jacq. See *L. perenne* ssp. *alpinum*.
***L. alpinum*** ssp. ***julicum*** (Hayek) Hayek. See *L. perenn* ssp. *alpinum*.
***L. angustifolium*** Huds. See *L. bienne*.
***L. bulgaricum*** Podp. See *L. tauricum*.
***L. collinum*** Guss. See *L. austriacum* ssp. *collinum*.
***L. julicum*** Hayek. See *L. perenne* ssp. *alpinum*.
***L. lewisii*** Pursh. See *L. perenne* ssp. *lewisii*.
***L. muelleri*** Moris. See *L. maritimum*.
***L. salsoloides*** Lam. See *L. suffruticosum* ssp. *salsoloides*.
***L. sibiricum*** DC. See *L. perenne*.
***L. trigynum*** Roxb. non L. See *Reinwardtia indica*.
For further synonymy see *Cathartolinum*.

**Liparis** Rich. (From Gk *liparos*, fat, greasy or shining, referring to the shiny surface of the leaves of many species.) Orchidaceae. About 250 species of terrestrial and epiphytic orchids, usually with pseudobulbs. Leaves 1 to several, thin-textured and plicate, or stiff, smooth and leathery. Raceme terminal, few- to many-flowered; flowers usually yellow-green or dull purple, usually fairly small; sepals and petals free, spreading or reflexed, lateral sepals sometimes adnate to each other; petals often linear; lip entire or bilobed, not spurred; column long, arched; pollinia 4, in 2 pairs. Pantropical and also temperate, with 1 species in GB. Z10 unless specified.

CULTIVATION The larger species from tropical and subtropical regions require shaded positions in the intermediate or warm house and a cultural regime similar to that of *Eria*. The remainder can be attempted in the alpine house or in sheltered, specially adapted corners of the bog or peat garden where they need painstaking establishment on living sphagnum combined with composted bark, soft water and a cool, humid atmosphere.

***L. atropurpurea*** Lindl. Terrestrial, to 30cm; pseudobulbs obscure. Lvs 3–4, 7.5–10cm with petiole 2–2.5cm, ovate or orbicular, asymmetrical at base. Raceme 10–20cm, laxly several-fld; fls dull purple; sep. linear, dorsal sep. 15mm, erect, lateral sep. slightly shorter, spreading; pet. about 15mm, narrowly linear, spreading; lip about 10×8mm, orbicular or obovate with 2 calli at base, fleshy, recurved, margin crenulate; column 8mm, slender, curved. Sri Lanka, S India.

***L. bowkeri*** Harv. Terrestrial or epiphytic, 12–30cm; pseudobulbs to 7cm, conic. Lvs 2–5; 6–12×3–6cm, lanceolate or ovate, plicate, light green. Raceme several-fld; fls yellow or yellow-green, turning buff-orange with age; sep. 6–11×1–4mm; pet. to 11mm, linear, deflexed; lip to 8×8mm, orbicular, with small bifid callus near base and metallic grey mid-line. Throughout much of tropical Africa; S Africa. Z9.

***L. caespitosa*** (Thouars) Lindl. Small, epiphytic, with ovoid pseudobulbs 1–2cm high set close together on a creeping rhiz. Lf 1, erect, coriaceous, light green, usually about 10×1cm, oblanceolate. Raceme to 15cm, densely many-fld; fls yellow or yellow-green, very small, non-resupinate; sep. 2–2.5mm, ovate, acute; pet. of similar length but narrower; lip 2.5×2mm, oblong, sometimes obscurely 4-lobed. Uganda, Tanzania, Malawi, Madagascar, Réunion, Sri Lanka and from NE India to Philippines, New Guinea, Solomon Is. and Fiji.

***L. condylobulbon*** Rchb. f. Epiphytic, forming dense clumps; pseudobulbs to 24×2cm, cylindrical but swollen at base. Lvs 2, to 20×2.5cm, narrowly lanceolate, thin-textured. Raceme to 22cm, fairly densely 15–35-fld; fls scented, cream to pale green, about 4mm diam.; sep. and pet. reflexed, sep. 2.5–3mm, dorsal sep. lanceolate, lateral sep. ovate, pet. 2–2.5mm, linear; lip erect at base then deflexed, 3×2mm, ovate, apex bifid, the edges toothed or ciliate. SE Asia, Polynesia, New Guinea, Australia.

***L. cordifolia*** Hook. f. Terrestrial pseudobulbs to 4cm, ovoid, compressed, clustered. Lf 1, to 13×10cm, broadly ovate, cordate, acuminate. Infl. of similar length to lf; fls green, to 18mm diam.; sep. linear-lanceolate, acute; pet. linear, spreading; lip wedge-shaped, almost trilobed at apex, the margin denticulate. Sikkim. Z9.

***L. elegans*** Lindl. Terrestrial, with slender, creeping rhiz.; pseudobulbs set 1–2.5cm apart, 2–3cm long, ovoid, 2-lvd. Lvs 12–25×2–3cm, oblanceolate, narrowed at base to broad 2–6cm stalk. Raceme erect, 25–35cm, densely many-fld; sep. and pet. pale yellow-green, lip orange to salmon; pedicel and ovary 4mm; bracts 5mm; sep. 4×1.5mm, backward-curving; pet. 4×0.5mm, spreading; lip 4×1.5mm, erect at base then bent down sharply at about halfway, oblong, apex finely toothed and bifid. Sumatra to Philippines (not Java), Malaysia.

***L. lacerata*** Ridl. Pseudobulbs 2–3cm, ovoid, 1-lvd. Lf to 18×4cm, lanceolate, narrowed to a stalk about 4cm long. Raceme about 20cm, densely many-fld; fls white with an orange lip; pedicel and ovary 8mm; bracts 3mm; dorsal sep. 6×2mm, lateral sep. slightly shorter; pet. 6×1mm; lip 8mm, narrow at base then abruptly widening to 6.5mm at apex, erect at base then sharply bent down, apex deeply bilobed, lobes divergent, each with about 6 narrow 1.5mm teeth. Malaysia, Borneo, Sumatra.

***L. latifolia*** (Bl.) Lindl. Pseudobulbs about 8×3cm, conical, with large red-brown sheaths at base, flattened, 1-lvd. Lf to 33×7.5cm, lanceolate, channelled at base. Raceme erect, of similar length to lf, many-fld; fls yellow with orange-brown lip; pedicel and ovary 15mm; bracts 8–10mm; sep. 8×3mm, reflexed; pet. of similar length but 1mm wide; lip 10×9mm, basal half narrow, erect, apical half turned down, deeply bilobed, lobes rounded, finely toothed. Malaysia, Sumatra, Borneo, Java.

***L. liliifolia*** (L.) Rich. ex Lindl. Terrestrial, to 25cm; pseudobulbs 2×1cm, ovoid, covered with dry sheaths, 2-lvd. Lvs to 18×6cm, ovoid or elliptic, glossy green, keeled below. Raceme several- to many-fld; sep. pale green, pet. purple, lip translucent light purple with darker veins; pedicel and ovary 15mm; sep. 10×2mm, oblong-lanceolate, the edges rolled under; pet. to 10mm, filiform; lip 10×8mm, recurved, obovate, apiculate; column 4mm. Late spring–summer. N America, Sweden. Z4.

***L. loeselii*** (L.) Rich. FEN ORCHID. Terrestrial, to 25cm; pseudobulbs 10×5mm, ovoid, covered with dry sheaths, 2-lvd. Lvs to 20×6cm, oblong or elliptic, acute or obtuse, keeled below, glossy green. Raceme laxly few- to several-fld; fls dull yellow-green; sep. 5×1mm, narrowly oblong, edges recurved; pet. 5mm, filiform; lip 5×3mm, obovate or oblong, recurved at about halfway; column 3mm. Summer. Northern Europe; N America.

***L. nervosa*** (Thunb.) Lindl. Terrestrial or lithophytic; pseudobulbs conical, to 4cm. Lvs 2–3, to 35×6cm, lanceolate, plicate, light green. Raceme densely many-fld; fls green or yellow-green, often with a maroon-purple lip; dorsal sep. about 6×2mm, oblong, reflexed, lateral sep. shorter, rolled up under lip; pet. to 6mm, linear, reflexed; lip 4×4mm, fleshy, recurved. Tropical Africa, tropical America, India to Japan and Philippines.

***L. nigra*** Seidenf. Terrestrial, usually about 35cm but occasionally reaching 1m; pseudobulbs about 20×1cm, cylindrical, enclosed in sheaths. Lvs about 5, to 15×6cm, ovate, plicate. Raceme 25–35cm, fairly densely many-fld; scape winged, dark red-purple; fls deep red-purple, 15mm diam.; pedicel and ovary arched, 15mm, red-purple; dorsal sep. 18×3mm, linear, reflexed, lateral sep. 15×5mm, falcate, hidden under lip; pet. 17mm, filiform, reflexed; lip 14×14mm, bent down in middle, obovate, mucronate, the margin denticulate; column 7mm, red-purple. Taiwan.

***L. nutans*** Ames. Terrestrial; pseudobulbs to 3cm, pear-shaped, with distichous sheaths, 1-lvd. Lf 18–30×1.5–3cm, narrowly oblong-lanceolate, acute. Infl. shorter than lf; peduncle winged, much longer than rachis; rachis nodding, covered with distichous bracts, to 5cm, densely many-fld; fls brick red; sep. 7×3mm; pet. linear, 7×0.5mm; lip 8×8mm, fan-shaped, fleshy and somewhat channelled below column, with a basal callus; column 6mm. Philippines.

***L. torta*** Hook. f. Terrestrial; pseudobulbs about 2cm, conical, 1-lvd. Lf 14–15×2.5–3.5cm, lanceolate, coriaceous. Raceme of similar length to lf, laxly few- to many-fld; fls cadmium yellow; pedicel and ovary 17mm; sep. 10–12mm, linear-oblong, recurved; pet. 9–10mm, linear; lip 9–10×8–9mm, obovate, with bilobed basal callus, apex obscurely wavy; column winged. India.

***L. tricallosa*** Rchb. f. Pseudobulbs conical, about 12×2cm, 1-lvd. Lf to 18×5.4cm, ovate. Raceme to 45cm, scape and rachis purple; sep. pale green, pet. purple, green towards base, lip pale green with purple-pink veins, becoming pink-tinged as fls age; dorsal sep. 20×2mm, lateral sep. slightly shorter; pet. 20mm, linear; lip about 18×18mm, broadly ovate, minutely toothed toward apex. Sumatra to Philippines.

***L. viridiflora*** (Bl.) Lindl. Epiphytic; pseudobulbs clustered, 1–9×1–2cm, ovoid or conical, 2–3-lvd. Lvs to 25×2.5cm, narrowly oblanceolate. Raceme pendent, 17–18cm, densely many-fld; fls green, very small; sep. 2–4×1–2mm, oblong; pet. 2–4mm, linear; lip 2–3×1.5–3mm, orbicular or ovate, recurved, fleshy; column arched, 2mm. Sri Lanka, India, Burma, Malaysia, China, Japan, Sumatra, Borneo, Philippines and Fiji.

***L. bituberculata*** (Hook.) Lindl. See *L. nervosa*.
***L. elata*** Lindl. See *L. nervosa*.
***L. guineensis*** Lindl. See *L. nervosa*.
***L. longipes*** Lindl. See *L. viridiflora*.
***L. macrantha*** Rolfe. See *L. nigra*.
***L. neglecta*** Schltr. See *L. bowkeri*.

**Lippia** L. (For Auguste Lippi, Italian naturalist and botanist born in Paris in 1678.) Verbenaceae. Some 200 species of herbs, shrubs or small trees, often aromatic, glabrous or pubescent. Leaves opposite or ternate, entire, dentate or crenate, usually petiolate. Inflorescence an axillary spike, short to elongate, many-flowered, usually with conspicuous bracts; calyx small, usually campanulate, membranous; corolla tube cylindrical, erect or curved, limb 4-lobed, slightly labiate; stamens 4, included or exserted, didynamous, inserted near middle of corolla tube, filaments short, anthers ovate; ovary bilocular, each locule with 1 ovule, style terminal, stigma obscurely bilobed. Fruit small, enclosed in persistent calyx. Tropical Africa, Americas.

CULTIVATION In their native regions, *Lippia* spp. have a variety of uses. *L. dulcis*, yerba dulce, a highly aromatic plant, is used medicinally in the treatment of bronchial ailments, particularly for whooping cough. *L. graveolens*, Mexican oregano, more pungent than common oregano, and *L. micromera,* Spanish thyme, are culinary herbs. They are more frost tender than the closely related *Aloysia*, and suitable for outdoor cultivation only in frost-free climates. Grown for their attractive and highly aromatic foliage, they are well suited to general shrub plantings and for the herb garden. Grow in full sun in any moderately fertile, well-drained soil. Under glass, admit full sun and and use a freely draining, medium-fertility, loam-based mix; maintain good ventilation, water moderately when in growth and keep almost dry in winter with a minimum temperature of 10°C/50°F. Propagate by seed, basal or nodal softwood cuttings, or semi-ripe cuttings in early summer, rooted in a closed case with gentle bottom heat.

***L. dulcis*** Trev. MEXICAN LIPPIA. Perenn. herb to 60cm, erect or decumbent, sometimes fruticose near base, glabrous or strigulose. Lvs to 5cm, ovate to rhombic, aromatic, acute or acuminate, sparsely to densely strigulose and obscurely glandular beneath, crenate-serrate; petiole to 1.5cm. Infl. with a solitary peduncle, to 5cm; bracts ovate-cuneate, abruptly acuminate; cal. minute, villous; cor. to 1.5mm, white. Mexico, Guatemala to Panama.

***L. graveolens*** HBK. Shrub to 2m, branches shortly pilose. Lvs to 6cm, elliptic to oblong or ovate-oblong, usually obtuse or rounded, densely and softly pilose above, glandular and densely tomentose or pilose beneath, finely crenate; petiole to 1cm. Infl. with 2–6 peduncles, to 12mm; bracts often in 4 rows, ovate to lanceolate, acute, densely pilose and glandular; cal. to 2mm, villous and glandular; cor. white, tube strigulose, to 3mm. Southern N America, Mexico, Guatemala, Nicaragua, Honduras.

***L. micromera*** Schauer. Shrub to 2m, aromatic, pilose-hirsute. Lvs to 1.5×0.8cm, chartaceous, narrowly obovate, acute to obtuse, glandular, sparingly strigose-hirsute above, hirsute beneath, entire or crenate; petiole to 1mm. Infl. with a solitary peduncle, to 4mm; bracts to 2mm, elliptic-lanceolate, obtuse, ciliate, sparingly pilose; cal. to 1mm, membranous, pilose; cor. white, exterior glandular, tube to 5mm, distally pubesc. Fr. glabrous. W Indies, Trinidad, Venezuela, Guyana.

***L. canescens*** HBK. See *Phyla canescens*.
***L. citriodora*** (Lam.) HBK. See *Aloysia triphylla*.
***L. montevidensis*** Spreng. See *Lantana montevidensis*.
***L. nodifera*** (L.) Michx. See *Phyla nodifera*.
***L. wrightii*** A. Gray. See *Aloysia wrightii*.
For further synonymy see *Phyla*.

**Liquidambar** L. SWEET GUM. (From Lat. *liquidus*, liquid, and *ambar*, amber, referring to the fragrant resin.) Hamamelidaceae. 4 species of deciduous trees to 44m. Leaves palmately 3–7-lobed, stipules small, similar to *Acer* but in alternate, not opposite, arrangement, shiny dark green, turning bright orange and red in autumn, margins serrate; petioles slender. Flowers monoecious, inconspicuous, green or yellow, in globose heads; male flowers in catkin-like racemes, 5–7cm, made up of stamens only; female flowerheads solitary, made up of fused calyx and carpels only. Fruit a globose head of many dehiscent capsules, each containing 1 or 2 winged seeds. N America, Eurasia, China.

CULTIVATION *L. styraciflua*, the most commonly cultivated species, is a stately tree with conical head and handsome, maple-like foliage, suitable for planting in parks, avenues and large gardens. It tolerates temperatures down to at least −15°C/5°F. The best forms produce brilliant autumn tints. Other spp. are often not hardy below −5°C/23°F. *L. formosana* Monticola Group is slightly more cold-tolerant and shows attractive purple-hued foliage in spring. Plant in autumn/winter on deep, fertile, well-drained but moisture-retentive soils in full sun, giving plenty of room for the development. *Liquidambar* resents transplanting and, if this essential, prepare by root-pruning a year in advance. Propagate from seed sown in autumn into outdoor seed beds or from stratified seed in spring: sometimes taking up to two years to germinate. Also from softwood cuttings in summer and by layering. Protect young plants from frost and plant out after the second year.

***L. formosana*** Hance. FORMOSAN GUM. Straight-trunked tree to 40m, young shoots often corky. Lvs 13×15cm, 3-lobed, sometimes with subsidiary lobes at base giving blade appearance of being 5-lobed, base cordate to truncate, lobe apices pointed, margins finely serrate, glabrous above, usually downy beneath; petioles to 6cm, glabrous or downy. Fr. cluster to 4cm diam., individual capsules beaked at tips, scales at base. S China, Taiwan. Z7. Monticola Group: plants originally introduced from China by E.H. Wilson, characterized by their large, glabrous, 3-lobed lvs colouring beautifully in autumn, and their cold-hardiness.

***L. orientalis*** Mill. ORIENTAL SWEET GUM. Slow-growing, bushy-headed, small tree to 7m in cult., to 30m in the wild; young shoots glabrous. Lvs usually 5-lobed, 5–7cm diam., lobes oblong and often reaching two-thirds of depth of blade, glabrous, margins coarsely toothed and glandular; petioles 2.5–5cm. Flowers at same time as young lvs open, rarely produced below zone 7. Fr. cluster to 2.5cm across. Spring. Asia Minor. Z8.

***L. styraciflua*** L. SWEET GUM; AMERICAN SWEET GUM; RED GUM. Tall, straight-trunked tree, to 45m in the wild, to 22m in cult., overall shape a narrow pyramid; young shoots smooth, often corky later. Lvs 5- or 7-lobed, 15cm diam., lobes triangular, shining dark green and glabrous above, hairy in vein axils beneath, autumnal colouring variable between individual specimens, but ranges between yellows, greens and almost mauve. Male fls in heads on hairy spikes to 8cm; female fls larger. Fr. cluster to 4cm diam. Spring. E US. 'Aurea': lvs mottled and striped yellow. 'Burgundy': autumn colour deep red, appearing later, persisting longer than other forms. 'Festival': erect habit; autumn shades of yellow, peach, pink. 'Golden Treasure': lf margins golden yellow. 'Lane Roberts': autumn colour deep black crimson-red. 'Moonbeam': lvs variegated cream; autumn colour vivid. 'Palo Alto': autumn colour orange-red. 'Pendula': upright, columnar; shoots pendent. 'Rotundiloba': lf lobes rounded. 'Variegata': lvs mottled yellow. 'Worplesdon': pyramidal; autumn tints red. Z5.

***L. formosana*** var. ***monticola*** Rehd. & Wils. See *L. formosana* Monticola Group.
***L. imberbe*** Ait. See *L. orientalis*.

**Liriodendron** L. (From Gk *lirion*, lily, and *dendron* tree.) Magnoliaceae. 2 species of deciduous trees, to 60m. Bark grey, becoming fissured. Leaves alternate, broadly oblong, apex wide-emarginate, truncate or retuse, base broadly 1–2-lobed on each side; stipules free, caducous. Flowers terminal, solitary, unscented; tepals 9, outer 3 tepals sepaloid, reflexed, inner 6 tepals petaloid, in 2 whorls of 3; stamens spirally arranged; gynoecia sessile, styles elongate. Fruit cone-like, fusiform, brown, winged, formed by imbricate samaras. Eastern N America, China, Indochina. Z5.

CULTIVATION A graceful, upswept branch system and unusual saddle-shaped foliage, which turns butter yellow in autumn, place *Liriodendron* in the first rank of specimen and avenue trees for parks, open spaces and larger gardens. The delicately scented, pale green flowers are usually visible only at close quarters but they are beautiful when cut and displayed where the elegant vase-shaped form and internal markings may be appreciated. Although *Liriodendron* spp. are tolerant of temperatures to at least −15°C/5°F, flowering is more profuse in hot summer climates. Once thought to be represented only by the American sp., the smaller *L. chinense* was discovered in central China in 1875: fossil records indicate a much wider distribution in preglacial times with evidence from Alaska, Greenland and Europe.

Plant in late spring in a sunny, open position on deep, moisture-retentive, fertile soils. *Liriodendron* spp. are gross feeders, and on rich soils growth is rapid. Limit young trees to a single leader as two or more are likely to incur structural weakness. Propagate from seed (a large proportion of which may be infertile) in the autumn or in spring by grafting selections on to *L. tulipifera* in a warm, closed propagating case. Grow on in low-fertility, loam-based medium before planting out into nursery beds for a further 3–4 years. Alternatively, by layering in spring, growing on young plants for two years before severing from the parent stock; also by air-layering.

On moist soils, summer leaf drop may cause maintenance problems, exacerbated by aphid and scale infestation with their accompanying honeydew drip. Bark-ringing by rabbits and hares is common; protect newly planted trees.

***L. chinense*** (Hemsl.) Sarg. CHINESE TULIP TREE. As for *L. tulipifera* but smaller, to 16m. Fls smaller, petaloid tepals to 4cm, green, veins yellow beneath; gynoecia protruding from perianth in fls. Fr. to 9cm. C China, Indochina. Z8.

***L. tulipifera*** L. TULIP TREE; YELLOW POPLAR; TULIP POPLAR; CANARY WHITEWOOD. Tree to 50m+. Bark grooved. Lvs to 12cm, bright green above, pale green below. Fls pale green, banded orange near base; inner tepals 6×3cm, sepaloid tepals tinged green, strongly reflexed; stamens included, fil. 15mm; gynoecia included at flower opening. Fr. to 7cm, samaras to 45mm, apices acute. Eastern N America. 'Aureomarginatum': lf margins yellow or green yellow. 'Contortum': lvs contorted, undulating. 'Fastigiatum' ('Pyramidale'): habit narrow-pyramidal; branches fastigiate. 'Integrifolium': lvs oblong, side lobes absent. Z4.

***L. figo*** Lour. See *Michelia figo*.
***L. tulipifera*** var. ***sinensis*** Diels. See *L. chinense*.

**Liriope** Lour. (After the nymph Liriope.) LILY TURF. Liliaceae (Convallariaceae). Some 5 species of perennial, evergreen, stemless, tufted or occasionally rhizomatous herbs, to 45cm. Leaves grass-like. Flowers white to dark mauve, grape-like, clustered in a scapose, elongated spike or raceme; tepals 6, free; stamens 6; ovary superior (cf. *Ophiopogon*), closely related except for half-inferior ovary). Fruit black, berry-like; seeds 1 or 2, fleshy. Japan, China, Vietnam.

CULTIVATION The most frequently seen species in cultivation, *L. muscari* is valued as fairly drought-tolerant evergreen groundcover, bearing its densely flowered spikes of lavender blue in late autumn. *L. spicata* is earlier in bloom, both are cold tolerant to −15°C/5°F, possibly more with shelter from cold drying winds. Cultivate as for *Ophiopogon*.

***L. exiliflora*** (L.H. Bail.) H. Hume. To 45cm high, rhizomatous. Lvs to 45cm, dark green. Fls mauve, in a lax raceme, emerging from violet rachis and violet-brown stalk. Japan, China. 'Silvery Sunproof' ('Ariake Janshige';): lvs boldly striped white to gold; fls violet-purple, abundant. Z7.

***L. graminifolia*** (L.) Bak. To 20cm, rhizomatous. Scape erect, black-purple. Lvs to 30cm, linear-lanceolate, basal, blunt-tipped, 3-nerved, with translucent, thin-textured auricles at base. Fls deep violet-purple to white, clustered 3–5 in an open, spike-like raceme 15–30cm long; tepals almost campanulate, free almost to the base, deep violet-purple. Japan, China. Material grown under this name is probably *L. muscari*. Z8.

***L. minor*** (Maxim.) Mak. Close to *L. muscari* but smaller and with fewer fls. Z6.

***L. muscari*** (Decne.) L.H. Bail. To 45cm, tufted, with thick, dark tubers. Lvs to 60×2cm, firm. Fls dark mauve, densely clustered. China, Taiwan, Japan. Over 30cvs; height 18–60cm, dwarf to sturdy; lvs deep green, occasionally variegated white or yellow; spikes with variable density; fls white to lilac, violet or dark mauve; cvs notable for habit include 'Grandiflora' (to 60cm; lvs narrow, arching; fls lavender); 'Christmas Tree' (to 20cm; fls large); for lvs: 'Variegata' (lvs boldly striped yellow at margin); 'Gold-banded' (compact; lvs wide, dark green edged gold, arching); 'John Burch' (lvs wide, yellow-green central stripe fls large, spike tall); 'Silvery Midget' (to 18cm; lvs variegated white); for fls: 'Monroe White' (fls large, pure white, abundant); 'Big Blue' (fls lavender, in dense spikes); 'Lilac Beauty' (stems stiff, tall; fls dark lilac, abundant); 'Curly Twist' (fls lilac flushed burgundy); 'Majestic' (tall; fls rich violet); 'Ingwersen' (fls deep violet); 'Royal Purple' (fls dark purple, profuse). Z6.

***L. spicata*** Lour. To 25cm, rhizomatous. Scape erect, light mauve-brown. Lvs to 35×0.5cm, grass-like, minutely serrate with translucent auricles. Fls pale mauve to nearly white; tube distinct; rachis mauve. China, Vietnam. 'Alba': to 22cm, spreading; lvs narrow, dark green; fls white. 'Silver Dragon': to 20cm, compact; lvs narrow, striped silvery white; fls pale purple; fr. white-green marked green. Z4. Z4.

***L. graminifolia*** hort. non (L.) Bak. See *L. muscari*.
***L. graminifolia*** var. ***densiflora*** Bak. See *L. muscari*.
***L. japonica*** hort. See *Ophiopogon japonicus*.
***L. muscari*** var. ***densiflora*** hort. See *L. muscari*.
***L. muscari*** var. ***exiliflora*** L.H. Bail. See *L. exiliflora*.
***L. platyphylla*** F.T. Wang & Tang. See *L. muscari*.

**Lisianthius** P. Browne. Gentianaceae. (From Gk *lysis*, loosening, and *anthos*, flower; meaning uncertain.) 27 species of glabrous herbs and shrubs. Leaves opposite, stalked or sessile, sometimes amplexicaul, ovate to lanceolate. Flowers in cymes, corymbs or umbels, subtended by involucre of leafy bracts, large, 5-merous, yellow, yellow-green, white or blue-black; corolla tube long, lobes spreading. Fruit a capsule. C & S America, Caribbean. The florist's *Lisianthius* is usually *Eustoma grandiflorum*. Z9.

CULTIVATION In temperate zones, *Lisianthius* requires the protection of the greenhouse or conservatory, with a winter minimum of 15°C/60°F. In exceptionally favoured areas, *L. nigrescens* may survive in a sheltered niche. Its erect stems carry slender trumpet-shaped, purple-black blooms which last well in water and are useful in flower arrangements. In Mexico, they are used for grave decoration, hence the common name. Grow in a well-drained medium of 2:1:1 loam, peat and sand, in clay pots. These may be moved to a sheltered spot outdoors in summer. Staking may be necessary. Sow seed in spring for flowers the following year.

Prone to red spider mite, especially in hot dry weather; spray at 10-day intervals, and ensure good ventilation.

***L. nigrescens*** Cham. & Schltr. FLOR DE MUERTO. Shrub to 2m; stems much-branched, terete. Lvs sessile, oblong-lanceolate, acuminate, 3–5-veined, nearly united at base. Infl. to 1m, terminal, diffuse; fls to 5cm, blue-black, nodding; cor. lobes spreading, recurved at tips; stamens not exserted beyond mouth of cor. tube. Summer. S Mexico, C America.

***L. exaltatus*** (L.) Lam. See *Eustoma exaltatum*.
***L. russellianus*** Hook. See *Eustoma russellianus*.
***L. russellianus*** Hook. See *Eustoma grandiflorum*.
***L. zelanicus*** Spreng. See *Exacum trinervium*.

**Lissochilus** R. Br.
***L. giganteus*** Welw. See *Eulophia horsfallii*.
***L. horsfallii*** Batem. See *Eulophia horsfallii*.
***L. krebsii*** Rchb. f. See *Eulophia streptopetala*.
***L. speciosus*** R. Br. ex Lindl. See *Eulophia speciosa*.

**Listera** R. Br. (For Michael Lister (1638–1712), British zoologist, physician to Queen Anne.) Orchidaceae. Some 25 species of herbaceous, terrestrial orchids. Rhizomes short, roots slender. Stem erect. Leaves 2, rarely 1 or 3, sessile, almost opposite, sited just below stem centre. Raceme spike-like, slender, cylindrical; petals and sepals almost equal, patent or convergent; lip deeply divided from apex, sometimes with 2 basal lobes, central furrow produces nectar, spurless. Late spring–summer. Temperate Asia, N America, Europe. Z6.

CULTIVATION See ORCHIDS, The Hardy Species.

***L. cordata*** (L.) R. Br. LESSER TWAYBLADE. To 20cm. Stem glabrous then minutely pubesc. toward infl., bronze at base; basal sheaths 1–2. Lvs 1–3cm, ovate-deltate or triangular. Raceme to 6cm, lax, 4–12-fld; bracts minute; sep. to 2.5mm, olive-green to rust-coloured, narrow-elliptic, obtuse; pet. 3–4.5mm rusty-green; lip green flushed mauve, linear, with 2 small lateral lobes near base and apical lobe cleft, spreading. Europe, Asia, N America, Greenland.

***L. ovata*** (L.) R. Br. TWAYBLADE. Stem pubesc. toward infl. Lvs 20–60cm, ovate to broadly elliptic; basal sheaths 2–3, brown. Raceme 7–25cm, bracts ovate-lanceolate; fls green, rarely tinged red-brown; pet. and sep. incurved, forming lax hood; lip 7–15mm, strongly decurved, apically cleft, lateral lobes absent or greatly reduced. Europe to C Asia.

**Listrostachys** Rchb. f. (From Gk *listron*, spade, and *stachys*, ear of corn or spike.) Orchidaceae. 1 species, an epiphytic orchid. Stems usually less than 6cm, rarely to 15cm, the lower part covered with overlapping leaf bases. Leaves 8–35×1–2cm, ligulate or linear-oblong, equally or unequally bilobed at apex, the lobes obtuse. Racemes erect or spreading, 10–25cm, densely many-flowered; flowers small, distichous, white, sometimes with small red spots toward base and with red spur; pedicel and ovary 2mm; bracts very short; sepals and petals free, similar, sepals 2–3mm, ovate, petals similar but slightly shorter and narrower; lip entire, 2–3mm, obovate or more or less quadrate, apiculate, spurred, the mouth of the spur some distance from base of lip and column; spur 3.5–5mm, stout, dorsally compressed, clavate at apex; pollinia and stipites 2, viscidium 1. W Africa to Zaire. Z10.

CULTIVATION As for *Angraecum*.

***L. pertusa*** (Lindl.) Rchb. f. As for the genus.

***L. monteiroae*** Rchb. f. See *Cyrtorchis monteiroae*.
***L. sedenii*** Rchb. f. Schltr. See *Cyrtorchis arcuata*.
For further synonymy see *Angraecum*.

**Litchi** Sonn. (Native Chinese name.) Sapindaceae. 1 species, a polygamous tree, 12–20m. Leaves spirally arranged, to 25cm, pinnate, pinnae 2–8, to 20cm, entire, thickly coriaceous, elliptic-oblong to lanceolate, tapering at both ends, glaucous beneath; petiole to 5cm. Panicles terminal, to 30cm, in upper leaf axils; flowers white tinged green or yellow, in 5–12-flowered cymes; calyx shallowly 4- or 5-lobed, segments rounded; petals absent, stamens usually 8, filaments hairy; disc annular, hairy to glabrous; style 2-branched; ovary in female flowers bilobed, to 5mm, bilocular, each locule with 1 ovule. Fruit a drupe, *c*3.5×3cm, bright red to purple when ripe, nearly smooth or scaly to densely set with flat, conical, acute warts; seeds single, large, with a white fleshy aril, separate from the seed coat. S China. Z9.

CULTIVATION In tropical and subtropical zones, *L. chinensis* is grown primarily for its fruit, rich in vitamin C, with a succulent, translucent white aril, eaten fresh, dried or preserved in syrup. They are grown extensively in their native southern China, in India, Japan, S Africa, Australasia and, to a lesser extent, in Florida, California and Hawaii. *L. chinensis* is a beautiful round-topped evergreen tree, slow to mature but long-lived, with attractive coppery-red young leaves and clusters of rosy fruits, and can be used as an ornamental specimen or in mixed plantings, in areas that are frost-free or almost so.

*Litchi* has been so long improved in cultivation that wild forms, aside from naturalized escapes, are thought to be unknown; cultivars of *Litchi*, were discussed in one of the earliest-known treatises on fruit cultivation, by the Chinese scholar T'sai Hsiang in 1079 AD. In the US, the most commonly grown cvs are 'Brewster' and 'Royal Chen' (possibly identical to the Chinese 'Chen T'sai'). Early-maturing cvs (e.g. 'Tai So', and 'Bengal') are more suited to warmer climates; 'Haak Yip' yields particularly high-quality fruit. Late-maturing cvs, such as 'No Mai Chee' and 'Wai Chee', require more chilling to fruit well.

In their natural range, climatic conditions are hot and humid for most of the year, with a winter that is cool, misty and frost-free. Litchi have a positive requirement for chilling (to 7–12°C/45°–54°F) and winter dormancy to induce flowering, and good fruiting relies on warm humid summers, with a minimum rainfall of 1200mm/47in. Old trees suffer injury at −4°C/25°F, although when young they will not tolerate temperatures below freezing. In temperate zones, *Litchi* can be grown in intermediate glasshouse conditions.

*L. chinensis* is tolerant of a range of soil types, if well-drained, but does best on deep, moist, acid soils that are rich in organic matter, since these provide optimum conditions for beneficial mycorrhizal associates. However, they have made good growth on limestone soils with the application of iron chelates, and will withstand wet soils, provided that the water is not stagnant. Plant at the beginning of the growing season, ensuring thorough soil preparation by incorporating organic matter; planting holes should be inoculated with soil from established trees to provide mycorrhizal fungi. If planting for fruit production, give a sheltered position and space at 8×8m/25×25ft (if spaced too closely, they may develop a narrower head and fruit only on the topmost branches). Protection from wind is essential, especially when young, so screen if necessary. *Litchi* is shallow-rooting; avoid surface cultivations and use a mulch to conserve moisture and suppress weeds. Irrigate in dry weather. Prune young trees only to establish a well-spaced framework. Older specimens may be rejuvenated by heavy pruning followed by the application of fertilizer. The scoring of branches in autumn is sometimes practised to induce heavier flowering the following spring. The fruit is harvested in entire panicles, about 100 days after blooming, and should be fully mature when picked since they will not ripen off the tree.

Propagate by air layering, grafting, or from greenwood cuttings under mist in summer. Propagation from seed is possible, but fruiting quality will be variable, and specimens may take up to 15 years to fruit. Seed quickly loses viability on removal from the fruit, and should be sown fresh, 1cm/½in. deep in a loamless propagating medium.

***L. chinensis*** Sonn. LYCHEE; LITCHEE. As for the genus. ssp. ***chinensis*** Sonn. Twigs slender, diam. to 3.5mm. ssp. ***philippinensis*** (Radlk.) Leenh. Lvs with pinnae in 1–2, rarely 3 pairs. 'Brewster': vigorous; fr. medium to large. 'Groff': fr. small but meaty, in large clusters. 'Kaimana': vigorous; fr. large, juicy. 'Haak Yip': compact; fr. small to medium, in large clusters. 'Tai Tso': vigorous; fr. medium, very juicy, clusters large. 'Wai Chee': compact; fr. and clusters small. ssp. ***javensis*** Leenh. Twigs thick, to 7mm. Fls in sessile clusters.

For synonymy see *Nephelium*.

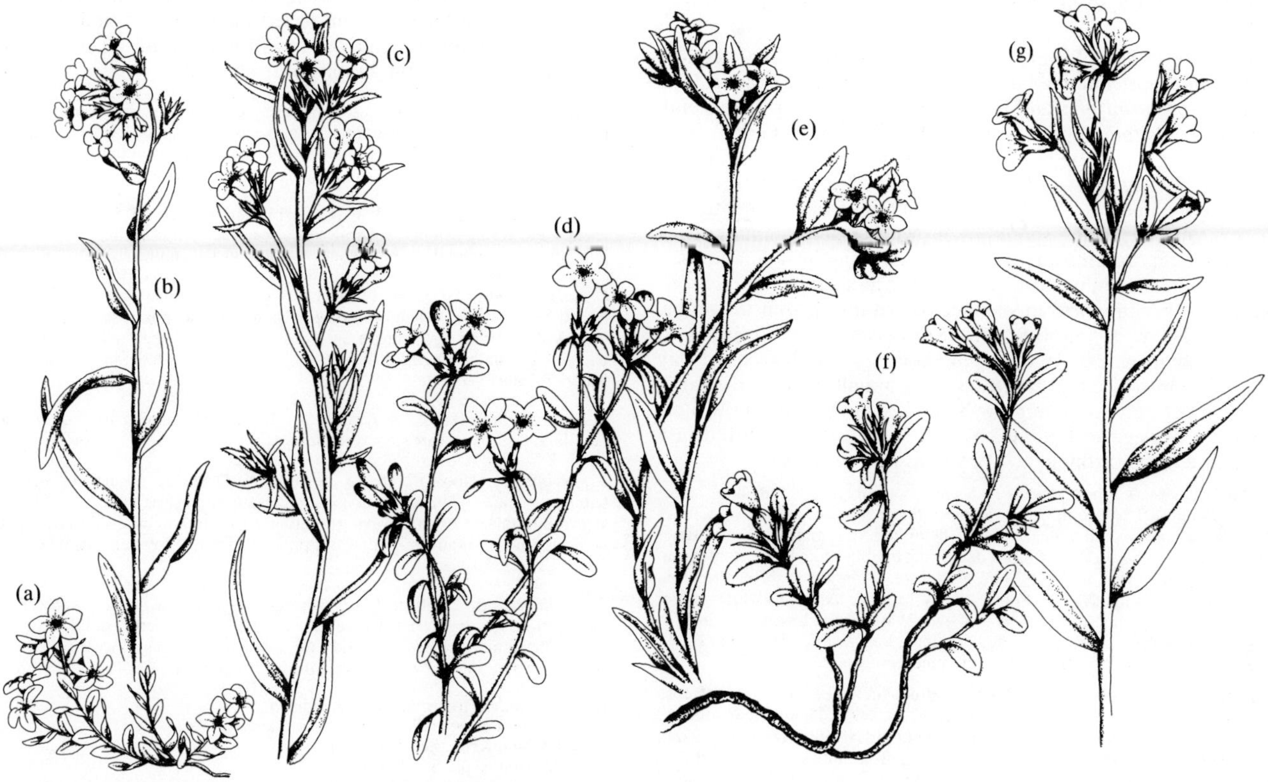


**Lithodora and Lithospermum** (×0.66) (a) *Lithodora diffusa* (b) *Lithospermum multiflorum* (c) *Lithodora rosmarinifolia* (d) *Lithodora fruticosa* (e) *Lithospermum canescens* (f) *Lithodora oleifolia* (g) *Lithospermum officinale*

**Lithocarpus** Bl. (From Gk *lithos*, stone, and *carpos*, fruit, alluding to the hard-shelled fruit.) TANBARK OAK. Fagaceae. 300 species of oak-like evergreen trees. Buds with a few, leaflike scales; terminal bud present. Leaves leathery, mostly entire, some species dentate. Male flowers in erect, simple or branched spikes, stamens 10–12; female flowers at the base of male spikes or in special catkins; calyx 4–6-lobed, without petals; styles 3, cylindrical, stigma only on the top of the style. Fruit a very hard-shelled, acorn-like nut in a calyx cupule; these with either imbricate, distinct or concentric rings of connate scales; mature in second year. SE Asia and Indonesia, 2 in Japan and 1 in western N America. Similar to *Quercus* but differs in the male flower being in erect spikes (pendulous in *Quercus*) and the acorns are borne few to many, often densely, on stout, stiff spikes.

CULTIVATION As for *Quercus*.

***L. cleistocarpus*** (Seemen) Rehd. & Wils. Tree to 20m+. Young shoots glabrous. Lvs 10–20×3–6cm, to 30×10cm on young plants, lanceolate or narrowly elliptic, long-acuminate, entire, grey-green, glabrous, vein pairs 9–12; petiole 1.5–2cm. Fr. 2–2.5cm thick, in dense clusters on stiff, 5–7cm long spikes; cupules thick and deep. C China. Z7.

***L. densiflorus*** (Hook. & Arn.) Rehd. TANBARK OAK. Tree to 30m, rarely 45m; bark thick, red-brown, furrowed. Young shoots densely white-woolly. Lvs 5–13cm, elliptic to oblong, acute, base round to broadly cuneate, stiff and leathery, with 12–15 vein pairs, these terminating in as many sharp teeth, loose stellate-pubesc. above at first, later glabrous grey-green, densely white tomentose beneath at first, green-brown, eventually nearly glabrous and grey-green. Male fls in erect, slender, 5–10cm spikes, with a disagreeable odour. Fr. 2–2.5cm, grouped 1–3; cupule covering basal quarter of acorn, scales short-spined. N America (California, SW Oregon). var. ***echinoides*** (R. Br.) Abrams. Shrub to 3m. Lvs only 3–5cm, obtuse. Z7.

***L. edulis*** (Mak.) Nak. Small tree to 10m+, often a shrub in cult.; young shoots glabrous. Lvs 7–15cm, narrowly elliptic to oblanceolate, entire, leathery, tapered toward apex, obtuse, glossy yellow-green above, grey-green beneath, vein pairs 9–11. Fr. 2.5×0.8cm, grouped 2–3 together on a glabrous axillary spike. Japan. Z7.

***L. glaber*** (Thunb.) Nak. Tree to 7m, or shrub; young shoots always tomentose. Lvs 7–14×2.5–4.5cm, elliptic-oblong to lanceolate, widest in the middle, leathery, tough, gradually acuminate, entire or occasionally with a few marginal teeth at the apex, glossy green and glabrous above, white-tomentose beneath, vein pairs 6–8. Fr. 1.5–2cm, sessile and pubesc. on terminal, 5–12cm spikes, ovoid, cup flat. Japan, E China. Z7.

***L. henryi*** (Seemen) Rehd. & Wils. Tree to 20m+ with a rounded crown; young shoots grey-brown, with white lenticels, soft pubesc. when young, soon glabrous. Lvs 10–25×3–5cm, elliptic-oblong, long-acuminate, entire, base cuneate, glossy green above, lighter green beneath, vein pairs 10–14, glabrous, leathery; petiole 2–2.5cm. Fr. usually well developed, 2cm, many, on stiff, 15cm, erect spikes; cupules thin and shallow. C China. Z7.

***L. pachyphyllus*** (Kurz) Rehd. Tree to *c*35m with outward spreading branches. Young shoots soft-pubesc. Lvs 10–23cm, elliptic-lanceolate, apex long acuminate, base cuneate, entire, leathery, tough, glossy dark green above, silvery-green stellate pubesc. beneath; petiole 6–12mm. Fr. in pairs or 3s, each with 3 acorns, in thick spikes to 15cm, about one third of the fr. sessile with the 6 or 9 acorn cups fused into a mass 3–4cm thick, acorns wider than high, nearly totally enclosed within the cup. E Himalaya. Z9.

***L. cordifolius*** (L. f.) L. Bol. See *Aptenia cordifolia*.

For illustration see FAGACEAE.

**Lithodora** Griseb. (From Gk *lithos*, stone, and *doron*, gift.) Boraginaceae. Some 7 species of shrublets and subshrubs. Leaves linear to elliptic to obovate, often setose, revolute or incurved, usually unveined. Cymes small, terminal, leafy, loosely 1–10-flowered; calyx deeply 5-lobed, lobes narrow, subequal, somewhat accrescent; corolla blue, purple or white, infundibular or hypocrateriform, throat without appendages, exterior glabrous or pubescent, interior glabrous, without a basal annulus, lobes ovate to suborbicular, ascending or spreading; stamens usually included, filaments filiform, anther oblong, obtuse or retuse; style filiform, simple or branched above, usually included, stigmas 2, terminal. Nutlets ovoid or ovoid-cylindric, smooth or minutely tuberculate or rugose, with a prominent ventral keel. SW Europe to Asia Minor.

CULTIVATION The flowers of *Lithodora* exhibit some of the clearest and most intense blues in the Boraginaceae, particularly fine in *L. rosmarinifolia* and in *L. diffusa* 'Grace Ward'; the pink buds of *L. oleifolia* open to a much paler blue. Given good drainage in a raised bed, *L. diffusa* will survive temperatures to about −15°C/5°F; most of the remaining species will tolerate cold to between −5 and −10°C/14–23°F, with the possible exception of *L. rosmarinifolia*, which should be grown in a hot, sunny crevice or, where temperatures fall below −5°C/23°F, in the alpine house.

Grow in full sun in perfectly drained but moisture-retentive soils that do not become arid in summer or wet and frozen in winter. *L. diffusa* needs a lime-free soil. Trim over after flowering to maintain compactness. In the alpine house, use well-crocked clay pots with a mix of equal parts loam, leafmould and coarse sand. Water moderately when in growth and keep almost dry in winter. Propagate by seed in autumn, by soft stem cuttings, rooted in a closed case with bottom heat, or by semi-ripe cuttings.

***L. diffusa*** (Lagasca) Johnst. Stems to 60cm, procumbent or straggling, setaceous. Lvs to 3.8×0.8cm, elliptic or oblong to linear, obtuse, margin sometimes inflexed, setose above and beneath. Cal. to 8mm; cor. to 21mm, blue, sometimes purple, exterior pubesc., throat with a dense ring of long white hairs; stamens inserted at unequal levels, anth. to 2mm. Nutlets to 4×2mm, pale brown to grey, oblong, subacute, smooth. NW France to SW Europe. 'Alba': fls white. 'Cambridge Blue': to 8cm high; fls light blue. 'Grace Ward': habit low and trailing, to 15cm high; lvs narrow, dark green; fls azure blue, long-lasting. 'Heavenly Blue': habit very low, to 8cm high; fls small, azure blue, profuse. Z7.

***L. fruticosa*** (L.) Griseb. Stems to 60cm, tufted; branches erect, white-setose when young, dark grey with age. Lvs to 2.5cm, linear or oblong-linear, obtuse, white-setulose throughout, margins tuberculate-hispid, strongly revolute. Cal. to 6mm, hispid; cor. to 15mm, exterior of blue or purple, lobes setulose; anth. to 3mm. Nutlets to 4×2mm, white, ovoid, constricted toward base. Spain, S France. Z8.

***L. oleifolia*** (Lapeyr.) Griseb. Stems to 45cm, slender, diffuse, ascending, leafless below. Lvs to 4×1.5cm, obovate or oblong-obovate, obtuse, slightly hispid above, white-sericeous beneath, clustered. Cymes 3–7-fld; cal. to 8mm, white-sericeous, lobes linear, subacute; cor. pink becoming blue, exterior sericeous, interior glabrous, tube to 12mm, lobes to 3mm, rounded. Nutlets to 3×2mm, ovoid, grey-white, smooth, with a short beak. E Pyrenees. 'Barker's Form': habit spreading, to 12cm high, very vigorous; fls pale sky blue. Z7.

***L. rosmarinifolia*** (Ten.) Johnst. Stems to 60cm, tufted; branches erect or pendent, grey-pubesc. above. Lvs to 6×1cm, narrowly lanceolate to linear, acute or subacute, dark green, glabrous or setulose above, densely grey-setose beneath, margin inflexed or strongly revolute. Cal. to 6mm, white-setose; cor. tube to 12mm, lilac, blue or white, exterior setulose, throat slightly glandular, limb to 17mm diam., lobes oblong, rounded. Nutlets white, smooth. S Italy, Sicily, NE Algeria. Z8.

***L. zahnii*** (Heldr. ex Hal.) Johnst. Stems to 60cm, tufted, much-branched; branches erect or ascending, densely leafy when young, sericeous, becoming black and leafless with age. Lvs to 4×0.4cm, coriaceous, narrow, elongate, linear or linear-oblong, obtuse, grey-green and hispid above, densely grey-setose beneath, strongly revolute. Cymes 1- to few-fld; cal. to 11mm, lobes linear, densely white-pubesc.; cor. white or blue, hypocrateriform, glabrous, tube to 10mm, limb to 15mm diam., lobes ovate, obtuse, patent; anth. to 2.5mm. Nutlets smooth, lustrous. S Greece. Z8.

***L. prostrata*** (Lois.) Griseb. See *L. diffusa*.
For further synonymy see *Lithospermum*.

**Lithophragma** (Nutt.) Torr. & A. Gray. (From Gk *lithos* stone and *phragma*, fence, referring to its habitat.) WOODLAND STAR. Saxifragaceae. 9 species of perennial herbs, to 85cm. Rosettes of leaves arise from fibrous rooted, subterranean bulbils. Leaves reniform to orbicular, 3-lobed or trifoliate with incised leaflets; petiole 1–25cm. Flowering stem simple or branching, one to several per rosette, bearing stipulate leaves; inflorescence racemose; flowers small, often replaced by bulbils, occasionally fragrant, floral parts fused at base to form a campanulate-conical floral cup (hypanthium); sepals 5, triangular; petals 5, spreading, white to pink, clawed, entire to 5-lobed, longer than sepals; stamens 10. Fruit a capsule; seed minute. Western N America. Z8.

CULTIVATION Mostly woodland natives for well-drained peaty soils and light shade. The foliage is visible only for a short growing season. Ensure moist conditions while in growth and allow soil to dry when dieback begins. May also be grown in the alpine house in pans of high-fertility loam-based medium with added grit and leafmould. Otherwise cultivation as for *Tellima*, but propagate in early spring by division, bulbils or from seed.

***L. affine*** A. Gray. To 55cm. Lvs pubesc., orbicular to reniform, 3–5-lobed, petiole to 22cm. Flowering stems several per rosette, simple, with 1–3 small lvs. Infl. 3–15-fld; pedicel shorter than fls; fls nodding; hypanthium conical; pet. widely spreading, ovate, 6–13mm, usually 3-lobed; ovary semi-inferior.

***L. bolanderi*** A. Gray. To 85cm. Lvs orbicular, pubesc., 3–5 lobed; petiole to 25cm. Flowering stems several per rosette, 2–3-branched; fls fragrant; hypanthium campanulate; pet. white, 4–7mm, usually entire.

***L. glabrum*** Nutt. To 35cm. Lvs sparsely pubesc., orbicular to trifoliate, often tinged red; petiole 1–4cm. Flowering stems several per rosette, occasionally branched, bearing 2–4 much-reduced lvs; stipules large; infl. 1–7-fld, erect; pedicels 2–4 times length of fl; fls often replaced by bulbils; pet. 3 pink, rarely white, 5–7mm, 5-lobed.

***L. heterophyllum*** (Hook. & Arn.) Torr. & A. Gray. Similar to *L. affine* except petiole to 8cm, flowering stem often many-branched, ovary superior.

***L. parviflorum*** (Hook.) Nutt. ex Torr. & A. Gray. To 50cm. Lvs 3-lobed to trifoliate, nearly glabrous to densely pubesc; petiole less than 6cm. Flowering stems unbranched, with 2–3 lvs, resembling rosette lvs; infl. 4–14-fld, nodding, pedicels shorter than fls; pet. white-pink 7–16mm, obovate, 3-cleft; ovary inferior.

***L. tenellum*** Nutt. To 30cm. Lvs 3–5 irregularly lobed or digitate, sparsely pubesc.; petiole less than 8cm. Flowering stems 1–3 per rosette, simple with lvs 2, palmatifid, much reduced; infl. 3–12-fld, compact; pet. pink, occasionally white, 3–7mm, ovate, 5-lobed; ovary semi-inferior to superior.

***L. anemonoides*** Green. See *L. parviflorum*.
***L. austromontanum*** Heller. See *L. parviflorum*.
***L. brevilobum*** Rydb. See *L. tenellum*.
***L. bulbiferum*** Rydb. See *L. glabrum*.
***L. rupicolum*** Greene. See *L. tenellum*.
***L. tenellum*** var. ***florida*** Suksd. See *L. glabrum*.
***L. thompsonii*** Hoover. See *L. tenellum*.
***L. trilobum*** Rydb. See *L. heterophyllum*.
For further synonymy see *Tellima*.

**Lithops** N.E. Br. (From Gk *lithos*, stone, and *opsis*, appearance.) LIVING STONES; FLOWERING STONES; PEBBLE PLANTS. Aizoaceae. 35 species of succulent, tufted, stemless perennials. Plant body swollen, obconic, composed of 2 lobes, united for most of their length and with a marked central fissure, the upper surface of each elliptic to reniform, concave, flat or convex, normally glaucous, with a range of stone-like characters — opaque with coloured fissures, pitting, rugae, dots or with a central panel of a different colour and usually semi-translucent, either clear or occluded to varying degrees by island-like markings or incursions of the marginal coloration, sometimes with blood-red spotting or veining within the fissures or panel. Flowers terminal, solitary, emerging from the fissure, yellow or white, sometimes yellow with a white centre. Midsummer–early winter. S Africa, Namibia. Z9.

In the following descriptions, the colour and texture of the upper surface is usually the same as that of the rest of the exposed body and the markings within the panel. The panel, of a different colour and texture, may be clear and unmarked, or have its edges channelled or eroded and its centre so cluttered with converging markings as to appear nothing more than a faint and broken network of slightly darker lines.

CULTIVATION *Lithops* spp. are found growing in sand, gravel or even clay soils among rocks and pebbles, with the surface of the leaves only exposed at the surface, many species retracting almost completely into the soils in the dormant season. The plants are extremely fascinating and attractive additions to a general collection of succulent plants because of their pebble-like appearance and great range of leaf surface colour and pattern. Their flowering period is normally late summer and early autumn.

For maximum control of soil moisture, grow under cover even in warm regions. In temperate regions they are best grown in a greenhouse; windowsill culture for prolonged periods generally causes excessive elongation of the plant bodies. They require full sun and a dry atmosphere at all times, possibly with light shading in the height of summer if ventilation is at all inadequate. Plants in their native habitat regularly withstand temperatures of 40–50°C/104–122°F, but temperatures of 30°C/86°C in the static air of a greenhouse can cause severe scorching or even death.

They will grow well in any well-drained, low-fertility potting medium but generally are longer-lived in a sandy/gritty loam-based medium. Although the plants are small they are best grown in relatively large pots or several together in a tray or pan as they have extensive roots, and this also allows the potting medium to keep a more uniform temperature. Water very sparingly from early summer to late autumn; keep dry during the winter and only syringe sporadically in spring. Watering should only begin in the summer when the old pair of leaves is almost totally shrivelled; this can vary considerably from species to species. Only water in the autumn during periods of dry sunny weather as plants that remain too wet for too long at that time of year can split their bodies or rot. Repotting is done when growth starts in late spring. Liquid feed should only be given to well-established plants, and then only a weak low-N fertilizer should be used. Excessive nutrition causes excessive growth and leaf development and a great tendency to rapid decay in the winter. Although in their native habitat these plants grow almost flush with the soil surface, it is safer in cultivation to raise them higher out of the growing medium and to have a 10mm layer of grit or gravel on top of the potting medium. Pest control and propagation as for *Conophytum*.

***L. aucampiae*** L. Bol. Body 20–32×20–53×16–37mm, fissure shallow, lobes unequal, upper surface elliptic-reniform, colour and patterning variable – dull brick to sandy brown or ochre with sienna to green-brown dots, these often joined by slender fissures or more expanded, sometimes to the point of forming a semi-lucent green-brown panel with blotches and a broken margin. Fls 3–5.2cm diam., yellow. Early autumn. NW Cape. 'Betty's Beryl': upper surface yellow-green, largely covered with an olive panel with many blotches and irregular margins; fls white. 'Storm's Snowcap': face pale ginger to sandy brown, marked darker brown; fls white. var. ***koelemanii*** (Boer) Cole. Upper surface pale rust to grey-brown, entirely covered with a pattern of fine, broken dark lines resembling hieroglyphs or cerebral folds. Fls 3–5.5cm., yellow. ssp. ***euniceae*** (Boer) Cole. Upper surface dove-grey to pale brown with a brown central panel broken by minute and sparse or large and congested blotches and spreading to margins as a close fringe of crazed veins. var. ***flaminalis*** Cole. Upper surface pale grey, sometimes with a faint pink tinge, panel translucent battleship-grey, irregular, often with small or obscure blotches and spreading almost to margins by dendritic fissures. Fls 2.5–4.5cm diam., yellow.

***L. bromfieldii*** L. Bol. Body 15–32×20–23mm, fissure shallow, lobes equal, upper surface elliptic-reniform, buff to grey with rugae sunken, irregular, dark red edged grey-green, rather brain-like. Fls 2.5–4.5cm diam., yellow. NW Cape. var. ***glaudinae*** (Boer) Cole. Upper surface dove-grey or dull olive, glaucous with many translucent olive or dark brown spots and figures, some appearing polished, metallic, the whole resembling a densely pitted, ore-bearing stone. var. ***insularis*** (L. Bol.) Fearn. Differing from var. glaudinae in the slightly concave (not flat) upper surface with larger, pitted dots merging to form a loose, obscure network of crazed bronze-green markings, none or very few of them lustrous. 'Sulphurea': upper surface dull mustard-yellow marked grey-green, otherwise as for var. *insularis*. var. ***mennellii*** (L. Bol.) Fearn. Upper surface dull dove-grey, often with a brown or pink tint, covered with deep, broken, chocolate to dark green fissures.

***L. comptonii*** L. Bol. Body 25–30×2–35×17–23mm, fissure deep, lobes divergent, equal or unequal, upper surface elliptic-reniform, rounded-convex, smooth, sublustrous, blue-grey to dull lilac-grey, panel slate-grey, semi-translucent with scattered blotches and crazed to fissured edges. Fls 2–3cm diam., yellow with white centre. Cape Province (Karroo). var. ***weberi*** (Nel) Cole. Body sides dove-grey, faces buff (as are numerous raised, scattered blotches) but largely covered by a translucent slate-grey panel with fissured edges.

***L. dinteri*** Schwantes. Body 20–30×20–30×15–20cm, fissure deep, lobes conjunct, unequal, upper surface elliptic-reniform, flat to convex, buff, panel semi-translucent, grey-green with an irregular but scarcely fissured or broadly lobed edge, a scattering of small milky blotches and several conspicuous blood-red dots or dashes. Fls 2–3, 2cm diam., yellow. S Namibia. 'Dintergreen': markings rather clouded, grey-green, red spots obscure. var. ***brevis*** (L. Bol.) Fearn. Body 15–20×18–21×12–15mm, upper surface buff to grey, panel translucent leaden grey, covering most of face with a relatively unbroken if cloudy edge, no blotches and few or no red dashes. NW Cape. ssp. ***frederici*** (Cole) Cole. Body 15–20×14–20×10–14mm, upper surface rather smooth and rounded, buff to pale grey, the panel so thickly crowded by blotches, lobes and dots as to be reduced to scattered, misshapen dark grey figures with embedded red flecks, the whole rather like a quail's egg. ssp. ***multipunctata*** (Boer) Cole. Body 20–30×20–33×15–20mm, upper surface mushroom-grey to pale buff, slightly darker toward centre where panel is massively occluded and shows only as irregular distinct hieroglyphs or blood-red spots.

***L. divergens*** L. Bol. Body 15–20×20–25×12–14mm, lobes widely divergent, fissure deep, upper surface oblong-reniform, dove-grey, sometimes suffused tan or rose, panel glossy, semi-translucent dark grey-green, filled with small dots and figures. Fls 1.5–2.7cm diam., yellow with a white centre. NW Cape. var. ***amethystina*** Boer. Body 20–25×23–35×13–20mm, still more broadly and deeply cleft than species type, the fissure and margins of upper surface strongly tinted lilac.

***L. dorotheae*** Nel. Body 20–30×20–23×13–16mm, fissure tight, shallow, lobes conjunct, upper surface convex, rounded, dark beige or buff, panel translucent grey-green or olive with jagged to deep lobed edges and large blotches (sometimes reducing it to a pattern or broad hieroglyphs), rusty red dots embedded in panel or lining markings. Fls 2.5–4.2cm diam., yellow. NW Cape.

***L. francisci*** (Dinter & Schwantes) N.E. Br. Body 15–30×24–30×17–20mm, fissure deep, lobes conjunct to divergent, very unequal, upper surface elliptic-reniform, flat to convex, dove-grey, panel remaining only as an obscure and slightly sunken pattern of darker grey fissures, the whole surface dotted dark grey-green, the dots sometimes coalescing. Fls 1.5–2cm, diam., yellow. C Namibia.

***L. fulviceps*** (N.E. Br.) N.E. Br. Body 25–30×25–30×23–27mm, fissure shallow, lobes conjunct, equal to subequal, upper surface oblong, reniform, flat, tawny, buff or grey tinted rose, covered with large or small, polished, raised, grey-green spots sometimes linked by blood-red sunken dots. Fls 2.5–3.5cm diam., yellow. S Namibia to NW Cape. var. ***lactinea*** Cole. Body strongly glaucous blue-grey, upper surface lilac-lined, spots many, blue-green, linked by sunken, blood-red rugae.

***L. gesineae*** Boer. Body 18–22×22–36×14–26mm, fissure deep, lobes somewhat divergent, reniform, unequal, upper surface flat to domed, dull tan to grey, panel translucent olive, largely occluded by crowded jigsaw-like blotches, thus appearing as a pattern of mossy green speckles or narrow dark fissures. Fls 2.5–4cm diam., yellow. Namibia var. ***annae*** (Boer) Cole. Larger than species type with markings darker, forming a denser pattern.

***L. geyeri*** Nel. Body 20–25×20–29×15–20mm, fissure deep, lobes conjunct or divergent, usually equal, upper surface elliptic, flat or slightly convex, pale buff, panel translucent, olive to mahogany, virtually entire and unblotched in a smooth half moon or closely occluded, forming a slightly blurred, crazed pattern. Fls 2.5–4cm diam., yellow, often with white centre. NW Cape.

***L. gracilidelineata*** Dinter. Body 15×35–50×25–38mm, fissure shallow, lobes conjunct, near equal, upper surface flat, rugose, reniform, pale grey overlaying a broken pattern of fine, sunken, black or cinnamon lines like veins in fat or cerebellum; in some forms, colour bleeds from the veins tinting much of the surface apart from the interstices a pale fleshy brown. Fls 2.5–4.5cm diam., yellow. Namibia. 'Fritz's White Lady': fls white. var. ***waldroniae*** Boer. Somewhat smaller. Upper surface pearly grey impressed with fine, intricately branching blood-red lines. Fls 1–2cm diam., yellow. ssp. ***brandbergensis*** (Boer) Cole. Body 15×36–48×28–36mm. Upper surface beige (not grey), darker toward centre, with obscure spots and chestnut dendritic lines.

***L. hallii*** Boer. Body 17–20×20–47×14–30mm, fissure shallow, lobes conjunct, usually unequal, upper surface flat grey assuming a buff tint, or pale brown, panel translucent dark olive to brown, often with bright red dots in marginal sinuses, the whole crowded and turned into a close network by many raised blotches. Fls 2.5–4.5cm diam., white. NW Cape. var. ***ochracea*** (Boer) Cole. Smaller than species type with lobes usually more unequal and tinted ginger, panel pale brick-red, unblotched with indented edges, each sinus containing a jasper-red spot or blotched and reticulate. Fls 2.5–4.7cm diam., white. NW Cape. 'Green Soapstone': upper surface lime-green, panel jade to olive.

***L. helmutii*** L. Bol. Body 20–25×23–30×15–20mm, fissure deep, lobes divergent, upper surface elliptic-reniform, strongly convex, battleship-grey marbled or closely speckled glossy, translucent grey-green (i.e. panel densely occluded). Fls 2.5–3.3cm diam., yellow with white centre. NW Cape.

***L. herrei*** L. Bol. Body 20–25×23–30×15–21mm, fissure deep, lobes conjunct to divergent, unequal, reniform, upper surface flat, dull grey, pale or grey tinted lilac, panel dark grey-green, open and translucent with scattered blotched and deeply lobed edges or virtually occluded, only a broken pattern of fine crazed lines. Fls 1.5–2.3cm diam., yellow or bronze-yellow with a white centre. NW Cape, S Namibia.

***L. hookeri*** (Berg) Schwantes. Body 20–23×30–46×23–35mm, fissure shallow, tight, lobes conjunct, usually unequal, upper surface flat, reniform-elliptic, buff to pale glaucous brown, panel rich brown, filled by many interlocking fleshy figures with deep dark intervening grooves, forming a vermiculate pattern. Fls 2.5–4.5cm diam., yellow. NW Cape. var. ***dabneri*** (L. Bol.) Cole. Upper surface pale grey, vermiculate patterning very close, dark grey or grey-green. var. ***elephina*** (Cole) Cole. Upper surface buff to tan with panel olive-green, fewer, broader blotches and a more open pattern resembling thick wrinkled hide. var. ***lutea*** (Boer) Cole. Differs in more open network of deep sunken, rusty-red grooves over a pale buff surface. var. ***marginata*** (Nel) Cole. Upper surface dull pink to ochre, minutely and intricately vermiculate, pattern dark grey-green to dull red. var. ***subfenestrata*** (Boer) Cole. Dull tan with panel olive to grey-green, somewhat lustrous and largely occluded by heavy-textured, vermiculate blotches. var. ***susannae*** (Cole) Cole. Body 15–20×22–28×17–20mm, upper surface pale grey, sometimes with an obscure, darker pale grey, markings dark, sunken, forming a broken network.

***L. julii*** (Dinter & Schwantes) N.E. Br. Body 20–30×25–38×20–25mm, fissure shallow, lobes conjunct then briefly divergent, equal or unequal, upper surface reniform, flat to slightly concave, colour variable, dove- to dark grey, panel dark brown to olive with minute red dots, eroded edges and many broad blotches, thus leaving a sunken pattern of loose crazed reticulation, often with a conspicuous brown stain on the inner lip of each lobe. Fls 2.3–4.3cm diam., white. Namibia. A pallid form exists, as yet unnamed, with a bold lip stain but patterning virtually obscured by a thin covering of the grey ground colour. 'Peppermint Crème': is a milky blue-green form of this variant with a pale grey panel and olive lip stains. ssp. ***fulleri*** (N.E. Br.) Fearn. Body 12–14×25–32×18–23mm, lobes markedly unequal, upper surface slightly rugose, colour variable, buff to dull grey, panel translucent grey, sometimes with pale fragment-like blotches, edges eroded and lobed to varying degrees, dark brown or red spots or dashes in sinuses. 'Fullergreen': body and markings pale grey-green, panel dull sap-green, eroded-reticulate. ssp. ***fulleri*** var. ***brunnea*** (Boer) Cole. Body 12–14×16×18–20mm, lobes near equal, upper surface slightly convex, buff, panel olive to chocolate-brown with few, minute or many, distinct markings, edges shallowly to deeply eroded with red-brown flecks in sinuses. var. ***rouxii*** (Boer) Cole. Body 15–20×30–40×20–25mm, lobes rather more closely conjunct, upper surface flat, reniform, pale grey or beige, sometimes tinted pink, panel paler still, slightly translucent, with obscure markings, edges only slightly eroded, outlined yellow or ochre with etched red dashes resembling stitches.

***L. karasmontana*** (Dinter & Schwantes) N.E. Br. Highly variable. Body 30–40×25–35×15–28mm, fissure deep, lobes conjunct then briefly divergent, lip-like, unequal to equal, upper surface elliptic-reniform, flat, concave or convex, rugose, dull grey or beige, panel dark brown, almost obscured by close markings leaving an impressed pattern of faint dendritic lines, or, in some variants, pale beige with upper surface rugose and entirely suffused pale brick-red. Fls 2.5–4.5cm diam., white. Namibia. var. ***lericheana*** (Dinter & Schwantes) Cole. Body 15–20×20–27×15–20mm, lobes near equal, buff, upper surface rounded, rugose, pink-tinted, pale olive to dull jade-green, markings few, large, edges deeply eroded with lobes irregular, projected into panel. var. ***tischeri*** Cole. Body 20–25×30–35×20–25mm, lobes rounded, strongly unequal, upper surface broadly reniform, flat, rugose, capped pale ginger, panel dark olive to chocolate, so obscured by markings and irregular marginal incursions as to be an open pattern of dull, impressed 'veins', resembling calf's liver. ssp. ***bella*** (N.E. Br.) Cole. Body 25–30×20–30×15–20mm, lobes rounded, strongly divergent, upper surface convex, grey to buff, panel dull olive reduced to an open, jagged-edged network by broad markings and marginal incursions. ssp. ***eberlanzii*** (Dinter & Schwantes) Cole. Body 25–30×25–38×20–25mm, close to ssp. *bella*, but with panel paler, markings larger, thus with a closer and more obscure network, often with conspicuous red dots and dashes in its bends and gulleys. 'Avocado Cream': pale grey capped buff tinted lime, network close, broken, dark olive.

***L. lesliei*** (N.E. Br.) N.E. Br. Body 20–45×30–49×23–33mm, fissure shallow, lobes congruent, then briefly divergent, with marked inner lips, equal to unequal, upper surface elliptic-reniform, flat to convex, grey-green to buff to pale terracotta, sometimes capped pale gold, panel pale to dark olive, with closely eroded edges and dense, dotted, irregular markings forming a fine, mossy, dendritic pattern. Fls 3–5.5cm diam., yellow. N Cape, Orange Free State, Transvaal. 'Albiflora': upper surface of lobes buff marked olive; fls white. 'Albinica': upper surface of lobes pale gold, panel dull olive, finely marked; fls white. 'Storm's Albinigold': close to 'Albinica' but with fls yellow. var. ***hornii*** Boer. Body 20–30×30–38×25–30mm, lobes grey-buff, upper surface beige to brick, capped pale ginger, pale olive-grey crowded by fine, irregular markings, edges with a regular line of minute branching channels. Often mistaken for *L. aucampiae*. var. ***mariae*** Cole. Body 20–30×30–38×25–30mm, lobes grey-buff, upper surface sandy gold, panel olive, but so finely and densely marked as to appear minutely green-gold speckled. var. ***minor*** Boer. Body 15–18×16–28×10–20mm, upper surface terracotta, panel dark green with minutely eroded margins and many, irregular, perforated (thus dotted) markings. var. ***rubrobrunnea*** Boer. Close to var. *minor* but larger, upper surface terracotta to dusty pink, more closely marked over olive panel. Fls yellow, 2.5–3.5cm diam. var. ***venteri*** (Nel) Boer & Boom. Body pale grey, panel dark grey to grey-green, unmarked with minutely eroded edges or with fine and dense markings leaving a mossy, dark, dendritic pattern. ssp. ***burchellii*** Cole. Body pale grey or buff, panel charcoal-grey with many fine markings creating an intricate, spreading network, or virtually unmarked, characterized by radiating marginal lines with expanded tips.

***L. marmorata*** (N.E. Br.) N.E. Br. Body 28–30×25–36×17–23mm, fissure deep, lobes strongly divergent, near-equal, upper surface narrow-reniform, deeply fissured, flat to convex, pale grey or beige sometimes tinted green or lilac, panel translucent, dark grey or grey-green, spreading outward from a clean arc on inner lip, closely and deeply marked with jagged edges, resembling a grey fissured stone with a partly worn, paler surface. Fls 2.5–4.5cm diam., white. NW Cape (Little Namaqualand). var. ***elisae*** (Boer) Cole. Body 15–25×24–36×15–25mm, usually buff or beige, panel so crowded with a few large markings as to appear a pale loose pattern of crazed and impressed veins.

***L. meyeri*** L. Bol. Body 20–30×25–35×28–24mm, fissure deep, lobes strongly divergent, unequal, upper surface elongate-elliptic to reniform, flat and smooth or slightly concave and wrinkled, pale lilac-grey capped dove-grey, with a slightly darker, semi-translucent, unmarked panel. Fls 2.5–4cm diam., yellow with a white centre. NW Cape. 'Hammeruby': lobes dull garnet.

***L. naureeniae*** Cole. Body 20–25×25–35×20–25mm, fissure deep, lobes divergent, upper surface reniform, slightly convex, grey to buff, panel olive, unmarked with a finely fringed edged or scattered with jigsaw-piece markings, edges deeply eroded and lobed. Fls 2.5–3.5cm diam., yellow with a white centre. NW Cape.

***L. olivacea*** L. Bol. Body 20×18–24×15–18mm, fissure deep, lobes conjunct, near-equal, upper surface flat, reniform with a straight inner margin, pale grey or beige, panel translucent, olive, edge slightly eroded, clear or with markings few, scattered raised. Fls 2.5–4cm diam., yellow with white centre. SW Cape.

***L. optica*** (Marloth) N.E. Br. Body 20–30×20–30×15–20mm, cleft deep, lobes unequal, divergent, rounded, upper surface reniform to broadly and unequally elliptic, convex, grey-green to dove-grey with a green or blue-green translucent panel, either unmarked with edges slightly eroded or closely marked, resembling a broad bean. Fls 1.2–2cm diam., white, often pink-tipped. Namibia. 'Rubra': lobes dull ruby-red, panel darker, unmarked.

***L. otzenia*** Nel. Body 25–30×25–30×18–20mm, fissure deep, lobes divergent, rounded, upper surface reniform-elliptic, convex, buff, panel dull olive-brown, semi-translucent with edges deeply eroded (lobes rounded) and a few broad, round to reniform intramarginal markings. Fls 2.3–5cm diam., yellow with white centre. NW Cape. 'Aquamarine': body and markings grey-green, panel dark blue-green.

***L. pseudotruncatella*** (A. Berger) N.E. Br. Body 25–30×25–50×20–35mm, fissure shallow, lobes conjunct, unequal, upper surface broadly reniform, flat to slightly concave, grey to buff, panel olive-brown, so obscured as to appear a fine network of dots and mossy 'veins', these terminating in dull red dashes, sometimes staining edges pale copper. Fls 2.5–5cm diam., yellow. Namibia var. ***elisabethiae*** (Dinter) Boer & Boom. Slightly smaller, body grey tinted lilac-blue or pink, markings dark grey, marginal dashes bright red. var. ***riehmerae*** Cole Slightly smaller than species type, body milky grey with a moonstone-like bloom near fissure on upper surface and a fine, moss-like, pale olive pattern. ssp. ***archerae*** (Boer) Cole. Lobes equal, conjunct then briefly divergent, inner margins lip-like, upper surface perfectly reniform, pale grey with a slightly darker central zone, faint, delicate radical fissures, obscure spotting and, sometimes, marginal red dots and dashes. ssp. ***dendritica*** (Nel) Cole. Close to ssp. *archerae* but with a more regular network of fine, dark brown or olive, hieroglyph-like markings, radiating from a distinct, straight line of colour at inner margin. ssp. ***groendrayensis*** (Jacobsen) Cole. Body 20–40×30–53×28–44mm, fissure shallow, lobes conjunct, upper surface elliptic-reniform, flat, slightly rugose, pale grey with the faintest blue-grey central zone, sometimes fissured, sometimes with a scattering of minute red dots. ssp. ***volkii*** (Schwantes ex Boer & Boom) Cole. Body 30–40×30–38×20–26mm, lobes unequal, upper surface rounded-reniform, pale milky grey with faint marbling or dots.

***L. ruschiorum*** (Dinter & Schwantes) N.E. Br. Body 20–45×20–38×20–27mm, fissure deep, lobes conjunct, then divergent, slightly unequal, very rounded, upper surface convex, pale grey or cream, glaucous, plain or with faint impressed dots or a broken network of crazed lines inlaid with dark rust dashes. Fls 1.5–3cm diam., yellow. Namibia. var. ***lineata*** (Nel) Cole. Lobes buff to beige with a close network of brown to red capillary-like lines.

***L. salicola*** L. Bol. Body 20–25×20–35×13–26mm, fissure shallow, lobes conjunct then divergent, unequal, upper surface reniform-elliptic, slightly convex, grey, panel translucent sap-green with eroded and red-dotted edges and obscure (embedded) markings or with many small, scattered markings, some superficial, of a golden hue, some embedded, cloudy. 'Malachite': body grey-green, panel olive edged ochre, ragged-edged, markings ochre or lime-green, some clouded.

***L. schwantesii*** Dinter. Body 30–40×25–40×20–30mm, fissure shallow, lobes conjunct, equal to unequal, upper surface flat, broadly oblong-reniform, rugose, grey or buff capped pale ginger, panel olive-grey with a broken network of erratic cinnamon lines. Fls 2.5–3.6cm diam., yellow. Namibia. var. ***marthae*** (Loesch & Tisch.) Cole. Body 20–30×20–26×15–18mm, lobes decidedly unequal, fawn to grey, panel grey edged ochre, markings few, vein-like, brick-red. var. ***rugosa*** (Dinter) Boer & Boom. Body 15–20×30–38×20–28mm, grey-buff to pale lilac, panel fleshy pink or sandy brown with a close network of deeply impressed brown lines and figures, appearing rugose, darkly dotted and organ-like. var. ***urikosensis*** (Dinter) Boer & Boom. Body 12–30×30–43×20–27mm, fissure deep, fawn capped pale ochre, closely netted burn sienna, the lines broken and sunken, thus often appearing dotted. ssp. ***genseri*** (Boer) Cole. Body 20–25×30–40×25–28mm, lobes strongly divergent at apex, grey-tan, capped pale brown with a deeply impressed close network of red-brown lines. ssp. *L. steineckeana* Tisch. Body 15×18–23×16–19mm, fissure shallow, often grey, lobes divergent at apex, rounded, upper surface semicircular, convex, grey-white suffused dirty cream, usually with a few scattered grey-green dots, panel small, opaque, seldom present. Fls 2–3.2cm diam. Habit unknown, possibly a garden hybrid. ssp. *L. terricolor* N.E. Br. Body

20–25×20–30×15–24mm, fissure deep, lobes conjunct, slightly unequal, upper surface oblong-reniform, slightly convex, buff to tan, closely spotted olive or mid-green. Fls 1.5–3.5cm diam., yellow, occasionally with a white centre. Cape (Karroo to Eastern Province). 'Silver Spurs': lobes rather golden, spotted olive; fls pure white. 'Speckled Gold': lobes grey-green, capped dull gold, spotted olive.

***L. vallis-mariae*** (Dinter & Schwantes) N.E. Br. Body 20–40×30–40×20–30mm, fissure shallow, lobes conjunct, unequal, upper surface flat, broadly reniform-elliptic, dove-grey with a free network of obscure, impressed, translucent grey lines, sometimes obliterated, appearing as scattered dots. Fls 2–3cm diam., straw-yellow, rarely orange-yellow, sometimes tinged pink or bronze. Namibia.

***L. verruculosa*** Nel. Body 20–30×23–34×18–20mm, fissure deep, lobes conjunct, briefly divergent at apex, strongly unequal, upper surface reniform-oblong to rounded-triangular, grey capped tan, sometimes with a darker grey translucent panel and small tan markings, closely and finely fissured, covered with raised red-brown dots, hence verruculose. Fls 2–3.5cm diam., very variable, mainly straw-yellow but also golden yellow, dark yellow, light orange, bronze, carrot and lime-yellow, shell-pink and rose, salmon, cream and near-white, frequently with a contrasting inner ring of orange, rose, mauve or magenta. NW Cape. var. ***glabra*** Boer. Body 20–25×25–30×17–20mm, grey edged buff, panel dark grey, edge eroded, with fewer red dots. Fls 2–3cm diam., white. ssp. ***deboeri*** (Schwantes) Cole. Has many more markings, occluding the panel with a deeply fissured network. ssp. ***kennedyi*** (Boer) Cole. Lobes dove-grey capped pale ginger, panel dull olive with scattered ginger markings.

***L. viridis*** H. Lück. Body 17–20×20–25×15–18mm, fissure deep, lobes divergent, equal to unequal, rounded, upper surface reniform to semicircular, convex, dull grey, panel translucent grey-green, usually clear and covering most of upper surface, edge slightly eroded. Fls 2.5–3.5cm diam., yellow with white centre. NW Cape.

***L. werneri*** Schwantes & Jacobsen Body 10–15×20–24×15–18mm, fissure deep, lobes conjunct then divergent, unequal, rounded, upper surface oblong-reniform, flat to slightly convex, pale grey, panel dark olive, usually obscured or underlying many dark dots fused to form a mossy, dendritic pattern branching divaricately toward outer margin. Fls 1.5–2.8cm diam., yellow. Namibia.

***L. alpina*** Dinter. See *L. pseudotruncatella.*
***L. annae*** Boer. See *L. gesineae* var. *annae.*
***L. archerae*** Boer. See *L. pseudotruncatella* ssp. *archerae.*
***L. aurantiaca*** L. Bol. See *L. hookeri.*
***L. bella*** N.E. Br. See *L. karasmontana* ssp. *bella.*
***L. bella*** var. ***lericheana*** (Dinter & Schwantes) Boer. See *L. karasmontana* var. *lericheana.*
***L. brevis*** L. Bol. See *L. dinteri* var. *brevis.*
***L. bromfieldii*** var. ***insularis*** f. ***sulphurea*** Y. Shimada):. See *L. bromfieldii* var. *insularis* 'Sulphurea'.
***L. christinae*** Boer. See *L. schwantesii* var. *urikosensis.*
***L. chrysocephala*** Nel. See *L. julii.*
***L. commoda*** Dinter. See *L. karasmontana.*
***L. comptonii*** var. ***viridis*** H. Lück.) Fearn. See *L. viridis.*
***L. dabneri*** L. Bol. See *L. hookeri* var. *dabneri.*
***L. dendritica*** Nel. See *L. pseudotruncatella* ssp. *dendritica.*
***L. dinteri*** var. ***marthae*** (Loesch & Tisch.) Fearn. See *L. schwantesii* var. *marthae.*
***L. dinteri*** var. ***multipunctata*** Boer. See *L. dinteri* ssp. *multipunctata.*
***L. eberlanzii*** (Dinter & Schwantes) Boer & Boom. See *L. karasmontana* ssp. *eberlanzii.*
***L. edithae*** N.E. Br. See *L. pseudotruncatella* var. *riehmerae.*
***L. edithiae*** L. Bol. See *L. karasmontana* ssp. *eberlanzii.*
***L. eksteeniae*** L. Bol. See *L. dorotheae.*
***L. elevata*** L. Bol. See *L. optica.*
***L. elisabethiae*** Dinter. See *L. pseudotruncatella* var. *elisabethiae.*
***L. elisae*** Boer. See *L. marmorata* var. *elisae.*
***L. erniana*** Tisch. & Jacobsen. See *L. karasmontana* ssp. *eberlanzii.*
***L. farinosa*** Dinter. See *L. pseudotruncatella* ssp. *dendritica.*
***L. fossulifera*** Tisch. nom. nud. See *L. karasmontana* var. *tischeri.*
***L. framesii*** L. Bol. See *L. marmorata.*
***L. frederici*** Cole. See *L. dinteri* ssp. *frederici.*
***L. friedrichiae*** (Dinter) N.E. Br. See *Conophytum friedrichiae.*
***L. fulleri*** N.E. Br. See *L. julii* ssp. *fulleri.*
***L. fulleri*** var. ***chrysocephala*** (Nel) Boer. See *L. julii.*
***L. fulleri*** var. ***kennedyi*** Boer. See *L. verruculosa* ssp. *kennedyi.*
***L. fulleri*** var. ***ochracea*** Boer. See *L. hallii* var. *ochracea.*
***L. fulleri*** var. ***tapscotti*** L. Bol. See *L. julii* ssp. *fulleri.*
***L. glaudinae*** Boer. See *L. bromfieldii* var. *glaudinae.*
***L. gulielmii*** L. Bol. See *L. schwantesii.*
***L. herrei*** var. ***geyeri*** (Nel) Boer & Boom. See *L. geyeri.*
***L. herrei*** f. ***albiflora*** Jacobsen. See *L. marmorata.*
***L. inae*** Nel. See *L. verruculosa.*
***L. inornata*** L. Bol. See *L. schwantesii* var. *marthae.*
***L. jacobseniana*** Schwantes. See *L. karasmontana.*
***L. julii*** var. ***brunnea*** Boer. See *L. julii* ssp. *fulleri* var. *brunnea.*
***L. julii*** var. ***littlewoodii*** Boer. See *L. julii.*
***L. julii*** var. ***pallida*** Tisch. See *L. julii.*
***L. kuibisensis*** Dinter & Jacobsen. See *L. schwantesii.*
***L. kuibisensis*** Dinter. See *L. schwantesii* var. *urikosensis.*
***L. latenitia*** Dinter. See *L. karasmontana.*
***L. lericheana*** (Dinter & Schwantes) N.E. Br. See *L. karasmontana* var. *lericheana.*
***L. lesliei*** var. ***applanata*** Boer nom. nud. See *L. lesliei.*
***L. lesliei*** var. ***luteoviridis*** Boer. See *L. lesliei.*
***L. lesliei*** f. ***albiflora*** Cole). See *L. lesliei* 'Albiflora':.
***L. lesliei*** f. ***albinica*** Cole):. See *L. lesliei* 'Albinica'.
***L. lineata*** Nel. See *L. ruschiorum* var. *lineata.*
***L. localis*** (N.E. Br.) Schwantes. See *L. schwantesii L. terricolor.*
***L. lydiae*** L. Bol. See *L. fulviceps.*
***L. marginata*** Nel. See *L. hookeri* var. *marginata.*
***L. marthae*** Loesch & Tisch. See *L. schwantesii* var. *marthae.*
***L. maughanii*** N.E. Br. See *L. julii* ssp. *fulleri.*
***L. mennellii*** L. Bol. See *L. bromfieldii* var. *mennellii.*
***L. mickbergensis*** Dinter. See *L. karasmontana.*
***L. nelii*** Schwantes. See *L. ruschiorum.*
***L. opalina*** Dinter. See *L. karasmontana.*
***L. orpenii*** L. Bol. nom. nud. See *L. lesliei.*
***L. peersi*** L. Bol. See *L. schwantesii L. terricolor.*
***L. pilarsii*** L. Bol. See *L. ruschiorum.*
***L. pseudotruncatella*** var. ***alta*** Tisch. See *L. pseudotruncatella.*
***L. pseudotruncatella*** var. ***edithae*** (N.E. Br.) Boer & Boom. See *L. pseudotruncatella* var. *riehmerae.*
***L. rugosa*** Dinter. See *L. schwantesii* var. *rugosa.*
***L. salicola*** var. ***reticulata*** Boer. See *L. hallii.*
***L. schwantesii*** var. ***begseri*** Boer. See *L. schwantesii* ssp. *genseri.*
***L. schwantesii*** var. ***nutupsdriftensis*** Boer. See *L. schwantesii* var. *urikosensis.*
***L. triebneri*** L. Bol. See *L. schwantesii.*
***L. turbiniformis*** (Haw.) N.E. Br. See *L. hookeri.*
***L. turbiniformis*** var. ***brunnes-violacea*** Boer. See *L. hookeri* var. *subfenestrata.*
***L. turbiniformis*** var. ***dabneri*** (L. Bol.) Cole. See *L. hookeri* var. *dabneri.*
***L. turbiniformis*** var. ***elephina*** Cole. See *L. hookeri* var. *elephina.*
***L. turbiniformis*** var. ***lutea*** Boer. See *L. hookeri* var. *lutea.*
***L. turbiniformis*** var. ***subfenestrata*** Boer. See *L. hookeri* var. *subfenestrata.*
***L. urikosensis*** Dinter. See *L. schwantesii* var. *urikosensis.*
***L. ursulae*** nom. nud. See *L. karasmontana.*
***L. vallis-mariae*** var. ***margarethae*** Boer. See *L. vallis-mariae.*
***L. vanzylii*** L. Bol. See *Dinteranthus vanzylii.*
***L. volkii*** Schwantes ex Boer & Boom. See *L. pseudotruncatella* ssp. *volkii.*
***L. weberi*** Nel. See *L. comptonii* var. *weberi.*
For further synonymy see *Mesembryanthemum.*

**Lithospermum** L. (From Gk *lithos*, stone, and *sperma*, seed, referring to the hard seeds.) GROMWELL'S PUCCOON. Boraginaceae. Some 60 species of annual or perennial herbs. Stems erect or decumbent, herbaceous or somewhat shrubby, simple or branched, hispid, strigose or villous. Leaves alternate, usually numerous, often unveined. Flowers in terminal racemes or solitary in leaf axils; pedicels short to elongate; bracts usually numerous, leafy; calyx usually 5-lobed, usually enlarged in fruit, lobes lanceolate or linear-cuneate, short to elongate; corolla white, yellow, orange or blue, infundibular to hypocrateriform, exterior pubescent, plicate or gibbous at throat, often with pubescent or glandular appendages, lobes equal, overlapping in bud, orbicular to ovate or obovate; stamens 5, included, anthers small, oblong, obtuse or apiculate; ovary 5-lobed, style usually filiform, usually included, stigmas 2, rounded, cleft Nutlets 4, ovoid or ellipsoid, stony, white or pale brown, smooth, rough or tuberculate. Cosmopolitan (except Australia).

CULTIVATION *Lithospermum* spp. are suited to the wild garden, herbaceous border and rock garden. *L. officinale*, the only European species and a rare British native, occurs in hedgerows and at the woodland edge; *L. canescens* is found in similar habitats. *L. caroliniense* inhabits sandy plains and pine barrens.

Grow in sun in moderately fertile and freely draining soils; *L. multiflorum*, which is particularly useful for plantings in dry sites, prefers calcareous soils. *L. canescens* requires a warm, lime-free, sandy soil or, in the alpine house, a freely draining mix of loam, leafmould and coarse sand; irrigate with lime-free water. Propagate by seed: *L. canescens* is best sown in a soilless propagating medium, and may be potted on directly into tufa rock half buried in potting mix and kept in semi-shade until established.

***L. canescens*** (Michx.) Lehm. PUCCOON; PAINT INDIAN. Perenn., canescent. Stems to 40cm, adpressed-pubesc. Lvs to 4×1cm, linear-oblong to ovate-oblong. Cal. lobes short, linear-lanceolate; cor. to 18mm, yellow or orange-yellow, infundibular, limb to 15mm diam., tube to 8mm, cylindrical, interior glabrous, with glandular appendages in throat; style to 9mm. Nutlets white, smooth. N America. Z3.

***L. caroliniense*** (Walter) MacMill. Perenn., hispid. Stems to 100cm, minutely adpressed-pubesc. Lvs to 4×1cm, numerous, cauline, lanceolate or linear-lanceolate, acute, hispid, sessile. Infl. terminal, loosely-fld; cal. to 8mm at anthesis, lobes lanceolate; cor. to 25mm diam., orange-yellow, salverform, exterior slightly villous-hispid, lobes ovate to suborbicular, tube to 13mm, throat appendages puberulent. Nutlets to 3.5mm, white, shiny, ovoid. Eastern N America. Z6.

***L. distichum*** (G. Don) Ortega. Perenn. Stems to 20cm, erect-ascending, often branched at base, sericeous. Lvs numerous, strigose; basal lvs to 8.5cm, oblong-lanceolate to spathulate, obtuse, base attenuate; cauline lvs to 3cm, lanceolate to oblong, subacute or obtuse, base cuneate or obtuse, sessile or subsessile. Cal. to 3mm at anthesis, to 6mm in fr., lobes oblong-linear to spathulate, acute or obtuse; cor. white, tube to 6mm, lobes to 4mm, rounded, anth. subsessile. Nutlets to 2.5mm, ovoid, lustrous. Mexico, Guatemala. Z9.

***L. incisum*** Lehm. Stems to 50cm, solitary to numerous, erect, usually strigose, becoming branched. Basal lvs to 12×1cm, oblanceolate, acute, petiolate; cauline lvs to 6×0.6cm, linear to linear-lanceolate, hispidulous toward base. Cal. to 12mm, lobes unequal, slender; cor. to 35mm, yellow, salverform, exterior slightly strigose, limb to 20mm diam., lobes to 7×7mm, ovate, erose-fimbriate, throat appendages slightly glanduliferous, truncate; anth. to 2.5mm; style elongate, slender. Nutlets to 3.5×2.5mm, back convex, usually smooth. Central N America. Z3.

***L. multiflorum*** Torr. Perenn., grey-pubesc. Stems to 50cm, few to numerous, erect, sometimes branched above. Lvs to 7×1cm, numerous, cauline, linear-lanceolate to lanceolate, sessile. Infl. terminal, erect, simple or forked, loosely fld; cal. to 6mm at anthesis, to 10mm in fr., lobes unequal, linear; cor. yellow-orange, infundibular above, interior glabrous, exterior somewhat villous, tube to 10×3mm, cylindric, limb to 9mm, lobes to 3.5mm, broadly ovate, obtuse or rounded, usually entire, throat appendages glandiferous; anth. to 2.5mm; style to 4mm in short-styled fls, to 9mm in long-styled fls. Nutlets to 3.5×2.5mm, white or brown, ovoid, usually smooth. Western N America. Z3.

***L. officinale*** L. Perenn. Stems to 100cm, solitary or numerous, erect, branched, covered with trichomes. Lvs to 8×2cm, lanceolate, acute, slightly revolute, entire, adpressed-bristly throughout. Cal. lobes to 4mm in fl., narrowly lanceolate, pubesc.; cor. green, yellow or yellow-white, to 6mm, hypocrateriform, tube to 4mm, limb to 4mm diam., lobes to 1.5mm, spreading, throat appendages trapeziform, glandiferous; style to 2mm. Nutlets to 4mm, ovate, lustrous, white, smooth. Europe, Asia. Z6.

***L. ruderale*** Douglas ex Lehm. Perenn. Stems to 60cm, usually numerous, erect or decumbent, green-grey adpressed-pubesc. Lvs to 10×2cm, numerous, linear-lanceolate to lanceolate, terminally clustered. Cor. pale yellow to yellow green, infundibular to campanulate, tube to 7mm, cylindric, limb to 13mm diam., lobes entire, ascending. Nutlets to 6mm, white to grey, ovoid, lustrous, smooth. Western N America. Z4.

***L. angustifolium*** Michx. See *L. incisum*.
***L. benthamii*** (Wallich ex G. Don) Johnst. See *Arnebia benthamii*.
***L. brevifolium*** Engelm. & Gray. See *L. incisum*.
***L. calycinum*** Morris. See *Amsinckia calycina*.
***L. decumbens*** Vent. See *Arnebia decumbens*.
***L. densiflorum*** Ledeb. ex Nordm. See *Arnebia densiflora*.
***L. diffusum*** Lagasca. See *Lithodora diffusa*.
***L. doerfleri*** hort. See *Moltkia doerfleri*.
***L. echioides*** Benth. See *Mertensia echioides*.
***L. elongatum*** Decne. See *Mertensia elongata*.
***L. ×froebelii*** Sünderm. See *Moltkia × intermedia* 'Froebelii'.
***L. fruticosum*** L. See *Lithodora fruticosa*.
***L. gastonii*** Benth. See *Buglossoides gastonii*.
***L. gmelinii*** Michx. See *L. caroliniense*.
***L. graminifolium*** Viv. See *Moltkia suffruticosa*.
***L. griffithii*** (Boiss.) Johnst. See *Arnebia griffithii*.
***L. hirtum*** (Muhlenb.) Lehm. See *L. caroliniense*.
***L. ×intermedium*** Froebel. See *Moltkia × intermedia*.
***L. linearifolium*** Goldie. See *L. incisum*.
***L. mandanense*** Spreng. See *L. incisum*.
***L. oleifolium*** Lapeyr. See *Lithodora oleifolia*.
***L. petraeum*** (Tratt.) DC. See *Moltkia petraea*.
***L. prostratum*** Lois. non Buckley. See *Lithodora diffusa*.
***L. purpurascens*** Gueldenst. See *Buglossoides purpureo-caeruleum*.
***L. purpureo-caeruleum*** L. See *Buglossoides purpureo-caeruleum*.
***L. rosmarinifolium*** Ten. See *Lithodora rosmarinifolia*.
***L. tinctorium*** L. See *Alkanna tinctoria*.
***L. zahnii*** Heldr. ex Hal. See *Lithodora zahnii*.
***L. zollingeri*** A. DC. See *Buglossoides zollingeri*.
For further synonymy see *Batschia*.

For illustration see LITHODORA.

**Lithrea** Miers ex Hook. & Arn. (From Gk *luthron*, black blood, referring to the black staining juice.) Anacardiaceae. 3 species of polygamo-dioecious trees. Leaves alternate, coriaceous, ternate or compound; leaflets 5; rachis alate. Inflorescence a panicle in axil of uppermost leaf, rarely terminal; bracts deltoid, caducous; pedicels glabrous above abscission plate; calyx 5-lobed, lobes semicircular or broadly deltoid, occasionally ciliate at margin; petals 5, valvate, lanceolate, glabrous; stamens 10, slightly shorter than petals, shorter and sterile in female flowers; disc 10-lobed, style 1, stigmas 3, hemispherical, ovary unilocular, ovule basal. Fruit an ivory drupe, mescocarp resinous. S America. Z9.

CULTIVATION *L. molleoides* has evergreen foliage and attractive clusters of fruit and is used as an ornamental in mild climates, such as southern California. *L. caustica* has a toxic sap, used in tanning and dyeing, but which causes extensive and painful swelling of the skin. In frost-free climates plant in any well-drained soil, in full sun. In temperate regions, grow in the intermediate glasshouse, as for *Pistacia*. Propagate from seeds or from root cuttings.

***L. caustica*** (Molina) Hook. & Arn. LITRE; LITHI. Shrub or small tree to 4m, evergreen. Bark green-brown becoming dark grey-brown. Lvs 21×33×45–55mm, simple, coriaceous, glabrous, broadly lanceolate to ovate, apex acute, obtuse or emarginate, base truncate or cuneate, veins white, prominent; petiole 3–15mm. Panicles 1–5, sparsely pilose; fls yellow, slightly inrolled at apex. Fr. 12×11mm, epicarp creamy yellow; seeds light brown, slightly rugose. C Chile.

***L. molleoides*** (Vell.) Engl. AROEIRA BRANCA; AROEIRA BRAVA. To 5m. Bark light brown, densely puberulent, becoming creamy-brown and glabrate. Lvs ternately compound, rarely 5-foliate; leaflets to 5×2cm, sessile, thinly coriaceous, terminal leaflet larger, ovate to ovate-lanceolate; petiole to 3cm. Panicles erect, shortly pilose, 5–6cm; pedicels to 1mm; pet. lanceolate to ovate. Fr. 5×5.5mm, epicarp cream, separating from resinous mesocarp; seed 3.5×2mm, brown, rough. Brazil, Argentina.

***L. aroeirinha*** Marchand ex Warm. See *L. molleoides*.
***L. laurina*** Walp.. See *Malosma laurina*.
***L. molle*** Gay. See *Schinus latifolius*.
***L. veneosa*** Miers. See *L. caustica*.
For further synonymy see *Duvana, Mauria, Persea, Rhus* and *Schinus*.

**Litsea** Lam.
***L. glauca*** Sieb. See *Neolitsea sericea*.

**Littonia** Hook. (For Dr S. Litton, former Professor of Botany in Dublin (mid-19th century).) Liliaceae (Colchicaceae). Some 8 species of perennial, rhizomatous, climbing herbs. Stems prostrate to erect, flexuous, simple. Leaves alternate or opposite above, ternate or quinate, often almost whorled below, lanceolate, tendrilous at apex, stalkless. Flowers orange, campanulate, nodding, axillary, solitary in leaf axils, with pedicel occasionally borne just below leaf; tepals 6, separate, free almost to the base, not spreading widely, with basal, nectar-bearing scale; stamens 6, anthers basifixed, versatile; style simple, straight. Fruit a loculicidal, 3-valved capsule; seeds globose, brown. S Africa, Arabia. Z9.

CULTIVATION Scrambling or climbing understorey herbs of woodland and scrub, grown for their deep golden flowers which are followed by attractive seed pods. In mild sheltered gardens, *L. modesta* will survive mild winters, or can be lifted and stored in frost-free conditions over winter, otherwise it needs protected cultivation as for *Gloriosa*.

***L. modesta*** Hook. Tuber 3cm diam. Stem to 1.2m, simple, slender, often prostrate or runner-like. Lvs bright emerald, linear to ovate-lanceolate, alternate or opposite and narrow above, whorled, glabrous, ending in tendril below. Fls bright orange; pedicels short, to 5cm; tepals orange yellow, lanceolate, tapering, sharply-tipped. S Africa. var. ***keitii*** Leichtlin. Stem branched, fls abundant.

**Livistona** R. Br. (For Patrick Murray, Baron of Livingstone, who before 1680 had a well-stocked garden which became the Edinburgh Botanic Garden.) Palmae. 28 species of pleonanthic, hermaphrodite, shrubby or arborescent palms to 25m. Stems solitary, erect, clothed with leaf sheaths, becoming bare and ringed or covered with leaf bases. Leaves palmate or costapalmate, marcescent; sheaths forming fibrous rust-brown mats; petiole to 2m, channelled or flat above, convex beneath, glabrous, sparsely hairy, margins armed with horizontal spines or unarmed, adaxial hastula prominent, abaxial hastula inconspicuous or absent; blade to 2m, divided into mostly single-fold segments, segments rigid or pendent, waxy beneath, midribs conspicuous. Inflorescences interfoliar, mostly solitary, branched ×5, amid tubular sheathing bracts; rachillae erect to pendent; flowers cream to yellow, arranged spirally, singly or in clusters to 5; calyx 3-lobed; petals valvate, grooved within; stamens 6, joined into ring; carpels 3. Fruit to 4cm, globose to ovoid or pyriform, green, red, blue-green to black or brown, with apical stigmatic remains. Asia, Australasia. Z10.

CULTIVATION Occurring in a diversity of habitats, but even in the drier tropics usually found where soil moisture is reliable and plentiful, *Livistona* spp. are elegant and graceful fan palms, especially attractive in flower and fruit, grown outdoors as specimens or in deep pots in the intermediate glasshouse or conservatory. Most thrive in tropical and subtropical climates; *L. australis, L. chinensis, L. decipiens* and *L. saribus* are also suitable for cultivation in warm temperate zones and will tolerate temperatures down to freezing point for short periods. Propagate by seed sown in deep containers to avoid constriction of the root; seed shows longer viability than is the case with most palms.

***L. australis*** (R. Br.) Mart. GIPPSLAND PALM; CABBAGE PALM; AUSTRALIAN PALM; AUSTRALIAN FAN PALM. Stem to 25m×30cm, spiny fibrous at first, becoming bare. Petiole edged with spines at first; blades to 1.75cm, green to brown, glossy, undulate, divided to two-thirds into seg., seg. to 70, with drooping, cleft tips Infl. equal to or shorter than lvs; bracts hairy chestnut brown; fls cream, occasionally males only. Fr. to 2cm, spherical, black, red-brown, waxy. E coastal Australia.

***L. chinensis*** (Jacq.) R. Br. ex Mart. CHINESE FAN PALM. Stem to 12m×30cm, swollen at base. Petioles shorter than lf blades, margins armed proximally with short spines; blades dull green-brown, cut to two-thirds, seg. deeply cut to base. Infl. far shorter than lvs; bracts green to grey-brown. Fr. to 2.5cm, ovoid to spherical, deep blue-green to grey-pink, glossy. S Japan, Ryuku, Bonin Is., S Taiwan.

***L. decipiens*** Becc. Resembles *L. australis* but shorter. Lvs to 2m, cut to halfway, seg. hanging like a curtain. Infl. bracts glabrous. Fr. glossy. Queensland.

***L. humilis*** R. Br. To 6m. Lvs divided to halfway into 30–35 seg., seg. deeply emarginate, rigid, to 45cm; petiole serrate, scurfy. Infl. exceeding lvs; bracts hairy; fls 2–4 per cluster. Fr. *c*1.5cm, obovoid-ellipsoid, black. N Australia.

***L. jenkinsiana*** Griff. To 9m. Lvs to 1.8m diam., pale beneath, divided into large, entire central portion and many deeply cleft seg. Infl. pubesc.; bracts hairy; fls 2 per cluster. Fr. deep blue, globose, *c*2.5cm. Himalayan foothills.

***L. mariae*** F. Muell. CENTRAL AUSTRALIAN FAN PALM. Stem to 30m×30cm, swollen at base, clothed with persistent lf bases. Lvs bronze-red to blue-green; petiole to 2m, edged with spines at base; blades to 2m, thick, prominently ribbed, coated with flaky wax beneath, cut to halfway, seg. deeply cleft with drooping tips. Infl. erect, white scaly; bracts green; fls crowded, cream-yellow. Fr. glossy, black, spherical to 2cm. Australia.

***L. merrillii*** Becc. To 18m. Lvs to 1.35m, pale beneath, seg. deeply emarginate, drooping at tips; petiole serrate below, densely matted-hairy. Fls solitary, to 0.35cm. Fr. globose, *c*2.5cm diam. Philippine Is.

***L. muelleri*** Bail. To 6m. Lvs green, rigid, divided to two-thirds depth into 50 seg., seg. shallowly emarginate; petiole serrate below. Infl. glabrous; fls 2–3 per cluster. Fr. black, globose to ovoid, *c*1.25cm. N Australia.

***L. robinsoniana*** Becc. Resembles *L. rotundifolia* but petioles arching to pendent; blades deep glossy green, thin; seg. shallowly cleft, pendent, apices truncate. Infl. shorter than lvs; bracts straw-yellow; fls yellow. Fr. to 1.5cm, orange. Philippines.

***L. rotundifolia*** (Lam.) Mart. Stem to 24m×20cm. Lvs erect to pendent; petioles spiny below; blades shorter than petioles, glossy deep green, seg. rigid, shallowly emarginate. Fr. to 2cm, spherical, scarlet to black. Philippines, Sabah, Sulawesi, Moluccas.

***L. saribus*** (Lour.) Merrill ex A. Chev. To 22.5m. Lvs to 1.5m, unevenly divided into several-fold seg., seg. further shallowly divided into deeply emarginate seg.; petiole coarsely and sharply toothed below. Infl. glabrous; fls in clusters of 3–5. Fr. to 1.25cm, globose, blue. SE Asia, Indonesia, Philippine Is.

***L. altissima*** Zoll. See *L. rotundifolia*.
***L. cochinchinensis*** (Bl.) Mart. See *L. saribus*.
***L. hoogendorpii*** Teijsm. & Binnend. ex Miq. See *L. saribus*.
***L. oliviformis*** (Hassk.) Mart. See *L. chinensis*.
For further synonymy see *Corypha* and *Latania*.

For illustration see PALMS.

**Llavea** Lagasca. (For M. la Llave, who discovered *L. cordifolia*.) Pteridaceae (Cryptogrammaceae, Cryptogrammataceae). 1 species, a calcicole, evergreen fern to 60cm. Rhizomes scaly, thick, short. Fronds to 60×30cm, lime to olive green, often glaucous beneath; pinnae to 5.25cm, ovate and sterile near base, becoming linear toward apex of blade, ultimately to 8cm, strongly reduced and revolute, these fertile, bearing sporangia over their surface along forking veins; stipes yellow, covered in large acicular scales. Mexico to Guatemala. Z9.

CULTIVATION As for *Davallia*, in cool glasshouse. The growing medium must be of alkaline reaction.

***L. cordifolia*** Lagasca. As for the genus.

**Lloydia** Salisb. ex Rchb. (For Edward Lloyd (1660–1709), keeper of the Ashmolean Collection, Oxford.) Liliaceae (Liliaceae). About 12 species of rhizomatous, creeping perennials to 15cm. Bulbs with a thin, brown papery tunic. Leaves basal and cauline, narrow-linear. Flowers 1–2, terminal, white or yellow; perianth segments 6, free, spreading, with a gland at base; stamens inserted at perianth base, anthers attached to filament at base; ovary trilocular, superior. Fruit a 3-grooved capsule; seeds several per chamber, in 2 ranks, roughly triangular. Temperate N Hemisphere. Z5.

CULTIVATION *L. serotina*, from arctic, tundra and rocky alpine habitats to altitudes of 3000m/9750ft, is a delicate species grown for its slender, thread-like leaves and small, bell-shaped, white flowers in summer. It is very cold hardy but sometimes proves difficult to maintain in cultivation. Grow in light shade or bright indirect light, in perfectly drained but moisture-retentive soil, so that bulbs receive adequate moisture in summer, when in growth, but can be drier in winter. A gritty or gravelly peaty soil that approximates to those of its native rock ledges is ideal. Propagated by seed sown when ripe in the cold frame or in spring.

***L. longiscapa*** Hook. Similar to *L. serotina* but fls larger, drooping; perianth seg. marked purple or red at base. Summer. Himalaya, W China.

***L. serotina*** (L.) Salisb. ex Rchb. SNOWDON LILY To 15cm. Bulb tunic fibrous. Basal lvs 2–3, stem lvs 2–5, to 20cm. Fls erect, to 1.5cm, white, pale yellow at base on exterior surface, veined red-purple; perianth seg. ovate-lanceolate, obtuse. Spring–summer. Temperate N Hemisphere.

**Loam**. A word which originally meant clay or mud, but has come to be used rather loosely for soils of good quality. 'Loams' are often regarded by gardeners as the best possible soil type, with the optimum combination of good drainage and moisture retention, and good nutrient-holding capacity. The term loam is used slightly differently by soil scientists. It denotes a soil texture class which has a balanced mixture of sand, silt and clay, and contains humus or decayed organic matter. While this helps to give good physical properties it is important to note that the levels of organic matter in the soil and the pH are ignored by this classification. In practice, both of these can have a profound implication on the fertility and ease of cultivation of a garden. One can thus speak of 'sandy loam' and 'clay loam', according to their predominant content. 'Fibrous loam' contains a high proportion of fibre in the form of partly decayed plant stems, especially grass. 'Chalky loam' is better referred to as marl.

Loam has been used as a component in potting mediums for centuries. The first standardized loam-based medium, the John Innes 'compost' developed in the 1930s, used topsoil that was taken from a turf ley. This was very rich in fibrous organic matter and therefore well structured. Before use it was stacked to let the living components of the organic matter decompose.

Plant pathogens and weeds are a problem in loam-based substrates and so a process of heat sterilization is usually applied. Some types of loam react poorly to this process and can give rise to manganese toxicity – these should not be used in potting mixes.

Obtaining loam of sufficient quality for use in potting mediums, as recommended for the original John Innes composts, is extremely difficult today. In the UK, legislation prevents the stripping of topsoil from agricultural fields and this is usually substituted by material from development sites. Sometimes the soil is too heavy or too light to be a true loam. Most often it is deficient in organic matter. By shredding and mixing with peat the soil can be given the appearance of good structure while in the bag, but this degenerates rapidly on watering, causing it to puddle.

Although the nutrient-holding and buffering qualities are still good, the aeration will be poor.

Loam is usually supplied from a loam stack, a heap of inverted turf allowed to break down over a year or more. On the small scale, at least, this system is efficient and renewable, with future sources of of sward carefully maintained and refurbished. A loam stack is made by stacking 100mm/4in.-thick turves, from a 3–4-year-old ley, grass-side down. The stack should be no more than 3m/10ft wide and 2m/6½ft high but can be of any length. The turves in the walls of the stack should overlap to improve the binding. Farmyard manure (FYM) may be used to bind the turves together. Broken turves should be laid in the centre of the stack. The loam will be ready for sterilizing and use in potting composts after twelve months.

See also POTTING MEDIUMS; SOIL; STERILIZATION.

**Loasa** Adans. (From the native name in S America.) Loasaceae. 105 species of annual, biennial or perennial herbs or subshrubs covered in stinging hairs. Habit bushy, decumbent or twining. Leaves entire, lobed or decompound. Flowers nodding to decurved, solitary and axillary or in short racemes or panicles; petals 5, spreading yellow, white or cinnabar-red, deeply concave above, carinate beneath (i.e. on upper surface), appearing saccate and inflated, each with a colourful basal nectar-scale. Mexico to S America. Z10.

CULTIVATION *Loasa* spp. bear their brightly coloured flowers over long periods in summer and are grown in the annual border, although since the foliage is clothed with stinging hairs they need careful handling. Sow seed *in situ* in spring or earlier under glass, setting out after danger of frost is past into a sunny situation in any moderately fertile and well-drained soil.

***L. acanthifolia*** Desr. ex Lam. Annual or short-lived perenn. to 1.5m. Stems erect, thickly covered in stinging bristles. Lvs to 10cm, opposite cordate, ovate, deeply and sinuately palmatifid to pinnatifid, the divisions acuminate, sharply and irregularly toothed. Fls to 2cm diam. yellow, solitary.

***L. canarinoides*** Britt. Annual or short-lived perenn. to 1.75cm. Stems closely divaricately branched, extremely bristly. Lvs to 10cm, cordate-oblong to lyrate, deeply pinnatifid, sharply toothed, with veins impressed and sharply bristly above, dark, shining green. Pet. to 3cm, deeply hooded and inflated, dull orange to cinnabar-red, on slender axillary pedicels, decurved at ovary. C America.

***L. triphylla*** Juss. Annual to 40cm. Stems erect to loosely twining. Lvs to 6cm, alternate, trifoliolate or simple in upper regions of plant, the lobes deeply and irregularly toothed or serrate. Fls to 1.8cm diam.; pet. white; nectar-scales yellow barred red and white, forming a crown of colourful concentric rings. S America. var. ***papaverifolia*** (HBK) Urban & Gilg. Lower lvs with 2–4 slender, irregularly toothed, pinnate lobes each side. Fls to 2.5cm diam. var. ***volcanica*** (André) Urban & Gilg Lvs more shallowly lobed than species type. Fls to 5cm diam.

***L. aurantiaca*** hort. See *Caiophora lateritia*.
***L. lateritia*** (Klotzsch) Gillies ex Arn. See *Caiophora lateritia*.
***L. volcanica*** André. See *L. triphylla* var. *volcanica*.

**LOASACEAE** Dumort. LOASA FAMILY. Dicot. 15 genera and 260 species of herbs, sometimes climbing, shrubs or small trees with coarse silicified or often calcified hairs, sometimes stinging, often gland-tipped. Leaves simple, often lobed, alternate or opposite; stipules absent. Flowers bisexual, regular, solitary or in cymes; calyx (4) 5 (–7) free sepals, convolute or imbricate, persistent; corolla (4) 5 (–7) petals (or 10 including 5 petaloid staminodes), free or lobes of a tube; stamens (10–) numerous or 5, free or with basal tube or in antepetalous bundles, sometimes the anthers ± sessile on corolla-tube, some often petaloid or nectariferous staminodes; ovary inferior, 3–5 (–&0 fused carpels, 1-loculed with parietal placentas, rarely plurilocular with axile placentas; ovules 1-numerous. Fruit a capsule, rarely dry-indehiscent; seeds in copious oily endosperm or endosperm absent. America, Africa, S Arabia. *Blumenbachia, Caiophora, Eucnide, Loasa, Mentzelia*.

**Lobb, William** (1809–1863) and **Thomas** (1820–1894). Plant collectors. William Lobb was born in Perran-ar-Worthall in Cornwall. He started his career as a gardener for John Williams at Scorrier House. In 1837 he joined the firm of Exeter nurserymen, Veitch & Co., along with his brother, and three years later he was sent to South America as their first plant collector. He explored the Argentine, the Andes and the Chilean forests, and subsequently popularized *Auracaria imbricata*, the monkey puzzle tree, and *Abutilon vitifolium*. In 1845 he made a second visit and travelled through Chile and Patagonia, finding *Lapageria rosea*. Other notable discoveries were *Tropaeolum speciosum*, *Nothofagus obliqua, Embothrium coccineum* and *Berberis darwinii*. He also sent back *Saxegothaea conspicua* and *Podocarpus nubigenia*, which provide excellent timber.

His final expedition in 1849 took him to Douglas's conifers in the Sierra Nevada, California, where he remained even after his employment with Veitch ended in 1857. His successes here included the Californian nutmeg, *Torreya californica*, *Dicentra chrysantha* and *Ceanothus lobbianus* as well as *Abies grandis, A. concolor* and *Thuja plicata*. After a visit to the Calaveras Grove in 1853, he was also responsible for the successful introduction of the giant redwood, *Sequoiadendron giganteum*. William Lobb died of paralysis in San Francisco.

Thomas Lobb was employed in 1837 by Veitch at the same time as his brother, eventually becoming their chief collector in the East Indies. In 1843 he explored Java and the adjacent islands. His first consignment included *Phalaenopsis* and *Vanda* spp. His second commission, in 1848, took him to Northeast India, covering the Khasia Hills, Assam, Burma and Malaya. He sent back more orchids, including *Paphiopedilum villosum* and *Aerides fieldingii*, and the important shrubs *Berberis wallichiana, Hypericum hookerianum* and *Rhododendron veitchianum*. In 1860, having lost a leg in the Philippines, he retired to Devoran, Cornwall, where he died.

The genus *Lobbia* commemorates the brothers, Thomas having discovered the type species, *L. dependens*, near Singapore. Many other plants commemorate the brothers, Thomas especially, at specific rank, for example *Bulbophyllum lobbii*. Their memorial in Cornwall refers to 'two collectors of plants from foreign countries who rendered distinguished service to British Horticulture'.

**Lobelia** L. (For Matthias de l'Obel (1538–1616), botanist and physician to James 1.) Campanulaceae. Some 365 species of annual or perennial herbs, shrubs and treelets, often with a milky, acrid sap. Leaves alternate, simple, often sessile. Flowers in racemes or solitary, sometimes bracteolate; calyx tube sometimes gibbous, lobes erect; corolla slit to the base on the upper side, bilabiate, with the lower 3 lobes large and spreading, and the upper 2 lobes small and recurved; stamens inserted at base of corolla, anthers connate, ciliate; style glabrous. Capsule loculicidal, apically dehiscent, 2-valved. Tropical to temperate climates, particularly America.

CULTIVATION *Lobelia* exhibits a huge diversity of form from montane tree species such as *L. aberdarica*, through a range of handsome perennials of varying hardiness to small species commonly grown as annuals, *L. erinus*, *L. tenuior*, and *L. gracilis*. The annual Lobelias are commonly grown as edging and in windowboxes, with trailing kinds, such as the Fountain series, well suited to hanging baskets. Valued for their (typically) rich, deep blue flowers, modern selections have extended the colour range to include pure white (*L. erinus* 'White Lady'), carmine pink (*L. e.* 'Rosamond') and pale lilacs, as in *L. e.* 'Lilac Fountain'.

North American species such as annual *L. inflata*, and the aquatic *L. dortmanna*, grown in native plant collections and wild gardens in conditions that approximate to habitat, are valued for interest rather than outstanding beauty. *L. siphilitica*, *L. cardinalis*, the more tender *L. splendens* and the tetraploid hybrids derived from them, *L.* × *speciosa* group, include some of the most beautiful of garden perennials bearing tall strong spikes of bloom with luminous colour in late summer. They are suited to the herbaceous border, and especially to the moist soils at stream and pond side; although sometimes grown as marginal water-plants, they are generally short-lived when submerged.

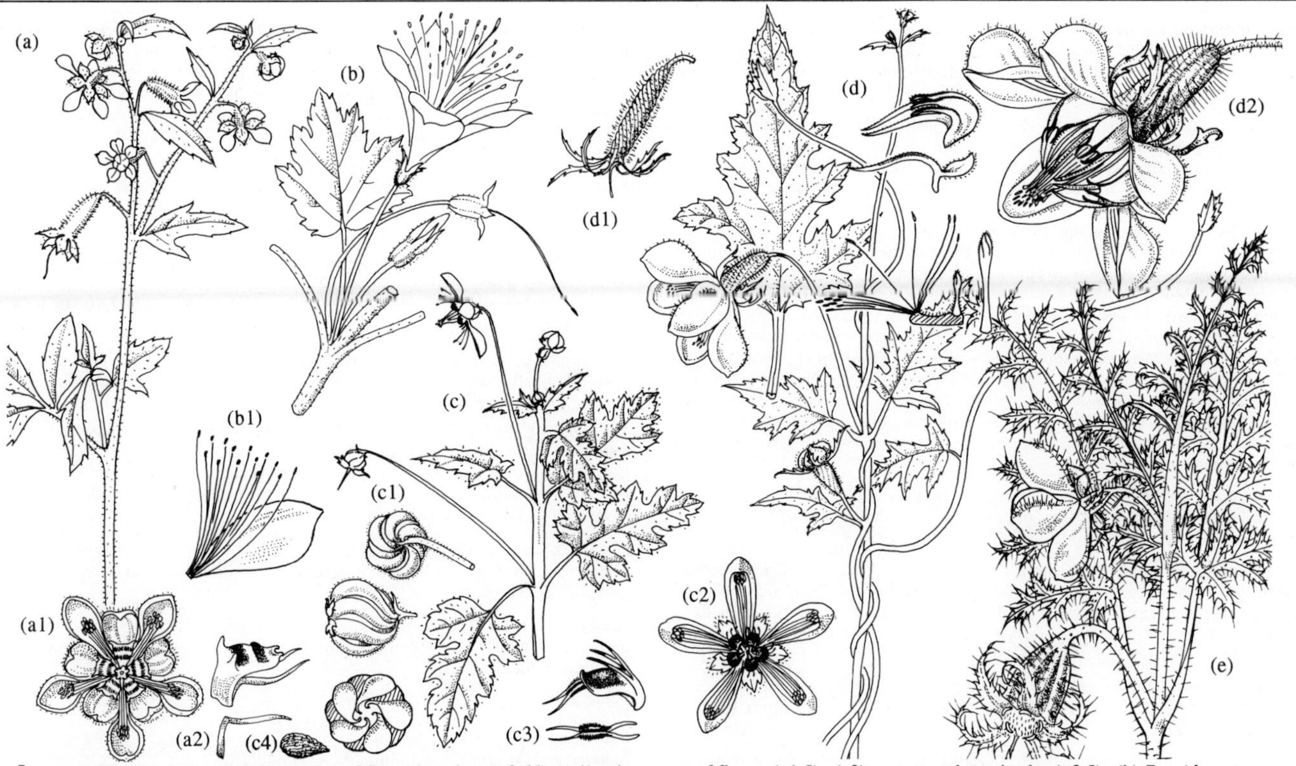


**Loasaceae** (a) *Loasa triphylla* portion of flowering plant (×0.66) (a1) enlargement of flower (×1.5) (a2) nectary and staminodes (×2.5) (b) *Eucnide bartonioides* portion of flowering plant (×0.66) (b1) petal showing stamens attached (×0.6) (c) *Blumenbachia insignis* portion of flowering plant (×0.6) (c1) separate drawings of fruit from two angles and sectioned to show chambers for seeds (c2) flower (×1.5) (c3) nectary and staminodes (×2) (c4) seed (×4) (d) *Caiophora lateritia* portion of flowering plant (×0.6) (d1) fruit (×0.6) (d2) flower (×1.5) with separate drawings of nectary and staminodes; section through part of flower showing stamens rising individually from within the petal while stigma is undeveloped; stigma when mature (e) *Caiophora* sp. flowering and fruiting plant (×0.6)

*L.* ×*speciosa* hybrids developed in Canada by Wray Bowden have markedly improved hardiness; a winter mulch of wheat straw is recommended where winter temperatures fall to −30°C/−22°F. The reputed tenderness of the perennial species appears to be derived in part from confusion in British gardens between the Mexican *L. splendens* and *L. cardinalis*, which occurs as far north as Ontario and New Brunswick, but also because, in regions with maritime mild winters, rosettes may by induced into premature growth in warm spells. This softer growth is almost inevitably more susceptible to frost. Other handsome perennials include *L. tupa*, with beautifully felted leaves, for a sunny position with winter protection at temperatures below −10°C/14°F, and the hardier, violet flowered *L.* ×. *girardii* group, needing straw mulch protection below about −15°C/5°F.

Grow in full sun or light shade in an open position, with some shelter from wind, in a permanently moist loamy soil, enriched with well-rotted manure in the autumn preceding planting; *L. siphilitica* and *L. cardinalis* occur in moist habitats and wilt quickly in dry conditions. *L.* ×*speciosa* hybrids tend to be gross feeders and on poorer soils benefit from fortnightly applications of 20:20:20 NPK fertilizer in spring and early summer; withhold nitrogen from mid summer onwards to allow growth to harden for the winter. Cut stems to ground level after flowering.

Propagate species by fresh seed in autumn. *Lobelia* spp. hybridize readily and may not come true. Divide rosettes in spring. Rosettes of more tender species like *L. fulgens* and *L. tupa* may be lifted and potted up in the cold frame as insurance against winter losses. *L. cardinalis* may be layered into moist sand, rooting at the nodes. Increase selected forms by leaf bud cuttings in mid summer; cut firm stems immediately above the node, with about 1cm/$\frac{1}{2}$in. of stem below, cut the stem longitudinally in half, and root in a mix of equal parts composted bark and sharp sand, under mist with bottom heat. Overwinter young plants in frost-free conditions.

Sow seed of annuals in late winter under glass at 15–18°C/60–65°F; lower temperatures to 10–13°C/50–55°F on germination and prick out seedlings in clumps, hardening off in the cold frame before setting out after danger of frost is passed. In mild damp winters crowns may be attacked by slugs and are susceptible to crown rots.

***L. aberdarica*** R.E. Fries & T.C.E. Fries. Narrowly columnar tree to 2.7m. Lvs to 35cm, crowded below infl., linear to linear-ovate. Fls in erect, terminal, bracteate, pyramidal panicles to 1.8m; cor. to 4cm, blue to white. Kenya, Uganda. Z10.

***L. amoena*** Michx. Perenn., to 1.2m. Lvs to 20cm, linear-lanceolate, dentate, glabrous. Fls in secund, many-fld racemes, pale blue. Summer. N America.

***L. anceps*** L. Perenn., stems prostrate. Lvs oblanceolate-obovate, narrower above. Fls axillary bracts entire; cor. blue, throat stained white or yellow. Summer. S Africa. Z9.

***L. aquatica*** Cham. Aquatic, prostrate herb; stems to 60cm, rooting at nodes or floating. Lvs to 2.5cm, lanceolate to oblong, subsessile to sessile. Fls solitary, axillary; cor. to 0.5cm, blue marked with white; anth. white-pubesc. W Indies, S America. Z10.

***L. cardinalis*** L. CARDINAL FLOWER; INDIAN PINK. Short-lived perenn. herb, to 90cm; stems usually glabrous, strongly tinged purple bronze. Lvs to 10cm, basal and rosulate or cauline and alternate, narrow-ovate to linear-oblong, acuminate, toothed. Fls in bracteate spikes; cor. to 5cm, bright scarlet. Capsule suborbicular. Summer. N America. 'Alba': fls white. 'Rosea': fls pink. Z3.

***L. comosa*** L. Glabrous perenn. herb to 60cm. Lvs to 5cm, linear to oblanceolate. Fls in lax spikes; cor. to 1cm, dark blue, throat dilated, tinged with yellow. Capsule obovoid. S Africa. Z9.

***L. coronopifolia*** L. Decumbent perenn. herb. Lvs narrow-ovate, irregularly dentate. Fls few, long pedicellate, clear blue. Summer. S Africa. Z9.

***L. davidii*** Franch. Small, erect shrub to 90cm. Lvs to 10cm, linear-elliptic to narrow-ovate, doubly serrate to serrulate, short-petiolate. Fls in long racemes; bracts foliaceous; cor. lobes to 2.5cm, linear-lanceolate, purple to violet; anth. bright blue. China, Burma.

***L. dortmanna*** L. WATER LOBELIA. Aquatic, glabrous, perenn. herb to 60cm; stems hollow, almost leafless. Basal lvs rosulate, oblong, sessile. Fls few, pendulous, hold above water in racemes; cal. lobes oblong; cor. to 2cm, pale mauve. Summer. N America, W Europe. Z4.

***L. erinus*** L. EDGING LOBELIA. Small perenn. herb; branches 8–15cm, slender, sprawling then ascending or cascading. Lower lvs ovate to obovate, toothed, petiolate, stem lvs linear, subsessile. Fls in lax spikes; cor. to 2cm, throat yellow to white, tube blue to violet; anth. exserted, blue. Summer. S Africa. 'Alba': fls white. 'Blue Moon': fls dark violet-blue. 'Blue Stone': fls intense sky-blue. Cascade Mixed: habit trailing; fls violet through blue to pink and white. 'Compacta': habit low, dense. 'Crystal Palace': habit very dwarf, densely branched; lvs obovate, minute; fls numerous, deep blue. 'Emperor William': fls globose, vivid blue. 'Erecta': habit erect, compact. 'Gracilis': stems slender. 'Kathleen Mallard': fls double, blue. 'Mrs Clibran Improved': fls deep blue with a white centre. 'Pendula': stems drooping. 'Pink Flamingo': habit erect, branching; fls bright pink. 'Pumila': habit dwarf. 'Rosamund': fls deep cherry-red with a white centre. 'Rosea': fls pink-violet. Royal Hybrids: habit compact, prostrate; fls blue or white. 'Sapphire': habit trailing; fls glossy deep blue with a white centre. 'Snowball': fls snow-white, occasionally pale blue. 'Speciosa': fls large, blue. 'Waverly Blue': habit compact; fls large, sky-blue. 'White Cascade': habit trailing; fls pure white.

***L. fenestralis*** Cav. Upright annual or perenn. herb, to 60cm. Lvs to 7cm, linear, serrate. Fls in spikes; cor. to 1cm, pubesc., blue, violet or white. Texas to New Mexico and Arizona south to Mexico. Z9.

***L. ×gerardii*** Chabanne ex Nicholas. *(L. cardinalis × L. siphilitica.)* Robust perenn., to 1.5m. Lvs ovate to elliptic in a basal rosette. Fls in dense, large racemes; cal. ciliate; cor. violet tinged with pink, to purple, lower lip with 2 deltoid white marks. Summer. Garden origin. 'Rosenkavalier': fls pure pink. 'Vedrariensis': lvs dark green, tinged red, fls dark violet. Z7.

***L. glandulosa*** Walter. Perenn., to 1.3m. Lvs narrow-ovate to linear, thickly dentate, glabrous, bright green. Fls blue in a lax raceme, sometimes secund. Autumn. S US. Z9.

***L. gracilis*** Andrews. Annual, to 60cm, glabrous. Lvs to 2cm, linear-ovate to oblong. Fls in lax, secund racemes; cor. to 1cm, upper lip densely pubesc., deep blue, throat yellow. Summer. S Australia.

***L. heterophylla*** Labill. non Lindl. Erect annual to 40cm. Lvs linear to filiform, entire, dentate, or pinnatisect. Fls in a secund raceme; bracteoles lanceolate; cal. scabrous, ribbed, lobes narrow-deltoid to subulate; cor. blue, often yellow in throat. Capsule obliquely ellipsoid, finely pubesc. Autumn and winter. Australia.

***L. holstii*** Engl. Perenn., ascending to 30cm. Lvs to 4cm, crowded near base, narrowly ovate, bluntly dentate, short-petiolate. Fls in lax raceme, long-pedicellate; cor. bilabiate, tube cylindric, larger lip 3-lobed, smaller lip 2-lobed, lobes obovate-oblanceolate to lanceolate-acuminate. Autumn. Tropical E Africa. Z10.

***L. ilicifolia*** Ker-Gawl. Prostrate perenn. to 15cm. Lvs narrow-ovate, remotely and deeply dentate, glabrous. Fls solitary, axillary; cor. pink inverted. Summer. S Africa. Z9.

***L. inflata*** L. INDIAN TOBACCO. Spreading, pubesc. annual, to 90cm. Lvs to 6cm, oblong, crenate to serrate. Fls in loose racemes; cal. inflated after anthesis; cor. to 1cm, blue, purple or tinged with pink. Summer–autumn. N America.

***L. kalmii*** L. Prostrate or creeping to upright perenn., to 30cm. Lower lvs obovate to spathulate, upper lvs linear to filiform. Fls in loose spikes, pedicels bracteate; cor. to 1cm, blue with prominent white eye, or all white. Summer. N America. Z4.

***L. laxiflora*** HBK. Perenn. herb or shrub to 90cm, branching, finely pubesc. Lvs to 8cm, lanceolate to elliptic, acuminate, serrate. Fls pendulous, long-pedicellate, bracteate; cor. red and/or yellow; anthers grey, tufted to hispid. Summer. Arizona, Mexico, Colombia. Z9.

***L. linnaeoides*** (Hook. f.) Petrie. Glabrous, perenn. herb; stems prostrate, slender. Lvs 0.8cm, orbicular, coarsely serrate-sinuate in upper half, thick, usually subsessile. Fls on slender pedicels; cal. split to almost half way, lobes narrow deltoid, acuminate; cor. elongated, lobes obovate to linear-oblong, white to pale blue, tinged with purple. New Zealand. Z8.

***L. pinifolia*** L. Shrub, to 60cm. Lvs to 2.5cm, many, filiform. Fls in narrow spikes; cor. blue-violet or occasionally pale pink; anth. included, brown, pubesc. S Africa. Z9.

***L. sessilifolia*** Lamb. Glabrous perenn. to 60cm; stems slender, simple, erect, leafy. Lower lvs lanceolate, attenuate, shallowly dentate, upper lvs gradually smaller, becoming bracteate, sessile. Fls in dense terminal spikes; cor. bilabiate, lobed to middle, violet. Summer. Taiwan, Korea, Manchuria, Japan. Z5.

***L. siphilitica*** L. GREAT LOBELIA; BLUE CARDINAL FLOWER. Perenn. herb to 60cm; stems erect, very leafy. Lvs to 10cm, ovate-lanceolate, somewhat pubesc., irregularly dentate, light green. Fls in dense spikes; pedicels with foliaceous bracts; cal. lobes with basal auricles; cor. to 2.5cm, blue. Summer–autumn. E US. 'Alba': fls white. 'Nana': habit rather smaller; fls blue. 'Nana Alba': habit compact; fls white. Z5.

***L. ×speciosa*** Sweet. *(L. cardinalis × L. splendens × L. siphilitica.)* Hispid perenn. Lvs oblong-obovate, acuminate, sessile. Cal. lobes with short basal auricles; cor. to 3cm, red or mauve tinged with purple or violet. Garden origin. 'Bees Flame': lvs bronze-red; fls scarlet. 'Brightness': fls brilliant red. 'Dark Crusader': fls blood-red. 'Jack McMasters': fls mauve. 'Queen Victoria': lvs beetroot-red; fls vivid red. 'Russian Princess': lvs tinged red; fls bright purple. 'Will Scarlet': lvs tinged red; fls bright scarlet. Z3.

***L. spicata*** Lam. PALE SPIKE. Perenn. or bienn., simple or branched, to 1.2m. Like *L. inflata*, but stems finely pubesc. at base; cal. partially dilated. N America (New Brunswick to Minnesota). Z4.

***L. splendens*** Willd. Perenn., closely related to *L. cardinalis*, but more slender in habit; lvs to 15cm, narrower, usually linear, subsessile; infl. often secund, glabrous; fls blood red. Texas, Mexico. 'Illumination': lvs dark green; fls scarlet, borne in large spikes. Z8.

***L. subnuda*** Benth. Annual. Lvs rosulate, cordate-lanceolate, pinnatifid, tinged purple beneath, veins prominent, green. Fls long-pedicellate, pale blue in lax racemes. Mexico. Z9.

***L. tenuior*** R. Br. Diffuse annual or perenn. herb to 60cm. Lower lvs small, oblong-obovate, deeply dentate, upper lvs narrower, pinnatifid to entire. Fls in loose racemes or panicles; cal. tube narrow; cor. lobes obovate, bright blue, throat with a white or yellow eye. Autumn. W Australia. 'Blue Wings': fls very numerous, cobalt-blue. Z9.

***L. tomentosa*** L. f. Perenn. shrublet, to 50cm, Lvs pinnatifid, lobes bifurcate, tomentose, involute. Fls blue to purple; cor. throat usually purple, hispidulous. Autumn. S Africa. Z9.

***L. tupa*** L. Perenn. to 2m; stems upright, robust, simple. Lvs to 30cm, lanceolate, decurrent, white to pale green velutinous. fls in terminal spikes, large, brick red. Autumn. Chile. Z8.

***L. angulata*** Forst. f. See *Pratia angulata*.
***L. campanulata*** Lam. See *Monopsis campanulata*.
***L. fulgens*** Hemsl. See *L. splendens*.
***L. heterophylla*** Lindl. non Labill. See *L. tenuior*.
***L. perpusilla*** Hook. f. See *Pratia perpusilla*.
***L. physaloides*** (A. Cunn.) Hook. f. See *Pratia physaloides*.
***L. plumieri*** L. See *Scaevola plumieri*.
***L. pratiana*** Gaudich. See *Pratia repens*.
***L. ramosa*** Benth. See *L. tenuior*.
***L. repens*** Thunb. See *Pratia repens*.
***L. triquetra*** L. See *L. comosa*.
For further synonymy see *Pratia*.

## Lobivia Britt. & Rose.

***L. allegraiana*** Backeb. See *Echinopsis hertrichiana*.
***L. andalgalensis*** (F.A. Weber ex Schum.) Britt. & Rose. See *Echinopsis huascha*.
***L. arachnacantha*** Buining & Ritter. See *Echinopsis arachnacantha*.
***L. backebergii*** (Werderm. ex Backeb.) Backeb. See *Echinopsis backebergii*.
***L. binghamiana*** Backeb. See *Echinopsis hertrichiana*.
***L. boliviensis*** Britt. & Rose. See *Echinopsis pentlandii*.
***L. breviflora*** Backeb. See *Echinopsis sanguiniflora*.
***L. bruchii*** Britt. & Rose. See *Echinopsis bruchii*.
***L. caespitosa*** Purpus. See *Echinopsis maximiliana*.
***L. chlorogona*** Wessner. See *Rebutia famatinensis*.
***L. chorrillosensis*** Rausch. See *Echinopsis haematantha*.
***L. chrysantha*** (Werderm.) Backeb. See *Echinopsis chrysantha*.
***L. chrysochete*** (Werderm.) Wessner. See *Echinopsis chrysochete*.
***L. cinnabarina*** (Hook.) Britt. & Rose. See *Echinopsis cinnabarina*.
***L. corbula*** Britt. & Rose. See *Echinopsis maximiliana*.
***L. cylindrica*** Backeb. See *Echinopsis aurea*.
***L. densispina*** (Werderm.) Wessner. See *Echinopsis kuehnrichii*.
***L. drijveriana*** Backeb. See *Echinopsis kuehnrichii*.
***L. ducis-pauli*** misapplied. See *Echinopsis longispina*.
***L. elongata*** Backeb. See *Echinopsis haematantha*.
***L. famatimensis*** (Speg.) Britt. & Rose. See *Rebutia famatinensis*.
***L. ferox*** Britt. & Rose. See *Echinopsis ferox*.
***L. formosa*** (Pfeiff.) Dodds. See *Echinopsis formosa*.
***L. glauca*** Rausch. See *Echinopsis marsoneri*.
***L. grandiflora*** Britt. & Rose. See *Echinopsis huascha*.
***L. grandis*** Britt. & Rose. See *Echinopsis bruchii*.
***L. grandis*** (Britt. & Rose) Backeb. See *Echinopsis bruchii*.
***L. haematantha*** (Speg.) Britt. & Rose. See *Echinopsis haematantha*.
***L. hermanniana*** Backeb. See *Echinopsis maximiliana*.
***L. higginsiana*** Backeb. See *Echinopsis pentlandii*.
***L. hualfinensis*** Rausch. See *Echinopsis haematantha*.
***L. huascha*** (F.A. Weber) W.T. Marshall. See *Echinopsis huascha*.
***L. incaiaca*** Backeb. See *Echinopsis hertrichiana*.
***L. jajoiana*** Backeb. See *Echinopsis marsoneri*.
***L. janseniana*** Backeb. See *Echinopsis chrysantha*.
***L. johnsoniana*** Backeb. See *Echinopsis pentlandii*.
***L. kieslingii*** Rausch. See *Echinopsis formosa*.
***L. kuehnrichii*** Fric. See *Echinopsis kuehnrichii*.

***L. kupperiana*** Backeb. See *Echinopsis lateritia*.
***L. larae*** Cárdenas. See *Echinopsis pentlandii*.
***L. lateritia*** (Gürke) Britt. & Rose. See *Echinopsis lateritia*.
***L. longispina*** Britt. & Rose. See *Echinopsis longispina*.
***L. maximiliana*** (Heyder ex A. Dietr.) Backeb. See *Echinopsis maximiliana*.
***L. muhriae*** Backeb. See *Echinopsis marsoneri*.
***L. nealeana*** Backeb. See *Echinopsis saltensis*.
***L. neohaageana*** Backeb. See *Rebutia pygmaea*.
***L. orurensis*** Backeb. See *Rebutia pygmaea*.
***L. pampana*** Britt. & Rose. See *Echinopsis pampana*.
***L. peclardiana*** Krainz. See *Echinopsis tiegeliana*.
***L. pectinata*** Backeb. See *Rebutia pygmaea*.
***L. pentlandii*** (Hook.) Britt. & Rose. See *Echinopsis pentlandii*.
***L. polycephala*** Backeb. See *Echinopsis sanguiniflora*.
***L. pseudocachensis*** Backeb. See *Echinopsis saltensis*.
***L. pugionacantha*** (Rose & Boed.) Backeb. See *Echinopsis pugionacantha*.
***L. pygmaea*** (R.E. Fries) Backeb. See *Rebutia pygmaea*.
***L. raphidacantha*** Backeb. See *Echinopsis pentlandii*.
***L. rebutioides*** Backeb. See *Echinopsis haematantha*.
***L. rossii*** (Boed.) Backeb. & F. Knuth. See *Echinopsis pugionacantha*.
***L. saltensis*** (Speg.) Britt. & Rose. See *Echinopsis saltensis*.
***L. sanguiniflora*** Backeb. See *Echinopsis sanguiniflora*.
***L. schieliana*** Backeb. See *Echinopsis schieliana*.
***L. schreiteri*** Cast. See *Echinopsis schreiteri*.
***L. silvestrii*** (Speg.) G. Rowley. See *Echinopsis chamaecereus*.
***L. steinmannii*** (Solms-Laubach) Backeb. See *Rebutia steinmannii*.
***L. sublimiflora*** Backeb. ex Wessner. See *Echinopsis haematantha*.
***L. tegeleriana*** Backeb. See *Echinopsis tegeleriana*.
***L. tiegeliana*** Wessner. See *Echinopsis tiegeliana*.
***L. varians*** Backeb. See *Echinopsis pentlandii*.
***L. vatteri*** Krainz. See *Echinopsis marsoneri*.
***L. walteri*** Kiesling. See *Echinopsis walteri*.
***L. walterspielii*** Boed. See *Echinopsis cinnabarina*.
***L. wegheiana*** Backeb. See *Echinopsis pentlandii*.
***L. westii*** Hutchison. See *Echinopsis maximiliana*.

**Lobularia** Desv. (Diminutive of Lat. *lobus*, referring to the small fruit.) Cruciferae. 5 species of annual or perennial hairy herbs. Leaves narrow, simple, entire. Flowers scented in compact terminal racemes, white; sepals 4; petals 4, ovate to spathulate, short-clawed; stamens 6, free. Fruit a silique, compressed elliptic to round. North temperate regions. Closely related to *Alyssum*.

CULTIVATION *L. maritima* occurs in dry, sunny, rocky and sandy habitats, especially on the coast. As a wild flower, it has a sprawling habit and may reach 30cm/12in. in height; it is better known in cultivation in dwarf colour selections ranging from pure white through pinks to deep violets, many of which retain the sweet fragrance of the type. Flowering profusely from early summer until autumn, *Lobularia* spp. are commonly used in bedding and edging, as temporary groundcover, and on dry walls. Double-flowered and variegated forms are sometimes grown as pot plants in the cold glasshouse. All are tolerant of maritime conditions.

Grow in full sun, in well-drained soils. Sow seed at 10–13°C/50–55°F, in later winter/early spring, and harden off in the cold frame before planting out in spring. Alternatively, sow thinly *in situ* in spring. Deadheading by trimming with scissors prolongs flowering. Plants may be attacked by slugs and flea beetles (*Phyllotreta* spp.), crucifer downy mildew (*Peronospora parasitica*), crucifer white blister (*Albugo candida*) and club root (*Plasmodioiphora brassicae*).

***L. maritima*** (L.) Desv. SWEET ALISON; SWEET ALYSSUM. Annual or perenn., 10–55cm. Stem much-branched from base. Lvs 8–35×1–4mm, linear, long drawn-out at base, somewhat silvery. Racemes elongating in fruit, to 18cm; pedicels to 10mm, horizontal to erect. Fls fragrant; sep. 1–5mm, hairy; pet. to 3.5mm, blade rounded. Fr. 2.5–3mm, elliptic; seed pale brown. S Europe, widely naturalized. Z7. 'Carpet of Snow': ground-hugging, to 10cm, to 15cm diam.; fls white. 'Little Dorrit': to 10cm; fls white. 'Navy Blue': to 10cm; fls deep purple. 'New Carpet of Snow': compact, to 10cm; fls pure white, free-flowering. 'Oriental Nights': spreading, to 10cm; fls rich purple, fragrant; early-flowering. 'Rosie O'Day': to 10cm, wide-spreading to 25cm diam.; fls rose-pink, later pink, long-lasting, fragrant. 'Royal Carpet': to 10cm; fls deep purple, fragrant. 'Snow Crystals': mound-forming, to 25cm diam.; fls bright white, florets double standard size (tetraploid). 'Sweet White': to 10cm; fls white, honey-scented. 'Wonderland Rose': compact, low-spreading; fls bold purple; early-flowering. 'Wonderland White': compact, low spreading; fls white; early-flowering.

For synonymy see *Alyssum* and *Clypeola*.

**Lockhartia** Hook. (For David Lockhart (fl.1827) Superintendent of the Trinidad Botanical Garden.) Orchidaceae. Some 30 species of epiphytic orchids. Rhizome short. Pseudobulbs absent. Stems simple, elongate, erect or pendent, leafy. Leaves numerous, distichous, erect or spreading, bases overlapping, equitant. Inflorescence a raceme or a panicle, lateral or terminal, few- to many-flowered; flowers small, mostly yellow to white; sepals subequal, free, spreading or reflexed; petals usually larger than sepals, otherwise similar; lip entire to 3(–5)-lobed, lateral lobes linear to spathulate, incurved or recurved, midlobe lobulate, disc callose; column stout, short, footless, bialate or biauriculate, anther terminal, operculate, incumbent, pollinia 2, waxy. Tropical America. Z10.

CULTIVATION Epiphytes for bright, humid positions in the intermediate house, distinguished by their slender stems closely clothed with leaves and bright, *Oncidium*-like axillary flowers. Establish in an open bark mix with additional rockwool or sphagnum in small pans or baskets. Syringe regularly when in growth. Decrease water supplies a little over the winter months. Propagate by division.

***L. acuta*** (Lindl.) Rchb. f. Lvs to 3×1cm, ovate-triangular, subacute or apiculate, coriaceous. Infl. to 9cm, paniculate, many-fld; peduncle filiform; fls to 1cm diam., white or pale yellow, sometimes marked pale brown; sep. to 4×3mm, ovate, obtuse, spreading; pet. to 5×3mm, elliptic-oblong, obtuse; lip to 6×4mm, yellow marked pale brown, lateral lobes linear, obtuse, midlobe subquadrate, obtuse, emarginate; callus 2-ridged, pilose, base tuberculate; column white, undulate, wings triangular. Panama, Trinidad, Venezuela, Colombia.

***L. amoena*** Endress & Rchb. f. Stems to 40×2.5cm, erect or pendent, laterally compressed. Lvs to 3.5×1cm, coriaceous, ovate-triangular, fleshy, subacute. Infl. to 3cm, a few-fld panicle; fls to 2cm; sep. and pet. bright yellow, sep. to 6×4mm, dorsal sep. ovate, obtuse, minutely apiculate, slightly reflexed, lateral sep. elliptic-lanceolate, subacute, strongly reflexed, pet. to 7×4mm, elliptic-oblong, obtuse, reflexed; lip to 10×8mm, bright yellow, slightly marked red-brown at base, complex, lateral lobes linear-ligulate, acute, incurved, midlobe subquadrate, truncate, undulate, 4-lobulate, basal lobules strongly reflexed, callus linear, slightly papillose; column with spreading wings. Costa Rica, Panama.

***L. elegans*** Hook. Stems to 30cm, erect to pendent, numerous. Lvs to 20×6mm, obliquely triangular, obtuse, subtruncate or retuse, coriaceous. Infl. usually an arching lateral raceme, 1- to many-fld; sep. and pet. pale yellow, sep. to 5×3mm, elliptic to ovate, apiculate, deeply concave, pet. to 5×3mm, obliquely ovate, obtuse to apiculate, slightly concave; lip to 6×5mm, yellow slightly marked purple-maroon, conspicuously 3-lobed, lateral lobes triangular, acute to obtuse, subentire, midlobe large, oblong-ligulate, rounded to emarginate, undulate, callus ligulate, obtuse or rounded, with 4 or 5 basal tubercles; column yellow, to 2mm, wings 2, subquadrate, denticulate. Colombia, Venezuela, Trinidad, Brazil.

***L. lunifera*** (Lindl.) Rchb. f. Stems to 35cm, slender, erect. Lvs to 20×7mm, narrowly triangular-ligulate, subtruncate, subcoriaceous, rigid. Infl. usually terminal, a raceme, 1- to few-fld, erect to arching; fls long-stalked; sep. and pet. golden yellow, sep. to 6×5mm, broadly obovate to oblong, acute or rounded, reflexed, pet. to 5×3mm, oblong, obtuse or retuse; lip to 8×4mm, golden yellow finely spotted purple, spreading, sessile, lateral lobes to 4mm, linear, acute, erect, midlobe subquadrate, obscurely 4-lobulate, emarginate, callus verrucose; column to 2mm, yellow spotted purple, erect, wings 2, dentate. Brazil.

***L. micrantha*** Rchb. f. Stems to 40cm, erect to pendent. Lvs to 2×1cm, narrowly triangular, coriaceous, obliquely truncate or obtuse. Infl. a raceme or a panicle, subterminal, 1- to few-fld; fls small, yellow; sep. to 4×3mm, ovate to elliptic, concave, acute, apiculate; pet. to 4×2mm, ovate to elliptic-ovate, obtuse; lip to 5×5mm, lateral lobes basal, linear-oblong or linear-ligulate, acute or obtuse, spreading or reflexed, midlobe subrhombic to obovate, deeply retuse, callus slightly concave, sometimes cleft; column short, wings 2, triangular to subquadrate. Nicaragua to Surinam, Brazil.

***L. oerstedii*** Rchb. f. Stems to 45cm, erect. Lvs to 4cm, triangular, acute to obtuse, suberect. Infl. to 3.5cm, a pendent, axillary raceme, 1- to several-fld; fls to 2cm, bright yellow; sep. to 8×5mm, narrowly ovate to suborbicular, rounded, reflexed, concave; pet. to 9×5mm, broadly elliptic to subquadrate, truncate, reflexed; lip to 14×14mm, bright yellow spotted and barred dark red below, complex, 5-lobed, basal lobes elliptic, apex denticulate, undulate, central lobes ovate-triangular, erect, broadly obtuse, apical lobe bilobulate, undulate, callus to 7×4mm, light brown, quadrate, pilose, with 4 central papillose keels; column to 4mm, fleshy, wings 2, subquadrate, denticulate, spotted red. Mexico to Panama.

***L. pittieri*** Schltr. Stems to 20×4.5cm. Lvs to 3.5×1cm, narrowly triangular to linear-lanceolate, acute to acuminate. Infl. axillary, 1-fld; fls to 1.5cm diam., yellow to yellow-orange; sep. to 5×2mm, elliptic-lanceolate, minutely apiculate; pet. to 5×3mm, suborbicular to oblong-elliptic, acute to obtuse; lip to 8×6mm, oblong-subquadrate, deeply emarginate, entire to obscurely 3-lobed, disc with an ovate-oblong callus, orange, slightly papillose, apex thickened, with an erect, median spur. Costa Rica, Panama, British Honduras.

***L. pallida*** Rchb. f. See *L. acuta*.
***L. robusta*** (Batem.) Schltr. See *L. oerstedii*.
For further synonymy see *Fernandezia*.

**Loddiges, Conrad** (*c*1739–1826). Nurseryman. Loddiges came to London from Hanover as a young man to work as a gardener. In 1771 he bought the Hackney garden of John Busch and started to develop a nursery that was to become one of the most famous most comprehensive in England, especially for rare and exotic plants.

At the centre of the Loddiges nursery was a huge domed iron-ribbed glass palm-house containing a vast collection of tropical exotics. This great hothouse was the largest in the world when it was built in 1817, heated by steam and watered by an overhead sprinkler system invented by Loddiges himself. There were also some twenty other hothouses and a number of greenhouses situated in the extensive grounds. The nursery was renowned in its day for its vast collection of palms (280 species by 1845), orchids and other tender plants, as well as camellias, yuccas, roses, willows, heaths, rhododendrons and azaleas. Plants from such eminent collectors as Bartram and Michaux were introduced at the nursery. The scale and profitability of Messrs Loddiges' nursery at Hackney reflected the growing demand for exotic plants in the early 19th century.

Loddiges managed the nursery with his two sons, William and George, who continued to run it after his death and also corresponded with plant collectors including James Drummond and Allan Cunningham. The latter referred to 'those truly excellent men, the Messrs Loddiges'. Their first catalogue appeared in 1777 and by 1823 was in its 13th edition. Also appearing regularly, and illustrating many of the plants in the garden, was the periodical the *Botanical Cabinet* (1817–1834), many of the 2000 drawings being the work of Conrad's son, George Loddiges (1784–1846), who 'conducted' (edited) the periodical from 1817 until 34.

**Loder, Gerald Walter Erskine**, 1st Lord Wakehurst (1861–1936). Plantsman and administrator. Educated at Eton and Trinity College, Cambridge, he was called to the Bar in 1888 and served as Conservative MP for Brighton from 1889 to 1905. In 1903 he bought Wakehurst Place, near Ardingly in Sussex, a beautiful Elizabethan house with extensive gardens, and a particularly mild climate. Here he indulged his passion for horticulture, creating formal gardens, parkland, woodland and planting trees and rare shrubs. In 1914 a 20-acre pinetum was laid out. Through his dedication he established Wakehurst as one of the most important collections of rare plants in Britain. He was especially interested in shrubs from New Zealand, conifers, and rhododendrons recently introduced from China, Northern Burma and Tibet. In 1921 he presented the Loder Cup to the Royal Horticultural Society to commemorate his brother Sir Edmund Giles Loder (1849–1920), who had had notable success in growing hybrid rhododendrons and conifers at Leonardslee. His collection of shrubs from New Zealand and other parts of Australasia was unique and he presented a cup to be awarded annually in New Zealand for the best collection of native plants.

Loder was involved in many horticultural organizations, serving on the Council of the Royal Horticultural Society from 1920 onwards and holding the Presidency from 1929 to 1931, as successor to Lord Lambourne. He resigned when appointed Chairman of the Southern Railway Company. He was elected Fellow of the Linnean Society in 1914, served on its council, and was Vice-President. Loder's interest in trees, particularly conifers, led to his election as President of the Royal Arboricultural Society from 1926 to 1927 and he was closely involved in the 1931 Conifer Conference. He was awarded the Royal Horticultural Society's Victoria Medal of Honour in 1936. He donated plants freely from his garden, especially during Kew's establishment of a National Pinetum at Bedgebury. Loder was raised to the peerage in 1934 and died at Wakehurst.

Wakehurst Place came under the direction of the Royal Botanic Gardens, Kew, in 1968. He was awarded the Royal Horticultural Society Victoria Medal of Honour in 1967, as was his wife in 1976.

**Lodoicea** Comm. ex DC. SEYCHELLES NUT; COCO DE MER; DOUBLE COCONUT. (For Louis XV of France (1710–1774).) Palmae. 1 species, a pleonanthic, dioecious palm, solitary-stemmed, to 30m. Trunk slightly swollen at base, faintly ringed. Leaves to 7m, costapalmate, rigid, marcescent; sheath splitting opposite petiole, a triangular hole forming in petiole base; petiole 4m, grooved above, rounded and black-dotted beneath, tomentose; costa acuminate, extending almost to end of blade; blade base cuneate, segments single-fold, shallowly emarginate, apices pendent, shiny above, dull and tomentose along ridges beneath. Inflorescences interfoliar, pendent, enclosed in 2 bracts; male flowers on rigid rachillae to 2m, sepals 3, connate, corolla lobes 3, tips overlapping, stamens 17–22; female flowers to 10cm, on flexuous spikes to 70cm, one per pit, sessile, ovoid, with 2 cupular bracts at base, sepals 3, free, coriaceous, imbricate, petals as sepals, stigmas 3, stout reflexed. Fruit to 50cm, ovoid-cordate, bilobed, resembling a giant wooden heart or the rear of a large woman, 1–3 seeded. Seychelles. Z10.

CULTIVATION Suitable for outdoor cultivation only in tropical climates, *L. maldivica* is too large for indoor cultivation in all but the largest hothouse. It is remarkable however for the size of its seed, contained in fruits which may weight 18kg/40lbs and more. On germination, the radicle may reach a length of almost one metre before the plumule emerges and constriction of either may result in death of the seedling. Success is most likely by germinating the seed in a clay drain pipe, or in one pot stacked upon another so that the radicle may push through into the bottom pot; keep in warm dark and moist conditions and pot on into a fertile loam-based mix with additional leafmould. Water plentifully and maintain high humidity at a temperature of 18°C/65°F.

***L. maldivica*** (Gmel.) Pers. As for the genus.

***L. sechellarum*** Labill. See *L. maldivica*.
For further synonymy see *Coco*.

**Logania** R. Br. (For James Logan (1674–1751), Irish writer botanist, William Penn's agent in US and Governor of Pennsylvania.) Loganiaceae. About 20 species of herbs or subshrubs, or rarely much-branched, spreading, tufted shrubs. Leaves opposite, entire; stipules occasionally present, narrow and small. Inflorescence a terminal or axillary cyme or head, or flowers solitary; flowers white or pink, 5- or sometimes 4-parted, often small; corolla campanulate or salverform, tube cylindrical. Fruit a capsule. New Zealand, Australia, New Caledonia. Z9.

CULTIVATION *L. populifolia*, from coastal woodland on limestone, and *L. albidiflora*, which occurs in forest on sandstone soils, are grown primarily for their sometimes sweetly scented flowers produced in spring; those of *L. albidiflora* last well when cut. In essentially frost-free zones, grow in well-drained but moisture-retentive soils in part shade. In zones with hot dry summers, in soils that are dry or impeccably drained, *L. albidiflora* has survived temperatures to −7°C/20°F. Under glass, grow in bright filtered light in a sandy, loam-based medium with additional leafmould or equivalent; water moderately when in growth and maintain a winter minimum of 5–7°C/40–45°F. Propagate by seed or by semi-ripe cuttings in sharp sand in a closed case.

***L. albidiflora*** (Andrews) Druce. To 1m. Lvs lanceolate, both ends narrowed, smooth; stipules very slender. Infl. axillary panicles, shorter than lvs; fls white. Spring–early summer. Australia.

***L. populifolia*** (Lam.) Leeuwenb. Erect shrub to 2m+, glabrous. Lvs elliptic, obovate or lanceolate, tips acuminate, 2.5–8×1–3.5cm, lateral veins conspicuous. Infl. leafy panicles of long-pedunculate cymes; fls small, white; cal. 2mm, black-green; cor. 5mm. Fr. rounded, to 6mm, apically pointed. W & S Australia.

***L. floribunda*** R. Br. See *L. albidiflora*.
***L. latifolia*** R. Br. See *L. populifolia*.

*L. longifolia* R. Br. See *L. populifolia*.
*L. vaginalis* (Labill.) F.J. Muell. See *L. populifolia*.

**LOGANIACEAE** C. Mart. (inc. Buddlejaceae & Retziaceae). BUDDLEJA FAMILY. Dicot. 29 genera and 600 species of trees, shrubs, lianes and herbs, sometimes accumulating aluminium, often with alkaloids. Leaves opposite, rarely spiral, simple, rarely ternate, entire or lobed; stipules present, sometimes with ocrea. Flowers usually bisexual, regular, in cymes, sometimes solitary; calyx 4 or 5 free sepals; corolla 4 or 5 (–16) petals, united into a tube; stamens inserted on corolla tube, equal in number to petals and usually alternate with them; ovary superior, sometimes half inferior, usually of 2 fused carpels, with as many locules; style terminal, sometimes apically lobed; ovules 2-numerous on axile placentas. Fruit a capsule, berry or drupe; seeds 1-numerous, sometimes winged; endosperm fleshy, starchy or horny. Mainly tropical, few temperate. Strychnine is obtained from *Strychnos*, which also yields timber. *Anthocleista, Buddleja, Desfontainia, Fagraea, Gelsemium, Geniostoma, Logania, Nuxia, Spigelia, Strychnos*.

**Loiseleuria** Desv. (For Jean Louise August Loiseleur-Deslongchamps (Loiseleur), (1774–1849), physician and botanist.) Ericaceae. 1 species, a small evergreen shrub, 7.5–20cm. Stems prostrate, forming expansive mats. Leaves 4–12×2–3mm, crowded, usually opposite, oval to oblong, entire, apex blunt, base tapered, margins strongly revolute, leathery, glossy glabrous above, midveins impressed, glabrous, glaucescent or tomentose beneath, midvein glabrous, conspicuous; petioles short, ascending, canescent. Flowers solitary or 2–5 in small, terminal, umbellate clusters; pedicels 2–10mm, glabrous, erect; bracts coriaceous, persistent, sharp-tipped; calyx campanulate, purple-tinted, deeply 5-lobed, half corolla length; corolla 4×6mm, rose-pink or white tinted rose, broadly campanulate to cupped, lobes 4–5, spreading, equalling corolla tube, triangular-ovate, overlapping in bud; stamens 5, alternate with corolla lobes, anthers dehiscing through slits (not through pores, as in *Rhododendron*); style persistent, shorter than fruit. Fruit a 2–3-celled dry capsule, 3–4mm, globose-ovoid, red. Spring–early summer. N America, Europe, Asia, in high alpine and subarctic regions. Z2.

CULTIVATION A creeping evergreen forming mats or mounds of foliage, *Loiseleuria* is grown for its rose-pink flowers carried at the stem tips in late spring and early summer, and is well suited to cool, damp positions on the rock garden. It is sometimes grown in the alpine house or frame, but flowers less freely when pot-grown. It is hardy at least to −30°C/−22°F, but thrives only in zones with cool humid summers. Grow in good light in moist but sharply drained, peaty, acid soils. Propagate by seed, or by semi-ripe heel cuttings in a closed case with bottom heat; also by simple layering.

*L. procumbens* (L.) Desv. ALPINE AZALEA; MOUNTAIN AZALEA; MINEZUO. As for the genus.

**Lolium** L. (Lat. name for a troublesome weed, *L. tomulentum*.) RYEGRASS; DARNEL. Gramineae. 8 species of annual or perennial grasses to 1m. Rhizomes spreading extensively; stems erect, tufted. Leaf blades not flat; sheaths auriculate; ligules obtuse, translucent, papery. Spike simple, flattened or cylindric, to 25cm; rachis scalloped; spikelets solitary, sessile, adpressed to hollows in rachis, opposite, distichous, few- to many-flowered, to 2.5cm; lower glumes reduced, upper glume exserted, stiff; lemmas dorsally convex, obtuse, acute or aristate, 5–7-ribbed, to 5mm. Summer. Eurasia. Z5.

CULTIVATION See LAWNS.

**Lomagramma** J. Sm. (From Gk *loma*, margin, and *gramma*, line, from the position of the sori.) Lomariopsidaceae. Some 18 species of large scandent ferns. Rhizome scandent. Fronds to 30cm, uniserial, pinnate or rarely bipinnate, membranous, flaccid, dimorphic; sterile pinnae to 20cm, numerous, lanceolate, serrate or entire, the base truncate, sessile, and articulate with the rachis, covered in numerous peltate scales; fertile fronds seasonal, often wanting, pinnae contracted, wholly sporangiferous, or sometimes the contraction only partial, and then the sporangia forming a broad marginal line, veins uniform, reticulate, areoles oblong, hexagonoid. SE Asia. Z10.

CULTIVATION As for *Bolbitis*.

*L. sorbifolia* (Willd.) Ching. Rhiz. wide-creeping or long-trailing. Sterile fronds to 1.8m, bright green; pinnae 15–20×4cm, ligulate, cut down to a narrow wing into undivided, close, obtuse lobes; fertile pinnae more distinct, 15–20×0.5cm. China, Solomon Is.

**Lomaria** Willd.
*L. alpina* Spreng. See *Blechnum penna-marina*.
*L. attenuata* Willd. See *Blechnum attenuatum*.
*L. gibba* Labill. See *Blechnum gibbum*.
*L. colensoi* Hook. f. See *Blechnum colensoi*.
*L. elongata* Bl. See *Blechnum colensoi*.
*L. falcata* Spreng. See *Blechnum discolor*.
*L. magellanica* Desv. See *Blechnum magellanicum*.
*L. niponica* Kunze. See *Blechnum nipponicum*.
*L. rigida* J. Sm. See *Blechnum durum*.
*L. rotundifolia* Colenso. See *Blechnum fluviatile*.
*L. speciosa* Bl. See *Photinopteris speciosa*.

**Lomatia** R. Br. (From Gk *loma*, edge, referring to the winged edge of the seeds.) Proteaceae. 12 species of woody evergreens to 12m. Stems ultimately glabrous, grey-brown, branching divaricately. Leaves alternate or paired, opposite, entire, toothed, pinnatifid or pinnately compound, often polymorphic. Flowers bisexual, paired in lax racemes or crowded terminal panicles, green, yellow-white or scarlet; perianth obliquely tubular, the limb splitting as 4 narrow twisted lobes. Fruit a tough follicle, bearing several seeds. Spring–summer. Australasia, S America.

CULTIVATION Ornamental evergreens, with dark, leathery, more or less divided leaves and young growth, which in most species is clothed in felted or silky down, red-brown in *L. ferruginea*. All have interesting and attractive flowers, the creamy white or pale yellow flowers of *L. myricoides*, *L. silaifolia* and *L. tinctoria* are sweetly scented; those of *L. ferruginea*, bicoloured in buff-yellow and scarlet, are extremely handsome. Although *Lomatia* make useful cut flowers, the slow growth of some spp. will limit cutting. Most are hardy to about −10°C/14°F. *L. dentata* and *L. myricoides* are slightly more tender, to −5°C/23°F, but all must be protected from cold drying winds. They will thrive in a sheltered and stable environment such as the woodland garden and are amenable to tub cultivation in the cool glasshouse or conservatory.

Grow in well-drained, preferably peaty soils with a pH 5–6, in sun or light dappled shade, with shelter from cold drying winds especially to the north and east. A dry mulch of bracken litter or straw at the base will give additional protection. Under glass (winter minimum 5–7°C/40–45°F), grow in a mix of equal parts loam, leafmould or equivalent, and sharp sand; water moderately when in growth, reducing as temperatures fall to keep almost dry in winter. *Lomatia* requires little pruning, but as new shoots emerge from the base, old growth may be removed to prevent overcrowding. Propagate by seed or from softwood or semi-ripe cuttings in sand, in a closed case with bottom heat at 19–22°C/66–72°F.

*L. dentata* R. Br. To 4m. Lvs to 8cm, holly-like, elliptic, strongly toothed, dark glossy green above, pale or grey-green below. Fls green-white. Chile. Z8.

*L. ferruginea* R. Br. To 7m. Stems erect, branching from base; young shoots rusty-sericeous. Lvs to 20×10cm, narrowly triangular in outline, pinnate; pinnae to 17, leathery, olive green above, tomentose beneath, coarsely pinnatifid, fern-like, particularly those in basal third. Racemes axillary, to 6cm; fls to 12 per raceme, scarlet fading at tips and centre to olive green. Chile, Patagonia. Z9.

*L. hirsuta* (Lam.) Diels. To 12m. Young stems puberulent. Lvs to 10×6cm, emerging golden or rusty-pubesc., hardening glabrous, shining dark green, broadly ovate, coriaceous, obtuse or abruptly acute, crenate; petiole brown-pubesc., to 3cm. Panicles axillary, to 7cm; fls olive green to ivory. Chile, Peru. Z8.

*L. myricoides* (Gaertn. f.) Domin. Broadly spreading shrub to 2.5m. Young growth ridged, brown-puberulent. Lvs to 12.5cm, narrow-linear to lanceolate,

**Lomatia and allies** (a) *Embothrium coccineum* fruit LS (b) *Lomatia ferruginea* fruit LS (c) *Gevuina avellana* (×0.33)

glabrous, tough, subentire to coarsely and remotely dentate in apical half, sessile or petiolate. Racemes to 15cm, terminal or axillary at ends of branches; fls ivory to yellow-green, fragrant, profuse, resembling *Grevillea*. SE Australia. Z8.

***L. silaifolia*** (Sm.) R. Br. Densely branched, spreading shrub to 1m. Young growth glabrous or silky-pubesc. Lvs to 20×20cm, pinnate, bipinnate or tripinnate; seg. lanceolate, acute, coriaceous, glabrous, dark green, somewhat revolute. Fls ivory in showy panicles. E Australia. Z8.

***L. tinctoria*** (Labill.) R. Br. Dense, suckering shrub to 75cm. Lvs to 8cm, pinnate or bipinnate; seg. linear-lanceolate, dark green, finer than in the closely related *L. silaifolia*. Racemes to 20cm, spreading, terminal; fls ivory to topaz, sweetly scented. Tasmania. Z8.

***L. obliqua*** (Ruiz & Pav.) R. Br. See *L. hirsuta*.

**Lomatophyllum** Willd. (From Gk *loma*, border, and *phyllon*, leaf, referring to the reddened margins.) Liliaceae (Aloeaceae). Some 12 species of perennial succulents, closely resembling *Aloe* and sometimes included within it. Stems thick, unbranched. Leaves in terminal rosettes, ligulate, coriaceous, long-acuminate, thin, serrate, spines upcurved, margins often thickened and red. Flowers tubular, in panicles. Fruit a plump fleshy berry (cf. dry capsule in *Aloe*). Indian Ocean Is. Z10.

CULTIVATION As for *Aloe*, with a winter minimum of about 10°C/50°F.

***L. occidentale*** Perrier. To 1m; trunk fleshy, to 10cm diam. Lvs 80–100×10–12cm, 15–20, long-acuminate, stiff, recurved, deeply channelled, sparsely spinose, spines to 4mm. Fls 2.5–3cm, deep pink. W Madagascar.

***L. purpureum*** (Lam.) Dur. & Schinz. Robust, to 2m; stem stout. Lvs 80×10cm, linear-lanceolate, channelled, margins thickened, red, spiny. Fls yellow to red. Mauritius.

***L. borbonicum*** Willd. See *L. purpureum*.

**Lonas** Adans. AFRICAN DAISY; YELLOW AGERATUM. Compositae. 1 species, an annual herb to 30cm. Leaves alternate, lower leaves, tripartite, petiolate, lobes dentate, upper leaves pinnatifid, sessile or short-petiolate. Capitula discoid, 2–10 in a dense, terminal corymb; receptacle elongate-conical, scaly; involucre campanulate, phyllaries in many series, margins scarious; florets hermaphrodite yellow. Fruit a prismatic, ribbed cypsela; pappus a corona. SW Mediterranean.

CULTIVATION As for *Acroclinium*.

***L. annua*** (L.) Vines & Druce. As for the genus.

***L. inodora*** (L.) Gaertn. See *L. annua*.

**Lonchitis** L. (From Gk name used by Dioscorides for plant with spear-shaped seeds, derived from *logche*, lance, spear; referring to the form of the fronds.) Dennstaedtiaceae. 2 species of terrestrial or epilithic ferns. Rhizomes short-creeping, fleshy, covered with trichomate hairs and massed roots. Fronds stipitate, uniform, few, 2–3-pinnate or -pinnatifid, ovate or deltoid to lanceolate, membranous, fleshy, more or less pubescent, especially below; veins free or anastomosing, in which case areolae without free, included veinlets; rachis and costa ridged below; stipes approximate, fleshy. Sori marginal, continuous on segments, on vascular connective comissure, linear to oblong; indusia formed from modified reflexed margin, kidney-shaped, opening inwards, membranous; paraphyses present or absent; spores globose to tetrahedral, trilete, somewhat granulate. Tropical America, Africa and Madagascar. Z10.

CULTIVATION As for *Hypolepis*.

***L. hirsuta*** L. Fronds to 2×1m, pubesc., uppermost pinnae reduced, petiolate, subopposite or alternate, ascending, ovate or deltoid to oblong, pinnules to 12×3cm or more, sessile, deltoid or linear to oblong, apex acute to narrowly acute, base more or less adnate, seg. to 9mm wide, subfalcate, oblong, apex obtuse, margin subentire to lobed; stipes to 1m, pubesc., straw-coloured. Tropical America (W Indies, Mexico to Bolivia, Brazil).

***L. currori*** (Hook.) Kuhn. See *Blotiella currori*.

*L. lindeniana* Hook. See *Blotiella lindeniana*.
*L. natalensis* Hook. See *Blotiella natalensis*.
*L. repens* L. See *Hypolepis repens*.
*L. tenuifolia* Forst. f. See *Hypolepis tenuifolia*.
For further synonymy see *Antiosorus*.

**Lonchocarpus** Kunth (From Gk *lonche*, lance and, *karpos*, fruit, referring to the shape of the fruit.) BITTER WOOD; TURTLE BONE; CABBAGE BARK; WATERWOOD. Leguminosae (Papilionoideae). Some 150 species of trees or shrubs. Leaves alternate, imparipinnate; leaflets opposite; stipules usually absent. Flowers in simple or paniculate racemes, white to violet; pedicels clustered or paired, rarely solitary; calyx cupulate, truncate or short-toothed; standard orbicular, often auricled at base, emarginate, wings obliquely oblong, keel obtuse, united along lower margin; stamens 10, 1 free at base, but united with the others from the middle, anthers versatile. Fruit oblong to suborbicular or elongate, flat, indehiscent, 1–4-seeded; seeds flat, reniform or round. Tropical America, Africa and Australia. Z10

CULTIVATION *Lonchocarpus* spp. range through a number of tropical and subtropical habitats from mangrove swamps, river banks in the Amazon basin, to open hillside and dry plains, to altitudes of 1000m/3250ft. Their toxic properties have long been exploited in their native lands, often for fish poisons and some have been commercially developed as sources for rotenone insecticides. In warm, essentially frost-free zones, with well-distributed rainfall, *Lonchocarpus* spp. make beautiful ornamental trees for parks and gardens, with a graceful habit, dense crowns of elegant, evergreen foliage, and handsome fragrant flowers, carried in profusion even on young plants. Mature specimens may survive occasional short-lived frosts, to about −4°C/25°F. Their use in temperate zones, where they require hothouse conditions, is limited by their size to large glasshouses where they can be planted out. Cultivate as for *Gliricidia*.

***L. domingensis*** (Pers.) DC. GENOGENO; CAPASSA. Tree to 15m. Branchlets initially pubesc. Leaflets to 12×7.5cm, 7–13, oblong to elliptic-oval, obtuse, leathery, glabrous to pubesc. Pedicels to 7mm; cal. 5mm, rusty-pubesc.; cor. pink to purple, standard 15mm, suborbicular, white at base, silky. Fr. to 12×3cm, linear-oblong, flat, to 12×3cm, brown-tomentose becoming glabrous, usually somewhat torulose. Tropical America and Africa, Caribbean.

***L. latifolius*** HBK. FORTEVENTURA; HEDIONDO; PALO HEDIONDO; PALO SECO. Tree to 16m. Branchlets tomentulose to glabrous. Leaflets to 24×12cm, 5–9, ovate to elliptic-oblong, to 24×12cm, short-acuminate to subobtuse at apex, rounded at base, glabrous above, pubesc. beneath. Racemes to 12cm, solitary, axillary; cal. 3mm, cupulate, brown-sericeous, 5-toothed; cor. purple, pink or yellow, standard 8mm, emarginate, sericeous. Fr. elliptic, to 9×2.5cm, papery, puberulous. Tropical America, Caribbean.

***L. punctatus*** Kunth. Close to *L. violaceus*, distinguished by leaflets in 2–4 pairs, ovate-oblong, pale green, to 5cm, lighter above, and pet. densely spotted. Trinidad, NE Venezuela.

***L. violaceus*** Benth. non hort. Small, glabrous tree. Leaflets to 9cm, in 3–5 pairs, ovate, translucent-dotted, dark green above. Racemes axillary; cal. truncate; cor. white outside, pale purple or pink inside. Fr. to 6×3cm, lanceolate. W Indies.

*L. griftonianus* (Baill.) Dunn. See *Millettia griftoniana*.
*L. maculatus* (Kunth) DC. See *Gliricidia sepium*.
*L. violaceus* hort. non Benth. See *L. punctatus*.
For further synonymy see *Dalbergia*.

**London, George** (*d*1713). Nurseryman and garden designer. London is first recorded as apprenticed to Charles II's gardener, John Rose, at St James's Park. After three or four years service Rose 'sent him into France for improvement', where he visited many of the great gardens and learnt the precepts of formal garden design, perhaps even being advised by André Le Nôtre. On returning to England, London became head gardener to Henry Compton, Bishop of London, at Fulham Palace. The expertise he gained through working with Compton's collection of exotic plants, or 'greens', was to prove useful when London established the Brompton Park nursery with his partners Cook, Lucre [Looker] and Field in 1681. He was joined by Henry Wise in 1688, and in the same year London assured himself of future royal favour when he helped his old ally and patron Compton escort the Protestant Princess (and later Queen) Anne from Kensington Palace to Nottingham. With the accession of William and Mary, London was made Deputy Superintendent of the Royal Gardens, Master Gardener and a page of the backstairs to the Queen.

By 1691, London and Wise were sole partners at Brompton Park, and their nursery rose to become the foremost in England. Their horticultural innovations and huge selection of plants were widely appreciated, as Stephen Switzer, an admiring pupil, records: 'twill be hard for any of posterity to lay their hands on a tree in any of these kingdoms, that have not been a part of their care'; they also received lavish praise from John Evelyn. By around 1700 Wise had largely taken charge of the landscape design part of the business, but London did play a major part in the design of formal gardens at Castle Howard, Longleat, Chatsworth, Badminton, Blenheim, and Melbourne Hall (where his design survives). On Queen Anne's accession in 1702 and Wise's appointment as Royal Gardener, London concentrated on supervising most of the other major gardens of England. In 1706 he began two major projects, the design of Wanstead, Essex, and Canons, near Edgware.

London is remembered first as a practical gardener who, in Switzer's opinion 'made the greatest figure that ever yet any gardener did': Loudon's legacy at at Brompton Park helped to provide 'the Nursery and Fund of Gardening and Plantation with which the nation was stocked'.

**Lonicera** L. (For Adam Lonitzer (1528–86), German naturalist, author of a herbal (*Kreuterbüch*) much reprinted between 1557 and 1783.) HONEYSUCKLE. Caprifoliaceae. About 180 species of deciduous or evergreen, bushy, scandent, twining or creeping shrubs. Bark often exfoliating. Leaves opposite, usually simple, entire, sometimes pinnately lobed, sessile or shortly petioled, sometimes with connate stipules, upper leaf pairs often fused, forming a disc. Flowers epigynous, paired and axillary or in usually 6-flowered whorls in terminal spikes or panicles, bracteate; sepals 5; corolla tubular to campanulate, tube often basally swollen, bilabiate with upper lip 4-lobed, or with regular 5-lobed limb and lobes imbricate; stamens 5, included or exserted; ovary inferior. Fruit a many-seeded berry, white, yellow, red or black. N Hemisphere.

CULTIVATION A large, diverse and generally long-lived genus, *Lonicera* spp. have a wide range of applications in the garden; most are grown for their attractive flowers, many of which are sweetly scented. The berries are often attractive to birds.

The bush or shrubby honeysuckles include many excellent plants for mixed and shrub borders; some – such as *L. xylosteum*, an under-used and easily propagated shrub, and *L. nitida* – can be used as informal hedges. *L. nitida*, the box-leaved honeysuckle, is a fast-growing shrub of dense and evergreen habit, which responds well to close clipping and is useful for more formal hedging and for topiary; 'Baggesen's Gold', an attractive clone of *L. nitida*, has yellow leaves which turn green in winter. It is now commonly used in urban massed plantings.

Those flowering in winter include *L.* ×*purpusii*, with fragrant cream-coloured flowers, and *L. fragrantissima*, its parent, which produces flowers continuously although not profusely throughout winter, followed by berries in spring. It is hardy to −25°C/−13°F and tolerant of city conditions.

The genus includes some of the hardiest shrubs, useful in very cold climates, some even in subarctic conditions; *L. chrysantha*, hardy to −40°C/−40°F, is one of the most attractive, the flowers cream at first, darkening to yellow, giving rise to coral red berries. *L. maackii* f. *podocarpa*, a graceful wide-spreading shrub, beautiful in flower and fruit, and the drought-resistant *L. tatarica*, with rose-pink flowers, are equally hardy.

For rockeries, smaller spp. include *L. albertii*, low-growing and procumbent, among the most handsome in bloom, and *L. pileata*, of neat habit and with dark shining leaves which can also be used for ground cover. The twining *L. japonica* 'Aureo-reticulata', its leaves netted with gold, is also used for groundcover but needs strict control, being a rampant species likely to swamp less vigorous neighbours.

The climbing and twining spp. are used for covering trelliswork, walls, fences, pergolas and old tree stumps. This group includes the woodbine, *L. periclymenum*, the common honeysuckle of hedgerow and woodland, and its cultivars, which are among the most fragrant of the genus, but there are many others worthy of cultivation. *L. tragophylla*, with showy bright yellow blooms, for shady positions, is hardy in southern New England, and *L.* ×*brownii*, the unscented scarlet trumpet honeysuckle, has a number of useful cvs including 'Dropmore Scarlet', which produces brightly coloured tubular flowers from summer to early autumn. *L. hildebrandtiana*, the frost-tender giant Burmese honeysuckle, is the largest; its creamy flowers fading to orange are up to 15cm/6in. long, followed by egg-shaped fruit up to 2.5cm/1in. in diameter. In colder climates, it is a subject for the large cool glasshouse or conservatory, minimum temperature 5°C/40°F, otherwise grow in full sun.

Plant the evergreen climbers in spring, deciduous species in their dormant season, in a moist but well-drained soil enriched with organic matter. Give climbers a light annual mulch of leafmould or well-rotted compost; excess nitrogen will generate vigorous foliar growth at the expense of flowers, in which case apply sulphate of potash at 14g/m$^2$($\frac{1}{2}$oz/yd$^2$) in spring.

*Lonicera* will grow in sun or part shade, although the bush species flower more profusely in sun. In habitat, the climbers generally grow with their roots in shade and their shoots reaching up to the sun, and in partial shade they appear to be less susceptible to attack by aphids. For hedges, plant 30–45cm/12–18in. specimens 30cm/12in. apart in spring, and cut back to half their height; tip back two or three times the first season to encourage bushiness. Plant glasshouse specimens in the border, using wires as support. Keep barely moist in winter with minimum temperature 5–7°C/40–45°F; water freely in the growing season and provide good ventilation throughout spring, summer and autumn. Prune young specimens by shortening stems to encourage branching and establish a good framework. Thereafter prune to keep within bounds, and thin out old wood to prevent excessive crowding after flowering, or for late summer-flowerers in early spring.

Propagate from semi-ripe cuttings in summer, or by hardwood cuttings in late autumn, as for *Weigela*, also by simple layering in late autumn. Some shrubby species can be divided in early spring. Aphid infestations cause distortion of flower trusses and young shoots.

***L. acuminata*** Wallich. Scandent or rarely creeping shrub. Branchlets pubesc. Lvs 10×4.5cm, oblong, long-acuminate, cordate at base, scattered-pubesc. or glabrescent; petioles 5mm, pubesc. Fls in terminal, many-fld capitula, and also often axillary 2-fld peduncles; bracteoles 1.5mm, ciliate; cal. tube glabrous, sep. glabrous or ciliate; cor. to 2cm, yellow to red; cor. tube funnelform, 8.5mm, setose-pubesc., lobes pubesc. or glabrous; style dense fulvous-pubesc. Fr. black. Summer. Himalaya (Nepal to Sikkim). Z5.

***L. affinis*** Hook. & Arn. Scandent, semi-evergreen shrub to 7m. Branches terete, glandular, white-puberulent when young. Lvs to 9×5cm, ovate or oblong-elliptic, acute or short-acuminate, rounded at base, glabrous above, glandular-pubesc. beneath; petioles to 1cm, glandular, white-puberulent when young. Fls white, becoming yellow, paired, terminal; peduncles to 7mm, axillary; bracts 2mm, lanceolate-deltoid, patent; bracteoles free, somewhat pilose; cal. glabrous, sep. narrow-deltoid; cor. bilabiate, narrow, to 6cm, glabrous outside; style glabrous. Fr. 7mm diam., glabrous, blue-black, white-pruinose. Spring–summer. Japan, China. Z6.

***L. albertii*** Reg. Low deciduous shrub to 120cm, of patent habit. Young branchlets slender, glabrous or glandular. Lvs to 3×0.3cm, linear-oblong, sessile, blunt, often few-toothed towards base, blue-green, glabrous above, white beneath; petioles very short. Fls rose-lilac, fragrant, 2cm diam., paired, axillary; peduncle 6.5mm; cor. tube cylindric, to 12.5mm, slender, pubesc. inside, glabrous outside, lobes patent, oblong; fil. to 2× anth. Fr. 8.5mm diam., maroon to white, pruinose, separate. Turkestan, Tibet. Z6.

***L. albiflora*** Torr. & A. Gray. WHITE HONEYSUCKLE. Of bushy habit, to 2.5m, somewhat scandent. Branches twining. Lvs to 3cm, rarely to 6.5cm, rigid, suborbicular to oval or obovate, broad-rounded, rounded to broad-cuneate at base, glabrous or pubesc., somewhat glaucous, uppermost pair connate at base. Fls 1.5–3cm, white or yellow-white, glabrous or pilose outside, cor. 1.5–3cm, bilabiate; style and fil. glabrous. Fr. orange. Spring. Southern N America. Z6.

***L. alpigena*** L. Deciduous shrub, 1m, of narrow upright habit. Branchlets green, sparsely glandular and pubesc. Lvs to 10cm, elliptic to oblong, apex acuminate, dark green and shiny above, paler and pubesc. initially beneath, margins ciliate. Fls yellow-green, tinged red, to 1.5cm, paired; peduncles erect, to 5cm; cor. 12.5mm, bilabiate, pubesc. inside; stamens pubesc. below. Fr. ovate-globose, to 13mm, shiny dark red. Spring. C & S Europe. 'Macrophylla': lvs large, glabrous, prophylls small; fls glabrous outside. f. ***nana*** (Carr.) Nichols. Dwarf shrub. Lvs scattered-pubesc. beneath, more densely on venation. Fls deep red. Z6.

***L. alseuosmoides*** Gräbn. Scandent evergreen shrub. Young branchlets slender, glabrous. Lvs to 6×0.85cm, narrow-oblong, apex and base acuminate, glabrous, margins recurved and adpressed-pubesc. Fls in short broad panicles; cor. 12.5mm, funnelform, tube exceeds limb, inside purple and pubesc., outside yellow and glabrous. Fr. to 6.5mm diam., globose, black, purple-pruinose. Summer–autumn. W China (Sichuan). Z6.

***L. altmannii*** Reg. & Schmalh. Deciduous shrub to 2.5m. Young branchlets purple-pubesc. Lvs to 5×3.5cm, ovate to elliptic, mostly acute, base rounded or acuminate, ciliate, apex usually pubesc.; petioles to 5mm. Fls white tinged yellow, paired; bracts 6.5mm; pedicel 6.5mm; cor. 12mm, tube slender, larger than lobes, gibbous, pubesc. Fr. 8mm, ellipsoid, orange-red. Spring. Turkestan. var. ***hirtipes*** Rehd. Lvs to 5cm, broad-ovate, hispid. Shoots and petioles densely setose-pubesc. Ovary often pubesc. Alatau Mts. var. ***pilosiuscula*** Rehd. Lvs ovate, to 4cm, sparsely pubesc. above, glabrous or venation pubesc. beneath. Branchlets and petioles fine-pubesc. and sparsely setose. Cor. and ovary glabrous. Alatau Mts. var. ***saravshanica*** Rehd. Shoots glabrous or fine-pubesc. Lvs to 2.5cm, densely grey-tomentose below, apex subobtuse. Saravshan, W Bukhara. Z5.

***L.* ×*americana*** (Mill.) K. Koch. (*L. caprifolium* × *L. etrusca.*) Resembles *L. caprifolium* in growth and foliage, but lower lvs more acute. Young stems purple, glabrous. Fls fragrant, yellow, tinted maroon, in crowded whorls from axils of connate lvs and small bracts, often in 25×20cm panicles; cor. 5cm, tube slender, glandular, pubesc. outside. Fr. red. Summer. S & SE Europe, NW Yugoslavia. 'Atrosanguinea': fls deep red outside. 'Quercifolia': lvs open emarginate, sometimes with yellow margin or red striped. 'Rubella': fls light purple outside, buds more deeply coloured. Z6.

***L.* ×*amoena*** Zab. (*L. korolkowii* × *L. tatarica.*) Vigorous deciduous shrub to 3m. Lvs to 4×2.5cm, ovate, slightly cordate at base, grey-green; petiole short. Fls 18mm diam., light pink or white, paired, crowded at shoot tips; cor. bilabiate. Summer. 'Alba': habit shrub-like, rounded; shoots more pubesc.; fls white, later tinted yellow, fragrant, abundant. 'Arnoldiana': habit open; shoots pendulous; lvs oblanceolate, grey-green; fls white, vertical pink tinting on opening, prolific. 'Rosea': fls pink, later yellowing, fragrant. Z5.

***L. angustifolia*** Wallich. Deciduous shrub to 2.5m, rounded. Outer branches pendent. Lvs to 5×1.25cm, elliptic-lanceolate, bright green and glabrous above, paler and lightly pubesc. beneath, especially on veins; petiole to 2mm, lanate. Fls pale pink, paired; peduncles to 1.5cm, slender, pendent; cor. 8mm, tubular, pet. equal; style short, included. Fr. red, joined in pairs, edible. Spring–summer. Himalaya, Kashmir. Z5.

***L. arborea*** Boiss. Erect deciduous shrub to 2m, sometimes a small tree. Shoots quadrangulate, grey white-pubesc. Lvs to 3.5cm, ovate to elliptic, apex rounded to slightly emarginate, base rounded to subcordate, grey-pubesc., becoming glabrous. Fls red; cor. 1.5cm, soft-pubesc. outside, glabrous or pubesc. inside, somewhat gibbous. Fr. orange-yellow. S Spain, N Africa. Z7.

***L. arizonica*** Rehd. Erect deciduous shrub. Lvs to 7cm, ovate to oval, apex rounded, base rounded to broad-cuneate, ciliate, deep green and glabrous above, lighter and often white-pubesc. beneath; petiole to 12mm. Fls in solitary whorls or subcapitate spikes; cor. to 4.5cm, orange inside, muddy red tinged outside, glabrous; style glabrous. Fr. red. Spring–summer. SW US (Arizona, New Mexico). Z6.

***L. balearica*** (DC.) DC. Like *L. implexa*, but lvs oval or obovate to oblong, lower lvs truncate to cordate at base. Whorls of fls fewer than *L. implexa*. Mediterranean. Z8.

***L.* ×*bella*** Zab. (*L. morrowii* × *L. tatarica.*) Intermediate between parents. Erect deciduous shrub. Lvs to 5cm, ovate, more acute, soon glabrous. Fls more red-coloured than parents, later yellow, paired; cor. 12.5mm, bilabiate. Fr. red. Summer. 'Atrorosea': fls deep pink to red; fr. dark red. 'Candida' ('Albida'): fls white. 'Chrysantha': fls yellow. 'Dropmore': habit pendulous, to 2m high; fls white, later yellow, abundant. 'Incarnata': fls red. 'Polyantha': fls pink-red, prolific. 'Rosea': fls pale pink, turning white, eventually yellow. Z4.

***L. biflora*** Desf. Deciduous shrub. Branchlets white-velutinous. Lvs to 6×4.5cm, ovate to ovate-elliptic, subobtuse, dark green and pubesc., soon glabrous above, grey-green and densely pubesc. beneath. Fls fragrant, yellow, axillary, paired; peduncle to 1cm; bracts and bracteoles ovate; cor. to 4cm, tube narrow, grey-puberulent; ovaries glabrous. Fr. globose, black. SE Spain, Sicily, N Africa. Z9.

***L. bracteolaris*** Boiss. & Buhse. Erect deciduous shrub. Lvs to 5cm, ovate to elliptic, apex obtuse, subacute, base round to somewhat cordate, blue-green above, paler beneath, glabrous or slightly ciliate; petiole to 5mm. Fls white, paired; bracts lanceolate, 6mm; cor. 12mm, glabrous, gibbous; stamens included, styles exserted. Fr. ovoid-rounded, 8mm diam., orange-red. Spring. Transcaucasus. Z5.

**Lonicera** (a) *L. albertii* (×0.6), flower (×1) (b) *L. spinosa* (×0.6), flower (×1) (c) *L. utahensis* (×0.6), flower (×1) (d) *L. caerulea* (×0.6), flower (×1) (e) *L. villosa* (×0.6), flower (×1) (f) *L. canadensis* (×0.6), flower (×1) (g) *L. tangutica* (×0.6), flower (×1) (h) *L. pileata* (×0.6), flower (×1) (i) *L. nitida* (×0.6) (j) *L. gynochlamydea* (×0.6) (k) *L. ferdinandii* var. *leycesterioides* (×0.6)

**Lonicera** (a) *L. fragrantissima* leaves (×0.6), flowers (×0.6) (b) *L.* × *purpusii* leaves and (above) flowers (×0.6) (c) *L. standishii* leaves (×0.6), flowers (×0.6) (d) *L. hispida* leaves (×0.6), flowers (× 1) (e) *L. bracteolaris* leaves (×0.6), flowers (× 1) (f) *L. altmannii* leaves (×0.6), flowers (× 1) (g) *L. strophiophora* leaves (×0.6), flower (× 1)

**L.×brownii** (Reg.) Carr. (*L.sempervirens* × *L.hirsuta.*) SCARLET TRUMPET HONEYSUCKLE. Resembles *L.sempervirens*. Scandent deciduous shrub to 3m. Lvs elliptic, blue-green and somewhat pubesc. beneath, uppermost leaf pairs connate; petiole glandular. Fls in capitula; cor. resemble those of *L.hirsuta*, bilabiate, glandular pubesc. outside. Spring–summer. 'Dropmore Scarlet': vigorous; fls long trumpet-shaped, bright scarlet, midsummer-early autumn, long lasting. 'Fuchsioides': fls orange-scarlet, bilabiate. 'Plantierensis': fls large, coral-red, cor. russet. 'Punicea': fls orange-red outside; slow-growing. 'Youngii': fls deep crimson. Z5.

**L.caerulea** L. Erect deciduous shrub to 2m, much-branched. Bark buff to rufous; branchlets glabrous or sparse-pubesc. Lvs to 8×3cm, elliptic, sometimes obovate, ovate or oblong, acute or subacute, glabrous or somewhat pubesc. beneath. Fls yellow-white, axillary, paired; peduncles to 11mm; cor. to 15mm, tube gibbous, pubesc.; bracts linear. Fr. globose, dark blue, pruinose, connate at base. Spring. NE Europe, Pyrenees to Bulgaria and SW Czechoslovakia. 'Globosa': fr. almost globose. 'Sphaerocarpa': fr. oval to globose. 'Viridifolia': habit shrub-like, erect; shoots red; lvs to 3cm, elliptic to obovate, strong green, paler beneath, pubesc.; cor. tube long, thick. var.*L.caerulea* var. *altaica* (Pall.) Sweet. Branchlets setose. Lvs to 7cm, pubesc. above and beneath; cor. pubesc. outside; stamens included. Z2.

**L.calcarata** Hemsl. Tall scandent shrub. Lvs to 14cm, ovate to elliptic-lanceolate, acuminate. Fls red-yellow, axillary, paired; cor. 3cm, with a 1.5cm spur; fil. pilose at base; style pilose at base; ovary 5-celled. China. Z6.

**L.canadensis** Bartr. FLY HONEYSUCKLE. Erect, deciduous shrub to 1.5m, broad. Branchlets rufous, glabrous. Lvs to 8cm, ovate to elliptic, pale green, ciliate. Fls yellow-white, tinged red, paired; cor. to 2cm, tubular to funnelform, glabrous outside. Fr. pale orange-red. Spring. N America (Canada to Michigan). Z3.

**L.caprifolium** L. ITALIAN WOODBINE; ITALIAN HONEYSUCKLE. Scandent deciduous shrub to 6m. Branchlets subglabrous. Lower lvs on short petioles, upper lvs sessile, to 10×5cm, obovate or oval, apex rounded, base acuminate, subglabrous, glaucous, especially beneath, blue-green beneath, terminal pair fused. Fls yellow-white, pink-tinged, fragrant, in 4–10-fld, sessile whorls from axils of terminal 3 pairs of lvs; cor. bilabiate, upper lip erect to reflexed, 4-lobed, to 5cm, tube slender. Fr. orange-red. Spring–summer. Europe, W Asia. 'Pauciflora': cor. tube to 3cm, purple or rose outside, off-white inside. 'Praecox': lvs grey-green; fls cream, often tinted light red, later turning yellow, early-flowering. Z5.

**L.caucasica** Pall. Erect deciduous shrub to 2m. Young branches glabrous. Lvs to 10×3cm, elliptic to ovate, apex acute or acuminate, base rounded to cuneate, glabrous; petioles short. Fls pink, paired, axillary, fragrant; peduncles to 14mm; bracts linear, to 5mm; bracteoles broad, 1mm, connate; cor. bilabiate, to 12mm, glabrous or pubesc.; tube expanded one side. Fr. globose, to 1cm diam., black, connate in pairs. Spring–summer. Caucasus. Z6.

**L.cerasina** Maxim. Deciduous small shrub. Bark brown, later grey; young branches light green, glabrous. Lvs to 12×4cm, elliptic-lanceolate, oblong-lanceolate or obovate-oblong, long-acuminate or -attenuate, apex obtuse, base broad-cuneate, glabrous or sparse-pubesc. above, glabrous beneath, ciliate at margins; petioles to 1cm, glabrous or sparse-glandular-pubesc. Fls yellow-white; peduncles to 12mm, glabrous; bracts linear; cor. 1cm, bilabiate, gibbous. Fr. ellipsoid, to 8mm, red; seeds to 6×3.5mm, broad-elliptic, shiny. Spring. Japan. Z7.

**L.chaetocarpa** (Batal. ex Rehd.) Rehd. Erect deciduous shrub to 2m. Branchlets setose, glandular. Lvs to 8cm, ovate to oblong, occasionally oval, truncate to acute, green above, grey-green beneath, setose, especially beneath. Fls yellow, solitary or paired, cream; peduncles to 2cm, pubesc.; bracts to 2.5cm, white, persistent; cor. tubular, 3cm, 5-lobed, lobes rounded and patent, pubesc. and glandular outside; ovary glandular and setose. Fr. bright red. Summer. W China. Z5.

**L.chamissoi** Bunge. Erect deciduous shrub to 1m, densely branched. Bark grey; young branches terete, glabrous, subglaucous. Lvs chartaceous to membranous, sessile, broad-ovate to elliptic, to 5×2.5cm, apex obtuse or rounded, base rounded, glabrous; petioles to 2mm. Fls deep red-violet, paired; peduncles to 14mm; bracts and bracteoles broad-ovate or orbicular, to 1mm; cor. 1cm, glabrous outside, gibbous; stamen and style included. Fr. subglobose, 8mm, scarlet, shiny; seeds oval or broad-elliptic, to 3×2mm. Summer. Japan, Kuriles, Sakhalin, Kamchatka, Amur. Z5.

**L.chrysantha** Turcz. Deciduous small tree to 4m. Bark fuscous-grey; young branches long-patent-pubesc. and minute-glandular-punctate. Lvs to 12×6cm, obovate, ovate-elliptic or oblong-ovate, apex strong-acuminate, base acute to rounded, pubesc. especially on veins beneath; petioles to 7mm. Fls pale yellow, paired; peduncles to 2cm, patent-pubesc. or subglabrous; bracts broad-linear; bracteoles elliptic, ciliate; cor. bilabiate, to 1.5cm, gibbous, upper lip divided to centre. Fr. globose, to 7mm diam., dark red; seeds broad-elliptic, 4×3mm. Spring–summer. NE Asia to C Japan. Z3.

**L.ciliosa** (Pursh) Poir. Twining evergreen shrub. Lvs to 10cm, ovate or oval, apex and base acuminate, ciliate, blue-green and glaucous beneath, terminal pair connate forming acute elliptic disc; petioles to 12.5mm. Fls to 4cm, yellow to orange-scarlet, pubesc. outside, in terminal, 1–3-whorled spikes; cor. more bilabiate than *L.sempervirens*, swollen at base. Fr. 5mm diam., red. Summer. North America. Z5. var. ***occidentalis*** (Hook.) Nichols. Fls slightly larger; cor.-tube glabrous, dark orange outside. Z5.

**L.confusa** (Sweet) DC. Twining deciduous to semi-evergreen shrub. Branchlets brown, soft short-pubesc. Lvs elliptic to oblong, to 7cm, pubesc. and ciliate, deep green above, becoming glabrous, grey-green beneath. Fls white, later yellow, fragrant, axillary and terminal, in short, dense panicles; bracteoles subulate; cor. 4cm, slender, glandular-pubesc. outside. Fr. black. Summer–autumn. E China. Z8.

**L.conjugialis** Kellogg. Straggling deciduous shrub to 1.5m, much-branched. Stem slender; branchlets strigulose. Lvs to 4cm, oblong-ovate to oblong-obovate, acute, slender, pale green and subglabrous above, lighter and pubesc. beneath, ciliate; petioles to 3mm. Fls dull purple, paired, axillary, on middle and upper part of branches; peduncles to 2.5cm, slender; bracts minute or absent, cal. teeth obsolete; cor. to 8mm, bilabiate, white-pubesc. Fr. to 6mm, bright red. Summer. W US (California). Z8.

**L.deflexicalyx** Batal. Deciduous shrub to 1.5m, spreading. Branches horizontal or cernuous; young branchlets purple, pubesc. Lvs to 8×2.3cm, narrow-ovate, to apex acute, base rounded, dull green and pubesc. above, grey and pubesc., especially when young, beneath; petioles 8.5mm. Fls yellow, paired, axillary; cor. to 1.5cm, outside pubesc., base gibbous; stamens pubesc. at base; style completely pubesc. Fr. pink-red. Spring–summer. China, Tibet. var. ***xerocalyx*** (Diels) Rehd. Lvs longer, to 10cm, narrower, slightly glaucous beneath. Ovaries enveloped by a cupule composed of the connate bracteoles. China (Yunnan). Z5.

**L.demissa** Rehd. Deciduous shrub to 4m, much-branched. Bark grey, exfoliating; young branches dark purple, ascending short-pilose. Lvs to 3.5×1.25cm, broad-oblanceolate to narrow-obovate, occasionally narrow-oblong, to apex obtuse, base acute, pubesc. and subglaucous beneath; petioles very short. Fls pale yellow, paired; peduncles to 1.5cm, slender; bracts membranous, linear; bracteoles suborbicular; cal.-tube minutely glandular-punctate, sep. short, obtuse; cor. bilabiate, to 12mm, short-pubesc. outside, gibbous; ovaries glandular-pubesc. Fr. to 6×8mm, globose, dark red, shiny; seeds to 3×2.5mm, rounded-ovate, red. Spring–summer. Japan. Z6.

**L.dioica** L. Patent or twining deciduous shrub to 1.5m. Stems glabrous when young. Lvs to 9×5cm, oval or oblong, apex and base acuminate, glabrous when young, intensely glaucous beneath, upper pairs connate into disc. Fls yellow-green, tinged purple, *c*1.5cm, in terminal clusters; cor. bilabiate, gibbous, glabrous outside; style usually glabrous. Fr. red. Spring–summer. Northeast America. Z5.

**L.discolor** Lindl. Erect deciduous shrub to 2m. Branchlets slender, glabrous; young shoots rufous. Lvs to 8cm, oblong to elliptic, rounded at base, deep green above, pale blue-green and glaucous beneath, glabrous. Fls on middle and upper part of branches, yellow-white, often tinted red outside, paired; peduncles 2–3cm, brown; bracts glandular-pubesc., cal. teeth linear-lanceolate; cor. to 3cm, tube short, gibbous, pubesc. inside, glabrous outside. Fr. globose, to 1cm diam., black, connate. Spring–summer. Kashmir to Afghanistan. Z6.

**L.etrusca** Santi. Scandent semi-evergreen shrub to 4m. Young shoots maroon, glabrous. Lvs to 8×5cm, oval or obovate, apex rounded, rounded or broad-tapered at base, glaucous, blue-green and usually pubesc. beneath, upper lvs connate. Infl. terminal spikes, often in groups of 3; fls closely packed in whorls, yellow tinted red, becoming deep yellow; peduncle to 4cm; bracteoles broad; cor. bilabiate, 5cm, tube narrow, occasionally glabrous or glandular; stamens much exserted. Fr. 6mm diam., red. Summer. Mediterranean region. 'Donald Waterer': fls red and white, yellowing with age, fragrant. 'Michael Rosse': fls cream and pale yellow, later darkening, slightly fragrant. 'Superba': shoots flushed red; fls cream, later orange, in large terminal panicles; strong-growing. Z7.

**L.ferdinandii** Franch. Robust deciduous shrub to 3m, patent. Shoots glandular and setose when young. Lvs 5×4.5cm, ovate, apex acuminate, rounded or cordate at base, dull green, pubesc., setose, paler beneath; petioles 6.5mm, adnate to stipules; stipules connate, forming disc surrounding stem at each node. Fls yellow, axillary, paired; cor. bilabiate, to 2cm, tube broad, saccate, dense-glandular and short-pubesc. outside. Fr. bright red, separate. Summer. Mongolia, N China. var. ***leycesterioides*** (Gräbn.) Zab. Branchlets often subglabrous. Lvs to 7cm, ovate-oblong to lanceolate. Cor. slightly setose-pubesc. or glabrous, eglandular. Mongolia. Z6.

**L.flava** Sims. YELLOW HONEYSUCKLE. Somewhat scandent deciduous shrub to 2.5m, often bushy. Stems glabrous; branchlets grey-green pruinose. Lvs to 8cm, broad-elliptic to elliptic, apex acute, bright green above, blue-green and densely pruinose beneath, uppermost pair connate into a disc. Infl. terminal, pedunculate, fls grouped in 1–3 superimposed and spreading whorls, fragrant, yellow, later orange; cor. bilabiate, upper lip 3-lobed, tubular not gibbous, 3cm. Fr. 6.5mm diam., red. Spring–summer. SE US (S Carolina). Z5.

**L.floribunda** Boiss. & Buhse non Zab., non Rehd. Low deciduous shrub, densely branched. Shoots fine-tomentose. Lvs to 3cm, broad-ovate to elliptic, apex obtuse to acute, truncate to slightly cordate at base, light green and somewhat pubesc. above, grey-green and dense soft-pubesc. beneath. Fls red; cor. broad-saccate; bracts subulate. Fr. yellow-red. Iran. Z8.

***L. fragrantissima*** Lindl. & Paxt. Evergreen to deciduous shrub to 2m, open, spreading. Young shoots glabrous, longer than *L. standishii* shoots, pruinose. Lvs to 7×3.5cm, oval, coriaceous, broad-cuneate apex and base, short setose-cuspidate, glabrous, setose on margins when young and on midrib, dark dull green above, blue-green and glaucous beneath; petiole to 3mm. Fls fragrant, cream, paired, axillary; cor. bilabiate, 12.5mm, tube short, glabrous outside. Fr. long-rounded, dull red. Winter–spring. China. Z5.

***L. giraldii*** Rehd. Scandent evergreen to 2m. Branches twining, tangled, dense yellow erect-pubesc. when young. Lvs to 7×2.5cm, narrow-oblong, acuminate, cordate at base, dense-pubesc.; petiole to 8.5mm, pubesc. Fls maroon, in capitate terminal clusters at branch tips; cor. 2cm, yellow-pubesc., tube slender, enlarged slightly at base. Fr. purple-black, pruinose. Summer. China (Sichuan). Z6.

***L. glaucescens*** (Rydb.) Rydb. Closely resembles *L. dioica*. Twining deciduous shrub. Shoots glabrous. Lvs to 8cm, elliptic to oblong, blue-green and pubesc. beneath, uppermost pair fused. Fls light yellow, red and short-pubesc. inside, 2cm, tube opening slightly to apex; style pubesc. Fr. pale red. Spring–summer. Northeast N America (Canada to Nebraska). Z3.

***L. glehnii*** F. Schmidt. Closely resembles *L. alpigena*. Deciduous shrub. Shoots glandular-pubesc. Lvs obovate, ovate or oblong-elliptic with cordate base, pubesc. beneath. Fls green-yellow; glabrous, anth. yellow. Japan, Sachalin, Hondo, Hokkaido. Z6.

***L. gracilipes*** Miq. Shrub to 180cm. Branches usually subadpressed curved-pubesc. Lvs to 6×5cm, broad-lanceolate to ovate to rhombic, apex often acute, usually cuneate at base, pubesc., blue-green beneath; petioles to 5mm. Fls pink to carmine, solitary, rarely paired, cernuous; peduncles to 3cm, thin, pendent, usually glabrous; bracts 1, rarely 2, narrow-lanceolate, to 7mm; bracteoles usually absent; cal. shallow-cupulate; cor. narrow-funnelform, to 2cm, short-lobed; style included. Fr. ellipsoid, 1cm, scarlet. Spring. Japan. 'Alba': fls white. Z6.

***L. griffithii*** Hook. f. & Thoms. Deciduous twining shrub to 5m. Bark exfoliating; young shoots glabrous. Lvs to 5×2.5cm, broad-ovate, oblong or rounded, green, glabrous, glaucous, margin often deeply lobed; petiole to 12.5mm. Fls rose to white, in terminal clusters of 2–3 whorls; sep. lanceolate, spreading, persistent; cor.-tube bilabiate, 2.5cm, fine-glandular-pubesc. outside; stamens glabrous; style villous. Spring. Afghanistan. Z9.

***L. gynochlamydea*** Hemsl. Erect deciduous shrub to 3m. Young shoots purple, glabrous. Lvs to 10×4cm, lanceolate, apex long-acuminate, base rounded to broadly acuminate, midrib lanate above and at base beneath; petiole 3mm. Fls white, pink-tinged, erect, paired; cal. produces collar covering cupule margin and united bracteoles; cor. bilabiate, to 12mm, tube short, broader at base, pubesc. outside; stamens and style lightly pubesc. Fr. white or purple-white, translucent, separate; seeds almost black. Spring. China (Hupeh, Yunnan). Z6.

***L. ×heckrottii*** Rehd. (? *L. sempervirens* × *L. ×americana*.) Scarcely scandent deciduous shrub, lax, spreading. Lvs to 6cm, subsessile, oblong or elliptic, glaucous beneath, uppermost pairs connate at base. Fls abundant, rich pink outside, sparsely pubesc. and yellow inside, 4cm, in whorls on terminal spikes; cor. bilabiate, tube slender. Fr. red. Summer. 'Goldflame': lvs dark green; fls yellow inside, flushed strong purple (a dark selection of the cross). Z5.

***L. henryi*** Hemsl. Scandent evergreen or semi-deciduous shrub. Shoots slender, dense-strigose. Lvs to 9×4cm, oblong-lanceolate to oblong-ovate, acuminate, rounded or cordate at base, deep green above, lighter and somewhat shiny beneath, ciliate, pubesc. on venation, occasionally subglabrous; petiole to 12.5mm. Fls 2cm, maroon or yellow, usually paired, crowded in panicles, spikes, or heads, axillary and terminal cor. bilabiate; fil. pilose at base. Fr. purple-black. Summer. W China. Z4.

***L. heteroloba*** Batal. Resembles *L. tatsiensis*, but lvs smaller, more densely pubesc., especially on midrib. Stamens shorter than anth. NW China.

***L. heterophylla*** Decne. Resembles *L. webbiana*, but branchlets glabrous, lvs to 9cm, elliptic to oblong-lanceolate, sometimes lobed, glabrous or subglabrous. Fls yellow, becoming tinted red, glandular-pubesc. outside. Himalaya. var. ***karelinii*** (Bunge) Rehd. Lvs to 8cm, thick, not lobed, dark green above, paler beneath, glandular-pubesc. on veins. Fls yellow-white, becoming tinted red, 1.5cm; cor. glandular outside. Fr. red. C Asia. Z5.

***L. hildebrandtiana*** Collett & Hemsl. GIANT BURMESE HONEYSUCKLE; GIANT HONEYSUCKLE. Vigorous scandent evergreen, sometimes semi-deciduous, to 25m. Lvs to 12×10cm, broad-ovate, oval or rounded-oval, apex abruptly acuminate, base broadly acuminate, deep green above, lighter and glandular beneath; petiole to 2cm. Fls cream white, later sparsely rich orange, fragrant, paired, axillary, or grouped in large infl.; cor.-tube narrow, to 16×10cm, bilabiate, upper lip 4-lobed, lower lip recurved. Fr. ovoid, to 2.5cm. Summer. China, SE Asia. Z9.

***L. hirsuta*** Eaton. HAIRY HONEYSUCKLE. Twining deciduous shrub. Young shoots slender, glandular-pubesc. Lvs to 10×5cm, oval, deep dull green above, grey beneath, pubesc., especially beneath, ciliate, upper lvs fused forming disc. Infl. terminal or axillary spikes of fls in 2–3 dense whorls; cor.-tube bilabiate, to 3cm, yellow-orange glandular-pubesc. outside, base saccate. Fr. yellow-red. Summer. NE America. Z3.

***L. hispida*** Roem. & Schult. Deciduous shrub to 1.5m. Young shoots hispid. Lvs to 8×3.5cm, ovate-oblong, short-acuminate or truncate, rounded or broad-tapered at base, setose-pubesc., especially on margins and veins beneath, deep green above, grey-green beneath; petiole 3mm. Fls yellow or yellow-white, paired, axillary, pendent; peduncles 1cm; cor. to 3cm, funnelform, enveloped by 2, ovate, persistent white bracts, to 2.5cm. Fr. oblong, 1.5cm, bright red. Spring–summer. Turkestan. Z6.

***L. hispidula*** Douglas ex Torr. & A. Gray. Procumbent, sometimes scandent, deciduous shrub. Branches sarmentose; branchlets usually hispid. Lvs to 6cm, oval-oblong, apex abrupt-acuminate or acute, rounded to subcordate at base, pubesc. to glabrous above, soft-pubesc. beneath, ciliate, uppermost leaf pair fused into disc. Infl. spikes of fls in close whorls; cor. white becoming red, bilabiate, tube 1.5cm, glabrous or slightly pubesc. Fr. red. Summer. Western N America (British Columbia to California). Z6.

***L. humilis*** Karel. & Kir. Erect dwarf shrub. Lvs 0.8–2cm, ovate or oval, coriaceous, apex acute, ciliate and sparsely adpressed-pilose. Fls at base of young branchlets, with or before lvs; peduncles short; bracts ovate; cor. tubular-campanulate, pilose, white to yellow-white, bilabiate; stamens included. Turkestan. Z6.

***L. iberica*** Bieb. Robust, erect deciduous shrub to 2m, dense, bushy. Young shoots pubesc. Lvs to 5×2.5cm, ovate, occasionally rounded, apex subobtuse, cordate at base, deep dull green above, grey beneath, pubesc. Fls pale yellow or white, 1.5cm, pubesc., axillary and terminal, paired; peduncles to 5mm; bracts oval-oblong, to 1cm, foliaceous; cor. bilabiate, tube strongly gibbous. Fr. to 8mm diam., bright red, puberulent. Summer. Caucasus, Persia, N Iran. 'Erecta': habit narrowly fastigiate, to 3m high; lvs to 2cm. 'Microphylla': habit prostrate, loose-growing; twigs drooping; lvs to 2cm, tinted blue. Z6.

***L. implexa*** Sol. MINORCA HONEYSUCKLE. Scandent evergreen 2.5m+. Young shoots slender, purple, glabrous or setose pubesc. Lvs to 7×2.5cm, sessile, elliptic to oblong, acuminate or blunt, glabrous, strongly glaucous beneath, leaf pairs on flowering shoots mostly fused into rhombic disc. Fls yellow, pink-suffused outside, white inside, becoming yellow, in the axils of the 3 uppermost leaf pairs; cor. to 4.5cm, tube pubesc. inside; style pubesc. above. Summer. Mediterranean. Z9.

***L. interrupta*** Benth. CHAPARRAL HONEYSUCKLE. Twining evergreen shrub, of bushy habit. Branchlets glabrous, glaucous. Lvs to 4cm, orbicular to elliptic, entire, glabrous or somewhat pubesc., green above, glaucous beneath, uppermost leaf pairs connate at base. Fls to 2cm, sessile, yellow, in interrupted spikes to 16cm; cor. funnelform, gibbous, glabrous outside; fil. pubesc. Fr. 5mm diam., subglobose, red. Summer. SW US (Arizona and S California). Z8.

***L. involucrata*** (Richardson) Spreng. TWINBERRY. To 90cm. Resembles *L. ledebourii*, but habit smaller. Lvs to 12.5cm, narrower, ovate to oblong-lanceolate, less pubesc., occasionally glabrous. Fls 12.5mm, yellow or red-tinged, paired; cor. tubular; stamens equal limb. Fr. 8mm diam., ovoid to globose, shiny purple-black, subtended by spreading bracts, later reflexed. Spring. Mexico, W North America, S Canada. var. ***flavescens*** (Dipp.) Rehd. Lvs to 12cm, oblong-lanceolate, green, glabrous or pale subglabrous. Cor. slightly gibbous at base. NW US (British Columbia to Oregon, Utah & Wyoming). Z4.

***L. japonica*** Thunb. JAPANESE HONEYSUCKLE; GOLD-AND-SILVER FLOWER. Scandent evergreen or semi-evergreen vigorous shrub. Branches terete, hollow, glandular, prominently patent-pubesc. when young. Lvs to 8×3cm, oblong to ovate-elliptic, apex acute or obtuse, mucronate, usually rounded at base, entire, often incised-sinuate when young, light green beneath, lanate, villous, sometimes glabrous, margins ciliate; petioles to 8mm. Fls white, becoming pink later yellow, paired, intensely fragrant; peduncles to 1cm; bracts foliaceous, ovate, to 2cm; bracteoles 1mm, elliptic, pilose; cal.-tube glabrous, sep. 1mm, ovate, ciliate; cor. to 4cm, bilabiate, soft-pubesc. outside, tube narrow. Fr. to 7mm diam., blue-black, separate. Spring–summer. Japan, Korea, Manchuria, China; naturalized SE US. var. ***repens*** (Sieb.) Rehd. Stems sometimes maroon. Lvs soon glabrous, often deeply lobed markedly purple-tinged on veins beneath. Fls white becoming yellow, upper lip lobed. 'Aureo-reticulata' ('Reticulata'): habit compact, ground-covering, to 3m high, to 3m wide; lvs small, bright green, golden reticulate venation, sometimes lobed; otherwise like var. *repens*. 'Dart's World': habit spreading and bushy, to 25cm high, to 1.2m wide; stems dark maroon; lvs to 7×3cm, ovate, dark green, tinted blue and pubesc. with red venation beneath; fls to 4cm, 2-lipped, interior white, exterior often flushed rosy red, later yellow and strong red, in pairs. 'Halliana': lvs pubesc. when young, rich green; fls white, sometimes tinted red, later yellow, upper lip divided almost to middle. 'Hall's Prolific': habit climbing, to 6m high, to 3m wide; lvs ovate; fls white, later cream to yellow, strongly scented, profuse. 'Purpurea': lvs tinted purple; fls maroon outside, white inside. 'Variegata': lvs variegated yellow. Z4.

***L. kesselringii*** Reg. Closely resembles *L. caucasica*, but lvs to 6×2cm, oblong or elliptic-lanceolate; peduncles to 8mm; fls pink, in pairs, smaller, and cor.-tube less swollen. Kamchatka. Z6.

***L. koehneana*** Rehd. Vigorous erect shrub to 3.5m. Lvs to 10cm, ovate or rhombic-ovate to obovate, acuminate, subglabrous above, villous-pubesc. and glaucescent beneath. Fls 2cm, yellow, paired; peduncles to 2.5cm slender, longer than *L. maackii*; cor. bilabiate, pubesc. outside; anth. pilose. Fr. dark red, rarely yellow. China. Z6.

**Lonicera** (a) *L. involucrata* leaves (×0.6), flowers (×1) (b) *L. arborea* leaf (×0.6), flowers (×1) (c) *L. nummulariifolia* leaf (×0.6), flowers (×1) (d) *L. oblongifolia* leaves (×0.6), flowers (×1) (e) *L. alpigena* leaves (×0.6), flowers (×1) (f) *L. webbiana* leaves (×0.6), flowers (×1) (g) *L. pyrenaica* leaves (×0.6), flowers (×1) (h) *L. orientalis* leaf (×0.6), flowers (×1) (i) *L. kesselringii* leaf (×0.6), flowers (×1) (j) *L. floribunda* leaves (×0.6), flowers (×1) (k) *L. caucasica* leaf (×0.6), flowers (×1) (l) *L. discolor* leaf (×0.6), flowers (×1) (m) *L. korolkowii* leaves (×0.6), flowers (×1) (n) *L. trichosantha* leaves (×0.6), flowers (×1) (o) *L. chaetocarpa* leaves (×0.6), flowers (×1)

***L. korolkowii*** Stapf. Deciduous shrub to 3m, lax, patent, graceful. Young shoots pubesc. Lvs to 3×2cm, ovate or oval, apex acuminate, usually tapered at base, light glaucous green, blue-green beneath, pubesc., especially beneath; petiole to 6.5mm. Fls pale rose, 1.5cm, paired, axillary; cor. bilabiate, tube narrow, pubesc. within. Fr. bright red. Summer. Mts of Soviet C Asia, Afghanistan, Pakistan. 'Aurora': to 2.5m high; twigs pendulous; lvs narrowly ovate, acute, small, velvety pubesc. beneath, green tinted grey, on elongated shoots; fls small, to 8mm long, to 18mm wide, shocking pink; fr. dark orange. 'Floribunda': lvs broadly ovate, obtuse, velvety pubesc.; cor. to 15mm, tube somewhat bulging, white. Z5.

***L. ledebourii*** Eschsch. Sturdy erect deciduous shrub to 2m. Young shoots stout, glabrous rarely pubesc. Lvs to 12×4.5cm, ovate-oblong, base acuminate or rounded, dull dark green above, brighter and lanate beneath, margins pubesc.; petioles 6.5mm. Fls deep orange-yellow, to 2cm; subtended by 2–4 purple-tinged and glandular cordate bracts; peduncles erect, to 4cm; cor. funnelform, glutinous-pubesc. outside. Fr. black, surrounded by persistent, red bracts. Summer. W US (California). Z6.

***L. maackii*** (Rupr.) Maxim. Deciduous erect shrub to 5m. Bark dark grey, exfoliating; young branches often dark purple, dense white-pubesc. Lvs 8×4cm, narrow-obovate to broad-lanceolate, apex long-acuminate or acute, cuneate at base, dark green and minute patent-pubesc. above, lighter and minute-pubesc., especially on veins, beneath; petioles to 5mm, purple, dense-pubesc. Fls white, later yellow, fragrant, axillary, paired on outer side of branchlets; peduncles to 4mm, glandular-punctate; bracts membranous, linear; bracteoles shallowly emarginate, ciliate; cal. to 3mm, cupulate; cor. 2cm, bilabiate, glabrous or lightly pubesc. outside. Fr. to 4mm diam., globose, dark red or black; seeds to 4×2.5mm, ovate or elliptic, light yellow. Spring–summer. Japan, Korea, Manchuria, N China, Amur, Ussuri. 'Erubescens': fls suffused pink; otherwise as f. *podocarpa*. 'Rem Red': habit upright and rounded, to 5m high; lvs dark green; fls white, later yellow; fr. 5mm diam., bright red. f. ***podocarpa*** Rehd. Shrµb to 3m, wide-spreading. Fls white to yellow. Fr. red. Z2.

***L. maximowiczii*** (Rupr.) Maxim. Erect deciduous shrub to 3m. Young shoots tinted purple, glabrous or somewhat setose. Lvs to 11.5×5.5cm, oval, dark green and glabrous above, lightly pubesc. beneath. Fls purple-red, 1cm, glabrous outside, paired; peduncles 2cm, glabrous; cor. bilabiate, tube enlarged at base. Fr. ovoid, red, connate. Spring–summer. Manchuria (Amurland), Korea, China. var. ***sachalinensis*** F. Schmidt. Lvs broad, apex less acute, dark green and glabrous above, markedly blue-green beneath. Fls dark purple, to 18mm; sep. acuminate. Fr. dark red, completely connate. Sachalin, Japan. Z4.

***L. microphylla*** Roem. & Schult. Sturdy deciduous shrub to 90cm. Branchlets short, glabrous, rigid. Lvs to 2.5×1.25cm, oval or obovate, apex obtuse or subacute, base acuminate, glaucous, finely pubesc., dull grey-green above, fine-lanuginose and distinctly veined beneath; petiole 1.5mm. Fls pale yellow, 1cm, glabrous to fine-pubesc. outside, paired; anth. slightly exserted. Fr. bright red, connate. NW Himalaya, Tibet, Siberia. Z3.

***L. ×minutiflora*** Zab. (*L. morrowii* × *L. xylosteoides*.) Erect deciduous shrub. Branchlets spreading, fine-pubesc. Lvs to 3cm, oval-oblong to oblong, obtuse, fine-pubesc. beneath. Fls white; cor. bilabiate upper lip deeply divided, 12mm, outspread, stamens included. Fr. red. Spring–summer. Z6.

***L. morrowii*** A. Gray Deciduous shrub to 2m, densely branched. Young branches obscurely 4-angled, dense short soft-pubesc. Lvs to 5×2.5cm, oblong or ovate to elliptic, apex obtuse, occasionally subacute, rounded at base, light green and pubesc. beneath. Fls white, later yellow, paired, axillary; peduncles to 1.5cm; bracts linear, somewhat foliaceous; bracteoles elliptic; sep. broad-lanceolate, to 1mm; cor. 13mm, pubesc. outside, upper lip divided to base, gibbous. Fr. to 7×8mm, depressed-globose, dark red, shiny; seeds to 3×2mm, oval or rounded-ovid. Spring–summer. Japan. 'Xanthocarpa': fr. yellow. Z3.

***L. ×muendeniensis*** Rehd. (*L. ×bella* × *L. ruprechtiana*.) Erect, deciduous shrub. Lvs to 7cm, ovate to lanceolate, apex acuminate, base acuminate or rounded, dark green above, pubesc. beneath. Fls white to yellow-white, sometimes tinted red, upper lip deeply incised; fil. pubesc. below. Fr. red. Spring. Z5.

***L. ×muscaviensis*** Rehd. (*L. morrowii* × *L. ruprechtiana*.) Erect deciduous shrub. Young shoots pubesc. Lvs to 5cm, ovate to oval-oblong, acuminate, dark green, sparse-pubesc. above, dense-pubesc. beneath. Fls white. Fr. bright red. Spring–summer. Z5.

***L. myrtilloides*** Purpus. Deciduous, finely branched shrub, to 1.5m. Young shoots glandular-pubesc. Lvs to 3cm, oblong to elliptic, pubesc. at least on midrib. Fls white, red at base, fragrant cernuous; peduncles 1cm; cor. pubesc. outside. Fr. red, connate. Spring–summer. Himalaya. Z6.

***L. myrtillus*** Hook. f. & Thoms. Deciduous shrub to 1m, compact, rounded. Branches stiff; young shoots pubesc. Lvs oval or ovate, to 2.5cm×6.5mm, glabrous, dark green above, paler and glaucous beneath, recurved at margins. Fls in pairs on short peduncles, fragrant yellow-white; cor. tubular-campanulate, to 8mm, glabrous; bracts narrow-oblong; ovaries connate, 2-, rarely 6-locular. Fr. 6.5mm diam., orange-red. Spring–summer. Himalaya, Afghanistan. var. ***depressa*** (Royle) Rehd. Peduncles equal lvs; bracts oval, broader. Himalaya (Nepal, Sikkim). Z6.

***L. nervosa*** Maxim. Deciduous shrub, erect, to 3m. Young shoots glabrous, spreading, tinged purple. Lvs to 6×2.5cm, oval to oblong, apex and base acuminate, glabrous, red at first, later bright green above, except on veins which remain red; petiole to 4mm. Bracts connate into cupule; fls pale pink, paired; cor. 1cm; style pubesc. to apex. Fr. black, separate. Spring–summer. China. Z6.

***L. nigra*** L. Deciduous shrub to 1.5m, rounded. Branches rigid. Lvs to 5cm, usually oval, bright green, glabrous or pubesc. on midrib beneath. Fls dusty pink, bilabiate, in axillary pairs; peduncles slender, pubesc. Fr. blue-black, connate at base. Spring–summer. Mts of C & S Europe. Z6.

***L. nitida*** Wils. Densely branched evergreen shrub to 3.5m. Young shoots thin, erect, purple, pubesc., sparse-setose. Lvs to 1.2cm thick, ovate to rounded, blunt, cordate at base, dark green and shiny above, lighter beneath, usually glabrous; petiole 1mm, minute-setose. Fls to 1cm, cream to white, paired on short, lateral shoots. Fr. 6.5mm diam., shiny blue-purple, transparent. Spring. China (W Sichuan, Yunnan). 'Aurea': habit erect; lvs gold. 'Baggesen's Gold': habit low, dense; branches nodding; lvs small, gold, later sulphur green; fls cream; fr. purple tinted blue. 'Elegant': habit shrub-like, to 1m high; twigs loose, spreading, sometimes almost horizontally; lvs small, to 1.5cm, mainly distichous, suborbicular to narrowly ovate, dull green; fls white, freely produced; fr. purple. 'Ernest Wilson': habit spreading; branches arching to drooping; lvs tiny, to 12mm, ovate, glossy green; a clone of *L. nitida*. 'Fertilis': habit erect, to 2.5m; stems upright or arching; lvs large, broadly ovate to elliptic; fls and fr. prolific. 'Graciosa': habit low and mat-forming, densely branched; shoots arching; lvs small; fls and fr. rare; a seedling of 'Elegant'. 'Hohenheimer Findling': habit shrub-like, to 1.25m wide; twigs nodding; lvs to 1.8cm, narrowly oval, strong green. 'Maygreen' ('Maigrün'): habit squat, compact, to 80cm high, to 80cm wide; lvs shiny, long-lasting. 'Yunnan': habit erect, wide, similar to 'Ernest Wilson'; shoots erect; lvs large, not usually distichous; fls abundant. Sometimes misnamed *L. yunnanensis*. Z7.

***L. ×notha*** Zab. (*L. ruprechtiana* × *L. tatarica*.) Vigorous erect deciduous shrub. Young shoots glabrous or subglabrous. Lvs to 6cm, ovate to lanceolate-elliptic, apex acuminate, at base rounded to truncate, lightly pubesc. to subglabrous beneath. Fls white, yellow or pink, paired; cor. 18mm, bilabiate, tube expanded. Fr. red. Spring–summer. 'Alba': fls white. 'Carneorosea': fls crimson. 'Gilva': fls pale yellow, edged pink. 'Grandiflora': fls large, white tinted yellow, later tinted pink; fr. maroon. 'Ochroleuca': fls flushed yellow; fr. orange. Z4.

***L. nummulariifolia*** Jaub. & Spach Erect shrub to 9m. Young branches puberulent or glandular-villous. Lvs to 5×3.5cm, ovate-lanceolate to suborbicular, obtuse, sparse-pubesc. or villous, sometimes glandular-pubesc. Fls pale cream to deep yellow, paired, axillary; peduncles to 3mm; bracts linear-lanceolate, 1mm; bracteoles 1mm, free; cor. to 2cm, pubesc., tube not expanded. Fr. yellow, glabrous or sparse-pubesc. Turkestan, S Greece, Crete. Z6.

***L. oblongifolia*** (Goldie) Hook. SWAMP FLY HONEYSUCKLE. Erect deciduous shrub to 1.5m. Branchlets fine soft-pubesc. Lvs to 8cm, subsessile, oblong to oblanceolate, obtuse, fine-pubesc., blue-green above, grey-green beneath. Fls to 1.5cm, yellow, paired; peduncles erect, to 2.5cm; bracts minute, caducous; bracteoles usually indistinct; cor. to 1.5cm, tubular, deeply-bilabiate. Fr. red; seeds 2mm, smooth. Spring. NE North America. Z3.

***L. obovata*** Royle. Erect deciduous shrub to 2m, bushy. Branchlets glabrous. Lvs to 1.2cm, obovate, subsessile, cuneate at base, glabrous or subglabrous, white beneath. Fls yellow-white, paired; bracts usually subulate; cor. 1cm, glabrous outside, base saccate; stamens equal limb. Fr. ellipsoid, blue-black. Spring. Himalaya to Afghanistan. Z5.

***L. orientalis*** Lam. Erect deciduous shrub to 3m. Branchlets glabrous. Lvs to 10cm, ovate to lanceolate, apex acute, usually rounded at base, dark green above, grey-green beneath, glabrous but veins pubesc. Fls pink to violet, paired; peduncles to 2.5cm; bracts subulate; cor. bilabiate, tubular, to 12mm. Fr. ellipsoid blue-black, connate. Spring–summer. Asia Minor. Z6.

***L. periclymenum*** L. WOODBINE; HONEYSUCKLE. Twining shrub to 4m. Young shoots glabrous or pubesc., hollow. Lvs to 6.5×4cm, ovate, oval or obovate, apex usually acuminate, occasionally obtuse, base acuminate, lightly pubesc. becoming glabrous, glaucous and blue-green beneath, uppermost pair separate. Fls fragrant, red and yellow-white, to 5cm, glandular-glutinous outside, in 3–5-whorled terminal spikes; cor. bilabiate. Fr. round, bright red. Summer. Europe, Asia Minor, Caucasus, W Asia. var. ***glauco-hirta*** Kunze. Lvs ovate to elliptic, acute, pubesc., blue beneath. Spain, Morocco. 'Aurea': lvs variegated yellow. 'Belgica': habit bushy, to 3m high, to 3m wide; lvs glabrous, thick, elliptic-oblong; fls white, flushed purple outside, later yellow, scented, in large clusters; fr. large, red, abundant. 'Belgica Select': a fast-growing selection of 'Belgica'. 'Berries Jubilee': lvs tinted blue, glaucous grey beneath; fls yellow; fr. bright red; vigorous grower. 'Graham Thomas': fls large, white, later yellow tinted copper, long-lasting. 'Quercina': lvs 'oak-like', sinuate, sometimes variegated white. 'Serotina': lvs narrow; fls dark purple outside, later fading, yellow inside, profuse; fr. red. 'Serotina Florida': habit compact; fls dark red outside, yellow and white inside, crimson in bud, scented; fr. translucent red; slow-growing. 'Serpentine': to 6m tall; branches and twigs slender, deep maroon when young; lvs narrow, tinted pale blue beneath; fls to 7cm, 2-lipped, upper lip wide and 4-lobed, lower lip narrow, interior cream, exterior light mauve with white edge, later yellow; buds deep maroon, in clusters to 10, arranged in rings; fr. red, profuse, dense. Z4.

***L. pileata*** Oliv. Low, often prostate, evergreen or semi-deciduous shrub. Branches often horizontal; young shoots purple, thickly pubesc. Lvs to

**Lonicera** (×0.6) (a) *L. tragophylla* (b) *L. caprifolium* (c) *L. periclymenum* (d) *L.* × *tellmanniana* (e) *L. splendida* (f) *L.* × *americana*

3×1.25cm, distichous, ovate-oblong or slightly lozenge-shaped, apex obtuse or rounded, tapered at base, subglabrous, shiny dark green. Fls yellow-white, in sessile pairs; bracts lanceolate-subulate; cal. produces collar covering the cupule margin; cor. to 8mm, funnelform, pubesc. outside, base tuberculate. Fr. 5mm diam., globose, amethyst-coloured, translucent, with outgrowth from cal. at apex. Spring. China. 'Moss Green': habit low-spreading, compact; lvs bright green; not vigorous. 'Royal Carpet': habit prostrate, to 45cm high, to 1.5m wide; branches straight, spreading; lvs glossy green; fr. purple. Z5.

***L. praeflorens*** Batal. Deciduous shrub to 2m. Bark grey-brown, exfoliating; young branchlets sometimes puberulent. Lvs to 6.5×4cm, membranous, broad-ovate, apex acute or abrupt acute, obtuse to rounded at base, pubesc., especially beneath, subglaucous; petioles to 4mm. Fls precocious; peduncles to 8mm, glabrous; bracts broad-lanceolate or narrow-ovate, ciliate; bracteoles absent; cal.-tube glabrous, sparse-glandular-pilose on margin; cor. to 1.5cm, white tinted yellow, funnelform, subactinomorphic, glabrous outside, tube straight; stamens exserted. Fr. 8mm diam., red. Spring. Japan, Korea, Manchuria, Ussuri. Z5.

***L. prolifera*** (Kirchn.) Rehd. GRAPE HONEYSUCKLE. Rarely scandent, deciduous shrub to 180cm, blue-pruinose of lax, patent habit. Lvs to 10×6.5cm, thick, oval, obovate or oblong, pruinose above, glaucous and lightly pubesc. beneath, upper lvs connate, forming round disc. Fls pale yellow, usually in 4 superimposed whorls; cor.-tube 3cm, pubesc. inside, glabrous outside, slightly expanded. Fr. to 12.5mm diam., scarlet. Summer. C North America (Ohio to Tennessee & Mo.) Z5.

***L. ×propinqua*** Zab. (*L. alpigena* × *L. ledebourii.*) Deciduous shrub. Two forms, one resembling *L. alpigena*, the other *L. ledebourii*. Cor. tawny, bilabiate, expanded; bracts densely glandular. Z6.

***L. prostrata*** Rehd. Procumbent deciduous shrub. Branches thin, hollow, forming a hemispheric mass; young shoots pubesc. and tinged purple. Lvs to 3×1.25cm, oval or ovate, apex acute-acuminate, base abruptly acuminate, pubesc. above, later glabrous, veins sparsely pubesc. beneath; petiole 2.5mm, pubesc. Fls pale yellow, axillary, paired; cor. bilabiate, 1.5cm. Fr. to 8.5mm, ovoid, red. Summer. W China. Z5.

***L. ×pseudochrysantha*** Barua. (*L. chrysantha* × *L. xylosteum.*) Most similar to *L. chrysantha* but with broader bracts. Z3.

***L. purpurascens*** Walp. Deciduous sturdy bush to 3m. Young shoots stiff, purple, soft fine-pubesc. Lvs to 4×2.5cm, oblong or slightly obovate, apex obtuse to acute-acuminate, base acuminate to rounded, pubesc. especially beneath, dull green above, grey beneath; petiole to 6.5mm, pubesc., purple. Fls purple, cernuous; cor. tubular-funnelform, 1.5cm, pubesc. outside, enlarged at base; anth. equal limb; style exserted. Fr. blue-black, connate. Spring. Himalaya, Kashmir, Afghanistan. Z6.

***L. ×purpusii*** Rehd. (*L. fragrantissima* × *L. standishii.*) Erect semi-evergreen shrub to 3m, densely branched. Branchlets arching, glabrous, sometimes light setose-pubesc. Lvs to 10cm, ovate-elliptic, dark green above, light green beneath, glabrous, pubesc. on veins beneath, margins setose. Fls fragrant cream-white, axillary, 2–4-clustered; cor. glabrous outside; fil. shiny white, anth. golden-yellow. Fr. red. Winter–spring. 'Winter Beauty': fls creamy white, very fragrant, winter-flowering. Z6.

***L. pyrenaica*** L. Erect deciduous shrub to 2m. Lvs to 4×1cm, sessile, obovate to oblanceolate, apex abrupt-acuminate, tapered at base, glaucous, paler and more glaucous beneath. Fls cream, rose-tinted, cernuous, paired; peduncles to 2cm; bracts foliaceous; cor. 2cm, funnelform-campanulate, tuberculate at base. Fr. globose, 6mm diam., red, connate at base. Spring–summer. E Pyrenees, Balearic Is. Z5.

***L. quinquelocularis*** Hardw. Deciduous shrub, sometimes a small tree, to 4m. Young shoots somewhat purple, thickly pubesc. Lvs to 5×4cm, oval, occasionally obovate or orbicular, apex short-acuminate, occasionally rounded, rounded or tapered at base, dull green and pubesc. initially above, grey and more pubesc. beneath. Fls cream white, later yellow, axillary, paired; cor. bilabiate, to 2cm, densely adpressed-pubesc. outside, tube slender, slightly expanded. Fr. round to oval, translucent white; seeds violet. Summer. Himalaya, China. f. ***translucens*** (Carr.) Zab. Lvs longer, base cordate. Cor. tube distinctly gibbous. Z5.

***L. reticulata*** Champ. Twining evergreen, rarely deciduous, shrub. Branches short-pubesc. or glabrous. Lvs to 7cm, oblong-ovate, obtuse, rounded to subcordate at base, glabrous above, tomentose and strongly reticulate beneath; petioles to 1.5cm. Fls in axillary pairs, usually in terminal panicles or racemes; bracts subulate; sep. ovate-lanceolate; cor. to 6cm; style glabrous; ovaries glabrous. Fr. usually black, with persistent cal. Hong Kong. Z10.

***L. rupicola*** Hook. f. & Thoms. Deciduous dense bush to 2.5m. Bark exfoliating; branches interlacing, forming a rounded, impenetrable mass; branchlets lightly pubesc. or glabrous when young. Lvs to 2.5×1.25cm, often 3 together, oblong or ovate, apex obtuse, base rounded or somewhat cordate, dull green and glabrous above, lighter and pubesc. beneath, often glabrous later; petiole to 3mm. Fls pale pink to lilac, fragrant, axillary, paired; cor. 5-lobed, lobes ovate, tube pubesc. outside. Fr. red. Spring–summer. Himalaya, Tibet. Z8.

***L. ruprechtiana*** Reg. Deciduous bushy shrub to 3m, sometimes to 6m. Young shoots pubesc. Lvs to 10×4cm, ovate to oblong, apex often slender-acuminate, tapered at base, dark green above, lighter beneath, pubesc. beneath and on sunken midrib above; petiole to 6.5mm. Fls white, later yellow, axillary, paired; peduncles to 2cm; cor. bilabiate, divided to half or two-thirds depth, 2cm, glabrous outside. Fr. 8.5mm diam., bright red, transparent. Spring–summer. NE Asia, Manchuria, China. 'Xanthocarpa': lvs densely pubesc.; fls small; fr. yellow. Z6.

***L. saccata*** Rehd. Shrub to 1.5m, of slender-branched habit. Lvs to 5cm, oblong, obtuse to acute, pubesc. beneath. Fls 12mm, white or yellow-white, paired; peduncles slender; bracts oblong, foliaceous; cor. tubular-campanulate, 5-lobed, tube enlarged at base. Fr. orange-red or scarlet. Spring. China. Z6.

***L. sempervirens*** L. TRUMPET HONEYSUCKLE; CORAL HONEYSUCKLE. Vigorous scandent evergreen shrub. Young shoots glabrous. Lvs to 8×5cm, oval or slightly obovate, deep green and glabrous above, blue-green, glaucous and often pubesc. beneath, 1–2 uppermost pairs of lvs connate, forming a circular or oblong disc; petiole to 6.5mm. Fls rich scarlet-orange outside, more yellow inside, in 3–4 superimposed whorls; cor. to 5cm with 5 equal lobes. Fr. bright red. Spring–autumn. E & S US (Connecticut to Florida & Texas). var. ***minor*** Ait. Semi-evergreen. Lvs elliptic to oblong-lanceolate. Fls more abundant orange-red to scarlet, smaller, narrower. 'Magnifica': fls red outside, interior yellow; semi-evergreen. 'Sulphurea' ('Flava'): to 10m; fls bright yellow, long- and late-flowering. 'Superba' ('Red Coral', 'Red Trumpet', 'Rubra', 'Dreer's Everlasting'): lvs ovate-elliptic, glabrous above; fls bright scarlet; deciduous. Z3.

***L. serotina*** (Ait.) Gand. Like *L. periclymenum* but lvs on longer petioles, elliptic to oblong, glabrous; fls dark purple becoming paler, abundant, produced later than *L. periclymenum*. Europe, N Africa. Z6.

***L. setifera*** Franch. Medium-sized shrub. Shoots setose-pubesc. Lvs to 7.5cm, oblong-lanceolate, soft-pubesc., margins usually coarse-dentate. Fls precocious, fragrant straw-yellow to pink, setose, in clusters; cor. to 8mm; ovaries glandular and setose. Fr. red, setose. Winter–spring. Himalaya, Assam, China. Z8.

***L. similis*** Hemsl. Scandent semi-evergreen shrub. C & W China (Hupeh, Sichuan), India, Burma. var. ***delavayi*** (Franch.) Rehd. Scandent, evergreen, glabrous shrub. Lvs to 6cm, lanceolate, apex acute, base round to cordate, bright green above, white lanate beneath. Infl. racemose at branchlet tips; fls to 8cm, in axillary pairs, white becoming yellow; cor. bilabiate; stamens and style strongly exserted, tube slightly expanded. Fr. black. SW China. Z9.

***L. spinosa*** (Decne.) Walp. Deciduous, often almost efoliate, shrub to 120cm. Branches armed with thorns. Lvs to 3cm, narrow-oblong, glabrous, occasionally 2-toothed. Fls 2cm, lilac-pink, paired; cor. tubular-funnelform, tube slender, limb spreading, apices oval, pubesc. inside, glabrous outside; stamens included or equal limb; styles exserted. Fr. white or purple, pruinose. NW Himalaya, Tibet, E Turkestan. Z6.

***L. splendida*** Boiss. Vigorous scandent evergreen. Lvs to 5cm, oval to oblong, glabrous, rarely pilose, glaucous, upper pair connate. Fls yellow-white, becoming maroon, in terminal, sessile clusters of densely compound whorls; cor. to 5cm, bilabiate, fine-pubesc. outside. Summer. Spain. Z9.

***L. standishii*** Jacq. Deciduous or semi-evergreen bush to 2.5m, sometimes 3.5m+. Bark exfoliating; young shoots tuberculate, setose. Lvs to 10×5cm, oblong-lanceolate, apex slender-acuminate, rounded or broad-cuneate at base, distinctly veined beneath, pubesc., setose on margins and midrib; petiole 3mm, setose. Fls fragrant, cream-white tinted palest pink, axillary, paired, usually pubesc. outside; bracts linear-lanceolate, pubesc., ciliate; cor. bilabiate. Fr. obcordate, red. Winter–spring. China. var. ***lancifolia*** Rehd. Lvs very narrow. Z6.

***L. strophiophora*** Franch. Deciduous shrub to 2.5m. Bark grey; young branches often dark purple-brown, light brown later, glabrous or scattered long-glandular-pubesc. Lvs to 8cm, membranous, broad-ovate to ovate-oblong, apex acuminate to acute, occasionally obtuse, base obtuse-rounded, coarse-pilose, especially on midrib beneath; petioles to 7mm, lax-pilose and sparse-glandular-pilose. Fls pale yellow, paired, cernuous; peduncles reflexed, to 2cm, lax-glandular-pilose; bracts to 1.5cm, membranous, ovate, subacute, light green, ciliate; bracteoles absent; cor. to 2cm, narrow-funnelform, glabrous. Fr. globose, red, pilose. Spring–summer. Japan. Z6.

***L. subaequalis*** Rehd. Scandent deciduous shrub. Branches glabrous. Lvs to 10cm, oval to oblong-obovate, apex obtuse, tapered at base, glabrous, uppermost pair connate into an elliptic disc; petiole short. Fls in sessile whorls; cor. to 3cm, funnelform, pubesc. inside, glandular outside; stamens inserted close to mouth of tube; fil. glabrous, anth. linear-oblong; style glabrous, exceeding the cor. W China (Sichuan). Z6.

***L. subspicata*** Hook. & Arn. Scandent evergreen shrub to 2.5m. Branchlets puberulent. Lvs to 4×1cm, linear-oblong to oblong, rounded both ends, entire, coriaceous, grey-pubesc., especially beneath, uppermost pairs connate into a disc; petioles to 5mm. Fls yellow or cream whorled in short, foliaceous spikes to 12cm; sep. broad-lanceolate, 1mm; cor. bilabiate, to 1cm, glandular-pubesc., tube gibbous; fil. pubesc. at base. Fr. to 7mm ellipsoid, yellow or red. Summer. W US (California). Z8.

***L. syringantha*** Maxim. Deciduous shrub to 3m, graceful, much branched. Young shoots thin, glabrous. Lvs in twos or threes, to 2.5cm×9.5mm, oblong or ovate, apex obtuse or broad-acuminate, rounded or somewhat cordate at base,

**Lonicera** (a) *L. henryi* leaf (×0.6), flowers (×1) (b) *L. giraldii* leaf (×0.6), flowers (×1). (c) *L. alseuosmoides* leaf (×0.6), flowers (×1) (d) *L. confusa* (×0.6) (e) *L. similis* var. *delavayi* (×0.6) (f) *L. biflora* leaf (×0.6), detached flowers (×1) (g) *L. japonica* 'Halliana' leaf (×0.6), detached flowers (×1) (h) *L. affinis* (×0.6) (i) *L. arizonica* (×0.6) (j) *L. glaucescens* leaf (×0.6), flower (×1) (k) *L. dioica* leaf (×0.6), flower (×1) (l) *L. japonica* (×0.6) (m) *L. ciliosa* leaf (×0.6), flower (×1)

dull green, somewhat glaucous, glabrous; petiole 2mm. Fls 12.5mm, paired, soft lilac, fragrant; sep. lanceolate; cor.-tube campanulate, to 8mm, pubesc. inside. Fr. red. Spring–summer. China, Tibet. 'Grandiflora': fls large. Z4.

***L. szechuanica*** Batal. Closely resembles *L. tangutica*, but lvs to 2.5cm, cuneate-obovate, apex obtuse, glabrous, glaucous and blue-green beneath, bracts subulate, shorter than ovaries, cor. 12mm, slender, and style glabrous. W China, (Sichuan, Kansu, Yunnan). Z6.

***L. tangutica*** Maxim. Low deciduous shrub. Shoots glabrous. Lvs to 3cm, obovate to oblong, apex mostly acute, base cuneate, ciliate, sparsely pilose above and on the veins beneath, otherwise glabrous beneath. Cor. to 1.4cm, narrow, base slightly swollen, white-yellow, becoming pink; bracts subulate; peduncles to 3cm. Fr. pendent, partly connate. Spring–summer. China (Kansu, Sichuan, Hupeh, Yunnan). Z6.

***L. tatarica*** L. Erect, deciduous shrub to 4m. Shoots grey, glabrous. Lvs to 6cm, ovate to lanceolate, apex acute, base rounded to subcordate, usually glabrous, rarely puberulent, glaucous beneath. Fls paired, axillary; peduncles to 2cm; cor. to 2.5cm, white to carmine, tube straight or base slightly swollen. Fr. globose, scarlet to yellow-orange. Spring–summer. S Russia to C Asia. Many cvs, ranging habit from dwarf to vigorous; lvs 4–10cm, green, blue tinted or variegated yellow; fls white to dark red; fr. yellow to bright red. Habit ranges from 'Grandiflora' (tall, vigorous; fls very large, pure white) to 'Nana' (dwarf; fls small, pink) and 'Louis Leroy' (low, rounded; lvs tinted blue; fls large, cor. lobes dusky pink, bordered white; fr. orange). 'Fenzlii' has lvs striped and speckled yellow. Cvs notable for fl. colour include 'Virginalis' (fls very large, white; fr. bright red), 'Discolor' (cor. pale pink inside, margin and dorsal side deep red; fr. orange), 'Latifolia' (syn. 'Grandiflora Rosea'; shoots thick; lvs large; fls pale pink with dark stripes), 'Rosea' (fls large, pale pink; fr. deep red), 'Sibirica' (syn. 'Rubra'; f. *sibirica* (Pers.) Rehd.) cor. lobes deep red, wide white border), 'Hack's Red' (fls dark pink-red), 'Arnold's Red' (habit dense and woody; branches arching; lvs tinted blue; fls darkest red, fragrant; fr. bright red); 'Zabelii': fls bright pink. Those notable for fruit include 'Lutea' (fr. yellow), 'Morden Orange' (fls light pink; fr. orange.). Z3.

***L. tatsienensis*** Franch. Erect, deciduous shrub, to 2m. Branchlets glabrous. Lvs to 4cm, ovate to oblong-ovate, apex acuminate, pilose, especially beneath; margin entire, rarely deeply lobed. Fls paired, axillary; peduncle to 3cm, glabrous; cor. to 1.2cm, bilabiate, deep purple; pilose at base; anth. included; style pilose. Fr. connate. Spring–summer. Tibet. Z6.

***L. ×tellmanniana*** hort. (*L. sempervirens* × *L. tragophylla.*) Vigorous, deciduous, scandent shrub. Branchlets glabrous, green-brown. Lvs to 10cm, ovate to oblong, becoming deep green above, white-pruinose beneath, upper pair fused into an elliptic disc. Infl. terminal whorls; cor. tube to 4.5cm, rich orange. Summer. Garden origin, Budapest, 1920s. In the US, this is known as 'Redgold'. Z5.

***L. tenuipes*** Nak. Erect, deciduous shrub, to 3m. Shoots yellow to rufous, pubesc., becoming glabrous. Lvs to 6cm, obovate to oblong-ovate, pubesc. above, brown-lanate beneath. Fls to 1.8cm, solitary, red, pubesc. outside, base gibbous; peduncles to 2cm. Fr. ellipsoid, red. Spring. Japan. Z6.

***L. thibetica*** Bur. & Franch. Deciduous shrub to 1.5m, erect to procumbent, loose-tomentose. Lvs to 3cm, oblong-lanceolate, often in groups of 3, apex acute, deep green, shining above, white-tomentose beneath. Fls paired, axillary; cor. 1.5cm, pale purple, erect, tubular-campanulate, 5-lobed, villous inside, often pubesc. outside; sep. lanceolate to ovate, apices acute; bracts linear-lanceolate; style half as long as tube. Fr. red. Summer. Tibet, China (Sichuan). Z4.

***L. tomentella*** Hook. f. & Thoms. Deciduous, spreading shrub, 1.5–3m. Branchlets rigid, densely tomentose, bark exfoliating. Lvs 1.5–4cm, almost distichous, oblong, apex acute, base rounded, pubesc. to glabrous above, villous beneath. Fls paired, axillary, cernuous; bracts leafy; bractlets fused into a cupule; cor. 1.6cm, tubular-campanulate, 5-lobed, lobes spreading, tinted pink, tube straight, pubesc. outside; stamens inserted in upper half of tube; style equals tube. Fr. 1cm, globose, blue-black. Summer. Himalaya, Sikkim. Z5.

***L. tragophylla*** Hemsl. Deciduous, vigorous, scandent shrub. Branchlets hollow; flowering shoots 15–20cm. Lvs to 14cm, sessile or subsessile, oblong, glaucous green and midrib pubesc. beneath, uppermost 1–3 pairs fused into elliptic or rhombic discs. Fls 1–2 whorls in a terminal head; infl. glabrous; cor. 7–8cm, tube 3× length of limb, lightly hairy inside, orange to yellow, often tinted red above. Fr. red, mesocarp fleshy; seeds smooth, yellow-white. Summer. China. Z6.

***L. trichosantha*** Bur. & Franch. Deciduous, erect, spreading shrub, to 1.5m. Branches slender, nearly glabrous. Lvs 2.5–4cm, broadly ovate, apex obtuse, mucronate, base rounded to subcordate, pilose especially on venation beneath. Fls paired, axillary; peduncles 0.3–1cm; cal. campanulate, truncate or faintly lobed; cor. 1.8–2cm, bilabiate, pubesc. outside, yellow or white becoming yellow, tube short, base gibbous; style pilose. Fr. bright red; seeds 2–4mm, yellow-brown. Summer. Tibet, W China. Z6.

***L. tschonoskii*** Maxim. Erect shrub. Branches slender, glabrous. Lvs 6–9cm, elliptic-oblong, apex and base acute. Fls on upper half of branches; peduncles 1.5–4cm; bractlets fused forming a cupule, often divided; cor. to 1cm, bilabiate, yellow-white, to pink or violet; cor. tube gibbous; stamens pubesc. in lower half. Fr. black. Summer. Japan. Z6.

***L. utahensis*** S. Wats. Closely related to *L. canadensis*. Low shrub to 1.5m. Lvs to 6cm, broad ovate to oblong, apex and base obtuse, glabrous, occasionally lightly hairy beneath, becoming glabrous. Fls in axils of lower lvs or basal bracts of branches; cor. to 2cm, tubular-campanulate, 5-lobed, yellow-white tinted red, base saccate. Fr. orange-red. Spring. Western N America (British Columbia to Oregon, Utah, Wyoming, Montana). Z4.

***L. venulosa*** Maxim. Closely related to *L. coerulea*. Lvs glabrous, occasionally lightly puberulent at first below, oval, apex obtuse. Cor. bilabiate, glabrous, tube longer than limb, venation reticulate, especially below; ovary 3-celled; cupule margin free. Fr. blue, juicy. Japan. Z6.

***L. vesicaria*** Komar. Related to *L. ferdinandii*. Robust shrub. Branches bristly. Lvs 5–10cm, ovate to ovate-oblong, midrib ciliate and hairy beneath, lvs becoming bract-like toward apex of branches. Fls in axils of upper lvs; cal. 5-dentate; cor. bilabiate, tube yellow, hairy outside; style pubesc. Fr. connate. Korea. Z5.

***L. villosa*** (Michx.) Roem. & Schult. Closely related to *L. caerulea*. Deciduous shrub, young shoots tomentose, branches diverging at 45° angle. Lvs villous above and beneath. Cor. funnelform, tube exceed limb, pilose outside. Fr. blue, edible. N America (Newfoundland to Alaska, to Pennsylvania, Wisconsin, California). var. ***solonis*** (Eaton) Fern. To 75cm, bark exfoliating. Lvs to 4cm, pubesc. to glabrous above, long-pubesc. beneath. Cor. white tinted palest yellow, narrow-campanulate, glabrous or pubesc. outside, long-pubesc. inside. Fr. ovate, blue-black, edible. Spring–summer. Minnesota to Newfoundland. Z2.

***L. ×vilmorinii*** Rehd. (*L. deflexicalyx* × *L. quinquelocularis.*) Resembles *L. quinquelocularis*. Lvs wider, shorter, apex more obtuse. Infl. shorter than in *L. quinquelocularis*. Cal. 5-lobed. Fr. yellow, tinted pink, spotted red. Garden origin, *c*1899. Z6.

***L. webbiana*** Wallich. Erect, deciduous shrub, to 3m. Lvs 6–10cm, ovate to oblong-obovate, apex acuminate, pubesc., often glandular. Fls on lower half of branchlets; peduncles and shoots glandular-pilose, rarely glabrous; cor. *c*1cm, bilabiate, tube gibbous, villous inside, white tinted yellow-green; ovaries distinct, joined at base to half length. Fr. connate or separate, scarlet; seeds to 0.6cm. Spring. SE Europe, Afghanistan, Himalaya. Z6.

***L. ×xylosteoides*** Tausch. (*L. tatarica* × *L. xylosteum.*) Erect, much branched, deciduous shrub, to 2m; branches rigid-pubesc. Lvs to 6cm, broadly elliptic, ovate or obovate, ciliate and pubesc. above and beneath, blue-green. Fls light red, pubesc., base swollen; peduncles to 1.5cm, glabrous; stamens included, base hairy; style hairy. Fr. fused at base, yellow to red. Spring–summer. Cult. before 1838, Czechoslovakia. Z6.

***L. xylosteum*** L. Erect, deciduous shrub to 3m. Lvs 3–7cm, ovate to obovate or oblong, apex acute or acuminate, pubesc. throughout. Fls in middle or lower half of branches; cor. 1cm, yellow-white, often tinted red, bilabiate, upper lip divided to one-quarter or one-third; stamens pubesc. at base, style pubesc. throughout. Fr. depressed-globose, red, rarely yellow. Summer. Europe, Caucasus, Siberia, China. 'Clavey's Dwarf' ('Claveyi'): habit globular, branched to the ground, to 1.5m high; lvs tinted blue-grey; fls white; fr. red; slow-growing. 'Compacta' ('Emerald Mound', 'Nana'): habit dense, mound-forming to hemispherical, to 1.2m high, to 1.8m wide; lvs tinted blue-grey; fls off-white; fr. dark red. 'Miniglobe': habit dwarf, compact; lvs strong green. 'Mollis': lvs more pubesc. Z3.

***L. yunnanensis*** Franch. Evergreen, scandent shrub, to 4m; shoots glabrous. Lvs 3–4cm, oblong to lanceolate, almost glabrous, uppermost pair fused into disc. Fls in whorls, gathered into spikes, occasionally solitary; cal. bilabiate; cor. to 2.5cm, yellow, glabrous, tube swollen, interior pubesc. China (Yunnan). var. ***tenuis*** Rehd. Smaller. Lvs to 3cm, lightly pubesc. beneath. Fls in single whorls; cor. to 2cm, white become yellow. SW China. Z7.

***L.* cultivars**. 'Freedom': to 3m high, vigorous; lvs tinted blue; fls white flushed pale pink; fr. red; resistant to honeysuckle witches, broom aphid. 'Hedge King': habit upright, rounded, to 1.5m high, to 1m wide; lvs tinted grey; fls white to yellow; fr. red; resistant to aphid. 'Hidcote': lvs tinted pale grey, deciduous; fls dark orange to red. Z6.

***L. alpigena*** var. ***glehnii*** (F. Schmidt) Nak. See *L. glehnii*.
***L. altaica*** Pall. See *L. caerulea* var. *altaica*.
***L. amherstii*** Dipp. See *L. strophiophora*.
***L. arborea*** var. ***persica*** (Jaub. & Spach) Rehd. See *L. nummulariifolia*.
***L. brachypoda*** DC. See *L. japonica* var. *repens*.
***L. brandtii*** Franch. & Savat. See *L. tschonoskii*.
***L. breweri*** A. Gray. See *L. conjugialis*.
***L. bungeana*** Ledeb. See *L. microphylla*.
***L. caerulea*** var. ***reticulata*** Zab. See *L. venulosa*.
***L. canescens*** Schousb. See *L. biflora*.
***L. caprifolium*** var. ***major*** Carr. See *L. ×americana*.
***L. chinensis*** Wats. See *L. japonica* var. *repens*.
***L. coerulea*** hort. non Hook. See *L. caerulea* var. *altaica*.
***L. coerulea*** Hook. non hort. See *L. villosa*.
***L. coerulea*** var. ***villosa*** (Michx.) Torr. & A. Gray. See *L. villosa*.
***L. coerulescens*** Dipp. See *L. ×xylosteoides*.
***L. delavayi*** Franch. See *L. similis* var. *delavayi*.
***L. depressa*** Royle. See *L. myrtillus* var. *depressa*.
***L. dumetorum*** Lam. non Moench. See *L. xylosteum*.
***L. dumetorum*** Moench non Lam. See *L. xylosteum*.

***L. diversifolia*** Wallich. See *L. quinquelocularis*.
***L. douglasii*** Koehne, non DC. See *L. glaucescens*.
***L. ebractulata*** Rydb. See *L. utahensis*.
***L. edulis*** Turcz. See *L. caerulea*.
***L. emphyllocalyx*** Maxim. See *L. caerulea*.
***L. etrusca*** var. ***brownii*** Reg. See *L.* ×*brownii*.
***L. flavescens*** Dipp. See *L. involucrata* var. *flavescens*.
***L. flexuosa*** Thunb. See *L. japonica* var. *repens*.
***L. gibbiflora*** Maxim. non Dipp. See *L. chrysantha*.
***L. glauca*** Hill. See *L. dioica*.
***L. gracilipes*** var. ***glandulosa*** Maxim. See *L. tenuipes*.
***L. grata*** Ait. See *L.* ×*americana*.
***L. hispanica*** Boiss. & Reut. See *L. periclymenum* var. *glauco-hirta*.
***L. hispida*** var. ***chaetocarpa*** Batal. ex Rehd. See *L. chaetocarpa*.
***L. ibotaeformis*** Nak. See *L. demissa*.
***L. implexa*** f. ***balearica*** DC. See *L. balearica*.
***L. involucrata*** var. ***ledebourii*** (Eschsch.) Zab. See *L. ledebourii*.
***L. italica*** Schmidt. See *L.* ×*americana*.
***L. japonica*** var. ***chinensis*** (Wats.) Bak. See *L. japonica* var. *repens*.
***L. japonica*** var. ***flexuosa*** (Thunb.) Nichols. See *L. japonica* var. *repens*.
***L. kaiensis*** Nak. See *L. praeflorens*.
***L. karelinii*** Bunge. See *L. heterophylla* var. *karelinii*.
***L. korolkowii*** var. ***zabelii*** (Rehd.) Rehd. See *L. tatarica* 'Zabelii'.
***L. leycesterioides*** Gräbn. See *L. ferdinandii* var. *leycesterioides*.
***L. ligustrina*** Wallich. See *L. nitida*.
***L. ligustrina*** var. ***yunnanensis*** Franch. See *L. nitida* 'Fertilis'.
***L. nepalensis*** Kirchn. See *L.* ×*xylosteoides*.
***L. occidentalis*** (Lindl.) Hook. See *L. ciliosa*.
***L. occidentalis*** Hook. See *L. ciliosa* var. *occidentalis*.
***L. ochroleuca*** St.-Lager. See *L. xylosteum*.
***L. odoratissima*** hort. ex Dipp. See *L. fragrantissima*.
***L. orientalis*** var. ***caucasica*** (Pall.) Rehd. See *L. caucasica*.
***L. orientalis*** var. ***discolor*** Clarke. See *L. discolor*.
***L. orientalis*** var. ***longifolia*** Dipp. See *L. kesselringii*.
***L. parvifolia*** Edgew. non Hayne. See *L. obovata*.
***L. periclymenum*** f. ***serotina*** Ait. See *L. serotina*.
***L. persica*** Jaub. & Spach. See *L. nummulariifolia*.
***L. phylomelae*** Carr. See *L. gracilipes*.
***L. pileata*** f. ***yunnanensis*** (Franch.) Rehd. See *L. nitida* 'Fertilis'.
***L. pilosa*** Maxim. See *L. strophiophora*.
***L. pubescens*** Stokes non Sweet. See *L. xylosteum*.
***L. pubescens*** Sweet non Stokes. See *L. hirsuta*.
***L. pyrenaica*** Kit. non L. See *L. xylosteum*.
***L. reticulata*** Maxim. non Champ. See *L. venulosa*.
***L. rubra*** Gilib. See *L. xylosteum*.
***L. rupicola*** var. ***thibetica*** (Bur. & Franch.) Zab. See *L. thibetica*.
***L. sachalinensis*** (F. Schmidt) Nak. See *L. maximowiczii* var. *sachalinensis*.
***L. sempervirens*** var. ***brownii*** (Reg.) Lav. See *L.* ×*brownii*.
***L. sericea*** Royle. See *L. purpurascens*.
***L. shikokiana*** Mak. See *L. cerasina*.
***L. sororia*** Piper. See *L. conjugialis*.
***L. spinosa*** var. ***albertii*** (Reg.) Rehd. See *L. albertii*.
***L. sullivantii*** A. Gray. See *L. prolifera*.
***L. tenuiflora*** Reg. & Winkl. See *L. altmannii*.
***L. uniflora*** Bl. See *L. gracilipes*.
***L. velutina*** DC. See *L. villosa*.
***L. vulgare*** Borkh. See *L. xylosteum*.
***L. vulgaris*** Roehl. See *L. xylosteum*.
***L. xerocalyx*** Diels. See *L. deflexicalyx* var. *xerocalyx*.

**Lopezia** Cav. (For Tomas Lopez (*c*1540), Spanish botanist who studied South American plants.) Onagraceae. 21 species of annual or perennial herbs; roots sometimes tuberous. Stems branched, sometimes woody, often tinged red, swollen. Leaves cauline, stipulate, in spirals or opposite. Inflorescences terminal racemes; bracts leaflike, subsessile, linear to narrowly lanceolate; flowers zygomorphic, floral tube present or absent; sepals 4, subequal, lanceolate; petals 4, often unequal, upper 2 free or partly fused with upper 3 sepals, purple-red to lilac or white; stamens 2, one usually sterile, staminode petaloid, sometimes enveloping fertile stamen and releasing it explosively, shedding pollen; pollen usually blue; stigma subcapitate, becoming papillose. Fruit a subglobose or club-shaped capsule, loculicidal; seeds tuberculate. C America. Z10.

CULTIVATION Grown as potplants and in the open in warm-temperate gardens, largely for their beautiful insect-like flowers, which resemble mosquitoes in shape and are produced in quantity over a long period. All are extremely easy of cultivation: plant in well-drained soil on a sunny site or in part-day shade. In cold areas, grow as potplants and in hanging baskets, maintaining a minimum night temperature of 10°C/50°F and planting into a medium-fertility loam-based mix; water moderately, and pinch for bushier specimens. Propagate from seed, sown with a little bottom heat (plants, due to their floral structure, are practically self-infertile) and by cuttings in spring.

***L. racemosa*** Cav. Variable annual or perenn., glabrous or strigulose, sometimes glandular-hairy. Stems to 1.5m, erect to decumbent. Lower lvs 1–8×0.5–4.5cm, ovate to lanceolate, mucronulate, serrate or with few teeth, upper lvs 0.5–5×0.15–2.5cm, ovate to narrow-lanceolate, serrate to entire. Sep. 3.5–7.5×0.5–2mm, hairy, sometimes glandular; pet. white to white tinted lilac, or purple, pink to red or vermilion, lower pet. 3.5–10×1.5–6mm, obovate to suborbicular, claw equals or exceeds blade, upper pet. 4–8.5×0.7–2mm, linear to oblong-lanceolate, claw shorter than blade; fertile anth. grey-green to blue-green; staminode white, tinted pink. Capsules 7×2–5mm, globose, pear-shaped to ellipsoid. Mexico, El Salvador. ssp. ***racemosa***. MOSQUITO FLOWER. Perenn., hairy, strigulose, sometimes glandular-hairy or subglabrous. Stems erect to decumbent. Lvs 0.5–8×0.15–4.5cm, not fleshy, pubesc. to subglabrous, ovate to lanceolate, serrate or with few teeth; pedicels 0.6–2.7cm.

***L. albiflora*** Schldl. See *L. racemosa* ssp. *racemosa*.
***L. angustifolia*** Robinson. See *L. racemosa* ssp. *racemosa*.
***L. axillaris*** Thunb. ex Schweig. See *L. racemosa* ssp. *racemosa*.
***L. cordata*** Hornem. See *L. racemosa* ssp. *racemosa*.
***L. corymbosa*** Sprague & Riley. See *L. racemosa* ssp. *racemosa*.
***L. elegans*** Rose. See *L. racemosa* ssp. *racemosa*.
***L. foliosa*** Brandg. See *L. racemosa* ssp. *racemosa*.
***L. glandulosa*** Rose. See *L. racemosa* ssp. *racemosa*.
***L. haematodes*** Kunze. See *L. racemosa* ssp. *racemosa*.
***L. hirsuta*** Jacq. See *L. racemosa* ssp. *racemosa*.
***L. integrifolia*** DC. See *L. racemosa* ssp. *racemosa*.
***L. lineata*** Zucc. See *L. racemosa* ssp. *racemosa*.
***L. mexicana*** Jacq. See *L. racemosa* ssp. *racemosa*.
***L. minima*** Lagasca ex Schrank. See *L. racemosa* ssp. *racemosa*.
***L. minuta*** Lagasca. See *L. racemosa* ssp. *racemosa*.
***L. oppositifolia*** Lagasca. See *L. racemosa* ssp. *racemosa*.
***L. parvula*** Rose. See *L. racemosa* ssp. *racemosa*.
***L. pringlei*** Rose. See *L. racemosa* ssp. *racemosa*.
For further synonymy see *Riesenbachia*.

**Lophanthera** A. Juss. (From Gk *lophos*, crest, and *anthera*, anther.) Malpighiaceae. 4 species of shrubs or small trees with abundant white latex. Leaves to 30cm, opposite, entire, elliptic to obovate; stipules present. Inflorescence a terminal thyrse, with many few-flowered branches; flowers very numerous, 300–500; bracts and bracteoles present, persistent; calyx 5-lobed, with 10 basal glands externally; petals 5, entire or minutely denticulate, deciduous, posterior petal differentiated from other 4; stamens 10 in single whorl, filaments free or connate at base, unequal; carpels 3 on glabrous or hairy receptacle, uniovulate, connate on central axis, styles 3. Fruit a dry, 1-seeded schizocarp. Northern S America. Z10.

CULTIVATION *L. lactescens* is an attractive evergreen, grown for its long panicles of small golden-yellow flowers; suitable for outdoor cultivation in humid tropical gardens, it is cultivated in the warm glasshouse or conservatory in cooler climates. Grow in a fertile, well-drained but moisture-retentive medium in sun; water plentifully when in growth, less at other times, and maintain a minimum temperature of 16–18°C/60–65°F. Propagate by seed, semi-ripe cuttings or by air layering.

***L. lactescens*** Ducke. Tree to 15m. Lvs 15–24×9–12cm, obovate, apex rounded or obtuse or apiculate, base decurrent, glandular beneath; petioles to 2.5cm, sericeous to glabrate; stipules 8–12mm, triangular, connate or free at apex. Infl. 30–40cm, pendulous, pubesc.; fls 300–500; pet. 5–7mm, yellow. Brazil.

**Lophocereus** (A. Berger) Britt. & Rose.
***L. australis*** (K. Brandg.) Britt. & Rose. See *Pachycereus schottii*.
***L. mieckleyanus*** (Weingart) Borg. See *Pachycereus schottii*.
***L. sargentianus*** (Orcutt) Britt. & Rose. See *Pachycereus schottii*.
***L. schottii*** (Engelm.) Britt. & Rose. See *Pachycereus schottii*.

**Lophochloa** Rchb.
***L. cristata*** (L.) Hylander. See *Rostraria cristata*.
***L. phleoides*** (Vill.) Rchb. See *Rostraria cristata*.

**Lophomyrtus** Burret. Myrtaceae. 2 species of shrubs or small trees. Leaves opposite, simple, leathery, dotted with glands. Flowers solitary, axillary, 4-merous, white; calyx tube not exceeding ovary, calyx lobes persistent; stamens numerous; ovary inferior, 2-celled, ovules numerous, attached to ribbon-like lobe of the placenta. Fruit a many-seeded berry. New Zealand. Z9.

CULTIVATION As for *Myrtus*.

***L. bullata*** (Sol. ex A. Cunn.) Burret. To 5.4m. Lvs to 5cm, broadly ovate to suborbicular, leathery, puckered, often tinged red. Fls *c*1.25cm diam. Fr. 1cm diam.

***L. obcordata*** (Raoul) Burret. To 4.5m. Lvs to 1.25cm, obcordate, cuneate, apically emarginate. Fls to 6.5mm diam. Fr. 6.5mm diam.

***L. ×ralphii*** (Hook. f.) Burret. (*L. bullata* × *L. obcordata*.) Intermediate between parents. 'Purpurea': lvs deep purple-red.

For synonymy see *Myrtus*.

**Lophophora** J. Coult. (From Gk *lophos*, crest, and *-phoros*, bearing, referring to the tufted areolar hairs.) Cactaceae. 2 species of almost geophytic cacti; rootstock napiform or carrot-like; stems depressed-globose, usually clustering, weakly tuberculate-ribbed, spineless. Flowers arising in the densely woolly stem apex, campanulate, self-fertile; pericarpel and tube naked; stamens sensitive, closing around the style when touched. Fruit cylindric to clavate, pink or red, naked, juicy when ripe, but soon drying; floral remnant deciduous; seeds broadly oval, 1.5×1.1mm, black-brown, matt, relief low-domed; hilum large, basal, impressed. E & N Mexico and S Texas.

CULTIVATION Grow in a cool frost-free greenhouse (min. 2–7°C)/35–40°F, use 'standard' cactus compost: moderate to high inorganic content (more than 50% grit), pH 6–7.5; full sun; low air-humidity; keep dry from mid-autumn until early spring, except for light misting on warm days in late winter.

***L. diffusa*** (Croizat) H. Bravo. Questionably distinct from *L. williamsii*, stem simple, 2–7×5–12cm, yellow-green; ribs absent or very poorly defined, flat; areoles irregularly and widely spaced. Fl. to 2.4×2.2cm; inner tepals 2–2.5mm wide, white, pale yellow or very pale pink. Summer. E Mexico (Querétaro). Contains only trace amounts of the intoxicating alkaloids found in *L. williamsii*. Z9.

***L. williamsii*** (Lem. ex Salm-Dyck) J. Coult. Stems 2–6×4–11cm, blue-green; ribs 4–14, more or less tuberculate; areoles on mature stems bearing tufts of wool, regularly spaced. Fl. to 2.4×2.2cm; inner tepals 2.5–4mm wide, pink with pale to white margins. Spring–autumn. N & NE Mexico, S Texas. Well-known as 'peyote' for its narcotic properties. Z9.

***L. echinata*** Croizat. See *L. williamsii*.
***L. lewinii*** (J. Coult.) Rusby. See *L. williamsii*.
***L. lutea*** (Rouhier) Backeb. See *L. diffusa*.
***L. ziegleri*** Werderm. ex Borg. See *L. diffusa*.
For further synonymy see *Echinocactus*.

For illustration see CACTI.

**Lophosoria** Presl. Lophosoriaceae. 1 species, a terrestrial tree fern. Rhizomes pale brown-pubescent, erect or creeping, covered in dense hairs and roots. Fronds to 4m, 2-, 3- or 4-pinnate to -pinnatifid, deltoid to ovate, pinnae, to 45cm, subsessile or petiolate, lanceolate to oblong or ovate, pinnules to 10×3cm, short-petiolate, oblong, acute to narrowly acute, truncate at base, deeply incised, final segments to 12mm, lanceolate-acute, deeply notched; stipes straw-coloured to brown. Sori circular. Tropical to temperate C & S America. Z9.

CULTIVATION *L. quadripinnata* is distributed through the Americas from Mexico to Chile. In favourable warm, damp forest habitats it produces a trunk up to one metre tall, but in colder regions trunk formation, if any, is slow. It is rarely grown outdoors in temperate regions but it is potentially hardier than many other tree-ferns, being able to survive a few degrees of frost; in cold areas some protection will be necessary. Even if no trunk is produced the glaucous undersides of the fronds merit its inclusion in any collection. Out of doors, *Lophosoria* should be grown in a sheltered sun less spot. Under glass in the cold or cool house it will thrive in low to medium light. Pot into a soilless potting medium with added leafmould – pH should be in the range 5–6.5 – and water plentifully. Plant out in late spring or early summer. Propagate by spores or occasionally by offsets which form around the main crown.

***L. quadripinnata*** (Gmel.) C. Chr. As for the genus.

***L. pruinata*** (Sw.) Presl. See *L. quadripinnata*.

**LOPHOSORIACEAE** Pichi Serm. See *Lophosoria*.

**Lophospermum** D. Don.
***L. scandens*** D. Don. See *Asarina lophospermum*.

**Lophostemon** Schott. (From Gk *lophos*, crest, and *stemon*, stamen.) Myrtaceae. 6 species of trees, occasionally arborescent shrubs. Leaves alternate and crowded at the ends of the branchlets in pseudoverticils around the bract-covered bud at the stem apex. Juvenile leaves opposite, leaf veins transparent, the broken petiole of young stem yielding a milky exudate. Inflorescence a dichasium, borne in lf axil of a leaf or bud scale; sepals mostly persistent; petals 5, white to cream; stamens in more than one whorl, filaments united into fascicles opposite the petals, inflexed to decumbent; ovary semi-inferior, 3-locular. Seeds linear-cuneate. N & E Australia, S New Guinea. Z10.

CULTIVATION In warm climates *Lophostemon* spp. are used as street and avenue shade trees, and in mild coastal and essentially frost-free zones can be grown in sheltered sites outdoors, but otherwise need cool glasshouse protection. *L. confertus*, grown in commercial forestry in Hawaii, is a rapidly growing, densely foliaged tree and is extremely tolerant of hard and repeated pruning. Treat as for *Callistemon*.

***L. confertus*** (R. Br.) P.G. Wils. & J.T. Waterhouse. BRUSH BOX. Usually 35–40m. Bark pink-brown, mostly deciduous on the upper branches with a rough 'sock' at the base of the trunk, rarely completely deciduous or full-barked. Lvs 7–15×2.5–4.5cm, lanceolate, acute; petioles to 2cm; pseudoverticils of 4 or 5 lvs. Infl. 3–7-fld, cymose, pedunculate, axillary, subtended by bract scales, rarely by lvs; sep. subulate, 4–5mm, caducous; pet. 6–9mm, orbicular; staminal fascicles 10–15mm, narrow, stamens numerous, mostly exceeding 70 per fascicle. Fr. turbinate to hemispherical, 10–15mm diam.; seed 2–3mm. E coast of Australia (Queensland, NSW). A variegated selection is also widely planted.

***L. lactifluus*** (F. Muell.) P.G. Wils. & J.T. Waterhouse. Bark red-brown, fibrous-papery, persistent; axes and lvs glabrous. Lvs to 15cm, elliptic to ovate-lanceolate, acute; pseudoverticils of 2 or 3 lvs; petioles long, about a quarter length of lamina. Fls small, very numerous in many-branched cymes borne in the axils of bud scales or lvs; sep. short, to 1mm, persistent; pet. 2–3mm; staminal fascicles 2–3mm, stamens 12–25 per fascicle. Fr. 3–16mm diam.; seeds 1–1.5mm. Australia (Northern Territory).

***L. suaveolens*** (Sol. ex Gaertn.) P.G. Wils. & J.T. Waterhouse. To 15m. Bark red-brown, fibrous-papery; shoots, lvs and infl. often villous-hairy. Lvs to 10cm, ovate to lanceolate, obtuse or acuminate; pseudoverticils of 3–4 lvs. Fls mostly 7–15 per infl., the cymes pedunculate, axillary, subtended by bud scales or lvs; sep. obtuse, 1mm, persistent; pet. 4–5mm; staminal fascicles, 3–5mm, stamens 30–50(–58) per fascicle. Fr. 6–8mm diam.; seeds 1.5–2mm. S New Guinea and E Australia (NSW).

***L. conferta*** R. Br. See *L. confertus*.
For further synonymy see *Melaleuca* and *Tristania*.

**Lophotocarpus** T. Dur.
***L. guyanensis*** (HBK) J.G. Sm. See *Sagittaria guyanensis*.

**LORANTHACEAE** Juss. MISTLETOE FAMILY. (Excluding Viscaceae.) Dicot. 70 genera and 940 species of photosynthetic hemiparasites, typically brittle shrublets on tree-branches, less often terrestrial shrubs, lianes or trees (*Nuytsia*) on host roots; haustorium 1 or several at ends of epicortical roots, plant rarely *Cuscuta*-like, haustoria usually promoting gall-like host growth; stem often dichasial but nodal constrictions absent. Leaves opposite or ternate, simple, entire, rarely scale-like; stipules absent. Flowers usually bisexual, regular, conspicuous, epigynous, frequently red or yellow, insect- or bird-pollinated, in dichasia sometimes resembling heads, racemes, umbels, etc.; calyx a toothed or lobed rim or cup at summit of gynoecium; corolla (3–) 5–6(–9) free petals, often with a basal tube, sometimes nectariferous at base; stamens equal to, opposite and adnate to corolla, staminal disc sometimes present; ovary inferior, of 3–4 fused carpels, usually 1-loculed; ovules 4–12. Fruit a berry or drupe with latex, 1–3-seeded, rarely dry indehiscent; seeds without testa but covered with viscous material, often with more than 1 embryo; endosperm copious, starchy. Tropical and temperate, especially southern. *Loranthus*, *Nuytsia*.

**Loranthus** Jacq. (From Gk *loros*, strap, and *anthos*, flower, referring to shape of sepals.) Loranthaceae. 1 species, a dioecious shrub to 1m, parasitic on members of the Fagaceae, especially *Fagus*, *Castanea* and *Quercus*. Stems dull brown, jointed. Leaves 1–5cm, opposite, deciduous, obovate-oblong, apex obtuse, dark green, coriaceous, short-petiolate, veins pinnate or slightly parallel. Inflorescence a terminal raceme or spike to 4cm; flowers actinomorphic, small, perianth 2-whorled, sepals 4, petals 4–6, green-yellow; stamens inserted at base of petals; ovary inferior, ovules several, not differentiated from placenta. Fruit a viscid berry, 1cm, pyriform-globose, yellow. C & SE Europe.

CULTIVATION A semi-parasitic species usually found on *Quercus* or *Castanea* spp., *L. europaeus* may be introduced to its host by inserting seed into the centre of a gently bruised bud on growth made the previous year.

***L. europaeus*** Jacq. As for the genus.

**Loropetalum** R. Br. ex Rchb. (From Gk *loron*, thong, and *petalon*, petal; the petals are long and narrow.) Hamamelidaceae. 2 species of evergreen, stellate-pubescent shrubs or small trees, to 3m. Leaves alternate, entire, ovate, somewhat asymmetrical at base, to 5cm. Flowers produced freely in clusters of 6–8, in terminal heads; calyx 4-lobed; petals 4, long and narrow, to 2.5cm, green-white; stamens 4; ovary inferior, horned, 2-celled. Fruit a woody capsule with 2 apical points; 1 seed per cell. Himalaya, China, Japan. Z9.

CULTIVATION Although tolerant of temperatures down to −5°C/23°F, *Loropetalum* flowers well only where temperatures seldom drop below 5°C/40°F: in colder regions it may be grown in the intermediate glasshouse in a well-drained but moisture-retentive, high-fertility, loam-based medium to which additional organic matter has been added. Cultivation otherwise as for *Hamamelis*.

***L. chinense*** (R. Br.) Oliv. Bushy, twiggy shrub, to 1m in cult., to 3m in the wild. Lvs to 4cm, dark green, margins fringed with bristly hairs, base oblique, tips acute, stellate-pubesc. throughout, but more so beneath; petioles short. Fls white to green; pet. 2cm, undulate-ligulate, altogether pet. give clusters a feathery appearance. Late winter–early spring. India, China, Japan.

***L. indicum*** Oliv. See *L. chinense*.

**Lotus** L. (From Gk name *lotos*, used by Dioscorides and Theophrastus for certain Leguminosae.) Leguminosae (Papilionoideae). Some 100 species of annual or perennial herbs. Leaves subpalmate or imparipinnate; leaflets 4–15, entire, lowest pair stipulate; stipules glandular, minute or absent. Inflorescence an umbellate raceme, axillary, 1- to many-flowered, commonly subtended by a bract; bracteoles absent; calyx campanulate, teeth sometimes equal, length variable; standard broad-ovate, claw usually cuneate or subulate, wings regularly or irregularly positioned, obovate or oblique-oblong, keel obtuse to acute, fused on 1 or both edges; stamens generally 10, diadelphous, anthers equal; pistil sessile, oblong, ovary 1- to many-ovuled, style glabrous, incurved, stigma minute and terminal. Fruit dehiscent, linear to oblong-falcate, beak short, upturned; seeds few to many; valves usually 2. Mediterranean Europe, south to Sahara Desert, west to Asia; W US; Australia; S Africa.

CULTIVATION *Lotus* spp. have a range of horticultural uses, in the wild garden, rock garden, shrub border, glasshouse and vegetable garden. *L. corniculatus*, a widespread wild flower found on poor sandy and chalky soils, is sometimes regarded as a lawn weed but becomes a valuable species in the flower meadow, since it is a nectar source for bees and butterflies and a food source for caterpillars. *L. tenuis* and *L. angustissimus* occur naturally in similar, dry grassy habitats.

*L. uliginosus*, which occurs in damp pastures, ditches and at freshwater margins, is suitable for naturalistic and conservation plantings in situations that approximate to its natural habitat. In New Zealand, it is used as a pioneer plant in reclamation of peat and pumice soils and on other wet acid soils unsuitable for the more commonly used *Trifolium* spp. *L. tenuis*, which grows at altitudes to 3100m/10075ft, *L. corniculatus*, especially in its double form 'Plenus', and *L. creticus* are all suitable for the rock garden.

The herbaceous *L. jacobaeus* and the softly shrubby *L. sessilifolius*, and *L. berthelotii* are more or less silvery-downy leaved plants with strongly coloured flowers and are suitable for planting outdoors in warm temperate climates that are frost-free or almost so; given shelter and perfect drainage, *L. jacobaeus* will probably tolerate temperatures to −5°C/23°F. In cool temperate zones, these species make beautiful specimens for the cool glasshouse or conservatory, *L. sessilifolius* and *L. berthelotii* are among the finest plants for hanging baskets.

*L. tetragonolobus*, the asparagus pea, is an attractive species grown for its edible pods, which when cooked whole have a flavour resembling that of asparagus. Seeds should be sown in a sunny position in fertile, well drained soil in late spring, or started under glass for planting out after danger of frost is passed. Plants require the support of twiggy pea-sticks, and are spaced 25–30cm/10–12in. apart, in rows 40cm/16in. apart. Harvest pods when young (3–5cm/1–2in. long) and eat raw or cooked. It is perhaps understandably confused with the asparagus bean or winged bean, *Psophocarpus tetragonolobus*, and the asparagus bean or asparagus pea, *Vigna unguiculata* ssp. *sesquipedalis*, both of which are described elsewhere.

With the exceptions of *L. formosissimus, L. pinnatus* and *L. uliginosus*, which thrive in damp soils, *Lotus* spp. are grown in any sharply draining, dry soil in full sun. Prune shrubby spp. when necessary, after flowering. Under glass, grow in direct sun, with a winter minimum temperature of 7°C/45°F and good ventilation; use a free-draining, medium-fertility loam-based mix, with additional sharp sand. Water moderately when in growth and keep almost dry in winter. Propagate by scarified seed in spring, by division of perennials and by semi-ripe cuttings in summer.

***L. angustissimus*** L. SLENDER BIRD'S FOOT TREFOIL. Procumbent annual, 5–50cm. Stems many, erect. Leaflets 8–12×2.5–4mm, obovate to oblong; stipules minute. Infl. 1–3-fld, on peduncles 3mm–2cm long; bracts 1–3, unequal; pedicels *c*1mm; cal. 6–7mm, campanulate, teeth exceeding tube; cor. 5–8mm, yellow, becoming pale red, standard more or less equal to keel, keel acuminate or beaked at apex; ovary 5–7mm. Fr. 1.5–3cm×1–1.5mm, terete, straight. Summer. Europe, naturalized US. Z6.

***L. argophyllus*** (Gray) Greene. Perenn., 10–60cm tall, spreading or sprawling; stems many. Lvs 8–15mm, silver-pubesc., imparipinnate to costapalmate. Petioles 2–10mm; leaflets 6–12mm, 3–7, lanceolate-elliptic to obovate. Fls 7–12mm, 4 or more on 1–3mm peduncles, yellow, becoming red or amber; keel ridged; ovary pubesc., 2–4-ovuled. Fr. short, not dehiscent, glabrous or pubesc.; seeds 1–2. Spring–summer. Europe, naturalized US. Z9.

***L. berthelotii*** Lowe ex Masf. CORAL GEM; PARROT'S BEAK; PELICAN'S BEAK. Low-growing or cascading perenn. subshrub, to 1m. Branches slender, downy, ash-grey, becoming woody. Lvs costapalmate, alternate, very short-stalked; leaflets 1–1.8cm, linear to filiform, 3–5, spreading, soft silver-grey. Infl. bunched at ends of branchlets, on short peduncles; cor. 2–4cm, orange-red to scarlet or purple, seg. narrow, standard linear, recurved, wing pubesc., narrow-lanceolate, keel longest, slender, prominently beaked, lobster claw-like, i.e. resembling *Clianthus*. Spring–summer. Canary Is., Cape Verde Is., Tenerife; naturalized US. 'Kew Form': lvs silver; fls red, summer-flowering, remontant.

***L. corniculatus*** L. BIRD'S FOOT TREFOIL. Perenn., 5–40cm, ascending or prostrate; stems several, solid or hollow. Lf stalk 2–7mm; leaflets 5–15mm, 3, obovate, odd-oblanceolate to oblong. Infl. 4–8-fld, erect or ascending, on long peduncles; pedicels 1–2mm; cal. tube 2.8–3.5mm, teeth 1.8–2.5mm, subulate; cor. 10–14mm, vivid yellow, darkening to red flecked orange, ascending, keel semi-auriculate, crescent-shaped and extended; ovary 20–40-ovuled. Fr. 1.5–3.5cm×2mm, thin-oblong, rounded, dehiscent, finely beaked. Spring–summer. Europe, Asia, naturalized US. 'Plenus' ('Flore Pleno', 'Pleniflorus'): habit mat-forming, vigorous; fls double, yellow, orange in bud. Z5.

***L. creticus*** L. Perenn., 30–60cm, woody-based, pubesc. Stems erect or prostrate, rigid. Lvs 1–3cm; leaflets 7–18×4–9mm, thick, upper leaflets obovate, densely sericeous. Racemes 3–6-fld, on thick peduncles; bracts 3, shorter than cal; cal. 7.5–9mm, campanulate or somewhat 2-lipped, with sharp-pointed lateral teeth, nearly equal to upper teeth in length; cor. 12–18mm, vivid yellow, standard entire, wings exceeding keel, keel with a long, purple-tipped beak. Fr. to 4cm×2mm, cylindrical. Spring–summer. Portugal, Mediterranean region. Z8.

***L. formosissimus*** Greene. Perenn., 10–40cm, glabrous, decumbent to ascending. Stems solitary or grouped. Leaflets 6–20mm, 5–7, obovate, at least in lower lvs; stipules 1.5cm, deltoid-ovate, sometimes reduced or absent, tough or withered. Infl. pedunculate; bracts 1–3-foliate; cal. tube indistinguishable from hypanthium; cor. 10–16mm, 3–8, bicoloured, standard pet. yellow, wings lilac becoming white, keel purple-tipped, incurved, ovary *c*23-ovuled. Fr. 2–3cm×2–3mm, beak short; valves glabrous. Spring–summer. Europe, US. Z6.

***L.jacobaeus*** L. Perenn., 30–90cm, grey-hirsute. Leaflets and stipules elongated or elongate to broad-ended, mucronate. Peduncles exceeding lvs; cor. dark maroon, standard yellow. Cape Verde Is. Z9.

***L.maritimus*** L. Perenn., 10–40cm, prostrate or ascending, glabrous or pubesc. Leaflets to 30×15mm, asymmetrical, ciliate; stipules smaller, ovate, acute, or obtuse. Peduncles exceeding lvs; bracts 3, narrowly oblong, smaller than leaflets; fls 2.5–3cm, usually solitary, cal. tube exceeding cal. teeth; cor. pale yellow, standard exceeding wings. Fr. 30–60×3–5mm, somewhat flattened, glabrous or slightly downy, 4-winged. W, C & S Europe, Ukraine, N Africa. Z6.

***L.ornithopoides*** L. Annual, 15–50cm, prostrate, pubesc. Stems few or numerous, erect. Lvs petiolate; upper leaflets 3, 8–18×4–10mm, obovate to rhombic, lower leaflets 2, generally slightly smaller, ovate. Infl. 7–10mm, 2–5-fld, on delicate peduncles, overlapping lvs; bracts 3, exceeding cal.; cal. 6–7mm, 2-lipped, lateral teeth short; cor. 7–10mm, yellow, standard equalling wings, keel shorter, curved, short-beaked. Fr. flattened, 20–40×2–3mm, moniliform. Spring. S Europe.

***L.palustris*** Willd. Perenn., to 1m, villous or pubesc., prostrate or ascending; young shoots glabrous. Leaflets 14–20×6–12mm, lanceolate-ovate to obovate. Infl. 2–4-fld, on peduncles raised clear of lvs; pedicels *c*1mm; cal. campanulate, teeth twice tube length, curved; cor. 6–10mm, yellow, keel generally equal to standard and wings, tip short, somewhat incurved. Fr. 12–30×2mm, linear, terete. Spring–summer. S & E Mediterranean regions. Z8.

***L.pinnatus*** Hook. Perenn., 20–40cm, glabrous; stems slender, ascending. Lvs 4–7cm; leaflets to 19mm, 5–9, obovate, obtuse or acute; stipules 3–5mm. Racemes 3–7-fld; peduncles exceeding lvs; bracts absent; pedicels to 1.5mm; cal. 2-lobed, tube 6–7mm; cor. 12–15mm, standard and keel yellow; wings white, obovate. Fr. linear, 40–60×1.5mm. Spring–summer. Europe, US. Z8.

***L.scoparius*** (Nutt.) Ottley. WILD BROOM; DEER CLOVER. Perenn., to 2m, erect or prostrate, glabrate or finely hispidulous. Branches bushy; stems green, grouped, furrowed. Lvs 1–2cm, usually small, caducous (new foliage borne with rains); lf stalk 2–8mm; leaflets 6–15mm, 3–6, oblong, oblanceolate; stipules black. Infl. sessile or subsessile. Fls 2–7; cal. tube 2–4.5mm, teeth to 1mm, subulate; cor. 7–11mm, yellow, becoming amber or red, seg. subequal, claws just projecting beyond cal. tube. Fr. 1–1.5cm, curved, not dehiscent, long-beaked, setulose or glabrate. Spring–summer. Europe, US. Z6.

***L.sessilifolius*** DC. Shrub, ashy-grey, sericeous, low-growing. Branches numerous, sprawling, downy. Lvs palmate, 5-foliolate, sessile; leaflets 5–10mm, oblong-lanceolate to elongated. Peduncles 1.5–2.5cm, extending to 4–8cm when in fruit, axillary or terminal; pedicels 0.5–1.5mm; fls 14–15cm, 3–5, vivid yellow about 7mm, ovary to bronze 27-30-ovuled, somewhat villous; style. Fr. 15–25×1.5mm, grouped 2–5, narrow-oblong, leathery, glabrous. Spring. Canary Is. Z9.

***L.tenuis*** Waldst. & Kit. ex Willd. NARROWLEAF TREFOIL. Perenn. herb, 20–90cm, glabrous or, rarely, puberulous. Branches delicate, usually twining. Lvs compound; leaflets linear, 5–15×1–4mm. Infl. 1–6-fld, long-stalked; bracts usually 3; cal. to 5mm, glabrous, teeth equal, tube usually exceeding teeth in length; cor. 6–12mm, yellow, standard 7–9×5–7mm, wings obovate to elongate, keel 6–7mm, long-beaked. Fr. 15–30×2–3mm, terete. Summer. Europe, naturalized US. Z4.

***L.tetragonolobus*** L. WINGED PEA; ASPARAGUS PEA. Annual to 40cm; stems sprawling or creeping. Leaflets to 2.5cm, 3, obovate to broadly elliptic. Fls to 19mm, crimson to maroon, on 1–2-fld peduncles exceeded by, or equal to lvs. Fr. to 76mm, tetragonal and conspicuously 4-winged. S Europe. Other legumes rejoicing in the name of winged or asparagus pea or asparagus bean are *Psophocarpus tetragonolobus* and *Vigna unguiculata* ssp. *sesquipedalis*: these crops are described separately.

***L.uliginosus*** Schkuhr GREATER BIRD'S FOOT TREFOIL. Perenn., 10–80cm, ascending or erect, glabrous to villous; stems tubular. Leaflets 8–25×3–15mm, blunt or terete, ovate-elliptic to elliptic, glaucous beneath; stipules minute. Infl. 8–12-fld, on 3–10cm peduncles, bracteate; pedicels 1–2mm; cal. tube 3–4mm, often slightly villous, teeth somewhat unequal, lanceolate; cor. 10–18mm, rich yellow, frequently dappled red, becoming darker, standard just exceeding wings, keel beak long, semi-incurved, barely exceeding wings; ovary about 50-ovuled, elongate. Fr. 20–30×2mm, cylindrical. Spring–summer. Europe, N Africa. Z6.

***L.alpinus*** (DC.) Schleich. ex Raym. See *L.tenuis*.
***L.mascaensis*** hort. non Burchard. See *L.sessilifolius*.
***L.pedunculatus*** Cav. See *L.uliginosus*.
***L.peliorhynchus*** Hook. f. See *L.berthelotii*.
***L.tenuis*** Waldst. & Kit. ex Willd. See *L.alpinus*.
For further synonymy see *Tetragonolobus*.

**Loudon, Jane Wells** (1807–1858). Writer and horticulturist. Jane Loudon, née Webb, is thought to have been born in Birmingham or at Kitwell House in Worcestershire. After the death of her father she earned her living by writing poetry and books for children, although her most remarkable publication, *The Mummy!* (1827), was a futuristic work about society in the twenty-second century, which makes reference to innovations such as steam-driven ploughs, milking machines and air conditioning. In 1830 she met the horticultural writer J.C. Loudon, who had favourably reviewed *The Mummy!* and requested to meet the anonymous author, whom he had assumed to be a man. They were married later that year, and Jane Loudon soon began to act as his amanuensis, assisting him in all his projects. From 1839–45 she wrote a number of botanical and horticultural works in her own right, developed her talents as a botanical illustrator, attended Lindley's lectures, and published book reviews, in Loudon's *Gardener's Magazine*. The majority of her works were of horticultural instruction written for women readers with little knowledge of science or the practice of gardening, and they were extremely popular; over a thousand copies of *Gardening for Ladies* (1840) were sold on the day of publication. *The Ladies' Companion to the Flower-garden* (1841) and *The Lady's Country Companion* (1845) were similarly received. Her writings often began with a simple explication of botanical theory and included guides for planting and maintaining gardens throughout the year. In her remarks on flower gardens she advocates geometrical designs, as promoted by her husband.

Jane Loudon travelled widely in Britain, examining gardens and country architecture with her husband and daughter Agnes. Widowed, she continued to earn her living by writing from her house at Porchester Terrace, Bayswater. Her nineteen books on natural history and botany, many of which she illustrated herself, include *The Ladies' Flower Garden of Ornamental Annuals* (1839–40); *Bulbous Plants* (1840); *Hardy Perennials* (1841); *British Wild Flowers* (1845); *The Ladies Flower Garden* (1839–48, 4 vols); *Botany for Ladies* (1842); *Amateur Gardener's Calender* (1847); and she was editor and founder of the journal *The Ladies' Magazine of Gardening* (1841–2).

**Loudon, John Claudius** (1783–1843). Writer, editor, landscape gardener and architect. Loudon was born in Cambuslang, Lanarkshire, Scotland, the son of a farmer. He was educated in Edinburgh and after leaving school was apprenticed to the nursery of Robert Dickson of Hassandeanburn. Here he began to study arboriculture. He taught himself French and Italian and in 1803 travelled to Loudon, where he introduced himself to Sir Joseph Banks and James Sowerby and began to write for journals on subjects related to horticulture, garden design and architecture. His first article, 'Hints...[on] laying out the grounds of the public squares in London' appeared as a letter in the *Literary Journal* in 1803. He praises the doctrines of the picturesque as expounded by Uvedale Price and advises the planting of flowering almond trees (not plane trees, an innovation he is often credited for). Loudon set up as a landscape gardener and received several commissions in Scotland, advising the Earl of Mansfield at Scone in 1804, and in 1806 published *A Treatise on Forming, Improving and Managing Country Residences*. In the same year he was elected Fellow of the Linnean Society and executed designs at Barnbarrow, Wigtownshire, and Ditchley, Oxfordshire. Loudon suffered severely from rheumatism while still in his twenties, and during his convalescence at Wood Hall Farm, Pinner in Middlesex, he put into practice Scottish farming methods which he believed could be profitable in southern England. Some five years later he bought Tew Park at Great Tew in Oxfordshire, where he put his agricultural innovations to the test on a larger scale (creating a celebrated *ferme ornée*) and instructed private pupils, effectively establishing the first agricultural college. He published his *Designs* (1811) and *Observations on laying out Farms, in the Scotch Style, adapted to England* (1812).

The venture was extremely successful and the sale of Tew Park in 1811 supplied Loudon with sufficient profits to make a tour of northern Europe (1813–15) including Sweden, Germany and Russia. He reached his destination, Moscow, with difficulty and found the city still burning in the wake of Napoleon's invasion. On his return to England he found himself in severe financial trouble, and in order to rectify the situation began to write again, first travelling to France and Italy in 1819 to gather information for his *Encyclopaedia of Gardening, Comprising the Theory and Practice of Horticulture, Floriculture, Arboriculture, and Landscape Gardening, including ... a General History of Gardening in all Countries* (1822). This work, the product of three years' intensive work, was the first truly comprehensive treatment of gardening, and was a massive success, going through eight editions in 12 years. Loudon wrote for a new audience, concentrating on the smaller domestic gardens of the middle class rather than large country estates. His *Suburban Gardener* (1828) and *Suburban Horticulturist* (1842) were also extremely popular. As a result of his experiences of European formal garden design, Loudon's abiding enthusiasm for the 'irregular' style had waned, and he advocated instead a geometrically symmetrical approach, stressing values such as 'dignity, refinement and appropriation to man' above 'picturesque beauty'; if gardens were to be regarded as works of art, then the artifice should not only be made apparent, but celebrated as such.

Loudon wrote a great deal on the subject, zealously promoting his views as 'conductor' of *The Gardener's Magazine*, founded in 1826. He visited many British gardens with his wife Jane. J.C. Loudon first used the phrase 'gardenesque' (as opposed to 'picturesque') in the *Gardeners' Magazine* of 1832. In its original sense, the 'gardenesque' style referred to the method of planting which had as its aim the full realization of plants as individual elements in design for their own sake, not only as ornamental features. Trees, shrubs and flowers were to be enjoyed botanically as well as aesthetically, and used collectively as part of a symmetrical design organized according to colour and shape. His own garden at Porchester Terrace, Bayswater, contained around 2000 different species, including 600 species of alpine plants in pots and hundreds of different bulbs planted on the lawn.

Loudon also produced designs for the Birmingham Botanical Gardens (1831) and two of the earliest public parks, the Terrace Garden at Gravesend (1835) and the Derby Arboretum (1839). In the *Gardener's Magazine* he campaigned for the provision of more parks in Loudon, and for green belts or 'breathing zones' at the edge of the city. At Kensington Gardens his suggestions for the planting of flowering trees and shrubs and the use of iron railings rather than high walls were accepted. In later life, his views on landscape design were influenced by Humphry Repton, and in 1840 he edited Repton's works.

Loudon was always a great advocate of mechanical innovations, such as the mowing-machine, and he popularized the greenhouse in the *Gardener's Magazine*, inventing a wrought-iron glazing bar to facilitate curvilinear glass roofs. He published several works on the subject: *Treatise on Hot-Houses* (1805), *Remarks on the Construction of Hot-Houses* (1817) and *The Greenhouse Companion* (1824).

His most famous work is perhaps the vast *Arboretum et Fruticêtum Britannicum* in eight volumes (1838), the publication of which plunged Loudon into debts which he failed to repay before his death. Loudon personally supervised his seven artists (who eventually produced around 3000 illustrations) and collated all the information gathered by himself and his 826 (named) correspondents.

Loudon was also influential in the field of architecture. He executed several designs after 1811 and included many illustrations of domestic architecture (principally in an Italianate style) in his *Encyclopaedia of Gardening*. He also launched *The Architectural Magazine* (1834), the first of its kind, and published an influential *Encyclopaedia of Cottage, Farm and Villa Architecture and Furniture* (1833). He founded the *Magazine of Natural History* (1828) and revolutionized cemetery design as a result of *On the Laying Out, Planting, and Managing of Cemeteries: and on the Improvement of Churchyards* (1843). He designed the cemeteries at Histon Road, Cambridge, the Common, Southampton, and the Abbey Cemetery, Bath.

Loudon's output was truly prolific (his writings total more than 60 million words) and he was possessed of apparently limitless energy. He successfully overcame an addiction to the laudanum he had been taking as a painkiller for his rheumatism, and, in 1825, reputedly returned to work in the afternoon after his broken right arm had been amputated.

His other publications include *Hints on the Formation of Gardens and Pleasure-grounds* (1812), *Encyclopaedia of Agriculture* (1825), *Encyclopaedia of Plants* (1825), *Hortus Britannicus* (1830), *Hortus Lignosus Londinensis* (1838) and *Self-instruction of Young Gardeners* (1845). The genus *Loudonia* was named in his honour.

**Lourea** Necker. See *Christia*.

**Loxoma** R. Br. (From Gk *loxos*, oblique, and *soma*, body, referring to the incomplete annulus of the sporangium.) Loxomataceae. 1 species, a temperate terrestrial fern. Rhizome stout, spreading, somewhat tortuous, about 5mm diam., densely hairy, hairs bristly, dark brown. Fronds 15–60cm, broadly deltoid-triangular, tripinnate, dark to light green above, glaucous to white or occasionally pale green beneath, glabrous, coriaceous; pinnae ascending, primary pinnae to 20cm, secondary pinnae to 10cm, veins free; pinnules oblong, subacute to acute, notched, to 5cm; stipes stout, 20–60cm, erect, pale to dark brown, glabrous except for bristles at base. Sori marginal, terminating veinlets, in sinuses of pinnules; sporangia pyriform to obovoid, shortly stalked; indusium to 1mm, urceolate, truncate at mouth; receptacle slender, hairy, 2–3mm, far-exserted when mature. New Zealand. Z10.

CULTIVATION As for *Davallia*.

***L. cunninghammi*** R. Br. As for the genus.

**LOXOMATACEAE** C. Presl. See *Loxoma*.

**Loxoscaphe** T. Moore.

***L. brachycarpa*** (Mett.) Kuhn. See *Asplenium brachycarpum*.

**Loxostigma** C.B. Clarke. (From Gk *loxos*, oblique, and *stigma*.) Gesneriaceae. 3 species of perennial herbs. Leaves in unequal, opposite pairs. Flowers axillary, several on pendent peduncles; corolla tubular, slightly inflated toward base, shallowly 2-lipped; stamens 4, inserted, anthers in coherent pairs; disc annular. Fruit a linear, valvate capsule. India (E Himalaya). Z10.

CULTIVATION As for *Streptocarpus*. See also GESNERIADS.

***L. griffithii*** (Wight) C.B. Clarke. Lvs to 17.5×8cm, ovate, short-pubesc.; sep. to 0.8cm, lanceolate; cor. to 3.5cm, pale yellow marked with brown. E Himalaya.

***L. kurzii*** (C.B. Clarke) B.L. Burtt. Lvs to 20×10cm, opposite or almost alternate, crowded on stem, elliptic, markedly dentate. Sep. to 1.5cm; cor. to 3cm, yellow, spotted rusty-red in throat. E Himalaya.

For synonym see *Briggsia* and *Chirita*.

**Lucilia** Cass. (From Lat. *lucidus*, bright.) Compositae. About 22 species of erect, more or less caespitose, rhizomatous perennial herbs. Stems simple or branched, lanate. Leaves almost decussate, scattered or rosetted, ovate, obovate, oblong or linear, sessile, basally adpressed to the stem, entire, mucronate, very densely lanate on one or both sides. Capitula radiate, rarely discoid, sessile, in leafy inflorescences, clustered or solitary; receptacle naked; involucre oblong at first, becoming obdeltate; phyllaries in 4 series, bright and scarious, rarely membranous and opaque, outer oval, rarely subcircular or oblong, frequently hairy on back, blunt, inner linear-obovate, usually glabrous, sharply acute; ray florets 9 to many, white, thread-like; disc florets 2–23, white. Fruit an oblong to oblong-elliptic, sericeous-pubescent or sparingly pilose, rarely glabrous cypsela; pappus of numerous rough white hairs. Throughout the Andes, and from S Brazil to NW Argentina. Z9.

CULTIVATION As for *Helichrysum*.

***L. chilensis*** Hook. & Arn. Caespitose herb to 5cm, forming silvery-white, dense or more or less lax cushions. Stems prostrate, branched. Lvs scattered, 3–10×1.5–3mm, oblong-obovate, attenuate at base, apex obtuse, lanate on both sides. Capitula radiate, in apparently racemose infl.; involucre 4–9×2–8mm;

phyllaries 14–21, outer 3.5–4.5×1.5–2.5mm, inner 4–9×0.3–1mm, grey-brown to dirty white; ray florets 12–25, minute; disc florets 3–5. Fr. to 2mm, oblong, sericeous-pubesc. or sparingly pilose; pappus hairs 3.5–8mm. Argentina, Chile.

For synonymy see *Gnaphalium*.

**Luculia** Sweet. (From the native name *luculi swa*.) Rubiaceae. Some 5 species or shrubs of small trees. Leaves petiolate, opposite; stipules interpetiolar, deciduous, cuspidate. Flowers in terminal, many-fld corymbs or panicles, white to pink, fragrant; bracteoles deciduous; calyx lobes 5, unequal, deciduous, linear or oblong to subulate; corolla salver-shaped, lobes 5, imbricate in bud, simple or appendaged at base; stamens 5, inserted at mouth of corolla tube, anthers linear, yellow; ovary 2-celled, style included, stigmas 2, linear, ovules many in each cell. Fruit a capsule, septicidally 2-valved, woody; seeds many, imbricate, testa winged and rough, endosperm fleshy. E Asia.

CULTIVATION Beautiful shrubs, widely cultivated in the subtropical regions of the world for their attractive evergreen foliage, and for the terminal clusters of fragrant pink or white flowers often produced in great profusion. In temperate zones, *Luculia* are suitable specimens for the cool glasshouse or conservatory, with a minimum temperature of 5–10°C/40–50°F. Grow in a medium-fertility, loam-based mix, with medium humidity and in direct sunlight. Water plentifully when in growth, and sparingly in winter. Cut back flowered stems to a framework in autumn or early spring. Propagate from softwood cuttings of new growth in spring, or from seed in spring.

***L. grandifolia*** Ghose. To 6m. Lvs to 35×25cm, ovate to elliptic, apex acute to narrowly acute, margin and veins red; petioles red. Fls in cymes to 20cm wide, white; cor. tube to 4cm, cylindric, lobes to 2cm. Bhutan. Z9.

***L. gratissima*** (Wallich) Sweet. To 5m. Stems lenticellate, red-pubesc.; branches spreading. Lvs to 20×10cm, ovate or lanceolate to elliptic or oblong, apex narrowly acute, base attenuate, leathery to membranous, pubesc. beneath, 9–12-veined; petioles to 2cm. Fls short-pedicellate, in many-fld, pubesc. corymbs to 20cm wide, pink; cal. tube to 6mm, pubesc., lobes to 13×3mm, subulate, glabrous or pubesc.; cor. tube to 3cm, lobes to 15×5cm, simple, spreading, obovate. Fr. to 16×8cm, obovoid. Autumn–winter. Himalaya. Z10.

***L. intermedia*** Hutch. To 7m. Stems verrucose. Lvs to 15×7cm, lanceolate to oblong, apex narrowly acute, 9–12-veined. Fls in cymes to 18cm wide, red; cor. tube to 35mm, cylindric, lobes appendaged. Winter. Yunnan. Z9.

***L. pinceana*** Hook. To 3m. Stems pubesc. Lvs to 15×5cm, ovate or lanceolate to elliptic, apex narrowly acute, base attenuate, leathery, sparsely pubesc. beneath, 12–14-veined; stipules to 15mm; petioles to 1cm. Fls in many-fld, glabrous corymbs, to 20cm wide, white and pink-flushed; cal. tube to 5mm, glabrous, lobes to 15×5mm, obovate; cor. tube to 5cm, interior pubesc., lobes to 5cm wide, 2-appendaged. Fr. to 15×10mm, obovoid, ribbed. Summer–autumn. Nepal to Yunnan. Z9.

***L. gratissima*** Wallich, non Sweet. See *L. pinceana*.
For further synonymy see *Cinchona* and *Mussaenda*.

**Lucuma** auct. non Molina.
***L. campechiana*** HBK. See *Pouteria campechiana*.
***L. mammosa*** auct. non (L.) Gaertn. f. See *Pouteria sapota*.
***L. nervosa*** A. DC. See *Pouteria campechiana*.
***L. salicifolia*** HBK. See *Pouteria campechiana*.

**Ludisia** A. Rich. (Derivation of name obscure, possibly after the subject of an elegy written by her widower.) Orchidaceae. 1 species, a terrestrial or lithophytic orchid. Stems succulent, prostrate to ascending, segmented, terete, pink to brown with paler flecks, branching and rooting at nodes. Roots adhesive, ciliate. Leaves scattered along creeping stems or in a loose rosette on ascending (flowering) stems, subcordate to broad-elliptic, acute, to 7.5cm, fleshy, narrowed to a clasping petiole, velvety-papillose, bronze to black with 5 longitudinal copper-red veins and broken venation between, underside pink to brown, glossy. Inflorescence a terminal, bracteate raceme to 15cm; axis pubescent, pink-green; flowers spiralling, numerous, sparkling white, to 2cm diameter; dorsal sepals and petals forming a hood, lateral sepals reflexed; lip basally saccate, tip cleft and frilled, limb twisted; column glossy golden-yellow, diverging from lip; ovary twisted, pubescent. SE Asia, China, Indonesia. Z9.

CULTIVATION A striking orchid grown for its beautifully patterned, velvety leaves and slender spikes of white flowers. It is the largest and most robust of the jewel orchids (see *Anoectochilus*) and, unlike its allies, will withstand almost any conditions provided some shade and temperatures over 10°C/50°F. Because of its meritorious flowers and foliage and ease of propagation (sections of rhizome will root and sprout freely if buried in a leafy/sandy mix, kept moist and given a little bottom heat). *Ludisia* is gaining popularity as a houseplant. Place the rhizomes, half-buried, in a mix of leafmould, coarse bark and charcoal in pans or half pots. Water freely, allowing a slight drying between each watering. Mist with soft water during warm weather. Ideally, maintain medium to high humidity, temperatures in excess of 15°C/60°F (if lower, reduce watering accordingly) and light to deep shade. Repot and divide after flowering, when the flowered growths will deteriorate.

***L. discolor*** (Ker-Gawl.) A. Rich. As for the genus. A highly variable species treated here as encompassing the many taxa named in *Haemaria* and recombined on rather questionable grounds in *Ludisia*. These are probably best treated as cultivars and include *L. dawsoniana*, a large plant (lvs to 12cm) of particular vigour, and *L. otletae* with finely patterned narrow-lanceolate lvs and sparsely flowered spikes.

For synonymy see *Goodyera* and *Haemaria*.

**Ludlow, Frank** (1885–1972) and **Sherriff, George** (1898–1967). Plant collectors. Ludlow was born in Chelsea and educated at Wellington School and Cambridge, where he gained a BA in natural sciences. He became vice-principal of Sind College, Karachi, and, after serving in World War One, the inspector of European schools in Poona and later headmaster of a Tibetan school. In 1927 he was awarded the OBE. He met Sherriff in 1929 on a shooting trip in Kashmir, where they planned the seven expeditions to the eastern Himalayas and south-eastern Tibet for which they are famous.

Sherriff, born in Stirlingshire and educated at Sedbergh and the Royal Military Academy, Woolwich, saw distinguished service in World War I and in the mountain artillery on the Northwest Frontier after the war. He then joined the consular service, eventually becoming British Consul in Kashgar until 1932.

Between 1933 and 1950 the two men systematically explored Bhutan and the outlying Himalayan regions, including Tibet. In 1938, travelling with Sir George Taylor, they found over 5000 specimens which were either new or found only in China and Sikkim, including *Paeonia lutea* var. *ludlowii*, the tall yellow tree peony, and of the 24,000 specimens gathered overall, 27 primula, 38 saxifraga and 23 gentians were entirely new. Ludlow and Sherriff were discerning collectors – their most notable finds include *Meconopsis superba, Meconopsis grandis, Luculia grandifolia* and *Primula ludlowii*.

War interrupted their efforts; Sherriff returned to military service, and in 1943 replaced Ludlow as Assistant Political Officer in charge of the British Mission at Lhasa, Tibet, where they rediscovered the Lhasa poppy, *Meconopsis torquata*. In 1946 they resumed their travels in Tibet and Pome. Although unable to explore the Tsangpogo Gorge, they found 23 species of rhododendron in a tiny area of Pemakochung alone. In 1949 they made their last collections in Bhutan, gathering 5000 species including *Lilium sherriffii* and *Euphorbia griffithii*.

They returned to England in 1950, Sherriff to Scotland where he created a fine Himalayan garden at Ascreavie in Kirriemuir, Ludlow to the British Museum where he worked on their collections and wrote on *Corydalis*, publishing a description of a new Himalayan and Tibetan species and subspecies with W.T. Stearn in 1975.

Volume 174 of the *Botanical Magazine* is dedicated to both. Sherriff was awarded the Royal Horticultural Society's Victoria Medal of Honour in 1953, and although Ludlow declined the medal, he did accept honorary fellowship of the society. Sherriff was also a fine photographer, and his work can be found in the British Museum.

**Ludvigia** L. See *Ludwigia*.

**Ludwigia** L. (For C.G. Ludwig (1709–1773), German botanist.) Onagraceae. 75 species of herbaceous to woody, erect plants, often floating or creeping; underwater parts sometimes swollen and spongy or bearing inflated white spongy pneumatophores, particularly in woody or semi-woody species. Leaves mostly alternate, sometimes opposite, simple. Flowers actinomorphic, yellow or white, solitary and axillary or in terminal clusters; sepals 4–5, somewhat persistent in fruit; petals absent or 4–5, deciduous, yellow, showy; stamens 4, or 10 in 2 whorls; ovary inferior, 4- or 5-locular. Fruit a cylindrical to obconical capsule, many-seeded. Cosmopolitan, especially in warmer regions.

CULTIVATION Floating aquatics and creeping, wet-soil perennials, largely of warm climates: the lower surface of the leaves of *L.palustris* are suffused purple or red (especially under good light conditions). The aquatics are grown in outdoor pools in warm temperate gardens or in aquariums in colder regions: plant in a dense loam-based medium, topped off with pea-shingle, or in shallow water on the muddy base of ponds; ensure strong, filtered light and minimum water temperatures of 13°C/55°F. Terrestrials are suitable for bog gardens and watersides in warm areas: give a sunny site and fertile soil. In colder gardens, plants grown in the open may be overwintered under glass and planted out after the last frosts: alternatively treat as frost-tender annuals. Forms of *L.palustris* (aquatic) and *L.alternifolia* (native to bog and wet woodland) which originate in northern America should be tolerant of more severe winter conditions. Propagate from seed, sown in spring at 15–21°C/60–70°F and covered lightly with sand; stand pots of terrestrials in shallow trays of water but plunge aquatics so that water covers the sand surface by 2–5cm/1–2in. Alternatively, increase by softwood cuttings in a closed case in early spring or by division in spring where this is possible.

***L.alternifolia*** L. RATTLE BOX; SEED BOX. Stems erect, branched, 45cm to 1m. Lvs 3.5–10cm, alternate, linear to linear-lanceolate, sessile or shortly petiolate. Fls solitary from upper lf axils; sep. ovate, 4; pet. 4, minute, yellow. Capsules *c*5mm, cubical, slightly wing-angled. E US. Z4.

***L.grandiflora*** (Michx.) Zardini, Gu & Raven. Very similar to *L.hexapetala* but distinguished by being a hexaploid species. SE US, S America. Z9.

***L.helminthorrhiza*** (Mart.) Hara. Floating herb rooting at nodes, with spongy pneumatophores. Lvs 1–5cm, rounded. Fls solitary in axils, mostly 5-merous; pet. to 1.3cm, broad, white with a basal yellow spot. Capsule nearly cylindrical. S Mexico to S America. Z9.

***L.hexapetala*** (Hook. & Arn.) Zardini, Gu & Raven. Long-hairy perenn. herb with decumbent rooting and more or less erect, leafy branches to 1.5m tall, with pneumatophores arising from underwater buried parts. Lvs 3–13×0.3–2.5cm, spathulate to oblanceolate; petioles 1–5(–25)mm. Fls borne singly in upper axils; sep. 5, rarely 6, 6–20×1.5–3mm, hairy; pet. 12–30×9–15mm, bright golden-yellow with a darker spot at base, obovate; stamens 10. Capsule light brown, with 10 conspicuous darker brown ribs, terete, 1.3–2.5cm, hairy. SE US to Argentina; introduced in Europe where it is naturalized in rivers and ditches in parts of S France and NE Spain. Z6.

***L.longifolia*** (DC.) Hara. Erect perenn. to 2m. Stems narrowly winged, glabrous. Lvs 10–20cm, lanceolate, much reduced up the stem. Fls solitary in upper axils; sep. 4, lanceolate, to 1.3cm; pet. to 2.5cm, pale yellow. Capsule elongate-pyramidal, 4-angled. Brazil to Argentina. May have been misidentified in gardens as *L.decurrens*, an annual species of N & S America.

***L.natans*** Elliot. Aquatic herb rooting at nodes. Lvs opposite, elliptic to obcordate, tinged purple beneath, petioled. Fls axillary; sep. 2–4mm, 4, triangular; pet. yellow, quickly shed. Capsule 3–6mm, 4-sided, tapering at base. N America and W Indies. Z9.

***L.octovalis*** (Jacq.) Raven. Robust well-branched herb, sometimes woody at base or even shrubby, to 4m. Lvs 0.7–14.5×0.1–4cm, linear to subovate, attenuate at apex; petioles to 10mm. Sep. 4, 3–15×1–7.5mm, ovate or lanceolate; pet. 3–17×2–17mm, yellow, broadly obovate or cuneate. Capsule thin-walled, 17–45cm×2–8mm, terete, pale brown with 8 darker ribs. Tropics. Z10.

***L.palustris*** (L.) Elliot. WATER PURSLANE. Stems weak, floating in shallow water or creeping in mud, to 50cm or longer, well-branched and forming mats. Lvs 0.7–4.5×0.4–2.3cm, opposite, lanceolate to elliptic-ovate, red or red-purple beneath; petioles about the same length. Fls axillary and usually paired; sep. 4, 1.4–2×0.8–1.8mm; pet. 0; stamens 4, green. Capsule 2–5×2–3mm, dull light brown, elongate-globose, obscurely 4-angled, with 4 longitudinal green bands. Americas, Europe and Asia. A sterile hybrid between *L.palustris* and *L.repens* is also sometimes cultivated. Z3.

***L.peploides*** (Kunth) Raven. Herb with stems sprawling and rooting at nodes or floating, usually ascending when flowering and up to 60cm. Lvs 1–9.5×0.4–3cm, elliptic; petioles 0.2–3cm. Fls borne singly in upper lf axils; flowering stem, cal. and capsule finely hairy to subglabrous; sep. 5, 4–12×1.5–2.5mm; pet. bright golden-yellow with a darker spot at the base, obovate, 7–17×4–13mm; stamens 10. Capsule light brown, with 10 conspicuous darker brown ribs, terete, 1–2.5cm. N & S America; naturalized in rivers in SW France. Z7.

***L.peruviana*** (L.) Hara. Shrub 0.5–3m tall, entirely covered with villous pubescence, long inflated pneumatophore arising from submerged, buried roots. Lvs 4–12×0.3–1.5cm, lanceolate to broadly lanceolate, apex acute to acuminate. Fls borne singly in upper lf axils; sep. 10–18×4–8mm, 4 or 5, lanceolate, irregularly serrulate, villous; pet. bright yellow, veiny, suborbicular, 15–24×16–26mm with a claw 1–3mm long; stamens twice as numerous as the sepals. Capsule 1.2–3×0.6–1cm, villous, light yellow-brown with 4 prominent dark brown ribs, 4-angled. SE US to S America; introduced in the Old World. Z9.

***L.uruguayensis*** (Cambess.) Hara. See *L.grandiflora*.
For further synonymy see *Jussiaea*.

**Ludwigiantha** (Torr. & A. Gray) Small. See *Ludwigia*.

**Lueddemannia** Lind. & Rchb. f. (Named in honour of M.E. Lueddeman (fl. 1854), who cultivated orchids in Paris.) Orchidaceae. Some 2 species of epiphytic orchids. Pseudobulbs clustered, ovoid to ovoid-oblong, usually apically bifoliate. Leaves rigid, erect, lanceolate to elliptic, plicate. Inflorescence from base of pseudobulbs, a lateral raceme, pendent, many-flowered; flowers often large, fleshy, rather spreading; sepals similar, free, ovate-elliptic to oblong-elliptic, lateral sepals oblique; petals smaller than sepals, oblanceolate to spathulate-elliptic; lip clawed, apex trilobed; lateral lobes erect, midlobe triangular; disc with an erect callus, crested or tuberculate; column clavate, arcuate, apex auriculate-alate, anther terminal, operculate, incumbent, unilocular, pollinia 2, compressed. Venezuela, Peru, Ecuador, Colombia. Z10.

CULTIVATION As for *Stanhopea*.

***L.pescatorei*** (Lindl.) Lind. & Rchb. f. Pseudobulbs to 13×7cm, slightly compressed, ovoid to ovoid-oblong, light yellow-brown. Lvs to 40×9cm, lanceolate to elliptic-lanceolate, acute. Infl. to 50cm; peduncle light green spotted dark purple; sep. to 27×14mm, ovate to ovate-elliptic, acute or obtuse, light red-brown finely spotted purple, interior bright red-maroon with pale brown margins; pet. to 23×9mm, spathulate-oblanceolate or oblanceolate, acute or subobtuse, bright golden-yellow, apical margins marked red; lip to 26×19mm, bright golden-yellow, fleshy, rigid, lateral lobes obliquely ovate-triangular, obtuse to subacute, midlobe minutely papillose, acute, disc central, with a warty callus, minutely papillose; column to 19mm, pale yellow-cream, apex winged, anth. pale yellow. Venezuela, Colombia, Ecuador, Peru.

***L.triloba*** Rolfe. See *L.pescatorei*.
For further synonymy see *Cycnoches*.

**Luetkea** Bong. (For Count F.P. Luetke, Captain of the fourth Russian expedition to circumnavigate the globe (early 19th century).) Rosaceae. 1 species, a tufted, procumbent, evergreen subshrub. Stems becoming woody, often creeping, flowering stems to 15cm, subglabrous. Leaves to 1.5cm, alternate, rigid, bright green, divided ×2–3 into linear pointed lobes. Flowers small, bisexual, in narrow racemes to 5cm; bracts entire to ternate; calyx tube hemispheric, lobes 2mm, ovate; petals to 3.5mm, 5, white, round-obovate; stamens 20, filaments basally connate; pistils 5. Follicles 5, coriaceous, smooth, 4mm, 1-seeded. Summer. Mts of NW America (Alaska to Oregon). Related to *Spiraea* but leaves ×2–3 ternately dissected and filaments connate into a short tube at base. Z3.

CULTIVATION Grown as evergreen groundcover, for banks, and in the rock garden or peat garden. Its dark green, deeply cut foliage is reminiscent of the mossy saxifrages; the short racemes of creamy white, woolly flowers are carried in summer. Hardy to 15°C/5°F. Grow in lime-free, well-drained but moisture-retentive soils rich in leafmould, in light shade, ensuring a cool, moist root run. Propagate by division, by seed in spring, or by soft tip cuttings in spring.

***L.pectinata*** (Pursh) Kuntze. As for the genus.

***L. caespitosum*** Kuntze. See *Petrophytum caespitosum*.
For further synonymy see *Saxifraga* and *Spiraea*.

**Luffa** Mill. (Arabic *louff*, name given to *L. cylindrica.)* LOOFAH; DISHCLOTH GOURD; RAG GOURD; STRAINER VINE. Cucurbitaceae. 6 species of annual climbers, occasionally trailing, monoecious or dioecious, scabrous or hairy. Tendrils 2–6-fid. Leaves simple, palmately angled or lobed, glandular; probracts glandular. Male inflorescence a raceme; flowers large, conspicuous, white to yellow; calyx tube campanulate, lobed; petals 5, free; stamens 3–5, filaments and anthers free; female flowers solitary, similar to male except staminodes absent; ovary ribbed, tuberculate or spiny; stigmas 3. Fruit elongate, cylindric, glabrous or spinose, fleshy becoming dry, dehiscent through terminal operculum; seeds compressed, black, narrowly winged. Pantropical, probably introduced to Americas. Z9.

CULTIVATION Annual climbers grown throughout the tropics for their large golden-yellow flowers and edible young fruits and commercially for their fibrous fruits ('loofah sponges') the exposed and dried vascular system of the dried fruit of *L. cylindrica* is the bathroom loofah. The young fruits of *L. acutangula* are eaten in the Orient. They occur in the wild in woodland and grassland. Cultivate as for *Trichosanthes* except that multiple planting and cross-pollination are not required. Prepare the sponges by steeping mature fruit in running water until the skin and seed contents have been washed away. Seed races vary and the largest-fruited must be selected out.

***L. acutangula*** (L.) Roxb. ANGLED LOOFAH; SING-KWA. Climber. Stem 4–5-angled. Tendrils 4–7-fid. Lvs palmate, glabrous, about 17×11cm; lobes 5–7, acuminate; petiole 8–12cm. Male infl. a raceme to 15cm, borne on long peduncle; female fls solitary; pedicels bracteate, bearing nectaries; cal. tube pubesc., 5-lobed; cor. yellow to 5cm diam., bearing nectaries in female; stamens 3; ovary 10-angled. Fr. deeply 10-angled, to 30cm or more, about 10cm diam.; seeds rugose, emarginate, to 12×8cm. Pakistan, widely cultivated throughout Tropics. var. ***amara*** (Roxb.) Clark. Lvs smaller, softly villous. Fr. to 8cm; seeds smaller. India, Pakistan, Yemen.

***L. cylindrica*** (L.) M. Roem. LOOFAH; VEGETABLE SPONGE. Climber or trailer to 15m. Stems finely pubesc. Tendrils 3 to 6-fid. Lvs palmate, ovate-cordate, 6–18×6–20cm, lobes 3–5, ovate, sometimes slightly lobulate, sparsely serrate or entire, midlobe largest. Male raceme glandular-bracteate, 12–35cm; female fls on peduncle to 3cm; cal. tube pubesc. within, lobes acute, to 12mm; pet. yellow, rounded, to 45mm; stamens 3 or 5, absent in female; ovary cylindric, densely pubesc., slightly 10-ribbed, absent in male. Fr. ellipsoid to cylindric, glabrous, to 50cm; seeds lenticular, to 12×8×3mm, smooth, narrowly winged. Tropical Asia and Africa.

***L. operculata*** (L.) Cogn. Stems climbing or trailing, striate. Tendrils bifid. Lvs palmate, subreniform, scabrous, to 15cm, lobes 3–5, narrowing at base, entire or slightly denticulate, midlobe largest. Male raceme 5–30-fld, to 20cm; pedicels glandular-bracteate, to 3m (female fls sessile); sep. triangular to ovate-acuminate, to 3mm; pet. 5, free, to 1cm; stamens 3, anth. sometimes partially connate, staminodes sometimes present in female; ovary fusiform, tomentose, spinose, absent in male; style linear, sometimes 3-parted. Fr. about 6cm, ellipsoid to fusiform, dry operculate, fibrous, slightly ribbed, spinose; seeds white to dark brown, compressed. Mexico to Colombia and Peru.

***L. aegyptiaca*** Mill. See *L. cylindrica*.
***L. amara*** Roxb. See *L. acutangula* var. *amara*.
***L. gigantea*** hort. See *L. cylindrica*.
***L. macrocarpa*** hort. See *L. cylindrica*.
***L. marylandica*** hort. See *L. cylindrica*.
For further synonymy see *Cucumis* and *Momordica*.

**Luina** Benth. (An anagram of *Inula*.) Compositae. 3 species of perennial herbs, with many erect, simple stems from a woody base. Leaves alternate, entire to deeply cleft. Capitula discoid, in terminal corymbs; receptacle naked; involucre oblong-campanulate; phyllaries in 1 series, equal, rather firm, somewhat herbaceous; florets all tubular, hermaphrodite, fertile, usually yellow. Fruit a prominently several-nerved cypsela; pappus of numerous, soft, white bristles. Western N America.

CULTIVATION Grow on the rock garden, as for *Inula*.

***L. hypoleuca*** Benth. LITTLE-LEAF LUINA. Stems 15–40cm, white-tomentose, leafy. Lvs 20–60×7–35mm, broadly elliptic or ovate, subentire, sessile, green and thinly tomentose glabrous above, white-tomentose beneath. Involucre 5–8mm high, thinly tomentose or becoming glabrous; receptacle to 1cm diam.; phyllaries 8–10; florets 10–17, dull yellow or cream. Fr. *c*2mm, brown, glabrous. Summer to early autumn. British Columbia to California.

***L. nardosmia*** (A. Gray) Cronq. See *Cacaliopsis nardosmia*.

**Luisia** Gaudich. (For Dom Luis de Torres, Portuguese botanist.) Orchidaceae. Some 30 species of epiphytic, monopodial orchids. Stems slender, terete, branching near base, thus appearing clump-forming. Leaves alternate, remote, dark green, tinted maroon in optimum conditions, fleshy, slender, terete, attached to cylindric sheathing base. Inflorescences numerous, axillary, short, clustered; sepals and petals obovate, acute, forward-pointing; lip prominent, lobed, coloured, fused to column base. Tropical Asia to Polynesia. Z9.

CULTIVATION As for *Papilionanthe*; the habit is, however, rather more compact than in that genus and the flowers (clustered, green and mauve) altogether less showy.

***L. psyche*** Rchb. f. Lvs blunt, erect, to 15cm. Fls pale yellow-green, lip violet-brown, chequered white or yellow; sep. concave, obtuse, to 1.5cm; pet. linear to obovate, to 4cm; lip to 2.5cm, ovate-oblong, basally saccate with 2 lobe-like appendages. Burma, Laos.

***L. teretifolia*** Gaudich. Lvs tapering to a point, curving upwards, to 20cm. Fls yellow, green, or pale pink, lip base green and purple or yellow; dorsal sep. elliptic, lateral sep. lanceolate, exterior keeled, apical point fleshy; pet. linear-oblong; lip trilobed, cordate above, almost square below, basally inflated, midlobe cordate, undulate, lateral lobes elliptic, undulate at tips. India, SE Asia to N Caledonia.

***L. alpina*** Lindl. See *Trudelia alpina*.

**Luma** A. Gray. (Native Chilean name.) Myrtaceae. 4 species of shrubs or small trees to *c*10m, weakly to strongly glandular, variously puberulent to villous. Leaves persistent, subcoriaceous to submembranous, mainly elliptic. Inflorescence 1-flowered, or a dichasium of 3 (rarely more) flowers; flowers tetramerous, the calyx lobes ovate-triangular to ovate-orbicular, concave. Fruit a fleshy, somewhat spongy berry. Seeds lenticular, 1–16 per fruit. Argentina, Chile. Distinguished from other South American Myrtaceae by its tetramerous flowers and relatively small, elliptic to suborbicular leaves with acute to apiculate apices. The name *Myrceugenella* has commonly been used for this genus since it was proposed by Kausel (1942). However, *Luma* has priority over *Myrceugenella*. Z9.

CULTIVATION Grown for the neat glossy evergreen foliage, carried in beautiful contrast to the slender red stems, *L. apiculata* becomes increasingly attractive as it matures, when the cinnamon-coloured bark flakes and peels away revealing the grey white trunk beneath. In warm maritime gardens, *Luma* spp. are tolerant of several degrees of frost (to about −10°C/14°F). Cultivate as for *Myrtus*.

***L. apiculata*** (DC.) Burret. ARRAYÁN; PALO COLORADO; TEMU; COLLIMAMOL. Shrub or small tree to *c*10m. Trunk smooth, appearing somewhat twisted. Bark grey to bright orange-brown; hairs off-white. Lvs 1–4.5×0.5–3.5cm, elliptic to suborbicular, less often ovate or lanceolate, glabrous or villous to puberulent along midvein and margins beneath; petiole 1–2mm. Infl. 1-fld or bearing a dichasium of 3 (rarely more) fls; peduncle 5–30cm; cal. lobes triangular-ovate to suborbicular, 2–3(–4)mm long and wide, ciliate; pet. suborbicular, 3–5mm, ciliate; stems 170–300, *c*5–7mm. Fr. subglobose, to 1cm diam., dark purple. Argentina, Chile. 'Glanleam Gold': fls striped yellow to cream; fls white. 'Penwith': lvs striped yellow to cream, tinged red; fls white.

***L. chequen*** (Molina) A. Gray. CHEQUÉN; ARRAYÁN BLANCO. Shrub or small tree up to *c*9m. Bark grey-brown; hairs off-white. Lvs 0.5–2.5(–4)×0.4–1.5(–1.8)cm, elliptic, ovate or lanceolate, rarely suborbicular, glabrous or pubesc. along midvein and margins beneath, acute or scarcely acuminate; petiole 0.5–2mm. Infl. 1-fld; peduncle 0.5–2.5cm; cal. lobes concave, ovate-orbicular, 1.8–3.2×2–3cm, ciliate; pet. suborbicular, *c*4–7mm, ciliate or glabrous; stamens *c*90–230, 3–7mm. Fr. subglobose, 0.6–1cm diam., dark purple. Chile.

For synonymy see *Eugenia*, *Myrceugenella* and *Myrtus*.

**Lunaria** L. (From Lat. *luna*, moon, alluding to the shape of the pod.) Cruciferae. 3 species of biennial or perennial herbs. Stems, erect, branching. Leaves simple, cordate, toothed, petiolate. Flowers large, in terminal racemes; sepals 4, erect; petals 4, long-clawed, purple, rarely, white. Fruit a silique, very compressed, oblong-elliptic to nearly round, septum white, papery. Spring–summer. C & S Europe. Z8.

CULTIVATION The spring-flowering perennial, *L. rediviva*, is found in damp and shady wooded habitats, especially on calcareous soils; *L. annua*, occurring on waste and cultivated land, often as a garden escape, is widely naturalized elsewhere, including parts of North America, where it was introduced in the 1930s. They are grown in flower and shrub borders, at the woodland fringe and in the wild garden. Both spp. are hardy to −15°C/5°F. The translucent septa, elliptical in *L. rediviva*, somewhat rounded in *L. annua*, held on bleached, dry branches, are popular with arrangers of dried flowers for their satiny, silver-white texture and their form. Harvest as pods turn brown; hang to dry and allow valves and seed to fall away.

Grow in moist fertile soils, in part shade or sun. Propagate from seed sown in autumn or spring; *L. rediviva* also by division. Plants may be affected by crucifer white blister (*Albugo candida*) and club root (*Plasmodioiphora brassicae*). A virus infection sometimes causes distortion and streaking in the flowers.

***L. annua*** L. HONESTY; SILVER DOLLAR; PENNY FLOWER. Bienn. to 1m. Lvs ovate-lanceolate, cordate, coarsely toothed, upper lvs sessile to subsessile. Fls unscented; pet. 15–25mm, purple-red. Fr. 20–70×15–35mm, oblong-round, blunt at apex and base, translucent when ripe. 'Alba': to 85cm; fls white. 'Alba Variegata': to 100cm; lvs suffused white; fls pure white. 'Haslemere': to 85cm; lvs green variegated off-white; fls purple, freely produced. 'Variegata': lvs green, variegated and edged cream. 'Violet': pods large; fls bright purple.

***L. rediviva*** L. PERENNIAL HONESTY. Similar to *L. annua* except perenn., lvs finely toothed, not sessile higher up the stem. Fls fragrant. Fr. tapering at base and apex.

***L. biennis*** Moench. See *L. annua*.

**Lupinus** L. (From Lat. *lupus*, wolf, referring to the belief that the plants take over the land, exhausting the fertility of the soil.) LUPIN. Leguminosae (Papilionoideae). Some 200 species of annual or perennial herbs or shrubs. Stems often pubescent. Leaves alternate, palmate, long-stalked; leaflets 5–15 per leaf; stipules slender, adnate to base of petioles. Flowers showy, in erect, terminal racemes or spikes, or whorled; bracts often caducous; bracteoles adnate to base of calyx; calyx bilabiate, lips entire or toothed, upper sometimes bifid; standard erect, orbicular or broad-ovate, margins reflexed, wings falcate-oblong or obovate, connate at apex, keel beaked; stamens 10, monadelphous, anthers alternately long and short; stigma terminal, style incurved, glabrous; ovary sessile, ovules 2 to many. Fruit an oblong, laterally compressed, dehiscent legume, usually sericeous or hirsute, somewhat torulose; seeds 2–12. Western N America, Mediterranean, S America, S Europe, N Africa.

CULTIVATION In the wild, *Lupinus* spp. occur predominantly, but not exclusively, in dry habitats, frequently on stony and low-fertility soils; species such as *L. polyphyllus*, *L. latifolius* and *L. nootkatensis* occur on moist soils, generally found where drainage is good. A large and horticulturally valuable genus, with species suited to a variety of situations in the garden, *Lupinus* is grown for its often beautiful foliage and sometimes fragrant spikes of showy flowers. The annuals include a number of species that are both beautiful and functional. The seeds of several species (e.g. *L. albus*) were formerly used by the Egyptians, Greeks and Romans to make a flour for bread and for medicinal purposes. The plants were also widely used for green-manuring (e.g. *L. luteus*) and land reclamation (e.g. *L. arboreus*). *L. albus*, *L. luteus* and *L. angustifolius* are used in the southern United States as winter cover crops for soils of low fertility, adding nitrogen and phosphates when dug into the soil. Some species are cultivated for fodder (e.g. *L. perennis*), but use of these plants for forage and fodder merits caution because of toxicity. The seeds of *L. albus* are edible if roasted and, like those of *L. luteus*, are sometimes ground and used as a coffee substitute. *L. mutabilis* is much used by the natives of South America as a substitute for edible beans; they are soaked overnight to remove toxic alkaloids and then cooked. *L. texensis*, which forms extensive carpets of blue in summer in its native Texas, *L. densiflorus* and *L. nanus* make beautiful additions to the wild garden and native plant collections, and are also suitable in more formal situations for border edgings.

Perennial species such as *L. polyphyllus* are also used in the wild garden, especially on stream banks and for flowering above rough grass, where they may be short lived but will self-seed. In drier conditions, in finer grasses in the orchard and especially on the dry gravelly soils that approximate to those of its native habitats, the shrubby *L. arboreus* can be used to similar effect; it has been used to stabilize sandy soils and dunes where it self seeds to form extensive ground cover.

Some low-growing species are suitable for the rock garden the most choice amongst these being *L. confertus*, *L. lyallii* and the exquisite *L. ornatus*, grown for their densely pubescent, silvery foliage and spikes of blue flowers. Although cold hardy, like many silver leaved subjects, they do not thrive in winter wet and, where this a grave problem, should be grown in pans in the alpine house or frame, and watered carefully and sparingly in winter.

The most commonly cultivated perennials are those derived mainly from *L. polyphyllus* and its crosses with *L. arboreus* and probably some of the annual species; young plants produce the best flowers and all are easily raised from seed. Some of the finest of these are the Russell Lupins, raised by George Russell of York over a period of 25 years and introduced in 1937. Named selections are chosen for colour and height, from dwarf races such as Garden Gnome, Minarette and Dwarf Gallery, which seldom exceed 45–60cm/18–24in., to the well-proportioned heights of *L.* Band of Nobles, which may achieve 150cm/5ft. The colour spectrum of hybrids ranges from cream and white shades through yellows in *L.* Chandelier, orange reds in *L.* Flaming June, carmine in *L.* The Pages to rich, deep violets in *L.* Thundercloud and includes strong primary colours and bicolours, as in *L.* The Châtelaine and *L.* The Governor. More subtle shades are found in *L.* Blushing Bride, ivory white, *L.* George Russell, creamy pink, *L.* Wheatsheaf, golden-yellow flushed pink. Those hybrids which are sold as mixed shades are at their most splendid when planted in groups of five or more, where maximum tonal contrasts are achieved. Most hybrids and species are not long-lasting when cut, but will survive longer if the cut stem is filled with water before arranging.

The shrub species, include *L. arboreus*, usually with yellow spikes of sweetly moss-scented flowers, and *L. albifrons*, with beautiful silky foliage. Although useful in the shrub border, both make fine additions to the herbaceous border. *L. arboreus* is well suited to naturalizing on rough banks and dry walls, especially on poor dry soils, and in maritime areas, where it will self sow. Given good drainage and shelter from cold winds, *L. arboreus* will tolerate temperatures to −15°C/5°F, *L. albifrons* is less hardy.

Grow *Lupinus* spp. in full sun, in deep, moderately fertile, well-drained soils that are slightly acid to neutral. Grow rock garden species in soils that are gritty or gravelly and impeccably drained. Repot alpine-house specimens each spring.

Sow annual species *in situ* in spring, as soon as the soil is workable. Sow perennials in pots and plant out when small; lupins are generally intolerant of root disturbance. Germination is quicker if seeds are pre-soaked for 24 hours in warm water. Sow *L. angustifolius* for green manure in spring and summer, spaced at 7cm/2½in. in rows 15cm/6in. apart; dig in about eight weeks after germination. Named varieties can be propagated by basal cuttings, taken with a small part of the rootstock attached, in sand in the cold frame.

The fungus *Pleiochaeta setosa* causes small black-purple spots which may enlarge so that the leaves shrivel and die. Spots may also occur on stems and pods. The disease can be controlled by copper-based fungicides. Lupins can also be affected by black root rot, *Thievaliopsis basicola*, crown gall, *Agrobacterium tumefaciens*, powdery mildew, *Erisyphe trifolii* and sclerotina rot, *Sclerotinia sclerotium*. Alfalfa mosaic virus and a strain of the bean yellow or pea mosaic virus group can cause various symptoms including vein banding, leaf yellowing and flower colour breaks; severely affected plants should be destroyed and replaced with healthy stock.

Lupins may become severely infested in both Europe and North America with the lupin aphid, *Macrosiphum albifrons*, and leaves and flowers can be damaged by woodlice. In North America, plants may be attacked by the capsid bug, *Poecilocapsus lineatus*.

***L. affinis*** J. Agardh. Annual, erect to 60cm. Stems several, strigose or short-villous. Leaflets to 4cm, 6–8, oblanceolate; petioles to 10cm. Fls deep blue, in racemes to 22cm of somewhat remote whorls; pedicels to 6mm; upper cal. lip to 5mm, lower to 6mm; pet. to 12mm, standard suborbicular, lighter in centre, keel not much curved, ciliate towards apex. Fr. to 5cm, villous-hirsute; seeds to 5mm, 5–8, subquadrate, dark brown, mottled. Spring. W US (California, Oregon).

***L. albifrons*** Benth. Shrub to 1.5m, habit rounded. Stems adpressed-sericeous. Leaflets to 3×1cm, 7–10, oblanceolate to spathulate, acute or rounded, silver-sericeous; petioles to 4cm. Fls blue to maroon or lavender, mostly whorled in racemes to 30cm; pedicels to 8mm, patent-pubesc.; bracts to 5mm, upper cal. lip bifid, lower entire, tapered at base. Fr. to 5cm, villous-strigose; seeds 4mm, 5–9, mottled or spotted. Spring–summer. W US (California). var. ***emineus*** (Greene) C.P. Sm. Fls slightly larger; pedicels sometimes adpressed-pubesc. Z8.

***L. albus*** L. WHITE LUPINE; FIELD LUPINE; WOLF BEAN; EGYPTIAN LUPIN. Annual to 120cm. Stems short-pubesc. Leaflets to 5cm×18mm, obovate or obovate-cuneate, mucronulate, subglabrous above, sparse-villous beneath. Fls white or tinted pale blue, alternate, in sessile racemes to 10cm; cal. to 9mm, upper and lower lips shallow toothed; cor. to 16mm, keel tipped pale blue. Fr. to 10cm, short-villous or subglabrous, rugulose, yellow; seeds to 14mm, 4–6, orbicular-oblong, flat, glabrous, dull light yellow or white. S Balkans, Aegean.

***L. angustifolius*** L. Annual to 50cm. Stem slender, hairy. Leaflets *c*3cm, 5–9 linear, apex obtuse, sericeous beneath. Fls blue. Fr. 6×1.5cm. Summer. Mediterranean.

***L. arboreus*** Sims. TREE LUPIN. Evergreen shrub to 3m. Branchlets rather woody, terete, dense, sericeous-pubesc. Leaflets to 5cm, 7–9×(–11), oblanceolate, acute or mucronate, glabrous above, lanuginose beneath, grey-green; stipules subulate. Fls sulphur-yellow, sometimes blue or lavender, in erect, lax, terminal racemes to 25.5cm; cal. upper lip emarginate, lower entire; cor. to 17mm, standard glabrous outside, keel curved, ciliate at apex. Fr. to 7.5cm, densely tomentose, brown, seeds to 5mm, 5–12 ellipsoid, dark brown, mottled spotted. Spring–summer. W US (California). 'Golden Spire': fls gold. 'Mauve Queen': fls lilac. 'Snow Queen': fls white. 'Yellow Boy': fls bright yellow. Z8.

***L. arcticus*** S. Wats. Very similar to *L. nootkatensis*, but with longer petioles and acute leaflets. N America S to Washington. Z4.

***L. argenteus*** Pursh. Erect perenn. to 60cm. Branches short-strigose. Leaflets to 4.5×0.5cm, 5–9, linear-oblanceolate, acute, subglabrous above, strigose beneath. Fls to 13mm, blue, lilac or lavender, less commonly white or rose, subverticillate, in lax racemes to 12cm; pedicels to 6mm; cal. upper lip 4mm, emarginate, lower 5mm, entire; standard suborbicular, pubesc. beneath, wings glabrous, keel strongly curved at apex, ciliate. Fr. to 2.5cm, strigose-sericeous; seeds 4mm, 2–4 light brown, unmottled. Summer–autumn. SW US (California, New Mexico). var. ***depressus*** (Rydb.) C. Hitchc. To 25cm. Fls crowded. Z4.

***L. benthamii*** Heller. Erect annual to 60cm. Stems villous. Leaflets to 5cm, 7–10, linear, villous; petioles to 12cm. Fls to 1.5cm, blue, in racemes to 20cm; pedicels to 6mm; bracts linear; cal. to 5mm, upper lip bifid, lower tridentate; standard to 1.5cm, suborbicular, with yellow spot, keel curved, ciliate below. Fr. to 3.5cm; seeds 2mm, 3–9, tawny, mottled brown. Spring. W US (California).

***L. bicolor*** Lindl. Erect annual to 40cm. Stems villous. Leaflets to 3cm, 5–7, oblanceolate to cuneate, villous; petioles to 7cm. Fls blue, 1–3-verticillate, in racemes to 7cm; pedicels to 3mm; bracts subulate, to 6mm; cal. upper lip to 4mm, lower tridentate to entire, to 6mm; standard to 9×8mm, oblong, truncate, reflexed, with purple-dotted white spot at centre sometimes spreading and wholly purple-red, keel slender, apex acute, ciliate. Fr. to 2cm, strigose; seeds to 3mm, 5–8, pale pink or somewhat grey. Spring–summer. Western N America (California to British Columbia).

***L. breweri*** A. Gray. Perenn. Stems tufted, decumbent or prostrate, silver-sericeous. Leaflets to 2cm, 7–10, oblanceolate to spathulate, silver-sericeous; petioles to 5cm. Fls to 9mm, violet, in dense-fld racemes to 5cm; pedicels to 3mm; cal. upper lip bifid, lower entire to tridentate, 3mm; standard rounded to obovate, white or somewhat yellow at centre, glabrous outside, keel glabrous or sparsely ciliate. Fr. to 16mm, sericeous; seeds to 4mm, 3–4, flesh-coloured, marked brown. Summer. W US (California, S Oregon, W Nevada). Z5.

***L. chamissonis*** Eschsch. Somewhat shrubby perenn., erect to 90cm. Young shoots sericeous-pubesc. Leaflets to 3cm×6.5mm, 5–7, lanceolate, abruptly acuminate, tapered at base, silver adpressed-pubesc.; petioles to 2.5cm. Fls blue or lilac, subverticillate, in erect racemes to 15cm; pedicels 6.5mm, sericeous; cal. 6.5mm; cor. 16mm, standard broad, blotched-yellow at base, pubesc. outside. Fr. to 3cm×6.5mm, sericeous. Summer–autumn. W US (California, Washington). Z8.

***L. confertus*** Kellogg. Thick-rooted, robust perenn. to 35cm. Stems several, dense white-sericeous. Leaflets to 4cm×8mm, usually 7, elliptic-oblanceolate, subacute, lax grey-sericeous; petiole to 9cm. Fls to 1.5cm, violet-purple, in dense racemes to 30cm; pedicels to 2mm; bracts subulate, to 9mm, persistent; cal. upper lip 5mm, lower 7mm; standard elliptic-obovate, lighter in centre, keel short-acuminate, somewhat curved, apex woolly. Fr. to 18mm, white sericeous-villous; seeds to 3mm, 2–5, pale, mottled. Summer. SW US (California, W Nevada). Z5.

***L. densiflorus*** Benth. Annual to 40cm. Stems simple or branched above, adpressed-pubesc. Leaflets to 2cm, 7–9, oblanceolate, obtuse to mucronate, glabrous above; petioles to 10cm. Fls white, violet- or rose- tinted or veined, 5–12-whorled in racemes to 20cm+; cal. 8mm, green, minutely pubesc., subtended by narrow reflexed bracts, lower lip 3mm diam., acute, slender bidentate; standard 14×8mm, keel slender, apex ciliate. Fr. 1.5cm, ovate-oblong, long-villous; seeds to 5mm. Spring–summer. W US (California). var. ***aureus*** (Kellogg) Munz. Fls pale yellow, sometimes bordered red. var. ***glareosus*** (Elmer) C.P. Sm. Fls 1.25cm, pet. pale blue, standard with white spot. var. ***lacteus*** (Kellogg) C.P. Sm. Stems and pedicels long-pubesc. Fls white, pale pink or lavender. 'Ed Gedling': fls gold.

***L. diffusus*** Nutt. Much-branched perenn. to 40cm+. Stems many, diffuse to spreading, rusty-pubesc. Leaflets to 12×5cm, solitary, oblong, elliptic, obovate or oblanceolate, acute to obtuse, mucronate, densely short-adpressed-pubesc.; petioles to 10cm. Fls light to deep blue, subverticillate, in many-fld racemes to 30cm; pedicels to 4mm, stout, densely short-rusty-pubesc.; bracts to 8mm, subulate, caducous, densely pubesc., subtending pedicels; cal. densely short rusty-adpressed-pubesc., tube 4mm, upper lip 4mm, lower trilobed, to 7mm; standard to 16mm, blotched cream. Fr. to 4.5cm, linear-oblong, densely adpressed-pubesc. SE US. Z7.

***L. excubitus*** Jones. Erect, freely branching, sericeous shrub to 1.5m. Leaflets to 3cm, 5–8, oblong-lanceolate to spathulate; petioles to 10cm. Fls to 12.5mm, blue, lilac or violet, in verticillate racemes to 25cm; pedicels to 6mm, strigose; bracts to 7mm, lanceolate, acuminate, deciduous; cal. upper lip emarginate, lower entire; standard suborbicular, glabrous or slightly pubesc. outside, yellow at centre, later somewhat red, wings broad, keel broad, apex curved, ciliate. Fr. to 5cm, densely sericeous-pubesc.; seeds 4mm, 6–8, pale brown, mottled. Spring–summer. W US (California). var. ***hallii*** (Abrams) C.P. Sm. Lvs less downy; fls longer. Z8.

***L. formosus*** Greene. Perenn. to 80cm. Stems decumbent or ascending, adpressed-sericeous. Leaflets to 7×1.5cm, 7–9, oblanceolate, sericeous; petioles to 7cm. Fls to 1.5cm, violet to blue, lilac, or white, in somewhat verticillate dense racemes to 25cm; pedicels to 4mm, patent-pubesc.; bracts to 7mm, linear-lanceolate, standard rounded, glabrous, keel slender, curved. Fr. to 3.5cm, sericeous-pubesc.; seeds to 4mm, 5–7, mottled grey. Spring–autumn. W US (California). Z8.

***L. grayi*** (S. Wats.) S. Wats. To 35cm. Stems ascending to decumbent, densely grey-tomentose and villous. Leaflets to 3.5cm×7mm, 5–11, oblanceolate, acute, tomentose; petioles to 12cm. Fls to 1.5cm, deep violet to lilac, in subverticillate racemes to 15cm; pedicels to 4mm; bracts to 5mm; cal. upper lip to 6mm, broad, deeply bidentate, lower lip 6mm+, entire to tridentate; standard rounded, yellow at centre, keel densely ciliate at apex and often toward base. Fr. to 3.5cm, strigose; seeds 4–6, mottled. Spring–summer. W US (California). Z8.

***L. hartwegii*** Lindl. Annual to 90cm. Stems tufted, much-branched, very densely pale-villous. Leaflets to 4.5×1.5cm, 7–9, oblong to oblanceolate, apiculate, densely pubesc. Fls 1.5cm, pale blue, in crowded elongate racemes to 20cm; pedicels 6mm; bracts slender, tufted at apex, pubesc.; cal. 12mm, densely pubesc., green, upper lip bifid; standard green-white above when young, later lilac-tinged, wings blue, keel white, tipped green; anth. orange. Fr. to 4.5cm, linear-oblong, grooved, densely white-pubesc.; seeds 4.5×2.5mm, 3–10, cream, dotted. Summer–autumn. Mexico.

***L. hirsutissimus*** Benth. Robust annual to 1m. Stems sparsely branched, densely tawny-hirsute. Leaflets to 5cm, 5–8 broad cuneate-obovate, pubesc.; petioles to 18cm. Fls to 1.5cm, red-violet to magenta, in racemes to 25cm; pedicels to 4mm; cal. to 1cm, upper lip bifid, lower entire to tridentate; standard suborbicular, usually blotched yellow, keel densely ciliate below. Fr. to 3.5cm, hispid-setose; seeds to 4mm, pale, mottled brown. Spring. W US (California), Baja California.

***L. latifolius*** Lindl. ex J. Agardh. Perenn. to 120cm. Stems erect, leafy, subglabrous to minutely strigose. Leaflets to 10×3cm, 7–9, broad-lanceolate, acute, occasionally obtuse, glabrous or subglabrous above; petioles to 20cm. Fls to 1.5cm, blue to purple, rarely somewhat yellow, verticillate or scattered, in lax racemes to 45cm; pedicels to 12mm, patent-pubesc.; bracts linear-subulate, to 12mm; cal. upper lip emarginate, lower entire; standard suborbicular, to 1cm diam., glabrous, wings truncate or incurved at base, keel curved, ciliate toward apex. Fr. 3cm, dark brown, pubesc.; seeds 4mm, 7–10, mottled deep brown. Spring–summer. W US (California to Washington). var. ***subalpinus*** (Piper & Robinson) C.P. Sm. Dwarf, 10–25cm, with long, soft red to white hairs. Z7.

***L. laxiflorus*** Douglas ex Lindl. Perenn. to 60cm. Leaflets to 5cm, 7–11, pubesc. or glabrous above, pubesc. beneath. Fls white, occasionally blue or purple-tinged, in short-stalked, lax racemes; standard pubesc. at base beneath. Fr. to 3cm. W US (California to Washington). Z8.

***L. lepidus*** Douglas ex Lindl. Perenn. to 30.5cm. Stems tufted, grey- to rusty-pubesc. Leaflets 5–9 densely pubesc. Fls to 12.5mm, violet-blue, in dense racemes to 15cm; standard glabrous. Fr. to 2cm, pubesc. N America (British Columbia and Wyoming to SW US). Z3.

***L. leucophyllus*** Douglas ex Lindl. Erect perenn. to 90cm. Stems stout, simple or branched, very leafy, grey lanate-villous. Leaflets to 6.5cm, 7–9, oblanceolate, acute, sericeous-velutinous; petioles to 15cm. Fls to 12mm, white, pink or blue-flushed, or purple, subverticillate, crowded; pedicels to 3mm; bracts to 4mm, linear-lanceolate, persistent; cal. gibbous, lips to 4mm, upper bidentate, lower subentire; standard pubesc. beneath, keel stout, ciliate towards apex. Fr. to 2.5cm, sericeous to lanate, seeds 3–6, rufous to somewhat grey, mottled. Spring–summer. W US (California to Washington and Montana). Z4.

***L. littoralis*** Douglas. Perenn. to 80cm. Roots bright yellow. Stems decumbent or prostrate, slender, branched, patent-villous, especially near nodes. Leaflets to 3.5cm, 5–9, oblanceolate, strigose; petioles to 5cm. Fls to 13mm, blue or lilac, in few-verticillate racemes to 15cm; pedicels to 12mm, patent-pubesc.; bracts subulate, to 5mm; cal. upper lip entire or emarginate, lower entire; standard broad, glabrous, wings broad, keel curved, apex ciliate. Fr. to 3.5cm, brown, lax-pubesc. to strigose; seeds 3mm, 9–14, linear-oblong, mottled. Spring–summer. Western N America (California to British Columbia). Z7.

***L. longifolius*** (S. Wats.) Abrams. Subshrub to 1.5m. Stems erect, adpressed-grey-pubesc. Leaflets to 6×1.5cm, 6–9, elliptic- or oblong-oblanceolate, obtuse, subsericeous; petioles to 7cm. Fls to 18mm, deep blue to violet, scattered or subverticillate, in racemes to 40cm; pedicels to 1cm, patent-pubesc.; bracts to 6mm; cal. upper lip bifid or bidentate, lower entire or bidenticulate; standard suborbicular, glabrous, blotched yellow at centre, wings broad, keel curved, apex ciliate. Fr. to 6cm, brown, pubesc.; seeds 6mm, 6–8, grey, somewhat mottled and lined brown. Spring–summer. W US (California), Baja California. Z9.

***L. luteus*** L. YELLOW LUPINE. Annual to 80cm. Stems densely pilose. Leaflets to 6cm×12mm, 7–11, obovate-oblong, mucronate, sparsely villous. Fls bright yellow, verticillate; peduncles to 12cm, pubesc.; cal. upper lip to 7mm, bifid, lower 1cm, tridentate; cor. to 16mm. Fr. to 5×1cm, black, densely villous; seeds to 8mm, 4–6, orbicular-oblong, flattened, smooth, dull black, mottled and lined white. Summer. Iberian Peninsula, Italy, W Mediterranean Is. Z6.

***L. lyallii*** Gray. Tufted, semi-prostrate perenn. to 12cm; stems silky, arising from a stout, woody base. Leaflets to 12mm, 5–6, oblanceolate, acute, adpressed-sericeous. Fls to 12mm, blue, in capitate racemes to 3cm; peduncles to 10cm, slender; bracts to 5mm, linear-lanceolate; cal. upper lip to 3mm, bifid, lower to 4mm, entire to tridentate; standard elliptic-obovate, deep blue, sometimes with pale spot at centre, keel straight. Fr. to 1.5cm, sericeous; seeds 2mm, 3–4, oblong, pale. Summer–autumn. W US (California to Washington). Z8.

***L. micranthus*** Guss. Annual to 40cm. Stems brown-hirsute. Leaflets to 7×1.5cm, 5–7, obovate-cuneate to obovate-oblong, mucronate, sparsely hirsute. Fls deep blue, alternate or irregular-verticillate, in racemes to 12cm; cal. upper lip 6mm, bifid, lower deep-tridentate, to 12mm; cor. to 14mm, standard 6.5mm, emarginate, with purple-dotted white spot at centre, keel dark violet toward apex. Fr. to 5cm, rusty-pubesc.; seeds to 8mm, 3–4, orbicular-oblong, flattened, smooth, dull pink-grey to -brown, dark-veined and -punctate. C & S Portugal, Mediterranean, Western N America (California to British Columbia.) Z8.

***L. mutabilis*** Sweet. Erect subshrub to 1.5m. Stems branched, glabrous. Leaflets 6×1.5cm, 7–9, oblanceolate, glabrous above, pubesc. and somewhat glaucous beneath. Fls 2cm, white; pedicels 9mm; cal. upper lip somewhat bifid or entire; standard retuse, white and blue, becoming blue and with a large yellow blotch at centre, sometimes violet-tinged, wings and keel white. Fr. to 7.5cm; seeds large. Summer. S America (Andes). var. ***cruckshanksii*** (Hook.) L.H. Bail. Fls large; standard shaded purple, wings deep blue. Peru. Z9.

***L. nanus*** Douglas. Erect annual to 50cm. Stems, simple or branched at base, villous and minute-pubesc. or strigulose. Leaflets to 3cm×5mm, 5–7, linear to spathulate, acute; petioles to 8cm. Fls rich blue, verticillate, in racemes to 24cm; peduncles to 14cm; pedicels to 5mm; bracts to 1cm, linear-lanceolate; cal. upper lip bifid, to 5mm, lower bi- or tridentate, to 5.5mm; standard suborbicular, to 11.5mm, reflexed, with purple-dotted white or yellow spot, wings ciliate toward slender apex, keel slender. Fr. to 3.5cm×5.5mm, strigose; seeds to 4cm, mottled brown or dark grey. Spring–summer. W US (California). 'Pixie Delight': to 45cm high; fls softly coloured; annual.

***L. nootkatensis*** Donn ex Sims. Closely resembles *L. perennis*, but stems usually stouter and villous or hirsute, lvs 6–8-foliolate, leaflets to 6×1.5cm, cal. upper lip 8mm and lower to 1cm. Northwest N America, NE Asia. Z4.

***L. ornatus*** Douglas ex Lindl. Herbaceous perenn. to 75cm; stem and lvs sericeous. Leaflets 4–7, rarely more. Racemes 15–30cm; fls *c*2cm, standard pink with pale centre, wings blue. Early summer–autumn. Z7.

***L. perennis*** L. SUNDIAL LUPINE; WILD LUPINE. Stout perenn. to 70cm. Leaflets to 5cm×12mm, 7–11, oblanceolate, obtuse, rarely acute, glabrous above, sparse-pubesc. beneath; petioles to 15cm. Fls to 16mm, violet, pink, white or multi-coloured, alternate or verticillate, in lax racemes to 30cm; peduncles to 10cm; pedicels to 1cm, slender; bracts to 6mm, subulate to linear, caducous; cal. upper lip to 6mm, emarginate, lower lip 8mm, entire; keel ciliate. Fr. to 5×1cm, short-pubesc. to villous, 4–6-seeded. Spring. Eastern N America (Maine to Florida). Z4.

***L. plattensis*** S. Wats. Perenn. to 60cm. Stems pubesc. Leaflets to 4cm, 7–9, thick, pubesc., slightly glaucous. Fls light blue, standard dark-spotted. Fr. to 3cm. Summer. W US (Wyoming, Colorado, Kansas). Z3.

***L. polyphyllus*** Lindl. Stout perenn. to 1.5m, usually unbranched. Stems minutely pubesc. Leaflets to 15×3cm, 9–17, obovate-lanceolate, acute, glabrous above, sparsely sericeous beneath. Fls to 14mm, blue, purple, pink or white, verticillate, in somewhat dense racemes to 60cm long; peduncles to 8cm; pedicels to 1.5cm; bracts 1cm, linear, caducous; cal. lips entire; keel glabrous. Fr. to 4cm, brown, lanate; seeds 4mm, 5–9, spotted. Summer. Western N America (California to British Columbia). 'Moerheimii': fls white and rose. var. ***burkei*** (S. Wats.) C. Hitchc. To 60cm. Stems, petioles and leaflets glabrous or white pubesc. Z3.

***L. pubescens*** Benth. Annual to 90cm. Stems soft-pubesc. Leaflets 7–9; stipules minute. Fls violet-blue, white at centre, verticillate, in long racemes. Fr. 2.5cm, dense-pubesc.; seeds small, pale. Mexico, Guatemala.

***L. rivularis*** Douglas ex Lindl. Closely resembles *L. latifolius*, but stems villous, petioles to 5cm, leaflets to 4cm, strigulose especially beneath. Fls to 16mm, keel ciliate. Fr. to 5cm, subadpressed-pubesc.; seeds to 4mm, 8–12, mottled. Spring–summer. Western N America (California to British Columbia). Z8.

***L. saxatilis*** Ulbr. Branched subshrub to 40cm. Stems densely hairy at first. Leaflets 1.25–3cm, 7, narrowly oblanceolate, silky-hairy beneath; petiole to *c*5cm. Racemes 12.5cm, whorls 4-fld; fls bright purple-blue, standard 1.25cm. Fr. silky. Peruvian Andes. Z9.

***L. sericatus*** Kellogg. Erect to decumbent perenn. to 50cm. Stems usually unbranched, densely and minutely downy. Leaflets to 4×2cm, 6–7, spathulate-obovate, obtuse or retuse, densely and minutely sericeous; petioles to 15cm. Fls to 16mm, violet to lavender, scattered or subverticillate, in somewhat dense racemes to 30cm long; peduncles to 12cm; pedicels to 5mm; bracts to 7mm, subulate, caducous; cal. to 7mm, strigose, upper lip bidentate, lower tridenticulate; standard rounded, pubesc. beneath, keel curved, ciliate. Fr. to 2.5cm, pubesc.; seeds 5–7, pale brown, mottled. Spring–summer. W US (N California). Z8.

***L. sparsiflorus*** Benth. Erect, branched annual to 40cm. Stems slender, strigose and villous. Leaflets to 3cm×3mm, 5–9, 5–9, linear to oblanceolate, subacute, strigose and villous; petioles to 8cm. Fls to 12mm, pale blue to lilac, in racemes to 20cm long; peduncles to 8cm; pedicels to 5mm; bracts to 4mm, linear-lanceolate, caducous; cal. 5mm, upper lip bifid, lower apiculate or tridentate; standard suborbicular, with yellow spot, keel curved, ciliate. Fr. to 2cm, strigose; seeds to 3mm, 5–7, light-mottled. Spring. W US (California, S Nevada, Arizona), Baja California. Z9.

***L. stiversii*** Kellogg. Freely branching annual to 45cm. Stems minutely pubesc. Leaflets to 4cm, 6–8, cuneate to obovate, strigose; petioles to 8cm . Fls to 1.5cm, bright yellow, in racemes to 3cm long; peduncles to 8cm; pedicels 2mm; cal. to 8mm, pubesc., upper lip bifid, lower entire; wings 1.5cm, rose-pink or purple, keel rather paler or white, ciliate at base. Fr. to 2.5cm, glabrous, several-seeded; seeds 2.5mm, compressed, pale, dark-spotted. Spring–summer. W US (California).

***L. subcarnosus*** Hook. TEXAS BLUEBONNET. Decumbent annual to 40cm, branched at base. Stems downy. Leaflets to 2.5cm×12mm, 5–7, oblanceolate, rounded, sometimes truncate or obtuse, glabrous or subglabrous above, sericeous beneath and on margins; petioles to 5cm. Fls to 13mm, bright blue, crowded, in several-fld racemes to 12cm long; peduncles to 8cm erect; pedicels to 6mm; bracts 6mm, lanceolate, deciduous; cal. upper lip bifid lower entire or acute-tridentate; standard broad, suborbicular, white at centre, turning purple, wings to 11×7mm somewhat inflated, keel slender-acuminate. Fr. stout, to 3.5cm×8mm; seeds 5mm diam., 4–5, grey or tawny, sometimes lightly spotted. Spring. SW US (Texas).

***L. succulentus*** Douglas ex K. Koch. Stout annual to 1m; stems succulent or fistulose. Leaflets to 7cm, 7–9, cuneate to cuneate-obovate, deep green, glabrous above, strigulose beneath; petioles to 12cm. Fls deep violet, verticillate, in racemes to 30cm long; peduncles to 10cm; pedicels to 6mm; bracts to 6mm, subulate, pubesc., caducous; cal. 8mm, substrigose, upper lip deeply cleft, lower lip entire to tridentate; standard to 14mm, yellow at centre, wings somewhat ciliate, keel curved, ciliate at base. Fr. to 5cm×8mm, thinly and weakly hairy, dark, several-seeded; seeds to 5mm, oblong, mottled dark brown. Winter–spring. W US (California), Baja California.

***L. sulphureus*** Douglas ex Hook. Perenn. to 1m, hairy. Leaflets to 5cm, 9–11, oblanceolate, apex subacute, glabrous or pubesc. above, pubesc. beneath. Fls small, yellow to blue-violet, standard glabrous, recurved. Fr. 2.5cm. British Columbia to California. Z8.

***L. texensis*** Hook. TEXAS BLUEBONNET. Closely resembles *L. subcarnosus*, but leaflets usually acute, wings deep blue and not inflated, and fr. somewhat white-pubesc. SW US (Texas).

***L. tidestromii*** Greene. To 30cm, branched. Roots yellow; stems slender, adpressed-sericeous. Leaflets to 2cm, 3–5, oblanceolate, silver-sericeous; petioles to 3cm. Fls to 13mm, blue, verticillate, in racemes to 10cm long; peduncles to 8cm; pedicels to 5mm; bracts 5mm, lanceolate-ovate, caducous; cal. 8mm, upper lip deeply bifid, lower entire or emarginate; standard rounded, glabrous, paler in centre, fading violet, keel curved, ciliate toward apex. Fr. to

2.5cm, somewhat yellow; seeds 3mm, 5–8, mottled black. Spring–summer. W US (C California). Z8.

***L. tomentosus*** DC. Perenn. to 1.5m. Base woody, stem much branched, sericeous. Leaflets 8–10, equalling petioles, sericeous. Racemes to 20cm; fls 2cm, straw-yellow striped light blue at first, darkening with age becoming blue-purple, variable. Summer. Peru. Z9.

***L. truncatus*** Nutt. ex Hook. & Arn. Branched annual to 70cm. Stems deep green, subglabrous to sparsely strigulose. Leaflets to 4cm, 5–7, linear, apices truncate to emarginate or dentate, subglabrous to sparse-strigulose; petioles to 10cm. Fls to 12mm, violet, deepening to red with age, in racemes to 15cm long; peduncles to 10cm; pedicels to 3mm; bracts to 4mm, subulate, persistent, cal. to 6mm, upper lip bifid, lower entire to tridentate; standard 1cm×9mm, keel ciliate. Fr. 3cm×6mm, villous; seeds 3mm, 6–7, rhomboid, pale flesh-coloured, mottled brown. Spring. W US (California). Z9.

***L. vallicola*** A.A. Heller. Erect annual to 35cm. Stems usually simple villous and minute-pubesc. or strigulose. Leaflets to 2.5cm×3mm, 6–8, linear. Fls to 1cm, bright blue, verticillate, in racemes to 10cm long; peduncles to 7cm; pedicels slender, to 5mm; cal. upper lip 2mm, lower 4mm; standard broad, paler at centre, scarcely reflexed, keel strongly curved, ciliate toward apex. Fr. to 2.5cm×5mm, sericeous; seeds 2.5mm, 3–6, pale flesh-coloured. Spring–summer. W US (California). Z8.

***L. villosus*** Willd. Decumbent, much-branched perenn. to 90cm. Stems many, villous. Leaflets to 15×6cm, 1 oblong or elliptic, obtuse to acute, apiculate, broad to rounded or tapered at base, densely villous; petioles to 1.5cm. Fls lilac to purple, subverticillate, crowded in erect racemes to 30cm, long; pedicels to 4mm, densely pubesc.; bracts to 12mm, linear-subulate, caducous; cal. upper lip truncate or somewhat emarginate, lower lip trilobed; standard deep maroon at centre. Fr. to 4.5cm, villous-pubesc. N America (N Carolina to Florida, west to Missouri). Z8.

***L. andersonii*** var. ***grayi*** Wats. See *L. grayi*.
***L. brittonii*** Abrams. See *L. albifrons* var. *eminens*.
***L. burkei*** S. Wats. See *L. polyphyllus* var. *burkei*.
***L. chamissonis*** var. ***longifolius*** S. Wats. See *L. longifolius*.
***L. cruckshanksii*** Hook. See *L. mutabilis* var. *cruckshanksii*.
***L. cytisoides*** J. Agardh. See *L. latifolius*.
***L. depressus*** Benth. See *L. argenteus* var. *depressus*.
***L. hirsutus*** sensu L. 1763 pro parte, et auct., non L. 1753. See *L. micranthus*.
***L. menziesii*** Agardh. See *L. densiflorus* var. *aureus*.
***L. subalpinus*** Piper and Robinson. See *L. latifolius* var. *subalpinus*.
***L. volcanicus*** Greene. See *L. latifolius* var. *subalpinus*.

**Luronium** Raf. (Name used by Dioscorides.) Alismataceae. 1 species, a monoecious, perennial, aquatic herb. Stems elongate, rising in water or creeping and rooting at nodes. Submerged leaves basal, linear, floating, aerial leaves elliptic to ovate, to 4×15cm, base rounded to cuneate, apex obtuse. Flowers axillary, long-pedunculate; petals 7–10mm, white, with a yellow spot at the base; stamens 6; carpels 6–15 in an irregular whorl, free, each with one ovule, styles apical. Fruitlets 2–5mm, achenical, with 12–15 longitudinal ribs and short apical beak. Summer. W&C Europe. Z8.

CULTIVATION As for *Alisma*.

***L. natans*** (L.) Raf. As for the genus.

For synonymy see *Alisma*.

**Luteola** (Tourn.) Webb & Berth.
***L. complicata*** (Bory) Webb. See *Reseda complicata*.

**Lutyens,** Sir **Edwin Landseer** (1869–1944). Architect and garden designer. Lutyens met Gertrude Jekyll in 1889, and they entered into a long and productive partnership, with Lutyens planning the building and garden layout, and Jekyll planning the planting schemes. Lutyens built a house for Jekyll at Munstead Wood, Surrey, where she had already been designing a garden, and her description of the result in her books helped to boost Lutyens's reputation. Some notable examples of their collaboration were Hestercombe, Somerset, and Marsh Court, Hampshire. For Edward Hudson, founder of *Country Life*, a magazine which did much to boost Lutyens's reputation, the pair worked on the Deanery Garden, Sonning, Berkshire; Lindisfarne Castle, Northumberland; and Plumpton Place, Sussex.

Not all Lutyens's gardens were planned with Jekyll. In 1901 he designed a new garden for Ammerdown House, Somerset, and the gardens for his house at Little Thakeham, Sussex, and The Salutation, Sandwich, Kent, have no documented contribution from Jekyll. His partnership with Jekyll ended about 1912. She was nearly 70 and severely myopic, and he was becoming involved in large public projects. The largest of these was the planning, with Sir Herbert Baker, of the city of New Delhi, where Lutyens designed a complex of grand buildings, spacious avenues and gardens with canals and fountains in a combination of western and Moghul styles. He was appointed architect to the Imperial War Graves Commission after World War I.

After the war, his work became more monumental and classical in style; he described classicism as 'the great game', and works such as his Cenotaph in Whitehall show him playing with the rules of classical architecture. At Gledstone Hall, Yorkshire, in 1923, he built a new house with a garden in the French classical style, with a long central canal. Tyringham, Buckinghamshire (1924), was a large formal garden with a sheet of water, water-jets, stone pavilions and topiary.

**Lutzia** Gand. (For Ludwig Lutz, president of the Société Botanique de France earlier this century.) Cruciferae. 1 species, a shrubby, evergreen, perennial herbs, to 30cm. Stems diffuse, much-branched and woody at base. Leaves silver-hairy, oblanceolate to obovate. Flowers in a raceme; sepals 4, equal, erect, 7–11mm; petals 4, golden yellow, oblong, obtuse, clawed, 12–20mm, entire; stamens 6, all filaments toothed or with appendages. Fruit a round to ovoid silicle, leathery, 10–15mm, valves without nerve, inflated, style long; seed brown. Crete, Greece Carpathian Mts. Z8.

CULTIVATION Found on cliffs and rocks, *Lutzia* is grown for its spreading tangle of silvery foliage and loose sprays of yellow flowers in spring. For the sunny rock garden and wall plantings. Cultivate as for *Alyssum*.

***L. cretica*** (L.) Greuter & Burdet. As for the genus.

***L. fruticosa*** Gand. See *L. cretica*.
For further synonymy see *Alyssoides* and *Alyssum*.

**Luzula** DC. (Classical Lat. name, possibly from *luciola*, glow-worm, from *lux*, light.) WOOD-RUSH. Juncaceae. 80 species of perennial or, rarely, annual herbs. Leaves mostly basal, grass-like, flat or with a longitudinal groove, soft, with long flexuous white hairs. Flowers inconspicuous, bracteolate, in umbel-like, paniculate, corymbose or congested inflorescences; perianth brown or green, sometimes white, with 6 free scarious segments. Fruit a 1-celled capsule; seeds 3, usually with a succulent basal appendage aiding ant dispersal. Cosmopolitan, especially temperate Eurasia. Z6.

CULTIVATION *Luzula* spp. most commonly cultivated in gardens are generally natives of open subalpine woodland, on both dry and moist soils. The rhizomatous and perennial species make effective groundcover in the moist and shaded conditions which may be unsuitable for more choice subjects. Their grass-like form and habit provides useful foliage contrasts, especially as they age, when they sometimes assume attractive parchment colours. All have light soft clusters of brown or creamy flowers in early summer, and leaves edged with hair, distinguishing them from *Juncus*.

Plant *L. maxima* in moisture-retentive soils on rough ground or in the wild garden, where the marginal bands of cream of its cv. 'Marginata' will lighten dark places; its creeping nature is also useful for stabilizing banks of heavy soil. The graceful *L. nivea*, has similar soil requirements to *L. maxima*, but will prove less invasive and appreciates a sunny aspect. *L. campestris*, although less decorative, can be used in drier woodland shade and may naturalize on well-drained soils. Plant in spring and propagate by division between autumn and spring; also by seed, sown in spring/summer.

***L. campestris*** (L.) DC. FIELD WOOD-RUSH. To 30cm, loosely tufted. Basal lvs to 4mm wide, sparsely ciliate, soft and flat. Infl. with 1 sessile and a few pedunculate clusters of 5–12 fls; peduncles straight, erect, but deflexed in fruit; perianth seg. to 4mm, brown; anth. to 6× length of fil. Capsule to 3mm; seeds to 1.3mm with a basal appendage to half the length of the seed. Europe as far north as Norway.

***L. lutea*** (All.) DC. To 30cm, loosely tufted. Basal lvs short, linear-lanceolate, to 6mm wide, glabrous; sheaths red-brown. Infl. erect, condensed into pedunculate clusters of fls; perianth seg. to 3mm, straw-coloured, equal; anth. equalling fil. Capsule 2.5mm, dark brown; seeds to 1.5mm, brown, oblong, basal appendage inconspicuous. S Europe.

***L. luzuloides*** (Lam.) Dandy & Willmott. To 65cm, loosely tufted. Basal lvs to 6mm wide, flat, with long hairs. Infl. corymbose, loose or condensed into clusters of 2–10 fls; perianth seg. to 3.5mm, dirty white or pink, the inner seg. longer than the outer, acute; anth. to 3× length of fil. Capsule ovoid; seeds to 1.2mm, dark brown. S & C Europe.

***L. maxima*** (Rich.) DC. To 80cm, loosely tufted, in large tussocks. Basal lvs to 30×2cm, channelled, with a few or many silky hairs. Infl. spreading, with many fls in groups of 2–5; bracteoles lacerate to ciliate; perianth seg. to 4mm, brown, the inner seg. longer than the outer; anth. to 6× length of fil. Capsule to 4.4mm; perianth seg. ovoid; seeds to 2mm, shiny. S, W & C Europe. 'Aurea': lvs broad, golden-yellow. 'Marginata': habit dense; lvs deep green edged white; spikelets gold and brown, hanging. 'Tauernpass': lvs very broad.

***L. multiflora*** (Retz.) Lej. MANY-FLOWERED WOOD-RUSH. To 30cm, densely tufted, erect. Basal lvs to 4mm wide, sparsely hairy. Infl. umbel-like, with to 10 clusters of to 18 fls each; fls sessile or pedunculate; perianth seg. to 3.5mm, brown; anth. slightly exceeding fil. Capsule to 3mm; seeds oblong, to 1.3mm; basal appendage to half length of the seed. Europe, America, Australia.

***L. nivea*** (L.) DC. SNOW RUSH. To 60cm, loosely tufted. Basal lvs linear, to 30×0.4cm, flat; stem lvs to 20cm. Panicle loose with to 20 clusters of fls; perianth seg. to 5mm, off-white, unequal, acute; anth. slightly shorter than fil. Capsule to 2.5mm, globose; seed 1.5mm, red-brown. Alps, C Europe.

***L. pilosa*** (L.) Willd. HAIRY WOOD-RUSH. To 35cm, tufted. Basal lvs to 10mm wide, flat, sparsely to densely hairy. Infl. with unequal spreading branches, deflexed in fruit; perianth seg. nearly equal, brown with broad hyaline margins; anth. exceeding fil. Capsule to 4.5mm, pear-shaped, light green; seeds to 1.8mm, pale brown, basal appendage to 1.5mm, hooked. Europe.

***L. cultivars***. 'Botany Bay': young lvs off-white, broad. 'Mount Dobson': hardy; dark brown cymes. 'N.Z. Ohau': habit large, hardy.

***L. albida*** (Hoffm.) DC. See *L. luzuloides*.
***L. campestris*** ssp. ***multiflora*** (Retz.) Buchenau. See *L. multiflora*.
***L. campestris*** ssp. ***occidentalis*** V. Krecz. See *L. multiflora*.
***L. cuprina*** Rochel & Steud. See *L. luzuloides*.
***L. nemorosa*** (Pollich) E. Mey. See *L. luzuloides*.
***L. subpilosa*** (Gilib.) V. Krecz. See *L. campestris*.
***L. sylvatica*** (Huds.) Gaudin. See *L. maxima*.

For illustration see ORNAMENTAL GRASSES.

**Luzuriaga** Ruiz & Pav. (For Don Ignatio M.R. de Luzuriaga (early 19th century), Spanish botanist.) Liliaceae (Luzuriagaceae). 4 species of trailing perennial herbs with rooting, rather shrubby stems, sometimes climbing, with simple or branched leafy lateral shoots. Leaves jointed to stems, very short-stalked, lower surface dark green, facing upwards because of twisted petiole, veins parallel, 3 to many, upper surface glaucous except for green veins (lowest leaves of lateral shoots often reduced to scales). Flowers showy, solitary or a few together, axillary, pedicels equalling perianth; tepals 6, free, white; stamens 6; ovary superior, 3-celled; style simple. Fruit a berry. Peru, Chile, Falkland Is., New Zealand. Floral parts spotted orange-brown when dry. Z9.

CULTIVATION Semi-woody trailing plants, sometimes climbing by means of rooting stems, *Luzuriaga* spp. are attractive in foliage and beautiful in flower. Although tolerant of light frost they are more frequently and safely grown in the cool glasshouse, in a moist, fibrous soilless medium, in shade. Propagate by semi-ripe cuttings in sand in a closed case with bottom heat.

***L. polyphylla*** Hook. f. Much-branched, shrub-like, scrambling or twining. Lvs 1.25–2.5cm, elliptic to oblong, alternate, mostly subtending fls. Fls to 2cm diam., white, sometimes spotted red-brown, broadly campanulate, solitary; fil. longer than anth., anth. dorsifixed, reflexed. Summer. Chile.

***L. radicans*** Ruiz & Pav. Stems slender, vining, sparsely branched. Lvs 1–3.5×0.3–1.2cm, linear-oblong to elliptic-ovate or ovate-lanceolate. Fls to 3.25cm diam., pure white, fragrant, star-shaped, spreading, solitary or 2–3 together, fragrant; fil. thick, anth. yellow, connivent, much longer than fil., basifixed, erect. Summer. Chile, Peru.

***L. erecta*** Kunth. See *L. polyphylla*.

**Lycaste** Lindl. (For Lykast, daughter of King Priam.) Orchidaceae. Some 35 species of epiphytic, terrestrial or lithophytic orchids. Rhizomes short. Pseudobulbs to 14cm, usually ovoid, slightly laterally compressed. Leaves 1 to several, at apex of each pseudobulb and sheathing base, lasting 1–2 seasons, plicate, lanceolate, acuminate, bright lustrous green. Flowers appearing with or shortly before new growth, usually borne singly on 1–10 erect or spreading, sheathed stalks arising, from base of pseudobulb, large, fragrant; sepals erect to spreading, subequal, lanceolate to elliptic-lanceolate, obtuse or acuminate, connate at base with column-foot, forming a saccate mentum; petals similar to sepals, shorter, enclosing column; lip articulate with column-foot, trilobed, midlobe spreading to decurved, pubescent, entire to fimbriate or undulate, lateral lobes erect, disc often pubescent, callused; column long, semi-terete, arcuate, produced into foot at base; anther terminal, 1-celled, pollinia 4. Mexico, C America, W Indies, S America. Z10.

CULTIVATION Robust plants for the cool or intermediate house. Squat pseudobulbs carry broad, ribbed leaves and a series of solitary waxen flowers from their bases, alongside new growth. With the exceptions of the smaller *Ll. aromatica, cruenta* and *deppei*, these plants are best maintained with 3–4 back bulbs at most and a vigorous lead. Pot in a mix of coarse bark, charcoal, sphagnum and leafmould, with a little dried FYM just prior to the end of the winter resting period. When in growth, water and feed freely and maintain in humid, buoyant conditions in light shade (avoid leaf scorch); aim to promote the largest and firmest possible pseudobulbs. Once growth is complete, reduce temperature and watering and increase light. Flowers and new growth tend to emerge simultaneously. In the three species mentioned above, flowers may well precede new shoots and water should be restricted until they are fully initiated.

***L. aromatica*** (Graham ex Hook.) Lindl. Pseudobulbs to 10×4.5cm, squat, dark green, obscurely ribbed. Lvs to 50×10cm, falling to leave 2 sharply-pointed remnants at apex of pseudobulb. Scapes to 17cm, fls to 8cm diam., bright yellow, sweetly scented; sep. to 4×2cm, green-yellow; pet. to 3.5×2cm, deep yellow; lip to 3cm, golden yellow, dotted orange, concave below, lateral lobes porrect, crenulate on front margin, midlobe marginally undulate, disc pubesc., callus flap-like, truncate, broadly cuneate, extending over base of midlobe; column to 2.5cm. Spring. Mexico, Honduras, Guatemala.

***L. barringtoniae*** (Sm.) Lindl. Pseudobulbs ellipsoid, to 9×5cm. Lvs to 50×12cm. Infl. several; scapes to 12cm; bracts loose; fls to 7cm, pendent, waxy, long-lived, olive green; sep. to 4.5×1.5cm, dorsal sep. narrower; pet. similar; lip light buff-brown, to 4.5cm, long-clawed, lateral lobes at claw-apex narrowly falcate, midlobe blunt, marginally fimbriate, callus broad, deeply furrowed. Spring–summer. Cuba, Jamaica.

***L. brevispatha*** (Klotzsch) Lindl. Pseudobulbs to 6.5×4cm, ellipsoid to ovoid. Lvs to 50×10cm. Scapes to 10cm, fls to 5cm diam.; sep. to 3×1.5cm, pale green, dotted pale rose; pet. to 2.5×1.5cm, white to rose; lip to 3cm, white, spotted rose to purple, concave below, lateral lobes incurved, forming tube; midlobe emarginate, disc slightly pubesc., callus tongue-shaped. Costa Rica, Nicaragua, Panama, Guatemala.

***L. ciliata*** (Ruiz & Pav.) Rchb. Pseudobulbs to 7cm, ovoid. Lvs to 25cm. Scapes numerous, to 10cm, fls to 10cm diam., not opening fully, nodding, waxy, deliciously fragrant, ivory tinted green, lip sometimes yellow, callus orange to yellow; sep. and pet. narrow-oblong, falcate, obtuse, pet. parallel to sides of column; lip midlobe fimbriate to ciliate. Spring. Peru.

***L. cochleata*** Lindl. & Paxt. Similar to *L. aromatica*. Fls to 5cm diam.; sep. green-yellow, slightly pubesc. above at base; pet. deep orange; lip basally saccate, midlobe rounded at tip, fimbriate, callus slightly grooved, tip rounded. Spring. Guatemala, Honduras.

***L. crinita*** Lindl. Resembles *L. aromatica* except disc of lip pubesc.; pseudobulbs and lvs more robust; scapes longer. Spring–summer. Mexico, Guatemala.

***L. cruenta*** (Lindl.) Lindl. Pseudobulbs ovoid-oblong, to 10×5cm. Lvs to 45×15cm, elliptic-lanceolate to broadly elliptic. Scapes to 17cm, fls to 10cm diam., spicily scented; sep. to 5×2.5cm, yellow-green; pet. to 4×2.5cm, bright yellow to yellow-orange; lip yellow, dotted maroon, spotted crimson at base, saccate, white hairs in saccate portion, midlobe emarginate, pubesc., disc corrugated at base, with small, subquadrate, truncate callus. Spring. Mexico, Guatemala, Costa Rica, El Salvador.

***L. denningiana*** Rchb. f. Pseudobulbs to 10×7cm. Lvs to 70×10cm. Scapes to 50cm×5mm, fls large, open; sep. fleshy, to 11×2.5cm, linear-falcate, light yellow-green; pet. to 5×2cm, green to cream, broadly falcate; lip bright orange, to 5×2.5cm, rigid, crispate, lateral lobes sharply recurved and folded back, midlobe rounded, sharply folded back, covering lateral lobes below lip and deeply grooved above; column cream, orange at base; anth. cream; pollinia yellow. Winter. Venezuela, Colombia, Ecuador.

***L. deppei*** (Lodd.) Lindl. Pseudobulbs and lvs similar to *L. aromatica* except more robust. Scapes to 17cm, fls nodding, to 9cm diam.; sep. to 6×2.5cm, pale green flecked or faintly lined oxblood to red; pet. to 4.5×2cm, white, flecked red at base; lip bright yellow with red dots, red lateral stripes at base, strongly veined, lateral lobes involute, midlobe strongly decurved, to 2cm, margins crenate, disc thickened in middle, callus small, rounded, sulcate. Spring–autumn. Mexico, Guatemala.

***L. fulvescens*** Hook. Allied to *L. longipetala*. Pseudobulbs to 10×5cm. Lvs to 80×8cm. Scapes to 25cm, fls nodding, to 10cm diam.; sep. and pet. yellow-green tinted bronze, sep. to 5.5×1.5cm, pet. shorter; lip to 2.5×1.5cm, lateral lobes small, orange-red, midlobe large with yellow, fimbriate margins, callus 2-lobed, front wider. Summer. Venezuela, Colombia.

***L. lasioglossa*** Rchb. f. Pseudobulbs to 10×4cm, ovoid. Lvs to 55×12cm, strongly veined. Scapes slender, to 25cm, fls to 11cm diam.; sep. to 7×2cm, red-brown; pet. to 4×2cm, bright yellow; lip to 4×2cm, yellow flecked and striped purple, tubular below, midlobe densely pubesc., callus ovate-triangular, notched at apex; column densely pubesc. in middle. Spring–winter. Guatemala, Honduras.

***L. leucantha*** (Klotzsch) Lindl. Pseudobulbs ovoid, to 7.5×3.5cm. Lvs to 65×6cm. Fls to 10cm diam.; sep. brown-green to apple green, to 4.5×2cm; pet. yellow-white, to 4×2cm; lip to 3×2cm, conspicuously nerved, lateral lobes yellow, midlobe cream-white, pubesc., margin denticulate, callus rounded; column yellow-white. Costa Rica, Panama.

***L. locusta*** Rchb. f. Similar in habit to *L. longipetala*, lvs smaller. Fls to 9cm; sep. and pet. sea-green, pet. smaller than sep.; lip dull green, margin white, midlobe large, oval, fimbriate; column slender, pubesc. Spring. Peru.

***L. longipetala*** (Ruiz & Pav.) Garay. Pseudobulbs to 15cm, oblong-ovoid, furrowed with age. Lvs to 80×9.5cm. Infl. robust; fls to 16cm diam.; sep. and pet. yellow-green, tinged brown, sep. to 8.5×3cm, pet. smaller; lip red-brown to violet-purple, lateral lobes short, midlobe oblong-ovate, margins denticulate or fimbriate. Summer. Ecuador, Peru, Colombia, Venezuela.

***L. macrobulbon*** (Hook.) Lindl. Resembles *L. longipetala* except more robust, pseudobulbs larger. Fls to 6cm diam.; sep. green-yellow; pet. white-yellow, shorter than sep.; lip yellow, sparsely spotted brown at base, lateral lobes very short, blunt, midlobe large, oval. Spring–summer. Colombia.

***L. macrophylla*** (Poepp. & Endl.) Lindl. Pseudobulbs to 7×4cm, ovoid. Lvs to 50×9cm, strongly ribbed. Scapes to 14cm, fls nodding, to 9cm diam.; sep. olive-green, edged pink-brown, to 4×2cm; pet. white, spotted rose-pink, to 3.5×2cm, parallel to column; lip white, margins dotted rose, midlobe spreading, ciliate, callus concave, margin dotted pink; column white, dark purple to red at base; pollinia yellow. Spring–summer. Costa Rica, Panama, Colombia, Venezuela, Brazil, Peru, Bolivia.

***L. powellii*** Schltr. Pseudobulbs ellipsoid-ovoid, smooth to rigid, to 7×3.5cm. Lvs to 45×8cm. Scapes to 15cm; fls to 10cm diam.; sep. pale translucent green marked chestnut brown or wine-red, margins yellow, wide-spreading; pet. cream-yellow to white, dotted pink or wine-red, parallel to column, tips reflexed; lip white, dotted red, midlobe short, spreading, callus ligulate, obtuse, concave. Summer-autumn. Panama.

***L. schilleriana*** Rchb. f. Allied to *L. longipetala*. Fls to 12cm; sep. pale olive green; pet. white, dotted brown; lip yellow-white, lateral lobes small, midlobe white, flecked rose-pink, margin fringed. Spring. Columbia.

***L. skinneri*** (Lindl.) Lindl. Pseudobulbs ovoid, to 10×3.5cm. Lvs to 75×15cm. Scapes to 30cm, fls to 14cm diam.; sep. white to violet-rose, to 8×3.5cm; pet. red-violet, often marked deep rose-crimson, to 7.5×4cm; lip white to pale rose, flecked red-violet, to 5cm, lateral lobes pubesc., midlobe strongly decurved, disc pubesc. at centre, callus fleshy. Autumn–spring. Guatemala, Mexico, Honduras, El Salvador. The fl. colour of this widely cultivated species is highly variable; numerous colour forms have been named, ranging from white to shell-pink to burgundy.

***L. tricolor*** (Klotzsch) Rchb. f. Pseudobulbs ovoid, to 8×3.5cm. Lvs to 35×7cm. Scapes to 11cm; bracts almost exceeding flower; sep. to 4×1cm, pale green, tinged rose-pink; pet. white to pink, dotted rose; lip white dotted pink, lateral lobes involute, midlobe suborbicular to obovate, margins denticulate; callus small, obovate. Guatemala, Costa Rica, Panama.

***L. xytriophora.*** Lind. & Rchb. f. Allied to *L. longipetala*, lvs shorter. Scapes to 12.5cm, fls to 10cm diam.; sep. green-brown, to 4×2cm; pet. yellow-green, tips white, to 3×2cm; lip white tinted rose-pink on interior surface, to 3×1.5cm, midlobe marginally undulate, callus very small, yellow, dotted red; column to 3cm, pubesc. in anterior portion. Spring–summer. Costa Rica, Ecuador.

***L.* grexes and cultivars** (see also under × *Angulocaste*).

*L.* Aquila: large plants with orange fls on tall stems; 'Detente' is a particularly fine clone.

*L.* Athena: plants with many fine dark pink fls.

*L.* Auburn: floriferous plants; fls in a wide range of colours, mostly whites pinks and reds, some orange and bicolors; there are numerous awarded clones of high quality.

*L.* Balliae: very floriferous plants; fls pink and pink-red; 'Superba' is a fine clone.

*L.* Brugensis: large plants; fls on erect stems, large, creamy yellow, yellow and orange shades with an orange lip.

*L.* Cassiopiea: compact plants; fls in attractive shades of peach-pink; several awarded clones.

*L.* Concentration: strong plants; fls bright yellow, long-lasting.

*L.* Guinevere: fls pale green on tall stems; flowering over a long season.

*L.* Hera: large plants and fls; apricot-yellow.

*L.* Imschootiana: large plants making fine specimens, very floriferous; fls cream or pale pink, freckled with fine red spots.

*L.* Jason: very floriferous plants; fls deep yellow-orange, often scented.

*L.* Koolena: well-shaped fls in shades of white, pink and red.

*L.* Libra: very free flowering, up to 30 fls per bulb; fls orange-brown with darker orange spots.

*L.* Macama: well-shaped fls in pink and red shades.

*L.* Neptune: fls fine, pale green.

*L.* Pink Dream: very floriferous, somewhat cup-shaped fls in a fine deep pink.

*L.* Queen Elizabeth: fine, pale green to white fls.

*L.* Vulcan: fine shaped fls, variable, white, pink and red, the best a glowing orange-red.

*L.* Wyldfire: the best of the deep red-flowered hybrids.

***L. bradeorum*** Schltr. See *L. tricolor*.
***L. candida*** Rchb. See *L. brevispatha*.
***L. consobrina*** Rchb. f. See *L. aromatica*.
***L. costata*** (Lindl.) Lindl. See *L. ciliata*.
***L. crocea*** Lindl. See *L. fulvescens*.
***L. dowiana*** Endl. & Rchb. f. See *L. macrophylla*.
***L. fimbriata*** (Poepp. & Endl.) Cogn. See *L. ciliata*.
***L. gigantea*** Lindl. See *L. longipetala*.
***L. leuco-flavescens*** hort. See *L. leucantha*.
***L. virginalis*** (Scheidw.) Lindl. See *L. skinneri*.

**Lychnis** L. (From Gk *lychnos*, lamp; the name *Lychnis* was used for these plants by Theophrastus, and refers to the use of the grey-felted leaves of *L. coronaria* as lamp-wicks.) CATCHFLY. Caryophyllaceae. About 20 species, mostly perennial herbs, differing from *Silene* only in the combination of 5 styles and a capsule opening with 5 teeth (most *Silene* species have 3 styles and a capsule opening with 6 teeth). Widespread in the N Temperate zone; several species grown in gardens.

CULTIVATION *Lychnis* spp. range through northern temperate regions in diverse habitats, from fenland, damp meadow and moist woodlands (*L. flos-cuculi*) to rocky or alpine meadow habitats (*L. alpina*, at altitudes of 3100m/10,075ft, frequently on siliceous substrates). Woolly or downy-leaved species such as *L. flos-jovis, L. coronaria* and *L. viscaria* are suited to dry borders or raised beds. *L. coronaria* self-seeds freely in gravelly soils; the vibrant magenta flowers of the species are beautiful but may demand careful placement. *L.c.* 'Oculata' has pale pink blooms with a darker eye. The white-flowered form should be grown in isolation if white-flowered offspring are desired, since the magenta colour is dominant. *L.* ×*haageana* and *L. chalcedonica* require more moisture to thrive; the latter is sometimes used in bog garden or streamside plantings with the roots above water level. *L.* ×*haageana* flowers in its first year from seed and may be grown as an annual.

*L. flos-cuculi* is eminently suitable for wild garden and meadow plantings that approximate to its habitat, there forming a valuable nectar source for bees and butterflies. *L. alpina*, whose natural populations have been much reduced by over-collecting, is a dwarf, mat-forming plant for the rock garden. Most tolerate temperatures below −15°C/5°F, although *L. flos-jovis* and *L.* ×*haageana* may not survive where temperatures fall below −10°C to −15°C (14–5°F).

Grow *L. coronaria* and *L. flos-jovis* in well-drained soils in full sun; give *L. viscaria* slightly more moisture. *L. chalcedonica, L.* ×*haageana* and *L. flos-cuculi* require fertile, moisture-retentive soils in sun or part shade. Deadhead to prolong flowering and provide taller species with shelter from strong winds. Propagate perennials by division in autumn or spring, or from seed sown when ripe or in spring.

***L. alpina*** L. Glabrous, tufted perenn. to 15cm. Lvs in rosettes, linear-spathulate. Infl. dense, more or less capitate, of 6–20 fls; cal. 4–5mm; pet. usually pale purple, deeply bifid. Summer. Subarctic regions and N Hemisphere mts. Variable in density of infl. and in size of fls. Dwarf, mat-forming rock plant growing best on siliceous rock. 'Alba': fls white. 'Rosea': fls rose pink. Z5.

***L. chalcedonica*** L. MALTESE CROSS. Stout, erect, hispid perenn. with simple stems to 50cm. Basal lvs ovate, acute; cauline lvs amplexicaul. Infl. capitate, 10–50-fld; fls large; cal. 14–18mm; pet. limb *c*15mm, bifid, bright scarlet. Summer. European part of USSR; widely cultivated. The scarlet-fld plant is an old cottage-garden favourite, but several colour-variants exist, including white and pink, and double-fld cvs are known. 'Alba': fls pale off-white. 'Flore Plena': fls double, red. 'Grandiflora': fls large, brilliant red. 'Red Tiger': fls bright scarlet. 'Rosea': fls rose. 'Salmonea': fls salmon pink. Z4.

***L. coronaria*** (L.) Desr. DUSTY MILLER; ROSE CAMPION. Stout, erect bienn. or short-lived perenn. to 80cm, covered with a dense grey-white tomentum. Lvs ovate-lanceolate. Infl. few-fld; fls large, long-stalked; cal. 15–18mm; pet. limb *c*12mm, entire or shallowly 2-toothed, purple-red. Summer. SE Europe, but locally naturalized elsewhere from widespread cultivation. An old cottage-garden plant, long cultivated in Europe. White and pale pink variants are widely cultivated. 'Alba': fls white. 'Angel Blush': fls large, white flushed pink. 'Atrosanguinea': lvs pale grey; fls deep carmine pink. 'Blood Red': fls red; early flowering. Dancing Ladies Mixed: fls white, carmine, often with dark eye. 'Flore Pleno': fls double. 'Oculata': fls white with cherry pink eye. Z4.

***L. coronata*** Thunb. Nearly glabrous perenn. to 60cm, Lvs ovate-elliptical, sessile. Infl. a few-fld cyme; fls large; cal. 25–30mm, tubular, with a pair of closely adpressed, lanceolate bracteoles; pet. claw exceeding cal., limb *c*20mm, orange-red, irregularly toothed, but not bifid or laciniate. Summer. E China; cultivated in Japan. Rarely seen in European or N American gardens. var. ***sieboldii*** (Van Houtte) Bail. See *L. sieboldii*. Z6.

***L. flos-cuculi*** L. RAGGED ROBIN. Sparsely hairy perenn. with decumbent non-flowering shoots and erect, branched, flowering stems to 75cm. Basal lvs oblanceolate to spathulate, stalked; cauline lvs linear-lanceolate, connate at base. Infl. a loose, few-fld cyme; fls large, on slender pedicels; cal. 5–6mm; pet. limb 12–15mm, pale purple, deeply 4-fid with narrow, unequal, spreading seg. Summer. Common in wet places throughout much of Europe; also Caucasus and Siberia. White- and pink-fld variants, both single and double, are known in cultivation. A dwarf variant not exceeding 15cm is sometimes grown in rock gardens. 'Alba': fls white. 'Alba Plena': fls double, white. 'Rosea Plena': fls double, pink. Z6.

***L. flos-jovis*** (L.) Desr. Densely white-tomentose perenn. with erect, usually unbranched stems to 80cm. Lvs lanceolate-spathulate. Infl. more or less capitate with 4–10 fls; cal. 10–12mm; pet. limb *c*8mm, scarlet, bifid with broad, often cut lobes. Summer. Native in European Alps, but long cultivated and locally naturalized elsewhere. Purple- and white-fld variants are in cultivation, but the scarlet plant is most popular. 'Alba': fls white. 'Hort's Variety': dense; fls rose pink. 'Nana' ('Minor'): habit dwarf, to 25cm; fls red. Z5.

***L. fulgens*** Sims. Sparsely white-hairy perenn. to 60cm. Lvs narrowly ovate, sessile. Infl. a few-fld cyme; cal. less than 20mm; pet. limb deep red, deeply bifid with shallowly toothed lobes. Summer. E USSR, Manchuria, Korea, Japan. Not commonly cultivated, but involved in the parentage of important garden hybrids: see *L. ×haageana*. Z6.

***L. ×haageana*** Lemoine. Short-lived perenn. with stems to 60cm clothed with downwardly pointing hairs. Lvs lanceolate, glandular-hairy. Infl. few-fld, glandular-hairy; cal. *c*18mm; pet. limb *c*20mm, broadly obovate, bifid, and usually with a narrow tooth on each side and variably toothed on lobe margins, scarlet or rich orange-red. This name can be used for a group of garden-hybrids of uncertain parentage but clearly involving Far Eastern species, especially *L. fulgens* and *L. sieboldii*. In recent years selections from crosses between these hybrids and *L. chalcedonica*, known as *L. ×arkwrightii* hort. have become very popular, especially the cv Vesuvius with dark foliage and very large orange-scarlet fls. These hybrids are best treated as summer annuals. 'Grandiflora': fls large, red. 'Hybrida': fls red. 'Salmonea': fls salmon pink. Z6.

***L. miqueliana*** Rohrb. ex Franch. & Savat. Sparsely hairy perenn.; flowering stems to 60cm. Lvs ovate or oblong, acute. Infl. few-fld; fls large; cal. 25–30mm, glabrous; pet. limb 25–30mm, cuneate-obovate, nearly entire, vermilion. Summer. Japan (mts). Z6.

***L. nivalis*** Kit. Dwarf, caespitose, glabrous perenn. with simple flowering stems to 20cm. Basal lvs crowded, oblong-lanceolate to spathulate; cauline lvs 1 or 2 pairs, usually linear. Fls 1–3 on short pedicels; cal. 10–12mm; pet. limb bilobed, pale purple or white. Summer. Restricted to the Muntiĭ Rodnei range in the Romanian Carpathians. Z5.

***L. sieboldii*** Van Houtte. Like *L. coronata*, and sometimes treated as a variety of that sp., but hairy, with a rather dense infl. and deep red, broadly cuneate pet., shallowly lobed with toothed lobes. Summer. Japan. Z6.

***L. viscaria*** L. Glabrous or sparsely hairy perenn. with stiff stems to 60cm, simple or slightly branched above, very sticky below the upper nodes. Lvs elliptic- to oblong-lanceolate. Infl. a narrow, interrupted, spike-like panicle of numerous fls; cal. 6–15mm, tinged purple; pet.-limb 8–10mm, entire or shallowly bifid, usually purple-red. Summer. Widespread in Europe and W Asia. 'Alba': fls white. 'Albiflora': fls double, white. 'Fontaine': vigorous; fls large, double, pale red. 'Kugelblitz': fls carmine pink. 'Nana': dwarf. 'Rosea': fls pink. 'Splendens Snow': fls white. 'Splendens Dwarf Fireball': to 30cm; fls red. 'Splendens Fire': fls bright red. 'Splendens Plena' (Flore Pleno'): lvs dark; fls double, bright magenta pink. 'Thurnau': fls brilliant red. 'Zulu': to 60cm; fls rich red. ssp. ***atropurpurea*** (Griseb.) Chater. Fls deep purple. Fr. with short carpophore when ripe. Balkan Peninsula. Z4.

***L. ×walkeri*** hort. (*L. coronaria* × *L. flos-jovis*.) Garden hybrid represented in cultivation by 'Abbotswood Rose', a neat grey-tomentose perenn. with stems to 40cm and ovate lvs. The fls are numerous, bright pink, in more compact infl. than in *L. coronaria*. Z6.

***L. wilfordii*** Reg. ex Maxim. Sparsely hairy perenn.; flowering stems to 60cm. Lvs narrowly ovate, clasping at base. Infl. few-fld, cal. less than 20mm, pet. limb *c*20mm, deep red, deeply and finely laciniate. Summer. E USSR, Manchuria, Korea, Japan. Z6.

***L. yunnanensis*** Bak. f. Small, hairy perenn.; flowering stems slender to 20cm. Lvs linear or linear-lanceolate. Fls solitary or few in a loose corymb; cal. glandular; pet. limb, bifid, white. Summer. SW China (Yunnan). Related to *L. flos-cuculi*. Z7.

***L. alba*** Mill. See *Silene latifolia*.
***L. coeli-rosa*** (L.) Desr. See *Silene coeli-rosa*.
***L. dioica*** L. See *Silene dioica*.
***L. grandiflora*** Jacq. See *L. coronata*.
***L. lagascae*** Hook. f. See *Petrocoptis glaucifolia*.
***L. oculata*** Backh. See *Silene coeli-rosa*.
***L. pyrenaica*** Bergeret. See *Petrocoptis pyrenaica*.
***L. vespertina*** Sm. See *Silene latifolia*.
For further synonymy see *Agrostemma* and *Viscaria*.

**Lycianthes** Hassl. (From *Lycium*, and *anthe*, flower.) Solanaceae. About 200 species of shrubs or vines. Leaves simple, generally entire. Inflorescence solitary or fascicled in leaf axils; flowers few to many; calyx campanulate-truncate, 10-ribbed, ribs toothed; corolla rotate, 5-lobed, plicate at base; stamens 5, filaments inserted on corolla tube; ovary 2-celled, ovules numerous; style simple, stigma small. Fruit is a berry, globose or pyriform; seeds numerous, compressed discs. Tropical America, East Asia. Z10.

CULTIVATION As for *Brugmansia*.

***L. rantonnetii*** Carr. BLUE POTATO BUSH. Shrub to 180cm, subglabrous, unarmed. Lvs to 10cm, ovate to lanceolate, undulate, usually acuminate, somewhat pubesc. beneath. Infl. axillary, cymose, 2–5-fld; cor. 10–25mm diam., dark blue or violet, paler blue or tinged yellow in centre. Fr. drooping, cordate, to 2.5cm, red. Argentina to Paraguay. 'Royal Robe': fls violet blue with yellow centres, fragrant, long-flowering.

**Lycium** L. BOXTHORN; MATRIMONY VINE. (From Gk *lykion*, from Lycia, Asia Minor; name of a species of *Rhamnus* transferred to this genus by Linnaeus.) Solanaceae. About 100 species of deciduous and evergreen shrubs, often spiny; stems slender, erect or spreading, often scrambling. Leaves alternate, often clustered, small, narrow, entire, grey-green; petioles short. Flowers solitary or clustered, many, small, dull white, green or purple, in leaf axils; calyx 3–5-toothed, bell-shaped; corolla funnel-shaped, 5-lobed; stamens 5, exserted, often with a circle of basal hairs; style 1. Fruit a showy bright red berry; seeds few to many. Cosmopolitan; temperate and subtropical regions.

CULTIVATION *Lycium* spp. are interesting if unspectacular flowering shrubs; *L. pallidum* is of special interest by virtue of its green flowers with violet-etched petals. Given a warm season to ripen fruit, they are primarily valued for their berries, providing a long-lasting display of colour in the autumn and early winter on an arching, elegant branch system. *L. chinense* is so prolific even in the cool British climate that it has become naturalized along the south coast of England from bird-sown seed. *L. pallidum* rarely berries well after cool British summers. They are remarkably tolerant of maritime conditions. *L. carolinianum*, *L. barbarum* and *L. afrum*, survive temperatures down to about −5°C/23°F; *L. pallidum* will tolerate temperatures down to about −17°C/1°F; and a final group includes the most commonly grown spp., *L. chinense* and *L. barbarum*, which usually withstand winter minimums of −23°C/−10°F. On the edge of their zones of hardiness, specimens often succeed when trained as wall plants or espaliers against a framework of wire. Many spp., notably *L. barbarum* and *L. chinense* make good informal hedges, withstanding shearing well and providing a thorny and impenetrable barrier; in South Africa, *L. afrum* is frequently used. Other garden uses include shrub plantings for stabilizing banks and clothing unsightly tree stumps and retaining walls.

In the open garden, plant in spring into any well-drained soil in a sunny position: impoverished soils and exposed locations are suitable, provided that plants are not at the extreme limit of their zone of hardiness. Avoid situations where the freely suckering rootstocks are likely to invade nearby flower borders. Prune in late winter or early spring to confine to the space allocated, or to thin old, crowded or weak wood; shear hedging plants two to three times in the growing season. Espaliers should be pruned after fruiting in winter or early spring. Propagate from seed sown in spring and by rooted suckers. Alternatively, by hardwood cuttings in autumn or spring, layering, or by semi-ripe cuttings rooted with gentle bottom heat in summer. *L. pallidum* is the most difficult to propagate, suckering only occasionally and being notoriously difficult to root from cuttings.

***L. afrum*** L. Erect, deciduous, rigid shrub, to 2m, with stout thorns. Lvs to 23×2mm, linear-spathulate, dark green above, paler beneath, glabrous. Fls solitary; cal. to 7mm, deeply 5-toothed; cor. to 22mm, tubular, purple-brown, lobes to 2mm, enclosing stamens; fil. densely hairy basally. Fr. to 8mm, red, becoming dark purple, ovoid, with a persistent cal. at the base. N & S Africa. Z9.

***L. barbarum*** L. COMMON MATRIMONY VINE; DUKE OF ARGYLL'S TEA TREE. Deciduous, erect or spreading shrub, to 3.5m. Branches usually spiny, arching or recurved, glabrous. Lvs to 5cm, narrowly oblong-lanceolate, acute or obtuse, cuneate grey-green. Fls in clusters of 1–4, on long pedicels; cal. with 2–3 obtuse lobes; cor. tube to 9mm, slightly exceeding lobes, dull lilac. Fr. to 2cm, ovoid, orange-red or yellow. SE Europe to China. A widespread and variable shrub, the taxa *L. chinense* and *L. europaeum* are maintained here as they represent distinct plants; however, both of these names are commonly applied to material typical of *L. barbarum*. Z6.

***L. carolinianum*** Walter. CHRISTMAS BERRY. Spiny shrub to 1.5m, evergreen, glabrous. Stems erect, branches spreading. Lvs to 2cm, clustered, clavate or spathulate-clavate, obtuse, entire, fleshy. Pedicels to 15cm; cal. to 4mm, lobes triangular-ovate, acute; cor. to 6mm, blue, mauve; occasionally white, lobes ovate to oblong-ovate, obtuse or notched, to 6mm; fil. villous at base. Fr. subglobose, to 12mm diam., red. S Carolina to Florida and Texas. Z8.

***L. chilense*** Bertero To 2m, deciduous, much-branched; branches often procumbent, mostly unarmed. Lvs to 2cm, oblong, base cuneate, sometimes glandular-pubesc. throughout. Fls usually solitary, to 1cm diam.; pedicels short; cal. 5-lobed, white-pubesc.; cor. to 8mm, yellow, pubesc. outside, lobes 5, purple within equalling tube. Fr. to 8mm diam., globose, orange-red. Chile. Z9.

***L. chinense*** Mill. CHINESE MATRIMONY VINE. Shrub to 4m, deciduous; branches arching or procumbent, usually unarmed. Lvs to 8cm, rhombic-ovate to ovate-lanceolate, acute or obtuse, cuneate, bright green, glabrous; petioles to 1cm. Fls 1–4; pedicels to 12mm; cal. 3 to 5-toothed, lobes acute; cor. purple, to 15mm. Fr. to 2.5cm, ovoid to oblong, scarlet to orange-red. China. See *L. barbarum*. Z6.

***L. depressum*** Stocks. Erect, deciduous, thorny shrub, to 3m. Lvs to 7cm, lanceolate, thick, grey-green above, paler or blue-green beneath, glabrous. Fls in clusters of 2–4, nodding; cal. 4–6-toothed, glabrous; cor. tube narrowly funnelform, to 10mm, twice as long as lobes, pink; fil. pubesc. Fr. small, globose, red. W & C Asia. Z5.

***L. europaeum*** L. Rigid deciduous shrub to 4m, with stout thorns. Lvs to 5×1cm, oblanceolate, grey-green, smooth, rarely with soft or stiff hairs. Fls solitary or in clusters of 2 or 3; cal. 3mm, 3-fid with unequally toothed seg.; cor. 11–13mm, narrowly funnelform, pink or white, lobes 3–4mm; stamens usually exserted, fil. not pubesc. Fr. to 8mm, globose to ovoid, red. Mediterranean, Portugal. See *L. barbarum*. Z9.

***L. pallidum*** Miers. Much-branched, erect, deciduous shrub to 2m; branches spreading, spiny. Lvs to 3cm, oblanceolate, thick, fleshy. Fls solitary or in pairs, nodding; pedicels short; cal. with 5 acute lobes; cor. to 2cm, pale yellow-green, pink at the base, lobes rounded, one third length of tube; stamens and styles exserted. Fr. to 1cm diam., globose, scarlet. Arizona and Utah to Mexico. Z6.

***L. ruthenicum*** Murray. Deciduous shrub, to 2m; twigs with narrow thorns. Lvs to 30×1.5mm, narrow-lanceolate, pale grey-green, smooth, fleshy. Cal. 3–4mm, bilabiate; cor. to 10mm, narrowly funnelform, pale violet with darker veins, lobes 2.3mm; stamens exserted, fil. pubesc. at base. Fr. black. C & SE Asia, W Kazakhstan. Z6.

***L. tetrandrum*** Thunb. Small, much-branched, thorny shrub; branches thick, leafless, but with lateral twigs leafy at the base, ending in a thorn. Lvs to 4cm, clustered, obovate, dark green above, pale green beneath, shiny. Fls solitary; cal. hemispherical, campanulate, 5-toothed, glabrous; cor. violet, cylindrical, tube curved, limb spreading; fil. glabrous. Fr. red, enclosed within the cal. Peru, Andes. Z9.

***L. carnosum*** hort., non Poir. See *L. chinense*.
***L. flaccidum*** Koch. See *L. barbarum*.
***L. glaucum*** Miers. See *L. ruthenicum*.
***L. gracile*** Meyen. See *L. chilense*.
***L. grevilleanum*** Miers. See *L. chilense*.
***L. halimiifolium*** Mill. See *L. barbarum*.
***L. horridum*** HBK. See *L. tetrandrum*.
***L. intricatum*** Boiss. See *L. europaeum*.
***L. mediterraneum*** Dunal. See *L. europaeum*.
***L. ovatum*** Lois. See *L. chinense*.
***L. rhombifolium*** Dipp. See *L. chinense*.
***L. turcomanicum*** Turcz. See *L. depressum*.
***L. vulgare*** Dunal. See *L. barbarum*.

**Lycopersicon** Mill. (From Gk *lykos*, wolf, and *persikon*, peach, probably referring to the fruit's inferiority to the peach (*Prunus persica*).) Solanaceae. 7 species of annual herbs, to 50cm or more. Stems erect, becoming decumbent, branched; base sometimes woody; indumentum glandular, aromatic. Leaves variably pinnate or pinnatifid, coarsely toothed. Inflorescence terminal, appearing extra-axillary or lateral; flowers in monochasial cymes; calyx deeply 5-lobed, accrescent, becoming reflexed in fruit; corolla rotate, yellow, limb to 5-, occasionally to 6-lobed; stamens attached to corolla throat, filaments very short. Fruit a mucilaginous berry, to 3- or more chambered; seeds elliptic, flattened. Western S America, Galapagos Is. Z9.

CULTIVATION See TOMATOES.

***L. esculentum*** Mill. TOMATO; LOVE APPLE. Coarse, aromatic, glandular-pubesc. perenn. herb, often grown as an annual, to 2m. Stems erect to scrambling, rooting at nodes. Lvs spirally arranged, ovate, to 20×25cm; pinnae to 9, to 8cm, irregularly dentate to curled; petiole to 6cm. Fls to 12 per cyme, to 2cm diam.; cal. to 9mm, pubesc., persistent; cor. 6-lobed, lobes acuminate, to 1cm, reflexed when mature, yellow; stamens 6; anth. yellow, to 1cm. Fr. globose to irregular cylindric or ovoid, to 15cm diam., fleshy, to 9-chambered, orange, yellow to red when mature, sometimes furrowed. Seeds to 5×4mm. var. ***cerasiforme*** (Dunal) A. Gray. CHERRY TOMATO. Fls more numerous. Fr. small, to 2.5cm diam., 2-chambered. var. ***pimpinellifolium*** (Jusl.) Mill. CURRANT TOMATO. Lvs to 20cm. Racemes often paired, to 25-fld. Fr. to 1cm diam., 2-chambered. var. ***pyriforme*** (Dunal) Alef. Fr. pear-shaped, to 5cm.

***L. peruvianum*** (L.) Mill. Aromatic herb. Stems tomentose. Lvs pinnatisect, tomentose. Resembles *L. esculentum* but infl. racemose; racemes paired, sometimes solitary. Fls yellow. Fr. long, villous, to 7mm diam. Andes.

***L. lycopersicum*** L. See *L. esculentum*.

**LYCOPODIACEAE** Mirb. in Lam. & Mirb. See *Lycopodium*.

**Lycopodium** L. CLUB MOSS. (From Gk *lykos*, wolf, and *podus*, foot; the rhizomes resemble a wolf's paw.) Lycopodiaceae. Some 450 species of evergreen terrestrial or epiphytic herbs. Stems erect or prostrate, branched. Leaves crowded, continuous with the stem, usually uniform and multifarious, rarely dimorphous and distichous, imbricate or subverticillate, entire or serrate, small, scale- or needle-like, 1-nerved, veins circinate. Sporophylls like other leaves or else modified and aggregated to form compact terminal strobili. Sporangia axillary, reniform, compressed, 1-loculed, coriaceous, dehiscing by a split down the apex from end to end; spores very numerous, all alike, minute. Gametophytes fleshy or tuberous, with or without chlorophyll. Cosmopolitan, mostly in temperate regions, or, usually, at altitudes in tropical regions.

CULTIVATION Fern allies resembling mosses, from a wide range of habitats: many are terrestrial on poor soils, especially swamps (e.g. *L. cernuum*), or at altitude (*L. alpinum*), but most are epiphytic or lithophytic in tropical or temperate rainforest, or at altitude in cloud forest. Of the terrestrials, *L. alpinum* and *L. selago* require alpine house treatment in an acid mix high in organic matter and kept wet by immersing the base of the container in water. All terrestrial spp. are difficult to establish: *L. cernuum* requires warm glasshouse conditions and is occasionally seen in cultivation in wet conditions in a growing medium low in nutrients in bright filtered sunlight (see *Dicranopteris*). Epiphytic spp. are more easily cultivated and well worth the effort of growing to specimen size, especially those from lowland tropics. *L. phlegmaria* is a superb, weeping, fir-like plant suited to basket cultivation in shady, humid, intermediate to warm conditions. Warm glasshouse conditions are required with high humidity and good air movement maintained at all times, and bright filtered sunlight. The root system is small and serves merely for anchorage and plants are best mounted on to cork or tree fern slabs or, better, hung up in teak baskets in pure sphagnum moss – preferably living. Experience has shown that watering to the roots should be kept to a minimum, the moss being kept just moist to avoid the sensitive root system from rotting off. Most of the water is taken in through the foliage as atmospheric moisture and daily syringing with mineral-free water, more frequently during hot weather, is required. All parts of the plant are very sensitive to mineral salts and metals (avoid wire baskets) but light feed may be given at monthly intervals through the growing season using seaweed-based liquid fertilizers at half strength applied as a foliar spray, and then purged with water afterwards. Overwintering of plants may be difficult in cold temperate areas and supplementary lighting is helpful. Healthy and well established plants need remounting only if absolutely essential, and a good root system should anchor the plant without extra support.

Propagation is by layering of the growing tips by anchoring onto the substrate. Plants will layer themselves in this way in the wild, forming serpentine colonies in time. Spores are produced in quantity, and are used for scientific research where a fine powder is required, but have rarely been raised successfully. The subterranean gametophyte generation of many terrestrial spp. may last for many years.

***L. alpinum*** L. Main stem wide-trailing, usually hypogeous, with lvs only rudimentary; branches ascending, lower copiously flabellulate-compound; branchlets nearly square, to 2mm diam. Lvs adpressed, ovate-lanceolate, entire, rounded on the back, green, thick; midrib hidden. Strobili sessile on the end of the leafy branchlets, cylindric, to 2.5cm; sporophylls ascending, imbricated, broad ovate, acute. Arctic zones and mts of the temperate zone in both hemispheres. Z2.

***L. annotinum*** L. Main stem trailing, caudate, very long; branches ascending, upper simple, lower copiously compound. Lvs to 6mm, moderately close, spreading or lower reflexed, lanceolate, mucronate, minutely dentate, green, firm, shortened and ascending at the nodes, midrib distinct. Strobili solitary, sessile at the end of leafy branchlets, often many to a branch, cylindric, to 36mm; sporophylls ascending, closely overlapping, broad ovate, shortly cuspidate, stramineous. Arctic zones and mts of the temperate zone of both hemispheres. Z2.

***L. carinatum*** Desv. Stems 30×0.5cm, pendulous, several times dichotomously branched. Lvs to 8mm, moderately close, ascending, lanceolate, acute, entire, green, rigid; midrib distinct. Strobili usually simple, square; sporophylls ovate, acute, sharp-keeled, 2–3mm, green, rigid; sporangia in the axils of sporophylls. SE Asia (Neilgherries, Malaysia, Philippines, Taiwan, Polynesia). Z10.

***L. cernuum*** L. Stems to 120cm, stiffly erect, simple towards base, copiously branched upwards, lower branchlets ascending or pendulous, copiously compound, short, divaricate. Lvs 3mm, crowded, linear, subulate with revolute edges, pale green, lower spreading; midrib prominently raised below. Strobili sessile at the end of branchlets, many per branch, cylindric, to 18mm; sporophylls ascending, broad ovate, densely ciliate, with a large cusp. Tropics of both hemispheres, extending to Japan, the Azores, Cape Province, New Zealand. Z10.

***L. clavatum*** L. GROUND PINE; RUNNING PINE. Main stem trailing, caudate, very long; lower branches copiously compound, to 12cm. Lvs to 4mm, crowded, loosely arcuate ascending, lanceolate with a distinct awn, often minutely dentate, green, firm, midrib distinct. Strobili 1–3 on a long common peduncle with distant adpressed sporophylls; sporophylls much imbricated, broad ovate with a distinct mucro, stramineous, rigid. Arctic and alpine zones of both hemispheres, mts of tropical Asia, Africa, America, Mascarene Is. and Polynesia. Z10.

***L. complanatum*** L. GROUND PINE; GROUND CEDAR. Main stem hypogeous, trailing, very long; branches ascending, copiously compound, branchlets 50×2mm. Lvs dimorphic, rigid, firm, those of the lower plane with a very decurrent adnate base and short ascending free lanceolate tip, those of the lower plane erect, adpressed, linear. Strobili several to a common peduncle from the axis of a branch, cylindric, 25–50×2mm; sporophylls ascending, broad ovate, short cuspidate. N temperate zones of both hemispheres, Madeira, Azores, Madagascar, Java, Sumatra, New Guinea, Tahiti, Tropical America. Z10. var. ***digitatum*** (A. Br.) A. Br. Main stem mostly epigeous; branches regularly flabellate, short; branchlets determinate, without annual constrictions. Strobili mostly 3–4. N America (Quebec and Newfoundland to Minnesota, south to Georgia, Tennessee and Iowa). Z3.

***L. dalhousieanum*** Spring. Stems 60×2.5cm, pendulous, little-branched, stramineous, robust. Lvs to 25mm, crowded, ascending or rarely spreading, lanceolate, entire, glaucous green, firm, midrib distinct. Strobili to 25cm, flexuous, simple; sporophylls ovate to ovate-lanceolate, to 14mm; sporangia in axils of sporophylls. Borneo and Malay Peninsula (mts). Z9.

***L. dendroideum*** Klotzsch non Michx. Main stem trailing, hypogeous; lower branches copiously compound, to 60cm; branchlets divaricate, short. Lvs to 4mm, crowded, loosely ascending, lanceolate, mucronate, green, firm; midrib obscure. Strobili several to each main branch, each sessile on the end to the branchlets, or 2–3 on a short peduncle ending its main axis, to 7.5cm; sporophylls much imbricated, broad ovate with a distinct mucro, rigid, stramineous. Ecuador (high Andes). Z8.

***L. lucidulum*** Michx. SHINING CLUB MOSS. Stems 15–30×1.2–1.8cm, suberect, 1–3 dichotomously forked. Lvs to 8mm, moderately crowded, lanceolate, entire, unequal, bright green, glossy, firm, upper lvs spreading, lower reflexed, midrib distinct. Sporangia in irregular zones in the axils of shorter leaves interspersed with longer ones the length of the stem. N America, Japan, China. Z5.

***L. obscurum*** L. GROUND PINE; PRINCESS PINE. Stems erect, simple at base, copiously branched upwards, to 45cm, with crowded mostly ascending branches and branchlets. Lvs 3mm, lax, erecto-patent, lanceolate, mucronate, green or tinged red, bright glossy, firm. Strobili 1–6, terminal on the upper branchlets, erect, sessile, cylindric, to 36mm; sporophylls ascending, imbricate, broad-ovate, acute, not cuspidate. N America (Newfoundland, Canada to Carolina), Japan, Kamschatka, Siberia. Z3.

***L. phlegmaria*** L. Stems to 60cm, pendulous, 2–4× dichotomously branched, stramineous. Lvs to 2cm, moderately close, spreading or ascending, ovate or ovate-lanceolate, rounded or cordate at base, entire, flat, firm, always green; midrib distinct. Strobili to 15cm×2mm, copious, usually forked at and above the base, rarely longer, flaccid; sporophylls ovate, wrinkled on the back, a little longer than the sporangia. Tropical Old World to E Himalayas, Australia (Queensland), New Zealand. Z10.

***L. phlegmarioides*** Gaudich. Stem to 45cm, pendulous, 2–4× dichotomously branched, pale. Lvs 6–8mm, lax, ascending, ovate, obtuse or subacute, entire, bright green, firm, rigid; midrib distinct. Strobili to 10cm, forked, very slender; sporophylls moderately dense, broad-ovate, little longer than the sporangia. Malay and Polynesia Is. Z10.

***L. polytrichoides*** Kaulf. Stems 30cm×1.5–2mm, very pendulous, several times dichotomously branched. Lvs to 3mm, dense, ascending, linear-subulate, entire, bright green, moderately firm, midrib distinct. Sporophylls ovate, green; sporangia in the axils of sporophylls of the branchlets. Sandwich Is. Z10.

***L. selago*** L. Stems to 23cm, erect, several times dichotomously forked; branchlets erect, 6mm diam., often short. Lvs to 6mm, crowded, ascending, lanceolate, entire or minutely dentate, green, glossy, moderately thick and firm, often with axillary gemmae; midrib obscure. Sporangia in the axils of unaltered lvs the length of the stem. Arctic and N temperate zones of both hemispheres. Z2.

***L. squarrosum*** Forst. Stems to 60cm; pendulous, 2–3× dichotomously branched; branches and branchlets long, to 2.5cm diam. Lvs to 18mm, crowded, spreading or loosely ascending, lanceolate, entire, dark green, moderately firm, midrib distinct. Strobili simple, long; sporophylls much reduced, to 6mm, erecto-patent, lanceolate, green; sporangia in axils of sporophylls. E Himalaya, Khasia, Sir Lanka, Malaysia, Philippines, Polynesia, Seychelles, Mascarene Is. Z10.

***L. taxifolium*** Sw. Stems to 60×1–2.5cm, generally pendulous, several times dichotomously branched. Lvs moderately dense, lanceolate, entire, rarely linear, always green, firm, lower generally spreading, upper loosely ascending, midrib distinct. Sporangia in the axils of unaltered lvs of the branchlets. Tropical America (Cuba and Mexico to S Brazil). Z10.

***L. tristachyum*** Pursh. Main stems wide-creeping, with distant scale-like lvs, erect stems repeatedly branched, to 30cm; branches subdichotomous, ultimate branchlets 1.5–3.5cm×1–2mm. Lvs in 4 ranks, lanceolate-subulate, sharply attenuate, entire, green tinged blue, those of the upper rank adpressed, those of the 2 lateral ranks subfalcate, with erect or incurved tips, larger; those of the lower rank adpressed, much smaller. Strobili 3–4, borne on elongate peduncles, 1.5–2.5cm×2.5–4mm, linear-cylindric; sporophylls subdeltoid, peltate, contracted suddenly at base, scarious erose margins, to 2.5mm, tinged yellow. N America (New Brunswick to Ontario, Michigan and Minnesota, south to Alabama and W Virginia). Z3.

***L. australe*** Willd. See *L. phlegmaria*.
***L. boryanum*** A. Rich. See *L. cernuum*.
***L. capillaceum*** Willd. See *L. cernuum*.
***L. dendroideum*** Michx. non Klotzsch. See *L. obscurum*.
***L. epiceaefolium*** Desv. See *L. squarrosum*.
***L. ericaefolium*** Presl. See *L. phlegmaria*.
***L. flagellaria*** Bory. See *L. carinatum*.
***L. juniperfolium*** Lam. See *L. annotinum*.
***L. laxum*** Presl. See *L. carinatum*.
***L. reflexum*** Sw. See *L. lucidulum*.
***L. rubellum*** Presl. See *L. obscurum*.
***L. spurium*** Willd. See *L. dendroideum*.
***L. ulicifolium*** Vent. See *L. squarrosum*.

## Lycopsis L.

***L. echioides*** L. See *Arnebia pulchra*.

***L. pulchra*** Willd. ex Roem. & Schult. See *Arnebia pulchra.*

**Lycopus** L. (From Gk *lykos*, a wolf, and *pous*, foot, an allusion to the rhizomes.) Labiatae. 14 species of perennial herbs. Verticillasters many-flowered, dense, remote; calyx campanulate, 13-veined with 5 equal teeth; corolla tube shorter than calyx, lobes 4, subequal, upper two lobes spreading; stamens 2, exserted, staminodes 2 or absent. Europe, N America, 1 sp. in Australia.

CULTIVATION These perennials add diversity in foliage and habit to wet places by streams or ponds or in damp meadows. Propagate by division of the rhizomes or from seed sown in a cold frame in spring.

***L. americanus*** Muhlenb. ex W. Barton WATER HOREHOUND. Glabrous perenn., 20–80cm; rhiz. elongate, not tuber-bearing. Stems simple or branching, hairy at nodes. Lvs 3–8×1–3.5cm, ovate-lanceolate, narrowly petiolate or subpetiolate, irregularly incised-dentate or subpinnatisect, reducing upwards. Cal. 1–3mm, 5-lobed, lobes deltoid, subulate with prominent midvein; cor. 2–3mm, scarcely exceeding cal., white or pink; stamens 2, exserted, staminodes clavellate, very small. N America. Z4.

***L. europaeus*** L. GYPSYWORT. Stems 20–120cm, sparsely to densely hairy, branches ascending. Lvs 3–10×1–5cm, ovate-lanceolate or elliptical, pinnatifid or pinnatisect at base, reducing to lobed or toothed at apex, upper leaves and bracts less divided or toothed. Bracts 3–5mm; cal. 3.5–4.5mm, teeth subulate about twice as long as tube; cor. 3–4mm, white, with a few small purple dots; staminodes very reduced or absent. Europe to NW Asia. Z5.

***L. virginicus*** L. BUGLEWEED. Perenn. with long, tuber-bearing, narrow rhiz. Stems 20–80cm, erect, puberulent, often tinged purple. Lvs 2–14×1–5cm, ovate, oblong-ovate to elliptic, apex acuminate, margins coarsely dentate, subpetiolate. Glomerules dense; cal. 1–2mm, tubular, lobes 4–5, broadly deltoid, oblong-lanceolate; cor. 1–2mm, scarcely exserted, white, lobes almost equal; stamens 2 included, staminodes much reduced. E US. Z5.

**Lycoris** Herb. (For a beautiful Roman actress, the mistress of Mark Anthony.) Amaryllidaceae. 10–12 species of bulbous perennial herbs. Bulbs ovoid to ellipsoid, short-necked, sheathed with membranous tunics. Leaves basal, linear or lorate, usually hysteranthous. Scape robust; inflorescence a terminal umbel, subtended by 2 free spathes on a solid peduncle; perianth bilaterally or radially symmetric, lobes 6, free, usually united into a short tube at base, spreading, strongly recurved, somewhat undulate, covered in minute scales; stamens 6, erect or ascending, inserted near throat of perianth tube, deflexed, anthers versatile. Fruit a spherical to ovoid capsule; seeds black-brown. China, Japan.

CULTIVATION Often found flowering in profusion at the edges of cultivated fields in China and Japan; *L. sanguinea* grows on sparsely wooded slopes and on mountain foothills. Sharing their common name of spider lily with the genus *Hymenocallis*, *Lycoris* spp. bear showy and elegant flowers with narrow reflexed petals in late summer and early autumn; the leaves emerge after the flowers, although sometimes, as in *L. squamigera*, not until spring. *L. aurea, L. radiata* and *L. squamigera* will tolerate temperatures to at least −15°C/5°F; *L. sprengeri* and *L. incarnata* are almost as hardy, and where conditions allow a period of dry warmth during their summer dormancy and winter wet is not excessive, they can successfully be grown out of doors. All are amenable to pot cultivation in the cool glasshouse or conservatory. *Lycoris* is particularly sensitive to root disturbance, and may take several years to become well established; topdressing is therefore preferable to repotting whenever possible, and plants may remain in the same pot for up to 4–5 years. Propagate by offsets or from ripe seed. Otherwise, cultivate as for *Amaryllis*.

***L. albiflora*** Koidz. Very similar to *L. radiata* and probably only a variety of that species. Lvs to 1.25cm across; fls white. Z7.

***L. aurea*** (L'Hérit.) Herb. GOLDEN HURRICANE LILY; GOLDEN SPIDER LILY. Bulb 5–6cm diam., ovoid. Lvs to 60×1.2–1.8cm, lorate, fleshy, glaucous. Scape to 60cm; spathes 3–5cm; peduncles 8–15mm; fls 5–6, erect; perianth 9.5–10cm, golden-yellow, funnelform, tube 1.5–2cm, lobes recurved at tips, margins very wavy; stamens slightly exserted. Spring–summer. China, Japan. Z7.

***L. incarnata*** Comes ex Spreng. Habit as *L. aurea* but scape to 45cm, fls fragrant, pale flesh-pink or rose, perianth lobes neither reflexed nor wavy. China. Z7.

***L. radiata*** (L'Hérit.) Herb. SPIDER LILY; RED SPIDER LILY. Bulb 2.5–3.5cm diam., broadly ellipsoid. Lvs 30–60×0.6–0.8cm, linear-lorate, dark green, somewhat glaucous. Scape to 50cm; spathes 2–4cm; pedicels 6–15mm; fls 4–6, nodding; perianth 4–5cm, rose-red to deep red, tube 6–8mm, lobes strongly reflexed and margins very wavy; stamens well exserted. Summer–autumn. Japan. The superficial resemblance of this plant to *Nerine sarniensis* has led to its confused naming in horticulture and may account for the enormous distribution long ascribed to the Guernsey Lily. 'Variegata': fls crimson, edged white as they fade. 'Alba': fls white, perianth lobes tinged yellow at base. Z3.

***L. sanguinea*** Maxim. Bulb 2.5cm diam., ovoid. Lvs *c*1cm wide, linear, dark green. Scape to 50cm; spathes 2–4cm; peduncle *c*5cm; fls 4–6, erect; perianth 5–6cm, dull red, funnelform, tube 12–15mm, lobes slightly recurved, margins not crisped; stamens not exserted. Summer. China, Japan. Z6.

***L. sprengeri*** Bak. Resembles *L. squamigera* but shorter, scape to 30cm; fls many, erect, perianth tube very short, margins of lobes not wavy. Japan. Z6.

***L. squamigera*** Maxim. MAGIC LILY; RESURRECTION LILY. Bulb 4–5cm diam., ovoid. Lvs 30×1.8–2.5cm, lorate, borne in spring. Scape to 70cm; spathes 2–4cm; pedicels 1–3cm; fls 6–8, slightly nodding, fragrant; perianth 9–10cm, pale rose-pink flushed or veined lilac or purple, funnelform, tube 2.5cm, lobes recurved at tips, margins slightly wavy; stamens not exserted. Summer. Japan. Z5.

***L. africana*** (Lam.) M. Roem. See *L. aurea.*

**Lygodium** Sw. (From Gk *lygodes*, flexible, twining, referring to the climbing habit.) CLIMBING FERN. Schizaeaceae. About 40 species of vine-like, scandent ferns. Rhizome subterranean, creeping, short to medium. Stipes long, twining. Fronds arising in 2 rows from upper surface of rhizome; rachises elongate, slender, winged, twining, wiry, pinnae borne in distant pairs on short stalks, pinnate or palmately lobed, pinnules entire or serrate. Sporangia arranged laxly in a row flanking midvein of sporangiophores (contracted marginal segments); indusium hood-shaped, opening longitudinally; annulus subapical, lateral; spores tetrahedral. Tropics. Z10 unless specified.

CULTIVATION Fern of wide distribution, inhabiting forests, their elongated fronds climbing through trees and shrubs by means of twining pinnules and rachis. Growth can be up to 10–12m/32–40ft. with the uppermost fronds frequently growing in full sun. Glasshouse protection is required in cold climates for all except *L. palmatum*. Lygodium spp. are useful for hiding unsightly structures, growing up trellises and supports and for providing shade for other plants. Rampant growth may smother other plants if allowed to grow through them in cultivation. *L. japonicum* is especially good for providing seasonal shade for cool growing orchids, as it is deciduous in winter (requiring a semi-dry rest), quickly forming a shady canopy in the glasshouse roof during the scorching summer months; the extensive and fibrous root system has properties similar to that of osmunda fibre, making a useful alternative as a growing medium. Most other spp. require warm glasshouse treatment and are evergreen throughout the year. The root system of all spp. is extensive and specimens are better planted out into a soil of neutral to slightly acid pH; they become stunted and less likely to climb if restricted in a container. Where plants are containerized, use a medium suitable for terrestrial ferns. High humidity, bright filtered sunlight and good air circulation ensures strong growth in the warm glasshouse. Water copiously throughout the growing season, and feed at two week intervals. Growth will slow in winter, so water moderately; growth of *L. japonicum* will cease altogether and fronds will die down during which time water should be applied sparingly to avoid rot. Mulch with organic matter before growth commences. Hard scale is a problematic pest on *Lygodium*, and emerging croziers must be protected from slugs and snails.

Propagate from spores or by division. Serpentine layering is also a possibility: an actively growing frond is pinned out or weighed down at each node onto the soil surface where it may root and shoot out as a new plant. Fronds may also be layered individually.

*L. palmatum* is occasionally attempted in cultivation and is hardy to −15°C/5°F. However, it requires extremely acid conditions (pH 5.5–4.5) to succeed – a difficult requirement to fulfill in cultivation.

***L. articulatum*** A. Rich. Sterile fronds bipinnatifid, seg. 5–7.5×1–1.5cm, 4, ligulate-oblong, obtuse at apex, distinctly auriculate at base, shortly petiolate, fertile fronds multi-dichotomous; sporangiophores short, densely clustered, lamina much reduced. New Zealand.

***L. circinatum*** (Burm. f.) Sw. Pinnules deeply digitate, into 5–6 lobes, or 1–2-forked, sterile pinnules with ultimate division 10–30×1–2cm; sporangiophores 2–4mm in short, densely clustered spikes, close-set in marginal rows. Tropical Asia and Australasia.

***L. flexuosum*** (L.) Sw. Pinnules linear-lanceolate, subacute at apex, articulate at base, shortly petiolate, terminal seg. 8–15×1–2cm, ligulate-oblong, with 3–4 similar seg. each side, occasionally hastate or pinnate below, fertile fronds smaller than sterile. Sporangiophores to 6mm, triangular, marginal; sporangia 3–5mm. Tropical Asia and Australasia.

***L. japonicum*** (Thunb.) Sw. Pinnules 10–20×8–18cm, deltoid, terminal seg. pinnatifid or hastate, lateral seg. 2–3 per side, very unequal, long-petiolate, pinnate in lower part, margins entire, serrate or minutely crenate. Sporangiophores to 12mm. Japan to Australia.

***L. microphyllum*** (Cav.) R. Br. CLIMBING MAIDENHAIR FERN; SNAKE FERN. Rhiz. creeping, densely brown- to black-pubesc. Fronds to 3m; primary rachis 1.5mm diam., secondary rachis 4mm, terminating in dormant bud, producing 1 pair of lateral branches, tertiary rachis to 15cm, pinnately branched, pinnules 3–6 each side, stalked, glabrous, sterile pinnules lanceolate-ovate, cordate at base, fertile pinnules ovate to deltate. Sporangiophores 4–6mm; spores reticulate. Tropics, widespread in Old World, naturalized Jamaica and Florida. Z6.

***L. palmatum*** (Bernh.) Sw. Rhiz. 1mm diam., terete, black. Fronds 40–90cm, sterile pinnae 2–4×3–6cm, on stalk to 2cm, deeply palmately lobed, deeply cordate at base, sinus nearly closed, glabrous, lobes to 25×12mm, to 6, entire, rounded at apex, fertile pinnae apical, dichotomously branched several times, axes naked or narrowly marginate, terminal seg. numerous, 3–5×1.5mm; rachis 1mm diam., dark brown at base, paler upwards, sparsely pilose at base. Sporangia 6–10 per seg. E US (New Hampshire to Florida).

***L. reticulatum*** Schkuhr. Pinnules 15–22×10–15cm, with terminal seg. and 6 subequal seg. each side, ligulate-oblong or cordate-haste, rounded or cordate at base, articulate at base, 5–7.5×1–2cm, lowest shortly stalked. Sporangia in close rows along seg. margins. Australia, Polynesia.

***L. volubile*** Sw. Rhiz. short-creeping, black-pubesc. Fronds several to numerous, thickly clustered, climbing to 10m+ in trees and bushes; stipes 1.5–3mm diam., tinged brown to yellow, as is primary rachis, secondary rachis rudimentary, tertiary rachis distantly alternately divided, narrowly marginate, minutely pubesc., ultimate sterile pinnules 4–10×0.5–1.5cm, alternate, 2–4 per side, oblong-lanceolate, cuneate or truncate at base, acute to acuminate at apex, margins minutely crenate-serrate, fertile pinnules usually shorter than sterile. Sporangiophores to 10mm, often very shortly pilose at base; spores minutely punctate, obscurely cristate-tuberculate. C America, W Indies, northern S America.

***L. dichotomum*** Sw. See *L. circinatum*.
***L. forsteri*** Lowe. See *L. reticulatum*.
***L. hastatum*** (Willd.) Desv. See *L. volubile*.
***L. pedatum*** Sw. See *L. circinatum*.
***L. pinnatifidum*** Sw. See *L. flexuosum*.
***L. scandens*** Sw. See *L. microphyllum*.

## Lygos Adans.

***L. sphaerocarpa*** (L.) Heyw. See *Retama sphaerocarpa*.

## Lyonia Nutt.

**Lyonia** Nutt. (For John Lyon (d. before 1818), enthusiastic collector of American plants, who introduced many into England.) Ericaceae. Some 35 species of evergreen or deciduous shrubs or small trees. Branches conspicuously angled. Leaves alternate, entire, obscurely toothed or serrate, sometimes scaly-downy, petiolate. Flowers densely packed in axillary fascicles or, more rarely, in short racemes; bracts solitary, bracteoles 2 or absent; calyx lobes, 4–8- persistent, valvate; corolla ovoid, campanulate, urceolate or cylindric, white to pink, lobes 4–7; stamens 8–16, filaments often hirsute, sometimes with 2 short appendages near apex, anthers oblong or obovoid, blunt, dehiscing through large terminal pores; ovary 4–5-celled, ovules many; style erect; stigma truncate. Fruit a subspherical or ovoid capsule, valves thickened and woody at sutures; seeds small, numerous, linear-oblong. US, E Asia, Himalayas, Antilles.

CULTIVATION Grown for their attractive shining, leathery foliage and dense, pendent clusters of flowers, those of *L. ovalifolia* being particularly useful, blooming in late summer. Cultivate as for *Leucothoë*.

***L. ferruginea*** (Walter) Nutt. RUSTY LYONIA. Evergreen, diffuse shrub or small tree to 5m, often lepidote, the scales ferruginous, occasionally becoming white with age. Lvs 1–9×0.5–4.5cm, elliptic to ovate or obovate, entire, margins usually revolute, leathery, apex blunt or sharp-tipped, densely lepidote beneath, initially so above; petiole 2–9mm. Fls 1–10 in axillary, pendulous fascicles; pedicels 4–14mm; bracteoles to 1.5mm, narrowly deltoid; cal. lobes 1–2×0.5–1.2mm, deltoid, sharp-tipped, lepidote; cor. 2–4×2–4mm, pitcher-shaped, fil. lacking appendages or exiguously spurred at apex. Fr. 3–6×3–4.5mm, ovoid to elliptic, downy, somewhat lepidote; seeds 2–3.5mm. Late winter–spring. SE US. Z9.

***L. fruticosa*** (Michx.) Torr. ex Robinson. STAGGER BUSH. Erect, evergreen shrub, 1.5–3m. Twigs somewhat angled, sparsely lepidote. Lvs 5–60×3–40mm, obovate or, more rarely, elliptic, apex sharp-tipped, leathery, lepidote beneath and, at first, above, the scales ferruginous; petiole 1–7.5mm, lepidote. Fls 1–10 in fascicles or short racemes; pedicels 3–15mm, lepidote; bracteoles 0.9–2mm, narrowly deltoid; cal. lobes deltoid, 1–1.5×0.5–1mm, usually lepidote, cor. 2.5–5×2.5–4mm, urceolate, white or tinged pink, lobes 4–6; fil. 1–2.5mm, lacking appendages or spurred at apex, anth. 0.8–1.5mm; ovary downy, sometimes lepidote. Fr. 3–5×2.5–4.5mm, ovoid to elliptic, somewhat downy, sparsely lepidote; valves with pale, thickened sutures; seeds 1.5–2.5mm. US Coastal Plain (S Carolina to Florida). Z8.

***L. ligustrina*** (L.) DC. MALE BERRY; HE HUCKLEBERRY; MALE BLUEBERRY; BIG BOY. Deciduous shrub to 4m. Branches many. Young twigs glabrous or lightly downy. Lvs 3–7cm, oblong, elliptic, lanceolate or obovate, tapering to base and apex, entire or finely serrate. Fls densely packed in downy, terminal panicles 8–15cm long; cal. lobes ovate-deltoid, downy, sharp-tipped; cor. *c*4mm, oval-urceolate to subspherical, off-white, downy, lobes small, broad, reflexed. Late spring–early summer. E US. Z3.

***L. lucida*** (Lam.) K. Koch. FETTER BUSH; SHINY LYONIA. Erect, glabrous, evergreen shrub to 2m. Branches conspicuously 3-angled. Lvs to 7.5cm, elliptic to oblong-ovate, entire, coriaceous, apex tapering to a point, base tapering, glabrous and lustrous above, finely nigrescent-punctate beneath. Fls in axillary, umbel-like clusters; cal. lobes 3–5mm, tinged red, lanceolate; cor. 3–9mm, oval-urceolate, white or, more frequently, tinged pink, lobes small, erect. Fr. a subglobose capsule, 5mm thick. Spring–summer. SE US. 'Rubra': fls dark pink. Z5.

***L. macrocalyx*** (Anthony) Airy Shaw. Shrub, evergreen. Young shoots glabrous, grey-brown. Lvs 5–10×3–5cm, ovate to oblong or oval-lanceolate, entire, apex tapering to a slender point, glabrous and vivid green above, glaucous beneath, finely brown setose-hirsute on both surfaces. Fls in drooping, axillary racemes 7–10cm long; cal. lobes 6mm; cor. 10mm, urceolate, lutescent white, apex 5-toothed, teeth deltoid. Summer. China (NY Yunnan), SE Tibet. Z8.

***L. mariana*** (L.) D. Don. STAGGER BUSH. Deciduous shrub to 1.5m. Twigs glabrous, cylindric. Lvs 3–6cm, oblong, elliptic or obovate, entire, coriaceous, turning red in autumn, glabrous above, brown glandular-punctate beneath. Fls in pendulous, axillary clusters, grouped into terminal racemes; cal. lobes green flecked red; cor. 7–9mm, ovate-cylindric, white to pale pink, 7–9mm long, ovate-cylindric. Late spring–late summer. E US. Z5.

***L. ovalifolia*** (Wallich) Drude. Deciduous or small tree to 12m. Branches terete. Lvs 6–10×2–6cm, ovate-elliptic, broad ovate or narrow ovate-oblong, leathery, apex sharp-tipped, base round to cordate, finely downy above and beneath, somewhat setose beneath. Fls in axillary and terminal, downy racemes 3–6cm; pedicels short; bracts and bracteoles falling early; cal. lobes lanceolate, apex sharp-tipped; cor. 8–10mm, more or less white, tubular pitcher-shaped, downy; ovary sparsely soft-hirsute. Fr. a glabrous capsule, 3–4mm diam. Late spring–late summer. China, Japan, Taiwan, Himalayas. var. ***lanceolata*** (Sieb. & Zucc.) Hand.-Mazz. Lvs elliptic-oblong to lanceolate, base usually cuneate, more rarely rounded. Himalaya, W China. var. ***elliptica*** (Sieb. & Zucc.) Hand.-Mazz. Lvs longer and narrower. Fls in short racemes. Z6.

***L. ferruginea*** var. ***arborescens*** (Michx.) Rehd. See *L. ferruginea*.
***L. ligustrina*** var. ***foliosiflora*** (Michx.) Fern. See *L. ligustrina*.
***L. racemosa*** D. Don. See *Leucothoe racemosa*.
***L. arborea*** (L.) D. Don. See *Oxydendrum arboreum*.
For further synonymy see *Andromeda* and *Pieris*.

## Lyonothamnus A. Gray

**Lyonothamnus** A. Gray. (For W.S. Lyon, early resident of Los Angeles who discovered the plant, and Gk *thamnos*, shrub.) CATALINA IRONWOOD. Rosaceae. 1 species, a slender evergreen tree to 15m; crown narrow; bark rufous to grey, exfoliating in narrow strips; branchlets pubescent. Leaves opposite, simple to pinnate, lanceolate-oblong, to 16cm, thick, glossy green above, pubescent beneath, entire to crenate-serrate or lobed toward base; stipules deciduous; petiole to 2cm. Flowers numerous, bisexual, in large, terminal, corymbose, compound panicles to 20cm diam.; pedicels short; calyx tube campanulate, subtended by 1–3 bracteoles; calyx lobes 5, persistent; petals 5, white, rounded, to 5mm; stamens 15, inserted on a lanate disc lining the calyx tube; carpels 2, distinct, each with 4 ovules; style stout; stigma subcapitate; ovary 4-ovulate. Fruit 2 small ligneous follicles to 4mm, glandular-pubescent, usually 4-seeded; seeds 2mm, oblong, flat, brown. Spring–summer. California (Santa Catalina Is.) Z9.

CULTIVATION *L.floribundus* ssp. *aspleniifolius* is a slender and graceful small tree, grown for its beautiful evergreen foliage, deeply cut and fern-like, dark green above and grey beneath, and for its shredding chestnut-brown bark. The clusters of creamy white flowers are carried in early summer. It grows best in mild maritime districts that suffer little frost, but will tolerate temperatures to −5°C/23°F. Protect roots from prolonged low temperatures with a thick mulch of well-composted organic matter, or evergreen branches. Grow in sun to semi-shade in fertile well-drained soil, with protection from cold drying winds. In regions at the limits of their hardiness, grow in a sheltered niche, facing south or southwest. Propagate by seed sown in autumn, by softwood cuttings in summer, or by semi-ripe basal cuttings. *Lyonothamnus* may prove difficult to propagate.

***L.floribundus*** A. Gray. As for the genus. ssp. ***aspleniifolius*** (E. Greene) Raven. Lvs broad-ovate, bipinnate, leaflets 2–7, to 11.5×1.5cm, then pinnatifid into many oblique lobes, to 13mm.

***L.aspleniifolius*** E. Greene. See *L.floribundus* ssp. *aspleniifolius*.

**Lyperanthus** R. Br. (From Gk *lyperos*, mournful, and *anthos* flower, referring to the dark colour of the dried flowers of *L.nigricans*.) Orchidaceae. Some 8 species of terrestrial herbaceous orchids, glabrous. Leaf solitary, basal, lanceolate or ovate. Flowers in an erect, terminal raceme on bracteate stem; dorsal sepal incurved or erect; lateral sepals and petals lanceolate, spreading or erect; lip entire or trilobed, papillose, sometimes with raised longitudinal lines. Summer–autumn. Australia, New Zealand, New Caledonia. Z9.

CULTIVATION See ORCHIDS.

***L.forrestii*** F. Muell. To 23cm. Lvs 3, pale green, lower lf ovate-lanceolate, coriaceous, spreading, middle lf smaller, lanceolate, upper lf reduced, acute. Fls to 4, white, tinted pink, spotted and striped deep crimson; dorsal sep. erect, forming a hood, lateral sep. spreading; pet. lanceolate to falcate, 3-veined, sometimes spotted: all 2.5cm; lip obovate, lower half erect, upper recurved, margins crenulate, longitudinal venation prominent. W Australia.

***L.nigricans*** R. Br. RED BEAK. To 20cm. Lf to 9cm, ovate-cordate. Fls 2–8, white lined crimson; sep. and pet. to 3.5cm, tipped dark red-brown; dorsal sep. broadly lanceolate, incurved, lateral sep. linear, spreading or deflexed; pet. similar to lateral sep.; lip crimson-veined, tipped purple, ovate-lanceolate, sessile, trilobed, fringed or minutely dentate, raised plate longitudinal. SE and central SW Australia.

***L.suaveolens*** R. Br. BROWN BEAKS. To 45cm. Lf to 20cm, linear-lanceolate, concave, margins incurved. Fls 2–8, sometimes fragrant, dark red to brown; dorsal sep. to 2.3cm, forming a hood, lateral sep. and pet. equal, slightly exceeding dorsal sep., linear; lip trilobed, lateral lobes obtuse, midlobe ovate-oblong, recurved, glandular bordered with scale-like glands, grouped in threes. SE Australia, Tasmania.

**Lysichiton** Schott. SKUNK CABBAGE. Araceae. 2 species of robust, clump-forming, deciduous perennial herbs. Rhizomes thick, sparsely branched. Leaves bold, ovate-oblong, base cordate-truncate, margins sometimes undulate, glabrous, bright green, rather soft-textured, produced in loose rosettes, 3–6 per lead shortly after flowers, semi-erect at first, ultimately appearing somewhat wilted, musky when bruised, prominently veined below (hence the common name); petioles short, pale, grooved above, winged. Spathe large, ovate-lanceolate, base sheathing, yellow or white, arising in late winter or early spring from the thick, dormant bud; peduncle stout, short at first, lengthening in fruiting stage; spadix cylindric, subtended by spathe, long-stalked; flowers bisexual, crowded, perianth segments 4. Fruit green. NE Asia, Western N America. Z6.

CULTIVATION Occurring in swamps and wet woodland soils, *Lysichiton* spp. are well suited to bog gardens, streamsides and other permanently damp habitats, where they will tolerate temperatures to at least −15°C/5°F. Grow primarily for their striking inflorescences which emerge in late winter/early spring, the lush foliage which follows the flowers effectively smothers weeds and has a distinctive musky odour, hence the common name. Slow to establish and commonly not flowering until their sixth year they will increase freely later by seed and may naturalize. Hybrids may occur where both species are growth together.

Grow in wet or damp deep humus-rich soils in sun or part shade. Plant 2–3 year old specimens in early summer. When used as a waterside marginal, prepare the planting site with rich loam to a depth of at least 30cm/12in., built up to water level. Propagate by division, removing young plants which form at the base of old rhizomes. Pot on into a high-fertility loam-based medium and keep watered and shaded until established. Alternatively, sow ripe seed in later summer and keep saturated by standing the base of the pot in clean water; pot on as necessary until large enough to plant out.

***L.americanum*** Hult. & H. St. John. Lvs 50–125×30–80cm. Spathe to 40cm, bright yellow. Western N America.

***L.camtschatcense*** (L.) Schott. Close to *L.americanum*, but more compact in all parts, the spathe white, not yellow. NE Asia.

**Lysidice** Hance. Leguminosae (Caesalpinioideae). 1 species, a shrub or tree, to 7.5m. Leaves to 15cm, pinnate, leathery, glabrous; leaflets to 12cm, 4–8, ovate to lanceolate. Inflorescence paniculate, bracts to 2cm, white to pink; calyx tube lobed, lobes 4, to 11mm, imbricate, reflexed; petals to 1.2cm, pink to purple, 5, 3 clawed, spoon-shaped, 2 inconspicuous; stamens 6, 4 fertile, 2 rudimentary, protruding; style circinnate when young. Fruit to 20×4cm, oblanceolate to oblong, occasionally asymmetric, becoming woody. Spring. S China, Vietnam. Z8.

CULTIVATION *L.rhodostegia*, a fast-growing species occurring at low altitudes in moist habitats, is suited to cultivation as a lawn or shrub border specimen, or for other situations where its spectacular white and violet flowerheads can be appreciated. The persistent white or pink bracts remain attractive even when flowering is over. Grow in a sunny position, sheltered from cold winds, in a moisture-retentive but free-draining soil. Propagate from seed or from softwood cuttings, under mist or in a closed case with bottom heat.

***L.rhodostegia*** Hance. As for the genus.

**Lysiloma** Benth. Leguminosae (Mimosoideae). (From Gk *lysis*, loosening, and *loma*, border.) 30 species of shrubs and trees; spines absent. Leaves alternate, bipinnate gland solitary between or below lowest pinnae; stipules persistent. Inflorescence axillary, fasciculate or heads or spicate racemes; flowers pentamerous; calyx wavy-dentate; corolla funnel-shaped, lobes shorter than tube; stamens many, 12–30, exserted, base joined. Fruit stipitate, linear, oblong, flat, thin; segments membranous, margins persistent, sinewy. Tropical and subtropical America. Z9.

CULTIVATION *Lysiloma* spp. occur in sheltered valleys, by lakesides and on lightly wooded dry, rocky slopes to altitudes of 1000m/3250ft. *L.latisiliqua*, grown as a shade tree in Southern Florida, has a pyramidal habit with branches slightly drooping at their tips. They are adaptable to a range of soil types. Propagate by seed.

***L.latisiliqua*** (L.) Benth. WILD TAMARIND. Glabrous tree, to 10m+. Pinnae 4–8-paired; leaflets to 1.5×0.5cm, 20–30, elliptic-oblong, paired. Infl. to 2cm diam., tinged white, borne to 3 in lf axils or in small racemes; cor. lobes frequently reflexed. Fr. to 10×4cm. Antilles, S Florida, Mexico. Z9.

***L.microphylla*** Benth. var. ***thornberi*** (Britt. & Rose) Isely. Shrub or small tree. Pinnae 8–14-paired; leaflets to 0.6×0.2cm, 30–40, short-oblong, paired; stipules visible on young shoots. Infl. to 1cm diam. Fr. to 12×1cm. Summer. S Arizona. Z9.

***L.sabicu*** Benth. SABICU. Shrub or small tree. Lvs glabrous; pinnae 4–8-paired; leaflets to 2.5×2cm, 8–12, paired, elliptic to obovate, paler green beneath; stipules frequently conspicuous. Infl. heads to 2.5cm diam. Fr. to 12×4cm. Spring. W Indies. Z10.

***L.bahamensis*** auct. See *L.latisiliqua*.
***L.thornberi*** Britt. & Rose. See *L.microphylla* var. *thornberi*.
***L.watsonii*** ssp. ***thornberi*** (Britt. & Rose) Felger & Lowe. See *L.microphylla* var. *thornberi*.

**Lysimachia** L. (From Gk *lysis*, releasing, and *mache*, strife: supposed to possess soothing qualities.) LOOSESTRIFE. Primulaceae. 150 species of erect or procumbent herbs, rarely dwarf shrubs. Leaves opposite, whorled or rarely alternate, entire or crenate. Fls 5-merous, axillary, solitary or clustered, or in terminal bracteate panicles or racemes; corolla rotate, lobes entire or dentate, often glandular above. Fruit a capsule, more or less globose, with 5 valves, seeds rugose, numerous. N America, Eurasia, S Africa.

CULTIVATION A cosmopolitan genus, found in damp grassland or swampy terrain and making easily grown subjects for moist borders in sun and part shade or at the waterside and in bog gardens. Those commonly cultivated are perennial and inclined to be invasive. *L. leschenaultii* (preferring lighter, sandy soils), *L. nutans* and shrubby *L. hillebrandii* will not withstand winter conditions in cool-temperate areas. Rampant *L. nummularia* makes a rapidly spreading, evergreen groundcover, while *L. vulgaris* and *L. punctata* (this last withstanding drier conditions than most) are resilient border plants. *L. clethroides* makes a graceful show of curving white racemes in late summer and does well in the semi-wild garden or in woodland, especially if given enough space for its running rootstock to form a large stand. The glaucous-leaved *L. ephemerum* is a non-invasive perennial for the grey border. *L. thyrsiflora* will grow in the shallow water of pond margins.

Plant in spring to autumn (22–45cm/9–18in. apart), incorporating farmyard manure, and divide when overcrowded. Topdress annually with bonemeal in spring: staking may be necessary in exposed positions and mulching is advisable to provide some frost protection in colder continental climates. Propagate from seed sown in a cold frame in late summer. Alternatively by division, autumn to spring, or from 10–12cm/4–5in. softwood cuttings of *L. nummularia* in late spring.

***L. atropurpurea*** L. Puberulent; stems 20–65cm, erect; branches few near base. Lvs to 8×1cm, rarely to 10×2cm, alternate, upper lvs sessile, lower lvs short-petiolate, linear or lanceolate to spathulate, irregularly crenate and undulate, glaucous. Infl. a terminal spike; cal. to 5mm; cor. to 5mm diam., dark purple, lobes oblong, spathulate; stamens longer than cor.; style to 5mm, persistent. Fr. to 5mm. Balkan Peninsula. Z6.

***L. barystachys*** Bunge. Puberulent; stems to 60cm, erect, simple or upper part branched. Lvs alternate, rarely opposite, to 80×15mm, linear-oblong to lanceolate, entire, sessile, pubesc., margin ciliate, apex acuminate, base narrowed. Infl. a terminal spike, reclinate at first, later erect; bracts linear, mucronate, ciliate; pedicels pubesc.; cal. campanulate, lobes ovate, margins membranous, glandular; cor. white, 3× longer than cal., lobes oblong or lanceolate, obtuse; stamens half as long as cor. lobes, fil. glandular, gradually enlarged to base; style subcapitate, persistent. Fr. to 5mm diam.; seeds black, trigonous, reticulate. USSR, China, Japan, Korea. Z5.

***L. ciliata*** L. Stems to 102cm, erect, glabrous. Lvs to 14×6cm, opposite or in whorls of 4, ovate to lanceolate, glabrous except for ciliate margin; petiole to 1cm. Fls solitary or paired, in axils of upper lvs; pedicels to 9× as long as cal.; cal. to 1cm, lobes lanceolate; cor. to 1cm diam., lobes obovate, yellow with red basal blotches; style to 5mm, filiform, persistent. Fr. to 5mm diam., ovoid or globose. N America, naturalized Europe. Z4.

***L. clethroides*** Duby. GOOSENECK LOOSESTRIFE. Stems to 1m, erect, simple. Lvs to 13×5cm, alternate, ovate or lanceolate, subsessile, sparsely pubesc., grey-green dotted with black glands. Fls in terminal racemes; pedicels to 3× as long as fls; cal. to 5mm, lobes ovate, obtuse, with white margins; cor. to 1cm diam., white, lobes lanceolate to spathulate, obtuse; stamens half as long as cor.; style stout, persistent. Fr. very small, subglobose. China, Japan. Z4.

***L. decurrens*** Forst. f. Glabrous; stems to 45cm, erect, simple or slightly branched. Lvs opposite or alternate, to 4cm, lanceolate or oblong-lanceolate, apex acute, base usually narrowed; petiole decurrent. Infl. racemose, fragrant; bracts subulate; pedicels to 1cm, recurved in fr.; cal. campanulate, lobes lanceolate, acuminate or acute; cor. pink or white, lobes obovate-spathulate, obtuse; stamens united at base; style filiform. E Asia (Himalaya to Macronesia). Z6.

***L. delavayi*** Franch. Glabrous; stems simple or weakly branched to 45cm. Lvs alternate, rarely opposite or ternate, to 8×1cm, narrow-lanceolate, apex acute, glaucous beneath, raised dots above, membranous. Infl. a long raceme, loosely fld at base; bracts subulate, to 15mm; pedicels slender; cal. lobes lanceolate, acute, glandular; cor. white, often tinged purple, to 1cm diam., lobes oblong, undulate. C China, Yunnan. Z6.

***L. ephemerum*** L. Glabrous; stems to 1m, simple, erect. Lvs to 15×3cm, opposite, linear or lanceolate to spathulate, amplexicaul, entire, grey-green, sometimes glaucous. Infl. a terminal raceme, rarely with smaller axillary racemes at base; bracts to 5mm; pedicels to 5mm; cal. to 5mm, lobes ovate, obtuse, margins white; cor. to 1cm diam., white, lobes lanceolate to spathulate, obtuse; stamens half length of cor.; style to 5mm, lengthening with age, persistent. Fr. to 5mm, globose. SW Europe. Z7.

***L. fortunei*** Maxim. Stems to 50cm, erect, sometimes branched in upper part, lower part sulcate, often leafless, red-brown, glabrous or slightly glandular-pubesc. toward infl. Lvs to 60×15mm, alternate, narrowly or broadly lanceolate, obtuse, subsessile, entire, glabrous, coriaceous, minutely black-dotted. Infl. a loose, many-fld raceme; bracts lanceolate to subulate, equalling or exceeding pedicels; cal. half length of cor., lobes broad-ovate, obtuse, margins white; cor. to 5mm diam., white to rose-pink, lobes broad-obovate, rounded; stamens half length of cor., fil. dilated at base; style thickened, base glandular. Fr. to 5mm, globose, style truncate. China, Japan. Z7.

***L. henryi*** Hemsl. Stems trailing, tips ascending, to 30cm high, upper part pubesc. Lvs thick, almost all opposite, some alternate, to 6×3cm, ovate-lanceolate; petiole 1–2cm. Infl. terminal; pedicels to 1cm; cal. lobes linear, acute, glabrous or nearly so; cor. yellow, lobes oblong-ovate, obtuse; stamens shorter than cor. lobes, unequal. Yunnan, Sichuan. Z7.

***L. hillebrandii*** Hook. f. ex Gray. Shrub to 2.5m, sometimes prostrate, densely branched, with rusty-tomentose young shoots. Lvs alternate, or more or less opposite, size very variable, lanceolate, ovate or linear, coriaceous; petiole to 5mm. Infl. 4–8-fld clusters, in axils of upper lvs; cal. campanulate, red-purple, lobes obovate, obtuse; fil. dilated at base, anth. erect, fixed at base. Fr. globose or ovoid, glabrous. Hawaii. Z10.

***L. japonica*** Thunb. Stems to 25cm, puberulent, simple or slightly branched, obscurely 4-angled, prostrate or erect, leafy. Lvs to 25×20mm, opposite, round-ovate or ovate, entire, apex obtuse or subacuminate, base sometimes somewhat cordate, pubesc., margins ciliate; petiole to 1cm. Fls solitary, or 1–3 in axils, erect (reclinate in fruit); pedicels shorter than or equal to cal.; cal lobes lanceolate, acute, pubesc., exceeding cor. lobes; cor. yellow, lobes lanceolate-ovate or ovate, crenate; stamens half length of cor., fil. dilated to base, connate in tube; style filiform, usually equalling stamens. Fr. pubesc. in upper part, shorter than cal. Eurasia. Z6.

***L. lanceolata*** Walter. Stem erect, glabrous, 4-angled, to 45cm. Lvs to 10cm, opposite, lower lvs spathulate, upper lvs lanceolate to linear, apex acute or acuminate, base usually narrowed, petiolate or nearly subsessile. Fls axillary, solitary or in panicles; pedicels to 3cm, drooping; cal. lobes lanceolate, acute or acuminate, nearly equal to or exceeding cor. lobes; cor. pale yellow, lobes erose and cuspidate-pointed. Fr. nearly equal to cal. lobes. E US. Z5.

***L. leschenaultii*** Duby. Erect, simple or slightly branched, glabrous. Lvs opposite or alternate, lanceolate, acuminate, 4–8mm; petiole to 1cm. Infl. racemose; bracts linear-subulate; pedicels 2–4× bracts; cal. campanulate, lobes linear-lanceolate, acute; cor. lilac, purple or red-purple, to 3× length of cal., lobes obovate, obtuse; stamens exserted; style filiform. SW Asia. Z9.

***L. lichiangensis*** Forr. Erect, glabrous, to 45cm; stems slightly branched from base. Lvs alternate, to 5cm, lanceolate, narrowed to base, often clasping stem, dotted and striped. Fls in terminal spikes; cor. pink, veined rose-pink, wide-campanulate, tube densely glandular, lobes entire; stamens exserted. Yunnan. Z8.

***L. lobelioides*** Wallich. Glabrous; stems to 25cm, branched from base. Lvs usually opposite, to 5cm, ovate or round, apex acute, entire, short-petiolate. Fls in loose slender racemes; bracts linear; cal. campanulate, lobes oblanceolate-spathulate, obtuse, margin membranous; cor. white, campanulate, lobes oblanceolate-spathulate. N India, W China. Z8.

***L. longifolia*** Pursh. Erect, glabrous, to 60cm. Lvs more or less erect, opposite, to 4cm, linear, entire, margin revolute, subsessile. Fls axillary; pedicels to 3cm; cal. lobes oblong-lanceolate, acute; cor. large, golden yellow, lobes broadly ovate, acuminate, sparsely toothed; anth. large. N US. Z5.

***L. mauritiana*** Lam. Glabrous herb or subshrub; stems simple or branching basally, usually erect, to 40cm. Lvs usually opposite, spathulate, lower lvs with short winged petiole, upper lvs sessile, margins revolute, apex obtuse. Infl. an apical raceme, sometimes a panicle; bracts leafy, lanceolate or linear; cal. campanulate, lobes lanceolate-ovate, obtuse, dotted; cor. white, tube deep yellow, lobes obovate, denticulate, erose. SE Asia, S Pacific. Z10.

***L. nemorum*** L. YELLOW PIMPERNEL. Evergreen, glabrous; stems to 45cm, procumbent. Lvs to 30×20mm, opposite, ovate to ovate-lanceolate, apex acute, short-petiolate. Fls solitary in axils of middle lvs; pedicels filiform, less than 1.5× length of subtending lvs; cal. to 5mm, lobes linear-lanceolate or subulate; cor. to 1cm diam., yellow. Fr. to 5mm, globose; style deciduous. W & C Europe. Z6.

***L. nummularia*** L. CREEPING JENNY; MONEYWORT. Evergreen, glabrous; stems to 50cm, prostrate fast-creeping, expansive and rooting at nodes. Lvs opposite, to 20×25mm, closely spaced, broad-ovate to suborbicular, apex obtuse, base rounded or cordate, short-petiolate, dotted with glands. Fls solitary, rarely in pairs, in axils of median lvs; pedicels stout, far shorter than or exceeding subtending lvs; cal. to 1cm, lobes ovate, acuminate; cor. to 2cm diam., yellow, lobes obovate, minutely glandular-pubesc., dotted with tiny black glands. Fr. to 5mm,

**Lysimachia** (× 1) (a) *L. clethroides* (a1) flower (b) *L. punctata* (b1) flower (c) *L. thyrsiflora* (d) *L. ephemerum* (e) *L. ciliata* (f) *L. nummularia*

globose, rarely produced in colder climates. Europe, naturalized eastern N America. 'Aurea': lvs golden yellow. Z4.

***L. nutans*** Nees. Erect, sparsely branched, to 60cm. Lvs opposite, to 8cm, lanceolate, apex acuminate, glabrous, base contracted to winged petiole. Fls in terminal racemes, dense at first, lax later; bracts linear-subulate, acute; pedicels variable, usually 10–15mm; cal. campanulate or tubular, lobes lanceolate or linear-lanceolate, obtuse; cor. purple, tube to 3cm, lobes obovate. S Africa. Z9.

***L. paridiformis*** Franch. Erect, glabrous; stems sometimes grooved, to 30cm. Lvs at stem apex 4, to 13cm, whorled, ovate, apex and base attenuate, margins cartilaginous; stem lvs ovate or lanceolate-ovate, opposite, sessile, to 15mm. Infl. many-fld, in head among apex lvs; bracts to 5mm, linear; cal. campanulate, lobes linear, acuminate, margins usually sparsely ciliate; cor. large, bright yellow, lobes lanceolate, acute. W China. Z7.

***L. phyllocephala*** Franch. Tufted, to 60cm, puberulent. Lvs variable in size, to 5cm, ovate or elliptic, crowded below infl. Infl. close terminal clusters, almost sessile; cor. bright yellow, to 2cm diam., shortly funnel-shaped, lobes obovate, with a few, scale-like glands on both surfaces. S & W China. Z8.

***L. pseudo-henryi*** Pamp. Similar to *L. henryi*, but puberulent. Lvs elliptic or ovate-elliptic. Fls to 2cm diam. China. Z8.

***L. punctata*** L. Puberulent; stems to 90cm, erect. Lvs to 75×35cm, opposite or in whorls of 3–4, petiolate, lanceolate to elliptic, apex acute, base rounded, ciliate, puberulent, dotted with glands beneath. Infl. usually 2-fld, in axillary clusters; pedicels to 3× length of cal., to 1cm; cal. lobes narrow-lanceolate, ciliate; cor. to 15mm diam., yellow, lobes ovate to lanceolate, glandular-pubesc. C Europe, Asia Minor, naturalised N America. Z5.

***L. ramosa*** Wallich ex Duby. Glabrous; stems erect, simple or slightly branched, 60–120cm. Lvs alternate, linear-lanceolate or oblong, acuminate, dotted with round glands; petiole 5–12cm. Fls axillary; pedicels 3–10cm; cal. half as long as cor., lobes ovate, acute; cor. yellow, lobes obovate, acute or obtuse. SE Asia. Z10.

***L. terrestris*** (L.) Britt., Sterns & Pogg. Glabrous herb, erect, to 80cm. Lvs to 90×15mm, opposite, lanceolate, apex acute, dotted with black glands, subsessile; usually with moniliform bulbils in axils. Infl. a terminal raceme, rarely produced in Europe; pedicels to 15mm; cal. to 5mm; cor. 5–10mm diam., yellow, lobes streaked and dotted with red or black; style persistent. Fr. globose. N America. Z5.

***L. thyrsiflora*** L. Usually glabrous, but pubesc. under dry conditions; stems to 70cm, erect. Lvs to 95×20mm, sessile, lanceolate, with numerous black glands. Infl. in dense axillary racemes; fls 7-merous; bracts to 5mm, linear-lanceolate; pedicels shorter than bracts; cal. to 5mm, lobes linear-oblong; cor. to 5mm diam., yellow, lobes linear-lanceolate; stamens longer than cor.; style to 10mm, persistent. Fr. very small. Europe. Z6.

***L. verticillata*** Spreng. Resembling *L. punctata* except lvs ovate-oblong, apex blunt, softly pubesc. below; petioles 1–2cm. Infl. axillary, many-fld; pedicels elongating in fruit. W Asia. Z8.

***L. vulgaris*** L. YELLOW LOOSESTRIFE. Pubesc., stoloniferous; stems 50–160cm, erect. Lvs to 90×35mm, opposite or in whorls of 3–4, ovate to lanceolate, acuminate, dotted with black or orange glands; petiole to 1cm. Infl. a terminal panicle, leafy at base; upper bracts linear, subulate; cal. half as long as cor., lobes triangular-lanceolate, margins red, minutely ciliate; cor. to 10mm diam., bright yellow; style deciduous. Fr. to 5mm, subglobose. Europe, Asia. Z5.

***L. azorica*** Hook. See *L. nemorum*.
***L. bulbifera*** Curtis. See *L. terrestris*.
***L. davurica*** Ledeb. See *L. vulgaris*.
***L. repens*** Stokes. See *L. nummularia*.

**Lysionotus** G. Don. (From the Gk *Lysis*, loosening, and *noton*, back; the capsule opens elastically from the dorsal suture.) Gesneriaceae. 20 species of evergreen shrubs or subshrubs, often epiphytic. Leaves often coriaceous, ternate, entire or toothed. Flowers in axillary and terminal cymes, occasionally solitary; calyx 5-partite, segments narrow, 2 anterior segments connate; corolla purple or violet, tube elongate, limb bilabiate, upper lip 2-lobed, lower lip 3-lobed; stamens 2, included, filaments with an apical hook exceeding anthers. Fruit an elongate-linear, 4-valvate capsule. E Asia, Himalaya.

CULTIVATION As for GESNERIADS.

***L. carnosa*** Hemsl. Dwarf shrub, glabrous, branches green, rigid. Lvs to 5cm in whorls of 3, short-petiolate, thick, fleshy, ovate, obtuse, rounded at base, pale green below, sparsely dentate. Fls to 3cm, borne in pairs in upper lf axils, white, tinged with lilac. Autumn. E Asia. Z9.

***L. pauciflora*** Maxim. Epiphytic, glabrous shrub to 20cm; stems usually unbranched, pale grey-brown. Lvs to 6×1.5cm, oblong-lanceolate, subobtuse, acute at base, sparsely mucronate-dentate. Fls solitary, axillary on peduncles to 1cm; sep. linear-lanceolate, to 3mm; cor. to 3cm, pale pink-mauve. Fr. pendulous, to 8cm; seeds with capillary appendages at apices. E Asia. Z8.

***L. serrata*** D. Don. Perenn., terrestrial herb; stem erect, to 60cm, cylindric, glabrous, subcarnose. Lvs to 25cm, ternate, in whorls, ovate-lanceolate, acuminate, coriaceous, serrate, bright green, reticulate-veined; petiole to 2.5cm, canaliculate. Fls 5–10 per peduncle; peduncle terete, glabrous; cal. campanulate, seg. lanceolate; cor. pale lilac or blue with purple veins, lobes rotund-ovate; stigma persistent in fruit. Fr. compressed, to 10cm. Himalaya. Z10.

**LYTHRACEAE** St-Hil. LOOSESTRIFE FAMILY. Dicot. 26 genera and 580 species of herbs, shrubs or trees, often with alkaloids. Leaves opposite, rarely whorled or alternate, simple; stipules vestigial or absent. Flowers bisexual, often heterostylous, solitary, in axillary fascicles, terminal racemes or panicles, regular or not, with conspicuous hypanthium, sometimes spurred or with epicalyx, usually 4- or 6-merous, less often 8–16-merous; calyx valvate lobes of hypanthium; corolla free, attached at summit of or within hypanthium, crumpled in bud; stamens usually twice calyx or corolla, in 2 whorls, inserted in hypanthium (1 in *Rotala*, numerous and centrifugal in *Lagerstroemia*); ovary superior, of 2–4 (–6) fused carpels, plurilocular, but partitions sometimes not reaching apex, surrounded by annular nectary disc; ovules usually numerous. Fruit usually a capsule, dehiscing variously; seeds usually numerous, sometimes winged; endosperm usually absent. Tropical, few temperate. *Cuphea, Heimia, Lagerstroemia, Lawsonia, Lythrum, Rotala, Woodfordia.*

**Lythrum** L. (From Gk *lythron*, blood, referring to the colour of the flowers.) LOOSESTRIFE. Lythraceae. 38 species of perennial or annual herbs or small shrubs to 120cm. Stem sharply 4-angled, slender or robust. Leaves opposite, alternate or whorled, sessile or subsessile, to 76×14mm, glabrous, rarely pubescent, ovate to linear, base acute, cordate to obtuse to lanceolate, entire. Flowers 6-merous, regular, either solitary, paired in leaf axils, or numerous in clusters on leafy terminal spike; pedicels to 3mm; calyx tube green, cylindric, to 8mm, lobes alternate with longer, shorter or equal appendages; petals 4–8, to 9mm, deciduous, rose-purple, pink or white; stamens 6 or 12, stamens and styles of unequal length, di- or trimorphic; ovary 2-valved, with or without thick hypogynous ring. Fruit a capsule, 2-valved, septicidal or septifragal; seeds many, small, ovate. N America, Europe, Old World. Z5.

CULTIVATION Perennials for the bog garden, water margin or sunny, moisture-retentive border. The long, upright wands of crumpled magenta flowers last for many weeks in late summer. Eye-catching autumn colour is a frequent bonus. Most commonly grown are *L. salicaria* and *L. virgatum*: *L. virgatum* is the more refined plant, suitable for controlled, smaller-scale plantings.

Plant in rich, moisture-retentive soil in full sun; *L. alatum* will prefer a sandier but still moist soil. Self-sown seedlings (particularly of *L. salicaria*) are plentiful and rapidly produce a tough rootstock; in formal herbaceous borders these may prove undesirable and can be avoided by deadheading. Propagate annuals and perennials from seed sown in spring or perennials by division, although they may be slow to re-establish. Alternatively, increase from softwood cuttings, rooted in a sandy propagating mix in spring/early summer.

***L. alatum*** Pursh. Erect perenn., to 1m, with basal offshoots, stem slender to robust, much-branched, virgate. Lvs oblong-ovate to linear-lanceolate, to 76×14mm, sessile, dark green above, grey-green beneath, apex acute, base subcordate or lanceolate, mostly alternate but lower lvs opposite. Fls solitary, axillary; cal. tube green, to 7mm, appendages 2× length of lobes; pet. to 6.5mm, purple; style and stamens dimorphic, either style or stamens exserted. Summer. E & C US. var. ***alatum*** Pursh. Stems slender, to 80cm. Lvs ovate to oblong, base subcordate to rounded. var. ***lanceolatum*** (Elliott) Torr. & Gray ex Rothr. Robust, to 1m. Lvs lanceolate, tapering at base. Z3.

***L. salicaria*** L. PURPLE LOOSESTRIFE; SPIKED LOOSESTRIFE. Erect, pubesc. perenn. to 120cm. Lvs opposite or whorled, lanceolate, to 10×1.5cm, base cordate to obtuse, sessile. Fls numerous in whorled clusters on leafy spikes; cal. tube to 6mm with appendages 2–3× lobe length; pet. pink-purple, to 9mm, trimorphic; stamens and styles of 3 lengths, stamens 12; hypogynous ring absent. Summer. Old World, naturalized NE US. 'Atropurpureum': fls dark purple. 'Roseum Superbum': fls larger, rose-pink. var. ***tomentosum*** (Mill.) DC. Cal. and bracts white-tomentose. 'Brightness': to 90cm; fls deep rose-pink. 'Feuerkerze' ('Firecandle'): to 90cm; spikes slender, rose-pink. 'Happy': dwarf to 60cm; lvs small; fls red. 'Lady Sackville': to 100cm; spikes deep pink. 'Pink Spires': spikes tall, bright pink. 'Purple Dwarf': dwarf; fls purple, abundant. 'Purple Spires': vigorous; fls rosy-purple, abundant. 'Red Gem': to 100cm; spikes long, red. 'Robert': to 90cm, habit neat; spikes bright pink. Z3.

***L. virgatum*** L. Similar to *L. salicaria* but lvs narrower, glabrous, base acute. Fls paired or clustered in leafy racemes; appendages equal or shorter than cal. lobes. Summer. Europe and Asia, naturalized New England. 'Dropmore Purple': fls purple. 'Morden Gleam': to 140cm, fls rose-pink. 'Morden Pink' fls magenta; hybridization of this mutant with *L. alatum* has produced. 'Morden Rose': compact, fls rose-red. 'Rose Queen': to 90cm; fls pink from purple buds. 'The Rocket': to 75cm; fls vivid rose-pink.

***L.* cultivars**. 'Croftway': to 1m; fls in spikes, large, bright red. 'Stichflamme' ('Flash Fire'): fls bright pink. 'Zigeunerblut' (Gypsy Blood'). Z4.

***L. cordifolium*** Nieuwl. See *L. alatum* var. *alatum*.
***L. dacotanum*** Nieuwl. See *L. alatum* var. *alatum*.
***L. fruticosum*** L. See *Woodfordia fruticosa*.
***L. lanceolatum*** Elliott See *L. alatum* var. *lanceolatum*.
***L. petiolatum*** L. See *Cuphea viscosissima*.

# M

**Maackia** Rupr. & Maxim. (For Richard Maack (1825–86), Russian naturalist.) Leguminosae (Papilionoideae). 8 species of deciduous shrubs or trees, closely related to and resembling *Cladrastis*, but leaf buds solitary, exposed, not hidden in leaf base (cf *Cladrastis*), leaves alternate, imparipinnate; leaflets subopposite; stipules absent. Inflorescence an erect, dense, paniculate raceme; calyx campanulate, shallowly 4-lobed, upper lobe bifid; petals subequal, standard obovate to cuneate, becoming reflexed; stamens 10, united at base. Fruit semi-elliptic to oblong, flat, dehiscent; seeds to 5. E Asia.

CULTIVATION *Maackia* spp. are small, slow-growing deciduous trees suitable for the border or as lawn specimens, grown for their foliage and late summer flowers. *M. amurensis*, with attractive peeling coppery bark and a much-branched shrubby habit, holds its dense spikes of blue-white blooms above the bold, deep green foliage, in late summer; flowers are carried even on young specimens. *M. chinensis* is smaller and of more upright habit; it is especially beautiful in late spring, when its silvery-downy young foliage is held in pleasing contrast to the deep blue-green of its young shoots. They will tolerate a range of soil types, including deep soils over chalk, and is hardy to −15°C/5°F. Unlike many leguminous plants, they transplant readily. Grow in a warm, sunny position in any fertile well-drained soil. Restrict pruning to young plants or to the removal of small branches; large wounds do not heal quickly. Sow seed in autumn pre-soaked in hot water at 90°C/195°F for 24 hours. Also by root cuttings.

***M. amurensis*** Rupr. & Maxim. Tree to 20m or more, often a shrub in cool climates. Rachis to 20cm; leaflets to 8×4.5cm, 7–11, ovate, short-acuminate or acute, glabrous; stipules absent. Infl. terminal; fls to 12mm; cal. to 5mm; cor. dull white or cream to yellow, becoming brown, standard obovate-cuneate, notched, wings elliptic-oblong. Fr. to 5×1cm spreading, flanged. Summer. E Asia. var. ***buergeri*** (Maxim.) Schneid. Leaflets pubesc. beneath. Z4.

***M. chinensis*** Tak. As for *M. amurensis*, but leaflets to 2cm, 11–13, downy; fr. to 7×2cm oblong to somewhat elliptic. Summer–autumn. China (Hubei, Sichuan). Z5.

***M. faurei*** (Lév.) Tak. As for *M. amurensis*, but smaller, to 8m; leaflets to 5cm, 9–13, ovate, obtuse, finely pubesc., becoming glabrous; fls to 9mm. Fr. to 4cm, semi-elliptic to short-rectangular, to 4cm, lower margin winged. Summer. Korea, C China. Z5.

***M. tenuifolia*** (Hemsl.) Hand.-Mazz. Shrub. Rachis 10cm; leaflets to 8cm, 3–7, elliptic to ovate, opposite, ciliate, becoming glabrous. Infl. to 8cm, axillary, to 20-fld; fls to 2cm; pedicels to 15mm; cal. to 8mm, cylindric; cor. yellow or white, standard entire. Fr. to 5cm×8mm, oblong, persistent, wings absent. China. Z6.

***M. honanensis*** Bail. See *M. tenuifolia*.
***M. hupehensis*** Tak. See *M. chinensis*.
For further synonymy see *Cladrastis*.

**Macadamia** F. Muell. (For John Macadam, M.D., secretary of the Philosophical Institute of Victoria.) Proteaceae. Some 10 species of trees or shrubs. Leaves whorled, entire or serrate. Inflorescence a simple raceme, terminal or axillary; flowers small, in pairs, pedicellate; bracts deciduous; perianth usually regular; nectary glands sometimes united around ovary; filaments short, anthers inserted slightly below lamina; ovary with 2 ovules, style ovoid or clavate at apex, stigma small, terminal. Fruit a hard, globular drupe, indehiscent; seeds 1 or 2. Madagascar to Australia. Z10.

CULTIVATION *Macadamia* spp. occur on alluvial silts and fertile volcanic soils, in upland tropical (to 1500m/4875ft) and subtropical climates in their native Queensland and New South Wales, although they are grown for their nuts in the southern US, West Indies, S Africa and are an important orchard crop in Hawaii, where a number of cultivars have been developed. Not all species give edible nuts; those of *M. ternifolia* give a positive cyanide reaction.

*Macadamia* spp. have long been grown as a homestead tree, for shade and ornament, in their native regions, and as a street for avenue tree, developing a clean straight trunk when given space. *M. integrifolia*, bears creamy white flowers attractive to bees, and a smooth-skinned fruit containing a sweet and crisp white kernel resembling a hazelnut in flavour. *M. tetraphylla* is similar, with pink flowers and a rough fruit, less commonly grown for commercial production. They are a drought resistant ornamentals with handsome glossy foliage, but for good fruiting require good drainage and a moderately fertile soil with about 1000mm/40in. rainfall per annum. Although *Macadamia* spp. may survive slight frosts, growth is optimal between 20–25°C/68–77°F, ceasing below 10°C/50°F and above 30°C/86°F; cold weather can result in loss of the entire crop. They are liable to wind injury when young and on shallow soils are easily uprooted in storms.

In temperate regions, *Macadamia* may be grown as a foliage ornamental in the cool to intermediate glasshouse, with minimum winter temperatures of 10–15°C/50–60°F. Grow in a well-drained, medium-fertility mix, preferably in a clay pot with crocks, and keep evenly moist, but not constantly wet when in growth. They stand cutting back well, and should be pruned, potted or top dressed in spring, and may be put outside in summer. *Macadamia* needs the space of the open garden to develop fruit.

Propagate by fresh husked seed which germinates freely with a bottom heat of 25°C/77°F. Desirable cvs are increased by wedge grafting on to seedling understock, or on to selected stocks which are more resistant to phytopthera root rots. Commercial stocks are expected to begin bearing reasonable crops at 7–8 years and continue to do so for 40–50 years; where commercial considerations are not important *Macadamia* may fruit for up to 100 years.

***M. integrifolia*** Maid. & Betche. MACADAMIA NUT. Medium tree to 20m. Lvs to 14cm, in whorls of 3, oblong to obovate, obtuse apex, young foliage serrate. Fls white in pendent, cylindrical racemes to 30cm; perianth hairy, to 12mm; style 15mm, tip ellipsoid; Fr. spherical, to 35cm diam.; seed hard and brown. Winter–spring. E Australia.

***M. ternifolia*** F. Muell. MAROOCHIE NUT. Small tree to 6m. Lvs 16cm, in whorls of 3, obovate to elliptical, irregularly toothed. Fls pink in 4–20cm, axillary racemes. Late winter–spring. E Australia.

***M. tetraphylla*** L. Johnson QUEENSLAND NUT. Bushy medium tree to 18m. Lvs to 20cm, oblong-obovate, in whorls of 4 (rarely 3 or 5). Fls creamy pink to purple, in cylindrical, pendulous, axillary racemes to 45cm; perianth hairy, to 9mm. Fr. globular, to 3.5cm diam. Winter–spring. E Australia.

**Macbridea** Elliott ex Nutt. (For Dr James Macbride of South Carolina (early 19th century).) Labiatae. 2 species of perennial herbs. Stems simple, rarely branched. Leaves opposite, blades puberulent, entire or repand-serrate. Flowers in axillary clusters sometimes forming contracted panicles; calyx membranous, campanulate, forming 3 lobes, upper lobe entire, lanceolate, lower lobes oblong, incised or entire; corolla white, pink or purple, tube inflated, 2-lipped, upper lip arching, concave, entire or incised, lower lip patent, broadly 3-lobed, lobes rounded, middle lobe largest; stamens 4, ascending under the upper lip. Nutlets smooth. SE US. Z9.

CULTIVATION *M. pulchra* is a plant of damp places in clearings in pine forests, occasionally cultivated under cool glasshouse conditions for its attractive, showy, purple flowers. It requires bright indirect or filtered sunlight and plenty of water in summer, and thrives in a fertile, loam-based, humus-rich compost. Although in its native habitat it grows in damp places all year round, *Macbridea* benefits in cultivation from a drier period when dormant. In winter, watering should be withheld and started only when growth resumes in early spring. It will not tolerate freezing conditions. Propagate from division of the rhizomes when dormant or from seed sown under glass in spring. Fungal and bacterial roots may be destructive to the dormant crowns in winter if excess moisture is present around the plant.

***M. alba*** Chapm. Like *M. pulchra*, but with fls white.

***M. pulchra*** Elliott. Stems 30–60cm, erect, usually simple, glabrous or sparsely pubesc. Lvs 4–8cm, elliptic, oblong or linear-elliptic, apex acute or acuminate, margin undulate or repand-serrate, lower lvs petiolate with thickened margins, upper lvs sessile. Infl. of 4-fld cymes forming axillary whorls; bracts ovate or oblong; cal. to 1cm, lobes entire; cor. 3–3.5cm, rose-purple striped white and purple, tube abruptly dilated near the middle, upper lip 1cm across, entire, lower lip with incised central lobe and truncate lateral lobes. Late summer. N Carolina, Florida, Alabama.

**Macfadyena** A. DC. (For James MacFadyen (1798–1850), Scottish botanist, author of *Flora Jamaica* (1837).) Bignoniaceae. 3–4 species of climbing vines. Branches slender, subterete with glandular patches between nodes. Leaves bifoliolate with terminal, trifid, claw-like tendril; pseudostipules small, subulate. Inflorescences axillary cymes or thyrses, often reduced to 1–3 flowers; calyx truncate to spathe-like, split at middle, or bilabiate to irregularly lobed, membranous; corolla yellow, tubular-campanulate, glabrous outside; anthers glabrous; ovary oblong, lepidote, puberulent or glabrescent; ovules 2–4-seriate; disc annular-pulvinate. Fruit a narrow linear capsule, flattened, valves parallel, smooth; seeds slender, 2-winged, wings brown or irregularly hyaline. Mexico, W Indies to Uruguay.

CULTIVATION Vigorous climbers grown for their yellow, foxglove-like flowers, *Macfadyena* spp. are suitable for outdoor cultivation in regions that are frost-free or almost so, although in California they have been known to tolerate several degrees of frost. *M. unguis-cati*, a spectacular plant when covered in its beautiful golden yellow blooms, has also been used as groundcover and in erosion control. They are handsome plants for the cool glasshouse or conservatory in cool temperate zones. Cultivate as for *Bignonia*. Under glass, cut back at planting to 60–100cm/24–39in., pinching out shoot tips as they reach 1.3–1.6m/4–5ft to build up a framework. Prune established plants immediately after flowering, remove overcrowded and outward-facing growth, and give stems the additional support of ties.

***M. unguis-cati*** (L.) A. Gentry. ANIKAB; BEJUCO EDMURCIELAGO; MANO DE LAGARIJA. Climber; stem *c*6cm diam., dependent on a tree for support; pseudostipules ovate, striate. Claws of lf tendrils swollen; young lvs 1–2×0.4–0.8cm, narrow-ovate to lanceolate, apex mucronate; adult lvs 5–16×1.2–6.9cm, narrow-ovate to ovate, membranous, lepidote, glabrous or puberulent especially on veins, glandular on veins beneath; petiole 1.1–4.7cm; petiolules 0.5–2.5cm. Infl. usually 1–3(–15)-fld; cal. 5–18×8–18mm, margin sinuate; cor. yellow striped orange in throat, 4.5–10×1.2–2.4cm at mouth, tube 3.3–6.9cm, lobes 1.2–3.1cm. Capsule 26–95×1–1.9cm, linear, apex tapered. Mexico and W Indies to Argentina. Z8.

For synonymy see *Bignonia, Doxantha* and *Microbignonia*.

**Machaeranthera** Nees. (From Gk *machaira*, sword, and *anthera*, anther, referring to the shape of the anthers.) Compositae. About 26 species of annual to perennial herbs, with branched stems. Leaves alternate, margin entire to pinnatisect or spiny-toothed, apex more or less spiny. Capitula usually radiate, solitary to numerous in panicles or cymes; phyllaries in many series, brown-white below, green toward apex; ray florets female, fertile, blue to purple or white. Fruit a cypsela; pappus of white to brown bristles. Western N America.

CULTIVATION Suited to naturalizing in the wild flower garden and other informal plantings and for inclusion in collections of native plants. Most species occur on plains, prairies and dry hills and other freely draining habitats. *M. tanacetifolia* is increasingly offered as an annual for cut flowers although it seldom blooms in great profusion in the wild. Most thrive in sun in any moderately fertile, well-drained but moisture-retentive soil. Propagate by seed, perennials also by division.

***M. bigelovii*** (A. Gray) Greene. Bienn. or perenn. to 35cm, puberulent below, glabrous above. Lvs to 8×1cm, linear-oblong to oblanceolate, entire or toothed, more or less glabrous. Capitula few to many in a cyme; involucre *c*12×23mm; phyllaries linear to lanceolate; ray florets violet or pink or purple. Fr. to 4mm; pappus bristles off-white. W US. Z8.

***M. blephariphylla*** (A. Gray) Shinn. Erect subshrubby perenn. to 30cm. Lvs to 2.5×1cm, oblong-spathulate to linear-lanceolate, obtuse, toothed, stem lvs scabrous and puberulent. Capitula solitary; involucre *c*12mm, phyllaries lanceolate, squarrose, white below, green above; ray florets white, tinged pink and violet. Fr. silky; pappus brown. Late summer. W Texas, New Mexico. Z9.

***M. canescens*** (Pursh) A. Gray. Bienn. to perenn. with several branched stems to 70cm. Basal lvs to 9×1.5cm, linear-oblanceolate, stem lvs smaller, linear or bract-like, grey-puberulent and spinulose, often glandular above. Capitula numerous; involucre *c*10mm, grey-hairy; phyllaries in 4–8 series; ray florets pale indigo. Summer–early autumn. British Columbia to Arizona. Z8.

***M. tanacetifolia*** (Kunth) Nees. TANSY LEAF ASTER. Glabrous to villous annual, to 50cm. Lvs to 14cm, 1–2 pinnatifid or pinnatisect, lobes setaceous. Capitula solitary or many in a cyme; involucre 12×20mm, phyllaries linear-lanceolate, green and reflexed at apex; ray florets pink-purple to blue-purple. Fr. *c*3mm, pilose; pappus bristles off-white. Winter. W US. Z8.

***M. tortifolia*** (Torr. & A. Gray) Cronq. & Keck. MOJAVE ASTER. Subshrubby perenn. with numerous branched stems, to 70cm. Lvs to 6×1.5cm, linear to lanceolate, spiny-toothed, often tomentose. Capitula solitary; involucre *c*12mm, usually tomentose; phyllaries in 4–5 series, scarious, fimbriate; ray florets blue-violet to lavender. Fr. silky; pappus bristles tawny. Spring–autumn. Utah to Arizona. Z5.

For synonymy see *Aster, Haplopappus* and *Xylorhiza*.

**Machaerocarpus** Small.
***M. californicus*** (Torr. ex Benth.) Small. See *Damasonium californicum*.

**Machaerocereus** Britt. & Rose.
***M. eruca*** (Brandg.) Britt. & Rose. See *Stenocereus eruca*.
***M. gummosus*** (Engelm. ex Brandg.) Britt. & Rose. See *Stenocereus gummosus*.

**Machairophyllum** Schwantes. (From Gk *machaira*, dagger, and *phyllon*, leaf.) Aizoaceae. 10 species of compact cushion-forming perennials ultimately attaining 120cm diam., vegetative parts smooth, shining, pale blue or white-grey, rarely tinged green; internodes enclosed by leaf bases. Leaves 2.5–10×2cm, linear-lanceolate, rarely oblong or more or less rhombic, carinate toward tip below, obliquely truncate in profile, acute. Flowers 1–3, usually solitary, 4–6.5cm diam., opening in the afternoon or at night, yellow or orange; stigmas 5–6. S Africa (Cape Province). Z9.

CULTIVATION As for *Pleiospilos*.

***M. acuminatum*** L. Bol. Lvs 40–45×8–11×6–10mm, pale green, triquetrous, long-tapered. Fl. solitary, 5cm diam., golden yellow, night-flowering. Cape Province: Humansdorp.

***M. albidum*** (L.) Schwantes. Lvs 7–100×20mm, incurved, carinate-triquetrous toward tip, off-white. Fls in threes, inside yellow, outside flushed red. Cape: Oudtshoorn District.

*M. cookii* (L. Bol.) Schwantes. Lvs 6 per stem, 35–80×9mm, crowded, spreading, triquetrous, tapered, blue-green. Fls 4.5cm diam., yellow. Cape Province: Barrydale.

For synonymy see *Bergeranthus, Carruanthus* and *Mesembryanthemum*.

**Mackaya** Harv. (For James Townsend Mackay (1775–1862), Scottish-born botanist and gardener.) Acanthaceae. 1 species, an evergreen, erect then spreading shrub to 1.5m. Leaves opposite, 7.5×12.5cm, elliptic, apex pointed, deep green, lustrous, margin sinuate-dentate; petiole short. Flowers borne in terminal, loose spikes; calyx deeply 5-lobed, lobes 6mm, linear-lanceolate; corolla 5cm, tubular-campanulate, pale violet, tube terete, lobes 5, large, flared, with darker veins; stamens 2, anther sacs 2; sterile stamens 2, ovary 2-locular with 2 ovules per locule. Fruit an oblong-ellipsoid capsule; pedicel long, woody; seeds 2, rough, ridged. Spring–autumn (winter). S Africa. Z9.

CULTIVATION As for *Justicia*.

*M. bella* Harv. As for the genus.

For synonymy see *Asystasia*.

**Macleania** Hook. (For Mr John Maclean of Lima, an English merchant and patron of botany.) Ericaceae. Some 40 species of evergreen shrubs. Branches slender, often pendulous. Leaves simple, alternate, coriaceous, often tinged red when young; petioles short. Flowers in terminal or axillary fascicles or racemes; calyx usually 5-toothed; corolla tubular, limb 5-lobed; stamens 10, connate or free; ovary inferior. Fruit a globose drupe. Tropical C & S America. Z10.

CULTIVATION Suitable for outdoor cultivation in frost free zones, in cool temperate climates *Macleania* spp. are grown for their clusters of pendent waxy flowers in spring or summer, and are attractive evergreens for the cool to intermediate glasshouse or conservatory. Grow in well-crocked pots with a freely draining, humus-rich, neutral to acid medium, in bright filtered light or part shade. Water moderately when in full growth reducing as light levels and temperatures fall to keep just moist in winter, with a minimum temperature of 10°C/50°F. Provide support for climbing species and cut back in winter or after flowering to shape and restrict shoot length as necessary. Propagate by seed, by semi-ripe cuttings or by simple layering.

*M. angulata* Hook. Shrub to 1m. Lvs 3–7×2–5cm, broadly elliptic-ovate, apex obtuse, base rounded, tinged red when young; petioles to 6mm. Fls 3 or more in axillary fascicles; pedicels *c*15mm; cal., pedicels and ovary green-tinged; cor. *c*20mm, flask-shaped, angular, scarlet, base swollen, tapering upwards towards lobes, lobes small, erect, yellow. Summer. Peru.

*M. cordifolia* Benth. Diffuse shrub, 1.2–2.4m. Branches drooping, slender. Lvs 3–10×2–4.5cm, oblong-ovate, coriaceous, apex blunt or subacute, base rounded or shallowly cordate, tinged red-purple when young; petioles 2–3mm. Fls 3–10 in short, axillary racemes, glabrous or finely downy; pedicels *c*17mm, red; cal. ovate, red; cor. scarlet or crimson, 19–25mm, cylindric, lobes white or lutescent-white, thickly white-hirsute inside mouth. Fr. *c*12mm diam., globose, tinged pink. Spring. Peru, Ecuador.

*M. insignis* M. Martens & Gal. Glabrous shrub to 1.8m; base woody and tuberous. Lvs 4–10×2–4cm, elliptic, coriaceous, apex blunt or subacute, base usually narrowly cordate or rounded, tinged red when young; petioles 2–3mm. Fls 1–4 in axillary fascicles; pedicels 7–20mm, glabrous or with stout, red hairs; cal. teeth not joined; cor. 22–37×*c*6mm, angled, orange to orange-scarlet at base, lobes diffuse, deltoid, finely soft-hirsute inside mouth. Summer. S Mexico, Honduras, Guatemala.

*M. longiflora* Lindl. Shrub to 1.5m; base woody, tuberous. Lvs 5–7.5×2.5cm, ovate-oblong or ovate-lanceolate, apex blunt to subacute, principal lateral veins inconspicuous; petioles very short. Fls 1–3 or several in lf axils; pedicels *c*6mm; cor. 22–26×6mm, dark and dull red, cylindric. Spring. Peru.

*M. ovata* Klotzsch. Shrub. Lvs 3–6×1–2.5cm, narrowly elliptic-oblong to broadly ovate, apex blunt or subacute, base narrowly cordate or rounded; petioles 1–4mm. Fls in glabrous fascicles; pedicels 4–7mm; cal. teeth joined, sometimes soft-hirsute; cor. 18–26mm, angled, orange to orange-pink, mouth finely soft-hirsute inside. Costa Rica, Panama.

*M. pulchra* Hook. f. Shrub. Branches long, drooping. Lvs 5–12.5×1.8–5cm, oval to oblong, somewhat cordate, red-tinged when young, becoming dark glossy green later. Fls axillary, drooping; pedicels *c*18mm, rich scarlet; cal. rich scarlet, lobes acuminate; cor. tubular, scarlet, *c*30×9mm, lobes lutescent, deltoid, diffuse. Spring. New Grenada.

*M. punctata* Hook. Low shrub. Shoots somewhat angular. Lvs 3.5–6×1.7–3cm, oval to cordate, coriaceous, red-tinged when young; petioles very short. Fls in large, terminal clusters; cor. *c*3cm, cylindric to urceolate, angular, dark rose-coloured, lobes lutescent-white. Fr. *c*15mm diam., globose-ovoid, grey tinged pink. Ecuador.

**Macleaya** R. Br. (For Alexander Macleay (1767–1848), Colonial Secretary for New South Wales.) Papaveraceae. 3 species of perennial herbs to 2.5m. Rhizomes creeping, sometimes invasive. Stems erect, rigid, glaucous; latex yellow. Leaves to 20cm across, shallow-palmatifid and palmately nerved, serrate. Flowers apetalous, numerous, small, in terminal, plume-like, branched, spreading racemes to 30cm. Fruit a papery, 1-chambered capsule, opening from apex downward; seeds 1–6, arillate. Late spring–summer. E Asia.

CULTIVATION Specimens for the large herbaceous or mixed border, *Macleaya* spp. are grown for their bold attractive habit, handsome foliage and light, plume-like panicles borne throughout summer. The flowers of *M. cordata* are pearly white over bronze-tinted glaucous foliage, those of *M. microcarpa* are bronze to pale buff on opening. Although they can be invasive, *M. cordata* is less so than *M. microcarpa*, and they can be checked by spading through their limits annually in spring; if grown as lawn specimens, mowing controls their spread.

Plant during the dormant season, in a sunny sheltered position and deep fertile soil, uniformly moist but well drained. They will tolerate light shade. *M. microcarpa* may need the support of twiggy sticks when half-grown. Remove flower heads after blooming and cut down to ground level in autumn. Propagate by division, in the dormant season, or by transplanting suckers in spring. Alternatively, make 5–8cm/2–3in. cuttings of basal shoots, and root in the cold frame, in a sandy propagating medium. Grow on in the nursery bed before planting out in autumn. Generally free of pests and diseases.

*M. cordata* (Willd.) R. Br. PLUME POPPY; TREE CELANDINE. To 2.5m. Lvs to 20cm across, somewhat reflexed, rounded-cordate, deeply obtusely toothed and lobed, grey to olive-green above, downy white beneath. Fls beige to cream-white, in plumed racemes to 1m; stamens 25–30. Fr. oblanceolate; seeds 4–6. China, Japan. 'Alba': fls white. 'Flamingo': stems grey-green; fls small, buff pink. var. ***thunbergii*** (Miq.) Miq. Lvs glaucous beneath. Z3.

*M.* ×*kewensis* Turrill. (*M. cordata* × *M. microcarpa*.) To 2.5m. Stems terete, yellow-green, glaucous. Lvs horizontal, almost right-angled, larger near base, ovate, 5–9-lobed, base subcordate, apex truncate. Infl. terminal, laterally branched, apical bracts linear-lanceolate; fls cream to buff. Garden origin. Z4.

*M. microcarpa* (Maxim.) Fedde. As for *M. cordata* except fls beige, flushed pink below; stamens 8–12. Fr. circular; seeds solitary. C China. 'Coral Plume': fls pinker than type. 'Kelway's Coral Plume': fls deep coral. Z5.

For synonymy see *Bocconia*.

**×Maclellanara**. (*Brassia* × *Odontoglossum* × *Oncidium*.) Orchidaceae. Trigeneric orchid hybrids tolerant of intermediate growing conditions. Plants consist of a group of compressed pseudobulbs growing from a basal rhizome, each with one or two leaves at its apex and two or more leaf-like sheaths arising at its base. Inflorescences arise in the axils of these sheaths and may be simple or branched. Flowers with narrow sepals and petals, lip large, conspicuously marked with brown spots.

×*M.* Pagan Lovesong: very large fls on tall spikes; fls cream or yellow-green with large brown spots, lip larger than other sep. and pet. but similar coloration; many outstanding clones have received awards.

**×Macludrania** André. Moraceae. (*Cudrania* × *Maclura*.)

CULTIVATION As for *Maclura*.

×*M. hybrida* André. (*Cudrania tricuspidata* × *Maclura pomifera*.) Small to medium-sized deciduous tree. Bark tinged yellow, furrowed; twigs dark brown, spiny. Lvs to 15cm, alternate, ovate, glabrous, long-acuminate, unlobed, violet beneath. Garden origin. Z6.

**Maclura** Nutt. (For William Maclure (*d*1840), American geologist.) OSAGE ORANGE; BOW WOOD. Moraceae. 12 species of dioecious shrubs, treelets or climbers, armed with spines. Leaves in spirals or sometimes subdistichous, pinnately veined; stipules lateral, free or connate spine-forming branchlets. Inflorescence in leaf axils, globose-capitate, bracteate, with yellow dye-containing glands embedded in the tepals and bracts; tepals 4, partly connate; stamens 4, inflexed in bud, pistillode present in staminate flower; ovary free, stigmas 1 or 2 (and then unequal in length), filiform, Fruiting perianth enlarged, fleshy, yellow to orange; fruit free, somewhat drupaceous; seed fairly small; cotyledons thin, equal, plicate. America, Asia, Africa (mostly warmer regions).

CULTIVATION The timber of *Maclura*, silky, lustrous and durable, is one of the many bearing the common name yellowwood; it was used by the indigenous Americans for bow-making, hence also, bow-wood. The roots yield a yellow dye. The primary horticultural interest of *M. pomifera* lies in its unusual but inedible fruits, about the size of an orange, produced when male and female plants are grown together. It also has attractive, ridged, deep orange-brown bark, develops clear yellow autumn colour, and, given space, develops an open and globular head. *Maclura* makes an effective windbreak and in central Europe and in the US it was frequently planted as a boundary hedge, valued for its ability to withstand hard shearing and as a thorny and impenetrable stock barrier. The miles of 'Osage Orange' fencing once common in the American Midwest have now been largely superseded by barbed wire.

Plant when dormant, in any well-drained soil, in full sun. Growth and hardiness develops best in areas experiencing hot, dry summers; *Maclura* tolerates temperatures down to −17 to −21°C/1.4 to −6°F, although young growth may be cut by frost. Cultivated specimens often achieve only half the stature of wild plants. Little maintenance is required, but when necessary, prune in winter; contact with the milky sap should be avoided, since it may cause contact dermatitis in some individuals. Propagate from fresh seed sown in an open seed bed in autumn, or from stored seed stratified for two months at 4°C/39°F. Plants of known gender are raised from semi-ripe cuttings in a closed frame of under mist in summer. Alternatively by layering in summer, or by root cuttings in winter.

***M. pomifera*** (Raf.) Schneid. Tree, to 18m (usually to 9m in cult.), deciduous, with rounded, irregular, open head, rugged; bark and branches orange-brown, juvenile green, thorns to 2.5cm+. Lvs 5–15cm, entire, alternate, ovate-acuminate, bright green, lustrous above, tomentose beneath; latex milky, clear yellow in autumn. Fls inconspicuous, green; male fls in 2.5–3.75cm racemes from short spur-like branchlets on previous year's shoots, stamens 4; female fls in dense spherical heads to 2.5cm diam., cal. 4-lobed, pet. lacking, stigma long, slender. Fr. in clusters *c*8.5–12.5cm diam., nearly globose, with coarse pebble-like surfaces, initially green, orange when ripe, inedible. Early summer. US (Arkansas to Texas) 'Inermis': twigs thornless. 'Pulverulentia': lvs white, powdery. 'Fan d'Arc': hardy growing; lvs large, dark. Z5.

***M. aurantiaca*** Nutt. See *M. pomifera*.
***M. excelsa*** (Welw.) Bur. See *Milicia excelsa*.
***M. tinctoria*** D. Don ex Steud. See *Chlorophora tinctoria*.
***M. tricuspidata*** Carr. See *Cudrania tricuspidata*.

**Macodes** (Bl.) Lindl. Orchidaceae. Some 10 species of evergreen, terrestrial orchids allied to *Anoectochilus* and *Ludisia* and closely resembling the latter except in its resupinate flowers. Summer. Malesia to Papuasia. Z10.

CULTIVATION As for *Anoectochilus*.

***M. petola*** (Bl.) Lindl. Rhiz. fleshy, creeping, slender, rooting and branching at nodes. Lvs to 8, spiralling in a loose rosette, to 9×6cm, elliptic to ovate, acute, fleshy, papillose appearing velvety, bottle green with 5 longitudinal veins and many finer reticulate golden veins in obscure transverse bands above, purple-green beneath; petioles grooved, clasping at base. Infl. an erect, terminal spike to 20cm; fls small, white, lip rusty brown. Sumatra to Philippines. var. ***javanica*** (Hook. f.) A.D. Hawkes. Lvs to 10cm, veins silver-green. Java.

***M. sanderiana*** Rolfe. Lvs to 7×4.5cm, broadly ovate to orbicular, emerald green with 5 very conspicuous, golden, longitudinal veins and finer crowded reticulation above, purple-green beneath. Fls brown-white, lip white. Papua New Guinea.

For synonymy see *Anoectochilus*.

**Macradenia** R. Br. (From Gk *makros*, large, and *aden*, gland, referring to the large gland to which the pollinia are attached.) Orchidaceae. Some 12 species of epiphytic orchids. Pseudobulbs small, cylindrical, apically unifoliate, clothed at base with grey-white, scarious sheaths. Leaves fleshy to coriaceous. Inflorescence from base of pseudobulb, a raceme, loosely few to many-fld, erect to pendent; flowers small; sepals equal, free, slightly spreading; petals similar to sepals; lip erect, continuous with column base, 3-lobed, lateral lobes erect, clasping column, midlobe short, spreading; column footless, wingless, slightly grooved below, anther erect, pollinia 2, attached to viscid disc or gland by long membranaceous narrow stipe. Florida, W Indies, Mexico, S America. Z10.

CULTIVATION Intermediate house orchids requiring sunny conditions and pot or basket culture in an open medium. See ORCHIDS.

***M. brassavolae*** Rchb. f. Pseudobulbs to 4.5×1cm, curved, slightly compressed. Lvs to 18×3cm, oblong or oblong-lanceolate, acute or obtuse, subcoriaceous. Infl. to 25cm, pendent, few-to many-fld; peduncle dark maroon-red; fls showy, maroon sometimes striped white, margins yellow-green; sep. and pet. to 20×5mm, lanceolate to linear-lanceolate, acuminate, slightly spreading; lip to 19×8mm, fleshy, lateral lobes short, suborbicular-obovate, midlobe linear-lanceolate, recurved, acute, disc with a narrow central keel; column to 7mm, clavate, fleshy, apex with 2 subquadrate auricles, apical margin erose. Mexico, C America, Colombia, Venezuela.

***M. lutescens*** R. Br. Pseudobulbs to 5×1cm, slightly compressed. Lvs to 16×3cm, oblong-lanceolate, acute, coriaceous. Infl. to 17cm, pendent, loosely few-fld; fls white-yellow or dull yellow marked brown-purple; dorsal sep. to 12×6mm, broadly elliptic-oblong, acute, deeply concave, lateral sep. to 12×4mm, obliquely elliptic-lanceolate, acute, subfalcate; pet. to 11×3mm, oblong-elliptic, acute; lip to 10×7mm, lateral lobes obcordate to suborbicular, incurved, midlobe narrowly linear-lanceolate, reflexed, margins revolute, disc with 3 central keels; column to 8mm, clavate, apex irregularly dentate. Winter. Florida, W Indies, Venezuela, Colombia, Guyana, Surinam.

**Macrobia** (Webb & Berth.) Kunkel. See *Aichryson*.

**Macropiper** Miq. Piperaceae. 9 species of shrubs or small trees. Branches often swollen at nodes. Leaves generally alternate, entire, with stipules united to petioles. Inflorescences axillary, unisexual, spikes, bracteate; flowers minute, crowded; male of 2–3 stamens, anther cells distinct; ovary superior, 1-celled, ovule 1. Fruit a small drupe, often connate to bracts and fleshy axis. S Pacific (Polynesia to New Guinea & New Zealand). Z10.

CULTIVATION Occurring in low-altitude humid forest, *M. excelsum* is grown for its large aromatic leaves, especially attractive in its variegated forms. Suitable for outdoor cultivation in frost-free zones, in cool temperate regions it requires the protection of the cool to intermediate glasshouse or conservatory. Grow in any freely draining and moderately fertile loam-based medium in bright indirect light or part shade; liquid feed fortnightly and water to keep evenly moist, but not constantly wet, when in growth, reducing in winter to keep just moist, with a winter minimum temperature of 10°C/50°F. It will tolerate quite severe pruning: cut back in spring to shape and restrict size. Propagate by seed, layers or by semi-ripe cuttings in sand in a closed case with gentle bottom heat.

***M. excelsum*** (Forst. f.) Miq. PEPPER TREE; KAWA-KAWA. Shrub or tree to 6m, glabrous throughout, aromatic; branches somewhat flexuous, dark. Lvs opposite, 7.5×9cm, broadly ovate to suborbicular, cordate at base, abruptly narrowed to obtuse apex, dark green to green tinged yellow, subcoriaceous; petioles 2.5cm, rufescent, stipules adnate. Spikes solitary or in pairs, 2–8cm, fls close-set, sessile; peduncles 1cm; bracts orbicular-peltate; male of 2, rarely 3 stamens; female of 3, rarely 4 stigmas. Fr. broadly obovoid, somewhat angular, 2–3mm diam., exocarp yellow to orange, succulent. Year-round. New Zealand.

**Macropodium** R. Br.
***M. laciniatum*** Hook. See *Thelypodium iaciniatum*.

**Macrosiphonia** Muell. (From Gk *makros*, large, and *Siphonia*.) Apocynaceae. 10 species of shrubby herbs and subshrubs close to *Mandevilla*, differing in their non-climbing habit and solitary flowers that open at dusk, with very long slender corolla tubes. Americas, warm temperate to tropical regions. Z9.

CULTIVATION As for *Mandevilla*.

***M. macrosiphon*** (Torr.) A.A. Heller. Erect perenn. subshrub to 40cm. Stems initially tomentellous. Lvs to 5cm, ovate-elliptic to rounded, thickly tomentose; petioles to 1cm. Fls solitary, terminal; cal. lobes leafy, thickly tomentellous; cor. to 10cm, funnelform, white, limb to 5cm diam., exterior somewhat downy. Fr. 10–25cm, slender. Texas to Mexico.

**Macrothelypteris** (H. Itô) Ching. (From Gk. *makros*, large, *thelys*, female, and *pteris*, fern.) Thelypteridaceae. Some 9 species of terrestrial ferns. Rhizomes suberect to creeping or short-creeping, branched; scales dense, ciliate at margin. Frond blades uniform, 2–3-pinnate to -pinnatifid, glandular with stalked glands, or pubescent with acicular, trichomate hairs, basal pinnae not, or only a little, reduced, pinnules adnate, veins running short of margin; rachis scaly, costa pubescent; stipes approximate and clustered, pubescent, scaly at base. Sori marginal, dorsal, on veins, circular; indusia (where present) persistent; paraphyses absent; sporangia glandular; spores reticulate and ridged. Mascarene Is., Tropical Asia to Polynesia, NE Australia; naturalized in tropical and warm Americas. Z10.

CULTIVATION As for *Christella*. Profuse, it can become a weed in the warm glasshouse.

***M. polypodioides*** (Hook.) Holtt. Rhiz. suberect and massive to short-creeping. Stipes to 1m, pubesc. and scaly, scales narrowly linear, to 2cm. Frond blades to 80cm, pinnae to 60×35cm, subsessile, deltoid, apex narrowly acute, pinnules narrowly acute at apex, lobed at margin, to 7×2cm; rachis scaly, scales narrowly lanceolate to ovate, ciliate, costa pubesc. Taiwan, Thailand, Philippines, New Guinea, Queensland, Polynesia.

***M. setigera*** (Bl.) Ching. Rhiz. suberect and massive to short-creeping; scales brown. Frond blades deltoid, to 1m, pinnae to 30×15cm, pinnules lanceolate, deeply lobed at margin, to 10×3cm; rachis densely scaly, costa white-pubesc. Malay Islands.

***M. torresiana*** (Gaudich.) Ching. Rhiz. short-creeping; scales very narrow, dark brown. Stipes to 50cm, glaucous to straw-coloured or brown with many dark narrow scales. Frond blades lanceolate, to 70×50cm, herbaceous deeply tripinnatifid, pinnae to 30×10cm, to 15 pairs, deltoid, pinnules oblique, deeply lobed at margin, to 8×3cm, lobes oblique, dentate, notched or somewhat lobed at margin, to 12×5mm, veins to 12-paired, pinnate; rachis and costa pubesc. below. Mascarene Is., Tropical Asia, Japan to Queensland and Polynesia.

For synonymy see *Alsophila, Dryopteris* and *Thelypteris*.

**Macrotyloma** (Wight & Arn.) Verdc. (From Gk *makros*, large, *tylos*, knob, and *loma*, border or margin.) Leguminosae (Papilionoideae). Some 24 species of annual or perennial herbs, some woody at base; stems pubescent, sprawling, prostrate or erect. Leaves 3-foliolate, rarely 1-foliolate; stipels linear-lanceolate or reduced, filiform; stipules deltoid. Flowers few, borne in axillary clusters or apical pseudoracemes, short-pedicellate; calyx campanulate, lobes 4–5, deltoid, 2 upper lobes partially fused in a bidentate lip; standard round to elliptic, with 2 parallel linear ears, wings narrow, keel straight; stamens diadelphous, anthers uniform; ovary narrow-oblong, ovules 3–13, style filiform, smooth or slightly pubescent, stigma ciliate. Fruit oblong, straight or falcate, laterally compressed; seeds compressed. E Africa, S Africa, India, Malaysia, W Indies, Australia. Z10.

CULTIVATION As for *Lens*.

***M. uniflorum*** (Lam.) Verdc. HORSE GRAM; POOR MAN'S PULSE. Climbing annual herb with slender, puberulent stems. Leaflets 3, oblong, obtuse, terminal leaflet 1.8–2.5cm. Fls axillary, yellow or green-yellow, 1–3 on very short pedicels. Fr. 2.5–5.5cm, linear-oblong, somewhat falcate, sessile, glabrous or puberulent; seeds 6–8, tipped with a persistent 6mm style. Range as for the genus.

For synonymy see *Dolichos*.

**Macrozamia** Miq. (From Gk *makros*, great, plus *Zamia*.) Zamiaceae. 12 species of cycads, perennial, evergreen gymnosperms, dioecious, bearing cones, arborescent and subterranean, palm-like in appearance, to 10m. Leaves borne annually in whorls at apex amid bracts, pinnate, glossy, coriaceous; pinnae numerous, opposite, with parallel venation; rachis arching, bisulcate, rarely armed or pubesc. Female strobili axillary (apparently terminal) among leaves. Sporophylls peltate, stipes angular to rounded, laterally expanded, some terminally compressed to a narrow transverse wing, bearing 2 ovules on inward-facing margins. Male strobilus narrower, longer. Sporophylls with sporangia in 2 separate areas, tip reflexed as erect spine. Seeds large, ovoid, in fleshy, brightly coloured coating. Australia. Z9.

CULTIVATION Large cycads suitable for tubs or landscaping outdoors in subtropical and tropical regions; elsewhere for containers and beds in cool or intermediate greenhouses, the home or for interior landscaping. Cultivation as for the SE Asia species of *Cycas*, although most will benefit from full sunlight. *M. spiralis* and *M. communis* are particularly fine, large plants, ideal for situations where a bold, palm-like form is needed. *M. pauli-guilielmi*, a smaller plant with spiralling glaucous foliage, is a striking curiosity for xeriscapes under glass.

***M. communis*** L. Johnson. BURRAWONG. To 3m. Stem largely below ground, to 60cm diam. Lvs borne in whorls to 50, to 2m; pinnae to 130, opposite to 25×1cm, coriaceous, rigid, widely spaced, linear, pungent with to 13 prominent veins, pale beneath; rachis bisulcate at pinna insertions, terete. Female strobili. cylindric to 45×20cm, glabrous. NSW.

***M. diplomera*** (F. Muell.) L. Johnson. Related to *M. communis*. To 2m. Stem subterranean. Lvs to 50, to 120cm; pinnae to 120, glossy to 20×1cm, dichotomously divided; stomata on both surfaces, each pinna segment 7-veined, pungent, basal portion narrowed to waxy yellow callosity. NSW.

***M. fawcettii*** C. Moore. Related *M. pauli-guilielmi*. To 1.5m. Stem ovoid, subterranean. Lvs to 1.20m, to 5 in whorl emerging woolly, later glabrous; pinnae linear-lanceolate, subfalcate, spirally twisted with a few teeth at tip, basal callosity red-green, to 25×1.5cm, to 13 veins; rachis terete, twisted spirally to 180°. NSW.

***M. heteromera*** C. Moore. var. ***heteromera*** (C. Moore) Maid. & Betche. Related to *M. stenomera*, from which it differs in having adaxial stomata. To 1m. Pinnae lobed, rigid, dull green, glaucous above, less so beneath; rachis slightly twisted. New South Wales.

***M. lucida*** L. Johnson. Related to *M. spiralis* from which it differs in its long, slender, untwisted rachis; pinnae 35×1.5cm, falcate, very glossy, basal zone white, callosity absent. S Queensland.

***M. miquelii*** (F. Muell.) A. DC. var. ***miquelii*** (F. Muell.) Schust. To 2.5m. Stem simple, mostly subterranean, ovoid, swollen, scarred, to 1.5m diam. Lvs to 100, to 2m long, downy at first, later glabrous; pinnae to 50 pairs, linear, falcate, pungent, tip sometimes toothed in juvenile foliage, 30×1cm, to 11 veins, somewhat glaucous, margins involute; basal callosity white to red. Queensland, NSW.

***M. moorei*** F. Muell. To 9m. Stem massive, columnar, exposed, to 7m tall, 71cm diam. Lvs to 3m, to 100, smooth, rigid, semi-erect; pinnae to 50 pairs, linear-lanceolate, to 30×1cm, pungent, somewhat glaucous with to 11 veins. Female strobili. to 4, cylindric, to 90cm. Male strob. to 20, narrow-oblong, to 30×5cm. Fr. ovoid, to 6×2cm, seed coating red. Queensland, NSW.

***M. pauli-guilielmi*** W. Hill & F. Muell. Variable. To 1.5m. Stem simple, swollen, ovoid, often subterranean, covered with scars and fibre of decayed lf bases. Lvs emerging woolly, later glabrous grey-green, to 1m, in whorls to 5; pinnae soft, densely set, to 120, erect, narrow-linear to filiform to 20×0.5cm, 3–10-nerved, entire; rachis flattened, very twisted, woolly at base. Queensland.

***M. riedlei*** (Fisch. ex Gaudich.) Gardn. To 5m. Stem exposed to 4m high, 120cm diam. Lvs to 100, at first erect, later arching to pendent, to 2m; pinnae to 150, spreading upwards, densely set, rigid, entire, linear to 35×1cm, reduced to spines in basal portion of rachis, to 15 prominent veins beneath, apex pungent, pinna base callous red-green, stomata on both surfaces, dull green. Rachis unarmed, basally woolly, terete, bisulcate. W Australia.

***M. secunda*** C. Moore Related to *M. spiralis* from which it differs in its concave rachis, rigid, narrow, apparently secund pinnae, held semi-erect, and close venation. Arid-growing, sclerophyllitic, glaucous. NSW.

***M. spiralis*** (Salisb.) Miq. To 2m. Stem subterranean. Pinnae dull-green, linear-falcate, pink-orange at base, to 25cm×10mm. Rachis subangular to terete. New South Wales.

***M. stenomera*** L. Johnson. To 1m. Stem subterranean. Stomata on abaxial surface of pinnae; pinnae lobed ×2–3, lax, dark green. Rachis twisting toward apex. NSW.

***M. denisonii*** C. Moore & F. Muell. var. ***hopei*** (W. Hill) Schust. See *Lepidozamia peroffskyana*.
***M. corallipes*** Hook. f. See *M. spiralis*.
***M. douglasii*** W. Hill. See *M. miquelii*.
***M. dyeri*** F. Muell. See *M. riedlei*.

**M. fraseri** Miq. See *M. riedlei*.
**M. heteromera** var. **tenuifolia** Schust. See *M. stenomera*.
**M. hopei** W. Hill ex Bail. See *Lepidozamia hopei*.
**M. oldfieldii** (Miq.) A. DC. See *M. riedlei*.
**M. plumosa** hort. See *M. pauli-guilielmi*.
**M. preisii** Lehm. See *M. riedlei*.
**M. spiralis** (Salisb.) Miq. See *M. heteromera*.
**M. spiralis** var. **cylindrica** Reg. See *M. communis*.
**M. tridentata** (Willd.) Reg. See *M. spiralis*.
**M. tridentata** ssp. **mountperryensis** (Bail.) Schust. See *M. miquelii*.

**Maddenia** Hook. f. & Thoms. (For Col. E. Madden (*d*1856), plant collector in India.) Rosaceae. 4 species of deciduous shrubs or trees. Leaves alternate, serrate; stipules paired, persistent. Flowers unisexual, in terminal racemes; pedicels short; sepals 10, very small; petals absent; stamens 25–40; carpels in staminate flowers solitary, sessile, with slender style and capitate stigma, in pistillate flowers 2, oblong, truncate, with sessile and oblique stigma; ovary 2-ovulate; ovules collateral, pendulous. Fruit a 1-seeded, oblong, subcompressed, fleshy drupe. Himalaya, China. Closely related to *Prunus*, but sepals 10.

CULTIVATION Grown for botanical interest rather than ornamental value; the inconspicuous flowers give rise to small black fruits. Grow in the shrub border or sunny woodland edge, in fertile well-drained soil; hardy to −15°C/5°F. Propagate by seed or semi-ripe cuttings.

**M. hypoleuca** Koehne. MADDEN CHERRY. Shrub or small tree to 6m; young branchlets dark brown, glabrous. Lvs to 12cm, ovate-oblong, long-acuminate, round at base, double-serrate, glabrous and dark green above, blue-white beneath, 14–18 pairs of veins. Flowers in dense racemes to 5cm, rufous, later green. Fr. ellipsoid, 8mm, black. Winter–spring. C & W China (Hupeh). Z5.

**M. hypoxantha** Koehne. Resembles *M. hypoleuca*, but lvs yellow beneath, slightly pubesc. on veins. W China (Sichuan). Z7.

**Madia** Molina. (From Chilean name for *M. sativa*.) Compositae. About 18 species of erect annual to perennial herbs. Leaves opposite or alternate, linear to elliptic-oblong, entire or toothed, aromatic. Capitula radiate, solitary or few to many clustered in loose panicles; receptacle scaly; involucre deeply grooved, phyllaries infolding; ray florets fertile, female, yellow; disc florets, usually male, often yellow. Fruit a laterally compressed cypsela, outer enveloped by phyllaries; pappus usually absent. Flowers open in the morning or evening, closing when exposed to bright sunlight. Western N America and Chile.

CULTIVATION As for *Encelia*.

**M. elegans** D. Don ex Lindl. COMMON MADIA; COMMON TARWEED. Annual to 1.5m. Stems branched, villous below, glandular above. Lvs alternate, to 14×1.5cm, linear or lanceolate, usually entire, basal lvs occasionally rosulate. Capitula in corymbs, long-pedunculate; ray florets 8–16, 1–2cm, sometimes with a red-brown spot near base; disc florets yellow or maroon. Fr. cylindrical. Summer. Western N America (Washington to Baja California).

**M. madioides** (Nutt.) Greene. Perenn. to 80cm. Stems simple, hirsute below, glandular-pubesc. above. Lvs mostly opposite, to 13×1.5cm, basal lvs rosulate, linear to linear-oblong, entire to toothed. Capitula in a raceme or cyme, usually shortly pedunculate; ray florets 8–15. Fr. hemispheric; pappus of 5–8 scales, to 1mm. Summer. Western N America (Vancouver Is. to California). Z8.

**M. sativa** Molina. CHILE TARWEED; COAST TARWEED; MADIA OIL PLANT. Annual to 1.3m. Stems branched above, glandular. Lvs to 20×1.5cm, fairly crowded, alternate, lanceolate to linear, broad at base, tar-scented, basal lvs opposite. Capitula in racemes, panicles or glomerules, short-pedunculate; ray florets 5–12, to 6mm. Fr. oblanceolate. Summer. Western N America, Chile.

**M. nuttallii** A. Gray. See *M. madioides*.
**M. viscosa** Cav. See *M. sativa*.

**Maesa** Forssk. (From Arabic *maas*, applied to a species of the genus not in general cultivation.) Myrsinaceae. About 100 species of woody, evergreen, perennial, erect or scandent shrubs and small trees to 10m. Leaves alternate, entire or toothed, simple, often gland-dotted. Inflorescence an axillary raceme or panicle; flowers small, white, on bracteate pedicels; calyx 5-lobed; corolla campanulate or almost so; stamens 5; ovary half-inferior. Fruit a fleshy drupe, calyx and style persistent at apex, many-seeded. Tropical and subtropical areas, excluding Americas. Z10.

CULTIVATION As for *Ardisia*.

**M. indica** (Roxb.) Wallich. Shrub or small tree, to 10m. Lvs to 18cm, elliptic-oblong to elliptic, toothed, coriaceous. Infl. a many-fld axillary or terminal raceme, fls white, fragrant. Fr. creamy-white, edible. Early winter. India.

**M. japonica** (Thunb.) Moritzi. Shrub or small tree, 1–5m. Lvs to 15cm, obovate or oblong-ovate to elliptic-lanceolate, glossy-green above, paler beneath, entire to serrate. Infl. a short, axillary raceme or racemose panicle, fls white. E Asia.

**Magnolia** L. (For Pierre Magnol (1638–1715), Professor of Botany and Director of Montpellier Botanic Gardens, France.) Magnoliaceae. Some 125 species of evergreen or deciduous shrubs or trees. Bark smooth to rough; buds silver to grey-pubescent, enveloped by stipular scales, abscising and leaving annular scars; young twigs smooth, glaucous, sericeous or hispidulous. Leaves alternate or clustered and appearing whorled, entire, broadly elliptic to ovate, glossy, glabrous or pubescent, sometimes emarginate at apex, attenuate, cordate, cuneate or rounded at base; stipules caducous; petioles with basal stipule scars. Flowers large, stellar or cupulate, terminal, solitary, appearing before leaves in some spp., often fragrant; perianth segments 6–33 in whorls of 3 or more, outer whorl often reduced, sepal-like, downy, caducous, others white or rose pink to purple, in some species yellow or green; stamens arranged spirally, soon abscising, pollen sacs narrow, dehiscing laterally or inwardly; gynoecium sessile or short-stipitate, cylindric to subglobose; carpels many, superior, spirally arranged, each with 2 ovules. Fruiting cones subglobose to cylindric, formed from the aggregation of free, longitudinally dehiscent follicles and often asymmetric due to ovule abortion; seeds 1–2 per follicle with an outer orange or pink arilloid layer, ultimately suspended on fragile threads. Japan, Himalaya, W Malesia (to Java), Eastern N America to Tropical America.

CULTIVATION *Magnolia* ranks amongst the most ancient of the Angiosperm genera; the fossil remains of the simple flowers found in the Tertiary rocks are immediately recognizable and their perfection has suffered little evolutionary change in 100 million years, showing a fascinating parallel with the beetles which are their major pollinators (*Nitidulidae* spp.), also found in abundance in the Tertiary period.

Magnolias are valued for their exceptional longevity and for their exquisite and fragrant blooms, which include some of the largest flowers of any tree or shrub grown in the gardens of temperate zones, often, as with the deciduous members of the section Yulania, carried precociously and conspicuously in advance of the foliage. With the notable exception of the American *M. grandiflora*, the Asiatics are nearly always superior in their flowering display to those from other regions; the majority, although slow to mature, become increasingly floriferous with age.

As with many plants used medicinally, their cultivation has a long history; both Asiatic and American species have been used in local herbal medicine for their aromatic, stimulant and tonic virtues. In China, where *M. denudata* is known to have been in cultivation for almost 1400 years, it had both medicinal and religious significance and many cherished and venerable specimens were grown in Temple gardens, symbolic of candour, purity and the feminine (Yin) principle.

With the exception of the few tropical species, mostly from high altitudes in the equatorial mountains of tropical America, the majority of *Magnolia* spp. occur in the northern hemisphere, usually in moist, humus rich soils. Some, such as *M. fraseri*, grow on river banks, in swamp and on moist bottomlands, whilst others, like *M. delavayi*, occur in relatively open habitats and in scrub on limestone or sandstone to altitudes of 1200–3300m/3936ft–10,824ft. They are, however, found predominantly in thicket, woodland and forest habitats throughout their natural range, from the low-altitude moist woodland of *M. virginiana* and coastal plain forests of *M. pyramidata* to the primeval forests of the Japanese Islands for the exotically fragrant *M. hypoleuca*. *M. campbellii* and its subspecies *M.c.* ssp. *mollicomata* are found at high altitudes in the Sikkim Himalaya, the last discovered by

**Magnolia** (×0.66) (a) *M.*× *soulangiana* (b) *M. acuminata* (c) *M. acuminata* var. *subcordata* (d) *M. liliiflora* (e) *M. denudata*

**Magnolia** (×0.4) (a) *M. fraseri* (b) *M. hypoleuca* (c) *M. macrophylla*

George Forrest in 1904, amongst the drifting snows of the Mekong valley in Yunnan, at altitudes of 3050m/10,000ft, in natural association with *Viburnum, Daphne* and *Rhododendron* spp.

Magnolias are not difficult to cultivate provided that certain fundamental conditions are satisfied in siting, planting and management. Most species are best sited with the maximum wind shelter possible since the branches tend to be brittle; this is especially important for the large leaved evergreens and for the spring-flowering species of the *Yulania* subgenus with their precocious flowers, so that the blooms are protected from bruising spring winds. A protective screen of conifers or other evergreens (which incidentally provide a dark background to enhance the display) is beneficial in this regard as well as helping to protect the flowers from damaging spring radiation frosts. In general, it is essential to survey and avoid likely frost pockets where cold air cannot drain freely away before planting any of the spring flowering species.

Given adequate moisture at the roots most enjoy full sun and indeed need it in most parts of the UK, as there is empirical evidence from the US and southern Europe that light levels and possibly spring temperatures both enhance the depth of flower colour. Conversely, the late spring and summer flowering species of the Oyama section, such as *Mm. wilsonii, sieboldii, sieboldii* ssp. *sinensis* and *globosa*, prefer light dappled shade or some shade for at least part of the day to grow freely and produce good quality flowers. They are woodland natives under natural conditions and their pendent flowers are seen at their best when the plants are drawn up a little by open woodland. They are also pliable enough to espalier on to a shady and wind-sheltered wall. (*M. stellata*, which responds well to spur pruning immediately after flowering is eminently suitable for similar treatment.) The tree Asiatics such as *Mm. campbellii, dawsoniana, sargentiana* var. *robusta* and their derivatives are well suited, wherever possible, to situations where their glamorous flowers can be viewed from above or at eye level and at close quarters, for example, below a terrace wall. The more compact *M. stellata* and its cvs are good at the pathside, where their fragrance can be readily appreciated. The low-growing species with small leaves frequently show remarkable tolerance of exposure although the blooms are just as sensitive to bruising by wind; with other deciduous species, they are very tolerant of atmospheric pollution, suiting them well to small urban gardens and courtyards. In Japan, *M. stellata* (shidekobushi) is often pot grown for house and garden decoration.

Magnolias thrive in a wide variety of soil types. Provided there is an adequate supply of moisture and drainage is good, most will at least tolerate alkaline conditions; given adequate reserves of humus in the soil, *Mm. acuminata, acuminata* var. *cordata, delavayi, kobus* and its cultivars, ×*loebneri, sieboldii, sieboldii* ssp. *sinensis* and *wilsonii* are amongst the most tolerant of soil alkalinity, and *M. grandiflora* has even been known to thrive in gardens with relatively shallow soils over chalk. The ideal soil is a medium, neutral to acid loam with plenty of organic matter to hold moisture and provide necessary good aeration for the wide-ranging, shallow roots.

Once established, magnolias are easy-going plants and will put up with a range of different climatic conditions. Several species have shown reliable tolerances to temperatures as low as −28°C/−18°F, including *Mm. acuminata, kobus* and *stellata*, along with *M.* ×*loebneri* (*M. kobus* ×*stellata*). In addition, in zones where normal winter temperatures fall to between −15 and −20°C/−4°F, *Mm. cylindrica, fraseri, hypoleuca, liliiflora, macrophylla,* ×*soulangiana,* and *virginiana* have grown well, suffering damage only in unusually cold seasons when temperatures as low as −35°C/−30°F were recorded. These temperatures are based on those at the George Landis Arboretum, Esperance, New York, and at Brookville, Pennsylvania, and it seems likely that such tolerance may be a function of a summer climate that allows good ripening of the wood. Similarly, *M. grandiflora* will tolerate temperatures as low as −17°C/1°F in the US and with shelter from cold, drying winds and protection from freezing at the roots it can be grown as far north as Philadelphia and New York State. In the British Isles, however, *M. grandiflora* requires wall protection at temperatures below −5°C/23°F to −10°C/14°F. Other records indicate that *Mm. cordata, denudata, liliiflora,* ×*thompsoniana* and *M. sieboldii* are hardy to −20°C/−4°F, *Mm. ashei, sargentiana, sieboldii* ssp. *sinensis* and *wilsonii* to −15°C/5°F. *Mm. campbellii, dawsoniana* and *globosa* are tolerant to −10°C/14°F; in all cases hardiness refers to survival of the specimen: those which flower early in spring are frequently subject to spoilage of the flowers by frost.

Although optimal rainfall is in the region of about 720mm/28in. per annum, magnolias tolerate drier climates and soils, and in the 1989 drought in southern England established *M.* ×*soulangiana* and Gresham hybrids that were well mulched continued to grow freely, whilst neighbouring *Rhododendron* spp. were burned and severely damaged.

Much of this tolerance is a function of care taken in planting, in preparing a generous pit excavated to about 1.5m/5ft diameter and with a trenched subsoil. Liberal quantities of humus in the form of leafmould, unlimed compost or turfsoil should be added to the excavated topsoil before it is returned. Deep planting is one of the most common causes of poor growth or even subsequent death in newly planted magnolias; since they are naturally surface rooting, planting too deep may lead to root suffocation. The collar must be well clear of the soil and the shoulders of the main roots where they join the stem barely below the surface, with a generous mulch of some loose, moisture retentive material preserving the aeration necessary for free and vigorous root growth. This is particularly important on heavier soils. With budded or grafted plants no attempt should be made to cover the point of union in the hope of stimulating roots from the scion as is the practice for example with tree paeonies. It will lead at best to weak and sullen growth and at worst to a slow and dwindling death. In any event the objective is highly unlikely to be achieved.

Magnolias may be moved bare-rooted though most are now containerized. To leave planting until the sap begins to rise as is sometimes advocated is doubtful advice. Container-grown plants may be planted at any time, provided that proper attention is paid to watering during establishment, and the best time for planting bare rooted or balled plants is early in the autumn to give them time to establish before the onset of hard weather. Most magnolias will take a season to settle in and with a generous mulch to maintain moisture levels during dry spells will grow on strongly; in prolonged periods of dry weather, irrigation must be thorough and plentiful. The best mulch is leafmould, but well-rotted farmyard or stable manure is good and even bark, although this lacks nutrients, is quite adequate to suppress weeds and conserve moisture; great care is necessary when weeding to avoid damage to the shallow root system and weed suppression is always to be preferred. Finally, staking is required to prevent wind rock and if a tree form is desired a tall stake is necessary *ab initio* to support a strong and dominant leader.

During the first year after planting a light surface dressing of general fertilizer can be applied, preferably incorporated with a bulky organic mulch but the best aid to rapid establishment and to optimum growth in the following year is foliar feeding on at least fortnightly intervals up to early autumn. Magnolias are sensitive to excessive applications of fertilizer which can cause leaf burn and even death. After establishment, however, surface applications are beneficial.

Pruning is generally a simple matter of shaping the plant at planting time by removing weak and badly placed growth and tipping back long shoots. Routine pruning is usually restricted to removing deadwood and watershoots, but where a specimen outgrows its allotted space, it can be pruned hard back immediately after flowering for deciduous species and in early spring for evergreens. It is important when removing larger branches to preserve the branch/bark ridge leaving the branch collar intact; if necessary apply an anti-fungal wound treatment based on *Trichoderma viride*. The mass of adventitious shoots which sometimes result can be rubbed out apart from the required replacement growth.

Magnolias have a reputation for being difficult to propagate. It is true that the great Asiatics will generally not root from cuttings

**Magnolia** (×0.66) (a) *M. grandiflora* (b) *M. virginiana* (c) *M. delavayi*

and need to be grafted or chip budded. While the care required and the level of success may not be favourable to nursery production in quantity, for the amateur who requires only small numbers it is a feasible proposition using the side veneer method, either in late winter or late summer under glass.

The Soulangianas, the De Vos and Kosar hybrids, and the early-flowering species of the Oyama section can be grown from softwood cuttings with mist and bottom heat at 21–24°C/70–75°F, or, with careful management from semi-ripe cuttings using the warm bench and polythene system or the closed case with bottom heat. Root in sharp sand or in a mix comprising two parts moss peat one part sharp sand. Light wounding and treatment with 0.8% I.B.A. are both advantageous. Cuttings will take 6–8 weeks to root in trays or pots and should be overwintered *in situ*, leaving potting on until growth has started in the following spring. They should be kept as dry as possible over winter and cool but frost free.

Simple layering in early spring is often a good alternative using standard procedures, although species with a stubby habit of growth like *M. stellata* may not produce suitable material and where specimens are large and high branching it may be awkward to effect. In commercial nurseries, it is common practice to stool stock specimens grown on good fertile soil to force them to produce long flexible growth from the base; stems tongued and pegged in spring will be ready to sever in the following spring, to be lined out in late autumn/early winter. Autumn layers of the current season's wood with the leaves removed are treated in a similar fashion, but will take two years to root. An alternative for the amateur gardener, though not for the timid, involves cutting a single stem hard back in early spring to force new growth suitable for layering in the following spring. Magnolias generally show good regeneration and often produce strong growth even from old wood.

The precocious flowering species and summer-flowering evergreens appear to need hotter summers than those usually experienced in the UK to set seed, although *M. sieboldii* ssp. *sinensis, M. wilsonii* and others of the Oyama section frequently produce abundant seed. When available, seed is an excellent method of propagation for the species and will yield strong young plants that grow away very quickly although they will show the normal range of variation and may take several years after first flowering to achieve good quality blooms. Seed should be sown fresh or vernalized for spring sowing; store cleaned seed for about 100 days at 2–4°C/36–39°F. Dried seed may germinate after a year's dormancy but frequently fails to do so.

Magnolias are remarkably trouble-free and most problems stem from defective planting or management. Chlorosis can be caused by excessive alkalinity and by both excesses and insufficiencies of potash, but should not be confused with the natural pallor of the young leaves on many species; lime-induced chlorosis is quickly remedied by foliar applications of iron chelates (sequestered iron). On alkaline soils, care must be taken to ensure that mulching materials such as leafmould and garden compost are lime free.

A black bacterial leaf blotch is probably caused by *Pseudomonas syringae*, controlled by copper-based fungicidal sprays although it may be best to destroy badly affected plants. Pale irregular spots on the leaves of *M. grandiflora* are caused by the fungus *Phyllosticta magnoliae* but its effects are usually cosmetic. *Magnolia* spp. are also affected by armillaria root rot, coral spot, and grey mould, whilst mottling and various other leaf patterns are possibly caused by cucumber mosaic virus.

Capsid bugs can cause unsightly puncturing of the foliage but these and the common army of fly, aphid and molluscs are easily controlled by a proprietary insecticide/molluscicide. In the US, *Magnolia* spp. are sometimes attacked by magnolia scale. Mealybug and red spider mite are the major pests under glass but biological control is now available for the latter, otherwise a suitable acaricide will curtail a particularly bad infestation.

**1** Undersurface of leaves glabrous.

1.1 Undersurface of leaves glaucous or glaucescent.
*M. delavayi.*

1.2 Undersurface of leaves green.
*M. coco.*

**2** Undersurface of leaves pubescent.

2.1 Undersurface of leaves more or less rusty-red or brown-pubescent.
*M. grandiflora.*

2.2 Undersurface of leaves silver-velvety pubescent (trees moreover sometimes erratically deciduous).
*M. virginiana.*

**3** Leaves in distinct clusters or rosettes.

3.1 Flowers appearing before leaves (leaves in rosettes only on short shoots; on main shoots leaves alternate); leaves relatively small.
*Mm. cylindrica, dawsoniana.*

3.2 Flowers appearing after leaves; leaves relatively large.

3.2.1 Leaves auriculate (with ear-like lobes) at base.
*Mm. fraseri, macrophylla.*

3.2.2 Leaves without distinct ear-like lobes at base.
*Mm. ashei,* 'Charles Coates', *hypoleuca, officinalis, pyramidata, tripetala.*

**4** Leaves alternate, not forming distinct clusters or rosettes.

4.1 Flowers precocious, appearing before leaves (or as leaves are appearing).

4.1.1 Leaves fairly obviously pubescent on undersurface.
*M. campbellii.*

4.1.2 Leaves minutely pubescent or glabrous on undersurface, the midrib and veins sometimes more conspicuously pubescent.

a. Leaves green beneath.
*Mm. biondii, cylindrica, dawsoniana, denudata* (*heptapeta* auct.), *kobus* (*praecocissima*), *liliiflora* (*quinquepeta* auct.), ×*loebneri,* ×*soulangiana, stellata* (*tomentosa*).

b. Leaves more or less glaucous beneath.
*M. acuminata* var. *cordata* (also flowering with or after the leaves), *M.* ×*proctoriana, M. salicifolia, M. sargentiana, M. sprengeri.*

4.2 Flowers appearing after development of leaves (or sometimes almost simultaneously).

4.2.1 Leaves softly pubescent on under surface, the hairs along the veins and midrib sometimes appearing brown when dry.
*Mm. globosa, sinensis, wilsonii.*

4.2.2 Leaves sparsely pubescent or glabrous on undersurface.
*Mm. acuminata, acuminata* var. cordata (leaves developing as flowers open, but sometimes flowering a second time late in the season), ×*wiesneri* (×*watsonii*).

***M. acuminata*** (L.) L. CUCUMBER TREE. Deciduous tree to 30m; habit conical at first, later candelabriform, bark brown suffused grey, grooved and coarse with age. Lvs to 24cm, ovate to elliptic or oblong-ovate, apex acute to acuminate, base often unequal, cuneate, truncate, dark green above, downy or glaucescent beneath; petioles to 3.5cm. Fls cupulate; erect; pedicels to 3cm, glabrous; seg. 9, grey-green tinged green to yellow-green, sometimes flushed glaucous maroon, oblanceolate to oblong-spathulate, to 9×3cm, outer 3 seg. to 3cm, becoming reflexed; stamens to 1cm. Cones ovoid to oblong-cylindric, asymmetric, green, later red-brown. Spring–summer. Eastern N America. 'Variegata': lvs stippled bright gold. f. ***aurea*** (Ashe) Hardin. Inner seg. golden yellow. var. ***subcordata*** (Spach) Dandy. YELLOW CUCUMBER TREE. Habit more shrubby, to 7.5m. Twigs densely sericeous. Lvs to 15cm, obovate-oblong, base ovate, seldom cordate, pubesc. beneath. Fls faintly scented; seg. to 7cm, lime-green to clear yellow; pedicels stout, velutinous. 'Butterflies': fls strong yellow, finely shaped. 'Golden Glow': fls yellow. 'Elizabeth' (*M. acuminata* × *M. denudata*): fls precocious, yellow fading to cream. 'Gold Star' (*M. acuminata* var. *subcordata* 'Miss Honeybee' × *M. stellata* 'Rubra'): densely branching shrub bearing yellow fls close in form and attitude to a gardenia, on bare twigs. 'Miss Honeybee': fls large, pale yellow, borne even on young plants; fr. vivid red. 'Yellow Bird' (*M. acuminata* × *M.* ×*brooklynensis*): fls yellow. 'Yellow Lantern' (*M. acuminata* × *M.* ×*soulangiana* 'Alexandrina'): habit upright, large; fls lemon yellow. Z4.

***M. amoena*** Cheng. Tree, 8–12m. Lvs 10–15×3.5–5cm. Fls 6cm diam., cupular, appearing before lvs, fragrant; seg. 9, oblanceolate or nearly spathulate, pale to mid-pink; fil. purple-red. E China. Z8.

***M. ashei*** Weatherby. As for *M. macrophylla* but smaller, to 10m. Twigs glaucous and downy at first. Lvs to 60cm, borne in pseudowhorls, broadly oblanceolate, basally cordate to auriculate, thin-textured, glossy pale green above, grey-green beneath, margins wavy; petioles with long stipule-scars. Fls smaller than *M. macrophylla*, to 13.5×6cm. Cones to 7cm, cylindric, ovoid. US (NW Florida). Z7.

***M. biondii*** Pamp. Closely related to *M. salicifolia* but lvs green beneath, vegetative buds and pedicels sericeous. Fls 9–10cm diam., lemon-scented; seg. 6, white flushed pink at base, outer 3 1.5× as wide as inner. Seeds strongly and unilaterally grooved. C China. Z8.

***M.*** **×*brooklynensis*** Kalmb. (*M. acuminata* × *M. liliiflora.*) Habit as for *M. acuminata*, the seed parent, but bark smooth, grey. Immature fl. buds rose to

**Magnolia** (×0.66) (a) *M. kobus* (b) *M. stellata* (c) *M. salicifolia* (d) *M.× loebneri*

purple, shaded yellow and green; fls campanulate, to 9cm across, erect; seg. 6. Spring–summer. Garden origin. 'Evamaria': fls purple washed with ochre. 'Woodsman': outer seg. green, otherwise purple and, at centre, soft pink fading to white. Z5.

***M. campbellii*** Hook. & Thoms. ssp. ***campbellii.*** Robust deciduous tree to 30m; twigs yellow-green, later grey to ochre. Lvs to 23×11cm, elliptic-ovate to oblong-lanceolate, acute to acuminate, base rounded to cuneate, unequal, pale green, glabrous or finely sericeous beneath, coriaceous, dark green above. Fls appearing before lvs, erect; seg. to 14×6cm, to 16, broad, fleshy, concave, white or crimson to rose-pink, paler above, inner whorls erect, enclosing gynoecium, outer whorls often reflexed. Cones to 15cm, erect, later pendent, cylindric. Early spring. Himalaya to China. Z9. 'Betty Jessel': fls bright red-pink, almost crimson. 'Darjeeling': fls very dark pink to claret. 'Ethel Hillier': vigorous and fast-growing; fls large, white, faintly flushed pink at base. 'Late Pink': fls late, pink. 'Sidbury': fls close to *M. campbellii* ssp. *campbellii* but earlier. 'Trewithen Dark Form': seg. light carmine beneath, dark pink above. 'Trewithen Light Form': seg. dark pink beneath, pink washed white above. var. ***alba*** Griff. Fls white. The form most often found in the wild. 'Maharaja': fls large, white, purple at base. 'Maharanee': fls white. 'Strybing White': fls large, white. ssp. ***mollicomata*** (W.W. Sm.) Johnstone. Twigs and pedicels thickly bronze-downy; buds narrow-ovoid. Hardier than *M. campbellii* spp. *campbellii* in northern temperate zones and will flower while still young. The fls are produced earlier than in ssp. *campbellii* and are usually bright pink beneath, white above. Z8. See also *M.* ×*raffillii*.

***M.* 'Charles Coates'.** *(M. sieboldii × M. tripetala.)* Small tree to 6m. Lvs 26×13cm, borne in whorls at branch apices, ovate, acute, base cuneate. Fls 10cm diam., fragrant, ivory-white with a showy central boss of red stamens, erect, dish-shaped. Z6.

***M. coco*** (Lour.) DC. Evergreen shrub to 120cm. Lvs to 26×8.5cm, elliptic, attenuate, glossy dark green, coriaceous; petiole to 15mm. Fls short lived, nocturnally very fragrant, nectar glands present in flowers, pedicel to 2cm; larger seg. 6–9, cupped, creamy white, often tipped pale rose. S China, Java. Z9.

***M. cylindrica*** Wils. Deciduous tree to 9m. Bark grey to buff. Twigs rusty brown, sericeous when young. Lvs to 15×6cm, obovate-elliptic, glabrous, dark green with distinctly reticulate venation above, paler beneath with adpressed pubescence on major veins; petiole to 2cm. Fls appearing before lvs, cupular, resembling *M. denudata*; seg. to 10×4cm, creamy-white tinged pink at base, usually 9, spathulate to obovate, outer 3 papery, brown. Cones to 8×3cm, cylindric. Spring. E China. Similar to *M. salicifolia* and *M. kobus* but cones cylindric. It has been suggested that plants as *M. cylindrica* show close affinities with *M. denudata* or *M. soulangiana* and are of hybrid origin; for a fuller discussion, see Treseder (1978). 'Albatross' (*M. cylindrica* × *M.* ×*veitchii*): fast-growing, erect tree; fls large, pure white, borne profusely in early spring. Z6.

***M. dawsoniana*** Rehd. & Wils. Deciduous tree or shrub to 12m. Branching pattern open, becoming twiggy; twigs glabrous or, rarely, sericeous. Lvs 13.5×8cm, obovate, occasionally elliptic, short-acuminate, occasionally emarginate, base unequal, rounded to cuneate, burnished dark green, midrib pubesc., coriaceous above, conspicuously reticulate, puberulent, pale green beneath; petioles to 3cm with a short basal stipule-scar. Fls borne before lvs, fragrant, held horizontally or nodding; pedicels to 1.5cm, pubesc. to glabrous; seg. 11×5cm, usually 9, recurving, ultimately drooping, oblanceolate to oblong-spathulate, white to pale rose, pale pink above; stamens to 1.8cm, scarlet. Spring. China (E Sikang). Easily distinguished from *M. sargentiana* by its bushier, free-flowering habit and clearly reticulate venation. 'Chyverton': hardier than the typical species and possibly a hybrid between *M. dawsoniana* and *M. sprengeri* 'Diva'; fls frost-tolerant, bright crimson, colouring more deeply in cold weather. 'Clark's Variety': fls deep pink, produced on young plants. Z9.

***M. delavayi*** Franch. Bold evergreen tree, to 10m, but often cut back by hard winters. Branches sparse, robust; bark grey, fissured; twigs simple, erect, glabrous blue-green, sometimes glaucous, terminating in a glabrous, sharply conical inrolled bud, reminiscent of larger-leaved *Ficus* spp. Lvs to 30×17cm+, ovate to oblong, sinuate, apex mucronate, base round to cordate, coriaceous, glabrous, deep sea-green above, grey-green, glaucescent beneath; petiole to 7.5cm, stout. Fls to 20cm across, slightly fragrant, short-lived; outer seg. 3, reflexed, green fading off-white, inner seg. 6–7, to 10×5cm in 2 whorls, fleshy, ivory to topaz, cupped. Cones to 20cm, ovoid-cylindric, erect. Late summer. SW China (Yunnan). Z9.

***M. denudata*** Desr. YULAN; LILY TREE. Deciduous tree to 15m, usually less in cult. Habit broadly pyramidal; branching frequent, divaricate then arching; young twigs pubesc. Lvs to 15cm, obovate to ovate, abruptly acute, base cuneate, softly pubesc. beneath; petioles to 2cm, basal scars short. Fls to 15cm diam. citrus-scented, appearing before lvs, goblet-shaped, erect; seg. to 7.5cm, 9, white to ivory. Cones to 15cm, fusiform, erect. E & S China. 'Purple Eye': habit broadly spreading; fls highly fragrant, inner seg. snow-white, flushed purple at base. Z6.

***M.* De Vos** and **Kosar Hybrids**. *(M. liliiflora* 'Nigra' × *M. stellata* 'Rosea'.) 'Anne': early flowering (mid April); fls erect, 6.5×10cm, seg. 6–8, dark claret. 'Betty': early flowering (mid April) and vigorous; fls very large, to 20cm diam., seg. to 19, dark claret beneath, cream above. 'Judy': fls small, to 7.5cm diam., seg. 10, red-purple beneath, cream above. 'Randy': erect and columnar, profusely flowering in late April, fls to 12.5cm diam., claret beneath, white above. 'Ricky': vigorous, erect, columnar; fls to 15cm diam., red-purple, late April. 'Susan': compact in habit; fls fragrant, seg. claret, slightly twisted, late April. *(M. liliiflora* 'Reflorescens' × *M. stellata* 'Waterlily'.) 'George Henry Kern': fls produced over a long period (spring to midsummer), seg. 8–10, strap-shaped, heavy-textured, rose-pink in bud, opening pale pink. In N America, colour is often deeper still. 'Jane': strong and vigorous, late flowering with small fls to 10cm diam., fragrant, red purple beneath, snow white above. 'Lilenny'; probably also belongs here. 'Pinkie': late-flowering, habit more spreading, fls to 18cm diam., seg. 12, pale, mauve beneath, white above. across, 12 tepals, claret outside, white inside. Z5.

***M. fraseri*** Walter. EAR-LEAVED UMBRELLA TREE. Erect deciduous tree to 10m, allied to *M. macrophylla*. Bark smooth, grey or brown; shoots glabrous, lf scars transverse-elliptic. Lvs to 27×18cm, borne in false whorls at branch tips, rather thin-textured, obovate, obtuse to acute, base deeply cordate or auriculate, glabrous light green throughout, sometimes glaucous beneath; petiole to 6cm+. Fls appearing after lvs, fragrant, tulip-shaped, expanding later, to 20cm diam.; pedicels to 3.5cm; seg. 9, inner seg. to 12×5cm, white tinted yellow at first, later ivory, spathulate to obovate, bases clawed, outer seg. deflexed, tinged green. Cones to 11cm, ellipsoid, bright red, later brown suffused purple. Spring. SE US (mts). Z6.

***M.* Freeman Hybrids**. *(M. grandiflora × M. virginiana.)* Plants arising from crosses made the US National Arboretum in 1930, they flower freely from May to July, often when still young, as do vegetatively propagated plants of *M. grandiflora*; they are also hardier in many areas of the US than *M. grandiflora*, the pollen-parent. The fls and lvs are generally somewhat smaller and tighter than in *M. grandiflora* and of a finer colour, the fls being virginal white, the lvs a strong glossy green. It is likely that these species hybridize naturally in the northernmost regions of *M. grandiflora's* range, also that *M. grandiflora* 'Exmouth' is in fact a hybrid. 'Freeman': hardy, early flowering; fls larger than in *M. virginiana*. 'Maryland': fls similar to 'Freeman' but larger, lemon-scented. 'Timeless Beauty': dense, upright habit, long-flowering; fls white to ivory, cupped, spicily fragrant. Z5.

***M. globosa*** Hook. & Thoms. Deciduous shrub or tree to 7m. Branches spreading; twigs brown, rusty-red pubesc., later glabrous. Lvs 21×9cm, elliptic to obovate, acute to curved, base rounded, grey-green and rusty- or golden-pubesc. at first, especially the midvein, later dark glossy green above, glaucous and finely pubesc. beneath; petioles with long basal stipule-scars. Fls to 12cm diam., pendent, opening after lvs, ovoid, subglobose or cupulate; pedicel to 6.5cm; seg. 9–12, ivory, inner seg. 7×3cm, spathulate to obovate or elliptic, apices rounded; stamens to 1.7cm, purple tinged red. Cones to 8cm, cylindric, pendent, pink, later crimson-brown. Summer. Sikkim, E Nepal, Bhutan, NE Assam to SE Tibet, Burma, W China. Indian forms of this species are taller and hardier than those plants originally collected by Forrest in the Tsarong region of SE Tibet. Z9.

***M. grandiflora*** L. LARGE-FLOWERED MAGNOLIA; BULL BAY; SOUTHERN MAGNOLIA. Evergreen tree, to 30m. Bark brown or grey; young shoots and buds rusty-tomentose. Lvs to 20×9cm, elliptic to ovate or subglobose, obtuse to short-acuminate, base attenuate, rounded or cuneate, stiffly coriaceous, glossy dark green above, rust-red pubesc. beneath, falling after 2 years; petioles to 3cm, robust, lacking stipule scars. Fls to 25cm diam. fragrant, erect; seg. 9–12, occasionally more, the 3 outermost seg. sepaloid, the others to 12×9cm, creamy white, obovate or spathulate, fleshy, cupped; stamens to 2cm, fil. purple. Cones to 7.5cm, ovoid; follicles puberulent. Summer–autumn. SE US. 'Angustifolia': lvs to 20×5cm, narrowly obovate-elliptic. 'Cairo': early and long-flowering, lvs pliable and glossy. 'Charles Dickens': lvs broad and blunt, fls large, fruit red. 'Edith Bogue': notable for hardiness. 'Exmouth' ('Exoniensis', 'Lanceolata', 'Stricta'): habit conic; lvs narrow, acuminate, finely pubesc. beneath, margins recurved; fls to 25cm diam.; possibly the result of *M. grandiflora* ×*M. virginiana*. 'Ferruginea': erect and compact, lvs rust-brown tomentose beneath, glossy dark green above. 'Galissonière': very hardy, regular in habit, lvs russet beneath. 'Gloriosa': habit compact; fls to 35cm diam. 'Goliath': habit bushy; lvs short, broad, obtuse, blistered, glabrous beneath. 'Little Gem': dwarf and slow growing (to 4m in 15 years); fls profuse, white, cup-shaped. 'Nantensis': fls profuse, double. 'Praecox': early and long-flowering. 'Praecox Fastigiata': early and long-flowering, narrow and erect in habit. 'Russet': early blooming, compact, upright and pyramidal growth, lvs long, dark green above, rusty and suede-like beneath, fls cream, fragrant, large to 25 by 30cm. 'Saint George': an American selection with a large number of seg. 'Saint Mary': free-flowering from early age, lvs long to 30cm, dark, rusty-tomentose beneath. 'Samuel Sommer': hardy, lvs russet-tomentose beneath, glossy green above, fls to 40cm across. 'Victoria': hardy, lvs rust beneath, fls small. See also Freeman hybrids. Z6.

***M.* Gresham Hybrids**. Strong, ascending, medium trees with scented fls composed of 12 seg., 8 reflexed at maturity, the inner 4 remaining erect. (i) Svelte Brunettes (*M. liliiflora* 'Nigra' × *M.* ×*veitchii*). 'Dark Raiment': fls to 12cm deep, red-violet. 'Heaven Scent': hardy, free-flowering, vigorous and spreading; fls to 12cm deep, flushed dark pink, honey-scented. 'Peppermint Stick': fls white, violet at base, heavily flushed deep pink, with a median longitudinal stripe of violet on the exterior. 'Raspberry Ice': fls lavender-pink, paler toward tips. 'Royal Crown': is also grown. (ii) Buxom Nordic Blondes (*M.* ×*veitchii M.* ×*soulangiana* 'Lennei Alba'). 'Manchu Fan': a popular selec-

**Magnolia** (×0.66) (a) *M. sargentiana* (b) *M. campbellii* (c) *M. cylindrica*

tion. 'Rouged Alabaster': fls white flushed clear pink. 'Sayonara': fls to 20cm diam., rounded, white flushed pink. 'Sulphur Cockatoo': fls large, fragrant, white, the inner seg. stained violet-pink at base. 'Tina Durio': vigorous fast-growing tree; fls very large, borne profusely, heavy-textured, white. (iii) *M.*×*veitchii* × *M.*×*soulangiana* 'Rustica Rubra' ('Todd Gresham', 'Darrell Dean', 'Joe McDaniel', 'Peter Smithers'): large, fast-growing trees with large cup- or bowl-shaped fls to 30cm diam., colours ranging from deep pink to rose-purple to claret. (iv) *M.*×*veitchii* 'Peter Veitch' × *M.*×*soulangiana* 'Lennei Alba'. 'Mary Nell': habit close to *M.*×*soulangiana*; fls to 25cm diam., produced relatively late in season, heavy-textured, white, stained claret at base. Z6.

***M. hypoleuca*** Sieb. & Zucc. Deciduous, to 30m, crown broadly pyramidal, branches spreading; bark pale grey; twigs smooth, tinted purple-red; buds ash-grey suffused black. Lvs to 40×20cm, obovate, base attenuate, apex obtuse, pale grey-green above, blue-green, pubesc. beneath, carried at branch tips in spreading pseudowhorls. Fls to 20cm diam., fragrant cup-shaped or spreading; seg. to 12, ivory flushed yellow-pink with age, fleshy; stamens crimson to blood-red. Cones to 20cm, oblong-cylindric, showy, red. Summer. Japan (Kurile Is.). cf. *M. officinalis*. Z6.

***M.* 'Kewensis'**. (*M. kobus* × *M. salicifolia.*) Broadly spreading small to medium tree. Lvs to 12.5×6cm, oblong-lanceolate to elliptic, resembling *M. salicifolia* but not anise-scented. Fls to 12.5cm diam., precocious, fragrant; seg. 6, snow white, spreading to nodding. Possibly a clone of *M. salicifolia*. Z6.

***M. kobus*** DC. Deciduous shrub or tree, to 30m. Habit variable, broadly spreading, conical or domed; twigs and shoots thick, congested (in types formerly described as var. borealis) or straight, slender (var. kobus). Lf buds pubesc.; lvs to 19×12cm, short-acuminate, occasionally wrinkled, veins pubesc. below. Fls to 10cm diam., appearing before lvs, erect; sepaloid seg. to 1.5cm, 3, soon abscising, petaloid seg. 7×3.5cm, usually 6, creamy white, often basally and marginally stained wine-red or pink, spathulate to obovate. Cones to 12cm, cylindric, symmetric, pink. Winter–spring. Japan (Honshu, Hokkaido). 'Wada's Memory': see *M. salicifolia*.

The typification of *M. kobus* is problematic. De Candolle based the name in part on Plate 42 of Banks's 1791 *Icones Selectae*, engraved from a drawing by Kaempfer. He also cites *M. gracilis* Salisb. in the synonymy of *M. kobus*, when this is clearly referrable to *M. liliiflora* Desr. Moreover, De Candolle's own specimen of '*M. kobus*' is also *M. liliiflora* (Koidzumi, 1929). Koidzumi rejected *M. kobus* as a confused name, proposing instead the name *M. praecocissima*. Thunberg's *M. tomentosa* (1794) is also based in part on Plate 42 of Banks's 1791 *Icones Selectae*. It also draws on foliage of an *Edgeworthia* shown fully developed alongside the flowers. This confusion led in some 19th-century texts (notably Johnson's *Gardener's Dictionary*), to the maintenance of both the names *M. gracilis* and *M. kobus*, where only *M. kobus* was meant, and, via *M. tomentosa*, to the notion that *M. kobus* was evergreen.

Veda (1986) urged the adoption of *M. praecocissima* for plants generally held to be *M. kobus* and argued that the Kaempfer/Banks plate in fact depicts *M. stellata*, to which the name *M. tomentosa* could now be properly applied. It is, however, likely that *M. kobus* and *M. stellata* will both become conserved names due to the conceptual clarity conferred on them by long use. Z5.

***M.* 'Lanarth'**. A highly distinctive plant introduced from NW Yunnan by Forrest as *M. mollicomata*. Habit vigorous, fastigiate. Lvs broad, oblong-obovate, thick. Fls close in form to *M. campbellii* ssp. *mollicomata* but opening a deep purple-red. This plant has given rise to a number of beautiful hybrids including 'Mark Jury' (*M. c.* spp. *mollicomata* 'Lanarth' group × *M. sprengeri* var. *robusta*): fls to 25cm diam., purple; 'Iolanthe' (*M.* 'Mark Jury' (Lanarth group) × *M.*×*soulangiana* 'Lennei'): fls soft violet, paler within, borne over a long season even on young plants. Z8.

***M. liliiflora*** Desr. MU-LAN; WOODY ORCHID. Deciduous shrub to 4m. Lvs to 20×10cm, elliptic to obovate, abruptly acute, sparsely pubesc., sap.-green above, slightly paler beneath with pubesc. veins; petioles to 2cm, stipule scars long, downy. Fls appearing with lvs and continuing while lvs emerge, goblet-shaped; seg. 9, the 3 outermost reduced, caducous, sepal-like, the inner 6 to 7.5cm, obovate-oblong, obtuse, concave above at tip, thick, white often flushed pink to claret above, pink to garnet beneath. Cones to 5cm, squat oblong, brown. Spring. China. The precise application of the name *M. liliiflora* has been rather confused: see *Taxon* 36:590–600 (1987), 'Rejection of the names *M. heptapeta* and *M. quinquepeta*/Magnoliaceae' for fuller discussion. 'Gracilis': habit and leaves slender and small. Fls deep purple. 'Holland Red': exceptionally dark. 'Nigra' 'Nigricans'; *M.*×*soulangiana* 'Nigra': seg. numerous, claret to amethyst above, paler below. 'O'Neill': vigorous; fls large, dark purple. *M. liliiflora* 'Nigra' has been crossed with *M. campbellii* to produce *M.* 'Star Wars', an exceptionally vigorous, well-shaped tree leaving abundant, large purple-pink fls with flamboyantly outspread seg. Z6.

***M.*×*loebneri*** Kache. (*M. kobus* × *M. stellata.*) Shrub or small tree, habit as for *M. stellata* but twigs velutinous, lvs 15×6cm, narrow-obovate, larger, fls larger with 12 spathulate seg. to 8×3cm, white, occasionally tinged pink beneath. Garden origin, *c*1910. 'Ballerina': slow-growing, late-flowering; fls fragrant, white flushed pink at base, seg. to 30. 'Leonard Messel' (possibly a hybrid of *M. kobus* × *M. stellata* 'Rosea'): hardy; fls to 13cm diam., seg. interior white, exterior lavender-purple. 'Merrill': vigorous; fls larger than *M. stellata*, semi-double, seg. 15. 'Neil McEacharn': attaining 4.5m after 15 years; fls borne in profusion, with many white and pink-flushed seg. 'Snowdrift': lvs and fls somewhat larger than typical *M.*×*loebneri*; a 12-tepalled clone. 'Spring Snow': seg. broad, white, tinted green at base. Z5.

***M. macrophylla*** Michx. LARGE-LEAVED CUCUMBER TREE; GREAT-LEAVED MACROPHYLLA; UMBRELLA TREE. Large deciduous shrub or tree to 20m; branches spreading, open; trunk to 45cm diam.; bark smooth. Lvs to 95×35cm, borne in dense false whorls, elliptic, oblanceolate to oblong-ovate, obtuse, base cordate to auriculate, pale green, glabrous above, downy white beneath. Fls fragrant, to 30cm+ diam., borne on leafy shoots; pedicels 5cm; seg. 6–9, 20×14cm, thick, matt ivory or cream, inner 3 spotted or tinged purple toward base, outer seg. narrow-spathulate, tinged green; stamens to 2cm. Cones to 9cm, ovoid to globose, rose pink; seeds red, appendaged along suture. SE US (Georgia, Alabama, north to Arkansas). Distinguished from the closely related *M. ashei* by its ovoid-globose (not ovoid-cylindric) fr. cones and its carpels, which bear an appendage along the suture. Z6.

***M.* 'Michael Rosse'**. (*M. campbellii* var. *alba* × *M. sargentiana* var. *robusta.*) Fls large, pale purple. Z9.

***M. officinalis*** Rehd. & Wils. Deciduous tree to 20m. Bark ash-grey, exfoliating in sheets; twigs initially yellow to grey-sericeous. Lvs to 40×20cm, obtuse, base attenuate, rounded, cuneate, occasionally acute, undulate, light green, glabrous above, glaucescent, downy beneath. Fls to 20cm diam., strongly fragrant; seg. cupped, 9–12, fleshy, outer 3 oblong-spathulate, thick, inner seg. 10×5cm, creamy white, bases clawed; stamens 1.5cm, numerous, red. Fr. to 15cm, oblong-ovoid, apex flattened, base rounded, basal follicles convex. W & C China. Easily distinguished from *M. hypoleuca* (which it resembles in foliage and habit) by its yellow-grey (not purple-tinged) young shoots and flat-topped fr. cones. var. ***biloba*** Rehd. & Wils. Distinguished, perhaps inadequately, from species type by its preponderance of emarginate lvs. Z8.

***M.* 'Princess Margaret'**. (*M. campbellii* var. *alba* ×*M. sargentiana* var. *robusta.*) Fls to 25cm diam., dark claret beneath, cream tinged purple above. Z9.

***M.*×*proctoriana*** Rehd. (*M. salicifolia* × *M. stellata.*) Broad, spreading, small tree to 7.5×6m. Lvs to 13×5cm, resembling *M. salicifolia* but paler beneath and less aromatic if crushed. Fls to 10cm diam., precocious, white tinted pink at base, somewhat fragrant, seg. 6–12, spreading to lax. 'Slavin's Snowy': fls fragrant, to 15cm diam., seg. 6–9, white, distinctively blotched pink at base. Z5.

***M. pyramidata*** Bartr. ex Pursh. Resembles *M. fraseri* but smaller in habit with lvs rhombic to pandurate. Cones to 5.5cm. SE US. Z8.

***M.*×*raffillii*** hort. (*M. campbellii* ssp. *campbellii* × *M. campbellii* ssp. *mollicomata.*) 'Charles Raffill': fl. buds stained claret; seg. purple-pink beneath, white stained pink at margin above. 'Kew's Surprise': fls darker pink than in 'Charles Raffill': 'Wakehurst': fls darker than in 'Charles Raffill'. Z8.

***M. salicifolia*** (Sieb. & Zucc.) Maxim.
ANISE MAGNOLIA; WILLOW-LEAF MAGNOLIA. Tree or shrub to 12m. Bark buff grey to brown tinged silver; twigs scented of lemon or anise, smooth at first, becoming somewhat warty in second season. Lvs to 12×5.5cm, narrow-oval to lanceolate, acute or rounded, base cuneate to rounded, glabrous, dull green above, pale green below, glaucous and sometimes initially finely downy. Fls precocious; pedicels glabrous; fl. buds shaggy; outer 3 seg. to 3.5×1cm, sepaloid, caducous, inner 6 seg. to 9×4cm, lanceolate to spathulate, white, occasionally tinged green or flushed pink at base beneath. Cones cylindric, to 6cm, symmetric, green, becoming purple-black; seeds scarlet, shallowly grooved. cf. *M. biondii*. Japan (Honshu, Shikoku, Kyushu). 'Else Frye': erect; lvs green above, blue-green beneath, thinly pubesc.; fls to 9cm diam., dark carmine at base fading to white at apex; fil. pink. 'Fasciata': narrowly upright in habit, with many dark shoots. 'Jermyns': slow-growing and late-flowering; lvs wider, fls larger than in type. 'Wada's Memory': small tree, habit upright, compact; lvs to 12.5×5.75cm, elliptic, green, flushed red-brown at emergence; fls to 17cm diam., fragrant white, seg. 6, at first borne horizontally, then drooping and fluttering; very possibly a natural hybrid between *M. kobus* and *M. salicifolia*. Z6.

***M. sargentiana*** Rehd. & Wils. Deciduous tree to 25m. Bark beige-grey; twigs glabrous, yellow-green at first, later grey or grey-brown. Lvs to 18×11cm, elliptic to obovate, occasionally oblong or suborbicular, apex rounded, emarginate or acuminate, base cuneate, deep glossy green above, paler, grey-pubesc. below, except on glabrous midrib; petioles glabrous, slender. Fl. buds ovoid-acute, grey-pubesc.; fls fragrant, precocious, pendent; seg. 10–14, to 9×3.5cm, spathulate or oblong-oblanceolate, white to pale purple-pink above, purple-pink below; stamens to 1.8cm. Cones cylindric, to 11cm, asymmetric, usually twisted due to erratic development of carpels; seed coat orange-red. Spring. W China (N Yunnan, Sichuan, E Sikang). 'Treve Holman': one of the many offspring arising from the union of *M. sargentiana* and *M. campbellii*. var. ***robusta*** Rehd. & Wils. Habit bushy. Lvs oblanceolate, to 21×9cm, emarginate. Fls to 30cm+ diam., initially rose-purple. 'Caerhays Belle' (*M. s.* var. *robusta* × *M. sprengeri* 'Diva'): seg. broad, pale carmine. Z9.

***M. sieboldii*** K. Koch. Deciduous shrub or tree to 10m; branches slender. Lvs 12×10cm, oblong to ovate-elliptic, abruptly acute, base cuneate to subcordate, deep green, subglabrous above, glaucescent, pubesc. beneath; petioles to 4.5cm, initially pubesc. Fls to 10cm, produced over long season, fragrant, cupulate, later dish-shaped, held more or less horizontally, not nodding as in *M. wilsonii* and *M. sieboldii* ssp. sinensis; pedicels 2.5–6cm, bowed upwards, pubesc.; seg. to 12, white, outer 3 reflexed, inner seg. obovate to spathulate, to 6×4.5cm; sta-

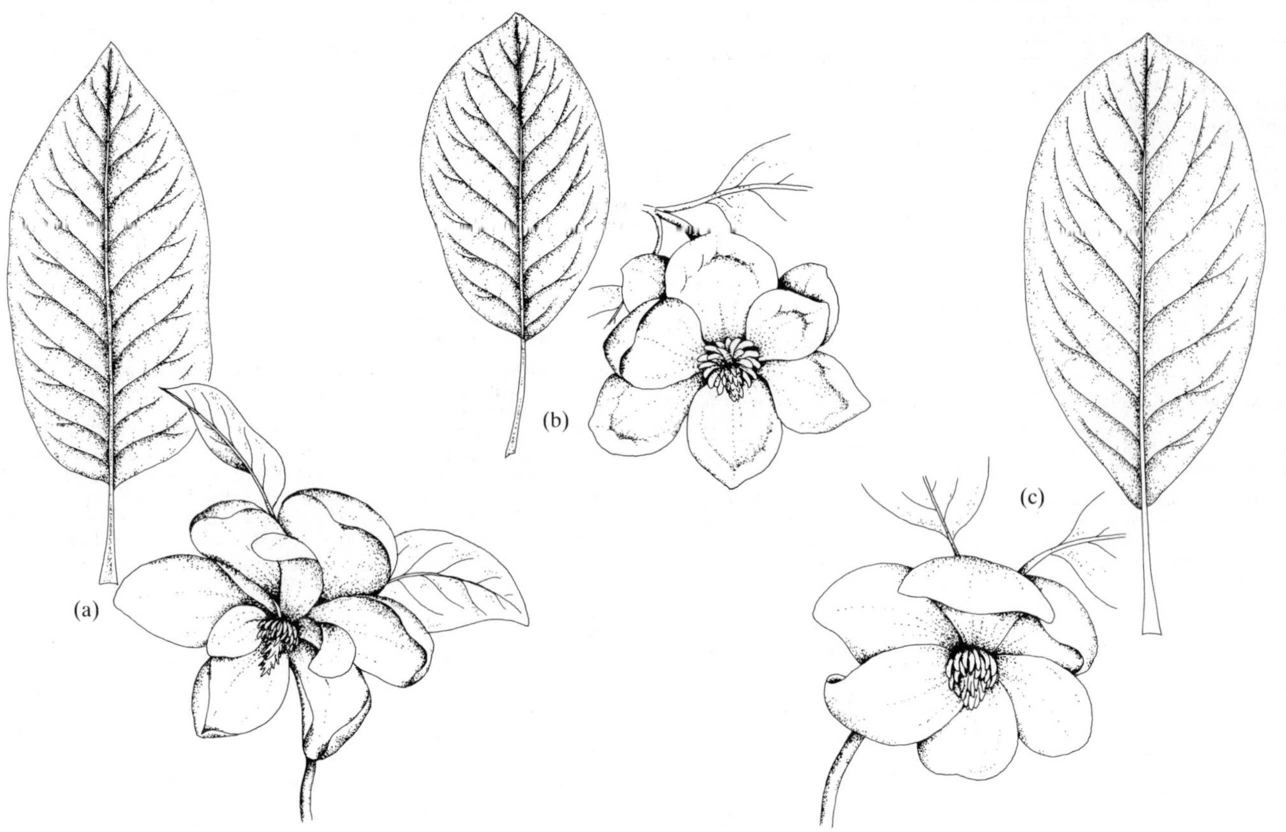


**Magnolia** (×0.66) (a) *M. wilsonii* (b) *M. sieboldii* (c) *M. sieboldii* var. *sinensis*

mens to 1.5cm, numerous, crimson, giving the appearance of a solid red wheel. Cones to 7cm, pendent, cylindric, pink, later dark brown tinged purple; seeds scarlet. Spring–summer. E Asia. 'Semiplena': fls semi-double. ssp. ***sinensis*** (Rehd. & Wils.) Spongb. CHINESE MAGNOLIA. Broadly branching shrub or tree to 6m. Branches spreading to ascending; young shoots initially yellow-brown-sericeous, later glabrous, grey-brown. Lvs 7.5–21×5–16cm, oval to oblong, obovate or suborbicular, obtuse or abruptly acute, base cuneate or rounded, glabrous, pea-green to grey-green above, glaucescent and, at first, velutinous beneath; petiole to 6.5cm, sericeous. Fls to 13cm diam., nodding, fragrant; pedicels to 5cm; seg. *c*9, 2.5–5cm across, white obovate, to oblong-spathulate; stamens bright crimson. Cones to 7.25×3.25cm; seed rose-pink turning orange, then red. Z7.

***M.*×*soulangiana*** Soul.-Bod. SAUCER MAGNOLIA; CHINESE MAGNOLIA. *(M. denudata × M. liliiflora.)* Deciduous shrub or tree to 10m; habit of *M. denudata* but more slender. Bark silver-grey; twigs purple-brown. Lvs to 16.5×12cm, broadly elliptic to suborbicular, short-acuminate, occasionally rounded, base often unequal, attenuate, dark shiny green above, often puberulent below, membranous to subcoriaceous. Fls precocious, erect; pedicels to 7mm; seg. 9, cupped, oblong-obovate, concave above at tip, white, variously marked rose-pink to violet-purple beneath, outer seg. often smaller, occasionally sepaloid, tinged green, 40×13mm, interior seg. spathulate to obovate, to 11×7cm+. Cones cylindric, 10cm, asymmetric; seed coat red. Spring. Garden origin. The most widely cultivated magnolia, its many cultivars are differentiated by colour – they range from white to claret – and whether early or late flowering. Of the white cvs, notable early-flowerers include the 5m 'Alba Superba', the slow-growing 'Amabilis' and the cream 'Sundew'; late-flowerers include 'Lennei Alba'. Of those with fls that are carmine at base, the vigorous 'Alexandrina', streaked with dark purple and with white above, is notable as an early flowerer; among the later-flowerers are the fast-growing 'Brozzonii', the fragrant 'Speciosa', 'Verbanica', and the warm pink of 'E. Soulange Bodin'. Of the darker-flowered cultivars, ranging from deep carmine to dark claret, the large-fld 'San Jose' and the flushed 'Just Jean' are notable early-flowerers. The inappropriately named 'Burgundy' has fls lavender-pink. Among the late cvs in this range are the fast-growing 'Lennei', the long-flowering 'Lombardy Rose', the slow 'Norbertii', the small-fld 'Rustica Rubra', the very dark burgundy of 'Vanhouttei' and 'Dark Splendour'. 'Variegata' has fls stippled with yellow. 'Picture' was used by Pickard's Magnolia Gardens to produce a wide range of fragrant large-fld hybrids, prominent among which are the carmine 'Pickard's Charm', the purple-claret 'Pickard's Ruby' and the deep burgundy 'Pickard's Garnet'. Z5.

***M. sprengeri*** Pamp. Deciduous tree to 20m. Bark pale grey, flaking; young shoots yellow-green, glabrous. Lvs to 13.5×7cm, obovate to lanceolate-elliptic, short-acuminate, occasionally rounded, base rounded or cuneate, glabrous, green above, pale green, glabrous to villous beneath; petioles to 25mm. Fls precocious, fragrant, dish-shaped; pedicels pubesc. becoming glabrous; seg. 12×5.5cm, 12–14, spathulate to oblong-ovate, white, occasionally tinged rosy red to pale pink; stamens to 1.5cm. Cones to 13cm, narrowly cylindric, asymmetric, green, becoming buff-pink, later brown. Spring. China (Honan, Hupeh, Sichuan). 'Burncoose': seg. rose-purple. 'Claret Cup': seg. claret beneath, fading to white above. 'Diva': seg. rosy red. 'Lanhydrock': seg. red-purple. var. ***elongata*** (Rehd. & Wils.) Stapf. Lvs twice as long or longer than wide. Seg. white. Z9.

***M. stellata*** (Sieb. & Zucc.) Maxim. STAR MAGNOLIA. As for *M. kobus* but smaller, to 7.5m. Twigs silky-pubesc. with bark muskily scented at first. Lvs 13.5×6.5cm, narrow-oblong to obovate. Fl. seg. 12–33, (the outer 3 reduced, sepaloid), laxly spreading, star-like, 6.5×1.5cm, snow white, faintly flushed pink with age; stamens purple. Spring–summer. Japan (S Honshu), possibly of garden origin and an escape in that area. 'Centennial': hardy, vigorous to 1.5m, fls white. 'Crysanthemumiflora': fls fully double, pale pink fading white. 'Dawn': seg. pale pink, up to 45 per fl. on a mature plant. 'George Henry Kern': small-fld and attractive, seg. mauve beneath, white above. 'Norman Gould': very slow-grower (5m after 35 years); fls to 15cm diam., white, precocious, borne profusely from an early age, seg. few. 'Rosea': fls tinged rose-pink fading to white. 'Rose King' ('King Rosea'): dense and twiggy in growth, buds soft rose-pink opening to white fls tinged pink at base. 'Rosea Massey': an American selection; fls pale pink fading white. 'Royal Star': fast-growing; fls open some 10 days later than species type, seg. to 30, snow white. 'Rubra': vigorous, to 2m, branches profuse; seg. stained purple-pink. 'Waterlily': seg. long and slender, pink in bud. Z4.

***M.*×*thompsoniana*** (Loud.) Vos. *(M. virginiana × M. tripetala.)* As for *M. virginiana* in habit, but pith only partially septate. Stems growing exceptionally vigorously, rangy. Lvs larger, to 18cm, obovate to, occasionally, elliptic, acuminate, base attenuate, glossy green above, glaucous beneath, falling erratically or persistent. Fls to 15cm diam., cream to primrose, produced on even young plants, fragrant, vase-shaped; seg. 12, 3 outer seg. sepaloid, persistent. Summer. Garden origin. 'Urbana': fully hardy. Z5.

***M. tripetala*** L. UMBRELLA TREE; ELKWOOD; UMBRELLA MAGNOLIA. Deciduous tree, to 12m. Crown open, broadly divaricate. Bark grey, shiny. Lvs 50×26cm+, crowded in umbrella-like pseudowhorls at ends of branches, oblanceolate, base tapering, pale green pubesc. below when young, conspicuously veined; petioles to 5cm. Fls creamy-white, erect, vase-shaped, somewhat asymmetric, muskily scented; seg. 9–12, oblong-spathulate, outer seg. sepaloid, inner seg. oblong-spathulate, fleshy; stamens to 2.2cm. Cones to 10cm, ovoid-cylindric to conic, red-pink; seeds red. Spring–summer. Eastern N America. 'Bloomfield': lvs to 70×30cm; fls very large. 'Silver Parasol' (*M. tripetala* × *M. hypoleuca*): bark silvery; lvs in showy umbrella-like whorls; fls close to *M. hypoleuca*. 'Woodlawn': cones to 12.5cm, bright red. Z5.

***M. ×veitchii*** Bean. (*M. denudata* × *M. campbellii*.) Deciduous tree, to 30m. Bark smooth, silver-tan; twigs at first tinted purple, adpressed-pubesc., later glabrous, grey-brown. Lvs 22×12cm, oblong to obovate, acute or short-acuminate, base unequal, cuneate or rounded, dark green above, veins pubesc. above, often tinted purple at first. Fls precocious, vase-shaped, erect; pedicels to 1.4cm, pubesc.; seg. 7–10, subequal, obovate to spathulate, 12.5×6cm, white tinged violet to pink beneath, pale pink above; stamens to 2.5cm. Cones to 10cm, asymmetric. Garden origin. 'Isca': fls borne early in season, off-white turning pale pink. 'Peter Veitch': fully hardy; fls white flushed pale garnet. 'Rubra': close to 'Peter Veitch' but hardier, with fls wine red in bud, borne even on young plants. Z7.

***M. virginiana*** L. SWEET BAY; SWAMP BAY; SWAMP LAUREL. Evergreen or erratically deciduous shrubs or trees, to 30m+. Frequently multi-stemmed; branches often spreading, straggly; bark ridged, grey-brown. Lvs 11×5cm, alternate, variable, narrow-oblong to occasionally suborbicular, rounded, attenuate, acute or obtuse, base acute to cuneate, shiny green above, glaucous, silver-velvety pubesc. beneath. Fls globose to cupulate, 6cm diam., white to ivory, produced sparingly over the season at tips of short branches among outspread lvs, highly fragrant; seg. 6–15, 3 outer seg. reflexed, inner seg. 5×2cm, obovate or suborbicular; stamens 1cm. Fr. 4.5cm, ellipsoid to subglobose. Summer–autumn. E US. 'Havener': fls large with many seg. 'Mayer': habit shrubby. See also Freeman hybrids. var. ***australis*** Sarg. A southern variant with a more arborescent habit and densely sericeous young stems. Carolinas, Florida. Z5.

***M. ×wiesneri*** Carr. (*M. hypoleuca* × *M. sieboldii*.) Distinguished from *M. sieboldii* by its larger, short-stalked fls and broader, tougher lvs with veins in 10–15. Tree or shrub to 7m+. Bark exfoliating in thin sheets; twigs pubesc. then glabrous. Lvs alternate, appearing whorled, obovate, attenuate, apex acute to rounded, base cuneate to acute, margin undulate, veins pubesc. above, green, glaucous beneath with midvein velvety pubesc., tinged. Fls spicily fragrant, cupulate, erect; seg. 9, 3 outer seg. reflexed, inner seg. 6×3.5cm, obovate, creamy white; stamens to 2cm, crimson. Garden origin. Z6.

***M. wilsonii*** (Finet & Gagnep.) Rehd. Closely related to *M. sieboldii*. Deciduous shrub or tree to 8m+. Bark brown; twigs purple-red, velvety-pubesc., later glabrous. Lvs 16×7cm, lanceolate to oblong-ovate, acute to acuminate, base truncate or rounded, matt green above, velvet-pubesc. beneath. Fls fragrant, cupulate, becoming saucer-shaped; pedicels to 45mm; seg. 9–12, inner seg. 6.5×4.5cm, white, spathulate to narrow-lanceolate, incurved; stamens 12mm, rose-purple. Cones to 10cm, cylindric, crimson. W China (E Sikang, W Sichuan, N Yunnan). Z7.

***M. zenii*** Cheng. Spreading deciduous tree to 7m; bark smooth, grey. Branchlets initially yellow-white, with scattered lenticels, becoming flushed purple. Buds with silky adpressed hairs. Lvs 7–16×3–7cm, oblong to oblong-obovate, apex abruptly acuminate, base wedge-shaped to rounded, pale green and glabrous above, paler beneath, 10–12 lateral veins each side, venation villous, prominent beneath; petiole 0.6–1.5cm, glabrous or hairy, grooved above. Fls 12cm diam., appearing before lvs, cupular, fragrant; seg. 9, 6.8–7.8×2.7–3.8cm, near spathulate with rounded to acute tips, white shaded and lined purple on basal half outside. Fr. 5–7×1–2.5cm, cylindrical; carpels woody; seeds 1–2, 1cm, obovoid, irregular, scarlet, outer coat blackened, apex rounded, base rounded to obtuse. E China. Z9.

***M. acuminata*** var. ***cordata*** Sarg. See *M. acuminata* var. *subcordata*.
***M. aulacosperma*** Rehd. & Wils. See *M. biondii*.
***M. auriculata*** Bartr. See *M. fraseri*.
***M. ×coatesii*** hort. See *M.* 'Charles Coates'.
***M. compressa*** Maxim. See *Michelia compressa*.
***M. conspicua*** Salisb. See *M. denudata*.
***M. conspicua*** var. ***soulangiana*** hort. ex Pamp. See *M. ×soulangiana*.
***M. cordata*** Michx. See *M. acuminata* var. *subcordata*.
***M. denudata*** var. ***purpurascens*** (Maxim.) Rehd. & Wils. See *M. sprengeri*.
***M. discolor*** Vent. See *M. liliiflora*.
***M. foetida*** Sarg. See *M. grandiflora*.
***M. fraseri*** var. ***pyramidata*** (Bartr.) Pamp. See *M. pyramidata*.
***M. glauca*** L. See *M. virginiana*.
***M. glauca*** var. ***major*** Sims. See *M. ×thompsoniana*.
***M. glauca*** var. ***thompsoniana*** Loud. See *M. ×thompsoniana*.
***M. fuscata*** Andrews. See *Michelia figo*.
***M. globosa*** var. ***sinensis*** Rehd. & Wils. See *M. sieboldii* ssp. *sinensis*.
***M. gracilis*** Salisb. See *M. liliiflora*.
***M. halleana*** Parsons. See *M. stellata*.
***M. heptapeta*** (Buc'hoz) Dandy. See *M. denudata*.
***M. ×highdownensis*** Dandy. See *M. wilsonii*.
***M. kobus*** var. ***borealis*** Sarg. See *M. kobus*.
***M. kobus*** var. ***loebneri*** (Kache) Spongb. See *M. ×loebneri*.
***M. kobus*** var. ***stellata*** (Sieb. & Zucc.) Blackburn. See *M. stellata*.
***M. macrophylla*** ssp. ***ashei*** (Weatherby) Spongb. See *M. ashei*.
***M. major*** C. Schneid. See *M. ×thompsoniana*.
***M. mollicomata*** W.W. Sm. See *M. campbellii* ssp. *mollicomata*.
***M. nicholsoniana*** hort. non Rehd. & Wils. See *M. sieboldii* ssp. *sinensis*.
***M. nicholsoniana*** Rehd. & Wils. non hort. See *M. wilsonii*.
***M. obovata*** Thunb. See *M. hypoleuca*.
***M. oyama*** hort. See *M. sieboldii*.
***M. parviflora*** Sieb. & Zucc. non Bl. See *M. sieboldii*.
***M. parviflora*** var. ***wilsonii*** Finet & Gagnep. See *M. wilsonii*.
***M. praecocissima*** Koidz. See *M. kobus*.
***M. pumila*** Andrews. See *M. coco*.
***M. purpurea*** Curtis. See *M. liliiflora*.
***M. quinquepeta*** (Buc'hoz) Dandy. See *M. liliiflora*.
***M. salicifolia*** var. ***fasciata*** Millais. See *M. salicifolia*.
***M. sinensis*** (Rehd. & Wils.) Stapf. See *M. sieboldii* ssp. *sinensis*.
***M. speciosa*** Geel. See *M. ×soulangiana*.
***M. taliensis*** W.W. Sm. See *M. wilsonii*.
***M. thuberi*** Parsons. See *M. kobus*.
***M. tomentosa*** Thunb. See *M. stellata*.
***M. tsarongensis*** W.W. Sm. & Forr. See *M. globosa*.
***M. umbrella*** Desr. See *M. tripetala*.
***M. verecunda*** Koidz. See *M. sieboldii*.
***M. ×watsonii*** Hook. f. See *M. ×wiesneri*.
***M. yulan*** Desf. See *M. denudata*.
For further synonymy see *Talauma*.

**MAGNOLIACEAE** Juss. MAGNOLIA FAMILY. Dicot. 7 genera and 200 species of trees and shrubs. Leaves spirally arranged, simple, entire (lobed in *Liriodendron*); stipules large, enclosing the terminal bud, deciduous. Flowers large, usually terminal and solitary, usually bisexual, regular, usually with long receptacle; perianth spiral or in 3 whorls, 6–18, often all petaloid; stamens numerous, spirally arranged, often strap-shaped; ovary of 2-numerous free or partly fused carpels, sometimes not completely closed but with more or less distinct style and terminal stigma; ovules 2-numerous on marginal placenta. Fruit a follicle or indehiscent and berry-like or samaroid (*Liriodendron*); seeds usually large; embryo very small in copious oil, proteinaceous endosperm. *Liriodendron, Magnolia* and *Michelia* yield valuable timber. Temperate and tropical E Asia and America. *Liriodendron, Magnolia, Manglietia, Michelia*.

**×Mahoberberis** Schneid. Berberidaceae. (*Mahonia* × *Berberis*.) 4 evergreen or semi-evergreen shrubs to 2m, resembling *Mahonia* in flower and unarmed stems and *Berberis* in their simple or tripartite leaves. These hybrids are of garden origin: the first ×*M. neubertii* was raised in Baumann's nursery *c*1850. Others have arisen since in Sweden and the US. Unlike both parents, ×*Mahoberberis* is reputedly immune from rust. Z6.

CULTIVATION Tough evergreens growing in any soil and any exposure. ×*M. aquisargentii* is an excellent boundary shrub with viciously spiny leaves which vary considerably on a single plant and strong upright growth; flowers and fruits only occur after a lengthy growing season. ×*M. miethkeana* is selected for winter interest: the leaves are tinted bronze in the colder months. ×*M. neubertii* and ×*M. aquicandidula* are more open-growing. Propagate from wounded nodal semi-ripe cutting taken in late summer or early autumn; treat with hormone rooting powder. Good success rates have been achieved with the use of plugs for rooting, which ensures minimal disturbance. Grow in a closed propagating case, misting to maintain the necessary humidity. Place potted cuttings in a cold frame over winter. All spp., except ×*M. aquisargentii*, are prone to powdery mildew; use an appropriate fungicide, particularly during hot dry spells.

**×*M. aquicandidula*** Krüssm. Evergreen shrub to 1m, low-growing, often rather weak and sparse. Lvs ovate, acuminate, to 4cm with to 4 prominent teeth per side, shining deep green above, white pruinose beneath, borne densely. Fls bright yellow. Late winter.

**×*M. aquisargentii*** Krüssm. Robust evergreen to 2m; stems upright. Lvs variable: those on unbranched, erect growth tripartite, sessile, coarse, semi-rigid, ovate, to 7cm, glossy above with to 6 spiny teeth per side, lateral pinnae smaller or reduced, spiny, those on older growth axillary, petiolate, flexible, simple or greatly reduced tripartite, closely, minutely serrulate; all pinnae become

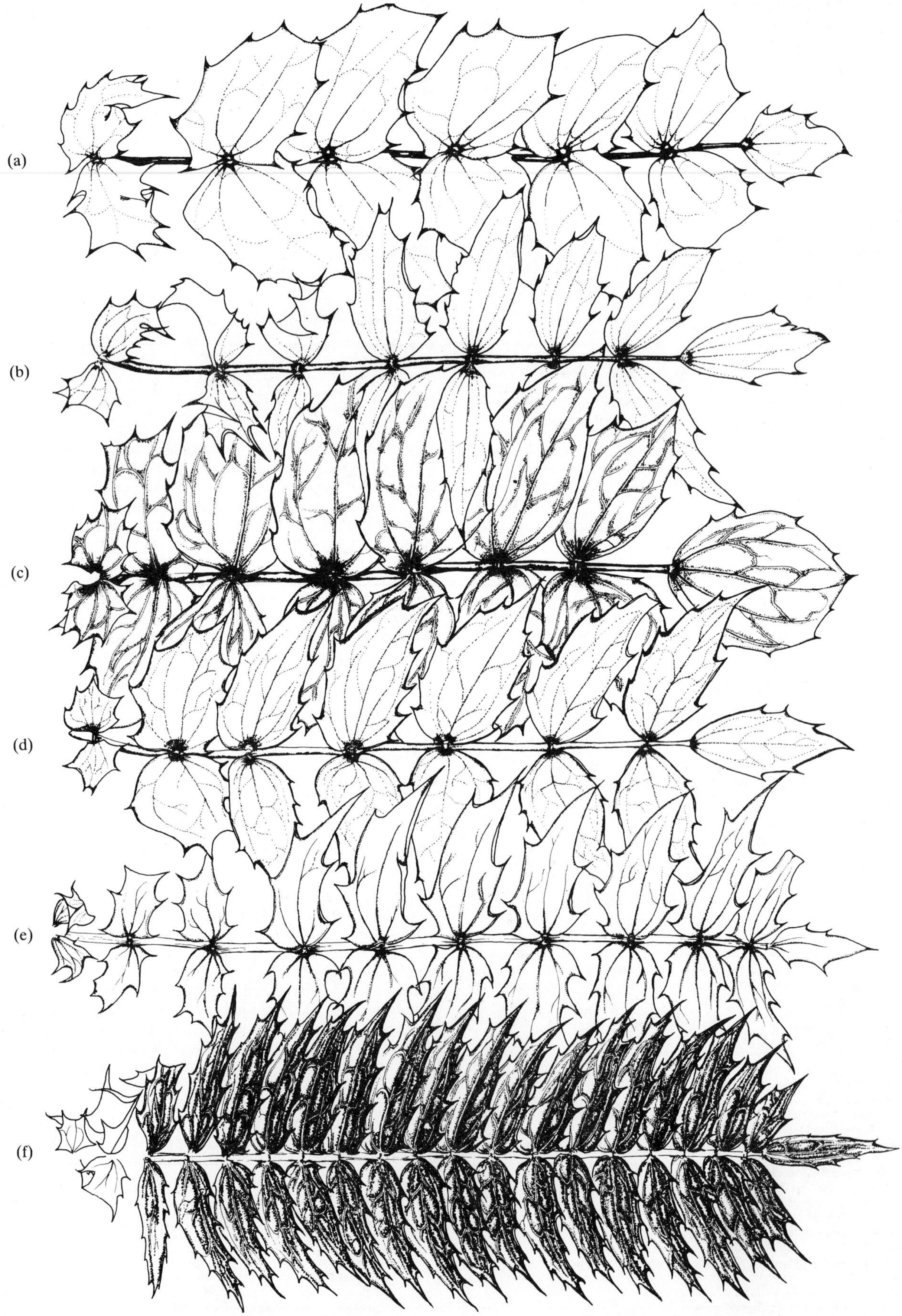


**Mahonia** (a) *M. napaulensis* (b) *M. napaulensis* × *M.japonica* (c) *M. bealei* (d) *M. japonica* (e) *M.* × *media* (f) *M. lomariifolia*

maroon-brown in winter. Fls rarely, borne in terminal panicles. Fr. black, glaucous. Late winter.

×***M. miethkeana*** Meland. & Eade. Robust, erect, seldom branching, to 2m. Lvs variable, as in ×*M. aquisargentii*, elliptic-lanceolate, dentate with large spines to 1.5mm, emerging yellow-bronze, hardening glossy dark green above, paler beneath, turning copper-red in autumn. Fls in sparse racemes, pale yellow. Late winter.

×***M. neubertii*** (Lem.) Schneid. Evergreen to 1m with expansive, open habit; stems rigid, erect. Lvs variable: simple, ovate to 7.5cm, serrulate, or, as in *Mahonia*, rigid, ovate-acute, tripartite, coarsely serrate. A mule. 'Latifolia': spreading, to 2×2m; lvs obovate, dull-green, somewhat glaucous.

**Mahonia** Nutt. (For Bernard McMahon, American horticulturist, *d*1816.) OREGON GRAPE; HOLLY GRAPE. Berberidaceae. 70 species of evergreen shrubs and small trees. Stems to 4m, erect or sprawling, simple or sparsely branched near base, thornless, scarred or sheathed by abscising or persistent petiole bases. Leaves to 1m, alternate or in whorls atop stems, imparipinnate or trifoliolate; leaflets sharply spiny-serrate, semi-rigid, sometimes glossy or glaucous, in opposite pairs, basal pair sometimes reduced, stipule-like. Flowers yellow unless white or maroon, sometimes sweetly scented, borne in fascicles of radiating short racemes, umbellate clusters or panicles. Fruits berry-like, plum-red to pruinose black. Asia, N & C America.

CULTIVATION Shrubs cultivated for their handsome evergreen foliage, their yellow or white, often fragrant flowers and their decorative pruinose fruits. The robust, taller-growing Asian species are usually native to damp woodlands, while the shorter, spreading, American species are plants of forest edges or dry scrub. Most are tolerant of a wide range of sites, given a free-draining soil. The larger Asiatics, notably *M. japonica, M. bealei, M. napaulensis, M. lomariifolia* and *M.* ×*media*, are particularly valued for their bold foliage and winter blooming. They are best used as specimen plants in a semi-shaded position in a woodland garden or mixed shrubbery. Provide a damp, slightly acid to neutral soil with a high humus content. Prolonged exposure to harsh winds and temperatures below −15°C/5°F is liable to cause leaf scorch and flower damage. *M. lomariifolia* requires a slightly sheltered site although its hybrids, *M.* ×*media*, are more resilient; *M. napaulensis* invariably underperforms in gardens where temperatures fall regularly below −10°C/14°F. *M. japonica* will tolerate −20°C/−4°F. Thin out only leggy, exhausted stems ('canes') in spring.

Low-growing species from NW America (*M. aquifolium, M. pinnata, M. repens* and their hybrid progeny) sucker profusely and are valuable medium-height groundcover. These are tolerant of a wider range of soils and climatic conditions than members of the first group and will adapt to most sites. They may sometimes become invasive, and should be held in check by the removal of unwanted offshoots; older portions of these subjects may lose vigour and become bare, in which case it may be necessary to reduce and replant them. Glaucous-leaved species from the southern US and Central America require dry, perfectly drained sites in full sun. They will suffer from wind scorch, winter wet and any exposure to temperatures below −10°C/14°F: dieback is a common occurrence in these species outside a mediterranean-type climate. Plant in gritty, slightly acid soil, preferably on a south-facing wall.

Propagate by fresh seed, having cleaned off the fleshy exterior, surface-sown on a sandy propagating mix under glass. Division of most species is possible where offshoots or basal branches have rooted; to this effect, stooling may be advantageous. Take leaf-bud cuttings of members of the first group in late winter. The suckering species may be readily divided. Mallet cuttings of the warmer-growing American species, taken in late winter and inserted around a sand-filled clay pot, may root in a cold frame. Alternatively, they may be grafted on to stocks of *Berberis thunbergii*. Hybridization is likely to occur among members of the same group. For diseases and pests, see *Berberis*.

**1** Shrubs, usually erect and sparsely branched, to 2m or more. Leaves to 1m; leaflets 7–41, dull grey-green to dark green, obscurely nerved above, semi-rigid. Inflorescence a cluster of fascicled racemes; bracts persistent, 1–4cm.
*Mm. bealei, confusa, fortunei, gracilipes, japonica,* ×*lindsayae, lomariifolia,* ×*media, napaulensis, nervosa.*

**2** Shrubs, erect or semi-prostrate, seldom exceeding 2m. Stems often slender, branching or suckering quite freely. Leaves to 40cm. Inflorescence many-flowered in fascicled or solitary racemes or panicles; bracts deciduous, 0.2–0.8cm.

2.1 Stems spreading, seldom exceeding 1.5m. Leaflets 5–13 with veins sunken above. Racemes dense, erect, 2–5 per fascicle.
*Mm. aquifolium, dictyota, eutriphylla, gracilis,* 'Heterophylla', *pinnata, pumila, repens,* ×*wagneri.*

2.2 Leaflets to 23. Inflorescence a solitary, loose, pendulous raceme or panicle.
*M. arguta.*

2.3 Leaflets 3–9, obscurely veined, rigid, often thick, glaucous. Inflorescence few-flowered, fascicled, umbellate or subumbellate.
*Mm. fremontii, haematocarpa, nevinii, swaseyi, trifolia, trifoliolata.*

***M. aquifolium*** (Pursh) Nutt. OREGON GRAPE. Shrub to 2m, usually less, sparingly branched above ground but suckering freely; stems smooth, grey-brown. Leaflets 5–13, sessile, variable, obliquely ovate, to 8×4cm, with to 12 spiny teeth per side, glossy, dark green turning purple-red in autumn and winter, grey-pruinose beneath at first, becoming olive, glabrous. Fls golden, slender-stalked, borne profusely on erect racemes to 8cm, 3–4-fascicled, produced beside terminal bud. Fr. globose, mauve-black, thickly glaucous; style absent. Late winter. NW America. 'Apollo': low-growing, expansive, to 60cm; lvs larger, dull, good winter colour. 'Atropurpurea': lvs red-purple in winter; fls in short racemes. 'Donewell': broad and arching to 1m; lvs long-thorned, tinted blue below; rachis red, fls yellow. 'Forescate': to 1m; lvs tinted blue beneath, spring, winter and young lvs tinted red. 'Orange Flame': low-growing, to 60cm; lvs robust, becoming bronze, tinted with orange-red after first season, dark red in winter; fls golden; susceptible to rust and mildew. *M. aquifolium* hybridizes freely in gardens with *M. repens* and *M. pinnata*. 'Smaragd': habit broad; fls profuse. Z5.

***M. arguta*** Hutch. Shrub to 2m. Lvs to 30cm; leaflets 9–23, to 9×2cm, lanceolate, base cuneate, margins serrate with up to 3 spiny teeth per side, lustrous, reticulate throughout. Fls to 60 in arching panicles to 40cm, panicle branches bearing to 4 fls each, pale yellow. Fr. globose to 8mm diam., blue-black; style absent. Late spring. C America. Z9.

***M. bealei*** (Fort.) Carr. Shrub to 2m. Lvs narrowly obovate, to 50×20cm; leaflets 9–15, widely spaced to 6cm intervals, rigid, ovate, attenuate toward apex, to 10×6cm, terminal leaflet large, wide, to 15×20cm, spiny-serrate with to 6 teeth per side, dull grey- or metallic green above, olive beneath. Fls in racemes, to 10cm, 6–9-fascicled. Fr. ovoid, 1×0.6cm, glaucous grey; style reduced or absent. Late winter. W China (Hubei). Scarcely distinct from *M. japonica* and usually treated at cultivar level, despite the anomaly of *M. japonica* being a cultigen and *M. bealei* a species recorded in the wild. It is distinguished by its dense, more luxuriant habit, darker lvs, broader leaflets (the terminal leaflet especially), more coarsely spiny stipules, shorter, crowded racemes, and fls wider by some 2mm. The diagnostic character most frequently quoted, erect racemes, is not useful; whilst *M. bealei* may flower before the racemes are fully elongated, the infl. is ultimately arching to pendent. A hybrid between this species and *M. napaulensis* has been offered under the name *M. japonica* 'Trifurca', an upright shrub with bold ruffs of outspread lvs, the leaflets broad and coarsely toothed, the fls pale yellow in short, erect, clustered racemes. A hybrid between *M. bealei* and *M. lomariifolia* has been recorded: *M.* 'Arthur Menzies' has an upright, compact habit, lvs to 45cm, leaflets to 19, deep blue-green, 3–4 spines per side, and lemon-yellow fls in erect racemes. Z6.

***M. confusa*** Sprague. Small shrub resembling *M. fortunei*. Leaflets to 20, narrow-lanceolate, spinose, sea-green to leaden grey, silvery beneath; rachis purple-tinted. Fls small, pale yellow in erect, slender racemes. Fr. pruinose, blue-black. Autumn to winter. China. Z8.

***M. dictyota*** (Jeps.) Fedde. Shrub to 1m. Lvs with 3 pairs overlapping leaflets; leaflets ovate, to 4×2.5cm, serrate with to 4 spiny teeth per side, glossy, reticulate above, dull with prominent venation beneath. Fls in racemes to 7cm. Fr. ellipsoid, glaucous dark blue, to 1cm long; style absent. Late spring. SW US. Z8.

***M. eutriphylla*** Fedde. To 1.5m. Lvs to 11×5cm; leaflets 3, 2, opposite, oblong-ovate, to 4×2cm broadly cuneate at base, apex acute, serrate with to 5 teeth per side, terminal leaflet petiolate, to 1cm, glossy, dark green, reticulate above, dull grey-green with more prominent venation beneath. Fls in racemes to 2cm. Fr. ovoid, to 1cm, blue-black, glossy; style reduced. Late spring. Mexico. Z9.

***M. fortunei*** (Lindl.) Fedde. To 2m. Stems erect, unbranched. Lvs to 25×18cm; leaflets 7–13, elliptic-lanceolate, long-acuminate, flexible, increasing in size from base, to 10×2.5cm, serrate with 10 teeth per side, apex acute, not cusped, dark matt green above, pale yellow-green with prominent reticulate venation beneath. Fls borne profusely on slender racemes to 5cm, 4–8-fascicled. Late autumn. China. Z7.

***M. fremontii*** (Torr.) Fedde To 4m. Lvs to 10cm; leaflets 3–7, to 6×1.5cm, oblong-lanceolate, thick, rigid, spiny serrate, sessile, mucronate, vivid, glaucous blue above, grey beneath, terminal leaflet petiolate, linear-lanceolate. Fls to 5 in a subumbellate cluster, to 5cm; pedicels slender, to 1.5cm, pale yellow. Fr. ovoid, to 1.5cm, purple-black, pruinose; style absent. Summer. SW US. Sometimes confused with *M. trifoliolata*, which differs in only ever bearing 3 leaflets per lf. Z8.

***M.gracilipes*** (Oliv.) Fedde. Suckering, to 1.5m. Lvs to 65×15cm; leaflets oblique, 5–7, widely spaced to 12×5cm, thick, semi-rigid, spiny-serrate in apical half, cusped, dull green above, bright glaucous grey becoming glabrous beneath, terminal leaflet petiolate, to 15×5cm. Fls in loose racemes to 50cm, 3-fascicled, lax; inner pet. white; outer sep. maroon. W Sichuan (Mt Omei). Z7.

***M.gracilis*** (Hartw.) Fedde. Leaflets 5–13, often overlapping, ovate, to 5×3cm, closely spiny-serrate, acute, shiny, light green above, paler beneath. Otherwise resembling *M. aquifolium* except fr. glaucous blue, ovoid, to 1.2cm; style persistent, to 1.5mm. Late winter. Mexico. Z8.

***M.haematocarpa*** (Wooton) Fedde. Stems slender, erect, usually simple, to 4m. Lvs with to 7 leaflets, lowest pair very close to base of rachis; stipules to 2mm; leaflets rigid, tough, oblong-lanceolate, to 4×1cm, serrate with to 4 spiny teeth per side, apex mucronate, cusped, blue-grey. Fls pale yellow, to 6 in narrow, loose, subumbellate racemes. Fr. globose, dark red; style absent. Late spring. W US. Distinguished from *M.fremontii* by its showy red fr. Z8.

***M.*'Heterophylla'.** To 1.5m. Stems red at first. Lvs to 30cm; leaflets to 7, lanceolate, to 9cm×1.5cm, margins subequal, entire or serrate with to 10 narrow teeth per side, sessile or petiolate, variable, often reflexed or twisted, dark glossy green throughout. Fls and fr. seldom produced. Garden origin. This plant is unlikely to be the result of *M. aquifolium* × *M. fortunei*, as Zabel suggested. It is more probably a hybrid seedling of *M. toluacensis* (Bean) Ahrendt, from which it differs in its polymorphic foliage. Z7.

***M.japonica*** (Thunb.) DC. Closely related to *M.bealei*. Stems to 2m, erect, branching little. Lvs to 45×15cm; 7–19, growing longer and narrower from base to apex, to ×3.5, tough, rigid, oblong-ovate at base to lanceolate at apex, base obtuse, serrate with to 6 spiny teeth per side, glossy grey-green above, often tinted red in winter, yellow-green beneath, terminal leaflet longer and broader than others. Fls yellow, highly fragrant, borne loosely on pendent racemes to 25cm, to 10-fascicled, on 1-year-old growth. Fr. ovoid to 9mm, mauve, glaucous grey; style greatly reduced. Late winter–early spring. Japan, in cult. only; possibly China, Taiwan. 'Hiemalis': lvs to 50cm, leaflets narrow, racemes to 35cm, flowering profusely in mid-winter. Z6.

***M.×lindsayae*** P.F. Yeo. *(M.japonica × M.siamensis.)* 'Cantab': medium-sized shrub, spreading. Lvs long, arching, deep green; leaflets to 15, remote, with to 6 spines per side; rachis and petiole tinted red in cold weather. Fls lemon yellow, large, fragrant on spreading or drooping racemes. Winter. Z7.

***M.lomariifolia*** Tak. Stems erect to 4m, to 10m in habitat, seldom branching. Lvs to 60×15cm, appearing whorled, held gracefully outspread, often curving upwards at tip; leaflets 18–41, regularly spaced, crowded, becoming larger, narrower and overlapping toward apex, median length 7cm, width decreasing from base, 1.5–0.7cm, oblong-ovate to oblong-lanceolate, serrate with to 7 spines per side, apex sharply acuminate, subfalcate, glabrous dark green throughout, sometimes slightly concave above. Fls crowded on erect spikes to 15cm, to 17-fascicled, terminal. Fr. ovoid, blue-black, glaucous; style reduced. Flowering time varies. Burma, W China. Z7.

***M.×media*** C. Brickell. *(M.japonica × M.lomariifolia.)* 'Buckland': infl. to 65cm diam., racemes to 14, branched, fls fragrant, pale yellow (1971). 'Charity': erect to 5m; lvs with to 21 leaflets, ovate-lanceolate, obtuse at base, long-acuminate at apex, to 3 teeth on upper margin, to 4 on lower, dark glossy green above, yellow-green beneath with prominent venation; fls deep yellow in erect racemes to 35cm, numerous, to 20-fascicled, terminal; winter. 'Faith': similar to *M.lomariifolia*, fls paler. 'Hope': fls densely set on the rachis, bright pale yellow. 'Lionel Fortescue': fragrant, erect infl. (1971). 'Underway': habit branching, bushy; fls autumn. 'Winter Sun': racemes horizontal rather than pendent; fls frost-resistant, topaz-yellow, first opening in autumn (1970).

***M.napaulensis*** DC. Shrub to 3m. Lvs to 50×15cm, oblong to lanceolate; leaflets to 11 pairs, upwardly overlapping toward apex, more widely spaced at base, 4.5×2cm at base, enlarging to 6.5×3.5cm at median, decreasing again at apex, terminal leaflet largest, to 7×4cm, all leaflets rigid, oblong-ovate, coarsely and sinuately spiny-serrate with 2–6 teeth on each side, dull green above, paler, veined beneath, often revolute or twisted; rachis patent, tinted pink with 2 clasping, spiny, orbicular stipules at base. Fls in dense, erect, terminal racemes to 10cm, 3–4-fascicled, pale yellow. Fr. ovoid to 1.2cm, purple, pruinose blue; style persistent, to 1.5mm. Winter–spring. Nepal, Sikkim, Assam. Z6.

***M.nervosa*** (Pursh) Nutt. To 1m, suckering. Lvs to 60cm; leaflets sessile, 11–23, thick, median length 7cm, base 4cm, apex 5cm, 3.5cm wide at base, decreasing toward apex to 2cm, changing upwards from ovate to oblong-lanceolate, closely serrate, grey-green above, yellow-green beneath. Fls in racemes to 20cm, to 4-fascicled. Fr. globose, to 8mm diam., glaucous blue; style absent. Late winter. NW America. Z6.

***M.nevinii*** (Gray) Fedde. Erect to 2.25m. Leaflets to 3×1cm, 3–7, narrow-lanceolate, rigid with to 6 spiny teeth per side, grey blue-glaucous above with white venation. Fls to 8 in loose subumbellate racemes. Fr. globose, to 6mm diam., black, blue-glaucous; style absent. Spring. California. Z8.

***M.pinnata*** (Lagasca) Fedde. Readily distinguished from *M.aquifolium* by its more erect, regular habit, more finely serrate leaflets and pet. shorter than inner sep. To 2.5m. Leaflets 5–9, subequal, to 6×1.5cm, ovate-lanceolate, base widely cuneate, apex acute, margins undulate, armed with to 13 slender, forward-pointing spines per side, dull green above, tinted maroon or red in winter, grey pruinose beneath, reticulate throughout. Fls axillary and terminal in racemes to 6cm, to 5-fascicled. Fr. ovoid to 6mm diam., glaucous blue; style absent. Spring. California. Z7.

***M.pumila*** (Greene) Fedde. Suckering, to 0.5m. Lvs to 14cm; leaflets 5–7, to 5×3cm, base broadly cuneate, apex acuminate, margins bearing to 8 spiny teeth per side, emerging red, then glaucous plum-purple, ultimately vivid or dull grey-green above, grey pruinose beneath, sparsely papillose. Fls in racemes to 4cm, to 5-fascicled. Fr. obovoid, to 1cm; style absent. Spring. W US. Z7.

***M.repens*** G. Don. Suckering, semi-prostrate shrub to 0.5m. Lvs to 25cm; leaflets usually 5, ovate, subequal, base subcordate, apex obtuse or very abruptly acute, dull green above, papillose beneath, glaucous at first, with 9–18 spiny teeth per side. Fls deep yellow, borne terminally in racemes to 8cm, to 6-fascicled. Fr. globose to 9mm diam., glaucous blue; style absent. Late spring. NW America. 'Rotundifolia': robust; lvs ovate, entire or serrulate. Z6.

***M.swaseyi*** (Buckley) Fedde. Closely resembling *M. nevinii*, differs in attaining 2.5m, its thick, reticulate lvs and narrower racemes to 6cm. Fr. globose, white-yellow, flushed red; style absent. Spring. Texas. Z8.

***M.trifolia*** Cham. & Schltr. Prostrate or erect to 5m. Leaflets to 7, ovate, thick, rigid, to 3×2.5cm, margins undulate and with to 3 spines per side, abruptly acuminate, dull grey-green above, paler beneath. Fls golden on short racemes to 2cm, to 3-fascicled. Fr. ovoid, glaucous blue; style absent. Spring. Mexico. Z8.

***M.trifoliolata*** (Moric.) Fedde. var. ***glauca*** I.M. Johnst. Erect to 2.25m. Leaflets 3, to 6.8cm, sessile, lanceolate-acute, rigid, undulate with 1–4 lobe-like marginal spines per side, apex pungent, blue-green, thickly white-glaucous. Fls in short corymbs. Spring. Mexico. Z7.

***M.×wagneri*** (Jouin) Rehd. A collective name for plants arising from *M. pinnata* × *M. aquifolium*. Late spring. Garden origin. 'Aldenhamensis': vigorous and erect to 1.5m; lvs large, tinted blue beneath, young lvs bronze; fls yellow. 'Fireflame': to 1.25m; leaflets 7, dull green or glaucous blue above, grey-green beneath, blood red to bronze in winter. 'Hastings Elegant': dense, compact and upright; lvs evergreen; fls in large heads, profuse, yellow 'King's Ransom': narrowly upright to 1.6m; young lvs pruinose, tinted dark blue; fls pale yellow; fr. pruinose, very dark blue. 'Moseri': erect to 80cm; young lvs tinged bronze-red, later dark green; fls yellow; fr. pruinose, blue-black. 'Pinnacle' ('Pinnata'): erect to 1.5m, vigorous; young and winter lvs tinted copper; fls yellow. 'Undulata': erect to 1.5m, vigorous; lvs very glossy, margins undulate, young and winter lvs tinted red-bronze; fls in dense racemes, pale yellow. 'Vicaryi': broadly erect to 1m; lvs small, some autumn lvs tinted red; fls in small dense racemes; yellow; fr. pruinose, very dark blue. Z7.

***M.acanthifolia*** G. Don. See *M.napaulensis*.
***M.alexandri*** Schneid. See *M.lomariifolia*.
***M.fascicularis*** DC. See *M.pinnata*.
***M.glumacea*** DC. See *M.nervosa*.
***M.herveyi*** Ahrendt. See *M.repens* 'Rotundifolia'.
***M.japonica*** 'Trifurca'. See *M.bealei*.
***M.pinnata*** var. ***wagneri*** Jouin. See *M.×wagneri*.
***M.schiedeana*** (Schldl.) Fedde. See *M.trifolia*.

**Maianthemum** Wigg. (From Gk *maios*, the month of May, and *anthemon*, blossom.) Liliaceae (Convallariaceae). 3 species of perennial, rhizomatous herbs. Rootstock slender, creeping. Stems erect, glabrous, or minutely pubescent, with basal scales. Leaves 2 or 3, alternate above. Flowers white, borne in terminal racemes; flower-stalks slender, bracted; tepals 4, free, spreading or deflexed, deciduous; stamens 4; ovary superior or 2-celled, with 2 ovules per cell; style simple, short; stigma slightly 2-lobed. Fruit a 1- or 2-seeded berry. Northern temperate regions.

CULTIVATION A charming native of humus-rich slightly acid soils in moist and shaded habitats, *Maianthemum* spp. make good groundcover in the wild and woodland garden although they may prove too invasive for more carefully manicured areas. They are tolerant of warm summers only with sufficient moisture at the root. Propagate by division.

***M.bifolium*** (L.) Schmidt. FALSE LILY OF THE VALLEY. Stems 5–20cm, upper part hairy. Lvs 3–8×2.5–5cm, broadly cordate-ovate, thinly-textured, with a broad sinus, apex acute to acuminate, persistent, distinctly stalked. Fls 8–20 per raceme, white; pedicels solitary or twin, slender, jointed near apex; tepals 1–3mm. Fr 5–6mm, pale green and spotted at first, eventually red. W Europe to Japan. Z3.

**Maihuenia** (Philippi ex F.A. Weber) Schum. (From *maihuen*, a local name for the plant.) Cactaceae. 2 species of low, caespitose shrubs; stems succulent, segmented; segments small, globose or short-cylindric. Leaves present, small, terete, persistent; spines usually 3. Flowers terminal, solitary; tube none; perianth spreading, yellow. Fruit obovoid or oblong, somewhat fleshy; floral areoles with small, persistent, leaves; seeds almost circular, 4.2×3.2mm, black-brown, shiny; relief low-domed; hilum small, oblique, superficial. Argentina and Chile.

CULTIVATION May be grown in an unheated greenhouse or out-of-doors with winter protection from rain; use 'standard' cactus compost: moderate to high inorganic content (more than 50% grit), pH 6–7.5; grow in full sun; keep dry from late autumn; if growing under glass, recommence light watering in late winter/early spring. These plants are winter-hardy in parts of Europe, given a well-drained soil and protection from excessive moisture.

***M.patagonica*** (Philippi) Britt. & Rose. Resembling *M.poeppigii*; stem-seg. cylindric, 2–8×1–1.2cm. Lvs ovate or subulate, 2–4mm; central spines 2–5cm. Fl. 4.5–5.5×3–4.5cm, white or pink. Fr. 2cm, globose. Summer. S Argentina. Z5.

***M.poeppigii*** (Otto ex Pfeiff.) Schum. Dwarf shrub, eventually forming low mounds; stem-seg. short-cylindric, 1.2–3×1–1.2cm. Lvs 4–6mm; central spine 1–1.5cm, white, laterals *c*4mm. Fl. 3–4.5×3cm, yellow, stigmas green. Fr. *c*1×1cm, obconic. Summer. S Argentina, S Chile. Z5.

**Maihueniopsis** Speg. See *Opuntia*.

**Mairia** DC. (For M. Maire, early 19th-century Prussian explorer.) Compositae. About 14 species of perennial herbs or subshrubs. Leaves alternate, often radical. Capitula radiate, solitary or few clustered in a corymb; phyllaries in 1 to few series, subimbricate; ray florets female, fertile, purple or white; disc florets hermaphrodite, fertile or sterile, yellow. Fruit a glabrous to sparsely pilose cypsela; pappus of plumose bristles. S Africa (S & SW Cape). Z7.

CULTIVATION As for *Gerbera*.

***M.crenata*** (Thunb.) Nees. Perenn. herb. Lvs radical, numerous, 8×2cm, obovate-oblong, bluntly toothed, more or less arachnoid. Capitula solitary, *c*2.5cm diam., on peduncle to 25cm, glabrous to tomentose; phyllaries pilose, membranous. S & SW Cape.

For synonymy see *Arnica* and *Aster*.

**Malachodendron** Cav.
***M.pentagynum*** (L'Hérit.) Small. See *Stewartia ovata*.

**Malachra** L. (A variant from Gk *malache*, mallow, applied to these tropical and subtropical plants.) Malvaceae. 6 species of hispid annual and perennial herbs or subshrubs. Leaves unlobed to palmately lobed or angulate. Flowers small, in terminal or axillary head-like clusters, subtended by conspicuous leaf-like bracts; epicalyx present or absent; calyx of 5 sepals, campanulate; petals 5, red, yellow or white; staminal tube short; styles 10, stigmas capitate; ovary 5-celled, each cell 1-ovuled. Fruit a schizocarp, mericarps 5, obovoid, 3-angled, indehiscent or partly dehiscent. Tropical & subtropical America, W Indies, some naturalized in the Old World. Z10.

CULTIVATION A frost-tender genus of coarse habit, not noted for exceptional beauty but sometimes grown as late blooming tender annuals in cool temperate zones. Cultivate as for *Anoda*.

***M.fasciata*** Jacq. Annual to 1.2m; stems woody at base, villous with simple and stellate hairs. Lvs to 15cm, suborbicular, 3–5-lobed, serrate, with simple spreading hairs; petioles with simple and stellate hairs; stipules 1.5–3cm. Fls in axillary, almost sessile, 5-fld heads, subtended by long-acuminate, often reflexed bracts; cal. 4–5mm; cor. 8–10mm, white turning pink. Mericarps 3–3.5mm, reticulate-veined, warted, glabrescent. Mexico to the Guianas and Paraguay, Cuba, Jamaica, Puerto Rico, Lesser Antilles, Trinidad and Pacific Is.

***M.radiata*** (L.) L. Herb or subshrub to 2.5m; stems erect, yellow-hispid. Lvs to 12cm, deeply 3–5-lobed; stipules to 1cm. Fls in terminal heads, subtended by bracts to 4cm; epicalyx to 9–12 lobes, 1–1.2cm, filiform; cal. 8–10mm; cor 1–1.2cm, pink. Mericarps to 4mm, glabrous, minutely warted. C & S America, W Indies, Tropical Africa.

For synonymy see *Sida*.

**Malacocarpus** Salm-Dyck non Fisch. & C.A. Mey. See *Parodia*.

**Malacothamnus** Greene. (From Gk *malache*, mallow, and *thamnos*, shrub.) CHAPARRAL MALLOW. Malvaceae. 20 species of suffrutescent perennials, shrubs or small trees. Stems densely stellate-tomentose with long, mostly flexuous branches. Leaves simple, petiolate, palmately lobed. Flowers in cymose clusters, forming loose or dense terminal heads, spikes, racemes or panicles, rarely solitary; epicalyx segments 3, filiform to ovate, free or united at base; sepals 5, united at base; petals 5, white to deep mauve; stamens united in a tubular column; styles as many as the mericarps, stigmas capitate. Fruit a schizocarp; mericarps 7–14, muticous, unarmed, 1-seeded, splitting at maturity into 2 valves. SW N America (California, Baja California). Z9.

CULTIVATION Ornamental shrubs for dry, warm temperate climates, grown for the densely flowered terminal spikes of rose pink or deep mauve blooms. Where long hot summers allow adequate ripening of the wood, *Malacothamnus* tolerates short-lived and sporadic frosts to about −5°C/23°F, perhaps even lower, but in cool temperate regions is more safely grown in the cool glasshouse or conservatory. Cultivate as for *Sphaeralcea*.

***M.davidsonii*** (Robinson) Greene. Shrub to 4m, densely stellate-tomentose, stems stout. Lvs 2.5–10cm diam., thick, rounded to cordate, 3-, 5- or 7-lobed; petioles to 3cm. Fls numerous, in short racemes forming panicles to 40cm, often many fls abortive; epicalyx to 3mm; sep. 5–8mm, free cal. lobes 2–4mm, densely tomentose; pet. 12–15mm, pink or rose. Mericarps 3mm, hairy at apical part. California (San Fernando Valley).

***M.fasciculatus*** (Nutt. ex Torr. & A. Gray) Greene. Shrub to 2m, branches slender, densely stellate-hairy. Lvs 2–4cm, as long as broad, unlobed or 3-, 5- or 7-lobed, subcoriaceous, greener above than beneath. Fls numerous, in interrupted spikes to open panicles; epicalyx 2–4mm; cal. 6–8mm, stellate-hairy, the free lobes deltoid; pet. 12–18mm, pale to deep mauve. Mericarps 2.5–3mm, apical part stellate-hairy; seeds 1.5mm. Coastal ranges of California and N Baja California.

For synonymy see *Malvastrum* and *Sphaeralcea*.

**Malaxis** Sol. ex Sw. (From Gk *malaxis*, softening, referring to the soft texture of the leaves of most species.) Orchidaceae. About 300 species of terrestrial, lithophytic or epiphytic orchids. Rhizome tuberous, creeping. Leaves 1 to several, thin-textured, plicate, almost always deciduous. Raceme terminal, usually densely many-flowered; flowers usually small, non-resupinate, green, buff, dull orange or dull purple; sepals and petals free, spreading; lip larger than tepals, entire or lobed, margin often denticulate; column short, stigma ventral; anther terminal; pollinia 4, in 2 pairs. Cosmopolitan, mainly tropical Asia. Z10.

CULTIVATION Largely terrestrial orchids with plicate leaves and slender spikes of curious flowers. Some of the American species, for example *M.macrostachya, M.spicata* and *M.unifolia*, are sometimes grown for their flowers in the cool house or outside in zones 8–10, where their requirements are close to those of the hardier *Calanthe* species. *M.calophylla* described below is one of several species including *Mm. discolor, metallica* and *scottii* from SE Asia valued for their beautifully bronzed and purple-flushed foliage. These require warm, humid and shaded conditions (min. temperature 15°C/60°F), a substrate of composted bark, charcoal, leafmould and sphagnum, and careful watering throughout the year. They are all suited to growing cases and are sometimes cultivated alongside *Anoectochilus, Lepanthes*, and other fragile orchids noted for their foliage.

***M.calophylla*** (Rchb. f.) Kuntze. Terrestrial, with short, erect stem, usually 3-lvd. Lvs 7–12×4.5cm, ovate, acute, yellow-green with bronze central patch and transverse lines, edge often undulate. Peduncle 5–8cm; rachis to 15cm; raceme many-fld; fls small, pale pink or creamy yellow; dorsal sep. 3–4mm, lateral sep. 2.5×1mm; pet. 3.5mm, narrowly linear; lip about 3mm with long auricles, apex emarginate. Malaysia, Thailand.

***M.ophioglossoides*** Muhlenb. ex Willd. See *M.unifolia*.

**Malcolmia** R. Br. (For William Malcolm, late 18th-century London nurseryman.) MALCOLM STOCK. Cruciferae. 35 species of annual to perennial herbs. Stems branching, often prostrate. Leaves alternate, entire or twice pinnately lobed, ciliate, hairs branched, occasionally simple. Flowers small, in loose racemes; sepals 4, erect; petals 4, white or purple to red, linear or awl-shaped. Fruit a silique, valves 3-veined, stigma sessile; seeds in 1 or 2 rows, not winged. Mediterranean to Afghanistan.

CULTIVATION *Malcolmia* ssp. are usually found in coastal habitats. *M. maritima*, the Virginia stock, occurring naturally on sands and sea cliffs of southwest Greece and southern Albania, is largely replaced in the eastern Aegean by *M. flexuosa*. Both spp. are widely naturalized in southern Europe. *M. graeca* and *M. littorea* flower in their first year from seed and are usually treated as annuals. They do not bloom well in zones with hot humid summers, especially where high temperatures are maintained at night. Grown for their colourful, lightly fragrant flowers, in informal drifts in the flower border and as edging. They are likely to self-seed. *M. maritima* is particularly rewarding for children, since it grows quickly, sometimes blooming within a month of sowing, and does well on the poor soils that often serve as children's gardens. Grow in well-drained neutral to alkaline soils, in sun or part day shade. Fertile soils produce lush foliage at the expense of flower. Sow seed thinly *in situ*, at six-week intervals, from early spring, until autumn for continuity of bloom.

***M. chia*** (L.) DC. Annual, to 30cm. Stem erect, rarely reclining, branching above. Lvs obovate to ovate, rarely lyrate, finely toothed. Raceme few-fld; fls 3–12mm across; pet. 6–10×1.5–2.5mm, pink to violet, claw long, tinged white or green; pedicel 4–10mm in fruit. Fr. 25–70×1mm, straight, spreading; seed mucilaginous. E Mediterranean, Greece, Turkey. Z9.

***M. flexuosa*** (Sibth. & Sm.) Sibth. & Sm. Similar to *M. maritima* except little-branched, branches short. Pedicel thickened at base. Fr. to 3mm diam. Aegean coast, Crete, Cyprus. Z9.

***M. graeca*** Boiss. & Sprun. Annual, 5–20cm. Stem branched from base. Lvs in dense rosettes, lanceolate-obovate, toothed, lyrate or pinnately cut. Fls scented, 4–16mm across; sep. hairy; pet. 8–17mm, purple-violet; pedicel thin, 4–10mm. Fr. 10–50mm; seed mucilaginous. Greece. ssp. ***bicolor*** (Boiss. & Heldr.) Stork. Fls clustered at top of raceme, pet. violet-pink, base yellow; pedicel very short. S Albania, Greece. Z9.

***M. littorea*** (L.) R. Br. Perenn., 10–40cm. Base woody. Lvs linear-lanceolate, roughly hairy, wavy-toothed, more or less sessile. Pet. 14–22mm, bright purple-pink. Fr. 30–65×1.5mm, tapering to apex, stigma 2–6mm. Summer. SW Europe. Z7.

***M. maritima*** (L.) R. Br. VIRGINIA STOCK. Annual, to 35cm. Stems diffusely branched. Lvs round to obovate-elliptical, tapering to base, branched-hairy, toothed or entire. Raceme many-fld, straight, lacking bracts; fls 8–20mm diam.; sep. two-thirds pet. length; pet. 12–25mm, red-purple, rarely violet, notched, long-clawed; pedicel 4–15mm. Fr. 35–80×1–2mm, stigma to 6mm; seed dark brown, wingless or winged. Spring–autumn. Mediterranean, widespread. A variable species. Compacta Mixed: compact, to 40cm; fls small, pink, white and red, fragrant; seed race. Z8.

***M. bicolor*** Boiss. & Heldr. See *M. graeca* ssp. *bicolor*.
For further synonymy see *Cheiranthus*.

**Malephora** N.E. Br. (From Gk *male*, armhole, and *phorein*, to bear.) Aizoaceae. 15 species of erect or creeping shrubby perennials. Leaves shortly united at the base, triquetrous-prismatic, long-semicylindric, soft-fleshy, slightly blue-pruinose, unspotted. Flowers axillary or terminal, short-pedicellate, golden yellow, yellow or pink, to 5cm diam.; sepals usually 4; stigmas to 8, feathery. Late summer–winter. S Africa (Cape Province, Orange Free State), Namibia. Z9.

CULTIVATION As for *Lampranthus*.

***M. crocea*** (Jacq.) Schwantes. Stems stout, more or less gnarled. Lvs 2.5–4.5cm×6mm, crowded together on short shoots, indistinctly triquetrous, pale green, pruinose. Fls solitary, 3cm diam., golden yellow inside, reddened outside. Cape: Fraserburg District. var. ***purpureo-crocea*** (Haw.) Jacobsen & Schwantes. Fls brilliant red. Cape: Laingsburg District, Little Namaqualand.

***M. engleriana*** (Dinter & A. Berger) Schwantes. Dense, soft shrub to 30cm tall and 50cm across. Lvs 2–4cm, obtuse-triquetrous, curved, obtuse above, green, slightly waxy, very soft. Fls 2cm across, glossy orange-yellow inside, orange-red outside. Namibia: Great Namaqualand.

***M. herrei*** (Schwantes) Schwantes. Mostly prostrate; stems often rooting. Lvs to 50×5mm, triquetrous, rounded-carinate, green. Fls axillary, 5cm diam., golden yellow, orange below. S Africa (Orange Free State).

***M. lutea*** (Haw.) Schwantes. Erect shrub with many short shoots. Lvs spreading, 25–45×4mm, compressed-triquetrous, yellow-green, white-pruinose. Fls 3–4cm diam., yellow. Cape: Little Karroo.

***M. thunbergii*** (Haw.) Schwantes. Stems prostrate, rigid, nodose. Lvs crowded, 5cm long or more, 6–8mm across below, semicylindric, bluntly triquetrous above, fresh green, spotted. Fls 3.5–4cm diam., yellow. SW Cape.

For synonymy see *Crocanthus, Hymenocyclus* and *Mesembryanthemum*.

**Malesherbia** Ruiz & Pav. Passifloraceae. Some 20 species of pubescent, perennial herbs with woody bases. Stems erect, branching sparsely. Leaves cauline, alternate, sessile, linear-lanceolate to spathulate, sometimes crenate-dentate or obscurely pinnatifid. Flowers in terminal clusters of loose panicles, showy, subtended by slender, leaf-like bracts; calyx tubular, straight or curved, campanulate to turbinate, lobes 5, valvate, oblong, abruptly acute; petals 5, oblong, abruptly acute; petals 5, oblong acute to spathulate, broader than calyx lobes; corona toothed, stamens 5. Peru, Chile, Argentina.

CULTIVATION Grow in a gritty, acid medium, min. temp. 10°C/50°F.

***M. linearifolia*** Poir. To 50cm. Lvs to 5cm, linear, obtuse, recurved. Panicle open or a loose arrangement of fls toward stem apex; cal. green flushed purple; cor. lilac to pale mauve. Autumn. Chile.

For illustration see PASSIFLORACEAE.

**Malformations**. Teratology is the study of malformations; in the present context, of malformations or monstrosities in plants. This implies that it is possible to define the 'normal', and that can be difficult. All species show variation to a greater or lesser extent. For example, altitude can have an influence on the size of plants, and any species at the limits of its natural range may show variations in size or form from the representatives of the main populations. Plants of some species become succulent, with thicker, more fleshy leaves, if grown in saline soils. Towards the end of a growing season, there can be extreme modification to inflorescence branching or size. There can be very large differences between size, range of leaf morphology and the age of maturity in weedy species growing in suitable or poor conditions.

Bearing in mind natural and environmentally induced variation, there are readily observed and not infrequent malformations in plants arising from other factors. These are seen as excessive or arrested growth, excessive or arrested development, or abnormal development both in form or position of parts.

The cause of each particular occurrence may need individual investigation, but it is now generally agreed that imbalance in hormone distribution or quantity can account for many of the instances. Auxin levels and distribution are particularly critical, and other non-specific hormones may play a part. Parasitism by mites, viruses, and so on can influence the production of hormones in the plant which regulate the formation of galls or witches' brooms, structures that the plant would not normally produce. Genetic changes, both minor and major, are also recognized as potential causes of abnormal growth.

Earlier workers thought that some of the changes seen, particularly in flowers, where parts may increase or decrease in relation to the normal or appear to grade one into another, could be taken as examples of reversion, or recapitulation of an ancestral state. They were prepared to build evolutionary sequences on such evidence. Little credence is now given to this line of argument, although one may search for evidence of homologies in these abnormalities. Minor changes brought about by genetic or environmental causes are thought by some to be able to bring about reversion to an ancestral condition.

Occasionally an unusually good supply of mineral nutrient, particularly nitrogen, can lead to luxuriant growth or hypertrophy. Changes in somatic chromosome number, of chromosomal

**Malformations** (a) Spiral fasciation (*Asparagus*) (b) Flat fasciation (*Asparagus*) (c) Multiple fasciation (*Pinus pinaster*) (d) Flat fasciation (*Salix sachalinense* 'Sekka') (e) Peloric foxglove (*Digitalis purpurea*) (f) 'Hen-and-chickens' proliferation (*Calendula*) (g) Flat fasciation with multiple flowers (florist's chrysanthemum) (h) Proliferation (rose) (i) Gamopetaly (*Papaver bracteatum*) (j) Petaloid calyx (*Mimulus*) (k) Sepals becoming leafy (*Primula vulgaris*) (l) Foliar proliferation above inflorescence (*Polyanthus primula*) (m) Phyllody - bracts replacing inflorescence (*Plantago major*) (n) Bifurcation of frond (*Asplenium scolopendrium*) (o) Cristation of frond (*Dryopteris filix-mas*) (p) Cristate inflorescence (*Celosia cristata*) (q) Cristate stem (*Mammillaria vaupelii* 'Cristata') (r) Monstrous growth (*Lophocereus schottii* 'Monstrosus')

From *Vegetable Teratology*, M. T. Masters, 1869; *The Principles of Vegetable Teratology*, W. C. Worsdell, 1915; and photographs.)

abnormality, can produce unusual growth forms. for example, autotetraploids are frequently larger than diploids of the same species, such as the grape cultivar *Vitis* 'Perlette', *Clematis montana* 'Tetrarose' and the majority of *Narcissus* cultivars. Wheat is a well known allopolyploid derived from three smaller species.

Plants, unlike animals, have open development. Their growing points (apical meristems) contain immature tissue, with the potential for growth. This growth is normally well ordered, but physical or chemical damage to an apical meristem can influence its future behaviour. The chance, or trauma induced, division of the apex into two independent meristems can lead to dichotomy – two shoots developing from one region. Breakdown in growth co-ordination can take place in the apex, often induced by hormonal imbalance. This can bring about abnormal branching or multiplication of shoots and bushy development, or unusual leaf arrangement (phyllotaxy), or clusters of leaves produced instead of flowers.

Plant parts can develop out of place; inflorescences that normally are of determinate or limited development, can suddenly revert to vegetative shoots, which are indeterminate, or open (a natural feature of some perennials – *Erica*, for example). In the abnormal cases, the cause is thought to be often of hormonal origin. Day-length, changes in temperature regimes or stage of maturity are factors though to influence the normal transition from vegetative to flowering apex. Unusual changes in temperature could cause abnormalities to arise during the delicately balanced transition period.

One of the most striking abnormalities is fasciation. This results from problems in the apical meristem. Sometimes there may be incomplete or incipient dichotomy; or the apical meristem may show lateral expansion. Familiar examples occur in *Ranunculus, Delphinium* and *Forsythia,* where wide, laterally branching stems, giving the impression of several normal stems fused together, can develop. Sometimes an abnormal number of flowers is produced on fasciated stems, as is sometimes seen in lilies. In 'ring fasciation' a ring of subsidiary flowers or flower-heads is produced around the normal central one. This occurs for instance in members of the Compositae, such as the daisy, where the resulting abnormal form is sometimes called 'hen-and-chickens'. Sometimes lateral buds develop on the thickened stem, and branches of normal dimension and appearance grow from it.

Some fasciated forms are cultivated. Thus 'Sekka' is a clone of *Salix sachalinensis*; the flattened, recurving stems are not regularly produced but are encouraged to form by hard pruning. Another familiar example is *Celosia cristata*, the cock's comb, a tetraploid cultigen derived from *C.argentea*, which can be seed-propagated; there are a number of cristate forms among cacti, forming fan-shaped or dense convoluted growths, and many ferns have cultivars in which the ends of fronds are crested. Such plants are often given names like 'Cristata' or 'Monstrosa'.

Where apparent cohesion or adhesion of plant parts occurs, in reality, developmental processes have failed to produce the normal separation. Leaves may fail to separate properly from stems; parts of flowers may appear to be stuck together; stamens to petals, petals to sepals and so on. In double flowers it is quite common to find adnate or even intermediate parts. Petaloid stamens are common in such flowers.

Another interesting change that can occur in flowers is from zygomorphy to actinomorphy – from bilateral symmetry to radial symmetry. This is probably the outcome of a small genetic change and is well investigated in *Antirrhinum* for example. The phenomenon is known as pelory or peloria. A well-known example is the foxglove *Digitalis purpurea* 'Monstrosa', in which a large, open, regular flower tops the spike of normal 2-lipped bell-shaped flowers; this is heritable from seed.

Freak plants produced artificially, by grafting, are sometimes regarded as teratological, but this is not strictly so. Unusual colour mutants, lacking chlorophyll, can sometimes be perpetuated by grafting, as for example *Gymnocalycium* in the Cactaceae. Unsuitable matching of stock and scion can bring about unusual forms. For example, the selection of a vigorous scion for a restricting rootstock in *Fraxinus* can lead to the scion bulging above the graft. The reverse is commonly seen in *Prunus* where a vigorous stock grows much wider than the scion grafted to it; in top-worked trees this can be grotesque.

**Mallotus** Lour. (From Gk *mallotos*, woolly; the fruit in some species is white-spiny.) Euphorbiaceae. About 140 species of deciduous, mostly tropical trees or shrubs. Leaves usually alternate, opposite on some species, wide, simple, palmately veined, petiolate, with stipules. Flowers dioecious, small, in spikes or panicles; calyx lobes valvate or imbricate; petals absent; stamens numerous; styles 3. Fruit a capsule. Old World Tropics.

CULTIVATION *M.japonicus* is an attractive foliage plant for essentially frost-free gardens, suited to a warm south- or southwest-facing wall where temperatures seldom fall much below freezing or otherwise for the cool glasshouse (min. 5–7°C/40–45°F). Grow on any well-drained but moisture-retentive soil, in full sun or light part day shade. Propagate by seed or semi-ripe cuttings.

***M.japonicus*** (Thunb.) Muell. Arg. Deciduous tree or shrub, 3–4m. Shoots rather thick, with a white pith, densely red stellate-pubesc. when young, later grey. Lvs 10–20×6–15cm, rounded-obovate to broadly ovate, long-acuminate, entire, 3-veined, yellow-green beneath with yellow translucent glands, 2 glands on the base; petiole very long. Fls inconspicuous, in 8–15cm long panicles, white-pubesc. Japan, China, Korea.

**Malope** L. (Name of Gk origin, used by Pliny for a mallow.) Malvaceae. 4 species of annual and perennial herbs. Leaves simple, unlobed or palmately lobed. Flowers axillary, solitary, on long pedicels; epicalyx segments 3, free, leafy, cordate-ovate, broader than the sepals; petals white, pink or violet; styles filiform, stigmas lateral, filiform, as many as the mericarps. Fruit a schizocarp, mericarps numerous, 1-seeded, indehiscent, glabrous, rugulose, irregularly superposed in a globose head. Mediterranean to W Asia.

CULTIVATION *M.trifida* occurs on sandy soils, often on cultivated land; *M.malacoides* is found on wasteland, on maritime sands and in thickets around the Mediterranean. They make substantial plants, grown for their profusion of showy, delicate flowers, carried in succession throughout the summer, in shades of pink, conspicuously veined with deeper shades. *Malope* spp. have long been grown as hardy annuals in cottage gardens and mixed borders for their flowers, which last well when cut; they perform best in regions with cooler summers and may fail in very hot, humid conditions. Grow in moderately fertile and humus-rich, sandy soils in full sun, and irrigate in summer as necessary. Dead-head regularly to extend flowering season.

Propagate from seed sown under glass in early spring, or *in situ*; sow successionally if grown for cutting. For winter and spring flowers, sow seed from late summer on, growing on in a well-drained, medium-fertility, loam-based mix, with a minimum temperature of 7–10°C/45–50°F in direct sunlight with low humidity. Sometimes infected by rust, *Puccinia malvacearum*, and by fungal stem cankers, *Colletotrichum malvarum*. Also by aphid.

***M.malacoides*** L. Annual or perenn. herb to 50cm; stems ascending, hispid mainly toward apex. Lvs 2–5×1–3.5cm, oblong-lanceolate to ovate, crenate, upper lvs often 3-lobed. Epicalyx 8–12×6–8mm during anthesis, longer and strongly accrescent in fruit, cordate-orbicular, acuminate; sep. acuminate, longer and narrower than epicalyx seg.; pet. 2–4cm, deep pink or purple. Mediterranean to W Russia. Z8.

***M.trifida*** Cav. Annual glabrescent herb to 1.2m; stems erect, stout, unbranched. Lvs to 10cm, long-petiolate, crenate-dentate, lower lvs suborbicular, upper lvs 3–5-lobed, lobes triangular. Epicalyx seg. 1.2–1.5cm, orbicular-cordate during anthesis, to 3cm in fruit; sep. lanceolate-ovate; pet. 4–6×2–4cm, deep purple-red. W Mediterranean. 'Alba': fls white. 'Grandiflora': fls large, dark rose. 'Rosea': fls rose red. 'Vulcan': fls large, bright red, free-flowering; tetraploid.

***M.grandiflora*** Dietr. See *M.trifida*.
***M.stipulacea*** Cav. See *M.malacoides*.

**Malortiea** H.A. Wendl.
***M.gracilis*** H.A. Wendl. See *Reinhardtia gracilis*.

***M. simplex*** H.A. Wendl. See *Reinhardtia simplex*.

**Malosma** (Nutt.) Engl. Anacardiaceae. 1 species, a small evergreen tree or shrub, to 4m. Branches slender, brown, glaucescent, glabrous. Leaves simple, alternate, ovate or elliptic, rarely lanceolate or oblong, coriaceous, glabrous, entire, tinged red above, paler beneath, margins white, slightly revolute; petioles 1–4cm. Inflorescence a thyrses, terminal, dense, glabrous, intricately branched, to 10cm; bracts spathulate; flowers functionally unisexual; sepals 5, imbricate; petals 5, white, spreading, elliptic; ovary unicarpellate by abortion, sessile on disc. Fruit a white drupe, almost symmetrical, somewhat flattened, about 1.5mm with sterile carpels forming a raised line on side of fruit. California. Z9.

CULTIVATION As for *Lithrea*.

***M. laurina*** (Nutt.) Nutt. ex Engl. As for the genus.

For synonymy see *Lithrea, Rhus* and *Toxicodendron*.

**Malpighia** L. (For Marcello Malpighi (1628–94), Italian naturalist, Professor at Bologna.) BARBADOS CHERRY; ACEROLA. Malpighiaceae. About 45 species of erect shrubs or small trees. Leaves opposite, ovate to lanceolate or linear-lanceolate, margins entire or dentate, glabrous or hairy, hairs often strongly irritant (rather than stinging as usually described); petioles short, eglandular; stipules minute, deciduous. Flowers in axillary or terminal umbellate clusters or corymbs, or sometimes solitary; sepals 5, with 6–10 glands on exterior; petals unequal, unguiculate, white, pink or red, fimbriate or ciliate at apex; stamens 10, filaments glabrous, free; ovary glabrous, 3-lobed, styles 3. Fruit a red, orange, scarlet or purple drupe with 3 stones, stones with 3–5 dorsal crests. Caribbean, tropical America. Z10.

CULTIVATION *M. glabra*, the Barbados cherry, widely planted in gardens throughout Jamaica, is a small evergreen native of the humid tropics. The smooth-skinned cherry-like fruits have a sweet, red juicy pulp with a flavour reminiscent of raspberries, reputed to be one of the richest natural sources of Vitamin C. Eaten fresh the fruit provides five times the recommended daily requirement of the vitamin, and until the advent of synthesized ascorbic acid, *M. glabra* was grown commercially in Hawaii to boost the vitamin content of other fruit juices. The fruit is also used in jams, jellies and in *doces* and *refrescos* (soothing and refreshing beverages). The potential of this species for repeated blooming, up to five flushes per annum, gives rise to an estimated commercial yield of 60 tonnes per hectare.

In tropical and frost-free subtropical areas (as far north as Texas), *Malpighia* spp. are also used as ornamentals in shrub borders, as lawn specimens, and as low hedges which stand shearing well. *M. coccigera* is particularly valued for its compact habit and holly-like leaves. Plant in fertile well-drained soil, on a sunny site with part day shade. Prune in winter only to shape or to limit size. In temperate climates grow in the glasshouse, with minimum night temperature 15°C/60°F, medium humidity and bright filtered light, in a sandy loam-based medium with additional organic matter. Propagate in summer by semi-ripe cuttings with entire leaves, rooted with bottom heat in a closed case or under mist. Also from seed.

***M. aquifolia*** L. Shrub to 2m, branches smooth. Lvs lanceolate, spiny-dentate, with decumbent irritant bristles beneath. Fls axillary, 1–2, pale pink. S America.

***M. coccigera*** L. MINIATURE HOLLY; SINGAPORE HOLLY. Shrub to 1m, branches elongate, often prostrate. Lvs 0.6–2.5×0.4–2.4cm, orbicular or broad-elliptic to obovate, base rounded, apex rounded, margin deeply sinuate, with lobes aristate-dentate, coriaceous, glabrate. Fls axillary, solitary or paired; pet. pink or lilac. Fr. subglobose, red, 5–15mm. W Indies.

***M. cubensis*** Kunth in HBK. LADY HAIR. Shrub to 2m. Lvs 1.5–2.5cm, narrow-oblong, obtuse or acute, densely covered on both surfaces by yellow irritant hairs. Fls 1 to few in glabrous umbel; cal. covered by glands; pet. 5–7mm, white or pale pink. Cuba, W Indies.

***M. emarginata*** Sessé & Moc. ex DC. BARBADOS CHERRY. Shrub or small tree 2–6m, much-branched, branchlets stiff. Shoots with internodes short, densely leafy, or internodes long. Lvs 2.5–7×1.4–3.3cm (to 10–15cm in cult.), ovate or elliptic or obovate, base cuneate to rounded, apex often emarginate and apiculate, or acute, margin entire. Fls 2–4, pink or purple; cal. with 6 glands; stamens unequal; 2 styles longer than third. Fr. red, to 1cm diam. W Indies, Mexico south to Venezuela and Peru.

***M. glabra*** L. BARBADOS CHERRY. Shrub to 3m. Lvs to 10cm, ovate-lanceolate or elliptic-lanceolate, cuneate, entire, glossy dark green above. Fls 3–5 in umbels, to 1.5cm across, red or rose; cal. with 8 glands, externally glabrous or sparsely hairy; stamens subequal; styles subequal. Fr globose, red, to 1cm diam. Texas to northern S America, W Indies. 'Fairchild': habit weeping; lvs small, pointed fls pink.

***M. mexicana*** A. Juss. Lvs ovate to obovate-lanceolate, acute to obtuse, glabrous to hairy. Fls in cymes, purple, to 2cm across; sep. densely hairy. Fr. globose, red. Mexico.

***M. suberosa*** Small. Lvs to 10cm, oblong to oblong-ovate, crenulate, bright green. Fls sessile, white or pink; sep. glabrous. Fr. yellow-red. Cuba.

***M. urens*** L. COWHAGE; COW ITCH CHERRY. Erect or scrambling shrub to 3m, branches smooth. Lvs oblong-ovate, glabrous above, with decumbent bristles beneath. Fls in clusters, solitary on peduncles, pink or pale purple. W Indies.

***M. angustifolia*** Hitchc. non L. See *M. cubensis*.
***M. punicifolia*** auct., non L. See *M. emarginata*.
***M. punicifolia*** L. See *M. glabra*.

**MALPIGHIACEAE** Juss. MALPIGHIA FAMILY. Dicot. 68 genera and 1100 species of small trees, shrubs, or lianes, often with unusual secondary growth, plant usually covered with branched unicellular hairs and sometimes with alkaloids. Leaves opposite, simple, entire, very often with 2 large fleshy glands on petiole or abaxial surface; stipules often large and united. Flowers bisexual, bilaterally symmetrical to regular, 5-merous, with 2-bracteolate pedicels, inflorescence racemose; calyx basally connate, often with 2 conspicuous glands at the base; corolla imbricate, often clawed, with ciliate to fringed margins; stamens in (1) 2 (3) whorls, some often sterile, filaments more or less basally connate; ovary superior, of (2) 3 (–5) fused carpels, plurilocular; placentation axile; styles usually distinct; ovule 1 per locule. Fruit a schizocarp of winged to nut-like mericarps, sometimes a nut or drupe; seeds with oily embryo; endosperm this or absent. *Bunchosia* and *Malpighia* have edible fruits. Tropical and warm regions, especially S America. *Acridocarpus, Bunchosia, Hiptage, Lophanthera, Malpighia, Sphedamnocarpus, Stigmaphyllon*.

**Malus** Mill. APPLE. (Lat. for apple-tree.) Rosaceae. Some 35 species of trees and shrubs, lateral shoots thorny. Leaves alternate, serrate, occasionally lobed, rolled or folded in the bud. Flowers in corymbs, hermaphrodite, white or pink; petals 5, obovate-orbicular; stamens 20, occasionally 15; carpels 5, rarely 3–4, basal portion fused, tufted. Fruit a pome, endocarp tough and parchment-like, locules with 2 ovaries producing 1–2 seeds, sometimes surrounded by persistent calyx. Europe, Asia, US.

CULTIVATION *Malus* spp. can are found throughout the temperate zones of the northern hemisphere; many in habitats similar to those of the European native *M. sylvestris*, the wild crab apple, which occurs in scrub, hedgerow and woodland (especially oak woodland) on neutral to calcareous soils. *M. pumila*, the orchard apple, is sometimes found naturalized in similar habitats but is distinguished by its larger and sweeter fruits. (For apple cultivation see APPLES.) Whilst the fruits of most species and cultivars are technically edible in that they are not toxic, many are unacceptably small, sour and/or bitter: those with larger and sweeter fruits must be selected where culinary use is the primary intention. These include the following cultivars: 'Cheal's Scarlet', 'Chilko', 'Crittenden', 'Dartmouth', 'Dolgo', 'Elise Rathke', 'Golden Hornet', 'Hopa', 'Hyslop', 'John Downie', 'Montreal Beauty', 'Red Silver', and 'Veitch's Scarlet'. Some species and cvs, notably *M. floribunda, M.* 'Aldhamensis', 'Golden Hornet', 'John Downie' and 'Winter Gold' can be used as (very effective) pollinators in fruit orchards.

The fruiting crabs, like other *Malus* spp., can provide ornamental interest throughout the year, especially in spring: the blossom, white in *M. hupehensis, M. florentina* and *M. sargentii*, pink in *M. floribunda*, or deep rose in *M. spectabilis* and *M.* ×*purpurea*, is often beautifully fragrant, notably in the violet-scented *M. angustifolia* and *M. coronaria* 'Charlottae'. The decorative fruit, with a colour range from clear yellow through bright reds to deep red-purple, often persists well into winter and even the fruit of American native species, which rarely colours well, makes a valuable food source to attract birds and other wildlife into the garden. Several species, such as *M. coronaria, M. glaucescens,* and *M. kansuensis*, colour well in autumn.

Taller species such as *M. floribunda, M. hupehensis* and *M. prattii*, when grown as standards, are suitable as lawn specimens, at the woodland edge, or in large borders. Smaller species or those grown as half-standards can be selected for the smaller garden or border. *M. tschonoskii* is a small conical tree, bearing few fruits but with brilliant autumn colours in orange, purple and scarlet, and is well suited to planting in public access areas.

*Malus* will tolerate light, dappled shade, although autumn colour and fruiting is better in sun and all are hardy to at least −15°C/5°F; these are records in the US of *Malus* growing satisfactorily where temperatures drop below −45°C/−49°F. Most species tolerate a range of fertile soils, although *M. ioensis* 'Plena' and *M.* ×*schiedeckeri*, of more delicate constitution, are unsuitable for chalk soils.

Grow in a sunny position, in moisture-retentive but not boggy soil. In very rich soil, vegetative growth is made at the expense of flowering. Prune in winter when necessary to remove dead, diseased, damaged or crossing wood. Untidy growth may also be removed after flowering. On grafted specimens, it may be necessary to remove suckers that occur below the graft union. Standard and half standard trees grown for ornamental purposes are often trained in the nursery with an open, wide-branching crown; for fruiting purposes it may be preferable to obtain a feathered maiden to form a central leader (spindlebush) tree, with a well-spaced framework of laterals as for apples.

Propagate species by seed, although species grown in close proximity may hybridize and not come true; *M. hupehensis* produces seed apomictically, and seedlings therefore come true. Sow seed in spring, following three months' cold stratification in damp peat at 1°C/34°F. Temperatures above 15–20°C/59–68°F in the sowing medium may induce secondary dormancy. Cultivars are T-budded, or whip and tongue grafted on to clonal rootstocks (in Britain often onto seedling rootstock derived from seed extracted in Europe during processing of fruit for juice or canning).

Pests and diseases affecting crab apples are similar to those of orchard apples. See APPLES.

***M.* ×*adstringens*** Zab. *(M. baccata* × *M. pumila.)* Lvs softly downy beneath. Fls pink, cal. and pedicel short tufted. Fr. 4–5cm, subglobose, short-stalked, cal. occasionally persistent, red, yellow, or green. 'Almey': habit rounded, upright, to 4m; lvs tinted purple when young, later bronzed; buds chestnut; fls profuse, deep purple, pet. lighter at base; fr. globose, to 2cm diam., orange with a red cheek, to completely red. 'American Beauty': habit upright, vigorous; lvs bronzed red when young, later bronzed green; fls double, clear red; fr. sparse. 'Crimson Brilliant': habit shrub-like, slow-growing; lvs bronzed purple; fls single to semi-double, carmine with a white star; fr. to 2cm diam., dark purple. 'Helen': habit shrub-like; twigs laterally spreading; lvs light red; fls single, purple; fr. purple stained red. 'Hopa': habit broad, loosely upright, to 4m; lvs oval-elliptic, bronzed red; fls profuse, red washed lilac; fr. clear orange to bright red, edible. 'Irene': lvs finely serrate, tinted red; fls profuse, single, purple; fr. to 2cm diam., maroon. 'Nipissing': habit shrub-like; fls carmine, later darker, soon fading; fr. orange to dark red, bronzed green on shaded side. 'Osman': habit large, shrub-like; fls single, pink washed white; fr. to 4cm diam., orange to red. 'Patricia': habit upright, to 5m; crown rounded; lvs bronzed; fls single, dark red, early; fr. to 2.5cm diam., dark red; seedling of 'Hopa'. 'Pink Beauty': fls single, dark carmine; fr. bright red. 'Pink Giant': fls simple, pink, later light pink washed lilac; fr. to 2cm diam., dark orange. 'Purple Wave': habit spreading, to 4m; lvs tinted red when young, later darker; fls single, purple; fr. purple. 'Radiant': habit dense, upright; lvs tinted red when young, later dark green; buds deep rd, fls profuse, single, dark pink; fr. small, to 13mm, light blackcurrant; seedling of 'Hopa'. 'Red Silver': lvs silver pubescent when young, later chestnut to bronzed red; fls single, dark pink, later fading; fr. maroon; from 'Niedzwetzkyana'. 'Red Splendor': fls dark pink, later lighter; fr. to 1.5cm diam., red; from 'Red Silver'. 'Robin': fls dark pink, soon fading; fr. to 4cm diam, sunset orange, edible. 'Simcoe': fls single, dark pink, soon fading; fr. to 2.5cm diam., dark orange; from 'Niedzwetzkyana'. 'Sissipuk': fls single, rich dark red, fading to light pink, late; fr. to 2.5cm diam., purple. 'Timiskaming': lvs red in autumn; fls single, rich purple; fr., to 2cm diam., maroon. 'Transcendent': habit broad, shrub-like; buds pink, fls white; fr. striped dark yellow and red, sour, edible. 'Vanguard': habit narrow and upright, later spreading; lvs tinted red when young, later dark green; fls profuse, single, light pink; fr. to 2cm diam., vivid red. 'Wabiskaw': habit columnar to narrow upright, vigorous; lvs tinted red when young, later bronzed; fls single to semi-double, dark red stained purple, anth. gold; fr. to 3cm diam., dark pink. Z3.

***M. angustifolia*** (Ait.) Michx. Shrub or small tree 5–7m, rarely to 10m, shoots slender, lightly downy at first, soon glabrous. Lvs 3–7cm, lanceolate-oblong to oval, pointed or blunt, coriaceous, widely cuneate, almost entire or deeply serrate, especially so on strong shoots, pale green above, smooth or felted beneath, persistent to semi-evergreen in mild localities. Fls 2.5cm diam., aromatic, in sparse corymbs; cal. lobes long, tapered; pet. narrow-obovate, white-pink, late flowering; style base downy-tufted. Fr. 1.5–2.5cm, slightly pyrimiform, apex and base depressed, yellow-green, aromatic. S US. 'Prince Georges' (*M. angustifolia* × *M. ioensis* 'Plena'): habit small, shrub-like upright, conic; twigs spreading, densely foliate; lvs persistent; fls fragrant, pink, very late; sterile. Z6.

***M.* ×*arnoldiana*** (Rehd.) Sarg. *(M. baccata* × *M. floribunda.)* Shrub to 2m, resembling *M. floribunda*, not robust. Shoots widely arching, soon glabrous. Lvs 5–8cm, elliptic to ovate, long-tapered, base rounded or tapered, roughly biserrate, slightly pubesc. when young, later glabrous except for veins beneath. Fls 4–6 in cymes; pedicel thin, red-brown; cal. lobes 5mm, lanceolate, red, abscising from fr.; pet. 3mm, carmine-red in bud later, pink becoming white, narrowly elliptic, clawed; styles 3–4, usually 3, basal third downy, fused. Fr. 15mm, globose, yellow-green. Garden origin. 'Linda': fls single, carmine, later light pink; fr. to 3cm diam., carmine. Z4.

***M.* ×*astracanica*** Dum.-Cours. *(M. prunifolia* × *M. pumila.)* Resembles *M. pumila*, differing in rougher, more deeply serrated lvs on longer petioles; fls bright red; fr. pruinose. Thought to have arisen in Asia. Z3.

***M.* ×*atrosanguinea*** (Späth) Schneid. *(M. haliana* × *M. sieboldii.)* Resembling *M. floribunda* in arching spreading habit, shoots slightly pendulous. Lvs ovate, serrate, basally lobed on strong shoots, dark green, waxy. Fls simple, deep carmine in bud and full flower. Fr. 1cm, globose, red or yellow flushed red. Garden origin. Z4.

***M. baccata*** (L.) Borkh. Tree or shrub to 5m, often confused with *M. robusta*, shoots slender, glabrous. Lvs 3–8cm, ovate, long-tapered, finely serrate, light green, glabrous above and beneath; petioles to 5cm. Fls 3–3.5cm diam., in small clusters, white; cal. glabrous, teeth long-tapered, abscising in fr. Fr. 1cm, globose, yellow and red. NE Asia to N China. 'Columnaris': habit narrow upright, to 8×2m; fls snow white; fr. yellow with red cheek. 'Dolgo': habit shrub-like, upright; fls single, white, early; fr. to 3cm diam., bright red. 'Gracilis': habit shrub-like, slow-growing; branches slender, dense; lvs small, narrow; buds pink, fls white, stellate; fr. small red. 'Lady Northcliffe': buds light pink, fls profuse, white; fr. to 1.5cm diam., dark orange. 'Macrocarpa': fr. large, to 3cm diam., glossy yellow stained red. 'Orange': habit large, shrub-like; buds light pink, fls white; fr. large, to 4cm diam.; red washed orange. 'Red River' ('Dolgo' × 'Delicious'): habit upright; fls single, pink; fr. large, to 5cm, bright red, edible. 'Rudolf': buds carmine, fls single, pink, later fading; fr. dark orange to red. 'Spring Snow': habit upright; fls large, white; fruitless; seedling of 'Dolgo'. var. ***himalaica*** (Maxim.) Schneid. Lvs wide, elliptic, roughly serrate, glabrous, veins on lower lf surfaces remaining downy. Fls 3cm diam., pink in bud. Fr. 1–1.5cm, yellow flushed red. W Himalaya, SW China. var. ***jackii*** Rehd. Crown broader than species type, branches stout. Lvs broadly elliptic. Fls 3–cm diam., white. Fr. 1cm, red, waxy. Korea. var. ***mandschurica*** (Maxim.) Schneid. Lvs broadly elliptic, margins with few fine serrations, lower surfaces and petioles downy at first. Fls to 4cm diam., white, aromatic, cal. and pedicel downy at first. Fr. 12mm, ellipsoid, bright red, ripening early. C Japan, C China. Z2.

***M. bracteata*** Rehd. Resembles *M. ioensis*, differing in less deeply incised serrations and smaller lobes, these often recurved. Small tree to 7m, shoots pubesc. at first becoming glabrous later. Lvs oval to ovate-elliptic, serrate, soon glabrous. Fls 3–5 in clusters, pink, pedicel with awl-shaped prophylls abscising soon after fls. Fr. 3cm, yellow. S US. Z6.

***M. brevipes*** (Rehd.) Rehd. Crown stiff, compact, usually shrubby. Lvs resemble those of *M. floribunda*, 5–7cm, finely serrate. Fls many, white-pale cream; pedicel glabrous. Fr. subglobose, on erect, rigid, red stalks, scarlet, slightly ribbed, cal. abscising. Z5.

***M. coronaria*** (L.) Mill. Small tree to 7m wide spreading, shoots stiff with numerous short-thorned laterals, tomentose at first, becoming glabrous. Lvs 5-10cm, ovate-oblong, pointed, roughly serrate, slightly lobed, more so on strong shoots, tomentose at first becoming glabrous and scarlet-orange. Fls 4–6 in clusters, to 4cm diam., pink; pet. suborbicular. Fr. 4cm, depressed globose, green, base slightly ribbed, aromatic. NE US. 'Charlottae' ('Charlotta'): lvs red stained orange in autumn; fls double, soft pink, fragrant. 'Kola': habit conic, later spreading; crown rounded; lvs tinted silver; fls pink, fragrant; fr. large, to 5cm diam., waxy, yellow and stained green. 'Nieuwlandiana': habit shrub-like, to 3×3m; fls in large hanging clusters, vivid pink, very fragrant; fr. as type but blue pruinose. var. ***dasycalyx*** Rehd. Lvs paler green beneath, venation only downy on strong shoots. Fls smaller than species type, 3.5cm diam., pink, highly aromatic; cal. downy. Fr. 4cm, yellow-green. N America (Ontario to Indiana). var. ***elongata*** (Rehd.) Rehd. Lvs larger, oval-narrow triangular or lanceolate, lobes reduced. Fls 3.5cm diam., pink. Fr. 3cm, green. US. Z4.

***M.*** **×*dawsoniana*** Rehd. *(M. fusca × M. pumila.)* Resembles *M. fusca*, differs in wider, more elliptic habit. Lvs 6–8cm, pointed, base rounded, margins roughly serrate, rarely lobed. Fls simple, 2.5–3.5cm diam., pale pink becoming white. Fr. 4×2.5cm, ellipsoid, yellow; cal. reduced, persistent. Late flowering. Garden origin. Z5.

***M.*** **×*denboerii*** Krüssm. *(M. ioensis × M. ×purpurea.)* Resembles *M. ioensis*, but growth vigorous, more upright. Lvs on strong shoots resemble *M. ioensis*, others elliptic, unlobed, bronze-purple becoming bright yellow, brown and purple on senescence. Fls 2.5cm diam., deep pink. Fr. 2.5cm, globose, red, with red flesh. Garden origin. 'Evelyn': habit upright, vigorous; lvs bronzed, tinted red in autumn; fls profuse, single, dark salmon; fr. to 3cm, tinted red. 'Lisa': less vigorous than 'Evelyn'; fls dark pink, later fading, fragrant; fr. small to 2.5cm diam., carmine, sometimes stained orange. Z4.

***M. florentina*** (Zucc.) Schneid. Shrub at first becoming a wide spreading tree 8×6m, shoots downy, fluffy. Lvs 5–7cm, broadly ovate, margins serrate, lobes incised, matt green above, yellow grey felted beneath becoming scarlet on senescence. Fls many, in downy clusters of 2–6. Fr. 1cm, ellipsoid, red. N Italy. Z6.

***M. floribunda*** Van Houtte. Shrub to 4m, or tree to 10m, crown dense, apex arched, shoot tips slightly pendulous, slender, downy. Lvs 4–8cm, folded in bud opening long-tapered, deeply serrate, slightly lobed on strong branches. Fls 2.5–3cm diam., abundant along whole length of branch, deep pink in bud fading to pale pink, white inside. Fr. 0.5cm, yellow. Japan. 'Peachblow': habit upright; buds dark pink, fls white; fr. to 1cm diam., red. Z4.

***M. formosana*** (Kawak. & Koidz.) Kawak. & Koidz. Tree or shrub to 12m, shoots downy grey, usually thorny. Lvs 8–15×2.5–5.5cm, ovate-oblong, apex pointed, base rounded or cuneate, margins unevenly serrate, veins in 9–11 pairs, soon glabrous. Fls 2.5cm diam., in small downy clusters; cal. lobes lanceolate, downy; pet. 5, 12mm, obovate. Fr. 4–5cm, ovoid, cal. persistent. China (Hainan), Taiwan. Z8.

***M. fusca*** (Raf.) Schneid. Shrub to 7m or tree to 10m, shoots downy at first. Lvs 3–10cm, long-oval to oblong-elliptic, pointed or long-tapered, deeply serrate, usually 3-lobed, at least on the strong shoots, upper and lower lf surfaces pale green, downy at first, becoming glabrous. Fls in clusters of 6–12, pink-white, soon fading; pedicels slender, downy. Fr. 1cm, ellipsoid, yellow or red, cal. absent. W US. Z6.

***M. glabrata*** Rehd. Resembles *M. glaucescens*, differs in green colouring of lower lf surfaces. Lvs fine, pale green, smooth, margins distinctly lobed, base cordate, basal vein pair arising from margin. Fls 3cm diam.; cal. red-brown, glabrous; pet. ovate, rounded, short-clawed, pink; styles 5. Fr. 3cm, depressed-globose, yellow-green, base distinctly ribbed. US (N Carolina to Alabama). Z6.

***M. glaucescens*** Rehd. Shrub or small tree, crown wide spreading, branches sometimes thorny. Lvs 5–8cm, oval-triangular, pointed, shallowly triangular lobed, pubesc. at first becoming glabrous, dark green above, blue-green beneath, becoming yellow and deep purple on senescence. Fls 3.5cm diam., in clusters of 5–7; cal. lobes lanceolate, exterior tufted downy, interior felted; pet. ovate, apex tapered to claw, white-pink. Fr. 3–4cm, depressed-globose, base and apex distinctly depressed, yellow, shiny, aromatic. E US. Z5.

***M.*** **×*gloriosa*** Lemoine. *(M. pumila* 'Niedzwetzkyana' × *M. schiedeckeri.)* Resembles *M. schiedeckeri* most closely, differs in bronze red young lvs, purple crimson fls to 4cm diam., sparsely displayed. Fr. to 3cm. Garden origin. 'Oekonomierat Echtermeyer': habit widely pendulous; lvs tinted red when young, later bronzed green; fls single, carmine; fr. to 2.5cm diam., brown tinted red. Z4.

***M. halliana*** Koehne. Shrub 2–4m, crown sparse, irregular. Lvs 4–8cm, oval-oblong, pointed, margins with shallow rounded notches, red-green at first, becoming dark green above, paler beneath, never hairy, petiole and venation remaining red-green. Fls 3–4cm diam., in small, often pendulous bunches of 4–7, red in bud opening deep pink, often semi-double on slender pedicels. Fr. 6–8mm, obovoid, red-brown ripening late, seeds large. China. 'Parkmanii': habit shrub-like; fls in hanging clusters, soft pink; fr. globose, to 1.5cm diam., red. var. ***spontanea*** (Mak.) Koidz. Short, wide-spreading, thick-set shrub. Lvs 3–4cm, elliptic to obovate. Fls to 3cm diam., smaller than type species, biennially borne. Fr. 1cm, yellow-green. Japan. Z5.

***M.*** **×*hartwigii*** Koehne. *(M. baccata × M. halliana.)* Branches ascending, forming a tight upright crown, shoots dark brown. Lvs 6–8cm, ovate, pointed, entire. Fls 4cm, semi-double, deep pink in bud fading white; cal. red, later abscising leaving a scar ring on fr. Fr. 1cm, globose to pyriform, yellow-green. Garden origin. 'Katherine': habit upright, slightly spreading; lvs acuminate; fls fully double, pink, later white; fr. to 1cm diam., yellow, sometimes tinted red. Z4.

***M.*** **'Henrietta Crosby'**. *(M. arnoldiana × M. pumila* 'Niedzwetzkyana'.) Vigorous. Fls single, pink. Fr. to 2.5cm diam., vivid red. Z4.

***M.*** **'Henry F Dupont'**. *(M. arnoldiana × M. purpurea 'Eleyi'.)* Habit spreading. Buds purple, fls single to semi-double, pink. Fr. to 12mm diam., red tinted brown, persistent. Z4.

***M.*** **×*heterophylla*** Spach. Resembles *M. soulandii* but lvs smaller, wider, with downy petioles; fls 4cm, pink in bud becoming white; fr. to 6cm, green. 'Red Tip': vigorous; lvs with red tips when young, orange in autumn; fls solitary, dark salmon; fr. large, to 4cm diam., yellow stained green. Z4.

***M. honanensis*** Rehd. Shrub closely resembling *M. kansuensis*, differs in reduced vigour, slender shoots. Lvs 6–8cm, rounded-ovate, downy, margins with 2–5 pairs of broadly ovate serrated lobes, autumn colour scarlet. Fls 2cm diam., in clusters of about 10, white, glabrous; styles 3–4. Fr. 1cm, pitted, yellow-green. NE China. Z6.

***M. hupehensis*** (Pamp.) Rehd. Tree or shrub, 5–7m; shoots rigid, spreading, soon glabrous. Lvs 5–10cm, ovate to oblong, long-tapered, base rounded-cordate, margins deeply incised, slightly downy beneath, young lvs red-green at first. Fls 4cm diam., in clusters of 3–7, pink fading to white, aromatic; cal. red-green, downy. Fr. 1cm, rounded, yellow-green, flushed red. India (Assam). 'Rosea': fls profuse, cherry blossom pink; fr. yellow, sometimes tinted red. Z4.

***M. ioensis*** (Wood) Britt. PRAIRIE CRAB. Small tree, branches well-spaced, felted at first, becoming glabrous, red-brown. Lvs 5–10cm, oblong-ovate, pointed, deeply serrate, dark green above, yellow-green felted beneath, becoming deep red or yellow on senescence. Fls 4cm diam., white tinged pink, aromatic, reminiscent of violets. Fr. 3cm, rounded, ellipsoid, occasionally rather pointed, shiny green, cal. persistent. C US. 'Fimbriata': lvs narrower then type; fls fully double, pink, fimbriate. 'Klehm's': vigorous; lvs large; fls fully double, pink, fragrant; fr. sparse, green. 'Nova': fls dark pink, sterile; mutation of 'Plena'. 'Plena': fls profuse, very large, fully double, soft pink; fr. to 3cm diam., green. 'Prairiefire': bark glossy dark red; lvs persistent; fls vivid red; fr. conic, maroon; disease and scab resistant. var. ***creniserrata*** Rehd. Habit rather columnar, twigs tufted downy at first, never thorned. Lvs elliptic-ovate to oval-oblong, margins scalloped or entire, almost biserrate on strong shoots; cal. felted. var. ***palmeri*** Rehd. Small tree, very similar to species type, differing in smaller, finer, more oblong lvs, these downy, only scalloped on flowering branches, apex rounded. var. ***spinosa*** Rehd. Small shrub 1.5–2.5m, shoots slender, with numerous thorns. Lvs small than type, serrate, lobes reduced and only present on strong shoots. Fls 3.5cm diam., pink. Fr. 3cm, green. var. ***texana*** Rehd. Shrub to 4m, shoots dense, first year wood felted, glabrous in subsequent year. Lvs smaller but broader than type species, lobes reduced or absent, retaining dense felt. Z2.

***M. kansuensis*** (Batal.) Schneid. Shrub or small tree to 5m, shoots lightly downy at first, becoming glabrous, red-brown. Lvs 5–8, ovate with 3 or 5 triangular lobes, margin with numerous serrations, dark green above, paler beneath, usually downy at least on veins; petiole variable, 1.5–4cm. Fls 1.5cm diam., in bunches of 4–10, white; cal. downy tufted. Fr. 1cm, ellipsoid, yellow to purple, lightly pitted. NW China. f. ***calva*** Rehd. Lvs, cal., petiole and new growth always glabrous; fr. deeper yellow than species type. NW China. Z5.

***M. lancifolia*** Rehd. Shrub or small tree to 6m, crown spreading, shoots thorned, downy at first. Lvs 3–7cm, oval-lanceolate, sometimes more rounded, apex pointed, margins biserrate to variable depths, rarely slightly lobed. Fls 3cm diam., in corymbs of 3–6, cal. and pedicel glabrous, styles 5; pet. rosy pink. Fr. 3cm in pendulous bunches, rounded, green, waxy. E US. Z5.

***M.*** **×*magdeburgensis*** Hartwig. *(M. pumila × M. spectabilis.)* Shrub or small tree, resembling *M. spectabilis*. Crown globose. Lvs 6-8cm, wider than *M. spectabilis*, elliptic, apex and base acuminate, downy beneath. Fls 4.5cm diam.; pet. 5–12, bright red in bud, opening deep pink; cal. and pedicel downy. Fr. 3cm, rounded, green-yellow flushed red. Garden origin (1850 Germany). Z4.

***M.*** **'Mary Potter'**. *(M. atrosanguinea × M. sargentii* 'Rosea'.) Habit low, broad, vigorous. Buds pink, fls white. Fr. to 1cm diam., bright red.

***M.*** **×*micromalus*** Mak. *(M. baccata × M. spectabilis.)* Shrub or small erect tree, 4×3m; shoots elongated, soon glabrous, dark brown. Lvs 5–10cm, elliptic-oblong, long-tapered, base triangular, coriaceous, margins closely small serrate, waxy green above becoming glabrous. Fls simple, 4.5cm diam., in clusters of 3–5, always pink, not fading. Fr. 1.5cm, rounded, slightly pointed, yellow, basal eye depressed, cal. absent. Japan. Z4.

***M.*** **×*moerlandsii*** Doorenbos. *(M. ×purpurea* 'Lemoinei' × *M. sieboldii.)* Tall shrub. Lvs green brown, slightly lobed, shiny. Fls red-pink, numerous. Fr. 1–1.5cm, rounded, purple. Garden origin (1938 Holland). 'Liset': habit shrub-like, upright, vigorous; lvs maroon, later glossy dark green; fls profuse, single, vivid purple-red; fr. to 15mm diam., dark brown. 'Nicoline': habit shrub-like, tall; lvs purple stained green; fls in clusters, small, dark maroon. 'Profusion': habit upright, to 4m; lvs tinted red, later bronzed green; fls single, light maroon with pink centre, late; fr. small, to 1.5cm diam., oxblood-red, pruinose. Z5.

***M.*** **×*platycarpa*** Rehd. *(M. coronaria × M. pumila.)* Tree to 6m, crown spreading, shoots without thorns, felted only at first. Lvs 5–8cm, ovate to elliptic, apex and base rounded, base rounded, base subcordate, margins roughly biserrate, occasionally triangularly lobed on strong shoots, veins on lower lf surfaces downy. Fls 3.5cm diam., pink in bud opening white; cal. and pedicel glabrous. Fr. 4–5cm, depressed-globose, yellow-green, rarely red, apex and base hollowed, waxy, aromatic. SE US 'Hoopesii': lvs unlobed or slightly lobed; fls pink washed white; fr. to 5cm diam., green. Z6.

***M. prattii*** (Hemsl.) Schneid. Erect shrub or small tree to 7m, shoots downy at first. Lvs 6–15cm, elliptic-oblong, long-tapered, margins finely biserrate, veins in 8–10 pairs, downy beneath. Fls 2cm diam., in clusters of 7–10; pet. rounded, white; styles 5. Fr. 1–1.5cm, rounded-ovate, red or yellow, pitted, cal. persistent, pedicel stout. China (Sichuan, Hupeh). Z6.

***M.prunifolia*** (Willd.) Borkh. Small tree to 10m, shoots lightly downy at first only. Lvs 5–10cm, elliptic or ovate, margins scalloped, lightly downy beneath. Fls 3cm diam., in clusters of 6–10, pink in bud opening white; cal. lobes lanceolate, white-felted, persistent. Fr. numerous, 2cm, ovate, yellow-green to red. Origin unknown (NE Asia). 'Cheal's Crimson': habit upright to broad, to 5m; buds pink, fls single, white; fr. prolific, to 2.5cm diam., light orange with scarlet cheek. 'Cheal's Golden Gem': fls single, white; fr. rounded, prolific, gold. 'Fastigiata': habit narrow upright, later spreading; fls white; fr. yellow and red. 'Hyslop': habit upright to spreading; crown broad; fr. globose, to 4cm diam., yellow stippled and blotched with light red, edible. 'Pendula': branches weeping. var. ***rinki*** (Koidz.) Rehd. Lvs downy beneath. Fls 5cm diam., pink; cal. tufted. Fr. 1.5–3cm, yellow-green, edible but bitter. Z3.

***M.pumila*** Mill. Tree, 5–7m, occasionally to 15m; trunk soon branching, crown globose, open; shoots felted, thornless. Buds downy. Lvs 4–10cm, elliptic-ovate, pointed or blunt, base cordate, margins scalloped, pubesc. at first, later glabrous; petiole to 3cm. Fls to 3cm diam., white, becoming pink; cal. lobes tapered, downy, as are pedicels and styles, the latter at least on basal portion. Fr. 2–6cm, rounded, green, indented at both ends. Europe, Asia Minor (Caucasus, Turkestan). var. ***paradisiaca*** Schneid. PARADISE APPLE. Commonly used as a rootstock for grafting. Over 30 cvs, several descended from 'Niedzwetzkyana' (fls and fr. dark red, fr. large to 5cm diam.) known as the Rosybloom Group. 'Aldenham Purple': fls lilac; fr. purple; 'Cowichan': fls white; 'Redford': fls and fr. red; 'Rosseau': lvs red; fls purple; fr. dark red; 'Scugog': fls pink; 'Sundog': fls pink; 'Thunderchild': fls pink; fr. purple. Other cvs notable for fl colour include; 'Dartmouth': fls white. 'Elise Rathke': weeping habit; fr. large, to 7cm diam., apple-shaped. 'Garry': fls purple; fr. carmine. 'Kingsmere': fls purple; fr. carmine. 'Montreal Beauty': fls white. 'Redfield': fls and fr. red. 'Trial': fls white. 'Translucent': fls white. 'Veitch's Scarlet': fls white; fr. bright scarlet. Z3.

***M.×purpurea*** (Barbier) Rehd. (*M.astrosanguinea* × *M.pumila* 'Niedzwetzkyana'.) Large shrub or small tree, vigorous, young shoots elongated, bark dark red-black. Lvs 8–9cm, ovate, pointed, scalloped, occasionally lobed on strong shoots, brown-red at first becoming green, shiny. Fls 3–4cm diam., purple-red, soon fading. Fr. 1.5–2.5cm, rounded, purple-red, cal. persistent, pedicel long. Garden origin (France 1900). 'Aldenhamensis': habit shrub-like, low-growing, to 3.5m; lvs bronzed red; buds deep red, fls profuse, maroon; fr. red tinted brown. 'Amisk': buds carmine, fls simple, pink; fr. conic, to 3cm diam., red and yellow. 'Chilko': fls single, light maroon, later darker; fr. scarlet. 'Eleyi': habit shrub-like, slightly spreading; lvs darker than type; fls single, maroon; fr. ovate, purple. 'Eleyi Compacta': habit compact, shrub-like; branches short; lvs, fls and fr. purple. 'Hoser': buds dark purple; fls pink; fr. pruinose purple. 'Jadwiga': habit pendulous; crown broad; buds maroon, fls pink; fr. conic, to 5cm diam., blackcurrant purple. 'Jay Darling': fls maroon; fr., to 2.5cm diam., purple. 'Kobendza': fls purple washed brown outside, pink inside; fr. globose, to 1.5cm diam., purple. 'Lemoinei': habit shrub-like, upright, vigorous; lvs dark purple, later bronzed or dark green; fls single to semi-double, maroon; fr. to 1.5cm diam., dark purple. 'Neville Copeman': fr. dark orange to vivid carmine; seedling of 'Eleyi'. 'Sophia': buds dark purple, fls fading to pink; fr. small, globose, pruinose purple. 'Szafer': buds violet, fls fading to lilac washed light pink; fr. small, to 12mm, globose, purple. 'Wierdak': buds oblong, rich purple, fls lilac washed pink; fr. to 1.5cm diam., glossy maroon. Z4.

***M.×robusta*** (Carr.) Rehd. (*M.baccata* × *M.prunifolia*.) Vigorous, erect, conical shrub or small tree, branches spreading, slightly pendulous at tips. Lvs 8–11cm, elliptic, pointed, base rounded, margins scalloped, bright green. Fls 3–4cm diam., in corymbs of 3–8, white occasionally pink. Fr. 1–3cm, ellipsoid to rounded, yellow or red, occasionally with blue bloom, on long slender pedicels, cal. either falling or persistent. Garden origin. 'Alexis': buds light pink, fls single, white; fr. to 3cm diam., vivid pink-red, pruinose. 'Beauty': habit narrowly upright; fls single, white; fr. to 3cm diam., scarlet. 'Erecta': habit narrowly upright when young, later spreading; fls single to semi-double, white stained light pink; fr. small, to 2cm diam., yellow with red cheeks, pruinose. 'Fairy': habit upright, vigorous; fls single, white; fr. large, to 4cm diam., scarlet. 'Joan': fls single, white, early; fr. large, to 35mm, scarlet, persistent. 'Red Sentinel': fls single, white, early; fr. glossy scarlet, persistent. 'Red Siberian': fr. bright red. 'Yellow Siberian': fr. yellow. var. ***persicifolia*** Rehd. Large shrub, branches slender, elongated. Lvs 5–10cm, oval-lanceolate, finely scalloped. Fls 4cm diam., numerous, pink in bud opening white. Fr. 2cm, abundant, rounded or oblong, red. N China. Z3.

***M.rockii*** Rehd. Resembles *M.baccata*, young shoots densely downy, tufted. Lvs to 12cm, elliptic to ovate, margins densely and shallowly serrate, base rounded, downy beneath, veins reticulate. Fls 2.5cm diam., red-pink in bud, opening white; pedicel and cal. tufted, pubesc. Fr. ovoid to globose, apex occasionally tapered, yellow flushed red, cal. persistent. W China. Z5.

***M.sargentii*** Rehd. Shrub to 2m, shoots wide spreading, almost horizontally, dense, thorny. Lvs 5–8cm, ovate, deeply serrate with 3 lobes, bright green becoming orange on senescence. Fls 2.5cm diam., abundant, biennially borne along whole length of shoot, buds pale pink, opening white. Fr. 1cm, globose, dark red, cal. falling, pedicel long, fr. often persisting until spring. ????. 'Rosea': buds dark pink, fls fading to white. Z4.

***M.×schiedeckeri*** Späth ex Zab. (*M.floribunda* × *M.prunifolia*.) Shrub to 3m, rarely tree-like, shoots tightly erect, downy at first. Lvs ovate, serrate, usually with a large tooth, bright green, paler downy beneath. Fls 4–5cm diam., semi-double, pale pink, deeper in bud; pet. 10. Fr. 1cm, yellow-orange, pedicel long, cal. persistent. Garden origin. 'Barbara Ann': lvs tinted red; fls semi-double, maroon fading to pink; fr. small, to 12mm diam., purple. 'Dorothea': habit shrub-like, low and slow-growing; fls semi-double to double, profuse at first, carmine to pink; fr. to 13mm diam., yellow. 'Exzellenz Thiel': branches vertically pendulous; buds pink, fls fading to white; fr. large, to 2cm diam., yellow and red; only available as a grafted cv. 'Hillieri': habit shrub-like, vigorous; fls semi-double, light pink; fr. globose, to 2cm diam., yellow and orange. 'Red Jade': twigs slender, hanging, almost to ground; buds pink, fls single, fading to white; fr. ovate, to 1.5cm, scarlet; probably a seedling of 'Exzellenz Thiel'. Z4.

***M.*'Selkirk'**. (*M.baccata* × *M.pumila*.) Vigorous; crown rounded. Fls in clusters, clear pink. Fr. bright scarlet. Z4.

***M.sieboldii*** (Reg.) Rehd. Shrub to 4m, shoots arched, wide spreading, black-brown. Lvs 3–6cm, ovate-elliptic, long-tapered, margin strongly dentate and 3–5-lobed, especially on strong shoots, dark green above, paler beneath, both surfaces downy, becoming red or yellow on senescence. Fr. 2cm diam., deep pink in bud, soon fading, eventually white; pet. obovate. Fr. 0.5cm, globose, red to yellow-brown, retained into winter. Japan. 'Fuji': habit low, broad, spreading; fls anenome-centred, white stained green, sometimes stained purple; fr. small, to 12mm, orange. 'Gorgeous': habit shrub-like, upright; fls soft pink, fading to white; fr. prolific, large, to 2.5cm diam., dark orange to light red. 'Henry Kohankie': branches becoming pendulous; fr. in clusters, to 4, large, to 3.5×3cm, scarlet; selected from *M.sieboldii* seedlings. 'Seafoam': habit nodding to pendulous; fls solitary, dark carmine, fading to white flushed with light pink. 'White Angel': habit upright, later nodding; fls in clusters, to 6, snow-white; fr. prolific, small, to 12mm diam., scarlet; seedling. 'Winterglod': habit shrub-like, upright to spreading; lvs irregularly serrate; buds pink, fls fading white; fr. gold, persistent. var. ***arborescens*** Rehd. Tree to 10m. Lvs large, less lobed than species type. Fls 3cm diam., white. Fr. 1cm, yellow-red. Korea. Z5.

***M.sikkimensis*** (Wenz.) Koehne. Tree, 5–7m, resembles *M.baccata*; shoots densely felted. Lvs 5–7cm, oval-oblong, apex long-tapered, margins deeply serrate, felted beneath. Fls 2.5cm diam, in clusters of 4–9, white, sometimes pale pink outside, cal. felted. Fr. 1.5cm, pyriform, yellow-red, pitted. N India. Z6.

***M.×soulardii*** (Bail.) Britt. (*M.ioensis* × *M.pumila*.) Tall shrub, most resembling *M.ioensis*. Lvs 5–8cm, broad-elliptic, roughly scalloped, slightly lobed, coriaceous, wrinkled above, downy beneath. Fls 3.5cm diam., pink, soon fading; pedicel stout, rigid. Fr. to 5cm, depressed-globose, yellow-green flushed red. US. 'Red Flesh': lvs bronzed red; fls single, carmine to light maroon, alternate years; fr. scarlet. 'Wynema': habit low, open, spreading, to 4m; fls single, salmon pink, later darker, late, alternate years; fr. large, to 5cm diam., scarlet, sometimes with red cheeks, edible. Z4.

***M.spectabilis*** (Ait.) Borkh. Large shrub or small tree to 8m, compact pyramidal at first, later spreading; shoots lightly downy at first, becoming red-brown. Lvs 5–8cm, elliptic-oblong, short-tapered, margins adpressed, dentate, waxy green above, paler downy beneath. Fls 4–5cm diam., single or semi-double, dark pink in bud, opening pale pink; pedicel 2–3cm, smooth or sometimes downy; cal. lobes ovate-triangular, glabrous. Fr. 2–3cm, rounded, apex not indented, yellow. China. 'Blanche Amis': habit shrub-like, upright; buds carmine, fls semi-double, white inside, dark carmine outside; fr. globose, small, to 8mm diam., yellow. 'Dorothy Rowe': fls single to semi-double, light cream, anthers yellow; fr. scarlet; seedling of 'Riversii'. 'Plena' ('Frau Luise Dittman'): fls profuse, double, pink, soon fading; fr. globose, to 2cm diam., yellow. 'Riversii': fls double, pink; fr. large, to 3.5cm diam., yellow. Z4.

***M.sublobata*** (Dipp.) Rehd. (*M.prunifolia* × *M.sieboldii*.) Tree; crown conical, shoots downy. Lvs 4–8cm, narrow-elliptic, lvs on strong shoots wider with 1–2 lobes, felted at first eventually downy only on lower surfaces. Fls to 4cm diam., pale pink, pedicel and cal. tufted; styles 4–5, rarely 3. Fr. 1.5cm, subglobose, yellow, cal. sometimes absent. Japan. Z6.

***M.sylvestris*** (L.) Mill. Tree or shrub to 7m, shoots short slightly thorny; buds tomentose. Lvs 4–8cm, oval to rounded, margins scalloped or roughly incised, subglabrous; petiole 2–4cm, half blade length. Fls to 4cm diam., pink-white outside, pinker within, pedicel glabrous; styles separate or slightly connate, smooth. Fr. 2–4cm, rounded, yellow-green flushed red, sour, pedicel short. C Europe. 'Plena': habit upright to spreading; fls double, soft pink, fading to snow white; fr. scarlet, sometimes blotched yellow; often incorrectly listed as *M.spectabilis alba plena*; it is in fact a double sport of the European wild apple, not the Asiatic apple. var. ***domestica*** (Borkh.) Mansf. The form giving rise to cultivated apples; see APPLES.

***M.toringoides*** (Rehd.) Hughes. Shrub or small tree to 8m, shoots soon glabrous. Lvs 3–8cm, ovate and crenately lobed or simple and elliptic (the latter less common and irregularly produced), glabrous except for downy venation beneath. Fls 2cm diam., in bunches of 3–6, white; pedicel virtually absent; cal. felted. Fr. numerous, 1.5cm, globose to pyriform, yellow flushed red, retained into winter. W China. Z5.

***M.transitoria*** (Batal.) Schneid. Closely resembles *M.toringoides*, differs in smaller, narrower habit; shoots felted when young; lvs 2–3cm, broadly ovate, margins deeply narrow lobed, densely downy; fls to 2cm diam., white; fr. 1.5cm, red. NW China. Z5.

***M.trilobata*** (Labill.) Schneid. Erect shrub or small tree. Lvs 5–8cm, distinctly 3-lobed, shiny green, soon glabrous, becoming intense red on senescence. Fls 3.5cm diam., in clusters of 6–8, white. Fr. 2cm, ellipsoid, red. W Asia. Z6.

***M.tschonoskii*** (Maxim.) Schneid. Tree to 12m, pyramidal at first, spreading later; shoots felted; buds red. Lvs 7–12cm, ovate-elliptic, roughly serrate to slightly lobed, white felted at first becoming dark green glabrous above, lightly felted beneath, autumn colour orange-red. Fls 3cm diam., in clusters of 2–5, white. Fr. 2 3cm, rounded, yellow green flushed red. Japan. Z6.

***M.* 'Van Eseltine'**. *(M.arnoldiana × M.spectabilis.)* Habit upright to columnar. Fls vivid pink. Fr. to 2cm diam., yellow with red cheek or completely yellow. Z4.

***M.yunnanensis*** (Franch.) Schneid. Compact, erect tree to 10m, shoots felted only a first. Lvs 6–12cm, broadly ovate, base rounded or cordate, margins roughly biserrate, occasionally with 3–5 pairs of shallow, broad lobes, felted beneath becoming red-orange on senescence. Fls 1.5cm diam., usually in crowded corymbs to 5cm, white, cal. and pedicel densely downy, tufted; styles 5. Fr. 1–1.5cm, red, pitted, cal. flattened. W China. var. ***veitchii*** Rehd.. Lvs ovate, base strongly cordate, margins slightly lobed, slightly tapered, becoming completely glabrous. Fls smooth, to 1.2cm diam. Fr. to 1.3cm, red with white pits. C China. Z6.

***M.×zumi*** (Matsum.) Rehd. *(M.baccata* var. *mandshurica × M.sieboldii.)* Small pyramidal tree, shoots lightly downy. Lvs 5–9cm, ovate, long tapered, margins scalloped to lobed on strong shoots, downy beneath at first. Fls 3cm diam., pink in bud, fading to white; cal. villous on the outside; pet. elliptic; styles 4–5. Fr. 1cm, rounded, red. Japan. var. ***calocarpa*** Rehd. Habit more spreading; lvs smaller, always entire on fruiting wood, distinctly lobed on strong shoots; fls rather smaller, white, styles only 3–4 winter. Fr. 1–1.3cm, prolific in crowded bunches, scarlet, retained into winter. 'Bob White': buds soft pink, fls single, fading to white; fr. small, to 1.5cm diam., muddy yellow, persistent throughout winter. 'Golden Hornet': fls white; fr. large, to 3cm diam., gold. 'Professor Sprenger': fr. small, to 1cm diam., orange, persistent throughout winter. Z5.

***M.*cultivars**. 'Adams': disease-resistant. 'Brandywine': rose-form pink fls and silver winter bark. 'Centurion': fls bright red. 'Coralburst': dwarf. 'Gibbs Golden Gate': late flowering, winter-persistent. 'Indian Magic': fr. prolific, scarlet. 'John Downie': fls large, white. 'Red Baron': fls and fr. dark red. 'Ormiston Roy': late flowering, winter persistent. 'Pink Spire': narrowly upright. 'Snowdrift': fls large, white. 'Strawberry Parfait': fls single, pink, fragrant. 'Sugar Tyme': disease-resistant.

***M.acerba*** Mérat. See *M.sylvestris*.
***M.asiatica*** Nak. See *M.prunifolia* var. *rinki*.
***M.cerasifera*** Spach. See *M.baccata* var. *mandschurica*.
***M.communis*** Poir. See *M.pumila*.
***M.crataegifolia*** Koehne. See *M.florentina*.
***M.dasyphylla*** Borkh. See *M.pumila*.
***M.diversifolia*** Roem. See *M.fusca*.
***M.domestica*** Poir. non Borkh. See *M.pumila*.
***M.domestica*** Borkh. non Poir. See *M.sylvestris* var.*domestica*.
***M.floribunda*** var. ***arnoldiana*** Rehd. See *M.×arnoldiana*.
***M.floribunda*** var. ***brevipes*** Rehd. See *M.brevipes*.
***M.hybrida*** var. ***gloriosa*** Lemoine. See *M.×gloriosa*.
***M.kaido*** hort. ex K. Koch. See *M.×micromalus*.
***M.ringo*** Sieb. ex Dipp. See *M.prunifolia* var. *rinki*.
***M.ringo*** var. ***sublobata*** Dipp. See *M.sublobata*.
***M.rivularis*** M. Roem. See *M.fusca*.
***M.sempervirens*** Desf. See *M.angustifolia*.
***M.sibirica*** Borkh. See *M.baccata*.
***M.sieboldii*** var. ***calocarpa*** Rehd. See *M.×zumi* var. *calocarpa*.
***M.sinensis*** Dum.-Cours. See *Pseudocydonia sinensis*.
***M.spectabilis*** 'Kaido'. See *M.×micromalus*.
***M.theifera*** Rehd. See *M.hupehensis*.
***M.toringo*** Sieb. See *M.sieboldii*.
***M.transitoria*** var. ***toringoides*** Rehd. See *M.toringoides*.
***M.yezoensis*** Koidz. See *M.prunifolia* var. *rinki*.
For further synonymy see *Eriolobus* and *Pyrus*.

**Malva** L. (From Lat. *malva*, mallow, from the Gk *malache*, probably derived from Gk *malachos*, soothing, referring to its medicinal properties.) Malvaceae. 30 species of annual or perennial herbs and subshrubs. Stems erect or decumbent, simple or branched. Leaves alternate, orbicular, suborbicular, cordate or reniform, entire to crenate or lobed. Flowers axillary, solitary or in clusters, small or showy; calyx 5-lobed, subtended, by epicalyx of 1–3 free segments, usually adnate to the base of the calyx; petals white, pink or purple, obcordate; central axis of receptacle usually inconspicuous, not raised above the level of the carpels; styles linear-filiform. Fruit a discoid schizocarp; mericarps numerous, reniform, 1-seeded, unbeaked. Europe, Asia, Tropical & S Africa, Indomalaya; widely introduced into temperate and tropical regions.

CULTIVATION Found in the wild in open sunny habitats, on waste ground, along roadsides and hedgebanks, and in pasture or grassy meadows. *M.nicaeensis* occurs on stony and rocky ground, *M.neglecta* on dry soils, frequently in coastal habitats, often naturalized on dry walls or as a garden weed. *Malva* spp. are undemanding in cultivation, grown for their spikes of bowl-shaped flowers, carried throughout the summer, in the herbaceous border or in native plant collections and other naturalistic plantings, as well as in collections of medicinal plants. *M.moschata* emits a sweet musky fragrance in warm weather and when bruised. *M.verticillata*, with its smaller, more delicate flowers, can be used as a temporary screen; *M.v.* 'Crispa', with extremely decorative foliage, is sometimes cultivated as a salad green. *Malva* is tolerant of temperatures to −15°C/5°F.

Grow in any reasonably drained and moderately fertile soil, in full sun. Staking with twiggy sticks may be necessary, especially on moist rich soils. Cut down flowered stems of *M.alcea* and *M.moschata* in autumn. Propagate by seed; sow annuals *in situ* in early spring, perennials in the cold frame or under glass at 16°C/60°F. Also by softwood cuttings in spring, in sand in a closed frame. Prone to infestations of rust; collect and burn all affected material in autumn and spring – chemical control is difficult.

***M.alcea*** L. Perenn. herb to 80cm; stems pilose with tuberculate-stellate hairs. Lower lvs suborbicular, crenate, upper lvs palmatisect. Fls solitary in lf axils at apical parts of stem and branches; epicalyx seg. ovate; sep. 4–6mm, triangular; pet. 2.5–4cm, pale red. Mericarps rugose, with a dorsal crest. S Europe, naturalized US. 'Fastigiata': to 1m, habit narrowly upright; fls deep pink. Z4.

***M.moschata*** L. MUSK MALLOW. Perenn. erect to 1m; stems branched, hirsute, with spreading simple hairs. Basal lvs reniform, shallowly 3-lobed, upper lvs deeply divided, 3-, 5- or 7-lobed, the lobes pinnatifid or bipinnatifid. Fls 2.5–5cm diam., axillary, with slender pedicels; pet. 2–3cm, white or pink. Mericarps hispid, white-pubesc. Europe, NW Africa, naturalized US. 'Alba': to 60cm; lvs deeply cut; fls silky white. 'Rosea': fls rose tinted purple. Z3.

***M.neglecta*** Wallr. COMMON MALLOW. Annual to 50cm; stems prostrate to ascending, branched, pilose, with simple and stellate hairs. Lvs long-petioled, suborbicular, shallowly lobed, crenate, pilose. Fls in axillary clusters; epicalyx seg. linear, almost equalling cal.; sep. 2–4mm, broadly triangular; pet. 8–12mm, hairy at base, pink or white. Mericarps pilose, smooth. Europe, NW Africa, SW Asia, naturalized US.

***M.nicaeensis*** All. Annual or short-lived perenn. to 50cm; stems ascending or erect, sparsely pilose. Lvs suborbicular to shallowly lobed, lobes 3, 5 or 7, crenate-dentate; petioles to 15cm, usually longer than lamina. Fls solitary or in axillary clusters of 3–5; epicalyx seg. to 2mm, oblong-elliptic; sep. broadly triangular; pet. 8–12mm, pink-lilac, hairy at base. Mericarps 2–3cm, reticulate, glabrous or hairy. Mediterranean, Arabia to Iran, S Russia; naturalized US. Z7.

***M.sylvestris*** L. TALL MALLOW; HIGH MALLOW; CHEESES. Perenn. to 1m; stems erect or ascending, pilose with tuberculate hairs. Lvs broadly cordate or suborbicular, to 10cm diam., 3-, 5- or 7-lobed; petiole to 15cm. Fls axillary, in clusters of 2–5 in upper lf axils; pedicels to 2cm, unequal; epicalyx seg. to 4mm, ovate-lanceolate, pubesc.; sep. 4–7mm; pet. 1.5–2cm, mauve, paler and hairy at base, notched at apex. Mericarps to 3mm, mostly 10, pale brown, glabrous or pubesc., rugose-reticulate on dorsal side. Europe, N Africa, SW Asia; introduced US as garden escape. 'Alba': to 75cm; fls pure white, along stems. 'Brave Heart': habit upright, to 90cm; lvs large; fls large, pale purple with dark eye. 'Cottenham Blue': to 75cm; fls pale blue, veins darker, early flowering. 'Primley Blue': habit prostrate, to 20cm; fls soft violet, veins darker. Z5.

***M.verticillata*** L. Annual or bienn. to 1.8m; stems erect. Lvs suborbicular, 5- or 7-lobed. Fls in dense axillary clusters; pet. 1–1.2cm, white or purple. Mericarps glabrous, transverse-ridged. Europe, Asia, naturalized US. 'Crispa': habit upright, 2m; lvs wavy-edged; fls small, pale lavender, grouped in leaf axils; annual or biennial. Z6.

***M.crispa*** (L.) L. See *M.verticillata*.
***M.involucrata*** Torr. & A. Gray. See *Callirhoë involucrata*.
***M.mauritiana*** L. See *M.sylvestris*.
***M.setosa*** Moench. See *M.nicaeensis*.

For illustration see HERBS.

**MALVACEAE** Juss. MALLOW FAMILY. Dicot. 116 genera and 1550 species of herbs, shrubs and some trees, usually with stellate hairs and parenchyma with scattered mucilage-cells, cavities or canals. Leaves spirally arranged, simple to dissected, usually palmately veined; stipules usually present. Flowers usually bisexual, epicalyx usually present, solitary and axillary or in cymes; calyx 5 free sepals, sometimes united at the base; corolla 5 free petals, often connate at the base of staminal tube; stamens 5

**Malvaceae** (×0.3) (a) *Callirhoe digitata* (b) *Malva alcea* (c) *Malva moschata* (d) *Callirhoe involucrata* (e) *Callirhoe triangulata* (f) *Abutilon megapotamicum* (g) *Sidalcea malviflora* (h) *Callirhoe papaver* (i) *Gossypium barbadense* (j) *Pavonia multiflora* (k) *Hibiscus cameronii*

to numerous but usually numerous, connate in a tube for most of its length, anthers monothecous, pollen spinulose; ovary superior, with 1 to numerous fused carpels but frequently 5; styles usually as many as carpels, usually united at the base, and as many locules with axile placentation; ovules 1 to numerous. Fruit a loculicidal capsule, schizocarp, rarely berry or samara; endosperm oily and proteinaceous, copious to absent. *Gossypium* provides cotton, while some species of *Abutilon*, *Hibiscus* and *Urena* yield useful fibres. *Abelmoschus esculentus* has edible fruit, okra; the leaves of *A. manihot* are eaten as a vegetable in some Pacific islands; the seeds of *A. moschatus* (ambrette) are grown for their musky flavour. Roots of *Althaea officinalis* (marsh mallow) are of medicinal value. Cosmopolitan, especially tropical. *Abelmoschus, Abutilon, Alcea, Alogyne, Althaea, Anisodontea, Anoda, Asterotrichion, Bakeridesia, Callirhoë, Eremalche, Goethea, Gossypium, Gynatrix, Hibiscus, Hoheria, Howittia, Iliamna, Kitaibela, Kokia, Kosteletzkya, Kydia, Lagunaria, Lavatera, Malachra, Malacothamnus, Malope, Malva, Malvaviscus, Napaea, Pavonia, Phymosia, Plagianthus, Radyera, Robinsonella, Sida, Sidalcea, Sphaeralcea, Thespesia, Wercklea.*

**Malvastrum** A. Gray.

***M. fasciculatum*** var. ***laxiflorum*** (A. Gray) Munz & I.M. Johnst. See *Malacothamnus fasciculatus*.
***M. hypomandarum*** Sprague. See *Anisodontea* × *hypomandarum*.
***M. rotundifolium*** A. Gray. See *Eremalche rotundifolia*.
***M. virgatum*** (Murray) A. Gray & Harv. See *Anisodontea capensis*. Malvaceae.

**Malvaviscus** Adans. (From Lat. *malva*, mallow, and *viscum*, glue, referring to the sticky seeds.) 3 species of shrubs, sometimes vine-like. Leaves simple, unlobed or palmately lobed. Flowers solitary in axils of upper leaves or in terminal few-flowered racemes or cymes; epicalyx segments 6–16; corolla funnelform; petals red with a prominent basal auricle; stamens united in a column, exceeding petals; style 10, stigmas capitate; ovary 5-celled, each 1-ovuled. Fruit a berry; seeds with red fleshy coat, soon drying. C & S America. Z9.

CULTIVATION Frost-tender shrubs grown for their brilliant and richly coloured bell-shaped flowers with conspicuous stamens protruding from the mouth of the bell; the flowers never open fully, hence the common name 'sleeping hibiscus'. In frost-free, warm temperate regions, grow in full sun in any well-drained soil. In cool temperate zones grow under glass with a minimum winter temperature of 10–15°C/50–60°F, in direct sunlight in well-crocked pots of a loam-based mix with additional organic matter. Water plentifully when in growth; keep just moist during the winter months. Cut flowered stems hard back in winter to maintain shape. Propagate by softwood or semi-ripe cuttings or by seed in spring. Prone to infestation by red spider mite and glass house whitefly.

***M. arboreus*** Cav. WAX MALLOW. Shrub to 4m, usually densely velvety-hairy. Lvs 6–12cm, broadly ovate or cordate to suborbicular, unlobed or 3-lobed, coarsely toothed, stellate-pubesc. above, softly downy below. Fls solitary; pedicel 2.5–7cm; cal. to 2cm; pet. 2.5–5cm, rich red. Mexico to Peru and Brazil. A variable species, comprising some infraspecific taxa previously treated as distinct spp. var. ***drummondii*** (Torr. & A. Gray) Schery. Lvs almost as long as broad, symmetrically lobed with simple prominent hairs above; pet. 2.5–3cm. Florida, Texas, Mexico. var. ***mexicana*** Schldl. TURK'S CAP. Almost glabrate; lvs lanceolate to ovate, unlobed to obscurely lobed. Pet. 2.5–5cm. Mexico to Colombia.

***M. candidus*** Moc. & Sessé ex DC. Differs from *M. arboreus* by the 5-lobed lvs, to 18cm, hairy on both surfaces; cor. to 8cm; staminal column 12–15cm, with anth. terminating a much longer free portion of the stamen. Mexico.

***M. conzatti*** Greenman. See *M. arboreus* var. *mexicana*.
***M. drummondii*** Torr. & A. Gray. See *M. arboreus* var. *drummondii*.
***M. grandiflorus*** Moc. & Sessé ex DC. See *M. arboreus* var. *mexicana*.
***M. mollis*** Ait. DC. See *M. arboreus*.

**Mamillopsis** (Morr.) Britt. & Rose.

***M. senilis*** (Salm-Dyck) Britt. & Rose. See *Mammillaria senilis*.

**Mammea** L. Guttiferae. About 50 species of evergreen trees or shrubs; stems contain copious white or yellow latex. Leaves opposite, entire, leathery to papery with translucent glands or secretory channels, venation pinnate, reticulate. Flowers polygamous, solitary or in short axillary cymes, sometimes cauliflorous, white or pink; calyx bilobed, persistent in fruit; petals 4, occasionally 5–6, caducous; stamens (in male flowers) numerous, fused at base, fewer or staminodal in female flowers; ovary 2–4-locular, ovules 4; stigma peltate, 2–4-lobed or denticulate. Fruit baccate or drupaceous, indehiscent. Tropical America (1), Africa (1), Madagascar, Indomalesia, Pacific. Z10.

CULTIVATION *M. americana* is a large heavy-branched and short-trunked tree, native to tropical America and the West Indies, where it is commonly planted as a dooryard tree. A beautiful tree, resembling an evergreen Magnolia, it is grown for the large fruits (sometimes the size of a child's head), which have thick firm flesh, with an aromatic flavour similar to that of apricot. They are eaten fresh, steeped in wine, or, being rich in pectin, as preserves.

In tropical areas, grow *Mammea* spp. in deep, rich, well-drained sandy loam. Seedlings will bear fruit within 6–10 years. In some individuals, flowers will be predominantly female, and the tree will bear heavily; in others the reverse will be true. Where frosts occur, grow under hot glasshouse conditions, in a medium of fibrous sandy loam, with a little leafmould. Propagate by greenwood cuttings with bottom heat in a closed case, of under mist. Also from seed, which may take two months to germinate.

***M. africana*** Sab. Tree, 30–45m; crown spreading, branches grey. Lvs oblong to elliptic, acuminate, 9–35×3–13cm, coriaceous, glossy dark green, lateral veins numerous. Bisexual fls solitary; sep. red, rounded, concave, to 15mm pet. white or yellow, elliptic to obovate, to 20mm; male fls smaller; stamens numerous; ovary ovoid; style 2mm, stigma 4–5mm across. Fr. orange, spotted brown, subglobose to pyriform, 10–18cm diam., pericarp thick, arils yellow. Tropical Africa.

***M. americana*** L. MAMMEE; MAMMEE APPLE; SOUTH AMERICAN APRICOT. Tree to 18m. Lvs obovate, obtuse, 25×10cm, glossy dark green, translucent-spotted. Fls solitary, axillary, fragrant, white, 2.5cm across. Fr. globose, to 15cm diam., pericarp russet, rough, thick and leathery; aril yellow, sweet and fragrant; seeds 1–4, bitter, poisonous to fish, chicks and some insects. Caribbean, S America.

***M. siamensis*** (Miq.) Anderson. Tree to 10m. Lvs linear-oblong to oblong-lanceolate, obtuse, 15–20×5–6cm, much veined. Fls axillary, solitary or paired, occasionally clustered, fragrant, 16mm across; sep. 2; pet. 4, rounded, white; stamens numerous. Fr. ovoid, mucronate, 3cm, glabrous. Thailand.

**Mammillaria** Haw. (From Lat. *mammilla*, little teat or nipple, referring to the tubercles (podaria).) Cactaceae. Some 150 species of low-growing cacti, simple or clustering, sometimes forming mounds to 1m across, sometimes almost geophytic; stems depressed-globose or globose to cylindric, tuberculate, some with latex; tubercles terete, conic, pyramidal or gibbous, not grooved; areoles bipartite, as in *Coryphantha* and *Escobaria*, but with no interconnecting groove; dorsal (distal) portion of areoles at tubercle-apex, spiny, normally non-flowering; ventral portion 'axillary', naked, felted, hairy, or with bristle-spines; gland-spines absent. Flowers arising singly at 'axillary' areoles, mostly small, campanulate to funnelform; pericarpel naked; tube usually short. Fruit berry-like, oblong or clavate, often bright red, rarely immersed in stem; seeds diverse (see conspectus). SW US, Mexico, C America, Caribbean region, Colombia, Venezuela.

CULTIVATION Grow in a cool frost-free greenhouse (min. 2–7°C/36–45°F), use 'standard' cactus compost: moderate to high inorganic content (more than 50% grit), pH 6–7.5; full sun; low air-humidity; keep dry from mid-autumn until early spring, except for light misting on warm days in late winter. A few species, like *M. beneckei* and *M. guerreronis*, need higher minimum temperatures.

Mammillaria has long been popular with collectors, and horticultural treatments list 250–350 species. Many of these (including some listed below) should probably be treated as varieties or local forms, leaving a more conservative estimate of the size of the genus as 100–150 species. Many names used by nurserymen and collectors are of disputed or uncertain application, or invalid, such as: *Mm. acanthoplegma, amoena, atroflorens, bachmannii, crinita, flavescens, fuscata, fuliginosa, knebeliana, haehneliana, kunzeana, multihamata, neocoronaria, pentacantha, pfeifferi, phaeacantha, phymatothele, obscura, orcuttii, pyrrhocephala, rosea, scheidweileriana, schelhasii, seideliana, seitziana, tiegeliana, tricha-*

*cantha, trohartii, verhaertiana, wagneriana, webbiana*. These are best discarded. Since 1987, many new species have been proposed and introduced to cultivation by W. Reppenhagen and others which are not treated here.

The genus is divisible into six subgenera, and the principal subgenus (*Mammillaria* itself) into three sections and about 14 series, mainly by features of the seeds and flowers. The subgenera are differentiated as follows:

**1** Seeds black; relief of testa-cells flat or domed, not pitted. Subg. **Mammilloydia** *M. candida*.

1.1 Seeds brown or black, if black then the testa-cells pitted (par-concave):

1.2 Tubercles relatively large and soft, cylindric or terete; latex absent; flowers relatively large (more than 2×2cm), bright yellow or orange, rarely cream.

1.3 Flowers salver-shaped, orange-yellow, the tube solid below the insertion of the stamens; fruit red; seeds 2–3mm, ruminate. Subg. **Oehmea** *M. beneckei*.

1.4 Flowers funnelform, pure yellow (cream in *M. carretii*), the tube solid only in the lower part; fruit green or brown-green; seeds less than 2mm, not ruminate. Subg. **Dolichothele** *Mm. baumii, carretii, longimamma, melaleuca, sphaerica, surculosa*.

**2** Tubercles various, if relatively large and soft then the flowers not as above; latex absent or present; flowers various, if large then not bright yellow or orange.

**3** Flowers at least slightly zygomorphic, scarlet, longer than broad; tube conspicuous, 2–4cm; stamens exserted; one or more of the central spines usually hooked; seeds black.

3.1 Perianth-limb strongly zygomorphic (bilabiate); stems cylindric. Subg. **Cochemiea** *Mm. halei, maritima, pondii, poselgeri, setispina*.

3.2 Perianth-limb regular or nearly so; stems globose. Subg. **Mamillopsis** *M. senilis*.

**4** Flowers regular, not scarlet or orange, usually broader than long or without a conspicuous tube; central spines hooked or not; seeds black or brown. Subg. **Mammillaria**

The three sections of subgenus *Mammillaria* are characterized as follows:

Sect. *Hydrochylus*: Latex (milky sap) usually absent, if present only slightly milky; flowers small to large; central spines hooked or not. Seed broadly oval to almost circular, 1.1–1.6×0.8–1.5mm, black-brown or rarely brown, shiny to matt, occasionally rugose; relief par-concave (pitted when seen under a strong hand-lens); cell-boundaries (when seen under the microscope) straight or rarely undulate; hilum medium to large, basal to oblique, superficial to impressed; strophiole or strophiolar pad sometimes present.

Sect. *Subhydrochylus*: Flowers small to medium-sized (usually less than 25mm). Latex often present, mainly in stem, but only slightly milky; central spines rarely hooked (some spp. of ser. *Polyacanthae*). Seed broadly oval, 1.0–1.4×0.7–1.1mm, brown, semi-matt; relief par-concave or concave; cell-boundaries undulate; hilum small to medium, oblique, superficial, appendages none.

Sect. *Mammillaria* (*Galactochylus*): Flowers small to medium-sized. Latex always present, milky; central spines not hooked (except *M. uncinata*). Seeds broadly oval, 0.9–1.2×0.7–0.9mm, brown, semi-matt; relief (appearing striate under a strong hand-lens), concave, the pits usually obscured by the undulate to strongly undulate cell-boundaries; hilum small to medium, oblique, superficial, appendages none.

*Synopsis of series and groups in subg. Mammillaria.*

Sect. *Hydrochylus*.

Series I. *Longiflorae*. Flowers large, more or less salver-shaped, or tubular-funnelform, pink or purple, 25mm or more diam., typically with a tube of about equal length. Fruit remaining more or less sunk in the stem, colourless; seeds black. Plants mostly clustering and caespitose; stems small; central spines hooked, straight or absent. S & NW Mexico.
*Mm. deherdtiana, dodsonii, goldii, longiflora, napina, saboae, theresae*.

Series II. *Ancistracanthae*. Flowers mostly rather large, often 2–3cm long, funnelform, pink, cream or white, the tube relatively short. Fruit exserted, often red; seeds black. Plants often densely clustering; stems slenderly columnar or cylindric; tubercles relatively stout, firm-textured; one or more hooked central spines usually present. W & NW Mexico, SW US.
*Mm. albicans, armillata, barbata, blossfeldiana, boolii, capensis, dioica, fraileana, goodridgei, grahamii, guelzowiana, heidiae, hutchisoniana, insularis, mainiae, mazatlanensis, milleri, multidigitata, neopalmeri, phitauiana, schumannii, sheldonii, swinglei, tetrancistra, thornberi, viridiflora, wrightii, yaquensis, zephyranthoides*.

Series III. *Stylothelae*. Flowers mostly small, averaging less than 20mm, funnelform or campanulate-funnelform, variously coloured, often creamy yellow. Fruit exserted, usually red, rarely nearly colourless; seeds brown or black. Plants usually freely clustering; stems globose or shortly cylindric; tubercles cylindric or terete, relatively slender, soft-textured; one or more hooked central spines nearly always present. Mexico.
*Mm. anniana, aurihamata, bocasana, bombycina, erythrosperma, glassii, jaliscana, leucantha, longicoma, mercadensis, moelleriana, painteri, pennispinosa, pubispina, pygmaea, rettigiana, sinistrohamata, stella-de-tacubaya, wildii, zeilmanniana*.

Series IV. *Proliferae*. Flowers mostly small, averaging less than 20mm, funnelform or campanulate-funnelform, variously coloured, often creamy yellow. Fruit exserted, usually red, rarely nearly colourless; seeds brown or black. Plants usually freely clustering; stems globose or shortly cylindric; tubercles cylindric or terete, relatively slender, soft-textured; hooked central spines absent; central and radial spines more or less intergrading. NE Mexico, SW US (Texas), Cuba, Hispaniola.
*Mm. albicoma, gracilis, picta, pilispina, prolifera, vetula*.

Series V. *Lasiacanthae*. Flowers mostly small, rarely exceeding 20mm, funnelform or campanulate-funnelform, pale pink, creamy yellow or white, rarely purple-pink. Fruit usually exserted, red, rarely more or less embedded in the stem and nearly colourless; seeds black. Plants usually clustering; stems depressed-globose to globose, completely hidden or almost so by the numerous radial spines; central spines absent. E Mexico.
*Mm. aureilanata, carmenae, dumetorum, herrerae, humboldtii, lasiacantha, laui, lenta, magallanii, pectinifera, plumosa, schiedeana*.

Series VI. *Sphacelatae*. Flowers small, less than 20mm, funnelform or narrowly so, pink or purple-red. Fruit exserted, red; seeds black. Plants clustering; stems cylindric or globose (but becoming clavate-cylindric); tubercles obtuse-conic or terete; central spines straight or rarely hooked. S Mexico.
*Mm. kraehenbuehlii, sphacelata, viperina*.

Series VII. *Leptocladodae*. Flowers small, c15mm, campanulate, creamy yellow or red. Fruit exserted, dull red; seeds brown or black. Plants mostly slender-stemmed, densely clustering; tubercles obtuse-conic; central spines straight or absent. C & N Mexico.
*Mm. densispina, elongata, microhelia, mieheana, pottsii*.

Series VIII. *Decipientes*. Flowers small, less than 20mm, funnelform, almost white, scented. Fruit exserted, green to pale pink; seeds brown. Plants clustering and caespitose; stems depressed-globose or eventually clavate-cylindric; tubercles elongate-terete; central spines straight or absent. EC Mexico.
*Mm. albescens, camptotricha, decipiens*.

Sect. *Subhydrochylus*.

Series IX. *Heterochlorae*. Flowers small, averaging less than 20mm, campanulate, purple-pink or rarely creamy yellow. Fruit dull purple-pink or green-tinged. Plants simple or sometimes clustering; stems globose to cylindric, sometimes stoutly so; tubercles terete; central and radial spines usually sharply differentiated by colour, or the radials reduced to bristles or absent; central spines straight or curved, never hooked. C Mexico, N of the Sierra Volcanica Transversal.
*Mm. calacantha, discolor, fera-rubra, kewensis, mollendorffiana, mundtii, polythele, pringlei, rhodantha, wiesingeri*.

Series X. *Polyacanthae*. Flowers small to medium-sized, averaging 20mm, campanulate, purple-pink or rarely small, creamy yellow. Fruit dull purple-pink or green. Plants simple or clustering; stems globose to cylindric, sometimes elongate; tubercles terete; central and radial spines sharply differentiated or intergrading, hooked central spines sometimes present, radial spines not lending the whole plant a white appearance. S Mexico, south of the Sierra Volcanica Transversal.
*Mm. backebergiana, bella, duoformis, eriacantha, guerreronis, hamata, magnifica, matudae, meyranii, nunezii, pilcayensis, rekoi, spinosissima*.

Series XI. *Supertextae*. Flowers small or very small, averaging 10–12mm, purple, pink or rarely yellow. Fruit bright red. Plants simple or offsetting and clustering, rarely dividing dichotomously; stems globose to cylindric; tubercles usually small, terete-conic; axillary bristles not conspicuous; central and radial spines sharply differentiated; central spines straight or rarely absent, radial spines often spreading-adpressed, obscuring the tubercles and giving the whole plant a white appearance. S Mexico.
*Mm. albilanata, columbiana, crucigera, dixanthocentron, haageana, supertexta*.

Sect. *Mammillaria (Galactochylus)*.

Series XII. *Leucocephalae*. Flowers small, 10–15mm, campanulate. Plants simple or clustering, mostly by dichotomous branching; tubercles usually small, terete-conic; axillary bristles often conspicuous; central and radial spines sharply differentiated; central spines straight or rarely curved, radial spines often spreading-adpressed, obscuring the tubercles and giving the whole plant a white appearance. NE Central Mexico.
*Mm. brauneana, bravoae, chionocephala, formosa, geminispina, hahniana, klissingiana, leucocentra, mendeliana, morganiana, muehlenpfordtii, parkinsonii, perbella, pseudoperbella, sempervivi, woodsii*.

Series XIII. *Mammillaria* (Macrothelae). Flowers medium-sized, averaging 20mm, often broadly campanulate, purple, pink, pale yellow or white. Plants simple or offsetting and forming mounds; tubercles conic to pyramidal or gibbous, often large; axillary bristles usually absent; spines variable, rarely obscuring the body, sometimes few in a single series. C & N Mexico, SW US, N South America, Lesser Antilles.
*Mm. arida, baxteriana, bocensis, brandegeei, canelensis, coahuilensis, compressa, craigii, gaumeri, gigantea, grusonii, gummifera, heyderi, johnstonii, lloydii, magnimamma, mammillaris, marksiana, melanocentra, nivosa, pe-*

*ninsularis, petrophila, petterssonii, roseoalba, rubida, scrippsiana, sonorensis, standleyi, tesopacensis, uncinata, winterae, zeyeriana.*

Series XIV. *Polyedrae.* Flowers medium-sized, averaging 15mm long, usually creamy yellow with red-tinged outer tepals, sometimes purple-pink. Plants simple, offsetting, or clustering by dichotomous branching; tubercles conic, often more or less angled, medium-sized; axillary bristles usually conspicuous; spines usually few, rarely obscuring the body, sometimes few in a single series. S Mexico, Guatemala.
*Mm. carnea, eichlamii, karwinskiana, mystax, nejapensis, polyedra, sartorii, voburnensis.*

***M. albescens*** Tiegel. Series *Decipientes*. Intermediate between *M. decipiens* and *M. camptotricha*, central spines 0, radial spines shorter and straighter than in *M. camptotricha*, white. Autumn. EC Mexico. Z9.

***M. albicans*** (Britt. & Rose) A. Berger. Series *Ancistracanthae*. Clustering; stem to 15cm or more ×4cm, cylindric; axils with wool (dense in the flowering zone) and bristles; central spines mostly 4–8, 7–10mm, straight, radial spines 14–21, 5–8mm. Fl. pink or nearly white with long purple stigmas. Fr. 10–18mm, clavate, red. Summer. NW Mexico (Is. in Gulf of California). Z9.

***M. albicoma*** Boed. Series *Proliferae*. Clustering; individual stems to 5×3cm; axils with hair-like bristles; central spines 0 or 3–4, 4–5mm, straight, white, tipped darker, radial spines 30–40, 8–10mm, soft, hair-like, white. Fl. 10–13mm diam., creamy. Spring. NE Central Mexico. Z9.

***M. albilanata*** Backeb. Series *Supertextae*. Simple or offsetting; stem to 15×8cm, shortly cylindric; tubercles short conic; axils with dense curly white hairs; central spines 2 or 4, very short or up to 7mm, white at first, yellow-brown or rusty tipped, radial spines 18–22, 2–6mm, white, brown at base. Fl. small, only 7.5mm, dark carmine red. Spring. SW Mexico. Z9.

***M. anniana*** Glass & Fost. Series *Stylothelae*. Clustering; individual stems to 3cm diam., tubercles 4–7×4mm, axils with 4–5 hair-like bristles to 13mm; central spines 5–9, 9–12mm, one often hooked in older specimens, others straight, only slightly stronger than the radials, yellow to golden amber, radial spines 13–14, 6–11mm, stiff, pale yellow-white. Fl. 8–12×6mm, necked above ovary, pale yellow. Fr. 10–15×1.5–3mm, red. Spring. NE Mexico. Z9.

***M. arida*** Rose ex Quehl. Series *Mammillaria*. Resembling *M. baxteriana*. Simple; central spines 4–7, 12–16mm, dark brown, finely acicular, radial spines *c*15, pale. Summer. NW Mexico (S Baja California). Z9.

***M. armillata*** K. Brandg. Series *Ancistracanthae*. Simple or clustering, narrowly columnar, to 30×4.5cm; tubercles firm-textured, somewhat ascending; axils sparsely woolly, with bristles; central spines 1–4, 10–20mm, one or more hooked, brown or yellow-brown, radial spines 9–15, 7–12mm. Fl. 1–2×2cm, pale yellow or flesh-coloured, stigmas 6–7, tinged pink. Fr. 15–30mm, clavate, red. Summer. NW Mexico (Cape region of Baja California). Z9.

***M. aureilanata*** Backeb. Series *Lasiacanthae*. Stem simple, base tuberous; tubercles cylindric, *c*10×7mm; axils naked; central spines 0, radial spines 25–30, setaceous to wool-like, transparent white, later pale yellow. Fl. 3cm, white to very pale pink. Fr. clavate, white, tinged pink. Spring. NE Mexico. Z9.

***M. aurihamata*** Boed. Series *Stylothelae*. Clustering; stem globose to ovoid; axils normally with about 8 white bristles; central spines 4, lowermost hooked, longer, 1.5–2.5cm, radial spines 15–20, to 8mm, yellow white, thin setaceous. Fl. 15×12mm, pale yellow. Fr. clavate, red. Spring. NC Mexico. Z9.

***M. backebergiana*** Buchenau. Series *Polyacanthae*. Usually simple; stem 4–6cm diam., cylindric; tubercles shortly pyramidal, not angled, 5mm; axils naked or very rarely with 1–3 bristles; central spines 1–3, 7–8mm, yellow-brown to brown, radial spines 10–12, 8–10mm, yellow-white, brown-tipped, later pale grey-brown. Fl. 18–20×10–13mm, purple-red, stigmas 4–6, green. Fr. 20mm, white below, dull green above. Spring. C Mexico (State of Mexico). Z9.

***M. barbata*** Engelm. Series *Ancistracanthae*. Simple or clustering; stem depressed-globose; tubercles 8×3mm; axils naked; central spines several, with 1–2 hooked, robust, erect, dark, radial spines numerous in several series, the outermost up to 40, hair-like, the inner 10–15, 6–8mm, stronger, tawny. Fl. 1.5–2×1.5–2cm; outer tepals somewhat ciliate, green, inner rose-red to straw coloured or pale green; stigmas 5–7 green-yellow. Fr. 10–12mm, oblong, green; floral remnant persistent. Spring. N Mexico (Chihuahua). Z9.

***M. baumii*** Boed. Series *Longimammae*. Densely clustering, stems to 6–7×5–6cm, subglobose to ovoid; tubercles cylindric, 8–10×5mm; areoles with white wool at first; axils soon naked; central spines 5–6(–8–11), up to 10–18mm, slender acicular, straight, pale yellow, radial spines 30–35(–50), up to 15mm, very thin, white. Fl. 25×28mm, funnelform; outer tepals tinged brown or green, inner bright yellow; stigmas 4–5, 5mm, green. Fr. up to 15×10mm, oblong to ovoid, grey-green. Spring. NE Mexico (Tamaulipas). Z9.

***M. baxteriana*** (Gates) Backeb. & F. Knuth. Series *Mammillaria*. Simple or occasionally clustering; stem to 10cm diam., depressed-globose; tubercles conic; axils with short white wool; central spines usually 1, 15–20mm, acicular, white with brown tip, becoming all white, radial spines 8–10, the lower longer, to 15mm, acicular, white, occasionally brown-tipped in youth. Fl. yellow with light red markings on outer tepals; stigmas 9, pale yellow. Fr. 15mm, clavate, red. Summer. NW Mexico (S Baja California). Z9.

***M. bella*** Backeb. Series *Polyacanthae*. Usually simple; stems to 15×9cm; tubercles conic, dark green; axils with bristles; central spines 4–6, *c*20mm lowermost to 30mm, sometimes hooked vitreous white, tipped red, radial spines up to 20, to 8mm glassy white. Fl. 20×18mm, carmine; stigmas pale green. Fr. clavate, at first green, later tinged pink. Summer. SW Mexico (Guerrero). Z9.

***M. beneckei*** Ehrenb. Subg. *Oehmea*. Simple or clustering; stems to *c*10×7cm, globose to short-cylindric, apex often oblique; tubercles soft-textured; central spines 2–6, 8–12mm, 1 or 2 longer, hooked, dark brown, radial spines 8–15, 6–8mm, pale. Fl. 2–2.5×3–4cm, salver-shaped, orange-yellow, tube solid below insertion of stamens. Summer. W Mexico. Z9.

***M. blossfeldiana*** Boed. Series *Ancistracanthae*. Simple or clustering; stems globose to short-cylindric, green, rootstock tuberous or not; axils sparsely woolly, without bristles; central spines 4, the upper like the radials, the lower porrect, hooked, 10(–12)mm, dark brown to black, radial spines 13–20, 5–7(–10)mm, pale yellow, tipped darker. Fl. 2cm diam.; tepals nearly white with rose-carmine stripe; stigmas 5–9, green, up to 10mm. Fr. clavate, orange-red. Summer. NW Mexico (C Baja California). Z9.

***M. bocasana*** Poselger. Series *Stylothelae*. Freely clustering; stems more or less globose, usually almost hidden by the spines; axils naked or with a few fine hairs or bristles; central spines 1(–5), 5–10mm, 1–2 hooked, red or brown, radial spines 25–50, 8–10(–20)mm, hairlike, pure white. Fl. 13–22× up to 15mm, creamy white; outer tepals with pale pink mid-stripe. Fr. up to 4cm, cylindric. Spring. C Mexico (San Luis Potosi). Z9.

***M. bocensis*** Craig. Series *Mammillaria*. Simple or clustering and forming mounds; stems depressed-globose to short cylindric; axils usually without bristles; central spines 1, 8–12mm, red-brown with darker tip, radial spines 6–8, 5–14mm, acicular, chalky white to red-tinged with darker tip. Fl. 15–20mm; tepals pale pink or green with brown mid-stripe; stigmas pale yellow-green. Fr. clavate, red-tinged. Summer. NW Mexico (Sonora). Z9.

***M. bombycina*** Quehl. Series *Stylothelae*. Clustering; stems to 20×7–8cm, short cylindric, tubercular axils white-woolly; central spines 4, the lowest longest, 20mm, hooked, yellow- or red-brown, radial spines 30–40, up to 10mm, stiff, glassy white. Fl. 15×15mm, carmine red. Fr. off-white. Spring. WC Mexico. Z9.

***M. boolii*** Lindsay. Series *Ancistracanthae*. Simple or rarely clustering; rootstock carrot-like; stem to 5cm diam., depressed-globose to globose, grey-green; axils naked; central spines 1, 15–20mm, hooked, yellow or horn-coloured with darker tip, radial spines about 20, 15mm, thin acicular, white. Fl. 25×24mm, pink or lavender pink; stigmas 4 pale green. Fr. 30mm, clavate, orange. Summer. NW Mexico (coast of Sonora). Z9.

***M. brandegeei*** (J. Coult.) K. Brandg. Series *Mammillaria*. Simple; stem globose to cylindric; axils densely woolly in youth; central spines (1–)3–4, 10–12mm, red-brown below, black-tipped, radial spines about 10, 7–10mm, slender, rigid white with dusky tips, spreading but not radiating. Fl. small, to 2cm, pale yellow, tinged green or brown. Fr. dull pink or purple, not scarlet red. Summer. NW Mexico (deserts of central Baja California). Z9.

***M. brauneana*** Boed. Series *Leucocephalae*. Simple; stem globose; axils with wool and bristles; central spines 2–4, 5–7mm, red-brown or horn-coloured, radial spines 25–30, up to 5mm, very thin. Fl. up to 13mm broad, red-violet. Fr. not described. Spring. NE Mexico. Plants under this name are frequently seen in collections, but the natural distribution of *M. brauneana* is undocumented. Z9.

***M. bravoae*** Craig. Series *Leucocephalae*. Resembling *M. hahniana*. Simple or later clustering; stems globose; axils with wool and bristles; central spines 2, 6–8mm, brown, tinged pink, paler at base, black tipped, radial spines 28–30, 4–7mm, slender acicular, white. Fl. 10×10mm, deep pink; stigmas pink-brown. Fr. clavate, carmine. Spring–summer. EC Mexico. Z9.

***M. calacantha*** Tiegel. Series *Heterochlorae*. Resembling *M. rhodantha*, but with strongly curved and more or less adpressed central spines. Simple; stem globose to short cylindric; axils with wool at first and sparse bristles; central spines 2 or 4, up to 15mm, acicular, at first red-brown with darker tip, becoming paler, radial spines usually 25, 5–6mm, pale yellow, shiny. Fl. 14mm, carmine; stigmas carmine. Summer. C Mexico. Z9.

***M. camptotricha*** Dams. Series *Decipientes*. Clustering; individual stems *c*4–7cm diam., globose; tubercles elongate, tapering, up to 20×7mm; areoles shortly woolly at first; axils sparsely hairy and with a few bristles; central spines typically 0, radial spines (2–)4–5(–8), up to 3cm, setaceous or finely acicular, almost straight to strongly curved or tortuous, typically pale yellow but varying from white to golden brown. Fls. small, up to 17mm, white, delicately scented. Fr. 20×4mm, pale pink to pale green at top, slender clavate. Autumn. EC Mexico. Z9.

***M. candida*** Scheidw. Subgenus *Mammilloydia*. Simple or clustering; individual stems to *c*14cm diam., depressed-globose to globose, in age stoutly cylindric and decumbent; tubercles broadly and obtusely cylindric, *c*10mm, blue-green; areoles with scant wool; axils with few to several fine white bristles; central spines 8–12, to 1cm, only slightly stronger than the radials, white or tipped pink or brown, radial spines numerous (up to *c*55), to 1.5cm, white. Fl. 2–3cm long, near apex, rose pink, stigmas purple-red. Fr. cylindric, pink; floral remnant deciduous. Spring. NE Mexico. The structure of the seed indicates that this is probably not a true *Mammillaria*. Z9.

***M. canelensis*** Craig. Series *Mammillaria*. Simple; stem globose; axils with dense wool and bristles; central spines 2–4, to 3cm, robust, straight to variously curved, yellow to orange-brown, radial spines 22–25, 5–15mm, very fine acicular, white. Fl. (see note). Summer. NW Mexico. The fl. of the original form were not described. Both red- and yellow-fld forms have been reported in cult. material. Z9.

***M. capensis*** (Gates) Craig. Series *Ancistracanthae*. Clustering; stems to 25×3–5cm, cylindric; axils naked or with 1–3 short bristles; central spines 1, 15–20mm long, hooked (or straight), white at base, shading through red-brown to black at tip, radial spines 13, 8–15mm, acicular. Fl. 2cm, pale pink; stigmas green-yellow. Fr. 2cm, clavate, orange-scarlet. Summer. NW Mexico (Cape region of Baja California). Z9.

***M. carmenae*** Castañeda. Series *Lasiacanthae*. Clustering; stems globose to ovoid; central spines 0, radial spines very numerous, more than 100, up to 5mm long, finely bristly, somewhat upstanding, white or pale yellow. Fl. 11×11mm, white, tinged pink (or cream); stigmas yellow. Fr. 6mm, pale green. Spring. EC Mexico. Z9.

***M. carnea*** Zucc. Series *Polyedrae*. Simple or more often clustering; stems to 85mm diam., globose to clavate-cylindric; tubercles pyramidal, 4-angled, to 13×8–10mm, mid-green, often red-brown towards tip; axils with wool but no bristles; spines usually 4, variable, all 6–15mm, or the uppermost longest, to 20mm, or the lowermost longest, to 50mm, pink-brown, tipped black. Fl. 15–20×12–15mm, flesh pink. Fr. red. Spring. S Mexico. Z9.

***M. carretii*** Rebut ex Schum. Series *Longimammae*. Simple or clustering; stems of cultivated form depressed-globose, tubercles 7–10×7mm; central spine 1, 14–18mm, hooked, brown, radial spines 12–14, to 13mm, pale yellow. Fl. 2.5×1.5cm, creamy white; inner tepals with pink mid-stripe. Fr. green. Spring. NE Mexico. Z9.

***M. chionocephala*** Purpus. Series *Leucocephalae*. Simple or rarely clustering; stem nearly globose to shortly cylindric; axils with copious wool and bristles up to 2cm; central spines 2–4 rarely 5–6, 4–6mm white or darker tipped, radial spines 22–24 up to 8mm, setaceous, white. Fl. nearly white or flesh-colour with red mid-stripe. Fr. 16–17mm, carmine. Spring. NE Mexico. Z9.

***M. coahuilensis*** (Boed.) Moran. Series *Mammillaria*. Simple; stem to 5cm diam., globose, tuberous at base and bearing dried remains of old tubercles; tubercles trigonous, blue-green; axils sparsely woolly; central spines 1, 6mm, straight, acicular, brown-tipped, radial spines *c*16(–25), somewhat weaker, grey-white, the lower longer, up to 6mm, all spines finely pubesc. Fl. 3cm diam.; outer tepals rose with pale brown mid-stripe, inner white with rose mid-stripe; stigmas pale yellow-green. Fr. clavate, red. Spring. N Mexico (Coahuila). Z9.

***M. columbiana*** Salm-Dyck. Series *Supertextae*. Simple or clustering; stems cylindric; axils woolly; central spines 3–7, 6–8mm, pale yellow to brown, radial spines 18–20(–30), 4–6mm, bristly, white. Fl. 7–8mm, pink. Fr. orange-red, clavate. Spring. SE Mexico (Yucatan), Guatemala, Jamaica, N or N South America. Z9.

***M. compressa*** DC. Series *Mammillaria*. Clustering to form mounds 60cm or more diam.; individual stems 5–8cm diam., clavate-cylindric; tubercles bluntly gibbous, angled, 4–6×8–15mm, light blue-green; axils with wool and bristles, the latter sometimes inconspicuous or lacking; spines 4–6, unequal, upper short, lowermost to 15–70mm, white to pale red with darker tip. Fl. 10–15×10–15mm, deep purple-pink. Fr. red. Spring. C Mexico. Z9.

***M. craigii*** Lindsay. Series *Mammillaria*. Simple, with fibrous roots; stems depressed globose; axils with wool but no bristles; central spine 1, up to 3cm, acicular, golden with brown tip, radial spines 8, similar to the centrals, up to 2.5cm. Fl. about 2×1.5cm, deep purple-pink; stigmas green-yellow. Fr. clavate, red. Summer. NW Mexico. Z9.

***M. crucigera*** Mart. Series *Supertextae*. Simple or branching dichotomously; stems cylindric or obovate; axils with white wool; central spines 4(–5), 2mm, rigid, waxy yellow or brown, radial spines 24 or more, 2mm, white, more slender than the centrals. Fl. purple; stigmas purple. Summer. S Mexico. Z9.

***M. decipiens*** Scheidw. Series *Decipientes*. Clustering; individual stems to 10×4–7cm, globose to clavate; tubercles cylindric-terete, 10–22×5–7mm, with a few fine axillary bristles; central spines 1–2, rarely none, to 18–27mm, straight, brown, radial spines 5–11, 7–15mm, straight, pale yellow or white. Fl. *c*15×10mm, white, slightly scented. Fr. *c*20×4mm, cylindric, green, tinged red. Autumn. EC Mexico. Z9.

***M. deherdtiana*** Farwig. Series *Longiflorae*. Simple; roots somewhat tuberous; stem 2.5×4.5cm, depressed-globose; tubercles conic, up to 10mm; axils slightly woolly or naked; central spines 0–6, 3–7mm long, nearly porrect, pale to dark red-brown or rarely yellow, radial spines (25–)33–36, 3–6mm, somewhat curved, at first yellow, soon white, sometimes tipped red-brown. Fl. up to 5cm diam.; tube to 2cm; inner tepals bright rose-violet; stigmas white. Fr. 3–4mm diam., globose, remaining half-embedded in the stem, pale green in exposed portion; fl. remnant persistent. Summer. SW Mexico (Oaxaca). Z9.

***M. densispina*** (J. Coult.) Orcutt. Series *Leptocladodae*. Usually simple; stem to 12×6(–10)cm, globose to short-cylindric; axils without bristles; central spines 5–6, 10–12(–15)mm, straight, more rigid and darker than the radials, black-tipped, radial spines about 25, unequal, 8–10mm, erect-spreading, slender but rigid, yellow. Fl. *c*10×15mm, pale yellow, Fr. pink, tinged green. Spring. C Mexico. Z9.

***M. dioica*** K. Brandg. Series *Ancistracanthae*. Simple or clustering, stems to 10–15×3–8cm, cylindric to columnar; axils with 4–15 bristles, as long as the tubercles; central spines 3–4, larger, to 15mm, hooked, dark brown, radial spines 11–22, bristly, off-white. Fl. creamy yellow, bisexual or female, the bisexual flowers usually larger, to 2.5×2cm, the female only 1–1.5×1–1.5cm, stigmas pale yellow or brown, tinged green. Fr. 1–2.5cm, clavate, scarlet. Summer. NW Mexico (Baja California), SW United States (SW California). Z9.

***M. discolor*** Haw. Series *Heterochlorae*. Simple, depressed-globose to short-columnar, some forms eventually 15×10cm or larger; tubercles cylindric-terete, 10–15×8–9mm, green or slightly glaucous; axils with scant wool or naked; central spines 4–8, lowest longest, to 22mm, amber yellow to dark brown, radial spines 16–28, to 8–9mm, glassy white or with slight yellow tinge. Fl. 20–25×10–15mm, varying from cream yellow through pale pink, tinged brown, to bright pink. Fr. 2–3cm, clavate, red. Spring. Mts of C Mexico. Z9.

***M. dixanthocentron*** Backeb. ex Mottram. Series *Supertextae*. Simple; stem to 30×7–8cm, stout-cylindric; tubercles *c*6mm; axils woolly; central spines 2, divaricate, the upper erect, *c*5mm, lower porrect or downward-pointing, to 15mm, pale yellow or brown; radial spines *c*19–20, 2–4mm, white. Fl. 8–10×8–10mm, pale clear red. Fr. 2cm, slender, orange-red. Spring. S Mexico (Oaxaca). Z9.

***M. dodsonii*** Bravo. Series *Longiflorae*. Resembling *M. deherdtiana*, but with longer and more regularly produced central spines, and fewer and longer radial spines. Simple or clustering; stem up to 3×4cm, depressed-globose; rootstock fibrous; tubercles conic, 5×4mm; axils naked; central spines 3–5, 1–2cm, red-brown, stronger than the radials, straight or slightly curved, radial spines 20–21, the lowest longest, up to 18mm, acicular, vitreous white. Fl. large, 4cm, purple; fil. cream, anth. intense yellow, style and stigmas purple. Fr. not described, enclosed in the stem at the base of the tubercles. Summer. SW Mexico (Oaxaca). Z9.

***M. dumetorum*** Purpus. Series *Lasiacanthae*. Clustering; individual stems depressed-globose, eventually cylindric-globose; tubercles 10×5mm, conic, dark green; axils with a few fine curly hairs; central spines 0, radial spines numerous, 4–6mm, the inner finely bristly and somewhat longer than the outer, white or pale yellow. Fls 18×18mm, white, tinged green. Fr. red. Spring (or autumn). EC Mexico. Z9.

***M. duoformis*** Craig & Dawson. Series *Polyacanthae*. Resembling *M. nunezii*, but stem to 9×3–4cm, more slender, elongate-cylindric; central spines 4, 10–12mm, upper three straight, lowermost longest, stout acicular, hooked or straight, pink-brown below, almost black above, radial spines 18–20, 5–7mm, slender acicular, straight, orange-tan at very base, chalky white to pale yellow above. Fl. 15×12mm, crimson. Fr. 18×4mm, dull pink-brown. Spring. SC Mexico (Puebla). Z9.

***M. eichlamii*** Quehl. Series *Polyedrae*. Clustering; stems cylindric to sub-clavate; axils with pale yellow wool at first and white bristles 1cm; central spine 1, 1cm, yellow at base, red-brown in upper half, radial spines 6, 5–7mm, the upper three shorter and weaker, all acicular, straight, pale yellow with darker tip. Fl. 2cm, yellow; outer tepals with brown-tinged mid-stripe. Summer. Honduras. Z9.

***M. elongata*** DC. Series *Leptocladodae*. Clustering; stems 1–3cm diam., cylindric, elongate; tubercles short; axils naked; central spines 0–3, to 15mm, pale yellow to dark brown, radial spines 14–25, 4–9mm, pale to golden yellow, regularly radiating. Fl. about 10×10mm, pale yellow or tinged pink. Fr. dull pink or red-tinged. Spring. C Mexico. Z9.

***M. eriacantha*** Pfeiff. Series *Polyacanthae*. Simple, sometimes clustering later; stem to 30(–50)×5cm, slender cylindric; tubercles 7×6mm; axils without bristles but often woolly in flowering zone; central spines 2, 8–10mm, golden yellow, minutely hairy, radial spines 20–24, 4–6mm, paler golden yellow, also minutely hairy. Fl. small, 10–12×12–14mm, yellow, tinged green. Fr. dull purple. Spring. E Mexico (Veracruz). Z9.

***M. erythrosperma*** Boed. Series *Stylothelae*. Resembling *M. zeilmanniana*; freely clustering, individual stems to 5×4cm; axils with hair-like white bristles; central spines 1–3, rarely 4, up to 10mm, the lowest hooked, pale yellow in the lower half, dark red-brown at the tip, radial spines 15–20, 8–10mm, very thin white. Fl. 15×15mm, clear dark red, including the stigmas. Fr. 2cm, clavate, carmine. Spring. EC Mexico (San Luis Potosi). A white-fld form is also grown. Z9.

***M. fera-rubra*** Craig. Series *Heterochlorae*. Resembling *M. rhodantha* but radial spines fewer, fl. smaller. Usually simple; stem 10×9cm, globose to short cylindric; tubercles 9×7mm; axils with short wool; central spines 6, occasionally 7, the seventh porrect, 12mm, orange brown, paler at base, radial spines 15–18, 3–7mm, upper shorter. Fl. *c*15×12mm. Fr. 20–6mm, scarlet. Spring–summer. Mts of WC Mexico. Z9.

***M. formosa*** Scheidw. Series *Leucocephalae*. Usually simple; stem to 15cm diam., depressed-globose to globose or short cylindric; tubercles crowded, obscurely 4-angled, light green, glabrous; axils white-woolly but without bristles; central spines usually 6, sometimes 4 (or 7), to 8mm, pink-brown, darker tipped, later grey brown, radial spines 20–25, 3–6mm, white. Fl. 10–18×10–15mm, pale pink or nearly white. Fr. red. Spring. NE Central Mexico. Z9.

***M.fraileana*** (Britt. & Rose) Boed. Series *Ancistracanthae*. Stems to 15×3cm or taller, cylindric; axils naked or with at most a single bristle; central spines 3–4, 10mm, one of them strongly hooked, dark brown, radial spines usually 11–12, 8–10mm. Fl. rather larger, pale pink; inner tepals acuminate, 2–2.5cm often lacerate towards the tip; fil. and style pink, the latter paler and much longer than the stamens; stigmas 6–7, long and slender, purple. Summer. NW Mexico (S Baja California). Z9.

***M.gaumeri*** (Britt. & Rose) Orcutt. Series *Mammillaria*. Clustering; stems to 15cm, globose to short cylindric; tubercles nearly terete, obtuse, 5–7mm; axils naked; central spines 1, porrect, usually brown, radial spines 10–12(–20), white with brown tips or the lower darker. Fl. 10–15mm, creamy white. Fr. 18–20mm, clavate, crimson. Spring. SE Mexico (Yucatan). Z9.

***M.geminispina*** Haw. Series *Leucocephalae*. Soon clustering and forming mounds; individual stems 6–8cm diam., becoming cylindric; axils with wool and short bristles; central spines 2 or 4, the uppermost 15–40mm, others 7–15mm, chalky white, tipped brown or black, radial spines 16–20, 5–7mm, chalky white. Fl. 15×15mm, deep pink. Fr. red. Summer–autumn. C Mexico. Z9.

***M.gigantea*** Schum. Series *Mammillaria*. Simple; stem to 30cm diam., depressed-globose to globose; tubercles to 10mm or more, dark green; axils woolly; central spines 4–6, robust, lowermost longest, to 2cm or more, yellow, brown or almost black at first, radial spines up to 12, less than 5mm, white. Fl. 15×15mm, pale yellow, tinged green. Fr. purple-red. Spring. C Mexico. Z9.

***M.glassii*** R.A. Foster. Series *Stylothelae*. Clustering; to 3×3cm, stems globose, eventually cylindric, to 10cm; tubercles terete, 7×2–3mm; axils with 20–30 bristly hairs to 25mm, white; central spines 1, 4–5mm, porrect, hooked (or straight), golden amber, 6–8 subcentral to 3mm, pale amber, difficult to distinguish from radials, radial spines 50–60, 10–15mm, hair-like, white, interlacing. Fl. to 14×3–5mm, opening completely only in bright sunlight; inner tepals light pink. Fr. to 20×3–4mm, green, turning pink before withering. Spring. NE Mexico. A number of larger-fld. varieties have been described which are of uncertain status. Z9.

***M.goldii*** Glass & Fost. Series *Longiflorae*. Resembling *M.saboae*, but less inclined to cluster, and with more numerous spines, etc.; individual stems small, to 25mm diam., subglobose; tubercles terete, 5–7mm; axils naked; central spines 0, radial spines 35–45, 2–3mm, thin, subpectinate, interlacing, glassy white. Fl. *c*3.5×3.5cm, funnelform; tube *c*18×2.5mm; inner tepals dark lavender pink; anth. orange yellow. Summer. NW Mexico (Sonora, Nacozari). Z9.

***M.goodridgei*** Scheer ex Salm-Dyck. Series *Ancistracanthae*. Clustering; stem to 10×4cm, erect, cylindric, axils naked; central spines 4, almost white below, brown above, upper 3 straight, lowermost hooked, radial spines 12, subpectinate, interlacing. Fl. 15×15mm, cream-coloured, funnelform; stigmas 6, to 3.5mm, olive green. Fr. to 2.5cm long, clavate, red; fl. remnant persistent. Summer. NW Mexico (Isla Cedros). Z9.

***M.gracilis*** Pfeiff. Series *Proliferae*. Offsetting very freely, the offsets easily detached; principal stems to 13×1–3cm, slender, cylindric; tubercles short, obtusely conic, 6×6mm; axils naked; central spines 0–2(–5), up to 10–12mm, stiffer than the radials, white or dark brown, radial spines 11–17, 3–8mm, bristly, chalky white. Fl. small, *c*12×8mm; tepals pale yellow with pink or brown midline. Fr. small clavate, to 12mm, red; fl. remnant caducous. Spring. EC Mexico. Z9.

***M.grahamii*** Engelm. Series *Ancistracanthae*. Simple or branched at base, 7.5–10×7.5–11cm, globose to ovoid, grey-green, from thickened roots; tubercles ovoid-cylindric, 6–12×4–5mm; axils naked; central spines 1–3, the longest hooked, to 18(–25)mm, dark brown, the hook 1.5mm across, the others when present straight, shorter, paler, radial spines 20–35, 6–12mm, white. Fl. 2.5–4.4cm diam., pink; outer tepals erose; stigmas pale green, to 8mm. Fr. 12–25×6mm, subglobose to barrel-shaped, red. Summer. SW US. Z9.

***M.grusonii*** Runge. Series *Mammillaria*. Mostly simple, globose and later cylindric, to 50×25cm; tubercles four-angled, 6–8mm; axils naked; central spines 2–3, 4–6mm, stronger than the radials, straight, red-brown at first, later snow white, one ascending, one descending, radial spines 12–14, 6–8mm, the upper shorter. Fl. 2.5×2.5cm, yellow. Fr. scarlet. Spring. N Mexico (Coahuila). Z9.

***M.guelzowiana*** Werderm. Series *Ancistracanthae*. Simple or eventually clustering; roots fibrous; stems to 7cm or more diam., flattened-globose; tubercles conic-cylindric, *c*12–13×4–5mm, flabby; axils naked; central spine 1(–3), 8–10mm, hooked, red or yellow, radial spines 60–80, 15–20mm, hair-like, tortuous, pure white. Fl. large, *c*5×6cm, campanulate-funnelform, intense purple-pink; stigmas green. Fr. 8×7mm, almost globose, tinged pink or yellow; seeds with corky strophiole. Summer. NW Mexico. Z9.

***M.guerreronis*** (Bravo) Backeb. & F. Knuth. Series *Polyacanthae*. Clustering; individual stems to 60×6cm, cylindric; tubercles cylindric, 8–10×4–5mm; axils with short wool and 15–20 white bristles; central spines usually 4 (2–5), upper straight, to 15mm, lowermost straight or often hooked, to 25mm, light (to dark) brown at first, later nearly white, radial spines 20–30, 5–10mm, bristly, white. Fl. small, red. Fr. to 25mm, cylindric-clavate, eventually tinged pink or purple. Summer. SW Mexico (Guerrero). Needs more warmth than most mammillarias, and seems reluctant to flower in European collections. Z9.

***M.gummifera*** Engelm. Series *Mammillaria*. Simple 7–10×7.5–12.5cm, hemispheric; tubercles pyramidal, 12–14×10–12mm; axils woolly at first; central spines 1–2, 4mm, dark, radial spines 10–12, upper 4–6mm, bristly, almost white, lower 12–14mm, stronger, dark. Fl. 3×1.2–2.4cm; tepals pink with darker midstripe. Summer. N Mexico. Closely allied to *M.heyderi*, but distinctive in appearance and spination, and more south-westerly in distribution. Z9.

***M.haageana*** Pfeiff. Series *Supertextae*. Usually simple (clustering in var. *schmollii* (Craig) D. Hunt), very variable, reaching 15×5–10cm in larger variants; tubercles small, crowded; axils often woolly and variants; tubercles small, crowded; axils often woolly and sometimes with bristles; central spines usually 2, sometimes 1 or 4, to 15mm, usually brown or dark brown, radial spines 15–25, 3–6mm, white. Fl. small, 12×10mm, deep purple-pink. Fr. red. Spring. SE C Mexico. Z9.

***M.hahniana*** Werderm. Series *Leucocephalae*. Simple or clustering; individual stems to 20×12cm; tubercles very numerous, triangular-conic, small, *c*5×2–3mm; axils with 20 or more long white bristles to 35–40mm; central spines 1(–4), up to 4mm, white with red-brown tip, radial spines 20–30, 5–15mm, hair-like, white. Fl. *c*12×12–15mm, deep purple-pink. Fr. small, 5–7mm, clavate, red. Spring. C Mexico. Z9.

***M.halei*** Brandg. Subg. *Cochemiea*. Resembling *M.poselgeri* but without hooked spines; clustering; stems cylindric, 30–50×5–7.5cm; tubercles short, rounded; axils woolly; central spines 3–4, 25mm, straight, radial spines 10–21, 12mm. Fl. 1.5–5cm, tubular, scarlet. Fr. 12mm, clavate, red. Summer. NW Mexico (islands off Baja California). Z9.

***M.hamata*** Lehm. ex Pfeiff. Series *Polyacanthae*. Clustering; stems cylindric, to 60×10cm or more; axils without bristles; central spines 3–4, lowest longest, usually hooked, to 3cm, brown, radial spines 15–20, white. Spring. SC Mexico (Puebla). The modern interpretation assumes that the poorly described *M.hamata* was the same as the plant earlier illustrated by Ortega as *Cactus cylindricus*. Z9.

***M.heidiae*** Krainz. Series *Ancistracanthae*. Resembling *M.zephyranthoides*. Simple or clustering: roots fibrous; stem *c*3×5.5cm; tubercles cylindric, 8–11×6mm; axils with 1–5 fine bristles to 10mm; central spines 0–2, *c*12mm, hooked, red-brown, pale yellow below, or only 1–2mm, straight, radial spines 16–24, to 11mm, bristly, glassy white. Fl. to 3×2.5cm, near apex, funnelform, yellow, tinged green; stigmas 6, emerald green. Fr. 7–8mm diam., globose to broadly ovoid, green, tinged brown. Summer. S Mexico (Puebla). Z9.

***M.herrerae*** Werderm. Series *Lasiacanthae*. Simple or clustering; stems usually 2–3cm in diameter, globose to cylindric, tubercles numerous, small, 5–6×2mm; axils naked; central spines 0, radial spines 60–100 or more, unequal, *c*1–5mm, bristly, almost white. Fl. 2–3.5×2.5–3cm, lavender pink or nearly white; stigmas green. Fr. 6mm diam., subglobose, colourless to pale green or dull pink. Spring. EC Mexico. Z9.

***M.heyderi*** Muehlenpf. Series *Mammillaria*. Stem 7.5–15cm diam., usually simple, depressed to subglobose; tubercles conic, elongate, 9–12×6mm; axils naked or woolly, without bristles; central spines 0–2, 3–10mm, brown, radial spines 9–22, 4–14mm, brown or white. Fl. usually 20–30×15–30mm, white, pale yellow or pale pink. Fr. obovoid, red. Spring. SW US, N Mexico. Z9.

***M.humboldtii*** Ehrenb. Series *Lasiacanthae*. Simple or clustering; individual stems to *c*7cm diam., depressed-globose or globose; tubercles cylindric, 4–13×2–3mm; axils with wool and white bristles shorter or longer than the tubercles; central spines 0, radial spines 80 or more, 4–6mm, unequal, snow-white. Fl. 2.5×1.5cm, bright purple-pink with green stigmas. Fr. clavate, red; fl. remnant caducous. Spring. EC Mexico. Z9.

***M.hutchisoniana*** (Gates) Boed. Series *Ancistracanthae*. Soon clustering; rootstock fibrous; stems to 15×4–6cm, cylindric; tubercles short, conic; axils without bristles; central spines 4, 7–10mm, light tan with purple tip, at least the lowermost hooked, radial spines 10–20, purple-tipped. Fl. about 2.5×2.5cm, pale pink or creamy white; outer tepals striped dull maroon or brown outside; stigmas 5mm, green or olive green. Fr. 2×1cm, clavate, scarlet. Summer. NW Mexico (Baja California). The earlier-described *M.goodridgei* Salm-Dyck (Cedros Island) may be conspecific. Z9.

***M.insularis*** Gates. Series *Ancistracanthae*. Simple or clustering; rootstock tuberous; individual stems to 6×5cm, depressed-globose; tubercles conic, 7×7mm, blue-green; axils naked or slightly woolly; central spines 1, 1cm, hooked, black-tipped, radial spines 20–30, 5mm, acicular, white. Fl. 15–25mm, funnelform; outer tepals light green, inner light pink with white mid-stripe. Fr. 1cm, clavate, orange red, tending to be hollow. Summer. NW Mexico (Los Angeles Bay area of Baja California). Z9.

***M.jaliscana*** (Britt. & Rose) Boed. Series *Stylothelae*. Clustering; stems 5cm diam., globose; tubercles 4–5mm; axils naked; central spines 4–6, one hooked, red-brown, darker tipped, radial spines 30 or more. Fl. 1cm diam., pale pink or tinged purple, delicately fragrant; stigmas white. Fr. 8mm, white. Spring. WC Mexico (Jalisco). Z9.

***M.johnstonii*** (Britt. & Rose) Orcutt. Series *Mammillaria*. Usually simple; stem eventually 15–20×10cm, globose to short-cylindric; tubercles 4-angled, 10–15mm, somewhat blue-green; axils naked; central spines usually 2, sometimes 4 or 6, 10–25mm, purple-brown to black, radial spines 10–18, 6–9mm, white, tipped brown. Fl. 2×2cm, white. Fr. red. Summer. NW Mexico (Sonora). Z9.

***M. karwinskiana*** Mart. Series *Polyedrae*. Simple at first, later dividing apically and/or offsetting; individual stems to 15×10cm, depressed-globose to short cylindric; tubercles pyramidal-conic, obscurely angled, 10×8–9mm; axils with bristles; spines 4–7, subequal 5–9mm, or the upper and lower longer, 10–12mm, occasionally one in addition porrect, to 25mm, all red-brown at first, fading to horn-coloured, tipped darker. Fl. 20–25×15–20mm, very pale yellow, often striped red on outer tepals. Fr. red. Spring or autumn. S Mexico. Z9.

***M. kewensis*** Salm-Dyck Series *Heterochlorae*. Very similar to *M. polythele*, but spines usually 6–8. Stem simple, subglobose to columnar; tubercles conic, deep green; axils woolly at first, later naked; spines (4–)6–8, radiating, somewhat recurved or adpressed, equal or unequal, the lateral 6–7mm, the upper and/or lower sometimes longer, straight, subulate, grey-white, dark red-brown or black. Fl. 15mm long, purple-pink. Fr. up to 2cm, clavate. Summer. C Mexico (Queretaro, Hidalgo). Z9.

***M. klissingiana*** Boed. Series *Leucocephalae*. Simple at first, eventually clustering; individual stems 16×9cm, globose to clavate; tubercles 5×2mm; axils with numerous white bristles to 10mm; central spines 2–4, 2mm, subulate, almost white, darker towards tip, radial spines 30–35, to 5mm, spreading, more or less straight, almost white. Fl. *c*10×8mm, rose pink, stigmas yellow. Fr. small, 5–6mm, clavate. Spring. NE Mexico (Tamaulipas). Z9.

***M. kraehenbuehlii*** (Krainz) Krainz. Series *Sphacelatae*. Densely clustering; individual stems 3–12×3.5cm, cylindric, softly fleshy; tubercles attenuate to conic, 5–10×*c*5–6mm; axils naked; central spines 0–1, thicker and longer than the radials, brown-tipped, radial spines 18–24, *c*3–8mm, very thin, mostly curving and interlacing, chalky white, brown-tipped. Fl. *c*18mm, lilac-carmine; stigmas 1.5mm, yellow-white. Fr. *c*20×5mm, clavate, dark carmine. Spring. S Mexico (Oaxaca). Z9.

***M. lasiacantha*** Engelm. Series *Lasiacanthae*. Usually simple; stem small, globose or globose-ovoid; tubercles cylindric, 4–6mm, axils naked; central spines 0, radial spines 40–80 in several series, 3–5mm, white, pubesc. or glabrous. Fl. *c*13×13mm; tepals white with red mid-stripe, stigmas 5, yellow-green. Fr. 12–20mm, obovate-clavate, scarlet; fl. remnant caducous. Spring. SW US (SC New Mexico and Texas), N Mexico. Z9.

***M. laui*** D. Hunt. Series *Lasiacanthae*. Clustering; individual stems to 6×4.5cm, depressed-globose to globose or shortly oblong; tubercles terete, 8×6mm, largely hidden by the spines; axils naked or sparsely woolly; central spines 0–numerous, more or less intergrading with the radials, radial spines 35–60 or more, in several series, *c*6–9mm, setaceous to hair-like, typically white, glabrous. Fl. *c*15×12mm, purple-pink, stigmas white. Fr. *c*1cm, cylindric-clavate, white or pale pink; fl. remnant persistent. Spring. EC Mexico. There are three named forms: f. *laui*, with up to 12 white central spines 7–10mm long intergrading with the radials; f. *subducta* D. Hunt, with up to 12 stronger pale yellow brown centrals 7–10mm; and f. *dasyacantha* D. Hunt, with very slender white centrals, scarcely or not distinguishable from the radials. Z9.

***M. lenta*** K. Brandg. Series *Lasiacanthae*. Branching dichotomously; individual stems 3–5cm diam., forming flat-topped clusters, in nature only 1–2cm high (above ground); tubercles slender conic, *c*1cm, light green; axils with short persistent wool and an occasional bristle; central spines 0, radial spines 30–40, 3–7mm, soft and fragile, white, or those at the centre tinged yellow. Fl. *c*2×2.5cm; tepals white with pink or pale purple mid-stripe; stigmas olive-green. Fr. 1cm, clavate, red. Summer. N Mexico. Z9.

***M. leucantha*** Boed. Series *Stylothelae*. Simple or rarely clustering; rootstock stout, napiform; stem up to 3.5cm diam., globose or somewhat elongate-globose; tubercles *c*7×2mm; axils sparsely woolly with fine white bristles 5mm; central spines 3–4, up to 5–6mm, dark amber-yellow, all hooked except the fourth when present, radial spines *c*18, up to 5mm, somewhat thinner than the centrals, white, often the upper tipped brown-yellow. Fl. 15mm, white. Seeds dark grey-brown. Spring. NE Mexico. Z9.

***M. leucocentra*** Berg. Series *Leucocephalae*. Resembling *M. geminispina*. Simple or clustering, globose to short-columnar, to *c*12×11cm; tubercles terete-conic, *c*8×9mm, glaucous green; axils with white bristles; central spines 4–6, to 12mm, white with dark tip, radial spines 30–35, *c*6mm, chalky white. Fl. as in *M. geminispina*. Summer. C Mexico. Z9.

***M. lloydii*** (Britt. & Rose) Orcutt. Series *Mammillaria*. Usually simple. Stem sometimes 10×6–7cm, depressed-globose to short-cylindric; tubercles 4-angled; axils only slightly woolly; central spines 0, radial spines 3–4, uppermost red or dark brown, others white, 2–5mm. Fl. 15×15mm; outer tepals dark red with light or coloured, inner white, with a tinge of red and dark red mid-stripe. Spring. NC Mexico (Zacatecas). Z9.

***M. longicoma*** (Britt. & Rose) A. Berger. Series *Stylothelae*. Resembling *M. bocasana*, but with more prominent central and stiffer radial spines. Clustering; individual stems 3–4cm diam.; tubercles conic, 4–5mm, dark green, obtuse; axils with long white hairs; central spines 4, 10–12mm, 1–2 hooked, brown above, paler below, radial spines 25 or more, weak and hair-like, more or less interlacing. Fl. white, outer tepals pink with darker mid-stripe; stigmas cream. Spring. C Mexico. Z9.

***M. longiflora*** (Britt. & Rose) A. Berger. Series *Longiflorae*. Usually simple; stems 3–9cm diam., globose; tubercles *c*1cm long, plump; central spines 4, the upper 3 straight, the lowermost strongly hooked, 11–25mm, dark brown to yellow or white, radial spines 25–30, 10–13mm, bristly, white. Fl. 2–3.5×2–3cm, funnelform, pink or purple-pink, with distinct tube; pericarpel and fruit immersed in the stem. Spring. Mts of NW Mexico. Z9.

***M. longimamma*** DC. Subgenus *Dolichothele*. Simple or clustering; rootstock tuberous; stems to 10–12cm diam.; tubercles oblong-terete, largest in the genus, 20–50×6–12mm, often widely separated; central spines 0–3, usually 1, bristly, protruding, to 25mm, radial spines 6–10, 12–18mm, all spines pale brown, pale yellow or white. Fl. large, 3–6×3–6cm, bright yellow. Fr. ovoid, green, tinged yellow or purple. Summer. EC Mexico. Z9.

***M. magallanii*** Schmoll ex Craig. Series *Lasiacanthae*. Simple, with large taproot; stem *c*6×4–5cm, cylindric-clavate; tubercles 6×4mm; axils with scant wool; central spines 0–1, 1–3mm, porrect, straight, curved or hooked, orange-tan at base, brown at tip, radial spines 70–75, 2–5mm, horizontal and interlacing, orange tan at base, becoming chalky white, brown at tip. Fl. 10×6mm; tepals cream with brown or pink mid-stripe. Spring. N Mexico (Coahuila). Z9.

***M. magnifica*** Buchenau. Series *Polyacanthae*. Clustering; individual stems to 40×5–9cm, cylindric; tubercles rounded pyramidal or conic, (3–)6–7×7–9mm; axils with bristles; central spines 4–5 or more, the lowest 15–55mm, hooked, remainder shorter, straight, all clear yellow-brown, radial spines 17–24, 3–8mm, glassy white or yellow. Fl. 17–20×11–15mm, pink-red. Fr. (9–)15–22mm, clavate, pink below, green at tip. Spring. SC Mexico (Morelos-Puebla border). Z9.

***M. magnimamma*** Haw. Series *Mammillaria*. Variable; usually clustering and forming mounds 50cm or more diam.; individual heads to 10–12cm diam.; tubercles dark green, pyramidal-conic but not sharply angled, *c*10×10mm; axils woolly in flowering zone; spines 3–6, usually 1 longer, to 5cm and stronger than the others and more or less curved. Fl. *c*2×2cm, pale yellow to deep purple-pink. Fr. red. Spring. C Mexico. Z9.

***M. mainiae*** K. Brandg. Series *Ancistracanthae*. Simple or clustering; stems to 10–12×6–7cm, globose; tubercles terete, 10–15(–18)×*c*10mm; axils naked, often red; central spines 1, *c*15mm, strongly hooked and somewhat twisted, brown below, tipped nearly black, or pale yellow with dark tip, sometimes 1–2 others present, weaker and shorter, radial spines 8–15, 6–12mm, the upper somewhat shorter, pale yellow, becoming white, dark-tipped. Fl. to 2cm, pale pink with darker mid-stripe; stigmas long, purple. Fr. globose to obovoid, shorter than the tubercles. Summer. SW US (Arizona), N Mexico. Z9.

***M. mammillaris*** (L.) Karst. Series *Mammillaria*. Simple or clustering; stem to 6×7cm or larger, globose to short cylindric; tubercles terete-conic, 7–12×4–8mm, glossy green; axils slightly woolly; central spines 3–5, 7–10mm, red-brown, darker tipped, radial spines 10–16, 5–8mm, tinged red-brown. Fl. small 8–12×6–10mm, pale yellow. Fr. 10–20×6–8mm, red. Summer. Dutch West Indies, Grenadines, Venezuela. Z9.

***M. maritima*** (Lindsay) D. Hunt. Subg. *Cochemiea*. Resembling *M. setispina*. Clustering and forming clumps to 1m diam.; stems 3–7cm diam., erect or decumbent, cylindric, blue-green; tubercles subconic, somewhat flattened laterally; fl. axils woolly; central spines 4, red-brown, upper 3 ascending, 1–2cm, straight, lowermost porrect, 2–5cm, hooked, radial spines 10–15, *c*1cm, acicular, red-brown. Fl. 3cm, trumpet-shaped, scarlet; tepals in 3 series, the uppermost flared and reflexed, the lower erect, adpressed to tube; stamens and style exserted. Fr. globose, red. Summer. NW Mexico (Baja California). Z9.

***M. marksiana*** Krainz. Series *Mammillaria*. Simple at first, later clustering; stems 6–15×5–12cm, broadly globose, apex woolly; tubercles gibbous-pyramidal, somewhat 4 or more sided, 7–10×10–14mm, light or yellow-green; flowering axils woolly, without bristles; spines (4–)9–11(–21), 8–11mm, few on main heads, more numerous on offsets, golden yellow or sometimes brown. Fl. *c*15×15mm, yellow. Fr. to 2×1cm, clavate, purple-red. Summer. NW Mexico. Z9.

***M. matudae*** H. Bravo. Series *Polyacanthae*. Simple or clustering; stems to 20cm or more ×3–5cm, elongate-cylindric; tubercles conic, 4.5×2.5mm; axils without wool or bristles; central spines 1, 4–5mm, ascending, pink-brown at first, later dirty white, radial spines 18–20, 2–3mm, translucent white. Fl. 12mm, light purple-red. Fr. 12mm, green, tinged red. Spring. C Mexico (State of Mexico). Z9.

***M. mazatlanensis*** Schum. ex Gürke. Series *Ancistracanthae*. Clustering; stems slender-cylindric, to 15×2–4cm; tubercles shortly conic, 4–8×10mm; axils naked or with 1–2 short bristles; central spines 3–4, the upper more or less in the plane of the radials, to 15mm, typically straight, but hooked in some plants, red-brown above, paler below, radial spines 13–15, 5–10mm, white. Fl. to 3–4×3cm, carmine red; stigmas 6mm, green. Fr. 2cm, clavate, tinged red. Summer. Coast of NW Mexico (Sonora-Michoacan). Z9.

***M. meiacantha*** Engelm. Series *Mammillaria*. Simple; stem depressed-globose; tubercles compressed, quadrangular-pyramidal, 14–16mm; axils naked; central spines 0–1, 3–7mm, ascending, radial spines 5–9, 6–10mm, all spines almost white to dirty yellow, brown-tipped, the central darker. Fl. *c*2.5cm; tepals pink or nearly white with pink mid-stripe. Fr. 2–3cm, scarlet, ripening the following season. Summer. SW US, N Mexico. Z9.

***M.melaleuca*** Karw. ex Salm-Dyck. Subg. *Dolichothele*. Simple or sometimes clustering; stem globose, tubercles ovoid-terete, *c*10×7mm, deep glossy green, axils naked. Central spine 1, sometimes lacking, brown, radial spines 8–9, 12–14mm, spreading-recurved, the upper 4 a little longer, typically dark brown, the lower white. Fl. *c*2cm, yellow. Fr. green, tinged red. Summer. NE Mexico. Z9.

***M.melanocentra*** Poselger. Series *Mammillaria*. Simple; stem to 15cm diam., depressed-globose, glaucous green; tubercles pyramidal, large, *c*1×14mm; axils woolly at first; central spines 1, to 3cm, stout, black, radial spines 7–9, unequal, 6–22mm, the lowest longest, black when young, later pale grey, black tipped. Fl. *c*2×2cm, deep pink. Fr. to 3cm, clavate, pink or red. Spring. N Mexico (Nuevo Leon). Z9.

***M.mendeliana*** (Bravo) Werderm. Series *Leucocephalae*. Resembling *M.hahniana*; axillary bristle-hairs 15–25mm; central spines (2–)4, the lowermost to 2cm, radial spines poorly developed or lacking. Spring. C Mexico (E Guanajuato). Z9.

***M.mercadensis*** Patoni. Series *Stylothelae*. Simple or clustering, stems 5–6cm diam., usually more or less globose; axils naked; central spines 4 or more, usually only one hooked, 15–25mm, varying from pale straw yellow to dark red-brown, radial spines 25–30, stiffly bristly, white or pale yellow. Fl. *c*15×15mm, pale pink; stigmas creamy white. Fr. red. Spring. Mexico (E flank of Sierra Madre Occidental). Z9.

***M.meyranii*** Bravo. Series *Polyacanthae*. Clustering; stems to 55×4–5cm, cylindric; tubercles conic, 8×2–3mm; axils with sparse wool at first, without bristles; central spines 2, divergent, 1cm or less, at first orange yellow with chestnut brown tip, later dirty white, radial spines 17–19, 3–6mm, white with yellow base. Fl. 18mm, purple; stigmas green. Fr. 20×5mm, clavate, light purple-pink with brown-green tinge, scented. Spring. Mexico (State of Mexico). Z9.

***M.microhelia*** Werderm. Series *Leptocladodae*. Simple or clustering; stems to 25×3.5–6cm, cylindric; tubercles shortly conic, 4×6mm; axils soon naked; central spines 0–4(–8), to 11mm, dark red-brown, radial spines (30–)50, 4–6mm, yellow, regularly radiating and often slightly recurved. Fl. about 15×15mm, creamy white to red or purple. Fr. *c*10×4mm, pale green or pink. Spring. C Mexico (Querétaro). Z9.

***M.mieheana*** Tiegel. Series *Leptocladodae*. Intermediate between *M.elongata* and *M.densispina*. Clustering; stems to 15×5cm, cylindric; tubercles shortly ovoid, 7×7mm; upper axils somewhat white-woolly; central spines 3–6, to 15mm, almost straight, honey-yellow or often brown, radial spines 18–20, similar, pale yellow, almost white on new growth. Fl. 15mm, yellow. Fr. 15mm, long-clavate, or ovate, 6–7mm, nearly white, translucent. Spring. C Mexico (Querétaro). Z9.

***M.milleri*** (Britt. & Rose) Boed. Series *Ancistracanthae*. Simple at first, later clustering; stems up to *c*15×4–8cm, cylindric, green; tubercles *c*10×10mm; axils naked; central spines 1(–2)(–4), the principal one 12–15mm, broadly hooked, black-purple, the second, where present, shorter, straight, paler, radial spines 18–28, 6–12mm, light brown to red. Fl. *c*2×2–3cm, lavender-pink with light green or pale brown stigmas. Fr. 20–25mm, dimorphic, either clavate, scarlet, or small, ovoid, green. Summer. SW US, N Mexico. Z9.

***M.moelleriana*** Boed. Series *Stylothelae*. Simple; stem to 11×10cm, globose to short cylindric; tubercles ovoid, *c*8×8mm; axils naked; central spines 8–10, the (2–)4 lowermost hooked, to 20(–30)mm, the upper somewhat shorter, straight, all honey yellow to dark red-brown; radial spines *c*30–40(–50), 7–9mm, white, faintly yellow at base. Fl. 15(–20)×15mm, more or less pale pink with darker mid-stripe according to the colour of the spines. Fr. 15mm, clavate, pale green. Spring. WC Mexico. Z9.

***M.mollendorffiana*** Shurly. Series *Heterochlorae*. Resembling *M.rhodantha*, but more slender, and with smaller flowers. Simple; stem to 35×6–12cm or taller, globose to cylindric; tubercles subcylindric, 6–8×4–6mm; axils woolly, and with 4–5 bristles in age; central spines 4–6, 6–14mm light yellow brown with darker tip, radial spines 18–28, 3–5mm, dull chalky or glassy white. Fl. 10–16×8mm, purple. Fr. 14mm, clavate, purple-red. Summer. C Mexico (Hidalgo). Z9.

***M.morganiana*** Tiegel. Series *Leucocephalae*. Simple at first, later dividing apically; individual heads globose, depressed at apex, to 8cm diam.; tubercles pyramidal, 10×5mm; axils with fine hairs to 2cm; central spines 4–6, 10mm, white, tipped brown, radial spines numerous (40–50), to 12mm, hair-like, white. Fl. *c*1×1cm; tepals pink with darker mid-stripe. Fr. red. Spring. C Mexico. Z9.

***M.muehlenpfordtii*** C.F. Först. Series *Leucocephalae*. Simple at first, often dividing apically later; individual heads depressed-globose, 10–15cm diam.; tubercles conic, 8–10×6mm; axils with fine bristles; young areoles with pale yellow wool; central spines 4(–7), the lowermost longest, 5–35mm, often strong and curved, remainder 4–14mm, pale to dark yellow, often tipped brown, radial spines 40–50, 2–8mm, glassy white. Fl. 15×10mm, deep purple-pink. Fr. red. Summer. C Mexico. Z9.

***M.multidigitata*** Radley ex Lindsay. Series *Ancistracanthae*. Freely clustering; individual stems 5–8(–20)×2–5cm, cylindric; tubercles obtuse, *c*5×3mm, green; axils slightly woolly; central spines usually 4, *c*8mm, straight, white with brown tip, radial spines 15–25, 6–8mm, white. Fl. 15mm, white, stigmas green. Fr. 15×4mm, clavate. Summer. NW Mexico (Isla San Pedro Nolasco). Z9.

***M.mundtii*** Schum. Series *Heterochlorae*. Simple; 6–7cm diam., stem depressed-globose; tubercles conic, 6–7mm, leaf-green; axils naked; central spines 2–4, straight, red-brown, radial spines 10–12, to 5mm, white. Fl. 2cm, carmine red. Fr. slender-cylindric, red. Summer. Mts of C Mexico (near Toluca). The above description follows current usage which may or may not be correct. Z9.

***M.mystax*** Mart. Series *Polyedrae*. Simple; stem to 15×7–10cm, globose to cylindric, eventually dividing apically; tubercles pyramidal, angled and keeled, 10–15×8mm; axils with bristles; spines variable; central spines 3–4, 15–20mm often one in addition porrect, to 7cm, tortuous, purple-brown at first, tipped darker, later grey, radial spines 3–10, 4–8mm, white, brown-tipped. Fl. 25×20mm, deep purple-pink. Fr. 2–2.5cm, red. Spring. S Mexico. Z9.

***M.napina*** Purpus. Series *Longiflorae*. Simple; root napiform; stem to *c*5cm diam., globose; tubercles conic, 8–10×7–8mm; axils somewhat woolly or naked. Spines about 12, usually all radial, 8–9mm, somewhat curved, glassy white or yellow at base. Fl. 4cm diam.; tepals pale pink with deeper mid-stripe. Fr. immersed between the tubercles, colourless. Summer. SW Mexico. Z9.

***M.nejapensis*** Craig & Dawson. Series *Polyedrae*. Resembling *M.karwinskiana*. Clustering; stems to 15×5–7.5cm, ovoid to cylindric-clavate; tubercles 5–8×6–8mm; axils with many tortuous white bristles; spines 3–5, upper shorter, 2–5mm, lowermost longest, to 25(–50)mm, white with red-brown tip. Fl. 18×10mm; tepals pale cream with brown red to scarlet mid-stripe. Fr. 20×6mm, slender clavate, bright red. Spring or autumn. SW Mexico. Z9.

***M.neopalmeri*** Craig. Series *Ancistracanthae*. Usually clustering; stems to 5×5cm, cylindric; tubercles cylindric, *c*4mm, glaucous; axils with dense wool and bristles; central spines 2–5, 6–8mm, straight or occasionally hooked, pale brown with darker tip, radial spines 15–20, 3–5mm, white. Fl. small, *c*12mm, nearly white. Fr. clavate, scarlet. Summer. NW Mexico (San Benito Island). Z9.

***M.nivosa*** Link ex Pfeiff. Series *Mammillaria*. Simple or clustering; stems globose to short-cylindric; tubercles obtusely conic, 10–15×10mm, dark green to bronze; axils densely woolly, without bristles; spines 7–14, longest to 2cm, bright yellow to dark brown. Fl. 15–20mm, yellow. Fr. red, clavate; fl. remnant caducous. Summer. West Indies (S Bahamas to Antigua). Z9.

***M.nunezii*** (Britt. & Rose) Orcutt Series *Polyacanthae*. Simple or later clustering; stems to 15×8cm, globose to cylindric; tubercles terete; axils with bristles; central spines 2–6, 10–12mm, all straight, or lowermost longer, hooked, brown, or glassy white with brown tip, radial spines 10–30, 5–8mm, bristly, white. Fl. 20×15–18mm, purple-pink. Fr. white or green, tinged pink. Spring. SW C Mexico (Guerrero). Z9.

***M.painteri*** Rose ex Quehl. Series *Stylothelae*. Simple at first, later clustering; stems 2cm diam., globose; tubercles terete; axils without bristles; central spines 4–5, to 1cm, 1 hooked, dark brown, puberulent, radial spines *c*20, to 5mm, bristly, white, puberulent. Fl. 15mm; outer tepals tinged brown, inner nearly white; stigmas cream. Fr. red. Spring. EC Mexico (Queretaro). Z9.

***M.parkinsonii*** Ehrenb. Series *Leucocephalae*. Simple at first, later dividing apically; individual stems 7–15cm diam.; tubercles pyramidal, 8–10×4–6mm; axils with wool and bristles; central spines 2–4, rarely 5, upper 6–8mm, lowermost variable, up to 3.5cm, often curved, white or red-brown, tipped dark brown, radial spines 30–35, white. Fl. 12–15×12–15mm, creamy yellow, tinged brown or pink. Fr. red. Spring. C Mexico. Z9.

***M.pectinifera*** F.A. Weber. Series *Lasiacanthae*. Simple; rootstock fibrous; stem to 3–5cm diam, globose to short-cylindric; tubercles small; axils naked; areoles elongate, spines 20–40, 1.5–2mm, bristly, pectinate, adpressed, white. Fl. to *c*25×25mm; tepals creamy yellow or pale pink with pale brown mid-stripe. Fr. 6mm, oblong, tinged green. Spring. SE C Mexico. Z9.

***M.peninsularis*** (Britt. & Rose) Orcutt. Series *Mammillaria*. Simple or clustering; stems depressed-globose, grey-green; tubercles erect, pointed, 4-angled, pale green; axils with long wool at first, later naked; spines 4–8, nearly erect, short and pale with brown tips, one sometimes nearly central. Fl. 1.5cm; outer tepals narrow, tinged red, inner narrow, acuminate, green or light yellow with erose margins; stamens pale; style longer than the stamens; stigmas green. Summer. NW Mexico (Cape Region of Baja California). Z9.

***M.pennispinosa*** Krainz. Series *Stylothelae*. Typically simple; rootstock stout; stem *c*3×3.5cm, depressed-globose, tubercles cylindric, 5–7×3mm; axils woolly at first, later naked; central spines 1(–3), 1 hooked, 10–12mm, yellow at base, brown-red above, pubesc., others when present ascending, similar to the radials, radial spines 16–20, 5–8mm, slender, straight, feathery-pubesc., grey-white. Fl. *c*15×15mm; tepals white with pale pink mid-stripe; stigmas pale yellow. Fr. 5mm, ovoid, green; seeds with corky strophiole. Spring. N Mexico (Coahuila). Z9.

***M.perbella*** Hildm. ex Schum. Series *Leucocephalae*. Clustering and forming low mounds by apical division; individual stems *c*5cm diam., depressed-globose; tubercles small, 5–7×3–4mm; axils with short bristly hairs; central spines usually 2, sometimes 1 or 0, 1–4mm, brown or white with red-black tip, radial spines 12–22, 1.5–4mm. Fl. *c*10×10mm, purple-pink. Fr. red. Spring. C Mexico. Z9.

***M.petrophila*** K. Brandg. Series *Mammillaria*. Simple; stem to 15×15cm; tubercles short with broad base; axils woolly; central spines 1–2, nearly 2cm, dark chestnut brown, radial spines *c*10, *c*1cm. Fl. 18–20mm; tepals yellow, tinged green, lightly erose; stigmas 6, green-yellow. Fr. red. Summer. NW Mexico (S Baja California). Z9.

***M.petterssonii*** Hildm. Series *Mammillaria*. Simple; stem to 30cm diam., subglobose; tubercles angled, *c*1×1cm, dark green; axils woolly; central spines 5–7, one to 45mm, porrect, the others shorter, brown at first, tipped darker, radial spines *c*10, 2–10mm, the uppermost shorter and weaker, white, all spines stiff and straight. Fl. 2–2.5cm, purple-pink. Spring. C Mexico (Guanajuato). Z9.

***M.phitauiana*** (Baxter) Werderm. Series *Ancistracanthae*. Clustering; roots fibrous; stems to 15–25cm, cylindric; tubercles conic, 4–6mm; axils with about 20 bristles; central spines 4, 4–6mm, all straight or 1 hooked in young plants, upper half brown, lower white, radial spines *c*24, 4–12mm, lower longest, white. Fl. 12–15mm, white, outer tepals with red midrib. Fr. *c*1cm, globose to clavate, red. Summer. NW Mexico (S Baja California). Z9.

***M.picta*** Meinsh. Series *Proliferae*. Usually simple; stem often *c*5×5cm; globose or ovoid, becoming tuberous at base; tubercles cylindric-terete; axils with fine bristles; spines 15–20, 10–12mm, in a graded series, pubesc.; central spines straight, porrect, darker than the radials, upper and lateral radials straight, dark tipped, lower slender, white. Fl. *c*20×15mm, white with pale green tinge. Fr. red. Spring. NE C Mexico. Z9.

***M.pilcayensis*** Bravo (as 'pitcayensis', orth. error). Series *Polyacanthae*. Resembling *M.spinosissima*. Simple or clustering; stems to 50×4–5cm, slender-cylindric; tubercles 5×2–3mm; axils woolly and with 8–10 slender bristles; central and radial spines similar, about 30, 5–6mm, bristly, pale glassy yellow. Fl. *c*2cm, purple-red. Spring. SW C Mexico (Guerrero, Barranca de Pilcaya). Z9.

***M.pilispina*** Purpus. Series *Proliferae*. Clustering; stems 4cm diam., subglobose; tubercles cylindric, to 10×6mm; axils with wool and a few long hair-like bristles; central spines 5–8, 6–10mm, brown in upper half, white or yellow below, radial spines *c*40, 7–10mm, fine, hair-like, pubesc., white, in a ring behind the other spines. Fl. 10–15×10mm, creamy white. Spring. EC Mexico. Z9.

***M.plumosa*** F.A. Weber. Series *Lasiacanthae*. Clustering to form mounds to 40cm or more diam.; individual stems to 6–7cm diam., globose, hidden by the spines; tubercles cylindric, to 2cm×2–3mm; axils woolly; spines up to 40, 3–7mm, feathery, white. Fl. small, about 15×12mm, creamy white or tinged brown-pink. Fr. pale pink to dull red. Winter. NE Mexico. Z9.

***M.polyedra*** Mart. Series *Polyedrae*. Simple at first, later clustering; stems to 30×10–12cm, subglobose; tubercles pyramidal-applanate, 6–7-sided; axils with wool and bristles; spines 4–6, 6–25mm, the uppermost longest and strongest, straight, horn-coloured, tipped dark purple. Fl. *c*25mm, pink. Spring. S Mexico. Z9.

***M.polythele*** Mart. Series *Heterochlorae*. Simple; stem to 30–80×8–12(–17)cm, cylindric; tubercles pyramidal-conic, 9–14×8mm, dark blue-green; axils woolly; central spines 2–4, 8–17(–25)mm, usually dark brown, in some variants yellow-brown, radial spines 0 or rudimentary. Fl. 15–19×10–14mm, purple-pink. Fr. dull purple. Summer. C Mexico (Hidalgo). Z9.

***M.pondii*** Greene. Simple or few-branched; stems to 30cm, cylindric; axils with bristles; central spines 4–5, the longest more than 25mm, rigid and strongly hooked, dark brown above the middle, radial spines 20–30, white, slender. Fl. nearly 5cm, bright scarlet. Summer. NW Mexico (Cedros Island). Z9.

***M.poselgeri*** Hildm. Branching from the base; rootstock becoming tuberous; stems to 0.3–2m×4–7cm, cylindric, elongate; tubercles wide-spaced, conic-pyramidal, rounded at apex, *c*1cm, upswept; axils woolly and rarely setose; central spines 1, 15–25mm, hooked, radial spines 7–9, 9–12mm, all spines white, brown tipped. Fl. 3cm or more, in upper axils; tube curved; limb oblique, with double ring of recurving tepals, bright scarlet; stamens and style well-projecting. Fr. 6–8mm diam., obovoid, red. Summer. NW Mexico (S Baja California). Z9.

***M.pottsii*** Scheer ex Salm-Dyck. Series *Leptocladodae*. Clustering; stems to 20×3cm, slender cylindric; axils without bristles; central spines *c*7, 7–12mm, uppermost longest, tipped dark brown, paler below, radial spines 40–45, about 6mm, bristly, chalky white. Fl. about 12×12mm, deep red. Fr. red. Spring. N Mexico, SW US (SW Texas). Z9.

***M.pringlei*** (J. Coult.) K. Brandg. Series *Heterochlorae*. Resembling *M.rhodantha* but yellow- or golden-spined. Simple or branching dichotomously; stems to 15×12cm, depressed-globose to globose; tubercles rounded-conic, 10–14×10–12mm, green, with watery sap; axils with fine bristly hairs to 1cm; central spines 6–8, 2–3cm, very stout, more or less flexuous, upper usually longest and recurved, radial spines 18–22, 7–9mm, fine acicular. Fl. 14–18mm, rose-purple with rose-purple or pale yellow stigmas. Fr. 2cm, green or tinged purple. Summer. C Mexico. Z9.

***M.prolifera*** (Mill.) Haw. Series *Proliferae*. Clustering freely and forming dense clumps; individual stems to *c*9×4.5cm, globose to cylindric-clavate; tubercles terete, to 10×4–5mm; axils more or less naked or with fine white hairs as long or longer than the tubercles; central spines 5–12, 4–9mm, straight, puberulent, white to yellow or red-brown, sometimes dark-tipped, radial spines intergrading with the centrals, 25–40, 3–12mm, bristle-like to hair-like, straight to tortuous, white. Fl. *c*10–18mm, creamy yellow, or tinged pink, outer tepals brown-striped. Fr. to 2cm, red. Spring. NE Mexico, SW US, Cuba, Hispaniola. Z9.

***M.pseudoperbella*** Quehl. Series *Leucocephalae*. Simple, or perhaps branching dichotomously; individual heads globose at first, later cylindric, 7–10×5–8cm, the apex sunken and woolly; tubercles cylindric, 6–7×2–3mm, leek-green, eventually losing the spines; flowering axils with wool and bristles, eventually becoming naked; central spines 2(–4), *c*3–5mm, thick, brown with black tip, the lower shorter, paler, radial spines 20–30, 2–3mm, pure white. Fl. 10–15mm, inner tepals with prominent pink mid-stripe. Fr. *c*15×4mm, clavate, deep pink. Summer. Presumably C Mexico. Z9.

***M.pubispina*** Boed. Series *Stylothelae*. Simple; stem to 4cm diam., globose; tubercles cylindric, *c*8×2mm; axils pale green or pink with fine tortuous bristles; central spines (3–)4, pubesc., the lowermost hooked, *c*9mm, tipped red- or black-brown, pale below, the upper 10mm, straight, pale or white, radial spines *c*15, *c*8–12mm, hair-like, more or less crooked and tortuous, pubesc., white. Fl. 18×15mm; outer tepals dirty pink with broad white edges, inner pure white or cream with delicate pink mid-stripe. Spring. C Mexico (Hidalgo). Z9.

***M.pygmaea*** (Britt. & Rose) A. Berger. Series *Stylothelae*. Simple or clustering, individual stems depressed-globose to ovoid-cylindric, to 6×5.5cm (larger in cult.); tubercles cylindric, 7–11×4–5mm; axils with bristly hairs; central spines 4, upper 3 straight, erect, 5–7mm, tinged pink at first, later straw yellow to red-brown, lowermost hooked, 5–6mm, all pubesc., radial spines 22–28, to 6mm, very fine, mostly radiating to sides, white, pubesc. Fl. *c*1cm; outer tepals apiculate, red tinged, inner creamy white. Fr. *c*1–5cm, slender cylindric, bright red. Spring. EC Mexico (Queretaro). Z9.

***M.rekoi*** (Britt. & Rose) Vaupel. Series *Polyacanthae*. Resembling *M.nunezii*, but spines typically stronger and one central consistently hooked. Simple; stem to 12×5–6cm, globose to short-cylindric; tubercles terete, 8–10mm; axils with wool and 1–8 long white bristles; central spines 4, 10–15mm, brown, the lower one sometimes hooked, radial spines *c*20, 4–6mm, white. Fl. 1.5cm, deep purple; stigmas pale green. Fr. 12mm, clavate, red. Spring. S Mexico (Oaxaca). Z9.

***M.rettigiana*** Boed. Series *Stylothelae*. Simple; stem depressed or elongate-globose; tubercles cylindric, 8–10mm; axils naked or with a little wool but no bristles; central spines 3–4, red-brown, the 2–3 upper straight, 12mm, the lowermost hooked, to 15mm, radial spines 18–20, to 10mm, thin acicular, smooth. Fl. *c*15mm diam., pale pink; stigmas almost white. Fr. clavate, small, red. Spring. C Mexico (SW Hidalgo). Z9.

***M.rhodantha*** Link & Otto. Series *Heterochlorae*. Usually simple, occasionally offsetting or branching dichotomously; stem to 40×12cm, cylindric; tubercles obtuse-conic to cylindric, to 16×9mm; axils woolly at first and with a few bristles; central spines 4–9, to 18(–25)mm, usually somewhat recurved, variable in colour, typically red-brown, radial spines typically 17–24, 4–9mm, glassy white to pale yellow. Fl. 20–25×15–18mm, purple-red; stigmas 1mm, usually purple. Fr. 15–25mm, cylindric-clavate, dull purple-red towards apex, often paler towards base. Summer. Mts of C Mexico. Z9.

***M.roseoalba*** Boed. Series *Mammillaria*. Simple; stem depressed-globose; tubercles angled, 10×8mm; axils densely woolly; spines 4–5(–6), to 8mm, somewhat unequal, spreading rather regularly and somewhat recurved, almost white, pink-brown towards base. Fl. 3cm; outer tepals pink, tinged brown, inner nearly white. Fr. 1.5cm, clavate, red. Spring–summer. NE Mexico. Z9.

***M.rubida*** Schwarz ex Backeb. Series *Mammillaria*. Simple; stem to 9×13cm, depressed-globose, blue-green at first, later dull red; tubercles pyramidal, only slightly angled; axils woolly; central spines 1, to 2cm, radial spines 8, to 1.5cm, all spines red-brown. Fl. *c*2.2cm; outer tepals with dull red mid-stripe, inner almost white, tinged green. Summer. W Mexico (Sinaloa). Z9.

***M.saboae*** Glass. Series *Longiflorae*. Clustering; individual stems 1–2×1–2cm, ovoid, from fleshy roots; tubercles small, rounded 2–5×5mm, smooth, green; axils naked; central spines 0, rarely 1, 2mm, straight, radial spines 17–25, 2mm, slender, glassy white, slightly curved, yellow at the base. Fl. to 4×4cm, funnelform, pink; anth. pale yellow. Fr. sunken in the stem; fl. remnant persistent; seeds 1mm. Spring. Mts of NW Mexico (SW Chihuahua, Sonora). Z9.

***M.sartorii*** Purpus. Series *Polyedrae*. Clustering; stems often 10×8–9cm tall, globose to somewhat cylindric-globose, rarely to 12cm diam., flat-topped, dark glaucous green; tubercles pyramidal, irregularly angled, *c*7–10×10–12mm; axils with dense white or pale yellow wool and sparse to numerous bristles; central spines 2–10, very variable, 0–2 porrect, only 1–2mm or rarely to 8cm, 2–8 spreading, 2–8mm, off-white or pale brown with brown tip, radial spines 0–12, rudimentary, 1–2mm, bristle-like. Fl. *c*2cm; tepals pale carmine with darker mid-stripe; stigmas 6, pale yellow or red-tinged. Fr. *c*1.5cm, red. Summer. SE Mexico (Veracruz). Z9.

***M.schiedeana*** Ehrenb. Series *Lasiacanthae*. Clustering; individual stems to 10×6cm, depressed-globose, becoming tuberous at base; tubercles cylindric-terete, 6–10×3–4mm, tapering to 1mm at tip, dark green; axils with white woolly hairs longer than the tubercles; central spines 0, radial spines very numerous, *c*80, 2–5mm, adpressed, minutely pubesc., white, pale yellow towards the base, golden yellow at the base, the tip usually hair-like. Fl. 10–15×10mm, creamy white. Fr. 12×2–3mm, slender-cylindric, bright carmine red. Autumn. EC Mexico (Hidalgo). Z9.

***M.schumannii*** Hildm. Series *Ancistracanthae*. Clustering; roots thickened; stems to 6–8×3–4cm, ovoid to short-cylindric; tubercles short, grey green; axils soon naked; central spine usually 1, 1–1.5cm, hooked, dark brown to white with dark tip, radial spines 9–15, 6–12mm. Fl. *c*2.5×2.5–4cm, lavender pink; stigmas tinged green or pale yellow. Fr. to 2cm, orange-scarlet at first, partly embedded in the stem and tending to break off when dry. Summer. NW Mexico (S Baja California). Z9.

***M.scrippsiana*** (Britt. & Rose) Orcutt. Series *Mammillaria*. Simple at first, later clustering; individual stems to 8cm diam., globose to short cylindric; tubercles blue-green; axils woolly; central spines 2, 8–10mm red-brown, radial spines 8–10, 6–8mm, off-white. Fl. *c*1cm; tepals pink with paler margins; stigmas about 6, pale yellow. Spring. WC Mexico (Jalisco). Z9.

***M.sempervivi*** DC. Series *Leucocephalae*. Simple at first, sometimes later dividing apically or offsetting; stems to 10cm diam., depressed-globose; tubercles angled-conic, to 10×7mm, dark blue-green; axils woolly; central spines usually 2, sometimes 4, to 4mm, brown or black, later grey, radial spines rudimentary, on juvenile stems only. Fl. 10–12×10–12mm, nearly white or pale pink. Fr. red. Spring. EC Mexico. Z9.

***M.senilis*** Salm-Dyck. Subg. *Mamillopsis*. Clustering; stems to 15×10cm, globular to cylindric; tubercles conic, obtuse, 3–4mm; axils with bristles; central spines 4–6, white, at least the upper and lower hooked, radial spines 30–40, 2cm, somewhat thinner than the centrals, white. Fl. 5–7×2–2.5cm, scarlet; tube straight, *c*4cm×10mm at base, widening to 15mm diam. at throat, with broadly rounded scales; limb spreading; tepals oblong-obtuse, denticulate; stamens and style 2–2.5cm, exserted. Fr. red. Spring. Mts of NW Mexico. Z9.

***M.setispina*** (J. Coult.) K. Brandg. Subg. *Cochemiea*. Clustering; stems to 30×3–6cm; tubercles short and broadly conic; axils woolly; central spines 1–4, 2–5cm, upper straight, lowest one longest, hooked, radial spines 10–12, very unequal, 10–34mm, slender, flexuous, white with black tips. Fl. *c*5cm. Fr. 3cm, obovate, scarlet. Summer. NW Mexico (Baja California). Z9.

***M.sheldonii*** (Britt. & Rose) Boed. Series *Ancistracanthae*. Clustering; stems *c*8cm, slender-cylindric; axils without bristles; central spine 1, hooked, radial spines 12–24, pale with dark tips, the 3 or 4 upper ones darker, a little stouter and 1 or 2 of them subcentral. Fls *c*2×3cm; tepals pale purple with paler margins; fil. and style light purple; stigmas green. Fr. 2.5 to 3cm, clavate, pale scarlet. Summer. NW Mexico (Sonora). Z9.

***M.sinistrohamata*** Boed. Series *Stylothelae*. Resembling *M.mercadensis*. Simple; stem to 4.5cm diam., globose; tubercles short-cylindric, 8×4mm; axils naked; central spines 4, lowest hooked, to 14mm, others straight, equalling the radials, pale yellow, radial spines *c*20, 8–10mm, glabrous, white. Fl. 15mm; tepals nearly white, tinged green, with pale green or red mid-stripe; stigmas nearly white. Fr. small, clavate, red. Spring. NC Mexico. Z9.

***M.sonorensis*** Craig. Series *Mammillaria*. Simple and later clustering; stems depressed-globose to stout cylindric; tubercles globose-quadrangular but not sharply angled, 8–15×8–18mm, dull blue-green; axils with wool, typically without bristles; spines variable; central spines 1–4, 5–20(–45)mm, red-brown, radial spines 8–10(–15), 1–20mm, upper shortest, slender acicular to acicular, off-white to cream, tipped red-brown. Fl. 20mm, usually deep pink; style and stigmas olive-green. Fr. 12–18×10mm, clavate, scarlet. Spring. NW Mexico. Z9.

***M.sphacelata*** Mart. Series *Sphacelatae*. Clustering and sometimes forming mounds 50cm or more diam.; individual stems 20cm or more ×15–30mm, cylindric, erect or decumbent; tubercles conic, *c*7×5–6mm; axils slightly woolly or naked; central spines (1–)3–4, 4–8mm, straight, ivory or chalky white, tipped or speckled red or black, radial spines (10–)11–14(–15), 5–8mm, similar to the centrals. Fl. purple-red, 15×10mm; stigmas pale yellow-green. Fr. clavate, scarlet. Spring. S Mexico (Puebla). Z9.

***M.sphaerica*** A. Dietr. Subgen. *Dolichothele*. Resembling *M.longimamma*, but tubercles generally smaller; radial spines more numerous. Clustering and forming low clumps to 50cm wide, individual stems subglobose, 5cm diam.; tubercles conic-cylindric, 12–16×5–6mm, flabby; axils slightly woolly; central spines 1, 3–6mm, yellow, radial spines 12–14, 6–9mm, off-white to pale yellow. Fl. 6–7cm diam., yellow. Fr. 10–15mm, tinged green or purple, with pleasant odour. Summer. NE Mexico, US (SE Texas). Z9.

***M.spinosissima*** Lem. Series *Polyacanthae*. Simple at first, later often clustering; stems cylindric, to 30×8cm; tubercles ovate-conic, 4–6×4mm; axils slightly woolly but without bristles; central spines 4–9 or more, 10–15mm, bristly, red-brown or pale yellow, radial spines 14–26, 4–10mm, bristly, nearly white. Fl. 15–20×15mm, purple-pink. Fr. green to dull purple. Spring. C Mexico. Z9.

***M.standleyi*** (Britt. & Rose) Orcutt. Series *Mammillaria*. Simple or sometimes clustering; stems to 9×12cm, depressed-globose, pale blue-green; tubercles obtuse, 8×12mm, pale blue-green; axils with wool and bristles. Central spines 4–5, 5–9mm, white, tipped red-brown, radial spines 13–19, 4–8mm, white. Fl. *c*12–18×12mm, purple-pink. Fr. red. Spring. NW Mexico (Sonora). Z9.

***M.stella-de-tacubaya*** Heese. Series *Stylothelae*. Simple, 4–5×3–4cm, bright green, covered with white spines; tubercles cylindric, *c*8×3–4mm; areoles elliptic, with white wool; axils sparsely woolly; central spines 1, 5–6mm, hooked, black, radial spines 35–40, 3–5mm, interlacing, white. Fl. *c*15mm; outer tepals with dark salmon-pink mid-stripe, inner nearly white; stigmas 6, tinged green. Fr. 2cm, red, appearing about 1 year after the flowers. Spring. N Mexico (Coahuila). Z9.

***M.supertexta*** Mart. ex Pfeiff. Series *Supertextae*. Simple; stem to 15×7cm, subglobose to cylindric or oblong; tubercles small, 2–4mm, crowded, conic, green; axils woolly; central spines 0–2, 3mm, white, sometimes tipped black, radial spines 16–18, to 5mm, white. Fl. lateral, small, 6–7mm, deep red or pink. Spring. S Mexico (Puebla, Oaxaca). Z9.

***M.surculosa*** Boed. Subg. *Dolichothele*. Freely clustering; rootstock tuberous; individual stems *c*3×2cm; tubercles cylindric; *c*8×4mm; axils naked. Central spine 1, to 2cm, slender, hooked, amber yellow, darker tipped, radial spines *c*15, 8–10mm, bristly, pale yellow. Fl. *c*2.5×2cm, funnelform, sulphur yellow; style and stigmas green-yellow. Fr. to 17mm, oblong-clavate, green, tinged brown. Spring. NE Mexico. Z9.

***M.swinglei*** (Britt. & Rose) Boed. Series *Ancistracanthae*. Stems 10–20×3–5cm, cylindric; tubercles *c*7×7mm; axils with bristles 4–5mm; central spines 4, ascending, dark brown or black, the lowest longest, 10–17mm, hooked or sometimes straight, radial spines 11–18, 5–8mm, dull white with dark tips. Fl. 2×2–3cm; outer tepals tinged green or pink, inner tepals nearly white with brown mid-stripe; stigmas green. Fr. 14–18mm, dark red, clavate. Summer. NW Mexico (Sonora). Z9.

***M.tesopacensis*** Craig. Series *Mammillaria*. Simple; stem to 18×13cm, globose to cylindric; tubercles pyramidal-conic, 10–12×7–8mm, blue-green; axils naked or with scant wool in the flowering area; central spines 1(–2), 10–12mm, red-brown at first, black-tipped, later ashy brown, radial spines 10–15, 4–7mm, slender acicular, same colour as centrals. Fl. 20×20mm; inner tepals cream with pink mid-stripe or deep purple-pink; stigmas pale green or yellow-green. Fr. 18×10mm, short-clavate, scarlet. Summer. NW Mexico (Sonora). Z9.

***M.tetrancistra*** Engelm. Series *Ancistracanthae*. Simple or clustering; rootstock tuberous; stems to 25×3.5–7.5cm, cylindric or ovoid-cylindric; tubercles cylindric, 8–14×*c*6mm; axils with bristles; central spines 3–4, the upper 2–3 to 14mm, straight or one or more hooked, 18–25mm, radial spines 30–60 in two series, the outer setaceous, *c*6–10mm, white, the inner stouter, longer and dark tipped or tinged purple. Fl. *c*2.5×2.5–3.5cm; tepals lavender, edged white; stigmas creamy white. Fr. 15–30×5–10mm, cylindric to clavate, red; fl. remnant caducous; seeds with a large, corky strophiole. Summer. SW US, NW Mexico. Z9.

***M.theresae*** Cutak. Series *Longiflorae*. Resembling *M.saboae* but stems larger, often tinged purple, radial spines plumose. Simple or sparingly clustering, subglobose to cylindric, to *c*4cm×10–25mm, from stout taproots; tubercles cylindric, 4–6×2–3mm, olive green, sometimes tinged purple; axils sparsely woolly; central spines 0, radial spines 22–30, 2mm, plumose, translucent white. Fl. 3.5–4.5×*c*3cm, funnelform; tube slender, *c*2cm×3mm; outer tepals green-brown, inner violet-purple; anth. deep yellow, stigmas pale yellow. Fr. *c*10mm, sunken in stem; seeds only *c*0.5mm. Spring. Mts of NW Mexico (Durango). Z9.

***M.thornberi*** Orcutt. Series *Ancistracanthae*. Clustering by suckers and lightly attached offsets; stems usually 5–10×1.5–2.5cm, slender-cylindric, tapered at base; tubercles 5–9×5–9mm; axils naked; central spines 1, 9–18mm, hooked, pale to dark red-brown, radial spines 13–20, 5–9mm, white or pale yellow, tipped red-brown. Fl. 15–30×15–20mm, purple-pink; stigmas red, 3–5mm. Fr. 9–15×4.5–7.5mm, red. Summer. SW US (Arizona) N Mexico. Z9.

***M.uncinata*** Zucc. ex Pfeiff. Series *Mammillaria*. Usually simple; stems usually 6–10×8–10cm, depressed-globose; tubercles obtuse-conic, somewhat angled, 8–10×8–12mm, dark blue-green; axils woolly at first, soon naked; central spines 1(–2), 7–10mm, hooked, red-brown, tipped darker, radial spines 3–7, to 5–6mm, rigid, subequal, the upper shorter, pink-tinged or off-white, darker-tipped. Fl. *c*1.5–2×1.5cm, white with brown-red mid-stripe. Fr. 1–2cm×4–6mm, clavate, purple-red. Spring. C Mexican plateau. Z9.

***M.vetula*** Mart. Series *Proliferae*. Resembling *M.gracilis*, but stems stouter, offsets more firmly attached. Clustering; stems to 4cm diam., globose to short-cylindric; tubercles to 8mm, obtuse-conic; axils slightly woolly or naked; central spines 1–7, *c*1cm, red-brown, radial spines 18–45, 4–12mm, white. Fl. 10–15mm, pale yellow; stigmas 5, white. Autumn. EC Mexico. Z9.

***M.viperiana*** Purpus. Series *Sphacelatae*. Resembling *M.sphacelata*. Clustering, with elongate, decumbent, cylindric stems usually 1.5–2cm diam.; tubercles to 5×3mm, short cylindric or globose; axils slightly woolly and sometimes with fine white bristles; spines numerous, to 5mm, fine, variable in colour from white to half-white and half-brown, to black-brown. Fl. red. Fr. cylindric-clavate, red. Summer. S Mexico (Puebla). Z9.

***M.viridiflora*** (Britt. & Rose) Boed. Series *Ancistracanthae*. Resembling *M.wrightii*, but with smaller, paler flowers and more numerous spines. Stem 5–10×5–7.5cm, simple or sometimes clustering, globose to short-oblong, obscured by spines; tubercles terete, *c*4.5×4.5mm; axils naked; central spines 1(–4), 1.5–3cm, 1 or more hooked, red-brown, radial spines 20–30, 10–12mm, bristle-like, white or pale brown, with brown tip. Fl. 1.5cm, narrowly campanulate, tinged green or pink. Fr. 10–22×4.5–13mm, globose to ovoid, green to dull purple, juicy. Spring. SW US, N Mexico. Z9.

***M.voburnensis*** Scheer. Series *Polyedrae*. Resembling *M.karwinskiana*. Clustering by offsets rather than apical division; individual stems 5–12×3–8cm, cylindric; tubercles 10–13×8–16mm, pyramidal, dark green, red towards apex; axils with wool and bristles; central spines 1–3, 12mm, rigid, straight, subulate, brown at first, radial spines 6–9, 5–9mm, nearly white. Fl. 15–20mm; tepals pale yellow, the outer with red mid-stripe. Autumn. S Mexico, Guatemala. Z9.

***M. wiesingeri*** Boed. Series *Heterochlorae*. Resembling *M. discolor* but with smaller fl. Simple; rootstock stout; stem to 4×8cm or larger, depressed-globose; tubercles *c*10×3–4mm, slender-pyramidal; axils naked or with occasional bristles; central spines 4(–6), 5–6mm, red-brown, radial spines *c*20, 5–6mm, glassy white. Fl. *c*12×10mm, carmine red; stigmas 5, short, white. Fr. 1cm, slender-clavate, carmine red. Summer. EC Mexico (Hidalgo). Z9.

***M. wildii*** A. Dietr. Series *Stylothelae*. Clustering; stems to about 12×5cm, globose to cylindric; tubercles to 10×4–6mm, terete, obtuse; axils with bristly hairs; central spines 4, 8–10mm, lowermost hooked, straw yellow to brown, radial spines 8–10, 6–8mm, bristly, pale yellow to white. Fl. 8–10mm, excluding the pericarpel; outer tepals nearly white with brown-red mid-stripe, inner transparent white; stigmas 5, pale yellow-green. Fr. red. Spring. C Mexico (Hidalgo). Z9.

***M. winterae*** Boed. Series *Mammillaria*. Simple; stem to 20–30cm diam., depressed-globose; tubercles to 15×15–25mm, quadrangular; axils naked at first, later rather densely white-woolly, without bristles; spines 4, the upper and lower to 30mm, the lateral to 15mm, all stout-acicular, straight or somewhat curved, pale grey or faintly red, tipped brown. Fl. *c*3×2.5cm; outer tepals pale yellow with brown-red mid-stripe, inner nearly white with pale sulphur-yellow mid-stripe; stigmas 5–9, pale green-yellow. Fr. clavate, pale red. Summer. NE Mexico. Z9.

***M. woodsii*** Craig. Series *Leucocephalae*. Resembling *M. hahniana*. Simple; stem 5×8cm, flattened globular to clavate; tubercles 7×6–7mm, angled and keeled below, nearly rounded at apex, dull grass-green; axils with dense wool in flowering zone and numerous white hair-like bristles to 25mm; central spines 2 (or 4), lowermost to 16mm, upper 4–5mm, dull chalky purple-pink with black tip, radial spines 25–30, 4–8mm, hair-like, tortuous, white. Fl. 10–12×12–15mm, pink. Fr. 15×6mm, clavate, deep pink. Spring–summer. C Mexico. Z9.

***M. wrightii*** Engelm. & Bigelow. Series *Ancistracanthae*. Usually simple; stem to 6cm diam., flattened-globose to short cylindric, tubercles *c*13mm, terete; axils naked; central spines 1-several, 1 or more hooked, 5–21mm, brown, radial spines bristle-like, 8–20 (averaging 13), white. Fl. 2.5–5×2.5–7.5cm, averaging 4.5×3.5cm, purple, pink or rarely white. Fr. up to 28×26mm (averaging 19×15mm), grape-like, dull purple. Spring. SW US, N Mexico, at 1500–2400m. var. ***wilcoxii*** (Toumey ex Schum.) W.T. Marshall. Central spines usually 1–2; radials 12–30 (averaging 20). Fl. somewhat smaller, *c*3.5×2.9cm. Fr. smaller, 6–15mm diam. SW US, N Mexico, at 1050–1500m. Z9.

***M. yaquensis*** Craig. Series *Ancistracanthae*. Resembling *M. thornberi*, but stems more slender. Clustering freely, joints very easily detached, to 7×1.5cm; tubercles 3×5mm, short conic; axils faintly woolly; central spines 7mm, hooked, red-brown, radial spines 18, 5–6mm, smooth, cream, tipped light brown. Fl. 2×2cm; inner tepals pale pink with deeper mid-stripe; stigmas 6, 5–7mm, purple-red. Fr. 9×5mm, elongate-globose to short clavate, scarlet. Summer. NW Mexico. Z9.

***M. zahniana*** Boed. Series *Mammillaria*. Resembling *M. winterae*, but with shorter, subulate spines and pure yellow flowers. Simple, to 6×10cm, depressed-globose; tubercles 2×2cm, pyramidal, tetragonal, dark leaf-green; axils with sparse wool; spines 4, straight, subulate, horny white, tipped black, the lowest 15mm, the upper 8mm. Fl. 20×25mm; outer tepals pale yellow, tinged green, with white margins and red mid-stripe, inner sulphur yellow to darker yellow with pale margins; stigmas 8–10, 4mm, pale green. Summer. NE Mexico. Z9.

***M. zeilmanniana*** Boed. Series *Stylothelae*. Freely clustering; individual stems to 6×4.5cm; tubercles subcylindric; axils naked; central spines 4, the upper 3 straight, the lowest hooked, slightly longer, all red-brown, radial spines *c*15–18, finely bristly, pubesc., white. Fl. to 2cm, violet-pink or purple, rarely white; stigmas pale yellow. Fr. pale pink or almost white. Spring. C Mexico (Guanajuato). Z9.

***M. zephyranthoides*** Scheidw. Series *Ancistracanthae*. Simple; rootstock stout; stem to 8×10–15cm, flattened-globose; tubercles to 25mm, slender, flabby; axils naked; central spines 1–2, to 14mm, hooked, red-brown or paler, radial spines 12–18, 8–10mm, hair-like, white. Fl. to 3×4cm, tube hollow above ovary; tepals white with pink mid-stripe; stigmas green. Fr. red, ovoid. Summer. C Mexico. Z9.

***M. zeyeriana*** Haage f. ex Schum. Series *Mammillaria*. Simple; stem to 20×20cm, globose to shortly cylindric, pale blue-green; tubercles 10–12mm, conic, lightly angled and obliquely truncate; axils naked; central spines 4, curved, red-brown, uppermost 2cm or more, lower shorter, radial spines *c*10, to 10mm, from upper part of areole, spreading, straight, white. Fl. *c*25×20–25mm, white or pale yellow, tinged pink-brown. Spring. N Mexico. Z9.

***M. aggregata*** Engelm. See *Echinocereus triglochidiatus* var. *melanacanthus*.
***M. alamensis*** Craig. See *M. sheldonii*.
***M. angularis*** Link & Otto ex Pfeiff. See *M. compressa*.
***M. applanata*** Engelm. ex Salm-Dyck. See *M. heyderi*.
***M. arizonica*** Engelm. See *Escobaria vivipara*.
***M. bogotensis*** Werderm. See *M. columbiana*.
***M. bucareliensis*** Craig. See *M. magnimamma*.
***M. bullardiana*** (Gates) Backeb. & F. Knuth. See *M. hutchisoniana*.
***M. bumamma*** Ehrenb. See *Coryphantha bumamma*.
***M. caerulea*** Craig. See *M. chionocephala*.
***M. caput-medusae*** Link & Otto ex Pfeiff. See *M. sempervivi*.
***M. celsiana*** Lem., misapplied. See *M. muehlenpfordtii*.
***M. centricirrha*** Lem. See *M. magnimamma*.
***M. cephalophora*** Quehl, not of Salm-Dyck. See *M. aureilanata*.
***M. ceratites*** Quehl. See *Neolloydia conoidea*.
***M. chapinensis*** Eichlam & Quehl. See *M. voburnensis*.
***M. chlorantha*** Engelm. See *Escobaria vivipara*.
***M. cirrifera*** Mart. See *M. compressa*.
***M. clava*** Pfeiff. See *Coryphantha octacantha*.
***M. collina*** Purpus. See *M. haageana*.
***M. collinsii*** (Britt. & Rose) Orcutt. See *M. voburnensis*.
***M. compacta*** Engelm. See *Coryphantha compacta*.
***M. confusa*** (Britt. & Rose) Orcutt. See *M. karwinskiana*.
***M. conoidea*** DC. See *Neolloydia conoidea*.
***M. conspicua*** Purpus. See *M. haageana*.
***M. cornifera*** DC. See *Coryphantha cornifera*.
***M. cowperae*** Shurly. See *M. moelleriana*.
***M. crocidata*** Lem. See *M. polythele*.
***M. dasyacantha*** Engelm. See *Escobaria dasyacantha*.
***M. dawsonii*** (Houghton) Craig. See *M. baxteriana*.
***M. dealbata*** A. Dietr. See *M. haageana*.
***M. denudata*** (Engelm.) A. Berger. See *M. lasiacantha*.
***M. deserti*** Engelm. See *Escobaria vivipara*.
***M. dietrichiae*** Tiegel. See *M. parkinsonii*.
***M. dolichocentra*** Lem. See *M. polythele*.
***M. durispina*** Boed. See *M. kewensis*.
***M. echinaria*** DC. See *M. elongata*.
***M. echinus*** Engelm. See *Coryphantha echinus*.
***M. elegans*** DC. misapplied. See *M. haageana*.
***M. elephantidens*** Lem. See *Coryphantha elephantidens*.
***M. emskoetteriana*** Quehl. See *Escobaria emskoetteriana*.
***M. erecta*** Lem. ex Pfeiff. See *Coryphantha erecta*.
***M. erectohamata*** Boed. See *M. aurihamata*.
***M. exsudans*** Zucc. See *Coryphantha ottonis*.
***M. fasciculata*** Engelm. ex B.D. Jackson. See *Echinocereus fendleri* var. *fasciculatus*.
***M. floribunda*** Hook. See *Neoporteria subgibbosa*.
***M. fragilis*** Salm-Dyck ex K. Brandg. See *M. gracilis*.
***M. fuauxiana*** Backeb. See *M. albilanata*.
***M. gabbii*** Engelm. ex J. Coult. See *M. brandegeei*.
***M. galeottii*** Scheidw. ex C.F. Först. See *M. polythele*.
***M. gasseriana*** Boed. See *M. stella-de-tacubaya*.
***M. glareosa*** Boed. See *M. baxteriana*.
***M. globosa*** Link. See *M. longimamma*.
***M. graessneriana*** Boed. See *M. columbiana*.
***M. guirocobensis*** Backeb. See *M. sheldonii*.
***M. hamiltonhoytea*** (Bravo) Werderm. See *M. gigantea*.
***M. haudeana*** Lau & Wagner. See *M. saboae*.
***M. heeseana*** McDowell. See *M. petterssonii*.
***M. hemisphaerica*** Engelm. See *M. heyderi*.
***M. hidalgensis*** Purpus. See *M. polythele*.
***M. hoffmanniana*** (Tiegel) Bravo. See *M. polythele*.
***M. inaiae*** Craig. See *M. swinglei*.
***M. kelleriana*** Craig. See *M. kewensis*.
***M. knebeliana*** Boed. See *M. pygmaea*.
***M. kunthii*** Ehrenb. See *M. haageana*.
***M. lanata*** (Britt. & Rose) Orcutt. See *M. supertexta*.
***M. lehmannii*** Link & Otto ex Pfeiff. See *Coryphantha octacantha*.
***M. leona*** Poselger. See *M. pottsii*.
***M. leucotricha*** Scheidw. See *M. mystax*.
***M. longiseta*** Muehlenpf. See *M. compressa*.
***M. macdougalii*** Rose. See *M. heyderi*.
***M. macracantha*** DC. See *M. magnimamma*.
***M. macromeris*** Engelm. See *Coryphantha macromeris*.
***M. martinezii*** Backeb. See *M. supertexta*.
***M. mexicensis*** Craig. See *M. grusonii*.
***M. microcarpa*** Engelm. provisional name. See *M. milleri*.
***M. microheliopsis*** Werderm. See *M. microhelia*.
***M. micromeris*** Engelm. See *Epithelantha micromeris*.
***M. microthele*** Muehlenpf. See *M. formosa*.
***M. missouriensis*** Sweet. See *Escobaria missouriensis*.
***M. mollihamata*** Shurly. See *M. pygmaea*.
***M. multiceps*** Salm-Dyck. See *M. prolifera*.
***M. multiformis*** (Britt. & Rose) Backeb. See *M. erythrosperma*.
***M. multiseta*** Ehrenb. See *M. karwinskiana*.
***M. mutabilis*** Scheidw. See *M. mystax*.
***M. nealeana*** Craig, invalid. See *M. muehlenpfordtii*.
***M. neopotosina*** Craig. See *M. muehlenpfordtii*.
***M. neumanniana*** Mart. See *M. magnimamma*.
***M. nickelsiae*** Brandg. See *Coryphantha nickelsiae*.
***M. nigra*** Ehrenb. See *M. polythele*.
***M. obconella*** Scheidw. See *M. polythele*.
***M. occidentalis*** (Britt. & Rose) Boed. See *M. mazatlanensis*.
***M. ochoterenae*** (Bravo) Werderm. See *M. discolor*.
***M. ocotillensis*** Craig. See *M. gigantea*.
***M. octacantha*** DC. See *Coryphantha octacantha*.
***M. oliviae*** Orcutt. See *M. grahamii*.

***M. ortizrubiana*** (Bravo) Werderm. See *M. candida*.
***M. ottonis*** Pfeiff. See *Coryphantha ottonis*.
***M. pacifica*** (Gates) Backeb. & F. Knuth. See *M. baxteriana*.
***M. pectinata*** Engelm. See *Coryphantha echinus*.
***M. phellosperma*** Engelm. See *M. tetrancistra*.
***M. potosina*** hort, non *M. potosiana* Jacobi. See *M. muehlenpfordtii*.
***M. pseudocrucigera*** Craig. See *M. sempervivi*.
***M. pseudomammillaris*** Salm-Dyck. See *M. discolor*.
***M. purpusii*** Schum. See *Pediocactus simpsonii*.
***M. pycnacantha*** Mart. See *Coryphantha pycnacantha*.
***M. radians*** DC. See *Coryphantha radians*.
***M. radiosa*** Engelm. See *Escobaria vivipara*.
***M. raphidacantha*** Lem. See *Coryphantha clavata*.
***M. recurvata*** Engelm. See *Coryphantha recurvata*.
***M. ritteriana*** Boed. See *M. chionocephala*.
***M. robustispina*** Schott ex Engelm. See *Coryphantha scheeri* var. *robustispina*.
***M. roseocentra*** Boed. & Ritter. See *M. magallanii*.
***M. ruestii*** Quehl. See *M. columbiana*.
***M. saffordii*** (Britt. & Rose) Bravo. See *M. carretii*.
***M. scheeri*** Muehlenpf. 1845, not Muehlenpf. 1847. See *Neolloydia conoidea*.
***M. schmollii*** (Bravo) Werderm. See *M. discolor*.
***M. shurliana*** (Gates) Gates. See *M. blossfeldiana*.
***M. similis*** Engelm. See *Escobaria missouriensis*.
***M. simplex*** Haw. See *M. mammillaris*.
***M. simpsonii*** (Engelm.) M.E. Jones. See *Pediocactus simpsonii*.
***M. solisii*** (Britt. & Rose) Boed. See *M. nunezii*.
***M. stella-aurata*** Mart. ex Zucc. See *M. elongata*.
***M. sulcolanata*** Lem. See *Coryphantha sulcolanata*.
***M. tetracantha*** Pfeiff. See *M. polythele*.
***M. tolimensis*** Craig. See *M. compressa*.
***M. tuberculosa*** Engelm. See *Escobaria tuberculosa*.
***M. turbinata*** Hook. See *Strombocactus disciformis*.
***M. vaupelii*** Tiegel. See *M. haageana*.
***M. viereckii*** Boed. See *M. picta*.
***M. villifera*** Otto ex Pfeiff. See *M. polyedra*.
***M. vivipara*** (Nutt.) Haw. See *Escobaria vivipara*.
***M. waltheri*** Boed. See *M. heyderi*.
***M. wilcoxii*** Toumey ex Schum. See *M. wrightii* var. *wilcoxii*.
***M. woburnensis*** auct. See *M. voburnensis*.
***M. yucatanensis*** (Britt. & Rose) Orcutt. See *M. columbiana*.
***M. zuccariniana*** Mart. See *M. magnimamma*.
For further synonymy see *Bartschella*, *Cochemiea*, *Dolichothele*, *Krainzia*, *Mamillopsis*, *Pelecyphora*, *Phellosperma* and *Solisia*.

For illustration see CACTI.

**Mandevilla** Lindl. (For H.J. Mandeville, British Minister at Buenos Aires, who introduced *M. suaveolens*.) Apocynaceae. Some 120 species of tuberous, perennial herbs, subshrubs and, more usually, lianes with milky sap. Leaves opposite, pinnately veined. Inflorescence a lateral raceme; calyx 5-parted; corolla funnelform to salverform, tube cylindric to ovoid, throat campanulate to oblong, lobes 5; stamens enclosed within throat, anthers connivent. Fruit, paired cylindric follicles. C & S America. Many species formerly known under the synonym *Dipladenia*. Z10 unless specified.

CULTIVATION Handsome climbers for warm climates on pergolas, arbours and as wall specimens with support, or in the glasshouse or conservatory border in cooler zones. *M. laxa*, showing some tolerance of frost, is suitable for a warm, sheltered wall in favoured temperate gardens; it breaks freely from old wood and given suitable protection (hessian, matting, etc.) may regenerate from the base even if cut by frost. *Mandevilla* spp. are grown for their showy, funnel-shaped, often sweetly scented blooms, produced over long periods in spring or summer.

Grow in a coarse, well-drained but moisture-retentive medium, rich in organic matter, with full sun but with shade from the strongest summer sun. *M. laxa* can be grown in the cold house, kept frost free; other species perform better at minimum temperatures of 7–10°C/45–50°F. Water plentifully and liquid feed occasionally when in growth and flower. Provide support and mist over frequently, especially in warm bright weather. Reduce water as light levels and temperatures drop in autumn to keep almost dry in winter. Prune in late winter/early spring to thin old and crowded growth and spur back remaining stems. Established plants greatly resent disturbance of the tuberous roots and most perform better in the border than in pots.

Propagate desirable varieties by semi-ripe stem cuttings in summer or by softwood nodal cuttings, 8–10cm/3–4in. long. Treat with 0.5% I.B.A., and root in a closed case with bottom heat at 20°C/68°F. Increase species by seed in spring sown at 18–23°C/65–75°F. *M. laxa* comes readily from seed. Red spider mite, mealybug and whitefly may be pests under glass.

***M. ×amabilis*** (hort. Buckl.) Dress. *(M. splendens × ?.)* Twiner to 4m. Lvs 10–20cm, oblong-acute, rugose, short-petioled. Fls 9–12.5cm diam., funnelform, rose pink, rosy crimson at centre, throat yellow, lobes rounded, short-acuminate. Garden origin.

***M. ×amoena*** hort. *(M. ×amabilis × M. splendens.)* A backcross with more abundantly produced, darker blooms to 10cm diam. Probably synonymous with *M.* 'Alice du Pont' and *M.* 'Splendens Hybrid' (sic.).

***M. boliviensis*** (Hook. f.) Woodson. WHITE DIPLADENIA. Slender-branched shrubby climber to 4m. Lvs to 10cm, glossy green, elliptic to obovate-elliptic, apex caudate-acuminate, base obtuse; petioles to 2cm. Fls 3–7 per raceme; cor. to 5cm, funnelform, white, throat golden yellow, lobes to 4cm, acuminate. Bolivia, Ecuador.

***M. laxa*** (Ruiz & Pav.) Woodson. CHILEAN JASMINE. Climber to 4m. Stems verruculose, wiry. Lvs 5–7cm, cordate-oblong, acuminate, glossy green above, purple or grey-green beneath with tufts of pale hair in axils; petioles 1.25–5cm. Fls highly fragrant; cor. to 5cm diam., white to ivory, tube downy within. Argentina. Z9.

***M. sanderi*** (Hemsl.) Woodson. Twining shrub to 5m. Lvs to 6m, broadly oblong-elliptic, apex briefly acuminate, base rounded, coriaceous, glabrous; petiole to 1cm. Raceme equalling lvs, 3–5-fld; cor. rose-pink, funnelform, throat to 4.5cm, lobes to 3.5cm, acuminate. Brazil. 'Rosea' (BRAZILIAN JASMINE): lvs to 5cm, ovate, lustrous green above, bronze-green beneath; fls to 8cm, salmon pink, throat and tube yellow within.

***M. splendens*** (Hook. f.) Woodson. Twining shrub to 6m. Stems initially downy. Lvs to 20cm, broadly elliptic, apex acuminate, base subcordate, thin-textured, very finely downy. Raceme equalling lvs, 3–5-fld; cor. 7.5–10cm diam., funnelform, rose pink, tube to 4cm, lobes to 3.25cm, briefly acuminate, spreading. SE Brazil. 'Rosacea': fls rose-pink, flushed and bordered deeper rose, tube yellow within, ringed bright rose at throat.

***M. suaveolens*** Lindl. See *M. laxa*.
***M. tweediana*** Gadeceau & Stapf. See *M. laxa*.
For further synonymy see *Dipladenia*.

**Mandragora** L. (Classical Gk name used by Hippocrates.) Solanaceae. 6 species of acaulescent or very short stemmed perennial herbs. Taproots stout, erect, fleshy, often branching, fusiform. Leaves simple, basal, in a dense rosette, ovate to lanceolate-obovate. Flowers axillary, solitary, actinomorphic, pale blue, violet, white or purple; calyx bell-shaped, 5-lobed, lobes overlapping, expanding after flowering; corolla bell-shaped, 5-lobed, persistent; stamens 5, slightly protruding; filaments thread-like; ovary surrounded by a basal glandular disc; stigma capitate. Fruit fleshy, 2-chambered, becoming 1-chambered by the destruction of the septum; seeds reniform. Mediterranean to Himalaya.

CULTIVATION *M. officinarum*, the mandrake, forms a wide rosette of wrinkled, malodorous leaves, from which emerge the short-stalked flowers followed by the aromatic, deep yellow poisonous fruits. It contains the medicinal alkaloid hyoscyamine. Because its taproot resembles the human form, the mandrake was said to possess magical powers. It could only be pulled out of the ground by a sorcerer's dog and would 'scream' when exposed to the air.

Grow in a warm, sheltered position, in deep, light, well-drained but moisture-retentive, circumneutral soil; will tolerate some shade. Propagate by seed sown ripe or in spring, also by root cuttings in winter.

***M. autumnalis*** Bertol. Resembles *M. officinarum*, but lvs oblong-lanceolate, ovate, subglabrous, to 25cm. Scape pale purple; fls violet or white; cal. conspicuously expanding after flowering; cor. spreading, to 3cm, lobes triangular. Fr. ellipsoid, to 3cm diam., orange to yellow. Winter–spring. E Mediterranean.

***M. officinarum*** L. MANDRAKE; DEVIL'S APPLES. To 30cm. Lvs ovate to lanceolate, veins villous when young, petiolate, entire, undulate. Pedicels shorter than lvs; cor. to 2.5cm, lobes triangular. Fr. globose, yellow. Spring. N Italy, W Yugoslavia.

***M. acaulis*** Gaertn. See *M. officinarum*.
***M. vernalis*** Bertol. See *M. officinarum*.

**Manettia** Mutis (For X. Manetti (*b*1723), Keeper of the botanic garden at Florence.) Rubiaceae. Some 80 species of evergreen herbs or subshrubs, usually climbing. Leaves opposite, petiolate, stipules generally attached to petioles, sometimes toothed, apex acute. Flowers axillary and solitary, or in pedunculate, few-flowered panicles or cymes, white or yellow to red; bracteate; calyx tube turbinate or obovoid to campanulate, limb persistent, lobed, lobes usually 4, often with intervening teeth; corolla tubular to funnelform, tube plane or curved; terete to 4-angled, interior and throat occasionally pubescent, lobes usually 4, erect or reflexed; stamens usually 4, inserted at throat, anthers oblong, included or exserted; ovary 2-celled, style filiform, stigma occasionally 2-lobed, club-shaped, ovules many. Fruit a capsule, obovoid to turbinate, 2-celled and -grooved, leathery to papery; seeds many, compressed, winged. Tropical America. Z10.

CULTIVATION Evergreen, twining climbers grown for their vibrantly coloured, tubular flowers and glossy foliage. *M. luteo-rubra* and *M. cordifolia* are both commonly known as the fire cracker vine, a reference to the bright orange and scarlet of the blooms, in the first tipped with yellow. Grow in bright, indirect light, on trellis or other support, in the glasshouse or conservatory, min. 7–10°C/45–50°F. Pot in a well-drained, medium-fertility, loam-based mix, with added leafmould. Water plentifully when in growth, reducing water as temperatures fall in autumn. Avoid persistent wetting of foliage especially in bright sunlight or cold weather. Cut back if necessary in spring. *Manettia* spp. are also grown in temperate zones as annuals, planted outside for summer display, in humus-rich soils with part shade in summer. Specimens of *M. luteo-rubra*, achieved by growing on three cuttings on a wigwam structure, soon make sturdy and highly decorative houseplants. Most will degenerate after a few years, making frequent propagation desirable: take softwood cuttings of new growth in spring, or semi-ripe cuttings in summer. Susceptible to attack by white fly, *Trialeurodes vaporariorum*.

***M. coccinea*** (Aubl.) Willd. Climbing herb to 2m. Stems 4-angled, glabrous to short-pubesc. Lvs to 10×5cm, ovate or lanceolate or oblong, apex acute or narrowly acute, base acute or obtuse and decurrent, thin-textured, lustrous, rough above, glabrous to short-pubesc. beneath; petioles to 14mm; stipules to 2mm, toothed. Fls axillary and solitary, or in pedunculate, few-fld cymes or racemes; peduncles to 5cm; cal. tube to 5mm, glabrous or pubesc., lobes to 14mm, linear to oblanceolate, attenuate, recurved, margin ciliate, glabrous or pubesc.; cor. salverform, pink to scarlet spotted red, tube to 23mm, exterior and throat yellow-pubesc., densely so within, lobes to 5mm, ovate or deltoid to oblong, apex acute, glabrous; anth. to 3mm. Summer. W Indies and Cuba to Northern S America.

***M. cordifolia*** Mart. FIRECRACKER VINE. Climbing herb, to 4m. Stems terete. Lvs to 8cm, variable, ovate to ovate-lanceolate, apex acute or narrowly acute, base obtuse to cordate, thin-textured, lustrous above, glabrous or pubesc. beneath; petioles short. Fls solitary or in a crowded leafy panicle (*M. micans*); cal. lobes lanceolate to oblong, apex acute; cor. to 5cm, vivid red or dark orange fading to yellow at lobes (*M. micans*), tubular, tube distended above, interior pubesc. Winter–summer. S America (Bolivia to Argentina, Peru).

***M. luteo-rubra*** Benth. BRAZILIAN FIRE CRACKER; TWINING FIRE CRACKER; FIRE-CRACKER VINE. Climbing perenn. herb or shrub to 4m in cult. Stems strongly twining, somewhat 4-angled, intricately branched, slender, shortly and coarsely pubesc. throughout, somewhat viscid, pale green. Lvs 2.5–10cm, ovate-rhombic to ovate-lanceolate, acute, pale to dark green, subcoriaceous. Fls solitary, rarely paired, axillary, short-stalked; cal. lobes to 1.25cm, foliose, erect to reflexed; cor. to 5cm, tube cylindric, bright red, hispidulous, lobes 4, yellow, short. Paraguay, Uruguay.

***M. reclinata*** L. Climbing herb to 1m. Stems terete, glabrous. Lvs to 7×3cm, ovate to elliptic, apex narrowly acute, base acute or obtuse, thin-textured, occasionally sparsely pubesc.; petioles to 1cm, pubesc.; stipules deciduous, deltoid. Fls axillary and solitary, or in umbellate panicles; pedicels to 3cm, peduncles to 35mm; cal. tube to 8×3mm, turbinate, pubesc., limb persistent, lobes to 9×2mm, unequal, linear to lanceolate, pubesc.; cor. red, tube to 2cm, exterior minutely pubesc., interior with winged hairs, lobes to 5×4mm, ovate, narrowly acute; stigma papillose. W Indies and Cuba, Mexico to Northern S America.

***M. asperula*** Benth. See *M. cordifolia*.
***M. bicolor*** Hook. f. non Paxt. See *M. luteo-rubra*.
***M. costaricensis*** Wernham. See *M. coccinea*.
***M. discolor*** hort. See *M. luteo-rubra*.
***M. glabra*** Cham. & Schldl. See *M. cordifolia*.
***M. grandiflora*** Vell. See *M. cordifolia*.
***M. inflata*** Sprague. See *M. luteo-rubra*.
***M. micans*** Poepp. & Endl. See *M. cordifolia*.

**Manfreda** Salisb. (For Manfred 'de Monte Imperiale', ancient author on simples.) Agavaceae. 18 species of perennial herbs, with succulent roots, fleshy subterranean stems or bulbous rootstocks. Stems very short or absent. Leaves rosulate, basal, flexible, margins often sinuate, small, green, often blotched with red, brown or purple, not evergreen. Inflorescence spike-like, lax, several-flowered; flowers bisexual, radially symmetric; perianth segments 6, united below to form a generally long and narrow tube, lobes subequal or equal, spreading or reflexed, green, yellow or tinged purple; stamens 6, filaments attached to perianth tube, long-exserted, anthers versatile; ovary inferior, 3-celled with numerous ovules in each cell; style club-shaped, 3-lobed at apex, long-exserted. Fruit an erect capsule, apically dehiscent; seeds copious, black. SE US to Mexico.

CULTIVATION The slender and scarcely succulent foliage of *Manfreda* spp. is usually marked with pink or brown, and is quite distinct from the firm fleshy leaves of the related *Agave*. *Manfreda* spp. require more water during the growing season, but otherwise cultivation is as for *Agave*. The foliage is softer than that of most of the *Agavaceae* and is more prone to red spider mite; spray regularly with clean water in summer to reduce risk of infestation.

***M. longiflora*** (Rose) Verh.-Will. Rootstock short, thick. Stems bulbous. Basal lvs 5–7, 10–25×2cm, spreading, elongate, linear, minutely serrate, spotted dark green or brown, stem lvs 2–3, bract-like. Flowering stems 30–100cm, erect, simple, green tinged purple; fls few, solitary in axils of bracts; perianth slender, salverform, white tinged green at first, brick red in age, tube 35mm, seg. spreading, oblong. Fr. small, subglobose, 35mm diam.; seeds flattened. Spring–summer. S Texas, N Mexico.

***M. maculosa*** (Hook.) Rose. Lvs 15–30×1–2cm, few, linear-lanceolate, recurved, concave, minutely irregularly dentate, margins hyaline, glaucous with brown or somewhat green markings, thick and fleshy. Flowering stem 90–120cm; infl. lax, 20–30cm; fls 10–18, subsessile, 4–5cm, fragrant; perianth lobes oblong, shorter than tube, white tinged green, flushed pink with age; stamens slightly exserted, fil. attached at top of perianth tube, anth. 9–16mm. Capsules 2–2.5×2–2.5cm. Spring–summer. Southern N America (Texas, Mexico).

***M. variegata*** (Jacobi) Rose. Lvs 20–45×2–4cm, few, lanceolate, slightly tapered to base, gradually tapered to apex, obtuse, margins incurved, glaucous with brown markings, succulent, deeply grooved. Flowering stem 90–130cm; fls 4cm, subsessile, fragrant; perianth lobes at least to length of tube, narrow, green tinged brown; stamens to 5cm, fil. attached at top of perianth tube, anth. 8mm. Fr. 15–22mm, much longer than broad. Spring. Southern N America (Texas, Mexico).

***M. virginica*** (L.) Salisb. Lvs 60×2.5–5cm, 6–15, oblong-spathulate, gradually tapered to base, abruptly tapered at apex, margins sinuate, dark green with red stripes, thick, flaccid, somewhat grooved. Flowering stem 80–180cm; infl. about 30-fld, 30–50cm; lower pedicels to 8mm; fls 2.5–5cm, fragrant; perianth seg. linear-oblong, yellow tinged green or brown; fil. attached to base of perianth tube, anth. 12mm. Fr. 1.5–2cm, longer than broad. Summer. S US (Maryland to Missouri, Florida & Texas).

For synonymy see *Agave*, *Polianthes* and *Runyonia*.

**Mangifera** L. (From *mangas*, the Hindi name for the fruit, and Lat. *ferre*, to bear.) MANGO. Anacardiaceae. About 35 species of andromonoecious trees. Leaves simple, alternate, exstipulate. Inflorescence a terminal or axillary panicle; pedicels articulate; calyx 4–5-lobed; petals 4–5, overlapping, sometimes with glandular ridges, usually free; disc usually extrastaminal, often lobed, notched or furrowed, sometimes obsolete in male flowers; stamens 1–12, usually 5, sometimes with staminodes, anthers dorsifixed; ovary superior, glabrous, unilocular, style eccentric or lateral, stigma simple. Fruit a fleshy, resinous, drupe; exocarp coriaceous, endocarp fibrous; seeds 1, sometimes polyembryonic, testa free. India to S China and Solomon Is., naturalized N Australia. Z10.

CULTIVATION *M. indica* was grown in India for 4000 years; from there it spread to Southeast Asia, Africa and South America. It now grows almost everywhere in the tropics and frost-free subtropics. India is the largest producer: nine million tonnes on a million hectares. The chief exporters, however, are Mexico and Mali. Mango is the most popular fruit of the Orient. Ripe fruit is eaten for dessert, or is canned or juiced; pickles and chutney are made from unripe fruit. The edible part contains about 15%

sugars, 0.5% protein and significant amounts of vitamins A, B and C.

The optimal climate for mango ranges from monsoon tropics to the frost-free subtropics, with a marked dry (or cool) season of at least three months. Light frost kills young trees, but older trees tolerate some frost when dormant. The optimum temperature is 25°C/77°F. The dry season of equatorial regions is too unreliable for commercial cultivation of mango.

Water needs depend on soil, climate and cultivar. About 1200mm, well spaced over eight months, is adequate on soil of good water holding capacity, otherwise, irrigation must be supplied. Low humidity and strong wind unduly raise $E_p$ and lead to severe wilting. A very fertile soil is not needed, but very poor and shallow land is unsuitable. A pH of 6–7 is ideal. At a higher pH, deficiencies of trace elements appear and will reduce growth and fruit production. A light slope furthers drainage, but steep slopes are unsuitable.

There are hundreds of cultivars in India and dozens more elsewhere. Good descriptions are often lacking. The monoembryonic cultivars from India and Florida are generally highly coloured and fibreless. 'Alphonso', 'Mulgoa' and 'Neelum' are well known for their high quality. 'Alphonso' prefers a humid climate and has small fruit (average 240g), the other two are more at home in a drier climate, have bigger fruit and mature later. The best Florida cultivars are – from early to late maturing – 'Irwin', 'Haden', 'Tommy Atkins', 'Kent', 'Zill' and 'Keitt'. Polyembryonic cultivars come from Indochina ('Cambodiana'), Indonesia ('Golek' and 'Arumanis'), the Philippines ('Carabao'), Hawaii ('Momi K' and 'Pope'), the West Indies ('Amélie' and 'Julie') and West Africa ('Améliorée du Cameroun'). Some cultivars are self-incompatible and must be planted in mixed stands, but self-compatible cultivars also benefit from cross-pollination.

Seeds are sown fresh. The taproot extends to 5m/16ft below surface unless checked by hardpans. Seedlings bear fruit after seven years but grafted trees may bloom in the third year. However, it is better to remove all panicles during the first four years. Bloom is initiated by drought or cold. The flowers are male or perfect, but few of the latter develop into mature fruit. Alternate bearing occurs frequently due to rain, mineral deficiencies and other factors. Bonfire smoke and a 1% $KNO_3$ spray promote flowering.

The general practice is to graft on polyembryonic stock. Well-known rootstocks are cultivars 'Pahutan', 'Goa', 'Golek', 'Arumanis', 'Carabao', 'Pico', 'Sabre', 'Carotte' and 'Maison-rouge'. The seeds are washed, dried in shade, and sown 5cm deep, convex side up, at 15×30cm. Germination of peeled seeds takes 18 days, or one month with the seed coat on. The cotyledons remain in the soil, the shoot is tinged with red. Hybrids must be removed; these seedlings are always at the micropylar end. Transplanting at 40×100cm takes place when seedlings are 10cm high; care is taken that roots and stems are not damaged. Stocks should be fed and irrigated frequently; weeds, pests and diseases must be controlled. Modern practice is to plant the seedlings in 15cm-deep bags.

Approach grafting on six-month to 1½-year-old stock is common in India; elsewhere budding is preferred as it takes less labour. The regular practice in Florida is chip budding on very young stocks. Cuttings, cut layers and stooling are possible methods of propagation.

Seedling trees are spaced at 10×10m or wider; grafted trees at 10×8m. If planted closer, thinning out will be required later. As this is usually delayed, or omitted, it is better to plant wide and grow an intercrop of banana or papaya for six years. Where strong wind may occur, a shelterbelt will be needed. Holes of 40cm³ are made on permeable soil and manure (50kg) and rock phosphate (1kg) are mixed with the soil before filling. Initial irrigation may be necessary. Weeds must be kept under control in the young orchard, but not by cover crops, which would dry out the soil. After some years the trees will shade out the weeds. Good drainage is essential. Young trees must be irrigated every two weeks during drought. Older trees need irrigation only when in fruit. Feeding with NPK 4:1:4 at 750g N per 12-year-old tree is advised in India; 1000kg NPKMg 10:3:12:6 per ha was needed in Venezuela. Trace elements should be added when necessary. Leaf analysis showed that a minimum of 15 ppm Zn is required. Only light pruning is needed for young trees. Older trees can be rehabilitated by top grafts.

Anthracnose, caused by *Colletotrichum gloeosporioides* var. *minor*, results in leaf spot and fruit rot. Control in the field can be achieved by frequent sprays of appropriate fungicides. 'Tommy Atkins', 'Keitt', 'Améliorée du Cameroun' and 'Alphonso' are resistant. Canker, gummosis, powdery mildew and storage rot are also caused by fungi. The cause of malformation is uncertain, but a 200 ppm spray of NAA cures it. A hopper attacks mango blossom in India; sooty mould develops on their honey-dew. Other pests are scales, fruit flies and nematodes.

An average yield in on-years is 500 fruits per tree. The fruit is harvested when the colour changes, or after some fruit has dropped. Picked fruit is immersed in water at 52°C for five minutes for protection against anthracnose. Exposure to sunlight is harmful. Then the fruit is cooled at 15°C, graded, sized, packed and stored or transported at 9°C and 85–90% relative humidity. For marketing, the fruit is ripened at 16–21°C for five days.

In temperate regions, grow in a lofty hot glasshouse (min. 16–18°C/60–65°F) in a sandy, loam-based medium. Keep evenly moist but not constantly wet. Maintain moderate humidity.

***M. caesia*** Jack. Tree to 35m. Trunk occasionally buttressed, bark grey-brown, fissured. Lvs coriaceous, elliptic, obovate, ovate, ovate-oblong or lanceolate, cuneate, short-acuminate or obtuse; petiole flattened, 2–6cm. Infl. a terminal panicle, pyramidal, 15–75cm, puberulent; bracts ovate-lanceolate or elliptic; disc pulvinate; stamens 5, 3–4 infertile; ovary subglobose. Fr. rough, brown to yellow-brown or pale green, ellipsoid, to 19×10cm. Sumatra, Malay Peninsula, naturalized elsewhere in Malaysia.

***M. foetida*** Lour. Tree to 40m. Bark green or red-brown, rough, fissured or scaly. Lvs 14–35×6–16cm, stiff, coriaceous, oblanceolate to elliptic, obtuse, sometimes emarginate, cuneate or attenuate, dark green, nerves raised above, prominent beneath. Panicles mostly terminal, pyramidal, glabrous, dense, 10–40cm; bracts ovate-lanceolate, to 5mm; fls pink to dark red; cal. 5-lobed, ovate; pet. narrowly lanceolate, to 9mm, 3-ridged; disc pulvinate; stamens 5; ovary subglobose. Fr. yellow or grey-green. Spring. Indochina, Malaysia.

***M. indica*** L. MANGO. Tree to 30m. Bark grey, fissured. Lvs to 30×7cm, subcoriaceous or papery, oblong-elliptic or oblong-lanceolate, acuminate or acute; petiole 2–6cm. Panicles tomentose; bracts triangular, to 5mm; sep. 5, ovate; pet. 5, oblong-ovate to obovate, ridged; disc thick, papillose; stamens 5, 1 fertile; ovary obliquely ovoid or subglobose; style to 2mm, rudimentary or absent in male fls. Fr. variably ovoid-oblong, 4–25×1–10cm, variably yellow, green or red, flesh yellow, endocarp thick, fibrous. Burma, widely naturalized throughout tropical Asia. Large numbers of cultivars exist locally. The following are grown in the US: 'Carrie': fr. medium-sized. 'Edgehill': fr. small to medium. 'Glenn': fr. large. 'Haden': fr. very large. 'Irwin': fr. medium, seed small. 'Julie': fr. medium. 'Keitt': fr. medium to large.

***M. ×odorata*** Griff. (*M. indica* × *M. foetida.*) Tree to 35m. Bark grey, smooth or fissured. Lvs to 35×10cm, coriaceous, elliptic-lanceolate or lanceolate, acuminate or acute, cuneate or obtuse; petiole 5–7cm, grooved above, convex beneath. Panicles terminal or sometimes in upper lf axil, pyramidal, 12–50cm, sometimes puberulous; bracts ovate to ovate-oblong, 1–2mm; cal. lobes ovate to elliptic, rarely lanceolate; pet. 5, exterior pale yellow, becoming red; stamens 5, 1 fertile; ovary subglobose; style eccentric, minute in male fls. Fr. dark green, obliquely ovoid to broadly ellipsoid, to 13×10cm, flesh yellow. Origin unknown, naturalized Malaysia.

***M. foetida*** Bl. non Lour. See *M. caesia*.
***M. foetida*** var. ***odorata*** Griff. See *M. ×odorata*.
***M. horsfieldii*** Miq. See *M. foetida*.
***M. indica*** Bl. non L. See *M. foetida*.
***M. kemanga*** Bl. See *M. caesia*.
***M. leschenaultii*** Marchand. See *M. foetida*.
***M. oblongifolia*** Hook. f. See *M. ×odorata*.
***M. pinnata*** L. f. See *Spondias pinnata*.
***M. verticillata*** C. Robinson. See *M. caesia*.

**Manglietia** Bl. (From the Malay name for one of the species.) Magnoliaceae. Some 25 species of shrubs or trees, as for *Magnolia*, but leaf petiole bases appearing swollen; flowers 9-lobed in 2 whorls, occasionally more; ovules to 6 per carpel (cf. *Magnolia*, with 2 ovules per carpel). Malesia to S China, E Himalaya. Z9.

CULTIVATION As for *Michelia*.

***M. insignis*** (Wallich) Bl. Tree, to 12m; young shoots grey-pubesc., becoming glabrous. Lvs to 20×6.5cm, oblong to elliptic, acute or short-acuminate, base cuneate, glossy green above, glaucous beneath, coriaceous, entire; petiole to 25mm. Fls solitary, erect, to 7.5cm diam., white tinged pink to rose-carmine, outer tepals sepaloid, inner tepals obovate. Fr. to 9cm, plum red. Spring. W China, Himalaya, Burma.

**Manihot** Mill. (The Brazilian name.) CASSAVA; MANIOC; YUCA; TAPIOCA PLANT. Euphorbiaceae. 98 species of monoecious trees, shrubs and herbs, with milky juice. Leaves alternate, usually palmately veined and digitately 3- to 7-lobed or parted, sometimes peltate, stalked. Flowers usually rather large, terminal or in the axils of upper leaves, in racemes or panicles; calyx campanulate, shortly or deeply 5-lobed, often coloured; stamens 10. Fruit a capsule. Tropical and warm temperate America. Z10.

CULTIVATION Although a number of species make attractive foliage specimens for the warm glasshouse, especially those with variegated cultivars, *Manihot* is of greater economic importance. *M. esculenta* is one of the most important tropical crops and is extensively cultivated in most lowland tropical regions. It is relatively immune to insect attack because of its high levels of cyanide, and is a reliable and important crop on somewhat impoverished soils with many cultivars with differing amounts of cyanide, removed by squeezing the ground tuber in water and by evaporation during drying. Cassava meal (Brazilian arrowroot) and tapioca are used in soaps, puddings etc., a glue form is used on postage stamps; sugar, alcoholic drinks and acetone are all derived from it; the evaporated toxic juice is cassareep, used for preserving meat and in table sauces. Unfortunately cassava is deficient in protein and where it forms a major part of the diet malnutrition often occurs.

Protect from strong bright sunlight in summer, which will scorch the foliage; otherwise cultivate as for *Hura*.

***M. dulcis*** (J.F. Gmel.) Pax SWEET CASSAVA. Distinguished from *M. esculenta* in having somewhat smaller roots, lvs 3- to 13-lobed, lobes lanceolate to obovate. Fr. cylindrical, not winged. S America.

***M. esculenta*** Crantz. BITTER CASSAVA; MANIOC; MANDIOCA; TAPIOCA; GARI. Shrubby tree to 3m, with long tuberous edible roots, and soft, brittle stems. Lvs deeply parted into 3–7 lobes, lobes spathulate or linear-lanceolate, acuminate. Fr. 12mm diam., 6-angled, narrowly winged. Brazil. 'Variegata': lvs bright green, variegated yellow along veins.

***M. glaziovii*** Muell. Arg. Tree to 10m, with forked branches. Lvs 15–20cm, numerous, ribs white; petiole 15–20cm. Fls in few-fld racemes or panicles from forks of young branches; male fls green-white with a purple tinge; female fls pale green-yellow, in lower part of raceme. Fr. not winged. Brazil.

***M. manihot*** (L.) Cockerell. See *M. esculenta*.
***M. utilissima*** Pohl. See *M. esculenta*.

For illustration see VEGETABLES.

**Manilkara** Adans. (From the Malay name for the genus.) Sapotaceae. 70 species of evergreen trees to 30m+, with milky latex. Leaves alternate, spirally arranged or rarely opposite or whorled, thick. Inflorescence axillary, flowers solitary or in clusters, bisexual; sepals (4–)6(–8), in 2 whorls; corolla 6(–9) lobed, tube usually much shorter than lobes, divided to base into 3 segments, central erect, narrow, clasping stamen, outer spreading, petaloid, entire, divided or laciniate; stamens 6(–12), usually alternate with (0–)6(–9) staminodes, ovary superior. Fruit a fleshy berry, ovoid or globose, 1-several seeded, seeds large, ellipsoid to obovoid, with a narrow elongate scar. Pantropical. Z10.

CULTIVATION *M. zapota* produces a milky exudate, *balata*, hard and brittle until chewed, the inelastic polymer originally used as the base for chewing gum. This species, in many areas tapped to exhaustion, no longer fulfills the requirements of the industry and other lactiferous members of the Sapotaceae, Moraceae, and Euphorbiaceae are used. *Manilkara* is native to lowland forests of central America, but is grown for chiclé especially in the Yucatan Peninsula of Guatemala and Mexico. It is also valued throughout the humid tropics for its delicious fruit, sapodilla, slightly larger than a plum, with an aromatic pulp reminiscent of honey and jasmine, very sweet and slightly acid, eaten perfectly ripe since it has a high tannin content. A good tree produces 300kg of fruit per annum.

*Manilkara* grows best in well-drained soils of pH 6–7, and is resistant to drought, wind and salt. In temperate regions it can be grown in hot glasshouse conditions in a rich sandy loam with bright filtered light, watering moderately to plentifully. Propagate from cuttings or from seed.

***M. bidentata*** (A. DC.) A. Chev. BALATA. Tree to at least 30m, with hard, purple wood. Lvs 6–21×2.3–8(–9.5)cm, on 1.5–4.5cm petioles, narrowly elliptic or oblong, coriaceous to chartaceous, glabrous. Infl. fasciculate, (2–)5–20-fld; sep. 4–6mm, outer whorl lanceolate, inner lanceolate or narrowly elliptic; cor. (3–)3.5–6(–6.5)mm, lobes 6; stamens 6, staminodes 6, 1–3.5mm. Fr. 1–3(–4)cm, ellipsoid to globose, smooth, glabrous, seeds 1–2, 0.9–2.6cm, glossy, brown. W Indies (Windward Is), Panama, Colombia, Venezuela, Peru, Brazil.

***M. zapota*** (L.) Royen. SAPODILLA; NISPERO; CHICLE. Tree to at least 30m. Lvs 6.6–14.4×2.1–5.2cm, on 1–3cm petioles, in clusters at twig apices, glabrous, elliptic to oblong-elliptic, ovate-elliptic or elliptic-lanceolate, subglabrous, chartaceous, vein pairs 15–23. Fls solitary, sep. 7–9.5mm, ovate to lanceolate, cor. 8–11mm long, lobes 6(-7), sometimes lacking outer seg.; stamens and staminodes 6, the latter (2–)2.5–5mm, oblong, elliptic or lanceolate, somewhat petaloid. Fr. 3.5–8×6cm, broadly ovoid or ellipsoid, rough and brown, pulp sweet, translucent, somewhat granular, pale yellow-brown; seeds 2–10, glossy black. Mexico to Costa Rica. 'Brown Sugar': fr. small to medium, very sweet. 'Prolific': fr. large.

For synonymy see *Achras*.

**Mansoa** DC. (For Antonio Luiz Patricio da Silva Manso (1778–1848), Brazilian botanist and author of works on medicinal plants.) Bignoniaceae. About 15 species of lianes. Branches subterete to tetragonal, glabrescent or pubescent, with or without glandular patches between nodes; pseudostipules subulate. Leaves trifoliate, terminal leaflet often replaced by simple tendril. Inflorescence axillary or terminal raceme or panicle; flowers with calyx cupular to tubular-campanulate, truncate or 5-ribbed with ribs ending in broad or subulate teeth *c*5mm, puberulent-lepidote; corolla white to purple-red, puberulent and glandular-lepidote; anthers glabrous or downy; ovary cylindrical, glandular-papillose; ovules 2–4-seriate. Fruit a linear-oblong capsule, flattened, valves parallel, woody, densely pubescent or tuberculate, tubercles to 5mm; seeds 2-winged, wings membranous, rarely absent. Mexico to Brazil. Z10.

CULTIVATION As for *Crescentia*.

***M. alliacea*** (Lam.) A. Gentry. BEJUCO DE AJO. Vegetation smells strongly of onions. Leaflets 5–10×1.5–5cm, ovate-elliptic, apex acuminate or obtuse, base truncate or attenuate, shining above; tendrils 5–10cm. Fls in groups of 6–25, dark to pale purple; cor. 4–6×0.5–2cm. Capsule 14–25×1.5–2cm, acuminate. Americas.

***M. difficilis*** (Cham.) Bur. & Schum. Leaflets 5–11×3–6cm, oblong-ovate, apex acute to acuminate, base rounded to cordate, leathery, shining, punctate; pseudostipules to 3mm. Cal. 5–13×4–7mm, leathery, margin ciliate; cor. 5.5–9cm, violet, purple or vermilion, limb 6.5cm diam., puberulent. Fr. 18–25×1.5–2.6cm, linear-oblong; valves convex, rugose, lenticellate; seeds 1.2–1.5×0.3–0.5cm, in membranous wings. Brazil.

***M. hymenaea*** (DC.) A. Gentry. Stem 5cm diam. Plant smells strongly of onions. Lvs 2-foliolate with trifid tendril or scar; leaflets 4.8–9.4×3.3–7.5cm, ovate to narrow-ovate, apex obtuse to acute, base truncate to cordate, usually glabrous; petiole 1.3–3.5cm; petiolules 1–2.6cm. Infl. branches puberulent; cal. 4–6mm; cor. 4.1–5×0.8–1.5cm at mouth, pale lilac to purple, pink or white, tube 3–3.6cm, lobes 0.6–1.3cm, tube glabrous, lobes puberulent. Fr. linear, 15–25×1.7–2cm, acuminate, smooth, glabrous, with central prominent rib; seeds 2-winged. Winter. Mexico to Brazil.

For synonymy see *Adenocalymma, Anemopaegma, Cydista, Pachyptera, Petastoma* and *Pseudocalymma*.

**Manulea** L. (From Lat. *manus*, a hand, represented by conformation of the corolla.) Scrophulariaceae. Some 60 species, annual or perennial herbs or subshrubs, glabrescent to tomentose. Leaves radical, rosulate, and cauline, usually opposite, sometimes alternate in upper reaches of plant, entire or denticulate; bracts inconspicuous, often absent. Inflorescence terminal, racemose or spicate or, frequently, compound, thyrsoid or paniculate; calyx deeply 5-cleft, rarely bilabiate, segments or lobes sublinear or ovate-lanceolate, persistent; corolla tubular-subcampanulate, limb spreading, lobes 5, broad-narrow, obtuse-acute, entire or cleft;

stamens didynamous, glabrous, inserted on throat or upper half of corolla tube, filaments threadlike, short, anthers by fusion 1-celled, upper pair fertile or barren, reniform, included or shortly exserted, lower pair fertile, oblong or reniform, included, ovary 2-celled, style threadlike, included or shortly exserted, stigma narrowly subclavate, obtuse. Fruit a septicidal capsule, valves bifid at apex; seeds numerous, rugose. S Africa (2 species Tropical Africa). Z10.

CULTIVATION *M. rubra* is treated as a frost-tender annual in cool temperate zones, grown for its flowers in a sunny situation in any moderately fertile and well-drained soil. *M. tomentosa* is a handsome specimen for the intermediate glasshouse or conservatory, valued for its brightly coloured flowers carried above the attractive grey-green foliage. Propagate by seed or softwood cuttings in a closed case with gentle bottom heat.

***M. rubra*** L. Annual or perenn. to 60cm. Stems herbaceous, basally decumbent to ascending, canescent. Lvs to 6cm, oblanceolate, dentate, basally attenuate, petiolate. Infl. an interrupted raceme, branched near base; bracts 4mm sublinear, obtuse; fls numerous, thyrsoid; pedicels very short, pubesc.; cal. 4mm, seg. linear, obtuse, ciliate; cor. tube 18mm, slender, ruddy, orange or golden yellow, exterior pubesc. above, limb 6mm diam., lobes oval-oblong, entire, obtuse; stamens included. Fr. 7mm, ovoid-oblong, glabrous. Summer. S Africa.

***M. tomentosa*** L. Hoary subshrub to 75cm; branches decumbent or ascending. Lvs 2–4×1–2cm, pale grey-green, opposite, occasionally alternate just below infl., fleshy or thin-textured, toothed, petiolate or subsessile, densely hairy (hairs short, stiff, glandular). Fls numerous, sessile or nearly so in clusters, in dense, terminal, racemes, to 8cm; cal. exterior hoary; cor. orange or yellow, exterior glandular-tomentose; stamens finely glandular-pubesc., anth. pallid, fil. very short; style almost glabrous. Spring–autumn. S Africa.

**Marah** Kellogg. (Derivation obscure.) BIGROOT; MANROOT. Cucurbitaceae. 7 species of monoecious, herbaceous vines. Tubers large, globose to cylindric. Tendrils simple to 3-fid. Stems striate. Leaves suborbicular, palmate, cordate, 5–7-lobed; petioles long. Male inflorescence a raceme or peduncle, axillary, deciduous; calyx teeth small or rudimentary; corolla campanulate to rotate, glandular, segments 4–8, usually 5; anthers 3; filaments fused; female flowers solitary, co-axillary with male; calyx and corolla similar to male except larger; ovary inferior; locules usually 4. Fruit a capsule, globose to fusiform, pendulous, often spinose, dehiscent, turgid becoming dry; seeds large. Western N America. Z8.

CULTIVATION As for *Coccinia*, but in cool intermediate conditions. Multiple planting is not required for fruit set.

***M. fabaceus*** (Naudin) Greene. Stems to 7m, sparsely pubesc. Lvs palmate, suborbicular, to 5–10×5–10cm, glabrous to scabrous, lobes 5–7, acute or obtuse, occasionally mucronate, 1–3cm deep. Male infl. 5–25cm; cal. teeth obscure; cor. green-white, to 5×10mm, with marginal trichomes; staminodes absent in female; ovary globose, tapering. Fr. globose, densely spinose, 4–5cm; seeds lenticular, light brown, ridged, to 24×20×15mm. California.

***M. macrocarpus*** (Greene) Greene. CHILICOTHE. Stems 1–7m, deeply striated. Lvs palmate, suborbicular, scabrous above, hispid beneath, lobes 5–7, acute or obtuse. Male infl. 5–40cm, cal. lobes 2.5mm, smaller in female, deltoid to linear-lanceolate, occasionally obsolete; cor. cupular, white; staminodes scale-like or absent in female. Fr. cylindric, beaked, 8–12×6–9cm, spines dense, flattened, 5–30mm; seeds oblong, somewhat flattened, brown with dark equatorial line, 9–25mm. California, Baja California.

***M. oreganus*** (Torr. & A. Gray) Howell. Stems 1–7m, often sparsely pubesc. Tendrils 2–3-fid. Lvs palmate, suborbicular, cordate, entire to subcrenulate or denticulate, glabrous to pubesc., 8–35cm diam., lobes 5–7, shallow, acute, obtuse or acuminate; petiole pubesc., 4–12cm. Cal. lobes broadly triangular to subulate; cor. to 12×17mm, white, male slightly smaller. Fr. striped, sparsely spinose, spines to 6mm; seeds discoid, to 20×12mm, red-brown. SW US to S Canada.

For synonymy see *Echinocystis* and *Sicyos*.

**Maranta** L. (For B. Maranti (*fl.* 1559), Venetian botanist.) Marantaceae. Some 32 species of herbaceous perennials, stems short, sparsely branched erect or scandent with basal and cauline leaves to highly branched with few or no basal leaves. Rhizome sometimes swollen, starchy. Leaves homotropic, rarely antitropic, obovate to elliptic, exhibiting 'sleep' movements; petioles slender; sheaths usually present, often auriculate. Inflorescences 2 to several per shoot, simple or sparsely branched with 2–6 pedicellate flower pairs (cymules); bracts persistent, papery, fibrous, secondary bracts absent; bracteoles sometimes present; flowers usually zygomorphic, occasionally actinomorphic; sepals thin; corolla tube green, 4–14mm, 2–10× longer than wide; outer staminodes 2, showy, callose staminodes fleshy, apically petaloid; stigmatic orifice funnel-shaped; ovary trilocular, ovules 1. Fruit a capsule with persistent sepals; seed single, arillate, with distally branching perisperm canal. Tropical C & S America. Z10.

CULTIVATION *Maranta* spp. are found on the moist soils of evergreen or deciduous forest, often in clearings where light levels are comparatively high. They may used as ornamental, spreading groundcover in tropical and subtropical gardens; the highly patterned foliage is particularly striking in dappled shade. *M. arundinacea* is cultivated in tropical lowlands for its thick, starchy rhizomes, ground to produce 'arrowroot', an important food crop.

In cool temperate areas, *Maranta* spp. are tolerant houseplants, raising their leaves into an erect 'prayer' position in the evening; the red herringbone pattern of *M. leuconeura* 'Fascinator' or 'Tricolor' is particularly attractive. Intense light, dry atmospheres and draughts cause curling of the foliage; in the home, regular syringing with soft water ensures the necessary humidity. Alternatively, grow in a hot glasshouse with minimum temperatures of 16°C/60°F (although plants will survive as low as 10°C/50°F). Give medium humidity (damping down regularly in warm weather) and bright filtered or indirect light – if grown in overly dark conditions, the foliage will be too 'soft'. Water plentifully in summer, sparingly when temperatures are low. Plants are vigorous and repotting into pans of a coarse, medium-fertility loam-based mix with the addition of bark chippings may be necessary 2–3 times during the growing season. Feed regularly with a dilute liquid fertilizer which is said to improve the leaf markings, as will a loam-rather than peat-based growing medium. Propagate by basal shoots removed with 2–3 leaves attached in a sandy rooted medium with 21°C/70°F bottom heat. Alternatively, by divisions rooted in a closed case in spring. Large plants with numerous crowns are most suitable for propagation purposes.

***M. arundinacea*** L. ARROWROOT; OBEDIENCE PLANT. Erect, branching, to 2m. Lvs to 25cm, lanceolate, pubesc., apex acuminate, base attenuate, sometimes varigated, basal lvs petiolate; pulvinus borne on leaf sheath. Infl. sparingly branched; fls white. Throughout genus range. 'Aurea': lvs golden, intermittently marked light green. 'Variegata': lvs sulphur green and dark green.

***M. bicolor*** Ker-Gawl. To 35cm with basal tubers and prostrate shoots. Lvs to 15×10cm, glaucous, elliptic to ovate, pale green spotted brown with paler central zone, purple beneath, inserted directly on sheath or with short petiole to 2cm. Infl. a solitary spike; bracts 4; fls white with purple-maroon lines. Northeast S America.

***M. leuconeura*** E. Morr. PRAYER PLANT; TEN COMMANDMENTS. Low-growing, rhiz. spreading, prostrate to suberect. Lvs to 12×9cm, elliptic, exceeding petioles, lustrous dark green, grey or maroon veined or zoned grey or red above, grey-green or maroon beneath. Infl. a slender, solitary spike; bracts 2; fls white or violet or spotted violet. Brazil. 'Massangeana': lvs tinted blue, dull rusty-brown toward centre, jagged silver band along midrib and silver lines along lateral veins. var. ***leuconeura***. Lvs broad-elliptic, dark green above with a pale, comb-like central zone and pinnate silver veins. var. ***kerchoveana*** (hort.) E. Morr. RABBIT'S FOOT. Lvs grey-green with a row of olive spots on each side of midrib.

***M. ruiziana*** Körn. Low, scandent. Runners farinose. Lvs to 7.5cm, pubesc., antitropic, ash-green, densely villous on midrib. Fls small; bracteoles ridged, rudimentary. Central & Northern S America.

***M. allouia*** Aubl. See *Calathea allouia*.
***M. kegeljanii*** E. Morr. See *Calathea bella*.
***M. argyraea*** hort. See *Calathea argyraea*.
***M. asymmetrica*** hort. See *Calathea taeniosa*.
***M. bachemiana*** hort. See *Calathea bachemiana*.
***M. baraquinii*** Lem. See *Calathea baraquinii*.
***M. bella*** Bull. See *Calathea bella*.
***M. compressa*** A. Dietr. See *Ctenanthe compressa*.
***M. cuspidata*** Roscoe. See *Marantochloa cuspidata*.
***M. cylindrica*** A. Dietr. See *Calathea cylindrica*.
***M. eximia*** Mathieu. See *Calathea exima*.
***M. fasciata*** Lind. See *Calathea fasciata*.
***M. glabra*** Körn. See *Ctenanthe glabra*.
***M. indica*** Tussac. See *M. arundianacea*.
***M. insignis*** H.W. Ward. See *Calathea lancifolia*.

***M. jacquinii*** Roem. & Schult. See *Stromanthe jacquinii.*
***M. kegeliana*** hort. See *Calathea bachemiana.*
***M. kummerana*** E. Morr. See *Ctenanthe kummerana.*
***M. legrelliana*** Lind. See *Calathea legrelliana.*
***M. leopardina*** Bull. See *Calathea leopardina.*
***M. lietzei*** hort. See *Calathea lietzei.*
***M. lubbersiana*** auct. See *Ctenanthe lubbersiana.*
***M. lushnathiana*** Reg. & Körn. See *Ctenanthe compressa* var. *lushnathiana.*
***M. lutea*** Aubl. See *Calathea lutea.*
***M. maculata*** Pav. See *Calathea pavonii.*
***M. makoyana*** E. Morr. See *Calathea makoyana.*
***M. mazellii*** hort. See *Calathea virginalis.*
***M. massangeana*** E. Morr. See *M. leuconeura.*
***M. medio-picta*** E. Morr. See *Calathea medio-picta.*
***M. micans*** Mathieu. See *Calathea micans.*
***M. oppenheimiana*** hort. See *Ctenanthe oppenheimiana.*
***M. oppenheimiana*** var. ***tricolor*** hort. See *Ctenanthe oppenheimiana* 'Tricolor'.
***M. orbifolia*** (Lind.) H. Kenn. See *Calathea orbifolia.*
***M. ornata*** Lind. See *Calathea majestica.*
***M. pilosa*** Schauer. See *Ctenanthe pilosa.*
***M. pinnato-picta*** hort. See *Calathea applicata.*
***M. porteana*** (Gris) Körn. See *Stromanthe porteana.*
***M. protracta*** Miq. See *M. arundinacea.*
***M. pruinosa*** Reg. See *Pleiostachya pruinosa.*
***M. pulchella*** E. Morr. non Lind. See *Calathea pulchella.*
***M. pulchella*** Lind. non E. Morr. See *Calathea zebrina* 'Humilior'.
***M. ramosissima*** Wallich. See *M. arundinacea.*
***M. roseo-picta*** Lind. See *Calathea roseo-picta.*
***M. sanderiana*** hort. See *Calathea* 'Sanderiana'.
***M. sanguinea*** hort. See *Stromanthe sanguinea.*
***M. setosa*** (Roscoe) A. Dietr. See *Ctenanthe setosa.*
***M. silvatica*** Roscoe. See *M. arundinacea.*
***M. smaragdina*** Lind. See *Monotagma smaragdinum.*
***M. splendida*** Lem. See *Calathea splendida.*
***M. tonckat*** Aubl. See *Stromanthe tonckat.*
***M. truncata*** Link. See *Calathea truncata.*
***M. veitchiana*** Van Houtte. See *Calathea veitchiana.*
***M. wallisii*** Lind. See *Calathea wallisii.*
***M. warscewiczii*** Mathieu. See *Calathea warscewiczii.*
***M. wiotii*** E. Morr. See *Calathea wiotii.*
***M. zebrina*** Sims. See *Calathea zebrina.*

**MARANTACEAE** Petersen. ARROWROOT FAMILY. Monocot. 31 genera and 550 species of rhizomatous perennial herbs, rhizomes sympodial and usually starchy. Leaves distichous with open sheath, petiole distinct and sometimes winged, lamina simple, rolled from 1 side in bud, with distinct pulvinus at the base, venation pinnate-parallel with prominent midrib. Flowers bisexual, 3-merous, in thyrses, sometimes on a separate shoot from the rhizome; calyx 3 non-petaloid sepals; corolla 3 petals with a basal tube, usually white, 1 petal often hood-like and larger; androecium united to the corolla, 1 fertile stamen, often petaloid; staminodes 2–4, petaloid but small; ovary inferior, of 3 fused carpels, 3-loculed; style 1, terminal; septal nectaries at ovary summit; each locule 1-ovuled. Fruit a capsule or berry. Starch is extracted from rhizomes of West Indian arrowroot (*Maranta arundinacea*). *Calathea* species provide leaves for basket-making and roofing, as well as some edible flowers and tubers. Tropical, especially American. *Ataenidia, Calathea, Ctenanthe, Donax, Ischnosiphon, Maranta, Marantochloa, Megaphrynium, Monotagma, Phrynium, Pleiostachya, Stachyphrynium, Stromanthe, Thalia, Thaumatococcus, Trachyphrynium.*

**Marantochloa** Brongn. & Gris. (From *Maranta*, which is superficially resembles, and Gk *chloe*, grass.) Marantaceae. About 3 species of perennial herbs. Stems and rhizomes somewhat hardened, branching or simple, glabrous or pubescent. Leaves alternate, homotropic or antitropic, asymmetric, 1 side curved, the other straight; midrib ridged above; petiole sheathing at base, non-callose part often swollen. Inflorescence simple or branching; bracts persistent, hooked, 1 per 2 or 3 cymules; peduncles usually long, pedicels variable; bracteoles and interphylls absent; sepals free, often chaffy, linear, fibrous, acute; corolla tubular, long, lobes acute; outer staminodes 2, petaloid, cucullate staminode with proximal appendage; ovary with 3 fertile uniovulate locules. Fruit a globose capsule, dehiscent or indehiscent; seeds arillate. Tropical Africa. Z10.

CULTIVATION As for *Calathea.*

***M. cuspidata*** (Roscoe) Milne-Redh. Stems erect, to 60cm. Lvs to 40×15cm, triangular-lanceolate, acuminate, subtruncate at base, glabrous above, pubesc. beneath, midrib pubesc.; petiole 15–20cm, sheathing. Infl. many slender racemes, terminal; peduncle about 15cm; bracts to 4×1cm, persistent, axillary, 1 per 2 cymules; pedicel 7–10mm; sep. scarious; cor. *c*2cm, yellow; ovary pubesc. Senegal to Ivory Coast.

***M. purpurea*** (Ridl.) Milne-Redh. To 1m, erect or climbing, branching, rhizomatous. Lvs to 45×18cm, ovate to ovate-oblong, narrowly acuminate, rounded at base, glabrous, pruinose beneath; petiole length variable. Infl. to 30cm, branched, rachis rose, pubesc., to 2cm; bracts to 3×0.6cm, caducous, 1 per 2 cymules, red; pedicel about 10cm; cal. and cor. rose-pink to light brown; outer staminodes white, inner staminodes yellow. W & C Africa to Angola.

***M. flexuosa*** (Benth.) Hutch. See *M. cuspidata* and *M. purpurea.*
For further synonymy see *Clinogyne, Donax, Maranta* and *Phrynium.*

**Marattia** Sw. (For the Italian botanist J.F. Maratti (*d*1777), who published *De Floribus Filicum* in 1760.) Marattiaceae. About 60 species of large evergreen ferns. Rhizome large, subtuberous, succulent; stipes succulent with adnate stipules at base. Fronds large, ovate, 2–3-pinnate; pinnules oblong, glossy. Sori large, 4–12 in continuous single submarginal row; syngania of 2 opposite rows of fused sporangia opening by slits down the inner face. Tropics. Prothalli are invaded by a symbiotic fungus.

CULTIVATION As for *Angiopteris*. *M. douglasii* and *M. salicina* require cool glasshouse conditions. The succulent rhizomes are used as a vegetable, boiled, roasted or baked, by the indigenous people of C & S America and New Zealand.

***M. alata*** Sw. Stipes 30–60×2.5+cm, paleate. Fronds 90–120cm, tripinnatifid, chaffy below; pinnae 12–18×6mm, lower pinnae largest, ultimate divisions oblong, serrate or crenate. Syngania copious, submarginal, sides erect, 1.5mm, attachment oblong or rather rounded. Tropical America, W Indies.

***M. attenuata*** Labill. Stipes 90–120cm, smooth. Fronds 90–120cm, 3-pinnate, glabrous; pinnae 45–60cm on stalk to 15cm; pinnules 2–3 each side; seg. 10–15×2.5–3.5cm, 3–4 each side plus terminal seg., serrate at apex, cuneate at base, lower short-stalked, rachis not winged. Australia.

***M. circutaefolia*** Kaulf. Stipes 30–60×2.5cm, smooth. Fronds 150–180cm, bipinnate, glabrous; lower pinnae 30–45×30cm; pinnules 10–15×2.5cm, oblong-lanceolate, cuneate or somewhat rounded at base, margins entire or minutely serrate; rachis narrowly winged near apex. Brazil.

***M. douglasii*** (Presl) Bak. DOUGLAS MULESFOOT FERN; PALA. Rhiz. surrounded by persistent succulent black auricles; stipes subterete, to 1.5m, pale green or foxy below, blackened at base, thick, smooth, rather succulent. Fronds to 120×150cm, deltoid, tripinnate, dark glossy green above, paler beneath, brittle and fleshy; pinnae oblong-lanceolate; pinnules 10–25×6–8mm, linear, shortly stipitate, rachis winged, ultimate pinnules ovate to oblong, bluntly serrate, veins simple or twice-forked, somewhat translucent. Hawaii.

***M. fraxinea*** (Poir.) Sm. KING FERN; PARA FERN. Stipes swollen below, 30–60×2.5–4cm, smooth, paleate. Fronds 2–5m, bipinnate or occasionally tripinnate, dark green, glabrous; pinnae 30–60×30cm; pinnules 10–15×1.5–4cm, oblong-lanceolate, acuminate at apex, cuneate to somewhat rounded at base, margins entire or minutely serrate. Asia, Africa, Tropical America, New Zealand.

***M. salicina*** J. Sm. POTATO FERN. Rhiz. short-creeping, stout, starchy; root numerous, branching, thick and succulent; stipes erect, succulent, dark and swollen at base, tuberculate, enclosed at base by a pair of ear-like stipules. Fronds arching, semi-weeping, pinnate when young, or bipinnate in mature plants, glossy green; pinnules alternate; rachis tuberculate, secondary rachis swollen at base. Tropical Asia, Australasia.

***M. smithii*** Mett. ex Kuhn. Large terrestrial fern; rhiz. erect, massive, globose; stipes stout, 1.5–2.5m. Fronds to 3×1.5m, bipinnate, dark green above, paler below, frond bases persistent; pinnae alternate, to 1m; pinnules 12–15×1.5cm, numerous, linear-oblong, acuminate at apex, unequally rounded at base, margins shallowly serrate, acutely so near apex, veins mostly simple, some forked near base, regularly spaced. Polynesia (New Hebrides, Fiji, Samoa).

***M. alata*** Hook. & Arn. non Sw. See *M. douglasii.*
***M. fraxinea*** Luerssen non (Poir.) Sm. See *M. smithii.*
***M. laevis*** Sm. See *M. alata.*
***M. sorbifolia*** Brackenr. non Sw. See *M. smithii.*

**MARATTIACEAE** Bercht. & J. Presl. *Angiopteris, Christensenia, Marattia.*

**Marcetella** Svent.
***M. moquiniana*** (Webb & Berth.) Svent. See *Bencomia moquiniana.*

**Margaritaria** L. (The name alludes to the characteristic pearly white endocarp of the fruit.) Euphorbiaceae. 14 species of dioecious shrubs or trees (rarely scandent), usually deciduous, new leaves appearing with flowers (or sometimes evergreen). Leaves distichous, entire; petioles short. Flowers in clusters at proximal axils of expanding leafy branches; sepals 4, often unequal; stamens 4. Fruit capsular, more or less irregularly dehiscent. Old and new World Tropics (except for Pacific Is.). Z10.

CULTIVATION As for the warm growing non-succulent species of *Euphorbia*.

***M.discoidea*** (Baill.) Webster. Shrub or tree to 20m (rarely 30m). Branchlets subterete or angled, glabrous or hirsutulous when young. Lvs 3–15×2–4(–5.5)cm, ovate-elliptic to obovate-oblanceolate, acute, thin, glabrous except on midribs, stalked. Fls dioecious, male fls in many-fld clusters, female fls in lf-axils. Fr. subglobose to oblate, scarcely to distinctly 3-lobed (5.5–)6–9(–11)mm diam. W to E & SE Africa.

For synonymy see *Phyllanthus*.

**Marginaria** Bory.
***M.augustifolia*** (Sw.) Presl. See *Campyloneurum augustifolium*.

**Margyricarpus** Ruiz & Pav. (From Gk *margaron*, pearl, and *karpos*, fruit, referring to the white fruit.) Rosaceae. 1 species, an evergreen, densely branched subshrub to 60cm; branchlets densely leafy. Leaves to 2cm, alternate, imparipinnate, the pinnae falling to expose a thorny rachis, sparsely pilose to glabrescent, usually 9-foliolate; petioles to 2mm; leaflets linear, to 10mm, glabrescent, margins involute and lanate. Peduncle to 5mm; bracts rhombic-elliptic to orbicular, to 5.5mm, acute to cuspidate, glabrescent to lanate at margins; flowers bisexual, small, 1–3 per axil or in sparse cymes; petals absent; stamens 1–3, anthers purple, ellipsoid to globose; style to 1mm; stigma white, orbicular. Fruit globose, to 7mm diam., leathery, fleshy, white with purple tints. Spring–summer. S America (Andes). Z9.

CULTIVATION Grown in the rock garden or alpine house for its finely divided, dark, evergreen leaves. In favourable seasons the inconspicuous flowers give rise to persistent, fleshy, round, white berries. Grow in well-drained, moisture-retentive, preferably lime-free soils in an open position, but with some shade during the hottest part of the day. Hardy to −5°C/23°F; protect from prolonged winter frosts. Grow in pans in the alpine house and water freely when in growth, keeping dry but not arid in winter. Propagate by softwood cuttings in early summer, by simple layering, or from seed sown in autumn.

***M.pinnatus*** (Lam.) Kuntze. PEARL FRUIT. As for the genus.

***M.setosus*** Ruiz & Pav. See *M.pinnatus*.
For further synonymy see *Empetrum*.

**Marianthus** Hueg. ex Endl. (From Maria and Gk *anthos*, flower, dedicating the flower to the Virgin Mary.) Pittosporaceae. 15 species of perennial, evergreen, procumbent shrubs or woody climbers, to 5m; stems slender. Leaves alternate, entire or with the lower leaves lobed. Inflorescence a terminal or axillary cluster; flowers 5-merous; petals connivent at base and appearing fused, red, blue or white. Fruit a capsule, compressed, membranaceous; seeds many, unwinged. Australia. Z8.

CULTIVATION As for *Billardiera*.

***M.erubescens*** Putterl. Climber to 5m. Lvs leathery, broad. Fls many, 2.5cm, brilliant red. Late spring. W Australia.

***M.ringens*** (J.L. Drumm. & Harv.) F.J. Muell. Climber to 3m. Lvs broad, leather, dark green. Fls many, *c*2.5cm; pet. orange, narrowly acuminate. Spring. W Australia.

**Mariscus** Vahl.
***M.cyperoides*** (L.) Urban. See *Cyperus cyperoides*.
***M.sieberianus*** Nees. See *Cyperus cyperoides*.

**Markea** Rich. See *Dyssochroma*.

**Markhamia** Seem. ex Schum. (For Sir Clements Robert Markham (1830–1916), explorer and writer.) Bignoniaceae. 12–13 species of trees. Leaves opposite, imparipinnate. Inflorescences terminal panicles; calyx spathaceous, usually finely acuminate; corolla yellow or ruddy-brown, tubular-campanulate; stamens didynamous, staminodes small; ovary linear-oblong, glabrous or scaly, disc present. Fruit linear, ribbon-like, valves parallel; seeds in hyaline wing. Africa, Asia. Z10.

CULTIVATION As for *Spathodea*.

***M.lutea*** (Benth.) Schum. 5–10m. Branches tetragonal, lenticellate. Leaflets 4.5–21×2–9cm, 7–13, oblong to ovate, apex acute to acuminate, base cuneate, margin usually entire, rarely irregularly dentate, pilose beneath; petiolules 11mm; rachis angled. Pedicels 0.5–1cm, scaly; cal. 1.8–2.6cm, mucron 1cm, scaly; cor. 4–7×1.7–2.6cm at mouth, yellow lined red in throat, tube 3–4.5cm, lobes 1–1.5cm, scaly outside. Fr. 33–47×1.3–5cm, linear, scaly. Ghana to Cameroun, Zaire, Burundi.

***M.obtusifolia*** (Bak.) Sprague. To 10m. Lvs to 42cm; leaflets to 15cm, 5–11, oblong-ovate to lanceolate. Cor. yellow striped brown in throat, lobes glandular. Fr. to 60cm, straight to curved, felty-tomentose. Africa.

***M.stipulata*** (Wallich) Seem. Leaflets to 30cm, oblong-elliptic, apex acuminate, margin entire, puberulent beneath. Racemes 20cm; cal. 5cm, leathery, rusty-tomentose; cor. yellow, twice cal. length, purple-red in mouth, lobes crenulate. Fr. 30×2.5cm, attenuate-acuminate, pendent. SE Asia.

***M.hildebrandtii*** (Bak.) Sprague. See *M.lutea*.
***M.platycalyx*** Bak. See *M.lutea*.
For further synonymy see *Dolichandrone, Muenteria* and *Spathodea*.

**Marniera** Backeb.
***M.chrysocardium*** (Alexander) Backeb. See *Epiphyllum chrysocardium*.

**Marrow** (courgette, zucchini). *Cucurbita pepo*. Cucurbitaceae. The marrow (often known as vegetable marrow) is a bush or trailing annual producing large, cylindrical, edible fruits. Immature marrows of some cultivars are called courgettes or zucchini. The centre of origin is considered to be northern Mexico and the Southern United States. It is now widely distributed in many tropical and subtropical regions and can be cultivated outdoors in temperate regions during the summer period. It is primarily a summer vegetable but can be stored for use during the winter.

Marrows require an open sunny site and a fertile, moisture-retentive but well-drained soil with a pH of 6.5–7.0. Well-rotted organic matter incorporated into the planting area will increase soil fertility and help retain sufficient moisture for growth. Excess manure, however, can lead to excessive leaf growth at the expense of fruit development. Marrows require a soil temperature of at least 13°C/55°F for germination and are best sown in small pots under protection in the spring for planting out 4–5 weeks later when temperatures are higher. This should only be carried out after the risk of frost has passed and plants should be hardened off first. Later direct sowings can be made in the open or under cloches, placing two or three seeds per site at a depth of 2.5cm/1in., thinning later to leave the strongest seedling. Spacing should be 90cm/36in. apart for the bush types and approximately 1.2m/48in. for the trailing types. Marrows must be kept very well watered at all stages but particularly during flowering. Mulching helps to reduce water loss from the soil surface.

Marrows produce separate male and female flowers; these are insect-pollinated. Under cool conditions it is sometimes advantageous to assist the process by hand pollinating, carried out most easily by taking off male flowers and dabbing their pollen into the females, which can always be recognized by the immature ovary just below the perianth. Liquid feeding is beneficial, particularly during fruit swelling. Regular harvesting enables plants to continue producing over a longer period and increases total yield. Courgettes (young fruit) should be cut when about 10cm/4in. long, but where marrows are required harvesting can start at between 15–20cm/6–8in. Marrows to be stored should be allowed to develop to their full size.

There are many vigorous, high-yielding cultivars suitable for courgettes. These include 'Early Gem', with dark green fruits which can also be grown on for marrows, and the yellow-fruited 'Gold Rush'. 'Long Green Trailing' produces large marrows with pale and dark green stripes, and 'Zebra Cross' has white-striped fruits. Some recommended cultivars (green unless specified) are 'Ambassador', 'Blondee' (cream-white), 'Brimmer', 'Burpee Golden', 'Zucchini' (yellow), 'Gold Rush' (yellow), 'Onyx' and 'Rondo de Nice', with ball-shaped fruits.

Relatively disease free when grown on a well-drained site. Seedlings should be protected from slug damage. Cucumber mosaic virus can present a problem in some seasons.

For summer squash, see PUMPKINS AND SQUASHES.

**Marrubium** L. (From Heb. *marrob*, bitter.) HOREHOUND. Labiatae. 40 species of perennial aromatic herbs to 50cm. Stems tetragonal, lanate or tomentose. Leaves opposite, ovate, pubescent, rugose, crenate or dissected. Inflorescence axillary spikes of dense-flowered whorls, often remote; bracteoles linear or subulate, rarely ovate; calyx campanulate, 10-veined, teeth 5–10, spiny, recurved in fruit; corolla bilabiate, upper lip bilobed, notched, erect, lower lip trilobed, depressed, tube included, stamens within tube, petals white. Fruit glabrous nutlets. Temperate Eurasia, 1 species adventive in N America. Distinguished from similar Labiatae by inclusion of corolla tube in calyx, absence of helm, leaves entire and calyx 10-veined. Z8.

CULTIVATION Grow in full sun and well-drained soils. Most will withstand temperatures to −10°C/14°F but they will not tolerate damp around their roots in winter. Propagate by rooted layers from established plants, or from softwood cuttings of new growth in spring or autumn. Also by seed sown in late spring, although germination may be erratic; thin to 20cm/8in. apart.

***M.cylleneum*** Boiss. & Heldr. To 50cm; stems lanate. Lvs obovate, crenate, tomentose, petiolate. Infl. tight whorls; bracteoles subulate; cal. tomentose, tube to 5.5mm; cor. to 12mm, yellow, upper lip spathulate, lower lip with midlobe larger than laterals. Greece, Albania. Z7.

***M.incanum*** Desr. To 50cm; stems white-tomentose with numerous short, vegetative branches. Lvs oblate to ovate, crenate to dentate, tomentose. Infl. dense whorls; bracteoles subulate, almost as long as cal.; cal. tube 7mm, teeth to 4mm; cor. white, upper lip ovate, all 3 lobes of lower lip equal. Italy, Balkans. Z7.

***M.kotschyi*** Boiss. & Hohen. To 40cm; stems many, simple. Lvs elliptic, crenate; petioles to 3cm. Infl 3–8-whorled; fls sessile, to 25 per whorl; bracteoles equal to cal. tube; cal. tube to 7mm, teeth to 2.5mm, apiculate, glabrous, purple; cor. red or purple, rarely white, 14mm. Summer. Iraq, Kurdistan. Z8.

***M.leonuroides*** Desr. To 45cm; stems green, tomentose. Lvs reniform, dentate, grey-pubesc. beneath. Infl. dense; bracteoles inconspicuous, subulate; cal. tube lanate, teeth 5, subulate; cor. twice length of cal. tube, pink or lilac. Crimea, Caucasus. Z6.

***M.libanoticum*** Boiss. Stems lanate, procumbent at base, ascending green-yellow. Lvs to 14mm, round or ovate, crenulate, petiolate; floral lvs longer than whorl. Bracts subulate to 5mm; cal. stellate, tomentose; cor. pink, slightly longer than cal. Summer–early autumn. Lebanon. Z8.

***M.supinum*** L. To 45cm; stems usually simple, lanate at base, tomentose toward apex. Lvs reniform, cordate at base, crenate. Bracteoles conspicuous; cal. to 7mm; cor. pubesc., pink to lilac, upper lip 2-lobed, spathulate, lower lip with larger midlobe. C & S Spain (mts). Z7.

***M.velutinum*** Sibth. & Sm. To 45cm; stems simple or short-branched, white-lanate. Lvs round, crenate, near glabrous above, tomentose beneath. Bracteoles subulate, to 4mm; cal. equal to brackets, pubesc., exceeding cor.; cor. yellow, pubesc. Summer. N & C Greece. Z8.

***M.vulgare*** L. COMMON HOREHOUND; WHITE HOREHOUND. To 45cm, thyme-scented; stem usually branched, white-pubesc. Lvs to 5cm, round to ovate, crenate, tomentose beneath, downy to near glabrous above, rugose. Infl. dense globose whorls, axillary on leafy stem; bracteoles subulate; cal. tube 3–4mm, faintly veined, teeth 10, hooked; cor. white, to 1.5cm, upper lip flat, bilobed. Summer. Europe, N Africa, Canary Is., Asia. A variegated form exists. Z3.

***M.astracanicum*** Jacq. See *M.kotschyi*.
***M.brachyodon*** Boiss. See *M.kotschyi*.
***M.candidissimun*** auct., non L. See *M.incanum*.
***M.goktschaicum*** N. Popov. See *M.kotschyi*.
***M.purpureum*** Bunge. See *M.kotschyi*.
For further synonymy see *Thymus*.

**Marsdenia** R. Br.
***M.erecta*** (L.) R. Br. See *Cionura erecta*.

**Marshallia** Schreb. (For Moses Marshall (*d*1813), American botanist.) Compositae. 10 species of erect perennial herbs. Leaves alternate, simple, entire, sessile or subsessile, stem leaves somewhat amplexicaul. Capitula discoid, numerous; receptacle convex to conic, usually hollow, scaly; involucre hemispheric or campanulate, phyllaries in 1–2 series, often imbricate; florets tubular, fertile, white, cream, pale lavender or purple. Fruit a turbinate or clavate cypsela; pappus of scales. N America.

CULTIVATION Most species will tolerate temperatures down to about −20°C/−4°F given good drainage. Grow in any gritty, moisture-retentive and well-drained soil that is rich in organic matter, in sun or light dappled shade. *M.trinervia* tolerates drier soils. Propagate by seed sown in autumn or spring and by division.

***M.caespitosa*** Nutt. ex DC. Stem very short. Lvs to 15×1cm, mostly basal, linear-lanceolate, glabrous. Peduncle to 30cm, glabrate beneath, white to tawny pubesc. beneath capitulum; involucre 15–25×6–12mm; phyllaries 6–10×1–2mm, linear-oblong, herbaceous, with white hyaline margins beneath; florets 10–12mm, white or cream, occasionally pale lavender; anth. white or cream, rarely tinged blue. Spring. US. Z6.

***M.grandiflora*** Beadle & F.E. Boynt. Stem to 50cm, glabrous, striate. Lvs 8–25×2–3cm, oblanceolate, elliptic or ovate-lanceolate, lower lvs with sheathing petioles, upper lvs sessile. Peduncle to 15cm; involucre 25×13mm diam.; phyllaries 7–12×2–3mm, ovate-lanceolate, with white hyaline margins; florets 10–15mm, purple; anth. purple. Summer. CE US (Pennsylvania through W Virginia to Tennessee). Z5.

***M.obovata*** (Walter) Beadle & F.E. Boynt. Stem to 50cm, leafy beneath. Lvs 5–12×0.5–2cm, oblanceolate to elliptic, glabrous. Peduncles to 35cm, involucre to 25×12mm; phyllaries to 10×3mm, oblong; florets 10–12mm, pale lavender to purple, cream, occasionally white; anth. tinged blue, rarely cream or white. Spring–early summer. SE US (Virginia southwards into W Florida). Z7.

***M.trinervia*** (Walter) Trel. ex Branner & Cov. Stem leafy, to 1m, often purple-tinged beneath, distinctly grooved toward apex. Lvs to 9×3mm, oblong to ovate-lanceolate, upper lvs sessile. Peduncles 10–20cm, pubesc. above; involucre to 20×10mm; phyllaries to 11×3mm, linear-lanceolate; florets 10–15mm, lilac-purple; anth. purple. Summer. SE US (Virginia to Mississippi). Z7.

**Marsilea** L. PEPPERWORT; WATER CLOVER; NARDOO. (For Luigi Ferdinando Marsigli of Bologna (1656–1730).) Marsileaceae. About 65 species of aquatic or marshy ferns. Rhizomes long-creeping, rooting at nodes, branched, slender, growing through mud with erect fronds or submerged with floating fronds; stipes long. Fronds dimorphic: sterile fronds of 2 pairs of leaflets, arranged like 4-leaf clover; veins numerous, radiating from leaflet base, forked. Sori linear, enclosed by a case of modified fronds (sporocarps) attached to the rhizome by a pedicel; sporocarps usually produced by plants in drying-out habitats. Tropical and temperate regions.

CULTIVATION Very adaptable in cultivation and deserving to be more widely grown as a marginal plant in tropical pools, as an aquatic in tropical aquariums, or as a pot plant if kept moist by immersing the base of the container in water. For cultivation see *Ceratopteris*, although plants must be anchored in substrate if grown aquatically. All spp. require full sun. *M.quadrifolia* may be grown in outdoor pools in cold climates, hardy down to −15°C/5°F.

Propagate by division or from spores: the sporocarps need to be lightly abraded before immersing in water where they expand and burst to release the spores. Germination is immediate and the highly reduced prothallus remains inside the large, seed-like spores. The gametophyte generation is complete within 24 hours, after which the first roots and shoots appear after 2–3 days and should be transplanted into a substrate. A mature, sporocarp-bearing plant can develop in as little as three months.

***M.drummondii*** A. Br. COMMON NARDOO. Rhiz. pubesc. near apex; stipes to 30cm, slender. Fronds arising singly from rhiz.; leaflets 12×9mm, broadly obovate-cuneate or fan-shaped, rather crenate or shortly lobed or occasionally entire, glabrous on floating plants, sericeous on terrestrial plants. Sporocarps solitary, more or less sericeous particularly when young; sporocarp to 9mm, usually smaller; pedicels unbranched, 2–8× length of sporocarp. Australia. Z9.

***M.fimbriata*** Schum. Fronds rather large, margins often crenate. Sporocarps subsessile or shortly, stoutly pedicellate, rather large. Ghana. Z10.

***M.hirsuta*** R. Br. Rhiz. densely ferruginous-villous near apex when young; stipes to 15cm, slender. Fronds arising singly at intervals along rhiz., leaflets narrowly oblong or obovate to broadly cuneate, more or less hirsute beneath, particularly when young. Sporocarps solitary or clustered, pubesc.; sporocarp small, subglobose; pedicel lacking at base of sterile fronds, or shorter than sporocarp, unbranched. Australia. Z9.

***M.mutica*** Mett. Stipes to 90cm, often much less, arising singly along rhiz. Leaflets broad, rounded at apex, 2×2.5cm, inner and outer zone 2 different shades of glossy green, separated by a brown or light green band, smooth, glabrous. Sporocarps to 4 per pedicel, 1–1.5mm; pedicels longer than sporocarp, branched 1–3 times, 2mm. Australia. Z9.

***M.quadrifolia*** L. Aquatic; stipes 8–15cm. Leaflets 12–18mm, deltoid, outer margin rounded, entire, glabrous. Sporocarps clustered; sporocarp rounded oblong, 3–4mm; pedicels 12–24mm, 2–4-ternate, erect, connate, adnate to base of stipe of sterile frond and upper part of sporocarp base; sori 16–20. Warm temperate Europe, N Asia, E US. Z5.

**Martynia** L. UNICORN PLANT; DEVIL'S-CLAW; ELEPHANT-TUSK; PROBOSCIS FLOWER. (For John Martyn FRS (1699–1768), Professor of Botany at Cambridge.) Pedaliaceae. 1 species, an annual or perennial herb, 1–2m, viscid-pubescent. Leaves opposite throughout, ovate to broadly deltoid, 5–7-lobed or rarely entire, irregularly dentate, cordate at base, to 25cm; petioles to 25cm. Inflorescence racemose, open, 7–20-flowered; pedicels 1.5–2cm; sepals 5, free, lanceolate, to 1.5cm; cor. 5–5cm long, cream to maroon, tube usually yellow-, orange- or red-spotted within, lobes blotched deep purple; fertile stamens 2, staminodes 2, sometimes with a further rudimentary filament. Fruit a pendulous capsule, ovoid, body 2.5–3.5cm, horns 2, curved, diverging after dehiscence, to 1cm. C America & W Indies, in highlands; naturalized in India and New Caledonia.

CULTIVATION Suitable for growing along trellis and fencing, or effective when allowed to sprawl through other plants in the hot sunny border, *M. annua* is valued for the creamy-white to red-purple bell-shaped flowers which are followed by unusual horned fruits. Sow seed in early spring under glass, germinate at 21°C/70°F, and prick out into individual pots. Pot on as necessary and grow on in full light, hardening off before planting out after danger of frost is passed, into any well-drained, fertile soil in full sun.

***M.annua*** L. As for the genus.

***M.angulosa*** Lam. See *M.annua*.
***M.arenaria*** Engelm. See *Proboscidea arenaria*.
***M.diandra*** Gloxin. See *M.annua*.
***M.fragrans*** Lindl. See *Proboscidea fragrans*.

**Mascarena** L.H. Bail.
***M.lagenicaulis*** L.H. Bail. See *Hyophorbe lagenicaulis*.
***M.revaughanii*** L.H. Bail. See *Hyophorbe lagenicaulis*.
***M.verschaffeltii*** (H.A. Wendl.) L.H. Bail. See *Hyophorbe verschaffeltii*.

**Masdevallia** Ruiz & Pav. (For Jose Masdevall (*d*1801), Spanish botanist and physician.) Orchidaceae. Some 300 species of tufted, evergreen, often diminutive, epiphytic or lithophytic orchids, lacking pseudobulbs; rhizome short-creeping. Secondary stems short, erect, apically unifoliate, thinly sheathed. Leaves fleshy, glabrous, coriaceous, dorsally carinate, erect or suberect, narrow-elliptic to obovate-spathulate, narrowed into a sulcate petiole at base, usually tridentate at apex. Inflorescence a terminal single or few-flowered raceme borne at junction of petiole and stem; peduncles erect, slender; flowers small or large, variously coloured, essentially triangular in outline due to showy, expanded sepals emerging from a papery bract; sepals showy, ovate to triangular, fused near base forming a narrow or cup-shaped tube, sometimes connate throughout, distal portions spreading, terminating in short to elongate tails, lateral sepals connate to base of lip forming a chin; petals much smaller than sepals, narrow, linear-oblong to subquadrate; lip small, articulated to column foot, sessile or short-clawed, often partially concealed within calyx; disc with or without calli; column short, erect to arching, apex entire or variously dentate, sometimes winged, foot short, anther operculate, unicellular, pollinia 2, pyriform, waxy. Mexico to Brazil and Bolivia. See also *Dracula, Dryadella, Scaphosepalum*. Z10.

CULTIVATION Cool-growing tufted orchids of diminutive stature and exhibiting a remarkable range of colour and form in their (generally) tricorn-like flowers, from the vivid flames and magentas of *M. veitchiana* and *M.coccinea* to the long-tailed lilac *M.caudata* and small, sinister *M.rolfeana*. Pot in a mix of fine bark, charcoal and sphagnum in small, well-crocked clays. Position in light shade in a buoyant, humid, cool environment – growth will deteriorate where temperatures depart from a day maximum of 25°C/75°F, night minimum 5°C/40°F. Although they should never be allowed to dry out, these plants are susceptible to damping off, and should therefore be watered carefully. An alternative, especially provided in a growing case, to which these orchids are perfectly suited, is to bed the pots together in a tray of living sphagnum; this will encourage searching development of their wiry roots. Propagate by division.

*Masdevallia* has been split: in the crudest morphological terms, species with pendulous scapes and motile lips can now be found in *Dracula*, very dwarf plants in *Dryadella*, and those with several small flowers carried on one scape in *Scaphosepalum*. Some of the cultigens listed below may, strictly, belong to or draw on these segregate genera.

***M.abbreviata*** Rchb. f. Densely caespitose. Lvs to 15×1.5cm, spathulate to oblong-oblanceolate, obtuse. Infl. to 18cm, slender, several-fld, erect or arcuate; fls small; sep. and pet. white spotted crimson; sepaline tube to 6mm, campanulate, dorsal sep. suborbicular-ovate or triangular-ovate, dentate, tail to 1.5cm, yellow, lateral sep. similar to dorsal sep., obliquely ovate; pet. spathulate-cuneate, retuse-apiculate, with anterior keel; lip to 5mm, pale yellow, oblong-pandurate, basal portion ovate, apical portion suborbicular or obscurely 3-lobed. Peru, Ecuador.

***M.amabilis*** Rchb. f. Lvs to 18×2.5cm, oblong to oblanceolate, obtuse, coriaceous, dark green. Infl. to 30cm, 1-fld; peduncle terete, slender; sepaline tube yellow-orange with crimson venation, to 2.5cm, narrowly campanulate-cylindrical, slightly curved, dorsal sep. free portion ovate to triangular, acuminate, orange-yellow or rose, with red venation, tails to 5cm, dull red, lateral sep. connate for half of length, ovate-triangular, orange-red tinged crimson, tails to 3.5cm; pet. to 6mm, narrowly oblong, apiculate, yellow streaked red; lip to 6mm, pandurate to oblong, apiculate, apex recurved and rounded, yellow-white. Peru.

***M.attenuata*** Rchb. f. Lvs to 13×2cm, linear-oblanceolate, bright lustrous green. Infl. 1-fld, usually shorter than lvs; fls somewhat campanulate, waxy, green-white, to 2.5cm long; sepaline tube sometimes streaked red, interior pubesc., tails to 1.5cm, orange-yellow, lateral sep. connate for basal third; pet. white edged green, oblong-lanceolate to subrhombic; lip to 5×2mm, white with brown apex, oblong-lanceolate to oblong-pandurate, with 2 longitudinal keels. Costa Rica, Panama.

***M.auropurpurea*** Rchb. f. & Warsc. Lvs to 12.5×2.5cm, oblong-oblanceolate, subacute or obtuse; petiole elongate. Infl. subequal to lvs, 1–3-fld; sepaline tube yellow tinged brown, to 1.5cm, dorsal sep. connate with lateral sep. for 1cm from base, free portion triangular, tail to 4cm, bright yellow, slender, lateral sep. deeply connate, free portion ovate-triangular, oblique, tail to 2.5cm, slender, bright yellow; pet. linear-oblong, acute or apiculate, with anterior keel; lip oblong-lanceolate, short-acuminate, base cordate, bicarinate, apex reflexed and papillose. Peru, Ecuador, Colombia, Bolivia.

***M.barlaeana*** Rchb. f. Stems very short, densely tufted. Lvs to 12.5×2.5cm, elliptic-oblanceolate or oblong, acute or obtuse. Infl. to 25cm, slender, erect, 1-fld; sepaline tube narrow, scarlet, campanulate-cylindric, slightly decurved, dorsal sep. to 4cm, red-orange with a median and marginal red lines, ovate-triangular to subquadrate, lateral sep. connate for two-thirds of length, bright carmine shaded scarlet, with 3 scarlet lines, elliptic-oblong, tails to 14mm, sometimes crossing each other; pet. minute, linear-oblong, minutely tridentate at apex, with longitudinal keel; lip white, with purple spot at apex, to 6mm, oblong-oblanceolate, longitudinally 2-keeled in centre, apex recurved. Peru.

***M.bonplandii*** Rchb. f. Lvs to 8×2cm, oblong-spathulate. Infl. to 20cm, erect, 1-fld; fls yellow-green; sepaline tube spotted brown-purple, to 2cm, sep. triangular to oblong-ligulate, acute, 2-keeled; pet. oblong, acute, slightly dilated toward middle, carinate; lip short-clawed; lamina oblong, apex broadly rounded, reflexed, papillose, bicarinate. Peru, Ecuador.

***M.caloptera*** Rchb. f. Lvs to 8×2cm, ovate-oblong to lanceolate, rounded to obtuse, older lvs tinged red-brown. Infl. to 15cm, erect, 2–5-fld; fls small; sep. white streaked and spotted rust to crimson, tails yellow-orange, dorsal sep. round-triangular, hooded, keeled below, minutely dentate, tail slender, erect, to 1cm, lateral sep. ovate-oblong, recurved, tails to 1cm, decurved; pet. minute, white with a prominent anterior crimson keel, oblong-spathulate, apiculate, apical margins dentate; lip yellow streaked crimson, slightly larger than sep., oblong to obscurely 3-lobed, lateral lobes oblong, erect, midlobe orbicular-obovate, apiculate; column pale green marked crimson, to 4mm. Ecuador, Colombia, Peru.

***M.calura*** Rchb. f. Lvs to 10cm, broadly oblanceolate, coriaceous, blue-green. Infl. to 10cm, erect or arcuate, 1-fld; fls to 10.5cm across, deep burgundy with a black hue; sep. apices yellow, sepaline tube to 1.5cm, cylindrical, curved, dorsal sep. triangular, tails to 5cm, filiform, lateral sep. connate for 2cm, ovate-oblong, reflexed, slightly papillose above, tails with triangular sinus, filiform, parallel; pet. rich crimson, apex white, to 8mm, ovate, apex triangular; lip deep crimson, pandurate, base bilobulate, apex rounded and deflexed, bicarinate; column white. Costa Rica.

***M.caudata*** Lindl. Lvs to 8×3cm, obovate-spathulate, obtuse, pale green, thinly coriaceous. Infl. subequalling lvs, suberect; peduncle terete, slender, 1-fld; fls broad, slightly fragrant, to 15cm across, usually smaller; sepaline tube short, broad, fleshy, cup-like, dorsal sep. lime to buff, spotted and lined lilac, lamina to 2.5×2cm, obovate, concave, tails to 6.5cm, slender, yellow, lateral sep. buff flushed or spotted lilac or rose, free portion to 1.5×1.5cm, obliquely ovate, tails to 5cm, pale green, slender, deflexed; pet. white, concealed in tube, minute, linear-oblong, apex obliquely dentate; lip white spotted mauve-purple, oblong, apex reflexed; column to 7mm, white spotted mauve-purple on margins, foot arcuate. Colombia, Venezuela, Ecuador.

***M.civilis*** Rchb. f. & Warsc. Lvs to 25×1.5cm, linear or linear-oblong, subacute. Infl. to 8cm, mottled purple-black, 1-fld; fls fleshy, strongly scented, polished; sepaline tube to 2.5cm, cylindrical, gibbous below, yellow-green spotted purple, interior minutely papillose, sep. yellow-green, deep purple at base, to 4cm, ovate-triangular, tails short, yellow, recurved; pet. white with central purple stripe, small, spathulate, acute; lip mottled and spotted purple, to 1.5cm, oblong, obtuse, apex recurved and papillose, 2-keeled. Peru.

***M.coccinea*** Lind. ex Lindl. Lvs erect, to 23×3cm, narrow-oblong to obovate-lanceolate, pale to deep glossy green. Infl. to 40cm, slender, suberect, 1-fld at apex; peduncle terete; fls large, showy, waxy, variable in colour; sep. deep crystalline magenta, crimson, scarlet, pale yellow or cream-white, sepaline tube to 2cm, campanulate-cylindric, slightly compressed, curved, sep. large, flattened, often longitudinally ridged, dorsal sep. to 8cm, narrowly triangular or linear, tail slender, erect or recurved, lateral sep. longer than dorsal sep., connate in basal third, ovate-attenuate, outer margin falcate, decurved with short tails; pet. to 1cm, usually off-white, translucent, linear, 2-lobed at apex with anterior, longitudinal keel; lip to 1cm, usually shorter, oblong, slightly pandurate above, bicarinate. Colombia, Peru.

***M.coriacea*** Lindl. Lvs to 20×2cm, linear-oblanceolate, coriaceous, erect, deep green above, pale green and keeled below. Infl. to 20cm, pale green flecked purple, 1-fld; sepaline tube to 1.5cm, pale yellow spotted purple along veins, broadly cylindrical, dorsal sep. to 4cm, same colour as tube, ovate-triangular, with short, broad tail, lateral sep. to 3.5cm, yellow, oblong, acuminate; pet. to 1.5cm, white with central purple stripe, oblong to spathulate, obtuse; lip to 1.5cm, yellow-green with central purple stripe and marginal spots, oblong, pubesc. above, reflexed; column to 1cm, pale green, minutely dentate at apex. Colombia.

***M.corniculata*** Rchb. f. Lvs to 25×4cm, oblong-lanceolate. Infl. to 10cm, erect, 1-fld; bract large, pale green, keeled; fls to 8cm across, pale yellow marked or suffused red-brown; sepaline tube broadly cylindrical, curved, gibbous below, to 2cm, dorsal sep. free portion triangular, tail to 5cm, slender, lateral sep. connate for 3cm, oblong, reflexed, tail shorter than dorsal tail, recurved, slender; pet. white, tipped yellow, ligulate; lip yellow spotted purple, subpandurate, apex verrucose. Colombia.

***M.davisii*** Rchb. f. Lvs to 20×2cm, narrowly oblong-oblanceolate, apex subacute, bright lustrous green, coriaceous. Infl. to 25cm, erect, 1-fld; peduncle slender, terete; fls large, showy, fragrant, bright orange-yellow; sepaline tube narrowly campanulate-cylindric, to 17mm, with a prominent keel above, dorsal sep. ovate-triangular, tail slender, to 2.5cm, lateral sep. exceeding dorsal sep., connate for half of length, obliquely ovate-oblong, tail to 7mm; pet. small, concealed within tube, oblong, apex bilobed, apiculate, with anterior, longitudinal keel; lip smaller than pet., concealed within tube, oblong-pandurate, apex reflexed, apiculate. Peru.

***M.floribunda*** Lindl. Lvs to 12×2cm, oblong-oblanceolate, obtuse, dark lustrous green, coriaceous. Infl. usually exceeding lvs, numerous, erect to decumbent, 1-fld; fls to 4cm across; sep. pale yellow or buff-yellow spotted brown-crimson, sepaline tube to 1.5cm, cylindrical, dorsal sep. free portion to 1cm, ovate-triangular, tail to 12mm, slender, recurved, lateral sep. free portion rotund to ovate, to 1.5cm, tail to 6mm, slender, recurved; pet. to 5×2mm, white, linear-oblong, apex dentate, with anterior keel; lip to 5×2cm, white with crimson-brown blotch at apex, linear-oblong to lanceolate-oblong, cordate at base, apex reflexed; column to 5mm, suberect. Mexico, Guatemala, Honduras, Costa Rica.

***M.ignea*** Rchb. f. Lvs to 23×5cm, elliptic-lanceolate or oblong-lanceolate, coriaceous, dark green, suberect. Infl. to 40cm, erect, 1-fld; peduncle slender, terete; fls to 8cm across; sep. scarlet to orange, often tinged crimson, sepaline tube to 2cm, cylindrical, hooded, curved, dorsal sep. free portion to 1cm, triangular, tail to 4cm, slender, strongly deflexed, lateral sep. connate for 2.5cm, broadly falcate-ovate, acute, divergent, 3-nerved, margin reflexed, tails short; pet. white with purple median line, to 8mm, linear-oblong, acute, anterior margin keeled; lip stained orange-red at apex, fleshy, oblong, sulcate, margins crenate, apex recurved, apiculate; column white, lined purple, to 1cm, apex dentate. Colombia.

***M.infracta*** Lindl. Lvs to 14×2.5cm, lanceolate to oblong, subobtuse, erect, coriaceous, bright lustrous green. Infl. to 25cm, erect, 1–5-fld; fls produced in succession, yellow-white to ochre, white at base of tube, flushing orange to blood-red, campanulate, pendent; sepaline tube to 13mm, cupped, curved, dorsal sep. free portion to 5cm, ovate to triangular, tail to 4cm, filiform, lateral sep. free portion to 5cm, rotund-oblong, connate for 2cm, tails to 4cm, strongly divergent, filiform; pet. to 8mm, obliquely linear, apiculate, white to pale pink; lip to 1cm, linear or slightly pandurate, apex reflexed, apiculate, bicarinate, spotted red-brown at apex. Brazil, Peru.

***M.ionocharis*** Rchb. f. Stems short. Lvs to 12×1.5cm, narrowly elliptic-lanceolate, acute. Infl. 1-fld; peduncle to 10cm, slender, terete; fls to 1.5cm diam., excluding sep. tails; sepaline tube campanulate, to 13mm, yellow-white, sep. free portion green-white blotched rose-purple, triangular-ovate, keeled behind, tails to 2cm, slender, yellow; pet. minute, triangular-oblong, acute; lip minute, clawed, oblong-pandurate, purple, apex reflexed. Peru.

***M.laucheana*** Bonhof. Lvs to 12.5×2.5cm, obovate-oblanceolate, dark green; petiole short. Infl. shorter than lvs, erect, 1-fld, slender, pale green; fls to 1.8cm diam., excluding tails; sepaline tube campanulate, white flushed rose to mauve at base, free portions white to buff, ovate-triangular, tails to 2cm, rigid, incurved, orange. Costa Rica.

***M.ludibunda*** Rchb. f. Lvs to 7.5×3cm, suberect, elliptic-spathulate, coriaceous, apex bifid. Infl. exceeding lvs, erect, 1-fld; peduncle slender, terete; fls to 7.5cm across, widely spreading; sepaline tube to 8mm, campanulate, dorsal sep. bright magenta with yellow base and margins, free portion obovate, concave, to 1.5cm, tails yellow, to 2.5cm, lateral sep. oblong, spreading, obtuse, white above, base magenta, margins recurved, tails yellow, slender, to 4cm; pet. white, linear-oblong, apiculate, anterior margin keeled, to 8mm; lip white, oblong, sulcate at base, apiculate, to 8mm; column to 8mm, white spotted purple marginally, foot and apex purple, apex dentate. Colombia.

***M.macrura*** Rchb. f. Stems clustered, to 15cm. Lvs to 37×7cm, elliptic-oblong, obtuse, coriaceous, lustrous green. Infl. usually equalling lvs, erect, 1-fld; fls large, to 25cm across, fleshy; sep. red to dull brown-yellow, studded with many maroon warts, sepaline tube to 1.5cm, cylindrical or flattened, ribbed, dorsal sep. free portion to 15cm, lanceolate to narrowly triangular, acuminate, tail long, erect, yellow-green, lateral sep. to 12.5cm, ovate to oblong, connate for basal 4cm, tail long, strongly decurved; pet. to 1cm, pale yellow-brown, oblong-curved; lip to 8mm, yellow-brown spotted purple below, oblong, papillose, bicarinate, apex reflexed; column to 8mm, yellow, spotted crimson on foot. Colombia, Ecuador.

***M.maculata*** Klotzsch & Karst. Lvs to 18×3cm, linear-lanceolate, acute, coriaceous. Infl. to 25cm, several-fld; peduncle triquetrous; fls produced in succession, showy, spreading; sep. yellow or yellow-green, spotted and tinged red, sepaline tube to 16mm, flattened-cylindrical, orange-yellow above, red below, dorsal sep. free portion ovate-triangular, tail slender, to 7cm, lateral sep. connate to middle, ovate-oblong, tails tapering strongly, pale yellow, parallel or divergent; pet. small, oblong-ligulate, apiculate, white; lip to 1cm, oblong, papillose and dentate at apex, dull purple, apex recurved; column to 6mm. Venezuela, Peru, Colombia.

***M.mejiana*** Garay. Lvs to 12×1.5cm, usually erect, oblong-lanceolate, obtuse, subcoriaceous. Infl. to 10cm, ascending, 1–2-fld; fls to 7cm across, white flecked pink, tails yellow-orange; sepaline tube campanulate, free portions spreading, broadly ovate, or wholly fused forming a cup, tails fleshy, divergent. Colombia.

***M.melanopus*** Rchb. f. Lvs to 12.5×1.5cm, oblong-spathulate or oblanceolate, obtuse. Infl. numerous, to 25cm, slender, erect, loosely 3–8-fld; fls secund, to 2.5cm across; sep. and pet. white minutely spotted and flecked purple; sepaline tube shortly campanulate, to 6mm, gibbous below, sep. free portion triangular or suborbicular, concave, keeled behind, tails to 13mm, bright yellow, slender; pet. minute, spathulate-cuneate, retuse-apiculate, with anterior keel; lip to 4mm, white spotted purple, apex rounded into a yellow terminal lobe, pandurate-oblong, anterior portion 2-keeled. Colombia, Ecuador, Peru.

***M.mooreana*** Rchb. f. Lvs to 20×3cm, linear-oblong, coriaceous, dark green, spotted purple below. Infl. to 10cm, erect, stout, green spotted dull purple; fls horizontal, to 9cm across, fleshy, solitary; sepaline tube broadly cylindrical, slightly ventricose below, sep. long, tapering, forward-pointing, dorsal sep. yellow-white streaked purple at base, triangular, tail yellow, linear, to 5cm, lateral sep. crimson to purple, interior surface covered with many black-purple papillae, connate almost to middle, triangular, acute, tail yellow toward apex; pet. white with a central purple stripe, oblong, acute; lip black-purple, oblong, pubesc. above; column green-white, margins black-purple. Colombia, Venezuela.

***M.nidifica*** Rchb. f. Stems short. Lvs to 5×7cm, spathulate or oblanceolate, acute to rounded, coriaceous. Infl. almost equalling lvs, 1-fld; peduncle filiform, dull green-crimson; fls small, variable in size and colour; sep. white, green-white or pale yellow, spotted and striped crimson, maroon to olive below, sepaline tube to 7mm, slightly inflated below, pubesc. within, dorsal sep. rotund to ovate-triangular, concave, pubesc. within, tails to 3cm, slender, crimson, lateral sep. ovate, tails similar to dorsal sep., yellow; pet. minute, cream with central purple streak, oblong, acute, keeled on anterior margin; lip to 4mm, yellow with 3 longitudinal purple lines, pandurate-oblong, acute to obtuse, curved; column to 4mm, pink marked crimson. Costa Rica, Peru, Ecuador, Colombia.

***M.pachyantha*** Rchb. f. Lvs to 20cm, oblanceolate, coriaceous, clustered, dark green. Infl. exceeding lvs, erect, 1-fld; fls large, to 12cm including tails; sepaline tube pale orange-yellow, broadly cylindrical, slightly curved, dorsal sep. pale yellow-green with brown-purple venation, triangular, keeled above, tail to 2.5cm, stout, erect, lateral sep. connate almost to middle, ovate-oblong, pale yellow-green heavily spotted rose-purple, tail bright yellow, shorter than dorsal tail; pet. white with brown-purple midline, ovate, acute; lip brown, dark brown-black toward apex, ligulate, apex reflexed; column green, margins purple-brown. Colombia.

***M.pandurilabia*** Schweinf. Lvs to 12×2.5cm, obovate, oblanceolate or elliptic, subacute to rounded, apex minutely tridentate; petiole to 5cm, slender. Infl. to 20cm, erect to arcuate, slender, 1-fld; fls small; sep. and pet. yellow-brown; sepaline tube to 5mm, interior pubesc., dorsal sep. suborbicular-ovate, tail slender, to 3.5cm, lateral sep. obliquely semiorbicular-ovate; tails similar to dorsal sep.; pet. minute, obliquely oblong-triangular, apex tridentate, base with a prominent lobule; lip to 4mm, ovate-pandurate, recurved, apiculate. Peru.

***M.peristeria*** Rchb. f. Lvs to 15×2.5cm, linear-lanceolate or oblong, coriaceous, deep blue-green. Infl. to 7cm, 1-fld; peduncle terete, pale green spotted crimson; fls to 12.5cm diam., fleshy, spreading; sepaline tube to 2cm, broadly cylindric, gibbous below, prominently ribbed, sep. yellow or yellow-green spotted crimson, reverse yellow-green, ovate-triangular, tails fleshy, to 3.5cm, triquetrous toward apex; pet. pale green-yellow, linear-oblong, acute, curved, minutely bidentate; lip to 1.5cm, green-white with purple papillae, oblong-pandurate, base sulcate, rounded to truncate, papillose, apex reflexed; column white-green, to 12mm, finely dentate. Spring–summer. Colombia.

***M.polysticta*** Rchb. f. non Hook. f. Lvs to 15×2.5cm, subspathulate or oblanceolate, apex rounded and minutely tridentate. Infl. to 25cm, pale green spotted dull purple, loosely 3–9-fld; fls to 5cm diam., white or pale lilac spotted dark red or purple; sepaline tube short, interior papillose, dorsal sep. free portion broadly ovate, cucullate, tail slender, to 2.5cm, lateral sep. narrowly oblong-lanceolate, oblique, with a yellow central line, margins reflexed and slightly ciliate, tail slender, to 2.5cm; pet. minute, spathulate-cuneate, retuse, apiculate, with anterior keel; lip minute, to 3mm, pandurate-oblong, keeled. Ecuador, Peru.

***M.pumila*** Poepp. & Endl. Lvs to 9×1cm, linear-oblanceolate or linear-spathulate, obtuse or subacute, apex minutely tridentate, lustrous green. Infl. to 3.5cm, filiform, 1-fld; fls small, pure white; sepaline tube to 5mm, cylindrical, dorsal sep. small, triangular-lanceolate, to 3cm including fleshy tails, lateral sep. large; pet. to 5mm, linear-ligulate, obtuse, falcate; lip to 5mm, narrow-clawed, ovate-oblong, apex rounded, base cordate. Peru, Venezuela.

***M.racemosa*** Lindl. Stems erect, at intervals of 3cm on rhiz. Lvs to 12.5×2cm, elliptic-oblong, obtuse, suberect, coriaceous, lustrous or red-green. Infl. to 35cm, erect or arcuate, slender, dull red-green, 4–15-fld; fls showy, to 6cm across; bright orange-scarlet shaded crimson, sometimes almost yellow; sepaline tube to 1.5cm, cylindrical, narrow, dorsal sep. smaller than lateral sep., free portion narrow ovate-triangular, acuminate, reflexed, tail to 6mm, suberect, lateral sep. connate for basal 2.5cm, broadly obcordate, spreading, apiculate, with dark longitudinal veins; pet. pale yellow, to 8mm, short-clawed, ovate; lip white, to 1cm, narrowly oblong, bicarinate; column pale yellow above, pink below, to 1cm. Colombia.

***M.reichenbachiana*** Endress. Lvs to 15×2.5cm, erect, oblanceolate-spathulate, acute, keeled below, coriaceous, tridentate at apex. Infl. exceeding lvs, slender, erect, 1–3-fld; peduncle terete, bright green; fls produced in succession, to 6cm across; sepaline tube white-yellow below, red-scarlet above, to 2.5cm, curved, funnel-shaped, hooded or almost closed at apex by concave, depressed dorsal sep., dorsal sep. sealing-wax red to pale yellow-white, lined red within, free portion to 12mm, triangular, tail to 5cm, slender, recurved, yellow, lateral sep. yellow-white, connate for half of length, ovate-triangular, decurved, keeled behind, tails to 3.5cm, slender, yellow; pet. white, to 8mm, ovate-oblong, truncate, dentate; lip white, to 6mm, oblong-pandurate, apex recurved; column white, to 8mm. Spring–autumn. Costa Rica.

***M.rolfeana*** Kränzl. Resembles *M. reichenbachiana* except smaller. Infl. shorter than lvs; fls to 5cm long, chocolate-brown to dark purple; sepaline tube yellow at base, to 12mm; lip red. Spring–summer. Costa Rica.

***M.rosea*** Lindl. Lvs to 20×3cm, elliptic-lanceolate to obovate, acute, clustered, dark green. Infl. slightly exceeding lvs, slender, erect or arcuate, 1-fld; sepaline tube to 2.5cm, compressed, scarlet and vermilion, dorsal sep. to 5cm, slender, tail-like, red above, yellow below, arching over broader, carmine, short, red-tailed lateral sep.; pet. to 5mm, white, oblong; lip white, to 5mm, oblong, shallowly pandurate, apex with many black papillae; column white, curved. Spring–summer. Colombia, Ecuador.

***M.schlimii*** Lind. ex Lindl. Lvs to 20×5cm, obovate to elliptic, rounded or obtuse, suberect. Infl. to 35cm, erect, to 8-fld; peduncle terete, light green; fls nodding; sepaline tube short-cylindrical, ochre or golden below, maroon within, dorsal sep. narrow-triangular, long-tailed, golden-green, decurved and arching over larger lateral sep., tail then becoming horizontal, to 4.8cm, lateral sep. to 3cm, decurved, oblong-ovate, fused, forming a heart-shaped shield covered with maroon papillae, tails to 4cm, yellow, slender, divergent; pet. white, to 6mm, falcate-oblong, acute; lip white marked with short maroon transverse bars, to 6mm, linear-oblong to pandurate, acute, with 2 converging ridges toward apex; column white, purple marginally, to 6mm. Spring. Colombia, Venezuela.

***M.schroederiana*** hort. Sander ex Garden. Lvs to 15×2.5cm, oblanceolate. Infl. to 21cm, erect, 1-fld; fls to 8cm across; sepaline tube short-campanulate, white, ribbed, expanding as a flattened oblong platform formed by fusion of lateral sep., pearly white flushed ruby red in upper portions and at dorsal sep., tails long, yellow, lateral tails held horizontally, dorsal tail erect; pet. to 8mm, fleshy, clawed, pale pink spotted rose-purple, oblong, obtuse, undulate; lip white rose spotted rose-purple, to 1cm, pandurate-oblong, obtuse, apex recurved, bicarinate; column apex dentate. Winter–summer. Peru.

***M.tovarensis*** Rchb. f. Stems short. Lvs to 14×2cm, erect, obovate to oblanceolate, obtuse, coriaceous, dark green. Infl. to 18cm, erect, 1–4-fld, flowering successively, often over several seasons; peduncle glabrous, triquetrous; fls to 3.5cm across, long-lived, pure crystalline white, tailed cream or jade; sepaline tube cylindrical, to 6mm, slightly gibbous below, dorsal sep. free portion to 40×6mm, filiform, tail erect, lateral sep. to 4×1cm, shaped like a lyre, connate for half of length, longitudinally ribbed, ovate-oblong, translucent, acuminate, tails short, pale yellow-green, often crossing over; pet. to 6×2mm, oblong, acute; lip to 6×2mm, oblong to spathulate, acute, recurved at apex with 2 central ridges; column purple with white base and apex, to 4mm, subterete, finely dentate. Venezuela.

***M.triangularis*** Lindl. Lvs to 15×3cm, obovate or elliptic oblong, obtuse, margins strongly recurved, coriaceous. Infl. to 15cm, erect, slender, 1-fld; fls broadly campanulate, spreading, to 12cm; sepaline tube broadly campanulate, sep. yellow-green heavily spotted purple-brown, free portion to 2cm, ovate-triangular, concave, keeled behind, tails to 4cm, purple, slender; pet. white, to 6mm, oblong, tridentate at apex; lip white flecked purple, to 6×3mm, oblong, 3-lobed near apex, lateral lobes obscure, midlobe orbicular, reflexed, apex purple-haired; column to 5mm, white. Colombia, Venezuela.

***M.triaristella*** Rchb. f. Dwarf to 8cm. Fls 1–2, buff stained chocolate-maroon; lateral sep. fused in a carinate blade with 2.5cm green divergent tails, dorsal sep. hooded, long-tailed. Costa Rica.

***M.trochilus*** Lind. & André. Lvs to 18cm, narrowly elliptic-lanceolate, clustered, erect, lustrous green. Infl. to 30cm, erect, 1–3-fld; peduncle stout, triquetrous; fls produced in succession, to 20cm; sepaline tube yellow, short, cylindrical, dorsal sep. interior tawny yellow, exterior yellow stained chestnut-brown, concave, suborbicular, keeled, tail yellow, to 8cm, reflexed, lateral sep. forming a chestnut-brown hemispherical cup, ribbed, tails similar to dorsal sep.; pet. white, linear-oblong, apex acute or tridentate; lip red-brown, clawed, oblong, apiculate, base auriculate, apex dentate; column white. Colombia, Ecuador.

***M.tubulosa*** Lindl. Lvs to 11×1.5cm, oblanceolate, obtuse, erect. Fls 1 per infl., 6–12cm, white to ivory; sep. narrow, forward-pointing, tubular. Colombia, Venezuela.

***M.veitchiana*** Rchb. f. Lvs to 25×2.5cm, oblong to narrowly oblanceolate, subacute, pale green, erect. Infl. to 45cm, erect, 1-fld; fls variable, to 8cm across, showy; sep. interior shining vermilion covered with many iridescent purple papillae, exterior tawny yellow with dark venation, sepaline tube to 3cm, campanulate-cylindrical, dorsal sep. free portion to 3cm, triangular-ovate, margins often recurved, tail slender, to 3.5cm, lateral sep. larger than dorsal sep., broadly ovate or triangular, acuminate, connate for 3cm, tails short, often forward-pointing or overlapping; pet. to 1.5cm, oblong, acute, keeled, white; lip to 1.5cm, oblong to obscurely 3-lobed, apex papillose, reflexed, white; column short, semi-terete, white. Peru.

***M.velifera*** Rchb. f. Lvs to 20×2.5cm, lanceolate or linear-elliptic, obtuse, clustered, bright green. Infl. to 10cm, stout, 1-fld; fls to 7.5cm, malodorous; sepaline tube to 2cm, broadly cylindrical, gibbous below, dorsal sep. yellow-brown spotted red-brown, triangular, concave, tail to 5cm, stout, lateral sep. connate for 5cm, similar colour to dorsal sep. or shiny red-brown, oblanceolate-oblong, tail yellow, stout; pet. green-white or green-yellow, to 12mm, linear-oblong; lip dark purple, oblong-subquadrate, papillose; column yellow or yellow-green spotted red, curved, triquetrous. Colombia.

***M.wageneriana*** Lindl. Lvs to 5×1.5cm, elliptic to spathulate, suberect, coriaceous, lustrous dark green above. Infl. suberect to spreading, 1-fld; peduncle to 5cm, slender; fls to 6cm; sep. light green-yellow or cream, orange-yellow toward base, spotted and streaked violet, sepaline tube short, dorsal sep. free portion broadly ovate-oblong, to 1×1cm, concave on inner side, tails slender, to 5cm, sharply recurved, lateral sep. similar to dorsal sep., connate for more than half of length; pet. minute, narrowly oblong, truncate, bidentate at apex; lip clawed, rhomboidal, margin reflexed, dentate, pale yellow-green or white, spotted purple; column to 5mm, semi-terete, pale violet or white, spotted violet. Venezuela.

***M.xanthina*** Rchb. f. Lvs to 7.5×2cm, obovate-oblong, petiole short. Infl. erect; peduncle to 8cm, slender, terete, pale green, 1-fld; fls spreading; sepaline tube obscure, sep. bright yellow or cream with dark yellow venation, dorsal sep. obovate-oblong, cucullate, recurved at base, tails orange-yellow, erect, to 3.5cm, lateral sep. with purple spot at base, lanceolate, tails to 33mm, orange-yellow, slender; pet. white, to 4mm, oblong, anterior margin keeled; lip pale yellow slightly spotted crimson, fleshy, oblong; column white marked purple, tridentate at apex. Colombia, Ecuador.

***M.* grexes and cultivars.**

*M.* Angel Frost: robust plants with mid-green lvs; fls large, tangerine orange or red with white or purple hairs.

*M.* Angel Tang: small plants to 10cm; fls light orange with purple hairs.

*M.* Confetti: small plants which are profuse bloomers; fls fragrant, pale, with yellow tails and covered with bright pink dots.

*M.* Copper Angel: robust plants to 20cm; fls large and flat, coppery-orange.

*M.* Diana: small plants with fls more than 2.5cm diam., white overlaid with red stripes and with long yellow tails.

*M.* Doris: plants up to 15cm with fleshy lvs and usually 2 fls per infl.; fls orange, minutely spotted on the outside and with crimson stripes within and short red tails.

*M.* Falcata: tall plant, to 35cm; fls brilliant orange with red in the centre and with red tails.

*M.* Freckles: small plants to 7.5cm; fls pink or beige, heavily spotted with lavender or crimson, and with long curved tails.

*M.* Harlequin: small plants to 12.5cm; fls white, cream or pale pink, heavily striped with wine red or purple and short tails.

*M.* Heathii: vigorous plants to 25cm; fls orange or orange red and held well above the foliage.

*M.* Kimballiana: vigorous plants to 15cm; fls tubular at base, then opening widely, orange or yellow with self-coloured tails; easy to grow and flower.

*M.* Marguerite: lvs light green on plants to 12cm; fls well above the foliage, coppery orange and covered with short purple hairs, tails orange.

*M.* Measuresiana: robust plant to 15cm with long slender infl. bearing 1–2 white or pale pink fls.

*M.* Prince Charming: lvs fleshy, dark green, often purple beneath; fls often below the lvs, large and fleshy, orange striped with red and long red-hued tails.

*M.* Redwing: small plants to 12.5cm; fls on long slender infl., brilliant magenta.

*M.* Snowbird: strong plants to 12.5cm; fls large, held above the foliage, white with yellow tails.

***M. acrochordonia*** Rchb. f. See *M. trochilus*.
***M. amethystina*** Rchb. f. See *Porroglossum amethystinum*.
***M. anchorifera*** Rchb. f. See *Scaphosepalum anchoriferum*.
***M. bella*** Rchb. f. See *M. Dracula bella*.
***M. biflora*** Reg. See *M. caloptera*.
***M. brevis*** Rchb. f. See *Scaphosepalum breve*.
***M. bruchmuelleri*** hort. See *M. coriacea*.
***M. calyptrata*** Kränzl. See *M. corniculata*.
***M. candida*** Klotzsch & Karst. See *M. tovarensis*.
***M. chestertonii*** Rchb. f. See *Dracula chestertonii*.
***M. chimaera*** Rchb. f. See *Dracula chimaera*.
***M. colibri*** hort. See *M. trochilus*.
***M. cyathogastra*** Schltr. See *M. nidifica*.
***M. dayana*** Rchb. f. See *Zootrophion dayanum*.
***M. echnida*** Rchb. f. See *Porroglossum echnidum*.
***M. edwallii*** Cogn. See *Dryadella edwallii*.
***M. elephanticeps*** Rchb. f. See *M. mooreana*.
***M. ephippium*** Rchb. f. See *M. trochilus*.
***M. erythrochaete*** Rchb. f. See *Dracula erythrochaete*.
***M. estradae*** Rchb. f. See *M. ludibunda*.
***M. fragrans*** Woolw. See *M. civilis*.
***M. fulvescens*** Rolfe. See *M. schroederiana*.
***M. galeottiana*** A. Rich. & Gal. See *M. floribunda*.
***M. gibberosa*** Rchb. f. See *Scaphosepalum gibberosum*.
***M. harryana*** Rchb. f. See *M. coccinea*.
***M. herzogii*** Schltr. See *M. auropurpurea*.
***M. inflata*** Rchb. f. See *M. corniculata*.
***M. klabochorum*** Rchb. f. See *M. caudata*.
***M. laucheana*** Kränzl. ex Woolw. See *M. attenuata*.
***M. lindenii*** André. See *M. coccinea*.
***M. longicaudata*** Lem. See *M. infracta*.
***M. militaris*** Rchb. f. See *M. ignea*.
***M. mordax*** Rchb. f. See *Porroglossum mordax*.
***M. muscosa*** Rchb. f. See *Porroglossum muscosum*.
***M. myriostigma*** Morr. See *M. floribunda*.
***M. normanii*** hort. See *M. reichenbachiana*.
***M. pulvinaris*** Rchb. f. See *Scaphosepalum pulvinare*.
***M. punctata*** Rolfe. See *Scaphosepalum anchoriferum*.
***M. shuttleworthii*** Rchb. f. See *M. caudata*.
***M. simula*** Rchb. f. See *Dryadella simula*.
***M. swertiifolia*** Rchb. f. See *Scaphosepalum swertiifolium*.
***M. tenuicauda*** Schltr. See *M. nidifica*.
***M. triglochin*** Rchb. f. See *Trisetella triglochin*.
***M. uniflora*** HBK. See *M. bonplandii*.
***M. vampira*** Luer. See *Dracula vampira*.
***M. verrucosa*** Rchb. f. See *Scaphosepalum verrucosum*.
***M. xipheres*** Rchb. f. See *Porroglossum muscosum*.
***M. zebrina*** Porsch. See *Dryadella zebrina*.

**Masson, Francis** (1741–1805). Plant collector. Masson was the first plant collector to be sent out by the royal gardens, Kew. Born in Aberdeen, he trained as a gardener and made his way to Kew, then under the directorship of William Aiton. It was Joseph Banks who persuaded George III to award a stipend to a collector of plants and seeds to be cultivated at Kew, and Banks was to handle Masson's financial affairs for the duration of his work as Royal Collector. Masson had shown himself to be an able gardener and was willing to undertake the long sea journeys which deterred a number of other contenders for the post; he was therefore sent to the Cape on board Cook's *Endeavour* in 1772, the first wholly botanical expedition with government sponsorship.

This was the beginning of a lifetime of collecting for Masson. He stayed in South Africa for two and a half years, and this was followed by six years in the Azores and the Canaries (1776–81), and a further three years in Spain and Portugal (1783–85) before he returned to the Cape (1786–95). Masson's first stay in South Africa included several lengthy journeys to the interior with Carl Thunberg, a pupil of Linnaeus, where they collected a great many notable plants (particularly pelargoniums and heaths) despite many hardships. Among their most significant finds were *Nerine sarniensis*, *Aloe dichotoma*, *Erythrina corallodendron* and *Gardenia stellata*. James Edward Smith was to credit Masson with providing the bulk of the 1700 species of Cape plants to be found in Kew by 1800, a considerable contribution. Some may still be seen at Kew, among them the ancient cycad *Encephalartos longifolius*, collected by Masson in the 1770s. Masson's expedition to the Lesser Antilles was botanically unprofitable (with the notable exception of the discovery of *Senecio cruenta*) due to extraneous circumstances; he fought the French at Grenada in 1779 and was captured in the trenches and imprisoned, and in 1780 he was victim of a hurricane on St. Lucia in which he lost all his possessions and specimens. As a result of his second journey to the Cape, Masson introduced some 100 new species.

Masson's final expedition was to North America, a mission commissioned from the Crown by Sir John Pringle. Masson had spent some three years in England at this juncture and was anxious to be exploring again. However, the climactic change was to prove too great for him. In 1797 he set out on his last expedition, covering large parts of both Upper and Lower Canada but producing relatively little (24 new species are listed in *Hortus* Kewensis) and exasperating Banks. He died in Montreal at the age of 65.

Reports of his work and travels indicate that Masson was well-liked and respected; his unrivalled field experience more than compensated for any lack of formal training. His letters to Linnaeus indicate the significance of his contribution: in 1775, only three years into his work, he is already able to boast of more than 400 species added to the Kew collection. He was elected Fellow of the Linnean Society in 1796. Masson was also a skilled artist and partly illustrated his monograph *Stapeliae Novae* (1796). Most of his collection is now held at the British Museum. The genus *Massonia* was named in his honour.

**Massonia** Thunb. ex L. f. (For Francis Masson (1741–1805), who collected in South Africa.) Liliaceae (Hyacinthaceae). 8 species of bulbous perennial herbs. Leaves 2, usually opposite, ovate, oblong or suborbicular, rather fleshy, spreading and lying close to or directly upon soil surface. Scape very short, barely emerging from leaf cleavage; flowers fragrant, in a rounded, corymbose umbel-like head, subtended by large scarious bracts; perianth tube erect, cylindric, lobes 6, spreading or reflexed; stamens attached to mouth of tube; ovary superior; style usually exceeding stamens. Fruit a winged or deeply lobed capsule, longitudinally dehiscent; seeds many, black. Late autumn–early winter. S Africa. Z9. cf. *Daubenya*.

CULTIVATION Late autumn and early winter-flowering bulbs for sunny rockeries in essentially frost-free, mediterranean-type climates, or for the cool glasshouse (min. 7°C/45°F), *Massonia* spp. are curious rather than beautiful, holding the almost stemless flowers close against the pair of leaves which lie on the soil surface. Grown in full sun in a sandy potting mix and water moderately when in growth, reducing water after flowering for a period of dry dormancy. Propagate by surface-sown seed or by removal of offsets when dormant.

***M.depressa*** Houtt. Bulb 2–3.5cm, ovoid. Lvs 7–15×4–10cm, orbicular to oblong, acute, glabrous or with sparse marginal hairs. Fls 20–30, green, yellow, white, cream or pink to red or brown, occasionally flecked purple; tube 1–1.5cm, lobes 0.8–1cm, linear-lanceolate; fil. as long as tube, cream, yellow or green, occasionally tinged red or purple, anth. 2.5–4mm, yellow or purple. Cape Province.

***M.echinata*** L. f. Bulb 1–2cm, ovoid. Lvs 2–8×1–4cm, ovate to oblong, acute or obtuse, usually hairy, at least on margins. Fls 5–20, yellow, white or pink; tube 0.5–0.7cm, lobes 0.4–0.8cm, lanceolate, reflexed; fil. white, anth. 0.5–1.25mm, yellow or purple. Cape Province.

***M.jasminiflora*** Bak. Bulb 1–2cm, ellipsoid. Lvs 3–6×1.5–5cm, ovate to broadly oblong, acute, glabrous or occasionally with marginal hairs, rarely papillose. Fls to 15 (usually fewer), fragrant, white or pink; tube 0.8–2cm, slender, lobes 0.4–0.8cm, reflexed; anth. 1–1.5mm, green, blue, dark purple or black. Cape Province, Orange Free State, Lesotho.

***M.pustulata*** Jacq. Bulb 1–2.5cm, ovoid or spherical. Lvs 3–10×2–7cm, ovate-orbicular to oblong, acute, pustular-papillose above, especially toward apex, margins often minutely ciliate or finely toothed. Fls 15–25, pink, white, yellow or tinged green; tube 0.6–1.1cm, lobes 0.45–1cm, linear-lanceolate, reflexed; fil. 0.4–1.2cm, white, anth. 1–1.75mm, yellow or tinged red. Cape Province. Close to *M.echinata* but distinguished by lvs papillose above.

***M.amygdalina*** Bak. See *M.echinata*.
***M.angustifolia*** L. f. See *Polyxena angustifolia*.
***M.bolusiae*** Barker. See *M.echinata*.
***M.bowkeri*** Bak. See *M.jasminiflora*.
***M.brachypus*** Bak. See *M.depressa*.
***M.ensifolia*** Ker-Gawl. See *Polyxena pygmaea*.
***M.latifolia*** L. f. See *M.depressa*.
***M.longifolia*** var. ***candida*** Ker-Gawl. See *M.echinata*.
***M.odorata*** Hook. f. See *Polyxena odorata*.
***M.sanguinea*** Jacq. See *M.depressa*.
***M.scabra*** Thunb. See *M.echinata*.
***M.violacea*** Andrews. See *Polyxena pygmaea*.

**Mastichodendron** (Engl.) H.J. Lam. (From Gk *mastiche*, mastic, a tree-derived gum or resin, and *dendron*, a tree, due to the latex produced by trees of this genus.) Sapotaceae. 6 species of evergreen trees with milky latex, to at least 25m. Leaves alternate to subopposite, entire. Inflorescence axillary, or at defoliated nodes, a many-flowered cluster; sepals 5, overlapping; corolla 5-lobed, lobes lacking appendages; stamens and staminodes 5; ovary superior, locules usually 5. Fruit 1-seeded, seed with a scar shorter than half its length. W Indies, C America, Mexico, US (Florida). Z10.

CULTIVATION An ornamental evergreen with lustrous foliage, grown for shade in frost-free warm temperate and subtropical climates, and valued for its tolerance of dry conditions and nutritionally poor and alkaline soils. Grow in any well-drained soil in sun. Propagate by seed.

***M.foetidissimum*** (Jacq.) H.J. Lam. MASTIC. Tree, 6–16(–25)m, with hard, heavy, bright orange wood. Lvs to 20cm, on slender pedicels to 7cm, oblong-ovate to broadly elliptic, apex blunt, glabrous. Fls to 4mm long, green-yellow. Fr. 1–2.5cm, yellow, later black, ovoid to pyriform, 1–3 seeded. Florida and W Indies to Belize and Mexico.

For synonymy see *Sideroxylon*.

**Matricaria** L. (From Lat. *mater*, mother, name given by the early herbalists who used the plant for treating diseases of the uterus.) Compositae. About 5 species of usually annual herbs. Stems erect or ascending, usually branched, leafy. Leaves alternate, finely 2–3-pinnatisect, segments numerous, narrowly-linear. Capitula discoid or radiate, solitary or in corymbs; receptacle hemispherical to conical, often hollow, naked; phyllaries in 2 to several series, imbricate, margins scarious; ray florets female, white; disc florets tubular, bisexual, yellow. Fruit a more or less laterally compressed, obovoid cypsela, with 3–10 ribs; pappus a small corona or absent. Eurasia.

CULTIVATION The aromatic *M.recutita*, often found in cornfields, is sometimes cultivated in herb gardens having similar fragrance and medicinal uses to chamomile, although it is more bitter to taste, and usually considered inferior in effect. Sow seed *in situ* in late summer, or under glass in spring, into a sunny position in any well drained soil.

***M.aurea*** (L.) Schultz-Bip. Annual herb, 4–25cm. Stems slender, decumbent or ascending, often flexuous, basally branched. Lvs 5–25×3–10mm; seg. with a sharp point. Capitula 1 to numerous, discoid, 4–7mm diam.; peduncles 0.5–2.5cm; receptacle conical, hollow; phyllaries with brown margins. Fr. 1mm, pale to dark brown; pappus 1mm, scarious. Spring. W Mediterranean, SW Asia to W Himalayas.

***M.matricarioides*** (Less.) Porter PINEAPPLE WEED. Annual herb, 5–45cm, strongly aromatic. Stems erect or ascending, much-branched above and often also from base, branches rigid. Lvs 2–6×1–2cm, crowded, glabrous; seg. flattened, acute, bristle-pointed. Capitula discoid, 1–40, occasionally to 1cm diam.; peduncles 0.2–3cm; receptacle conical, hollow; phyllaries with colourless margins; florets green-yellow. Fr. to 2mm, pale brown; pappus membranous. Summer. NE Asia, elsewhere introduced.

***M.recutita*** L. SWEET FALSE CHAMOMILE; WILD CHAMOMILE; GERMAN CHAMOMILE. Annual herb, sweetly scented, 15–60cm. Stems erect or ascending, usually much-branched above. Lvs 4–7cm; seg. acute, well-separated. Capitula radiate, 1 to 120, 1–2.5cm diam.; peduncles 3–10cm; receptacle conical, hollow; phyllaries with pale margin; ray florets 10–20, white, soon deflexed, 6–9×2–3mm, occasionally absent. Fr. 1mm, pale grey; pappus very small or absent, rarely conspicuous. Summer. Europe, W Asia to India.

***M.africana*** P. Bergius. See *Oncosiphon africanum*.
***M.asteroides*** L. See *Boltonia asteroides*.
***M.capensis*** L. See *Oncosiphon africanum*.
***M.capensis*** hort. See *Tanacetum parthenium*.
***M.caucasica*** (Willd.) Poir. See *Tripleurospermum caucasicum*.
***M.chamomilla*** L. See *M.recutita*.
***M.coreanum*** Lév. & Vaniot. See *Dendranthema coreanum*.
***M.globifera*** (Thunb.) Fenzl ex Harv. See *Oncosiphon piluliferum*.
***M.grandiflora*** hort. See *Tripleurospermum inodorum*.
***M.grandiflora*** (Thunb.) Fenzl ex Harv. See *Oncosiphon grandiflorum*.
***M.inodorum*** L. See *Tripleurospermum inodorum*.
***M.maritima*** L. See *Tripleurospermum maritimum*.
***M.oreades*** Boiss. See *Tripleurospermum oreades*.
***M.parthenium*** L. See *Tanacetum parthenium*.
***M.perforata*** Mérat. See *Tripleurospermum inodorum*.
***M.suffructicosa*** Fenzl ex Harv. See *Oncosiphon suffructicosum*.
***M.tchihatchewii*** (Boiss.) Voss. See *Tripleurospermum oreades* var. *tchihatchewii*.

For further synonymy see *Chamomilla* and *Cotula*.

**Matteuccia** Tod. (For C. Matteucci (1800–1868), Italian physicist.) OSTRICH FERN. Dryopteridaceae (Athyriaceae). About 4 species of medium-sized, terrestrial perennial ferns. Stock erect, stout, clothed with persistent leaf bases. Fronds dimorphic, tufted, glabrous, with free veins, fertile fronds smaller, more erect, darker green and longer-petioled than the sterile; petiole expanded at the base; sori globose, contiguous in rows, covered by the revolute leaf margin. Temperate N America, Europe, E Asia.

CULTIVATION *M.struthiopteris* is one of the most popular garden ferns, ideal for damp situations. It spreads by underground rhizomes to form colonies of tall yellow-green 'shuttlecocks'. The foliage is a delightful feature in the garden in spring but can become rather ragged late in a dry season. The fertile fronds are produced after the first flush of vegetative fronds and persist throughout the following winter. Spores are shed in mid-winter. *M.pennsylvanica* (Willd.) Raymond, the American ostrich fern, is now included in *M.struthiopteris* (the European form), the two forms are, however, slightly different; *M.pennsylvanica* has a steely blue rachis and pinnae contracted from the midpoint but not to the base. *M.orientalis* is a rare garden plant with spreading leaves. Both species are hardy to −20°C/−4°F, and prefer a damp situation, although *M.orientalis* is more tolerant of drought. Leaves of *M.struthiopteris* will turn yellow and burn if planted in full sun. *M.struthiopteris* can be invasive, therefore be prepared to prune off unwanted side crowns. Propagate by separating these side crowns, or by spore in mid-winter.

Ostrich ferns are not normally grown as pot plants, but if this is preferred use a loamless potting mix and water plentifully. Optimum pH is 5–6.5. Plant out in late spring.

***M.orientalis*** (Hook.) Trev. Sterile fronds to 60cm, arched, petiole one-third as long as lamina, lamina triangular, to 15cm wide, pinnate, bright green, pinnae pinnatifid, crenately lobed, coriaceous, the lowest pair deflexed; fertile fronds to 30cm, dull green becoming dark brown, pinnae distant, linear, margins revolute. India (Sikkim), W China, Japan.

***M.struthiopteris*** (L.) Tod. OSTRICH FERN; SHUTTLECOCK FERN. Stock with long underground rhizomes. Sterile fronds to 170×35cm, herbaceous; petiole very short with large, lanceolate scales at the base, pale upwards; lamina to

120×40cm, broadly lanceolate, pinnate, soft, bright green, pinnae 30–70, alternate, narrowly lanceolate, pinnatifid; fertile fronds to 60×6cm, persistent, becoming dark brown, lamina to 25×8cm, oblanceolate, pinnate, olive green, pinnae to 6cm, linear, obtuse, subcylindric because of their revolute margins; indusium cup-shaped, thin, not persisting. Europe, E Asia, E N America. Z2.

For synonymy see *Onoclea* and *Struthiopteris*.

**Matthiola** R. Br. (For Pierandrea Mathioli (1500–77), Italian physicist and botanist.) STOCK; GILLYFLOWER. Cruciferae. 55 species of annual or perennial herbs, occasionally subshrubs, to 80cm. Leaves usually simple, sometimes pinnatifid, entire or toothed. Inflorescence a terminal raceme, dense to lax, elongating in fruit; flowers often nocturnally fragrant; sepals 4, erect, saccate at base; petals 4, long-clawed, obtuse; stamens 6, filaments free, some winged. Fruits a silique, linear, terete or laterally compressed, often with 2 horn-like projections on either side of stigma; seed usually winged. W Europe, C Asia, S Africa. Z6.

CULTIVATION *Matthiola* spp. have long been appreciated for the strong and sweet fragrance of their blooms, and are grown for bedding and as long-lasting cut flowers, under glass and outdoors.

The night-scented stock, *M. longipetala* (sometimes sold as *M. bicornis*), is grown for its delightful scent rather than ornamental merit; sow in small drifts *in situ* in spring, in sun or part shade, in an unobtrusive position where their perfume can be appreciated. They are sometimes grown in association with *Malcolmia maritima*, the Virginia stocks, or *Lobularia maritima*, sweet alyssum, to provide a more attractive combination of scent and colour than either species achieves alone.

The genus has been the subject of much horticultural improvement as a florist's flower, one of the primary aims being the production in each generation of a high percentage of the superior double blooms, which having neither pistils nor stamens are completely sterile. Some are selected for double flowers, the genetic factor for doubling is linked to cotyledon colour. This seed may bear the prefix Hansen, from the Copenhagen nursery that introduced them. Double flowers in strains of the Stockpot types are identified by the distinctive notching in the seed leaves.

Modern selections of garden stocks, largely derived from *M. incana* and *M. sinuata*, are available in an enormous range of size, from the 20cm/8in. dwarf Stockpots, to the Column types approaching a metre in height, and in colours from soft pastel pinks to deep blues and carmines, and in shades of yellow, copper and gold. They are classified horticulturally into a number of groups, the major divisions in cultural requirements being between the annuals, the biennials and the intermediate types.

The annuals are by far the largest group, and include the Ten-week (flowering ten weeks from sowing) and the dwarf, bushy Trisomic seven-week races. Trisomic individuals have an additional chromosome, and are frequently less fertile than diploids.

Annuals are classified into a number of strains of different form, habit, and garden use, thus: (a) Ten-week Dwarf Large-flowering: compact, free flowering, to 30cm/12in., excellent for bedding purposes. (b) Ten-week Excelsior (Column): of upright habit, to 80cm, producing the single columnar densely flowered spike valued by florists; for cultivation in the glasshouse or outdoors and excellent for cutting. The Pacific strain is also of this columnar type, and better suited to outdoor cultivation. (c) Ten-week Giant Imperial: of bushy and branching habit, to 60cm/24in., with long well-shaped spikes; for cutting and bedding. (d) Ten-week Giant Perfection: of erect and bushy habit, to 70cm/28in., with long spikes of large flowers. For bedding cutting and exhibition. (e) Ten-week Mammoth or Beauty: erect, bushy and compact, to 45cm/18in., producing several spikes of large flowers; for bedding, cutting and for glasshouse cultivation for winter bloom. (f) Perpetual-flowering, or All the Year Round: dwarf, vigorous plants, with large spikes of pure white flowers, excellent for cutting, and pot culture. The other major divisions comprise the Brompton stocks, erect and bushy biennials, to 45cm/18in., used for bedding. The Intermediate, or East Lothian stocks which, when treated as annuals, flower to follow on from the Ten-week stocks, are also grown as biennials for flowering in spring and early summer.

Grow all types in sun, in a fertile, well-drained, neutral or slightly alkaline soil. Sow seeds of annuals in early spring under glass, at 15°C/60°F. Grow on in well-ventilated conditions at 10°C/50°F; water moderately, allowing to become almost dry between waterings. Harden off and plant out after danger of frost is passed; stake tall varieties. In zones that do not experience hot humid summers, seed may be sown *in situ*, in spring.

To ensure double flowers, seed stock must be from a selected race, sown at 13–18°C/55–65°F. On emergence of the first pair of leaves, the temperature is dropped to at least below 10°C/50°F, and preferably to 7°C/45°F. The genetic difference in cotyledon colour should then be quite distinct; those with yellow green, or pale coloured cotyledons are double-flowered, dark green seedlings may be discarded. In the Trisomic seven-week strains, after pricking out and growing on in the usual way, doubles should become apparent at four-leaf stage, although the difference is less clear cut; the sturdier seedlings are likely to be double. Stocks of the 'Stockpot' type, a dwarf strain grown for bedding, cutting and pot plants, exhibit notched seed leaves in double-flowered plants.

For glasshouse flowers, sow from late summer, in succession through till mid-winter, spacing in the glasshouse border at 15–20cm/6–8in., or given a final pot size of 10–15cm/4–6in. Use a porous, medium-fertility, loam-based propagating mix. Maintain a temperature of about 10°C/50°F; at temperatures above 15°C/60°F bud initiation may be inhibited, so keep cool and well ventilated. Liquid feed weekly, as the roots fill their pots.

Sow biennials in summer, in a seed bed or lightly shaded frame, and overwinter in the cold glasshouse or frost-free frame, and plant out in early spring. Provide cloche protection if overwintering outdoors, in all but the mildest area.

A bacterial leaf spot, leaf rot and stem rot of stocks is caused by *Xanthomonas incamae*. The disease is seed-borne and subsequently spread by water splash. It can be controlled by soaking seed in hot water (54°C/130°F for 10/33ft minutes) but is not common in UK so treatment is not usually necessary. The disease known as canker (*Leptosphaeria maculans*, conidial state *Phoma lingam*) causes damping off as well as stem canker. Elongated sunken lesions develop at ground level and are dotted with the black pycnidia of the fungus; small, circular, brown leaf spots also occur. The disease is seed-borne but commercial seed will usually be from healthy plants and treated with a fungicide. Stocks can also be affected by black root rot (*Thielaviopsis basicola*), club root (*Plasmodiophora brassicae*), damping-off, foot and root rot (*Phytophthora* spp. *Phythium* spp. *Rhizoctonia solani*) and downy mildew (*Peronospora parasitica*). Flower colour breaks, leaf distortion and mottling can be caused by viruses including cucumber mosaic virus.

Stocks can become infested in Europe and North America by polyphagous species of aphids, caterpillars of the diamond-back moth (*Plutella xylostella*), flea beetles (*Phyllotreta* spp.) and a root fly, namely cabbage root fly (*Delia brassicae*).

***M. fruticulosa*** (L.) Maire. Perenn. Base woody. Lvs oblanceolate-linear, somewhat white-hairy, entire to wavy-toothed. Sep. 6–14mm; pet. 12–28mm, yellow-purple. Fr. 25–12×1–3mm, cylindrical; stigma usually horned. S Europe.

***M. incana*** (L.) R. Br. BROMPTON STOCK. Bienn. subshrub, 30–80cm. Stems woody at base, erect, branching. Lvs lanceolate, coarsely hairy, rarely wavy-toothed. Sep. 9–15mm; pet. 2–3cm×4–12mm, usually purple, sometimes pink or white. Fr. 4.5–16cm×3–5mm, somewhat compressed. Summer–autumn. S & W Europe. 'Annua': early-flowering; annual.

***M. longipetala*** (Vent.) DC. NIGHT-SCENTED STOCK. Annual, 8–50cm. Stems simple or many-branched. Lvs oblong-linear, simple or pinnatisect, entire or toothed. Raceme lax; sep. 10mm, densely stellate-pubesc., hooded at tip; pet. 1.5–2.5cm×2–7mm, oblong-ovate to linear, yellow, green or pink. Fr. 4.5–15cm×1–2.5mm, narrow-linear, slightly compressed, ascending, hairy, horned. Greece to SW Asia, S Ukraine.

***M. odoratissima*** (Bieb.) R. Br. Evergreen subshrub, 30–60cm. Stem erect, branching, woody at base. Lvs white downy, toothed or pinnatifid. Fls sweet-scented in the evening; sep. 20–30×3–5mm, pale buff becoming mauve-bronze. Fr. 8.5–18×2–4mm, compressed, not horned. Summer. Bulgaria, Caucasus, Iran.

***M. tricuspidata*** (L.) R. Br. Annual, 7–35cm. Lvs oblong, obtuse, wavy-toothed, lvs on flowering stems wavy to pinnatifid. Racemes flexuous, many-fld; sep. 7–11mm; pet. 15–22mm, bright lilac, paler near base. Fr. 2.5–10cm×2–3mm, cylindrical, horizontal or deflexed, 3-horned. Summer. Mediterranean.

***M. annua*** Sweet. See *M. incana*.
***M. fenestralis*** R. Br. See *M. incana*.
***MM. scabra*** L. See *Guettarda scabra*.
***M. tristis*** R. Br. See *M. fruticulosa*.
For further synonymy see *Cheiranthus*.

**Mattiastrum** (Boiss.) Brand.
***M. himalayense*** (Klotzsch) Brand. See *Paracaryum himalayense*.
***M. lithospermifolium*** (Lam.) Brand. See *Paracaryum lithospermifolium*.
***M. racemosum*** (Schreb.) Brand. See *Paracaryum racemosum*.

**Matucana** Britt. & Rose (After Matucana, a village in Peru.) Cactaceae. 7 or more species of low, simple or clustering terrestrial cacti; stems globose to short-cylindric; ribs few to numerous, broad, low, more or less tuberculate; spines numerous, fine, to few or absent. Flower subapical, funnelform to narrowly tubular-funnelform, diurnal, in various colours; floral areoles naked or hairy; limb usually more or less zygomorphic, often narrow, rarely regular (*M. aureiflora*): filaments of lower stamens coalescent at base to form a diaphragm over the nectar-chamber (except in *M. madisoniorum* and *M. oreodoxa*); staminodal hairs sometimes also present. Fruit hollow, splitting longitudinally from the base, the pericarpel somewhat fleshy at first, later dry; seeds broadly oval to hat-shaped, 1.2–1.6×1.4–2mm, black-brown, more or less shiny, ruminate or not; relief low-domed; hilum large, basal, impressed or deeply impressed; micropyle sometimes projecting. Peru. The genus, which is only weakly differentiated (mainly by habit) from *Oreocereus*, has been divided into four groups on details of seed structure (hilum-micropylar region; Bregman et al., in *Succulenta* 69: 139–142. 1990).

CULTIVATION Grow in a cool frost-free greenhouse (min. 2–7°C/35–45°F), use 'standard' cactus compost: moderate to high inorganic content (more than 50% grit), pH 6–7.5; full sun; low air-humidity; keep dry from mid-autumn until early spring, except for light misting on warm days in late winter.

***M. aurantiaca*** (Vaupel) F. Buxb. Simple or clustering; stems to 15×15cm, flattened-globose to globose or short-cylindric, epidermis dark shiny green; ribs usually about 16, often somewhat spiralled, tuberculate; areoles to 8(–15)mm, elliptic, elongate, ending in a groove to the base of the tubercle above; spines red-brown below and yellow-brown above at first; central spines 3–7, up to 4.5cm, suberect or horizontal, radial spines *c*16–18, 0.5–2.5cm, subpectinate and recurved. Fl. 7–9×5–7cm, tubular-funnelform, orange-red; tube slightly curved, relatively thick, 12–17mm diam.; scales numerous; areoles densely hairy with dark brown hairs to nearly naked; limb slightly to strongly oblique; anth. yellow; stigmas yellow-green. Fr. 1–2cm diam., globose, red-tinged yellow with red-brown scales, splitting longitudinally. N Peru. Very variable in habit, spination and flowers. A large number of introductions have been described as separate species, such as *M. ritteri* and *M. weberbaueri*. Z9.

***M. aureiflora*** Ritter. Simple; stem to 13cm diam., flattened-globose; ribs 11–27, tuberculate, shiny grey-green; areoles oval, 5–8×*c*2mm, 7–11mm apart; spines *c*10–12, 7–18mm, subpectinate, yellow- or yellow-brown above, darker below, 1–4 more central developed on old plants only, to 2.5cm. Fl. 3–4.5×4–5cm, regular, funnelform, bright golden yellow; tube slender, flared; floral areoles sparsely hairy; tepals broadly spreading; stigmas pale green or nearly white. Fr. *c*14×10mm, ovoid, red-green or tinged purple, drying and splitting longitudinally. Peru (Cajamarca). Z9.

***M. haynei*** (Otto ex Salm-Dyck) Britt. & Rose. Usually simple but some forms clustering; stem to 60×10cm, globose to short-cylindric; ribs 25–30, tuberculate; areoles small, close-set, woolly at first, eventually glabrous; central spines usually 3, 3.5–5cm, dark-tipped, developed on plants of flowering size, radial spines *c*30, to 2cm, bristly, glassy white to yellow-brown. Fl. 6–7×3.5cm, apical, nearly regular, scarlet to purple-crimson; scales small; floral areoles naked; limb scarcely oblique, the seg. acute; anth. yellow; stigmas green. Fr. globose, small. N Peru. Z9.

***M. madisoniorum*** (Hutch.) G. Rowley. Simple; stem to 10(–30)×8–15cm, globose to shortly columnar, epidermis papillose, grey-green, viscid; ribs 7–12, obscure; areoles 2–2.5cm apart; spines absent or 1–3 on mature plants, 4–5 on cultivated seedlings, equal, 5–6cm, curved or twisted irregularly, dark brown to almost black at first. Fl. 8–10×4.5–5cm, apical, erect, almost regular, orange-red; tube straight or slightly curved; scales distant; floral areoles with dark brown hairs; limb spreading, not or only slightly oblique; staminal diaphragm absent; anth. and stigmas yellow. Fr. *c*2cm diam., globose, splitting longitudinally. N Peru (Amazonas). Z9.

***M. myriacantha*** (Vaupel) F. Buxb. Usually simple; stem to 30×7–12cm, globose to short-cylindric, green; ribs 30–40, straight, tuberculate; tubercles conic, 5–8mm; areoles 4–7mm apart, round to oval, 2.5–4mm; spines 25–50, 1–3cm, yellow or white to red-brown, the most central porrect. Fl. 5–7×4–5.5cm, tubular-funnelform; pericarpel *c*8mm diam.; tube deep pink; floral areoles described as with bearing numerous red-brown hairs to 2cm, but naked or with sparse hairs in cultivated forms; limb slightly to strongly oblique; tepals varying from deep pink to almost white. Fr. *c*1cm diam., globose, green. Peru (Amazonas). Z9.

***M. oreodoxa*** (Ritter) Slaba. Usually simple; stem to 8cm diam., globose, grass-green to dark green; ribs 7–12, 3–6mm high, with low, rounded tubercles; areoles 8–15mm apart, round to oval, 1–3mm; spines pale brown, straight or curved; central spines 0–2, 1.5–4cm, radial spines 4–10, 1–3cm. Fl. 4–6×3cm, regular, slender funnelform, orange-yellow; tube slender, flared; floral areoles sparsely hairy or naked; tepals broadly spreading; nectar-chamber open, not closed by the lower fil. bases. Fr. *c*14×8mm, ovoid, red-green to pink. Peru (Ancash). Z9.

***M. paucicostata*** Ritter. Clustering from the base; stems 7–15×4–7cm, globose to ovoid, dark green; ribs 7–11, broad, straight, with conic tubercles; areoles 1–1.5cm apart, round or oval, 2–3mm; spines red-brown at first, later grey, curved, persistent; central spines 0–1, to 3cm, radial spines 4–8, 5–30mm. Fl. 6×3cm, red; pericarpel 6mm diam., with white hairs; tube curved; limb oblique. Fr. *c*8×11mm, depressed-globose, green. Peru (Ancash). Z9.

***M. ritteri*** Buining. Resembling *M. aurantiaca*; to 3–5×5–10cm, depressed-globose, becoming taller in cult.; epidermis very dark green; ribs 12–22, 1cm broad; areoles 1–2cm apart, oval, 5–10×3–6mm; spines black-brown at first, later grey; central spines 1–2(–5), 2–4cm, radial spines 7–10(–14). Fl. 7–9×4.5–5cm; pericarpel 4mm diam.; tube slender, 5–6mm diam.; floral areoles with tepals carmine-red, edged violet, paler towards base. Fr. 1–1.5cm diam., shiny red, tinged green. May/June. Peru (La Libertad). Z9.

***M. weberbaueri*** (Vaupel) Backeb. Resembling *M. aurantiaca*; usually simple; stem to 20×12cm, depressed-globose to short-cylindric, green; ribs 18–30, somewhat spiralled, tuberculate; areoles *c*10mm apart, round to elliptic, to 7mm; spines 25–30, 1–5cm, golden yellow to dark brown. Fl. 6×3cm; tubular-funnelform, yellow or orange-red; pericarpel *c*8mm diam.; limb slightly to strongly oblique. Fr. *c*8mm diam., ovoid, green and red. NE Peru (Amazonas). Z9.

***M. icosagona*** (Kunth) F. Buxb. See *Cleistocactus icosagonus*.
For further synonymy see *Borzicactus*.

**Maughaniella** L. Bol.
***M. luckhoffii*** (L. Bol.) L. Bol. See *Diplosoma luckhoffii*.

**Maurandya** Ortega.
***M. barclaiana*** Lindl. See *Asarina barclaiana*.
***M. erubescens*** (D. Don) A. Gray. See *Asarina erubescens*.
***M. lophospermum*** L.H. Bail. See *Asarina lophospermum*.
***M. purpurea*** hort. See *Asarina purpusii*.
***M. scandens*** (D. Don) A. Gray non (Cav.) Pers. See *Asarina lophospermum*.
***M. scandens*** (Cav.) Pers. See *Asarina scandens*.

**Mauria** Kunth.
***M. schickendantzii*** Hieron. ex Engl. See *Schinus latifolius*.
***M. simplicifolia*** Humb. & Kunth ex Hook. & Arn. See *Lithrea caustica*.

**Maxillaria** Ruiz & Pav. (From Lat. *maxilla*, jaw, referring to the supposed resemblance of the column and lip to the jaws of an insect.) Orchidaceae. Over 300 species of epiphytic, occasionally lithophytic, rarely terrestrial orchids, variable in size. Rhizome long or short, horizontal or ascending. Pseudobulbs large, small or almost absent, usually 1-leafed at apex and usually enclosed in sheaths, some of which may be leaf-bearing. Inflorescence always single-flowered; peduncles arising singly or in groups from base of pseudobulbs or axils of sheaths; flowers red, brown, yellow, white or mottled; sepals subequal, the lateral sepals joined at base to the column foot and forming a mentum with it; petals similar to sepals but usually smaller; lip attached to column foot, concave, entire or trilobed; column erect with a short foot, stout, anterior surface concave; anther terminal, with an operculum; pollinia 4, ovoid, attached to oblong stipe. Capsule erect, ovoid or obovoid. Tropical America from W Indies and Mexico to Brazil, with 1 species in Florida. Z10.

CULTIVATION Cool or intermediate-growing orchids requiring an open bark mix, a brief winter rest, and light shade. See ORCHIDS.

***M. acicularis*** Herb. Pseudobulbs 1.5–2cm, clustered, ribbed, 2-lvd. Lvs to 7cm, acute, the midvein impressed above. Fls wine red, lip dark purple; sep. and pet. elongated, subacute; lip obscurely trilobed; column yellow. Brazil.

***M. alba*** Lindl. Rhiz. ascending; pseudobulbs 4–5×2cm, ellipsoid, compressed, 1-lvd. Lvs to 30×1.5–2cm, ligulate, obtuse, slightly bilobed at apex, light green. Peduncles with several scarious bracts, arising in axils of sheaths on new growths; fls white; sep. 20×5–6mm, oblong-ligulate, acuminate; pet. 16–18×4–5mm, oblong-elliptical, acute; lip 11–12×4.5–6mm, fleshy, obscurely trilobed with callus running from base to about middle, midlobe oblong-ovate, thickened at apex; column 8–9mm; ovary 2–3cm. Throughout most of tropical America.

***M. arachnites*** Rchb. f. Epiphytic or lithophytic; pseudobulbs small, compressed, 1–3-lvd. Lvs 15–25×3cm, lanceolate, acute, light green. Infl. to 15cm; fls fragrant, sep. yellow-green, pet. white, lip golden yellow, all flushed with maroon; sep. 55–57×9mm, lanceolate, acuminate, margins recurved; pet. 45×13mm, lanceolate, acuminate, incurved, margins only slightly recurved; lip 17×10mm, trilobed towards apex, lateral lobes erect, midlobe truncate, all lobes with denticulate margin; column about 7mm. Venezuela, Colombia, Ecuador.

***M. arbuscula*** Rchb. f. Rhiz. slender, branched, with or without pseudobulbs. Lvs distichous, 2cm, linear-ligulate, unequally bilobed at apex. Peduncles axillary; fls somewhat globose, 1cm diam.; sep. and pet. white sometimes spotted with red, lip deep red; sep. and pet. ligulate; lip ligulate with a slight constriction just before the enlarged and fleshy apex and a linear callus in the centre. Peru, Ecuador.

***M. aurea*** hort. ex Rchb. f. Terrestrial; rhiz. creeping or ascending; pseudobulbs ovoid, set 6–10cm apart, with numerous basal sheaths, some leaf-bearing. Lvs 15–25×2–3cm, linear-elliptic. Infl. in clusters from axils of basal sheaths; fls yellow, the lip with brown marks; sep. 10–15mm, lanceolate-elliptic; pet. slightly smaller; lip recurved. Colombia.

***M. callichroma*** Rchb. f. Pseudobulbs clustered, to 5×1.5cm, ovoid, compressed, dark brown, enclosed in long sheaths, 1-lvd. Lvs 30–45×4–5cm, with folded, petiolate base about 8cm. Infl. arising from base of pseudobulb; peduncle covered with loose sheaths, pale green with dark scales; fls yellow and white flushed with dark red; dorsal sep. to 55×8mm, lanceolate, mucronate, lateral sep. slightly shorter; pet. to 52×5mm, lanceolate, acute; lip to 24×14mm, trilobed in apical half, the base, lateral lobes and callus pubesc., lateral lobes erect, midlobe about 9×8mm, fleshy, ovate. Venezuela, Colombia.

***M. camaridii*** Rchb. f. Rhiz. to 150cm, covered in grey sheaths, branched, pendent, straggling, the ends upturned; pseudobulbs to 8×2.5cm, ovoid, compressed, 1–2-lvd, set close together at base of plant, 5–12cm apart further up. Infl. arising from axils of sheathing lvs towards end of rhiz.; fls white, the lip yellow on midlobe, sometimes with transverse streaks of red-brown; dorsal sep. 26×7mm, oblong or oblanceolate, obtuse, lateral sep. slightly shorter and wider; pet. 24×6–7mm, oblong; lip 13×13mm, trilobed, with toothed, glandular-hairy callus towards base, lateral lobes erect, midlobe truncate. C America, W Indies, Venezuela, Colombia, Brazil, Peru.

***M. cobanensis*** Schltr. Dwarf, epiphytic, 4–10cm; rhiz. short; pseudobulbs densely packed, 15–20×4–5mm, cylindrical but narrowing toward apex, slightly compressed, 1-lvd. Lvs erect or slightly spreading, 3.5–6×1–1.5cm, elliptic-ligulate, obtuse. Infl. short, arising at base of pseudobulb; fls dull pink-tan, veined with red-brown; sep. spreading, to 14mm, ligulate, apiculate, the lateral sep. oblique and forming short, obtuse mentum with column foot; pet. slightly shorter, ligulate-spathulate, obtuse, projecting forwards; lip 10×5.5mm, with longitudinal ridge from base to middle, concave, obovate, obscurely trilobed, lateral lobes rounded, midlobe quadrate, slightly emarginate; column slender, 7mm, column foot 2.5mm; ovary 7mm. Summer. Mexico to Costa Rica.

***M. coccinea*** (Jacq.) L.O. Williams ex Hodge. Robust, to 50cm; rhiz. covered with overlapping, papery sheaths; pseudobulbs to 4cm, ovoid, compressed, 1-lvd. Lvs to 35×2.5cm, linear-oblong, acute or obtuse, folded at base. Infl. clustered; peduncles wiry, 6cm; fls bright rose-pink, carmine or vermilion; sep. to 12mm, spreading, fleshy, ovate-lanceolate, acuminate, concave; pet. to 8mm, ovate or ovate-lanceolate, acute or acuminate; lip to 8mm, fleshy, trilobed, lateral lobes erect, midlobe more or less ovate, recurved; column short. Capsule beaked. Greater & Lesser Antilles.

***M. consanguinea*** Klotzsch. Rhiz. creeping; pseudobulbs elongated, somewhat compressed, ribbed, 2-lvd. Lvs oblong-lanceolate, cuspidate, folded and narrowed toward base. Peduncles clustered, to 6cm; sep. yellow, margins red, pet. pale yellow, lip yellow-white with purple spots; sep. about 25×6cm, lanceolate, acute, spreading; pet. shorter and narrower, acuminate; lip 25×10mm, trilobed with a tongue-shaped callus between the lateral lobes, lateral lobes rounded, erect, midlobe ovate, obtuse, recurved; column arched. Brazil.

***M. crassifolia*** (Lindl.) Rchb. f. Rhiz. short and stout; pseudobulbs 1.5–3×0.5–1.5cm, oblong, compressed, 1-lvd at apex, covered with sheaths, some leaf-bearing. Lvs to 45×4cm, somewhat fleshy, linear to linear-oblong, obtuse or subacute, folded at base. Infl. 1–3 from lf axils; peduncle about 1cm with a scarious bract about half way; fls campanulate, fleshy, yellow to orange, usually with purple marks; pedicel and ovary 1–2cm; sep. 14–18×5–6mm, lanceolate, acute, concave; pet. 12–15×3–3.5mm, linear-oblanceolate, sometimes curved, the edge entire or denticulate; lip 13–15×6.5–8mm, elliptic, obscurely trilobed with longitudinal, hairy callus in basal half, margins entire or denticulate; column arched, 8–10mm. US (Florida), C America, W Indies, Venezuela, Brazil.

***M. crassipes*** Kränzl. Rhiz. creeping; pseudobulbs to 25×10mm, conical, set 1–1.5cm apart, 2-lvd at apex. Lvs to 9×1.5cm, lanceolate, acute, petiolate, fleshy-coriaceous. Infl. to 12cm; fls yellow edged with red, apex of lip purple, column tinged lilac; sep. 25×5mm, ovate-lanceolate, acuminate; pet. 18×3mm, ligulate-lanceolate, acute; lip 15×7–8mm, trilobed in apical half, lateral lobes erect, midlobe oblong, the edge undulate; column arched, 8mm. Brazil.

***M. cucullata*** Lindl. Pseudobulbs 4–5cm, elliptic, 1-lvd. Lvs to 20cm, ligulate, obtuse. Peduncle to 13cm, stiffly erect; fls dingy dark brown; sep. and pet. 25–28mm, lanceolate, acute; lip 23mm, trilobed, lateral lobes small. Mexico.

***M. curtipes*** Hook. Pseudobulbs clustered, 3.5–4×2cm, 1-lvd. Lvs about 15×2cm, broadly linear-lanceolate, acute. Infl. arising from base of pseudobulb; fls buff-yellow, underside of lip speckled with red; sep. and pet. 13–16×5mm, oblong, subacute; lip oblong in outline, obscurely trilobed with a shiny, purple-brown callus between the lobes, midlobe slightly reflexed; front of column shiny red-brown. Mexico.

***M. densa*** Lindl. Rhiz. ascending, covered with brown, scarious sheaths; pseudobulbs to 8cm, oblong, compressed, 1-lvd. Lvs to 40×5cm, linear to oblong-lanceolate, obscurely bilobed at apex. Peduncles clustered, axillary; fls variable in colour, green-white, yellow-green, white tinged with purple, dark maroon or red-brown; sep. about 10mm, linear-lanceolate, acuminate, keeled; pet. slightly smaller; lip obscurely trilobed, oblong, concave and clasping the column at base, apex channelled and recurved. Mexico, Guatemala, Honduras, Belize.

***M. desvauxiana*** Rchb. f. Epiphytic, occasionally lithophytic; rhiz. stout, creeping; pseudobulbs set close together, to 4×2.5cm, ovoid, somewhat compressed, 1-lvd. Lvs to 45×4.5cm, including folded, petiolate base to 10cm, blade elliptic, acute. Infl. arising from base of pseudobulb; peduncle 3cm, covered with overlapping, loose, tubular sheaths; fls fleshy, sep. dull apricot-yellow with maroon flush at base and apex, pet. maroon, the margins paler, lip mostly pink, deep maroon in centre, edge of midlobe almost white; sep. 25–35×13–18mm, ovate, apiculate; pet. to 30×18mm, obovate, rounded at apex; lip to 25mm, 20mm across lateral lobes, with smooth, longitudinal callus towards base, midlobe 8mm diam., the edge thin and undulate, the central part fleshy and verrucose. Guyana, French Guiana, Surinam, Venezuela, Brazil.

***M. discolor*** (Lodd.) Rchb. f. Pseudobulbs clustered, to 7cm, ovoid, compressed, 1-lvd at apex. Lvs to 35×6cm, ligulate, unequally bilobed at apex. Peduncles 4–5cm, arising from base of pseudobulb; fls waxy, sep. and pet. apricot, variably spotted maroon, lip orange with deep maroon spots; sep. 22×7mm, lanceolate, acute, rather fleshy, the margins recurved; pet. 18×4mm, oblanceolate, acute; lip 13×7mm, obscurely trilobed, fleshy, with longitudinal, glandular-hairy callus running for most of its length. Guyana, French Guiana, Venezuela.

***M. echinochila*** Kränzl. Pseudobulbs clustered, 30–35×10mm, long-ovoid, 2-lvd at apex. Lvs to 10×0.5cm, linear, acute. Fls brown; sep. 20×5–6mm, oblong, acute, lateral sep. somewhat curved; pet. similar but slightly narrower; lip 15×8mm, entire, obovate, edge undulate. Brazil.

***M. elegantula*** Rolfe. Rhiz. stout, creeping; pseudobulbs to 6cm, narrowly ellipsoid, compressed, 1-lvd at apex, with several large, distichous, basal sheaths, the uppermost usually leaf-bearing. Lvs to 30×5.5cm, oblong-elliptic, acute, petiolate; petiole to 20cm. Peduncles to 25cm, almost covered with tubular sheaths; fls large, white tinged with purple-brown; sep. and pet. spreading, sep. 25–45×15mm, oblong, acute or subacute, lateral sep. slightly longer than dorsal sep., pet. slightly shorter and narrower than dorsal sep., obliquely lanceolate, acute or acuminate; lip 17×12mm, oval in outline, obscurely trilobed, apex obtuse, recurved; column about 1cm. Peru, Ecuador.

***M. equitans*** (Schltr.) Garay. Stems almost erect, clustered, to 30cm, leafy along length when young; when older, leafy at apex and the lower part covered in grey lf-bases. Lvs to 10cm×8mm, fleshy, bilaterally flattened, straight or recurved, with purple streak near edge of sheathing base. Peduncles covered with white sheaths, arising from lf axils; sep. and pet. cream, sep. flushed with pink, lip violet-purple with white apical margin; sep. 14–15×5–6mm, oblong, acute, spreading, rather fleshy; pet. 13×3mm, narrowly lanceolate, parallel to column; lip 14×6mm, fleshy, with median callus, obscurely trilobed, midlobe 4mm diam., apex recurved. Venezuela, Guyana, Brazil, Colombia, Peru.

***M. ferdinandiana*** Barb. Rodr. Rhiz. 10–25cm, creeping, branched; pseudobulbs well spaced, ovoid, compressed, 1-lvd at apex. Lvs 6–9cm×6–8mm, linear-lanceolate, acute. Infl. 5–15mm; sep. and pet. green-white, spotted purple on outer surface, lip white with purple spots; sep. and pet. about 10×2.5–4mm, oblong, acute; lip erect, 10×8mm, broadly ovate in outline, obscurely trilobed, lateral lobes erect, midlobe suborbicular. Brazil.

***M. fletcheriana*** Rolfe. Pseudobulbs clustered, 3–5cm, oblong-ovoid, fairly compressed, 1-lvd at apex, with a pair of distichous, leaf-bearing sheaths. Lvs to 24×5.5cm, oblong or elliptic, petiolate; petiole 5–12cm. Peduncles 25–35cm, almost covered in loose sheaths; fls white or yellow with purple lines; sep. recurved or spreading, to 45×25mm, ovate, acute; pet. shorter and narrower, obliquely ovate-lanceolate, shortly acuminate, projecting forwards over column;

lip to 50×30mm, obovate in outline, with oblong, fleshy callus above middle, obscurely trilobed, lateral lobes erect, midlobe suborbicular, recurved, undulate, trilobulate; column about 1.5cm, column foot 4cm. Peru.

***M.friedrichsthalii*** Rchb. f. Rhiz. erect or pendulous; pseudobulbs clustered, to 5cm, elliptic-oblong, slightly flattened, the upper pair of sheaths usually leaf-bearing. Lvs usually 2–3, 3–18cm, ligulate, obscurely bilobed at apex. Infl. 1 to several, about 3cm; fls variable in colour and size, often not opening wide, yellow-green to green-mauve; sep. to 30mm, linear-lanceolate, acute or acuminate; pet. similar but slightly smaller; lip entire, narrowly oblanceolate, thickened at apex. Mostly summer. Mexico and Belize to Panama and Colombia.

***M.gracilis*** Lodd. Pseudobulbs clustered, 20–25×10–13mm, ovoid, compressed, 2-lvd at apex. Lvs 10–20×1–1.5cm, linear-ligulate, acute. Infl. to 10cm; fls scented, yellow, sep. and pet. flushed with purple on outer edge, lip with purple marks; sep. 17–22×5–7mm, fleshy, narrowly lanceolate, acute; pet. 12–20×2–3mm, narrowly linear-lanceolate, acute; lip erect, 12–15×7–9mm, deeply trilobed in apical half, lateral lobes erect, midlobe oblong, edge undulate-denticulate. Brazil.

***M.grandiflora*** (HBK) Lindl. Pseudobulbs to 6cm, oblong-ovoid, compressed, 1-lvd at apex, when young surrounded by distichous, overlapping sheaths of which some are leaf-bearing. Lvs 11–28×5cm, elliptic to ligulate, acute, petiolate; petiole 3–10cm, laterally compressed. Peduncles 1–2, 12–25cm, with several loose, tubular sheaths; fls slightly nodding, milk-white, scented, fleshy, 10cm diam.; sep. spreading, dorsal sep. 35–45×20mm, ovate-oblong, acute, concave, lateral sep. slightly longer and wider forming conical mentum with column foot; pet. slightly shorter and narrower than dorsal sep., elliptic-lanceolate; lip parallel to column, recurved, 25×15mm, ovate in outline, obscurely trilobed, lateral lobes erect, apex fleshy; disc with 3 calli; column arched, 12–13mm. Summer. Ecuador, Peru, Colombia, Venezuela, Guyana.

***M.juergensii*** Schltr. Rhiz. with short, erect branches so that plant eventually forms a dense mound; pseudobulbs 1cm, ribbed. Lvs needle-like, 3–4cm. Fls 12mm diam., very dark red, almost black, the lip with wet-looking surface; sep. and pet. about 6mm, ovate, obtuse; lip tongue-like. Autumn–winter. Brazil.

***M.kautskyi*** Pabst. Slender, tufted, epiphytic, with very short rhiz.; pseudobulbs 15×15mm, globose, wrinkled, 4-angled, 2-lvd. Lvs 17–25×4–5mm, narrowly linear, acute, midvein prominent below. Infl. very short, arising from base of pseudobulb; fls spreading or erect, yellow, lip spotted with dark purple towards apex; sep. 13–15×5mm, narrowly oblong, acute, lateral sep. slightly oblique; pet. linear, acute; lip 12×8.5mm, broadly elliptic in outline, shortly clawed at base, trilobed in apical quarter, lateral lobes small, rounded, midlobe 3×4mm, oblong; column 8mm, slender, curved; ovary 12mm. Brazil.

***M.lepidota*** Lindl. Epiphytic or terrestrial; pseudobulbs clustered, to 5×1.5cm, ovoid, covered with sheaths of which 1 may be leaf-bearing, 1-lvd at apex. Lvs linear-ligulate, to 35×2cm including folded petiolate base 2–4cm long. Peduncles arising from base of pseudobulb, to 12cm, red towards base, covered with loose, tubular sheaths; sep. and pet. yellow, marked with red at base, lip creamy yellow with maroon marks; sep. to 60×7mm, lanceolate, acuminate, dorsal sep. projecting forwards, lateral sep. spreading; pet. to 45×4mm, curved-lanceolate, acuminate, projecting forwards; lip 20×12mm, fleshy, with raised central callus bordered with hairs, obscurely trilobed, midlobe covered with yellow-green farina, apex dorsally keeled, mucronate. Venezuela, Colombia, Ecuador.

***M.linearis*** C. Schweinf. Rhiz. erect, elongated, with very short branches, covered with overlapping, tubular, warty sheaths. Lvs in groups of 4–6, 13.5–40×0.5cm, narrowly linear, acuminate, the margins rolled back. Peduncles spreading, to 7cm, covered with tubular sheaths, arising in clusters from axils of leaf-bearing sheaths towards apex of stem and on branches; dorsal sep. 26×3.5mm, linear, acute, mucronate, lateral sep. slightly wider and curved; pet. like lateral sep. but smaller; lip parallel to column, recurved, 10mm, with longitudinal callus in basal two-thirds, trilobed near apex, lateral lobes erect, semi-elliptic, midlobe about 2mm, fleshy, narrowly triangular; column 5mm. Peru.

***M.luteo-alba*** Lindl. Epiphytic or terrestrial; pseudobulbs clustered, ovoid, compressed, dark brown, covered with scarious sheaths, 1-lvd at apex. Lvs to 50×5cm, including folded, petiolate base, linear-ligulate, rigid, midvein prominent below. Peduncles to 12cm, covered with green sheaths spotted with brown; fls white and yellow, side lobes of lip with purple-brown veining; sep. 52×8mm, lanceolate, acute, margins recurved, lateral sep. somewhat curved; pet. 46×6mm, projecting forwards, lanceolate-falcate, margins recurved; lip 25×14mm, with longitudinal, pubesc. callus, thick-textured, lateral lobes small, midlobe broadly ovate. Costa Rica, Panama, Venezuela, Colombia, Ecuador.

***M.macrura*** Rchb. f. Pseudobulbs compressed, spherical, forming row on rhiz. Lvs ligulate, acuminate. Peduncles clustered; fls pink-tan, lip with red longitudinal streaks, to 12cm diam.; sep. and pet. linear-lanceolate, caudate; lip trilobed, shortly clawed at base, oblong in outline, with oblong callus between lobes. Mexico.

***M.marginata*** Fenzl. Very similar to *M.picta*, differing mainly in rather smaller fls; sep. dull yellow with brown margin and tinged with brown towards apex; lip short, white, edged and irregularly spotted with brown, margin slightly undulate, lateral lobes short. Brazil.

***M.meleagris*** Lindl. Rhiz. short; pseudobulbs clustered, 2–5.5×1–2cm, ellipsoid or ovoid, compressed, 1-lvd at apex. Lvs 15–40×0.5–2cm, linear, obtuse, coriaceous. Infl. to 8cm, arising from base of new growth; fls scented of coconut, variable in size and colour, buff-orange, buff-olive or flesh-coloured, marked with dark red, lip dark red; sep. 12–30×4–7mm, elliptic, acute, acuminate or obtuse; pet. similar but shorter and adnate to dorsal sep.; lip 7–16×4–8mm, trilobed towards base, recurved, with transverse ridge between the small, erect, lateral lobes, midlobe fleshy, ovate-orbicular to elliptic. Mexico, Guatemala, Panama.

***M.mosenii*** Kränzl. Rhiz. stout, 1cm diam.; pseudobulbs set obliquely, about 2cm apart, 4–4.5cm×3.5–5mm, 4- or 8-angled, enlarged at apex, glossy green-black, 2-lvd at apex, with large basal sheaths. Lvs 10–15cm×6–7mm, linear-lanceolate, long-acuminate, rigid. Peduncles solitary, of similar length to pseudobulbs, with large, almost transparent brown sheaths; fls yellow-brown, spotted with dull lilac inside; dorsal sep. 20×4mm, lanceolate, acute, concave, lateral sep. 20×5mm, oblong-lanceolate, forming short, obtuse mentum with column foot; pet. 15×4mm, obovate-oblong, obtuse; lip 17×6–7mm, almost entire. Brazil.

***M.nasuta*** Rchb. f. Pseudobulbs to 9×4cm, bilaterally flattened, clustered. Lvs to 60×4cm, linear, unequally bilobed at apex, glossy bright green. Peduncles about 8cm, arising at base of pseudobulbs; fls yellow-green flushed with maroon, lip mostly maroon or red, with yellow apex; sep. 32–37×7–8mm, lanceolate, acuminate, rather fleshy, margins somewhat recurved, apices stiff and keeled; pet. 25×6mm, oblanceolate, acute; lip 18×7mm, with a sticky, longitudinal callus towards base, obscurely trilobed, apex thick and keeled. Guatemala, Costa Rica, Venezuela, Colombia, Brazil.

***M.nigrescens*** Lindl. Pseudobulbs long-ovoid, compressed, the base covered with grey sheaths, 1-lvd. Lvs to 35×3.5cm, linear, rigid, folded and petiolate at base, the margins somewhat recurved. Peduncles to 14cm, covered with green sheaths marked with brown; sep. and pet. maroon-red, orange-maroon at apex, grading to yellow at base of sep., lip maroon-black; sep. 45–60×7–10mm, lanceolate, acute, dorsal sep. erect, lateral sep. spreading or reflexed; pet. 40–55×6mm, falcate-lanceolate, somewhat spreading; lip to 17×12mm with longitudinal callus at base, obscurely trilobed, apex fleshy. Venezuela, Colombia.

***M.ochroleuca*** Lindl. var. ***longipes*** Sander. Usually terrestrial, sometimes epiphytic; pseudobulbs clustered, to 8×4cm, ovoid, very compressed, ribbed, 1-lvd at apex and with 1–2 leaf-bearing sheaths at base. Lvs to 45×3cm, linear, keeled, unequally bilobed at apex. Peduncles arising in clusters from axils of sheathing lvs, to 16cm, with several sheaths; fls strongly scented, sep. and pet. white turning to yellow in apical half, lip white with orange midlobe; sep. 32×3.5mm, narrowly lanceolate, acute; pet. 29×2mm, narrowly lanceolate, acuminate; lip 11×6mm, with sparsely hairy callus in basal half, trilobed about halfway, lateral lobes erect, obtuse, sparsely hairy, midlobe fleshy, rough-textured, with scattered hairs below; ovary to 2cm. Venezuela, Brazil.

***M.pachyphylla*** Schltr. Epiphytic; rhiz. pendent, usually curving up at tip, covered with brown sheaths; pseudobulbs set close together obliquely on rhiz., 25–35×7–9mm, cylindrical to conical, ribbed, 1-lvd. Lvs 10–15×1cm, spreading, oblanceolate, acute, thick-textured. Peduncles very short, about 15mm including ovary; fls pale yellow, lip yellow streaked with rose-pink near margin; sep. 18×10mm, ovate-oblong, acute, the lateral sep. oblique and forming blunt mentum with column foot; lip 17×17mm, with linear callus in basal third, trilobed, clawed at base, apex enlarged and obtuse, lateral lobes rounded; column 10mm, slightly curved, column foot 4mm. Brazil. var. ***brunneo-fusca*** Hoehne. Fls deep yellow-brown.

***M.parkeri*** Hook. Pseudobulbs clustered, 3.5×2–3cm, ovoid to subglobose, somewhat compressed, with large, spotted, grey-brown sheaths with incurved margins at base, 1-lvd at apex. Lvs with petiolate base about 5cm long, blade to 45×4cm, linear-ligulate, acute. Peduncles to 7cm, covered with sheaths; sep. yellow, pet. white with maroon veining towards base, lip orange-yellow, lateral lobes maroon-veined, midlobe margin white, column maroon with white apex; sep. 32–33×18–20mm, ovate, obtuse, rather fleshy, margins recurved, dorsal sep. erect, lateral sep. spreading; pet. 28×10mm, lanceolate, acute, projecting forwards; lip 23×16mm with a hairy longitudinal callus in basal half, trilobed about halfway, lateral lobes erect, obtuse, midlobe oblong-ovate, fleshy; column 10–12mm. Guyana, Surinam, Venezuela, Peru.

***M.pendens*** Pabst. Rhiz. to 2m, sometimes branched; pseudobulbs set well apart, to 6×4cm, ovoid, somewhat compressed, 1–2-lvd at apex and with 2 or more leaf-bearing sheaths with persistent bases at base of pseudobulb. Lvs to 25×5cm, lanceolate, acute, keeled. Peduncles to 5cm, arising in clusters from axils of sheathing lvs; ovary about 2cm; fls cream flushed with pink, sep. yellow at apex; sep. 16–21×4–5mm, lanceolate, acute; pet. 13–16×3–4mm, oblong, mucronate; lip difficult to flatten, 12×9mm, with basal callus with keeled veins radiating from it, trilobed about halfway, apex of midlobe deeply emarginate, erose. Guyana, Venezuela, Colombia, Brazil.

***M.picta*** Hook. Pseudobulbs clustered or set a short distance apart, to 6cm, ovoid, compressed, ribbed, 1–2-lvd at apex. Lvs to 30cm, ligulate, acute. Peduncles clustered, 12–20cm; fls large, golden yellow inside, cream-yellow outside, cross-banded and flecked with purple-brown, lip yellow-white or cream spotted with red, column red-violet; sep. about 30mm, oblong, acute, curved forwards; pet. slightly shorter and narrower, parallel to column; midlobe tongue-shaped, deflexed, lateral lobes erect. Winter. Brazil.

***M.plebeja*** Rchb. f. Rhiz. ascending; pseudobulbs oblong, compressed. Lvs ligulate, acute, keeled below apex on outer surface, folded at base. Peduncles short; fls pale yellow, the lip darker, sep. and pet. sparsely spotted with dark purple; sep. ovate, acute; pet. ligulate, acute; lip oblong in outline, obscurely trilobed in middle, with an oblong, waxy callus in basal half. Brazil.

***M.porphyrostele*** Rchb. f. Pseudobulbs clustered, to 4.5cm, broadly elliptic, 2-lvd. Lvs to 20×1.5cm, linear-ligulate, obtuse. Peduncles clustered, to 8cm; fls yellow, about 4cm diam.; sep. about 20mm, lanceolate, the tips incurved; pet. similar but shorter. Winter–spring. Brazil.

***M.reichenheimiana*** Rchb. f. Pseudobulbs clustered, to 1.5cm, subglobose but fairly compressed, 1-lvd at apex and sometimes with a leaf-bearing sheath. Lvs to 4×2.5cm, elliptic, obtuse, apiculate, fleshy, blue-green mottled with grey, sometimes with white dots on upper side, slightly tinged with maroon on edge and underneath. Peduncles to 5cm, covered with brown sheaths; sep. orange, tinged with maroon, pet. yellow-orange, lip with yellow midlobe and callus, lateral lobes dark maroon; sep. and pet. lanceolate, acuminate, projecting forwards, sep. 32–35×6mm, pet. 25×5mm; lip 15×8.5mm, with scattered glandular hairs and a longitudinal callus in basal half, trilobed in apical third, lateral lobes rounded, erect, midlobe fleshy, ovate, edge undulate; column about 5mm, apex fringed with glandular hairs. Trinidad, Costa Rica, Venezuela.

***M.ringens*** Rchb. f. Pseudobulbs set close together, to 4×2.5cm, ellipsoid or ovoid, compressed, 1-lvd. Lvs to 54×5cm (usually smaller), elliptic-oblong, petiolate; petiole to 13cm. Peduncles to 18cm, covered with green sheaths spotted with maroon; sep. and pet. yellow-cream, tinged with orange-pink at apex, lip cream, underside of apex dark maroon; sep. 18–40×6–8mm, oblong, acute, spreading; pet. to 26×5.5mm, narrowly lanceolate, obtuse; lip 13–17×6–11mm, with a longitudinal callus with scattered white hairs in basal half, trilobed in apical third, lateral lobes rounded, erect, midlobe fleshy, truncate, edge undulate; column 6–7mm. Mexico to Panama; Venezuela to Peru.

***M.rufescens*** Lindl. Very variable; rhiz. creeping; pseudobulbs usually clustered, 1.5–6cm, varying from small, subglobose, compressed to long-ovoid and 4-angled, sheaths sometimes caducous, sometimes persistent. Lvs 4–30×3–6cm, elliptic, oblong or ligulate, sometimes with petiole to 4cm. Fls variable in colour, from green-brown and cream to dull yellow or orange flushed with maroon, or maroon and white; sep. spreading, dorsal sep. 9–24×3–10mm, oblong, concave, lateral sep. similar but wider; pet. slightly shorter than dorsal sep., obliquely oblong or lanceolate; lip 8–20×6–12mm with longitudinal callus in basal half, trilobed about halfway, lateral lobes erect, midlobe truncate; column 7–16mm. Widespread in Tropical America.

***M.sanderiana*** Rchb. f. Epiphytic or lithophytic; rhiz. short or long; pseudobulbs clustered, to 5cm, subglobose to ovoid, compressed, 1-lvd. Lvs to 40×5.5cm, narrowly oblong, acute or cuspidate, leathery, petiolate; petiole to 20cm. Peduncles basal and axillary, sometimes clustered, to 25cm, covered with tubular sheaths; fls large, fleshy, sep. and pet. white flecked with violet-purple, lip dull yellow with red markings, dark purple on outer surface; dorsal sep. 60–75×20mm, oblong or oblong-lanceolate, lateral sep. wider and slightly longer, forming a conical mentum; pet. somewhat shorter; lip 30–35mm, ovate in outline, obscurely trilobed in basal half, lateral lobes erect, midlobe ovate to suborbicular, apex rounded and margin crisped; column about 15mm, the foot longer. Peru, Ecuador.

***M.sanguinea*** Rolfe. Rhiz. creeping, covered with overlapping sheaths; pseudobulbs 1–2.5cm, ellipsoid, slightly compressed. Lvs 25–40×0.4cm, narrowly linear, subacute. Peduncles short, about equalling pseudobulb; sep. red-brown, apices yellow, pet. pale yellow with red-brown spots, lip carmine-red or crimson-purple with black-purple crest; sep. 12–16×4–5mm, oblong, obtuse; pet. linear-oblong, obtuse; lip 12–14×6mm, almost entire, oblong, obtuse, with a shiny, linear callus; column 12mm, clavate. C America.

***M.seidelii*** Pabst. Dwarf epiphyte to 5cm; rhiz. ascending; pseudobulbs minute, erect, linear or linear-oblong, 2-lvd. Lvs 2.5–3cm×7–8mm, erect, awl-shaped with a groove above. Peduncles solitary, about same length as lvs, with 3 sheaths; fls white, erect; sep. 8–8.5×1.5mm, ligulate, acute, margins reflexed, lateral sep. oblique; pet. 7×1.5mm, ligulate, acute, somewhat oblique; lip 7mm, fleshy at base, lateral lobes obscure, densely puberulous, midlobe 2mm diam., narrowly obovate; column 3mm, club-shaped, curved, column foot 2mm. Brazil.

***M.sophronites*** (Rchb. f.) Garay. Rhiz. long, creeping, covered in brown sheaths; pseudobulbs 1–1.5cm, subglobose when young, later slightly compressed, dull brown, 1-lvd, set 2–4cm apart on rhiz. Lvs to 2×1cm, elliptic, unequally bilobed at apex, fleshy, light glossy green. Sep. and pet. orange-red, lip midlobe yellow with cream edge, lateral lobes cream; fls rather cup-shaped; sep. 11–13×7mm, ovate, apiculate; pet. 8×5.5mm, ovate, apiculate; lip 7×7mm, not including basal claw, with smooth callus in basal half, trilobed toward base, lateral lobes erect, rounded, with erose margins, midlobe ovate, obtuse, glandular-tubercular with erose margin. Venezuela.

***M.striata*** Rolfe. Pseudobulbs clustered, 4.5–8cm, oblong to ovoid, fairly compressed, with several pairs of sheaths, some leaf-bearing, 1-lvd at apex. Lvs to 24×4–6cm, oblong to elliptical, leathery, petiolate; petiole to 10cm. Peduncles to 30cm, covered with tubular sheaths; fls large, green-yellow with purple-red stripes, lip white, lateral lobes veined with red-purple; dorsal sep. 45–70×12mm, oblong-lanceolate, acute, concave, lateral sep. of similar length but oblique and much wider at base and acuminate, forming conical mentum about 25mm long with column foot; pet. shorter and narrower than dorsal sep., obliquely lanceolate, acuminate, tips recurved; lip 35–40mm, with linear callus in basal half, obscurely trilobed near apex, lateral lobes erect, rounded, midlobe ovate-lanceolate, recurved, margins undulate; column 11mm, column foot about 20mm. Peru.

***M.tarumaensis*** Hoehne. Pseudobulbs to 3cm, somewhat compressed. Lvs to 50×2.5cm, ligulate, folded at base. Peduncle to 5cm; sep. and pet. yellow-brown, lip purple-red with longitudinal green stripe; sep. 14×6mm, oblong-elliptic, obtuse; pet. similar but narrower and acute; lip 13×7mm, obscurely trilobed, elliptic in outline, with raised, sticky callus. Brazil, Venezuela.

***M.tenuifolia*** Lindl. Rhiz. ascending; pseudobulbs about 2.5cm, ovoid, set 2.5–5cm apart. Lvs 20–35×1cm, linear, midvein impressed. Peduncles several, to 5cm; fls with a strong coconut scent, to 5cm diam., deep red mottled with yellow towards base of sep. and pet., lip mainly yellow, marked with dark red, column pale yellow, the front spotted with dark red; sep. spreading, 20–25mm, lanceolate or ovate, margins recurved; pet. shorter, projecting forwards; lip about 16×10mm, obscurely trilobed, midlobe tongue-shaped, deflexed. Spring–summer. Mexico to Honduras and Nicaragua.

***M.triloris*** E. Morr. Pseudobulbs clustered, to 6×5cm, ovoid, compressed, with grey, scarious sheaths towards base, 1-lvd at apex. Lvs to 40×6cm, linear-ligulate, with dorsal keel. Fls fragrant, sep. and pet. yellow, white at base, with maroon patch on reverse, lip lateral lobes white with maroon veins, midlobe yellow with white margin; sep. 65–70×13–20mm, lanceolate or oblanceolate, spreading, stiff in texture, margins recurved; pet. 60×12mm, lanceolate, acute, projecting forwards; lip 28×16mm, stiff, with hairy longitudinal callus at base, trilobed at about halfway, lateral lobes erect, midlobe oblong, thickened, sparsely pubesc., reflexed, the edge undulate, usually with a minute, spur-like projection on the underside near the apex; column 12mm. Venezuela.

***M.uncata*** Lindl. Rhiz. to 80cm, pendent, covered with red-brown sheaths; pseudobulbs obscure, to 5mm, largely hidden by sheaths, set about 2cm apart, 1-lvd. Lvs to 8cm×3mm, stiff, linear, margins incurved. Peduncles arising among sheaths, to 1cm; fls green-cream, sometimes tinged with light maroon; sep. and pet. projecting forwards, sep. 11–14×3–5mm, ovate, apiculate, lateral sep. oblique, pet. to 9×4mm, obliquely ovate, apiculate; lip to 13×5mm, with smooth callus in middle, obscurely trilobed in apical half, midlobe slightly emarginate; column 11mm, including foot, with hook-like processes below apex. Mexico to Brazil and Peru.

***M.valenzuelana*** (A. Rich.) Nash. Pendulous, lacking pseudobulbs. Lvs several, forming fan, to 18×1.5cm, fleshy, bilaterally flattened. Peduncles arising from lf axils, about 5cm; fls small, about 2.5cm diam., sep. and pet. yellow-green, lip light brown with purple spots; sep. 11–14×5–6mm, ovate, acute or apiculate, rather fleshy, dorsal sep. erect, lateral sep. semi-spreading; pet. 9×3mm, oblong-lanceolate, projecting forwards; lip 10×5mm, callus consisting of a line of white, glandular hairs broken into basal, median and apical strips, obscurely trilobed, fleshy. C America, W Indies, Venezuela, Colombia, Ecuador, Brazil.

***M.variabilis*** Lindl. Often terrestrial; rhiz. elongated, creeping or ascending; pseudobulbs set 3–6cm apart, 2–4cm high, cylindrical, flattened, 1-lvd at apex, with numerous basal sheaths, some leaf-bearing. Lvs 15–25cm, oblong-linear, leathery. Peduncles 2–3cm, in groups of 2–3; fls varying in colour from pale yellow to dark red; sep. spreading, elliptic-lanceolate; pet. similar but projecting; lip slightly shorter, tongue-shaped, reflexed, with dark red central callus. Throughout the year. Mexico to Panama.

***M.venusta*** Lindl. Pseudobulbs 4–5cm high, ovate, somewhat flattened, 1-lvd. Lvs to 30cm, ligulate, acute. Peduncles to 15cm, covered in red-tinged sheaths; fls somewhat nodding, to 15cm diam., sep. and pet. milk-white, lip yellow with 2 red spots, margins of lateral lobes red; sep. to 75mm, lanceolate, acute, dorsal sep. concave, lateral sep. somewhat curved; pet. similar but slightly shorter; lip fleshy, trilobed, midlobe triangular, recurved. Winter–spring. Colombia.

***M.villosa*** (Barb. Rodr.) Cogn. Pseudobulbs clustered, to 8cm, cylindrical to oblong-ovoid, 1-lvd at apex, with several pairs of overlapping sheaths, the upper ones leaf-bearing. Lvs to 44×5cm, ligulate to oblong, leathery, petiolate; petiole to 9cm. Peduncles to 8cm, arising from base of pseudobulb, covered with loose, tubular sheaths; fls small, bell-shaped, yellow, yellow-brown or orange, lip sometimes white; sep. 15–20×8mm, ovate-oblong, acute, concave, lateral sep. oblique and forming a low mentum; pet. shorter and narrower than sep., lanceolate or oblanceolate; lip erect, parallel to column, somewhat recurved, 13–15×8mm, oblong-ovate in outline, obscurely trilobed above middle, lateral lobes erect; column to 10mm, column foot short. Peru, Brazil, Guyana.

***M.vittariifolia*** L.O. Williams. Pseudobulbs clustered, 5–6mm diam., subglobose. Lvs about 9cm, narrowly ligulate, arching. Fls 10cm diam., milk-white, lip with yellow lateral lobes and red midlobe. Summer–autumn. Costa Rica, Panama, Colombia.

***M.abelei*** Schltr. See *M. rufescens.*
***M.acutifolia*** Lindl. See *M. rufescens.*
***M.amparoana*** Schltr. See *M. ringens.*

***M.angustifolia*** Hook. See *M.variabilis*.
***M.articulata*** Klotzsch. See *M.rufescens*.
***M.boothii*** Lindl. See *Nidema boothii*.
***M.bractescens*** Lindl. See *Xylobium bractescens*.
***M.brevipedunculata*** Ames & Schweinf. See *M.nasuta*.
***M.concava*** Lindl. See *Xylobium foveatum*.
***M.coriacea*** Barb. Rodr. See *M.desvauxiana*.
***M.cyanea*** (Lindl.) Beer. See *Warreella cyanea*.
***M.decolor*** Lindl. See *Xylobium palmifolium*.
***M.densa*** Lindl. See *Ornithidium densum*.
***M.dichroma*** Rolfe. See *M.elegantula*.
***M.elongata*** Lindl. & Paxt. See *Xylobium elongatum*.
***M.foveata*** Lindl. See *Xylobium foveatum*.
***M.fuscata*** Klotzsch. See *M.picta*.
***M.heuchmannii*** Hook. See *M.variabilis*.
***M.hirtilabia*** Lindl. See *M.parkeri*.
***M.iridifolia*** Rchb. f. See *M.valenzuelana*.
***M.jugosa*** Lindl. See *Pabstia jugosa*.
***M.kegelii*** Rchb. f. See *M.parkeri*.
***M.kreysigii*** Hoffsgg. See *M.picta*.
***M.lactea*** Schltr. See *M.ringens*.
***M.leontoglossa*** Rchb. f. See *Xylobium leontoglossum*.
***M.leucochila*** Hoffsgg. See *M.picta*.
***M.lindeniana*** A. Rich. See *M.meleagris*.
***M.longifolia*** (Barb. Rodr.) Cogn. See *M.tarumaensis*.
***M.loretoensis*** Schweinf. See *M.parkeri*.
***M.lorifolia*** Rchb. f. See *M.parkeri*.
***M.lutescens*** Scheidw. See *M.camaridii*.
***M.macleei*** Batem. ex Lindl. See *M.uncata*.
***M.mattogrossensis*** Brade. See *M.equitans*.
***M.monoceras*** Klotzsch. See *M.picta*.
***M.nana*** Hook. See *M.uncata*.
***M.nasalis*** Rchb. f. See *M.nasuta*.
***M.oxysepala*** Schltr. See *M.nasuta*.
***M.pachyacron*** Schltr. See *M.reichenheimiana*.
***M.pallidiflora*** Hook. See *Xylobium pallidiflorum*.
***M.palmifolia*** (Sw.) Lindl. See *Xylobium palmifolium*.
***M.pertusa*** Lindl. See *M.lepidota*.
***M.petiolaris*** A. Rich. ex Rchb. f. See *M.desvauxiana*.
***M.pubilabia*** Schltr. See *M.ringens*.
***M.punctata*** Lodd. See *M.gracilis*.
***M.punctostriata*** Rchb. f. See *M.meleagris*.
***M.punktulata*** Klotzsch. See *M.marginata*.
***M.revoluta*** Klotzsch. See *M.variabilis*.
***M.rollissonii*** Lindl. See *Promenaea rollissonii*.
***M.rousseauae*** Schltr. See *M.ringens*.
***M.rubrofusca*** Klotzsch. See *M.nigrescens*.
***M.rugosa*** Scheidw. See *M.rufescens*.
***M.saxicola*** Schltr. See *M.lepidota*.
***M.serotina*** Hoehne. See *M.consanguinea*.
***M.setigera*** var. ***angustifolia*** Klinge. See *M.callichroma*.
***M.squalens*** (Lindl.) Hook. See *Xylobium variegatum*.
***M.squamata*** Barb. Rodr. See *M.uncata*.
***M.stapelioides*** Lindl. See *Promenaea stapelioides*.
***M.stenobulbon*** Klotzsch. See *Xylobium pallidiflorum*.
***M.stenostele*** Schltr. See *M.uncata*.
***M.superba*** La Ll. & Lex. See *Govenia superba*.
***M.tricolor*** Lindl. See *M.marginata*.
***M.tuerckheimii*** Schltr. See *M.ringens*.
***M.vandiformis*** (Schltr.) C. Schweinf. See *M.equitans*.
***M.vanillodora*** A. Rich. ex Rchb. f. See *M.rufescens*.
***M.variegata*** Ruiz & Pav. See *Xylobium variegatum*.
***M.xanthina*** Lindl. See *Promenaea xanthina*.

**Maximiliana** Mart. (For Maximilian zu Wied-Neuwied, plant collector, *d*1867.) MARIPA; INAJA; CURCURITA PALM. Palmae. 1 species, a monoecious palm to 22m. Stem solitary, to 18m tall, to 50cm diam., erect or procumbent, becoming bare and ringed. Leaves pinnate, to 6m; sheaths fibrous; pinnae emerging scurfy, later glabrous, narrow, lanceolate, acute, to 1m×5cm, semi-rigid, in whorls of up to 5 held at differing planes along rachis, longest near base; petioles flattened above, bisulcate, flattened beneath. Flowers on bisexual spikes, branching ×350, amid 3 bracts, the uppermost woody, furrowed and persistent, splitting longitudinally; female flowers at base of branchlets, ovoid, sepals 3, overlapping, petals 3, staminodal ring pubescent, carpels 3, fused; male flowers near apex of branchlets, sepals 3, imbricate, shorter than petals; stamens 6, exserted, exceeding petals; pistillode absent. Fr. ovoid, 3-seeded, with stigmatic remains and persistent perianth. Northern S America, W Indies. Z10.

CULTIVATION Handsome hot glasshouse specimens in temperate zones. *M.regia* is particularly decorative as a young plant. Leaves and fibre used a heavy-duty weaving material. Woody bract used as a container; mesocarp provides 'milk' for drinking; seeds oil-yielding, edible if roasted. For cultivation see PALMS.

***M.maripa*** (Corr.) Drude. As for the genus.

***M.caribaea*** Griseb. & H.A. Wendl. See *M.maripa*.
***M.martiana*** Karst. See *M.maripa*.
***M.regia*** Mart. See *M.maripa*.
For further synonymy see *Englerophoenix*.

**Maximowicz, Carl Johann** (1827–1891). Botanist and plant collector. He was brought up in St Petersburg and in 1844 went to the University of Dorpat, where he became the director's assistant in the botanic garden. At the age of only 24 he was appointed Conservator of the Imperial Botanic Garden at St Petersburg, and in that capacity in 1853 he embarked as plant collector on an expedition which passed through Rio de Janeiro, Valparaiso and Honolulu, before being forced to stop at De Castries in Manchuria due to the outbreak of war. Maximowicz used this opportunity to make a three-year study and collection of the flora and geography of the area around the Amur and Ussuri rivers, sending back, amongst about 100 other plants, *Paeonia obovata*, before returning to St Petersburg via Siberia in 1857. His *Primitiae Florae Amurensis* (1859) was a great success and, despite the hardship involved, Maximowicz was encouraged to undertake another journey. After travelling across Siberia and through Manchuria in 1859 and 1860 (resulting introductions include *Celastrus orbiculatus* and *Lonicera maximowiczii*), he explored Japan for three and a half years. With the help of a Japanese assistant he collected many plants, seeds and bulbs (although most of the latter were lost), sending them back to St Petersburg for cultivation. Among his finds were *Stewartia pseudo-camellia, Acer capillipes, Ligularia dentata, Magnolia stellata, Hypericum patulum* and *Rhododendron brachycarpum*, although only a form of *Rosa rugosa* was widely disseminated.

Maximowicz returned in 1864 subsequently, and with a cargo of 72 boxes of specimens, about 400 living plants and 300 kinds of seed, after a visit to England during which he suffered from a fever caught in Japan, he became Chief Botanist at St Petersburg. He held this post from 1869 until his death, producing a vast amount of work as the authority on the flora of eastern Asia and studying the specimens sent back by other collectors such as Potanin and Prjevalsky.

**Maytenus** Molina. (From Chilean vernacular name.) Celastraceae. Some 255 species of shrubs or small trees, usually glabrous, stems sometimes spinose. Leaves alternate, often distichous, entire or dentate, membranous to fleshy-coriaceous, persistent; petiole short; stipules absent or minute and caducous. Flowers clustered in axillary dichasial cymes, short thyrses, racemes or compact fascicles, 4–5-merous; sepals persistent; petals spreading, green-white to red; disc conspicuous, usually flattened, annular and adnate to ovaries. Fruit a capsule, ellipsoid to obovoid, loculicidally, 2–5-valved, coriaceous; seeds usually 3, ovoid-ellipsoid, covered partially or entirely by a fleshy red or white aril. Tropical and subtropical regions.

CULTIVATION Grown for their evergreen foliage, which in *M.boaria* weeps gracefully and in *M.ilicifolia* is distinctly holly-like. There is a further attraction in the ripe fruit which splits open to reveal colourful seeds, in red, scarlet or orange-yellow. If frost-free conditions cannot be guaranteed for *M.ilicifolia* and *M.serratus*, their cultivation should be restricted to a border in the glasshouse where a minimum temperature of 5°C/40°F can be maintained. With the exception of *M.boaria*, which will tolerate temperatures to −10°C/14°F, remaining species are only hardy in mild areas, with a minimum temperature of −5°C/23°F, where they are best grown against a sunny wall or, in the case of *M.chubutensis*, in the shade of other plants or on a north wall. The soil should be well drained but on no account allowed to dry out. Propagate from semi-ripe cuttings taken in summer rooted with the aid of mist and gentle bottom heat.

***M. boaria*** Molina. MAYTEN. Evergreen shrub or tree to 24m, glabrous throughout; branchlets drooping, slender. Lvs 2.5–5×2cm, lanceolate or narrowly ovate to narrowly elliptic, attenuate at both ends, closely and finely serrate, mid-green above, paler below; petioles slender, very short. Fls mostly unisexual, both sexes on the same plant, clustered 2–5, small and inconspicuous, white tinged green. Fr. 2-valved, yellow, coriaceous; seeds 2, aril scarlet. Spring. Chile. Z8.

***M. chubutensis*** (Speg.) Lourteig, O'Donnell & Sleumer. Dwarf evergreen shrub to 60cm. Lvs 1×0.5cm, broad-elliptic to broad-ovate, shortly and stiffly pubesc. above. Fls solitary or in clusters, small, pale red. Argentina. Z9.

***M. ilicifolia*** Reisseck ex Mart. Shrub or tree to 5m, dioecious. Lvs holly-like, 2–15×1–7cm, elliptic or oblong, spiny-dentate, with 4–7 teeth per side, base cuneate. Fls in crowded fascicles, small; pedicels to 4mm; sep. suborbicular, tinged red; pet. elliptic or ovate, yellow. Fr. 2-valved, to 11mm, tinged red; seed 1–4, tinged red, aril thin. S America (Bolivia, Paraguay, S Brazil, east to Argentina). Z10.

***M. magellanica*** (Lam.) Hook. f. Tree or shrub to 7m, main stem to 25cm diam., brown to pale grey; twigs glabrous. Lvs 1.5–9.5×2.5–3.5cm, ovate to lanceolate, acute to acuminate, rarely obtuse, attenuate at base, margin serrate and thickened, pale green, glabrous; petiole to 1cm; stipules minute, brown, caducous. Fls 5-merous in fascicles of few to many; pedicels to 4mm; cal. lobes to 1mm, rounded, convex; pet. to 2mm, ovate, obtuse, erose, red with white margin, punctate. Fr. to 6mm orbicular-obcordate, seeds 2, ellipsoid, with fleshy aril at base. Autumn. Southern S America (S Chile, S Argentina, Tierra del Fuego). Z9.

***M. phyllanthoides*** Benth. Low shrub or tree to 3m+; shoots glabrous, pale grey. Lvs to 3cm, oblong-ovate, obscurely crenate, obtuse, cuneate, glabrous, veins reticulate; petiole to 6mm. Fls to 3mm diam., solitary or in sparse clusters, apparently perfect. Fr. to 8mm, obovate, 3–4-angled; seed 1–3, arils red. Southern N America (Florida, Mexico). Z9.

***M. serratus*** (Hochst. ex A. Rich.) R. Wilcz. Evergreen shrub to 2m+, sometimes spiny. Lvs to 7.5cm, elliptic to ovate to oblanceolate, finely dentate. Fls in branching clusters, pale white. Fr. 3-valved. Ethiopia. Z10.

*M. chilensis* DC. See *M. boaria*.
For further synonymy see *Gymnosporia*.

**Mazus** Lour. (From Gk *mazos*, breast, referring to the protuberances in the corolla throat.) Scrophulariaceae. Some 30 species of low-growing, annual or perennial herbs, usually creeping or prostrate rooting at nodes. Leaves dentate or sinuate, lower leaves opposite or rosulate, upper leaves usually alternate. Inflorescence a terminal almost one-sided raceme or flowers solitary; calyx campanulate, 5-lobed; corolla blue-mauve or white, tube short, 2-lipped, upper lip erect, 2-lobed, lower lip larger, spreading, 3-lobed, with 2 distinct breast-shaped eruptions in the throat; stamens 4, didynamous, anther cells divergent; style slender, stigma equally 2-lamellate. Fruit a capsule, loculicidal; seeds numerous. SE Asia, China, Taiwan, Malay Archipelago, Australasia.

CULTIVATION Charming dwarf groundcover for sheltered, slightly acid positions in the rock garden. Protect during winter with evergreen branches or salt hay, and as insurance against loss, overwinter stock plants in frost-free conditions. Otherwise, as for *Lagotis*.

***M. pumilio*** R. Br. Perenn., almost tufted, rhizomatous; branches leafy to 7cm, almost prostrate, at nodes. Lvs 2–5cm, rosulate, narrowly obovate-spathulate, apex obtuse, entire or sinuately toothed, membranous, glabrous or almost so. Peduncle slender, 1–6-fld; pedicels curved, bracteate; cal. narrow campanulate, lobes narrow, acute; cor. white or blue, throat yellow, lobes 6–12mm diam., broad, obtuse. Capsule subglobose, included in persistent cal. Summer. Australasia. Z7. 'Albus': fls white.

***M. radicans*** (Hook. f.) Cheesem. Perenn.; stem robust, creeping, sometimes subterranean, rooting at nodes; branches to 5cm leafy, almost erect. Lvs crowded, linear-obovate, obtuse, almost entire, usually pilose. Peduncles 1–3-fld, erect, glabrous-pilose; bracts 1 or 2, linear-subulate; cal. hairy; cor. 12–18mm, white, throat yellow, lips sometimes blotched purple; stamens 4, upper pair shorter than cor. tube, lower pair equalling cor. Capsule 9mm, ovoid, included in persistent cal. Summer. New Zealand. Z6.

***M. reptans*** N.E. Br. Perenn.; stems slender to 5cm, prostrate, rooting. Lvs to 10mm, lanceolate to elliptic, coarsely toothed. Racemes 2–5-fld; cor. purple-blue, lower lip blotched white, yellow and red-purple. Summer. Himalaya. Material grown as *M. rugosus* (syn. *M. japonicus*) is usually *M. reptans*. 'Albus': fls white. Z3.

For synonymy see *Mimulus*.

**McMahon, Bernard** (*c*1775–1816). American nurseryman. McMahon was born into a prosperous family in Ireland but was forced to leave for America in 1796 as a result of his involvement in an unsuccessful revolutionary plot. There, in 1809, he set up a botanic garden in Pennsylvania. As a good gardener and a man of education, he was friendly with President Jefferson and with members of the botanical circle in Pennsylvania, and it is said to have been at his house that the Lewis and Clark expedition across the continent was planned. McMahon's fame is linked with the fact that the first American seed catalogue was produced for his nursery. He wrote the *American Gardener's Calender* (1806), updated under the same title for many years after his death. He grew 30 species of native oak his garden at Upsal, and Nuttall recognized his contribution in naming the North American shrub *Mahonia* in his honour.

**Mecodium** C. Presl. ex Copel.
***M. australe*** (Willd.) Copel. See *Hymenophyllum australe*.
***M. flabellatum*** (Labill.) Copel. See *Hymenophyllum flabellatum*.

**Meconella** Nutt. (Lat. diminutive of Gk *mekon*, poppy.) Papaveraceae. Some 3–4 species of annual herbs. Stems erect, dichotomously branching, glabrous, somewhat glaucous. Leaves mostly basal, opposite, usually spathulate. Flowers solitary, terminal on axillary peduncles; sepals 3, slightly hairy; petals 6, rarely 5, white to cream; stamens 6–12; carpels 3. Fruit a linear capsule, opening from apex to base, valves 3, spiralling once open. Spring–summer. Western N America. Z6.

CULTIVATION Native to Pacific N America from California and Oregon to British Columbia, *Meconella* is an annual closely related to *Platystemon* and thrives in areas of cool summers; the flowers deteriorate rapidly in hot humid weather. They are used for edging borders, or grown in informal drifts in the rock garden. They prefer a sandy soil, otherwise cultivate as for *Papaver rhoeas*.

***M. linearis*** (Benth.) Nels. & Macbr. To 25cm. Lvs to 7cm, basal, linear. Fls cream.

***M. oregana*** Nutt. ex Torr. & A. Gray. To 10cm. Stems filiform. Basal lvs spathulate, to 1.5cm, stems lvs to 1cm, oblong-lanceolate to ovate-lanceolate, obtuse. Fls to 0.5cm diam.; sep. ovate-lanceolate; pet. oblong-cuneiform, cream with an ivory patch at base; stamens 6. Fr. to 1cm.

**Meconopsis** Vig. (From Gk *mekon*, poppy, and *opsis*, appearance.) ASIATIC POPPY. Papaveraceae. 43 species of annual, biennial or perennial herbs, often monocarpic. Sap yellow. Stems scapose and simple, or branched and leafy. Leaves often in a basal rosette, occasionally on stem, usually entire, sometimes lobed or dissected, glabrous or with simple or barbellate hairs. Flowers usually solitary or in racemes, yellow, blue, white or tinged red; sepals 2, caducous; petals 4, rarely 5–9; stamens 20+; ovary 1-chambered, stigma usually 4–6-lobed, rarely 2–3-lobed, usually capitate or clavate, with decurrent rays, rarely depressed with widespread rays. Fruit a capsule, usually ovoid or oblong, rarely narrowly cylindric, opening via apical valves. Himalaya to W China, W Europe.

CULTIVATION A group of hardy and semi-hardy biennials and perennials which with one exception (*M. cambrica*) are native to the Himalayas and mountains of China and Tibet. Many are monocarpic although they may take between two and four years before first flowering. Cultivated for their beautiful nodding poppy-like flowers, the basal rosettes of some species (e.g. *M. grandis*, *M. quintuplinervia* and *M. chelidonifolia*) are extremely handsome, and those of the monocarpic species may also be winter-persistent, as in *M. napaulensis*, *M. paniculata* and *M. regia*. They are plants for the woodland garden, peat terrace and shady herbaceous border. Although tall, many are suitable for the rock garden if provided with moist crevices with perfect drainage out of direct sun; for this purpose, *M. villosa*, *M. cambrica*, *M. integrifolia* and *M. quintuplinervia* are of suitable scale. Except for a few favoured parts of North America where cool moist summers and relatively mild winters prevail (e.g. the Pacific Northwest) they are not generally suitable for American gardens.

Nearly all grow best in part shade, and this is important to ensure and preserve good flower colour. They require shelter from summer heat and strong winds, and a moist but not stagnant root-run, in soil that is quick draining especially in winter, when even the hardiest species will rot if water accumulates around the collar. In very wet areas protect winter green species with open cloches or panes of glass. *M. cambrica* will grow in virtually any soil, in any position.

Plant in spring in a humus-rich, lime-free soil. Deadhead to prolong flowering and cut down perennial species in autumn. Some species, e.g. *M. grandis, M. sheldonii, M. quintuplinervia*, can be divided in spring or autumn although some growers divide immediately after flowering. Lift and divide perennial species every three years to prevent deterioration.

All can be seed-propagated. Sow ripe seed (late summer) in equal parts peat and sand. Prick out into boxes and overwinter in a well-ventilated cool greenhouse or frame. Germination is slower in spring, when they will require a temperature of 13–16°C/55–60°F.

Plants may suffer from downy mildew (*Peronospora* spp.), which is grave at seedling stage and should be treated with appropriate fungicide. The perennial species are thought to be longer-lived if they develop several crowns before being allowed to flower – for example, *M. betonicifolia* will be monocarpic if flowered as a biennial but may flower over several seasons if raised slowly (in cool conditions) and stopped in the first two years to induce offsetting.

***M. aculeata*** Royle. Monocarpic perenn., to 60cm. Lvs in a basal rosette and on stem; basal lvs and lower stem lvs petiolate, to 27.5×5cm; irregularly pinnatifid or pinnatisect, with yellow-brown bristly spines; lobes oblong, obtuse to rounded, or deltoid, acute; upper stem lvs sessile. Fls solitary on axillary pedicels to 22.5cm, with bract-like lvs near apex; pet. 4, rarely 6, to 3×3cm, sky blue, rarely mauve or red; stamens many, anth. yellow. Fr. subglobose to elliptic-oblong, densely spiny, opening by 3–8 apical valves. Summer. W Himalaya. Z7.

***M. ×beamishii*** Prain *(M. grandis × M. integrifolia.)* To 1.2m. Basal lvs to 25cm, oblanceolate, acute, tapering to the petiole. Fls yellow, pet. base often blotched yellow; pet. 6–8, obovate, to 7.5×6.5cm. Garden origin.

***M. bella*** Prain. Perenn., to 15cm. Stems short, densely covered in old petioles. Lvs in a dense basal rosette, pinnate or pinnatifid, to 17.5×2.5cm, glabrous to sparsely setose; lobes obovate to oblong, obtuse, ultimate lobes trifid. Fls to 18, all solitary on flimsy setose scapes; pet. 4, rarely 5–6, obovate to suborbicular, to 3×3cm, pink, pale blue or purple; anth. yellow-orange, stigma 4–7-lobed, capitate. Fr. pear-shaped or obovoid, 4–7-valved. Summer. Himalaya. Z8.

***M. betonicifolia*** Franch. BLUE POPPY. Short-lived perenn., to 2m. Stems rigid, erect, glabrous or with scattered hairs. Basal and lower stem lvs to 35×7.5cm, petiolate, oblong to ovate, truncate to cordate at base, obtuse at apex, roughly serrate, sparsely setose throughout; petiole sheathing at base, upper stem lvs sessile, amplexicaul, uppermost lvs in a pseudowhorl, subtending fls. Fls to 6, in somewhat drooping cymes on axillary scapes to 25cm; pet. 4, obovate to suborbicular, obtuse, to 5×5cm, mauve-pink to bright sky blue; anth. orange or orange-yellow. Fr. oblong to oblong-elliptic, glabrous to densely bristly; valves 4–7, opening along one-third of length. Summer. China. 'Alba': to 110cm; fls white. Harlow Carr Strain: perenn.; fls blue. Z7.

***M. cambrica*** (L.) Vig. WELSH POPPY. Perenn. to 60cm. Stems erect, branching, foliose, glabrous or sparsely hairy. Basal lvs deeply pinnatisect toward base, pinnatifid toward apex, to 20cm, glabrous to sparsely hairy above, seg. pinnatifid or irregularly lobed, lower seg. distant; upper stem lvs subsessile. Fls solitary, in axils of upper stem lvs; pedicels to 25cm; pet. 4, or double in cultivars, obovate to suborbicular, to 3×3cm, yellow; anth. yellow. Fr ellipsoid-oblong, 4–7-ribbed; valves splitting along a quarter of length. Summer. W Europe. var. ***aurantiaca*** hort. ex Wehrh. Fls orange. 'Frances Perry': fls scarlet. 'Flore-Pleno': fls semi-double, yellow or orange. Z6.

***M. chelidonifolia*** Bur. & Franch. Perenn., to 1m. Stems erect, branching, grooved with closely adpressed, sparse bristles. Basal lvs pinnatisect; seg. distant, pinnatisect to pinnatifid, bristly throughout, glaucous beneath; upper stem lvs sessile, trifid, pinnatisect; seg. pinnatifid. Fls on flimsy, axillary pedicels; pet. 4, obovate or suborbicular, to 2.5×2.5cm, yellow; anthers yellow. Fr. ellipsoid; valves apical, 5–6. Summer. China (W Sichuan). Z8.

***M. ×cookei*** G. Tayl. *(M. punicea × M. quintuplinervia.)* Lvs basal, elliptic to oblanceolate, acute, entire, to 15×2cm. Scape to 40cm; fls pendent, ruby-red; pet. 4, ovate, to 5×4cm. Garden origin. Z7.

***M. delavayi*** (Franch.) Franch. ex Prain. Perenn., to 27.5cm. Stems branching, caespitose. Lvs all basal, ovate to narrowly oblanceolate, acute to rounded at apex, entire, to 15×3cm, sparsely setose throughout, glaucous beneath. Fls somewhat drooping, solitary, on flimsy terminal scapes; pet. usually 4, occasionally 6 or 8, ovate, obovate or orbicular, acute to rounded at apex, to 3×2.5cm, deep purple, rarely deep pink; anth. orange. Fr. narrowly oblong or cylindric, to 6cm; valves 3–5 at apex. Summer. China (Yunnan). Z8.

***M. dhwojii*** G. Tayl. ex Hay. Monocarpic perenn., to 60cm. Stems branching in upper part. Basal and lower lvs petiolate, pinnatisect toward base, pinnatifid toward apex, to 32.5cm, seg. obtusely or acutely lobed, sparsely setose throughout, bristles dark purple at base; upper stem lvs smaller. Fls numerous, borne in branching racemes, lower branches to 5-fld, upper branches 1-fld; pet. 4, obovate to orbicular, to 3×3cm, yellow; anth. orange-yellow. Fr. ellipsoid to oblong, opening by 5–6 apical valves. Summer. Nepal. Z8.

***M. ×finlayorum*** G. Tayl. *(M. integrifolia × M. quintuplinervia.)* Lvs basal, elliptic to broadly lanceolate, 6.5–8×2–3.5cm, tapering to a winged petiole. Peduncles to 36cm, bristly; pet. white, 4–6, ovate, 3–3.5×2–2.5cm, base cuneate, apex acute. Garden origin. Z7.

***M. gracilipes*** G. Tayl. Monocarpic perenn., to 60cm. Stems branching, sparsely setose, becoming near-glabrous. Basal lvs to 25cm, rosulate, bristly, deeply cut throughout, upper lvs sessile, auricled at base, amplexicaul. Fls on flimsy, axillary branches to 35cm; lower branches 3-fld, upper branches 1-fld; pet. 4, yellow, obovate or orbicular, to 3×2.5cm; stamens orange-yellow becoming dark brown. Fr. ellipsoid or oblong-ellipsoid, bristly, opening by 4–7 apical valves. Summer. Nepal. Z8.

***M. grandis*** Prain. Perenn., to 120cm. Stem erect, densely retrorse-setose. Basal and lower stem lvs to 30cm, narrowly oblanceolate to elliptic-oblong, irregularly serrate, broadly crenate, setose throughout, acute at apex, tapering into petiole at base; petiole to 17.5cm. Fls 3+, on axillary pedicels to 45cm; pet. usually 4, often to 9, suborbicular or broadly ovate, to 6×5.5cm, purple or deep blue; anth. yellow. Fr. narrowly ellipsoid to oblong, opening by 4–6 apical valves. Summer. Himalaya. 'Miss Dickson' ('Puritan'): fls white. Z5.

***M. horridula*** Hook. f. & Thoms. Short-lived perenn., to 80cm. Stems prickly, with persistent petioles at base. Basal rosette and lower stem lvs elliptic to narrowly obovate, apex abruptly acute, tapering to petiole at base, entire or sinuate, to 25×3cm, grey-green with purple or yellow spiny bristles throughout; upper stem lvs sessile, uppermost lvs reduced. Fls 1–2, nodding, on axillary pedicels to 22.5cm, covered with dense spiny bristles; pet. 4–8, ovate to suborbicular, minutely toothed at apex, 4×3cm, cobalt blue to violet or white; anth. buff, becoming dark grey. Fr. ellipsoid-oblong or subglobose, covered with dense, spreading, closely adpressed bristles, opening by 4–9 apical valves. Summer. Himalaya to W China (high altitudes). Z6.

***M. integrifolia*** (Maxim.) Franch. Short-lived perenn., to 90cm, covered with downy, orange-red hairs. Stem striated, densely hairy. Basal lvs in a dense rosette, entire, oblanceolate to obovate or almost linear, tapering towards base, acute to obtuse at apex, to 37.5×5cm, densely hairy throughout; petioles broadly linear; upper stem lvs subsessile, narrowly elliptic to linear; uppermost stem lvs in a pseudowhorl. Fls 4–5, solitary on axillary pedicels to 45cm, rarely on simple basal scapes; pet. 6–8, suborbicular to obovate, to 3×3cm, yellow or rarely white; anth. orange or yellow, becoming black. Fr. ellipsoid-oblong, opening by 4–9 valves along one-third of length. Summer. Tibet, Upper Burma, W China. Z7.

***M. latifolia*** (Prain) Prain. Short-lived perenn., to 120cm. Basal and lower stem lvs oblong to ovate or broadly lanceolate, cuneate to obtuse at base, to 20×3cm, with yellow-brown spines throughout, crenate or deeply serrate; upper stem lvs sessile. Fls many, solitary on spiny, usually bracteate, pedicels to 2.5cm; pet. 4, obovate or suborbicular, rounded and entire at apex, to 3×2.5cm, usually pale blue, rarely white; fil. deep blue, anth. orange-yellow. Fr. ellipsoid-oblong, with dense spreading spines, opening by 4–7 apical valves. Spring–summer. N Kashmir. Z7.

***M. ×musgravei*** G. Tayl. *(M. betonicifolia × M. superba.)* To 62cm. Basal lvs oblong, pubesc., base cuneate to cordate, margins densely serrate, to 7.5cm; stem lvs oblong to triangular-lanceolate. Pet. white, ovate to suborbicular, to 5×5cm; fil. white, anth. orange-yellow. Garden origin. Z7.

***M. napaulensis*** DC. SATIN POPPY. Perenn., to 2.6m. Stems branching. Basal lvs in a dense rosette, pinnatisect, to 50×10cm; seg. pinnately lobed, setose, lobes acute to rounded, lower stem lvs with shorter petioles, upper stem lvs sessile, lanceolate, entire or pinnatifid, cuneate to auricled at base. Fls drooping, in branched cymes, to 17-fld; pedicels sparsely setose, to 7.5cm; pet. 4, obovate to suborbicular, to 4×3cm, red to purple or blue, rarely white; anth. orange-yellow. Fr. ellipsoid-oblong to oblong, densely covered with closely adpressed bristles, splitting by 5–8 apical valves. Spring–summer. C Nepal to SW China (Sichuan). 'Alba': fls white. Z8.

***M. paniculata*** (D. Don) Prain. Short-lived perenn., to 2m. Stem branching. Basal lvs in a rosette, pinnatisect, villous and setose throughout, seg. lanceolate, oblong or deltoid, acute to rounded at apex, lobed or entire, upper stem lvs sessile, amplexicaul. Fls solitary on axillary pedicels from upper lvs and in 2–6-fld racemes; pet. 4, ovate to suborbicular, to 5×5cm, yellow; fil. pale yellow; anth. orange-yellow; stigma 6–12-lobed, purple. Fr. ellipsoid-oblong, stellate-hairy, opening by 6–12 apical valves. Spring–summer. E Nepal to NE Assam. Z8.

***M.punicea*** Maxim. Perenn., to 75cm. Lvs to 38×3cm, in a basal rosette, oblanceolate, tapering to petiole throughout; petiole sheathing at base. Fls solitary, somewhat drooping, on 6 simple, ribbed scapes with reflexed bristles; pet. usually 4, occasionally 6, rhombic-elliptic, acute to rounded to 10×5cm, deep red; fil. tinged red; anth. yellow. Fr. ellipsoid-oblong, glabrous to densely bristly, opening by 3–5 apical valves. Spring–summer. NE Tibet, China (Kansu, Sichuan). Z7.

***M.quintuplinervia*** Reg. Perenn., to 30cm. Stems erect to ascending, densely covered in old leaf bases and bristles at base. Lvs to 25×3cm, golden to rusty-setose throughout, in a basal rosette, obovate to narrowly oblanceolate, acute or obtuse, with 3–5 longitudinal ribs. Fls solitary, pendent on 3 ribbed, retrorse-hispid scapes; pet. 4, occasionally 6, obovate or orbicular, rounded at apex, to 3×3cm, pale mauve-blue or light violet, rarely white; anth. pale yellow or buff. Fr. erect, ellipsoid or oblong-ellipsoid, opening by 3–6 apical valves. Spring–summer. NE Tibet, China. Z8.

***M.regia*** G. Tayl. Perenn., to 60cm, with soft, white or pale yellow hairs. Stems branching. Basal lvs to 40×9cm, in a dense rosette, persisting through winter, narrowly elliptic, tapering at base and apex, serrate, covered with dense silver-grey or golden silky hairs, upper stem lvs sessile, amplexicaul, less densely hairy. Fls many, borne on axillary branches from upper lvs; branches 1–4-fld; pet. 4, rarely 6, suborbicular, to 6×5cm, yellow; anth. deep orange. Fr. oblong to ellipsoid, with dense, closely adpressed bristles, opening by 7–12 apical valves. Spring–summer. C Nepal. Z8.

***M.×sarsonii*** Sarsons. (*M.betonicifolia* × *M.integrifolia.*) Close to *M.betonicifolia* in habit, to *M.integrifolia* in fl. shape and colour. Garden origin (1930).

***M.×sheldonii*** G. Tayl. (*M.betonicifolia* × *M.grandis.*) *Interrupt oblong-lanceolate, bristly throughout, serrate; upper lvs sessile, amplexicaul. Fls solitary on axillary pedicels from upper stem lvs; pet. 4, obovate to suborbicular, to 3cm, blue.* Garden origin. 'Branklyn' lvs coarsely toothed; fls to 20cm diam. Crewdson Hybrids: fls blue-green. 'Ormswell': to 80cm; fls deep blue. 'Slieve Donard': to 1m; fls blue-green. Z6.

***M.simplicifolia*** (D. Don) Walp. Perenn., to 80cm. Stems stout and robust. Lvs to 37×5cm, in a dense basal rosette, interspersed with barbellate hairs, subsessile or petiolate, oblanceolate to ovate, tapering gradually at base, acute to rounded at apex, with long flimsy bristles throughout, entire or irregularly serrate to lobed; petioles to 20cm, linear, widening at base. Fls solitary; pedicels 1–5, to 70cm, retrorse-setose; pet. 5–8, obovate, to 5×4cm, purple to light blue; fil. purple to light blue; anth. orange. Fr. erect, narrowly oblong to oblong-ellipsoid, glabrous to densely retrorse-setose, opening by 4–9 valves along one-third of length. Spring–summer. C Nepal to SE Tibet. Z7.

***M.sinuata*** Prain. Annual, to 75m. Basal lvs to 17.5×3cm, few, usually withered by flowering time, obovate to oblanceolate, tapering into petiole at base, rounded at apex, sharply setose, deeply lobed; petioles flattened; lower stem lvs narrowly oblanceolate to oblong; upper stem lvs sessile, auricled and amplexicaul at base. Fls 4–8, solitary on axillary pedicels to 22.5cm; pet. 4, obovate, emarginate, to 3×2cm, blue, purple or mauve, anth. orange-yellow. Fr. to 5×1cm, narrowly obovoid to oblong-ellipsoid, 3–4-ribbed, with spreading spines, opening by 3–4 apical valves. Spring–summer. Nepal to Bhutan. Z8.

***M.superba*** King ex Prain. As for *M.regia* except lvs more roughly hairy. Fls solitary on main axis, white. Summer. Tibet, W Bhutan. Z7.

***M.villosa*** (Hook. f.) G. Tayl. Perenn., to 60cm. Stem simple, with dense, spreading bristles. Basal lvs to 12.5×12cm, forming a tuft, soon withering, petiolate, ovate to suborbicular, 3–5-lobed, sparsely setose throughout, glaucous beneath, lobes subacute to rounded; petioles to 20cm, setose; stem lvs wide-spread on stem, to 10×10cm. Fls 1–5, solitary; pedicels axillary, setose, to 14cm; pet. 4, suborbicular to ovate, obtuse, to 2.5×3cm, yellow; fil. orange-yellow, anth. yellow, becoming brown. Fr. narrowly oblong to cylindric, to 9×0.5cm, opening by 4–7 valves along half its length. E Nepal to Bhutan. 'White Swan': to 90cm; fls white. Z7.

***M.baileyi*** Prain. See *M.betonicifolia*.
***M.cathcartii*** hort. See *M.villosa*.
***M.wallichii*** Hook. See *M.napaulensis*.

**Medeola** L. (Named for the mythical sorceress, Medea.) Liliaceae (Trilliaceae). 2 species of perennial herbs. Rhizomes horizontal, thick, tuberous. Stems slender. Leaves in 2 whorls. Inflorescence a terminal umbel; flowers few, sessile; tepals similar, separate, recurved; filaments slender, anthers oblong, versatile; ovary ovoid, 3-celled, each cell containing several ovules; styles separate almost to base, recurved-spreading, stigmatic along inner side. Fruit a few-seeded berry. NE America.

CULTIVATION Native to eastern temperate North America, where it occurs in woodland and on shady banks, *Medeola* is used in the wild garden, or in similar informal situations in shade. *M.virginiana*, has a habit of growth resembling the related *Paris*, but it bears 3–9 pale green flowers in a nodding umbel at the top of each stem, in early summer, followed by purple berries which ripen in autumn. The rhizomes are crisp and edible, resembling cucumber. Plant in semi-shade in slightly acid soils enriched with leaf mould. Propagate from ripe seed in autumn; sow after removal of the flesh, into a well-drained, soil-less propagating medium, in the cold frame.

***M.virginiana*** (L.) Merrill. INDIAN CUCUMBER ROOT. Rhiz. 3–8cm. Stems 30–70cm, erect, lanate when young, persistently so around leaf-bases. Lvs of lower whorl 6–12×1.5–4cm, 5–11, oblong-lanceolate, base and apex acuminate, lvs of upper whorl 3–6×1.5–4cm, usually 3, ovate, base rounded, apex acuminate. Infl. 3–9-fld; pedicels spreading or deflexed, 1.5–2.5cm; tepals to 8mm. Fr. dark purple. Summer. E Canada, E US (Nova Scotia & Quebec to Minnesota, S to Tennessee, to Alabama & Georgia in mts). Z3.

***M.asparagoides*** L. See *Asparagus asparagoides*.

**Medicago** L. MEDIC; MEDICK. (From *Medike*, name given by Dioscorides to a grass.) Leguminosae (Papilionoideae). Some 56 species of annual or perennial herbs or small shrubs. Leaves 3-foliate, stipulate; leaflets finely dentate; stipules united to petioles. Racemes short, axillary; calyx campanulate, teeth 5, subequal; stamens 10, 9 united, 1 free. Fruit longer than calyx, usually indehiscent, curved or spirally twisted, sometimes falcate, reniform or nearly straight, often spiny. Europe, Mediterranean, Ethiopia, S Africa, Asia.

CULTIVATION *Medicago* spp. occur in a range of habitats, from rocky Mediterranean hillsides (*M.arborea*) to grassland (*M.lupulina* and *M.falcata*); some occur in sandy and rocky maritime habitats. They often grows on calcareous soils. The shrubby *M.arborea*, hardy to about −10°C/14°F, has attractively downy foliage and bears a succession of yellow flowers throughout the summer, followed by curious snail-shaped pods. In regions at the limits of its hardiness, it requires the protection of a south wall, but is resistant to salt spray and wind. The low-growing, silvery shrub *M.cretacea* is as hardy. *M.intertexta* and *M.scutellata* are sometimes used as cover for dry, sunny banks; *M.falcata* is grown in similar situations and in borders.

Species that hail from grassland may be grown in the wild flower meadow; they have deeply penetrating root systems and are tolerant of cutting; *M.sativa* and *M.lupulina* are a valuable source of nectar and pollen for bees and butterflies. *M.sativa* (alfalfa, lucerne) produces high-quality forage even on relatively poor land since, in the presence of appropriate *Rhizobium* spp., it fixes nitrogen very effectively. It can be used in gardens as green manure: the extensive and penetrating root system (to 6m/20ft) will also bring up trace elements and improve soil aeration. Sow at about 15–20g/m$^2$, in spring or late summer; inoculation with rhizobium before sowing ensures nodulation and subsequent nitrogen fixation. *M.sativa* matures in about 14 weeks and can be turned to provide a complete fertilizer that includes calcium, magnesium, potassium, nitrogen and trace elements. It is also grown for sprouted seeds; germinate in moist, dark conditions at 16–20°C/60–68°F, rinse daily and consume at 4–6 days, as green shoots appear.

Propagate from seed, sown in autumn or spring; stratification or scarification may improve germination. Propagate perennials also by division. Take softwood or semi-ripe cuttings of shrubs in summer and root in a closed case with bottom heat.

***M.arborea*** L. MOON TREFOIL. Evergreen shrub, 1–2m, finely grey-pubesc.; wood black, hard. Lvs 2.5–3cm; leaflets 6–18mm, 3, obovate, branchlets sericeous beneath, finely toothed at apex; stipules lanceolate, entire. Racemes short, subcapitate, 4–8-fld; fls 12–15mm, yellow. Fr. 12–15mm, in spiral of 1–1.5 turns, not spiny, reticulately veined. Late spring–early autumn. S Europe. Z8.

***M.cretacea*** Bieb. Ascending shrub to 25cm. Branches sparsely adpressed-pubesc. Leaflets to 8mm, broad-ovate, rounded and mucronate at apex, entire or nearly so, pubesc. throughout. Racemes subcapitate, many-fld., on peduncles shorter than lvs; fls to 7mm, yellow; cal. villous. Fr. to 1cm, falcate, compressed, adpressed-pubesc. or glabrescent. Summer. SE Europe to Crimea. Z9.

***M.falcata*** (L.) Arcang. SICKLE MEDICK. Herbaceous perenn.; stems prostrate, 60cm–1.2m. Leaflets oblong, toothed only at apex. Racemes short, dense;

peduncles longer than lvs; fls pale yellow, sometimes violet and green; cor. 5–8mm. Fr. almost straight to falcate. Summer. Europe (inc. GB), N Asia, India. Z7.

***M. intertexta*** (L.) Mill. CALVARY CLOVER. Nearly glabrous procumbent or ascending annual to 50cm. Leaflets obovate, cuneate, denticulate, sometimes with a dark spot; stipules ovate to ovate-lanceolate, incised. Racemes 1–7- or 10-fld; fls 6–9mm, yellow. Fr. 12–15mm diam., in a spiral of 3 or 6–10 turns, ovoid, cylindric or rarely discoid, both ends convex, glabrous or pubesc. on spines, transversely veined, spines usually 3–4mm, curved and adpressed to fr. Mediterranean, Portugal. The common name refers to the red spots on the lvs, said to represent stigmata, and the spiny seed pods the Crown of Thorns.

***M. lupulina*** L. BLACK MEDICK, HOP CLOVER, NONSUCH, YELLOW TREFOIL. More or less pubesc. annual or short-lived perenn., 5–60cm. Leaflets orbicular, obovate, or rhombic- or oblong-cuneate, rounded to emarginate, usually apiculate; stipules lanceolate to ovate, serrate or entire. Racemes 10–50-fld; fls 2–3mm, yellow. Fr. 1.5–3mm, reniform, black when ripe, transverse veins strongly curved, slightly anastomosing and forming an elongated network. Europe (except extreme N), naturalized N America. Z5.

***M. marina*** L. Procumbent, white-tomentose, densely leaf perenn., 20–50cm. Leaflets obovate, cuneate at base, denticulate at apex; stipules ovate, acuminate, entire or toothed. Racemes almost capitate, 5–12-fld; fls 6–8mm, pale yellow. Fr. 5–7mm, in a spiral of 2–3 turns with a small hole through the middle, cylindric, densely white-tomentose, submarginal and marginal veins thick, with 2 rows of short conical spines. European Mediterranean, Black Sea and Atlantic coasts. Z8.

***M. orbicularis*** (L.) Bartal. Glabrous or sparsely pubesc. procumbent annual, 20–90cm. Leaflets obovate-cuneate, dentate at apex or in upper part; stipules laciniate. Racemes 1–5-fld; fls 2–5mm, yellow. Fr. 10–17mm diam., in a spiral of 4–6 turns, lenticular, convex on both faces, glabrous or somewhat glandular-pubesc., not spiny; transverse veins with a few, usually weak, anastomosing branches. S Europe, W Asia.

***M. polymorpha*** L. Glabrous or pubesc. annual to 40cm. Leaflets obovate to obcordate, cuneate, dentate near apex. Stipules lanceolate to ovate-lanceolate, laciniate. Racemes 1–5-fld; fls 3–4.5mm. yellow. Fr. 4–8mm diam., in a lax spiral of 1.5–6 turns, usually glabrous and spiny, transverse veins strong, anastomosing freely, submarginal veins conspicuous, separated from marginal vein by deep groove, margin with 3 keels separated by 2 grooves, spines absent or exceeding diam. of fr. Europe, Asia.

***M. sativa*** L. ALFALFA; LUCERNE. More or less pubesc. perenn. to 80cm. Leaflets obovate to almost linear, long-cuneate, dentate at apex; stipules lanceolate to linear subulate, entire or dentate at base. Racemes 5–40-fld; pedicels short, stout, erect in fr.; fls 6–11mm, blue to purple. Fr. nearly straight, falcate, or in a spiral of 1–3 twists with a hole through the centre, glabrous, pubesc. or glandular, not spiny, transverse veins anastomosing and forming transversely or radially elongated network. SW Asia, naturalized in US, Europe. Z5.

***M. scutellata*** (L.) Mill. More or less densely glandular-pubesc. annual, 20–60cm. Leaflets obovate to elliptical, cuneate, dentate in upper part; stipules ovate-lanceolate to lanceolate, incised-dentate. Racemes 1–3-fld; fls 6–7mm, yellow. Fr. 9–18mm diam., in spiral of 4–8 pelviform, overlapping turns, glandular-pubesc., not spiny, transverse veins numerous, conspicuous, freely anastomosing and joining strong marginal vein. S Europe.

***M. denticulata*** Willd. See *M. polymorpha*.
***M. echinus*** Lam. See *M. intertexta*.
***M. hispida*** Gaertn. See *M. polymorpha*.

**Medinilla** Gaudich. (For J. de Medinilla de Pineda, Governor of the Marianne Islands in 1820.) Melastomataceae. Some 150 species of evergreen shrubs, some climbing or epiphytic. Leaves opposite or whorled, in some species unequal, solitary and alternate, simple, entire, leathery or fleshy, conspicuously 3–9-nerved. Flowers white, rose or flamingo-pink in panicles or cymes, these sometimes pendulous and bracteate, appearing whorled; bracts, where present, sometimes large and rosy; calyx entire or 4- or 6-toothed, persisting in fruit; petals 4–5 or 6, ovate, oblong or obovate, acute. Fruit a spherical or ovoid berry. Tropical Africa, SE Asia, Pacific. Z10.

CULTIVATION *M. magnifica* is one of the most beautiful of tropical evergreens, grown for its lush foliage and huge panicles of brilliantly coloured blooms, which retain their perfection over long periods. Suitable for outdoor cultivation only in the humid tropics; grow in the warm glasshouse or conservatory in cooler regions (min. 15–21°C/60–70°F). Grow in bright filtered light, ensuring shade from the hottest summer sun, in a fertile, open and porous medium enriched with leafmould and with additional sharp sand. Provide buoyant high humidity, syringe frequently, water plentifully and feed fortnightly when in full growth. During the winter months, a slight temperature drop to the lower end of this range and a period with just sufficient water to prevent wilting will help promote flowering. Prune to shape as necessary and repot immediately after flowering. Propagate by semi-ripe cuttings in a sandy propagating mix in a humid closed case with bottom heat; pinch out young plants to encourage branching.

***M. magnifica*** Lindl. Robust epiphytic shrub to 3m. Branches stout, tetragonal to prominently winged, strongly and regularly divaricate, jointed, faintly lenticellate, silver-green in first season, hardening rusty brown. Lvs 20–30cm, broadly ovate, acute, opposite, deep glossy green, sessile or subsessile. Panicle to 40cm, strongly pendulous, terminal; axil stout, pink; bracts large, pink, leaf-like, paired, concave above, initially overlapping, ultimately remote except for apex; fls to 2.5cm diam., pink to coral-red, clustered within bracts. Philippines.

**Mediocactus** Britt. & Rose in part.
***M. coccineus*** Britt. & Rose, not. See *Selenicereus setaceus*.
***M. megalanthus*** (Schum. ex Vaupel) Britt. & Rose. See *Selenicereus megalanthus*.

**Mediolobivia** Backeb. See *Rebutia*.

**Mee, Margaret Ursula** (1909–1988). Artist. Margaret Brown was born in Chesham, Buckinghamshire. She displayed an early interest in painting, but only began study at St Martin's School of Art at the age of 38. She went on to Camberwell School of Art, where Victor Pasmore was teaching, and there met her second husband Greville Mee. They then moved to São Paulo in Brazil in 1952, where she began teaching. Mee soon began to explore the indigenous flora of the Brazilian Amazon, a task which was to be her passion for the next thirty years. Starting in the now much-depleted Atlantic Coast rainforest, she journeyed through many remote and dangerous areas, often alone, collecting and sketching specimens before producing finished paintings in her studio. Many of the species she found were on the verge of extinction – what had begun for her as a celebration of the Amazon and its flowers looked as if it might become only a record, as the destruction of the rainforest accelerated. With this in mind, she eschewed her earlier classical style and, as can be seen in her *Flowers of the Brazilian Forests* (1968), *Flores de Amazonas* (1980) and *In Search of the Flowers of the Amazon Forest* (1988) set her flower portraits in luxuriant habitat, compositions to stress her outspoken commitment on conservation.

Her work, resulting from 15 expeditions, has proved invaluable to botanists as an unrivalled survey of Amazonian plant life. She discovered many new species, and some were named after her including the orchids *Sobralia margaretae* and *Catasetum meeae*, and the bromeliads *Neoregelia margaretae* and *Aechmea meeana*.

Margaret Mee died as the result of a car accident in 1988, but not before the launch of the Margaret Mee Amazon Trust, an organization dedicated to preserving the artist's work and to furthering research and education in Amazonian plant life and conservation.

**Meehania** Britt. (For Thomas Meehan (1826–1901), writer and nurseryman.) JAPANESE DEAD NETTLE. Labiatae. 6 species of creeping stoloniferous perennial herbs. Leaves opposite, petiolate, toothed. Verticils few-flowered, distant; bracts leaflike, bracteoles small; calyx campanulate or tubular-campanulate, 15-nerved, 2-lipped, upper lip 2-lobed, lower lip 3-lobed, the teeth deltoid; corolla tube gradually expanding, limb 2-lipped, upper lip 2-lobed, concave, lower lip 3-lobed; stamens 4 in two rows. Nutlets ovate, smooth. Asia, N America.

CULTIVATION All species of *Meehania* occur in rich deciduous woodlands. The genus is closely related to *Glechoma* (wall ivy), differing in the arrangement of the anthers and the more robust nature of *Meehania*. They form large patches of ground cover in dappled shade or in exposed but sunless areas. They flower from mid to late summer giving a display of lilac or blue flowers on rather untidy running stems which may form dense clumps. Most species are frost-hardy to –15°C/5°F. Propagate from severing rooted stolons and replanting or from seed sown in a cold frame in spring.

***M.cordata*** (Nutt.) Britt. MEEHAN'S MINT; CREEPING MINT. Stoloniferous, finely pubesc. herb. Stems 10–20cm, scattered with rough hairs. Lvs 2.5–6×2–4cm, broadly cordate, apex blunt to acute, margins crenate; petioles 2–3cm. Fls 3–6 in terminal verticillasters; cal. 1cm, puberulent; cor. 2.5–3.5cm, broadly expanding, lavender or lilac blue, hairy in the throat. E US. Z4.

***M.fargesii*** (A. Lév.) C.Y. Wu. Stoloniferous, finely pubesc. herb. Stems 15–40cm, scattered with glandular hairs at nodes. Lvs 2.5–6.5×2–4.5cm, deltoid-subcordate, petiolate, finely pubesc. on both surfaces, scattered with long glandular hairs, apex acute, margins irregularly serrate; petioles 2–3cm. Fls 2–6 in distant terminal and axillary verticils; pedicels 5mm; cal. tubular-funnelform, glandular pubesc. and strongly aromatic, lobes acute, upper 3 lobes longest; cor. tube widely expanding, 2-lipped, upper lip hooded, 2-lobed, lobes entire, lower lip patent, recurved, 3-lobed, middle lobe largest, distinctly bearded with white hairs on upper surface, margin erose, lateral lobes entire; cor. 2.8–4.5cm, long, blue streaked purple, lobes white; stamens attached to the upper lip. W China. Z7.

***M.urticifolia*** (Miq.) Mak. Stoloniferous, pubesc. herb. Stems 15–30cm. Lvs cauline, 2–5×2–3.5cm, deltoid-cordate to ovate-cordate, membranous, apex acute, margin coarsely obtuse-serrate; petioles 2–5cm. Fls 3–12 in loose terminal one-sided spikes; bracts 7–15mm, ovate; cal. 1cm, tubular-funnelform; cor. 4–5cm, blue-purple, upper lip 8–10mm, suberect, lower lip with midlobe largest, 2 lateral lobes spreading, spotted dark purple. Japan, NE China, Korea. Z5.

For synonymy see *Dracocephalum* and *Glechoma*.

**Megacarpaea** DC. (From Gk *megas*, great, and *karpos*, fruit.) Cruciferae. 7 species of large, perennial herbs. Roots very thick. Leaves pinnately cut, lobes lanceolate-oblong or linear, entire or toothed. Inflorescence paniculate, elongating in fruit; flowers large, sometimes monoecious or reduced; sepals 4, equal at base, broadly elliptic; petals 4, white, yellow-white or violet, obovate, slightly longer than sepals; stamens 6–16, free, not toothed. Fruit a silicle, large, winged, compressed, 2-lobed, breaking in half on ripening, 1 seed per locule. Europe to C Asia and China. Z7.

CULTIVATION Rare and beautiful crucifers, grown for their foliage; that of *M.polyandra* is arching, divided and, although finer, architectural in the manner of the cardoon, *Cynara cardunculus*, and a foil for the large panicles of flowers. It occurs on open slopes and in light forest at 3000–4300m/9750–13975ft in the Himalaya from Kashmir to Nepal. Grow in sun, in light well-drained soils. Propagation is usually from seed, but root cuttings may also succeed.

***M.bifida*** Benth. Similar to *M.polyandra* except lf seg. entire, fls yellow, 5mm across; stamens 7–11. Fr. very deeply notched, 4–5×6–7cm, wing 1.5cm wide. Early summer. Himalaya.

***M.megalocarpa*** (Fisch.) Schischkin. 20–40cm. Root to 3cm thick. Stem branched above. Lvs 15–16×10cm, white-hairy, lobes irregular. Fls small, yellow-green; lower fls on each raceme lacking sep., pet. and stamens; upper fls have undeveloped ovaries; sep. green, linear; pet. white-yellow, linear, stamens 6. Fr. develop from lower fls only, notched above and below, 18×22–32mm. Spring. Mongolia.

***M.polyandra*** Benth. 1–2m. Stems 6–12cm thick at base. Lvs 15–30cm, lobes 10–20×1–5cm, becoming reduced higher up the stem, sharply or bluntly toothed. Raceme dense, 20cm; fls 1cm across; sep. 5–5.5×2–3mm; pet. 4.5–6×2–3mm, yellow-white; stamens 8–16. Pedicel 2cm long in fruit; fr. nearly round, 3–3.5×3.5–5cm, deeply notched at apex; seed wingless, 10mm across. Spring–summer. Himalaya.

***M.laciniata*** DC. See *M.megalocarpa*.
For further synonymy see *Biscutella*.

**Megacodon** (Hemsl.) H. Sm. (From Gk *megas*, large, and *kodon*, bell.) Gentianaceae. 1 species, a perennial herb, differing from *Gentiana* in the elongated style. Stems robust, erect, to 2m in fruit. Basal leaves 30×10cm, elliptic, 5-veined, petiolate, cauline leaves 10–15cm, paired, basally united. Flowers few, often paired, short-stalked, nodding in upper axils (pedicels becoming erect in fruit); calyx tube 1.5cm, funnel-shaped, lobes 2cm ovate, obtuse; corolla 6–8cm, broadly campanulate, pale yellow, netted green within, lobes broadly ovate, overlapping, recurved, much longer than tube; anthers free. Capsule to 5cm, sessile, cylindric. Summer. C Nepal to SW China. Z7.

CULTIVATION A spectacular perennial from streamsides and damp pastures in the Himalayas, it creates a dramatic effect if planted in groups. Plant in dappled sunlight with a cool, moist root-run, in a sheltered position at the margins of ponds or streams (though not at the water's edge) or in the peat, bog or woodland garden; a humus-rich soil is essential. Protect the crowns with bracken during the winter. Propagate by division. Prone to attack by slugs.

***M.stylophorus*** (C.B. Clarke) H. Sm. As for the genus.

For synonymy see *Gentiana*.

**Megalopanax** Ekman. See *Aralia*.

**Megaphrynium** Milne-Redh. (From Gk *mega*, great, and *phrynion*, a name used by Dioscorides.) Marantaceae. About 5 species of tall perennial herbs. Leaves basal, petiolate, broadly elliptic. Inflorescence a panicle; bracts caducous; cymules 1 per node; bracteole fleshy; sepals free, sometimes adnate to corolla; corolla tube very short, lobes oblong, longer than calyx; outer staminodes linear-lanceolate, subulate, sometimes 1 absent; ovary trilocular. Fruit a subglobose capsule, grooved, tardily dehiscent, exocarp fleshy; seeds arillate. W Africa. Z10.

CULTIVATION As for *Calathea*.

***M.macrostachyum*** (Benth.) Milne-Redh. To 2m. Lvs to 50×30cm, glabrous, elliptic to ovate-oblong, acuminate, rounded at base; sheath leathery. Panicle to 20cm; peduncle to 5cm; bracts 10+, to 2.5cm, leathery, ovate, acute; cymules sessile; sep. to 1mm, ovate; cor. tube yellow, violet at base, lobes to 1cm; outer staminodes 2, callose staminode to 6mm, downy. Capsule polished red, to 2cm diam.; seeds wrinkled. Togo, Guinea.

For synonymy see *Phrynium*.

**Megaskepasma** Lindau. (From Gk *megas*, large, and *skepasma*, covering or shelter.) Acanthaceae. 1 species, an evergreen shrub to 3m. Stems downy then gland-dotted, stout, obscurely 4-angled. Leaves 12–30cm, ovate-elliptic to oblong-elliptic, acute, dark green, midrib and petiole tinted rose. Inflorescence a terminal spike to 30cm; bracts to 3.25cm, broadly ovate, crimson, showy; calyx lobes 5, equal; corolla to 7.5cm, white or shell pink, tube slender, limb 2-lipped. Fruit a 4-seeded, oblong capsule. Venezuela. Z10.

CULTIVATION Grow in full sun with some shade from intense summer sun, in a high-fertility loam-based mix, with a minimum temperature of 15–18°C/60–65°F and controlled high humidity. Water plentifully but carefully and feed weekly when in full growth allowing the surface of the medium to dry between waterings; keep almost dry in winter. Cut hard back after flowering. Propagate by seed or by greenwood or semi-ripe cuttings in a closed case with bottom heat.

***M.erythrochlamys*** Lindau. BRAZILIAN RED CLOAK; RED JUSTICIA. As for the genus. Sometimes misnamed *Adhatoda cydoniifolia* in gardens.

**Meiracyllium** Rchb. f. (From Gk *meirakyllion*, little fellow or stripling, referring to the low creeping habit.) Orchidaceae. 2 species of epiphytic orchids. Rhizomes creeping, sheathed. Stems short or absent, thickened, single-leaved. Leaf fleshy, coriaceous, broad, sessile. Infl. several-flowered, terminal, flowers large for the plant size, sepals erect, spreading, similar, lateral sepals oblique, petals broader than sepals; lip fused to the column foot, saccate or gibbous. C America. Z9.

CULTIVATION Grow in baskets or on rafts in semi-shaded, humid conditions in the intermediate house. Syringe frequently.

***M.trinasutum*** Rchb. f. Rhiz. terete, sheathed when young. Stems obscure. Lvs orbicular to elliptic, broad, sessile, obtuse or rounded, coriaceous to fleshy, 2.8–5×1.5–3.5cm. Infl. several-fld; bracts triangular, acute; fls red-purple; sep. oblong-elliptic, shortly acuminate or acute, margins reflexed; pet. elliptic, oblique, 0.7–1×0.3cm; lip ovate-cordate, fleshy, sessile, saccate-hooded, margins lobed at base. Mexico, Guatemala.

***M.wendlandii*** Rchb. f. Rhiz. stout. Stems ascending, curved, to 1cm. Lvs obovate, or oblong, obtuse or rounded, fleshy, coriaceous, to 5×2.3cm. Infl. single-fld; bracts ovate, acute; fls purple, base yellow; dorsal sep. oblong-elliptic, concave, acute 1–1.7×0.4cm, lateral sep. oblong-lanceolate, margins minutely dentate; lip obovate or flabellate, concave, margins upturned, apex decurved, acuminate, 1–1.3×0.7cm. Mexico, Guatemala.

***M. wettsteinii*** Porsch. See *Neolauchea pulchella.*

**Melaleuca** L. (From Gk *melas*, black, and *leukos*, white, in allusion to the often black trunk and white branches.) HONEY MYRTLE; BOTTLEBRUSH; PAPERBARK. Myrtaceae. Over 150 species of evergreen trees and shrubs. Bark usually of numerous, thin, paper-like, corky layers, sometimes scaly or hard and furrowed. Leaves usually alternate, sometimes opposite or whorled, usually subsessile, entire, flat, concave or semicylindrical, usually small and crowded, firm in texture, may be dotted with oil glands. Inflorescence usually axillary; flowers perfect or male, sessile, in heads or cylindrical spikes, the axis usually growing beyond into a leafy shoot; calyx tube 4-lobed; petals 5, concave, usually with a short claw; stamens conspicuous, numerous, much longer than petals, in 5 bundles opposite petals, the united basal part of each bundle flattened into a short or long claw. Fruit small, sessile or very shortly pedicellate, sometimes embedded in thickened stem, woody, 3-celled capsule, usually remaining on stem. Mainly Australian; also New Caledonia, New Guinea and Malesia. Z9. In *Melaleuca* the stamens are longer than the petals and this character is used to separate it from many genera; it is similar to *Callistemon* and *Kunzea* but differs in having the stamens united in bundles opposite petals.

CULTIVATION As for *Callistemon.*

***M. acuminata*** F. Muell. Shrub to 4m. Bark layered, scaly, rough. Branches rather slender, wand-like. Lvs 5–10×2–4mm, opposite, decussate, flat or concave, ovate, acute, often pungent; petiole to 1mm. Infl. 1- or few-fld axillary clusters on previous year's branchlets; fls single within each bract; pet. pink or white, nearly circular, shortly clawed, *c*2mm; stamens white, fil. 9–17, free part to 3mm. Fr. cup-shaped, 3–4×4–5mm. NSW, Victoria, S & W Australia.

***M. armillaris*** (Sol. ex Gaertn.) Sm. BRACELET. Shrub to 0.5m to tree to 8m, glabrous except for the young shoots. Lvs (9–)14–28(–35)×0.7–1.3mm, spirally arranged, linear or narrowly elliptic to compressed or semiterete. Infl. of 25–70 densely arranged monads; sep. triangular, 0.7–1mm, often persistent on mature fr.; stamens 6.5–12.5mm, 10–16(–20) per bundle, fil. white to rarely mauve. Fr. often deeply immersed in an inflated rachis, globose or shortly rounded-cylindrical, 3–4×4–7mm, smooth, entire to moderately toothed. NSW, Victoria, S Australia.

***M. biconvexa*** Byrnes. Shrub or small tree to 10m. Bark layered, papery. Lvs 7–18×2–4mm, opposite, channelled above, keeled beneath, broadly to narrowly ovate, acute, sometimes apiculate, villous, soon glabrous; petiole to 1mm. Infl. a few-fld, dense, terminal head or short spike; fls single within each bract. Petals broadly ovate to nearly circular with distinct narrow claw, 5–6mm; stamens white or pale yellow. Fr. campanulate to urceolate, 4–5mm long and wide. NSW, Australia.

***M. cajuputi*** Powell. Shrub or usually a tree to 25m. Bark layered, fibrous and papery. Lvs 45–120×8–20mm, scattered, narrowly to broadly ovate or obovate, acute; petioles to 7mm. Infl. a many-fld terminal or upper-axillary spike, usually single, sometimes 2–3 together; fls in triads; pet. broadly obovate, clawed, to 2.5mm; stamens white. Fr. cup-shaped to globose, to 3×4mm. Australia to Malesia.

***M. coccinea*** A.S. George. Openly branched shrub to 2.7m, tomentose on all parts with lvs soon glabrescent but stems remaining sparsely hairy. Lvs 5.6–20×0.9–4.4mm, decussate, very narrowly triangular or ovate to very broadly ovate, usually somewhat reflexed. Infl. a spike of (22–)30–38 fls; sep. broadly ovate, 1.5–2mm, persistent to fr. maturity; stamens red, 11–26mm, 9–18 per bundle. Fr. compressed barrel-shaped, 2.8–3.1×4–7mm, papery in texture. W Australia.

***M. cordata*** Turcz. Shrub to 3m. Lvs to 12mm, alternate, ovate-cordate, somewhat clasping, several-nerved from base. Infl. in terminal, dense, globose heads; fls red-purple; cal. densely tomentose-villous. W Australia.

***M. cuticularis*** Labill. SALT-WATER PAPERBARK. Shrub 1.5–3m. Bark deciduous, in paper-like layers. Branches rigid, tortuous. Lvs 6–10×2–3mm, linear-oblong or narrow-lanceolate. Fls 1–3, in small terminal clusters, cream-white; pet. reflexed; stamens numerous. W & S Australia.

***M. decora*** (Salisb.) Britt. Shrub or tree to 12m. Bark many-layered, papery, fibrous. Lvs 15–16×1–2mm, scattered, flat or concave above, linear, oblong or narrowly elliptic, acute, with prominent midrib, 3-veined, narrowed at base; petiole very short *c*1mm. Infl. a many-fld, open, upper axillary or terminal spike (sometimes leafy so flowers appear axillary). Fls solitary within each bract to triads; pet. white, broadly ovate-elliptic with a long claw, 2–3mm; stamens white, fil. 20–40, free part to 3.5mm. Fr. cup-shaped or truncate-ellipsoid, 2–3mm long and wide. Queensland, NSW.

***M. decussata*** R. Br. ex Ait. f. Shrub to 4m. Bark rough, fissured. Lvs 4–15×3mm, opposite, decussate, narrowly obovate to linear, usually obtuse, faintly 3-nerved; petiole very short, to 1mm. Infl. a many-fld usually dense, axillary (rarely terminal) spike. Fls single within each bract, opposite; pet. purple-pink, ovate, truncated to short claw, *c*2mm; stamens purple, fil. 10–25 in 2 series on each claw margin, free part to 5mm. Fr. truncate-conical, partially embedded in the expanded rachis, 3–5mm diam. Victoria, S Australia.

***M. densa*** R. Br. Shrub to 2m. Lvs to 3mm, opposite, overlapping, ovate. Infl. short spikes. W Australia.

***M. diosmifolia*** Andrews. Shrub to 3m. Lvs 9–13×3–5mm, spiral, elliptic, somewhat spreading, flat, obtuse to almost acute; petiole 1.3–1.8mm. Infl. a spike of *c*20–30 monads; sep. transversely triangular, 1.3–2mm, sometimes persistent to fr. maturity; stamens green, 3–5 per bundle. Fr. 5–8×9–12mm, compressed-globular, papery in texture. W Australia.

***M. elliptica*** Labill. Shrub to 3m. Bark thinly furrowed, peeling in strips. Lvs up to 5–6mm, opposite, ovate to suborbicular, closely set, leathery. Infl. in oblong or cylindrical spikes; stamens *c*16mm, red. W Australia.

***M. ericifolia*** Sm. SWAMP PAPERBARK. Shrub to small tree to 8m. Bark layered, corky. Lvs scattered, or sometimes ternate or few opposite pairs, 7–15(–18)×*c*1mm, linear, shallowly concave above, acute, 1–3 veined. Infl. a dense, rarely open, terminal spike; fls single within each bract; pet. white, circular with short claw, *c*1mm; stamens white, fil. 7–13, free part to 6mm. Fr. campanulate to cylindrical, 2.5–4mm long and wide, usually in dense spike. NSW, Victoria, Tasmania.

***M. fulgens*** R. Br. Shrub, 0.4–2.6m, glabrous except for the young tomentose shoots. Lvs 8.3–35×1–4.3mm, decussate, narrowly elliptic or slightly obovate, acute to acuminate; petiole very short or sessile. Infl. a spike of 6–20 fls; sep. very broadly transversely ovate, 1–3mm; stamens scarlet or deep pink (rarely white), numerous. Fr. urceolate, 4.8–8.8×7.5–13.5mm, rough and wrinkled in texture to almost papery. W & C Australia. ssp. ***steedmanii*** (C. Gardn.) Cowley. Distinguished by its obovate flat lvs.

***M. gibbosa*** Labill. Shrub to 3m. Bark rough, fissured. Lvs 2–6×1–4mm, opposite, decussate, concave above, keeled beneath, usually reflexed at tip, broadly ovate to broadly obovate; petiole absent or very short. Infl. a few- or many-fld axillary spike or cluster; fls single within each bract, opposite; pet. pink, ovate-truncate, clawed, 2–2.5mm; stamens purple to pink, glabrous, fil. 12–20, free part to 4mm. Fr. truncate-conical or cylindrical, partially embedded in expanded rachis, 3–4mm diam. S Australia and Tasmania.

***M. glaberrima*** F. Muell. Shrub 0.5–2m, glabrous except for the sparsely lanuginose young shoots. Lvs 5–10×0.5–1mm, spirally arranged, slightly spreading and sometimes subfalcate, semiterete to terete especially toward apex, obtuse to acute; petiole 0.5–1mm. Infl. of 10–40 moderately densely arranged monads; sep. triangular, 1–1.5mm, persistent to mature fr.; stamens 5.5–12mm (6–)8–16(–20) per bundle, fil. mauve, pink or purple. Fr. occasionally partially immersed in an inflated rachis, globose, sometimes compressed by mutual pressure, 3–4×3–4mm. W Australia.

***M. huegelii*** Endl. HONEY MYRTLE. Nearly glabrous shrub to 3m. Bark firm, pale. Lvs to 6mm, alternate, spirally arranged, overlapping, ovate-acuminate, striate with 3–7 nerves. Infl. a dense narrow spike to 13cm; fls white, pink in bud; staminal bundles to 12mm. W Australia. Distinguished by the whipcord branches with small overlapping, adpressed lvs, and the axis continuing to grow before flowering is over.

***M. hypericifolia*** Sm. Shrub or small tree to 6m. Bark layered, hard and somewhat papery. Lvs 10–40×4–10mm, opposite, biconvex or flat, narrowly elliptic to obovate; petiole *c*1mm. Infl. a many-fld, dense axillary spike; fls single within each bract; pet. red, broadly elliptic, *c*5mm; stamens crimson-red, to 14mm. Fr. broadly ovate to campanulate, to 7×9mm. NSW.

***M. incana*** R. Br. Shrub to 3m, pubesc. Lvs to 12mm, alternate or subopposite, spreading, linear or linear-lanceolate, narrowed to very short petiole, obscurely 1-nerved. Infl. in terminal, dense, ovoid to oblong spikes, the axis rarely growing out until after flowering; fls off-white; staminal bundles usually less than 12mm. W Australia.

***M. lanceolata*** Otto. Shrub or rounded tree to 8(–12)m, rarely prostrate and less than 1m. Young shoots tomentose with crisped or straight hairs. Bark firm, fibrous and grey. Lvs 3.8–12.2×0.7–1.9mm, alternate, spirally arranged, linear to elliptic, flat to terete. Infl. a leafy spike; fls in 6–20 triads; sep. very transversely ovate or broadly to narrowly triangular, 0.5–1.1mm, persistent to young fr.; stamens white or cream, 6–14 per bundle. Fr. barrel-shaped, ovoid or globose, 2.3–4.8×2.5–5.2mm, smooth to papery. S Australia.

***M. lateritia*** A. Dietr. ROBIN-REDBREAST BUSH. Shrub, 1–3m. Bark soft-corky, becoming fibrous. Lvs 13×2mm, alternate, scattered, linear. Infl. in showy cylindrical or oblong spikes; stamens scarlet-red, *c*15mm. W Australia.

***M. laxiflora*** Turcz. Shrub 0.5–1(–2)m. Lvs 15–20×2–4mm, spirally arranged, narrowly obovate, flat, acute to acuminate. Infl. of (6–)10–15(–20) loosely arranged monads; sep. triangular, 1–1.5mm, persistent to mature fr.; stamens 10–18 per bundle, fil. pink to mauve. Fr. somewhat pyriform. W Australia.

***M. leucadendra*** (L.) L. RIVER TEATREE; WEEPING TEATREE; BROAD-LEAVED PAPERBARK; PAPERBARK; BROAD-LEAVED TEATREE. Tree to 30m. Bark layered, papery. Lvs scattered, 8–23×0.9–4cm, narrowly ovate to elliptical, acute, widest below middle, thinly leathery; petioles 6–12mm. Infl. a many-fld, open to distant-fld, upper-axillary or terminal spike; fls in triads; pet. white, obovate to nearly circular with a short, broad claw, 2–4mm; stamens white, fil. 5–10, free part to 12mm. Fr. cup-shaped or cylindrical, 4–5mm long and wide. N Australia, W Australia, Queensland, also in Malesia and New Caledonia.

***M. linariifolia*** Sm. Shrub or small tree to 10m. Bark layered, papery. Young parts somewhat pubesc. Lvs 10–30×1–3mm, mostly opposite, rigid, linear or narrowly elliptic, midrib prominent beneath; petioles absent or very short. Infl. a many-fld, usually open terminal or subterminal spike; fls usually opposite, solitary within each bract; pet. white, broadly elliptic to nearly circular, 2–3mm; stamens white, fil. 30–60, free part to 3mm. Fr. turbinate or cylindrical, 2.5–3.5mm long and wide. Queensland, NSW, Northern Territory and north-eastern S Australia.

***M. macronychia*** Turcz. Multi-stemmed shrub to 3m, glabrous except for the young shoots. Lvs 8.7–27×4.5–12.6mm, spiral, broadly elliptic or obovate to broadly obovate, acute; petiole 0.7–2.5mm or sometimes almost sessile. Infl. a spike of 30–65 fls; sep. very broadly ovate, 1.2–2.6mm, persistent to young fr.; stamens red, 20–34 per bundle. Fr. compressed barrel-shaped, 3.5×4.6–5.1mm, papery in texture. W Australia.

***M. microphylla*** Sm. Shrub. Lvs alternate, scattered, spreading or recurved, to 10mm, linear. Infl. in short spikes. Flowers off-white. W Australia.

***M. nesophila*** F. Muell. WESTERN TEA MYRTLE. Shrub or small tree to 7m or more. Bark thick, spongy, peeling in broad strips. Lvs to 23mm, alternate, obovate-oblong to oblong-cuneate, obscurely 1–3-nerved. Infl. in terminal dense heads to 23mm across; fls lavender or rose-pink; staminal clusters to 12mm, claws short. W Australia.

***M. nodosa*** (Gaertn.) Sm. Shrub to 7m. Bark layered, papery. Lvs alternate, 15–40×1–3mm, terete or linear ovate, acute, cuspidate with straight tips; petioles to 1mm. Infl. dense with few to many male or perfect fls in axillary and terminal shortly pseudo-pedunculate heads; fls single, pairs or triads within each bract; rachis growing out after anthesis; pet. yellow-white, circular with or without claw, 1–1.5mm; stamens yellow, fil. 3–5, free part to 5mm. Fr. compressed angular-turbinate, *c*3mm long and wide. Queensland, NSW.

***M. preissiana*** Schauer PREISS'S PAPERBARK. Small to medium-sized tree, 9–13m, with a zig-zag appearance. Bark white, papery. Lvs with nearly parallel sides and blunt more or less callose tip. W Australia.

***M. radula*** Lindl. Shrub 0.3–2.4m, glabrous except for the young shoots. Lvs 13–41.5×0.8–1.3mm, decussate, very narrowly elliptic, flat but with margins strongly recurved and appearing almost linear, acute to acuminate; petiole very short or sessile. Infl. a spike of 2–8(–10) fls; sep. to 1mm, very broadly transversely ovate, weakly persistent to very early fruiting stages; stamens purple, mauve, lilac, pink or white, 30–90 per bundle. Fr. globular, 5.2–8.2×7–10.8mm, smooth or slightly wrinkled but not papery in texture. W Australia.

***M. spathulata*** Schauer. Shrub to 1m. Lvs to 7mm, alternate, obovate, narrowed at base. Infl. in terminal globose clusters. Fls pink or red; staminal bundles 7mm, claws less than half as long. W Australia.

***M. squamea*** Labill. Shrub to 3m, rarely to 6m. Bark corky. Lvs scattered, flat or concave above, 4–10×1–3mm, lanceolate, acute, incurved towards apex, 3-sometimes 5-nerved; petioles to 1.5mm. Infl. a few-fld terminal head or short spike; fls single within each bract; pet. pink-purple, rarely nearly circular with a short claw, 2–3mm; stamens purple, pink or rarely white, fil. 4–9, free part to 6mm. Fr. urceolate to ovoid, 5–7mm long and wide. NSW, Victoria, Tasmania.

***M. squarrosa*** Sm. Shrub or small tree to 15m. Bark layered, papery. Lvs 5–15×4–7mm, opposite or subopposite, decussate, ovate to very broadly ovate, acute to acuminate, almost pungent; petiole very short, *c*1mm. Infl. a many-fld, usually dense terminal spike; fls mostly in triads; pet. white or tinged pink, ovate to nearly circular with short claw, 1.5–2mm; stamens white or pale yellow, fil. 6–12, free part to 6mm. Fr. cup-shaped, *c*4mm long and wide. S & SE Australia.

***M. styphelioides*** Sm. Shrub or small tree, rarely to 20m. Bark layered, papery or hard and scaly. Lvs 4–25×2–6mm, scattered, sessile, flat, often more or less twisted, ovate to broadly ovate, acute, tapering to a short rigid point, striate with 15–30 fine veins. Infl. a few- to many-fld, dense, sometimes leafy, upper-axillary terminal or subterminal spike; fls in triads, sometimes single; pet. white, nearly circular, shortly clawed, 1–2mm; stamens white, fil. 12–26, free part to 6mm. Fr. cup-shaped to ovoid, 2–3.5×2–3mm, in open or dense spikes. E Australia.

***M. tenella*** Benth. Shrub to 5m. Lvs to 5mm, alternate, linear. Infl. in terminal globose or short-cylindrical spikes; fls white. W Australia.

***M. teretifolia*** Endl. Tall shrub. Lvs to 5cm, alternate, linear-subulate, cylindrical. Infl. in sessile head, axillary or lateral; fls white. W Australia.

***M. thymifolia*** Sm. Shrub usually 1m, rarely to 6m, commonly multi-branched from lignotuber. Bark corky, flaky. Lvs 5–15×1–3mm, opposite or subopposite, flat or concave above, stiff, narrowly elliptic, acute; petioles to 1mm. Infl. usually a few-fld, dense axillary spike usually on older wood; fls single within each bract; pet. pink to purple, ovate with a distinct claw, 4–5mm; stamens pink to purple, fil. 40–60, free part of 4mm. Fr. cup- or barrel-shaped, 4–5m long and wide. Queensland, NSW.

***M. viridiflora*** Sol. ex Gaertn. Shrub or tree to 25m. Bark layered, papery and fibrous, loose to tight and hard. Lvs 5–22×0.6–7cm, scattered, narrowly to broadly obovate, sometimes elliptic or broadly ovate, acute to obtuse; petioles 4–20mm. Infl. a many-fld, dense to moderately open, upper-axillary or terminal spike, often 2–4 together; fls in triads; pet. white or red, obovate, with short claw 2–5mm; stamens white, yellow, green, pink or red, glabrous. Fr. shortly barrel-shaped, 2.5–5×4–6mm. New Guinea, New Caledonia, Australia. var. ***rubriflora*** Brongn. & Gris. Distinguished by its thinner and shorter lvs and shorter stamens.

***M. wilsonii*** F. Muell. Shrub to 1.5m. Bark compact, rough, fissured. Lvs 8–15×1–2mm, opposite, decussate, flat or concave above, ovate, acute, cuspidate, often recurved or twisted, glabrous or woolly then glabrescent early; petiole to 1mm. Infl. 1- or few-fld axillary (sometimes terminal) clusters on previous years' wood; fls single within each bract; pet. white often tinged pink, nearly circular, shortly clawed, *c*2mm; stamens pink, fil. 7–15, free part to 6mm. Fr. cup-shaped, 3–4×4–5mm, borne in small clusters. Victoria, S Australia.

***M. abietina*** Sm. See *M. cuticularis*.
***M. alba*** hort. ex Steud. See *M. armillaris*.
***M. callistemonea*** Lindl. See *M. lateritia*.
***M. chlorantha*** Bonpl. See *M. diosmifolia*.
***M. coronata*** Andrews. See *M. thymifolia*.
***M. corrugata*** J.M. Black ex Eardley. See *M. fulgens*.
***M. crassifolia*** Benth. See *M. laxiflora*.
***M. curvifolia*** Schldl. See *M. lanceolata*.
***M. diffusa*** Forst. f. See *Metrosideros diffusus*.
***M. erubescens*** Otto. See *M. diosmifolia*.
***M. foliosa*** Dum.-Cours. See *M. diosmifolia*.
***M. genistifolia*** Sm. See *M. decora*.
***M. juniperina*** Sieb. ex Rchb. f. See *M. nodosa*.
***M. laurina*** Sm. See *Tristaniopsis laurina*.
***M. longicoma*** Benth. See *M. macronychia*.
***M. magnifica*** Specht. See *Asteromyrtus magnifica*.
***M. nummularia*** Turcz. See *M. elliptica*.
***M. parviflora*** Lindl. non Rchb. f. See *M. laxiflora*.
***M. pauciflora*** auct. non Turcz. See *M. biconvexa*.
***M. pubescens*** Schauer. See *M. lanceolata*.
***M. quinquenervia*** (Cav.) S.T. Blake. See *M. viridiflora* var. *rubriflora*.
***M. seorsiflora*** F. Muell. See *M. lanceolata*.
***M. steedmanii*** C. Gardn. See *M. fulgens* ssp. *steedmannii*.
***M. suaveolens*** Sol. ex Gaertn. See *Lophostemon suaveolens*.
***M. symphyocarpa*** F. Muell. See *Asteromyrtus symphyocarpa*.
***M. trinervia*** Sm. See *Leptospermum trinervium*.

**Melampodium** L. (From Gk *melas*, black, and *pous*, foot; application unclear.) Compositae. About 37 species of annual to perennial herbs and subshrubs, to 1m. Leaves linear to ovate, pinnatisect to dentate or entire. Capitula radiate; involucre cup-shaped; phyllaries *c*5, herbaceous or margins scarious; ray florets usually white to pale yellow; disc florets usually yellow. Fruit a linear, cylindrical cypsela. Tropical and warm America.

CULTIVATION Tolerant of drought and nutritionally poor soils, they bear creamy white daisy flowers over long periods, from spring often into autumn; suitable for sunny banks, rockeries and native plant gardens. Grow in full sun in any deep, well-drained soil. Propagate by seed; *Melampodium* are taprooted and division is not recommended.

***M. cinereum*** DC. Subshrub to 20cm, strigose. Lvs to 5×1cm, linear-oblong, entire to pinnately 10-lobed. Capitula to 2cm diam.; ray florets to 6×2mm, cream; disc florets yellow. Fr. to 2mm. Spring–autumn. Texas, N Mexico. Z9.

***M. leucanthum*** Torr. & A. Gray. Subshrub, to 60cm, strigose. Lvs to 4×1cm, linear-oblong, entire to pinnately 6–lobed. Capitula to 3.5cm diam.; ray florets to 12×6mm, cream; disc florets yellow. Fr. to 2.5mm. Spring–autumn. Mexico to Colorado. Z4.

**Melandrium** Röhling. Caryophyllaceae. This generic name has been widely used especially in European Floras for some plants now generally included within the genus *Silene*. In this treatment we have followed *Flora Europaea* in treating all *Melandrium* species as *Silene*. The most important synonymy is as follows.

***M. album*** (Mill.) Garcke. See *Silene latifolia*.
***M. californicum*** (Dur.) Rohrb. See *Silene californica*.
***M. dioicum*** (L.) Casson & Germaine. See *Silene dioica*.
***M. elisabethae*** (Jan) Rohrb. See *Silene elisabethae*.
***M. keiskii*** (Miq.) Ohwi. See *Silene keiskii*.

*M.rubrum* (Weigel) Garcke. See *Silene dioica*.
*M.virginicum* (L.) A. Braun. See *Silene virginica*.
*M.zawadskii* (Herbich) A. Braun. See *Silene zawadskii*.

**Melanoselinum** Hoffm. (From Gk *melas*, black and *Selinum*.) Umbelliferae. To 7 species of monocarpic, shrubby herbs; stems palm-like. Leaves few times pinnatisect to pinnate. Involucre of irregularly cut bracts; petals notched, white or tinged purple. Fruit pubescent, dark brown-black; mericarps with toothed wings. Madeira and Azores. Z9.

CULTIVATION Grow in full sun in any moderately fertile and well-drained soil. Propagate by seed.

***M.decipiens*** (Schräd. & Wendl.) Hoffm. BLACK PARSLEY. Bienn. or monocarpic perenn. to 2.5m; stem erect, slightly woody, simple. Lvs *c*40×30cm, in terminal rosette, 2–3-pinnate, seg. ovate to lanceolate, sharply serrate, 2–12cm, bright green-yellow, smooth, except midribs and rachis pubesc.; petiole inflated, smooth. Umbels centrally depressed, numerous in crowded, pubesc. infl. to 90cm; rays *c*30, to 5cm; involucral bracts 10–12, irregularly cut to pinnatifid, to 3cm; involucels numerous, lanceolate, tinged purple; fls fragrant. Fr. oblong, to 14mm; mericarps with toothed, lateral wings to 1.5mm. Spring–summer. Madeira.

**Melanthium** L. (From Gk *melas*, black, and *anthos*, flower; the persistent perianth segments become dark after flowering.) Liliaceae (Melanthaceae). 5 species of rhizomatous perennial herbs; rhizomes thick; roots fibrous. Leaves linear to oblanceolate, basal leaves sheathing. Inflorescence a large, open, terminal panicle, with axils and pedicels roughly hairy; flowers small, bisexual and male flowers in the same inflorescence; perianth segments 6, free, spreading, persistent, clawed, exterior ciliate, with 2 dark spots at base of blade; stamens 6, adnate to claws of perianth segments; ovary superior, trilocular; styles 3, free, spreading. Fruit a capsule; seeds flat, winged. Summer. N America.

CULTIVATION *M.virginicum* is suitable for acidic soils in the bog garden and in streamside plantings, and requires slightly damper conditions than *Veratrum*, which it otherwise resembles in its cultural requirements.

***M.hybridum*** Walter. To 150cm, slender. Lvs to 7.5cm wide, oblanceolate, tapering to base. Fls green; perianth seg. 0.6cm, suborbicular, undulate, claw as long as blade. E US (Connecticut to Georgia). Z6.

***M.virginicum*** L. BUNCHFLOWER. To 170cm. Lvs to 30×3cm, linear, conduplicate, grassy, those on stem narrower. Flowering stem stout; panicles 15–45cm diam. Fls cream at first, later green-yellow, darkening to brown with age; perianth seg. 0.8cm, broadly oblong-cordate to ovate, margins flat, 2–3× longer than claw. E US (New York to Florida, Texas, Indiana). Z5.

*M.latifolium* Desr. See *M.hybridum*.
*M.massoniifolium* Andrews. See *Whiteheadia bifolia*.
For further synonymy see *Helonias*.

**Melasphaerula** Ker-Gawl. (From Gk *melas*, black, and *sphaerula*, a Latinized diminutive of a sphere, referring to the corms.) Iridaceae. 1 species, a perennial herb. Corms to 1cm diam., globose or conical, often with cormlets at base, with dark, leathery fibrous tunic. Stem 20–50cm, straggling, branched, branches to 7cm. Leaves 5–25×1cm, 6–7 lanceolate, grass-like, sheathing the basal half of stem. Spikes flexuous, laxly 3–7-flowered; flowers small, irregular, white or cream, usually purple-veined; perianth segments 6, 10–15×2–4mm, joined for 1mm at base, either spreading and stellate or 2-lipped; stamens short, arched; style 6mm, 3-branched, branches 2mm; ovary sharply 3-angled. Close to *Sparaxis*, differing in the angled ovary. S Africa (SW Cape). Z9.

CULTIVATION As for *Ixia*.

***M.ramosa*** (L.) N.E. Br. As for the genus.

*M.graminea* Ker-Gawl. See *M.ramosa*.

**Melastoma** L. (From Gk *melas*, black, and *stoma*, mouth; the mouth is stained black by the berries.) Melastomataceae. Some 70 species of evergreen shrubs, often erect, strigose. Leaves oblong or lanceolate, opposite, entire, leathery, 3–7-veined, stalked. Inflorescence cymose, terminal, few- to many-flowered; flowers showy, 2-bracteate, calyx stiffly hairy, calyx lobes alternating with bristle-tipped appendages (cf. *Medinilla*); petals usually 5, obovate or unequal-sided, sometimes ciliate at base, white, pink or purple; stamens 10, rarely 14, dimorphic. Fruit a leathery or fleshy berry, breaking irregularly into 5–7 cells with many spiral seeds. SE Asia. Z10.

CULTIVATION As for *Medinilla*.

***M.candidum*** D. Don. Shrub, to 1.2–2.5m; branches hoary, bluntly 4-angled, at first strigosely scaly, scales dense, adpressed, brown. Lvs 5–15cm, ovate, acute, 7-veined, densely bristly above, hairy beneath; pedicels 0.6–2cm, villous. Infl. a 3–7-fld cyme, 2.5–7.5cm diam.; fls fragrant; cal. grey-hairy; pet. 3–4cm, pink or white; bracts densely hairy. Taiwan and Ryuku Is. to SE Asia and Philippines.

***M.malabathricum*** L. INDIAN RHODODENDRON. Spreading shrub to 1.8–2.5m; branches subterete, densely covered with adpressed scales. Lvs 7.5–10cm, ovate to broadly lanceolate, 3–5-veined, base obtuse, apex acute, strigose. Fls 1–5 in a corymb; pet. to 1.5cm, purple; bracts to 1.5cm. Fr. to 0.8cm, pulp red. India, SE Asia.

***M.sanguineum*** Sims. Shrub 2–6m; branches covered with long red hairs. Lvs to 20cm, oval-oblong, slender-pointed, 5-veined, usually glabrous, bristly above, pale beneath, usually glabrous. Fls few, 5–8cm diam.; cal. densely hirsute, lobes lanceolate; pet. purple. Fr. to 1cm diam. Malaysia to Java.

***M.villosum*** Aubl. & Sims. Shrub, 90–120cm; branches terete, hairy. Lvs ovate, acute, entire, 5-veined, hairy. Fls rose-pink, in few-fld clusters; pet. obovate, retuse, mucronate. Spring. S America.

*M.banksii* A. Cunn. ex Triana. See *M.malabathricum*.
*M.decemfidum* Roxb. See *M.sanguineum*.
*M.septemnervium* Lour. non Jacq. See *M.candidum*.
For further synonymy see *Tibouchina*.

**MELASTOMATACEAE** Juss. MELASTOMA FAMILY. Dicot. 215 genera and 4750 species of shrubs, herbs and less often trees or lianes, stems often 4-angled. Leaves opposite, rarely alternate, simple, often with several prominent sub-parallel veins; stipules rare. Flowers bisexual, insect-pollinated, in cymes, usually perigynous, regular or slightly zygomorphic, (3) 4 or 5 (–10)-merous; calyx lobes valvate or a rim on hypanthium, sometimes a calyptra; corolla usually free, convolute in bud; stamens usually 2 whorls, often dimorphic, filaments often twisted at anthesis bringing anthers to 1 side of the flower, connective often with appendages; ovary (2) 3–5 (–15) fused carpels, with as many locules, or sometimes partitions not developing and 1-loculed; style terminal; ovules (1–) numerous per locule, on axile placentas. Fruit a loculicidal capsule or berry; seeds usually small; endosperm absent. Some produce edible fruits (*Conostegia, Heterotrichum, Melastoma*), or timber (*Astronia*), while *Clidemia* is an important weed in some Pacific islands. Tropical and warm, especially S America. *Bertolonia, Centradenia, Dissotis, Heterocentron, Medinilla, Melastoma, Memecylon, Monolena, Osbeckia, Rhexia, Sonerila, Tibouchina*.

**Melia** L. (Gk name for the ash.) Meliaceae. 5 species of deciduous or semi-evergreen trees or shrubs. Buds small, rounded, with few outer scales, these sometimes superposed. Leaves alternate, pinnate or 2-pinnate, leaflets entire to serrate. Flowers in axillary panicles; calyx 5- or 6-lobed, small, imbricate; petals 5–6, free, imbricate in bud; stamens united in a cylindrical, erect tube, with 10–12 lobes at apex and bearing 10–12 anthers between the lobes on the inside; ovary on a short disc. Fruit drupaceous. Old World Tropics, Australia.

CULTIVATION *M.azederach* is a rapidly growing tree, often used in its native regions for reafforestation. It is valued as an ornamental for its dense, rounded crown and fragrant blooms; the yellow berries are toxic. Other species are suitable for outdoor cultivation only in essentially frost-free zones. They tolerate a range of well-drained soils and hot dry conditions, self-seeding in profusion where conditions suit. Propagate by seed.

***M.azederach*** L. CHINABERRY; PERSIAN LILAC; PRIDE OF INDIA; BEAD TREE. Deciduous tree to 15m with furrowed bark. Lvs to 80cm, leaflets to 5cm, ovate to elliptic, acute, sharply serrate or lobed, glabrous. Fls 2cm diam., lilac, in loose panicles 10–20cm long; pet. 5mm wide, spreading or decurved; staminal tube erect, violet. Fr. 1–5cm diam., round-ovate, yellow. Summer. N India, China.

'Floribunda': bushy, very floriferous. 'Umbraculiformis' (TEXAN UMBRELLA TREE): branches radiating in a dense, flattened, spreading head.

***M.azadirachta*** A. Juss. Tree to 16m. Lvs to 5cm, simple pinnate, leaflets 2.75–1.3cm, 9–15, ovate-lanceolate, slender-pointed, unequal sided, toothed or lobed, glabrous. Fls white, in axillary panicles 15–22.5cm long; pet. ciliate. Fr. 1–7mm, oval, purple. Late spring–early summer. E Indies. Z10.

***M.dubia*** Cav. Large tree. Lvs 23–60cm, doubly pinnate, leaflets 3.5–5cm, ovate to oval-lanceolate, slender-pointed, entire or toothed. Fls 1cm diam., green-white, in crowded downy panicles 12–20cm long, near the end of shoots. E Indies. Z10.

***M.composita*** Willd. See *M.dubia*.
***M.japonica*** G. Don. See *M.azederach*.
***M.sempervirens*** Sw. See *M.azederach*.

**MELIACEAE** Juss. MAHOGANY FAMILY. Dicot. 51 genera and 575 species of trees, often pachycaul, rarely shrubs or suckering shrublets, dioecious, polygamous, monoecious or with only bisexual flowers; bark bitter and astringent. Leaves pinnate, bipinnate, unifoliolate or simple, alternate, rarely decussate, sometimes spiny; stipules absent. Flowers regular, often with rudiments of opposite sex if unisexual, in spikes or thyrses, axillary; calyx (2) 3–5 (–7) free sepals, sometimes bracteole-like; corolla 3–7 (–14) free petals, in 1 (–2) whorls, sometimes basally connate; stamens usually atop a tube, with 3–19 (–30) anthers in 1 (–2) whorls, nectary usually a disc around the ovary; ovary superior (1) 2–6 (–20) fused carpels, with as many locules; placentation axile, sometimes 1-loculed with intruded parietal placentas, e.g. *Heckeldora*; ovules 1-numerous per locule. Fruit a capsule or drupe; seeds winged, or with corky outer layers, or with fleshy sarcotesta or aril; endosperm absent. Many are important timber trees, notably species of *Cedrela, Dysoxylum, Entandrophragma, Khaya, Lovoa, Melia* and *Swietenia* (mahogany). Some provide oil-seeds, like *Chisocheton* and *Trichilia*, or have edible fruits like *Aglaia cucullata* and *Lansium domesticum* (langsat). Tropical, few subtropical. *Aphanamixis, Melia, Toona, Turraea*.

**MELIANTHACEAE** Link. MELIANTHUS FAMILY. Dicot. 2 genera and 8 species of trees and shrubs. Leaves pinnate, alternate; stipules connate, intrapetiolar. Flowers bisexual, resupinate through twisting of pedicel, in racemes; calyx 5 free sepals, sometimes 2 fused or all 5 connate at the base; corolla 5 free petals, imbricate and unequal or 1 much reduced, nectary-disc extrastaminal; stamens 4 or 5, sometimes connate at the base; ovary superior, of 4 (5) fused carpels, plurilocular, each locule with 1 (*Bersama*) or 2–5 (*Melianthus*) ovules. Fruit a capsule; seeds 1 or 2 per loculed; endosperm copious, oily or starchy. Tropical and S Africa. *Melianthus*.

**Melianthus** L. (From Gk *meli*, honey, and *anthos*, flower; the calyces are filled with nectar.) Melianthaceae. 6 species of shrubs with robust, sparsely branched stems, often following a semi-herbaceous habit in colder locations, otherwise evergreen, becoming woody, especially the basal portions and aromatically scented in all parts. Leaves alternate, imparipinnate with conspicuous stipules, leaflets toothed. Flowers in erect axillary and terminal racemes, showy, profusely nectariferous, irregular; sepals and petals 5, the uppermost usually partly fused into a hooded tube, the lowermost forming a short spur; stamens 4, exserted. Fruit a 4-lobed, winged and papery capsule, containing many, shining black seeds. S Africa; *M.major* naturalized in India. Z9.

CULTIVATION *M.major* is a magnificent plant grown for its blue-green, architectural foliage in sheltered locations in Zone 8 and over, and also used as a dot plant in bedding schemes.

Grow in full sun or light shade in moisture-retentive but freely draining soils; fertile soils give good foliage effects although flowering is better on poor soils. Mulch with a thick layer of bracken litter or conifer branches in autumn in areas where frosts are prolonged. Top growth will be cut back by frost, but given root protection will resprout from the base in spring. In containers use a loam-based potting mix; water moderately when in growth and maintain a minimum winter night temperature of 5–10°C/40–50°F. Propagate by seed in spring, greenwood stem tip cuttings in summer rooted in a closed case with bottom heat, or by removal of suckers in spring. Red spider mite may be a problem under glass.

***M.major*** L. HONEY FLOWER. To 2.25m. Stems thick, terete, translucent sea-green and thickly glaucous at first and ridged to winged at internodes, becoming woody in second season. Lvs to 50cm, semi-erect then arching, or spreading, glabrous, vivid glaucous blue; leaflets 5–13×2.5–6cm, 9–11, ovate-oblong, coarsely serrate; petiole strongly winged, amplexicaul; stipules to 10cm. Racemes to 80cm; fls brown-red.

***M.minor*** L. To 2m, less robust in all parts than *M.major*, also predominantly downy, not glaucous. Lvs to 20cm; leaflets 4–5.25×1.25–2cm, 9–13, oblong-lanceolate, serrate, grey-green and rather coarsely pubesc. above, paler beneath; petiole winged. Fls brick-red in racemes to 38cm.

**Melica** L. (From Lat. *melica in varro*, a kind of vessel or amphora, alluding to the swollen stem bases.) MELIC. Gramineae. 70 species of perennial grasses to 150cm. Rhizomes creeping; stems flimsy to stout, erect, clumped, often bulbous at base. Leaf blades linear, flat or involute, arching; sheaths clasping. Panicles open or contracted, rarely compound; spikelets 2- to several-flowered, somewhat laterally compressed; rachilla usually disarticulating above glumes and between fertile florets; glumes unequal, obtuse or acute, membranous, 3–5-ribbed; lower 1–3 florets bisexual; lemma dorsally convex, 5–13-ribbed, papery, with scarious margins, aristate; palea 2-keeled; upper florets vestigial, sterile, rarely with a small bisexual floret enclosed in overlapping lemmas forming a clavate structure. Summer. Temperate regions (except Australia).

CULTIVATION Grow in sun or dappled shade in a light, moisture-retentive, sandy or loamy soil, most species perform well on calcareous soils. *M.ciliata* is more tolerant of dry soils. Propagate by seed or division.

***M.altissima*** L. SIBERIAN MELIC. To 150cm. Rhiz. creeping. Lf blades acute, to 22.5×1cm, scabrous; ligules to 5mm. Panicles erect, secured, dense, interrupted at base to 25×2.5cm; spikelets oblong, to 1cm; fertile florets 2; fertile lemmas acute, finely scabrous. C & E Europe. 'Alba': spikelets very light green. 'Atropurpurea': spikelets deep mauve, sweeping downwards and overlapping. Z5.

***M.ciliata*** L. SILKY-SPIKE MELIC. To 75cm. Stems densely tufted, erect, flimsy, grey-green. Lf blades involute and filiform or flat and broader, acute, to 17.5cm, grooved, ligules to 2mm, split. Panicles spike-like, nodding, cylindric, 15×1cm, silky, pale green or tinged purple; spikelets subsessile, elliptic-oblong, to 0.5cm; glumes ovate, acute, to 0.8cm; lemma narrowly ovate, acute, to 0.5cm, silky white-ciliate. Europe, N Africa, SW Asia. Z6. 'ALba': florets white.

***M.nutans*** L. MOUNTAIN MELIC; NODDING MELLIC. To 60cm. Stems clumped or solitary, slender, tetragonal in section. Lf blades to 20×0.5cm, green, pubesc. above; sheaths tubular; ligules obtuse, to 0.1cm. Panicles secund, loose, nodding to 15cm; spikelets to 1cm, elliptic-oblong, obtuse, purple or maroon; fertile florets 2–3, on thread-like peduncles to 1.5cm; glumes elliptic, obtuse, papery; fertile lemmas dorsally convex, obtuse, finely scabrous; palea elliptic, keels winged. Europe, N & SW Asia. Z6.

***M.transsilvanica*** Schur. As for *M.ciliata* except to 1m; lvs flat, to 0.6cm wide, midrib prominent; fls in a shorter panicle; glumes distinctly unequal, upper twice as long as lower. Eurasia. Z6.

***M.uniflora*** Retz. WOOD MELIC. To 60cm. Stems loosely, tufted. Lf blades acute to 20×0.8cm, pubesc. above, fresh green; sheaths tubular, mucronate at apex, sparsely hairy or glabrous. Panicles lax, sparsely branched, to 20×10cm; spikelets obovate, to 0.8cm, purple or tinged brown, on threadlike peduncles to 0.5cm; fertile floret solitary; glumes equal; fertile lemmas obtuse, smooth. Europe, SW Asia. 'Alba': very pale green form with white fls. 'Aurea': lvs tinted gold. 'Variegata': very small; lvs longitudinally striped with cream and green; more often cultivated than type. Z7.

For illustration see ORNAMENTAL GRASSES.

**Melicocca** L.
***M.bijuga*** L. See *Melicoccus bijugatus*.
***M.*** L.

**Melicoccus** P. Browne. (From Gk *meli*, honey, *kokkos*, kernel: the fruit is very sweet.) Sapindaceae. 2 species of glabrous polygamous or dioecious trees. Leaves alternate, equally pinnate, pinnae sessile, in 2–3 pairs, almost opposite. Inflorescence a many-flowered raceme or panicle; flowers regular; petals 4 or 5;

stamens 8. Fruit a drupe; single seed surrounded by a large fleshy aril. Tropical America, W Indies. Z10.

CULTIVATION An American relative of the litchi, *M. bijugatus* is a large spreading tree native to the tropics of Central and South America. They are grown for their fruits, collected and sold only locally, which consist of a sweet and gelatinous pulp surrounding a single large seed, enclosed in a thin green rind. When ripe, they have a grape-like flavour; the seeds are also eaten roasted. A decoction of the bark is used throughout its native region in the treatment of dysentery.

*Melicoccus* thrives in tropical lowlands which receive heavy rainfall, and are intolerant of frost, Key West in Florida probably representing its northern limit. In temperate regions, slow growth and small stature make it a suitable subject for the hot glasshouse, in a medium-fertility loam-based mix with additional leafmould. Propagate from seed (although fruiting is variable in seedlings) or by air layering; alternatively, from greenwood cuttings with bottom heat in a closed case, or under mist.

***M. bijugatus*** P. Browne. SPANISH LIME; HONEY BERRY; MAMONCILLO; GENIPE. Slow-growing tree to 18m. Lvs to 15cm, pinnae 4–6, to 10cm, elliptic-lanceolate, glabrous. Fls fragrant, white tinged yellow. Fr. to 3cm diam., globose, green, leathery, pulp juicy, translucent, tinged yellow.

For synonymy see *Melicocca*.

**Melicope** Forst. & Forst. f. (From Gk *meli*, honey, and *kope*, a division, referring to the 4 honey-glands at the base of the ovary.) Rutaceae. Some 150 species of trees or shrubs. Leaves opposite or alternate, simple or trifoliate, gland-dotted. Flowers in cymes or panicles, sometimes solitary, small, bisexual or unisexual; sepals minute; petals apically inflexed; stamens 8, inserted at base of disc, filaments subulate; ovary 4-lobed, 4-locular. Fruit of 4, 1-seeded cocci, testa lustrous. Tropical Asia to Australia. Z10.

CULTIVATION As for *Boronia*.

***M. ternata*** Forst. & Forst. f. Shrub or small tree to 6m, glabrous, spreading. Lvs to 10×4cm, opposite, trifoliate, ovate or obovate-oblong to elliptic, entire; petiole to 5cm. Infl. of axillary cymes; peduncles to 2cm; pedicels to 5mm; fls to 10mm diam.; sep. to 1.5mm, ovate-oblong, gland-dotted; pet. to 5mm, green or green-white, ovate-oblong, gland-dotted; ovary glabrous. Cocci to 5mm, pale brown, seeds black. New Zealand.

**Melicytus** Forst. & Forst. f. (From Gk *meli*, honey, and *kytos*, a hollow vessel, referring to the staminal nectaries.) Violaceae. 4 species of dioecious shrubs or trees, to 10m+. Leaves alternate, obovate to lanceolate, minutely stipulate. Flowers regular, borne in fascicles to 12, occasionally solitary; calyx 5-lobed; petals 5, spreading; anthers 5, sessile, united by a toothed membrane or free; ovary 1-chambered. Fruit a berry. Spring. New Zealand, Norfolk Is., Fiji, Solomon Is. Z9.

CULTIVATION Occurring in lowland forest, at forest margins and in subalpine scrub, *M. ramiflorus* is extremely decorative in fruit, the grey-white stems stems clothed thickly in lustrous blue-violet berries. At the warmer end of its natural range, *M. ramiflorus* often blooms twice in the year, in spring and again at the end of the summer, so that the fruits of the first flowering sometimes overlap with the second blooming, although the tiny flowers are not very conspicuous.

Hardiness is not well tested and seems likely to vary with provenance, some specimens, with shelter and good drainage, have survived several degrees of frost without injury (to about −5°/23°F) and seem likely to tolerate lower ambient temperatures given wall protection and shelter from cold drying winds. Grow in the cool, well-ventilated greenhouse in a moderately fertile, loam-based mix with direct sun or bright filtered light. Water moderately when in growth, sparingly in winter. Propagate by seed sown when ripe or in spring.

***M. lanceolatus*** Hook. f. To 5m+. Bark grey-brown. Lvs membranous, oblong to lanceolate, to 16×3cm, serrulate; petioles to 15mm. Fls in fascicles to 6, 3–5mm diam.; pet. tinged purple; pedicels to 1cm. Fr. to 6mm diam., stained dark purple. New Zealand.

***M. ramiflorus*** Forst. & Forst. f. WHITEY WOOD. Tree, to 10m+. Bole branching from base; bark grey-white. Lvs submembranous, to 15×5cm, coarsely serrate, apex highly variable, even on same plant; petioles to 2cm. Fls in fascicles to 10, to 4mm diam.; cal. lobes tiny; pet. yellow-green; stigma 4–6-lobed. Fr. obovoid to subglobose, lavender to violet, dark blue or purple. Distribution as for the genus.

**Meliosma** Bl. (From Gk *meli*, honey, and *osme*, scent, alluding to the honey-scented flowers.) Sabiaceae. 20–25 species of deciduous or evergreen pubescent to glabrous trees or shrubs to 25m. Leaves alternate, simple or pinnate with subopposite leaflets, margins serrate or entire, petioles short, often swollen at base, conspicuously longitudinally grooved above. Inflorescence a large, pyramidal, terminal or axillary panicle; flowers small, fragrant, bisexual, sessile or short-pedicellate; sepals 5, occasionally 4, imbricate, unequal; petals 5, very unequal, outer 3 concave orbicular, imbricate, inner 2 much smaller than outer, bifid or scale-like, sometimes adnate to fertile stamens; stamens 5, outermost sterile, reduced to cupular staminodes, inner whorl fertile, filament short, enlarged at apex and surrounding base of anther; ovary superior, 2(–3)-locular, surrounded by disk at base, ovules 1. Fruit a 1-seeded black or red drupe; embryo with twisted radicle. Tropical America, tropical and temperate Asia. Hardy species from Japan and China, all deciduous.

CULTIVATION Grown for their attractive habit, handsome foliage and conspicuous panicles of sweetly scented flowers, *Meliosma* spp. are undemanding in cultivation. Grow in sun in deep, moisture-retentive, moderately fertile, circumneutral soils. Propagate by seed, layers or from softwood cuttings under mist.

***M. alba*** (Schldl.) Walp. Deciduous tree to 25m, trunk to 2m diam. Lvs to 30cm, pinnate, leaflets 5–13, usually 9, ovate to elliptic or oblong, acute, attenuate to base, upper leaflets 2.5–15×2.5–6cm, smaller below, margin sparsely fine-toothed or entire, chartaceous, somewhat shining above, dull pale green beneath where pubesc. in vein-axils. Flowering before lvs appear; panicles axillary, to 20×10cm; fls to 6mm across, cream-white. Fr. 6mm, globose, black. Late spring. Mexico, China (Hubei, Sichuan). Z8.

***M. dilleniifolia*** (Wight & Arn.) Walp. Deciduous shrub or tree to 10–15m, twigs pubesc. Lvs 3–24×1.5–12cm, obovate to elliptic or obovate-oblong or oblong, apex acute, base cuneate or attenuate, margin aristate-serrulate, somewhat scabrous above, subglabrous to pubescent beneath, lateral veins in 8–30 pairs. Panicle terminal, erect or deflexed 10–50cm; fls white. Fr. 4–5mm, globose. Himalaya to China and Japan. ssp. ***dilleniifolia.*** Lvs 7–30×4–15cm, pubesc., margin finely dentate, lateral vein pairs 13–27. Panicle erect, to 28cm. S Himalaya (Punjab to N Burma). ssp. ***cuneifolia*** (Franch.) Beus. Lvs 3–24×1.5–10cm, subglabrous to pubesc., especially in vein axils beneath, margin closely to remotely dentate, lateral vein pairs 10–30. Panicle erect, to 50cm; fls to 4mm, yellow-white, becoming pure white, very fragrant. Fr. 6mm, globose, black. Summer. W China. ssp. ***flexuosa*** (Pamp.) Beus. Shrub to 5m; young shoots purple-hairy. Lvs 4–16×2–8cm, subglabrous to sparsely pubesc. beneath, margin closely to remotely dentate, lateral vein pairs 12–21. Panicles terminal, erect or deflexed, 7–22cm; fls 4mm, white. Summer. EC China. ssp. ***tenuis*** (Maxim.) Beus. Deciduous shrub or small tree; young shoots purple, pubesc. Lvs 3–16×1.5–7cm, subglabrous to sparsely pubesc. beneath, hairy in vein-axils beneath, margin coarsely dentate, lateral veins pairs 8–14. Panicles erect to deflexed, to 15cm; fls 4mm, yellow-white. Summer. Japan. Z9.

***M. myriantha*** Sieb. & Zucc. Deciduous shrub or small tree, 6.5–15m, branches spreading. Lvs 5–25×2–10cm, apex short-acuminate, base broad-cuneate or rounded, margin regularly dentate, petiole and midrib covered by red-brown hairs, lateral veins in 24–30 pairs. Panicles terminal, 15–20cm; fls 3mm, yellow-white, very fragrant. Fr. small, dark red. Summer. Japan, Korea. Z9. Sometimes mislabelled *M. meliantha.*

***M. parviflora*** Lecomte. Deciduous tree to 8m; stems hairy. Lvs 6.5–8×2.5–3.5cm, simple, obovate, apex obtuse, tip acute or shortly acuminate, attenuate to narrowly cuneate base, glabrous except on veins and vein-axils beneath, veins in 8–12 pairs, terminating in mucronate teeth. Panicles terminal, 20–30cm, with axes red-pubesc.; fls very small, white. Fr. 3mm, globose, red. Summer. W & C China. Z9.

***M. pinnata*** (Roxb.) Walp. Deciduous tree, 20–40m; young shoots stout, glabrous, pale grey. Lvs 17.5–35cm, pinnate, leaflets 5–13, lowermost 2.5×2cm, orbicular to ovate, becoming ovate to obovate above, terminal leaflet 7.5–14×3–6.5cm, acute, dentate, pubesc. above when young, pubesc. in vein axils beneath. Panicles terminal, 15–30cm; fls to 6mm, pure white. Fr. to 6mm. Summer. Korea, China. Z9.

***M. simplicifolia*** (Roxb.) Walp. Evergreen shrub or tree to 20m. Lvs 3–50×1–18cm, elliptic or obovate to lanceolate, apex acute to acuminate, base acute or attenuate to cuneate, somewhat coriaceous, glabrous to densely pubesc.

beneath, especially in vein axils, margin entire or spinous-dentate, lateral veins in 7–25 pairs. Panicles terminal, erect, 10–60cm; fls small. Fr. 4–10mm, globose. S & SE Asia (Sri Lanka to Indonesia). ssp. ***pungens*** (Walp.) Beus. Small tree; shoots red-pubescent. Lvs 5–20×2–8cm, oblong or lanceolate, acute to acuminate, coriaceous, coarsely dentate, lateral vein pairs 7–18. Panicles 10–55cm; fls large. Fr. 8mm, globose. Sri Lanka, India. Z10.

***M. veitchiorum*** Hemsl. Deciduous tree to 50m; branches stout, rigid, erect. Lvs 45–75cm, pinnate, leaflets 8.5–17.5–4–8.5cm, 7–9, ovate or oblong, apex obtuse to shortly acuminate, sometimes subcordate at base, margins entire or sparsely toothed, midrib pubesc. beneath, veins pairs 10–15. Panicles terminal, to 45×30cm, fls to 6mm, cream white. Fr. 6–8mm, subglobose, rich violet to black. Late spring. W China. Z8.

***M. beaniana*** Rehd. & Wils. See *M. alba*.
***M. cuneifolia*** Franch. See *M. dilleniifolia* ssp. *cuneifolia*.
***M. dilatata*** Diels. See *M. parviflora*.
***M. flexuosa*** Pamp. See *M. dilleniifolia* ssp. *flexuosa*.
***M. oldhamii*** Maxim. See *M. pinnata*.
***M. parvifolia*** hort. See *M. parviflora*.
***M. pendens*** Rehd. & Wils. See *M. dilleniifolia* ssp. *flexuosa*.
***M. pungens*** (Wallich ex Wight & Arn.) Walp. See *M. simplicifolia* ssp. *pungens*.
***M. rhoifolia*** Maxim. See *M. pinnata*.
***M. sinensis*** Nak. See *M. pinnata*.
***M. stewardii*** Merrill. See *M. myriantha*.
***M. tenuis*** Maxim. See *M. dilleniifolia* ssp. *tenuis*.

**Melissa** L. (From Gk *melissa*, bee: the plant is attractive to bees.) Labiatae. 3 species of perennial deciduous herbs, to 1.5m. Leaves ovate, short-petioled. Inflorescence whorled; calyx campanulate, bilabiate with 13 veins, upper lip flat, 3-toothed, lower lip 2-toothed; corolla bilabiate, upper lip erect, lower lip 3-lobed. Fruit a nutlet. Mediterranean Europe, garden escapee in N Europe and N America.

CULTIVATION *Melissa* is grown as a herb for its lemon-scented leaves, used in *pot-pourri*, and as a drought-tolerant border plant. Grow in any well-drained soil, in an open sunny site, with shelter from strong winds. Golden-leaved cvs benefit from light shade and should be cut back after flowering to produce new growth of better colour. Plants for culinary used should be cut back regularly to maintain a supply of fresh shoots; older leaves deteriorate in aroma and develop a stale and musty flavour. Propagate by division in spring or autumn, or by seed sow *in situ* in spring, thinning to 30cm/12in. Germination may be slow.

***M. officinalis*** L. BEE BALM; LEMON BALM. Erect, branched, tufted, semi-deciduous. Stems glandular, hirsute. Lvs crenate, lemon-scented, with impressed veins. Fls 4–12 per axillary whorl; cal. glandular-pubesc., teeth of lower lip lanceolate; cor. to 15mm, pale yellow. Late summer. S Europe. 'All Gold': lvs golden yellow; fls palest lilac. 'Aurea': lvs golden. ssp. ***altissima*** (Sibth. & Sm.) Arcang. Lvs foetid. Z4.

***M. grandiflora*** L. See *Calamintha grandiflora*.
***M. umbrosa*** Bieb. See *Clinopodium umbrosum*.

For illustration see HERBS.

**Melittis** L. (From Gk *melissa* or *melitta*, bee: the plant is attractive to bees.) BASTARD BALM. Labiatae. 1 species, a deciduous perennial herb to 50cm. Stems erect, hairy. Leaves petiolate, oval, to 8cm, crenate, hispid, honey-scented when fresh. Flowers to 6 per whorl; pedicel to 10mm; bracteoles absent; calyx wide, campanulate, bilabiate, upper lip with 2–3 small teeth, lower lip bilobed; corolla to 40mm, white, pink or purple or with large purple blotch on lower lip. Summer. WC & S Europe to Ukraine. Z6.

CULTIVATION Found in open woodlands, *Melittis* is useful for the front of a herbaceous border and for herb gardens. Plant in any moisture-retentive soil with added leafmould, preferably in light, woodland shade. Propagate by division in spring. When dried, *Melittis* retains its fragrance for long time.

***M. melissophyllum*** L. As for the genus. ssp. ***melissophyllum***. Lvs to 7cm with to 20 large teeth on each side. ssp. ***albida*** (Guss.) P.W. Ball. Stem densely covered with stalked glands. ssp. ***carpatica*** (Klokov) P.W. Ball. Lvs to 15cm with to 32 large teeth on each side.

**Melo** Mill. See *Cucumis*.

**Melocactus** Link & Otto (From Lat. *melo*, melon, and *Cactus*, referring to the shape; a pre-Linnaean name and variant of *Echinomelocactus*. Linnaeus, followed by Britton & Rose, used the contraction *Cactus*, but this usage is rejected under modern rules.) Cactaceae. About 30 species of simple globose cacti, rarely more than 1m high, only branching if damaged; stem depressed-globose to cylindric, strongly ribbed, spiny. Flowering zone an apical cephalium with wool and usually bristles; flower small, tubular, red to pink, more or less immersed in the cephalium; pericarpel and tube naked. Fruit a juicy berry, usually clavate, red, pink or white; seeds 0.8–1.2×0.6–1.5mm, broadly oval, black-brown, more or less shiny; relief flat to domed (tuberculate); hilum medium, basal, impressed. Tropical America, especially E Brazil and Amazonia, Peru, Venezuela, Central America and the Caribbean.

CULTIVATION Grow in a heated greenhouse (min. 10–15°C/50–60°F), use 'acid standard' cactus compost: moderate to high inorganic content (more than 50% grit), below pH 6; grow in full sun; maintain low humidity; water very sparingly in winter (to avoid shrivelling). With the exception of *M. matanzanus*, the Brazilian species are those most frequently seen in cultivation, the others generally being more difficult to cultivate (some requiring a minimum temperature of 15°C/60°F throughout the year). Flowering can occur at any time of the year when the plant is growing.

***M. ×albicephalus*** Buining & Brederoo. Resembling *M. ernestii* but ribs more acute and spines much shorter. Cephalium with white wool; bristles very short and hidden. E Brazil (Bahia). (A natural hybrid of *M. ernestii* and *M. glaucescens*.) Z9.

***M. azureus*** Buining & Brederoo. Stem to 13–45×14–19cm, green, grey-green or intensely glaucous; ribs 9–10, acute; areoles 2.8–3.5cm apart; central spines 1–4, 2–5.3cm, radial spines 7–11, stout, lowermost longest, to 5.3cm. Cephalium to 3.5–12×7–9cm, with white wool and pale brown felt-like tufts or conspicuous red bristles; fl. 19–23×8–11.5mm, magenta-pink. Fr. to 17×6mm, white to rather pale pink; seeds 1–1.7×0.9–1.5mm, testa almost smooth. E Brazil (C N Bahia). Z9.

***M. bahiensis*** (Britt. & Rose) Lützelb. Stem 9.5–21×11–21cm, depressed-globose to conic; ribs 8–14, acute to rounded; areoles to 2.4cm apart; central spines 1–4, 1.7–5cm, porrect, radial spines 7–12, 2–6cm, mostly straight, the lowermost longer than the others. Cephalium rarely more than 5×6.5–8.5cm, with white wool and dark red-brown bristles; fl. 20–23×10–12.5mm. Fr. to 25×9mm, clavate, red to crimson; seeds 1–1.3×1mm; testa somewhat tuberculate. E Brazil. Z9.

***M. broadwayi*** (Britt. & Rose) A. Berger. Stem 10–20cm tall, ovoid, yellow-green; ribs 14–18, rounded; areoles 1cm or more apart; central spines 1–3, brown, porrect, radial spines 8–10, 1.0–1.5cm, incurved. Cephalium 2–3×6–7cm; bristles soft, brown; fl. purple. Fr. to 2.5cm, magenta. Tobago, Grenadines, St Vincent. Z9.

***M. concinnus*** Buining & Brederoo. Intermediate between *M. violaceus* and *M. zehntneri*. Stem 8–12×11–16cm, depressed-globose to globose; ribs 8–12, acute; areoles 1.3–2cm apart; central spine 1, 1.0–1.9cm, ascending, curved, radial spines 6–8, to 1.5–2.6cm. Cephalium 2.5–5.5×4–9cm, with white wool and pink-red bristles; fl. 20–23×6–12mm, pink. Fr. 13–18×5–8.5mm, pink; seeds 1.1–1.3×0.9–1.3mm; testa strongly tuberculate at end opposite hilum. E Brazil (Bahia, N Minas Gerais). Z9.

***M. conoideus*** Buining & Brederoo. Stem to 10–17cm, strongly depressed to hemispheric; ribs 11–14; areoles to *c*15mm apart; central spine 1, 2.0–2.2cm, radial spines 8–11, lowermost 2–3.5cm, recurved at apex. Cephalium to 4×7.5cm; fl. *c*22×10mm, magenta-pink. Fr. *c*18×5–6mm, lilac-magenta; seeds to 1.25mm; testa tuberculate. E Brazil (SE Bahia). Z9.

***M. curvispinus*** Pfeiff. Very variable; stem 6–30×8–27cm, depressed-globose, globose or ovoid; ribs 10–16, more or less acute; central spines 1–4(–5), to 5.2cm, diverging, radial spines 7–11(–15), 1.6–4.2cm, more or less curved, rarely all straight. Cephalium usually 2–6×3–10cm, with white wool and red-brown bristles. Fl. 20–43×16–25mm; tepals widely spreading. Fr. rather large, 20–60×8–16mm, clavate, bright red; seeds 1.2–1.6mm; testa more or less smooth. C America & N South America (SW & E Mexico to Colombia and Venezuela), Cuba. Z9.

***M. ernestii*** Vaupel. Stem 9–45×7–22(–35)cm, subglobose to short-cylindric; ribs 9–13, more or less rounded; areoles to 2.8cm apart; central spines 4–8, to 3.2–9cm, radial spines 7–13, lowermost 4.5–15cm, flexible, slender. Cephalium to 6×13cm; fl. 20–29×9–18mm. Fr. 14–45×5–12mm; seeds to 1.35×1mm; testa tuberculate. E Brazil. Z9.

***M. glaucescens*** Buining & Brederoo. Stem to 13–18×14–24cm, globose to slightly pyramidal, grey-green to grey-blue; ribs 8–15, acute; areoles 1–2cm apart; central spines 1–2, ascending, to 2cm, radial spines 5–8, the lowermost to

2cm. Cephalium to 10×6.5–7cm, with short creamy white wool, bristles very short, hidden; fl. 25×15.5mm, lilac-magenta. Fr. 9.5–16×5–7mm; seeds 1.1–1.3×0.9–1.15mm; testa strongly tuberculate at end opposite hilum. E Brazil (C Bahia). Z9.

***M. harlowii*** (Britt. & Rose) Vaupel. Stem to 25(–30)×6–16cm, ellipsoid to cylindric, light green, ribs 10–13; areoles closely set, usually less than or *c*1cm apart; central spines (1–)3–4, to 5cm, radial spines *c*12, 1–2(–3)cm, slender. Cephalium 1–15×3–7.5cm with wool and bristles; fl. to 20(–30)×10–25mm. Fr. 12–22×5–11mm, obovoid, pink to white. SE Cuba. Z9.

***M. intortus*** (Mill.) Urban. Stem to 60(–90)×30cm, globose to tapered-cylindric; ribs (9–)14–27, rounded, thick; central spines 1–3, radial spines 10–14, 2–7cm, stout, more or less straight. Cephalium eventually to 50cm or more high, cylindric, with white wool and numerous red bristles; fl. 15–20×7–10mm, pink. Fr. 10–25×5–10mm, pink to red. West Indies (Turks & Caicos southwards to Martinique). Z9.

***M. levitestatus*** Buining & Brederoo. Stem 15–60×14–30cm, globose to cylindric; ribs 9–15, to 8cm broad at base; areoles 3–4.2cm apart; spines to 3.3cm, brown-red; central spines 1–4, radial spines 7–10. Fl. to 20–27×6–9mm, red. Fr. 12–20×7–12mm; seeds 1.35–1.75mm, smooth. E Brazil (W & CS Bahia, N Minas Gerais). Z9.

***M. macracanthos*** (Salm-Dyck) Link & Otto. Very variable; stem 9–30cm diam., usually depressed-globose, green; ribs 11–23, rounded-tuberculate; central spines 1–4(–6), to 7cm, porrect, much longer and stouter than the radials, red, brown or yellow, radial spines 9–17, very fine-acicular. Cephalium to 23×4–11cm; fl. *c*20mm. Fr. 15–20mm; seed *c*1mm. Netherlands Antilles. Z9.

***M. matanzanus*** León. Resembling *M. violaceus* and *M. neryi*, but ribs 8–9. Cephalium with dense orange-red bristles. Seeds *c*1mm. N Cuba (Matanzas & Las Villas Provinces). One of the smallest and most popular species. Z9.

***M. neryi*** Schum. Resembling *M. violaceus*, but stem dark blue-green; spines curved, sometimes longer. Venezuela, Surinam, N Brazil (Amazonas). Z9.

***M. oreas*** Miq. Stem 8–15(–35)×10–18cm, depressed-conic to elongate; ribs 10–16, somewhat rounded to obtuse; areoles 1–1.8cm apart; central spines 1–4, 2–4.5cm, radial spines mostly 8–11, slender, the lowermost to 4.8cm. Cephalium 12×4–8cm, with dark red-brown bristles; fl. 17–22×7–10mm. Fr. to 28×5–9mm, clavate, bright red or crimson-red, often somewhat flattened, especially below apex; seeds 1–1.2×0.8–1.1mm; testa slightly tuberculate. E Brazil (Bahia, Pernambuco). Z9.

***M. peruvianus*** Vaupel. Stem to 20(–40)×20cm, globose to pyramidal or cylindric; ribs 8–16, more or less acute, low; central spines absent or 1–4 to 6cm, radial spines (4–)6–10(–14), to 6cm, straight to strongly curved. Cephalium to 20×8cm, with wool and bristles; fl. to 23×10(–15)mm, purple-red. Fr. 10–25×5–10mm, red; seeds *c*1mm; testa finely tuberculate. Peru, SW Ecuador. Z9.

***M. salvadorensis*** Werderm. Stem 12–20×12–25cm, depressed-globose, grey-green or glaucous; ribs 8–14, acute; areoles 2–3cm apart; central spines 1–4, 1.5–3cm, radial spines 7–10, lowermost 2–4.6cm. Cephalium to 15×10cm, with dense pale red bristles; fl. to 25×12mm, pink. Fr. *c*17×6.5–9mm, lilac-magenta. E Brazil (S & E Bahia). Z9.

***M. violaceus*** Pfeiff. Stem 5–18×6–17m, depressed-globose to subpyramidal; ribs 8–15, acute; areoles 0.6–1.8cm apart; central spine 0–1, ascending, shorter than the longest of the radials, radials 5–9(–11), to 1–2.4cm, straight. Cephalium to 5.5×3.7–8.5cm, with wool and bristles; fl. 15–25×6–13.5mm, deep pink. Fr. 12.5–19×5.5–7.5mm, pink or white; seeds 1.2–1.5×1.1–1.4mm; testa tuberculate at end opposite hilum. E Brazil (mainly from coastal region, Rio de Janeiro northwards to Natal). *M. melocactoides Hoffsgg.* has been used for the plant treated as *M. violaceus Pfeiff.* here. Its typification is problematical (see Taylor, N.P., in Cactus & Succulent Journal of Great Britain 42: 67 (1980)). Z9.

***M. zehntneri*** (Britt. & Rose) Lützelb. Stem 11–48×9–25cm, depressed-globose to short cylindric, dark or grey-green to blue-green; ribs 10–16(–22), acute; areoles 2–4cm apart; central spines (0–)1–2(–4), 1.5–4cm, ascending, radial spines 7–11, 1.9–3.9cm, rather stout. Cephalium to 11(–30)×6–10cm, with white wool and red bristles; fl. to 25×2–13mm, pink. Fr. 12–20mm×5–9mm, pink; seeds 1–1.4×0.8–1.35mm; testa strongly tuberculate at end opposite hilum. NE Brazil. Z9.

***M. amoenus*** Hoffsgg. See *M. intortus*.
***M. amoenus*** hort. non Hoffsgg. See *M. curvispinus*.
***M. amstutziae*** Rauh & Backeb. See *M. peruvianus*.
***M. antonii*** (Britt.) F. Knuth. See *M. intortus*.
***M. brederooianus*** Buining See *M. bahiensis*.
***M. caesius*** Wendl. See *M. curvispinus*.
***M. communis*** (Ait.) Link & Otto. See *M. intortus*.
***M. curvicornis*** Buining & Brederoo. See *M. zehntneri*.
***M. depressus*** Hook. See *M. violaceus*.
***M. jansenianus*** Backeb. See *M. peruvianus*.
***M. maxonii*** (Rose) Gürke. See *M. curvispinus*.
***M. melocactoides*** Hoffsgg. See *M. violaceus*.
***M. oaxacensis*** (Britt. & Rose) Backeb. See *M. curvispinus*.
***M. obtusipetalus*** Lem. See *M. curvispinus*.
***M. trujilloensis*** Rauh & Backeb. See *M. peruvianus*.

For further synonymy see *Cactus*.

For illustration see CACTI.

**Melons**. The sweet melon (*Cucumis melo* ssp. *melo*) is an annual, prostrate herb, assumed to have originated in Africa, where more than 40 species of *Cucumis* are native to tropical and subtropical areas. The species is very variable. It is thought to have been introduced to Asia relatively recently and produced many subspecies in that favourable environment, so that there are secondary sources of origin in south Russia, India, Iran, and China. Collections from India possessing resistance to powdery mildew were used to save the melon industry in the US earlier this century.

Melons were known to the Romans, but seem to have been little valued by them, probably due to poor fruit quality. In the 15th century melons were brought from Turkish Armenia to the papal estate of Cantaluppe near Rome, and by that time fruit quality must have improved, for they were distributed from there to the rest of the Mediterranean area, Western Europe and North America (by Columbus on his second voyage).

Melons are a warm-season crop and, according to cultivar, need 85–125 days without frost from sowing to fruit maturity. They are day-neutral. In colder climates they need protection for all or part of the growing period, but with adequate heat can be grown over a long period. In Britain, by the end of the 17th century, the cultivation of melons was widespread in glasshouse hot beds made up for manure which during fermentation provided the necessary heat. In North America most of the early cultivars had green flesh, but those with orange flesh were selected around the middle of the 19th century and became popular. In these colder climates, in the 19th and early 20th centuries, there was a considerable glasshouse industry growing melons for local markets, but this declined with increased fuel costs and improved transport from more favourable climates; small areas are still grown in the Netherlands and France.

There are many cultivars of melons which are grouped according to fruit character. The Cantalupensis Group, the cantaloupes, including Charentais types, have ovoid or round fruits with a ridged rind; they are grown in the Mediterranean region and include the well-known 'Ogen'. The Reticulatus Group, the musk melons, have net markings on the rind, orange flesh and are widely grown in the US, in the Mediterranean area and under glass in the north. The Inodorus Group, winter melons, includes honeydew melons with a harder rind (thus facilitating longer storage).

Melons are now largely grown in warm dry climates of the tropics and subtropics; warm humid climates are less suitable as melons are susceptible to foliage diseases and fruit quality is reduced. Spain produces most melons in Europe; France also has a flourishing industry, with further production in Italy, Israel and Greece, and smaller melon-growing areas in Kenya and North Africa. Melons are widely grown in Asia, largely for home consumption. In the US they are grown in the southern states, both east and west. Melons can be grown throughout the year in favourable climates, depending on choice of cultivar. Almost all melons are eaten fresh; there are minor uses for the fruits in yoghurt and as frozen melon balls.

Flowers are, according to cultivar, either monoecious (staminate or pistillate) or andromonoecious (some staminate and some hermaphrodite); most American cvs are andromonoecious and give a better set than European cultivars, which are usually monoecious. However, help with pollination is usually recommended, by introducing hives of bees in commercial crops, in the open or under glass. Hand pollination is recommended on a small scale. Hermaphrodite flowers produce round fruits; pistillate flowers elongated ones.

Plants and flowers are killed by frost, and melons are hardly grown at altitudes above 500m/1640ft. Plastic tunnels may be used to protect plants from temperatures lower than optimum, either in the early stages or throughout the season.

The best soils are well-drained fertile loams (pH 5.5–7.0), with a minimum depth of 40cm/16in. In acid soils there is a risk of molybdenum deficiency. Lighter soils are used for earlier crops, but there is some loss of fruit quality. Soil preparation is started in the autumn before planting, with thorough cultivation to remove weeds, and also if necessary to incorporate manure, to maintain soil structure and improve moisture retention. The soil is allowed to settle before the final cultivation prior to sowing or planting. In some areas, melons are grown on ridges, and soil may be covered with a warming plastic mulch before sowing in rows or ridges.

Seeds are sown 1.2–3.7cm/½–1½in. deep in rows spaced at 1.2–2m/4–6½ft or in hills 60–120cm/2–4ft apart. Plants may also be raised in pots or boxes under protection before transplanting when two or three true leaves have formed. The minimum soil temperature for germination is 15°C/60°F and the optimum for seedling growth is about 30°C/85°F. Plants sown in rows are thinned to 30cm/12in. apart, although precision sowing will eliminate this operation. In cooler climates young plants may be protected by individual tents glassine or translucent paper or grown under low plastic tunnels.

Generous amounts of organic material in the soil benefit melons, supplemented by a complete fertilizer before planting. Rates vary with soil type, water availability and type of culture. Weeds are controlled by shallow hoeing or chemical herbicides until the plants cover the ground, or by black plastic film laid as a mulch. Open-grown plants in the US are not stopped; regular picking allows fruiting to continue. In Europe, each grower has his own system.

Water demand is high when plants are growing fast and fruits are swelling, but is reduced just before fruits start to mature. Trickle irrigation is commonly used in the open, as the most efficient system. Fruits which are allowed to ripen develop the best flavour, and picking is done at regular intervals to obtain fruits at the right stage. In most cultivars of the musk melon group this is when the fruit separates easily from the stem, which is called 'full-slip'. Cantaloupes signal maturity by a change in rind colour and, in certain cultivars, by the development of a scent and of fine circular cracks at the base of the stem. In melons picked on hot days field heat must be removed as quickly as possible before sending to market. Some trials in California with picking at night have been successful in obtaining cool fruit of the right quality. Mechanical harvesting has not been successful, although conveyor belts are often used to accelerate transport between field and packing shed. Storage is relatively short-term, and musk melons can be kept for 6 to 12 days at 3–4°C/37–39°F (RH 85–90%). Honeydew melons can be kept longer; for 14–90 days since they have a hardier, less permeable rind at 10–15°C/50–60°F.

In colder climates, with a shorter frost-free period, melons are grown with protection for all or part of the season: they take 3–4 months to reach maturity, and warm dry conditions are essential for ripening. In France, where there are several climatic areas, different cultural systems are practised: in heated glasshouses in soil or soilless culture (vermiculite or perlite), in plastic tunnels (high or low) or in the open air (with or without irrigation). In northern Europe melons are still grown in gardens in small houses of glass or plastic.

In greenhouses they may be grown in beds, or in raised troughs and boxes (30cm/12in. deep, 46cm/18in. wide), in a high-fertility loam-based medium with well-rotted manure; good basal drainage is essential. They can be grown all year round with heat, but the usual time for sowing is spring. Seeds are sown singly in pots or soil blocks, at a temperature of 16–18.5°C/60–65°F and after the seedlings have emerged at 13–15°C/55–60°F. When true leaves appear, melons are transplanted in the greenhouse bed at 45–60cm/8–24in. apart along the side walls. When about 10–15cm/4–6in. tall the growing point is pinched out, which stimulates the production of two shoots, to be trained up wires on the side walls. A temperature of 16–27°C/60–80°F is maintained with ventilation when temperatures rise above this. When each shoot has produced five leaves, the growing tip is again removed to stimulate side shoots on which the flowers are produced. When three leaves are produced on each of these side shoots the tips are pinched out. Six to eight flowers are selected on each plant and are hand pollinated: once they have set, four fruits of uniform size are selected (not more than one per lateral) for growing on, and the others removed.

Plants should be kept well watered, and given a weekly liquid feed from the stage when the fruits are about the size of a walnut. Stop the fruit-bearing laterals at the first joint beyond the fruit when it begins to swell. As the fruits grow they need to be supported by nets tied to the wires. Leaves and laterals are thinned out as necessary. When the fruit has reached full size humidity levels are lowered for ripening; feeding is stopped and watering reduced to keeping the medium just moist to avoid rind splitting. Signs of ripening are as already described. Most will break cleanly from the vine; others, like honeydew melons, must be cut.

For early crops, on hotbeds in frames, the growing medium must be of sufficient depth to maintain a temperature of about 18.5°C/65°F. In frames, two plants are positioned in the centre of each frame and two shoots from each are led to the corners of the frame. When each shoot has produced 6–8 leaves the growing tips are cut back to four leaves. The side shoots thus stimulated are next stopped at three leaves and the flowers subsequently produced are hand-pollinated, eventually allowing two fruits to develop per plant for main crops, and one for early and late crops. A flat stone may be placed under each fruit to keep them clean and to aid uniform ripening.

Recommended cultivars. *Cantaloupe*: 'Charentais', 'Early Sweet', 'Sweetheart' (good under glass in cooler climates). *Musk melons* (netted or nutmeg melons); green-fleshed: 'Emerald Gem', 'Gaylia Fl Hybrid', 'Jenny Lind', 'Ogen' ('Haogen'), 'Rocky Ford', 'Rocky Sweet'; salmon-fleshed: 'Ambrosia', 'Banana', 'Burpee Hybrid', 'Hearts of Gold', 'Iroquois', 'Musketeer' (bush); red- or orange-fleshed: 'Blenheim Orange-Superlative', 'Minnesota Midget' (very compact bush), 'Resistant Joy N22 Fl Hybrid' (very early); white-fleshed: 'Gold Crispy', 'Hero of Lockinge'. *Winter melons* (late-ripening, can be stored): 'Golden Beauty' (Casaba type, rough-skinned), 'Earli-Dew', 'Green Fleshed', 'Orange-fleshed' (honeydew types). Others: 'Sugar Baby' (small, light green flesh), 'Crenshaw' (warm climate), 'Early Crenshaw' (very large), 'Honeyshaw' (very early), 'Yellow Canary'.

Melons are susceptible to collar-rot, hence mound and ridge cultivation is advised. A further precaution is to plant seedlings with soil balls emerging from the medium surface. Overwatering in dry periods may cause splitting: wait until slight foliage wilt is apparent before watering. Other susceptibilities, common to all cucurbits, are to *Botrytis cinerea, Erysiphe chichoracearum*, bacterial canker (*Bacterium carotovorum*), leaf blotch (*Cercospora melonis*) and root rot (*Fusarium vasinfectum, Verticillium albo-atrum*) and cucumber mosaic virus. Grafting on to a resistant rootstock is sometimes practised to prevent infection by root disease.

**Melothria** L. (From Gk *melothron*, bryony.) Cucurbitaceae. About 10 species of monoecious or dioecious climbers or trailers, herbaceous, perennial, occasionally annual. Tendrils simple. Leaves entire or palmately lobed, often scabrid or hispidulous. Male inflorescence a raceme or corymb; male flowers small, pedicellate; receptacle campanulate; sepals small, denticulate; corolla white, yellow or pale green, deeply divided; stamens 3, usually free, anthers occasionally coherent; pistillode globose; female inflorescence a cluster or solitary; flowers similar to male except staminodes 3, ovary globose to fusiform, triloculate with disc at base of style. Fruit a berry, long-stalked, small, indehiscent; seeds many, compressed, often emarginate, smooth or rugose, cream-white. Subtropical and tropical Americas. Z10.

CULTIVATION As for *Coccinia*, but multiple planting is not required for fruit set.

***M.pendula*** L. Scandent. Stems slender, often rooting at nodes. Lvs slender, pubesc., ovate-cordate to triangular, angulate, entire or, sometimes, shallowly lobulate, acuminate, scabrous above, paler and pubesc. beneath. Male raceme 2–7-fld; female fls solitary on filiform pedicels; cor. yellow; ovary oblong; stigma slightly lobed. Fr. subglobose to ellipsoid or ovoid, to 2cm, purple dappled green; seeds obovate, to 4mm. S US to S America.

***M. indica*** (L.) Lour. See *Zehneria indica*.
***M. japonica*** (Thunb.) Maxim. See *Zehneria indica*.
***M. maderspatana*** (L.) Cogn. See *Mukia maderaspatana*.
***M. punctata*** Cogn. See *Zehneria scabra*.
***M. scabra*** (L. f.) Naudin. See *Zehneria scabra*.

**Memecylon** L. Melastomataceae. Some 150 species of shrubs or trees. Leaves opposite. Inflorescence an axillary or terminal and panicled cyme, few- to many-flowered, flowers 4-merous, white or blue; stamens 8; ovary inferior, 1-celled. Fruit a berry. Tropical Africa, Asia, Malay Archipelago.

CULTIVATION As for *Medinilla*.

***M. floribundum*** Bl. Shrub to 3m. Lvs to 18×2.5–7.5cm, ovate-elliptic, coriaceous, obtuse; petiole to 0.6cm. Pet. 5–6mm, exterior tinged red, interior purple-blue. Fr. 1.5cm, ovoid. Java.

***M. umbellatum*** Burm. f. Small tree to 7.5m; stems and branches densely lenticellate. Lvs 7.5–15cm, oblong-ovate, acuminate, coriaceous. Infl. an axillary cyme 2.5–5cm, borne on old wood; fls numerous, deep blue to purple. Fr. globose, 0.6–1.5cm diam., purple to black. India, SE Asia, N Australia.

***M. caeruleum*** Jack. See *M. floribundum*.

**Mendoncella** A.D. Hawkes. (For Luis Mendonca, editor of the orchid journal *Orquidea*.) Orchidaceae. Some 4 species of epiphytic orchids allied to *Zygopetalum*. Rhizome short. Pseudobulbs ovoid to cylindrical, short, often clustered, base enveloped by several overlapping bracts and leaf sheaths, apex 1–2-leaved. Leaves lanceolate, petiolate, plicate, prominently veined. Inflorescence a basal raceme, erect or nodding, short to elongate, 1- to few-flowered; flowers often large; sepals subsimilar, free or slightly connate at base, spreading, lateral sepals oblique, articulated to column foot forming a short mentum; petals wider than sepals; lip articulated to column foot, trilobed, lateral lobes erect, often fimbriate, midlobe large, spreading, entire to fimbriate, apex recurved, disc with a fleshy, sulcate callus, dentate; column short, stout, curved, apex winged or auriculate, anther terminal, operculate, incumbent, subglobose, pollinia 4, waxy, pyriform, strongly compressed. Mexico to Guyana, Brazil, Peru. Z10.

CULTIVATION As for *Zygopetalum*.

***M. burkei*** (Rchb. f.) Garay. Pseudobulbs to 12×3cm, oblong-cylindrical. Lvs to 45×2cm, coriaceous, oblong-lanceolate or linear-elliptic, acute or acuminate, suberect. Infl. to 60cm, loosely few-fld; fls to 5cm diam., fragrant, waxy, long-lived; tepals to 3.5×1.5cm, pale brown, marked chestnut-brown, often edged green, the lip white marked violet on callus; sep. ovate-oblong to elliptic-lanceolate, acute or acuminate, pet. obliquely ovate-oblong to oblong, acute or apiculate; lip to 25×22mm, interior densely pubesc., clawed, obovate to obovate-suborbicular, undulate or denticulate, rounded and apiculate, apex recurved, callus semicircular, closely toothed; column to 15mm, clavate, bi-auriculate. Venezuela, Guianas, Brazil, Surinam.

***M. grandiflora*** (A. Rich.) A.D. Hawkes. Pseudobulbs to 8×3cm, narrowly ovoid. Lvs to 50×7cm, lanceolate to elliptic-lanceolate, acute or acuminate. Infl. to 20cm, 2- to several-fld; fls to 8cm diam., showy, waxy, fragrant, long-lived, green or yellow-green, broadly striped red-brown, the lip white streaked red; sep. to 5×1.5cm, lanceolate, acuminate, apex recurved; pet. to 4.5×1.5cm, obliquely falcate, acuminate, apex recurved; lip to 3×2cm, erose, lateral lobes erect, obliquely ovate, basally carinate, midlobe obovate to ovate-rhombic, arcuate, slightly concave, apex strongly recurved, callus erect, lunate, denticulate; column to 3cm, white or pale yellow, streaked red, bialate, apex ciliate. Mexico, Guatemala, Costa Rica, Panama, Colombia, British Honduras.

***M. jorisiana*** (Rolfe) A.D. Hawkes. Pseudobulbs to 10×2cm, ovoid-oblong. Lvs to 27×6cm, oblanceolate, acute. Infl. to 27cm, suberect, few-fld, pale green marked dark green or purple-green, the lip white, darkening to pale yellow at midlobes and marked purple on callus, fleshy-rigid; dorsal sep. to 30×12mm, oblong-lanceolate, acute or subobtuse, lateral sep. to 34×14mm, ovate-lanceolate, acute to acuminate; pet. to 26×10mm, obliquely oblong-lanceolate; lip to 20×19mm, fimbriate, elliptic to suborbicular-obovate, lateral lobes small, auriculate, midlobe large, elliptic-orbicular to subquadrate, apex rounded or truncate; callus large, carinate; column light yellow-green striped maroon, anth. white tinged pink. Venezuela, Brazil.

For synonymy see *Batemannia, Galeottia* and *Zygopetalum*.

**Meniscium** Schreb. Thelypteridaceae. Some 20 species of terrestrial ferns. Rhizomes creeping, dictyostelic, woody or fleshy, sparsely scaly. Fronds stipitate, uniform or slightly dimorphous, pinnate or, rarely, simple, glabrous or trichomate-hairy; pinnae entire to saw-toothed or notched at margin, veins anastomosing in angular or arching pairs, with free veinlet excurrent from their union. Sori medial, transverse across anastomoses and often continuous, linear to arching, lacking indusia; paraphyses present or absent; sporangia glabrous or pubescent to setose; annulus approximately 18-celled; spores often oblong, reticulate to ridged or tuberculate. Tropical America. Z10.

CULTIVATION As for *Christella*.

***M. angustifolium*** Willd. Rhiz. short-creeping, covered with massed roots as well as many scales. Lamina to 50×30cm, erect, slightly dimorphous (sterile pinnae smaller than fertile), oblong; pinnae 8–22 lateral and 1 apical, to 16×2cm, petiolate, spreading, linear to lanceolate, narrowly acute to attenuate at apex, cuneate at base, more or less entire at margin, rachis grooved above, minutely pubesc.; veins to 2mm distant, with to 12-rowed areolae; stipes to 45cm, minutely pubesc. W Indies, Central America south to Bolivia.

***M. reticulatum*** (L.) Sw. Rhiz. short-creeping, somewhat woody; scales in upper part lanceolate, toothed at margin, russet. Lamina to 120×60cm, erect, slightly dimorphous (sterile pinnae shorter-petiolate than fertile), pinnate, lanceolate or oblong to deltoid; pinnae to 30×10cm, narrowly lanceolate or deltoid to strap-shaped, narrowly acute and caudate at apex, cuneate to obtuse at base, entire to notched or undulate at margin; stipes to 1m, minutely pubesc. Florida, W Indies, Central America south to Peru.

***M. triphyllum*** Sw. See *Pronephrium triphyllum*.
For further synonymy see *Dryopteris* and *Thelypteris*.

**MENISPERMACEAE** Juss. MOONSEED FAMILY. Dicot. 78 genera and 520 species of usually dioecious lianes and scandent shrubs, rarely trees or herbs, usually with bitter poisonous sesquiterpenoids and alkaloids; stems often with unusual secondary thickening and becoming flattened. Leaves simple, rarely trifoliolate, alternate, rarely lobed; stipules absent. Flowers usually regular, rarely brightly coloured, 3-merous, often with 2 whorls of calyx, corolla and androecium, usually in thyrses, rarely solitary or on old wood; calyx (1–) 6 (–12) free sepals; corolla often 6, sometimes more or fewer or absent; stamens (1–) 6 (–40), often opposite petals; filaments sometimes connate, anthers usually introrse; females with (1) 3 (6–30) free carpels in 1 or more whorls, often held on a gynophore, each with 2 (1 soon aborting) ovules. Fruit a head of drupes or nuts, usually curved; seeds often horseshoe-shaped; endosperm oily, proteinaceous, sometimes ruminate or absent. Many have local medicinal uses, in the preparation of curare *Chondrodendron tomentosum* provides one of its ingredients. Tropical and warm, few temperate. *Cocculus, Menispermum*.

**Menispermum** L. (From Lat. *menis*, a tiny half-moon-like device inscribed at the opening of books, and *spermum*, seed, referring to the shape of the seed.) Menispermaceae. 2 species of woody-based dioecious twiners. Stems slender, tangled, rampant, suckering, pale green, frequently persisting for a few seasons and becoming woody, otherwise performing as an herbaceous perennial. Leaves variable in shape, obscurely 5–7-lobed, peltate, petiole long, inserted near basal sinus. Flowers inconspicuous, yellow-green in axillary stalked racemes or panicles; sepals 4–10, exceeding petals; petals 6–9; stamens in male flowers 9–24, in females, 6, sterile; carpels 2–4. Fruit to 1cm diam., dark red-purple to black, subglobose, hanging in grape-like bunches; seeds crescent-shaped. Eastern N America, E Asia.

CULTIVATION Vigorous, suckering climbers forming a dense tangle of twining shoots clothed in attractive foliage, suitable for walls (with support), trellis and for growing up and through trees, although they require thoughtful placement if they are not to outcompete less vigorous neighbours. Where both genders are grown together, *Menispermum* produces long racemes of small, glossy, black fruits containing the crescent-shaped seed that gives rise to the common name, moonseed. Although in habitat *M. canadense* may experience temperatures to −30°C/−22°F and below, in mild maritime climates *M. canadense* may produce softer growth that is cut to the ground where winter temperatures fall much below −5 to −10°C/23–14°F; this is not necessarily disadvantageous, since they will re-sprout from the base in spring, and where not cut by frost may need to be kept in check by pruning to the base in late autumn or early spring. Grow in partial shade or full sun in any moderately fertile soil that does not dry out excessively in summer. Propagate by seed, by removal of suckers, or by ripewood cuttings in the cold frame or cool glasshouse in autumn.

***M. canadense*** L. YELLOW PARILLA. Stems to 6m, usually persistent. Lvs 5–20cm, ovate-cordate to suborbicular, entire or obscurely 5–7-lobed, dark green above, somewhat paler and initially downy beneath. Racemes long. Fr. pruinose purple-red to blue-black. Eastern N America. Z5.

***M. davuricum*** DC. Distinguished from *M. canadense* by its annual, or rarely persistent aerial stems, its shorter, more crowded and frequently paired racemes, lvs to 10cm, more evidently peltate and sharply lobed and larger, black fr. E Asia. Z4.

***M. dauricum*** auct. See *M. davuricum*.

**Mentha** L. (For Xaverio Manetti (1723–1785), botanist and director of the Botanic Garden in Florence.) MINT. Labiatae. 25 species of aromatic herbaceous perennials or occasionally annuals. Rhizomes fleshy and creeping. Stems erect, branching. Flowers small, purple, pink or white in axillary verticils often forming an interrupted spike; calyx regular or weakly 2-lipped, tubular or campanulate, 10–13-veined with 5 or 4 subequal teeth; corolla weakly 2-lipped with 4 subequal lobes, upper lobe usually broader, often emarginate, tube shorter than calyx; stamens 4, diverging more or less equal, usually exserted but included in many hybrids. Nutlets ovoid, smooth. Eurasia, Africa.

CULTIVATION Nearly all mints are invasive creeping plants grown for their aromatic foliage and have long been cultivated for their culinary, antiseptic and aromatic qualities. They will tolerate a large range of soils and habitats, thriving in hot, well-drained places where plenty of moisture is available to them. The running fleshy rhizomes of some species, notably *M. spicata* and *M. suaveolens*, can spread yards underground, lifting paths and invading other plants if left unchecked. These can be grown in isolated borders or in areas where the rhizomes will remain hemmed in such as in the gaps of a terrace or planted in deep chimney pots plunged into the ground. *M. pulegium* is a much smaller plant and thrives in moist places either in full sun or in partial shade. *M. requienii* is a tiny mat-forming plant requiring similar conditions, its existence strongly witnessed if accidentally walked on or bruised under foot. Due to its tiny size *M. requienii* is often grown as a pan plant kept in a cold frame during winter; although small, it seeds itself readily.

Mints can be easily propagated by removal of the rhizomes to be replanted before they suffer drying. Many mints are infertile and so this is the only safe method of their reproduction. Others are so prone to hybridize that seed if set is often of hybrid origin. *M. pulegium* and *M. requienii* may be propagated from seed.

Many mints are prone to attack from mildew in dry weather and from rust fungi. These, although rarely fatal, are unsightly and can be cured by spraying with a suitable fungicide.

***M. aquatica*** L. WATERMINT. Subglabrous to tomentose perenn. Stems 15–90cm, simple or branched, often red-purple. Lvs 2–6×1–4cm, usually ovate to ovate-lanceolate, petiolate, margins serrate. Infl. a terminal head comprising 2–3 verticillasters sometimes with 1–3 axillary verticillasters below; bracts inconspicuous, lanceolate; pedicels and cal. hairy, cal. 3–4mm, tubular, veins distinct, teeth subulate; cor. lilac. Nutlets pale brown. Eurasia. A variable species parenting various hybrids. Z6.

***M. arvensis*** L. CORN MINT. Variable perenn. 10–60cm. Stems hairy, erect or ascending, simple or branched. Lvs 2–6.5×1–2cm, elliptic-lanceolate to broadly ovate, base narrowing to a petiole, margins shallowly crenate or serrate, hairy on both surfaces. Fls in remote axillary verticillasters; bracts decreasing in size upwards, longer than fls; cal. 1.5–2.5mm, campanulate, hairy, teeth deltate; cor. lilac, pink or rarely white, hairy outside. Nutlets pale brown. GB, Europe, N Asia, Himalaya, Japan. var. ***piperascens*** Malinv. Lvs ovate, gland-dotted, distinctly petioled. Cal. teeth long-acuminate. Japan, Korea, Sakhalin. var. ***villosa*** (Benth.) Stewart. Lvs lanceolate, cuneate at base, pubesc., angles of stems distinctly pubesc. Cor. white or pink. N America. Z4.

***M. cervina*** L. Subglabrous perenn., 10–40cm, with scent of penny-royal. Stems procumbent and rooting below, erect above. Lvs 1–2.5×0.1–0.4cm, linear-oblanceolate, glabrous, base attenuate, margins entire or obscurely dentate, sessile. Bracts leaflike, bracteoles digitately lobed; verticillasters many-fld; cal. tubular, teeth 4, deltoid with white apical awns, throat hairy within; cor. tube straight, lilac or white. SW Europe. Z7.

***M. ×gracilis*** Sole. *(M. arvensis × M. spicata.)* GINGERMINT; REDMINT. Variable perenn., 30–90cm. Stems erect, usually glabrous, sometimes sparsely pubesc., often tinged red. Lvs 3–7×1.5–4cm, ovate-lanceolate, lanceolate, oblong or elliptic, shortly petiolate, apex acute, margin entire or remotely serrate, both surfaces glabrous or sparsely pubesc., undersurface sometimes with hairs on the veins. Fls in distant verticillasters; bracts leaflike, decreasing in size upwards, uppermost sometimes shorter than fls; cal. 2–3.5mm, campanulate, glabrous below, teeth subulate, ciliate; cor. lilac, stamens usually included within the tube. N Europe including GB, widely cultivated. 'Aurea': to 30cm; spreading; lvs gold, strongly fragrant. 'Variegata': vigorous; lvs flecked gold, scent fruity, flavour ginger. Z6.

***M. longifolia*** (L.) Huds. HORSEMINT. Creeping perenn., 40–120cm, strongly scented. Stems tomentose, rarely subglabrous. Lvs sessile or rarely petiolate, linear, linear-lanceolate to oblong-elliptic, apex acute, margin sharply serrate, irregular, smooth to slightly rugose above, green- to grey-tomentose, rarely white-tomentose, beneath. Verticillasters many, congested, forming a tapering often much-branched spike; cal. 1–3mm, narrowly campanulate, hairy; cor. white, lilac or mauve, 3–5mm. Nutlets red-brown, reticulate. Europe, W Asia, C Russia, Ethiopia, S Africa. 'Variegata': lvs grey splashed with yellow, hairy. ssp. ***capensis*** (Thunb.) Briq. Lvs 5–10×1–2cm, linear-lanceolate, densely pubesc. on both surfaces. S Africa, Lesotho, Zimbabwe. ssp. ***noeana*** (Boiss. ex Briq.) Briq. Lvs with distinct petioles. Iraq, NW Iran, SE Turkey. ssp. ***polyadena*** (Briq.) Briq. Lvs 3–8×1–1.5cm, oblong-lanceolate, glabrous or sparsely hairy. S Africa. ssp. ***typhoides*** (Briq.) Harley. Lvs less than 5×2cm, concolorous on both surfaces. Infl. slender, lateral branches pedunculate. SE Europe, SW Asia. ssp. ***wissii*** (Lanert) Codd. Lvs linear, less than 5mm wide. Namibia. Z6.

***M. ×piperita*** L. *(M. aquatica × M. spicata.)* PEPPERMINT. Perenn., 30–90cm, usually glabrous, occasionally hairy, often tinged red-purple. Lvs 4–9×1.5–4cm, ovate-lanceolate to lanceolate, petiolate, margins serrate, apex acute, usually glabrous or thinly hairy. Infl. of congested verticillasters forming a terminal oblong spike; bracts lanceolate; cal. 3–4mm, tubular, the tube usually glabrous, teeth ciliate; cor. lilac-pink; stamens included. Europe. 'Candymint': stems tinted red; lvs sweetly fragrant. 'Citrata': LEMON MINT; EAU DE COLOGNE MINT: lvs aromatic, ovate, glabrous; infl. smaller. 'Crispa': to 50cm; lvs crinkled. 'Lime Mint': lvs scented lime. 'Variegata': lvs deep green mottled cream, peppermint flavour. Z3.

***M. pulegium*** L. PENNYROYAL. Subglabrous to tomentose perenn., 10–40cm. Stems procumbent or upright. Lvs 5–30×4–12mm, shortly petiolate, narrowly elliptical to oval, margins entire or with to 6 teeth on each side, upper surface usually glabrous, lower sparsely to densely pubesc. Verticillasters distant; bracts leaflike, becoming smaller upwards; cal. 2–3mm, teeth ciliate, lower teeth subulate, upper teeth shorter; cor. 4–6mm, lilac; stamens exserted or included. Nutlets pale brown. SW & C Europe to GB. 'Cunningham Mint' ('Dwarf Pennyroyal'): low; lvs oval, light green. Z7.

***M. requienii*** Benth. CORSICAN MINT. Glabrous or sparsely hairy procumbent perenn. Stems 3–10cm, creeping and rooting at the nodes forming cushions or mats. Lvs and bracts 2–7mm, ovate orbicular, entire or sinuate. Cal. 1–2mm, teeth deltoid, subulate; cor. scarcely exserted, lilac. Nutlets pale brown, smooth. Corsica, Italy, Sardinia. Z6.

***M. ×smithiana*** R.A. Graham. *(M. aquatica × M. arvensis × M. spicata.)* Robust perenn., 50–150cm, subglabrous and conspicuously red-tinged, sweetly scented. Lvs 3–9×2–4cm, ovate, base rounded, sparsely hairy to subglabrous, petiolate. Verticillasters remote, sometimes crowded at stem apex; bracts decreasing upwards, longer than fls, suborbicular, cuspidate at apex, margins serrate; cal. 5-lobed, tubular, glabrous or sparsely hairy, teeth to 1.5mm, weakly ciliate; stamens usually exserted. N & C Europe. Usually sterile. Z6.

***M. spicata*** L. SPEARMINT. Perenn., 30–100cm. Lvs 5–9×1.5–3cm, lanceolate or lanceolate-ovate, smooth or rugose, serrate with regular teeth, glabrous to densely hairy, sessile or nearly so, apex acute. Infl. a terminal cylindrical spike, 3–6cm long; cal. 1–3mm, campanulate, glabrous or hairy, teeth subequal; cor. lilac, pink or white. Nutlets reticulate in hairy plants, smooth in glabrous ones. S & C Europe. 'Chewing Gum': lvs deep mahogany, bubble gum scent. 'Crispa': lvs strongly curled around the margins. 'Kentucky Colonel': lvs large, ruffled, richly scented. Z3.

***M. suaveolens*** Ehrh. APPLEMINT. Perenn., 40–100cm. Stems sparsely to densely white-tomentose, apple-scented. Lvs 3–4.5×2–4cm, sessile or shortly petiolate, rugose, pubesc. on both surfaces, apex obtuse, cuspidate, rarely acute, margins serrate with 10–20 teeth. Verticillasters many, usually congested, forming a terminal spike 4–9cm long, often interrupted below and branched; cal. 1–2mm, campanulate, hairy, teeth subequal; cor. white or pink. S & W Europe. Often found under the name of *M. rotundifolia*. 'Variegata' (PINEAPPLE MINT): lvs streaked, sweet and fruity fragrance. Z6.

***M. ×villosa*** Huds. *(M. spicata × M. suaveolens.)* A variable hybrid with plants representing both parents and many intermediates. *M. ×villosa* 'Variegata' is often found as *M. rotundifolia* 'Variegata'. var. *alopecuroides* (Hull) Briq. Middle cauline lvs 4–8×3–6cm, broadly ovate or orbicular, softly hairy, margins serrate. Infl. robust; cal. 2mm, cor. pink. Garden origin, much cultivated. Also much cultivated is another sterile hybrid *M.* ×*villosonervata* Opiz, distinguished as *M. spicata* × *M. longifolia*; this plant has narrower lvs with rather widely spreading teeth along the margins and very few hairs on the surfaces. Z5.

***M. canadensis*** L. See *M. arvensis* var. *villosa*.
***M. cardiaca*** (S.F. Gray) Bak. See *M.* ×*gracilis*.
***M. crispa*** L. See *M. spicata*.
***M.* ×*gentilis*** L. See *M.* ×*gracilis*.
***M. hirsuta*** Huds. See *M. aquatica*.
***M. incana*** Willd. See *M. longifolia*.
***M. insularis*** Req. See *M. suaveolens*.
***M. macrostachya*** Ten. See *M. suaveolens*.
***M. nigricans*** Mill. See *M.* ×*piperita*.
***M. odorata*** Sole. See *M.* ×*piperita* 'Citrata'.
***M. rubra*** Sm. non Mill. See *M.* ×*smithiana*.
***M. sylvestris*** L. See *M. longifolia*.
***M. viridis*** (L.) L. See *M. spicata*.

For illustration see HERBS.

**Mentocalyx** N.E. Br.
***M. muirii*** N.E. Br. See *Gibbaeum schwantesii*.
***M. velutinum*** (L. Bol.) Schwantes. See *Gibbaeum velutinum*.
***M. velutinus*** (L. Bol.) N.E. Br. See *Gibbaeum velutinum*.

**Mentzelia** L. (For Christian Mentzel (1622–1701), German botanist.) Loasaceae. 60 species of annual, biennial or perennial herbs or shrubs, lacking stinging hairs. Leaves alternate, coarsely toothed or pinnatifid. Flowers solitary or in short racemes or cymes, sometimes fragrant, nocturnal or opening only in bright sunlight; petals ovate-elliptic, orange, yellow or white, free; stamens free. Americas

CULTIVATION Grown for their simple flowers and attractive foliage, suitable for the annual border and for naturalistic plantings in the wild garden. *M. lindleyi* is well sited where the fragrance may drift through open doors and windows on summer evenings; it is tolerant of poor gravelly soils. Sow seed *in situ* in spring in warm, sunny and sheltered position in any moderately fertile, well-drained soil.

***M. lindleyi*** Torr. & A. Gray. Annual to 0.6m. Lvs pinnatisect to pinnatifid. Fls to 5cm diam., grouped 2–3 at summits of stems, golden, stained orange-red at base, fragrant, nocturnal. California.

***M. livicaulis*** (Douglas) Torr. BLAZING STAR. Bienn., to 1.25m. Stems lustrous-white. Lvs sinuately toothed. Fls 5–10cm, pale yellow, opening in early morning. SW US.

***M. aurea*** hort. non Nutt. See *M. lindleyi*.
For further synonymy see *Bartonia* and *Nuttallia*.

**MENYANTHACEAE** Dumort. BOGBEAN FAMILY. Dicot. 5 genera and 40 species of aquatic or marsh plants, with intercellular canals and spaces in stems. Leaves simple (3-foliolate in *Menyanthes*), cordate to reniform or linear, spirally arranged; petiole sheathing at the base; stipules absent, or petioles with winged margins. Flowers bisexual, regular, solitary or in various inflorescence types; calyx 5 free or connate sepals; corolla 5 petals united into a tube, with valvate to imbricate lobes and crested or fringed margins; filaments attached to the corolla-tube and alternate with the lobes, nectary disc often around the ovary; ovary of 2 fused carpels, superior to half-inferior, 1-loculed; style terminal; ovules numerous on 2 parietal placentas. Fruit a capsule, variously dehiscent, or a berry; seeds with copious, firm, oil endosperm. Cosmopolitan. *Menyanthes, Nephrophyllidium, Nymphoides, Villarsia*.

**Menyanthes** L. (Possibly derived from *menanthos*, 'moonflower', a name used by Theophrastus for a plant growing on lake Orchomenos (Gk *men*, moon), or a reference to the month-long flowering period of these plants (Gk *men*, month.) BOG BEAN; BUCK BEAN; MARSH TREFOIL. Menyanthaceae. 1 species, a perennial aquatic and marginal herb, often rooting at water margin and spreading across surface, growth emersed. Rhizomes creeping, then ascending, thick, branching freely, rooting at nodes, covered with leaf sheaths toward tips. Leaves trifoliolate, glabrous; leaflets 3–6cm, elliptic to obovate, obtuse or abruptly acute, entire, spreading; petioles 7–20cm, sheathing at base, winged, slightly inflated. Inflorescence an erect, scapose, axillary raceme, 12–25cm, 10–20-flowered; flowers to 2.5cm, white flushed pink, short-lived, 5-parted, the petals heavily fringed and bearded. Fruit a capsule. Circumboreal. The rhizomes provided a tonic infusion thought effective against fever and gout, also ground by the Inuit to make a flour. The leaves are used in Sweden to make a bitter-tasting beer. Z3.

CULTIVATION Plant in submerged lily baskets in ponds in cool temperate regions or establish at margins where the rhizomes can spread freely across the water surface.

***M. trifoliolata*** L. As for the genus.

***M. crista-galli*** Menz. ex Hook. See *Nephrophyllidium crista-galli*.

**Menzies, Archibald** (1754–1842). Plant collector. Menzies was born in Aberfeldy, Perthshire, Scotland, educated locally, and first worked in the gardens of Menzies Castle. At the age of 14 he entered the Royal Botanic Garden, Edinburgh as an apprentice gardener under Professor John Hope, who encouraged him to train as a surgeon while also nurturing his interest in botany. In 1778 he went on a collecting trip to the Highlands, and his resultant findings were published by Fothergill and Pitcairn. After qualifying in medicine at Edinburgh (1781) and practising briefly as a surgeon's assistant in Caernarvon, Wales, he joined the Royal Navy (1782) as an assistant surgeon. He saw action in the West Indies against the French in 1782, and from 1782–6 was stationed at Halifax, Nova Scotia. Menzies sent a collection of seeds from Nova Scotia and Labrador to Sir Joseph Banks at Kew in 1784, and Banks commissioned him as naturalist on a naval expedition to collect furs, chiefly of the sea otter, from 1786–9, the first of his two voyages around the world. The *Prince of Wales* sailed to Nootka Sound via Cape Horn, and Menzies collected, amongst other plants, *Cupressus nootkaensis, Rosa nutkana* and *Rubus nutkanus*.

Menzies's most important discoveries were made while he was naturalist on Captain George Vancouver's circumnavigation of the globe in Cook's old ship, the *Discovery*, from 1791–5. Menzies was charged by Banks to study and record in his journal the flora, fauna, mineralogy and anthropology of all the areas visited, with a view to colonization. A Wardian case was provided for the transportation of live plant specimens. Accompanied by the *Chatham*, the *Discovery* travelled to the Cape of Good Hope, Australia (where Menzies collected *Banksia menziesii* and *Drosera menziesii*) and New Zealand (where he collected many ferns and mosses at Dusky Sound), before going on to Tahiti, Hawaii and up the west coast of America. The expedition continued by open boat via the Straits of Juan de Fuca and Puget Sound, Menzies noting *Rhododendron californicum, Cornus nuttallii, Arbutus menziesii* and *Abies grandis*, before reaching the site of the city of Vancouver. The expedition arrived at Nootka in 1792, and went on to San Francisco, Monterey (where Menzies found *Sequoia sempervirens* and *Pinus radiata*) and Hawaii, before spending three seasons (1792–4) charting 1800 miles of the Alaskan coast, Menzies collecting *Abies menziesii, Nemophila menziesii, Menziesia ferruginea* (named in his honour by J.E. Smith) and many other plants. On the return journey the expedition stopped at Valparaiso, Chile, and Menzies travelled inland to Santiago, where he pocketed some unusual nuts, served with dinner at Spanish Viceroy's residence, which proved to be *Araucaria araucana*, the monkey-puzzle tree.

On returning to England, Menzies gave his collections to Kew; his other discoveries included *Ribes speciosum* and *Lupinus arboreus*. In 1799 he was again posted to the West Indies as ship's surgeon, but was forced to retire (to Notting Hill, London) in 1802 due to asthma. He had been elected Fellow of the Linnean Society in 1790. He bequeathed his herbarium (chiefly cryptogams) to Edinburgh University.

**Menziesia** Sm. (For Archibald Menzies (1754–1842), botanist and naval surgeon.) Ericaceae. 7 species of deciduous shrubs, hairless or soft-hirsute. Leaves alternate, elliptic, entire, petiolate, membranous, teeth usually absent. Flowers drooping in terminal umbels or racemes; pedicels long, usually rough-hirsute; calyx very short, usually rough-hirsute, lobes 4 or 5; bracts soon falling; corolla campanulate, urceolate or cylindric, finely pubescent within, lobes 4 to 5, overlapping in anthesis; stamens 5–10, not exserted, anthers linear, dehiscing through apical pores, lacking appendages, filaments slender, flattened; style filiform. Fruit a capsule, oblong to virtually spherical, coriaceous, erect, 4–5-valved; seeds numerous, exiguous, linear, somewhat tapering to base and apex. US, E Asia.

CULTIVATION Grown for their pendent clusters of small flowers in the woodland garden, shrub border and large rock garden; *M. ciliicalyx, M. pilosa* and *M. purpurea* are also amenable to pot cultivation in the alpine house or cold glasshouse and/or plunge frame, as for *Leucothoë*. Most species are tolerant of temperatures to −20°C/−4°F.

Grow in dappled shade in moist but free-draining soil, that is lime-free and humus-rich; maintain an acidic organic mulch and protect from cold dry winds and late frosts. Remove fading flowerheads and prune only to remove deadwood after flowering. *Menziesia* blooms on the previous season's wood. Propagate from greenwood cuttings in summer in a closed case with bottom heat, or from seed sown in autumn at about 13°C/55°F.

***M. ciliicalyx*** (Miq.) Maxim. Erect branched shrub, 30cm–1m. Young branchlets glabrous or sparsely downy. Lvs 2.5–5×1.5–2.5cm, obovate or ovate-oblong, more rarely oblong, apex acute to blunt, tapering to base, margins loosely soft-hirsute, glaucous and adpressed coarse-hirsute on midrib beneath; petioles 2–4mm. Fls 3–8, somewhat oblique, in umbels; pedicels generally 2–3cm, glandular soft-hirsute; cal. with a wavy surface, lobes absent; cor. 13–17mm, yellow or green-white, purple-tipped, tubular to urceolate, white-downy inside, lobes 4 or 5, small; stamens 8 or 10, pubesc., anth. *c*4mm, slender; ovary sparsely glandular-hirsute; style 10–14mm. Fr. *c*4mm, valves 5. Late spring–early summer. Japan (Honshu). var. ***multiflora*** (Maxim.) Mak. Fls 6–10 in umbels; cal. lobes 4–6mm, elongate, lanceolate to linear-lanceolate, ciliate; cor. usually purple-tinted, subcampanulate anth. 2–3mm, style 7–10mm. Japan (Hokkaido, Honshu, Shikoku). var. ***purpurea*** Mak. Lvs coarsely long- and soft-hirsute above; pedicels glandular- and eglandular-hirsute; cal. lobes 1–2mm; cor. purple. Summer. Japan (Honshu). var. ***bicolor*** Mak. Umbels usually lacking axis; cal. lobes 1–2mm, rounded to elliptic; anth. *c*2mm. Late spring–summer. Japan (Honshu, Hokkaido, Shikoku). Z6.

***M. ferruginea*** Sm. RUSTY LEAF; FOOL'S HUCKLEBERRY. Suberect, deciduous shrub, 50cm×2m. Young branches finely downy and somewhat soft glandular-hirsute. Lvs 2–6×1.2–2cm, elliptic-ovate to elliptic-obovate, apex acute, tapering to base, margins serrate, adpressed-ferruginous downy above and on midrib beneath. Fls 2–5 in umbels; pedicels 1–2cm, soft-hirsute to glandular-setose; cal. downy to glandular-ciliate, lobes tapering to a point at apex; cor. 6–8mm, lutescent-red, cylindric, lobes 4, diffuse; stamens 8, fil. glabrous or hirsute at base; ovary glabrous, to sparsely soft glandular-hairy. Fr. 5–7mm, ovoid. Late spring–summer. W US (N California to Alaska, Oregon). var. ***glabella*** (Gray) Beck. Usually to 1m, rarely more. Lvs 2.5–6cm, bluntly inverse-ovate, margins ciliate and finely serrate, slightly downy to subglabrous. Fls in small, drooping clusters; cal. lobes ovate, ciliate, apex acute; cor. 7–9mm, cream-coloured, ovoid-campanulate bell-shaped, lobes 4. Late spring. N America (British Columbia to Idaho). Z6.

***M. pentandra*** Maxim. Soft-hirsute shrub, 70cm–1.2m. Lvs 2.5–5×1–2.5cm, flat, narrowly elliptic, sharp-tipped at base and apex, membranous, green above, paler beneath, coarsely hirsute above and on midrib beneath. Fls 3–6 in umbels; pedicels 15–30mm, downy and soft glandular-hirsute; cal. 2–3mm, glandular-ciliate, lobes 5; cor. 5–7mm, yellow-white, obliquely urceolate, downy inside tip and on lobes; stamens 5, hairless, *c*1.5mm diam., anth. broadly lanceolate; ovary downy and glandular soft-hirsute; style *c*4mm. Fr. 3–4mm diam., ovoid-globose; valves 5. Late spring–early summer. Japan (Hokkaido, Shikoku, Honshu, Kyushu, Sakhalin, S Kuriles). Z6.

***M. pilosa*** (Michx.) Juss. MINNIE BUSH. Erect shrub, 1–2m; twigs somewhat downy. Lvs 2–5×1–2.5cm, elliptic to inversely ovate, apex abruptly tapering to a sharp tip, somewhat adpressed downy above and on margins, sparsely hirsute on midrib beneath. Fls few in small umbels; pedicels 6–20mm, glandular-downy, decurved; cal. lobes small, ovate, ciliate, sharp-tipped at apex; cor. *c*6mm, campanulate, ivory to orange-pink; stamens 8, hairless; style equal to cor. length. Fr. *c*6mm, glandular-hirsute. Late spring–early summer. E US (Pennsylvania to Alabama). Z4.

***M. purpurea*** Maxim. Deciduous shrub, 70cm–2.4m; shoots slender, glabrous. Lvs 2.5–4×1.2–2.2cm, oval-elliptic to oblong or inversely ovate, apex rounded with an exiguous tip, tapering to base, sparsely setose above and on midrib beneath; petiole *c*5mm; cal. lobes 4 or 5, ovate-oblong, *c*4mm long, glandular-ciliate. Fls 4–8 in terminal umbels; pedicels slender, 12–18mm, glandular-hirsute; cor. 12–16×*c*6mm, tubular-campanulate, red to purple, lobes 4 or 5, ciliate; stamens 4–10, densely hirsute; ovary glandular-hirsute. Late spring–early summer. Japan. Z6.

***M. azorica*** hort. See *Daboecia cantabrica.*
***M. bryantha*** Sw. See *Bryanthus gmelinii.*
***M. globularis*** Salisb. See *M. pilosa.*
***M. lasiophylla*** Nak. See *M. ciliacalyx* var. *multiflora.*
***M. multiflora*** Maxim. See *M. ciliacalyx* var. *multiflora.*
***M. polifolia*** Juss. See *Daboecia cantabrica.*

For illustration see *Ericaceae.*

**Merendera** Ramond. (From *quita meriendas*, Spanish for *Colchicum.*) Liliaceae (Colchicaceae). Some 10 species of perennial, stemless herbs to 4cm; corm oblong to ovoid, sometimes with a neck, enclosed by a leathery or thin-textured, black or dark brown tunic. Leaves 3–15, usually to 6, basal, linear to linear-lanceolate, partially developed at flowering. Flowers white or magenta or mauve, solitary or grouped, emerging from spathaceous bracts; tepals 6, linear to narrowly obovate with a long narrow claw, initially valvate, later spreading; stamens borne near base of tepals, anthers versatile or basifixed, pollen yellow; ovary subterranean, styles 3, free to base (cf. *Colchicum, Bulbocodium*). Mediterranean, N Africa, W Asia, outliers in Middle East and NE Africa.

CULTIVATION With the possible exception of *M. montana*, which is amenable to outdoor cultivation in cool temperature zones, the remaining species are more safely grown in the bulb frame or in pans in the alpine house where the flowers and dormant bulbs can be protected from rain. Propagate by seed, when ripe for spring-flowering species, or in spring for those which bloom in autumn.

***M. androcymbioides*** Valdes. Close to *M. attica* but with anth. yellow and lvs slightly broader. Balkan Peninsula, Turkey. Z8.

***M. attica*** (Tomm.) Boiss. & Sprun. Corm 1.5–2×1–2cm, oblong-ovoid, tunic leathery, black-brown to black, neck 1–2cm. Lvs to 18×0.3–0.8cm after flowering, 2–6, linear to linear-lanceolate. Fls 2–6, white to lilac; tepals 15–27×2.5mm, linear to narrow-elliptic, usually with basal teeth; fil. to 8mm, anth. 2–4mm, black, deep purple-black or green-white, versatile. Autumn. Balkan Peninsula, Turkey. Z8.

***M. filifolia*** Cambess. Corm 1.5–2×1.2cm with long neck 1–5cm. Lvs 15×0.1–0.3cm, 5–15, linear, glabrous, developing after flowers or as they fade. Fls solitary, rose to red-purple; tepals 20–40×2–8mm, narrow-elliptic to narrow oblong-elliptic; fil. 4–7mm, anth. yellow, basifixed. Capsule to 12mm, ellipsoid-oblong. Spring. SW Europe, W Mediterranean, N Africa. Z8.

***M. hissarica*** Reg. Close to *M. robusta*, from which it differs in its solitary white fls and 2 lvs per corm. Z8.

***M. kurdica*** Bornm. Corm 2–4×1.5–2cm, oblong-ovoid, narrow, almost horizontal, tunics brown, thin-textured. Lvs 4–12cm at flowering, expanding to 17cm, 3, lanceolate to narrow-lanceolate. Fls 1–2, pale to deep purple; tepals 3–3.5×0.5–1cm with basal auricles; fil. to 9mm, anth. 3–4mm, yellow. Capsule 2–3cm, ellipsoid. Spring. SE Turkey, NE Iraq. Z8.

***M. montana*** Lange. Corm 2–3×1.5–2.75cm, tunic leathery, dark brown, neck to 2cm. Lvs to 44×0.4–1cm, 3 or 4, appearing after flowers, linear, channelled, somewhat falcate. Fls 1–2, pale magenta to rosy purple; tepals 26×3–11mm, narrow-elliptic to narrow oblong-oblanceolate, subacute, erect to spreading; fil. 4–6mm, anth. 5–10mm, yellow, basifixed. Capsule to 2.5cm, ellipsoid-oblong. Autumn. Iberian Peninsula, C Pyrenees. Z6.

***M. robusta*** Bunge. Corm 3–6×2–3cm, tunics tough, dark brown, neck 1–3cm. Lvs to 5cm at flowering, to 25cm at maturity, 3–6, linear-lanceolate, concave above, dark green. Fls 1–4, deep pink to pale lilac or white, flask-shaped, fragrant; tepals 18–40×2–9mm, oblong-elliptic to linear-elliptic, keel tinted red to orange below; anth. 8–12mm, green-yellow, basifixed. Capsule to 3cm, oblong-ovoid. Spring. C Iran, S USSR, N India. Z8.

***M. sobolifera*** Mey. Corm 2–8cm, small and narrow, borne at the end of a horizontal shoot, tunics brown. Lvs linear, 3, 2–10cm at flowering, 10–21×0.3–1.3cm thereafter. Fls 1, occasionally black-violet, versatile. Capsule to 2cm, ovoid-oblong. Spring. E Europe, Iran and adjacent USSR. Z6.

***M. trigyna*** (Adams) Stapf. Corm to 3.5×2cm, oblong-ovoid; tunics black or black-brown, coriaceous; neck 2–3cm. Lvs to 17×0.3–1.8cm, 3, narrow lanceolate, emerging at flowering, glabrous, blunt-tipped, tapering into tube. Fls 1–3, rose to white; tepals 20–30×4–9mm, free, erect, disintegrating after spreading, oblong or narrow-elliptic, usually toothed at base; anth. 2–4mm, brown to yellow, versatile. Capsule to 3cm, ovoid-ellipsoid. Spring. E Turkey, Iran, Caucasus. Z7.

*M. aitchisonii* Hook. See *M. robusta*.
*M. brandegiana* Markgr. See *M. attica*.
*M. bulbocodium* Ramond. See *M. montana*.
*M. caucasica* Bieb. See *M. trigyna*.
*M. eichleri* Boiss. See *M. trigyna*.
*M. linifolia* Munby. See *M. filifolia*.
*M. manissadjiania* Aznav. See *M. trigyna*.
*M. navis-noae* Markgr. See *M. trigyna*.
*M. persica* Boiss. & Kotschy. See *M. robusta*.
*M. pyrenaica* (Pourr.) Fourn. See *M. montana*.
*M. raddeana* Reg. See *M. trigyna*.
*M. rhodopea* Velen. See *M. attica*.
For further synonymy see *Bulbocodium* and *Colchicum*.

**Merinthosorus** Copel. (From an artificial Gk word *merinthos*, divided, and *sorus*.) Polypodiaceae. 1 species, an epiphytic fern. Rhizomes to 3cm wide, short-creeping, occasionally branching, stout, dictyostelic, fleshy; scales many, to 15mm, dentate, apex narrowed. Fronds to 120×30cm+, broadly lanceolate, short-stipitate, uniform: lower part sterile, deeply pinnatifid, pinnately lobed at base, lobes broadly lanceolate, entire, eventually detachable from rachis, basal lobes dilated, scarious, collecting plant-litter, papery to thinly leathery or membranous; central sterile lobes to 20×3cm, oblong, apex narrowly acute; upper part fertile, pinnate, pinnae to 30×3cm, sessile, narrowly elongate-linear, entire, thinly leathery; veins prominent, reticulate, with free, included veinlets. Sori uninterrupted, forming soral patch entirely covering lower surface of apical pinnae, on each side of costa; paraphyses absent. Malaysia to Polynesia. Z10.

CULTIVATION As for *Drynaria*, but only one type of frond is produced, possessing tassel-like fertile pinnules near the tip; spores are shed quickly, and the dead tassels can be messy when shed.

*M. drynarioides* (Hook.) Copel. As for the genus.

For synonymy see *Acrostichum*.

**Merremia** Dennst. (For the German naturalist, Blasius Merrem (*d*1824).) Convolvulaceae. 60–80 species of perennial, herbaceous of woody climbers, occasionally erect to procumbent, a few cm high to 20cm+. Leaves petiolate, entire, lobed or compound with 7 leaflets. Inflorescence axillary, 1- to few-flowered, with lanceolate or linear bracts; sepals usually subequal; corolla campanulate or funnel-shaped, entire or lobed, white, yellow or purple; filaments glandular at base, anthers spirally twisted after dehiscence; stigma globose or biglobose. Fruit a dry capsule; seeds 1–6, pubescent or glabrous. Pantropical. Separated from *Ipomoea* largely on the basis of its smooth (rather than spinulose) pollen grains, visible with a hand lens due to the large size of the grains. Z9.

CULTIVATION *M. tuberosa* is a rampant plant, best used on garden boundaries or to cover unsightly garden structures; the fruits are useful in dried flower arrangements. Cultivation as for *Ipomoea*; most easily propagated from seed.

*M. aurea* (Kellogg) O'Donnell. Slender, tuberous climber to 2.5m. Lvs compound, ovate to orbicular in outline, axils hairy, leaflets 5, 2–4×0.5–2cm, entire, subsessile. Fls solitary, on glabrous pedicel; sep. to 1cm, oblong to oval, blunt, unequal; cor. 5–10cm diam., 3–8cm long, funnel-shaped, golden-yellow, midpetaline areas darker. Fr. subglobose; seeds 1–4, black, densely short-pubesc. Mexico (Baja California).

*M. dissecta* (Jacq.) Hallier f. Herbaceous climber to at least 8m; stems hairy at first, later glabrous. Lvs divided almost to base into 7–9 10cm, lanceolate lobes, glabrous or sparsely hairy, margins coarsely and sinuately toothed. Infl. 1–4-fld, on a 5–7cm peduncle; pedicel clavate; sep. 1.8–2.5cm, oblong, mucronate, glabrous; cor. 3–4.5cm long, to 5cm diam., broadly funnel-shaped, white with a purple or magenta tube. Fr. 1.5cm diam., globose, surrounded by persistent cal; seeds 8mm, black, glabrous. S US to Tropical S America.

*M. tuberosa* (L.) Rendle. WOOD ROSE; YELLOW MORNING GLORY; SPANISH WOODBINE. Large, stout woody climber to 20m. Lvs 8–15cm, deeply 7-lobed almost to base, glabrous, lobes elliptic to lanceolate, entire, apices acuminate; petioles long. Infl. 1- to several-fld; peduncles 10–20cm; fls on 1–2cm, club-shaped pedicel; sep. to 3cm, unequal, oblong, blunt with a small mucro; cor. 5–6cm, campanulate, bright yellow. Fr. 1–4-seeded; seeds to 1.7cm diam., densely short-pubesc. Mexico to Tropical S America, introduced in many other tropical regions.

For synonymy see *Ipomoea*.

**Mertensia** Roth. (For Francis Karl Mertens, (1764–1831), Professor of Botany, Bremen.) Boraginaceae. Some 50 species of perennial herbs, caulescent, glabrous or pubescent. Stems solitary to numerous, erect to decumbent. Leaves alternate, linear to cordate, entire, sessile or petiolate. Cymes usually terminal, scorpioid, often becoming paniculate with age; bracts absent; calyx deeply 5-lobed, sometimes campanulate; corolla blue, pink or white, tubular, campanulate, cylindrical or infundibular, usually with 5 scales in the throat; stamens included or slightly exserted, inserted below throat; style included or exserted, stigma small, entire or obscurely lobed. Nutlets 1–4, fleshy-coriaceous, angled, smooth or rugose. N Temperate.

CULTIVATION *Mertensia* includes alpine species such as *M. alpina, M. echioides* and *M. primuloides* which, with other low-growing species, are suited to cool, moisture-retentive situations on the rock garden in light, neutral to slightly acid soils with good light but shade from hot sun. All require good drainage, emphatically so for those species from higher altitudes such as *M. alpina, M. primuloides* and *M. elongata*. In the alpine house grow in deep pots, in a lean gritty mix with additional leafmould.

*M. maritima*, uncommon and declining in the wild on the coastal shingles of northern Europe, thrives in sun in nutritionally poor, gravelly or sandy soils is best suited to maritime gardens. *M. virginica*, from moist woodland, and *M. paniculata* from damp streamside habitats, prefer deep, moist but well-drained soils that are rich in organic matter and these are well suited to naturalizing in open woodland in shade or semi-shade. The foliage of *M. virginica* dies back in summer, leaving a conspicuous gap when used in border plantings. Most species are tolerant of cold to −15°C/5°F; *M. sibirica, M. maritima* and *M. virginica* grow in zones where temperatures may fall below −25°C/−13°F.

Propagate from seed sown rip in the cold frame, protect young plants from direct sun. Also by careful division in early autumn or spring; *M. maritima* resents root disturbance and is more reliably propagated by seed.

*M. alpina* (Torr.) G. Don. Stems to 30cm, erect or ascending, glabrous. Lvs strigose above, glabrous beneath, basal lvs to 7×3cm, linear-lanceolate to oblong, cauline lvs to 6×2cm, elliptic or lanceolate. Infl. becoming slightly paniculate; pedicels to 10mm, strigose or glabrous; cal. to 5mm, lobes linear-lanceolate to oblong, acute to obtuse, ciliate; cor. dark blue, tube to 6mm, interior glabrous, limb to 6mm; scales conspicuous; style equalling cal. Nutlets to 2mm, rugose. N America (Wyoming, Colorado, New Mexico, Idaho).

*M. bakeri* Greene. Stems to 40cm, simple to slightly branched, erect or ascending, pubesc. Lvs densely hoary-pubesc., basal lvs to 11×3.5cm, ovate-elliptic to linear-lanceolate, petiolate, cauline lvs to 8×2.5cm, ovate to linear-lanceolate, sessile or subsessile. Infl. a panicle, loosely to densely-fld; pedicels to 1.5cm, usually grey-white pubesc., often reflexed; cal. to 5mm, lobes lanceolate to linear-lanceolate, acute, exterior pubesc.; cor. blue, tube to 9mm, with basal ring of hairs, limb to 6mm, scales usually conspicuous, glabrous to pubesc. or papillose; anth. to 2mm. Nutlets to 3.5mm, rugose. N America (Colorado and Utah to New Mexico).

*M. ciliata* (James) G. Don. Stem to 120cm, erect or ascending. Lvs ciliate, often papillose above, basal lvs to 15×10cm, ovate or lanceolate to oblong, base subcordate; cauline lvs to ovate to lanceolate, obtuse or acuminate, base attenuate to subcordate, sessile or subsessile. Infl. axillary, elongate with age; cal. lobes to 3mm, subacute or obtuse, margins ciliate or papillose, exterior glabrous, interior strigose; cor. bright blue, to 8mm, interior glabrous or crisped-pubesc., scales conspicuous, glabrous to pubesc. or papillose; anth. to 2.5mm. Nutlets rugose. N America (Montana to New Mexico). Z4.

*M. echioides* (Benth.) Benth. & Hook. f. Stems to 30cm, erect, sometimes decumbent, pubesc. Basal lvs to 9×2.5cm, lanceolate or ovate to elliptic-lanceolate, subobtuse to acute, petiolate, cauline lvs subsessile. Infl. to 13cm, scorpioid, elongate, densely many-fld; pedicels to 5mm; cal. to 4mm, lobes linear, pilose; cor. deep blue to blue-purple, to 7mm, infundibular to subcylindrical, lobes erect, scales inconspicuous or absent; fil. linear, anth. to 2mm, oblong, exserted; style to 15mm, stigma capitate. Nutlets to 2.5mm, ovoid-triagonal, usually white, lustrous. Pakistan, Kashmir, Tibet. Z6.

*M. elongata* (Decne.) Benth. & Hook. f. Stems to 25cm, simple, erect, green-white, adpressed-pubesc. Lvs with adpressed, tuberculate-based bristle hairs throughout; basal lvs to 60×12mm, oblong to oblong-lanceolate or elliptic-

**Mertensia** (×0.6) (a) *M. virginica* (b) *M. lanceolata* (c) *M. alpina* (d) *M. sibirica* (e) *M. primuloides* (f) *M.maritima*

lanceolate, acute, ciliate, petiolate; cauline lvs to 70×12mm, lanceolate, sessile or subsessile. Infl. solitary, elongating with age, densely many-fld; pedicels to 6mm, pubesc, suberect; cal. to 5mm; lobes linear, acute, erect, sparingly strigose; cor. blue to deep purple-blue, to 9mm, campanulate to cylindric-campanulate, lobes to 3.5×3mm, subrotund, spreading, scales usually inconspicuous; anth. to 2mm, oblong, acute, subsessile. Nutlets to 2.5×1.5mm, ovoid-triagonal, usually white, glabrous, lustrous. Pakistan, Kashmir. Z6.

***M. lanceolata*** (Pursh) A. DC. Stem to 45cm, erect or ascending. Basal lvs to 14×4cm, ovate-lanceolate, glabrous to short-strigose or pustulate above, glabrous beneath; cauline lvs to 10×3cm, elliptic-oblong to lanceolate to linear, acute to obtuse, pubesc., sessile. Infl. scorpioid, paniculate with age; cal. to 9mm, lobes to 6mm, triangular to lanceolate, acute or obtuse, exterior glabrous, ciliate; cor. blue, tube to 6.5mm, interior with a basal ring of hairs, limb to 9mm, usually campanulate, scales glabrous or puberulent; anth. to 2mm. Nutlets to 3mm, usually rugose. N America (Saskatchewan to New Mexico). Z4.

***M. longiflora*** Greene. Stem to 35cm, erect. Lvs glabrous to hirsute above, glabrous beneath; basal lvs to 5×2.5cm, spathulate to ovate, petiolate, cauline lvs to 8×4.5cm, ovate-elliptic to oblong-lanceolate, obtuse. Infl. short, mostly dense; pedicels to 6mm, glabrous to pubesc.; cal. to 6mm, lobes to 4.5mm, linear-lanceolate to lanceolate, acute, glabrous, ciliate; cor. bright blue, tube to 15mm, interior glabrous or basally puberulent, limb to 7mm, scales prominent, mostly glabrous; fil. to 2mm, anth. to 2mm. Nutlets to 4mm, rugose. N America (British Columbia, to N California). Z3.

***M. maritima*** (L.) S.F. Gray. OYSTER PLANT. Stem to 100cm, decumbent or spreading. Lvs to 10×5cm, fleshy, spathulate to ovate, acuminate or obtuse, petiolate, glaucous sea green papillose above. Pedicels to 3cm; cal. to 6×4mm, lobes triangular to oblong, acute; cor. pink becoming blue, tube to 5mm, limb to 4mm; scales inconspicuous or absent; stamens to 1mm; style to 5mm. Nutlets rotund, acute, smooth. N America (Alaska to Massachusetts), Greenland, Eurasia. Z3.

***M. oblongifolia*** (Nutt.) G. Don. Stem to 30cm, erect or ascending. Lvs strigose above, glabrous beneath; basal lvs to 8×2cm, narrowly elliptic-oblong to oblong or spathulate, obtuse, cauline lvs to 8×1.5cm, elliptic-oblong to linear, sessile or subsessile. Infl. dense, ultimately branching pedicels to 1cm, glabrous to strigose; cal. to 7mm, lobes ovate-triangular to linear, acute, ciliate; cor. blue, tube to 12mm, interior glabrous, limb to 7mm, scales conspicuous, glabrous to puberulent; fil. to 4mm, anth. to 2mm, oblong. Nutlets to 4mm, rugose. N America (Montana to N California). Z4.

***M. paniculata*** (Ait.) G. Don. Stem to 75cm, erect. Lvs scabrous and adpressed-pubesc. above, spreading-pubesc. beneath, basal lvs to 20×14cm, ovate-subcordate to elliptic-lanceolate, acute to acuminate, petiole to 25cm, cauline lvs to 18×8cm, ovate to lanceolate, acuminate, sessile or subsessile. Infl. scorpioid; peduncle to 3cm, strigose, becoming reflexed; cal. to 7mm, glabrous or pubesc., lobes triangular to narrowly lanceolate, acute; cor. pink when young, blue with age, sometimes white, tube to 7mm, interior glabrous or pubesc., limb to 9mm, scales prominent, glabrous or puberulent; fil. to 3mm, anth. to 3mm. Nutlets rugose. Canada, N US. Z4.

***M. platyphylla*** Heller. Stem to 90cm, erect. Lvs minutely strigose above, somewhat hirsute beneath; basal lvs to 12×10cm, ovate-subcordate, acute or acuminate, petiole to 25cm, cauline lvs to 14×7cm, ovate to lanceolate, acuminate, sessile or short-petiolate. Infl. scorpioid; pedicels to 4cm, strigose; cal. to 12mm in fr., lobes to 1mm, lanceolate to linear, acute, ciliate, exterior usually glabrous; cor. blue, sometimes white, tube to 6mm, interior glabrous or puberulent, limb to 9mm, scales prominent, usually glabrous; fil. to 2.5mm, anth. to 5mm. Nutlets to 7mm, somewhat rugose. N America. Z4.

***M. primuloides*** (Decne.) Clarke. Stem to 15cm, strigose, densely leafy below. Basal lvs to 7×1cm, lanceolate to oblong or linear-lanceolate, acute or obtuse. Infl. solitary, short, few-fld; pedicels to 3.5cm; cal. to 4mm, lobes oblong or linear to linear-lanceolate, pilose; cor. deep blue to white or yellow, to 15mm, hypocrateriform, tube cylindrical, limb to 10mm diam., scales conspicuous; anth. subsessile. Nutlets to 3mm, brown, ovate, carinate. Afghanistan, Pakistan, Tibet. Z5.

***M. sibirica*** (L.) G. Don Stems to 45cm, erect, unbranched. Basal lvs suborbicular to broadly elliptic or cordate; cauline lvs ovate, acute. Infl. a terminal raceme; fls blue-purple. Eurasia. 'Alba': fls white. Z3.

***M. umbratilis*** Greenman. Stem to 60cm, erect or ascending. Lvs glabrous or sparingly strigose above, glabrous beneath; basal lvs to 11×6cm, ovate to ovate-oblong, obtuse, base decurrent, petiole to 8cm, cauline lvs to 10×5cm, oblong to ovate-oblong, acute or obtuse, ciliate, sessile or subsessile. Infl. axillary, scorpioid; pedicels to 10mm, glabrous or papillose; cal. to 8mm, glabrous, ciliate, lobes triangular-lanceolate or lanceolate, acute; cor. blue, tube to 14mm, interior glabrous, limb to 9mm, scales conspicuous, glabrous or puberulent; fil. to 5mm, anth. to 2.5mm. Nutlets to 4mm, rugose. N US (Washington to Oregon). Z6.

***M. virginica*** (L.) Pers. ex Link. Stem to 70cm, erect. Basal lvs to 20×12cm, elliptic to ovate, glabrous to slightly papillose above, long-petiolate; cauline lvs to 12×9cm, elliptic-oblong to ovate, glabrous, sessile or short-petiolate. Infl. axillary, scorpioid; pedicels to 10mm; cal. to 10mm, lobes oblong-lanceolate or lanceolate, acute or obtuse; cor. blue, sometimes pink or white, tube to 21mm, interior with a dense basal ring of hairs, limb to 13mm, campanulate, scales mostly inconspicuous; fil. to 8mm, anth. to 2mm, oblong-linear. Nutlets to 3mm, rugose. N America. 'Alba': fls white. 'Rubra': fls pink. Z3.

***M. viridis*** (A. Nels.) A. Nels. Perenn. to 30cm. Basal lvs to 10×3cm, elliptic to oblanceolate, glabrous or shortly pubesc. above and beneath, petiolate; cauline lvs to 7×2.5cm ovate to linear, sessile or short-petiolate. Fls erect to pendent; cal. to 6mm, lobes linear-lanceolate to ovate, acute to obtuse, glabrous to pubesc.; cor. deep to light or white, tube to 9mm, interior densely pubesc., limb to 9mm, glabrous or pubesc. Nutlets to 3mm, minutely tuberculate, wrinkled. Montana, Colorado, Utah. Z3.

***M. pterocarpa*** (Turcz.) Tatew. & Ohwi. See *M. sibirica*.
***M. pulchella*** Piper. See *M. longiflora*.
***M. tibetica*** (Decne.) Clarke. See *M. primuloides*.
***M. tweedyi*** Rydb. See *M. alpina*.
For further synonymy see *Eritrichium, Lithospermum, Pseudomertensia* and *Pulmonaria*.

**Meryta** Forst. & Forst. f. (From an artificial Gk word *merytos*, meaning growing together; the male flowers in some species forming a knob or head.) Araliaceae. 25–30 species of small to medium evergreen, generally pachycaulous, dioecious trees of oceanic climates. Leaves simple, spirally arranged, more or less tufted, large, somewhat coriaceous; in at least one species juvenile leaves markedly differing from adults. Inflorescences terminal, to 3 times compound; flowers in heads or umbels on the spreading primary branches. Pacific Is. (Micronesia through Vanuatu to New Zealand and SE Polynesia). Z10.

CULTIVATION *Meryta* spp. make small, round-headed trees, grown for their glossy foliage in essentially frost free warm-temperate zones and particularly in maritime exposures where they show marked resistance to salt-laden winds. Plant in fertile, deep, moisture-retentive soils. In colder areas, grow in the cool to intermediate glasshouse, in large tubs in a medium fertility, loam-based mix with additional organic matter. Give strong, filtered to indirect light and water moderately. Propagate from seed in autumn, by semi-ripe cuttings rooted with bottom heat or by air-layering. As only female plants of *M. denhamii* are known in cultivation, this must be propagated by eye cuttings in later winter. It is sometimes used as an understock for grafts of *Schefflera veitchii*. In addition to the species described below, *M. latifolia* (Endl.) Seem. from Norfolk Island and *M. sonchifolia* Lind. & André, from New Caledonia with very large pinnatifid leaves, are sometimes cultivated.

***M. denhamii*** Seem. Tree to 10m, becoming strongly branched when well-grown, the crown dense. Juvenile lvs membranous, linear-elliptic, dark green, to 30×1.3cm; adult lvs rather larger, elliptic, to 125×22cm, apex acute to obtuse, base narrowed, margin with coarse, rounded teeth. Infl. small, stout, with few heads; fls in heads. New Caledonia (Isle of Pines). Only females known in cult.

***M. sinclairii*** (Hook. f.) Seem. PUKA. Round-headed tree to 8m, without distinct juvenile foliage. Lvs oblong-obovate, to 50cm, apex obtuse, margins entire. Infl. to 45cm; fls green-white, in dense umbels. Fr. black, fleshy, to 13mm or less. New Zealand (Three Kings, Hen & Chickens).

For synonymy see *Aralia* and *Oreopanax*.

**Mesembryanthemum** L. emend. L. Bol. (From Gk *mesembria*, midday, and *anthemon*, flower, due to the flowers opening only in bright sunlight.) Aizoaceae. 40–50 species of annuals or biennials, more or less conspicuously glossy-papillose throughout. Stems usually erect, thick, fleshy, often with a basal rosette of leaves; branches often prostrate, creeping or ascending. Leaves alternate or opposite, shortly united, cylindrical or flat, expanded. Flowers solitary or numerous in more or less elongated inflorescences, white, pink or red, rarely yellow. S Africa, Namibia. Z9.

CULTIVATION This once enormous genus now contains only a few species of mainly annuals and biennials and can be treated as for *Dorotheanthus*. Their flowers are, however, rather smaller and less brightly flowered. The leaves of many species are highly attractive and very delicate and so are best handled as little as possible and even then with great care.

***M. aitonis*** Jacq. Lvs obovate-spathulate, 5×2.5cm, somewhat obtuse. Fls red. E Cape.

***M. barklyi*** N.E. Br. To 60cm, blue-green, tinged purple; stem 4-angled. Lvs expanded-spathulate, lower lvs to 28cm long, 18cm wide midway, with prominent veins and undulating margins, upper lvs smaller. Fls 3.6cm diam., white. Cape: Little Namaqualand; Namibia: Great Namaqualand.

***M. cryptanthum*** Hook. f. Prostrate; stems thick, cylindrical. Lvs 3–4×0.6–0.8cm, lower lvs opposite, flat, thick and fleshy, lvs on flowering stems more or less cylindrical, elliptical and clavate, green or red, sometimes waxy yellow. Fls 1–2cm diam., sessile, axillary, white to deep pink or yellow. Namibia, Red Sea coast.

***M. crystallinum*** L. Stems spreading, densely papillose. Lvs ovate or ovate-spathulate, thick-fleshy, very papillose with undulating margins. Fls 3–5 together, 2–3cm diam., white. Namibia, E Cape, introduced Mediterranean, Canary Is., California.

***M. guerichianum*** Pasc. Highly succulent; stems 5–8mm thick, cylindrical. Basal and lower cauline lvs in several opposite and decussate pairs, basal lvs 15×8cm, ovate to rhombic, narrowed teretely below, upper lvs smaller. Fls 2.5–4cm diam., white or green to yellow-white and pink to light red, pedicels 1–4cm. Cape Province, Namibia.

***M. hypertrophicum*** Dinter. Forming flat cushions; stems spreading, prostrate. Lvs 1–1.3cm thick, digitate to hemispherical, soft, very fleshy. Fls 4–6cm diam., white or red, very numerous on ageing stems. S Namibia, Little Namaqualand.

***M. inachabense*** Engl. Soft-fleshy, prostrate, erect or curved ascending, basally branching. Basal and lower cauline lvs 2–5×1–2cm, oblong-spathulate to obovate. Fls 1–1.5cm diam., very numerous, fragrant, yellow, occasionally white; pedicels 5–15mm; stigmas red. Cape Province: Kenhardt District; Namibia: Great Namaqualand.

***M. intransparens*** L. Bol. Robust; main stem erect to 50cm, flowering stems elongated, prostrate, to 1m long, 18mm diam., hexagonal. Lvs 11×9cm, ovate, acute, margins undulating. Fls 4cm diam., 30 together, white. Cape Province: Clanwilliam and Laingsburg Districts.

***M. macrophyllum*** L. Bol. Covered with short papillate hairs, velvety; stems to 70cm, prostrate, 4-angled. Lvs 40×23×0.5cm (the largest lvs in the Aizoaceae), to 32, rosulate, oblong-ovate, margins undulating, lower surface keeled and long-hirsute. Infl. 50×50cm; fls 4–5cm diam., numerous, mauve-pink. Cape Province: Little Namaqualand.

***M. nodiflorum*** L. To 20cm, grey-green with large papillae. Lvs 1–2.5cm×1–2mm, linear, ciliate below. Fls white. Cape: Little Namaqualand and southwards, introduced S Europe, N Africa, Arabia, Iran, Iraq, Pakistan, Atlantic Is., California, Baja California.

***M. aduncum*** Jacq. See *Ruschia schollii*.
***M. alkalifugum*** Dinter nom. nud. See *M. barklyi*.
***M. altile*** N.E. Br. See *Conophytum ficiforme*.
***M. angulatum*** Thunb. See *M. aitonis*.
***M. aquosum*** L. Bol. See *M. hypertrophicum*.
***M. arenarum*** (N.E. Br.) L. Bol. See *M. inachabense*.
***M. astridae*** Dinter. See *Titanopsis hugo-schlechteri*.
***M. aureum*** L. See *Lampranthus aureus*.
***M. bellum*** (N.E. Br.) Dinter. See *Lithops karasmontana* ssp. *bella*.
***M. bergerianum*** Dinter. See *Hereroa hesperanthera*.
***M. bicolor*** Curtis. See *Lampranthus coccineus*.
***M. bicolorum*** (L.) Rothm. See *Lampranthus bicolor*.
***M. bidentatum*** Haw. See *Glottiphyllum semicylindricum*.
***M. bigibberatum*** Haw. See *Glottiphyllum semicylindricum*.
***M. brachyphyllum*** Pax. See *Drosanthemum paxianum*.
***M. caducum*** Auct. non Ait. See *M. inachabense*.
***M. calycinum*** Ecklon & Zeyh. See *Sphalmanthus canaliculatus*.
***M. canaliculatum*** Salm-Dyck. See *Sphalmanthus salmoneus*.
***M. candidissimum*** (Haw.) N.E. Br. See *Cheiridopsis denticulata*.
***M. canum*** (Haw.) Berger. See *Aloinopsis peersii*.
***M. carinatum*** Vent. See *Semnanthe lacera*.
***M. caulescens*** Mill. See *Lampranthus deltoides*.
***M. clavatum*** Haw. See *Dorotheanthus gramineus*.
***M. claviforme*** DC. See *Dorotheanthus gramineus*.
***M. copticum*** L. See *M. nodiflorum*.
***M. corallinum*** Haw. See *Lampranthus coralliflorus*.
***M. crystallinum*** Auct. non L. See *M. guerichianum*.
***M. crystallophanes*** Ecklon & Zeyh. See *M. aitonis*.
***M. cultratum*** Salm-Dyck. See *Glottiphyllum latum* var. *cultratum*.
***M. cupreum*** L. Bol. See *Cephalophyllum caespitosum*.
***M. dactylindum*** Welw. ex Oliv. See *M. cryptanthum*.
***M. damarum*** N.E. Br. See *Lithops karasmontana*.
***M. demissum*** Willd. See *Disphyma australe*.
***M. densum*** Haw. See *Trichodiadema densum*.
***M. dentatum*** Kerner. See *Semnanthe lacera*.
***M. depressum*** Haw. See *Glottiphyllum depressum*.
***M. didymaotum*** Marloth. See *Didymaotus lapidiformis*.
***M. digitiforme*** Thunb. See *Dactylopsis digitata*.
***M. dinterae*** Dinter. See *Chasmatophyllum musculinum*.
***M. divergens*** Kensit. See *Gibbaeum fissoides*.
***M. diversifolium*** Haw. See *Cephalophyllum diversiphyllum*.

***M. dubium*** L. Bol. See *Cephalophyllum decipiens*.
***M. eberlanzii*** Dinter & Schwantes. See *Lithops karasmontana* ssp. *eberlanzii*.
***M. echinatum*** Ait. See *Delosperma pruinosum*.
***M. educale*** var. ***virescens*** Haw. Moss. See *Carpobrotus virescens*.
***M. emarcidum*** Thunb. See *Sceletium emarcidum*.
***M. evolutum*** N.E. Br. See *Ruschia evoluta*.
***M. exacutum*** N.E. Br. See *Ruschia acuminata*.
***M. exile*** hort. ex Haw. See *Carpobrotus aequilaterus*.
***M. expansum*** L. See *Sceletium expansum*.
***M. falcatum*** Thunb. See *Semnanthe lacera*.
***M. falcatum*** var. ***galpinii*** L. Bol. See *Lampranthus falcatus* var. *galpinii*.
***M. fenchelii*** Schinz. See *M. guerichianum*.
***M. ferrugineum*** Schwantes. See *Lithops lesliei*.
***M. fibulaeforme*** Haw. See *Conophytum fibuliforme*.
***M. filamentosum*** DC. See *Erepsia mutabilis*.
***M. fimbriatum*** Sonder. See *Ruschia pygmaea*.
***M. flanaganii*** Kensit. See *Delosperma tradescantioides*.
***M. flexile*** Haw. See *Lampranthus emarginatus*.
***M. forficatum*** Jacq. See *Erepsia mutabilis*.
***M. forskahlii*** Hochst. See *M. cryptanthum*.
***M. francisci*** Dinter & Schwantes. See *Lithops francisci*.
***M. fulleri*** (L. Bol.) L. Bol. See *M. inachabense*.
***M. fulviceps*** N.E. Br. See *Lithops fulviceps*.
***M. garicusianum*** Dinter. See *M. guerichianum*.
***M. gibbosum*** Haw. See *Gibbaeum gibbosum*.
***M. glaciale*** Haw. See *M. crystallinum*.
***M. gladiatum*** Jacq. See *Semnanthe lacera*.
***M. glaucinum*** Haw. See *Erepsia mutabilis*.
***M. grandifolium*** auct. non Schinz. See *M. barklyi*.
***M. grandifolium*** Schinz ex Range. See *M. guerichianum*.
***M. gratum*** N.E. Br. See *Conophytum gratum*.
***M. heathii*** N.E. Br. See *Gibbaeum heathii*.
***M. hispidum*** var. ***pallidum*** Haw. See *Drosanthemum floribundum*.
***M. hooker*** Berg. See *Lithops hookeri*.
***M. imbricans*** Haw. See *Lampranthus emarginatus*.
***M. imbricatum*** var. ***rubrum*** Haw. See *Ruschia tumidula*.
***M. incurvum*** var. ***roseum*** DC. See *Lampranthus roseus*.
***M. insititium*** Willd. See *Malephora crocea*.
***M. julii*** Dinter & Schwantes. See *Lithops julii*.
***M. karasbergensis*** (L. Bol.) Friedrich. See *Hereroa hesperanthera*.
***M. karasmontanum*** Dinter & Schwantes. See *Lithops karasmontana*.
***M. laeve*** Thunb. See *Malephora thunbergii*.
***M. lanceolatum*** sensu lato Haw. See *M. aitonis*.
***M. lepidum*** Haw. See *Lampranthus productus* var. *lepidum*.
***M. lericheanum*** Dinter & Schwantes. See *Lithops karasmontana* var. *lericheana*.
***M. lesliei*** N.E. Br. See *Lithops lesliei*.
***M. leve*** N.E. Br. See *Ruschia mollis*.
***M. linguiforme*** var. ***latum*** Salm-Dyck. See *Glottiphyllum latum*.
***M. locale*** N.E. Br. See *Lithops schwantesii*.
***M. longispinulum*** Sonder. See *Sphalmanthus canaliculatus*.
***M. magnipunctatum*** Haw. See *Pleiospilos compactus* ssp. *canus*.
***M. marmoratum*** N.E. Br. See *Lithops marmorata*.
***M. micans*** Thunb. non L. See *Delosperma expersum*.
***M. minusculum*** N.E. Br. See *Conophytum minusculum*.
***M. minutum*** Haw. See *Conophytum minutum*.
***M. multipunctatum*** Salm-Dyck. See *Cheiridopsis rostrata*.
***M. muricatum*** Haw. See *Lampranthus deltoides*.
***M. nigrescens*** Haw. See *Carpobrotus aequilaterus*.
***M. nobile*** Haw. See *Pleiospilos compactus* ssp. *canus*.
***M. obtusum*** Haw. See *Gibbaeum fissoides*.
***M. opticum*** Marloth. See *Lithops optica*.
***M. paxii*** Engl. See *Drosanthemum paxianum*.
***M. perviride*** Haw. See *Gibbaeum gibbosum*.
***M. pinque*** L. Bol. See *M. barklyi*.
***M. polyphyllum*** Haw. See *Lampranthus emarginatus*.
***M. ponderosum*** Dinter sub. nud. See *Juttadinteria longipetala*.
***M. pseudotruncatellum*** A. Berger. See *Lithops pseudotruncatella*.
***M. pugioniforme*** L. non DC. See *Conicosia pugioniformis*.
***M. pugioniforme*** L. Bol. See *Herrea robusta*.
***M. pyropaeum*** Haw. See *Dorotheanthus gramineus*.
***M. ramulosum*** Haw. See *Cheiridopsis rostrata*.
***M. recumbens*** N.E. Br. See *Chasmatophyllum musculinum*.
***M. recurvum*** Haw. See *Ruschia schollii*.
***M. reflexum*** Willd. See *Sphalmanthus canaliculatus*.
***M. ringens*** var. ***caninum*** L. See *Carruanthus ringens*.
***M. roseum*** Haw. See *Drosanthemum striatum*.
***M. rostellatum*** DC. See *Ruschia rostella*.
***M. rubrocinctum*** Ecklon & Zeyh. See *Carpobrotus acinaciformis*.
***M. ruschii*** Dinter & Schwantes. See *Lithops ruschiorum*.
***M. ruschiorum*** Dinter & Schwantes. See *Lithops ruschiorum*.
***M. salmoneum*** Haw. See *Sphalmanthus salmoneus*.
***M. sarcocalycanthum*** Dinter & Berger. See *M. cryptanthum*.
***M. saxetanum*** N.E. Br. See *Conophytum saxetanum*.
***M. scalpratum*** Haw. See *Glottiphyllum linguiforme*.
***M. sexipartitum*** N.E. Br. See *Delosperma lehmannii*.
***M. spathulatum*** L. Bol. See *Drosanthemum uniflorum*.
***M. spathulifolium*** Willd. See *Dorotheanthus bellidiformis*.
***M. squamulosum*** (Dinter) Dinter. See *M. barklyi*.
***M. steingroeveri*** Pax ex Engl. See *Ruschia odontocalyx*.
***M. stellatum*** hort. See *Erepsia gracilis*.
***M. stenophyllum*** L. Bol. See *Ruschia stenophylla*.
***M. stramineum*** Willd. See *Cephalophyllum tricolorum*.
***M. suavissimum*** Dinter. See *Juttadinteria suavissimum*.
***M. subrostratum*** Willd. See *Cephalophyllum subulatoides*.
***M. torquatum*** Haw. See *Drosanthemum floribundum*.
***M. tortuosum*** DC. See *Sceletium expansum*.
***M. tortuosum*** L. See *Sceletium tortuosum*.
***M. tricolor*** Jacq. See *Erepsia mutabilis*.
***M. tricolorum*** Haw. See *Cephalophyllum tricolorum*.
***M. trigonum*** N.E. Br. See *Cerochlamys pachyphylla*.
***M. truncatellum*** Hook. f. See *Lithops hookeri*.
***M. truncatellum*** Dinter. See *Lithops pseudotruncatella*.
***M. turbiniformis*** Haw. See *Lithops hookeri*.
***M. vallis-mariae*** Dinter & Schwantes. See *Lithops vallis-mariae*.
***M. varians*** Haw. See *Sceletium tortuosum*.
***M. vernae*** Dinter & A. Berger. See *Malephora engleriana*.
***M. vescum*** N.E. Br. See *Cheiridopsis cigarettifera*.
***M. violaceum*** DC. See *Lampranthus emarginatus*.
***M. volckameri*** Haw. See *M. aitonis*.
For further synonymy see *Amoebophyllum, Cryophytum, Halenbergia, Hydrodea, Opophytum* and *Platythyra*.

For illustration see AIZOACEAE.

**Mesospinidium** Rchb.
***M. cochliodum*** Rchb. f. See *Symphyglossum sanguineum*.

**Mespilus** L. (The Latin name for this fruit.) MEDLAR. Rosaceae. 1 species, a deciduous tree or shrub, to 5m. Bark grey-brown, fissured, sometimes flaking. Branches arching, divaricate; branchlets light brown-tomentose at first; thorny in the wild, usually thornless in cultivation. Leaves to 12cm, alternate, oblong-lanceolate, short-acuminate, dull green above, tomentose beneath, serrate, yellow and rufous in autumn; petioles very short. Flowers white, to 5cm wide, usually solitary, sometimes paired; pedicels lanuginose; calyx tomentose, lobes 5, pubescent, lanceolate-acute, incurved, persistent; petals 5; stamens usually 25–40. Fruit turbinate, to 2.5cm, brown when ripe, crowned with the 5 calyx lobes, showing the transecting ends of the bony seed vessels. Spring–summer. Europe, Asia Minor. Related to *Crataegus* and *Cotoneaster*, but flowers large and solitary, and fruit with 5 carpels.

CULTIVATION The medlar, *Mespilus germanica*, is indigenous through much of Europe and is thought to have originated from Transcaucasia. It is occasionally found growing wild in hedges and thickets, even in southern England, but this is considered likely to have resulted from garden escapes. Only ever of minor horticultural importance, it was grown in Asia Minor, Greece and Rome whose ancient writings occasionally make reference to it. The French introduced it to North America in the 17th century and medlars are sometimes used for garden hedging in Florida, where escapes are also found in the wild.

Charlemagne's list of fruits in the year 800 includes the medlar, and in England it appears in some Westminster Abbey records for 1270 and again in others connected with Henry VIII. There is a German reference (*Heresbachins* 1577) to the wood of the medlar being used for making wheel spokes. Greater use of medlar fruits appears to have occurred on the European continent, particularly in the Middle Ages, than in Britain, and this still holds good though on a reduced scale. In France they were the main ingredient of a much-prized preserve, whereas in Britain they were preferred following a meal and complemented by port wine. The fruit, which is flattened, apple-shaped and with a wide, open eye, should be kept until part-rotten (bletted) to enjoy maximum flavour, one which is an acquired taste. Picking should be delayed until late October or early November and the fruit stored eye downwards in dark, cool conditions for a short while to ripen fully.

Only three cultivars are widely listed: 'Dutch' with large flowers and foliage and fruits up to 6.5cm in diameter and markedly flattened, but with only fair flavour; it dates at least from the 17th century. The smaller-fruited 'Nottingham' has a finer flavour and more upright growth; it is thought to be one of the earliest selections of the common wild medlar. Little if any attention has ever been given to breeding new cultivars, the only notable introduction being 'Royal', introduced by Rivers from France in 1860; it has medium-sized fruits. There is a seedless cultivar called 'Stoneless', but its fruits are very small and of poor flavour.

Medlar trees will succeed on any reasonable moisture-retentive soil; an organic mulch annually in spring gives best results. Tree size will be medium (approx. 5.5–6m/18–20ft) on quince rootstock, perhaps 7–7.5m/23–25ft on seedling pear. A bush is the most practical tree-type, trained as for bush apple although it is also grown as a round headed standard, which will need staking for several seasons until established. Occasional tidying and thinning of branches is the only pruning necessary on established trees, with particular attention to removal of the crossing branches which seem to arise as a consequence of the natural habit of the species.

Apart from the use of the fruit, the medlar tree is particularly attractive as an ornamental. It has a twisted yet spreading habit, even drooping in the large-fruited 'Dutch', 'Breda Giant' and 'Large Russian'. The flowers are large and pink-white and the foliage develops glorious orange-gold tints in the autumn. Where space allows, a half-standard or even full-standard form will allow the tree to show its natural form and grace. Many carry large spines on older wood but those selected as the best cultivars for fruiting tend to have fewer spines.

Cultivate as for APPLE. Large, dark brown blotches on the leaves, which may spread into the shoot, are caused by the fungus *Sclerotinia mespili*. Spores growing on the blotches are spread by insects to infect the flowers which develop into 'mummies' rather than fruits. Affected leaves should be burnt and regular sprays with a systemic fungicide may be necessary to control the disease. Medlars may sometimes be affected by brown rot (*Sclerotinia fructigena*) and powdery mildew (*Podosphaera leucotricha*). May be attacked by the apple grass aphid (*Rhopalosiphum insertum*) and by various defoliating caterpillars.

***M.germanica*** L. As for the genus. 'Dutch': fr. to 6.5cm diam., flattened. 'Nottingham': more upright, well flavoured. 'Royal': fr. medium size. 'Stoneless': fr. small.

***M.acuminata*** Lodd. See *Cotoneaster acuminatus*.
***M.amelanchier*** L. See *Amelanchier rotundifolia*.
***M.arborea*** Michx. f. See *Amelanchier arborea*.
***M.arbutifolia*** L. See *Aronia arbutifolia*.
***M.arbutifolia*** var. ***melanocarpa*** Michx. See *Aronia melanocarpa*.
***M.canadensis*** L. See *Amelanchier canadensis*.
***M.crenulata*** D. Don. See *Pyracantha crenulata*.
***M.flabellata*** Spach. See *Crataegus flabellata*.
***M.fontanesiana*** Spach. See *Crataegus fontanesiana*.
***M.grandiflora*** Sm. See × *Crataemespilus grandiflora*.
***M.japonica*** Thunb. See *Eriobotrya japonica*.
***M.oliveriana*** Dum.-Cours. See *Crataegus oliveriana*.
***M.pruinosa*** Wendl. See *Crataegus pruinosa*.
***M.prunifolia*** Marshall. See *Aronia prunifolia*.
***M.pyracantha*** L. See *Pyracantha coccinea*.
***M.racemiflora*** Desf. See *Cotoneaster racemiflorus*.
***M.sorbifolia*** Poir. See × *Sorbaronia sorbifolia*.
***M.tanacetifolia*** Lam. See *Crataegus tanacetifolia*.

**Mestoklema** N.E. Br. (From Gk *mestos*, full, and *klema*, a small branch.) Aizoaceae. About 7 species of small, branched shrubs or trees, usually with a tuberous caudex; young stems papillose. Leaves opposite, united at the base, triquetrous or cylindrical, minutely papillose or glistering, leaf bases persisting as a thorn after leaf fall. Flowers produced in a small branched terminal inflorescence, small, white to shades of red and yellow, pedicels becoming blunt thorns. Capsule with 5 lidded cells. S Africa (Cape Province) Namibia, Réunion Is. Z9.

CULTIVATION Pot deeply to accommodate taproot, otherwise as for *Pleiospilos*.

***M.arboriforme*** (Burchell) N.E. Br. Tree-like, 30–45cm, with a distinct trunk 2.5cm thick, freely branching above; shoots roughly hirsute. Lvs 12×2×2mm, minutely hirsute. Infl. 5–8cm diam.; fls 5mm diam., yellow to orange. Cape Province (West Griqualand and Philipstown Districts), Namibia (Great Namaqualand).

***M.macrorhizum*** (DC.) Schwantes. Caudex tuberous; stems 2.5–7.5cm. Lvs crowded, obtusely triquetrous. Fls 1–3 together, small, white. Réunion Is.

***M.tuberosum*** (L.) N.E. Br. Much-branched shrub, 50–70cm, caudex large, hemispherical or tuberous. Lvs 10–15×2–3mm, triquetrous, minutely papillose, light green. Fls 7–8mm diam., red-yellow. Cape Province, Orange Free State, Namibia.

For synonymy see *Delosperma* and *Mesembryanthemum*.

**Mesua** L. (For Johannes Mesue of Damascus (777–857), physician and botanist.) Guttiferae. 3 species of evergreen trees or shrubs. Leaves opposite, crowded on stems, narrow, leathery, often with translucent spots; venation distinct, many parallel laterals diverging from midrib. Flowers polygamous or bisexual, solitary, axillary, large and showy; sepals and petals 4; stamens very numerous; ovary bilocular, ovules 2 per locule; style long, stigma peltate. Fruit with woody rind, 1-celled, 4-valvate; seeds 1–4, not arillate. Indomalesia. Z10.

CULTIVATION *M.ferrea* is a handsome evergreen tree planted frequently in Sri Lanka, India and Malaya near Buddhist temples and as a garden ornamental. In subtropical gardens it is an attractive specimen tree with deep red young foliage and a succession of fragrant white blossom produced through late winter and early spring. Cultivation as for *Calophyllum*.

***M.ferrea*** L. IRONWOOD; NA. Tree to 13m; trunk erect, straight. Lvs linear-lanceolate to oblong-lanceolate, acute, to 15cm, deep red when young, becoming glossy dark green, glaucous below. Fls terminal, solitary or paired, white, to 7.5cm across, fragrant; stamens deep yellow. Fr. subglobose, ovoid-conic, to 5cm. Summer. India to Malaysia.

**Metapanax** Frodin. (From Gk *meta*, between, among, and *Panax*, referring to the shifting generic position of this group of species.) Araliaceae. Species of glabrous evergreen shrubs or trees of bushy habit, with relatively slender branches. Leaves simple or palmately lobed or compound, without stipules, lobes broadly and shallowly toothed to almost entire. Inflorescence terminal, paniculate, 1–2× compound, pyramidal to conical in outline, fairly slender; main axis to 18cm, longer than the lowest primary branch; primary branches few to several; flowers in small umbels at ends of main axis, branches and peduncles, the umbels dispersed throughout the inflorescence; calyx subentire to minutely 5-toothed; petals 5, abutting one another, free; stamens 5; ovary 2-locular, the disk slightly to strongly elevated, the styles partially or mostly united into a column. Fruit drupaceous, compressed, thin-walled, expanding entirely or mostly below the disk, more or less transversely oblong or ellipsoid at maturity, the stylar column and arms persistent. China, N Vietnam.

CULTIVATION As for *Pseudopanax*.

***M.davidii*** (Franch.) Frodin. Shrub or tree to 12m. Lvs simple, entire or trilobed or trifid, or 2–3-foliolate; petioles to 20cm; blades when lvs entire narrowly lanceolate to narrowly ovate, to 15×6cm, apex acute, base cuneate to rounded, broadly toothed; simple lvs trinerved at base; lobes of compound lvs sessile. Infl. to 18cm; umbels 12–15-fld, about 18mm across; fls green-yellow. Fr. black, to 6mm across; styles to 2mm. Summer. W & C China, N Vietnam. Z7.

***M.delavayi*** (Franch.) Frodin. Shrub to 5m. Lvs usually 3–5-foliolate, occasionally 2-foliolate or simple; petiole to 12cm; leaflets oblong-lanceolate, to 12×2.5cm, sessile or shortly stalked, the base cuneate, broadly toothed or subentire. Infl. to 15cm; umbels as in *M.davidii* but slightly larger. Fr. to 5mm diam.; styles to 3mm. Summer. SW China, N Vietnam. Less hardy than *M.davidii*, and distinguished from it mainly by its smaller, usually 3–5-foliolate lvs. Z9.

For synonymy see *Nothopanax*, *Panax* and *Pseudopanax*.

**Metasequoia** Miki ex Hu & Cheng. (From Gk *meta*, with, and *Sequoia*.) Cupressaceae. 1 species, a deciduous, monoecious conifer, fast-growing, to 45m+. Bole to 2m diameter, deeply ridged and buttressed at base. Bark deeply furrowed, fibrous, flaking in long shreds, rust coloured. Crown conic, becoming columnar. Branches ascending, or level, often twisted. Shoots in 2 rows, opposite, glabrous, green, becoming orange-brown, weak shoots without buds, falling in autumn, green. Leaves opposite, distichous, horizontal, subsessile, linear, flexible, bright green above, lighter, with 2 stomatal bands beneath, 2–2.5cm long, becoming yellow, red and finally foxy brown when falling in autumn. Male 'cones' in terminal or axillary racemes to 30cm long, only produced in areas with hot summers. Female cones with seed scales 14–28, decussate, basal and apical scales sterile; mature cones ripe in 6–7 months on 2–4cm stalks, globose to ovoid and acute at apex, dark brown, 1.5–3×1.5–2cm; seed scales bearing 5–8 brown seeds to 5mm, each with 2 surrounding narrow wings. W China (E Sichuan, W Hubei). Originally described from fossils as *Taxites* Brongn. Z5.

CULTIVATION Plant in a damp soil within reach of water and with side shelter as high as possible but in full light. Avoid dry sites and frost pockets where first growth will be scorched, but the tree is fully hardy to −30°C/−22°F. Soil pH has little effect, until about 3.5. Like *Taxodium*, it can be planted beside or even in shallow standing water. Warm summers are needed for good growth; in Britain the best trees are in SE England, and it grows very poorly in Scotland. First 'discovered' in 1941, though long cultivated in its native region, where it is planted to stabilize river banks and paddyfield walls.

A superb specimen tree, rapidly growing to a great size. Pruning basal branches is often advisable and decreases irregularities (flutes and pockets) in the trunk.

***M. glyptostroboides*** Hu & Cheng. DAWN REDWOOD. As for the genus. 'Emerald Feathers': lvs very bright green, luxuriant; vigorous. 'National': crown narrowly conic.

For illustration see *Taxodium* and allies.

**Methysticodendron** R.E. Schult.
***M. amesiomium*** R.E. Schult. See *Brugmansia* × *candida*.

**Metrosideros** Banks ex Gaertn. (From *metra*, middle, and *sideros*, iron, in reference to the hard wood of the genus.) Myrtaceae. 50 species of aromatic shrubs, trees or woody climbers. Leaves opposite, simple, pinnately veined, gland-dotted. Flowers red, pink, white or occasionally yellow, in axillary or axillary and terminal, cymose, usually pedunculate inflorescences, these sometimes reduced to a single flower, often aggregated into compound inflorescences, sometimes ramiflorous; sepals 5, imbricate; petals 5; stamens numerous, 2 or more times as long as petals, rarely less; ovary 3-celled. Fruit a leathery capsule; seeds narrowly linear to filiform. S Africa, Malesia, Australasia, Pacific Is. Z9.

CULTIVATION Grown for the leathery aromatic foliage and the attractive and brilliantly coloured flowers, large specimens are amongst the most spectacular of woody flowering plants. *M. excelsus* often forms a multi-stemmed tree with a wide spreading crown smothered in crimson flowers in summer (i.e. Christmas in its native lands). *M. umbellatus* is smaller with a more rounded habit, equally generous in bloom, with the additional interest of coppery young foliage. In favoured maritime climates, that are frost free or almost so, the climbing species will scramble over tree stumps or up and through other supports. The tree species make beautiful specimens or may be used as hedging, and since most bloom even as young plants, in cooler temperate zones make excellent subjects for large pots and tubs in the cool glasshouse or conservatory, to be moved outdoors for the summer months. *M. excelsus* can be attempted outdoors in sheltered maritime climates in Zone 8 and over.

Grow in a freely draining but moisture retentive, medium to high fertility potting mix with additional leafmould; *M. excelsus* is useful in soils of lower fertility. Most are tolerant of some lime, but are unsuitable for shallow soils over chalk. Grow in full sun with protection from the hottest summer sun under glass and maintain good ventilation with moderate humidity. Water plentifully when in growth, less at other times. Provide a winter minimum temperature of 7–10°C/45–40°F. Prune immediately after flowering to restrict size and to remove old weak and overcrowded growths. Propagate species by seed sown in spring, desirable varieties by semi-ripe cuttings in summer rooted in a closed case with bottom heat.

***M. carmineus*** Oliv. Liane to 15m+. Branchlets, infl. and receptacle setose to pubesc. Lvs 15–35×7–10–(20)mm, elliptic to ovate-oblong to broad-ovate, obtuse to subacute, coriaceous; petioles 1mm. Infl. in terminal compound cymes; fls numerous, bright carmine; pedicels 5mm; sep. broad-oblong, 2mm; pet. suborbicular, shortly clawed, 5×4mm, margins usually toothed; stamens 10–15mm. Capsule subglobose, 6–7–(9)mm diam. New Zealand.

***M. colensoi*** Hook. f. Slender liane to 6m+. Branchlets subterete, setose to pubesc. Lvs to 15–20×7–10mm, ovate-lanceolate, acute to acuminate, densely pubesc. when young, subsessile. Infl. of terminal and lateral, small, few-fld cymes; pedicels usually setose, 3mm; receptacle *c*5mm, more or less funnelform, pubesc.; sep. narrow-triangular, acute; pet. pink to white, orbicular; stamens *c*10cm. Capsule subglobose, 3-ribbed, to 4mm diam., often less. New Zealand.

***M. collina*** (Forst. & Forst. f.) A. Gray. Tree or shrub, 1–20m. Branchlets subterete to subquadrangular. Lvs 4–8.5×1.5–6cm, elliptic-lanceolate to oblong or obovate-elliptic, coriaceous, copiously glandular-punctate; petioles (2–)4–12mm. Conflorescences with 3–5 pairs of uniflorescences; peduncles 3–20mm; sep. 2×3mm; pet. obovate to orbicular, to 4mm long and wide; stamens 12–20mm. Fls and fr. conspicuous throughout the year. Samoa and SE Polynesia. 3 varieties are currently recognized.

***M. diffusus*** Forst. f. SMALL RATA VINE. Slender liane to 6m+. Branchlets indistinctly 4-angled, finely pubesc. Lvs 7–8–(25)×3–8mm, oblong to ovate-lanceolate to ovate-oblong, usually acute to apiculate, somewhat pubesc. when young, subsessile. Infl. of few-fld lateral cymes, usually below lvs; pedicels to 5mm, pubesc.; receptacle turbinate, *c*3mm, abruptly expanded above; sep. ovate-triangular; pet. suborbicular, white to pink; stamens slender, 7–9mm, white to pink. Capsule subglobose, 3–4mm. New Zealand.

***M. excelsus*** Sol. ex Gaertn. CHRISTMAS TREE; POHUTUKAWA. Tree to 20m. Branchlets stout, tomentose. Lvs 5–10×2.5–3.5cm, elliptic to oblong, acute or obtuse, coriaceous, thick, white-tomentose beneath. Infl. of broad, compound cymes; pedicels stout, tomentose; receptacle obconical; sep. deltoid; pet. crimson, oblong; stamens crimson, 30–40mm. Capsule 7–9mm, distinctly exserted, tomentose. New Zealand.

***M. fulgens*** Sol. ex Gaertn. Liane to 10m+; bark separating in flakes. Lvs 35–60–(75)×25mm, elliptic-oblong, obtuse, glabrous; petiole stout, 2–5mm. Infl. of terminal cymes; receptacle obconical to urceolate, glabrous, *c*12mm, ribbed; sep. oblong, obtuse; pet. suborbicular, orange-red; stamens scarlet, 20–25mm. Capsule deeply immersed, *c*10×10mm, dehiscing irregularly. New Zealand.

***M. kermadecensis*** Oliv. KERMADEC POHUTUKAWA. Tree to 30m. Branchlets densely white-tomentose. Lvs 2–5×1–2cm, broadly ovate to elliptic-ovate, coriaceous, margins recurved, densely white-tomentose beneath; petioles 5mm. Infl. terminal compound cymes; pedicels stout, to 10mm; receptacle obconical; sep. deltoid to triangular, gland-tipped; pet. oblong, pubesc.; crimson; stamens crimson, 12–20mm. Capsule 6mm, distinctly exserted, woody, white-tomentose. New Zealand (Kermadec Is.). Has been confused in cult. with *M. excelsus* but the lvs are of a different shape.

***M. parkinsonii*** Buch. Straggling shrub or tree up to *c*7m. Branchlets 4-angled. Lvs 35–50×15–20mm, ovate-lanceolate, rather abruptly narrowed to obtuse or subacute apex, coriaceous; petiole 2mm. Infl. in compound cymes, usually below lvs; fls many, bright crimson; receptacle turbinate; sep. ovate-triangular; pet. oblong, somewhat toothed; stamens 20–25mm. Capsules 6–7mm. New Zealand.

***M. perforatus*** (Forst. & Forst. f.) A. Rich. FLOWERY RATA VINE. Rather slender liane to 15m+. Branchlets terete, somewhat setose. Lvs 6–12×5–9mm, broad-ovate to broad-oblong to suborbicular on same plant, glabrous, pale beneath and more or less setose, margins recurved, subsessile. Infl. of axillary few-fld cymes, crowded toward apex of branchlets; peduncles and pedicels pubescent to setose; receptacle broad-turbinate; sep. broad, obtuse; pet. suborbicular, white or pink; stamens 8–10mm, white to pink. Capsule subglobose, 4–5mm diam., exserted. New Zealand.

***M. polymorphus*** Gaud. LEHUA. Small erect to prostrate shrub to tall tree. Bark usually rough and fissured, separating in thick flakes, sometimes smooth and separating in long thin strips. Lvs 1–8×1–5.5cm, obovate to orbicular, sometimes elliptic, broadly ovate or ovate, apex rounded or obtuse to acute, base cuneate to cordate, lower surface glabrous or woolly or adpressed-pubesc., margins revolute to flat; petioles 1–16mm. Fls red, in infl. of 2–5-pairs of cymules, glabrous or adpressed or woolly pubesc.; peduncles 7–18mm; pedicels 2–8mm; sep. rounded to triangular, 1.5–4×1.5–3mm; pet. obovate to orbicular, 2.5–5×2–4.5mm; stamens 10–30mm. Hawaii. A number of varieties are recognized.

***M. robustus*** A. Cunn. RATA; NORTHERN RATA. Tree to 25m+. Branchlets 4-angled, puberulous. Lvs 25–50×15–20mm, elliptic to ovate-oblong, obtuse, glabrous, coriaceous; petioles stout, more or less 2mm. Infl. a many-fld terminal cyme; pedicels to 5mm; receptacle obconical, to 9mm; sep. broad-triangular; pet. oblong, *c*3mm; stamens red, *c*30mm. Capsule oblong, 6–9mm, distinctly exserted. New Zealand. In nature originates usually as an epiphyte, gradually spreading into its host but apparently never actually superseding it. Has been confused in cult. with *M. umbellatus*.

***M. umbellatus*** Cav. SOUTHERN RATA. Tree to 15m+. Branchlets subterete, glabrous. Lvs 30–50×15–20mm, glabrous, coriaceous; petiole 5mm. Infl. of terminal cymes; peduncle to 10mm; receptacle obconical, silky; sep. oblong-triangular to ovate, *c*3mm; pet. light red, suborbicular, 5mm; stamens light red, *c*20mm. Capsule urceolate, 8–9mm, exceeded by receptacle. New Zealand (to Stewart & Auckland Is.)

*M. aurea* hort. See *M. fulgens*.
*M. collinus* ssp. *polymorphus* (Gaud.) Rock. See *M. polymorphus*.
*M. floridus* Sm. See *M. fulgens*.
*M. lucidus* (Forst. f.) A. Rich. See *M. umbellatus*.
*M. scandens* (Forst. & Forst. f.) Druce. See *M. fulgens*.
*M. speciosus* sensu Colenso. See *M. fulgens*.
*M. tomentosa* A. Rich. See *M. excelsus*.
For further synonymy see *Melaleuca*.

**Metroxylon** Rottb. (From Gk *metra*, heart of a tree, and *xylon*, wood, referring to the large pith.) Palmae. Some 6 species of erect, monocarpic palms. Stems ringed, rough. Crownshaft absent. Leaves numerous, densely clustered; petioles smooth, rigid; pinnae opposite, linear-lanceolate, tapered to the apex. Flowers paired, 1 male and 1 female together, subtended by small bracts; sepals 3, united at base; petals 3, valvate in bud; stamens 6; pistil 3-celled, with 3 ovules; stigmas 3-lobed. Fruit ellipsoid or subglobose, 1-seeded; seed with non-ruminate endosperm. Malaya to Fiji. Z10.

CULTIVATION See PALMS. *M. sagu* is the sago palm: sago is extracted from the trunks which are crushed and washed, having been felled shortly before flowering.

*M. sagu* Rottb. SAGO PALM. Stems to 10m, roughly ringed. Lvs to 7m, arching; petioles long, robust, clasping stem at base; pinnae long, tapering at the apex, margins occasionally prickly. Inflorescences to 7m. Fr. globose, yellow-brown. Malaya.

**Meum** Mill. (From *meon*, name used by Dioscorides.) Umbelliferae. 1 species, a glabrous, aromatic perennial to 60cm. Stems striate, with crowded, fibrous petiole remnants at base. Leaves mostly basal, 3–4-pinnate, segments crowded, filiform, to 5mm. Umbels compound, rays 3–15, to 5cm; involucres few or absent; involucel of few bracteoles; calyx teeth absent; flowers white or tinged purple; petals ovate with slightly inflexed apex. Fruit to 7mm, ovoid, slightly compressed; mericarps with thick prominent ridges; vittae 3–5 per furrow. Summer. Europe. Z7.

CULTIVATION A native of rough, rocky grassland, usually on limestone, *Meum* is grown for its fresh green fennel-like foliage and clean white flowers. Suitable for the front border or for naturalizing in the sunny wild garden, it is easily grown in any well-drained, moderately retentive, fertile soil in sun. Propagate by fresh seed or division.

*M. athamanticum* Jacq. BALDMONEY; MEU; SPIGNEL. As for the genus.

**Mexicoa** Garay. (For the country.) Orchidaceae. 1 species, a diminutive orchid, allied to and formerly included in *Oncidium*. Pseudobulbs to 4×2cm, ovoid to pyriform, apically unifoliate or bifoliate. Leaves to 15×1.5cm, equitant, thinly coriaceous, linear to linear-lanceolate, acute or subacute, arcuate. Inflorescence to 20cm, a basal raceme, seldom exceeding leaves; tepals white or yellow-tinged and veined rose; sepals to 14×4mm, elliptic or narrowly oblanceolate, subacute; petals to 12×4mm, obliquely oblong-oblanceolate to obovate, subacute; lip to 17×11mm, yellow, ovate, deflexed, lateral lobes spreading, elliptic, midlobe to 12×7mm; callus yellow-orange, linear, bifid; column to 5mm, strongly incurved. Mexico. Z10.

CULTIVATION As for *Oncidium*.

*M. ghiesbreghtiana* (A. Rich. & Gal.) Garay. As for the genus.

For synonymy see *Oncidium*.

**Meyer, Frank Nicholas** (1875–1918). Plant collector. Born Frans Meijer in Amsterdam, at the age of 14 he became a gardener's assistant at the Amsterdam Botanical Garden. In his eight years there under Hugo de Vries he rose to be head gardener in charge of the experimental garden. His prevailing *Wanderlust* held sway, however, and he journeyed, on foot as always, around Europe and the Alps before going to America in 1901 and working for a year in the glasshouses of the US Department of Agriculture in Washington DC. He periodically made solo expeditions to study plants in the field and spent time in Mexico, California and Cuba. In 1904–5 he worked at the Missouri Botanical Garden until David Fairchild and the USDA chose him to be their collector of economic plants in eastern Asia, with grains, fruit and timber-trees as his primary objectives. He was immediately despatched to China on the first of four expeditions (1905–8, 1909–11, 1912–15 and 1916–18) which were to take him as far west as Russian Turkestan and east into Manchuria, Korea and Kansu. Meyer was a difficult character, prone to fits of depression and always remaining distant from the Chinese, but he skilfully packaged and sent back many valuable economic plants including soy beans, new types of grain, fruit, vegetables, bamboos, Chinese cabbage, elms, bean sprouts, bamboo shoots and water chestnuts. Among his 2500 plant introductions were some notable ornamentals like *Syringa meyeri, Juniperus squamata* var. *meyeri, Ulmus parvifolia, U. pumila, Pyrus calleryana, Castanea mollisima, Rosa xanthina* and *Pistacia chinensis*. He died in mysterious circumstances during a journey down the Yangtze River.

**Meyerophytum** Schwantes. (For Pastor G. Meyer of Steinkopf, South Africa, who discovered the type species and Gk phyton, plant.) Aizoaceae. 4 species of succulent perennials, slender, freely branched, 7–8cm, papillose. Stems to 3mm thick, the lower part often clothed with the crowded remains of leaves, internodes enclosed, annual growth consisting of 2–3 pairs of dimorphic leaves, axillary buds present in the lower leaf and in the first pair of the upper leaves, the lower leaves thicker, united for half their length or more to 1cm, upper leaves united for a third of their length or less, 15–25×2–3×2–3mm. Flowers solitary, to 3.5cm diam., rose-purple; pedicels to 3.5cm. S Africa (Cape Province). Z9.

CULTIVATION As for *Mitrophyllum*.

*M. meyeri* (Schwantes) Schwantes. Highly succulent, forming dense mounds. Lvs 10×4mm, united to form small, plump, round, scarcely cleft bodies alternating with larger ones, dark green-yellow, becoming red-tinged. Fls flame-coloured. Cape: Little Namaqualand.

For synonymy see *Mitrophyllum*.

**Meziothamnus** Harms. See *Abromeitiella*.

**Mibora** Adans. (Name invented by Michel Adanson (1727–1806).) EARLY SAND-GRASS; SAND BENT. Gramineae. Monospecific genus of annual grasses to 3cm, rarely to 15cm. Stems very slender. Leaves tufted, arching, glabrous grey-green; blades flat or rolled, to 2.5cm, very narrow; sheaths overlapping; ligules obtuse, translucent, papery. Raceme spike-like, secund, erect to drooping, to 2cm, tinged red or purple; spikelets subsessile, distichous, overlapping, laterally compressed, oblong, obtuse, 1-flowered, to 3mm; glumes equal, 1-veined, membranous; lemmas shorter than glumes, 5-ribbed, densely pubescent; palea equals lemma. Late winter–spring. Mediterranean, coastal W Europe. Z7.

CULTIVATION *M. minima* is one of the smallest of grasses, one of the earliest to emerge and in bloom in early winter; on moist soils, it retains its bright foliage well into the season and may produce a second flush of flowers in autumn under favourable conditions. *M. minima* is sometimes used to provide shade at the roots of terrestrial orchids and in the rock garden. Grow in damp but light sandy soils in light shade or in sun. Propagate by seed; *M. minima* may self-sow where conditions suite.

*M. minima* (L.) Desv. As for the genus.

*M. verna* P. Beauv. See *M. minima*.

**Michaux, André** (1746–1802) and **François André** (1799–1855). Botanists and plant collectors. Born at Sartory, Versailles, André Michaux was expected to take over the running of the estate managed by his father. However, after the death of his wife in childbirth, the disconsolate Michaux took up botany, first under le Monnier at Montreuil and, in 1777, under Bernard de Jussieu at Le Trianon near Versailles. On his appointment as collector for the Jardin du Roi in Paris, Michaux went first to England to collect seeds, then to Auvergne and the Pyrenees, and between

1781 and 1784 he travelled extensively in Persia, where he found *Rosa persica, Dionysia michauxii* and *Michauxia campanuloides*. On his return to France, he was commissioned to go to North America to seek out suitable trees for shipbuilding to replace France's depleted timber stocks. He arrived at New York in 1785 with his son François André, a servant and Pierre Paul Saulnier, a journeyman gardener. Within three days he was collecting in New Jersey and within a month he had sent back five boxes of seeds, including red and white oaks, horse chestnuts, tulip trees, laurels and azaleas. This prolific output proved sustainable and, during his eleven years in North America, Michaux shipped some 60,000 plants and 90 boxes of seed to France. He established two nurseries as his headquarters: one in New Jersey under Saulnier's direction, and one near Charleston in South Carolina overseen by his son.

His most concentrated exploration was in the mountain wilderness of North Carolina but he travelled throughout the United States (even when his funds from France were cut off after the Revolution), notably in Florida, the Mississippi, Illinois, and even into Canada and the Bahamas. In the Carolinas alone, Michaux is credited as the authority for 26 genera, 188 species and four varieties, including *Rhododendron calendulaceum, Shortia galacifolium* and *Pyrularia pubera*, and also for 95 other species and varieties elsewhere in the US. As well as shipping back thousands of young trees to Europe, he made many important introductions to the US via his Charleston nursery, including *Ginkgo biloba, Albizia julibrissin* and *Lagerstroemia indica*.

Michaux's return to France in 1796 was marred by a shipwreck off the Netherlands in which much of his material was lost. Unable to obtain funding for another trip to North America, he joined Baudin's expedition to Australia, but left it in 1801 at Mauritius so as to explore Madagascar, where he died of a fever the following year. His two published works, *Histoire des chênes de l'Amérique septentrionale* (1801) and *Flora boreali-americana* (1803) – the first Flora of the area, with all the plants personally collected by Michaux – were illustrated by Redouté. The genus *Michauxia* was named in his honour.

François Michaux accompanied his father on his American mission and oversaw the Charleston nursery. After a brief return to Paris in 1803–4 he went back to the US for another two years, collecting trees for the French government in the east and mid-west. In 1809 he returned to France and acted as a Franco-American scientific intermediary, recommending French botanical books to his American contacts and maintaining an extensive correspondence with Benjamin Vaughan and other members of the American Philosophical Society. From 1814 he worked on his *North American Sylva* (1817–18) and in 1822 bought a site at Vauréal, Val d'Oise, where he built a garden. In 1828 he accepted the post of administrator at Harcourt in Eure, west of Paris and here he put his sylvan knowledge to good use in the management of the estate's forests and the establishment of the Forest Tree Arboretum. His published works include *Voyage à l'ouest de mont Alleghanys* (1804), *Mémoire sur la naturalisation des arbres forestiers* (1805) and *Mémoirs sur les causes de la fièvre jaune* (1852).

**Michauxia** L'Hérit. (For André Michaux (1746–1802), French botanist.) Campanulaceae. Some 7 species of short-lived robust perennial herbs. Leaves generally linear-lanceolate, irregularly dentate, pinnately lobed or lyrate, petiolate. Flowers borne in dense spikes, racemes or panicles, 8–10-merous; calyx with reflexed appendages between lobes; corolla white; stamens free, filaments basally dilated; style thick, rigid, pubescent. Fruit a capsule, 8-ribbed, dehiscing by 3 valves at base; seeds small, ellipsoid. E Mediterranean, SW Asia. Z7.

CULTIVATION *Michauxia* spp. are stately specimens for herbaceous and mixed borders. Treated as biennials or short-lived perennials in cultivation, they bloom in their second or third year from seed and usually die after flowering. Grow in moderately fertile, freely draining, gritty soils in a warm, sunny site sheltered from wind; protect in winter with a layer of evergreen branches. Propagate from seed down *in situ* in spring.

***M. campanuloides*** L'Hérit. ex Ait. Stem stout, to 1.75m, thick at base, hispid, branched near top. Lvs lyrate or pinnatifid, lobes ovate, lower lvs with long winged petiole, upper lvs sessile. Fls pendulous, borne along stems and branches, pedicellate; cal. lobes to 1cm, ciliate; cor. lobes ligulate, recurved, suffused purple. Summer. Syria, E Mediterranean.

***M. laevigata*** Vent. Stout, to 2m, usually glabrous. Lower lvs oblong lanceolate, doubly serrate, pubesc., long-petiolate, upper lvs sessile. Fls in lax racemes; cal. lobes to 0.6cm, ciliate, cor. lobes spreading, recurved. Summer. N Iran.

***M. tchihatchewii*** Fisch. & C.A. Mey. Stout to 2m. Lvs pubesc., long-petiolate, lower lvs oblong, upper lvs broadly ovate. Fls pendulous, in a dense spike, pedicellate; cal. lobes to 12mm; cor. campanulate. Summer. E Mediterranean.

For synonymy see *Mindium*.

**Michelia** L. (For P.A. Michel (1679–1737), Florentine botanist.) Magnoliaceae. Some 45 species of evergreen or deciduous shrubs or trees, as for *Magnolia* but flowers axillary, tepals 6–21, subequal in 2 or more whorls, carpels 1 to many, gynoecia prominently stipitate. SE Asia, India, Ceylon. Z9.

CULTIVATION *Michelia* spp. thrive best in those subtropical and warm-temperate gardens where temperatures rarely fall to freezing point. Grown for their glossy evergreen foliage and the strongly scented waxen flowers, which are followed by decorative seedheads. They are suited to pot cultivation in the cool to intermediate glasshouse or conservatory. *M. compressa, M. doltsopa* and *M. figo* have survived outdoors in sheltered situations in southern Britain.

Grow in humus-rich, well-drained, neutral to alkaline soils, in direct light or partial shade. Water pot-grown specimens plentifully during the growing season, sparingly in winter. Prune only if necessary to restrict growth. Propagate from seed sown ripe in autumn, or in spring; or by greenwood cuttings in summer under mist, or with bottom heat in a closed case.

***M. champaca*** L. CHAMPACA. Evergreen tree, to 25m. Bark pale grey, smooth; twigs closely pubesc. Lvs to 28×11cm, lanceolate, ovate, acuminate, base acute or cuneate, pubesc. below; petiole to 4cm. Fls highly fragrant, orange to white; lobes to 20, to 3cm×5mm. India, China, Himalaya.

***M. compressa*** (Maxim.) Sarg. Erect, evergreen, tree-like shrub, to 12m. Branches and buds brown-pubesc. Lvs to 10×4cm, oblong or oblong ovate, shiny deep green above, pale green below, coriaceous; petioles to 3cm, pubesc. Fls fragrant, to 3cm diam., occasionally more; lobes 12, oblanceolate, to 2.5cm, white, exterior purple at base, fls frequently tinged pale yellow. Fr. to 5cm. Japan.

***M. doltsopa*** Buch.-Ham. ex DC. Tree, to 12m. Twigs grey brown; buds red-pubesc. Lvs to 18×8cm, oblong-lanceolate, acute or short acuminate, base cuneate, glossy green above, grey-sericeous, leathery, entire; petiole to 3cm. Fls to 5×4cm, ovoid to globose, short-stipitate, fragrant, lobes oblong-lanceolate, base attenuate, white. SW China, E Himalaya, E Tibet.

***M. figo*** (Lour.) Spreng. BANANA SHRUB. Evergreen shrub to 4.5m. Bark dark grey; branches many, twigs yellow-brown pubesc. Lvs 10×5cm, elliptic-oblong, dusky green above; petiole to 0.5cm. Fls to 3cm, cupulate, scented of banana, ivory tinged yellow, base and margins tinged rose to purple; carpels 25+. Fr. conic. China.

***M. nilagirica*** Zenk. Shrub or medium-sized tree. Stems white; twigs erect; buds silky-pubesc. Lvs to 15cm, elliptic, blunt-acuminate, hard, shiny, glabrous, or pubesc. only on veins beneath. Fls white or creamy, to 10cm across, perianth parts 9–12, obovate, short-lived. Seeds scarlet, smelling of mango. S India.

***M. sinensis*** Hemsl. & Wils. Tree to 15m. Bark dark grey. Lvs to 14×5cm, ovate-oblong or oblanceolate, acute, base cuneate, glossy above, glaucous beneath, coriaceous, entire. Fls ivory white; sep. 3; pet. 9–11. Fr. borne in spikes to 15cm, stipitate; peduncle short, erect. W China (Yunnan).

***M. velutina*** DC. As for *M. doltsopa*, but lvs narrower, to 25×6cm, grey-pubesc. beneath; petiole to 2cm. Fls to 5cm across, perianth seg. oblanceolate, to 3.5cm×7mm. India (Bhutan, Sikkim).

***M. excelsa*** (Wallich) Bl. ex Wallich. See *M. doltsopa*.
***M. fuscata*** (Andrews) Wallich. See *M. figo*.
***M. glauca*** Wight. See *M. nilagirica*.
***M. lanuginosa*** Wallich. See *M. velutina*.
***M. ovalifolia*** Wight. See *M. nilagirica*.
***M. pulneyensis*** Wight. See *M. nilagirica*.
***M. wilsonii*** Finet & Gagnep. See *M. sinensis*.
For further synonymy see *Liriodendron, Liriopsis* and *Magnolia*.

**Micranthemum** Michx. (From Gk *mikros*, small, and *anthemon*, flower.) Scrophulariaceae. 3 species of short-lived aquatic herbs. Leaves opposite; petioles absent. Flowers red to purple, solitary, borne in axils; calyx 4-partite; corolla 1- to 2-lipped; stamens 2, from throat; styles bifid. Capsule enclosed in calyx. Summer. Americas. Z9.

CULTIVATION Slender creeping plants found on the damp, shaded soils of forest floors, in marshes and as submerged aquatics. In temperate areas they may be grown under intermediate glasshouse conditions in a medium of equal parts loam, leafmould and sand. They are also suitable for cultivation in subtropical aquaria (grow in the same medium as above), although under these conditions they are often eaten by vegetarian fish or snails and are susceptible to heavy algal growth.

***M. micranthemoides*** (Nutt.) Wettst. Stems to 20cm, sprawling or floating, then ascending. Lvs 0.5cm, elliptic, entire. Cor. white, lip 3-lobed. E US.

***M. umbrosum*** (J.F. Gmel.) S.F. Blake. Stems sprawling, to 30cm. Lvs to 1cm, elliptic to orbicular. Cor. 2-lipped, white. SE US, C & S America.

**Micranthocereus** Backeb. (From Gk *mikros*, small, *anthos*, flower, and *Cereus*.) Cactaceae. A genus of 9 species of sub-shrubby to tall columnar cacti, unbranched or branching from the base; stems cylindric, ribbed; ribs 10–30 or more, narrow; areoles close-set, with spines and sometimes long wool. Fertile zone a continuous or discontinuous, superficial or sunken, woolly/bristly cephalium; flower from the cephalium, tubular, diurnal or partly nocturnal; pericarpel and tube naked except for minute scales; tepals short, erect or spreading, variously coloured. Fruit indehiscent, red, conspicuous or disintegrating in the cephalium; floral remnant tardily deciduous or persistent, rarely blackening; pulp scanty, nearly white; seeds broadly oval, 1–2mm, black-brown; relief convex or flat; hilum oblique or hilum region greatly expanded; appendages none. CE Brazil.

CULTIVATION Grow in a heated greenhouse (min. 10–15°C/50–60°F), use 'acid standard' cactus compost: moderate to high inorganic content (more than 50% grit), below pH 6; grow in full sun; maintain low humidity; water very sparingly in winter (to avoid shrivelling).

***M. polyanthus*** (Werderm.) Backeb. Shrub to 1.2m, branching from base; stems 3.5–5cm diam.; ribs *c*15–20; non-flowering areoles *c*1cm apart, with dense woolly hairs 1–2cm covering the stem; central spines *c*3–7, with 1–3 stronger, up to 3cm, golden yellow, light brown or occasionally red-brown, radial spines *c*20–30, 5–12mm, white to golden yellow. Cephalium lateral, white, the wool intermixed with long bristly spines; fl. numerous, only 16–18mm, tubular; tube pink-red; tepals erect, 2–3mm, the outer pink, the inner creamy white. Fr. 5–7mm, pink-red. E Brazil (S Bahia). Z9.

For synonymy see *Arrojadoa*.

**Micranthus** (Pers.) Ecklon. (From Gk *mikros*, small, and *anthos*, flower.) Iridaceae. 3 species of perennial herbs. Corms small, globose, with tunics of coarse, matted fibres. Leaves 3–5, partly sheathing. Spikes distichous, flowers numerous, small, blue, irregular, closely imbricate; tube slightly curved, widened towards throat, lobes more or less equal, obtuse, spreading; stamens inserted near top of tube, usually arched; style branches 6, short. S Africa (SW Cape). Z9.

CULTIVATION As for *Watsonia*.

***M. junceus*** (Bak.) N.E. Br. 20–70cm, usually unbranched. Lvs 3–4, the 2 lowest long, terete, 1–2mm diam., the lowest with axillary bulbils. Spike to 25cm, often with bulbils in the bracts in the basal half; fls slightly scented, pale to deep blue; tube 4–5mm, lobes 5–6mm, oblong. Similar to *M. plantagineus*, except for lvs. Summer.

***M. plantagineus*** (Pers.) Ecklon. 25–40cm, sometimes branched. Lvs 3, the 2 lowest usually 10–25×0.5–1cm, the blade flat, but in some populations longer and only 2–3mm wide, lowest lf often with bulbils at base. Spike to 20cm; fls slightly scented, pale to deep blue, outer lobes sometimes tipped with red; tube 4–5mm, lobes 5–6mm, oblong. Summer.

***M. tubulosus*** (Burm.) N.E. Br. Corms 1–1.5cm diam., with short neck. Plants 20–35cm, stem unbranched. Lvs 3–5, usually brown at flowering time, the lowest 2–3 with tubular, inflated blades 5–15cm×3–7mm. Spike 7–17cm, often with bulbils in lower bracts; fls scented, blue, sometimes almost white; tube 5–6mm, lobes 5–6mm, oblong. Summer.

**Microbiota** Komar. (From Gk *mikros*, small, and *Biota* (syn. of *Platycladus*), the closest relative of this species.) Cupressaceae. 1 species, an evergreen, monoecious, spreading shrub, 40cm to rarely 70cm high, to 2m or more across. Bark brown tinged grey, scaly. Foliage pale green, bronzed red or purple above in winter; resin fragrant; branches stout; twigs rhombic. Foliage in flat sprays, curving downwards, bright green turning bronze in cold conditions, leaves to 3×1mm, facial leaves triangular or needle-like, lateral leaves convex, apices incurved; glands visible on lower part of leaves. Male cones ovoid, yellow, 2mm. Female cones terminal, on short twigs, globose, 2×3mm, opening to ×6mm; scales to 4, coriaceous to woody with sharp 1mm bract, only one scale fertile. One seed per cone, 2mm, filling the cone, smooth ovoid, pointed at apex, unwinged, as in *Platycladus*. SE Siberia. Z3.

CULTIVATION A valuable prostrate evergreen for rockeries and dwarf conifer collections, exceedingly hardy and site tolerant. Only recently introduced and not yet widely available, despite the ease of propagation. Cultivate as for *Juniperus*. Propagation by cuttings; roots very easily; seeds are also produced.

***M. decussata*** Komar. As for the genus.

**Microcachrys** Hook. f. ex Hook. (From Gk *mikros*, small, and *kachrys*, catkin, referring to the tiny cones.) Podocarpaceae. 1 species, an evergreen, monoecious or dioecious spreading shrub, to 1m. Branches procumbent, thin, whip-like, rhombic in section. Leaves arranged in decussate pairs, overlapping, persistent, scale-shaped, 1.5–3mm long, margins finely pubescent under lens, incurved, apex blunt. Male cones, terminal, 3mm, ovoid. Female cones ovoid to globose, 5–8×5mm, fertile scales spirally arranged, 15–30, fleshy, blunt triangular, 2mm, red when mature, translucent, overlapping; ovule inverted. Seeds 1 per fertile scale, 0.5–1mm, united to the upper side of the scale; wings absent. W Tasmania. Z8.

CULTIVATION An interesting low shrub for the dwarf conifer garden; hardy in all but the coldest areas of Britain, but requires moist soil and very high humidity with plenty of rain. In drier areas plant in a shady site near water with protection from dry winds. Rarely more than 50cm/20in. tall, but spreading 1–2m/3–6½ft, rarely to 3m/10ft on oldest plants; also suitable for bonsai. Propagation as *Podocarpus*.

***M. tetragona*** Hook. f. As for the genus.

**Microcitrus** Swingle. (From Gk *mikros*, small and *Citrus*.) Rutaceae. 5 or 6 species of shrubs or small trees, armed or unarmed; twigs very minutely pubescent; spines single or paired, slender, in leaf axils. Leaves dimorphic, on young seedlings small cataphylls, merging into small linear-elliptic leaves and finally to characteristic species foliage; mature leaves glabrous but for base of main vein, coriaceous, strongly veined; petioles short, flattened, wingless, finely pubescent. Flowers small, 4–5-merous; stamens free; ovary 4–8-locular, ovules 4–8+ per locule. Fruit rounded ovoid to cylindric; pulp vesicles generally rounded or ovoid, noncoherent, full of acid pulp with minute acrid oil droplets along axis; seeds ovate, small. Australia, New Guinea. Z10.

CULTIVATION As for *Citrus*.

***M. australasica*** (F. Muell.) Swingle. FINGER LIME. Tall shrub or small tree; twigs of seedlings horizontal, of older plants upright; spines to 1cm. Lvs of seedlings 4×3mm, ovate, shortly petiolate, of older plants to 2.5×1.5cm, lozenge-shaped, obscurely dentate above, truncate at base, truncate or emarginate at apex, those on lateral twigs smaller; petiole articulate. Fls generally solitary, usually 5-merous, subglobose in bud; pedicel 1–2mm; sep. free, small, concave; pet. oblong, 7–8mm; stamens 20–25; pistils short, stout, ovary 5–7-locular, ovules 8–16 per locule. Fr. 7–10×2cm, cylindric-fusiform, often slightly curved, yellow tinged green, peel rough, pulp vesicles loosely cohering; seeds numerous, 6–7mm. Australia (coasts of S Queensland & N NSW).

*M.australis* (Planch.) Swingle. AUSTRALIAN ROUND LIME; NATIVE ORANGE. Tree, 9–18m, armed with spines to 1cm. Lvs 3–4×2–3cm, entire, obovate to obcordate, cuneate at base, those of lateral twigs rhombic, 2–3×1.5cm; petioles 2–3mm, pubesc. Fls solitary, 10–15mm diam.; stamens 16–20. Fr. 2.5–5cm, globose, locules 6, pulp vesicles firm-textured, very pale green near peel, grass-green near centre, containing strong-flavoured oil; seeds flattened. NE Australia.

*M.papuana* H.F. Winters. Shrub to 2.5m, foliage slightly lime-scented when crushed; spines present, generally solitary. Lvs 15–25×2–6mm, linear to elliptic or obovate, minutely crenate, emarginate at apex, tapered to base, dark green, distinctly black glandular punctate beneath; petiole 1mm. Fls axillary, generally solitary, near branch apex, 8mm diam., cream, faintly fragrant; cal. lobes 5; pet. 5–12, white within, yellow-green-glandular without. Fr. 5–8×1cm, cylindric, beaked at apex, green maturing to yellow, seg. 3–5, pulp acid, peel thin and granular, with oil glands; seeds ovoid, 6mm, generally 5 per seg. New Guinea.

*M.warburgiana* (Bail.) Tan. Twigs very slender; spines 4mm. Lvs 4–6×1–2cm, rhombic-lanceolate to elliptic, margins minutely crenate, rounded or emarginate at apex, cuneate at base; veins reticulate; petioles 2–3mm, pale, very narrowly winged. Fr. 2cm diam., globose, 6-locular, peel thin, with numerous oil glands, on stout peduncle to 3mm. SE New Guinea.

**Microcycas** (Miq.) A. DC. (From Gk *mikros*, small, and *Cycas*.) Zamiaceae. 1 species, a perennial, evergreen, arborescent, dioecious cycad to 20m. Stem columnar, simple, irregularly swollen, uppermost regions clothed with persistent leaf-bases, these falling to leave thin bark furrowed and scarred. Leaves pinnate in terminal crowns to 50 in number, to 2m, emerging annually, downy at first; pinnae to 80 pairs, to 20cm, lanceolate, glossy, reflexed. Female strobilus borne annually, 1 or 2, among terminal bracts, to 70×15cm with a great many peltate, hexagonal sporophylls, russet, felty, each with a convex swelling. Seed to 3cm, with pink peach fleshy coating. Cuba (Pinar del Rio). Z10.

CULTIVATION As for the tropical *Zamia* spp.

*M.calocoma* (Miq.) A. DC. PALMA CORCHO. As for the genus.

**Microglossa** DC.
*M.albescens* (DC.) Benth. ex C.B. Clarke. See *Aster albescens*.

**Microgramma** Presl. (From Gk *mikros*, small, and *gramma*, letter.) Polypodiaceae. Perhaps 20 species of epiphytic ferns. Rhizomes long-creeping, occasionally branching, dictyostelic, covered with roots as well as scales; scales usually lanceolate to awl-shaped, not clathrate, peltately attached. Fronds stipitate, dimorphous, simple, entire, stiff, leathery, glabrous, pubescent, or scaly; sterile fronds ovate, fertile narrower; stipes distant, jointed to basal phyllopodia. Sori superficial or somewhat sunken, uniserial on each side of costa, discrete, on or terminating veinlets, circular to elongate; paraphyses (where present) filiform; annulus 12–20-celled; spores ellipsoid to kidney-shaped, glassy. Tropical America, Africa. Z10.

CULTIVATION As for *Pyrrosia*.

*M.ciliata* (Willd.) Alston. A poorly distinguished species allied to *M.piloselloides*, distinctive for its narrowly linear fronds. Sori many, developed over margins. Tropical America.

*M.heterophyllum* (L.) Wherry. Epiphytic or epilithic fern. Stems climbing or wide-creeping, almost filiform, 1mm wide; scales to 7mm, linear to subulate, attenuate, toothed, rusty or tawny. Fronds variable, membranous, glabrous: sterile fronds to 10×2cm, oval or elliptic to broadly lanceolate or linear-lanceolate, apex and base attenuate, entire to undulate or notched or, occasionally, pinnatifid; fertile fronds to 16cm, narrower; veins anastomosing, 1-rowed major areolae with free, included veinlets; stipes to 2cm, glabrous. Florida, W Indies.

*M.lycopodioides* (L.) Copel. Epiphytic or epilithic fern. Rhiz. wide-creeping, much-branched; scales to 1cm, dense, linear to lanceolate or subulate, apex attenuate and acute, margin ciliate, light brown or rusty, but eventually white or grey. Fronds sessile or short-stipitate: sterile fronds to 15×2.5cm, strap-shaped to linear-lanceolate, apex attenuate and acute or obtuse or truncate, base attenuate and decurrent, margin cartilaginous and entire or somewhat undulate, often scaly on costa; fertile fronds to 20×1.5cm, linear to oblong or elliptic; costa prominent, veins indistinct, reticulate, with several-rowed or irregular discrete areolae, most with 1 or more free, included veinlets; stipes to 15mm. Tropical America, Africa.

*M.nitida* (J. Sm.) A.R. Sm. Epiphytic fern. Rhiz. long-creeping, much-branched, to 7mm wide; scales to 7mm, sparse, adpressed, lanceolate or ovate, more or less entire, light brown or tawny to grey. Fronds sessile or short-stipitate: sterile fronds to 15×4cm, lanceolate or elliptic, apex obtuse, base cuneate, margin entire and somewhat cartilaginous, stiff, glabrous, lustrous; veins reticulate; fertile fronds, linear to oblong, apex acute; veins reticulate, with several-rowed or irregular and discrete areolae; stipes 1cm. C America, W Indies.

*M.owariensis* (Desv.) Alston. Related to *P. lycopodioides*, but with sterile fronds oval or ovate, obtuse at apex, smaller, wider. Tropical Africa.

*M.piloselloides* (L.) Copel. SNAKE POLYPODY. Epiphytic fern. Rhiz. wide-creeping or climbing, much-branched filiform, 1mm wide; scales to 4mm, linear to lanceolate, apex attenuate, margin recurved, pale brown. Fronds stipitate, scaly: sterile fronds to 5×2cm, ovate or obovate or, occasionally, lanceolate or elliptic, apex acute or narrowly acute; fertile fronds to 9×1cm, linear to lanceolate, occasionally dentate, scales deciduous, adpressed; veins indistinct, reticulate, with costal and few marginal areolae; stipes to 2cm, glabrous or scaly. Tropical America.

*M.squamulosa* (Kaulf.) Sota. Epiphytic fern. Rhiz. creeping; scales bleached to brown or rusty. Fronds to 8cm, stipitate, virtually uniform, erect, linear-lanceolate to oblong-elliptic, apex acute, base attenuate, dull; veins variable, areolae with or without free, included veinlets, these often divaricate. Tropical America.

*M.vacciniifolia* (Langsd. & Fisch.) Copel. Epiphytic fern. Rhiz. wide-creeping or climbing, much-branched scales to 5mm, dense, lanceolate or awl-shaped to filiform, margin ciliate, white or grey to light yellow-brown or rusty. Fronds sessile or short-stipitate, leathery: sterile fronds to 5×1cm, rounded or ovate to elliptic, apex obtuse; fertile fronds to 10×0.7cm, linear to strap-shaped, apex acute or truncate, base attenuate and long-decurrent, margin entire and often revolute at margin; veins indistinct, reticulate, with costal areolae and few marginal areolae with or without free, included veinlets. W Indies, Tropical S America.

*M.bifrons* (Hook.) Lell. See *Solanopteris bifrons*.
*M.piloselloides* (L.) Copel. See *Drymoglossum piloselloides*.
For further synonymy see *Phlebodium* and *Polypodium*.

**Microlepia** Presl. (From Gk *mikros*, small, and *lepis*, scale, referring to the indusia.) Dennstaedtiaceae. Some 45 to 50 species of terrestrial or, rarely, epilithic ferns. Rhizomes short- to long-creeping, solenostelic, subterranean, covered with trichomate hairs or bristles and massed roots. Fronds stipitate, uniform, anadromous and spreading to ascending, 1–4-pinnate or -pinnatifid, ovate to deltoid, thin-textured, pubescent, lowest pinnae often reduced, usually oblique, base often basiscopically auriculate, margin of segments notched to lobed; veins free, terminating submarginally; rachis and costa grooved; stipes distichous, approximate or distant, erect or suberect, not jointed, usually short-pubescent. Sori medial to submarginal or marginal, terminating veins, often superficial; indusia basally or laterally attached, cup- or half-cup-shaped, opening outwards; paraphyses present or absent; annulus 16–20-celled; spores globose to tetrahedral, trilete, smooth to echinate or tuberculate. Tropics & subtropics. Z10.

CULTIVATION As for *Hypolepis*.

*M.firma* Mett. Rhiz. erect. Fronds to 80cm, erect to arched, 2–3-pinnate or -pinnatifid, deltoid, sparsely pubesc., especially above, firm-textured, pinnae to 20×10cm, opposite, oblique, ovate to deltoid, apex acute to narrowly acute, margin of pinnules notched to lobed; rachis and costa densely pubesc. above; stipes to 40cm, brown. Tropical Asia (Indochina).

*M.hirta* Presl. Rhiz. creeping. Fronds to 1.8m×60cm, 3–4-pinnate or -pinnatifid, ovate to deltoid, more or less densely pubesc., pinnae to 30×10cm, opposite, ovate or deltoid to lanceolate, pinnules lanceolate, seg. oblong, margin toothed to lobed; rachis and costa pubesc.; stipes to 80cm, pubesc. Tropical Asia (India, Sri Lanka).

*M.marginata* (Panz.) C. Chr. Rhiz. long-creeping, brown-pubesc. Fronds to 55×40cm, 1–2-pinnate or -pinnatifid, ovate to lanceolate, pubesc., esp. below and on veins above, pinnae to 20×3cm, linear, base basiscopically auriculate, margin notched to lobed or pinnatifid, seg. oblong, apex obtuse; stipes to 50cm, rough and pubesc. Tropical Asia (Indochina, Sri Lanka, to Taiwan, Japan).

*M.platyphylla* (D. Don) J. Sm. Rhiz. creeping, brown-pubesc. Fronds to 1.4m, 2–3-pinnate or -pinnatifid, ovate to deltoid, leathery, lustrous, glabrous, pinnae to 40×20cm, lanceolate, pinnules to 12cm, petiolate, distant, oblique, linear to lanceolate, margin cartilaginous, apex of seg. obtuse, margin toothed; stipes to 1m, stiff, glabrous, lustrous, straw-coloured. Tropical Asia (Indochina, Sri Lanka, to Taiwan, Philippines).

*M.pyramidata* (Wallich) Lacaita. Rhiz. creeping. Fronds to 1.8m×60cm, 3–4-pinnate or -pinnatifid, deltoid, pubesc. on veins beneath, pinnae to 30×10cm, ovate to lanceolate, pinnules lanceolate, seg. oblong, margin toothed; rachis and costa pubesc.; stipes to 60cm. Sori 2–20 per seg. Tropical Asia (China).

***M. speluncae*** (L.) Moore. Rhiz. to 1cm; hairs dense, jointed, green. Fronds to 1.5×1m, erect or suberect to ascending, 3–4-pinnate or -pinnatifid, deltoid, papery, pubesc. on veins, pinnae to 50×20cm, short-petiolate, deltoid or lanceolate to oblong, apex narrowly acute, pinnules to 80×25mm, lanceolate to deltoid, apex narrowly acute, seg. to 4mm wide, approximate or distant, oblique, oblong, margin toothed or notched to lobed, veins forked; rachis and costa rough; stipes to 50cm, to 2cm distant, grooved above, rough, sparsely short-pubesc., green to purple or brown. Tropics.

***M. strigosa*** (Thunb.) Presl. Rhiz. to 5mm, creeping, brown-pubesc., hairs to 2mm. Fronds to 80×30cm, erect to arched, 2–3-pinnate or -pinnatifid, ovate to lanceolate, short-pubesc. on veins, pinnae to 20×4cm, lowest reduced, alternate, to 5cm distant, linear to lanceolate, apex and base attenuate, pinnules to 25×10mm, sessile, approximate to imbricate, oblique, rhomboid or parallelogram to oblong, apex obtuse, base cuneate, margin notched at apex or toothed or, occasionally, lobed, lobes approximate, apex obtuse, margin notched; veins prominent, especially below; stipes to 35cm, grooved, rough, pubesc. Tropical Asia (India to Japan, Sri Lanka to Polynesia).

***M. galeottii*** Fée. See *Saccoloma inaequale*.
***M. grandissima*** Hayata. See *M. platyphylla*.
***M. hirsuta*** Presl. See *Davallodes hirsutum*.
***M. hirta*** sensu auct., non Presl. See *M. pyramidata*.
***M. inaequale*** (Kunze) Presl. See *Saccoloma inaequale*.
***M. jamaicensis*** (Hook.) Fée. See *M. speluncae*.
For further synonymy see *Acrophorus, Aspidium, Davallia, Scypholepia* and *Trichomanes*.

## Micromeles Decne.

***M. keissleri*** Schneid. See *Sorbus keissleri*.
***M. rhamnoides*** Decne. See *Sorbus rhamnoides*.

## Micromeria Benth.

**Micromeria** Benth. (From Gk *mikros*, small, and *meris*, part, referring to the usually very small flowers.) Labiatae. Some 70 perennial, rarely annual, herbs or dwarf shrubs to 50cm. Stems tetragonal, erect. Leaves opposite, entire, revolute, short-petiolate or sessile. Inflorescence a spike of short-stalked whorls of few flowers; calyx tubular to campanulate, 13–15-veined, teeth 5, equal, throat often pubescent; corolla bilabiate, white to purple, naked within, upper lip erect, lower lip 3-lobed, tube straight; stamens 4, convergent. Fruit 4 nutlets. Mediterranean, Caucasus, SW China. Closely related to *Satureja*, distinguished by convergent stamens. Z7 unless specified.

CULTIVATION Often aromatic and resembling *Thymus* spp., they are widely distributed in temperate and warm temperate regions, mostly occurring on dry, rocky, exposed habitats. *M. marginata* is the most decorative species, suitable for rock gardens on open, sunny sites and in poor, well-drained soils. Propagate by softwood or semi-ripe heel cuttings, in spring and summer.

***M. chamissonis*** (Benth.) Greene. YERBA BUENA. Perenn. with stems trailing and rooting, to 70cm. Lvs to 3.5cm, ovate, obtuse, crenate, glabrous, petiolate. Infl. of solitary axillary fls on large stalk; cal. to 5mm; cor. twice as long, white or purple. Spring and autumn. W US.

***M. croatica*** (Pers.) Schott. Densely pubesc. tufted shrub to 20cm. Lvs to 1×0.8cm, ovate, acute, entire. Whorls to 12-fld; cal. 15-veined; cor. to 15mm, violet. Yugoslavia.

***M. dalmatica*** Benth. Perenn. herb, pubesc. to 50cm. Stems erect, simple or branched. Lvs to 2×1.5cm, ovate, obtuse, obscurely dentate, punctate beneath. Whorls dense, short-stalked axillary, to 60-fld; cal. to 3mm, puberulent; cor. to 6mm, white or pale lilac. Balkans. Z6.

***M. graeca*** (L.) Benth. Dwarf shrub to 50cm. Stems many, erect, simple. Lvs to 1.2×0.7cm, ovate, becoming narrower toward apex, sessile, revolute. Infl. loose; fls to 18 per whorl; cal. villous at throat, to 5mm, teeth lanceolate, subulate; cor. to 13mm, purple. Mediterranean. Divided into 7 mainly geographical ssp: ssp. ***graeca.*** Wider middle and upper lvs. ssp. ***consentina*** (Ten.) Guinea. Autumn-flowering. ssp. ***fructicosola*** (Bertol.) Guinea. Axillary lf fascicles; calcicole. ssp. ***garganica*** (Briq.) Chater. Upper lvs linear. ssp. ***imperica*** Chater. Linear middle and upper lvs. ssp. ***longiflora*** (C. Presl) Nyman. Peduncles rigid. ssp. ***tenuifolia*** (Ten.) Nyman. Whorls to 4-fld.

***M. juliana*** (L.) Benth. SAVORY. Dwarf pubesc. shrub, to 40cm. Stems numerous, erect, mostly simple. Lvs to 1.3cm, ovate to linear-lanceolate, entire, revolute, sessile. Whorls to 20-fld, sessile; cal. to 3.5mm, straight, teeth subulate; cor. slightly exceeding cal., purple. Mediterranean.

***M. marginata*** (Sm.) Chater. Dwarf shrub to 20cm. Stems puberulent, ascending, mostly simple. Lvs to 1.2×0.5cm, ovate, entire, obtuse, puberulent or glabrous beneath. Whorls lax, to 12-fld, pedunculate; cal. to 8mm, 12-veined, throat downy; teeth half as long as tube; cor. to 16mm, purple or violet. Maritime Alps.

***M. thymifolia*** (Scop.) Fritsch. Perenn. to 50cm. Stems woody at base, ascending, glabrous or puberulent. Lvs to 2×1.2cm, ovate to oblong, obtuse, petiolate, punctate beneath. Whorls dense, to 30-fld, with short pedicels; cal. to 3mm, teeth triangular; cor. to 9mm, white or violet. Balkans, S Italy, Hungary. Z6.

***M. varia*** Benth. Procumbent perenn. to 30cm. Stems woody at base. Lvs ovate to lanceolate, revolute. Whorls to 10-fld; fls small, subsessile; cor. slightly larger than cal., purple. Summer. Madeira. 'Aurea': lvs golden.

***M. alternipilosa*** K. Koch. See *Satureja spicigera*.
***M. corsica*** (Benth.) Lév. See *Acinos corsicus*.
***M. douglasii*** (Benth.) Benth. See *M. chamissonis*.
***M. ericifolia*** (Roth) Bornm. See *M. varia*.
***M. piperella*** (Bertol.) Benth. See *M. marginata*.
***M. rupestris*** (Wulf. ex Jacq.) Benth. See *M. thymifolia*.
For further synonymy see *Satureja* and *Thymus*.

## Micropropagation

**Micropropagation**. Micropropagation uses plant tissue culture techniques to propagate plants, usually vegetatively, although this approach can be successfully used for germination of seed, as is the case in orchid growing. Plant tissue culture consists of growing isolated parts of whole plants *in vitro* (literally 'in glass') under aseptic conditions. The growth of plant tissues is controlled by regulating the constituents of the growth medium and the environment, principally light and temperature. While micropropagation uses smaller portions of plant tissue than most other forms of propagation, it rarely uses the microscopic portions implied in its name.

Plant tissue culture techniques were conceived by research biologists during the early part of the 20th century as a means of studying the functioning and development of tissues, and ultimately cells, in isolation from the whole organism. Although initial attempts were not successful, by the close of the 1930s, aseptic cultures of isolated roots of a number of plant species had been established. Subsequent developments resulted in a considerable body of knowledge being built up and the techniques were extended to a wide range of species. As these developments occurred the opportunities for applying techniques to horticultural situations became apparent, at least in theory. The earliest horticultural application of the technology came as early as the 1920s, when Prof. Knudson developed a method for the non-symbiotic germination of orchid seeds on a simplified tissue culture medium. Ripe but ungerminated seeds, after sterilizing the seed coat to remove natural contaminants, were seeded on to a sterilized nutrient medium in a test tube or flask. The seeds were found to germinate and develop through the protocorm stage to form rooted plantlets which could be transferred to compost. This method avoided the variable response achieved when orchid seed was sown directly on to compost. Although many modifications to this procedure have been made, Knudson's method still forms the basis of seed raising in the orchid industry.

Many of the initial applications of plant tissue culture to propagation resulted from the development of techniques which had arisen in fundamental research studies in botanical sciences. Early observations during tissue culture work noted that small pieces of tissue from shoot tips, approaching a meristem in size, were often free of virus. This had led to the use of meristem culture to produce virus-free individual plants. By modifying the medium upon which these plantlets were grown *in vitro*, principally by the addition of plant growth regulators, it became apparent that axillary buds could be stimulated to give multiple shoot plantlets. These multiple shoots could then be divided and transferred to a fresh medium (sub-cultured) at regular intervals to achieve the rapid multiplication in plant material which characterizes micropropagation.

Micropropagation is now widely used in the production of orchids, pot plants and cut-flower crops, with increasing use being made of the technique in the propagation of trees, shrubs and plantation crops. Plant breeders also use tissue culture techniques to assist in breeding programmes, producing clonal parental lines, embryo rescue, the creation of haploid plants, genetic transformations or to introduce cultivars more rapidly.

PRINCIPLES OF MICROPROPAGATION. Several features characterize the micropropagation process. A thorough knowledge of these is essential so as to understand the technique and the factors which may require modification in order to develop a viable micropropagation system for a given plant species or cultivar.

*Asepsis* (freedom from micro-organisms). Good sterile technique is essential to success in micropropagation. The medium upon which plant tissues are cultured will also support the growth of a range of micro-organisms. If these organisms become established they can contaminate the culture severely, resulting in the death of the plant tissue. Contamination can arise either from the plant, its surfaces and internal tissues, or from the working environment, including the medium and containers in which the plant tissue is being grown. In nature, plant surfaces carry a significant population of micro-organisms which are not pathogenic to the plant but which will grow rapidly if present within *in vitro* cultures, inhibiting plant growth, and which can result in plant death. Several precautions are taken to control this source of contamination. First, the stock plant should be grown in a manner which will reduce the surface population of micro-organisms. Growing stock plants in containers within a glasshouse with scrupulous attention to hygiene and pest and disease control will lower the population of surface microbes. Overhead watering should be avoided, as this results in splash of microbes from the medium to the aerial parts of the plant. Secondly, when plant material is excised from the stock plant for micropropagation it is taken through three surface sterilization steps, comprising a prewash in 70% alcohol or sterile water to which 0.1% wetting agent has been added, followed by immersion of the explant, for 2–30 minutes in a sterilant. A number of chemicals can be used at this stage but formulations of sodium hypochlorite (domestic bleach) are most commonly used at an appropriate dilution. The higher the concentration of chemical and the longer the exposure time the greater will be the 'kill' of microbes. Too high a concentration or exposure time will, however, result in death of plant tissues. The anatomy of plants will affect the concentration of chemical used and the exposure time; some are very delicate whilst others might possess surface hairs or exudates which retain contamination. Lastly, the plant tissue is rinsed two or three times in sterile water to remove any residual sterilant, prior to insertion into the growing medium. Each of these steps is carried out in a clean air environment, usually created by a laminar flow cabinet.

All mediums and glassware or plastic containers in which plant tissues will be grown must be sterilized. An autoclave is essential for sterilizing mediums and can be used for glassware. Plastic culture vessels are usually bought in ready-sterilized. Autoclaves are operated for 15–20 minutes at 121°C/250°F and 1.05kg/cm$^3$ to give adequate sterilization. The exact time required can vary with the volume of media being processed.

The main part of the micropropagation process is the initiation of plant tissues and their subsequent regular division and transfer to fresh medium. The clean environment necessary for these operations is created within laminar flow cabinets, where filters remove contaminants and give a clean non-turbulent air stream within which to work. Contamination can also arise from the instruments used to handle and divide plants. Initially instruments can be sterilized by heat in an oven or autoclave. During working, instruments are periodically sterilized by flaming or suitable alternative treatment.

*Culture Medium*. Micropropagation is a closed growing system where the medium must supply all the plant tissue's requirements for nutrients, vitamins and moisture to sustain growth and development *in vitro*. A source of carbon, usually sucrose or a related sugar, is needed. Various organic compounds or plant extracts have been included in the medium as they can often enhance the quality of growth *in vitro* by supplying trace elements, vitamins or other growth factors in small balanced amounts. All mediums are made up using pure water, which is created by distillation or passing through a deionizer: this avoids the risk of introducing unknown levels of some nutrients into the medium. While in culture, plant tissues often require a support to prevent their becoming submerged in the liquid medium. In the majority of instances the medium is solidified by the use of an appropriate concentration of agar. Occasionally, stationary liquid cultures can be advantageous, with plant tissue supported on an absorbent support, often a filter paper bridge, which acts as a wick to conduct nutrients to the tissues while keeping them in the gas phase. More usually, liquid cultures are mechanically agitated in some way to facilitate gaseous exchange. Enhanced growth rates are possible in such a system but the response between species can vary considerably.

A wide range of culture mediums has been used for growing and propagating plants, most being variations of a limited range which have been developed. The most commonly used basic nutrient formulation was devised by Murashige and Skoog in the 1960s for use in a bioassay for plant growth regulator activity, involving tobacco callus. This medium has also proved to be successful for a wide range of herbaceous plants. Woody plants in general appear to favour lower nutrient concentrations, typically one third of that which is found in Murashige and Skoog medium, as are contained in media similar to that devised by Anderson in the mid-1970s. After all the constituents have been added, the pH of the medium is adjusted to 5.6–6; however, ericaceous plants will require a lower pH.

The development of plant tissues *in vitro* also usually requires the incorporation of some plant growth hormones, and in micropropagation the levels and balance of these is used to control the rate of multiplication and the initiation of rooting. Two classes of hormone are used: cytokinins, which favour shoot development, and auxin, which stimulates rooting. A high proportion of cytokinin relative to auxin will favour shoot development while the reverse of high auxin and little or no cytokinin favours rooting. Increasing levels of cytokinins result in increasing shoot numbers but decreasing shoot length and an inhibition of root initiation and root expression. There is also some evidence of increasing growth disorders and genetic instability in plant tissues grown at very high levels of cytokinin. Three cytokinins are widely used in micropropagation, kinetin, 6-benzylaminopurine (BAP) and 6(yy-dimethylallyl amino)-purine (2-iP). Indole-3-acetic acid (IAA) is a naturally occurring auxin which has been used, but its instability has led to the use in cultures of two synthetic analogues, indole-3-butyric acid (IBA) and naphthylacetic acid (NAA). Occasionally, benefit is derived from the inclusion of other plant growth regulators in the medium, such as gibberellic acid (GA3), which aids shoot elongation.

*Culture Environment*. During micropropagation, *in vitro* cultures are grown within a controlled temperature room at between 20°C/68°F and 28°C/82°F, depending upon species, in long days (16 hours) under banks of fluorescent lights giving intensities of 1000–5000 lux. Species and cultivars can respond to different conditions for optimum *in vitro* growth and development. Increasing temperature increases growth up to the point of stress and ultimately death. Temperature can also affect root initiation, root number and survival after rooting. In some bulb crops low temperatures may sometimes be necessary in order to break dormancy, which can gradually become apparent *in vitro*. While photosynthesis appears to take place at relatively low rates in culture, light is required to sustain that which does occur and to ensure proper plant development. Decreasing light levels result in etiolation of shoots and an increase in petiole length. Increasing light can enhance leaf size and the survival of species when they are transferred to compost. Short day lengths can result in less leaf lamina development, lower chlorophyll content of leaves, and poorer shoot quality with a reduction in multiplication rates. There is also the possibility that short days in some crops can be used to manipulate physiology *in vitro* such as stimulating minituber formation in potato cultures. Complete darkness can result in an absence of chlorophyll and atypical growth, but can be useful for a short period, particularly in some woody plant species, stimulating the initiation of roots.

Within *in vitro* cultures humidity is naturally high, with most closures to culture vessels allowing only minimal gaseous exchange. Prolonged exposure to these high levels results in plant tissues having reduced cuticular wax, stomata with slow closure response and other transient anatomical changes which significantly affect water loss from tissues when micropropagated plantlets are weaned from *in vitro* growing conditions. The limited gaseous exchange can also lead to a build up of detrimental gases such as ethylene. Some crops are particularly sensitive to ethylene, with high levels adversely affecting growth and causing death of tissues in extreme cases. It is therefore important to use closures to culture vessels which, while excluding microbes, still allow some gaseous exchange to take place. Only rarely have the optimum *in vitro* culture conditions been determined for a plant species or cultivar. The requirements of species differ and there can also be significant differences in the requirements of cultivars within a species.

## PATHWAYS OF MICROPROPAGATION

Theoretically, it should be possible to take any part of a plant, establish it within an *in vitro* culture system, multiply the tissues and regenerate complete plantlets. While this is not practical there are a number of routes which can be successfully used, although only three have wide uses for micropropagation.

*Meristem Culture*. This method is generally adopted with the aim of producing virus-free plants. Considerable skill is required to excise meristems successfully before they are established on a sterile medium for growth into a plantlet capable of being established in potting medium and indexed to ensure virus elimination. Although principally used for the production of virus-free plants, meristems can provide a starting-point for a system of micropropagation, as is the case in strawberry. The stolon tip of the plant provides a convenient source of explant, which when the outer scales are dissected away gives a meristem which can be established *in vitro* to form a proliferating crown, which can be divided to generate large numbers of plants.

*Shoot Tip Culture*. The most frequently used route in micropropagation commences with a shoot tip. A small softwood cutting, 2–5cm/1–2in. in length, is excised from the stock plant and, after surface sterilization, placed onto an appropriate culture medium. The explant can take several weeks to become conditioned to the *in vitro* environment. In many woody plants, tissues undergo a phase change to a growth form which is more juvenile in appearance. The medium is formulated to induce the lateral buds on these shoots to grow to the point where the shoot system can be divided and individual shoots transferred to a fresh medium, where the process is repeated. A series of proliferating cultures is established which can yield large numbers of shoots over a relatively short time for subsequent transfer to a root-including medium and ultimately establishment in compost.

*Organ Culture*. It is possible for other organs to be used as a starting point for micropropagation. While any organ could theoretically be taken successfully into culture, those which are naturally more regenerative are chosen, often reflecting the conventional method of propagating the plant. Thus leaf tissue is used for micropropagation of *Saintpaulia* spp. (leaf lamina) and *Begonia* spp. (leaf petiole). Other organs used for other species include bulb scales, internodal stem sections and parts of the flower. Anthers and pollen can be of particular interest to plant breeders in creating haploid lines. In some species, embryoids develop directly from pollen, and, under suitable *in vitro* conditions, develop into whole plants. More usually, organ explants produce minimal callus within which shoot primordia develop and grow; these can then be divided and subcultured to achieve rapid multiplication rates.

*Callus Culture*. In any organ explant excessive callus formation can be stimulated by the incorporation of higher levels of auxin in the culture medium than would otherwise be desirable. The resulting mass of unorganized cells can be increased in culture, with the formation of shoots and ultimately whole plants being stimulated by a change in the composition of the medium. Some plants naturally produce callus in culture without recourse to high auxin levels, and occasionally callus can regenerate shoots spontaneously, without external stimulation. These methods of culture present a problem to the propagator, as large amounts of callus tend to favour a higher frequency of genetic instability in the regenerated plants than is found in culture systems based on shoots alone. Such genetic variability can be exploited in plant breeding, where the soma-clones which arise can be tested in their own right or incorporated into a crossing programme.

*Cell Culture*. An alternative pathway is to transfer callus, created in culture, to a liquid medium which, given the correct formulation and agitation, can result in the mass of cells breaking up to give either suspensions of single cells or small clusters of cell aggregates. Cell suspensions can be maintained indefinitely using culture techniques similar to those used for bacterial culture, although there are a number of differences between the response of plant cells and microbial fermentations. The use of this form of culture system for the propagation of plants is very limited at present. Researchers are examining the conditions under which cells form embryo-like structures (embryoids) which have not originated by sexual fertilization. These have been described as 'naked', asexual, clonal or somatic seeds. It could be possible to combine this approach with fluid-drilling technology, developed for conventional seed, to give a system for the multiplication and delivery of clonal seed.

Cell suspensions also offer the possibility to plant breeders of applying selection pressures, for resistance or tolerance to a wide range of conditions, to a large *in vitro* population of cells. Cells from suspensions can also be used in genetic engineering studies. Many plants produce useful or potentially useful chemicals by their natural metabolism. These chemicals can also be produced by the metabolism of cells in culture, with culture conditions modified to increase the chemical yield.

Choosing the most appropriate pathway for micropropagation requires a clear objective and knowledge of the plants to be propagated. The potential problems are illustrated by the variegation that occurs in some ornamental plants, where the ornamental feature can either be the result of a chimaera or a beneficial virus infection (e.g. in pelargoniums). By use of a shoot-tip or meristem culture a beneficial virus could be eliminated, while a chimaera would not be affected. However, by using an organ explant from a leaf petiole the beneficial virus could be retained but the chimaera lost. Careless use of pathways could therefore result in large numbers of plants which do not possess the ornamental feature for which they are being grown.

## PROCESS OF MICROPROPAGATION

The process of micropropagation is described in five main stages, commencing with the stock plant and concluding with the weaning of plantlets from *in vitro* conditions.

*Stage 0: Stock Plant*. Micropropagation is capable of producing very large numbers of plants. It is therefore essential that the best stock plant selection is made from which the initial cultures are established. The stock plant must be true to type and free from pests and disease. Ideally it should be grown in a container under glass and managed in such a way as to minimize the risk of severe contamination of the explants when they are taken into culture. There may be an opportunity in some species to manipulate the stock plant by controlling the nutrition or environmental conditions in which it is grown in a way which will increase the success of explant establishment *in vitro*. Material can if necessary be taken directly from field-grown stock but the level of initial contamination is likely to be higher.

*Stage I: Initiation*. Appropriate explants are collected from the stock plant, surface-sterilized to remove microbes, and inserted into the culture medium after the removal of any damaged or superfluous tissues. Any gross contamination of the cultures will become apparent within five days and these cultures are discarded. In some plants exudates (phenols and tanins) can be produced in culture, often as a reaction to tissue damage, which can inhibit establishment and growth *in vitro*. Growth of cultures in this initial stage can sometimes be improved by decapitation of shoot tips to remove apical dominance, or by changing the orientation of the explant in the medium. The initiation medium can be a basic formulation with a low auxin level and low to moderate cytokinin. Too high an auxin level can result in excessive callus. Plant tissues can take 4–16 weeks to become acclimatized to the *in vitro* environment, during which time transfer to a fresh medium without dividing the tissues may be necessary. For many woody plants a phase change occurs to a more juvenile type of growth. When growth and development has begun tissues can be transferred to the multiplication stage.

*Stage II: Multiplication*. During the multiplication cycle a rapid increase in plant material occurs. The culture medium for multiplication frequently has an increased level of cytokinin, with optimum rates determined to give the highest shoot proliferation consistent with good shoot quality. Too high a cytokinin level, while increasing shoot numbers, results in very compact growth with an increasing incidence of abnormalities in growth. The optimum levels of cytokinin and auxin will frequently vary between cultivars. Cultures which are growing rapidly are routinely divided and transferred to fresh mediums at regular intervals (serially subcultured). The subculture process can be as frequent as every two weeks for some herbaceous plants, or at 8–10-week intervals for wood plants. Typically, many plants can be subcultured on a four-week cycle. At each subculture at least a doubling of shoot numbers is aimed for, although increases of five- or ten-fold can occur. This reaction, like many others *in vitro*, is species dependent; nevertheless, the enormous potential for producing large numbers of plantlets can be seen in this regular cycling of multiplication, especially as, in theory at least, it can continue indefinitely. Prolonged cycling can however result in an increasing incidence of growth abnormalities, genetic aberrations and off-types. In order to control these the number of subculture cycles is limited. Shoots generated in the multiplication stages can be transferred to a rooting medium as one batch or in smaller numbers over an extended period, depending upon individual requirements.

*Stage III: Rooting*. The rooting or root initiation medium is based upon that used for multiplication with cytokinin omitted but auxin retained and sometimes increased in concentration. A reduction in the total strength of nutrients to one third or half the level in multiplication may also be beneficial. Where high levels of cytokinin were required in the multiplication stages a residual effect may carry over into the rooting stage; this may be corrected by the incorporation of activated charcoal into the rooting medium. Ideally, roots should be initiated but should not emerge at this stage, as root systems which develop *in vitro* are somewhat atypical and may not function fully when transferred to a potting medium. For some plants which root and establish easily and rapidly in potting medium, it may be possible to avoid this rooting stage and transfer shoots from multiplication medium directly to potting medium.

*Stage IV: Weaning or Acclimatization*. Micropropagated plantlets develop a distinctive morphology in response to the *in vitro* environment in which they have grown. Micropropagated plants immediately from culture frequently have a juvenile or seedling appearance, together with the associated growth characteristics which are generally transitory but can be used to advantage. They also have reduced surface wax on the leaves, a modified internal structure to the leaf, and poor stomatal response, all of which contribute to high water loss so that micropropagated plants can therefore easily desiccate. Changes of this type to the leaf surface can also make micropropagated plants more susceptible to damage from scorch and from pest, disease and crop-protection chemicals. During weaning, conditions must be created to minimize water loss and stress while allowing root development in the potting medium until the plantlets establish and assume their normal morphology. It is therefore essential to wean in conditions of uniform high humidity (95%), shade and even temperatures (18–20°C/65–68°F). Mist propagation systems and polythene propagation covers under shaded glass have been used to create these conditions and are useful for some crops; fog propagation systems, especially those capable of giving a uniform distribution of a 'dry' fog, have proved successful in weaning a wide range of micropropagated material. The droplet size created in a dry fog, approximately 10 micron, is capable of remaining suspended in the air for some time. Good control of the fogging by humidistat is essential and electronic devices are the most satisfactory.

For some species, base heat and supplementary lighting during weaning are beneficial at certain times of the year. Lighting in particular can extend the weaning season and improve plant quality. There is often considerable variability in the size of plantlets within the culture vessel and this is also present immediately prior to weaning. This leads to variable rooting and establishment upon transfer to the potting medium. It is therefore essential to grade plantlets before weaning in order to achieve a more uniform establishment and growth. Grading criteria will depend upon the species being grown but will usually be based on some facet of plant size. In general, larger propagules wean more successfully, root faster and grow away more quickly than the smaller grades. The smallest grades often remain highly variable and are usually best discarded at an early stage. It is not uncommon for only 50% of propagules immediately from culture to come within the first grade, and effort directed to modify the *in vitro* culture conditions to increase this percentage is beneficial. The influence of these grades can be carried through to establishment and growing on after potting.

Soilless mediums are suitable for weaning, with both perlite and rockwool also being useful in some circumstances. The nutritional requirement during weaning is species-dependent and three groupings of plants can be identified based upon response to feed in the compost. For some plants, such as *Kalmia*, inclusion of any fertilizer during weaning is detrimental, rooting and growth being severely depressed. However, once rooted and hardened off, a dilute liquid feed programme prior to potting can improve plant survival and quality. In the second group, the availability of fertilizer during weaning, while not essential or detrimental, will improve plant quality and early growth, e.g. *Rhododendron*. The last group comprises plants such as *Rosa* and *Magnolia* spp. where nutrients are an essential component in the production of plants that establish and grow away rapidly on potting. These nutrient requirements can be met by the use of liquid feeds or the incorporation of an appropriate formulation of slow-release fertilizer into the medium.

POTENTIAL OF MICROPROPAGATION. Rapid clonal propagation is a major advantage of micropropagation. This basic benefit makes possible the rapid propagation and introduction of new cultivars in substantial numbers. Similarly, the production and dissemination of disease-free plant material can be speeded by micropropagation, for not only can large numbers be produced, but as micropropagation takes place *in vitro* plant material is exposed to lower risk of reinfection than might otherwise be the case. Producing disease-indexed plants requires skill and appropriate testing facilities, as plants are not necessarily disease-free simply because they have been micropropagated. Rapid propagation can also be of particular interest for plants that are difficult to propagate by other means, and micropropagation may make more widely available a number of plants which would otherwise be restricted in cultivation. Major crop plants required in large numbers can also be micropropagated to advantage, enabling growers to respond more quickly to changes in demand.

Since micropropagation stages in culture are independent of season it is possible to propagate all the year round and to programme production. Season can, however, become important both at the initiation stage, when the stock plant must be in the correct condition for excision, and at weaning and growing on. The effect of season can be mitigated to some extent in many species by use of temperature control and supplementary lighting.

Compared with conventional propagation, relatively few stock plants are needed for micropropagation; this can result in considerable savings in both space and the maintenance necessary to hold stock. While in theory only one stock plant is required from which to initiate cultures – and indeed may be all that is available of a rare plant or new cultivar – for large-scale production it is prudent to use a larger number in order to spread the genetic base and risk. Plant material grown *in vitro* can often be more easily exchanged between countries than if grown in soil or compost, although plant health regulations do apply to micropropagated material and must be complied with. Micropropagated material is frequently used as a route for international exchange between botanic gardens and other research institutes. Many advantages of micropropagation can be exploited in the conservation of plants and their reintroduction. Whether the starting point is a single rare plant or a small amount of seed, *in vitro* culture techniques can increase the possibility of achieving successful propagation of species which often present considerable difficulties to conventional propagation.

PROBLEMS OF MICROPROPAGATION. One major problem arising from the use of micropropagation is the risk of off-types occurring, as a result of either transient phenotypic changes or permanent genetic changes. A number of risk factors have been identified which can affect the rate at which such aberrations occur. Generally, the more callus produced, the higher the risk; similarly, high auxin concentrations (which increase callus) and/or high cytokinin levels increase risk. The longer the time for which plant material is exposed to these conditions, and especially the more serial subcultures through which the material is taken, the greater the risk of off-types. Each of these factors can interact with species and cultivar to limit or increase the risk. Some plants are more prone than others to spontaneous mutation, which if it occurs in culture cannot be as readily identified as in the conventional propagation system. It is therefore an important aspect of quality control in commercial situations to grow on a proportion of micropropagated plants in order to test trueness to type. The occurrence of off-types and mutations in well-regulated micropropagation systems is however rare. Slight alterations in growth habit after micropropagation are more common and are usually transient. Given that reasonable precautions are taken, the rate at which mutations or off-types occur in micropropagation should be similar to the incidence in any other propagation system for a given plant.

An aura of scientific mystique can surround micropropagation facilities as a result of preconceptions which arise from the image of expensively equipped plant science laboratories. Horticultural micropropagation laboratories do not need all of this sophisticated equipment to produce plants satisfactorily. Nevertheless, micropropagation can be a costly technique, partly as a result of the development work which can be required to devise a method for a new species or cultivar which has not previously been propagated by the method. Many of the basic principles of general propagation apply equally to micropropagation.

Despite all the research which has taken place within the field of plant tissue culture, there are still considerable gaps in knowledge. The increased understanding of the utilization of nutrients and growth regulators by *in vitro* shoot systems could enable a wider range of plant species to be micropropagated satisfactorily. Shoot development can be very asynchronous, and unusual bacterial problems can be encountered *in vitro*. Nevertheless, micropropagation has gained a significant place within horticulture as a means of rescue for rare or endangered species, rapid introduction of new cultivars, the creation and dissemination of disease-free plants and for the propagation of plants where other means pose some constraints. For a number of crop plants micropropagation has become the accepted main method of plant production.

**Micropterum** Schwantes.
***M.cuneifolium*** (Jacq.) Schwantes. See *Dorotheanthus bellidiformis*.
***M.limpidum*** (Ait.) Schwantes. See *Dorotheanthus bellidiformis*.

**Microsorium** Link. (From Gk *mikros*, small, and *sorus*.) Polypodiaceae. Perhaps 40 species of, usually, epiphytic ferns. Rhizomes short- or long-creeping, or climbing, occasionally branching, dictyostelic; scales deciduous or persistent, usually more or less lanceolate, entirely or at least centrally clathrate. Fronds stipitate, uniform, simple or pinnatifid or, rarely, pinnate, entire, leathery to herbaceous or papery and thin-textured, glabrous or, occasionally, pubescent; main veins often prominent, veins irregularly reticulate, anastomosing into areolae with free, simple or divaricate, included veinlets, these with terminal hydathodes, stipes distant, jointed to rhizome, occasionally winged. Sori superficial or somewhat sunken and pustulate, 1–3-serial at union of veinlets, or 2-serial between main lateral veins, or irregularly dispersed over surface, round to oval or, occasionally, elongate, spreading; paraphyses usually absent; annulus 14–16-celled; spores often smooth. Tropical Africa to Asia, Australasia, Polynesia. Z10.

CULTIVATION Glasshouse cultivation as for *Polypodium*. *M.pteropus* can be grown as a submerged aquatic.

***M.diversifolium*** (Willd.) Copel. KANGAROO FERN; HOUND'S TONGUE FERN. Epiphytic or epilithic fern. Rhiz. long-creeping, to 8mm wide, fleshy, glaucous; scales to 10×2mm, adpressed, deciduous, ovate to lanceolate, narrowly acute and, occasionally, hair-tipped at apex, clathrate, lustrous brown. Fronds many, arching to pendent, unusually polymorphous, leathery, glabrous, lustrous, bright green: simple fronds to 25×5cm, linear to oblong, elliptic, or lanceolate, apex acute or obtuse, margin entire or somewhat undulate; irregularly pinnatifid fronds to 30×15cm, seg. to 10×3cm, broadly lanceolate to oblong; regularly and deeply pinnatifid fronds to 45×22cm, seg. to 15×2.5cm, narrowly linear to oblong, apex acute; veins prominent, reticulate, areolae with free, included veinlets; stipes to 20cm, mostly glabrous, grooved, lustrous pale brown. Australia, Tasmania, New Zealand.

***M.fortunei*** (Moore) Ching. Rhiz. to 4mm wide; scales ovate, torn at margin, clathrate, brown. Fronds to 60×5cm, simple, narrowed at apex and base, margins somewhat undulate; costa prominent, veins indistinct, reticulate, areolae with free, divaricate, included veinlets; stipes 2cm distant, to 25cm, mostly glabrous. China, Taiwan.

***M.linguaeforme*** (Mett.) Copel. Epiphytic fern. Rhiz. creeping; scales brown. Fronds to 50×9cm, sessile or short-stipitate, erect, simple, apex obtuse or narrowly acute, base enlarged, scarious, collecting plant-litter, margin entire or somewhat undulate, papery and thin-textured, dark green, brown at base; veins prominent, reticulate, areolae with free, included veinlets. Philippines, Borneo, to New Guinea, Fiji.

***M.membranaceum*** (D. Don) Ching. Rhiz. creeping, to 1cm wide; scales ovate, narrowly acute at apex, entire at margin, brown to dark green. Fronds to 1m×15cm, simple or, occasionally, pinnatifid, elliptic to lanceolate, apex attenuate, base attenuate and long-decurrent, margin entire or somewhat undulate, membranous, seg. narrowed; veins prominent, main lateral veins parallel, distant (at 1cm intervals), areolae with free, divaricate, included veinlets; stipes to 12cm, winged in decurrent part of frond. Asia (India, Sri Lanka, to China, Taiwan, Philippines).

***M.musifolium*** (Bl.) Ching. Epiphytic or epilithic fern. Rhiz. short-creeping, covered with roots as well as scales; roots massed, brown-woolly; scales to 4mm, ovate, apex narrowly acute, margin dentate, clathrate, dark brown. Fronds to 1m×12cm, sessile, erect, simple, ovate to oblong or strap-shaped, apex obtuse or narrowly acute, attenuate toward but dilated at base, margin entire, firmly papery to leathery; veins prominent, areolae with free, included veinlets. Malaysia, Indonesia, Philippines to New Guinea, Polynesia.

***M.nigrescens*** (Bl.) Copel. PIMPLE FERN. Epiphytic or epilithic fern. Rhiz. creeping, fleshy; scales caducous, adpressed, ovate, dark brown. Fronds to 80×45cm or more, deeply pinnatifid, oblong, apex narrowly acute, base cuneate and decurrent, membranous, glabrous, dark blue-green, seg. to 30×4cm, opposite, to 23, lanceolate, to oblong or linear, apex narrowly acute, margin entire or somewhat undulate; veins prominent, reticulate, areolae with free, included veinlets; stipes to 50cm, lustrous brown to straw-coloured. S India, Sri Lanka, Malaysia, to Australia (Queensland), Polynesia.

***M.normale*** (D. Don) Ching. Epiphytic fern. Rhiz. long-creeping or climbing, to 5mm wide; scales deciduous, awl-shaped, clathrate, hairy at base. Fronds to 60×5cm, simple lanceolate to strap-shaped, apex narrowly acute, base attenuate and long-decurrent, margin entire or somewhat undulate, membranous and thin-textured, glabrous; veins somewhat indistinct, main lateral veins absent, areolae irregular, with free, included veinlets; stipes approximate, to 5cm, straw-coloured. Asia (N India to S China, Malaysia) to New Guinea, Australia.

***M.novae-zelandiae*** (Bak.) Copel. Epiphytic fern. Rhiz. long-creeping or climbing, to 1cm wide, woody; scales to 1cm, dense, spreading, ovate to lanceolate, pale tawny-brown. Fronds to 120×35cm, deeply pinnatifid, lanceolate to oblong, apex narrowly acute, firmly leathery, glabrous, dark green, seg. to 20cm×15mm, opposite, to 20 pairs, lanceolate to linear or oblong, apex narrowly acute, base often attenuate, entire to somewhat undulate at base; veins somewhat indistinct, reticulate, areolae with free, included veinlets; stipes to 30cm, glabrous, lustrous, light brown. New Zealand.

***M.pappei*** (Mett. ex Kuhn) Tard. Epiphytic or epilithic fern. Rhiz. creeping, to 3mm wide; scales to 3.5cm, deciduous, ovate to lanceolate, apex narrowly acute, entire, dark brown. Fronds to 70×8cm, simple, elliptic, apex narrowly acute, base attenuate and decurrent, entire to somewhat undulate, leathery to membranous, glabrous, dark green; costa prominent, veins indistinct, main lateral veins to 1cm apart, areolae with free, simple or divaricate, included veinlets, stipes to 15cm, mostly glabrous, light green. Tropical Africa, Madagascar.

***M.parksii*** (Copel.) Copel. Epiphytic or terrestrial fern. Rhiz. creeping, to 5mm wide; scales adpressed, clathrate. Fronds to 45×30cm, deeply pinnatifid to almost pinnate, erect, papery, glabrous, lustrous, seg. to 20cm×15mm, opposite, to 12 pairs, apex narrowly acute, attenuate toward and dilated at base, margin somewhat undulate; veins indistinct, reticulate, areolae with free, included veinlets; stipes to 60cm, to 10cm distant, glabrous, straw-coloured. Fiji.

***M.pteropus*** (Bl.) Copel. Epilithic, amphibious fern. Rhiz. creeping, to 3mm wide, fleshy, green; scales deciduous, linear to lanceolate, clathrate, dark brown. Fronds erect, simple or trilobate, entire at margin, membranous and thin-textured: simple fronds to 20×4cm, lanceolate to obovate, apex narrowly acute, fronds at base attenuate and decurrent; trilobate to 40×5cm, terminal lobe narrowly acute at apex, lateral lobes similar but smaller; costa scaly and main veins prominent beneath, veins reticulate with oblong areolae and 1–2-rowed minor areolae; stipes to 20cm, 2cm distant, scaly, winged in upper part. Asia (India, Malaysia, to S China, Taiwan, Philippines).

***M.punctatum*** (L.) Copel. CLIMBING BIRD'S-NEST FERN. Epiphytic fern. Rhiz. medium-creeping, to 12mm wide, woody to fleshy, covered with massed, hairy roots as well as scales, green; scales to 3mm, apex acute, base obtuse, margin dentate or ciliate, centrally clathrate, dark brown. Fronds to 120×8cm, short-stipitate, simple, lanceolate, obtuse or narrowly acute at apex, attenuate and decurrent at base, entire at margin, leathery and fleshy, glabrous, light yellow-green; veins indistinct, main veins 2.5cm distant, joined by arcuate veinlets, reticulate into irregular areolae with free, included veinlets; stipes approximate, to 1cm. Tropical Africa, Asia, Australasia, Polynesia. 'Cristatum': fronds erect, tipped with a crest, pale green. 'Grandiceps': fronds pendent, crested, spreading and branched at apex, leathery.

***M.rubidum*** (Kunze) Copel. Epiphytic fern. Rhiz. wide-creeping, to 1cm wide, fleshy; scales adpressed, ovate, brown. Fronds 1m×30cm, pinnatifid almost to rachis, narrowly oblong, narrowly acute at apex, leathery, seg. to 25×1.5cm, to 40 or more, more or less erect, narrowly oblong, apex narrowly acute to obtuse, base decurrent, margin entire to somewhat undulate or swollen; veins somewhat prominent below, areolae with free, included veinlets; stipes to 50cm. Asia (N India, Malaysia) to Polynesia.

***M.scandens*** (Forst. f.) Tind. FRAGRANT FERN. Epiphytic fern. Rhiz. long-creeping and climbing, to 7mm wide, much-branched, fleshy to woody; scales to 6×1mm, persistent, lanceolate, narrowly acute at apex, widened at base, margin dentate, papery, lustrous dark brown. Fronds to 35×1cm, polymorphous, membranous and thin-textured, glabrous, musk-scented, dull dark green: simple narrowly lanceolate or elliptic to linear, apex and base attenuate, margin entire; deeply and irregularly pinnatifid fronds to 50×15cm, seg. to 10×1.5cm, opposite, to 21 pairs, remote, erecto-patent or, occasionally, spreading, linear to lanceolate, or oblong, or ovate, apex narrowly acute. Stipes to 10cm, grooved, more or less glabrous, lustrous brown. Australia, New Zealand.

***M.scolopendrium*** (Burm. f.) Copel. WART FERN. Rhiz. long-creeping, to 1cm wide, fleshy, green to brown; scales to 5mm, caducous, ovate to lanceolate or deltoid, apex narrowly acute, clathrate, dark brown. Fronds to 40×30cm, deeply pinnatifid, oblong to ovate, base attenuate and decurrent, or, rarely, simple, lanceolate, smaller, leathery to papery, glabrous, lustrous, light green, seg. to 15×3cm, opposite, to 5 pairs, spreading, lanceolate to linear, oblong, or strap-shaped, apex narrowly acute to obtuse, margin entire to thickened and somewhat falcate, terminal seg. elongate; stipes to 30cm, 8cm distant, glabrous, lustrous, stramineous. Tropical Africa, Asia, Australasia, Polynesia.

***M.steerei*** (Harrington) Ching. Rhiz. to 12mm wide; scales lanceolate, entire to somewhat toothed at margin, clathrate, brown. Fronds to 40×8cm, elliptic or lanceolate to oblong, entire, firmly membranous; costa and main lateral veins prominent below, veins obscure; stipes approximate. E Asia (China, Taiwan, SE Asia).

***M.superficiale*** (Bl.) Ching. Epiphytic fern. Rhiz. long-creeping or climbing, woody; scales sparse, lanceolate, lustrous brown. Fronds to 30×5cm, simple, lanceolate to oblong or linear, apex narrowly acute, base attenuate and decurrent, margin entire, firmly membranous; stipes to 15cm, remote, erect to somewhat falcate, glabrous; costa prominent, costules absent, areolae irregular, with free, simple or divaricate, included veinlets. Asia (N India, Indonesia, Japan), to Australia.

***M.alternifolium*** (Willd.) Copel. See *M.nigrescens*.
***M.ensato-sessilifrons*** (Hayata) H. Itô. See *Colysis hemionitidea*.
For further synonymy see *Acrostichum, Drynaria, Phymatodes, Phymatosorus, Pleopeltis* and *Polypodium*.

**Microstrobos** J. Garden & L. Johnson. (From Gk *mikros*, small and Lat. *strobus*, cone.) Podocarpaceae. 2 species of dioecious shrubs, to 60cm, rarely 2m, spreading. Leaves densely spirally arranged, imbricate, in 4–5 ranks, scale-like, 1.5–2.5mm wide, resembling *Dacrydium* in shape, apex incurved. Male cones ovoid or subglobose, erect, to 3mm; 10–15 scales. Female cones terminal, to 3mm, with 4–8 scales; scales 1–1.5mm, thick based with acuminate tip, containing 1 seed, 1mm long; green-brown, dry, not fleshy. SE Australia, Tasmania. Z8.

CULTIVATION Very rarely seen in cultivation, both species are hardy in wetter maritime climates; *M.niphophilus* the hardier. Both have very high moisture requirements; *M.fitzgeraldii* grows in the spray zone of waterfalls. A useful addition to the dwarf conifer collection, tolerating wetter sites than any other dwarf conifers, and also shade tolerant. Propagate as *Podocarpus*; layers and cuttings root easily.

***M.fitzgeraldii*** (F. Muell.) J. Garden & L. Johnson. BLUE MOUNTAIN PINE. Semi-prostrate shrub, to 60cm×1m. Twigs to 5mm diam., pendent. Lvs subulate, loosely overlapping, olive green; stomatal bands white below, to 3mm; apex incurved. Male cones terminal; seed cones ovoid to subglobose, to 3mm. New South Wales, by waterfalls. Z8.

***M.niphophilus*** Garden & Johnson. TASMAN DWARF PINE. Shrub to 2m. Branches short, stiff. Bark grey, tinged purple, slightly ridged. Lvs densely arranged, scale-like, 1.5–2×1.5mm, keeled, green. Male cones to 3mm; apex obtuse; female cones to 3mm. Tasmania (Mount Field, Lake St Clair). Z8.

For synonymy see *Pherosphaera*.

**Microterangis** Schltr. ex Sengh. (From Gk *microteros*, smaller, and *ankis*, spur, referring to the spur on the tiny flowers.) Orchidaceae. 4 species of epiphytic orchids. Short-stemmed, densely leafy. Leaves usually oblong or obovate, unequally and obtusely bilobed at apex. Racemes many-flowered; flowers small, 2–3mm diam., dull yellow, yellow-orange or red-brown; sepals and petals free, similar; lip entire or dentate at apex, spurred; spur of about the same length as the lip; column straight, very short; pollinia 2, with communal stipe and very small viscidium. Madagascar, Mascarene Is., Comoros Is. Z9.

CULTIVATION As for *Aerangis*.

***M.boutonii*** (Rchb. f.) Sengh. Stem short; roots slender, numerous. Lvs to 13×3cm, oblanceolate, unequally and obtusely bilobed at apex, 1 lobe often virtually absent. Raceme to 17cm, densely many-fld; peduncle very short, to 3cm; fls small, 2–3mm diam.; sep. and pet. ovate-triangular, pet. slightly shorter than sep.; lip tridentate at apex; spur filiform, of similar length to lip. Comoros Is.

***M.hariotiana*** (Kränzl.) Sengh. Stem 4–5cm, often less. Lvs 4–7, 5–15×1.5–4cm, obovate-oblong. Racemes numerous, pendent, sometimes 2–3 arising together; peduncle 1–4cm; rachis 10–20cm, densely many-fld; fls red-brown; pedicel and ovary 2mm; sep. and pet. 1–2mm, ovate, obtuse; lip entire, subcordate at base, similar to tepals but slightly wider; spur 2mm, apex swollen. Comoros Is.

***M.hildebrandtii*** (Rchb. f.) Sengh. Stem short; roots slender. Lvs ligulate, unequally and obtusely bilobed at apex. Raceme laxly many-fld; fls small, yellow-orange; sep. and pet. 2–3mm, ligulate, apex rounded; lip 2–3mm, oblong, acute; spur 2–3mm, filiform but swollen at apex. Comoros Is.

For synonymy see *Angraecopsis, Angraecum* and *Chamaeangis*.

**Microtis** R. Br. (From Gk *mikros*, small, and *ous* ear.) Orchidaceae. Some 12 species of herbaceous terrestrial orchids. Leaf solitary, elongate. Fls in dense spike; dorsal sepal incurved, erect, lateral sepals oblong or lanceolate; petals narrower than sepals, spreading, incurved; lip sessile, oblong, orbicular or ovate, disc with 2 basal calli, rarely 1 at apex. E Asia, Australia, New Zealand. Z9.

CULTIVATION See ORCHIDS, The Hardy Species.

***M.unifolia*** (Forst. f.) Rchb. f. To 50cm. Lf rounded, elongate. Fls golden to pale green; dorsal sep. to 2mm, forming a hood, lateral sep. shorter, oblong, decurved or deflexed; pet. oblong, partly obscured by dorsal sep.; lip green, edged pale yellow, crenate, obtuse, calli 2, dark green. Late autumn–winter.

**Mikania** Willd. (For J.G. Mikan (1743–1814), Professor of Botany at Prague, or his son J.C. Mikan (*d*1844), plant collector in Brazil.) Compositae. About 300 species of evergreen, perennial, woody or herbaceous lianes. Leaves usually opposite, entire to dentate. Capitula discoid, small, clustered in spikes, racemes or panicles; involucre cylindric to ovoid; phyllaries 4–5, usually striate; florets hermaphrodite, pink, white or tinged purple, occasionally lime green or blue. Fruit a 5-angled cypsela; pappus bristles usually white or tinged yellow, scabrid. Tropics, especially New World.

CULTIVATION As for *Delairea*. Most species are frost tender and need glasshouse protection in cool temperature zones.

***M. dentata*** Spreng. Woody, clothed in purple hairs. Lvs palmately lobed, 5–7, oblong-rhombic to oblanceolate-rhombic, entire to pinnatifid or 3-lobed, dark green above, purple beneath. Capitula clustered in lax corymbs; florets white tinged yellow. Pappus off-white. C & S Brazil. Z10.

***M. hemisphaerica*** Schultz-Bip. ex Bak. Herbaceous, glabrous throughout. Lvs to 10cm, simple, ovate, cordate at base, acuminate, margins serrate-dentate; petiole to 5cm. Capitula in a corymbose panicle; florets white flushed with pink. Pappus rufescent. Brazil. Z10.

***M. parviflora*** (Aubl.) Karst. Herbaceous to woody. Lvs large, ovate, entire to remotely dentate, apex acuminate, base acute or decurrent, glabrous or nearly so. Capitula in cymes; florets pale lime green or pale blue. Pappus pale brown. C & Tropical S America. Z10.

***M. scandens*** (L.) Willd. WILD CLIMBING HEMP-WEED; CLIMBING HEMP-VINE. Herbaceous, subglabrous. Lvs to 10cm, triangular to hastate, base deeply cordate, margins entire or remotely repand-dentate, apex acuminate, glabrous to slightly scabrous or pubesc.; petioles long. Capitula in dense corymbs, strongly vanilla-scented; florets white, tinged yellow, or lilac to purple. Pappus off-white. Summer. Tropical America. Z4.

***M. amara*** Willd. See *M. parviflora*.
***M. apiifolia*** DC. See *M. dentata*.
***M. ternata*** (Vell.) Robinson. See *M. dentata*.

**Mila** Britt. & Rose. (Anagram of Lima, capital of Peru.) Cactaceae. 1 species, a variable cactus, low, clustering; rootstock stout; stems 30×(1–)1.5–2.5(–4)cm, short-cylindric; ribs 10–13, 3–5mm high; areoles 2–5mm apart, at first densely brown-felted; spines variable in number, length, texture and colour, usually more than 20, centrals 1–8, 1–3cm, radial spines 10–40, 5–20mm. Flower 2–3.5×2–3cm, subapical, small funnelform-campanulate, yellow; scales of pericarpel and tube small, narrow; floral areoles with woolly or bristly axillary hairs. Fruit small, to 12–15mm, globose, fleshy, red-tinged, with scales and woolly hairs; seeds *c*1.0×0.8mm, broadly oval, black-brown, matt, periphery keeled; relief low-domed; hilum medium, basal, superficial. C Peru. Z9.

CULTIVATION Grow in a cool frost-free greenhouse (min. 2–7°C/37–45°F), use 'standard' cactus compost: moderate to high inorganic content (more than 50% grit), pH 6–7.5; full sun; low air-humidity; keep dry from mid-autumn until early spring, except for light misting on warm days in late winter.

***M. caespitosa*** Britt. & Rose. As for the genus.

***M. kubeana*** Werderm. & Backeb. See *M. caespitosa*.
***M. nealeana*** Backeb. See *M. caespitosa*.

**Milicia** (Sim) C. Berg. Moraceae. 2 species of dioecious trees. Leaves distichous, pinnately veined; stipules semi-amplexicaul, free. Inflorescences in leaf axils, spicate, bracteate. Male flowers: tepals 4, basally connate; stamens 4, inflexed in bud, pistillode present; female flowers 5–15, tepals 4, basally connate; ovary free, stigmas 2, filiform, very unequal in length. Fruiting perianth enlarged, more or less fleshy, green; fruit free, slightly drupaceous; seed small, with endosperm; cotyledons thin, equal, plane. Tropical Africa. Z10.

CULTIVATION As for *Artocarpus*.

***M. excelsa*** (Welw.) C. Berg. Tree, to 30(–50)m. Lvs 6–20×3.5–10cm, coriaceous, chartaceous at first, elliptic to oblong, apex acuminate, base cordate to obtuse, margin repand to subentire, when juvenile serrate to crenate-dentate, hirtellous to tomentose, becoming entire, puberulent to pubesc. on main veins only, especially beneath; petiole 1–5cm; stipules 0.5–5cm, caducous. Male infl. a spike, 8–20×0.5cm; female infl. a spike, 2–3×0.5cm, to 5×1.5cm in fruit; stigmas to 7mm. Fr. 2.5–3mm, ellipsoid. Tropical Africa.

***M. africana*** Sim. See *M. excelsa*.
For further synonymy see *Chlorophora*, *Maclura* and *Morus*.

**Milium** L. (Lat. *milium*, millet.) Gramineae. 6 species of annual or perennial grasses to 2m. Stems in loose tussocks, flimsy to stout. Leaf blades flat; ligules papery, translucent. Panicles loose or contracted; spikelets single-flowered, somewhat longitudinally flattened; glumes subequal, obtuse, 3-ribbed; lemma shorter than glumes, elliptic, dorsally convex or flattened, 5-ribbed, stiff, shining, not awned; palea obtuse, 2-ribbed, not keeled, rigid. Summer. Eurasia, N America. Z5.

CULTIVATION *M. effusum*, found in oak and beech woodland frequently on damp, heavy humus rich lime soils, has been widely planted in English woodlands as a food source for game birds. Grown as ornamentals for flowers and foliage, the golden and variegated forms making extremely useful and beautiful ground cover in semi-shade or in the dappled sunlight of the woodland garden. The fresh spring leaves of *M. e.* 'Aureum' are also useful in floral arrangements. Hardy to temperatures of −20°C/−4°F and below. Grow in fertile, moist but well-drained soil. Propagate by seed and division, *M. e.* 'Aureum' comes true from seed. *Milium* will self sow but seldom to the point of nuisance.

***M. effusum*** L. WOOD MILLET. Perenn. to 180cm. Lf blades 30×1.5cm, glabrous, undulate; sheaths smooth; ligules obtuse, to 1cm. Panicles to 30×20cm, lax, lanceolate to ovate or oblong, nodding, branched, light green or tinged purple; branches in whorled cluster, flexuous; spikelets to 5mm. 'Aureum' ('Bowles' Golden Grass'): lvs and spikelets yellow; more often cultivated than type. 'Variegatum': lvs bright green with white longitudinal stripes; weak growing. Z6.

***M. multiflorum*** Cav. See *Oryzopsis miliacea*.

**Milla** Cav. (For Juliani Milla, gardener to the Spanish court in Madrid, 18th century.) Liliaceae (Alliaceae). 6 species of perennial herbs. Corm small, with thinly-textured coat, roots fleshy. Stem erect. Leaves 2–7, linear, flat to almost terete. Inflorescence erect to spreading, umbelliferous. Flowers 2–4 per umbel, rarely solitary, with long pedicels; scape naked, subtended by 4 chaffy spathes; tepals united to above the middle, forming a long tube, striped green on white, pink, or blue; lobes 6, shorter than tube; stamens 6, emerging at mouth of tube, protruding beyond corolla; ovary 3-celled, borne on a long stalk. Fruit a loculicidal capsule; seeds black, flat. S US, C America. Former species of *Milla* now found mostly under *Brodiaea* and *Leucocoryne*.

CULTIVATION As for *Ipheion*.

***M. biflora*** Cav. To 30cm. Lvs 2–7, 10–50cm, narrow-linear, channelled above and rounded beneath to almost terete, blue-green. Fls 1–6, occasionally 8, to 20cm, snow-white within, green without, fragrant, sessile; perianth seg. 6, 1.5–3.5cm, erect to spreading, overlapping to form a long, campanulate tube 10–20cm long, white or tinged with lilac, with 3, 5, or 7 green central veins or 1 broad central stripe. SW US, C America.

***M. uniflora*** Graham. See *Ipheion uniflorum*.

**Miller, Philip** (1691–1771). Gardener and writer. Miller was born in Deptford or Greenwich and was educated in European languages and the sciences by his father. At an early age he worked in his father's market garden and nursery at Deptford and soon established his own florist's business in St George's Fields in Pimlico. In 1722 Sir Hans Sloane recommended him for the post of Curator of the Chelsea Physic Garden, and Miller held the post for 22 years. Through Miller's work the garden acquired an international reputation for its collection. Miller also undertook a number of pioneering experiments in horticulture; he was the first to discover a method of raising tropical seeds such as the coconut, and he grew flowering plants, including tulips and narcissi, in water-filled bottles. He was also responsible for providing cotton-seed for the cotton plantations of Georgia.

In 1731 Miller published his great *Gardeners Dictionary*, which went through eight editions. It contained descriptions, classifications and histories of plants as well as notes on cultivation and pertinent criticism of contemporary agricultural methods. Miller's concepts of genera and species were largely taken from Tournefort and Ray and, until the publication of the edition of 1768, he did not wholly accept Linnaeus's system of binomial nomenclature.

However, the latter praised Miller's work highly, visited the Physic Garden on three occasions, and named the genus *Milleria* in his honour.

Miller engaged in a voluminous correspondence with native and European botanists, writing to Gilbert White on the subject of melon culture, helping Alexander Pope choose pear trees for his garden, and advising the Duke of Bedford, among others, on garden design. He was a Fellow of the Royal Society and a Member of the Botanic Academy at Florence. Miller gave a number of lectures to the Royal Society and his other publications include *A Gardener's Kalendar* (1732) and, possibly, contributions to the Society of Gardeners' *Catalogus Plantarum* (1730).

**Millettia** Wight & Arn. (For J.A. Millett, 18th-century botanist who made the first collection of *Millettia* in Canton, China.) Leguminosae (Papilionoideae). Some 90 species of lianes, shrubs or trees. Leaves imparipinnate; stipules small, subulate or acicular, caducous, stipels present; leaflets in few to several pairs, opposite or alternate, oblong-lanceolate, generally evergreen, texture often coriaceous. Fls usually in terminal and lateral panicles or racemes; bracts and bracteoles usually falling before anthesis; calyx campanulate, either truncate or with 5 teeth, upper dental pair connate; petals 5, violet, blue, lilac, pink or white, standard large, reflexed or diffuse, glabrous or sericeous, keel blunt, incurved, clawed, wing oblong-falcate, usually auricled and clawed; stamens 9, usually monadelphous, anthers equal, ovate; ovary thread-like, occasionally hirsute, usually sessile, ovules 3–11, style downy at base, glabrous at apex, stigma terminal, small. Fruit linear or oblong, swollen or flat, valves 2, ligneous or coriaceous; seeds 1 to few, reniform or orbicular. E Asia, India, Africa, Madagascar. Z10 unless specified.

CULTIVATION Bearing long pendulous racemes of bloom which much resemble those of *Wisteria*, the tree species are handsome flowering ornamentals, used as lawn and avenue specimens in warm temperate and subtropical climates. *M. stuhlmannii* has been used in street plantings. *M. dura* is a fast growing and floriferous species with good drought resistance, although the wood is somewhat brittle and prone to wind damage. Cultivate as for *Bauhinia*. The climbing *M. reticulata*, bearing dense and fragrant racemes of lavender blue or darker pink-purple flowers, has withstood hard frosts, and with wall protection may be grown where winter temperatures may fall to −15°C/5°F and below.

***M. dura*** Dunn. Small tree or shrub to 13m. Young stems brown-pubesc. Lvs initially rusty-pubesc.; stipules to 8mm; petiole 3–5cm; leaflets 8–9×2–3cm, 15–19, lanceolate-oblong, apex tapering to a point, glabrous above except on midrib and margins, downy beneath. Fls in rusty-pubesc., drooping panicles 10–20cm long; peduncle to 5cm; pedicels to 1.3cm; bracts 1–2mm, oval; bracteoles *c*1mm, oblong; cal. rusty-pubesc., tube 6mm, teeth *c*1mm long, tapering to a point; cor. mauve, standard *c*2.5cm, keel downy beneath, *c*2.4cm; stamens 2–2.4cm, anth. *c*1mm; ovary *c*1.8cm, downy, ovules 8–11. Fr. 14–20×2.1cm, flat, linear-oblong, glabrous. E Africa.

***M. grandis*** (E. Mey) Skeels. Evergreen or deciduous tree to 12m, bark flaky, pale brown. Lvs *c*15cm×10–13cm; petioles velvety, red; leaflets *c*7×1.9cm, in 5 or 6 or, more rarely, 7 pairs, oblong or broadly lanceolate, apex acute, base rounded, glabrous above, thinly sericeous beneath; stipules present, stipels 2 at base of each leaflet stalk. Fls purple. Fr. 15×4cm, erect, rusty-villous then woody. Spring. S Africa (Transkei, Natal).

***M. griftoniana*** Baill. To 17m. Leaflets to 10cm, in 3–4 pairs, oval, apex acuminate, fls in erect racemes to 15cm, deep purple. Fr. 7.5cm or more, narrowly lanceolate. Tropical W Africa.

***M. nitida*** Benth. Tall liane. Branchlets initially rusty-pubesc. Leaflets 0.5–7.5cm, usually 5, ovate or elliptic-oblong, apex tapering to a short tip, leathery, glabrous, lustrous above; petioles 5–10cm. Fls large, densely packed in downy panicles; cal. rusty-pubesc.; cor. purple, standard *c*2.5cm, sericeous beneath, keel long, curved. Fr. 7–10×1–1.5cm, rusty-pubesc., torulose. S China, Hong Kong, Taiwan. Z8.

***M. ovalifolia*** Kurz. Glabrous tree of medium height. Lvs to 45cm; leaflets in 3 pairs, ovate-elliptic, apex tapering to a point, somewhat glaucous beneath. Fls in solitary or grouped, delicate racemes to 7.5cm long; cor. blue, standard to 0.6cm. Fr. to 5cm, rather woody. Burma.

***M. reticulata*** Benth. Tall ascending shrub. Lvs persistent; leaflets 3–9×1.5–5.5cm, 5–9, lanceolate to elliptic, apex blunt, base cordate, glabrous, subcoriaceous; petiolules 2–3mm. Fls large, densely packed in erect, terminal, glabrous or downy panicles 15–20×*c*20cm; cor. rose to blue, standard to 1cm, keel curved. Fr. to 12×1.5cm, elongate. S China, Taiwan. Z8.

***M. stuhlmannii*** Taub. Tree to 20m. Bark smooth, yellow or grey-green. Stipules *c*10×3mm; leaflets to 13×1cm, 7–9, elliptic-obovate, apex rounded or notched, base rounded or cuneate, subglabrous above, sparsely downy beneath. Fls in minutely grey-velutinous, drooping panicles to 25cm long; pedicels to 9mm; cor. glabrous, lilac and somewhat white at base, standard 2.5cm diam., keel 2.2×1.1cm, wings 2.3×1.1cm; fil. sheath 2–2.5cm, anth. to 0.2cm; ovary thickly sericeous, ovules 8–10. Fr. 25–35×3.5–4.7cm, yellow-brown. Malawi, Mozambique.

**Milligania** Hook. f. (For Dr Milligan, 19th-century South African botanist.) Liliaceae (Asphodelaceae). 4–5 species of perennial herbs. Rhizomes short, thick. Stems simple or branched, more or less pilose. Basal leaves tufted, linear-lanceolate, shortly imbricate, coriaceous, usually woolly, widened into thick, prominent sheaths below; stems leaves few, becoming smaller toward apex. Flowers small, campanulate, in a terminal panicle; pedicels short; lower bracts leafy, upper bracts small; perianth segments 6, spreading, subequal, ovate or oblong, shortly united into a tube; stamens fixed to throat of tube, shorter than perianth segments, filaments subulate, anthers ovate, dorsifixed; ovary trilocular; style columnar, trifid above. Fruit a subglobose capsule; seeds angular, black shiny. Tasmania. Z9.

CULTIVATION As for *Ophiopogon*.

***M. densiflora*** Hook. f. Lvs 20–25cm, sparsely covered with white silky hairs. Stems stout, woolly, many-branched. Fls 1.25cm diam. in dense racemes; perianth seg. 0.6cm, white, sometimes flushed mauve; stamens well exserted, anth. yellow. Midsummer.

***M. johnstonii*** Muell. Dwarf. Lvs to 10cm, 5–6, white-woolly, basally sheathing, covering stem. Corymbs small, just exceeding lvs; fls 3–6; fls 0.7cm, erect, white, tube as long as seg., seg. narrowly oblong, obtuse, ascending; stamens shortly exserted from tube, anth. yellow. Midsummer.

***M. longifolia*** Hook. f. Densely tufted. Stems 30–60cm, to 5cm diam., stout, villous, branches ascending. Lvs to 60cm, grass-like, sparsely villous beneath, margin ciliate, closely sheathing at base, bright green. Panicles large, many-fld; bracts large, villous, exceeding pedicels; pedicels arched, covered with silky hairs; fls small, horizontal or ascending; perianth white, tube one-third length of seg., seg. oblong, obtuse, 0.6cm; anth. yellow. Summer.

**Millingtonia** L. (For Thomas Millington (1628–1704), English botanist who wrote on plant physiology and is reputed to have discovered plant sexuality.) Bignoniaceae. 1 species, an evergreen or deciduous tree to 25m. Trunk to 30cm diam., bark cracked, corky. Leaves to 1m, opposite, 2–3-pinnate, pinnae to 6×3cm, lanceolate-elliptic, with pubescent domatia around venation below, apex acuminate, margin entire, undulate or crenate. Flowers white, nocturnal, fragrant in terminal, erect, 10–40cm thyrses; calyx to 4mm, campanulate, truncate, 5-lobed, lobes ovate, acute; corolla 5-lobed, tube to 8cm, base 2mm diam., widening to 5cm diam. at apex, lobes ovate, acute, 1.5cm; stamens 4, unequal, 1 or 1.4cm, inserted at base of throat, slightly exserted; style to 8cm. Capsule to 35×1.75cm, linear, valves flat; seeds to 3.5×1.5cm, discoid, enclosed in wing. SE Asia and E Java through Lesser Sunda Is. and S Celebes. Z10.

CULTIVATION One of the handsomest of tropical flowering trees, *Millingtonia* is widely used in avenue plantings in India. Its strongly fragrant tubular flowers, which resemble those of *Nicotiana*, open pure white and age to pale yellow. Cultivation as for *Jacaranda*.

***M. hortensis*** L. As for the genus.

***M. dubiosa*** Span. See *M. hortensis*.
***M. pinnata*** Blanco. See *Radermachera pinnata*.
***M. quadripinnata*** Blanco. See *Radermachera pinnata*.

**Miltonia** Lindl. (For Lord Fitzwilliam Milton (1786–1857), landowner and orchidologist.) PANSY ORCHID Orchidaceae. Some 20 species of epiphytic orchids allied to *Brassica, Oncidium* and *Odontoglossum*. Rhizome long and creeping or short. Pseudobulbs with 1 or 2 apical leaves, enveloped below by one to several pairs of distichous, often foliaceous sheaths. Leaves linear to elliptic-lanceolate or oblong, subcoriaceous, thin, glabrous, pale to dark green, sometimes fluorescent; petioles short or elongate. Inflorescence axillary, a raceme or rarely a panicle, erect or arching, loosely 1 to many-flowered; flowers small to large, showy, widely spreading; sepals subequal, free or lateral sepals shortly connate at base; petals similar to sepals or often wider; lip broadly spreading from column base, simple or pandurate, base sessile or shortly clawed; disc inconspicuous or lamellate at base; column short, footless, bi-alate or bi-auriculate at apex, bilobed or truncate; anther terminal, opercular, incumbent; pollinia 2, ovoid, waxy. Costa Rica to Ecuador and Brazil. Z10.

CULTIVATION See ORCHIDS.

***M. candida*** Lindl. Resembles *M. clowesii* except sep. and pet. oblong-obtuse; lip shorter than other seg., clasping column at base. Autumn. Brazil.

***M. clowesii*** Lindl. Allied to *M. candida* and *M. cuneata*. Pseudobulbs to 10cm, ovate-oblong, compressed. Lvs to 45×2.5cm, pale green, linear-ligulate, acute. Infl. a raceme, to 45cm, several-fld; fls to 8cm diam.; tepals yellow, heavily blotched and barred chestnut-brown; sep. to 4×1cm, lanceolate, acuminate, slightly undulate; pet. to 3.5×1cm, similar to sep.; lip white at tip, deep purple at base, to 4×2cm, flat, subpandurate, caudate; callus white or yellow with 5–7 keels of unequal length. Autumn. Brazil.

***M. cuneata*** Lindl. Similar to *M. clowesii*. Lvs dark green. Tepals chocolate-brown tipped and barred yellow-green; lip obovate, slightly undulate, white-cream; callus basal, 2-keeled, spotted rose-purple. Winter–spring. Brazil.

***M. flavescens*** Lindl. Rhiz. creeping. Pseudobulbs to 12×2.5cm, ovate-oblong, compressed. Lvs to 35×1.5cm, acute, apiculate, pale green. Infl. a raceme, to 10-fld; peduncle with distichous, pale brown sheaths; bracts to 6.5cm, straw-coloured, glume-like; fls fragrant, to 7.5cm diam., straw-yellow; tepals to 50×5mm, linear-oblong to linear-lanceolate, acute; lip to 2.5cm, yellow, spotted blood-red, ovate-oblong, acute, undulate, base pubesc., transversed by 4–6 radiating lines. Summer–autumn. Brazil.

***M. regnellii*** Rchb. f. Pseudobulbs to 9×1cm, ovate-oblong, compressed, amethyst, pale yellow-green. Lvs to 30×1.5cm, linear-ligulate, acute, bright green. Infl. a raceme, to 40cm, 3–5-fld; fls to 7.5cm diam.; tepals cream suffused rose to lilac or pale amethyst; sep. to 3×1cm, oblong-lanceolate, recurved at apex; pet. wider than sep. elliptic-oblong; lip to 3.5×3.5cm, pale rose streaked lilac or amethyst, margins white, rotund, obscurely trilobed; callus of several radiating yellow lines. Early autumn. Brazil. Darker 'purple-blue' variants are sometimes described as 'Purpurea'.

***M. russelliana*** Lindl. Pseudobulbs ovate-oblong, to 7.5cm, laterally compressed, clustered. Lvs to 25×2.5cm, linear-oblong to linear-lanceolate. Infl. a raceme, to 30cm, erect, several-fld; fls to 5cm diam.; tepals to 3cm, ovate-oblong, red-brown, margins green-yellow; lip oblong, concave, rose-lilac, apex white or pale yellow; disc purple, with 3 raised ridges. Winter–spring. Brazil.

***M. schroederiana*** (Rchb. f.) Veitch. Pseudobulbs to 5cm, ovoid-oblong. Lvs to 20cm, linear-oblong, acute. Infl. a raceme, erect, to 50cm, several-fld; fls fragrant, to 6cm diam.; tepals chestnut brown, marked and tipped pale yellow; sep. to 30×5mm, linear-lanceolate, acute, margins revolute; pet. similar to sep., to 25×5mm, inclined on either side of dorsal sep.; lip rose-purple at base, white above to 2.5×1.5cm, subpandurate, slightly convex; callus of 3 protuberances; column white, yellow dorsally, wings narrow. C America.

***M. spectabilis*** Lindl. Rhiz. stout, creeping. Pseudobulbs to 7×2.5cm, spaced at short intervals, strongly compressed, pale green-yellow, ovate-oblong. Lvs to 13×2cm, linear-ligulate, thin, apex rounded, pale yellow-green. Infl. to 25cm, erect, enclosed by imbricate, flattened sheaths; fls solitary, flat, to 10cm diam.; sep. to 4×1.5cm, white, often tinged rose at base, lanceolate-oblong; pet. similar to sep. with white patch at base, to 3.5×1.5cm; lip rose-violet, margins white or pale rose, to 5×4.5cm, obovate-orbicular; callus yellow with pink axial lines, 3-keeled, column white, pink-violet at apex; anther white; pollinia yellow. Autumn. Brazil. var. ***bicolor*** hort. Fls larger than species type; lip with large blotch of violet on upper half. var. ***moreliana*** (Warn.) Henfr. Fls deep plum-purple; lip streaked and shaded rose, deeply veined. This form more usually encountered in cultivation.

***M. warscewiczii*** Rchb. f. Rhiz. abbreviated. Pseudobulbs to 12.5×2.5cm, oblong-cylindric, strongly compressed, dark green. Lvs to 33×3.5cm, linear-oblong, acute or obtuse, bright green. Infl. a panicle or rarely a raceme, to 54cm, suberect to arcuate, exceeding lvs, often loosely branched, many-fld; fls widely spreading; tepals cinnamon, white or yellow at apex, to 2.5×1.5cm, oblong-spathulate, margins undulate; lip to 3×2.5cm, rose-purple, tinged yellow and red-brown, margins white, ovate-suborbicular or suborbicular-obovate, deeply bilobed at apex; disc with 2 small yellow teeth; column short, stout, wings rounded. Peru, Colombia, Costa Rica.

***M.* grexes and cultivars** (see also under *Colmanara, Miltassia, Miltonidium* and *Odontonia*).

*M.* Alexandre Dumas: pale green lvs; fls magnificent clear yellow with red-brick centre.

*M.* Anjou 'St Patrick': pale green lvs; fls deep crimson with some white stripes spreading from the centre.

*M.* Anne Warne: yellow-green lvs and pseudobulbs; sep. and pet. shiny maroon red, raspberry red lip with darker veins; warm growing.

*M.* Bleuana: one of the early primary hybrids; fls white, deep pink spots at the base of the pet. and orange mask on the lip.

*M.* Bluntii: lvs and pseudobulbs yellow-green; fls lilac pink with a darker lip.

*M.* Brutips: very floriferous grex; fls dark red with white border to all parts, mask on the lip darker red and bordered in white.

*M.* Charlesworthii 'Raphael': an early primary hybrid; fls white with deep spots at the base of the pet.; lip with a dark red mask; many other clones in pale colours but with the spots at the base of the pet.

*M.* Celle 'Wasserfal': pale green lvs; fls deep red-purple, lip streaked with lines and dots in white giving a waterfall-effect.

*M.* Derek Strauss: pale green lvs; fls very large, pastel shades including yellows and pinks; several awarded clones.

*M.* Edwige Sabourin 'Neige': pale green lvs; pure white fls, very large and prolific.

*M.* Emotion: pale green lvs; there are many clones of white, pink, lavender and various shades of pink-orange fls; 'Monique' has very large fls and 'Red-breast' is white with a brick red mask.

*M.* Eros 'Kensington': pale green lvs; rich red-purple fls with a white border.

*M.* Gascogne 'Vienne': pale green lvs; fls pink with a crimson mask outlined in white.

*M.* Gattonense: an old hybrid but still producing fine progeny; white fls with yellow mask on lip.

*M.* Guanabara: yellow-green lvs and pseudobulbs; flowers in long spikes, with straw-coloured sep. and pet. and pink lip.

*M.* Hamburg: pale green lvs; fls with deep red sep. and pet. and a much paler lip, bordered in white and with a yellow and white mask.

*M.* Hannover 'Mont Millais': pale green lvs; fls bright red outlined in white, with yellow mask.

*M.* Hyeana: an early hybrid with well-shaped fls which are white with yellow mask.

*M.* Jean Sabourin 'Vulcain': pale green lvs; prolific bloomer with many deep burgundy-red fls with brown mask.

*M.* Jersey: pale green lvs; brilliant red fls.

*M.* Lambton Castle 'Cooksbridge': shapely fls in deep raspberry red, the small orange-red mask outlined in white.

*M.* Lyceana 'Stamperland': pale green lvs; fls prolific, white with large purple spots at base of the pet., yellow mask on lip.

*M.* Piccadilly 'Micheline': pale green lvs; fls deep rich red with mask outlined in white.

*M.* Robert Strauss Ardingly: white or creamy yellow fls with small red spots at the base of the pet. and orange-brown mask on the lip.

*M.* Saint Helier 'Trinity': lvs pale green; fls raspberry red with a very dark mask on the lip outlined in white.

*M.* Seine Diamant 'Medellin': pale green lvs; pure white fls with a faint touch of pink at the centre.

*M.* Storm 'La Tuilerie': pale green lvs; rich red fls with a yellow mask outlined in white.

*M.* Violet 'Tears': large fls with raspberry pink sep. and pet., lip white with pink border and large red mask which continues with spots and streaks across the lip.

***M. endresii*** (Rchb. f.) Nichols. See *Miltoniopsis warscewiczii*.
***M. moreliana*** Warn. See *M. spectabilis* var. *moreliana*.
***M. phalaenopsis*** (Lind. & Rchb. f.) Nicols. See *Miltoniopsis phalaenopsis*.
***M. roezlii*** (Rchb. f.) Nichols. See *Miltoniopsis roezlii*.
***M. superba*** Schltr. See *Miltoniopsis warscewiczii*.
***M. vexillaria*** (Rchb. f.) Nichols. See *Miltoniopsis vexillaria*.

**×Miltonidium**. *(Miltonia × Oncidium.)* Orchidaceae. Intergeneric orchid hybrids most of which will tolerate intermediate conditions. Plants consist of a group of compressed pseudobulbs growing from a basal rhizome, each with one or two leaves at its apex and two or more leaf-like sheaths arising at its base. Inflorescences arise in the axils of these sheaths and may be simple or branched. Flowers very varied in shape and often conspicuously marked in a variety of colours.

×*M.* Richard Peterson: erect branching sprays of many medium size fls; sep. and pet. yellow heavily dotted with brown, lip large, clear bright yellow with some brown spots around the crest.

**Miltoniopsis** Godef.-Leb. Orchidaceae. 5 species of epiphytic or lithophytic orchids closely allied to *Miltonia*. Rhizome short. Pseudobulbs clustered, unifoliate, subtended basally by many distichous, imbricate, foliaceous sheaths. Leaves narrowly linear to elliptic-lanceolate. Inflorescence a raceme, axillary, erect to arcuate, 1- to few-flowered; flowers large, showy, flattened; tepals spreading; petals reflexed near middle; lip large, flattened, basally auriculate, joined to column base by central keel; column short with dorsal keel, wingless, footless; anther incumbent, subglobose, pollinia 2, obpyriform; stigma orbicular to subquadrate; rostellum bifid, broadly triangular. Costa Rica, Panama, Venezuela, Ecuador, Colombia. Z10.

CULTIVATION See ORCHIDS.

***M. phalaenopsis*** (Lind. & Rchb. f.) Garay & Dunsterv. Pseudobulbs to 3.5cm, ovoid, strongly compressed, pale green-grey. Lvs to 22×0.5cm, pale green or glaucous, linear, acuminate. Racemes shorter than lvs, slender, 3–5-fld; fls to 6.5cm diam.; tepals pure white; sep. to 2×1cm, elliptic-oblong, acute; pet. wider than sep., elliptic, obtuse; lip to 2.5×3cm, white blotched and streaked purple-crimson or pale purple, 4-lobed, lateral lobes rounded, midlobe emarginate, flabellate; callus of 3 small, blunt teeth with yellow spot on either side. Late spring. Colombia.

***M. roezlii*** (Rchb. f.) Godef.-Leb. Pseudobulbs to 6.5cm, ovoid-oblong, compressed. Lvs to 30×1.5cm, pale green with dark green longitudinal lines below, linear, acute. Racemes to 30cm, slender, 2–5-fld; fls to 10cm diam.; sep. to 5×2cm, white, ovate-oblong, acuminate; pet. similar, to 5×2.5cm, white blotched deep wine-purple at base; lip to 5×5.5cm, white, orange-yellow at base, widely obcordate, sinus apiculate, either side of base with corniculate auricle, 3 raised ridges on disc with 2 small dorsal teeth. Colombia.

***M. vexillaria*** (Rchb. f.) Godef.-Leb. To 30cm. Pseudobulbs to 6×2cm, oblong-ellipsoid, strongly compressed, grey-green. Lvs to 25×2.5cm, linear-oblong to linear-lanceolate, acute, pale green. Racemes to 30cm, lateral from base of pseudobulb, loosely 4–6-fld; fls large, to 10cm diam.; tepals rose-pink or white flushed rose-pink; sep. to 3×1.5cm, obovate-oblong, recurved above; pet. similar to sep., often slightly wider, margins white; lip much larger than sep., white or pale rose, deep rose on disc, suborbicular or reniform, with deep, triangular apical sinus, biauriculate at base; callus yellow, small, tridentate, bilobed at base; column short, wingless. Colombia, Ecuador.

***M. warscewiczii*** (Rchb. f.) Garay & Dunsterv. Pseudobulbs to 6cm, ovate-oblong, grey-green, compressed, distant on rhiz. Lvs to 30cm, linear-oblong or linear-lanceolate, acute, pale green. Racemes to 30cm, loosely 3–6-fld; fls to 7cm diam., cream-white, each seg. with a rose-purple blotch at base; sep. and pet. to 3×1.5cm, ovate-elliptic, acute; lip to 3.5×3.5cm, widely pandurate, dilated, with 2 small, rounded basal lobes, midlobe emarginate; callus yellow, with 3 short pubesc. ridges; column wings pale rose, narrow. Winter. Costa Rica.

For synonymy see *Miltonia* and *Odontoglossum*.

**Mimetes** Salisb. (From Gk *mimetes*, mimic, on account of it resemblance to other species.) Proteaceae. 12 species of erect or decumbent undershrubs. Stems simple, tomentose or villous. Leaves oblong-elliptic or ovate, entire or 3-dentate at apex, densely adpressed silky-tomentose or villous. Capitula sessile, solitary in upper leaf-axils, 3–12-flowered; involucral bracts usually shorter than flowers, frequently coloured, membranous or coriaceous, often villous or tomentose; receptacle densely setose; perianth tube very short or absent, perianth segments 4, filiform or linear-filiform, often villous, limb linear or oblong-linear, villous or occasionally glabrescent; stamens 4, filaments short and fleshy, often fused with perianth; ovary solitary, pubescent; style usually glabrous, more or less jointed or sinuate at junction with stigma; ovule solitary. Fruits ovoid, glabrescent, pericarp slightly hardened. S Africa (S & SW Cape). Z9.

CULTIVATION As for *Protea*.

***M. cucullata*** R. Br. Stems 120–150cm, sometimes decumbent, branches densely tomentose. Lvs 3–7.5×0.4–1.2cm, oblong or oblong-lanceolate, obtuse at base, 3–5-fid at apex, or occasionally entire, coriaceous, pubesc. when young, glabrous when fully mature, indistinctly 3-veined. Capitula sessile, 5cm long, 4–10-fld, axillary toward branch apices; involucral bracts 3–4-seriate, linear or lanceolate, acuminate, minutely pubesc. to subglabrous; receptacle long-setose; perianth tube 4mm, pubesc. within, seg. filiform, 3mm, pilose, limb 5–6mm, linear, villous; style more or less flattened, 5cm. S Africa (Cape Province).

***M. lyrigera*** Knight. See *M. cucullata*.

**Mimosa** L. (From Gk *mimos*, mimic; the leaves of many species resemble animals in their sensitivity.) Leguminosae (Mimosoideae). Some 400 species of spiny herbs, shrubs or small trees; stems divaricate, climbing, trailing or erect, thorns internodal to subnodal and paired, usually laterally compressed, curved, broadened at base, usually armed. Leaves clustered from spurs and/or alternate, bipinnate often exhibiting steep movements and sensitive to touch; leaflets numerous, symmetric or asymmetric; stipules acicular to lanceolate, usually inconspicuous, not spiny; petioles usually pulvinate. Flowers sessile, white, pink or lilac, mostly 4–5-merous, in stalked, rounded heads or, less frequently, spikes or racemes, from spurs or leaf axils; calyx tubular to campanulate, lobes 4–6, narrow, usually bristly; petals 4 or 5, valvate, somewhat connate or free; stamens to 10; ovary sessile, stipitate, 2- to many-ovuled, sometimes villous, style filiform, oblique, stigma small, terminal. Fruit dehiscent, oblong, compressed, straight to curved or twisted, margins straight, undulate or torulose to moniliform, often prickly, persistent, valves 2, opening separately from sutures either as a unit or segments; seeds flat, orbicular. C & S America, S US, Asia, Tropical & E Africa. Z9.

CULTIVATION Frost-tender plants grown for their finely divided foliage and flowers, they are suitable for outdoor cultivation only in subtropical and warm temperate zones but are amenable to pot cultivation under glass in cool temperate areas. *M. argentea* is an attractive climber, especially effective where the silvery grey undersides of the leaves can be seen from below. The long slender shoots of the prostrate *M. marginata* are also seen to best advantage if allowed to trail from the heights of a large hanging basket.

*M. pudica* is cultivated as a home, greenhouse and experimental novelty; it exhibits 'sleep movements' at night, when its leaflets fold together and petioles droop: this condition can be quickly induced by touching the plant or producing a rapid drop in temperature or air pressure. The contact stimulus is transmitted through the phloem of the petiole pulvinus, which contains fibres of living wood. The reaction may be the result of loss of turgor in pulvinus cells or the work of contractile proteins. Similar movements can be observed in *M. polycarpa* and *M. sensitiva*. Maximum sensitivity is displayed at temperatures between 25–30°C/77–86°F. Grow under glass in a loam-based medium with additional sand and leafmould or equivalent, with bright filtered light, medium humidity and a minimum temperature of 13–16°C/55–60°F. Water plentifully and apply liquid feed to established plants weekly when in growth; water just moderately in winter. Damp down and ventilate freely at temperatures above 18–21°C/65–70°F. Give climbing species the support of canes or wires.

Propagate by seed, pre-soaked in hot water and sown uncovered in early spring at 18–21°C/65–70°F. Shrubby species can also be propagated by semi-ripe cuttings in sand in a closed case with bottom heat.

Susceptible to dry atmospheres and to cold draughts and prone to infestations of mealybug and red spider mite.

***M. argentea*** hort ex L.H. Bail. Climber. Young shoots flushed pink. Lvs with 2–3 pairs of pinnae; leaflets 40, tipped pink, silvery grey flushed pink beneath. Fls red. Summer. Brazil.

***M. marginata*** Lindl. non Lam. Prostrate shrub with long, slender shoots. Leaflets ciliate. Fls purple, the heads on long stalks. Subtropical S America.

***M. pigra*** L. Prickly, thicket-forming, pubesc. shrub, 1–4m; prickles nearly straight, broad, white, primarily on stems. Pinnae 4–6 pairs; leaflets 3–4mm, 15–25 pairs, crowded, oblong, nearly symmetric. Racemes axillary and terminal; fl. heads to 1cm diam., fascicled, fragrant, bright lilac pink fading to white, ovoid to capitate; cal. 1mm; cor. 2mm. Fr. 4–6×1cm, oblong, straight; valves conspicuously hispid and velvety, dehiscing as 7–15 narrow seg. leaving the persistent, empty margins. S Texas, tropics and warm regions of both hemispheres.

***M. polycarpa*** Kunth. Much-branched thorny shrub or subshrub, to 3m rather like a taller and coarser *M. pudica*. Lvs sensitive, 1 pair of pinnae; leaflets to 1.6cm. Fls pink to lilac in globose heads to 2.5cm diam. Fr. usually hairy on face and marginally bristly. S America. var. ***spegazzinii*** (Pirotta) Burkart. Leaflets 1.25cm, minutely downy.

***M. pudica*** L. SENSITIVE PLANT; TOUCH-ME-NOT; SHAME PLANT; LIVE-AND-DIE; HUMBLE PLANT; ACTION PLANT. Prostrate or semi-erect herb, 0.3–0.8m, often forming small compact bush to 0.6m; branches glabrous or pubesc., heavily armed with broad-based, white then black-tipped recurved thorns. Lvs small, sensitive, bipinnate; leaflets 10–25 pairs, grey-green, soft-textured, oblong; petioles to 4cm. Infl. axillary or terminal; fls pale pink to lilac, in stalked heads to 2cm diam.; cor. lobes 4; stamens 4. Fr. 1.3–1.8cm×3mm, oblong, prickly margined, ultimately separating into 1-seeded seg. Summer. S Mexico to C America, W Indies, Hawaii, Fiji, Australia. Z9.

***M. sensitiva*** L. SENSITIVE PLANT. Semi-climbing, prickly evergreen shrub to 2m. Lvs composed of 2 unequal pinnae; leaflets ovate, acute, glabrous above, adpressed-hairy beneath. Fls purple. Tropical America.

***M.contorti-siliqua*** Vell. See *Enterolobium contortisiliqua.*
***M.cyclocarpa*** Jacq. See *Enterolobium cyclocarpa.*
***M.fagifolia*** L. See *Inga laurina.*
***M.illinoensis*** Michx. See *Desmanthus illinoensis.*
***M.inga*** L. See *Inga vera.*
***M.juliiflora*** Sw. See *Prosopis juliiflora.*
***M.laurina*** Sw. See *Inga laurina.*
***M.natans*** L. f. See *Neptunia oleracea.*
***M.nemu*** Poir. See *Albizia julibrissin.*
***M.plena*** L. See *Neptunia plena.*
***M.spegazzinii*** Pirotta. See *M.polycarpavar. spegazzinii.*
***M.ynga*** Vell. See *Inga edulis.*

**Mimulus** L. (Perhaps a diminutive of Lat. *mimus*, a mimic actor, referring to a fanciful resemblance of the markings of the corolla to a grinning face; or from *mimo*, ape, referring to gaping mouth of corolla.) MONKEY FLOWER; MUSK. Scrophulariaceae. 150 species of annual or perennial herbs, of erect or diffuse habit, or rarely shrubs. Leaves opposite, entire to dentate or occasionally laciniate. Flowers axillary or on spike-like raceme, bracteoles absent; sepals 5, generally united almost throughout, tube usually inflated and plicate-angled, teeth equal or uppermost longest; corolla 2-lipped, throat open or closed by a palate, yellow, red, purple or violet; filaments 4, didynamous, all antheriferous; stigmas distinct and lamelliform, or adhering by margins into funneliform structure. Capsule cylindric, loculicidal, septum unruptured to deeply splitting in dehiscence; seeds wingless, tinged yellow, reticulate to almost smooth. Mostly America, also South Africa & Asia.

CULTIVATION Taller herbaceous species are best suited to informal plantings in damp border, woodland, bog garden and by ponds where their invasive habit will not overtake more delicate plants; smaller spp., including alpines such as *M.primuloides*, which occur at fairly high altitudes on wet, rocky mountain terrain, are suitable as edging or ground-cover in moist border, rock garden or by small pools. *M.guttatus* and the less invasive *M.ringens* are particularly successful when grown as marginals or in shallow water. Included within this group of damp-soil lovers are the garden hybrids (*M.×hybridus*), derived primarily from *M.luteus* and *M.guttatus*, although tending to be more compact than their parents. A very few spp., including *M.cardinalis* and *M.lewisii*, tolerate slightly drier but nevertheless rich soils in light woodland shade: some, like the annuals *M.brevipes* and *M.fremontii*, prefer dry soils; the desert-native, *M.fremontii*, demands them. These spp. are useful for dry situations in shade or sun.

The shrubby spp. (e.g. *M.aurantiacus*) are frost-tender inhabitants of chaparral vegetation in California and Baja California: these are grown under glass in cold areas or in the open garden where winters are mild, given the protection of a warm wall and a dry, sunny spot. Many of the herbaceous spp. (among them some of the showiest garden hybrids) are not reliably frost-hardy, particularly where the ground freezes hard: those from the west coast of the US and from South America are most vulnerable. *M.cardinalis* and *M.ringens* are tolerant of temperatures to −7°C/19°F; *M.moschatus* to −15°C/5°F, *M.guttatus* to temperatures almost as low. Some, although frost-tender, may self-sow and perpetuate themselves in this way.

Where winters are severe, *Mimulus* spp. are best treated as annuals for summer bedding display or flowering pot-plants for windowsills and cool glasshouses: *M.×hybridus*, *M.×burnettii*, *M.cupreus*, *M.luteus*, *M.moschatus*, *M.variegatus* and their cvs are particularly successful when used in this way. Where grown in the open garden in cold areas, take softwood cuttings in summer as an insurance policy or protect plants in the open with cloches. Plant out in late spring after the last frosts, into moist soils in a partly shaded position, incorporating additional organic matter: where the ground is perpetually moist or boggy, *Mimulus* spp. thrive with full exposure to the sun. Grow alpine spp. in a cool, moist position, in gritty soils. Divide frequently, and trim in late summer when necessary. Prune pot-grown specimens in late winter; repot, and start into growth at 13°C/55°F, ventilating freely whenever possible: water plentifully when growing strongly and plunge in the open during the summer months. Feed fortnightly with a dilute liquid fertiliser when the roots fill the pots.

Sow seed of all spp. at 13–16°C/55–60°F under glass and covered very lightly with grit or sieved soil. *M.cupreus*, *M.luteus* and *M.variegatus* sown in late winter, will flower in the same year. Other spp. are sown in spring. For winter/spring flowering annuals in pots, sow in the autumn and overwinter under glass. Seed may also be sown *in situ* after the last frosts. Increase herbaceous spp. and cultivars by division in spring or by 5cm/2in. softwood cuttings in spring and summer. Propagate shrubby spp. by semi-ripe cuttings in late summer, rooted in a closed propagating case. Susceptible to *Botrytis cinerea*: spray fortnightly in winter with an appropriate fungicide and pick over regularly in winter to remove diseased and dying foliage.

***M.alsinoides*** Douglas ex Benth. CHICKWEED MONKEY FLOWER. Annual herb, often tinged purple, somewhat glandular-pubesc. to glabrescent. Stems 5–25cm, ascending or decumbent, very slender, often much-branched. Lvs 1–2.5cm, ovate to oblong, minutely dentate, rounded or truncate at base, petioles approximately length of lamina, veins palmate. Pedicels 1–3cm; cal. 6–8mm, slightly plicate-angled, upper lobes acute to 0.5mm, lower generally rounded, slightly longer; cor. 10–12mm, yellow, throat narrowly campanulate, ventrally flattened, faintly 2-ridged, glabrous, orifice open, upper lobes ascending, lower longer with large dark purple or crimson spot at base of central lobe; anth. glabrous. Capsule 5–6mm, not dehiscing though septum apex. Spring–early summer. America, Vancouver Is. to California.

***M.aurantiacus*** Curtis. BUSH MONKEY FLOWER; ORANGE BUSH MONKEY FLOWER. Glutinous shrub. Stems 60–120cm, much-branched, woody, finely glandular-pubesc. Lvs 3–7cm, oblong or lanceolate-oblong, serrate, tapered to base, sessile, green and glabrous above, paler and finely pilose beneath. Pedicels 7–15mm, finely glandular-pubesc.; cal. 2–2.5cm, tube ridged and slightly winged on angles, distally somewhat inflated, lobes lanceolate, uppermost 7mm, others half that; cor. 3.5–4.5cm, orange or deep yellow, glutinous without, throat campanulate-funneliform, about as long as narrow tube, with 2 ventral low orange, minutely pubesc. ridges, lobes rounded or erose; anth. glabrous; stigmas rather unequal, minutely fimbriate. Capsule 20mm, dehiscing throughout, splitting septum to base. Spring–summer. S Oregon to California. Z8.

***M.brevipes*** Benth. WIDE-THROATED YELLOW MONKEY FLOWER. Annual herb, more or less minutely glandular-pubesc. Stems erect, 40–100cm. Lvs to 10cm, basal lvs broadly oblong to obovate, stem lvs elliptic-lanceolate or linear-lanceolate, apex acute to attenuate, attenuate at base to sessile, minutely dentate to entire, bright green, veins pinnate. Pedicels 0.5–1cm; cal. 2–2.5cm, green plicate-ridged, troughs paler, lobes lanceolate, acuminate to attenuate, uppermost sep. 9–12mm, distally upward-curving, lowest pair 3–5mm; cor. 2.5–4cm, funneliform, clear yellow with maroon spots within, particularly ventrally, glabrous without, pubesc. within on 2 ventral ridges and at base of lowest lobe, lobes broadly rounded; anth. glabrous; stigmas minutely ciliate. Capsule 9–13mm, dehiscing dorsally and ventrally, splitting septum. Spring–summer. California & Baja California.

***M.×burnetii*** hort. *(M.cupreus × M.luteus.)* Perenn. herb. Stems tufted, to 30cm. Lvs ovate to oblong, palmately veined. Fls copper-yellow; cor. throat yellow, palate spotted. Garden origin (Aberdeen, *c*1901). Z7.

***M.cardinalis*** Douglas. SCARLET MONKEY FLOWER. Perenn. herb. Stems 40–120cm, erect, freely branched, hirsute, scarcely glandular. Lvs ovate to oblong-elliptic, minutely sharply sinuate-dentate, glandular-pubesc., upper amplexicaul at base, largest 7–11cm, veins 3–5, longitudinal. Pedicels 5–8cm; cal. 2.5–3cm, angular-winged, lobes almost equal, acute, 3–5mm; cor. 4.5–5cm, strongly bilabiate, upper lip arched and ascending, lower lips decurved-reflexed, lobes scarlet, throat narrow, tinged yellow, with 2 ventral yellow hairy ridges; stamens ciliate, exserted; stigmas minutely fimbriate. Capsules 16–18mm, dehiscing through apex of septum. Summer. Oregon to California and Nevada, Baja California. 'Aurantiacus' ('Orange Perfection'): fls fiery orange-red. 'Grandiflora': fls dark red. 'Roseus': fls very large, pink with dark spots. 'Roseus Superbus': fls large, dark pink-red. Z7.

***M.cupreus*** Dombrain. Annual herb, compact or more or less dwarf, glabrous or minutely pubesc. Stems 10–30cm, freely branched from base terete. Lvs 15–30×8–15mm, elliptic to subrhombic-ovate, irregularly coarsely serrate, sessile or subsessile, veins 3–5, diverting from base. Fls copious; pedicels generally shorter than subtending lvs, occasionally much longer; cal. campanulate, more or less red-spotted, lobes acute-triangular, upper largest, obtuse; cor. 2.5–3.5cm, tube yellow, throat dilated, lower side of lower lip spotted red, lobes spreading, golden yellow ageing to brilliant copper. Capsule constricted at base; seeds longitudinally striate. Summer. S Chile. Cvs listed under this name are now listed under *M.×hybridus*.

***M.fremontii*** (Benth.) A. Gray. Annual herb, glandular-pubesc. to glandular-villous. Stems 5–20cm, erect. Lvs to 2.5cm, spathulate to oblanceolate or oblong-lanceolate, obtuse, shallowly dentate to entire, cuneate at base, sessile, veins longitudinal. Pedicels 2–4mm; cal. strongly winged on ridges, 8–10mm, lobes acuminate to somewhat cordate, uppermost 2–3mm, others 1.5–2mm; cor.

2–2.5mm, broadly funneliform, crimson or deep pink tinged purple, pubesc. without, glabrous within except for ventral ridges, ventral ridges 2, yellow, minutely pubesc.; throat deep purple except ventrally, where yellow with purple spots, lobes rounded-truncate, slightly retuse; anth. glabrous; stigmas equal, minutely ciliate. Capsule 8–10mm, dehiscing throughout dorsally, splitting septum to base. Spring–summer. California to N Baja California.

***M. guttatus*** Fisch. ex DC. COMMON LARGE MONKEY FLOWER. Annual or occasionally bienn. herb, glabrous except for infl. Stems 40–100cm, erect or decumbent, branched, sometimes stoloniferous. Lvs variable, 1.5–15cm, mostly obovate to subrotund, minutely sinuate-dentate or sometimes pinnatifid-dentate towards base, lower lvs on petioles sometimes longer than lamina, upper sessile. Infl. a several-fld raceme, finely glandular-pubesc.; pedicels 2–6cm; cal. 2cm, strongly plicate-angled, lobes broadly triangular, acute, uppermost 4–6mm, lower shorter, lowest pair finally upcurved; cor. 3–4.5cm, bright yellow, throat with ventral pair of large red to purple-brown-spotted hairy ridges joining distally to form palate almost or totally closing orifice, lower lip longer, its lobes deflexed-spreading; anth. glabrous; stigmas minutely fimbriate. Capsule 10–12mm, stalked, not dehiscing through septum apex. Spring–summer. Alaska to Mexico. 'A.T. Johnson': to 15cm; fls yellow spotted red. Z6.

***M. ×hybridus*** hort. ex Siebert & Voss. *(M. luteus × M. guttatus.)* Fls large, colour variable. 'Andean Nymph': fls pink with cream-tipped pet. 'Bee's Dazzler': brilliant crimson-red. 'Brilliant': fls deep purple-crimson. Calypso Hybrids: fls large, burgundy, scarlet and gold. 'Duplex': calyx enlarged, colourful. 'Fireflame': bright flame red. 'Highland Pink': fls rich pink. 'Highland Red': fls deep red. 'Highland Yellow': fls yellow. 'Hose in Hose': fls soft tan, one sitting inside the other. 'Inschriach Crimson': dwarf, carpet-forming; fls crimson. 'Leopard': yellow, spotted rust. 'Malibu': to 25cm, growth strong; fls orange. 'Mandarin': fls bright orange, abundant. 'Nanus': habit dwarf; lvs glossy; fls bright orange to gold, with red throat. 'Old Rose': to 15cm; fls bright red. 'Queen's Prize': dwarf; fls large, in bright colours, many spotted and blotched. 'Royal Velvet': to 20cm; fls large velvety, mahogany red with gold throats speckled mahogany. 'Roter Kaiser' ('Red Emperor'): to 20cm high, fls crimson to scarlet. 'Shep': fls large, yellow splashed brown. 'Whitecroft Scarlet': fls vermilion. 'Wisley Red': to 15cm; fls velvety blood red. Z6.

***M. lewisii*** Pursh GREAT PURPLE MONKEY FLOWER. Perenn. herb, glandular-pubesc. Stem erect, 30–90cm. Lvs 3–7cm, oblong-elliptic, sinuately minutely dentate, lower obscurely petiolate, others tapered to amplexicaul base, veins 3–5, longitudinal. Pedicels stout, 3–10cm; cal. angular-ribbed, 2–3cm, lobes almost equal, triangular-aristate, 4–6mm; cor. 2–5cm, lobes scarcely differentiated, magenta or rarely white, throat campanulate with 2 ventral yellow hairy ridges and maroon spots; anthers ciliate; stigmas minutely fimbriate. Capsule 14mm, dehiscing through apex of septum. Summer. NW America (Alaska to California, east to Montana & Colorado). 'Albus': fls white. Z5.

***M. longiflorus*** (Nutt.) Grant. SALMON BUSH MONKEY FLOWER. Glutinous shrub. Stems 30–90cm or more, much-branched, woody, pubesc. Lvs 4–8cm, lanceolate or oblanceolate, minutely serrate to entire, margins sometimes revolute, tapered to base, glutinous-pubesc., paler beneath. Pedicels 2–7mm, glutinous-pubesc.; cal. 2.5–3.5cm, ridged, tube inflated, lobes linear-lanceolate, uppermost 7–9mm, others half that; cor. 5–6cm, cream to yellow tinged salmon, glandular or glutinous without, glabrous within, throat campanulate-funnelform, about as long as narrow tube, with 2 ventral low orange ridges, lobes rounded; anth. glabrous; stigmas almost equal, minutely ciliate. Capsule 15mm, dehiscing throughout, splitting septum to base. Spring–summer. S California to N Baja California. Z9.

***M. luteus*** L. MONKEY MUSK; YELLOW MONKEY FLOWER. Perenn. herb, usually without distinct rootstock, glabrous. Stems 10–30cm, prostrate or decumbent to rarely ascending, robust, hollow, sometimes glandular but not clammy, rooting at lower nodes. Lvs 2–3cm, numerous, broadly ovate to oblong, dentate, veins 5–7, palmate. Cal. 5-angled, 5-dentate; cor. 2–5cm, yellow, with deep red or purple spots. Summer. Chile; naturalized elsewhere, including GB. Dwarf perenn. with densely matted stolons; stems 2.5–5cm; fls 2–3cm, generally solitary, rarely to 4. Z7.

***M. moschatus*** Douglas. MUSK FLOWER; MUSK PLANT. Perenn. herb, glandular-pilose; rhiz. creeping, spreading. Stems 10–40cm, decumbent to diffuse. Lvs to 2.5cm, lanceolate-ovate to oblong-ovate, entire to remotely sinuate-dentate, truncate or rounded at base, shortly petiolate, thin, veins pinnate. Pedicels filiform, 1–4cm; cal. winged on angles, 8–11mm, lobes lanceolate, 2–4mm, somewhat unequal, throat oblique; cor. 18–25mm, pale yellow, throat tubular, finely brown-spotted and streaked with black, with 2 ventral ridges, pilose, lobes similar, spreading; anth. scarcely pubesc. Capsule 6mm, not dehiscing through septum. Summer. British Columbia to Newfoundland, S to W Virginia and California. Traditionally this plant was cult. for its distinctive musky scent, but since about 1914 clones in cultivation are odourless. 'Harisonii': fls larger than type, 3.5–4cm diam. Z7.

***M. primuloides*** Benth. Perenn. herb, rhizomatous, rosulate or short-stemmed, downy. Stems erect or ascending, often stoloniferous, scape-like, to 10cm. Lvs to 1–4.5cm, oblanceolate to elliptic-obovate, entire to distally dentate or minutely dentate, cuneate to sessile at base, glabrous or villous above, veins 3, longitudinal. Fls solitary, small; cal. slightly ridged, 6–7mm, lobes 1–2mm, minutely mucronate, ciliate; cor. 15–20mm, yellow, throat narrowly campanulate, palate deeper yellow and densely hairy, ventral side freely brown-spotted, spots mostly small, one sometimes larger, orifice open, lobes notched and spreading; anth. ciliate. Capsule 6–7mm, dehiscing through apex of septum. Summer. Washington to California, east to Idaho, Utah and Arizona. Z4.

***M. puniceus*** (Nutt.) Steud. RED BUSH MONKEY FLOWER. Glutinous shrub. Stems 60–150cm, erect or ascending, much-branched, woody, minutely pubesc. Lvs 3–10cm, lanceolate, entire or lower undulate-serrate, tapered to base, sessile, slightly paler beneath, minutely pubesc. Pedicels 10–25mm, finely pubesc.; cal. 2–2.5cm, ridged, distally somewhat wider, lobes linear, uppermost 6–8mm, others half that; cor. 3.5–4.5cm, scarlet to carmine or salmon-orange, minutely pubesc. and somewhat glutinous without, glabrous within, throat narrowly campanulate, about 1.5× length of narrow tube, with 2 ventral narrow orange to flame-scarlet ridges, lobes truncate, emarginate or slightly lobed; anth. glabrous; stigmas rather unequal, minutely ciliate. Capsule 20mm, dehiscing throughout, splitting septum to base. Spring–summer. California to N Baja California. Z9.

***M. ringens*** L. ALLEGHENY MONKEY FLOWER. Perenn. herb, glabrous. Stems to 1m, simple or branched above, 4-angled or very narrowly winged. Lvs 5–10cm, lanceolate to narrowly oblong or oblanceolate, acute or acuminate at apex, tapered or rounded at base, sessile and amplexicaul, margins obscurely crenate, reduced upwards, ultimately merely to bracts on some specimens. Pedicels solitary in upper axils, divergent, erect or upcurved when mature, 2–4cm; bractlets absent; cal. 10–15mm, lobes short, broadly ovate to semicircular at base, abruptly prolonged into short sublinear tip; cor. 25–30mm, violet-blue, rarely pink or white, throat very narrow. Summer. N America. Z3.

***M. tilingii*** Reg. LARGER MOUNTAIN MONKEY FLOWER. Perenn. herb, forming dense mats, glabrous or almost so; rhizomes slender. Stems 5–30cm, decumbent, somewhat stoloniferous. Lvs 1–3cm, ovate to oval, generally obtuse or sometimes somewhat acute at apex, rounded to cuneate at base, sinuate-dentate, shortly petiolate or upper lvs sessile, veins 3–5, palmate. Fls terminal, 1–3, occasionally to 5; pedicels 2.5–5cm; cal. 1.5–2cm, strongly plicate-angled, lobes acute, uppermost 3–5mm, lower shorter, lowermost pair finally upcurved; cor. 2.5–3.5cm, yellow, throat ventrally deeper coloured, with 2 red to brown-spotted hairy ridges joined distally into a palate that almost or totally closes orifice, upper lip with ascending-erect lobes, lower lip longer, lobes deflexed-spreading; anth. glabrous; stigmas somewhat minutely fimbriate. Capsule 7–8mm, slightly stiped, not dehiscing through septum apex. Summer. W US. var. ***caespitosus*** Grant. Smaller than species type, finely pubesc. in distal parts. Stems 3–10cm, crowded. Lvs 5–12mm, narrowly elliptic to ovate, entire to minutely dentate. Cal. 11–15mm; cor. 2–3cm, with palate only partially closing orifice. Washington to British Columbia. Z7.

***M. variegatus*** Lodd. Similar to *M. luteus*, but more dwarf. Fls larger; cor. with 2 yellow ventral ridges with brown spots, throat yellow, lobes crimson purple, violet on back. Chile. Z8.

***M. caespitosus*** Greene. See *M. tilingii* var. *caespitosus*.
***M. glutinosus*** Wendl. See *M. aurantiacus*.
***M. glutinosus*** var. ***brachypus*** A. Gray. See *M. longiflorus*.
***M. glutinosus*** var. ***puniceus*** A. Gray. See *M. puniceus*.
***M. grandiflorus*** T.J. Howell. See *M. guttatus*.
***M. hirsutus*** Bl. See *Torenia flava*.
***M. langsdorfii*** Donn ex Greene. See *M. guttatus*.
***M. luteus*** var. ***cuprea*** Hook. in Curtis. See *M. cupreus*.
***M. luteus*** var. ***variegatus*** Hook. See *M. variegatus*.
***M. radicans*** Hook. f. See *Mazus radicans*.
***M. roseus*** Douglas ex Lindl. See *M. lewisii*.
***M. tigrinus*** hort. See *M. ×hybridus*.
For further synonymy see *Diplacus*.

**Mimusops** L. (From Gk *mimo*, an ape, and *opsis*, resemblance: the corolla lobes are said to look like the upper body of an ape.) Sapotaceae. 57 species of evergreen, woody shrubs and trees, to at least 20m. Leaves thick, leathery, mostly obovate to elliptic, closely-veined. Inflorescence an axillary cluster, flowers white or almost so; sepals 6–8, in 2 whorls; corolla 6–8 lobed, each lobe with 2 petaloid appendages, stamens and staminodes 8, ovary superior, 8-locular. Fruit a berry with 1-several large seeds, ovoid to globose; seeds with a small circular scar at base. Tropical Africa, 1 species India to Malaysia, Burma and Pacific Is. Z10.

CULTIVATION As for *Chrysophyllum*.

***M. elengi*** L. SPANISH CHERRY; MEDLAR; TANJONG TREE. Tree to at least 20m, with a dense, spreading, rounded crown. Lvs 5–16×2–7.5cm, in 1.2–2.5cm petioles, alternate or in lax spirals, elliptic or ovate to oblong-elliptic, obtuse or bluntly acute, margins upcurled, wavy. Fls 1–1.5cm diam., white, later brown, very fragrant, short-pedicellate; pet. caducous, acute. Fr. 2.5–3.5×1.2–1.6cm, ovoid or oblong, smooth, orange-red when mature, pulp yellow, floury, edible; seed 1, large, hard, dark brown. India to Burma, Malaysia and Pacific Is.

**Mina** La Ll. & Lex.
***M. lobata*** Cerv. See *Ipomoea lobata*.

**Minuartia** L. (For Minuart, 18th century Spanish botanist, contemporary of Linnaeus.) SANDWORT. Caryophyllaceae. About 100 species of perennial, more rarely annual, herbs, often with linear leaves and mat-forming habit. The technical difference from *Arenaria* is in the ripe capsule, where the teeth are the same number as the styles (usually 3). In the descriptions, sepals and petals are 5 unless otherwise stated. Widely distributed in temperate and arctic N hemisphere. Z5 unless specified.

CULTIVATION As for *Arenaria*. Propagate by seed in spring, species such as *M. cherleroides, M. graminifolia* and *M. verna* by division immediately after flowering. Desirable cultivars also by greenwood cuttings in mid summer.

***M. cherlerioides*** (Hoppe) Bech. Dense cushion-plant with closely-packed, oblong-elliptic, fleshy, usually glabrous lvs to 3mm. Fls solitary on very short stalks; sep. 4, 2–4mm, 3-veined, lanceolate, acute; pet. 4, 2–4mm, lanceolate. Summer. C & E European Alps.

***M. graminifolia*** (Ard.) Jáv. Cushion-plant with linear-lanceolate, rigid leaves to 4cm, usually glandular-hairy, and flowering stems to 14cm. Infl. a 2–7-fld cyme; sep. 6–10mm, 5–7-veined, lanceolate; pet. 8–10mm, narrowly obovate. Summer. S Europe (mts).

***M. laricifolia*** (L.) Schinz & Thell. Loosely tufted, with a woody stock, and glabrous flowering stems to 30cm. Lvs linear, rigid, often falcate, to 10mm. Infl. a few-fld cyme, somewhat hairy on pedicels and sep.; sep. 4–7mm, 3-veined, oblong-lanceolate; pet. 6–10mm, obovate, Summer. Mts of S & C Europe.

***M. obtusiloba*** (Rydb.) House. Resembles *M. laricifolia*, but is mat-forming, with trailing non-flowering stems and usually solitary fls on stems to 6cm. It is best distinguished by the ovate, very obtuse, purple-tipped sep. and the narrowly oblanceolate pet. Summer. Western N America (Alaska to Oregon). Grows and flowers freely in cult. in N America. Z3.

***M. recurva*** (All.) Schinz & Thell. Densely tufted with woody stock and flowering stems to 15cm. Lvs falcate, glandular-hairy, to 10mm. Infl. 2–8-fld or fls sometimes solitary; sep. 3–6mm, 5–7-veined, ovate-lanceolate; pet. 4–8mm, ovate. Summer. Mts of S & C Europe.

***M. sedoides*** (L.) Hiern. Glabrous cushion-plant with densely packed, somewhat fleshy, linear-lanceolate lvs to 15mm, and solitary, almost sessile fls. Sep. 5, 2–5mm, 3-veined, ovate; pet. (if present) small, not longer than sep., tinged yellow. Summer. European mts from Pyrenees to Carpathians; also in Scotland. The plants are often dioecious, and female plants are usually apetalous, so the male plant is more showy preferred in cult.

***M. verna*** (L.) Hiern. Loosely-tufted perenn., usually glandular-hairy, with flowering stems to 15cm and linear-subulate lvs to 2cm. Infl. a loose few-fld cyme; sep. 3–5mm, 3-veined, ovate-lanceolate, spreading in flower; pet. 4–6mm, obovate. Summer. Widespread in Europe. A very variable plant; variants with larger pet. (ssp. *verna* and ssp. *grandiflora* (Presl) Hayek) are preferred in cultivation. The plant commonly grown under the name of *M. verna* 'Aurea' seems to be, at least for the most part, *Sagina subulata* 'Aurea'. Z2.

***M. aretioides*** (Sommerauer) Schinz & Thell. See *M. cherlerioides*.
For further synonymy see *Alsine, Alsinopsis* and *Arenaria*.

**Mirabilis** L. (From Lat. *mirabilis*, wonderful.) UMBRELLAWORT; MARVEL OF PERU. Nyctaginaceae. Some 50 species of annual or perennial herbs, to 1.5m. Roots tuberous, elongate, attaining a weight of 20kg in cult. Stems regularly 2–3-branched, forked, glabrous to glandular-pubesc., sometimes viscid. Leaves opposite, ovate, often sessile on upper stem. Inflorescence an axillary corymb, fragrant; flowers 1 to several, red, magenta, yellow, white or variegated, subtended by a 5-lobed, calyx-like involucre; involucral bracts connate, persistent or marcescent; perianth tubular to campanulate, constricted above the ovary, limb spreading, 5-lobed, plicate, deciduous; stamens 5–6, unequal, exserted, filaments incurved, united into a fleshy base. Fruit an achene, enclosed in hardened base of perianth and surrounded by persistent staminal cup. Summer. SW US, S America. Z8.

CULTIVATION Undemanding plants for the mixed and herbaceous border where the climate is dry and virtually frost-free. *M. jalapa*, the most commonly cultivated, has fragrant evening- and night-opening blooms; in suitable conditions it self-seeds freely and may become difficult to eradicate due to its deep-rooting habit. Tubers often survive winters where temperatures do not fall much below –5°C/23°F, provided that plants are given a warm, sheltered position in very well-drained soils. Alternatively, lift and overwinter in a frost-free place as for *Dahlia*. Grow in fertile, well-drained soils in full sun or part-day shade. In colder areas, grow as annuals; *Mirabilis* flower in one year from seed. Dwarf cvs of *M. jalapa* may be grown in a medium-fertility, loam-based mix in a cool but frost-free glasshouse. Propagate from seed sown at 16°C/60°F in spring: harden off young plants before planting out. Sow also *in situ* after danger of frost: self-sown seedlings are easily transplanted. Also by division of tuberous rooted spp. in spring. Young growth is particularly susceptible to aphid.

***M. dichotoma*** L. To 60cm. Lvs ovate, acute, rounded at base. Fls yellow. Mexico.

***M. ×hybrida*** hort. (*M. jalapa* × *M. longiflora*.) To 60cm. Lvs cordate, sometimes basally truncate, sinuate, short-petioled. Infl. dense, fls white, perianth tube glabrous or pubesc., lobes spreading. Garden origin.

***M. jalapa*** L. MARVEL OF PERU; FOUR-O'-CLOCK; FALSE JALAP. Erect perenn., to 60cm. Stems glabrous or short-pubesc. Lvs 5–10cm, ovate, entire, cordate at base, apex acuminate; petioles 2.5–5cm. Fls fragrant, opening in the late afternoon, 1 per involucre, involucre campanulate, to 1.5cm; perianth 3–5cm, purple, crimson, yellow or white, often striped or mottled, limb 2.5cm diam. Peru, garden escape in N America.

***M. laevis*** Curran. To 1m, many-branched, stems often decumbent, viscid-pubesc. Lvs 1–3.5cm, ovate to linear-ovate, subglabrous to pubesc.; petioles to 1.5mm. Fls 1–3 per involucre, perianth 1–1.5cm, rose to purple-red, lobes subovate. California.

***M. linearis*** (Pursh) Heimerl. To 60cm+. Stems glabrous or pubesc. below, viscid above. Lvs to 10cm, linear to linear-lanceolate, sessile or subsessile. Fls 3 per involucre, pale pink to maroon. S Dakota to Mexico.

***M. longiflora*** L. To 1m. Stems glandular-pubesc., viscid. Lvs ovate-cordate to ovate-lanceolate, slender-acuminate, short-petioled to subsessile. Fls 3 or more per involucre, perianth tube to 15cm, white, sometimes tinged pink or violet, viscid-pubesc., nocturnally fragrant. W Texas, Arizona, Mexico. var. ***wrightiana*** (A. Gray) Kearney & Peebles. To 120cm. Stems puberulent. Lvs distinctly petioled.

***M. multiflora*** (Torr.) A. Gray. Much-branched, to 1m. Lvs ovate to ovate-linear, grey-green, glaucous. Fls 6–8 per involucre, bracts maroon, perianth tube to 5cm, pink to purple. Utah, Colorado to Texas. var. ***pubescens*** Zipp. ex Span. in L. Glandular-pubesc.

***M. nyctaginea*** Michx. To 1m+. Stems subglabrous. Lvs to 10cm, deltoid to linear-ovate, petiolate. Fls 3 per involucre, white to pale pink; involucre enlarging in fruit. Wisconsin to Mexico.

***M. viscosa*** Cav. To 1m, viscid-pubesc. Lvs to 10cm, ovate, usually cordate at base, apex acute, petiolate. Fls usually 1 per involucre, perianth 1.5cm, funnel-shaped, purple, red, pink or white; involucre enlarged and pendent in fruit. Mexico, Colombia, Ecuador, Peru.

***M. californica*** A. Gray. See *M. laevis*.
***M. froebelii*** Greene. See *M. multiflora* var. *pubescens*.
***M. uniflora*** Schrank. See *M. jalapa*.
***M. wrightiana*** A. Gray. See *M. longiflora* var. *wrightiana*.
For further synonymy see *Alliona, Hesperonia* and *Oxybaphus*.

**Miscanthus** Anderss. (From Gk *mischos*, stalk, and *anthos*, flower, referring to the stalked spikelets.) Gramineae. 17 species of perennial grasses, to 4m. Rhizomatous; stems reed-like, strong, clumped. Leaf blades narrow, to 120cm, not rolled but somewhat folded, gracefully arching; ligules short, membranous. Panicle terminal, oblong-elliptic or obtusely pyramidal, composed of arching, spike-like, pubescent racemes to 20cm; rachis continuous; spikelets in pairs, equal, with a ring of long hairs at base, stalks of pairs unequal, 2-flowered; upper floret hermaphrodite, lower sterile; glumes equal, stiff, awnless; lemmas papery, translucent; lemma of fertile floret softly aristate, shorter than lemma of sterile floret. Old World Tropics, S Africa, E Asia.

CULTIVATION Found predominantly in moist soils in meadow and sometimes in marshland, *Miscanthus* spp. are valued for their robust clump-forming habit, late summer flowers and good foliage colours. This is especially fine in the variegated cultivars of *M. sinensis* such as 'Zebrinus' notable for the distinctive horizontal banding; specimens may also give a brief flush of russet in autumn. *Miscanthus* spp. are used as screening and wind filters, may be given back border placement in larger herbaceous border; if grown as lawn specimens any invasive tendencies will be strictly confined by mowing. *Miscanthus* is also used at the water's edge at pond and stream side but here should be given sufficient space to develop; *M. s.* 'Zebrinus' and 'Variegatus' in particular may suffer from overcrowding from other larger vigorous waterside grasses. Grow in sun or light shade in deep fertile soils that remain moist when plants are in growth. Protect young plants by mulching in zones where frosts are prolonged. Propagate by division in early autumn or spring, species also by seed.

***M. floridulus*** (Labill.) Warb. Robust, tufted, evergreen perenn. Culms stout, to 2.5m, glabrous. Lvs elongate, to 3cm diam., light glaucous green, scabrous at margins, pubesc. above towards base; ligules truncate, to 2mm; sheaths glabrous. Infl. erect, pyramidal panicles to 50cm, white, puberulent-scaberulous, with axillary tufted-pubesc.; racemes many, to 20cm, slender, branched at base, subsessile; spikelets obliquely patent, lanceolate, to 3.5mm, acute, with tufted-pubesc. to 6mm at base; glumes herbaceous, glabrous; awn to 1cm. Summer. Ryukyus, Taiwan, Pacific Is. Z6.

***M. sacchariflorus*** (Maxim.) Hackel. AMUR SILVER GRASS. To 3m. Rhiz. creeping, roughly bumpy. Lf blades spreading, linear, acute, flat, stiff, to 90×3cm, smooth, margins rough, midrib very pale green to silver-white; sheaths beige. Panicles finely hairy, to 40×13cm, very pale green, tinged red or purple; racemes many, to 30cm, flimsy; spikelets narrow, to 5mm, dull beige, with long silky hairs twice length of spikelet from base. Late summer–autumn. Asia; escaped in US. 'Aureus': small, not vigorous, to 1.5m; lvs striped gold. 'Robustus': habit large, vigorous, to 2.2m 'Variegatus': lvs narrowly striped white. Z8.

***M. sinensis*** Anderss. EULALIA. To 4m. Rhiz. short, not stoloniferous; stems in large clumps, rigid, erect, smooth. Lf blades mostly basal, erect or arching, linear, acute, flat, to 120×1cm, glabrous to sparsely hairy above, blue-green; sheaths stiff, rolled, minutely serrate; ligule silky-haired. Panicles obpyramidal, branching, to 40×15cm, light grey, tinged purple-brown or maroon; racemes erect or spreading, to 20cm; spikelets lanceolate to 5mm, with a ring of long, silky, white or purple hairs at base; upper, fertile lemma with awn to 1cm. Summer. E Asia. Many cultivars: habit ranges from erect to gently arching or fountain-like; height of foliage from 0.85–2.00m; height of fl. panicle 1.2–2.7m; lvs narrow to wide, green, or finely or boldly variegated in white or yellow, striped or banded, autumn colour inconspicuous to deep red tinted bronze; fls early to late, plumes silver to flushed pink, red or bronze. *Habit* 'Goliath': large, to 2m. 'Gracillimus': all parts more slender than type; lvs with a white midrib. 'Grosse Fontaine': fountain-like; early-flowering. 'Strictus': as for 'Zebrinus', but of smaller stature; very erect; lvs banded yellow at intervals. 'Yaku Jima': very dwarf, to 85cm; lvs narrow, arching. *Lvs striped* 'Cabaret': lvs wide, broad central creamy white band and dark green edge, flushed pink in autumn; panicles copper. 'Goldfeder': lvs edged and striped yellow. 'Morning Light': lvs narrow, arching, neatly edged white; panicles red-bronze. 'Sarabande': lvs with wide central silver stripe. 'Variegatus': lvs with longitudinal white or cream-white stripes. *Lvs banded* 'Tiger Tail': lvs banded cream. 'Zebrinus' ZEBRA GRASS: lvs with horizontal bands of white or yellow. *Lvs with autumn colour* 'Graziella': lvs narrow, somewhat arching, burgundy and orange with bronze tints in autumn; panicles large, white, nodding. 'Purpureus' ('Purpurascens'): small; lvs with pink-tinted central vein, browns and orange-reds in autumn; panicles oatmeal flushed pink. *Flowers* 'Flamingo': panicles tinted flamingo pink. 'Kleine Fontaine': lvs arching; fls early. 'Malepartus': robust; lvs burgundy in autumn; panicles large, copper to silver tinted mauve. 'Rotsilber': panicles tinted red. 'Silberfeder': upright; lvs narrow; stems slender; panicles loose, silver occasionally flushed pink. Z4.

***M. tinctorius*** (Steud.) Hackel. Tufted perenn. Culms to 1m. Lvs flat, broad-linear, to 40cm×12mm, scabrous on margins, with slender midrib, mostly glabrous, pilose towards base; ligules semi-rotund or truncate, to 3mm; sheaths sometimes sparse-pilose. Infl. erect, exserted corymbs, with a very short axis; racemes 2–12, to 15cm; spikelets to 6mm, acute, tufted-pubesc. at base to 3mm; awn absent; glumes coriaceous, acute, long-pilose, rather brown, the first bi-dentate, scabrous on the 2 ribs above. Autumn. Japan. 'Variegatus': dwarf, to 20cm; lvs streaked cream. Z6.

***M. transmorrisonensis*** Hayata. Similar to *M. floridulus* but with graceful, golden, sparsely branched panicles. Taiwan.

***M. formosanus*** A. Camus. See *M. floridulus*.
***M. japonicus*** Anderss. See *M. floridulus*.
***M. sieboldii*** Honda. See *M. tinctorius*.
***M. zebrinus*** (Beal) Nak. ex Matsum. See *M. sinensis* 'Zebrinus'.

For illustration see ORNAMENTAL GRASSES.

**Misopates** Raf. WEASEL'S SNOUT. Scrophulariaceae. Some 6 species of annual herbs similar to *Antirrhinum*. Stems to 60cm. Leaves elliptic to lanceolate, entire, subsessile or sessile, opposite at base, alternate toward apex. Flowers 3–4 in spike-like racemes; calyx lobes unequal, longer than corolla; corolla tube pink to white. Fruit a capsule. Summer. Mediterranean, W Atlantic Is., SW & C Asia. Z6.

CULTIVATION *M. orontium* occurs as a wildflower on roadsides, wasteland and as an arable weed, although its numbers have declined with the use of agricultural herbicides. Resembling a slender and delicate *Antirrhinum*, the lesser snapdragon is suitable for the wild garden and other informal planting; grow as for *Antirrhinum*.

***M. orontium*** (L.) Raf. Stem erect, simple, to 50cm, glabrous to densely pubesc. Lvs elliptic, linear or lanceolate, 20–50×2–7mm; petiole short. Raceme terminal, lax, clothed with leaflike bracts diminishing toward apex; cor. pink sometimes white, 10–15mm, shorter or equal to cal.; cal. lobes 10–17mm; pedicel 0–2.5mm. Fr. 8–10mm, ovoid, glandular-pubesc. Summer. SW & C Europe, naturalized in temperate zones.

For synonymy see *Antirrhinum*.

**Mitchella** L. (For Dr John Mitchell (1676–1768), correspondent of Linnaeus and botanist in Virginia.) PARTRIDGE BERRY. Rubiaceae. 2 species of evergreen herbs. Stems trailing, mat-forming, glabrous. Leaves opposite, petiolate, round-ovate, glossy, glabrous, dark green; stipules minute. Flowers in scarcely peduncled pairs, terminal, white, fragrant; calyx 4-toothed; corolla funnelform, lobes 4, spreading, valvate, interior densely pubescent: stamens 4, exserted or included; ovaries united; style 1, included or exserted; stigmas 4, linear. Fruit a 2-eyed, berry-like drupe, crowned by persistent calyx teeth, scarlet or, rarely, white; seeds 8. N America, Japan.

CULTIVATION *Mitchella* spp., occurring in sandy substrates on wooded hillsides, are creeping evergreens with trailing stems which root where they touch the ground. They are grown as groundcover, particularly in woodland, or on the peat terrace or rock garden. The flowers, although not conspicuous, are pleasantly fragrant in *M. repens*; the decorative berries are edible, but not particularly well-flavoured, except perhaps to partridge. Hardy to −20°C/−4°F. Grow in humus-rich, neutral to acid soils, in shade. Propagate by removal of rooted branches in spring or from seed, removed from the berry and sown in a soilless propagating mix.

***M. repens*** L. PARTRIDGE BERRY; TWO-EYED BERRY; RUNNING BOX. Stems creeping, rooting, to 30cm, glabrous or puberulent. Lvs obtuse at apex, truncate or sub-cordate at base, to 2cm, often veined white; petiole puberulent above. Fls very occasionally united, often tinged purple; cor. to 12mm, lobes ovate. Fr. globose, to 8mm wide, throughout winter. Spring–summer. N America. f. ***leucocarpa*** Bissell. Fr. white. Z3.

***M. undulata*** Sieb. & Zucc. Lvs to 2.5cm, ovate to lanceolate, acute, glabrous, margins undulate; petiole 3mm. Cor. cylindric, to 1.5cm, pink, lobes white-fringed; cal. 3mm, 4-lobed. Summer. Japan, S Korea. Z6.

***M. repens*** var. ***undulata*** (Sieb. & Zucc.) Mak. See *M. undulata*.

**Mitella** L. (Diminutive of Lat. *mitra*, thus a small cap or mitre, alluding to the shape of the fruit.) BISHOP'S-CAP; MITREWORT. Saxifragaceae. 20 species of perennial, minutely pubescent herbs, to 45cm. Rhizomes short, sometimes stoloniferous. Leaves ovate, cordate at base, lobed, crenate; petiole long, slender. Flowering stem with to 3 sessile leaves; racemes slender, usually secund; flowers small, green or yellow, nodding; sepals 5, fused into a saucer at base; petals 5, pinnately fringed or lobed; stamens 5, rarely 10, usually opposite sepals; ovary partially inferior; styles 2, short. Fruit a capsule, apically dehiscent, seeds numerous, shiny black. Late spring–summer. N America, NE Asia.

CULTIVATION A dainty plant resembling a small *Tiarella*, native to woodlands, meadows, and swamps, its attractive foliage makes good groundcover in moist woodland or pockets in the rock garden. Cultivation as for *Heuchera*. *Mitella* will self-sow in moist rich soil and *M. nuda* may colonize by stolons.

***M. breweri*** Gray To 10cm. Lvs cordate to reniform, 4–10cm broad, glabrous to coarsely hairy, margin very shallowly 5–11-lobed and 1–2×toothed. Flowering stem leafless or with thin bracts. Fls 20–60, green-yellow; cal. cup-shaped, 3–3.5mm broad; pet. 1–2mm, divided into 5–9 seg.; ovary almost inferior. British Columbia south to Sierra Nevada, east to NW Montana and Idaho. Z5.

***M. caulescens*** Nutt. Flowering stem 1–3-leaved. Fls to 25 borne loosely and opening from apex of downy raceme, yellow; pet. purple at base. Western N America. Z5.

***M. diphylla*** L. Flowering stems to 40cm with a single pair of opposed short-stalked or sessile lvs; racemes to 20cm; fls to 6mm diam.; pet. white, deeply fringed. N America. f. ***oppositifolia*** (Rydb.) Rosend. Lvs on flowering stem distinctly stalked. Z3.

***M.diversifolia*** Green Lvs cordate, ovate, 3–6cm broad, 5-lobed, entire to shallowly crenate. Fls 8–35; cal. campanulate 2.5–3.5mm; pet. 2mm, white suffused pink or purple, long-clawed, blade oval with a 3–5-lobed tip. Cascade Mts. Z5.

***M.nuda*** L. To 20cm. Usually stoloniferous. Lvs subreniform, 1–3cm; margin double crenate. Flowering stem leafless, or with a single sessile leaf at base. Fls 3–12; cal. 3mm, fused for up to half its length; pet. green-yellow, 4mm, pinnately divided into 8 seg.; stamens 10. Northern N America, E Asia. Z4.

***M.ovalis*** Green. To 30cm. Lvs cordate-oblong, 2–4×3–6cm, shallowly 5–9-lobed; ten finely toothed. Flowering stem leafless. Fls crowded, 20–60, green-yellow, 1cm across; pet. pinnately divided into 4–7 unpaired seg. Western N America, BC to California. Z7.

***M.pentandra*** Hook. To 40cm. Lvs 2–5cm broad, 5–9-lobed, twice crenate. Flowering stem naked or with 1–2 small scales. Fls 6–25; cal. 3–4mm broad; pet. green, 2–3mm, pinnately divided into 8 seg. NW America (Alaska to California). Z3.

***M.stauropetala*** Piper. To 50cm. Lvs 2–8cm wide, 5–7-lobed, often suffused purple, once or twice crenate. Flowering stems several, leafless; fls crowded 10–35, cal. campanulate 4–6mm, lobes tinged white or purple; pet. white or purple, 2–4mm, 3-lobed, sometimes entire. Montana to Colorado, west to Washington, Oregon. Z4.

***M.trifida*** Graham. To 40cm. Lvs 2–6cm broad, indistinctly 5–7-lobed, crenate. Fls to 20; cal. 1.5–3.5mm, campanulate; pet. white to purple 1.5–2.5 mm long, 3-lobed or entire. BC to California, E to Rocky Mts. Z6.

***M.grandiflora*** Pursh. See *Tellima grandiflora*.
***M.hallii*** Howell. See *M.ovalis*.
***M.micrantha*** Piper. See *M.trifida*.
***M.oppositifolia*** Rydb. See *M.diphylla* f. *oppositifolia*.
***M.stenopetala*** Piper. See *M.stauropetala*.
***M.violacea*** Rydb. See *M.trifida*.

**Mitragyna** Korth. (From Gk *mitra*, mitre, and *gyne*, woman, referring to the shape of the stigma.) Rubiaceae. Some 12 species of trees or shrubs; branches terete. Leaves opposite, petiolate; stipules intrapetiolar, conspicuous, oblong-spathulate, caducous. Flowers in dense terminal or axillary, solitary or cymose heads, pedunculate, bracteate and bracteolate; bracts 2, leaflike; bracteoles many, pubescent; calyx tube turbinate or truncate, limb tubular, abbreviated or absent, lobes 5, valvate; corolla tube cylindric to funnelform, glabrous or pubescent at throat, lobes 5, valvate; stamens 5, inserted at throat of corolla, filaments short, anthers oblong, short-tipped; ovary 2-celled; style filiform; stigma exserted, mitre-shaped, hollow-based, bifid at apex; ovules many. Fruit many capsules in globose heads, dehiscent into 2 cocci; seeds many, oblong, winged. Tropical Africa and Asia. Z10.

CULTIVATION Tropical Old World trees and shrubs occasionally cultivated for their funnel shaped flowers. Cultivate as for *Bouvardia*.

***M.inermis*** (Willd.) Kuntze. Tree, to 15×2m, usually smaller; bark dark grey, smooth; branchlets pubesc. Lvs to 12×8cm, elliptic or obovate, narrowly acute at apex, obtuse at base, red to green, pubesc., 6–9-veined; petioles to 3.5cm; stipules oblong-lanceolate, 1.5cm. Fls in dense globose heads 3cm wide, white or cream to yellow, fragrant; stamens and style exserted. Summer–winter. Africa (Mauritania to Sudan).

***M.parvifolia*** (Roxb.) Korth. Bark light grey. Lvs to 11×7cm, very variable, elliptic, oval, obovate or orbicular, obtuse to narrowly acute at apex, acute, obtuse or heart-shaped at base, pubesc. beneath, 6–8-veined; petioles to 2.5cm; stipules to 12mm. Fls in heads 2.5cm wide, pale yellow, sessile or pedunculate; peduncles to 8cm; cor. to 8mm; stigma white. Summer–autumn. N India, Sri Lanka.

***M.africana*** Korth. See *M.inermis*.
For further synonymy see *Nauclea*.

**Mitraria** Cav. (From Lat. *mitra*, mitre, referring to the shape of the fruit.) Gesneriaceae. 1 species, a climbing or straggling, evergreen perennial herb or subshrub; stem villous to glabrous, obscurely tetragonal becoming somewhat woody at base, branching dense, tangled. Leaves to 2cm, opposite in equal pairs, ovate, acute, dentate, lustrous dark green, coriaceous, hairy. Flowers solitary on arching axillary, tomentose to pubesc. peduncles; floral bract 1, bilobed; calyx 4- or 5-lobed, lobes to 1.2cm, lanceolate, free, slightly enclosed by floral bract; corolla to 3cm, tubular, scarlet or orange-red, inflated about halfway up, narrowing to mouth, pilose, limb lobed, lobes to 0.7cm, rounded, slightly reflexed; stamens 4, anthers united in pairs; ovary superior. Fruit a capsule, green flushed red. Summer–autumn. Chile. Z10.

CULTIVATION As for *Asteranthera*.

***M.coccinea*** Cav. As for the genus.

**Mitriostigma** Hochst. (From Gk *mitra*, mitre, and *stigma*, referring to cap-like stigma.) Rubiaceae. 5 species of shrubs and small trees. Leaves simple, opposite; stipules deltoid, acute. Flowers subsessile, 3 or more in dense or loose, axillary or lateral cymes; calyx tube ovoid or obconical, 5-lobed; corolla cylindric to bell- or funnel-shaped, glabrous or pubescent at throat, lobes 5, spreading or erect; stamens 5, inserted, anthers subsessile, included or exserted; ovary 1–2-chambered; stigma clavate, mitre-shaped, included or exserted. Fruit drupaceous, crowned with persistent calyx. Subsaharan Africa.

CULTIVATION Closely related to *Gardenia*, *M.axillare* is a desirable and slow-growing evergreen shrub, bearing long-lived and sweetly scented white flowers. Grow in the intermediate glasshouse (min. 12°C/54°F), in a neutral to acid soilless medium, with medium humidity and in bright indirect light. Water plentifully when in growth, sparingly in winter. Propagate from ripe-wood cuttings in autumn.

***M.axillare*** Hochst. Compact, evergreen shrub or small tree, 3–4m. Lvs to 15×5cm, lanceolate, elliptic-lanceolate, or ovate, apex attenuate to acute, base obtuse, entire, dark green, glabrous, prominently veined beneath; petioles to 1cm; stipules triangular or subulate, narrowly acute, conspicuous, deciduous. Fls in secund axillary cymes, white, occasionally pink-flushed, to yellow, fragrance reminiscent of orange-blossom. Fr. ovoid, to 3cm, orange. Spring. S Africa (Natal, Transvaal).

For synonymy see *Gardenia*.

**Mitrophyllum** Schwantes. (From Gk *mitra*, bishop's hat, and *phyllon*, leaf, referring to the shape of the plant bodies.) Aizoaceae. 6 species of highly succulent shrubs, 12–70cm. Stems branching, 5–15mm thick, occasionally to 10cm long, internodes short, enclosed by persistent leaf bases. Leaves trimorphic, the third type present only during flowering; sterile branches and shoots with 2 pairs of leaves, the first pair forming the 'mitre' or cone, the second much smaller and united for a quarter or up to the entire length forming a sheath, anchoring the following seasons's cone leaves, the united leaf pair borne in the axils of the cone leaves persists until the sheath is paper thin, allowing the free part to harden off; leaves on flowering shoots form the last 2 leaf pairs and have elongated internodes. Flowers short-pedicellate, white, pink or yellow. Growing season very short, late summer–early autumn. S Africa (Cape Province). Plants previously referred to *Conophyllum* are now included here. Z9.

CULTIVATION These succulent plants originate in winter rainfall areas and will only grow when the day length is short. They endure a dry summer resting period without water, when the previous season's green leaves dry up. No amount of watering will start growth during long-length days. In autumn, the stems plump up after the first watering. When the new leaves are obvious, water freely every 1–2 weeks. In pot cultivation in a greenhouse, remove the remains of old leaves adhering to the soft new leaves. In winter, reduce the frequency of watering if temperatures fall below 10°C/50F. Water throughout spring, but no new leaves should grow. As days lengthen, the leaves dry up and watering should be very infrequent until autumn. Growth is vigorous during the autumn and these plants need a rich but gritty, well-drained potting mix. Keep in full sun. Propagate from seed. Flowering is difficult.

***M.mitratum*** (Marloth) Schwantes. Forming mats of thick, soft stems, becoming woody, nodes annularly thickened. Cone lvs 7–8cm long, 2cm thick, the free parts 10–12mm long, bluntly triquetrous, second lvs 8–10cm long, 10mm thick below, light green, glossy-papillose. Fls 2.5–3cm diam., white, reddened at tips. Cape: Little Namaqualand.

***M.chrysoleucum*** (Schltr.) Schwantes. See *Monilaria chrysoleuca*.

***M. meyeri*** Schwantes. See *Meyerophytum meyeri*.
***M. pisiforme*** (Haw.) Schwantes. See *Monilaria pisiformis*.
For further synonymy see *Conophyllum* and *Mesembryanthemum*.

For illustration see AIZOACEAE.

**Modecca** Lam. See *Adenia*.

**The modern garden**. The modern garden is a term which is already out of date, as it has been before. In this case it refers to a concept of what a garden should be and look like which emerged in the 1920s as a result of developments in art and architecture with which it was inevitably associated. It evolved over the ensuing half century into a prototype as recognizable as the Medieval, Islamic, Italian Renaissance and other clearly defined garden styles. It is a small garden even within large properties, clearly related to the house in style and function, satisfying the physical and aesthetic needs of an expanding middle-class segment of society within a Euro-American context.

In the early years of the 20th century the idea of what a garden should be had been distilled from a major origin in Repton's theory that the surroundings of the house should accommodate people in comfort, as well as collections of plants (in compartments) within a larger picturesque landscape. After an acrimonious argument between Reginald Blomfield and William Robinson over the contrasting virtues of architectural and natural gardens, a compromise type which combined the two emerged. Typified in England by the early work of Jekyll and Lutyens or in the United States by the gardens of Farrand and Platt, the Arts and Crafts garden was smaller than both Repton's landscapes and the extensive formal layouts of Kemp or Paxton. It was a garden of architectural enclosures and terraces around the house with a wild garden beyond, representing exactly what its title implies – a blend of artistic composition with the traditions of stonework and horticultural practice in the spirit of the movement dedicated as it was to simplicity, a back-to-nature lifestyle and the promotion of craftsmanship in architecture and gardening. The gardens of owner designers such as Lawrence Johnson (Hidcote) and Vita Sackville West (Sissinghurst) in England or Beatrix Farrand's garden for Ambassador and Mrs Bliss at Dumbarton Oaks in Washington, D.C. are classic examples of the type.

What factors would contribute to a change in this well-established and popular concept? As in previous eras, garden design was susceptible to the influences of time, place and people. Place, though important, becomes for better or worse, the least critical factor in the concept of the modern garden as we shall see in an international context. Time, the social and intellectual characteristics of a period – the state of science, the arts, the economy and political structure – is more critical. People – both the designers of gardens (their sources of form and inspiration) and those for whom the gardens are made (their lifestyle and preferences) – are and were in turn influenced by time and place.

In architecture, the Arts and Crafts philosophy reintroduced the idea of the master designer (a familiar role in the Renaissance) and the idea that everything from silverware, furniture, house and garden should be designed in concert. Voysey and Mackintosh in Britain, Wright and the Green brothers in the US were masters of this concept. But as Euro-American society developed after World War I, a new industrial, professional, socially conscious middle class emerged and the Bauhaus school of design in Germany focused the arts and crafts into a simple, economic but also artistic approach to building which would make good-quality, functional housing available to all. Cubism and subsequent abstraction in the arts was included in the architectural developments, but garden designers were reluctant participants. It was the architects who set the pace, either regarding the landscape as a romantic setting for their pristine white boxes or including it within an architectural extension of the house. Both ideas were clearly articulated in Corbusier's Villa Savoie (1931) which sat like a factory in an agricultural landscape but held within it a 'garden' on the second floor. These two attitudes, a romanticized nature and a garden as an extension of the house, responded to a sense of time, place and people in the 1930s.

By the 1920s, in the fine arts, Europe and specifically France had become the centre of new ideas in painting, sculpture, music and literature. The 1925 Exposition of Decorative Arts held in Paris featured gardens which were said to reflect the joy of the present and the needs of modern life through the influx of cubism and new industrial materials. This new modern French school produced gardens which were either tableau-objects that ignored the context and the presence of the house, or they followed the modernist premise of the garden as a continuation of the house. Whatever the objective, the gardens tended to be small paved places in which nature was subdued. Trimmed boxwood and coloured gravels in geometric patterns and zigzags articulated the ground plane. Mirrors reflected minimalist compositions. Designed by such architects as the Vera brothers, Moreux and Guvrekian, or artists such as Legrain (whose famous Tachard garden of 1925 was essentially a bookbinding design laid out on the ground), the French gardens of the late 1920s and early 1930s presented the public with a new idea of what a garden might be. The tableau-object type was short lived, but the modern architect's belief in the garden as an outdoor room persisted and became the model for gardens of the post-World War II period.

The Architekturgarten in Germany, a product of the Jugendstil movement, was a reaction (as in England and America) to the landscape garden in its reduced form surrounding suburban villas. In the early years of the century the architect Muthesius argued that the relationship between house and garden was so intimate that they should be designed by one person. Thus the title garden architect was coined. The form of the garden was discussed in terms of the social, economic and functional determinants which resulted in its small size and geometric appearance. Symmetry was no longer the central source of layout and the German and Northern Europeans' irrepressible love of perennial plants reintroduced a soft counterpoint to the architectural structure.

The Scandinavians' reverence for nature and the outdoors during their short summers combined with a tradition of excellence in domestic architecture that fitted well with the concept of the garden as a sunny uncluttered extension of the house. The work of C. Th. Sorensen, whose book *About Gardens* was published in 1939, typifies the modern garden in Scandinavia in pre- and post-war years. Often small, the gardens incorporated the new geometry of abstract art with planting drawn from a limited selection of hardy plants while serving the function of an outdoor room.

The British, whose strong garden traditions had dominated Europe for over a hundred years and whose Arts and Crafts garden seemed the perfect answer to the question of combining gardening with history, avoided the ugly questions raised by modern society. The British public slept through the artistic revolution in garden design and all but ignored the new architecture which opted to take over the garden. Modern architecture which flourished in Europe and Scandinavia was slow to gain popularity in the UK. But with the closure of the Bauhaus in 1933, some refugee architects stopped long enough on their way to the United States to influence young architects and garden designers in England.

Perhaps the best-known of the latter, because of his contemporary writing as much as his practice, was Christopher Tunnard. His *Gardens in the Modern Landscape* (1938) advocated the infusion of modern art and function into garden design and the important unity between garden and architecture; modern surroundings for a modern house. Two examples, Halland in Sussex (1936) and St Ann's Hill, Chertsey (1937) illustrate the concept. White concrete and glass international-style houses sit in English landscape gardens composed of woods and glades. Adjacent to the building are paved terraces and semi-enclosed 'garden' spaces. These projections form sheltered sunny usable areas and serve as a physical and visual link between the architecture and the land. Introduced planting is minimal. The inclusion of sculpture in both gardens manifested the modernist's belief in the benefits to be gained from the interrelationship of architecture, sculpture and painting.

The role of plants in the modern garden can be judged by a section in Tunnard's book (2nd edition, 1948). Titled Architect's Plants, it features species chosen for their structural rather than floral interest, including hardy exotics such as *Yucca gloriosa, Phormium tenax* and *Cordyline australis*; variegated evergreens such as *Vinca major*; conifers such as *Araucaria imbricata* and grey foliage plants such as *Hosta fortunei*.

It can be seen by now that the commonly held belief that the modern garden was of American origin is a myth. It is true, however, that the new garden type reached its zenith in the United States in the post World War II years (1946–60). This was a result or a product of a prosperous and large middle class, the relocation of the epicentre of 'modern' architecture in the United States, and a few other favourable factors. Since the concept of a garden as outdoor room depended so much on a climate and lifestyle which permitted its use on a regular basis, it is not surprising to find its realization in a geographical location where the essential criteria of Time, Place and People coincided. Such a place was the coastal zone of California, enjoying what is often referred to as a Mediterranean climate. Temperatures in this zone range from the 50s (F) in winter to the 70s (F) in summer, hotter in the south, cooler in the north, rarely dropping below freezing. Rainfall is limited to the winter from November to April and typically amounts to 25 inches, often less. Predictable patterns of rainfall, warm temperatures, sunny skies, low humidity and a dearth of flies and mosquitoes results in a climate conducive to outdoor living and makes a swimming pool a worthwhile investment. The relatively new geology of the Coast Ranges around San Francisco and running through Los Angeles provided sites for urban and suburban homes on steep hillsides with views. Native evergreen oaks, madrone, Ceanothus and chaparral and the introduced Australian Eucalyptus covered the hills. This landscape of slopes, views and existing vegetation was embraced as counterpoint by the designers of the modern California garden.

To date in California, garden design had followed first, Spanish/Mexican precedent, then the 19th-century landscape style and through the Arts and Crafts ideal to a small garden related to its bungalow for people of modest means. As in Europe, the United States experienced an eclectic revival in architecture and garden design in the first three decades of the 20th century. California had its share, but by the 1930s a simpler lifestyle lead to the new problem of the small garden usually, but not always, in town which would provide maximum delight and use and minimum maintenance. It was seen that the small garden could not be natural if it was to serve as an extension of the house. Nor could the heroic proportions of the classic formal garden fit into a limited area.

Californians had always been obsessed with the outdoors. A tradition of eating outside dating back to the rancho barbecue and the informal entertaining which it inspired was a major theme of the influential *Sunset* magazine. An influx of population after the war, with young children, mobile, active, interested in sports and leisure, saw the garden as an extra room for the shrinking house. The idea was to make the garden as usable as the living room. In the typical modern California garden there would be direct indoor-outdoor connections and a predominant use of hard surfaces. Grass, if any, would be confined to a small irrigated area. On sloping sites wooden decks would extend usable level space and provide views. Swimming pool, barbecue and provision for other recreational pursuits were often included. The limited space was divided and structured with fences, walls and screens creating privacy and hiding utilities with immediate effect (essential for mobile families). Shade was provided by the inclusion of existing trees into the design or by a constructed overhead trellis. Wherever possible, views of distant hills were brought in to give a sense of space to otherwise small gardens. Parking space, especially in the country, was a major component of the design, often exceeding the size of the house in area. And of course there would be plants, the quantity and variety depending on the owners' interest; a lemon in a pot, espaliered fruit trees, geraniums or special collections. Although each one is different, reflecting site, architecture, owner's preferences and designer's approach, these are the basic characteristics of the modern California garden.

As in Europe, it was architects who fostered the concept of the modern garden in California either by including it in their own purview like Richard Neutra, or by encouraging and working with young landscape architects willing to break with tradition. Two who fall into the latter category and who became early exponents of the modern garden are Thomas Church and Garrett Eckbo.

Church's point of departure in garden design included the Mediterranean tradition, the architecture of the house, the site, and the preferences of the client. His orientation was European but his context was California and a new socio-economic class structure. The new house and its small garden, he argued, 'must go to work for us, solving our living problems while it also pleases our eyes and our emotional psychological needs. The lines of the modern garden must be moving and flowing so that it is pleasing when seen from all directions both inside and out.' In the catalogue for a 1939 Exhibition of Landscape Design in San Francisco, which featured Church's work, it was suggested that the creation of a garden fell halfway between the making of painting and the making of a house. The early products of Church's extensive practice were published in his *Gardens Are for People* in 1955.

Garrett Eckbo, ten years younger than Church but equally Californian, followed in Church's footsteps to Harvard Graduate School of Design in the late 1930s, where he found entrenched traditionalism and reverence for Frederick Law Olmsted in the landscape department, while in architecture (upstairs) there had been a conversion to radical modern theories. The Bauhaus had arrived in America. Eckbo 'defected' to the new ideas (new forms to solve new problems) and published an article in 1937 titled 'Small Gardens in the City', in which bilateral symmetry and design rules were uncompromisingly rejected and denounced in favour of 'no rules, [of] forms which come out of the situation and artistic expression; dynamic, not static. Let there be rhythm, life and action...This is the USA 1937 AD,' exclaimed Eckbo passionately. 'Automobiles, airplanes, streamlined trains, mass production, the machine, new materials, new thoughts, new social concepts, a more abundant life – all of these suggest a new kind of garden for the modern age'. Eckbo argued that gardens were places where people live out of doors, where people not plants were the important thing. They should be backgrounds to life. 'But more than an outdoor living room they are places of delight, fantasy, illusion, imagination and adventure.' The astonishing article was accompanied by drawings of 16 versions of small town gardens on small urban lots. Special attention was paid to counteracting the restrictions of a small garden in a variety of ways; partial screening of areas, creative use of levels, de-emphasis of enclosing lines and walls through the use of murals, glass blocks and mirrors.

Church and Eckbo essentially defined the modern garden in the post war years using California as its environment. Others such as Halprin, Osmundson and Staley, Royston and Baylis developed and proliferated the concept in California to the point that it became identified with the modern garden.

In other parts of the world, designers such as Roberto Burle Marx in Brazil and Louis Barragán in Mexico, both influenced by modern art and architecture, contributed to the body of work embraced by the term the modern garden. Burle Marx, an artist/ botanist, emphasized the role of indigenous plants, Barragán, the contrast between architecture and nature. Their gardens, however, tended to be large scale for wealthy clients, and although embracing the functional outdoor room, they could more appropriately be described as works of arts, crossing new frontiers in the continuing and evolving relationship between society and nature. They may better be thought of as laying the ground work for post-modern garden design, as Gaudi and Saarinen had done, in their own individualistic way, for post-modern architecture.

**Moehringia** L. (For Paul Moehring (1710–1792), German naturalist.) SANDWORT. Caryophyllaceae. About 20 species differing from *Arenaria* only in the presence of an appendage (strophiole) on the seed, but mainly easily distinguished by having 4- (not 5-) petalled flowers (a rare condition in *Arenaria*). Widely distributed in temperate and arctic N Hemisphere. Z5.

CULTIVATION Of delicate appearance, *M. muscosa* is grown for the bright mossy foliage that is studded throughout summer with a profusion of tiny starry white blooms. Grow on the rock garden, scree or in crevices in a lean and gritty calcareous soil rich in moisture-retaining organic matter. Propagate by seed sown in early spring or by division in autumn.

***M. muscosa*** L. Glabrous, loosely matted plant with thin, intertwining stems and linear lvs to 4cm. Fls in a very loose cyme on a long slender pedicel; sep. usually 4, about 3mm, lanceolate, acute; pet. usually 4, 4–5mm, ovate-lanceolate; styles usually 2. Summer. Mts of C & S Europe.

**Mohavea** A. Gray. (For Mohave Creek, California, the first recorded location of this genus.) Scrophulariaceae. Some 2 species of annuals. Aerial parts pubescent, viscid, branches erect or ascending. Leaves simple, linear to ovate, entire, opposite or alternate toward stem apex. Inflorescence a dense leafy raceme; calyx 5-lobed; corolla yellow, lips fan-shaped; palate pubescent, almost choking throat; stamens 2. Summer. SW US. Z7.

CULTIVATION Desert annuals closely related to *Antirrhinum*, and suitable for cultivation on rock gardens, at border fronts and for naturalizing in wild gardens where summers are hot and dry. They will tolerate extremely poor soils, provided these are light and sandy or gravelly. Sow *in situ* in a sunny, open position in spring (or autumn in areas experiencing little or no winter frost) and thin to 10cm/4in. apart.

***M. confertiflora*** Jeps. Stems to 60cm, glandular-pubesc., viscid, simple or branched. Lvs linear-lanceolate to ovate-lanceolate, fleshy. Cal. lobes lanceolate; cor. paler yellow than palate, both spotted red-brown; stamens 2.

**Mohria** Sw. (For David Mohr (*d* 1808), German botanist.) Schizaeaceae. 4 or more species of terrestrial fern; rhizome prostrate, clad in scales. Fronds erect, bipinnate, clad in small brown scales below. Sporangia at apices of segments of fertile lamina; indusium wanting. African mainland and islands.

CULTIVATION A sweetly scented fern for the cool to intermediate glasshouse, *M. caffrorum* requires an open and porous medium comprising leafmould and sharp sand, exposure to full light and moderate watering, ensuring that water does not come into contact with the foliage. Propagate by spores.

***M. caffrorum*** (L.) Desv. SCENTED FERN. Rhiz. to 10mm diam., clad in brown scales. Fronds tufted, erect; blade 20–58×5–11cm, narrowly oblong to elliptic, bipinnate to pinnatifid, pinnae pinnatifid to bipinnate, margins crenate. Tropical & Subtropical Africa and adjacent islands.

**×Mokara**. *(Arachnis × Ascocentrum × Vanda.)* Orchidaceae. The introduction of *Ascocentrum* features to the *Aranda* crosses has produced a range of more compact Scorpion orchids of brilliant colours which are very popular as cut flowers in the Far East. Plants compact, upright, with long stems bearing alternate leaves in two rows. Inflorescences axillary, upright, with many brightly coloured flowers; sepals and petals fuller than the *Aranda* parents, lip small.

× *M. Khaw Phiak Suan:* dense infl. of many fls, bright yellow with few orange spots near the base, lip orange.

×M. Mak Chin On: tall plants with many upright spikes; fls intense imperial purple or cerise pink, very fine; many awarded clones.

×M. Panni: upright spikes of closely arrange fls; fls yellow with dense covering of red spots, lip brick-red.

×M. Walter Oumae: fls white, pink-mauve at the tips of the sep. and pet., covered with fine mauve spots, lip pink-mauve.

**Molineria** Colla.
***M. capitulata*** (Lour.) Herb. See *Curculigo capitulata*.
***M. latifolia*** (Dryand.) Herb. See *Curculigo latifolia*.
***M. plicata*** Colla. See *Curculigo capitulata*.
***M. recurvata*** (Dryand. in Ait.) Herb. See *Curculigo capitulata*.

**Molinia** Schrank. (For J.I. Molina (1740–1829), writer on the natural history of Chile.) Gramineae. 2–3 species of perennial grasses to 120cm. Stems tufted, lax; basal internode bulbous. Leaves flat; ligule a row of hairs. Panicles narrow-lanceolate, loose; spikelets laterally compressed, 1–4-flowered; glumes subequal, acute, papery, translucent, lower glumes 1-nerved, upper glume 3-nerved; lemma obtuse, 3-nerved, convex on dorsal surface, glabrous; palea equals lemma. Eurasia. Z5.

CULTIVATION *Molinia* occurs on open moorland, in moist, humus rich infertile, base-poor soils; in the wild plants act as secondary host to the ergot fungus, which infects cultivated rye. The species is used in waterside and other informal naturalistic plantings, the variegated and coloured cvs in the border – all are attractive when in bloom, especially in the purple-flowered forms. Grow in moisture-retentive, humus-rich acid or neutral lime-free soils in an open position in sun. Propagate by division in early autumn and spring, species also by seed.

***M. caerulea*** (L.) Moench. PURPLE MOOR-GRASS. To 120cm. Lf blades to 45×1cm, deciduous; ligules densely hairy. Panicles dense, spike-like to 40×10cm, purple to olive-green; spikelets to 1cm; lemmas acute or obtuse, to 5mm; anth. purple-brown; stigmas mauve. Summer–autumn. 'Dauerstrahl' ('Ramsey'): stems tall, tinted yellow. 'Edith Buksaus': to 1m; stems strong; panicles dark, long-lasting. 'Heidebraut' ('Heatherbride'): stems soft straw yellow, to 1.5m; spikelets tinted yellow, forming a glistening cloud. 'Moorhexe' ('Bog Witch'): narrowly upright; stems slender, to 50cm; fls dark. 'Moorflamme': to 70cm; lvs coloured well in autumn; infl. dark. 'Nana Variegata': dwarf form of 'Dauerstrahl', to 80cm. 'Overdam': to 60cm; stems strong; lvs fine. 'Strahleonguelle' ('Fountain Spray'): stems curving. 'Variegata': tufted, compact; stems slender and upright, bright ochre, to 60cm; lvs striped dark green and cream-white; panicle oatmeal, spikelets tinted purple; slow-growing. ssp. ***arundinacea*** (Schrank) H. Paul. To 2.5m. Lvs to 12mm diam. Infl. panicle with long, patent to erecto-patent branches; lowest lemma long-acute, to 6mm. W Europe. 'Altissima': to 1m; lvs golden-yellow in autumn. 'Bergfreund' ('Mountain's Friend'): lvs strong yellow in autumn; panicles brown. 'Fontäne' ('Fountain'): stems inclining, forming a fountain. 'Karl Foerster': tall, lvs to 80cm. 'Skyracer': tall, lvs to 1m, clear gold in autumn. 'Transparent': spikelets sparse, giving the whole infl. a light, spacious, transparent quality. 'Winspiel' ('Windplay'): stems slender, swaying; plumes gold-brown, dense.

***M. altissima*** Link. See *M. caerulea* ssp. *arundinacea*.
***M. arundinacea*** Schrank. See *M. caerulea* ssp. *arundinacea*.
***M. litoralis*** Host. See *M. caerulea* ssp. *arundinacea*.

For illustration see ORNAMENTAL GRASSES.

**Molle** (Tourn.) Adans. See *Schinus*.

**Mollet family**. Royal gardeners and garden designers. The Mollet family was unrivalled until the advent of André Le Nôtre, and central to the development of the French formal style. The first was Jacques Mollet, head gardener to the Duc d'Aumale at the Château of Anet in the 1580s. His son Claude Mollet (*c*1563–1648) worked under him at Anet as a young man. In 1582 Claude came under the instruction of the architect Etienne du Pérac (*d*1601) after the latter's return from Italy. According to Claude's own account, under du Pérac at Anet, he created the first parterres and *compartments de broderie*, the designs made by the use of box and coloured earth for which the Mollet family were to become famous. After this he moved into the service of Henri IV and in 1595 was commissioned to lay out a garden at Saint-Germain-en-Laye, where he designed intricate parterres using box. He also made designs for Montceaux-en-Brie and for an island garden at Fontainebleau. At the Tuileries, as 'Premier Jardinier aux Tuileries', he was mainly responsible for the new garden east of the palace and for the avenue of mulberries in the Grand Jardin. Claude's book *Théâtre des plans et jardinages*, published posthumously in 1652 and illustrated by his sons Claude, André, Jacques and Noël, was an early standard work on gardening, also containing autobiographical details. Olivier de Serres' folio work *Le Théâtre d'agriculture et mesnage des champs* (1600), dedicated to Henri IV, contains woodcuts of garden designs by Claude Mollet.

Of Claude's sons, André Mollet (*c*1600–*c*1665), is the most famous, renowned for his book *Le jardin de plaisir* (1651), published in Stockholm in French, German and Swedish editions. With autobiographical details in the preface, this work disseminated the family style, a strictly geometric plan comprising features such as parterres, avenues and *bosquets*, throughout virtually the whole of Northern Europe. In about 1629 André was working for Charles I in England, moving into the service of Prince Frederik Hendrik of Orange in 1633 and remaining there until 1635. In England *c*1629–1633 he laid out the gardens at St James's Palace, returning to England in 1642 to do the same for Wimbledon House at the request of Queen Henrietta Maria, replacing the Elizabethan gardens with four parterres, a maze and a wilderness. In the Netherlands André provided the designs for two parterres at Honselaarsdijk, near the Hague, these appearing in his book. He produced similar designs at Buren. After working in Holland, André returned to France where he became 'Premier Jardinier du Roi', living near the Tuileries gardens. In 1646 a Swedish delegation visited France and managed to persuade Mollet to enter the service of Queen Christina of Sweden. He was finally appointed in 1648 and left France with various trees and shrubs. He worked in Stockholm from the year of his arrival until 1653 as head of the royal gardens, modernizing the King's Garden by creating orangeries and a *parterre de broderie*. He had four French garden assistants, one of whom was his son Jean, who remained in charge when André left. Jean's work was in great demand and he remained in the country until his death.

André was in England again in 1658 together with his relative Gabriel Mollet (*d*1663). Both were appointed King's Gardeners to Charles II at the palace of St James in 1661 and imported trees and flowers from France. After Gabriel's death, André became gardener in chief at St James's. His brother Pierre Mollet (*d*1659) took over one of his father's jobs at the Tuileries, as head of the Grand Jardin. Another brother, Claude Mollet (*d*1664) was appointed head of the new garden in the east. In 1639 he designed the first *parterre de broderie* at Versailles and also worked on the new Louvre garden in about 1656. He may also have been responsible for the designs in Boyceau's *Traité du jardinage* (1638). In 1645 he occupied the post of 'Desseignateur des Planz et Jardins du Roy'. The other of André's brothers, Jacques Mollet (*d c*1622), worked at Fontainebleau from at least 1612, continuing the design tradition of his father. The younger Claude's son Charles Mollet succeeded his father at the Tuileries and is recorded as redesigning the orangery at Fontainebleau in 1671. The post at the Tuileries then passed to his son Armand-Claude Mollet in 1692.

**Moltkia** Lehm. (For Count Joachim Gadake Moltke of Denmark, *d*1818.) Boraginaceae. Some 6 species of perennials. Stems herbaceous or shrubby, densely leafy, strigose. Leaves alternate. Cymes short, solitary or terminally crowded, bracteate; calyx deeply 5-lobed, linear, equal or subequal; corolla blue, purple or yellow, infundibular, tube cylindrical, glabrous, lobes equal or subequal, erect, overlapping, rounded, usually glabrous, lacking throat scales; stamens exserted, filaments equal or unequal, short to elongate, anthers oblong to lanceolate; style exserted, slender, filiform, stigma entire or emarginate. Nutlets 4, ovoid to ovoid-trigonal, smooth to minutely tuberculate or papillate, ventral keel usually prominent. N Italy to N Greece, SW Asia.

CULTIVATION *Moltkia* spp. occur in freely draining limestone soils, frequently in rock crevices receiving full sun. *M. doerfleri*, suited to mixed and herbaceous borders and the rock garden, may prove invasive. The shrubby *M.* ×*intermedia* is useful groundcover. *Moltkia* prefers approximately neutral to alkaline soils but otherwise has similar garden uses and cultural requirements to *Lithodora*. Propagate also by layering.

***M. caerulea*** (Willd.) Lehm. Perenn., adpressed-pubesc. Stems to 20cm, simple, erect or ascending. Basal lvs to 8cm, oblanceolate, obtuse, base attenuate; cauline lvs to 3.5cm, oblong, acute, sessile. Cymes 2 or 3, terminal, elongate in fr.; bracts ovate-lanceolate, acute; pedicel short; cal. to 4mm in fl., to 8mm in fr., lobes acute; cor. to 19mm, blue, tube cylindrical or cylindrical-campanulate, glabrous, lobes to 2mm, somewhat recurved, interior sparsely adpressed-pubesc., exterior glabrous; fil. to 7mm, anth. to 2.5mm; style exceeding fil. Nutlets to 4mm, obliquely ovoid, minutely papillate, punctate to tuberculate. W Asia.

***M. doerfleri*** Wettst. Perenn. Stems to 50cm, simple, erect, from stout rhiz., adpressed-setulose. Lvs lanceolate, acute, adpressed-setulose. Cal. to 10mm; cor. to 22mm, elongate, deep purple, lobes to 2.5×4mm, rounded, broad; fil. to 2mm, compressed, anth. to 3.5mm, yellow. Nutlets to 4mm, minutely blotched purple. Albania.

***M.* ×*intermedia*** (Froebel) J. Ingram. (*M. petraea* × *M. suffruticosa.*) Closely resembles *M. suffruticosa* except larger and more shrubby. Lvs broader. Fls deep bright blue, in spreading heads. Europe to Asia. 'Froebelii': fls azure-blue. Z6.

***M. petraea*** (Tratt.) Griseb. Shrub to 40cm. Branches numerous, erect, slender, densely white-adpressed setose. Lvs to 50×6mm, oblanceolate or oblong-lanceolate to linear, subacute or obtuse, sparsely setose above, densely white-setose beneath, margins revolute. Cymes short, compact; cal. to 4mm; cor. to 8mm, blue or violet-blue, lobes to 1.5mm; fil. to 8mm, anth. to 2mm, blue, apex rounded; style to 4mm. Nutlets to 4mm. Yugoslavia to C Greece. Z6.

***M. suffruticosa*** (L.) Brand. Shrub to 25cm. Stems erect, caespitose, slender, adpressed-setose, loosely branched. Lvs to 150×3mm, elongate, linear, acute, sparsely setose above, densely white-setose beneath, sometimes revolute. Cymes short, dense, clustered in corymbs; cal. to 6mm, hispid; cor. to 17mm, blue, elongate, lobes to 3.5mm, elliptic, rounded; fil. to 3mm, anth. to 3mm, yellow, unequal; style exceeding cor. Nutlets to 3mm, ovoid. N Italy. Z8.

***M. graminifolia*** (Viv.) Nyman. See *M. suffruticosa*.
For further synonymy see *Echium*, *Lithospermum*, *Onosma* and *Pulmonaria*.

**Moluccella** L. (From the original collection region, the Moluccas.) Labiatae. 4 species of glabrous, annual or short-lived perennial herbs. Stems tetragonal, to 1m. Leaves opposite, crenate, petiolate. Inflorescence composed of axillary whorls; bracteoles subulate; calyx bilabiate, tube campanulate, 5–10 veins with 5–10 spiny teeth, expanding at fruiting to become papery and conspicuously reticulate; corolla white, fragrant, insignificant, bilabiate, upper lip hooded, lower lip 3-lobed. Mediterranean to NW India. Z7.

CULTIVATION Noble annuals producing tall stems of small lilac flowers enclosed in greatly enlarged calyces, excellent for the flower border and, later, for drying. Treat as half-hardy, sowing seed under glass in early spring at 15°C/60°F, or, later, *in situ*, in sunny well-drained borders.

***M. laevis*** L. BELLS OF IRELAND. Annual. Stems multiple, erect to 60cm. Lvs to 6cm, ovate light green, deeply crenate. Infl. whorled; bracteoles axillary; cal. light green, white-reticulate, campanulate or saucer-shaped. Late summer. W Asia.

***M. spinosa*** L. Glabrous annual, erect to 1m. Lvs to 6cm, ovate to cordate, deeply serrate or lobed. Whorls distant; bracts spiny, subtending fls; cal. bilabiate, upper lip erect with strong spine, lower lip 7–10-spined; cor. white, to 40mm, velvety. Late summer. Mediterranean.

**Momordica** L. (From Lat. *mordere*, to bite; the seeds have praemorse tips.) Cucurbitaceae. 45 species of monoecious or dioecious, annual or perennial scramblers. Tendrils simple or bifid. Leaves palmate or pedate with 3–7 lobes or leaflets, dentate or undulate. Flowers solitary (males sometimes in corymbs or racemes); peduncle of male flower conspicuously bracteate; calyx tubular; corolla showy, rotate or campanulate, yellow or white, deeply lobed; stamens 3, occasionally 2, free, inserted in throat of tube, anthers flexuous, partially coherent, absent in female; ovary oblong or fusiform, usually ribbed, tuberculate or papillose. Fruit pendulous, ripening yellow or orange, bursting and expanding in a starlike configuration at maturity, oblong, dehiscent or indehiscent, tuberculate or ridged; seeds compressed with grooved margin, often glossy red, suspended in a white, pulpy mass. Africa, Indomalesia, naturalized Americas. Z9.

CULTIVATION Perennial tendril climbers from the moist tropics of the Old World, particularly Africa and found in bushland, savannah and sometimes colonizing disturbed ground. Grown for their tuberculate fruit, splitting in several species to reveal showy, scarlet-pulped seeds. *M. balsamina* and *M. charantia* bear fruits which are edible when green and are cultivated for fruit production. *M. cochinchinensis* has showy, hooded flowers and *M. charantia* flowers which are strongly vanilla-scented in the morning.

In temperate zones all need glasshouse cultivation as annuals in hot conditions, high humidity and bright filtered light. The potting compost must be well-drained but rich – 2:2:1:1 sterilized loam/well-rotted manure/peat/grit is ideal. Plant in early spring. *M. cochinchinensis* and *M. rostrata* are dioecious, and six plants are needed to ensure a plant of each sex for seed production. Water plentifully throughout growth and liquid feed fortnightly, training the growth on to wires or a trellis. Control red spider mite as described under *Trichosanthes*. Collect seed in the autumn for spring sowing with bottom heat at 20°C/68°F.

***M. balsamina*** L. BALSAM APPLE. Climber or trailer to 1.5m. Tendrils simple. Lvs broadly ovate to reniform, cordate, pubesc., deeply and acutely palmately lobed, to 90–120mm, sharply dentate; petiole pubesc., 4–60mm. Fls solitary; bract ovate-cordate, veined, attached to upper part of peduncle; pet. yellow with green venation, to 15×12mm; ovary fusiform, beaked. Fr. to 7cm, ovoid or ellipsoid, tapering at both ends, covered with ridged, irregular protuberances, green ripening orange and bursting. E Indies, widely naturalized.

***M. cardiospermoides*** Klotz. Climber to 6m, perenn.; rootstock tuberous. Lvs biternately 9–15-foliolate, leaflets ovate-oblong, 5–30×4–20mm, acute, apiculate. Fls solitary; male bract usually larger; pet. yellow, 19–26×10–15mm; ovary slightly tuberculate, 10–12×4–4.5mm. Fr. ellipsoid, irregularly tubercled; seeds rugose or ridged, to 14×9×4mm. Southern Africa.

***M. charantia*** L. BALSAM PEAR; BITTER GOURD; BITTER CUCUMBER; LA-KWA. Annual, climbing to 5m. Stems rigid. Tendrils simple. Lvs deeply 3–7-lobed, pubesc. on nerves, lobes obovate to rhombic, acute and apiculate. Fls solitary; bract mucronate, entire; pet. pale yellow to orange, to 22×15mm, bearing basal scales; ovary ovoid, beaked. Fr. oblong or ovoid, orange yellow, strongly rugose-tuberculate, dehiscent, 7–25cm; seeds sculptured, to 11×6×4mm, with grooved margins, embedded in red pulp. Tropics, introduced to Americas.

***M. cochinchinensis*** (Lour.) Spreng. SPINY BITTER CUCUMBER. Climbing annual. Lvs orbicular, 3–10cm across, cordate, glabrous, lobes 5–9, deeply divided, acute, apiculate, sometimes obscurely pinnatifid. Fls solitary; bract entire, inserted half way on peduncle; cor. yellow, lobes to 2cm; ovary fusiform, muricate. Fr. oblong or oval, tapering, ribbed and warty to subspinose, dehiscent, to 20cm; seeds red. India to Japan and New Guinea.

***M. foetida*** Schumacher. Dioecious perenn. climber or trailer, to 4.5m, base becoming somewhat woody, Lvs ovate-cordate, simple, apiculate, subentire to dentate, sometimes tomentose on nerves beneath, 1–16×1–17cm. Male fls 1–9 per fascicle; cal. ciliate, dark purple in male; pet. caducous, white to pale yellow, obovate, darker with scales at base; ovary ovoid, beaked, softly papillose-spinose. Fr. ellipsoid, softly spiny, to 1.5cm; seeds brown, oblong, about 10×6×3mm. Tropical Africa and America.

***M. involucrata*** E. Mey. Climber. Stems glabrous. Tendrils simple. Lvs palmate, glabrous, lobes 5, dentate, teeth obtuse, to 2.5cm, mucronate. Fls solitary; bracteole reniform, entire, to 1cm across, inserted near fl.; sep. obtuse-orbicular, about 5mm; pet. at least 1cm; stamens 3, free, anth. coherent. Fr. globose-ovoid, attenuate, rugose, orange, about 3cm diam. S Africa (Natal).

***M. rostrata*** Zimm. Dioecious perenn. climber; rootstock tuberous. Stems to 7m with pubesc. tufts at nodes, becoming woody. Lvs compound, pedate, biternate; leaflets usually 9, elliptic to suborbicular, serrate or dentate, to 5×3cm. Male infl. subumbellate; female fls subsessile, solitary, occasionally paired; bract white-pubesc., to 10×12mm, usually much smaller, especially female; pedicel white-pubesc.; cal. lobes subtriangular; pet. oblong-ligulate, to 13×8mm, orange-yellow, darker with 2 scales toward base; stamens 3; ovary slightly ridged. Fr. ovoid, beaked, slightly ridged, scarlet; seeds coated with yellow pulp. E Africa.

***M. brachybotrys*** Poepp. & Endl. See *Cyclanthera brachybotrys*.
***M. cylindrica*** L. See *Luffa cylindrica*.
***M. elateria*** L. See *Ecballium elaterium*.
***M. lanata*** Thunb. See *Citrullus lanatus*.
***M. operculata*** L. See *Luffa operculata*.

**Monachosorum** Hance.
***M. maximowiczii*** (Bak.) Hayata. See *Ptilopteris maximowiczii*.

**Monadenium** Pax. (From Gk *monos*, single and *aden*, gland.) Euphorbiaceae. Some 50 species of monoecious perennials, from acaulescent succulents to arborescent shrubs, to 5.5m, as for *Euphorbia*, but inflorescence cyathia zygomorphic; involucre bracteate, cupulate, apex truncate; involucral gland horseshoe-shaped, with a wide rim; bracts persistent behind rim. C, SW, mainly tropical E Africa. Z10.

CULTIVATION As for the succulent species of *Euphorbia*, adapted according to altitude of natural habitat, and habit of growth. Those occurring above 2000m/6565ft (*M. rhizophorum*) need temperate glasshouse conditions with a minimum temperature of 7–10°C/45–50°F, lower-altitude species requiring higher temperatures and dry conditions as for other succulents. Species with a herbaceous habit, where the stems die back during dormancy, are kept dry when leafless; all need dry conditions in winter.

***M. cannelli*** Leach. As for *M. spinescens*, but smaller, to 1.5m. Spines solitary. Infl. peduncles prominently ridged; involucral appendages wider at apex; styles to twice length of *M. spinescens*, to 6mm. Fr. pubesc. Angola.

***M. coccineum*** Pax. Perenn., to 1m+. Stems unarmed, solitary or 2, erect or creeping, simple or branched, to 130×1.5cm, 5-sided, glabrous green, occasionally tinged purple. Lvs alternate, oblanceolate to obovate, 85×35mm, acute or mucronate, base attenuate, fleshy, glabrous, midrib keeled, margin serrate; stipules deciduous, scale-like. Infl. cymes borne in upper lf axils, forked, forming heads to 4cm diam.; peduncles fleshy, scarlet above, pale green below, to 7cm; bract cup scarlet; involucre to 5mm diam., pale yellow; glandular rim wrinkled. Tanzania. Z9.

***M. echinulatum*** Stapf. Somewhat prickly succulent, to 70cm. Stems simple, to 1cm diam., glabrous or prickly. Lvs alternate, to 45mm distant, elliptic to elliptic lanceolate, short-stipitate, to 12×6.5cm. Infl. cymes axillary, to 5× dichotomous; peduncles to 10cm; bract cup oblique, to 21mm diam.; involucre to 7×4mm, cupulate, green, occasionally flushed pale pink; ovary protruding. Tropical W Africa, Tanzania. f. ***glabrescens*** Bally. Glabrous apart from peduncles. Infl. cymes 1–2× dichotomous.

***M. elegans*** S. Carter. Small tree or arborescent shrub, to 3.5m; bark shiny, exfoliating in flakes; branches becoming pendulous, to 15mm diam.; spines in groups of 3, central spine to 18mm, lateral to 10mm. Lvs spathulate, to 4×3cm, glabrous, apex rounded, base attenuate below median point. Infl. peduncle to 35mm, ridged longitudinally, beset with slender paired spines to 5mm; cyathia 8×5mm; involucre keg-shaped, gland rim white, bordered red, segmented, seg. 5–7, pubesc. below. Tanzania.

***M. invenustum*** N.E. Br. Perenn. herb, to 80cm. Stems 1–2 erect, unarmed, glabrous, glaucous; lf scars to 4cm distant. Lvs fleshy, variably orbicular ovate, to 4×3.5cm, dark green above, pale green, slightly pubesc. below, margin occasionally crenulate; petiole to 6mm. Infl. cymes axillary; peduncles to 15mm; bract cup to 6mm, oblique, bikeeled below, dark green, banded paler green; involucre funnel-shaped, to 5mm; gland yellow-white, somewhat discoid. Kenya. var. ***angustum*** Bally. Lvs oblanceolate.

***M. laeve*** Stapf. Perenn. herb. Stems 1 to several, erect to procumbent, to 1m. Lvs alternate, elliptic-ovate to oblanceolate, acute, to 17×7cm, base cuneate, attenuate; petiole to 2cm, winged. Infl. cymes axillary; peduncles to 10cm, 2–4× dichotomous; bract cup pendent, to 14×16mm, margin undulate; cyathia 4×5mm; involucre cupulate, 4mm. Fr. exserted, pedicel reflexed. Tanzania, N Malawi.

***M. lugardae*** N.E. Br. Perenn. herb, to 60cm. Stems 1 to several, to 60cm, to 3cm diam., appearing hexagonal to pentagonal paved. Lvs borne terminally or on upper portion of stems, obovate, to 9×4cm, acute, margin crenate to serrate; stipules slightly spiny. Infl. cymes solitary, borne in upper lf axils, to 13mm; peduncles to 6mm; bract cup oblique, to 7mm, apex notched; involucre pendent, exterior pale green, interior yellow or orange brown; ovary winged, wings serrate. Bechuanaland, Natal, S Zimbabwe.

***M. magnificum*** E.A. Bruce. Shrub. to 1.5m. Stems 1 to several, to 4cm diam. Stem branches 4–5 sided, spiny, spines clustered, borne on margins, in fascicles to 3×3mm. Lvs sessile, elliptic to obovate, to 15×10cm, fleshy, reflexed, glabrous, dark green, later tinged red. Infl. cymes axillary; peduncles to 14cm, to 7mm diam., beset with red small spines; involucral bracts fleshy; involucre keg-shaped, pale green, lobed, lobes fringed, rhombic. Tanzania.

***M. rhizophorum*** Bally. Succulent glabrous herb, to 10cm. Stems to 10cm, to 7cm diam., borne at the apices of rhizome, to 10cm apart. Lvs borne apically, obovate to spathulate, to 3.5×2.5cm, apex mucronate, base attenuate, sessile. Infl. cymes axillary, forming (usually solitary) bracteate heads; peduncle to 6mm, pale green-white, striped dark brown; bract cup oblique, to 7×5mm; involucre to 5mm, green tinged yellow, glandular rim sturdy, yellow. Fr. exserted, peduncle reflexed. Kenya.

***M. ritchiei*** Bally. Succulent perenn. herb, to 40cm. Stems to 3cm diam., warty, warts to 7mm, prominent, bearing spines to 2mm. Lvs ovate to subcircular, sessile, apex apiculate, to 27×20mm, dark green above, paler below. Infl. cymes few, consisting of few, asymmetrically arranged, bracteate heads; bract cup oblique, to 8mm; involucre to 6×5mm, fleshy, glandular rim scarlet. Kenya. ssp. ***marsabitense*** S. Carter. Stems decumbent, to 2cm diam.; warts densely spirally arranged. Lvs puberulous; bract cup grey-green, occasionally flushed pink. ssp. ***nyambense*** S. Carter. Lvs glabrous; bract cup vivid pink.

***M. rubellum*** (Bally) S. Carter. Glabrous perenn. herb. Stems fleshy, erect, to 5cm, or decumbent, to 25cm, to 5mm diam., ridged, striped green-purple. Lvs lanceolate, to 4.5×1cm, entire, tinged purple, apex acute. Infl. peduncle to 17mm, forked once; stipules scale-like, 1–4-dentate, brown; bract cup to 6×4mm, pink tinged rose; cyathia 5mm; involucre keg-shaped. Kenya.

***M. schubei*** (Pax) N.E. Br. Succulent perenn. herb, to 45cm. Stems erect, to 4cm diam., dark green, warty, warts to 1cm, prominent; spine shields bearing sharp spines to 2mm, central spine longest, red-brown, becoming grey. Lvs oblanceolate, to 6.5×2cm, acute, base attenuate, sessile. Infl. cymes axillary, 1–2× dichotomous; peduncle to 6mm; bract cup to 6×5mm green, margin white, occasionally tinged pink, veins dark green; involucre cupulate, 4mm, rim white-green or light pink. Tanzania, S Zimbabwe.

***M. spectabile*** S. Carter. Succulent shrub, to 3m. Stems simple or sparsely branched. Stem to 5cm diam., somewhat 5-sided, pale green, waxy bloomed; spines to 6mm. Lvs sessile, obovate, to 33×23cm, fleshy. Infl. bright red, spiny; peduncle to 15cm; bract cup to 6×8mm. Infl. cyathia 6×4mm; involucre keg-shaped. Fr. exserted; pedicel to 7mm. Tanzania.

***M. spinescens*** (Pax) Bally. Tree, to 6m; bark yellow brown, exfoliating in flakes. Branches to 2.5cm diam., warty; spines borne below lf scars, in groups of 3, central spine to 14mm. Lvs alternate, oblanceolate to obovate, to 9×4cm, glabrous, acute, base cordate, dark green above, lighter below, midrib prominent, keeled. Infl. cymes crowded at branch apices, 7× dichotomous or more, forming heads to 7cm diam.; involucral bracts to 10×7mm, pale green tinged pink; involucre to 9×5mm, lobed, lobes bearing threadlike processes; styles to 3mm. Tanzania.

***M. stapelioides*** Pax. Cushion-forming perenn., to 15cm. Stems erect, to 15cm+, longer stems becoming decumbent, glabrous; warts spirally arranged, rhomboid or hexagonal. Lvs borne on uppermost warts, obovate to rhombic or spathulate, to 3cm×18mm, acute. Infl. cymes solitary, borne in upper lf axils; peduncles to 2cm, fleshy, pale green flushed pink; involucre cylindric or urn-shaped, to 7×5cm; gland red or brown. Kenya, N Tanzania.

***M. stoloniferum*** (Bally) S. Carter. Glabrous perenn. herb. Stems to 15cm, procumbent. Lvs ovate, to 5×2.5cm, entire, apex acute, base attenuate, green tinged purple. Infl. peduncle to 15mm, once or twice forked; bract cup to 6×4cm, dark green, midrib white; cyathia 6×4mm; involucre keg-shaped, glandular rim yellow. Fr. exserted on a pedicel to 5mm. Kenya.

***M. torrei*** Leach. As for *M. spinescens*, but smaller, to 3m; young branches more warty; spines borne on wart apices, solitary. Lvs deciduous, obovate to spathulate or cuneate, acute, occasionally obtuse, midrib keeled below. N Mozambique, Tanzania.

***M. montanum*** var. ***rubellum*** Bally. See *M. rubellum*.
***M. rhizophorum*** var. ***stoloniferum*** Bally. See *M. stoloniferum*.
***M. subulifolium*** Chiov. See *Kleinia subulifolia*.
***M. succulentum*** Schweick. See *M. stapelioides*.

**Monanthes** Haw. Crassulaceae. 12 species of herbs or shrubby annuals and perennials. Leaves succulent, entire, opposite or alternate, in dense rosettes at the ends of branched stems. Inflorescence a raceme or cyme, 5–9-branched; flowers small; sepals 6–8, usually joined at base; petals 6–8, linear, free; stamens twice as numerous as petals; carpels free, as many as petals, with a whorl of large nectiferous scales at their base. Fruit a dry capsule; seeds very small. Summer. Canary Is. and N Africa. Z8.

CULTIVATION Dwarf shrubby plants, with minute and often interestingly textured leaves carried in dense rosettes. They carry dull-coloured flowers on slender stems, and should be rested during the summer months. Cultivate as for *Cotyledon*.

***M. anagensis*** Praeger. Similar to *M. laxifolia* except lvs 2.5cm, opposite although appearing alternate, linear-lanceolate, thin, green, often tinged red; sep. narrow. Tenerife.

***M. brachycaulon*** (Webb & Berth.) Lowe. Erect, stolon-forming perenn. Stem simple, bulb-like. Lvs 14–20×5×2.5mm, in rosettes of *c*20, papillose, oblanceolate, blunt, very fleshy, green, mottled purple towards base. Infl. 5–7-fld; pedicel 10mm, hairy, thin; fls green-purple, to 10mm across. Spring. Tenerife and Salvage Is.

***M. laxiflora*** (DC.) Bolle. Perenn. herb, hanging or diffuse, irregularly branching. Stem woody at base, grey. Lvs 1.2–1.6cm, opposite, very thick, oval, fleshy, usually silvery or dark green, very variable. Infl. 6–10-fld, lax; fls purple to yellow, spotted red, nectar scales small. Spring. Canary Is. A very variable species.

***M. muralis*** (Webb & Bolle) Christ. Erect subshrub, tree-like, to 8cm. Stems much-branched, grey-red. Lvs 6×3×2mm, in dense terminal rosettes, obovate, very thick, mottled purple. Infl. 3–7-fld, terminal; fls white; sep. 6, spotted red; pet. 6, spotted and veined red. Spring. Canary Is.

***M. pallens*** (Webb & Christ) Christ. Roots fibrous. Stems short, thick, bulbous. Lvs in dense rosettes of 40–80, 3–5cm diam., ovate-round, tapering at base, pale green, densely papillose. Infl. many-fld, leafy; fls small, yellow; pet. white, lined red. Spring. Canary Is.

***M. polyphylla*** Haw. Minute, mat-forming perenn. Stems thin, horizontal. Lvs in dense rosettes, 1–2cm across, round in cross section, blunt, light green, papillose at apex otherwise glabrous. Flowering stem glabrous. Fls 1–4, red; sep. and pet. covered in white hairs. Spring. Canary Is.

***M. subcrassicaulis*** (Kuntze) Praeger. Similar to *M. polyphylla* except lvs not dense rosettes but rather long elongate rosettes. Flowering stems hairy. Canary Is.

***M. agriostaphys*** Christ. See *M. laxiflora*.
For further synonymy see *Sempervivum*.

**Monarda** L. (For Nicholas Monardes (1493–1588), Spanish botanist and physician, author of the first medicinal flora of North America (1571) translated 1577 as *Joyfull Newes*.) WILD BERGAMOT; HORSEMINT; BEEBALM. Labiatae. 16 species of aromatic annual or perennial herbs. Stems erect, simple or branched variously pubescent. Leaves sessile or petiolate, simple, ovate, lanceolate, elliptical or linear, margin usually serrate. Flowers borne in dense glomerules, terminal and solitary or in an interrupted spike, subtended by an involucre or usually foliar bracts; calyx tubular, 13–15-veined, often hairy within, teeth 5, equal or subequal; corolla strongly 2-lipped, upper lip either erect and linear or plicate and hooded, lower lip spreading, 3-lobed, lateral lobes reduced, ovate, apex obtuse; stamens 2, seated within funnel-shaped throat, ascending under the upper lip, exserted or included; style exserted, posterior branch shorter. Nutlets 4, oblong, smooth. N America.

CULTIVATION *M. didyma* has long been cultivated for oil of bergamot extracted from young leaves, for dried leaves in pot-pourri, and for the high nectar yield useful for bees. The annual species are usually grown for their sweet scent and for nectar production for bees. The perennial species, particularly the many showy forms of *M. didyma*, make first-rate clump-forming plants for the herbaceous border. The annual species tend to grow best on sandy rather acidic soils in full sun. The herbaceous species will thrive in any soil, growing best if a good mulch of manure or garden compost is incorporated into the soil. The herbaceous species prefer full sun, also attracting bees while they flower in the latter part of the summer. The clumps will expand by means of creeping rhizomes below ground, which will need to be kept in check.

Propagate annual species from seed sown direct *in situ* in late spring. Propagate herbaceous species either from seed sown in a cold frame in spring or from division of established clumps during the dormant period. Various mildew fungi can be a nuisance, especially in hot dry summers. This can be curtailed by removal of infected debris and burning it during the winter and applying a systematic fungicide at the first signs of infection.

Other perennial species occasionally cultivated are *M. russeliana*. Nutt. (*M. bradburiana* Beck), flowers pink with purple spots; *M. bartlettii*, Standl., flowers magenta; and *M. pringlei* Fern., with vermilion flowers.

***M. citriodora*** Cerv. ex Lagasca. Annual, 30–60cm. Stem unbranched or branched at the infl., pubesc. Lvs 3–6cm, lanceolate or oblong, evenly puberulent throughout, margins remotely serrate or ciliate; petioles to 3cm. Glomerules 1.5–3.5cm across, subtending outer subfoliar bracts, inner bracts oblong, occasionally lanceolate, 5–9mm broad, abruptly acuminate to a spinose bristle 2–5mm long, inner surfaces canescent often purple, outer surfaces pubesc.; cal. tube 6–13mm, puberulent, mouth bearded, teeth 2–7mm, aristate, hirsute; cor. white or pink, dotted with purple, tube 7–19mm long, throat funnel-shaped, upper and lower lips equal. C & S US, N Mexico.

***M. clinopodia*** L. Perenn. to 1.25m. Stems simple or branched, glabrous or thinly pubesc. Lvs ovate to deltoid 5–13×3–6cm, hirsute above, more densely so beneath, margins serrate; petioles 1–3cm. Glomerules 1.5–3cm, across, outer bracts subfoliar, green with purple midveins; cal. 6–10mm, green, tube and teeth slightly hairy or glabrous, teeth 1mm, mouth with a few patent hairs; cor. white with purple spots, 1.4–3cm, glabrous or short-pubesc., upper lip, not bearded; stamens seated 1mm within cor. tube, tube 8–20mm long, gradually expanded upward. N America (New York to Illinois and mts of Alaska). Z5.

***M. didyma*** L. BEE BALM; BERGAMOT; OSWEGO TEA. Perenn. herb, 70–120cm. Stems simple or branched, glabrous or thinly pilose. Lvs 6–14×3–8cm, ovate, deltoid to ovate-lanceolate, margin serrate, thinly hirsute above, more hirsute beneath, especially on veins; petioles 1–4cm. Glomerules terminal, 2–4cm across, outer bracts subfoliar, membranous, tinged red, spreading or reflexed; cal. 9–14mm, usually crimson, glabrous or puberulent, teeth 1–2mm, mouth glabrous; cor. bright crimson, 3–4.5cm, tube 2–3cm, usually 2× length of cal., upper lip hirtellous not bearded; stamens seated 2–4mm within tube. Canada, US. 'Alba': fls white. 'Cambridge Scarlet': fls red. 'Croftway Pink': fls rose-pink. 'Salmonea': fls salmon pink. 'Burgundy': fls dark blue-purple. Z4.

***M.fistulosa*** L. Perenn. herb, 35–120cm. Stems usually branched, pubesc. in upper parts or rarely glabrous. Lvs 4–10×1.3–5cm, ovate or lanceolate, margins serrate to nearly entire, pubesc. throughout or rarely glabrous; petioles 8–15mm. Glomerules 1.5–3cm across, outer bracts subfoliar, frequently pink tinted, reflexed; cal. 7–10mm, puberulent, teeth 1mm, long-acuminate, mouth hirsute within; cor. lavender, lilac or pink, 2–3cm, pubesc., upper lip comose, tube 1.5–2cm, gradually expanded upward; stamens seated 1mm within the tube. Canada, US, Mexico. Plants described as *M.fistulosa* var. *purpurea* Pursh and *M.fistulosa* var. *rubra* Gray are probably natural hybrids with *M. didyma*. Z4.

***M.menthifolia*** Graham. MINT-LEAVED BERGAMOT. Perenn. herb, 30–75cm. Stems simple, rarely branched, glabrous or pubesc. above. Lvs 3.5–9×3–5cm, ovate or lanceolate, margins serrate or subentire, glabrous or softly hirtellous above, usually pubesc. beneath; petioles 2–5mm. Glomerules terminal, 1.5–2.5cm across, outer bracts subfoliar, frequently tinted pink, reflexed; cal. 7–10mm, occasionally tinted pink, puberulent, teeth 1mm, acuminate, mouth hirsute; cor. lavender or rose-purple, 2.5–3.5cm, pubesc., upper lip comose, tube 1.6–2.5cm, 2× length of cal., gradually expanded upward; stamens seated 1–3mm within the tube. Canada, US. Z3.

***M.pectinata*** Nutt. PLAINS LEMON MONARDA. Annual, 15–30cm, branched several times. Stems pubesc. Lvs 2–5×0.6–1.2cm, oblong-lanceolate or oblong, glabrous to puberulent throughout, margins remotely serrate to subentire; petioles 2–15mm. Glomerules 1.5–2.5cm across, outer bracts foliar, inner bracts oblong, 2–7mm wide, acuminate to a spinose bristle, midvein conspicuous, margins ciliate, surfaces glabrous (bracts 2 or rarely 4); cal. tube 6–8mm, puberulent or glabrous, mouth hirsute, teeth aristate, slender, 2–3mm, hirsute, often pink or red; cor. pink or nearly white, tube 8–14mm, including funnel from throat, lips equal, shorter than tube. S US.

***M.punctata*** L. A polymorphic species, perenn., bienn. and annual. Stems sparingly branched, 30cm–1m, variously pubesc. Lvs 1.5–9.5cm, lanceolate to oblong, petiolate, margins serrate to subentire. Glomerules 1.5–2.5cm across; bracts spreading or reflexed, subglobose to oblong, green-white or tinged purple, entire, sometimes ciliate; cal. teeth deltoid, acuminate or subspinose, not aristate; cor. yellow or pink, usually dotted purple. US. ssp. ***punctata.*** Perenn. or bienn., 25–85cm. Stem pubesc., without bristles. Lvs 3–7×0.5–1.5cm, upper surface sparsely puberulent, lower, pubesc. especially on veins; petioles to 2cm. Cal. 6–9mm, teeth 1mm, mouth glabrous or hispid; cor. yellow or rarely white with purple spots; unexpanded part of tube 6–8mm. E US, along seaboard. ssp. ***arkansana*** Epling. Perenn. herb, 50–115cm. Stems pubesc., with bristles. Lvs 4–10×1.2–2.5cm, upper surface sparingly pubesc., lower pubesc., especially along veins; petioles to 2.5cm. Cal. 5–8mm, teeth 1mm, mouth glabrous or hispid; cor. yellow with purple spots, unexpanded part of tube 4–6mm. Arkansas. ssp. ***coryi*** Epling. Perennial herb, 40–60cm. Stems pubesc. Cal. tube 5–8mm long, glabrous, mouth glabrous or sparingly hispid; cor. pink without purple dots, unexpanded part of the tube 5–8mm. Texas. ssp. ***intermedia*** Epling. Perenn. herb, 40–60cm tall. Stems pubesc. Lvs 5–7×1–2cm, surfaces evenly pubesc.; petioles to 1.8cm. Cal. tube 5–8mm, teeth 1mm, sometimes sparsely hairy on margin, mouth glabrous or hispid; cor. yellow with purple dots, unexpanded part of the tube 5–8mm. Texas. ssp. ***occidentalis*** Epling. Annual, 30–40cm. Stems simple or branched, pubesc. Lvs 2.5–5×1–1.7cm, surfaces evenly pubesc., petioles to 1.5cm. Cal. 4–7mm, pubesc., teeth 1m, ciliate with silky hairs; cor. white or pink, sometimes dotted purple, unexpanded part of the tube 4–7mm. US, Mexico. ssp. ***stanfieldii*** (Small) Epling. Perenn. herb, 35–75cm. Stems canescent with short hairs. Lvs 6–9×1.5–3cm, upper surfaces puberulent, lower surfaces evenly pubesc.; petioles to 2.5cm. Cal. 7–10mm, evenly pubesc., teeth 1mm, margins densely hispid, mouth densely bearded; cor. yellow with purple dots, unexpanded part of tube 8–11mm. Texas. ssp. ***villicaulis*** Pennell. Perenn. herb, 20–70cm. Stems simple or branched, densely hairy. Lvs 3.5–8×7–2cm, upper surface pubesc., lower surface densely tomentose, silvery; petioles to 2cm, cal. 5–7.5mm, teeth 1mm, mouth glabrous or hispid; cor. yellow with purple dots, unexpanded part of tube 5–7mm. E US. Z6.

***M.*cultivars**. Over 50 cvs, either selections or hybrids of *M.didyma* and *M.fistulosa*; those with zodiacal names may be mildew-resistant. Habit dwarf to tall, height from 60–90cm; fls white to red or deep blue. 'Beauty of Cobham': tall; fls lilac-pink. 'Blue Stocking' ('Blaustrumpf'): tall; fls brilliant deep violet. 'Capricorn': fls purple. 'Croftway Pink': fls clear rose pink. 'Kardinal': tall; fls red tinted purple. 'Loddon Crown': fls maroon. 'Mahogany': tall; fls deep wine red. 'Pisces': fls strong pink, cal. green. 'Prairie Night' ('Prarienacht'): fls rich violet. 'Snow Queen': low; fls creamy white. Z4.

***M.allophylla*** Michx. See *M.clinopodia*.
***M.aristata*** Nutt. See *M.citriodora*.
***M.coccinea*** Michx. See *M.didyma*.
***M.cornata*** Rydb. See *M.menthifolia*.
***M.dispersa*** Small. See *M.citriodora*.
***M.kalmiana*** Pursh. See *M.didyma*.
***M.lasiodonta*** Small. See *M.punctata* ssp. *villicaulis*.
***M.lutea*** Michx. See *M.punctata* ssp. *punctata*.
***M.mollis*** L. See *M.fistulosa*.
***M.nuttallii*** A. Nels. See *M.pectinata*.
***M.oswegoensis*** Barton. See *M.didyma*.
***M.penicillata*** Gray. See *M.pectinata*.
***M.punctata*** var. ***humilis*** Torr. See *M.pectinata*.
***M.punctata*** var. ***lasiodonta*** Gray. See *M.punctata*.
***M.punctata*** var. ***occidentalis*** Palmer & Steyerm. See *M.punctata* ssp. *occidentalis*.
***M.ramaleyi*** A. Nels. See *M.menthifolia*.
***M.scabra*** Beck. See *M.fistulosa*.
***M.stanfieldii*** Small. See *M.punctata* ssp. *stanfieldii*.
***M.stricta*** Wooton. See *M.menthifolia*.
***M.tenuiaristata*** Gray. See *M.citriodora*.

For illustration see HERBS.

**Monardella** Benth. (Diminutive of *Monarda*, a closely allied genus.) Labiatae. 19 species of annual or perennial herbs, often with creeping stems and fragrant foliage. Leaves small, entire or serrate. Inflorescence of terminal, globose, bracteate glomerules; calyx narrow, tubular, 10–15-nerved, teeth 5, deltoid, subequal, erect, throat without hairs; corolla small, often purple to rose, bilabiate, upper lip 2-lobed, lower lip 3-lobed, lips subequal, plane, lobes linear-oblong; stamens 4, all fertile, didynamous, the anterior pair more prominent but not much exserted. Nutlets smooth, oblong-oval. Western N America.

CULTIVATION Attractive aromatic annuals and perennials ideally suited for a well-drained rock garden or for pot display in the alpine house. Some species, e.g. *M.odoratissima*, have long been grown locally for medicinal teas. The annuals may be sown *in situ* in late spring in a fertile soil in full sun; the best-grown plants may need some watering in dry summers, although this is not necessary for their survival. The perennial species grow in full sun over rocks, preferring sandy soils and resenting excessively cold, damp soils during winter. They also make attractive pan plants for cold alpine house display. A loam-based medium-fertility potting compost with added sand is a good growing medium. Plants of the decumbent species may be put into a 25cm/10in. half pot. Watering should be reduced during winter.

Propagate from seed sown in a pot placed in a cold frame in spring, or from division of established clumps or semi-ripe cuttings taken in summer. Pot-grown plants may suffer from root mealybug, for which a systematic insecticide will probably be the only effective cure.

***M.lanceolata*** A. Gray. Erect annual to 50cm. Branching stems puberulent, tinted purple. Lvs 3–4cm, lanceolate, entire, apex obtuse, puberulent; petiole to 1.5cm. Glomerules 1.5–3cm diam.; bracts ovate-lanceolate, acute, exceeding cal. green, scabrous, reticulate-veined with prominent costate veins; cal. 6–8mm, glabrous, 13-veined, teeth ovate-deltoid, hirsute within; cor. rose-purple, 12–15mm, tube exserted, puberulent, limb 3–5mm, upper lip shortest. Nutlets oblong-oval. California, Nevada, Arizona. var. ***microcephala*** A. Gray. Glomerules reduced to 1cm across or less, all floral parts subsequently reduced. Stems and branches more divaricate than in species type. California, Baja California.

***M.linioides*** A. Gray. Decumbent shrubby perenn. Stem branching, 30–50cm, pubescence close, silvery. Lvs 1–4cm, narrowly oblong to narrowly lanceolate, apex acute or obtuse, margin entire, both surfaces covered in a minute silvery pubescence; petiole 2–5mm. Glomerules 2–3cm diam., bracts ovate to lanceolate, acuminate, equalling or exceeding cal., scarious, white-puberulent or tinged rose to purple; cal. 6–10mm, 13-nerved, rather slender, puberulent to hirsute; cor. 12–15mm rose to purple, the lobes slender, tube puberulent inside and out, lips subequal. California, Nevada, Arizona, Baja California. ssp. ***eulinoides*** Epling. Bracts ovate to rotund, off-white. California, Baja California. ssp. ***stricta*** (Parish) Epling). Bracts lanceolate, purple coloured. California, Baja California, Nevada, Arizona.

***M.macrantha*** A. Gray. Decumbent subshrubby perenn., emerging from slender rhiz. Stems 10–30cm, seldom branching, pubesc. or villous. Lvs 0.5–3cm, subcoriaceous, variable. Glomerules 2–4cm diam.; bracts oblong-elliptical, equal to cal., acute, membranous, sparsely villous; cal. variable, 1.2–2.5cm, sometimes tinged purple, teeth acute, villous within; cor. scarlet to yellow, puberulent, tube much exserted, limb 5–11mm, upper lip longest. California, Baja California. ssp. ***eumacrantha*** Epling. Lvs 1–3cm, glabrate above, pubesc. beneath. 25mm long. Glomerules 3–4cm diam.; bracts seldom equalling cal. purple; cal. 20–25mm; cor. usually 35–45mm. California, Baja California. ssp. ***nana*** (A. Gray) Epling. Lvs 0.5–1.5cm, ovate, glabrous or sparsely villous. Glomerules 2–3.5cm diam., bracts usually longer than cal., often tinged white; cal. 12–15mm; cor. usually 25–30mm. California, Baja California. Z9.

***M.odoratissima*** Benth. A polymorphic species. Perenn. with a woody decumbent stem; branches erect or ascending, 10–60cm, pubescence never silvery, often glaucous or cinereous. Lvs 1–3cm, ovate-lanceolate to oblong-lanceolate, entire, rarely obscurely serrate, pubesc. or glabrate; sessile or petiole to 3mm. Glomerules 1–5cm diam.; bracts membranous ovate or rotund, purple, densely short villous or tomentose, ciliate; cal. 6–10mm, 13-nerved, teeth ovate, hirsute within; cor. 1–2cm, rose-purple to pallid, tube retrorsely puberulent, lobes lanceolate not linear oblong. Nutlets oval-oblong. W US (Mts). ssp. ***australis*** (Abrams) Epling. Lvs 1–2.5cm, lanceolate or oblong, often acute, green or cinereous. Bracts lanceolate, exceeding cal., acuminate, slightly hairy; cor. 1.5cm, lobes slender, slightly tapering. ssp. ***discolor*** (Greene) Epling. Lvs 2cm, ovate, distinctly hoary-pubesc. Bracts ovate, equal to cal.; cal. woolly-pubesc.; cor. about 13mm, lobes slender. ssp. ***euodoratissima*** Epling. Lvs 2cm, appearing nearly glabrous. Bracts ovate to rotund, pubesc., about equal to cal.; cal. woolly-pubesc. around teeth; cor. 15mm, lobes slender. ssp. ***glauca*** (Greene) Epling. Lvs 1.5–4cm, ovate lanceolate, elliptical or oblong, glabrate appearing glaucous. Bracts ovate to orbicular slightly hairy, purple; cal. hirsute around the teeth, seldom woolly; cor. 1–2cm, lobes tapering. ssp. ***pallida*** (Heller) Epling. Lvs 2–3cm, lanceolate-oblong, cinereous; petiole margined. Glomerules compact; bracts inconspicuous, usually shorter than cal., broadly ovate, often woolly and tinged purple; cal. short, often densely woolly, cor. 1–1.5cm, pallid, lobes noticeably tapering. ssp. ***parvifolia*** (Greene) Epling. Lvs 1–2cm, lanceolate or oblong, cinereous; petiole margined. Glomerules small, 1–2cm, diam.; bracts inconspicuous, ovate, acute, usually shorter than cal.; cal. pubesc., sparingly hairy about the teeth; cor. usually less than 1cm. ssp. ***pinetorum*** (Heller) Epling. Leaves softly pubesc., subvillous beneath, ovate to lanceolate, 1.5–2.5cm long, margin usually revolute. Bracts inconspicuous, equalling, ovate, short pubesc., tinged purple. Cal. pubesc.; cor. rose-coloured 1–1.5cm, lobes tapering. Z8.

***M. villosa*** Benth. Perenn. from decumbent stems, woody at base, variable in stature, 10–60cm, subglabrous to pubesc. Lvs 1–3cm, ovate to lanceolate or rotund, apex obtuse, margins entire, obscurely crenate-serrate or dentate-serrate, usually villous or villous-tomentose; petiole to 1cm. Glomerules compact, 2–4cm across, bracts leaflike; cal. 7–10mm, 13-nerved, shaggy villous above, teeth deltoid-ovate; cor. 10–18mm, pale rose to rose-purple, lobes linear-oblong and very narrow; stamens equal to length of lobes. California, Oregon. 'Sheltonii': to 60cm, well-branched; fls small, light purple. ssp. ***neglecta*** (Greene) Epling. Stems puberulent to glabrous, tinted purple. Lvs to 1.5cm, ovate, margins serrate, base cuneate. Bracts ovate, acute, membranous, outer bracts leaflike, inner purple, ciliate; cal. 6–8mm; cor. 12–14mm, rose-purple. California. Z8.

***M. acuta*** Greene. See *M. lanceolata.*
***M. australis*** Abrams. See *M. odoratissima* ssp. *australis.*
***M. discolor*** Greene. See *M. odoratissima* ssp. *discolor.*
***M. glabra*** Nutt. See *M. odoratissima* ssp. *euodoratissima.*
***M. glauca*** Greene. See *M. odoratissima* ssp. *glauca.*
***M. ingrata*** Greene. See *M. odoratissima* ssp. *glauca.*
***M. modocensis*** Greene. See *M. odoratissima* ssp. *glauca.*
***M. muriculata*** Greene. See *M. odoratissima* ssp. *parvifolia.*
***M. nana*** A. Gray. See *M. macrantha* ssp. *nana.*
***M. nervosa*** Greene. See *M. odoratissima* ssp. *discolor.*
***M. odoratissima*** Howell non Benth. See *M. odoratissima* ssp. *euodoratissima.*
***M. ovata*** Greene. See *M. odoratissima* ssp. *glauca.*
***M. pallida*** Heller. See *M. odoratissima* ssp. *pallida.*
***M. parvifolia*** Greene. See *M. odoratissima* ssp. *parvifolia.*
***M. peninsularis*** Greene. See *M. lanceolata* var. *microcephala.*
***M. pinetorum*** Heller. See *M. odoratissima* ssp. *pinetorum.*
***M. purpurea*** Howell. See *M. odoratissima* ssp. *glauca.*
***M. rubella*** Greene. See *M. odoratissima* ssp. *glauca.*
***M. sanguinea*** Greene. See *M. lanceolata.*

**Moneses** Salisb. (From Gk *monos*, single, and *esis*, delight, alluding to the beauty of the single flower.) WOOD NYMPH; ONE-FLOWERED WINTERGREEN. Pyrolaceae. 1 species, a perennial, evergreen, glabrous, stoloniferous, dwarf herb to 10cm, resembling *Pyrola*. Leaves opposite or in threes, whorled, ovate to obovate, to 2.5cm, minutely toothed, dark green, glabrous, paler below; petioles to 8mm. Flowers terminal, solitary, nodding; sepals 5, fringed, persistent; petals 5, to 1cm, orbicular, entire or finely fringed, spreading, waxy white to shell pink; stamens 10; ovary subglobose, 5-celled, style straight, elongate, stigma distinctly 5-lobed. Fruit an erect, apically dehiscent capsule, to 8cm wide. N temperate. Z2.

CULTIVATION Found in moist, usually coniferous woodland on mossy ground or on nurse logs, on lime free soils to altitudes of 2100m/6825ft.; in Britain wild populations are rare and decreasing; even those which remain in Scotland are threatened, usually by commercial forestry. Cultivate as for *Pyrola*.

***M. uniflora*** (L.) A. Gray. As for the genus.

For synonymy see *Pyrola*.

**Monilaria** Schwantes. (From Lat. *monile*, a string of pearls.) Aizoaceae. 5 species of low-growing, clump-forming succulents; stems short and thick, often jointed like a string of beads. Leaves heterophyllous, one pair only united at the base, more or less semicylindric with bright papillae, the other alternating pair united into smooth subglobose bodies. Flowers long-pedicellate, white, tinged yellow, or red. S Africa (Cape Province). Z9.

CULTIVATION As for *Mitrophyllum*.

***M. chrysoleuca*** (Schltr.) Schwantes. Stems fleshy, 6–10cm. Lvs 30–50×5mm, cylindrical, obtuse, minutely papillose, second pair globose, smooth. Fls 3cm diam., snow-white or pink-purple. Cape: Van Rhynsdorp District and Little Namaqualand.

***M. moniliformis*** (Haw.) Schwantes. Stems and branches 7.5–10cm×8–11mm. Body lvs oblong to rounded, spherical, 12mm, dark green, secondary lvs united for 12mm within body, 10–15cm×4–5mm, semicylindric, soft, papillose at first. Fls around 3cm diam., white. Cape: Van Rhynsdorp District.

***M. pisiformis*** (Haw.) Schwantes. Freely branched; short stems 2–3cm. Body lvs very short, pea-sized, secondary lvs 5–6cm×3–4mm, more or less cylindric, glossy-papillose. Fls 3cm diam., yellow or flushed red with a white border. Cape: Van Rhynsdorp District.

***M. luckhoffii*** (L. Bol.). See *Diplosoma luckhoffii.*
***M. peersii*** L. Bol. See *M. moniliformis.*
For further synonymy see *Conophyllum, Mesembryanthemum, Mitrophyllum* and *Schwantesia*.

**MONIMIACEAE** Juss. MONIMIA FAMILY. Dicot. 35 genera and 450 species of trees, shrubs or lianes, often with alkaloids; twigs often flattened at nodes. Leaves leathery, evergreen, usually opposite, simple, often with gland-dots and contain aromatic oils; stipules absent. Flowers small, usually unisexual, regular to oblique, usually perigynous with concave hypanthium, solitary or in cymose inflorescences; calyx 2+2 free sepals, fleshy, decussate; corolla 7–20 (or more) free petals, or perianth not differentiated into calyx and corolla, reduced or absent; male flowers with numerous stamens, in 1 or 2 series, with short filaments and basal nectaries; females with usually superior ovary, of (1–) numerous free carpels, with short styles and terminal stigmas; carpels sometimes sunk in receptacle, with 1 ovule. Fruit a head of drupes or nuts, often enclosed in hypanthium; seed with copious oily endosperm. Some are timber trees, such as *Doryphora, Hedycarya, Peumus,* others are medicinal and produce scents; for example *Laurelia*, the source or Peruvian nutmeg. Tropical and warm, especially southern, mainly Madagascar, Australia and Polynesia. *Atherosperma, Hedycarya.*

**Monizia** Lowe. (For J.M. Moniz (*fl.* c1856), Madeiran botanist.) Umbelliferae. Monospecific genus of woody-based herbs to 1m, arising from a thick black taproot. Leaves to 30cm, mostly basal, triangular in outline, 3–4-pinnatisect, terminal segments narrow-oblong or linear, bright green, incised-serrate, petiole sheathing, finely pubescent; upper stem leaves 2–3-pinnatisect. Umbels compound, compact, with 20–25 rays; involucral bracts 6–10, linear-lanceolate; involucel similar to involucre; flowers dull white; petals slightly pilose. Spring. Madeira. Z9.

CULTIVATION As for *Melanoselinum*.

***M. edulis*** Lowe. CARROT TREE; DESERTA CARROT. As for the genus.

For synonymy see *Melanoselinum*.

**Monochoria** C. Presl. Pontederiaceae. (From Gk *monos*, single and *chorizo*, to separate; the front stamen differs from the other five.) About 5 species of annual or perennial aquatic herbs. Rhizome short and creeping or absent; stems erect or creeping. Leaves emergent on long sheathing petioles, basal or alternate on short erect stem, sagittate, cordate-ovate to lanceolate. Inflorescence with solitary, terminal, sheathing leaf enclosing membranous spathe at base of peduncle; flowers in elongate racemes; perianth segment 6, subequal, oblong, free, blue, often spotted red; stamens 6, inserted on perianth tube, anthers oblong, basifixed, unequal, one large, blue, the other 5 smaller, yellow; ovary sessile, 3-locular; style filiform, apex trifid or 6-fid. Fruit capsular with numerous seeds. Africa, Asia to Australia. Z10.

CULTIVATION As for *Pontederia* and *Heteranthera* in tropical or subtropical pools or indoor aquaria.

***M. vaginalis*** (Burm. f.) Kunth. Rhiz. short. Stems creeping, rooting from nodes. Lvs long-petiolate, linear to ovate or ovate-cordate, to 10cm. Infl. erect, to 60cm, raceme subspicate; fls variable in size, to 15mm across, few to many on short pedicels, upper fls opening first; perianth seg. unequal, 3 larger seg. obovate, 3 smaller seg. oblong, blue, spotted red; anth. unequal, largest blue, others yellow. Summer. S & SE Asia. Spp. from Africa have erroneously been attributed to *M. vaginalis*.

**Monodora** Dunal. Annonaceae. 20 species of evergreen trees and shrubs. Leaves alternate, entire, petiolate. Flowers showy, pendulous, solitary or paired, fragrant, long-stalked, bisexual; sepals somewhat swollen; petals 6, in 2 whorls, basally fused, undulate to crisped, the inner petals converging at apex; stamens short, crowded; pistils numerous; ovaries unilocular, ovules numerous; carpels initially free but fusing to form a fleshy subglobose syncarp; seeds woody. Tropical Africa, Madagascar. Z10.

CULTIVATION As for *Artabotrys*.

***M. myristica*** (Gaertn.) Dunal CALABASH NUTMEG; JAMAICA NUTMEG. To 8m. Lvs 10–35×8–18cm, obovate-oblong to elliptic; petioles 2cm, basally cordate, pale green, veins prominent beneath. Pedicels 12–20cm, pendulous; fls fragrant; sep. 1.5–3cm; pet. 6–10cm, broadly elliptic, yellow marked purple, the inner pet. much shorter, obovate, off-white, downy beneath, yellow spotted crimson above. Fr. 15cm diam., many-seeded. Tropical W Africa south to Angola.

**Monolena** Triana. (From Gk *monos*, one, and *olene*, arm, referring to the arm-like process at the base of the anther.) Melastomataceae. Some 8 species of evergreen and deciduous fleshy, glabrous herbs. Aerial stems virtually absent, consisting of short, ring-scaled excrescences on the surface of a large, somewhat misshapen and crisply succulent rhizome. Leaves in clusters, rather fleshy, oblong, cordate or orbicular, entire or shallow-toothed, petiolate. Flowers pink or white, subsessile in slender scorpioid cymes; calyx tube fleshy, turbinate, withering in fruit; petals 5, rounded-obovate to spathulate. Tropical S America.

CULTIVATION A curious fleshy-rooted herb with attractive pink flowers. Conditions as for tropical rhizomatous *Begonia* spp. Increase by portions of the rhizome, the wounds dusted with sulphur.

***M. primuliflora*** Hook. f. Rhiz. to 13×8cm, exposed, smooth, golden-brown, often with numerous concavities and irregularities. Lvs to 18cm, semi-deciduous, ovate-elliptic, acuminate, semi-erect, thinly fleshy, finely sinuate-toothed, ciliate, lustrous light green, distinctly nerved above, pink-tinted and initially thinly scurfy beneath; petioles to 10cm, slender, flushed pink. Cymes to 15cm; fls to 2.5cm diam., candy-pink, centre white; anth. yellow. Colombia.

For synonymy see *Bertolonia*.

**Monolopia** DC. (From Gk *monos*, single, and *lopos*, covering, referring to the uniseriate involucre.) Compositae. 4 species of erect, annual herbs, floccose. Leaves opposite below, alternate above, simple, entire or toothed sessile. Capitula radiate, rather large, terminal, pedunculate; receptacle conic; involucre hemispherical or campanulate; phyllaries free or connate into a cup, usually with black hairs at apex; ray florets female, fertile, yellow, disc florets hermaphrodite, fertile, yellow. Fruit an oblanceolate, acutely 3–4 angled cypsela, somewhat compressed; pappus absent. SW US (California).

CULTIVATION For the cut flower border and for native plant collections, especially on sunny banks that approximate to habitat, *Monolopia* spp. are undemanding annuals for any well-drained soil in sun; sow *in situ* in spring or earlier under glass.

***M. lanceolata*** Nutt. Stems to 60cm, hollow, simple to diffusely much-branched, densely lanate, becoming glabrate below. Lvs to 10cm, broadly lanceolate to linear, entire to undulate-dentate. Peduncles to 12cm; involucre to 1cm, broadly campanulate to depressed hemispheric; phyllaries free, lanceolate to ovate-lanceolate, densely white-lanate below, black-lanate at apex; ray florets to 2cm. Fr. to obcompressed, grey-strigose. Spring. California.

***M. major*** DC. Similar to *M. lanceolata* but stems to 1m, sparingly branched, involucre to over 1cm, phyllaries connate in lower half. Fr. strongly obcompressed, 4mm, glabrate or strigose toward apex. Spring. California.

***M. major*** var. ***lanceolata*** A. Gray. See *M. lanceolata*.

**Monopanax** Reg.
***M. ghiesbreghtii*** (Versch. ex E. Morr.) Reg. See *Oreopanax xalapensis*.

**Monopsis** Salisb. (From Gk *monos*, one, and *opsis*, face; the flowers are regular, not bilabiate.) Campanulaceae. Some 18 species of small, annual herbs. Similar to *Lobelia*. Leaves sessile. Flowers solitary axillary, stalked; calyx tube oblique, lobes spreading; corolla slit to the base on the upper side, tube longer than the short lobes; stamens inserted at base of corolla, anthers connate in an erect ring; style filiform; stigma of 2 curved filiform branches. Tropical S Africa.

CULTIVATION Undemanding annuals for zones with cool moist summers, for the flower border and as edging, in any moderately fertile, well drained soil in sun or semi-shade. Sow seed *in situ* in spring or earlier under glass.

***M. campanulata*** (Lam.) Sonder. Prostrate annual to 25cm. Lvs to 1.5cm, obovate-lanceolate, entire to irregularly denticulate, grading to linear-lanceolate above. Fls borne on erect pedicels; cor. to 1.5cm, deep blue; anth. bright yellow. S Africa.

***M. debilis*** (L. f.) C. Presl. Slender, erect annual herb to 20cm, usually glabrous, occasionally pubesc. Lvs to 4cm, linear, dentate. Fls small, on long pedicels; cal. to 0.2cm, obliquely obovate to obtriangular, minutely pubesc., conspicuously veined, lobes lanceolate; cor. to 0.7cm, lobes ovate, dark blue. Autumn. S Africa, naturalized W Australia.

***M. unidentata*** (Ait. f.) F. Wimm. Prostrate perenn., generally glabrous. Lvs to 2cm, opposite, alternate or whorled, lower lvs oblong-orbicular, upper lvs linear, irregularly dentate, recurved. Fls usually solitary, pedicellate; cor. bilabiate, violet to blue. S Africa.

For synonymy see *Dobrowskya* and *Lobelia*.

**Monopyle** Moritz ex Benth. & Hook. f. (From Gk *monos*, single, and *pyle*, door; the capsule opens by one dorsal slit.) Gesneriaceae. 8 species of perennial herbs; stems sparsely branched, marked red. Leaves paired, opposite, often markedly unequal, the smaller leaf often reduced to a stipule, serrate. Flowers many in a paniculate inflorescence; calyx lobes 5, entire, equal; corolla white and purple, open-campanulate, exterior minutely strigillose, limb broad with spreading, subequal lobes; stamens 4, anthers connate, filaments inserted on corolla; staminode 1. Fruit a linear-oblong capsule. S America. Z10.

CULTIVATION See GESNERIADS.

***M. racemosa*** Benth. Softly pubesc.; stem cylindric, dark brown-purple. Lvs closely arranged in opposite, equal pairs, ovate-lanceolate, acuminate, serrulate, subacute at base, bright green above; petiole to 1cm, flushed maroon-red with a pale green, purple-maculate blotch at base. Fls in a many-fld terminal raceme; pedicels to 0.8cm; cal. tube hemispheric, lobes unequal, broadly ovate; cor. to 2.5×2cm, white, tube ventricose, interior faintly spotted pink, limb to 2cm across, 5-lobed, lobes broadly truncate, lower 3 lobes irregularly deeply toothed. Colombia.

**Monostiche** Horan.
***M. colorata*** (Hook.) Körn. See *Calathea colorata*.
***M. daniellii*** Horan. See *Thaumatococcus daniellii*.

**Monotagma** Schum. (From Gk *monos*, single, and *tagma*, series; the flowers are borne singly.) Marantaceae. About 20 species of perennial herbs. Rhizomes spreading. Stems erect. Leaves rosulate, homotropic, unequal; petioles long, often annulate at base. Inflorescence a terminal, usually densely branched, panicle; bracts tough, rolled, green or brightly coloured, diverging from rachis in flowering to give a comb-like appearance; bracteoles absent; prophylls membranous; flowers slender, borne singly; sepals short, linear, thin, membranous; corolla tube longer with slightly hooded lobes; outer staminode 1, petaloid, coloured, callose staminode bilobed, firm and fleshy, cucullate staminode with short simple appendage; stigmatic orifice often funnel-shaped; ovary unilocular, glabrous to apically pubescent. Fruit a capsule with thin, toughened pericarp; seeds long, black, arillate. Tropical America (Matto Grosso to Peru). Z10.

CULTIVATION As for *Calathea*.

***M. smaragdinum*** (Lind.) Schum. Erect, showy, about 40cm. Lvs basal, lanceolate to oblong-lanceolate, acuminate, emerald-green with dark green pubescence along midrib above, pale green, minutely pubesc. beneath. Infl. a spike to 13cm; bracts to 3cm, oblong-acute, papery; fls 4–8; sep. lanceolate; cor. lobes lanceolate; outer staminode obovate. Ecuador.

For synonymy see *Calathea, Ischnosiphon* and *Maranta*.

**Monsonia** L. (For Lady Ann Monson, a correspondent of Linnaeus.) Geraniaceae. Some 25 species of prostrate to upright herbs or subshrubs, similar to *Sarcocaulon*, but stems more or less herbaceous, and without spines. Stems few to several, some woody at base. Leaves stipulate, almost opposite to opposite, unequal, simple or divided, margins toothed, veins pinnate or palmate. Flowers bisexual, solitary or in many-flowered umbels, axillary in leaf axils, 5-parted, regular; sepals overlapping, free or fused, margins membranous, apex mucronate; petals free, overlapping or twisted, veins palmate; stamens 15, in groups of 3 or rarely 5, groups fused at base, middle filament long, outer filaments shorter, filaments awl-shaped, base flattened, ciliate; anthers glabrous, dorsifixed, 2-celled; ovary superior, beaked, 5-lobed, ovules 2 per lobe. Fruit a schizocarp, splitting into 5, 1-seeded mericarps, mericarp tail helically twisted, crested; seeds brown. Africa, Madagascar, SW Asia. Z10.

CULTIVATION In temperate climates, grow in the intermediate glasshouse with good light and low humidity, in a well-drained, medium-fertility loam-based mix, with up to one quarter by volume of sharp sand or fine shingle. A layer of sharp sand or fine grit at the top of the pot helps reduce the risk of stem rot; crocking is also beneficial. May be grown in a clay land-drain to accommodate the taproot. Water sparingly, except at flower-bud formation, and apply half-strength liquid feed during the growing season. With shelter from wind, specimens may be put outside on warm summer days. Propagate from seed sown in spring at 15–20°C/60–68°F, in a mix of equal parts propagating medium and sharp sand. Pollinate by hand to ensure seed set. Also by root cuttings, and nodal cuttings, during the growing season, in 40:60 sieved sphagnum and sharp sand or vermiculite, in a closed case with bottom heat at 18°C/64°F. Some authorities recommend that the bases of nodal cuttings dry for 2–3 days, to allow wounds to seal. *Monsonia* is prone to rots if overwatered. Draughts and overfeeding cause browning of the leaf margins. Young plants may suffer sun scorch.

***M. speciosa*** L. Evergreen, perenn. subshrub to 30cm, with or without woody rhiz. Branches to 16cm, glabrous or pubesc. with pale hairs and glandular hairs. Lf petiole hairy as stem, lower lvs rosulate or alternate, upper lvs opposite, lamina to 60×60cm, palmately deeply or shallowly divided into 5 or 7 lobes, lobes finely pinnately lobed or simple, margins toothed to crenulate, downy and glandular-hairy beneath, densely pubesc. above, apex obtuse to acute, base truncate to cordate. Fls solitary, 5cm diam.; peduncles to 30cm, pedicels to 100cm; involucral bracts 6; sep. green, purple or red, joined at base, to 3×1cm; pet. to 6.5×4cm, rose, crimson, purple, base and veins darker, streaked with black lines at base, exterior tinged green, glabrous or sparsely glandular-hairy, apex 5-toothed. Fr. to 10cm, mericarp base to 1.6cm, beak to 8cm. Spring. S Africa (SW Cape).

***M. lobata*** Montin. See *M. speciosa*.

**Monstera** Adans. (From Lat. *monstrum*, a marvel, or *monster*, possibly alluding to curious shape of leaves.) SWISS-CHEESE PLANT; WINDOWLEAF. Araceae. 22 evergreen, epiphytic, perennial lianes, to 20m+. Aerial roots often present, long, corky, negatively phototropic. Stems stout, fibrous, ascending or sprawling. Leaves in 2 ranks, dimorphic with juvenile and adult phases; juvenile foliage often entire, sometimes overlapping, close to tree-bark, when known as shingle plants (also occurring in other genera of Araceae, as well as other families); adult leaves to 90×75cm, entire or pinnatifid, more or less oblong, unequal, often perforated, coriaceous, bright to dark green; petioles long, exceeding lamina, pulvinate at apex, sheathed below. Peduncle short; spathe large, to 45cm, cymbiform, deciduous, usually white or cream; spadix densely covered by hermaphrodite flowers, shorter than spathe; perianth absent; stamens 4; ovary 2-locular, ovules 2 per locule; sterile flowers sometimes present among others, with rudimentary parts. Fruit of clustered white berries, sometimes edible when mature, aromatic; seeds soft. Tropical America.

CULTIVATION *Monstera* spp. are usually vining climbers of humid tropical America, found scrambling up tall trees. In temperate zones, they are most commonly grown as houseplants, or in hot glasshouses. Under such conditions, poles of sphagnum moss are often provided in imitation of natural hosts, dampened to improve atmospheric humidity and to provide a moist medium for the running aerial roots. Since the natural tendency of the plants is to grow upwards or to sprawl, specimens in cultivation may be reluctant to make the bushy plants that growers prefer. Species such as *M. standleyana* are thicker stemmed and mounding in habit, growing naturally without support. The leaf perforations of many species, absent in young leaves, make them particularly elegant and attractive subjects, but if the necessary draught-free conditions of filtered light and high humidity are not provided, these perforations may fail to develop. Too much or too little water will cause rapid leaf yellowing. Plants will benefit from frequent sponging of leaves to remove dust.

*M. deliciosa*, that most popular of houseplants, was once grown in English hothouses for its large, cone-shaped compound fruit, known as ceriman, with a flavour described as somewhere between a pineapple and a banana. The fruits are consumed when completely ripe and are used in fruit salad and for drinks and ices. Fruit is produced only under perfect growing conditions, in a warm moist climate, and plants fruit better when allowed to sprawl along the ground. In the US, vines are cultivated in Florida, under half shade, as for pineapple.

Propagate from seed, which must not be allowed to dry out; by internodal cuttings, or from cuttings made from growing tips with one leaf attached, rooted with bottom heat in a sandy propagating mix. Alternatively, propagate by air-layering.

Cultivation otherwise as for *Philodendron*.

***M. acuminata*** K. Koch. SHINGLE PLANT. Stems flattened. Lvs to 28×13cm, ovate, very unequal, base cordate, entire or pinnatifid with 1–2 segments to 5cm wide, coriaceous; petioles to 15cm, sheath broad, membranous, persistent. Peduncle to 5cm; spathe to 7.5cm, spadix 5cm, oblong-ovate. C America.

***M. adansonii*** Schott. To 8m. Lvs to 90×25cm, ovate to oblong-ovate or -elliptic, very unequal, larger half rotund-truncate at base, other half subcuneate, perforations irregular, large, elliptic-oblong, in single series on one or both sides of midrib, seldom breaking margin; petioles shorter than lamina, sheath extending to pulvinus, green, persistent. Spathe to 20cm, white, spadix to 10cm, slender. Northern S America. var. ***laniata*** (Schott) Madison. Lvs 22–55×15–40cm, ovate, membranous with many perforations; petiole sheathe deciduous. Spadix to 13×2cm, yellow. Costa Rica to Brazil.

***M. deliciosa*** Liebm. CERIMAN; SWISS-CHEESE PLANT. To 20m. Stems stout, climbing or sprawling; aerial roots present, long. Lvs 25–90×25–75cm, orbicular-ovate, cordate, entire when juvenile, regularly pinnatifid to halfway to midrib when adult, seg. curved, oblong, with one vein, also usually perforate with elliptic to oblong holes between base of marginal perforation and midrib, coriaceous, glossy dark green, veins paler green; petioles equalling or exceeding lamina, sheath becoming scarious, deciduous, pulvinus flattened, winged. Spathe to 30cm, cream, persistent; spadix to 25×3cm, swelling in fruit, cream-coloured, aromatic and tasting of banana and pineapple when mature. Mexico to Panama. 'Albo-variegata': lvs large, partly rich deep green with other sections a contrasting creamy-white. 'Variegata': lvs irregularly variegated cream or yellow.

***M. dubia*** (HBK) Engl. & K. Krause. Adult lvs to 130×60cm, oblong, base truncate, regularly pinnatisect, seg. 12–20, linear; juvenile forms shingle plant, with lvs silver-variegated. Petioles to 45cm, sheath deciduous. Spathe large, white; spadix to 42.5cm, white. C America (Nicaragua, Costa Rica).

***M. epipremnoides*** Engl. Large climber. Adult lvs to 90×55cm, ovate- to oblong-elliptic, base truncate or weakly cordate, pinnatifid, seg. to 3.5cm across, perforate with 2–3 ranks of elliptic to linear-oblong holes, outermost holes large, reaching or cutting margin; juvenile lvs broad-ovate, smaller; petioles sheathing nearly to pulvinus, sheath persistent, expanded at apex. Spathe to 40cm, white, spadix to 19cm. Costa Rica.

***M. karwinskyi*** Schott. Stems to 4m+. Lvs 55–85×33–55cm, entire, ovate to oblong-elliptic, base truncate, coriaceous, perforate with 1 narrow-oblong hole between main lateral veins; petioles to 55cm, sheathed to pulvinus, sheath soon becoming scarious, deciduous. Spathe green externally, white within; spadix to 14cm, shorter than spathe, thick, cream-coloured. Tropical Mexico.

***M. obliqua*** (Miq.) Walp. Plant small, stems climbing. Lvs to 20×7cm, entire, elliptic to oblong-lanceolate, sometimes much-perforated, with holes covering more area than laminal tissue, or not perforate, bright green. Peduncle to 7.5cm; spathe short, spadix to 3.5cm, with few fls. Northern S America.

***M.punctulata*** Schott. Resembling *M.deliciosa* but lvs 120×60cm, ovate- to oblong-elliptic, petioles much spotted with white, pulvinus subcylindric; scarious cataphylls persistent on stem; juvenile phase a shingle plant, lvs ovate, base oblique. Spathe to 14cm, pink-buff externally, white within. Tropical Mexico.

***M.standleyana*** Bunting. Juvenile phase with slender stems; lvs to 20×5cm, narrow-oblong-lanceolate, main lateral veins emerging from midrib at acute angle; petioles to 12.5×1.5cm. Adult stems stout, lvs to 60×33cm, entire, oblong-ovate, base obtuse, not perforate, very dark green, lateral veins prominent beneath; petioles 50cm, broadly winged. Peduncle to 30cm; spathe 28cm, cream-coloured; spadix 15cm, cream. Costa Rica.

***M.subpinnata*** (Schott) Engl. Lvs to 33cm, orbicular-ovate, pinnatifid with 3–4 pairs of widely separated narrowly oblanceolate seg., each 15×2.5cm, with 1 main lateral vein and several parallel subsidiary veins; petiole to 25cm, sheath deciduous. Spathe to 15cm, dull yellow, spadix to 10cm. Peru.

***M.falcifolia*** Engl. See *M.obliqua*.
***M.guttifera*** hort. See *M.standleyana*.
***M.latiloba*** K. Krause. See *M.subpinnata*.
***M.leichtlinii*** hort. See *M.epipremnoides*.
***M.nechodomii*** hort. See *Epipremnum pinnatum*.
***M.pertusa*** (L.) De Vriese, non Schott. See *M.adansonii*.
***M.uleana*** Engl. See *M.subpinnata*.
For further synonymy see *Philodendron* and *Raphidophora*.

**Montanoa** La Ll. & Lex. (For the Mexican politician Don Luis Montanoa.) Compositae. About 20 species of vines or pachycaul treelets and trees. Stems terete to tetragonal, herbaceous parts green to purple or brown, woody parts with sticky resinous sap. Leaves opposite, entire to serrate or pinnatifid, rarely pinnatisect, petiolate. Capitula usually radiate, in corymbs or panicles; receptacle slightly to strongly convex, scaly; involucre subcylindric to hemispheric; phyllaries in 1–2 series; ray florets sterile, white or cream to rose or purple; disc florets hermaphrodite, usually fertile, yellow to grey-green or black. Fruit cypsela, narrowly obpyramidal, laterally compressed; pappus absent. Tropical America. Z10.

CULTIVATION A frost-tender genus, grown for its flowers and for the handsome foliage, often with a fresh resinous fragrance; *Montanoa* spp. make striking and fast-growing specimens for the shrub borders of frost-free zones but are also cultivated as annuals for their attractive foliage, or as potplants for the warm glasshouse in cool temperate zones; containerized specimens may be moved out of doors for the summer. Treat as for *Bartlettina*. Propagation is also possible by root cuttings.

***M.bipinnatifida*** (Kunth) K. Koch. Shrub or tree to 10m. Lvs to 30×40cm, broadly ovate to ovate-lanceolate, serrate to deeply 1–2-pinnatifid, entire above, seg. acute to acuminate, dark green, hairy; petioles to 20cm, auriculate. Capitula radiate, pendulous, 2–4cm diam., in terminal clusters of over 20 heads; phyllaries 6–8mm, 8–9, in 2 series; ray florets 10–12, white; disc florets numerous yellow. Late autumn–winter. S Mexico.

***M.hibiscifolia*** Benth. Shrub to 6m; stems terete, light brown. Lvs to 40×30cm, ovate to pentagonal, deeply 3–5-lobed, occasionally subentire to serrate, pubesc. beneath; petioles to 6cm, usually auriculate. Capitula radiate, pendulous, 1–2cm diam., numerous, in compound corymbs; phyllaries 5–7, in 1 series; ray florets 7–8, white; disc florets numerous, yellow. Autumn–winter. S Mexico to Guatemala and Costa Rica.

***M.mollissima*** Brongn. & Groenl. Shrub to 2m, downy at first. Lvs to 17×10cm, lanceolate to triangular, entire to irregularly dentate to 3-lobed, base cordate, subglabrous above, softly downy beneath, sessile or petioles to 6cm, usually winged and auriculate. Capitula radiate, erect, 1–2cm diam., in compound corymbs; phyllaries 4–7mm, 6–8, more or less in 1 series; ray florets 8–12, white; disc florets numerous, yellow. Autumn. Mexico.

***M.tomentosa*** Cerv. ZOAPATLE. Shrub to 3m, densely branched, downy. Lvs to 20×15cm, triangular-ovate, entire to serrate, irregularly dentate or lobed, base cordate to cuneate, downy beneath; petiole to 4cm. Capitula usually radiate, erect, 3–8mm diam., numerous, in a broad, compound panicle to 40cm diam.; phyllaries 3–5mm, 4–6, in 1 series; ray florets *c*6, 3–5mm, cream to white or absent; disc florets few, light to dark yellow. Autumn. Mexico.

**Montbretia** hort.
***M.crocosmiiflora*** Lemoine. See *Crocosmia* × *crocosmiiflora*.
***M.pottsii*** (Bak.) Bak. See *Crocosmia pottsii*.

**Montezuma** Moc. & Sessé ex DC. (For Montezuma, 16th-century Aztec king.) Bombacaceae. 1 species, an evergreen tree to 16m; trunk to 45cm diam., bark deeply furrowed, grey or brown; branches spreading. Leaves 5–20cm, alternate, simple, cordate, ovate to orbicular, acute to acuminate, coriaceous, green to yellow-green; petioles to 12.5cm. Flowers axillary, solitary; pedicels long, to 14cm; calyx truncate, to 2.5cm, transversely dehiscent after anthesis; petals 5, 6–11×7.5cm, somewhat sinuate, pink to crimson on inner side, externally tan to orange, densely stellate pubescent; stamens united into column to 7cm, filaments white; ovary 5-locular, style to 5.5cm, white, stigmata 3–4, yellow. Fruit ovoid, indehiscent, dry when mature, somewhat succulent when young; seeds few, brown. Puerto Rico (originally thought to occur in Mexico). Z10.

CULTIVATION As for *Durio*.

***M.speciosissima*** Moc. & Sessé ex DC. As for the genus.
For synonymy see *Thespesia*.

**Montia** L. (For Giuseppe Monti (*d* 1760), Italian botanist.) MINER'S LETTUCE; WINTER PURSLANE. Portulacaceae. 15 species of small, soft, hairless, often glaucous annual or perennial herbs. Basal leaves petioled, rather fleshy; stem leaves often several and alternate, or only 2 and then opposite, usually sessile. Flowers small, white or pink, usually several in simple to compound, axillary or terminal racemes; sepals 2, persistent and often of unequal size; petals 2–5 (rarely 6); stamens as many as petals; style 3-branched. Fruit a 3-valved capsule, spherical or ovoid; seeds 1–3, usually black and glossy. N temperate regions, S America, tropical Africa and Asia. Closely related to *Claytonia* from which it differs in the number of ovules in the ovary.

CULTIVATION *Montia* spp. occur predominantly on acidic sandy soils, *M.perfoliata* on dunes and waste ground, *M.sibirica* in moister and more shaded woodland and streamside habitats; both species are suited to naturalizing in conditions approximating to those in habitat. *M.chamissoi* is native of wet waterside soils, and useful in wilder areas of the bog and pondside garden; with roots in moist soil the slender creeping stems will extend outwards over the surface of the water. *M.sibirica* is particularly valued for the long succession of delicate bloom in the deep shade of the wild and woodland garden, being self perpetuating there by seed when conditions suit, although seldom to the point of nuisance. *M.perfoliata* is also occasionally grown as a salad herb, with a mild, slightly acid flavour, eaten raw or cooked as for spinach. It can be cropped year-round with cloche protection in cooler climates. Sow *in situ* in drills, or in blocks to space at 15cm/6in. within rows; spring sowing for summer crops, mid-summer sowings for over-wintering.

***M.chamissoi*** (Ledeb. ex Spreng.) T. Dur. & B.D. Jacks. Floating or creeping perenn., rooting at nodes. Stem lvs to 5cm, in several opposite pairs, spathulate to oblanceolate. Fls to 5mm, pale rose, 1–9 in a raceme at or near the ends of the shoots. N America (Alaska south to California and New Mexico). Z3.

***M.perfoliata*** (Donn) J.T. Howell. MINER'S LETTUCE; WINTER PURSLANE; CUBAN SPINACH. Annual, glabrous, bright green, 10–30cm or more. Lvs basal, rhombic-ovate to lanceolate, long-petioled. Infl. subtended by a perfoliate disc-like organ; fls white. N America, naturalized GB. A complex assemblage of variable forms. f. ***parviflora*** (Douglas ex Hook.) J.T. Howell. Basal lvs linear to oblanceolate. Infl. elongate; fls with sepals only *c*3mm.

***M.sibirica*** (L.) J.T. Howell. SIBERIAN PURSLANE. Annual or of longer duration, to 40cm. Basal lvs usually many, rhombic-ovate to lanceolate, petioles 2–3× as long as blades, some becoming fleshy at base or having bulbils in the axils; stem lvs 2, opposite, sessile to short-petioled. Fls white to pink, in many-fld terminal racemes to 30cm. N America (Alaska south to California, and from Iowa to Minnesota). Z3.

***M.flagellaris*** (Bong.) Robinson. See *Claytonia parvifolia* var. *flagellaris*.
***M.parviflora*** (Douglas) J.T. Howell. See *M.perfoliata* f. *parviflora*.
***M.parvifolia*** (Moc. ex DC.) Greene. See *Claytonia parvifolia*.
***M.parvifolia*** ssp. ***flagellaris*** (Bong.) Ferris. See *Claytonia parvifolia* var. *flagellaris*.
For further synonymy see *Claytonia*.

**Monvillea** Britt. & Rose.
***M.campinensis*** (Backeb. & Voll) Backeb. See *Cereus campinensis*.

***M. cavendishii*** sensu Britt. & Rose. See *Cereus saxicola*.
***M. diffusa*** Britt. & Rose. See *Cereus diffusus*.
***M. haageana*** Backeb. See *Cereus haageana*.
***M. insularis*** (Hemsl.) Britt. & Rose. See *Cereus insularis*.
***M. lindenzweigiana*** (Gürke) Backeb. See *Cereus spegazzinii*.
***M. marmorata*** (Zeissold) Frič & Kreutz. See *Cereus spegazzinii*.
***M. phatnosperma*** (Schum.) Britt. & Rose. See *Cereus spegazzinii*.
***M. rhodoleucantha*** (Schum.) A. Berger. See *Cereus saxicola*.
***M. smithiana*** (Britt. & Rose) Backeb. See *Cereus smithianus*.
***M. spegazzinii*** (F.A. Weber) Britt. & Rose. See *Cereus spegazzinii*.

**MORACEAE** Link. MULBERRY FAMILY. Dicot. 40 genera and 1200 monoecious, dioecious trees, shrubs, lianes, stranglers and herbs, usually with lactifers with milky latex (absent in *Fatoua*) and sometimes alkaloids. Leaves alternate or opposite, usually simple, often with cystoliths, cell walls with silica or calcium carbonate; stipules present, sometimes minute. Flowers unisexual, small, wind-pollinated (insect-pollinated in *Ficus*), in axillary inflorescences with the axis often thickening to form a head or invaginated receptacle or almost closed syconia (*Ficus*); calyx (0–) 4–5 (–8) sepals, connate at the base, sometimes in 2 whorls; corolla absent; stamens as many and opposite sepals; ovary superior or inferior, of 2–3 fused carpels, with 1 often rudimentary, 1 (2)-loculed, with usually 2 styles and 1 ovule. Fruit a drupe, sometimes with dehiscent exocarp, receptacle often becoming fleshy; seeds often with unequal cotyledons; endosperm oily or absent. Some are important fruit trees, such as bread-fruit, *Artocarpus*; fig, *Ficus carica*; mulberry, *Morus*, or useful timber trees, such as *Chlorophora, Ficus* and *Maclura*. *Ficus elastica*, rubber plant, is an important source or rubber, while *Broussonetia papyrifera*, paper mulberry, provides the tapa or kapa cloth of Polynesia. Tropical and warm, few temperate. *Antiaris, Artocarpus, Brosimum, Broussonetia, Castilla, Chlorophora, Cudrania, Dorstenia, Ficus,* × *Macludrania, Maclura, Milicia, Morus*.

**Moraea** Mill. (For Robert More, 18th-century botanist and natural historian. Originally spelt *Morea*, but changed to *Moraea* by Linnaeus in 1762, possibly in honour of his father-in-law Johan Moraeus, a Swedish physician.) Iridaceae. About 120 species of perennial herbs, usually deciduous, rarely more or less evergreen. Rootstock a corm rooting from apex, covered with membranous, fibrous or almost woody tunics. Leaves 1 to several, basal or borne on stem. Stem simple or branched; inflorescence of one to several flowers in terminal clusters enclosed by paired spathes. Flowers usually yellow or purple-blue but sometimes white, cream, pink, orange or red, often with nectar guides of a contrasting colour at base of outer, and sometimes also inner, tepals; tepals 6, free; outer 3 usually with a more or less erect claw with nectary at base and spreading or reflexed blade, inner 3 sometimes similar to outer 3 but smaller, sometimes tricuspidate, occasionally much reduced or even absent; stamens 3, lying opposite outer tepals, filaments free or partly joined, usually forming column surrounding style, anthers adpressed to style branches; style with 3 branches, usually flat and petaloid, each with pair of terminal, projecting crests. Fruit a globose or cylindrical capsule. Subsaharan Africa from Ethiopia to S Africa. Z9 unless specified.

CULTIVATION *Moraea* spp. occur in coastal and mountain habitats in the Cape, Natal and the Transvaal, with a number of species occurring in more tropical climates. Those from tropical Africa and Madagascar require glasshouse temperatures of 12–15°C/53–60°F, those species from the Southwest Cape, which grow in winter and flower in spring or early spring, also need protection from frost in cool temperate climates but are well suited to cultivation in the cool glasshouse or conservatory. In general, species from the Eastern Cape, which flower in summer, are frost hardy, withstanding winter temperatures between −5 and −10°C/23–14°F.

All need full sun and a fertile, sandy and well drained medium with plentiful moisture when in growth, and to be kept dry when dormant. Propagate by seed, sown in spring for species that grow during summer, in autumn for winter-growing species.

***M. alpina*** Goldbl. Dwarf to 12cm, sometimes branched. Lf 1, absent or starting to develop at flowering time, terete, less than 1mm diam. Fls violet to deep blue with orange-yellow nectar guides on outer tepals; outer tepals 12–18mm, the blade 6–10×5–7mm; inner tepals 11–13mm, lanceolate, usually reflexed; style branches 6–8mm, crests 2–3mm. Spring–summer. S Africa (Natal, Drakensberg), Transkei, Lesotho. Z8.

***M. angusta*** (Thunb.) Ker-Gawl. 20–40cm, unbranched. Lf 1, arising from stem just above ground, longer than plant, stiff, terete. Fls pale yellow, usually brown- or grey-tinged, or grey-blue; outer tepals with yellow nectar guides; outer tepals 30–50mm, the claw longer than blade, inner tepals 25–35mm long, at first erect, reflexing later; style branches to 20mm long, crests of similar length or longer. Late winter–summer. S Africa (SW Cape).

***M. aristata*** (Delaroche) Asch. & Gräbn. 25–35cm, sometimes with 1 branch. Lf 1, basal, longer than plant, to 5mm wide, linear, glabrous. Fls white, outer tepals with concentric crescents of green, blue-violet or black at base; outer tepals 30–35mm, claw to 12mm, hairy, blade about 20×15mm, horizontal, inner tepals 15–20mm, tricuspidate with long, central cusp; style branches 7–8mm, crests 6–7mm. Spring. S Africa (Cape Town, almost extinct in wild).

***M. bellendenii*** (Sweet) N.E. Br. 50–100cm, usually branched. Lf 1, basal, longer than plant but not erect, to 10mm wide, linear, glabrous. Fls yellow speckled with brown-purple in centre; outer tepals 22–33mm, claw 9–13mm, blade 14–18mm long and wide, the edges curving up, inner tepals tricuspidate, 8–10mm long, not including central cusp 2–4mm long, coiled inwards; style branches 6mm, crests 3–8mm. Spring. S Africa (SW Cape, east to Plettenberg Bay).

***M. caeca*** Barnard ex Goldbl. Slender, 20–40cm, occasionally 1-branched. Lf 1, longer than plant, to 3mm wide, linear, channelled, glabrous. Fls lilac-purple, the outer tepals with yellow claws and yellow or black nectar guides at base of blades; outer tepals 23–28mm, claw 8–12mm, pubesc., blade not quite so long and 18–22mm wide, horizontal, inner tepals spreading, tricuspidate, to 18mm including central cusp 5–8mm long; style branches 5mm, crests to 7mm. Spring. S Africa (SW Cape).

***M. calcicola*** Goldbl. Slender, 30–40cm, stem slightly pubesc., sometimes with 1 branch. Lf 1, basal, longer than stem but usually trailing, 3–5mm wide, linear, channelled, hairy on outer side. Fls slightly scented, blue-violet, outer tepals with triangular blue-black nectar guides; outer tepals 25–35mm, claw 8–10mm, hairy, blade to 25×32mm, spreading, inner tepals 14–22mm, tricuspidate, the central cusp long, narrow and spreading; style branches 6–8mm, crests about 4mm. Spring. S Africa (W Cape).

***M. ciliata*** (L. f.) Ker-Gawl. Dwarf, 2.5–20cm, unbranched, the stem subterranean. Lvs 3–4, arising at ground level at base of infl., erect, usually longer than infl., 3–35mm wide, usually pubesc., the edges ciliate, often undulate or crisped. Fls scented, white, yellow, pale brown or blue with yellow nectar guides on outer tepals, opening midday and over in evening; outer tepals 20–35mm, blade 10–25mm, slightly reflexed, inner tepals 16–30mm, erect or spreading, linear or narrowly lanceolate; style branches 7–15mm, crests of similar length. Winter–spring. S Africa (Cape Province).

***M. fugax*** (Delaroche) Jacq. 12–50cm, branched. Lvs 1 or 2, subopposite, arising on stem just below lowest branch, usually longer than stem, trailing, linear or filiform, channelled. Fls scented, white, yellow or blue, opening midday and fading in evening; outer tepals 20–40mm, blade horizontal or reflexed, of similar length to claw, inner tepals 20–35×5–8mm, blade spreading or erect; style branches 12–20mm, crests 6–18mm. Late winter–spring, occasionally to summer. S Africa (S & W Cape). ssp. ***fugax***. Lvs 1 or 2, linear, channelled. Fls yellow, white or deep blue; outer tepals 27–40mm; spathes 35–65mm. ssp. ***filicaulis*** (Bak.) Goldbl.. Lvs 2, filiform. Fls white or cream sometimes tinged with pink or violet, or deep violet; outer tepals 20–26(–35)mm; spathes 20–40mm.

***M. gawleri*** Spreng. To 45cm, usually with 3–5 branches. Lvs 1–3, 1 or 2 basal, the topmost borne at lowest branch, shorter than stem, 1–6mm wide, linear, erect or spreading and coiled, the edges sometimes wavy or crisped. Fls cream, yellow or brick-red, often with darker veins, sometimes with style branches and crests paler; outer tepals 12–28mm long, the blade more than twice as long as claw, 5–14mm wide, reflexed, inner tepals 10–20mm long, reflexed; style branches 5–8mm, crests erect, lanceolate. Winter–spring. S Africa (Cape winter rainfall area).

***M. gigandra*** L. Bol. 20–40cm, occasionally with 1 branch; stem pubesc. Lf 1, basal, as long as or longer than stem, linear, glabrous or somewhat pubesc. Fls large, most often blue-purple with bright blue nectar guides bordered with white at base of outer tepals, rarely orange or white with nectar guides of a different colour; outer tepals 30–45mm long, claw 6mm, blade horizontal, to 35mm wide, inner tepals 9–15mm, tricuspidate, the central cusp long and narrow; style branches to 6×2mm, crests short; anth. large, 13–15mm, overtopping style crests. Spring. S Africa (SW Cape), almost extinct in the wild.

***M. gracilenta*** Goldbl. 30–80cm, with many branches. Lf 1, longer than stem but trailing, linear, channelled, arising at base of lowest branch. Fls scented, opening mid to late afternoon, fading by early evening, mauve-blue; outer tepals 20–30mm, blade of similar length to claw, 6–8mm wide, reflexed, inner tepals 18–28×5–6mm, the blade spreading; style branches 7–9mm, crests 7–12mm, linear-lanceolate. Spring–summer. S Africa (SW Cape).

***M. huttonii*** (Bak.) Oberm. Robust plants to 1m, occasionally with 1–2 short branches, forming clumps. Lf 1, usually longer than stem, 0.5–2.5cm wide, linear. Fls scented, yellow with darker yellow marks at base of outer tepals; style crests with brown or purple blotch; outer tepals to 55mm, blade to 35×20mm, spreading, inner tepals to 45mm, lanceolate, erect; style branches to 15×8mm, crests 10–13mm. Spring–early summer. S Africa (E Cape, Natal, SE Transvaal, Transkei), Lesotho.

***M. insolens*** Goldbl. To 35cm tall, usually branched, forming small clumps. Lf 1, usually longer than stem, 2–4mm wide, linear, channelled. Fls bright orange-red or rarely cream, claws and nectar guides dark brown; outer tepals to 30mm long, blade to 20mm wide, much longer than claw, spreading or slightly reflexed, inner tepals similar but smaller, to 25×15mm; style branches 4mm long, crests 1–2mm, triangular; anth. 8mm, overtopping style crests. Spring. S Africa (SW Cape); only 1 small population is known in the wild.

***M. loubseri*** Goldbl. 15–20cm, usually with 1 branch; stem finely pubesc. Lf 1, basal, usually longer than plant, 2–3mm wide, linear, channelled, pubesc. on outer side. Fls violet-blue, black and bearded in centre, with dark blue nectar guides on outer tepals; outer tepals 20–24mm, claw to 10mm, covered with black hairs, inner tepals 15–20mm, tricuspidate, the central cusp long and slender; style branches 6mm, crests 1–2mm, triangular. Very rare in wild. Late winter–spring. S Africa (W Cape).

***M. moggii*** N.E. Br. Slender, to 70cm, unbranched. Lf 1, longer than stem, to 1.5cm wide, linear, flat or channelled above, channelled beneath. Fls white, cream or yellow, the outer tepals with bright yellow nectar guides bordered with purple veins; outer tepals 40–75mm, blade to 50×33mm, reflexed; inner tepals to 60×25mm, erect; style branches to 20mm, crests 10–20mm. Summer–autumn. S Africa (E Transvaal, NE Natal), Swaziland.

***M. natalensis*** Bak. 15–45cm, branched. Lf 1, arising near top of stem, to 20cm, narrowly linear to subterete. Fls lilac to violet-blue, outer tepals with yellow nectar guides bordered with purple; outer tepals 14–20mm, blade to 14×10mm, reflexed, inner tepals to 15mm, linear-lanceolate, blade also reflexed; style branches, including crests, to 11mm. Summer. S Africa (Natal, Transvaal), Zimbabwe, Zambia, Malawi, Mozambique, Zaire.

***M. neopavonia*** R. Fost. Slender, 30–60cm, sometimes with 1 branch, the stem pubesc. Lf 1, basal, longer than plant, 3–5mm wide, linear, channelled, pubesc. on outer side. Fls large, 6–8cm diam., orange, rarely orange-red, the outer tepals with deep blue nectar guides, sometimes speckled, the claws speckled with deep blue; outer tepals 22–40mm, claw 10–12mm, blade 20–28×12–18mm, inner tepals entire or tricuspidate; style branches 5–8mm, crests 1–2mm; anth. 9–12mm, overtopping style branches and crests. Spring. S Africa (W Cape).

***M. papilionacea*** (L. f.) Ker-Gawl. 10–15cm, usually with few to several branches. Lvs 2–4 arising near base, of similar length to plant, sometimes longer, to 7mm wide, linear, usually hairy, the edges ciliate. Fls scented, pale yellow or salmon-pink, the outer sepals with yellow nectar guides edged with yellow, green or red; outer tepals 22–28mm, claw 8–10mm, blade 8–14mm wide, spreading or reflexed; inner tepals 20–22mm, blade 5–8mm wide, reflexed; style branches 5–8mm, crests 8–15mm long, lanceolate. Late winter–spring. S Africa (SW Cape).

***M. polyanthos*** L. f. 10–45cm, usually branched in upper half. Lvs 2–3, the lowest basal, longer than stem, 3–6mm wide, linear, channelled. Fls scented, white, lilac or pale to deep purple-blue, all tepals with yellow nectar guides; claws forming cup, holding stamens; outer tepals 23–40mm, claw 10–12mm, blade 8–10mm wide, obovate, spreading or slightly reflexed, inner tepals 18–55×6–10mm, blades also spreading, style branches 4–5mm long, the apices forked; crests absent. Winter–spring. S Africa (Cape winter rainfall area).

***M. polystachya*** (Thunb.) Ker-Gawl. To 80cm, branched; corm to 5cm diam. Lvs 3–5, as long as or longer than stem but usually trailing, 6–20mm wide, linear, flat or channelled. Fls pale blue or violet with yellow or orange nectar guides on outer tepals; outer tepals 36–55mm, claw 15–20mm, blade 13–25mm wide, spreading or reflexed; inner tepals 30–45×15mm, blade erect or reflexed; style branches about 10mm long, crests about 20mm; ovary often veined with red. Autumn–winter. S Africa (Cape, W OFS, W Transvaal), Namibia, Botswana.

***M. ramosissima*** (L. f.) Druce. Large, branched, 50–120cm; corm to 18mm diam., surrounded by small cormlets; roots spiny; stem with axillary cormlets towards base. Lvs numerous, mostly basal, 30–50×1.5–3cm, somewhat channelled. Fls bright yellow, outer tepals with darker yellow nectar guides, opening late morning and fading in late afternoon; outer tepals 30–40mm, blades about 15mm wide, reflexed, inner tepals to 35mm, also reflexed; style branches 20–25mm, crests prominent. Spring–summer. S Africa (S & W Cape).

***M. schimperi*** (Hochst.) Pichi-Serm. 20–50cm, unbranched, often forming clumps. Lf 1, 9–15mm wide, linear, channelled below, shorter than stem at flowering, later much longer. Fls purple-blue, outer tepals with yellow nectar guides; ovary usually maroon-red; outer tepals 40–65mm, claw and blade of similar length, blade spreading or slightly reflexed, inner tepals 35–45mm, lanceolate, erect; style branches 15–20mm, crests 10–20mm. Spring–early autumn. Widespread in tropical Africa.

***M. serpentina*** Bak. 4–20cm, usually with several branches. Lvs 1–5, usually basal but occasionally borne on stem, linear, sometimes pubesc., wavy or coiled. Fls white to yellow, inner tepals sometimes flushed with violet or mauve-pink, outer tepals with large, deep yellow nectar guides; outer tepals 24–30mm, blade 14–20×15–24mm, somewhat reflexed, inner tepals 20–30mm long, erect, oblanceolate; style branches about 6mm, crests 4–8mm, lanceolate. Spring. S Africa (NW Cape).

***M. spathulata*** (L. f.) Klatt. Robust, 50–90cm, usually unbranched, often forming clumps. Lf 1, basal, longer than stem, to 1.5cm wide, linear, flat or channelled. Fls yellow, outer tepals with darker yellow nectar guides; outer tepals 35–50mm long, blade 20–35mm, spreading or reflexed, inner tepals erect, 30–40mm; style branches to 18mm, crests to 10mm. Flowering time variable. S Africa (Cape summer rainfall area, E Transvaal, Transkei), Lesotho, Swaziland, Zimbabwe, Mozambique. Z8.

***M. speciosa*** (L. Bol.) Goldbl. 40–75cm high, branching toward apex; corm large, to 4cm diam. Lvs several, basal and cauline, about half length of stem, to 4cm wide, channelled, the edges undulate. Fls erect or drooping, pale blue-mauve, all tepals with yellow nectar guide; tepal claws forming cup including fil., outer tepals 30–45mm, claw 12–15mm, blade to 17mm wide, spreading or reflexed, inner tepals similar but blades slightly narrower; style branches 2–6mm; crests absent. Winter–spring. S Africa (S & W Cape).

***M. stricta*** Bak. 15–25cm, usually with 3–6 branches; corms to 3cm diam., often with cormlets attached. Lf 1, basal, usually absent at flowering time, later about 60cm long, 1.5mm wide, terete. Fls lilac or violet-blue, outer tepals with yellow or orange nectar guides; outer tepals to 24mm, blade 11–14×5–8mm, lanceolate or obovate, reflexed, inner tepals 15–18×2–4mm, more or less erect, linear or lanceolate; style branches 7–8mm, crests 3–6mm. Winter–spring. E Ethiopia to E Cape. Z8.

***M. thomsonii*** Bak. Slender, 15–30cm, usually with 3–6 branches. Lf 1, basal, usually absent or just starting to grow at flowering time, to 60cm long, 1.5mm wide, terete. Fls pale blue-violet, all tepals with yellow nectar guide; outer tepals 20–24mm, claw 9–10mm, blade 11–14×5–8mm, spreading, lanceolate or obovate, inner tepals 16–18mm, blade about 7mm wide, lanceolate, spreading; style branches 7–8mm, crests very small. Winter–spring or early summer. Tanzania, Malawi, S Africa (E Transvaal).

***M. tricolor*** Andrews. Small plants 5–15cm, unbranched. Lvs usually 3, slightly shorter than plant, glabrous or pubesc., the margins ciliate. Fls yellow, pink, red or pale purple, outer tepals with yellow nectar guides sometimes bordered with maroon; opening mid morning, fading late afternoon; outer tepals 20–25mm, blade 8–13mm, spreading, lanceolate; inner tepals similar but narrower; style branches to 5mm, crests 8–10mm long, triangular. Winter–spring. S Africa (SW Cape).

***M. tripetala*** (L. f.) Ker-Gawl. 10–50cm, sometimes branched. Lf 1, rarely 2, basal, usually longer than stem and trailing, linear or lanceolate, sometimes pubesc. Fls usually pale to deep blue or purple, sometimes yellow or pale pink, outer tepals with white or yellow nectar guide; outer tepals lanceolate, 20–35mm, claw to 15mm, hairy, blade spreading or reflexed; inner tepals very small, usually filiform but sometimes tricuspidate, occasionally absent; style branches 7–10mm, crests linear-lanceolate, 5–15mm. Late winter–summer. S Africa (Cape winter rainfall area).

***M. vegeta*** L. 10–30cm, usually with several branches. Lvs several, longer than plant, linear, glaucous grey-green. Fls relatively small, dull-coloured, yellow, brown, pink or blue, outer tepals with yellow nectar guide; outer tepals lanceolate, 20–25mm, blade to 18mm, reflexed, inner tepals similar but smaller; style branches 7–8mm, crests 7–10mm. Spring. S Africa (SW Cape).

***M. villosa*** (Ker-Gawl.) Ker-Gawl. 15–40cm, stem hairy, branched or unbranched. Lf 1, basal, as long as or longer than plant, linear, channelled, pubesc. on outside. Fls white, cream, pink, lilac, orange or purple, outer tepals with yellow nectar guides edged with 1 or 2 broad outer bands of darker colour; outer tepals 28–40mm, claw 8–12mm, blade suborbicular, 20–28mm long and wide, spreading horizontally or slightly reflexed, inner tepals 16–30mm, tricuspidate, the central cusp long, narrow and spreading; style branches 5–7mm long, to 8mm wide, crests 5–8mm, erect. Late winter–early spring. S Africa (W Cape). ssp. ***villosa***. Stem usually branched. Fls pink, blue or purple (rarely cream or green); outer tepals 30–40mm, blades more or less horizontal. ssp. ***elandsmontana*** Goldbl. Stem usually unbranched. Fls orange, nectar guides edged with dark blue (rarely white with brown nectar guides); outer tepals 28–31mm, blades curved up, rather cup-shaped.

***M. arenaria*** Bak. See *M. serpentina*.
***M. bicolor*** Steud. See *Dietes bicolor*.
***M. catenulata*** Lindl. See *Dietes iridioides*.
***M. edulis*** (L. f.) Ker-Gawl. See *M. fugax*.
***M. filicaulis*** Bak. See *M. fugax* ssp. *filicaulis*.
***M. glaucopis*** (DC.) Drapiez. See *M. aristata*.
***M. iridioides*** L. See *Dietes iridioides*.
***M. pavonia*** (L. f.) Ker-Gawl. See *M. neopavonia*.
***M. ramosa*** (Thunb.) Ker-Gawl. See *M. ramosissima*.
***M. robinsoniana*** (F. Muell.) Benth. & F. Muell. See *Dietes robinsoniana*.
***M. spathacea*** (Thunb.) Ker-Gawl. See *M. spathulata*.
***M. trita*** N.E. Br. See *M. stricta*.

## Morangaya G. Rowley.

***M. pensilis*** (K. Brandg.) G. Rowley. See *Echinocereus pensilis*.

**Morawetzia** Backeb.
***M. doelziana*** Backeb. See *Oreocereus doelzianus*.

**Moricandia** DC. (For Etienne Moricand (1779–1854), Italian botanist, author of *Flora Veneta*.) VIOLET CABBAGE. Cruciferae. 8 species of annual or perennial herbs. Stock often woody, branching. Foliage dense; leaves simple, ovate, sessile, fleshy, glabrous, usually entire; flowering stem leaves sessile, clasping. Inflorescence a loose raceme; flowers large; sepals 4, inner sepals saccate at base; petals 4, purple-violet or white; stamens 6. Fruit a silique, valves with prominent midveins, style very short; seed narrowly winged or wingless. Mediterranean, on calcareous soils.

CULTIVATION Natives of fields, wayside and other uncultivated ground, usually on calcareous soils, *Moricandia* spp. are grown for their large violet flowers, carried over glaucous and fleshy foliage. Although they may form a perennial rootstock or woody base, they flower in their first year from seed, and are usually treated as annuals or biennials. Grow in sun, in light, well-drained soil. Propagate from seed in spring.

***M. arvensis*** (L.) DC. To 60cm. Lvs glaucous, entire, obovate, obtuse, tapering at base; flowering stem lvs cordate, clasping, acute. Fls 10–20 in a loose raceme; pet. 2cm, violet. Fr. 30–80×2–3mm, compressed, angled in section; seed wingless, brown. W Mediterranean. Z8.

***M. moricandioides*** (Boiss.) Heyw. Similar to *M. arvensis* except lvs sometimes toothed. Fls more numerous; pet. violet. Fr. round in section; seed winged. SC & E Spain. Z8.

***M. hesperidiflora*** DC. See *Diplotaxis acris*.
***M. ramburii*** Webb. See *M. moricandioides*.
For further synonymy see *Brassica*.

**Morin family**. Nurserymen. René Morin (*d*1657?) and Pierre Morin (*d*1658?) were brothers who flourished separately as nurserymen in Paris, making their fortunes by satisfying the immense demand for bulbs in Europe at the time. René Morin was less well-known than his younger brother Pierre, 'the famous florist', but he was admired by Tradescant (who ordered bulbs from him), Cornut and others for his skill in propagating and promoting bulbs, exotics and other new plants from China and North America, including *Pelargonium triste*, varieties of *Tulipa serotina*, *Viburnum opulus* var. *sterilis* (the 'Guelder rose' or 'Sambucus rosea'), *Rhus typhina*, *Lobelia cardinalis* and *Lilium canadense*. René Morin also published in 1621 a catalogue, including 45 varieties of tulip, which is notable for its use of Latin nomenclature.

Pierre Morin was even more successful than his brother: his catalogue of 1651 comprises four separate lists of ranunculus, irises, anemones and more than 100 tulips. Sir Thomas Hanmer was one of Pierre Morin's many foreign correspondents – he ordered bulbs from him, and John Evelyn visited the Paris nursery twice. The need for an international system of classification was recognized by Pierre Morin, and in his *Remarques necessaires pour la culture des fleurs* (1688), written when he was gravely ill, he avoids the usual vernacular and uses a simple Latin terminology. The work is a lucid and useful horticultural manual and floricultural calendar, with information on soil and climatic conditions and a particularly innovative system for describing irises. Like his brother, Pierre Morin propagated mainly bulbs for sale but he also raised new plants, including from North America *Tradescantia virginiana* and *Eupatorium purpureum*.

Jean Morin, 'the Englishman', was probably related to René and Pierre (as a nephew or younger brother), and became famous for his introduction of *Nerine sarniensis*, the Guernsey lily, which bloomed in 1634, and about twenty years later for his cultivation of the *Brunsvigia* of Heister, the candelabra flower.

**Morina** L. (For Louis Morin (1636–1715), French botanist.) Morinaceae. 4 species of perennial, prickly herbs. Leaves mostly basal, tufted, oblong, undulate and spiny-toothed (rarely entire), progressively reduced on flowering stems to whorled, foliose and spiny bracts subtending flowers packed in marked verticillasters on a terminal spike. Calyx 2-lipped, enclosed within bristle-tipped involucel; corolla tubular, 5-lobed, with a spreading, somewhat bilabiate limb, pink, red, yellow or white. E Europe to Asia. Z6.

CULTIVATION Grown for the low, faintly aromatic basal rosettes of glossy, spined foliage as for the long elegant flowering stems carrying whorls of beautiful waxen textured flowers in summer. The flowers of *M. longifolia*, white on emergence, flush pink then crimson after fertilization, the pale yellow blooms of *M. persica* blush red.

Given perfect drainage, *M. longifolia*, will tolerate temperatures to −17°C/1°F without damage, although as with other species, specimens quickly deteriorate in wet soils; in damp conditions slug grazing at the root may lead to fatal infection by root rotting pathogens. Grow in any fertile, humus-rich, well-drained but moderately moisture-retentive, sandy or gritty soil in sun.

Fresh ripe seed germinates freely in an open, gritty propagating mix and is best sown in individual pots to avoid damage to the tap root. Overwinter young plants in the well ventilated cold frame. Also by root cuttings. Division is possible but risky and divided plants are often extremely slow to re-establish.

***M. coulteriana*** Royle. To 80cm. Lvs narrowly oblong-lanceolate, margins spiny. Fls to 1.75cm, pale yellow. W Himalaya.

***M. longifolia*** Wallich ex DC. WHORLFLOWER. To 1.3m. Lvs to 30×4cm, dark glossy green, narrowly oblong, undulate to pinnatifid, spiny-toothed. Fls to 2.25cm; cor. white, flushing shell pink, then bright crimson, particularly the limb; fertile stamens 2, exserted. Himalaya.

***M. persica*** L. Robust, 30–90cm. Lvs 15–20×1–2cm, linear to elliptic, dentate to pinnatifid, glabrous. Fls in somewhat distant verticillasters; bracts 2–4.5×1cm, ovate-triangular, with marginal spines up to 1cm long; cal. lobes subequal, entire or emarginate; cor. tube 3cm, villous, lips patent, pink. Balkan Peninsula. Z6.

**MORINACEAE** J. Agardh. MORINA FAMILY. Dicot. 3 genera and 13 species of perennial herbs with persistent leaf-bases. Leaves opposite or whorled, often spiny; stipules absent. Flowers bisexual, zygomorphic, in verticillasters, sometimes subcapitate; epicalyx of 4 fused bracteoles; calyx cupular, 2-lobed or with oblique mouth; corolla more or less 2-lipped; stamens 4, one pair above the other near corolla mouth, or 2 fertile+2 staminodes in the tube; ovary inferior, of 3 fused carpels, 1-loculed, with 1 pendulous ovule and slender style. Fruit dry-indehiscent, enclosed in the epicalyx and topped by the calyx. Balkans to Himalaya and China. *Morina*.

**Morinda** L. (From Gk *moron*, mulberry, and *inda*, Indian.) Rubiaceae. Some 80 species of shrubs, erect or climbing, or trees. Stems usually glabrous; branches and branchlets terete or 4-angled. Leaves opposite or, rarely, in whorls of 3; stipules united at base, occasionally sheathing with petioles. Flowers hermaphrodite or polygamo-dioecious, long- or short-peduncled or, rarely, sessile, axillary or terminal in dense, often paniculate or umbellate clusters, often united by calyces; calyx tube obovoid or urn-shaped or hemispheric, limb truncate or minutely toothed; corolla tube funnel- or salver-shaped, white or red, lobes 4–7, usually 5, valvate in bud, leathery; stamens 4–7, usually 5, inserted in tube or at throat of corolla, anthers dorsifixed, included or exserted, usually oblong or linear; ovary 2–4-celled (occasionally spuriously), style included or exserted, 2-branched or, rarely, entire; ovules solitary in each cell. Fruit a syncarp, fleshy; pyrenes many, 1-seeded, hard; seeds obovoid or reniform. Tropics.

CULTIVATION Commonly called 'Indian mulberry', a reference to the resemblance of thc aggregated fruits to the mulberries of the Moraceae family, *Morinda* spp. are grown for their dense clusters of creamy or reddish coloured flowers. In *M. jasminoides* the cream or buff coloured flowers are sweetly fragrant. *M. citrifolia* 'Variegata' has white-marbled, pendent foliage. Cultivate as for *Hamelia*.

***M. citrifolia*** L. non Bedd. INDIAN MULBERRY; AWL TREE; PAINKILLER. To 6m+; branches and branchlets 4-angled, glabrous; bark smooth, brown or grey. Lvs to 25×12cm, petiolate, oblong to elliptic, usually acute or narrowed at apex and base, sublustrous and dark green above, pale beneath; petioles to 2cm; stipules oblong, entire or 2–3-fid, caducous, to 1cm, glabrous. Fls sessile, few to several in heads, these axillary, solitary or 2–3; peduncles lf-opposed, to 3cm; cor. tube

1cm, pubesc. at throat, white or green. Fr. ovoid, to 4×3cm, pale yellow or green to white; seeds 4mm. Spring. Tropical Asia, Australia and Polynesia; widely naturalized in Tropical America, W Indies. 'Potteri': to 4m; lvs mottled white. 'Variegata': lvs marbled white. var. ***bracteata*** Roxb. Fls occasionally bracteate; cal. with spathulate or lanceolate, leaflike, white-lobed, to 8cm; anth. included. India, Sri Lanka.

***M.jasminoides*** Cunn. Shrub, to 6m, glabrous. Lvs to 8cm, petiolate, ovate to oblong-lanceolate or elliptic, apex narrowly acute, base narrowed, occasionally wavy; stipules united, deciduous. Fls to 12 or more in heads; peduncles axillary, 2 together; cal. united or in capitula; cor. buff; ovary 4-celled, style cleft. Fr. globose, 1cm wide. Spring. Australia.

***M.tinctoria*** Roxb. Tree; branches and branchlets pubesc.; bark soft, grey to yellow. Lvs to 25cm, petiolate, oblong to elliptic-obovate or lanceolate, acute or narrowed at apex and base or, rarely, cordate at base, dull, glabrous or, rarely, pubesc. beneath; petioles to 3cm. Infl. solitary, axillary or lf-opposed, or, rarely, terminal, panicled; fls white, jasmine-scented; cor. tube to 2cm, exterior hairy; anth. included or exserted. Fr. ovoid or globose, to 2.5cm wide, green. India, SE Asia.

***M.umbellata*** L. Shrub, erect or trailing or climbing, divaricately branched, to 1m or, when vine-like, 6m high. Branches terete, glabrous or pubesc. at first. Lvs to 10×5cm or more, oblong to elliptic, acute at apex, narrowed or acute or obtuse at base, occasionally membranous, glabrous or pubesc. beneath, veins 5–6, conspicuous; petioles to 1cm; stipules acute, united or sheathing. Fls in terminal, umbellate heads; peduncles to 10, to 4cm, glabrous or pubesc.; cor. rotate, to 6mm, hairy at throat. Fr. globose, to 12mm wide, orange-red. Tropical Asia, Australia.

***M.citrifolia*** Bedd. non L. See *M. tinctoria*.
***M.citrifolia*** var. ***potteri*** Deg. See *M. citrifolia* 'Potteri'.
***M.exserta*** Roxb. See *M. tinctoria*.
***M.quadrangularis*** hort. See *M. citrifolia*.
***M.royoc*** hort. See *M. umbellata*.

**Moringa** Adans. (From local Malabar name.) Moringaceae. 14 species of deciduous, somewhat succulent trees; trunk thick, bark smooth. Leaves large, alternate, 2–3-pinnate; stipules absent or small, on base of petiole and pinnae. Flowers in axillary racemes or panicles, zygomorphic, bisexual, white or red; sepals and petals 5, free; stamens 10; carpels 3 on short gynophore; ovary 1-celled. Fruit a pod-like capsule; seeds many, globular or ovoid, sometimes winged. Africa, Madagascar, India, Arabia. Z10.

CULTIVATION Valued as ornamentals for their foliage and long racemes of fragrant flowers, and grown as specimens and as informal hedging in tropical and subtropical regions. *M. oleifera* is also of commercial value for its seeds, which yield an edible oil used in perfumery, for the edible roots used as a relish, and for the bark, which yields a gum used in similar fashion to gum tragacanth. All species tolerate a wide range of soil types and are easily grown in full sun. In temperate zones they require warm glasshouse protection; grow in a sandy loam-based mix with additional leafmould. Propagate by seed or semi-ripe cuttings in a closed case with gentle bottom heat.

***M.longituba*** Engl. Small bush with a large rootstock. Lvs bipinnate. Fls precocious, coral red; cor. irregular; pet. glabrous; ovary glabrous; receptacle narrow, tubular, to 8mm. Seeds to 2.5cm. W Somalia, Kenya.

***M.oleifera*** Lam. HORSERADISH TREE; BEN; OIL OF BEN TREE. Tree, to 8m. Lvs to 60cm, 2–3-pinnate, petiolate; pinnae elliptic, to 2.5cm, dark green above, pale green below. Fls cream, 2.5cm diam., fragrant, in loose panicles to 15cm; sep. pale green, to 1.2cm; pet. unequal, slightly larger than sep. Fr. to 50×1.5cm, 9-ribbed, light brown; seeds round, 3-angled, winged, black, oily. Arabia and India; naturalized W Indies, S Asia and Africa.

***M.ovalifolia*** Dinter & A. Berger. AFRICAN MORINGO. To 7m; trunk squat, bark pale grey to coppery, containing stored water. Lvs to 60cm, bipinnate with 4–7 pairs of pinnae, each with 2–7 pairs of opposite leaflets; leaflets to 2.5×1.8cm, ovate, glabrous, light green, entire, stalked. Fls to 3mm diam., many, in panicles; pet. 4–5, white. Fr. to 40cm, 3-sided, flattened, pale green to grey-pink; seeds winged. Namibia.

***M.pterygosperma*** Gaertn. See *M. oleifera*.

**MORINGACEAE** Dumort. See *Moringa*.

**Morisia** Gay. (For Giuseppe Giacinto Moris (1796–1869), Professor of Botany at Turin.) Cruciferae. 1 species, a hairy perennial herb. Leaves 5–8cm, borne in crowded rosettes from a buried stem, oblong-lanceolate, pinnatisect, bright glossy green, veins pubescent beneath. Flowers 8–16 per rosette, solitary on erect pedicels, golden-yellow, to 2cm across; sepals 4; petals 4. In fruit pedicel arches, burying silique. Silique 2-jointed; lower section nearly spherical, 3–5-seeded, dehiscent; upper section ovoid-conical, indehiscent, 1–2-seeded. Spring–early summer. Corsica, Sardinia. Z7.

CULTIVATION On the rock garden and scree, or in pots in the alpine house, *Morisia* requires poor, gritty and perfectly drained soils to maintain its flat and neat rosettes, and in these conditions will tolerate temperatures to −15°C/5°F. In rich soils growth becomes coarse, soft, and susceptible to winter cold and damp; this genus is intolerant of warm humid conditions in summer, and in the US its cultivation is probably restricted to the Pacific Northwest.

Propagate from seed in autumn, sown directly into deep, soil-filled crevices in the rock garden, or in pans of a sandy propagating medium in the cool glasshouse or cold frame. Also by root cuttings in winter in sand. Water sparingly.

***M.monanthos*** (Viv.) Asch. As for the genus. 'Fred Hemingway': fls larger.

**Mormodes** Lindl. (From the Gk *mormo*, goblin, and *-eides*, resembling, referring to the grotesque appearance of the flowers.) Orchidaceae. Some 20 species of epiphytic orchids allied to *Catasetum*. Rhizome short. Pseudobulbs fleshy, cylindrical to fusiform, enveloped at base by several overlapping sheaths. Leaves distichous, sheathing base of pseudobulb and apical, plicate, elongate, articulated, usually thin-textured, persisting for one season. Inflorescence a lateral raceme, from nodes of pseudobulbs, erect to arching, loosely few to many-flowered; flowers showy, fleshy, often spreading, bisexual or unisexual; sepals and petals similar, free, spreading or reflexed, often narrow, lateral sepals oblique; lip very fleshy, adnate to column base, often reflexed, glabrous or pubesc., simple to 3-lobed; column stout, erect, obliquely twisted, wingless, footless, anther terminal, operculate, incumbent; pollinia 2 or 4, waxy, ovoid-oblong. C & S America. Z9.

CULTIVATION See *Catasetum*.

***M.aromatica*** Lindl. Pseudobulbs to 15×3cm, fusiform, compressed. Lvs to 60×6cm, lanceolate to linear-lanceolate, distinctly 3-nerved. Infl. to 32cm, ascending, many-fld; peduncle terete, to 6mm diam.; fls to 4cm diam., green-brown to purple-brown spotted dark purple, spicily fragrant; sep. to 32×15mm, fleshy, ovate-elliptic, acute; pet. to 16×18mm, darker than sep., elliptic-ovate, acute, finely dentate; lip to 25mm, fleshy, lateral lobes apiculate, midlobe triangular, acuminate, long-apiculate; column to 16mm. Mexico, El Salvador, Honduras.

***M.buccinator*** Lindl. Pseudobulbs to 20×4cm, oblong-ellipsoid to ovoid, clustered, slightly compressed. Lvs to 40×6cm, oblong to narrowly lanceolate, acuminate. Infl. to 50cm, erect to arching, few to many-fld; fls to 6.5cm diam., the colour widely variable – green flushed pink with an ivory lip, bright lime green to pale yellow, the lip lemon yellow, wholly deep yellow-orange (var. *aurantiaca* Rolfe), maroon with a somewhat paler lip, bronze with a rose-pink lip or wholly white; sep. to 3×1.5cm, linear to oblong-lanceolate, acute to acuminate, reflexed; pet. subequal to sep., obliquely linear to oblong-lanceolate, acute, slightly reflexed; lip to 3×3cm, strongly curved over column, slender-clawed, obovate or ovate-elliptic, apiculate, reflexed, apex truncate; column to 18mm, semiterete. Mostly late winter. Mexico, Guatemala, Panama, Colombia, Venezuela, Guyana.

***M.colossus*** Rchb. f. Pseudobulbs to 30×4.5cm, subcylindrical. Lvs to 30cm, ovate-elliptic. Infl. to 60cm, arcuate, densely many-fld; fls to 12cm diam., long-lived, fragrant, usually spreading, olive green to yellow tinted rose at base, the lip bronze to bright yellow with a few red spots at base; sep. to 50×8mm, linear-lanceolate, acuminate; pet. to 45×10mm, lanceolate, acuminate; lip to 5×2.5cm, short-clawed, simple, ovate-rhombic to ovate-elliptic, acute or acuminate, lateral margins strongly recurved; column to 17mm. Spring. Costa Rica, Panama.

***M.hookeri*** Lem. Pseudobulbs to 10cm, cylindrical to fusiform. Lvs linear-lanceolate, acuminate. Infl. short, erect, few-fld; fls to 4cm diam., fragrant, red to deep red-brown; sep. to 20×6mm, lanceolate, acuminate, strongly reflexed; pet. similar to sep. but somewhat shorter; lip to 16×16mm, obovate, truncate, apiculate, obscurely 3-lobed, lateral lobes strongly reflexed, pubesc. Winter. Costa Rica, Panama.

***M.igneum*** Lindl. & Paxt. Pseudobulbs to 35×5cm, cylindrical. Lvs lanceolate, acuminate, prominently veined. Infl. to 60cm, solitary or several produced in succession, arching, few to many-fld; fls to 5cm diam., fragrant, long-lived, variable in colour – yellow, olive-green or tan to red, often spotted red-brown, the lip white, yellow, olive, tan or brick red sometimes; sep. to 28×7mm, lanceolate, acuminate, sparsely spotted red, reflexed; pet. to 25×8mm, elliptic-lanceolate, acute, reflexed; lip very fleshy, clawed, subrotund, shortly apiculate, lateral margins reflexed. Spring. Costa Rica, Panama, Colombia.

***M. maculatum*** (Klotzsch) L.O. Williams. Pseudobulbs to 15cm, cylindrical to fusiform, clustered, several-lvd. Lvs to 38×3cm, linear-lanceolate, acuminate. Infl. to 40cm, arching to horizontal, densely many-fld; fld to 4cm, long-lived, fragrant, pale tawny-yellow spotted red-chocolate; sep. and pet. subsimilar, to 3.5×1cm, upcurved, ovate, acuminate; lip to 24×16mm, lateral lobes acuminate, midlobe large, acuminate; column to 18mm, semiterete. Autumn–early winter. Mexico. var. ***unicolor*** (Hook.) L.O. Williams. Fls clear pale yellow.

***M. rolfeanum*** Lind. Pseudobulbs to 10cm, ovoid-fusiform to fusiform. Lvs to 38×5cm, lanceolate to elliptic-lanceolate, acuminate, pale green spotted dark green below. Infl. to 15cm, erect, loosely few-fld; fls to 10cm, pale green to golden-yellow marked red, the lip sometimes heavily stained dark red-brown within; sep. to 4.5cm, ovate to lanceolate, obtuse to acuminate; pet. subequal to sep., elliptic-oblong to obovate, obtuse or apiculate; lip subequal to sep., simple, obovate-oblong to elliptic, revolute, apex recurved, acute; column to 2.5cm, white tinged red, acuminate. Peru.

***M. warscewiczii*** Klotzsch. Pseudobulbs to 16×5cm, cylindrical to fusiform, slightly compressed. Lvs to 23×4.5cm, elliptic-lanceolate to linear-lanceolate, acuminate. Infl. to 50cm, slender, several-fld; fls polymorphic, very fleshy or thickened, particularly at apices, variable in colour – maroon, olive or yellow-green mottled maroon or striped and spotted rusty red, the lip maroon, green-white or yellow sparsely spotted purple or red-brown; sep. to 35×12mm, lanceolate to oblong-lanceolate, acute or acuminate, reflexed; pet. to 32×13mm, elliptic-lanceolate, acuminate, reflexed, undulate; lip to 32×13mm, pubesc., lateral lobes linear-oblanceolate, acute to subobtuse, twisted, midlobe linear to subtriangular, apex truncate or rounded, slightly reflexed; column to 27mm, arcuate, sulcate. Mexico, Guatemala, Honduras.

***M. atropurpureum*** Hook. See *M. hookeri*.
***M. histrio*** Lind. & Rchb. f. See *M. warscewiczii*.
***M. macranthum*** Lindl. & Paxt. See *M. colossus*.
***M. pardina*** Batem. See *M. maculatum*.
***M. pardina*** var. ***unicolor*** Hook. See *M. maculatum* var. *unicolor*.
***M. vernixium*** Rchb. f. See *M. buccinator*.
***M. wendlandii*** Rchb. f. See *M. colossus*.
For further synonymy see *Catasetum*.

**Mormolyca** Fenzl. (From Gk *mormolyka*, hobgoblin, apparently referring to the bizarre profile of the flower and its sinister hue.) Orchidaceae. Some 6 species of epiphytic orchids. Rhizome short, sometimes creeping. Pseudobulbs fleshy, subglobose to ellipsoid-cylindrical, apically unifoliate. Leaves large, coriaceous, erect, elliptic-oblong to ligulate, sessile or shortly-petiolate. Inflorescence basal, 1-flowered; peduncle slender; flowers fleshy; sepals similar, free, spreading, lateral sepals oblique; petals subsimilar to sepals, smaller; lip erect, 3-lobed, lateral lobes erect, small, midlobe large, ovate to subquadrate, decurved, disc callose; column arcuate, wings absent, footless; anther terminal, opercular, incumbent, pollinia 4, ovoid. C America, northern S America.

CULTIVATION As for *Encyclia*.

***M. gracilipes*** (Schltr.) Garay & Wirth. Pseudobulbs to 3×1cm, ovoid-oblong to cylindrical, compressed. Lvs to 8×2cm, elliptic-oblong or ligulate, acute, sessile, light green, rugulose. Infl. to 23cm, usually exceeding lvs; sep. and pet. yellow-brown; sep. to 34×13mm, lanceolate to ovate-lanceolate, apical margins involute, long-acuminate; pet. to 17×2mm, obliquely linear or linear-lanceolate, acute, base twisted; lip to 11×8mm, yellow-brown finely marked dark purple-brown, obovate or obovate-rhombic, abruptly acute, lateral lobes indented; column yellow, to 8mm, clavate, slender, arcuate. Venezuela, Colombia, Ecuador, Peru.

***M. peruviana*** Schweinf. Pseudobulbs to 2m, clustered, ellipsoid. Lvs to 14×1cm, ligulate or narrowly oblong, subacute, sessile. Infl. to 12cm, several, slender, erect; fls to 3cm diam., yellow; sep. to 20×5mm, oblong-lanceolate, mucronate; pet. to 19×4mm, linear-oblong, acute or apiculate; lip to 15×7mm, parallel to column, ovate-subquadrate, lateral lobes porrect, triangular-lanceolate, acuminate, midlobe subquadrate, truncate or rounded, callus ovate, concave, porrect, trilobulate; column to 13mm, slender, clavate. Peru.

***M. ringens*** (Lindl.) Schltr. Rhiz. slender, creeping. Pseudobulbs to 4×3cm, ellipsoid to subspherical, compressed. Lvs to 35×4cm, narrowly lanceolate to ligulate, acute to obtuse. Infl. to 35cm, usually equalling lvs; fls fleshy, yellow to lavender; sep. to 19×8mm, lined purple, elliptic-oblong, obtuse; pet. to 15×6mm, elliptic-oblong, obtuse or rounded, convex; lip to 10×5mm, oblong-elliptic to ovate-elliptic, pilose, ciliolate, lavender to maroon, 3-lobed, lateral lobes minute, acute to obtuse, midlobe suborbicular, decurved; callus fleshy, tridentate; column to 10mm, pilose. Mexico to Costa Rica.

***M. lineolata*** Fenzl. See *M. ringens*.
For further synonymy see *Trigonidium*.

**Morren, Charles Jacques Edouard** (1833–1886). Botanist, horticulturist and artist. Edouard Morren was born in Ghent and educated at the University of Liége, where his father, Charles François Antoine Morren, was professor of physics and (later) botany. As an undergraduate Edouard Morren studied philosophy and fine arts, but he took his doctorate in natural sciences. Deciding to pursue a career as a botanist and horticulturist, Morren visited all the great botanical gardens of Europe and began contributing articles and paintings to periodicals, notably *La Belgique horticole*, which had been founded by his father. Morren specialized in bromeliads: he produced an influential monograph on the family; contributed around 250 paintings of them to *La Belgique horticole*, and built up a massive collection (the largest then in cultivation), which was ultimately purchased by Kew in 1886.

Due to his father's failing health, Morren took up the chair of botany at Liége in 1855, simultaneously becoming editor of *La Belgique horticole* – positions he held until his death. He produced a wealth of publications, established the city of Liége's botanical gardens, and in 1883 founded a new Botanical Institute for the university. His son became a famous hybridizer. Edouard Morren's published works include *Plantes de Serres* (1867); *La digestion végétale* (1876), *Principes élémentaires de physiologie végétale* (1877) and *La sensibilité et la mobilité des vegetaux* (1885).

**Morus** L. (From Lat. *morus*, mulberry.) MULBERRY. Moraceae. About 12 species of fast-growing, short-lived, deciduous, monoecious or dioecious trees and shrubs to 20m. Crown dense, rounded, often rugged; bark brown, rough, often burred. Shoots green soon becoming brown; exuding white latex when cut; buds ovoid-conic, 3–6 outer scales, terminal bud absent; stipules small, caducous. Leaves alternate, distichous, mostly cordate and serrate, simple or 2–5-lobed, turning yellow in autumn, venation sub-trinerved; petiole short. Inflorescences of bracteate unisexual catkins in leaf axils, green, short, capitate, calyx membranaceous, in male divided into 4 imbricate segments, 4 tepals, connate at base, 1 stamen, filaments free, inflexed in bud, pistillode present; in female ovary enclosed within calyx, ovoid or subglobose; ovule solitary, pendulous, 2 stigmas, linear-subulate, sessile or on a short style, subequal in length, the calyx becoming succulent in the fruit. Fruit superficially resembling a raspberry but structure differs: 20–100 per catkin, closely packed but separate, drupaceous, enclosed in persistent fleshy calyx forming a syncarp, green at first, ripening through orange or white to red or deep purple; seed within testa; ripe late summer to mid-autumn of same year. W N America and S Europe east to Japan, south to lowland tropics in C Africa.

CULTIVATION The mulberry belongs to the same family as the fig, the Moraceae. It is the black mulberry, *Morus nigra*, that is prized for its fruit; that of the white mulberry, *M. alba*, is considered more insipid but the leaves of this species are renowned as food for silk-worms. It is thought to have originated in China where for over 5000 years it has been grown and used in silk production. The black mulberry's origins are not precisely known but it is likely that it came from the Caucasus or possibly from mountainous regions further east. Both the black and the white mulberry were grown in Mesopotamia and ancient Egypt and the mulberry is mentioned several times in the Bible. It spread to ancient Greece and Rome and thence, with the Roman legions, across Europe to Britain and subsequently to many other parts of the world. Another species, *M. rubra*, is native to the northeast United States.

The black mulberry would almost certainly have been planted in Britain by the Romans and since the trees are slow-growing and can be very long-lived (several hundred years) it is possible that some specimens survived from Roman times until the Middle Ages. The tree can attain a height of 9m/30ft or more, with attractive gnarled bark and spreading head. Very old trees can occasionally be seen and attain most unusual, artistic outlines. There are a number of references to mulberries from the 13th century and the Tudor period. James I tried unsuccessfully to encourage silk production, even establishing a mulberry garden on the site now occupied by Buckingham Palace. Many thousands of trees were planted, but they were all *M. nigra*, which proved to be unsatisfactory for silk production. The growing of mulberries in Britain subsequently declined and the trees have long since been planted as much for their decorative effect as for any culinary use.

In other parts of the world the black mulberry has long since become established and popular. It is quite widely grown in Australia, South Africa and southern Europe, in those regions where the climate is reasonably cool and temperate and with winters that will satisfy the tree's comparatively high chilling requirement. Some seedless cultivars are now grown in Iran and neighbouring areas. Named Western cultivars include 'Cooke', 'Chelsea', 'Illinois Everbearing', and 'Wellington'. 'White' is white-fruited and therefore non-staining. If fruit production is the primary aim it is important to obtain a selection known for its large, juicy fruits since many exist that produce only small, seedy fruits. In many parts of the Mediterranean, like Greece, mulberries are commonly used as street trees, being severely pollarded every spring to produce long stiff branches with large shade-producing leaves.

The flowers are unisexual and are carried on inconspicuous catkins. The trees are self-fertile. Leafing and flowering is late, normally with little risk of frost damage, but leaf-fall is often early, the foliage soon succumbing to the first autumn frosts. Even in warm climates the tree is therefore bare for a large part of the year but its bark and shapeliness are the compensation. The fruit is actually formed from a cluster of individual flowers, each ultimately forming part of the whole collective fruit. At first green it gradually turns to pink, then red and finally to deepest crimson, almost black. The juice stains badly and is particularly difficult to remove.

Trees for fruit should be planted in a sheltered, sunny situation in good soil conditions and preferably with short grass beneath to aid harvesting; in colder climates spring planting is advised to take advantage of a warming soil. Only in southern Britain is success likely; further north wall protection, using fan-trained trees, is advisable. Specimen trees will require sufficient headroom to allow for cultivations beneath them and support for half-standard or standard forms is wise until the tree is firmly rooted. Small trees can be maintained in large pots or tubs using a high-fertility soil-based medium. Any pruning should be done in winter merely to keep tree shape and to avoid crossing branches but kept to a minimum because of the tree's propensity to bleeding. Should any large cut continue to bleed, it should be cauterized with a red-hot poker. Roots are similarly vulnerable should larger ones happen to be broken.

The fruit ripens in late summer and should be used immediately as it is very soft. That from a good selection will be equivalent to a large loganberry is size. Fruit can either be gathered up from short-mown grass or shaken on to sheets to ensure cleanliness, and has a number of culinary uses including jam, colouring and flavouring other preserves, and also for making wine. The ripe fruit is sweet yet with marked underlying tartness.

Nutritional needs are minimal unless soil conditions demand occasional applications of a compound fertilizer (preferably one higher in nitrogen) at 4.5–5.0g/m$^2$. Mulching of newly established trees is recommended and irrigation is essential during dry periods.

Propagation is either by layering in autumn or more usually by hardwood cuttings of well-ripened young shoots approximately 18cm/7in. long with a heel of two-year-old wood. These are taken either in autumn or early spring and are inserted in a shady border or in a cold frame with all but the top 5cm/2in. below ground. Seedlings take too long to mature; grafting is difficult because of excessive sap flow (bleeding). Quite large branch portions will take root in the open under favourable weather and soil conditions.

Bacterial blight (*Pseudomonas mori*) results in small, angular, black spots on the leaves and lesions on the shoots which can cause dieback. Affected shoots should be removed and burned in the autumn. Small, dark brown leaf spots on which black pycnida appear are caused by the fungus *Phloeosporella maculans*. Regular sprays with a copper-based fungicide may be needed to control both of these diseases. Canker and a resultant dieback of young shoots is caused by *Gibberella moricola* (syn. *G. baccata*); red pustules of *Fusarium* spores (the conidial state of this fungus) form on the dead twigs and around the edges of the cankers; affected shoots should be cut out. Mulberry may also be affected by coral spot (*Nectria cinnabarina*) and powdery mildew (*Phyllactinia crylea*). The principal pests are birds, against which netting may be essential.

***M. alba*** L. WHITE MULBERRY. Tree to 16m, crown rounded. Young shoots downy at first, glabrous by autumn. Lvs 8×6–20×12cm, broad ovate-cordate, margin coarsely dentate, apex rounded to acute, often bi- or tri-lobed with irregular sinuses; glossy light green above, glabrous beneath except for veins; petiole 1–2.5cm. Fls pale green cylindrical heads 8–14×6mm on a 12mm pedicel; stigma sessile on female fls. Fr. clusters 1–2.5cm, green-white ripening pink to dark red; sweet but poor flavour. China. Z5. 'Aurea': lvs and bark yellow. 'Chaparral': vigorous growth; branches slender, drooping; lvs bright green; no fruit. 'Constantinopolitana': compact, thickly branched tree; lvs ovate, to 15cm long, leathery, coarsely serrate, dark green and glossy above, lighter beneath. 'Fegyvernekiana': dwarf, to 80cm. 'Fruitless': sterile, fast-growing, to 18m, crown rounded; lvs oblong-acute, glossy. 'Kingan': sterile; suitable where fruit drop a nuisance. 'Laciniata': lvs deeply lobed and toothed. 'Macrophylla': lvs mostly large, 20×15cm. 'Multicaulis': suckering shrub; lvs to 35cm; fr nearly black when ripe. Probably more than one clone involved. 'Nana': habit dwarf, shrubby, rounded; lvs regularly lobed. 'Nigrobacca': fr ripen dark purple. 'Pendula': shoots hanging; crown weeping if trained or grafted high on stem of type. 'Pyramidalis': conic. 'Striblingii': male fls falling early; no fruit. 'Venosa': lvs slender-tapered, with conspicuous pale downy veins. var. ***tartarica*** (Pall.) Ser. Lvs and fr. smaller than type. Z4.

***M. australis*** Poir. Tree or shrub to 8m; young shoots glabrous. Lvs variable, 5×3–15×10cm, mostly cordate-ovate, serrate, often deeply 3–5-lobed, scabrous green above, thinly pubesc. beneath at first, soon glabrous. Fls as in *M. alba* but with style longer. Fr. 1.5cm, deep red, sweet, setose from styles. E Asia. Z6.

***M. cathayana*** Hemsl. Tree to 15m; young shoots downy. Lvs 7×5–15×12cm (to 20cm on vigorous shoots), cordate, blunt-serrate, apex cuspidate, simple, to 3-lobed on strong shoots, scabrous above, pubesc. beneath; petiole 2cm. Male fls 2cm. Fr. 2.5cm, pale green ripening red to dark purple. C China. Z6.

***M. macroura*** Miq. Tree to 10m. Lvs 7–20cm, cordate or rounded at base, sparsely pubesc.; petiole 2.5cm, downy. Himalaya, Burma, S China. Z8.

***M. microphylla*** Buckl. TEXAS MULBERRY. Tree or shrub to 6m; shoots nearly glabrous. Lvs 3–7cm, commonly 2–5-lobed or simple, glossy green above, finely pubesc., soon glabrous beneath. Fr. 1–1.5cm, globose to short-ovate, dark purple, sweet. Arizona to W Texas and N Mexico. Z6.

***M. nigra*** L. BLACK MULBERRY. Tree to 15m; shoots tomentose, green soon brown. Lvs mostly 8×6–12×8cm, simple broad ovate-cordate, to 22×15cm and often 2–3-lobed on strong shoots, coarsely, often double-serrate, rough scabrous deep green above, paler and pubesc. beneath; petiole pubesc., 2cm. Fls pale green catkins, males 2–2.5cm, females 1–1.5cm. Fr. 2–2.5cm on a 1cm peduncle, green ripening through orange and red to deep purple, sweet, richly flavoured. Probably SW Asia, but extensive early cultivation has obscured range. Z5.

***M. rubra*** L. RED MULBERRY. Tree to 15m, rarely 20m, dense, rounded crown. Shoots slender, brown, thinly pubesc. Lvs mostly 8×6–12×8cm, simple sub-orbicular to slightly cordate (not strongly as in *M. nigra*) at base, to 20×18cm and often 2–3-lobed on strong shoots, coarsely serrate, rough scabrous dark blue-green above, paler and pubesc. beneath; petiole pubesc., 2cm. Fls pale green, males 2–4cm, females 2–2.5cm. Fr. 2.5–3cm on a 1cm peduncle, green ripening through orange and red to purple, sweet, good flavour. E US, extreme SE Canada. Z5. 'Nana': dwarf, slow-growing; lvs smaller, 3–5-lobed.

***M. acidosa*** Griff. See *M. australis*.
***M. alba*** var. ***latifolia*** Burret. See *M. alba* 'Multicaulis'.
***M. alba*** var. ***multicaulis*** (Perrott.) Loud. See *M. alba* 'Multicaulis'.
***M. alba*** var. ***stylosa*** (Ser.) Bur. See *M. australis*.
***M. bombycis*** Koidz. See *M. alba*.
***M. celtidifolia*** Sarg. See *M. microphylla*.
***M. excelsa*** Welw. See *Milicia excelsa*.
***M. indica*** Roxb. non L. See *M. australis*.
***M. japonica*** Bail. See *M. alba*.
***M. kagayamae*** Koidz. See *M. alba*.
***M. laevigata*** Wallich ex Brandis. See *M. macroura*.
***M. mongolica*** (Bur.) Schneid. See *M. alba*.

***M. stylosa*** Ser. See *M. australis*.

**Moscharia** Ruiz & Pav. (From Gk *moschos*, musk, referring to the musky odour.) Compositae. 2 species of pubescent annual herbs. Stems erect, branched above. Leaves alternate, lower leaves elliptic, pinnate, petiolate, upper leaves entire or lobed, sessile, amplexicaul. Capitula discoid, terminal, sessile, in a many-branched, flat-topped cyme of many smaller heads surrounding a central, solitary, larger head; receptacle convex; phyllaries 1–7, lanceolate, scarious; florets hermaphrodite, bilabiate, outer lip larger. Fruit a fusiform cypsela; pappus a single row of short scales. S America (Chile). Z10.

CULTIVATION As for *Monolopia*.

***M. pinnatifida*** Ruiz & Pav. Stem to 70cm. Basal lvs to 18×3cm, seg. dentate, stem lvs lanceolate. Infl. hemispherical, to 8×10mm; phyllaries to 5mm; florets white to pale rose, outer lip to 5×3mm. Fr. to 1mm; pappus scales white, present only in outer capitula of infl. Spring. C Chile.

**Mucuna** Adans. (Brazilian name for these plants.) Leguminosae (Papilionoideae). Some 100 species of woody lianes, climbing herbs and erect shrubs. Leaves trifoliolate; leaflets stalked; stipules caducous; stipels frequently present. Flowers large in axillary clusters or racemes, often long-peduncled and pendulous; calyx bilabiate, lobes 4–5, upper pair united union; standard rounded, exceeded by other petals, keel hardened at apex, sharply beaked; ovary sessile, ovules few to several. Style filiform, stigma tiny, terminal. Stamens 10, vexillary stamen free, anthers 2 types, 5 larger, glabrous, basifixed, alternate with 5 shorter, versatile, filaments distended at apex. Fruit ovoid, torulose to linear, often sharply bristly or velvety (causing irritation), thick, usually dehiscent; seeds oblong or spherical, with a hilum and rim-aril, or a longer hilum and no aril. Widespread in the tropics and subtropics of both hemispheres. Z10.

CULTIVATION As for *Camoensia*.

***M. bennettii*** F. Muell. NEW GUINEA CREEPER. Woody climber to 20m. Stems rugose, mostly glabrous. Petioles 5–12cm; leaflets 11–13.5×5–7.5cm, elliptic, apex acute, base rounded, glabrous. Fls to 8.5cm, vivid scarlet or flame-coloured, in short infl.; cal. orange, pubesc. and setose, tube 8–10×20mm; keel curved, 11mm diam. New Guinea.

***M. novoguineensis*** R. Scheff. Liane to 30m; stems to 5cm diam., initially densely hirsute, later glabrous. Leaflets 10–19×8.5–13.5cm, elliptic, glabrous or pubesc. throughout. Fls 5–8cm, showy, flame-coloured to scarlet, in pendulous, conical infl., 7–60cm long; cal. 6–13×9–22mm diam., yellow-hued, red-brown pubesc.; keel 4–7mm diam., strongly curved. Fr. 16–27×4–6cm, linear-oblong, torulose. New Guinea.

***M. pruriens*** (L.) DC. VELVET BEAN. Semi-woody, climbing herb, short-lived perenn. or annual, to 4m. Stems rugose, initially thickly hirsute, later glabrous. Lvs to 46cm; stipules 3–4×1mm, hirsute; leaflets 5–19×3.5–17cm, ovate, obovate, rhomboid or elliptic, grey-hirsute; petioles 2–40cm. Racemes to 30cm; fls 3–4cm, damson coloured to pale purple or white; cal. densely pale brown hirsute, tube 0.5×1cm; standard ovate, 1.7–2×1.5cm, keel 2.8–4cm, curved wings 2–4×1.2cm. Fr. 5–9×0.8–2×0.5cm, oblong, thickly amber- or brown-setose or velutinous, sometimes rugose. Asia; naturalized elsewhere. var. ***utilis*** (Wallich ex Wight) Bak. ex Burck. VELVET BEAN; FLORIDA BEAN; BENGHAL BEAN. Racemes to 30cm, pendulous; standard purple flushed green, wings dirty red. Fr. darkly velutinous.

***M. sempervirens*** Hemsl. Vigorous evergreen climber to 12m. Lvs prominently reticulate-veined; terminal leaflet to 12cm. Fls waxy, bruised purple-black, malodorous, borne in short nodding racemes, often several from one axil on old wood; keel 6–8cm, strongly curved. Fr. to 30cm, velutinous. Spring. China (W Hubei, Sichuan).

***M. aterrima*** (Piper & Tracy) Holland. See *M. pruriens* var. *utilis*.
***M. cochinchinensis*** (Lour.) A. Chev. See *M. pruriens*.
***M. deeringiana*** (Bort) Merrill. See *M. pruriens* var. *utilis*.
***M. kraetkei*** Warb. See *M. novoguineensis*.
***M. nivea*** DC. See *M. pruriens*.

**Muehlenbeckia** Meissn. (For H.G. Muehlenbeck (1798–1845), Swiss physician.) Polygonaceae. 15 species of largely dioecious, evergreen climbing or procumbent subshrubs and shrubs. Stems initially robust, erect or stoloniferous, simple, later densely branched with dark, slender, interlacing branchlets. Leaves small, alternate, occasionally absent, petiolate; stipules sheathing. Flowers minute, occasionally fertile and unisexual flowers on same plant, axillary or terminal and clustered, white-green; perianth deeply 5-lobed; stamens 8; styles 3; ovary 3-angled. Fruit a 3-angled achene, surrounded by enlarged fleshy perianth, white. S America, New Zealand, Australia, New Guinea.

CULTIVATION Grown for their intricate habit, minute foliage and small but very sweetly fragrant flowers, *Muehlenbeckia* spp. are suitable for covering tree stumps and rocky banks, or for scrambling through shrubs. *M. complexa* is also amenable to hanging basket cultivation, forming a mass of intricately tangled dark wiry stems if unsupported and bearing fleshy white fruits where plants of both genders are grown together.

Given a position sheltered from cold, drying winds, *M. axillaris* will tolerate temperatures of −15°C/5°F and below. With the exceptions of *M. adpressa* and *M. gunnii*, which require cool glasshouse protection (5°C/40°F) in cool temperate zones, the remaining species show similar cold tolerance. Grow in well-drained soil in sun to part shade. Prune only to restrict to allotted space. Propagate by semi-ripe cuttings in summer, or by seed, *M. axillaris* also by division.

***M. adpressa*** (Labill.) Meissn. Spreading or climbing shrub, often twining over other plants, to 2m, glabrous. Lvs orbicular to ovate, cordate at base, 1–6cm, margins minutely crisped, petiolate. Fls in axillary racemes, 2.5–8cm; perianth seg. 2.5–3mm. Fr. perianth enclosing 3-angled ovoid achene. Australia. Z9.

***M. australis*** (Forst. f.) Meissn. Stout dioecious vine to 10m; stems much-branched, interlacing, branchlets slender. Lvs ovate to nearly orbicular, 2–8×1–3cm; petioles to 25mm; stipules 4–5mm. Fls 4–5mm diam., in branched panicles to 5cm, tinged green. Fr. glossy, black. Summer–early autumn. New Zealand. Z8.

***M. axillaris*** (Hook. f.) Walp. Small deciduous prostrate or straggling shrub, forming clumps to 1m across, stems and branches rooting at nodes, shoots thin, wiry, gold to black, finely grey-pubesc. Lvs oblong to nearly orbicular, 5–10×3–6mm, glabrous, dark green above, ashy grey beneath; petiole to 3mm; stipules 2–3mm. Fls 1 or 2 in lf axils, to 4mm diam., yellow-green. Fr. 3mm, glossy, black. Summer–early autumn. Australia, Tasmania, New Zealand. Z8.

***M. complexa*** (Cunn.) Meissn. MAIDENHAIR VINE; WIRE VINE; MATTRESS VINE; NECKLACE VINE. Deciduous liane, creeping or climbing to 5m; stems interlaced forming dense tangles without support, branchlets slender, wiry, soft, gold-red, white-pubesc. when young, later brittle, bark red-brown. Lvs bright green above, purple or silver beneath, variable on same plant, oblong to circular or pandurate, rounded or cordate at base, 5–20mm, glabrous; petiole to 1cm. Fls small, green-white, in axillary or terminal spikes, 2.5–3cm. Fr. 2–2.5mm, black, enclosed in fleshy white cup of perianth. Summer. New Zealand. 'Nana': dwarf; lvs pandurate. var. ***microphylla*** (Colenso) Ckn. Dense shrub to 60cm. Lvs few, rounded, small. var. ***triloba*** (Colenso) Cheesem. Lvs pandurate, deeply lobed, 1.5–3.5×1.5–2.5cm. Z8.

***M. ephedroides*** Hook. f. Prostrate to sprawling shrub, forming a thicket; stems to 1m, rush-like, deeply grooved, glabrous. Lvs linear to sagittate, 8–25mm, often absent, dark to grey-green, sessile; stipules 1–2mm. Fls in small axillary clusters or small spikes, occasionally with a few fertile fls; perianth seg. 2–3.5mm, narrow-triangular. Fr. 3×1.5mm, shiny black. Summer. New Zealand. var. ***muriculata*** (Colenso) Cheesem. Small shrub. Stems very slender, almost thread-like. Lvs smaller than species type, 3–12mm. Perianth seg. becoming membranous in fr. Z8.

***M. gunnii*** (Hook. f.) Walp. Climbing shrub, resembling *M. adpressa* but stems to 10m; lvs broadly lanceolate-hastate, acute or short-acuminate, 3–8×1–3cm; petiole 5–15mm. Perianth seg. 4–5mm. Fr. ovoid-oblong, 5mm. Australia. Z9.

***M. sagittifolia*** (Ortega) Meissn. Liane or climbing shrub. Lvs variable, sagittate or lanceolate, acuminate, 4–9×1.5–2.5cm, upper lvs narrow, linear; petiole 5–15mm, with extra-floral nectaries near insertion; stipules short, membranous. Fls in a slender raceme, white-green, resembling *M. complexa*; perianth seg. reflexed. Fr. 3–4mm. Summer. S America (Brazil, Paraguay, Uruguay). Z9.

***M. adpressa*** var. ***hastata*** Meissn. See *M. gunnii*.
***M. muriculata*** Colenso. See *M. ephedroides* var. *muriculata*.
***M. nana*** Thurst. See *M. axillaris*.
***M. platyclada*** (F. Muell.) Meissn. See *Homalocladium platycladum*.
***M. triloba*** Colenso. See *M. complexa* var. *triloba*.
***M. varians*** Meissn. See *M. complexa* var. *triloba*.

**Mueller, Ferdinand von** (1825–1896). Botanist. He was born in Rostock, Germany, and at the age of 15 was apprenticed to a chemist in Husum, Schleswig-Holstein. He studied the local flora, established a large herbarium at the back of the chemist's shop and went on to Kiel University, becoming a Doctor of Philosophy at the age of 21. In 1847 he emigrated to Australia with suspected phthisis and found a job as a chemist's assistant in Adelaide. He systematically explored the indigenous flora and wrote his first monograph on Australian plants in 1852, when he moved to Victoria. Mueller was appointed as the first Government Botanist for Victoria in 1853 after being recommended by Hooker (he retained close links with Kew all his life) and kept the post until his death. By 1863 he had made botanical and geographical expeditions all over Australia. He published his *Fragmenta Phytographiae Australiae* from 1858 to 1882; monographs on *Eucalyptus*, *Acacia*, *Myoporinae* and *Salsolaceae*; the economically useful *Select Extra-Tropical Plants*, (1871) and a *Systematic Census of Australian Plants* (2nd ed, 1889).

Mueller unselfishly sent his entire Australian herbarium to Bentham at Kew to help in his work on the *Flora Australiensis*, having accepted that he could not undertake the work himself without the use of the European herbaria. He was Director of Melbourne Botanic Gardens from 1857 to 1873, when he was relieved of the position owing to a lack of success with landscape design. He bitterly resented the decision and never entered the gardens again, although he worked in the adjoining herbarium and library.

Ferdinand von Mueller was an enthusiastic correspondent and an advocate of Australian flora. He was solely responsible for the popularization and cultivation of many Australian plants, and he investigated, named and described an estimated 2000 species. Several genera, including *Muellerera, Muellerella* and *Muellerina*, were named in his honour.

**Muenteria** Seem.
***M. lutea*** (Benth.) Seem. See *Markhamia lutea*.
***M. platycalyx*** (Bak.) Sprague. See *Markhamia lutea*.

**Muilla** S. Wats. (Anagram of *Allium*.) Liliaceae (Alliaceae). 5 species of herbaceous perennials to 60cm, resembling *Allium* but lacking characteristic odour. Corms covered with fibrous tunics, developing from subterranean stems. Leaves few, nearly terete. Flowers numerous, stellate in scapose umbels with more than 1 spathe; tepals 6, white to green with darker midrib, bases united, forming perianth tube, upper parts free; stamens 6, inserted at base of perianth tube; ovary with many ovules. Fruit globular, 3-ridged. SW US, Mexico. Z9.

CULTIVATION As for *Allium*.

***M. maritima*** S. Wats. To 50cm high. Corm to 2cm diam. Lvs to 60cm. Fls 4–70; spathes 3–6, lanceolate; pedicels 1–5cm; tepals 3–6mm, white, tinged with green, midrib brown; anth. purple. Fr. 5–8mm. Spring–summer. US (California), Mexico. Z9.

***M. serotina*** Green. See *M. maritima*.
For further synonymy see *Allium, Bloomeria, Hesperoscordum* and *Nothoscordum*.

**Muiria** N.E. Br. (For Dr John Muir of Riversdale, Cape Province.) Aizoaceae. 1 species, a clump-forming leaf succulent with short fibrous roots, related to *Gibbaeum*, forming a large almost spherical body with a pair of leaves united completely except for a tiny slit. One of the most highly developed leaf-succulents in the world, the entire central tissue is composed of large water-storing cells when are highly water retentive even when removed from the plant body, and small amounts of connective tissue which appears to absorb waste products. Leaf bodies completely united except for a small fissure offset at the tip of the bodies; body more or less compressed, ovoid to spherical, sometimes rather angular, soft-fleshy, light green, densely covered with velvety hairs. Flowers solitary, rupturing the cells at the top of the body, pink-white, 8–20mm diam., only just projecting from the body at the apex, bractless; calyx 6-lobed; petals free. Capsule 6–7-celled with 6–7 stigmas which are not united to the base. Growing season very short, summer–early autumn. S Africa (Cape Province: Riversdale District). Z9.

CULTIVATION As for *Gibbaeum* but a difficult plant in cultivation. It has a very short growth period from midsummer to early autumn and must not be given water at other times, but spray freely in spring and late autumn. Keep in a full sun all year and in a minimum temperature at 10°C/50°F.

***M. hortenseae*** N.E. Br. As for the genus.

For illustration see AIZOACEAE.

**Mukdenia** Koidz. (From the Chinese city, Mukden.) Saxifragaceae. 2 species of deciduous perennial herbs, to 60cm. Rhizomes short, creeping, scaly. Leaves peltate, round to reniform, cordate at base, deeply, palmately, 5–9-lobed, bronze-green, glabrous or nearly so, irregularly dentate; petioles long. Flowering stem leafless, taller than leaves; racemes paniculate; pedicels of unequal length; flowers numerous, small, white, campanulate; sepals 5, twice petal length; petals 5, oblong; stamens 5; ovary semi-inferior. Fruit a capsule, globose, with 2 persistent styles. Spring. N China, Manchuria, Korea. Z7.

CULTIVATION Deciduous groundcover for woodland fringe and other highly shaded locations; cultivate as for *Heuchera*.

***M. rossii*** (Oliv.) Koidz. As for the genus.

For synonymy see *Aceriphyllum* and *Saxifraga*.

**Mukia** Arn. Cucurbitaceae. 4 species of monoecious climbers. Stems hispid, becoming somewhat woody at base. Tendrils simple. Leaves palmate, ovate to cordate, triangular, petiolate. Inflorescence a sessile cluster; flowers small, unisexual, yellow, subsessile or pedicellate; calyx campanulate, lobed; petals joined at base; male flowers with 3 stamens inserted on calyx and an elevated disc; female flowers sometimes solitary; stigmas 2–3; ovary ellipsoid or globose; staminodes present or absent; disc annular. Fruit a berry, small, subsessile, ellipsoid to globose, sometimes hispid at first, red when ripe, smooth; seeds small, subelliptic, margins raised. Old World Tropics. Z9.

CULTIVATION As for *Momordica*.

***M. maderaspatana*** (L.) Roem. Climber or trailer, perenn., to 3m. Rootstock woody. Stems bristly. Lvs ovate, hastate, sagittate, usually cordate, sometimes dentate or lobulate, 1.5–11×1.5–11cm, midlobe triangular, lateral lobes ovate-triangular; petiole rough-pubesc., to 8cm. Fls pedicellate; cal. to 2cm, lobes 1mm; pet. about 2×1mm, yellow; ovary green, globose, slightly beaked, bristly. Fr. subsessile, in clusters, scarlet, glabrous, smooth; seeds ovate. Spring–late summer. Africa, India to China and Malaysia, Australia.

For synonymy see *Cucumis* and *Melothria*.

**Mulch**. A covering placed on the surface of cultivated soil, a mulch has several distinct objects, the main one being to conserve soil moisture and reduce the need for watering in dry weather. Mulches insulate the soil in winter, help to maintain consistently high temperatures in spring (accelerating seed germination), and keep the soil surface cooler in summer, encouraging beneficial soil bacteria and deterring certain pests. Mulches also smother annual weeds and may add nutrients to the soil and improve its structure.

They usually consist of fairly bulky organic materials such as partly decayed animal manures, chopped straw, spent mushroom compost, spent brewery hops, peat, crushed bark, and garden compost. Lawn mowings can be used – but not in wet weather, when they form too dense and close a layer and impede soil aeration. Fallen leaves constitute a natural mulch and can be left in place provided one is reasonably confident that they will neither cause an allelopathic reaction (*Juglans*, for example), nor promote overdamp conditions likely to encourage pests and diseases. For basic soil insulation and weed suppression, mulches can be made with loose material such as chaff or chopped bracken, or by making a layer of loose soil with a Dutch hoe. Bulky materials which do not enhance soil texture or nutrition but do conserve moisture include pea gravel and flat stones; the latter are also highly decorative. Black polythene or similar plastic sheet is a fairly recent mulching material which represses weed growth and conserves moisture whilst achieving rapid soil-heating. The sheet can be held down by stones or by burying the edges in a narrow trench. Vegetables or other seedlings can then be planted through holes in the sheet. Alternatively a finely perforated translucent sheeting can be laid over soil which has already been sown with seed or where young plants have been planted; the sheeting warms up the soil and then floats on top of the crop as it grows.

Before any kind of mulch is applied to it, the soil should be free of perennial weeds; it should be at field capacity (holding the maximum amount of water it can) and should be neither frozen nor compacted. To avoid the infertile or compacted layer between mulch and soil that can develop over successive years of mulching, fork the mulched soil lightly before applying a further layer in another season. The normal times for application are spring and autumn. Most bulky mulches should be at least 10cm/4in. deep if they are to smother weeds.

Mulches have certain disadvantages: some plants may react adversely to materials like spent mushroom compost which is usually alkaline; manure may contain weed seeds and straw and, if poorly rotted, traces of harmful ammonia. Straw used alone may have been treated with a hormone weedkiller which may, no matter how residual, affect plant growth. Garden compost, if it has not become sufficiently heated while decomposing, may still contain viable weed seeds. Mulches absorb so much moisture and can form such a close seal on the soil surface that they can prevent light rain or watering from reaching plant roots: if water must be supplied to mulched plants it should be in good quantity. In very cold conditions temperatures over mulches tend to be lower than they would be over bare soil; where they fall below freezing, it may be advisable to protect emerging shoots and flowers borne near the surface (e.g. in strawberries) with additional straw, bracken or a clôche.

See also COMPOST HEAP.

**Mulgedium** Cass.
***M. bourgaei*** Boiss. See *Cicerbita bourgaei*.
***M. macrorhizum*** Royle. See *Cephalorrhynchus macrorhizus*.
***M. uralense*** Rouy. See *Cicerbita macrophylla* ssp. *uralensis*.

**Mundulea** (DC.) Benth. Leguminosae. 15 species of small trees or shrubs. Leaves imparipinnate; stipules minute or absent; leaflets entire, usually obovate, with reticulate venation. Inflorescences terminal pseudoracemes; flowers purple-blue; standard sericeous pubescent outside with a short, distinct claw; wings and keel glabrous except on margins at base; stamens 10, fused together but one free at base; style glabrous; stigma minute, glabrous. Fruit a many-seeded, usually indehiscent, densely pubescent pod; seeds not arillate. Madagascar and Old World Tropics. Z10.

CULTIVATION As for *Podalyria*.

***M. sericea*** (Willd.) A. Chev. Shrub or small tree, 2–7m; young branches pubesc. Lvs to 10cm; leaflets to 4×1.4cm, opposite, in *c*6 pairs, oblong ovate, elliptic or lanceolate, apex rounded, minutely pubesc. above and beneath or glabrescent above. Fls paired; cal. 6mm; standard 2.1×1.5cm, including claw; keel 1.8cm, including claw. Fr. to 8×0.8cm, base tapered, apex acute, yellow-brown, softly pubesc., constructed between seeds; seeds 4–9. Old World Tropics. Probably originally from Madagascar like the rest of the genus, but its natural range much extended because of its use as a fish poison.

**Munnozia** Ruiz & Pav. Compositae. About 40 species of annual to perennial herbs and subshrubs, with milky sap. Leaves opposite, base rounded to hastate, minutely serrate to pinnatisect, tomentose to pilose above, tomentose beneath; petioles often winged or auriculate. Capitula radiate, pedunculate, in a terminal, corymbose panicle; receptacle scaly; involucre broadly campanulate; phyllaries in 2–4 series, ovate to oblong; ray florets yellow, occasionally white or lavender; disc florets yellow. Fruit a ribbed, usually hairy cypsela; pappus of bristles and scales. Tropical S America, particularly Andes. Z10.

CULTIVATION A frost-tender perennial requiring the protection of the cool, well-ventilated glasshouse in temperate climates, in a freely draining mix of loam, sharp sand and leafmould. Propagate by division in spring.

***M. maronii*** (André) H. Robinson. Perenn. herb to 60cm, mostly white-hairy. Lvs to 12×10cm, triangular-hastate to triangular-cordate, remotely dentate, densely lanate. Capitula in long-pedunculate corymbs. Fr. usually hairy. Brazil.

For synonymy see *Liabum*.

**Muntingia** L. (For Abraham Munting (1626–83), Professor of Botany at Gröningen, Holland.) Elaeocarpaceae. 1 species, an evergreen tree to 12m. Leaves to 12.5cm, oblong-lanceolate, acuminate, serrate, alternate, tomentulose beneath. Flowers ephemeral, axillary, solitary or in clusters; sepals to one-third length of petals, ovate-lanceolate to subulate, green, downy, alternating with petals; corolla to 2.5cm diam., rotate, petals white, 5, spreading, broadly obovate, narrowing to a short claw, crepe-like; stamens numerous in a central boss arising from an annular disc, anthers yellow; ovary superior, 5-celled, stigma squat, 5-lobed, rugulose. Fruit a berry to 1.5cm diam., globose, white, fleshy. Tropical America. Sometimes included in Flacourtiaceae. Z10.

CULTIVATION *M. calabura* is a rapidly growing evergreen, occasionally cultivated for its edible fruits, used in preserves and eaten fresh. The flowers are carried over long periods, even on young plants. Suitable for outdoor cultivation in zones that are essentially frost free; in cooler climates, grow in the warm glasshouse in a sandy loam-based medium with additional leafmould or equivalent. Prune hard back when necessary to confine to bounds. Propagate by seed or semi-ripe cuttings in sand in a closed case with bottom heat.

***M. calabura*** L. CALABURA; JAMAICAN CHERRY. As for the genus.

**Murdannia** Royle, nom. cons. (In compliment to Murdan Aly, a plant collector and keeper of the herbarium at Saharunpore.) Commelinaceae. 40–45 species of annual or perennial herbs. Cincinni borne in panicles or verticils or solitary; flowers zygomorphic or nearly actinomorphic; sepals 3, equal, free; petals 3, subequal, free; stamens 3–6, the outer whorl usually fertile, sometimes 1 staminodal or absent, the inner whorl staminodal or rarely 1 or more absent, staminodes with hastate or trilobed antherodes; ovary 3-locular. Capsule subequally 3-valved; seeds with a punctiform to linear hilum and dorsal to lateral embryotega. Old World tropics. Z10.

CULTIVATION Requires warm greenhouse treatment, good light, and a rich, light, well-drained potting mix. Propagate annuals by seed, perennials by cuttings or seed.

***M. nudiflora*** (L.) Brenan. Weak, prostrate or decumbent annual herb, rooting at the nodes. Lvs 3–6×0.3–0.7cm, narrowly lanceolate or linear, rounded-acute at the apex, subamplexicaul at base, sparsely hairy or glabrous. Cincinnus usually solitary with *c*5–8 fls, stalk 2–5cm or more, pedicels *c*3mm at anthesis, 4–5mm in fruit, rigid, glabrous; fls *c*4mm diam., white, blue or purple-pink; fertile stamens 2, sterile stamens 2–4, fil. bearded. Capsule 3–4mm; valves apiculate, persistent. Flowering sporadic over year. Asia, widely naturalized in tropical America. Z9.

***M. simplex*** (Vahl) Brenan. Fleshy-rooted perenn. Lvs to 30×1–2cm, mostly basal, forming a loose rosette, linear-lanceolate, acuminate, channelled, glabrous or with margins ciliate towards base. Flowering stem to 1m, infl. a lax panicle of several-fld cincinni, axes of cincinni notched with close-set scars of fallen fls; fls 1–1.5cm diam.; pet. pale to dark blue or purple; stamens 2, bearded, anth. white; staminodes 3, glabrous, with trilobed antherodes. Spring–summer. Tropical Asia, Africa. Z9.

For synonymy see *Aneilema*.

**Murraya** Koenig ex L. (For John Andrew Murray (1740–41), pupil of Linnaeus and Professor of Medicine and Botany at University of Göttingen.) Rutaceae. 5 species of unarmed trees. Leaves odd-pinnate; leaflets alternate. Inflorescence axillary or terminal, of large panicles; flowers 5-merous, rather large, cylindric or elongate-ovoid in bud; calyx divided almost to base into lanceolate sepals; petals lanceolate or linear, imbricate; stamens 10, free, elongate; ovary ovoid, 2–5-locular, generally 2 ovules per locule; style long, slender. Fruit a small berry, ovoid to subglobose, pulp mucilaginous. Asia (India and China south to Australia). Z10.

CULTIVATION Grown in their native regions as border specimens or as screens and hedging, in cool temperate climates *Murraya* spp. are handsome specimens for tubs or large pots in the glasshouse or conservatory. Grown for their large panicles of bloom and rich green, aromatic foliage, *M.paniculata* produces several flushes of deliciously fragrant blooms throughout the year followed by small decorative fruits.

Grow in a fertile moisture-retentive but well-drained medium, that is rich in organic matter, with full sun to part shade. Water plentifully and liquid feed fortnightly when in full growth, moderately at other times. Maintain a winter minimum of 10–30°C/50–55°F. Prune if necessary in early spring. Propagate by seed in spring or by semi-ripe cuttings in a closed case with gently bottom heat. Whitefly may be a troublesome pest under glass.

***M.alata*** Drake. Shrub to 1m; branches glabrous, bark yellow. Lvs to 10cm, 5–7-foliolate, glabrous, leaflets 3–4×1–2cm, oblong or rhombic, subacute to acute at apex, entire or obscurely crenate, coriaceous; rachis winged; petiole very short, winged, minutely pubesc. Infl. axillary, cymose, few-fld, 2–3cm, minutely pubesc.; pedicels 6mm; sep. acute, 1.5mm, pubesc. without; pet. erect, obovate, 1–1.5cm; fil. linear; ovary 2-locular. Fr. ovoid, red, fleshy; seeds 1–2. N Vietnam, Hainan Is.

***M.koenigii*** (L.) Spreng. CURRY LEAF; KARAPINCHA. Evergreen tree, 4.5–6m, trunk to 3m×45cm, glabrous or slightly minutely pubesc. Lvs odd-pinnate, pungently aromatic, leaflets 2.5–4cm, 5–10 each side, oblong-lanceolate to ovate, subfalcate, oblique at base, acuminate at apex, more or less minutely serrate, membranous, glabrous or minutely pubesc. on midvein beneath; petiolules short, minutely pubesc.; rachis more or less pubesc., occasionally glabrous. Infl. terminal, corymbose; pet. 4–6mm, oblong-lanceolate, acute, white or tinged yellow; alternate stamens shorter; style short, thick. Fr. 8–10mm, ellipsoid, apiculate at apex, dark blue tinged black; seeds 1–2. Asia.

***M.ovatifoliolata*** (Engl.) Domin. Very similar to *M.paniculata*, but habit more straggling; twigs hirsute; lvs 3–9-foliolate, leaflets broadly ovate; cal., pet. and ovary hirsute. Australia (Queensland).

***M.paniculata*** (L.) Jack. ORANGE JESSAMINE; SATIN-WOOD; COSMETIC BARK TREE; CHINESE BOX. Tree or shrub, 4.5–7.5m, evergreen; trunk to 2.5m×60cm, twigs minutely pubesc. when young. Lvs pinnate or occasionally 3-foliolate, glabrous and glossy, leaflets 2.5–4cm, alternate, cuneate-obovate to obliquely rhombic, coriaceous, shortly petiolulate; rachis sometimes minutely pubesc. Infl. terminal, corymbose, small, dense, subsessile, fragrant; pet. 12–18mm, recurved, white; stamens 10, alternate ones shorter; ovary 2-celled. Fr. to 12mm, oblong-ovoid, bluntly acuminate, orange to red; seeds 1–2, villous. Flowers several times per year. China and India south to Australia.

***M.stenocarpa*** (Drake) Swingle. Small tree, to 1m, glabrous throughout. Lvs to 4–12×3–5cm, 1-foliolate, elliptic or oblanceolate, cuneate at base, narrowed to obtuse or almost emarginate at apex, serrate, glossy, subcoriaceous, oil glands distinctly visible particularly on margin; petiole 2–3.5cm. Infl. axillary, cymose, few-fld; fls small, to 2.5×1.5mm in bud; cal. lobes ovate, acute, small; pet. oblong; fil. ciliate; ovary oblong, substipitate, ovules 2. Fr. 1.5cm, oblong, attenuate at apex, red, fleshy. Distribution as for the genus.

***M.exotica*** L. See *M.paniculata*.
***M.paniculata*** var. ***ovatifoliolata*** Engl. See *M.ovatifoliolata*.

**Musa** L. (From Arab. *mauz*, banana, or for Antonius Musa, physician to Octavius Augustus, first Roman emperor.) BANANA; PLANTAIN; MANILA HEMP. Musaceae. About 40 species of large, rhizomatous or stooling herbs, to 6m. Leaves large to gigantic, oblong or elliptic, entire but often tearing, pinnately parallel-veined, margin often red, spirally arranged, midrib with deep rounded groove above; sheaths tightly clasping, forming pseudostem. Inflorescence a terminal spike, pendulous or erect, peduncle often pubescent, emerging from centre of pseudostem; flowers in clusters subtended by coloured bracts, female or hermaphrodite at base, male toward apex of inflorescence; bracts often roll back to reveal flowers, in single or double ranks; tepals 2, one tubular and compound with 3 lobes and 2 accessory lobes, the other free and inserted, opposite; stamens 5, rarely 6; ovary inferior, trilocular with many ovules. Fruit a many-seeded berry, seeds subglobose, lenticular or cylindrical, less than 7mm in diameter, arillate and black. Tropical Africa, Indian subcontinent, SE Asia, N Queensland.

CULTIVATION Some of the smaller ornamental spp. such as *M.auriantiaca, M.uranoscopus* and *M.velutina* are suitable for the intermediate glasshouse in temperate regions where space allows, and are also valued as foliage and flowering plants for home and conservatory. *Musa* spp. grow extremely rapidly under favourable conditions and it is not uncommon that the larger species outgrow their allotted space by their second or third season from seed; the foliage is extremely attractive however, and *Musa* spp. are sufficiently easy to grow that they can be replaced regularly as necessary. In tropical and frost-free subtropical gardens *Musa* spp. are often grown for foliage effects, and in temperate regions, *M.basjoo* is occasionally used as a dot plant in frost-tender bedding, overwintered in the cool glasshouse; they need a site with full protection from wind which quickly shreds the leaves. Of the larger species with edible fruits, *M.acuminata* and *M.*×*paradisiaca* are the most likely to succeed under glass, although they will require spacing of at least 2.4×2.4m/8×8ft and 3m/10ft of headroom, in the open border or in containers of at least 60cm/24in. diam. Grow other species in the glasshouse border or in large tubs or pots in an open, freely draining, high-fertility, loam-based medium, pH 6–7.5.

As ornamentals, *M.acuminata* will grow with a minimum temperature of 10°C/50°F, *M.velutina* at 16°C/60°F; any flowering and fruiting growths should be removed as they shrivel. For fruit production the optimal temperature is about 27°C/80°F but, especially during the ripening stage, the night temperature should not fall much below 18°C/65°F, since cooler conditions greatly impair fruit flavour and texture; surplus suckers should be removed frequently, root formation ceases as flowering begins and the number allowed to fruit is governed by available space at the root. The period between flowering and harvest will vary between 80 and 120 days, depending largely on temperatures (*Musa* fruits are always harvested green in commerce, ripened after transport in warmth and with ethylene treatment and high humidity). Each shoot bears one bunch of fruit and then dies, the perennial corm will then produce further suckers. Admit bright filtered light, maintain high humidity but with a buoyant atmosphere, ventilating where this is possible without a marked fall in temperature. Water plentifully and apply a liquid feed weekly when in full growth; water sparingly in winter. Propagate by seed in spring, germinate at 21°C/70°F, or by division of suckers with a portion of rhizome.

***M.acuminata*** Colla. Pseudostems to 7m or more, green blotched brown or black. Rhiz. short. Lvs erect or ascending to 3×0.7m, rounded at base, green sometimes dark-flecked above, green or purple beneath; sheath upper edge with papery margin. Infl. pendulous; peduncle brown-pubesc.; bracts acute, grooved, exterior bright red to purple or yellow, interior paler; female fls in 2 rows in each lower bract; terminal male bud acute. Fr. to 12×2.5cm, glabrous bright yellow, pulp white to yellow; seeds angular, depressed. Flowering irregular. SE Asia, N Queensland. 'African Rhino Horn': slender plant, fr. to 60cm long. 'Dwarf Orinoco' and 'Orinoco' ('Bluggoe'): fr. very thick with pink-tinted flesh. 'Manzano' ('Silk'): plump short fr. of dessert quality when ripe. 'Mysore': tall, disease-resistant, fr. medium-sized, dessert quality when ripe. 'Puerto Rican Dwarf': short plant, fr. very large in small bunches. Z9.

***M.aurantiaca*** G. Mann. Pseudostems many, closely grouped, to 3m. Infl. erect; bracts red or yellow; fls bright yellow. Fr. green. Assam. Z9.

***M.balbisiana*** Colla. Pseudostems clustered, to 7m and 28cm diam., green or yellow-green. Rhiz. short. Lvs to 3m, green, glaucous beneath; sheath waxy. Infl. pendulous; peduncle glabrous; female fls clustered; male bud obtuse; bracts obtuse, grooved, exterior purple, crimson inside; male fls in 2 rows, to 20 per bract. Fr. to 10×3cm, pale yellow, indehiscent, pulp cream; seeds subglobose. Indian subcontinent, S China, Philippines, New Guinea. Z10.

***M.basjoo*** Sieb. & Zucc. JAPANESE BANANA. To 5m, stoloniferous; pseudostem green, waxless, glabrous. Lvs 2m×70cm, oblong-lanceolate, thin, bright green; petiole stout, to 30cm. Infl. horizontal to pendulous; peduncle downy; bracts grooved, downy, outside yellow-green or tinged brown, inside pale yellow, biseriate; male fls about 20 per bract. Fr. sessile, to 6×2.5cm, yellow-green with white pulp; seeds black, compressed. Japan, Ryuku Is. 'Variegata': lvs banded or flecked lime green, cream and white. Z8.

***M.mannii*** H. Wendl. To 1.5m, stoloniferous; pseudostem slender, about 70cm, tinged or blotched black. Lvs *c*80×20cm, oblong. Infl. erect, to 14cm; bracts red-purple, slightly grooved; fls yellow, female fls in clusters of 3. Fr. green, small. Spring. NE India. Z9.

***M.ornata*** Roxb. FLOWERING BANANA. Stem slender, 2–3m, glaucous, waxy green. Lvs to 2m×35cm, slightly glaucous, sheath margins adpressed to stems. Infl. erect; fls orange-yellow, in single row; male bud slender; bracts pale purple, grooved, occasionally slightly revolute. Fr. about 6×2cm, yellow; seeds black, angular depressed, 5mm. Flowering irregular. Bangladesh, Burma. Z10.

***M.*×*paradisiaca*** L. (*M. acuminata* × *M. balbisiana.*) EDIBLE BANANA; FRENCH PLANTAIN. To 8m, stoloniferous; pseudostem terete, 14cm diam. at base. Lvs to 2.5m×70cm, oblong, green. Infl. pendulous, to 15.m. Fr. usually seedless, often yellow, pulp white. Tropics. Z9. There may be as many as 300 cultivars of edible banana worldwide. The leading commercial cultivar was for a century 'Gros Michel' ('Bluefields') now being phased out owing to susceptibility to destructive Panama disease. It has largely been replaced by Cavendish cultivars. Recommended cultivars of dessert bananas (*M.* ×*paradisiacum* and *M. troglodytarum*) include 'Cocos': medium-height, short fr. 'Dwarf Cavendish' ('Basrai'): short plant, fr. medium-length. 'Dwarf Jamaican Red' and Jamaican Red': fr. purple-red till ripe. 'Giant Cavendish' ('Grande Naine'): tall, large fr. in large bunches. 'Haa Haa': short plant, fr. medium-sized. 'Hua Moa': tall, fr. rounded, flesh pink-tinged. 'Ice Cream' ('Blue Java'): medium-sized plant, fr. stout, medium-sized. 'Koae': lvs striped laterally white and pale green on dark green, young fr. variegated, later yellow. 'Lacatan': very tall, fr. medium-sized in large bunches. 'Lady Finger': tall plant, fr. small, sweet. 'Valery': semi-dwarf, fr. long, in large bunches. 'Vittata': lvs variegated pale green and white, midrib white, edged red.

***M. sanguinea*** Hook. Similar to *M. uranoscopus* except pseudostem to 1.5m, slender; lvs to 90×15cm; infl. and rachis red; bracts strongly revolute; peduncle pubesc.; fls yellow to green-yellow, spotted red. NE India. Z9.

***M. textilis*** Née. MANILA HEMP; ABACA. Pseudostems to 6m, clumped, green to purple-green. Stoloniferous. Lvs to 2m, glabrous, oblong, basally deltoid, bright green, often spotted brown above, glaucous beneath, conspicuously veined; petiole to 30cm, sheathing. Infl. a horizontal to pendulous spike; fls biseriate; pedicel short; outer sep. bearing horns; male bracts persistent, polished, revolute, outside red to purple, inside paler. Fr. indehiscent, glabrous, to 7cm; seeds subglobose, black, dorsiventrally compressed. Philippines. Z9.

***M. troglodytarum*** L. FE'I BANANA. Confused names encompassing a range of seedless and seeded cultigens grown throughout Polynesia and Melanesia, notably cvs Aiuri, Borabora, Rureva and Soaga. Pseudostems to 7m, clumped, dark green, becoming maroon or violet-blue at base or wherever cut. Lvs to 4×3m, sap green, sometimes stained or flushed violet to maroon. Infl. erect; female fls to 12 per cluster; male fls ivory tinted maroon, to 4 per bract; bracts glabrous green. Fr. to 14cm, orange-brown, pulp sour unless cooked. Distribution described originally as Sumatra for *M. troglodytarum* and Tahiti for *M. fehi.* Z10.

***M. uranoscopus*** Lour. Pseudostem to 1m, terete, glossy red-green, becoming papery with age. Lvs to 75×30cm, oval to elliptic, abruptly acute, glossy light green above, somewhat waxy beneath, conspicuously pinnately veined, midrib green to rose-pink, sunken above, prominent below. Infl. to 0.75m, erect; bracts magenta to scarlet, to 15×8cm, fleshy, barely reflexed or revolute, often tipped green, persistent, shiny; fls 2 per bract. Fr. oblong to cylindric, to 5×2.5cm, rose-pink to green, downy, later yellow-brown; seeds spherical, black. Indochina. Z10.

***M. velutina*** Wendl. & Drude. Pseudostems to 1.5m, yellow-green to purple-green; rhiz. short. Lvs to 1m, dark green above, paler with red midrib beneath, venation conspicuously pinnate. Infl. erect; peduncle pubesc., white; fls bisexual, in monoseriate clusters; male bud acute to acuminate; bracts not grooved, outside purple-haired, inside darker. Fr. to 9×3cm, pink, pubesc., indehiscent, pulp white; seeds black, to 5mm. Flowering irregular. NE India. Z9.

***M. arnoldiana*** De Wildeman. See *Ensete ventricosum.*
***M. cavendishii*** Lamb. ex Paxt. See *M. acuminata.*
***M. chinensis*** Sweet. See *M. acuminata.*
***M. coccinea*** Andrews. See *M. uranoscopus.*
***M. ensete*** J. Gmel. See *Ensete ventricosum.*
***M. fehi*** Bertero ex Vieill. See *M. troglodytarum.*
***M. japonica*** Thiéb. & Ketel. See *M. basjoo.*
***M. nana*** auct. non Lour. See *M. acuminata.*
***M. paradisiaca*** var. ***sanguinia*** Welw. See *M. sanguinea.*
***M. religiosa*** Dyb. See *Ensete gilletii.*
***M. rosacea*** hort. non Jacq. See *M. ornata.*
***M. sapientum*** L. See *M.* ×*paradisiaca.*
***M. superba*** Roxb. See *Ensete superbum.*

**Musanga** R. Br. (W African vernacular name.) UMBRELLA TREE. Cecropiaceae. 2 species of evergreen trees. Leaves alternate in terminal compound rosettes, divided almost to base; segments entire, narrow, cuneate, abruptly acuminate; stipules large, connate, deciduous, enclosing young inflorescence. Female inflorescence solitary or in pairs, flowers in small round heads, bracts slender-stalked, perianth obovoid-tubular, stamens 1, anther short, ellipsoid; male inflorescences in pairs, flowers minute borne on oblong disc, bract threadlike, perianth tubular, narrow, basally constricted; stigma fimbricate; ovary ovoid. Fruit in persistent perianth, succulent; seed hard, shiny. W & C Tropical Africa. Z10.

CULTIVATION As for *Cecropia.*

***M. cecropioides*** R. Br. UMBRELLA TREE; CORK WOOD; PARASOLIER. To 20m, usually much less. Trunk short and slender; bark green-brown to grey with prominent lenticels. Cylindric stilt roots formed later. Petiole pubesc., to 70cm; leaf seg. 12–15, entire, to 45×10cm, grey-hairy beneath; stipules red, 15–20cm, densely pubesc. Male infl. to 4cm; female infl. to 2cm. Fr. yellow. W Africa to Angola and Uganda.

**Muscadinia** (Planch.) Small.
***M. rotundiMichxfolia*** (Michx.) Small. See *Vitis rotundifolia.*

**Muscari** Mill. (From Gk *moschos*, musk, alluding to the scent of some species.) GRAPE HYACINTH. Liliaceae (Hyacinthaceae). 30 species of bulbous perennial herbs. Bulbs tunicated, ovoid, sometimes producing offsets. Leaves 1–4, basal, linear, sometimes sulcate, rather fleshy. Inflorescence a dense, scapose, terminal raceme, uppermost flowers often sterile, forming a tuft (coma); bracts minute; perianth united into a tube, cylindric, campanulate, tubular or urceolate, blue to yellow to white, limb comprising 6 small lobes, acute, reflexed, often of a different colour; stamens 6, anthers included; ovary superior, 3-celled. Fruit a 3-angled capsule; seeds 2 per cell, black, shiny or wrinkled. Spring. Mediterranean, SW Asia.

CULTIVATION Early spring-flowering bulbs, they are well suited to naturalizing at woodland edge and for lining borders or paths in full exposure. Many species can be treated as temporary bedding plants for spring display; the more choice and unusual species deserve positions on rock gardens or on the tops of banks and walls, where the sweet musky fragrance from which they derive their name can be appreciated at close quarters. *M. macrocarpum* and *M. muscarimi* are both powerfully scented; these two Asian spp. must have good drainage and full sun to flower well, and may be pot grown in a medium-fertility, loam-based mix, to be brought indoors when in full bloom.

*M. comosum* is a large and beautiful Mediterranean species, made conspicuous by the coma of sterile florets above the fertile flowers; in the form *M. c.* 'Plumosum' the inflorescence consists of finely shredded, violet blue, sterile florets. Amongst the easiest and most prolific species are *M. armeniacum, M. aucheri, M. botryoides, M. comosum, M. latifolium* and *M. neglectum*, these last two, in some forms, with particularly beautiful, deep navy blue flowers. These vigorous species may become invasive but in any case look best in large, bold groups.

Topdress established clumps with bonemeal in spring; lift and divide when overcrowded, incorporating fresh top soil before replanting. Propagate by offsets after flowering or by seed sown when ripe.

***M. armeniacum*** Bak. Lvs to 30×6cm, 3–5, sometimes to 7, linear to linear-oblanceolate, sometimes paler above. Racemes 2.5–7.5cm, fls crowded and overlapping; fertile fls 3.5–5.5×2.3–3.5mm, obovoid to oblong-urceolate, azure, sometimes flushed purple, rarely white, lobes paler than tube or white, sterile fls few, smaller and paler than fertile, rarely of the same colour. SE Europe to Caucasus. 'Album': fls white. 'Argaei': fls bright blue. 'Argaei Album': fls white; spike small; late-flowering. 'Blue Spike': to 15cm, vigorous; infl. branched, fls large, fully double, profuse, soft blue. 'Cantab': strong-growing; stalks short; fls pale Cambridge blue. 'Dark Eyes': fls bright blue, rimmed white. 'Heavenly Blue': fls vivid blue. 'Saphir': fls dark blue, rim white, long-lasting, sterile. 'Sky Blue': fls pale turquoise, rim white, compact. Z4.

***M. aucheri*** (Boiss.) Bak. Lvs 5–20×0.2–1.5cm, usually 2, erect to spreading, falcate to narrowly spathulate, pale green and glaucous above, tip hooded-incurved. Raceme dense, ovoid or cylindric; fertile fls 3–5×2–5mm, subspherical or ovoid, bright azure, rarely white, lobes paler blue or white, sterile fls paler, as many as fertile fls or fewer. Turkey. The variant formerly known as *M. tubergenianum* is commonly cultivated and has a prominent coma of pale sterile fls. Z6.

***M. azureum*** Fenzl. Lvs 6–20×0.3–1.5cm, 2–3, erect to spreading, narrowly oblanceolate, tip often incurved, glaucous and paler above. Racemes 1.5–3cm, dense, ovoid; fertile fls 4–5mm, campanulate, not constricted, bright blue with a darker stripe on the lobes, sterile fls few, smaller and paler than fertile; anth. blue. E Turkey. 'Album': fls pure white. 'Amphibolis': fls pale blue, larger, earlier. Z8.

***M. botryoides*** (L.) Bak. Lvs 5–25×0.5–1.3cm, 2–4, erect, spathulate, often ribbed above, apex abruptly contracted, hooded or tapering. Raceme dense at first, later loose and cylindric; fertile fls 2.5–5mm, subspherical, azure, rarely white, lobes white. C & SE Europe. 'Album': fls pure white, sweetly scented. 'Caeruleum': fls bright blue. 'Carneum': fls flesh pink. Z3.

***M. comosum*** (L.) Mill. TASSEL HYACINTH. Bulbs to 3.5cm, without offsets, tunics pink. Lvs 3–7, erect to spreading, linear, channelled. Raceme loose; fertile fls 5–9mm, oblong-urceolate, brown-olive, lobes cream or yellow-brown, sterile fls subspherical or obovoid, rarely tubular, bright violet, on fleshy, bright violet, ascending pedicels, forming a conspicuous terminal tuft. S & C Europe, N Africa, SW Asia; naturalized Europe. 'Plumosum' ('Monstrosum'): inflorescence much-branched, consisting only of sterile fls and their stalks, all mauve blue. Z4.

***M. latifolium*** T. Kirk. Lvs 7–30×1–3cm, 1, rarely 2 together, erect, broadly oblanceolate, apex acuminate, often hooded. Raceme dense at first, becoming loose; fertile fls 5–6mm, oblong-urceolate, tube strongly constricted toward apex, deep violet, lobes concolorous, recurved; sterile fls blue. S & W Asia. Z4.

***M. macrocarpum*** Sweet. Bulbs 2–4cm diam., roots thick. Lvs to 30cm. Racemes loose, 20–30-fld; fertile fls 8–12mm, oblong-urceolate, blue-violet at first becoming yellow, expanded toward apex to form a brown or yellow corona, sterile fls tinged purple, few or absent. Aegean Is., W Turkey. Z7.

***M. massayanum*** Grunert. Bulbs 2–6cm diam., without offsets, tunics ivory. Lvs to 25×1–2.5cm, linear, falcate or sinuous, thick, glaucous, apex incurved. Flowering stem to 22cm, stout, tinted mauve; raceme dense, cylindric; fertile fls to 1.1cm, pink to violet at first, later pale green- or yellow-brown, lobes dark brown, sterile fls pink or violet on ascending to spreading pedicels, forming a dense tuft. E Turkey. Z7.

***M. muscarimi*** Medik. Bulb 2–4cm diam., roots thick. Lvs 10–20×0.5–1.5cm, pale grey-green. Flowering stem erect to prostrate, not exceeding lvs; fls muskily scented, fertile fls 8–14mm, narrowly urceolate, purple at first, becoming pale green to ivory, strongly contracted toward apex, then expanded to form a brown corona, sterile fls purple-tinged, rarely present. SW Turkey. Long cultivated in Turkey and in Holland by Clusius as early as 1596. Z6.

***M. neglectum*** Guss. ex Ten. COMMON GRAPE HYACINTH. Bulb 1–2.5cm diam., sometimes with offsets. Lvs 6–40×0.2–0.8cm, erect and spreading to prostrate, channelled to subterete, bright green, sometimes red-brown at base. Raceme dense in flower, loose in fruit; fertile fls 1.5–3.5×3.5–7.5mm, ovoid to oblong-urceolate, strongly constricted toward apex, deep blue-black, lobes white, recurved, sterile fls smaller and paler blue, rarely white. Europe, N Africa, SW Asia. A very variable species. Z4.

***M. pallens*** Bieb. Bulb ovoid, small. Lvs to 20cm+, equalling to exceeding scape, linear, acute, becoming enlarged above. Flowering stem 15–20cm; raceme short, oblong, dense; pedicels short; fls nodding, oval, white or blue tinged violet, teeth reflexed; sterile fls small, capsule compressed, valves obcordate. Caucasus.

***M. tenuiflorum*** Tausch. Like *M. comosum* but with 3–7 narrower lvs; fls fewer, pale grey-brown, lobes pale cream, sterile fls bright violet. C Europe (Germany). Z5.

***M. atlanticum*** Boiss. & Reut. See *M. neglectum*.
***M. cyaneo-violaceum*** Turrill. See *M. armeniacum*.
***M. luteum*** Tod. See *M. macrocarpum*.
***M. moschatum*** Willd. See *M. muscarimi*.
***M. paradoxum*** misapplied. See *Bellevalia pycnantha*.
***M. pinardii*** Boiss. See *M. comosum*.
***M. racemosum*** Lam. & DC. See *M. neglectum*.
***M. szovitsianum*** Bak. See *M. armeniacum*.
***M. tubergenianum*** Turrill. See *M. aucheri*.
For further synonymy see *Bellevalia*, *Botryanthus*, *Hyacinthella* and *Leopoldia*.

**Mushrooms**. From time immemorial edible fungi have been collected from the wild but few species have been brought into cultivation. This is due to the complex and specific microbial processes and associations involved in their growth and development, and to the technical problems in developing substrates on which they will grow and fruit. About ten species are cultivated on a significant scale world-wide. In order of importance these are *Agaricus bisporus* (including *A. bitorquis*), *Lentinus edodes* (shiitake mushroom), *Volvariella volvaceae* (Chinese mushroom, straw mushroom), *Flammulina velutipes* (winter mushroom), *Pleurotus* spp. (oyster mushroom), *Pholiota nameko* (nameko or viscid mushroom), *Auricularia* spp. (Jew's ear) and *Tremella fuciformis* (snow mushroom). All the cultivated species are Basidiomycetes with *Auricularia* and *Tremella* belonging to the Tremellales and the others to the Agaricales.

Cultivation of the different species is not distributed uniformly across the world. Production in a particular region is influenced by ethnic tastes and preferences, the natural environment and the availability of suitable substrates. In the West, cultivation is dominated by *Agaricus* with a very small but increasing interest in other species. By way of contrast, *Lentinus* is the most important species in the Far East, with a significant interest in a range of other species. *Agaricus* accounts for two-thirds of the world production of cultivated fungi and is the only species of significance cultivated in the British Isles. Mushroom cultivation is unique in that it provides the only profitable process for converting waste lignocellulose from agriculture and forestry into a useful, edible product.

*Mushroom kits*. It is very difficult for private gardeners to prepare composts on which mushrooms can be grown with a reasonable expectation of success. There are, however, a number of mushroom-growing kits available. These consist of prepared compost which has already been spawned and a bag of casing material. The packaging may be a plastic bag, a water-resistant cardboard or rigid plastic box, or a rigid plastic tub. This packaging doubles as a growing container and the purchaser simply follows the instructions enclosed.

*A. bisporus* is cultivated on substrates prepared from cereal straw, that from wheat being preferred. Preparation involves two phases. In Phase I the straw or strawy horse manure is wetted, mixed with chicken manure and activators, and built into stacks. These activators provide a source of nitrogen and soluble carbohydrate which promotes the microbial breakdown of the straw in the stack. The commonly used activators are chicken manure and molassed malt waste. Fermentation develops and the stacks are turned at intervals of 2–4 days over a period of 7–14 days to maintain aeration and ensure uniformity. In Phase II the fermenting compost is transferred to a facility in which it is pasteurized at 55–60°C/130–140°F over a period of 4–8 days in a process known as 'peak heating'. At the end of this period the compost is cooled at 25°C/77°F and inoculated with a pure culture of *Agaricus* mycelium (spawn) grown on cereal grain. The spawned compost is maintained at 25°C/77°F for 10–14 days during which it is colonized by the fungal mycelium (spawn-running). The upper surface of the colonized compost is then covered with a layer of peat/chalk (casing) and the temperature lowered to 16–18°C/60–65°F. The mycelium continues to colonize the compost and also invades the casing layer. After 18–21 days fruit bodies are initiated (pinning) and develop into the typical gilled caps. The crop is produced in flushes at intervals of 7–10 days over a period of 30–35 days. Production is then terminated by heating to at least 60°C/140°F with live steam (cooking out), the spent compost removed and the facility cleaned in preparation for the start of the next cycle. The production cycle takes 12–14 weeks.

The microbiology of the substrates used for *Agaricus* has been intensively researched and is better understood than those for other cultivated fungi. Cultivation requires accurate control of the environment and particularly of temperature, $CO_2$ level, ventilation rate and evaporative capacity of the air at different stages in the production cycle. 25°C/77°F is optimum for mycelial development but a lower temperature of 16–20°C/60–68°F is required for sporophore initiation and development. High $CO_2$ levels are necessary to promote mycelial growth but they must be lowered for sporophore initiation and the correct development of the cap and stipe.

The crop may be cultivated in purpose-built sheds, in insulated 'tunnels' covered with plastic film, or in caves. The substrate may be contained and the crop produced in ridged beds on the floor, in tiered wooden trays, on metal shelves, in deep troughs or in open-topped plastic bags. The several processes in the preparation and handling of compost, filling of trays and shelves, spawning, casing, watering and clearance of the used compost are all highly mechanized.

*Agaricus* is subject to attack by a range of pests and diseases. The common pests are eelworms and the larvae of sciarid, cecid and phorid flies. The important diseases are fungal viruses, the bacterial pathogen *Pseudomonas tolassi* and the fungal pathogens *Verticillium* and *Mycogone*. Pests and diseases are controlled initially by the pasteurizing process in Phase II, by strict attention to hygiene and by the manipulation and accurate control of the growing environment supplemented as necessary by appropriate insecticidal, fungicidal and biological controls.

*Lentinus edodes* or *shiitake* is the second most important cultivated fungus though it only accounts for 16% of total production. It is most important in Japan, where it is used both fresh and dried, and is also grown in the US, where over 40 strains are available. In nature the fungus attacks the wood of broad-leaved trees, mainly oak. For cultivation, trees are felled in the autumn and limbs 5–15cm/2–6in. diameter cut into 1m lengths. These are stored for 30–60 days and then inoculated with *Lentinus* mycelium cultured on sawdust or on small wooden wedges. 15–20 inoculations are made in each log after which they are first placed in a 'laying ground' for about a year and then at the onset of winter in a 'raising ground'. The latter is usually a shaded glade with a constant high humidity and a temperature range of 12–20°C/55–68°F. Fruit bodies start to appear the following spring. These are two flushes each year, in spring and autumn, and production is maintained over a period of 3–6 years.

More recently the fungus has been grown on mixtures of sawdust, soya bean meal and rice bran. Although yields are less than in the traditional method the production cycle is reduced to 6–8 months. Greater control is possible and the system lends itself to greater mechanization.

*Volvariella volvaceae* is regarded as an expensive delicacy in China and other Asian countries; it is also grown in Nigeria and Madagascar. The substrates used are either fermented rice straw or composted cotton waste. Traditionally the crop was grown in the open but it is now most commonly grown in film plastic structures using cotton waste as substrate. The waste is first composted and then filled into tiered beds each about 10cm/4in. deep. These are inoculated with pure culture spawn and the temperature maintained at 35°C/95°F. The substrate is colonized in about five days. No casing is needed but sporophore initiation is light-dependent. Fruit bodies appear in about five days and develop to harvest in four days. The first flush lasts 3–4 days and a second can sometimes be obtained about a week later. The product is highly perishable and has to be marketed quickly. The production cycle takes 5–6 weeks.

*Flammulina velutipes* is of about the same economic importance as *Volvariella*. In nature it is a wood-destroying species attacking broad-leaved trees such as aspen, willow and elm. The species is widely distributed through Europe, the Far East, Africa, North America and Australia. It was gathered wild in Japan for centuries but it is now cultivated on sterilized mixtures of sawdust and rice bran. The substrate is filled into 1l/1¾ UK pt/2¼ US pt polypropylene jars, sterilized and then inoculated with pure culture spawn. Colonization takes 20–25 days at 22–25°C/72–77°F. Fruiting is controlled by adjusting the temperature and humidity first to 10–12°C/50–55°F and 80–85%RH until the first fruit bodies appear. The temperature is then dropped to 3–5°C/37–40°F until the fruit bodies are 2cm/1in. long, when the temperature is raised to 5–8°C/40–46°F and the RH lowered to 75–80%. The developing fruit bodies in the neck of the jar are supported by a cylinder of waxed paper. At harvest the wax paper is removed, the clump cut and marketed whole. The production cycle takes 12–20 weeks.

*Pleurotus ostreatus*, the oyster mushroom, is a wood-degrading saprophyte widely distributed through the temperate regions. It is popular in Japan and Central Europe. The substrate is prepared from chopped straw supplemented by corn cobs and soya bean flour. The mixture is packed into trays or boxes and pasteurized at 70–80°C/160–175°F for 24 hours. After cooling the substrate is packed into boxes or plastic bags, inoculated with grain spawn and kept at 25–30°C/77–86°F in a dark room. Colonization takes 2–3 weeks, after which the blocks of substrate are removed from their containers and stacked in tiers so as to expose the maximum vertical surface for fruit body development. Fruit body initiation is light-dependent and the crop is lit with fluorescent tubes on a 12-hour cycle. During cropping the temperature is maintained at 10–12°C/50–55°F. The production cycle takes about 70 days.

*Pholiota nameko*, together with *Lentinus*, *Flammulina* and *Pleurotus*, is among the four most important fungi cultivated in Japan. The species was originally grown on hardwood logs of *Fagus* (beech) or *Quercus* (oak) partly embedded in the soil. This has given place to culture on sterilized mixtures of sawdust and rice bran, a technique developed in Japan and Taiwan. Two strains of the fungus are used, a high-temperature strain growing at 15°C/60°F and above which fruits in midsummer and a low-temperature strain growing below 15°C/60°F and cropping in late summer–early autumn.

*Auricularia* is popular in China, where it is cultivated on logs of broadwood trees in a similar manner to *Lentinus*, the logs cropping for a period of 3–6 years. In Taiwan cultivation has been developed on a sawdust/rice bran substrate. This is compressed into plastic bags to form a cylindrical cake. These cakes are sterilized, cooled, inoculated with mycelium and maintained at 28°C/82°F or less. When the blocks are colonized they are removed from the bags and stacked in frames to give a vertical wall of substrate on which the fruit bodies develop. The harvesting period is shorter than on logs but 3–4 flushes are obtained in each cropping cycle. The crop is dried and not sold fresh.

*Tremella fuciformis* is popular in China, Japan and Taiwan. Cultivation is on logs, using a technique similar to that for *Lentinus* and *Auricularia*. Gelatinous fruit bodies appear about eight weeks after inoculation and cropping continues for about seven months of each year for a period of 3–6 years. The mushrooms are washed after picking. Some are sold fresh but most are dried; they are usually stewed with fruit.

*Tuber*, the highly prized truffles belonging to the Ascomycetes, develop from a mycorrhizal association between the fungus and the appropriate trees, oaks, beech and hazel in particular. They are not cultivated in the same sense as the fungi described above, but methods have been developed in which tree seedlings are inoculated in a nursery to establish the mycorrhizal association, following which the 'truffled seedlings' are planted in suitable areas, such as old vineyards, for which a number of criteria have to be met. Truffles of different kinds can be grown in parts of France, Italy and Spain, and presumably in Portugal, Bulgaria and Yugoslavia where they also exist naturally. Harvesting is still carried out with pigs or dogs since digging up tree plots disturbs the mycorrhizal association and may destroy productivity, so that yields depend on the skill of the harvester as well as the weather and the age and management of the plot.

PESTS. The stalks and caps of mushrooms may be tunnelled by the maggots of various flies including those of fungus gnats (Sciaridae), gall midges (Cecidomyidae), often referred to as cecids and phorid flies (Phoridae). The larvae of fungus gnats have conspicuous black heads and are up to 5mm/1/5in. long; those of phorids are a little shorter and thicker with the head end tapering and a blunt hind end; the larvae of cecids are much smaller, with two spots behind the head and the body tapering at both ends. Mushroom may also be attacked by various mites including tarsonemid mites namely the mushroom mite (*Tarsonemus myceliophagus*); red pepper mites (*Pygmephorus* spp.) with minute yellow- to red-brown mites that can swarm in vast numbers over the beds; and tyroglyphid mites, with soft translucent white bodies clothed with long hairs, that cause pits to develop on the stalks and caps. Other pests injurious to mushrooms include the mushroom eelworms (*Aphelenchoides composticola* and *Ditylenchus myceliophagus*), woodlice, millepedes and slugs.

**Mussaenda** L. (From the Sri Lankan name.) Rubiaceae. Some 100 species of shrubs, subshrubs and herbs, sometimes twining. Stems erect or climbing, branched, terete. Leaves ovate or elliptic to oblong, apex more or less acute, subsessile or petiolate, opposite or 3-whorled, membranous, glabrous or pubescent; stipules interpetiolar, persistent or deciduous, truncate or 2-lobed, occasionally connate. Flowers pedicellate in axillary or terminal, few- to many-flowered panicles or cymes; bracts and bracteoles deciduous; calyx tube turbinate to ovoid or oblong, lobes 5, linear or spathulate to lanceolate, often one developed into an enlarged, showy limb; corolla tubular to funnelform, tube pubescent at throat, lobes 5, spreading, valvate in bud and often connate, pubescent; stamens 5, attached at throat, anthers dorsifixed, included, linear; ovary 2–4-celled, style occasionally 2-branched, stigma 2-

lobed, included or exserted, ovules many. Fruit a berry, globose to ellipsoid, 2-celled, indehiscent, fleshy, occasionally crowned by persistent calyx limb; seeds many, flat, testa reticulate to spinulose, endosperm fleshy. Tropical Old World. Z10.

CULTIVATION Grown for their colourful enlarged leaf-like sepals, more conspicuous than, but sometimes in vibrant contrast to the flower, as in *M. erythrophylla* with bright red sepals and yellow petal lobes, and *M. frondosa* with orange flowers and white sepals. *M.* 'Aurorae' is a particularly good form.

Grow in the hot glasshouse (min. 16–18°C/60–65°F) in a pH-neutral mix of equal parts loam, peat and leafmould with added sharp sand, with direct sunlight. Water plentifully when in growth, sparingly in winter. Provide support for climbing specimens, and thin out crowded stems or prune to a framework in spring. Propagate from semi-ripe cuttings or air layering in summer, or by seed in spring.

Susceptible to attack by white fly, *Trialeurodes vaporariorum*; control with the parasitic *Encarsia formosa*, or with a contact or systemic insecticide. Also by red spider mite, *Tetranychus urticae*; control with predator mite, *Phytoseiulus persimilis*.

***M. arcuata*** Poir. Shrub, to 7m. Stems erect or climbing, viscid, glabrous or short-pubesc., indistinctly lenticellate. Lvs to 20×10cm, obovate or elliptic to suborbicular, apex narrowly acute to caudate, base obtuse or acute to cuneate, lustrous and leathery glabrous above and sparsely pubesc. beneath, 5–7-veined; petioles to 2cm; stipules to 1cm, deciduous, truncate or 2-lobed, glabrous. Fls yellow, fragrant in loose or dense, few-fld panicles or cymes; pedicels to 7mm, peduncles to 4cm; bracts to 25×2mm; cal. tube turbinate to ellipsoid, to 4mm, limb deciduous, lobes to 15×3mm, linear or spathulate, margin toothed; cor. tube to 25mm, glabrous or pubesc. at throat, lobes to 2×1cm, ovate or elliptic to oblong, apex acute, red stellate-pubesc. Fr. to 3×2cm, globose to ellipsoid, yellow to green. Tropical Africa, Madagascar.

***M. erythrophylla*** Schumach. & Thonn. Shrub, to 8m. Stems erect or climbing, red-pubesc. and, occasionally, white-lenticellate. Lvs to 18×11cm, ovate or elliptic to suborbicular, apex acute or narrowly acute, base cuneate or obtuse to cordate, pubesc., 7–10-veined; petioles to 5cm; stipules to 1cm, persistent, 2-lobed, pubesc. Fls in dense, pedunculate panicles or cymes, pink to red and white to yellow; pedicels to 1cm, peduncles to 3cm, both pubesc.; bracts to 2cm, glabrous; cal. tube to 5mm, obovoid, pubesc., limb deciduous, lobes to 2×3mm, lanceolate, enlarged lobes to 6 per infl., ovate to orbicular, bright scarlet, pubesc.; cor. tube to 3mm, pubesc., lobes to 1×1cm, partially connate, orbicular, apex obtuse, glabrous or pubesc. Fr. to 3×2cm, ovoid to ellipsoid, pubesc., yellow. Tropical Africa. 'Queen Sirikit': branches drooping; lvs broad, wavy, head of bright pseudo lvs, bracts deep pink to ivory.

***M. frondosa*** L. Shrub, to 3m. Stems erect, glabrous or pubesc. to tomentose. Lvs to 15cm, ovate, lanceolate or elliptic to oblong, apex narrowly acute, tomentose beneath, sessile or petiolate; stipules to 6mm, 2-lobed. Fls yellow in dense, terminal corymbs; cal. to 2cm, enlarged lobe to 5cm, white; cor. funnel-shaped, tube to 25mm, pubesc., lobes ovate, apex acute or narrowly acute. Fr. to 1cm, globose to obovoid, areolate, glabrous to sparsely pubesc. Summer–autumn. Tropical Asia (Indochina to Malaysia).

***M. glabra*** Vahl. COMMON MUSSAENDA. Shrub, to 3m. Stems ascending to diffuse, more or less glabrous, lenticellate. Lvs to 15×8cm, oblong to lanceolate or elliptic, apex narrowly acute, base attenuate, lustrous and leathery, sparsely pubesc. on veins beneath, 5–6-veined, short-petiolate; stipules truncate to 2-lobed, lanceolate, apex acute. Fls in terminal, branched, many-fld cymes, orange to red; bracts persistent, lanceolate, apex subulate; cal. to 6mm, tube campanulate, limb deciduous, lobes lanceolate, apex subulate, developed lobe to 10cm, white, apex acute, base obtuse, glabrous; cor. tube to 25mm, glabrous or pubesc., apex of lobes acute. Fr. to 1cm, globose, glabrous. Tropical Asia (India to Malaysia).

***M. incana*** Wallich. Shrub, to 1m. Stems erect, simple or branched, pubesc. Lvs to 15×8cm, ovate or elliptic to oblong, apex acute or subacute, base acute or obtuse, rigid, pubesc., 9–10-veined, subsessile to short-petiolate; stipules 2-lobed, apex attenuate. Fls in subsessile corymbs, chrome yellow; cal. lobes filiform, developed lobe to 7cm, pubesc., white to cream or yellow; cor. to 2cm, lobes ovate, apex narrowly acute. Fr. globose, pubesc. to glabrous. Tropical Asia (India to Malaysia).

***M. macrophylla*** Wallich. Shrub, to 2m. Stems climbing, simple, sparsely pubesc. Lvs to 25×10cm, ovate to oblong, apex acute to narrowly acute, base obtuse or acute to cuneate, sparsely pubesc. on veins; petioles to 4cm; stipules 2-lobed, deltoid. Fls orange in dense, short-stalked, terminal cymes; cal. tube to 2mm, limb deciduous, lobes lanceolate to oblanceolate, apex obtuse, developed lobe to 12cm, rhomboid, white to yellow; cor. to 3cm, tube pubesc., lobes orbicular. Fr. to 2×1cm, ellipsoid, pubesc. Summer. Tropical Asia (India to Taiwan, Malaysia, Philippines).

***M. pubescens*** Ait. f. Shrub to 2m. Stems erect to climbing, pubesc. Lvs to 8×4cm or more, ovate or elliptic to oblong, apex acute to narrowly acute, base acute or obtuse, papery, pubesc., short-petiolate; stipules to 1cm, 2-lobed, connate at base, deltoid or lanceolate to linear. Fls yellow in dense, terminal cymes or corymbs; bracts linear; cal. tube to 3mm, pubesc., lobes to 6mm, erect, linear, pubesc., developed lobe to 9×5cm, ovate to elliptic, white; cor. tube to 3cm, pubesc., lobes to 6mm, ovate to deltoid or lanceolate, apex narrowly acute, pubesc. Fr. to 1cm, subglobose to ellipsoid, glabrous or pubesc., black. Tropical Asia (China, Taiwan). Often confused in cultivation with *M. frondosa*.

***M. roxburghii*** Hook. f. Shrub to 4m. Stems erect, pubesc. Lvs to 30×5cm, lanceolate or elliptic to oblong, apex narrowly acute to caudate, base attenuate, membranous, glabrous to pubesc. beneath, 8–10-veined; petioles to 25mm; stipules deltoid to lanceolate. Fls in dense, many-fld cymes or corymbs; cal. limb persistent, lobes filiform, pubesc., developed lobe to 7cm, glabrous, white; cor. tube to 2cm, silky, lobes filiform, pubesc. Fr. globose to ellipsoid, glabrous. Tropical Asia (Himalaya).

***M. sanderiana*** Ridl. Shrub, to 2m. Stems erect to creeping. Lvs lanceolate, base cordate, sericeous, subsessile. Fls in terminal cymes, yellow; developed lobe to 8cm, white, sericeous; cor. tubular. Tropical Asia (Indochina).

***M. cultivars.*** 'Aurorae': lvs to 15cm long, wavy, softly haired; fls gold.

***M. abyssinica*** Chiov. See *M. arcuata*.
***M. albiflora*** Hayata, non Merrill. See *M. pubescens*.
***M. coccinea*** Poir. See *Warszewiczia coccinea*.
***M. formosa*** Jacq. See *Randia formosa*.
***M. kotoensis*** Hayata. See *M. macrophylla*.
***M. luculia*** Buch.-Ham. ex D. Don. See *Luculia gratissima*.
***M. parviflora*** Kanehira, non Miq. See *M. pubescens*.

**Mutisia** L. f. (For José Celestino Mutis of Cadiz (1732–1808), teacher of anatomy and student of South American plants.) Compositae. About 60 species of glabrous to tomentose shrubs or lianes. Leaves alternate, simple or pinnate, often terminating in a tendril. Capitula radiate, medium to large, terminal, solitary, pedunculate, erect to pendulous; receptacle flat to convex; involucre cylindric to oblong-campanulate; phyllaries imbricate, in several rows, broadly lanceolate, often with leafy appendage; ray florets few, female, purple, rose, yellow, scarlet or orange, rarely white; disc florets numerous, hermaphrodite, fertile or sterile, usually yellow. Fruit a cylindric-fusiform to turbinate, glabrous cypsela; pappus of long, stiff, plumose, tawny or white bristles. S America. Z9 unless specified.

CULTIVATION Given the protection of a south- or southwest-facing wall and good drainage *M. oligodon* will tolerate temperatures to about −15°C/5°F and *M. decurrens* to about −10°C/14°F; *M. clematis*, *M. ilicifolia*, *M. spinosa* var. *pulchella* and *M. subulata* are almost as hardy.

Grow in deep, well-drained, moderately fertile soils, in a position with shade at the roots but where top growth will receive full sun; a large rock or deep organic mulch placed over the roots will provide the necessary protection and help conserve moisture when in growth. Provide support by means of wire or trellis. Under glass water moderately when in growth, maintain good ventilation with a minimum winter temperature of 7–10°C/40–50°F. Prune to remove weak and overcrowded growth after flowering or in spring in cool climates. Propagate by stem cuttings in summer rooted in sand in a closed case with gently bottom heat, by simple layering or by removal of suckers in species like *M. decurrens*. Also by seed in spring.

***M. acuminata*** Ruiz & Pav. Much-branched shrub to 1m; branches flexuous. Lvs 8–10cm, pinnatisect, terminating in a trifid tendril; leaflets to 4×1cm in 9–14 pairs, opposite or alternate, elliptic-lanceolate, acuminate, base decurrent, glabrous. Capitula on peduncles to 12cm; involucre cylindric; phyllaries in 6–7 series, ovate to oblong, innermost to 5cm, outer much shorter, grey, tinged red; ray florets 5–8, bright red or scarlet. Fr. to 2cm; pappus to 2cm. Andes (Peru to Bolivia).

***M. clematis*** L. f. Liane to 10m; branches angular, minutely tomentose at first. Lvs 5–10cm, pinnate; with a long, trifid, terminal tendril, leaflets to 7×3cm, in 4–5 pairs, lowermost reduced to stipules, otherwise opposite, elliptic, tomentose beneath and sometimes also above. Capitula to 6cm diam., pendulous, shortly pedunculate; involucre campanulate; phyllaries in 4–5 series, lanceolate, acute, inner to 4.5cm, outer shortest; ray florets 9–10, bright orange to scarlet or maroon. Fr. 1.5cm; pappus to 1.7cm. Summer–autumn. N Andes (C Colombia and Ecuador).

***M. decurrens*** Cav. Much-branched, rhizomatous subshrub to 2m. Lvs to 10×2cm, lanceolate, sessile, acute at apex with long, bifid, terminal tendril, decurrent at base, entire or sharp-toothed, main vein prominent. Capitula to 12cm diam., on peduncles to 10cm; involucre campanulate; phyllaries in 4–5 series, outer *c*1cm, broadly oval, with short linear appendage, inner to 3.5cm, oblong-ovate, acute; ray florets 10–15, brilliant orange. Fr. to 1cm; pappus to 2.5cm, plumose. Summer. S Andes (Chile, Argentina). Z8.

***M. ilicifolia*** Cav. Branched shrub to 3m; branches glabrous or somewhat lanate above. Lvs to 6×4cm, ovate to ovate-elliptic, sessile, with a long, simple, terminal tendril, base cordate and semi-amplexicaul, margin spinose-dentate with 10–12 pairs of triangular teeth, subcoriaceous, glabrous above, tomentose or glabrescent beneath. Capitula 2–3cm diam., on peduncles to 4cm; involucre campanulate; phyllaries in 5–6 series, outer reduced to an acute, lanceolate appendage, to 13mm, densely tomentose below, middle almost semicircular with lanceolate appendage, inner broadly oblong-ovate, to 1.5cm, somewhat tomentose near apex, otherwise glabrous; ray florets *c*8, pale pink. Fr. to 1cm, cylindric-fusiform; pappus to 1.8cm, off-white. Chile.

***M. latifolia*** D. Don. Shrub to 1.5m; branches 2–3-winged, ascending or sprawling, densely leafy. Lvs to 5.5×3.5cm, ovate or elliptic, sessile, apex truncate, base cordate and semi-amplexicaul, spinose-dentate with 10–15 pairs of teeth each side, midrib conspicuously prolonged into a terminal tendril, subcoriaceous, tomentose or glabrescent above, densely tomentose or occasionally subglabrous beneath. Capitula to 7.5cm diam., on peduncles to 4cm; involucre campanulate; phyllaries in 5–7 series, outer broadly ovate-lanceolate, to 1.5cm, acute, tomentose on back, middle semicircular with ovate-lanceolate appendage, inner broadly elliptic, to 2cm, without appendage, glabrous; ray florets 10–15, lilac or deep rose. Fr. glabrous; pappus to 1.8cm, dusky white. Autumn. C Chile.

***M. linearifolia*** Cav. Dwarf creeping shrub to 30cm; branches densely leafy, ribbed. Lvs to 3×0.5cm, linear, sessile and decurrent, acute and shortly mucronate, entire, strongly revolute, glabrous. Capitula to 6cm diam., shortly pedunculate; involucre campanulate; phyllaries in 4–5 series, ovate to elliptic, shortly mucronate, outer to 0.5cm, occasionally suborbicular, inner to 2cm, tinged red; ray florets 8–10, red. Fr. striate; pappus to 2.5cm, white to pale grey. S Andes (N Argentina, C Chile).

***M. oligodon*** Poepp. & Endl. Straggling shrub or liane to 1m, decumbent or ascending; branches gently undulate. Lvs to 3.5×1.5cm, oblong to elliptic, acute or obtuse, sessile, base cordate, usually remotely 1–2-dentate near apex, upper lvs few, terminating in a tendril, glabrous above, densely tomentose beneath. Capitula to 7cm diam. on peduncles to 5cm; involucre campanulate; phyllaries in 5–6 series, outer shortest, semicircular with a lanceolate, reflexed, apical appendage, inner oblong, to 2cm, obtuse; ray florets *c*10, bright red. Fr. 12–14mm, cylindric, somewhat tapered to apex; pappus 18mm, off-white. S Chile, S Argentina.

***M. sinuata*** Cav. Low shrub to 30cm, often creeping; branches flexuous, narrowly winged. Lvs close-set, to 3×0.6cm, lanceolate, sessile, acute, base attenuate and decurrent, margins revolute, with 6–8 triangular teeth, glabrous above, minutely tomentose or glabrescent beneath, upper lvs usually terminating in a simple tendril. Capitula to 5cm diam., shortly pedunculate; involucre campanulate; phyllaries in 4–5 series, broadly ovate to oblong, outer to 1cm with a lanceolate terminal appendage, inner minutely mucronate; ray florets 8–10, to 2cm, white to light yellow above, pink or grey below. Fr. cylindric-fusiform, to 15mm; pappus to 15mm, white. S Andes (C Chile and Argentina).

***M. speciosa*** Ait. Shrub to 6m; branches prominently ribbed, occasionally narrowly winged. Lvs 4–12cm, pinnate, terminating in a trifid tendril, leaflets in 4–7 pairs, opposite or alternate, lanceolate, generally acute, base cuneate, lowermost leaflets reduced. Capitula to 8cm diam., usually on peduncles to 1.5cm; involucre campanulate; phyllaries in 5–7 series, ovate-lanceolate, outer recurved, inner mucronate; ray florets 13–20, pink to red. Fr. 2.5cm, cylindric-fusiform, glabrous; pappus to 2.5cm, white. Andes of Ecuador, S Brazil.

***M. spinosa*** Ruiz & Pav. Liane to 6m; young branches spinose-winged. Lvs to 6×3.5cm, elliptic to ovate-elliptic, sessile, base cordate and semi-amplexicaul, usually entire or with 1–2 pairs of spinose teeth near apex, terminating in a long simple tendril, glabrous above, sparsely lanate or glabrous beneath. Capitula to 6cm diam., on peduncles to 8cm; involucre campanulate; phyllaries in 5 series, outer semicircular, with a linear-lanceolate, generally reflexed, apical appendage, inner to 1.5cm, oblong; ray florets 8–10, pale pink. Fr. to 1.5cm, cylindric, somewhat attenuate toward apex; pappus 2cm, white, tinged grey. S Argentina, Chile. var. ***pulchella*** (Speg.) Cabr. Lvs persistently white-tomentose beneath.

***M. subulata*** Ruiz & Pav. Low, often creeping shrub to 50cm; stems cylindric, undulate. Lvs to 7×0.1cm, linear-subulate, with apical spine or tendril of variable length, sessile, margin revolute, entire, glabrous. Capitula to 7.5cm diam., shortly pedunculate; involucre cylindric; phyllaries in 7–8 series, outer ovate, to 1cm, with short, linear, apical appendage, inner oblong, to 3cm, obtuse; ray florets *c*10, brilliant red to scarlet. Fr. to 1cm; pappus 2–2.5cm, plumose, white. S Andes (C Chile).

***M. arachnoidea*** Mart. ex D. Don. See *M. speciosa*.
***M. breviflora*** Philippi. See *M. ilicifolia*.
***M. pulchella*** Speg. See *M. spinosa* var. *pulchella*.
***M. retusa*** Rémy. See *M. spinosa* var. *pulchella*.
***M. versicolor*** Philippi. See *M. subulata*.
***M. viciaefolia*** Cav. See *M. acuminata*.

**MYOPORACEAE** R. Br. MYOPORUM FAMILY. Dicot. 5 genera and 220 species of small trees and shrubs. Leaves simple, usually gland-dotted, alternate, rarely opposite. Flowers bisexual, regular or irregular, solitary or in axillary cymes; calyx 5 fused sepals, lobes open or imbricate; corolla 5 fused petals, often bilabiate, lobes imbricate; stamens 4, upper posterior staminode or absent, rarely 5, alternate with corolla-lobes on corolla-tube; ovary superior, of 2 fused carpels with terminal style, 2-loculed; ovules (1) 2 per locule, or 4–8 superposed in pairs, or the locule subdivided into 4–10 uniovulate compartments. Fruit a drupe or separating into 1-seeded drupe-like segments; seeds with almost straight embryo; endosperm scanty or absent. Some provide timber (*Eremophila, Myoporum*), others provide locally eaten fruits. Australia (mostly), Pacific, Indian Ocean, S Africa and few W Indies. *Bontia, Eremophila, Myoporum*.

**Myoporum** Banks & Sol. ex Forst. f. (From Gk *myo*, to close, and Lat. *porum*, a pore, due to the densely glandular-punctate leaves.) Myoporaceae. About 30 species of perennial, evergreen trees and shrubs, often of ericoid appearance, to about 10m. Leaves alternate, entire or serrate, glandular-punctate with pellucid glands. Inflorescence an abbreviated cyme or single-flowered; flowers small, often white; calyx 5-lobed; corolla campanulate-hypocrateriform with a short tube, lobes 5, patent; stamens 4, ovary 2–4 loculed, with 1(–2) ovules per locule. Fruit a more or less fleshy drupe. Australia and New Zealand to E Asia and Mauritius.

CULTIVATION In warm, essentially frost-free, mediterranean-type climates, the taller species are tolerant of clipping and make good windbreaks and boundary hedging in coastal gardens; the colourful fruits are decorative. In similar climates, smaller species such as *M. debile* are suitable for the rockery or sunny banks, especially valuable in dry soils. In cooler zones, grow in a sandy loam-based mix in the cool, well-ventilated glasshouse or conservatory. Propagate by simple layers, by semi-ripe cuttings or by seed.

***M. debile*** (Andrews) R. Br. Low, spreading shrub, with slender, semi-prostrate branches, twigs tinged red. Lvs 4–8×0.5–1cm, sessile, narrowly linear-lanceolate, subacute, margins with small, acute teeth near base and apex only. Fls 1–2, axillary, on 4–5mm pedicels; cal. lobes 5–7mm, narrowly lanceolate; cor. 6–8mm, pink to purple, campanulate, lobes shorter than tube, villous inside; stamens 4. Fr. subspheroidal, *c*9×10mm, white below, maroon above. Australia, New Zealand. Z9.

***M. insulare*** R. Br. BOOBYALLA. Tree or large shrub to 10m. Lvs to 7.5cm, obovate to lanceolate, thick, usually glabrous, margins entire or with few teeth. Infl. axillary, 2–4 fld; cor. to 6mm, white with pink spots. Fr. to 6mm diam., globose, blue-purple. Australia. Z9.

***M. laetum*** Forst. f. Tree to 10m, smaller in exposed sites, bark brown, twig apices and buds sticky. Lvs 4–10×(1–)2–3cm, on flattened petioles to 3cm long, lanceolate to oblong-lanceolate or oblong to obovate, somewhat fleshy, bright green, glabrous, teeth variably crenate to sinuate. Infl. a reduced axillary cyme, 2–6-fld, peduncle to 15cm; cal. lobes 2mm, narrowly lanceolate, cor. *c*1cm diam., campanulate, white with purple spots, lobes villous above. Fr. 6–9mm, narrowly ovoid, pale to dark maroon. New Zealand. Z9.

***M. parvifolium*** R. Br. Low, spreading, glabrous shrub to 50cm. Lvs 1–2.5×2–3cm, dense, linear, apex broader, Infl. 1–3-fld, axillary, on peduncles to 1cm, honey-scented, cor. to 1cm wide, deeply 5-lobed. Summer. Australia. Z9.

***M. sandwiciense*** (A. DC.) A. Gray BASTARD SANDALWOOD; NGAIO; NAIO. Tree to 20cm, wood dark yellow-green, hard, smelling of sandalwood. Lvs to 15cm, ovate-lanceolate. Fls to 8mm diam., white or pink; cor. lobes 5–6(–7), stamens equalling cor. lobes. Fr. white. Hawaii. Z9.

***M. tenuifolium*** Forst. f. Round-crowned to 8m, bark grey-brown. Lvs 4.5–10(–17)×1.5–3(–5)cm, on 0.5–1cm petioles, lanceolate, apex acuminate, base cuneate, entire, glossy-green above. Infl. a dense (1–)5–9-fld cyme, fls on slender pedicels to 12cm; cal. 2–3mm, lobed divided for half their length; cor. tube 4–5mm, limb 10–12mm diam., white with purple spots. Fr. 7–9mm, ovoid, very dark purple when mature. Early summer. Australia, introduced in SW Europe. Z9.

***M. tetrandrum*** (Labill.) Domin Erect shrub or small tree of variable habit, twig tips not sticky. Lvs 2.5–5×1–2.5cm, elliptic-oblong to lanceolate, obtuse and mucronate or obtuse, toothed to entire, glabrous. Infl. 2–6-fld, axillary; cal.

lobes lanceolate; cor. to 9mm diam., white with pink, stamens 5. Fr. 4–6mm, globose. Australia, introduced Portugal. Z9.

***M. acuminatum*** R. Br. See *M. tenuifolium*.
***M. serratum*** R. Br. See *M. tetrandrum*.

**Myosotidium** Hook. (From *Myosotis* and *eides*, resembling, referring to the flowers which resemble those of *Myosotis*.) Boraginaceae. 1 species, a perennial or biennial herb. Stems to 1m, succulent, stout. Basal leaves to 30cm, clustered, fleshy, reniform to broadly ovate or ovate-cordate, obtuse, lustrous bright green, glabrous above, slightly retrorse-pubescent beneath, long-stalked; cauline leaves oblong, sessile. Inflorescence a dense corymbose cyme, to 15cm; flowers dark to pale blue; pedicels to 1cm; calyx deeply 5-lobed, lobes oblong, obtuse, adpressed-pubescent; corolla tube short, throat with 5 protuberances, lobes 5, rounded, spreading; stamens 5, short, inserted within tube; ovary 4-lobed, style short, stigma capitate. Fruit of 4 nutlets, nutlets compressed, to 15mm diam., alate. New Zealand. Z8.

CULTIVATION Endemic to rocky and sandy coastal habitats on the Chatham Islands and naturalized on seaside shingle in Northern Europe, *Myosotidium* is now rare and vulnerable in the wild. It is grown for its glossy, deeply veined, fleshy foliage and dense heads of large forget-me-not-blue flowers in summer. In coastal gardens with cool summers and little winter frost, it is suitable for the front of borders or the rock garden. Where temperatures fall to about −17°C/1°F, protect with evergreen branches or dry bracken litter, otherwise grow in the cold glasshouse. Plant in a cool position in semi-shade, sheltered from wind, in freely draining, humus-rich soils. Mulch with seaweed. Propagate from seed sown ripe in autumn or by careful division.

***M. hortensia*** (Decne.) Baill. As for the genus.

***M. nobile*** Hook. See *M. hortensia*.
For further synonymy see *Myosotis*.

**Myosotis** L. (From the Gk *mys*, mouse, and *ous*, ear, referring to the appearance of the leaves.) FORGET-ME-NOT; SCORPION GRASS. Boraginaceae. Some 50 species of annual, biennial or perennial herbs, pubescent. Leaves alternate. Flowers usually in paired cymes, mostly white, blue or purple usually with a conspicuous white or yellow eye; bracts usually absent; calyx 5-lobed, often accrescent in fruit; corolla rotate or salverform, lobes 5, obtuse, spreading, faucal scales 5, distinct, usually included, papillose; stamens 5, usually included, filaments inserted near middle of tube, anthers ovate, obtuse; ovary 4-lobed, style filiform, included, stigma small, capitate. Nutlets 4, ovoid, erect, usually compressed, shiny, smooth, glabrous, black to brown. Temperate distribution, mainly Europe, New Zealand.

CULTIVATION *M. sylvatica* and *M. alpestris* occur in damp woodland and meadow, the latter on basic rock formations. Their many cultivars are grown as hardy annuals or biennials (tolerating winter temperatures of at least −15°C/5°F); these are available in compact dwarf cultivars, such as 'Ultramarine' with deep indigo blue flowers, 'White Ball' compact with white blooms, and the taller rose pink flowered 'Rose'. Traditionally used in spring bedding and as border edging, they are also suited to window boxes and to pot cultivation in the cold glasshouse for winter and early spring blooms. The wild species of *M. sylvatica* and its forms are especially suitable for naturalizing in informal areas, where they will self-seed.

*M. scorpioides, M. laxa*, and *M. palustris*, found in wet habitats at water margins and in marshy ground, are suited to pond edge and other damp sites, in mud or very shallow water, especially in wilder areas of the garden; *M. palustris* is vigorous and invasive, sometimes occurring as a lawn weed (or used in the wild flower lawn).

The alpine New Zealand species *M. explanata* and *M. colensoi* are found in moist, rocky habitats, *M. australis* occurs at higher altitudes in exposed situations, *M. colensoi* on limestone scree. Grow these in gritty, moderately fertile and perfectly draining soils in sun or in light, partial shade; *M. australis* and *M. colensoi* are particularly well suited to scree plantings. *M. explanata* needs protection from the brightest sun and plentiful water when in flower. In the alpine house use a mix of equal parts loam leafmould and sharp sand.

Propagate by seed or division. Powdery mildew may seriously reduce flowering of annual/biennial spp. Myosotis smut shows as off-white spots on the leaves, and often occurs on plants allowed to self-sow. Aphids are particularly damaging if allowed to infest alpine spp.

***M. alpestris*** F.W. Schmidt. Tufted perenn. Stems to 30cm, erect, simple or branched, usually pubesc. below. Basal lvs to 8×1.5cm, oblong, ovate-oblong or lanceolate, obtuse, petiolate or subsessile, sparsely or densely pubesc.; cauline lvs to 2.5cm, sessile. Fls bright or deep blue; pedicels to 5mm in fr.; cal. to 7mm in fr., with adpressed, spreading or sometimes uncinate hairs; cor. to 9mm diam., lobes rounded, spreading. Nutlets to 2.5mm, ovoid to ellipsoid, dark brown, with a distal rim. Europe, Asia, N America. Z4.

***M. alpina*** Lapeyr. Perenn. Stems to 12cm, densely tufted. Basal lvs lingulate, sessile, glabrous beneath. Fls bright or deep blue; pedicels to 2mm; cal. to 7mm, densely covered with uncinate hairs; cor. to 8mm diam. Nutlets to 2×1mm, narrowly ovoid. Europe. Z6.

***M. arvensis*** (L.) Hill. Annual or bienn. Stems to 50cm, erect, often with many slender branches near base, sparsely to densely pubesc. Basal lvs to 8×1.5cm, oblanceolate, short-petiolate to subsessile; cauline lvs lanceolate, sessile. Fls bright blue to dark purple, ebracteate; pedicels to 1 cm; cal. to 7mm in fr., lobes incurved, densely covered with uncinate hairs; cor. to 3mm diam., campanulate, limb ascending or spreading. Nutlets to 2.5×1mm, ovoid, acute, black, with a rim. Europe, NE Africa, Asia; naturalized N America. Z6.

***M. australis*** R. Br. Perenn. Stem branched near base; branches to 30cm, few to many, erect or ascending. Basal lvs to 6cm, elliptic or spathulate, apex rounded, with spreading hairs above and short retrorse hairs beneath; petiole to 6cm; cauline lvs to 1.5cm, oblong or spathulate, adpressed-pubesc.; sessile. Fls white or yellow; bracts absent; pedicels short; cal. to 4mm, covered with uncinate hairs; cor. lobes rounded, concave. Nutlets acute, somewhat carinate. Australia, Tasmania, New Zealand. Z8.

***M. azorica*** H. Wats. Perenn. Stem to 60cm, much-branched, with white, retrorse hairs below. Lvs to 10×2cm, narrowly obovate or oblanceolate, densely pubesc. Fls blue with a white eye; cal. to 5mm in fr., lobes narrowly linear, with straight, deflexed hairs at base; cor. to 6mm diam. Nutlets to 1.5×1mm, ovoid, obtuse, rimmed. Azores, Canary Is., Algeria. Z9.

***M. caespitosa*** Schultz. Perenn. Stems to 60cm, simple or branched, erect or suberect, sparingly covered with white, adpressed hairs. Basal lvs to 4×1cm, ovate-oblong, subobtuse or rounded, sparsely adpressed-pubesc. above, often glabrous beneath; cauline lvs to 6×1cm, obovate-oblong to lanceolate-oblong, obtuse to subacute. Fls blue; bracts absent; pedicels to 10mm in fr., hispid; cal. to 4mm in fr., lobes short, erect, sparsely adpressed-pubesc.; cor. to 3mm, limb to 4mm diam., lobes ovate-spreading. Nutlets to 1.5×1mm, broadly ovate, apex rounded, dark brown. Europe, Asia, N Africa, N America. Z6.

***M. colensoi*** (T. Kirk) Macbr. Stem short-branched, decumbent. Basal lvs to 3×1cm, lanceolate, subacute, adpressed-pubesc., sometimes glabrous beneath, short-petiolate; cauline lvs to 1×0.3cm, oblong, sessile or subsessile. Cymes few to many-fld; fls white, short-pedicellate; bracts to 10×3mm, oblong; cal. to 7mm in fr., densely adpressed-pubesc., lobes subacute; cor. to 8mm diam., tube to 5mm, cylindrical, lobes rounded. Nutlets to 1.5×1mm, acute. New Zealand. Z8.

***M. dissitiflora*** Bak. Closely resembles *M. sylvatica* except lower in habit, pubesc. Fls deep sky blue. Nutlets stalked. Switzerland. Z6.

***M. explanata*** Cheesem. Perenn. Stem to 30cm, white-pubesc., ascending, slightly branched; branches to 20cm, erect. Basal lvs to 7×1.5cm, obovate to linear or spathulate, rounded, pubesc.; petiole to 6.5cm; cauline lvs to 3×1cm, oblong-lanceolate, acuminate, adpressed-pubesc., sessile. Fls white; bracts absent; pedicels minute; cal. to 10mm in fr., lobes to 5mm, obtuse, covered with spreading or retrorse hairs; cor. to 10mm diam., tube to 10mm, lobes rounded. Nutlets to 2.5mm, oblong. New Zealand. Z8.

***M. laxa*** Lehm. Annual to perenn. Stems to 50cm, cylindrical, branched near base, decumbent, adpressed-pubesc. Lvs to 8×1.5cm, lanceolate to spathulate. Fls bright blue with a yellow eye; pedicels to 25mm in fr.; cal. to 8mm in fr., lobes narrowly triangular, without uncinate hairs; cor. to 5mm diam. Nutlets to 2×1.5mm, ovoid, obtuse, dark brown. Europe, N America. Z6.

***M. lithospermifolia*** (Willd.) Hornem. Perenn., densely pubesc. Stems to 40cm, much-branched near base, grey-green. Basal lvs to 6×1cm, narrowly elliptic or obovate, obtuse, petiolate; cauline lvs to 4×0.5cm, numerous, narrowly obovate to linear, obtuse. Infl. much-branched, many-fld; fls bright blue; pedicels to 6mm; cal. to 5mm in fr., densely covered with patent to deflexed uncinate bristles; cor. to 6mm diam., rotate. Nutlets to 2×1mm, narrowly ovoid, black-grey. W Asia. Z6.

***M. lyallii*** Hook. f. Stem slightly branched; branches to 8cm, decumbent. Basal lvs to 3.5×1cm, ovate-spathulate to elliptic, obtuse, pubesc., sometimes glabrous beneath; petiole to 3.5cm; cauline lvs smaller, subacute. Cymes to 2cm, mostly simple, few-fld; fls white; cal. to 6mm, lobes to 3mm, subacute, pubesc.; cor. to 8mm diam., tube cylindrical, lobes to 3mm, oblong. Nutlets to 1.5×1mm, acute. New Zealand. Z8.

***M. macrantha*** (Hook. f.) Benth. ex Hook. f. Stem slightly branched; branches to 30cm, erect to ascending. Basal lvs to 12×2cm, spathulate-lanceolate to obovate, subacute, with adpressed or spreading hairs above and sparse retrorse hairs beneath; petiole to 11cm; cauline lvs to 2×0.6cm, oblong or lanceolate, subacute, truncate at base, adpressed-pubesc. above, sparsely spreading-pubesc. beneath. Cymes mostly simple, many-fld; fls yellow to brown-orange, short-pedicellate; bracts absent; cal. to 8mm, lobes to 5mm, obtuse, pubesc.; cor. to 8mm diam., infundibular, tube to 10mm, lobes rounded, scales inconspicuous. Nutlets to 3×1.5mm, oblong. New Zealand. Z8.

***M. palustris*** (L.) Nath. Closely resembles *M. caespitosa* except cal. to 3mm in fl., to 5mm in fr., lobes triangular; cor. to 8mm diam. Europe, Asia, N America. 'Alba': fls white. 'Mermaid': stems thick; lvs dark green; fls deep blue, eye yellow.

***M. rehsteineri*** Wartm. Resembles *M. scorpioides* except smaller, caespitose. Stems to 10cm, adpressed-pubesc. Lvs to 2.5×1cm. Cal. to 5mm in fr.; pedicels to 7mm in fr.; cor. to 10mm, pink to bright blue. Europe. Z6.

***M. scorpioides*** L. FORGET-ME-NOT. Perenn. Rhiz. creeping. Stems to 100cm, erect to ascending, angled, glabrous or patent-pubesc. near base. Lvs to 10×2cm, oblong-lanceolate to oblanceolate, usually adpressed-pubesc., sometimes glabrescent. Fls bright blue, with white, yellow or pink eye; cal. to 6mm in fr., with short, adpressed setae; cor. to 8mm diam., limb flat. Nutlets to 2×1mm, ovoid, somewhat rimmed. Europe. 'Sapphire': fls bright sapphire blue. 'Semperflorens': habit dwarf, to 20cm; fls in summer. 'Thuringen': fls sky blue. Z5.

***M. stricta*** Link ex Roem. & Schult. Annual. Stems to 40cm, erect to ascending, much-branched below, covered with white uncinate hairs at base. Basal lvs to 4×1cm, oblong to oblong-spathulate or lanceolate, obtuse to rounded, with spreading and some uncinate hairs; cauline lvs few, ovate-lanceolate, sessile. Infl. to 20cm in fr., densely fld toward apex; fls minute, pale to bright blue; pedicels to 1.5mm, suberect, pubesc.; cal. to 4mm in fr., with deflexed uncinate hairs and adpressed straight hairs at base; cor. to 2mm diam., tubular-campanulate. Nutlets to 1.5×1mm, ovate, subacute, dark brown, conspicuously rimmed, carinate at apex. N Africa, Europe, W Asia. Z6.

***M. sylvatica*** Ehrh. ex Hoffm. GARDEN FORGET-ME-NOT. Bienn. to perenn. Stem to 50cm, solitary to few, erect or suberect, usually much-branched, covered with adpressed or spreading hairs. Basal lvs to 11×3cm, elliptic-oblong to oblong-lanceolate, obtuse to rounded, petiolate; cauline lvs sessile. Infl. to 15cm in fr.; fls bright blue, purple or white-blue varying to pink with a yellow eye; pedicels 10mm, suberect; cal. to 5mm in fr., lobes lanceolate to linear, densely covered with straight or uncinate hairs; cor. to 8mm diam., lobes rounded, spreading. Nutlets to 2×1.5mm, ovoid, acute, black-brown, somewhat rimmed. N Africa, Europe, W Asia. 'Blue Ball': small and compact; fls rich indigo. 'Blue Basket': compact; fls indigo. 'Blue Bird': tall; fls deep blue. 'Carmine King': erect; fls rosy carmine. 'Compacta': dense and low. 'Fischeri': dwarf; fls blue tinted pink. 'Pinkie': fls bright pink, long-lasting. 'Royal Blue': tall; fls indigo, early-flowering, abundant. 'Robusta Grandiflora': vigorous; fls large. 'Rosea': tall; fls soft pink. 'Stricta': branches erect and straight. 'Tall Blue': to 45cm; fls light blue, early. Victoria Mixed: fls blue, pink, rose, white; seed race. 'White Ball': small and compact; fls large, white. Z5.

***M. traversii*** Hook. Stem branched, branches to 15cm, erect or ascending. Basal lvs to 7×1cm, spathulate, pubesc.; cauline lvs to 2cm, oblong, rounded. Fls white to lemon-yellow, short-pedicellate; cal. to 5mm in fl., densely adpressed-pubesc., sparsely covered with uncinate hairs; cor. to 4mm diam., tube to 5mm, cylindric, lobes rounded. Nutlets to 2.5×1mm, oblong. New Zealand. Z8.

***M. uniflora*** Hook. Perenn., tufted. Stems to 5cm, erect, much-branched. Lvs to 5×1.5mm, closely imbricate, membranaceous, triangular to subulate, subacute, adpressed-pubesc. Fls yellow; cal. to 3mm, interior glabrous, exterior adpressed-pubesc.; cor. to 5mm diam., tube to 5mm, cylindric, lobes to 2mm, orbicular. Nutlets to 2×1.5mm, dark brown. New Zealand. Z8.

***M. welwitschii*** Boiss. & Reut. Annual to bienn. Stems to 60cm, robust, with somewhat deflexed hairs at base, branched at base. Lvs to 7×1.5cm, elliptic or ovate-lanceolate, pubesc. Infl. adpressed-pubesc., often much-branched; fls bright blue with a yellow-white eye; cal. to 6mm in fr., campanulate; cor. to 10mm diam. Nutlets to 2×1mm, ovoid, black, acute, rimmed. Spain, Portugal, Morocco. Z9.

***M. decora*** T. Kirk ex Cheesem. See *M. colensoi*.
***M. hortensia*** Decne. See *Myosotidium hortensia*.
***M. macrophylla*** Adams. See *Brunnera macrophylla*.
***M. oblongata*** Link. See *M. sylvatica*.
***M. pyrenaica*** Pourr. See *M. alpina*.
***M. scorpioides*** ssp. ***caespititia*** (DC.) Baumann. See *M. rehsteineri*.
***M. scorpioides*** var. ***arvensis*** L. See *M. arvensis*.
***M. scorpioides*** var. ***lithospermifolia*** Willd. See *M. lithospermifolia*.
***M. scorpioides*** var. ***palustris*** L. See *M. palustris*.
***M. sylvatica*** ssp. ***alpestris*** (F.W. Schmidt) Gams. See *M. alpestris*.
For further synonymy see *Exarrhena*.

**Myrceugenella** Kausel.
***M. chequen*** (Molina) Kausel. See *Luma chequen*.
***M. gayana*** (Barnéoud) Kausel. See *Luma chequen*.

**Myrceugenia** Berg. Myrtaceae. Trees to *c*10m or much-branched shrub less than 1m. Leaves opposite (rarely ternate or sub-opposite), variously shaped, usually not strongly aromatic. Inflorescence axillary, uniflorous or a dichasium with 1–3 levels of bifurcation, the peduncles borne in the axils of leaves or small bracts, solitary or superimposed in rows of 2–4. Fruit a berry, yellow, orange, red or dark purple; seeds usually 1–5. SE Brazil to Chile and Argentina. Z9.

CULTIVATION As for *Myrtus*.

***M. exsucca*** (DC.) Berg. Tree to *c*12m. Bark light grey, rough with longitudinal fissures, hairs red-brown to yellow-brown. Lvs to 2–7.5(–12.5)×1.5–3.5(–5)cm, suborbicular, elliptic, elliptic-obovate or elliptic-ovate, dark or light grey green to red-brown above, lightly yellow green to red-tan beneath, dull, strongly discolorous; petiole 1.5–6mm. Infl. a solitary fl., a dichasium or, less often, a bracteate shoot, the multiflorous infl. 3–10cm, bearing to 10 fls; cal. lobes ovate to ovate-oblong, concave, 1.6–2.8mm, strongly reflexed after flowering; pet. suborbicular, 2–4mm diam.; stamens 170–275, 3–10mm. Fr. globose, *c*6–8mm diam. Chile, Argentina.

***M. planipes*** (Hook. f. & Arn.) Berg. Small tree to *c*8m. Bark grey, often persisting as strips beneath the leaf base, hairs white-yellow, or less often red-brown. Lvs 2.2–8×1–3cm, elliptic, acuminate; petiole 2–6mm. Peduncles strongly flattened, to 3cm, solitary or to 3(–4) in the axils of lvs or, less often, of bracts; cal. lobes broadly ovate, concave, 1.8–3×2.5–4mm; pet. suborbicular, 3–6mm diam.; stamens 120–220, 7–12mm. Fr. globose, 0.8–1cm diam., purple-black. Chile, Argentina.

***M. rufa*** (Colla) Skottsb. Shrub, 1–2m. Bark splitting in a reticulate fashion, white-grey, the new inner bark at first red-brown, becoming white-grey; hairs red-brown to off-white. Lvs 0.5–1.8×0.2–0.5cm, broadly to narrowly elliptic, ovate or oblong, light blue-green to yellow-green, puberulent and often lustrous above, red-brown to white-yellow and densely strigose-pubesc. beneath; petiole densely pubesc., 1–2mm. Peduncles uniflorous, slightly flattened, 1–4mm, densely pubesc., solitary or 2–3 in a row in the axils of lvs; cal. lobes ovate to suborbicular, 1.2–2.6mm long and wide; pet. more or less orbicular, 2–3mm diam., stamens 60–100, 3–6mm. Fr. 4–8mm diam., yellow to orange, pubesc. Chile. Easily distinguished by its small thick lvs that have revolute margins and show little or no venation.

***M. apiculata*** (DC.) Niedenzu. See *Luma apiculata*.
***M. ferruginea*** (Hook. f. & Arn.) Reiche. See *M. rufa*.

**Myrcia** DC. ex Guillem.
***M. lechleriana*** Miq. See *Amomyrtus luma*.

**Myrciaria** O. Berg. Myrtaceae. 40 species of evergreen trees or shrubs. Leaves opposite, simple. Flowers subsessile, clustered in leaf axil or on trunk and branches; calyx tubular, 4-lobed, tube prolonged above the ovary, circumscissile at base after flowering; petals 4, small; stamens many. Fruit a globose berry. Americas (primarily tropical). Related to *Eugenia* but differs in having the calyx tube prolonged above the ovary. *M. cauliflora* cultivated for edible fruit. Z10.

CULTIVATION *M. cauliflora*, the Brazilian grape tree, is an evergreen native of Brazil, where it is grown for its fruit. Rich in vitamin C, the fruit is eaten fresh, in jellies, or made into wine. In warm tropical and subtropical areas with light rainfall, it will produce up five or six crops per year. It is frost tolerant; if grown in cooler areas such as southern Florida, specimens are usually smaller. *M. floribunda*, and *M. myriophylla*, are smaller-growing species requiring similar conditions. All species have a high iron requirement and best results are obtained on deep, fertile, leafy soils, and in loamless potting media. In less favourable soils, the application of iron frits will help prevent chlorosis. Propagate from seed, which should germinate in one month, by side-veneer grafting and by cuttings.

***M. cauliflora*** (DC.) O. Berg. JABOTICABA. Tree to 13m. Lvs to 10cm, lanceolate or somewhat broader, acuminate. Fls white, in clusters along the trunk and branches. Fr. globose, 1.5–3.5cm diam., white to purple, edible. S Brazil.

***M. edulis*** (Vell.) Skeels. Tree to 7m. Branches pendent. Lvs 5–7.5cm, willow-like, rusty-pubesc. when young. Fls 13mm diam., in axillary or terminal clusters. Fr. pear-shaped, *c*5cm, orange-yellow, downy, ill-smelling. Brazil. Material cult. under this name may be *Eugenia aggregata*.

***M.floribunda*** (West ex Willd.) O. Berg. Tree to 10m. Lvs to *c*7cm, lanceolate to ovate-lanceolate, acuminate. Fls white, sessile, 2–5 in lateral clusters. Fr. globose, to 13mm across, red or yellow, edible. W Indies, S Mexico to C America, Guyana and Brazil.

***M.myriophylla*** (Casar.) O. Berg. Much-branched shrub. Lvs very narrow and crowded (at least on juvenile plants), to 4cm or more, midrib obscure above but prominent beneath. Fls white, solitary on axillary peduncles. Brazil.

For synonymy see *Eugenia*.

**Myrica** L. (From Gk *myrike*, the Homeric name for tamarisk.) Myricaceae. Around 35 species of deciduous or evergreen shrubs or small trees. Leaves alternate, simple, entire or toothed, exstipulate, usually oblanceolate, subsessile or short-petiolate. Flowers unisexual: male inflorescence a catkin, narrow-ellipsoid to cylindric, very rarely branching, perianth absent, stamens 2–8, filaments free or partially united at base; female inflorescence usually ovoid and sessile, ovary unilocular, subtended by 2 or more rounded bracteoles. Fruit an ovoid or spherical drupe, grey-green to purple, sometimes resinous or waxy-pruinose. Subcosmopolitan (not Mediterranean, Australia; Europe 2).

CULTIVATION *Myrica* is a useful genus suited to a wide range of soil types and locations. *M.pensylvanica*, grown for its aromatic foliage and off-white, waxy fruits, is suited to dry and maritime sites and is tolerant of road salt; as with *M.cerifera*, it is useful for informal hedging. The suckering *M.gale*, also grown for its sweetly fragrant foliage, has a dense and upright habit and bears golden-brown catkins in spring; it is grown in the peat terrace, bog garden and moist border and is often included in naturalistic and native plantings. *M.californica*, *M.faya*, *M.heterophylla* and *M.rubra* are all persistent and attractive in fruit, and berried branches can be cut for indoor decoration in winter. In areas that experience winter frosts, *M.faya* and *M.rubra* can be grown in the cool glasshouse. *M.gale* and *M.pensylvanica* are remarkably hardy, surviving temperatures in their native habitats down to −40°C/−40°F and below; the remaining species are less hardy.

Plant in an open position in sun or light shade, in well-drained soil; *M.cerifera* and *M.californica* prefer moist soils and *M.gale* is perfectly adapted to boggy sites. Prune to restrict size when necessary in late winter or early spring; remove weak and straggling growth of *M.gale* and *M.cerifera* at ground level.

Propagate from seed; remove seed from pulp when ripe and sow outdoors in a sheltered nursery bed. Soak seed of *M.pensylvanica* in hot water prior to sowing to remove its protective wax coat. Alternatively, increase by simple layering in spring, or by removal of suckers in *M.gale*.

***M.californica*** Cham. CALIFORNIA WAX MYRTLE; CALIFORNIA BAYBERRY. Evergreen shrub or small tree to 10m. Lvs 6–10cm, narrow-elliptic to oblanceolate, apex acute, base acuminate, margins with forward-pointing teeth. Male infl. to 2cm, borne in axils of older lvs, female infl. to 10mm, borne in axils of younger growth. Fr. to 6mm diam., spherical, deep purple, waxy. Coastal US (California to Washington). Z7.

***M.cerifera*** L. Evergreen shrub or tree to 12m. Lvs 3–9cm, oblanceolate, entire or serrate in apical half, apex acute, base acuminate. Male infl. to 2cm, borne below lvs, female infl. to 1cm. Fr. to 3mm diam., spherical, grey-white, waxy-pruinose. US (New Jersey to Florida and Texas). Z6.

***M.faya*** Ait. CANDLEBERRY MYRTLE. Evergreen shrub or small tree to 8.25m. Lvs to 10.8cm, oblanceolate. Male infl. 2cm, often branched; female infl. usually simple. Fr. to 5mm diam., red to black, waxy and fleshy, to 0.6cm diam. Canary Is., Madeira, S Portugal. Z9.

***M.gale*** L. SWEET GALE; BOG MYRTLE; MEADOW FERN. Deciduous shrub to 2m, usually shorter. Branches ascending. Lvs 2–6cm, oblanceolate, apex obtuse to abruptly acute, base acuminate, toothed in apical half. Infl. on 1-year-old wood, males to 1.5cm, crowded, females to 6mm, extending to 1cm in fruit. Fr. to 3mm diam., yellow-brown, dotted with resin, enclosed by 2 fused bracteoles. N America, Europe to Japan. Z1.

***M.heterophylla*** Raf. Similar to *M.pensylvanica* and *M.cerifera* but lvs 5–12cm, deciduous, oblanceolate. Fr. 2–4mm diam., grey-white, waxy-pruinose. E US. Z6.

***M.pensylvanica*** Lois. BAYBERRY; CANDLEBERRY; SWAMP CANDLEBERRY. Deciduous or semi-evergreen shrub to 2.75m. Lvs 2–8cm, broadly oblanceolate, apex obtuse or abruptly acute, base acuminate, entire or sparsely toothed in apical half. Infl. borne under lvs, males to 1.5cm, females to 1cm. Fr. to 4mm diam., globose, grey-white, with a dense covering of rough white wax. Eastern N America. Z2.

***M.rubra*** Sieb. & Zucc. Small evergreen tree, exceptionally attaining 20m. Lvs 6–12cm, oblanceolate to obovate, usually obtuse, entire or toothed in apical half. Fr. 1.5–2.5cm diam., dark purple-red, succulent. E Asia. Z10.

***M.caroliniensis*** auct. non Mill. See *M.pensylvanica*.
***M.caroliniensis*** Mill. See *M.cerifera*.

**MYRICACEAE** Bl. WAX MYRTLE FAMILY. Dicot. 3 genera and 50 species of aromatic trees and shrubs, with long colourless unicellular hairs and peltate usually yellow multicellular glands; roots usually nitrogen-fixing bacteria. Leaves simple, alternate; stipules only in *Comptonia*. Flowers small, wind-pollinated, usually unisexual, sometimes bisexual, in simple or compound spike; perianth absent; males often with 2 bracteoles as well as a bract; stamens (2–) 4 (–6), at summit of ovary in bisexual flowers; females with 2 bracteoles, sometimes sepaloid; ovary superior, of 2 fused carpels, 1-loculed, with distinct styles and 1 basal ovule. Fruit a drupe or nutlet, sometimes with accrescent bracteoles; seeds with straight embryo; endosperm absent. *Myrica* provides timber and edible fruits and some of the fruits are a source of wax. Subcosmopolitan. *Comptonia, Myrica*.

**Myricaria** Desv. (Adapted from *Myrike*, the Homeric name for tamarisk.) FALSE TAMARISK. Tamaricaceae. 10 species of deciduous shrubs or subshrubs. Leaves small, scale-like, imbricate. Flowers in long, terminal and axillary, narrow racemes; calyx and corolla 5-parted; stamens 10, the filaments connate at the base or to past the middle; ovaries with 3, nearly sessile stigmas. Fruit a conical, acuminate, 3-valved, dehiscent capsule; seeds with pubescent tufts. S Europe, Asia, China, Siberia. Closely akin to *Tamarix* from which their flowers differ in having 10 united stamens (free and only 4–8 in *Tamarix*).

CULTIVATION Tolerant of chalk soils, otherwise as for *Tamarix*.

***M.davurica*** (Willd.) Ehrenb. Very similar to *M.germanica*; racemes usually axillary; bracts oblong-ovate, obtuse, with an encircling, membranous margin, shorter than the fl. buds; fil. often only one-third connate. USSR. Z5.

***M.germanica*** (L.) Desv. Shrub, narrowly upright, 1–2m, shoots grey-brown, the young shoots blue-green or grey-green, later more yellow, very densely foliate. Lvs scale-like, blue-green, linear-lanceolate, imbricate. Fls bright-red, in 10–15cm, spike-like racemes, mostly terminal, occasionally some lateral; bracts oval-oblong, long-acuminate, with a broad membranous margin. Stamens connate to about the mid-point. C & S Europe. Z6.

For synonymy see *Tamarix*.

**Myriocarpa** Benth. (From Gk *myrios*, very many, and *karpos*, fruit.) Urticaceae. Some 15 species of small trees or shrubs, usually dioecious, rarely monoecious. Leaves alternate, dentate, pinnately veined; stipules often 2-lobed. Flowers scattered along the thread-like branches of the inflorescence in slender axillary racemes or spikes, males more densely clustered, sessile, with 4–5-lobed perianth, females lacking perianth or with 2 opposite bracts, sometimes stalked; stamens 4–5; ovary compressed. Fruit an achene. C & S America. Z10.

CULTIVATION Grown in the gardens of the humid tropics and subtropics as an ornamental evergreen, in cooler climates *M.stipitata* makes a handsome foliage specimen for tubs and large pots in the intermediate to warm glasshouse or conservatory. Valued primarily for the large, finely quilted, blue-green leaves, brushed silver at the margins and with contrasting pale undersides, the long racemes of bloom are also attractive.

Grow in bright, filtered light in a porous, loam-based mix with additional sharp sand and screened, well-rotted organic matter; provide moderate humidity, water plentifully when in growth and liquid feed as roots fill the pots. Maintain a winter minimum temperature of 13–16°C/55–60°F. Plants will become leggy under glass as they mature; cut back after flowering, repot in early spring and/or replace with young plants every second or third year. Propagate by seed, by air layering or by greenwood or semi-ripe cuttings in a closed case with bottom heat.

***M. stipitata*** Benth. Shrub or small tree to 12m. Lvs 10–30×10–20cm, ovate or obovate-elliptic, apex obtuse or slender-acuminate, densely pubesc. when young, margins usually toothed, often silver. Fls green-white, in long racemes. Summer. S America.

For synonymy see *Boehmeria*.

**Myriophyllum** L. (From Gk *myrios*, many, and *phyllon*, leaf, referring to the leaves which are much divided.) MILFOIL. Haloragidaceae. Some 45 species of aquatic or terrestrial herbs, usually monoecious, glabrous, perennial or sometimes annual. Stems slender, usually branched, erect or decumbent-ascending, often floating in aquatic plants. Leaves usually dimorphic in aquatic plants; emergent lvs whorled or alternate, entire or slightly dentate; submerged lvs usually whorled, pinnatifid into filiform segments. Flowers usually in terminal spikes, sessile or subsessile, minute; sepals 4 or absent, erect; petals 2 to 4 or absent; stamens 4 or 8, anthers large, often mucronate; ovary 2 to 4-locular, styles 2 to 4. Fruit splitting into 2 to 4 nutlets; nutlets 1 seeded. Cosmopolitan.

CULTIVATION *M. verticillatum* and *M. spicatum* occur in waters from calcareous sources, *M. alterniflorum* in still and slow moving waters of a peaty nature. *M. alterniflorum, M. spicatum* and *M. verticillatum* are useful as oxygenators and as shelter for fish spawn in cold water pools and aquaria; *M. pinnatum* and *M. hippuroides* are grown in heated aquaria, the latter frequently used in fish breeding tanks. *M. aquaticum* and *M. pinnatum* require minimum water temperatures of 18–24°C/65–75°F.

Grow in a sandy medium rich in decaying organic matter in full light. Remove excess growth as necessary. *M. alterniflorum* requires cool, lime-free water. *M. verticillatum* will survive in ponds in zones where winter temperatures fall as low as −15°C/5°F; *M. aquaticum* will not tolerate temperatures much below freezing. Frost tender species may be overwintered as rooted pieces in a moist medium in the frost free glasshouse. Propagate by stem cuttings rooted directly into the growing medium or by division.

***M. alterniflorum*** DC. Stems to 120cm. Lvs to 2.5cm, in whorls of 3 to 5; submerged lvs pinnatifid, seg. 6–18. Infl. to 3cm; male fls in opposite or alternate pairs, sometimes solitary; female fls in whorls of 2–4 or solitary; pet. to 2.5mm, yellow streaked red; stamens 8. Fr. to 2×1.5mm, subcylindrical, slightly tuberculate. NE America, Europe. Z6.

***M. aquaticum*** (Vell.) Verdc. PARROT FEATHER; DIAMOND MILFOIL. Stems to 2m, woody at base. Lvs subsimilar, in whorls of 4 or 5, to 4cm, pinnatifid, seg. short, bright yellow-green or blue-green. Fls solitary, axillary; bracts pinnatifid; sep. to 2mm, narrowly triangular, acute; pet. absent in female fls, 4 in male fls, to 4mm; stamens 8. Fr. to 2×1mm, ovoid, minutely tuberculate, 4-sulcate. S America, Australia, New Zealand, Java. Z10.

***M. elatinoides*** Gaudich. Stems to 120cm. Lvs in whorls of 3 to 5, emergent lvs to 8×5mm, ovate-oblong, obtuse, subentire to entire, submerged lvs to 2cm, finely pinnatifid. Fls in axils of upper lvs, solitary; bracteoles to 2mm, lanceolate; sep. triangular; pet. to 2mm, pink; stamens 8. Fr. to 1.5mm, red-brown. Mexico, S America, New Zealand, Australia. Z10.

***M. heterophyllum*** Michx. Stems to 1m. Emergent lvs lanceolate to oblong or linear, sharply dentate, submerged lvs to 5cm, crowded. Infl. to 50cm, erect to pendent, simple or branched; male fls to 3mm diam.; pet. 4, oblong to ovate-oblong; stamens 4 to 6. Fr. to 2.5mm, carinate. NE America. Z6.

***M. hippuroides*** Nutt. ex Torr. & A. Gray. WESTERN MILFOIL. Stems to 60cm, simple or branched. Lvs in whorls of 4 or 5, pale green, emergent lvs linear to lanceolate, entire to serrate, submerged lvs to 2cm. Fls in axils of emergent lvs; pet. white, obovate. N America (California to Washington). Z7.

***M. pinnatum*** (Walter) BSP. Stems to 60cm. Lvs in whorls of 4 or 5, emergent lvs linear, pectinate or serrate, submerged lvs to 2cm, segments 6 to 10. Infl. to 20cm, simple, erect; male fls to 2.5mm diam.; pet. 4; stamens 4 to 8. Fr. to 2mm, ovoid, carinate. N America. Z6.

***M. spicatum*** L. Stems to 3m, much branched. Lvs to whorls of 4 to 5, emergent lvs to 10×2mm, ovate to obovate, obtuse, usually entire, submerged lvs to 2.5×2cm, with 7–11 pairs of filiform seg. Infl. to 7.5cm; fls solitary in lf axils; bracteoles ovate, obtuse; sep. ovate to triangular, mucronate, absent in female fls; pet. 4, wine red, caducous, reduced in female fls; stamens 8. Fr. to 3×3mm, finely tuberculate. N America, Europe, Asia, N Africa. Z6.

***M. verticillatum*** L. MYRIAD LEAF. Stems to 1m, simple or branched. Emergent lvs to 1cm, pectinate-pinnatifid, submerged lvs to 4×4cm, in whorls of 4 to 6, with 8 to 16 pairs of opposite seg. Infl. to 15cm, erect; bracteoles suborbicular, digitate; sep. to 1cm, triangular, acute, serrate; pet. to 4mm, rose, caducous, absent in female fls; stamens 8. Fr. to 3×3mm, ovoid, smooth. Northern N America, Europe, Asia. Z3.

***M. brasiliense*** Cambess. See *M. aquaticum*.
***M. proserpinacoides*** Gillies ex Hook. & Arn. See *M. aquaticum*.
***M. scabratum*** Michx. See *M. pinnatum*.

**Myristica** Gronov. (From Gk *myristikos*, smelling of myrrh.) Myristicaceae. Some 100 species of large, evergreen, dioecious trees. Leaves usually waxy white or glaucous below, veins slightly depressed above. Flowers in axillary racemes or clusters, the males subtended by a bracteole; calyx teeth 3–5; stamens 6+, filaments united, anthers large, united. Fruit large, succulent, arillate. Asia, Australasia; cultivated throughout the Tropics. Z10.

CULTIVATION A handsome and strongly aromatic evergreen grown in coastal regions of the humid tropics both as an ornamental and commercially as the source of nutmeg and mace, the major producers being Indonesia, Granada (West Indies) and Sri Lanka. The fleshy yellow fruit holds the kernel closely wrapped in the waxy red network of the aril (i.e. mace), the kernel contains the glossy, oil-rich and fragrant nutmeg. In cool temperate zones *Myristica* is frequently included in collections of economically important plants, in the hot glasshouse (min. 16–18°C/60–65°F). Grow in bright filtered light, in a freely draining, high-fertility, loam-based mix with additional sharp sand; maintain high humidity and water plentifully when in growth. Propagate from fresh seed, which germinates in about 5–6 weeks, and must be transplanted carefully to avoid damage to the delicate taproot, or by semi-ripe cuttings in sand in a closed case with bottom heat; also by grafting known female plants on to seedling understock.

***M. fragrans*** Houtt. NUTMEG. To 10m. Young branches glabrous with scattered lenticels. Lvs to 12cm, alternate, oblong, entire, initially covered with short-lived silvery scales, aromatic. Fls to 1cm, pale yellow; cor. absent. Fr. to 5cm, splitting longitudinally; albumen (nutmeg) brown, tough, mottled, enclosed by a thin, pink-scarlet perisperm (mace). Indonesia.

**MYRISTICACEAE** R. Br. NUTMEG FAMILY. Dicot. 19 genera and 440 species of dioecious or monoecious trees, usually with spherical ethereal oil-cells, often with the aromatic phenolic myristicin; bark typically with coloured sap when slashed. Leaves simple, entire, alternate, often gland-dotted; stipules absent. Flowers in cymes or racemes; calyx (2) 3 (–5) fused sepals, with valvate lobes; corolla absent; stamens 2-numerous, with more or less united filaments and often laterally connate anthers; ovary superior, with 1 unclosed carpel, stigma rarely with style and 1 almost basal ovule. Fruit fleshy to leathery, usually dehiscent along 2 sutures; seed endotestal, with conspicuous, copious, oily aril; endosperm ruminate; embryo small; cotyledons sometimes basally connate. Seeds of *Myristica fragrans* are the source of nutmeg (the kernel) and mace (the aril). Some provide timber, especially *Virola*. Tropical. *Myristica*.

**Myrmecodia** Jack. (From Gk *myrmex*, ant; ants nest in the rhizomes.) ANT-PLANTS. Rubiaceae. 45 species of epiphytic woody shrubs inhabited by ants usually of the genus *Iridomyrmex*. The hypocotyl swells to form tuber in which a series of cavities develop by the death of pockets of tissue which have become surrounded by meristem-derived suberized layers. Such cavities form in the absence of ants, but the dead material is usually excavated and removed by ant activity in a wild situation. The cavities are of several species and are used by ants for different purposes; smooth-lined cavities are used as brood chambers, while those with a papillose surface are used to deposit waste material, from which the plant absorbs nutrients in a nutrient-poor environment. The cavities may be several centimetres in diameter; the proportion of cavity to tissue varies between the species. Tuber rounded or cylindric, often pendent. Stems highly modified, 1 to few, with very short internodes, covered with shield-like outgrowths (clypeoli), or thickened by fleshy development of cortex, usually heavily armed with leathery stipules and many spines both on tuber and stems; spines simple to highly branched, sometimes

**Myrmecophilous plants** (a) *Solanopteris bifrons* (×0.1) (a1) LS of modified rhizome showing roots in cavity (×0.5) (b) *Lecanopteris carnosa* (×0.1) (b1) rhizome LS (×0.8) (c) *Codonanthe crassifolia*, with a section of 'ant garden', a nest supported by the root system (×0.15) (d) *Dischidia rafflesiana* (×0.1) (d1) modified leaf sac LS (×0.4) (e) *Hydnophytum* sp. (×0.1) (e1) caudex LS (×0.4) (f) *Myrmecodia tuberosa* (×0.1) (f1) caudex LS (×0.4) (g) *Schomburgkia tibicinis* (×0.1) (g1) pseudobulb LS (×0.2) (h) *Acacia cornigera* (×0.8) (h1) enlargement of Beltian bodies on pinnae tips and foliar nectary on rachis (i) *Acacia drepanolobum* (×0.8) (j) *Iridomyrmex cordatus* (×5)

stellate, derived from modified roots, serving to protect ants moving over surface below. Leaves ovate, acute. Flowers sessile, sunken in tissue between clypeoli, subtended by scarious, hairy bracts; corolla tubular, 4-lobed, white, very small, tube-mouth closed by inward pointing hooks; anthers and stigma enclosed in tube. Fruit a fleshy berry with 1–10 seeds. Indonesia to Fiji, especially New Guinea. Z10.

Very seldom cultivated. See MYRMECOPHILOUS PLANTS.

**Myrmecophilous plants**. Like the carnivores and caudiciform succulents, certain myrmecophilous genera have excited much horticultural interest on account of their remarkable adaptation. The swollen and chambered stems of *Hydnophytum* and *Myrmecodia*, the gouty rhizomes of *Lecanopteris* and the inflated leaf sacs of *Dischidia* place these plants in the first rank of horticultural curiosities.

Myrmecophytes are plants which live in symbiosis with ants. The plant usually forms a hollow structure, the domatium, in which the ants nest. In ant-garden plants (e.g. *Codonanthe*), the roots of the plant make a scaffolding for the ant nest. In other ant-epiphytes, the domatia are enclosed, as in the fern *Lecanopteris*, which has a hollow rhizome, or the main rhizome is hollow, or in *Solenopteris*, where the large lateral branches are excavated by the ants. In *Dischidia* the domatia are inflated leaves with numerous stomata on the inner surface, through which the plants utilize the $CO_2$ respired by the ants, thus greatly reducing water loss to the plant. As these domatia age, the ants remove their brood and use the old domatia as middens, which are penetrated by adventitious roots. In the orchid *Schomburgkia*, ants enter the hollow pseudobulbs by a narrow slit at the base; they also collect the nectar secreted from the tips of the corolla lobes and their presence protects the developing seeds from predation.

Most specialized of the ant epiphytes are members of the Hydrophytinae, a subtribe of the Rubiaceae. Here, the meristem within the tuber develops layers of tissue which form chambers with absorptive surfaces that can take in nutrients deposited by the ants. In *Hydnophytum*, the chambers may be smooth-walled or warty; in *Myrmecodia*, they are particularly complex, and may be honeycombed and superficial or deeper and shelf-like.

In the wild, the main advantage for plants of domatia inhabited by ants is defence; the ants attack any insect or vertebrate which ventures on to the plant. In many savanna acacias, the swollen stipular spines are hollowed out and inhabited by ants, which gain nutrients from the plant and not only attack insect predators but also chew at any plant which touches the acacia. This behaviour is effective at reducing predators of the ant colony and for the plants is invaluable not only in reducing competition from other plants but also in reducing access for leafcutter ants.

In other species, such as *Cecropia* in the New and *Macaranga* in the Old World tropics, ants derive food bodies from the hollow-stem domatia; in contrast, a number of understorey trees (e.g. *Cordia* and *Clidemia*) have invaginated domatia and produce no food, but the ants raise homopteran insects in the domatia. This indirect way of feeding may be more efficient for the ants, as it is more difficult for other insects to 'steal' the food, and food is not released at all if ants happen to be absent.

*Dischidia* ssp. will succeed as houseplants if potted fairly tightly in a mixture of coarse bark and leafmould. Situate in bright filtered light with a minimum night temperature of 13°C/55°F. Water liberally with soft water, but avoid sodden root conditions. Mist frequently and apply a weak foliar feed when the plant is in full growth. Encourage the slender trailing stems to cascade or train them on canes. In well-grown specimens, the massive leaf sacs may overburden the stems, at which point it is advisable to attach them to a cork slab, preferably padded with moss or palm fibre.

The two rubiaceous genera and *Lecanopteris*, a charming if bizarre fern, are best cultivated under glass and accorded a regime suitable for intermediate-growing epiphytic orchids. Seedlings of *Hydnophytum* and *Myrmecodia*, should be grown in high temperatures on beds of sphagnum or perlite before removal to very open bark-based mediums or mounting on rafts or cork. *Lecanopteris* will thrive in a shady, humid, warm house either as a basket plant or tied to tree-fern slabs or dead boughs. All should be watered and syringed freely when conditions are optimal and growth most luxuriant; at other times, heed must be paid to these plants' susceptibility to botrytis. Each of these ornamental myrmecophytes is sparse-rooting: the roots we actually see are little more than anchors – pot-grown *Hydnophytum* spp. may seem simply to sit on the substrate – which stresses the need for perfect drainage and carefully judged ambient conditioning.

Myrmecophytes make fascinating additions to any predominantly epiphytic collection – they should be considered by orchid and bromeliad enthusiasts. They adapt readily to terrarium culture and, of course, have great value as educational display plants.

**Myrobalanus** Gaertn.
***M.bellirica*** Gaertn. See *Terminalia bellirica*.
***M.chebula*** (Retz.) Gaertn. See *Terminalia chebula*.

**Myroxylon** L. f. (From Gk *myron*, myrrh, and *xylon*, wood, referring to the resinous, sweet-scented timber.) Leguminosae (Papilionoideae). 3 species of evergreen trees, to 12m+. Leaves imparipinnate; leaflets alternate, glandular-punctate; stipules caducous. Inflorescences a terminal or axillary raceme; bracts inconspicuous, coriaceous; calyx campanulate, lobes subequal; standard wide, clawed, keel and wings similar; stamens 10, free; pistil winged. Fruit flat, 2-winged; seed solitary. Tropical Northern S America, naturalized Old World. Z10.

CULTIVATION Sometimes planted as ornamentals in tropical zones; *M.balsamum* is tapped for its sweet, citrus-flavoured balsam, the balsam of Tolu used to flavour medicines, ointments and perfumes. In temperate zones, grow under glass with a minimum night temperature of 16–18°C/60–65°F, in a loam-based mix with added sharp sand and leafmould. Water plentifully when in growth. Propagate from semi-ripe cuttings in a closed case with bottom heat, or by seed.

***M.balsamum*** (L.) Harms. TOLU BALSAM TREE. To 12m. Bark fragrant. Rachis to 15cm; leaflets to 1.2×0.3cm, 5–13, elliptic-oblong or ovate, coriaceous, shiny. Infl. congested; pedicels to 8mm; cal. to 6mm, shallow-cupulate; cor. to 1cm+, white, standard ovate, long-clawed; stamens protruding, anth. conspicuous. Fr. to 11×2.5cm, oblong to oblanceolate, coriaceous, winged, wings papery. Mexico to Northern S America, Venezuela to Peru. var. ***pereirae*** (Royle) Harms. BALSAM OF PERU. Fr. attenuate. Leaflets smaller. Z8.

***M.pereirae*** Royle. See *M.balsamum* var. *pereirae*.
***M.peruiferum*** auct. See *M.balsamum*.
***M.senticosum*** (Hance) Warb. See *Xylosma congestum*.
***M.toluiferum*** A. Rich. See *M.balsamum* var. *balsamum*.

**Myrrhis** Mill. (Name used by Dioscorides.) Umbelliferae. 1 species, an aromatic, perennial herb to 2m; stems hollow, puberulent. Leaves 2–3-pinnate, segments 1–3cm, oblong-lanceolate, pinnatifid or deeply toothed, pale beneath, often blotched white. Umbels compound with 4–20 pubescent rays 1.5–3cm; involucre usually absent; involucel of some 5 slender bracteoles; flowers white, male and bisexual on terminal umbel, male only on some lateral umbels; petals cuneate-obovate, the outermost radiating. Fruit 15–25mm, linear-oblong; mericarps sharply ridged, dark brown, with bristly hairs. Early summer. Europe. Z5.

CULTIVATION Grown for its sweetly aromatic and fern-like leaves which emerge in late winter and very early spring (persisting until the following early winter) and for its umbels of clean white flowers in early summer, sweet cicely has a number of applications in the garden. It is grown in the herb garden for its culinary and medicinal virtues, and is well suited to naturalizing in woodland walks and for plantings in the shrub border. If cut back periodically in the herbaceous border, its fresh green foliage makes an admirable foil for other plants, and may be used to cover ground previously occupied by bulbs or early perennials that have died back and left unsightly gaps. It is hardy to at least −15°C/5°F.

Grow in any deep, moisture-retentive soil, in sun or dappled shade. *M.odorata* self-seeds freely, and must be dead-headed where this is likely to be a nuisance. Propagate from ripe seed, by careful division or by root cuttings, in spring or autumn.

***M.odorata*** (L.) Scop. SWEET CICELY; GARDEN MYRRH. As for the genus.
For illustration see HERBS.

**MYRSINACEAE** R. Br. MYRSINE FAMILY. Dicot. 37 genera and 1250 species of trees, shrubs, lianes, few subherbaceous, usually with secretory ducts or cavities with resins. Leaves alternate, simple, usually entire, with gland dots and dashes, or glandular hairy; stipules absent. Flowers usually regular, bisexual, small, in usually ebracteolate inflorescences; calyx (3)4 or 5(6) free sepals, often basally connate; corolla same but rarely free; stamens opposite corolla-lobes and usually adnate to tube with filaments sometimes basally connate; ovary superior, rarely half-inferior (*Maesa*), of 3–5(6) fused carpels, 1-loculed, with terminal style and few-numerous ovules. Fruit a berry or drupe, rarely a 1-seeded capsule; seeds with oily endosperm. Tropical and warm regions, few temperate Old World. *Ardisia, Maesa, Myrsine.*

**Myrsine** L. (Name given by Dioscorides to the myrtle, *Myrtus communis.*) Myrsinaceae. 5 species of evergreen, perennial trees and shrubs, to 6m. Leaves alternate, leathery, usually entire. Inflorescence a sessile or pedunculate, axillary or lateral umbel or cluster, flowers small, dioecious-polygamous, 4–5 merous; corolla lobes imbricate in bud, stamens 4–5. Fruit a small drupe, dry or fleshy, 1-seeded. Azores to China and New Zealand. There is taxonomic debate over whether *Rapanea* and *Suttonia*, treated here as synonyms of *Myrsine*, are distinct genera.

CULTIVATION Grown for their often aromatic foliage, but also for the attractive fruits, in warm mediterranean-type climates *Myrsine* spp. are sometimes used as hedging and as specimens for the shrub border. Given good drainage and shelter from cold drying winds, the aromatic *M.africana* may tolerate several degrees of short-lived frost, and is suitable for the sunny rock garden; in cooler zones young plants are grown as houseplants for the sunny windowsill. The hardier *M.nummularia* is also suited to the rock garden or to the cool, well-ventilated glasshouse or conservatory. Grow in full sun or part shade in any fertile, well-drained, circumneutral soil. Propagate by seed or semi-ripe cuttings.

***M.africana*** L. CAPE MYRTLE; AFRICAN BOXWOOD. Shrub, 0.5–1.5m, densely leafy, young shoots softly hairy. Lvs 6–20×6–12mm, on petioles to 2mm, narrowly obovate to elliptic, apex rounded or truncate, glabrous, glossy green above, sparsely toothed toward apex. Infl. a sessile, axillary cluster, 3–6-fld, fls unisexual, pale brown. Fr. 6mm diam., globose, blue-lilac. Late spring. Azores, Montane E & S Africa, Himalaya, China. Z9.

***M.chathamica*** F. Muell. Shrub, 0.5–1.5m, densely leafy, young shoots softly hairy. Lvs 6–20×6–12mm, on petioles to 2mm, narrowly obovate to elliptic, apex rounded or truncate, glabrous, glossy green above, sparsely toothed toward apex. Infl. a sessile, axillary cluster, 3–6-fld, fls unisexual, pale brown. Fr. 6mm diam., globose, blue-lilac. Late spring. Azores, montane E & S Africa, Himalaya, China. Z9.

***M.chathamica*** F. Muell. Tree to *c*6m, with dark bark, twigs densely covered in short, stiff hairs. Lvs 2–7.5×1.5–4cm, on petioles to *c*5mm, obovate or elliptic or broadly elliptic, entire, leathery, apex blunt or occasionally emarginate. Fls unisexual, in a group of clusters or solitary, *c*3mm diam. on pedicels to 6.5mm; cal. lobes 4, deltoid, margins ciliolate; pet. 4, oblong, free, with fimbriate margins. Fr. (5–)6–9mm diam., purple. New Zealand (Chatham Is.). Z8.

***M.nummularia*** Hook. f. Prostrate to scandent shrub to 30cm, twigs red-brown. Lvs 4–10×4–10mm, on petioles *c*1mm long, obovate to suborbicular or obovate oblong, margins slightly recurved, ciliolate when young, apex minutely apiculate or rarely retuse. Fls solitary or in small clusters, tiny; cal. lobes 4, ovate; pet. 4, obovate, free, ciliolate. Fr. 5–6.5mm diam., globose, blue-purple. New Zealand. Z7.

***M.retusa*** Ait. See *M.africana*.
For further synonymy see *Rapanea* and *Suttonia*.

**MYRTACEAE** Juss. MYRTLE FAMILY. Dicot. 120 genera and 3850 species of trees and shrubs, with abundant scattered secretory cavities, pith characteristic with internal phloem, usually with ectotrophic mycorrhizae. Leaves usually opposite, often leathery; stipules rudimentary or absent. Flowers bisexual, regular, with hypanthium extended beyond ovary, with conspicuous bracts, calyx, corolla or stamens attractive to animals especially birds, usually on cymes (solitary in *Myrtus communis*); calyx (3)4 or 5(6) free or connate sepals, sometimes much reduced or splitting at anthesis or forming calyptra; corolla similar (a calyptra in *Eucalyptus*); stamens numerous, free or in bundles, usually bent inwards in bud; ovary inferior or half-inferior, of 2–5(–16) fused carpels, with as many locules; style terminal (stigma sessile in *Psiloxylon*); placentation axile; ovules 2-numerous per locule. Fruit a berry, capsule or drupe; seeds few-numerous, endosperm often absent. Many provide timber (*Eucalyptus*), edible fruits such as guava (*Psidium guajava*), jaboticaba (*Myrciaria cauliflora*), pineapple guava (*Feijoa sellowiana*), rose apple (*Syzygium jambos*) and Surinam cherry (*Eugenia uniflora*), oils and spices such as allspice (*Pimenta dioica*), clove (*Syzygium aromaticum*) and cajuput oil (*Melaleuca cajuputi*). Tropical and warm, and warm Australia. *Acmena, Actinodium, Agonis, Amomyrtus, Angophora, Asteromyrtus, Backhousia, Baeckea, Beaufortia, Callistemon, Calothamnus, Calytrix, Chamelaucium, Darwinia, Eucalyptus, Eugenia, Feijoa, Homoranthus, Hypocalymma, Kunzea, Leptospermum, Lophomyrtus, Lophostemon, Luma, Melaleuca, Metrosideros, Myrceugenia, Myrciaria, Myrtus, Pileanthus, Psidium, Regelia, Rhodomyrtus, Syzygium, Tristania, Tristaniopsis, Ugni, Verticordia.*

**Myrtillocactus** Console. (Name suggested by Schumann, presumably from *Vaccinium myrtillus*, which has similar-looking fruits, and *Cactus*.) Cactaceae. 4 closely related species of arborescent or shrubby cacti; branches numerous, ascending, few-ribbed, spiny. Flowers diurnal, small, up to 9 per areole; scales small; floral areoles slightly woolly; tube very short; perianth rotate; stamens relatively few. Fruit small, globose, berry-like, fleshy; seeds 1.6×1.3mm, broadly oval, black-brown, dull; relief low-domed; hilum large, basal, impressed. Mexico, Guatemala. The edible fruits are harvested and sold in Mexican markets as *garambullos*.

CULTIVATION Grow in an intermediate greenhouse (min. 10–15°C/50–60°F), use 'standard' cactus compost: moderate to high inorganic content (more than 50% grit), pH 6–7.5; shade in hot weather; maintain low humidity; keep dry from mid-autumn until early spring, except for light misting on warm days in late winter.

***M.cochal*** (Orcutt) Britt. & Rose. Resembling *M.geometrizans*, but stems green, spines fewer; tree to 3m with short trunk to 30cm diam.; branches numerous; ribs 6–8, obtuse; spines nearly black at first; central spine 0–1, 2cm, radial spines 3–5, short. Fl. 2.5×2.5cm; tepals pale yellow, tinged green. Fr. 12–18mm diam., globose, dark red. NW Mexico (Baja California). Z9.

***M.geometrizans*** (Mart. ex Pfeiff.) Console. Tree 4–5m, with short trunk; branches numerous, upcurving, 6–10cm diam., blue-green; ribs 5–6; areoles 1.5–3cm apart; central spine 1, 1–7cm, dagger-like and sometimes 6mm broad at the base, almost black, radial spines 5–9, 2–10mm, red-brown at first, fading to grey. Fl. *c*2×2.5cm, creamy white. Fr. 1–2cm diam., dark red or purple. C & S Mexico. Z9.

***M.schenckii*** (Purpus) Britt. & Rose. Resembling *M.geometrizans*, but stems dark green, ribs 7–8, areoles 5mm apart, black-felted; central spine 1, 2(–5) cm, radial spines 6–8, 5–12mm. S Mexico (Oaxaca). Z9.

***M.pugionifer*** (Lem.) A. Berger. See *M.geometrizans*.
For further synonymy see *Cereus*.

**Myrtus** L. (Gk name for this plant.) Myrtaceae. 2 species of evergreen shrubs. Leaves opposite, entire, with aromatic oil glands, pinnately-veined. Flowers white or pink, actinomorphic, solitary in axils; calyx (4–)5-lobed, lobes separate, persistent; petals 4, white, spreading. Stamens numerous, longer than the petals. Fruit a berry, crowned by persistent calyx lobes. Mediterranean, N Africa. Z8.

CULTIVATION *M.communis*, typically found in maquis and garigue scrub communities, has long been valued for its aromatic evergreen foliage and fragrant flowers, traditionally used in triumphal garlands and bridal wreaths. In mild coastal climates

*M. communis* is grown as a specimen and sometimes as hedging. Its tolerance of clipping suits it well to training as an espalier or fan against warm, south- or southwest-facing wall. In cooler, drier inland gardens, or in areas experiencing prolonged hard frost, traditional pot-grown forms of round-headed standards or pyramids, are moved into the cool glasshouse for the winter months. Given shelter from cold drying winds and good drainage, *M. communis* may tolerate temperatures to between −10°C and −15°C/14–5°F, the smaller leaved cultivar *M.* 'Tarentina', to −15°/5°F.

Grow in full sun in a moderately fertile, well-drained soil enriched with leafmould or other well-composted organic matter. In pots, use a freely draining, medium-fertility, loam-based mix, water moderately when in growth, reducing as light levels and temperatures fall to keep just moist in winter at a minimum temperature of 5°C/40°F. Repot every other year in early spring. Prune in spring to maintain size and shape and to remove frosted growth. Propagate by semi-ripe nodal cuttings in summer rooted in sand in a closed shaded frame or in a closed case with bottom heat. Also by basal cuttings of the current year's growth taken in late autumn and rooted in a shaded frost-free frame, or by simple layering.

***M. communis*** L. MYRTLE. Much-branched erect shrub to 5m with dense foliage. Lvs to 5×1.5cm, ovate-lanceolate, acute, entire, coriaceous, dark lustrous green, transparently dotted, firm, entire, strongly scented when crushed. Flowers white or pink-white, to 3cm diam., fragrant; pedicels long and slender, to 3cm; cal. lobes usually 5; pet. suborbicular, white. Fr. subglobose, 7–10×6–8mm, blue-black when ripe. Mediterranean and southwest Europe; widely cultivated since ancient times, the native range is therefore uncertain. Cvs include 'Albocarpa': fr. white. 'Buxifolia': lvs elliptic. 'Compacta': habit dwarf, dense. 'Flore Pleno': fls double, white. 'Leucocarpa': fr. white. 'Microphylla': habit dwarf, densely leafy; twigs brown; lvs less than 2.5cm, linear-lanceolate, overlapping, needle-like, glossy black-green; fls white, fragrant. 'Microphylla Variegata': lvs striped white. 'Minima': dwarf habit, lvs small. 'Tarentina': habit compact, rounded; lvs needle-like; fls cream-white, fragrant. 'Variegata': habit small; lvs with white margins or stripes, pointed, leathery. var. ***acutifolia*** L. Habit erect. Shoots tinged red. Lvs lanceolate, long-acuminate, with cuneate base. Stalk tinged red. Sep. large, obtuse. var. ***italica*** L. Branches and shoots narrowly upright. Lvs 3×1cm, oval-lanceolate. var. ***latifolia*** Tinb. & Lagasca. Lvs 2–3×1–1.5cm, oval-oblong to oblong-lanceolate, acuminate. var. ***romana*** Mill. Lvs 3–4.5×1–1.5cm, broadly ovate, strongly acuminate, light green, mostly borne in whorls of 3–4.

***M. boetica*** Mill. See *M. communis*.
***M. bullata*** (Sol.) A. Cunn. See *Lophomyrtus bullata*.
***M. buxifolia*** Raf. See *M. communis* 'Buxifolia'.
***M. gayana*** (Barnéoud) Berg. See *Luma chequen*.
***M. italica*** Mill. See *M. communis*.
***M. latifolia*** (Berg) Badillo. See *M. communis*.
***M. minima*** Mill. See *M. communis* 'Minima'.
***M. obcordata*** (Raoul) Hook. f. See *Lophomyrtus obcordata*.
***M. romana*** Hoffsgg. See *M. communis*.
***M. samarangense*** Bl. See *Syzygium samarangense*.
***M. tomentosa*** Ait. See *Rhodomyrtus tomentosa*.
***M. ugni*** Molina. See *Ugni molinae*.

**Mystacidium** Lindl. Orchidaceae. About 11 species of small epiphytic orchids. Stem short; roots numerous. Leaves distichous, usually ligulate. Inflorescences racemose, axillary or arising from stem below leaves, few to several-flowered; flowers white, green or yellow-green; sepals and petals free, similar; lip entire or lobed at or near the base, spurred; column short and stout; rostellum trilobed; pollinia, stipites and viscidia 2. Tropical & S Africa. Z10.

CULTIVATION As for *Angraecum*.

***M. brayboniae*** Summerh. Stem very short; roots 3–4mm diam., grey-green with white streaks. Lvs 3–4, 2–5×1cm, elliptic, slightly bilobed at apex. Racemes 1–2, arising below lvs, 2.5–3.5cm, 5–8-fld; fls white, about 2cm diam., slightly cup-shaped; sep. and pet. 7–8×2mm, lanceolate, acute; lip trilobed toward base, 8mm long, 4mm wide across lobes, midlobe 3×2mm, ovate, obtuse; spur 19–21mm, tapering from a wide mouth. S Africa (E Transvaal).

***M. capense*** (L. f.) Schltr. Stem short; roots 3–5mm diam., grey-green with white streaks. Lvs 4–10, 8.5–13×1–1.5cm, ligulate, dark green, unequally and obtusely bilobed at apex. Racemes axillary or arising below lvs, 6–12-fld; fls white, 1.5–2.5cm diam.; sep. 8–12×2–3mm, lanceolate, acute; pet. slightly shorter and narrower; lip trilobed at base, 8–12×3mm, lanceolate, acute; spur 4–6cm, straight, slender, tapering. S Africa, Swaziland.

***M. millari*** Bol. Stem short; roots numerous, 4mm diam., grey with white streaks. Lvs 2–6, to 12×1.5cm, ligulate, unequally bilobed at apex, leathery, dark green with prominent reticulate venation, glabrous but with a rather velvety appearance particularly when young. Racemes pendent, arising below lvs, 2–5cm, fairly densely 7–10-fld, the fls somewhat drooping; fls white with green anther-cap; 8–12mm diam.; pedicel and ovary 9–11mm; dorsal sep. 6–7×3mm, obovate, lateral sep. slightly longer, oblanceolate; pet. like dorsal sep.; lip 5–6mm, oblong-obovate, recurved at tip; spur 20mm, funnel-shaped in basal quarter, narrowing fairly abruptly to become slender. S Africa (Natal, Eastern Cape).

***M. tanganyikense*** Summerh. Dwarf; stem very short; roots 1mm diam. Lvs 3–4, to 5×1cm, oblanceolate, unequally and obtusely bilobed at apex, dark green with raised reticulate venation. Racemes arising at base of stem, to 6cm, laxly or densely several-fld; fls pale green or creamy white; pedicel and ovary 6–7mm; sep. and pet. spreading, lanceolate, acute; dorsal sep. 4×1mm, lateral sep. slightly longer and oblique; pet. slightly shorter; lip entire, similar to pet.; spur 10–20mm, tapering, slender, straight or slightly incurved. Tanzania, Malawi, Zambia, Zimbabwe.

***M. venosum*** Harv. ex Rolfe. Stem very short; roots numerous, 4–5mm diam., grey-green, streaked white. Lvs 3–4, to 6×1cm, ligulate, unequally bilobed at apex, sometimes with darker reticulate venation, usually deciduous in resting season. Racemes arising among roots at base of stem, 5–8.5cm, 4–7-fld; fls white, 17–20mm diam; sep. and pet. lanceolate, acuminate, recurved at tips; sep. 7–9×2–3mm; pet. 7×2mm; lip 9×2mm, lanceolate, with 2 small, rounded lobes at base; spur 3–4.5cm, slender, tapering. S Africa, Swaziland.

***M. filicorne*** Lindl. See *M. capense*.
For further synonymy see *Angraecum*.

# N

**Nabalus** Cass. (From Indian name for rattlesnake root, in modern Lat.) RATTLESNAKE ROOT; DROP-FLOWER. Compositae. About 15 species of perennial herbs. Stems usually simple, sometimes purple. Leaves alternate, to dentate or pinnatifid, mostly petiolate below, auriculate and amplexicaul above. Capitula ligulate, small, numerous, in open or spike-like terminal panicles and drooping axillary corymbose clusters; receptacle flat, naked; involucre hemispherical to narrowly cylindric; phyllaries in 1–2 series, subequal, outer most smaller; florets truncate, white to yellow or pink. Fruit an oblong or narrowly columnar, truncate, usually terete, often ribbed cypsela; pappus of copious, rigid bristles. N America, temperate E Asia.

CULTIVATION As for *Cicerbita*.

***N. albus*** (L.) Hook. WHITE LETTUCE. To 1.5m, usually glabrous and glaucous. Stem unbranched, to 20cm, often purple. Lvs unbranched to 20cm, more or less triangular-hastate, sinuate-dentate or pinnatifid, usually petiolate, uppermost lanceolate and entire. Capitula *c*6mm diam., pendulous, in paniculate or thyrsoid, often axillary, clusters; phyllaries 6–8, white, tinged green and purple; florets white, tinged, green or yellow, fragrant. Pappus cinnamon brown. Summer. Northeast N America. Z5.

***N. asper*** (Michx.) Torr. & A. Gray. To 1.5m, scabrous or pubesc. Stem unbranched. Lvs to 8cm, ovate to oblong or oblanceolate, basal attenuate, winged-petiolate, commonly obtuse, stem lvs acute, dentate, uppermost entire. Capitula 6–8mm diam., erect, spreading or slightly drooping, in a long narrow thyrse; phyllaries 8–10, densely hirsute; florets pale yellow to cream. Pappus stramineous. Late summer–early autumn. EC S E US. Z6.

***N. autumnalis*** (Walter) C. Jeffrey To 1m, glabrous, somewhat glaucous. Stem usually unbranched. Lvs to 25cm, lanceolate to oblanceolate, sinuate-pinnate or pinnatisect, lobes entire or dentate, distant, petiolate, progressively reduced upwards, upper lvs entire, sessile. Capitula to *c*4mm diam., pendulous, in a terminal, narrow, simple or branched, often unilateral thyrse; phyllaries *c*8, tinged purple; florets white or pale pink. Pappus stramineous. Autumn. E US. Z5.

***N. serpentarius*** (Pursh) Hook. LION'S FOOT; GALL-OF-THE-EARTH. To 1.5m, glabrous or sparsely pubesc. Stem often branched above, green or purple tinged. Lvs to 20cm, pinnatifid or pinnately to palmately divided, dentate or entire, thick, rigid. Capitula *c*6mm diam., pendulous, in paniculate axillary clusters; phyllaries *c*8, green, or purple tinged, bristly-hispid; florets white, cream or pink, rarely yellow. Pappus light brown or stramineous. Autumn. E US. Z5.

For synonymy see *Prenanthes*.

**Nageia** Gaertn. (From the Japanese name for this plant, nagi.) Podocarpaceae. 5 species of evergreen, dioecious, occasionally monoecious trees. Crown columnar. Leaves in opposite, decussate pairs, broad lanceolate, apex acuminate, base cuneate, flattened, lacking midrib, rigid, coriaceous; petiole short, twisted. Male cones solitary or in groups of up to 6, ovoid-cylindric, to 2cm×8mm, subtended by sterile scales; peduncle axillary, naked. Female cones terminal, solitary or paired, borne on short axillary peduncles; ovule single, inverted, enclosed by a thinly fleshy layer; seed to 2cm diameter, pruinose blue-black. S Japan, NE India, SE China, Taiwan to Malaysia, Philippines, Moluccas, New Guinea. Easily told from all other genera in *Podocarpaceae* by the absence of a midrib, but superficially similar to *Agathis*.

CULTIVATION *N. nagi* is hardy in winter to about −20°C/−4°F, but requires a four-month hot, humid summer for successful growth. The other species are similar but less winter hardy. They are decorative trees for warm continental areas, including SE US, E Australia and New Zealand North Island, as well as their native areas. Propagation as for *Podocarpus*.

***N. fleuryi*** (Hickel) Laub. Tree to 10m+. Lvs broad lanceolate, decussate, coriaceous, 10–18×3.5–5cm, apex acuminate, base attenuate. Male cones sessile, axillary, 3-fascicled, long-cylindric, to 3.5cm×4mm, subtended by overlapping keeled bracts. Female cones on axillary scaly peduncle; ovule inverted in axil of a subterminal bract. Seeds globose, to 2cm diam. China (Guangdong, Guangxi) to Vietnam & Kampuchea. Z9.

***N. nagi*** (Thunb.) Kuntze. NAGI. Tree to 25m. Bark dark brown to grey. Lvs glossy dark green, broad lanceolate, 4–8×1.5–3cm, acuminate, glaucous beneath, decussate. Male cones cylindric, grouped 1–5, to 2cm, subtended by a lanceolate scale to 6mm; peduncles axillary, scaly, to 1cm. Seed cones axillary; peduncle to 1cm; fertile scale blue-black; seeds globose, 10–15mm, receptacle not swollen, small. S China to Taiwan & S Japan. Z8.

***N. wallichiana*** (Presl) Kuntze. Tree to 40m. Bark beige or grey, smooth. Lvs decussate, broad lanceolate, 10–15×3–5cm, to 22×7cm on vigorous trees, parallel-veined, acute to acuminate; petiole to 10mm. Male cones grouped 1–7 on 2–10mm peduncles, to 2cm×5mm. Female cones axillary, 12–20mm; scales to 7, lanceolate, fleshy, abscising; fertile bracts subterminal. Seeds globose, smooth, covered by thin fleshy layer, to 2cm diam., with slightly swollen receptacle. Assam & Burma to New Guinea. Z9.

***N. formosensis*** (Dümmer) Page. See *N. nagi*.
***N. mannii*** (Hook. f.) Laub. See *Afrocarpus mannii*.
For further synonymy see *Decussocarpus* and *Podocarpus*.

**Nageliella** L.O. Williams. (For Otto Nagel, who collected species in Mexico.) Orchidaceae. 2 species of epiphytic or terrestrial orchids. Rhizome short-creeping. Pseudobulbs short, semiterete, clavate, striate, apex thickened, unifoliate. Leaves apical, semi-erect, fleshy, thickly coriaceous, subsessile, ovate-lanceolate to oblong-lanceolate, often flushed red-purple, mottled or spotted white and rugulose, tongue-like in appearance, sometimes with midrib obscurely impressed above and keeled below. Inflorescence terminal, a nodding to semi-erect raceme, panicle or subumbellate, few to many-flowered; branches short; flowers small, pink, magenta or red; sepals erect, connivent, dorsal sepal free, lateral sepals adnate to column foot forming a mentum; petals linear to lanceolate; lip adnate to column, basally swollen or saccate, simple to obscurely 3-lobed; column slender, arcuate, apex biauriculate, anther operculate, incumbent, pollinia 4, waxy. C America. Z10.

CULTIVATION Small epiphytes for the cool and intermediate house, grown for their slender stems of magenta flowers and (*N. purpurea*) the attractively patterned fleshy foliage. Pot in half pots or pans of medium- to fine-grade bark mix; position in light shade or, for better leaf colour, full sunlight; water freely throughout the growing season, very sparingly at cooler times of the year.

***N. angustifolia*** (Booth ex Lindl.) Ames & Correll. Pseudobulbs to 7cm, terete. Lvs to 10×2cm, erect, linear-lanceolate to oblong-lanceolate, acute to obtuse, marked dark red-brown. Infl. to 30cm; peduncle terete, filiform; fls produced in succession, nodding, bright magenta; dorsal sep. to 7×3mm, elliptic-oblong, subacute, lateral sep. obliquely ovate-elliptic, rounded to acute; pet. to 7×2mm, linear to linear-lanceolate, obtuse, finely denticulate; lip to 9mm, simple, basal portion geniculate, apical portion suborbicular, obscurely 3-lobed, deeply concave, retuse, crenate; column deep pink, slender. Guatemala.

***N. purpurea*** (Lindl.) L.O. Williams. Pseudobulbs slender, erect, to 8cm, strongly striate. Lvs to 12×3cm, lanceolate to ovate-lanceolate, often spotted brown-purple, subacuminate. Infl. to 50cm, erect; peduncle semi-terete to compressed; fls red-purple; dorsal sep. to 9×4mm, elliptic, acute, lateral sep. to 10×2mm, ovate to oblong-lanceolate, acute to obtuse; pet. subequal to lateral sep., elliptic-lanceolate, acute to obtuse, minutely fimbriate; lip simple, to 11mm, apical portion deflexed, ovate-suborbicular, obtuse to acute, slightly concave, basal portion geniculate; column to 7mm, subterete, slender. Mexico, Guatemala, Honduras.

For synonymy see *Hartwegia*.

**NAJADACEAE** Juss. See *Najas*.

**Najas** L. (Name from Gk *naias*, water nymph.) NAIAD; WATER NYMPH. Najadaceae. 35 species of monoecious or dioecious submerged aquatic herbs, inhabiting fresh or brackish water. Stems elongate to short, to 60cm+, filiform, much branched, smooth or muricate. Leaves opposite, alternate or whorled, linear to narrowly oblong, entire or toothed or spined, dilated at base to form conspicuous sheaths that are sometimes auriculate, with 2 minute scales within each sheath. Flowers solitary or fascicled in sheath-axils, minute, pedunculate or subsessile; male flowers of single stamen enclosed by perianth-like spathe; female flowers naked, ovary solitary with short style, stigmas 2–4, ovule 1. Fruit an achene, loosely surrounded by membranes; seeds ovoid to elliptic. Cosmopolitan.

CULTIVATION As for *Zanichellia*.

***N. flexilis*** (Willd.) Rostk. & W.L.E. Schmidt. Lvs to 2.5×0.1cm, in whorls of 3, linear, minutely denticulate, sheaths not auriculate. Monoecious; male fls with spathe; female with 3–4 stigmas. Achene elliptic, acute, to 3mm. Eastern N America, N & C Europe. Z5.

***N. graminea*** Delile. Lvs to 4×0.1cm, whorled, linear or subulate, acuminate, minutely denticulate, sheaths with long-triangular auricles. Monoecious, fls fascicled; males lacking spathe. Achene to 2.25mm. S Europe, Asia, Australasia, N & E Africa. Z8.

***N. guadalupensis*** (Spreng.) Morong. Lvs 2.5×0.1cm, linear, acute to acuminate, minutely denticulate, sheath not auriculate. Monoecious; male fls with spathe; stigmas 2–3. Fruit ellipsoid, 1.6mm. California to S America, including Galapagos. Z9.

***N. indica*** (Willd.) Cham. Lvs to 4.5cm, linear, minutely spinulose, sheath with overlapping edges, sometimes auriculate. Monoecious; fls solitary; males with sheath. Achenes to 2.5mm. India, Malaysia to Philippines and Japan. Z10.

***N. minor*** All. Lvs to 3×0.1cm, linear, minutely spinose-dentate, sheath with rounded-truncate auricles. Monoecious; fls fascicled; males with spathe. Fruit 2–3mm. Europe, Asia, N & C Africa. Z6.

***N. falciculata*** A. Braun. See *N. indica*.
***N. kingii*** Rendle. See *N. indica*.
***N. microdon*** A. Braun. See *N. guadalupensis*.

**Namibia** Schwantes. (For the Namib desert, the plant's native habitat.) Aizoaceae. 2 species of succulent perennials, closely allied to *Juttadinteria*, forming dense hemispherical clumps. Shoots with 1–2 pairs of highly succulent, thick, soft, finely rough leaves. Flowers sessile or short-stalked; calyx with 5 sepals, not 4 as in *Juttadinteria*, violet or white. Namibia (S Namib). Z9.

CULTIVATION As for *Lithops*.

***N. cinerea*** (Marloth) Dinter & Schwantes. Lvs 13×10–12×12mm, rounded-triangular on upper surface, more or less recurved at tip, lower surface navicular and rounded-carinate, grey-green, rough with white dots. Fls 3cm diam., violet.

***N. pomonae*** (Dinter) Dinter & Schwantes. Forming dense cushion 20×10cm. Lvs 30×15–18×12–14mm, united for 10–12mm, crowded, broadly navicular, angles distinct, keel obtuse, apiculate, white-grey or light grey. Fls 3cm diam., white.

***N. ponderosa*** (Dinter) Dinter & Schwantes. See *Juttadinteria longipetala*.
For further synonymy see *Juttadinteria*.

**Nananthus** N.E. Br. (From Gk *nanos*, dwarf, and *anthos*, flower.) Aizoaceae. 10 species of very tuberous, dwarf, tufted, glabrous succulents. Stems caudiciform, tuberous, to 13×4.5cm. Leaves 4–6 per stem, opposite, ascending or spreading, 1.5–5cm, widened in the upper half, widest in the middle, above that square, oblong, linear, ovate or broadly ovate, subobtuse, acute to acuminate, sometimes conspicuously aristate, lower surface obtusely keeled upwards, often white-punctate. Flowers solitary with 2–3 series of petals, yellow, with or without a red median stripe; pedicel short with 2 basal bracts. S Africa (Cape Province, Orange Free State), Botswana. Z9.

CULTIVATION As for *Pleiospilos* but needs a deep pot for its tap-root.

***N. aloides*** (Haw.) Schwantes. Lvs 5cm, usually 6 per shoot, obliquely lanceolate or narrowly rhombic, often flat-furrowed, carinate-triquetrous above, dark green with numerous white, prominent, tuberculate dots and rough angles. Fls 2.5–3.5cm diam., yellow, sometimes with a darker yellow stripe. Cape (W Griqualand), Botswana.

***N. transvaalensis*** (Rolfe) L. Bol. Similar to *N. vittatus* but lvs 2–3×1–1.3cm, with large tubercles crowded toward lf margins. Fls 2–3cm diam., light yellow. Transvaal: Boshof District.

***N. vittatus*** (N.E. Br.) Schwantes. Lvs 2–3cm long, 6–8mm wide midway, 6–8 per shoot, opposite, unequal, obliquely lanceolate, acute, shortly apiculate, semicylindric, expanded above, dull green with tuberculate raised dots. Fls 2–2.5cm diam., light yellow with a thin red median stripe. Orange Free State: Fauresmith District.

***N. wilmaniae*** (L. Bol.) L. Bol. Caudex tuberous. Lvs 2.2×1.3×0.6cm, 2 pairs per stem, base oblong, broadening midway, ovate at tip, acute, lower surface carinate, compressed toward tip with pallid dots, dirty olive green. Fls 2cm diam., yellow with red longitudinal stripes. Cape Province: West Griqualand.

***N. albipunctus*** (Haw.) N.E. Br., also (Haw.) Schwantes. See *Rabiea albipuncta*.
***N. cradockensis*** L. Bol. See *Aloinopsis jamesii*.
***N. crassipes*** (Marloth). L. Bol. See *Aloinopsis spathulata*.
***N. dyeri*** L. Bol. See *Aloinopsis rubrolineata*.
***N. jamesii*** (L. Bol.) L. Bol. See *Aloinopsis jamesii*.
***N. lodewykii*** (L. Bol.) L. Bol. See *Aloinopsis lodewykii*.
***N. luckhoffii*** (L. Bol.) L. Bol. See *Aloinopsis luckhoffii*.
***N. malherbei*** L. Bol. See *Aloinopsis malherbei*.
***N. orpenii*** (N.E. Br.) L. Bol. See *Aloinopsis orpenii*.
***N. peersii*** L. Bol. See *Aloinopsis peersii*.
***N. rubrolineatus*** (N.E. Br.) N.E. Br. See *Aloinopsis rubrolineata*.
***N. schooneesii*** (L. Bol.) L. Bol. See *Aloinopsis schooneesii*.
***N. soehlemannii*** F.A. Haage. See *Aloinopsis peersii*.
***N. villetii*** L. Bol. See *Aloinopsis villetii*.
For further synonymy see *Aloinopsis* and *Mesembryanthemum*.

**Nandina** Thunb. (From Japanese name, *nandin*.) HEAVENLY BAMBOO. Berberidaceae. 1 species, an evergreen or semi-deciduous shrub to 2m. Stems erect, clumped, usually simple, slender, to 3.75cm diam., grey-brown, woody, scarred or sheathed (near apex) by leaf bases, cane-like. Leaves alternate, clustered toward summit, bi- to tripinnate, to 90cm, held semi-erect or horizontal; pinnae to 7cm, elliptic, lanceolate or narrow-rhombic, entire, glabrous, subcoriaceous, emerging slightly glaucous, lime green tinted rose, hardening sap-green, paler beneath, becoming red to purple in autumn, midvein conspicuous, depressed; petioles slender, glossy, basally clasping. Inflorescence a terminal panicle, erect to arching, to 40cm; flowers white, to 7.5mm diam.; sepals in concentric whorls increasing in size toward centre; petals 3–6; stamens 6; ovary with abrupt conical stigma. Fruit a bright red berry, to 1cm diam., usually smaller. Summer. India to Japan. Z7.

CULTIVATION An upright and elegant evergreen, used extensively in Japanese gardens for the striking effects of its foliage, flushed red when young and colouring red-purple at the end of the season. The flowers are carried in a profusion of large panicles, followed by decorative fruits, pea-sized, red and persistent, although not always freely produced. *Nandina* may also be used successfully in indoor planting schemes, given good access to water, direct sunlight and protection from excessive draughts.

Plant in a humus-rich, moist but well-drained soil, in a cool but sunny position, sheltered from cold winds. Well-ripened wood is frost hardy but young tips may be damaged by severe frosts. Remove damaged foliage by cutting shoots right back to the base, the retain the upright form of the clump. Rejuvenate leggy, older shrubs on the same principle, in summer, taking out a few of the oldest stems to the ground. Plant in groups: male and female flowers are borne on the same plant but group plantings will increase the likelihood of berries.

Take single node cuttings in midsummer; root in a closed case with bottom heat in a sandy mix; maintain high humidity. Alternatively, in late autumn or early winter, insert 10–18cm/4–7in. nodal or heeled cuttings in a cold frame, in late autumn or early winter; lift and pot the following autumn. Seeds do not germinate freely but may be successful if sown when ripe.

***N. domestica*** Thunb. As for the genus. Cultivars abound, particularly in Japan, where some 60 are named. The most commonly found include: 'Firepower': dwarf, strong autumn colours, crimson and green. 'Flora': fr. golden yellow. Little Princess': strong colour in spring and autumn; fls white. 'Longifolia': pinnae narrow-oblong, to 10cm. 'Nana Purpurea' ('Purpurea'): to 1.25m; lvs shorter, sparsely bipinnate; pinnae broader, fewer, softer, retaining purple-red flush throughout season and colouring brilliantly in autumn. 'Richmond': vigorous; fr. scarlet in winter. 'Variegata': lvs, petioles and young stems variegated white, cream and candy pink. 'Woods Dwarf': vigorous, low-growing; lvs light gold, tinted red in winter. var. ***leucocarpa*** Mak. ('Alba'). Fr. dull white. Japan.

**Nannoglottis** Maxim. (From Gk *nannos*, dwarf, and *glotta*, tongue.) Compositae. About 8 species of erect, perennial herbs, to 1m. Stems subsimple, sparsely to moderately leafy. Leaves elliptic to oblong or oblanceolate, entire or toothed, membranous, lower petiolate, upper winged, decurrent. Capitula heterogamous, radiate, solitary, or few in a lax corymb; receptacle convex, nude; involucre hemispherical; phyllaries in *c.*2 series, subequal, oblong, acuminate, outer few, leaf-like, inner membranous; florets yellow, numerous; ray florets female, ligule reflexed, oblong; disc florets hermaphrodite, campanulate. Fruit angled, oblong to linear, 8–10-ribbed, hairy or glabrate; pappus of scabrid, plumose, unequal hairs. W China, Himalaya. Z8.

CULTIVATION As for *Cicerbita*.

***N. hookeri*** (C.B. Clarke ex Hook. f.) Kit. Robust herb, to 80cm. Stems simple or slightly branched, sparsely softly villous. Lvs to 15×15cm, elliptic to oblanceolate, obtuse or acute, entire or irregularly toothed, basal lvs absent or soon withering, stem lvs 4–6. Capitula few, 3–4.5cm diam., long-pedunculate; phyllaries *c.*6mm, ovate-lanceolate, acuminate, glandular-hairy; ray florets to 13mm. Pappus short, red. W China to Nepal.

**Nanodes** Rchb. (From Gk *nanodes*, pygmy.) Orchidaceae. 3 species of diminutive epiphytic orchids formerly included in *Epidendrum*. Stems tufted, cane-like, ascending to arching-pendulous, densely clothed in overlapping leaf sheaths. Leaves 2-ranked, near-opposite, glossy pale green, rather fleshy with conspicuous stem-encircling sheaths. Flowers solitary or paired, borne terminally, small, waxy, translucent with a simple lip. C & S America. Z10.

CULTIVATION As for *Epidendrum pseudepidendrum*.

***N. discolor*** Lindl. Stems 6.5–10cm, densely clustered, completely concealed by lf sheaths. Lvs 1.75–3×0.5–1cm, fleshy, recurved or spreading, elliptic to linear-oblong, obtuse, apiculate, dorsally carinate, light green. Fls to 1.5cm diam., usually paired, born terminally, translucent yellow-green or green-brown to pale pink-purple; dorsal sep. 1.2–1.8×0.3–0.4cm, lanceolate to oblanceolate, acute to acuminate, lateral sep. obliquely elliptic-lanceolate, acute or acuminate; pet. shorter than sep., narrowly elliptic to linear-lanceolate, acute, denticulate; lip 0.7–0.9×0.9–1.1cm, simple, reniform to ovate-suborbicular, apiculate, erose-ciliate, short-clawed; column to 6mm, slightly recurved. C & S America.

***N. mathewsii*** Rolfe. Stems to 10cm. Lvs 1.5–2×0.7–0.9cm, fleshy, oblong, obtuse or retuse. Fls solitary, light purple-green; sep. 1–1.2×0.35–0.5cm, narrowly elliptic-lanceolate, acute; pet. 1–1.4×0.1cm, narrowly linear, obtuse; lip 0.75–1×1–1.8cm, fleshy, adnate to column, transversely oblong, decurved, callus fleshy, trilobulate. Mexico to Panama, Venezuela to Peru.

***N. medusae*** Rchb. f. Stems to 25cm, densely clustered, somewhat pendulous. Lvs 4–7×1.5–3cm, narrowly ovate-oblong, fleshy, apex bilobed, blue-green. Fls usually solitary, born terminally, to 8cm; sep. and pet. yellow-green tinged red-brown, 2.8–4.2×1–1.5cm, oblong or oblong-lanceolate, acute; lip 3–4.5×4–5.5cm, deep maroon, green at base, transversely oblong, emarginate, deeply lacerate-fimbriate; column to 13mm, fleshy. Ecuador.

For synonymy see *Epidendrum* and *Neolehmannia*.

**Napaea** L. (Probably from Gk *napaios*, belonging to a wooded vale or dell, as the plant grows in valleys and lowlands.) GLADE MALLOW. Malvaceae. 1 species, a perennial, dioecious, coarse herb, to 2.5m; stems erect. Leaves to 60cm, palmately 5–11-lobed, lobes serrate to pinnately divided. Flowers in cymose panicles; epicalyx absent; calyx to 6mm; petals of male flowers to 1.2cm, slightly longer than those of female flowers; anthers 15–20, at the tip of staminal column; female flowers with styles enclosed and subtended by a ring of sterile anthers; styles 10. Fruit a schizocarp, mericarps 10, rarely dehiscent, 1-seeded. E & C US (Ohio to Illinois and Minnesota). Z4.

CULTIVATION *N. dioica* is found in the wild in moist alluvial soils of valleys and bottomlands. Achieving heights of 2.7m/9ft, it makes a statuesque, roughly pubescent perennial, bearing small but numerous white flowers in branched clusters at the top of the stem. Cultivate as for *Iliamna*.

***N. dioica*** L. GLADE MALLOW. As for the genus.

For synonymy see *Sida*.

**Napoleonaea** P. Beauv. (For Napoleon Bonaparte (1769–1821).) Lecythidaceae. Some 10 species of evergreen trees or shrubs. Leaves alternate, elliptic-oblong, ovate or obovate, glabrous, apex acute, usually entire, margin glandular beneath; petiole to 9mm. Flowers solitary or, rarely, in panicles, showy, often brightly coloured, borne in leaf axils or on trunk or branches, subsessile or short-pedicellate, bracteate; calyx 5-lobed; petals absent; stamens many, borne in 4 whorls on a glandular disc, those of the outer 3 whorls sterile and united to form a wheel-shaped pseudocorolla and corona, those of the innermost whorl sterile or fertile; stigmas 5; ovary inferior, 5-locular. Fruit a berry, smooth or spiny, sometimes lobed, seeds to 20. W & C Africa. Z10.

CULTIVATION Tropical trees of the rainforest understorey, *Napoleonaea* spp. are interesting and ornamental garden specimens in the humid subtropics but require warm glasshouse treatment in cooler zones. Grown for their showy, saucer-shaped flowers, exotically coloured and beautifully constructed, and sometimes carried on trunk and branch. Grow in a mix of equal parts fibrous loam, leafmould or equivalent and sharp sand, with a minimum temperature 16–18°C/60–65°F, as for *Barringtonia*.

***N. imperialis*** P. Beauv. Shrub to 7m. Lvs to 22×9cm, elliptic to obovate, acuminate, entire or undulate, glands at the base and the apex. Fls subsessile, solitary or clustered in twos and threes in lf axils or on old wood; bracts to 3×4mm, glandular; cal. 16–20mm diam.; corona 35–40mm diam. Fr. to 3.5×4.5cm. Nigeria (Benin), Equatorial Guinea (Bioko Is.).

***N. cuspidata*** Miers. See *N. imperialis*.
***N. miersii*** Hook. f. See *N. imperialis*.

**Naravelia** DC. (From a Singalese name.) Ranunculaceae. Some 5 species of woody climbers, closely allied to *Clematis*. Leaves opposite, pinnate, lower leaflets normal, others transformed into tendrils at end of rachis. Flowers actinomorphic, in terminal panicles; calyx of, usually 4, valvate, petaloid sepals, purple-green to yellow; corolla 9–14 staminodes, linear to clavate; stamens numerous. Fruit a narrow achene with plumose style and twisted ovary, sometimes beaked, not twisted. India to Malaya. Z10.

CULTIVATION A climber for the intermediate glasshouse in a light, loamy medium. Propagate as for *Clematis*.

***N. zeylanica*** DC. Climbing shrub. Lvs trifoliolate, lower 2 leaflets ovate, acute, glabrous above, sericeous beneath, 5-veined, entire, or 1–2-toothed, central leaflet transformed to tendril, 3-fid at apex; petiole long. Fls yellow, sep. ovate-lanceolate, caducous; pet. 6–12, linear-spathulate, exceeding sepals. Fr. slightly hairy. Autumn–winter. Tropical India, Malaya, Sri Lanka.

For synonymy see *Atragene*.

**Narcissus** L. (A Gk plant-name said to be derived from *narke*, numbness, torpor, from its narcotic properties; in Gk mythology the youth Narcissus, who fell in love with his own reflection in a pool, was turned into a lily by the gods.) DAFFODIL. Amaryllidaceae. About 50 species of perennial bulbous herbs.

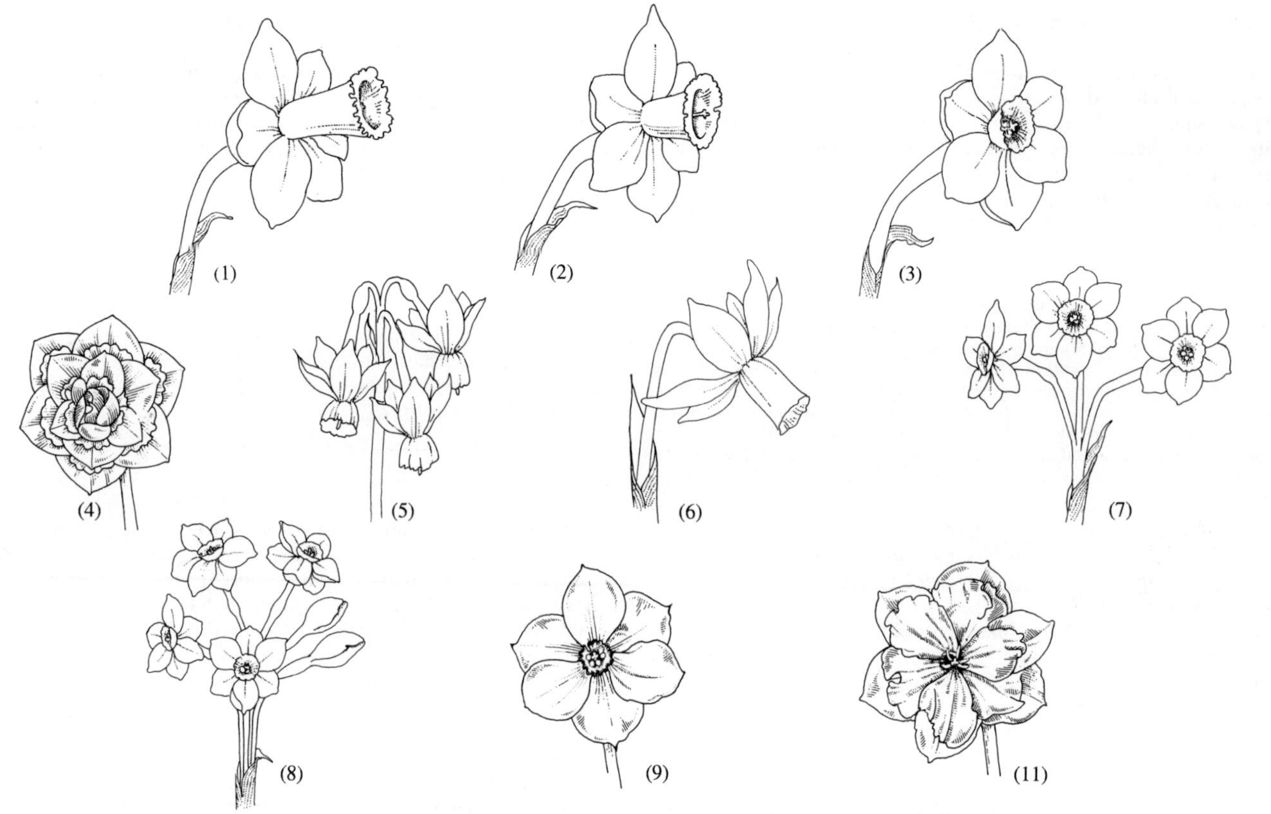


**Daffodils** (Numbers refer to the divisions of the official Classification) (1) Trumpet (2) Large-cupped (3) Small-cupped (4) Double (5) *N. triandrus* derivatives (6) *N. cyclamineus* derivatives (7) Jonquils (8) *N. tazetta* derivatives (9) *N. poeticus* derivatives (11) Split-cupped
These relate to cultivars of garden origin. Div. 10 comprises the wild species, and Div. 12 miscellaneous cultivars.

Leaves 1 to several, lasting from late winter to early summer, basal, erect, spreading or prostrate, linear, rush-like or strap-shaped. Flowers yellow or white, sometimes fragrant, erect to drooping, solitary or in an umbel of 2–20, subtended by a one-valved, usually scarious membranous spathe, borne on a leafless scape; perianth tubular at the base, with 6 segments, almost always with a conspicuous corona in the form of a trumpet or a smaller ring or cup, often a different colour from the segments; stamens 6, usually in 2 whorls, attached to the perianth tube; ovary 3-celled, with many ovules. Fruit an ellipsoid to almost spherical capsule; seeds many, sometimes with an appendage. S Europe and Mediterranean; also N Africa, W Asia, China and Japan.

CULTIVATION Narcissi (which include all daffodils; see classification below) are among the most popular garden plants, capable of being grown in beds and borders, rock gardens, in grass and woodlands, and in pots. They are also excellent as cut flowers. Their flowering period extends from late autumn to early summer (longer still if the species are included) though the main flowering period is in spring. In the wild, species are found in cool-temperate climates in a great variety of habitats including coastal areas, meadows, woodlands, river banks, rocks and alpine turf, at altitudes from sea level to over 3000m/9840ft.

Most daffodils of garden origin will grow in almost any soil or situation, though their preference is for soil which stays moist but well-drained during the growing season. Full sun or some sun during parts of the day is usually desirable but most cultivars will tolerate some shade provided that it is not dense or continuous. Light shade from deciduous trees or shrubs suits most cultivars, and is preferable to full sun for late-flowering cultivars in warmer areas. Most daffodils are hardy enough to survive even when the ground is frozen solid to a depth of several centimetres in midwinter, but benefit from the insulating effect of being covered by snow or a mulch of leaves. They are also tolerant of quite severe frost on leaves and even flowers, but members of the Tazetta division are less hardy and need protection in colder areas.

Generally, bulbs should be planted to one-and-a-half times their own depth. In light soils they can be planted rather deeper. Shallow planting produces more increase and smaller bulbs; deeper planting less increase but larger bulbs. The soil, unless recently dug to a depth greater than planting depth, should be loosened with a fork to allow penetration by roots, and the bulbs then pressed firmly in. Bulbs should be divided by pulling them apart at the basal plate before planting. For clumps it is advisable to plant bulbs at least 15cm/6in. from their neighbours in every direction. Bulbs can be established in sward either by removing the turf before planting or by using a bulb planter. Clumps in borders rarely need to be lifted for three years after planting, and can often be left much longer. Bulbs in grass can be left undisturbed for many years.

Most cultivars are tolerant of either acid or alkaline soils. Species will, of course, favour a soil type close to that of their habitat – e.g. acid to neutral soils, pH 5.5–7.0, for most forms of *Narcissus bulbocodium, N. triandrus, N. asturiensis* and *N. cyclamineus*; alkaline, ph 7.0–8.0, for *N. jonquilla* and *N. tazetta*. Where the right conditions can be provided many species will colonize by offsetting and self-seeding.

When daffodils are grown in grass it is advisable not to cut the grass until 4–6 weeks after the flowers have faded, but it can then be cut with little damage to the bulbs, even if the leaves are still green. Lift bulbs when the leaves turn yellow. Unless replanted immediately they should be dried off and stored in single layers in a cool, dry, dark place. Care should be taken not to damage or bruise the bulbs, and they should not be exposed to strong sunlight or damage will follow. When dry, the bulbs should be cleaned of old tunics and soil, any showing signs of damage or disease should be discarded, and offsets should be detached for propagation. The best time for planting is late summer or very early autumn, or even earlier for *N. poeticus* and its hybrids, which have virtually no resting period. Later planting, even until late autumn, reduces the length of the growing season but can give reasonable results. When possible bulbs should be planted in soil which has been well cultivated. They should not be allowed to come into contact with fresh farmyard manure, but ground which has had well-rotted manure or compost incorporated can be used if a crop has first been taken, and the bulbs will benefit from the humus.

Daffodils are well suited to pot cultivation, either for exhibition or decorative purposes. Deep pots should be used to allow plenty of room for roots. Either soil-based or soilless potting medium can be used. The medium needs to be free-draining, and perlite can usefully be added. Four or five double-nosed bulbs can be put in a 25cm/10in. pot, three double-nose or 4–5 single-nosed in a 22cm/9in. pot. Bulbs should be pressed in firmly and the medium over and around the bulbs should also be pressed firm. A mass of flowers can be produced by 'double-banking' the bulbs, placing one layer half way down the pot, infilling with soil, and placing another layer between the noses of the lower ones (see also BULBS).

After planting the pots should be stood outdoors for at least 12 weeks, and should be plunged and covered with a protective layer. The plunge bed should allow free drainage. The protective layer should provide insulation, but should be of a substance through which shoots can grow without obstruction such as light soil, leached ash, straw or pine needles. Bulbs should be kept adequately watered while in the plunge bed, but not too wet. The time for taking them out depends on when flowers are required and the conditions to which they are moved, for example whether to a heated or unheated greenhouse or indoors. It is essential that they should be kept cool, especially at first, otherwise they will grow lax and the flowers may abort. If plastic pots are used, special care must be taken not to allow the soil to overheat. Leaves and stems may well require staking. After removal from the plunge, pots should be watered frequently and never be allowed to become dry, and can be fed with weak tomato (high potash) fertilizer. Humidity needs to be medium to high. After flowering, unless the bulbs are discarded, they should be carefully removed from their pots and planted with as little disturbance of their roots as possible in a lightly shaded place outside and kept well watered. They can then be lifted in the normal way and replanted in the garden. The bulbs are unlikely to be suitable for growing in pots again until they have had a season to recover.

For home decoration, bulbs can be grown in bulb fibre, but this provides no nutrient at all and the bulbs will be exhausted unless they are planted out as above after flowering. The fibre should be kept moist at all times. For very early flowering in pots, bulbs which have been specially prepared by pre-cooling should be obtained.

The smaller species and miniature hybrids perform especially well in pots, either in the cold or alpine house or in frames. A high-fertility soil-based potting medium is suitable for most, preferably mixed with coarse grit or fine chippings in the proportion two parts medium to one of grit. An ericaceous mix with extra bulky material is best for species which grow in acid soils. Small bulbs (e.g. *N. bulbocodium*) can be planted 12 to a 12cm/5in. pot, about 7cm/3in. deep. Good ventilation is essential throughout the growing season. Bulbs should be started into growth by watering plentifully in late summer or early autumn. They should then be kept moist through the winter and again watered copiously through the spring until the leaves begin to yellow, after which little or no water will be required. Species from hotter areas can be 'baked', i.e. given full sun exposure and minimal moisture; they are still best plunged, however, in summer. Those from cooler regions are better left outside, plunged in a shady place and uncovered.

For daffodils in the garden, two parts bonemeal and one part hoof-and-horn meal are beneficial to provide slow-release phosphate and some nitrogen. This mixture may be combined with the soil at planting time or scattered at any time afterwards at 175–225g/m$^2$. Alternatively, a slow-release nitrogen compound can be used as an autumn dressing. Wood ash applied in early spring is useful for providing potassium. In spring a balanced liquid fertilizer or one containing extra potash may be used, but is rarely necessary for bulbs grown outside. In normal seasons rainfall will provide all the water needed, but daffodils need moisture in early autumn to initiate growth, and they appreciate abundant water in the period of rapid growth up to and through flowering.

Propagation of daffodil cultivars is achieved by letting the bulbs divide naturally, which is a slow process. It can be speeded up by twin-scale propagation, a time consuming method. The bulb is sterilized for five minutes in 1% formaldehyde and then cut into segments, usually 36 or 48 for a good-sized bulb. Each segment is then cut so that pairs of fleshy leaf scales are created, attached to their own portion of basal plate. The twin scales are further disinfected by dipping for 30 minutes in a weak solution of fungicide (e.g. 0.2% benomyl). They are then placed in polythene bags containing damp vermiculite. The bags are sealed with an air space above the vermiculite and stored at 20°C/68°F for 12 weeks, by which time small bulbs should have formed. These can then be grown on like daffodil seedlings and should reach flowering size in 3–4 years. Some cultivars respond to this method better than others. It has not been used for species to any extent. Most species are slow to increase by division and are propagated by seed.

Most cultivars readily set seed if hand-pollinated, but will not breed true. The seed should be collected when the capsule begins to turn yellow or the old flower falls away. Seed should be sown immediately or in early autumn at the latest. It is best sown in pots or boxes which are at least 15cm/6in. deep, in a light sandy medium and shallowly covered. Germination occurs in winter and the first leaf appears in late winter or early spring. The seedlings should be kept watered to prolong their growing season, and are better not planted out into open ground until the end of their second growing season. Two-year-old bulbs can be planted out about 10cm/4in. deep and about 10cm/4in. apart. They can then be left undisturbed until they flower, usually in their fourth or fifth year, and for a year or two after so that selections can be made. It is unwise to give names to new cultivars until they have flowered several times so that their consistency can be assessed. Names should be registered with the Royal Horticultural Society as International Registration Authority.

The smaller species can easily be raised from seed in the same way, but the sowing containers should be shallower and the medium grittier. If thinly sown they can be left in their original pot until they flower, after three or four years in good conditions.

Over the last century, breeders have greatly widened the colours and combinations of colours as well as the sizes and shapes available. Although yellow trumpet daffodils are perhaps still the most popular, pure white daffodils are now common, cultivars with deep red or orange cups are often sunproof or nearly so, and cultivars with deep pink cups or cups paler than the perianth are no longer novelties. Many cultivars bred from *N. cyclamineus, N. triandrus* and members of the Jonquil and Tazetta divisions are attractive and satisfactory garden plants.

Miniature daffodils are increasingly popular. There is no universally accepted definition of a miniature. The Royal Horticultural Society defines them for exhibition purposes as having flowers no more than 5cm/2in. in diameter when flattened out. Other societies issue what they call Approved Lists. Some of the best miniatures for garden purposes are now propagated commercially on a very large scale. Daffodils larger than miniatures but less than standard size are now being termed intermediates, but again there is no generally accepted definition.

Daffodils are increasingly popular for competitive exhibition. The qualities sought after are poise, horizontally held flowers on stiff upright stems, broad flat untwisted petals of tough substance and satin-smooth quality, strong colours or pure whites, symmetry and consistency.

CLASSIFICATION. Although the usage of the cut flower trade and of some bulb catalogues is to call narcissus cultivars with long coronas (or 'trumpets') daffodils, and those with short coronas (or 'cups') narcissi, this is not a tenable distinction when so many have coronas of medium length. Narcissus and daffodil are treated here as synonyms.

The RHS has pioneered classification of daffodils since 1908 and since 1955 has been International Registration Authority for the genus. Under the current (1989) system of classification daffodils fall into 12 divisions. Within each division daffodils are further distinguished by code letters for their colours: White or Whitish = W; Green = G; Yellow = Y; Pink = P; Orange = O; Red = R.

The colour code consists of two letters or groups of letters separated by a hyphen. The letter(s) before the hyphen describe the perianth segments (or 'petals'), the letter(s) following it describe the corona. For purposes of colour coding perianth segments and coronas are divided into three zones, none of which need be in specific proportions. If the perianth segments are substantially of a single colour one letter is used. If they are of more than one colour two or three letters are used, describing the outer zone before the midzone and/or base. If the corona is substantially of a single colour one letter is again used. Otherwise three letters are always used, describing the eye zone before the midzone and rim. In double daffodils the code letter(s) before the hyphen describe not only the outer whorl of perianth segments but also any extra perianth segments (of the same colour) interspersed with the corona segments.

The full classification consists of the division followed by the colour code. For example a daffodil with yellow petals and yellow trumpet is 1 Y–Y; one with mainly yellow petals having a white base and a medium cup having a white eye zone and midzone and a yellow rim is 2 YW–WWY; and one with white petals and a short cup having a green eye zone, yellow midzone and orange rim is 3 W–GYO.

Division 1. *Trumpet daffodils of garden origin.* One flower to a stem; corona ('trumpet') as long as, or longer than the perianth segments ('petals'). 'Arkle' (1Y-Y): fls yellow, trumpet deep yellow. 'Ballygarvey' (1W-Y): petals wide and pointed, trumpet rich chrome. 'Bravoure' (1W-Y): perianth pure white, trumpet long, yellow. 'By Jove' (1Y-Y): fls vivid gold, petals broad, trumpet narrow. 'Dutch Master' (1Y-Y): stem thick; fls golden yellow, trumpet frilled. 'Empress of Ireland' (1W-W): fls very large, white. 'Hero' (1Y-O): perianth rich gold, trumpet orange. 'Honeybird' (1Y-W): perianth pale lemon flushed white, trumpet white with yellow base and rim. 'King Alfred' (1Y-Y): tall; fls golden yellow. 'Little Gem' (1Y-Y): dwarf, to 12cm; fls yellow. 'Lunar Sea' (1Y-W): perianth light lemon, trumpet fades to white. 'Mount Hood' (1W-W): perianth wide, white, trumpet ivory; long-lasting. 'Primeur' (1Y-Y): fls gold. 'W.P. Milner' (1W-W): dwarf, to 20cm; perianth frilled, soft cream, trumpet white flushed lemon.

Division 2. *Large-cupped daffodils of garden origin.* One flower to a stem; corona ('cup') more than one-third, but less than equal to the length of the perianth segments ('petals'). 'Ambergate' (2O-O): perianth vibrant tangerine, cup strong orange. 'Ann Abbott' (2W-P): fls delicate, perianth white, cup pale pink touched yellow, darker pink at rim. 'Apropos' (2W-YYP): perianth white, cup orange-yellow with frilled salmon pink edge. 'Binkie' (2Y-W): perianth sulphur yellow, cup becoming pale cream edged yellow. 'Camelot' (2Y-Y): perianth rounded, thick, cup frill-edged. 'Carlton' (2Y-Y): tall; perianth clear yellow, cup lighter. 'Ceylon' (2Y-O): perianth yellow, cup orange turning brilliant red. 'Charter' (2Y-W): tall; perianth lemon, cup yellow turning white. 'Dailmanach' (2W-P): fls large, perianth white, cup long, apricot pink. 'Daydream' (2Y-W): perianth pale yellow, cup white with cream edge. 'Desdemona' (2W-W): fls purest white, stamens pink. 'Falstaff' (2Y-R): perianth metallic gold, cup deep orange-red. 'Fortune' (2Y-O): tall, to 45cm; perianth bright yellow, cup long, vivid red-orange. 'Golden Aura' (2Y-Y): fls large, brilliant yellow. 'Ice Follies' (2W-W): perianth soft white, cup wide and crinkled, pale primrose fading to white. 'Passionale' (2W-P): tall, to 40cm; perianth snow white, cup soft pink. 'Professor Einstein' (2W-R): perianth white, cup flat and frilled, brilliant orange. 'Red Hill' (2W-R): perianth white, flushed yellow at centre, cup orange-red. 'Salome' (2W-PPY): perianth white, cup long, deep pink finely edged yellow. 'Satin Pink' (2W-P): perianth white, cup pale creamy pink. 'Silver Standard' (2W-Y): perianth white, cup crinkled, creamy yellow fading with age. 'Stainless' (2W-W): fls delicate, pure white. 'Vulcan' (2Y-O): perianth yellow, cup deep scarlet.

Division 3. *Small-cupped daffodils of garden origin.* One flower to a stem; corona ('cup') not more than one-third the length of the perianth segments ('petals'). 'Amor' (3W-YYO): perianth white, cup wide, primrose shading to orange at rim. 'Audubon' (3W-WWP): perianth white, cup cream with coral pink band. 'Barrett Browning' (3W-O): perianth rounded, white with a flush of lemon at centre. 'Birma' (3Y-O): perianth golden yellow, cup deep orange. 'Doctor Hugh' (3W-GOO): perianth white, cup orange with a green hue at base. 'Edward Buxton' (3Y-OOR): perianth white, cup orange. 'Gold Frills' (3W-WWY): perianth white, cup open and crinkle-edged, white with fine yellow rim. 'Lollipop' (3W-Y): tall; perianth, rounded, white, cup frilled, pale lemon. 'Lovable' (3W-W): fls pure white, cup neat.

Division 4. *Double daffodils of garden origin.* One or more flowers to a stem, with doubling of the perianth segments or the corona or both. 'Acropolis' (4W-R): tall; white with occasional orange-red segments. 'Cheerfulness' (4W-Y): creamy white, centre segments yellow, fragrant. 'Dick Wilden' (4Y-Y): tall; yellow, centre segments darker, early-flowering. 'Double Event' (4W-Y): fls rounded, pure white with yellow segments interspersed in centre. 'Erlicheer' (4W-Y): white with centre segments yellow, long-lasting. 'Eystettensis' (4Y-Y): to 20cm; double, segments regularly arranged, pale yellow; corona absent. 'Pencrebar' (4Y-Y): dwarf to 20cm; camellia-form, yellow. 'Petit Four' (4Y-PPY): tall; perianth pale cream, centre segments soft pink-apricot. 'Rip van Winkle' (4Y-Y): dwarf to 12cm; sunny yellow. 'Swansdown' (4W-W): perianth white, cup full of delicate white segments. 'Tahiti' (4Y-O): tall; perianth golden, centre segments brilliant red-orange. 'Unique' (4W-Y): perianth white, centre segments wavy, yellow. 'White Lion' (2W-Y): white petals interspersed with buff to yellow segments.

Division 5. *Triandrus daffodils of garden origin.* Characteristics of *N. triandrus* clearly evident: usually two or more pendent flowers to a stem; perianth segments reflexed. 'April Tears' (5Y-Y): fls yellow, cup lighter coloured. 'Arish Mell' (5W-W): tall; fls pure white. 'Hawera' (5Y-Y): to 7 fls per stem; fls bright yellow. 'Ice Wings' (5W-W): fls snow white, trumpet long. 'Liberty Bells' (5Y-Y): tall; to 3 fls per stem; fls rich lemon. 'Thalia' (5W-W): tall, to 40cm; 3 or more fls per stem; fls pure white. 'Tuesday's Child' (5W-Y): to 3 fls per stem; perianth white, cup sulphur.

Division 6. *Cyclamineus daffodils of garden origin.* Characteristics of *N. cyclamineus* clearly evident: usually one flower to a stem; perianth segments reflexed; flower at an acute angle to the stem, with a very short pedicel ('neck'). 'Beryl' (6W-YYO): perianth primrose, cup orange. 'Charity May' (6Y-Y): fls vivid pure yellow, long-lasting. 'Dove Wings' (6W-Y): perianth clear creamy yellow ageing to white, cup yellow. 'February Gold' (6Y-Y): perianth clear yellow, cup deeper yellow, profuse. 'February Silver' (6W-W): perianth white, cup creamy white. 'Foundling' (6W-P): perianth recurved, white, cup deep rose. 'Jack Snipe' (6W-Y): perianth creamy white, cup yellow. 'Jenny' (6W-W): perianth white, cup narrow, pale yellow, becoming white. 'Jetfire' (6Y-R): perianth yellow, cup red and deepening with age. 'Jumblie' (6Y-O): to 3 fls per stem; perianth yellow, cup yellow-orange. 'Peeping Tom' (6Y-Y): perianth deep yellow, cup yellow. 'Tête-à-Tête' (6Y-Y): dwarf, to 20cm, multi-headed; fls bright yellow.

Division 7. *Jonquilla daffodils of garden origin.* Characteristics of the *N. jonquilla* group clearly evident: usually 1–3 flowers to a rounded stem; leaves narrow, dark green; perianth segments spreading not reflexed; flowers fragrant. 'Baby Moon' (7Y-Y): fls rich yellow. 'Bellsong' (7W-P): perianth opening blush pink fading to ivory, cup bright pink. 'Bobbysoxer' (7Y-YYO): perianth yellow, cup yellow with orange rim. 'Lintie' (7Y-O): perianth yellow, cup dark orange. 'Pipit' (7Y-W): perianth pale lemon, cup fading to white. 'Pueblo' (7W-W): fls white. 'Sugarbush' (7W-YYW): perianth white, cup yellow and white. 'Suzy' (7Y-O): to 4 fls per stem; perianth yellow, cup intense orange. 'Sweetness' (7Y-Y): fls rich gold, petals pointed. 'Trevithian' (7Y-Y): to 3 fls per stem; fls lemon.

Division 8. *Tazetta daffodils of garden origin.* Characteristics of the *N. tazetta* group clearly evident: usually 3–20 flowers to a stout stem; leaves broad; perianth segments spreading not reflexed; flowers fragrant. 'Avalanche' (8W-Y): to 15 fls per stem; fls white, cup soft yellow. 'Chinita' (8Y-YYR): perianth rounded, primrose, cup shallow, yellow with wide red rim. 'Cragford' (8W-R): perianth white, cup vibrant orange. 'Geranium' (8W-O): perianth soft white, cup rich orange, scented. 'Grand Soleil d'Or' (8Y-O): to 5 fls per stem; perianth gold, cup orange, strongly scented. 'Minnow' (8Y-Y): to 20cm high; to 5 fls per stem; perianth creamy yellow, cup flat, pure yellow. 'Paper White' (8W-W): to 5 fls per stem; fls pure white. 'Scarlet Gem' (8Y-O): perianth yellow, cups rich red-orange. 'Silver Chimes' (8W-W): perianth white, cup white with a strong cream flush from the base.

Division 9. *Poeticus daffodils of garden origin.* Characteristics of the *N. poeticus* group without admixture of any other: usually one flower to a stem; perianth segments pure white; corona usually disc-shaped, with a green or yellow centre and a red rim; flowers fragrant. 'Actaea' (9W-GWO): fls large, perianth wide, white, cup canary yellow edged in red, flush of green at base. 'Cantabile' (9W-GGR): perianth white, cup green with fine red rim. 'Felindre' (9W-GYR): perianth white, cup green and yellow, edged red.

Division 10. *Species, wild variants and wild hybrids.* All species and wild or reputedly wild variants and hybrids, including those with double flowers. Species and natural varieties.

Division 11. *Split-corona daffodils of garden origin.* Corona split rather than lobed and usually for more than half its length. 'Baccarat' (11Y-Y): fls rich lemon yellow, corona darker. 'Broadway Star' (11W-W): fls white, cream streaked orange and yellow. 'Canasta' (11W-Y): perianth white, corona very large, rich yellow. 'Cassata' (11W-W): perianth white, corona white with hint of lemon. 'Orangery' (11W-OOY): perianth cream-white, corona orange with yellow rim. 'Pearlax' (11W-P): perianth white, corona apricot-pink. 'Valdrone' (11W-Y): perianth white, corona lemon.

Division 12. *Miscellaneous daffodils.* All daffodils not falling into any one of the above divisions. 'Nylon' (12W-W): fls creamy white. 'Tarlatan' (12W-W): fls soft white.

PESTS AND DISEASES. Most narcissus pests are common to both Europe and North America. These include bulb flies (*Merodon equestris* and *Eumerus* spp.), the stem eelworm (*Ditylenchus dipsaci*), the root lesion eelworm (*Pratylenchus* spp.), the bulb mite (*Rhizoglyphus* spp.), the bulb scale mite (*Steneotarsonemus laticeps,* a tarsonemid mite), slugs and millepedes. In some areas, particularly those in the vicinity of oil seed rape crops, narcissus blooms may become invaded by pollen beetles. Bulbs may be eaten by mice in the field and during storage where they may also become infested with the tulip bulb aphid (*Dysaphis tulipae*).

A basal rot, caused by the fungus *Fusarium oxysporum* f. sp. *narcissi*, is the most important disease of narcissi in Britain. During the growing season the fungus enters the bulbs through the roots or root plate and there may be some yellowing of the leaf tips. The main problem occurs during storage: a chocolate-brown soft rot spreads up through the scales from the base and a mass of pink spores may be produced on the basal plate. In leaf scorch, caused by the fungus *Stagonospora curtisii*, there appears a red-brown leaf tip necrosis as well as brown spots elsewhere on the leaf and on the spathes, flower stalks and flowers. Most of the infection takes place as the shoot passes through the neck of the bulb because the fungus survives in the bulb scales.

Narcissus smoulder disease, caused by the fungus *Sclerotinia narcissicola* (conidial state *Botrytis narcissicola*), also causes brown spots on the leaves and flowers. In wet conditions a grey mould growth appears on the spots and produces conidia which spread the disease further. It is small black sclerotia between the bulb scales and in the soil which cause the primary infection as the shoots emerge. Narcissus fire is caused by the fungus *Sclerotinia polyblastis* (conidial state *Botrytis polyblastis*) which overwinters as sclerotia on plant debris. The flowers are disfigured and eventually destroyed by small brown spots, while elongated red-brown blotches later form on the leaves to result in the 'fire' phase of the disease. As with smoulder disease, conidia produced on the dead tissue continue to cause secondary infections during the growing season.

Narcissus white mould (*Ramularia vallisumbrosae*) causes sunken, grey or yellowed spots and streaks on the leaves, which become covered with powdery masses of white spores. These spores spread the disease during the growing season and the fungus overwinters by producing small, black sclerotia in the infected tissue.

Narcissi can be affected by grey bulb rot caused by *Rhizoctonia tuliparum*, which is mainly known as a serious disease of tulips. This is a dry rot which progresses from the neck of the bulb downwards and the shoots are unlikely to emerge at all. As in so many of these diseases the fungus persists in the soil as sclerotia.

Most of the diseases can be controlled to some extent during the growing season by removing heavily infected leaf tissue and spraying with dithiocarbonate or other fungicides. But selection of healthy bulbs, routine dormant bulb treatment (dips in systemic fungicides or in hot water (44.4°C/112°F for three hours) plus formalin (0.2% commercial formaldehyde), careful handling and proper storage conditions are the main control measures. Narcissi can also be affected by blue mould (*Penicillium* spp.) and white root rot (*Rosellinia necatrix*), as well as several virus diseases, including those caused by narcissus degeneration virus, narcissus latent virus, narcissus mosaic virus, narcissus tip necrosis virus, narcissus yellow stripe virus, arabis mosaic virus and cucumber mosaic virus. Some of the viruses are transmitted by aphids, some by eelworms and some by contact. The gardener should obtain virus-free stocks and discard any obviously affected plants.

***N. assoanus*** Dufour. RUSH-LEAVED JONQUIL. Bulb to 3cm, subglobose, dark. Lvs to 20×0.2cm, cylindric, slightly striate on outer surface, spreading or prostrate, green. Scape 7–25cm, terete, smooth; pedicels 1.5–2cm, included in spathe; fls 2–3, to 2.2cm diam., horizontal or slightly ascending, yellow, fragrant; perianth tube 1.2–1.8cm, straight; seg. obovate, 0.7–1×0.7cm patent, incurved, imbricate at base; corona cup-shaped conic, 0.5×1.1–1.7cm, crenate, deeper yellow than seg. S France, S & E Spain. Z7.

***N. asturiensis*** (Jordan) Pugsley. Bulb to 2cm, globose, pale. Lvs 8×0.6cm, glaucous-green, spreading, channelled. Scape 7–14cm, not erect, nearly terete, striate, solid; fl. solitary, to 3.5cm across, usually drooping, soft yellow; spathe to 2.8cm, remaining green; pedicel to 10mm; perianth tube to 8mm, green-yellow; seg. to 1.4×0.4cm, usually twisted, deflexed; corona 1.7cm, widened below, constricted at middle, mouth spreading, fimbriate. N Portugal, NW & NC Spain. 'Giant': larger in all parts, to 20cm. Z4.

***N. bicolor*** L. Bulb to 3cm with short neck, pale. Lvs 30–35×1.1–1.6cm, green or glaucous, erect, flat. Scape 35cm, compressed, sharply 2-edged; fl. solitary, horizontal or ascending; spathe to 54cm, scarious; pedicel 2–2.5cm; perianth tube 1cm, green- to orange-yellow, broad; seg. 3.5–4cm, cream or pale sulphur-yellow, spreading or deflexed, imbricate, not twisted; corona to 4cm, yellow, almost parallel, 1.5–2cm diam., mouth with little or no flange, lobed or dentate. Pyrenees and Corbières. Z6.

***N. broussonetii*** Lagasca. Bulb to 4cm, neck long, brown. Lvs 4, 28×0.9cm, glaucous, erect, lightly striate but keel absent. Scape to 40cm, compressed, lightly striate; fls 1–8, ascending, white, to 3.5cm diam., fragrant; pedicel 1cm; perianth tube to 2.8cm, funnel-shaped, white; seg. 1.6×1.2cm, patent or incurving, slightly imbricate; corona rudimentary; stamens exserted, bright yellow. Autumn. Morocco. Z8.

***N. bulbocodium*** L. HOOP PETTICOAT DAFFODIL; PETTICOAT DAFFODIL. Centre of an extremely variable complex in which many minor variants have received unwarranted taxonomic distinction, although some are horticulturally valuable. *N. cantabricus* and *N. romieuxii* are closely related. ssp. ***bulbocodium.*** Bulb to 2×1.5cm, globose, pale to dark. Lvs 10–30(–40)cm×1–5mm, semi-cylindric, erect, ascending or prostrate, dark green. Scape 2.5–20cm, terete, faintly striate; fl. solitary, horizontal, pale yellow to deep golden-yellow, often green-tinged, to 4.5cm diam.; spathe to 3.5cm; pedicel 2.5–20mm, or absent; perianth tube 6–25mm, yellow, often tinged green, especially below; seg. much shorter than corona, 0.6–2cm×0.5–5mm, often tinged green; corona funnel-shaped, 0.9–3.2×0.7–3.4cm, yellow, margin of mouth spreading or incurved, entire to dentate or crenate; anth. included in corona or slightly exserted; style and filaments usually concolorous with corona, style sometimes long-exserted. W

**Narcissus** (×1) (a) *N. papyraceus* (b) *N. poeticus* (c) *N. cyclamineus* (d) *N. pseudonarcissus* (e) *N. bicolor* (f) *N. pseudonarcissus* ssp. *nobilis* (g) *N. pseudonarcissus* ssp. *moschatus* (h) *N. asturiensis* (i) *N. viridiflorus*

France, Spain, Portugal, N Africa (usually on acidic soil in habitat). var. ***bulbocodium*** including *N. bulbocodium* 'Tenuifolius'. Plants usually dwarf; bulb dark. Lvs 2–3, prostrate or spreading. Fls golden-yellow; pedicel 0.4–2cm, perianth to 3cm long. Range of ssp. var. ***conspicuus*** (Haw.) Bak. Plant robust. Lvs erect. Fls dark yellow to citron, 3–3.5cm long, corona 2cm diam. Includes var. *citrinus* hort., loosely applied to large-flowered pale yellow plants, but not var. *citrinus* Bak. ssp. ***obesus*** (Salisb.) Maire. Bulb globose, dark. Lvs to 30×0.2cm, more or less prostrate, sinuous, channelled on inner surface, lightly striate on outer. Scape 10cm, terete, smooth; pedicel 7mm; fl. to 3.5cm diam., horizontal or ascending, bright yellow; perianth tube to 2.5cm, conic, yellow; seg. 1.4×0.5cm, patent, twisted; corona to 1.8×2cm, mouth crenate or slightly incurved, deeper yellow than seg.; anth. biseriate, upper 3 in corona. WC Portugal. Z6.

***N. cantabricus*** DC. WHITE HOOP PETTICOAT DAFFODIL. ssp. ***cantabricus.*** Bulb to 2.5×2cm, globose, dark. Lvs 2, or 4–5 in var. *foliosus* (Maire) Fernandes, ascending or spreading, to 15cm×1mm, semicylindrical, slightly channelled and faintly or not striate. Scape 5–10cm, terete; fl. solitary, ascending, to 40mm diam., pure- or milk-white, fragrant; pedicel absent or 5–17mm; perianth tube to 2.4×1.2cm, funnel-shaped, white, green below; seg. 1.2×0.5cm, white, nearly patent; corona to 1.5×4cm, entire or crenate or undulate; anth. included, yellow, style and filaments white, style exserted. S Spain, N Africa (Morocco, Algeria). var. ***petunioides*** Fernandes. Scape 6cm; fls pure white, horizontal; corona nearly flat, 3–4cm diam., deeply crenate, margin recurved. Algeria. ssp. ***monophyllus*** (Dur.) Fernandes. Differing from ssp. *cantabricus* in lf solitary, 27cm×1mm. Scape 3–8cm; pedicel absent; fl. horizontal or ascending, to 4.5cm diam. S Spain, N Africa. Z8.

***N. cyclamineus*** DC. Bulb to 15mm, globose, pale. Lvs 12(–30)cm×4–6mm, bright green, spreading, keeled. Scape to 20cm, terete, smooth; fl. solitary, drooping or pendent, deep yellow; spathe green, becoming scarious; pedicel 10mm; perianth tube 2–3mm, green; seg. sharply reflexed, obscuring ovary 2×0.4cm, twisted or not twisted; corona 2cm, slightly constricted just below flared margin, 12-lobed or fimbriate. NW Portugal, NW Spain. Z6.

***N. dubius*** Gouan. Bulb to 3cm with distinct neck, dark. Lvs 50cm×7mm at flowering, spreading, dark green, inner face flat, outer striate. Scape 15–25cm+, elliptic; fls 2–6, ascending, 16mm diam., white; spathe to 4cm; pedicel 4.5cm; perianth tube 1.6×0.2cm, green, white at distal end; seg. 7×6mm, apiculate, patent, slightly imbricate; corona 4×7mm, cup-shaped, crenate; anth. biseriate. S France, SE Spain. Z7.

***N. elegans*** (Haw.) Spach. Bulb to 3.5×3cm, globose, dark. Lvs 12–25cm×3–5mm, erect, glaucous, striate on outer surface, apex hooded. Scape 20cm+, compressed, striate, scabrid; fls 2–7, horizontal, 2.5–3.5cm diam., fragrant; spathe 4cm, scarious; pedicels unequal, to 5cm; perianth tube 1.6×0.2cm, green; seg. 1.5×0.3–0.7cm, white, patent, becoming twisted with age, slightly imbricate; corona 1×2mm, green, becoming dull orange; anth. biseriate. Autumn. W & S Italy, Sicily, Corsica, Sardinia, N Africa (Morocco to Libya). Z8.

***N. fernandesii*** Pedro. Close to *N. wilkommii* and *N. gaditanus*. Bulb small, globose, dark. Lvs 33cm×3mm, green, erect to spreading or prostrate, finely striate, channelled at base. Scape 17cm, terete, finely striate; fls 1–5, ascending, 2.8cm diam., yellow; pedicel 2–4cm, exceeding spathe; tube 2×0.3cm, sometimes slightly curved, green except for distal end; seg. 1.2×0.7cm, apiculate, patent but reflexed at base, imbricate at base; corona 6×8mm, slightly deeper yellow than seg., parallel sided above, crenate; anth. biseriate. C Portugal, SW Spain. Z8.

***N. gaditanus*** Boiss. & Reut. Bulb small to medium-sized, globose, dark. Lvs 20cm×2mm, ascending or prostrate, dark green, tip rounded, channelled at base, outer surface striate. Scape 9–14cm, terete, finely striate; fls 1–3, ascending, 1.4–1.6cm, diam.; pedicel 1.5cm; perianth tube 1.5×0.3cm, green or yellow, straight or slightly curved; seg. 5×4mm, apiculate, yellow, reflexed, slightly imbricate at base; corona 3–5×6–7mm, yellow, cup-shaped, entire; anth. biseriate. S Portugal, S Spain. Z8.

***N. hedraeanthus*** (Webb & Heldr.) Colmeiro. Bulb to 1.5×1cm, globose, dark. Lvs 2 or more, to 6×0.1–0.15cm, erect to spreading, dark green. Scape shorter than lvs, curved or ascending; fl. solitary, horizontal or ascending, pale yellow, 2.4cm diam.; spathe dark brown; pedicel absent; perianth tube 1.4×0.5cm, pale yellow, base green; seg. 1.2×0.2cm, patent or spreading, not twisted; corona 0.7×1cm, margin often slightly expended, crenate; anth. exserted; style and filaments concolorous with corona, style long exserted. S Spain. Z8.

***N. humilis*** (Cav.) Traub. Bulb to 1.5cm, globose, dark. Lvs to 20×0.1cm, solitary or occasionally 2, usually not produced by flowering bulbs, erect, channelled at base. Scape 7–20cm, slender; pedicel 0.6–1.6cm; fl. solitary, 2.5cm diam., ascending, yellow; perianth tube absent; seg. 1–1.8×0.2–0.3cm; corona absent; fil. spreading, anth. uniseriate. Autumn. S Spain, Algeria, Morocco. Z8.

***N. ×incomparabilis*** Mill. (*N. poeticus* × *N. pseudonarcissus.*) Bulb to 3cm(+)cm. Lvs to 35×1.2cm, glaucous, linear, flat. Scape to 45cm, compressed; spathe to 3.5cm; fl. solitary, to 8cm diam.; perianth tube to 2.5cm, narrowly obconic, widening to throat; seg. narrow-obovate, 2.5–3×1.2–1.6cm, patent, pale yellow; corona to 2.2×2cm, deep orange-yellow, margin undulate, lobulate. Wild in S & SC France, also of garden origin and widely naturalized. Z4.

***N. ×intermedius*** Lois. (*N. jonquilla* × *N. tazetta.*) Lvs 4, subcylindric, to 45×0.8cm, deeply channelled, bright green. Scape to 40cm, subterete; spathe to 4cm, scarious; pedicels to 4cm; fls 3–6, to 3.5cm diam., fragrant; perianth tube to 2cm, tinged green; seg. ovate, to 1.4cm, imbricate, bright lemon-yellow; corona 4mm high, orange yellow. W Mediterranean. Z8.

***N. jonquilla*** L. JONQUIL. Bulb to 3×2.5cm, globose, dark, with short neck. Lvs 2–4, erect to spreading, to 40–45×0.8cm, channelled at base, cylindric towards apex, striate, green. Scape to 40cm, terete or subterete, finely striate; spathe to 5cm, scarious; pedicels 4.5–9cm; fls 1–6, to 3cm diam., ascending; perianth tube to 3cm, slightly curved, pale green , seg. elliptic, to 1.3cm, apiculate, patent, imbricate, yellow; corona cup-shaped, 7–10×2–4mm, yellow, margin shallowly lobed or somewhat crenate. S & C Spain, S & E Portugal, naturalized elsewhere. var. ***henriquesii*** Fernandes. Lvs to 25×0.3cm. Scape to 21cm; pedicel to 3.5cm; fls 1–2, to 3.8cm diam., horizontal; perianth tube to 1.8cm, straight; seg. to 1.7cm, patent, not imbricate, margins curving inwards; corona cup-shaped, parallel-sided near margin, to 0.6×1cm, 6-lobed. C Portugal. Z4.

***N. longispathus*** Pugsley. Bulb to 3cm, dark, with neck. Lvs 20–40(–60)×1cm, erect, striate, glaucous. Scape 10–45(–175)cm, compressed, striate; spathe to 10cm, green; pedicel 5cm; fls 1–3, 4–9cm diam., ascending; perianth tube 1.5cm, green; seg. 2–3cm, patent, sometimes twisted, slightly imbricate, yellow; corona subcylindric, margin expanded, crenate, yellow. SE Spain. Z8.

***N. ×medioluteus*** Mill. (*N. poeticus* × *N. tazetta.*) PRIMROSE PEERLESS. Bulb to 6×4.5cm. Lvs to 70×1cm, glaucous, flat. Scape to 60cm, compressed; pedicels to 3.5cm; fls 2, occasionally 1 or 3, 3–5cm diam., fragrant; perianth tube to 2.5cm, cylindric, broader at throat; seg. broad-obovate to 2.2cm, white; corona to 5×12mm, bright yellow, margin crenate, white-scarious. S France, naturalized elsewhere. Z7.

***N. minor*** L. Bulb to 3cm, globose, pale brown, with neck. Lvs 3–4, erect, 8–15×0.4–1cm, sage-green or glaucous, flat or channelled. Scape 14–20cm, terete; spathe to 4cm, scarious; pedicels 7–12mm; fl. solitary, to 3.7cm diam., horizontal or ascending; perianth tube 1–1.8cm, yellow or green-yellow; seg. ovate-lanceolate, 1.5–2.2cm, somewhat twisted, drooping, yellow, often with deeper median streak; corona 1.7×2.5cm, plicate, dilated at mouth, margin frilled. Pyrenees, N Spain. Z4.

***N. ×odorus*** L. CAMPERNELLE JONQUIL. (*N. jonquilla* × *N. pseudonarcissus.*) Bulb to 3cm. Lvs to 50×0.8cm, strongly keeled, bright green. Scape to 40cm, terete or nearly so; spathe to 7cm, scarious; pedicels to 3cm; fls 1–4, ascending, bright yellow, very fragrant, perianth tube to 2cm; seg. to 2.5×1.3cm; corona to 1.8×2cm, regularly lobed to subentire. Garden origin; naturalized S Europe. 'Rugulosus': selected cv, larger than the type. 'Plenus': fls double, regular to form. Z6.

***N. pachybolbus*** Durieu. Bulbs 10×5–7cm, globose, dark. Lvs 7, to 50×3.8cm, flat or slightly twisted, finely striate on both surfaces, pale green. Scapes to 7 per bulb, 30(–50)cm, compressed; pedicels to 4cm; fls 3–17, to 1.8cm diam., white; perianth tube 1.4cm; seg. ovate-oblong, 7mm, obtuse, imbricate; corona 2–3mm high, entire. Morocco, Algeria. Z9.

***N. papyraceus*** Ker-Gawl. PAPER-WHITE NARCISSUS. Bulb to 5×3.5cm, globose, dark. Lvs to 30×1.7cm, erect, keeled, glaucous. Scape to 40cm+, sharply keeled, striate; spathe to 5cm, scarious; pedicels 4cm; fls 2–20, 2.5–4cm, diam., ascending, fragrant; perianth tube 15×3mm, green below, white above, seg. white, to 1.8cm, ovate, apiculate, imbricate; corona cup-shaped, 3–6×8–11mm, entire or slightly notched, white. Winter–spring. ssp. ***polyanthus*** (Lois.) Asch. & Gräbn. Lvs green, to 25×1.5–2cm. Scape subterete; pedicels to 4.5cm; fls 3–12(–20), 2.5–4cm diam., horizontal; corona entire, pale sulphur-yellow when young, becoming white. W Mediterranean. ssp. ***panizzianus*** (Parl.) Arcang. Lvs to 55×1cm, erect, glaucous. Scape to 28cm, compressed; pedicels 3cm; fls 2–8, 2–2.5cm diam. SE France, SW Spain, Portugal. Z8.

***N. poeticus*** L. POET'S NARCISSUS; PHEASANT'S-EYE NARCISSUS. Bulb to 4×3.5cm, pale, with long neck. Lvs 4, to 45×0.6–1cm, erect, channelled, green or somewhat glaucous. Scape 35–50cm, compressed, striate; spathe to 5cm, scarious; pedicel 2.5cm; fl. solitary, 4.5–7cm diam., horizontal to ascending, fragrant; perianth tube cylindric, 2.5×0.4cm, green; seg. suborbicular to cuneate, to 3×2.2cm, more or less patent, imbricate, white, yellow at base externally; corona flat and discoid, to 2.5×14mm, yellow with red frilled margin; anth. biseriate, upper 3 exserted. Capsule broadly ellipsoid. Late spring. France to Greece. var. ***recurvus*** (Haw.) Fernandes PHEASANT'S EYE NARCISSUS. Perianth seg. strongly reflexed, pure white; corona discoid, with throat green, margin red. Capsule spherical. Late spring. var. ***hellenicus*** (Pugsley) Fernandes. Lvs 50×1cm, erect, pale green. Scape to 50cm; fl. 4.5cm diam., somewhat ascending; seg. rounded, becoming reflexed; corona 3mm high, yellow, throat green, margin scarlet. Greece. ssp. ***radiiflorus*** (Salisb.) Bak. Lvs 5–8mm wide. Perianth seg. to 3cm, narrow, green-white, unguiculate, scarcely imbricate; corona to 2.5×10mm, shortly cylindric, sometimes wholly red (var. *poetarum* Burb. & Bak.); stamens all partially exserted. S & C Europe, W Balkans. Z4.

***N. pseudonarcissus*** L. WILD DAFFODIL; LENT LILY; TRUMPET NARCISSUS. Bulb 2–5cm, pale brown, with neck. Lvs 8–50×0.5–1.5cm, erect, ligulate, usually glaucous. Scape 12–50(–90)cm, erect, 2-edged, striate; spathe to 6cm, scarious; pedicel 2–20mm; fl. usually solitary, occasionally 2–4, horizontal to drooping, sometimes ascending, concolorous or bicoloured, fragrant; perianth tube 1.5–2.5cm; seg. 1.8–4cm, patent to erect-patent, sometimes twisted, white to

**Narcissus** (×1) (a) *N. requienii* (b) *N. bulbocodium* (c) *N. cantabricus* (d) *N. jonquilla* (e) *N. hedraeanthus* (f) *N. romieuxii* (g) *N. triandrus* (h) *N. rupicola* (i) *N. rupicola* ssp. *watieri*

deep yellow; corona 1.5–4.5cm, white to deep yellow; margin subentire to 6-lobed. W Europe to N England. A very variable species presented considerable taxonomic difficulties that are compounded by the presence in cultivation of numerous selected variants of poorly understood provenance, and by the occurrence of naturalized populations. Until this situation is better understood it seems best to treat distinct regional populations as subspecies. ssp. ***pseudonarcissus.*** Lvs 12–35×0.6–1.2cm, erect, glaucous. Scape 20–35cm; pedicel 3–12mm; fl. solitary, horizontal or drooping, to 6.5cm diam.; perianth tube 1.5–2.2cm, yellow, usually tinged green; seg. 2–3.5cm, twisted, deflexed, slightly imbricate, white to sulphur yellow, usually darker than seg. W Europe except Portugal & S Spain. ssp. ***major*** (Curtis) Bak. Lvs 20–50×0.5–1.5cm, erect, twisted, glaucous blue. Scape to 50cm; pedicels 0.8–3cm; fl. solitary, to 9.5cm diam., concolorous, deep yellow; perianth tube 1.8cm, green-yellow; seg. 1.8–4cm, twisted, inner deflexed, outer reflexed; corona 2–4cm, margin expanded. Spain, Portugal, S France, naturalized elsewhere. ssp. ***moschatus*** (L.) Bak. Lvs 10–40×0.5–1.2cm, erect, glaucous. Scape 15–35cm; pedicel 1–2.5cm; fl. solitary, 5–6cm diam., horizontal or drooping, usually uniform sulphur-white; perianth tube 8–15mm, green; seg. 2–3.5cm twisted; corona 3–4cm, slightly flanged at margin. Pyrenees. ssp. ***nevadensis*** (Pugsley) Fernandes. Lvs 12–30×0.5–1cm, erect, glaucous. Scape to 30cm, somewhat compressed; pedicel 2–3.5cm; fls 1–4, 5cm diam., ascending; perianth tube 1.5cm, green-yellow; seg. 1–2×1cm, deflexed, not twisted, slightly imbricate, white with yellow central streak; corona 1.5–2.5cm, subcylindric, margin slightly expanded, yellow. S Spain (Sierra Nevada). ssp. ***nobilis*** (Haw.) Fernandes. Lvs 15–50×0.8–1.5cm, glaucous. Scape 15–30cm, somewhat compressed, striate; pedicel 8–15mm; fl. solitary, horizontal or ascending, 8–12cm diam.; perianth tube to 2.5cm, bright yellow; seg. 3–4cm, more or less patent, twisted, imbricate, white with yellow mark at base on reverse; corona 3–4cm, margin expanded, deeply dentate. N Portugal, NW & NC Spain. ssp. ***obvallaris*** (Salisb.) Fernandes. TENBY DAFFODIL. Lvs 30×0.6cm, erect, glaucous. Scape 20cm; pedicel 2mm; fl. solitary, 4cm diam., horizontal; perianth tube 1cm, yellow with green stripes; seg. to 3cm, nearly patent, slightly twisted, yellow; corona to 3.5cm, margin dilated, 6-lobed, sometimes reflexed. S Wales but true origin unknown; similar plants recorded from C Spain. ssp. ***pallidiflorus*** (Pugsley) Fernandes. Lvs 15–40×0.5–1.2cm, erect, slightly glaucous. Scape 30cm; pedicel 2mm; fl. solitary, horizontal or drooping, 7.5cm diam.; perianth tube 2.5cm, green, with yellow streaks; seg. 3–4cm, twisted, slightly imbricate, pale yellow with darker median streaks; corona 3–4cm, margin expanded, recurved, pale yellow, slightly deeper than seg. Pyrenees, Cordillera Cantabrica. ssp. ***portensis*** (Pugsley) Fernandes. Lvs 8–12×0.5–0.7cm, suberect, nearly flat, glaucous. Scape 12–20cm, compressed, 2-edged; pedicel 0.5–1.5cm; fl. solitary, drooping, horizontal or ascending, concolorous, deep yellow; perianth tube to 2.2cm, green; seg. 2–3cm, narrow, deflexed, median veins green; corona obconic, 2.5–3.5cm, margin 6-lobed or crenulate, but not expanded. N Portugal, NW & C Spain. Z4.

***N. romieuxii*** Braun-Blanquet & Maire. ssp. ***romieuxii.*** Bulb 1cm, globose, dark. Lvs to 20×0.1cm, erect or spreading, dark green, weakly striate. Scape 10–20cm, terete; spathe scarious, usually brown; pedicel absent; fl. solitary, 2.5–4cm diam., horizontal or ascending, pale to medium yellow; perianth tube to 2.5cm, green at base, yellow above; seg. to 1.3×0.4cm, nearly patent; corona 1.5×3cm, margin 6-lobed and crenate; anth. exserted, exceeded by style, pollen bright yellow, fil. and style yellow. N Africa. var. ***mesatlanticus*** Maire. Indistinguishable from ssp. *romieuxii*; the plant in commerce under this name has pale yellow flowers. 'Julia Jane': Selected form with wide corona, resembling *N. cantabricus* ssp. *cantabricus* var. *petunioides*, but fl. pale yellow. ssp. ***albidus*** (Emberger & Maire) Fernandes. Bulb globose, dark. Lvs to 22cm, subterete with shallow channel, erect, green. Scape to 9cm, terete; pedicel 4mm; fl. solitary, to 3cm diam., ascending; perianth tube 1.7cm, green at base, white above; seg. 9×3mm, patent, white; corona 0.9×2cm, margin crenate, white; stamens widely separated, slightly exceeded by style, fil. and style white. Algeria. Z7.

***N. rupicola*** Dufour. ssp. ***rupicola.*** Bulb to 2.5cm, globose, pale. Lvs 18×0.3cm, erect, 2-keeled, glaucous. Scape 14–23cm, terete, striate; pedicel absent or very short; fl. solitary, to 3cm diam., ascending; perianth tube 2.2cm, green or green-yellow; seg. to 1.5×1.1cm, patent, imbricate, apiculate, yellow; corona 3–5×6–18mm, conic or reflexed, deeply 6-lobed to crenate or subentire, yellow; anth. and style included in tube. Spain, Portugal. ssp. ***watieri*** (Maire) Maire & Weiller. Fls white; pedicel 2mm. Morocco (High Atlas). Z8.

***N. scaberulus*** Henriq. Bulb to 2.2×1.8cm, globose, pale. Lvs 7–30×0.2cm, erect or prostrate and sinuous, 2-keeled, margin often scabrid, glaucous. Scape 5–25cm, terete, striate; pedicel to 2.5cm; fls 1–5, 1.8cm diam., ascending; perianth tube to 1.4cm, green; seg. to 7×5mm, apiculate, patent or slightly reflexed, slightly imbricate, deep orange-yellow; corona cup-shaped, 5×7mm, margin often incurved minutely crenulate or entire, deep yellow; anth. biseriate. NC Portugal. Z8.

***N. serotinus*** L. Bulb 1.5–2cm, globose, dark. Lvs 1–2, 10–20×0.1–0.5cm, erect or spreading, dark green, sometimes with longitudinal white stripes, absent from bulbs that have flowered. Scape 13–30cm, terete, finely striate; spathe 1.5–3.5cm, tubular below, hyaline; pedicel 7–2cm; fls solitary or occasionally 2–3, to 3.4cm diam., ascending, fragrant; perianth tube to 2cm, dark green; seg. oblong-lanceolate, to 1.6×0.7cm, patent or sometimes recurved, twisted, white; corona minute, to 1.5×4mm, 6-lobed, dark yellow to orange. Autumn. Mediterranean. Z8.

***N. tazetta*** L. BUNCH-FLOWERED NARCISSI; POLYANTHUS NARCISSI. Extremely variable and many variants have been named; as with *N. pseudonarcissus* the situation is confused by horticultural selection and naturalization. ssp. ***tazetta.*** Bulb to 5×3.5cm, globose, dark. Lvs 20–50×0.5–2.5cm, erect, twisted, keeled, glaucous. Scape 20–45cm, stout, slightly compressed; spathe to 5cm, scarious; pedicels unequal, 2.5–7.5cm; fls 1–15, 4cm diam., horizontal, fragrant; perianth tube cylindric, 2cm, pale green; seg. broad-ovate, 0.8–2.2cm, patent, incurving, white; corona cup-shaped, 0.5×1cm, bright to deep yellow; stamens biseriate, upper 3 included in corona. S Portugal, Mediterranean, east to Iran, probably introduced further east, where fully naturalized in Kashmir, China and Japan. ssp. ***aureus*** (Lois.) Bak. Perianth seg. deep yellow to golden yellow; corona deep yellow to orange. SE France, Italy, Sardinia, Algeria, naturalized elsewhere. ssp. ***corcyrensis*** (Herb.) Bak. Fls 1–2; perianth seg. narrow, sometimes reflexed, pale yellow; corona yellow. Corfu. ssp. ***italicus*** (Ker-Gawl.) Bak. Perianth seg. cream or very pale yellow; corona deeper yellow. NE Mediterranean, N Africa. 'Canaliculatus': to 20cm; lvs narrow, erect, glaucous, striate; fls small; seg. white, corona ochre yellow; sometimes shy-flowering, origin unknown. Z8.

***N. ×tenuior*** Curtis. (*N. jonquilla* × *N. poeticus*.) Close to *N. jonquilla*. To 30cm. Lvs linear, flat. Fls 2–3, to 5cm diam.; corona flat, to 5mm, deeper yellow than perianth seg. Probably garden origin. Z4.

***N. triandrus*** L. ANGEL'S TEARS. Bulb to 2×1.7cm, globose, dark. Lvs 15–30×1.5–5mm, keeled or striate, flat or channelled, erect or decumbent, sometimes curled at tip, green, or slightly glaucous. Scape 20–30cm, elliptic, slightly keeled; spathe to 4cm; pedicel to 4cm; fls 1–6, pendulous, white to bright yellow, usually concolorous; perianth tube 1.5cm, green below, yellow above; seg. sharply reflexed, lanceolate to linear-oblong, 1–3cm, often with deeper median streak; corona cup-shaped, 0.5–1.5(–2.5)×0.7–2.5cm, entire, somewhat undulate; anth. biseriate, upper 3 exserted beyond corona. Spain & Portugal, NW France. Probably best treated as a single variable species: many variants have been described, based on flower colour, number of flowers and size of floral parts, but these do not seem to be reliable field characteristics. var. *albus* (Haw.) Bak. is typical of wild populations and should not be separated from the species, while var. *concolor* (Haw.) Bak. is probably only an extreme form with fls deep yellow and lvs 2mm wide; the name is loosely applied in horticulture to any yellow-flowered plant. Z4.

***N. viridiflorus*** Schousb. Bulb to 3×3cm, globose, very dark. Lvs 30–60×0.4cm, cylindric, hollow, erect or spreading, striate, glaucous dark green, not usually produced by flowering bulbs. Scape 9–25(–40)cm, terete or elliptic, striate; spathe to 5cm; pedicel to 7cm; fls 1–5, ascending, 2.5cm diam., dull green, malodorous; perianth tube 1.5cm; seg. linear-oblong, 1–1.6×0.2cm, acute, patent or reflexed; corona 1×4mm, 6-lobed; stamens bright yellow, upper 3 included in corona, pollen bright yellow. SW Spain, Morocco. Z8.

***N. willkommii*** (Samp.) Fernandes. Bulb to 3×2.5cm, globose, dark. Lvs to 37×0.3cm, erect, flattened at base, rounded above, glaucous dark green. Scape to 18cm, terete, smooth; pedicels to 2.2–4cm; fls usually solitary, 3cm diam., horizontal; perianth tube to 1.6cm, straight, green-yellow; seg. broad-elliptic, 0.6–1.3×0.7cm, apiculate, patent, or reflexed and curving inwards, slightly imbricate, yellow; corona cup-shaped, 0.6×1cm, deeply 6-lobed, yellow. S Portugal, SW Spain. Z8.

***N. abscissus*** (Haw.) Schult. & Schult. f. See *N. bicolor*.
***N. albescens*** Pugsley. See *N. pseudonarcissus* ssp. *moschatus*.
***N. alpestris*** Pugsley. See *N. pseudonarcissus* ssp. *moschatus*.
***N. aureus*** L. See *N. tazetta* ssp. *aureus*.
***N. barlae*** Parl. See *N. papyraceus* ssp. *panizzianus*.
***N. bertolonii*** Parl. See *N. tazetta* ssp. *aureus*.
***N. ×biflorus*** Curtis. See *N. ×medioluteus*.
***N. bulbocodium*** ssp. ***romieuxii*** (Braun-Blanquet & Maire) Emberger & Maire. See *N. romieuxii*.
***N. calathinus*** L. See *N. ×odorus*.
***N. campernelli*** hort. ex Haw. See *N. ×odorus*.
***N. canaliculatus*** hort. See *N. tazetta* 'Canaliculatus'.
***N. cavanillesii*** A. Barra & G. Lopez. See *N. humilis*.
***N. clusii*** Dunal. See *N. cantabricus* ssp. *cantabricus*.
***N. confusus*** Pugsley. See *N. pseudonarcissus* ssp. *major*.
***N. corcyrensis*** (Herb.) Nyman. See *N. tazetta* ssp. *corcyrensis*.
***N. cupularis*** (Salisb.) Schult. See *N. tazetta* ssp. *aureus*.
***N. ×gracilis*** Sab. See *N. ×tenuior*.
***N. hispanicus*** Gouan. See *N. pseudonarcissus* ssp. *major*.
***N. italicus*** Ker-Gawl. See *N. tazetta* ssp. *italicus*.
***N. italicus*** ssp. ***lacticolor*** (Haw.) Bak. See *Narcissus tazetta* ssp. *italicus*.
***N. jonquilloides*** Willk., non Willk. ex Schult. f. See *N. willkommii*.
***N. juncifolius*** auct. See *N. assoanus*.
***N. juncifolius*** ssp. ***rupicola*** Dufour. See *N. rupicola*.
***N. ×leedsii*** hort. See *N. ×incomparabilis*.
***N. lobularis*** hort. See *N. minor*.
***N. major*** Curtis. See *N. pseudonarcissus* ssp. *major*.
***N. maximus*** hort. See *N. pseudonarcissus* ssp. *major*.
***N. minimus*** hort. See *N. asturiensis*.
***N. minutiflorus*** Willk. See *N. gaditanus*.
***N. moschatus*** L. See *N. pseudonarcissus* ssp. *moschatus*.
***N. nanus*** Spach. See *N. minor*.
***N. ×nelsonii*** hort. ex Bak. See *N. ×incomparabilis*.
***N. nevadensis*** Pugsley. See *N. pseudonarcissus* ssp. *nevadensis*.
***N. nobilis*** Haw. See *N. pseudonarcissus* ssp. *nobilis*.

***N. obesus*** Salisb. See *N. bulbocodium* ssp. *obesus*.
***N. obvallaris*** Salisb. See *N. pseudonarcissus* ssp. *obvallaris*.
***N. ornatus*** Haw. See *N. poeticus*.
***N. pallens*** Freyn ex Willk. See *N. assoanus*.
***N. pallidiflorus*** Pugsley. See *N. pseudonarcissus* ssp. *pallidiflorus*.
***N. panizzianus*** Parl. See *N. papyraceus* ssp. *panizzianus*.
***N. ×poetaz*** hort. ex L.H. Bail. See *N. ×medioluteus*.
***N. poeticus*** ssp. ***angustifolius*** (Haw.) Hegi. See *N. poeticus* ssp. *radiiflorus*.
***N. polyanthus*** Lois. See *N. papyraceus* ssp. *polyanthus*.
***N. portensis*** Pugsley. See *N. pseudonarcissus* ssp. *portensis*.
***N. provincialis*** Pugsley. See *N. minor*.
***N. pumilus*** Salisb. See *N. minor*.
***N. radiiflorus*** Salisb. See *N. poeticus* ssp. *radiiflorus*.
***N. requienii*** Roem. See *N. assoanus*.
***N. tenuifolius*** Salisb. See *N. bulbocodium* var. *bulbocodium*.
***N. tazetta*** ssp. ***papyraceus*** (Ker-Gawl.) Bak. See *N. papyraceus*.
***N. tortuosa*** Haw. See *N. pseudonarcissus* ssp. *moschatus*.
***N. watieri*** Maire. See *N. rupicola* ssp. *watieri*.
For further synonymy see *Braxireon*, *Carregnoa* and *Tapeinanthus*.

**Nardostachys** DC. (From Gk *nardos*, fragrant shrub, *stachys*, spike.) Valerianaceae. 2 species of perennial herbs. Root thick, fibrous, very fragrant. Leaves opposite, entire, mostly basal. Flowers red or tinged purple, in dense, terminal, head-like cymes; calyx 5-lobed, enlarging in fruit; corolla 5-lobed, stamens 4; ovary inferior, 3-celled. Fruit 1-seeded. India, Himalaya, China.

CULTIVATION Suitable for the rock garden and herb gardens (the root yields a fragrant essential oil used in perfumery and medicinally). Cultivate as for *Valeriana*. Propagate by seed.

***N. grandiflora*** DC. SPIKENARD. Root fusiform, inclined; stock 7.5cm, ascending, simple or branched; stem to 25cm. Leaves to 10cm, mostly basal, elliptic-lanceolate or spathulate, acute, narrowed to a stalk. Fls pale rose-purple, in very dense cymes in a terminal panicle; cor.-tube cylindrical, gibbous at base, short; lobes rounded. Himalaya.

**Narthecium** Moehr. (From Narthex, ancient name for *Ferula*.) BOG ASPHODEL. Liliaceae (Melanthiaceae). 8 species of herbaceous, rush-like, rhizomatous, plants of marshy places; roots fibrous. Leaves distichous, equitant, basal and clothing stem, linear, often falcate, rigid, striate, rush-like. Flowers in a scapose raceme; bracts as long as pedicels; perianth segments 6, equal, linear, yellow, green beneath, spreading in flower, erect and persistent in fruit; stamens 6, versatile, filaments woolly; ovary superior, trilocular, ovules numerous; style simple. Fruit a many-seeded, septicidal capsule; seeds with bristle appendages. Summer. N temperate regions.

CULTIVATION Occurring in acid bogs and on heath and moorland to 1200m/4000ft, the bog asphodel *N. ossifragum* is occasionally grown in the bog garden, and in other situations approximating to those in habitat. Propagate by division or seed.

***N. americanum*** Ker-Gawl. YELLOW ASPHODEL. To 45cm. Lvs to 20×6cm, linear. Fls 0.5–0.6cm in dense racemes to 5cm; pedicels 0.6cm; perianth seg. linear; anth. yellow. E US (New Jersey to Delaware and S Carolina). Z6.

***N. asiaticum*** Maxim. To 60cm. Lvs to 25×1cm, linear. Fls 1cm in racemes to 12cm; pedicels 1.5cm; perianth seg. linear; anth. pale yellow. Japan. Z7.

***N. californicum*** Bak. To 50cm. Lvs to 30×0.6cm, linear. Fls 1cm in racemes to 15cm; pedicels to 1.5cm; perianth seg. linear-lanceolate; anth. red. W US (SW Oregon to C California). Z7.

***N. ossifragum*** (L.) Huds. BOG ASPHODEL. To 40cm; stems and floral axis becoming deep orange after flowering. Lvs to 30×0.5cm, rigid, often curved, strongly ribbed. Perianth seg. 0.6–0.8cm, linear-lanceolate, becoming deep orange after flowering; anth. orange. W Europe (Scandinavia to N Spain and Portugal). Z6.

**Nassauvia** Comm. ex Juss. Compositae. About 40 species of perennial herbs, often woody at base, or dwarf shrubs. Leaves alternate, small, simple, usually rigid and spinulose. Capitula discoid, usually sessile, solitary or grouped in dense, globose to ovoid inflorescences; receptacle flat; phyllaries in 2 series; florets hermaphrodite, 2-lipped, outer lip larger than inner. Pappus of caducous scales or plumose bristles. Southern S America. Z8.

CULTIVATION *Nassauvia* spp. occur in high alpine screes, amongst the quartz rock slides and boulder fields of the high Andean peaks, to altitudes of 4000m/1300ft, and are fascinating and challenging plants for cultivation in the alpine house. The neat and compressed columns of growth are tightly wadded with dense white hair on the underside of the leaves. *N. lagascae* bears heads of sweetly scented white flowers, on hirsute stems that grow wider and woollier below the flat flowerhead; those of *N. revoluta* are more rounded. Grow in a lean and gritty alpine mix, with a topdressing of grit and a wedge of small stones to keep the neck clear of the medium surface. Double potting facilitates watering without wetting the foliage. Propagate by seed.

***N. lagascae*** (D. Don) F. Meigen. Perenn. herb to 8cm. Stems procumbent to ascending, sparingly branched. Lvs to 13×4mm, densely imbricate, oblong, recurved, apex 5–9-dentate, subglabrous above, densely lanate beneath. Capitula numerous, in a dense, globose spike to 4cm; phyllaries to 8mm, outer linear, inner elliptic to acute or mucronate; florets white or mauve. Pappus of plumose bristles. Summer. W Argentina, E Chile.

***N. revoluta*** D. Don. Dwarf shrub to 20cm. Stems numerous, ascending, branched, densely leafy. Lvs to 10×6mm, imbricate, ovate to ovate-lanceolate, recurved above, mucronate-dentate. Capitula in dense glomerules to 2.5cm diam.; phyllaries to 5mm linear to lanceolate, acute; florets white. Pappus of white scales. Patagonia.

**Nasturtium** R. Br. (From Lat. *nasus*, nose, and *tortus*, twist; used by Pliny for a pungent plant.) WATERCRESS. Cruciferae. 6 species of perennial, often semi-aquatic herbs, to 80cm. Rhizomes frequently formed. Leaves pinnate, with simple hairs, or glabrous. Flowers small, in a raceme, sepals 4, spreading, slightly saccate at base; petals 4, yellow or white; stamens 6, filaments free. Fruit a silique, terete or laterally compressed. Europe to C Asia, N Africa and N America. Z6.

CULTIVATION Aquatic and wet soil perennials in shallow freshwater habitats throughout Europe, especially on those chalk and limestone formations that give rise to the springs of uncontaminated water at constant temperature (about 10°C/50°F) they prefer. They are very sensitive to pollution. Grown as a salad vegetable and garnish, with the piquant flavour of many of the edible crucifers, *Nasturtium* is exceptionally rich in vitamins and minerals, especially iron. In commercial production, watercress is grown in beds, constructed to allow the inflow and outflow of natural spring or bore-hole water, whose pH (optimum 7.2), temperature (10–11.5°C/50–53°F) and microbiological quality is carefully monitored. While the best results are obtained by growing in running water, this must be absolutely clean and uncontaminated by livestock or sewage. For this reason, there may be health risks attached to the consumption of wild watercress. Where such clean water is unavailable, cultivation in shallow trenches is perfectly adequate for home consumption, given good light and shelter from cold winter winds.

Prepare a trench 30cm/12in. deep and 60cm/24in. wide, with a 10–15cm/4–6in. layer of compost or well-rotted manure at the bottom, covered with a 10cm/4in. layer of fertile soil. In spring, plant rooted trimmings 15cm/6in. apart; these may be from good-quality, shop-bought stock, which roots easily in water. Alternatively, sow seed in drills, thinning to 15cm/6in. Keep constantly moist, pinch out tips to encourage branching and remove flowerheads; their formation reduces vegetative growth. A 5cm/2in. layer of sharp sand or grit on the bed will protect foliage from soil splash. With judicial cutting in their first year of establishment, harvesting thereafter encourages prolific branching.

For glasshouse or frame cultivation, pot rooted cuttings in high-fertility loam-based mix, crocking with a layer of gravel. Between spring and autumn, seed will germinate in the cold glasshouse; in winter, sow at 18–21°C/65–70°F. The normal recommendation is to keep evenly moist by standing the pot in cool fresh water, changing daily in summer, and on alternate days in winter. In practice, watercress in pots in the glasshouse will continue to thrive given moderate watering in the normal way, although such plants will develop a hotter flavour.

*Nasturtium* spp. are tolerant of temperatures as low as −15°C/5°F, but unless given the protection of cloche or low tunnel, growth will cease during winter, and badly frosted material will probably be inedible. *N. microphyllum*, whose leaves become brown-purple in winter, is the hardier species. Until the end of

World War II, the hybrid brown cress, *N. officinale* × *N. microphyllum*, was commercially cultivated, but the vegetatively propagated stock became so badly infested with crook root and virus disease that it has now been superseded by stock of *N. officinale* with deep green round leaves, originating in the US.

*Nasturtium* is attacked by various aphid spp., notably *Aphis nasturtii* (controlled by specific aphicide) and the small striped flea beetle, *Phyllotreta undulata*. However, where cultivation in running water is practised, insecticides pose a potential danger to fish and other wild life and in this situation their use may be prohibited by law, and should in any case be checked with the Regional Water Authority. Plants may be attacked in Europe and North America by caterpillars of the diamondback moth (*Plutella xylostella*); tarsonemid mites, namely the strawberry mite (*Tarsonemus pallidus*); and by leaf beetles (*Phaedon* spp.), including the mustard beetle (*N. cochleariae*) in Europe and the watercress beetle (*N. aeruginosus*) in North America.

Crook root disease (infection by a water borne-fungus, *Spongospora subterranea* f. sp. *nasturtii*) causes crooked and swollen roots, leading to loss of vigour and eventual death. Treatment is available only to commercial growers. Turnip mosaic virus, spread by the aphids *Myzus persicae* and *Brevicoryne brassicae*, causes mottling and yellow leaf spots; propagate only from green, symptom-free material, or from seed, which will not carry the virus. In commercial production the disease is controlled by applying zinc sulphate to the water to give a zinc concentration of 0.1 ppm. Pale yellow, circular leaf spots are caused by the fungus *Septoria sisymbrii* and this fungus as well as downy mildew (*Peronospora parasitica*) can cause the leaves to turn yellow and collapse. Severely affected aerial growth should be removed; fungicides should not be applied to watercourses.

***N. microphyllum*** (Boenn.) Rchb. Similar to *N. officinale* except fls larger; pedicel to 15mm. Fr. 16–24mm, seeds in one row. W Europe.

***N. officinale*** R. Br. COMMON WATERCRESS. 20–80cm. Stems creeping, becoming erect, often floating. Lvs petiolate; lateral leaflets in 3–5 pairs, wavy to entire, terminal leaflet much larger. Pet. 4–6×2mm, white; pedicel 6–12mm. Fr. 11–18×2mm, straight to curved; seeds in 2 rows per locule. Spring–early summer. Europe to SW Asia, introduced N America and elsewhere.

***N. amphibium*** (L.) R. Br. See *Rorippa amphibia*.
***N. armoracia*** (L.) Fries. See *Armoracia rusticana*.
***N. fontanum*** (Lam.) Asch. See *N. officinale*.
For further synonymy see *Cardamine*, *Rorippa* and *Sisymbrium*.

**Nauclea** L. (From Gk *naus*, ship, and *kleio*, to close; the fruit cells resemble a ship's hull.) Rubiaceae. Some 10 species of shrubs or trees. Leaves petiolate, opposite; stipules persistent or deciduous, terminally adpressed, keeled and flat, ovate or obovate to elliptic. Flowers terminal or lateral and solitary, or in pedunculate, globose heads; bracts present; calyx glabrous or pubescent, limb often obsolete, persistent, lobes 4–5, deltoid to oblong, obtuse; corolla funnelform, tube glabrous at throat, lobes 4–5, overlapping in bud, oblong; stamens 4–5, inserted at throat, anthers basifixed, ovate; ovaries 2-celled, connate in bud, style exserted, stigma fusiform, ovaries many. Fruit a berry, globose, 2-celled, indehiscent, pyrenes 2; seeds compressed, ovoid to ellipsoid, testa crusty, endosperm fleshy. Tropical Africa, Asia to Polynesia. Z10.

CULTIVATION Small trees and shrubs with smooth leathery evergreen leaves, sometimes cultivated in the tropics for their fragrant flowers and edible red fruits. Cultivate as for *Cinchona*.

***N. diderrichii*** (De Wildeman) Merrill. Tree, to 40m. Stems glabrous, bark furrowed, grey to brown. Lvs to 40×20cm, elliptic, apex obtuse or narrowly acute, base obtuse or cuneate, glabrous; petioles to 2cm; stipules to 5cm, elliptic to oblong, glabrous. Fls in terminal heads to 3cm wide; peduncles to 2cm; cal. lobes to 2mm, club- or prism-shaped, apex obtuse; cor. funnel-shaped, white or yellow or green, tube to 8mm, lobes to 3×1mm, elliptic to oblong. Fr. to 4cm, globose, succulent, ribbed, white or grey to pale brown. Tropical Africa.

***N. officinalis*** (Pierre ex Pitard) Merrill ex Chun. Tree, to 30m. Lvs to 25×14cm, obovate to elliptic, apex acute, base acute or obtuse, leathery to papery, glabrous, 4–10-veined; petioles to 2cm; stipules to 25×14mm, ovate to elliptic. Fls in terminal heads; cal. lobes to 1mm, pubesc.; cor. tube to 4mm, glabrous, lobes to 1mm. Tropical Asia (Indochina to Malaysia, Indonesia).

***N. orientalis*** (L.) L. Tree, to 12m. Branches whorled, bark furrowed, grey to brown. Lvs to 25×15cm, ovate, apex acute, base obtuse, margin undulate, glabrous, 7–9-veined; petioles to 4cm, grooved above; stipules persistent, not keeled. Fls in heads; cal. lobes spathulate; cor. tube to 8mm. Tropical Asia to Australia, Polynesia.

***N. cordata*** Roxb. See *N. orientalis*.
***N. esculenta*** (Sab.) Merrill. See *Sarcocephalus latifolius*.
***N. latifolia*** Sm. See *Sarcocephalus latifolius*.
***N. parvifolia*** Roxb. See *Mitragyna parvifolia*.
***N. undulata*** Roxb. See *N. orientalis*.
For further synonymy see *Cephalanthus* and *Sarcocephalus*.

**Nauplius** (Cass.) Cass. Compositae. About 8 species of subshrubs or annuals. Stem erect to ascending, branched, striate, glandular. Leaves alternate, sessile, spathulate, oblong or linear, entire to pinnatifid, often succulent, sometimes auriculate. Capitula radiate, solitary, terminal; receptacle convex to flat; involucre to campanulate; phyllaries imbricate in 3 series, outer phyllaries spreading often toothed, foliaceous, with a more or less yellow base, inner smaller, entire, with scarious margins; ray florets female, oblong, yellow to white, sometimes tinged purple beneath; disc florets hermaphrodite, yellow. Fruit an obovate, rough cypsela; pappus free, brown to colourless scales. Mediterranean and Macronesia. Z9.

CULTIVATION Treat *N. aquaticus* as a hardy annual for the flower border. *N. sericeus* is suitable for the rockery or mixed border in warm, dry, frost-free climates, otherwise grow in containers in the cool glasshouse, to move outdoors for the summer. It requires similar treatment to the tender species of *Euryops*.

***N. aquaticus*** (L.) Cass. Annual to 50cm, fragrant. Stems often purple-tinged. Lvs to 8×2cm, oblong to ovate-oblong, base auriculate, folded along pale midrib, pubesc., densely glandular. Capitula to 2cm diam.; receptacle flat; phyllaries to *c*35, outer to 2cm, conspicuous, much longer than ray florets, pubesc.; ray florets to 30, yellow, to 7mm. Fr. densely strigose-hispid. Spring–summer. W Mediterranean, Canary Is.

***N. sericeus*** (L. f.) Cass. Subshrub to 1m, fragrant. Stems glandular, grey-tinged, becoming brown below. Lvs to 6×2cm, densely set, spathulate, silver grey-pilose. Capitula to 5cm diam.; receptacle convex; phyllaries more than 50, not exceeding ray florets, outer to 2.5cm, silky-hairy; ray florets more than 30, yellow, to 20mm. Fr. moderately hispid. Canary Is.

For synonymy see *Asteriscus*, *Buphthalmum* and *Odontospermum*.

**Nautilocalyx** Lind. ex Hanst., emend. Wiehler. (From Gk *nautilos*, sailor, and *calyx*, probably referring to the boat-shaped floral bracts.) Gesneriaceae. About 38 species of mostly terrestrial, perennial herbs and subshrubs. Stems erect, ascending or creeping, succulent, branching at base. Leaves rarely rosulate, usually opposite in pairs, sometimes cuneate or winged at base. Flowers axillary, solitary or several clustered in cymes, usually subtended by 2 or more floral bracts; sepals unequal, rarely connate; corolla tubular with an apical limb and basal spur, limb 5-lobed, lobes nearly equal; stamens 4, united at base and continuous with corolla for part of their length; anthers in connivent pairs; ovary superior. Fruit a bivalved capsule. Tropical America. Z10.

CULTIVATION See GESNERIADS.

***N. adenosiphon*** (Leeuwenb.) Wiehler. Stems to 20cm, creeping or ascending, tomentose at apex, otherwise glabrescent. Lvs to 4×2.8cm, in unequal pairs, ovate, obtuse or acute at apex, rounded to obcordate at base, crenate-serrate, adpressed-pubesc. above, minutely pilose beneath. Fls solitary, axillary; sep. to 12×6mm, ovate to narrowly ovate, serrate, dorsal sep. curled around spur; cor. to 3.5×0.5cm, white, pilose; lobes suborbicular, to 8mm. Venezuela.

***N. bicolor*** (Hook.) Wiehler. Stems short, hairy, creeping and procumbent. Lvs ovate to cordate, spreading, acute, serrate, coarsely reticulate, pubesc., margin ciliate. Fls erect or inclined in axillary clusters; sep. nearly erect, linear-lanceolate, curved at apex; cor. tube white, gibbous, spotted with purple inside, limb white with a broad purple border; lobes suborbicular; stamens inserted; style included. Colombia.

***N. bracteatus*** (Planch.) Sprague. Stems simple, pubesc. Lvs sessile, ovate, acuminate, irregularly serrate, attenuate at base. Fls solitary; pedicels short; floral bracts acuminate, serrate, flushed with purple; sep. connate to middle, erect, narrowly linear, dentate, purple-flushed above, white-veined; cor. to 3.5cm, white; limb broad. Colombia.

***N. bullatus*** (Lem.) Sprague. Stems to 60cm, erect. Lvs to 23×8cm, elliptic, bullate, attenuate at base, dark green above, purple beneath; petiole winged. Fls

8–10 in axillary cymes; pedicels very short; floral bracts 2, green; sep. to 2.5cm, equalling cor. tube, pale green, rarely marked with purple, dentate; cor. to 3.2cm, densely pilose, pale yellow, lobes to 1.2cm. Peru.

***N.forgetii*** (Sprague) Sprague. As for *N. lynchii* except lvs bright green, marked with red on veins, margin markedly undulate; petiole to 5cm, villous, not winged; sep. much shorter than cor. tube, often tinged red. Peru.

***N.glandulifer*** Wiehler. Stems to 20cm, erect or ascending, pilose-hirsute, with long maroon hairs. Lvs in equal pairs, oblanceolate, crenate-undulate, cordate-auriculate, flushed with maroon above, wine-red beneath; petiole to 2cm. Fls in axillary cymes of 2–6; floral bracts yellow-green, oblanceolate; sep. lanceolate, pilose below, glabrous above; cor. to 4.2cm, cream-white, sericeous, lobes to 6×5mm, upper lobes speckled with maroon, striped with maroon inside. Ecuador.

***N.hirsutus*** (Sprague) Sprague. Stems to 50cm, erect, villous. Lvs to 16×6cm, oblanceolate, acuminate and recurved at apex, cuneate at base, somewhat bullate, villous on veins beneath; petiole to 3cm. Fls 4–8 in axillary cymes; floral bracts to 2×0.6cm, villous beneath; sep. to 2cm, ovate-lanceolate, acuminate, cor. to 3cm, pale yellow, glandular-pilose, limb to 1.5cm across, lobes elliptic. Peru.

***N.lucianii*** (Fourn.) Wiehler. Stems stout at base. Lvs ovate, succulent, dark green with pale veins above, flushed with red beneath. Fls in axillary clusters; sep. linear-lanceolate; cor. rose-red, outside red-pilose, narrowed above, lobes rounded. Colombia.

***N.lynchii*** Hook. f. Stems to 6 0cm, erect. Lvs elliptic-lanceolate, dentate, attenuate at base, dark green and nearly glabrous above, puberulent beneath. Fls 2–3 in axillary cymes; floral bracts lanceolate; sep. to 2.5×1cm, ovate, flushed with maroon; cor. to 3cm, pale yellow, outside red-pilose, inside marked with purple flecks, lobes to 1.2cm. Colombia.

***N.melittifolius*** (L.) Wiehler. Stems trailing, rooting at nodes. Lvs to 25×10cm, ovate, crenate, sparsely adpressed-hairy above, puberulent beneath. Fls several in a loose axillary cyme; sep. to 1.1cm, narrowly ovate, puberulent; cor. to 2cm, pilose, cherry-red, lobes to 0.7cm. Lesser Antilles.

***N.pallidus*** (Sprague) Sprague Stems to 50cm, usually erect, pilose. Lvs to 25×10.5cm, ovate-lanceolate, acute, recurved at apex, tapered at base, pale green, glabrous except for sparse pubesc. on veins, margins crenate-serrate, sparsely ciliate; petiole to 2cm. Fls in axillary cymes of 3–6; floral bracts 2, lanceolate, sparsely ciliate beneath; sep. to 1.7cm, ovate, acuminate, rounded to subcordate at base, sparsely puberulent below; cor. to 5cm, cream-white, glandular-pilose, inside spotted and lined purple, limb to 3cm across, lobes to 1.2×1.6cm, elliptic. Peru.

***N.panamensis*** (Seem.) Seem. Stems to 20cm, tetragonal, villous. Lvs to 10×5.5cm, ovate-acuminate, sparsely pilose above, almost glabrous beneath, margins crenate-serrate. Fls in axillary fascicles; pedicels to 2cm, tomentose; sep. to 1cm, ovate-lanceolate, remotely toothed; cor. to 3cm, erect, cylindric, pale yellow, lobes suborbicular. Mexico, Panama, Colombia.

***N.picturatus*** (L.) Skog. Stems to 20cm, erect, densely branched from base. Lvs to 14×5cm, elliptic, denticulate, rugose, dark green with pale veins and pubesc. above, marked with maroon and pubesc. beneath. Fls in axillary clusters; floral bracts obovate; cal. lobes to 1.5cm, pubesc.; cor. to 3cm, white, purple-striped, hairy outside. Peru.

***N.pictus*** (Hook.) Sprague. Stems to 30cm, purple or green, creeping or ascending, glabrescent. Lvs to 22.5×10cm, often bullate, oblong-elliptic or oblong-lanceolate, acuminate at apex, cuneate at base, crenate-serrate. Fls solitary or in axillary cymes; sep. green, linear-lanceolate, long-acuminate, toothed, dorsal sep. curled around spur; cor. to 4.5cm, outside pilose, to 3.5cm, cream or pale yellow, limb to 2cm. Fr. to 1cm diam., globose. N Brazil, Guyana.

***N.speciosus*** Wiehler. Stems branching at base, erect, to 25cm, rose-pink; young shoots sericeous. Lvs 9–13×4.5–6cm, in equal to subequal pairs, oblanceolate, acuminate, serrate, green and glabrous above, pale green, sometimes marked with pink and sericeous beneath; petiole 4–10cm. Fls in axillary cymes of 4–6; floral bracts 1.9×0.8cm, ovate-lanceolate, acute, pink; pedicels to 3cm, pink, sparsely sericeous; cor. to 5cm, spurred, white, sericeous, lobes subequal, to 11×11mm, marked with purple on veins; stamens 4, not exserted; style white. Panama.

***N.villosus*** (HBK) Sprague. Stems erect or ascending, purple or green, glabrescent. Lvs to 16×8.5cm, elliptic or oblong-elliptic, acuminate at apex, cuneate at base, coarsely serrate or crenate-serrate. Fls 1-several; pedicels villous, to 2cm; sep. connate at base, linear-lanceolate, sparsely toothed, long-acuminate; cor. to 5.5×1.5cm, white, outside pilose, inside marked with purple; ovary hirsute, ovoid. Venezuela, Guyana.

For synonymy see *Alloplectus* and *Episcia*.

**Navarretia** Ruiz & Pav. (For Dr. F. Navarrete, Spanish physician.) Polemoniaceae. About 30 species of erect to branching, rigid-stemmed, annual herbs, to 50cm. Leaves alternate, usually pinnate or bipinnate, rarely palmate or entire, spine-tipped or acerose towards apex. Inflorescence a densely bracteate, spiny head; flowers 4- or 5-merous, sessile or subsessile; calyx divided to base, lobes entire to toothed, unequal, acerose, sinuses quarter to two-thirds filled by scarious membrane; corolla hypocrateriform to funnelform, purple, blue or pink to yellow or white; stamens and style included or exserted, stigma entire to 2–3-lobed. Fruit a capsule, obovoid to ovoid, 1–3-loculed, 3–8-valved, membranaceous to chartaceous; seeds usually brown, often with tiny pits. Western N America, Chile and Argentina. Z7.

CULTIVATION As for *Gilia*.

***N.mellita*** E. Greene. Erect, branching, glandular-pubesc., to 20cm tall, with a honey-like scent. Lvs irregularly and pinnately or bipinnately lobed, lobes lanceolate, rigid. Infl. a cluster or fls solitary; cal. 8–12mm, glandular-pubesc. cor. 6–7mm, lobes *c*1.5mm, pale blue, throat with purple veins. Fr 3–4mm, ovoid. Spring–summer. California.

***N.squarrosa*** (Eschsch.) Hook. & Arn. Erect, branching, to 50cm, glandular-pubesc., with an unpleasant, skunk-like smell. Lvs irregularly and pinnately or bipinnately lobed, lobes lanceolate, rigid. Infl. a cluster or fls solitary; bracts 1–1.5cm, pinnate to palmate; cal. 8–12mm, glandular-pubesc.; cor. 1–1.2cm, broadly funnelform, blue to purple, lobes 2–3mm; stamens and style included, stigma 3-lobed. Fr. 3–4mm, ovoid. Summer. California to British Columbia.

For synonymy see *Gilia*.

**Navia** Mart. ex Schult. f. (Named for Bernard Sebastian von Nau (1766–1845), German naturalist and physicist.) Bromeliaceae. 74 species of much-branched to cushion-forming perennials herbs, often lying flat on the ground, to 4m high in flower, though many species are low and short-stemmed. Leaves forming a rosette, or in a dense spiral along stem, sheaths large, blades narrow, entire or toothed. Inflorescences terminal, sometimes compound panicles, but usually with flowers aggregated into a compound head (capitulum); scape usually absent; flowers actinomorphic, sessile or subsessile; sepals free or fused, coiled, overlapping; petals fused to form a slender tube. Fruit a capsule, seeds more or less naked. SE Colombia, N Brazil, E Venezuela and Guyana. Z10.

CULTIVATION See BROMELIADS.

***N.acaulis*** Mart. ex Schult. f. Short-stemmed, sometimes branched. Lvs to 12cm, glabrous, densely toothed, apex sharply acute. Infl. globose, sessile, sunk in rosette centre; floral bracts 5mm, lanceolate, acuminate; sep. 4–6mm, slightly fused, posterior winged and keeled; stamens exserted. Fr. broadly ellipsoid, woody to leathery. S. Colombia.

***N.arida*** L.B. Sm. & Steyerm. Stemless or with short, unbranched, erect stem. Lvs about 20, in a rosette, sheaths small, blades to 38cm long, linear, spreading, caudate-attenuate, green above, white-scaly below, laxly toothed, with spreading, 2mm spines. Infl. sessile, central, simple, densely capitate; outer bracts few, more or less leaflike, tinged red; floral bracts about 2.5cm, very narrowly triangular, red, white-scaly, membranous; pedicel stout, 5mm; sep. 3.5–4cm, very narrowly triangular, thin, keelless; pet. yellow, tips pink. Fr. ovoid, 8mm. S Colombia.

For synonymy see *Dyckia*.

**Neanthe** P. Browne.
***N.bella*** Cook. See *Chamaedorea elegans*.

**Nectaroscordum** Lindl. Liliaceae (Alliaceae). 3 species of onion-scented, herbaceous perennials to 120cm, resembling *Allium* but outer tepals with 3–7 veins; pedicel apices swollen beneath flowers; ovary many-ovuled. Bulbs solitary, subterranean, tunics membranous. Leaves linear, sheathing base of stem. Flowers numerous in a scapose umbel with deciduous spathe atop a solitary stem; perianth segments free; stamens 6; ovaries with 5 or more ovules per cell. S Europe, W Asia, Iran. Z7.

CULTIVATION Suitable for naturalizing in open woodland or in the herbaceous border, but care should be taken in siting, as in full sun they will become invasive. Colouring is subtle rather than showy, but the umbels of pendent flowers, carried in summer are nonetheless attractive. The strap-shaped leaves, which emerge in spring, die back at or shortly after flowering. As the generic name suggests, the whole plant smells strongly of garlic when crushed. Hardy to at least −13°C/5°F. Grow in any light, well-drained soil that is neither excessively dry nor waterlogged, in sun or part shade. Propagate from seed in early spring; in suitable conditions seed may be sown *in situ*. Also from offset bulbils.

***N. siculum*** (Ucria) Lindl. SICILIAN HONEY GARLIC. Bulbs solitary, ovoid, to 3cm diam., tunics membranous. Lvs 3–4, 30–40×1–2cm; basal lvs deeply channelled, keel sharp-edged. Scapes to 120cm; fls 10–30, 1.5–2.5×2cm, bell-shaped, pendulous, in loose umbels; pedicels unequal, pendent at first, erect on fruiting; tepals to 15×9mm, typically nearly white, flushed flesh-pink and dark red, green toward base below, ovary tinted pink. Spring–summer. France, Italy. ssp. ***bulgaricum*** (Janka) Stearn. Tepals white to yellow, flushed pale pink and green above, edged white, flushed green below. E Romania, Bulgaria, Turkey, Crimea. Z6.

***N. bulgaricum*** Janka. See *N. siculum*.
For further synonymy see *Allium*.

**Neillia** D. Don. (For Patrick Neill (1776–1851), Scottish naturalist, Secretary of the Caledonia Horticultural Society.) Rosaceae. Some 10 species of suffrutescent herbs or, more often, arching shrubs to 6m; branching flexuous in shrubby species. Leaves alternate, usually 3-lobed, irregularly serrate; stipules entire or dentate. Buds in leaf-axils of long shoots often multiple, one above the other. Flowers in racemes or panicles; calyx tube cylindric to campanulate, lobes 5, pubescent inside; petals 5, white or pink, short-clawed; stamens 10–30; carpels usually 1, to 5, free when 1+, each carpel 2–10-ovulate. Fruit 1 or more follicles, dehiscent along the ventral suture, several-seeded; seeds glossy, pale brown. E Himalaya to China and W Malaysia.

CULTIVATION In their native regions, *Neillia* spp. are found in scrub and in rocky places by streams. They are suitable for the shrub border and are grown for their profuse clusters of flowers in summer and for their gracefully arching habit, the long stems exhibiting a zig-zag mode of growth similar to that seen in *Stephanandra incisa*. The dark glossy leaves are attractively textured. Grow in moist, well-aerated soil, in sun to part-shade. They are hardy to −20°C/−4°F, but in areas where low temperatures are prolonged, protect the roots with a deep mulch; if the plant is cut to the ground it may then shoot from the base.

With the exception of *N. thyrsiflora* (which flowers on the current season's growth and is pruned in late winter or early spring), prune after flowering, cutting out all old stems at ground level to encourage young growth and maintain the graceful habit. Propagate by semi-ripe cuttings in a closed case with bottom heat, by softwood cuttings in early summer, by removal of suckers in autumn, or by seed.

***N. affinis*** Hemsl. Shrub to 2m; young shoots glabrous, angular. Lvs to 9cm, ovate to oval-oblong, long-acuminate, cordate at base, small-lobed, slightly pubesc. on veins beneath; petiole to 2.5cm. Fls pink, in elongate, 10+-fld racemes to 8cm; cal. tube campanulate, finely pubesc., with stalked glands; cal. teeth to 4mm, shorter than cal. tube; stamens 25–30; carpels usually more than 1, villous. Follicle villous. Spring–summer. W China (Sichuan). var. ***pauciflora*** (Rehd.) J.E. Vidal. Raceme contracted, to 4cm, 5–10-fld; fls fascicled at the end of the axis. SW China (Yunnan). Z6.

***N. sinensis*** Oliv. Shrub to 3m; branchlets brown, glabrous, with exfoliating bark. Lvs to 8cm, oval-oblong, long-acuminate, incised-serrate and lobed, teeth sharp, pubesc. on veins beneath, later entirely glabrous, light green; petiole 1cm; stipules entire. Fls in cernuous, 12–20-fld, simple racemes to 6cm; pedicels to 1cm; cal. white-pink, tubular, to 12mm, glabrous, with a few glandular setae; cal. teeth triangular, long-acuminate; carpels 1–2, 4–5-ovulate. Spring–summer. C China. var. ***ribesioides*** (Rehd.) J.E. Vidal. Cal. tube less than 6.5mm. Summer–autumn. Z6.

***N. thibetica*** Bur. & Franch. Shrub to 2m; branchlets subcylindric, fine-pubesc. Lvs to 8cm, ovate, long-acuminate, subcordate at base, biserrate and lobulate, later glabrous above, finely and densely pubesc. beneath; petiole to 1.5cm; stipules ovate, serrate. Fls pink to white, in short, dense, 8–15cm racemes; pedicels to 4mm; cal. tubiform, finely pubesc.; carpels 1. Follicle villous at apex. Summer. W China (Sichuan). Z6.

***N. thyrisflora*** D. Don. Shrub to 3m. Lvs to 12×6cm, ovate, acuminate, rounded or shallow-cordate at base, irregularly serrate, usually shallowly trilobed; petiole to 1cm; stipules ovate, 7mm, serrate. Fls in large, terminal panicles; cal. cup 2.5mm, adpressed-pubesc., at fruiting bearing stiffly stalked capitate 1.5mm glands, lobes triangular, to 3.5mm, erect; pet. white, elliptic, to 5mm; stamens 8–10, fil. 1mm; carpel ovoid, 2mm; style 2mm. Follicle 5mm, 8–10-seeded. Himalaya to W China, Burma, south to Indonesia. Z8.

***N. uekii*** Nak. Shrub to 3m. Branches and infl. axis with an indumentum of sparse, eventually deciduous, hairs stellate. Lvs 5-lobed, glabrous above, sparsely pubesc. beneath; petiole 5mm; stipules entire or dentate. Pedicels to 4mm, glandular; cal. tube campanulate, sparsely pubesc., glandular; pet. usually pink; carpels 1–2, usually glabrous, later villous. Follicle villous at apex. Korea. Z9.

***N. amurensis*** (Maxim.) Bean. See *Physocarpus amurensis*.
***N. bracteata*** (Rydb.) Bean. See *Physocarpus bracteatus*.
***N. capitata*** (Pursh) Greene. See *Physocarpus capitatus*.
***N. longiracemosa*** Hemsl. See *N. thibetica*.
***N. malvacea*** Greene. See *Physocarpus malvaceus*.
***N. millsii*** Dunn. See *N. uekii*.
***N. monogyna*** (Torr.) Greene. See *Physocarpus monogynus*.
***N. monogyna*** var. ***alternans*** Jones. See *Physocarpus alternans*.
***N. opulifolia*** (L.) Brewer & S. Wats. See *Physocarpus opulifolius*.
***N. pauciflora*** Rehd. See *N. affinis* var. *pauciflora*.
***N. ribesioides*** Rehd. See *N. sinensis* var. *ribesioides*.
***N. tanakae*** Franch. & Savat. See *Stephanandra tanakae*.
***N. torreyi*** of *Bot. Mag.* t. *7758*, non S. Wats. See *Physocarpus malvaceus*.
***N. torreyi*** S. Wats. See *Physocarpus monogynus*.

**Neltuma** Raf.
***N. constricta*** (Sarg.) Britt. & Rose. See *Prosopis constricta*.
***N. glandulosa*** Torr. Britt. & Rose. See *Prosopis glandulosa*.
***N. neomexicana*** Britt. See *Prosopis neomexicana*.

**Nelumbium** Juss.
***N. luteum*** Willd. See *Nelumbo lutea*.
***N. speciosum*** Willd. See *Nelumbo nucifera*.

**Nelumbo** Adans. (Name used in Sri Lanka for *N. nucifera*.) LOTUS. Nelumbonaceae. 2 species of perennial rhizomatous aquatic herbs. Rhizome cylindrical, spongy, horizontal, wide-spreading, swollen. Leaves long-petiolate, usually emergent, occasionally floating, blades peltate, carried horizontally, concave-orbicular, veins radiate; cataphylls present on rhizome. Peduncle radical, slender, equalling or exceeding leaves arising from cataphyll-axil; flowers solitary, bisexual, emergent from water, large and showy, yellow, pink or white; sepals 4–5, imbricate; petals numerous, spirally arranged; stamens 200–400, filaments slender; ovaries 12–40, in distinct whorls, sunken within swollen fleshy receptacle, with 1 ovule. Fruit of separate hard-walled nuts, pitted on the dorsal surface of an accresent, obturbinate receptacle; endosperm absent; seeds with extreme longevity, surviving several hundred years in river-mud. Eastern N America, warm Asia to Australia.

CULTIVATION Extraordinarily beautiful aquatics for the still water pool, valued for their wax-bloomed foliage, their fragrant and exquisite chalice-shaped flowers and for the decorative seed heads which can be air-dried for winter decoration. In warm climates, they have long been grown for culinary use: the leaf stalks, rootstock and seed are all edible. Deep water cultivation, where the leaf stalks will reach their potential height of 2.5m/8ft is generally practicable only in warm subtropical climates or in the tropical house pool; in cooler zones shallow water heats up more quickly to provide the warmth necessary for good growth and flowering. Grow in tubs, baskets or beds in heavy, loam enriched with well-rotted farmyard manure or compost; set rootstocks horizontally at about 25mm/1in. deep and gradually increase the depth of water from 5–8cm/2–3in. to between 40–60cm/16–24in. as growth proceeds. Remove any fading foliage during the growing season and as temperatures begin to fall in late summer and autumn, gradually reduce the water level and mulch deeply with leafmould/compost, or lift, wash and store roots in moist sand in a cool frost-free place for the winter.

The sacred lotus is usually treated as a tender aquatic below Zone 9. Some of its cultivars, especially those of Far Eastern provenance, prove perfectly hardy, however, in outdoor pools in places as far north as New York City. The lotus should also be considered for tub cultivation on terraces, where few plants are so striking in leaf and bloom in high summer – establish rhizomes on a loamy rich mix in the lower two-thirds of wooden or glazed tubs, fill the remainder with water. As frost kills foliage, remove tubs to shelter (in a cold greenhouse or garden shed) and keep just moist. Move outside and replenish water in late spring.

In the heated glasshouse pond, treat *N. nucifera* as for the tropical species in *Nymphaea*. Propagate by division of the rhizome, deeply resentful of disturbance, potting up in individual pots with the terminal buds facing upwards. Chip seed before sowing in small pots of rich loamy medium in early spring; set in an aquarium or warm glasshouse, covered with a depth of 5cm/2in. of water and maintain a temperature of 25–30°C/77–86°F. Pot on and gradually acclimatize to greater depths of water, set out in late spring/early summer after danger of frost is passed. Seed grown plants will flower in their third year.

***N. lutea*** (Willd.) Pers. WATER CHINQUAPIN; AMERICAN LOTUS; YANQUAPIN. Lvs emergent, to 2m above surface, lamina 50cm across, glaucous, blue-green, glabrous above, pubesc. and lepidote beneath, veins prominent beneath. Peduncles equalling petioles; fl. 10–25cm across, pale yellow; pet. concave, obovate, obtuse; anth. with hooked appendage. Fr. obconic or hemispheric, to 10cm diam.; seeds nearly globular. Summer. Eastern N America. 'Flavescens': lvs splashed red in centre; fls small, free-flowering. Z4.

***N. nucifera*** Gaertn. SACRED LOTUS. Lvs emergent, to 2m above surface, lamina to 80cm across, glaucous, margin undulate; petioles and peduncles with short fleshy prickles. Infl. exceeding lvs; fls pink or white, sometimes double in selected cvs, very fragrant, to 30cm diam.; sep. caducous, green; pet. to 12×7cm, oblong or elliptic, obtuse; anth. yellow. Receptacle 10×10cm in fr., seeds, to 2cm, ellipsoid. Summer. Asia from Iran to Japan, south to Australia; introduced to the Nile *c*500BC, but now extinct there. 'Alba': lvs large, pea-green; fls large, white, fragrant. 'Alba Grandiflora': lvs deep green; fls white. 'Alba Plena': fls large, double, cream tinged green, later pure white, scented. 'Alba Striata': sepals white edged pale pink. 'Charles Thomas': fls deep pink tinged lavender. 'Chawan Basu': habit semi-dwarf; fls white edged pink, abundant. 'Empress': petals white fringed crimson. 'Lotus Blossom': fls white heavily tipped pink. 'Maggie Belle Slocum': fls large, pink, held above lvs, fragrant. 'Momo Botan': lvs medium-sized. 'Mrs. Perry D. Slocum': fls large, deep pink turning cream-yellow. 'Pekinensis Rubra': fls carmine-pink. Pekinensis Rubra Plena': fls double, large, carmine-pink. 'Red Lotus': fls deep red, petals large. 'Rosea Plena': fls double to 30cm across, rose-pink, fragrant. 'Shiroman': fls double, large, cream acquiring green centre, later pure white. 'Speciosum': fls single, light pink. 'Shirokunshi': to 45cm; fls tulip-shaped. 'Tulip': habit dwarf; fls pure white, tulip-shaped. Z5.

***N. pentapetala*** (Walter) Fern. See *N. lutea*.
***N. speciosa*** auct. See *N. nucifera*.
For further synonymy see *Nelumbium*.

**NELUMBONACEAE** Dumort. See *Nelumbo*.

**Nemastylis** Nutt. (From Gk *nema*, thread, and *stylos*, column, referring to slender style.) Iridaceae. 7 species of perennial herbs; rootstock a tunicate bulb. Leaves long, linear, plicate. Flowers short-lived, in few-flowered clusters subtended by spathes; tepals 6, similar; stamens 3, filaments separate or joined only at base; style short, with 6 long, spreading, divided branches. N & Tropical America. Z9.

CULTIVATION As for *Tigridia*.

***N. acuta*** (Bartr.) Herb. PRAIRIE IRIS. 15–60cm, sometimes branched; bulb to 2cm diam., globose or ovoid, with dark brown, scaly tunic. Lvs 3–4, to 30cm. Infl. 2–3-fld; fls 4–6cm diam., blue-violet, opening in early morning; tepals spreading, obovate. Spring. Southern US.

***N. floridana*** Small. To 1.5m but often less, sometimes branched. Lvs to 45cm, narrowly linear. Fls to 5cm diam., violet, white in centre, opening in afternoon. Late autumn. SE US (Florida).

***N. tenuis*** ssp. *pringlei* (Wats.) Goldbl. Stem unbranched. Fls scented, pale blue; outer tepals obtuse, inner acute. Mexico.

***N. geminiflora*** Nutt. See *N. acuta*.

**Nematanthus** Schräd. (From Gk *nema*, thread, and *anthos*, flower, referring to the thread-like pedicels.) Gesneriaceae. Some 30 species of epiphytic climbing or trailing subshrubs; stems often woody at base, rooting at nodes, to 1.5m, glabrous to densely pubescent. Leaves opposite-decussate, elliptic to obovate, 1.5–16×1.8cm, acute to acuminate, sometimes cuspidate, glabrous to densely pubescent, often tinged purple beneath, entire to sparsely dentate; petiole to 7cm, often purple. Flowers 1–8 per cyme, usually resupinate, subtended by 2 elliptic bracts; pedicel usually filiform, green or tinged purple, glabrous to densely pubescent; calyx lobes green, orange or red- or purple-tinged, linear to ovate, often reflexed, enclosing corolla tube; corolla to 5.5cm, yellow, orange, pink or purple, glabrous to pubescent, cylindric or tubular, often curved and pouched, graduating into 5 lobes, lobes often mixed in colour; stamens 4, coherent, forming a rectangle; ovary superior, glabrous or pubescent. Fruit a capsule, dehiscing to produce a coloured placental mass; seeds on funicles. S America. Z10.

CULTIVATION See GESNERIADS.

***N. corticola*** Schräd. To 1.2m. Lvs to 15×5cm, variable, elliptic-ovate, pale green below, entire, veins purple beneath; petiole to 2cm, sparsely pubesc. Fls solitary on pedicels to 20cm; cal. to 1.5cm, purple at base, pubesc., lobes ovate-elliptic, reflexed at apex; cor. to 5cm, pink except at white base, inner surface tinged yellow, lobes to 7×5mm; ovary tinged purple, glabrescent. Fr. to 2cm, placental mass cream. Northern S America.

***N. crassifolium*** (Schott) Wiehler. Stem climbing or pendent, to 1.5m. Lvs to 15×4cm, variable, ovate-elliptic, apex cuspidate, succulent, pale green below, rarely purple-tinged, sparsely hairy, margin entire, ciliate; petiole to 2cm. Fls 1–2 per axillary cyme; pedicel to 2cm; peduncle to 16cm; cal. to 3.5cm, purple toward apex, glabrescent to pubesc., lobes ovate-acuminate, serrate; cor. to 5cm, bright red, marked with white within, lobes deltoid-obtuse, revolute, to 1–3×0.8cm; ovary densely hairy toward apex. Fr. to 3×2cm, mauve, ovoid, placental mass cream. Eastern S America.

***N. fissus*** (Vell. Conc.) Skog. Stems trailing to ascending, to 0.6m, densely pubesc. toward tips. Lvs to 9×4cm, obovate, base asymmetric, apex acute to cuspidate, succulent, sparsely to densely hairy above, pale green with purple midrib and densely pubesc. beneath, somewhat serrate; petiole to 2cm, green to red, densely pubesc. Fls 2–4 per cyme; cal. to 1.8cm, green, often tinged red, densely pubesc., lobes ovate, entire; cor. to 3.5cm, expanded, saccate, then constricted, bright red, occasionally marked with yellow, densely pubesc., lobes broadly ovate. Fr. yellow, glabrescent, broadly ellipsoid, to 2×1.5cm, placental mass pale yellow. Eastern S America.

***N. fluminensis*** (Vell. Conc.) Fritsch. Stem erect or pendent, woody at base, to 1.5m, glabrous. Lvs 5–17×2.5–6cm, ovate or obovate, cuspidate, succulent, green and glabrous above, spotted purple below, margin entire. Fls 1–2 per axil; pedicels to 4cm, tinged purple, pubesc.; cal. to 2.5cm, often tinged purple, densely hairy, lobes ovate-acuminate, serrate toward apex, to 0.5cm; cor. 4–5cm, yellow, densely pubesc., recurved, lobes revolute, deltoid-obtuse, to 11×8mm, tube to 7mm; ovary glandular-pubesc. Spring–autumn. S America.

***N. fornix*** (Vell. Conc.) Charteris. Stems climbing, shrubby at base, to 70cm. Lvs to 6×2.5cm, elliptic, acute, fleshy, sparsely hairy above, pale green beneath; petiole to 1cm, pubesc. Fls solitary; pedicel to 2cm, sparsely pubesc.; cal. to 2cm, marked with red, sparsely pubesc., lobes ovate, acute; cor. to 3cm, bright red, lobes ovate-oblong, to 2.2mm. Fr. cream, ovoid-conic, to 1.5×1cm, placental mass white. Eastern S America.

***N. fritschii*** Hoehne. Stems pendent, to 1.5m, densely pubesc. Lvs to 13×5cm, ovate-elliptic, apex slightly cuspidate, base obtuse, succulent, bright green above with a large dark patch beneath, veins densely pubesc. Fls solitary on axillary pedicels to 10cm; cal. to 3cm, tinged purple, pubesc., lobes ovate, serrate; cor. to 4.5cm, resupinate, pouched, outer surface pink, inner surface white and mauve, lobes reflexed, oblong-ovate, to 0.5×0.4cm; ovary tinged purple. Fr. mauve, sparsely pubesc., ovoid, to 3×1.5cm, placental mass white. Eastern S America.

***N. gregarius*** Denh. Stems climbing or pendent, to 80cm. Lvs to 3×1.7cm, elliptic to ovate, subobtuse at base and apex, fleshy, glabrous; petiole to 0.3cm. Fls 1–3 per cyme; pedicel to 1.5cm; cal. to 1.5cm, marked orange at apex, lobes ovate, to 0.8cm wide; cor. to 2.5cm, bright orange with a purple-brown stripe leading to each lobe, lobes obtuse, to 2×2mm. Fr. to 1×0.8cm, yellow-orange, placental mass pale cream. Eastern S America. 'Variegata': lvs spreading, glossy, green with yellow centre; fls orange.

***N. hirtellus*** (Schott) Wiehler. Stem woody at base, to 80cm, glabrous. Lvs to 16×6cm, ovate, asymmetric, apex slightly cuspidate, somewhat fleshy, sparsely pubesc. above, pale green and with red pubesc. veins beneath, entire; petiole to 7cm, red-carmine. Fls 1–4 per cyme; pedicel to 0.6cm; cal. to 2cm, orange-green tinged purple, lobes ovate-angular; cor. to 3.5cm, yellow striped purple throughout, densely pubesc., lobes slightly reflexed. Fr. to 2cm, tinged purple, glabrescent, placental mass cream. Eastern S America.

***N. lanceolatus*** (Poir.) Charteris. Stem woody at base, to 1.5m. Lvs to 12×4cm, obovate-elliptic, slightly cuspidate at apex, succulent, red-veined, finely pubesc.; petiole to 4.5cm, carmine. Fls 1–6 per cyme; pedicels to 0.5cm, red-purple; cal. to 1cm, tinged red, lobes ovate-orbicular; cor. to 3cm, red-orange, densely pubesc., lobes glabrous, slightly reflexed, yellow. Eastern S America.

***N. strigilosus*** (Mart.) H.E. Moore. Stem climbing, woody at base, to 1.5m. Lvs to 3.5×1.8cm, obovate, obtuse, sparsely pubesc. above, pale green and densely pubesc. on veins beneath, entire; petiole to 0.5cm. Fls solitary; pedicel to 1cm; cal. to 1cm, green to red-brown, abruptly expanded, pouched, lobes ovate, acute; cor. to 2cm, tube orange, limb yellow, lobes ovate, to 3×2mm. Fr. ovoid-orbicular, to 1.2×1cm, sparsely hairy. Eastern S America.

***N. wettsteinii*** (Fritsch) H.E. Moore. Stem usually pendent, to 50cm, becoming glabrescent. Lvs to 2.5×1cm, elliptic-ovate, subobtuse, fleshy, bright green and glabrous above, pale green and marked with red beneath, entire; petiole to 0.3cm. Fls 1–2 in axils; pedicels to 0.8cm, sparsely hairy; cal. to 0.7cm, sparsely pubesc., lobes linear-lanceolate; cor. to 2.4cm, orange, tube abruptly expanded, lobes yellow, rounded, not reflexed; style glabrous, white. Fr. conic, obtuse at apex, to 1.5×1cm, bright orange, placental mass pale orange. Eastern S America.

***N.* cultivars**. 'Bijou': lvs dull red beneath; fls pendent, pink. 'Black Gold': fls copper-orange, calyx dark orange. 'Black Magic': lvs small, dark, glossy, dark green; fls orange with yellow tip. 'Candy Corn': lvs small, thick, glossy, dark green; fls orange with yellow tip. 'Freckles': lvs dark green; fls yellow, flecked with red. 'Jungle Lights': habit compact and trailing; lvs small, glossy, tinged dark-purple; fls orange and pink. 'Tropicana': habit erect, freely branching; lvs dark green, glossy; calyx bright red, cor. yellow with maroon stripes.

***N. chloronema*** Mart. See *N. crassifolium*.
***N. dichrus*** (Spreng.) Wiehler. See *N. hirtellus*.
***N. ionema*** Mart. See *N. corticola*.
***N. radicans*** C. Presl. See *N. strigilosus*.
***N. radicans*** (Klotzsch & Hanst. ex Hanst.) H.E. Moore non C. Presl. See *N. gregarius*.
***N. longipes*** DC. See *N. crassifolium*.
***N. nervosus*** (Fritsch) H.E. Moore. See *N. fornix*.
***N. perianthomegus*** (Vell. Conc.) H.E. Moore. See *N. hirtellus*.
***N. selloanus*** (Klotzsch & Hanst.) H.E. Moore. See *N. fissus*.
For further synonym see *Alloplectus, Columnea and Hypocyrta*.

**Nemesia** Vent. (Name used by Dioscorides.) Scrophulariaceae. About 65 species of annual or perennial herbs or subshrubs. Leaves opposite. Flowers axillary or in short terminal racemes; calyx 5-lobed; corolla bilabiate, tube very short, produced into spur or pouch at front, upper lip 4-lobed, lower entire or bilabiate, with palate almost closing throat; stamens 4, filaments of lower pair sometimes curved around those of upper. Fruit is a capsule, laterally compressed; seeds flattened, conspicuously winged. S Africa. Z9.

CULTIVATION Commonly used as frost-tender annuals for summer bedding, mixed borders and pot-plant display in cool glasshouses. *N. strumosa* and its offspring are the most often seen and the least affected by hot humid summers; however, given a continental climate, most are more successful when grown as glasshouse pot-plants sown in the autumn and overwintered at a minimum temperature of 10°C/50°F for flowering in spring. In cooler climates they may be grown on for bedding out in late spring. Plant out after last frosts (spacing 10–15cm apart) into a medium to light, slightly acidic soil to which additional organic matter has been added for moisture-retention: give a sunny position. After the first flush of flower, trim back to give a second display and water well in dry weather since a check to growth gives weak, spindly plants. Sow seed in autumn/spring at 15°C/60°F and lightly covered: harden off before planting out into the open garden. Grow on pot-plants in a medium-fertility loam-based mix, pricking out three seedlings to a pot: give sunny, cool, well-ventilated conditions and water plentifully during the summer; stake to give the brittle stems support and feed fortnightly with a dilute liquid fertilizer. Susceptible to foot and root rots.

***N. azurea*** Diels. Annual herb, glandular-pilose; stems 10–20cm, branched at base or rarely simple. Lvs ovate to linear-oblong, minutely dentate to entire, subglabrous. Infl. racemose; pedicels 5–10mm, glandular; sep. 2–2.5×1–1.5mm, elliptic; cor. purple to violet without, azure-blue within, palate yellow, lobes of upper lip 5–6×2.5mm, lower lip 6–7×5.5mm, emarginate. Fr. ovate, slightly 2-horned at apex, 5mm. Summer. S Africa.

***N. barbata*** (Thunb.) Benth. Annual herb to 50cm, glabrous or nearly so, rather glossy; stems simple or branched near base, 4-angled. Lvs 1–3cm, ovate to lanceolate, coarsely dentate to subentire. Infl. racemose, terminal, to 10cm; cal. glandular; cor. 1.5cm, blue, upper lip pale blue within with white margin and purple lines, white without, with short, obtuse lobes, lower lip longer than upper, broadened toward obtuse apex, entire or nearly so, deep blue, lower part white striped red without, palate pilose, spur conical, straight, shorter than lower lip, striped purple; lower stamens with larger anthers than upper. Fr. slightly narrowed to both ends, with 2 acute points at apex; seeds white, wing vertical, continuous, with irregular outgrowths both sides. S Africa.

***N. chamaedrifolia*** Vent. Perenn. herb, to 50cm; stems freely branched. Lvs ovate, dentate, acute, glabrous or pubesc. Fls in upper lf axils; cal. glandular; cor. white or flushed pale pink, lower lip simple, obtuse, approximately same length as upper, spur about as long as lips. Fr. suborbicular; seeds with 2 wings, with prominent outgrowths both sides, pale brown. S Africa.

***N. cynanchifolia*** Benth. in Hook. Annual herb, 15–60cm; stems profusely branched, ascending or diffuse, 4-angled, pubesc. to glabrous. Lvs 1.2–3×0.3–1.6cm, ovate-lanceolate to lanceolate, obtuse at apex, rounded at base, sinuate-dentate; petioles to 1cm, smaller toward summit of stem. Infl. subcorymbose, generally dense, 3–15cm; pedicels to 3cm, slender, glandular-pubesc.; cal. minutely pubesc., seg. 2–4mm; cor. lilac-blue to purple, upper lip 6–9mm, lower lip emarginate, 6–8mm, palate hairy, spur 6–8mm, cylindric. Fr. 9–10×6–8mm, broadly oblong, not or scarcely horned. Summer. S Africa.

***N. floribunda*** Lehm. Annual herb, erect, glabrous below, somewhat pilose above, shining, pallid; stems 15–40cm, branched from base or subsimple, 4-angled. Lvs 1–4×0.1–1.6cm, ovate or upper lanceolate, obtuse or rounded at apex, subtruncate at base, subentire to dentate, sessile or lower shortly petiolate. Infl. lax, subcorymbose, 3–12cm, fls fragrant; pedicels slender; cal. minutely pubesc., seg. 3–4mm; cor. white or very pale, upper lip 3–4mm, lower lip 5–6mm, bilobed, palate shortly hirsute, spur 5mm, conic. Fr. obovate-oblong, broadly notched, not horned at apex. S Africa.

***N. foetens*** Vent. Perenn. herb to 60cm, somewhat shrubby, glabrous or almost so; stems erect, branched, slightly woody at base. Lvs to 4cm, linear to lanceolate, entire or dentate. Infl. racemose, terminal; cal. hairy or glabrous; cor. to 1.5cm, lips and spur approx. equal lengths, colour various, pale blue, pink, lavender or white, with spur, crest and throat yellow. Fr. broadly ovate, glabrous or viscid-pubesc. S Africa.

***N. grandiflora*** Diels. Erect herb, subglabrous; stems 30–50cm, simple or branched. Basal lvs 2×0.5cm, oblong, cuneate at base, on petioles to 1cm, stem lvs 2–5×0.1–0.3cm, linear, remotely dentate, sessile. Infl. glandular; cal. seg. 4mm, linear-lanceolate; cor. lobes oblong, upper 5–6×4–5mm, lower scarcely emarginate, 9–12×20mm, throat bearded, palate hirsute, spur to 4mm, conic, short. Fr. 9–12×6–8mm, ovate, contracted with 2 short apical horns. S Africa.

***N. lilacina*** N.E. Br. Minutely glandular-pubesc. perenn.; stems to 35cm, freely branched. Lvs to 3.5cm, narrowly lanceolate, dentate. Infl. racemose, to 30cm, lax; pedicels slender; cor. small, lilac, upper lip to 4mm, with purple stripes, lower lip to 4mm, palate with yellow markings, spur short, white. S Africa (SW Cape).

***N. linearis*** Vent. Perenn. herb; stems to 60cm, branches ascending. Lvs linear-lanceolate, entire or remotely dentate. Cor. purple, upper and lower lips approx. same length, spur straight, shorter than lips. Spring–early autumn. S Africa.

***N. macroceras*** Schldl. Annual herb, erect, slender; stem to 30cm, simple or sparingly branched, shining and subglabrous. Lvs remote above, lanceolate to linear, more or less dentate, lowest to 7×1cm, reduced upwards. Infl. lax, fls slightly fragrant; pedicels minutely glandular-pubesc.; cal. seg. 2–4mm, oblong to lanceolate, minutely glandular-pubesc.; cor. with upper lip white, lobes 6–7×2mm, lower lip 6mm, emarginate, yellow, spur deflexed, cylindric, 8mm. Fr. 6–8mm, obovate-oblong, broadly notched at apex, not horned, rounded and oblique at base, glabrous. S Africa.

***N. pageae*** L. Bol. Plant 22–30cm, bushy, stems branched. Fls small; cor. bright cherry red, lower lip rich yellow. Summer. S Africa.

***N. strumosa*** Benth. in Hook. Annual herb, 15–60cm, erect, glabrous below, somewhat glandular-pilose above; stems quadrangular, branched from base, leafy at least below. Lvs to 7.5cm, oblanceolate-spathulate, entire to dentate, stem lvs sessile, becoming lanceolate then linear, reduced ultimately to 1.5cm. Infl. 5–10cm, compactly subcorymbose in fl., elongating in fr.; pedicels to 4cm; cal. lobes 4–6mm, linear, pilose; cor. colour various, yellow or purple to white, often veined purple without, throat yellow with darker markings, upper lip 6–9×16–24mm, lower lip 2–3cm broad, notched at apex, bearded within. Fr. ovoid, 8–12mm; seeds numerous, tuberculate, winged. S Africa.

***N. versicolor*** E. Mey. ex Benth. Annual herb, to 50cm, glabrous or subglabrous; stem simple or branched near base. Lvs to 5cm, ovate to broadly elliptic to linear, somewhat sinuate or dentate, lower petiolate, upper sessile. Infl. terminal, racemose, to 7.5cm; cor. to 12mm, colour variable, blue, mauve, yellow or white, lips often different colours, upper lip with obtuse oblong lobes, lower lip approx. same length as upper, broad, obtuse, shortly bilobed, palate broad, scarcely lobed, spur almost straight or slightly incurved, approximately same length as lower lip. Fr. broadly oblong, with small scarcely spreading tips; seeds white, wing continuous, covered by prominent outgrowths. S Africa. f. ***compacta*** Voss Plants more compact, 20–30cm; fls profuse, white, rose, violet and blue.

***N.* cultivars** and hybrids. Mostly derived from *N. strumosa* and *N. versicolor*, these are the nemesias popular for summer bedding. 'Blue Gem': habit bushy, to 20cm; cloud of sky-blue fls. Carnival Hybrids: compact bushes to 30cm; very floriferous. 'Funfair': to 25cm; fls brilliant colours; seed race. 'Grandiflora': fls large. 'Mello Red and White': fls raspberry red and white. 'Mello White': fls white. 'Nana Compacta': habit dwarf. 'Suttonii': to 50cm; fls irregularly shaded, with broad lip in front and pouch at base, from carmine, through yellow and pink to white. 'Tapestry': to 25cm, habit upright; fls richly coloured.

***N. compacta*** hort. ex Vilm. See *N. versicolor* f. *compacta*.
***N. macrocarpa*** (Ait.) Druce. See *N. chamaedrifolia*.

**Nemopanthus** Raf. (From Gk *nema*, thread, *pous*, foot, and *anthos*, a flower, referring to the very slender pedicels.) MOUNTAIN HOLLY. Aquifoliaceae. 1 species, a deciduous, stoloniferous shrub to 3.5m, closely allied to *Ilex* but differing in the much reduced calyx and free petals. Leaves alternate, oblong-ovate, to 6×3cm, entire or slightly serrate. Flowers 4–5-merous, green-yellow. Fruit spherical, red; pyrenes 3–5. Eastern N America. Z5.

CULTIVATION As for *Ilex*.

***N. mucronatus*** (L.) Trel. As for the genus. The plants sold as the above species in the British Isles this century should be called *Ilex collina* Alexander (*Nemopanthus collinus* (Alexander) Clark).

***N. collinus*** (Alexander) Clark. See *Ilex collina*.
For further synonymy see *Ilex*.

**Nemophila** Nutt. (From Gk *nemos*, grove, and *philos*, loving, in reference to the habitat of some species.) Hydrophyllaceae. 11 species of annual glabrous, downy or hispidulous herbs. Stems delicately branched and spreading, somewhat succulent and easily broken. Leaves opposite or alternate, usually pinnatifid. Flowers usually solitary, stalked, sometimes in racemose cymes; calyx deeply 5-lobed, appendage in each sinus spreading to reflexed, more rarely vestigial; corolla campanulate, cylindrical or rotate, usually exceeding calyx, petals blue or white; stamens 5, glabrous, included; style bifid. Fruit a 1-celled, hairy capsule; seeds 2–10. Western N America.

CULTIVATION Fast-growing annuals used for border edging, window boxes and other containers, suitable for north-facing sites with good light. They are sometimes grown in pots in the cool glasshouse or conservatory. Grow in moisture-retentive soils in sun or part shade with shelter from wind. Support with peasticks if necessary. Sow *in situ* in spring or autumn. The soft foliage is particularly attractive to aphids, treat with a specific aphicide.

***N. maculata*** Benth. ex Lindl. FIVE SPOT. To 30cm, glabrous to hispidulous. Stems erect to semi-prostrate, spreading. Lvs opposite, 4–7-lobed. Fls to 4.5cm diam., solitary, long-stalked, axillary; pet. white, each with a deep violet blotch near or at the apex, sometimes faintly veined or tinted mauve-blue. C California.

***N. menziesii*** Hook. & Arn. BABY-BLUE-EYES. To 12cm, hirsute. Stems to 30cm, spreading-procumbent, bluntly angular. Lvs 3.5–6cm, 9–11-lobed, rarely entire. Fls to 4cm diam., solitary, long-stalked, axillary; pet. broadly obovate, rounded, spreading, highly variable in colour: white to sky-blue, often with a white or yellow-stained centre, or spotted or stained darker blue or purple-black. California. 'Alba': fls white with a black centre. 'Crambeoides': fls pale blue veined purple, unspotted. 'Coelestis': fls white edged sky-blue. 'Grandiflora': fls pale blue with a white centre. 'Insignis': fls pure blue. 'Marginata': fls blue edged white. 'Occulata': fls pale blue with a purple-black centre. 'Purpurea Rosea': fls purple-pink. var. ***atromaria*** (Fisch. & C.A. Mey.) Chandl. Fls white spotted black-purple. var. ***discoidalis*** (Lem.) Voss. Fls bronze-purple edged white.

***N. aurita*** Lindl. See *Pholistoma auritum*.
***N. insignis*** Douglas & Benth. See *N. menziesii*.

**Neoabbottia** Britt. & Rose. See *Leptocereus*.

**Neoalsomitra** Hutch. (From Gk *neos*, new, and *Alsomitra* a closely allied genus.) Cucurbitaceae. 12 species of dioecious climbers. Tendrils simple or bifid. Leaves simple or 3–5-foliolate. Male flowers in panicles or loose axillary racemes; peduncles very slender; calyx cup-shaped, lobes 5, oblong to oblong-lanceolate; corolla rotate, deeply 5-lobed, lobes oblong; stamens 5, free, with short filaments, anthers oblong, curved; female flowers in racemes; ovary 1–3-locular, ovules numerous, styles 3–4. Fruit clavate to cylindric, terete to bluntly triangular in section, 3-valved; seeds compressed, wing membranous (if present), with sinuate-tuberculous margin. Indomalaya to Australia and W Pacific. Z10.

CULTIVATION As for *Trichosanthes*.

***N. podagrica*** Steenis Stems to 30m, glabrous, base fleshy, thickened, fusiform, to 100×10cm, with hard, green spines 1.5–5cm (adapted lvs) in basal regions; branches also thickened at base. Leaflets obovate, blunt, base cuneate, middle leaflet 6–11×4–7mm, petiolule to 2cm, lateral leaflets 5–10×3–6cm, petiolule to 1.5cm; outermost leaflets smaller, from petiolule of lateral leaflets. Male fls green-yellow, in panicles to 40cm, female fls on pedicels *c*1mm. Fr. in panicles, tubular to cup-shaped, to 1.5–2cm; seeds flat, 4–5×3–3.5mm, with a delicate wing. S Malaysia.

**Neobakeria** Schltr.
***N. angustifolia*** Schltr. See *Polyxena angustifolia*.
***N. namaquensis*** Schltr.. See *Polyxena angustifolia*.

**Neobathiea** Schltr. (For M. Henri Perrier de la Bâthie (1873–1958), a French botanist who worked mainly on Madagascan orchids.) Orchidaceae. 6 species of epiphytic orchids. Stems usually short. Leaves ligulate, elliptic or oblanceolate. Raceme 1- to few-flowered; flowers white; sepals and petals free; lip trilobed, spurred, with the mouth of the spur immediately below the column, spur slender; column short, with 2 arms at the base tightly enclosing, and joined to, the sides of the mouth of the spur. Madagascar. Z9.

CULTIVATION As for *Angraecum*.

***N. filicornu*** Schltr. To 6cm. Lvs 4–5, 4–5×1cm, narrowly elliptic. Flowers solitary, pure white; peduncle 2–2.5cm; pedicel and ovary 12mm; sep. 13×2.5mm, narrowly oblanceolate; pet. similar but slightly shorter and narrower; lip 20×10mm, trilobed at base, midlobe ovate-lanceolate, acute, lateral lobes subcordate; spur pendent, 14cm, becoming filiform from a funnel-shaped mouth; column 3.5mm, stout.

***N. perrieri*** (Schltr.) Schltr. Small, almost stemless. Lvs 4–6, 3.5–7×1–2cm, oblong-spathulate, undulate. Fls 1–2, white; peduncle 6–12cm; pedicel and ovary 25mm; sep. 22mm, narrowly oblanceolate, acute; pet. similar but slightly smaller; lip trilobed at about halfway, 20mm×20mm, lateral lobes diverging, ovate, midlobe ovate, acute, twice as large as lateral lobes, the whole lip shaped like a spear-head; spur 7–10cm, filiform from a funnel-shaped mouth, curving forward, then pendent; column very short.

**Neobenthamia** Rolfe. (From Gk *neos*, new, and for George Bentham (1800–1884), British botanist.) Orchidaceae. 1 species, a terrestrial or lithophytic orchid. Roots fleshy. Stems clustered, branched, leafy, 90cm to 2m tall. Leaves linear-lanceolate, grass-like, distichous, to 28×2cm. Inflorescence terminal, racemose or paniculate, densely many-flowered; flowers white, the lip with a pubescent yellow centre edged with pink dots; sepals and petals spreading, similar, subequal, sepals 10–12mm, oblong-elliptic, petals 9–10mm, oblong-spathulate; lip entire, fleshy, 11×7mm, oblong-obovate, margin undulate; column short and thick, 2–3mm; anther-cap dull purple; pollinia in 2 pairs of 2. Tanzania. Z10.

CULTIVATION Intermediate to warm-growing orchids. Culture similar to that of *Sobralia*.

***N. gracilis*** Rolfe. As for the genus.

**Neobesseya** Britt. & Rose.
***N. asperispina*** (Boed.) Boed. See *Escobaria missouriensis*.
***N. missouriensis*** (Sweet) Britt. & Rose. See *Escobaria missouriensis*.
***N. notesteinii*** (Britt.) Britt. & Rose. See *Escobaria missouriensis*.
***N. rosiflora*** Lahman ex G. Turner. See *Escobaria missouriensis*.
***N. similis*** (Engelm.) Britt. & Rose. See *Escobaria missouriensis*.
***N. wissmannii*** (Hildm. ex Schum.) Britt. & Rose. See *Escobaria missouriensis*.
***N. zilziana*** (Boed.) Boed. See *Escobaria zilziana*.

**Neobuxbaumia** Backeb. (For F. Buxbaum (1900–79), Austrian cactologist, with the Gk prefix *neo-*, new, to distinguish it from *Buxbaumia* Hedw., a genus of mosses.) Cactaceae. 8 species of massive columnar or tree-like cacti, simple or branched; stems stout cylindric, ribbed; ribs 8 to very numerous, usually low. Fertile zone usually unmodified, or apical, with larger areoles with numerous bristles and bristly spines; flower tubular-campanulate or tubular-funnelform, nocturnal; scales fleshy; floral areoles naked or with a few weak bristles. Fruit ovoid with non-juicy, white, pulp, dehiscent by vertical slits; seeds broadly oval, 2.0–2.8×1.6–1.9mm, black-brown, shiny; relief flat; hilum medium, oblique, superficial; appendages none.

CULTIVATION Grow in an intermediate greenhouse (min. 10–15°C/50–60°F), use 'standard' cactus compost: moderate to high inorganic content (more than 50% grit), pH 6–7.5; shade in hot weather; maintain low humidity; keep dry from mid-autumn until early spring, except for light misting on warm days in late winter. The most commonly grown species, *N.polylopha*, is a valuable, fast-growing subject for outdoor displays in frost-free areas. This genus may be better united with *Carnegiea*, but is here maintained, partly for the practical reason that several of the species do not have names in that genus, and partly because the relationships of the individual species with both *Carnegiea* and *Pachycereus* are not yet fully elucidated. The species fall into two groups. In one the species are branched and flower at the stem apices, and in the other they are normally unbranched and flower laterally.

***N.euphorbioides*** (Haw.) F. Buxb. Simple, columnar, 3–5m; stem 10–15cm diam., dark green or blue-green, sometimes tinged red; ribs usually 8–10, 3cm high, rounded-acute, somewhat tuberculate; areoles *c*1cm apart; central spines 1(–2), to 4cm, dark grey, radial spines 1–10, 4–26mm. Fl. 6–8cm, funnelform, pale to deep red-pink; tube and outer tepals wine-red; scales decurrent; throat cream. Fr. 6cm, oblong, yellow-green; fl. remnant caducous at maturity. E Mexico (Tamaulipas to Veracruz). Z9.

***N.macrocephala*** (F.A. Weber ex Schum.) Dawson. Tree with main axis to 7–15m and trunk 30–60cm diam.; lateral branches few to several, 30–40cm diam., erect, dark green; ribs 17–26, low, obtuse; spines pink or red at first, becoming grey or nearly black; central spines 1–3, radial spines 8–12. Flowering zone apical; areoles larger, with abundant yellow wool and numerous translucent pink bristles and bristly spines; fl. 4–5×2–3cm, nocturnal, narrowly campanulate-funnelform; pericarpel 12–16×10–12mm, globose; scales of pericarpel and tube broad, imbricate, purple-brown, fleshy; areoles of pericarpel felted and with bristly spines, those of tube glabrous; outer tepals purple-red, reflexed at anthesis, inner white, with red tip and pale red mid-stripe. Fr. 2cm, globose, deep purple-red, with curly bristles. S Mexico (Puebla). Z9.

***N.mezcalaensis*** (Bravo) Backeb. Columnar; stem unbranched, to 5–10m×13–30(–40)cm, light green; ribs 13–25, 18–25mm high; areoles 18–26mm apart; spines white or pale yellow, tipped red or brown; central spines 1–4, somewhat longer than the radials, radial spines 5–9, 8–20mm. Fl. 5.5cm, lateral, tubular-funnelform; scales of pericarpel and tube tinged red, green or yellow; floral areoles naked; outer tepals coloured like the scales, inner white, sometimes tinged green or pink. Fr. 3–4cm, globose or obovoid; areoles persistent, with felt and spines. SW Mexico. Z9.

***N.polylopha*** (DC.) Backeb. Columnar, to 15m×50cm, normally unbranched; ribs 22–36 or more; areoles 8–11mm apart; spines 7–9, 1–3cm, bristly, yellow. Fl. 5–8×3.5–4.5cm, shortly campanulate-funnelform; scales of pericarpel and tube glandular, dull purple-brown; floral areoles almost naked; inner tepals pink. Fr. 2.5–4×2–3.5cm, ovoid, scaly and with a few bristles, olive green. C Mexico. 1828. Z9.

***N.tetetzo*** (F.A. Weber ex Schum.) Backeb. Columnar, to 15m tall, usually branched; trunk to 60cm diam.; branches few, erect, light grey-green; ribs 13–17 or more; areoles 7–35mm apart; central spines 1–3, the longest to 3–4cm, dark brown to black, radial spines (0–)7–12, 5–20mm. Flowering zone apical, unmodified; fl. 5.5cm, tubular-funnelform; scales of pericarpel narrow, not imbricate; fl. areoles with wool and short bristles, accrescent in fruit; inner tepals white, tinged green. Fr. *c*4×3cm, ovoid, green, tinged red. S Mexico (Puebla, Oaxaca). Z9.

For synonymy see *Carnegiea*, *Cephalocereus*, *Cereus*, *Lemaireocereus* and *Pachycereus*.

**Neocabreria** R. King & H. Robinson. (From Gk *neos*, new, and for Angel L. Cabrera, Argentine botanist.) Compositae. 3 species of erect subshrubs. Stems sparingly branched, pubescent. Leaves opposite, rather crowded, oblong to elliptic, crenate or serrate, cuneate at base, shortly petiolate, pubescent above, glabrous beneath. Capitula discoid, in a corymbose panicle, shortly pedunculate; receptacle flat to convex; phyllaries in 2–4 series, imbricate, oblong to linear, 4-ribbed, tinged brown or yellow; florets white to rose-purple. Fruit a prismatic, ribbed cypsela; pappus of bristles, scabrid. Tropical S America. Z10.

CULTIVATION As for *Bartlettina*.

***N.serrulata*** (DC.) R. King & H. Robinson. Lvs to 6×1.5cm, lanceolate, toothed. Capitula numerous; involucre ovoid; phyllaries in 2–3 series. Brazil.

For synonymy see *Eupatorium*.

**Neocallitropsis** Florin. (From Gk *neos*, new, *Callitris* and *-opsis*, resemblance; new name based on the illegitimate name *Callitropsis*, resembling *Callitris*.) Cupressaceae. 1 species, an evergreen, probably dioecious conifer to 10m, allied to *Libocedrus* and *Callitris*. Bark grey-brown, resinous. Crown conic; branches spreading, horizontal, not segmented; branchlets divided. Leaves dimorphic, 8-ranked in decussate whorls of 4, densely arranged, superficially similar to *Araucaria heterophylla*; juvenile leaves acicular, to 1.5cm, outspread; adult leaves 6×3mm, tough, incurved, acute, minutely denticulate, dorsal surface keeled. Male cones terminal, borne on long branchlets. Female cones terminal, borne on short branchlets; scales 8, in 2 decussate whorls of 4, long-acuminate, apices with a long reflexed acuminate spine; seeds with minute wings. New Caledonia, rare and endangered. Z10.

CULTIVATION Frost tender, and requiring high humidity. Found on well-drained mineral-rich serpentine soils, *N.pancheri* it is tolerant of very alkaline conditions. Propagate by cuttings or seed, though seed rarely available and often absent even in wild.

***N.pancheri*** (Carr.) Laub. As for the genus.

***N.araucarioides*** (Compton) Florin. See *N.pancheri*.

**Neocardenasia** Backeb.
***N.herzogiana*** Backeb. See *Neoraimondia herzogiana*.

**Neochilenia** Backeb. ex Dölz. See *Neoporteria*.

**Neocogniauxia** Schltr. (From Gk *neos*, new, and for M.A. Cogniaux (1841–1916), Belgian botanist.) Orchidaceae. Some 2 species of epiphytic orchids. Rhizome creeping. Secondary stems short, slender, terete, erect, enveloped by 1–3 tubular sheaths, apically unifoliate. Leaves coriaceous, erect or suberect, linear-oblong to linear-lanceolate. Inflorescence terminal, slender, surpassing leaves, erect to arching; fls solitary, showy, orange to scarlet; sepals and petals subequal, subsimilar, free, spreading; lip small, enveloping and parallel to column, simple to obscurely trilobed, often papillose; column short, subterete, arching, footless, clinandrium denticulate, pollinia 8, waxy, ovoid. Jamaica, Cuba, Haiti, Dominican Republic. Z10.

CULTIVATION Epiphytes for bright positions in the intermediate house. See ORCHIDS.

***N.monophylla*** (Griseb.) Schltr. Secondary stems to 9cm, enveloped by flecked sheaths. Lvs to 25×1cm, linear-oblong or linear-elliptic, obtuse, suberect. Infl. to 30cm, arching; bracts sheathing, spotted purple; fls to 5cm diam., showy, bright orange-scarlet; sep. to 22×8mm, elliptic-oblong or ovate-oblong, obtuse; pet. to 17×9mm, obovate-elliptic or elliptic-oblong, obtuse; lip to 9mm, ovate or obovate, apiculate, 3-lobed, midlobe cordate-semicircular, papillose, disc 3-ridged, with a sac-like growth on the central keel. papillose; column to 9mm, orange, auriculate, anth. purple. Autumn–winter. Jamaica.

For synonymy see *Laelia* and *Trigonidium*.

**Neocussonia** Hutch.
***N.umbellifera*** (Sonder) Hutch. See *Schefflera umbellifera*.

**Neodawsonia** Backeb.
***N.apicicephalium*** (Dawson) Backeb. See *Cephalocereus apicicephalium*.

**Neodonnellia** Rose. See *Tripogandra*.

**Neoevansia** W.T. Marsh.
***N.striata*** (Brandg.) Sanchez-Mej. See *Peniocereus striatus*.

**Neofinetia** Hu. (For Achille Finet (1862–1913), French botanist.) Orchidaceae. 1 species, an epiphytic, monopodial orchid, to 15cm. Stems short, branching basally, appearing tufted. Leaves to 10cm, alternate, in two ranks, basally overlapping and clothing stem, narrow-ligulate, falcate to recurved, tapering, fleshy, centrally grooved and folded above. Inflorescence axillary, a raceme, ascending; flowers to 10, white; sep. and pet. to 1cm spreading, linear-oblong to linear-lanceolate; lip to 10mm, obscurely 3-lobed, recurved, midlobe ligulate, lateral lobes erect, obtuse, spur very slender; column fleshy, winged. China, Japan, Korea. Z9.

CULTIVATION Small and graceful epiphytes for humid, semi-shaded situations in the cool house. Pot in a fine bark mix and water throughout the year, allowing a slight drying between waterings.

*N.falcata* (Thunb.) Hu. As for the genus. Variegated forms occur and are valued bonsai subjects.

**Neogaerrhinum** Rothm.
*N.filipes* (A. Gray) Rothm. See *Antirrhinum filipes*.

**Neogardneria** Schltr. ex Garay. (From Gk *neos*, new and *Gardneria*.) Orchidaceae. Some 3 species of epiphytes. Pseudobulbs ovoid. Foliage lanceolate, plicate. Inflorescence lax; sepals and petals similar, free; lip subsessile, trilobed, midlobe narrow, abruptly deflexed, lateral lobes erect, callus fan-shaped, crested, irregularly furrowed. NE Tropical America. Z10.

CULTIVATION Epiphytes for the intermediate house. See ORCHIDS.

*N.murrayana* (Gardn.) Garay. Pseudobulbs ovate, grooved to 7.5cm. Lvs lanceolate, membranous, acute, furrowed. Scapes shorter than lvs; fls pale yellow-green, lip white, lateral lobes streaked dark-purple; tepals ovate-lanceolate, acute, spreading, bases fused, subequal; lip trilobed, midlobe similar to lateral lobes, reflexed, lateral lobes oblong, erect, incurved, callus between lateral lobes crested, fleshy, recurved, furrowed. Brazil.

For synonymy see *Zygopetalum*.

**Neoglazovia** Mez. (For A. Glaziou (1828–1906), French plant collector and landscape architect, and Gk *neos*, new.) Bromeliaceae. 2 species of perennial, terrestrial herbs, spreading via rhizomes, stems short. Leaves narrow, longer than inflorescence, in a bundle-like rosette, blades linear, scarcely distinct from sheaths. Inflorescence simple, loosely racemose, erect, terminal, bracteate; lower floral bracts linear, upper triangular, shorter; sepals free, nearly symmetric; petals free, symmetric, ligulate. Fruit fleshy. NE Brazil. Z10.

CULTIVATION See BROMELIADS.

*N.concolor* C.H. Wright. To 1m in flower. Lvs 40–60cm, 5–8, densely white-scaly, long-acuminate, distant-serrate with curved, 4mm-long spines. Infl. 30cm; scape slender, canescent; lower floral bracts longer than fls; pedicel slender, 5–7mm; sep. broadly ovate, obtuse, red; pet. 2cm, bright purple, with 2 fimbriate basal scales.

*N.variegata* (Arruda) Mez. Lvs to 150cm, glabrous above, with broad white crossbands beneath, pungent, margins incurved. Infl. to 25cm, lower floral bracts equal fls; sep. 6–7mm, suborbicular, blunt or with a small mucro; pet. 13mm, blunt, with 2 subentire basal scales.

**Neogomesia** Castañeda.
*N.agavoides* Castañeda. See *Ariocarpus agavoides*.

**Neohenricia** L. Bol. (From Gk *neos*, new, and *Henricia*.) Aizoaceae. 1 species, a very small leaf-succulent related to *Stomatium* and *Rhinephyllum*, differing on account of their papillose leaf surface (smooth in *Stomatium*, rugose in *Rhinephyllum*). Stems freely branched, creeping, densely mat-forming. Leaves 4 together on a shoot, 10mm long, 2mm wide below, 5mm wide and convex above, with many tiny white tubercles. Flowers pedicellate, 14×12mm, white, nocturnal, strongly fragrant. S Africa (Orange Free State: Fauresmith District). Z9.

CULTIVATION As for *Pleiospilos*.

*N.sibbettii* (L. Bol.) L. Bol. As for the genus.

For synonymy see *Henricia*.

**Neolauchea** Kränzl. (From Gk *neos*, new, and for Herr Friedrich Wilhelm George Lauche (1827–1883), German dendrologist and gardener.) Orchidaceae. 1 species, an epiphytic orchid. Rhizome elongate, creeping, branched. Pseudobulbs 1.8–2.5cm, borne at short intervals on rhizome, narrowly ovoid, enveloped by fibrous sheaths, 1-leaved at apex. Leaves 4–6cm, coriaceous, narrowly linear, subterete. Inflorescence to 5cm, terminal, slender, erect or arching, 1-flowered; flowers small, rose-red or lilac; dorsal sepal broadly ovate, apiculate, concave, lateral sepals shortly connate, adnate to column foot forming a sac-shaped mentum; petals larger than sepals, spreading, ovate-oblong; lip broadly ovate-oblong, concave, with 2 teeth near base; column short. S Brazil. Z10.

CULTIVATION Epiphytes for the intermediate house; see ORCHIDS.

*N.pulchella* Kränzl. As for the genus.

For synonymy see *Mieracyllium*.

**Neolehmannia** Kränzl.
*N.porpax* (Rchb. f.) Garay & Dunsterville. See *Nanodes mathewsii*.

**Neolitsea** (Benth.) Merrill. (From its relation to *Litsea*.) Lauraceae. Some 60 species of evergreen, dioecious trees and shrubs. Leaves alternate, petiolate, entire, usually 3-nerved, leathery. Inflorescence umbellate, subsessile, bracteate; male flowers with 6 fertile stamens in 3 rings, the outer 4 without glands, the 2 inner with one gland on either side; female flowers with 6 staminodes. Fruit a red or black berry. E & SE Asia, Indomalaysia.

CULTIVATION As for *Laurus*, but calcifuge.

*N.sericea* (Bl.) Koidz. Evergreen tree to 6m. Branches tinged green when young. Lvs to 18×7cm, oblong or ovate-oblong, obtuse, 3-veined from the base, densely yellow-pubesc. like soft suede above when young, becoming glabrous, dark green above, glaucous and white beneath, aromatic when crushed; petiole to 3cm. Fls yellow. Fr. to 1.5cm, ellipsoid, red. Temperate E Asia. Z9.

*N.glauca* (Sieb.) Koidz. See *N.sericeae*.
*N.sieboldii* (Kuntze) Nak. See *N.sericea*.
*N.latifolia* Koidz. non S. Moore. See *N.sericea*.
For further synonymy see *Litsea*.

**Neolloydia** Britt. & Rose. (For Professor F.E. Lloyd (fl. 1922), with the Gk prefix, *neo-*, new, to distinguish the name from *Lloydia* Salisb. ex Rchb.) Cactaceae. 14 species of low-growing or dwarf cacti, simple or clustering; rootstock fibrous to napiform; stems depressed-globose to short cylindric, tuberculate; areoles usually entire, apical, rarely bipartite, with apical and axillary portions connected by a groove (*N.conoidea*); spines various but never hooked. Flowers mostly small, short funnelform, at upper edge of areole (axillary in *N.conoidea*); pericarpel naked or rarely with 1–2 small scales; tube narrow, short. Fruit globose to turbinate, naked or almost so, dry or slightly fleshy, splitting vertically or disintegrating to release the seeds; seeds 1.2–1.9×0.9–1.3mm, nearly circular to broadly oval, black-brown or brown, matt, not wrinkled or ridged, periphery keeled or not; relief low- to high-domed; hilum medium to large, basal or oblique, superficial or impressed. E & NE Mexico and SW Texas.

CULTIVATION Grow in a cool frost-free greenhouse (min. 2–7°C/36–45°F), use 'standard' cactus compost: moderate to high inorganic content (more than 50% grit), pH 6–7.5; full sun; low air-humidity; keep dry from mid-autumn until early spring, except for light misting on warm days in late winter. Probably related to *Thelocactus*, but with smaller stems and flowers, and with the pericarpel and tube usually naked, not conspicuously scaly. Many are semi-geophytic in nature.

*N.conoidea* (DC.) Britt. & Rose. Very variable; simple or clustering; stem 5–24×3–6cm, globose-ovoid to shortly cylindric, grey to blue-green or slightly yellow-green; tubercles large, 3–10×6–10×5–9mm, ascending, grooved; areoles bipartite, apical (abaxial) portion vegetative, bearing spines and offsets, axillary (adaxial) portion flower-bearing; central spines 0–6, 5–30mm, black to red-brown, projecting, straight, radial spines 8–28, to 5–13mm, almost white or dark tipped. Fl. 2–3×4–6cm; tepals to 30×9–10mm, magenta. Summer. E & NE Mexico, SW US (SW Texas). Z9.

*N.gielsdorfiana* (Werderm.) F. Knuth. Simple, rarely clustering; stem to 5–7×4.5–5cm, globose to ovoid or short cylindric, light blue- to grey-green or somewhat yellow-green; tubercles 6–10×3–5×3–5mm; central spines 0–1, to 20mm, white, dark tipped or nearly black, curved upwards, radial spines 5–7, to 20mm. Fl. 1.3–2.4×1.5–2cm; tepals to 13×4mm, pale yellow with faint red-brown mid-stripe. NE Mexico (SW Tamaulipas). Z9.

*N.horripila* (Lem.) Britt. & Rose. Simple or often clustering; stems 7–10(–18)×4–9cm, globose or elongate, yellow- to olive- or blue-green; tubercles 7–9×5–7×5–7mm; central spines (0–)1(–3), 12–42mm, straight, white to tinged yellow, dark tipped, radial spines 12–14, 9–41mm. Fl. 2.2–4×2.5–4cm; tepals to 23×6mm, magenta, paler to white near base. Spring. E Mexico (Hidalgo). Z9.

***N. knuthiana*** (Boed.) F. Knuth. Usually simple; stem 3–6×3.5–7cm, slightly depressed-globose, blue-green; tubercles 4–5×5–7×5–7mm; central spines 1–2, to 10–16mm, white, radial spines 14–20, 6–8mm. Fl. 2.3–3×1.8–2.5cm; tepals to 19×5mm, pale pink with darker mid-stripe. E Mexico (San Luis Potosi). Z9.

***N. laui*** (Glass & Fost.) E.F. Anderson. Simple; stem 0.5–1.5×1.2–3.5cm, depressed-globose, yellow-green; tubercles 2–3×3–10mm; central spines 0, radial spines 6–8, 12–22mm, pale brown. Fl. to 3.5cm diam.; tepals to 19×5mm, pale pink with darker mid-stripe; fil. red. Summer. E Mexico (San Luis Potosi). Z9.

***N. lophophoroides*** (Werderm.) E.F. Anderson. Simple; rootstock tuberous; stem depressed-globose to ovoid; tubercles 9–12×10–12mm, areoles densely woolly; central spine 0–1, to 11mm, nearly white or grey with dark tip, radial spines 2–5(–6), 2–9mm. Fl. to 3.5cm diam.; tepals to 20×5mm, silvery-white to pale pink. Summer. E Mexico (San Luis Potosi). Z9.

***N. mandragora*** (Fric ex A. Berger) E.F. Anderson. Simple; rootstock large, napiform, junction with stem neck-like; stem 3–7×3–6cm, globose to ovoid, green to grey-green; tubercles 3–4×3–4×3–5mm; central spines 1–2, 10–22mm, white, darker at base or tip, straight, radial spines 8–25, 3–15mm, white. Fl. 2–3×1.5–3.5cm; tepals to 25×5mm, white, mid-stripe tinged green, brown or magenta. Spring. NE Mexico (S Coahuila, S Nuevo León). Z9.

***N. pseudomacrochele*** (Backeb.) E.F. Anderson. Simple, rarely clustering; stem 2–4×2.5–3.5cm, globose to short-cylindric, dark blue-green; tubercles 6–8×7–10×3–5mm; spines 5–8, to 15–30mm, dirty white below, black-brown to grey above, slender, bristly, curved and twisted. Fl. 2.5–3.2×3–3.5cm; tepals to 27×5mm, creamy white or pink with darker mid-stripe; stigmas white. Summer. EC Mexico (Querétaro). Z9.

***N. pseudopectinata*** (Backeb.) E.F. Anderson. Simple; stem 2–3×2–3.5cm, depressed-globose, covered by spines; tubercles 3–3.5×2–3mm, laterally compressed; areoles linear; central spines absent, radial spines *c*50, 1–2mm, white, pectinate, adpressed, not plumose. Fl. like those of *N. valdeziana* or slightly larger. NE Mexico (SW Tamaulipas, S Nuevo León). Z9.

***N. saueri*** (Boed.) F. Knuth. Simple; stem 3–5×4–7.5cm, depressed-globose, grey- to blue-green; tubercles 9–10×7–9×2–5mm; central spines 1–3, 10–20mm, grey-black, curving slightly upwards, radial spines 7–14, 5–15mm, white. Fl. 1.5–2.3×2–2.5cm; tepals to 12×3.5mm, white with pale pink mid-stripe. NE Mexico (SW Tamaulipas). Z9.

***N. schmiedickeana*** (Boed.) E.F. Anderson. Simple or clustering in cult.; stem 1–3×1.5–5cm, depressed-globose to globose or short-cylindric, dark blue to grey-green; tubercles 1.5–7×3–18×2–8mm; spines absent or 1–8 or more, diverse, 1–30mm, straight or curved, flattened and papery, or flexible and acicular. Fl. 1.5–2.6×1–3.2cm; tepals to 27×7mm, white, yellow or pink to magenta. Spring. NE Mexico (S Nuevo León, SW Tamaulipas, San Luis Potosi). var. ***schmiedickeana.*** Stem dull dark green; tubercles 3–4×5–7×4–5mm; spines 2–4, 15–22×1mm, dark brown to grey, flattened, curved and sometimes twisted. Fl. 2–2.7×1.8–2.8cm; tepals white to pink with magenta mid-stripes; stigmas white. NE Mexico (SW Tamaulipas). var. ***dickinsoniae*** (Glass & Fost.) E.F. Anderson. Stem dark green; central spines 1–3, 13–22mm, grey-brown, cylindric, slightly curved, radial spines 18–20, *c*2.5mm, white. F. 2×1.7cm; tepals white with pale red-brown mid-stripe; stigmas white. NE Mexico (S Nuevo León). var. ***flaviflora*** (G. Frank & Lau) E.F. Anderson. Stem grey-green; spines 4–6, to 30mm, brown, flattened, curved towards stem apex. Fl. 1.5×1–1.5cm; tepals pale yellow; stigmas off-white. E Mexico (San Luis Potosi). var. ***gracilis*** (Glass & Fost.) E.F. Anderson. Stem grey-green; tubercles slender, 1.5–1.9×3–5×7–8mm; central spine 1, 18–23×1–2mm, thin and papery, curved near apex, flexible, radial spines, 1–3, 2mm, white. Fl. 2×1.5cm; tepals white, sometimes with faint pink mid-stripe; stigmas off-white. NE Mexico (S Nuevo León). var. ***klinkeriana*** (Backeb. & Jacobsen) E.F. Anderson. Stem blue-green to grey-green or tinged brown; tubercles 3–6×5–9×5–8mm; spines 1–3, 7–8×1mm, dark brown then pale grey, cylindric, curved upward. Fl. 1.5–2.3×1–2.7cm; tepals white with magenta mid-stripe; stigmas white. E Mexico (San Luis Potosi). var. ***macrochele*** (Werderm.) E.F. Anderson. Stem grey-green to yellow-green; tubercles 6–8×12–18×2–4mm; spines rarely absent, usually 1–4(–6), to 20–27×1–1.5mm, pale brown, strongly curved and twisted. Fl. 2–2.6×2.3–3.2cm; tepals white with faint brown to pink mid-stripe; stigma pink. E Mexico (N San Luis Potosi). var. ***schwarzii*** (Shurly) E.F. Anderson. Stem grey-green; tubercles flattened, 5–7×6–8×2–3mm; spines absent or 1–3, to 10–14mm, light brown, paler at base, darker at apex, flattened, curved towards stem apex. Fl. 2–2.5×2.5–3.2cm; tepals white with faint pink mid-stripe; stigmas pink. E Mexico (N San Luis Potosi). Z9.

***N. smithii*** (Muehlenpf.) Klad. & Fittkau. Simple; stem mostly 7–12×4–9cm, globose to short-cylindric, grey- or blue-green; tubercles 3–5×3–4×2–3mm; central spines 1–4, to 12–30mm, white to yellow-brown, darker towards apex, straight, radial spines 12–27, 3–18mm, white, darker tipped, later tinged yellow. Fl. 1.8–3.5×1.2–4cm; tepals to 29×7.5mm, magenta with paler margins. Spring. NE Mexico (SE Coahuila, Nuevo León, N San Luis Potosi). Z9.

***N. valdeziana*** (H. Möller) E.F. Anderson. Simple; rootstock napiform; stem 1–2.5×1.5–2.5cm, depressed-globose to ovoid, bright green but hidden by the spines; tubercles 2–3×1–2×2–3mm; areoles circular; central spines 0, radial spines *c*25–30, 1–2mm long strongly adpressed, plumose, white. Fl. 2–2.5×2.2–2.5cm; tepals to 12×6mm, white with pale pink mid-stripe, or magenta with paler margins. Spring. NE Mexico (SE Coahuila, S Nuevo León). Z9.

***N. viereckii*** (Werderm.) F. Knuth. Simple or clustering; stems 2–7×3–6.5cm, globose to globose-cylindric, blue-green; tubercles 4–6×8–15×5–6mm; areoles with abundant wool; central spines 3–5, 15–20mm, dark brown towards apex, radial spines 13–22, 8–13mm. Fl. 1.5–3.5cm diam.; tepals white or magenta and white near base. NE Mexico (S Nuevo León, SW Tamaulipas). Z9.

***N. beguinii*** Britt. & Rose, nom illegit. See *N. smithii*.
***N. ceratites*** (Quehl) Britt. & Rose. See *N. conoidea*.
***N. clavata*** (Scheidw.) Britt. & Rose. See *Coryphantha clavata*.
***N. durangensis*** (Runge) L. Bens. See *Sclerocactus unguispinus*.
***N. erectocentra*** (J. Coult.) L. Bens. See *Sclerocactus erectocentrus*.
***N. grandiflora*** (Pfeiff.) F. Knuth. See *N. conoidea*.
***N. intertexta*** (Engelm.) L. Bens. See *Sclerocactus intertextus*.
***N. johnsonii*** (Engelm.) L. Bens. See *Sclerocactus johnsonii*.
***N. macdowellii*** (Quehl) H.E. Moore. See *Thelocactus macdowellii*.
***N. matehualensis*** Backeb. See *N. conoidea*.
***N. odorata*** (Boed.) Backeb. See *Coryphantha odorata*.
***N. subterranea*** (Backeb.) H.E. Moore. See *N. mandragora*.
***N. texensis*** Britt. & Rose. See *N. conoidea*.
***N. unguispina*** (Engelm.) L. Bens. See *Sclerocactus unguispinus*.
For further synonymy see *Gymnocactus*, *Mammillaria*, *Pelecyphora*, *Strombocactus*, *Thelocactus*, *Toumeya* and *Turbinicarpus*.

**Neomacfadya** Baill. See *Arrabidaea*.

**Neomarica** Sprague. (From Gk *neo-*, new, plus *Marica*.) Iridaceae. 15 species of rhizomatous, herbaceous perennials. Rhizomes short, creeping. Leaves tough, ensiform, copiously veined or strongly ribbed, equitant, carried in a basal fan. Flowering stems erect, somewhat compressed, bearing a single terminal leaf and 1–4 long-stalked axillary bracts, plantlets sometimes forming in axils, notably in *Nn. northiana* and *gracilis*; flowers clustered, short-lived; pedicels compressed, winged; perianth radially symmetric, outer segments 3, lanceolate-ovate, broadly clawed, erecto-patent, inner segments 3, far smaller than outer segments, erect then reflexed, brightly coloured; filaments free; style branches cleft or trifid, opposing stamens. Fruit a capsule. Tropical America, W Africa. Z10. Plants in this genus were formerly named in *Marica* (Ker-Gawl.) Herb., a name applied to species now placed in *Cipura* Aubl.

CULTIVATION Undemanding, tender perennials grown for their iris-like flowers, sometimes fragrant as in *N. northiana* and *N. caerulea*, and often exquisitely and intensely coloured with contrasting cross-veining and banding. In temperate zones grow in the warm glasshouse, with a minimum temperature of 15°C/60°F; *N. gracilis* and *N. caerulea* will grow in a slightly lower temperature regime, minimum 10°C/50°F. Grow in bright filtered light or full sun, in a well-drained, fertile, loam-based mix with additional organic matter and sharp sand. Water moderately when in growth, reducing in autumn and winter to keep fairly dry during the short days. Propagate by division of the rhizomes, growing on with gentle bottom heat until established; also by seed.

***N. brachypus*** (Bak. f.) Sprague. Lvs to 50×4cm, ensiform. Fls to 8cm diam., yellow banded chestnut at base; style branches trifid. Summer. W Indies.

***N. caerulea*** (Ker-Gawl.) Sprague. Lvs to 160cm, narrowly acuminate, obscurely ribbed. Flowering stems to 60cm; fls many, 8–10cm diam., outer perianth seg. pale blue to lilac, inner seg. deep blue, the claws and blade bases of all yellow-white banded brown and orange-yellow; style branches cleft with a flattened, horn-like basal appendage. Summer. Brazil.

***N. gracilis*** (Hook.) Sprague. Closely related to *N. northiana*, from which it differs in its flowering stems seldom exceeding 60cm, fls to 5.75cm diam., style branches with 3 (not 2) erect teeth. Summer. S Mexico to N Brazil.

***N. longifolia*** (Link & Otto) Sprague. Closely related to *N. brachypus*. Lvs to 30×2.5cm. Flowering stems 30–90cm, narrowly winged, bearing 3 long-stalked clusters of fls toward the summit; fls to 5cm diam., yellow banded brown. Summer. Brazil.

***N. northiana*** (Schneev.) Sprague. Lvs to 60×5cm, conspicuously ribbed. Flowering stems to 90cm, viviparous; fls 6–8cm diam., scented; outer perianth seg. white to yellow mottled crimson or maroon at base, inner seg. curved, barred or stained violet to blue at apex, veined red at base; style branches trifid, lateral teeth 3, 2 erect, 1 reflexed. Spring–summer. Brazil.

**Neomirandea** R. King & H. Robinson. (From Gk neos, new and for Faustino Miranda (1905–64), Mexican botanist.) Compositae.

Some 24 species of large perennial herbs, shrubs or small trees, often epiphytic; stems somewhat branched, often hollow. Leaves usually opposite, elliptic to deltoid, base cuneate to cordate, margins entire to pinnatifid dentate, sometimes glandular-punctate beneath, petiolate. Capitula discoid, in a broad, corymbose panicle; receptacle more or less flat; involucre cylindric; phyllaries in 3–4 series, imbricate; florets white, lavender, pink or maroon. Fruit a ribbed, glabrous to hairy cypsela; pappus of persistent, scarcely scabrid bristles. Mexico to Ecuador. Z10.

CULTIVATION As for *Bartlettina*.

***N. araliifolia*** (Less.) R. King & H. Robinson. Epiphytic shrub to 4m. Lvs to 16×7cm, opposite, ovate-elliptic, base cuneate, somewhat fleshy, glabrous; petiole to 6cm. Capitula to 1cm high; phyllaries to 7mm, lanceolate to ovate, inner longer; florets white. Fr. minutely pubesc.; pappus to 6mm. Panama to Mexico.

For synonymy see *Eupatorium*.

**Neomoorea** Rolfe. (For F.W. Moore (1857–1950), orchid specialist and sometime Curator of Glasnevin Botanic Garden, Dublin.) Orchidaceae. 2 species of epiphytic orchids. Pseudobulbs ovoid, stout. Leaves 2, borne at apex of pseudobulbs, elliptic-lanceolate, plicate, acute or pungent. Inflorescence basal, erect or arched; flowers showy, waxy, fragrant; sepals free, spreading; petals similar, base narrower; lip deeply trilobed, mobile, attached to the column foot, midlobe lanceolate, concave, acuminate, basal crest shortly pedicellate, wings 2, lateral, spreading or erect, lateral lobes subreniform, spreading. Columbia, Panama. Z10.

CULTIVATION Epiphytes for the intermediate house. See ORCHIDS.

***N. irrorata*** (Rolfe) Rolfe. Roots dimorphic: long, creeping and short, erect. Pseudobulbs ovoid, compressed, furrowed, 4–11×2.5–6cm. Lvs 45–75×10–13cm. Infl. arched or erect, few- to 12-fld, 15–45cm; sep. and pet. red-brown, base white, lip pale yellow, banded and marked brown-purple, midlobe yellow, spotted red; sep. elliptic-lanceolate to elliptic-ovate, acute, concave, spreading, 2–2.8×1–1.8cm; pet. elliptic-obovate, acute; lip midlobe acuminate, callus crested.

**Neomortonia** Wiehler. (From the Gk *neos*, new, and *Mortonia*.) Gesneriaceae. 1 species, a herbaceous, perennial epiphyte. Stems to 60cm, slender, pendent or climbing, branching at base, pilose, often purple-flushed. Leaves opposite in equal pairs, to 3×1.5cm, ovate, broadly elliptic or obovate, acute to obtuse, dentate, crenate, often flushed with purple. Fls solitary, axillary, pilose; calyx to 1cm, lanceolate, dentate, often flushed with purple, pilose; corolla to 3cm, spurred, white, tube funnel-shaped, inflated at base, flushed with pink, throat marked with orange-brown, limb 5-lobed, lobes to 10×8mm, subequal; stamens 4, anthers coherent in pairs; stigma mouth-shaped. Fruit a pilose, ovoid, bright orange berry to 11×8cm; seeds on light yellow funicles. Colombia, Panama, Costa Rica. Z10.

CULTIVATION As for *Aeschynanthus*. See GESNERIADS.

***N. rosea*** Wiehler. As for the genus.

**Neopanax** Allan.
***N. arboreus*** (Murray) Allan. See *Pseudopanax arboreus*.
***N. colensoi*** (Hook. f.) Allan. See *Pseudopanax colensoi*.
***N. kermadecensis*** (Oliv.) Allan. See *Pseudopanax arboreus*.
***N. laetus*** (T. Kirk) Allan. See *Pseudopanax laetus*.
***N. simplex*** (Hook. f.) Allan. See *Pseudopanax simplex*.

**Neoporteria** Britt. & Rose. (For Carlos Porter, Chilean entomologist; the Gk prefix *neo*-, new, distinguishes the name from *Porteria* Hook.) Cactaceae. Some 25 species of cacti, mostly rather small, simple, rarely clustering, sometimes geophytic; stems globose to short-cylindric, ribbed; ribs usually divided into prominent tubercles; areoles centrally placed, oval, depressed, felted. Flower arising at the apex or crown, tubular-funnelform, broadly funnelform or campanulate; tube distinct or very short, with small scales; floral areoles variously felted and hairy or bristly, the uppermost more strongly developed; tepals spreading, or the outermost spreading and the inner erect, concealing the stamens; stamens inserted in the throat and tube in one series. Fruit globose to ovoid, sometimes balloon-like (*N. islayensis*); pericarp initially fleshy but the interior always dry when mature, and usually releasing the seeds through a basal opening; seeds 1.3–1.8×1.0–1.4mm, broadly oval, black-brown, matt, ruminate or not; relief low-domed; hilum medium to small, basal or oblique, impressed. Chile, S Peru and W Argentina.

CULTIVATION Grow in a cool frost-free greenhouse (min. 2–7°C/36–45°F), use 'standard' cactus compost: moderate to high inorganic content (more than 50% grit), pH 6–7.5; full sun; low air-humidity; keep dry from mid-autumn until early spring, except for light misting on warm days in late winter. Following Donald & Rowley (l.c.), the genus is nowadays taken to comprise a number of subgenera and sections corresponding to segregate genera proposed by Backeberg and others. An alternative treatment, submerging *Neoporteria* as a whole into *Eriosyce* Philippi, could be defended taxonomically, but would have the disadvantage of introducing new names for all the species. The component groups are distinguished as follows:

1 *Pyrrhocactus* group: Flowers funnelform to urceolate, yellow or tinged red; pericarpel and tube woolly, sometimes with bristles. Fruit globose or ovoid, thin-walled, only slightly elongating when ripe, then drying out and sometimes more or less disintegrating; seeds large, 1.6–2.3mm, dark brown or black; hilium micropylar region (HMR) relatively large, deeply impressed, oval to keyhole-shaped, micropyle not clearly separated.
*Nn. bulbocalyx, strausiana, umadeave*.

2 *Islaya* group: Stem apex densely woolly. Flowers wide funnelform, usually small, sulphur yellow; pericarpel and tube densely woolly; areoles of pericarpel with or without bristles. Fruit clavate, thin-walled, red, greatly elongating and balloon-like when ripe, the seeds contained in a sac-like structure in the apex; seeds 0.75–1.5mm, black; cells isodiametric, sometimes slightly elongate and then more or less in rows; relief domed; HMR relatively large, impressed, keyhole-shaped, micropyle not clearly separated.
*N. islayensis*.

3 *Neochilenia* group: Flowers funnelform; pericarpel and tube somewhat woolly, sometimes with weak bristles; tepals spreading, yellow, pink or white. Fruit oval to sometime clavate, thick- to thin-walled, red or red-green, elongating 1.2–4 times when ripe; seeds 0.7–1.5mm, black or brown, sometimes keeled; relief domed, HMR relatively small, not impressed, always keyhole-shaped, micropyle in a clearly defined groove, sometimes completely surrounded by testa-cells.
*Nn. aricensis, chilensis, curvispina, horrida, jussieui, paucicostata*.

4 *Neoporteria* group: Similar to *Neochilenia* group, but flowers adapted to humming-bird pollination, tubular or narrow funnelform; inner tepals erect or slightly incurved, not spreading, carmine red. Fruit ovoid, thin-walled, red, elongating when ripe; seeds as in *Neochilenia* group.
*Nn. clavata, nidus, subgibbosa, wagenknechtii*.

5 *Thelocephala* group: Geophytic species with large, tuberous rootstock; stem very small, to 1–5cm diam. Flowers pale yellow or pink; pericarpel and tube densely woolly; floral areoles with stiff, porrect bristles. Fruit ovoid, thin-walled, soon dry after ripening, with long porrect bristles; seeds resembling those of *Islaya* group; black, relief domed; HMR large, micropyle not always clearly defined.
*Nn. napina, occulta, odieri, reichei*.

***N. aricensis*** (Ritter) Donald & G. Rowley. Simple; stem to 55×10cm; globose at first, eventually cylindric and decumbent; ribs 13–21, 5–10mm high; spines yellow-brown or rarely black-brown, becoming grey; central spines 5–12, 1–3cm, upcurved, radial spines 10–16, *c*8–15mm. Fl. *c*2×2cm; tube very short; floral areoles densely woolly; perianth pale yellow, style and stigmas yellow. Fr. 1–2×1–1.5cm, dark red or red-brown. Chile (S Africa). Z9.

***N. bulbocalyx*** (Werderm.) Donald & G. Rowley. Simple; stem eventually 50×12cm, globose to short-cylindric, dull grey-green; ribs 12–17, swollen beneath the large areoles; central spines usually 4, *c*2cm, stout, upcurved, pale yellow or dark brown to grey, radial spines *c*7–12, 1.5–2cm, similar to the centrals or paler. Fl. 4–4.5cm, urn-shaped; scales with dense wool and several bristles; perianth yellow with red throat. Fr. small, globose, dry. N Argentina (Catamarca, La Rioja). Z9.

***N. chilensis*** (Hildm. ex Schum.) Britt. & Rose. Simple or clustering from the base; stem globose to short-columnar, woolly at apex; ribs 20–21, crenate, pale green; central spines 6–8, 2cm, radial spines *c*20, 1cm, glassy white. Fl. 5cm diam., funnelform; floral areoles with wool and long white hairs; tepals pink or pale yellow; style and stigmas pale yellow. Chile. Z9.

***N. clavata*** (Söhr.) Werderm. Resembling *N. subgibbosa*. Stem to 60×8–12cm, globose to elongate-cylindric, glaucous green; ribs 9–18, tuberculate; central spines 1–4, 3–5cm, almost black, or grey, radial spines 6–16, 1–2.5cm. Fl. variable, 2–7cm; tepals purple pink, paler below, the inner erect, acute, concealing the stamens. Fr. 2–4cm, yellow or red. Chile. Z9.

***N. confinis*** (Ritter) Donald & G. Rowley. Stem 6–12cm diam., semi-globose to cylindric, green, apex naked to spiny; ribs 13–21, narrow, obtuse, crenate-tuberculate; spines pale yellow to grey-brown or almost black, slightly curved; central spines 3–7, 2–4cm, radial spines 8–12, 1–2.5cm. Fl. 3–4.5cm diam., funnelform; floral areoles with white wool; tube olive-green, uppermost areoles with a few thin, white bristles; outer tepals red with pale margins, inner tepals white with pale red mid-stripe; style and stigmas red. Fr. 1.5×1cm, hollow, red-green; pericarp fleshy, dehiscent by a basal pore. Chile (Copiapo). Z9.

***N. curvispina*** (Bertero) Donald & G. Rowley Variable; simple; stem to 15–30cm diam., globose, grey-green; ribs 13–16 or more, 1–3cm high, transversely grooved or notched; central spines usually 2–4, to 3cm, stout, upcurved, radial spines usually 8–12, 1–2cm. Fl. to 5.5×4–6cm; broadly funnelform, tepals pale yellow with narrow to broad red mid-stripe; stigmas cream to pale red. Fr. 1.5×1.4cm, ovoid, almost glabrous, tinged red or green, thick-walled, without pulp. Chile (Santiago area). Z9.

***N. horrida*** (Rémy & Gay) D. Hunt. Simple or sometimes clustering; stem to 10cm diam. or more, short-cylindric, dark green to blue-green; ribs 14–20, thickened and strongly tuberculate around the areoles; areoles white, to 1.5cm; central spines 1–5, to 2.5cm, strong, subulate, black or brown and yellow below, radial spines 8–12, later more, subulate. Fl. 4.5–5×3.5–4cm; pericarpel and tube green; scales minute; areoles woolly; outer tepals with red-brown mid-stripe, inner white or dingy yellow; stigmas tinged red or purple. Fr. almost glabrous. Chile (Valparaiso). Z9.

***N. islayensis*** (C.F. Först.) Donald & G. Rowley. Very variable; simple; stem usually 10–15(–75)×10cm, globose to short-cylindric, apex densely woolly; ribs 12–21, more or less strongly tuberculate; areoles conspicuously white-woolly; spines numerous, variable, usually scarcely differentiated into central and radial. Fl. 1.5–2.5×1.5–2.5cm, rarely to 4×4cm; floral areoles with dense woolly hairs; perianth and style yellow. Fr. to 3–4cm, when ripe inflated, balloon-like, pink or red. S Peru, N Chile. Z9.

***N. jussieui*** (Monv. ex Salm-Dyck) Britt. & Rose. Simple; stem globose or short-cylindric, dark or grey green to almost black; ribs 12–17, rather stout, divided into prominent tubercles; central spines 1–2, 2.5cm, radial spines 7 or perhaps more, dark brown. Fl. 3–3.5cm; floral areoles woolly; perianth pale pink or yellow; stigmas red. Chile. Z9.

***N. napina*** (Philippi) Backeb. Variable; simple; stem to 10×5cm, globose to ovoid, grey-green or tinged red; ribs *c*14, more or less distinctly tubercled; areoles slightly felted or glabrous; central spines 0–1, almost black, radial spines usually 3–9, up to 3mm, black. Fl. 3–3.5cm; upper floral areoles with long hairs and dark curly bristles; perianth pale yellow or the outer tepals tinged pink; style purple; stigmas yellow. Fr. globose to ovoid, moderately woolly. Chile (Huasco). Z9.

***N. nidus*** (Söhr.) Britt. & Rose. Simple; stem to 30×5–9cm, globose to short-cylindric; ribs 16–18, rounded, tuberculate, hidden by the spines; spines *c*30, to 3–5cm, weak and tortuous, interlaced and covering the apex, brown (at least the central), yellow or almost white. Fl. 4–6×2.5cm, tubular-funnelform, pink; inner tepals more or less erect, narrow, acute. Chile. Z9.

***N. occulta*** (Philippi) Britt. & Rose. Usually simple; rootstock tuberous, without neck; stem 3–8cm diam., depressed-globose to globose, dark grey-green or tinged maroon; ribs 12–14 or more, tubercled and notched; areoles elongate; spines usually lacking, or 4–8; central spines 0–1, 1–5mm, radial spines 4–7, 3–11mm, slightly curved, adpressed, black or dark brown. Fl. 2.3–4cm, campanulate-funnelform; floral areoles with scant wool and bristles; tepals nearly white with pale red mid-stripe; stigmas orange-red. Fr. red, woolly. Chile (Taltal). Z9.

***N. odieri*** (Lem. ex Salm-Dyck) Backeb. Similar to *N. napina*, but the floral areoles with conspicuous bristles to 1cm. Simple or clustering, depressed-globose, to 6cm diam., dark red-brown or nearly black; ribs 8–13, conspicuously tubercled; areoles with scant wool; central spines 0–1, to 15mm or more, radial spines 6–10, to 5mm, thin, almost black or red-brown. Fl. 2.5–5cm, white, yellow or pale pink; floral areoles with white wool and conspicuous fine bristles to 1cm. Chile (Copiapo to Huasco). Z9.

***N. paucicostata*** (Ritter) Donald & G. Rowley. Simple; stem *c*15–30×6–8cm, hemispheric at first, later cylindric, pale grey-green; ribs 8–13, 1–2cm high, with chin-like tubercles; areoles 10–15mm apart, 5–8×3–5mm, white-felted, not sunken; central spines 1–4, to 4cm, grey-brown, tipped black, radial spines 5–8, 1.5–3cm, somewhat recurved, off-white. Fl. 3–5×3–5cm; floral areoles woolly; outer tepals pink-tinged, inner white, style red. Fr. 1.5–2×1–1.5cm, red or tinged green. Chile. Z9.

***N. reichei*** (Schum.) Backeb. Simple; depressed-globose, grey-green; ribs resolved into spirally arranged tubercles 4–5mm diam.; areoles elliptic, 2mm; spines 7–9, to 3mm, equal, spreading, hyaline or white at first, later grey. Fl. 2.5–3.3×4cm, campanulate; floral areoles with woolly hairs and bristles; tepals yellow; style red; stigmas 10–12, red. Chile. The identity of Schumann's type is disputed, and modern usage of the name may be incorrect. Z9.

***N. strausiana*** (Schum.) Donald & G. Rowley. Simple; stem to 20×8–15cm, globose to elongate, black-green, apex without wool; ribs 12–14, 1cm high, obtuse, notched; spines almost black, tinged purple, upcurved; central spines 6–8, 3–4cm, radial spines 12–14, 2.5–3cm. Fl. 4×5cm, broadly funnelform; floral areoles with wool and bristles; tepals pale yellow or tinged red; stigmas pale yellow. Fr. 0.7–1cm, globose, green, thin-walled, becoming hard and dry when ripe and dehiscing by a basal pore. W Argentina. Z9.

***N. subgibbosa*** (Haw.) Britt. & Rose. Variable; simple; stem eventually to 1m×10cm, globose to short cylindric at first, green to grey-green; ribs 16–20, more or less tuberculate; areoles large; central spines 4–8, to 4cm, strong, yellow, brown or nearly black at first, radial spines 16–24, 1–3cm, amber-yellow. Fl. 3–6cm, pink, paler towards the throat; inner tepals erect, acute, concealing the stamens. Fr. 1.5–2×1cm, red or red-green. Chile. Z9.

***N. taltalensis*** (Werderm.) Hutchison. Simple; stem to 8cm diam., globose, dull dark green; ribs 10–16, with chin-like tubercles; areoles with pale yellow-brown felt at first; central spines to *c*6, to 3cm, dark grey-brown to almost black, radial spines merging with the centrals, *c*6–20, 3–20mm, curving to tortuous, brown, fading to white. Fl. 3×2.5cm or larger, fuchsia-purple, yellow or white. Chile (Taltal). The names *N. fobeana* (Mieckley) Backeb., *N. fusca* (Muehlenpf.) Britton & Rose and *N. hankeana* (C.F. Först.) Donald & Rowley may be referable here, but are very uncertain. Z9.

***N. umadeave*** (Fric ex Kreutz.) Donald & G. Rowley. Simple; stem to 40×10–20cm, globose to slightly elongate, dark green; apex without wool; ribs *c*18–21 or more, *c*1cm, deeply notched, about 1cm high; areoles large, elongate, with white wool; spines 20–35 or more, to 45mm, more or less upcurved, white or tinged violet. Fl. 3–3.5cm, funnelform; upper floral areoles with wool and 1 or more bristles 1.5cm; tepals and stigmas pale yellow. Fr. 3–4×1.5–2cm, elongate, light brown, woolly. NW Argentina (Jujuy). Z9.

***N. villosa*** (Monv.) A. Berger. Simple; stem to 15×8cm, short-cylindric, grey-green, becoming tinged purple-black; ribs 13–15, divided into prominent tubercles with large, felted areoles; central spines 4, to 3cm, bristly, dark, radial spines numerous, grading from bristly to hair-like, pale brown or off-white. Fl. *c*2cm, pink with white throat. Chile (Huasco). Z9.

***N. wagenknechtii*** Ritter. Simple; stem to 30×11cm, globose to cylindric, grey-green; ribs 11–17, very obtuse, with chin-like projections; areoles 3–10mm apart, 6–13×7mm; central spines 3–6, 2–3cm, almost black at first, later grey-brown, radial spines 10–20, 1.5–2.5cm, straight, dark grey. Fl. 2.2cm, purple. Fr. barrel-shaped, green or red-tinged. Chile (La Serena). Z9.

***N. acutissima*** (Otto & Dietr.) Borg. See *N. subgibbosa*.
***N. atrispinosa*** (Backeb.) Backeb. See *N. villosa*.
***N. bicolor*** (Akers & Buining) Donald & G. Rowley. See *N. islayensis*.
***N. castaneoides*** (Cels ex Salm-Dyck) Werderm. See *N. subgibbosa*.
***N. cephalophora*** (Backeb.) Backeb. See *N. villosa*.
***N. froehlichianus*** (Schum.) Backeb. See *N. horrida*.
***N. gerocephala*** Y. Ito. See *N. nidus*.
***N. heteracantha*** (Backeb.) W.T. Marshall. See *N. subgibbosa*.
***N. krainziana*** (Ritter) Donald & G. Rowley. See *N. islayensis*.
***N. kunzei*** sensu Ritter, non (C.F. Först.) Backeb. See *N. confinis*.
***N. kunzei*** (C.F. Först.) Backeb. See *N. curvispina*.
***N. litoralis*** Ritter. See *N. subgibbosa*.
***N. nigricans*** (Linke) Ritter. See *N. horrida*.
***N. nigricans*** (Linke) Britt. & Rose. See *N. horrida*.
***N. nigrihorrida*** (Backeb.) Backeb. See *N. clavata*.
***N. pilispina*** Ritter. See *N. taltalensis*.
***N. polyrhaphis*** (Pfeiff. ex Salm-Dyck) Backeb. See *N. villosa*.
***N. senilis*** (Philippi) Backeb. See *N. nidus*.
***N. subcylindrica*** (Backeb.) Backeb. See *N. subgibbosa*.
***N. tuberisulcata*** (Jacobi) Donald & G. Rowley. See *N. horrida*.
***N. tuberisulcatus*** (Jacobi) A. Berger. See *N. horrida*.
For further synonymy see *Mammillaria*, *Neochilenia* and *Pyrrhocactus*.

**Neoraimondia** Britt. & Rose (In honour of Antonio Raimondi (1825–90), 'the great geographer and naturalist of Peru'; the Gk prefix *neo-*, new, distinguishes the name from *Raimondia* Safford.) Cactaceae. 2 species of shrubby or arborescent cacti, much branched from the base or with a definite trunk; stems erect, few ribbed; non-flowering areoles large, brown-felted, usually spiny and one or more of the spines very long; flowering areoles enlarged, felted, nearly spineless, gradually prolonged into a spur, flowering annually. Flowers 1–2 per areole, small, the pericarpel and tube bearing small scales and felted areoles with or without bristles; limb short; stamens inserted in the upper part of the tube. Fruit globose to oblong, felted and more or less spiny; seed 1.7–1.9×1.2mm, broadly oval, black-brown or brown, semi-matt, rugose or ruminate; relief low-domed; hilum medium, oblique, impressed, mucilage-sheath present, covering entire seed. Peru, N Chile, Bolivia.

CULTIVATION Grow in an intermediate greenhouse (min. 10–15°C/50–60°F), use 'standard' cactus compost: moderate to high inorganic content (more than 50% grit), pH 6–7.5; shade in hot weather; maintain low humidity; keep dry from mid-autumn until early spring, except for light misting on warm days in late winter.

***N. arequipensis*** (Meyen) Backeb. Robust shrub, branching from the base; stems columnar, to 10m×20–40cm; ribs 4–10; areoles 1–4cm apart, large, the flowering enlarging over several years to become a globose or cylindric felted spur up to 10cm long; spines variable, up to 12 or more, very unequal, the longest up to 25cm. Fl. 2.5–4×2–4cm; pericarpel and tube felted; perianth rotate, pink, purple-red or white with green tinge. Fr. to 7cm diam., dull purple, shedding the areoles when ripe; seeds dull black. Coastal belt of Peru, N Chile. Z9.

***N. herzogiana*** (Backeb.) F. Buxb. Eventually a tree 7–10m, with a distinct trunk 1–2m×50cm; stems 15–20cm diam.; ribs sometimes 5 at first, later 6–7; spines as in *N. arequipensis*. Fl. 7–7.5×5–6cm; floral areoles with dense bristly spines 1–2cm; tepals purple with paler or white margins. Fr. *c*5cm diam., yellow, tinged red; areoles and spines; seeds somewhat smaller than in *N. arequipensis*, dark brown. Bolivia. Z9.

***N. gigantea*** Backeb. See *N. arequipensis*.
***N. macrostibas*** (Schum.) Backeb. See *N. arequipensis*.
***N. roseiflora*** (Werderm. & Backeb.) Backeb. See *N. arequipensis*.
For further synonymy see *Neocardenasia*.

**Neoregelia** L.B. Sm. (For E.A. von Regel (1815–92), German botanist and Director of the Imperial Botanic Gardens, St Petersburg, 1875–92.) Bromeliaceae. 71 species of mostly terrestrial, perennial herbs, to 60cm in flower. Leaves firm, in a dense, funnel-shaped or tubular rosette to 1m diameter, toothed and spinose, sometimes tipped, spotted, banded or flushed red, attenuate to rounded, abruptly acute. Inflorescence hidden in rosette centre, usually simple, dense, capitiform, corymbose or umbellate, on a short, enclosed scape, scape bracts bright pink, red or purple, involucrate; flowers perfect, pedicellate; sepals asymmetric, erect, acute, basally fused; petals violet, blue or white (rarely red), spreading, free or fused into a tube, stamens and stigma usually not exserted. S America. Distinguished from the closely-related *Nidularium* by its simple inflorescence and pedicellate flowers. Z10.

CULTIVATION See BROMELIADS.

***N. carolinae*** (Beer) L.B. Sm. BLUSHING BROMELIAD. Lvs 40–60cm, innermost with pink, vermilion or purple bases when in flower, ligulate, sparsely scaly beneath, closely toothed, spines 1mm. Infl. crowded, outer bracts bright red, papery; pedicels to 7mm; sep. 16–20mm, fused for 5mm, green; pet. to 3cm, lavender blue, fused for half their length. Brazil. f. ***tricolor*** (M.B. Fost.) M.B. Fost. ex L.B. Sm. Lf blades with longitudinal pink, white and green stripes. Garden origin.

***N. chlorosticta*** (Bak.) L.B. Sm. Lvs 20–30cm, outer green, inner dark purple blotched pale green, sometimes banded silver beneath; sheaths ovate or elliptic, forming an inflated tank; blades linear, abruptly acute, spiny-denticulate. Infl. red-purple, simple, few-fld; outer bracts hyaline, broad, shorter than sep.; floral bracts hyaline, spathulate; pedicels to 10mm, slender; sep. to 18mm, elliptic, fused for 2–7mm; pet. 10–15mm, blue-violet, elliptic, acute; stamens exserted. Brazil.

***N. compacta*** (Mez) L.B. Sm. Lvs to 26cm, erect, in a dense rosette, blades ligulate, green, the innermost red when in flower, margins red or denticulate. Infl. many-fld, simple; outer bracts broadly ovate, apex triangular to pungent, upper bracts longer than fls, sparsely scaly; floral bracts linear, thin; pedicels to over 5mm; sep. 30mm, fused for 10mm, sublanceolate, not incurved; pet. red. Brazil.

***N. concentrica*** (Vell.) L.B. Sm. Spreading via stout basal rhiz. Lvs to 40cm, green, purple or purple-spotted, tipped red, scurfy, toothed, spines 4mm, stout, black. Infl. many-fld; outer bracts broadly ovate, shorter than sep., yellow-white flushed with violet or purple, papery, apex scaly, rounded, mucronate; floral bracts linear, incurved, pale green, thin; pedicels slender, 10–18mm; sep. 22–30mm, usually free, subelliptic, long-attenuate, green; pet. longer than stamens, white or blue. Brazil.

***N. cruenta*** (Graham) L.B. Sm. Lvs 30–90cm, rigid, inner red in flower, green banded mahogany beneath with a large blood-red spot at apex, abruptly acute, densely toothed, spines bright red, straight, stout; sheaths flushed purple, scaly. Infl. many-fld; outer bracts very broadly ovate, green, mucronate, scaly, upper bracts almost as long as sep.; floral bracts narrowly ovate, keeled, blunt, green or white; sep. pale green, fused for 3mm, straight; pet. blue or purple with a pale line, ligulate, spreading. Brazil.

***N. fosteriana*** L.B. Sm. Lvs to 30cm, copper-red with a few green spots, pale grey-scaly, apex dark red, margins laxly toothed, spines 1mm. Infl. compound, red, on a short scape; outer bracts broadly ovate, becoming papery, equalling sep., denticulate; floral bracts narrowly lanceolate; pedicels slender, 5mm; sep. 15mm, fused for 2mm, lanceolate, floccose above; pet. 19mm, red, acuminate. Brazil.

***N. kautskyi*** Pereira. Stoloniferous. Lvs to 30cm, papery, in sparsely scaly, inner lvs green, outer chartreuse-green, with dense red-brown blotches, laxly denticulate. Infl. simple, 30-fld, corymbiform, scape 35mm; lower bracts rounded, green, upper bracts triangular, green, papery, involucrate; floral bracts lanceolate; pedicel 10mm; sep. 20mm, green, nearly free; pet. 35mm, fused for 5mm, white, apex violet. Brazil.

***N. macwilliamsii*** L.B. Sm. Lvs 30cm or more, entire, pale-scaly, base of blade red with green spots, apex green. Infl. dark red, 30-fld; scape 3cm; floral bracts thin, lanceolate, equalling sep.; pedicels slender, to 5mm; sep. 32mm, fused for 5mm, lanceolate, acute. Brazil.

***N. marmorata*** (Bak.) L.B. Sm. MARBLE PLANT. Lvs to 60cm, margins laxly toothed, spines 1mm; sheaths broadly elliptic, purple spotted pale green; blades ligulate, blotched purple, apex with a bright red spot. Infl. many-fld; outer bracts pale green, broadly ovate, papery; floral bracts linear; pedicels slender, to 15mm; sep. 19–24mm, green, slightly fused; pet. 24mm, white tinged pink, much longer than stamens. Brazil.

***N. melanodonta*** L.B. Sm. Lvs 15–20cm, scurfy throughout, sheaths broadly elliptic, yellow-green, blotched purple; blades broadly ligulate, blotched magenta, apex spiny, retuse, with a magenta spot, margins with black, lax, teeth to 1.5mm. Infl. few-fld, narrowly ellipsoid, on a very short scape; outer bracts ovate, denticulate, densely scaly, cuspidate, floral bracts narrower; pedicels 20mm, slender; sep. 23mm, fused at base, apex inrolled, with a fine, sharp point; pet. light blue. Brazil.

***N. pineliana*** (Lem.) L.B. Sm. Stem short, erect. Lvs to 50cm, densely scaly; sheaths broadly ovate, purple; blades linear, green and less scaly above, copper-green beneath, denticulate. Infl. surrounded by reduced, carmine inner lvs, occasionally replaced by a cluster of bright red, sterile bracts; floral bracts oblong; pedicels slender, long; sep. to 20mm, fused for 4mm, subelliptic; pet. to 4cm, violet, apex dark blue, linear, fused for almost their whole length. Brazil.

***N. princeps*** (Bak.) L.B. Sm. Stemless. Lvs 20–50cm laxly toothed spines to 0.5mm; sheaths orbicular, large, green, densely scaly; blades ligulate, green, grey-scaly beneath, inner reduced, bright red in flower. Infl. many-fld; floral bracts oblong, thin, keeled; pedicels to 10mm; sep. 24mm, fused for 2mm; pet. 35mm, white tipped dark blue, linear, almost entirely fused. S Brazil.

***N. spectabilis*** (Moore) L.B. Sm. PAINTED FINGERNAIL; FINGERNAIL PLANT. Stemless. Lvs 40–45cm, in an open, funnel-shaped rosette, grey-scaly, banded white beneath; sheaths 15cm; blades ligulate, outer green with a bright red apical spot, inner wholly red, subentire or denticulate. Infl. many-fld; outer bracts red or purple, broadly ovate, papery, floral bracts elliptic, brown-scaly; pedicels to 6mm; sep. 18–23mm, fused for 2mm, subelliptic, with a semiorbicular wing, blade linear, hooked, apex red-brown hairy; pet. 2–3cm, ligulate, spreading, violet-blue. Brazil.

***N. tristis*** L.B. Sm. Lvs 20–60cm, in a slender, funnel-shaped rosette; sheaths elliptic, large, dark brown with pale spots; blades ligulate, green and glabrous above, banded red-brown and pale-scaly beneath, toothed, spines 0.5mm. Infl. many-fld; outer bracts brown-purple, broadly ovate; floral bracts oblong, dark purple, thin; pedicels 4–10mm; sep. 16mm, fused for 3mm; pet. lavender tipped blue, slightly fused. CE Brazil.

***N. cultivars.*** 'Amazing Grace': lvs dark green striped red and pale green. 'Cathryn Wilson': to 50cm across; lvs broad, vivid maroon mottled green; fls tinted blue. 'Marcon' (*N. marmorata* × *N. spectabilis*): lvs brassy yellow, blotched maroon. 'Marconfos' (*N. marmorata* × *N. concentrica*): lvs wide, deep maroon with fresh green freckles and tipped plum, edged with brown spines; infl. low, fls lilac. 'Vulcan' (*N. concentrica* × *N. johannis*): compact; lvs wide, thick, blotched, tinted purple in centre.

For synonymy see *Nidularium*.

**Neotchihatchewia** Rausch. (For Count Pierre de Tchihatchef (1808–90), Russian traveller and writer.) Cruciferae. 1 species, a perennial herb to 25cm. Stem erect. Leaves 2.5–7cm, narrow-elliptic, hairy, toothed, lower leaves petiolate. Flowers vanilla-scented, in rounded corymbs 10cm across; sepals 4, 6–8mm; petals 4, clawed, red-purple. Fruit compressed, indehiscent, pendulous, winged, hairy, becoming glabrous. Spring. Armenia, W Turkey. Z7.

CULTIVATION A sturdy short-lived perennial with a thick rootstock, grown for its vanilla-scented, bright rosy-lilac flowers. Grow in the alpine house, or in a sheltered and sunny situation on the rock garden. Propagate from fresh seed, or sow in spring and prick off into small pots of well-drained, sandy propagating medium, since it resents root disturbance.

***N. isatidea*** (Boiss.) Rausch. As for the genus.

For synonymy see *Tchihatchewia*.

**Neottopteris** J. Sm.
***N. antiqua*** (Mak.) Masam. See *Asplenium antiquum*.
***N. australasica*** J. Sm. See *Asplenium australasicum*.

**Neowerdermannia** Backeb. (For Erich Werdermann (1892–1959), author of papers on cacti and latterly Director of the Botanical Museum and Herbarium at Berlin; the Gk prefix *neo-*, new, distinguishes the name from *Werdermannia* O. Schulz.) Cactaceae. 2 closely allied species; plants small, simple, with stout taproot; stems more or less globose; ribs indistinct, *c*16, spiralling, deeply divided into triangular tubercles; areoles at base of upper side of tubercles. Flower funnelform with spreading limb, white or lilac-pink. Seed 2.2×1.4mm, broadly oval, black-brown, matt, ruminate; relief low-domed; hilum medium, oblique, impressed. N Argentina, S Bolivia, Peru, N Chile.

CULTIVATION Grow in a cool frost-free greenhouse min. 2–7°C/36–45°F; use 'standard' cactus compost: moderate to high inorganic content (more than 50% grit), pH 6–7.5; full sun; low air-humidity; keep dry from mid-autumn until early spring, except for light misting on warm days in late winter.

***N. chilensis*** Backeb. Resembling *N. vorwerkii*, but fl. creamy white, fr. dehiscing by a lateral fissure. N Chile (Iquique) to border with Argentina. Z9.

***N. vorwerkii*** Fric. Stem broadly flattened-globose; tubercles spirally arranged, bluntly conic, 3-sided, flattened above, keeled below, with the areoles situated in the depressions between; spines up to 10, lowest directed downwards, almost hooked at tip, to 4cm, nearly black at first, remainder to 1.5cm, off-white. Fl. *c*2 cm diam.; tepals white with light lilac-pink mid-stripe, or pale lilac. Fr. deep-seated between the tubercles, tearing open apically when ripe. N Argentina, S Bolivia, Peru, N Chile. Z9.

**NEPENTHACEAE** Dumort. See *Nepenthes*.

**Nepenthes** L. (Name used by Homer, meaning grief-assuaging, applied because of supposed medicinal properties.) PITCHER PLANT; TROPICAL PITCHER PLANT. Nepenthaceae. 70 species of climbing or scrambling, terrestrial or epiphytic dioecious carnivorous perennial shrubs or semi-woody herbs to 15m. Leaves loosely spiralling, ligulate to lanceolate, entire, coriaceous, with midrib prolonged into clasping tendril terminated by swollen pitcher; petiole distinct, sometimes winged, or absent; pitchers to 35cm, held upright from end of pendulous tendril, hollow and usually containing water, cylindric to rounded, often with unequal sides and sometimes sigmoidally curved, usually green with red spots or suffusion, mouth of pitcher with thickened, ribbed and often colourful rim, the peristome; apex prolonged to form a fixed 'lid' projecting over pitcher-mouth, often brightly coloured and with nectar-secreting glands, acting as insect lure and partial shield against excessive entry of water to pitcher; 2 wings or ridges present on side of pitcher opposite to insertion of lid, often undulate and usually toothed or fringed. Pitchers often dimorphic depending on location on plant (i.e. equal and borne on basal leaf 'whorls' or slender on scrambling stems); all effective insect traps with complex trapping mechanisms; insects are attracted by bright colours and secretions of lid and peristome, enter pitcher but cannot obtain a grip on smooth waxy surface of upper part of inner wall and fall into the liquid below where death and digestion occurs. Inflorescence an ebracteate raceme or thyrse; flowers small, to 3mm across; regular; sepals 4, in 2 whorls of 2, glandular on inner surface, green, bronze or dull red-brown; corolla absent; stamens 8–25, united in column; ovary inferior, 3–4-locular, ovules many, stigma sessile. Fruit a dehiscent leathery capsule, seeds numerous, usually filiform. Madagascar, Seychelles, Tropical Asia to Australia (northern Queensland). Z10.

CULTIVATION The tropical pitcher-plants fall into two groups, those occurring in the wild below 1000m/3250ft, the 'lowland' species, and the 'highland' species from above this altitude, which in cultivation differ in their temperature requirements. Lowland species require a minimum winter temperature of 18.5°C/65°F, with diurnal temperatures exceeding 27°C/80°F; in summer the nightly minimum should be 21°C/70°F, with diurnal temperatures rising to 38°C/100°F. This also applies to lowland hybrids and hybrids with highland species. A winter nocturnal minimum of between 8.5–12°C/47–54°F is suitable for the highland species with diurnal temperature between 18–22°C/64–72°F: in summer the maximum daytime temperature should not exceed 21°C/70°F, with a nocturnal minimum of 12–15°C/54–60°F. Basic cultivation is similar for the two groups. The compost must be well drained; two parts bark, two parts perlite and one part moss peat is a standard compost. Ample moisture and high humidity are required but free drainage is essential; lattice or basket pots are recommended for this reason. Liquid fertilizer is beneficial, applied to the roots or as a foliar feed. Old plants benefit from heavy pruning in spring. Propagation is best performed by air layering, as cuttings seldom succeed.

***N. alata*** Blanco. To 3.5m. Pitchers numerous, weakly dimorphic; lower 6.5–13cm, cylindric above, constricted at centre, inflated at base, light green with red flecks, or heavily suffused red, mouth oblique, oval, peristome green or occasionally red, lid elliptic with glandular crest at base of inner surface; wings prominent, fimbriate; upper pitchers elongate with wings reduced to ribs. Highland. Philippines, Malaysia, Borneo, Sumatra.

***N. albomarginata*** Lobb. To 2m. Lvs 20×2.5cm. Pitchers to 12.5cm, cylindric, narrowed to base where it becomes upcurved, green, sometimes spotted red, or pink, with conspicuous white band immediately below peristome, mouth oblique, oval, peristome finely ribbed, narrow, lid oblong, rounded, green, spotted red, wings narrow, sparsely toothed. Lowland. Malaysia, Sumatra, Borneo.

***N. ampullaria*** Jack. Tall climber, producing pitchers only at base. Upper lvs to 17.5×5cm, oblong, tendril to 7.5cm. Pitchers produced from subterranean rhiz. or rosettes of basal lvs with lamina to 5cm; pitchers similar, to 5cm, rounded, squat, green spotted and blotched deep red, or entirely green or deep red, mouth horizontal, oval to round, peristome with narrow rim, but descending vertically into pitcher-mouth, lid to 3.5cm, narrow, reflexed from mouth, wings broad, widely spreading, strongly toothed. Lowland. Malaysia, Borneo, Sumatra to New Guinea.

***N. bicalcarata*** Hook. f. Tall climber to 14m. Pitchers dimorphic; lower to 10cm, rounded, green, sometimes suffused rust-red or entirely rust-red, mouth somewhat oblique, round, peristome inclined into pitcher, green, lid well raised above pitcher, reniform, with ends of peristome forming 2 distinct walrus-like tusks pointing downwards, wings broad, toothed; upper pitchers to 13cm, campanulate to funnel-shaped, wings replaced by ribs. Lowland. Borneo.

***N. burbidgeae*** Burb. Tall climber to 10m. Lvs to 40×10cm, oblong to lanceolate, tendril to 60cm. Pitchers dimorphic; lower to 18×12cm, ovate, pale green to white with red blotches, mouth oblique, round, peristome broad, yellow-white with red bands, lid orbiculate, glandular at base below, margin undulate, wings narrow, toothed; upper pitcher to 13×7cm, funnel-shaped, contracted just below mouth, mouth horizontal, wings reduced to prominent ribs with very short teeth. Highland. Borneo (Mt Kinabalu).

***N.* ×*chelsonii*** hort. Veitch ex Mast. *(N.* ×*dominii* × *N.* ×*hookeriana.)* Intermediate between parents. Pitchers broadly ovoid, yellow-green spotted purple-red, mouth oblique, oval, peristome dark purple, wings broad, toothed. Lowlands. Garden origin (GB 19th century).

***N.* ×*coccinea*** hort. *(N.* ×*dominii* × *N. mirabilis.)* Pitchers to 15×7.5cm, yellow-green heavily marked purple-red, inflated below middle, cylindric in upper part, mouth oblique, oval, peristome with red and black ridges, lid ovate-oblong, green with red markings, wings broad, toothed. Lowland. Garden origin.

***N.* ×*dominii*** Veitch. *(N. rafflesiana* × *N. gracilis.)* Tall climber. Pitchers to 15cm, light green, heavily marked dark red, cylindric but tapering upwards, mouth oblique, oval, peristome narrow, pale green, lid green, suffused red, wings broad, spreading, toothed. Lowland. Garden origin.

***N.* ×*dormanniana*** hort. *(N. mirabilis* × *N.* ×*sedenii Veitch (N. gracilis* × *N. lkhasiana).)* Pitchers 15×7.5cm, green with many red spots and blotches, flask-shaped, somewhat inflated below middle, mouth oblique, oval to rounded, peristome broad, green, finely ridged, lid broadly ovate, wings broad, undulate, toothed. Lowland. Garden origin.

***N. gracilis*** Korth. Stems slender, prostrate or climbing, to 2m. Lvs to 12.5×2.5cm, linear to elliptic, tendril to 7.5cm. Pitchers dimorphic, numerous; lower to 7.5cm, shortly flask-shaped, rounded below, light green with dark red spots, or suffused pink, or dark maroon to almost black, mouth slightly oblique, oval to rounded, peristome narrow, green; lid orbicular, dark red, wings narrow, shortly toothed; upper pitchers elongated, to 15cm, constricted at middle and

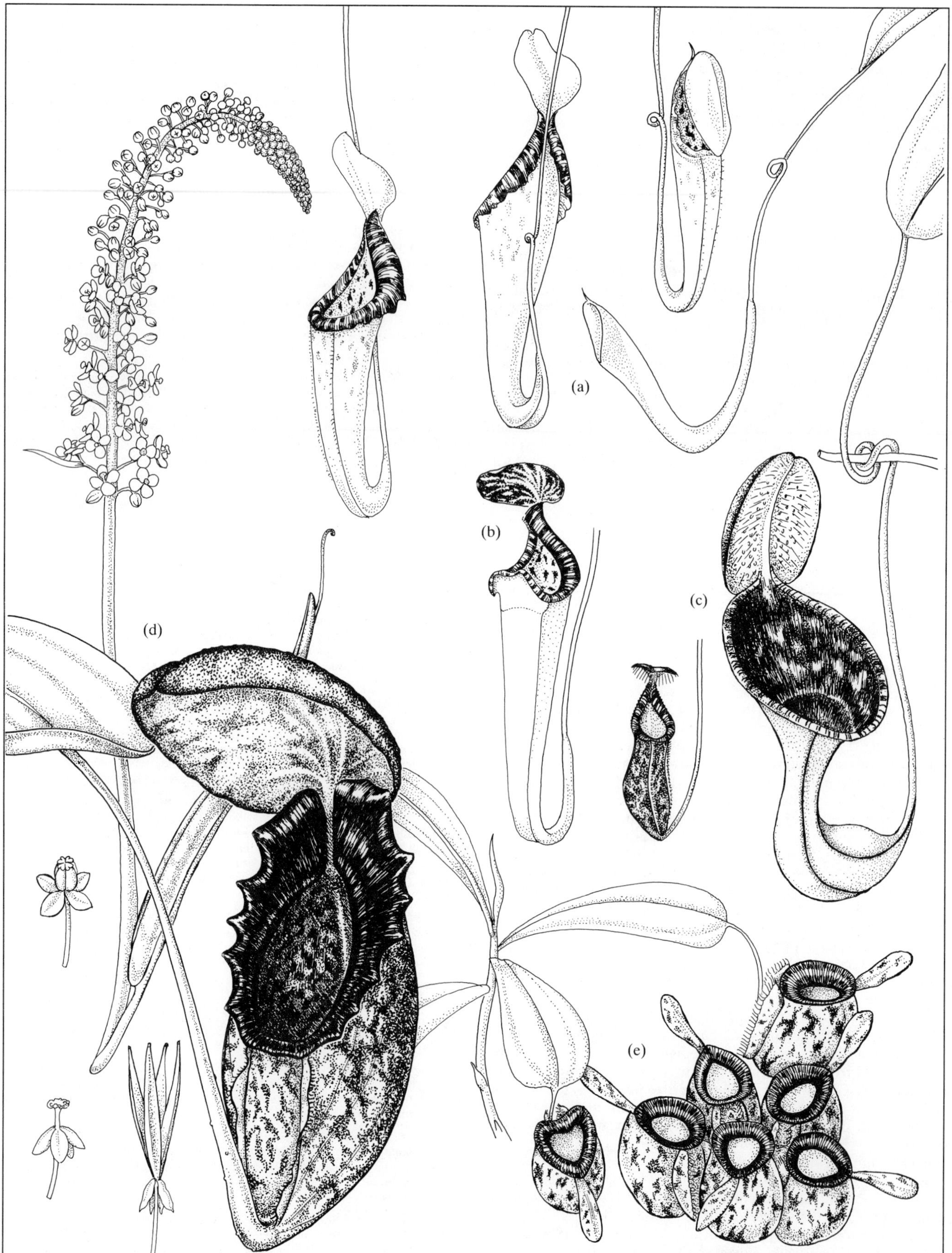


**Nepenthes** (a) *N.* × *mixta* upper pitchers (×0.25) and developing pitchers (×1) (b) *N. rafflesiana* upper pitcher (×0.25) (c) *N. lowii* upper and lower pitchers (×0.25) (d) *N. rajah* pitcher and male inflorescence with immature leaf (×0.2), female and male flowers and fruit (×2) (e) *N. ampullaria* rosette pitchers (in basal cluster) and climbing stem with pendent pitchers (×0.25)

somewhat inflated at base, dark mahogany-red or red-brown, with peristome green to red-brown, wings reduced to ridges, interior white or pink-white. Lowland. Indonesia (Borneo to Sulawesi), Philippines.

***N.*×*henryana*** Nichols. (*N. hookeriana* × *N.* ×*sedenii.*) Pitchers to 15cm, irregularly flask-shaped, inflated below with long cylindric neck, predominantly red-purple with few green flecks, mouth oblique, oval, peristome broad, crimson shaded violet, interior green with violet spots, wings narrow, toothed. Lowland. Garden origin (GB 19th century).

***N.* ×*hookeriana*** Lindl. (*N. rafflesiana* × *N. ampullaria.*) Natural hybrid. Pitchers dimorphic; lower to 11cm, ovoid, pale green with dark red spots, or sometimes heavily blotched red, mouth oblique, round, peristome broad, descending into pitcher, green, lid flat, obovate, wings broad, strongly fimbriate; upper pitchers to 12.5×2.5cm, funnel-shaped, wings reduced to ridges. Lowland. Malaysia, Sumatra, Borneo.

***N.*×*intermedia*** hort. Veitch. (*N. gracilis* × *N. rafflesiana.*) Pitchers to 15×6.5cm, green heavily blotched red, subcylindric, tapering gradually above; mouth oblique, ovate, peristome dark red, lid with distinct column, ovate, obtuse, wings broad, long-toothed. Lowland. Garden origin.

***N. khasiana*** Hook. f. Tall climber to 10m+. Lvs sessile, lanceolate. Pitchers dimorphic; lower 7.5–17.5cm, inflated below, tapering above, green, tinged pink, upper pitchers to 20cm, cylindric, slightly inflated at base, green with red markings, mouth oblique, oval, peristome dark red, lid oval, green externally, red within, wings reduced to ridges. Highland, winter maximum 8°C. Assam (Khasi hills).

***N. madagascariensis*** Poir. Low shrub, rarely climbing, to 2m. Lvs to 28×8cm, ovate to lanceolate. Pitchers dimorphic; lower to 13cm, squat-cylindric, red or green, spotted red, mouth oblique, ovate, peristome ribbed, red, lid curved over pitcher mouth, orbiculate to reniform; upper pitchers to 17cm, funnel-shaped, bright yellow-green, sometimes suffused red, mouth horizontal, lid erect; wings reduced to ridges. Highland. Madagascar.

***N.*×*mastersiana*** hort. Veitch ex Mast. (*N. sanguinea* × *N. khasiana.*) Pitchers 11×3cm, cylindric with slight constriction at middle, deep claret-red with deeper purple spots, thinly hairy, mouth oblique, ovate, peristome red, interior pink-cream, spotted red, lid rounded, wings narrow, sparsely toothed in lower pitchers, reduced to ridges in upper pitchers. Highland. Garden origin (GB before 1881).

***N. maxima*** Reinw. ex Nees. Lvs to 20cm, glandular beneath. Pitchers dimorphic; lower to 20×6.5cm, cylindric, pale green, longitudinally streaked red, mouth oblique, ovate, peristome wide, dark red, lid somewhat cordate, green, mottled purple, wings narrow, toothed; upper pitchers to 30×7.5cm, trumpet-shaped, wings reduced to ridges. Highland. Indonesia (Borneo, Sulawesi) to New Guinea.

***N. mirabilis*** (Lour.) Druce. MONKEY CUP. Shrub or climber to 10m. Lvs to 40×8cm, oblong to lanceolate, margin entire or minutely dentate. Pitchers cylindric or slightly inflated at base, to 18cm, pale green with red spots, or sometimes wholly red, mouth oblique, round, peristome broad, flattened, striped red, lid orbicular to ovate, wings present in lower pitchers, toothed, reduced to prominent ridges in upper pitchers. Lowland. S China, SE Asia to New Guinea and Queensland.

***N.*×*mixta*** Mast. (*N. northiana* × *N. maxima.*) Pitchers weakly dimorphic, 10–35×3.5–7.5cm; lower cylindric, pale green, spotted purple-red, mouth oblique, oval, peristome broad, strongly ribbed, glossy ruby red, lid finely spotted red, wings narrow, toothed; upper pitchers funnel-shaped, with wings reduced to ridges. Lowland. Garden origin (GB 1893).

***N. northiana*** Hook. f. Pitchers to 30×8.5cm, cylindric, pale green, heavily spotted purple, mouth oblique, oval, peristome very broad, outer margin undulate, yellow, striped purple, lid ovate-oblong, glossy, spotted black on lower surface, wings narrow, toothed. Lowland. Borneo.

***N. rafflesiana*** Jack. Tall climber, to 9m. Lvs to 25cm, oblong, tendril to 30cm. Pitchers dimorphic; lower to 12.5×7.5cm, ventricose, rounded at base, green, heavily spotted red, mouth oblique, oval, peristome broad, crimson, strongly ribbed, narrowing upwards to form elongate process to lid, spiny above, lid oblong-orbicular, wings to 2.5cm broad, spreading, teeth incurved; upper pitchers to 23×7.5cm, funnel-shaped, curved and narrowing to base, wings reduced to ridges. Lowland. Malaysia, Sumatra, Borneo.

***N. rajah*** Hook. f. KING MONKEY CUP. Stems prostrate. Tendrils emerge from underside of lamina below apex. Pitchers dimorphic, largest in genus; lower to 35×15cm, rounded, capable of capture and digestion of prey to rat-size, green lightly spotted red, or entirely red to purple externally, spotted red and purple-black within, mouth oblique, oval, peristome broad, outer margin projecting beyond pitcher-walls, undulate, strongly ribbed, crimson with darker bands, lid large, exceeding mouth, ribbed below, wings narrow, toothed; upper pitchers funnel-shaped, but shape has been likened to that of a lavatory, narrowing to base, wings reduced to ridges. Highland. Borneo (Mt Kinabalu).

***N. reinwardtiana*** Miq. Tall climber, to 10m. Lvs to 20×3cm, linear-lanceolate, sessile. Pitchers to 20×5cm, cylindric, somewhat inflated at base with slight constriction at middle, green externally, glaucous blue-green within, mouth oblique, ovate, peristome very narrow, green, lid elliptic, almost flat, to 4cm across; untoothed ridges present. Lowland. Borneo.

***N. stenophylla*** Mast. Tall climber. Pitchers dimorphic; lower to 15cm, narrow-cylindric, pale yellow-green, longitudinally flecked purple; mouth oblique, oval, peristome narrow, banded red, lid rounded, with narrow connective neck, wings very narrow, sparsely toothed; upper pitchers to 28cm, funnel-shaped, tapering to base, wings reduced to ribs. Highland. Borneo.

***N. tentaculata*** Hook. f. Stems prostrate, to 2m. Lvs to 18×3cm, lanceolate, sessile. Pitchers dimorphic; lower to 7×3cm, squat flask-shaped, inflated below, cylindric above, pale green to white, heavily marked with red-purple; mouth oblique, oval, peristome narrow, red, lid with distinct upright bristles on upper surface, wings narrow, toothed; upper pitchers to 15cm, elongate flask-shaped, purple-green to dark-red; wings present, narrow, toothed. Highland. Borneo.

***N. veitchii*** Hook. f. Epiphytic. Pitchers to 20cm, cylindric, pale green, mouth oblique, ovate, peristome broad, strongly ribbed, canary-yellow, lid small, oblong, wings broad, toothed. Highland. Borneo.

***N. ventricosa*** Blanco. Terrestrial or epiphytic; stems short. Pitchers numerous, to 18cm, inflated at base with middle constricted, pale to white-green, sometimes flecked red; mouth shallowly oblique, ovate, peristome broad, strongly ribbed, red, or green with red bands; lid ovate; wings absent. Highland. Philippines.

***N.* cultivars**. Many of the hybrids and selections popular in the last century are now lost to cultivation; among those still grown are 'Courtii': lvs leathery; pitchers marbled wine-red towards apex, wings fringed. 'Dir. G.T. Moore': lvs to 45cm; pitchers purple-red marbled green, wings prominent, rim lined purple. 'Henry Shaw': pitchers large, solid, pale green spotted wine-red. 'Lieut. R.B. Pring': pitchers pear-shaped, red-purple acquiring green marbling with age, wings prominent with purple hairs. 'St. Louis': pitchers pear-shaped, dark red becoming paler with age, slightly marbled green, wings mottled. 'Superba': vigorous; lvs deep green, long; pitchers variable from urn-shaped to funnel-shaped, green tinged yellow and splashed maroon, rim ribbed in maroon and crimson, lid striped red, fringe with red hairs.

***N. curtisii*** Mast. See *N. maxima*.
***N.* ×*dominiana*** Nichols. See *N.* ×*dominii*.
***N. phyllamphora*** Willd. See *N. mirabilis*.

**Nepeta** L. (Named used by Pliny, probably after Nepi in Italy.) Labiatae. About 250 species of perennial, rarely annual herbs, often aromatic. Leaves opposite, entire, crenate to serrate; floral leaves reduced. Flowers hermaphrodite or unisexual in distant or close verticillasters, 6 to many-flowered, frequently forming dense spikes or heads, rarely in racemes or panicles; calyx 15-nerved, teeth 5, subequal; corolla tubular-campanulate or funnel-shaped, bilabiate, tube long, slender at base, upper lip patent, 2-fld, lower lip 3-lobed, patent, middle lobe largest; stamens 4, in pairs, parallel, ascending under upper lip of corolla, upper pair longest, anther cells divergent; style branches subequal. Fruit 4 ovoid or ellipsoid nutlets, smooth or tuberculate. Summer. Eurasia, N Africa, mts of tropical Africa. Z9.

CULTIVATION *Nepeta* spp. are used predominantly in the herbaceous border and as edging plants. With the exception of the pale yellow-flowered *N. govaniana*, the herbaceous species have blue or white flowers. In *N. camphorata* and *N.* ×*faassenii* they are complemented by aromatic silvery foliage, while the flowers of *N. nuda, N. sibirica,* and *N. grandiflora* are a particularly attractive rich deep blue; these three are tall plants and may need staking to prevent flopping. *N. nervosa, N. nepetella* and *N.* ×*faassenii* are more compact and are suitable for edging, as well as being more tolerant of poor soils; if regularly clipped back, they will make tight clumps with a succession of flowers. The flowers are particularly attractive to bees. *N. cataria* is said to repel rats; its essential oils, released on bruising, are extremely attractive to cats. A few small species, such as *N. phyllochlamys*, are alpines from high mountains or dry cliff faces and are grown in hot dry situations in crevices, on the rock garden.

Grow in well-drained soils in sun; fertile soils generate bushier growth. Vigorous herbaceous species can be kept in check by spading around the edge of the clumps. Propagate by division in spring or autumn, or by stem tip or softwood cuttings in spring or summer. Sow seed of species *in situ* in autumn, thinning to 45cm/18in. apart. Germination of spring-sown seed is more erratic. In hot dry seasons, herbaceous species may be infected with powdery mildew (*Erysiphe* spp.).

***N. camphorata*** Boiss. & Heldr. Stems to 45cm, lanate, viscid. Lvs to 2cm, ovate, cordate at base, crenate, lanate, viscid, smelling of camphor when crushed. Bracteoles 2.5–4×0.25–0.5mm, linear, half length of cal. Fls in distant verticillasters; cal. grey, tube straight, teeth much shorter than tube, upper teeth not exceeding lower; cor. to 12mm, white spotted purple. S Greece. Z8.

***N. cataria*** L. CATNIP; CATMINT. Stems to 1m, branched, erect, grey-pubesc. to tomentose. Lvs 3.5–8×2–5mm, ovate, cordate at base, serrate, grey-tomentose beneath; petioles to 40mm. Bracteoles 1.5–3mm, linear-subulate. Fls to 35 in spike-like infl., lower verticillasters distant; cal. 5–6.5mm, ovoid, tube curved, teeth patent, unequal; cor. 6–10mm, white spotted blue-violet, tube shortly exserted from cal. Europe (widely naturalized), SW & C Asia. 'Citriodora': lemon-scented. Z3.

***N. ×faassenii*** Bergmans ex Stearn. *(N. racemosa × N. nepetella.)* Sterile garden hybrid resembling *N. racemosa*. To 60cm, short-pubesc. Stem branching at base. Lvs to 3cm, narrow-lanceolate to oblong-ovate, obtuse, truncate at base, deeply crenate, silver-grey, lower lvs petiolate; bracts short, linear-lanceolate. Fls in elongate or remote raceme; cal. as long as cor. tube, white-pubesc., teeth short, acute; cor. to 12mm, pale lavender with darker spots. 'Blue Wonder': compact, to 35cm high; fls blue, long-lasting. 'Dropmore': upright, fls deep lavender, in tall spikes. 'Little Titch': dwarf, to 15cm high. 'Porzellan': lvs narrow, grey; fls soft porcelain blue. 'Six Hills Giant': taller and tougher than type of species; fls in large sprays, lavender-blue. 'Snowflake': low and spreading; lvs tinted grey; fls snow white. 'Souvenir d'André Chaudron': roots invasive; lvs grey-green; fls large, tubular, rich lavender-blue. 'Superba': spreading; lvs tinted grey; fls dark blue, abundant. 'Walker's Low': to 75cm; stems arching. Z3.

***N. govaniana*** Benth. Stem erect, branching, somewhat pubesc. Lvs large, ovate-oblong or oblong-elliptic, rounded at base, crenate, short-petioled. Bracts small. Fls in elongated, lax racemes, verticillasters remote; cal. elongated, curved, mouth oblique, teeth subequal, lanceolate; cor. yellow, 4× length of cal., tube very thin, much exserted, expanded above. W Himalaya. Z5.

***N. grandiflora*** Bieb. Stems erect to 40–80cm, branched, glabrous or minutely pubesc. Lvs to 10cm, ovate, cordate at base, crenulate, glabrous; bracteoles 2–3mm, linear-subulate. Fls in elongated, interrupted spikes; cal. 9.5–11mm, often blue, teeth 1.5–2mm, lanceolate; cor. 14–17mm, blue, tube exserted. Caucasus, E and EC Europe (locally naturalized). Z3.

***N. laevigata*** (D. Don) Hand.-Mazz. Stems to 90cm, branches often spreading. Lvs to 10cm, ovate or triangular-cordate, serrate, petiolate. Fls pale blue in oblong or cylindric spike. W Himalaya. Z5.

***N. melissifolia*** Lam. Stems 20–40cm, ascending, pubesc. to villous. Lvs 1.5–3.5cm, ovate, cordate at base, coarsely crenate, pubesc.; bracteoles linear. Infl. elongate, racemose; cal. 8–10mm, curved, teeth 2–3.5mm; cor. 12–15mm, blue spotted red. S Aegean.

***N. nepetella*** L. Variable. Stems to 80cm, branched, minutely pubesc. Lvs to 4×2cm, lanceolate to oblong-lanceolate, truncate at base, crenate to dentate, pubesc. to lanate, green to glaucous; petioles to 15mm. Bracts leafy below, bracteoles 2–4mm, linear-lanceolate. Infl. many-fld verticillasters, usually branched; cal. 5–8mm, often tinged pink or blue, teeth triangular; cor. 10–12mm, cylindric-campanulate, pink or white, tube curved, exserted. SW Europe to S Italy. ssp. ***amethystina*** (Poir.) Briq. Cor. blue-violet. N Africa, Iberian Peninsula. Z8.

***N. nervosa*** Royle ex Benth. To 60cm, subglabrous. Lvs to 10cm, linear-lanceolate, entire or somewhat dentate, strongly veined; lower lvs short-petioled, upper lvs sessile. Infl. a dense, cylindric raceme 15cm long, cal. half length of cor., teeth subulate, ciliate, equally tube; cor. to 12mm, blue or yellow. Kashmir. Z5.

***N. nuda*** L. Variable. Stems to 1.2m, glabrous to minutely pubesc. Lvs 1.5–7×1–3.5cm, ovate to ovate-oblong, base cordate, upper lvs sessile; bracteoles 2–3mm, linear to linear-lanceolate. Infl. many-fld paniculate verticillasters, rarely spike-like; cal. 4–6mm, tube straight, teeth 1–2, equal, subulate, erect, upper teeth not exceeding lower; cor. 6–10mm, white or violet-blue. Fr. glabrous. S Europe, Asia. ssp. ***nuda***. Lower lvs distinctly petiolate. Infl. lax, cal. teeth linear-lanceolate, green or blue tinged; cor. pale violet. Europe to C Russia. ssp. ***albiflora*** Gams. Lower lvs subsessile or sessile. Infl. compact; cal. teeth lanceolate, white-tinged; cor. white. Greece, Yugoslavia, SW Asia. Z6.

***N. phyllochlamys*** P.H. Davis. Stems to 25cm, many, decumbent, densely tomentose or villous. Lvs 7–14×5–12mm, triangular-ovate, truncate or subcordate at base, crenulate, grey-white, felty; petioles to 12mm; bracts leaflike. Infl. simple, composed of distant verticillasters; cal. 8.5mm, slightly curved, teeth linear-lanceolate, subequal, shorter than tube; cor. 10mm. Fl. colour unknown in 1982; the closely related *N. isaurica* has cor. lilac-pink. E Mediterranean. Z8.

***N. prattii*** Lév. Stems erect to 90cm. Lvs to 40–50cm, ovate-lanceolate, crenate, upper lvs sessile. Infl. dense verticillasters; cal. to 8mm; cor. to 25mm, blue-violet. W China. Z6.

***N. racemosa*** Lam. Aromatic. Stems to 30cm, many, decumbent, ascending or erect, densely tomentose. Lvs 1–3×0.5–2.5cm, ovate, cordate at base, petiolate, veins prominent; bracteoles 2–3mm, linear-lanceolate. Fls in distant, many-fld verticillasters, lower pedunculate; cal. 6–10mm, strongly curved, densely violet-tomentose, teeth 1–2mm, linear-lanceolate, upper exceeding lower; cor. 10–18mm, deep violet to lilac-blue, curved. Caucasia, N & NW Iran. Plants in cultivation under this name are usually *N. ×faassenii*. Z4.

***N. raphanorhiza*** Benth. Stem to 45cm, somewhat glabrous. Lvs to 12mm, ovate to ovate-cordate. Fls in dense avoid raceme to 12mm; cal. half as long as cor., teeth lanceolate; cor. to 6mm, purple-blue. W Himalaya. Z5.

***N. sibirica*** L. To 1m, glabrous to subglabrous. Lvs 5–9cm, oblong-lanceolate, cuneate or cordate at base, dentate, petiolate, dark green and minutely pubesc. above, glandular-punctate beneath. Infl. to 12 many-fld verticillasters in racemes to 25cm; cal. 10mm, mouth oblique, teeth short, acute; cor. 25–30mm, blue or lavender, exterior pubesc., tube straight. Siberia. Z3.

***N. stewartiana*** Diels Differs from related *N. sibirica* in its smaller fls and curved cor. tube. China. Z6.

***N. tuberosa*** L. Variable. Rhizome tuberous. Stems to 80cm, simple, pubesc. to lanate. Lvs to 8cm, ovate-lanceolate to oblong, cordate at base, subglabrous to villous, lower lvs petiolate; bracts and bracteoles 8–16×3–8mm, ovate to lanceolate, papery, green-white tinged pink or red-purple. Fls in a simple spike; cal. 8–11mm, slightly curved, teeth 2.5–3mm, upper slightly exceeding lower; cor. 9–12mm, violet or purple. Spain, Portugal, Sicily. Z8.

***N. ucranica*** L. Stems to 50cm, erect, branched, subglabrous. Lvs to 4cm, oblong-lanceolate, crenate-serrate, glabrous; petioles to 15mm. Bracteoles 6–7mm, linear. Fls in numerous, lax, 3–5-fld cymes; cal. often tinged blue, equalling cor., teeth linear or linear-lanceolate, exceeding tube; cor. 7–9mm, blue-violet, slightly exserted. SE Europe, Asia. Z9.

***N. veitchii*** Duthie. Resembles *N. sibirica*. Lvs dentate or subentire, sessile or subsessile; bracts linear or subulate. Fls 30mm wide; upper verticillaster condensed; cor. tube straight. China (Sichuan, Gansu). Z6.

***N. wilsonii*** Duthie. Resembles *N. sibirica*. Lvs oblong, obtuse, regularly crenate, upper lvs sessile or subsessile; bracts lanceolate, to elliptic. Fls to 25mm; cor. tube much curved. China (Sichuan, Yunnan). Z6.

***N. amethystina*** Poir. See *N. nepetella*.
***N. aragonensis*** Lam. See *N. nepetella*.
***N. boissieri*** Willk. See *N. nepetella*.
***N. erodifolia*** Boiss. See *Lallemantia royleana*.
***N. glechoma*** Benth. See *Glechoma hederacea*.
***N. hederacea*** (L.) Trev. See *Glechoma hederacea*.
***N. incana*** Thunb. See *Caryopteris incana*.
***N. macrantha*** Fisch. ex Benth. See *N. sibirica*.
***N. marifolia*** Boiss. & Huet. See *N. racemosa*.
***N. murcica*** Guirão ex Willk. See *N. nepetella*.
***N. mussinii*** hort. non Spreng. See *N. ×faassenii*.
***N. mussinii*** Spreng. in Henck. See *N. racemosa*.
***N. pannonica*** L. See *N. nuda* ssp. *nuda*.
***N. pseudomussinii*** Floto. See *N. ×faassenii*.
***N. spicata*** Benth. See *N. laevigata*.
For further synonymy see *Dracocephalum*.

**Nephelaphyllum** Bl. (From Gk *nephale*, cloud, and *phyllon*, leaf.) Orchidaceae. Some 17 species of terrestrial orchids. Rhizomes creeping, fleshy. Pseudobulbs 1-leaved, some rudimentary. Leaves convolute, ovate-triangular to cordate, fleshy. Racemes erect; flowers 5–15; sepals and petals similar; lip trilobed or entire, interior ridged; spur short. Indonesia, Philippines, Hong Kong, India, China. Z10.

CULTIVATION As for the warm-growing, evergreen *Calanthe* spp.

***N. pulchrum*** Bl. Pseudobulbs subterete, dull purple, to 2.5cm, apex narrow. Lvs ovate to cordate, 6–10×4–6cm, olive green mottled grey to bronze above, deep green below with prominent venation, often flushed red-purple. Racemes dense, 3–5; fls fragrant; sep. and pet. pale green, exterior veined purple, lip white, base pale green and purple with yellow ridges; tepals sublinear, deflexed, to 1.5cm; lip elliptic, entire, ridges longitudinal, papillose; spur inflated, base constricted. Java.

## Nephelium L.

***N. litchi*** Cambess. See *Litchi chinensis*.
***N. longana*** Lour. See *Dimocarpus longan*.
***N. rubrum*** G. Don. See *Lepisanthes senegalensis*.

## Nephrodium Michx.

***N. banksiaefolium*** Presl. See *Osmunda banksiaefolia*.
***N. beddomei*** Bak. See *Parathelypteris beddomei*.
***N. calanthum*** Endl. See *Lastreopsis calantha*.
***N. canum*** Bak. See *Pseudocyclosorus canus*.
***N. chinense*** Bak. See *Dryopteris chinensis*.
***N. cicutarium*** (L.) Bak. See *Tectaria cicutaria*.
***N. decompositum*** R. Br. See *Lastreopsis decomposita*.
***N. glabellum*** Cunn. See *Lastreopsis glabella*.
***N. gymnosorum*** Mak. See *Dryopteris gymnosora*.

***N. lancilobum*** Bak. See *Lastreopsis decomposita*.
***N. microsorium*** Endl. See *Lastreopsis microsora*.
***N. pennigerum*** Hook., nom. nud. See *Sphaerostephanos penniger*.
***N. pentangularum*** Colenso. See *Lastreopsis microsora*.
***N. sherringiae*** Jenman. See *Tectaria trifoliata*.
***N. sparsum*** Hamilt. ex D. Don. See *Dryopteris sparsa*.
***N. velutinum*** (A. Rich.) Hook. f. See *Lastreopsis velutina*.

**Nephrolepis** Schott. LADDER FERN, SWORD FERN; BOSTON FERN. (From Gk *nephros*, kidney, and *lepis*, scale, alluding to the common form of the indusia.) Oleandraceae. Some 30 species of epiphytic or terrestrial ferns. Rhizomes short and erect, usually with spreading, wiry stolons; scales peltate. Fronds erect to arching or pendent, the blades linear to linear-oblong, the apex often of indeterminate growth, 1-pinnate, pinnae numerous, sessile and jointed to rachis or deciduous, numerous, basal pinnae reduced, veins free, 1–4-forked, oblique. Sori terminal on the first distal vein; indusia circular to lunate, persistent. Pantropical. Z10.

CULTIVATION In the wild, terrestrial forms of *Nephrolepis* rapidly form large stands of bright green, upright or arching fronds from the germination of a single spore and rapid vegetative spread by wiry rhizome or stolon: many are therefore considered weeds in tropical gardens and their cultivars (e.g. *N. cordifolia* 'Duffii' or 'Plumosa' and *N. exaltata* 'Hillii') are grown in preference.

*N. biserrata* occurs on wet boggy ground, but most are tolerant of fairly strong light and a dryish growing medium. Their drought tolerance, marked in *N. cordifolia* and *N. acutifolia*, makes epiphytic spp. undemanding in cultivation if given a humid atmosphere; those with arching fronds (e.g. *N. exaltata* 'Elegantissima', *N. falcata, N. pendula* and *N. davallioides*) are particularly good as basket plants or for cultivation on pads of tree-fern fibre. In humid, virtually frost-free zones, grow *Nephrolepis* spp. in the open garden as epiphytes (generally preferring palm hosts) or as spreading groundcover in part shade or sun: lacy cvs are unsuitable and vigorous spp. such as *N. exaltata* will swamp more delicate plants.

*N. exaltata* and *N. cordifolia* are remarkably tolerant houseplants; the huge range of *N. exaltata* cultivars has arisen from the original 'Boston Fern' (*N.e.* var. *bostoniensis*), a 19th-century mutation with markedly drooping fronds. Many of these cultivars, particularly those with thickly layered or lacy foliage (e.g. 'Childsii' and 'Smithii'), resent very moist conditions and are more susceptible to a range of pests and diseases.

In cool-temperate areas, grow *N. cordifolia, N. exaltata* and *N. hirsutula* in the cool glasshouse, *N. biserrata* in the intermediate glasshouse and *N. davallioides* and *N. pectinata* in tropical conditions. *Nephrolepis* is adaptable to cultivation in large containers, pans or beds, and all but the lacy spp. (which will not tolerate moisture on their foliage) are suitable for growing below glasshouse or staging shrubs.

Grow in a coarse, fast-draining fern mixture, preferring a soilless mix based on coarse sand and tree-fern fibre or bark clippings for the delicate cvs: these are best underpotted. Give bright filtered light and a moist but buoyant atmosphere, ventilating whenever possible. Syringe daily in hot weather, providing that the foliage will dry within an hour. Water evergreen spp. moderately in summer, sparingly in winter; keep deciduous species fairly dry during dormancy. Propagate by division in late winter/spring; young plantlets formed on spreading stolons generally make better plants when rooted. Also from spores; many cvs are either sterile (e.g. *N. cordifolia* 'Duffii') or will not come true. Commercially, *Nephrolepis* is now propagated by tissue culture rather than division, since huge quantities of plants may be raised in a comparatively short time. Generally fairly pest and disease resistant, but cvs are particularly susceptible to fern scale, whitefly, *Botrytis cinerea* and slugs and snails. Extreme sensitivity to chemical damage, especially in lacy cvs, means that sprays must be carefully chosen and tested.

***N. acutifolia*** (Desv.) Christ. Rhiz. very long-creeping, stolons short, branched; scales *c*5mm, margins short-ciliate, dark brown; stipes 15–30cm, with dense covering of pale brown scales when young. Stipes to 15cm, deciduously scaly, pale brown; frond-blade to 100cm or more ×*c*12cm, suberect, narrowly elliptic, acute, herbaceous, pinnae to 6×1.5cm (sterile) or 7×1cm (fertile), to 65 pairs, short-petiolate, oblong, apex acuminate, base obtuse or truncate, slightly auricled on acroscopic side, entire or dentate, sparsely pubesc., veins obscure. Tropical Africa, SE Asia to Polynesia.

***N. biserrata*** (Sw.) Schott. BROAD SWORD FERN. Rhiz. erect, to 2.5mm diam., scales to 10mm, crowded, spreading, lanceolate, ciliate, hair-pointed. Stipes 12–60cm, to 5mm diam., with pale brown flexuous linear scales; frond-blade to 3×0.3m, pendent, linear-oblong or broadly linear; pinnae numerous, 7–15×1.2–2.5cm, short-petiolate, linear-oblong, apex acute to acuminate, base unequal and truncate to cuneate and sometimes subauriculate acroscopically, margins finely dentate-serrulate on sterile pinnae to crenate on fertile ones, the crenations often minutely toothed, tissue sparsely to densely hairy on underside. Pantropical.

***N. cordifolia*** (L.) Presl. ERECT SWORD FERN; LADDER FERN. Rhiz. to 12mm wide, erect or suberect, with stolons, occasionally bearing scaly tubers; scales to 10mm, attenuate scales with long hair-like apices, orange-brown. Stipes 4–20cm, densely but deciduously clothed with many lax filiform, pale brown scales; frond-blade to 60×5cm, erect, arching or pendent, lanceolate to linear, apex acute or acuminate, leathery or membranous, pinnae to 20×9mm (sterile) or 30×5mm (fertile), to 70 pairs, short-petiolate, deciduous, crowded to overlapping, horizontal, alternate, oblong to linear, apex acute and attenuate or obtuse and toothed, base unequal and cordate to obtuse, entire or dentate and notched, veins sunken. Pantropical. 'Duffii' DUFF'S SWORD FERN: rachis usually forked one or more times, pinnae orbicular-crowded, attached in more than one plane, plants usually sterile. 'Plumosa': pinnae lobed at margin.

***N. davallioides*** (Sw.) Kunze. Rhiz. short and erect; scales to 3mm, adpressed, dark brown; stipe 15–30cm, the base densely covered with scales similar to rhiz. Frond blade to 2×0.3m, arching to pendent, linear to lanceolate, apex attenuate to narrowly acute, pinnae to 12×2cm (sterile pinnae) or 12–20×1.5cm (fertile pinnae), linear to lanceolate, acute at apex, truncate to cuneate to obtuse at base, crenate (sterile) or lobed to a depth of 2–3mm (fertile), lobes oblique, deltoid, obtuse, veins distinct; rachis scales numerous, with spreading hairs on them. Malay Peninsula & Philippines to New Guinea.

***N. exaltata*** (L.) Schott. BOSTON FERN. Rhiz. short, suberect, with slender stolons; scales to 7mm, lanceolate to linear-filiform, pale brown. Stipes 6–20cm, with deciduously linear pale brown spreading scales. Frond-blade linear, 50–250×6–15cm, erect, crowded together, often borne in false rosettes along stolons, pinnae numerous, 2–8×0.7–1.3cm, close, with auricle overlapping rachis, apex acute or subacute, base subcordate with auricle on acroscopic side; rachis fibrillose-scaly; margins bluntly serrulate to crenate, tissue deciduously fibrillose-scaly, veins 1 or 2-forked. Pantropical. 'Bostoniensis': fronds erect to pendent, pinnate, wide; the 'original' Boston Fern, which has produced, among others the following sports: 'Childsii': fronds approximate and overlapping, to 4-pinnate, deltoid. 'Elegantissima': fronds 2-pinnate. 'Fluffy Ruffles': fronds dense, to 3-pinnate, deltoid. 'Hillii': fronds 2-pinnate or -pinnatifid, to 1m, pinnae lobed and undulate at margin. 'Rooseveltii': fronds pinnate, pinnae unequal and auriculate at base, undulate. 'Smithii': fronds finely 3-pinnate, lace-like. 'Teddy Junior': fronds dense, pinnae undulate. 'Verona': fronds dense, pendent, to 4-pinnate. 'Whitmannii': fronds to 3-pinnate.

***N. falcata*** (Cav.) C. Chr. Rhiz. short and erect; scales to 4mm, closely imbricate, dark brown to black with pale edges. Stipes 10–20cm, scaly, purple to brown; frond-blade to 2m×10cm, arching to pendent, pinnae set close together, markedly falcate, apex acute or obtuse, base slightly auricled, basiscopic base subtruncate, minutely crenate, *c*5.5×1.3cm (sterile) or 55×10cm (fertile); rachis scaly and pubesc. Sori submarginal. Ceylon, Maldives, Burma, Indochina to Philippines & New Guinea. f. ***furcans*** Moore. FISHTAIL FERN. Pinnae bifid at apex.

***N. hirsutula*** (Forst.) Presl. Rhiz. short and erect with many long slender stolons; scales to 4mm, adpressed and overlapping, lanceolate, aristate. Stipes to 25cm or more, erect, clothed near base with scales similar to those of rhiz. Frond-lamina to 100×16cm, arching, pinnae to 8×2cm (sterile) or 8×1cm (fertile), close and overlapping, apex attenuate to acute, acroscopic base truncate and auricled, margins crenate, pubesc., veins obscure; rachis scales with hairy margins. Tropical Asia to Polynesia.

***N. multiflora*** (Roxb.) Jarrett ex Morton. ASIAN SWORD FERN. Rhiz. erect, with wiry stolons; scales 2–3mm×0.5–1mm, acuminate, dark brown or black with narrow, white, finely ciliate margins. Stipes stout, 5–30×0.4cm diam.; frond-blade 30–100×7–20cm, linear-lanceolate, narrowed towards the base, rachis densely clothed with pale brown, tortuous, filiform scales, these laxly long-ciliate near the base of the scale, pinnae 3.5–10×0.5–1.3cm, linear-oblong, acute to long-acuminate at apex, slightly unequal at base, the basiscopic side rounded, truncate or short-auriculate, the acroscopic side with a narrow, acute auricle, margins crenate to sharply and deeply serrate, tissue and costa abaxial with many pale brown, loosely adpressed, attenuate scales which are fimbriate-ciliate at the base. India & tropical Asia, widely naturalized in Florida, W Indies, C & S America.

***N. pectinata*** (Willd.) Schott. BASKET FERN; TOOTHED SWORD FERN. Rhiz. erect, abundantly stoloniferous; scales to 3mm. Stipes 10–20cm; frond-blades to 30–45×2.5–4cm, elliptic or linear, thin-textured, glabrous, pinnae close, 40–50 pairs per frond, parallel-sided, apex obtuse, base auriculate on acroscopic side, lower pinnae deflexed at base, margin shallowly crenate; rachis glabrous, indusia reniform to semiorbicular. S Mexico to Peru & Brazil, W Indies.

***N.pendula*** (Raddi) J. Sm. Rhiz. suberect to short-creeping, bearing numerous stolons; scales linear, almost black, with white cilia on margins. Stipe 10–35cm; frond-blade 30–150×3.5–7cm, pendent, glabrous, pinnae sessile or subsessile, apex obtuse, acroscopic base with rounded auricle, margin entire or slightly crenate, veins obscure; rachis glabrous except at pinna bases. S Mexico to Bolivia & Brazil.

***N.acuminata*** (Houtt.) Kuhn. See *N.davallioides*.
***N.barbata*** Copel. See *N.falcata*.
***N.duffii*** Moore. See *N.cordifolia* 'Duffii'.
For further synonymy see *Aspidium, Davallia, Polypodium* and *Tectaria*.

**Nephrophyllidium** Gilg. (From Gk *nephros*, kidney, and diminutive of *phyllon*, leaf.) Menyanthaceae. 1 species, a perennial herb. Rhizomes thick, creeping. Leaves 5–10cm diam., reniform, sometimes emarginate, crenate, distinctly veined; petioles 20–30cm, basally clasping. Inflorescence an erect, terminal cyme or corymb; corolla to 1.25cm diam., white, lobes 5, lanceolate, with a low medial crest and crisped margins. Japan to Northwest N America. Z3.

CULTIVATION As for *Menyanthes*.

***N.crista-galli*** (Menz. ex Hook.) Gilg. DEER CABBAGE. As for the genus.

For synonymy see *Fauria, Menyanthes* and *Villarsia*.

**Nephrosperma** Balf. f. (From Gk *nephros*, a kidney, and *sperma*, seed; the seeds are sometimes kidney-shaped.) Palmae. 1 species, a pleonanthic, monoecious palm to 10m. Stem erect, to 15cm diam., bare and ringed. Crownshaft absent. Leaves pinnate, to 2m, tinged red when young, neatly abscising; sheaths tomentose, densely covered at first with black spines, margin tattering; petioles channelled above, convex beneath, white-pubescent, sparsely scaly, bristled near base; pinnae 25–40, regularly spaced along each side of rachis, to 1m, 1–3-fold, glabrous above, scaly beneath, midrib clothed with ramenta. Inflorescences interfoliar, to 4m, branched once; peduncle to 3× length of rachis, erect, becoming curved, scaly, amid 2 deciduous, scaly and spiny bracts; rachillae lax, crowded, arranged spirally on rachis, bearing minute flowers arranged in triads (2 male, 1 female), with solitary or paired male flowers at tips: male flowers symmetrical; sepals 3, overlapping, petals 3–4× sepals, 3, valvate, stamens 40–50, pistillode ovoid; female flowers globose, sepals 3, overlapping, petals 3, overlapping, staminodes 6, tooth-like, pistil 1-celled, 1-ovuled. Fruit to 1cm across, spherical to reniform, red, with lateral stigmatic remains and resistant perianth, smooth, glossy. Seychelles.

CULTIVATION *N.vanhoutteanum* is most frequently found in humus-rich detritus in rocky fissures and crevices; it is a slender and elegant feather palm, especially attractive when young and suitable for the warm glasshouse, conservatory or atrium. Propagate by seed. See also PALMS.

***N.vanhoutteanum*** (H.A. Wendl. ex Van Houtte) Balf. f. As for the genus.

For synonymy see *Oncosperma*.

**Nephthytis** Schott. (For Gk mythological figure *Nephthys*, mother of *Anubis*, wife of *Typhonis*, all commemorated in aroid genera.) Araceae. 7 species of rhizomatous perennial herbs. Rhizomes short, horizontal, internodes short. Leaves to 35cm, sagittate or hastate with large basal lobes, main lateral veins united with marginal vein, minor veins reticulate; petioles long, terete, shortly sheathed. Peduncle subequal to or much shorter than petiole, with sheathing cataphylls at base; spathe expanded, erect, flat, hooded or reflexed, green, persistent; spadix sessile or shortly stipitate; flowers unisexual, male and female zones adjacent; perianth absent; stamens 1–4; stigmata sessile or with style present, ovules 1–2. Fruit an orange berry in clusters. Tropical W Africa.

CULTIVATION *Nephthytis* spp. require a coarse, open, low-fertility and very acid medium of leafmould, charcoal and composted bark in shaded, humid positions in the warm glasshouse. Propagate by division in spring or summer or by fresh seed, cleaned from the pulp; germinate at 18–23°C/65–75°F.

***N.afzelii*** Schott. Lvs 35×25cm, sagittate, lobes acute, lateral lobes ovate, longer than triangular median lobe; petiole to 50cm. Peduncle slightly shorter than petioles, to 45cm; spathe to 7×1cm, oblong, incurved, green; spadix subsessile, to 6cm; stamens 4; stigma discoid. Berries ovoid, 9mm, orange.

***N.poissonii*** N.E. Br. Close to *N.afzelii*, but lvs narrow-acuminate. Spathe oblong-ovate to ovate, abruptly acuminate, to 5cm across, finely spotted; spadix shortly stipitate; style present. Berries to 3cm, ellipsoid.

***N.gravenreuthii*** Engl. See *N.poissonii*.

**Neptunia** Lour. (From Neptune, Roman god of the sea, rivers and fountains; referring to the aquatic habit.) Leguminosae (Mimosoideae). Some 12 species of spreading, prostrate or, occasionally, floating (marginal) perennial herbs and shrubs, often stoutly taprooted. Stems terete, sometimes armed, angled when young, sparsely branched, forming and distorted by massive ribbons of subcuticular aerenchyma in semi-aquatic spp. Leaves alternate, bipinnate; stipules paired, lanceolate or lanceolate-acuminate, with 'sleep movements' (cf. *Mimosa pudica*); leaflets alternate, asymmetric, small, occasionally mucronate, glabrous or margins sparsely ciliate, surface appearing minutely punctate; rachis angled, prolonged into a linear leaflike projection, glabrous, thickly pulvinate at base and rachillae axils. Inflorescence a crowded spike, capitate to subspicate, yellow to green-yellow; flowers mimosoid, dimorphic, in solitary, axillary, globose heads, lower flowers staminate or barren with long, petal-like staminodes; calyx campanulate, 5-lobed or entire; corolla 5-merous; stamens free, exserted, regular, 5-merous, to 10, anthers bilocular; ovary glabrous, stipitate. Fruit broad-oblong, flat, dehiscent, to 20-seeded. Cosmopolitan. Z7.

CULTIVATION *Neptunia* spp. are frequently aquatic although a number of species are found on dry land. *N.oleracea* is found free-floating in slow-moving, still or stagnant waters in the tropics, often as a weed of irrigation channels. *N.plena* roots in moist soils at the margins of pools and swamps so that the prostrate stems float out on to the water's surface. They are grown for their pale yellow or green flowers and finely divided foliage which in some species, especially *N.plena*, is sensitive to the touch in the manner of *Mimosa pudica*; their spongy, floating stems are also a botanical curiosity. Adding much interest, as one of the few available aquatic shrubs, to the tropical aquarium or to tubs or tanks in the hot glasshouse.

In humid tropical zones, plant *N.plena* in full sun in moist waterside soils so that the trailing stems float on the water's surface. Care should be taken not to introduce this shrub where it is likely to escape and become a pernicious weed. Under glass, maintain a minimum temperature of 16–18°C/60–65°F, with high humidity; plant in turfy loam mixed with sharp sand, bonemeal, hoof and horn and charcoal, into clay pans topdressed with fine gravel or alpinist's grit. At first, plunge in water to half depth of container; within a few months, established plants may be submerged to the root collar. Propagate by seed or cuttings the latter usually by detaching rooted, floating branches.

***N.lutea*** (Leavenw.) Benth. Pubesc., perenn. herb. Stems prostrate or spreading, slender, to 2m+, compressed when young, often conspicuously hairy. Lvs with 3 to 11, pairs of pinnae; stipules to 4×2mm, lanceolate, persistent, membranous; leaflets to 8×3mm, some 20 pairs per pinna, short-oblong, obtuse or broadly acute; fls to 50 per dense, ovoid to short-cylindric head, bright yellow to 2×1.5cm; lower fls without sterile stamens; cal. acute, some 2mm; cor. to 4mm; stamens to 1cm. Fr. to 5cm×15mm, rounded or with small, broad apical point. Late spring–early summer. Southern N America (E Texas to C Oklahoma). Z7.

***N.oleracea*** Lour. Perenn. herb or subshrub, floating or prostrate near water's edge. Stems to 1.5m, becoming detached from the primary root system, in water developing dense white spongy tissue between the nodes; pinnae to 4 per lf; stipules to 15×5mm; leaflets to 18×3.5mm, to 20 pairs per pinna, oblong, obtuse to broadly acute. Fls to 50 per capitate spike, sessile, green; cal. to 3mm, entire; cor. to 4mm; staminodes 10, petal-like, to 16×1mm, yellow, anth. to 1mm, lacking terminal gland; ovary 2mm. Fr. to 3×1cm. Pantropical (Tropical Asia, Africa, and C and S America). Z9.

***N. plena*** (L.) Benth. Similar in general habit to *N. oleracea*, from which it may be distinguished by lvs with 5 pairs pinnae; stipules to 12×6.5mm; leaflets slightly smaller, to 38 pairs per pinna, oblong, obtuse to broadly acute. Fls 60 per capitate spike, yellow; cal. to 3mm; cor. to 5mm; staminodes to 9mm. Fr. to 5.5×1cm. Summer. Originating in coastal regions of C America, now widespread throughout the tropics and subtropics. Z10.

***N. natans*** (L.) Druce. See *N. oleracea*.
***N. tenuis*** Benth. See *N. lutea*.
For further synonymy see *Acacia* and *Mimosa*.

**Nerine** Herb. (From Gk Nereis, the name of a sea nymph.) Amaryllidaceae. About 30 species of bulbous perennials. Bulb globose or ovoid-pyriform, tunicated, sometimes produced into a neck. Lvs strap-shaped appearing with or soon after the flowers. Flowers 4–20+ on a slender or stout scape, often curiously scented; perianth funnel-shaped, usually zygomorphic, white, pink or bright red, erect or decurved, lobes 6, free, narrow-oblong to linear-lanceolate, falcate, more or less crisped, tips usually strongly recurved and rolled; stamens 6 inserted at the base of the perianth lobes, suberect or declinate, 2 lengths; style filiform, straight or declinate, stigma simple or trifid; ovary globose, 3-lobed. Fruit a globose, 3-celled capsule; seeds 1 or a few to a cell, globose. S Africa, Lesotho, Botswana, Swaziland. Z9 unless specified. The mistaken distribution of *N. sarniensis* can be traced to Robert Morison, Professor of Botany at Oxford, who in 1680 suggested it had become naturalized on the coast of Guernsey, the bulbs having been cast away from a ship coming from Japan, an interpretation accepted by Linnaeus. Since the true habitat of the plant is South Africa, this explanation could only be defended if the ship had revictualled at the Cape en route from Japan. The first illustration of *N. sarniensis* ('Narcissus Japonicus Rutilo Flore') was based by Cornut on a plant growing in the garden of Jean Morin in Paris in 1634; its alleged Japanese origin may have been due to ignorance or deception by the importer. In England, the 'golden tulip' (a soubriquet that suggests the cultivation of colour variants even at this early date) was in the Wimbledon garden of Cromwell's Major-General John Lambert in the 1650s. After the Restoration, Lambert was exiled to Guernsey and it is likely that he took the plant with him. Morison, a Royalist, may have falsified its origin to conceal any association with Lambert.

CULTIVATION *Nerine* is a genus of predominantly frost-tender bulbs grown for their long-lived, autumn blooms, carried in delicate umbels, each flower having the characteristically narrow, undulate perianth segments that give the spider-like appearance also seen in the related genera *Hymenocallis* and *Lycoris*. In many species, notably *N. sarniensis*, the flowers have a beautiful iridescent quality. The flowers last well when cut, and *Nerine* spp. are grown commercially on a large scale for this purpose. The leaves emerge after flowering, and persist over winter into the following spring or summer.

In cool-temperate zones, most species are cultivated in the cool glasshouse, since they are not tolerant of temperatures below freezing; *N. masonorum*, a dainty species for warm sheltered pockets in the rock garden in areas with mild winters, is well suited to cultivation in the alpine house in cooler zones. *N. bowdenii* will grow where winter temperatures drop to −15°C/5°F, although it will not tolerate these low temperatures in combination with winter wet, and in regions at the limits of its hardiness should be grown at the base of a south-facing wall in perfectly drained soil, with the additional protection of a dry mulch of bracken litter or leafmould. In northern Britain, large and well established clumps are most commonly seen at the base of south facing house walls, in the rain shadow of the eaves. *N. sarniensis* may be treated similarly.

***N. bowdenii*** Will. Wats. Bulb to 6×5cm, ovoid-pyriform, neck sometimes attaining 6cm. Lvs to 30×3cm, pale to dark green, glossy, appearing after fls. Scape to 45cm, hollow toward apex, spathe valves 2, thin; fls 6–7, muskily scented; pedicels to 5cm; perianth lobes to 7×0.8cm, candy pink to deep rose, rarely white, darker at midrib, margins undulate; stamens shorter than lobes; style equalling lobes, stigma obscurely 3-lobed; ovary glabrous. Fr. to 1cm diam., irregularly 3-lobed. S Africa (E Cape, Natal). 'Alba': fls white with a blush of pink. 'Hera' (*N. bowdenii* × *N. sarniensis*): fls rich pink. 'Mark Fenwick' ('Fenwick's Variety'): vigorous; fls soft cyclamen pink, early-flowering. 'Pink Triumph': fls deep pink. 'Wellsii': fls dark pink, seg. crinkled. Z9.

***N. duparquetiana*** Bak. Lvs usually prostrate, slender. Scape to 25cm; fls to 13; pedicels to 6cm, slender; lobes to 4.5×0.5cm, white, suffused or ribbed red-pink and sometimes tinted yellow, conduplicate, strongly recurved and twisted; stamens exceeding lobes, strongly forward-projecting. S Africa (N Cape, Kalahari).

***N. filamentosa*** Barker. Bulb to 2.7cm diam., subglobose to ovoid-pyriform with a slender neck to 2.5cm. Lvs to 10cm, 3–5, very slender, lax, sometimes sprawling and curling at tips, appearing with fls. Scape to 20cm, usually shorter, to 0.45cm diam.; spathe valves to 4.5cm, narrow; fls to 8; lobes to 2cm, bright rose, narrow-lanceolate, strongly recurved and rolled at tips; fil. far exceeding perianth, anth. dark red to black-purple. S Africa (E Cape).

***N. filifolia*** Bak. Bulb to 2.5cm diam., globose, with pale tunic overtopping the neck. Lvs to 20cm, 6–10, appearing with fls, slender, suberect. Scape to 30cm, slender, somewhat glandular-pubesc.; spathe valves to 2.5cm; fls 8–10; pedicels to 3.5cm; perianth 2.5cm, deflexed, white, rose pink, magenta or bright crimson, lobes to 3cm wide, oblanceolate, clawed, crisped; stamens declinate, shorter than lobes, anth. red; style equalling the longer stamens; ovary hairy. S Africa (E Cape, Transkei, Orange Free State, Swaziland, E Transvaal).

***N. flexuosa*** Herb. Bulb subglobose, to 3.5cm. Lvs to 2cm wide, 4–6, appearing with the fls, linear-lorate, arching, bright green, sometimes rough and pustular. Scape to 1m, slender, slightly glaucous, flexuous; spathe valves and pedicels to 5cm; fls 10–20, pale pink or white; lobes to 3×0.4cm, crisped, oblanceolate; stamens declinate, shorter than the lobes, anth. to 4mm, claret red; style declinate, equalling the stamens. 'Alba': fls white, edges somewhat ruffled. S Africa.

***N. fothergillii*** M. Roem. Bulb subglobose with membranous red-tinged tunics. Lvs 6–8, falcate, obtuse, glabrous, base canaliculate. Scape to 60cm with sheathing leaf bases, erect, glabrous; spathe to 3.5cm, valves acute, red; fls 15, scarlet; lobes 2cm, subundulate, strongly recurved, somewhat spiralling; filaments erect, scarlet, slightly exceeding perianth, anth. deep. violet; style filiform, suberect. S Africa.

***N. humilis*** Herb. Bulb to 3.5cm diam.; ovoid, tunics membranous. Lvs to 30×1.5cm, about 6, appearing with the fls, linear, suberect, channelled above. Scape to 35cm, slender, slightly glaucous; spathe valves to 3.5cm, green, equalling pedicels; fls 10–20, bright pale pink to deep rose; lobes to 3cm, oblanceolate, acute, crisped; stamens declinate, the longer 3 equalling the lobes, anth. 3mm, purple; style declinate, equalling the lobes. S Africa (W, SW & S Cape).

***N. masonorum*** Bol. Dwarf. Bulb short-necked. Lvs to 20cm×1.5mm, thread-like. Scape to 30cm, downy; pedicels to 3cm, densely pubesc.; fls 4–15; perianth pale to deep rose-pink, lobes to 1.5cm, recurved, undulate, with a deep pink longitudinal stripe; stamens deflexed, with 2 lanceolate processes at the base; style deflexed; ovary glabrous. S Africa (Cape Province).

***N. sarniensis*** Herb. GUERNSEY LILY. Bulb 5cm diam., ovoid, tunic pale brown. Lvs to 30×2cm, about 6, appearing after fls, suberect, not curved, bright green, glabrous. Scape to 45cm, somewhat compressed; spathe valves to 5cm, crimson; pedicels to 5cm; fls to 3.8cm, 10–20, erect, pale rose-red to scarlet, pink, rarely white, scarcely zygomorphic, lobes to 3.5×1.3cm, lanceolate, strongly recurved at tips, only slightly crisped; fil. boldly erect, bright red, 1.2cm longer than lobes, anth. usually pale; styles to 5cm, straight; ovary glabrous. Coastal S Africa. 'Kirstenbosch White': fls pure white. Z8.

***N. undulata*** Herb. Bulb to 2.5cm diam., ovoid; tunics membranous, pale. Lvs to 45×1.2cm, 4–6, appearing with the fls, linear, bright green. Scape to 45cm, slender; spathe valves to 3.5cm, equalling pedicels; fls 8–12, pale candy pink or rose; lobes to 2×0.2cm, oblanceolate, strongly crisped; stamens declinate, equalling lobes, anth. ultimately dark; style declinate. Fr. to 6mm diam., deeply lobed; seeds 1 per cell. S Africa.

***N.* cultivars**. The range of cvs reflects the diversity found amongst the species. Stem length can exceed 90cm, but new dwarfs are under 15cm. The most usual hybrids of *N. sarniensis* range between 30cm and 60cm. The range of colours shows a preponderance of red in great variety; there are no blue or yellow fls but excellent white and pink, through to very dark red and the most brilliant scarlet. Bicolours, mostly pink and white are increasingly common. Flowering season extends from June (with some of the progeny of *N. hirsuta*) to late November and, with suitable treatment, into December. *N. sarniensis* hybrids peak in mid-October, *N. flexuosa* hybrids in late October and November. The number of florets in the head varies widely, again reflecting the range found amongst the species. Selective breeding has given emphasis to larger flowerheads with more individual florets. While 10–15 florets is normal for the better varieties more recent forms may have as many 24, giving a more rounded head.

*Very short*. 'Hero': to 34cm; flowerheads 16cm diam.; florets 12, 7cm wide, red-violet. 'Hotspur': to 34cm; flowerheads 10cm wide; florets 13, 6cm wide, deep magenta. 'Ixanthia': to 30cm; flowerheads 5.5cm wide; florets 11, 5cm wide, pink-carmine. 'Kate Cicely': to 30cm; florets 8, 8cm wide, flame. 'Latu': to 36cm; flowerheads 14cm wide; florets 14, 6cm wide, white, red-ribbed. 'Patina': to 38cm; flowerheads 11cm wide; florets 11, 5cm wide, pale pink. 'Phoebe': to 30cm; flowerheads 13cm wide; florets 6, 5.5cm wide, blue-violet. 'Priscilla': to 37cm; flowerheads 13cm wide; florets 13, 6cm wide, pink. 'Pym': to 36cm; flowerheads 12cm wide; florets 7, 6.5cm wide, pink.

*Very early* (July-August). 'Anna Fletcher': to 51cm; flowerheads 12.5cm wide; florets 11, 6cm wide, apricot. 'Catherine': to 51cm; flowerheads 17cm wide; florets 14, 5cm wide, light red. 'Diana Wharton': to 42cm; flowerheads 13cm wide; florets 8, 6.5cm wide, mid-red. 'Fothergillii Major': to 51cm; florets 12, 14cm wide, florets 12, 6cm wide, deep orange-red. 'Glensavage Gem': to 78cm; flowerheads 21cm wide; florets 13, crimson. 'Hera': to 90cm; flowerheads 21cm wide; florets 16, 8cm wide, rose-carmine. 'Miss Eva Godman': to 42cm; flowerheads 16cm wide; florets 8, 6cm wide, light red. 'Mrs Bromely': to 60cm; flowerheads 12cm wide; florets 11, 6cm wide, red-orange. 'Paula Knight': to 60cm; florets 12, 7cm wide, china rose. 'Plymouth': to 60cm; flowerheads 16cm wide; florets 12, 7cm wide, mid-red.

*Very tall*. 'Blush Beauty': to 120cm; flowerheads to 16cm wide; florets 14, 7cm wide, very pale pink. 'Guy Fawkes': to 72cm; flowerheads 15cm wide; florets 14, 6½cm wide; light cerise. 'Kilwa': to 84cm; flowerheads 17cm wide; florets 14, 7cm wide; magenta. 'Kingship': to 75cm; flowerheads 15cm wide; florets 17, 5cm wide; cerise-purple. 'Mansellii': to 72cm; flowerheads 16cm wide; florets 18, 6cm wide; mid-cerise. 'Mischief': to 75cm; flowerheads 14cm wide; florets 14, 7cm wide; cerise-mauve. 'Namba': to 120cm; flowerheads 19cm wide; florets 17, 4cm wide; mid-pink. 'Parbet II': to 123cm; flowerheads 19cm wide; florets 10, 7½cm wide; pink, deep pink. 'Rushmere Star': to 72cm; flowerheads 16cm wide; florets 10, 7cm wide; bright magenta. 'Supremo': to 108cm; flowerheads 24cm wide; florets 15, 7cm wide; white/pale pink.

*Very late* (late October and November). 'Ancilla': to 66cm; flowerheads 12cm wide; florets 15, 6cm wide; purple-red. 'Bennet Poe': to 54cm; flowerheads 13cm wide; florets 13, 6½cm wide; mid-cerise. 'Cranfield': to 75cm; flowerheads 15cm wide; florets 16, 6cm wide; cerise. 'Konak': to 75cm; flowerheads 14cm wide; florets 12, 5cm wide; white/purple. 'Koriba': to 66cm; flowerheads 12cm wide; florets 12, 7cm wide; cerise. 'Kymina': to 75cm; flowerheads 14cm wide; florets 14, 7cm wide; pale pink. 'Mansellii': to 72cm; flowerheads 16cm wide; florets 18, 6cm wide; mid-cerise. 'Namba': to 120cm; flowerheads 19cm wide; florets 17, 4cm wide; mid-pink. 'Pink Triumph': to 60cm: flowerheads 15cm wide; florets 15, 6cm wide; fuschia pink. 'Wombe': to 57cm; flowerheads 16.5cm wide; florets 14, 6cm wide; orange-red. 'Zeal Giant': fls vivid deep pink, in large heads.

***N. curvifolia*** Herb. See *N. fothergillii*.
***N. veitchii*** hort. See *N. bowdenii*.

**Nerium** L. (Name used by Dioscorides.) OLEANDER; ROSE BAY. Apocynaceae. 1 species, a glabrous evergreen shrub, 2–6m. Branches spreading to erect. Leaves 10–22cm, usually in whorls of 3 or paired, opposite, lanceolate, acute, sharp-tipped, coriaceous, dark green, midrib prominent above; petiole short. Inflorescence a terminal, broad, compound cyme to 80-flowered; flowers showy, bisexual, often fragrant (a character formerly used to distinguish *N. odorum* from *N. oleander*); calyx lobes 5, to one quarter length of corolla; corolla funnelform, white to deep pink or yellow, tube slender-cylindric, throat dilated, limb 2.5–5cm diam., spreading, deeply 5-lobed, encircling a crown of 5 cleft or ragged segments at throat; stamens attached below throat, included, anthers plumose, slender; ovaries 2. Fruit a follicle. Mediterranean to W China, widely naturalized. All parts extremely toxic. Z8.

CULTIVATION *N. oleander* occurs in damp valleys and seasonally dry watercourses in gravelly soils. The highly toxic foliage may cause skin irritation on contact and death if eaten, nevertheless this beautiful genus is tolerant, grows rapidly, and is widely planted in warm temperate and subtropical regions as a border specimen or for screening and informal hedging. Given a sheltered sunny position, *N. oleander* may tolerate temperatures to −10°C/14°F for short periods, although in cool climates *Nerium* is more commonly grown in tubs in the glasshouse or conservatory, to be moved outdoors for the summer months.

Grow in full sun in a fertile, well-drained, loam-based medium with additional leafmould. The oleander is lime tolerant. As growth commences, maintain good ventilation and a temperature of about 10–13°C/50–55°F. Syringe occasionally and water plentifully. In late autumn withhold water for a short period after flowering and keep almost dry in winter, when temperatures may be allowed to fall to 5–8°C/40–46°F. Pinch out stem tips of young plants to encourage bushy habit, and prune established specimens in later winter to shape and restrict size; remove old and weak growths and shorten the previous season's flowered shoots by up to two thirds. Propagate cultivars by semi-ripe cuttings of terminal shoots, or by stem sections in summer after flowering. Increase species also by seed in spring. Under glass, scale insects, mealybug, red spider mite and aphids may be pests. Leaf spot disease and a bacterial gall may be damaging, remove and burn affected parts.

***N. oleander*** L. As for the genus. Over 400 cultivars have been recorded. For a checklist, see F.JJ. Pagen, *Agricultural University Wageningen Papers*, 87–2 (1987). These are variously scented or unscented, conform to one of three corolla types, single, superposed (hose-in-hose) and fully double, and range in colour from white to cream, pink, lilac, red, carmine, purple, yellow, salmon, apricot, flesh, copper and orange. Several have leaves variegated with white or yellow and, usually, rose pink, double flowers.

***N. indicum*** Mill. See *N. oleander*.
***N. odorum*** Sol. See *N. oleander*.

**Nertera** Banks & Sol. ex Gaertn. (From Gk *nerteros*, lowly, alluding to the habit.) Rubiaceae. Some 15 species of diminutive, perennial herbs, prostrate or creeping, rooting at nodes, somewhat foetid. Leaves minute, sessile or short-petiolate, opposite, usually ovate to lanceolate; stipules interpetiolar. Flowers hermaphrodite or polygamo-dioecious, sessile or short-pedicellate, axillary or terminal, solitary, inconspicuous; calyx truncate, or obscurely lobed or toothed; corolla tube funnelform or campanulate, lobes 4–5, valvate in bud; stamens 4–5, inserted at or near base of corolla tube, filaments filiform, long-exserted, anthers exserted; ovary 2-celled, style 2-lobed almost to base, lobes filiform, hairy, ovules solitary in each cell. Fruit a drupe, sometimes colourful, fleshy or, rarely, dry; pyrenes 2, 1-seeded. S China and SE Asia to Australia, New Zealand, Polynesia, Antarctic and Hawaii to C & S America, Tristan da Cunha. Z9.

CULTIVATION Grown for their masses of tiny bead-like fruits over low mats or hummocks of mossy foliage, *Nertera* spp. are suitable for pans in the cool glass or alpine house, as houseplants, or in regions where frosts are light and short lived, as ground cover in the rock garden; *Nertera* spp. are intolerant of excessive winter wet. Grow in a sandy/gritty, moisture-retentive and freely draining soils, with shelter from cold winds in a semi-shaded situation. Under glass maintain good ventilation, with a minimum temperature of 5–7°C/40–45°F. Propagate by careful division, by tip cuttings or by seed in spring in a sandy propagating mix in the shaded cool glasshouse or frame.

***N. balfouriana*** Ckn. Forming mats to 25cm wide. Lvs to 5×4mm, usually broad-ovate or -oblong, or obovate, obtuse at apex and base; petioles to 4mm, striate; stipules to 1mm, triangular. Fls sessile, axillary and terminal; cal. reduced, truncate; cor. funnel-shaped, tube to 3mm, glabrous, lobes 4, triangular, margins protuberant; stamens erect, 5mm; style falcate. Fr. to 1cm, squat-pyriform, yellow-orange. New Zealand.

***N. ciliata*** T. Kirk. Forming mats to 20cm wide. Stems and branches glabrous or pilose. Lvs to 5×5mm, ovate, apex acute or obtuse, base cuneate and obtuse, ciliate at margins; petioles to 3mm, often ciliate; stipules truncate or triangular, glabrous. Fls sessile; cal. truncate and ciliate; cor. funnel-shaped, to 4mm, glabrous, lobes 4–5, falcate, linear; anth. exserted; style occasionally 3-lobed. Fr. 4mm diam., globose, minutely pubesc., orange. New Zealand.

***N. cunninghamii*** Hook. f. Forming mats to 20cm wide. Lvs to 8×3mm, narrowly ovate, apex narrowed and acute, base narrowed and obtuse; petioles to 3mm, filiform; stipules triangular, acute. Fls sessile or subsessile, axillary and terminal; cal. to 2mm, truncate or obscurely 4-toothed; cor. campanulate, to 2mm, lobes 4; anth. and style short-exserted. Fr. to 4mm diam., globose, red. New Zealand.

***N. granadensis*** (Mutis) Druce. BREAD PLANT; CORAL MOSS; ENGLISH BABYTEARS. Forming patches to 40cm wide or more. Stems obscurely 4-angled. Lvs to 8×5mm, broad-ovate to rhomboid or orbicular, apex obtuse or acute, base narrowed and obtuse or subcordate, falcate and, occasionally, undulate at margins, membranous; petioles to 8mm; stipules broadly triangular. Fls sessile, axillary and solitary; cal. obsolete, truncate; cor. 3mm, campanulate, glabrous, lobes 4; style short-exserted. Fr. 5mm wide, globose or ovoid, depressed, glabrous, orange to dark red. S America, Taiwan and SE Asia, Australia and Tasmania, New Zealand. cf. *Soleirolia soleirolii* (*Helxine soleirolii*) in Urticaceae, for which this plant is sometimes mistaken when not in fruit.

***N. depressa*** Banks & Sol. ex Gaertn. See *N. granadensis*.

**Nervilia** Comm. ex Gaudich. (From Lat. *nervus*, a vein, alluding to the prominently veined lvs of many species.) Orchidaceae. About 80 species of terrestrial orchids arising from small, more or less globose tubers. Leaf broad, usually cordate, often pleated and lustrous, solitary, erect or prostrate, appearing after flowering. Inflorescence racemose, 1- to many-flowered; scape with 3–4 sheathing leaves, usually elongating after fertilization; flowers white, pink, dull purple, brown, green or yellow, sometimes fragrant; sepals and petals similar, lanceolate, spreading or projecting forwards; lip entire or trilobed, with or without a spur; column somewhat clavate; anther terminal; pollinia 2, granular. Arabia, mainland Africa, Madagascar, Mascarene Is., India, SE Asia to Japan, Pacific Is. and Australia. Z10.

CULTIVATION Curious orchids for damp, shady positions in the warm house, particularly for their pleated, heart-shaped leaves. Regime as for *Phaius* but with higher temperatures.

***N. bicarinata*** (Bl.) Schltr. To 75cm; tubers globose, about 2.5cm diam. Lf lamina to 17×22cm, reniform, apiculate, cordate at base, dark green, pleated, on petiole 18–20cm long, sometimes just starting to appear at flowering time. Raceme laxly 4–12-fld, the fls pendent, thin-textured, green, lip creamy white, veined purple; sep. and pet. 20–30×4mm, ligulate-lanceolate, acute, projecting forwards; lip 28–30×20–24mm, obscurely trilobed, with 2 fleshy ridges running from base to junction of lobes, midlobe ovate, acute, the apex recurved, lateral lobes erect; column 12–14mm, arched. Widespread in tropical Africa; Arabia.

***N. kotschyi*** (Rchb. f.) Schltr. 10–28cm; tubers to 2cm diam., ovoid or ellipsoid, pubesc. Lf 3–12×4–13cm, prostrate or erect, thick-textured, broadly cordate or broadly ovate, acute, ribbed, the veins usually with a jagged keel on the upper surface. Raceme 2–7-fld, the fls horizontal or pendent, veined green-brown, lip white or pale yellow purple; sep. and pet. 14–20×2–3mm, linear-lanceolate, acute, projecting forwards; lip 14–18×9–12mm, rather obscurely trilobed at about half-way, lateral lobes triangular, acute, midlobe ovate, undulate, the front margin reflexed, pubesc. between 2 longitudinal, fleshy ridges; column arched, 7–9mm. Tropical Africa (widespread). Z10.

***N. purpurata*** (Rchb. f. & Sonder) Schltr. To 22cm. Lf erect, lamina to 10×4cm, ovate or elliptic, green above, purple beneath with prominent veins, borne on petiole to 15cm. Raceme 2–4-fld; fls horizontal or pendent, green or yellow-green, the lip veined with purple; sep. and pet. 18×22×4mm, linear-lanceolate, acute, projecting forwards; lip 18×13mm, obscurely trilobed, pubesc. between 2 longitudinal fleshy ridges, midlobe triangular-ovate, obtuse, somewhat reflexed, lateral lobes erect, oblong; column 10mm, arched. Zaire, Zambia, Tanzania, Angola, S Africa.

***N. umbrosa*** (Rchb. f.) Schltr. See *N. bicarinata*.

**The Netherlands**. Gardening in the Netherlands, as in most of Europe, had its earliest expression in abbey and monastery gardens of the Middle Ages where vegetables, fruit and herbs were cultivated within the walls. Small gardens were made in the centre of a cloister walk, inside castle walls, and sometimes in towns, attached to private houses or to hospitals.

The layout of a medieval garden usually consisted of a square or slightly elongated rectangle, its exact form determined by the shape of the buildings around it. Courtyard gardens usually consisted of a more or less square space divided by a cross-shaped path. A feature – perhaps water or a tree – often marked the centre of the cross. It is likely that the courtyard was planted with grass rather than herbs, unless it was the only garden within the monastery complex. The vegetable gardens and orchards within the monastery walls were also of a mainly square or rectangular shape, usually subdivided into a number of smaller beds in which the vegetables, culinary and medicinal herbs, ornamental flowers for the altar, and fruit trees were grown.

The medieval castle garden or pleasure garden consisted of an enclosed space within the castle walls. The 13th-century Dominican monk, Albertus Magnus, described a square lawn surrounded by aromatic herbs and a variety of flowers, with trees and vines planted against the southern and western walls. Water from a well was channelled towards the centre where seating was placed in the form of a so-called turf bench, a bench constructed of masonry on top of which turf and wild flowers were laid to form a soft cushion. Illustrations of this kind of garden can be found in manuscripts such as the *Roman de la Rose* and in paintings of the Flemish Primitives, in which the Madonna is often portrayed seated on a turf bench. Plants were selected for cultivation because they were either useful – medicinal and kitchen herbs, vegetables and fruit from the orchard – or ornamental, cultivated because of their Christian symbolism – the rose, the white lily, the blue iris and the columbine, for example.

After the long struggle for independence from Spain, and particularly with the final retreat of Spanish troops in 1609, gardens in the Netherlands became more open in aspect, since castle and monastery walls were no longer needed to serve a defensive function. Houses and castles were built outside the town walls, often surrounded by a canal, with vegetable gardens and orchards beyond, separated from the surrounding agricultural land by another canal or moat. The *Nieuwe Cronyk van Zeeland* of 1696 includes many illustrations of castles with gardens exposed to the surrounding countryside. Gardens were designed on a rectangular pattern and divided into small, separate, square and rectangular areas; the axis of the garden was usually not related to the building or to an overall plan. The structural elements comprised leafy walks between the various subdivisions of the garden, which were delineated by railings, walls or hedges. Also featured were *parterres de broderie,* arbours at the crossing-points of paths, fountains, and mazes formed by low beds with ornamental flowers.

In the illustrations of Vredeman de Vries (1527–1604) bulbs are often depicted in smaller gardens. Bulbs were widely introduced at the end of the 16th century and became something of a status symbol, giving rise to the frantic speculation in the 1630s known as 'tulipomania'. Speculation in tulips was forbidden by the State in 1637. Other plants portrayed in illustrations of the day included sunflowers, African marigolds, tobacco plants, carnations, poppies and roses. Designers who created such gardens in the Netherlands between 1500 and 1650 included the Italian Vincidor de Bologna, the South Netherlander Jacob de Gheijn II, and the town architect of Groningen, G. Peters. Notable examples include the Castle of Breda (1536), Muiderslot (1609), Goudesteijn (1628), Castle Zuylestein (1632), the educational gardens of Leiden (1590) and Groningen (1642), as well as the strictly mannerist gardens of the Nassau family such as the Princesses-garden (1609), close to the present-day Paleis Noordeinde, Het Buitenhof (*c*1620), the inner gardens of Castle Buren (*c*1620), and Het Prinsenhof at Groningen (1626).

With the increasing prosperity from trade, shipping and industry in the northern Netherlands in the early 17th century, many newly rich merchants began to build country houses and lay out gardens. The increasing number of young Netherlanders who embarked on a 'Grand Tour' to complete their education developed a taste for the Italian style which influenced the development of both architecture and landscape gardening in the Republic of the Netherlands. Treatises by the Italian designers Alberti, Serlio, Vignola, Palladio and Scamozzi were translated into Dutch and contributed to the creation of a new garden architecture, a Dutch interpretation of the classical style with its emphasis on proportion, symmetry and harmony.

The Dutch classical style generally decreed that garden layout be a rectangle, usually in the classic proportions of 4:3, or sometimes 2:1 as advocated by the architect Philip Vingboons (1607–78). The axis of symmetry, usually the longitudinal axis, divided this rectangle into two equal parts to either side of the centre of the house. The whole of the rectangular garden was then enclosed by tree-lined canals, as are common in the polder landscape. The total area of the garden was often further subdivided into separate square gardens, parterres and beds of flowers.

The structural elements of the Dutch classical garden in the second half of the 17th century comprised an outer walled enclosure, perhaps dating from earlier times, or a hedge or planting of trees along the canals, with a divided interior of mazes, parterres and low ornamental plantings of subjects such as thyme, carnations, camomile and other flowering plants in tubs on tiles, with box hedges, leafy walks and arbours and mazes. Water played a more modest role than in the Italian gardens, although there were fountains and small water features with an element of surprise (*bedriegertjes*). Few garden statues were used although sundials were beginning to make their appearance. The plants used at this time are described in *Die Nederlandse Hovenier* written by Jan van der Groen in 1669. Van der Groen was gardener to the Prince of Orange and worked from 1659 to 1665 at the Oude Hof (today the Palace Noordeinde) and probably at the Huis ten Bosch. From 1665 to 1670 he worked at Honselersdijk and in 1671 at Huis ter Nieuwburg. Many of the plants he describes would have been growing in these gardens; they include bear's breeches, marsh mallow, yellow asphodel, larkspur, wild pink, common lavender, love-in-a-mist, auriculas and many more. The best-known houses and gardens in this style are the palaces built by Prince Frederik Hendrik, namely Honselersdijk (1621), Huis ter Nieuwburg (1630) and Huis ten Bosch (1647). Constantine Huygens and Jacob Cats followed him with Hofwijck (1640) and Sorgvliet (1651). All are in the vicinity of The Hague.

In other parts of the Republic, too, large country estates were laid out. Popular locations were along the large waterways such as the Haarlemmermeer and the Wijkermeer or in the new polders such as the Beemster, the Diemermeer and the Zeeland polders. The dunes were also favoured because of their proximity to the hunt. Medieval and 16th-century country houses of the nobility in and their gardens laid out in the classical style, the gardens being carefully designed to enhance and harmonize with the house.

In the province of North Holland gardens, laid out on classical lines were created at the Hof te Bergen (1642), De Nijenburg, Frankendael, Trompenburg (*c*1680), Elswout (1645), Hartenkamp (1691), Manpad, Kruidberg (*c*1660) and Beeckestein; in the province of South Holland, in addition to those already mentioned around The Hague, classical gardens were laid out at Duivenvoorde, Warmond (1632) and Keukenhof (1641), in Utrecht at Renswoude (1654), Geerestein and Soestdijk (1676) and in Gelderland and Overijssel at Slangenburg (1675), Oldenaller (1655), Weldam (1645) and Schoonheten (1640). One can still clearly see the Dutch classical division of the grounds at Weldam, Beeckestein (the first part behind the house), Schoonheten and the Hof at Bergen. The most important designers of the Dutch classical style were Jacob van Campen (1595–1657) and Pieter Post (1608–69).

From about 1680 the layout of Dutch country-house gardens was strongly influenced by the French baroque. The rectangular classical Dutch garden, enclosed by canals, was modified so that the main axis seems to extend beyond the outer perimeter of the garden into the landscape beyond; the main axis was often continued into the countryside with a lane. Gardens were still subdivided into symmetrical sections aligned along the central axis, but the central garden was often enclosed in the classical half-circle manner. Daniel Marot (1661–1752), the garden architect and author of *Nouveaux Livre de Parterres* (1703), liked to work with the half-circle enclosed in the form of a leafy walk or colonnade, and often used this Serliana-form in his parterre decorations.

Variety and liveliness were characteristic of the baroque gardens of the time. This was achieved by variation in all the structural elements, in scent and colour, the appearance and sounds of water – tumbling from fountains or trickling over water steps – and in the profusion of statues, depicting figures from Greek mythology and symbolizing the life or character of the owner or his wife. The water in the fountains and cascades, in the absence of a spring or different ground levels, was often propelled by a small windmill. The details of these various garden conceits – buildings, waterworks and decorative elements – were described in detail in design books of the day.

The principal structural elements of these French classical gardens consisted of parterres, woods with axes in the shape of a star, galleries, cabinets and wildernesses, mazes, hedges, cupolas and colonnades, orchards and vegetable gardens with serpentine walls. Water, as well as spouting from fountains and 'surprise' sources, was also employed for its reflective function in the waterway around the central part of the garden and in the perspective waterways. Statuary, sundials, shell grottoes and galleries, arbours and latticework all added to this rich picture. Further interest was added by menageries, aviaries and orangeries. From 1720 to 1750 the plethora of decorative elements was constantly increasing, while the paths in the woods and coppices became more winding and irregular – a reaction away from the heaviness of the baroque. Further variation took the form of additional axes radiating from other focal points, as well as so-called over-gardens and side-gardens outside the original design. Planting, too, became more varied. The exotic plant collections of Sorgvliet, Honselersdijk, Gunterstein, Leeuwenhorst and Het Loo were well known and favoured hothouse plants of the day included citrus trees, pomegranates, olives, oleanders, myrtles, laurels, laurustinus, strawberry trees, lilacs, Judas trees, agaves and aloes.

Examples of gardens laid out in the French classical manner along a long symmetrical axis, or which were later modernized to include a perspective lane in the distance or a perspective canal, include Slot Zeist (1677), Clingendaal (1680), Leeuwenburgh (1686), Het Loo (1689), Fraylemaborg (1690), The Voorst (1695), Kasteel Heemstede (*c*1700), Renswoude (1708), Beeckestein (*c*1730) and Meerenberg Heemstede (1732). The most important designers in the French classical style were Jakob Roman and Daniel Marot.

Along the rivers, such as the Vecht, gardens could not be as deep, so that designs based on a long perspective line from the centre of the house were not usually seen in these situations. These gardens were, however, richly provided with a wide range of garden decoration, large pools, clipped hedges and topiary. Shell grottoes from this period survive in the gardens of Castle Rosendael and Nienoord at Leek.

The newly fashionable winding path through wilderness and coppice to some extent heralded the landscape style that was to develop in the latter half of the 18th century. Examples of this can be found at Beeckestein (after 1723), Renswoude (1729), Duin en Berg (*c*1730), Manpad (*c*1730) and Huis ten Bosch (*c*1730).

The classical style of the Republic of the Netherlands was highly influential abroad, making a deep impression on garden design in England, Germany and Russia in particular. Several leading Dutch landscape designers went abroad to work and a number of Dutch handbooks were translated into French, German and English.

The early landscape style in the Netherlands (1750–1800) was characterized by its smaller scale and more contained character than the closely allied but wider, more undulating English landscape style. It had its origins in a reaction against the strict formality and artificiality of the classical genre combined with a wide appreciation of 17th-century landscape painters – Rosa, Lorrain and Poussin – who portrayed an idealized landscape, and the influence of writers such as Pope, Rousseau and Delille who were exploring the relationship between nature and society. This style applied in the Netherlands to country houses and public 'woods' such as the Alkmaarder Hout. These new ideas also followed on directly from those that inspired the winding coppice paths of the early 18th century, which were still popular after 1750 and were used at Nieuw Amelisweerd, Oostbroek, Gooilust, Huis ten Donck, Mildenburg, Hulshorst and Oldenaller. In the early days of the Dutch landscape style we can, in fact, talk of a transitional style which was initially applied within the confines of the earlier rigidly formal lines. Garden ornaments from the earlier period were generally taken over and included in the new layout.

Traveller's tales of the palaces and gardens of the emperor of China also became known at this time, and landscape designers were intrigued by capriciously romantic, small-scale landscapes such as those of the Summer Palace in Peking. This whimsicality was popularly applied in the early landscape style, as was the use of Chinese temples, shell houses and pagodas. The discovery of Herculaneum and Pompeii in about 1740 also influenced garden architecture. Roman ruins were recreated in Dutch gardens, as in English, and neoclassical buildings started to make their appearance in some early landscape parks. At Bloemendaal neoclassical cupolas were built at Wildhoef and de Rijp and a temple was built at Ter Hooge in Middelburg.

A walk through the parks of this period could be imagined as a meandering stroll of discovery along winding paths. The final destination of these paths was often unclear. On the way one might come across Chinese, neoclassical and, under English influence, neogothic buildings or a ruin or hermitage, either as solid structures or depicted in paintings on wooden hoardings. At Biljoen in Velp texts in verse by classical writers were set up on boards to inspire contemplation; such texts were designed to reinforce the experience of the ideal landscape.

The favoured planting of this period is best described in the book by J.C. Krauss entitled *Illustrations of the Most Beautiful and Exotic Trees and Shrubs which Used to Decorate English Woods and Gardens and Can be Planted in Our Soil and Be Cultivated Here* (1802). He describes, for example, *Rhododendron ponticum, Catalpa bignonioides, Campsis radicans, Cercis siliquastrum, Liriodendron tulipiferum* and *Euonymus americanus*. Another important book, published in the same year, was G. van Laar's *Magazine of Garden Decorations* – the standard work for the Netherlands.

Among the more important garden designers working in the early landscape style were J.G. Michael, J.D. Zocher Sr., J.P. Posth and P.W. Schonk. Examples of estates which were partly redesigned to incorporate the landscape style included Groenendaal (*c*1750) and Over-Holland (1755); shortly after that in South Kennemerl and Huis te Bennebroek (*c*1761); Beeckestein (*c*1770) and Manpad (1767) and in South Holland, Huis ten Donck (1765). After these Amelisweerd (1770) and Hardenbroek (1772) followed in Utrecht, and in South-Holland De Paauw (1770) and De Keukenhof (1772). The first parks adapted in Gelderland were most likely Verwolde (1776), Biljoen (*c*1780) and Rosendael (*c*1780). About 1780 an important contribution was made by Michael in South-Kennemerl and when designing Elswout (1781), Waterland (1781), possibly Velserbeek (1775) and Welgelegen (Haarlemmerhout, 1788). J.D. Zocher Sr. is first mentioned in relation to Meerenberg, Heemstede (1794). In Overijssel the landscape layout was first seen at Twickel (1780) and Het Nijenhuis Diepenheim. Bingerden, Horssen, Hulshorst and Oldenaller are late 18th-century examples in Gelderland.

After the creation of the Kingdom of the Netherlands in 1814, the first public parks and walkways were established. Country estates were opened to the public for walking and recreation, Soelen for example, or were reorganized as public parks, such as the Park at Rotterdam or the Prince's Garden at Leeuwarden. New species, particularly those from China and Japan such as rhododendrons and azaleas, were planted in the landscape gardens. During this late landscape period (1800–1870), the character of gardens changed for a third time, this time from an enclosed to an open aspect. The first such change had occurred during the Renaissance when a relation with the surrounding countryside was sought through the concept of the 'villa suburbana', the second time during the French classical period when the axis of symmetry was extended to such an extent that the transition into the surrounding countryside became invisible, and the third time when the transition was made from early to late landscape style, from an enclosed to an open aspect. The enclosed, small-scale park was opened up with the creation of large, open meadows and lakes, and vistas across these open spaces towards points outside the park itself. The view from De Paauw across a large lawn towards Raaphorst opposite, the perspective axis between Zeist and Blikkenburg and Wulperhorst, or the view from Beverweerd across the Kromme Rijn, are a few interesting examples of this.

Most of the old features characteristic of French classical garden architecture – the straight lines, perspective canals and formal decorative features such as the statuary – disappeared during this period, being replaced by a landscape of open meadows with trees planted singly or in clumps, backed by the surrounding parkland generously endowed with lakes. Trees would also form a backdrop to the house. These were the elements that dominated fashionable landscape design from 1800 onwards. The natural landscape, of course, played an important role in the creation of a design as, for instance, at Kasteel Nieuwburg (Neuborg) where the waterfall forming part of the South Limburg landscape was incorporated into the design.

The structural elements of the later landscape style comprised curving pathways, long vistas, open meadows planted with single specimen trees, or clumps, and bordered by a backdrop of trees, large expanses of water, waterfalls and running streams, artificially created differences in levels, and meadows where animals could graze. The decorative elements now consisted predominantly of neoclassic and neogothic garden houses and orangeries, and shelters for animals built in Swiss chalet-style.

The most important designers working in the 19-century landscape style in the Netherlands were J.D. Zocher Sr. and Jr., J.P. Posth, C.E.A. Petzold, L.P. Roodbaard, and H. and S.A. Van Lunteren. Country estates which were laid out in the characteristic manner of the late landscape style include Zypendaal (1802–4), Sonsbeek (1806 and 1821), Het Loo (1807 and 1808), Verwolde (1810), Haagse Bos (1819), Twickel (1833), De Paauw (1830), Zeist (1830), Velserbeek (1832), Clingendaal (1838), Duivenvoorde (1844), Oldenaller (1850), Nieuw-Amelisweerd (1860) and Ruurlo (1868 and 1880). New public parks included De Plantage at Schiedam (1826), the Stadspark in Maastricht (1837), De Plantage in Culemborg (1850) and the Vondelpark (1864). The first pinetum, at Schovenhorst, was planted in 1848.

From 1870 onwards, the increasingly prosperous merchants built new villas within the towns and in rural places accessible by rail. Small parks were also designed for the health and enjoyment of factory workers, such as the Sarphatipark in Amsterdam and the 'people's parks' in Dordrecht and Enschede. From 1890 various town councils took over this initiative and created further parks, and later, in the 1930s, further park projects were undertaken to help combat unemployment. The Amsterdamse Bos was one such example.

After 1870 too, a more mixed style of landscaping developed, incorporating a number of elements from the earlier styles. In England the garden architects Repton, Loudon and Paxton had developed a style that incorporated a formal layout near the house with a gradual transition into parkland beyond. Paxton's design for the landscaping of the Crystal Palace in London (1852), with its combination of formal and landscape styles, incorporating elements of the classical garden art of Italy and France, was a notable influence on the direction of the new mixed style. This style was introduced into the Netherlands by the German architect H.H.A. Wentzel who designed the flower-garden at the Princessetuin at De Paauw (1853), and by the Frenchman E.F. André, who designed new layouts for Weldam and Twickel executed by the Dutch landscape architect H.A.C. Poortman. Country estates which had been laid out in the landscape style now acquired, as new parterres, colourful enclosed flower gardens and rose gardens near the house, their form inspired by the classical principles of proportion, symmetry and harmony. These gardens were generally hedged or walled to give them some protection from the wider landscape and were sometimes sunken. At the foot of the walls and hedges were colourful and scented borders of perennials and the flower beds generally were further enhanced by decorative stone troughs, balustrades and statuary. These richly decorative inner gardens also displayed pergolas, arches in walls and hedges, wall niches for statues and hanging baskets for annuals. This style was not only applied in villa gardens but also in small gardens within public and private parks. Rock gardens also became popular at this time, either as part of the garden as at Warnsborn (*c*1900), or as an entity in itself.

The most influential designers working in the Netherlands between 1870 and 1940 were H. Copijn, H.A.C. Poortman, L.A. Springer and D.F. Tersteeg. Country estates which had flower and rose gardens added included Weldam (1886), Middachten (1901), Staverden (1907), De Voorst (1908), Duin en Kruidberg (1908), De Wiersse (1910), Menkemaborg (1921), Verwolde (1926) and Het Warmelo (1929). New layouts in the mixed or decorative style were applied at De Haar (1894), Rams-Woerthe (1899), Huis te Maarn (1907), Hooge Vuursche (1910), Remmerstein (1912) and Vredespaleis (1913).

Public parks laid out during this period include the Volkspark Enschede (1872), Sarphatipark (1885), G.J. van Heekpark (1918), Stadspark Groningen (1920) and Zuiderpark's-Gravenhage

(1920). After the Second World War, and the population increase that followed it, there was a great need for large-scale recreation grounds and these were generally laid out in the mixed style, incorporating both landscape and formal elements. The aim was to build a Dutch landscape rather than an exotic one. These generous sites comprise a number of different areas – lawns, lakes, playing areas – surrounded by woods with walks, bridle paths and cycle ways. Flowers and statuary are seldom used. There is also a recognized demand in Holland for small-scale wild or nature parks. As elsewhere in Europe, wild plants are endangered as a result of pollution and the inadequate maintenance of nature reserves. L.G. Le Roy pleads for letting nature run its course: he dislikes artificial fertilizers and pesticides and does not allow the clearance of dead plant material. In his wild gardens, man creates the environment – planting a wood, creating a marshland or building a rockery – nature does the rest. After several years, he claims, a natural balance of vegetation will occur. The application of Le Roy's theories may be seen at Lewenborg Groningen and Kennedy-Plantsoen Heerenveen, and elsewhere.

The 'heem' garden is a further reaction to the disappearance of wild species. Heem gardens are intended to be educational gardens where the visitor can become familiar with wild plants and the environment in which they grow. The best-known are J.P. Thijsse's gardens at Bloemendaal (1925) and De Braak in Amstelveen (1939); others can be found at Thijssepark Amstelveen (1940), and Tenellaplas Rockanje (1949).

A number of private gardens follow the ideas of Mien Ruys, who likes to feature hedges, pergolas, flower borders, brick and stonework, lawns and small lakes. Her perennial flower borders, rather in the style of Gertrude Jekyll, are arranged according to colour, height and flowering period: Walenburg is a good example of this style. Other well-known architects of public parks include J.T.P. Bijhouwer, C. Sipkes, L.G. Le Roy W.C.J. Boer, P.A.M. Buijs, P. Blaauboer, J. Bergmans and H. Warnau.

The successful restoration of the palace gardens at Het Loo (1978–84) evoked much interest. Garden architecture in the Netherlands at the end of the 20th century has shown a trend towards geometric lay-outs and the restoration of historic gardens – Arcen Castle gardens at Limburg (by the architect N. Roozen) and Het Marxveld in Vollenhove are recent examples.

**Neviusia** A. Gray. (For the Rev. Ruben Denson Nevius (1827–1913) of Alabama, who discovered the plant.) SNOW WREATH. Rosaceae. 1 species, an erect, deciduous, extremely stoloniferous shrub to 1.5m, of broad-growing habit. Shoots delicate, terete, lanuginose, soon glabrous. Leaves to 7cm, alternate, subdistichous, oval or oblong, fine-pubescent, later glabrous, doubly serrate above middle; petiole to 8.5mm, lanuginose. Flowers white to light green, bisexual, to 2.5cm diam. in short, open cymes; petals absent; stamens conspicuous to 8.5mm, exceeding calyx lobes, filaments white, patent, anthers yellow. Fruit 2–4 drupaceous achenes, oblique-ovoid, acute, turgid, enclosed by a persistent calyx; seeds pendulous. Summer. SE US (Alabama). Z5.

CULTIVATION *N. alabamensis* is indigenous to the cliff faces above the Black Warrior River in Alabama, US. Grown for their beautiful spring flowers with numerous white spreading stamens, they make spreading, multi-stemmed, small shrubs, suited to the shrub border and to sunny woodland edges and other informal plantings. The flowers (filaments) are creamy white in cool temperate climates, but if grown under glass, or brought indoors to open, they develop the pure white coloration more typical of their state in habitat. Hardy to −20°C/−4°F. Grow in moderately fertile, well-drained soil; water in periods of drought. Prune after flowering to remove old or dead wood; cut back to the base or to a suitable outward-facing bud. Propagate by division, by softwood cuttings with bottom heat in a closed case, by semi-ripe cuttings, and from seed.

***N. alabamensis*** A. Gray. As for the genus.

**Newbouldia** Seem. Bignoniaceae. (For the Rev. William Newbould (1819–1896), British botanist.) 1 species, a tree 3–10m. Branches terete to triangular, glabrous. Leaves subsessile, in groups of 3, imparipinnate; pinnae 5–28×1.5–11cm, 7–11, elliptic to narrow-obovate, apex acute to acuminate, base cuneate, entire to dentate, glabrous above, scaly beneath. Pedicels 1cm; calyx 1.6–2×0.8–1.1cm, often emarginate at apex, glabrous, glandular; corolla 4–6.5×1.8–2cm, pale purple-red or pink with darker streaks, tube 3–4cm, lobes 1–2cm, glabrous except at base of stamens; stamens didynamous; pistil 2.5–3.5cm; ovary cylindrical, glabrous, glandular; disc pulvinate, 5-lobed. Fruit 1.6–32× 1.3–1.6cm, linear, scaly; seeds 0.7–1.4×3.5–5cm. Senegal to Cameroun and Gabon. Z10.

CULTIVATION *N. laevis*, from the secondary and dry forests of West Africa, is a common species of regenerating forest; an erect and graceful tree, it is often used as living fence posts in its native regions. Cultivate as for *Spathodea*.

***N. laevis*** (P. Beauv.) Seem. ex Bur. As for the genus.

***N. pentandra*** (Hook.) Seem. See *N. laevis*.
For further synonymy see *Spathodea*.

**Neyraudia** Hook. f. Gramineae. Some 6 species of perennial grasses, resembling *Phragmites* in general appearance, to 3m. Culms filled with pith. Leaves linear. Inflorescence an open, many-flowered panicle; spikelets 4–8-flowered, stipitate. Inflorescence rachilla jointed midway between florets, glabrous below joint, pubescent above; glumes persistent, membranous, unequal; lemma ovate-lanceolate, apex bilobed, awn recurved, margins long soft-pubesc. Old World Tropics. Z9.

CULTIVATION As for *Thysanolaena*.

***N. reynaudiana*** (Kunth) Keng ex A. Hitchc. BURMA REED. Stems to 3m. Lvs flat, to 1m×4cm, midrib green, acute; lf sheaths ciliate or glabrous, ligule a dense ciliate fringe. Panicle pendent, to 80cm; spikelets to 9mm, short-stipitate, awn flat, recurved. S Asia.

For synonymy see *Arundo*.

**Nicandra** Adans. (For Nikander of Colophon, (*c*150AD), Greek botanist and medical writer.) Solanaceae. 1 species, a glabrous annual herb, to 130cm. Stems erect, branching. Leaves to 10×6.5cm or more, alternate, simple, elliptic-lanceolate to rhombic-ovate, apex obtuse to acute, rarely acuminate, base truncate to cuneate, margins wavy-toothed to slightly lobed. Flowers to 3.5cm, solitary, stipitate; pedicels to 3cm; calyx to 2cm, 5-lobed, accrescent, later scarious, to 3cm; corolla broadly campanulate, to 4cm diam., corolla tube white, limb lilac-purple to blue and white; stamens 5, attached to corolla. Fruit a 3–5-chambered subglobose berry, to 15mm diam., brown, enclosed by green calyx; seeds to 4×4mm, in some cases lacking a chromosome and capable of dormancy lasting several decades. Summer–autumn. Peru. Z8.

CULTIVATION A sturdy, freely-branching annual grown for its blue, bell-shaped flowers, produced freely throughout late summer and autumn, although opening fully for only a few hours at midday; the attractive fruit are enclosed in purple calyces and, resembling those of *Physalis* (although larger), last well for use in dried arrangements. It may self-sow freely in the garden, and is well suited to informal plantings. It will withstand poor weather conditions well and does not require staking. Sow *in situ* after the last frosts on to any rich, well-drained soil in full sun and thin to 30–60cm/12–24in. Alternatively, sow under glass in spring, at 16–18°C/60–65°F, and harden off before planting out.

***N. physaloides*** (L.) Gaertn. SHOO FLY; APPLE OF PERU. As for the genus. 'Violacea': upper section of corolla indigo, lower white.

**Nicarago** Britt. & Rose.
***N. vesicaria*** (L.) Britt. & Rose. See *Caesalpinia vesicaria*.

**Nicodemia** Ten.
***N. diversifolia*** (Vahl) Ten. See *Buddleja indica*.

**Nicolaia** Horan.
*N.* ***elatior*** (Jack) Horan. See *Etlingera elatior.*
*N.* ***speciosa*** (Bl.) Horan. See *Etlingera elatior.*

**Nicotiana** L. (For Jean Nicot (1530–1600), French consul in Portugal, who introduced *Nicotiana* to France.) TOBACCO. Solanaceae. Some 67 species of mostly clammy to viscid, aromatic, annual or perennial herbs and shrubs. Leaves alternate, simple, sessile to subsessile. Inflorescence terminal, paniculate; flowers actinomorphic to zygomorphic, stipitate, opening at night; calyx tubular to subglobose, or campanulate, pentamerous, persistent, accrescent; corolla tubular to funnelform, limb 5-lobed; stamens 5, unequal, included to slightly exserted; stigma capitate. Fruit a capsule, 2–4-chambered. Tropical America, Australia, Namibia.

CULTIVATION Grown for their pale, luminous flowers in milk-white, cream, subtle reds and green-yellows, the ornamental *Nicotiana* spp. are often overwhelmingly perfumed on warm, still summer evenings, and are invaluable as border annuals, preferably planted in close proximity to open doors or windows. Most keep their flowers partly closed during the day, but *N. rustica*, *N. tabacum* and *N. ×sanderae* provide colour even at noon, as do the modern bedding hybrids such as Sensation Mixed and the Nikki Hybrids. The flowers of *N. alata* and *N. sylvestris* will remain open during cloudy weather or when grown in shade. Larger spp. like *N. sylvestris*, *N. tomentosa* and *N. tabacum* create lush, foliage effects and provide height in bedding displays.

The felted green petals of *N. alata*, 'Lime Green' and 'Nikki Green' are valued by flower arrangers, but generally *Nicotiana* make short-lived cut flowers. *Nicotiana* spp. range in height from the compact bedding hybrids to tall, stately *N. sylvestris* and *N. glauca* (which may also be used in borders of grey-leaved plants): most tolerate part shade. *N. suaveolens* and *N. sylvestris* thrive in shade.

All species are poisonous, the poisonous alkaloid contained in *N. tabacum* and *N. rustica* being nicotine; (tobacco proper) cultivars of tobacco suitable for cultivation on a domestic scale have been developed, but curing the leaves in cool climates such that of Great Britain is problematic. *N. tabacum* is a cultigen grown in tropical America since pre-Columbian times. Its many forms are used for different purposes, e.g. Havana tobacco for cigars, Virginia tobacco for cigarettes, etc. *N. rustica*, the species originally introduced into Europe, is now grown as a source of insecticidal poison (e.g. the horticulturally important nicotine wash) in Europe and Asia.

Although some spp. are perennial, in cool-temperate areas *Nicotiana* spp. are generally treated as frost-sensitive annuals. In sheltered gardens *N. alata* and *N. sylvestris* may survive temperatures down to about −5°C/23°F, shooting in spring from dormant buds on their thick rootstocks: under such conditions *N. sylvestris* and *N. tabacum* may also be used as biennials. *N. glauca*, which can achieve almost tree-like proportions, is almost as hardy. Plant out in late spring in rich, moisture-retentive, but well-drained soil; stake tall plants in exposed places, with the possible exception of stout-stemmed *N. sylvestris*. Deadhead bedding plants to maintain flowering. Some, particularly *N. alata* cvs and *N.* × *sanderae*, are suitable for pot culture in the intermediate greenhouse: seedlings sown in autumn/late winter are overwintered at minimum night temperature of 10°C/50°F, in a coarse, well-drained, medium-fertility, loam-based mix. Ventilate freely and give strong, filtered light: water moderately and feed fortnightly with a dilute, liquid fertilizer.

To propagate, surface sow the fine seed in spring at 18°C/65°F, about ten weeks before setting out; modern hybrids may be sown in late spring for planting out in summer, to follow earlier flowering biennials. Harden off in cold frames before planting out. Young plants are susceptible to aphid. All are liable to the viruses common among Solanaceae, in particular those producing mosaic and mottling symptoms on foliage: see virus disease of *Petunia*.

*N.* ***acuminata*** (Graham) Hook. Annual, to 2m. Stem viscid, branched, purple when young. Lvs foetid, broad-ovate to lanceolate or triangular-lanceolate, to 25cm, petiolate, apex slender, entire, undulate. Infl. paniculate, few-fld; fls white tinged green, lined dark green or violet-red; cor. tube cylindric, to 8cm, limb to 18mm diam., lobes entire to shallow-notched, spreading; stamens included. Summer. Chile, Argentina. var. ***acuminata.*** Cor. 5–9cm. var. ***compacta*** Goodsp. Lvs sessile. Cor. 2.5–4cm. var. ***multiflora*** (Philippi) Reiche. Lvs petiolate. Cor 2.5–4cm.

*N.* ***alata*** Link & Otto. JASMINE TOBACCO; FLOWERING TOBACCO. Perenn., to 1.5m. Stems viscid, sparsely branched. Lvs spathulate-ovate, to 25cm, apex obtuse, base decurrent, attenuate, petiole winged; upper lvs sessile, auriculate, base encircling the stem. Infl. laxly racemose; fls exterior green-white, interior white, nocturnally fragrant; cal. to 2.5cm, tubular to campanulate; cor. tube funnel-shaped, to 10cm, pubesc., throat to 8mm diam., exterior green, limb to 2.5cm diam., viscid, seg. 5, blunt-acuminate; anth. purple. Fr. ovoid, to 18mm, not protruding; pedicel to 2cm. Summer. NE Argentina to S Brazil. Z7.

*N.* ***attenuata*** Torr. ex S. Wats. Annual, to 140cm. Stems solitary or many, erect, simple or branched, sticky pubesc. Lvs elliptic, to 10cm, viscid, upper lvs narrower, smaller. Infl. short-racemose or paniculate; fls white tinged rose; cal. to 7mm; cor. cylindric, tube to 27mm, interior white, limb to 13mm diam., lobes shallow, upper lobes somewhat reflexed; stamens included. Fr. ovoid, to 12mm, protruding; pedicel to 4mm. SW US, Mexico. Z8.

*N.* ***bigelovii*** (Torr.) S. Wats. Annual, to 2m. Stems clammy-pubesc., branches ascending. Lvs foetid, oblong-lanceolate, to 20cm, upper lvs smaller, to 8cm, apex obtuse. Infl. racemose, racemes lax; pedicels to 10mm, later to 15mm; cal. to 20mm+, 10-ridged; cor. to 5cm, white tinged green, limb to 3cm+ diam., lobed, lobes triangular-ovate; fil. to 15mm. Fr. narrow ovoid to globose, to 2cm+. Summer. W US (California to S Oregon). Z6.

*N.* ***forgetiana*** hort. Sander ex Hemsl. Annual or short-lived perenn., to 90cm. Stems erect or spreading, slender, pubesc., branched from base. Lvs oblong, pubesc., to 30cm, papery, apex obtuse, lower lvs tapered to a Z-winged stalk, upper lvs decurrent. Infl. a panicle, sticky-pubesc.; fls stipitate; pedicels slender, to 13mm, rose pink; cor. narrow, funnelform, to 3cm, to 2.5cm diam., tube interior pale green, exterior purple-red, limb to 1.5cm diam., scarlet; stamens subequal, fil. purple. Fr. ovoid to ovoid-oblong, to 13mm. Brazil. Z8.

*N.* ***fragrans*** Hook. Perenn., to 2m. Stems soft-pubesc, occasionally sticky-pubesc. Lvs in apical clusters, narrow-linear to oblanceolate, to 20cm. Infl. a lax panicle; fls fragrant; cal. cylindric, to 2cm, inflated; cor. tube to 10cm×3mm, white, tinged green, limb spreading, to 12mm diam., white, lobed, lobes unequal, acute or emarginate to obtuse; fil. to 2cm. Fr. globose to ovoid, to 10mm diam. S Pacific, Polynesia. Z10.

*N.* ***glauca*** Graham. TREE TOBACCO; MUSTARD TREE. Shrub, to 6m+. Stems erect, soft-woody, glabrous, glaucous. Lvs unequal, elliptic to lanceolate or cordate-ovate, glaucous, rubbery; apex acute, weakly sinuate; petiole unwinged. Infl. paniculate, terminal, lax; fls cream yellow-green, exterior pubesc.; cal. to 1.5cm, dentate, teeth triangular; cor. tube slightly curved, to 4.5cm, limb to 4mm, terete to 5-ridged, lobes short, throat slightly inflated. Fr. ellipsoid, included, to 1.5cm. Autumn. S Bolivia to N Argentina, naturalized US. Z8.

*N.* ***langsdorffii*** J.A. Weinm. Annual, to 1.5m+. Stems erect, branched, viscid-pubesc. Lvs ovate, undulate, apex blunt, base attenuate, upper lvs lanceolate, decurrent, apex acute. Infl. a secund, nodding panicle; fls stipitate; pedicels to 12mm, branched; cal. to 1cm, seg. triangular-acuminate; cor. tube subcylindric, to 2.5cm, viscid, fresh green, limb pleated, lobes triangular, acuminate. Fr. ovoid, to 1cm. Summer. Brazil. Z9.

*N.* ***longiflora*** Cav. Annual, to 1.5m. Stems slender, sparsely stiffly pubesc. Lvs lanceolate to spathulate, sessile, undulate, upper lvs stipitate, cordate to lanceolate, apex slender. Infl. laxly racemose; fls stipitate, opposite bracts, violet, exterior green or pearly violet; pedicel to 12mm; cal. to 2cm, 10-ridged; cor. tube to 12cm×3mm, exterior yellow, or grey to purple, pubesc., limb to 4cm diam., lobes ovate-lanceolate, to 13mm acuminate. Fr. ovoid, to 16mm; seeds elliptic. Autumn. Texas to Chile, Argentina. Z8.

*N.* ***noctiflora*** Hook. Perenn., to 90cm+. Stems slender, erect to procumbent, pubesc., branched. Lvs oblong-lanceolate, undulate, apex acute. Infl. paniculate, terminal, similar to *N. glauca*; fls interior white, exterior green tinged purple; pedicel to 1cm; cal. to 12mm; cor. cylindric, to 4× length of cal., limb to 15mm diam., lobes equal, oblong, obtuse, emarginate. Fr. elliptic, to 1.5cm. Autumn. Chile. Z8.

*N.* ***rustica*** L. TOBACCO; WILD TOBACCO. Annual, viscid-pubesc., to 1.5m. Lvs ovate to ovate-obtuse or elliptic, to 30cm+; petiole unwinged. Infl. paniculate, lax to crowded; fls to 18mm, tinged, yellow or green, opening during the day; cal. to 1.5cm, tubular to narrow-funneliform, dentate, teeth triangular, acute, unequal; cor. to 2cm, yellow tinged green, limb to 6mm+ diam., lobes obtuse, apex abruptly acute or obtuse; stamens 4, unequal, slightly protruding. Fr. subglobose to elliptic-ovoid, to 2cm. Summer–autumn. S America (Andes, Ecuador to Bolivia), Mexico. Z8.

*N.* ×***sanderae*** hort. Sander ex Will. Wats. *(N. alata* × *N. forgetiana.)* Shrubby, viscid-pubesc. annual to 60cm+. Lvs spathulate, undulate, upper lvs oblong-lanceolate. Infl. a loose panicle; cor. tube green-yellow at base; cor. to 3× length of cal., limb oblique, to 4cm+ diam., red, occasionally white to rose-carmine or purple, lobes acute. Garden origin. 'Breakthrough': dwarf, compact, fls fragrant in a range of colours; early flowering. 'Crimson King': fls deep crimson. 'Daylight Sensation': fls day-blooming in shades of lavender, purple, white and rose. 'Dwarf White Bedder': habit low, bushy; fls pure white, fragrant. 'Fragrant Cloud': fls pure white, large, fragrant at night. 'Grandiflora': fls large, corolla throat large, widely dilated. 'Lime Green': fls bright yellow tinged green, abundant. 'Nana': habit dwarf. Nikki Hybrids: habit bushy, hardy; fls in range of colours including white, shades of pink, red and yellow. 'Rubella': fls rose-red. Sensation Hybrids: fls in range of colours including pink, red and white, fragrant. 'Sutton's Scarlet': cor. dark red. 'White': fls heavily scented. Z7.

***N. suaveolens*** Lehm. Annual, to 1.5m. Stems numerous, densely pubesc. below, glabrous above. Lvs stipitate, oblanceolate to ovate-lanceolate, to 25cm, lower lvs stipitate, upper lvs subsessile; petiole winged. Infl. paniculate, terminal; fls pendent, exterior green-purple, interior white; pedicel to 15mm, later to 2cm; cal. to 16mm; cor. tube slender, to 45mm, limb to 35mm diam., lobes small, unequal, obtuse, entire to emarginate; stamens 4. Fr. narrow-ovoid to oblong, to 1cm. Summer. SE Australia. Z8.

***N. sylvestris*** Speg. & Comes. Annual, to 1.5m. Stems robust, branched, base woody. Lvs ascending, sessile, elliptic to elliptic-ovate, to 5cm, wrinkled, pinnatifid, terminal lobe enlarged, lateral lobes smaller, to 30cm+. Infl. short, paniculate racemes; fls declinate to pendent, fragrant; pedicel to 2.5cm; cor. tube spindle-shaped, to 8.5cm, swollen above, to 7× length of cal., exterior pubesc., limb to 3cm diam. Fr. ovoid, to 18mm; seeds ovoid. Summer. Argentina. Z8.

***N. tabacum*** L. TOBACCO; COMMON TOBACCO. Annual or bienn., viscid-pubesc., to 120cm. Stems often becoming woody at base. Lvs ovate to elliptic or lanceolate, to 25cm. Infl. paniculate or racemose, pendent; fls green-white to rose; cal. tubular to narrow-campanulate, dentate, teeth triangular, equal; cor. tube inflated, unequally swollen, to 5.5cm, white tinged green, exterior soft pubesc., limb to 1.5cm, lobed, lobes acuminate; stamens 4, unequal, anth. slightly protruding. Fr. elliptic to globose, to 2cm. Summer. NE Argentina, Bolivia. var. ***macrophylla*** Schrank. Lvs to 40cm, undulate, ovate or cordate. Fls rose to carmine red. Z8. 'Variegata' ('Connecticut Shade'): to 2.5m; lvs to 30cm, membranous, variegated irregularly cream with green; fls white tinged pink.

***N. tomentosa*** Ruiz & Pav. Shrub, to 7m. Stems to 3, branched, branches ascending. Lvs ovate to lanceolate, to 11cm, viscid; petiole winged, upper lvs occasionally sessile. Infl. branches to 60; pedicel to 12mm, later to 2cm; cal. to 2cm, dentate, teeth unequal; cor. interior glabrous, exterior glandular-pubesc., to 35cm, pale green-yellow, limb pink to red or white. Fr. ovoid-oblong, to 2cm, woody. S & C Peru, WC Bolivia. Z9.

***N. wigandioides*** Koch & Fintelm. Perenn. shrub, habit as for *N. tomentosa*, sticky-pubesc., to 3m. Stems white-pubesc. Lvs stipitate, ovate, to 50cm, undulate, pubesc. above, apex acute or acuminate; petiole to 12cm. Infl. paniculate, pendent; fls white, tinged yellow or green; cal. to 1cm; cor. salverform, to 15mm, limb to 13mm diam., lobes reflexed. Summer. Bolivia. Z9.

***N. affinis*** hort. ex T. Moore. See *N. alata*.
***N. axillaris*** Lam. See *Petunia axillaris*.
***N. persica*** Lindl. See *N. alata*.
***N. ruralis*** Vell. See *N. langsdorffii*.
***N. torreyana*** Nels. & Macbr. See *N. attenuata*.
***N. undulata*** Vent. See *N. suavolens*.

**Nidema** Britt. & Millsp. (Derived from *Dinema*.) Orchidaceae. 2 species of epiphytic orchids. Rhizome elongate, creeping, enveloped by papery bracts. Pseudobulbs fusiform to cylindrical, conspicuously stalked, apically unifoliate, usually widely spaced on rhizome. Leaves coriaceous, linear-ligulate to linear-lanceolate, articulated. Inflorescence a terminal raceme, few-flowered; flowers small; bracts conspicuous, acuminate, lanceolate; sepals free, subequal, usually linear to lanceolate; dorsal sepal erect, lateral sepals arched; petals subsimilar to sepals, oblique, smaller than sepals; lip articulated to column base, simple, acute or acuminate, sometimes papillose, disc with a grooved callus; column arching, with a short foot, wingless, anther terminal, operculate, incumbent, 4-celled, pollinia 4, waxy. Tropical America. Z10.

CULTIVATION Epiphytes for the intermediate house. See ORCHIDS.

***N. boothii*** (Lindl.) Schltr. Pseudobulbs to 6cm, cylindrical to narrowly ovoid, slightly compressed. Lvs to 25×1.5cm, linear-ligulate to narrowly lanceolate, acute or obtuse, lustrous bright green. Infl. to 15cm, loosely few-fld; fls white-green or ivory, fragrant; sep. to 20×4mm, linear-lanceolate to lanceolate, acute or acuminate, recurved; pet. to 15×4mm, elliptic-lanceolate to elliptic-ovate, acuminate, recurved; lip to 11×4mm, oblong-oblanceolate to linear-spathulate, subacute to rounded, serrulate, disc with 2 yellow, linear calli; column to 8mm. Mexico to Panama, W Indies, Northern S America.

***N. ottonis*** (Rchb. f.) Britt. & Millsp. Pseudobulbs to 4cm, cylindrical to narrowly ellipsoid, slightly compressed. Lvs to 19×1cm, linear to linear-ligulate, acute or obtuse. Infl. to 11cm, erect, slender; fls white or cream, sometimes tinged yellow or green; sep. to 11×3mm, lanceolate or oblong-lanceolate, acuminate, concave; pet. to 7×2mm, lanceolate, elliptic-lanceolate or oblanceolate, acute or acuminate; lip to 7×2mm, fleshy, rigid, linear-oblong, apiculate, incurved, canaliculate, disc 2-ridged; column to 4mm, pale cream or cream-green. W Indies, Panama, Colombia, Peru, Brazil, Nicaragua, Venezuela.

For synonymy see *Epidendrum* and *Maxillaria*.

**Nidularium** Lem. (From Lat. *nidulus*, a little nest, due to the large inflorescence bracts surrounding the flowers.) Bromeliaceae (Bromelioideae). 23 species of stemless, perennial, terrestrial or low-growing epiphytic herbs to 50cm in flower. Leaves in a flat rosette to 80cm diameter, the innermost reduced, bright red or pink in flower, outer leaves often banded or spotted with purple; leaf-sheaths large, forming funnel-shaped tanks, blades ligulate, often finely toothed. Inflorescence compound; flowers sessile in flat fascicles, surrounded by showy bracts; scape short, bracteate, floral bracts hidden; sepals more or less fused, unarmed or mucronate; petals fleshy, erect, fused into a tube, keeled, stamens not exserted, filaments fused to upper part of petals. E & SE Brazil. Differentiated from *Neoregelia* by its compound inflorescence and sessile flowers. Z10.

CULTIVATION See BROMELIADS.

***N. billbergioides*** (Schult. f.) L.B. Sm. To 40cm in flower. Lvs 30–70cm, green, in a dense, funnel-shaped rosette; sheaths 10cm, broadly elliptic, brown-scaly; blades sparsely scaly, laxly toothed, spines 0.5mm. Infl. *c*8cm; scape slender, erect; bracts elliptic, acute, green to orange and red-brown at infl. apex; floral bracts broad-ovate, papery; sep. to 15mm, fused at base; pet. 2cm, white, erect, fused for two-thirds of their length. var. ***citrinum*** (Burchell ex Bak.) Reitz. Infl. bracts bright yellow.

***N. burchellii*** (Bak.) Mez. Lvs to 50cm; sheaths broadly elliptic, brown-scaly, blades dark green and glabrous above, flushed purple and slightly scaly beneath, spiny-denticulate. Infl. 25–55mm, orange, crowded, subglobose, red-tomentose; fascicles few-fld; scape short, red-brown, scurfy, bracteate; floral bracts green, ovate, toothed recurved at apex; sep. 10mm; pet. 18mm, fused at base, white, elliptic, patent.

***N. ×chantrieri*** André. (*N. innocentii* × *N. fulgens*.) Lvs dark green, mottled maroon, with maroon margins and spines. Infl. bracts bright cerise; pet. white. Garden origin.

***N. fulgens*** Lem. Lvs to 40cm in a broad, spreading rosette, pale green with darker mottling, pungent, slightly scaly beneath, laxly toothed, spines 4mm. Infl. crowded, domed, on a very short scape; bracts bright cerise, broadly ovate, coarsely toothed; floral bracts white, lanceolate, sparsely brown-scaly; fls fascicled; sep. 20–24mm, slightly fused, red, narrow-lanceolate; pet. 5cm, fused for almost their whole length, tube white, apices dark blue, with white margins.

***N. innocentii*** Lem. Lvs 20–60cm, in a dense, spreading rosette; sheaths conspicuous, pale green or purple, brown-scaly; blades glabrous magenta to blood-red beneath or throughout, shiny, toothed, short spines. Scape short; infl. bracts red tipped green, large, toothed, brown-scaly, broad-ovate; floral bracts white, papery; fls 4–6 per branch; sep. to 30mm, fused for 3–9mm, white or pink; pet. to 50mm, fused, white with green bases. var. ***lineatum*** (Mez) L.B. Sm. Lf blades pale green with many fine, longitudinal white lines. Infl. bracts green, apices brick-red. Known only in cult. var. ***paxianum*** (Mez) L.B. Sm. Lf blades green, with a single, large, median white stripe. Infl. bracts green, tipped red. var. ***striatum*** Wittm. Lf blades green, with longitudinal white stripes. Infl. bracts carmine. Known only in cult.

***N. microps*** E. Morr. ex Mez. Spreading via slender rhiz. to 14cm. Lvs to 25cm, channelled, toothed, spines 0.5mm. Infl. subsessile, crowded, capitate, rusty-tomentose; infl. bracts purple, ovate, large, with dense, tiny teeth; floral bracts papery, elliptic; sep. dark red, to 14mm, fused for 3mm, ovate, mucronate; pet. 20–25mm, fused for half their length, white, elliptic, spreading.

***N. seidelii*** L.B. Sm. & Reitz. To 45cm in flower, spreading readily via offsets. Lvs to 80cm, slightly scaly. Infl. to 15cm, subcylindric; scape erect, 30×0.6, rusty-tomentose, later glabrous, with 2 remote bracts; infl. bracts to 6cm, yellow to purple, imbricate, concealing fls; branches few-fld, pulvinate; floral bracts thin, elliptic, sparsely scaly; sep. 14mm, fused for 2.5mm, spathulate, nerved, brown-tomentose at base; pet. 10mm, white, fused by claws only.

***N. 'Souvenir de Casmir Morobe'***. (*N. rutilans* × *N. marechalii*.) Large. Lvs broad, lush green with light marbling, inner rosette brilliant red.

***N. lindenii*** Reg. See *Canistrum lindenii*.
***N. lineatum*** Mez. See *N. innocentii* var. *lineatum*.
***N. makoyanum*** E. Morr. ex Mez. See *N. innocentii* var. *striatum*.
***N. marechalii*** hort. (Makoy) ex Bak. See *Neoregelia princeps*.
***N. mooreanum*** hort. (Haage & Schmidt). See *Neoregelia pineliana*.
***N. paxianum*** Mez. See *N. innocentii* var. *paxianum*.
***N. pictum*** hort. ex Bak. See *N. fulgens*.

***N. princeps*** E. Morr. ex Bak. See *Neoregelia princeps*.
***N. spectabile*** hort. ex Bak. See *Neoregelia princeps*.
For further synonymy see *Aechmea*.

**Nierembergia** Ruiz & Pav. (For John Eusebius Nieremberg (1595–1658), Spanish naturalist.) CUPFLOWER. Solanaceae. Some 23 species of annual or perennial herbs or subshrubs. Stems slender, creeping, spreading or erect. Lvs alternate, simple, entire. Flowers solitary, terminal or in cymes; calyx tubular to campanulate, 5-lobed, lobes spreading; corolla tubular, limb spreading, 5-lobed; stamens 4, attached to corolla; staminode 1. Fruit a 2-chambered capsule. S America. Z8 unless specified.

CULTIVATION *Nierembergia* spp. are slender-stemmed, graceful plants, generally found growing wild in moist but sunny situations in the temperate regions of South America: the upturned, bell-like flowers last from summer until well into the autumn and, in creeping spp., nestle against a backdrop of spreading, dark green foliage. None is reliably hardy where temperatures drop below about −12°C/10°F, but the hardiest species, *N. repens*, has survived winters in New York State when planted out into a sheltered warm garden: it creeps and spreads by underground runner at pond margins, on rock gardens and in the moist cracks between paving stones although also tolerating quite dry positions happily. Fairly aggressive if conditions are favourable, it should not be grown in close association with weaker plants: use also for flowering in pans in the alpine house. Other spp. may be used at border fronts, on the rock garden and raised beds.

In colder areas they are used as bedding annuals or pot plants for summer colour, since they flower in the first year from seed. Plant out in a sunny position after the last frosts into any gritty but moisture-retentive and reasonably fertile soil. Give a sheltered position as flowers are easily damaged if exposed to wind and rain: deadheading is not necessary since flowers dry cleanly on the plants. Clip back *N. hippomanica* and other shrubby to subshrubby spp. lightly after flowering. Those spp. at the borderline of their zones of hardiness may be lifted and overwintered in frost-free conditions or divisions/cuttings kept as an insurance against winter losses; alternatively, some protection may be offered in the open garden with propped panes of glass.

Grow under glass in a sharply draining, medium-fertility, loam-based mix: *N. gracilis* makes a particularly good pot-grown specimen. Pinch lateral growths several times; *N. scoparia* in particular benefits from 'stopping'. Give bright, airy conditions with some shade against strong summer sun: water plentifully in summer, sparingly in winter. Propagate from seed sown at 15°C/60°F in spring. Alternatively, divide creeping perennials in spring and take 5cm/2in. heeled cuttings of subshrubby spp. in summer. Root cuttings in a sharply draining sandy medium in a cold frame or closed propagating case; and overwinter in well-ventilated but frost-free conditions, watering sparingly. Harden off seedlings and cuttings in a cold frame before planting out.

***N. calycina*** Hook. Procumbent shrublet. Stems glandular pubesc. Lvs to 2×1.3cm, alternate to opposite, obovate to spathulate, apex and base obtuse; petiole to 3mm. Fls solitary, yellow at base; cal. campanulate, to 7mm, lobes obovate, revolute; cor. tube to 6cm, limb white; stamens touching. Autumn. Uruguay, Argentina.

***N. frutescens*** Durieu. Shrublet to 80cm. Stems profusely branched. Lvs to 5cm, sessile, linear to narrow-spathulate. Fls numerous, to 2.5cm wide; cal. 10-lobed; cor. tube yellow, limb pale blue, fading to white at margin; ovary 2-chambered. Summer–autumn. Chile. 'Albiflora': fls white. 'Atroviolacea': compact; fls deep purple. 'Grandiflora': fls large to 3cm wide. 'Purple Robe': mat-forming, dense to 15cm; fls rich violet-blue, cup-shaped.

***N. gracilis*** Hook. Perenn. herb, many-stemmed. Stems softly pubesc., to 45cm; branches ascending, to 45cm. Lvs to 3×0.5cm, lanceolate, obtuse, pubesc. to glabrous; petiole to 1cm. Fls terminal, white streaked purple toward centre; cal. to 5mm, funnel-shaped, lobes to 7mm, lanceolate; cor. tube to 1.5cm, limb to 4cm diam. Fr. cylindric, attenuate. Summer. Paraguay, Argentina. Z7.

***N. hippomanica*** Miers. Herb to 30cm+. Stems stiffly erect, densely branched, stiffly white-pubesc. Lvs to 8×2mm, spathulate, pubesc., green, acute. Fls numerous, blue tinged violet, tube to 9mm, to 18mm diam., slender, yellow, lobes unequal; cal. to 4mm, lobes to 3mm. Summer–autumn. Argentina. var. ***violacea*** Millán. Lvs longer than species type, to 2.5cm. Fls violet blue.

***N. linariifolia*** Graham. Herb to 30cm. Stems slender, erect, glandular-pubesc. Lvs scattered, spreading, linear-lanceolate, apex acute or obtuse. Fls solitary, borne opposite lvs, lilac, throat yellow, cor. exterior glandular-pubesc., interior glabrous, tube purple, lobes irregular-cordate, overlapping. Spring. Argentina.

***N. repens*** Ruiz & Pav. WHITECUP. Spreading procumbent perenn. herb. Stems slender, glabrous to pubesc., smooth. Lvs spathulate, obtuse. Fls campanulate, to 2.5cm diam.; petiole to 4cm; cal. glabrous to pubesc.; cor. tube cylindric, to 6cm×1mm, white, tinged yellow or rose pink at base. Summer. Andes, warm temperate S America. 'Violet Queen': fls rich purple-blue. Z7.

***N. scoparia*** Sendt. TALL CUPFLOWER. To 50cm. Stems densely branched, subglabrous, glaucous green. Lvs to 2×0.3cm, clumped, spathulate, obtuse. Fls stipitate, to 3mm; cal. tube to 4mm, lobes lanceolate; cor. violet, pilose, tube to 15mm, limb to 3cm diam. Brazil, Uruguay, Argentina. var. ***glaberrima*** Millán. Pedicel to 6mm; fls smaller, to 8mm long.

***N. veitchii*** Hook. Prostrate herb. Stems slender, branching, glabrous to sparsely pubesc. Lvs to 3.5×1.7cm, alternate to opposite, ovate to oblong. Fls pale lilac to violet; cal. to 13mm, funnel-shaped, lobes lanceolate to obovate; cor. tube slender, campanulate, to 3.5cm, pubesc.; fil. touching. S America.

***N. angustifolia*** HBK. See *N. scoparia*.
***N. caerula*** Sealy. See *N. hippomanica* var. *violacea*.
***N. filicaulis*** Lindl. See *N. linariifolia*.
***N. hippomanica*** hort. See *N. calycina*.
***N. rivularis*** Miers. See *N. repens*.

**Nigella** L. (From diminutive of Lat. *niger*, black, referring to the seed.) FENNEL FLOWER; WILD FENNEL; LOVE-IN-A-MIST; DEVIL-IN-A-BUSH. Ranunculaceae. Some 14 annual herbs. Stems erect, usually simple. Leaves alternate on stem, 1–3-pinnatisect, segments linear to very slender, uppermost leaves sometimes 3-parted or entire. Flowers bisexual, solitary, terminal and axillary, showy, white, pink, blue or yellow, in some species subtended by a ruff-like involucre of conspicuously veined leaves terminating in hair-like divisions; sepals 5, petaloid, deciduous in fruit; petals 5–10, smaller than sepals, 2-lipped, with outer lip 2-lobed or 2-fid and a hollow nectariferous claw; stamens numerous; carpels 2–10, commonly 5, partially or entirely connate. Fruit composed of united follicles forming a capsule, ultimately inflated with persistent horn-like styles; seeds numerous. Eurasia.

CULTIVATION Occurring in subalpine meadows, *Nigella* spp. are grown for their feathery foliage and long-lasting blue haze of summer flower, with the added interest of inflated and strongly ribbed brown seedheads to follow. Both flowers and seedheads are used, fresh or dried, in flower arrangements. Cultivation as for *Consolida* although seedlings of *Nigella* transplant more readily. Dead-heading increases later flower size but plants allowed to self-sow with perpetuate themselves in the following years.

***N. arvensis*** L. WILD FENNEL. To 50cm. Lvs pinnatisect, 3-parted or entire, segments filiform. Fls 2–3cm diam., pale blue, lacking an involucre; sepals ovate, cordate at base and narrowed into claw, limb acuminate; pet. upper lip 2-partite, lower linear, shorter. Fr. follicles united for two-thirds of length, 3-veined, with long, beak-like style. Summer. Europe. ssp. ***aristata*** (Sibth. & Sm.) Nyman. Lvs glaucescent, rigid, seg. narrower than in species type; uppermost lvs forming an involucre. Greece (Cyclades).

***N. ciliaris*** DC. Resembling *N. orientalis*. All parts sparsely villose. Fls yellow-white; sep. hispid; pet. unguiculate, the lower lip of pet. cuneate, bifid, with 4 long linear lobes; carpels 5–15, flattened, connate for one-third their length, prominently 3-veined. Syria.

***N. damascena*** L. LOVE-IN-A-MIST. Annual to 50cm, stems simple or branched. Involucral lvs finely divided, seg. filiform. Fls white, rose pink, pale or purple-blue, 3.5–4.5cm diam.; sep. broadly ovate, clawed; carpels entirely united. Fr. a smooth, subglobose inflated capsule, 10-locular, outer 5 sterile. Summer. S Europe, N Africa. 'Blue Midget': to 25cm; fls blue. 'Cambridge Blue': stems long; fls double, large, blue. 'Dwarf Moody Blue': dwarf, neat; fls semi-double, violet turning sky-blue. Miss Jekyll Hybrids: tall; fls semi-double in variety of colours including white, pink and blue. 'Mulberry Rose': fls double, large, pale pink. 'Oxford Blue': fls double, large, dark blue. Persian Jewels: fls white, pink, red and purple. 'Red Jewel': fls deep rose.

***N. hispanica*** L. FENNEL FLOWER. Stems 20–40cm, branching. Lf seg. slender but not filiform as in the closely related *N. arvensis*. Fls 4–5cm diam., solitary or paired, lacking involucre, bright blue; sep. short-clawed; stamens red. Follicles ribbed, almost entirely fused, densely glandular, styles spreading. Summer. Spain, S France. 'Alba': fls white. 'Atropurpurea': fls purple. 'Curiosity': fls deep blue, centre black, stamens maroon.

***N. integrifolia*** Reg. Stem to 25cm, pubesc., simple or much branched. Lower lvs linear-lanceolate to oblong-lanceolate, entire, 2–3cm; stem lvs palmatiparite,

**Nigella** (×1) (a) *N. damascena* (a1) cultivar (b) *N. ciliaris* (c) *N. hispanica* (d) *N. nigellastrum* (e) *N. arvensis*

seg. linear, sessile. Fls pale blue, in cymes; involucre of lvs exceeding fl.; sep. oblong, 5–8mm; pet. slightly shorter than sep. Fr. follicles 3, connate most of length, capsule 8–12mm, with short beak, hairy. Summer. Turkestan.

***N. nigellastrum*** (L.) Willk. Stems 20–40cm, slightly branched. Lvs very finely divided into long, linear seg. Fls 10mm diam., white-green tinged red; sep. 3–4mm, ovate-elliptic, shorter than pet.; pet. with lower lip cuneate-oblong, deeply 2-lobed. Fr. follicles 2–3, connate at base. Summer. Mediterranean to SW Asia.

***N. orientalis*** L. Stems 10–90cm. Lf segments linear, somewhat glaucous. Fls yellow-white, spotted red, involucre absent; sep. to 1.5cm, ovate, narrowed to short claw; pet. with upper lip broad ovate, lower lip ovate, 2-fid. Fr. of 2–14 follicles, united to middle, divergent above, beak erect, shorter than follicle. Spring–summer. SW Asia.

***N. sativa*** L. BLACK CUMIN; NUTMEG FLOWER; ROMAN CORIANDER. Stems to 30cm, erect, branched, pubesc. Lvs 2–3cm, seg. linear to oblong-lanceolate, short. Fls 3.5–4.5cm diam., white tinged blue, without involucre; sep. ovate, 1–1.5cm, with short claw. Fr. inflated, follicles 3–7, fused to base of outspread styles. Summer. SW Asia, cultivated Europe and N Africa.

***N. aristata*** Sibth. & Sm. See *N. arvensis* ssp. *aristata*.
***N. diversifolia*** Franch. See *N. integrifolia*.

**Nigritella** Rich. (Diminutive of Lat. *niger*, black, referring to the flower colour.) Orchidaceae. 1 species, a herbaceous, terrestrial orchid. Tubers 2, digitately lobed. Stems 5–30cm, angled, slender. Leaves linear to linear-lanceolate, channelled, minutely dentate, green. Spike 10–25cm, dense, conical becoming ovoid; flowers black-crimson, vanilla-scented; sepals and petals almost equal, lanceolate to triangular, spreading; lip subtriangular or ovate-lanceolate, entire, crenulate or trilobed, spur short, saccate, obtuse. Summer. Scandinavia to Greece. Z7.

CULTIVATION See ORCHIDS, The Hardy Species.

***N. nigra*** (L.) Rchb. f. As for the genus.

**Niphaea** Lindl. (From Gk *niphos*, snow, referring to the white flowers.) Gesneriaceae. 5 species of herbs; stems short, erect. Leaves often crowded near stem apex, ovate to elliptic, dentate or serrate, thin, petiolate. Inflorescences axillary; pedicels 2-several in each leaf axil; calyx turbinate-campanulate, 5-lobed; corolla subrotate, tube very short, lobes 5, broad, white; stamens 4–5, sometimes 4+1 staminode, filaments short, anthers oblong; ovary half-inferior, style stout, curved. Fruit is a capsule, half-inferior, free part conic, bivalved; seeds copious. C & S America. Z10.

CULTIVATION See GESNERIADS.

***N. oblonga*** Lindl. Small herb; stems slender, 3–15cm, rufescent, villous. Lvs few, crowded near stem apex, 7×5cm, ovate, obtuse or acute at apex, rounded to cordate at base, coarsely serrate to biserrate, hirsute; petioles 3cm. Pedicels 2-several in upper lf axils; cal. tube densely villous, lobes acutely lanceolate, 5mm, green, accrescent; cor. deeply lobed, lobes broadly rounded, tube 4mm, lobes 9mm, limb to 25mm diam., white, more or less villous without; stamens 4. Winter. Guatemala.

***N. roezlii*** Reg. Dwarf herb, compact, white- to rufescent-hairy throughout. Lvs ovate, obtuse, crenate, 5cm, dark green, rugose. Fls small; pedicels arising in upper lf axils, purple, glandular-hairy.

For synonymy see *Phinaea*.

**Niphidium** J. Sm. (So called from its resemblances to *Niphibolus* and *Pleuridium crassifolium*.) Polypodiaceae. Some 10 species of epiphytic, lithophytic or terrestrial ferns. Rhizomes short- to long-creeping, usually covered with roots as well as scales; scales occasionally peltate, clathrate, entire or dentate. Fronds stipitate, uniform, simple, attenuate at apex and base, entire, leathery, glaucous, glabrous or sparsely scaly, veins anastomosing areolae with free, included veinlets; stipes close and clustered, or remote, jointed to short phyllopodia. Sori superficial, at union of veins, 2-serial or more (1 row between veins), circular to oblong, lacking indusia; paraphyses present or absent; sporangia occasionally setose; spores ellipsoid, bilateral, monolete, smooth. Tropical America. Z10.

CULTIVATION As for *Campyloneurum*.

***N. crassifolium*** (L.) Lellinger. Rhiz. to 12mm wide, short-creeping, woody; scales to 7×2mm, entire, membranous at margin, light brown. Fronds to 90×13cm, ovate or lanceolate to elliptic, narrowly acute at apex, veins oblique, parallel, distinct; rachis sparsely scaly; stipes to 30cm, erect. C to S America.

***N. longifolium*** (Cav.) C. Morton & Lellinger. Scales entire. Fronds to 60×2cm, linear, apex narrowly acute, glabrous and lustrous above, stellate-pubesc. beneath; costa prominent below; stipes to 10cm, clustered. S. America.

***N. americanum*** (Hook. J. Sm. See *N. longifolium*.

**Nippocalamus** Nak.
***N. argenteostriatus*** (Reg.) Nak. See *Pleioblastus argenteostriatus*.
***N. argenteostriatus*** var. ***distichus*** (Mitford) Nak. See *Pleioblastus pygmaeus* var. *distichus*.
***N. chino*** (Franch. & Savat.) Nak. See *Pleioblastus chino*.
***N. chino*** var. ***akebono*** (Mak.) Mak. See *Pleioblastus akebono*.
***N. fortunei*** (Van Houtte) Nak. See *Pleioblastus variegatus*.
***N. humilis*** (Mitford) Nak. See *Pleioblastus humilis*.
***N. pygmaeus*** (Miq.) Nak. See *Pleioblastus pygmaeus*.
***N. simonii*** (Carr.) Nak. See *Pleioblastus simonii*.

**Nipponanthemum** Kitam. (Kitam.) (From Nippon and Gk *anthemon*, flower.) Compositae. 1 species, a perennial herb or subshrub to 1m. Leaves to 9×2cm, alternate, spathulate, crenate-dentate, minutely pubescent, lustrous, sessile. Capitula radiate, to 6cm diam., solitary, long-pedunculate; receptacle shortly conic, naked; involucre hemispheric, imbricate; phyllaries in 4 series, ovate to narrowly oblong, obtuse, margins lacerate and brown-scarious; ray florets to 3cm, white; disc florets yellow. Fruit a 3–4mm, 10-ribbed cypsela; pappus a lacerate corona. Japan. Z8.

CULTIVATION Found in the wild in coastal habitats, *N. nipponicum* is amongst the loveliest and most elegant of late-flowering perennials, bearing beautifully textured, pure white single flowers in late autumn over a mound of persistent, dark and lustrous foliage. Grow in full sun in very well-drained and moderately fertile soil; given a sheltered position against a south- or southwest-facing wall, the best of the bloom may be had before the onset of severe weather. Where winter temperatures fall much below −10°C/14°F, protect roots with a deep mulch of leafmould or bracken litter and foliage with evergreen branches. Plants cut back to the ground in winter may regenerate from the roots. Propagate by seed or division.

***N. nipponicum*** (Franch. ex Maxim.) Kitam. As for the genus.

For synonymy see *Chrysanthemum* and *Leucanthemum*.

**Nitella** Agardh. STONEWORT. Characeae. About 100 species of fragile aquatic plants. Plant a thallus with the slender axis erect, anchored to substrate by rhizomes, with limp and flexible, regular and symmetrically whorled, filiform branches of unlimited growth; branchlets leaf-like. Corona of oogonia 10-celled. Cosmopolitan. Superficially resembles *Equisetum*. Z6.

CULTIVATION See AQUARIUM PLANTS.

***N. flexilis*** (L.) Agardh. Branches in whorls of 6–8, straight or slightly incurved, 1.5–2 times longer than internodes of axis, the primary branches about twice as long as the secondary branchlets. N America, Eurasia, in still water.

***N. gracilis*** (Sm.) Agardh. Usually less than 10–15m. Branches in whorls of mostly 5–8, straight, sometimes condensed into heads, mostly shorter than internodes. Cosmopolitan.

**Nivenia** Vent. (For David James Niven (1774–1826), Scottish gardener at Edinburgh and Syon House; collector in S Africa 1798–1812.) Iridaceae. About 9 species of evergreen, shrubby perennials, closely related to *Aristea*. Leaves linear or sword-shaped. Flowers blue, solitary or in corymbs; perianth tube relatively long, slender, tepals 6, spreading; filaments short, anthers small. S Africa (S & SW Cape). Z9.

CULTIVATION As for *Aristea*.

***N. corymbosa*** Bak. Branched shrub, 0.5–2m. Lvs stiff, glaucous, arranged in a fan. Corymbs flattened; fls dark blue, *c*2cm diam. Summer–autumn.

***N. fruticosa*** (L. f.) Bak. Dwarf shrub 9–20cm tall; fls pale blue. Summer.

***N. stokoei*** N.E. Br. Dwarf shrub, 40–60cm. Lvs stiff, arranged in a fan. Fls dark blue, about 5cm long, 3cm diam. Summer–autumn.

For synonymy see *Aristea* and *Witsenia*.

**Noccaea** Rchb.
*N. alpina* (L.) Rchb. See *Pritzelago alpina*.

**Nolana** L. f. (From Lat. *nola*, a little bell, alluding to shape of corolla.) Nolanaceae. 18 species of glandular annual or perennial herbs or subshrubs. Leaves simple, alternate or verticillate, in unequal pairs in inflorescence, often somewhat succulent, subsessile or shortly petiolate, stipules absent. Flowers solitary or clustered, axillary, bisexual, heterostylous, actinomorphic with a tendency toward zygomorphy, calyx tubular-campanulate, lobes 5, imbricate; corolla campanulate, 5-lobed, plicate between lobes, sometimes bilabiate, blue to purple-blue, pink or white; stamens 5, inserted on corolla-tube alternate with corolla lobes, unequal, filaments slender or enlarged towards base, often hairy; carpels more or less united, sometimes in multiple ranks of 5, ovules several. Fruit a cluster of 3 to many distinct nutlets attached to receptacle; seeds 1 to several. Chile to Peru, Galapagos. Z10.

CULTIVATION Annuals with bell-shaped flowers easily grown outdoors in any moderately fertile soil in sun, or as pot plants in the cool glasshouse. Sow seed *in situ* in spring.

***N. humifusa*** (Gouan) Johnst. Annual or perenn. herb or subshrub, to 15cm, often more or less decumbent, stickily glandular-pubesc. Basal lvs to 2.5×1cm, elliptic or spathulate, petiolate, cauline lvs oblanceolate, sessile. Cal. campanulate, lobes 6mm, lanceolate-acuminate or ovate-acuminate; cor. 12–17mm, funnel-shaped, lilac with throat white, streaked violet or purple; fil. enlarged toward base, pubesc. Summer. Peru. 'Shooting Star': highly floriferous, stems trailing; fls lilac to lavender, streaked dark purple; suitable for baskets.

***N. paradoxa*** Lindl. ssp. ***paradoxa***. Annual or perenn.; stems 15–25cm, usually decumbent, puberulent to glandular. Basal lvs in rosette, cauline lvs opposite, 5.5×2cm, all ovate to elliptic, obtuse, somewhat succulent, petiolate, with lamina decurrent on petiole. Cal. to 2cm, campanulate or turbinate, lobes acuminate; cor. to 3.5×5cm, funnel-shaped, bright dark blue, throat yellow or white; fil. enlarged. Summer. Chile. 'Blue Bird': fls deep sky-blue with white throats, trumpet-shaped, abundant. 'Cliff Hanger': habit trailing; lvs bright green; fls cornflower blue, pale yellow throats. ssp. ***atriplicifolia*** (D. Don) Mesa. Stems to 10cm. Basal lvs spathulate, petiolate, cauline lvs to 8.5×1.5cm, elliptic to linear, acuminate, sessile. Cal. to 1.5cm, lobes acuminate; cor. to 3×4cm, blue, violet or white, with tube yellow or white. Summer. Peru, Chile.

***N.×tenella*** Lindl. (*N. humifusa* × *paradoxa*.) Intermediate between parents. Cor. pale purple-blue, throat white, veined purple. F1 hybrid; F2 and succeeding generations very variable. Summer. Garden hybrid.

***N. acuminata*** (Miers) Miers ex Dunal. See *N. paradoxa* ssp. *atriplicifolia*.
***N. atriplicifolia*** D. Don ex Sweet. See *N. paradoxa* ssp. *atriplicifolia*.
***N. grandiflora*** Lehm. ex G. Don. See *N. paradoxa* ssp. *atriplicifolia*.
***N. lanceolata*** (Miers) Miers ex Dunal. See *N. paradoxa* ssp. *atriplicifolia*.
***N. prostrata*** L. f. See *N. humifusa*.
***N. rupicola*** Gaudich. See *N. paradoxa* ssp. *atriplicifolia*.

**NOLANACEAE** Dumort. See *Nolana*.

**Nolina** Michx. (For P.C. Nolin, 18th-century French agriculturalist.) Agavaceae. Some 24 species of xeromorphic, evergreen perennials related to *Yucca* and *Dasylirion*. Caudex rarely absent, more often swollen and conical, flask-shaped or globose at base, succulent. Bark thick, corky. Leaves linear, tough and fibrous, glabrous, often serrulate with a broad sheathing base, margins and apex sometimes splitting-fibrous. Flowers produced usually only in advanced maturity, small, numerous on tall panicles; flowers of one sex often shed, some species dioecious; tepals 6, cream-white flushed mauve; stamens 6; ovary superior; stigma subsessile, 1–3-valved. Fruit a dehiscent capsule, papery, 3-lobed or alate; seeds 1–3, spherical, pale. S US, Mexico to Guatemala. Z10.

CULTIVATION *Nolina* is adapted to outdoor cultivation only in frost-free desert and semi-desert regions; elsewhere they are usually grown as part of a greenhouse selection of succulents. Narrow leaves, often glaucous, emerge from the woody stem to form large spiky 'mop heads'. *N. recurvata* is increasingly used as a major feature of interior landscapes, where it proves resilient and is valued for its massively swollen stem bases giving rise to slender trunks crowned with graceful foliage. Cultivation as for desert yuccas. Grow in a porous, well-drained soil or potting medium and provide a minimum temperature of 10–15°C/50–60°F. Water plentifully in summer and sparingly in winter. Propagate in spring by seed or offsets.

***N. bigelowii*** (Torr.) Wats. Stem 1–3m, base expanded. Lvs in terminal rosettes, to 12×3.5cm, rigid, persisting brown and deflexed around the trunk, margins smooth, splitting into fibres. Infl. dense, 1–3m. Arizona to Baja California.

***N. erumpens*** (Torr.) Wats. Stem 60–150cm. Lvs to 9×1cm, thick, straight, rigid, channelled, apex brushlike. W Texas, N Mexico.

***N. georgiana*** Michx. Stem straight, cylindric. Lvs narrow strap-shaped, serrulate, from a large bulb-like rosette. Fls off-white, showy; pedicel to 90cm. Georgia.

***N. gracilis*** (Lem.) Cif. & Giac. Similar to *N. stricta* but lvs glaucous with rougher margins.

***N. guatemalensis*** (Rose) Cif. & Giac. Tree to 6m or more. Trunk tapered, branching. Lvs in dense rosettes, to 1m×2.5cm, recurving, base broad, edges smooth. Panicle 75–110cm; pedicel short; fls 3mm. Guatemala.

***N. hartwegiana*** Hemsl. Trunk to 6m, base greatly enlarged. Lvs tufted, to 60×0.4cm, linear, entire, rough. Panicle 30–45cm; pedicel very short. Fr. thick-walled. Mexico.

***N. hookeri*** (Trel.) G. Rowley. Dioecious. Stem an irregular, swollen caudex to 1m wide; bark cork-like; branches short or absent. Lvs to 90cm, wiry, glaucous, grass-like in tufts on caudex. Panicle 10–30cm; fls tinged purple. Fr. subglobose. EC Mexico

***N. lindheimerana*** (Schelle) Wats. Stem absent or very short. Lvs 60–90×0.5cm, grasslike, wiry, flat, in rosettes of 15–20, apex entire. Panicle 60–120cm. Texas.

***N. longifolia*** (Schult.) Hemsl. Trunk to 2m or more, base broadened, tapering, with short branches. Lvs to 1m×2.5cm, thin, dark green with rough margins, recurved and hanging in dense rosettes, apex twisting. Panicle to 2m; fls white. Mexico.

***N. microcarpa*** S. Wats. BEARGRASS; SACAHUISTA. Stemless. Lvs 60–120×0.6–1.2cm, grasslike, densely tufted, arching, serrulate, apex brushlike. Fls minute on stout, erect panicle to 2m tall. SW US, Mexico.

***N. parryi*** S. Wats. Similar to *N. bigelowii* but lf margins serrulate, not fibrous. SW US.

***N. recurvata*** (Lem.) Hemsl. BOTTLE PALM; ELEPHANT FOOT TREE; PONY TAIL. Trunk flask-shaped, to 8m, swollen to 2m diam. at base, sparingly branched. Lvs in terminal rosettes, to 1.8×2cm, linear, channelled, recurved, serrulate. Panicle 90–112cm; fls 1.5mm diam. SE Mexico.

***N. stricta*** (Lem.) Cif. & Giac. Stem stout, to 6m or more, somewhat branched. Lvs to 1m×0.8–1.4cm, channelled, rigid, straight, glaucous, coarse, pale green with yellow-green margins. Mexico.

***N. tuberculata*** hort. See *N. recurvata*.
For further synonymy see *Beaucarnea, Calibanus, Dasylirion* and *Yucca*.

**Noltea** Rchb. (For E.F. Nolte, Professor of Natural History at Kiel University (early 19th century).) Rhamnaceae. 2 species of evergreen shrubs, to 4m. Leaves alternate, simple, toothed. Inflorescence axillary or terminal, corymbose, few-flowered; calyx 5-lobed, lobes triangular-ovate, erect or recurved, acute; petals 5, orbicular, hollow, inserted in sinuses between calyx lobes, nectariferous disc thin; stamens 5, as long as petals; stigma 3-lobed. Fruit a drupe-like berry, ovoid, 3-lobed, basal part surrounded by calyx tube. Late spring. S Africa. Z9.

CULTIVATION An attractive, glossy evergreen, sometimes used as hedging in essentially frost-free zones otherwise in large pots in the cool glasshouse or conservatory. Cultivate as for *Phylica*.

***N. africana*** (L.) Rchb. Erect, glabrous shrub to 4m. Lvs 4–6cm, with auriculate stipules with glandular, red margins, elliptic to oblong-lanceolate, margins toothed, dark glossy green above, pale beneath. Infl. small, 1–1.5cm wide, fls white. Fr. globose, 6mm diam., dry. S Africa.

**Nomocharis** Franch. (From Gk *nomos*, pasture, and *charis*, loveliness, referring to the plant's beauty.) Liliaceae (Liliaceae). 7 species of bulbous perennial herbs, to 1.3m. Bulb squamose, ovate to oblong, 1–3.5×1.–2.5cm, composed of several scales; scales erect, lanceolate, overlapping, fleshy, pale yellow. Bracts 1–4, remote, oblong to lanceolate, leafy, to 5cm in lower of part of stem. Leaves in 2–9 whorls of 3–9 on upper half of stem with 1 or 2 leaves between each whorl, or scattered along stem in pairs or triads toward apex, linear to lanceolate or oblong-ovate, acute to acuminate, 2–13×0.5–3cm. Flowers 1–9, terminal in uppermost leaf axils, flat to bowl-shaped, 5–10cm across, white to pink or

**Nomocharis** (a) *N. aperta* flowering stem (×0.5) (a1) stigma and style (×2) (a2) petal (×0.5) (b) *N. meleagrina* inner petal (×2) (c) *N. farreri* flowering stem (×0.5) (c1) inner petal (×0.5) (c2) stamen and style (×1) (d) *N.* × *finlayorum* (×0.5) (e) *N. pardanthina* f. *punctulata* inner petal (×1) (f) *N. pardanthina* flowering stem (×0.5) (f1) inner petal (×0,5) (f2) stamen (×2) (f3) stigma (×1.5) (g) *N.* × *notabilis* flowering stem (×0.5) (h) *N. saluenensis* inner petal (×1) (h1) stigma (×3) (h2) stamen (×3)

pale yellow, often spotted purple or maroon; perianth segments 6, not united, margins entire to subserrate or fimbriate; inner segments grooved, with basal nectary; stamens 6; filaments often fleshy, to 1.5cm long; anthers fixed laterally on a fine acicular appendage at filament apex; stigma 3-lobed. Fruit a chambered capsule, 1.5–3×1.5–2cm; seeds many, ovate, narrow-winged. Summer. W China, SE Tibet, Burma, N India. Z7.

CULTIVATION Most species require acid woodland conditions, similar to those given for the woodland species of *Lilium*; they are well suited to the peat terrace and woodland garden, where the optimal cool, humid and stable conditions prevail. Grow in light dappled or semi-shade in well-drained, peaty or leafy soils, with plenty of cool, fresh moisture at the roots. Propagate by seed, which has epigeal germination; see *Lilium*.

***N. aperta*** (Franch.) Wils. To 80cm. Bulbs elliptic, to 3.5cm. Lvs scattered along stem, 6.5–10×1–2cm, sessile, elliptic to lanceolate, acute, sometimes slightly pubesc. Fls flattened, to 10cm across, pale pink to red; outer perianth seg. 2–5×1–2cm, entire, pink to deep pink, spotted red in lower half, usually blotched maroon at base and pale green near tip, nectaries with fleshy excrescence; inner perianth seg. 2.5–4×1.3cm, always blotched; fil. to 1.5cm, maroon tipped yellow, anth. to 6mm; style to 1.3mm. Fr. cylindric, 2×2cm. Summer. W China (Yunnan, Sichuan).

***N. farreri*** (W.E. Evans) R. Harrow. To 1m. Bulb elliptic or subspherical, to 4cm. Lvs whorled, 3.5×2cm, linear to lanceolate, acuminate, dark green above, paler beneath. Fls to 20, saucer-shaped, drooping at first, later flattened and upright or horizontal, white to pink; outer perianth seg. elliptic to ovate, 2.5–5.5×1–2.5cm, entire, blotched dark maroon at base and pale green toward centre; inner perianth seg. ovate to broadly ovate, 2.5–5.5×1.5–3.5cm, entire or subserrate, maroon at base with a pale green patch toward centre and a few finer blotches; nectaries grooved; fil. to 11mm, purple, anth. to 6mm; style to 15mm. NE Burma.

***N.* ×*finlayorum*** Synge. *(N. farreri × N. pardanthina.)* Garden hybrid to 70cm. Lvs 4–12 per whorl. Fls 2–7, white to pink; perianth seg. outspread, usually red-maroon spotted only in lower half, occasionally spotted throughout, entire to subserrate.

***N. meleagrina*** Franch. To 85cm. Bulb ovoid, to 3.5cm. Lvs in 3–6 whorls, lanceolate, acuminate, to 13×3cm, dark green above, paler beneath; margins sometimes slightly hispid. Fls nodding, flattened, to 9.5cm diam., white, occasionally flecked pink below, blotched purple above; outer perianth seg. to 5.5cm, blotched purple at base; inner perianth seg. to 6cm, entire to fimbriate, purple at base; gynoecium sometimes absent. W China (Yunnan, SE Xizang).

***N.* ×*notabilis*** Sealy. *(N. saluenensis × N. farreri.)* Garden hybrid to 42cm. Bulb ovoid, to 2.5cm. Lvs scattered, elliptic to ovate, acute, 4–5×1–3cm, lustrous green above, paler below. Fls nodding, saucer-shaped, to 6cm diam., pink to mauve, spotted maroon, usually in lower half; outer perianth seg. with a deep crimson basal blotch and smaller markings above this; inner perianth seg. similar to outer seg. in colour; nectaries with black markings; stamens purple, light yellow at apex, to 12mm, anth. to 6mm; style to 12mm.

***N. pardanthina*** Franch. To 90cm. Bulb ovoid, to 3cm. Lvs whorled, sessile, elliptic to lanceolate, 2.5–10.5×0.5–2.5cm. Fls 1–24, nodding to erect, flattened, to 8.5cm diam.; outer perianth seg. 2.5–4.5×1.5–2.5cm, entire, white to pink, blotched purple, dark maroon at base; inner perianth seg. 2.5–4.5×2.5–3.5cm, blotches more numerous than outer seg.; fimbriate in apical portion; fil. to 8mm, purple, anth. to 4mm, red-maroon; style to 1cm. Fr. cylindric, 2.5–3×2–2.5cm, brown. W China (Yunnan, Sichuan). f. ***punctulata*** Sealy. Perianth seg. less densely spotted, spots only at base, margins shallow-fimbriate to subserrate. W China (W Yunnan).

***N. saluenensis*** Balf. f. To 85cm high. Bulb ovoid, to 3cm. Lvs scattered along stem, sessile, elliptic to elliptic-oblong, 2–4cm long, dark green above, pale green beneath, veins distinct. Fls 2–5, horizontal or drooping, saucer-shaped, to 6.5cm diam.; outer perianth seg. 3.5–4.5×1.5–2.5cm, entire, rose pink, paler in lower part, dark maroon patch at base with small spots over lower half; inner perianth seg. 4–4.5×1.5–2.5cm, entire; fil. to 11mm, purple, anth. to 8mm, green-blue; style to 6mm. W China (Yunnan, SE Xizang), NE Burma.

***N. synaptica*** Sealy. Similar to *N. saluenensis*. Fls white, tinted purple, spotted dark maroon throughout; perianth seg. with a dark purple, yellow-fringed, basal blotch. India (Assam).

***N. mairei*** Lév. See *N. pardanthina*.
***N. nana*** Wils. See *Lilium nanum*.
***N. oxypetalum*** Royle. See *Lilium oxypetalum*.

**Nopalea** Salm-Dyck.
***N. auberi*** (Pfeiff.) Salm-Dyck. See *Opuntia auberi*.
***N. cochenillifera*** (L.) Salm-Dyck. See *Opuntia cochenillifera*.
***N. dejecta*** (Salm-Dyck) Salm-Dyck. See *Opuntia dejecta*.

**Nopalxochia** Britt. & Rose (From the ancient Mexican name *nopalxochiquetzaltiquizi*, meaning cactus with scarlet flowers.) Cactaceae. 3–4 species of epiphytic cacti; stems terete at base, flattened above, margins crenate, spineless except the young growth; areoles with sparse wool. Flower solitary, diurnal, funnelform or campanulate-funnelform, pink or red; tube shorter than or equalling the limb; floral areoles with short bristles or naked. Fruit globose or ellipsoid, areolate and with or without bristles; seeds oval, *c*2–2.5×1.3–2mm, black-brown, shiny; relief flat; hilum medium, oblique, superficial; mucilage-sheath present, covering entire seed. S Mexico. Z10.

CULTIVATION Grow in an intermediate heated greenhouse (min. 10–15°C/50–60°F), 'epiphyte' compost: equal parts organic/inorganic matter, below pH 6 (essential); shade (11:00–15:00 hrs) all summer; maintain high humidity; reduce watering in winter and rest winter-flowering species in late summer. Closely related to *Heliocereus*, but here upheld pending definitive reclassification of the epiphytic cacti.

***N. ackermannii*** (Haw.) F. Knuth. Freely branching, mainly from the base; stems to 20–70(–100)×5–7cm, lanceolate, flat and crenate above, with terete base to 18cm×4–7mm, obscurely 3-ribbed. Fl. 12–14×10–14cm, curved-funnelform, pericarpel and tube 5–7×0.7–1cm, pale yellow-green; floral areoles, except the uppermost, with short wool and 0–5 bristly spines 3.5(–5)mm, pale yellow; perianth orange-red; tepals 7–10cm; staminal throat-circle present; fil. declinate, white to pale yellow at base, orange to scarlet above; style pale pink to magenta at base and apex, otherwise orange-scarlet; stigmas purple-red. Fr. 4×2–3cm, ovoid-oblong, shiny, green to brown-red, with low ribs, scales and pale brown spines; pulp white or pale pink, fragrant. Spring. S Mexico. Z9.

***N. conzattiana*** MacDougall. Resembling *N. ackermannii*, and perhaps only a variety of it. Fl. smaller, 11–12×5–6cm; tepals 4–6cm. S Mexico (Oaxaca). Z9.

***N. macdougallii*** (Alexander) W.T. Marshall. Stems 15–45×2–5cm, linear-oblong, 2-winged, 4–6mm thick, crenate, terete at base and apex. Fl. 7–8×*c*6.5cm, tubular-funnelform; pericarpel and tube 4–4.5×*c*1cm, brown-green; floral areoles almost naked; tepals purple-pink, the inner spreading, 3–3.5cm. Fr. 3.5cm, ovoid, green, with low ribs, scales and short hairs; pulp translucent white. Spring. SE Mexico (Chiapas). Z9.

***N. phyllanthoides*** (DC.) Britt. & Rose. Primary stems up to 40×0.6cm, terete below, flattened at apex, laterals lanceolate, flat, with terete stalk-like base, 15–30×2.5–4cm overall, crenate. Fl. 8–10×7–9cm, campanulate-funnelform; tube 2.5–5×0.7–1cm, pale green; floral areoles naked; perianth pink; outer tepals opening irregularly before anthesis, then spreading widely, inner remaining suberect; stamens, style and stigmas almost white. Fr. 3–4cm, ellipsoid, with low ribs, green at first, later red; pulp red, odourless. Spring. S Mexico. Z9.

For synonymy see *Epiphyllum*.

For illustration see CACTI.

**Normanbya** F. Muell. ex Becc. (For the Marquis of Normanby.) BLACK PALM. Palmae. 1 species, an unarmed, pleonanthic, monoecious palm to 20m. Stem solitary, erect, ringed, grey, swollen at base. Crownshaft conspicuous, pale grey, apex brown. Leaves to 2.5m, pinnate; petiole short or absent, white-tomentose with scattered brown scales; rachis curved, densely brown scaly; pinnae cuneate, dark green above, glaucous and scaly beneath, single-fold, divided to base into 7–9 linear, lax segments, hanging in several planes. Inflorescences to 450cm, infrafoliar, branched ×2, amid 2 tubular deciduous bracts; rachillae stout, bearing triads (2 male and 1 female) of flowers at base and female flowers at apex: male flowers symmetrical, sepals 3, overlapping, petals 3, free, stamens 24–40, pistillode flask-shaped; female flowers ovoid, sepals 3, imbricate, margins fringed, petals 3, staminodes 3, pistil 1-celled, stigmas 3. Fruit ovoid to obpyriform, dull pink to purple-brown, with apical stigmatic remains. N Queensland. Z10.

CULTIVATION Occurring in low altitude, high rainfall, tropical forest, in moist but well-drained alluvial soils, *N. normanbyi* is a tall, slender and distinctive feather palm, suitable for outdoor cultivation in shaded and sheltered situations in humid tropical gardens. In cooler zones, it is a handsome specimen for deep pots in the warm glasshouse or conservatory. Propagate by seed, which germinates very quickly if sown fresh. See also PALMS.

***N. normanbyi*** (W. Hill) L.H. Bail. As for the genus.

***N. merrillii*** Becc. See *Veitchia merrillii*.

**North, Marianne** (1830–1890). Botanical artist. Born in Hastings, Sussex, she had little formal education, spending only eighteen months at a school in Norwich. On her return from a tour of the Continent (1847–50), she took lessons in flower painting. In 1854 her father, a friend of such progressive figures as Charles Darwin, was elected Liberal MP for Hastings. The following year her mother died and the family moved to London. From 1860 onwards father and daughter made various trips abroad to the Continent and beyond. After her father's death in 1869, Marianne decided to continue her floral painting further afield, usually travelling alone. From 1871–72, she toured Canada, the United States and Jamaica, and in subsequent years travelled to most parts of the world. In 1876 she visited Ceylon and was photographed by Julia Margaret Cameron. In 1880 she visited Australia, at Darwin's suggestion, to paint the plant life there. In the early 1880s she exhibited at Conduit Street. The popularity of her work and its positive reception in the press encouraged her to display her paintings at Kew Gardens. She presented the paintings to Kew and even offered to build a gallery at her own expense. Her friend, James Fergusson (1808–1886), was employed to produce the designs and the gallery was finished by the time she returned from Australia in June 1881. It was opened in July 1882 and was an instant success with 2000 catalogues being sold within the first month.

Marianne North continued to travel and in 1884–85 made what was to be her last trip, to Chile, to paint the monkey-puzzle tree. Her health was declining from a fever first contracted in Borneo, and in 1886 she moved to Alderley in Gloucestershire where she died in 1890. Some 800 of her works, painted in oil, are in the North Gallery at Kew. The highly coloured paintings, tightly packed together, depict a wide variety of plants in their native environment, frequently in panoramic settings or surrounded by lush foliage. A genus she discovered in the Seychelles, *Northea seychellana*, is named after her, as is the pitcher plant, *Nepenthes northiana*. Her autobiographical works, *Recollections of a Happy Life* (2 vols, 1892) and *Further Recollections of a Happy Life* (1893), were edited by her sister.

**Notechidnopsis** Lavranos & Bleck. (Name establishing distinction of this genus from *Echidnopsis*.) Asclepiadaceae. 2 species of dwarf, succulent, leafless herbs, to 8cm. Stems prostrate to ascending, to 12cm×13mm, 6–10-angled, glabrous, sometimes burrowing, with tubercles giving a tessellated appearance, and soft, green teeth. Fls 5–15, in clusters toward stem apex; pedicels 2–5mm; sepals 5, small, fleshy; corolla about 9mm in diameter, flat, mauve, tube shallow, filled by corona, exterior sparsely short-pubescent, interior densely bristly, corona 2-whorled, not cup-shaped, extending above corolla, sulphur-yellow, sometimes ringed white, outer corona 10-lobed, inner whorl 5-lobed. Fruit a follicle. S Africa (Cape Province). Z10.

CULTIVATION As for *Stapelia*.

***N. columnaris*** (Nel) Lavranos & Bleck. Stem erect, 15–18×2–2.5cm, green-grey, simple or with 2–3 shoots from base, columnar, 8-angled, teeth curving downward. Cor. 4–8mm diam., lobes 2mm long, 4mm wide, ovate, pointed, exterior blotched red, interior white-hairy, yellow-green with red spots. S Africa (Cape Province, Little Namaqualand).

***N. tessellata*** (Pill.) Lavranos & Bleck. As for the genus.

For synonymy see *Echidnopsis* and *Trichocaulon*.

**Nothofagus** Bl. (From Gk *nothos*, false, and *Fagus*, to which it is related.) SOUTHERN BEECH. Fagaceae. About 40 species of monoecious, evergreen and deciduous trees and shrubs to 55m. Bark smooth purple-brown with distinct pale lenticels, becoming thick and scaly to furrowed on old trees. Shoots slender, glabrous or pubescent; stipules mostly caducous; buds short-acute, scales numerous; terminal bud absent. Leaves alternate, 0.8–20cm, ovoid to oblong or trullate, 4–22 pairs of veins, margin entire, waved or toothed, 0–8 teeth for each main vein, number of veins and teeth valuable for identification; glabrous to thinly pubescent above and beneath. Flowers unisexual; male flowers axillary, in groups of 1–3, stamens 3–90; female flowers axillary, solitary, rarely to 3-grouped, with 3(–7) styles; largely wind pollinated. Fruit solitary; an ovoid involucre, 5–25mm, covered with entire or branched, often sticky lamellae; mature in 5–8 months, (2–)4 valves splitting open to release the (1–)3(–7) nuts; nuts variable in size, 3–20mm, ovoid-acute, two end nuts triangular, middle one flattened, with narrow wings along edges, pale buff to brown with a small pale basal scar. Temperate southern S America, New Zealand, E Australia, and tropical high altitude New Caledonia and New Guinea. Closely related to *Fagus*, but differing in the many-seeded involucre and the lack of a true terminal bud; in these aspects showing a relationship to *Castanea*. All can be recognized by their distinctive herring-bone branching pattern; some are otherwise superficially similar to some *Alnus* and *Carpinus* spp.

CULTIVATION The deciduous species favour cool, wet summers in maritime temperate climates, where *N. procera* in particular grows rapidly into a very large, well-shaped tree. The evergreens are similarly adapted; *N. dombeyi* is notably fast growing. None is very tolerant of winter cold; the hardiest, *N. antarctica* and *N. pumilio*, are hardy only to zone 7, in Europe growing as far northeast as S Sweden. All other temperate species are killed or injured by −20°C/−4°F, in some −10°C/14°F; they are not suitable for frost-prone central areas in England, and should only be planted on sites with good air drainage. Hot humid summers are also avoided, and in N America they are confined to the Pacific coast from C California to SE Alaska. *N. obliqua* is well adapted to a Mediterranean climate with as little as 400mm/16in. rain; *N. alessandri* and *N. glauca* are nearly as well-adapted, but the other species all require year-round rainfall, from 800–4000mm/32–160in. annually. The tropical species are from high-altitude cloud forest are difficult to cultivate, needing constant cool humid conditions; they can only be grown in areas like the uplands of Queensland and, with care, New Zealand North Island.

Propagation is by seed, available from forestry sources in their native countries and British plantations; hybrids may be produced from garden-collected seed. The large-seeded *N. glauca* should be treated as for *Fagus*; the rest are better treated like *Betula* or *Alnus*, and like theirs the seed can be stored for long periods dried at 2°C/35.6°F. Moisten and chill at 1–5°C/34–41°F for 2–3 months before planting. The roots are very susceptible to desiccation and extreme care should be taken in moving plants. Plant when two years old and 30–80cm tall, though larger trees to 4m/13ft can be successfully established. All are light-demanding from an early age and need full sun, and require moist soils with reasonable drainage and pH5–7; they are poor on alkaline sites and deep acid peats. Only *N. antarctica* and *N. gunnii* tolerate exposure. All are suitable for bonsai; *N. antarctica* particularly so with its fragrant glossy foliage and naturally contorted form. This and *N. gunnii* are the only species suited to small gardens; like all the deciduous species they have excellent autumn colours.

Few pests and diseases; root rot caused by *Heterobasidion annosum* (*Fomes annosus*) has caused serious losses on alkaline soil, and phytophthora root rot (*Phytophthora* spp.) can kill both mature trees and nursery stock. Trees are able to recover well from partial defoliation by moth larvae. Frost damage is the commonest problem; symptoms are unusual as the shoots are more cold-tolerant than the bark; mature trees can be girdled at the base in severe winters, and leaf out the next spring only to die as the water supply from the roots is lost. More commonly patchy bark death causes stem cankers. Unlike *Fagus*, they do not suffer from bark damage by squirrels.

The genus is divided into evergreen and deciduous species. The 16 New Guinea and 5 New Caledonia species, all evergreen, are not in cultivation to any extent and are not covered here; typified by *N. brassii* Steenis, they differ from the other evergreen species in larger leaves and cupules with only 2 valves. The 3–4 named hybrids are included in the key; others occur both in the wild and cultivation.

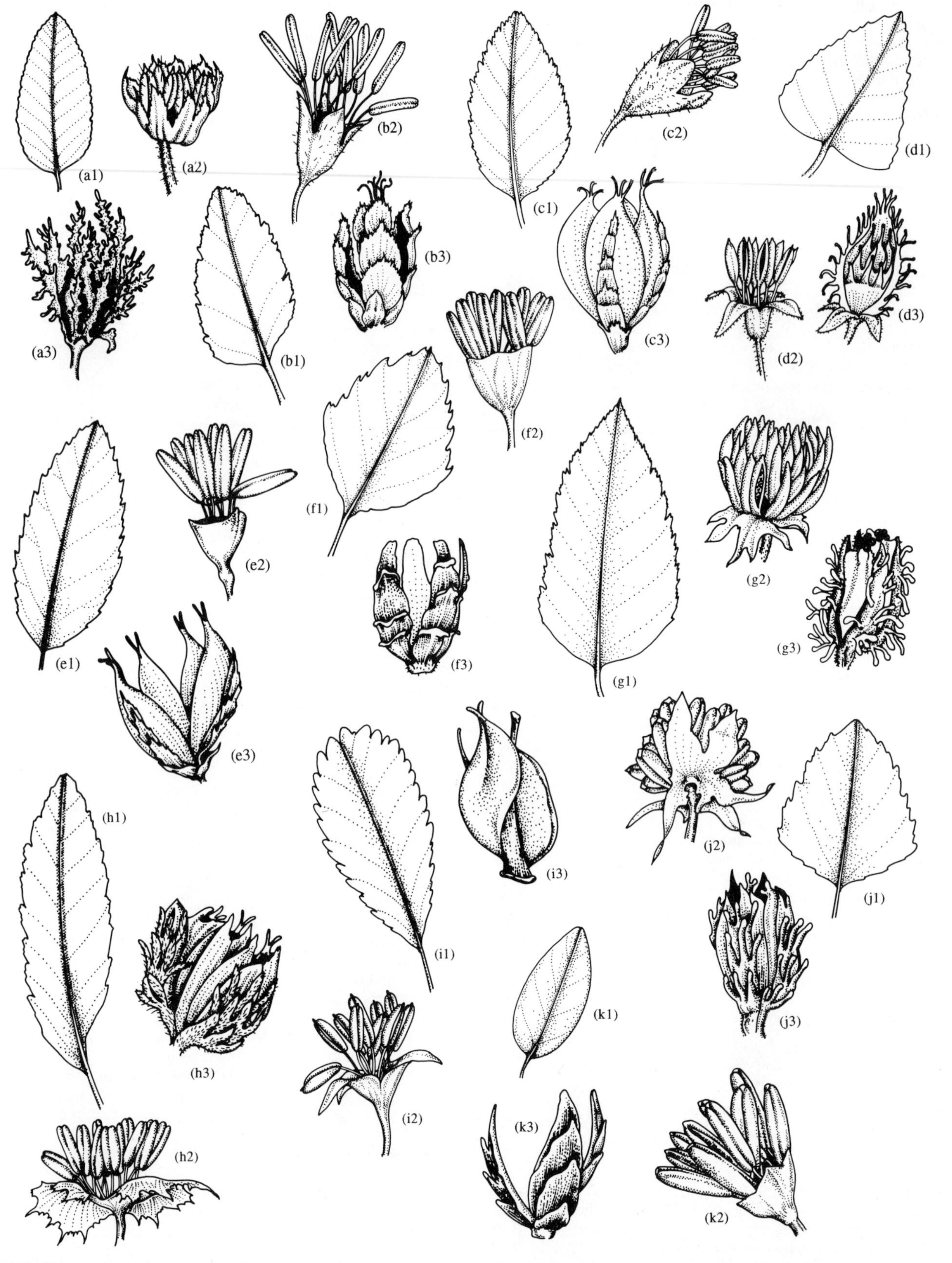


**Nothofagus** (a) *N.* × *alpina* (a1) leaf (×0.5) (a2) male flower (×4) (a3) female cupule (×3) (b) *N. antarctica* (b1) leaf (×2) (b2) male flower (×7) (b3) female cupule (×4) (c) *N. betuloides* (c1) leaf (×3) (c2) male flower (×4) (c3) female cupule (×4) (d) *N. cunninghamii* (d1) leaf (×4) (d2) male flower (×4) (d3) female cupule (×3) (e) *N. dombeyi* (e1) leaf (×3) (e2) male flower (×7) (e3) female cupule (×4) (f) *N. furca* (f1) leaf (×2) (f2) male flower (×6) (f3) female cupule (×3) (g) *N. menziesii* (g1) leaf (×4) (g2) male flower (×4) (g3) female cupule (×6) (h) *N. moorei* (h1) leaf (×1) (h2) male flower (×4) (h3) female cupule (× 1) (i) *N obliqua* (i1) leaf (i2) male flower (i3) female cupule (×3) (j) *N. pumilio* (j1) leaf (×1) (j2) male flower (×6) (j3) female cupule (×4) (k) *N. solanderi* (k1) leaf (×3) (k2) male flower (×6) (k3) female cupule (×4)

1 Evergreen; leaves folded along midrib in bud.
*Nn. ×apiculata, betuloides, ×blairii, cunninghamii, dombeyi, fusca, menziesii, moorei, nitida, solanderi, truncata.*

2 Deciduous; leaves plicate in bud.
*Nn. alessandri, × alpina, antarctica, glauca, gunnii, × leonii, obliqua, procera, pumilio.*

***N. alessandrii*** Espin. RUIL. Deciduous tree to 30m. Lvs 6–14×5–9cm, ovate to subcordate, 11–13 pairs of veins, finely serrate; bright green above, paler blue-green beneath, thinly glandular-pubesc. Male fls in groups of 3, yellow, stamens 10–20. Fr. a 4-valved, 10–13mm cupule, lamellae entire; nuts (5–)7, 7mm. C Chile. Z9.

***N. ×alpina*** (Poepp. & Endl.) Krasser. *(N. procera × N. pumilio.)* Similar to *N. procera* but lvs very small, 2–3×1–1.5cm. Possibly only a dwarfed mountain form of *N. procera*; if synonymous with *N. procera*, name *N. alpina* has priority. C Chile. Z7.

***N. antarctica*** (Forst.) Ørst. NIRE. Twisted small deciduous tree or shrub to 17m; crown irregular, open. Shoots glabrous, green, tinged red above. Lvs 1.5–4cm, oblong, finely but irregularly toothed, with 4 pairs of non-parallel veins and 3–8 small teeth between the veins; glossy rich green above, paler beneath, often sweetly aromatic, glabrous except a few hairs on veins. Male fls solitary, 8–13 stamens. Fr. green, tipped red, a 4-valved 5–7mm cupule, lamellae entire; nuts 3, 6mm. Tierra del Fuego to Chile. var. ***uliginosa*** A. DC. Lvs more pubesc. 'Benmore' ('Prostrata'): low-spreading form with interlacing branches in a dense mound. Z7.

***N. ×apiculata*** (Colenso) Krasser. *(N. solanderi × N. truncata.)* Natural hybrid intermediate between parent species. New Zealand. Z8.

***N. betuloides*** (Mirb.) Bl. COIGUE DE MAGELLANES; GUINDO BEECH. Evergreen tree to 25m, or shrub in exposure; crown more dense than *N. dombeyi*. Shoots orange-brown, glandular-pubesc. Lvs 1–3cm, ovoid, regular crenate, apex blunt acute, glossy dark green, slightly sticky, finely freckled white glands beneath, veins often pink; petiole 3mm. Male fls solitary, red, stamens 10–16. Fr. a 4-valved, 8mm cupule with glandular bristles; nuts 3. Chile, W Argentina, from 40°–55°S. Z7.

***N. ×blairii*** (T. Kirk) Ckn. *(N. fusca × N. solanderi* var. *cliffortioides.)* Natural hybrid intermediate between parent species. New Zealand. Z8.

***N. cunninghamii*** (Hook. f.) Ørst. MYRTLE BEECH. Evergreen tree to 55m, related to *N. menziesii*. Shoots slender, brown, pubesc. Lvs 6–10×4–9mm, deltoid or trullate to nearly orbicular, irregularly singly blunt-toothed, apex blunt-acute, glossy green, without pits beneath; petiole 2mm. Male fls solitary, 8–12 stamens. Fr. a 4-valved, 6–8mm, red cupule with recurved glandular lamellae; nuts 3. Tasmania. Z9.

***N. dombeyi*** (Mirb.) Bl. COIGUE. Evergreen tree to 50m, trunk to 4m diam.; crown regular ovoid-conic. Shoots red-brown above, green beneath, pubesc. Lvs 2–4cm, ovoid-acute to lanceolate, irregular-serrate, glossy dark green above, matt and pale beneath, finely freckled black (under lens); petiole 2–3mm. Male fls in groups of 3, bright red, stamens 8–13. Fr. solitary or to 3-grouped, a 4-valved, 8mm cupule with glandular bristles; nuts 3. Chile, Argentina. Z8.

***N. fusca*** (Hook. f.) Ørst. RED BEECH. Evergreen tree to 35m. Shoots red-brown, pubesc., often zig-zag. Lvs 3–5×2–3cm, broad-ovate, with 4–8 large, acute teeth on each side, thin, papery texture, veins 3–5 pairs, often branched near lf margin, matt yellow-green to dark green above, shiny beneath with minute pits at base, turning bright red before falling in second year. Male fls grouped 1–3, stamens 8–11. Fr. a 4-valved, 12mm cupule with entire lamellae; nuts 3. New Zealand. var. ***colensoi*** (Hook. f.) Ørst. Lvs thicker and stronger, margin with finer, blunter teeth. Z9.

***N. glauca*** (Philippi) Krasser. Deciduous tree to 30m; bark red-brown, flaky. Lvs 5–8×3–5cm, broad-oblong, base cordate, 10 pairs of veins, margin undulate, crenulate, glaucous green above, pale glaucous beneath with hair tufts in vein axils; petiole 5mm. Male fls solitary, stamens 40–90. Fr. a 4-valved 20–25mm cupule with glandular lamellae, 1cm-pedunculate; seeds 3, 15–19×10mm, nut-brown. C Chile. Z9.

***N. gunnii*** (Hook. f.) Ørst. TANGLEFOOT BEECH. Low to prostrate deciduous shrub to 3m, rarely a small tree. Shoots yellow-pubesc. Lvs 1–4cm, crinkled, nearly orbicular, 5–7 pairs of veins, similar to *N. pumilio*, but lobes between the veins not notched. Male fls solitary. Fr. a 4-valved, 8–9mm cupule with entire lamellae; nuts 3. Tasmania (mts). Z8.

***N. ×leonii*** Espin. *(N. glauca × N. obliqua* var. *macrocarpa.)* Deciduous tree. Lvs to 10×4cm, ovate, obtuse, margin doubly serrate, denticulate, base cuneate to truncate; petiole to 1cm. Chile Z7.

***N. menziesii*** (Hook. f.) Ørst. SILVER BEECH. Evergreen tree to 30m, bark variable, pale silvery to shiny red-brown with conspicuous lenticels. Shoot slender, dark brown-pubescent. Lvs 1–1.5cm, orbicular to broadly ovoid-acute, apex obtuse or acute, margin double-crenate, silvery grey on young trees, glossy dark green on older trees, coriaceous, glabrous except for two hair-filled pits in vein axils at base of blade; petiole 2mm. Male fls solitary, 30–35 stamens. Fr. a 4-valved, 6–9mm cupule with scale-like lamellae; nuts 3, 5mm with wings prolonged 1mm beyond nut apex. New Zealand. Z9.

***N. moorei*** (F. Muell.) Krasser. AUSTRALIAN BEECH. Evergreen tree to 35m. Shoots brown, pubesc. Lvs 3–8×2–4cm, rarely 11.5cm, ovate-lanceolate, glabrous, glossy dark green above, paler beneath, apex acuminate, margin finely sharp-serrate, 9–16 pairs of veins; petiole 5mm, pubesc. Male fls solitary, stamens 15–20. Fr. a 4-valved, 8–10mm cupule with scaly lamellae in V-pattern; nuts 3. Australia (NE NSW, SE Queensland). Z9.

***N. nitida*** (Philippi) Krasser. COIGUE DE CHILOE. Evergreen tree to 40m. Lvs 2.5–4×2–3cm, trullate, coarsely serrate, apex acute, coriaceous, dark glossy green tinged brown above, paler beneath. Male fls in groups of 3, stamens 3–8. Fr. a 4-valved, 5mm cupule with glandular bristles; nuts 3(–5), very small, 3mm. W Chile. Z7.

***N. obliqua*** (Mirb.) Bl. ROBLE BEECH. Deciduous tree to 40m, trunk to 2m diam., bark grey, shallow-fissured and plated. Shoot slender, red-brown above, green beneath, thinly pubesc.; bud 5mm, ovoid. Lvs 3–8×1.7–3cm, ovoid-oblong, mid-green above, paler beneath, glabrous, base slightly oblique, apex acute, margin double toothed; veins 7–12 pairs, regular and straight, 6–7mm apart, impressed above and prominent beneath, each vein ending in a large 4–8mm lobe-like tooth, itself 1–3-toothed each side; petiole 5–10mm. Male fls solitary, stamens 30–40. Fr. a buff, 4-valved, 7–9mm cupule with simple lamellae; nuts 3, 5–7×3mm, buff. Chile, W Argentina. The hybrids *N. obliqua × N. procera* and *N. obliqua × N. menziesii* have occurred in Britain; they are as yet unnamed. var. ***macrocarpa*** A. DC. Fr. larger, cupule to 12mm; nuts 10mm. Z8.

***N. procera*** (Poepp. & Endl.) Ørst. RAULI BEECH. Deciduous tree to 40m, trunk to 2m diam., bark dull green-grey with shallow vertical fissures. Shoot green, soon brown, warty, pubesc.; buds 1cm, narrow-conic. Lvs 4–15×3–8cm, to 20cm on vigorous young trees, ovoid-lanceolate to trullate, matt green and thinly pubesc. on both sides, apex blunt-acute, margin slightly scalloped, finely crenate-serrate; veins 15–22 pairs, very regular and straight, 7mm apart, impressed above and prominent beneath, each vein ending in a slight sinus with a 2–3mm tooth and 3–4 1mm teeth before the next vein sinus; petiole 5–10mm. Male fls grouped 2–3, stamens 20–30. Fr. an orange-buff, 10–17mm cupule covered in 3–9mm branched sticky glandular lamellae; nuts 3, 8–9×6mm, pale brown. Chilean Andes. Z7.

***N. pumilio*** (Poepp. & Endl.) Krasser. LENGA. Deciduous tree to 40m. Shoot brown, pubesc., with scattered warts; buds 3mm, ovoid. Lvs 2–4×1.5–2.5cm, broad-oval to ovoid, glossy green above, paler beneath with scattered adpressed long hairs on veins, apex rounded, margin ciliate, lobed; veins 5–7 pairs, prominent beneath, each ending in a 2mm deep sinus with a single, 1mm-notched lobe between (appearing as 2 crenate teeth, 3 on basal lobe where 2 notches); petiole 3–5mm. Male fls solitary, stamens 10–15. Fr. a 12mm cupule, 2-, not 4-valved; nuts 1(–2), 9–10×8mm, brown. Tierra del Fuego to Chilean Andes. Z7.

***N. solanderi*** (Hook. f.) Ørst. BLACK BEECH. Tree to 30m. Shoots slender, wiry, red-brown, tomentose. Lvs 7–13×6–7mm, very regular ovoid, entire, flat, coriaceous, apex mostly obtuse, glossy dark green above with scattered hairs at first, soon glabrous, thinly pale green-tomentose beneath (to glabrous on shaded shoots); petiole 2mm, red-brown. Male fls grouped 1–3, red, stamens 8–14. Fr. a 3-valved, 7mm cupule with entire lamellae; nuts 3. New Zealand. The spelling *solandri*, found in most texts, is an orthographic error. var. ***cliffortioides*** (Hook. f.) Poole. MOUNTAIN BEECH. Tree to 30m or shrub at high altitude. Lvs twisted and buckled with margins bent down and acute tip bent up. Intermediates with type common. New Zealand (mts). Z8.

***N. truncata*** (Colenso) Ckn. HARD BEECH. Evergreen tree allied to *N. fusca*, but lvs more coriaceous with 5–6 pairs of veins, margin with 8–12 shallow blunt teeth, blade without pits. Fls and fr. as *N. fusca.*. Possibly better treated as a variety of *N. fusca*. New Zealand. Z8.

***N. cliffortioides*** (Hook. f.) Ørst. See *N. solanderi* var. *cliffortioides*.
***N. nervosa*** (Philippi) Dimitri & Milano. See *N. procera*.
***N. solanderi*** var. ***cliffortioides*** (Hook. f.) Poole. See *N. cliffortioides*.

## Notholaena R. Br.

***N. bonariensis*** (Willd.) C. Chr. See *Cheilanthes bonariensis*.
***N. candida*** (Mart. & Gal.) Hook. See *Cheilanthes candida*.
***N. newberryi*** D.C. Eaton. See *Cheilanthes newberryi*.
***N. parryi*** D.C. Eaton. See *Cheilanthes parryi*.
***N. laevis*** Mart. & Gal. See *Cheilanthes sinuata*.
***N. pruinosa*** Fée. See *Cheilanthes sinuata*.
***N. trichomanoides*** (L.) R. Br. See *Cheilanthes trichomanoides*.
***N. candida*** Mart. & Gal. See *Cheilanthes candida*.
***N. canescens*** Kunze. See *Cheilanthes lasiophylla*.
***N. distans*** R. Br. See *Cheilanthes distans*.
***N. newberryi*** D.C. Eaton. See *Cheilanthes newberryi*.
***N. sinuata*** (Lagasca ex Sw.) Domin. See *Cheilanthes sinuata*.
***N. vellea*** R. Br. See *Cheilanthes vellea*.

**Notholirion** Wallich ex Boiss. (From Gk *nothos*, false, and *leirion*, lily; these plants have been placed in both *Lilium* and *Fritillaria* but are now considered separate from both.) Liliaceae (Liliaceae). 4 species of bulbous perennials to 1.5m. Bulb composed of pale, fleshy scales enclosed in a thin, brown, ribbed tunic formed from the bases of the previous year's leaves, bulbiliferous. Leaves produced in autumn and winter, basal and cauline, linear-lanceolate, to 45cm. Racemes 1–30-flowered, subtended by a short, linear bract; flowers trumpet-shaped to spreading, to 5cm, red, pink or pale purple, sometimes tipped green; perianth segments 6, free, tips recurved, occasionally spotted green; stamens 6, anthers versatile; stigma distinctly trifid. Fruit a 3-chambered capsule; seeds small, wingless. Summer. Afghanistan to W China. Z7.

CULTIVATION Grown for their delicate, trumpet-shaped flowers, usually in shades of blue-lilac and pink, carried on slender stems. *N. thomsonianum*, found in scrub and rocky habitats to altitudes of 2300m/7475ft in the western Himalaya, is prone to frost damage, since it leafs up early in the season, and for this reason in cool temperate zones it is more commonly cultivated in large containers, 25–30cm/10–12in. pans, in the cool glasshouse. Use a potting mix of rich woodland soil with silver sand and leafmould; grow in bright, filtered light and water plentifully when in full growth. Withold water when dormant but keep just sufficiently moist to avoid desiccation. *N. macrophyllum, N. campanulatum* and *N. bulbuliferum*, which come into growth later, are more hardy and appear to grow better where summers are reasonably cool. Grow in well-drained, humus-rich soils in light, dappled shade. Seed, which have epigeal germination, is the best means of increase, despite the plentiful production of bulbils, as for *Lilium* (see LILIES).

***N. bulbuliferum*** (Lingl.) Stearn. To 1.5m. Lvs 7–13, to 45×1cm. Fls horizontal, trumpet-shaped, to 4cm, pale lilac; perianth seg. recurved, spreading, the upper 3 ascending, 2 horizontally outspread, 1 descending, 2–4×1–1.5cm, tipped green. Nepal to W China.

***N. campanulatum*** Cotton & Stearn. To 80cm. Lvs 8–13, to 30cm. Fls to 20, pendulous, to 5cm, crimson to maroon; perianth seg. tipped green. N Burma, W China (Xizang, Yunnan).

***N. macrophyllum*** (D. Don) Boiss. To 40cm. Stems flimsy. Lvs 3–5 linear-lanceolate, to 45×2.5cm. Fls 1–7, horizontal to nodding, trumpet-shaped, to 5cm, pale pink to light mauve throughout; perianth seg. widespread. Himalaya.

***N. thomsonianum*** (Royle) Stapf. To 1m. Lvs 8–12, to 45×2cm. Fls 10–30, horizontal to ascending, trumpet-shaped, to 6.5cm, pale mauve; perianth seg. reflexed at tips, 5–6.5×0.5cm. W Himalaya, Afghanistan.

***N. hyacinthinum*** (Wils.) Stapf. See *N. bulbuliferum*.

**Nothopanax** Miq.
***N. arboreus*** (Murray) Seem. See *Pseudopanax arboreus*.
***N. cochleata*** (Lam.) Miq. See *Polyscias scutellaria* 'Cochleata'.
***N. colensoi*** (Hook. f.) Seem. See *Pseudopanax colensoi*.
***N. crispatus*** (Bull) Merrill. See *Polyscias* 'Crispata'.
***N. davidii*** (Franch.) Harms ex Diels. See *Metapanax davidii*.
***N. delavayi*** (Franch.) Harms ex Diels. See *Metapanax delavayi*.
***N. elegans*** (C. Moore ex Muell.) Seem. See *Polyscias elegans*.
***N. fruticosus*** (L.) Miq. See *Polyscias fruticosa*.
***N. fruticosus*** var. ***plumatus*** (Bull) Merrill. See *Polyscias* 'Plumata'.
***N. guilfoylei*** (Bull) Merrill. See *Polyscias guilfoylei*.
***N. laetus*** (T. Kirk) Cheesem. See *Pseudopanax laetus*.
***N. linearis*** (Hook. f.) Harms. See *Pseudopanax linearis*.
***N. ornatus*** (Bull) Merrill. See *Polyscias filicifolia* 'Ornata'.
***N. pinnatus*** (Lam.) Miq. See *Polyscias cumingiana*.
***N. sambucifolius*** (Sieb.) K. Koch. See *Polyscias sambucifolia*.
***N. simplex*** (Hook. f.) Seem. See *Pseudopanax simplex*.
***N. sinclairii*** (Hook. f.) Seem. See *Pseudopanax simplex* var. *sinclairii*.
***N. tricochleatus*** Miq. See *Polyscias scutellaria* 'Tricochleata'.

**Nothoscordum** Kunth (From Gk *nothos*, false, and *scordon*, garlic.) FALSE GARLIC; GRACE GARLIC. Liliaceae (Alliaceae). 20 species of herbaceous perennials to 70cm, resembling *Allium* but lacking characteristic odour. Bulbs tunicate. Leaves basal. Flowers numerous in loose umbels; spathe 1, 2-lobed; tepals 6, persistent, united at base, free at apex; ovary superior, cells with several ovules, style terminal. Fruit a 3-celled capsule; seeds black, angular. Americas.

CULTIVATION *Nothoscordum* spp. usually have white flowers, sometimes with a marked brown line running down each petal. *N. bivalve* is non-invasive and will grow in damp exposed places, tolerating temperatures to –10°C/14°F. *N. gracile* has deliciously scented flowers above straggling glaucous foliage and may be considered one of the most persistent and invasive weeds introduced to British gardens. It produces many tiny offset bulbils which fall off into the soil when the bulb is dug up; it also provides copious fertile seed which germinates readily in the poorest of soils. Grow in wild, distant areas of the garden where few other species will grow and where its inevitable spread will not cause nuisance.

***N. bivalve*** (L.) Britt. To 20cm. Lvs 3–4, to 4mm wide. Fls 4–8, almost stellate, tepals white to yellow, midrib green, lanceolate, spreading widely, united for a very short distance. Spring. S US. Z5.

***N. gracile*** (Ait.) Stearn. 30–75cm; bulbs ovoid, tunics membranous. Lvs 6–8, 20–40cm×7mm+. Fls 8–15, fragrant, funnel-shaped; tepals 9–15mm, white to lilac, streaked brown and pink below, midrib pink or mauve, obtuse, united in a short tube, ascending. Fr. 6–10mm. Spring–summer. S America, Mexico. Z7.

***N. fragrans*** (Vent.) Kunth. See *N. gracile*.
***N. maritimum*** Hook. f. See *Muilla maritima*.
***N. neriniflorum*** (Herb.) Traub. See *Caloscordum neriniflorum*.
***N. striatum*** (Jacq.) Kunth. See *N. bivalve*.
For further synonymy see *Allium*.

**Nothotaxus** Florin.
***N. chienii*** (Cheng) Florin. See *Pseudotaxus chienii*.

**Nothotsuga** Hu ex Page. (From Gk *nothos*, spurious, and *Tsuga*.) Pinaceae. 1 species, a monoecious, coniferous, evergreen tree, to 35m. Shoots slender, glabrous to sparsely pubescent, pendulous of tips. Winter buds ovoid-conic, acute to acuminate. Leaves narrowly linear-elliptic, 1–2.5cm×1–2mm, petiolate, dark green above, paler green beneath, entire, midrib conspicuous, ridged above and beneath, apex acute, base attached to cushion-like, persistent pulvinus. Male cones clustered, terminal. Female cones stalked, erect, resembling a miniature *Keteleeria fortunei*, cone, solitary, oblong-ovoid, 3–6×1–2cm closed; scales thinly woody, rhombic to ovate; bracts lanceolate, exserted 2–3mm; peduncle stiff, leafy. S China. Z8.

CULTIVATION Not yet cultivated outside of China, discovered 1930. Closely related to *Keteleeria* and to *Tsuga*, it will grow best under the same conditions as these. It can be expected to grow in the milder parts of Britain, but not to grow vigorously as summer temperatures are too low. Good growth can be expected in SE US, California, Mediterranean Europe, S Japan, N New Zealand and the moister regions of Australia. Propagation by seed, or grafting on to *Tsuga, Keteleeria* or *Pseudolarix*.

***N. longibracteata*** (Cheng) Hu. As for the genus.

For synonymy see *Tsuga*.

**Notobuxus** Oliv. (From Gk *nothos*, false, and *Buxus*.) Buxaceae. 7 species of shrubs or small trees formerly included in *Buxus*. Leaves opposite, entire, papery or leathery. Inflorescence fasciculate or a short cyme; male flowers with sepals 4, stamens 6, rudimentary ovary absent; female flowers with sepals 4, styles 3. Fruit a loculicidal capsule; seeds keeled. Tropical and South Africa; Madagascar. Z10.

CULTIVATION *N. macowanii* is very similar in appearance and habit to the common box, *Buxus sempervirens*, although it is not frost hardy. It is used in its native regions as a slow-growing hedge plant, and is sometimes grown in the intermediate glasshouse or conservatory as a pot plant. Grow in well-drained and moderately fertile soils in sun or light shade. Propagate by seed or semi-ripe cuttings.

***N. macowanii*** (Oliv.) Phillips. CAPE BOXWOOD. Shrub or small tree to 9m, slow-growing. Stems slender, green-brown, to 30cm diam.; young shoots pubesc. becoming glabrous. Lvs 1.5–2.5×0.4–1.7cm, glabrous, dark green, opposite, elliptic, apex obtuse, base narrowly-cuneate, midrib prominent above, lateral venation obscure. Fls unisexual, green: females solitary or with several male flowers; males in axillary cymes. Fr. ovoid; seeds trigonal, black, shiny. Winter. S Africa.

**Notocactus** (Schum.) Frič.
***N. alacriportanus*** (Backeb. & Voll) F. Buxb. See *Parodia alacriportana*.

*N.apricus* (Arech.) A. Berger. See *Parodia concinna*.
*N.arachnites* Ritter. See *Parodia crassigibba*.
*N.arechavaletae* (Speg.) Herter. See *Parodia ottonis*.
*N.concinnus* (Monv.) A. Berger. See *Parodia concinna*.
*N.corynodes* (Otto ex Pfeiff.) Krainz. See *Parodia erinacea*.
*N.crassigibbus* Ritter. See *Parodia crassigibba*.
*N.erinaceus* (Haw.) Krainz. See *Parodia erinacea*.
*N.floricomus* (Arech.) A. Berger. See *Parodia mammulosa*.
*N.fricii* (Arech.) Krainz. See *Parodia erinacea*.
*N.graessneri* (Schum.) A. Berger. See *Parodia graessneri*.
*N.grossei* (Schum.) Frič. See *Parodia schumanniana*.
*N.haselbergii* (Ruempl.) A. Berger. See *Parodia haselbergii*.
*N.herteri* (Werderm.) Buining & Kreuzinger. See *Parodia herteri*.
*N.leninghausii* (Schum.) A. Berger. See *Parodia leninghausii*.
*N.mammulosus* (Lem.) A. Berger. See *Parodia mammulosa*.
*N.minimus* Frič & Kreuzinger. See *Parodia caespitosa*.
*N.mueller-melchersii* Backeb. See *Parodia mueller-melchersii*.
*N.muricatus* (Pfeiff.) A. Berger, misapplied? See *Parodia concinna*.
*N.ottonis* (Lehm.) A. Berger. See *Parodia ottonis*.
*N.pauciareolatus* (Arech.) Krainz. See *Parodia erinacea*.
*N.rutilans* Daeniker & Krainz. See *Parodia rutilans*.
*N.schumannianus* (Nicolai) Frič. See *Parodia schumanniana*.
*N.scopa* (Spreng.) A. Berger. See *Parodia scopa*.
*N.submammulosus* (Lem.) Backeb. See *Parodia mammulosa*.
*N.tabularis* (Ruempl.) A. Berger. See *Parodia concinna*.
*N.uebelmannianus* Buining. See *Parodia crassigibba*.
*N.velenovskyi* (Frič) Frič. See *Parodia mammulosa*.
*N.vorwerkianus* (Werderm.) Krainz. See *Parodia erinacea*.
*N.werdermannianus* Herter. See *Parodia werdermanniana*.

**Notonia** DC.
*N.abyssinica* A. Rich. See *Kleinia abyssinica*.
*N.amaniensis* Engl. See *Kleinia amaniensis*.
*N.grandiflora* DC. See *Kleinia grandiflora*.
*N.grantii* Oliv. & Hiern. See *Kleinia grantii*.
*N.gregorii* S. Moore. See *Kleinia gregorii*.
*N.hildebrandtii* Vatke. See *Kleinia abyssinica* var. *hildebrandtii*.
*N.madagascarensis* Humbert See *Kleinia madagascarensis*.
*N.petraea* R.E. Fries. See *Kleinia petraea*.

**Notospartium** Hook. f. (From Gk *notos*, southern, and *spartion*, broom.) PINK BROOM; SOUTHERN BROOM. Leguminosae (Papilionoideae). 3 species of shrubs and trees. Mostly leafless in the adult plant with slender, flattened, weeping, branchlets, distinguished from the leafless species of *Carmichaelia*, and from *Chordospartium*, by the torulose linear pods. Flowers in pendulous lateral racemes; calyx bell-shaped, teeth 5, short, mostly uniform; standard obovate-obcordate, tapering to a short claw, wings oblong, shorter than keel, auricled at base, keel hatchet-shaped, obtuse; stamens 10, 1 free. New Zealand (South Is.). Z8.

CULTIVATION A rare plant in its native habitat, *N.carmichaeliae* grows in the damp shingle and sandy soils of submontane river valley sides at 250–650m/800–2110ft; it is also found on drainage terraces. Amongst the most attractive of New Zealand native shrubs, it is a graceful plant with smooth, arching, green stems, and a profusion of lilac-pink pea-flowers carried over long periods in summer. *N.glabrescens* makes a larger specimen of more lax habit, with pendulous, whip-like branches. Hardy to about −10°C/14°F, *Notospartium* spp. are suitable for a warm sheltered border or for the base of a sunny wall; protect at all costs from prolonged wet and cold winds.

Grow in a well-drained but moisture-retentive, humus-rich soils. *N.carmichaeliae* is tolerant of chalk soils. Provide support for older plants and protect young plants from prolonged winter frost using bracken litter or evergreen branches. Prune old and overgrown plants back to suitable new growth. Propagate from seed sown in the cold frame or glasshouse in spring or by semi-ripe cuttings in summer in a closed case with bottom heat.

*N.carmichaeliae* Hook. f. Shrub to 5m. Lvs to 0.6cm, present only on young plants, simple, obcordate or orbicular, emarginate to entire; branchlets rush-like, slightly flattened or subcylindrical, grooved, glabrous, to 5mm wide. Racemes to 5cm, 12–20-fld, sericeous, many, crowded; fls to 1cm, light purple to pink; axillary; cal. teeth triangular. Fr. to 2.5cm, slender, 3–8-seeded. Summer.

*N.glabrescens* Petrie. Resembles *N.carmichaeliae*, but larger with fls deeper purple, racemes more open, fr. larger. Round-headed tree to 9m. Upper branches ascending, lower pendulous; branchlets weeping, fine flattened, slightly grooved, glabrous, finally cylindric and tapering. Lvs triangular, inconspicuous scales. Fls in a crowd of axillary racemes, to 5cm long toward the end of the branchlet, each raceme carrying 15–25 blossoms, fls to 1cm; standard to 13mm diam., oval, erect, emarginate, white to purple-pink with a conspicuous purple blotch radiating from base, wing petals and keel oblong, much smaller than standard. Fr. to 2.5cm, 4–8-seeded. Late spring–early summer.

*N.torulosum* T. Kirk. Resembles *N.carmichaeliae* but of weaker, more slender habit, fls deeper purple, narrower, and never crowded on the sparse racemes with pedicels and cal. glabrous.

*N.exsul* F. Muell. See *N.carmichaeliae*.

**Notothlaspi** Hook. f. (From Gk *notos*, southern and *Thlaspi*.) PENWIPER PLANT. Cruciferae. 2 species of fleshy alpine herbs. Long taproot often produced. Leaves spathulate, petiolate, basal. Inflorescence a corymbose raceme; flowers large, fragrant; sepals 4; petals 4, white. Fruit a silicle, obovate-oblong, much compressed, broadly winged; seeds very numerous. Summer. New Zealand (South Is.). Z8.

CULTIVATION Grow in the alpine house, in a mix of 3:1 silver sand and flaked leafmould. *Notothlaspi* may appreciate a layer of small stones around its neck. Water moderately during growth and flowering, and keep dry, but not completely so, in winter. Move to a part-shaded frame in the hottest period of summer. Propagate from seed, sown ripe, in a mix of equal parts rubbed leafmould and fibrous loam, with 2 parts fine silver sand. Pot seedlings on directly to their permanent position, to minimize root disturbance.

*N.rosulatum* Hook. f. Erect, pyramidal herb, 7–25cm. Lvs radical, in a rosette or cushion, very numerous, overlapping, fleshy, white-hairy at first, becoming glabrous or nearly so, toothed. Flowering stem stout; fls white, crowded, in pyramidal raceme.

**Notylia** Lindl. (From Gk *notos*, back, and *tylos*, hump, referring to the recurved column apex.) Orchidaceae. Some 40 species of epiphytic orchids with or without pseudobulbs. Rhizome short. Pseudobulbs small, compressed, clustered, basally sheathed by leaves, apically unifoliate. Leaves fleshy or coriaceous, distichous, imbricate or equitant. Inflorescence a lateral raceme or panicle, arching to pendent, few- to many-flowered; flowers small; sepals subsimilar, free or connate at base, narrow, erect or spreading; petals similar to sepals, smaller, oblique; lip sessile or clawed, entire or obscurely lobed, disc callose or carinate; column slender or stout, footless, wingless, erect, with a long erect rostellum, anther erect, oblong, pollinia 2, waxy, ovoid. Tropical C & S America. Z10.

CULTIVATION Grow in intermediate conditions: see ORCHIDS.

*N.barkeri* Lindl. Pseudobulbs to 3×1cm, oblong to ellipsoid, compressed. Lvs to 20×4cm, coriaceous, broadly elliptic to ligulate, subacute to obtuse, pale green, apex obliquely tridenticulate. Raceme to 30cm, arching to pendent, many-fld; fls white to green-white, sometimes spotted yellow, faintly scented; sep. to 7×3mm, linear-lanceolate to elliptic-lanceolate, subacute to obtuse, concave, slightly inflexed, lateral sep. often connate forming a cleft synsepalum; pet. slightly shorter, narrower than sep.; lip to 6×2mm, short-clawed, ovate to narrowly triangular, subobtuse to acuminate, disc usually with a carinate callus; column to 3mm. Mexico to Panama.

*N.bicolor* Lindl. Pseudobulbs to 10×5mm, ovoid, compressed. Lvs to 5×1cm, linear-lanceolate to elliptic-lanceolate, fleshy, acuminate. Raceme to 10cm, few- to many-fld; peduncle very slender, erect to pendent; sep. to 15×2mm, white, linear-lanceolate, spreading, lateral sep. connate at base, falcate; pet. to 13×2mm, white to purple-lavender spotted dull purple, obliquely lanceolate; lip to 9×2mm, white to purple-lavender, short-clawed, basal portion linear, apical portion dilated, erose, spreading, disc with a grooved callus, spotted dark purple; column to 5mm, erect, glabrous, anth. large. Summer. Mexico, Guatemala, Costa Rica.

*N.bungerothii* Rchb. f. Pseudobulbs to 3×1cm, oblong, rugose. Lvs to 20×7cm, oblong, acute to obtuse, dark to olive green. Raceme to 45cm, pendent, densely many-fld; fls pale green to green-yellow; dorsal sep. to 8×2mm, lanceolate, curved, obtuse, lateral sep. to 7×3mm, connate, oblique, similar to dorsal sep.; pet. to 7×2mm, white marked yellow, linear-lanceolate, subacute; lip 6×2mm, white, short-clawed, ovate, base rounded or truncate, disc carinate; column to 3mm, pale green, terete, minutely pilose. Venezuela.

*N.carnosiflora* Schweinf. Pseudobulbs to 1cm, compressed to subcylindrical, apex unifoliate. Lvs to 6.5×2cm, oblong-elliptic, cuneate beneath. Infl. a basal raceme, arcuate, several-fld; fls fleshy, spreading; dorsal sep. to 7×3mm, oblong, acute, concave; lateral sep. connate, oblong; pet. to 5×1mm, oblanceolate-oblong, acute; lip to 4×2mm, ovate-triangular, unguiculate; disc slightly puberulent; column to 3mm, stout. Peru.

***N. mirabilis*** Schweinf. Pseudobulbs reduced to absent. Lvs to 14×3mm, equitant, obliquely linear-oblong to linear-elliptic, acute to subobtuse, fleshy. Panicle to 3.5cm, 1- to few-fld; peduncle very slender; fls membranous, spreading, pale lilac and dark violet; dorsal sep. to 4×2mm, ovate-oblong to ovate-elliptic, concave, acute, lateral sep. free, obliquely lanceolate, acute; pet. resembling lateral sep.; lip to 4×2mm, long-clawed, simple, ovate or obovate, apiculate, base auriculate; column to 2mm, erect, slender, clavate. Venezuela, Peru.

***N. pentachne*** Rchb. f. Pseudobulbs to 3×1cm, oblong to ovate-oblong, compressed. Lvs to 20×5cm, coriaceous, ligulate to oblong-lanceolate or elliptic, subacute to obtuse. Raceme to 35cm, pendent, slender, elongate, many-fld; sep. and pet. pale green to yellow, dorsal sep. to 10×3mm, lanceolate or oblanceolate, acute or acuminate, lateral sep. connate forming a synsepalum, bifid, acute or acuminate, recurved, pet. to 8×2mm, sometimes with a few orange spots, obliquely lanceolate, acute or acuminate lip to 6×3mm, white, long-clawed, dilated, to trulliform, acuminate, callus short, carinate; column to 5mm, slender, papillose. Panama, Colombia, Venezuela.

***N. rhombilabia*** Schweinf. Pseudobulbs to 20×6mm, narrowly cylindrical. Lvs to 14×2cm, linear to linear-oblong or elliptic-linear, acute to rounded, coriaceous, light green. Raceme to 25cm, many-fld, arching; fls pale yellow-green, fleshy; dorsal sep. to 8×3mm, deeply concave, oblong-lanceolate, acute, lateral sep. to 8×4mm, connate forming a synsepalum, oblong-elliptic, deeply concave; pet. to 8×2mm, linear to linear-oblanceolate, acute, falcate, reflexed-spreading; lip to 7×5mm, white, waxy, sessile, rhombic or ovate-rhombic, acute to acuminate, base rounded or cuneate, disc with a shallow longitudinal keel; column to 5mm, cream-white. Peru, Venezuela.

***N. sagittifera*** (HBK) Link & Klotzsch. Pseudobulbs to 15×6mm, inconspicuous, oblong. Lvs to 18×5cm, oblong or oblong-elliptic, obtuse, subcoriaceous, rigid, light green. Raceme to 30cm, arching, many-fld; fls clear green, the pet. with 2 round yellow spots; sep. to 7×3mm, membranous, deeply concave, linear-lanceolate, acute (lateral sep. connate forming a synsepalum), margins revolute; pet. to 6×2mm, linear-lanceolate, acute; lip white, to 5×2mm, fleshy, long-clawed, ovate-triangular, acute to acuminate, base truncate or cuneate; column to 3mm, pale green, apex geniculate. S America to Peru.

***N. wullschlaegeliana*** Focke. Pseudobulbs to 5×4mm, inconspicuous, ellipsoid to suborbicular. Lvs to 30×5mm, equitant, fleshy, obliquely oblong-lanceolate or elliptic-lanceolate, acute or subacute. Raceme to 5cm, subumbellate, basal, few-fld, arching; peduncle very slender; fls pale yellow-green or white marked purple, translucent, spreading; sep. to 7×2mm, lanceolate or linear-lanceolate, concave, acute, lateral sep. free; pet. to 6×2mm, obliquely linear-lanceolate, acuminate; lip to 6×1mm, short-clawed, oblong-linear at base to ovate-acuminate at apex, lateral margins irregularly toothed; column to 6mm, pale green, filiform, apex strongly recurved. S America to Peru.

***N. yauaperyensis*** Barb. Rodr. Pseudobulbs to 6×3mm, obliquely oblong. Lvs to 15×2cm, coriaceous, oblong to linear-oblong, obtuse. Raceme to 12cm, arching to pendent; fls white; dorsal sep. to 5×2mm, oblong or lanceolate to oblong-lanceolate, acute or subacute, lateral sep. linear to linear-lanceolate, basally connate, obtuse; pet. to 4×2mm, obliquely lanceolate to oblong-lanceolate, acute; lip to 4×2mm, fleshy, long-clawed, pubesc., ovate, obtuse, cordate at base, glabrous; column to 3mm, erect. Venezuela, Brazil.

***N. albida*** Klotzsch. See *N. barkeri*.
***N. bipartita*** Rchb. f. See *N. barkeri*.
***N. multiflora*** Lindl. See *N. sagittifera*.
***N. tridachne*** Lindl. & Paxt. See *N. barkeri*.

**Nouletia** Endl.
***N. pterocarpa*** (Cham.) Pichon. See *Cuspidaria pterocarpa*.

**Nuphar** Sm. (From *naufar*, Arabic name for Nymphaea.) COW LILY; SPATTERDOCK; YELLOW POND LILY; WATER COLLARD. Nymphaeaceae. Some 25 species of perennial, aquatic herbs. Rhizomes stout, creeping. Leaves large, entire, narrowly ovate to orbicular, with a basal sinus; floating lvs coriaceous; submerged lvs membranous. Flowers held above water surface, yellow and green, sometimes tinged purple, subspherical, solitary; sepals 4 to 6, coriaceous, broadly ovate to orbicular, inner sepals yellow, sometimes tinged green or red, outer sepals green; petals numerous, yellow, oblong or linear, smaller than sepals; stamens numerous, in several rows, inserted below ovary; ovary of 5–20 fused carpels, ovules numerous, style short or absent, stigma disc-like. Fruit berry-like, ovoid or conical, maturing above water, many-seeded. Temperature regions of N Hemisphere.

CULTIVATION Found predominantly in still and slow moving water, with *N. pumila* in the swamps of western Siberia, *Nuphar* spp. have similar requirements in cultivation to those of the hardy species of *Nymphaea*, although in general *Nuphar* spp. are more tolerant of shade and water movement and can become invasive where conditions suit. *N. japonica* is suitable for the large aquarium. *N. kalmiana* and *N. pumila* suit a water depth 30–45cm/12–18in., *N. japonica* requires depths to 75cm/30in., while the vigorous *N. lutea* thrives in depths to 2.4m/8ft.

***N. advena*** (Ait.) Ait. Lvs to 33×25cm, erect, usually standing above water surface, sometimes floating, broadly ovate to oblong, broadly rounded, lustrous green; sinus to 10cm, lobes triangular, spreading at right angles. Fls to 4cm diam.; sep. usually 6, to 35mm, broadly ovate to suborbicular pet. *c*20, to 8×5mm, yellow tinged red; stamens *c*200, usually 7 rows, fil. to 10mm, dull red; stigmatic disc with 10–24 rays. Fr. to 50mm diam., subglobose, green. E & C US, Mexico, W Indies. Z3.

***N. japonica*** DC. Floating lvs to 40×12cm, narrowly ovate to oblong, basally sagittate, glabrous above, pubesc. beneath when young; submerged lvs narrow, undulate, translucent. Fls to 5cm diam., yellow; sep. 5, to 2.5cm; pet. to 8mm, spathulate or oblong; stigmatic disc with some 11 rays. Japan. Z6.

***N. kalmiana*** Ait. Floating lvs to 10×7.5cm, broadly oblong to suborbicular, broadly rounded, glabrous above, slightly pubesc. beneath; sinus to 3.5cm, narrowly triangular; submerged lvs orbicular, thin. Fls to 18mm diam.; sep. 5, to 10×8mm, yellow, elliptic or obovate; pet. 7–10, to 6×3mm, orange, margins yellow, spathulate; stamens *c*35, in 3 rows; stigmatic disc with 6–10 rays. Fr. to 10mm diam., ovoid, usually red. E US. Z5.

***N. lutea*** (L.) Sm. YELLOW WATER LILY. Floating lvs to 40×30cm, ovate-oblong to suborbicular; sinus to 20cm; submerged lvs broadly ovate to orbicular. Fls to 6cm diam., malodorous; sep. 5, to 3cm, interior bright yellow, broadly ovate; pet. 18–20, to 10mm, spathulate; stigmatic disc with 15–20 rays. Fr. to 6cm. E US, W Indies, N Africa, Eurasia. Z4.

***N. polysepala*** Engelm. Lvs usually floating, to 40×25cm, ovate to oblong, broadly rounded, glabrous, dull green; sinus to 10cm, V-shaped, lobes acute or rounded. Fls to 7cm diam; sep. usually 9, to 5.5cm, oblong to orbicular, retuse or truncate, outer sep. green, interior tinged purple-brown; fil. yellow-green, anth. purple. Fr. to 6cm diam., ovoid to subcylindrical, light apple green to yellow. Northern N America. Z4.

***N. pumila*** (Timm) DC. Resembles *N. lutea*, except floating lvs to 14×13cm, broadly ovate to suborbicular. Fls to 3cm diam.; sep. 4 or 5, orbicular; pet. shorter, rounded; stigmatic disc with 8–10 rays. Fr. to 4.5cm. Europe, USSR, Japan. Z4.

***N. sagittifolium*** (Walter) Pursh. Floating lvs to 28×10cm, coriaceous, narrowly oblong to oblong-lanceolate; sinus to 3.5cm, V-shaped; submerged lvs to 36×7cm, undulate. Fls to 3cm diam.; sep. 6, to 2.5×2cm, oblong to orbicular, canary yellow tipped green; pet. and stamens pale yellow; stigmatic disc with 10–14 rays. Fr. to 3cm diam., lustrous apple green. SE US (Carolina). Z8.

***N. variegatum*** Engelm. Floating lvs to 28×22cm, ovate or oblong; sinus to 7.5cm, submerged lvs similar to floating lvs when present, thin. Fls to 4.5cm diam.; outer sep. green, inner sep. lemon yellow, tinged red toward base; pet. usually 16, subspathulate, clear yellow or sometimes bright green; stamens *c*150, usually in 6 rows, bright yellow; stigmatic disc with 7–25 rays. Fr. to 3cm diam., ovoid, green tinged red. N America. Z4.

***N. microphylla*** (Pers.) Fern. See *N. kalmiana*.

**Nutrients and plant nutrition**. Nutrients are mineral ions used by plants as building blocks to construct the proteins, fats and other compounds needed for growth. The essential nutrients required by plants are divided into the macronutrients – those needed in relatively large amounts (10s or 100s of kg/Ha), which are Nitrogen (N), Phosphorus (P), Potassium (K), Magnesium (Mg), Calcium (Ca) and Sulphur (S) – and the trace elements which are no less important but are only needed in g/Ha. These are Iron (Fe), Manganese (Mn), Copper (Cu), Zinc (Zn), Boron (Bo), Molybdenum (Mb) and Chlorine (Cl). There may be other trace elements that are needed in such small amounts that it is effectively impossible to prove the requirement, given that the uptake from sources such as the atmosphere and from water is inevitable.

Contrary to popular folklore it is too simplistic to say that 'nitrogen is for shoot growth, phosphorus is for roots and potassium for fruits and flowers'. There are many instances where nitrogen has promoted root growth on deficient soils, and vice versa with phosphorus and shoot growth. While it is true that different crops often give maximum performance when given different nutrients, (for example, leaf vegetables benefit from high-nitrogen feeds), all of the above elements are needed for building plant cells and must be supplied in adequate amounts.

In addition to these essential nutrients there are some 'beneficial elements' which can improve the growth of certain plants. The most commonly encountered example is sodium. This element can usefully be applied to plants from the beet and cabbage families which have developed from seaside habitats. However, sodium can be damaging to soil structure and should not normally be applied as a fertilizer without good reason.

NUTRIENTS IN SOILS. Very few soils are actually deficient in total amounts of plant nutrients. Deficiency symptoms more commonly arise because of some shortfall in the way, or the rate, at which the nutrients are made available. Resolving nutrient problems requires an understanding of how these nutrient-supply mechanisms work and of the implications of what may at first appear to be unrelated cultural operations.

Nutrients are taken up by plants as mineral ions dissolved in soil water. For prolonged growth and vigour there must be a constant supply of these nutrient ions. They originate in the following ways.

(a) *Weathering of soil minerals*. Mineral-rich rocks break down by the action of frost, water and organic acids. Rocks are the ultimate source of most soil nutrients but nitrogen is an important exception.

(b) *Breakdown of organic matter*. Organic matter from dead plant and animal remains is gradually broken down by soil organisms to release the constituent mineral nutrients. This process is called mineralization and is the source of a regular supply of nitrogen ions in particular.

(c) *Inputs from the atmosphere*. Many nutrients fall to earth dissolved in rain. This input, while low, is of great importance in some ecosystems. Inputs of nutrients are greater in areas with high levels of pollution. Nitrogen-fixing plants, including most legumes such as peas, can greatly increase the fertility of a soil by taking nitrogen from the soil air and converting it to organic matter.

Nutrient ions in solution are prone to leaching and would be very quickly lost from the soil unless there were some form of temporary storage. The most important mechanisms by which this is achieved are as follows.

(a) *Cation Exchange Capacity* (CEC). Cations (positively charged ions) are held by electrostatic charges on the surface of clay particles and organic matter. These stored nutrients are in equilibrium with those held in the soil solution so that, within broad limits, as the concentration in solution falls more ions are released from the store.

(b) *Chemical complexes between the ions*. Nutrient ions can combine with other nutrients or other soil minerals to form relatively insoluble salts. These can in turn break down again to release ions if the equilibrium with the soil solution changes. The relative solubility of different mineral elements changes dramatically with soil pH.

Plants quickly deplete nutrients from the soil solution that is immediately in contact with the roots. Ultimately these elements are replenished, quickly or slowly, from the soil stores, but continued plant growth depends initially on the transfer of ions in solution from elsewhere. There are two important mechanisms by which this is achieved.

(a) *Mass flow*. In this, dissolved nutrients travel with soil water as it drains or is taken up by plant roots. This mechanism is important for supplying the nutrients Ca, Mg, S, B, Cu, Zn, Fe, Cl, and N but does not supply sufficient P and K.

(b) *Diffusion*. Whenever nutrient uptake is greater than can be matched by the supply from mass flow, a concentration gradient is set up in the soil solution. Ions then move by the process of diffusion to maintain the supply to the plant roots.

Any problem that interferes with or slows the normal movement of water through the soil, such as drought or compaction, or any problem that breaks the continuous water connections through the soil, notably drought again, can severely limit the availability of nutrients to the plant. Water shortage can also limit nutrient uptake by restricting root growth.

Nitrogen is held primarily in organic matter and is therefore often concentrated in the top few centimetres of the soil. Summer drought can lead to nutrient shortages for deep-rooted plants long before they suffer from the direct effects of water shortage.

NUTRIENT LOSSES. Nutrients can be lost from the soil/plant system by leaching. This is where water draining through the soil takes dissolved mineral salts with it. It is only serious if the mineral ions move out of the root zone. Leaching into lower soil levels can actually be beneficial if it allows plants to continue nutrient uptake when there is surface drought.

Some elements are much more mobile than others. Nitrogen ions are prone to leaching, whereas phosphorus moves extremely slowly in soil. Leaching is worse on coarse soils where the drainage rate is high and the CEC is low. Leaching rates can therefore be reduced by increasing the CEC or by reducing the rate of water movement down the profile by improving structure and water retention. Adding clay or organic matter can help to meet both objectives. Vegetation also restricts leaching by recovering and recycling ions and by reducing water drainage, whereas leaving land fallow can deplete it of readily available nutrients. Reducing leaching is one of the benefits of green manures on unused land.

On sandy soils soluble fertilizers such as ammonium nitrate can be lost in just a few days of wet weather, making this an ineffective and uneconomic fertilizer. Slow-release fertilizers are often much better value on sands, even though they appear to cost more.

Fire is another means by which nutrients can be lost. If vegetation is burnt, certain elements such as nitrogen and sulphur form gases which join the atmosphere. Not all nutrients behave in the same way and a notable exception is potassium which is left behind in ashes (hence potash fertilizers).

Nitrogen can also be lost from the soil back to the atmosphere by the process of denitrification, which occurs as the result of bacterial action in waterlogged or anaerobic soils. A similar loss can occur by ammonia volatization, which happens when fertilizers or manures rich in ammonium compounds are applied to soils which are well aerated and have a high pH or have recently been limed.

The most obvious means by which nutrients are lost from a soil is by uptake into vegetation. Nutrients can be locked up in the biomass of large long-lived plants, especially trees, and it can be centuries before these enter the soil again. When plants are harvested, grazed or mown the nutrients removed can represent a loss from the system unless replaced as compost.

UPTAKE AND USE OF NUTRIENTS BY PLANTS. It is a truism that deficiencies only exist when there are insufficient nutrients to meet the demands of a given plant. However, different species vary in their demands and some show nutrient deficiencies more readily than others. Many crop varieties in particular have been bred to give high productivity, but this growth rate often relies on unusually high nutrient levels and they can therefore do poorly on a soil which would be perfectly adequate for most ornamentals and wild plants.

Plants can also show symptoms of nutrient deficiency if there is any problem associated with the health or vigour of root growth. This is particularly the case with immobile nutrients such as phosphorus – for adequate uptake the root system must explore the soil extensively.

NUTRIENT ANTAGONISMS. One of the most complex problems of plant nutrition is that not only are the absolute levels of a given nutrient important but also the relative proportions of two or more elements can affect plant growth and yield or influence the availability of other minerals. For example, adding extra nitrogen to a soil which is already deficient in phosphorus can increase the severity of the deficiency. Similarly, high potassium levels aggravate magnesium deficiency. Other antagonisms include N/K; K/Mg; Mg/K; P/K; P/Zn; Na/Ca; K/Ca; Mg/Ca; Ca/Mn; Cu, Zn, Co and Ni/Fe.

The opposite phenomenon is seen when addition of one nutrient improves the uptake or efficiency of use of another. These are called synergisms and include N/Mg and K/Fe.

DAMAGE FROM NUTRIENTS. Nutrients are not always beneficial and problems can arise if levels are too high. Firstly there can be an effect of salinity from excessive concentrations of any dissolved salt. Because of the quantities needed, this problem is most likely to occur when using soluble NPK fertilizers.

Some nutrients, notably zinc, copper and boron, can prove directly toxic at very much lower levels than would cause salinity effects. Boron in particular shows a very fine distinction between soil levels that are adequate as a nutrient, and levels which begin to reduce growth in sensitive plants. Fertilizing with this element should therefore not be undertaken too liberally, or without firm evidence that deficiencies do exist.

It is possible to see damage on some sensitive species at what would normally be regarded as relatively low levels of a given nutrient. For example, many Australasian plants are adapted to soils which are extremely deficient in phosphorus, and these suffer toxicity when planted in more ordinary substrates.

Nutrients can also sometimes produce undesirable growth responses in plants without actually being toxic. Nitrogen in excess is said to lead to a delay in flowering and fruiting, enhanced vegetative growth, a reduced root:shoot ratio and decreased winter-hardiness.

Excess nutrients, particularly nitrates, that leach from the soil can lead to problems of pollution of watercourses. This occurs when there are soluble ions in the soil, little or no root uptake and a large amount of soil water. It can arise from the addition of soluble fertilizers when crops are very small, especially on sandy soils, or from bare soil in winter. The problem of nutrient pollution is very much worse in areas where arable crops are grown.

### IDENTIFICATION OF NUTRIENT DEFICIENCIES

Identifying nutrient deficiencies can be very challenging. Often it relies upon the appearance of visual symptoms on the plant. However, while some symptoms are very diagnostic on some crops, in the majority of cases, particularly at low levels of deficiency, the visual clues can vary according to the availability of other nutrients and the type of plant. Confusion may also result because many other problems can cause similar symptoms, such as virus infection, physical root damage, waterlogging and herbicide damage.

Deciding which nutrient is causing a deficiency problem can also be difficult, although there are clues related to the mobility of the nutrients within the plant, and it is important to note whether the symptoms are affecting old or young leaves and the leaf margins or leaf veins.

The major problem with visual deficiency symptoms is that growth and yield can be affected long before there are obvious signs. Many farmers and vegetable growers therefore apply fertilizers annually, without waiting to see whether deficiency develops or not. This can however be expensive and may contribute towards pollution.

If more precision is required an assessment of the current nutrient status of the soil can be made by soil analysis. This can be achieved by laboratory tests, by the use of portable electrodes or with soil testing kits.

Soil analysis relies on the use of chemical extractants which remove nutrients at levels which are roughly equivalent to the amounts taken up by plant roots. Although a broad indication of fertility can be obtained, there are drawbacks to this approach as well, particularly concerning the interpretation of the results. Levels of nitrogen are particularly difficult to interpret, as the amount that is available in the soil after a cold wet winter tells us nothing about the likely levels in the summer. In addition, most soil test kits will only give readings for nitrogen as the nitrate ion. For vegetables grown at high pH this will be adequate, but it will be of no value for plants growing on acid ground where ammonium is important.

A soil is only deficient when the plant in question cannot obtain enough nutrients: both the demands and the root systems of a mature tree will be very different from those of a small vegetable seedling, for example. In addition, the more unusual the soil type to be tested the less certainty there is with regard to the accuracy of the tests.

Foliar analysis can be a more reliable technique as it gives a measure of how much nutrient has actually reached the plant. However, there has to be a comparison with the levels that would be expected in the leaves of a healthy plant of the same type and for many ornamentals this essential reference work is not readily available. The nutrient content of leaves is also affected by the age of the plant, the time of year, the leaf position and so on; there can be quite strong restrictions on the time of year the test is made. Foliar analysis can be difficult for amateur gardeners to carry out.

Some assessment of the status of new soil can be obtained by looking for 'indicator species'. Certain weeds and wild plants are much more likely to be present when nutrient levels are high. For example in Britain, stinging nettle is associated with soils that are high in phosphorus, whereas colonies of lupins, vetches or other legumes often denote nitrogen deficiency.

In practice it is often best to to understand the patterns of nutrient availability that are likely to operate on a given soil and to identify which crops and which seasons are likely to exhibit particular deficiencies. By combining moderate levels of precautionary feeding with an eye for possible deficiency symptoms, complicated tests are usually unnecessary.

### MACRONUTRIENT DEFICIENCIES

NITROGEN. Nitrogen is in many ways the most challenging plant nutrient to manage. It is also the nutrient needed in the greatest quantity by most plants. The only way that nitrogen can be stored in soils in the long term is as organic matter. This organic nitrogen is not available to plants until it is mineralized to inorganic ions by the activity of soil bacteria.

Because it relies on living organisms, the mineralization process is controlled by environmental factors such as water and oxygen supply, the presence of other nutrients, temperature, and pH. The breakdown is also affected by the chemical nature of the organic matter itself, notably the carbon:nitrogen ratio. To make cell material bacteria need these two elements in certain proportions. Any organic material that has a high C:N ratio, notably woody debris like sawdust, or straw, can be slow to decompose. To complete the breakdown under these conditions, mineralizing bacteria will take up free nitrogen from the soil, so adding some types of organic matter to a garden can actually reduce the nitrogen levels in the short term. It is for similar reasons that it is necessary to add nitrogen compounds to compost heaps when breaking down garden refuse.

During mineralization organic matter is first broken down into ammonium ions which, although soluble, are fairly well retained by soils with a good CEC. However, on substrates with a high pH, ammonium is rapidly converted by bacteria to the nitrite and nitrate anions (negatively charged ions) which are very soluble and are easily leached and lost from the soil. (Other soil elements that occur predominately in an anionic form, notably phosphate and sulphate, form strongly binding chemical complexes in soils which make them less soluble and less mobile.) Most plants seem to have little preference for ammonium or nitrate forms of nitrogen, although there is a tendency for those from habitats which have a low pH to respond better to ammonium fertilizers, and vice versa.

Nitrogen-fixing plants short-cut the above process by obtaining nitrogen directly from the air. The organic matter that they create is added to the soil when they die. In suitable conditions these plants can contribute as much or more N than would be added in a standard fertilizing regime. This organic matter also has a low C:N ratio and breaks down rapidly.

Nitrogen deficiency may occur under several circumstances. First, it may occur when land is low in organic matter, especially newly exposed subsoils, industrial spoil and sandy, droughted land. In extreme cases adding soluble fertilizers is only a short-term solution and may need to be repeated indefinitely. Overall applications of organic matter, or growing nitrogen-fixing plants, can resolve the problem more effectively. Secondly, it may exist on waterlogged soil and on topsoil which has been stored in heaps for a long time. The mineralization process will have been inhibited by anaerobic conditions and much of the free nitrogen will have been lost through denitrification. Thirdly, it can be found in spring following wet, cold winters when free nitrogen has been leached but the soil is still too cold for effective mineralization. Lastly, there may be a nitrogen deficiency following addition of large amounts of organic matter with a low C:N ratio.

*Deficiency symptoms.* Shoot growth is small and shoots are relatively few, thin, upright, and stiff; tillering and lateral growths are suppressed; the amount of foliage is small, and leaves are pale and yellow-green, developing high tints of yellow, orange, red, or purple as they mature; defoliation is premature. Flower-bud formation is reduced, and opening of the buds may be delayed; fruiting and tuber formation are poor, and fruits are generally small, highly coloured, sweet or 'woody' to taste, and store well; the barks of trees are often red-brown.

PHOSPHORUS. Phosphorus naturally originates from the weathering of rock minerals. It is stored without leaching on most soils, but it forms insoluble compounds at pH extremes which can lead to crop deficiency. This liming can increase phosphorus uptake on acid soils which may be directly the result of pH shift, a better root system, or more rapid organic matter breakdown. However, overliming can also cause deficiency by again immobilizing the phosphorus ions.

Induced deficiencies are very hard to correct by fertilizing because the added nutrients can themselves by rendered immobile. However, with phosphorus this process can take some time and soluble fertilizers can be effective in boosting plant uptake before the nutrient is converted to insoluble forms.

Plants vary in their need for phosphorus. Many legume crops, for example, have a high demand. The most important factor controlling the efficiency of phosphorus recovery is often the extent that the root system explores and ramifies through the soil. Phosphorus supply therefore varies dramatically from crop to crop and with different ages of any one crop. Young transplants can be prone to phosphorus shortages when mature plants would find an adequate supply. Symbiotic mycorrhiza are often important to plants on deficient soils, to extend the root system and to make phosphate uptake more efficient.

Some phosphorus is held in organic matter where it is slowly mineralized in a similar way to nitrogen. Because the mechanisms of phosphate release and availability are different, organic fertilizers can be of great importance on some soils and deficiencies may be corrected by adding manures.

Because of its immobility, relatively little of the phosphorus added in a fertilizer is either taken up by that year's crop or lost by leaching. Soils that have been fertilized for years have usually been slowly accumulating levels and therefore phosphorus deficiencies are becoming increasingly rare in intensively farmed areas.

*Deficiency symptoms.* Many of the effects are similar to those of nitrogen deficiency. Shoots are small, thin, and upright, and tillers and lateral growths are few; leaf characters may be similar to or differ markedly from those of nitrogen deficiency; colour may be bluish-green and dull purple or bronzed tints may develop, but tints may be lacking and older leaves may show marginal scorching, as in potato, or brown spotting, as in blackcurrant. Flower-bud formation, fruiting, seed and tuber formation are poor, and flowers may open late, all these points resembling nitrogen deficiency effects, fruits are often of variable colour, soft, markedly acid, and unpleasant to taste.

POTASSIUM. Potassium is a simple cation that is highly mobile in soils. It is effectively held by the CEC of most soils, but it does have a tendency to leach and become deficient on free-draining, acidic and sandy substrates. It is a fairly simple process to correct a deficiency through fertilization.

During the winter exchangeable potassium in the soil is replenished from mineral reserves. At this time plant growth and potassium uptake is slow, soil water deficiencies do not limit the movement of the ions to cation exchange sites, and weathering processes, frost and rainfall in particular, are more active. Potassium deficiency is therefore less likely to be seen in the spring. Potassium is not stored to any appreciable degree in organic matter.

*Deficiency symptoms.* In the early stages of potassium deficiency, shoot growth is restricted and thin, and later the internodes become progressively shorter and the plants may appear squat; in fruit trees, shoot dieback is serious in acute instances. Leaves may be blue-green or somewhat chlorotic, and the margins or tips usually die and turn brown or grey-brown (leaf scorch and tip burn); on some plants (clovers and potato) the leaves show characteristic spotting patterns as well as marginal effects. Flowering is not greatly reduced in the early stages, as occurs with nitrogen and phosphorus deficiencies, and lateral growths may appear excessive, giving plants a bushy appearance; flowers may open early and fruits set normally, but they drop excessively and cropping is poor; fruits are notably small and may appear immature, texture often being woody and flavour subacid and sweet.

CALCIUM. Calcium is rarely deficient or rendered unavailable in soils. However it is not very mobile, so deficiencies can arise if there is some problem with root growth. The effect of calcium as a plant nutrient is usually dwarfed by its effect as a modifier of soil pH; the relative absence or abundance of calcium has a profound impact on the availability of other nutrients.

*Deficiency symptoms.* The effects of calcium deficiency are mainly evident at growing points, such as the tips of shoots, and root development is especially poor. Other common effects are collapse of leaf margins or mesophyll tissues, wilting of shoots, petioles, or pedicels, and die back of shoots and flower trusses. Tuber formation is severely affected and tubers, if formed, may be deformed and useless, as in potato.

MAGNESIUM. Magnesium deficiency is uncommon but can occur on sandy acid soils or, because of poor availability of the nutrient, on very highly calcaereous soils. Magnesium is mobile on acid soils but if the pH is above 6.5 it becomes fairly immobile. Deficiencies on perennial plants on limy soil can thus be hard to treat.

*Deficiency symptoms.* The main effects of magnesium deficiency are shown in the foliage and in premature defoliation. The leaf effects are generally very striking and even beautiful. The leaves may become yellow (chlorotic) or they may develop characteristic tinting patterns, either centrally between the veins, with the marginal areas remaining green, or around the margins, when the effects spread inwards towards the leaf centre; necrosis may follow tinting, and chlorosis, or necrotic areas may develop without these effects. The older leaves are first to be affected, and the symptoms often spread rapidly to the younger leaves. Affected leaves defoliate prematurely, and defoliation may progress extremely rapidly.

SULPHUR. Sulphur is only deficient on a few fairly unusual soils. The problem can be aggravated by the burning of vegetation in these areas. It has never been shown to be deficient in the UK and is unlikely to become so in industrial regions while pollution has increased the amount of sulphur that falls to earth dissolved in rain.

*Deficiency symptoms.* The effects of this deficiency are generally similar to those of nitrogen deficiency, leaves being small, pale green, and in some plants developing bright tints.

SODIUM. Though possibly not essential for any plant, sodium is certainly beneficial for some crops, including beets, celery and turnips. The effect is more marked if potassium is limited, especially on cabbages, cereals and peas. Sodium is usually well retained in accessible form in soils, but leaches more readily than potassium. Although harmful in association with chloride (as common salt) an excess of sodium alone seldom occurs, except as an accumulation from irrigation in semi-arid areas.

*Deficiency symptoms*. In plants of the beet family sodium deficiency produces effects suggesting lack of water. Thus the leaves wilt readily in hot weather and dry out around the margins, and the old foliage often withers and falls.

### MICRONUTRIENT DEFICIENCIES

Micronutrients are needed in such small amounts by plants that true deficiencies are rare. Most soils have more than enough of the nutrients to supply crops indefinitely, even if no more were ever added. However, micronutrient deficiency can readily be induced by drought and high pH, especially on sandy soils which have comparatively low nutrient supplies and a poor buffering ability.

Excesses of micronutrients are common on unusual soils such as mine spoils or where pollution has occurred. Chlorine damage is common where road salt has been applied near trees. Again plants can differ in their susceptibility to these problems.

*Manganese* deficiency can occur on overlimed sandy soil, especially if much organic matter has been added. Manganese toxicity can occur on soils with a low pH.

The effects of manganese deficiency vary according to the crop. Chlorosis of the leaves is common in trees and shrubs, and the condition can usually be readily distinguished from iron deficiency chlorosis in two ways: first, the effects for manganese are usually more severe on older leaves than on the young tip leaves; second, the chlorosis begins near the margins of the leaves and progresses intervenally in a V-shaped pattern towards the midrib; as for iron, severe chlorosis may be followed by dieback of shoots. On brassicas the chlorosis develops as an intervenal mottle and may be indistinguishable from iron deficiency effects. On some crops (potato and beet) characteristic lesions and spots are developed on the leaves, and on peas and many kinds of beans the flat surfaces of the cotyledons of the seeds show characteristic brown lesions, known in peas as Marsh Spot.

*Iron* deficiency is common on limy soils and chalks, especially on plants adapted to acid soils. The characteristic effect of iron deficiency is chlorosis of the young leaves at the tips of shoots, the condition decreasing progressively down the shoots; the chlorosis develops as a well-defined pattern over the leaf surface, in which the small veins remain green and are all clearly visible in the early stages (cf. manganese); shoot tips often die and shoot and branch dieback may be serious in trees; fruits are highly flushed and have a pale 'ground' colour, while sugar content may be low.

*Copper* deficiency can occur where much lime and organic matter has been added, but only if the soil levels are low in any case. If the levels are high deficiencies cannot be induced. The main effects of copper deficiency occur at growing points, where the tissues may either fail to develop properly or die back; leaves may be dull, blue-green, or chlorotic. In trees, shoot and branch die-back may be accompanied by gumming (e.g. *Prunus*, etc.), and deformed, swollen growths and bark tissues may separate from the wood. The dying back of shoots from copper deficiency in apples and pears is known as 'summer dieback' since the shoots make normal growth each spring and dieback follows during the summer. Plants tend to develop vegetative growths rather than flowers.

*Boron* deficiency occurs on droughted, sandy soils when they are limed. Many crops receive adequate boron even from these soils. Brassicas show the greatest tendency to become deficient. This deficiency results in lack of differentiation of meristematic tissues, leading to death of growing points and deformation of developing tissues. The positions of affected tissues differ for different plants, and the various characteristic effects produced in crops have been given descriptive names by growers (e.g. 'crown rot' and 'canker' of beet, 'hollow stem' and 'curd browning' of cauliflower, 'cracked stem' of celery, 'brown heart' of swedes and turnips, 'top sickness' of tobacco, 'hen and chicken' in grapes, and 'drought spot', 'cork', and 'corky core' in apples). Crops affected with boron deficiency are generally unsightly and commercially useless.

*Chlorine* deficiency is very rare in natural soils, although some crops such as barley and tobacco sometimes show improved yield or quality following additions. Deficiency has been reported in man-made potting composts. Symptoms of this deficiency so far have only been determined for tomato. On this plant the first effect to be observed is wilting of leaf tips, which is followed by chlorosis, bronzing and necrosis of the leaves. These symptoms progress basipetally. The growth of leaves, stems, and roots may be severely depressed and with acute deficiency the plants may fail to produce fruit.

*Molybdenum deficiency* is rare in the UK but more common in some other countries such as Australia, especially in pasture crops. Molybdenum differs from most other elements in that it becomes more available under alkaline conditions, and hence deficiencies can often be cured by liming.

The effects of molybdenum deficiency have still to be determined for many plants and most is known regarding the effects on brassicas, lettuce, tomato and poinsettias. Deficiency effects on brassicas and lettuce are shown by death of growing points and chlorotic mottling of the leaves, together with marginal cupping or failure of the laminae to develop ('whip-tail' of cauliflower). On tomatoes, leaves show chlorotic mottling and margins roll forward. Legumes may show nitrogen deficiency effects as the nodule bacteria are unable to fix nitrogen. Most other plants examined show death of the marginal tissues of the leaves.

*Zinc* deficiency can occur on limed acid sands but also on some organic soils. The symptoms are aggravated by excessive additions of phosphorus. This deficiency is characterized by dwarfing of shoots, due to shortened internodes, and leaves which are often small and narrow ('little leaf' effect) may become crowded to produce 'rosette' effects; some foliage develops chlorotic mottling, as in *Citrus* species ('mottle leaf'), or intervenal chlorotic patterns or bronzing tints.

NUTRIENT TOXICITY SYMPTOMS. The effects that an excess of any particular element may produce are very variable, especially as they typically depend on the supply of other elements. The effects recorded below are the more common ones observed, and concern elements producing important effects in practice.

*Nitrogen*. The main effects are succulent vegetative growth, dark green foliage, lack of flowering and fruiting, delayed ripening of growth, and promotion of deficiency effects of nutrients in short supply.

*Phosphorus*. Early ripening and inducing of deficiencies of other nutrients, particularly potassium and trace elements (e.g. iron, copper and zinc).

*Calcium* (as distinct from excess lime). Deficiencies of other basic nutrients, especially potassium, and to less extent magnesium, and trace elements (e.g. manganese).

*Sodium*. Deficiency of calcium.

*Iron*. Deficiency of phosphorus and may reduce levels of trace elements, particularly manganese.

*Manganese*. Excess of manganese is an important cause of crop failures on strongly acid soils. It may cause direct toxic effects or induce a deficiency of iron. In instances of toxicity, foliage may show chlorotic mottling or spotting or brown lesions, these effects often resembling those resulting from a deficiency of the element. Other leaf effects include lateral restriction of laminae, incurling and necrosis of leaf margins and discoloration of veins; petioles and stems may develop lesions with subsequent collapse and dying of leaves.

*Aluminium*. Excess of this element also causes injury on acid soils. The effects on above-ground portions of affected plants resemble those due to phosphorus deficiency, and aluminium may, in fact, induce this deficiency. Root growth is poor, and the roots appear swollen and stubby and lack fibre.

*Boron*. Marginal and intervenal scorching of older leaves are common effects. In *Citrus* spp., leaves may show irregular, orange-coloured areas, and small raised brown spots resembling gum pockets occur on the under surfaces of the tinted areas.

*Heavy metals* (copper, zinc, cobalt, nickel, chromium, lead, etc.). These metals all produce severe chlorosis and intervenal necrotic patterns, and in some instances leaves may be deformed and pigmented. The chlorosis may be largely or wholly due to induced iron deficiency.

*Chlorine*. In the form of the chloride iron, this element often produces brown marginal scorching similar to potassium deficiency (e.g. on red currant).

MANAGING NUTRIENT SUPPLY

The immediate response of many gardeners faced with a nutrient deficiency is to add fertilizer. However, if the real problem is linked to poor nutrient availability rather than low levels, fertilizing may be of limited or no benefit or alternative feeding strategies may be needed. For example, iron is present in huge amounts in soil yet deficiencies can result from a high pH. This can be corrected by foliar feeding, using special sequestrene compounds that remain soluble at high pH, or by adding bulky organic manures (which slightly acidify the soil and also produce their own natural sequestrenes).

The nutrient status of crops can also be modified, deliberately or accidentally, by many cultural practices. Mulching or irrigating reduces drought and improves nutrient movement, although over-irrigation can encourage leaching. Mulches or cloches will increase soil temperature and bacterial activity early in the year. Cultivating and aerating the soil increases the rate of organic matter breakdown and also influences the rooting depth and extent of the plants. Marling a sandy soil (i.e. adding soil rich in clay and chalk) or adding organic matter can improve structure, water retention and Cation Exchange Capacity.

When growing fruit the choice of rootstock affects the extent of rooting and hence the likelihood of nutrient deficiencies. The presence of grass in an orchard can also influence nutrient availability. Above all modifying the soil pH is one of the most powerful means available for altering nutrient availability of gardens.

*Reducing fertility*. It is not always desirable for soils to have high nutrient levels. In nature very fertile soils are dominated by a very few aggressively competitive plants. The decline of wildflowers in countryside areas can often be directly attributed to the increased use of fertilizers, particularly in species-rich grassland where the more attractive plants are outcompeted by vigorous grasses.

When growing crops or garden plants, competitors are removed by weeding and the desired plants are able to take advantage of the nutrients, but where this husbandry is not possible reducing the fertility can help to keep aggressive species under control. In particular, when creating new wildflower gardens, removing the topsoil before sowing the seed mix has often proved very beneficial, although the effect can look rather patchy for the first year or two.

**Nuttall, Thomas** (1786–1859). Botanist and plant collector. Born in Yorkshire, he was brought up by his widowed mother and, after a modest education, was apprenticed to his uncle, a printer, in Liverpool. He enjoyed a friendship with a doctor who was an amateur botanist and they walked the moors together. At 21, he went to the United States and settled in Philadelphia, working as a printer. He spent all his leisure time travelling, studying botany, collecting and naming the rich New World flora. As a result, he became acquainted with William Bartram, and Professor Barton at Philadelphia University.

In 1810, he made his first major expedition (financed by Barton) with the plant collector, John Bradbury. They travelled to the Great Lakes and St Louis and penetrated west of the Mississippi. The journey was fraught with dangers, including hunger, illness and hostile Indians but they returned in 1812 with a fine collection of plants, including *Yucca glauca* and *Ratibida columnifera*. Nuttall then went to England, published their findings in *Curtis's Botanical Magazine* and donated plants to the Liverpool Botanic Garden, but returned to the US in 1815. Back in Philadelphia, he published, in two volumes, the *Genera of North American Plants* (1818). This was a milestone in the recording of American flora and established his reputation as a botanist. Another major expedition in the southern United States, from 1818 to 1820, was equally arduous. He travelled over 5000 miles in 16 months in hot, humid conditions and suffered fevers which damaged his health. Amongst the plants he found on this journey were *Coreopsis tinctoria* and *Penstemon cobaea*.

From 1822 to 1834, Nuttall was curator of Harvard Botanic Garden. He continued his studies, particularly ornithology, and gave lectures, but found the settled academic existence tame and went on several plant-hunting trips, including Wyeth's expedition across the Rockies to California (1833–36). They were the first to describe many of the North American alpine flora – Nuttall found *Cornus nuttallii* near Fort Vancouver, and also collected Pacific flora on the Sandwich Islands. For long periods grizzly bear was the only food, and again Nuttall came close to death by starvation.

Reluctantly, in 1841, he left his adopted country to live, as he said, 'almost an exile' at Nutgrove, near Wigan, Lancashire, where he had become heir to his uncle's estate. He lived here for the rest of his life, barring one visit to the US in 1847, and worked on the culture of rare plants, especially rhododendrons.

He is remembered as a father of American botany and a self-taught scientist who found, collected and described many North American genera in a precise, fine literary style. His other publications include *Journal of Travels into Arkansas Territory* (1821); *An Introduction to Systematic and Physiological Botany* (1827) and *North American Sylva* (1842). He was elected Fellow of the Linnean Society in 1813. Torrey and Gray named the genus *Nuttallia* in his honour.

**Nuttallia** Raf.
***N. cerasiformis*** Torr. & A. Gray. See *Oemleria cerasiformis*.

**Nuxia** Comm. ex Lam. Loganiaceae. 15 species of trees and shrubs with fibrous bark. Leaves opposite or arranged in whorls of 3, elliptic, tip subacute to rounded, base cuneate, hairy or glabrous, sometimes tomentose below, often leathery, entire or saw-toothed. Flowers numerous, small, 4-parted, usually white, in terminal, round-topped panicles resembling those of *Buddleja saligna*; lower bracts usually leaflike, others small; calyx 5mm, subcylindrical, exterior an indumentum of minute hairs to thick pubescence, interior pubescent; corolla tube cylindrical, usually shorter than calyx, lobes recurved; stamens protruding. Fruit a bivalved capsule; seeds small. Arabia to Tropical Africa, Mascarene Is., S Africa.

CULTIVATION A highly ornamental shade tree for parks and gardens in frost-free zones, sometimes used in street and avenue plantings. In areas with dry winters it may tolerate light frosts, but in cool temperate zones needs the protection of the cool glasshouse or conservatory, as for *Logania*. Growth is slow in cool areas and *N. floribunda* does not tolerate drought. Plant on rich deep soils that retain moisture throughout the year, in sun or dappled shade. Propagate by semi-ripe cuttings in a closed case with bottom heat, or from seed, which is less reliable.

***N. floribunda*** Benth. KITE TREE. Tree or shrub 2–25m, with conspicuous leaf scars. Lvs 4–16×1–7cm, oblong-elliptic, entire, crenate or toothed; petioles 3–55mm. Fls white, fragrant. Fr. brown, usually longer than cal., glabrous. Tropical & S Africa. Z9.

**Nuytsia** R. Br. ex G. Don f. (For Pieter Nuyts, Dutch explorer of coastal southwestern Australia 1626–27.) FIRE-TREE; FLAME-TREE; CHRISTMAS TREE. Loranthaceae. 1 species, a terrestrial glabrous evergreen shrub or small tree to 7m, parasitizing the roots of grass. Leaves 2.5–10×0.3–0.6cm, opposite, subopposite or occasionally lanceolate, apex acute to rounded, narrowing to base, whorled, sessile, veins pinnate. Inflorescences terminal, clustered in fascicles, axis to 25cm; flowers unisexual in crowded triads, sessile, bracteate, with median flower bisexual, lateral flowers male; calyx to 1.5mm, toothed; petals 6–8, to 1.5cm, linear, erect, free, brilliant orange-yellow; stamens 6–8, unequal; ovary unilocular, ovules several. Fruit 1cm, brown dry, 3-winged; seeds viscous. W Australia. Z9.

CULTIVATION Unusual in its family in that it is terrestrial and not parasitic, *Nuytsia* requires glasshouse treatment in cool temperate zones similar to that described for *Acacia* and establishment on a grass host.

***N. floribunda*** (Labill.) R. Br. ex G. Don f. As for the genus.

**NYCTAGINACEAE** Juss. FOUR O'CLOCK FAMILY. Dicot. 34 genera and 350 species of trees, shrubs and herbs, often with unusual secondary growth with concentric rings of vascular bundles or alternative rings of xylem and phloem. Leaves opposite, simple; stipules absent. Flowers usually bisexual, often in cymes, subtended by large and often coloured involucre and when reduced giving a 1-flowered pseudanthium with calyx-like involucre and corolla-like calyx; calyx (3–)5(–8) fused sepals, tubular, with valvate to plicate lobes, often corolla-like; corolla absent; stamens (1–) as many as calyx (–30); filaments of unequal length, sometimes basally connate; annular nectary-disc often around ovary; ovary superior, of 1 carpel; style long, slender; ovule 1, basal. Fruit an achene or nut, often enclosed in persistent base of calyx-tube; seed with large embryo, endosperm absent; perisperm copious, starchy. Some are edible or have medicinal uses such as *Mirabilis, Neea, Pisonia. Tropical and warm regions, especially Americas, few temperate. Abronia, Bougainvillea, Mirabilis, Nyctaginia, Pisonia.*

**Nyctaginia** Choisy. (From Gk *nyx*, night, and *gignomai*, I become.) Nyctaginaceae. 1 species, a viscid, branched, perennial herb, erect or decumbent, to 40cm. Roots tuberous. Leaves to 9×6.5cm, opposite, ovate to triangular, usually sessile. Flowers hermaphrodite in long-peduncled, capitate cymes, subtended by involucral of bracts; calyx funnel-shaped, limb 5-lobed, patent; perianth to 4cm; deep red, stamens 5–8. Fruit a turbinate, ribbed achene, involucral bracts persistent. SW US, N Mexico. Z9.

CULTIVATION From arid soils and dry rocky slopes, *Nyctaginea* is cultivated as for *Mirabilis*.

***N. capitata*** Choisy. SCARLET MUSK FLOWER. As for the genus.

**Nycteranthus** Necker.
***N. canaliculatus*** (Haw.) Schwantes. See *Sphalmanthus canaliculatus*.
***N. salmoneus*** (Haw.) Schwantes. See *Sphalmanthus salmoneus*.
***N. splendens*** (L.) Schwantes. See *Sphalmanthus splendens*.

**Nycterinia** D. Don.
***N. capensis*** (Walp.) Benth. See *Zaluzianskya capensis*.
***N. lychnidea*** D. Don. See *Zaluzianskya lychnidea*.
***N. maritima*** Benth. See *Zaluzianskya maritima*.
***N. villosa*** (F.W. Schmidt) Benth. See *Zaluzianskya villosa*.

**Nyctocalos** Teijsm. & Binnend. (From Gk, *nyx*, night, and *kalos*, beautiful, referring to the nocturnal flowers.) Bignoniaceae. 3 species of climbers. Leaves pinnately 3-foliolate, or pinnate with 5 pinnae, pinnae elliptic, glandular-punctate above, apex acuminate, margin entire. Flowers erect, fragrant, opening at night; calyx cupular, truncate, 5-toothed; corolla nearly actinomorphic, tube long, narrow, swollen at throat, 5-lobed, lobes overlapping; stamens 4 or 5, equal or unequal, filaments glabrous; style filiform. Fruit a flat capsule, apex acuminate, edges parallel; seeds orbicular in wing. SE Asia. Z10.

CULTIVATION As for *Macfadyena*.

***N. cuspidata*** Miq. Pinnae 6–18×3.5–10cm, ovate or obovate or oblong, apex acuminate to cuspidate, base rounded; petiole to 5cm; rachis to 3.5cm. Fls cream; pedicels to 1cm; cal. 6mm; cor. tube 15–19cm, to 6cm across at widest, lobes rounded, to 2cm; stamens 4, unequal, sometimes with rudimentary fifth stamens. Capsule 16–24×4.75cm; seed and wing to 4×3cm. Assam, Philippines, Celebes.

***N. assamica*** Hook. f. See *N. cuspidata*.
***N. brunfelsiaeflorus*** Miq. See *N. cuspidata*.
***N. macrosiphon*** Teijsm. & Binnend. See *N. cuspidata*.
***N. thomsonii*** Hook. See *N. cuspidata*.

For further synonymy see *Tecoma*.

**Nyctocereus** (A. Berger) Britt. & Rose.
***N. serpentinus*** (Lagasca & Rodriguez) Britt. & Rose. See *Peniocereus serpentinus*.

**Nymphaea** L. WATER LILY. (From Gk *nymphe*, a water-nymph, referring to the habit.) Nymphaeaceae. Some 50 species of aquatic, perennial herbs. Rhizomes erect or horizontal, submerged, sometimes tuberous, stoloniferous. Leaves usually floating, alternate, simple, broadly ovate to orbicular, subcoriaceous, entire to dentate, glabrous or pubescent, base deeply cleft into 2-lobes, subpeltate; petioles usually elongate, glabrous or pubescent. Flowers solitary, floating or emergent, bisexual, showy, fragrant, opening diurnally or nocturnally; sepals usually 4, free; petals many, free, mostly white, red, yellow or blue, grading into stamens; stamens numerous, multiseriate, anthers bilocular; ovary of 5–45 fused carpels, with stigmatic rays. Fruit berry-like, subglobose, many-seeded, maturing under water; seeds with a floating aril. Cosmopolitan distribution.

CULTIVATION Species from cooler regions are suitable for permanent positions in the pools and lakes of temperate gardens, one of the most important factors for success being the selection of appropriate species and cvs for the given depth of water. Depth requirements range from 15–30cm/6–12in. for *N. tetragona* and its hybrids, making them suitable for even the smallest stretches of water, including half barrels in the patio or courtyard garden. The majority of *N.* Laydeckeri Hybrids are grown at 30–60cm/12–24in, and those of *N.* Marliacea at 90cm/36in., although the tiny 'Mary Patricia' requires only 15–30cm/6–12in., and the more robust 'Carnea' and 'Rosea' need up to 1.2m/48in. of water above the crown, as does *N. tuberosa* and its cultivars.

Deep-water species, at depths of 2–2.5m/6–8ft for larger-scale plantings, include *N. alba* cultivars and hybrids such as 'Gladstoniana', with semi-double, starry white flowers. A similar diversity is seen in tropical species. *N. mexicana, N. sulfurea, N. heudelotii, N. elegans* and its variety 'Nana', are suited to tropical glasshouse; most other species, in similar protected environments, require a depth of 45–75cm/18–30in. Grow vigorous hybrids such as 'Ted Uber' and 'Yellow Dazzler' in 105cm/42in. of water and provide *N. gigantea* with a depth of 120cm/48in.

A number of species make attractive cut flowers, especially those where blooms are held clear of the water surface, as in *N. odorata* 'Eugene de Land' and 'William B. Shaw', both highly fragrant. Cut with 5–10cm/2–4in. of stem and apply a small spot of wax at the petal bases to prevent their closing at night.

Plant in baskets or into the pond floor into a low-fertility, loamy medium with a low fresh organic matter content, in water with a pH 6.0–7.0. Position with full sun away from disturbance by waterfalls, fountains and pumps. When necessary feed with a slow-release fertilizer placed into the baskets or in the near vicinity of root systems. At planting time remove adult leaves and damaged roots and treat cut surfaces with charcoal. With rhizomatous species and their hybrids, set tubers vertically with the fibrous roots spread out beneath. In both cases, the crown must be just at the surface of the medium, when topped with the final layer of pea gravel. Lower into the water slowly to expel air, and gradually increase depth as growth progresses to the appropriate level. In larger expanses of water, plant roots into a packet of soil wrapped in hessian, place carefully in water and allow to sink. Temperate species are generally cold hardy where temperatures fall to −15°C/5°F and below, provided that they have the protection of a sufficient depth of water above the crown (about 22–30cm/9–12in.) to protect from freezing. Alternatively, tubers can be lifted and stored in cool conditions if kept moist and protected from vermin. Most of the frost-tender species may be treated as annuals in temperate gardens.

Grow tropical species with a water temperature of 18–21°C/65–70°F in summer, 10°C/50°F in winter. Large tubers may not be easy to overwinter but most can grown on annually from smaller basal tubers, which have been stored in moist sand at 10°C/50°F over winter and brought into growth in full sun in spring. As the first floating leaves emerge plant into their flowering site, gradually increasing the depth of water over the crown.

Propagate temperate spp. by division in late spring/early summer. When plants become overcrowded, flowers are smaller and fewer and foliage is lifted out of the water. Division is usually necessary every third or fourth year, at slightly longer intervals with smaller and less robust varieties. Remove and replant vigorous side growths. Propagate tropical spp. by division or by removal of pieces of rhizome with a sprouting eye; pot up into a small immersed pot, pot on until roots fill a 10cm/4in. pot and then plant out. Increase viviparous tropical types by removal of young plantlets borne in the leaf blade sinus, potting up into a sandy medium immersed in water at 15–18°C/60–55°F. Pot on and sustain growth throughout their first winter.

Increase *N. tetragona*, *N. t.* 'Alba' and species also by seed. After pollination the developing seed head will sink; enclose in a light muslin bag to ensure that no seed is lost. Gather seed after about 10 days immersion, or immediately as it resurfaces. Sow with the surrounding pulp in a finely graded propagating mix, covered by about 2.5cm of water. Prick out as the first floating leaves appear and gradually raise the water level as growth proceeds. Sow tropical species at 23–27°C/75–81°F and grow on through their first winter.

Waterlily beetle, *Galerucella nymphaeae*, can be a destructive pest, adults overwinter amongst pondside vegetation, laying eggs on upper leaf surfaces in late spring. The emerging larvae feed on foliage and flowers eating holes in the blade and around the margin. Pupation usually takes place on the foliage and depending on conditions 2–3 generations may be produced in a season. Hosing down foliage, so that adults and larvae can be consumed by fish, and maintaining good winter hygiene at the pond edge offer some measure of control. The waterlily aphid, *Rhopalosiphum nymphaea*, attacks many soft-leaved aquatics during the summer, distorting foliage and flower stems and discolouring flowers. Eggs overwinter on *Prunus* spp., especially plum and blackthorn, but also on flowering cherries; large-scale landscape plantings with *Prunus* spp. at the waterside will almost certainly engender difficulty in maintaining a healthy population of *Nymphaea* spp. A tar oil winter wash on nearby *Prunus* spp. may help reduce aphid populations; hose down aphids into the water. Other pests include the China mark moth, *Nymphula stagnata* and *N. nympheata*, which shred the leaves; also affected by false leafmining midge and caddis fly.

Waterlily leaf spot, *Ovularia* and *Cercospora* spp. being causal agents, shows as dark rotting patches on leaves which eventually disintegrate. Remove and destroy affected parts. The precise cause of crown rot in water lilies is not well defined at present; the syndrome, whereby the crown suffers a putrid rot and rapidly collapses, is sometimes devastating of stock, and although affected plants may regenerate they remain a potential source of infection. The syndrome appears to be multifactorial and stress related; a number of pathogens have been isolated that seem likely to be involved; these include *Phytopthera, Phythium* and *Fusarium* spp., and gram negative rod bacteria. Whilst fungal agents have been controlled by routine micropropagation procedures of sterilization and disinfection, the bacterial associations are a limiting factor in the production of clean stock by micropropagation; the successful production of clean stock demands isolation and precise identification of the causal strains of bacteria and fungus followed by selection of specifically effective antibiotics and fungicides; this research is ongoing.

***N. alba*** L. EUROPEAN WHITE LILY. Robust herb. Lvs to 30cm diam., broadly ovate to suborbicular, entire, dark green above, red-green to yellow beneath, crowded on rhiz. Fls to 20cm diam., white, opening diurnally, floating, only faintly fragrant; sep. lanceolate, green tinged red-brown; pet. 20–25, broadly ovate; anth. yellow to orange; carpels 10–20, stigma yellow. Eurasia, N Africa. Z5.

***N. amazonium*** Mart. & Zucc. Lvs to 32×26cm, broadly ovate to elliptic, entire or subentire, green spotted purple-brown above,, purple-brown beneath, lobes usually overlapping; petioles purple, apex pubesc. Fls to 12cm diam., floating, cream-white or pale yellow; sep. to 8×3cm, dark green lined purple; pet. 16–28, to 5.5×2.5cm; stamens to 200, pale yellow; carpels 20–38. C America, Tropical S America. Z10.

***N. ampla*** (Salisb.) DC. Robust herb. Lvs to 40cm diam., suborbicular, subentire, green spotted purple-black above, red-purple spotted black beneath, lobes acute. Fls to 13cm diam., white; sep. ovate-lanceolate, exterior green, lined black; pet. 7–21, ovate-lanceolate, outer pet. tinged yellow-green; stamens to 190, yellow; carpels 14 to 23. Tropical & subtropical America. Z10.

***N. blanda*** G. Mey. Lvs to 21×19cm, broadly elliptic to suborbicular, chartaceous, entire, glossy green above, paler green beneath, lobes distant, subacute. Fls to 10cm diam., floating, cream-white to pale yellow; sep. to 5cm, ovate-oblong, green; pet. 12–20, in whorls of 4, to 3.5cm, ovate to oblong; stamens to 100, cream-white or yellow; carpels 20–40. C America, northern S America. Z10.

***N. caerulea*** Savigny. BLUE LOTUS. Lvs to 40cm diam., orbicular or suborbicular, entire or undulate, green above, green spotted purple beneath, sinus usually closed, lobes subacute. Fls to 15cm diam., pale blue, emergent, opening diurnally; sep. broadly lanceolate, green lined and spotted purple-black; pet. 14–20, lanceolate; stamens to 75; carpels 14–21. N & tropical Africa. Z10.

***N. calliantha*** Conard. Lvs to 28×23cm, ovate to suborbicular, entire, green above, green with purple margin beneath, deeply cleft. Fls to 15cm diam., light blue, pink or violet; sep. to 7cm, lanceolate, green with few black spots near margin; pet. *c*17, lanceolate; stamens to 100, yellow. C & SW Africa.

***N. candida*** Presl & C. Presl. Closely resembles *N. alba* except all parts similar. Lf lobes touching, lowest pair of lobes beneath curved toward each other. Fls to 7.5cm diam., scentless, line of sep. attachment sharply angular; pet. 15–18; stamens 30–70; carpels 14–25. N Eurasia. Z4.

***N. capensis*** Thunb. CAPE BLUE WATER LILY. Lvs to 40cm diam., floating, orbicular or ovate-orbicular, strongly dentate-undulate, green, spotted purple beneath when young, lobes acute, overlapping. Fls to 20cm diam., bright blue, opening diurnally, sweetly fragrant, emergent; sep. narrowly ovate-triangular, green, spotless; pet. 20–38, elliptic-lanceolate, shorter than sep.; stamens 120–220; carpels 24–30. S & E Africa, Madagascar. 'Eastoniensis': lvs serrate; fls steel blue. var. *zanzibariensis* (Casp.) Conard. Lvs smaller, tinged purple beneath; fls larger, to 30cm diam., deeper blue. 'Azurea': fls light blue. 'Jupiter': fls large, dark violet blue, scented, sepals purple interior. 'Rosea': lvs tinted red beneath; fls pale pink flushed red. Z10.

***N. ×chrysantha*** Marliac. (*N. rubra* × *N. mexicana.*) Lvs green mottled brown above. Fls yellow to yellow-vermilion; stamens bright orange. Garden origin.

***N. citrina*** Peter. Closely resembles *N. mexicana* except fls larger, to 15cm diam., fragrant, stellate. Lvs to 25cm diam., suborbicular, green above and beneath, lobes rounded. Pet. *c*22; stamens to 125; carpels *c*23. E Africa. Z10.

***N. colorata*** Peter. Resembles *N. stellata*. Rhizome short, erect. Lvs to 12.5cm diam., suborbicular, dark green with pale green venation above, green-brown beneath, strongly dentate-sinuate towards base, lobes overlapping. Fls to 10cm diam., light blue; sep. bright blue towards apex, obtuse; anth. violet. Tanzania. Z10.

***N. ×daubenyana*** hort. (*N. caerulea* × *N. micrantha.*) Lvs viviparous. Fls 5–18cm diam., 20cm above the water, blue, opening in the morning. Garden origin.

***N. elegans*** Hook. Lvs to 18cm diam., suborbicular or broadly ovate, thin, entire or slightly undulate, dark green above marked purple-black when young, bright red-purple beneath spotted blue-purple, lobes broadly separated. Fls to 13cm diam., pale violet, opening diurnally, fragrant; sep. lanceolate, dark green, dotted and lined black; pet. 12–24, lanceolate, exterior surface green; stamens 80–145, yellow, apices blue; carpels 15–25. Texas and N Mexico to Guatemala. Z9.

***N. fennica*** Mela. Lvs to 12×9cm, elliptic-cordate, lobes acute or obtuse, sometimes overlapping. Fls to 7cm diam., white to rose-pink, cupular; sep. ovate-elliptic, forming sharp angle at line of insertion; pet. 10–15, lanceolate, concave; stamens *c*50, anth. to 3mm. Finland. Z4.

***N. flavovirens*** Lehm. Vigorous. Lvs to 45cm diam., suborbicular to ovate, subentire to deeply sinuate, green above, pale green or sometimes red beneath. Fls to 20cm diam., white, strongly fragrant, opening diurnally, emergent; sep. green, sometimes lined black, lanceolate; pet. 16–20, acuminate, exterior surface tinged green; stamens *c*60, deep yellow; carpels 12–15. Mexico, S America. Over 20 cvs and close hybrids. 'Astraea' (*N. astraea*): fls star-shaped, blue shading to white centre, stamens yellow. 'Mrs C.W. Ward' ('Red Star'): fls rosy red, stamens golden yellow tipped pink. 'Purpurea' ('Blue Star'): fls vivid purple, centre gold. 'Stella Gurney' ('Pink Star'): fls large, pale pink. 'William Stone': fls large, dark blue, violet at centre, stamens gold tipped blue. Z10.

***N. gardneriana*** Planch. Rhiz. ovoid. Lvs to 21×15cm, suborbicular to elliptic, entire, green above, green mottle rusty brown beneath, lobes acute to rounded. Fls cream-white, floating; sep. to 8cm, ovate-oblong, green; pet. 16–28, in distinct whorls of 4, to 6cm; stamens 45–125, cream-white; carpels 13–35. S America. Z10.

***N. gigantea*** Hook. AUSTRALIAN WATER LILY. Tuberous. Lvs to 60cm diam., ovate to orbicular, undulate, dentate, green above, green tinged pink to purple beneath, lobes often overlapping, finely dentate. Fls to 30cm diam., sky blue to blue-purple, scentless, opening diurnally, emergent; sep. ovate to elliptic, green, margins and exterior surface often blue; pet. 18–50, exceeding sep., obovate; stamens 350–750, bright yellow; carpels 12–20. Tropical Australia, New Guinea. Z10.

***N.×helvola*** hort. *(N. tetragona × N. mexicana.)* Hardy. Lvs to 6cm, red blotched brown above and beneath; fls to 5cm diam., canary-yellow, sterile. Garden origin. Z6.

***N. heudelotii*** Planch. Lvs to 11cm, ovate to orbicular, entire or subentire, green above, red-purple flecked black beneath. Fls to 5cm diam., blue-white; sep. ovate-lanceolate, exterior lined purple and spotted black, pet. 5 to 8, lanceolate, acute; stamens 11–16; carpels 4–10. Angola. Z10.

***N. jamesoniana*** Planch. Rhiz. ovoid to cylindrical, stolons absent. Lvs to 24×20cm, elliptic, entire, green sometimes flecked black above and beneath, lobes acute, obtuse or rounded. Fls cream-white, floating; sep. to 6.5cm, ovate, green; pet. 12–20 in distinct whorls of 4, to 4.5cm; stamens 35–85, cream-white; carpels 19–33. Tropical & subtropical Americas. Z10.

***N. lotus*** L. EGYPTIAN WATER LILY; LOTUS; WHITE LILY. Robust. Lvs to 50cm diam., suborbicular, undulate-serrate, dark green above, green or brown and usually pubesc. beneath, lobes sometimes overlapping. Fls to 25cm diam., white, sometimes tinged pink, opening diurnally or nocturnally, slightly fragrant, emergent; sep. broadly ovate, exterior surface with white venation; pet. *c*20, rounded; carpels *c*30. Egypt to tropical & SE Africa. var. ***dentata*** (Schum. & Thonn.) Nichols. Lvs glabrous; fls white; pet. narrow; fil. with an apical purple spot. C Africa. Z10.

***N. mexicana*** Zucc. YELLOW WATER LILY. Rhiz. tuberous, spreading by runners. Lvs to 18cm diam., floating or emergent, ovate to orbicular, subentire to dentate-undulate, green blotched brown above, green-purple to deep purple beneath, lobes acute or obtuse, sometimes overlapping. Fls to 13cm diam., pale to bright yellow, slightly fragrant, floating or emergent; sep. lanceolate to elliptic, green, margins pale brown; pet. 12–23; stamens *c*50; carpels 7–10. Florida, Texas and Mexico. Z9.

***N. micrantha*** Guill. & Perrott. Vigorous. Lvs to 7×5cm, round-cordate, entire, pale green above, red dotted violet-black beneath, lobes acuminate, spreading. Fls to 23cm diam., white to bright blue; sep. narrow lanceolate; pet. 10, narrow lanceolate; stamens numerous, fil. white. W Africa. Z10.

***N. odorata*** Ait. FRAGRANT WATER LILY; POND LILY. Hardy. Rhiz. horizontal. Lvs to 25cm diam., orbicular, entire, dull dark green above, usually purple and rough beneath, lobes obtuse. Fls to 15cm diam., white, usually floating, sweetly fragrant, opening diurnally; sep. ovate-lanceolate, green, exterior surface tinged red-brown; pet. 23–32, ovate to lanceolate; stamens 55–105; carpels 13–25. E US. Over 20 cvs and close hybrids: 'Eugene de Land': fls pale orange-pink, stamens gold, scented, held above water. 'Exquisita': fls small, star-shaped, rose. 'Helen Fowler': fls large, deep pink, very fragrant, held above water. 'Roswitha' ('Buggele'): fls rich rose red. 'Sulphurea Grandiflora' (*N. odorata × N. mexicana*): lvs dark green, marbled; fls very large, stellate, bright rich yellow. 'William B. Shaw': fls large, flat, creamy pink, internal zone of dark red fine petals. var. ***rosea*** Pursh. Fls to 10cm diam., deep pink, strongly scented. E US. Prolifera': fls abundant. Z3.

***N. pubescens*** Willd. Lvs to 25cm, ovate or broadly oblong, floating, dark green above, dull purple-green and pubesc. beneath, undulate. Fls to 20cm diam., white, opening in evening; sep. to 9cm, obtuse, exterior surface green with white venation; pet. broadly ovate. India to Philippine Is, south to Java and Australia. Z10.

***N. rubra*** Roxb. INDIA RED WATER LILY. Closely resembles *N. lotus* except lvs to 45cm diam., dark bronze-red, pubesc. beneath; fls to 25cm diam., deep red-purple. India. 'Rosea': fls soft red, abundant. Z10.

***N. rudgeana*** G. Mey. Lvs to 36cm diam., suborbicular, irregularly dentate, green or sometimes purple above, green or purple-brown beneath, lobes dentate. Fls cream-white to light yellow, sometimes tinged pink, emergent or sometimes floating; sep. to 8cm, ovate, green or yellow-green; pet. 12–29, to 5.5cm; stamens 40–185, white-cream to light yellow; carpels 11–31. Northern and eastern S America. Z10.

***N. stellata*** Willd. Lvs to 15cm diam., suborbicular to elliptic, irregularly dentate-sinuate, bright green sometimes blotched brown above, pink to purple beneath. Fls to 12cm diam., pale blue to pink or white, emergent, opening diurnally; sep. exterior light green, interior blue-white; pet. 11–14, lanceolate; stamens 33–54, pale yellow with blue apices; carpels 10–17. S & SE Asia. 'Berlin': fls large, sky blue. Z10.

***N. stuhlmannii*** (Schweinf.) Gilg. Lvs to 25×21cm, ovate to orbicular, entire, green above and below, lobes obtuse, diverging. Fls to 15cm diam., bright yellow, sweetly fragrant; sep. obovate, yellow-green; pet. *c*22, broadly obovate; stamens *c*125, orange-yellow; carpels *c*23. Africa. Z10.

***N. sulfurea*** Gilg. Rhiz. erect, stout. Lvs to 5.5cm, broadly ovate to suborbicular, entire, red-green above, dark red beneath. Fls to 7cm diam., deep sulphur-yellow, fragrant, opening diurnally; sep. lanceolate, tinged purple; stamens 40–50, anth. bright yellow; carpels 12–14. Angola. Z10.

***N. tetragona*** Georgi. PYGMY WATER LILY. Hardy. Lvs to 10×7.5cm, ovate, entire, dark green blotched brown when young above, dull red beneath, lobes acute, diverging. Fls to 5cm diam., white or sometimes faintly lined purple, floating, slightly fragrant; sep. ovate to oblong, exterior surface green; pet. 8–17, ovate to oblong; stamens *c*40, anth. golden yellow; carpels 6–8. NE Europe, N Asia to Japan, N America. 'Alba': lvs small, oval, purple beneath; fls to 2.5cm diam., white. 'Helvola' ('Pygmy Yellow'): lvs dull green marbled brown; fls vivid yellow, stamens orange. 'Hyperion': fls dark amaranth. 'Johann Pring': fls to 5cm diam., rich pink, inner ring stamens light orange, outer ring dark pink. 'Rubis': fls deep red, lacking white dots on outer petals. 'Rubra': lvs tinted purple, red beneath; fls dark red, stamens orange. Z2.

***N. tuberosa*** Paine. Robust, hardy. Rhiz. horizontal. Lvs to 38cm diam., orbicular, entire, green above and beneath, lobes acuminate. Fls to 23cm diam., pure white, floating or emergent, sometimes faintly scented, opening diurnally; sep. rounded, green; pet. *c*20, obovate or subspathulate; stamens 50–100; carpels *c*14. NE US. Z3.

***N. cultivars.*** TROPICAL DAY-BLOOMING HYBRIDS. (white): 'Alice Tricker' (improved form of 'Mrs George H. Pring'): vigorous; fls large, pet. broad, white. 'Mrs George H. Pring' ('White Star') *('Mrs Edward Whitaker' × N. ovalifolia)*: lvs large, blotched rich brown; fls to 25cm diam., star-shaped, white with a hint of cream, stamens yellow tipped white, scented. (yellow): 'Trailblazer': lvs bright green, tinted purple below; fls star-shaped, deep yellow. 'Yellow Dazzler': lvs very large, fls large, flat, stellate, lemon yellow, held high, abundant. (pink): 'Afterglow': fls combine pink, orange and yellow. 'Enchantment': lvs oval, dotted; fls rich salmon pink, scented. 'General Pershing' *('Mrs Edwards Whitaker' × 'Castaliiflora')*: lvs pink, large, tinted purple; fls large, deep pink, fragrant, held to 30cm above water. 'Pink Pearl': fls vivid silvery pink, stamens yellow tipped pink, held above water. 'Pink Platter': lvs bright green marbled rich brown; fls open, soft pink; viviparous. (red): 'American Beauty' *(N. flavovirens 'Williams' × N. colorata)*: lvs large, orbicular, edges waved, veined; fls large, soft magenta, centre yellow. 'Jack Wood': lvs dotted brown; fls raspberry red, centre gold, scented. (purple): 'Mrs Martin E. Randig': lvs bronze beneath; fls dark purple, sep. pink, scented; viviparous. 'Panama Pacific': lvs bronze, veins marked red; fls deep plum, stamens gold, anth. purple. (blue): 'August Koch' *('Mrs Woodrow Wilson' × 'Blue Beauty')*: lvs dark green, flushed pink beneath; fls to 25cm diam., blue, stamens orange, fls held above water. 'Blue Beauty' ('Pennsylvania', 'Pulcherrima') *(N. caerulea × N. capensis* var. *zanzibariensis)*: lvs very large, long-lobed, edges waved, dark green spotted brown; fls deep blue with central gold disc, stamens yellow, anthers violet, scented, sepals marked black. 'Henry Shaw' (form of 'Castaliiflora'): lvs soft green, spotted brown above, tinted pink beneath; fls soft blue, scented, stamens yellow tipped blue. 'Leopardess': lvs dark green, splotched deep brown; fls cobalt blue, scented. 'Margaret Randig': vigorous; lvs dark green spotted bronze; fls large, petals wide, rich deep blue, scented. 'Mrs Edwards Whitaker' ('Castiflora' × *N. ovalifolia)*: lvs orbicular, margins waved; fls large, to 30cm diam., lavender blue, fading to silver, stamens yellow.

TROPICAL NIGHT-BLOOMING HYBRIDS. (white): 'Missouri' *('Mrs George C. Hitchcock' × 'Sturtevantii')*: lvs marbled purple, edges indented; fls very large, to 40cm diam., petals wide, snow white, held above water. 'Sir Galahad': vigorous; lvs large, waxy; fls star-shaped, cool white, stamens yellow. 'Wood's White Knight' *('Sir Galahad' × 'Missouri')*: fls light cream, stamen deep yellow. (pink): 'Mrs George Hitchcock' *('Omarana' × 'Omarana')*: lvs tinted copper, edges wavy; fls large, clear pink, stamens orange. 'Rosa de Noche': lvs large, tinted red; fls pink shading to apple blossom toward yellow centre. 'Sturtevantii' *(N. lotus × 'Devoniensis')*: lvs tinted red to copper, undulating; fls large, pearl pink, scented, held above water. (red): 'Emily Grant Hutchings': lvs small, edges wavy, flushed bronze; fls large, to 30cm diam., cupped, rich pink-red, stamens purple. 'Mrs John A. Wood': lvs tinted deep red; fls star-shaped, burgundy. 'Red Flare': lvs rich mahogany; fls star-shaped, vivid red, scented.

HARDY HYBRIDS. (white): 'Gladstoniana' ('Gladstone') *(seedling of N. tuberosa × N. alba)*: lvs round, dark red; fls very large, snow white, pet. thick, incurving, stamens gold. 'Hermine' ('Hermione') *(selection of N. alba)*: lvs ovate, dark green; fls white, pet. long, sep. bright green. 'Gonnere' ('Crystal White', 'Snowball') *(N. tuberosa 'Richardsonii' × ?)*: lvs large; fls large, round, pure white, sep. green. 'Gloire de Temple-sur-Lot': large; fls very double, blush pink aging to white, pet. incurving, stamens yellow. 'Virginalis': lvs tinted purple; fls semi-double, pure white, stamens yellow, sep. tinted pink. (yellow): 'Charlene Strawn': fls yellow, held above water, scented. 'Solfatare': lvs dark green marbled dark red; fls star-shaped, soft yellow with red hues. 'Sunrise': lvs elliptic, sometimes marked brown, tinted red beneath; fls to 20cm diam., bright yellow, scented. (sunset): 'Comanche': lvs purple when young; fls small, rich orange turning copper, held above water. 'Graziella': lvs dull green marked purple and brown; fls very small, orange-red, stamens orange. 'Sioux': lvs bronze, marbled brown; fls buff yellow turning peach then deep orange-red. (pink): 'Amabilis' ('Pink Marvel'): lvs large, rich green; fls large, to 25cm diam., star-shaped, flesh pink, darkening later, stamens gold, later orange. 'Fire Crest': fls deep pink, stamens red, petals pointed, very profuse, well scented. 'Lustrous': lvs copper when young; fls silky pale pink, stamens yellow, sepals pink inside, profuse. 'Pink Opal': lvs tinted bronze; fls double, cupped, soft pink to coral red, held above water, buds globose. 'Pink Sensation': lvs rounded; fls to 20cm diam., petals oval, stellate, rich pink, held above water. 'Ray Davis': fls very double, delicate, stellate, shell pink. 'Rene Gerard': fls open, rose pink with crimson marks near centre. 'Rose Arey': lvs tinted red; fls large, star-shaped, rose pink, stamens yellow, anise scented. (red): 'Attraction': lvs large; fls large, to 25cm diam., vivid red dotted white, stamens deep red-brown with gold top, sepals tinted pink. 'Charles de Meurville': strong-growing; lvs olive green; fls large, deep claret, striped white from tip. 'Ellisiana': fls small, claret, stamens orange, profuse, early-flowering. 'Gloriosa' ('Glory'): large; lvs tinted bronze; fls large, to 15cm diam., deep red. 'James Brydon' ('Brydonia Elegans'): large; lvs tinted purple, sometimes spotted dark red; fls large, double, cupped, bright red with metallic sheen, stamens deep orange tipped yellow, scented. 'Splendida' ('Splendide'): lvs dull green; fls ruby red, darkening with age, stamens orange. 'William Falconer': lvs purple when young, green with red venation; fls erect, blood red, stamens yellow.

***N.flava*** Leitn. See *N.mexicana*.
***N.pygmaea*** Ait. See *N.tetragona*.
***N.venusta*** Hentze. See *N.alba*.
***N.zanzibariensis*** Casp. See *N.capensis* var. *zanzibariensis*.

**NYMPHAEACEAE** Salisb. WATER LILY FAMILY. (including Barclayaceae (End.) Li). Dicot. 6 genera and 60 species of aquatic herbs, with rhizomes or tubers, often with alkaloids; vessels absent; root hairs from specialized cells and scattered vascular bundles (like many monocots) or a single ring. Leaves alternate on rhizome, usually rounded cordate and floating; stipules median-axillary or absent. Flowers solitary, bisexual, regular, aerial, insect-pollinated, hypogynous to epigynous; calyx 4–8(–14) free sepals, sometimes petaloid (*Nuphar*), corolla (0–) 8-numerous free petals, inserted around top of ovary, often passing into stamens; stamens numerous, spirally arranged and usually free and laminar, with elongate microsporangia, or transitional to forms with differentiated filaments and anthers; ovary superior to inferior, of (3–)5–35, more or less fused carpels; ovules numerous; placentation parietal. Fruit berry-like, often irregularly dehiscent through swelling of mucilage within; seeds arillate, with hooked hairs or glabrous; cotyledons 1 or 2, distinct or arising as lobes from common primordium. Some have edible seeds and rhizomes, i.e. *Euryale*. Cosmopolitan. *Euryale, Nuphar, Nymphaea, Victoria*.

**Nymphoides** Hill. (From Gk *nympha*, nymph, and *-oides*, resembling.) FLOATING HEART. Menyanthaceae. 20 species of aquatic perennial herbs. Rhizomes creeping; stems elongate. Leaves floating, long-stalked, ovate to orbicular, deeply cordate at base, margins entire or undulate. Flowers yellow or white, axillary or 1 to many on slender stalks arising from petioles, the flowering nodes sometimes with clusters of tuberous, short spur roots; corolla subrotate, lobes 5, entire or fringed; stamens 5, inserted at base of corolla; stigma bifid; ovary 1-celled. Fruit a capsule. Cosmopolitan.

CULTIVATION *N.peltata*, with beautifully marked leaves and lemon-coloured flowers, is a useful plant for colonizing large areas of water; the slightly more tender *N.aquatica* and *N.cordata* are more suitable as floating aquatics for smaller ponds or containers. Cultivate as for *Nymphaea* in full sun. *N.indica* is frost sensitive and is best in indoor aquaria (temperature 18°C) with high light levels in cool-temperate regions. Propagate by division in spring or by separation of young plantlets in autumn; sow seed as for *Nymphaea*. Easily damaged or killed outright by formalin when this is used against algae.

***N.aquatica*** (Walter) Kuntze. BANANA PLANT; FAIRY WATER LILY. Lvs 3.5–15cm diam., suborbicular to reniform, thickly fleshy, reticulate and pitted beneath, entire or repand. Flowering nodes with clusters of short, swollen roots. Fls 1.2–1.75cm diam., white; pet. unfringed. Seeds rough-textured. Eastern N America. Z6.

***N.cordata*** (Elliott) Fern. Lvs 2–2.5cm diam., ovate, deeply cordate at base, obscurely pitted beneath. Flowering nodes with clusters of slender tuberous roots. Fls to 1.2cm diam., cream or white, borne in umbels; pet. unfringed. Seeds smooth. Eastern N America. Z5.

***N.indica*** (Thwaites) Kuntze. WATER SNOWFLAKE. Lvs to 15cm diam., usually far smaller, orbicular, pale glossy green. Fls borne in profusion, ephemeral; pet. to 1cm, white stained deep yellow at centre, covered in white glandular hairs or densely papillose, margins fringed. Tropics. Z10.

***N.peltata*** (S.G. Gmel.) Kuntze. YELLOW FLOATING HEART; WATER FRINGE. Freely stoloniferous. Lvs 5–10cm diam., ovate-orbicular, repand, mottled. Flowering nodes lacking spur roots, with 2 opposite lvs. Fls to 2.5cm diam., sometimes more, bright gold-yellow, long-stalked, held above water in umbels; pet. short-fringed. Europe, Asia; naturalized US. Z6.

***N.lucunosa*** (Vent.) Kuntze. See *N.aquatica*.
***N.nymphaeoides*** Britt. See *N.peltata*.
For further synonymy see *Limnanthemum* and *Villarsia*.

**Nypa** Steck. (The vernacular Moluccan name for this palm.) MANGROVE PALM. Palmae. 1 species, an unarmed, pleonanthic, monoecious palm. Stem subterranean, immersed or prostrate, dichotomously branched. Leaves pinnate, erect, to 7m; petioles terete; rachis terete, angled distally; pinnae single-fold, reduplicate, coriaceous, to 90cm, regularly spaced along rachis, midrib prominent, chestnut brown, with papery scales beneath. Inflorescence interfoliar, erect, 5–6×branched: male flowers borne on pendent branches, yellow, perianth segments 6, similar, stamens 3; female flowers borne on apical branches forming a globose head, perianth segments 6, similar, free; carpels 3, separate. Fruits developing from 1 carpel, smooth, angled, with stigmatic remains, fibrous, to 12.5cm in terminal cluster, dispersed by sea. Malay Archipelago to Bay of Bengal, Solomon and Ryuku Is., tropical Australia. Z10.

CULTIVATION *N.fruticans* occurs in mangrove swamp, in tidal estuaries and in brackish waters, where it grows in water or is subjected to daily inundation. It has been used in its native regions in erosion control, and is widely grown for thatch and basket-making and for the sap, fermented as palm wine. Fresh seed needs warm and permanently moist conditions for germination. See also PALMS.

***N.fruticans*** Wurmb. As for the genus.

For illustration see PALMS.

**Nyssa** L. (For Nyssa, a water nymph: *N.aquatica* grows in swamps.) TUPELO. Nyssaceae. 5 species of deciduous trees, to 30m. Leaves alternate, lacking stipules, entire or toothed. Flowers unisexual, in pedunculate unisexual or bisexual heads at base of new growth; calyx minutely lobed; petals 5, small, green; stamens 10, surrounding a grey-blue nectary disc. Fruit usually a 1-seeded drupe. Early summer. Eastern N America, E Asia.

CULTIVATION Naturally gregarious in their native American wetland or swamp habitats. *Nyssa* spp. are best planted in groups for their brilliant autumn colours and attractive, drooping winter framework. They look particularly effective reflected by the water of ponds or lakes. *N.sylvatica* is tolerant of pollution, maritime areas and shade. Plant when dormant in deep, moisture-retentive, neutral to alkaline soil on sheltered sites in sun or part shade. Use container-grown plants or small specimens (up to 30cm/12in. high) with a large rootball as root disturbance is much resented. Propagate from stratified seed (5°C/40°F for three months), or by layers and semi-ripe cuttings in late summer.

***N.sinensis*** Oliv. CHINESE TUPELO. Similar to *N.sylvatica* but 10–15m and more spreading. Lvs oblong-lanceolate, apex acuminate, base broad-cuneate to rounded, to 20×7.5cm, sparsely pubesc. throughout and tinged red when young, becoming nearly glabrous. Autumn colour brilliant red and yellow, usually surpassing that of *N.sylvatica*. C China. Z7.

***N.sylvatica*** Marshall. BLACK GUM; PEPPERIDGE; SOUR GUM. Broadly columnar to conical, to 20–30m, lower branches often drooping. Lvs variable, ovate to elliptic or obovate, apex abruptly acuminate, base cuneate, to 15×7cm, entire, downy on the veins beneath at least when young; petiole to 3cm, downy. Male heads 2cm across with numerous short-pedicelled fls; female heads smaller, with 2–4 fls. Fr. ovoid, 1cm, blue-black. Lvs colour brilliant red and orange in autumn. Eastern N America. 'Jermyns Flame' and 'Sheffield Park' selected for autumn colour. var. ***biflora*** (Walter) Sarg. SWAMP TUPELO. To 15m, base of trunk swollen when growing in water. Lvs to 9×3.5cm, more leathery than typical variety, oblanceolate. Female fls borne in pairs. SE US. Z3.

**NYSSACEAE** Dumort. TUPELO FAMILY. (Including Davidiaceae.) Dicot. 3 genera and 8 species of deciduous trees. Leaves alternate, simple; stipules absent. Flowers more or less regular, small, bisexual or unisexual (plants polygamo-dioecious, subdioecious or monoecious), in heads or racemes or solitary; calyx a 5-toothed rim or almost absent; corolla 5 (–10) petals; nectary disc usually present (absent in *Davidia*); stamens (8–) 10 (–15), usually in 2 whorls, outer opposite petals, in bisexual flowers usually as many as and alternate with petals; ovary inferior, of 1–2 fused carpels, 1–2-loculed, with 1–2 basally united styles; ovule 1 per locule, apical, pendulous, anatropous. Fruit a drupe, the endocarp with 1-several locules; seed with straight embryo; endosperm oily with hemicellulose. Some yield timber and edible fruits (*Nyssa*). N America and E Asia. *Davidia, Nyssa.*

# O

**Oakesia** Wats. See *Uvularia*.

**Oakesiella** Small. See *Uvularia*.

**Oberonia** Lindl. (From Oberon, the fairy-king; an allusion to the quaint and variable forms of this plant.) Orchidaceae. Some 330 species of epiphytic orchids, lacking pseudobulbs. Stems absent or very short, obscured by a laterally compressed fan of overlapping, fleshy leaf bases. Leaves flattened, carinate-conduplicate, oblong or linear, sword-shaped, acuminate. Inflorescence terminal, usually incurved, usually arched, flowers very small, crowded; sepals subequal, often reflexed; petals narrower, sometimes dentate; lip sessile from column base, usually trilobed, spreading, base concave, lateral lobes often enveloping the column. Old World Tropics. Z10.

CULTIVATION Curious epiphytes grown for their flattened fans of sword-shaped leaves and short racemes of green flowers. Because of their growth habit, cultivation in sphagnum-lined pouches of a fine bark mix attached to vertically suspended rafts is advised. All species require light shade and buoyant, humid, intermediate conditions. Water and syringe throughout the year except in cold weather.

***O. disticha*** (Lam.) Schltr. Lvs to 3.5×1cm. Spike slender, pendent, 4–5cm; fls bright ochre to orange-yellow; sep. ovate to triangular, broad; pet. linear; lip loosely enveloping column, base saccate, apex bilobed, margins serrate. E & W Africa.

***O. iridifolia*** (Roxb.) Lindl. Lvs 4–6, 5–25×1–2.5cm. Infl. dense, decurved, to 18cm; fls to 1mm diam., pale green or brown; sep. subequal ovate, reflexed; lip orbicular, midlobe broad, rounded, bilobed, entire or erose, apex cleft, lateral lobes fringed. Himalaya, Burma, Philippines, Pacific.

***O. kanburiensis*** Seidenf. Lvs to 8.5×10cm. Infl. equalling or exceeding lvs. Bracts irregularly fringed; fls ochre to yellow, pet. pale yellow; sep. entire, to 1mm; pet. larger, ovate, coarsely fringed; lip to 1.3mm, lobes fringed, midlobe 1–2mm wide, bilobed. Thailand.

***O. brevifolia*** Lindl. See *O. disticha*.

**Obregonia** Fric. (For Alvaro Obregon, President of Mexico.) Cactaceae. 1 species, low-growing cactus; stem mostly simple, 5–20(–30)cm diam., depressed, pale green or tinged brown, tuberculate, becoming tuberous at base and with carrot-like taproot; tubercles 5–15×7–15mm, triangular, arranged as in a rosette, acuminate; areole apical; spines 0–5, to 15mm, pale, weak, soon deciduous. Flowers 2–3.6×2.5cm, in woolly stem-apex, almost white; pericarpel and tube well-developed, naked; tepals narrow, 1–1.5mm wide; stamens sometimes sensitive as in *Lophophora*; filaments pink. Fruit 16–25×3–6mm, clavate, white, fleshy then dry; floral remnant deciduous; seed almost circular, *c*1.3×1.5mm, black-brown, shiny; relief low-domed; hilum medium, oblique, impressed. Summer. NE Mexico (Tamaulipas). Z9.

CULTIVATION Grow in a cool frost-free greenhouse (min. 2–7°C/36–45°F), use 'standard' cactus compost: moderate to high inorganic content (more than 50% grit), pH 6–7.5; full sun; low air-humidity; keep dry from mid-autumn until early spring, except for light misting on warm days in late winter.

***O. denegrii*** Fric. As for the genus. The wild populations of this interesting species have been heavily exploited by commercial collectors and importation of habitat-collected specimens is now prohibited. The species can be propagated easily, if slowly, from seed.

For illustration see CACTI AND SUCCULENTS.

**Ochagavia** Philippi. (For Sylvestris Ochagavir, Minister of Education in Chile in 1853.) Bromeliaceae (Bromelioideae). 3 species of stiff, shrubby, perennial herbs, often more or less erect-stemmed. Leaves many, linear, toothed and spinose, in a utricular rosette. Inflorescence on a short scape, globose or in a subracemose head, short, many-flowered, sunk into rosette centre; sepals symmetric or almost so, free, with a short mucro; petals rose-pink or yellow, free, symmetric, narrowly elliptic or suboblong, stamens exserted or equalling petals. Fruit swollen, crowned by persistent sepals. C Chile. Z10.

CULTIVATION See BROMELIADS.

***O. carnea*** (Beer) L.B. Sm. & Looser. To 60cm. Lvs 20–50cm, deflexed, 30–50 in a dense rosette; sheaths triangular or ovate, toothed; blades stiff, white or ash-grey scaly below, shiny above, toothed, with 5mm spines. Infl. many-flowered, globose, on a short peduncle; outer bracts bright rose-pink, broadly obovate, cuneate, margins laciniate, forming an involucre; floral bracts similar but lanceolate, white or pale brown-scaly; fls 4–5.3cm; sep. 1.2–2.7cm, narrowly elliptic, translucent when dry, pet. 2–3cm, pink to lavender, apex with a small mucro, stamens bright yellow, exserted. Fr. 1.3–1.8cm, ellipsoid. Coastal C Chile.

***O. lindleyana*** Mez. See *O. carnea*.
For further synonymy see *Bromelia*.

**Ochna** L. BIRD'S EYE BUSH. (From Gk *ochne*, name used by Homer for the wild pear, the leaves of which are said to resemble those of some species in this genus.) Ochnaceae. 86 species of deciduous or partially or partially evergreen trees and shrubs. Leaves alternate, leathery, glossy, usually minutely toothed. Flowers solitary or in racemes, panicles or umbels; sepals 5, persistent, usually enlarged and flushed red in fruit; petals 5–10; stamens numerous; ovary 3–10-lobed, the lobes developing into distinct 1-seeded drupes attached to an enlarged, lobed receptacle. Old World Tropics. Z10.

CULTIVATION Grown for their lustrous evergreen foliage, attractive flowers, and curious fruits, *Ochna* spp. are suitable for outdoor cultivation in subtropical and frost-free warm temperate climates, where they are grown as specimens in the shrub border. Since they flower when relatively young they are also suitable for the intermediate glasshouse or conservatory. Grow in full sun in any well-drained and fertile soil. Under glass, provide moderate humidity, water plentifully and feed fortnightly when in full growth; maintain a winter minimum temperature of 10°C/50°F. Prune in early spring if necessary to shape or confine to bounds. Propagate by seed or semi-ripe cuttings.

***O. atropurpurea*** DC. Shrub to 2m. Lvs ovate, sharply toothed. Fls solitary; cal. dark purple in fruit, lobes ovate, becoming enlarged; pet. yellow. S Africa. Plants grown of this species are usually *O. serrulata*.

***O. kirkii*** Oliv. Glabrous shrub to 5m. Lvs 5–8cm, obovate-elliptic to broadly oblong, base cuneate to cordate, apex blunt, often mucronate, margin entire or minutely ciliate-toothed. Infl. a short, laterally borne panicle; cal. red-purple, becoming enlarged and outspread to recurved in fr.; pet. 2cm, yellow. Drupes 8–12. Tropical Africa.

***O. mossambicensis*** Klotzsch. Shrub to 3.5m. Lvs to 25cm, obovate to oblanceolate, rigid, apex abruptly apiculate, base narrow-cuneate, margin serrulate. Panicles densely fld, borne on lateral branches; cal. lobes red, developing and spreading in fr.; pet. to 2cm, yellow. Drupes 8–10. Mozambique.

***O. serrulata*** (Hochst.) Walp. MICKEY-MOUSE PLANT; BIRD'S EYE BUSH. Shrub or small tree to 2.25m. Branches closely lenticellate, golden-brown to bronze. Lvs to 6cm, narrowly elliptic, serrulate, glossy mid-green. Fls solitary or clustered, on lateral branchlets; cal. lobes yellow-green becoming enlarged, reflexed and bright red in fruit; pet. obovate, yellow, caducous. Drupes to 1cm diam., to 5, ripening glossy black. on a large red receptacle. S Africa.

***O. japonica*** hort. See *O. serrulata*.
***O. multiflora*** hort. non DC. See *O. serrulata*.
***O. serratifolia*** hort. non Bak. See *O. serrulata*.

**OCHNACEAE** DC. OCHNA FAMILY. Dicot. 37 genera and 460 species of evergreen trees and shrubs, few herbs, usually glabrous; young stems usually with cortical and sometimes medullary vascular bundles. Leaves usually simple, with many parallel lateral veins; stipules present. Flowers bisexual, more or less regular, in inflorescences of various types; calyx (3–) 5 (–12) free sepals, often persistent; corolla (4) 5 (–10) free, convolute petals; stamens (5, 10–) numerous, sometimes in 3–5 whorls, associated with 5 trunk-bundles, sometimes on long androgynophore, staminodes sometimes internal to stamens or a tube or lobed disc around the ovary; ovary superior, of (1) 2–15 of free carpels below with the common style, partitioned, with more or less distinctly axile placentation or deeply lobed that carpels appear distinct, when receptacle often enlarging in fruit; each locule with 1-numerous ovules. Fruit of distinct 1-seeded drupelets, sometimes a capsule, nut or berry; seeds often winged; endosperm oily and proteinaceous. Tropical especially Brazil. *Ochna*.

**Ochrocarpus** A. Juss. See *Mammea*.

**Ochroma** Sw. (From Gk *ochros*, pale yellow, alluding to flower colour.) BALSA; DOWN-TREE. Bombacaceae. 1 species, a rapidly growing tree to 30m, trunk smooth, often buttressed, to 1m diam.; branches spreading horizontally; wood very light. Leaves alternate, simple or palmate with 5–7 lobes or angles, broad-ovate to rounded in outline, cordate, to 30cm+ across, stellate-pubescent beneath; petioles long, equalling lamina, stipulate at base. Flowers solitary on stout axillary peduncles; calyx to 5cm, campanulate, lobes 5, unequal, brown-green, somewhat fleshy; petals 5, dull white to yellow or yellow-brown, to 15cm; stamens numerous, united below, exceeding petals; ovary 5-locular; style to 11cm long. Fruit an elongate angular capsule to 25cm; seeds numerous, surrounded by brown fibres. Seeds need very high temperatures to germinate. Lowland tropical America. Z10.

CULTIVATION A tropical forest native, young specimens can be accommodated in the warm glasshouse in cool temperate zones only if given sufficient headroom. *Ochroma* may be restricted for relatively short periods in containers or planted out into deep loam enriched with plentiful organic matter, although growth is extremely rapid when conditions are optimal. Cultivate as for *Durio*. Propagate by seed.

***O. lagopus*** Sw. As for the genus.

***O. pyramidale*** (Cav.) Urban. See *O. lagopus*.

**Ochrosia** Juss. (From Gk *ochros*, pale yellow, referring to the colour of the flowers.) Apocynaceae. 23 species of trees or shrubs with milky sap. Leaves usually in whorls, rarely opposite slender, pinnately nerved, entire. Inflorescence a cyme, terminal or in axils of upper leaves; flowers bisexual, regular; calyx 5-lobed; corolla funnelform, limb flaring, 5-lobed; stamens carried on corolla, anthers free, lanceolate, included; ovaries 2. Fruits made up of 1 or 2 small, 1-seeded drupes, fleshy or fibrous, slightly compressed; seeds flat. Malesia and Pacific Is., Australia. Z10.

CULTIVATION As for *Cerbera*.

***O. elliptica*** Labill. POKOSOLA. Tree to 6(–12)m. Lvs in whorls, 7.5–15cm, elliptic, leathery, apex acute or obtuse. Fls fragrant, in small dense, stalked corymbs in upper lf axils; cor. ivory, tube 1cm, lobes 6mm, linear. Fr. 5cm, oval, angled, bright red; seeds orbicular, narrowly winged. New Caledonia to Australia.

***O. mariannensis*** A. DC. Small tree. Lvs in whorls, coriaceous, elongate-oblanceolate, green and shiny. Fls small, white. Fr. red, compressed. Pacific Is.

**Ocimastrum** Rupr. See *Circaea*.

**Ocimum** L. (Plant name used by Theophrastus.) Labiatae. 35 species of aromatic annuals, perennials and shrubs. Stems erect, usually branching. Leaves opposite, petiolate or rarely sessile. Inflorescences of 6-flowered verticillasters arranged in a lax or dense spike; bracts small or large, occasionally brightly coloured, sometimes forming a terminal coma; calyx persistent, bilabiate, tubular, upper lip large, entire, accrescent, lower lip subequally 4-lobed, teeth of lateral lobes lanceolate or deltoid; corolla bilabiate, white, green or pink, tube straight or funnelform, subequal to calyx or exserted, upper lip subequally 4-lobed, lower lip entire; stamens 4 declinate, exserted from corolla tube. Nutlets brown or black, ovoid or round. Old World Tropics. Z10.

CULTIVATION *O. basilicum* is one of the most important culinary herbs; the leaves are used in salads, casseroles, sauces and certain liqueurs. *O. tenuiflorum* is a Hindu sacred herb, used in funeral rites as an emblem of good luck, and widely cultivated for anti-malarial fumigation. Other species are useful in cooking but are also medicinal having antiseptic and febrifugal properties. Although most species are more or less perennial, in cool temperate climates the basils are best treated as tender annuals sown under glass in spring, potted on under glass and planted out once summer is well under way. *O. basilicum* and its cultivars may be sown into a soilless compost and grown on in a similar medium benefiting from the water-retentive properties of such a compost in its formative months. In hotter climates two or more crops per year are possible.

Mildew can be a problem in hot dry summers, for which a suitable specific fungicide may be applied. Aphids are attracted by the succulent new growth and can cause unsightly distortion of the plants by damaging the growing points. Care should be given when spraying insecticides as *O. basilicum* is susceptible to phytotoxicity; pyrethrum-based insecticides are fairly safe.

***O. americanum*** L. Aromatic annual or short-lived perenn., 15–70cm. Stems erect or ascending, woody at base, epidermis sometimes peeling in strips, branched above; stem and infl. axis covered in long or short patent hairs. Lvs 1–8×0.4–4cm, narrowly ovate or elliptic, margin entire to shallowly serrate, apex acute, upper surface glabrous, lower surface glabrous or with hairs on the veins; petiole to 2cm. Infl. lax, verticillasters 10mm apart; bracts often erect, flattened, curved; cal. straight or downward-pointing, 2mm long enlarging in fruit to 5mm, covered in long hairs and sessile glands, inside of tube with a dense ring of hairs at the throat; cor. 4–6mm, white or pale mauve, tube straight or funnelform; stamens exserted from cor. by 1–3mm. Nutlets black, mucilaginous when wet. Tropical & S Africa, China and India. var. ***americanum.*** Stem indumentum of short retrorse, adpressed hairs. Lvs less than 2.5cm long. var. ***pilosum*** (Willd.) Paton. Stem indumentum of long spreading hairs. Lvs usually longer than 2.5cm. Tropical Africa.

***O. basilicum*** L. COMMON BASIL; SWEET BASIL. Aromatic annual or short-lived perenn., 20–60cm. Stems erect or ascending, woody at base, branching, glabrous, minutely pubesc. on infl. axis. Lvs 1.5–5×0.5–2cm, narrowly ovate to elliptic, margins entire to serrate, apex acute to acuminate, surfaces glandular punctate; petiole to 4cm. Infl. lax, verticillasters 8–20mm apart; bracts 3–8mm, deciduous or persistent, narrowly ovate to elliptical; cal. 2–3mm, enlarging in fruit to 6mm, more or less downward-pointing, upper lip glabrous, lower lip pubesc., gland-dotted, tube pilose with a ring of hairs in the throat; cor. 5–8mm, pink, white or creamy yellow, tube straight, scarcely exserted from cal. Nutlets black, mucilaginous when wet. Tropical Asia. 'Citriodorum': lvs lemon-scented.

'Crispum': lvs curled around the edges. 'Minimum' BUSH BASIL; GREEK BASIL: 15–30cm; lvs very small, less than 1cm long, ovate. 'Purple Ruffles': lvs purple, curled around the edges. 'Purpureum' ('Dark Opal'): lvs red-purple, clove-scented. 'Spicy Globe': compact and globose; lvs small; fls white.

***O. gratissimum*** L. Aromatic shrubby perenn., 60–250cm. Stems erect, much-branched, woody at base, epidermis often peeling in strips. Stems glabrous, pubesc. at the nodes and on infl. axis. Lvs 1.5–15×1–8.5cm, elliptic or ovate, sometimes glandular-punctate, pubesc. on both surfaces, upper surface darker green, margins serrate, apex acute to acuminate; petioles to 3cm. Infl. lax or dense; bracts 3–12mm, erect, ovate or narrowly ovate, acuminate, sometimes cucullate, erect above and forming a small green terminal coma; cal. 2–3mm, horizontal, downward-pointing or reflexed, pubesc. or tomentose, enlarging in fruit to 6mm; cor. 3–5mm, green, dull yellow or white, tube straight or funnelform. Nutlets brown, not mucilaginous when wet. India, W Africa, or Tropical Africa to Namibia and Natal. ssp. ***gratissimum.*** Infl. wider than 1cm; fruiting cal. horizontal or slightly downward-pointing, never strongly reflexed. var. ***glabrum*** Paton. Plant without hairs. India, W Africa. ssp. ***cylindraceum*** Paton. Infl. 0.7–1cm wide; fruiting cal. strongly reflexed. Tanzania.

***O. tenuiflorum*** L. HOLY BASIL. Aromatic woody or suffrutescent herb to 1m. Stems erect, branched, woody at base, covered in spreading hairs. Lvs 1.5–3×1.1–2cm, broadly elliptical, petiolate, margin serrate, both surfaces covered in short hairs, petiole 7–15mm. Infl. lax; cal. 1mm enlarging in fruit to 3mm, throat open and glabrous; cor. to 3mm, pink or white, tube parallel-sided, lower pair of stamens ciliate near bases. Nutlets brown, mucilaginous when wet. India and Malaysia.

***O. africanum*** Lour. See *O. americanum* var. *pilosum*.
***O. canum*** Sims. See *O. americanum*.
***O. citriodorum*** Vig. See *O. basilicum*.
***O. crispum*** Thunb. See *Perilla frutescens* var. *nankinensis*.
***O. frutescens*** L. See *Perilla frutescens*.
***O. frutescens*** var. ***crispum*** (Benth.) Decne. See *Perilla frutescens* var. *nankinensis*.
***O. fruticulosum*** Burchell. See *O. americanum*.
***O. graveolens*** R. Br. See *O. americanum* var. *pilosum*.
***O. lanceolatum*** Schumacher & Thonn. See *O. basilicum*.
***O. madagascariense*** Pers. See *Plectranthus madagascariensis*.
***O. pilosum*** Willd. See *O. americanum* var. *pilosum*.
***O. pusillum*** Forst. See *Plectranthus forsteri*.
***O. sanctum*** L. See *O. tenuiflorum*.
***O. scutellarioides*** L. See *Solenostemon scutellarioides*.
***O. simile*** N.E. Br. See *O. basilicum*.
***O. stamineum*** Sims. See *O. americanum*.
***O. suave*** Willd. See *O. gratissimum*.
***O. verticillatum*** L.f. See *Plectranthus verticillatus*.
***O. viride*** Willd. See *O. gratissimum*.

For illustration see HERBS.

**Octoclinis** Muell. See *Callitris*.

**Octomeria** R. Br. (From Gk *octo*, eight, and *meros*, a part, referring to the 8 pollinia which characterize the genus.) Orchidaceae. Some 50 species of epiphytic or terrestrial orchids. Rhizome short or elongate, creeping. Secondary stems often tufted, elongate, erect, enveloped by several tubular sheaths, apically unifoliate. Leaves erect, fleshy to coriaceous, sessile or short-petiolate, elliptic-oblong or linear to terete. Inflorescence 1 to many, axillary, densely clustered to subcapitate, 1- to many-flowered; flowers often small; sepals subsimilar, free to shortly connate, spreading; petals shorter than sepals and usually similar to them in form; lip articulate to column base, shorter than petals, entire or obscurely 3-lobed, apex spreading or reflexed, disc with a shortly bilamellate callus; column short, subterete, incurved, with a short foot at base, wingless, anther terminal, operculate, incumbent, bilocular, pollinia 8, oblong-clavate. C & S America, W Indies. Z10.

CULTIVATION Intermediate-growing orchids suitable for baskets or mounting on rafts in brightly lit, humid conditions.

***O. complanata*** Schweinf. Secondary stems to 8.5cm, numerous, slender. Lvs to 4cm, subterete to triquetrous-subulate, slightly arching. Infl. several, 1-fld; fls to 17mm, pale golden-brown to dark maroon-red; dorsal sep. to 8×3mm, elliptic-lanceolate to oblong-lanceolate, concave, acute; lateral sep. to 9×2mm, shortly connate, narrowly oblong to oblong-lanceolate, subacute, carinate; pet. to 5.5×2mm, elliptic-lanceolate to oblong-lanceolate; lip to 3.5×2.5mm, ovate-oblong, lateral lobes small, narrowly lanceolate-triangular, edged red-maroon, incurved, midlobe ovate, disc bicarinate, keels basal, yellow, short; column to 2mm, slender, arched, white suffused red. Venezuela, Peru, Brazil.

***O. diaphana*** Lindl. Secondary stems to 8cm, erect, slender, subcylindrical. Lvs to 6×1.5cm, ovate to oblong-lanceolate, acute, fleshy, sessile, ascending to erect, convex. Infl. to 5mm, 1-fld; fls translucent white, unscented; sep. to 10mm, elliptic-lanceolate, acute or acuminate, concave, thin-textured; pet. to 10mm, linear-lanceolate, acute or acuminate; lip to 7mm, obscurely trilobed, yellow-white flecked red-maroon, ovate-oblong, base cuneate, dentate, slightly crisped, apex truncate, disc with 2 short lamellae. E Brazil.

***O. erosilabia*** Schweinf. Secondary stems to 19cm, subterete to tetragonal, 3–5-jointed. Lvs to 17×1cm, linear-elliptic or linear-oblong, acute or subacute, lustrous pale green, slightly recurved, subsessile or petiolate. Infl. numerous, subcapitate, 1- to few-fld; tepals pale cream-white to cream-yellow, subtranslucent, sep. to 7×2.5mm, lanceolate or oblong-lanceolate, acuminate, pet. to 6×1.5mm, similar to sep.; lip to 3×2mm, yellow with 2 small bright purple marks, ovate-oblong, lateral lobes auriculate, midlobe ovate or ovate-oblong, truncate, erose-dentate, disc with 2 fleshy keels; column to 2mm, cream-white, stout. Venezuela, Guyana.

***O. graminifolia*** (L.) R. Br. Secondary stems to 5cm, remote, erect-ascending. Lvs to 11×1cm, narrowly linear-lanceolate to linear-oblong, erect, fleshy, sessile. Infl. 1- or 2-fld; fls pale yellow to yellow-green; sep. to 10×3mm, ovate or ovate-lanceolate, acuminate; lip to 6×3mm, fleshy, short-clawed, lateral lobes subquadrate to suborbicular, midlobe ovate, acute or acuminate, denticulate, disc with 2 oblique, fleshy, purple lamellae; column to 3mm, arched. Early winter. W Indies to Colombia & Brazil.

***O. grandiflora*** Lindl. Secondary stems to 20cm, terete or subterete, compressed above. Lvs to 20×1.5cm, coriaceous or subcoriaceous, linear-rhombic to linear-lanceolate, green-purple. Infl. 1- or 2-fld; fls to 2cm diam.; tepals translucent, white to straw-yellow, sep. to 13×3mm, narrowly elliptic-lanceolate, acute; lip to 8×6mm, yellow marked purple, short-clawed, lateral lobes erect, rounded, midlobe obovate to cuneate-flabellate, deeply emarginate, erose, disc bicarinate; column white marked red, short, stout, anth. white. Venezuela, Trinidad, Brazil, Surinam, Bolivia, Paraguay.

***O. integrilabia*** Schweinf. Secondary stems to 5cm. Lvs to 50×5mm, linear or linear-oblong to terete, acute, fleshy. Infl. 1- or 2-fld; fls rose to straw-yellow; sep. to 6×3mm, narrowly lanceolate to ovate-lanceolate, acute or shortly acuminate; pet. oblong-lanceolate to elliptic-lanceolate, acute or acuminate; lip to 3×3mm, simple or obscurely 3-lobed, ovate-elliptic or elliptic to suborbicular, emarginate, base cordate, disc with 2 central keels; column to 2mm, arched. Guyana, Venezuela.

***O. nana*** Schweinf. Secondary stems to 2.5cm. Lvs to 40×6mm, linear-lanceolate or linear-oblong, acute, fleshy-coriaceous, sessile, apex minutely denticulate. Infl. few-fld; fls produced in succession, thin-textured, pale translucent brown-yellow, the lip pale yellow; sep. to 4×2mm, elliptic-ovate, acute or subacute, concave; lip to 3×2mm, simple, elliptic to suborbicular, shortly acute or emarginate, base rounded-cuneate, disc with a short central callus; column to 1.5mm, cream. Venezuela.

***O. oxycheila*** Barb. Rodr. Secondary stems to 11×2cm, terete, erect to slightly arched. Lvs to 8×1.5cm, fleshy, lanceolate or oblong-lanceolate, erect-spreading, acute, sessile. Fls spreading to pendent, yellow-white, faintly scented; sep. to 5×1.5mm, fleshy, lanceolate or oblong-lanceolate, acute; pet. broadly ovate-rhombic, acute; lip to 4×2.5mm, ovate-oblong, narrowly clawed, lateral lobes small, erect, suborbicular, midlobe oblong-rectangular, apex tridentate, truncate, disc with 2 central calli, apex with a fleshy keel; column short. Brazil.

***O. saundersiana*** Rchb. f. Stems to 25cm. Lvs to 6cm, terete, subulate. Infl. fasciculate; fls yellow striped purple; sep. and pet. membranous, triangular, acute; lip 3-lobed, lateral lobes triangular, obtuse; midlobe oblong, acute; disc carinate; column incurved, clavate. Brazil.

***O. steyermarkii*** Garay & Dunsterville. Secondary stems to 5.5cm. Lvs to 5×1cm, lanceolate or narrowly lanceolate, acute, coriaceous, minutely tridenticulate. Infl. 1-fld; fls variable in colour, cream tinged pink, or pink to dark puce; dorsal sep. to 10mm, narrowly linear-lanceolate or lanceolate, apex produced into filiform tail, lateral sep. to 15mm; pet. to 8mm, lanceolate, with filiform tails; lip to 4×4mm, simple, broadly ovate to ovate-elliptic, disc with 2 central, lamellate calli; column to 2.5mm, dark purple, anth. yellow-cream. Venezuela.

***O. surinamensis*** Focke. Secondary stems to 10cm, numerous, base terete, apex compressed, 3- or 4-jointed. Lvs to 14×2cm, linear to oblong-elliptic, acute or obtuse, fleshy or subcoriaceous, pale dull green above, green to red-maroon below, usually petiolate. Infl. several, 1- to few-fld; fls yellow-white to pale yellow; sep. to 7×3.5mm, oblong-lanceolate to elliptic-lanceolate, acute or acuminate; pet. to 6.5×3mm, oblong-lanceolate, acuminate; lip to 4×4mm, lateral lobes small, broadly falcate-subovate, obtuse, midlobe obovate, denticulate, apex tridentate, disc with 2 short, dark maroon keels; column to 4mm, slender, arched, brown flushed pink-maroon, anth. pale yellow-brown. Peru, Brazil, Guianas, Venezuela, Colombia.

**Odontadenia** Benth. (From Gk *odons*, tooth, and *aden*, gland; referring to the 5-toothed glands.) Apocynaceae. 30 species of climbing shrubs closely related to *Mandevilla*. Leaves opposite, pinnately veined. Flowers borne in large, loose cymes, yellow, showy; calyx 5-lobed; corolla funnelform or slightly salverform. Tropical America. Z10.

CULTIVATION Given moderate watering when in growth and a winter minimum temperature of 15–21°C/60–70°F, cultivation essentially as for *Allamanda*. Propagate by cutting of young shoots rooted in a closed case with bottom heat, or by seed.

***O. macrantha*** (Roem. & Schult.) Markgr. Woody vine. Lvs to 15cm, oblong-ovate, apex acute, smooth, dark green, leathery. Fls to 8cm diam., delicately scented; cor. bright yellow shaded orange, tube 3.5–5cm. Costa Rica to Peru and N Brazil.

***O. grandiflora*** (G. Mey.) Kuntze. See *O. macrantha*.
***O. speciosa*** Benth. See *O. macrantha*.

**× Odontioda**. *(Odontoglossum × Cochlioda.)* Orchidaceae. The earliest of the intergeneric crosses in the *Oncidium* alliance; the first hybrid was registered in 1904. Plants consist of a group of compressed pseudobulbs growing from a basal rhizome, each with one or two leaves at its apex and two or more leaf-like sheaths arising at its base. Inflorescences arise in the axils of these sheaths and may be simple or branched. Flowers very varied, many with rounded shape and wide sepals and petals, lip large or small depending on the ancestry; flowers of many colours often conspicuously marked in a variety of colours, the bright red of so many crosses inherited from the *Cochlioda* parent. Most of these hybrids are 'cool' growers though a few are tolerant of warmer conditions.

× *O.* Astmo 'Lyoth Zebra'*:* very large and fine fls on a tall spike; sep. and pet. chestnut brown edged with yellow and with some white patches towards the centre, lip white apically, with some brown patches in the centre and a yellow crest at the base.

× *O.* Durham Castle 'Lyoth Supreme'*:* very fine round fls, intense clear red.

× *O.* Durham Supreme 'Lyoth Galaxy'*:* very fine round fls of large size; fls pale pink, heavily overlaid with wine red spots that coalesce, lip with broad red band and yellow around the basal crest.

× *O.* Eric Young: large white fls of excellent form, heavily marked with deep red.

× *O.* Golden Rialto 'St Helier'*:* fls rather crowded on upright spikes; fls white with few large clear yellow spots on all sep. and pet. and centre of lip; the clone 'Lyoth Sunny' is a clear bright yellow, paler towards the centre, with two brown spots on the lip which is edged with white.

× *O.* Harrods Forever 'Lyoth Dresden'*:* superb round fls of pastel pink with few brown-red spots, lip with a broad brown-red band across the centre and yellow basally.

× *O.* Heatonensis: primary hybrid made at the turn of the century; fls star shaped with elongated sep., pale pink with red spots, lip paler, white in the centre and with yellow in the throat.

× *O.* Ingmar: fine shaped fls of luminous orange red with lilac mauve tips to the sep. and pet., lip red basally with yellow crest, white flushed rose towards the apex.

× *O.* Joe's Drum: small to medium fls of fine shape, clear bright red.

× *O.* Keighleyensis: primary hybrid with small bright orange red fls of starry shape on short sprays.

× *O.* Lippestern: branching sprays bearing very round fls; sepals and petals a rich red-brown margined with white and with white tips, lip small but similar with yellow crest.

× *O.* Lynx: startling large fls; sep. and pet. with a yellow base and many large bright brown spots, lip white streaked and spotted with brown.

× *O.* Matanda: small to medium fls of intense cerise red, some spotting in darker red on the dorsal sep. and lip.

× *O.* Petit Port: very fine shaped fls of medium size; fls pale yellow-green, margined and striped with bright red, lip paler with fewer spots towards the base and cream flushed rose towards the tip.

× *O.* Red Rum: very fine fls in bright clear red.

× *O.* Saint Clement: very fine round fls of excellent substance; fls pink with dark red spots, lip paler with yellow crest; many fine awarded clones.

× *O.* Shelley: delightful fls of medium size, white flushed pink and with darker pin spots.

× *O.* Trixon: very fine fls in upright spikes; fls bright red with lilac tips to the sepals and lip, crest yellow; several awarded clones.

**Odontites** Ludw. (From Gk *odous*, tooth.) Scrophulariaceae. Some 30 species of semi-parasitic annuals or dwarf shrubs. Leaves opposite, sessile, narrow, entire or dentate. Racemes spike-like, terminal; calyx campanulate; corolla tube upper lip entire to bilobed, lower lip 3-lobed, entire or slightly emarginate; stamens 4, anthers villous or glabrous; stigma capitate. Fruit a capsule. W & S Europe to W Asia. Z6.

CULTIVATION As for *Bartsia*.

***O. verna*** (Bellardi) Dumort. RED BARTSIA. Annual, to 50cm. Stem erect, branching or simple. Lvs lanceolate to linear-lanceolate, sessile. Cal. campanulate; cor. tube 5–6mm, pubesc., mauve-pink, lower lip deflexed. Fr. oblong, 6–8mm, pubesc. Summer. Europe.

***O. rubra*** Gilib. See *O. verna*.
For further synonymy see *Bartsia*.

**× Odontobrassia**. *(Brassia × Odontoglossum.)* Orchidaceae. Intergeneric orchid hybrid. Plants consist of a group of compressed pseudobulbs growing from a basal rhizome, each with one or two leaves at its apex and two or more leaf-like sheaths arising at its base. Inflorescences arise in the axils of these sheaths and may be simple or branched. Flowers mostly with long narrow sepals and petals, lip large or small depending on the ancestry, often contrasting with the sepals and petals. Tolerant of intermediate conditions.

× *O.* Gordon Dillon: upright spikes of attractive fls; fls with curved sep. and pet., yellow or cream overlaid with deep chocolate, lip oval, bright red.

**× Odontocidium**. *(Odontoglossum × Oncidium.)* Orchidaceae. Intergeneric orchid hybrids. Plants consist of a group of compressed pseudobulbs growing from a basal rhizome, each with one or two leaves at its apex and two or more leaf-like sheaths arising at its base. Inflorescences arise in the axils of these sheaths and may be simple or branched. Flowers very varied, many with rounded shape but others have long narrow sepals and petals, lip large or small depending on the ancestry; flowers of many colours often conspicuously marked in a variety of colours. Most of these hybrids are 'cool' growers though a few are tolerant of warmer conditions.

× *O.* Crowborough 'Spice Islands'*:* branching spikes with many fls; fls golden yellow and orange with dark brown spits, lip large, white with yellow crest at the base.

× *O.* Jacobert: tall sprays of large fls often branching: fls rich coppery orange shades, some solid colours others patterned like odontoglossums, lip usually bright yellow or outlined in yellow; warm growing.

× *O.* Selsfield Gold: very large spikes bearing numerous fls; sep. and pet. bright yellow with brown blotches, lip primrose yellow, spotted with orange.

× *O.* Tiger Butter: large branching sprays bearing many small to medium fls; several awarded clones.

× *O.* Tigersun: tall sprays of large bright yellow fls but a tendency to fade with age; fls yellow throughout with chestnut brown spots on sep. and pet. and base of large yellow lip; several awarded clones.

**Odontoglossum** HBK. (From Gk *odontos*, tooth, and *glossa*, tongue, referring to the tooth-like processes of the lip.) Orchidaceae. Some 100 species of epiphytic or lithophytic orchids. Rhizome short or creeping. Pseudobulbs variously compressed, usually ovoid or elliptic-oblong, 1–3-leaved at apex, enveloped at base by distichous, leaf-bearing sheaths. Leaves coriaceous or fleshy, variously shaped. Inflorescence basal, a raceme or a panicle, erect or arching, few- to many-flowered; bracts minute to conspicuous; flowers usually large and conspicuous, sometimes small; sepals subequal, spreading, free or lateral sepals basally connate; petals similar to sepals, often shorter; lip simple or 3-lobed, basal portion often claw-like and usually parallel with column, sometimes adnate to column, lateral lobes spreading or erect, midlobe deflexed, entire or emarginate, disc variously lamellate, cristate or callose, sometimes with radiate keels; column long, slender, footless, apex sometimes auriculate; anther terminal, operculate, incumbent, pollinia 2, waxy, entire or sulcate. C & S America. Z10.

CULTIVATION A genus of great horticultural importance, *Odontoglossum* has spawned countless hybrids, many of them intergeneric and has, since the last century when vast sums changed hands for a single growth of *O. crispum*, enjoyed a popularity with orchid growers outdone only by that of *Cymbidium*. These plants are cool-growing and demand buoyant, freely ventilated and humid atmospheres in light shade. Their roots are comparatively fine: a correspondingly fine bark mix is advised, containing rockwool or sphagnum. Water and syringe freely when in growth, and impose drier cooler conditions when at rest. Never syringe in cold weather. The inflorescences of some will require training. Propagate by division.

Some of the most striking and widely grown *Odontoglossum* species (for example the showy clown orchid, *O.grande*, the eminently dependable *O.bictoniense*, the delicate white *O.convallarioides*, or nodding, rose *O.pendulum*, the diminutive *O.rossii* and *O.cervantesii*, with disproportionately large white flowers spotted chocolate and tinted rose) are now treated under segregate genera and can be located through the synonymy below. Their cultural requirements are largely the same as those described here, likewise the needs of many of the intergeneric hybrids, although ×*Wilsonara* and ×*Vuylstekeara* both have grexes that will tolerate even neglect in the home. See ORCHIDS.

***O.angustatum*** Lindl. non Batem. Pseudobulbs cylindric to elliptic or ovoid, to 8cm, 1-lvd at apex, with 4 accessory lvs at base. Lvs to 42×4.5cm, oblanceolate or oblanceolate-oblong, sessile. Panicle short- or long-branched, usually exceeding lvs; sep. to 35×8mm, green, marked brown, linear-lanceolate, long-acuminate, undulate; pet. yellow, transversely barred brown, lanceolate to ovate-lanceolate, broader than sep., margins undulate; lip to 2.5×1cm, white, ovate to ovate-oblong or oblong, basal portion short-clawed, anterior portion barred brown, basal crest closely and sharply toothed; column small, to 1.2cm, dilated at apex, wingless. Ecuador, Peru.

***O.aureo-purpureum*** Rchb. f. Pseudobulbs to 6×4cm, oblong-ovoid, remote on tough rhiz., apically bifoliate. Lvs to 70×3cm, linear-oblong or oblong, acute or acuminate, coriaceous. Panicle much-branched, erect, to 160cm, many-fld; fls large, wide-spreading, golden-yellow marked and spotted purple, red or brown; sep. to 3.5×1cm, linear-lanceolate to ovate-lanceolate, long-acuminate, undulate-crisped, recurved, with long, fleshy claws; pet. shorter and broader than sep.; lip to 2.5×1cm, golden-yellow with brown base and remainder spotted brown, fleshy, lanceolate, strongly recurved, margins crenate and undulate at base, disc with yellow basal callus of 2 fleshy keels; column yellow, to 1cm. Venezuela, Colombia, Ecuador, Peru.

***O.blandum*** Rchb. f. Pseudobulbs to 3×2cm, ellipsoid, apically bifoliate. Lvs to 25×2.5cm, linear-lanceolate, acute or subacute. Fls showy, crowded near apex of 25cm, arching raceme, sep. and pet. white, heavily spotted maroon-crimson, to 25×3mm, lanceolate, long-acuminate; lip to 23×10mm, white spotted purple, clawed, ovate, emarginate, acuminate, erose-dentate, callus yellow, 2-keeled, terminating in 2 slender, erect teeth, pubesc.; column with 3 or 4 apical cirri on each side. Colombia.

***O.cariniferum*** Rchb. f. Pseudobulbs to 12×8cm, ovoid to elliptic-oblong, apically bifoliate. Lvs to 45×4cm, linear-ligulate, acute, coriaceous. Panicle to 1m, stout, erect or arcuate, many-fld, usually branched, branches spreading, fractiflex; fls to 5cm diam., fleshy, sep. and pet. deep chestnut-brown edged yellow, lanceolate, acute or acuminate, keeled on reverse; sep. to 25×5mm; pet. shorter than sep., sometimes incurved; lip white, pale yellow with age, long-clawed, to 1.5×2cm, reniform, apiculate, callus rose-mauve, consisting of 2 rhomboid, toothed keels; column white flushed purple, winged. Spring. Costa Rica, Panama, Venezuela.

***O.cirrhosum*** Lindl. Pseudobulbs to 8cm, oblong-ovoid, apically unifoliate. Lvs 30×3cm, linear-ligulate, acute. Raceme or panicle to 60cm, arching; sep. and pet. white variously blotched red-brown; sep. to 4×0.7cm, narrowly lanceolate, long-acuminate, terminating in a recurved point; pet. rhombic-lanceolate, long-acuminate, shorter and broader than sep.; lip to 3cm, white with red-brown blotches on midlobe, base yellow, 3-lobed, lateral lobes rounded, denticulate, erect to spreading, midlobe recurved, narrow-lanceolate, long-acuminate, disc with 2 horn-like keels; column to 1cm, with 2 hair-like auricles near apex. Spring. Ecuador, Peru, Colombia.

***O.constrictum*** Lindl. Pseudobulbs to 7.5cm, ovoid, ribbed, apically bifoliate. Lvs to 40×2cm, linear-lanceolate, acute. Raceme or lightly branched panicle to 60cm, arching, sep. and pet. yellow or pale olive blotched and banded red-brown, to 20×5mm, oblong-lanceolate; lip to 2.5×1cm, white blotched pale red before callus, pandurate, apiculate, callus 2-keeled with erose margins; column white. Autumn–winter. Venezuela, Colombia, Ecuador.

***O.crispum*** Lindl. Pseudobulbs to 7.5cm, ovoid, apically bifoliate. Lvs to 40×3cm, linear-lanceolate to linear-elliptic, acute. Raceme or (rarely) panicle, arching, to 50cm; fls to 8.5cm diam., very variable, showy usually sparkling white or pale rose, variously spotted or blotched red or purple, sep. and pet. spreading, ovate-elliptic to oblong-elliptic, obtuse or acute to acuminate, undulate or finely and irregularly dentate; lip to 3×1.5cm, usually white or pink with a few red spots and a yellow disc, short-clawed, oblong, acute, undulate, finely dentate, callus fleshy, 2-lobed at apex; column lightly arcuate, with 2 lacerate wings. Winter. Colombia.

***O.cristatum*** Lindl. Pseudobulbs to 10cm, ovoid to oblong-ellipsoid, apically bifoliate. Lvs to 22×2cm, ligulate, acute. Raceme to 50cm, arching, sep. and pet. to 3×1cm, fleshy, cream-yellow with deep chestnut-brown blotches and markings, elliptic-lanceolate or ovate-lanceolate, acuminate; lip white or cream-yellow with few brown spots, fimbriate-dentate, disc with a basal callus of many long tooth-like projections; column to 1.5cm, arching, with 2 rounded, fimbriate wings above. Colombia, Ecuador, Peru.

***O.dormannianum*** Rchb. f. Pseudobulbs to 6×3cm, ovoid to ellipsoid, often spotted purple, usually apically bifoliate. Lvs to 25×4cm, oblong to linear-lanceolate, acute. Raceme or short-branched panicle, ascending to arching; sep. and pet. pale yellow to yellow-brown spotted dark brown or chocolate-brown; sep. to 35×5mm, linear-lanceolate to lanceolate, acuminate; pet. to 30×7mm, linear-lanceolate to ovate-lanceolate, subacuminate; lip to 26×7mm, clear yellow blotched dark brown near callus, lanceolate, subacuminate, callus white, 2 parallel plates, papillose or pubesc.; column to 12mm, white, narrow-winged. Colombia, Venezuela.

***O.edwardii*** Rchb. f. Pseudobulbs to 10cm, ovoid-pyriform, apically bifoliate. Lvs to 25×3cm, ligulate, subcoriaceous. Panicle much-branched, suberect, far exceeding lvs; fls to 2.5cm, fragrant, sep. and pet. bright magenta or mauve-purple, oblong, undulate; lip similar to sep. and pet., short, tongue-shaped, with yellow callus. Spring. Ecuador.

***O.epidendroides*** HBK. Pseudobulbs to 6cm, ovate-oblong, apically bifoliate. Lvs to 30×3cm, lanceolate to oblong-elliptic, acute. Panicle or raceme to 45cm, slightly arching; sep. and pet. bright yellow with 3–5 carmine spots; sep. to 35×7mm, lanceolate, acuminate, slightly undulate; pet. slightly wider than sep., suboblique; lip white spotted purple, shorter than sep., clawed, elliptic-oblong, sharply reflexed, margins crenate-undulate, callus linear-oblong, tridentate with 1–3 minute dentate calli on each side at base; column clavate, with 2 rounded auricles at apex. C America.

***O.hallii*** Lindl. Rhiz. short. Pseudobulbs to 10cm, ovoid or oblong-ovoid, apically unifoliate or bifoliate. Lvs to 30×4.5cm, elliptic-oblong or oblong-lanceolate, acute. Raceme (rarely a panicle) to 90cm, erect or arching; sep. and pet. pale yellow blotched chocolate-brown or purple-brown; sep. to 5.5×1cm, lanceolate or elliptic-lanceolate, long-acuminate; pet. ovate-lanceolate, shorter and broader than sep.; lip white blotched purple-brown, callus deep yellow, shortly clawed, lamina oblong, dentate to lacerate, basal portion crenulate, disc with large callus of several tooth-like keels; column to 2cm, arching, auricles divided into tooth-like processes or tendrils. Spring. Colombia, Ecuador, Peru.

***O.harryanum*** Rchb. f. Pseudobulbs to 8cm, ovoid-oblong, furrowed with age, apically bifoliate. Lvs to 44×4cm, oblong to oblong-elliptic, acute to obtuse, petiolate. Raceme to 1m, erect, 4–12-fld; fls variable; sep. to 4.5×2.5cm, buff to chestnut brown with vein-like streaks of yellow, elliptic-oblong, acute, undulate; pet. to 4×2cm, chestnut brown, white at base with broad, irregular lines of mauve-purple; lip 3-lobed, lateral lobes white striped purple, midlobe white to pale yellow disc with a prominent yellow, fimbriate callus; column to 1.5cm, with small, finely dentate auricles. Summer. Colombia, Peru.

***O.hennisii*** Rolfe. Pseudobulbs to 4cm, oblong-ovoid. Lvs to 15×2cm, linear-oblanceolate, acute. Infl. to 20cm, laxly 6-fld; sep. to 2.5cm, yellow spotted and blotched brown, lanceolate, acuminate, larger than similar pet.; lip to 2cm, spotted white and blotched red-brown, short-clawed, spreading, 3-lobed, lateral lobes dentate, rounded, midlobe narrow-ovate, long-acuminate; column to 1.5cm, clavate, yellow-white, apex dentate, acute. Peru, Ecuador.

***O.hunnewellianum*** Rolfe. Pseudobulbs to 5cm, ovoid, apically bifoliate. Lvs to 30cm. Raceme to 40cm, branched, arching, loosely many-fld; fls to 5cm diam., fleshy, round, sep. and pet. yellow with large brown blotches, broadly lanceolate to ovate, acute; lip cream-white spotted red-brown, obovate-elliptic, margins crenulate to undulate, callus yellow, dentate; column wings entire. Autumn–spring. Colombia.

***O.kegeljani*** Morr. Pseudobulbs to 8×3cm, pyriform, apically bifoliate. Lvs to 35×3cm, linear-lanceolate, mucronulate. Raceme to 40cm, arching, several-fld; sep. and pet. lemon-yellow blotched chestnut-brown, acute; sep. to 4.5×1.5cm, slightly longer than pet.; lip to 4×2.5cm, white blotched red-chestnut on apical lobe, narrowly clawed, oblong to suborbicular, crisped, callus consisting of 2 large, sharp, divergent teeth with some smaller teeth near base; column to 2.5cm, white blotched brown, anth. dark brown. Spring. Venezuela, Colombia, Ecuador, Peru.

***O.lindenii*** Lindl. Pseudobulbs to 6×5cm, ovoid, apically bifoliate. Lvs to 35×2cm, narrow-linear, erect, thin, margins revolute. Panicle short-branched, to 60cm, 5–7-fld; fls bright yellow; sep. to 2×1cm, short-clawed, lanceolate to oblanceolate, strongly undulate; pet. shorter, elliptic-spathulate, strongly undulate; lip to 1.5×1cm, ovate-lanceolate, callus prominent, fleshy, consisting of 2 erect plates clasping side of column with several long, toothed projections in front; column terete, yellow. Spring. Jamaica, Venezuela, Colombia, Ecuador.

***O.lindleyanum*** Rchb. f. Pseudobulbs to 7.5×3cm, ovoid to ovoid-oblong, apically bifoliate. Lvs to 30×2cm, linear-oblong to linear-lanceolate, acute. Raceme or panicle loosely several-fld, arching; fls fragrant, star-shaped, sep. and pet. to 30×5mm, yellow with central cinnamon-brown blotch and red-brown spots at base, linear-lanceolate, long-acuminate; lip to 3×1cm, red-brown tipped yellow, white at base spotted purple, lateral lobes small, midlobe linear-lanceolate, reflexed; column to 2cm, straight, with 2 narrow apical wings. Spring–summer. Colombia.

***O.lucianianum*** Rchb. f. Pseudobulbs to 4×2cm, pyriform, apically unifoliate or bifoliate. Lvs to 16×2.5cm, linear-oblanceolate, acute. Raceme to 40cm, erect;

sep. and pet. to 18×8mm, yellow-brown spotted red-brown, lanceolate or narrowly ovate, subacute or acute; lip subequal to sep., yellow or yellow-white with large chestnut-brown blotch in front of callus, triangular-lanceolate, basal portion subquadrate, callus white, pubesc., apex bilobulate; column to 7mm, wings linear-filiform. Venezuela.

***O. luteo-purpureum*** Lindl. Variable in size and colour. Pseudobulbs to 7×3cm, ovoid, apically bifoliate. Lvs to 60×2.5cm, oblanceolate or linear-lanceolate, acute, somewhat rigid. Raceme to 1m, suberect, loosely many-fld; sep. and pet. bright chestnut-brown tipped and marked yellow, ovate-lanceolate, acute or acuminate, undulate and, sometimes, fringed; sep. to 5×1.5cm; pet. to 4×1cm; lip to 3×2cm, yellow-white spotted brown, long-clawed, lateral lobes small, midlobe reniform, emarginate, fringed, callus golden-yellow, dentate; column wings dentate. Spring. Colombia.

***O. naevium*** Lindl. Pseudobulbs to 4×2.5cm, ovoid, grooved, apically bifoliate. Lvs to 35×2.5cm. Raceme arching; fls star-shaped, showy, to 6cm diam., sep. and pet. white blotched deep red-brown or red-purple, lanceolate, acuminate, margins undulate; lip white spotted red-brown, shorter than sep., linear-lanceolate, pubesc., disc yellow; column white, wings long-fimbriate, anth. white. Spring–summer. Venezuela, Colombia, Ecuador, Guianas.

***O. nevadense*** Rchb. f. Pseudobulbs to 10×5cm, ovoid, apically bifoliate. Lvs to 30cm, linear-lanceolate or ensiform, coriaceous. Raceme exceeding lvs, arching, to 15-fld; fls to 8.5cm diam., sep. and pet. similar, cinnamon edged yellow, sometimes longitudinally barred yellow at base, narrowly lanceolate or ovate-lanceolate, acuminate; lip shorter than sep., white barred chestnut-brown, triangular, acuminate, slightly recurved, deeply fimbriate or dentate, lateral lobes erect, parallel with column, semilunate, callus bilamellate; column to 6.5mm, white. Spring–summer. Colombia, Venezuela.

***O. nobile*** Rchb. f. Close to *O. crispum*. Pseudobulbs to 9cm, ovoid, speckled brown, apically bifoliate. Lvs to 20cm, ligulate, acute. Raceme or panicle to 60cm, usually branched, erect or arching, 10–100-fld; fls to 6cm diam., orbicular, lightly fragrant, sep. and pet. usually snow-white, sometimes tinged pale rose, ovate-elliptic or ovate-oblong, acute, margins undulate; lip white blotched purple-crimson at base, pandurate, undulate, midlobe cordate with an apical cusp, callus yellow. Spring. Colombia.

***O. odoratum*** Lindl. Pseudobulbs to 7.5cm, ovoid, apically bifoliate. Lvs to 30×4cm, lanceolate, acute. Raceme or panicle to 75cm; fls to 6.5cm diam., fragrant, pale to deep yellow dotted and blotched chocolate-brown; sep. to 35×7mm, ovate-lanceolate, acute or acuminate, apex reflexed; pet. to 30×6mm, lanceolate, long-acuminate, undulate; lip to 2.5×1cm, white at base, short-clawed, lateral lobes erect, rounded, lanceolate to oblong-elliptic, acuminate, striate at base, apical portion recurved, callus bidentate; column wings lanceolate, long-acuminate. Spring. Colombia, Venezuela.

***O. praestans*** Rchb. f. & Warsc. Pseudobulbs to 6cm, ovoid or pyriform-cylindrical, mottled purple-brown, apically bifoliate. Lvs to 23×1.5cm, linear-lanceolate or linear-oblong, acute, sessile or shortly petiolate. Panicle or raceme to 30cm, few- to many-fld; fls large, spreading, yellow-green spotted cinnamon-brown or purple; sep. to 4×1cm, lanceolate or linear-lanceolate, acuminate; pet. shorter and slightly wider than dorsal sep., lanceolate or ovate-lanceolate, acuminate; lip to 2.5cm, simple, lanceolate, long-acuminate, apex slightly recurved, short-clawed, callus with 4 longitudinal keels, irregularly dentate; column to 1cm, wings porrect, decurved, lacerate. Peru.

***O. ramosissimum*** Lindl. Pseudobulbs to 12×5cm, ovoid to ovoid-oblong, apically, unifoliate. Lvs to 60×5cm, linear-lanceolate, acute. Panicle to 1.5m, erect, apex much-branched, densely many-fld; fls to 5cm diam., fragrant, sep. and pet. white spotted violet, undulate and reflexed, narrowly lanceolate, acuminate; lip to 18×7mm, white blotched violet at base, cordate or deltoid, acuminate, undulate, callus white, bilamellate, multidentate dorsally. Spring. Venezuela, Colombia, Ecuador.

***O. ramulosum*** Lindl. Pseudobulbs to 12×5cm, ovoid, usually pale brown, apically bifoliate. Lvs to 60×4cm, linear to linear-oblanceolate, acute, coriaceous. Panicle to 1m, erect or arching, short-branched, many-fld; sep. and pet. yellow, base marked deep brown; sep. to 15×6mm, acute to subobtuse, dorsal sep. obovate-oblong or spathulate, undulate, lateral sep. free, undulate; pet. to 12×6mm, spathulate to elliptic-obovate, acute to apiculate; lip to 10×5mm, yellow marked brown, sessile, ovate or ovate-oblong to elliptic-oblong, acute to obtuse, convex, callus yellow or pale yellow, 4–7-lobed; column brown, to 5mm. Colombia, Venezuela, Ecuador.

***O. retusum*** Lindl. Pseudobulbs to 5cm, narrowly ellipsoid to ovoid, apically unifoliate. Lvs to 30×2cm, linear-lanceolate to elliptic-linear, obtuse to subacute. Panicle to 60cm, slender, short-branched, erect, loosely many-fld; sep. and pet. orange-red tinged yellow; sep. to 16×5mm, broadly oblanceolate to narrowly obovate, acute, concave, laterals oblique, dorsally carinate; pet. smaller than sep., narrowly oblong-obovate, acute; lip to 10×7mm, golden-yellow, sessile, oblong-subquadrate, recurved above, simple or slightly 3-lobed, retuse, disc with sulcate callus or 2 ridges to middle; column to 3mm, with prominent margin on each side. Ecuador, Peru, Colombia.

***O. rigidum*** Lindl. Pseudobulbs to 3.5cm, ovate or pyriform, apically unifoliate. Lvs to 15×1.5cm, linear-ligulate, acute, carinate. Panicle far exceeding lvs, loosely branched toward apex; sep. and pet. bright canary-yellow; dorsal sep. to 15×5mm, spreading, ovate-lanceolate, acuminate, concave, lateral sep. longer and narrower than dorsal sep.; pet. similar to dorsal sep., slightly wider; lip to 2×1cm, deep yellow, narrow-clawed, subquadrate, apex recurved, prominently apiculate, callus on claw, bilamellate, dentate in front; column clavate, wings irregularly lacerate. Peru, Ecuador.

***O. sanderianum*** Rchb. f. Pseudobulbs to 8×4cm, ovoid, apically bifoliate. Lvs to 25×3cm, narrow-linear, subacute. Panicle short-branched, suberect, arching, many-fld; sep. and pet. light ochre marked brown, lanceolate, acuminate; sep. to 35×8mm, longer than pet.; lip to 2.5×1cm, white with large purple-crimson mark below callus, clawed, subpandurate, acute, undulate, callus papillose; column white tipped pale yellow, with 2 subulate cirri at apex, anth. yellow. Venezuela, Colombia.

***O. schillerianum*** Rchb. f. Pseudobulbs to 7×3.5cm, ovoid, apically unifoliate or bifoliate. Lvs to 30×3cm, thin, minutely apiculate. Raceme erect, surpassing lvs, several- to many-fld; fls fragrant, sep. and pet. yellow blotched brown or maroon, elliptic-lanceolate, acute to acuminate; sep. to 2.5×1cm; pet. slightly smaller, finely pubesc.; lip to 2×1cm, white at base, centre purple-brown tipped yellow, clawed, deflexed, lateral lobes small, erect, midlobe oblong, acute, undulate, pubesc., disc with 2 blunt calli; column green-cream. Winter–spring. Venezuela, Colombia.

***O. tripudians*** Rchb. f. & Warsc. Pseudobulbs to 10cm, oblong-ovoid or ellipsoid, apically bifoliate. Lvs to 25×2.5cm, bright green, oblong-lanceolate, acute or acuminate. Raceme arching, far exceeding lvs, sometimes branched, many-fld; sep. to 3.5×1cm, maroon-brown, yellow at base and tips, elliptic-lanceolate to elliptic-oblong, acuminate; pet. smaller than sep., golden-yellow blotched maroon-brown near base; lip to 2.5cm, white or cream blotched rose or purple-red, with short claw parallel to column, subquadrate to pandurate, dentate, disc white with 10-keeled calli, spotted purple-red; column to 1.5cm, arching, with 2 tridentate wings above. Colombia, Ecuador, Peru.

***O. triumphans*** Rchb. f. Pseudobulbs to 10×4cm, ovoid-ellipsoid, apically bifoliate. Lvs to 40×4cm, oblong-lanceolate, coriaceous, acute, petiolate. Raceme or panicle to 90cm, erect to arching, 5–12-fld; fls to 10cm diam., sep. and pet. golden-yellow variously spotted rich chestnut-brown; sep. to 5.5×1.5cm, oblong-lanceolate, acute or acuminate; pet. to 4.5×1.5cm, elliptic-lanceolate, acute, undulate; lip to 3.5×2cm, white apically blotched red-brown, short-clawed, oblong-ovate, long-apiculate, lacerate, crest bidentate; column to 3cm, arcuate, with finely toothed auricles. Spring. Colombia, Venezuela.

***O. wallisii*** Lind. & Rchb. f. Pseudobulbs to 9cm, ovoid, apically unifoliate. Lvs to 25×1.5cm, linear, acute or acuminate. Raceme or panicle arching, to 50cm or more; fls to 5cm diam., fleshy, sep. and pet. to 6.5×3.5cm, golden-yellow blotched cinnamon-brown, oblong-lanceolate, acute or apiculate; pet. with fewer markings and slightly smaller than sep.; lip white streaked rose-purple near apex, long-clawed, midlobe oblong-ovate or oblong-elliptic, tip sharply reflexed, fringed, callus linear, grooved, terminating in 2 teeth; column short, broadly winged. Colombia, Venezuela, Peru.

***O.* grexes and cultivars** (see also × *Odontioda,* × *Odontonia,* × *Odontocidium,* × *Colmanara,* × *Wilsonara*); many plants which have received awards are clones of the species *O. crispum*.

*O.* Aloretus 'Roke': very large fls, white with maroon blotches attractively arranged on the sep. and pet., brown markings on the lip.

*O.* Ardentissimum: early hybrid, mostly white with deep red markings.

*O.* Buttercrisp: lovely pale yellow fls with red markings on the white-bordered lip.

*O.* Costro: fls large, mauve-red.

*O.* Coupe Point 'Mont Millais': fls large with white pet., sep. flushed with rose, sep. and lip marked with brown.

*O.* Cristor: outstanding white fls.

*O.* Durham Pancho: fls large lemon yellow with deep gold markings on all parts.

*O.* Goldrausch: fls brilliant golden yellow with brown markings.

*O.* Grouville Bay 'Mont Millais': lovely white fls of good shape boldly marked with bright red.

*O.* Hambuhren Gold: fls rich golden with dark chestnut markings.

*O.* Incaspum: fls shapely white with spots and striped of dark red on all the parts.

*O.* Kopan: large branched spikes of yellow fls with mahogany spotting.

*O.* Lemon Drop: fls deep canary yellow with a few golden-brown markings on the lip.

*O.* Moselle: fls yellow with brown markings.

*O.* Nicky Strauss: fls well-shaped, white, heavily marked with red.

*O.* Pescalo: lovely whites of good shape, some with red markings.

*O.* Pumistor: fls large, white with red spots on the pet. and lip.

*O.* Rialto: lovely white with yellow markings.

*O.* Robesca: fls large, white with red markings.

*O.* Royal Occasion: lovely white with yellow markings on the lip.

*O.* Royal Wedding: lovely white with yellow markings.

*O.* Saint Brelade 'Jersey': a new line of breeding from *Lemboglossum rossii*, fls well shaped, deep red outline in white with a wide mottled margin on the lip.

*O.* Spendidum: small flowered white but very prolific on branching spikes.

*O.* Stonehurst Yellow: strong plants with large spikes of golden yellow fls marked with deeper yellow.

*O.* Stropheon: fls large of heavy texture, usually with white backgrounds heavily overlaid with deep purple-red; many clones have been awarded.

*O.* Tontor: outstanding white fls.

***O. alexandrae*** Batem. See *O. crispum*.
***O. bictoniense*** (Batem.) Lindl. See *Lemboglossum bictoniense*.
***O. brachypterum*** Rchb. f. See *Otoglossum brevifolium*.
***O. brevifolium*** Lindl. See *Otoglossum brevifolium*.
***O. cervantesii*** La Ll. & Lex. See *Lemboglossum cervantesii*.
***O. chiriquense*** Rchb. f. See *Otoglossum chiriquense*.
***O. cimiciferum*** Rchb. f. See *Oncidium cimiciferum*.
***O. citrosmum*** Lindl. See *Cuitlauzina pendula*.
***O. compactum*** Rchb. f. See *O. aureopurpureum*.
***O. convallarioides*** (Schltr.) Ames & Correll. See *Osmoglossum convallarioides*.
***O. cordatum*** Lindl. See *Lemboglossum cordatum*.
***O. coronarium*** var. ***chiriquense*** (Rchb. f.) Veitch. See *Otoglossum chiriquense*.
***O. egertonii*** Lindl. See *Osmoglossum egertonii*.
***O. erosum*** Rich. & Gal. See *Lemboglossum stellatum*.
***O. gloriosum*** Lind. ex Rchb. f. See *O. odoratum*.
***O. grande*** Lindl. See *Rossioglossum grande*.
***O. grande*** var. ***williamsianum*** Rchb. f. See *Rossioglossum williamsianum*.
***O. hastilabium*** Lindl. See *Oncidium hastilabium*.
***O. hastilabium*** var. ***fuscatum*** Hook. See *O. cariniferum*.
***O. hookeri*** Lem. See *Lemboglossumcordatum*.
***O. hystrix*** Batem. See *O. luteo-purpureum*.
***O. insleayi*** (Barker ex Lindl.) Lindl. See *Rossioglossum insleayi*.
***O. koehleri*** Schltr. See *O. aureopurpureum*.
***O. krameri*** Rchb. f. See *Ticoglossum krameri*.
***O. lawrenceanum*** hort. See *Rossioglossum insleayi*.
***O. laxiflorum*** (Lindl.) Rchb. f. See *Gomesa laxiflora*.
***O. lueddemanni*** Reg. See *Lemboglossum cordatum*.
***O. maculatum*** La Ll. & Lex. See *Lemboglossum maculatum*.
***O. madrense*** Rchb. f. See *Lemboglossum maculatum*.
***O. majale*** Rchb. f. See *Lemboglossum majale*.
***O. membranaceum*** Lindl. See *Lemboglossum cervantesii*.
***O. oerstedii*** Rchb. f. See *Ticoglossum oerstedii*.
***O. pendulum*** (La Ll. & Lex.) Batem. See *Cuitlauzina pendula*.
***O. pescatorei*** Lindl. See *O. nobile*.
***O. planifolium*** (Lindl.) Rchb. f. See *Gomesa planifolia*.
***O. platycheilum*** Weatherby See *Lemboglossum majale*.
***O. polyxanthum*** hort. See *O. kegeljani*.
***O. pulchellum*** Batem. ex Lindl. See *Osmoglossum pulchellum*.
***O. purum*** Rchb. f. See *O. wallisii*.
***O. radiatum*** Rchb. f. See *O. luteo-purpureum*.
***O. recurvum*** (R. Br.) Lindl. See *Gomesa recurva*.
***O. rossii*** Lindl. See *Lemboglossum rossii*.
***O. spectatissimum*** Lindl. See *O. triumphans*.
***O. stellatum*** Lindl. See *Lemboglossum stellatum*.
***O. tetraplasium*** Rchb. f. See *O. angustatum*.
***O. uro-skinneri*** Lindl. See *Lemboglossum uro-skinneri*.
***O. warscewiczii*** Rchb. f. See *Miltoniopsis warscewiczii*.
***O. williamsianum*** Rchb. f. See *Rossioglossum williamsianum*.
For further synonymy see *Oncidium*.

**Odontoloma** J. Sm., nom. nud. See *Lindsaea*.

**Odontonema** Nees. (From Gk *odous*, tooth, and *nema*, thread, referring to the peduncles of *O. schomburgkianum*, which appear toothed with the falling away of the flowers.) Acanthaceae. 26 species of robust herbs and shrubs. Leaves opposite, entire. Inflorescence a terminal raceme or racemose panicle; flowers short-stalked; calyx lobes 5; corolla long-tubular, 5-lobed or bilabiate; stamens 2 attached above middle of corolla tube. Fruit a capsule. Tropical America. Z10.

CULTIVATION As for *Eranthemum*.

***O. callistachyum*** (Schldl. & Cham.) Kuntze. Evergreen pubesc. shrub to 4m. Stems 4-angled. Lvs to 30cm, ovate-oblong, acute, rugulose, stalked. Infl. a terminal racemose panicle, strongly erect; cal. downy, lobes bristly; cor. to 3cm, red, exterior glabrous, tube glandular within and on lobes, lower lip deflexed. Mexico.

***O. schomburgkianum*** (Nees) Kuntze. Evergreen shrub, erect to 2m. Stems leggy, woody in basal third, obscurely ridged, sparsely branched. Lvs to 22cm, oblong-lanceolate, acuminate, pale green, glabrous or sparsely downy at first, veins impressed above. Racemes to 90cm, very slender, pendulous, produced from upper lf axils; fls opposite, short-stalked; bracts narrow, inconspicuous; cal. to one-fifth length of cor., lobes slender; cor. to 3cm, crimson to scarlet, narrowly tubular, slightly swollen at base, then constricted, widening toward limb, lobes small, equal, rounded, semi-erect. Colombia.

***O. strictum*** (Nees) Kuntze. Evergreen glabrous shrub to 2m. Stems rigid, erect, usually simple. Lvs to 15cm, oblong, acuminate, somewhat undulate, glossy deep green. Infl. to 30cm, erect, slender, compact; cor. to 2.5cm, crimson, waxy, lobes small. C America. Sometimes misnamed *Justicia coccinea*.

For synonymy see *Thyrsacanthus*.

**× Odontonia**. *(Odontoglossum × Miltonia.)* Orchidaceae. Intergeneric hybrids of pastel colours with great charm. Plants consist of a group of compressed pseudobulbs growing from a basal rhizome, each with one or two leaves at its apex and two or more leaf-like sheaths arising at its base. Inflorescences arise in the axils of these sheaths and are usually simple. Flowers very varied, many with rounded shape but others with larger lip depending on the ancestry. Most of these hybrids are 'cool' growers though a few are tolerant of warmer conditions.

× *O.* Berlioz 'Lecoufle': large fls on tall infl; fls delicate mauve-pink on a white background with distinctive purple markings radiating from around the centre of the fl; several other clones have been awarded.

× *O.* Boussole 'Blanche': very floriferous hybrid often bearing two spikes at once; fls pure white with two very small maroon spots in the centre; long lasting.

× *O.* Debutante: semi-erect, branching sprays of medium-size fls; sep. and pet. are chocolate coloured with yellow tips, lip pure white; several awarded clones.

× *O.* Diane: unusual yellow fls in this generic cross; fls bright yellow with distinctive brown spots on the sep. and lip; several named clones, some awarded.

× *O.* Lulli 'Menuet': unusual white fls edged with mauve and with dark red spots towards the centre, lip large with a few orange dots in the throat.

× *O.* Molière: very large fls of splendid shape; fls white, sometimes flushed pink, margined with mauve and with purplish spots or lines on sep. and pet.; several awarded clones including 'Elite' and 'Lanni' which is almost pure white or very fine.

× *O.* Salam: vigorous plants with large fls; sep. and pet. deep peony purple-red, margined with white, lip broad and marked with a white border and yellow crest; several awarded plants including 'Fanion'.

**Odontophorus** N.E. Br. (From Gk *odous*, tooth, and *phoros*, bearing, referring to the presence of teeth on the leaves.) Aizoaceae. 3 species of leaf-succulents vegetatively similar in appearance to *Stomatium* but more closely allied to *Cheiridopsis* and *Cephalophyllum*, differing only in capsule detail. Low, shrub-forming plants with fleshy roots; stems ascending or prostrate and forming mats. Leaves 1–2 pairs per shoot, very thick, soft-fleshy, grey-green, tuberculate, pubescent, dentate. Flowers pedicellate, yellow or white. S Africa (Cape Province). Z9.

CULTIVATION As for *Argyroderma*.

***O. angustifolius*** L. Bol. Lvs 2.5–3.2cm, 4 per stem, oblong-linear to linear-tapered, tip rhombic and dentate with 3–4 marginal teeth. Fls 6mm diam., lemon yellow. Cape: Little Namaqualand.

***O. marlothii*** N.E. Br. Short-stemmed, with 2–3 lf pairs per stem. Lvs 25–35×7–8×7–8mm, somewhat swollen at base, side angles with 6–7 thickened, awned teeth, grey to dark green with prominent rounded tubercles tipped with fine white hairs. Fls 3cm diam., yellow. Cape: Little Namaqualand.

***O. nanus*** L. Bol. Low-growing, compact. Lvs crowded, 15×10×7–9mm, more or less ovate on upper surface, sides expanded and tuberculate, margins with stiff teeth, green to appearing green-white because of the hair-tipped tubercles. Fls to 43mm diam., white. Cape: Little Namaqualand.

***O. areolatus*** Marloth nom. nud. See *O. nanus*.

For illustration see AIZOACEAE.

**× Odontorettia**. *(Odontoglossum × Comparettia.)* Orchidaceae. Intergeneric orchid hybrids with small plants. Pseudobulbs very small, usually with one apical leaf and two sheath like leaves at the base. Inflorescences long and slender, bearing relatively large, brightly coloured flowers. These hybrids require intermediate or warm conditions.

× *O.* Mandarine: small plants with upright sprays of brilliant orange fls.

× *O.* Violetta: small plants with upright sprays of pink and purple spotted fls.

**Odontosoria** Fée BRAMBLE FERN. (From Gk *odous*, tooth, and *sorus*.) Dennstaedtiaceae. Some 12 species or more of terrestrial or lithophytic ferns. Rhizomes short- to long- or wide-creeping, covered with many dense roots and trichomes as well as, or instead of, scales. Fronds stipitate, erect to flexible or scandent, rampant, uniform, to 5× pinnate, frequently lanceolate to deltoid, glabrous; pinnules wedge-shaped, entire to lobed or otherwise incised at margin; rachis flexible, spiny, often grooved above, somewhat woody; veins forked, free; stipes approximate and clustered to distant, spiny. Sori sunken, marginal, terminating veinlets; indusia basally and laterally attached, forming oblong or urceolate involucrate cyst; paraphyses absent; sporangia stalked; annulus 18–22-celled; spores globose to oblong or tetrahedral, trilete, smooth or rough. Tropics. Z10.

CULTIVATION As for *Hypolepis*.

***O. aculeata*** (L.) J. Sm. Rhiz. short-creeping, woody to fibrous. Fronds flexible and scandent, to 3-pinnate, membranous; primary pinnae lanceolate to ovate, acute at apex, to 45×15cm, secondary pinnae lanceolate, acute at apex, to 8×3cm, final seg. narrowly wedge-shaped, to 4-lobed at margin, to 4mm wide; rachis spiny; stipes to 2m. W Indies.

***O. fumarioides*** (Sw.) J. Sm. Rhiz. short-creeping, to 6mm wide, woody to fibrous; scales to 2mm, spreading, linear to lanceolate. Fronds to 3m, flexible and scandent, to 5× pinnate, membranous; primary pinnae to 55×30cm, opposite, deltoid to lanceolate, secondary pinnae alternate or opposite, similar to primary, tertiary pinnae alternate, final seg. deeply lobed or fan-cut; stipes to 1m, spiny. W Indies.

***O. chinense*** (L.) J. Sm. See *Sphenomeris chinensis*.
***O. clavata*** (L.) J. Sm. See *Sphenomeris clavata*.
For further synonymy see *Davallia*.

**Odontospermum** Necker ex Schultz-Bip.
***O. aquaticum*** (L.) Schultz-Bip. See *Nauplius aquaticus*.
***O. maritimum*** (L.) Schultz-Bip. See *Asteriscus maritimus*.

**Oeceoclades** Lindl. (From Gk *oikeios*, private, and *klados*, branch.) Orchidaceae. About 30 species of terrestrial orchids related to *Eulophia*. Pseudobulbs well developed, on woody rhizome, 1- to several-leaved at apex. Leaves usually stiff, leathery or fleshy, usually conduplicate, often variegated, petiolate, the petiole articulated above the pseudobulb. Inflorescence racemose or paniculate, arising from base of pseudobulb; flowers resupinate, thin-textured; sepals and petals almost similar, free, spreading; lip 3- or 4-lobed, usually spurred, often with a callus at the mouth of the spur; column short, erect; pollinia 2. Tropical & S Africa, Madagascar, Mascarene Is., Seychelles, Comoros Is., India to New Guinea, Polynesia and Australia, Florida, Caribbean, C & S America. Z10.

CULTIVATION A most attractive genus of intermediate to warm-growing terrestrial orchids. In addition to the erect spikes of bloom, several of these species bear beautifully mottled leaves, particularly those from Madagascar which show the characteristic colouring of smaller semi-xerophytes in this region – dull pink and brown/green banding and spotting (cf. *Aloe bakeri*). Pot in deep, heavily crocked clays containing a mixture of coarse bark, garden compost, leafmould, sharp sand and a little dried FYM. Maintain light shade (full sunlight for spp. with coloured leathery leaves); reduce water during the winter months, misting to prevent shrivelling.

***O. angustifolia*** (Sengh.) Garay & P. Tayl. Pseudobulbs 2×2cm, ovoid or pear-shaped, 1-lvd, occasionally 2-lvd, at apex. Lvs more or less erect, to 10cm×7mm, petiolate, linear, acute, dull green mottled with purple. Infl. erect, racemose or with a few branches, to 30cm, 5–15-fld; sep. green-white below, brown above, pet. white with green stripes, lip white, edge of midlobe ochre yellow, lateral lobes and disc spotted with red, spur green; sep. 8×3mm, oblanceolate or elliptic, acute; pet. 6×4.5mm, elliptic; lip 10–12×14–16mm, trilobed, lateral lobes erect, midlobe obovate, bilobed; callus bilobed; spur globose or subglobose, slightly incurved, 3mm. Madagascar.

***O. ecalcarata*** (Schltr.) Garay & P. Tayl. Pseudobulbs 4–6×1.5cm, ovoid or ellipsoid, set close together on rhiz., 4–5-lvd, the lvs fully developed at flowering time. Lvs 20–25cm×7–8mm, linear, acute, deciduous. Infl. racemose or paniculate with a long peduncle, laxly many-fld; sep. and pet. green dotted with red, lip golden yellow with red spots; pedicel and ovary 10mm; sep. 7–8mm, ovate, obtuse; pet. similar but slightly broader; lip 7mm, trilobed, lateral lobes erect, obtuse, midlobe like a transverse bow with sharp angles, rounded and apiculate in front; spur absent; column 4.5mm. Madagascar.

***O. maculata*** (Lindl.) Lindl. Pseudobulbs 2–4×1.5–2cm, obliquely conical, sometimes slightly ribbed, 1-lvd. Lvs 8–32×2–5.5cm, lanceolate, stiff, leathery, pale grey-green mottled with darker green, tapering to a short petiole. Raceme to 35cm, about 12-fld; sep. and pet. green-pink, lip white with 2 purple-pink blotches in throat and purple-veined lateral lobes; pedicel and ovary 12mm; sep. and pet. 9–10×3–4mm, lanceolate, pet. slightly wider, lateral sep. spreading and curving down; lip 9×8mm with 2 white, erect calli in throat, trilobed, lateral lobes rounded, erect, midlobe obovate, bilobed, lobes rounded; spur 4–5mm, bulbous at tip; column 3–4mm. Tropical Africa (widespread), Florida, Caribbean, C & S America.

***O. pulchra*** (Thouars) Clements & Cribb. Robust, to 1m; pseudobulbs 12–16×1–1.5cm, spindle-shaped, surrounded with remains of fibrous sheaths, 2–3-lvd. Petiole 12–20cm; lf blade 20–70×3–6cm, lanceolate, fairly thin-textured. Raceme lax, to 1m; peduncle more than twice as long as rachis; fls yellow-green with small red-purple lines on pet. and lip, throat orange-yellow; pedicel and ovary 2–3cm; sep. 11×3mm, lanceolate, acute, lateral sep. curved and slightly narrower than dorsal sep.; pet. 9×4mm, oblong, acute; lip 6–7×12–15mm with a bifid callus 2mm long in the throat, trilobed, lobes obovate, lateral lobes obscure, midlobe deeply bilobed; spur short, globose, sometimes slightly bifid; column 4–5mm. Madagascar, Mascarene Is., Comoros Is., Asia and SE Asia to New Guinea, Polynesia and Australia.

***O. roseovariegata*** (Sengh.) Garay & P. Tayl. Pseudobulbs 2.5×2.5cm, ovoid, clustered, violet-brown, 2-lvd. Lvs prostrate, to 4×3.5cm, ovate, acuminate, margins undulate, dark purple-black mottled with pink. Infl. erect, racemose or slightly branched, to 55cm, laxly many-fld; sep. and pet. green flushed with purple outside, lip white, densely red-spotted, column yellow-green, anth. white; sep. 5–6×2mm, oblanceolate, obtuse, lateral sep. slightly curved; pet. 4–5×3mm, oblong-lanceolate, obtuse; lip 3.5–4×7–8mm, trilobed, lateral lobes erect, truncate, midlobe recurved, more or less quadrate, emarginate; spur 5mm, pendent, cylindrical. Madagascar.

***O. saundersiana*** (Rchb. f.) Garay & P. Tayl. Pseudobulbs 6–20×1.5–2cm, conical or cylindrical, clustered, 1–3-lvd. Lf blade 10–22×4–8cm, glossy green, leathery, narrowing abruptly to a channelled petiole almost as long as blade. Raceme longer than lvs, 20–40-fld; fls yellow-green flushed with purple-brown and with purple-brown veins; sep. 10–20×5–6mm, oblanceolate; pet. 10–15×8mm, ovate; lip 15–20mm with 2 calli at base, 4-lobed, lobes rounded; spur 5–6mm, straight, cylindrical, obtuse. Tropical Africa (widespread).

For synonymy see *Eulophia*.

**Oemleria** Rchb. (For Herr Oemler, of Dresden, a friend of Nuttall, Elliott and Torrey, who supplied many rare plants to Reichenbach.) OSO BERRY; OREGON PLUM. Rosaceae. 1 species, a deciduous shrub to 5m; bark smooth, grey or rufous. Stems rather straight, slender; branchlets glabrous, bright green. Leaves to 10×3cm, alternate, oblong to oblanceolate, glossy dark green above, grey and pubescent beneath, simple, entire; stipules small, abscising; petiole 6.5mm. Flowers dioecious, 6.5mm diam., white, fragrant, in short, nodding, 10cm-racemes terminating leafy branchlets; calyx green, tube turbinate-campanulate, 5mm, deciduous; sepals 5, 3mm; petals 5, obovate to narrow-obovate, to 6mm, patent in staminate flowers, smaller and erect in pistillate flowers; stamens 15 in 3 rings, abortive in pistillate flowers; carpels 5, free, glabrous; style short. Fruit 1–5 drupes, oval, black, glaucous, 1-seeded, with thin pulp and bony endocarp. Spring. Western N America. Related to *Prunus*, but pistils 5, free. Z6.

CULTIVATION Native to the moist, rich woodlands of the west coast of North America, *Oemleria* is a suckering shrub suitable for the woodland garden, or for damp, shaded shrub borders. *O. cerasiformis* is grown primarily for its almond-scented white flowers, opening in late winter and early spring and most freely borne on male plants, although on female plants they are followed by attractive sloe-black, plum-like fruits. *Oemleria* is hardy to −20°C/−4°F, and although tolerant of a range of soil types, will become chlorotic on shallow chalk soils. Grow in well-drained, moisture-retentive soils, in shade. Prune after flowering, to thin out old shoots and to relieve overcrowding. Old plants may be rejuvenated by cutting hard back.

***O. cerasiformis*** (Torr. & A. Gray) Greene. As for the genus.

For synonymy see *Nuttallia* and *Osmaronia*.

**Oenanthe** L. (From Gk *oinanthe*, inflorescence of the grape-vine.) Umbelliferae. 30 species of glabrous perennial herbs. Leaves usually pinnate. Umbels compound, usually with numerous bracts and bracteoles; flowers white; calyx teeth acute; petals emarginate, apex incurved; style conical, narrow. Fruit ovoid or oblong, terete, with a broad flat commisure; seeds flattened. N Hemisphere, S Africa, Australia.

CULTIVATION Found predominantly in marshland, water meadows and other damp habitats, *Oenanthe* spp. are suitable for naturalizing in damp fertile soils in the wild garden and other informal situations. *O. javanica* 'Flamingo' is a brightly variegated groundcover plant ideal for wet situations or use in containers and bedding. Propagate by stem tip cuttings, division or by simple layering (the last tends to occur spontaneously in any case). *O.javanica* is cultivated and collected from the wild and eaten as a vegetable in its native regions; it much resembles celery. Propagate by seed. *O.crocata* L., the hemlock water dropwort, is extremely poisonous in all its parts, and with *Conium maculatum*, hemlock, and *Cicuta virosa*, cow bane, accounts for about 10% of livestock poisonings in the UK.

***O.javanica*** (Bl.) DC. Stems 20–40cm, erect, angled, striate, from a branching base. Lvs 7–15cm, deltoid or deltoid-ovate, 1–2× pinnate, petiolate, terminal seg. 1–3×0.7–1.5cm, ovate or narrow-ovate, acute or subacuminate, irregularly toothed, sometimes deeply lobed. Umbels opposite lvs, pedunculate, 5–15 rayed, umbellets 10–25-fld; pedicels 2–5mm; fls white. Fr. 2.5mm, ellipsoid. Summer. India to Japan, Ryukyu, Taiwan, Malaysia, N Australia (Queensland). 'Flamingo': lvs splashed and zoned pale pink, cream and white. Z10.

***O.pimpinelloides*** L. Perenn., 30–100cm; roots with ovoid tubers towards ends. Stems solid, erect, branched, grooved. Lvs bipinnate, seg. 0.5–3cm, ovate to lanceolate, linear-lanceolate or linear, lobes usually entire. Umbel terminal, to 5cm across; rays 6–15, 1–2cm, stout; fls white. Fr. 3.5mm, cylindric, strongly ribbed. W & S Europe to SW Asia. Z8.

***O.japonica*** Miq. See *O.javanica*.
***O.stolonifera*** var. ***japonica*** (Miq.) Maxim. See *O.javanica*.

**Oenothera** L. (Name used by Theophrastus.) EVENING PRIMROSE; SUNDROPS; SUNCUPS. Onagraceae. 124 species of annual, biennial or perennial herbs. Stems erect, ascending, rarely decumbent and sometimes rooting at nodes, with taproot or fibrous roots, rarely rhizomatous. Leaves sometimes in basal rosette, otherwise alternate, sessile or petiolate, entire and dentate or pinnatifid; stipules absent. Flowers usually large and showy, solitary in leaf axils or gathered into corymbose, racemose or spicate inflorescences, actinomorphic, 4-merous, opening at dawn or dusk, soon fading; floral tube cylindrical, apex flared, deciduous; petals white, yellow or purple, rarely red or with a red spot, becoming orange and purple, obovate or obcordate; stamens 8 in 2 whorls; ovary 4-locular. Fruit an elongate capsule, terete to quadrangular or winged, straight or curved, sessile or constricted at base; seeds many, in 1–3 rows. N & S America, many naturalized elsewhere, usually on disturbed ground. Cultivated ornamentals include the evening primroses, which are generally evening-flowering, and the sundrops or suncups, which are day-flowering. Seeds of *O.biennis* are a source of gammalinoleic acid, which is important in the production of fatty acids and prostaglandins, used medicinally.

CULTIVATION Some of the 'evening' primroses are day-flowering, but some bear fragile and often scented blooms at night, which wither and die in the morning sun. Cultivated types are generally tap-rooted plants of stony and well-drained soils or mountainous country, preferring a dryish, sunny site in the garden: heavy clay soils may induce winter rots even in normally persistent spp. such as *O.macrocarpa*. A small group including *O.californica*, *O.pallida* ssp. *trichocalyx* and *O.deltoides* are challenging but interesting desert growers with little frost tolerance and requirements for extremely rapid drainage; these are grown more successfully under alpine house or frame conditions, in deep pots of a gritty, low fertility loam-based medium. Many spp. are variable in their perennating habit, influenced by climate and soil type in the speed with which they began to flower, seed and senesce: certain perennial spp. are therefore often best treated as annuals/biennials when gardening on heavy soils or in cold areas such as north eastern America (e.g. *O.acaulis*, *O.speciosa*, *O.rosea*). The most popular tall-growing spp. are *O.biennis* and *O.glazioviana*, prolific seeders which are useful for naturalizing in wild areas where their abundant seed will be devoured by small birds, particularly finches. The young shoots of *O.biennis* are sometimes eaten raw in salads or the roots cooked as for salsify. The colour interest provided by the red-flushed stems and calyces of *O.glazioviana* 'Afterglow' and the mahogany-tinted spring foliage of garden cvs of *O.fruticosa* spp. *glauca* make these excellent plants for informal borders. Low-growing spp. such as *O.acaulis*, *O.caespitosa* *O.macrocarpa* and *O.speciosa* make good front border or scree plants. *O.speciosa* and *O.caespitosa* produce invasive rootstocks which usually require curbing on the rock garden. Propagate annuals and perennials by seed, in a sandy medium in early spring or sow annuals in situ, autumn to spring. Sow biennial seed from late spring to early summer. Propagate perennials by division, or by softwood cuttings taken in spring before flowering. Grow on in individual pots of a low-fertility, loam-based medium and plant out the following spring while still small to allow undisturbed development of the taproot.

***O.acaulis*** Cav. Tufted perenn. or bienn., to 15cm, sessile or short-stemmed, branches angled, becoming zig-zag. Lvs 12–20cm, oblanceolate, irregularly pinnatifid, hairy, terminal lobe enlarged. Fls 5–8cm diam.; floral tube slender, 5–12cm; pet. emarginate, white ageing rose, evening-flowering. Capsule obovoid, 1cm, 4-winged, woody. Chile. 'Aurea': to 15cm, with prostrate branches; fls large, 5–8cm, yellow. Z5.

***O.albicaulis*** Pursh. Decumbent annual or bienn., 15–30cm. Stems white-pubesc. Rosette lvs 2.5–5cm, spathulate to obovate, stem lvs lanceolate, pinnatifid. Fls solitary, axillary, 5–7.5cm diam., evening-flowering; floral tube 2.5cm; pet. obcordate, 1–3cm, white ageing pink. Capsule cylindrical, 2.5–3cm. Western N America (Rocky Mts). 'Mississippi Primrose': fls pure white ageing through cream to shell-pink, fragrant. Z5.

***O.argillicola*** Mackenzie. Bienn. to perenn., fleshy, glabrous. Stems 60–120cm. Rosette lvs 15–20cm, oblanceolate-linear, stem lvs linear-lanceolate. Infl. terminal, evening-flowering; floral tube 3–5cm; pet. 2.5–3cm, yellow ageing vermilion. Capsule attenuate, spreading, woody at base. Eastern N America (Appalachians). Z5.

***O.biennis*** L. COMMON EVENING PRIMROSE; GERMAN RAMPION. Erect, annual or bienn.; roots fleshy. Stems erect, branched, 10–150cm, without red spots, hairy. Lvs green or blue-green, shallow-dentate, mature lvs red-veined, rosette lvs 10–30cm, oblong-lanceolate, stem lvs 8–15cm, lanceolate. Infl. erect, elongate, spicate or branched, evening-flowering, fls 4–5×4cm; floral tube 18–44mm; pet. 18–25mm, yellow, ageing gold. Capsule attenuate, 1.5–4cm. Eastern N America, naturalized in Europe (except extreme N & S) and elsewhere. Z4.

***O.brachycarpa*** A. Gray. Perenn., glabrous to tomentose, subsessile. Lvs 5–15cm, tufted, grey-green, narrow, entire to sinuate-pinnatifid, usually with a terminal lobe. Evening-flowering; floral tube 10–22cm; pet. broadly rhombic-ovate, 2.5–5cm, pale yellow, ageing lavender. Capsule 2.5cm, ovoid to sub-cylindrical, winged, sometimes only winged above. W Texas to SE Arizona and New Mexico. Z6.

***O.caespitosa*** Nutt. Tuft-forming bienn. to perenn. Stems 1 to several, 10–40cm, subglabrous, strigulose or hirsute to villous. Lvs in a rosette, 2–25×1–4cm, oblanceolate to rhombic or spathulate, irregularly sinuate-dentate, apex acute to rounded, base attenuate; petiole winged. Fls fragrant, evening-flowering, several opening together; buds erect; floral tube yellow-green, sometimes tinged red, 4–14cm; sep. green-red with prominent red veins; pet. 2–5×0.5–1cm, white ageing pink. Capsule 1.5–5cm, cylindrical to ellipsoid, straight to curved, sometimes sigmoid, tapering to a sterile beak. Western N America (Washington). ssp. ***caespitosa.*** Floral tube 3.5–7.5cm; pet. fading rose-purple. Capsule falcate, base distinctly asymmetric. ssp. ***crinata*** (Rydb.) Munz. Many-branched, forming dense mats. Floral tube 3.5–7.5cm; pet. fading rose or deep purple. ssp. ***macroglottis*** (Rydb.) W.L. Wagner, Stockhouse & Klein. Stems 4–8cm. Lvs oblanceolate to spathulate, glandular-pubesc., dentate. Floral tube 7.5–11cm; pet. fading pink to pale rose. Capsule subfalcate. ssp. ***marginata*** (Nutt. ex Hook. & Arn.) Munz. Lvs oblanceolate to lanceolate or elliptic, pinnately lobed. Floral tube 8–14mm; pet. fading pink to lavender. Capsule straight. Z4.

***O.californica*** S. Wats. Perenn. with creeping rhiz. Stems erect, 7–10cm. Lvs narrow-lanceolate, toothed or pinnatifid, strigose or hairy. Fls fragrant, evening-flowering, 5cm diam., white to pale pink with yellow centre. California. Z7.

***O.coryi*** W.L. Wagner. Tuft-forming perenn., sessile or subsessile. Rosettes 10–60cm across. Lvs to 16×0.7cm, linear to narrowly lanceolate, densely strigillose, lower half remotely pinnately lobed. Fls 1–3, slightly fragrant, evening-flowering; floral tube 5.5–12.5cm; pet. to 4×4cm, yellow, fading orange, drying lavender to purple, broadly obovate, sometimes with an apical tooth. Capsule 2.5–3cm, ovoid, abruptly constricted to apical beak, marginal wings to 6mm wide. WC Texas. Z7.

***O.deltoides*** Torr. & Frém. DESERT EVENING PRIMROSE. Annual, 5–25cm, branching from base, pubesc. above. Lvs 5–10cm, crowded, rhombic-ovate to rhombic-lanceolate, entire to pinnatifid. Evening-flowering; fls solitary, axillary, white, ageing pink, 4–8cm diam. Capsule 2.5–8cm, woody, spreading to reflexed. California (deserts). Z9.

***O.drummondii*** Hook. Erect to procumbent annual or perenn., densely strigillose, sometimes villous; taproot to 2cm. Stems 10–50cm, stiff, sometimes flushed red, simple or branched. Lvs grey-green, densely hairy to glandular-puberulent, remotely shallowly toothed to subentire, basal lvs 5–14×1–2cm, narrowly oblanceolate to elliptic, apex acute, stem lvs to 8×2.5cm, elliptic to obovate, sometimes lyrate. Fls 1 per spike, evening-flowering; floral tube 2–5cm; sep. to 3cm, green to yellow-green, flushed and edged red, tips free; pet. 2–4.5×2.5–5cm, yellow, broadly obovate, truncate to emarginate. Capsule

2–5.5cm, ellipsoid. N America (Atlantic coast and Pacific coast to Baja California). Z6.

***O.elata*** ssp. ***hookeri*** (Torr. & A. Gray) W. Dietr. & W.L. Wagner. HOOKERS EVENING PRIMROSE. Erect bienn. to perenn., to 80cm, with a basal rosette, stem and capsule with erect pubescence and glandular hairs in the region of the inflorescence. Lvs 5–12.5cm, lanceolate. Fls many in terminal spikes; cal. tube 2–5cm; sep. flushed with red, with distinct red pustulate hairs. Capsules 2.5–4cm, gradually narrowed upwards. N Western America. ssp. ***hirsutissima*** (A. Gray ex S. Wats.) Dietr. Stem flushed with red, without glandular hairs in the region of the inflorescence; the free tips of the capsule distinct. Z7.

***O.flava*** (A. Nels.) Garrett. Perenn.; stemless, caespitose. Lvs to 20cm, oblong-linear to oblanceolate, runcinate-pinnatifid. Cal. tube to 12cm, sep. tips free in bud, 1–2(–5)mm; pet. (0.7–)1–2.6(–3.8)cm, pale yellow to white, usually obovate with a terminal tooth. Capsule 4-winged. Washington south to California, Arizona and Mexico. ssp. ***taraxacoides*** (Wooton & Standl.) W.L. Wagner. MOUNTAIN DANDELION. Sep. often flecked with red-purple splotches and with free sep. tips in bud (1.7–)2.5–10(–12)mm; pet. (2.5–)3–4.5(–5)cm, usually obcordate. New Mexico, Mexico. Z8.

***O.fruticosa*** L. SUNDROPS. Bienn. or perenn., 30–80cm. Stem unbranched or branched, strigose to hairy overall, tinged red. Basal lvs 3–12×0.5–3cm, oblanceolate to obovate, toothed, stem lvs 2–11×0.2–5cm lanceolate. Day-flowering; sep. 0.5–2cm; pet. 1.5–2.5cm, suborbicular, shallow-toothed, deep yellow. Capsule clavate (because the basal portion is sterile), without glandular hairs. Eastern N America. 'Fireworks' ('Feuerwerkeri'): lvs tinged purple; fls yellow. 'Golden Moonlight': to 80 cm high; fls large, bright yellow. 'Highlight' ('Hoheslicht'): fls yellow. 'Illumination': lvs leathery, tinged bronze; fls large, deep yellow. 'Lady Brookborough': fls yellow. 'Silvery Moon': to 80cm high; fls large, pale yellow. 'Sonnenwende': to 60cm; lvs red in autumn; fl. buds red-orange. 'Yellow River': stems brick red; fls bright canary yellow. 'Youngii': to 50cm; fls large, bright yellow. 'Youngii-lapsley': to 60cm; fls yellow. ssp. ***glauca*** (Michx.) Straley. Lvs broader, usually relatively glabrous and sometimes glaucous or more dentate. Capsule oblong to oblong-ellipsoid, but not clavate, sometimes with glandular hairs. Z4.

***O.glazioviana*** Micheli ex Mart. LARGE-FLOWERED EVENING PRIMROSE. Hirsute bienn., to 1.5m. Stems erect, spotted red, hairs triangular, base red. Lvs broadly lanceolate, crispate, basal lvs in a rosette, upper lvs decreasing in size, midvein white above, red beneath. Fls 5–8cm, evening-flowering; buds erect; sep. flushed or striped red; stigma exceeding anth. Capsule hairy, red at base. NW Europe, widely naturalized panglobally, except Antarctica. Possibly a garden hybrid between *O.grandiflora* and *O.elata*. Z3.

***O.jamesii*** Torr. & A. Gray. Similar to *O.elata* ssp. *hookeri* but cal. tube 7–10cm. Oklahoma to New Mexico.

***O.kunthiana*** (Spach) Munz. Perenn. Stems slender, to 60cm. Basal lvs 2–10cm, oblanceolate, sinuate-pinnatifid; stem lvs reduced. Fls few, evening-flowering; pet. to 1.5cm, white to pink. Capsule 1–1.5cm, obovoid, 4-winged above. Texas to Guatemala. Z8.

***O.laciniata*** Hill. Erect to procumbent annual or short-lived perenn., usually rosette-forming. Stems to 1m, green or flushed red, simple to much-branched, covered with stiff, straight hairs. Lvs villous to strigillose, rosette lvs 4–15×1–3cm, linear-oblanceolate to narrowly oblanceolate, deeply lobed or dentate, stem lvs 2–10×0.5–3.5cm, narrowly oblanceolate to narrowly elliptic. Fls 1 per spike, evening-flowering; floral tube 12–35×1mm, yellow, often flushed red, sparsely villous to glandular-pubesc.; mature buds narrowly oblong-ovoid, upward curving; sep. to 1.5cm, green to yellow-green, edged or flushed red, tips spreading; pet. 0.5–2.2×0.7–2cm, broadly ovate, yellow to pale yellow, truncate to emarginate. Capsule 2–5cm, cylindrical. US (N Dakota south to Texas and east to Atlantic Coast), naturalized in California and W Europe. Z3.

***O.longissima*** Rydb. Similar to *O.elata* ssp. *hookeri* but ashy-strigose, with cal. tube 7–10cm. SW US.

***O.macrocarpa*** Nutt. OZARK SUNDROPS. Perenn., subacaulescent to caulescent, branched from base, decumbent to erect, pubesc. Lvs 2–8cm, lanceolate to ovate or obovate, subentire to dentate, dark green with silver midribs, narrow. Fls opening in the evening, yellow, to 10cm diam; cal. tinted red. Capsule large, winged. SC US. 'Greencourt Lemon': fls yellow. Z5.

***O.nuttallii*** Torr. & A. Gray. Perenn., 30cm–1m, from subterranean rootstock, glabrous on stems but glandular-pubesc. in infl. Lvs 2–7.5cm, oblong-linear to lanceolate, usually entire, glabrous above, strigose beneath. Fls, white, 3.5–5cm diam., opening in the evening; cal. tube *c*2.5cm. Capsule *c*2.5cm, straight. Northwest N America. Name also applied to *O.albicaulis*. Z5.

***O.pallida*** Lindl. Glabrous, rhizomatous perenn., 20–50cm, freely branching, branches spreading. Lvs 2.5–7cm, lanceolate, subentire or undulate. Evening-flowering; fls fragrant; sep. tips free in bud; perianth tube 2.5–5cm; pet. 1–2.5cm, white ageing to pink. Capsule cylindrical. Western N America. ssp. ***trichocalyx*** (Nutt. ex Torr. & A. Gray) Munz & W. Klein. Lvs grey-green, usually sinuate-dentate. Sep. tips fused in bud. Z4.

***O.perennis*** L. SUNDROPS Perenn., 10–50cm. Stems slender, simple or few branched. Basal lvs 2.5–5cm, spathulate to oblanceolate, mostly entire, finely strigulose. Fls in a loose, leafy spike; buds nodding; pet. 6–8mm, yellow. Capsule ellipsoid to oblong. Eastern N America. Z5.

***O.pilosella*** Raf. SUNDROPS. Erect perenn., 10–50cm, covered in spreading hairs. Basal lvs obovate to oblanceolate, stem lvs 2.5–10cm, lanceolate. Pet. 1–2.5cm, yellow, prominently veined. Capsule linear-clavate. Central N America. Z3.

***O.primiveris*** A. Gray Stemless winter annual, hairy. Lvs 2–10cm, oblanceolate, deeply pinnatifid, lobes toothed or lobed. Pet. 2–4cm, yellow ageing orange. Capsules to 2.5cm, gradually tapering upward, leathery to almost woody, hairy. SW US. Z8.

***O.rhombipetala*** Nutt. ex Torr. & A. Gray. Erect, strigillose, rosette-forming bienn. Stems 30–150cm, simple or branched, densely to sparsely hairy. Rosette lvs to 20×2cm, narrowly oblanceolate, bluntly dentate to lobed, apex acute, gradually narrowing to petiole, stem lvs to 15×2.5cm, narrowly lanceolate to narrowly oblanceolate, sessile or short-petiolate. Spikes elongated, densely-fld; floral tube 3–4.5cm, yellow, broadly elliptic to rhombic-elliptic, apex acute. Capsule 12–25mm, narrowly ellipsoid. N America (Great Plains). Z4.

***O.rosea*** L'Hérit. ex Ait. Erect, strigulose perenn., occasionally annual, 15–60cm. Lvs oblong-ovate to oblanceolate, basal lvs 2–5cm, entire to coarsely pinnatifid; petioles 1–2cm; stem lvs 1.5–3cm, subentire to pinnatifid, especially at base. Infl. spicate; floral tube 4–8mm; pet. 4–10×3–4mm, pink to red-violet. Capsule clavate, attenuate at base, ribbed or winged. N & S America (Texas to Peru), naturalized S Europe. Z6.

***O.speciosa*** Nutt. WHITE EVENING PRIMROSE. Perenn., erect, 30–60cm, strigose; rhiz. creeping. Lvs oblong-lanceolate to obovate, remotely toothed or pinnatifid, with basal rosettes. Day-flowering; floral tube 1cm; buds nodding; fls from upper axils, white ageing rose, sometimes pink when young; pet. 2–2.5cm. Capsule 2.5×1cm, upper part enlarged, lower part narrowing to cylindrical base. SW US to Mexico. 'Rosea': to 30cm; fls pale pink, opening during the day. Z5.

***O.stubbei*** Dietr., Raven & W.L. Wagner. Rosette-forming perenn. Stems 30cm–3m, several, decumbent, often with secondary branches, rooting at nodes, usually flushed red, sparsely to moderately hairy, young parts villous. Lvs pale green, remotely dentate, pubesc., stem lvs 2–7×0.5–15cm, narrowly elliptic to narrowly lanceolate, apex acute, base attenuate, rosette lvs 8–23×0.5–2cm. Fls erect; floral tube 10–15cm, flaring at mouth, sparsely villous or glandular-pubesc., glabrous within; sep. usually edged red-purple, 3–5cm; pet. 3–5×3.5–5cm, yellow, fading orange, drying red-purple. Capsule 25–35×4–5mm, cylindrical, base falcate. Mexico (Sierra Madre). Z8.

***O.tetraptera*** Cav. Branched annual, to 40cm, hairy. Lvs to 9×2.5cm, lanceolate to oblanceolate or narrowly elliptic, sinuate to sinuate-pinnatifid. Evening-flowering; buds erect; cal. tube to 3.5cm; pet. to 3.5cm, white, fading to pink. Texas south to S America.

***O.triloba*** Nutt. Sparsely hairy annual or bienn. Sessile or stems to 15cm. Lvs 5–20cm, tufted, oblanceolate, deeply pinnatifid. Evening-flowering; fls 1–2×2.5cm, pale yellow; pet. suborbicular with apical sinus and sometimes with dentate midlobe. Capsule 1cm, hard, ovoid, 4-winged. Central N America (Kansas to Texas). Z5.

***O.amoena*** Lehm. See *Clarkia amoena*..
***O.berlandieri*** (Spach) Walp. See *O.speciosa* non *Calylophus berlandieri*.
***O.biennis*** var. ***hirsutissima*** A. Gray ex S. Wats. See *O.elata* ssp. *hirsutissima*.
***O.brachycarpa*** var. ***typica*** sensu Munz. See *O.coryi*.
***O.childsii*** hort. See *O.speciosa*.
***O.cheiranthifolia*** Hornem. See *Camissonia cheiranthifolia*.
***O.clutei*** Nels. See *O.longissima*.
***O.densiflora*** Lindl. See *Boisduvalia densiflora*.
***O.erythrosepala*** Borb. See *O.glazioviana*.
***O.fraseri*** Pursh. See *O.fruticosa* ssp. *glauca*.
***O.glauca*** Michx. See *O.fruticosa* ssp. *glauca*.
***O.graciliflora*** Hook. & Arn. See *Camissonia graciliflora*.
***O.grandiflora*** (Lindl.) Nutt. See *Clarkia amoena* ssp. *lindleyi*.
***O.heterantha*** Nutt. See *Camissonia subacaulis*.
***O.hookeri*** Torr. & A. Gray. See *O.elata* ssp. *hookeri*.
***O.lamarckiana*** De Vries, non Ser. See *O.glazioviana*.
***O.lavandulifolia*** Torr. & A. Gray. See *Calylophus lavandulifolius*.
***O.leucocarpa*** Comien ex Lehm. See *Calylophus serrulatus*.
***O.lindleyi*** Douglas. See *Clarkia amoena* ssp. *lindleyi*.
***O.linearis*** Michx. See *O.fruticosa*.
***O.marginata*** Nutt. ex Hook. & Arn. See *O.caespitosa* ssp. *marginata*.
***O.missouriensis*** Pursh. See *O.macrocarpa*.
***O.muricata*** L. See *O.biennis*.
***O.ovata*** Nutt. ex Torr. & A. Gray. See *Camissonia ovata*.
***O.pratensis*** (Small) Robinson. See *O.pilosella*.
***O.primuloidea*** H. Lév. See *Camissonia ovata*.
***O.pumila*** L. See *O.perennis*.
***O.pusilla*** Michx. See *O.perennis*.
***O.riparia*** Nutt. See *O.fruticosa*.
***O.rubicunda*** Lindl. See *Clarkia rubicunda*.
***O.serotina*** Lehm. See *O.fruticosa* ssp. *glauca*.
***O.serrulata*** Nutt. See *Calylophus serrulatus*.
***O.sinuata*** L. See *O.laciniata*.
***O.spinulosa*** Nutt. ex Torr. & A. Gray. See *Calylophus serrulatus*.
***O.subacaulis*** (Pursh) Garrett. See *Camissonia subacaulis*.
***O.taraxifolia*** Sweet. See *O.acaulis*.

***O. tenella*** Cav. See *Clarkia tenella*.
***O. tetragona*** Roth. See *O. fruticosa* ssp. *glauca*.
***O. trichocalyx*** Nutt. ex Torr. & A. Gray. See *O. pallida* ssp. *trichocalyx*.
***O. whitneyi*** A. Gray. See *Clarkia amoena* ssp. *whitneyi*.
***O. youngii*** hort. See *O. fruticosa* ssp. *glauca*.
For further synonymy see *Anogra, Lavauxia, Pachylophus* and *Raimannia*.

For illustration see HERBS.

**Oenotrichia** Copel. Dennstaedtiaceae. Some 4 species of terrestrial, epiphytic or lithophytic ferns. Rhizomes creeping, solenostelic, red-pubescent. Fronds stipitate, uniform, finely pinnatifid, deltoid, pubescent, thin-textured, final segments incised at margin, veins free; stipes erect, pubescent. Sori submarginal, dorsal, terminating veinlets; indusia semicircular to reniform, attached basally by sinus, free at margin; paraphyses present; annulus 12–28-celled, interrupted; spores tetrahedral, tuberculate. Australia. Z10.

CULTIVATION As for *Hypolepis*. Should be kept underpotted.

***O. tripinnata*** (F. Muell.) Copel. HAIRY LACE FERN. Rhiz. short-creeping. Fronds erect or suberect, 20×15cm or more, 3-pinnate or 2-pinnatifid, all divisions falcate, pinnae lanceolate or oblong, pinnules deeply lobed, lobes to 4, obovate, obtuse; rachis and costa pubesc.; stipes wiry, to 15cm, sulcate, pubesc. Australia (Queensland).

For synonymy see *Davallia*.

**Oeonia** Lindl. (From Gk *oionos*, a bird of prey.) Orchidaceae. About 6 species of epiphytic orchids, most with long, thin, branched stems. Racemes laxly few- to many-flowered; flowers green or white, the lip often spotted with red or rose pink; sepals and petals free; lip with 3–6 spreading lobes, enfolding column at base; anterior edge of anther toothed or bifid; pollinia 2. Madagascar, Mascarene Is. Z10.

CULTIVATION As for *Angraecum*, but with very frequent misting.

***O. oncidiiflora*** Kränzl. Stem to 80cm, pendent or ascending, sparsely branched, thin, bearing numerous roots and lvs. Roots 1.5–2.5mm diam., mostly aerial. Lvs 2–5×1–2.5cm, ovate-oblong or elliptic, clasping stem at base, bright green. Raceme to 15cm, laxly 2–7-fld; fls 25mm diam., green or yellow-green, lip white spotted with bright red in the throat; pedicel and ovary 15–20mm; sep. 10×4mm, obovate or oblong, obtuse; pet. similar but 2–3mm wide; lip 20–25×25mm, 4-lobed, the lower lobes 5×7mm, rounded, apical lobes 14–15mm wide, fan-shaped, throat scattered with small hairs; spur 7–20mm, tapering from a wide mouth then somewhat swollen at apex; column 2–3mm. Madagascar.

***O. volucris*** (Thouars) Dur. & Schinz. Stems long, thin and branched, pendent or ascending. Lvs about 25×8mm, ovate or elliptic, spread along stem. Racemes 30–35cm, laxly few-fld; fls white; dorsal sep. 12–15×5–6mm, obovate-oblong, lateral sep. 24×8mm, oblanceolate; pet. 12–15×10–12mm, obovate; lip 25–30mm, papillose in throat, trilobed, lateral lobes small, inrolled, midlobe obovate, deeply emarginate or bilobed with a tooth between the lobes; spur 6mm, tapering gradually from mouth to apex; column very short. Madagascar, Mascarene Is.

**Oeoniella** Schltr. (Diminutive of *Oeonia*.) Orchidaceae. 2–3 species of epiphytic orchids. Stems long and leafy. Racemes long or short, laxly few- to several-flowered; flowers mainly white; sepals and petals free; lip cone-shaped at base, surrounding the column, trilobed at apex; spur short; pollinia and stipites 2, viscidium 1. Madagascar, Mascarene Is., Seychelles. Z10.

CULTIVATION As for *Angraecum*, but with frequent misting.

***O. polystachys*** (Thouars) Schltr. Stem usually to 15cm, rarely to 60cm, branched, leafy; roots numerous, 2–3mm diam. Lvs 3–11×1.5–2cm, ligulate or oblong. Racemes arising from stem opposite lvs, erect, 15–25cm, 7–15-fld; fls white; pedicel and ovary 8mm; sep. 12–18×3mm, linear-lanceolate, acuminate, the lateral sep. longer than the dorsal; pet. 15–16mm, linear; lip 16–18mm, cone-shaped, trilobed at apex, lateral lobes broad, margin crenulate, midlobe linear, acuminate; spur 4mm, tapering to apex; column very short. Range as for the genus.

**Oerstedella** Rchb. f. (For Anders Sandoe Ørsted (1816–72), Danish botanist.) Orchidaceae. Some 25 species of epiphytic or terrestrial orchids allied to *Epidendrum*. Rhizome short. Stems clumped, cane-like, simple or branched, leafy, enveloped by numerous verrucose leaf-sheaths. Leaves numerous, distichous, coriaceous. Inflorescence a terminal (rarely axillary) raceme or a panicle, usually many-flowered; flowers showy; sepals broadly linear-lanceolate to oblong-lanceolate; petals subsimilar to sepals, oblique; lip clawed, adnate to column, 3-lobed, lateral lobes obtuse or acuminate, midlobe large, oblong to oblong-lanceolate, entire to crenulate, callus papillose; pollinia 4, waxy, viscidium absent. Tropical America. Z10.

CULTIVATION As for *Epidendrum pseudepidendrum*.

***O. endresii*** (Rchb. f.) Hagsater. Stems to 30cm, erect, tightly clustered, rigid, simple or branched. Lvs to 4.5×1.5cm, elliptic to oblong-lanceolate, obtuse. Raceme, to 15cm, erect, loosely few to several-fld; fls to 2.5cm diam., fragrant, opal-white tinged lavender to rose-purple; sep. to 11×5mm, elliptic to ovate-oblong, acute, pet. subequal to sep., oblanceolate to obovate-spathulate, obtuse; lip to 12×10mm, white blotched violet-purple, lateral lobes subtriangular, acute or obtuse, midlobe bilobulate, lobules spreading, callus submamillate; column subclavate, anth. purple-violet. Winter. Costa Rica, Panama.

***O. schumanniana*** (Schltr.) Hagsater. Stems to 50cm, erect or bowed, clustered, leafy toward apex, covered with verrucose lf-sheaths. Lvs to 9×2.5cm, lustrous, lanceolate to elliptic-oblong, subacute or obtuse. Infl. to 60cm, erect, a raceme or a panicle, loosely many-fld; fls to 2.5cm diam., fragrant, long-lived, fleshy; sep. and pet. yellow spotted red-brown, sep. to 12×5mm, oblanceolate to ovate, acute or obtuse, pet. to 15×8mm, obovate or obovate-spathulate, obtuse; lip to 15×12mm, dark lavender, lateral lobes oblong, obtuse, spreading, midlobe cuneate-obovate, bifid, entire to crenulate; disc with 2 submamillate basal calli. Costa Rica, Panama.

***O. schweinfurthiana*** (Correll) Hagsater. Stems slender, simple or branched toward apex. Lvs 11×2cm, elliptic-lanceolate, acute or obtuse. Raceme, to 10cm, few-fld; sep. and pet. brown, sep. to 12×7mm, elliptic to obovate-elliptic, obtuse, fleshy, pet. to 13×10mm, obovate-cuneate, rounded to truncate; lip to 15×18mm, deeply 3-lobed, lateral lobes bilobulate, lobules obcordate-ovate, midlobe deeply bilobulate, lobules obovate, crenulate, apex rounded, callus to 2mm, oblong, channelled, with 2 papillae; column to 6mm, apex bilobulate, lobules undulate-crenate. Guatemala.

***O. verrucosa*** (Sw.) Hagsater. Stems to 120×1cm, stout, reed-like. Lvs to 23×4cm, narrowly lanceolate to linear-lanceolate, acute, erect-ascending. Infl. to 40cm, usually a panicle, many-fld, erect; fls fragrant, long-lived, white to cream-yellow; sep. spreading, to 10×4mm, elliptic-oblong to elliptic-obovate, concave, subacute to obtuse; pet. to 10×3mm, oblanceolate to linear-spathulate, obtuse to subacute; lip to 12mm, deeply 3-lobed, lateral lobes obliquely oblong to elliptic-subquadrate, obtuse to truncate, apex crenulate, midlobe bilobulate, lobules cuneate to broadly subquadrate-flabellate, truncate, apex fimbriate, callus yellow, grooved, apex trilobulate; column to 5mm, clinandrium with 4 truncate lobes. Summer. C America, W Indies.

***O. wallisii*** (Rchb. f.) Hagsater. Stems slender, to 70×1cm, erect, spotted purple. Lvs to 11×2.5cm, oblong-lanceolate, acute, curved to deflexed. Raceme arching to pendent, terminal or axillary, several-fld; fls to 4.5cm diam., fragrant, long-lived; sep. and pet. yellow to deep golden-yellow, spotted crimson, sep. to 25×11mm, spathulate, obtuse, pet. to 20×9mm, obovate, obtuse; lip to 25×28mm, white marked red-purple, cuneate-flabellate, 3-lobed, with radiating tuberculate lines; column to 6mm, stout. Autumn–early winter. Panama, Colombia.

For synonymy see *Epidendrum*.

**Oldenburgia** Less. (For S. Oldenburg, collector for Kew, 1772–3.) Compositae. About 4 species of shrubs, subshrubs or dwarf herbs, densely lanate below. Leaves rosulate, simple, sessile, obtuse, coriaceous, glabrous above, densely pubescent beneath. Capitula radiate, large, solitary; receptacle naked; phyllaries linear, acuminate, inner phyllaries herbaceous; florets hermaphrodite; ray florets purple and white, bilabiate, outer lip much larger; disc florets deeply 5-fid. Fruit a turbinate cypsela; pappus of mostly plumose bristles. S Africa (Cape Province). Z9.

CULTIVATION In warm, dry and essentially frost-free zones, *Oldenburgia* spp. make striking specimens, becoming increasingly rugged as they slowly reach maturity. They are grown for the large domed thistle-like blooms in a handsome combination of silver-grey and deep maroon and for the huge and heavily felted leaves; the rosettes of young growth are densely white woolly in beautiful contrast with the smooth upper surfaces sides of older foliage below. Suitable for the large rockery or for other hot dry positions in the garden, although plants generally perform better on good soils with irrigation when in growth. In cool temperate zones, *Oldenburgia* spp. require the protection of the cool glasshouse. Grow in full sun with good ventilation in well-crocked clay pots using a mix of fibrous loam, leafmould and sharp sand; water moderately when in growth, keep almost dry in winter and maintain a winter minimum at about 7–10°C/45–50°F. Propagate by seed or from semi-ripe cuttings in sand in a closed case.

***O.grandis*** (Thunb.) Baill. Shrub to 3m. Lvs crowded at apices of sterile branches, 15–25×8–14cm, obovate-oblong, cuneate at base, convex above, margins subrevolute, stiff, coriaceous, glabrous above, densely white-lanate beneath, lvs of flowering branches alternate, petiole lanate. Capitula to 10cm diam., peduncles to 50cm; phyllaries tomentose at base, becoming subglabrous toward apex. Fr. elongate, glabrous. S Africa.

***O.paradoxa*** Less. Dwarf, to 4cm. Lvs of sterile stems tufted at apex, 15–25×8–14cm, obovate-oblong, cuneate at base, margins strongly revolute, glabrous above, tomentose beneath, lvs of fertile stems 5–6×0.5–1cm, narrowly lanceolate, petiole densely pubesc. Capitula at first sessile among lf tufts, peduncles finally elongating to 30cm; phyllaries densely pubesc. at base, subglabrous at apex. Fr. short, silky-villous.

***O.arbuscula*** DC. See *O.grandis*.

**Oldenlandia** L. (For H.B. Oldenland, Danish botanist.) Rubiaceae. Some 300 species of annual or perennial herbs and shrubs. Stems erect or decumbent, simple or dichotomously and diffusely branched, glabrous or pubescent. Leaves petiolate or sessile, opposite; stipules interpetiolar, adherent to petiole or leaf, acute, entire or fringed, occasionally setose. Flowers bisexual, occasionally heterostylous, solitary or, more usually, in cymes or panicles, white, pink, or pale blue; calyx tube subglobose or obovoid to top-shaped, limb persistent, 4- or, occasionally, 5–8-toothed, teeth erect, usually distant; corolla cylindric, funnel- or salver-shaped, often pubescent at throat, 4–5-lobed; stamens 4 or 5, anthers usually exserted, dorsifixed, oblong; ovary 2-celled, style exserted or included, filiform, 2-lobed, ovules many in each cell. Fruit a capsule, globose, ovoid or turbinate, loculicidally dehiscent and 2-valved from apex. Tropics and subtropics. Z9.

CULTIVATION As for *Pentas*.

***O.natalensis*** (Hochst.) Kuntze. Shrub, to 50cm. Stems erect, branched, somewhat pubesc. Lvs to 8×2cm, short-petiolate, ovate to lanceolate, apex attenuate to acute; stipules setose. Fls in terminal, few-fld, umbellate clusters, pale blue to lavender or mauve; cor. funnel-shaped, tube to 12mm, lobes to 4mm. S Africa.

***O.umbellata*** L. CHAY; INDIAN MADDER. Annual herb. Stems erect, 4-angled, woody, glabrous or pubesc.; branches spreading. Lvs to 12cm, ovate or lanceolate or deltoid, margin reflexed; stipules setose. Fls in terminal or axillary, to 7-fld umbellate clusters, white; cal. lobes lanceolate. Fr. to 1mm. Tropical Asia.

**Olea** L. (From Gk *elaia*, the olive.) OLIVE. Oleaceae. Some 20 species of long-lived evergreen trees and shrubs, to 20m. Stems smooth or rough to spiny, glossy, golden-glabrous to silver-grey, slender and pliable at first, later becoming fissured and rigid and, in advanced maturity, blackened and contorted. Leaves opposite, entire or, rarely, irregularly toothed and lobed, ovate to elliptic, to 8cm long, grey to dark green, glabrous above, coriaceous and somewhat thickened; paler beneath, often glandular or silver-scurfy. Axillary or terminal panicles of white or off-white flowers borne in summer. Flowers inconspicuous, seldom over 1cm, with a musty fragrance, unisexual or bisexual; calyx and corolla short, 4-lobed; stamens 2; ovaries usually 2. Fruit carried in clusters, ovoid or globose drupes containing a single, ellipsoid stone to 1.5cm. Temperate and tropical Old World.

CULTIVATION One of the most important economic plants of semi-dry and dry regions, the olive provides fruit, oil, timber and emblems of peace. It also stabilizes the dusty, often hilly soils on which it grows and appeals to the gardener through its fine silvered foliage, its longevity and, eventually, its splendidly gnarled habit.

*Olea europaea* var. *europaea* and its cultivars, which bear the superior-quality fruit of commercial cultivation, are grown in orchards throughout the Mediterranean, in the southwestern US, South America, South Africa and Australia. Young bare-rooted trees are pruned hard at planting, and their stems whitewashed to reflect light and heat, to reduce sun scorch. They begin to bear at about six years of age, with an expected commercial lifespan of about 50 years. Flower initiation is dependent upon a 12–15-week period of diurnally fluctuating temperatures, with at least two months of average temperatures below 10°C/50°F. The flowers, which may be perfect or male only, are wind-pollinated, and moderate levels of humidity are necessary for good fruit set.

Although the olive is naturally drought-resistant and survives in infertile soils, heavy cropping is linked to annual rainfall levels of 60–75cm/24–30in. and a regime of feeding and irrigation, coupled with systematic thinning to 3–4 fruits per 30cm/12in. of branch; this may be achieved by means of hormone sprays, or by hand. Table olives are harvested in autumn, with the main crop following in winter, raw olives being processed by soaking in sodium hydroxide (caustic soda), to remove bitter principles, and preserved in brine or olive oil.

*Olea* generally requires a frost-free environment – even mature plants will be badly damaged by temperatures lower than −10°C/14°F. Most species, however, will tolerate short exposures to freezing conditions and *O.europaea* will grow in Zone 8, afforded the shelter of a wall and full sunlight, although good fruiting can be expected only in warm-temperate regions with moist winters and hot dry summers. Plant in a deep fertile soil, with perfect drainage, incorporating rubble and sharp sand where necessary. The weighting or arching of branches will encourage fruiting, but pruning may stimulate the overproduction of non-fruiting water shoots. In cool-temperate zones, *O.europaea* can be grown in the cool greenhouse, in the border, or in a well-crocked large pot, with a free draining mix of loam based potting medium with sharp sand. Its slender branches clothed with silvery foliage (and considerable drought tolerance) make it a good choice for a large interior with dry air.

Propagate by seed sown in gentle heat in spring, by semi-ripe cuttings in summer, or by layering. Grafting on to stock of *Osmanthus* may have a useful dwarfing influence. Susceptible to scale insect (*Saissetia oleae*), peacock spot fungus, (*Cycloconium oleaginum*), verticillium wilt (resistant rootstocks are available) and the bacterial disease 'black knot' (*Pseudomonas savastanoi*).

***O.capensis*** L. BLACK IRONWOOD. To 20m. Stems muricate. Lvs broad-lanceolate to obovate with basal portion cuneate, to 10cm, dark, shining, coriaceous above, paler beneath, with short petiole to 1cm. Fls white, to 0.5cm across, crowded in terminal panicles. Fr. globose, black, 1cm. Spring. S Africa. Z9.

***O.europaea*** L. var. ***europaea.*** COMMON OLIVE; EDIBLE OLIVE. Much-branched tree to 7m. Stems semi-terete. Lvs to 8cm, elliptic to lanceolate, grey-green above, scurfy, silver-green beneath. Fls off-white, fragrant, in axillary panicles to 5cm. Fr. subglobose, ripening red to purple-black, to 4cm. Summer. Mediterranean. *O.europaea* var. *europaea* is the fruit and oil-yielding cultigen. Cvs include: (*oil-producing*) 'Cipressino' ('Pyramidalis'): pyramidal in growth; fr. profuse when young. 'Coratina': self-fertile, erect habit. 'Frantoio' ('Frantoiana', 'Corregilo', 'Razzo'): shoots pendulous; fr. large, fleshy, ovate. 'Leccino': large mauve fr. carried on drooping branches, semi-hardy. 'Moraiolo': hardy and strong-growing. (*edible*) 'Ascolana': large, yellow. 'Cucco': fr. black, prolific. 'El Greco': fr. large, stones small. 'Manzanillo': crown rounded, open-branched; lvs leathery; fr. black. 'Mission': vigorous, prolific, very cold resistant. 'Santa Caterina': fr. large, ovate. 'Uovo di piccione': purple-red, very sweet. (*ornamental*) 'Little Ollie': bushy dwarf, fast-growing when young; lvs very dark green, no fls; heat- and drought-resistant. 'Majestic Beauty': open and refined in growth; lvs lighter and narrower, no mature fr. 'Picholine': vigorous, medium-sized, cured olives with nut-like flavour. var. ***oleaster*** (Hoffm. & Link) DC. WILD OLIVE. To 5m with ridged, spinose stems; fr. small, to 1.5cm, subglobose, thinly fleshed, inedible. ssp. ***africana*** (Mill.) P. Green. Resembling *O.europaea* var. *europaea* but fr. smaller, harder. To 8m with warty grey stems. Lvs to 10cm, linear-lanceolate with yellow scurf beneath. Fls in axillary panicles to 5cm. Fr. globose, to 0.5cm. S Africa. ssp. ***cuspidata*** (Wall ex DC.) Cif. To 9m. Lvs 5–10cm, oblong-lanceolate, acuminate, glossy above, red-brown and scaly beneath. Fls off-white in axillary cymes 2.5–5cm, cor. deeply lobed. Fr. ovoid, black, to 0.8cm. NW Himalaya, Arabia. Z8.

***O.chrysophylla*** Lam. See *O.europaea* ssp. *cuspidata*.
***O.communis*** Steud. See *O.europaea* var. *europaea*.
***O.laurifolia*** Lam. See *O.capensis*.
***O.undulata*** Jacq. See *O.capensis*.
***O.verrucosa*** (Willd.) Link. See *O.europaea* ssp. *africana*.

**OLEACEAE** Hoffsgg. & Link. OLIVE FAMILY. Dicot. 24 genera and 900 species of trees and shrubs, few lianoid, usually with peltate secretory hairs. Leaves opposite (spiral in *Jasminum*), simple, pinnate or 3-foliolate, exstipulate. Flowers usually bisexual, regular, in cymose inflorescences or solitary; calyx 4 (–15)-lobed (absent in *Fraxinus*); corolla 4 (–12)-lobed (absent in

*Fraxinus*), imbricate, valvate or convolute; stamens typically 2, rarely 4, attached to the corolla tube; ovary superior, 2-loculed, with terminal style, each locule with 2 ovules, rarely 1–4 or many; ovules in axile placentas. Fruit a capsule, berry, drupe or samara; seeds with straight embryo; endosperm oily or absent. The olive tree (*Olea europaea*) is a major source of fruit and oil. Flowers of *Jasminum* and *Osmanthus* are used for scent manufacture and for flavouring tea. Subcosmopolitan, especially temperate and tropical Asia. *Abeliophyllum, Chionanthus, Fontanesia, Forestiera, Forsythia, Fraxinus, Jasminum, Ligustrum, Olea, Osmanthus, Phillyrea, Schrebera, Syringa.*

**Oleandra** Cav. (Alluding to the supposed similarity of the leaves to those of *Nerium oleander*.) Oleandraceae. Some 40 species of epiphytic or terrestrial ferns. Rhizomes dictyostelic, rigid, often becoming woody, forming interwoven mats, then ascending (new growths) or scandent, scaly and pubescent, becoming bare, rooting freely; scales adpressed or spreading, often deciduous, peltate, overlapping, apex attenuate to acute, often ciliate, brown. Fronds stipitate, uniform or dimorphous (fertile elongate to linear, narrower than sterile), simple, entire, lanceolate to elliptic, cartilaginous at margin, firm-textured, glabrous to pubescent or scaly, veins free, forked or simple, with terminal, submarginal hydathodes; rachis occasionally scaly; stipes clustered or remote, often both together, i.e. clustered at growth tips, jointed to phyllopodia. Sori superficial, dorsal, on veins, uniserial each side of and near to costa, circular; indusia usually persistent, reniform to circular; paraphyses absent; annulus 12–14-celled; spores globose, monolete, bilateral, smooth or angular. Tropics. Z10.

CULTIVATION Epiphytic ferns of tropical rainforest: entire fronds are produced from branching aerial rhizomes supported by aerial roots giving an overall shrubby appearance, and forming quite dense thickets in the wild. Requiring warm glasshouse cultivation; high humidity, copious watering and bright indirect light during the summer growing season; with *O. neriiformis* watering should be moderate during winter when more than half the foliage may be shed. Difficult to contain, they are best grown in a hanging basket where the rhizomes are free to wander, or mounted on bark or tree fern where frequent syringing is required. Propagation is by division of the rhizomes, layering, or from spores.

***O. articulata*** (Sw.) Presl. Rhiz. scandent to long-creeping; scales spreading, persistent, lanceolate to linear, ciliate, pale red-brown. Fronds to 35×5cm, arching, lanceolate, apex caudate to narrowly acute, base cuneate, glabrous, olive green, thin-textured to leathery; stipes remote, to 20cm, phyllopodia to 3cm. W Indies, C to S America.

***O. neriiformis*** Cav. Rhiz. to 5mm wide, suberect or scandent, rigid; scales adpressed, overlapping, ciliate. Fronds to 30×3cm, linear to lanceolate, attenuate to caudate at apex, glabrous or pubesc., leathery; rachis and costa sparsely scaly at base, veins distinct, forked; stipes remote or clustered, to 2cm. Asia to Polynesia.

***O. wallichii*** (Hook.) Presl. Rhiz. to 5mm wide, long-creeping; scales spreading, lanceolate, hair-tipped, entire, brown. Fronds to 40×4cm, oblong, apex attenuate to caudate, base obtuse or acute, pubesc. beneath; rachis prominent, sparsely scaly, pubesc. or glabrous, veins free, forked; stipes to 5cm. India, China, Taiwan.

***O. mollis*** Presl. See *O. neriiformis*.
***O. nodosa*** (Willd.) Presl. See *O. articulata*.
For further synonymy see *Ophiopteris* and *Neuronia*.

**OLEANDRACEAE** (J. Sm.) Ching ex Pichi-Serm. *Arthropteris, Oleandra.*

**Olearia** Moench. (For Adam Olschlager [Olearius], German botanist (*d*1671), not for resemblance to olive.) DAISY BUSH. Compositae. About 130 species of herbs, evergreen shrubs or small trees. Leaves alternate or opposite, simple, leathery, usually white- or buff-tomentose beneath. Capitula radiate or discoid, solitary or few to several and variously compound; receptacle flat or convex; phyllaries imbricate in several series, margins dry or scarious; ray florets female, white, purple or blue or absent; disc florets hermaphrodite, tubular, yellow, white or purple. Fruit a ribbed or striate cypsela, usually pubescent to pilose; pappus of unequal barbellate bristles, often slightly thickened at apex. Australasia. Z9 unless specified.

CULTIVATION Grown for their handsome, sometimes pleasantly aromatic foliage, their attractive rounded form and for the masses of daisy flowers carried in profusion in summer, especially in seasons following long hot summers the previous year. With several notable exceptions most species are not reliably hardy where temperatures fall much below −5°C/23°F, unless given warm wall protection, although as a genus *Olearia* is extremely valuable in mild maritime gardens, showing good resistance to salt-laden winds and maintaining a characteristically dense and compact habit when grown in full sun and exposure. Several are of particularly dense habit and especially suitable for hedging, including *O. macrodonta, O. avicennifolia* and *O.* ×*haastii*, the two last also tolerate urban pollution. With *O. nummulariifolia, O. virgata, O.* ×*mollis* and *O. ilicifolia*, these three are amongst the hardiest, tolerating temperatures to −15°C/5°F; *O.* ×*scilloniensis* and *O.* 'Talbot de Malahide' are almost as hardy, to about −10°C/14°F.

Grow in any well-drained, moderately fertile soil, including chalky soils, in full sun. Almost without exception *Olearia* spp. respond well to hard pruning, breaking freely from older wood, and old leggy specimens may be rejuvenated by cutting hard back in spring; in zones that experience late frosts, delay removal of winter damaged wood until the pattern of new growth becomes clear. Otherwise prune after flowering. Propagate by semi-ripe cuttings in summer or by heeled ripewood cuttings of lateral shoots in the cold frame in early autumn. Softer-leaved types such as *O. phlogopappa* can be increased by softwood cuttings treated with 0.8% I.B.A. and rooted in a closed case or under mist in spring.

| | | |
|---|---|---|
| **1** | Leaves alternate, or in alternate fascicles | **2** |
| | Leaves opposite, or in opposite fascicles | **86** |
| **2** | Capitula radiate | **3** |
| | Capitula discoid | **83** |
| **3** | Ray and disc floret corollas white | **4** |
| | Ray and disc front corollas not both white | **27** |
| **4** | Leaves to 3cm, never decidedly longer | **5** |
| | At least some leaves 4cm or longer | **16** |
| **5** | Ray florets 10 or more; capitula usually *c*2cm diameter or greater | **6** |
| | Ray florets fewer than 10; capitula *c*105cm diameter or less | **9** |
| **6** | Leaves mostly linear or linear-obovate | **7** |
| | At least some leaves obovate to elliptic | **8** |
| **7** | Ray florets rarely more than 10; leaves pungent | *O. pinifolia* |
| | Ray florets to 15; leaves not or scarcely pungent, producing viscid yellow exudates | *O. ericoides* |
| **8** | Shrub, rarely more than 1.5m tall, glandular; few if any leaves greater than 10mm long; florets at least 8, often as many as 30 | *O. ramulosa* |
| | Shrub or tree, to 5m; at least some leaves to *c*3mm; florets few, usually less than 8 | *O. fragrantissima* |
| **9** | At least some leaves deltoid, generally broadest near base | *O. algida* |
| | Most leaves linear to elliptic, cuneate, obovate or oblong, generally broadest at or above middle | **10** |
| **10** | Ray florets mostly less than 5 per head | **11** |
| | Ray florets mostly 5 to 10 | **12** |
| **11** | Capitula solitary | *O. nummulariifolia* |
| | Capitula in compound inflorescence | *O. fragrantissima* |
| **12** | Leaves all linear | **13** |
| | Leaves ovate, oblong, cuneate or obovate, rarely and then only few linear | **14** |
| **13** | Plants generally glabrous, though margins of leaves and phyllaries often ciliate | *O. teretifolia* |
| | Plants more or less hairy, leaves generally villous or tomentose, at least beneath | *O. pinifolia* |
| **14** | Leaves cuneate, generally broadest toward apex | *O. obcordata* |
| | Leaves ovate to oblong or obovate, generally broadest near middle or below | **15** |

**15** Leaves to 3cm or more long, generally broad — *O. allomii*
Leaves rarely more than 1cm long, usually narrow — *O. ramulosa*

**16** Ray florets mostly 10 or more; capitula usually greater than *c*1.5cm diameter — **17**
Ray florets mostly less than 10; capitula *c*1.5cm diameter or less — **18**

**17** Leaves to 7.5cm, ovate-cordate to oblong; capitula very large, at least 2.5cm diameter — *O. pannosa*
Leaves to 10cm, lanceolate; capitula *c*1.5cm diameter — *O. ×mollis*

**18** Leaves mostly linear, linear-lanceolate or linear-oblong — **19**
Leaves mostly obovate to elliptic or oblong — **21**

**19** Capitula many, in corymbose inflorescences; leaves greater than 5cm long — **20**
Capitula usually solitary and axillary; leaves 2.5–4.5cm — *O. pinifolia*

**20** Leaves distinctly toothed — *O. ilicifolia*
Leaves entire — *O. lacunosa*

**21** Leaves toothed — *O. ×excorticata*
Leaves entire — **22**

**22** Infl. very broad; capitula *c*1.5cm long; phyllaries or more, in 4–5 series — *O. pachyphylla*
Infl. smaller; capitula much shorter; phyllaries few, in few series — **23**

**23** Capitula mostly with 6 or less florets — **24**
Capitula mostly with at least 10 florets — **26**

**24** Leaves elliptic-lanceolate, margins flat — **25**
Leaves oblong to broadly elliptic, margins undulate — *O. albida*

**25** Leaves tapered at base and apex; ray florets 0–2 — *O. avicennifolia*
Leaves somewhat obtuse at apex, base rounded; ray florets 3–6 — *O.* 'Talbot de Malahide'

**26** Leaves very leathery, width mostly greater than $\frac{1}{2}$ length, entire — *O. allomii*
Leaves more or less leathery, width rarely greater than $\frac{1}{2}$ length, more or less sinuate-dentate — *O. ×excorticata*

**27** Leaves to *c*3cm, never decidedly longer — **28**
At least some leaves 4cm or longer — **50**

**28** Ray florets mostly 10 or more; capitula sometimes *c*2cm diameter or greater — **29**
Ray florets fewer than 10; capitula *c*1.5cm diameter or smaller — **36**

**29** Leaves mostly linear to linear-obovate or oblong-linear — **30**
Leaves obovate to oval or elliptic — **33**

**31** Plants glabrous, sometimes leaf-margins ciliate — **31**
Plants with leaves tomentose beneath — **32**

**31** Involucre hemispherical; phyllaries narrow, usually acute — *O. ciliata*
Involucre ovoid or turbinate, rarely hemispherical; phyllaries usually obtuse — *O. glandulosa*

**32** Indumentum of leaves of centrally-attacked or T-shaped hairs, otherwise simple; ray florets white — *O. ledifolia*
Indumentum of leaves of stellate hairs; ray florets blue or purple — *O. asterotricha*

**33** Disc florets yellow — **34**
Disc florets purple — *O. iodochroa*

**34** Ray florets usually 40 or more — *O. frostii*
Ray florets rarely to 20, usually 16 or fewer — **35**

**35** Leaves to 3cm or more long; capitula *c*2.5–3cm diam. — *O. phlogopappa*
Leaves to 1.5cm; capitula to 1.5cm diam., usually less — *O. moschata*

**36** Ray florets mostly 5–10 per head — **37**
Ray florets mostly less than 5 per head — **44**

**37** Ray florets white, disc florets yellow — **38**
Ray and disc florets not in above combination — **43**

**38** Capitula solitary — *O. tasmanica*
Capitula in a compound inflorescence — **39**

**39** All or most leaves less than 2cm long — **40**
All or most leaves greater than 2.5cm long — **42**

**40** Leaves submembranous; tomentum adpressed, satiny; corymb loose, with long slender peduncles — *O. capillaris*
Leaves leathery; tomentum soft, dull; corymb compact, with short peduncles — **41**

**41** Leaves dark glossy green, glabrous above — *O. ×haastii*
Leaves green tinged grey scurfy above — *O. moschata*

**42** All or most heads with 6 or fewer florets — *O. ×haastii*
All or most heads with 10 or more florets — *O. allomii*

**43** Leaves 2.5–5cm long, obliquely ovate-oblong; inflorescence corymbose; ray florets 5–10 — *O. allomii*
Leaves to 3cm long, ovate to suborbicular; inflorescence racemose; ray florets 3–6 — *O. lepidophylla*

**44** Most leaves *c*1.5cm long or less — **45**
At least some leaves more than 2cm long — **46**

**45** Low and straggling or densely bushy shrub; leaves 6–12mm, obovate or rarely oval, dentate; capitula 3–5 in axillary clusters — *O. myrsinoides*
Shrub to 2m; leaves 2–3mm, oblong or oblanceolate, more or less entire; capitula numerous in larger pyramidal panicles — *O. floribunda*

**46** Leaves lanceolate, length/width ratio 3.5–4:1; capitula usually solitary or 2–5 in a panicle — *O. erubescens*
Leaves suborbicular to oblong, obovate, elliptic or ovate, length/width ratio less than 3:1; capitula usually more than 5 in corymbs — **47**

**47** Leaves of 2 kinds: sun leaves 5–15mm diam., broad-ovate to suborbicular, shade leaves to 3cm long, more oblong — *O. capillaris*
Leaves of 1 kind — **48**

**48** At least some leaves broadest above middle — **49**
Leaves broadest at middle or below — *O. ×haastii*

**49** Fruit pilose; leaves white-tomentose beneath; capitula fragrant — *O. fragrantissima*
Fruit pubescent; leaves white to fawn tomentose beneath; capitula not fragrant — *O. persoonioides*

**50** Ray florets mostly 10 or more; capitula frequently *c*2cm diam. or more — **51**
Ray florets mostly fewer than 10; capitula *c*1.5cm diam. or less — **70**

**51** Ray florets white — **56**
Ray florets not completely white — **64**

**52** Leaves linear to lanceolate — **53**
Leaves elliptic, oblong, ovate to suborbicular — **56**

**53** Disc florets yellow — **54**
Disc florets purple — *O. angustifolia*

**54** At least some leaves to *c*9cm, length/width ratio over 3:1 — **55**
Leaves to 7cm, length/width ratio less than 2.5:1 — *O. nernstii*

**55** Leaves rugose or reticulate above; capitula in dense round terminal clusters — *O. lirata*
Leaves more or less smooth above; capitula in lax corymbs — *O. cheesemanii*

**56** Disc florets purple or brown — **57**
Disc florets yellow — **59**

**57** Leaves to 3–8cm long — **58**
Leaves 10cm or longer — *O. ×traillii*

**58** Leaves mostly broadest at middle or above, base gradually tapered; ray florets to 15mm — *O. chathamica*
Leaves mostly broadest below middle, base often cordate; ray florets to 25mm — *O. pannosa*

**59** At least some leaves to 10cm long — **60**
Leaves to 8cm long, often much shorter — **61**

**60** Ray florets numerous, in 2 or more rows; capitula solitary — *O. insignis*
Ray florets 10–15, in 1 row; capitula numerous in corymbs — *O. ×scilloniensis*

**61** At least some leaves broadest above middle, margin toothed — **62**
At least some leaves broadest towards base, margin toothed or entire — **63**

**62** Capitula to 3cm diam.; infl. an erect, loose corymb; leaves less than 1.5cm wide — *O. phlogopappa*
Capitula to 6cm diam., solitary; leaves at least 2cm wide — *O. oporina*

**63** Leaves entire, ovate-cordate to oblong — *O. pannosa*
Leaves toothed, ovate to suborbicular — *O. tomentosa*

**64** Ray florets blue, purple, brown, or white tinged purple; disc florets never yellow — **65**
Ray florets various; disc florets always yellow — **68**

65 Leaves 10–25cm long — *O. lyallii*
Leaves to 8cm long, often much smaller — **66**

66 Leaves scabrous above — *O. asterotricha*
Leaves glabrous, smooth, often rugose — **67**

67 Leaves elliptic-lanceolate to oblong-obovate — *O. chathamica*
Leaves narrow-lanceolate — *O. semidentata*

68 Ray florets usually 20+; leaves 3–7cm, ovate to suborbicular — **69**
Ray florets 16 or fewer; leaves 1.5–5cm, oblong to narrowly-obovate — *O. phlogopappa*

69 Ray florets blue or mauve — *O. tomentosa*
Ray florets pale rose — *O. rotundifolia*

70 Leaves linear to lanceolate — **71**
Leaves ovate, oblong, elliptic, oblanceolate or obovate — **75**

71 Ray florets white or cream — **72**
Ray florets indigo — *O. hookeri*

72 Leaves 4cm long or less; phyllaries pilose — *O. erubescens*
Leaves over 5cm long; phyllaries ciliate, at least at apex — **73**

73 Leaves distinctly toothed — **74**
Leaves entire — *O. cheesemanii*

74 Leaf-teeth rather distant, not spinose, margins flat — *O. cheesemanii*
Leaf-teeth rather close-set, very sharp to spinose, margins more or less crisped — *O. ilicifolia*

75 Leaves mostly less than 5cm long — **76**
Some leaves at least 5cm long, often much longer — **78**

76 Capitula many to numerous in corymbose clusters; leaves glabrous above — **77**
Capitula borne singly in axils of upper leaves; leaves rusty above — *O. tasmanica*

77 Ray florets less than 5; leaves longitudinally symmetrical — *O. persoonioides*
Ray florets 5 or more; leaves oblique — *O. allomii*

78 Florets 15–20; ray florets white or blue; disc florets yellow — **79**
Florets fewer than 15; ray florets white or cream; disc florets yellow, red or cream — **80**

79 Capitula *c*1.5cm diameter; ray florets 7 or more, white; fruit pilose — *O. arborescens*
Capitula *c*2.5cm diameter; ray florets 6 or fewer, white or blue; fruit subglabrous — *O. speciosa*

80 Disc florets white, cream or yellow — **81**
Disc florets red — *O. macrodonta*

81 Leaves slightly tomentose above, margin toothed — *O. argophylla*
Leaves glabrous above, margins entire to subentire, rarely toothed — **82**

82 Inflorescence very broad; capitula *c*1.5cm long; phyllaries 35+ in 4–5 series — *O. pachyphylla*
Inflorescence smaller; capitula much shorter; phyllaries few, in fewer series — *O. furfuracea*

83 Inflorescence a raceme; capitula large; florets usually numerous, dark red to dark brown; leaf-teeth distinct — *O. colensoi*
Inflorescence a panicle; capitula small; florets few, white or yellow; leaves entire to obscurely toothed — **84**

84 Florets 2–4 or more per head; leaves lanceolate — *O. avicennifolia*
Florets 1 per head; leaves broad-oblong — **85**

85 Leaves rather thinly leathery, *c*3–5cm long, margins usually strongly undulate — *O. paniculata*
Leaves thickly leathery, usually not greater than 2cm long, margins usually only slightly undulate to flat — *O. coriacea*

86 Capitula radiate — **87**
Capitula discoid — **100**

87 Ray and disc florets white — **91**
Ray and disc florets not both white — **91**

88 Leaves minute, rarely to 5mm long — **89**
Leaves larger, at least some 1–10cm long — **90**

89 Leaves deltoid; ray florets usually 3 or 4 — *O. algida*
Leaves linear; ray florets usually more than 4 — *O. teretifolia*

90 Leaves 5–20mm, usually broadest above middle — *O. virgata*
Leaves 5–10cm, broadest at middle or below — *O. megalophylla*

91 Leaves rarely to 5cm long, usually much less; capitula various — **92**
Leaves more than 5cm long; capitula numerous — **99**

92 Leaves linear to lanceolate — **93**
Leaves obovate, oblong, elliptic to linear-obovate — **95**

93 Ray florets more than 10, white, mauve, blue or white tinged blue — **94**
Ray florets 3–5, white — *O. erubescens*

94 Low shrub to 30cm, rarely more; ray fls 12–15mm long; leaves 1–1.5cm long — *O. ciliata*
Shrub to 1–2m; ray florets *c*4mm long; leaves 1.5–5cm long — *O. glandulosa*

95 Florets white, cream or yellow — **96**
Florets grey-brown — *O. odorata*

96 Leaves broad-elliptic or -obovate, many greater than 10mm long, usually distinctly petiolate — **97**
Leaves linear to narrow-elliptic, not greater than 7mm long, sessile or subsessile — **98**

97 Capitula appearing before leaves; leaves glabrous above — *O. hectoris*
Capitula appearing with leaves; leaves rusty above — *O. tasmanica*

98 Leaves yellow-tomentose beneath; capitula solitary — *O. solandri*
Leaves white- or buff-tomentose beneath; capitula fascicled — *O. virgata*

99 Leaves lanceolate, viscid smooth above, white beneath — *O. viscosa*
Leaves oblong, densely tomentose beneath — *O. megalophylla*

100 Leaves acute, usually apiculate, 2.5–3cm wide, silky-white tomentose beneath — *O. traversii*
Leaves obtuse, 3–6.5cm wide, thinly tomentose beneath — *O. buchananii*

***O. albida*** Hook. f. Shrub or small tree to 5m, branchlets grooved, angular, loosely white-tomentose. Lvs 7–10×2.5–3.5cm, alternate, oblong to ovate-oblong, glabrous above when mature, with white adpressed tomentum beneath, margins flat to undulate; petioles to 2cm. Capitula to 7mm, radiate, very numerous, narrow, on short sulcate; outer phyllaries ovate, pubesc., inner linear-oblong, ciliate; florets 3–10 per capitulum, ray-florets 1–5, white, disc florets white. New Zealand.

***O. algida*** Wakef. Shrub, to 1.5m, much-branched; branches numerous slender, slightly tomentose. Lvs 2–3mm, in dense lateral fascicles, deltoid, broadest at base, revolute, glaucous, fleshy. Capitula radiate, solitary, to 1.5cm diam.; ray florets 3–4, white; disc florets white. Spring. SE Australia.

***O. allomii*** T. Kirk. Shrub to 1m; branchlets stout, smooth, silvery tomentose. Lvs 2.5–5×2–4cm, alternate, obliquely ovate-oblong, coriaceous, glabrous above when mature, adpressed silvery-tomentose beneath, entire. Capitula radiate, 1.5cm diam., in branched corymbs; peduncles to 2cm; phyllaries imbricate, broadly lanceolate, tomentose below; florets 14–20, ray florets 5–10. New Zealand.

***O. angustifolia*** Hook. f. Shrub or small tree to 6m, branches more or less tomentose. Lvs 7–15×1–2cm, alternate, narrowly lanceolate, acuminate, subsessile, finely crenate-dentate, becoming glabrous above, teeth callused. Capitula radiate, 2.5–5cm diam.; peduncles with many foliaceous bracts, tomentose; phyllaries in 2 series, outer tomentose below; ray florets white, disc florets purple. Summer. New Zealand.

***O. arborescens*** (Forst. f.) Ckn. & Laing. Shrub to 4m; branchlets angular, pale brown-tomentose. Lvs 4–8×2–4cm, alternate, broad- to elliptic-ovate, acute, margins sinuate-dentate to subentire, subcoriaceous, sparsely tomentose beneath. Capitula to 1.5cm diam., in large corymbs; peduncles slender, pubesc.; phyllaries elliptic-oblong, obtuse to subacute, outer pilose below, inner glabrous except at apex and margins; florets 15–20, ray florets 7–10, white, disc florets pale yellow. Summer. New Zealand.

***O. argophylla*** (Labill.) Benth. MUSKWOOD. Tree or shrub to 15m, trunk to 30cm diam.; young shoots slightly ribbed, grey-tomentose. Lvs 5–15×2.5–6cm, alternate, oblanceolate or ovate, tapered at apex and base, usually denticulate, grey-green, slightly tomentose above at first, especially on midrib, grey-tomentose silvery tomentum beneath; petiole to 2.5cm, grooved. Capitula numerous, in clustered corymbs to over 25cm diam.; ray florets 5mm, 3–5, narrow, cream; disc florets 6–8, yellow. Summer. S & SE Australia. 'Variegata': lvs edged yellow.

***O. asterotricha*** (F. Muell.) F. Muell. ex Benth. Shrub to 1m, branches more or less grooved and tomentose. Lvs to 4×2cm, alternate, oblong-linear, somewhat sinuate-dentate, scabrous above. Capitula radiate, large, solitary, terminal or few in a terminal corymb; florets blue or purple; ray florets 20+. Spring. S & SE Australia.

***O. avicennifolia*** (Raoul) Hook. f. Shrub or small tree to 7m; young shoots ribbed, scurfy. Lvs 5–10×2–4cm, alternate, ovate-lanceolate, tapered at base and apex, entire, grey-white, glabrous above, white- or pale yellow-tomentose beneath; petiole to 2cm. Capitula cylindric, 0.5cm, in erect, rounded, terminal corymbs to 5–8cm diam.; peduncles to 8cm, slender; involucre narrow, phyllaries few, glabrous to pubesc.; florets 2–3, white; ray florets 0–2. Summer.

New Zealand (South Is.). 'White Confusion': lvs large, slightly waxed; fls profuse, white. Z8.

***O.buchananii*** T. Kirk. Shrub or small tree to 6m; branchlets with red bark, glabrous. Lvs 5–7.5×3–6.5cm, opposite, elliptic-lanceolate, obtuse, entire, attenuate, glabrous above, thinly white-tomentose beneath; petiole short. Capitula discoid, 6–7mm, clustered in small corymbs; peduncles very slender, pubesc.; phyllaries *c*10, outer pubesc., inner glabrous except at apex; florets 6–8. New Zealand.

***O.capillaris*** Buch. Shrub to 2m, densely branched; branchlets slender, zigzagging with pale buff tomentum; bark furrowed, pale-papery, flaking. Lvs silvery-tomentose beneath, sun lvs 0.5–1.5cm diam., broad-ovate to suborbicular, entire, coriaceous, shade lvs to 3cm, more oblong, sinuate, membranous. Capitula radiate, 5–11, in lax corymbs; peduncles to 1cm; phyllaries subglabrous; florets 8–12, ray florets white, disc florets yellow. Summer. New Zealand.

***O.chathamica*** T. Kirk. Shrub, to 2m, more or less densely branched. Lvs 3–8×2–4cm, alternate, oblanceolate to elliptic, acute, tapered at base, regularly and obtusely dentate, glabrous above, midrib raised beneath; petioles to 8cm. Capitula to 4.5cm diam., solitary; peduncles to 25cm; phyllaries 8mm, linear, acute, woolly above; ray florets numerous, 1.5cm, linear, acute, white, occasionally tinged purple; disc florets dark purple. Summer. New Zealand (Chatham Is.).

***O.cheesemanii*** Ckn. & Allan. Erect shrub or small tree to 4m, much-branched, bark somewhat flaking; branchlets grooved with dense, buff tomentum. Lvs 5–9×2–3cm, alternate, linear to narrowly lanceolate, margins sinuate, apex subacuminate, thinly coriaceous, pilose above at first, becoming pale buff-tomentose; petioles 2cm, more or less winged, tomentose. Capitula 8–9mm in lax corymbs to 15cm diam.; peduncles very slender, densely tomentose; phyllaries 3–4mm, linear-lanceolate, ciliate; ray florets white; disc florets yellow. Spring–summer. New Zealand.

***O.ciliata*** (Benth.) F. Muell. ex Benth. Shrub to 30cm, branches shortly scabrous-hairy. Lvs in fascicles, 1–1.5cm, linear, rigid, mucronate, margins strongly revolute, scabrous-ciliate, glabrous or scabrous above, minutely tomentose beneath. Capitula 5–13cm, radiate, solitary, terminal; peduncles wiry, rufescent; phyllaries acute, ciliate; ray florets *c*20, white, mauve or blue; disc florets 50–80, yellow. Spring. Australia (temperate regions, including Tasmania).

***O.colensoi*** Hook. f. Shrub to 3m; branchlets stout, white- to buff-tomentose. Lvs 8–20×3–6cm, alternate, obovate, acute to subacute, irregularly serrate, glabrous, rugose above, densely tomentose beneath; petiole to 5mm. Capitula discoid, 2–3cm diam., dark brown to purple, in racemes of 5–8 heads to 20cm long; peduncles subtended by lanceolate tomentose bracts; phyllaries to 1cm, in 1–2 series, linear, mostly glabrous; florets dark brown to purple tubular, outer row female. New Zealand.

***O.coriacea*** T. Kirk. Shrub to 3m, branchlets stout, rigid, pubesc. Lvs 1–2×0.8–1.5cm, alternate, broadly ovate to suborbicular, coriaceous, subglabrous above, densely pale brown-tomentose beneath, margins somewhat revolute and undulate. Capitula discoid, narrow, in small corymbose panicles; peduncles short; phyllaries imbricate in several series, outer short, glabrous to pubesc., viscid-glandular; florets tubular, white. New Zealand (South Is.)

***O.ericoides*** (Steetz) Wakef. Shrub to 1m, much-branched, shoots very viscid. Lvs to 0.6cm, alternate, linear to linear-obovate, tomentose beneath, with viscid yellow exudates, margins strongly recurved; petioles short. Capitula radiate, solitary, terminal, 2cm diam.; ray florets to 15, white or tinged blue, linear; disc florets white. Spring. Tasmania.

***O.erubescens*** (DC.) Dipp. Shrub, to 1.5m, branches rufescent. Lvs 2–4×0.5–1.5cm, lanceolate, acute, sinuate-dentate, glabrous, reticulate above, subsessile. Capitula 2.5cm diam., solitary or 2–5 together in a leafy, oblong panicle to 45cm; phyllaries linear-lanceolate, pilose, outer obtuse; ray florets 3–5, white; disc florets 6–8, yellow. Spring–summer. NSW, Victoria, Tasmania. var. ***ilicifolia*** (DC.) Bean. As for *O.ilicifolia* except lvs less spiny, broader, and capitula more numerous.

***O.×excorticata*** Buch. *(O.arborescens × O.lacunosa.)* Shrub or small tree to 4m, trunk to 30cm diam.; branchlets white-tomentose; bark loose, brown, papery. Lvs to 10×2.5cm, elliptic, obscurely sinuate-dentate, acuminate, glabrous above, white-tomentose beneath; petioles short. Capitula radiate, 3–4mm, numerous, in rounded corymbs; peduncles short; phyllaries few, outer minute, pubesc. at tips; florets *c*12, ray florets 5–7, disc florets exserted. Spring. New Zealand (North Is.).

***O.floribunda*** (Hook. f.) Benth. Shrub to 2m, branchlets slender, tomentose at first. Lvs 2–3mm, alternate, in loose lateral clusters, oblanceolate or oblong, margins flat or narrowly recurved, bright to dark green, tomentose beneath. Capitula radiate, narrow, numerous, in large pyramidal panicles; phyllaries subglabrous; ray florets 3–5, white; disc florets 3–6, yellow. Summer. SE Australia.

***O.fragrantissima*** Petrie. Shrub or tree to 5m; branchlets rigid, flexuous, striate; bark dark red-brown. Lvs 0.8–3×0.5–1cm, alternate, elliptic to obovate, entire, membranous, becoming glabrous above, white-tomentose beneath; petiole to 3mm. Capitula radiate, to 2cm diam., sessile or subsessile, in alternate clusters of 12; phyllaries in 2–3 series, oblong, tomentose; florets 4–8, fragrant. New Zealand (South Is).

***O.frostii*** (F. Muell.) J.H. Willis. Straggling subshrub. Lvs 1–2.5×0.5–1cm, alternate, obovate, entire or bluntly sinuate-dentate in upper part, densely stellate-pubesc., dark green above, paler beneath. Capitula radiate, solitary and terminal or 2–3 together, axillary, pedunculate, 2–3cm diam.; ray florets 40–50, pale mauve or lilac; disc florets numerous, yellow. Victoria.

***O.furfuracea*** (A. Rich.) Hook. f. Shrub or tree to 5m, branchlets grooved, white-pubesc. at first becoming brown-pubesc. Lvs 5–10×3–6cm, alternate, ovate to elliptic-oblong, subentire to crenate-dentate, coriaceous, glabrous, dark glossy green above, lustrous brown-tomentose beneath, margin somewhat undulate; petioles to 2.5cm. Capitula to 1.5cm diam., many, in large corymbs to 12cm diam.; peduncles slender; phyllaries lanceolate to elliptic-oblong, pubesc. to pilose; ray florets 2–5, 3–6mm, oblong, white; disc florets 3–7, yellow. Spring. New Zealand.

***O.glandulosa*** (Labill.) Benth. Aromatic shrub or subshrub, 1–2m, glandular-tuberculate at first. Lvs 1.5–5×0.1cm, narrowly linear, acute, spreading, grooved above, convex beneath, margins glandular-tuberculate. Capitula small, radiate, in corymbose panicles; peduncles short; phyllaries lanceolate; ray florets 12–20, 4mm, white or tinged blue; disc florets *c*20, yellow. Summer. SE Australia.

***O.×haastii*** Hook. f. Shrub, 1–3m, much-branched, branchlets white- to grey-tomentose at first. Lvs 1–2.5×0.5–1cm, crowded, alternate, oval or ovate, entire, dark glossy green, glabrous above, white-tomentose beneath; petiole 3mm. Capitula 8mm diam., in corymbose clusters 5–8cm diam.; ray florets white; disc florets yellow. Summer. New Zealand. Z8.

***O.hectoris*** Hook. f. Shrub to 5m; branchlets slender, grooved, subglabrous, bark dark red-brown. Lvs 2–5×0.5–2cm, in opposite fascicles of 2–4, broadly elliptic, submembranous, glabrous above, thinly tomentose beneath; petioles slender, to 5mm. Capitula produced before lvs, radiate, 5mm diam., in fascicles of 2–5; peduncles to 1.5cm, slender, drooping, silky-pubesc.; phyllaries in 2 series, laxly imbricate, spreading, oblong, obtuse, pilose; florets 20–25; ray florets to 15, narrow, tinged yellow; disc florets yellow. New Zealand (South Is.).

***O.hookeri*** (Sonder) Benth. Shrub to 1m, branches numerous, slender, viscid, glabrous. Lvs 3–6×1cm, alternate, narrow, grooved above, convex beneath, margins revolute. Capitula radiate, solitary, sessile; ray florets 8–10, indigo; disc florets 8–12, yellow. Summer. Tasmania.

***O.ilicifolia*** Hook. f. Tree or shrub to 5m, with musky fragrance; branchlets stout, pubesc. at first. Lvs 5–10×1–2cm, alternate, linear-oblong to lanceolate, acute to acuminate, coriaceous to glabrous above, white- to yellow-tomentose beneath, margins undulate, acutely serrate-dentate; petiole to 2cm. Capitula radiate, fragrant, 1–1.5cm, many, in large corymbs to 10cm diam.; phyllaries rather lax, spreading, outer villous below, inner ciliate at apex; ray florets 10–15, white. Summer. New Zealand. Z8.

***O.insignis*** Hook. f. Spreading shrub, to 2m; young branchlets stout white- or pale brown-tomentose. Lvs 8–16×4–8cm, alternate, crowded at shoot apices, entire, oval or obovate, coriaceous, becoming glabrous above except on midrib and margins; petiole stout, 1.5–5cm. Capitula terminal, solitary, 3–6cm diam.; peduncles to 20cm; phyllaries in many series, woolly; ray florets 12mm, numerous, in *c*2 rows, linear, emarginate, 12mm, white; disc florets crowded, yellow. Summer. New Zealand.

***O.iodochroa*** (F. Muell.) F. Muell. ex Benth. Bushy shrub to 2m, much branched. Lvs to 1cm, alternate, linear to almost obovate, entire or emarginate, recurved. Capitula radiate, solitary or few in a terminal corymb; inner phyllaries with coloured margins; ray florets 15–20, white; disc florets purple. Spring. SE Australia.

***O.lacunosa*** Hook. f. Shrub to 5m; branchlets numerous, densely tomentose. Lvs 7–16×1–2.5cm, alternate, linear to linear-oblong, acute to acuminate, coriaceous, rugose, midrib yellow above, subrevolute, minutely sinuate-dentate; petiole to 1cm. Capitula many, radiate, to 1cm, in corymbs; peduncles slender; phyllaries in 3–4 lax series, tomentose below, outer ovate, inner oblong; florets 8–12, white. New Zealand.

***O.ledifolia*** (DC.) Benth. Shrub to 60cm, forming rounded clumps. Lvs 0.5–3cm, alternate, crowded, oblong-linear, obtuse, silver- or rusty-tomentose beneath, revolute. Capitula solitary, radiate; peduncles short; phyllaries narrowly oblong, tomentose; ray florets 10–12, white; disc florets yellow. Tasmania.

***O.lepidophylla*** (Pers.) Benth. Shrub, 1–2m, stout, erect, rigid; branches white-tomentose. Lvs to 3cm, alternate, clustered, ovate to suborbicular, tomentose beneath, revolute. Capitula radiate, small, in more or less racemose clusters; inner phyllaries tomentose toward apex; ray florets 3–6, white; disc florets 5–10, violet. Summer. SE Australia.

***O.lirata*** (Sims) Hutch. Shrub or small tree, to 3m; branches usually tomentose at first. Lvs 8–12×1.5–3cm, alternate, lanceolate, acuminate, entire, rugose or reticulate, shiny light green above, tomentose beneath crenately undulate. Capitula 2cm diam., in dense, rounded terminal clusters; ray florets 10–14, white; disc florets yellow. Spring. Victoria, NSW, Queensland, Tasmania.

***O.lyallii*** Hook. f. Shrub or tree to 10m, trunk to 60cm diam.; branchlets stout, densely white-tomentose. Lvs 10–25cm, alternate, elliptic-ovate to ovate-orbicular, abruptly acute to acuminate, irregularly crenate, densely white-tomentose beneath; petiole to 5mm. Capitula radiate, 3–4cm diam., clustered in racemes to 25cm; peduncles to 8cm; phyllaries many, in several series, linear-oblong, acute, glabrous except at margins; florets dark brown. New Zealand (Auckland Is.).

***O.macrodonta*** Bak. Shrub or tree to 6m, bark peeling in long strips; branchlets slender, angular, tomentose. Lvs 5–10×2.5–4cm, alternate, ovate-oblong, acute to acuminate, dark glossy green above, silver-tomentose beneath, musk-scented when crushed, margins undulate, acutely dentate-serrate; petiole to 15mm. Capitula radiate to 1cm, many in corymbs 8–15cm diam.; phyllaries few, narrow, pubesc. to villous; ray florets 10+, rays short, narrow, white; disc florets few, rufescent. Summer. New Zealand. 'Major': lvs and fls large. 'Minor': dwarf: lvs and fls small. Z8.

***O.megalophylla*** (F. Muell.) F. Muell. ex Benth. Shrub to 1m; branchlets grey- or brown-tomentose at first. Lvs 5–10×1–4.5cm, opposite, elliptic to oblong, reticulate above, grey- or brown-tomentose beneath; petiole short. Capitula radiate, large, numerous, in terminal corymbs; phyllaries many, outer shorter; ray florets 7–12, white. Summer. Victoria, NSW.

***O.×mollis*** (T. Kirk) Ckn. *(O.ilicifolia × O.lacunosa.)* Shrub to 3m; branches white-tomentose at first. Lvs to 10×1.5cm, alternate, lanceolate, spinulose, rounded at base, veins sunken above, very prominent beneath, almost perpendicular to midrib, densely white- to pale yellow-tomentose beneath, margins revolute; petiole very short. Capitula to *c*15cm diam., radiate, many, in corymbs; phyllaries rather lax, spreading; ray florets 8–15, white. New Zealand. 'Zennorensis': shrub to 2m; lvs narrow, acute, sharply dentate, 10×1–1.5cm, dark olive green above, white-tomentose below. Z8.

***O.moschata*** Hook. f. Shrub to 4m, slightly viscid, branches tomentose at first. Lvs 0.8–1.5×0.5cm, alternate, crowded on branches, oval to obovate, green, tinged grey, scurfy above, tomentose below, subsessile. Capitula radiate, 1cm diam., in axillary corymbs of 20–30; peduncles to 5cm, slender, tomentose; phyllaries in 2–4 series, ovate to narrowly oblong, to 4mm, pilose; ray florets 7–9, linear, white; disc florets 4–12, yellow. Summer. New Zealand (South Is.).

***O.myrsinoides*** (Labill.) Benth. Low and straggling shrub; branches numerous, angled, with silver-grey scurf at first. Lvs 0.6–1.2×0.3–0.6cm, alternate, obovate, occasionally narrowly oval, dentate, glossy green, glabrous above. Capitula radiate, 3–5 in axillary clusters; peduncles to 2.5cm; ray florets 2–3, white; disc florets 2–5, yellow. Victoria, Tasmania.

***O.nernstii*** (F. Muell.) F. Muell. ex Benth. Shrub to 2m; branches viscid, usually sparsely tomentose, at least at first. Lvs 3–7cm, alternate, oblong-lanceolate, narrow, acute, submembranous, glabrous and glossy green above, loosely stellate-tomentose beneath. Capitula radiate, in terminal clusters; ray florets 15–20, white; disc florets yellow. NSW, Queensland.

***O.nummulariifolia*** (Hook. f.) Hook. f. Shrub to 3m; branches sparsely white- to yellow-tomentose at first. Lvs 0.5–1×0.4–0.6cm, densely alternate, ovate to suborbicular, glabrous above white- to buff- or yellow-tomentose beneath, margins recurved; petiole *c*1mm. Capitula solitary, 3–5mm diam., fragrant, on short peduncles; phyllaries in several series, viscid pubesc.-pilose to subglabrous; florets 5–12, cream or pale yellow; ray florets 3–5. Summer. New Zealand. var. ***cymbifolia*** Hook. f. Lvs to 14mm, narrow-ovate, very viscid, revolute almost to midrib. Z8.

***O.obcordata*** (Hook. f.) Benth. Straggling shrub to 90cm. Lvs 6–9mm, alternate, cuneate, entire, apex truncate, bluntly 3–5-dentate, pale above, silver-grey beneath. Capitula radiate, solitary, axillary; florets few, white; ray florets 5 or 6. Fr. smooth. Summer. Tasmania.

***O.odorata*** Petrie. Sparse shrub to 3.5m, branches terete, wiry. Lvs 1–3×0.3–0.6cm, opposite or in opposite fascicles, subsessile, spathulate, bright green, glabrous above, silver-tomentose beneath. Capitula radiate, 6mm diam., in opposite fascicles of 2–5, on short branches, scented; phyllaries in 3–4 series, linear-oblong, obtuse, brown, viscid-glandular; florets dull grey-brown, ray florets to 20, short, disc florets to 20, cor. viscid-glandular. Fr. compressed, striate, 1–2mm, pilose; pappus 2–3mm. New Zealand (South Is.)

***O.oporina*** (Forst. f.) Hook. f. Like *O.chathamica*, except ray florets white, disc florets yellow. Summer. New Zealand (South Is.).

***O.*** Rowallan Hybrids. *(O.arborescens × O.macrodonta.)* Lvs sharply toothed. Capitula pendulous.

***O.pachyphylla*** Cheesem. Shrub to 3m, branchlets stout, grooved, pale brown-tomentose at first. Lvs 7–13×5–6.5cm, alternate, ovate to ovate-oblong, glabrous above, densely silver- to pale brown-tomentose beneath, entire, undulate; petiole stout, grooved, to 4mm. Capitula radiate, to 2cm, many in corymbs; phyllaries 35–40, in 4–5 series, to 4mm, tomentose; florets 7–10, white to cream. New Zealand (North Is.).

***O.paniculata*** (Forst. & Forst. f.) Druce. Shrub or tree to 6m; branchlets grooved, angular, dark brown-tomentose. Lvs 4–9×2.5–4.5cm, alternate, elliptic- and ovate-oblong, glabrous above, white- to buff-tomentose beneath, margins entire, undulate. Capitula discoid, narrow, in pyramidal panicles to 5cm long; phyllaries erect, imbricate, outer shorter, dull white, glabrous or nearly so, viscid-glandular; florets solitary, tubular, 0.5cm, dull white, fragrant. Autumn. New Zealand.

***O.pannosa*** Hook. Shrub to 1.2m, branches occasionally lanate. Lvs 5–7.5cm, alternate, ovate-cordate to oblong, petiolate, entire, veins often depressed above. Capitula radiate, large; peduncles thickened at apex; phyllaries, acute; ray florets to 2.5cm, white. Spring. SE & S Australia.

***O.persoonioides*** (DC.) Benth. Shrub to 3m; branchlets numerous, white- to fawn-tomentose, at least at first. Lvs 1.5–5×0.5–2.5cm, alternate, elliptic to obovate, obtuse, entire, tapering toward base, glabrous above, white- to fawn-silky-tomentose beneath. Capitula radiate, numerous, in small groups, forming terminal clusters, pedunculate; ray florets 3–4, white, disc florets yellow. Summer. Tasmania.

***O.phlogopappa*** (Labill.) DC. Aromatic shrub to 3m, much-branched, branches tomentose at first. Lvs 1.5–5×0.4–1.2cm, alternate, oblong or narrowly obovate, margins sinuous or shallowly toothed, dark dull green above, white- or grey-white-tomentose beneath; petiole short. Capitula 2.5–3cm diam., in erect, loose corymbs; peduncles slender; ray florets 10–16, white, occasionally pink, mauve or blue, disc florets yellow. Spring. Tasmania, Victoria, NSW. 'Coomber's Blue', 'Coomber's Mauve', 'Coomber's Pink': fls respectively blue, mauve and pink. 'Rosea': fls pale pink. 'Splendens': fls blue, lavender or rose; seed race. var. ***subrepanda*** (DC.) J.H. Willis. Lvs obovate, to 12mm. Capitula often solitary; peduncles very short, leafy.

***O.pinifolia*** (Hook. f.) Benth. Shrub to 1.5m; branches slender, more or less tomentose at first. Lvs 2.5–4cm, alternate, narrowly linear, rigid, pungent, margins revolute. Capitula radiate, usually solitary, axillary; florets numerous, white; ray florets 8–10. Tasmania.

***O.ramulosa*** (Labill.) Benth. Shrub to 1.5m; branches numerous, arching, somewhat bristly, tomentose, glandular. Lvs 2–10×2mm, alternate, crowded, linear to linear-obovate, glabrous above, tomentose beneath, margins revolute; petiole to 3mm. Capitula radiate, solitary, sessile, 1.5cm diam.; phyllaries 12–16, obtuse; ray florets 3–15, linear, white, occasionally pale blue or pink; disc florets white. Summer. S Australia, Tasmania. 'Blue Stars': lvs small; fls blue, star-like, profuse.

***O.*'Rossii'**. *(O.argophylla × O.macrodonta.)* Vigorous. Lvs ellipsoid, green above, silver-pubesc. beneath.

***O.rotundifolia*** (Less.) DC. Stout, much-branched shrub, branches tomentose at first. Lvs 3–6×1.5–3cm, alternate, ovate, acute or obtuse, subentire, to 4–6-dentate, dark green and rough above, tomentose beneath; petiole 1.5cm. Capitula 2.5–6cm, 9–12 in a terminal panicle; phyllaries very numerous in several rows, linear, acute, tomentose as shoots; ray florets numerous, linear, often emarginate, pale rose; disc florets yellow. Spring–summer. E Australia.

***O.×scilloniensis*** Dorrien-Sm. *(O.lirata × O.phlogopappa.)* Shrub to 3m; branches numerous, tomentose at first. Lvs to 11cm, alternate, elliptic-oblong, obtuse, deep green and reticulate above, pale green and closely tomentose beneath, margins sinuate; petioles to 6mm. Capitula radiate, 4–6cm diam., numerous, in corymbs; phyllaries densely tomentose; ray florets 10–15, pure white; disc florets yellow. Spring. Garden origin. 'Master Michael': lvs tinted grey; fls blue, profuse. Z8.

***O.semidentata*** Decne. Rounded shrub to 3.5m; branchlets slender, white-tomentose. Lvs 3.5–7×0.6–1cm, alternate, linear to lanceolate, distantly serrate in upper half, rugose, glabrous above, white-tomentose beneath, subsessile. Capitula radiate, solitary, terminal, to 5cm diam.; peduncles slender, to 8cm, tomentose, with many lanceolate bracts; phyllaries linear, acute, to 1cm, pilose; ray florets 2×0.5cm, spreading or slightly decurved, numerous, 2×0.5cm, pale purple; disc florets darker violet-purple. Summer. Chatham Is., New Zealand.

***O.solandri*** (Hook. f.) Hook. f. Shrub or small tree to 4m; branchlets angular, viscid, yellow-tomentose. Lvs to 1.5cm, opposite or in opposite fascicles, midrib depressed, linear-spathulate to linear-obovate, subcoriaceous, glabrous above, white- to yellow-tomentose beneath, margins slightly revolute; petioles *c*1mm. Capitula radiate, solitary, sessile, 10×5–7mm; phyllaries many, in 3–4 series, bright tawny yellow, viscid-pubesc.; florets 8–20, pale yellow. Summer–autumn. New Zealand. 'Aurea': lvs strongly tinged gold.

***O.speciosa*** Hutch. Straggling shrub to 1m; branches densely tomentose. Lvs to 10×3cm, alternate, oblong-elliptic, stout and coriaceous, brown-tomentose beneath, margins revolute, dentate. Capitula radiate, 2.5cm diam., in loose corymbs to 20cm across; peduncles to 5cm; phyllaries oblong, pubesc.; ray florets 5–6, white or blue, disc florets 10–12, yellow. Summer. Victoria.

***O.*'Talbot de Malahide'.** Very similar to *O.avicennifolia*, except lvs more obtuse at apex and base, capitula to 1cm, ray florets 3–6. Z8.

***O.tasmanica*** Curtis. Shrub to 1m; branches numerous, twiggy, tomentose at first. Lvs 1–4×0.5–2cm, alternate, elliptic to obovate, obtuse, entire, rusty above, pale-tomentose beneath. Capitula radiate, solitary in axils of upper lvs, forming terminal clusters; ray florets 5–6, white; disc florets yellow. Tasmania.

***O.teretifolia*** (Sonder) F. Muell. ex Benth. Shrub to 1.5m; branches slender, glabrous, glutinous. Lvs 2–5×1mm, alternate, linear, erect, adpressed, obtuse. Capitula small, radiate, terminal, in a long, narrow panicle; ray florets 4–9, 5–6mm, white; disc florets 5–10, white. Summer. SE Australia.

***O. tomentosa*** (Wendl.) DC. ex Steud. Shrub to 2m; branches slender, numerous, tomentose at first. Lvs 3–7cm, alternate, ovate to suborbicular, dentate, fleshy, rough or pubesc. above, tomentose beneath, petiolate. Capitula radiate, solitary or few in a terminal corymb; ray florets many, white to blue or mauve; disc florets yellow. Spring. SE Australia.

***O. ×traillii*** T. Kirk. *(O. angustifolia × O. colensoi.)* Like *O. colensoi* but to 6m, lvs, 10–15×2–3cm, capitula radiate, with white ray florets. Summer. New Zealand (South Is., Stewart Is.).

***O. traversii*** (F. Muell.) Hook. f. Shrub or tree, to 10m; trunk to 60cm diam.; bark pale, branchlets 4-angled, silky white-tomentose. Lvs 4–6.5×2.5–3cm, opposite, oblong to ovate-oblong, acute, usually apiculate, entire, glabrous bright dark green above, silky white-tomentose beneath; petiole to 6mm. Capitula discoid, 6mm, many, in axillary panicles of 5–12 2.5–5cm; phyllaries few, linear-oblong; florets 5–15, tubular outermost female, dull grey. New Zealand. 'Variegata': dwarf form; lvs variegated green and gold.

***O. virgata*** (Hook. f.) Hook. f. Shrub to 5m forming dense tangled bushes; branchlets slender, wiry, usually glabrous. Lvs 0.5–2×0.3–1cm, opposite or in opposite fascicles, narrowly obovate, glabrous above, white-tomentose beneath, short-petiolate or sessile. Capitula 8–9mm diam., radiate, in opposite clusters to 4cm diam.; phyllaries in 3 series, linear, usually silky-downy; florets 5–12, yellow to white, ray florets 3–6, white. Summer. New Zealand. var. ***lineata*** T. Kirk. Shrub to 2m; branchlets slender, pendulous, pubesc. Lvs 2–4×0.1–0.2cm, in sparse fascicles, narrowly linear, margins strongly revolute. Capitula radiate, on slender peduncles to 4cm; phyllaries more or less villous; ray florets 8–14; disc florets 6–10. Z7.

***O. viscosa*** (Labill.) Benth. Shrub, 1–2m; branchlets viscid. Lvs 5–7cm, opposite, petiolate, thin, oblong-lanceolate, silver-white-tomentose beneath. Capitula radiate, numerous in irregular panicles; phyllaries few, viscid; ray florets 1–2, cream-white; disc florets 3–5, yellow. Summer. SE Australia.

***O.* 'Waikariensis'.** Hybrid of unknown origin. As for *O. ×haastii* except compact shrub to 2.5m. Lvs to 7.5cm, elliptic, obtuse, silver-white-tomentose beneath.

***O.* 'Zennorensis'.** *(O. ilicifolia × O. lacunosa.)* To 2m. Lvs dark olive above, white beneath; young stems and petioles brown-pubesc.

***O. albida*** hort., non Hook. f. See *O.* 'Talbot de Malahide'.
***O. alpina*** Buch. See *O. lacunosa*.
***O. cunninghamii*** hort. See *O. cheesemanii*.
***O. cymbifolia*** (Hook. f.) Cheesem. See *O. nummulariifolia* var. *cymbifolia*.
***O. dentata*** Hook. f. non hort. See *O. macrodonta*.
***O. dentata*** hort. non Hook. f. See *O. rotundifolia*.
***O. forsteri*** Hook. f. See *O. paniculata*.
***O. gunniana*** (DC.) Hook. f. ex Hook. See *O. phlogopappa*.
***O. ilicifolia*** var. ***mollis*** T. Kirk. See *O. ×mollis*.
***O. lineata*** (T. Kirk) Ckn. See *O. virgata* var. *lineata*.
***O. lyrata*** (Sims) Hutch. See *O. lirata*.
***O. ×mollis*** hort. See *O. ilicifolia*.
***O. nitida*** (Hook. f.) Hook. f. See *O. arborescens*.
***O. oleifolia*** hort. See *O.* 'Waikariensis'.
***O. rani*** hort. See *O. cheesemanii*.
***O. stellulata*** hort. See *O. phlogopappa*.
***O. subrepanda*** (DC.) Hutch. See *O. phlogopappa* var. *subrepanda*.
***O. tomentosa*** hort. See *O. rotundifolia*.
For further synonymy see *Arnica, Aster, Eurybia, Pachystegia* and *Solidago*.

**Olfersia** Raddi. (For J.F. Olfers (early 19th century), Prussian administrator in Rio de Janeiro.) Dryopteridaceae. 1 species, a terrestrial fern. Rhizomes to 2cm, long-creeping; scales to 20×1mm, tufted, linear to lanceolate, apex twisted and hair-like, margin subentire, gold to pale brown. Fronds stipitate, dimorphous, leathery and firm-textured, sterile fronds to 85×35cm, pinnate, ovate or lanceolate to oblong, glabrous, pinnae to 25×9cm, terminal pinna 1, lateral pinnae 4–12 pairs, subopposite or alternate, ascending, ovate or lanceolate to oblong, apex narrowly acute, base unequal and cuneate, margin entire or notched, cartilaginous, fertile fronds 2-pinnate, pinnae smaller than sterile, often reduced to narrow laminar material, ephemeral, pinnules to 10×3mm, base adnate, margin entire, veins free, single or forked, parallel, oblique; rachis and costa grooved above, costa occasionally sparsely pubescent below; stipes to 50cm, approximate and clustered, scaly at base, straw-coloured. Tropical America. Z10.

CULTIVATION As for *Polybotrya*. *O. cervina* produces the occasional frond with a deeply serrate margin.

***O. cervina*** (L.) Kunze. As for the genus.

For synonymy see *Acrostichum, Osmunda* and *Polybotrya*.

**Oliverella** Rose.
***O. elegans*** Rose. See *Echeveria harmsii*.

**Olmsted, Frederick Law** (1822–1903). Landscape architect. Olmsted was born in Hartford, Connecticut, and educated privately due to illness, training as a civil engineer and early becoming interested in landscape design. Following brief periods as a clerk in New York and as a apprentice seaman, in 1844 Olmsted took up farming, first in Connecticut and after 1848 on Staten Island. His views on landscape design were decisively influenced by the writings of Uvedale Price and William Gilpin and by a visit to England in 1850 (chronicled in *Walks and Talks of an American Farmer in England*, 1852), in which he was impressed by the picturesque style and by the notion of the public park or 'People's Garden' epitomized for him by Paxton's Birkenhead Park, Liverpool. Shortly after returning to America, Olmsted gave up farming and pursued a journalistic career with the *New York Daily Times*, travelling extensively in the US and particularly in the south.

In 1855 he established a publishing firm which went bankrupt in 1857, after which took up employment as the first superintendent of Central Park, New York. He began by employing 900 men to clear the 770 acres of waste ground. In 1858 Olmsted collaborated with the architect Calvert Vaux, his partner until 1872, on their successful design for Central Park, 'Greensward'. Although Central Park owes something to the English Picturesque tradition. Olmsted's view of garden design was conservative. His achievement was to integrate landscape and the city by means as radical as routing traffic through a park and conserving pre-existing elements, such as rock outcrops, that recall the city's origins in the wilderness.

After 1859 Olmsted's career was interrupted by illness and a visit to Europe to recuperate. During the Civil War, he worked for the Sanitary Commission from 1861 to 1863, and from 1863 he was manager of a mining company in California, when he succeeded in preserving the Yosemite Valley area as a public reservation.

In 1866 Olmsted and Vaux were reappointed as landscape architects for Central Park and produced plans for the spacious Prospect Park, Brooklyn, considered by many to be Olmsted's finest individual achievement. His most ambitious project, however, was the 'Emerald Necklace' parks system for Boston, executed between 1878 and 1895. This was a grand conception involving 2000 acres of open land for five large parks, connecting parkways, harbour and riverfront improvements, smaller parks and playgrounds. It reflected Olmsted's conception of the public park itself and the surrounding urban areas as part of the same landscape design. Aside from the many parks, Olmsted also produced designs for community subdivisions, one of the earliest and most notable being Riverside, near Chicago, designed in 1869, an early example of the garden suburb. Olmsted also created plans for university campuses, the most complete being that for Stanford University in Palo Alto, California. His activities also extended to the creation of a programme for the administration of the Yosemite Wilderness reservation, created in 1864. In this range of activities Olmsted defined a profession which he himself termed landscape architecture.

**Olsynium** Raf. (From Gk meaning hardly united, referring to the stamens.) Iridaceae. About 12 species of perennial herbs with fibrous roots closely related to *Sisyrinchium*. Leaves mostly basal, usually linear or lanceolate. Flowers enclosed in spathes; perianth bell-shaped; tepals equal, 6; stamens joined only at base; style with 3 short branches. Fruit a capsule; seeds brown, seeds brown, more or less angular. N & S America. Z9.

CULTIVATION Graceful perennials for cool, semi-shaded positions in peat pockets on the rock garden or peat bed. They will survive frosts to −20°C/4°F and become dormant in late spring, but nonetheless require permanent moisture.

***O. biflorum*** (Thunb.) Goldbl. Stem 10–70cm. Basal lvs 1–5, 4–22cm×1–2.5mm, linear, cauline lvs 1–3. Infl. 2–7-fld; fls scented, cream, striped with maroon; tube

7–20mm, cylindrical to cup-shaped; tepals 10–18×5–7.5mm, oblong-ovate. Spring. Patagonia.

***O. douglasii*** (A. Dietr.) E. Bickn. GRASS WIDOW; PURPLE-EYED GRASS. Stems 15–30cm high, flattened but not winged. Basal lvs bract-like, stem lvs to 1cm. Spathes terminal, 2–3-fld; fls pendent, bell-shaped, 15–20mm, wine-red, purple-pink or white; tepals oblong-obovate. Western N America.

***O. filifolium*** (Gaudich.) Goldbl. Stem 15–20cm; lvs rush-like. Fls erect, white with red-purple lines. Spring. Falkland Is.

***O. grandiflorum*** (Douglas ex Lindl.) Raf. See *O. douglasii*.
***O. inflatum*** Suksd. See *O. douglasii*.
For further synonymy see *Phaiophleps, Sisyrinchium* and *Synphyostemon*.

**Omphalodes** Mill. (From Gk *omphalos*, navel, and *-oides*, like, referring to the nutlets which apparently resemble a navel.) NAVELWORT; NAVELSEED. Boraginaceae. Some 28 species of annual, biennial or perennial herbs, glabrous or minutely pubescent. Leaves simple, alternate, oblong to ovate; basal leaves long-petiolate. Flowers usually in terminal cymes, sometimes solitary and axillary, white or blue, sometimes bracteate; calyx 5-parted, accrescent in fruit; corolla 5-lobed, subrotate or subcampanulate, tube short, throat with 5 saccate invaginations forming an eye, frequently paler than the rest of the corolla; stamens 5, included, inserted near middle of tube; style included, stigma capitate. Fruit of 4 horizontal nutlets, depressed-globose, usually smooth, sometimes pubescent, alate. Europe, N Africa, Asia, Mexico.

CULTIVATION *O. luciliae*, which occurs in cliff face crevices, requires a sunny position with its roots in light, moist, sharply drained soils, with additional limestone chippings. Hardy to about −5°C/23°F, it dislikes winter wet and may be more safely grown in the alpine house. The annual species such as *O. linifolia*, with white blooms that last well when cut, are sown *in situ* in spring, in sun and well-drained soil. The remaining species are suitable for cool positions in the rock garden or for naturalizing in light, open woodland with treatment as for *Mertensia*. All species dislike root disturbance; divide carefully.

***O. cappadocica*** (Willd.) DC. Perenn. to 28cm, erect or ascending, from a creeping rhiz. Basal lvs to 10×4.5cm, ovate to cordate, acute or acuminate, finely pilose, long-petiolate; cauline lvs smaller, short-petiolate or subsessile. Fls bright blue with a white eye; bracts absent; pedicel to 3mm in fl., to 10mm in fr., arcuate-recurved; cal. lobes oblong-ovate, acute; cor. tube to 2mm, limb to 5mm diam. Nutlets to 3×2mm, elliptic, entire, margin pubesc. Asia Minor. 'Cherry Ingram': vigorous, to 25cm; fls deep blue. Z6.

***O. japonica*** (Thunb.) Maxim. Perenn., spreading-hirsute, from a short, stout rhiz. Stems to 20cm, ascending from a decumbent base, sometimes slightly branched toward base. Basal lvs to 15×2.5cm, oblanceolate, acute, base attenuate, pubesc. above and beneath; cauline lvs to 6cm, few, sessile or subsessile. Infl. a simple raceme, somewhat bracteate near base; pedicels to 15mm in fl., deflexed; cal. lobes to 8mm in fr., narrowly ovate; cor. to 10mm diam., blue. Nutlets to 3mm, smooth. Japan. Z7.

***O. krameri*** Franch. & Savat. Perenn., with white spreading hairs, from a short stout rhiz. Stems to 40cm, solitary to few, simple, erect. Basal lvs to 15×3.5cm, broadly oblanceolate, acute, long-petiolate; cauline lvs short-petiolate to sessile. Infl. erect, forked; bracts usually absent; fls to 15mm diam., blue; pedicel to 15mm; cal. lobes to 8mm in fr., narrowly ovate. Nutlets to 3.5mm diam., rotund, slightly depressed. Japan. Z7.

***O. linifolia*** (L.) Moench. Annual. Stems to 40cm, sometimes slightly branched near base, erect. Basal lvs to 10×2cm, linear-lanceolate to spathulate, sparingly strigose-ciliate, petiolate; cauline lvs smaller, linear to lanceolate, sessile. Infl. terminal, loosely 5 to 15-fld; bracts absent; fls to 12mm diam., white or blue; pedicel to 5mm in fl., to 20mm in fr.; cal. lobes to 3mm in fl., to 7mm in fr., ovate to lanceolate; cor. to 10mm in fr. Nutlets to 4mm, sometimes hirsute, margins lobed, dentate or crenate. SW Europe.

***O. luciliae*** Boiss. Perenn., to 25cm, tufted, glabrous. Basal lvs to 10×3.5cm, ovate or elliptic to oblong, obtuse or rounded, petiolate; upper cauline lvs smaller, sessile. Infl. terminal, bracteate; fls to 12mm diam., rose becoming blue; cal. lobes narrowly elliptic, subacute, glabrous; cor. tube to 4mm, limb to 8mm diam., flat to concave. Nutlets to 2.5×1.5mm, narrowly winged, entire. Greece, Asia Minor. Z7.

***O. nitida*** Hoffsgg. & Link. Perenn. to 65cm, erect, branched, sparingly setose. Basal lvs to 20×3.5cm, lanceolate or oblong-lanceolate, acute or acuminate, glabrous above, slightly strigose beneath; long-petiolate; cauline lvs smaller, short-petiolate to sessile. Infl. terminal, bracteate near base; fls to 10mm diam., blue, centre yellow-white; pedicels to 20mm in fr.; cal. lobes to 4mm in fl., to 7mm in fr., lanceolate to oblong or ovate; cor. to 9mm. Nutlets to 2.5mm, pubesc., margin dentate. Spain, Portugal. Z7.

***O. verna*** Moench. CREEPING FORGET-ME-NOT. Perenn. to 20cm, stoloniferous. Basal lvs to 20×6cm, ovate or ovate-lanceolate to cordate, mucronate to acuminate, sparingly hirsute, long-petiolate; cauline lvs smaller, ovate to elliptic, short-petiolate to sessile. Infl. terminal, bracteate near base; fls to 12mm diam., blue; pedicels to 12mm in fl., to 30mm in fr.; cal. to 4mm, lobes elliptic, pubesc.; cor. to 10mm. Nutlets to 2mm, pubesc., margin entire. Europe. 'Alba': fls white. Z6.

***O. lusitanica*** (L.) Pourr. ex Lange. See *O. nitida*.
For further synonymy see *Cynoglossum*.

**Omphalogramma** (Franch.) Franch. (From Gk *omphalos*, navel, and *gramma*, line.) Primulaceae. 15 species of perennial, usually rhizomatous, herbs, similar to *Primula*. Leaves arising from a sheath of scales, with round, amber, sessile glands, especially beneath. Scapes and outside of corolla tube covered with long articulate, glandular hairs. Flower lacking bracts, 6–8-merous, solitary; corolla infundibuliform, tube longer than calyx or lobes; stamens in posterior side of tube erect, those anterior bent across tube, filaments 10mm+. Fruit a 6–8-valved capsule, the upper quarter extruding from calyx, dehiscing from apex to nearly to base; seeds flattened, with broadly winged aril. Early summer. Himalaya, W China. Z7.

CULTIVATION Plants of mountain woodland (largely on limestone), or of damp, open, alpine slopes. Like *Meconopsis* and some *Corydalis* spp., they grow best in areas with cool moist summers, such as those of Northern Britain. *O. vinciflorum*, with tubular and solitary flowers of intense blue-violet, is probably the easiest species in cultivation, and suits the shady rock garden with gritty, moist but well-drained lime-free soil. Otherwise provide conditions similar to those enjoyed by the smaller, alpine spp. of *Primula* in the alpine house or cold frame, in pans of a gritty alpine mix with added leafmould. Propagate from seed or by division in spring.

***O. delavayi*** Franch. Rhiz. scales forming a collar around base of petioles and infl. Lvs to 10×7cm, broadly ovate to oblong or suborbicular, slightly crenulate, more or less glabrous, margins ciliate; petiole pubesc., to 3× longer than lamina. Scape 6–15cm, pubesc., especially towards apex, 20–30cm in fruit; cal. to 15mm, broadly campanulate, lobes pubesc., oblong to lanceolate, apex acute, obtuse or even-lobed, denticulate; cor. pale to deep rose-purple, 30–35mm diam., infundibuliform, tube to 5cm, base yellow, lobes ovate or oblong, deeply incised; anth. to 5mm, fil. to 1cm; style glandular-pubesc. Fr. 20–35mm. China (Yunnan), NE Upper Burma.

***O. elegans*** Forr. Rhiz. scales not forming collar. Lvs to 10×4cm, ovate to ovate-lanceolate, apex obtuse, base cuneate to round or cordate, usually entire, sometimes minutely denticulate, pubesc. above, hairs white, articulate, less pubesc. beneath, hairs confined to midrib and lateral veins; petiole subequal to twice as long as lamina, pubesc., base sheathing. Scape to 15cm in flower to 75cm in fruit, densely pilose, especially toward apex; cal. to 1cm, lobes narrowly-lanceolate, acute, tinged red, 3-veined, pubesc., clasping base of cor. tube; cor. deep-violet to dark blue-purple, to 6cm diam., tube to 35mm, colourless or creamy at base, with 6 or 7 cream bands running into upper portion, limb almost regular or slightly 2-lipped, with 3 lobes forming upper lip, 3 or 4 forming lower lip, lobes to 15×25mm, oblong to broad-obovate, to elliptic, bilobed, entire or slightly toothed; anth. to 5mm, fil. to 1cm, all except 1 bent, pressing anth. against stigma, other 1 lying along middle of lower half of cor. tube; style glabrous, slightly bent. Fr. to 2×1cm, cylindrical. SE Tibet, NW Yunnan, Upper Burma.

***O. elwesianum*** (King ex G. Watt) Franch. Scales embracing petiole bases. Lvs to 10×3cm, oblanceolate, apex round or obtuse, entire or obscurely denticulate and faintly cartilaginous at margin, base tapering, glabrous; petiole broadly winged, subequal to lamina. Scape to 12cm in flower, to 40cm in fruit, apex green, with crimson hairs, base tinged red, with white hairs; calyx to 1cm, green, pubesc., lobes lanceolate; cor. purple, infundibuliform, limb to 3cm diam., lobes oblong to obovate, emarginate, slightly dentate, margins pubesc., tube pale lemon inside, to 35mm, outside with crimson hairs; anth. to 5mm, fil. to 5mm, glabrous; style glabrous. Fr. to 2cm long. Sikkim, SE Tibet.

***O. farreri*** Balf. f. Scales forming collar, surrounding peduncles then petioles. Lvs to 10×5cm, round to cordate, apex obtuse, rounded, or acute, base deeply cordate, slightly crenulate, pubesc.; petiole to twice length of lamina. Scape to 12cm in flower, to 40cm in fruit; cal. to 2cm, broadly campanulate, lobes lanceolate, acute, usually entire, pubesc., tinged green; cor. deep rose-purple or violet, tube base yellow, 4–6cm diam., infundibuliform, outside covered with articulate hairs, lobes oblong or ovate, irregularly dentate, the upper 3 reflexing backwards along tube when mature, lower lobes projecting slightly forward;

anth. to 5mm, fil. to 1cm; style glabrous, or occasionally long-haired. Fr. to 25mm, veins slightly spirally twisted. NE Upper Burma.

***O.souliei*** Franch. Scales oblong, forming collar to 10cm, sheathing peduncle and petioles. Lvs to 30×7cm, ovate to elliptic or oblong, apex acute or obtuse, base tapering gradually, entire or remotely denticulate, usually glabrous, occasionally pubesc., rather fleshy; petiole broadly winged, distinct, subequal to half again as long as petiole. Scape to 35cm in flower, to 60cm in fruit, stiff, erect, apex covered in red, septate glandular-hairs; cal. to 1cm, campanulate, glandular-pilose outside, lobes ovate-lanceolate, acute or obtuse, clasping swollen base of cor. tube; cor. deep red-purple or blue-purple, tube base yellow with yellow bands inside, tube 2–4cm, glandular-pilose outside, limb 4–6cm diam., lobes spreading, broad-obovate or oblong, deeply or slightly bilobed, entire or irregularly toothed; anth. to 5mm, fil. to 1cm, glandular; style glabrous, slightly curved; stigma reaching beyond anth., exserted from mouth of cor. Fr. 2–3cm, broad-cylindrical. NW Yunnan, SE Tibet.

***O.vinciflorum*** (Franch.) Franch. Puberulent, with little or no or no woody rootstock, with large resting bud to 3cm diam., scales surrounding base of plant. Lvs to 20×5cm, variable, scarcely differentiated as bladed petiole and broadly oblanceolate or obovate, or blade distinct from petiole and ovate-oblong to oblong, apex round, entire to crenulate, base tapering gradually, or abruptly cuneate, round or cordate, glandular-pubesc. throughout. Scape to 20cm, later to 80cm, apex tinged purple, pilose, white below, red above, all tipped with red glands; cal. to 10mm, campanulate, lobes linear-oblong, glandular-pilose, clasping or spreading; cor. deep indigo-blue or purple, to 35mm, outside glandular-pubescent, limb 3–5cm diam., lobes narrow or broad-obovate, entire, faintly or deeply emarginate, apex crenate or toothed, upper lobes reflexed, lower lobes pointing forward; upper stamens erect, lower stamens bent backwards; fil. to 5cm, glabrous, anth. very short, forming cone behind style, reaching mouth or protruding just beyond; styles glabrous. Fr. to 2cm. China (Yunnan, Sichuan).

***O.rockii*** W.W. Sm. See *O. vinciflorum*.

**ONAGRACEAE** Juss. EVENING PRIMROSE FAMILY. Dicot. 24 genera and 650 species of herbs and shrubs, rarely trees, often with epidermal oil-cells, usually with internal phloem. Leaves whorled, opposite or alternate, simple, entire to pinnatifid; stipules sometimes present. Flowers usually bisexual, regular, solitary or in spikes to panicles, usually with long hypanthium nectiferous within, bird or insect (not beetle) – or self pollinated; calyx 4 free sepals, lobes often valvate on hypanthium; corolla 4 free petals, often clawed, rarely absent; stamens 4+4 or 4–2–1, within hypanthium or on disc; ovary inferior, of 4 fused carpels and 4-loculed, or half inferior and 2-loculed; placentation axile or parietal; ovules few to numerous per locule. Fruit a capsule, berry or nut; seeds usually numerous; endosperm absent; embryo straight, oily. Cosmopolitan, especially temperate and warm America. *Boisduvalia, Calylophus, Camissonia, Circaea, Clarkia, Epilobium, Fuchsia, Gaura, Hauya, Lopezia, Ludwigia, Oenothera.*

**×Oncidioda**. *(Cochlioda × Oncidium.)* Orchidaceae. Intergeneric orchid hybrids requiring cool growing conditions. Plants consist of a group of compressed pseudobulbs growing from a basal rhizome, each with one or two leaves at its apex and two or more leaf-like sheaths arising at its base. Inflorescences arise in the axils of these sheaths and may be simple or branched. Flowers have narrow sepals and petals, lip large or small depending on the ancestry; flowers of many colours often conspicuously marked.

**×*O.* Charlesworthii**: branching sprays of small fls borne in profusion; fls bright red with pink and yellow lip.

**Oncidium** Sw. (From Gk *onkos*, mass, body, referring to the fleshy, warty calli on the lip of many species.) Orchidaceae. Some 450 species of epiphytic, lithophytic or terrestrial orchids closely allied to *Odontoglossum, Brassia, Miltonia* and *Psychopsis*. Rhizome short to long and creeping, enveloped at base by papery bracts. Pseudobulbs large and conspicuous to minute, variously shaped, subtended by distichous sheaths, 1–4-leaved. Leaves equitant, fleshy, coriaceous or soft, oblong-lanceolate to terete; in the softer-leaved species a basal pair of leaves often sheaths the pseudobulbs in its first season prior to abscising to leave the bulb apically bifoliate. Inflorescence a lateral raceme or panicle, often branching and elongated, erect, arching or pendent, loose or dense, few- to many-flowered; flowers variously coloured, often yellow or brown, large and showy to inconspicuous; sepals usually subequal, spreading or reflexed, free or with lateral sepals connate almost to apex; petals similar to dorsal sepal or larger; lip adnate to base of column, entire to 3-lobed, lateral lobes porrect, spreading or reflexed, small and auriculate to large, midlobe showy, spreading, emarginate or bifid, central portion usually with an isthmus – disc with cristate or tuberculate basal callus; column short, stout, footless, with a fleshy plate below stigma, with prominent, variously shaped wings or auricles on either side; anther terminal, incumbent, operculate, pollinia 2, waxy, deeply sulcate, affixed to a stipe. Subtropical & Tropical America. Z10.

CULTIVATION A large genus of cool and intermediate-growing orchids. They differ greatly in habit, but are easily recognized by their slender, branching sprays of small flowers in shades of yellow and brown. Some of the most well-known species, for example *O.papilio*, are now include in separate genera (see synonymy). The smaller species with pronounced pseudobulbs and relatively soft growth require dappled sunlight and a humid, buoyant atmosphere in the cool house. Water and feed freely in the growing season, at other times only to prevent shrivelling. Pot in fine to medium grade bark-based mix in clay pans or baskets. The larger species with reduced pseudobulbs and massive, leathery, 'mule's ear' leaves should be mounted on bark or planted in baskets and afforded maximum light and humidity throughout the year. Their water requirement is not so great as that of the first group but they tend to favour a warmer and steamier situation. The inflorescences of species such as *O.cavendishianum* may attain two metres and require some training or, even, tying in to a trellis or the glasshouse framework. *O.pusillum*, a tiny plant with overlapping fleshy leaves and charming, large yellow flowers, needs to be treated as for the smaller *Laelia* species. Propagate by division. See ORCHIDS.

***O.abortivum*** Rchb. f. Pseudobulbs to 4×2.5cm, ellipsoid, clustered, strongly laterally compressed, unifoliate. Lvs to 16×2.5cm, oblong to oblong-lanceolate, acute, thin. Panicle to 30cm, many-fld, composed of fertile and abortive fls, branches 2-ranked; abortive fls consisting of linear seg., to 8mm, fertile fls 1–2, situated at branch apices, bright yellow banded dark purple-brown; dorsal sep. to 12×4mm, lanceolate to linear-lanceolate, acute, lateral sep. longer than dorsal sep.; pet. to 10×4mm, lanceolate to oblong-lanceolate, acute, oblique; lip bright yellow marked brown in centre, to 1.5×2mm, 3-lobed, lateral lobes subrotund, midlobe smaller than lateral lobes, triangular or ovate-triangular to lanceolate, acute, callus pale yellow, tubercles conical or cylindrical; column to 5mm, wings ligulate or deltoid, apical margins dentate. Venezuela.

***O.altissimum*** (Jacq.) Sw. non Lindl. Pseudobulbs to 10×5cm, ovoid-oblong, compressed, unifoliate or bifoliate. Lvs to 20×3cm, oblong or oblong-ligulate, acute. Panicle to 3m, short-branched toward apex, each branch 3–5-fld; fls to 3.5cm diam.; sep. and pet. yellow-green barred and blotched maroon, fleshy, narrow-lanceolate or oblanceolate, to 2×0.5cm, dorsally keeled, undulate; lip bright yellow, blotched maroon at base of midlobe, to 1×1cm, lateral lobes small, oblong, midlobe reniform, clawed, emarginate, callus with 10 tubercles; column to 5mm, slightly arching, with small, entire, rounded auricles. W Indies.

***O.ampliatum*** Lindl. Pseudobulbs to 10×8cm, ovoid to suborbicular, tightly clustered on short rhiz., lustrous green spotted purple-brown, strongly compressed, unifoliate to trifoliate. Lvs to 40×10cm, elliptic-oblanceolate to ligulate, obtuse or broadly rounded, fleshy-coriaceous. Raceme or panicle to 60cm, few- to many-fld; fls to 2.5cm diam.; sep. bright to pale yellow spotted chocolate-brown, to 10×7mm, obovate-spathulate, concave, incurved; pet. to 10×9mm, yellow with a few brown spots, flat, suborbicular, basally clawed, rounded at apex; lip bright yellow, paler below, to 2.5×3cm, deeply 3-lobed, lateral lobes small, subauriculate, midlobe broadly oblong or reniform, cleft or bilobed, callus pale cream marked yellow, fleshy, 3-lobed, midlobe trituberculate; column to 4mm, wings denticulate or lobulate. Guatemala to Peru, Venezuela, Trinidad.

***O.ansiferum*** Rchb. f. Pseudobulbs to 14×7cm, ovate-elliptic or elliptic-oblong, strongly compressed, unifoliate or bifoliate. Lvs to 45×5.5cm, elliptic-oblong to elliptic-oblanceolate, subcoriaceous. Panicle to 1m, solitary or paired, much-branched; fls to 3cm diam.; sep. and pet. red-brown edged yellow, sep. to 17×6mm, short-clawed, elliptic-oblong to lanceolate, spreading-reflexed, strongly undulate, pet. wider than sep., elliptic-oblong to elliptic-lanceolate, obtuse to subacute, strongly undulate; lip bright yellow with yellow-brown claw, to 18×13mm, pandurate, lateral lobes short, suborbicular, auriculate, midlobe broadly reniform to semi-orbicular to bilobulate with broadly triangular claw, callus yellow-white spotted pale brown, fleshy, obovate, 5-lobed, puberulent, ending in a central, porrect tooth; column to 6mm, stout, wings dolabriform, dentate-crenulate. Costa Rica, Guatemala, Panama, Nicaragua.

***O. anthocrene*** Rchb. f. Pseudobulbs to 15×5cm, ovoid-oblong, compressed, ridged, unifoliate or bifoliate. Lvs to 38×5cm, oblong-ligulate to oblong-lanceolate, obtuse or slightly retuse, coriaceous. Raceme rarely branching, to 1.2m, many-fld; fls to 6.5cm diam., waxy; sep. and pet. brown marked yellow, undulate, usually clawed; lip with central red-brown claw, pandurate, 3-lobed, lateral lobes small, yellow often spotted red-brown, midlobe bright yellow, cuspidate, bilobulate, callus yellow, toothed; column scarcely winged. Panama, Colombia.

***O. ascendens*** Lindl. Pseudobulbs to 2×1cm, ovoid, unifoliate or bifoliate. Lvs to 80×1cm, terete, lightly sulcate. Raceme to 50cm, simple or branched; fls small, yellow marked and stained red-brown; sep. spreading-reflexed, to 10×5mm, deeply concave, obovate; pet. resemble sep. in size, elliptic to subquadrate, apex rounded to truncate, lip yellow marked red near callus, larger than sep., lateral lobes obliquely oblong, small, erect, midlobe transversely elliptic to semi-orbicular, emarginate, callus erect, with suborbicular central keel flanked by several tubercles; column to 5mm, stout, wings narrow, falcate, incurved. C America, Mexico.

***O. auriferum*** Rchb. f. Pseudobulbs to 6×4cm, ovoid, clustered, compressed, unifoliate. Lvs to 25×2.5cm, linear, coriaceous. Panicle to 40cm, loosely many-fld, branches small, spreading; fls to 2.5cm diam.; sep. and pet. yellow with 2 or 3 pale brown bands, dorsal sep. to 10×4mm, elliptic or elliptic-oblong, obtuse, laterals ligulate to linear-ligulate, obtuse; lip golden-yellow with a blotch of pale red-brown either side of disc, to 15×20mm, pandurate, lateral lobes small, oblong, margins revolute, midlobe transversely oblong to reniform, apex cleft, margins wavy, separated from lateral lobes by broad claw, callus white, triangular, dentate; column wings broad, dolabriform, dentate. Venezuela, Colombia.

***O. barbatum*** Lindl. Pseudobulbs to 6.5×3.5cm, ovate to ovate-oblong with well-defined central ridge, unifoliate. Lvs to 10×2.5cm, linear-lanceolate to ovate-oblong, acute or emarginate. Panicle to 50cm, short-branched, loosely few-fld; fls to 2.5cm diam., waxy; sep. and pet. yellow barred chestnut-brown, sep. to 1.4×0.5cm, clawed, ovate-lanceolate to elliptic-oblong, undulate, lateral sep. connate in basal half, pet. slightly shorter and broader than sep., clawed, obliquely oblong; lip to 1×2cm, bright yellow, spotted red on callus, lateral lobes equal midlobe, obovate, obtuse, midlobe obovate, emarginate to apiculate, callus orbicular, fimbriate, 5-toothed; column wings suborbicular to subquadrate. Brazil.

***O. baueri*** Lindl. Rhiz. long-creeping. Pseudobulbs to 15×4cm, oblong-ovoid to cylindric, strongly compressed, usually bifoliate. Lvs to 78×6cm, ligulate to linear-oblong, acute to short-acuminate, slightly coriaceous. Panicle to 3m, much-branched, many-fld; fls to 3cm diam., waxy, long-lived; sep. and pet. green-yellow to bright yellow barred brown, sep. to 17×5mm, elliptic-lanceolate to obliquely linear-lanceolate, acute or short-acuminate, lateral sep. free, recurved at apex, pet. to 12×3mm, elliptic-lanceolate, acute with recurved apex; lip to 2×1cm, yellow with red-brown central blotch, pandurate to 3-lobed, lateral lobes small, midlobe transversely reniform, emarginate, broadly clawed, callus consisting of many teeth in 3 series, terminating in 3 subequal teeth; column to 6mm. Peru, Brazil, Bolivia, Ecuador.

***O. bicallosum*** Lindl. Resembles *O. cavendishianum* except infl. racemose, fls larger, yellow with green-brown suffusion, unspotted, lip lateral lobes smaller, callus bituberculate. Mexico, Guatemala, El Salvador.

***O. bicolor*** Lindl. Pseudobulbs to 7×3cm, ovoid, compressed, sharply ridged, unifoliate or bifoliate. Lvs to 18×6cm, oblong or oblong-elliptic, acute, base attenuate, coriaceous. Panicle to 1m, much-branched; fls numerous, small; sep. and pet. brown-yellow marked dark red-brown, dorsal sep. to 10×5mm, ovate to obovate, acute to rounded, concave, lateral sep. to 13×4mm, connate to middle or less, free portion oblong, acute, pet. to 12×6mm, narrowly obovate, acute to rounded, slightly undulate; lip bright yellow, to 2.5×3cm, pandurate, emarginate, callus white marked dark red-brown, pubesc., broadly triangular, tuberculate; column to 6mm. Venezuela, Brazil.

***O. bifolium*** Sims. Pseudobulbs to 9cm, ovoid or ovoid-oblong, clustered, grooved with age, bifoliate, rarely unifoliate. Lvs to 14×1.5cm, linear-ligulate, acute, subcoriaceous, often tinged bronze. Infl. simple, sometimes branched, to 35cm; fls 5–20, to 2.5cm diam.; sep. and pet. yellow marked red-brown, sep. ovate-elliptic, rounded, to 9×4mm, lateral sep. exceeding dorsal sep., pet. to 7×6mm, ovate, rounded or emarginate; lip rich golden-yellow, to 2×2.5cm, deflexed, lateral lobes small, triangular, midlobe large, short-clawed, reniform, strongly emarginate; callus yellow marked red-brown, tuberculate in front; column short, wing margins denticulate. Brazil, Uruguay, Argentina, Bolivia.

***O. boothianum*** Rchb. f. Pseudobulbs to 8cm, ellipsoid, strongly compressed, glossy green, unifoliate or bifoliate. Lvs to 30×9cm, ligulate, subacute, subcoriaceous. Panicle to 2m, arcuate to pendent, much-branched, many-fld; fls to 3cm diam.; sep. and pet. yellow marked red-brown, narrowly oblong, to 9×4mm; lip to 2×1cm, golden yellow marked red-brown, lateral lobes rounded, midlobe long-clawed, reniform, emarginate, larger than lateral lobes, callus white, verrucose, shortly pubesc. at base; column yellow, wings large, fringed. Venezuela.

***O. brachyandrum*** Lindl. Pseudobulbs to 8×4.5cm, ovoid to ellipsoid, clustered, compressed, often spotted purple, bifoliate or trifoliate. Lvs to 30×2cm, grassy, ligulate to linear-lanceolate. Raceme or panicle slender, elongated, few- to many-fld; sep. and pet. yellow or yellow-green mottled red-brown, sep. to 15×7mm, elliptic-oblong to elliptic-oblanceolate, acute to obtuse, concave, lateral sep. oblique, free or slightly connate, pet. smaller than sep., elliptic-oblanceolate to elliptic-oblong, rounded to subacute; lip yellow, to 2.5×2.5cm, broadly pandurate, emarginate, apical margin decurved, callus yellow marked red-brown, linear, fleshy, 3-keeled; column to 7mm, yellow spotted brown at apex, wings small, auriculate. Mexico, Guatemala, Honduras.

***O. bracteatum*** Warsc. & Rchb. f. Pseudobulbs to 7.5×3.5cm, linear to ovoid-oblong, strongly compressed, bifoliate, rarely unifoliate. Lvs to 40×3cm, linear-ligulate, obtuse, coriaceous. Panicle to 120cm, short-branched, conspicuously bracteate; fls usually 3, to 2.5cm diam.; sep. and pet. bright yellow-green heavily blotched and spotted brown-purple, sep. to 15×5mm, free, undulate, lateral sep. linear, prominently keeled below, dorsal sep. oblong-lanceolate, acute, pet. to 14×4mm, linear-oblong, acute, undulate; lip bright to pale yellow with red-brown claw, to 13×15cm, obscurely 3-lobed, midlobe oblong, emarginate, disc fleshy, with erect, toothed callus; column to 6mm, narrowly winged. Costa Rica, Panama, Nicaragua, Colombia.

***O. brevilabrum*** Rolfe. Pseudobulbs to 5.25cm, ovoid. Lvs to 32cm, linear. Panicles crowded; fls to 2cm diam., golden-yellow banded chocolate brown. S America.

***O. cabagrae*** Schltr. Pseudobulbs to 11×3cm, ovoid-elliptic to sublinear, strongly compressed, spotted black-brown, usually bifoliate. Lvs to 25×3cm, linear-ligulate, acute, subcoriaceous. Panicle to 80cm, loosely many-fld; fls to 2.5cm diam., long-lived; sep. and pet. yellow, heavily blotched deep chestnut-brown, sep. to 12×6mm, clawed, elliptic-lanceolate, acute, apices recurved, lateral sep. keeled below, pet. broader than sep., elliptic-oblanceolate, undulate; lip bright yellow with red-brown claw, lateral lobes small, semi-orbicular, midlobe reniform, emarginate, callus white spotted brown, erect, fleshy, truncate, bidentate; column to 5mm, wings broad, bilobed, minutely dentate. Costa Rica, Panama.

***O. caminiophorum*** Rchb. f. Pseudobulbs to 4×3cm, suborbicular to narrowly ovoid, compressed, unifoliate. Lvs to 12cm, oblong or linear-oblong. Panicle to 50cm, branched from base, many-fld; fls to 2.5cm across; sep. bright yellow, brown in basal half, free, to 8×3mm, lanceolate to obovate-oblong, acute, lateral sep. reflexed at apex; pet. resembling sep. in colour but obovate-oblong, obtuse; lip bright yellow spotted red, with chestnut-brown band, to 1×1cm, pandurate, lateral lobes ovate, rounded, midlobe transversely elliptic to subrotund, apex cleft, separated from lateral lobes by narrow claw, callus subquadrate with 3 small teeth on each side at base; column wings small, truncate. Venezuela.

***O. cardiochilum*** Lindl. Pseudobulbs to 10×2.5cm, ovoid-cylindric, compressed, concealed by sheathing lf bases, bifoliate. Lvs to 75×6cm, linear-ligulate to narrowly oblanceolate, acute to acuminate, slightly conduplicate, subcoriaceous. Panicle to 2m, loosely many-branched, rachis distinctly fractiflex; fls to 2cm across, lilac-scented; sep. and pet. red-brown tipped and marked green-white, sep. free, linear-lanceolate to linear-elliptic, acute or acuminate and recurved at apex, to 20×5mm, lateral sep. oblique, dorsally strongly carinate, pet. shorter and wider than sep.; lip white tinged and spotted red-purple, to 17×15mm, broadly pandurate, 3-lobed, callus spotted brown, with several small tubercles on either side and a large terminal tubercle; column to 6mm, marked red-brown, wings reduced. Guatemala, Peru, Costa Rica, Panama, Colombia.

***O. carthagenense*** (Jacq.) Sw. Pseudobulbs absent or to 2.5cm, unifoliate, sheathed. Lvs to 50×7cm, broadly lanceolate to oblong-elliptic, acute or sub-acuminate, rigid and coriaceous, green spotted red-brown, keeled below toward base. Panicle to 2m, many-fld; fls to 2.5cm across, showy, pale yellow or white, variously blotched and spotted rose-purple; sep. to 1.5×1cm, clawed, rounded, undulate-crisped; pet. clawed, oblong to elliptic-oblong, obtuse, undulate-crisped; lip to 16×14mm, pandurate, 3-lobed, callus prominent, fleshy, erect, tuberculate; column to 4mm, fleshy, with large, bilobulate, lateral wings. Florida and W Indies, Mexico to Venezuela and Brazil.

***O. cavendishianum*** Batem. Pseudobulbs to 2cm or absent, unifoliate. Lvs to 45×13cm, elliptic-oblong or broadly lanceolate, acute to subobtuse, usually yellow-green, flushed blood red in strong sunlight, thickly coriaceous, keeled below. Panicle to 2m on a stout erect scape, usually branched, many-fld; fls to 4cm diam., showy, fragrant, waxy; sep. and pet. yellow or green-yellow variously spotted and blotched red or brown, sep. to 1.5×1cm, obovate or sub-orbicular, obtuse or rounded, concave, undulate, dorsal sep. cochleate forming hood over column, pet. similar to sep., smaller, shortly clawed; lip deep yellow, larger than sep., deeply 3-lobed, undulate, callus white flecked red-brown, tubercled; column to 1cm, wings yellow spotted red, deflexed, falcate. Mexico, Honduras, Guatemala.

***O. cebolleta*** (Jacq.) Sw. Pseudobulbs to 1.5×1.5cm, conical to subspherical, concealed by large white sheaths, unifoliate. Lvs to 40×2.5cm, subcylindric to terete, sulcate, erect or suberect, dull grey-green sometimes spotted purple, tapering to sharp apex. Raceme or panicle simple or short-branched, to 150cm, many-fld; peduncle green spotted dark purple; fls to 3.5cm diam.; sep. and pet. green-yellow marked deep red-brown, sep. to 1.5×1cm, obovate, obtuse, spreading-reflexed, undulate, pet. slightly smaller than sep., oblong, rounded to subacute, undulate; lip bright yellow spotted red-brown, to 2×2.5cm, deeply 3-lobed, lateral lobes large, obovate, entire to crenulate, midlobe reniform-flabellate, emarginate, callus spotted red-brown, a sharp projecting keel with several tubercles on either side; column to 5mm, wings small, spreading, subquadrate or bilobulate. Mexico and W Indies to Paraguay.

***O. cheirophorum*** Rchb. f. COLOMBIA BUTTERCUP. Dwarf epiphyte. Pseudobulbs to 2.5×1.5cm, ovoid to suborbicular, tightly clustered, unifoliate. Lvs to 15×1.5cm, oblanceolate to linear-ligulate, subacute, thin. Panicle to 20cm, slender, densely many-fld; fls to 1.5cm diam., fragrant, bright yellow; dorsal sep. erect, short-clawed, to 5×3mm, deeply concave, obovate, minutely apiculate, lateral sep. to 6×3mm, obovate, recurved; pet. smaller than sep., short-clawed, rotund; lip larger than sep., lateral lobes erect, spreading, subquadrate to suborbicular, lower margin recurved, midlobe sessile, oblong to rotund, emarginate, margins upcurved, callus white, fleshy, with 3–5 apical teeth; column short, erect, wings obovate, porrect. Colombia, Panama, Costa Rica.

***O. chrysomorphum*** Lindl. Pseudobulbs to 5cm, ovoid, compressed, clustered, bifoliate or trifoliate. Lvs to 23cm, linear, subacute, slightly coriaceous. Panicle to 55cm, erect, branched from middle, densely fld, branches short, distichous, alternate, recurved; fls to 2cm across; sep. and pet. similar, golden yellow, to 10×2mm, oblong-lanceolate or spathulate, obtuse to acute or apiculate, reflexed, undulate; lip pale yellow, to 10×7mm, pandurate, 3-lobed, lateral lobes rounded, midlobe transversely elliptic to elliptic-reniform, clawed, obscurely 2-lobed, callus oblong, with 2 dorsal teeth and 2 teeth on each side; column wings obsolete. Colombia, Venezuela.

***O. cimiciferum*** (Rchb. f.) Lindl. Pseudobulbs to 10×4cm, oblong-cylindrical, compressed, deeply grooved, unifoliate or bifoliate. Lvs to 65×5cm, linear-oblong to narrowly lanceolate, acute or acuminate. Panicle to 3m with many short branches; fls small, brown or green-yellow banded brown, reflexed, undulate; dorsal sep. to 12×4mm, spathulate to elliptic-lanceolate, acute, lateral sep. longer, obliquely oblong-oblanceolate, acute; pet. to 1×6mm, elliptic-obovate, acute; lip to 8×8mm, simple, ovate-triangular, subtruncate, convex, callus bright yellow, multilobulate; column to 4mm, wings obscure, broad, anth. brown, pollinia elongate, yellow. Venezuela, Colombia, Ecuador, Peru.

***O. citrinum*** Lindl. Resembles *O. altissimum* vegetatively. Infl. simple or slightly branched, to 40cm, slender, several-fld; fls to 3.5cm diam.; sep. and pet. pale yellow or green-yellow faintly marked brown, to 12×3.5mm, spreading, ovate-oblong or ligulate, acute; lip clear yellow spotted and marked pale red-brown on callus, to 12×9mm, rounded-pandurate, 3-lobed, lateral lobes short, midlobe deeply emarginate, callus prominent, complex, bluntly dentate with short glandular hairs on central portion; column yellow blotched maroon, anth. pale yellow, unicellular. Trinidad, Venezuela, Colombia.

***O. concolor*** Hook. Pseudobulbs to 5×2.5cm, ovate-oblong, clustered, furrowed, usually bifoliate. Lvs to 15×2.5cm, ligulate-lanceolate, acute, subcoriaceous. Raceme to 30cm, pendent, loosely few- to many-fld; fls to 4cm diam., bright golden-yellow; sep. narrowly obovate-oblong, acute, to 2×1cm, concave, lateral sep. connate for half of length, longer and narrower than dorsal sep.; pet. elliptic-oblong, to 2×1cm, minutely apiculate, slightly undulate; lip to 3.5×3cm, prominently clawed, slightly convex, cuneate-orbicular, emarginate, callus bilamellate; column wings linear, tooth-like, spreading. Brazil.

***O. cornigerum*** Lindl. Pseudobulbs to 10cm, subcylindrical, sulcate, compressed, unifoliate. Lvs to 15cm, fleshy, broadly ovate or elliptic-oblong, subacute, dark green. Panicle to 30cm; fls to 2cm diam., crowded in upper reaches of infl.; sep. and pet. bright yellow spotted and banded red-brown, dorsal sep. curved over column, concave, ovate, lateral sep. connate to middle or more, ovate-oblong, pet. clawed, obovate, obtuse, incurved; lip bright yellow, pandurate, lateral lobes narrow, horn-like, curved upwards and inwards, midlobe oblong-orbicular, crisped, callus corniculate, tubercled; column wings spreading, linear-triangular. Brazil.

***O. crispum*** Lodd. Pseudobulbs to 10×5cm, oblong or ovoid, clustered, compressed, wrinkled with age, dark brown, bifoliate or trifoliate. Lvs to 20×5cm, oblong-lanceolate, acute, subcoriaceous. Panicle to 110cm, erect to pendent, strongly branched, many-fld; peduncle glaucescent, often mottled dull crimson; fls to 10cm across, showy, all seg. strongly crisped-undulate; sep. and pet. chestnut-brown or copper-brown sometimes spotted yellow, sep. clawed, obovate-oblong, to 2.5×1.5cm, acute, lateral sep. connate towards base, pet. slightly wider than sep., short-clawed, ovate, rounded at apex; lip chestnut-brown or copper-red with yellow base and callus, short-clawed, deflexed, to 3×3cm, obscurely 3-lobed. Brazil.

***O. crista-galli*** Rchb. f. Diminutive epiphyte. Pseudobulbs to 1.5×1cm, ovoid, clustered, concealed by several leaflike bracts, terminated by an abortive lf, 1.5×1cm; leaflike bracts to 8×1cm, flat, thin, linear-ligulate to narrowly elliptic, acute. Infl. 1–4, slender, equalling lvs, filiform, 1- to few-fld; fls to 2cm diam.; sep. yellow-green, spreading, dorsal sep. to 6×4mm, elliptic-ovate or elliptic-lanceolate, slightly concave, acute or apiculate, keeled below, lateral sep. narrower than dorsal sep., obliquely elliptic-lanceolate, acute; pet. to 10×5mm, obliquely ovate-oblong, bright yellow barred red-brown; lip bright yellow marked red-brown on disc, complexly 3-lobed, lateral lobes spreading, obovate-spathulate, short-clawed, crispate, midlobe large, short-clawed, 4-lobed, apical lobules projecting, ovate to oblong, lateral lobules rounded, callus large, flat, lobulate with 1 or more papillae on each side; column to 4mm, wings fleshy, rounded to obliquely ovate. Mexico to Colombia, Peru, Ecuador.

***O. cryptocopis*** Rchb. f. Pseudobulbs to 12cm, narrowly ovoid-conic, bifoliate. Lvs to 50×3cm, ligulate or linear-oblong, acute. Panicle to 2m, cascading, branches remote, short, few-fld; fls to 7.5cm across; sep. and pet. chestnut-brown edged golden-yellow, clawed, dorsal sep. to 2×2.5cm, short-clawed, broadly ovate, acute, apex recurved, margins undulate, lateral sep. long-clawed, exceeding dorsal sep., obliquely elliptic-ovate, acute or acuminate, apex recurved, pet. narrower than dorsal sep., ovate-lanceolate, obtuse, undulate-crisped, recurved, short-clawed; lip smaller than pet., chestnut-brown, pandurate-trilobed, lateral lobes small, triangular, reflexed, midlobe yellow, long-clawed, transversely oblong, retuse, central keel callused, papillose; column to 1cm, with 2 parallel, decurved horns in front, wings spreading, margins ciliate. Peru.

***O. cucullatum*** Lindl. Pseudobulbs to 5cm, ovoid to oblong, unifoliate or bifoliate. Lvs to 20×3.5cm, linear-ligulate or narrow-lanceolate, acute, dark green. Raceme or panicle slender, to 50cm, few- to many-fld; fls to 3.5cm diam.; sep. dark chestnut-brown or olive-green sometimes with yellow margin, to 12×6cm, ovate-oblong, concave, lateral sep. connate, bifid at apex; pet. similar to dorsal sep.; lip white to rose-purple spotted purple-crimson, to 2.5×3.5cm, basally 3-lobed, callus bright orange-yellow, with 5 tubercles; column short, stout, hooded. Colombia, Ecuador.

***O. dasystyle*** Rchb. f. Pseudobulbs to 5cm, oval, clustered, compressed, furrowed with age, unifoliate or usually bifoliate. Lvs to 15×2.5cm, narrowly lanceolate, subacute, bright green, keeled. Raceme or panicle to 40cm, sparsely branched, several-fld; peduncle slender; fls to 4cm diam.; sep. and pet. subequal, pale yellow blotched purple-brown, to 1.5cm, ovate-lanceolate, lateral sep. connate to middle; lip pale yellow, short-clawed, undulate, midlobe broadly reniform, large, callus dark purple, cordate, 2-lobed; column wings quadrate-orbicular, anth. beaked. Brazil.

***O. deltoideum*** Lindl. Pseudobulbs to 7.5cm, ovoid, compressed, bifoliate or trifoliate. Lvs to 25×3cm, linear or oblong-lanceolate, acute, subcoriaceous. Panicle to 80cm, branches spreading, loosely many-fld; fls to 2.5cm diam., pale golden-yellow, sometimes spotted red; sep. to 12×6mm, spathulate to oblong-oblanceolate, acute or obtuse, clawed, apex recurved; pet. shorter and wider than sep., ovate-spathulate, subacute to rounded, apex recurved, undulate; lip shorter and wider than sep., simple, cordate-reniform, subacute or apiculate, callus pale yellow surrounded by red band, toothed and verrucose; column to 6mm, wings broadly semi-ovate, entire to minutely dentate. Peru.

***O. divaricatum*** Lindl. Pseudobulbs to 4cm, subspherical, strongly compressed, yellow-green, unifoliate. Lvs to 30×8cm, oblong, coriaceous, obtuse. Panicle to 2m, much-branched, many-fld; peduncle dull purple; fls to 2.5cm; sep. and pet. yellow blotched chestnut-brown, sep. to 12×6mm, spathulate, pet. larger than sep., short-clawed, oblong, obtuse; lip yellow spotted chestnut-brown, to 1.5×1.5cm, lateral lobes large, rotund, midlobe small, transversely oblong, emarginate, undulate, callus 4-lobed, cushion-like; column glabrous, wings rounded. Brazil.

***O. ensatum*** Lindl. Pseudobulbs to 10×5cm, ovoid or ellipsoid, pale blue-green, slightly compressed, bifoliate. Lvs to 100×3cm, yellow-green, linear-lanceolate, long-acuminate, subcoriaceous, carinate below. Panicle to 2m, many-fld; fls to 3cm diam.; sep. and pet. clear yellow or yellow marked olive-brown, spreading-reflexed, undulate, short-clawed, sep. to 15×5mm, oblanceolate, acute; lip bright yellow, broadly pandurate, to 18×13mm, lateral lobes small, obtuse or auriculate, margins recurved, midlobe separated from lateral lobes by broad claw, transversely subreniform to suborbicular-cordate, emarginate, callus white, prominent, fleshy; column short, wings broad, crenulate. British Honduras to Panama.

***O. excavatum*** Lindl. Pseudobulbs to 18cm, ovoid-oblong, slightly compressed, clustered, lustrous green, unifoliate or bifoliate. Lvs to 50×4cm, linear to linear-ligulate, long-attenuate. Panicle to 1.5m, stout, many-fld; fls to 3.5cm diam.; sep. and pet. golden yellow, spotted and barred red-brown basally, strongly undulate, dorsal sep. to 1.5×1cm, obovate-oblong or oblanceolate, acute, lateral sep. narrower, oblong-oblanceolate, acute, pet. larger than sep., obovate-oblong, apex retuse; lip to 2×2cm, lateral lobes small, rounded, red-brown, midlobe short-clawed, transversely oblong, emarginate, yellow, red towards base, callus consisting of 5 lines of tubercles with a decurrent plate on either side; column to 5mm, wings oblong, porrect, slightly notched. Ecuador, Peru.

***O. falcipetalum*** Lindl. Pseudobulbs to 15×5cm, oval or ovoid-oblong, unifoliate or bifoliate. Lvs to 60×5.5cm, oblanceolate to lanceolate-ligulate. Panicle to 6m, short-branched, flexuous; fls to 7cm diam.; sep. russet-brown edged yellow, to 3×2.5cm, clawed, strongly undulate, dorsal sep. rounded, lateral sep. ovate, subacute; pet. yellow blotched chestnut-brown, smaller than sep., ovate-lanceolate, acute, strongly undulate; lip green-brown or purple-brown with yellow base and shiny brown sides, to 12×5mm, linear, lateral lobes triangular, reflexed, midlobe lanceolate to oblong-obovate, acute, callus bright yellow, fleshy, tubercled and ridged; column yellow-brown, spotted yellow-brown near base, to 1cm, wings small, horn-like. Venezuela, Colombia, Ecuador, Peru.

***O. flexuosum*** Sims. Pseudobulbs to 9×3cm, often remote, ovoid-oblong, strongly compressed, often yellow-green, bifoliate or rarely unifoliate. Lvs to 22×3cm, oblong-ligulate or linear-lanceolate, acute, subcoriaceous, bright green. Panicle to 1m, usually many-fld; fls to 2cm diam.; sep. and pet. bright yellow blotched and barred red-brown, dorsal sep. to 4×2mm, obovate-oblong, obtuse, concave, lateral sep. similar, base connate, apex bifid, pet. similar to dorsal sep., slightly larger; lip bright yellow marked red-brown on callus, to 13×15mm, clawed, lateral lobes auriculate, midlobe broadly reniform, emarginate, callus cushion-like, with 3 denticulate lobes in front; column wings subquadrate, curved forward. Brazil, Argentina, Paraguay, Uruguay.

***O.forbesii*** Hook. Resembles *O.crispum* except infl. simple, sep. and pet. rich chestnut-brown with yellow-marbled margins, column wings entire, spotted red. Brazil.

***O.gardneri*** Lindl. Resembles *O.crispum* except sep. and pet. brown striped yellow marginally, oblanceolate, lip with very small lateral lobes, midlobe yellow spotted red-brown marginally, brown at base, column wings entire. Brazil.

***O.globuliferum*** HBK. Rhiz. to 5m, slender, flexuous. Pseudobulbs remote, to 2.5×2cm, suborbicular to elliptic, unifoliate. Lvs to 6×2cm, elliptic-oblong, coriaceous. Infl. to 9cm, 1-fld; fls to 3.5cm; sep. and pet. basally spotted red or red-brown, dorsal sep. to 16×7mm, elliptic-oblong, acute, undulate, lateral sep. similar, obliquely lanceolate to oblong, short-clawed, pet. wider than sep., short-clawed, elliptic-oblong, subacute, undulate; lip to 3×4cm, bright yellow marked red-brown on claw and callus, lateral lobes small, midlobe large, spreading, deeply bilobed, undulate, callus small, triangular, tubercled; column wings spreading, green-yellow. Colombia, Venezuela, Costa Rica, Panama.

***O.haematochilum*** Lindl. Vegetatively similar to *O.lanceanum*. Panicle to 60cm, many-fld; fls to 5cm diam., long-lived, fragrant; sep. and pet. yellow-green blotched rich cinnamon, clawed, to 2.5cm, dorsal sep. suborbicular, lateral sep. free, oblong, pet. obovate-oblong, undulate; lip bright crimson, margin yellow spotted red, broadly clawed, base biauriculate, lamina transversely oblong, emarginate, callus bright crimson, 5-parted, verrucose, central portion a raised subtriangular plate; column wings rose-purple, reniform, recurved. Colombia, Trinidad.

***O.harrisonianum*** Lindl. Pseudobulbs to 2.5×2cm, subspherical, compressed, unifoliate. Lvs to 15×3cm, rigid, fleshy, linear-oblong, acute, recurved, grey-green. Panicle to 30cm, many-fld; fls to 1.5cm diam.; sep. and pet. golden-yellow blotched red or red-brown, dorsal sep. obovate, subacute, to 10×5mm, concave, recurved, lateral sep. spathulate, slightly wider than dorsal sep., pet. similar to lateral sep., smaller; lip golden-yellow, larger than sep., spreading-deflexed, 3-lobed, lateral lobes small, faintly striped chocolate-brown, subquadrate, midlobe clawed, transversely oblong or reniform, emarginate, callus 5-lobed; column short, fleshy, wings falcate. Brazil.

***O.hastatum*** (Batem.) Lindl. Pseudobulbs to 11×6cm, ovoid-conical, compressed, bifoliate. Lvs to 43×3cm, linear to lanceolate, acute or acuminate. Panicle to 1.5m, loosely branched, branches suberect, 6- or more fld; fls to 4cm diam.; sep. and pet. yellow-green or yellow, heavily spotted and barred deep maroon, sep. to 24×7mm, narrowly lanceolate, acuminate, undulate, pet. shorter than sep., lanceolate, acuminate; lip to 2×1.5cm, lateral lobes white, rotund-subquadrate or oblong, midlobe tinged and blotched rose-purple, short-clawed, ovate-elliptic, acuminate, callus white lined rose-purple, 4-lobed, lateral lobes short; column wings incurved, subquadrate-rounded. Mexico.

***O.hastilabium*** (Lindl.) Garay & Dunsterv. Pseudobulbs to 6×4cm, ovoid, compressed, unifoliate or bifoliate. Lvs to 35×4cm, oblong-lanceolate, obtuse or mucronate, pale green. Panicle to 80cm, many-fld; fls to 7.5cm diam., opening in succession, fragrant, long-lived; sep. and pet. pale cream-yellow or pale green, banded chocolate-brown, sep. to 4×1cm, linear-lanceolate, long-acuminate, keeled below, pet. smaller than sep.; lip white with rose-purple base, to 3.5×2cm, triangular, lateral lobes small, porrect, falcate, midlobe narrowly clawed, cordate or suborbicular, acute or apiculate, callus 3-keeled, median keel trilobulate at front; column lavender, bright yellow at base, narrowly winged. Venezuela, Colombia, Peru.

***O.heteranthum*** Poepp. & Endl. Pseudobulbs to 5×3cm, ovoid or ellipsoid, slightly compressed, clustered, light green, bifoliate, rarely unifoliate. Lvs to 20×3.5cm, narrowly linear to elliptic-lanceolate, acute or acuminate, subcoriaceous, keeled below. Panicle to 1m, erect to pendent, branches short, with 1–3 fertile fls toward apex, lower fls abortive; sterile fls broadly spreading, seg. linear to oblanceolate, lip usually entirely aborted; fertile fls to 1cm diam.; sep. and pet. pale yellow-green marked red-brown, sep. to 10×3mm, free, elliptic-lanceolate to ligulate, obtuse to subacute, often undulate, pet. wider than sep., obovate-oblong, obtuse to subacute; lip bright yellow slightly marked red-brown, to 1.5×1.5cm, broadly pandurate, lateral lobes broadly triangular, margins recurved, midlobe sessile to shortly clawed, transversely reniform, deeply bilobed, callus white marked brown, toothed and crested; column to 4mm, erect, wings transversely oblong, often recurved. Costa Rica, Panama, Venezuela, Colombia, Ecuador, Peru, Bolivia.

***O.hians*** Lindl. Pseudobulbs to 1.5cm, ovoid-subrotund, compressed, unifoliate. Lvs to 7×1cm, ovate to linear-oblong, acute to subobtuse, coriaceous. Infl. simple or slightly branched, to 25cm, very slender, few-fld; fls to 1cm diam., wide-spreading, ochre; sep. to 5×3mm, obovate, rounded; pet. broadly oblong, smaller than sep.; lip larger than sep., yellow with some red-brown spots, obovate-subquadrate, sessile, retuse, callus white, large, with 4 red-spotted, fleshy, finger-like lobes; column to 2mm, white, broadly winged. Brazil.

***O.hookeri*** Rolfe. Pseudobulbs to 6×1.5cm, narrowly conical, clustered, ridged, bifoliate. Lvs to 20×1.5cm, linear-ligulate or oblanceolate, apex rounded. Panicle to 45cm, many-fld; fls to 1cm diam.; sep. and pet. yellow flushed orange-brown, to 5×1mm, oblong, acute, reflexed; lip yellow marked orange or pale chestnut at base, to 6×5mm, lateral lobes linear-oblong, spreading, midlobe clawed, broadly obovate-cuneate, callus with 5 flattened lobes; column to 2mm, wingless. Brazil.

***O.hyphaematicum*** Rchb. f. Pseudobulbs to 10cm, oblong, clustered, compressed, unifoliate. Lvs to 30cm, oblong-lanceolate or ligulate, subacute, subcoriaceous. Panicle much-branched, to 1.5m, loosely many-fld; fls to 3.5cm diam., stained red below; sep. and pet. red-brown blotched deep red-brown, tipped yellow, ovate-lanceolate to oblong-lanceolate, acute, strongly undulate; lip canary-yellow, pale yellow below flushed and spotted crimson, broadly clawed, reniform, lateral lobes subreniform, midlobe reniform, emarginate, callus 5-keeled; column pale yellow, wings hatchet-shaped. Ecuador.

***O.incurvum*** Barker ex Lindl. Pseudobulbs to 10×3cm, ovoid, ribbed, compressed, bifoliate or trifoliate. Lvs to 40×2cm, linear-ligulate, acute, dark green. Panicle to 2m, branches numerous, distichous, many-fld, arcuate; fls to 2.5cm diam., fragrant; sep. and pet. white streaked and blotched lilac and rose-pink, undulate, dorsal sep. to 12×3mm, linear-oblanceolate, acute, lateral sep. longer than dorsal sep., curved, pet. to 14×3mm, linear-lanceolate, subacute; lip rose-pink blotched white, to 1.5×1cm, pandurate, lateral lobes small, suborbicular to oblong, midlobe clawed, suborbicular, apiculate, callus yellow marked brown, 5-toothed; column to 7mm, white, bidentate, wings tinged pink. Mexico.

***O.insculptum*** (Rchb. f.) Rchb. f. Pseudobulbs to 12.5×5cm, ovoid, compressed, clustered, bifoliate. Lvs to 45cm, ensiform to narrowly linear, acute to acuminate. Panicle loosely branched in upper half, pale green-brown, flexuous, branches short, few-fld; fls to 3.5cm diam., polished, dark cinnamon; sep. and pet. edged yellow-white, clawed, crisped-undulate, to 1.5cm, dorsal sep. suborbicular, lateral sep. ovate-oblong, pet. broadly ovate; lip narrowly oblong, reflexed, concave, lateral lobes small, apex blue-grey, callus triangular, prominent, dentate towards front; column narrowly winged. Ecuador.

***O.isthmii*** Schltr. Pseudobulbs to 12×4cm, narrowly ovoid to linear-oblong, compressed, longitudinally ridged, usually bifoliate. Lvs to 45×3cm, linear-lanceolate, acute, suberect, subcoriaceous. Panicle to 1m, many-fld; fls to 2.5cm diam., yellow marked copper-brown; sep. free, clawed, dorsal sep. to 12×5mm, oblanceolate, undulate, shorter than lateral sep., obliquely oblong, acute, undulate; pet. to 12×5mm, oblong-oblanceolate, subacute, undulate; lip spreading-deflexed, pandurate, lateral lobes auriculate, suborbicular, midlobe narrowly clawed, transversely reniform, emarginate, callus fleshy, brown, 7-lobed; column to 4mm, wings prominent. Costa Rica, Panama.

***O.jonesianum*** Rchb. f. Pseudobulbs to 1×1cm, ovoid, unifoliate. Lvs to 40×1.5cm, terete, pendent, grooved, fleshy. Raceme to 50cm, usually pendent, to 15-fld; fls to 7.5cm diam., showy, long-lived; sep. and pet. yellow-white spotted chestnut-brown, ovate-oblong, to 2.5×1cm, rounded, spreading, undulate; lip to 2×1cm, clawed, lateral lobes yellow-orange, auriculate, spreading, midlobe white spotted crimson, transversely oblong, emarginate, undulate, callus fleshy, lobed and tubercled; column white spotted red, to 7mm, wings oblong. Brazil, Paraguay, Uruguay.

***O.kienastianum*** Rchb. f. Pseudobulbs to 8cm, oblong-ovoid, bifoliate. Lvs to 50×2.5cm or more, oblong-oblanceolate, acute or acuminate. Panicle long-scandent, short-branched above, few-fld; fls large; sep. and pet. rich chocolate-brown edged pale yellow, undulate, dorsal sep. to 1.5×1cm, short-clawed, ovate-triangular, acute, lateral sep. exceeds dorsal sep., long-clawed, oblong-cuneate, acute, pet. similar to dorsal sep., apex reflexed; lip to 15×12mm, lateral lobes yellow spotted brown, small, midlobe brown, ovate-triangular, undulate to crisped, recurved above, callus yellow, 3-keeled, lateral keels with 3 lamellae on each side; column wings minute, curved. Peru, Colombia.

***O.lanceanum*** Lindl. Pseudobulbs reduced or absent. Lvs to 50×10cm, elliptic-oblong to lanceolate-oblong, acute, thickly coriaceous, dark green spotted maroon. Panicle to 30cm, few- to many-fld; fls to 6cm diam., fragrant, long-lived, waxy; sep. and pet. yellow or green-yellow, heavily spotted purple-brown or chocolate-brown, sep. to 3.5×2cm, short-clawed, elliptic-oblong, obtuse, undulate, shorter than lateral sep., pet. slightly narrower than sep., obovate-spathulate, obtuse; lip pale purple, base deep rose-purple, larger than sep., lateral lobes small, basal, triangular-oblong, midlobe broadly clawed, spathulate, callus deep rose-purple, 3-lobed; column to 7mm, pale yellow-green below, dark purple above. Colombia, Venezuela, Brazil, Trinidad, Guianas.

***O.leopoldianum*** (Kränzl.) Rolfe. Rhiz. long-creeping. Pseudobulbs to 2.5cm, ovoid-oblong to ovoid-cylindrical, unifoliate or bifoliate. Lvs to 16×2cm, oblanceolate, acute. Panicle to 2.5m, scandent, many-branched; fls to 4cm diam., spreading; sep. and pet. white with purple central portion, sep. short-clawed, to 2.5×1cm, broadly elliptic, obtuse, pet. smaller than sep., subsessile, elliptic-ovate, subacute; lip purple-violet, smaller than pet., deltoid, slightly 3-lobed, callus yellow; column yellow. Peru.

***O.leucochilum*** Batem. ex Lindl. Pseudobulbs to 13×6cm, ovoid, compressed, furrowed with age, unifoliate or bifoliate. Lvs to 60×4.5cm, dull green, ligulate, acute or obtuse, coriaceous. Panicle to 3m, strongly branched, many-fld; fls to 3.5cm diam.; sep. and pet. bright green to white-green blotched and barred deep red-brown or green-brown, to 2.5×1cm, elliptic-oblong to oblanceolate, acute to obtuse, slightly undulate; lip white tinged pink or yellow, to 2.5×2.5cm, pandurate, lateral lobes small, ovate to oblong, obtuse, margins reflexed, midlobe narrowly clawed, transversely oblong or reniform, emarginate, margins undulate, callus tinged purple, oblong, terminating in 5–9 slender teeth, 3 apical teeth recurved; column to 8mm, fleshy, wings rose-pink to rose-magenta. Mexico, Honduras, Guatemala.

***O. lietzii*** Reg. Pseudobulbs conical or subfusiform, to 12×2cm, lustrous green, unifoliate or bifoliate. Lvs to 20×5cm, ligulate or elliptic-oblong, acute, recurved. Raceme or panicle to 70cm, arching; peduncle purple spotted white; fls to 3.5cm diam.; sep. and pet. yellow or green-yellow barred bright red-brown, dorsal sep. to 15×8mm, spathulate, obtuse, concave, lateral sep. connate to near apex, shorter than dorsal sep., emarginate, pet. to 16×9mm, spathulate, obtuse, incurved; lip to 1×1cm, slightly convex, lateral lobes incurved, narrowly oblong, yellow with few chocolate-brown spots, margins recurved, midlobe chocolate-brown, callus pale orange-brown, large, verrucose-tuberculate; column to 5mm, pubesc. Brazil.

***O. longicornu*** Mutel. Pseudobulbs to 7×2cm, oblong-conical, clustered, slightly compressed, unifoliate or bifoliate. Lvs to 20×3cm, oblong to oblong-lanceolate, acute. Panicle to 45cm, branches elongate, slender, 2-ranked; fls to 2cm across; sep. pale green or red-brown, dorsal sep. to 6×3mm, elliptic-oblong, acute, concave, lateral sep. to 6×2mm, connate to middle, oblong; pet. red-brown, tipped yellow, subequal to sep., oblong, reflexed, undulate; lip to 11×8mm, apical half yellow, basal half red, lateral lobes oblong, margins recurved, midlobe flabellate, emarginate, callus red, a long, incurved horn; column yellow-green, to 5mm, subclavate, slightly incurved, wings absent. Brazil.

***O. longipes*** Lindl. & Paxt. Pseudobulbs to 2.5cm, ovoid-pyriform, clear green, 2–4-foliate, remotely or erratically spaced along a slender creeping rhiz. Lvs to 15×2cm, linear-lanceolate or oblong, soft, pale green, basally conduplicate. Raceme to 15cm, erect, loosely 2–6-fld; fls to 3.5cm diam., usually smaller, long-lived; sep. and pet. yellow-brown or pale red-brown spotted and streaked yellow, yellow-tipped, sep. to 16×4mm, oblong to spathulate, acute, undulate, apex reflexed, lateral sep. connate at base, pet. similar to sep., shorter and broader, obtuse; lip rich deep yellow, lateral lobes oblong-rounded with pale red-brown claw, margins undulate, midlobe reniform or transversely oblong, emarginate, callus white-spotted with 2 very prominent teeth in front; column wings narrow, inconspicuous. Brazil.

***O. loxense*** Lindl. Pseudobulbs to 12.5×4cm, ovoid to pyriform, slightly compressed, furrowed, unifoliate. Lvs to 40×5cm, narrowly lanceolate or ligulate, acute or acuminate. Panicle to 1.8m, vine-like, several-fld; fls to 7.5cm diam., borne at irregular intervals, fleshy; sep. cinnamon-brown barred bright or pale yellow, to 2.5×1cm, clawed, ovate-oblong, subacute, undulate; pet. wider than sep., obtuse; lip to 2×2.5cm, bright orange, pale yellow-orange on disc, lateral lobes reduced to minute auricles, midlobe spathulate, callus crimson-spotted, consisting of 4 shallow plates behind and a central, fringed plate with many bristles on each side; column wings obscure. Ecuador, Peru.

***O. lucasianum*** Rolfe. Pseudobulbs to 5cm, ovoid, slightly compressed, bifoliate. Lvs to 20cm, linear-lanceolate, acute. Panicle to 1m, arcuate, few- to many-fld; fls to 3cm diam., golden-yellow; dorsal sep. to 17×8mm, obovate-oblong, undulate, lateral sep. similar to dorsal sep., free or connate in basal half; pet. wider than sep., short-clawed, broadly oblong; lip pandurate-trilobed, to 2×2cm, lateral lobes small, midlobe suborbicular-reniform, cordate, bilobulate, callus 5-lamellate, verrucose; column short, wings semi-ovate, erose. Peru.

***O. luridum*** Lindl. Pseudobulbs to 1.5cm. Lvs solitary, borne from stout rhiz., to 85×15cm, oval to elliptic-oblong, acute to obtuse, coriaceous, light green spotted pale purple-brown. Panicle to 1.5m, short-branched; fls to 4cm diam.; sep. and pet. usually yellow-brown or red-brown variously marked and spotted yellow, sep. to 2×1cm, clawed, spathulate to obovate or suborbicular, strongly undulate, pet. shorter than sep. and somewhat oblong, otherwise similar; lip equals pet., broadly pandurate, lateral lobes small, revolute, midlobe rounded, short-clawed, entire or crenulate, emarginate, callus white or yellow spotted purple, composed of 5 fleshy, tuberculate lobules; column to 5mm, white, wings pale pink. Florida, W Indies and Mexico and Guyana and Peru.

***O. macranthum*** Lindl. Pseudobulbs to 15cm, ovoid to oblong-conical, bifoliate. Lvs to 55×5cm, oblong to linear-oblanceolate, acute. Panicle to 3m, short-branched, lax or twining, each branch 2–5-fld; fls to 10cm diam., long-lived, showy; sep. dull yellow-brown, to 4.5×3cm, clawed, strongly undulate, oblong-suborbicular; pet. golden-yellow, to 3.5×3cm, suborbicular-ovate, short-clawed, strongly undulate-crisped; lip smaller than sep. and pet., obscurely 3-lobed, white bordered with violet-purple, triangular, callus white, 6-toothed; column to 1cm, wings brown-purple, flabellate, bilobed or retuse. Ecuador, Peru, Colombia.

***O. maculatum*** Lindl. Pseudobulbs to 10×4cm, ovoid, clustered, strongly compressed, bifoliate. Lvs to 25×5cm, linear-ligulate to oblong-elliptic, coriaceous. Raceme or panicle to 1m, erect, many-fld; fls to 5cm diam., fragrant; sep. and pet. similar, bronze to yellow blotched dark chestnut-brown, to 3×1cm, oblong-elliptic to elliptic-lanceolate, obtuse to acuminate, apex often reflexed, spreading; lip to 3×2cm, white marked red-brown, obscurely 3-lobed, midlobe ovate-oblong, truncate, apiculate, undulate, callus 4-keeled, slightly puberulent. Mexico, Guatemala, Honduras.

***O. marshallianum*** Rchb. f. Pseudobulbs to 15×4cm, ovoid-oblong, clustered, slightly compressed, furrowed with age, bright green, bifoliate. Lvs to 30×4cm, bright green, ligulate-lanceolate, acute, subcoriaceous. Panicle to 1.8m, many-fld; fls to 5.5cm diam., variable; sep. to 2×1cm, dull yellow, barred pale red-brown, obovate-oblong, rounded, concave, lateral sep. longer and narrower than dorsal sep., connate in basal third, almost concealed by lip; pet. to 2.5×2cm, canary-yellow spotted pale red-brown towards centre or base, broadly obovate-oblong, emarginate, undulate; lip to 4×4cm, clawed, lateral lobes bright yellow spotted red, small, midlobe large, broadly subreniform, emarginate, bright yellow, claw and callus spotted red-orange; column to 7mm, wings oblong-subquadrate, entire. Brazil.

***O. meirax*** Rchb. f. Pseudobulbs to 2.5×1.5cm, ovoid to ovoid-oblong, compressed, unifoliate. Lvs to 7.5×1.5cm, lanceolate or oblong-lanceolate to linear-lanceolate, acute or obtuse, base attenuate and conduplicate. Raceme or panicle to 25cm; peduncle compressed at apex, basal portion triquetrous; sep. and pet. yellow unevenly flushed maroon, linear or linear-oblanceolate to oblanceolate-spathulate, dorsal sep. to 9×3mm, lateral sep. to 11×3mm, free, oblique; lip yellow tipped maroon, simple, to 9×7mm, ovate to ovate-triangular, acute, base cordate, callus a raised plate, tubercled; column to 5mm, wings absent. Colombia, Venezuela, Ecuador, Peru.

***O. microchilum*** Batem. & Lindl. Pseudobulbs to 3.5×3cm, ovoid or spherical, compressed, unifoliate. Lvs to 30×6.5cm, elliptic or elliptic-oblong, acute, coriaceous, olive, keeled below. Panicle to 1.5m, erect, much-branched, few- to many-fld; fls to 2.5cm diam., long-lived; sep. pale brown marked yellow, short-clawed, suborbicular to elliptic-oblong, to 1.5×1cm, concave, keeled below; pet. chestnut-brown or purple-brown barred and edged yellow, smaller than sep., oblanceolate, obtuse, undulate, incurved; lip smaller than pet., broadly triangular, lateral lobes white flecked maroon-purple, suborbicular, revolute, midlobe white with a purple spot, obscure, apiculate, sharply decurved, callus central, tubercled, yellow spotted purple above, purple below; column to 6mm, deep red, slightly pubesc., wings white, curved. Guatemala, Mexico.

***O. nanum*** Lindl. Pseudobulbs to 1.5×1cm, unifoliate. Lvs to 20×4cm, dull green with liver red spots, elliptic to elliptic-oblanceolate, acute. Panicle to 25cm, short-branched, few- to many-fld; fls to 1.5cm diam.; sep. and pet. ochre spotted rust, to 10×5mm, spathulate to obovate, obtuse, cucullate-concave; lip bright yellow, transversely oblong, larger than sep., lateral lobes marked red-brown, small, semi-orbicular, revolute, midlobe large, transversely oblong or reniform, emarginate, callus honey-brown, tuberculate, with 2 perpendicular ridges; column ochre flushed maroon, to 4mm. Venezuela, Peru, Brazil, Guianas.

***O. nigratum*** Lindl. & Paxt. Pseudobulbs to 12×6cm, ovoid to ovoid-oblong, strongly compressed and furrowed, pale brown or yellow-green, bifoliate. Lvs to 35×6cm, linear to narrow-lanceolate, coriaceous. Panicle to 1.8m, arcuate, lightly to much-branched, many-fld, branches to 60cm; sep. and pet. white or cream heavily banded and marked deep red-chocolate, undulate, sep. free, to 20×4mm, lanceolate, acute, lateral sep. oblique, pet. to 15×5mm, similar to sep.; lip yellow-brown or clear yellow, marked purple-brown, to 13×10mm, ovate, apex recurved, conspicuously to obscurely 3-lobed, callus yellow spotted red, erect, multituberculate, basal tubercles arranged in 2 transverse series; column to 5mm, curved, wings semi-rotund or triangular, white. Venezuela, Colombia, Guyana.

***O. nubigenum*** Lindl. Resembles *O. cucullatum* except smaller, fls smaller, lip white with violet spot in front of callus. Ecuador, Peru, Colombia.

***O. oblongatum*** Lindl. Pseudobulbs to 10×3.5cm, ovoid to ellipsoid, compressed, bifoliate. Lvs to 45×2.5cm, ligulate to linear-lanceolate, conduplicate, subcoriaceous. Panicle to 1.4m, erect, short-branched, many-fld; fls to 3cm diam., bright yellow spotted red-brown at base of seg.; sep. to 15×5mm, elliptic-oblanceolate, acute to subobtuse; pet. wider than sep., obliquely elliptic-oblanceolate, rounded, slightly undulate; lip to 2.5×1.5cm, pandurate, lateral lobes small, triangular, reflexed, midlobe with short, narrow claw, subreniform, deeply retuse, slightly undulate, callus fleshy, 4-lobed below, with 3 teeth at apex; column to 7mm, stout, wings auriculate, rounded. Mexico, Guatemala.

***O. obryzatum*** Rchb. f. Pseudobulbs to 10×4cm, ovoid, elliptic-oblong or suborbicular, compressed, ridged, glossy, unifoliate. Lvs to 45×4cm, linear-elliptic to linear-oblong, subacute. Panicle to 1m, many-fld; fls variable, to 3.5×2.5cm, yellow marked chocolate-brown; sep. to 15×5mm, obovate-spathulate, truncate or obtuse, clawed; pet. wider than sep.; lip larger than sep. and pet., pandurate, lateral lobes small, narrowly short-clawed, midlobe dilated, reniform, with a deep central sinus, callus white or yellow sparsely spotted chocolate-brown, surrounded by red-brown blotch, consisting of a number of toothed lobes; column to 4mm, wings prominent, porrect, erose. Colombia, Venezuela, Peru, Ecuador, Panama, Costa Rica.

***O. onustum*** Lindl. Pseudobulbs to 4cm, ovoid to oblong, compressed, unifoliate or bifoliate. Lvs to 12.5×2cm, linear-oblong or oblong, acute. Raceme or panicle to 40cm, often secund; fls to 2.5cm across, deep golden-yellow; sep. to 8×6mm, ovate to elliptic, cucullate, lateral sep. apiculate; pet. twice as large as sep., rotund, undulate; lip exceeds pet., rounded, deeply 3-lobed, lateral lobes small, spreading, midlobe round, callus 3-lobed, lateral lamellae cochleate, large; column to 2mm, wings crescent-shaped, obtuse. Panama, Colombia, Ecuador, Peru.

***O. ornithorhynchum*** HBK. Pseudobulbs to 6×3cm, ovoid to pyriform, smooth, semi-lucent pale grey-green, compressed, usually bifoliate. Lvs to 35×3cm, linear-lanceolate to ligulate, acute, pale or grey-green, soft. Panicle to 50cm, strongly arching, many-fld; fls to 2.5cm, fragrant, showy en masse; sep. and pet. white, pink or lilac, short-clawed, to 11×6mm, narrow-oblong to elliptic; lip darker than sep. and pet., pandurate, lateral lobes small, recurved, midlobe clawed, obovate, emarginate, upper margins recurved, callus golden-yellow or deep orange, consisting of 5 toothed lamellae with 2 horn-like tubercles in front; column to 5mm, wings broadly triangular, erose, anth. strongly beaked. Mexico, Guatemala, Costa Rica, El Salvador.

***O. panamense*** Schltr. Pseudobulbs to 16×6cm, ovoid-oblong, ridged, compressed, bifoliate. Lvs to 75×4cm, linear-lanceolate, acute, subcoriaceous; petioles elongate. Panicle to 3.5m, erect to pendent or scandent, many-fld; fls to 2.5cm diam.; sep. and pet. yellow blotched and barred olive to brown, slightly undulate, sep. short-clawed, to 13×5mm, elliptic-ovate, acute, pet. similar to sep., tips recurved; lip to 1.5×1.5cm, yellow blotched red-brown to yellow-brown below callus, obscurely 3-lobed, rounded, cleft, emarginate, callus white, erect, 4-keeled, tridentate at apex; column to 5mm, wings prominent, usually serrate. Panama.

***O. phalaenopsis*** Lind. & Rchb. f. Allied to *O. cucullatum*. Lvs narrow. Raceme to 25cm, slender, few-fld; fls to 3cm across; sep. and pet. white, barred and spotted dark purple; lip white tinted rose-purple, spotted purple around callus, midlobe reniform. Ecuador.

***O. phymatochilum*** Lindl. To 60cm. Pseudobulbs to 12.5×2.5cm, ovoid-oblong, often purple-brown, slightly compressed, unifoliate. Lvs to 35×7.5cm, elliptic to oblanceolate, acute to acuminate, coriaceous. Panicle to 60cm, pendent, loosely many-fld; fls to 5cm diam., showy; sep. to 35×3mm, pale yellow marked red-brown, sometimes white spotted red-orange, delicate, narrow, spreading-reflexed, undulate, keeled below; pet. shorter than sep. and broader; lip to 18×11mm, white spotted red-orange on callus, pandurate, lateral lobes auriculate, spreading-reflexed, undulate, midlobe clawed, ovate-cordate, apiculate, undulate, callus fleshy, triangular with a basal dentate flap on each side, 3-tubercled at apex; column to 5mm, slender, wings broad, dentate, white spotted red. Mexico, Guatemala, Brazil.

***O. pubes*** Lindl. Pseudobulbs to 7×1.5cm, subcylindrical, slightly compressed, clustered, unifoliate or bifoliate. Lvs to 12×3cm, lustrous dark green above, narrowly oblong-lanceolate, acute, subcoriaceous. Panicle to 60cm, branches alternately 2-ranked; fls to 2.5cm diam.; sep. and pet. usually chestnut to brick red banded and spotted yellow, dorsal sep. and pet. to 12×8mm, obovate or obovate-oblong, subtruncate, lateral sep. connate almost to apex, linear-ligulate, smaller than pet., recurved, subacute; lip red-brown edged yellow, slightly shorter than sep., lateral lobes small, linear, reflexed, midlobe large, suborbicular, emarginate, recurved, callus pubesc., tuberculate, dentate in front; column white, to 4mm, wings subfalcate, with villous hairs around stigma. Brazil, Paraguay.

***O. pulchellum*** Hook. Pseudobulbs absent. Lvs to 20×1.5cm, equitant, flattened laterally or triquetrous, linear-ligulate, keeled. Raceme or panicle to 50cm, erect or arcuate, many-fld; fls to 2.5cm diam., variable in size and colour, usually white, tinged pink or lilac-rose; sep. to 10×4mm, ovate, oblong or spathulate, cuneate, concave, lateral sep. concealed by lip, connate almost to apex, tip cleft; pet. wider than sep., obovate, apex rounded or apiculate, undulate; lip to 2.5×3cm, subquadrate, lobes 4, large, rounded, callus yellow, 3-lobed; column to 2mm, wings triangular-oblong or falcate. Jamaica, Guianas, Cuba, Hispaniola.

***O. pulvinatum*** Lindl. Pseudobulbs to 5cm diam., suborbicular-oblong, compressed, unifoliate. Lvs to 30×8cm, oblong, acute, fleshy, erect, yellow-green. Panicle to 3m, flexuous, many-fld, loosely branched, branches often further branched; fls to 2.5cm diam.; sep. and pet. yellow with red-brown or red-orange base, sep. to 13×6mm, ovate-spathulate, subacute to obtuse, undulate, dorsal sep. bent forward, concave, pet. similar to sep., obtuse-truncate; lip pale yellow spotted red or red-orange, wider than sep., lateral lobes suborbicular, fimbriate-undulate, midlobe subreniform, emarginate, callus white spotted red, cushion-like, papillose; column to 4mm, clavate, wings rounded. Brazil.

***O. pumilum*** Lindl. Pseudobulbs small or absent, unifoliate. Lvs arising from creeping rhiz., oblong to ligulate, acute, to 12×3.5cm, coriaceous. Panicle to 15cm, short-branched, densely many-fld; fls to 1cm diam., slightly campanulate; sep. and pet. somewhat incurved, straw-yellow spotted red-brown, obovate-oblong, obtuse; lip pale yellow marked red either side of callus, larger than sep. and pet., lateral lobes largest, ovate-oblong, midlobe subquadrate, curved forwards, callus 2-ridged; column oblong, acute, decurved. Brazil, Paraguay.

***O. pusillum*** (L.) Rchb. f. Diminutive epiphyte to 7cm. Lvs to 6×1cm, fleshy, narrow-oblong or elliptic, broad at base, apex sharply acuminate, equitant, conduplicate, the bases overlapping to form a flattened fan, through which wiry roots sometimes emerge. Infl. to 6cm, axillary; fls 1–4, to 2.7×1.5cm, yellow marked rusty-red. C & S America, W Indies.

***O. pyramidale*** Lindl. Pseudobulbs to 7cm, ovoid to cylindrical, compressed, unifoliate to trifoliate. Lvs to 20×3cm, oblanceolate to elliptic-oblong, acute or acuminate. Panicle to 50cm, erect to pendent, loosely many-fld, branches short, often compound; fls to 2.5cm diam., fragrant, canary-yellow, often spotted red; sep. and pet. reflexed, dorsal sep. to 7×3mm, oblanceolate-oblong, obtuse, lateral sep. slightly longer than dorsal sep., free, linear-oblanceolate, acute, pet. wider than dorsal sep., ovate-oblong, acute or apiculate; lip to 12×12mm, sessile, pandurate, lateral lobes small, rounded, reflexed, midlobe clawed, reniform or obovate-reniform, bilobulate in front, callus tubercled; column to 3mm, sigmoid, wings bilobed, divergent. Peru, Ecuador, Colombia.

***O. raniferum*** Lindl. Pseudobulbs to 6.5×2cm, ovoid to oblong, bifoliate. Lvs to 17×1.5cm, linear to narrow-oblanceolate, thin. Panicle to 35cm, erect, branches to 11cm, spreading; fls to 1.5cm across; sep. and pet. pale or bright yellow spotted red-brown, sep. minute, oblong-elliptic, pet. similar to sep., smaller; lip yellow, to 4×3mm, lateral lobes small, linear-oblong, spreading, midlobe obcordate, partially crenulate, callus red-brown, large, obscurely 2-lobed; column short, erect, narrow-winged. E Brazil.

***O. reflexum*** Lindl. Pseudobulbs to 8×5cm, ovoid to broadly ellipsoid, compressed, unifoliate or bifoliate. Lvs to 35×4cm, linear-lanceolate, acute, chartaceous. Panicle to 75cm, slender, straggling, loosely branched; fls to 4cm diam.; sep. and pet. pale yellow-green speckled dull red-brown, spreading, strongly reflexed, undulate, sep. elliptic-oblanceolate or linear-oblong, to 15×5mm, pet. linear-oblong, acute, slightly larger than sep.; lip to 2×2.5cm, bright yellow spotted red at base, pandurate, lateral lobes small, suborbicular, strongly revolute, midlobe clawed, transversely oblong, apically cleft, callus keeled with c8 tubercles; column to 5mm, stout. Mexico, Guatemala.

***O. robustissimum*** Rchb. f. Pseudobulbs short, broadly elliptic, compressed, unifoliate. Lvs to 40cm, ovate-elliptic or oblong, fleshy, keeled below, olive-green. Panicle to 2m, branches to 15cm, numerous, spreading; fls to 2.5cm diam.; sep. and pet. tipped yellow, red-brown at base, to 1.2×0.4cm, sep. cuneate-oblong or cuneate-obovate, apex rounded, pet. subequal to sep., oblong-oblanceolate, obtuse or truncate; lip yellow spotted or striped cinnamon, to 1×1cm, lateral lobes rounded, serrate, midlobe flabellate, emarginate, callus pulvinate, pilose. Brazil.

***O. sanderae*** Rolfe. Pseudobulbs to 6cm, ovoid, slightly compressed, unifoliate. Lvs to 45×8cm, elliptic to oblong, acute to rounded. Infl. to 80cm; fls produced in succession, large, showy, spreading; dorsal sep. red-brown, to 10×1cm, linear-oblanceolate, acute, lateral sep. to 7×2cm, yellow marked red, oblong-lanceolate, acute, decurved, undulate; pet. similar to dorsal sep., smaller; lip to 4×3.5cm, pale yellow, lateral lobes semi-orbicular, undulate-crisped, pale yellow spotted red-brown, midlobe clawed, suborbicular, undulate-crisped, pale yellow spotted red-brown near margin, callus 5-lobed; column to 1cm, wings with gland-tipped cilia. Peru.

***O. sarcodes*** Lindl. Pseudobulbs to 14×3cm, subfusiform, clustered, slightly compressed, dark green, bifoliate, rarely trifoliate. Lvs to 25×5cm, oblong, acute or obtuse, coriaceous, glossy green. Panicle to 1.8m, short-branched above; fls to 5cm diam., long-lived; sep. and pet. glossy, deep chestnut-brown edged yellow, dorsal sep. to 15×13mm, obcordate to obovate, concave, lateral sep. smaller, obovate-oblong, keeled below, slightly undulate, pet. larger than sep., obovate, obtuse, undulate; lip bright yellow spotted red-brown at base, to 2×2cm, lateral lobes small, oblong or suborbicular, margins reflexed, midlobe transversely elliptic, emarginate, undulate, callus an oblong lobed plate with a central tooth at each side. Brazil.

***O. schillerianum*** Rchb. f. Pseudobulbs to 5cm, ovoid-oblong, distant on rhiz., bifoliate. Lvs to 15×3cm, oblong. Panicle to 1.2m, scandent, loosely branched, branches short, often compound, few-fld; fls small, yellow-green barred brown; sep. to 15×5mm, oblong to oblanceolate, acute or apiculate; pet. wider than dorsal sep., acute or obtuse, undulate; lip to 2×2cm, pandurate to 3-lobed, lateral lobes semi-triangular or semi-ovate, short-clawed, midlobe large, cordate-reniform, retuse, callus multituberculate, tipped with 3 prominent tubercles; column dilated towards base, wings broadly dolabriform, dentate. Peru, Brazil.

***O. serratum*** Lindl. Pseudobulbs to 12cm, oblong-ovoid, compressed, bifoliate. Lvs to 55×4cm, narrowly linear-oblanceolate, acute. Panicle to 4m, loosely branched above, twining, many-fld; fls to 7.5cm diam., wide-spreading; sep. long-clawed, bright chestnut-brown edged yellow, dorsal sep. to 2.5×3.5cm, suborbicular, crisped-undulate, serrate, lateral sep. exceeds dorsal sep., ovate-oblong, obtuse, deflexed, margins strongly undulate and serrate; pet. chestnut-brown tipped bright yellow, smaller than sep., short-clawed, ovate-oblong, obtuse, strongly crisped and fimbriate; lip purple-brown with white margin and callus, to 1.5×1cm, hastate, callus consisting of a central plate with 2 acute teeth in front and a notched plate on each side; column to 8mm, wings narrowly cuneate, dentate at apex. Ecuador, Peru.

***O. sessile*** Lindl. ex Paxt. Pseudobulbs to 10×4cm, ovoid-oblong, compressed, bifoliate. Lvs to 38×3cm, linear to narrow-oblong, subacute to acute. Panicle to 60cm, branched above middle, erect, branches short, spreading; fls to 3.5cm diam., spreading, canary-yellow centrally spotted red-brown; sep. free, oblong-elliptic to oblong-obovate, to 17×5mm, obtuse, slightly undulate; pet. shorter and wider than sep.; lip to 2×2.5cm, sessile, pandurate-trilobed, callus 3-lobed, anterior portion bilamellate; column short, dilated near base, wings broad, dentate, truncate. Venezuela, Colombia, Peru.

***O. sphacelatum*** Lindl. Pseudobulbs to 15×5cm, ovoid-ellipsoid, compressed, sharp-edged, bifoliate or trifoliate. Lvs to 100×3.5cm, linear-ligulate or linear-lanceolate, acute, subcoriaceous. Panicle to 1.5m, short-branched; fls to 3cm diam.; sep. and pet. bright yellow blotched and spotted red-brown, often short-clawed, elliptic to obovate, acute and reflexed at apex, undulate; lip golden-yellow marked red-brown in front of callus, to 18×17mm, pandurate, lateral lobes small, rounded, midlobe transversely oblong, undulate, emarginate, callus fleshy, trilobed and toothed, white or yellow spotted orange-brown; column white spotted crimson on margins, to 6mm, subclavate, wings edged brown, oblong, with erose-crenate margins. Mexico to El Salvador.

***O. sphegiferum*** Lindl. Pseudobulbs to 4cm diam., broadly oval to subrotund, clustered, strongly compressed, unifoliate. Lvs to 20×4cm, elliptic-oblong, acute, pale green. Panicle to 1.2m, many-fld; fls to 2.5cm diam., bright orange, each seg. stained red-brown at base; sep. clawed, ovate; pet. clawed, oblong, apiculate; lip subpandurate, lateral lobes suborbicular, dentate, midlobe transversely oblong, emarginate, pale orange to bright orange, callus cushion-like, oblong, slightly papillose; column narrow-winged. Brazil.

***O. spilopterum*** Lindl. Pseudobulbs to 4×2.5cm, clustered, ovoid-compressed, becoming deeply sulcate, apex bifoliate. Lvs to 20×2.5cm, subcoriaceous, linear-lanceolate, acute. Infl. to 40cm, erect to pendent, simple, loosely several-fld; fls pendent; sep. and pet. violet-brown marked yellow-green; dorsal sep. to 10×5mm, ovate-oblong, acute, lateral sep. to 14×4mm, oblong, acute, basally connate; pet. to 10×6mm, ovate-subquadrate, base shortly unguiculate; lip to 2.5×3cm, sulphur-yellow, basally 3-lobed, lateral lobes oblong, auriculate, midlobe reniform, emarginate, crisped-undulate; callus violet-purple, fleshy, densely tuberculate; column fleshy, wings quadrate. Brazil, Paraguay.

***O. splendidum*** A. Rich. ex Duchartre. Pseudobulbs to 5×4.5cm, rotund, compressed, dull brown-green or purple-green, unifoliate. Lvs to 30×4.5cm, elliptic-oblong, subcoriaceous, V-shaped in cross section, often tinged purple. Panicle to 1m, erect, many-fld; peduncle glaucous; fls to 6cm diam., showy, long-lived; sep. and pet. bright yellow blotched and spotted rich red-brown, sep. to 2.5×1cm, elliptic-lanceolate, slightly apiculate, undulate, reflexed at apex, pet. to 3×1cm, elliptic-oblong, obtuse, reflexed at apex; lip golden-yellow, spreading, pandurate, to 4×2cm, lateral lobes small, rounded, tinged lavender, midlobe short-clawed, subreniform, emarginate, undulate, callus 3-lamellate; column to 1cm, wings rounded, concave. Guatemala, Honduras.

***O. stelligerum*** Rchb. f. Pseudobulbs to 8×3.5cm, ovoid-ellipsoid, compressed, bifoliate. Lvs to 16×3.5cm, elliptic-oblong, subacute, coriaceous. Panicle to 80cm, several-branched; fls large, stellate; sep. and pet. yellow spotted brown, to 2.5×1cm, spreading, oblong-ligulate or elliptic-lanceolate, subacuminate; lip yellow-white with dark yellow callus, to 2×1.5cm, pandurate, lateral lobes narrowly clawed, short, spreading-reflexed, obliquely semi-orbicular, midlobe cordate to suborbicular, shortly and abruptly cuspidate, undulate, callus keeled; column to 1cm, stout, wings subquadrate-rounded. Mexico, Guatemala.

***O. stenotis*** Rchb. f. Pseudobulbs to 14×4cm, linear-oblong, compressed, unifoliate or bifoliate. Lvs to 60×5cm, cuneate-oblong to linear-oblong, obtuse to subacute, subcoriaceous. Panicle to 1.5m, short-branched, usually densely many-fld; fls to 3cm diam.; sep. and pet. yellow blotched and barred red-brown, spreading, undulate, with recurved apices, sep. to 20×8mm, dorsal sep. oblong-lanceolate, apiculate, lateral sep. lanceolate to linear-lanceolate, acute, pet. to 16×6mm, lanceolate, acute; lip to 2×1.8cm, bright yellow with brown claw, pandurate, lateral lobes short-clawed, subquadrate to suborbicular, midlobe transversely subreniform, dilated, emarginate and bilobulate, callus erect, fleshy, multidenticulate; column to 7mm with 2 parallel, fleshy lobules below stigma. Costa Rica, Panama, Nicaragua.

***O. stipitatum*** Lindl. Pseudobulbs to 1×1cm, broadly truncate at apex, unifoliate. Lvs to 70×1cm, cylindrical, becoming pendent with age, acuminate, sulcate. Panicle slender, equalling lvs, pendent, many-fld; fls to 2cm diam.; sep. and pet. yellow marked or tinged red-brown, sep. subequal, to 7×4mm, spreading, short-clawed, dorsal sep. obovate-spathulate, obtuse, concave, lateral sep. obliquely obovate, acute, pet. to 8×3cm, elliptic-oblong, obtuse, undulate; lip bright yellow, to 2×2cm, pandurate, lateral lobes falcate, obliquely obtuse, midlobe narrowly clawed, transversely semi-orbicular to oblong, abruptly dilated, bilobulate, undulate, callus an elevated, rounded-transverse plate, terminating in an erect, rounded tubercle; column to 2.5mm, narrow-winged. Panama, Nicaragua, Honduras.

***O. stramineum*** Lindl. Pseudobulbs inconspicuous, unifoliate. Lvs to 20×4cm, oblong-lanceolate, obtuse or subacute, suberect, coriaceous, rigid; petiole short, stout. Panicle stout, exceeding lvs, short-branched; fls to 2cm diam.; sep. and pet. white or straw-coloured, sep. to 8×6mm, subrotund, widely spreading, emarginate, concave, lateral sep. speckled red, pet. narrower than sep., short-clawed, oblong-suborbicular; lip white or straw-coloured, speckled red, wider than sep., short-clawed, lateral lobes spreading, oblong, obtuse, slightly incurved, midlobe reniform, broadly clawed, emarginate, callus of several, plate-like keels; column white, wings marked purple, broad. Mexico.

***O. superbiens*** Rchb. f. Pseudobulbs to 10×3.5cm, elongate-ovoid, compressed, unifoliate or bifoliate. Lvs to 60×6cm, oblong-ligulate or linear-oblanceolate, acute, subcoriaceous. Panicle to 4m, twining, irregularly branched, branches to 15cm, few-fld; fls to 8cm diam.; sep. red-brown tipped yellow, to 3.5×2.5cm, clawed, undulate, rounded at apex, dorsal sep. suborbicular to ovate, base subcordate, lateral sep. longer than dorsal sep., briefly fused at base; pet. smaller than dorsal sep., ovate-oblong, yellow banded brown toward base, undulate, apex reflexed; lip purple or maroon, shorter than pet., short-clawed, perpendicular to column, oblong, auriculate, recurved, callus yellow, fleshy, with a central ridge and a prominent acute tubercle on each auricle; column to 1cm, wings small, falcate, either side of stigma. Colombia, Venezuela, Peru.

***O. teres*** Ames & Schweinf. Vegetatively similar to *O. stipitatum*. Panicle to 45cm, many-fld; fls to 1.5cm across; sep. and pet. yellow, heavily spotted red-brown, sep. free, to 6×4mm, short-clawed, suborbicular, concave, pet. subequal to sep., obovate-oblong, undulate; lip bright yellow, spotted red-brown below, to 8×8mm, pandurate, lateral lobes small, ligulate or oblong-spathulate, acute to obtuse, separated from midlobe by short claw, midlobe dilated, transversely reniform, obscurely bilobulate, callus yellow spotted red-brown, prominent, fleshy, tuberculate; column to 3mm, wings acute, incurved. Panama.

***O. tetrapetalum*** (Jacq.) Willd. Pseudobulbs absent. Lvs in tufts of 4 or more, to 20×0.5cm, triquetrous, sharp-edged, linear-ligulate, sulcate. Raceme sometimes branched, exceeding lvs, erect, usually dark purple, many-fld; fls to 2.5cm diam., variable in colour; sep. and pet. usually chestnut to rusty red barred and marked yellow or purple-rose, sep. to 8×3mm, spathulate, acute, keeled, lateral sep. largely connate, pet. wider than sep., broadly elliptic, broadly clawed, acute, undulate; lip white or pink blotched red to fore of callus, to 13×16mm, broadly clawed, lateral lobes small, obovate-oblong, midlobe transversely reniform, broadly emarginate, callus of 7 tubercles; column to 4mm, wings falcate, pale rose spotted yellow. W Indies to Colombia and Venezuela.

***O. tigratum*** Rchb. f. & Warsc. Pseudobulbs to 10×4cm, variable in shape, dull green, compressed, bifoliate. Lvs to 20×3.5cm, dull green. Panicle to 40cm, short-branched, branches loosely several-fld, fractiflex; fls to 2.5cm diam., showy; sep. and pet. spreading or reflexed, deep yellow marked brown or crimson, dorsal sep. to 9×3cm, cuneate-oblong, apiculate, lateral sep. slightly longer than dorsal sep., oblique, pet. shorter and wider than sep., flabellate, rounded and often apiculate; lip to 12×8mm, bright yellow banded brown basally with white callus, short-clawed, pandurate, lateral lobes auriculate, midlobe cordate-reniform, retuse, callus verrucose, apex with variable projection flanked by 2 teeth; column yellow tinged purple at apex, recurved, clavate below, wings yellow marked red-brown, broad, cleft. Venezuela, Colombia, Peru.

***O. tigrinum*** La Ll. & Lex. Pseudobulbs to 10×6cm, subglobose, compressed, bifoliate or trifoliate. Lvs to 45×2.5cm, narrowly oblong, acute, coriaceous, bright green. Panicle to 90cm, stout, usually erect, loosely branched, many-fld; fls to 7.5cm diam., violet-scented, long-lived; sep. and pet. bright yellow heavily blotched deep brown, similar, narrowly oblong, acute, reflexed at apex, undulate, sep. to 2.5×1cm, pet. shorter; lip bright yellow, to 3.5×4cm, with narrow claw, often tinged brown, spreading, lateral lobes small, rounded, midlobe transversely broad-oblong, emarginate, callus 3-keeled, terminating in 3 blunt teeth; column wings oblong, entire. Mexico.

***O. triquetrum*** (Sw.) R. Br. Pseudobulbs absent. Lvs 4 or more, triquetrous, to 15×1.5cm, linear-ligulate, acute, sulcate. Raceme to 20cm, slender, simple or slightly branched above, 5–15-fld; fls to 1.5cm diam., long-lived; sep. and pet. white-green spotted dark purple or rose, margins white, deeply tinged and spotted crimson, sep. broadly lanceolate, acute, lateral sep. connate, bifid at apex, slightly concave, to 10×4mm, pet. broader than sep., triangular-ovate, apiculate, clawed, undulate; lip usually white spotted and streaked purple or red-purple, to 1.5×1cm, lateral lobes small, rounded, midlobe large, cordate-ovate, apiculate, callus orange-yellow, small, subglobose; column to 4mm, wings triangular-oblong, acute at apex, outer margin crenulate. Jamaica.

***O. varicosum*** Lindl. Pseudobulbs to 12cm, ovate-oblong, compressed, clustered, often ribbed, bifoliate or trifoliate. Lvs to 25cm, rigid, ligulate, acute, dark green. Panicle to 1.5m, loosely branched, usually pendent, many-fld; fls to 3cm diam.; sep. and pet. yellow-green spotted and barred pale red-brown, sep. to 7mm, obovate, concave, lateral sep. connate for half of length, pet. narrowly oblong, undulate-crisped; lip bright yellow, much larger than sep., spreading, lateral lobes small, suborbicular, slightly crenate in front, midlobe to 4×5.5cm, transversely reniform, 2–4-lobed, callus fleshy, multidentate; column wings oblong. Brazil.

***O. variegatum*** (Sw.) Sw. VARIEGATED ONCIDIUM. Pseudobulbs much reduced with aborted apical lf. Lvs 4–6, distichous, lanceolate, acute, recurved, conduplicate, serrulate, dark green, to 15×1.5cm. Raceme or panicle to 45cm, slender; fls to 2cm diam., long-lived, white to pink richly stained brown or crimson-purple; dorsal sep. to 9×3mm, short-clawed, concave, broadly spathulate, subacute, lateral sep. larger than dorsal sep., oblanceolate to narrow-spathulate, connate almost to apex; pet. wider than sep., short-clawed, obovate to suborbicular, obtuse, sometimes emarginate, crenulate-undulate; lip to 1.5×2cm, pandurate, lateral lobes obovate to suborbicular, reflexed, erose-dentate, midlobe broadly oblong or reniform, deeply emarginate, crenulate, callus white-yellow, tuberculate; column to 3mm, wings broad, toothed. Florida, W Indies.

***O. volubile*** (Poepp. & Endl.) Cogn. Pseudobulbs to 5cm, narrowly oblong-cylindrical, clustered, slightly compressed, bifoliate. Lvs to 45×4cm, linear-oblanceolate, acute or acuminate. Panicle to 7m, scandent, branches loose, short, simple, few-fld; fls to 5cm diam., spreading; sep. light violet-purple or cinnamon-brown, free, to 2.5×1.5cm, long-clawed, dorsal sep. ovate-suborbicular, obtuse, lateral sep. oblique; pet. pale cinnamon or pale violet, white above middle, shorter than sep., short-clawed, obliquely ovate, acute; lip deep maroon, base yellow or white, to 1.5×1.5cm, pandurate-obovate, sessile, callus small, 3-toothed, tubercled; column to 5mm, clavate, wings absent. Peru.

***O. volvox*** Rchb. f. Pseudobulbs to 7×5cm, ovoid or oblong-pyriform, clustered, slightly compressed, furrowed, bifoliate. Lvs to 36×3cm, linear to oblong or narrow-lanceolate, obtuse, coriaceous. Panicle to 5m, loosely branched; fls to 2.5cm diam.; sep. and pet. yellow or yellow-brown, spotted and marked red-brown, sep. to 17×6mm, free, oblong, narrow-elliptic or oblong-lanceolate, acute to acuminate, undulate, pet. similar to sep., slightly undulate; lip to 18×16mm, bright yellow marked dark brown, pandurate-trilobed, lateral lobes small, subtriangular, midlobe transversely elliptic or reniform, emarginate or bilobulate, short-clawed, callus composed of 4 toothed plates; column to 7mm, yellow, wings dolabriform, entire or crenulate. Venezuela.

***O. waluewa*** Rolfe. Pseudobulbs to 7×1.5cm, oblong-cylindrical, grooved, slightly compressed, unifoliate. Lvs to 9×1cm, lanceolate, acute, petiolate, subcoriaceous. Infl. pendent, to 10cm, slender, densely fld above; fls 6–20, to 2cm diam.; sep. green white or cream, strongly concave, dorsal sep. to 10×4mm, oblong-spathulate, curved over column, lateral sep. shorter and wider than dorsal sep., connate almost to apex; pet. white to green-white barred purple, wider than sep., obovate, obtuse; lip similar in colour to pet., to 8×6mm, narrow at base, rhomboid, deeply 3-lobed above, lateral lobes rounded, reflexed, midlobe reniform, cleft, callus purple, linear, tubercles forming the image of an insect; column wings narrowly linear, curved forwards. Brazil, Paraguay.

***O. warscewiczii*** Rchb. f. Pseudobulbs to 8×3cm, ovoid, compressed, unifoliate or bifoliate. Lvs to 30×3.5cm, cuneate-ligulate, subcoriaceous; petiole conduplicate. Raceme to 50cm, to 15-fld; fls to 3cm diam., golden-yellow; bracts conspicuous, papery, spathaceous; dorsal sep. to 12×6mm, oblong, obtuse, slightly undulate, lateral sep. connate almost to apex, obovate, bifid, keeled below, to 15×10mm; pet. similar to dorsal sep., larger; lip to 2×2cm, pandurate, lateral lobes small, auriculate, midlobe suborbicular to oblong at base, apex bilobed, callus fleshy, narrow, terminating in 5 short, divergent teeth; column to 1cm, apex dilated, wings narrow. Costa Rica, Panama.

***O. wentworthianum*** Batem. ex Lindl. Pseudobulbs to 10×4.5cm, ovoid-ellipsoid, dark green mottled brown, compressed, bifoliate. Lvs to 35×3cm, ligulate, acute, subcoriaceous. Panicle to 1.5m, pendent, short-branched, many-fld; fls to 3cm diam.; sep. and pet. deep yellow blotched red-brown, spreading-reflexed, undulate, sep. to 2×1cm, elliptic or elliptic-obovate, rounded to acute, pet. shorter than sep., obliquely ovate-elliptic, rounded to subtruncate; lip to 2.5×2.5cm, transversely oblong, deflexed, lateral lobes pale yellow, small, rounded, curved forward, crenate, midlobe pale yellow blotched red-brown, obcordate to obreniform, emarginate, undulate, callus fleshy, spotted red-brown, triangular, with 3 teeth flanked by ridges; column to 7mm, wings triangular, crenulate, often spotted red-brown. Mexico, Guatemala.

***O. xanthodon*** Rchb. f. Pseudobulbs to 12cm, ovoid to ellipsoid, compressed, unifoliate. Lvs to 60×6cm, oblanceolate, acute or acuminate. Panicle to 2.7m, slender, climbing, loosely many-branched, branches slender, few-fld; fls to 5cm diam.; sep. and pet. deep brown edged yellow, wide-spreading, recurved, undulate, sep. to 2×2cm, ovate-oblong, acute, clawed, lateral sep. longer than dorsal sep., pet. similar to but smaller than dorsal sep.; lip smaller than pet., rich chocolate brown with yellow callus, pandurate-trilobed, basal portion subquadrate with reflexed lateral lobes, midlobe spathulate, recurved, acute, callus 1-keeled, tuberculate; column adnate to base of lip, wings minute. Ecuador, Colombia.

***O. zebrinum*** (Rchb. f.) Rchb. f. Pseudobulbs remotely spaced on rhiz., ovoid, slightly compressed, smooth, bifoliate. Lvs to 50×5cm, ligulate or elliptic-lanceolate, acute or acuminate. Panicle to 4m, much-branched, branches few- to several-fld; fls to 3.5cm diam.; sep. and pet. white barred red to violet, sep. to 2×1cm, elliptic-lanceolate or oblanceolate, acute or acuminate, undulate-crisped, pet. smaller than sep., obliquely oblong-ovate, acuminate, undulate-crisped; lip white, yellow-green at base, smaller than pet., triangular-lanceolate, spreading from base then strongly reflexed, callus yellow, often marked red, 3-lobed above with a central, apically dentate keel; column to 6mm, wings minute, lanceolate, anth. yellow-brown marked pink or maroon-brown. Venezuela.

***O.* grexes and cultivars** (see also × *Odontocidium*, × *Maclellanara* and × *Wilsonara*).

*O.* Boissiense: large golden yellow blooms marked with chestnut.

*O.* Ella 'Flambeau': the best of the varicosum type; fls bright lemon yellow with chestnut callus.

*O.* Fantasy 'Orchidglade': equitant; stunning colours rich green-yellow overlaid with maroon-red.

*O.* Fire Opal: equitant, rich pink shades over creamy white, sep. and pet. darker than lip; rich chestnut callus and shield on lip contrasts with white column.

*O.* Goldiana: thin leaved type; long branching sprays of small golden fls.

*O.* Green Gold: mule ear type; large fls clear green covered with brown spots contrasting with bright yellow lip, long-lasting.

*O.* Guinea Gold: thin leaved type; long branching sprays of bright golden fls.

*O.* Gypsy Beauty: white and burgundy red with raspberry lip apex.

*O.* Hawaiian Adventure: mule ear type; large sprays of rich brown and yellow fls.

*O.* Red Belt: equitant; lovely red fls on branching sprays.

*O.* Spanish Beauty: equitant; branching sprays of red fls, lip white spotted with red.

*O.* Sultamyre: superb example of the varicosum type of breeding; large yellow fls; many clones of which the best are 'Louis d'Or' and 'Thérèse'.

*O.* William Thurston: equitant, long branching sprays; fls in a wide range of colours in yellow, beige and dark brown.

***O. acrobotryum*** Klotzsch. See *O. harrisonianum*.
***O. altissimum*** Lindl. non (Jacq.) Sw. See *O. baueri*.
***O. aurosum*** Rchb. f. See *O. excavatum*.
***O. bernoullianum*** Kränzl. See *O. ampliatum*.
***O. bicornutum*** Hook. See *O. pubes*.
***O. bifrons*** Lindl. See *O. warscewiczii*.
***O. brenesii*** Schltr. See *O. obryzatum*.
***O. bryolophotum*** Rchb. f. See *O. heteranthum*.
***O. candidum*** Lindl. See *Palumbina candida*.
***O. carinatum*** Lindl. See *Leochilus carinatus*.
***O. cariniferum*** (Rchb. f.) Beer. See *Odontoglossum cariniferum*.
***O. celsium*** A. Rich. See *O. bifolium*.
***O. cerebriferum*** Rchb. f. See *O. ensatum*.
***O. ciliatulum*** Hoffsgg. See *O. barbatum*.
***O. ciliatum*** Lindl. See *O. barbatum*.
***O. cirrhosum*** (Lindl.) Beer. See *Odontoglossum cirrhosum*.
***O. citrosmum*** (Lindl.) Beer. See *Cuitlauzina pendula*.
***O. confusum*** Rchb. f. See *O. ensatum*.
***O. convolvulaceum*** Lindl. See *O. globuliferum*.
***O. corynephorum*** Lindl. See *O. volubile*.
***O. crispum*** var. ***forbesii*** (Hook.) Burb. See *O. forbesii*.
***O. cristatum*** (Lindl.) Beer. See *Odontoglossum cristatum*.
***O. cucullatum*** var. ***nubigenum*** (Lindl.) Lindl. See *O. nubigenum*.
***O. cucullatum*** var. ***phalaenopsis*** (Lind. & Rchb. f.) Veitch. See *O. phalaenopsis*.
***O. decipiens*** Lindl. See *O. crista-galli*.
***O. delumbe*** Lindl. See *O. ansiferum*.
***O. diadema*** Lindl. See *O. serratum*.
***O. dielsianum*** Kränzl. See *O. cheirophorum*.
***O. digitatum*** Lindl. See *O. leucochilum*.
***O. echinatum*** HBK. See *Erycina echinata*.
***O. egertonii*** (Lindl.) Beer. See *Osmoglossum egertonii*.
***O. epidendroides*** (HBK) Beer. See *Odontoglossum epidendroides*.
***O. fimbriatum*** Hoffsgg. See *O. barbatum*.
***O. flexuosum*** Lindl. non Sims. See *O. cimiciferum*.
***O. fulgens*** Schltr. See *O. obryzatum*.
***O. galeottianum*** Drapiez. See *Cuitlauzina pendula*.
***O. ghiesbreghtiana*** A. Rich. & Gal. See *Mexicoa ghiesbreghtiana*.
***O. graminifolium*** Lindl. See *O. brachyandrum*.
***O. guttatum*** (L.) Rchb. f. See *O. luridum*.
***O. haematochrysum*** Rchb. f. See *O. flexuosum*.
***O. haematoxanthum*** Rchb. f. See *O. flexuosum*.
***O. hallii*** (Lindl.) Beer. See *Odontoglossum hallii*.
***O. hebraicum*** Rchb. f. See *O. baueri*.
***O. holochrysum*** Rchb. f. See *O. onustum*.
***O. insleayi*** (Barker & Lindl.) Lindl. See *Rossioglossum insleayi*.
***O. ionops*** Cogn. & Rolfe. See *O. heteranthum*.
***O. iridifolium*** Lindl. See *O. crista-galli*.
***O. janeirense*** Rchb. f. See *O. longipes*.
***O. kramerianum*** Rchb. f. See *Psychopsis krameriana*.
***O. kymatoides*** Kränzl. See *O. carthagenense*.
***O. labiatum*** (Sw.) Rchb. f. See *Leochilus labiatus*.
***O. lacerum*** Lindl. See *O. stipitatum*.
***O. lankesteri*** Ames. See *O. ansiferum*.
***O. leucostomum*** Hoffsgg. See *O. hians*.
***O. limminghei*** E. Morr. ex Lindl. See *Psychopsis limminghei*.
***O. longifolium*** Lindl. See *O. cebolleta*.
***O. lunatum*** Lindl. See *Solenidium lunatum*.
***O. luteo-purpureum*** (Lindl.) Beer. See *Odontoglossum luteo-purpureum*.
***O. macrantherum*** Hook. See *Leochilus oncidioides*.
***O. massangei*** Morr. See *O. sphacelatum*.
***O. megalous*** Schltr. See *O. heteranthum*.
***O. microglossum*** Klotzsch. See *O. barbatum*.
***O. monoceras*** Hook. See *O. longicornu*.
***O. naevium*** (Lindl.) Beer. See *Odontoglossum naevium*.
***O. naranjense*** Schltr. See *O. ansiferum*.
***O. nodosum*** E. Morr. See *Psychopsis krameriana*.
***O. obryzatoides*** Kränzl. See *O. obryzatum*.
***O. ochmatochilum*** Rchb. f. See *O. cardiochilum*.
***O. oerstedii*** Rchb. f. See *O. carthagenense*.
***O. pachyphyllum*** Hook. See *O. cavendishianum*.
***O. papilio*** Lindl. See *Psychopsis papilio*.
***O. papilio*** var. ***kramerianum*** Lindl. See *Psychopsis krameriana*.
***O. patulum*** Schltr. See *O. nanum*.
***O. pelicanum*** Lindl. See *O. reflexum*.
***O. powellii*** Schltr. See *O. anthocrene*.
***O. quadricorne*** Klotzsch. See *O. hians*.
***O. quadripetalum*** Sw. See *O. tetrapetalum*.
***O. racemosum*** (Lindl.) Rchb. f. See *Solenidium racemosum*.
***O. rechingerianum*** Kränzl. See *O. cabagrae*.
***O. rigbyanum*** Paxt. See *O. sarcodes*.
***O. scansor*** Rchb. f. See *O. globuliferum*.
***O. suave*** Lindl. See *O. reflexum*.
***O. superfluum*** Rchb. f. See *Capanemia superflua*.
***O. tricolor*** Hook. See *O. tetrapetalum*.
***O. trilingue*** Sander. See *O. kienastianum*.
***O. uaipanese*** Schnee. See *O. nigratum*.
***O. unguiculatum*** Lindl. See *O. tigrinum*.

***O. unicorne*** Lindl. See *O. longicornu*.
***O. vexillarium*** Rchb. f. See *O. bifolium*.
***O. werckleri*** Schltr. See *O. globuliferum*.
For further synonymy see *Leochilus, Odontoglossum, Psygmorchis* and *Waluewa*.

**Oncoba** Forssk. (From *onkob*, the Arabic name of the N African species *O. spinosa*.) Flacourtiaceae. 39 species of shrubs or small trees, sometimes spiny, Leaves alternate, leathery or thin. Flowers white, red or yellow, terminal or axillary, solitary or in inflorescences, bisexual; sepals 3–5; petals 5–20, spreading, stamens numerous, in many rows borne on a fleshy ring. Fruit a leathery, pulpy berry, with many seeds. Tropical & S Africa; Brazil.

CULTIVATION Grown for their dark evergreen foliage, often deep green when young and bronzed in winter, and their fragrant flowers; those of *O. spinosa* are individually short-lived but are carried in succession over a long period. *O. spinosa* is sometimes used in frost-free zones as a prickly hedge or barrier in large gardens. *O. kraussiana*, once popular in England as a potplant for the warm glasshouse, is grown as a border specimen in subtropical regions. *Oncoba* will shed their leaves when temperatures fall below freezing, although in regions where long hot summers prevail, *O. spinosa* is frost-tolerant to between −5°C/23°F and −7°C/20°F. In temperate zones under glass, overwinter *O. spinosa* and *O. routledgei* in frost-free conditions; for *O. kraussiana*, maintain a winter minimum temperature of 5°C/40°F. As for *Flacourtia*.

***O. echinata*** Oliv. Glabrous shrub. Lvs to 15×6cm, thin, oblong; petiole to 12mm. Fls white, to 12mm diam., borne on the branch below the leaves, solitary or in twos and threes on short peduncles. Fr. round, to 25mm diam., densely spiny, with many seeds. Upper Guinea. Z10.

***O. kraussiana*** (Hochst.) Planch. Much-branched thornless evergreen shrub, to 4.5m. Lvs to 6×2.5cm, elliptic-oblong, downy, entire. Fls 5cm diam., white, solitary or in twos and three; pedicels to 8cm; sep. round, concave; pet. exceeding sep., spreading. Fr. orange, smooth, to 5cm diam. S Africa. Z9.

***O. routledgei*** Sprague. Spiny shrub or small tree, to 60m. Lvs ovate, crenate. Fls 5cm diam., fragrant, white, solitary or in pairs on old wood. Tropical Africa. Closely related to *O. spinosa*. Z9.

***O. spinosa*** Forssk. Glabrous shrub with spines to 5cm. Lvs to 9×5cm, thin or leathery, elliptic, with a rounded base, serrate. Fls 5cm diam., showy, white, fragrant, resembling a gardenia or camellia, terminal or lateral; cal. 4-lobed, persistent; pet. twice as long as sep. and variable in number. Fr. round, to 5cm diam., shiny, rusty brown, smooth with a hard shell. Africa, Arabia. Z9.

***O. monacantha*** Steud. See *O. spinosa*.
For further synonymy see *Xylotheca*.

**Oncosiphon** Källersjö. (From Gk *onkos*, bulk or mass, and *siphon*, tube, referring to the conspicuously swollen corolla tube.) Compositae. About 7 species of glabrous or pubescent, annual herbs. Leaves alternate, pinnatisect. Capitula subglobose, radiate or discoid, solitary or in corymbs; receptacle flat-convex or conical-globose, naked; phyllaries obtuse or acute, with scarious margins; ray florets disc florets, female, fertile, white bisexual 4-lobed, tube conspicuously swollen, campanulate. Fruit a terete cypsela, tapering at base, 4-ribbed, yellow-brown; pappus a small entire or dentate crown. S Africa and Namibia.

CULTIVATION As for *Chrysanthemum*.

***O. africanum*** Källersjö. Erect or spreading, to 30cm. Lower lvs 2.5–5cm, bipinnatisect, glabrous or sparsely pubesc., lobes narrow. Capitula solitary, radiate; receptacle conical-globose; phyllaries glabrous; ray florets white; disc florets yellow or tinged red. Pappus well-developed, apically dentate. S Africa.

***O. grandiflorum*** (Thunb.) Källersjö. Erect, much-branched, to 45cm. Stems pubesc., corymbosely branched. Lvs to 6cm, bipinnatisect, lobes narrow. Capitula 7mm diam., solitary, discoid; receptacle flat to slightly convex; phyllaries densely tomentose; florets yellow, lobes short. Pappus small, entire. S Africa.

***O. piluliferum*** (L. f.) Källersjö. STINK-NET. To 45cm, foul-smelling. Stems much-branched. Lvs to 4.5cm, bipinnatisect, lobes narrow. Capitula variable in size, solitary, discoid; receptacle conical-globose; phyllaries glabrous; florets yellow, lobes short. Pappus small, apically dentate. S Africa.

***O. suffructicosum*** (L.) Källersjö. Erect, to 45cm, strongly aromatic. Stems corymbosely branched, rather woody. Lvs to 4cm, bipinnatisect, lobes narrow. Capitula to 6mm diam., discoid, in dense, many-headed corymbs; receptacle conical; phyllaries subglabrous; florets bright yellow, lobes short. Pappus small, apically dentate. S Africa.

For synonymy see *Cotula, Matricaria* and *Tanacetum*.

**Oncosperma** Bl. (From Gk *onkos*, tumour, and *sperma*, seed, referring to the globose seed.) Palmae. 5 species of pleonanthic, monoecious palms, to *c*25m. Stems erect, clustered, sometimes branched, becoming bare, ringed, armed with deciduous, robust, black spines between rings, pointing downwards. Crownshaft tomentose and armed with spines of different lengths. Leaves to 5m, pinnate, neatly abscising; petiole flat or concave above, convex beneath, spiny and clothed with indumentum; pinnae single-fold, acute, acuminate, regularly spaced along rachis and held in one plane, pendent or rigid, or clustered and held in differing planes along rachis, unarmed, with bands of scales above and sometimes beneath, midrib clothed with ramenta beneath. Inflorescences to *c*60cm, infrafoliar, erect becoming horizontal, branched ×2 at base, ×1 toward summit; peduncle tomentose, unarmed or with straight spines; bud enclosed in 2 woody bracts, armed with straight or twisted spines; rachillae flexuous and pendent; bracteoles spirally arranged on rachillae, subtending triads of flowers (2 male, 1 female), or solitary or paired male flowers distally; male flowers asymmetrical, sepals 3, petals 3, exceeding sepals, stamens 6–9, pistillode trifid; female flowers smaller than male, globose, sepals 3, overlapping, petals 3, distinct; staminodes 6, toothlike. Fruit spherical, smooth or pebbled, to 2cm diam., purple-black, 1-seeded, with lateral to apical stigmatic remains. SE Asia and Malay Archipelago from Sri Lanka to Indochina and the Philippines. Z10.

CULTIVATION Native to humid tropical climates, with *O. tigilarum* found in brackish water swamp and creeks. *Oncosperma* spp. are suitable for outdoor cultivation in the humid tropics, especially effective in waterside plantings, otherwise requiring hot glasshouse conditions. Propagate by seed or suckers. See PALMS.

***O. fasciculatum*** Thwaites. Stems to 12m, clustered, densely spiny. Lvs to 2.4m; pinnae clustered in groups and held in differing planes along rachis, ascending but apices pendent. Infl. to 60cm, bracts unarmed; male fls 0.6cm, stamens 9. Fr. 1.25cm, black-purple. Sri Lanka.

***O. tigilarum*** (Jack) Ridl. NIBUNG PALM. Stems to 25m×20cm, densely clustered, smooth and grey near base. Lvs 3.5–6m with spiny bracts; pinnae pendent. Male fls golden yellow, 0.6cm, fragrant; stamens 6. Fr. blue-black, 1.25cm. Malay Peninsula, Borneo, Sumatra, Philippines.

***O. filamentosum*** Bl. See *O. tigilarum*.
***O. vanhoutteanum*** H.A. Wendl. & Van Houtte. See *Nephrosperma vanhoutteanum*.

**Onion**. *Allium cepa*. Liliaceae (Alliaceae). The onion is a biennial grown as an annual for the edible bulb, which has a usually strong pungent flavour. The leaves and immature bulbs are also edible. The onion probably originated in the regions of Iran and western Pakistan. It no longer occurs in the wild, although there are other members of the genus having a similar form and flavour which are native to more northern temperate regions. Its use can be traced back to 3200 BC, when it was an important food crop for the Egyptians. Onion production in India dates back to about 600 BC and there are records of the crop's use by Greeks and Romans about 400–300 BC. By the early Middle Ages, onions had reached northern Europe. Today the onion is cultivated on a large scale throughout most temperate and tropical regions of the world.

The onion is best adapted to a Mediterranean-type climate where the hot dry summers are ideal for bulb maturation. However, there are a large number of cultivars suited to a range of growing conditions, including cool-season production in tropical regions. For high yields, however, cool weather is desirable during the early stages of growth. The crop is tolerant of frost, but prolonged exposure to temperatures below 10°C/50°F will vernalize plants and cause them to bolt. Optimum seedling growth occurs in the range 20–25°C/68–77°F and declines rapidly at temperatures above 27°C/80°F. Once young plants are large enough, bulb formation is able to take place in response to long-day conditions. For this reason most cultivars grown in temperate climates will bulb during early summer, producing a late summer harvest. However, cultivars have been selected to produce bulbs over a wide range of long-day conditions ranging from 12 to more than 16 hours, thus making it possible to manipulate crop development in different regions. In all instances the bulbing response is to long days, although the cultivars sensitive to the lower end of the range are often erroneously referred to as short-day selections. Bulbing is also advanced to some extent by higher temperatures and also nitrogen deficiency. As leaves die back, the bulb enters a period of dormancy which can be prolonged by storing under conditions of low temperature (1°C/34°F) and low relative humidity.

Using an appropriate choice of cultivars along with storage, onions can be available from summer through winter until the following spring. Immature salad onions can be harvested throughout most of the year. Onions can be served cooked to provide flavour in a wide range of dishes or in soups. Salad onions trimmed and served entire, sliced bulbs and leaves are all served raw in salads. Small onions are also used for pickling.

Onions require an open site and a fertile well-drained soil. Soil pH should be at least 6.5 and more acid soils will require liming. Well-rotted organic matter will help improve the moisture retention characteristics of the soil. Onions are susceptible to a number of soil-borne pest and disease problems and for this reason a long period (at least four years) is desirable between successive crops to prevent their build-up.

Bulb onions can either be propagated from seed or vegetatively, using small bulblets referred to as sets. Maincrop onions should be sown in a well-prepared seedbed during early spring. Germination is poor in cold wet soils and, where possible, cloches should be used to warm the soil for early sowings in cold areas. Seed, preferably treated with a fungicidal dressing, should be sown thinly in 2cm/¾in.-deep drills in rows 30cm/12in. apart. Once established, the within-row spacing can be adjusted to 4cm/1½in. between plants by thinning. The size of the bulbs at harvest time is strongly influenced by competition between neighbouring plants and if larger bulbs are required the within-row spacing should be increased to up to 10cm/4in. Similarly, where small bulbs are required for pickling, plant populations can be arranged to give approximately 300 plants per square metre.

Weed control is important, particularly during the early stages of growth when the crop is building up its leaf area. During dry weather additional water may be necessary, but should not be applied too late during development as it may delay maturity and impair the keeping quality of bulbs.

Onions are ready to harvest when the leaves start to die back and fall over. They should be lifted at this stage and dried and cleaned thoroughly if required for storage. They may either be tied in ropes and hung up after drying in a cool dark shed or, alternatively, stored in net bags or shallow trays. Damaged and thick-necked bulbs do not store well.

The growing season can be extended by raising transplants under protection for earlier planting in spring or by sowing suitable cultivars outside in autumn to mature during early summer the following year, ahead of spring-sown crops. Transplants can be raised in seed trays in gentle heat under protection during late winter, for planting out after hardening off in early spring. Modular-raised transplants can be raised with a single seedling in each but it is more economical to produce multi-seeded blocks containing up to six seedlings which are planted out as a cluster. Provided the average space available to each seedling is similar for single and multi-seeded transplants, final bulb size will not be significantly affected.

The cultivation of an autumn-sown crop is more difficult. A suitable hardy cultivar should be selected which is capable of earlier bulbing the following year. The sowing date is also critical and depends on local climatic conditions. If plants are sown too early they may become large enough to be vernalized by the low winter temperatures, which will cause them to bolt in spring. Conversely, if sown too late they may be too small to survive the winter. As a rough guide the sowing date should be adjusted to enable the seedlings to reach a height of 15–20cm/6–8in. before the onset of winter.

The simplest technique for onion raising is to use sets. They are less prone to disease, will give a reasonable crop even in poor soil conditions, and mature earlier than seeded crops. Cultivars are available for both spring and autumn planting. They should be planted firmly with their tips at soil level 5cm/2in. apart in rows spaced at 25cm/10in. apart. If extra-large bulbs are required these spacings should be increased.

For salad use it is possible to use the thinnings removed during the production of maincrop onions. For continuity of production it is, however, preferable to sow specific cultivars (usually referred to as spring onions or scallions in the US) from spring to midsummer at intervals of two to three weeks. These can be followed by over-wintered sowings of extra-hardy cultivars for harvesting in the spring. In cold areas the overwintered crop is best protected by cloches. Salad onions should be sown at a fairly high density of around 300 plants per square metre, either in rows spaced at 10cm apart or in bands 8cm/3in. wide with 15cm/6in. between bands. Thinning should not be necessary and onions can be harvested by pulling as required.

Onion cultivars are available for a wide range of environmental conditions and uses. Most are brown- or yellow-skinned but red cultivars are also available. In cool climates, spring and autumn sowing are practised, though many cultivars can be sown at either time. In warm climates the equivalent criterion is long-day or short-day cultivars depending on locality. Recommended spring-sown cultivars: 'Ailsa Craig' (large, consistent, long-keeping, a standard exhibition cv.), 'Bedfordshire Champion', (large, globe-shaped, long-keeping, exhibition standard), 'Caribo' (straw-coloured), 'Early Yellow Globe' (mild, stores well), 'Hygro' (vigorous, globe-shaped), 'Lancastrian' (globe-shaped), 'North Holland Blood Red', 'Red Baron', 'Red Torpedo', 'Rijnsburger-Balstora' (dark thick skin), 'Rijnsburger-Robusta' (dark straw-coloured), 'Ringmaster' (very large, mild, good for onion rings), 'Southport Red Globe' (purple-red, globe-shaped), 'Southport White Globe' (pure white, globe-shaped), 'Sweet Sandwich' (light brown, globe-shaped, sweet pale yellow flesh), 'White Sweet Spanish' (white, globe-shaped, mild, also used for bunching), 'White Sweet Spanish Jumbo' (very large), 'Yellow Bermuda' (pale straw colour, mild and sweet).

For autumn sowing: 'Buffalo' (globe-shaped, high-yielding), 'Burgundy' (large flattened globe, dark red), 'Express Yellow' (globe-shaped), 'Keepwell' (globe-shaped, dark straw colour), 'Imai Early Yellow' (globe-shaped), 'Senshyu Semi-Globe Yellow' (high yield), 'Sturon' (flattened bulbs, good yield, long keeper), 'Texas Supersweet' (very large and sweet), 'Vidalia' (large, yellow, globe-shaped, very sweet), 'Walla Walla Sweet' (large, globe-shaped, brown, possibly the sweetest onion), 'White Bermuda' (semi-flat, white, very mild), 'White Granex' (large, flat, white, mild), 'Yellow Granex' (large, flat, pale yellow, very mild).

For salad onions the main cultivar is 'White Lisbon'; 'Winter Hardy White Lisbon' is a frost resistant selection. Although less winter hardy, the bunching onion (*A. fistulosum*) is an attractive and more pungent alternative to the salad onion. Available cultivars include: 'Yoshima', 'Hikari Bunching', 'Ishikura', 'Nebuka' and 'Hardy Long White'. Pearl or pickling onions, also called baby onions or boilers, are harvested when very small. Most are white-skinned; these include 'Aviv' (almost round), 'Barletta' (nearly round, used as cocktail onion), 'Crystal Wax' (flattened, very mild, 'Paris Silverskin' (flat), 'Purplette' (purple-red), and 'Wonder of Pompeii' (silvery).

The Egyptian onion (*A. cepa* var. *aggregatum*) produces small elongated bulbs in place of flowers on 1m tall stems. These can be harvested and planted in summer when they are ready for use during the following year. Their culinary uses are similar to those of ordinary onions.

Leaf blotch, caused by the fungus *Cladosporium alliicepae*, results in eye-shaped, white lesions, the centres of which become brown when spores are produced. If the infection is widespread the numerous white lesions resemble damage caused by droplets of a herbicide such as paraquat. Leaf rot, caused by *Botrytis squamosa*, also produces white lesions on the leaves and these tend to be concentrated around the tips, resulting in a dieback. Under moist conditions a grey mould growth develops on the shrivelled tissue. Another *Botrytis* species, *B. cinerea*, invades seedlings soon after emergence and subsequently causes a collar rot. Fungicide sprays may be necessary to control the leaf blotch, leaf rot and collar rot diseases.

Smut, *Urocystis cepulae*, is soil borne and the mycelium from germinating spores infects young seedlings. The first symptoms are lead-coloured streaks and spots; eventually the leaves become swollen and distorted and split to expose black, powdery spore masses. The spores can survive in the soil for up to 20 years so it is important not to grow *Allium* species on contaminated land although soil fumigation and fungicide seed treatments may give some control. White rot, caused by *Sclerotium cepivorum*, is another soil-borne disease. Affected plants are stunted and yellow, and black sclerotia form amongst the white fungal growth which rots the base of the plant. The sclerotia are resting bodies which persist in the soil. Mercurous chloride, calomel, applied in the drill or as a seed dressing, is the traditional control measure for this disease. Shanking is the name given to the disease caused by *Phytophthora* spp. These soil-borne fungi attack the roots and bulbs so that the leaves turn yellow and shrivel. There are no specific control measures but crop rotation should help.

Onions can also be affected by downy mildew (*Peronospora destructor*) and storage rots caused by bacteria (*Erwinia carotovora*) and fungi (*Botrytis allii*, the cause of neck rot, *Aspergillus* and *Penicillium* spp.). The aphid-transmitted onion yellow dwarf virus results in small bulbs and yellow, distorted leaves; onions are less frequently affected than shallots and leeks. Diseased plants should be destroyed and if possible, certified virus-free sets should be used.

The diseases referred to above affect, to same extent, other *Allium* spp. including chives, garlic, shallots and the ornamentals.

**Onobrychis** Mill. (Name used by Dioscorides; from Gk, *onos*, an ass, and *bryche*, bellowing, braying, referring to the fact that some species are used for forage; asses are said to bray for it.) SAINFOIN: SAINTFOIN; HOLY CLOVER. Leguminosae (Papilionoideae). Some 130 species of annual or perennial herbs, subshrubs or, rarely, spiny shrubs. Leaves alternate, imparipinnate; stipules free or united; leaflets entire, stipules absent. Flowers in axillary racemes or long-stalked spikes; calyx campanulate with 5 equal teeth; corolla white, pink or purple, rarely yellow; stamens 10, 1 free. Fruit compressed, suborbicular, indehiscent, margin usually toothed, sides pitted to reticulate-veined, veins and ridges often toothed; seeds 1–3. Summer. Temperate Eurasia. Z7.

CULTIVATION *O. viciifolia*, once cultivated as a fodder crop and now naturalized in parts of Britain and North America in grassland habitats on calcareous soils, is an important source of honey on the English chalk uplands. *O. arenaria* is found in freely draining stony habitats in central Europe, to altitudes of 2500m/8125ft. *O. viciifolia* is well suited to the wild garden and for naturalizing in turf, particularly on soils that approximate to those of their natural habitats, where it forms a valuable nectar source for bees. *O. montana* is suitable for the larger rock garden. Cultivate as for *Ononis*.

***O. arenaria*** (Kit. ex Schult.) DC. Resembles *O. viciifolia*, but cal. teeth with short, adpressed hairs, fr. shorter, with fewer teeth. Perenn. herb, to 80cm, pubesc. or subglabrous. Leaflets usually 3–12 pairs, narrow-oblong to elliptic, glabrous to pubesc., green or grey-green. Fls in very slender racemes; cal. pubesc. or glabrous; cor. to 1cm, pink veined purple. Fr. minutely pubesc., usually armed, teeth 3–8, to 4mm. Temperate Eurasia. Z6.

***O. caput-galli*** (L.) Lam. Annual to 90cm, sparsely pubesc. or glabrous. Leaflets to 2×0.6cm, 4–7 pairs, obovate to linear, mucronate, hairy; peduncles usually equalling lvs. Racemes to 8-fld; fls pale pink; cal. teeth to 4× longer than tube; cor. to 8mm, red-purple. Fr. to 1cm, teeth narrow triangular to subulate, to 5mm. Mediterranean to C Bulgaria.

***O. crista-galli*** (L.) Lam. Annual, resembling *O. caput-galli* but fr. longer. Peduncles often shorter than lvs. Racemes 2–8-fld; cal. teeth to 5× longer than tube; cor. to 8mm. Fr. to 14mm, teeth 3–5, broadly triangular. to 6mm. Mediterranean, N Africa, Asia Minor.

***O. laconica*** Orph. ex Boiss. Stemless sericeous perenn. to 30.5cm. Leaflets in 7–9 pairs, linear-elliptic. Fls bright pink, large, in a dense oblong-cylindric spike; peduncles very long. Levant. Possibly only a variant of *O. viciifolia*.

***O. montana*** DC. Perenn. herb to 50cm, sparsely pubesc. to subglabrous. Stipules usually united; leaflets 5–8 pairs, elliptic or ovate to oblong, green or grey-green beneath. Fls in racemes, usually 10+-fld; cal. sparsely pubesc., hairs adpressed or spreading to erect; cor. to 14mm, pink usually purple veined, standard to 2mm+ shorter than keel, wings to 7mm+ shorter than cal. Fr. to 12mm, pubesc., margins 4–8-toothed or unarmed, teeth to 4mm. Mts of C Europe, Italy and the Balkan Peninsula, possibly Pyrenees. Z5.

***O. radiata*** Steud. Erect herb, to 46cm tall. Leaflets ovate, obtuse, mucronate, hairy beneath. Fls yellow-white, lined red, standard spotted yellow; cal. hairy; spikes cylindric. Fr. roughly hairy. Iberian Peninsula.

***O. viciifolia*** Scop. SAINFOIN; HOLY CLOVER; ESPARCET. Closely resembles *O. montana*, but fr. shorter, marginal teeth shorter. Perenn. herb to 80cm, pubesc. to subglabrous. Leaflets to 3.5×0.7cm, in 6–14 pairs, ovate to oblong, rarely linear; peduncles longer than lvs. Racemes to 9cm, many-fld; fls to 1cm+; cal. to 8mm, pubesc., teeth to 3× longer than tube, long hairy; cor. to 14mm, pink veined purple. Fr. to 8mm, pubesc., margin usually 6–8-toothed, teeth to 2mm. C Europe. Z6.

***O. alba*** Boreau. See *O. viciifolia*.
***O. alectorocephale*** St.-Lager. See *O. caput-galli*.
***O. alectorolopha*** St.-Lager. See *O. crista-galli*.
***O. carnea*** Schleich. See *O. arenaria*.
***O. ochinata*** St.-Lager. See *O. caput-galli*.
***O. sativa*** Lam. See *O. viciifolia*.
***O. trilophocarpa*** (Coss. & Durieu. See *O. crista-galli*.

**Onoclea** L. (From Gk *onos*, vessel, and *kleio*, to close, referring to the closely rolled fertile fronds; Dioscoridean name.) Dryopteridaceae (Athyriaceae). 1 species, a coarse, terrestrial, perennial fern. Rhizomes creeping. Fronds dimorphic, arising singly, with anastomosing veins; sterile fronds to 1m, pinnately divided, glabrous, deciduous, petiole longer than lamina, lamina broadly ovate-triangular, pinnae 8–12 pairs, to 8cm wide, deeply lobed to sinuate or entire, rachis broadly winged; fertile fronds to 60cm, stiffly erect, lanceolate, bipinnate, becoming dark brown; pinnules with margins revolute, enclosing groups of sori in bead-like lobes; sori globose, borne on veins; indusium thin, membranous, caducous. Eastern N America, E Asia. Z4.

CULTIVATION A beautiful spreading fern producing carpets of pale green fronds (bronze-pink to ruby on emergence). It will colonize most locations provided they are not too dry and are sheltered from harsh winds. It is most usually, however, cultivated in bog and woodlands gardens or damp leafy soils, or at the margins of ponds and lakes where the spreading rhizomes may actually grow outwards, covering the water's edge with a dense undulating blanket. Over winter, the persistent erect black sporing fronds are a curiosity. Sterile fronds die down at the first frost. *O. sensibilis* can become invasive in suitable conditions. It is hardy to −30°C/−22°F. Plant in a damp site in part shade with, preferably, only two to three hours sun daily. Soil pH should be acid to near neutral, 5.0–6.5, with a high organic content. This fern is not recommended as a pot plant or for greenhouse culture. Plant out in early summer and water plentifully. Propagate by division.

***O. sensibilis*** L. SENSITIVE FERN; BEAD FERN. As for the genus. Occasionally naturalized in W Europe.

***O. orientalis*** Hook. See *Matteuccia orientalis*.
***O. struthiopteris*** (L.) Hoffm. See *Matteuccia struthiopteris*.

**Ononis** L. (Name used by Theophrastus.) REST-HARROW. Leguminosae (Papilionoideae). Some 75 species of annual or perennial herbs or dwarf shrubs, usually with glands, hairy. Leaves 3-foliolate, sometimes simple or imparipinnate; stipules adnate to the petiole; leaflets variable in shape, commonly toothed. Flowers in panicles, spikes or racemes; calyx campanulate, rarely tubular; corolla yellow, pink or purple, rarely white, keel ending in a beak; stamens 10, united. Fruit oblong or ovate, dehiscent. Summer. Canaries, Mediterranean, N Africa, Iran.

CULTIVATION *Ononis* spp. occur in dry, rocky or grassy habitats, often on calcareous soils; *O. natrix* is found to altitudes of 2100m/6825ft. They are small, generally summer-blooming plants grown for their loose racemes or slender panicles of flowers often carried over long periods; those of *O. speciosa*, considered the loveliest of the genus, are of a rich golden yellow, veined with dark red-purple; the flowers of the vigorous but short-lived *O. rotundifolia* are bright rose pink, the standard similarly streaked red. *O. fruticosa* is a compact, mound-forming shrub bearing its pretty soft pink blooms throughout the summer. *O. fruticosa, O. rotundifolia* and *O. speciosa* are suitable for the shrub and mixed borders; *O. natrix, O. aragonensis* and *O. repens* are particularly useful for planting on the tops of walls or on dry banks. Most are suitable in scale for the rock garden, although those species such as *O. repens*, which spreads by underground runners, are best confined to the wild garden, wild flower meadow and other naturalistic plantings; *O. repens* is a food plant for the Common Blue butterfly. *O. spinosa* is sometimes cultivated in the herbalist's garden.

*O. fruticosa, O. natrix* and *O. rotundifolia* are hardy to −15°C/5°F, *O. speciosa* to about −10°C/14°F. Grow in well-drained, neutral to alkaline (including shallow chalk) soils in full sun, giving *O. fruticosa* a sheltered position. Minimize root disturbance when planting. Propagate from scarified seed sown in spring or when ripe in autumn. Take care not to damage the developing taproot when pricking out. Alternatively, take softwood cuttings of the shrubby species in early summer and root in a closed case with bottom heat. Divide perennials shortly before growth recommences.

***O. aragonensis*** Asso Perenn. dwarf subshrub, to 30cm. Stems often tortuous, densely hairy above, sometimes with scattered short glandular hairs intermixed. Leaflets to 1cm, elliptic or suborbicular, obtuse or emarginate, leathery. Fls in long, loose, terminal panicles, primary branches 1–2-fld; pedicels to 4mm when present and jointed at base; cal. glandular-hairy, persistent, teeth 1.5–2.5× as long as tube; cor. to 18mm, yellow. Fr. to 8mm, ovate or rhombic, erect or spreading, glandular-hairy. Pyrenees, E & S Spain, Algeria. Z8.

***O. arvensis*** L. Resembles *O. aragonensis*, but pedicels not jointed, and cal. teeth 2.5–4× longer than tube. Perenn. herb to 1m, sometimes spiny, unarmed. Stems variably hairy, usually erect or ascending, not rooting at nodes. Lvs obtuse or acute, without glands beneath; leaflets to 2.5cm, elliptic to ovate. Fls borne usually in pairs at each node of the dense terminal raceme; cor. to 2cm, pink, standard hairy. Fr. to 9mm, about equal to the cal. Norway, E Germany, Albania. Sometimes considered synonymous with *O. spinosa* and united with it under the name *O. campestris*. Z6.

***O. cristata*** Mill. Perenn. to 25cm. Leaflets small, obovate,, margin denticulate. Fls solitary rose pink; peduncles much exceed lvs, glabrous. Fr. *c*1.2cm, slightly inflated. Summer. S Europe. Z7.

***O. fructicosa*** L. Resembles *O. rotundifolia*, but terminal leaflets subsessile. Dwarf shrub to 1m. Stems erect to 1m, usually many-fld, young stems short-pubesc. Lvs subsessile; leaflets to 2.5cm, oblong-lanceolate, subcoriaceous, glabrous. Infl. primary branches to 3cm; pedicels to 5mm; cor. to 2cm, pink. Fr. to 22mm. C & E Spain, C Pyrenees, SE France. Z7.

***O. minutissima*** L. Resembles *O. aragonensis* and *O. speciosa*, but pedicels not jointed, and cal. teeth 2.5–4× longer than tube. Deciduous dwarf shrub to 30cm. Stems often prostrate and rooting at nodes, subglabrous. Leaflets to 6mm, sessile oblong-oblanceolate to obovate. Infl. a dense terminal raceme with fls stalked, 1 per axil; cal. tube white, teeth long subulate, glabrous or short, glandular-hairy; cor. to 1cm, shorter than or equal to cal., yellow, standard glabrous. Fr. to 7mm; seeds 3–6, 2mm, smooth, brown. W Mediterranean to Yugoslavia. Z6.

***O. natrix*** L. Perenn. dwarf shrub, erect, many-branched. Stems to 60cm, woody at base, with dense glands and hairs. Lower lvs sometimes pinnate; leaflets variable, ovate to long and narrow. Fls in loose, leafy panicles, primary branches 1-fld; cor. to 2cm, yellow, often with violet or red veins. Fr. to 2.5cm. S & W Europe, N Spain. Z7.

***O. repens*** L. Closely resembles *O. spinosa*, but stems usually prostrate and ascending, often rooting. Leaflets usually ovate, obtuse or emarginate, to 3× longer than wide. Fls single, rarely paired, at each node, in loose leafy racemes; cal. densely hairy; cor. to 2cm, usually far exceeds cal., pink or purple. Fr. to 7mm. W & C Europe, E Sweden to Estonia, N Balkan Peninsula. Z6.

***O. rotundifolia*** L. Perenn. dwarf shrub, to 50cm, erect, branched. Stems villous and glandular. Leaflets 2.5cm, elliptic to orbicular, obtuse, roughly toothed, sparsely glandular, terminal leaflet with long petiolule. Infl. a panicle, branches to 6cm in fruit; pedicels to 0.6cm; cor. to 2cm, pink or white. Fr. to 3cm. Mainly mts, SE Spain to E Austria and C Italy. Z7.

***O. speciosa*** Lagasca. Closely resembles *O. aragonensis*, but leaflets shorter, and fls in dense spike-like panicle. Dwarf shrub, to 1m, erect or ascending. Stems with very short, dense, glandular hairs. Leaflets to 23mm, elliptic to suborbicular, subcoriaceous, glabrous, sticky, with sessile glands. Infl. a dense, oblong panicle, primary branches 1–3 fld, axis glandular-hairy; pedicels to 6mm; cor. to 2cm, golden-yellow. Fr. some 6mm. S Spain. Z7.

***O. spinosa*** L. Closely resembles *O. arvensis* but usually spiny, and fls usually 1 per node of the raceme. Dwarf shrub to 80cm. Stems usually spiny, sparsely glandular. Leaflets of variable shape. Fls single, rarely paired, at each node, in loose racemes; cal. glandular-pubesc., with short hairs at the mouth; cor. to 2cm, pink or purple, usually much exceeding cal. Fr. to 1cm. W, C & S Europe, S Norway, NW Ukraine. Z6.

***O. viscosa*** L. Annual to 80cm. Stems erect, eglandular, densely covered with soft hairs. Leaflets to 2cm, usually elliptic to obovate, obtuse. Infl. a panicle, primary branches 1-fld, to 2cm; cal. teeth 3-veined; cor. to 12mm, yellow, standard often veined red, wings with tooth on inner margin. Fr. to 2cm, flat or slightly inflated. Mediterranean, Portugal.

***O. altissima*** Colmeiro. See *O. arvensis*.
***O. antiquorum*** Willk. See *O. arvensis*.
***O. caduca*** Vill. See *O. arvensis*.
***O. campestris*** Koch and Ziz. See *O. spinosa* and *O. arvensis*.
***O. cenisia*** L. See *O. cristata*.
***O. dumosa*** Lapeyr. See *O. aragonensis*.
***O. hircina*** Jacq. See *O. arvensis*.
***O. procurrens*** Wallr. See *O. repens*.
***O. spinosa*** spp. *procurrens* (Wallr.) Briq. See *O. repens*.

**Onopordum** L. (Also spelt *Onopordon*; Latinized form of a Gk name, *Onopordon*.) Compositae. About 40 species of spiny, arachnoid biennials. Stem usually spiny-winged. Leaves armed, alternate, simple, pinnatilobed, pinnatifid to pinnatisect, rarely subentire. Capitula discoid, solitary or corymbose; involucre globose to hemispherical; phyllaries many in series, imbricate, spine-tipped, often recurved, leathery, glabrous to pubescent, sometimes glandular; florets tubular, hermaphrodite, maroon, rarely pink or white. Fruit a tetragonal, 4–5-ribbed, glabrous cypsela; pappus of rough or soft, deciduous hairs. Europe, Mediterranean, W Asia.

CULTIVATION *Onopordum* usually occurs in sunny and well-drained habitats; *O. acanthium* is found on slightly acid to calcareous soils, in hedgerow and on waste and cultivated ground to altitudes of 1500m/4875ft. They are magnificent biennials grown for their rosettes of viciously spiny but beautiful, densely downy foliage and for the imposing candelabra of nectar-rich, thistle flowers carried in the summer of their second year. *O. acaulon*, being stemless, is less imposing, but forms a fine low rosette of densely white woolly leaves, holding the white flowers at their centre. Given good drainage, most will tolerate temperatures to −15°C/5°F.

Grow in any fertile, well-drained, preferably slightly alkaline soil, in full sun. *O. acanthium* prefers heavier soils and will tolerate light shade. Unless deadheaded *Onopordum* spp. will self-seed, sometimes to the point of nuisance, however self-sown seedlings can provide a valuable source of replacement stock if moved when small. Propagate from seed in autumn or spring, sown *in situ* or in the cold frame; pot-grown plants should be planted out before the roots fill the pot, to avoid damage to the taproot. Slugs and snails may wilfully damage the leaves.

***O. acanthium*** L. To 3m. Stem yellow, pubesc., wings 2–4, with spines to 11mm. Lvs to 35×20cm, oblong-ovate to lanceolate or ovate, sessile, sinuate-dentate or pinnatilobed, lobes triangular, with an apical spine to 1cm, grey-green tinged grey and sparsely lanate above. Capitula solitary or in leafy, terminal clusters of 2–7; involucre to 3×6cm; phyllaries gradually tapering to a 5mm spine, minutely pubesc.; florets to 2.5cm, white or purple. Fr. 4–5mm; pappus 7–9mm, rough, pale-rufescent. Summer. W Europe to C Asia. Z6.

***O. acaulon*** L. Stem absent. Lvs to 40×12cm, in rosettes, oblong-oblanceolate to elliptic-lanceolate, petiolate, shallowly lobed to pinnatisect, lobes with apical spine to 1cm, white- to grey-lanate above, densely white-tomentose beneath. Capitula solitary or in clusters of 2–6, peduncles to 30mm; phyllaries to 4mm wide, ovate-lanceolate, apical spine to 12mm, glabrous; florets 2–2.5cm, white. Fr. 4–5mm; pappus 2–3cm, rough pale. Summer. Spain (mts), NW Africa. Z8.

***O. bracteatum*** Boiss. & Heldr. To 180cm. Stem white or tinged yellow, pubesc., wings 6–12, palmately spiny, spines to 7mm. Lvs to 30×8cm, oblong-lanceolate, sessile, pinnatisect to pinnatilobed, lobes triangular, palmate to dentate with an apical spine to 8mm. Capitula solitary or 2–4, peduncles to 4cm; involucre to 4×6cm; phyllaries to 1cm wide, broadly lanceolate, acuminate, apical spine to 8mm; florets 3–4cm, purple. Fr. 5–6mm; pappus 8–10mm, soft. Summer. E Mediterranean. Z6.

***O. illyricum*** L. To 130cm. Stems tinged yellow, pubesc., wings 2–12, spines to 7mm. Lvs to 55×15cm, sessile, oblong-lanceolate, pinnatifid to pinnatisect, lobes triangular-cuneate, entire lobulate or toothed, spiny. Capitula 1–4, peduncles 5–15cm; involucre to 5×6cm; phyllaries to 8mm wide, broadly lanceolate, tinged pink, attenuate to a 3–5mm spine, outer and middle phyllaries somewhat reflexed; florets 2.5–3.5cm, purple. Fr. 4–5mm; pappus 10–12mm soft. Summer. S Europe. Z7.

***O. macracanthum*** Schousb. To 1.5m. Stem white-lanate, wings to 10mm wide, spines to 5mm. Lvs 40×20cm, ovate-lanceolate to lanceolate, sessile, pinnatifid, lobes triangular-acute, each with apical spine to 6mm, densely tomentose, tinged grey above, white beneath. Capitula subglobose; involucre to 6cm; phyllaries 5–6mm wide, ovate-lanceolate, acuminate, spine to 7mm; florets 3cm, purple. Fr. 4–5mm; pappus 7–9mm, rough-rufescent. Summer. SE Portugal and S Spain. Z8.

***O. nervosum*** Boiss. To 3m. Stem tinged yellow, densely pubesc., wings to 2cm wide, densely reticulate-veined, spines to 1cm. Lvs to 50×20cm, oblong-lanceolate, sessile, strongly reticulate-veined beneath, veins pale, pinnatifid, lobes triangular, apical spine to 1cm, subglabrous above, sparsely wispy-hairy below. Capitula conical-ovoid; involucre to 5×5cm; phyllaries 4–6mm wide, ovate to lanceolate, acuminate, apical spine to 4mm; florets 3–3.5cm, pink. Fr. 4–5mm; pappus 8–10mm, soft. Summer. Portugal and Spain. Z8.

***O. salteri*** hort. To 2m, more or less viscid. Stem yellow-brown, wings 2–4 to 1.5cm wide, spines to 15mm. Lvs 25×10cm, oblong-lanceolate, sessile, pinnatilobed to pinnatifid, lobes triangular, remote apical spine to 8mm, rarely much longer, dark green, sparsely pubesc. above, more densely so beneath, especially on veins. Capitula in compound corymbs of 2–6; phyllaries 4–7mm wide, tapering to rigid spine to 4mm, outer usually deflexed; florets 2.5–3cm, purple-pink. Fr. 5–6mm; pappus 8–10mm, rough. Summer. SE Europe. Z8.

***O. arabicum*** hort. See *O. nervosum*.
***O. deltoides*** Ait. See *Synurus deltoides*.
***O. virens*** DC. See *O. tauricum*.

**Onosma** L. (From Gk *onos*, ass, and *osme*, smell: the plant is said to be liked by asses.) Boraginaceae. Some 150 species of hispid biennial and perennial herbs, often woody-based. Leaves usually numerous. Inflorescence of terminal cymes, usually branched, bracteate; calyx deeply 5-lobed, often accrescent, lobes equal, linear-lanceolate to ligulate or oblanceolate; corolla yellow, blue or purple, sometimes white or red, tubular to tubular-campanulate, shortly 5-lobed, with a basal annulus, throat scales absent; stamens included or exserted, inserted in corolla tube, anthers elongate, sagittate at base, terminated by elongate appendages; styles exserted, stigmas 2, capitate to bifid. Nutlets 4, erect, ovoid or triangular, acute or beaked, smooth or tuberculate. Mediterranean to E Asia.

CULTIVATION *Onosma* spp. dislike wet summers; those with hairy foliage are particularly prone to rot; care should be taken in the alpine house to avoid water on the foliage. *O. stellulatum, O. albo-roseum* and possibly other species with hairy leaves, may cause skin irritation in sensitive individuals; although the latter certainly deserves a place in sunny dry spots as an excellent ground cover with soft grey foliage and multi-coloured pastel flowers.

***O. albo-roseum*** Fisch. & Mey. Perenn. Stems to 25cm, erect or ascending, sometimes branched, setose. Lvs to 6×1.2cm, spathulate-lanceolate to obovate or oblong, acute to obtuse, green-white, densely setose, basal lvs petiolate, cauline lvs sessile. Infl. dense; bracts lanceolate to lanceolate-cordate; pedicels to 3mm; cal. to 16mm, lobes linear-lanceolate, densely pubesc.; cor. to 30mm, white to pink-purple, becoming deep purple or violet-blue, tubular-campanulate; anth. usually included. SW Asia. Z7.

***O. arenarium*** Waldst. & Kit. Perenn. or bienn. Stem to 70cm, much-branched, puberulent, setose. Basal lvs to 18×1.5cm, spathulate-oblong, densely setose and puberulent above. Infl. branched; pedicels to 4mm; cal. to 12mm in fl., to 18mm in fr.; cor. to 17mm, pale yellow, glabrous to puberulent. Nutlets to 3mm, lustrous, smooth. SE & C Europe. Z6.

***O. bourgaei*** Boiss. Perenn. Stems to 50cm, solitary to several, sometimes branched, patent-setose. Lvs oblong-spathulate to oblong-linear, subacute to obtuse, downy, basal lvs to 15×2cm, petiolate, cauline lvs to 9×1cm, sessile. Infl. of usually 2 cymes, weakly branched; bracts lanceolate, base cordate; pedicels to 1cm; cal. to 10mm in fl. lobes linear to linear-lanceolate, densely pubesc.; cor. to 15mm, pale yellow, cream or white, campanulate-clavate, pubesc.; anth. included. Nutlets to 3×2.5mm, ovoid, beaked, dark brown, dorsal keel inconspicuous. SW Asia. Z7.

***O. cassium*** Boiss. Perenn. Stems to 60cm, solitary, densely patent-setose, branches numerous. Lvs to 7×3cm, oblong to oblong-lanceolate, acute, densely patent-setose, white-tuberculate, cauline lvs sessile. Infl. elongate, subcorymbose; pedicels to 3mm in fl., to 10mm in fr.; cal. to 12mm in fl., to 16mm in fr., lobes linear, densely setose; cor. to 16mm, yellow, glabrous, subcylindrical, lobes revolute; anth. usually included. Nutlets to 5mm, pale brown, ovoid, subacute. SW Asia. Z8.

***O. echioides*** L. Perenn. Stems to 30cm, erect, tufted, sometimes slightly branched, stellate-setose, puberulent. Basal lvs to 6×0.7cm, oblong-linear or linear, subglabrous to densely stellate-setose, setae white, yellow or grey. Fls short-pedicellate; cal. to 10mm in fl., to 15mm in fr., tubercular-setose; cor. to 25mm, pale yellow, pubesc., base narrowed, apex cylindrical. Nutlets to 2.5mm, lustrous, smooth. SE Europe. Z7.

***O. emodi*** Wallich. Perenn. Stems to 50cm, usually several, decumbent or ascending, simple or branched above, hirsute. Lvs to 15×20cm, lanceolate or oblanceolate, acute, hispid, minutely strigose, cauline lvs sessile. Cymes clustered, usually forked; pedicels to 10mm, slender; cal. to 10mm, lobes triangular or triangular-lanceolate, acute; cor. to 13mm, base tubular, exterior hispid or villous, lobes to 1.5×2mm, recurved; fil. to 2mm, anth. to 5.5mm, included. Nutlets to 3mm, dull, tuberculate, minutely papillose. Himalaya. Z7.

***O. frutescens*** Lam. Perenn. Stems to 40cm, numerous, erect or ascending, simple, puberulent, patent-setose. Lvs to 7×1cm, lanceolate to oblong-lanceolate or linear, acute to obtuse, revolute, puberulent, patent-setose, sessile or short-petiolate. Infl. of 1 or 2 cymes, simple or slightly branched; pedicels to 5mm in fl., to 10mm in fr.; cal. to 15mm in fl., to 20mm in fr., lobes lanceolate, acute, hispid-setose; cor. to 20mm, pale yellow tinged purple, red or brown, campanulate-cylindric, glabrous; anth. exserted. Nutlets to 4mm, brown, ovoid, minutely beaked, smooth. SW Asia. Z8.

***O. helveticum*** (A. DC.) Boiss. Perenn. Stems to 50cm, several, erect, simple or branched above, puberulent, stellate-setose. Basal lvs to 7×0.6cm, spathulate-oblong, stellate-setose, puberulent. Fls short-pedicellate; cal. to 12mm in fl., to 17mm in fr., stellate-setose; cor. to 24mm, pale yellow, puberulent; anth. to 8mm. Nutlets to 4mm, lustrous, smooth. C Europe. Z6.

***O. heterophyllum*** Griseb. Perenn. Stems to 40cm, several, simple or branched, stellate-setose, puberulent. Basal lvs to 15×1cm, oblong to oblong-linear, stellate-setose throughout. Infl. of 1 to several cymes; pedicels to 2mm; cal. to 12mm in fl., to 15mm in fr., lobes linear-lanceolate, with simple and stellate setae; cor. to 30mm, pale yellow, tapered, puberulent; anth. included. Nutlets to 3mm, lustrous, smooth. SE Europe to SW Asia. Z6.

***O. hookeri*** Clarke. Perenn. Stems short, several, simple, hispid or hispid-villous. Basal lvs to 15×1.5cm, oblanceolate, acute, revolute, hispid or hispid-villous above, villous beneath, cauline lvs to 12×1.5cm, lanceolate or linear-lanceolate, acute or obtuse, base rounded. Cymes usually solitary, simple or forked; pedicels to 10mm; bracts lanceolate or subulate, inconspicuous; cal. to 22mm, lobes subulate, hispid or hispid-villous; cor. to 28mm, blue, sometimes purple or red, exterior villous; fil. to 6mm, linear, anth. to 8mm; style to 30mm, glabrous. Nutlets to 30mm, slightly rugose. Himalaya. Z7.

***O. nanum*** DC. Perenn. Stems to 18cm, erect, simple, puberulent, patent-setose. Basal lvs to 5.5cm, petiolate; cauline lvs to 2cm, linear to linear-spathulate, acute to obtuse, setose, velutinous, sessile. Infl. of 1 or 2 cymes; pedicels to 2mm; bracts ovate-lanceolate; cal. to 20mm, lobes linear, subacute; cor. to 25mm, white to yellow, becoming pink to blue or blue-purple, campanulate-cylindric, glabrous; anth. usually included. Nutlets to 3mm, pale grey, short-beaked. Turkey. Z8.

***O. pyramidale*** Hook. Bienn. Stems to 60cm, several, erect or ascending, branched above, hispid. Basal lvs to 20cm, oblanceolate, hispid; cauline lvs to 8×1.5cm, lanceolate, acute. Cymes simple or forked; pedicels 20mm, slender, hispid; cal. to 11mm, lobes linear-lanceolate, acute, hispid; cor. to 13mm, red, exterior minutely pubesc., interior mostly glabrous, lobes to 1×2mm, recurved; fil. to 6mm, subulate, basally villous, anth. to 5mm; style to 12mm, glabrous. Nutlets to 2mm, shiny, minutely rugose. Himalaya. Z7.

***O. sericeum*** Willd. Perenn. Stems to 30cm, 1 to several, erect or ascending, usually simple. Lvs to 10×3cm, lanceolate or obovate, acute; cauline lvs sericeous, sessile. Infl. of scorpioid cymes, becoming elongate; pedicels to 5mm in fr.; bracts to 7mm, linear to linear-lanceolate; cal. to 16mm in fl., to 30mm in fr., lobes lanceolate; cor. to 20mm, yellow, infundibular to clavate, puberulent; anth. included, truncate. Nutlets to 5×3.5mm, ovoid or ellipsoid, acute, smooth or minutely rugose. SW Asia. Z7.

***O. setosum*** Ledeb. Bienn. Stems to 60cm, erect, much-branched, hispid. Basal lvs to 10×1cm, linear to linear-lanceolate, densely setose. Infl. much branched; pedicels to 5mm; cal. to 30mm in fr.; cor. to 25mm, cream or pale yellow, glabrous. Nutlets to 6mm, minutely tuberculate. S Russia, Caucasus. Z6.

***O. sieheanum*** Hayek. Perenn. Stems to 45cm, erect, simple or branched above, patent-setose. Basal lvs narrowly lanceolate, attenuate, petiolate; cauline lvs to 6×0.6cm, linear-lanceolate or linear, acute, revolute, adpressed-setose. Cymes terminal or lateral, scorpioid; pedicels to 6mm; bracts narrowly linear-lanceolate; cal. to 17mm in fl., patent-setose; cor. orange or pale yellow, short-pubesc., lobes suberect; anth. included or exserted. Turkey. Z8.

***O. stellulatum*** Waldst. & Kit. Perenn. Stems to 25cm, simple, short-pubesc., stellate-setose. Basal lvs to 14×1.5cm, spathulate-oblong, sparingly stellate-setose. Pedicels to 14mm in fl.; cal. to 9mm, with simple or stellate setae; cor. to 18mm, light yellow, glabrous. Nutlets to 3mm, lustrous, smooth. Yugoslavia. Z6.

***O. tauricum*** Pall. ex Willd. Perenn. Stems to 30cm, several, tufted, usually simple, puberulent, stellate-setose. Lvs stellate-setose, puberulent, often white-green, basal lvs to 12×1cm, linear-oblong, acute, attenuate, petiolate, cauline lvs linear-oblong to linear-lanceolate, obtuse, sessile or subsessile. Cymes 1 or 2, terminal, pedicels to 5mm, cal. to 10mm in fl., to 18mm in fr., lobes linear, setose; cor. to 30mm, white to pale yellow, campanulate, glabrous; anth. included. Nutlets to 4mm, lustrous brown, smooth, short-beaked. SE Europe to SW Asia. Z6.

***O. tenuiflorum*** Willd. Perenn. Stems to 25cm, simple, ascending, pubesc. Lvs to 4×0.4cm, linear, obtuse, puberulent, setose. Cymes 1 or 2, terminal, many-fld; pedicels to 2mm; bracts linear, subacute; cal. to 8mm, lobes narrowly linear, densely pubesc.; cor. to 12mm, pale yellow, cylindrical, lobes acute, suberect, glabrous; anth. included. Nutlets to 3×2mm, grey to white-brown, slightly beaked. Caucasus, Turkey. Z6.

***O. caeruleum*** Willd. See *Moltkia caerulea*.
***O. decipiens*** Schott & Kotschy ex Boiss. See *O. nanum*.
***O. rupestre*** Bieb. See *O. tenuiflorum*.
***O. tubiflorum*** Velen. See *O. heterophyllum*.

**Onychium** Kaulf. (From Gk *onychion*, little claw, referring to the shape of the pinnae.) CLAW FERN. Pteridaceae (Cryptogrammataceae). Some 6 species of small terrestrial ferns. Rhizome creeping, or more often short and compact, paleate. Fronds 3–4-pinnate, finely cut, giving an open, lacy appearance, broad at base, ultimate pinnae reduced, glabrous, soft or subcoriaceous, veins frees except for a fertile commisure connecting tips. Sori continuous along both margins, covered by scarious, introrse marginal or submarginal indusium, so broad as to meet at the midrib, lacking paraphyses. Old World Tropics and Subtropics. Z10.

CULTIVATION Ferns for the frost-free glasshouse in bright filtered sunlight, best accommodated in shallow pans, or planted out where they will quickly colonize areas in the shade of other plants. For cultivation see FERNS. Growth is vigorous during summer, but many fronds will yellow and be shed during the autumn and winter months. Propagate by division, and will volunteer prolifically from spores where conditions are favourable.

***O. japonicum*** (Thunb.) Kuntze. CARROT FERN. Rhiz. to 4mm diam., creeping, often becoming invasive; scales to 3mm, broadly lanceolate, brown, membranous. Fronds 30+×15cm, triangular ovate-acuminate, 4-pinnatifid, deep green above, paler beneath, glabrous; stipes to 10–50cm, 1.5–3mm diam. near base, slender, pale green to straw-yellow, smooth, striate on upper side, tinged purple-brown toward base; lower pinnae to 15cm, obliquely ascending, alternate, gradually reduced toward apex, lanceolate-deltoid, long-acuminate, pinnules to 8mm, numerous, usually deltoid, ultimate divisions linear-mucronate, veins simple on sterile pinnules, pinnate on fertile. Japan.

***O. lucidum*** Spreng. Fronds 30cm+, ovate-acuminate, 3–4-pinnatifid, somewhat coriaceous, glossy; pinnules nearly uniform, narrow-linear, gradually acuminate, tapering below. E India, Nepal.

***O. siliculosum*** (Desv.) C. Chr. Rhiz. stout, scales lanceolate, spreading, brown. Fronds to 40cm, ovate, finely 3- or 4-pinnate, ultimate pinnules numerous, small and narrow, usually spathulate when sterile, to 5mm, often dentate at apex, small than fertile pinnules, linear, entire, acuminate. India to China, south to Malaya, Philippines.

***O. auratum*** Kaulf. See *O. siliculosum*.

**Oophytum** N.E. Br. (From Gk *oon*, egg, and *phyton*, plant, referring to the egg-shaped plant bodies.) Aizoaceae. 2 species of highly succulent perennials, distinguished from *Conophytum* by the fleshy, not membranous, calyx tube, forming dense mats of closely packed, soft, ovoid bodies which are concealed during the resting period by the dry white membranes of the old leaves. Flowers mostly white. S Africa (Cape Province). Z9.

CULTIVATION As for *Conophytum*.

***O. nanum*** (Schltr.) L. Bol. To 2cm; bodies spherical, 5–7mm across, minutely papillose. Fls 1cm diam., white with reddened tips. Cape: Van Rhynsdorp District.

***O. oviforme*** (N.E. Br.) N.E. Br. Bodies 12–20mm tall, olive-green, often flame-coloured, glossy-papillose; fissure 10–12mm across, small and only slightly gaping. Fls 22mm diam., white below, purple-pink above. Cape: Van Rhynsdorp District.

For synonymy see *Conophytum*.

**Ophiocolea** H. Perrier. (From Gk *ophis*, snake; this genus differs from *Colea* in its elongate fruit.) Bignoniaceae. 5 species of shrubs closely related to *Colea*. Stems simple or little-branched. Leaves imparipinnate, in whorls of 3–7 with smaller whorls of leafy bracts on stem above leaves. Flowers in racemes or panicles of cymes, usually borne on stem; corolla tubular-campanulate; stamens 4, didynamous, with a fifth minute staminode; disc cupular, thick; ovary linear, smooth, bilocular; ovules 2-seriate. Fruit 40–60cm, cylindrical, fleshy, pendent, undulate, many-seeded. Madagascar, Comoro Is. Z10.

CULTIVATION As for *Crescentia*.

***O. floribunda*** (Bojer ex Lindl.) H. Perrier. To 12m. Pinnae 15cm, 7–17 per lf, on lvs in terminal whorls from stem, subsessile, entire. Infl. borne on old wood just above previous year's lf scars, infl., cal., cor. and young fr. pubesc., sometimes glabrous, cor. tube hairy inside at base of stamens; cal. 4–6mm; cor. 2–5cm, tubular-campanulate, gradually or suddenly expanded from narrow tube, tube bright orange-yellow, lobes often white. Madagascar.

For synonymy see *Colea*.

**OPHIOGLOSSACEAE** (R. Br.) Agardh. See *Botrychium*, *Helminthostachys*, *Ophioglossum*.

**Ophioglossum** L. ADDER'S TONGUE FERN. (From Gk *ophis*, a snake, and *glossa*, tongue, referring to the shape of the fertile spikes.) Ophioglossaceae. 30–50 species of largely terrestrial ferns, several tropical species epiphytic. Rhizomes short, bulbous. Fronds solitary or few, erect, or in epiphytic species, dangling, simple, succulent. Sporangia in 2 ranks or tiered on a long-stalked, flattened spike, coalescent with age, spike forming an offshoot of the sterile frond or entirely separate from it. Cosmopolitan. Prothalli of this genus are invaded by a symbiotic mycorrhizal fungus in the same way as are *Botrychium* prothalli.)

CULTIVATION Fern allies distributed throughout the world in a wide range of habitats, from alpine grassland to tropical rainforest as terrestrials or epiphytes, in full sun or shade. Originating from such a wide range of habitats, a single formula for growing this genus is difficult to give. *O. palmatum* and *O. pendulum* are epiphytic and require warm glasshouse conditions. Both resent disturbance and find their way into cultivation on their support plant, usually *Platycerium*. It is thought that both are highly dependent upon a mycorrhizal association. *O. lusitanicum* and *O. vulgatum* are terrestrial in grassland, and hardy to −15°C/5°F. Growing through the winter months, they may naturalized in meadowland, or can be cultivated in the border where they must be left undisturbed; they can be difficult to establish. *O. petiolatum* and *O. reticulatum* are pantropical terrestrials colonizing grassland and verges. Easily cultivated in the warm glasshouse in shallow pans of terrestrial ferns mix. Their fronds are irresistible to insect and mollusc pests, and hanging the containers out of reach is often their only escape. Propagation is by division of the brittle rhizomes. Spores have rarely been successfully germinated.

***O. engelmannii*** Prantl. Terrestrial fern, 5–20cm. Rhizome sheathed by persistent old frond bases; stipes to 10cm, usually about 5cm. Fronds 2–5, usually 5–7×2–3cm, elliptic to oblong, acute at each end, apiculate, veins forming large areoles. Fertile panicle 1–3.5cm×3mm, on peduncle 6–9cm; sporangia to 0.5–1mm diam. N America (S Canada to Mexico). Z4.

***O. lusitanicum*** L. Rhiz. somewhat tuberous. Fronds 12–24×4mm, with sterile portion lanceolate to linear-lanceolate, rather obtuse at apex, cuneately narrowed towards base; fertile spike 6–12mm, linear, on firm peduncle 1–4cm when mature, arising nearly at base of sterile portion. Mediterranean and Caucasus. Z6.

***O. palmatum*** L. Epiphytic. Rhiz. cylindric, 1–2.5cm long, densely clothed with yellow-brown hairlike scales bearing many fleshy roots; stipes flaccid, succulent, 15–30cm. Frond blades 20–75cm, arching-pendent, obdeltate, palmately lobed, lobes 2–10, often unequal, simple and entire or occasionally forked, bright green; veining irregularly hexagonal. Sporophylls to 15 per frond, in a row towards top of stipe below sterile lamina, on individual stalks to 5cm bearing linear-oblong spikes to 3cm; sporangia 10–60 per fertile spike; spores tinged yellow. Tropical America, Madagascar, SE Asia. Z10.

***O. pendulum*** L. RIBBON FERN. Epiphytic, rhiz. creeping, white. Fronds 30cm–4.5m×3–8cm, pendent, strap-like, simple or forked, generally exceeding fertile spike, fleshy, brittle, generally twisted, lacking a distinct stem. Fertile spike pendent, inserted near base of sterile blade, generally solitary, cylindric, 5–15cm, succulent, ribbed, peduncle shorter than spike. Australasia, Asia, Polynesia. Z10.

***O. petiolatum*** Hook. Rhiz. erect, fleshy; stipes 10–20cm, occasionally to 30cm. Fronds 1.5–6×1–3cm, simple or occasionally forked at apex, ovate to broadly ovate or oblong, entire, veins reticulate, areoles rather large without intermediate veinlets. Fertile spike terminal, simple, pedunculate; sporangia marginal, coalescent in 2 ranks. Summer. Tropical Asia, Japan, Korea, Polynesia, Tropical America. Z10.

***O. reticulatum*** L. Rhiz. erect, cylindric, 0.5–2cm long, bearing persistent thick roots. Fronds 5–8×4–5cm, solitary or occasionally in pairs, deltate-ovate to reniform, cordate-lobed at base, veins distinct. Fertile spikes inserted above middle of sterile blade, 2–5cm long, on slender peduncle 7–15cm, greatly exceeding sterile portion; sporangia 20–60 pairs per fertile spike. Pantropical. Z10.

***O. vulgatum*** L. Terrestrial fern to 35cm; rhiz. not tuberous; stipes 5–12cm. Fronds 15–22cm, sterile portion 5–10×2–5cm, ovate to oblong-elliptic, sessile or distinctly stalked, venation regularly areolate. Fertile spike 1–4cm×2–3mm, inserted near middle of sterile frond, greatly exceeding sterile frond when mature, on 7–14cm peduncle; sporangia 1mm diam. Europe, W Asia, N America.

**Ophionella** P.V. Bruyns.
***O. arcuata*** (N.E. Br.) P.V. Bruyns. See *Pectinaria arcuata*.

**Ophiopogon** Ker-Gawl. (From Gk *ophis*, serpent, and *pogon*, beard.) Liliaceae (Convallariaceae). 4 species of perennial, evergreen herbs. Leaves linear, grasslike, usually sessile. Flowers white to lilac, numerous in racemes; tepals 6, overlapping, white, blue, lilac or lilac-tinted, tube obconical, adnate to inferior ovary (cf. *Liriope*); stamens 6, joined at base to tepals, filaments very short, anthers pointed. Fruit blue, berry-like.

CULTIVATION The clump-forming *O. jaburan*, especially attractive in its variegated forms 'Aureo-variegatus' and 'Argenteo-vittatus', is suitable for border edging and for rock gardens in essentially frost-free zones. In cooler areas it may be used as seasonal bedding, lifted before first frosts and stored cool and almost dry for the winter, or grown permanently as a pot plant for the windowsill or cool glasshouse. *O. japonicus* and *O. planiscapus*, with the black-leaved *O. p.* 'Nigrescens', are hardier, with shelter and good drainage surviving outside in zones where winter temperatures may fall to −15°C/5°F and occasionally to −20°C/−4°F and below; although they may suffer cosmetic damage in winter grow usually resumes unchecked in spring. They are grown as dense groundcover and are particularly valuable for erosion control. *O. japonicus* is also grown as a submerged, but then non-flowering aquatic.

Grow in sun, where soils remain sufficiently moist during the growing season, or in partial shade, in any moderately fertile, well-drained soil. Plants for groundcover require spacings at 15–20cm/6–8in. apart. Under glass, grow *O. jaburan* in a porous potting medium, water moderately and maintain a winter minimum temperature of 5–10°C/40–50°F. Propagate by ripe seed sown fresh in a sandy propagating mix in the cold frame, or by division.

***O. intermedius*** D. Don. Tufted. Lvs to 60×0.5cm, linear, margins serrulate toward base. Flowers 1cm wide, white to lilac, numerous, in a loose raceme. China. 'Argenteomarginatus': lvs edged white; fls white.

***O. jaburan*** (Kunth) Lodd. Close to *O. japonicus*, but more robust. Plants tufted, roots cord-like, not tuberous. Lvs to 60×0.5cm, linear, sometimes variegated white. Flowering stem to 60cm; fls tinted lilac or white in a dense raceme 7.5–15cm long. Fr. violet-blue, oblong. Japan. 'Aureo-variegatus': lvs striped yellow. 'Caeruleus': fls violet. 'Crow's White': lvs variegated white; fls white. 'Vittatus' ('Argenteo-vittatus', 'Javanensis', 'Variegatus'): lvs symmetrically arranged, pale green striped and edged creamy white; fls white. 'White Dragon': lvs boldly striped white, almost no green. Z7.

***O. japonicus*** (L. f.) Ker-Gawl. Stolons large, subterranean; roots tuberous. Lvs to 40×0.3cm, base narrow-linear, rather rigid, dark green, somewhat curved. Flowering stem 5–10cm, fls white to light lilac in a loose, short raceme. Fr. blue, 0.5cm diam. Japan. 'Albus': fls white. 'Compactus': miniature, dense, to 5cm. 'Kyoto Dwarf': tightly clumped, to 4cm; lvs narrow, dark green. 'Minor': compact, to 8cm; lvs curling, black-green. 'Nanus': small, to 12cm. 'Silver Dragon': lvs variegated white. Z7.

***O. planiscapus*** Nak. Often stoloniferous; root thickened. Lvs to 35×0.3–0.5cm, linear. Fls white or lilac, 6.5cm, in racemes. Fr. dull blue. Japan. 'Nigrescens' ('Arabicus', 'Black Dragon', 'Ebony Knight'): to 15cm; lvs curving, purple-black, lined silver-green at base when young; fls white tinted pink to lilac; fr. black. Z6.

***O. intermedius*** var. ***argenteomarginatus*** D. Don. See *O. intermedius* 'Argenteomarginatus'.
***O. spicatus*** D. Don. See *O. intermedius*.
For further synonymy see *Liriope*.

**Ophrys** L. (From Gk *ophrys*, referring to a plant with two leaves.) Orchidaceae. Some 30 species of terrestrial, herbaceous orchids. Tubers 2–3, smooth, fleshy, globose or ovoid. Leaves in a loose basal rosette and on flowering stems. Spike erect, clothed with, ultimately, bract-like leaves; sepals 3, glabrous, green-yellow to rose or white, spreading or reflexed, oblong or ovate; petals 2, usually narrower than sepals; lip flat, concave or convex, entire to trilobed, velvety above often with glabrous, shiny, mirror-like patch (speculum), sometimes with swelling below and apical appendage, spurless. Europe, N Africa, W Asia. Pollination is by pseudo-copulation: male insects are attracted by the highly-specialized mimicry of the flowers and a scent resembling female pheremones. Tubers used for salep in E Europe, Middle East.

CULTIVATION See ORCHIDS, The Hardy Species.

***O. apifera*** Huds. BEE ORCHID. Stems to 50cm. Basal lvs ovate to lanceolate, acute. Spike lax, 2–11-fld; sep. 8–15mm, oblong-ovate, spreading or deflexed, green or purple-violet, rarely white, with green longitudinal veins; pet. green or purple, triangular to linear-lanceolate or oblong, slightly revolute; lip 10–13mm, trilobed, central lobe broadly ovate, convex, margins dark red-brown, sometimes ochre or bicolour, recurved, velvety, appendage deflexed, yellow, sometimes absent, lateral lobes to 3mm, triangular-ovate, villous, speculum red-brown with yellow apical spots and margins. Mid spring–mid summer. W & C Europe. Z7.

***O. araneola*** Rchb. To 45cm. Lvs 5–9, ovate-lanceolate. Bracts exceed ovary; fls 6–10; sep. 6–10mm, green, revolute; pet. 4–8mm, green single-veined; lip 5–8mm, obscurely trilobed, pale to dark brown or olive green, entire, velvety, speculum blue, glabrous, loosely H-shaped. Spring–early summer. S & SC Europe. Z7.

***O. bertolonii*** Moretti. To 35cm. Leaves 5–7, ovate-lanceolate to lanceolate, acute. Spike 3–8-fld; sep. 8–10mm, deep pink-lilac, basally tinted green; pet. 4–6mm, linear-lanceolate, lilac; lip 10–13mm, entire or trilobed, concave, deep purple-black, velvety, speculum blue-violet, paler at edges; apical appendage yellow, margins glabrous. Late spring. S & C Europe. Z7.

***O. bombyliflora*** Link. Stems to 25cm. Basal lvs 4–6, oblong-lanceolate. Spike lax, 5–14-fld; sep. 9–12mm, green, ovate, obtuse, lateral sep. spreading or deflexed; pet. 3–4mm, triangular, purple at base, green at apex, velvety; lip to 10mm, trilobed, lobes deflexed appearing globose-inflated at tips, dark brown, velvety, speculum blue-violet with paler margin. Late spring–early summer. Mediterranean. Z8.

***O. fusca*** Link. Stems to 40cm. Basal lvs 4–6, oblong-lanceolate to ovate. Spike lax, 1–10-fld; sep. 9–11mm, oblong or ovate, dorsal slightly incurved forming loose hood, lateral sep. spreading, green to yellow-green, rarely pink; pet. linear to linear-oblong, two-thirds sep. length, green, yellow or light brown; lip 10–15mm trilobed, flat or convex, lateral lobes oblong-ovate (sometimes obscure), central lobe reniform, ovate, notched or bilobed, maroon, velvety above, speculum 2-segmented, iridescent blue, violet or brown, margin sometimes white or yellow. Mid–late spring. Mediterranean, SW Romania. Z7.

***O. holoserica*** (Burm. f.) Greuter. LATE SPIDER ORCHID. Stems to 55cm. Basal lvs 3–7, ovate-oblong. Spike lax, 6–14-fld; bracts exceeding ovary; sep. 9–13mm, ovate-oblong, dorsal slightly incurved, bright pink to magenta or white with green mid-vein; pet. triangular, rarely linear-lanceolate, half sep. length, pink to rose-purple, velvety; lip 9–16mm, ovate to obovate, entire, rarely incised or trilobed, dark brown to dark maroon or ochre, velvety, sometimes edged yellow, central projections minute, appendage upcurved, often 3-toothed. Late spring–mid summer. Europe, Mediterranean, USSR. Z6.

***O. insectifera*** L. FLY ORCHID. Stems to 50cm, slender. Lvs 7–9, linear-lanceolate, along ascending stem. Spike lax, 2–14-fld; bracts exceeding ovary; sep. 6–8mm, oblong-ovate, slightly concave, spreading, dorsal incurved; pet. 4–6mm, linear, revolute, violet-black, velvety; lip 9–10mm, trilobed, central lobe emarginate, flat or concave, ovate, violet-black or purple, paler at tip, sometimes with yellow margin, lateral lobes spreading, speculum reniform or rectangular, pale blue or violet. Late spring–summer. Europe inc. Scandinavia. Z6.

**Ophrys** (×1) (a) *O. vernixia* (a1) ssp. *lusitanica* (b) *O. lutea* (b1) ssp. *melena* (b2) ssp. *murbeckii* (c) *O. fusca* (c1) ssp. *omegaifera* (c2) *O. iricolor* (c3) *O. fusca* ssp. *durieui* (d) *O. sphegodes* (d1) ssp. *planimaculata* (d2) ssp. *aesculapii* (d3) *O. araneola*, (d4) *O. sphegodes* ssp. *provincialis* (d5) ssp. *atrata* (d6) ssp. *mammosa* (d7) ssp. *spruneri* (e) *O. ferum-equinum* (f) *O. bertolonii* (g) *O. argolica* (h) *O. reinholdii* (h1) ssp. *straussii* (i) *O. cretica* (j) *O. scolopax* (j1) ssp. *apiformis* (j2) ssp. *cornuta* (j3) ssp. *heldreichii* (k) *O. carmeli* (l) *O. holoserica* (l1) ssp. *maxima* (l2) ssp. *candica* (l3) ssp. *oxyrrhynchos* (l4) ssp. *exaltata* (m) *O. arachnitiformis* (3 forms) (n) *O. apifera* (o) *O. tenthredinifera* (p) *O. bombyliflora* (q) *O. insectifera*

***O. iricolor*** Desf. To 30cm. Basal lvs 3–4, ovate to ovate-lanceolate. Spike 1–4-fld; sep. to 12mm, oblong to ovate, yellow-green; pet. to 9mm, ligulate, olive or bronze, sometimes with small projections; lip to 25mm, trilobed, slightly convex, margins recurved, lateral lobes deep maroon, velvety, brown, glabrous beneath, speculum iridescent metallic blue. Late winter–late spring. Mediterranean. Z8.

***O. lutea*** Cav. YELLOW BEE ORCHID. To 40cm. Basal lvs 3–5, ovate or ovate-lanceolate, acute. Spike lax, 1–7-fld; bracts exceeding ovary; sep. 9–10mm, green, ovate to oblong-ovate, dorsal sep. incurved; pet. linear-oblong, obtuse, yellow-green, one-third to half sep. length; lip 12–18mm, oblong, dark brown to purple-black with a flat, yellow border to 3mm deep, lateral lobes ovate, mid-lobe reniform, emarginate to spreading-emarginate, speculum entire or bilobed, iridescent metallic grey-blue. Late winter–late spring. Mediterranean. Z8.

***O. scolopax*** Cav. WOODCOCK ORCHID. To 45cm. Basal lvs 5–6, lanceolate to oblong-lanceolate. Spike 3–10-fld; sep. 8–12mm, oblong to ovate, pink to mauve; pet. lanceolate to triangular, pink or red, one-fifth to half sep. length; lip 8–12mm, midlobe ovate, brown to black-purple, velvety, margins recurved, glabrous, lateral lobes triangular, dark brown with basal projections, speculum circular or loosely X-shaped, blue or violet, edged yellow or white, spotted dark brown. Early–late spring. S Europe. Z8.

***O. sphegodes*** Mill. EARLY SPIDER ORCHID. Stems 10–45cm. Basal lvs 5–9, ovate-lanceolate. Spike to 10-fld, lax; sep. 6–12mm, oblong-ovate to lanceolate, dorsal sep. narrowest, green, rarely white or purple; pet. half sep. length, oblong-triangular to lanceolate, green to purple-green or brown-red, 1–3-veined, often undulate; lip ovate, rich maroon-chocolate brown, velvety, margins patent or deflexed, speculum H-shaped, maroon or deep indigo, often bordered yellow. Spring. Europe. Z6.

***O. tenthredinifera*** Willd. SAWFLY ORCHID. To 45cm. Basal lvs 3–9, ovate to lanceolate. Spike lax, 3–8-fld; sep. 6–14×10mm, ovate, concave, lilac to pale rose, often veined green; pet. triangular, one-third to half sep. length, rose purple to pink, velvety, obtuse; lip 8–14mm, entire or obscurely trilobed, obovate or oblong with basal swelling, brown-purple, velvety, margin hirsute, yellow to green, pale brown or maroon, speculum small, grey-blue bordered yellow or white, bilobed, sometimes spotted brown. Late spring–early summer. Mediterranean. Z8.

***O. vernixia*** Brot. To 50cm. Basal lvs 3–5, oblong-lanceolate. Fls 2–15; sep. 6–8mm, oblong, green to purple-brown, forming hood; pet. purple-brown, lanceolate, one-third to half sep. length; lip to 13mm, trilobed, round or linear, margins revolute, brown to brown-purple, villous, speculum almost covering lobes, glabrous iridescent blue bordered yellow. Late spring–early summer. Mediterranean, N Africa. Z8.

***O. arachnites*** (L.) Reichard. See *O. holoserica*.
***O. ciliata*** Biv. See *O. vernixia*.
***O. fuciflora*** (F.W. Schmidt) Moench. See *O. holoserica*.
***O. fusca*** ssp. ***iricolor*** (Desf.) K. Richt. See *O. iricolor*.
***O. litigiosa*** Camus. See *O. araneola*.
***O. muscifera*** Huds. See *O. insectifera*.
***O. speculum*** Link. See *O. vernixia*.
***O. sphegodes*** ssp. ***litigiosa*** (Camus) Bech. See *O. araneola*.

**Ophthalmophyllum** Dinter & Schwantes.
***O. schlechteri*** Schwantes. ex Jacobsen. See *Conophytum maughanii*.
***O. triebneri*** Schwantes. ex Jacobsen. See *Conophytum friedrichiae*.

**Opithandra** B.L. Burtt. (From Gk *opithe*, behind, and *aner*, man, stamen; only the postero-lateral stamens are fertile.) Gesneriaceae. 6 species of acaulescent herbs. Leaves radical, usually dentate, petiolate. Flowers in an umbellate inflorescence, on scape-like, axillary peduncles; calyx 5-partite, segments lanceolate; corolla purple-violet, tube elongate, limb 2-lipped, upper lip 2-lobed, lower lip 3-lobed, lobes spreading or erect; stamens 2, extrorse, included, filaments straight, inserted on corolla tube; ovary superior, stigma 2-lobed. Fruit a capsule. E Asia. Z10.

CULTIVATION See GESNERIADS.

***O. primuloides*** (Miq.) B.L. Burtt. Densely pubesc. rhizomatous perenn. Lvs to 10×7cm, ovate, elliptic or orbicular, obtuse, cordate at base, grey-green, sharply toothed. Fls in a 10-fld infl. on peduncles to 20cm; pedicels to 3cm; cal. to 5mm, seg. linear-lanceolate; cor. to 2cm, pale purple-violet, purple-striate, exterior downy, tube slightly recurved at base, upper lobes erect or reflexed. Fr. to 4.5cm, glabrous. Summer. Japan.

**Oplismenus** Palib. (From Gk *hoplismenos*, armed, referring to the awned spikelets.) Gramineae. Some 5 species of trailing annual or perennial grasses. Stems flimsy, leafy. Leaves lanceolate to ovate, flat; ligules very short, ciliate. Inflorescence unilateral, few to several, spicate racemes on a common axis; spikelets paired, 2-flowered, laterally flattened, lower spikelet reduced, abscising at maturity; upper flower hermaphrodite, lower flower sterile or male; glumes subequal, to half length of spikelet, awned, awns sticky; lower lemma acute to awned, upper lemma crested, acute, flexible. Tropics, subtropics. Most species formerly in *Panicum* L. Z9.

CULTIVATION Found in forest shade in tropical zones, *Oplismenus* spp. are grown in temperate areas in hanging baskets and as low edging in the warm glasshouse or conservatory. *O. hirtellus* 'Variegatus' is the most commonly grown in these situations and an excellent plant for glasshouse bedding and underplanting. Grow in any moderately fertile and moisture-retentive potting mix in bright indirect light or filtered light and water plentifully when in growth. Maintain a minimum temperature of 15°C/60°F. *O. undulatifolius* is the hardiest species, grown in favoured gardens outdoors, tolerating several degrees of short-lived frost. Propagate by division of rooted stems.

***O. burmannii*** (Retz.) Palib. Annual, glabrous to pubesc., to 50cm. Stems leafy, slender, procumbent. Lvs lanceolate to elliptic, to 6cm×1.8cm, acuminate. Infl. to 10cm; racemes to 8, tightly clustered, bristled, erect or spreading; spikelets oblong-lanceolate, to 0.3cm; glumes awned, to 1cm. Summer–winter. Tropics. 'Albidus': lvs white with a pale green median stripe.

***O. compositus*** (L.) Palib. Creeping, procumbent perenn., resembling *O. hirtellus* but stems more robust, spikelets longer. Lvs narrow-elliptic to ovate, to 15×2.5cm. Infl. racemose, to 30cm; spikelets borne in fascicles to 10, to 10cm; glumes subequal, lanceolate to lanceolate-oblong. Africa, Asia, Polynesia.

***O. hirtellus*** (L.) Palib. Evergreen perenn., to 90cm+. Stems procumbent, flimsy, becoming erect, rooting at nodes. Lvs narrow-lanceolate to ovate, to 5cm×1.3cm, acuminate, pubesc.; sheaths glabrous to pubesc. Infl. to 15cm; racemes to 10, densely arranged, to 2.5cm; spikelets lanceolate-oblong to oblong, to 0.3cm, glabrous to sparsely pubesc.; lower glume awned, awn to 1cm; upper glume short-awned. Summer–winter. Tropical America, Africa, Polynesia. 'Variegatus' ('Vittatus'): lvs striped white, sometimes tinted pink.

***O. undulatifolius*** (Ard.) Beauv. Lvs small, ovate, strongly undulate to puckered. Tropics & Subtropics.

***O. bromoides*** (Lam.) Palib. See *O. burmannii*.
***O. imbecillus*** Roem. & Schult. See *O. hirtellus*.
***O. loliaceus*** (Lam.) HBK. See *O. hirtellus*.
For further synonymy see *Panicum*.

**Oplopanax** (Torr. & A. Gray) Miq. (From Gk *hoplon*, a weapon, and *Panax*, referring to the spiny stems.) Araliaceae. 3 species of deciduous, densely spiny, coarse suckering shrubs, with branching stems to 1m or so; prickles to 1.3cm. Leaves simple, bright green, palmately veined and more or less lobed, variously toothed, glabrous above, usually slightly hairy beneath. Inflorescences near branch ends, paniculate, at least partly racemiform, 1× compound, narrowly conic, woolly, peduncles gradually shortening towards its apex, each with a papery bract at base; flowers green-white, in small umbel-like clusters; calyx rim very short, obscurely 5-toothed; petals 5, valvate; stamens 5; ovary 2-locular, the styles mostly free, incurved at the tip, arising from a flattened disc. Fruit drupaceous, red, round, laterally somewhat compressed, smooth, remaining inferior through maturity; pyrenes 2; endosperm uniform. Late spring and early summer. NE Asia, N America. Z5.

CULTIVATION *O. horridus* is the most commonly cultivated species, hardy down to at least −15°C/5°F, although the young growth is likely to be cut back by spring frosts. It will tolerate maritime exposures. On cool moist soils it forms tall, impenetrable thickets of bold, rather maple-like foliage adorned with attractive red fruits. Site this species where its exotic foliage can be seen to best effect but its irritant spines are out of reach, preferably in semi-wild, damp and shady regions of a large plot. It resents neither disturbance nor pruning. Plant in sun or part-shade and propagate from seed in autumn, by sucker and root cuttings.

***O. elatus*** (Nak.) Nak. Lvs 5–7-lobed, to 30cm diam.; petiole to 16cm; lobes relatively shallow, as in some states of *O. horridus*, closely double-serrate, venation bristly-pubesc. beneath. Infl. to 18cm; peduncles to 6cm; pedicels finally to 10mm. Fr. obovate in outline, to 12mm, with persistent style branches. China (Kirin), Korea, Soviet Far East (Primorya). Z5.

***O. horridus*** (Sm.) Miq. DEVIL'S-CLUB. Stems often forming dense thickets. Lvs shallowly or deeply 5–13-lobed, to 35×40cm, conspicuously and irregularly serrate. Infl. somewhat shorter than lvs, to 20cm; peduncles to 5cm; pedicels finally to 8mm. Fr. to 7mm diam. Central & western N America (especially Pacific Coast). Z4.

***O. japonicus*** (Nak.) Nak. As *O. horridus* but lvs somewhat smaller and more deeply lobed, with the base sometimes peltate; lobes long-acute and sinuses deep. Japan. Z6.

For synonymy see *Echinopanax*.

**Oophytum** N.E. Br.
***O. aquosum*** (L. Bol.) N.E. Br. See *Mesembryanthemum hypertrophicum*.
***O. dactylinum*** (Welw. ex Oliv.) N.E. Br. See *Mesembryanthemum cryptanthum*.
***O. forskahlii*** (Hochst.) N.E. Br. See *Mesembryanthemum cryptanthum*.

**Opsiandra** Cook.
***O. maya*** Cook. See *Gaussia maya*.

**×Opsistylis**. *(Vandopsis × Rhynchostylis.)* Orchidaceae. These intergeneric crosses can be large or small plants depending on which *Vandopsis* species is used as the parent. Stems upright, leaves alternate, in 2 rows, narrowly channelled. Inflorescences axillary, on upright spikes, flowers round with flat sepals and petals and a small lip, usually very intensely coloured. The plants need bright light, high humidity and warm temperatures to grow and flower well. They grow extremely well out of doors in the humid tropics but are less easy in the glasshouse. The large plants in which *Vandopsis gigantea* is a parent soon become unwieldy, while those bred from *Vandopsis parishii* are much smaller and have very desirable flowers.

× *O.* Kultana: spreading or upright infl. of many well-spaced fls; fls basically ochre-yellow overlaid with coalescing spots of deep wine red, white surrounding the mauve column, lip bright mauve-purple.

× *O.* Lanna Thai: small plants; upright spikes of small fls, intense burgundy red with white centre surrounding the column.

**Opthalmophyllum** Dinter & Schwantes.
***O. acutum*** Tisch. See *Conophytum acutum*.
***O. carolii*** (Lavis) Tisch. See *Conophytum carolii*.
***O. edithae*** (N.E. Br.) Tisch. See *Conophytum pillansii*.
***O. friedrichiae*** (Dinter) Dinter & Schwantes. See *Conophytum friedrichiae*.
***O. herrei*** Lavis. See *Conophytum longum*.
***O. littlewoodii*** L. Bol. See *Conophytum devium*.
***O. longum*** Tisch. See *Conophytum longum*.
***O. lydiae*** Jacobsen. See *Conophytum lydiae*.
***O. maughanii*** (N.E. Br.) Schwantes. See *Conophytum maughanii*.
***O. noctiflorum*** L. Bol. See *Conophytum maughanii*.
***O. verrucosum*** Lavis. See *Conophytum verrucosum*.

**Opulaster** Medik. ex Rydb.
***O. alternans*** Heller. See *Physocarpus alternans*.
***O. bracteatus*** Rydb. See *Physocarpus bracteatus*.
***O. glabratus*** Rydb. See *Physocarpus glabratus*.

**Opuntia** Mill. (A pre-Linnaean name for some kind of spiny plant associated with the ancient Greek town of Opus, or the surrounding region, known as Eastern or Opuntian Locris, between Thermopylae and Thebes.) PRICKLY PEAR; TUNA. Cactaceae. Over 200 species of trees and shrubs, some low and caespitose; stems segmented; segments cylindric, club-shaped, subglobose, or more or less flattened, sometimes tuberculate, very rarely ribbed; leaves present, terete or subulate, usually small, caducous; glochids present; spines acicular, subulate or papery, usually 1 to many, sometimes sheathed and barbed, rarely 0. Flowers lateral or subterminal, rarely terminal, usually solitary, diurnal; floral areoles with leaves, areoles, glochids and often spines; ovary inferior; epigynal tube absent (but the pericarpel often produced beyond the ovary); perianth rotate or spreading, rarely erect, yellow, pink, red or off-white; stamens sometimes touch-sensitive; style often more or less expanded near base. Fruit fleshy or dry, umbilicate; seeds circular to broadly oval, 3–9mm; aril present, enclosing entire seed; aril pale brown to off-white, surface bony, trichotomous or alveolate. Throughout America, from S Canada to Patagonia.

CULTIVATION *Opuntia* spp. are generally easy to grow (though relatively few, even among the smaller-growing species, flower freely in cultivation), but vary in their requirements according to their geographical and altitudinal origin. A few species are hardy (listed below), and some from lowland tropical areas require higher minimum temperatures, but the great majority can be grown in a cool frost-free greenhouse (min. 2–7°C/35–45°F); use 'standard' cactus compost: moderate to high inorganic content (more than 50% grit), pH 6–7.5; full sun; low air-humidity; keep dry from mid-autumn until early spring, except for light misting on warm days in late winter. In general, *Opuntia*, spp. especially those with flat stem-segments, do best when given ample root-space and generous watering during the summer. Hardy species include: *Opuntia compressa, O. erinacea* (not var. *ursina*), *O. fragilis, O. howeyi, O. imbricata, O. littoralis, O. macrorhiza, O. phaeacantha* and *O. polyacantha*.

Various spp. of sect. *Opuntia* are grown for forage or edible fruits and some of those introduced to Australia and South Africa have become noxious pests. Some species are attractive to look at, but all contact should be avoided, and the plants kept out of reach of small children and animals. The numerous, minutely barbed glochids are easily detached from the plant but difficult to see and remove from the skin, where they will cause irritation, or from clothes and gloves. When repotting, hold the plants with folded newspaper etc., which can be disposed of after use.

There is no recent, conservative and comprehensive treatment of the genus, though there are useful regional accounts for several countries. The genus is divisible into 11 principal groups, sometimes treated as separate genera. They can be distinguished as follows.

**1a** Stem-segments globose, cylindric, ribbed or tuberculate, never appreciably compressed or flattened. **2**

**b** At least some segments compressed or flattened. **8**

**2a** Spines sheathed. N American spp. (Cylindropuntia)
*Oo. acanthocarpa, arbuscula, bigelovii, burrageana, cholla, echinocarpa, fulgida, imbricata, kleiniae, leptocaulis, munzii, parryi, prolifera, ramosissima, rosarica, rosea, santamaria, spinosior, tesajo, tunicata, versicolor, whipplei*.

**b** Spines not sheathed, or the sheath separating at the tip only. **3**

**3a** Flowers terminal; roots tuberous; seeds kidney-shaped. N American spp. (Marenopuntia)
*O. marenae*.

**b** Flowers rarely terminal; roots usually fibrous; seeds not kidney-shaped. **4**

**4a** Stem-segments ribbed. N American spp. (Grusonia)
*O. bradtiana*.

**b** Stem-segments terete or tuberculate, never ribbed. **5**

**5a** Tree-like or shrubby spp; stem-segments indeterminate, often elongate. S American spp. (Austrocylindropuntia)
*Oo. clavarioides, cylindrica, exaltata, miquelii, pachypus, subulata, verschaffeltii, vestita*.

**b** Shrubby or caespitose; stem-segments determinate, usually short. **6**

**6a** Stem-segments clavate, strongly tuberculate; spines sheathed at tip. N American spp. (Corynopuntia)
*Oo. bulbispina, clavata, invicta, moelleri, parishii, schottii, vilis*.

**b** Stem-segments oblong or globular, not compressed nor conspicuously tuberculate. S American spp. **7**

**7a** Mound-forming plants; stem-segments oblong; areoles more or less exposed; glochids usually yellow; fr. fleshy, indehiscent; seed-aril hard, smooth. (Maihueniopsis)
*Oo. boliviana, floccosa, glomerata, lagopus, nigrispina, ovata, pentlandii, platyacantha*.

**b** Laxly branched subshrubs; stem-segments globose to oblong; areoles deeply sunken; glochids red-brown; fr. dry, indehiscent; seed-aril spongy. (Tephrocactus)
*Oo. alexanderi, aoracantha, articulata, kuehnrichiana, molinensis, sphaerica*.

**8a** Perianth erect; stamens and style conspicuously exserted; stamens not touch-sensitive. Mexico; one sp. naturalized elsewhere. (Nopalea)
*Oo. auberi, cochenillifera, dejecta*.

**b** Perianth more or less spreading, urceolate to rotate; stamens not or scarcely exceeding the perianth, often touch-sensitive. **9**

**9a** Tree-like spp.; stem-segments dimorphic, those of the main axis elongate eventually cylindric, forming a continuous trunk. **10**

**b** Shrubby or rarely tree-like species; trunk, if developed, usually visibly jointed; stem-segments relatively uniform. Opuntia (Platyopuntia)
*Oo. arenaria, atrispina, aurantiaca, austrina, azurea, basilaris, beckeriana, bergeriana, bravoana, cantabrigiensis, chlorotica, compressa, corrugata, crassa, curassavica, decumbens, erinacea, ficus-indica, fragilis, hyptiacantha, lanceolata, leucotricha, lindheimeri, littoralis, macrocentra, macrorhiza, marnieriana, maxima, microdasys, mieckleyi, monacantha, pailana, paraguayensis, phaeacantha, picardoi, pilifera, polyacantha, puberula, pubescens, pycnantha, quimilo, repens, retrorsa, robusta, rufida, salmiana, scheeri, schickendantzii, soehrensii, stenarthra, stenopetala, streptacantha, stricta, strigil, sulphurea, tomentosa, tuna, velutina.*

**10a** Ultimate stem-segments thick, plate-like. N American and Caribbean spp. (Consolea)
*Oo. falcata, macracantha, moniliformis, rubescens, spinosissima.*

**b** Ultimate joints thin, almost leaf-like. S America spp. (Brasiliopuntia)
*O. brasiliensis.*

***O. acanthocarpa*** Engelm. & Bigelow. Shrub or tree to 3m; stem-seg. cylindric, 12–50×2–3cm, with elongate, laterally compressed tubercles; lvs *c*12×1.5mm; glochids minute; spines sheathed, 6–25, to 2.5cm, tinged red to white, or straw-coloured like the sheath. Fl. 4–6×4–5.5cm, red, purple or yellow. Fr. spiny, to 4cm, tinged brown. SW US & adjacent Mexico. Z9.

***O. alexanderi*** Britt. & Rose. Subshrub to 50×50cm; stem-seg. globose to elongate, to 9×3–5.5cm, tuberculate; areoles small; glochids to 4mm, pale yellow; spines 4–15, to 4cm, white, tipped darker, or violet-grey, downcurved at first. Fl. *c*6cm, pink. Fr. spiny, red, dry. NW Argentina. Z9.

***O. aoracantha*** Lem. Erect, to 60cm, simple or branched at or above ground; stem-seg. ovoid, 4–10×2–7cm, strongly tuberculate, grey-blue to olive-green; areoles 4–10mm diam., deeply sunken; glochids forming a ring around areoles periphery, to 5mm, red; spines 2–7, 5–16(–23)cm×2–3mm, flattened, flexible, yellow-brown then grey. Fl. 5–7cm, white. Fr. spiny, nearly globose, 2.5–3cm, disintegrating. NW Argentina. Z9.

***O. arbuscula*** Engelm. Dwarf tree or shrub to 1.2(–3)m; stem-seg. cylindric, 5–15cm×6–9(–12)mm, smooth, tubercles inconspicuous; lvs to 9mm; areoles 6–7.5mm apart, elliptic 3–4.5mm; spines sheathed, 1–4, 1–4cm, red- or purple-brown, the sheath conspicuous and persistent, light brown. Fl. 2.5–4.5×2–3.5cm, green, yellow or tinged brown. Fr. spineless, to 4×2cm. Arizona & NW Mexico. Z9.

***O. arenaria*** Engelm. Small creeping shrub, forming groups to 15×300cm, with rhizome-like regenerative roots to 100cm; stem-seg. flattened, narrowly obovate-oblong, 5–7.5×2–2.5×0.6–1.2cm, glaucous; areoles 4.5–6mm apart; glochids to 3mm, pale brown; spines 5–7, the longest 2.5–3.5cm, white to grey or red-brown. Fl. to 4.5(–6)×6cm, yellow. Fr. spiny, 2.5–3×0.9–1.2cm. SW US (near the Rio Grande) and Mexico (Chihuahua). Z9.

***O. articulata*** (Pfeiff.) D. Hunt. Dwarf shrub with brittle erect branches to 20–30cm; stem-seg. globose to oblong, usually 2.5–5×2.5–5cm, easily detached; spines lacking or 1–4, to 5cm or more ×7mm wide, flat, paper or raffia-like, pale brown or white. Fl. 3–4cm diam., white or pale pink. Argentina. Z9.

***O. atrispina*** Griffiths. Sprawling subshrub, 45–60×60–100cm; stem-seg. flattened, rounded to obovate, *c*10×7.5cm; areoles 12–20mm apart, to 4.5mm diam.; glochids yellow; spines 4–7, variable in size, to 4cm, almost black. Fl. to 5×6cm, yellow. Fr. spineless, to 20×12mm, red-purple. S Texas and adjacent NE Mexico. Z9.

***O. auberi*** Pfeiff. Resembling *O. cochenillifera*. Stem-seg. narrower; spines usually present, 2–3, to 3cm, off-white, tipped brown. Fl. *c*9cm, dull red; stamens tinged pink; stigmas green. S Mexico. Z9.

***O. aurantiaca*** Lindl. Low spreading shrub to 30cm; stem-seg. almost terete at base, somewhat compressed above, to 15×1.5×1cm, not tubercled, easily detached; spines usually 2–3, 1–3cm, pale brown. Fl. 2.5–4cm diam., orange-yellow. Fr. to 3cm, purple-red, spiny. Uruguay and adjacent Argentina. Z9.

***O. austrina*** Small. Resembling *O. compressa*; stem-seg. obovate to elliptic, 7.5–10(–14)×5–9(–12.5)cm; spines 3–5.6cm. SE US (Texas to Florida). Z9.

***O. azurea*** Rose. Shrub, 1–2m; stem-seg. flattened, circular to obovate, 10–15cm diam., glaucous green; areoles *c*2cm apart, lowermost on each joint spineless; spines 1–3, unequal, to 3cm, reflexed, eventually almost black. Fl. intense yellow; tepals carmine tipped. Fr. spineless, subglobose to ovoid, carmine, juicy and edible. NC Mexico. Z9.

***O. basilaris*** Engelm. & Bigelow Forming clumps 30–60cm or more tall; stem-seg. obovate to nearly orbicular, often truncate to retuse at apex, usually 8–20×6–15cm, blue-grey and often tinged purple around the edges and areoles, velvety; glochids red-brown, deciduous; spines usually 0, or 1(–5), short. Fl. 5–7.5×5–7.5cm, usually deep purple-red. Fr. dry, globose to obovoid, umbilicate. SW US, NW Mexico (Sonora). Z9.

***O. beckeriana*** Schum. Low shrub, freely branching; stem-seg. to 10cm, grass-green; spines 2–6, straight, yellow or with darker bands, or nearly white. Fl. 7–8cm diam., deep yellow. Origin unknown. Based on material cult. in Italy. Z9.

***O. bergeriana*** F.A. Weber. Tree-like or thicket-forming, much-branched, 1–3.5m, with a trunk 30–40cm diam.; stem-seg. narrowly oblong, to *c*25cm; spines 2–5, to 4cm, more or less flattened, brown or yellow below. Fl. deep red. Fr. to 4cm, red. Spring–summer. Origin unknown. Naturalized in parts of the French and Italian Riviera. Z9.

***O. bigelovii*** Engelm. TEDDY-BEAR CHOLLA. Small tree to 1.5(–2.5)m, with a well-developed trunk; stem-seg. cylindric-ellipsoid, 7.5–12.5(–20)×3.8–6cm, readily detached, tuberculate; areoles 3–6mm apart, 3mm diam.; spines sheathed, *c*6–10, to 2.5cm, pink- to red-brown, sheath straw-coloured, persistent. Fl. 3–4×2.5–4cm, pale green to yellow, striped with lavender. Fr. spineless, yellow, tuberculate, to 2cm. SW US, NW Mexico. The plant is picturesque and famous for its shimmering coat of pale yellow spines, but they are sheathed and vicious, and belie the common name. Z9.

***O. boliviana*** Salm-Dyck. Subshrub to 30cm; stem-seg. ovoid-oblong, 5–6.3×2–2.5cm, smooth; areoles sunken; spines 1–4, to 10cm, erect, translucent pale yellow. Fl. 2–3×5cm, yellow to orange. Mts of Bolivia, N Argentina. Z9.

***O. bradtiana*** (Coult.) K. Brandg. Spreading subshrub, to 1×5m or more; stem-seg. cylindric, ribbed like a cereoid cactus, 4–7cm diam.; ribs 8–10, low; leaves linear, fleshy, 8mm, soon deciduous; spines 15–25, 1–3cm, off-white except when young. Fl. very short, to 4cm diam., deep shiny yellow; fil. brown. Fr. spiny, ellipsoid. NE Mexico (Coahuila). Z9.

***O. brasiliensis*** (Willd.) Haw. Tree-like, to 6–9m or more, with cylindric, unjointed trunk and branches; ultimate stem-seg. flat and somewhat leaf-like, obovate to oblong-lanceolate, to 15×6cm, 4–6mm thick, eventually deciduous; lvs small, subulate, caducous; spines 1–3, to 15mm, on young growth, more numerous on the trunk, or lacking. Fl. *c*5×5cm, pale yellow; staminodal hairs present. Fr. globose, 2.5–4cm diam. Eastern S America. Z9.

***O. bravoana*** Baxter. Shrub to 2×2m; stem-seg. flattened, oblong, to 36×14cm, green with purple markings beneath the areoles; glochids yellow; spines 0–5, 2–6cm, pale yellow to grey, darker at base. Fl. to 8cm diam., yellow. NW Mexico (S Baja California). Z9.

***O. bulbispina*** Engelm. Dwarf mat-forming shrub, to 120cm diam.; stem-seg. ovoid, 20–25×10–12mm, tuberculate; spines 12–16, to 12mm, off-white, bulbous at base. Fl. purple. N Mexico. Z9.

***O. burrageana*** Britt. & Rose. Sprawling shrub, less than 1m; stem-seg. cylindric, to 15cm, tuberculate, often deciduous; areoles very close-set; glochids short, pale yellow, sometimes lacking; spines sheathed, numerous, to 2cm, sheaths pale yellow. Fl. 3–4cm diam., tinged pink or brown with a green centre. Fr. spiny, 2cm diam., tuberculate. NW Mexico (S Baja California). Z9.

***O. cantabrigiensis*** Lynch. Densely branched shrub, forming thickets 1.2×4m; stem-seg. flattened, 16–24×12–17cm, slightly glaucous; spines 1–3, 1–2cm, white. Fl. 9–14cm diam., yellow. Fr. spineless, ovoid, 4cm, glaucous red. Summer. Known for certain only from cultivation, where it was found to be hardy in a sheltered position at the Cambridge University Botanic Garden, England, for many years. Z9. The name is used here in its original, strict sense. Various authorities have identified it with a wild plant from central northern Mexico, but this seems improbable in view of its apparent hardiness and other differences.

***O. chlorotica*** Engelm. & Bigelow. Tree or shrub to 2×1.2m; stem-seg. flattened, rounded to broadly obovate, 15–20×12.5×17cm; areoles *c*2cm apart, elliptic; glochids to 4.5mm, yellow; spines 1–6, to 4cm, deflexed, pale yellow. Fl. 5–7.5×4–6cm, yellow. Fr. spineless at maturity, 4–6×2–3.5cm, grey-purple. SW US, NW Mexico. Z9.

***O. cholla*** F.A. Weber. Small tree, to 5m; stem-seg. cylindric, 5–30×2–3cm, tuberculate; glochids numerous, yellow; spines sheathed, 5–13, 3–25mm, yellow then grey, sheaths golden. Fl. 2.5–3cm diam., purple-pink. Fr. spineless, obovoid, green, 3–5×2–3cm, proliferous. Spring. NW Mexico (Baja California). Z9.

***O. clavarioides*** Pfeiff. Low shrub, much branched from tuberous roots; stem-seg. obconic, truncate or concave, often cristate at apex, to *c*2×1.5cm, not tubercled; lvs 1.5mm, tinged red, caducous; spines 4–10, minute, adpressed, white. Fl. *c*5cm diam., tinged brown, rarely seen in cult. Argentina. A curious species, usually grafted on other species of *Opuntia*, or *Cereus* or *Harrisia spp.* Z9.

***O. clavata*** Engelm. Low mat-forming shrub, 7.5–10×100–200cm; stem-seg. cylindric-clavate, 4–5×2–2.5cm, tuberculate; areoles *c*6mm apart; glochids pale yellow, 6mm; spines sheathed, 10–20, to 2.5cm, deflexed, dagger-like, grey. Fl. 5–6×3–5cm, yellow. Fr. spineless, yellow, 4×2cm. US (Arizona, New Mexico). Z9.

***O. cochenillifera*** (L.) Mill. Shrub or tree to 4m or more; stem-seg. elliptic to obovate, 8–25×5–12cm, dark green; areoles wide-spaced, *c*2.5cm apart; spines usually lacking, rarely 1(–3), less than 1cm. Fl. 5–6×1.2–1.5cm; perianth erect, bright red; stamens and style exserted, pink. Fr. ellipsoid, 2.5–3.8×2.5–3cm, fleshy, red. Mexico. Long cultivated in tropical America and elsewhere, formerly as a host for the cochineal insect. Commonly confused (since it rarely flowers in cultivation) with *O. paraguayensis* Schum. or an allied species. Z9.

***O. compressa*** (Salisb.) Macbr. Shrub, forming clumps or mats 10–30cm×2m or more; stem-seg. elliptic to obovate to orbicular, 5–12.5×4–10cm; green, often tinged purple; lvs subulate 4–7mm, caducous; spines usually 0, sometimes 1–2, especially on marginal areoles, to 2.5cm, terete, not flattened. Fl. 4–6×4–6cm, yellow, often with red centre. Fr. obovoid, 2.5–4×2–3cm, fleshy, purple or red. Summer. E & C US. Naturalized in Switzerland and hardy as far north as England. Z8.

***O. corrugata*** Salm-Dyck. Low creeping shrub, to 10cm tall; stem-seg. obliquely ovate or elliptic to orbicular, flattened but not strongly so, to 5×2.5×1.5cm, with low tubercles, pale blue green; lvs subulate, 2mm, tinged red; spines several, 8–12mm, often with 1–2 much longer. Fl. red, 6×5cm; stigmas green. NW Argentina. Z9.

***O. crassa*** Haw. Resembling spineless forms of *O. ficus-indica*; described as 1–2m tall, with thick, glaucous stem-seg. *c*8–12.5cm, usually spineless. Fl. and fr. not described. Origin uncertain. Reported by various authors as cultivated in tropical America, but of very uncertain status. Z9.

***O. curassavica*** (L.) Mill. Low shrub, spreading to cover large areas; stem-seg. somewhat flattened, 2–5cm, easily detached; glochids poorly developed; spines 4 or more, to *c*2.5cm, pale yellow at first, fading to white. Fl. 5cm diam., yellow, streaked red. Netherlands Antilles, N Venezuela. Z9.

***O. cylindrica*** (Lam.) DC. Becoming a small tree 3–4m; stems cylindric, unsegmented, 3–5cm diam., with low tubercles, green; lvs terete, acute, 10–13mm, deciduous; spines 2–6, to 1cm, off-white, or lacking, usually mixed with fine hair-like glochids. Fl. *c*2.5cm diam., red. Ecuador. Z9. A cristate form is also cultivated.

***O. decumbens*** Salm-Dyck. Spreading subshrub, to 40cm; stem-seg. flattened, 10–20cm, pubesc.; areoles circular with red markings beneath; spines 1–3, to 4cm, yellow. Fl. 4×5cm, plain yellow or tinged red. Fr. spineless, 3cm, purple-red. S Mexico. Z9.

***O. dejecta*** Salm-Dyck. Shrub to 2m; stem-seg. somewhat flattened, lanceolate, 10–15×3–6cm, green to grey-green; spines 2, or more at old areoles, to 4cm, tinged red at first, later yellow to grey. Fl. to 5cm, red; tepals erect. Fr. spineless, dark red. C America. Z9.

***O. echinocarpa*** Engelm. & Bigelow. Shrub to 1.5m; stem-seg. cylindric, 5–15(–40)×2(–4)cm, tuberculate; areoles circular, 1–2cm apart, 4–5mm; spines sheathed, 3–12, to 3.8cm, pale yellow to silvery, sheaths similar, persistent. Fl. 3–4.5×3–6cm, yellow-green. Fr. spiny, 1.2–2.5×1.2–2cm. SW US, NW Mexico. Z9.

***O. erinacea*** Engelm. & Bigelow. Similar to *O. polyacantha*, but with at least some of the spines flattened basally. SW US. Benson, *The Cacti of the United States and Canada* (1982), treats several popularly cultivated plants as varieties of *O. erinacea*, notably the following. var. ***ursina*** (F.A. Weber) Parish. Stem-seg. oblong or oblong-elliptic, 5–10×2.5–6cm; spines numerous, from all areoles, to 10cm, very slender and flexuous. Fl. orange or pink. var. ***utahensis*** (Engelm.) L. Bens., not Stem-seg. obovate, 5–8.5×5–7.5cm; areolar areas often purple-brown; spines from upper areoles only, 3(–10cm). Fl. 7–8×7–8cm, purple-red or pink. Z9.

***O. exaltata*** A. Berger. Resembling *O. subulata* and perhaps only a cultivar of it. Tree to 5m with a trunk 5–30cm diam. when well-grown; stems somewhat glaucous; leaves terete, acute, 1–7cm; spines pale brown. Mts of Peru, Bolivia, where it is grown as a hedge plant. Z9.

***O. falcata*** Ekman & Werderm. Resembling *O. moniliformis* but smaller, to 1.5m, stem-seg. narrower, 35×9cm, spines to 4cm. Fl. red. Haiti. Z9.

***O. ficus-indica*** (L.) Mill. INDIAN FIG; BARBARY FIG. Large shrub or small tree to 5(–7)m with a trunk sometimes 1m diam.; stem-seg. obovate to oblong 20–60×10–40cm, green or blue-green; spines variable, 1–2 or more, the longer to 2.5cm, white or off-white, or lacking. Fl. 6–7×5–7cm, yellow. Fr. 5–10×4–9cm yellow, orange, red or purple in different cultivars. Mexico. Long cultivated in warmer regions for the fruits, and widely naturalized. Z9.

***O. floccosa*** Salm-Dyck. Low caespitose shrub forming mounds eventually 2m diam.; individual stem-seg. to 10×3cm, densely clothed with long white areolar hair; lvs terete, 8–13×2–3mm, persistent; spines 1–3, 1–3cm, pale yellow. Fl. *c*3×3.5cm, yellow or orange. Mts of Peru and Bolivia. Z9.

***O. fragilis*** (Nutt.) Haw. Low shrub, forming clumps 5–10cm high and 30cm or more diam.; stem-seg. variable in shape, 2–4.5×1.2–2.5(–3.8)×1.2–2.5cm; spines 1–6(–9). Fl. 3–4×4.5cm, yellow or tinged green. Fr. obovoid, 12–15×9–12mm, green or red-green. US, Canada. Z8.

***O. fulgida*** Engelm. Small tree, to 3.5m; stem-seg. cylindric, 5–15×3–5cm, readily detached as propagules, tuberculate, light green; areoles elliptic, *c*4.5mm, 9–12mm apart; glochids pale yellow, to 2mm; spines sheathed, 6–12, to 3cm, pink to red-brown. Fl. *c*2.5×2cm, pink to off-white. Fr. usually sterile, proliferating, green. SW US, NW Mexico. Z9.

***O. glomerata*** Haw. Low caespitose shrub, forming dense mounds; stem-seg. terete-conical, to 4×2cm; spines always present, more or less flattened. Fl. yellow (rarely seen). N Argentina. Z9.

***O. hyptiacantha*** F.A. Weber. Small tree, to 4m; stem-seg. flattened, oblong or obovate, 20–30cm; areoles small, 2–3cm apart; glochids dark; spines 1 at first, later to 6, to 2cm, pale. Fl. red. Fr. spineless, globose, yellow to purple. C Mexico. Z9.

***O. imbricata*** (Haw.) DC. Eventually a small tree, to 3m; larger stem-seg. 12–38×2–3cm, strongly tuberculate; lvs to 15mm, caducous; spines 8–30, to 3cm, sheath dull brown. Fl. *c*6×6cm, purple. Fr. nearly globose, 3cm, yellow, spineless. Mexico, SW US. Z9.

***O. invicta*** Brandg. Low shrub, 20–50cm, eventually forming colonies 2m diam.; stem-seg. obovoid to clavate, 6–10×2–6cm, strongly tubercled; lvs subulate, 8–14, tinged red, deciduous; spines formidable, *c*16–22, to 3.5cm, flattened, not sheathed, tinged red at first, becoming dull brown. Fl. 5cm diam., yellow. NW Mexico (Baja California). Z9.

***O. kleiniae*** DC. Shrub to 2m; stem-seg. cylindric, 10–30×0.5–1cm, tuberculate, tinged purple-red; areoles 6–12mm apart; glochids tinged red; spines sheathed, 1–4, to 2.5cm, grey-pink, sheaths pale brown. Fl. 3–4.5×3–5cm, red-bronze to purple. Fr. spineless, red. SW US, N Mexico. Z9.

***O. kuehnrichiana*** Werderm. & Backeb. Low-growing, caespitose; stem-seg. globose to slightly oblong, to 8cm, grey-green; areoles off-white, lowermost spineless; spines 5–12, to 3.5cm, off-white. Fl. to 3cm diam., yellow. Fr. depressed-globose. Peru. Z9.

***O. lagopus*** Schum. Mat-forming shrub; stem-seg. cylindric, 10–25×3–8cm, hidden by the extremely long glochids; glochids to 1.5cm, dense, pale yellow; spines 1, 2cm, white. Peru. Z9.

***O. lanceolata*** Haw. Perhaps only a form of *O. ficus-indica*. Stem-seg. rhomboid or lanceolate, 20–30×6–8cm. Origin uncertain. Z9.

***O. leptocaulis*** DC. Brittle, thin-stemmed bush shrub to 50cm or more, sometimes developing a thin truck; stem-seg. slender-elongate, often 5–15cm×3.5mm, scarcely tuberculate, branching more or less at right-angles, easily detached; lvs to 12mm, caducous; spines usually 1, 1–5cm, slender, sheathed, the sheath yellow-brown to off-white. Fl. 2cm, pale green or pale yellow. Fr. globose to obovoid, 10–18mm, orange, red or yellow, often proliferous. Mexico, SW US. Z9.

***O. leucotricha*** DC. Becoming a small tree 3–4m; terminal stem-seg. oblong to broadly ovate, to 25×12cm, about 1cm thick, velvety; lvs small, subulate caducous; spines 1–6, to 7.5cm, becoming longer and more numerous on older seg., setaceous or hair-like, white, almost covering the stem. Fl. *c*5×5cm, yellow. Mexico. Z9.

***O. lindheimeri*** Engelm. Shrub, 1–3×1–5m; stem-seg. flattened, rounded to elongate, 15–25(–120)×12–20cm; leaves 3–9mm; areoles elliptic, 4.5×3mm, 2.5–4cm apart; glochids yellow, becoming brown; spines 1–6, to 4cm, yellow or paler. Fl. 5–8×5–7.5(–10.5)cm, yellow, rarely red. Fr. almost spineless, 3–7cm, purple. Z9.

***O. littoralis*** (Engelm.) Cockerell. Sprawling shrub, 30–60×60–120cm; stem-seg. flattened, obovate, elliptic or nearly rounded, 7.5–25×7.5–10cm or more, glaucous; areoles 1.5–3mm diam., 1.5–3cm apart; glochids yellow to brown; spines 0–11, to 5cm, brown, pink or grey. Fl. to 7.5×7.5cm, yellow with a red centre. Fr. spineless, obovoid, to *c*4cm, red-purple. SW US, NW Mexico. Z9.

***O. macracantha*** Griseb. Small tree; trunk cylindric, to 15cm diam.; ultimate stem-seg. flattened, oblong or ovate; areoles 2–3cm apart; glochids abundant, brown; spines 1–4, to 15cm, off-white. Fl. orange-yellow. Cuba. Z9.

***O. macrocentra*** Engelm. Usually a sprawling shrub, 0.6–2m, sometimes tree-like; stem-seg. nearly orbicular, *c*10–20×10–20cm, persistently purple-tinged; areoles typically 1.5–2.5cm apart; spines absent or 1(–3), often restricted to upper margins of seg., to 10(–17)cm, not flattened at base. Fl. 7.5–9×7.5–9cm; inner tepals bright yellow, red at base. Fr. 2.5–4×2cm, red or purple-red. SW US, N Mexico. Z9.

***O. macrorhiza*** Engelm. Low shrub to 12×180cm: rootstock usually tuberous; stem-seg. flattened, rounded to obovate, 5–10×5–6cm, glaucous; lvs to 7.5mm; areoles 1–2cm apart; glochids yellow to brown; spines 1–6, to *c*5.5cm mostly deflexed, off-white. Fl. to 6×6cm, yellow or yellow with a red centre. Fr. spineless, to 4cm, red-purple. US & N Mexico. Z9.

***O. marenae*** S.H. Parsons. Low shrub, 15–60cm; rootstock tuberous; stem-seg. to 20cm×8–15mm, faintly tubercled; lvs 5–10mm, caducous; spines several adpressed 3–10mm, fine white, and 1–2 or more stronger, projecting downwards, to 2cm. Fl. terminal, rotate, 6–8cm diam., satiny white; stamens sensitive. Fr. not externally visible until tip of stem splits. NW Mexico (Sonora). Z9.

***O. marnieriana*** Backeb. Resembling *O. stenopetala*. Low shrub; stem-seg. flattened, ovate to oblong, to 18×14cm, blue-green; spines usually 2, 1–3cm, more or less strongly flattened and curved, red-brown, tipped brown, sometimes accompanied by 1–2 shorter spines. Fl. unisexual, orange-red; tepals very narrow, suberect. Mexico. Z9.

***O. maxima*** Mill. Resembling *O. ficus-indica*, but stem-seg. elongate, more or less spathulate, to 35×10–12cm. Fl. 8cm diam., orange-red. Known only in cult. A species of very uncertain status. Z9.

***O. microdasys*** (Lehm.) Pfeiff. Shrub, forming thickets 40–60cm or more tall; stem-seg. oblong, obovate or suborbicular, 6–15×6–12cm, green, velvety; glochids typically yellow, or white; spines 0, rarely 1, very short. Fl. *c*4×4cm, yellow, outer seg. often tinged red. Fr. nearly globose, *c*3cm diam., fleshy, red or purple-red. C & N Mexico. Z8. Decorative and popular, despite the glochids which easily detach in large numbers and lodge in the skin if the plant is touched. The variant with white glochids is 'Albispina'. A similar species with brown glochids is *O. rufida* Engelm.

***O. mieckleyi*** Schum. Erect shrub; stem-seg. flattened, narrowly oblong, 15–25×4–6cm, dark green, tuberculate; areoles large, white-woolly; spines 0–2, to 5mm, dark. Fl. 6cm diam., brick-red; pericarpel spineless. Paraguay. Z9.

***O. miquelii*** Monv. Spreading shrub to *c*1×5m; stem-seg. cylindric, *c*8–20×5–6cm, tuberculate, strongly glaucous; glochids abundant, brown; spines 10 or more, short at first but eventually to 10cm, off-white. Fl. 4–8cm, magenta. Fr. larger, off-white. N Chile. Z9.

***O. moelleri*** A. Berger. Dwarf caespitose shrub; stem-seg. cylindric-clavate, 4–7×3–4cm, tuberculate; central spines 6, to 16mm, thickened at base, flattened, off-white; radial spines numerous. Fl. to 6×5cm, yellow-green; pericarpel spiny. NE Mexico (Coahuila). Z9.

***O. molinensis*** Speg. Similar to spineless forms of *O. articulata*, but seg. much smaller, and with conspicuous tufts of red-brown glochids. N Argentina. Z9.

***O. monacantha*** (Willd.) Haw. Erect shrub, to 2m, sometimes with a short trunk; stem-seg. oblong to obovate, tapered towards the base, 10–30×7.5–12.5cm; spines 1 or 2, unequal, longer to 4cm, brown towards tip and base, off-white between, more numerous on trunk. Fl. 5–7.5×7.5–10cm, yellow or orange-yellow; outer tepals tinged red. Fr. pear-shaped, 5–7.5×4–5cm, red-purple. SE Brazil to Argentina, naturalized in various warm countries. Z9.

***O. moniliformis*** (L.) Haw. Tree, with trunk 3–4m; ultimate stem-seg. flattened, 10–30×13cm; areoles elevated on small tubercles; glochids to 8mm, brown; spines 3–6 or more in age, to 2.5cm, pale yellow. Fl. *c*2.5cm diam., orange-yellow. Fr. oblong-ovoid, *c*6cm. Hispaniola to Puerto Rico. Z9.

***O. munzii*** C. Wolf. Tree to 5m; stem-seg. cylindric, 10–25×2.5cm, tuberculate; areoles 6–9mm apart; spines sheathed, 9–12, to 2cm yellow like the sheaths. Fl. to 5×5cm, yellow-green, sometimes tinged red. Fr. spineless, often sterile, yellow. SW US (S California). Z9.

***O. nigrispina*** Schum. Dwarf, mound-forming shrub, to 10cm; stem-seg. cylindric to ellipsoid, 2–3.5×1–1.5cm, tuberculate when young, yellow-green; glochids brown; spines 2–5, the 1–2 largest to 2.5cm, violet-black, rough, others paler. Fl. yellow. NW Argentina. Z9.

***O. ovata*** Pfeiff. Dwarf, caespitose or mound-forming shrub, to 12cm; stem-seg. ovoid, 3–4×1.5–2cm, not tuberculate; areoles 8mm apart; spines 7–8, unequal, stiff, straight, 4–10mm, white at first. Fl. 2.5–3cm diam., pale golden yellow. N Argentina. Z9.

***O. pachypus*** Schum. Simple, or branching candelabra-like, to *c*1m; stem cylindric, unsegmented, 3–5cm diam., tuberculate; leaves subulate, 4mm, caducous; areoles at upper edge of tubercles, 4mm diam., arranged in dense spirals; glochids yellow; spines 20–30, 5–20mm. Fl. tubular, 7cm, red; pericarpel spiny. Peru. A choice, slow-growing species. Z9.

***O. pailana*** Weingart. Erect, branched shrub; stem-seg. flattened, rounded to obovate, 10–14×9cm, blue; areoles 2cm apart; glochids yellow-grey; spines 3–8, 2–3cm, white at first, later brown. NW Mexico (Coahuila). Z9.

***O. paraguayensis*** Schum. Stem-seg. oblanceolate or narrowly elliptic, to 30×8×2cm, dark glossy green; spines absent or 1, to 1cm, pale yellow. Fl. *c*10×6.5cm, orange. Paraguay. Z9.

***O. parishii*** Orcutt. Mat-forming or caespitose shrub, to 15cm; stem-seg. cylindric to narrowly obovoid, 7.5–15×1.5–4cm, tuberculate or sometimes ribbed; lvs to 6mm; areoles 2–2.5cm apart; spines mostly at areoles on upper part of seg., sheathed, 16–33, the longest directed down, to 5cm, yellow, brown or red. Fl. 5–7.5×2.5–5cm, yellow or tinged red. Fr. spiny, to 8×2cm, yellow. SW US, N Mexico. Z9.

***O. parryi*** Engelm. Sprawling shrub to 40cm; stem-seg. cylindric, 7–45×1.8–2.5cm, strongly tuberculate; leaves 4.5–7.5mm; areoles 9mm apart, 6–7.5mm diam.; glochids red-brown; spines sheathed, 7–20, to 1.5(–3)cm, grey to red-brown, sheaths sometimes paler. Fl. 3–3.5×3–4cm, yellow or yellow-green, tinged purple. Fr. spiny. S California and adjacent Mexico. Z9.

***O. pentlandii*** Salm-Dyck. Dwarf shrub forming mounds eventually 1m diam.; stem-seg. globose to cylindric or obovoid, 2–10×*c*4cm; spines variable in number and length, acicular (not flattened), more or less deflexed, sometimes absent. Fl. yellow, orange or red, rarely seen in cultivation. Bolivia. Z9.

***O. phaeacantha*** Engelm. Sprawling and spreading shrub 0.3–1m tall; stem-seg. obovate or orbicular 10–40×7.5–22.5cm, blue-green, sometimes tinged purple; spines 1–8 or more, to 6cm, flattened or elliptic in section, brown or red-brown, sometimes confined to upper part of seg., rarely lacking. Fl. 6–8×6–7.5cm, yellow, sometimes red-tinged within. Fr. pear-shaped, 4–8×2–4cm, purple. SW US, N Mexico. Z9.

***O. picardoi*** Marn.-Lap. Low creeping shrub; stem-seg. flattened, obliquely oval, to 7×3.5cm, glossy green; spines to 10, very short, white, tipped yellow. Fl. 4cm diam., red. N Argentina. Z9.

***O. pilifera*** F.A. Weber. Small tree, to 5m; stem-seg. flattened, rounded, 12–35cm, pale or glaucous-green; areoles 2–3cm apart, with long white hairs to 2cm or more (hence the specific epithet), very abundant on young seg.; spines 3–6(–9), to 1.5cm, white. Fl. 6cm diam., deep pink; pericarpel white-bristly. Fr. 4–5cm, red, juicy. S Mexico. Z9.

***O. platyacantha*** Pfeiff. Low shrub, freely branched; stem-seg. cylindric, 2.5–7.5×1.6–2cm, tinged brown, scarcely tuberculate; spines diverse, the upper 2–3 longer, 1.2–2.5cm, flattened, pale yellow-grey with darker bands, the lower 3–4 shorter, 6–8mm, thin, adpressed. Origin uncertain (Argentina or Chile). Known only in cultivation. Z9.

***O. polyacantha*** Haw. Low shrub, forming mats or clumps 15cm×0.3–1m or more; stem-seg. orbicular to broadly obovate, 5–10×4–10cm, blue-green; spines 5–10, unequal, the longest to 5cm, not markedly flattened in section, mostly deflexed and largely covering the seg. Fl. 4.5–8×4.5–6cm, yellow. Fr. dry, spiny. Canada, US, N Mexico. Z3.

***O. prolifera*** Engelm. Small tree to 2.5m; stem-seg. cylindric, elongate-ellipsoid, 7.5–14×4–5cm, detaching readily, tuberculate; areoles 5–9mm apart; spines sheathed, 6–12, to 3cm, red-brown, later grey, sheaths pale yellow to rust-coloured. Fl. to 3×2.5cm, magenta. Fr. often sterile, proliferating. SW US (S California) and adjacent Mexico. Z9.

***O. puberula*** Pfeiff. Resembling *O. decumbens*. Low shrub, 40–70cm, sometimes with a definite trunk; stem-seg. flat but thick, elliptic to obovate, 7.5–12.5(–18)×5–7.5cm, pubesc.; areoles with purple markings beneath; spines usually 0, or 2–4, to 8mm, off-white. Fl. 4–5cm, plain yellow or tinged red. Fr. spineless, 3cm, purple-red. S Mexico. Z9.

***O. pubescens*** Wendl. ex Pfeiff. Brittle prostrate shrub, densely branched, to 40cm; stem-seg. nearly terete, 2–8×1–3cm or when young flattened and 2–3cm broad; spines 2–5 or more, 5–20(–30)mm, brown to black. Fl. yellow. Fr. spiny, 2–2.5cm, red. S Mexico, Ecuador, Peru. Z9.

***O. pycnantha*** Engelm. Low-growing, spreading shrub; stem-seg. flattened, rounded, 10–18×8–13cm, puberulous; areoles close-set, 4–8mm apart, large, to 7mm diam.; spines 7–12, 5–30mm, yellow or red-brown. Fl. 4–6cm diam., yellow, often tinged red. Fr. very spiny, red. NW Mexico (Baja California islands). Z9.

***O. quimilo*** Schum. Small tree, to 5m; stem-seg. flattened, elliptic to obovate, 50×25×2–3cm, grey-green; spines 1–3, to 14.5cm. Fl. 7cm diam., red. Fr. pear-shaped to globular, 5–7cm, yellow-green. N Argentina. Z9.

***O. ramosissima*** Engelm. Shrub to 60(–150)cm, profusely branched; stem-seg. cylindric, 5–10×0.6cm, with diamond-shaped, flattened tubercles, forming a distinctive pattern; spines sheathed, 1–3, to 5.5cm. Fl. on short lateral branches, 3–4.5×1.2cm, deep yellow to brown or some tepals lavender to red. SW US, N Mexico. Z8.

***O. repens*** Bello. Thicket-forming shrub, to 50×400cm; stem-seg. flattened, oblong or linear, 5–16×3.5cm, sometimes pubesc.; spines numerous, to 3.5cm, pink to brown at first, later paler. Fl. 4cm diam., yellow, fading to orange-pink. Fr. spineless, 2–3cm, red, few-seeded. Puerto Rico and nearby islands. Z9.

***O. retrorsa*** Speg. Creeping shrub; stem-seg. somewhat flattened, linear-lanceolate; areoles with purple markings beneath; spines 1–3, reflexed, white, tipped pink. Fl. 4–5cm diam., pale yellow. Fr. 2cm, purple. N Argentina. Z9.

***O. robusta*** Wendl. & Pfeiff. Shrub to 2m or more; stem-seg. orbicular or nearly so, massive, to 40×40cm or more, waxy pale blue; spines 2–12, unequal, longest to 5cm, white, pale brown or yellow below, terete. Fl. 5×5–7cm, yellow. Fr. globose to ellipsoid, 7–8cm, deep red. Summer. C Mexico. Z9.

***O. rosarica*** G. Lindsay. Caespitose shrub, to *c*1×1m, rooting on contact with the ground; stem-seg. 10–25×2–5cm, cylindric, tuberculate, the tubercles arranged into 8–12 false, spiralled ribs; areoles 5–9×4mm; spines sheathed, 4–15, the central(s) 2.5–5cm, red-black. Fl. 4.5cm, yellow, tinged red. Fr. spiny, dry. NW Mexico (Baja California). Z9.

***O. rosea*** DC. Resembling *O. imbricata* but smaller and more compact, more freely branched, spination denser, pale yellow. Fl. rose pink. C Mexico. Z9.

***O. rubescens*** Salm-Dyck. Tree to 6m; ultimate stem-seg. flattened, thin, oblong to obovate, to 25cm; areoles 1–1.5cm apart; spines to 6cm, white, sometimes lacking. Fl. 2cm diam., yellow, orange or red; pericarpel to 5cm, tuberculate. Fr. spiny, obovoid or subglobose, 5–8cm diam., red. Lesser Antilles. Z9.

***O. rufida*** Engelm. Very similar to *O. microdasys* but glochids red-brown. SW US (Texas), N Mexico. Z9.

***O. salmiana*** Pfeiff. Shrub 30–50cm or more, much branched; stem-seg. slender-cylindric to 25×1cm, not tuberculate, often tinged red; leaves very small, 1–2mm, tinged purple, caducous; spines 3–5, to 15mm, or lacking. Fl. produced rather freely, 2–3.5cm diam., pale yellow; stamens sensitive. Fr. oblong-ellipsoid, *c*1cm diam., red, barren in cultivated plants, but proliferous. S Brazil to Argentina. Z9.

***O. santamaria*** (Baxter) H. Bravo. Resembling *O. rosarica* but stem tubercles shorter, spines numerous, to *c*20. NW Mexico (S Baja California). Z9.

***O. scheeri*** F.A. Weber. Shrub to 1m; stem-seg. oblong to orbicular, 15–30×9–22cm, blue-green; spines 8–12, to 1cm, yellow, intermixed with long white or yellow hairs. Fl. large, to 10cm diam., yellow at first, fading to salmon-pink. C Mexico. Z9.

***O. schickendantzii*** F.A. Weber. Resembling *O. aurantiaca* but to 1–2m; stem-seg. larger, somewhat tuberculate, grey-green. N Argentina. Z9.

***O. schottii*** Engelm. Mat-forming or caespitose shrub, to 10×300cm; stem-seg. cylindric-clavate, 4–6×1.5–2.5cm, tuberculate; areoles *c*6mm apart, elliptic; spines 6–12, longest in uppermost areoles, to 2.5–5cm, tinged brown, yellow or red, flattened. Fl. *c*5cm diam., yellow. Fr. spineless, 4–5.5cm, yellow. SW US, N Mexico. Z9.

***O. soehrensii*** Britt. & Rose. Prostrate shrub, forming mats to 1m diam.; stem-seg. erect at first, somewhat flattened, rounded, 4–6cm diam., tuberculate, often tinged purple; spines up to 8, to 5cm, yellow or brown. Fl. 3cm, light yellow. Fr. spineless, 3cm. W Argentina. Z9.

***O. sphaerica*** C.F. Först. Low shrub, forming colonies; stem-seg. at first ovoid, eventually globose, to 5cm diam.; areoles close-set, shortly woolly; spines few to many, unequal, 1–4cm, brown at first, fading to grey. Fl. 4cm, deep orange. Peru. Z9.

***O. spinosior*** (Engelm.) Toumey. Shrub or tree to 2m; stem-seg. cylindric, 12.5–30×1.5–2.2cm, tuberculate; lvs 9–12mm; areoles 6–9mm apart; glochids minute; spines sheathed, 10–20, to 1.5cm, grey, pink at apex, sheaths pale brown. Fl. 5–6×4.5–5cm, purple, red, yellow or white. Fr. spineless, bright yellow. SW US, N Mexico. Z9.

***O. spinosissima*** (Martyn) Mill. Tree to 5m with densely spiny trunk to 20cm diam.; stem-seg. flattened, narrowly oblong, 12–40×5–10cm, 6–9mm thick; areoles with conspicuous glochids and several spines, the longest to 8cm, directed downwards; flowering seg. usually spineless. Fl. with short, orange perianth *c*2cm diam.; pericarpel 4–5cm. Jamaica. Z9.

***O. stenarthra*** Schum. Low shrub, creeping to 2m or clambering to 80cm; stem-seg. narrowly oblong, 8–25×2.5–5(–7)cm; spines 0–3, 0.6–3.5cm, pale brown to almost white. Fl. to 3cm, lemon-yellow. Fr. pear-shaped, to 2.5cm. Paraguay. Z9.

***O. stenopetala*** Engelm. Creeping shrub, with some erect branches; stem-seg. flattened, rounded to obovate, 10–25cm, grey-green; areoles 1–3cm apart; spines 2–6, to 5cm, red-brown to black. Fl. unisexual, 2.7–3.2cm, orange-red, tepals nearly erect. Fr. globose, 3cm diam. N Mexico. Z9.

***O. streptacantha*** Lem. Tree to 5m; stem-seg. flattened, obovate to rounded, to 30cm, dark green; spines numerous, white. Fl. 7–9cm diam., yellow to orange. Fr. globose, 5cm diam., dark red or yellow. Mexico. Z9.

***O. stricta*** Haw. Sprawling or erect shrub, 0.5–2m; stem-seg. obovate to oblong, 10–40×7.5–25cm, blue-green; spines few or lacking in var. *stricta*, up to 11 in var. *dillenii* (Ker-Gawl.) L. Bens., usually 1.5–4cm, stout, straight or commonly curved, flattened, yellow or with brown bands. Fl. *c*5–6×5–6cm, yellow. Fr. globose to pear-shaped 4–6×2.5–3cm, fleshy, purple. SE US to N Venezuela, naturalized in various tropical countries. Z9.

***O. strigil*** Engelm. Erect or sprawling shrub, 60–10×130–200cm; stem-seg. flattened, obovate, 10–12.5×8–10cm; areoles *c*9mm apart; glochids 6mm, red-brown; spines 1–8, directed down, one much longer, to 4cm, red-brown, tipped yellow. Fl. *c*4.5×6cm, creamy white. Fr. spineless, globose, 1.2–1.9cm, red. SW US (Texas), N Mexico. Z9.

***O. subulata*** (Muehlenpf.) Engelm. Becoming a small tree, 2–4m, or with several branches near the base; stems cylindric, unsegmented, 5–7cm diam., with low tubercles, green; lvs terete, acute, 5cm or more, persisting more than a year; spines 1–2 (or more on older growth), pale yellow. Fl. red, 7cm. S Peru. Z9.

***O. sulphurea*** G. Don. Low shrub, to 30×200cm; stem-seg. flattened, oblong to obovate, 12–25cm, tuberculate; spines 2–8, 3–10cm, brown or red-brown or paler. Fl. *c*4cm, yellow. Fr. only 1cm. Argentina. Z9.

***O. tesajo*** Engelm. Resembling *O. ramosissima* but stem tubercles elongate. Fl. to 2cm diam. Fr. red. NW Mexico (Baja California). Z9.

***O. tomentosa*** Salm-Dyck. Small tree 3–5m; stem-seg. flattened, oblong, 10–60cm, pubesc.; spines absent or 1–3, pale yellow. Fl. 4–5cm, orange. Fr. ovoid, red. C Mexico. Z9.

***O. tuna*** (L.) Mill. Shrub to 90cm; stem-seg. flattened, obovate to oblong, to 16cm but usually smaller, light green, tinged brown above the large areoles; spines 2–6, pale yellow. Fl. *c*5cm diam., pale yellow tinged red. Fr. obovoid, *c*3cm, red. Jamaica. Z9.

***O. tunicata*** (Lehm.) Link & Otto. Shrub, to 60cm, densely branched; spines 6–10, to 5cm, sheath conspicuous, yellow or off-white. Fl. yellow, 3×3cm. Mexico, SW US, and naturalized in parts of S America. Z9.

***O. velutina*** F.A. Weber. Shrub to tree to 4m; stem-seg. flattened, obovate, oblong or pear-shaped, rounded above, cuneate below, 15–30×8–15cm, pubesc.; areoles 2–3cm apart; glochids numerous, to 3mm; spines absent or 1–6, variable in size, to 4cm, pale yellow. Fl. to 3×3cm, yellow, orange or red. Fr. small, sub-globose, dark red. S Mexico. Z9.

***O. verschaffeltii*** Cels. Low shrub, forming clumps; stem-seg. usually elongate in cult., 6–20×1–1.5cm, with low tubercles; lvs terete, to 3cm, persistent; spines 1–3 or more, 1–3cm, setaceous, or absent. Fl. orange to deep red. Bolivia, N Argentina. Z9.

***O. versicolor*** Engelm. & J. Coult. Shrub or small tree to 2.5(–4.5)m; stem-seg. cylindric, 12.5–35×1.5–2cm, tuberculate, tubercles elongate; areoles elliptic, 12–15mm apart; spines sheathed, 7–10, to 1.5cm, red, tipped yellow, sheaths soon deciduous. Fl. 3–4×3–5.5cm, very variable in colour (hence the specific epithet), red, lavender, purple-pink, orange, yellow, green etc. Fr. spineless, sometimes proliferous. SW US (S Arizona), N Mexico (Sonora). Z9.

***O. vestita*** Salm-Dyck. Low, fragile-stemmed shrub; stem-seg. to 20×1–2cm, largely hidden by soft white areolar hair; lvs *c*1cm; spines 4–8, usually short and weak but sometimes to 15mm. Fl. 3.5×3cm, violet-red. Bolivia, N Argentina. A monstrose form is commonly grown. Z9.

***O. vilis*** Rose. Resembling *O. bulbispina* but stem-seg. clavate, to 5cm. N Mexico. Z9.

***O. whipplei*** Engelm. & Bigelow Mat-forming shrub, usually 30–60cm×1–2m, rarely erect, to 2m tall; stem-seg. cylindric, erect, densely arranged, 7.5–15×1–2cm, tuberculate; spines sheathed, 4–14, to 2.5(–5)cm, pale pink to pink-brown, sheaths silvery, conspicuous. Fl. 3–4×2–3cm, pale yellow. Fr. spineless, to 3×2cm, yellow. SW US. Z9.

***O. aciculata*** Griffiths. See *O. lindheimeri*.
***O. albispina*** hort. See *O. microdasys*.
***O. andicola*** Pfeiff. See *O. glomerata*.
***O. arborescens*** Engelm. See *O. imbricata*.
***O. aurea*** Baxter. See *O. basilaris*.
***O. brachyarthra*** Engelm. & Bigelow. See *O. fragilis*.
***O. bruchii*** Speg. See *O. alexanderi*.
***O. camanchica*** Engelm. & Bigelow. See *O. phaeacantha*.
***O. covillei*** Britt. & Rose. See *O. littoralis*.
***O. diademata*** Lem. See *O. articulata*.
***O. dillenii*** (Ker-Gawl.) Haw. See *O. stricta*.
***O. engelmannii*** Salm-Dyck. See *O. ficus-indica*.
***O. engelmannii*** auctt., non Salm-Dyck. See *O. phaeacantha*.
***O. fuscoatra*** Engelm. See *O. compressa*.
***O. gosseliniana*** F.A. Weber. See *O. macrocentra*.
***O. grahamii*** Engelm. See *O. schottii*.
***O. grandiflora*** Engelm. See *O. macrorhiza*.
***O. hamiltonii*** (Gates) G. Rowley, invalid name. See *O. rosarica*.
***O. hickenii*** Britt. & Rose. See *O. glomerata*.
***O. hoffmannii*** H. Bravo. See *O. pubescens*.
***O. humifusa*** (Raf.) Raf. See *O. compressa*.
***O. humilis*** Haw. See *O. tuna*.
***O. hystricina*** Engelm. & Bigelow. See *O. erinacea*.
***O. inermis*** (DC.) DC. See *O. stricta*.
***O. kunzei*** Rose. See *O. parishii*.
***O. laevis*** J. Coult. See *O. phaeacantha*.
***O. linguiformis*** Griffiths. See *O. lindheimeri*.
***O. mackensenii*** Rose. See *O. macrorhiza*.
***O. mamillata*** Schott. See *O. fulgida*.
***O. margaritana*** (J. Coult.) Baxter. See *O. pycnantha*.
***O. megacantha*** Salm-Dyck. See *O. ficus-indica*.
***O. mesacantha*** Raf. See *O. compressa*.
***O. microdasys*** var. ***rufida*** (Engelm.) Schum. See *O. rufida*.
***O. missouriensis*** DC. See *O. polyacantha*.
***O. mojavensis*** Engelm. See *O. phaeacantha*.
***O. occidentalis*** Engelm. & Bigelow. See *O. ficus-indica*.
***O. paediophila*** Cast. See *O. aoracantha*.
***O. pallida*** Rose. See *O. rosea*.
***O. papyracantha*** Philippi. See *O. articulata*.
***O. pestifer*** Britt. & Rose. See *O. pubescens*.
***O. pollardii*** Britt. & Rose. See *O. austrina*.
***O. polyantha*** Haw. See *O. tuna*.
***O. polycarpa*** Small. See *O. austrina*.
***O. pottsii*** Salm-Dyck. See *O. macrorhiza*.
***O. rafinesquei*** Engelm. See *O. compressa*.
***O. rauppiana*** Schum. See *O. sphaerica*.
***O. rhodantha*** Schum. See *O. erinacea* var. *utahensis*.
***O. rutila*** Nutt. See *O. polyacantha*.
***O. santa-rita*** Rose. See *O. macrocentra*.
***O. schweriniana*** Schum. See *O. fragilis*.
***O. serpentina*** Engelm. See *O. parryi*.
***O. setispina*** Engelm. See *O. macrorhiza*.
***O. spegazzinii*** F.A. Weber. See *O. salmiana*.
***O. stanlyi*** Engelm., invalid name. See *O. parishii*.
***O. strobiliformis*** A. Berger. See *O. articulata*.
***O. subinermis*** Backeb. See *O. pentlandii*.
***O. tardospina*** Griffiths. See *O. lindheimeri*.
***O. tenuispina*** Engelm. & Bigelow See *O. macrorhiza*.
***O. teres*** Cels ex F.A. Weber. See *O. vestita*.

***O. tetracantha*** Toumey. See *O. kleiniae*.
***O. tortispina*** Engelm. & Bigelow See *O. macrorhiza*.
***O. treleasei*** J. Coult. See *O. basilaris*.
***O. turpinii*** Lem. See *O. articulata*.
***O. ursina*** F.A. Weber. See *O. erinacea* var. *ursina*.
***O. vaseyi*** (Coult.) Britt. & Rose. See *O. littoralis*.
***O. violacea*** Engelm., invalid name. See *O. macrocentra*.
***O. vivipara*** Rose. See *O. arbuscula*.
***O. vulgaris*** Mill., confused name. See *O. compressa*.
***O. vulgaris*** auct., misapplied. See *O. monacantha*.
***O. wrightiana*** Baxter. See *O. parishii*.
***O. xanthostemma*** Schum. See *O. erinacea*.
For further synonymy see *Austrocylindropuntia*, *Cereus*, *Grusonia*, *Nopalea*, *Platyopuntia* and *Tephrocactus*.

For illustration see CACTI AND SUCCULENTS.

**Orbea** Haw. (From Lat. *orbis*, a disc, referring to the annulus at the mouth of the corolla tube.) Asclepiadaceae. 20 species of short, leafless, perennial herbs closely related to and often included in *Stapelia*, to about 10cm. Stems branching from the base, clump-forming, mostly tetragonal in section, erect to decumbent, acutely and prominently toothed, teeth conical or flattened deltoid, spreading. Leaves rudimentary, caducous. Flowers mostly basal, unscented or slightly malodorous, solitary or in a few-flowered cyme; corolla large, usually flattened, with a thickened annulus surrounding corona, more or less glabrous, lobes transversely rugose, margins often with motile, club-shaped cilia; corona 2-whorled, or outer whorl absent in some species, both whorls 5-lobed, inner corona lobes usually 2-horned. Fruit a spindle-shaped follicle, borne in pairs. S, E Africa. Z9.

CULTIVATION As for *Stapelia*.

***O. ciliata*** (Thunb.) Leach. Stems 3–6cm, mat-forming, ascending, glabrous, suffused red-green, teeth pointed, stout-conical. Fl. solitary; pedicel 1–2.5cm; cor. 7–8cm diam., bowl-shaped, pale green with tiny red-purple spots below, smooth, interior pale yellow-green, densely covered in a maroon-tipped, papillose verrucae above, tube short, annulus cup-shaped, dark purple, rough, margin thickened, lobes 3–3.2cm, ovate-acute, spreading, margins densely covered in flattened, club-like, highly motile white cilia; outer corona pale yellow sparsely dotted purple, lobes 2-toothed or emarginate, inner whorl buff minutely dotted purple, lobes pressed against annulus. Cape Province.

***O. cooperi*** (N.E. Br.) Leach. Stems to 5cm, erect or ascending, glabrous, grey-green or green, with brown or dark green spots and lines, teeth conical, very acute, spreading. Fls 1–3, in a sessile basal cyme; pedicel 6–12mm; cor. to 3.5cm diam., flat, glabrous, pale purple with many dull to pale yellow transverse rugae above, annulus to 9mm diam., pink-purple, tuberculose, lobes 1–1.4cm, ovate, acute, spreading or recurved, star-like, margins recurved, base purple-ciliate; outer corona dark maroon, saucer-shaped, lobes bifid or emarginate, inner corona pale yellow with small purple spots. Cape Province, Orange Free State.

***O. irrorata*** (Masson) Leach. Closely related to *O. verrucosa*. Stems to 10cm, ascending, to 10mm diam., green, glabrous, teeth conical, acute, to 6mm. Fls solitary to few; pedicel to 2.5cm; cor. 3.5cm diam., broadly campanulate, annulus indistinct (a concentration of rugae), pale yellow-green spotted dark red, tube 1cm, more densely spotted lobes 1.2cm, triangular, slightly recurved, cilia absent; outer corona glossy black to purple-brown, lobes bifid, spreading, to 2mm, inner corona orange-yellow, lobes ovate-lanceolate, bordered maroon. Cape Province.

***O. lepida*** (Jacq.) Haw. Stems 4–7cm, glabrous, 1cm diam. Fls 1–2, basal; cor. 3.5cm diam., exterior rough, interior glabrous, sulphur-yellow with small, irregular, purple-brown spots, annulus paler than lobes, tuberculose, lobes 1.2cm, broadly ovate, acute, margins eciliate; lobes of outer corona green or green-yellow, broadly oblong, emarginate or bifid, lobes of inner corona pale yellow or green, sometimes dotted purple-brown, 2-horned. Known only in cult.

***O. longidens*** (N.E. Br.) Leach. Stems 6–15×1cm, erect, bluntly 4-angled, glabrous green tinged red, teeth long-tapered, 12–15mm, soft, fleshy. Fls 3.5–4cm diam., 3 together, tube campanulate, lobes 14–16×9–10mm, ovate-lanceolate, pointed, pale green-yellow blotched red-brown, denser toward tips. Mozambique.

***O. macloughlinii*** (Verdoorn) Leach. Stems 4–8×1.2cm, much-branched from base, obtusely 4-angled, green, glabrous, teeth 3–6mm, pointed. Cor. to 5cm diam. with a distinct raised annulus around the corona which gradually merges, along its outer edge, into three disc, lobes broad-deltoid, yellow marked red. S Africa (E Cape).

***O. maculata*** (N.E. Br.) Leach. Stems to 7cm, stout, green spotted maroon, teeth prominent, deltoid, acute, to 1.5cm. Fls 1–3, around mid-point of stem; pedicel to 5cm; cor. very deeply 5–6-lobed, green-yellow with small maroon spots, more densely spotted towards apex, annulus small, lobes to 2.5cm, oblong, subacute, slightly rugulose, margins reflexed, cilia 3mm, club-shaped, white; corona dark maroon, outer whorl entire, basin-shaped, lobes of inner corona spathulate-oblong. S Africa, Botswana, Zimbabwe.

***O. namaquensis*** (N.E. Br.) Leach. Stems 3–8cm, prostrate to decumbent, glabrous, to 1.5cm, green finely striped red, teeth 5mm. Fls 1–4, basal; pedicel to 3.7cm; cor. 8–10cm diam., flat, pale green-yellow, banded or blotched purple, annulus prominent, thick, fleshy, 5-angled, margins recurved, tube with dense, stiff purple hairs at base, lobes 2.5–3cm, broadly ovate, recurved, long-attenuate, with dense transverse rugae, papillose, lobes of outer corona yellow with small purple-brown spots, linear or linear-lanceolate, inner lobes filiform, tips clavate, recurved. Cape Province, Namaqualand.

***O. paradoxa*** (Verdoorn) Leach. Stems less than 1cm thick, obtusely 4-angled, teeth 1–2cm with 2 very small lateral teeth below the tip, green to grey-green, glabrous, spotted purple. Fls to 5 together; cor. 2–2.4cm diam., tube 8mm, urn-shaped below the annulus, cup-shaped above it, dark glossy red, 4mm deep with stiff red hairs below, annual glossy dark red, outer margins blotched white, spreading part of disc green-white banded dark red, lobes 6×6mm, ovate to acute, green-white with dark red blotches in transverse lines, margins with red, motile, clavate hairs. Mozambique, Natal.

***O. prognatha*** (Bally) Leach. Stems to 6cm, erect to prostrate, with stiff, 2mm-thick adventitious roots, teeth sharp, fleshy. Fl. solitary, in axils of teeth, pedicel 8–10mm; cor. 1.5–3cm diam., livid blue-purple, tube shallowly saucer-shaped, densely papillose, annulus thick, fleshy, lobes broadly triangular, tips recurved, margins ciliate; outer corona dark purple, disc-like, inner corona pale yellow-brown, lobes fleshy, narrowly triangular. N Somalia.

***O. pulchella*** (Masson) Leach. Stems prostrate to ascending, 5–8×1cm, 4-angled, light green, teeth pointed, projecting. Fls several together; cor. rotate, 4.5cm diam., lobes triangular-ovate, tapered, minutely transversely wrinkled with minute brown spots, annulus small, minutely tuberculate with brown spots and ciliate margin. S Africa (E Cape).

***O. rangeana*** (Dinter & A. Berger) Leach. Stems 7cm, numerous, branching from base, green with red-brown markings, 4-angled, teeth 2–6mm. Cor. 4cm diam., glabrous, deeply 5-cleft, lobes 18×10mm, oblong to oblong-spathulate, yellow-green spotted wine red. Namibia.

***O. semota*** (N.E. Br.) Leach. Stems to 7.5×2cm, smooth, spotted red-brown, teeth 6–12mm, conical-deltoid, spreading. Fls 1–3; pedicel 2–3.5cm; cor. 3.5–4.5cm diam., flat, golden yellow with chocolate-brown markings, annulus 5-angled, dark red-brown, about 1cm diam., lobes about 1.5cm, ovate-lanceolate, attenuate, spreading or slightly reflexed, marginal cilia 3mm, dark red, motile; corona glabrous, lobes of outer whorl subtruncate or emarginate, lobes of inner whorl lanceolate or ovate-lanceolate. Tanzania, Kenya.

***O. speciosa*** Leach. Stems 90×6–8mm, erect or decumbent, basally branching, light green, obtusely 4-angled, teeth 1cm. Fls 1–3 together; cor. 3.5–5cm diam., exterior glabrous, interior minutely tuberculate, yellow with purple-red markings which are denser toward lobe tips, margins with red, clavate hairs, annulus small but distinct, lobes slight recurved. S Africa (Natal).

***O. tapscottii*** (Verdoorn) Leach. Stems 12×1cm, branching from base with 4 rounded angles, green to grey-green with darker blotches, teeth 2cm, acute, 2 smaller teeth at tip. Fls 3–4 together; cor. 5cm diam., lobes 2×1cm, ovate, tapered, red with white markings and several hairs, annulus 1cm diam. Botswana, S Africa (W Cape).

***O. umbracula*** (Henderson) Leach. Stems 17×1cm, branching from base, erect, bright with olive green or pink markings, 0.5cm thick at base, pointed, 2 small lateral teeth 6mm below tip. Fls solitary or several together; cor. 2.5–3cm diam., recurved from small prominent annulus, thick, fleshy, glabrous, annulus 7.5×3–5mm, annulus and lobes terracotta to tan, lobe tips transversely wrinkled. marked yellow-green. Cape Province.

***O. variegata*** (L.) Haw. TOAD CACTUS; STARFISH CACTUS. Very variable. Stems 5–10cm, erect, mat-forming, glabrous, grey-green, often tinged red-purple, teeth sharp, projecting, conical. Fls 1–5, pedicel 2.5–5.5cm; cor. 5–9cm diam., flat, exterior smooth, glabrous, pale green, purple-hued, interior densely rugose, pale yellow to sulphur with dark brown blotches and transverse lines, the blotches sometimes coalescing into 6 or 7 longitudinal rows, annulus circular or slightly 5-angled, broad, often revolute, pale yellow with small blotches, lobes broad, ovate, spreading, 5–7-veined; corona lobes yellow, with fine maroon spots, lobes of outer whorl linear-oblong, with 3 tiny, blunt apical teeth, lobes of inner corona 2-horned. Cape Province. 'Decora': fl. base yellow, delicate claret spots and cross lines.

***O. verrucosa*** (Masson) Leach. Stems 4–8×2cm, ascending, glabrous, green, teeth 3–6mm. Fls 1–3, basal; pedicel to 3cm; cor. 4.5–6cm diam., flat to saucer-shaped, lobed for about half its radius, pale yellow with brown and blood-red spots, annulus 5-angled, slightly hairy, with dense, small spots, furrowed toward angles, lobes deltoid-ovate, sharply tapering, recurved or spreading, rough, with dense and irregular transverse rugae, papillose; outer corona dark chocolate-brown, lobes acutely bifid, margins yellow, lobes of inner corona ovate-lanceolate, yellow, edged maroon. Cape Province. var. ***fucosa*** (N.E. Br.) Leach. Stems 4–6×0.6–0.9cm, erect, branching from base, dark green blotched purple-brown, very obtusely 4-angled, teeth pointed. Cor. 3cm diam., exterior smooth, interior wrinkled, glabrous, flat below, annulus 5-angled, 8–9mm diam., lobes triangular, 9–10×4–10mm with 1mm dark red blotches, annulus with denser confluent blotches, margins deep red. S Africa (SE Cape).

***O. woodii*** (N.E. Br.) Leach. Stems 4–8×1–1.5cm, branching from base, erect, 4-angled, teeth 6–12mm. Fls 3 to several together, 4cm diam., rotate lobes ovate, tapered, dark brown sparsely blotched yellow, very wrinkled, centre ciliate, margins recurved. S Africa (Natal).

***O. aperta*** (Masson) Sweet. See *Tridentea aperta*.
For further synonymy see *Caralluma, Diplocyatha, Podanthes, Stapelia* and *Stultitia*.

For illustration see *Hoodia*.

**Orbeanthus** Leach. (From Lat. *orbis*, globe, and Gk *anthos*, flower: the flowers are globe-shaped.) Asclepiadaceae. 2 species of succulent, sprawling perennials; stems smooth, horizontally spreading, with 4 blunt angles bearing short, tuberculate teeth, exstipulate. Flowers large, lacking cilia; corona finely hairy, encircled by annulus. S Africa. Z9.

CULTIVATION As for *Stapelia*, except that a winter minimum of 10°C/60°F is safer. The prostrate habit necessitates the use of wide shallow pans and an open growing medium.

***O. conjunctus*** (A. White & B.L. Sloane) Leach. Stems prostrate, sprawling, to 15cm, succulent, branching, 4-angled, to 8mm thick, glabrous, grey-green mottled dark brown-green on exposed surfaces, teeth conical, 10–16mm apart. Fls 2 or more from within the angle formed by the teeth; cor. subglobose-campanulate, glabrous, base with a shallow tube, constricted at the mouth into a fleshy pentagonal annulus, upon which the cup-shaped limb rests, tube 5mm deep, 14mm diam., annulus 8mm diam., limb 25mm diam., united portion 16mm deep, lobes 3×10mm, interior of tube, annulus and bottom of limb bright maroon, remainder of limb cream-white. Transvaal.

***O. hardyi*** (R.A. Dyer) Leach. Stems succulent, sprawling, arching, to 30cm, rooting at intervals, branching freely, forming a tangled mass, obtusely 4-angled, 6–9mm thick, toothed on angles with a groove between, green mottled purple. Fls solitary or several toward tips of young branches; cor. united 5–6mm beyond annulus, lobes expanding over a period of 3–4 days to 6mm across, exterior glabrous, annulus cushion-shaped, to 4mm high, 1.8–2mm across with central depression containing the corona, lobes ovate-acuminate, 2–2.5×1.3–1.8cm, minutely papillose except toward tips, mainly liver-coloured, rim of annulus paler. Transvaal.

For synonymy see *Stultitia*.

**Orbeopsis** Leach. (From Lat. *orbis*, a disc, like the closely related genus *Orbea*, with Gk suffix *opsis*, appearance.) Asclepiadaceae. 10 species of dwarf, succulent, leafless herbs, to about 25cm. Stems clump-forming, bluntly 4–5-angled, teeth conical or flattened deltoid, acute. Flowers mostly basal, in umbellate clusters, few to many, most malodorous; corolla usually flat, annulus absent, deeply lobed, rugulose or warty; corona more or less cup-shaped, 2-whorled, outer lobes broad, spreading, resting on tube mouth or included, inner lobes recurved, much longer than anthers. Fruit a spindle-shaped follicle, in pairs. S Africa to Angola and Mozambique. Z9.

CULTIVATION As for *Stapelia*, but with a winter minimum of 10°C/50°F.

***O. albocastanea*** (Marloth) Leach. Stems 6–8×1.4cm, branching, curved, almost square in cross section, dark green spotted red, teeth 3–5mm. Fls 3–6; pedicel 4–6cm, upward-curving; cor. 2.5cm diam., ivory, densely spotted purple-brown with coarse rugae, tube 8mm diam., cup-shaped, shallow, spots smaller, lobes 1cm, subacute, margins with clavate cilia, apices recurved; corona dark brown, outer lobes 2mm, linear, inner lobes to 5mm, subulate to filiform, with a long, acute dorsal inner horn. S Namibia.

***O. caudata*** (N.E. Br.) Leach. Stems to 7.5cm, erect, glabrous, 6mm diam., angles rounded, teeth 1cm, straight, spiny. Fls several, in sessile clusters, pedicel erect, 2cm; cor. very deeply lobed, yellow, mottled purple, tube shallow, saucer-shaped, 5–6mm diam., minutely papillose within, lobes 3–4.5cm, spreading, glabrous, margins with sparse, motile, clavate purple cilia, tips filiform; corona yellow, outer lobes 1.5mm, bifid, fused at base, inner lobes 1.5–2mm, linear, blunt. Zimbabwe, Namibia, Malawi.

***O. gerstneri*** (Letty) Leach. Clump-forming; stems 6–7×2.5–3cm, arising from subterranean stolons, 4-angled, deeply furrowed, teeth 13mm, 2 small lateral teeth near the tip. Fls 2–6 in clusters; cor. 3.5cm diam., tube cupular, exterior pale cobalt-green, interior purple-red, velvety, lobes 1.5×0.8cm, upper surface parchment-coloured with dark red spots, rough velvety, glossy, margins purple-ciliate. Natal. ssp. ***elongata*** (Dyer) Leach. Cor. lobes 2.5–3cm. Transvaal.

***O. gossweileri*** (S. Moore) Leach. Clump-forming; stems 10×1.5cm, stout, somewhat prostrate, blue-green lightly mottled purple, 4-angled, teeth 2cm, 7.5mm thick at base, 2 small lateral teeth at the tip. Fls 6–15 together, malodorous; cor. 10cm diam., lobes 4.5×1.2cm, tapering, margins recurved, upper surface minutely pubesc., base transversely rough, granular towards the tips. Angola, Zimbabwe, Zambia.

***O. huillensis*** (Hiern) Leach. Forming dense, broad cushions 6–7cm high, thick, clavate, 4-angled, soft-velvety, teeth compressed. Fls 6–10 in clusters; cor. 9cm diam., lobes 3–4cm, linear-lanceolate, dark red, exterior finely pruinose, interior glabrous, rough. Angola.

***O. knobelii*** (E. Phillips) Leach. Stems to 10×2cm, spreading, acutely angled, glabrous, teeth 6mm, conical, stout. Fls about 10; pedicel 1cm; cor. 3.5cm diam., white densely blotched black-purple, tube 5-angled, shallow, 1cm diam., lobes 1.3cm, ovate, tips green, reflexed when old, cilia motile, club-shaped, dark purple; outer corona basin-shaped, 5-angled, 8mm diam., lobes 4-angled, striped, inner corona lobes 4mm, filiform. Botswana.

***O. lutea*** (N.E. Br.) Leach. Variable. Stems 4–10×2cm, green blotched purple, glabrous, acutely angled, teeth 6–8mm, stout, acute. Fls 3–26, in a dense cluster; pedicel 1.2–2.5cm; cor. 4–7.5cm diam., deeply lobed, yellow to maroon, rugulose, tube 6–8mm diam., shallow, lobes 2–3.5cm, narrow-lanceolate, attenuate, cilia club-shaped, motile, purple; corona yellow, outer whorl cup-shaped, lobes 2mm, contiguous, 4-angled, inner lobes 2mm, filiform. Southern Africa. ssp. ***vaga*** (N.E. Br.) Leach. As for type but cor. lobes much broader and 1.5–2.5× longer than broad. Namibia, Angola, W Cape.

***O. melanantha*** (Schltr.) Leach. Stems 8–10×2cm, glabrous, strongly toothed, teeth 6–10mm, acute. Fls 3–5, per cluster; pedicel to 4.5cm, erect; cor. 5cm diam. tube absent, dark black-purple, densely rugulose, with dense, tiny, erect hairs inside, lobes 1.6–1.8cm, deltoid-ovate, acute, spreading, cilia long, motile, clavate, purple; outer corona brown-purple, lobes 4mm, flat, inner corona dark purple, lobes 4mm, apex bifid. Transvaal, Mozambique.

***O. tsumebensis*** (Oberm.) Leach. Stems to 25cm, 4 or 5-angled, branched, to over 3cm diam., pale green spotted red, glabrous, teeth triangular, to 3cm, flattened. Fls many, in sessile bundles; pedicel about 1.5cm; cor. about 6cm diam., exterior distinctly veined, interior smooth, dark chocolate-brown, glabrous, tube 7×12mm, campanulate, lobes 2.5cm, lanceolate, acute; outer corona cup-shaped, lobes 4-angled, inner lobes with a 3mm horn. N Namibia.

***O. valida*** (N.E. Br.) Leach. Forming loose clumps; stems 10–50×1.5cm, prostrate, tips ascending, green mottled purple, teeth stout, pointed, to 1.5cm. Fls in dense clusters of 20–40; cor. 4–6cm diam., deep chocolate or blood red, lobes 15×25×5–9mm, narrowing toward tips, surface very rough, densely covered with 3mm motile, clavate hairs. Botswana, Transvaal, Zimbabwe, Zambia.

For synonymy see *Caralluma* and *Stapelia*.

For illustration see *Hoodia*.

**Orbignya** Mart. ex Endl. BABASSU PALM. (For A.D. d'Orbigny, French naturalist of the 1900s who collected in tropical Latin America, and became Professor at the Jardin des Plantes, Paris.) Palmae. About 20 species of unarmed, pleonanthic, monoecious or androecious palms. Stem subterranean to erect, becoming bare and marked with irregular scars. Crownshaft absent. Leaves pinnate, erect to arching, marcescent; sheaths thick, margins fibrous; petiole thick and broad, channelled above, convex beneath, tomentose; pinnae crowded, single-fold, regularly spaced or clustered along rachis, linear-lanceolate, apices unequal or cleft, margins scaly; midrib prominent above. Spikes interfoliar with entirely male or entirely female flowers, or with flowers of both sexes, erect to pendent, branched once, amid 2 persistent bracts; inner bract larger, woody: male flowers in spirals or 2 rows with sepals 3, basally connate, petals (2)3–(5), exceeding sepals, ovate, rarely terete, stamens 6–30, included, pistillode small or absent; female flowers larger than males, sepals 3, ovate, overlapping, petals 3 exceeding sepals, leathery, glabrous or tomentose, staminodes united into large, leathery ring, stigmas 3–7, erect. Fruit ovoid, 1 to several-seeded, with persistent perianth and staminodal ring, epicarp scaly, mesocarp hard and fibrous or soft and pulpy, endocarp bony; seed endosperm homogeneous, often with hollow centre. S Mexico to subtropical S America. Z10.

CULTIVATION Occurring predominantly in forest but in high rainfall tropics also in more open habitats, *Orbignya* spp. are imposing but slow-growing feather palms grown as specimens in humid tropical gardens. The kernel oil is used in the manufacture of soap and margarine. Propagate by seed. For cultivation see PALMS.

***O. cohune*** (Mart.) Dahlgr. ex Standl. COHUNE PALM. To 13.5m. Trunk to 30cm diam. Lvs to 9m, pinnae regularly spaced along rachis. Infl. to 1.35m; male fls 1.6×1cm, in spirals, cream, pet. oblanceolate. Fr. 7.5×5cm, 1–3-seeded. C America.

***O. guayacule*** (Liebm.) E. Hern. Resembles *O. cohune* but male pet. spathulate, 1×0.5cm. Fr. 7×4cm. W Mexico.

***O. phalerata*** Mart. BABASSU; COCO DE MACAO. Stem to 30m×50cm diam. Lvs 10–25; sheath 40–120cm; petiole 8–42cm, channelled above; rachis to 8.5m, orange-brown scaly; pinnae 185×83×1–6cm, clustered at base of rachis, regularly spaced above, shining above, glaucous beneath. Infl. 1–3.5m; male fls yellow-cream, in rows; stamens 21–30. Fr. 7–13×4–10cm, 1–3 seeded. Brazil.

***O. spectabilis*** (Mart.) Burret. Trunk short or absent. Lvs erect, pinnae regularly spaced, linear-acuminate. Fr. ellipsoid, 5×3cm, 2–3 seeded. Brazil.

***O. barbosiana*** Burret. See *O. phalerata*.
***O. macropetala*** Burret. See *O. phalerata*.
***O. martiana*** Barb. Rodr. See *O. phalerata*.
***O. speciosa*** (Mart.) Barb. Rodr. See *O. phalerata*.

**ORCHIDACEAE** Juss. ORCHID FAMILY. Monocot. 796 genera and 17,500 species of perennial, mycotrophic, epiphytic or terrestrial herbs, rarely lianes, sometimes without chlorophyll, very rarely completely subterranean; roots usually with multi-layered velamen, in terrestrial species often swollen into tubers, or stems forming corms or rhizomes; stems of epiphytic species often thickened to form pseudobulbs with adventitious roots. Leaves entire, alternate, distichous, rarely opposite or whorled, sometimes scale-like, often fleshy and basally sheathing. Flowers usually bisexual, 3-merous, epigynous, irregular, in racemes or panicles to solitary, often resupinate; perianth 3+3 segments, usually petaloid, outer 3 sometimes green, inner 3 usually larger and of different colour from laterals forming labellum, the laterals often like outer perianth segments, nectaries various, sometimes hollow spur from base of labellum, or a cup on or embedded in the ovary, or extrafloral; stamens 1 (–3) all opposite labellum, when 1 united with style forming gynostemium (column) and truly median stamen of outer whorl, other 2 laterals of inner sometimes staminodal; ovary inferior, of 3 fused carpels, 1-loculed, rarely 3-loculed, with marginal placentas, gynostemium usually subtended by enlarged stigma-lobe (rostellum) to which caudicles often attached and from which a sticky viscidium is removed when pollinia taken by pollinators; ovules minute, numerous (to several million), with minute undeveloped embryo, endosperm formation arrested at 2–4 (–16)-nucleate stage, only testa usually persisting. Fruit a capsule; seeds numerous (to several million), with hygroscopic hairs often between seeds, these expelled by irregular movements of hairs when wetted; seeds usually germinating only in presence of appropriate fungus, forming a protocorm with basal rhizoids, no radicle and usually no cotyledon, the protocorm eventually giving rise to apical leaves. Vanilla is extracted from the cured fruit pods of *Vanilla planifolia*. Cosmopolitan. *Acacallis, Acampe, Acanthephippium, Aceras, Acianthus, Acineta, Acriopsis, Ada, Aerangis, Aeranthes, Aerides, Aganisia, ×Alexanderara, ×Aliceara, Amblostoma, Amesiella, Amitostigma, Anacamptis, Ancistrochilus, Ancistrorhynchus, Angraecopsis, Angraecum, Anguloa, ×Angulocaste, Anoectochilus, Ansellia, Arachnis, ×Aranda, Arethusa, Arpophyllum, Arthrochilus, Arundina, ×Ascocenda, ×Ascofinetia, Ascocentrum, Ascoglossum, ×Asconopsis, Aspasia, Barbosella, Barbrodria, Barkeria, Barlia, Batemannia, Bifrenaria, Bletia, Bletilla, Bollea, Bonatea, Brachycorythis, Brassavola, Brassia, ×Brassocattleya, ×Brassoepidendrum, ×Brassolaeliocattleya, Bromheadia, Broughtonia, Bulbophyllum, Cadetia, Caladenia, Calanthe, Calopogon, Calypso, Calyptrochilum, Capanemia, Catasetum, Cattleya, Cattleyopsis, ×Cattleytonia, Caularthron, Cephalanthera, Chamaeangis, Chaubardia, Chiloglottis, Chondrorhyncha, ×Christieara, Chysis, Cirrhaea, Cleisostoma, Cleistes, Clowesia, Cochleanthes, Cochlioda, Coelia, Coeliopsis, Coeloglossum, Coelogyne, Comparettia, Comperia, Constantia, Coryanthes, Corybas, Corymborchis, Cribbia, Cryptostylis, Cuitlauzina, Cycnoches, Cymbidiella, Cymbidium, Cynorchis, Cypripedium, Cyrtidium, Cyrtopodium, Cyrtorchis, Cyrtostylis, Dactylorhiza, Dendrobium, Dendrochilum, ×Dialaelia, Diaphananthe, Dichaea, Dimerandra, Dimorphorchis, Diplocaulobium, Diplomeris, Dipodium, Dipteranthus, Disa, Disperis, Diuris, Domingoa, ×Doritaenopsis, Doritis, Dracula, Dressleria, Dryadella, Dyakia, Elleanthus, Elythranthera, Encyclia, ×Epicattleya, Epidendrum, ×Epiphronitis, Epigeneium, Epipactis, Eria, Eriochilus, Eriopsis, Erycina, Esmeralda, Euanthe, Eulophia, Eulophiella, Eurychone, Flickingeria, Galeandra, Gastrochilus, Geodorum, Glossodia, Gomesa, Gongora, Goodyera, Grammangis, Grammatophyllum, Graphorkis, Grobya, Grosourdya, Gymnadenia, Habenaria, Hexadesmia, Hexisea, Himantoglossum, Holcoglossum, Houlletia, Huntleya, Ionopsis, Isabelia, Isochilus, Jacquiniella, Jumellea, Kefersteinia, Kegeliella, Kingidium, Koellensteinia, Laelia, ×Laeliocattleya, Laeliopsis, Lanium, Lemboglossum, Leochilus, Lepanthes, Lepanthopsis, Leptotes, Leucohyle, Liparis, Listera, Listrostachys, Lockhartia, Ludisia, Lueddemannia, Luisia, Lycaste, Lyperanthus, ×Maclellanara, Macodes, Macradenia, Malaxis, Masdevallia, Maxillaria, Mendoncella, Mexicoa, Microterangis, Microtis, Miltonia, ×Miltonidium, Miltoniopsis, ×Mokara, Mormodes, Mormolyca, Mystacidium, Nageliella, Nanodes, Neobathiea, Neobenthamia, Neocogniauxia, Neofinetia, Neogardneria, Neolauchea, Neomoorea, Nephelaphyllum, Nervilia, Nidema, Nigritella, Notylia, Oberonia, Octomeria, ×Odontioda, ×Odontobrassia, ×Odontocidium, Odontoglossum, ×Odontonia, ×Odontorettia, Oeceoclades, Oeonia, Oeoniella, Oerstedella, ×Oncidioda, Oncidium, Ophrys, ×Opsistylis, Orchis, Ornithidium, Ornithocephalus, Ornithophora, Osmoglossum, Otochilus, Otoglossum, Otostylis, Pabstia, Palumbina, Panisea, Paphinia, Paphiopedilum, Papilionanthe, Papperitzia, Paraphalaenopsis, Pecteilis, Peristeria, Pescatorea, Phaius, Phalaenopsis, Pholidota, Phragmipedium, Platanthera, Platystele, Plectorrhiza, Plectrelminthus, Pleione, Pleurothallis, Podangis, Pogonia, Polycycnis, Polystachya, Pomatocalpa, Ponerorchis, Porpax, Porroglossum, ×Potinara, Prasophyllum, Promenaea, Psychopsis, Pterostylis, Rangaeris, ×Renanopsis, ×Renantanda, Renanthera, ×Renanthopsis, Restrepia, Restrepiella, Rhinerrhiza, Rhyncholaelia, Rhynchostylis, ×Rhynchovanda, Robiquetia, Rodriguezia, Rossioglossum, Sarcochilus, ×Sarconopsis, Satyrium, Scaphosepalum, Scaphyglottis, Schoenorchis, Schomburgkia, Scuticaria, Sedirea, Seidenfadenia, Selenipedium, Serapias, Sievekingia, Sigmatostalix, Smitinandia, Sobralia, Solenangis, Solenidium, ×Sophrocattleya, ×Sophrolaelia, ×Sophrolaeliocattleya, Sophronitella, Sophronitis, Spathoglottis, Spiranthes, Stanhopea, Stelis, Stenia, Stenoglottis, Stenorrhynchos, ×Stewartara, Summerhayesia, Sunipia, Symphyglossum, Taeniophyllum, Tainia, Telipogon, Tetramicra, Teuscheria, Thelymitra, Theodorea, Thrixspermum, Thunia, Ticoglossum, Trias, Trichocentrum, Trichoceros, Trichoglottis, Trichopilia, Trichosalpinx, Trichotosia, Tridactyle, Trigonidium, Trisetella, Trudelia, Vanda, Vandopsis, Vanilla, ×Vascostylis, ×Vuylstekeara, Warmingia, Warrea, Warreella, ×Wilsonara, Xylobium, Ypsilopus, Zeuxine, Zootrophion, Zygopetalum, Zygosepalum, Zygostates.*

**Orchidantha** N.E. Br. (From Orchid and Gk *anthos*, flower, referring to the orchid-like flowers of this genus.) Lowiaceae. 7 species of low-growing rhizomatous perennial herbs. Leaves distichous, sheathing at base. Flowers malodorous, solitary or paired in bracteate, axillary cymes or panicles; calyx 3-lobed, tubular; corolla 3-lobed, 2 small, 1 enlarged, forming a lip; stamens 5. SE Asia. Z10.

CULTIVATION As for *Heliconia*.

***O. maxillarioides*** (Ridl.) Schum. To 40cm. Lvs to 25×10cm, oblong, coriaceous, tufted; petioles to 10cm. Fls borne in a 2–3-branched panicle; cal. lobes to 3.75cm, flushed purple-violet, tipped green; lip to 2.5cm, green marked purple. Malaysia.

**Orchids**. Orchids have been grown under glass in temperate regions for more than two hundred years and are not difficult to maintain if the correct environmental conditions are provided. A major problem in small glasshouses is the excessively high

**Orchidaceae** (a) *Stanhopea oculata* (b) *Masdevallia caudata* (c) *Ludisia discolor* (d) *Corybas fimbriatus* (e) *Vanda tessellata*

temperatures that can develop in summer – so much more shading is required for orchids than is used for other greenhouse plants (see below under Orchid House).

Orchids that are not frost-hardy originate from tropical parts of the world and depending on their altitudinal range in nature are usually designated 'warm', 'intermediate' or 'cool' in their growing requirements. Briefly, each can be defined by the minimum night temperature provided during the winter months. If three or four separate houses, or compartments in a large house, are available, each with different night temperatures, a wide range of orchids can be grown. Where only one glasshouse is available, it is necessary to select those orchids that grow under similar conditions and are suitable for the degree of warmth that can be provided in winter.

'Warm-growing' orchids are those that in the wild occur at sea level or at low altitudes in tropical regions, and hybrids derived from these wild species. These grow and flower best where there is a minimum night temperature of *c*20–24°C/68–75°F throughout the year. *Phalaenopsis* spp. and hybrids, *Vanda* and many others including the larger *Angraecum* spp., *Catasetum*, a few *Paphiopedilum* spp. and some of the larger *Dendrobium* spp. do best under this regime.

'Intermediate-growing' orchids are those from moderate altitudes where the minimum night temperature in the glasshouse falls to *c*58–60°F during the winter months but may be slightly higher during the summer. A wide range of orchids can be grown under these conditions, including *Cattleya* spp. and their relatives and hybrids with *Laelia, Brassavola, Oncidium, Brassia,* some *Coelogyne* spp., many *Paphiopedilum, Dendrobium* and *Bulbophyllum* spp.

'Cool-growing' orchids are those from medium or high altitudes in the tropics which grow and flower best where the minimum night temperature drops to *c*10–13°C/50–55°F during the winter months or even lower for short periods. Slightly higher minimum temperatures are beneficial during the summer. Many kinds of orchids tolerate these temperatures or flourish under them, including *Cymbidium, Paphiopedilum* spp. of montane origin, *Coelogyne* spp. from higher altitudes, *Masdevallia, Odontoglossum* and their hybrids, many central American and Andean species including *Lycaste, Laelia, Oncidium* and *Maxillaria* spp., New Guinea and Australian species, and many epiphytes from eastern Africa.

Some of these orchids can be grown as house plants in a suitable windowsill, or under artificial light in specialized growth rooms or cabinets (see below). Orchids of temperate origin do not thrive in heated greenhouses and are usually treated as alpines. They can also be grown in pots in unheated conservatories or as garden plants.

TENDER ORCHIDS. Some *Paphiopedilum* and *Cymbidium* spp. are grown for cut-flower production in greenhouse beds, but most orchids are grown in containers placed on the staging or suspended from the walls or special framework within the glasshouse. Clay or plastic pots are used more frequently, but baskets made of wire or wooden slats are usually used for some of the pendulous kinds and for *Stanhopea, Acineta* and *Dracula*, whose flowers grow downwards.

In choosing a pot or slab for mounting an orchid, the need for perfect drainage should be borne in mind. It is usually necessary to enlarge the drainage holes provided with a hammer or hole saw even if a very loose compost is used. While orchids can be grown with a mixture of other tropical plants, they are usually kept separate as this makes the control of greenhouse pests easier. In either case, it is very important to pay careful attention to greenhouse hygiene, removing dead leaves and faded blooms regularly as well as unsightly moss and other weeds, and to ensure the correct environmental conditions are maintained (see below under Orchid House).

*Composts*. The compost in which orchids are grown has the dual function of supporting the plant in its container and providing the roots with a medium which is well aerated yet moisture-retentive. It is seldom replaced more than once a year, and often at longer intervals, so it must decompose slowly. Composts in use today are usually mixtures of natural materials, such as pieces of pine or fir bark, coarse grit, fibrous peat, chopped dried leaves of sphagnum, and inert materials like perlite, perlag, pieces of horticultural grade charcoal and sometimes pieces of polystyrene. Individual growers and nurserymen each have their favourite mixes which are successful in their greenhouses and with their different watering regimes. A mix containing large particles with large spaces between them will need watering more frequently than a close mix with particles of small size.

Many growers add bone meal, dried blood or hoof and horn meal to these mixtures when plants are potted. Others prefer a compost which is completely inert so that they can supply known quantities of liquid fertilizer to the plants as a dilute feed on a regular basis throughout the growing season. Two tried and tested compost mixes are given below, but each can be modified to suit individual orchids.

*Basic epiphyte mix*: 3 parts washed bark chips, medium grade; 1 part coarse perlag; 1 part charcoal, horticultural grade; 1 part fibrous peat or broken leaves or chopped sphagnum.

*Basic mix for terrestrial orchids*: 3 parts fibrous peat; 2 parts coarse perlite; 2 parts coarse grit; 1 part charcoal, horticultural grade.

A fairly new medium for orchid growing is made up of water-repellent rockwool mixed with perlite. In effect it provides a substrate very similar to that of the mossy branches of trees in tropical forests, with a surface of springy, wet, air bubbles surrounding the plant roots. A carefully controlled system of watering and feeding is obviously necessary with this medium, a different system from that undertaken with conventional composts. It is therefore not convenient to use both rockwool and other composts for plants in a mixed collection. On the commercial scale the provision of water and nutrients is usually computer-controlled.

POTTING. Choosing the right size of pot is the first essential when potting an orchid. Its roots need to have ample space within the container, allowing enough space for at least one year's growth. Trying to save time by putting plants of small or medium size in a large pot is usually detrimental because too much compost can cause poor drainage. Weak roots need to be restricted and the base of the plant kept dry until healthy new roots develop. Many orchids do best in rather small pots. To ensure that drainage is efficient the container is often filled one third full with pieces of polystyrene, crock or large stones. The crocks can be packed vertically to fill the bottom quarter or third of the pot where perfect drainage is at a premium. Stones are particularly useful in plastic pots as the extra weight provides stability.

Fresh compost is essential for each session of potting or repotting is essential. It is usually necessary to soak pine bark before using, and peat and other components are moistened slightly before use. The synthetic materials such as perlite and rockwool are also more pleasant to use if slightly damp.

The technique of potting is simple. The plant is held in the pot with one hand so that the crown of the plant, the base of the pseudobulbs, or the part of the plant from which the roots emerge is just below the level of the rim. Compost is filled in around the roots with the other hand and gently shaken into the spaces between them by tapping the pot gently on the bench several times. Small plants or those with a poor root system may need to be tied to a stake, a short piece of cane or stiff wire, until they become established.

After potting the compost is usually watered thoroughly, sometimes on two or three consecutive days, to make use that the constituents are completely moistened. Newly potted plants are then kept dry for two or three weeks to allow the roots to settle. During this time the plants must be kept in a humid place and misted over frequently to make sure that the leaves do not become desiccated.

*Repotting*. Orchid plants need repotting from time to time. After a good season they may begin to grow over the edge of the pot or root growth may be so vigorous that the whole plant is pushed up out of the pot, although the presence of adventitious and escaping roots is quite normal in many genera (particularly *Phalaenopsis* and the *Laelia* alliance) and overgrown plants often fare best when left undisturbed for many seasons. In some genera (e.g. *Coelogyne* and *Eria*), the pot may serve as little more than a focus for cascading rhizomes, while *Vanda* and its allies may use the pot as little more than an anchor. Large plants of most genera may nonetheless need dividing or potting on into a larger container. Plants that have died off in the middle or on one side may need rejuvenating.

The commonest reason for repotting is that the compost has deteriorated. If there is difficulty getting a well-grown plant out of the old pot, it is sometimes helpful to leave it in a bucket of water for an hour or two. The saturated plant then slides out easily. Where a thick and adhesive rooted plant has attached itself to the inside of a clay, more drastic action may be needed, i.e. breaking the pot. Plants grown in rockwool have the advantage that repotting is required much less frequently.

During repotting all the old compost is removed and discarded. Dead roots, which are soft and brown, should be removed carefully, as near as possible to the point where they emerge from the upper parts of the plant. It is a good idea to use sterile tools for this operation in order to avoid spreading viruses. Healthy roots will be white and should be damaged as little as possible. They are rather brittle, but if they crack no harm will be done. Without compost and with clean healthy roots, the plant can then be carefully examined for any sign of scale insects, treated if necessary, and divided or reshaped as required. Old leafless pseudobulbs can be removed for propagation before the tidy plant is repotted in a clean pot with fresh compost as described above. Likewise, monopodial genera whose basal portions have become bare and which carry a greater number of aerial roots than potted roots can be rejuvenated by having their stems shortened to below the healthy aerial roots. These are then planted.

Some orchids resent disturbance and take a long time to reestablish after repotting. For some of the larger orchids in the *Vanda* alliance, including *Angraecum* spp., repotting is rarely necessary as very coarse bark pieces are used in the compost mix and these take a long time to deteriorate unless the plants are frequently over-watered.

*Mounted plants*. Many epiphytes also grow well mounted on slabs of cork oak bark of suitable size or firmly attached to chunks of tree fern fibre. At first, they must be tied firmly to the surface, usually with coarse nylon thread, plastic tape or copper wire, but new roots will soon grow and attach them to the mount. Mounted plants on bark or tree fern slabs may not need further attention for many years. If they become loose it may be desirable to transfer them to a fresh mount. Sometimes a thick growth of moss develops around mounted plants and this may need to be removed from time to time, to make sure the roots do not lack air.

*Watering and spraying*. Orchids need to dry out periodically and many adapt well to a weekly watering regime. A few need watering or misting every day, especially those which are mounted, while others grow best with a long moist growing season followed by a dry period of several months. The best approach for the new grower is to try to find out as much as possible about the natural habitat of the different kinds of orchids and find ways of imitating the wild environment in the management of the greenhouse. Rainwater is best, but it should be stored in a dark tank in the greenhouse so that it stays clean and is the right temperature for the plants.

After repotting, plants will need very little water in the pot because their roots are inactive. Swamping them at this stage may damage those roots which remain. During a period of a month or two the plants' moisture needs can be met by spraying or misting over the leaves, early in the day or, on sunny days, several times during the day. It is best to make sure that moisture does not lodge in leaf axils or the apex of new shoots over-night when temperatures drop, as the recently established plants may be more susceptible to water-borne disease. Misting over the leaves is always a useful exercise on sunny days as it helps to ensure high humidity in the greenhouse and also lowers the leaf temperature.

Once the plants are properly established in their pots or baskets and new root growth is visible, a regular watering regime can begin. On each occasion plants should be heavily and thoroughly watered, so that the compost is really wetted. If a hose is used, it is helpful to fit a water breaker to it, or to use a watering lance with a fine rose. This ensures a gentle flow of water so that the loose compost is not washed out of the pot. The frequency of watering will depend on the size of the pot and the kinds of compost used, as well as on the weather. There is really no substitute for daily inspection of the plants. The need for water can often be assessed by the weight of the pots once one becomes used to handling them. Once or twice a week is a good routine, but daily watering may be necessary in summer. In the winter, watering is usually reduced to once every week or two, and for a few plants water is given only monthly. Some growers prefer to water their plants early in the day so that the foliage will have dried off by nightfall when temperatures drop. In the tropical habitats of many orchids, however, storms arise at midday or in the afternoons and the plants are frequently still wet at night. Some growers make a habit of watering their plants in the late afternoon and, provided there is sufficient air movement within the glasshouse to prevent stagnation and inhibit pathogens, many plants grow under this regime.

*Feeding*. Because orchid composts are relatively inert, it is very beneficial to feed the plants during their growing season. If they are potted in rockwool, coarse bark or perlite only, this is essential. A dilute liquid fertilizer is the most convenient form to use as it can be applied with watering. Many of the proprietary brands of liquid fertilizer are suitable, but they need to be diluted to quarter or half the strength that is recommended for other pot plants. Little and often is a good maxim, but only when the plant is in active growth. Foliar feeding is sometimes recommended, but uptake through the leaves of many orchids is rather limited.

Many growers prefer to use a high-nitrogen fertilizer (30.10.10) early in the summer to encourage maximum growth while temperatures are high and days are long. Once the growths have matured, it is a good idea to change to a fertilizer that will encourage flowering, such as some of those sold for tomato crops, which are high in potash (10:10:30). Other growers prefer to use more natural fertilizers such as chicken maure or a liquid feed prepared from seaweeds. Great care must be taken to ensure that whatever is used is sufficiently dilute or the orchid roots can be damaged.

*Resting*. Many terrestrial orchids with storage organs undergo a long dormant season, when their pseudobulbs or tubers wait underground until favourable conditions for growth return. The season may be inimical because it is too hot or too cold but it is nearly always dry. Similarly, many of the epiphytic orchids (i.e. those with pseudobulbs or succulent rigid leaves) are structurally adapted to withstand a period of drought. This often coincides with lower temperatures. Except for the species which grow in swamps or in equatorial or cloud forests where some rain falls in every month, orchids need to dry out and 'rest' at some stage during their annual growth cycle.

In cultivation this need must not be forgotten. It is no use continuing to give water and fertilizer to dormant plants and may actually be harmful. At best it will lead to the production of weak non-floral growth. The resting period may be only a few weeks. In the Indian *Dendrobium* spp., for example, it is recognizable at its start by the withering of leaves and at the end by the development of new shoots. As soon as a new pseudobulb begins to grow, plants should be watered freely again: until then, only enough water need be given to prevent excessive shrivelling of the old pseudobulbs or corms. In many Mexican orchids, especially those at high altitude, the dry season lasts for several of the winter months and plants often flower during this period. The days are short and, with less light and lower temperatures, growth is minimal. Nevertheless, plants must be maintained in a humid environment, particularly at night, or they will become too desiccated. If the leaves begin to fall or pseudobulbs become wrinkled, a little water can safely be given.

*Staking and flowering*. Most orchids flower once a year according to the season, although some hybrids flower more frequently. *Odontoglossum* spp., for example, will flower at ten-month intervals under ideal conditions and *Phalaenopsis* hybrids twice a year. Many orchid genera produce long inflorescences bearing many flowers, but most plants of *Paphiopedilum* and *Lycaste* species and hybrids bear flowers singly.

For attractive presentation, whether in the glasshouse or home or on the show bench, nearly all inflorescences need some kind of training. It is best to place a cane of suitable size and length adjacent to each flower spike soon after it appears. A pointed cane or stiff wire can be pushed into the compost, not too close to the side of the pot where active roots could be damaged, and not too close to the base of the plant where new roots might be squashed. Indicating the emergence of spikes in this way also prevents accidental damage to them during routine work in the glasshouse. Young flower spikes can be tied to the cane as they develop, starting when they are 10–15cm/4–6in. high.

Orchids which naturally produce arching or pendulous spikes are best trained in their natural shape with stiff wire supports. The support should be kept to a minimum, depending on the length of the spray. Solitary flowers often need only a single tie, just below the pedicel, and multi-flowered orchids should have the top tie just below the first flower.

The presentation of flowers and spikes is best when plant are not moved, or even turned around, while the buds are developing, because they often re-orient themselves in relation to the strongest source of light when they have been moved. This can result in bent and twisted spikes instead of gracefully arching ones.

*Cultural problems*. Discoloration of leaves can be caused by mineral deficiencies. They will disappear when the plants are given adequate and properly balanced fertilizer. It is well worth giving suspect plants a teaspoon or two of epsom salts (magnesium sulphate), sprinkled on the surface of the compost and watered in, once or twice a month.

Stunted growth may also indicate a lack of nutrients, particularly nitrogen. Lack of flowers or fewer flowers than expected can also be due to an unbalanced fertilizer programme and indicate a need for a higher concentration of potassium or phosphorus in the feeding programme.

Too much fertilizer, especially nitrogen, is likely to promote very long but weak growths and thin leaves. Plants will need extra staking to prevent them breaking should this occur. Over-feeding can also result in loss of leaves. Salts dissolved in the water supply, as well as chemical fertilizers or a build-up of excess salts in the potting medium, can cause leaf tip die-back and root death. A generous flushing of the compost with plain water every month or so is very beneficial.

Distortions of the foliage sometimes occur on young growths, particularly in members of the *Oncidium* alliance, and also in *Cymbidium* and *Paphiopedilum*. This usually occurs as a result of a severe check, such as dryness or low temperatures, during the early development of the shoot, and can be avoided by greater attention to these details for subsequent growths. It can also be a genetic effect, and, if too unsightly, plants which regularly grow in an ugly way should be abandoned.

PESTS AND DISEASES. Orchids are not prone to attack by pests and diseases any more than other greenhouse plants. Provided their growing conditions are hygienic and buoyant, most plants will never need treatment with sprays or insecticides.

A greenhouse should always be kept clean and tidy with benches and pots free from weeds. Dead leaves and dying flowers should be removed regularly. New plants should be inspected most carefully before they are added to a collection: they may be harbouring pests which should be destroyed rather than introduced to a new collection. All insecticides and other chemicals should be used with the greatest care, wearing gloves, and strictly following the maker's instructions. They must only be used in the correct concentration and can be harmful to the plant if applied in bright sunlight or used when temperatures are high.

*Pests*. Aphids are often a nuisance on young shoots and on flower buds, especially during the winter months. Unless they are very numerous they can usually be gently removed with finger and thumb, or killed off by spraying with soapy water. Malathion is the safest general purpose insecticide for greenhouse use and is effective against aphids and many kinds of scale insects. Mealybugs are more resistant because of their water-resistant outer covering. These sap-sucking insects lurk on the undersides of leaves, under the sheaths on pseudobulbs and stems and within the bracts supporting the flowers. Regular inspection and treatment is the best means of keeping insect pests down to negligible proportions. Insecticides are best used as wettable powders rather than as liquids which have xylene as a solvent. There is no danger of foliage burn with the wettable powders, but they may leave an unsightly deposit.

Insects which eat parts of orchid plants, especially the flowers, include vine weevils and cockroaches. Both are nocturnal and the best way of dealing with them is to catch them in the act of feeding. Apart from catching pests, it can be a pleasure to be in a greenhouse in the evening – some orchids are powerfully scented then, and others have colours which glow under artificial light. Caterpillars and other insect larvae can be voracious and cause devastation even in a single night. Woodlice are sometimes a problem in bark composts as they feed on decaying plant material and sometimes turn their attention to young roots. They are not easy to eradicate, but can be controlled by careful attention to good hygiene, regular cleaning of the greenhouse and the use of a suitable powder sprinkled around the door and on the floor where they may enter. Slugs and snails can do considerable damage to buds, flowers and young shoots. Mice are also heavy feeders on young buds and shoots if they intrude into a greenhouse.

Red spider mites and several species of false spider mites are probably the worst pests of orchid plants and they are very difficult to eradicate. Small pits or tiny silver spots on the lower surface of the leaves are evidence of their presence. Other mite species make irregularly shaped depressions in the leaf surface which are often yellowish brown in colour. They multiply rapidly in warm and dry conditions. This is usually the key to their control. If mites are present in a greenhouse, it means that the environment is not quite humid enough for orchids. A heavy infestation of mites can be controlled with a miticide. Either of these should be used in cool weather and at least two applications should be made at ten day intervals in order to ensure that all stages of the mites' life cycle are killed.

*Fungus and bacterial diseases*. Black or brown spots on leaves and flowers and watery patches in leaf tissue are a sure sign that a pathogen has invaded the plant. Very often this is because of wrong or careless treatment of the plant. Over-watering, careless repotting, direct sunlight on a wet leaf, low temperatures, poor ventilation and stagnant air can all precipitate fungal or bacterial invasion. A number of fungi have been identified as orchid pathogens, particularly in tropical countries. Usually the rot or infection has gone too far for treatment by the time it becomes obvious. The best method of dealing with it is to remove the affected tissue and about 1cm (0.5in.) of adjacent healthy tissue, and disinfect the cut surface with flowers of sulphur. Damaged parts should be removed and burned to avoid infecting other plants. Badly affected plants should be abandoned and burned for the sake of the rest of the collection.

*Virus diseases*. A number of different virus diseases have been identified in cultivated orchids. The symptoms of virus infection are pale patches, often in the form of an irregular mosaic pattern, on the young shoots and leaves. These become brown or black as the plant ages. The most common orchid virus is Cymbidium mosaic virus (CyMV) which is particularly common in collections of *Cymbidium* but has also been identified, with slightly different symptoms, on other orchids including *Phalaenopsis* species and hybrids, *Angraecum*, and various members of the *Cattleya* and *Oncidium* alliances. It is hardly worth keeping suspect plants, which often grow weakly and flower poorly, as they can be a source of infection to other plants through insect bites or cutting tools. There is no cure for virus infections in orchid plants at present.

PROPAGATION. Orchids can be increased by division of mature plants, by activating dormant buds on 'backbulbs', by taking stem or inflorescence cuttings, and by hand pollinating the plants to obtain seeds. Each of these techniques is somewhat specialized and they are reviewed briefly below.

*Divisions and 'backbulbs'*. Large plants are easily divided into two or more parts when they are repotted. Sometimes a plant will

**Orchidaceae** I Growth and flowering habits (a) sympodial pseudobulbous (a1) basal inflorescence (a2) pseudobulb (b) monopodial (b1) axillary inflorescence (b2) aerial root thickly coated with velamen (c) sympodial non-pseudobulbous (c1) apical inflorescence II Variation in stem and foliage forms (a) 'chain-linked' pseudobulbs *(Otochilus)* (b) pseudobulb with leafy basal sheaths *(Odontoglossum)* (c) semi-cane type pseudobulb *(Cattleya)* (d) globose unifoliate pseudobulb on running rhizome *(Bulbophyllum)* (e) lageniform pseudobulb *(Pleione)* (f) bifoliate pseudobulb *(Coelogyne)* (g) *Polystachya* (h) cane-type pseudobulb *(Dendrobium)* (i) stem with imbricate leaves *(Lockhartia)* (j) cane stem *(Epidendrum)* (k) reed stem *(Sobralia)* (l) swollen leaf (stem short or absent) *(Dendrobium)* (m) narrow leaf (stem short or absent) *(Scutecaria)* (n) leaf enlarged (stem short or absent) *(Oncidium)* (o) tufted *(Masdevallia)* (p) fan-leaved *(Huntleya)* (q) monopodial (stem short or absent) *(Phalaenopsis)* (r) fleshy rhizomatous *(Anoectochilus)* (s) tuberous *(Calopogon)* (t) tuberous *(Calypso)* III The orchid flower (a) *Masdevallia* (synsepalum) (b) *Paphiopedilum* (b1) synsepalum (b2) staminode (b3) saccate labellum (c) *Cattleya* (c1) dorsal sepal (c2) lateral sepals (c3) petals (c4) labellum (c5) callus (c6) column (c7) anther cap (c8) stigmatic surface (c9) ovary (d) *Catasetum* (resupinate flower)

literally fall apart into several pieces. Other plants have pseudobulbs which are joined to each other by a tough rhizome which needs to be cut with a sterile knife or secateurs. It is a mistake to make too many divisions in the interests of rapid multiplication of plants as they may then be too small to survive. For most orchids two or three growths should be retained in each division. *Cattleya* and its allies need at least one leafy pseudobulb on the back growth, with a prominent dormant bud at its base, to have a chance of success. For *Lycaste* and members of the *Odontoglossum* alliance, two or three pseudobulbs are usually separated together. *Cymbidium* spp. are the easiest to propagate from old leafless pseudobulbs removed from the back of the plant. All loose sheaths should be removed and the cut base of each pseudobulb allowed to dry. Then it can be immersed up to a third of its height in sharp sand or grit and kept moist in a cool corner of the greenhouse. Within two or three months a new shoot will appear above the surface. After a further two or three months the shoot will have its own roots and be potted up, preferably with the old pseudobulb attached for the first year. New plants propagated in this way may reach flowering size in two or three years.

*Cuttings*. The pseudobulbs, stems and inflorescence stalks on some orchids make suitable propagating material when they are divided into cuttings. Each section must contain one or more dormant buds, and when it is detached from the rest of the plant and kept in suitably humid surroundings, such as laid on a bed of damp moss or inserted in a pan of moist grit, these buds will form new plantlets. After a few months they can be removed from the old piece of plant and potted up individually. The cane-like stems of *Epidendrum* and *Dendrobium* yield new plants in this way. The inflorescence stalks of *Phalaenopsis, Phaius* and *Calanthe* also have a few dormant buds which will each make a new plantlet under appropriate conditions. On many pseudobulbs, dormant buds will occasionally develop little plants, sometimes known as 'keikis', quite spontaneously; this is particularly obvious is a genus like *Pleione*. These can be removed and potted up as soon as they have a few roots to support their independent growth.

*Seeds*. Orchid seeds are extremely minute. Each consists of a tiny embryo surrounded by a single layer of protective cells. They are so small that the food reserves in the embryo are inadequate, by themselves, for the early development of the new plant. In nature most orchid seeds begin life in a partnership with a symbiotic fungus. The fungal hyphae, which are present in the soil or on the bark of a host tree, invade the seed and enter the cells of the embryo. The orchid soon begins to digest the fungal tissue and obtain nutrients from it, thus using the fungus as an intermediary in obtaining nutrients from decaying material in the soil.

In the laboratory, this process can be imitated by sowing sterilized seeds with a culture of the fungus on a suitable jelly-like medium called agar with the addition of porridge oats which the fungus can utilize. A simpler method is to use a medium containing all the mineral nutrients, water and sugar that the germinating seed needs and dispense with the fungus. All these techniques must be carried out in sterile conditions – otherwise it is extremely easy for the nutrient medium to become infected with unwanted micro-organisms that develop at the expense of the orchid. The work can be carried out in the kitchen, using a domestic pressure cooker to prepare sterile glassware and media. A sterile box or even a large polythene bag can be used as a cover for the operation which should be carried out as speedily as possible. However, it is much easier, and success is more assured, if the technique is carried out in a specialised laboratory on a laminar flow bench.

Conical flasks or sterile bottles containing the newly sown seeds are kept under controlled conditions while the embryo grows out through the seedcoat to form, first, a rounded protocorm covered in rhizoids and then a small plantlet. Sometimes the containers need to be kept in the dark for the first few months, but the epiphytic orchids develop green protocorms almost immediately and are kept under artificial light for 12–16 hours per day. Although the flasks are sealed, the medium will become too solid through dehydration after a few months and the plantlets will need to be transferred to freshly prepared medium in a new container. These techniques must also be carried out under sterile conditions. Eventually, about six to twelve months after sowing, the plantlets are large enough to be taken out of the flask, washed carefully to remove all traces of agar, and then potted up in a fine compost mix. For their first few weeks in the greenhouse they need special care. Extra warmth and humidity, such as can be provided in a small propagating case, is often beneficial.

Different kinds of orchids develop at different rates. Some of the quickest are the *Phalaenopsis* species and hybrids which can grow from seeds to flowering size in a little as 18–20 months. Others take much longer. Four to six years is an average length of time for most orchids.

*Meristem propagation*. A feature of orchid culture, both commercially and as a hobby, is the high value that is placed on plants which have received Awards from the Royal Horticultural Society (RHS), American Orchid Society (AOS) and other award-giving bodies around the world. Many people would like to have divisions of such desirable plants, and the demand makes their price high. The advent in 1960 of techniques for the culture and multiplication of the apical meristem of a young shoot, and the various forms of tissue culture which have been developed since then, have been extremely successful and have made it possible for many people to own and enjoy some of the best plants at the same price that they would have to pay for seedlings. The technique of growing new plants in this way is very similar to propagation from seeds, but, since the starting material is already mature, the protocorms which are obtained by this method develop into new, flowering size plants, far more quickly. Sterilised conditions, containers and plant material are used, and a warm growth chamber is necessary for the young plants on agar. After they are transferred to a normal orchid compost in the greenhouse, they grow away very rapidly. This technique is not difficult and modifications of it are carried out today in many parts of the world for a wide range of orchids.

*Use of colchicine*. The poisonous alkaloid colchicine can be used to change the chromosome constituents in the cells of orchid protocorms. The concentration and duration of the application of the chemical to plantlets in flasks must be carefully and accurately monitored. Colchicine treatment has a pronounced effect on the appearance of the adult plant which will usually have larger leaves and flowers of superior shape, but the plants grow to flowering size more slowly and may have fewer flowers. If colchicine is incorrectly applied, monstrosities may result.

Colchicine has been used successfully with many of the free-flowering *Cymbidium* hybrids, to produce flowers with better form and to promote fertility in some of the more unusual crosses. Recently it has been tried with some of the *Paphiopedilum* protocorms which have also developed into fertile plants with superior flowers.

HYBRIDIZATION. The first artificial hybrids among the orchids were made in the 1850s at the Veitch nursery in Exeter. The first seedlings that germinated were of the genus *Cattleya*, but the first orchid hybrid to flower was a *Calanthe* in 1856. Following this success, many seed capsules were produced from a wide variety of crosses. Germination of the seeds was not easy, but a few plants of various genera were raised, usually on the compost surrounding the mother plant. Advances were made when the process of symbiotic germination was developed by Bernard and Burgeff at the turn of the century. Thereafter orchid seeds were germinated on an agar medium infected with a mycorrhizal fungus. The greatest discovery, however, was the demonstration by Knudson in 1922 that the fungus could be dispensed with and that orchid seeds would germinated on an entirely artificial medium which combined suitable basic chemicals with agar and a supply of sugar, usually sucrose. This development precipitated an enormous increase in the number and variety of orchid hybrids made, which continues to this day.

ORCHID HYBRID AND CULTIVAR NOMENCLATURE. It was decided at an early stage in orchid hybridization that precise records should be kept of crosses made and the fertile hybrids that resulted. From 1871 the *Gardeners' Chronicle* published new hybrids and *The Or-*

*chid Review* also published new hybrids from its inception in 1893. In 1895 Messrs Sander & Sons, Orchid Growers, of St. Albans, England, instituted a system for the registration of orchid hybrids and in due course published in 1906 the first issue of *Sander's List of Orchid Hybrids*. Subsequently at intervals several volumes of addenda have been published, and orchid hybridists throughout the world remain greatly indebted to the Sander family for the initiative taken in providing a most valuable service.

These duties were taken over by The Royal Horticultural Society with effect from 1 January 1961, and in accordance with obligations accepted as International Registration Authority, the Society has agreed to publish, from time to time, a list of all registrations accepted after 31 December 1960. In order to maintain continuity, the title *Sander's List of Orchid Hybrids* is retained. The most recent volume appeared in 1991. A listing of nearly 100,000 orchid hybrids made and registered up to 1 December 1990 is thus available in the printed volumes and on a compact disk for use on a personal computer.

The Royal Horticultural Society has carried out the task of International Registrar of Orchid Hybrids in accordance with a set of rules agreed by the International Orchid Commission (IOC) following those of the International Code of Nomenclature for Cultivated Plants (ICNCP). In 1969 the IOC published a *Handbook on Orchid Nomenclature and Registration* (third edition, 1985) which outlines the general principles of plant nomenclature, the rules as they affect the nomenclature of wild and cultivated orchids, and the requirements for the registration of orchid hybrids.

Orchid hybrids are distinguished from the wild species and from the hybrids in many other groups of plants by a system of naming at two or three levels, for example, in the hybrid *Cattleya* Bow Bells 'White Wings', the name of the genus is *Cattleya*, the name of the grex is *Cattleya* Bow Bells and the name of the cultivar is *Cattleya* Bow Bells 'White Wings'.

The term *grex* denotes a group of individual plants of an artificial hybrid all bearing the same *grex name*. This grex name is applied to all the progeny directly raised from two parent plants which bear the same name (species or hybrids), regardless of which cultivar or colour form was used and regardless of which was used as the seed or pollen parent. The term grex name used in this way is unique to the orchids and is covered by the term *collective name* in the ICNCP. Thus *Sander's List of Orchid Hybrids* is a Register of grex names.

A *cultivar* in orchids is a clone, that is, a genetically similar assemblage of individuals derived originally from a single seedling individual by vegetative propagation. Cultivar epithets are fancy names enclosed in single quotes, e.g. 'White Wings' in the example given above. Grex and cultivar epithets cannot be used singly. The full name of an individual plant of this hybrid orchid is thus *Cattleya* Bow Bells 'White Wings'. Similarly, orchid species can be given cultivar epithets to distinguish particularly remarkable individual plants, e.g. *Paphiopedilum insigne* 'Harefield Hall'.

Further details and the rules regarding the registration of orchid hybrids can be found in the Handbook referred to above which is available from the Royal Horticultural Society.

*Merit Awards*. The system of giving awards to particularly meritorious plants was started in England by the Manchester and North of England Orchid Society and followed shortly thereafter by the Royal Horticultural Society. Since 1889 the RHS has had an Orchid Committee which makes recommendations for awards to Council. The importance of the cultivar epithet in an orchid name becomes apparent, as awards are given to individual plants. Awards are usually abbreviated to just the first letters of each word and the name of the body which makes the Award, e.g. FCC/RHS (First Class Certificate/Royal Horticultural Society), AM/AOS (Award of Merit/American Orchid Society). They are usually written after the orchid name and followed by the year of the award, e.g. *Lycaste* Wyld Fire 'Blaze of Tara' AM/RHS 1988.

There are now more than 40 orchid societies and associations giving a variety of awards around the world. A complete list is available in the Handbook on Orchid Nomenclature and Registration (see above).

*Sources of Plants*. Orchid plants are available from a wide range of specialist nurseries who advertise in the horticultural press and specialist magazines such as *The Orchid Review*, the orchid journal of the Royal Horticultural Society, *Die Orchidee*, the official journal of the Deutsche Orchideen-Gesellschaft, the *American Orchid Society Bulletin* and many others. Many hybrids which are now propagated in bulk are also available from garden centres. The British Orchid Growers' Association and the British Orchid Council combine to produce a leaflet annually in which details of the major producers and growers in UK are listed.

Wild orchid plants are specially protected in most countries and should not be collected without permission. The Convention on International Trade in Endangered Species of Wild Fauna and Flora (CITES) controls the import and export of orchid species through a permit system administered by each of the signatory nations.

THE HARDY SPECIES. A number of orchid genera whose species are amenable to cultivation occur mainly in the mountains of subtropical regions and in temperate areas. They may require frost-free conditions or a completely dry period during the cool weather when they are dormant. They are most easily accommodated in a cold frame or unheated glasshouse and can be treated in exactly the same way as many bulbs and alpine plants.

The most well-known group of temperate orchids from tropical regions comprises the species and hybrids of the genus *Pleione*. They grow best in shallow pans and need repotting annually into a fine, fast-draining but moisture-retentive compost. Repotting should be carried out in late winter, just as the new flowering shoots begin to emerge. The plants grow well in warm and humid conditions during the summer, but need to be dried off as the leaves turn yellow and fall in the autumn and kept very cool during the winter months.

European orchids, including the genera *Orchis, Ophrys* and *Dactylorhiza*, can also be grown very easily in pots in an alpine house. Similarly, some of the Australian terrestrial genera, particularly the greenhoods, *Pterostylis* species and hybrids, make attractive displays when in flower and need a pronounced dry season while the tubers are below ground. Some of the north American and Asiatic species of *Cypripedium* also respond well to pot grown culture, but require shadier conditions than other temperate orchids. Some of the Japanese species and hybrids of *Calanthe* are also very tolerant of this treatment and some forms of *Bletilla striata* are widely grown.

When purchasing terrestrial orchids it is important to be sure that they have originated as nursery-propagated plants and have not been taken directly from the wild which may be illegal.

ORCHIDS IN THE GARDEN. Some very attractive terrestrial genera from the northern temperate areas of the world are completely deciduous during the cold weather. They do not begin their annual cycle of growth until temperatures begin to rise in spring and they flower during late spring or mid-summer, set seeds during the late summer and autumn, and die down again before the first frosts of winter. The genera include some of the species of the lady's slipper genus, *Cypripedium*, and also a number of species of *Dactylorhiza*, both of which can make a spectacular addition to the woodland border. They require a humus-rich, moisture-retentive soil, which should not become waterlogged nor be allowed to dry out completely. Any good garden loam can be made suitable by the incorporation of leafmould and composted bark into the top 30cm (12in.) of soil. The dormant rhizomes or tuberous roots can be planted in this mixture. Dappled shade, or a position which is sunny for only part of the day, is suitable for several of the species. A few species prefer calcareous soils, including the European *Cypripedium calceolus*, and a suitable niche for this species can be prepared by adding some pieces of chalk or limestone to the prepared site.

Some of the orchids which normally grow in grassland habitats, including species of *Orchis* and *Ophrys*, grow well in lawns in various parts of the country. The only special care required is that they should not be mown early in the early in the year, before or immediately after flowering. They should also be established while the tubers are dormant, and, because they come into growth rather earlier than the woodland species, it is probably best to introduce the tubers during the autumn. Each should be set in a small cavity lined with sharp sand, at least 5cm/2in. below the surface of the ground.

ORCHID HOUSE. When choosing a greenhouse specifically for orchid growing it is important to bear in mind that small houses are much more difficult to keep cool in summer, without losing some of the essential humidity, than larger ones. The cost of heating a small structure in winter is proportionally greater because of its large surface area. For heat conservation it is wise to choose a 'plant house' type of structure, with solid walls up to the level of the staging, rather than the 'glass-to-ground' style which is more suitable for tomatoes. Sometimes orchid glasshouses are partially sunk below ground level and this can be very satisfactory in improving heat conservation and maintaining high humidity. For good air movement and ventilation it is desirable to have the eaves as high as possible at least 2m/6.6ft above ground level, and a pitched roof above the plants so that there is plenty of space for heated air to accumulate and escape through the ventilators.

*Size*. The minimum size for efficiency in a small orchid greenhouse is 3×2.4m/10×8ft. If the width can be increased to 3.8m/12ft, it will be possible to fit in a centre bench, as well as benches along the sides, and many more plants can be accommodated.

*Site*. Siting a greenhouse for orchid growing in a small garden can present problems. It will need the maximum amount of light possible during the winter months, so should not be shaded by trees or buildings on the south side. Making provision to shade the greenhouse by artificial means is much more satisfactory than trying to arrange shading from permanent features of the plot or boundary such as deciduous trees. The orientation of a small orchid house is not important but for larger collections a house that is aligned east-west is best. With the longest side of the house facing south, the maximum amount of light will enter during the winter. Similarly a conservatory for orchid growing should be on the south side of the house for maximum winter light and warmth. Connecting electricity, heating appliances and water to a conservatory attached to the house is no problem, and it may be wise to site a free standing greenhouse as near as possible to a dwelling for the same reason and for ease of access during the winter months.

*Structure*. Orchid houses have traditionally been built of wood with large panes of horticultural glass. Cedar is the most suitable wood available today as it requires little or no maintenance compared with softwoods that need repainting regularly. Metal houses are now used increasingly, particularly those made of aluminium which do not corrode or rust, and are equally satisfactory.

Several different kinds of glazing materials are currently used successfully in orchid houses. The most common is horticultural glass in large panes that permit the glazing bars to be spaced at least 60cm/2ft apart. Rippled glass is also very suitable but it is heavier and more expensive. Its use is therefore limited to strongly built structures where cost is not significant. Acrylic panels marketed as Plexiglass are becoming popular, though more expensive than glass. Being constructed in two layers they provide excellent insulation for the plants but slightly less light than glass. Polyethylene sheeting is not suitable for permanent structures as the material currently available has a relatively short life and the heat loss is much greater than through glass.

*Staging*. Open staging made of slats of wood or galvanised mesh will promote air circulation around the plants but it should not be too widely spaced or small pots will fall over. In old houses it was traditional to build a 'moisture staging', a solid framework containing gravel or perlite, just below the slats on which the plants stand. Surplus water draining from the plants at each watering ensures that the material remains moist and enhances the humidity in the vicinity of the plants. Many orchids are grown successfully without this refinement, however, and the cool-growing ones in particular benefit from a more open type of staging, such as that provided by wire mesh, where there is good air circulation around the pot and plant.

In addition to formal, table-like staging, which can be tiered to make plants easier to reach on wide benches, space must be arranged for mounted plants and epiphytic plants in baskets to hang, so that water will not drip from them on to the plants beneath. A piece of stout mesh along one end of the house is often a very useful area for hanging small plants.

*Floor*. It is helpful to have an earth or gravel-covered floor beneath the benches. Constant evaporation from this surface, and the ferns and other plants which may be encouraged to grow in it, helps to maintain high humidity. It has the disadvantage that it may provide a home for slugs and other pests and some growers prefer to have a hard surface throughout the house. It is always helpful to have a gravel or concrete path or stepping stones between the benches, but these should have a rough surface so that they do not become slippery as a result of algal growth in the humid conditions.

*Environmental factors*. In the wild orchids grow in competition with other plants whether it is in the canopy of trees, among rocks or in open grasslands. A study of the details of their environment will reveal the kind of conditions that are best for them in a greenhouse: shading from direct sunlight, moderate to warm temperatures but not excessively high, good drainage, high relative humidity coupled with good air movement, and plenty of rain water during the growing season. It is not always easy, in a greenhouse, to provide all these features at optimum levels in combination, but it is important to achieve the best possible balance of humidity, light, warm temperatures and air movement for healthy growth and maximum flowering. A greenhouse full of plants is usually a well balanced one, and there are many other plants whose growing requirements are compatible with those of orchids. Begonias, hoyas, columneas, bromeliads, peperomias, ferns and other tropical plants can all find a place in a heated greenhouse and help to provide the right atmosphere for orchids.

*Shading*. Orchids have a wide range of light requirements. Some, such as *Ludisia* and some of the paphiopedilums, grow in the deepest shade of tropical forests, while there are others, some of the laelias and encyclias, for example, which grow naturally in full sunlight. By arranging the plants carefully in relation to each other in the greenhouse their individual needs can be met. But there are also big seasonal differences in the amount of light available in temperate regions. For part of the year it will be necessary to have some means of excluding some of the incident light because it greatly increases the temperature in enclosed glass structures.

This can be achieved in various ways. The simplest method is to apply a coat of temporary greenhouse paint, such as 'Summer Cloud', to the outside of the glass as soon as the days become appreciably longer and brighter in spring. By early summer this may need to be removed and replaced with a thicker coat. This can be removed in one or two steps during the autumn when more light is again required.

It is also useful to have some form of additional shading over the glass during the brightest summer months. Laths or blinds giving about 50 per cent shade and raised 20–30cm/10–12in. above the glass are ideal. Such shading not only cuts down the amount of light entering the house through the roof but also provides a layer of insulation above the glass, thus helping to keep temperatures inside the house somewhat lower.

A thermal screen material installed inside the house for insulation during winter nights can also be used to provide shading during the summer. This is not so effective in lowering the temperature as shading material on the outside of the house.

*Heating and cooling*. Many orchids are adaptable to a wide range of temperature conditions within certain minima and maxima. Keeping up the required night time temperatures is often only a problem of expense. It is best achieved by using water-filled pipes that are warmed by an outside boiler or electric fan heaters which are stationed so that they do not blow warm air directly on to the plants. Any approved greenhouse heating system can be used, but oil or solid fuel burners must be carefully ventilated as there is always a danger that fumes from the heater will cause bud-drop or premature ageing of the flowers. Conveniently situated greenhouses can be connected to a domestic central heating source.

In many greenhouses, particularly the smaller ones, the main difficulty is not in keeping the house warm enough in winter but in keeping the temperatures down in summer. Some of the cooler growing orchids, masdevallias and odontoglossums, for example, grow poorly if temperatures exceed 25°C/75°F, and all orchids are under stress if the temperature exceeds 32°C/90°F. These temperatures are easily passed inside a small glass structure on a hot summer day. Plenty of ventilation is essential, but opening all the windows and doors can result in a sudden lowering of humidity which is undesirable.

Cooling can be effected by increasing the water content of the air. The well known practice of 'damping down', by spraying water on the benches and floors, both increases the humidity inside the house and lowers the temperature. Misting over the plants can also have a cooling effect on their tissues on a hot day. Some form of shading over the outside of the glass, and continuously running greenhouse fans are also extremely useful, both for their cooling effect and in keeping the air fresh and buoyant. In dry climates an evaporative cooling system can be very effective and sometimes a refrigerative air conditioning unit can be employed.

*Ventilation*. Anyone who has travelled in tropical countries, especially at medium or higher altitudes where orchids grow, notices how comfortable the atmosphere is, despite the temperature and humidity, because of the constant breeze. The need for constant fresh and moving air in the greenhouse where orchids are grown cannot be stressed too strongly. Ventilators should be open when ever the outside temperatures are warm enough. This can be arranged automatically by a simple device which has thermostatic controls. Fans especially designed for greenhouse use are invaluable. Anyone who has tried to grow orchids without one notices an immediate response in the growth of the plants when a fan is installed.

*Insulation*. Many small glasshouses are lined with one or more layers of plastic or 'bubble plastic' for all or part of the year. This achieves the same effect as double glazing, which is used in some expensive installations, and is very cost effective in retaining heat in the house. However, it also reduces the amount of light reaching the plants, and care must be taken that it is kept free of algae and replaced as soon as it becomes discoloured.

*Humidity*. Most orchids grow where humidity levels are high at night as well as during the day. The optimum relative humidity for most orchids is 65–75 per cent at midday, but for *Phalaenopsis*, *Vanda* and their relatives it can be higher. Damping down several times a day and in the evening is effective. A more sophisticated system, using a humidistat among the plants to operate an automatic under bench sprayline, is very useful for those who are away from their plants during the day. Sometimes the humidity is more difficult to regulate during the winter months, especially at night when heating systems are working full time. Damping down last thing at night is a very useful exercise.

ORCHIDS UNDER ARTIFICIAL LIGHT. Orchids can be grown without a garden or greenhouse in a special area of the home where extra artificial light can be provided together with enhanced humidity. Sometimes orchids grown in this way are superior to those in a greenhouse as they can be provided with the same quality of light for 12 hours or more every day, as in the tropics, instead of having to survive short winter days.

Fluorescent tubes of the 'warm white' variety are the best source of light. They can be erected in banks of four or more over a growing area of trays containing gravel or charcoal on which the plants are set. The leaf surface of the plant needs to be kept 15–45cm/16–18in. below the lights – nearer will be too hot and further away not light enough. Sometimes a growing area is enclosed in a glass case, or in a recess, where it is much easier to maintain the best humidity levels for orchids. Specially designed plant cases, in modern or traditional style, can be very attractive pieces of furniture and very suitable for paphiopedilums, phalaenopsis and other orchids with low light requirements.

ORCHIDS FOR THE WINDOW SILL. Many of the tropical orchids which have been cosseted in greenhouses in the past will do equally well in a window sill if a few basic rules are observed. The most important are ensuring that there is enough light for the plants, without too much heat, and also that there is adequate humidity in the immediate surroundings.

During the winter months a south facing window sill, or a table in the curve of a bay window, is probably the best place in the home for orchids, but this might prove too hot in the summer even when the plants are protected by a sun-filtering curtain. For the summer they are probably best in an east facing window sill where they will receive the morning sun. A deep window sill is ideal as it can be fitted with a polypropylene tray containing about 2–3cm/1in. of some other clean, moisture-retentive material. The contents of the tray should be kept moist but not waterlogged, and there will always be a suitably humid atmosphere around the orchid pots placed on top.

Orchids with 'intermediate' or 'warm' temperature requirements do best in modern, centrally heated homes. Many *Phalaenopsis* and *Paphiopedilum* species and hybrids give pleasure with their long-lasting flowers and a wide variety of species can be grown successfully with patience and understanding.

**Orchis** L. (From the Gk word for testicle, referring to the oblong tuberous roots of some species.) Orchidaceae. Some 35 species of deciduous, terrestrial orchids. Tubers entire, globose to elliptic, 2–3. Leaves linear-lanceolate to oblong-ovate, basal or almost basal, often spotted with spathe-like leaves sheathing emerging spike. Inflorescence an erect, crowded terminal raceme; flowers purple, red, yellow, or white; bracts membranous; petals and sepals equal, or petals sometimes smaller, incurved, forming a hood, or lateral sepals sometimes spreading; lip entire or trilobed, central lobe entire or divided, papillose or glabrous above; spur slender or saccate; ovary cylindric, twisted. Spring–summer. Temperate N Hemisphere. Z5.

CULTIVATION See ORCHIDS, The Hardy Species.

***O. collina*** Banks & Sol. Tubers ovoid. Stems 10–40cm, erect. Basal lvs 2–4, sometimes spotted, oblong-ovate to oblong-ligulate. Infl. cylindric or oblong, 2–15 fld; dorsal sep. 10–12mm, incurved, ovate-oblong, forming hood with pet., lateral sep. spreading or erect; pet. oblong-lanceolate, dark olive green to red; lip to 10mm, ovate to obovate, undulate, green-pink often blotched white; spur conical, short, decurved. Late winter–mid spring. Mediterranean.

***O. coriophora*** L. BUG ORCHID. Tubers ellipsoid. Stems 15–60cm. Basal lvs 4–10, linear to linear-lanceolate. Infl. oblong or cylindric, dense; bracts lanceolate equalling or exceeding ovary; pet. and sep. to 10mm, ovate-lanceolate, forming a violet-brown hood; lip trilobed, incurved, dark purple-red to purple-green, basally paler, sometimes spotted dark purple, lateral lobes denticulate, slightly shorter than central lobe of lip; spur conical, decurved, apically incurved. Mid spring–early summer. SC & E Europe. ssp. ***fragrans*** (Pollini) Sudre. As *O. coriophora* but central lobe exceeds laterals, spur equals or exceeds lip, fls paler, fragrant, bracts white.

***O. italica*** Poir. Tubers ellipsoid. Stems 20–45cm, erect. Lvs 5–10, oblong-lanceolate, margins undulate, sometimes spotted dark purple-brown. Infl. dense, conical, becoming ovoid or globose, upper fls opening first; sep. and pet. to 10mm, ovate-lanceolate, incurved, forming hood, lilac-rose beneath, sometimes striped red; lip pink, trilobed, to 16mm, rose-white above, often spotted purple, central lobe divided, lobules, 2, linear-elongate, lateral lobes linear, red or magenta towards tip; spur cylindric, decurved. Summer. Mediterranean.

***O. lactea*** Poir. As *O. tridentata* except stem to 20cm, lvs oblong-lanceolate, infl. dense, sep. spreading, veined green below, basally flushed green; lip linear-oblong to square, central lobe apically finely dentate, white, spots purple, sometimes forming a continuous line. Summer. Mediterranean.

***O. laxiflora*** Lam. Tubers ellipsoid or globose. Stem to 120cm, usually shorter, erect. Lvs 3–8, lanceolate or linear, patent. Infl. lax, ovoid or cylindric, 6–20-fld; bracts 3–7-veined, lanceolate, tinted red-purple; sep. rose pink, lilac or red, oblong, spreading, lateral sep. deflexed, dorsal sep. almost erect; pet. oblong, incurved, forming hood; lip trilobed, centre sometimes white, lateral lobes oblong, reflexed, midlobe reduced or absent; spur cylindric, horizontal or vertical. Spring–early summer. Europe, Mediterranean.

***O. longicornu*** Poir. Tubers subglobose. Stem 10–35cm. Lvs 6–8 in a basal rosette, oblong-lanceolate. Infl. dense, oblong, lax; bracts lanceolate, veined, tinged green or red; sep. to 6mm (pet. smaller), oblong, incurved, forming hood, white to pale pink or maroon; lip shallowly trilobed, midlobe white, spotted purple, lateral lobes larger than central lobe, recurved, deep purple-violet to

**Orchis** (×1) (a) *O. papilionacea* and variants (b) *O. morio* and variants (c) *O. longicornu* and variants (d) *O. coriophora* and (beneath) ssp. *fragrans* (e) *O. sancta* (f) *O. ustulata* (g) *O. italica* (h) *O. militaris* (i) *O. simia*

**Orchis** (×1) (a) *O. lactea* (b) *O.tridentata* and (below) ssp. *commutata* (c) *O. purpurea* (d) *O. collina* (e) *O. mascula* (f) *O. pallens* (g) *O. provincialis* and (right) ssp. *pauciflora* (h) *O. quadripunctata* (i) *O. anatolica* (j) *O. laxiflora* and (right) ssp. *palustris*

pink or red; spur cylindric, patent or upcurved, to 1.6cm. Late winter–mid spring. W Mediterranean.

***O. mascula*** L. EARLY PURPLE ORCHID. Tubers ellipsoid. Stems 20–60cm, erect. Lvs 3–5 in lower half of stem, becoming sheaths above, oblanceolate to linear-lanceolate, glossy, often spotted dark purple. Infl. dense, cylindric or ovoid, 6–20-fld; bracts lanceolate, tinted purple, 1-3-veined; fls purple; sep. 6–8mm, oblong-lanceolate or ovate, lateral sep. spreading or reflexed, dorsal sep. and pet. forming hood; lip 8–15mm, trilobed, white, centrally spotted purple or crimson, lateral lobes slightly deflexed or flat, midlobe apically notched, 1–1.5 times length of laterals; spur horizontal or vertical. Mid spring–mid summer. Europe.

***O. militaris*** L. MILITARY ORCHID. Stems 20–45cm, erect. Basal lvs 3–5, oblong-lanceolate to ovate. Infl. dense, conical, becoming cylindric as fls open; bracts ovate-lanceolate, tinted purple; sep. and pet. to 15mm, ovate-lanceolate, forming white to grey-pink hood, veined purple above; lip to 15mm, trilobed, white to dark purple (central lobe lighter), spotted red, lateral lobes linear, falcate, midlobe narrow, becoming triangular, apically bilobed, lobes oblong or ovate, with short dentations between; spur cylindric, decurved. Mid spring–mid summer. Europe, Mediterranean, USSR.

***O. morio*** L. GREEN-WINGED ORCHID. Stems 5–50cm. Basal lvs 5–9, oblong-lanceolate to oblong-ovate, becoming sheaths on stem. Infl. pyramidal or oblong, apical fls opening last; bracts lanceolate, veined; fls white to green or violet-red; sep. and pet. oblong-ovate, forming hood (sep. larger); lip to 10mm, trilobed, recurved, midlobe apically notched, truncate, sometimes dark-spotted, lateral lobes smaller, veined, tinged green; spur cylindric, patent, horizontal or upcurved, equal or exceeding lip. Spring–mid summer. Europe, Mediterranean.

***O. pallens*** L. Stem 15–40cm. Lvs 4–6, oblong or oblong-ovate, becoming sheaths. Infl. dense, ovoid or oblong; fls yellow; bracts single-veined, olive green; sep. 7–9mm, lateral sep. deflexed, ovate-oblong, dorsal sep. erect, forming hood with oblong pet.; lip trilobed, lateral lobes orbicular, midlobe truncate, slightly emarginate; spur patent, horizontal to ascending. Mid spring–early summer. C & SE Europe.

***O. palustris*** L. Stems 80–100cm. Lvs 4–6, linear to linear-lanceolate, keeled. Infl. cylindric, slightly lax; fls purple or pink; lateral sep. oblong, erect, patent; lip to 10mm, flabellate-cuneate, trilobed, midlobe equal or exceeding rounded-rectangular lateral lobes, centre white, dotted purple (rarely entire, dark purple); spur tapering or parallel, ascending. Mid spring–mid summer. N Europe, USSR.

***O. papilionacea*** L. BUTTERFLY ORCHID. Stems 15–40cm, angular, erect. Basal lvs lanceolate to linear-lanceolate, erect. Infl. lax, ovoid, 2–8-fld (rarely cylindric, dense); bracts tinted red, lanceolate, 3–4-veined; fls purple, rarely red or brown; sep. and pet. to 18mm, forming a lax hood, deep red or purple, prominently veined; lip 12–25mm, entire, cuneate or fan-shaped, remotely dentate, rose to red, dark-spotted or longitudinally striped, or absent; spur cylindric, descending. Spring–early summer. Mediterranean.

***O. provincialis*** Balb. PROVENCE ORCHID. Tubers ovoid. Stem 15–35cm. Lvs 2–5, oblong-lanceolate or lanceolate, dark-spotted or plain. Infl. lax to dense, cylindric, 7–20-fld; bracts lanceolate, 1–3-veined; fls pale yellow or white, lip deeper, centre orange-yellow, spotted maroon; sep. 9–11mm, ovate-oblong, lateral sep. spreading, deflexed, middle erect; pet. smaller; lip round-ovate, trilobed, lateral lobes ovate to round, midlobe smaller, truncate, rounded; spur cylindric, patent. Mid spring–early summer. S Europe. var. ***pauciflora*** (Ten.) Camus. As *O. provincialis* except with lvs sparsely spotted or unspotted, fls 3–7, spike lax, ovary exceeds bracts, lip 13–15mm, trilobed, lateral lobes recurved, midlobe incised. Mid spring–early summer. EC Mediterranean.

***O. purpurea*** Huds. LADY ORCHID. Tubers ellipsoid. Stem 30–80cm. Lvs 3–6, oblong to oblong-ovate, glossy. Infl. dense, cylindric, many-fld; bracts ovate-lanceolate; sep. 12–14mm, forming hood with pet., brown-purple or pink beneath, sometimes spotted purple, rarely pale green with white lip; lip to 15mm, trilobed, lateral lobes linear, midlobe obcordate or triangular, often with small dentation, pale rose or white, spotted purple; spur decurved. Mid spring–mid summer. Europe, Mediterranean.

***O. quadripunctata*** Ten. Tubers ovoid. Stems straight or flexuous, slender, 10–40cm. Lvs 2–4, linear to oblong-lanceolate, usually spotted purple. Spike lax, ovoid or cylindric, to 20-fld; bracts lanceolate, 1–3-veined; fls pink to violet, red or white; dorsal sep. 3–5mm, ovate, lateral sep. spreading, dorsal sep. recurved, erect, forming a lax hood with pet., to 5mm; lip orbicular, trilobed or entire, lateral lobes 4–7mm, oblong-ovate, midlobe oblong, basal blotch white with 2–6 purple spots. Late spring–early summer. Mediterranean.

***O. sancta*** L. As *O. coriophora* except lvs 6–12, oblong-lanceolate to linear, persisting longer than in other ssp. Lower bracts 3–5-veined, fls pink to lilac-red; median sep. 9–12mm, elongate, patent, apically ascending; lip flat, incurved, lateral lobes rhombic, 3–4-dentate, midlobe entire; spur narrowing apically, incurved. Mid spring. E Mediterranean.

***O. simia*** Lam. MONKEY ORCHID. Tubers ovoid. Stems 20–45cm. Lvs 3–5, oblong-lanceolate to ovate. Infl. dense, broadly cylindric to ovoid, lower fls open last; bracts one-fifth to half ovary length, ovate-lanceolate; sep. and pet. to 10mm, ovate-lanceolate, to 10cm, forming hood, pale pink to red beneath, often streaked red, interior spotted or veined red; lip trilobed, to 20mm, white to rose pink, dotted purple, lateral lobes linear, slender, obtuse, midlobe deeply divided, lobules 2, linear, slender, magenta toward apex; spur decurved, cylindric. Early spring–early summer. Europe.

***O. tridentata*** Scop. TOOTHED ORCHID. Tubers ellipsoid. Stems 15–45cm, erect. Lvs 3–4, oblong to ovate-lanceolate, largely basal, a few sheathlike higher on stem. Infl. conical to ovoid, fls white to rose-pink to violet, lip spotted maroon; bracts lanceolate, single-veined; sep. and pet. ovate-oblong (sep. tapering, acuminate), forming veined hood; lip length exceeds width, trilobed, lateral lobes incurved, falcate, truncate, dentate, midlobe triangular, twice length of laterals, bilobed or notched, lobules minutely dentate; spur cylindric, decurved. Mid spring–early summer. C & S Europe.

***O. ustulata*** L. BURNT ORCHID. Stems erect, 12–35cm. Lvs 2–3, oblong Infl. dense, ovoid, becoming cylindric; fls scented, buds dark purple; bracts single-veined, ovate to lanceolate; sep. and pet. 3–3.5mm, forming hood, brown-purple beneath, pink above; lip 4–8mm, trilobed, lateral lobes spreading, oblong, midlobe bilobed or entire, white to pale pink, spotted red; spur cylindric, decurved. Mid spring–late summer. Europe, USSR.

***O. aristata*** Fisch. ex Lindl. See *Dactylorhiza aristata*.
***O. comperiana*** Steven. See *Comperia comperiana*.
***O. coriophora*** ssp. ***sancta*** (L.) Hayek. See *O. sancta*.
***O. elata*** Poir. See *Dactylorhiza elata*.
***O. iberica*** Willd. See *Dactylorhiza iberica*.
***O. incarnata*** Soó. See *Dactylorhiza incarnata*.
***O. longicurris*** Link. See *O. italica*.
***O. maculata*** L. See *Dactylorhiza maculata*.
***O. maderensis*** Summerh. See *Dactylorhiza foliosa*.
***O. praetermissa*** Druce. See *Dactylorhiza praetermissa*.
***O. purpurella*** T. & T.A. Stephenson. See *Dactylorhiza purpurella*.
***O. saccata*** Ten. See *O. collina*.
***O. saccifera*** Brongn. See *Dactylorhiza saccifera*.
***O. sambucina*** L. See *Dactylorhiza sambucina*.
***O. sesquipidaliensis*** Willd. See *Dactylorhiza elata*.
***O. traunsteineri*** Rchb. See *Dactylorhiza traunsteineri*.

**Oreocallis** R. Br. Proteaceae. 5 species of evergreen trees or shrubs. Leaves alternate, simple or pinnate. Flowers paired in solitary or clustered racemes, pedicelled; perianth tube cylindrical, limb 4-lobed; anthers sessile; ovary stalked. Fruit unilocular, seeds numerous, winged. S America, Australia, Malay Archipelago. Z9.

CULTIVATION Beautiful ornamental trees rarely seen in cultivation mainly because of the difficulty of growing them on, especially in cooler climates or in areas with low summer humidity. They require a well-drained soil. Propagate by fresh seed sown in warm conditions, as it then germinates readily; also from semi-hardwood cuttings.

***O. pinnata*** (Maid. & Betche) Sleumer. DORRIGO OAK. Medium to tall tree to 25m. Lvs entire to pinnately lobed with adult lvs entire, lanceolate, to 15cm. Fls pink-red, in short terminal racemes; pedicel 4cm, red; perianth 3cm, smooth. Spring–early summer. E Australia.

**Oreocarya** E. Greene.
***O. celosioides*** Eastw. See *Cryptantha celosioides*.
***O. sheldonii*** Brand. See *Cryptantha sheldonii*.

**Oreocereus** (A. Berger) Riccob. (From Gk *oros*, mountain, and *Cereus*, from its Andean habitat.) Cactaceae. A genus of 5–7 species, mostly shrubby; stems erect or ascending, cylindric; areoles often developing long white hairs, especially the flowering, and densely spiny. Flowers diurnal, usually orange or red or purple, more or less zygomorphic, tubular-funnelform, straight to somewhat curved; floral areoles numerous, more or less hairy; perianth-limb narrow, oblique; upper tepals suberect, lower spreading or recurved; stamens numerous inserted in the throat and tube, the lowermost filaments coalescent at the base to form a diaphragm over the nectar-chamber, sometimes the diaphragm invested with staminodal hairs; style and stamens exserted. Fruit globose to ovoid, hollow, dehiscing by abscission at the base; pericarp fleshy; pulp none (except in *O. fossulatus*); seeds 1.2–2.0×1.1–1.7mm, broadly oval, black-brown, shiny or semi-matt, ruminate; relief low-domed; hilum large, basal or oblique, impressed. W South America (Andes of S Peru, S Bolivia, N Chile and N Argentina).

CULTIVATION Grow in a cool frost-free greenhouse (min. 2–7°C/35–45°F), use 'standard' cactus compost: moderate to high inorganic content (more than 50% grit), pH 6–7.5; full sun; low air-humidity; keep dry from mid-autumn until early spring, except for light misting on warm days in late winter.

***O. celsianus*** (Cels ex Salm-Dyck) Riccob. Shrub to 1–3m, mainly branching near base; stems to 12–20cm diam.; ribs 10–17, tuberculate, the sinuses relatively deep; areoles 10–18mm apart, large, with woolly hairs to 5cm long; central spines 1–4, to 8cm long, stout, straw yellow to dark brown; radial spines *c*9, to 2cm. Fl. 7–9×3cm, dull pink; tube slightly curved; limb oblique; tepals obtuse; anth. violet; stigmas well-exserted, yellow-green. Fr. globose, yellow-green. Mts of NW Argentina & Bolivia. Z9.

***O. doelzianus*** (Backeb.) Borg. Shrubby, branching from the base; stems to 1m×6–8cm; ribs 10–11; areoles 1.5cm apart, densely to sparsely hairy, or hairs absent; spines variable, up to 20, to 3cm, yellow to dark brown, 4 longer centrals sometimes developing later. Fr. to *c*10×3cm, arising in an apical tuft of bristles and hairs, deep purple-pink; floral areoles with numerous lax hairs; limb oblique; tepals obtuse. Fr. ovoid-globose, yellow-green. C Peru. Z9.

***O. hempelianus*** (Gürke) D. Hunt. Stem simple or branched from the base, globose at first but eventually short-cylindric, erect or decumbent, to 60×10–15cm, usually grey- or blue-green; ribs 10–20; areoles large, 5–15mm apart; spines very variable; centrals 3–10, up to 5cm, often curved, white, brown, or nearly black, radials 8–30, 1–3cm, needle-like to finely bristly, pale yellow to glassy white. Fl. 5–7.5×2.5–3.5cm, arising near apex, scarlet to purple-red; tube slightly curved; floral areoles densely and softly hairy; limb more or less oblique; tepals acute. Fr. *c*2cm diam., globose to ovoid, pale yellow, thin-walled. Mts of S Peru, N Chile. The name *Echinocactus leucotrichus* (properly of Philippi) has been misapplied to this species. Z9.

***O. leucotrichus*** (Philippi) Wagenkn. Shrub to 1–2m, branching from base; stems 6–12cm diam., grey-green; ribs 10–18, *c*1.5cm high, obtuse; areoles large, with numerous white, brown or almost black hairs; spines pale yellow or yellow-brown to orange-red; central spines 1–4, up to 5–8cm, radial spines 5–10, shorter. Fl. 8–9.5cm, arising near apex, scarlet to purple-red; tube straight or slightly curved; floral areoles densely hairy; limb more or less oblique; tepals obtuse. Fr. *c*4–6cm diam., globose to ovoid, green-yellow, thin-walled. S Peru, N Chile. Z9.

***O. pseudofossulatus*** D. Hunt. Resembling *O. celsianus*, but stems more slender and eventually taller. Shrub to 4m, branching up to halfway up; stems usually 5–6cm diam.; ribs 10–13, prominently tubercled; areoles *c*1cm diam., usually with numerous (40–60) white trichomes to 5cm; central spine 1, 2–5cm, straw yellow to red-brown, sometimes accompanied by shorter subsidiary centrals; radial spines usually 10–14, to 6mm. Fl. to 9cm, pink, tinged green, to mauve. Fr. *c*5cm diam., pale green. Bolivia. Z9. This species has been incorrectly known for more than half a century as *O. fossulatus*, based on a misidentification.

***O. trollii*** (Kupper) Backeb. Resembling *O. celsianus*, but lower-growing, to 1m; stems branching from base, *c*10cm diam. Fl. said to be only 4cm. S Bolivia, N Argentina. Z9.

***O. crassiniveus*** Backeb. See *Oreocereus trollii*.
***O. fossulatus*** sensu Backeb. non *Pilocereus fossulatus* Labouret. See *O. pseudofossulatus*.
***O. hendriksenianus*** Backeb. See *O. leucotrichus*.
***O. neocelsianus*** Backeb. See *O. celsianus*.
***O. rettigii*** (Quehl) F. Buxb. See *O. hempelianus*.
For further synonymy see *Arequipa*, *Borzicactus*, *Cleistocactus* and *Morawetzia*.

**Oreocharis** Benth. (From Gk *oros*, mountain, and *charis*, beauty, from the habitat.) Gesneriaceae. 27 species of perennial herbs. China and Japan

CULTIVATION See GESNERIADS.

***O. aurantiaca*** Franch. Rootstock short, straight, Lvs 3.5–5cm, in rosette, lanceolate or oblong-elliptic, rarely blunt, more or less leathery, green above, ciliate, cinnamon hairy beneath; petiole to 4cm. Peduncles 2–5, to 12.5cm, tinged red or purple; pedicels *c*2cm, slender; cal. red; cor. yellow, 2-lipped, white-hairy outside, seg. narrow. Yunnan.

***O. forrestii*** (Diels) Skan Lvs 3.5–14cm, in a rosette, ovate-oblong, coarsely toothed, blunt, densely rusty-hairy at least at first, main veins 5–7, prominent beneath. Scapes 4–10 or more, erect, 6–12cm; fls pale yellow, nodding, in loose 4–7-fld cymes; cor. tube widely cylindrical; limb slightly 2-lipped, lobes usually 4, rather spreading; stamens 4. Yunnan.

**Oreodoxa** auct. non Willd.
***O. borinquena*** Reasoner. See *Roystonea borinquena*.
***O. caribaea*** Becc. non Dammer & Urban. See *Roystonea borinquena*.
***O. caribaea*** Dammer & Urban non Becc. See *Roystonea oleracea*.
***O. princeps*** Becc. See *Roystonea princeps*.
***O. regia*** HBK. See *Roystonea regia*.

**Oreopanax** Decne. & Planch. (From Gk *oros*, mountain, and *Panax*; many species inhabit mountain regions.) Araliaceae. 80–100 species of unarmed, dioecious or polygamo-dioecious, evergreen, hairy or glabrous, sometimes epiphytic shrubs or trees, some with distinct kinds of foliage in different life-stages. Leaves clustered towards the ends of branches, simple, palmately lobed, palmatifid or digitately compound; stipular appendages poorly developed or absent. Inflorescences terminal, paniculate, 1–2× compound, usually pubescent but sometimes glabrescent, the main axis elongate; flowers in heads, each sessile or very short-stalked bracteoles 2–3 per head, more numerous in male than in female or hermaphrodite plants; heads stalked or sessile; petals usually 5 (rarely 4–6), white or tinged green, valvate in bud; stamens as many as petals; styles in male flowers 1–2; ovary in perfect or female flowers 3–12-locular; styles rather long, free or more or less united at base. Fruit berry-like, remaining inferior through maturity, the styles often falling; endocarp thin, the seeds with smooth or ruminate endosperm. Middle and South America.

CULTIVATION *Oreopanax* spp. are fairly common and conspicuous inhabitants of wet or dry montane woodland, sometimes to be found on steep, well-drained slopes. They are valuable bold, evergreen foliage shrubs or small trees for tropical and subtropical gardens: *O. echinops*, *O. peltatus* and *O. xalapensis* are particularly ornamental- the last is used as a specimen tree in the public parks of Central America. *O. peltatus* and *O. sanderianus* are used as pot plants in North America. Cultivation as for Trevesia, except that lower temperatures may be tolerated in dry conditions. In addition to species described below, *O. platanifolius* auct. non (Kunth) Decne. & Planch., Belgium 1859 (Lind.), with palmately lobed leaves, is occasionally cultivated in the south of France.

***O. andreanus*** Marchal. Shrub or small tree to 4m; stem simple or slightly branched. Shoots, petioles and lf undersurfaces covered with deciduous, rusty hair. Lvs on parts of shoots approaching flowering entire or somewhat 3-lobed, elliptic, trinerved at base, rounded and more or less cordate in overall outline, elsewhere palmately lobed with pinnatifid seg. Infl. terminal, to 30cm, erect, paniculate, 1–2× compound; heads in male infl. numerous. Ecuador (Andes). Z9.

***O. capitatus*** (Jacq.) Decne. & Planch. CABALLERA DE PALO; COAMATL. Tree to 18m, sometimes beginning life as an epiphyte; in cult. more commonly a shrub. Lvs to 25×18cm (commonly to 12.5cm), simple (occasionally tripartite), ovate or elliptic to oblong-elliptic, entire, base rounded or cordate, dark green above, pale grey beneath, sometimes with small scale-like hairs. Infl. 2× compound, finely hairy when young, later merely scaly-hairy or glabrous, the main axis to 18cm; fls in male heads 10–20 or more, in perfect heads, 5–12; pet. white; styles in male fls 1–2; ovary in perfect fls 5–12-locular, the styles short, mostly free, recurved. Fr. white-yellow, later darkening, round, 3–5mm diam. Spring and summer. Throughout range of the genus except at high altitudes. Rather variable. A related species is *O. obtusifolius* L.O. Williams (*O. guatemalensis* Decne. & Planch.: lvs rounded or very obtuse at apex, sometimes almost as broad as long; peduncular bracts longer than in *O. capitatus*. Middle America (Mexico, Guatemala, Belize, Honduras). Z9.

***O. dactylifolius*** Lind. ex Williams. Shrub or small tree, the stems, petioles and undersurfaces of the lvs rusty-hairy. Lvs in young plants to 45cm across, deeply palmatifid; seg. usually 7, deeply pinnately lobed; lvs in fertile shoots smaller, usually moderately to deeply 5-lobed, lobes entire or few-toothed, smooth, deep green above. Infl. as *O. andreanus* but lower part 2× compound. Origin reported as Mexico but more likely from Andean S America. Z9.

***O. echinops*** (Schldl. & Cham.) Decne. & Planch. CASTAÑO; CINCO HOJAS. Few-branched, coarsely hairy shrub or tree to 12m, the hairs often somewhat yellow. Mature lvs digitately 5-foliolate (becoming 5-lobed below infl.); leaflets sessile or very shortly stalked, thin, softly textured, obovate or oblong-obovate, to 45×22cm but commonly rather smaller, apex sharply pointed, juvenile lvs trilobed. Infl. 1× compound, the main axis to 32cm; heads large, many-fld on stout peduncles; style in male fls 1; ovary in perfect fls 4–7-locular, the styles short, mostly free, recurved. Individual fr. to 10mm across. Summer–autumn. Middle America (Mexico, Guatemala).

***O. epremesnilianus*** (André) André. Shrub or tree. Lvs pseudo-digitately compound, long-petioled, appearing peltate, seg. 7–9 radiating, the outer oblong or lanceolate, the middle coarsely pinnatifid, apices acute, bases tapering. Infl. as *O. andreanus*. Autumn. Origin undetermined. Similar to *O. floribundus* (Kunth) Decne. of Colombia and Ecuador. Well-grown plants resemble *Fatsia japonica*. Z9.

***O. nymphaeifolius*** (Lind. ex Hibb.) Gentil. Vigorous tree to 5.5m. Lvs glabrous, ovate to broadly ovate, to 30cm, entire, bright green above, paler beneath, palmately 3-veined, veins prominent beneath, apex slenderly pointed, base obtuse to rounded. Infl. 2× compound, with 7–9 primary branches; fls inconspicuous. Summer. Origin undetermined, possibly Guatemala (Zander). Possibly conspecific with *O. capitatus*. Z9.

***O. peltatus*** Lind. ex Reg. MANO DE LEON. Shrub or tree to 15m, crown ultimately large; young branches and other parts densely rusty-hairy. Adult lvs palmately lobed, sometimes peltate, to 50cm or more across, pubesc. throughout, darker above and sometimes glabrescent with age, base truncate or cordate, lobes usually 5–7, oblong or oblong-elliptic, coarsely toothed, more or less pointed, the sinuses moderately deep; juvenile lvs peltate. Infl. 2× compound, to 45cm, with many branches ascending from a short main axis; heads stalked; fls green-white; styles in male fls 1; ovary in perfect fls 2–3-locular, the styles mostly free. Fr. black at maturity, to 6mm across. Autumn. Middle America (Mexico, Guatemala). The similar *O. geminatus* Marchal (*O. lachnocephalus* Standl.) has sessile or subsessile heads. Z10.

***O. sanderianus*** Hemsl. COHETE; TRONADOR. Shrub or small tree, with habit of *Fatsia japonica* when young; vegetative parts glabrous. Lvs usually long-petiolate, to 25cm across, bright green, glossy, mostly 3–5-partite (those directly below infl. entire), base obtuse, truncate or deeply cordate; lateral lobes mostly small, widely set, often at a right angle to the midrib, midlobe usually largest, triangular. Infl. as *O. capitatus*; heads rather few-fld. Fr. white, about 5mm across. Middle America (Mexico to Honduras). Z10.

***O. xalapensis*** (Kunth) Decne. & Planch. BRAZIL; MACUILILLO MANO DE LEON; PATA DE GALLO. Dioecious shrub or tree to 18m×45cm, mostly glabrous. Adult lvs digitately 5–10-foliolate, long-petiolate, leaflets shortly stalked, narrowly oblong-lanceolate to obovate, to 30×7cm, lustrous green above, paler beneath, margins entire or somewhat toothed; juvenile lvs simple, broadly cordate-ovate; intermediate lvs deeply lobed or with 3 leaflets. Infl. 1× compound, more or less hairy, the main axis to 40cm; heads racemosely arranged; fls tinged green; style in male fls 1; ovary in female fls 5-locular, the styles more or less free. Fr. white, finally violet to black, ellipsoid, 5–7mm across, very juicy. Most of year. Middle America (Mexico to Panama), Revillagigedo Is. (Socorro). Z10.

***O. catalpaefolius*** (Willd. ex Roem. & Schult.) Decne. & Planch. See *O. capitatus*.
***O. dactyliferus*** auct. See *O. dactylifolius*.
***O. dactylifolius*** var. ***epremesnilianus*** André. See *O. epremesnilianus*.
***O. jaliscanus*** S. Wats. See *O. peltatus*.
***O. langlassei*** Standl. See *O. xalapensis*.
***O. reticulata*** hort., non (Willd.) Decne. & Planch. See *Meryta denhamii*.
***O. salvinii*** Hemsl. See *O. peltatus*.
***O. thibautii*** Versch. ex Hook. f. See *O. xalapensis*.
For further synonymy see *Aralia*, *Monopanax* and *Sciadophyllum*.

**Oreopteris** Holub. (From Gk *oros*, mountain, and *pteris*, fern.) Thelypteridaceae. 3 species of terrestrial ferns. Caudex suberect. Stipes tufted, short, clad with elongate translucent scales. Fronds pinnate, glandular below; pinnae deeply lobed, middle pinna longest; veins simple or forked, grooved and sparsely hairy above, scaly or pubesc. below. Sori submarginal; indusia present, sometimes very minutely hairy; sporangia short-stalked; spores openly reticulate. N Hemisphere.

CULTIVATION A small genus, formerly included in *Thelypteris*, *Oreopteris* includes the common European mountain fern, *O. limbosperma*, a fern of open moorland where soils are acid and rainfall moderately high. Rarely grown in gardens, it is a deciduous species, at its best in spring and early summer, the fragrant lemon scent given off when its leaves are bruised justifies its inclusion in the fernery. *O. limbosperma* is hardy to −30°C/−22°F at least. Site in a moist spot in acid soil (pH 4.0–6.0) in bright light with up to about 4 hours direct sunshine daily. If grown under glass use a soilless potting medium and water plentifully. Plant out in early summer. Propagate by spores, which ripen in late summer.

***O. limbosperma*** (All.) Holub. MOUNTAIN FERN. Caudex stout, branched, 10cm, older parts clad with dead frond bases, younger parts brown-scaly; stipes 5–15cm, sparsely scaly. Fronds fragrant with balsam-like scent when bruised; lamina 25–75×8–25cm, lanceolate, tapered, bright green tinged yellow, golden-glandular beneath; pinnae 20–30 each side, opposite to subopposite near base, alternate towards apex, basal pinnae shortly deltoid, others linear-lanceolate, pinnatifid, sessile; seg. oblong, acute with incurved apex, shallowly crenate; rachis and midribs white glandular-pubesc., and sparsely scaly toward base. Europe (Sweden to Pyrenees and N Italy, west to GB, east to Caspian Sea). Many cultivars of this fern were known in the past but today we have only two of note: (Angustifrons group) 'Radnor': recent wild find, frond narrow with elongate tip, very rare, 50cm. (Cristata-gracile group) 'Fernworthy': recent wild find, frond and pinnae lightly crested, pinnae curve towards apex of frond, very rare, 40–50cm.

For synonymy see *Dryopteris*, *Lastrea* and *Thelypteris*.

**Organic gardening**. A school that has developed (as a branch of organic agriculture) since just before the middle of the 20th century, in opposition to the increased use of manufactured pesticides and fertilizers by so-called 'high-input' agriculture. The principles of organic agriculture are basically the same as those regarded as good husbandry in the first half of the century, before farmers were encouraged to grow food as economically as possible for large urban populations.

When inorganic fertilizers began to be widely used this was usually without using any bulky organic materials at all. The result was rapid deterioration of soil structure and consequent erosion. The modern world probably first became aware of the devastating consequences of such practices when the dust bowls of the American Middle West were created in the 1930s. In these areas the natural vegetation had been removed for growing crops, mostly cereals. A relatively short period of heavy cropping, stimulated by massive fertilizer applications, and annual ploughing turned the soil into dust which simply blew away. Despite this clear warning farmers the world over continue to use inorganic fertilizers without replenishing the humus-producing, soil-binding organic materials, and also by replacing ploughing in of cereal stubble by burning (swaling). These continued assaults on natural good husbandry were the beginnings of the organic gardening (and in some degree agricultural) reaction.

Further reaction occurred when Rachel Carson, in her influential book *Silent Spring* (1962), showed that excessive amounts of chemical were applied by farmers in the US; many of these chemicals polluted the environment with long-term consequences, such as destroying many beneficial insects along with the harmful ones, thus upsetting the natural balance of populations. The same faults occurred in other parts of the world. It is now generally agreed that blanket applications of chemicals is usually dangerous as well as wasteful, and that they must be applied in a selective and economical manner.

Rudolf Steiner was an early preacher (1924) on organic agriculture and his principles for biodynamic farming and gardening have a firm hold in parts of Germany and Switzerland. Another movement is for 'holistic' agriculture, which aims to avoid any pollution of the environment from cultivation technique. The Rodale Organization was started in the US during World War II and its magazine *Organic Gardening* has reached a circulation of 750,000. In the UK the stimulus for organic gardening was the Henry Doubleday Research Association founded in 1954 by Lawrence Hills; it became the largest organization of amateurs for organic gardening in the world, and with such backing was able to establish a National Organic Gardening Centre near Coventry in 1985.

The main rule of organic gardening is 'to feed the soil not the plant', that is, to maintain and improve soil fertility with organic materials so that there is no need to depend on fast-acting (artificial) fertilizers to boost plant growth. This is done by regular application of bulky organic materials such as garden compost, farmyard manure, used mushroom compost, spent hops, seaweed and leafmould. These are broken down by soil micro-organisms into humus, a colloid material that improves soil structure (by encouraging the aggregation of soil particles) and as a result the soil's ability to hold nutrients in the root-feeding area of the plants. Both are vital characters of a fertile soil. However, nutrient contents of bulky organic materials are generally variable and unlikely to be sufficient to feed short-term, quick-growing vegetables, but will be adequate for the flower garden. To maintain humus in a soil producing food crops, an annual application of 5–6kg/m$^2$(9–11lbs/yd$^2$) is required, which is a considerable quantity for owners of small gardens to obtain, whether it be made at home or bought in.

These bulky materials almost always need to be supplemented by fertilizer application to provide the extra nutrients required, certainly by fruit and vegetables. Some organic fertilizers release their nutrients relatively slowly, such as bone meal, hoof and horn; others, such as dried blood and seaweed meal, are fast-acting. Many such organic fertilizers are more expensive per unit of nutrient than inorganic types, but it cannot be emphasized too strongly that using either without adding humus to the soil will result in deteriorating soil structure and poor plant growth.

Regular recycling of plant waste from garden and kitchen to make compost is an important habit for gardeners. This vegetable material is collected and stored outside, while it decomposes into a moist, crumbly state easily digested by soil micro-organisms. The breakdown occurs with or without oxygen. Compost made without oxygen (anaerobically) takes longer to reach the right state (about a year), but is less work (no turning and no activators). Aerobically made compost is ideally made in a heap of at least one metre in each direction, so that the material, during the composting process, will generate enough heat to kill all weed seeds. Such a heap needs careful mixing of different materials to ensure that the ratio of carbon to nitrogen is about 25:1. Carbon is high in, for instance, shrub prunings, and nitrogen is high in fresh nettles; lawn mowings and annual weeds have equal amounts of carbon and nitrogen. To generate adequate seed-killing heat, the heap is best constructed at one time, but collection of materials in a small garden is usually gradual and needs organization to build a successful heap. The solution is to collect all the material over days and weeks, storing it in plastic bags, until enough has accumulated for the heap. The material is then built up in layers, starting with one of about 15cm/6in. thickness, then a sprinkling or a thinner layer of an activator (e.g. seaweed meal, dried blood, urine), and another 15cm/6in. layer of vegetable waste, a sprinkling of activator and so on. The final covering is a piece of old carpet to keep in the heat. The heap heats up to about 19°C/66°F after about two weeks (in summer); five or so weeks later it is 'turned', bringing the material from the edge to the centre and vice versa. There is then a second period of reheating. On average the compost is ready in about 3–4 months after construction – faster in warm weather, slower when cold. Gardens are rarely self-sufficient in compost, and other humus-containing materials can be bought in according to circumstances.

There are advocates of non-cultivation in organic gardening schools, preaching 'no digging'. This technique, also known as organic surface cultivation, follows nature in that the soil remains undisturbed and organic materials are laid on the soil surface each year to be drawn down by earthworms and micro-organisms. This can be successful on soils with a good structure, but where the soil structure is initially weak, it may deteriorate further. Another system that avoids some digging is to construct deep beds, which are cultivated without being walked on. The beds are made about 120cm/4ft wide so that they can be tended from the paths at each side. Double digging is necessary in preparation, but with no further compaction by treading deep beds will continue to grow plants satisfactorily without regular digging.

Organic gardeners control pests, diseases and weeds chiefly by cultural methods; these include hygiene. Weeds can be prevented from growing (depriving them of light) by laying black plastic film (especially useful in the kitchen garden) or applying a thick mulch of organic material on the soil (suited to the flower garden). Hoeing or hand pulling of weeds when young, and certainly before they seed, prevents their multiplication. A flame gun can be used on vacant ground to burn off weeds; and using wide-spreading perennial plants as groundcover in the flower garden eventually suffocates weeds.

For controlling pests and diseases there are several strategems. Rotation of vegetable crops will prevent a build-up of harmful agents in the soil and avoid depletion of a particular nutrient. The scheme for rotation of vegetables – for three of four years – is based on groupings of potatoes, roots, brassicas, and legumes and onions. The vegetable plot is divided into 4 equal areas and each group is grown in one area and then rotated to the next area in the next year, so that no crop of one group grows in the same soil in successive years. If there is a vacant area, especially over winter, a green manure can be sown to 'trap' the nutrients in the soil (usually nitrogen) and prevent them from being washed out by heavy rain. Green manures, such as winter tares, grazing rye or lupins, are cut down well before flowering and dug into the soil to return the nutrients to the soil for the next crop.

Organic gardeners actively encourage natural predators, by growing their food plants, for example *Calendula* and *Limnanthes* for hoverflies, which also eat aphids. Biological control is another technique increasing in use and scope. Predators and parasites can be brought in and placed in the crop, to control such difficult pests as whitefly (*Encarsia formosa*) and spider mite (*Phytoseiulus persimilis*). On a less commercial scale, companion planting may reduce pest attack; it is said that planting carrots in rows next to onions prevent each from being attacked by their specific fly, and there are other quoted combinations. Carrot fly can be defeated by growing plants within a 75cm/30in. high screen; the adult will not fly above this height so does not find its food. Another method for preventing attack by carrot fly is to avoid the need for thinning (the fly is attracted by the smell of bruised tissues) by sowing very thinly. Sowing a very early stump-rooted cultivar (for example, 'Rondo') in soil blocks and transplanting is another way of avoiding thinning. Other physical barriers that can be used with other crops are to cover brassica seedlings with a thin plastic film to prevent flea beetle attack and to place greased paper strips round the trunks of apple trees to catch adult winter moths as they climb into the trees to layer their eggs. Slugs and snails can be destroyed by preparing beer traps in which they drown. Hand picking of such pests as gooseberry sawfly can be very effective.

Too many manufactured insecticides, particularly in the past, have destroyed beneficial as well as harmful pests. Many insecticides of natural origin, although less efficient, are less harmful to other animal life than inorganic types, and are not persistent. Organic pesticides most frequency recommended include soft soap (an old remedy which resurfaced in the 1990s), derris (poisonous to fish), pyrethrum (from *Tanacetum cinerariifolium*), and quassia chips (from *Picrasma excelsa*). However, pyrethrum has been largely replaced by synthetically made equivalents. In some warm countries, azadirachtin, derived from *Melia* has proved an effective insecticide. Some home-made insecticides prepared from rhubarb, elder and wormwood leaves and from garlic or garlic in oil, have been recommended, although their use is no longer legal in the EC. Nicotine was earlier recommended but in high concentrations it is very toxic to warm-blooded animals and is no longer approved.

Although some plant materials such as gooseberry, horsetail and garlic have been recommended as infusions for fungicides, their efficacy is dubious. An extract from beans known as wyerone has been shown to be an effective fungicide but its use has not been developed.

See also COMPOST; DIGGING; NUTRITION; SUBSTRATES AND SOIL AMELIORANTS; VEGETABLE CULTIVATION and (for Biological Control and Integrated Pest Management) the Glossary of PESTS, DISEASES and DISORDERS at the end of this work.

**Origanum** L. (From Gk *oros*, mountain, and *ganos*, joy.) MARJORAM; OREGANO. Labiatae. Some 20 species of subshrubs or perennial herbs, to 1m. Stems quadrangular in section, often pubescent, generally rhizomatous. Leaves usually simple, opposite, aromatic, petiolate, over 1cm wide. Inflorescence a spike-like arrangement of whorled flowers appearing paniculate or corymbose; bracts conspicuous, imbricate, usually coloured; calyx campanulate or funnel-shaped, pubescent, generally actinomorphic and 5-toothed or 1–2-lipped; corolla 2-lipped, upper lip entire, lower lip 3-lobed; stamens 4, 2 long and projecting; style single, arising from a depression in the middle of 4-lobed ovary. Fruit a 1-seeded nutlet. Mediterranean to E Asia.

CULTIVATION Native to the mountains of the Mediterranean, *Origanum* was cultivated as a culinary and medicinal herb in Ancient Egypt. In the garden, it is also used as low ground cover in borders or scree beds. Choicer alpine species like *O. amanum* and *O. rotundifolium* are grown on sunny screes or in the alpine house in pans of equal parts loam, leafmould and sharp sand. Plant 30cm/12in. apart in spring in any well-drained soil, in an open sunny site. *O. rotundifolium* must have lime-free soil; other species prefer slightly alkaline conditions. Trim back after flowering. Mulch *O. majorana* in cold winter areas. Harvest for freezing or drying just before the flower buds open. Propagate from seed in early spring, sown at 10–13°C/50–55°F, or later in drills in the open ground, thinning to 30cm/12in. Alternatively, take 5–8cm/2–3in. softwood cuttings in early summer, pot on individually, overwinter in frostfree conditions and plant out the following spring. Winter supplies for the kitchen may be taken as cuttings in summer and overwintered at a minimum of 10°C/50°F.

1 Calyx with 5 more or less equal teeth.
*Oo. laevigatum, vulgare.*

2 Calyx 1- or -2 lipped.
2.1 Calyx 1.5–3.5mm long; bracts 1–5mm, herbaceous, green, hairy.
*Oo. majorana, majoricum, microphyllum, onites, syriacum.*
2.2 Calyx 4–12mm, bracts 4–25mm, membranous, purple-yellow green, more or less glabrous.
*Oo. acutidens, amanum, calcaratum, dictamnus, leptocladum, libanoticum, rotundifolium, scabrum, sipyleum.*

***O. acutidens*** (Hand.-Mazz.) Iets. Stems to 50cm, glabrous, 10 pairs of branches per stem. Lvs to 3×2.4cm, ovate, subsessile, glaucous, obtuse. Fls to 12 per whorl; bracts yellow-green; cor. white or tinged with pink, to 16mm, twice cal. length. Summer. Turkey. Z9.

***O. amanum*** Post. Stems to 20cm, hirsute to scabrous. Lvs to 1.9×1.4cm, subsessile, cordate. Fls to 10 per whorl; bracts ovate, 2×1.5cm, vivid purple; cor. pink with lips at right angle to tube; cal. to 12mm. Late summer and autumn. E Mediterranean, Turkey, on calcareous rocks. Z8.

***O. calcaratum*** Juss. Subshrub to 35cm, lanate, hirsute, occasionally subglabrous. Lvs 6–30×5–25mm, subsessile, suborbicular to ovate or cordate, apex obtuse or acute, margins entire, surfaces lanate to glabrous and glaucous. Spikes often pyramidal, to 4cm, erect and crowded at ends of stems; bracts 5–12×4–10mm, suborbicular to elliptic, acute; cal. 5–10mm, upper lip subentire, lower very small (or absent), 2-lobed; cor. to 18mm, pink. Islands of S Aegean.

***O. dictamnus*** L. DITTANY OF CRETE; HOP MARJORAM. Dwarf shrub, stems to 30cm. Lvs 1.3–2.5×1.2–2.5cm, woolly-white, ovate to round, entire, veins prominent, lower lvs petiolate. Fls densely whorled in lax panicles; bracts hop-like, rose-purple; cal. 2-lipped, lower lip shallowly toothed; cor. pink, tube twice as long as cal. tube. Mid–late summer. Crete. Z7.

***O. ×hybridum*** Mill. *(O. dictamnus × O. sipyleum.)* Tufted perenn. subshrub to 25cm. Lvs to 2.5cm, downy, ovate, grey-green. Fls pink, 12mm, solitary or in threes, drooping, in hop-like cluster of bracts. Late summer–autumn. Levant. Z8.

***O. laevigatum*** Boiss. Stems to 70cm, glabrous, 12 branches per stem. Lvs to 3×1.7cm, petiolate or subsessile, ovate to elliptic, subcoriaceous. Cal. to 6mm; cor. purple, to 16mm. Spring, summer, early autumn. Turkey, Cyprus. 'Hopleys': to 75cm; fls large, strong pink, bracts large. 'Herrenhausen': upright, to 45cm; lvs and shoots flushed purple when young and during winter; fls pale lilac, in large clusters. Z8.

***O. leptocladum*** Boiss. Stems to 65cm, glabrous, to 10 pairs of branches per stem. Lvs to 1.7×1.5cm, sessile, cordate or ovate, glaucous, acute. Fls 2 per whorl; bracts lanceolate 5×3mm; cal. 2-lipped, to 5mm; cor. pink, to 14mm, lower fil. to 5mm, upper fil. 1.5mm. Autumn. Turkey. Z8.

***O. libanoticum*** Boiss. Stems to 60cm, pubesc. at base. Lvs 1.2cm, ovate, obtuse, petiole short. Fls in nodding spikes; bracts deep pink; pet. to 2cm, pink. Summer. Lebanon. Z8.

***O. majorana*** L. SWEET MARJORAM; KNOTTED MARJORAM. Annual, bienn. or perenn. herb to 60cm. Stems glabrous or tomentose, red. Lvs to 2cm, opposite, ovate, grey, pubesc. Infl. a dense terminal panicle; bracts grey-green, to 4×3mm, elliptic, obtuse; fls tubular, white, mauve or pink, to 8mm; cal. untoothed, 2-lobed. Late summer–autumn. Originally Mediterranean and Turkey, now widespread in Europe as escapee. Z7.

***O. majoricum*** Cambess. Stems to 60cm, pubesc. Lvs to 2.5cm, ovate to lanceolate, upper lvs sessile. Fls in terminal panicles; bracts exceeding cal.; cal. to 4mm; cor. pink, twice length of cal., campanulate. SW Europe. Possibly the sterile result of *O. vulgare × O. majorana*. Z7.

***O. microphyllum*** (Benth.) Boiss. Stems to 50cm; branches slender, rectangular. Lvs to 0.8cm, ovate, pubesc., petiolate. Fls in lax terminal panicles; bracts 4mm, spathulate; cal. 2mm, ciliate at mouth; cor. 5mm, purple. Summer. Mediterranean.

***O. onites*** L. POT MARJORAM. Mound-forming dwarf shrub to 60cm. Stems red, pubesc. and warty. Lvs to 2.2×1.2cm, ovate, rounded to cordate at base, bright green, aromatic, entire, becoming sessile toward apex. Infl. terminal, corymbose; bracts to 3mm, extending slightly beyond cal.; cal. 1-lipped, deeply split on one side; cor. to 6mm, mauve or white. Late summer. Mediterranean. 'Aureum': tall; lvs gold. Z8.

***O. rotundifolium*** Boiss. Subshrub to 30cm, spreading by rhizomes. Stems pubesc. with 5 pairs of branches. Lvs to 2.5×2cm, subsessile, suborbicular or cordate, stem-clasping, blue-grey. Infl. nodding, hop-like, 2–16 fls per whorl; bracts reniform to 25×27mm, bright pale green tinged purple-pink; cal. upper lip ovate, lower lip shorter with 2 teeth or ovate; cor. to 16mm, white or pale pink. Late summer, early autumn. Armenia, Georgia, Turkey. Z8.

***O. scabrum*** Boiss. & Heldr. Perenn. to 45cm. Stems rhizomatous, then erect and glabrous. Lvs 3cm, ovate, sessile, margins scabrous. Fls in lax nodding panicles; bracts to 10mm, conspicuous, purple, glabrous; upper lip of cal. 3-toothed; cor. pink, twice length of cal. S Greece (mts). ssp. ***pulchrum*** Boiss. & Heldr. Lf margin smooth. Cal. upper lip almost same length as lower. Z8.

***O. sipyleum*** L. Subshrub to 80cm. Stems tomentose at base, otherwise glabrous, branching freely. Lvs to 2.4×1.5cm, petiolate or subsessile, elliptic or cordate, usually glaucous. Fls paired in spicules to 28mm; cal. 2-lipped, toothed; cor. pink, to 11mm. Turkey. Z8.

***O. syriacum*** L. var. ***bevanii*** (Holmes) Iets. Subshrub to 90cm. Stems pubesc. with 10 pairs of branches. Lvs to 3.5×2.5cm, ovate, petiolate or subsessile. Infl. paniculate; bracts obovate, 2.5×3.5mm; cal. 2.5mm; cor. twice length of cal. Late spring, early summer. Cyprus, Turkey. Z8.

***O. vulgare*** L. WILD MARJORAM; OREGANO; POT MARJORAM. Rhizomatous, woody, branched perenn. herb to 90cm, strongly aromatic. Lvs to 4cm, short-petiolate, round to ovate, entire or slightly toothed, spotted-glandular beneath. Infl. a loose panicle or corymb; bracts to 10mm, twice length of cal., violet-purple or green, ovate-elliptic; pet. purple, to 4mm. Late summer and autumn. Almost all Europe in open woodland, generally on lime-rich soils. 'Album': to 25cm, bushy; lvs light green; fls white. 'Aureum': to 30cm, spreading; lvs small, gold in summer, burn in sun; fls lavender. 'Aureum Crispum': lvs golden, curly. 'Compactum': to 15cm, compact and cushion-forming; lvs small, round, dark green; fls pink tinted violet, profuse. 'Compactum Nanum': to 10cm, compact; lvs dark green, purple in winter; fls lilac. 'Gold Tip': lvs tipped in yellow. 'Heiderose': to 40cm, bushy, upright; fls pink. 'Heideturum': to 50cm; fls light pink. 'Nanum': dwarf, to 20cm; fls purple. 'Roseum': fls pink. 'Thumble's Variety': to 35cm; lvs large, pale yellow later yellow-green, non-burning; fls soft white, inconspicuous. 'Tracy's Yellow': vigorous; lvs gold. ssp. ***vulgare***. Lvs and cal. not usually glandular-punctate, stems and lvs pilose, bracts partly purple often glabrescent. Cor. pink. Mediterranean, E to S China. ssp. ***hirtum*** (Link) Iets. Lvs and cal. usually glandular-punctate, stems lvs and cal. densely hirsute, bracts green-hirsute, cor. white. Infl. usually compact, branches and spikes short. Greece, Turkey, Aegean Is. ssp. ***gracile*** (K. Koch) Iets. Lvs and cal. usually glandular-punctate, stems lvs and cal. glabrescent to puberulent, lvs more or less glaucous, bracts green, glabrescent. Infl. usually lax, branches and spikes slender. E Anatolia. ssp. ***viride*** (Boiss.) Hayek. Lvs and cal. not usually glandular-punctate, stems and lvs pilose, bracts green, rarely purple tinged, often puberulent. Cor. white or rarely pale pink. N & C Turkey. Z5.

***O. cultivars***. 'Barbara Tingey': fls pink, drooping, bracts green. 'Bucklands': upright; fls large, pink, bracts flushed pink. 'Entedank': to 50cm, loosely bushy; lvs tinted blue; fls small, lilac-pink, late-flowering. 'Kent Beauty': fls small, pink to mauve, bracts pink. 'Kent Pride': to 15cm; fls green flushed purple.

***O. bevanii*** Holmes. See *O. syriacum* var. *bevanii*.
***O. pseudo-onites*** Lindb. See *O. syriacum* var. *bevanii*.
***O. tournefortii*** Ait. See *O. calcaratum*.
For further synonymy see *Amaracus*.

For illustration see HERBS.

**Orites** R. Br. (From Gk *oreites*, mountain-dwelling, from its habitat.) Proteaceae. 6 species of shrubs or trees. Leaves alternate, entire, dentate or sometimes lobed, petiolate. Inflorescence a terminal or axillary spike; flowers in pairs within each bract; bracts concave; perianth segments usually free, lamina short, concave; nectary glands linear, obtuse; filaments short, anthers borne below lamina; ovary sessile, with 2 ovules, style filiform, terminal, stigma small. Fruit a coriaceous follicle, obliquely acute, navicular; seeds compressed, with a terminal wing. E Australia.

CULTIVATION *Orites* spp. occur either in rainforest (*O. excelsa*) or in alpine habitats (*O. lancifolia*); they are not yet common in cultivation although a number of warm-climate species have potential as foliage houseplants. *O. excelsa* requires good drainage and a sunny position, with some protection from strong sun when young and shelter from strong winds, and in cool temperate climates needs glasshouse protection and cultural conditions similar to those for *Banksia*. They require good drainage. *O. lancifolia* needs a well-drained loamy soil with a cool root run and in habitat is tolerant of light frost. Species have proved difficult to establish in the open ground and even then may be extremely slow growing. Propagate by semi-ripe cuttings or from fresh seed.

***O. excelsa*** R. Br. PRICKLY ASH. Tall tree, to 30m. Lvs 15–20cm, juvenile lvs tinted red, deeply pinnate with prickly toothed margins, adult lvs simple. Fls white in 10cm axillary spikes; follicle boat-shaped, to 25mm long. Late winter–early spring. E Australia. Z10.

***O. lancifolia*** F. Muell. ALPINE ORITES. Spreading medium shrub, 1.5 high and wide. Lvs 3cm, oblong-lanceolate, thick. Fls creamy white, in erect, 5cm spikes. Summer. E Australia. Z9.

**Orixa** Thunb. Rutaceae. 1 species, a deciduous, unarmed, dioecious shrubs to 3m; young branches and leaves aromatic, puberulous. Leaves 5–12×3–7cm, alternate, shortly petiolate, obovate, rhombic-ovate or elliptic, entire, apex abruptly acute, puberulous. Inflorescence axillary on previous year's branches, solitary and racemose, 2–3cm; flowers small, 3–5mm, green, bracts membranous, deciduous, pistillate flowers solitary; sepals 4, ovate, connate at base; petals 3mm, 4, elliptic, spreading; stamens 4; ovary and stigma 4-lobed. Fruitlets 4, each 1-seeded; seeds round, black. Japan, Korea, China. Z6.

CULTIVATION A tough subject that survives in fairly dry shady conditions or in full exposure, *Orixa* is used as hedging in Japan. It is not showy but will form a dense light green barrier in less than five years. It is indifferent to soil type. Propagate by removal of layered branches or from seed sown outside in spring.

***O. japonica*** Thunb. As for the genus. 'Variegata': lvs tinted silver, shading to a white edge.

For synonymy see *Othera*.

**Ormiscus** Ecklon & C. Zeyh.
***O. amplexicaulis*** (L. f.) Ecklon & C. Zeyh. See *Heliophila amplexicaulis*.

**Ormocarpum** P. Beauv. (From Gk *hormos*, necklace, and *karpos*, fruit.) Leguminosae (Papilionoideae). Some 20 species of tropical shrubs or small trees. Leaves alternate or clustered, imparipinnate or, paripinnate, or with 1 leaflet only; stipules striped. Flowers axillary, solitary, or in short, axillary racemes or clusters, yellow, white, pink, lilac, or purple-striped; stamens basally united; bracts and bracteoles persistent. Fruit flat, linear or curved, constricted into 2+ indehiscent, oblong or ellipsoid segments with conspicuous veins, often papillose, with long hairs or minute warts. Tropical Asia, Africa, Mexico, Caribbean. Z9.

CULTIVATION *Ormocarpum* spp. are frost-tender ornamentals grown for their loose clusters of large beautiful flowers; they occur in a variety of habitats, near coasts and fresh water, on savannah and dry, open slopes. In temperate zones, grow in the intermediate glasshouse (min. 13–16°C/55–60°F), in direct sunlight in a moisture-retentive but free-draining, loam-based mix, with additional leafmould. Propagate by semi-ripe cuttings in sand in a closed case with bottom heat.

***O. sennoides*** DC. Evergreen shrub to 2m. Branchlets with overlapping scales at base. Leaflets in 7–10 pairs the lvs ending in a long spine; stipules spiny, erect. Racemes loosely 3–7-fld; fls opposite, long-stalked, yellow. Summer. Caribbean (St Thomas Is.)

***O. trichocarpum*** (Taub.) Engl. Shrub or small tree to 4.5m. Leaflets to 1.1×0.5cm, in 7–13 pairs, ending in a terminal leaflet, elliptic to narrow oblong, apex sharply tipped, base rounded, margin entire; petioles and peduncles with soft, brown bristles. Fls in clusters of 1–4 along the stems, violet, cream, blue or mauve-pink, veined deep purple, standard to 16mm. Fr. to 5cm, covered with long, stiff, gold-yellow hairs. Autumn. Uganda, Kenya, S Africa.

**Ormosia** Jackson. NECKLACE TREE; BEAD TREE. (From Gk *hormos*, necklace, referring to the use of the ornamental seeds of several species in necklaces.) Leguminosae (Papilionoideae). Some 100 species of tropical trees. Leaves alternate, usually imparipinnate; leaflets large, proximal smallest, leathery, usually glabrous above and without stipels; stipules inconspicuous, caducous. Flowers in clustered racemes or, usually, in downy terminal panicles, yellow, white, lilac or dark purple; bracts usually inconspicuous, often caducous, bracteoles subtending calyx; calyx with 5 subequal, broad lobes with or without tube, or upper lobes fused; standard broad, other petals narrow; stamens to 10, free, unequal or in two sets, anthers small, versatile; ovules mostly 2–6, style filiform, proximally pubescent, stigma usually lateral and bifurcate. Fruit oblong or ovoid, laterally compressed or turgid, dehiscent, initially fleshy, becoming leathery or woody; seeds, few, circular, large, often red, or red and black. Tropical Asia, America, Madagascar. Z9.

CULTIVATION Usually fast-growing trees, native to rain forest on mountain slopes to altitudes of 2000m/6500ft, with South American species also found in the dry savannahs. In their native lands, most spp. have proved economically important as sources of timber and medicines and the seeds of *O. coccinea* are used as brilliant beads. In cooler zones, grow in the hot glasshouse in a well-drained medium of sandy loam and leafmould. Propagate by seed or semi-ripe cuttings in a closed case with bottom heat.

***O. calavensis*** Azaola in Blanco. Glabrous tree. Petioles to 14cm; leaflets to 14×3.5cm, in 2–3 pairs, opposite, elliptic or elliptic-oblong, acute glabrous, leathery. Infl. a bushy, rusty-tomentose, corymbiform panicle; pedicels *c*2mm, minutely bracteolate; cor. dull violet or purple-white, to 1.8cm. Fr. *c*3×1.5cm, subsessile, often rhomboid-elliptic, acute, glabrous, black, valves woody and glabrous, 1-seeded, or 2-seeded and elongate; seeds about 8mm diam., red. Summer. Philippines, naturalized in Florida.

***O. coarctata*** Jackson. BARACARO; JUMBIE BEAD. Resembles *O. monosperma*, but leaflets oblong-elliptic and shorter, most parts rusty-pubesc. Tree to some 30m. Lvs 5–11-foliolate; petiole to 7cm; leaflets to 15cm. Infl. some 4×1mm; fls to 15mm; cal. to 9mm; pet. dark purple. Fr. some 4×2cm, 1–3-seeded; seeds to 13×11mm, red and black. Guyana, Trinidad.

***O. coccinea*** (Aubl.) Jackson. PANACOCO; AGUI. Tree to 30m. Lvs imparipinnate; leaflets to 11.5cm, in 3–5 pairs, ovate to oblong, thick, glossy above, main veins very prominent beneath, sometimes hairy; petiole to 7cm. Infl. a panicle; cal. to 0.9cm, yellow or rusty downy; cor. to 1.5cm, dark purple. Fr. to 6×3cm, glabrous at maturity, shining, black or dark brown, 1–4-seeded; seeds to 15×12mm, 1–4, scarlet with black spot at one end. Amazon Basin, Guyana.

***O. emarginata*** (Hook. & Arn.) Benth. Glabrous tree. Leaflets to 7.5cm, mostly 5–7, obovate-oblong, blunt or emarginate. Panicles small; fls to 13mm; cal. black in contrast to pale pet. Fr. to 5cm; seeds to 1cm, ovoid to elliptic, shiny, scarlet. Hong Kong.

***O. krugii*** Urban. BOIS NAN-NON; PALO PERONIA; PERONILA. Resembles *O. monosperma*, but leaflets to 20×14cm, obtuse or abruptly acuminate, on petiolules to 13mm+. Tree to 25m. Lvs 5–9 foliolate; petiole to 28cm; leaflets sericeous beneath, often suborbicular. Cal. to 15mm, dark violet; pet. some 13mm. Fr. to 10×2.5cm, sericeous, pointed at either end, constricted between the seeds, brown; seeds 13×13mm, 4–6 red or spotted black. Hispaniola, Puerto Rico, Lesser Antilles.

***O. monosperma*** Urban. NECKLACE TREE; SNAKEWOOD; CACONIER. Tree to 6m. Leaflets 15–20cm, 7–9, oblong to obovate-oblong, slender-pointed, gradually acuminate, strongly nerved; petiolules elliptic or elliptic-oblong, to 4mm. Panicles, cal. and fr. rusty-blue or purple; cor. to 2cm. Fr. to 4cm, obovate, beaked, velutinous; seeds about 1.5cm, black or scarlet with black spot. Summer. Lesser Antilles, NE Venezuela.

***O. panamensis*** Benth. PERONIL; CORONIL. Tree to 15m. Leaflets 10×5cm, 5–7 pairs, elliptic-oblong, acuminate, pubesc. Racemes simple, gold or tawny, densely pubesc.; cal. to 1cm, densely tawny-sericeous; cor. to 2cm, lilac. Fr. to 7×5cm, sericeous, tawny-brown; seeds to 17×10mm, 1–4, dark red. Panama.

***O. acuta*** Vogel. See *O. monosperma*.
***O. glaberrima*** Wu. See *O. emarginata*.
***O. minor*** Vogel. See *O. monosperma*.
***O. stipitata*** Schery. See *O. panamensis*.
For further synonymy see *Layia*.

**Ornamental grasses, sedges and rushes**. In gardening the term 'grasses' usually embraces not only the true grasses (Gramineae) but also the sedges (Cyperaceae) the rushes and the reed maces (Typha), and the word is so used in this entry. The bamboos, which are true grasses, are considered elsewhere. The individual genera are described in their alphabetical positions.

Annual grasses or those treated as annuals, may be sown directly into the ground where they are to grow once all danger of frost is past, or they may be sown in seed trays under glass and planted out once frosts are over. Seed should be sown shallowly, either broadcast or in drills, and lightly covered, perhaps with silver sand, and protected from birds with chicken wire or cotton threads. Seed should be sown under glass 3–5 weeks earlier. Annuals should be set out 10–30cm/4–12in. apart, depending on species. Nearly all need to be grown in good, fertile soil in a sunny situation.

**Grasses** (a) *Typha latifolia* (b) *Cortaderia selloana* (c) *Miscanthus sinensis* 'Zebrinus' (d) *Carex pendula* (e) *Panicum virgatum* (f) *Molinia caerulea* (g) *Eragrostis curvula* (h) *Stipa calamagrostis* (i) *Coix lacryma-jobi* (j) *Histrix patula* (k) *Leymus arenarius* (l) *Briza maxima* (m) *Cyperus longus* (n) *Zea mays* (o) *Juncus effusus* f. *spiralis* (p) *Pennisetum villosum* (q) *Lagurus ovatus* (r) *Luzula maxima* (s) *Cynodon dactyion* (t) *Eriophorum latifolium* (u) *Bouteloua gracilis* (v) *Melica uniflora* (w) *Scirpus tabernaemontani*

The following annual grasses have ornamental spikelets: *Agrostis nebulosa, Aira elegantissima, Apera spica-venti, Avena sterilis, Briza maxima, B. minor, Bromus macrostachys, B. madritensis, Coix lacryma-jobi, Eragrostis* species, *Lagurus ovatus, Lamarckia aurea, Pennisetum* spp. (most species treated as annuals in colder parts of North America), *Phalaris canariensis, Phleum pratense, Rhynchelytrum repens, Setaria italica, Zea mays*.

Perennial grasses have the same general cultural requirements as most herbaceous border perennials, i.e. a well-drained sunny position. Sedges generally require damper and more shaded conditions, while many of the rushes need to be grown as pool marginals; some can also be grown with their roots covered by 10cm/4in. of water, as can the reed-maces. The smaller grasses need to be planted into ground that has been thoroughly prepared, but the larger ones such as *Arundo, Cortaderia, Saccharum* and *Miscanthus* generally require individual planting holes such as one would provide for trees or shrubs – that is the hole should be excavated 50cm/20in. deep and 1m/39in. across, the bottom of the hole covered with 10cm/4in. of farmyard manure and the back-fill soil enriched with leafmould or garden compost. The plants should be well firmed and watered in. Planting should be done in spring or early summer, never in autumn or winter.

Subsequent routine maintenance consists of regular annual grooming, designed to clear a crown of dead leaves and flowering culms. This is most usually done by cutting the top-growth to the ground in earliest spring, but alternatively the old leaves may be raked out. Tough gloves should be worn when dealing with *Cortaderia* and *Miscanthus* as these have saw-toothed leaf edges which can inflict very deep cuts.

A less regular requirement is the division of the plants. Several small grasses, especially the various blue-leafed bun-forming fescues, tend to die from the middle outwards after some years, and need to be lifted and divided and their dead centre discarded. Division can usually be effected by tearing the plants apart by hand but with larger and tougher grasses a knife or secateurs may be required. The largest grasses (*Arundo, Cortaderia, Saccharum, Miscanthus*) are best divided by lifting the entire plant out of the ground and then effecting division by means of an axe or bow-saw. All such dividing should be done in the spring, never in the autumn. Most of these plants can also be easily raised from seed.

The tallest grasses, such as *Arundo donax* and both *Miscanthus sacchariflorus* and *M. floridulus*, may be used for screens 2.4m/8ft tall or more. Smaller screens may be made using *Saccharum ravennae* and *Miscanthus sinensis* cultivars. Although these die down in winter they achieve their full height very rapidly each season.

All of the above, together with *Arundo plinii* and the more robust cultivars, of *Miscanthus sinensis*, as well as most *Cortaderia selloana* cultivars are also suitable for use as specimens on lawns. They have sufficient vigour to hold their own if used in shrub borders. *Cortaderia selloana* is only hardy to zone 7; being liable to damage in severe long cold winters as in the US and central Europe. In colder areas *Saccharum ravennae* may be used to similar effect in sheltered places.

Ornamental grasses may be planted with other perennials in beds and borders. When so used they associate particularly well with plants with bold foliage such as *Acanthus, Bergenia* and *Hosta*. In general individual grasses should not be crowded but given sufficient space for their overall form or outline to be seen. Grasses such as *Molinia caerulea* 'Variegata', which do not start into growth until June, may be planted to follow spring bulbs. Grasses also have a long season of blooms and by careful selection of species it is possible to achieve a succession of flowerings, as for example by using *Pennisetum alopecuroides* to follow *Deschampsia caespitosa*. Deliberate contrasts and harmonies can be created, for instance by planting *Hakonechloa macra* 'Albo Aurea' with *Hosta* 'Halcyon' or harmonizing hostas of the Tardiana Group with the different shades of blue to be found among the cultivars of *Festuca ovina* or *Poa colensoi*. Bronze-leafed grasses associate well with pale pink flowers or more arrestingly with yellow coreopsis and heleniums. Grasses suitable for the flower border in varying climates may be found in the following genera: *Agrostis, Alopecurus, Andropogon, Arrhenatherum, Bothriochloa, Bouteloua, Brachypodium, Briza, Bromus, Calamagrostis, Carex, Chasmanthium, Chionochloa, Cortaderia, Deschampsia, Eleusine, Elymus, Eragrostis, Festuca, Glyceria, Hakonechloa, Helictotrichon, Hystrix, Imperata, Koeleria, Melica, Milium, Miscanthus, Molinia, Oryzopsis, Panicum, Pennisetum, Phalaris, Phleum, Poa, Rhynchelytrum, Setaria, Spartina, Spodiopogon, Stipa, Uniola*. Several of these have attractive variegated forms.

Grasses can also be used in plantings on their own, the plants graded from tall to small as would be done with other perennials. Particular attention should be paid to plant form and seasonal variation. The plant form may be tufted (*Helictotrichon sempervirens*), mound-forming (*Pennisetum alopecuroides*), narrowly upright (*Calamagrostis* × *acutiflora* 'Karl Foerster'), fountain-shaped (*Miscanthus sinensis* 'Gracillimus') or irregular (*Phalaris arundinacea* 'Picta'), and these shapes may be used to complement each other. Tall grasses belong at the back or high point of a border, but many, especially the miscanthus, tend to loose their lower leaves and this needs to be concealed by grasses of intermediate size. The flowering season starts in early spring and runs through till mid autumn, but most grasses flower from mid summer till early autumn, so that a variety of effects can be achieved. Several also contribute autumn colour, especially *Chasmanthium latifolium, Imperata cylindrica, Miscanthus sacchariflorus, Panicum virgatum, Pennisetum alopecuroides, Schizachyrium scoparium, Sorghastrum nutans, Spartina pectinata* and *Stipa arundinacea*. Some evergreen grasses (evergreen to Zone 5) such as *Carex pendula, C. morrowii* and cultivars, *Deschampsia caespitosa, Festuca ovina* and cultivars, *Helictotrichon sempervirens, Holcus mollis* 'Albo-variegatus' and *Koeleria glauca* can be used to give winter interest. Grasses with coloured leaves can be used in much the same way as heathers in a heather garden, in bold drifts and groups, associated either with larger grasses as specimens or with dwarf conifers. A drift of *Festuca* 'Silver Seas' next to a drift of *Imperata cylindrica* 'Red Baron', separated from a group of *Hakonechloa macra* 'Albo-aurea' by a carpet of the bright green *Festuca eskia* with clumps of *Cortaderia selloana* 'Aureo-lineata' or *Miscanthus sinensis* 'Morning Light' could be highly effective.

In any planting composed wholly or almost wholly of grasses there is a danger of producing a wispy and insubstantial effect, little better than a wilderness. Such plantings need bulk to hold them together visually. This may be achieved by using the grasses in groups or drifts of not less than three or five for many of each species, and by using larger grasses (again in groups of three or five) to give a focal point to the general planting.

In such plantings the weed-suppressing qualities of grasses may be exploited. Although not usually thought of as groundcover plants many grasses naturally form impenetrably dense clumps and when planted close together in drifts are highly effective as ground cover. Especially useful are *Arrhenatherum elatius* ssp. *bulbosum* 'Variegatum', *Carex morrowii* and cultivars, *C. caryophyllea, C. elata* and *C. e.* 'Bowles Golden', *C. pendula, C. plantaginea, Cortaderia fulvida, C. selloana* and cultivars, *Dactylis glomerata* 'Variegata', *Deschampsia caespitosa* and cultivars and *D. flexuosa, Saccharum ravennae, Festuca* species and cultivars, *Imperata cylindrica* 'Red Baron', *Luzula nivea, L. maxima* and *L. m.* 'Marginata', *Miscanthus sinensis* and cultivars, *Molinia caerulea* 'Variegata', *Pennisetum* species and *Stipa gigantea*. Several grasses of running habit may also be effective as for example *Carex muskingumensis, Leymus arenarius, Glyceria maxima* and *G. m.* var. *variegata, Milium effusum* and *M. e.* 'Aureum' and *Phalaris arundinacea* 'Picta'. These running grasses should be cut nearly to the ground two or three times in their first two or three seasons to make them grow more densely.

More intimate plantings, either of grasses alone or of mixed plants, can be achieved in the pebble or scree gardens so popular in New Zealand and Australia. In these the bare earth is covered in a weed-suppressing mulch of pea-grit or, for pebble gardens, larger rounded stones. The New Zealand sedges (*Uncinia* spp.)

**Ornamental grasses** (a) *Arundo donax* 'Versicolor' (b) *Cortaderia selloana* (c) *Deschampsia caespitosa* (d) *Phalaris arundinacea* 'Picta' (e) *Holcus mollis* 'Albo-variegatus' (f) *Hakonechloa macra* 'Aureola' (g) *Festuca ovina*

and sedges such as *Carex buchananii, C. petriei* and *C. plagellifera*, look particularly well in these settings, but so too do *Helictotrichon sempervirens, Festuca ovina* and cultivars, the *Deschampsia* spp. and cultivars as well as the New Zealand species of *Cortaderia* and many *Miscanthus*.

Relatively few ornamental grasses are suitable for the rock garden, but the following may be useful, depending on the scale of the garden: *Alopecurus pratensis* 'Aureus', *A. lanatus, Bouteloua gracilis, Briza minor, Carex berggrenii, C. brunnea, C. conica* 'Variegata', *C. firma* and *C.f.* 'Variegata', *C. ornithopoda, C. plantaginea, C. siderosticha, C. umbrosa, C. uncifolia, Chionochloa flavescens, Hakonechloa macra, Holcus mollis* 'Albo-Variegatus', *Lagurus ovatus* 'Nanus', *Mibora minima, Oreobolus pectinatus* and *Luzula celata*.

Many grassy plants lend themselves to waterside planting where their refinement affords an excellent foil for the bold foliage of other waterside subjects. *Carex riparia* 'Variegatus', *C. grayi*, all the *Cyperus* species, *Phragmites australis* and *P.a.* 'Variegatus', as well as all the typhas and several ornamental *Juncus*, may be grown with as much as 10cm/4in. of water covering their roots, while the following are better grown as marginals: *Arundo donax, Carex elata* 'Bowles Golden', *C. pendula, C. siderosticha* 'Variegata', *Calamagrostis epigejos, Deschampsia caespitosa, Glycera maxima, Juncus effusus* and cultivars, *Miscanthus sacchariflorus, M. sinensis* and cultivars, *Molina caerulea* and cultivars, *Panicum virgatum, Phalaris arundinacea* 'Picta', *Spartina pectinata* and *Zizania aquatica*. Modern ponds are often made with liners which leave the ground immediately round the pond dry and the following grasses are especially useful in such situations: *Deschampsia caespitosa* and cultivars, *Helictotrichon sempervirens, Miscanthus sinensis, Pennisetum* spp. and *Spartina pectinata* 'Aureomarginata'.

Several ornamental grasses are effective in shade and in woodland gardens, including most of the sedges, *Brachypodium sylvaticum, Bromus ramosus, Calamagrostis epigejos, Chasmanthium latifolium, Coix lacryma-jobi, Deschampsia caespitosa, D. flexuosa, Festuca gigantea* and *F. tenuifolia, Hystrix patula*, all *Luzula* spp., *Melica altissima, M. uniflora* and *M.u.* 'Variegata', *Milium effusum, Molinia caerulea* 'Variegata', *Poa chaixii* and *P. nemoralis* and *Stipa pennata*. *Luzula maxima* and *L.m.* 'Marginata', together with *Carex morrowii* and its cultivars, will tolerate dry shade.

The inflorescences of many grasses are valued for picking and drying for floral arrangements. Many of the inflorescences naturally shatter to aid the dispersal of seed so it is important to pick the heads before seed develops, at the very latest once the anthers appear. The picked heads should be hung upside-down in a cool, draughty place to dry. The following are especially suitable: *Agrostis nebulosa, Aira elegantissima, Apera* species, *Avena* species, *Briza* species, *Bromus* species, *Calamagrostis epigeous* and *C.* × *acutiflora, Cortaderia* species and cultivars, *Deschampsia* species and cultivars, *Eragrostis* species, *Hordeum* species, *Hystrix patula, Lagurus ovatus, Leymus arenarius, Milium effusum, Miscanthus* species and cultivars, *Panicum virgatum, Pennisetum* species, *Phalaris canariensis, Polypogon monspeliensis, Rhynchelytrum repens, Setaria italica, Stipa* species, *Uniola* species and *Zizania aquatica*.

Some tender grasses may be grown to great effect in conservatories, including the giant *Arundo donax* 'Variegata', the various *Cymbopogon* spp. grown for their fragrance such as *C. citratus* (lemon grass) and *C. nardus* (citronella grass), *Echinochloa crus-galli*, several spp. and cultivars of *Cyperus, Gynerium sagittatum*, the trailing *Oplismenus compositus* and *O. hirtellus* 'Variegatus' (both known as basket grass), and *Stenotaphrum secundatum* 'Variegatum', also a grass of trailing habit. Under glass, grasses should be kept well-watered and be fed regularly through the growing season. The *Cyperus* species may be stood in water or grown in the conservatory pool. Minor infestations of pests such as white fly, aphids and red spider mite may be cleared up with suitable insecticides.

Many grasses may be grown to good effect in pots or tubs. *Hakonechloa macra* 'Albo-aurea' and *Leymus arenarius* both look particularly fine in terracotta pots. *Stenotaphrum secundatum* 'Variegatum' is much used in summer bedding arrangements and may also be used in pots on its own, especially where its trailing habit can be exploited.

**Ornithidium** Salisb. (From Gk *ornis*, bird, and *eidos*, resemblance, referring to the upper lip of the stigma, which resembles a beak.) Orchidaceae. Some 20 species of epiphytic orchids closely allied to *Maxillaria*. Rhizome elongate, enveloped by distichous overlapping sheaths, sometimes ascending and stem-like. Pseudobulbs scattered or clustered on rhizome, enveloped at least initially by leafy sheaths, apically unifoliate to bifoliate, reduced or absent in some species. Apical leaves subcoriaceous, elongate, sheathing leaves, short, distichous. Flowers solitary on clustered stalks borne basally, usually somewhat cupped with tepals incurved, small; sepals subequal, free, erect or spreading, lateral sepals adnate to column foot forming an inconspicuous mentum; petals similar to sepals, smaller; lip continuous with column foot or shortly connate, erect, unguiculate, 3-lobed, lateral lobes often clasping column, erect, parallel; midlobe spreading; column short, stout, sometimes with short foot, wingless, anther terminal, operculate, incumbent, galeate, pollinia 4, waxy, ovoid. Tropical America. Z10.

CULTIVATION Intermediate-growing epiphytes requiring partial shade and a light winter rest. See ORCHIDS.

***O. densum*** (Lindl.) Rchb. f. Rhiz. to 1cm diam. Pseudobulbs to 7×2.5cm, yellow-green, compressed, ovate-oblong to elliptic-oblong, unifoliate. Lvs to 40×4cm, linear to linear-oblong, retuse, olive-green. Infl. to 5cm; fls variable, grey to green-white tinged purple to red-brown or maroon; sep. to 9×3mm, elliptic-linear to elliptic-lanceolate, acute to acuminate; pet. to 7×3mm, elliptic-lanceolate, acute; lip to 4mm, continuous with column foot, lateral lobes small, basal, suborbicular, clasping column, midlobe ovate to suborbicular, obtuse, recurved, disc with concave obtuse callus; column to 4mm. Mexico, Honduras, Guatemala, Honduras.

For synonymy see *Maxillaria*.

**Ornithocephalus** Hook. (From Gk *ornis*, bird, and *kephale*, head, referring to the rostellum, which resembles a bird's bill.) Orchidaceae. Some 50 species of epiphytic orchids. Rhizome short, concealed by overlapping leaf sheaths. Pseudobulbs absent. Leaves jointed to leaf sheaths, distichous, overlapping, fleshy to subcoriaceous, arranged in a fan. Inflorescence a raceme, lateral, few- to many-flowered; flowers small; sepals subequal, free, spreading or reflexed, concave; petals larger than sepals, concave, short-unguiculate; lip entire or trilobed, sessile or subsessile; disc with a basal fleshy callus; column short, wingless, footless, anther terminal, incumbent, operculate, pollinia 4, waxy, borne on a slender stipe, rostellum long, slender, beak-shaped. Tropical America. Z10.

CULTIVATION As for *Oberonia* but with bright light and a slight winter rest. See ORCHIDS.

***O. bicornis*** Lindl. Lvs to 7×12cm, lanceolate to oblong-lanceolate, acute or apiculate, rigid, erect-spreading. Infl. seldom exceeding lvs, few- to many-fld; peduncle slender, flexuous, densely lanuginose; fls small, to 5mm diam., white-green or white-yellow; sep. to 3×2mm, suborbicular, spreading, apiculate, hispid below; pet. subequal to sep., suborbicular-flabellate, oblique, base cuneate, erose; lip to 7mm, lateral lobes inconspicuous, linear-spathulate, recurved, midlobe linear-oblong or oblong, acute to rounded, dorsally carinate; column to 5mm, slender. Guatemala, Honduras, Panama, Costa Rica.

***O. bonplandii*** Rchb. f. Lvs to 20×6mm, fleshy, lanceolate or oblong-lanceolate, acute, deep green. Infl. to 4cm, few-fld; peduncle minutely denticulate; sep. to 3×2mm, pale green, elliptic to elliptic-ovate, apiculate, lateral sep. oblique; pet. slightly larger than sep., pale green, flabellate to ovate-flabellate, truncate or rounded; lip to 5×2mm, white, margins, yellow-green toward base, entire, narrowly oblong, acute, disc with 2 large, yellow-green, fleshy, alate calli; column to 2mm, yellow-green, rostellum to 4mm. Venezuela, Colombia.

***O. gladiatus*** Hook. Lvs to 60×7mm, oblanceolate to oblong, acute to acuminate. Infl. to 7cm, suberect to arching, loosely few to several-fld; peduncle glabrous, narrowly winged; fls small, pale cream-green or white marked green; sep. to 4×2.5mm, elliptic-oblong to suborbicular, deeply concave, margins slightly erose, slightly recurved; pet. to 4×4mm, cuneate-obovate or flabellate, rounded or truncate, slightly erose; lip to 7×3mm, entire, linear-oblong, acute to rounded, base cordate-triangular, callus large, suborbicular-ovate; column to 1mm, cream-green, anth. cream-green, base yellow-green. Mexico, C America, Grenada, Tobago, Trinidad to Brazil, Peru, Bolivia.

***O. grandiflorus*** Lindl. Lvs to 15cm, few, narrowly oblong, obtuse. Infl. surpassing lvs, arcuate, densely many-fld.; fls to 18mm diam.; sep. and pet. white, with bright green basal spot, concave; lateral sep. smaller, reflexed; lip saccate, strongly carinate beneath; callus horse shoe-shaped, green; column white. Brazil.

***O. iridifolius*** Rchb. f. Lvs to 85×6mm, fleshy, linear-ensiform, acute or acuminate. Infl. to 8cm, spreading, loosely many-fld; peduncle slender, fractiflex, winged; fls small, white; sep. to 3×2mm, elliptic to suborbicular, spreading, ciliate; pet. to 4×5mm, broadly flabellate, base cuneate, apex rounded, ciliate; lip to 5.5×6mm, spreading, lateral lobes fleshy, suborbicular to subquadrate, apex rounded, midlobe ovate, suborbicular, concave; column to 3mm, fleshy. Mexico, Guatemala.

***O. myrticola*** Lindl. Lvs to 25×1cm, narrowly linear-lanceolate to ligulate-lanceolate, falcate, acute or acuminate. Infl. to 8cm, ascending, arching, densely many-fld; peduncle glandular-pubesc.; fls small, lemon-scented, exterior glandular-pubesc., white and green; sep. to 4×2mm, ovate, rounded, dentate; pet. to 4.5×4.5mm, almost transparent, suborbicular, entire to undulate-crisped; lip to 5×2.5mm, entire, reflexed, ligulate-oblong, acute, base cordate, disc with 5 fleshy calli, papillose; column to 2mm, erect. Brazil, Bolivia.

***O. inflexus*** Lindl. See *O. gladiatus*.
***O. navicularis*** Barb. Rodr. See *Zygostates lunata*.
***O. planifolius*** Rchb. f. See *Dipteranthus planifolius*.

**Ornithogalum** L. (Name used by Dioscorides, from Gk *ornis*, bird, and *gala*, milk.) Liliaceae (Hyacinthaceae). Some 80 species of bulbous perennial herbs. Bulbs usually subterranean, globose, tunics white or brown, rarely part-exposed, green and fleshy. Leaves in a rosette, linear to lanceolate or obovate, sometimes with a silver-white median stripe above, margins smooth or hairy. Inflorescence a scapose raceme or corymb, pyramidal to subcylindric, 2- to many-flowered; bracts usually conspicuous; tepals 6, equal or unequal in 2 distinct whorls, white, rarely yellow, orange or red, outside usually marked with a green stripe, usually widely spreading, rarely erect; stamens 6, filaments flattened, often broadened at base, sometimes winged; ovary superior, cylindric to spherical, yellow-green or purple-black; style terminal. Fruit a trilocular, many-seeded capsule. S Africa, Mediterranean.

CULTIVATION *Ornithogalum* has two main centres of distribution, in South Africa and around the Mediterranean, but includes a number of more northerly European natives which are robust and cold-hardy in cultivation, some of which may become invasive where conditions suit, such as *O. umbellatum* and *O. nutans*. The South African species are generally frost-tender and are planted temporarily in the summer borders of cool temperate gardens or grown in pots in the cool glasshouse. They include a number of species that are extremely valuable as long-lived cut flowers, especially *O. thyrsoides* which, if arranged when in bud, may last for several weeks in a cool room.

Vigorous species like *O. nutans*, *O. umbellatum* and *O. montanum* are suitable for naturalizing in short turf or thin grass or beneath shrubs. Taller species such as *O. pyrenaicum* and *O. nutans* also suited to the wild garden or other naturalistic plantings. The hardiest species, *O. umbellatum* and *O. pyrenaicum*, withstand temperatures to between −15 and −20°C/5 of to −4°F; *O. montanum*, *O. nutans* and *O. orthophyllum* are almost as tolerant, surviving temperatures at the warmer end of this range. *O. pyramidale*, *O. narbonense*, *O. oligophyllum* are hardy where temperatures seldom fall below −10°C/14°F. The beautiful *O. arabicum*, once widely cultivated as a cut flower crop, suits warm sunny borders, but where temperatures fall much below freezing are more satisfactory in containers of medium-fertility, loam-based mix in the cold glasshouse.

Grow in any moderately fertile, well-drained soil in sun; *O. nutans* and *O. umbellatum* tolerate partial shade. Propagate by seed sown when ripe in the cold frame; sown thinly they can remain *in situ* during their first summer dormancy and may be planted out as small bulbs form in their second or third year. Also by offsets when dormant.

***O. apertum*** (Verdoorn) Oberm. Lvs 10–20, glaucous, flat, narrow, tightly spiralled and coiled. Scape to 20cm, 8–20-fld; tepals white or yellow, with broad green central band. S Africa (Namaqualand, SW Cape Province). Z9.

***O. arabicum*** L. Bulb subterranean, broadly ovoid, bearing numerous bulblets. Lvs to 60×2.5cm, 5–8, broadly linear, more or less erect, dark green, thickly textured. Scape 30–80cm; raceme cylindric to subspherical, 6–25-fld, fls fragrant; tepals 1.5–3.2cm, white or cream, withering but not reflexing in fruit; fil. broadening below; ovary black or purple-black. cf. *O. saundersiae*. Mediterranean. The name *O. corymbosum* or var. *corymbosum* is usually applied to exceptionally floriferous specimens, bearing larger fls in corymbose racemes; the hardiness and vigour of such plants is often superior. Z9.

***O. conicum*** Jacq. Very similar to *O. thyrsoides* but flowering stems 40–100cm, lvs with smooth margins, fil. barely expanded at base. Early spring. S Africa (Cape Province). Z9.

***O. dubium*** Houtt. Bulb subterranean. Lvs to 10×2cm, 3–8, lanceolate to ovate-lanceolate, yellow-green, margins hairy. Scape to 30cm; raceme crowded, corymbose, cylindric to subspherical, 20+-fld; tepals 1.2cm, orange, red, yellow or, rarely, white, often tinged green or brown at base within; ovary yellow-green. Winter–spring. S Africa (Cape Province). Z9.

***O. longibracteatum*** Jacq. SEA ONION; FALSE SEA ONION; GERMAN ONION. Bulb with upper part exposed; tunics green and fleshy, bearing many bulblets. Lvs to 60×4cm, 8–12, strap-shaped, long-acuminate fleshy, flaccid, pale green, scapes 1–1.5m; raceme triangular to cylindric, 60–300-fld; bracts far exceeding fls; tepals to 9mm, white, outside with a green stripe; fil. broadening toward base; ovary yellow-green. S Africa (Cape Province, Natal). Z9.

***O. maculatum*** Jacq. SNAKE FLOWER. Lvs to 15cm, fleshy, blue-green. Scape 10–50cm, usually *c*15cm; infl. to 8-fld; tepals yellow or orange, but outer whorl often with tips blotched black or brown. Spring. S Africa (SW Cape). Z9.

***O. montanum*** Cyr. Bulb to 2.5cm diam., ovoid, subterranean, tunics usually brown. Lvs linear, 10–15cm, several, pale green usually with a white line above. Scape to 60cm; raceme to 10cm broad, somewhat corymbose, cylindric, 10–20-fld, fls drooping; tepals 2–3cm, not widely spreading, translucent white, outside with a broad green stripe; fil. of inner 3 stamens winged; ovary green, shorter than style. Europe (Balkans, Italy), SW Asia. Z6.

***O. multifolium*** Bak. Bulb *c*1.25cm diam. Lvs to 7cm, *c*10, slender, terete, glabrous, somewhat twisted. Scape to 25cm, usually *c*15cm; infl. 5–10-fld; fls fragrant, bright yellow to orange yellow. Spring. S Africa (Cape Peninsula).

***O. narbonense*** L. Lvs to 90×1.25cm, linear. Scape to 90cm; fls to 5cm diam. in loose, many-fld racemes; tepals keeled, milk white, midvein green. cf. *O. pyramidale*. Spring. Mediterranean, Caucasus, NW Iran. Z7.

***O. nutans*** L. Bulb to 4cm diam., ovoid, subterranean, bulblets numerous. Lvs 30–40cm, lorate, rather limp, several, pale green, with a white line above. Scapes to 60cm; raceme cylindric, 1-sided, 10–20-fld; fls nodding; tepals 2–3cm, translucent, white, broadly striped green outside, not widely spreading; fil. of at least 3 inner stamens winged, wings terminating in teeth at either side of anth.; ovary green; style shorter than ovary. Spring. Europe, SW Asia, naturalised in E US. Z6.

***O. oligophyllum*** Clarke. Bulb subterranean. Lvs to 15cm, linear-lanceolate to narrowly obovate, broad and blunt at apex, somewhat glaucous. Racemes corymbose, 2–5-fld; tepals 1–1.6cm, white to ivory edged pure white with a broad yellow-green stripe outside; pedicels 1–3cm, erect to spreading in fruit. Spring. Balkans, Turkey, USSR (Georgia). Z6.

***O. orthophyllum*** Ten. Similar to *O. umbellatum* but not producing bulblets; pedicels spreading to ascending in fruit, the lower 2–3.5cm. Spring. S & C Europe to N Iran. Z6.

***O. pruinosum*** F.M. Leighton. CHINCHERINCHEE. Lvs to 17cm, to 6, deep blue-green. Scape to 35cm, occasionally to 60cm; infl. a dense, many-fld spike, usually 35cm; fls white, fragrant. S Africa (Namaqualand, SW Cape Province). Z9.

***O. pyramidale*** L. Bulb to 3.7cm diam., ovoid, subterranean. Lvs to 45×1.25cm, glossy green, glaucous, withering before flowering ends. Scape 30–120cm; raceme cylindric to pyramidal, 30–50-fld; tepals 1.1–1.5cm, translucent white with a green stripe outside; ovary green; style shorter than ovary, base thickened and conical. Spring. C Europe, Yugoslavia, Romania cf. *O. narbonense*. Z6.

***O. pyrenaicum*** L. BATH ASPARAGUS; PRUSSIAN ASPARAGUS; STAR OF BETHLEHEM. Close to *O. pyramidale* but smaller and more delicate; tepals 9–13mm, pale yellow with a narrow green stripe outside; style longer than ovary. Spring. Europe, W & S Turkey, Caucasus. Z6.

***O. saundersiae*** Bak. GIANT CHINCHERINCHEE. Bulb large, globose, subterranean. Lvs 60×5cm, 6–8, erect to flaccid, lorate, dark green and glossy above. Scape 30–100cm; raceme corymbose, pyramidal, many-fld; pedicels long; tepals 1–1.5cm, white or cream; fil. conspicuously broadened below; ovary black or green-black, persistent and reflexed in fr. Early spring. S Africa (E Transvaal, Natal, Swaziland) cf. *O. arabicum*. Z9.

***O. thyrsioides*** Jacq. CHINCHERINCHEE; WONDER FLOWER. Bulb subterranean. Lvs to 30×5cm, 6–12, linear to narrow-lanceolate, ascending, withering before flowering ends, margins ciliate. Raceme corymbose, pyramidal to subspherical, many-fld; fls very long-lasting; tepals 1–2cm, translucent white to ivory tinted bronze or green at base; fil. of inner stamens broadly expanded at base; ovary yellow-green; style as long as ovary. Spring–early summer. S Africa (Cape Province). 'Album': fls snow white, with a somewhat darker 'eye' crowded in showy raceme. 'Aureum': fls topaz to golden. 'Flavescens': fls golden. 'Flavissimum': fls golden to ochre. Z9.

***O. umbellatum*** L. STAR OF BETHLEHEM. Bulb to 3.25cm diam., subglobose, subterranean, bulblets numerous. Lvs to 30×8cm, several, linear, tapering to apex, with a broad white line on midvein. Raceme broad corymbose, 6–20-fld; tepals 1.5–2.2cm, lustrous pure white with a green stripe outside; pedicels becoming horizontal, rigid in fruit, the lower 5–9cm. Spring. Europe, N Africa, Middle East. Z5.

***O. aurantiacum*** Bak. See *O. multifolium*.
***O. aureum*** Curtis. See *O. dubium*.
***O. balansae*** Boiss. See *O. oligophyllum*.
***O. caudatum*** Ait. See *O. longibracteatum*.
***O. corymbosum*** Ruiz & Pav. See *O. arabicum*.
***O. dichotomum*** Labill. See *Thysanotus dichotomus*.
***O. flavescens*** Lam. See *O. pyrenaicum*.
***O. lacteum*** Jacq. See *O. conicum*.
***O. miniatum*** Jacq. See *O. dubium*.
***O. tenuifolium*** Guss. See *O. orthophyllum*.

**Ornithophora** Barb. Rodr. (From Gk *ornis*, bird, and *phoros*, bearing, referring to the birdlike appearance of the column from one side.) Orchidaceae. 2 species of dwarf epiphytic orchids. Pseudobulbs sited along slender rhizomes, compressed ovoid-pyriform, glossy, apex 2-leaved; sheaths 1–2, leafy. Leaves linear-lanceolate, channelled, acute, suberect. Inflorescence basal, erect, lax, racemose; tepals oblong-lanceolate, reflexed to spreading, free; lip clawed, lamina transversely semicircular with acute, erect, lateral lobes, callus on claw fleshy, trilobed, at lip base with 4 fan-shaped ridges; column arcuate. Brazil. Z10.

CULTIVATION Dwarf epiphytes for the cool or intermediate house, they form large colonies of small pseudobulbs and grass-like foliage. The flowers, equally small, are delicate, pale and charming seen *en masse*. To accommodate the spreading habit, establish on rafts or slabs of fern or palm fibre suspended vertically in a bright, airy place. Spray over at least once daily except at coolest times of the year.

***O. radicans*** (Lind. & Rchb. f.) Garay & Pabst. Pseudobulbs oblong-ligulate, compressed, basal sheaths distichous, leaf-bearing, apex 2-leaved. Lvs linear-ligulate, grassy, cuneate, acute, 10–18×0.2–0.4cm. Infl. 7–15cm; fls white-green or green-yellow, lip white, callus yellow; dorsal sep. oblong-spathulate, narrow, acute, 4×1mm, lateral sep. ovate-falcate, narrow; pet. oblong-spathulate, apex rounded to subtruncate; lip trilobed, claw narrow, margin weakly undulate, midlobe saggitate to semi-round, apex notched, lateral lobes basal, long, acuminate, narrow; disc base crested.

For synonymy see *Sigmatostalix*.

**OROBANCHACEAE** Vent. BROOMRAPE FAMILY. Dicot. 17 genera and 230 species of herbaceous root-parasites without chlorophyll; stems usually fleshy, the radicle becoming a haustorium penetrating host-root. Leaves usually alternate scales, with often disorganized stomata; stipules absent. Flowers bisexual, in terminal bracteate racemes or spikes, solitary in *Phelipaea*; calyx (1–) 4 or 5 fused sepals, open or valvate; corolla 5 fused petals, more or less bilabiate, often curved; stamens 4, with adaxial 1 staminodal or absent, epipetalous and alternate with lobes; ovary superior, of 2(3) fused carpels; style thin with 2--lobed stigma, 1-loculed with parietal placentas; ovules numerous. Fruit a loculicidal capsule, each of the 2(3) valves, typically with 2 placentas; seeds minute; embryo undifferentiated; endosperm oily. N hemisphere, especially temperate and subtropical Old World. *Aeginetia, Orobanche*. Broomrapes (*Orobanche*) can cause damage to crop plants, especially in the Mediterranean and Middle East.

**Orobanche** L. (Name used by Dioscorides.) BROOMRAPE. Orobanchaceae. 150 species of annual and perennial herbs, lacking chlorophyll, fully parasitic, attached by haustoria to the roots of the host. Tubers subterranean, short-lived. Aerial stems erect, scaly-bracteate, leafless. Flowers sessile in compact, terminal spikes; calyx 2-lipped, 4–5-toothed; corolla tubular, curved, 2-lipped, lower lip 3-lobed, upper lip 2-lobed. Fruit a dehiscent 2-valved capsule; seeds numerous, small. Temperate regions, notably Europe. Some species are limited to a particular host genus, e.g. *O. hederae* on ivy. Spring–summer. Z6.

CULTIVATION The broomrapes have a curious beauty, particularly striking when seen as a large colony on an isolated stand of host plant. Fresh seed, mixed with silver sand and finely sifted loam, should be incorporated around the fibrous roots of potential hosts in late summer. Most conditions will suit – including deep shade for *O. hederae* – but soils must be well-drained.

***O. alba*** Stephan ex Willd. THYME BROOMRAPE. Parasitic on Labiatae and Leguminosae. Variable in height and fl. colour. Stems 8–35cm, stout, dull red, tinted ochre. Bracts similar in colour to stems, alternate on stems and densely clustered at base, glandular-pubesc. Infl. lax, few-fld; fls to 2cm, scented of cloves, pale yellow tinted red to deep mauve-red. Europe.

***O. flava*** Mart. YELLOW BROOMRAPE. Parasitic on Compositae, especially *Petasites*. Stems 15–60cm, stout, dull yellow-brown. Bracts same colour as stem, sparse, slender. Fls to 2cm, ochre, the upper lip stained red-brown. Europe.

***O. hederae*** Duby. Parasitic on *Hedera*. Stems 15–60×0.3–0.8cm, usually strongly swollen at base, glandular-pubesc., yellow to red-purple. Bracts 12–22mm, lanceolate-acuminate. Spike 10–40×2.5–4cm, lax, glandular-pubesc.; cor. 10–22mm, dull cream, red-purple at base. Europe.

***O. purpurea*** Jacq. PURPLE BROOMRAPE. Parasitic on Compositae. Stems 15–45cm, stout, blue-grey, sometimes branched at base, glandular-pubesc. toward apex, sparsely slender-scaly at base. Fls to 3cm, in a lax spike, dull violet, cream to yellow at base of cor. Europe.

***O. arenaria*** auct. ex Wallr. See *O. purpurea*.
***O. caerulea*** Vill. See *O. purpurea*.
***O. epithymum*** DC. See *O. alba*.
***O. rubra*** Sm. See *O. alba*.

**Orobus** L.
***O. cyaneus*** Steven. See *Lathyrus cyaneus*.
***O. gmelinii*** Fisch. ex DC. See *Lathyrus gmelinii*.
***O. luteus*** L. See *Lathyrus gmelinii*.
***O. myrtifolius*** (Muhlenb.) Hall. See *Lathyrus palustris*.
***O. myrtifolius*** Alef. See *Lathyrus palustris*.
***O. niger*** L. See *Lathyrus niger*.
***O. roseus*** (Steven) Ledeb. See *Lathyrus roseus*.
***O. venetus*** Mill. See *Lathyrus venetus*.
***O. vernus*** L. See *Lathyrus vernus*.

**Orontium** L. GOLDEN CLUB. Araceae. 1 species, an aquatic, perennial herb. Rhizomes thick, rooting into muddy bed, margins or (in cultivation) a basket, the branches clothed and terminating in alternate or tufted leaves. Leaves to 25×8cm, oblong to narrow-elliptic, submerged or aerial, sometimes floating, deep sage green with a thick glaucous silvering above, often purple-tinted beneath; petiole to 35cm, sometimes red-tinted. Spathe subtending spadix, green, bract-like, very small, soon withering; spadix to 18cm, narrowly cylindric, bright yellow, fading to ivory at the base and merging into the long, white stalk, upcurved and breaking the surface of the water. E US. Z7.

CULTIVATION Occurring in streams, shallow lakes and ponds, *O. aquaticum* is suitable for cultivation in large tubs and as a marginal plant in water from 10–45cm/4–18in. deep, hardy to about −15°C/5°F. Grow in fertile loamy soil in full sun; use containers 30×30×30cm(12in.$^3$), where necessary to limit spread. Propagate by division in spring or by seed fresh in submerged containers (seeds develop underwater, in small green berries).

***O. aquaticum*** L. As for the genus.

**Orostachys** (DC.) Fisch. (From Gk *oros*, mountain, and *stachys*, spike.) Crassulaceae. 10 species of biennial succulent herbs, 5–30cm. Leaves fleshy, in a dense hemispherical to globose basal rosette with cartilaginous spiny tips; flowering stem leaves alternate. Inflorescence on a tall, terminal flowering stem produced in second year; flowers subsessile, in a raceme, yellow-green or white to red; sepals 5, fleshy, around half petal length; petals 5, free, pointed, lanceolate, spreading; stamens 10, filament thin; nectary scales 5, small; carpels 5, free. Fruit a follicle, many-seeded, dehiscent. N Asia to Europe. Close to and sometimes included in *Sedum*. Z7 unless specified.

CULTIVATION Closely resembling *Sedum, Orostachys* spp. are short-lived rosette-forming plants that carry a dense tapering spike of star-shaped flowers in spring or summer, usually in their third year. They die after flowering but produce large numbers of seeds, which germinate readily. Grow in full sun, in a well-drained, gritty potting medium, with good ventilation and a winter minimum temperature of 8°C/46°F. *Orostachys* spp. may prefer frame cultivation rather than the glasshouse. Propagate from seed, or by division in spring and summer.

***O.aggregata*** (Mak.) Hara. Similar to *O.iwarenge* except lvs only 20–40×10–20mm, green, tips rounded. Japan (Honshu).

***O.chanetii*** (Lév.) A. Berger. Similar to *O.fimbriata* except lvs linear with a small cartilaginous spine; infl. somewhat pyramidal, to 20cm; pet. to 10mm, white-pink. Autumn. China.

***O.erubescens*** (Maxim.) Ohwi. Monocarpic perenn. to 25cm. Stem densely leafy, 6–15cm. Lvs dimorphic: winter lvs 15–30×4–7mm, spathulate, fleshy, spine tipped, sparsely toothed, cartilaginous; summer lvs lacking cartilaginous margin. Raceme many-fld, 40–100×15–20; fls subsessile, 6–8mm; anth. red turning purple. Autumn. Japan, Korea, N China.

***O.fimbriata*** (Turcz.) A. Berger. To 15cm. Rosette crowded. Flowering stem 10–15cm. Lvs 25×5mm, oblong, tip cartilaginous with a long spine; flowering stem lvs 10–30mm, linear-lanceolate. Raceme dense, branched; bracts spiny; pedicel long; sep. 1–3mm; pet. 5–6mm, fused at base, tinged red; stamens not exceeding pet. Follicles slender, beaked. Tibet, Mongolia, Japan, China.

***O.furusei*** Ohwi. Perenn. Sterile stems short, thin, erect or decumbent. Lvs 10–20×5–10mm, fleshy, obovate, flat. Racemes 5–10cm, many-fld; fls sessile; sep. 3.5mm; pet. 4.5–5mm, narrow-ovate, pale green; style 1mm; follicles equal pet. Autumn. Japan (Hokkaido).

***O.iwarenge*** (Mak.) Hara. Monocarpic perenn., to 45cm. Stem 10–25cm. Lvs 30–70×7–28mm, numerous, densely packed, glaucous, spathulate-oblong, blunt. Raceme 5–20cm, many-fld, dense; fls subsessile, white; sep. half pet. length; pet. 5–7mm. Autumn. China. Z6.

***O.malacophylla*** (Pall.) Fisch. Rosette crowded. Lvs lacking spiny tips, blunt, lanceolate-oblong or elliptic; flowering stem lvs alternate, to 7mm. Raceme elongated, many-fld, occasionally branched; bracts covering fls; sep. 3–4mm, pointed, fused at base; pet. 4–6mm, pale green-yellow, fused at base; stamens exceeding pet., anth. yellow. Late summer. Mongolia, China, Japan. Z6.

***O.spinosa*** (L.) C.A. Mey. To 35cm. Rosette crowded, 2–7cm across. Flowering stem 10–30cm. Lvs 15–25×3–5mm, oblong, apical spine white, 2–4mm, margin white; flowering stem lvs 10–25×2–5mm, sessile, spine-tipped. Raceme many-fld, compact; pedicel 1mm or absent; bracts oblong; sep. 3mm; pet. 6–9mm, yellow-green; stamens exceeding pet., anth. yellow. Follicles 5–6mm. E USSR to N & C Asia. Z4.

***O.japonica*** A. Berger. See *O. erubescens*.
For further synonymy see *Cotyledon, Sedum* and *Umbilicus*.

**Oroxylum** Vent. MIDNIGHT HORROR; TREE OF DAMOCLES; KAMPONG; KI TONG TOKANG. (From Gk *oros*, mountain, and *xylon*, wood, referring to one of several habitats of this tree.) Bignoniaceae. 1 species, a glabrous semi-deciduous tree, 6–27m. Trunk to 40cm diam., bark grey, scarred, branchlets becoming hollow, lenticellate. Leaves 2–4-pinnate at branchlet tips; petiole 0.5–2m; leaflets 4–15×3–9cm, ovate to oblong, apex acuminate, base cuneate, rounded to reniform, venation reticulate, conspicuous beneath. Flowers nocturnal, foetid, in terminal erect racemes, 0.25–1.5m; pedicels long, 2–4cm; calyx leathery becoming woody in fruit, truncate or irregularly split, 2–4×1.5–2cm, brown-purple; corolla purple-red to brown outside, yellow to pink inside, 7–10cm, lobes subequal, crisped or crenate, glandular-hairy inside, tube widened to base, *c*1.5cm; stamens hairy at base; style to 6cm, violet. Fruit a pendent capsule, 45–120×6–10cm, subulate, valves flat, becoming black, many-seeded; seeds 5–9×2.5–4cm, including wing. Ceylon through Himalaya to SE Asia and China. Z10.

CULTIVATION A handsome specimen tree for subtropical and tropical gardens, grown for bold glossy foliage, and for the extremely long and substantial fruits, hence the common name, tree of Damocles. The flowers open at night with a musty fragrance attractive to bats. *O. indicum* has a curious habit of growth, growing quickly to 5–10m/16–33ft; it then flowers and further upward growth ceases, the lower buds breaking to give rise to stiffly erect branches. Cultivate as for *Radermachera*.

***O.indicum*** (L.) Kurz. TREE OF DAMOCLES. As for the genus.

***O.flavum*** Rehd. See *Radermachera pentandra*.
For further synonymy see *Arthrophyllum, Calosanthes* and *Spathodea*.

**Oroya** Britt. & Rose. (After Oroya, Peru.) Cactaceae. 2 species of low-growing cacti; stem simple or offsetting, flattened-globose to very short cylindric, many-ribbed; areoles elongate; spines pectinate. Flower subapical, from the upper edge of the areoles, shortly funnelform or campanulate, regular, yellow to red; tube very short; scales small; floral areoles sparsely woolly; outer tepals spreading, inner suberect; stamens inserted in the throat and tube, the lowermost on a collar partly enclosing the nectar-chamber; filaments and style not exserted beyond the perianth. Fruit obovoid, slightly fleshy with small scales; seeds almost circular, 1.6×1.5mm, black-brown, semi-matt, not wrinkled or ridged, periphery keeled; relief low-domed; hilum large, basal, impressed. Peru.

CULTIVATION Grow in a cool frost-free greenhouse (min. 2–7°C/35–45°F), use 'standard' cactus compost: moderate to high inorganic content (more than 50% grit), pH 6–7.5; full sun; low air-humidity; keep dry from mid-autumn until early spring, except for light misting on warm days in late winter.

***O.borchersii*** (Boed.) Backeb. Resembling *O.peruviana*, but stems broader, spines yellow, fl. wholly yellow-green to yellow. N Peru. Z9.

***O.peruviana*** (Schum.) Britt. & Rose. Variable; stems to 40×20cm, simple or clustering, depressed-globose to very short cylindric, with up to 35 ribs; areoles to 1.5cm long; central spines 0–5, to *c*2cm, porrect, radial spines pectinate, *c*10–30, to 1.5cm, pale yellow to red-brown. Fl. 1.5–3×1.5–2.5cm, pale to deep pink-red, usually yellow inside. Mts of C Peru. Z9.

***O.gibbosa*** Ritter. See *O.peruviana*.
***O.neoperuviana*** Backeb. See *O.peruviana*.

**Orphium** E. Mey. (After Orpheus of Classical myth.) Gentianaceae. 1 species, an erect, slightly downy shrub to 60cm. Leaves to 5cm, linear to oblong, thick, sessile, opposite. Flowers solitary or clustered, terminal or in upper axils, 5-merous; calyx 1.5cm, tubular, loosely enclosing corolla tube, lobes oblong, obtuse; corolla to 4cm/1½in. diam., pink to red, subrotate, tube short, lobes 5, broadly rounded, mucronulate; anthers slightly twisted. Fruit a capsule. S Africa. Z9.

CULTIVATION As for *Chironia*.

***O.frutescens*** (L.) E. Mey. As for the genus.

For synonymy see *Chironia*.

**Ortegocactus** Alexander. (For the Ortega family of San José Lachiguiri, Oaxaca, Mexico, who assisted in the discovery of the plant.) Cactaceae. 1 species, a low-growing cactus, allied to *Escobaria* and *Mammillaria*; stems 3–4cm diam., clustering, reminiscent of *M. schumannii*, globose to short-cylindric, pale grey-green, tuberculate; tubercles low, rhomboid, 10–12mm diam., minutely punctate, the flowering grooved or not; areoles bipartite as in *Mammillaria*, the flowering sometimes grooved between the abaxial vegetative part and the adaxial floriferous part, as in *Escobaria*; spines, at least the tip, almost black; central spine 1, 4–5mm, radial spines 7–8, 5–10mm. Flowers axillary, diurnal, funnelform, 2–3×1.8–2.5cm; pericarpel without scales, but immersed in areolar wool; tube short, pale green; tepals yellow, or the outermost tinged purple outside; stigmas deep green. Fr. globose-ellipsoid, dull red, soon dry; floral remnant persistent; seed almost globose, 0.8–0.9×0.7mm, black-brown, matt; relief par-concave; hilum large, basal, superficial. S Mexico.

CULTIVATION Grow in a heated greenhouse (min. 10–15°C/50–60°F), use 'acid standard' cactus compost: moderate to high inorganic content (more than 50% grit), below pH 6; grow in full sun; maintain low humidity; water very sparingly in winter (to avoid shrivelling).

***O.macdougallii*** Alexander. As for the genus. S Mexico (Oaxaca). Z9.

**Orthilia** Raf. (From Gk *orthos*, straight, and *helix*, spiral, referring to the 1-sided raceme.) Pyrolaceae. 1 species, a shrubby, perennial, evergreen, rhizomatous herb to 20cm. Leaves 1.5–6cm, whorled, thinly coriaceous, ovate-elliptic, entire to finely round-toothed. Raceme secund, drooping, densely papillose, 8–15-flowered; bracts membranous, broadly oblanceolate to broadly lanceolate, 3–5mm, abruptly acute; flowers campanulate; pedicels 5–15cm, recurved, becoming erect in fruit; sepals orbicular, minutely toothed; petals pale green to ivory; styles exserted; filaments tapering, smooth. Fruit a capsule, 4mm diam. Summer. N temperate regions (in damp, coniferous woodlands). Z5.

CULTIVATION As for *Pyrola*.

***O. secunda*** (L.) House. As for the genus.

For synonymy see *Pyrola*.

**Orthiopteris** Copel.
***O. inaequalis*** (Kunze) Copel. See *Saccoloma inaequale*.

**Orthocarpus** Nutt. (From Gk *orthos*, upright, and *karpos*, fruit, referring to the symmetric seed capsules.) Scrophulariaceae. Some 27 species of annuals. Leaves alternate, 3–5-partite, lanceolate, irregularly divided. Spike terminal, bracts often coloured; calyx 2-lobed, campanulate; corolla tube 2-lobed, yellow, rose-crimson, cream, white or purple, upper lip entire, lower lip 3-lobed; stamens 4. Summer. W US, S America. Z9.

CULTIVATION Semi-parasites of upland prairie, dry grassland and open woodland, *Orthocarpus* spp. are annuals related to *Castilleja* and often share with this genus the same colourfully bracted inflorescence; as annuals, they are more easily managed than perennial semi-parasites and may be useful for sowing *in situ* in spring in informal flower borders. Also of use as a cut flower. Give an open, sunny site and a well-drained, moderately fertile soil, thinning to 10–15cm/4–6in. apart. In mild areas where temperatures do not fall much below freezing, sow during the autumn.

***O. erianthus*** Benth. Stems to 30cm, erect. Lvs incised at apex. Cor. tube pubesc., pale yellow, 15–20mm. W US. var. ***roseus*** A. Gray. Cor. rose to cream, becoming rose-purple. W US.

***O. imbricatus*** Torr. ex S. Wats. Stems to 30cm, erect, slender, pubesc. Lvs to 4cm, linear-lanceolate or linear. Infl. bracts entire, ovate, closely overlapping, purple-tipped; cor. to 13mm, rose-purple, lower lip tipped white; to 13mm. SW US.

***O. lithospermoides*** Benth. CREAM SACS. Stems erect, 25–60cm. Lvs pubesc., lower lvs entire, lanceolate, upper lvs pinnate, oblong, 20–65mm. Infl. bracts palmatifid; cor. tube 2.5–4cm, pale yellow to cream, lower lip with 2 purple blotches, dilated towards mouth. SW US.

***O. purpurascens*** Benth. ESCOBITA. Stems to 45cm, purple-flushed, pubesc., erect or basally branching. Lvs linear to pinnatifid, often tinged brown. Infl. bracts tipped rose-purple; cor. purple or crimson, tip of lower lip white with purple and (or) yellow spots or markings. SW US.

***O. tenuifolius*** (Pursh) Benth. Stem to 30cm, pubesc., branched toward apex. Lvs lanceolate, entire, upper lvs with 3–5 thread-like seg. Infl. bracts to 1.5cm, elliptic, entire or with side lobes, tipped purple; cor. yellow, purple-tipped or wholly purple, minutely pubesc. SW US.

For synonymy see *Triphysaria*.

**Orthophytum** Beer. (From Gk *orthos*, straight, and *phyton*, a plant, referring to the straight, erect inflorescence.) Bromeliaceae (Bromelioideae). 17 species of semi succulent, stemless or short-stemmed, perennial herbs. Leaves numerous, in many rows, forming a rosette, green or copper-green; sheaths large, clasping; blades serrate, narrowly triangular, long-attenuate, softly spiny. Inflorescence usually bipinnate, with several dense heads, rarely simple, on an erect scape, sometimes sessile in centre of rosette; inflorescence bracts leaflike, spreading; floral bracts large, pungent; flowers perfect, sessile or on short pedicels; sepals erect or suberect, free, symmetric or almost so; petals white, free, with 2 scales; inner staminal whorl fused to petals. Fruit berrylike, seeds lacking appendages. E Brazil. Z9.

CULTIVATION See BROMELIADS.

***O. navoides*** (L.B. Sm.) L.B. Sm. To 40cm, spreading via long stolons, whole plant brilliant red at floral maturity. Lvs 30cm, in dense rosette, sparsely scaly, fairly densely toothed, spines 1mm, upward-curving. Infl. densely capitate, sunk into rosette centre; floral bracts narrowly triangular, with small teeth; fls sessile; sep. to 3cm, free, narrowly triangular, straight; pet. white.

***O. saxicola*** (Ule) L.B. Sm. To 13cm in flower, stoloniferous. Lvs 3–6cm, suberect, in a dense rosette, pale green, fleshy and leathery, laxly toothed, with recurved 2–3mm spines. Infl. few-fld, compact, sessile or on a short scape; floral bracts leafy, reduced; fls sessile, sep. to 14cm, green with white, papery margin, pet. 13–14mm, free, white, blades oblong, spreading, with 2 lacerate scales above the base; stamens exserted.

***O. vagans*** M.B. Fost. Branching rhiz. forming extensive mats. Lvs to 12cm; sheaths nearly encircling rootstock, suborbicular, thin; blades green, deeply channelled, scaly beneath, toothed, spines 2mm. Infl. terminal, dense, sessile; bracts leaflike, bright red or orange, decreasing to 20mm at apex; branches 8–15-fld at apex; floral bracts narrowly lanceolate-triangular; fls subsessile, erect; sep. 12–15mm, narrowly triangular, tomentose; pet. 21mm, apple-green, linear, with 2 lacerate scales 2mm above the base.

**Orthrosanthus** Sweet. (From Gk *orthros*, morning, and *anthos*, flower; the flower opens early in the morning.) Iridaceae. 7 species of evergreen perennial herbs. Rhizome very short, woody. Leaves narrowly ensiform to linear, rigid and pliable or grassy, equitant at base or 1–2 reduced on flowering stem. Inflorescence simple or branched; flowers 2 to many per spathe, short-stalked or sessile, in clusters forming a loose panicle on slender erect stalk, ephemeral and only 1 in each cluster open at any time; bracteoles small, subtending each flower; perianth radially symmetric, tube short, segments ovate or oblong, spreading; filaments free, inserted on throat, anthers slender; style short, branches linear to oblong, entire. Tropical America, Australia. Z9.

CULTIVATION *Orthrosanthus* spp. usually occur on sandy well-drained soils; they are grown for their delicate clusters of symmetrical blue flowers carried in loose panicles on tall slender stems in summer; the flowers are very short-lived, lasting only a few hours although the clusters open in succession. In cool temperate zones, *Orthrosanthus* is best grown in the border or in pots in the cool glasshouse or conservatory, although *O. chimboracensis*, found at altitudes of up to 3000m/7475ft in the Andes, may be grown outside in favoured areas where temperatures do not drop much below zero, and *O. multiflorus* will tolerate slightly lower temperatures. Grow in a light, fertile, humus-rich and well-drained soil in sun. Under glass use a mix of fibrous loam, with additional leafmould and sharp sand. Water carefully and moderately when in growth, keeping almost dry at other times. Propagate by careful division of established plants or by seed, which germinates readily although seedlings develop slowly.

***O. chimboracensis*** (HBK) Bak. Basal lvs to 40×1cm, ribbed, margins minutely toothed, rough to the touch. Flowering stems 25–60cm, sparingly branched; fls lavender-blue, to 4cm diam., in a loose panicle composed of 3–4-fld clusters. Summer. Mexico to Peru.

***O. multiflorus*** Sweet. Basal lvs to 45×0.4cm, linear-ensiform, acute, rigid, equalling flowering stem, margins smooth. Fls pale blue (perianth seg. with a darker midvein), 3–4cm diam. on very short pedicels in 5–8-fld sessile or subsessile clusters forming a narrow panicle; spathes to 1.5cm with scurfy apices. Spring–summer. SW Australia.

***O. ocisapungum*** Ruiz. ex Diels. See *O. chimboracensis*.
For further synonymy see *Sisyrinchium*.

**Orychophragmus** Bunge. (From Gk *oryche*, pit, and *phragmos*, septum, from the pitted septum.) Cruciferae. 2 species of annual or biennial herbs. Stems simple or branching at base, glabrous or hairy. Leaves thin, lyre-shaped, pinnatifid, toothed, stem leaves entire. Sepals 4, narrow, linear, blunt; petals 4, violet, long-clawed, lamina broadly obovate, obtuse; stamens 6, free. Fruit a silique, linear, compressed, dehiscent, deeply pitted; seed 2mm. C Asia, China. Z7.

CULTIVATION The broad, pale green leaves of *O. violaceus* are eaten as a vegetable in China; in the West, it is more commonly grown as an ornamental annual or biennial, in the flower border or cool greenhouse, for its clusters of large lavender-blue flowers.

Grow in fertile well-drained soils, in full sun. Sow seed *in situ* in spring, or early summer. It will overwinter outdoors where temperatures do not fall below −5°C/23°F.

***O. violaceus*** (L.) Schultz. 10–15cm. Stem erect. Lvs variable, much divided near base of stem, becoming smaller, entire, cordate, sessile, clasping higher up. Sep. 12–16mm; pet. to 30mm, violet. Fr. 70–120×3mm. China.

**Oryza** L. (From Gk *oryza*, for the rice plant and its grain.) RICE. Gramineae. Some 19 species of annual or perennial rhizomatous grasses. Stems flimsy to robust. Leaves linear, flat; ligules subcoriaceous to papery. Inflorescence a panicle, loose or dense; spikelets laterally compressed, 3-flowered, upper flower fertile, lower flowers sterile; lodicules 2; glumes obscure; sterile lemma lobed, attached to base of fertile flower, fertile lemma keeled, rigid, awned; palea 3–7-ribbed, equal to lemma, tightly enclosing grain; stamens 6. Tropical Asia, Africa. Z10.

CULTIVATION The staple food of up to 50 percent of the world's population, many cultivars of rice have been developed to suit a wide diversity of climates and soil types; most are adapted to tropical and subtropical conditions and to the wet system of cultivation used in tropical lowlands; at higher altitudes, cultivars adapted to dry systems are more commonly used. In the wet system, flooding usually occurs after germination; seed may also be broadcast directly into shallow water or, in some regions, introduced as sprouts into wet mud. Rice is capable of germination either in the soil, or on the soil surface underwater; it is seldom successful sown in soil *and* underwater. It is grown as an ornamental for the dark foliage (in some cultivars) and for the inflorescence, attractive if dried once the seed grains have swollen, although in cool temperate zones this may only occur if grown under glass.

Treated as a frost-tender annual, *O. sativa* may be introduced to pond margins after the danger of frost has passed, thus ensuring the necessary constantly moist soil. It is sometimes cultivated in collections of economic crops. Under glass, grow in clay pans or in shallow (*c*15–20cm/6–8in.) fibreglass trays with a drain hole, which will allow periodic flooding and draining. Use a heavy and fertile loam-based medium, preferably with a high proportion of clay and silt, and sow seed thinly in late winter/early spring; cover with about 2cm/¾in. of coarse sharp sand and submerge to a depth of 2.5cm/1in. of water. Alternatively, germinate seed in moist soil and transplant sprouts into pans of soil covered by about 2.5cm of water. Grow in full sunlight and with moderate to high humidity; the application of a balanced general fertilizer is beneficial. The optimum water temperature is between 20–30°C/68–86°F; temperature above and below this range adversely affect growth. As growth proceeds the depth of water is gradually increased to 15–30cm/6–12in. Provided the soil is kept continuously moist, flooding is not strictly necessary; periodic drainage and re-flooding will reduce algal infestation and the harmful build-up of salts in the water. Rice will take between 90–260 days to mature, depending on cultivar, climate or environmental conditions, and from flowering to seed-ripening takes about 30 days, with a range of 15–60 days. Water should be drained off about a month before harvest to allow ripening; at this stage, the roots will have formed a dense mat at or near the soil surface, sometimes covered by green algae; although unsightly, this is seldom harmful. Rice is usually grown as an annual, but in favourable conditions a second ratoon crop is sometimes taken from the re-growth of stubble after the primary harvest.

***O. sativa*** L. Annual, to 180cm. Stems stout, upright, arching. Lvs elongate, to 150×2.5cm, usually smaller. Panicle arching to pendent, to 45cm; spikelets to 1cm; palea scabrous, mucronate to long-awned; lemma scabrous. SE Asia. 'Nigrescens': lvs dark purple. var. ***rufipogon*** (Griff.) Watt. Awns long, red; ornamental.

**Oryzopsis** Michx. (From Gk *oryza*, rice, and *opsis*, appearance, due to its similarity to *Oryza*.) RICE GRASS. Gramineae. Some 35 species of perennial grasses. Stems clumped. Leaves flat to rolled; ligules membranous. Inflorescence paniculate; spikelets stipitate, 1-flowered; flower narrow-lanceolate to ovate; lodicules to 3; callus short, obtuse; glumes persistent, papery; lemma leathery to rigid, brittle, convex, shorter than glumes, 5-ribbed, awn deciduous, straight; palea leathery, 2-ribbed, acute. N Hemisphere, temperate and subtropics. Z8.

CULTIVATION Native to woods and hills in subtropical and temperate climates, *Oryzopsis* spp. are grown for its light, open flowering panicles and slender graceful habit. Grow in full sun in any moderately fertile, moisture-retentive soil. Propagate by division or by seed sown *in situ* in spring.

***O. hymenoides*** (Roem. & Schult.) Ricker. SILKGRASS; INDIAN MILLET. To 60cm. Stems clumped. Branches, panicle, pedicels flexible. Lvs slender, margins inrolled. Panicle to 15cm, branches spreading; spikelet glumes to 6mm; lemma to 3mm, fusiform, straight, pilose, caducous, awn to 3mm. SW US, N Mexico.

***O. miliacea*** (L.) Asch. & Schweinf. SMILO GRASS. To 1.5m. Stems loosely clumped, rigid, smooth. Lvs flat, to 30×1cm, smooth; ligule very short. Panicle linear to oblong, pendent, to 30cm; spikelets short-stipitate, numerous, to 4mm, occasionally tinged purple; glumes distinctly striped green; lemmas smooth, awn to 8mm. Summer–autumn. Mediterranean.

For synonymy see *Milium* and *Piptantherum*.

**Osbeckia** L. (For Rev. Peter Osbeck (1723–1805), Swedish naturalist.) Melastomataceae. Some 40 species of herbs, subshrubs and shrubs, usually erect and bristly hairy. Leaves somewhat leathery, 3–7-veined, usually entire. Flowers showy, pink, violet or red, terminal, solitary, in loose heads or panicles; calyx scaly or hairy; petals 5, rarely 4, obovate, often ciliate. SE Asia, China, Japan, Australia, some spp. in Africa. Z9.

CULTIVATION As for *Melastoma*.

***O. chinensis*** L. Shrub, 30–60cm. Lvs lanceolate-oblong, 3-veined, hispidulous, slightly toothed, subsessile. Fls purple, in few-fld terminal cymes; pet. long-acuminate, exceeding stamens. Summer. China.

***O. glauca*** Benth. Shrub, about 60cm. Lvs elliptic, narrowed at base and apex, softly hairy, 3–5-veined. Fls red or purple; cal. with small, scattered, stellate hairs; pedicels short, on a terminal subracemose infl. Summer. India.

***O. nepalensis*** Hook. Shrub to 35cm, branched. Lvs lanceolate, often spotted brown, sessile. Fls large, purple-rose, in terminal and axillary panicles or corymbs; pet. obovate-orbicular, spreading. Early summer. Nepal. 'Albiflora': fls white.

***O. parvifolia*** Arn. Shrub, 30–60cm. Lvs ovate, acute, reflexed, 3-veined, strigose, sessile. Fls rather large, subsessile, in threes; cal. with stalked, stellate, red hairs; pet. rose. Summer. Sri Lanka.

***O. rostrata*** D. Don. Shrub; stems terete. Lvs oblong-lanceolate, slender-pointed, bullate, subsessile. Fls in terminal cymes, rose-pink; anth. long, curved, exserted. Bengal.

***O. rubicunda*** Arn.. Shrub. Lvs oblong, acute. Fls 5cm across, terminal on short stalks, solitary or in clusters, deep purple; anth. yellow. Sri Lanka.

***O. stellata*** Wallich. Shrub, 90–180cm. Lvs 6–15cm, thin, somewhat hispidulous, ciliate, 5-veined, long-acuminate. Fls lilac-red, clustered in terminal, few-fld cymes; cal. urceolate, pale green, seg. 4, sharply toothed, with stellate hairs becoming larger toward apex, rays 8 per hair, tinged red; pet. 4cm, broad-ovate or orbicular; stamens 8. Summer. India to China.

***O. wightiana*** Benth. Erect shrub; stems hairy. Lvs ovate, small, hairy. Fls large, purple, fugacious in close heads. India.

***O. yunnanensis*** Franch. ex Craib. Shrub, 30–90cm; stems terete, bristly, often tinged red. Lvs 5.5–9cm, ovate to oblong-ovate, dark green, sparsely bristly; stalk tinged red. Fls 4-merous in a few-fld panicle and solitary in upper axils, 2–5cm diam., bright magenta. W China.

***O. zeylanica*** Ker-Gawl. See *O. parvifolia*.

**Oscularia** Schwantes.
***O. caulescens*** (Mill.) Schwantes. See *Lampranthus deltoides*.
***O. pedunculata*** (N.E. Br.) Schwantes. See *Lampranthus deltoides*.
***O. deltata*** Schwantes. See *Lampranthus deltoides*.
***O. deltoides*** (L.) Schwantes. See *Lampranthus deltoides*.

**Osmanthus** Lour. (From Gk *osme*, fragrance, and *anthos*, flower.) DEVILWOOD; SWEET OLIVE; CHINESE HOLLY. Oleaceae. 30 species of evergreen shrubs or small trees, to 20m. Leaves opposite, glabrous, leathery, lanceolate to obovate, entire to sharply toothed, sometimes crenate, glossy green above, spotted below with numerous glandular depressions; petioles short; petiole and midrib occasionally downy. Flowers sometimes uni-

**Osmanthus** (a) *O. fragrans* (×0.75), flower enlarged (b) *O. heterophyllus* (×0.75), fruits (c) *O.* × *burkwoodii* (×0.75) (d) *O. delavayi* leaf (×0.75) (e) *O. decorus* leaf (×0.75) (f) *O. serrulatus* leaves (×0.75) (g) *O. yunnanensis* leaves (×0.75) (h) *O. armatus* leaves (×0.75)

sexual, clustered in leaf axils or, rarely, in terminal panicles, white to yellow, usually highly fragrant; calyx 4-toothed; corolla bell-shaped to tubular, limb 4-lobed; stamens 2. Fruit a single-seeded, hard-shelled drupe, dark-blue to purple, oval. S US, Middle East, most garden subjects from China, Japan.

CULTIVATION Valuable for their dark, leathery, evergreen foliage, *Osmanthus* spp. make dignified specimens in the shrub border, or as a backdrop for bulbs and perennials. They are grown primarily, however, for their richly fragrant flowers, borne even on quite young specimens. The elegant *O.* ×*burkwoodii*, a dense and compact shrub, and *O. heterophyllus*, hardier and more vigorous, are also useful for hedging; clipped over after flowering, they flower freely the following season.

All species described will grow in a range of fertile, well-drained soils, preferably neutral to acid, but some lime is tolerated and *O.* ×*burkwoodii*, *O. delavayi* and *O. yunnanensis* thrive in chalky conditions. With the exception of *O. decorus* and *O. heterophyllus*, all the species here need a site sheltered from freezing winds, and in regions of prolonged winter frost *O. fragrans* and *O. serrulatus* need the protection of a cool, airy greenhouse (minimum 4–10°C/39–50°F) in winter. Both sun and partial shade are acceptable. Remove straggly or winter-damaged growth. Propagate in late summer by semi-ripened cuttings in a propagating case with bottom heat. Ripe growths may be rooted in autumn in a cold frame. Layering can be carried out in autumn or spring. Seed should be sown in a cold frame on ripening. Susceptible to scale insect.

***O. armatus*** Diels. Shrub, 2–4m. Resembles *O. serrulatus* and *O. yunnanensis*. Young growth densely pubesc., bark turning grey-white in autumn, slightly warty. Lvs 7–14cm, oblong-ovate, thick leathery, spiny, strongly toothed, cordate at base, sometimes entire; petiole red-green. Fls off-white, clustered in lf axils. Fr. deep violet, to 2cm. Autumn. W China. Z7.

***O.*** ×***burkwoodii*** P. Green. *(O. delavayi* × *O. decorus.)* Small shrub, compact habit, 2×2m. Lvs 2–4cm, ovate-elliptic, serrate, acute, short-petioled; stem downy. Fls 5–7, clustered in axils; cor. 5mm; anth. slightly exserted; style 2mm; cal. 2mm, green-white. Late spring. Z6.

***O. decorus*** (Boiss. & Bal.) Kasapl. Broad, bushy shrub, to 3m. Lvs to 12×4cm, entire, oblong, tapering, dark green above, yellow beneath; growth glabrous and rigid. Fls white, small clusters, profuse. Fr. ovate, to 1.5cm, blue-black. Spring. Caucasus, Lazistan. 'Baki Kasapligil': slow-growing, more hardy, lvs narrower. Z7.

***O. delavayi*** Franch. Stocky shrub, 2×2m. Lvs to 3cm, ovate, finely toothed; dark green, glossy above, minutely spotted beneath, smaller than allies. Fls to 8 clustered in axils or terminal, white; cor. tubular, to 12mm. Spring. W China. Z7.

***O.*** ×***fortunei*** Carr. *(O. fragrans* × *O. heterophyllus.)* Expansive shrub, to 3m, taller in mild areas. Lvs to 10cm, more robust and armed than parents, oval, acuminate, teeth to 10, large, triangular or lvs entire on basal portions of growth. Fls white, fragrant, to 10 at axils; cor. 5mm, lobes larger than tube. Late summer. Garden hybrid, originally. orig. Japan, remade in US as × 'San Jose'. 'Variegatus': slow-growing; lvs variegated cream. Z7.

***O. fragrans*** Lour. FRAGRANT OLIVE; SWEET TEA. Shrub or small tree to 12m. Lvs to 10cm, oblong-lanceolate; entire or finely toothed, distinctly veined below. Fls white, solitary or few in stalked clusters; cor. 1cm, waxy, divided more or less to base; most fragrant. Summer. Himalaya, Japan, China. f. ***aurantiacus*** (Mak.) P. Green. Lvs entire; fls orange. Z9.

***O. heterophyllus*** (G. Don) P. Green. HOLLY OLIVE; CHINESE HOLLY; FALSE HOLLY. Erect dense shrub, to 5m. Lvs variable, to 6cm, entire, elliptic-oblong or with large teeth, often dimorphic, coriaceous, glossy green above, more yellow beneath, venation reticulate. Fls white, fragrant, 5mm wide. Fr. ovate, 12mm, blue; stone scarcely ribbed. Late summer. Japan, Taiwan. 'Aureus': lvs bordered yellow. 'Goshiki': compact, erect; leaves thorny, cream and bronze variegated, young growth rose pink. 'Gulftide': dense in habit; lvs slightly tortuous, conspicuously green, teeth sharp. 'Myrtifolius': a propagule of mature growth, habit very spreading; lvs ovate, pungent, entire. 'Purpureus': the most hardy cv., new growth purple-red. 'Rotundifolius': lvs obovate, undulate, entire; slow-growing. 'Variegatus': lf margins cream-white. Z6.

***O. serrulatus*** Rehd. Shrub, to 3m. Young growth finely pubesc.; lvs resemble *O. yunnanensis*, but broader with finer, forward-pointing teeth or sometimes entire. Fl. clusters 4–9, white. Spring. W China (Sichuan, Kwangsi). Z8.

***O. suavis*** King ex C.B. Clarke. Resembles *O. delavayi*, but lvs larger. Shrub or small tree to 3m. Young lf growth grey, downy; lvs to 6cm, oblong lanceolate, finely crenate. Fls white, to 8 in axils and terminally; cor. lobes rounded, bell-shaped; cal. ciliate. Himalayas to Yunnan. Z8.

***O. yunnanensis*** (Franch.) P. Green. Most closely related to *O. serrulatus*, lvs widest at median, prominently reticulate, teeth larger, to 3mm. Tall shrub to 5m. Young growth glabrous, yellow-grey. Lvs to 20cm, ovate-lanceolate, narrow-acuminate, base wedge-shaped, glabrous above, spotted black below with numerous depressions, to 30 sharp teeth on either side or entire. Fls waxy, off-white to light yellow, to 7 in axillary clusters, very fragrant. Fr. ovoid, to 15mm, dark purple, pruinose. W China. Z7.

***O. aquifolium*** Sieb. & Zucc. See *O. heterophyllus*.
***O. aurantiacus*** (Mak.) Nak. See *O. fragrans* f. *aurantiacus*.
***O. forrestii*** Rehd. See *O. yunnanensis*.
***O. ilicifolius*** (Hassk.) hort. ex Carr. See *O. heterophyllus*.
***O. rehderianus*** Hand.-Mazz. See *O. yunnanensis*.
For further synonymy see × *Osmarea* and *Phillyrea*.

**× Osmarea** Burkw. & Skipw.
×***O. burkwoodii*** Burkw. & Skipw. See *Osmanthus* × *burkwoodii*.

**Osmaronia** Greene.
***O. cerasiformis*** See *Oemleria cerasiformis*.

**Osmia** Schultz-Bip.
***O. odorata*** (L.) Schultz-Bip. See *Chromolaena odorata*.

**Osmoglossum** Schltr. (From Gk *osme*, odour, and *glossa*, tongue or lip, referring to the sweet fragrance of the type species.) Orchidaceae. 7 species of epiphytic orchids, formerly included in *Odontoglossum*. Rhizome short; roots clay-white. Pseudobulbs clustered, ovoid to elliptic-ovoid, enveloped by several distichous, overlapping leafy sheaths, apex usually bifoliate. Leaves erect to spreading, linear-ligulate, acute, coriaceous, base conduplicate. Raceme produced from axil of last basal leaf; peduncle compressed; bracts triangular-lanceolate, scarious, acute to acuminate; flowers usually small, fleshy, white, often tinged purple; sepals free, usually concave; lip sessile, porrect to sharply curved, entire, subequal to sepals and petals, fused to column foot, callus fleshy, 3-keeled; column short, winged, stigma transversely reniform; anther incumbent, galeate, usually white, pollinia 2, obpyriform. Mexico, Guatemala, El Salvador, Honduras, Costa Rica. Z10.

CULTIVATION As for *Odontoglossum*.

***O. convallarioides*** Schltr. Pseudobulbs to 8.5×3cm, ovoid to ovoid-elliptic. Lvs to 40×1cm, linear-ligulate. Infl. to 40cm, erect, few-fld; fls to 1.5cm diam., fragrant, white, sometimes tinged pink or lavender; sep. to 10×7mm, elliptic to oblong-elliptic, acute to subacute, concave; pet. wider than sep., suborbicular to obovate, obtuse or minutely apiculate; lip to 10×8mm, often spotted purple-red, obovate, apex subacute to obtuse, concave, callus yellow-orange, to 3.5×3.5cm, consisting of 3 fleshy ridges, lateral ridges terminating in a triangular tooth, middle ridge narrowly triangular; column to 4mm, apex obscurely 3-lobed, lobes entire. Spring. Mexico, Guatemala, Honduras, Costa Rica.

***O. egertonii*** (Lindl.) Schltr. Pseudobulbs to 10×3cm, ovoid or elliptic-oblong, usually glossy yellow-green. Lvs to 50×1.5cm, thin, narrowly linear-ligulate. Infl. erect, to 40cm, 5–10-fld; fls to 2cm diam., white marked lilac; dorsal sep. to 15×6mm, ovate-oblong to elliptic-oblong, acute to subobtuse, lateral sep. connate almost to apex, broadly elliptic, apex bifid; pet. subequal to sep., oblique, ovate to broadly elliptic, concave, margin crisped; lip to 12×9cm, oblong-subquadrate or oblong-elliptic, apiculate, concave, apex sometimes reflexed; callus to 5×5mm, yellow spotted brown, quadrate, with 3 fleshy ridges, lateral ridges terminating in a triangular tooth, middle ridge narrowly triangular; column to 4mm, 3-lobed, lobes lacerate-dentate. Usually spring. Mexico, Guatemala, Honduras, Costa Rica.

***O. pulchellum*** (Batem. ex Lindl.) Schltr. LILY OF THE VALLEY ORCHID. Pseudobulbs to 10×3.5cm, ovoid to ovoid-elliptic, furrowed. Lvs to 35×1.5cm, linear-ligulate. Infl. to 50cm, erect or slightly pendent, loosely 3–10-fld; fls to 3cm diam., fragrant, long-lived; sep. and pet. white above, tinted rose below; dorsal sep. to 2×1.5cm, obovate to elliptic, concave, apiculate, lateral sep. to 2×1cm, connate at base, oblique, broadly elliptic, apiculate; pet. to 2×1.5cm, suborbicular to obovate, subobtuse, apiculate, concave, margin often crisped; lip to 2×1cm, white, pointing upwards in flower, abruptly decurved at apex of callus, pandurate, apex recurved, margins crisped; callus to 7×5mm, yellow spotted red, with 3 fleshy ridges, oblong-quadrate, middle ridge narrowly triangular; column to 5mm, white, apex 3-lobed, lobes sharply dentate. Autumn–winter. Mexico, Guatemala, El Salvador.

***O. anceps*** Schltr. See *O. egertonii*.
For further synonymy see *Odontoglossum* and *Oncidium*.

**Osmorhiza** Raf. (From Gk *osme*, an odour, and *rhiza*, root.) SWEET CICELY; SWEET JARVIL. Umbelliferae. Some 10 species of perennial herbs, with thick, fleshy roots. Leaves 2–3-ternate or 2-pinnate, segments lanceolate to orbicular, serrate to pinnatifid; petioles sheathing. Umbels compound, rays glabrous; involucral bracts few or absent; involucel of several, narrow bracteoles, or absent; flowers white, green-yellow or purple; petals spathulate to obovate. Fruit linear-oblong, subcylindrical to clavate, hispid to glabrous; mericarps with filiform ribs; vittae obscure or absent. Americas, Asia. Z6.

CULTIVATION *Osmorhiza* spp., native to moist open woodlands in North America, are sweetly aromatic perennials suited to naturalistic plantings in the woodland and wild garden, and in collections of native plants. They are hardy to −20°C/−4°F. Propagate by seed. Otherwise, cultivate as for *Myrrhis*.

***O. brachypoda*** Torr. To 80cm, most parts pubesc. Lvs 8–25×10–18cm, ternate-pinnate, seg. ovate, 2–6×1–4cm, coarsely serrate to deeply pinnatifid; petiole to 20cm. Rays 2–5 per umbel, 2.5–10cm; involucre often absent; involucel of ciliate, linear bracteoles, to 1cm; fls green-yellow. Fr. oblong-fusiform, to 2cm, with narrow beak; mericarps with prominent, bristly ribs. US (California, Arizona).

***O. chilensis*** Hook. & Arn. Variable, 30–100cm, hispid. Lvs 5–15cm, 2-ternate, seg. ovate-lanceolate to orbicular, obtuse or acute, 2–6×1–4cm, hispid, serrate, incised or lobed; petiole to 16cm. Umbels with 3–8, spreading rays; involucre and involucel absent; fls green-white occasionally tinged pink. Fr. linear-fusiform to linear-oblong, to 2cm, beaked. E & W US, S America.

***O. claytonii*** (Michx.) C.B. Clarke. WOOLLY SWEET CICELY; SWEET JARVIL. To 1m, hairy. Lvs 10–30cm, ternate-pinnate, pubesc., seg. ovate to lanceolate, 3–7cm; petiole 5–12cm. Rays 3–5 per umbel, 1.5–8cm; bracts usually absent, sometimes 1–2 per umbel; involucel of several, reflexed bracteoles, to 8mm; fls white, 4–7 per umbellule, male fls 7–17 per umbellule, styles to 1.5mm. Fr. oblong-fusiform, *c*2cm, tapering to attenuate beak; mericarps with slightly hispid ribs. Eastern N America.

***O. longistylis*** (Torr.) DC. SMOOTH SWEET CICELY; ANISEROOT. To 1m. Lvs 8–25cm, 2-ternate or ternate-pinnate, seg. serrate, cut or deeply pinnatifid, ovate, 3–10cm, hirtellous; petioles 5–16cm. Umbels congested, with 3–6 spreading rays, to 5cm; involucral bracts 1 to several, ciliate; involucel of several bracteoles; fls white. Fr. oblong-fusiform, to 2cm. N America.

***O. occidentalis*** (Nutt.) Torr. To 120cm; stems robust, clustered. Lvs 10–20×6–15cm, 2-pinnate, seg. ovate to oblong-lanceolate, 2–10cm, serrate and incised or lobed; petiole 5–30cm. Rays 5–12 per umbel, 2–13cm; involucre and involucel commonly absent; fls yellow to green-yellow, male fls 90–225 per umbel. Fr. linear-fusiform, to 2cm, glabrous. Western N America.

***O. brevistylis*** DC. See *O. claytonii*.

**Osmoxylon** Miq. (From Gk *osme*, scent, and *xylon*, wood; the wood and foliage of the Ambonese *O. umbelliferum* are scented.) Araliaceae. About 50 species of unarmed, glabrous or hairy evergreen shrubs and trees. Leaves simple or variously palmately lobed, palmatifid or digitately compound, the bases and sometimes also the lower parts of the petioles with ring or spirally arranged fringe-like collars or crests of appendages; stipular ligules also present. Inflorescences terminal, umbelliform, generally 2× compound, with 10–60 primary rays diverging from a short main axis, each ray terminating in a umbel of sterile berry-like fls and bearing below it a pair of secondary branches, these terminated by heads or umbels with fertile flowers; petals 4–8, more or less united, the lower part tubular; stamens 4–30; ovary 1- to many-celled, the stigmata radiating from a short column. Fruit drupaceous. Borneo and Taiwan (Lanyu) to Micronesia and south and southeast to Vanuatu; especially numerous in the Philippines, Moluccas and New Guinea. Z10.

CULTIVATION *O. eminens* inhabits forest slopes, along streams and in damp, shaded ravines at low to medium altitudes. A bold, glossy-foliaged tree, it is suitable for cultivation in the humid tropics and is particularly striking in flower. In addition to the species described below, *O. borneense* Seem. from Borneo, a riverbank shrub with 9 narrow leaf-segments, and *O. lineare* (Merrill) Philipson from Luzon (Philippines), with 4–7 linear, all but discrete leaf-segments, have been introduced in Europe. *O. palmatum* (Lam.) Philipson, from the Moluccas, and *O. novoguineense* (R. Scheff.) Becc., from New Guinea, are occasionally cultivated in the US. Cultivation as for Trevesia.

***O. eminens*** (Bull) Philipson. Tree to 12m; branches few, stout, glabrescent. Lvs in terminal rosettes, glabrescent; petiole stout, to 1m; blade to 60cm, 9–19-lobed, dark glossy green above, the sinuses reaching to near the base; lobes lanceolate to oblong, to 15cm wide, lorate to irregularly pinnatisect, the central lobe sometimes 3-parted, margins coarsely and irregularly toothed. Infl. stout, hairy, 40cm diam.; primary rays many, to 13cm, dull red-brown, the sterile umbel to 5cm diam., secondary rays to 12cm, the fertile fls 50–60, light orange, in heads to 2cm diam.; ovary 5–6-locular. Fr. indigo-black, 9×5mm, remaining sessile. Micronesia (Caroline Is.); Philippines (widely distributed). Z10.

For synonymy see *Boerlagiodendron* and *Trevesia*.

**Osmunda** L. (For the Nordic god Thor, also called Osmunder; alternatively, from the Lat. *os*, mouth, and *mundare*, to clean.) FLOWERING FERN. Osmundaceae. About 12 species of rather coarse terrestrial ferns, deep-rooted. Fronds in large crowns, bipinnate or bipinnatifid, richly coloured when dying in the autumn. Sori on strongly contracted fertile pinnules, either separate on entirely fertile fronds or found in the middle or towards the end of sterile fronds; sporangia 2-valved, with opening across top. Temperate & Tropical E Asia, N & S America.

CULTIVATION Cosmopolitan terrestrial ferns inhabiting boggy areas or at the edge of water, or in rainforest. All are characterized by the profusion of roots surrounding the surface rhizome; the roots of *O. regalis* are the source of osmunda fibre, once widely used as a potting medium for orchids and other epiphytes. Adaptable to an enormous range of temperatures and situations, copious water should be supplied at all times, and many, especially *O. regalis*, make a bold feature near water where they will thrive in full sun. Also effective planted in moist and shady situations in between shrubs and in the fern border, or in containers in the conservatory or cool greenhouse. Only *O. banksiifolia* and *O. javanica* require cool glasshouse protection, others are hardy down to −20°C/−4°F and are deciduous in cold winter areas. Seasonal variation is a feature of some, e.g. *O. cinnamomea*: fronds emerge glaucous green and will fade to cinnamon brown with age, while those of *O. regalis* emerge tinged brown or purple (cv. Purpurascens), are green throughout summer and give golden yellow and brown autumn colour. The emerging croziers of all spp. are covered in loose woolly scales which fall away as the frond matures. Potting mix should be that recommended for terrestrial ferns, of acidic reaction: specimens growing in the ground or are too large to repot benefit from an annual topdressing with organic matter. The root system is extensive and wiry, and should be provided with a large container. Feed containerized plants at monthly intervals with a high-N liquid fertilizer while actively growing. *O. banksiifolia* is of tropical rainforest and requires conditions in cultivation as for *Todea*, it is susceptible to mealybug.

Propagation is by division of the rootstock (quite a strenuous undertaking due to the mass of roots), or from spores: the spores are produced over a short period on separate fertile fronds or pinnae and should be sown fresh – viability of the spore decreases exponentially three days after harvest. Spores are green and require light to germinate, developing rapidly, cultivars coming true.

***O. banksiifolia*** (Presl) Kuhn. Rhiz. erect or ascending, stout, sparsely ferruginous-lanate when young: stipes winged near base, lustrous brown. Fronds 1–1.5m, tufted, oblong-lanceolate, pinnate; pinnae in 10–20 pairs, 15–25×1–2cm, obliquely spreading, linear-lanceolate, tapered-acuminate, acutely coarsely dentate, coriaceous, lustrous, glabrous, margins thickened, tinged white, veins forked ×1–4, parallel, obliquely spreading; fertile pinnae 7–10cm, central, linear-cylindric, dark brown. E Asia (S China, Japan, Indochina, Malaysia). Z10.

***O. cinnamonea*** L. CINNAMON FERN; FIDDLEHEADS; BUCKHORN. Whole plant densely ferruginous-tomentose when young; stipes densely tufted, of sterile fronds 30–45cm, of fertile fronds shorter. Fronds dimorphic: sterile fronds 60–90×15–20cm, pinnate, pinnae 8–10×2–2.5cm, close-set, ligulate-lanceolate, cut almost to rachis; fertile fronds central, much smaller, becoming cinnamon brown as spores mature, pinnae lanceolate. N & S America, W Indies, E Asia. Z3.

***O.claytonia*** L. INTERRUPTED FERN. Stipes tufted, 30cm+, tomentose when young. Fronds 30–60×20–30cm, pinnate to pinnatifid, central pinnae-fertile; sterile pinnae 10–15×2.5cm, lanceolate, cut almost to rachis; fertile pinnae similar but much smaller; pinnules dense, cylindric. N America, Himalaya, China. Z3.

***O.japonica*** Thunb. Rhiz. ascending, short, stout, covered with withered frond remains, cinnamon-brown to black lanate when young; stipes winged at base, stramineous, smooth. Fronds to 1m, tufted, ovate to triangular-ovate, bipinnate; pinnae 20–30cm, oblong-ovate; pinnules 4–10×1–2.5cm, oblong to broadly lanceolate, obliquely truncate at base, minutely dentate, sessile, green above, glaucescent beneath; veins forked ×1–3, parallel, spreading; fertile fronds rising amongst sterile fronds to 50cm; sporophylls erect, laxly paniculate, cinnamon brown. Japan, China, Himalaya. Z6.

***O.javanica*** Bl. Stipes 15–30cm, tufted, erect, naked, firm. Fronds 30–90×20–30cm, pinnate, lower or central pinnae fertile; sterile pinnae 10–20×1–2cm, cuneate at base, entire or acutely dentate, occasionally slightly petiolate, fertile pinnae shorter, of numerous close-set, distinct oblong, sessile clusters. Borneo, Sumatra, Java. Z10.

***O.lancea*** Thunb. Fronds dimorphic: sterile fronds to 1m, oblong, tripinnate, shortly acuminate, pinnae 20–30cm, oblong, acuminate, stalked, lower shorter, pinnules 5×0.3cm, linear-lanceolate to broadly lanceolate, tapered to both ends, acuminate to cuneate at base, slightly dentate in upper part; fertile fronds 20–50cm, amongst sterile fronds; sporophylls loosely paniculate, erect, cinnamon-brown. Japan. Z6.

***O.regalis*** L. ROYAL FERN; FLOWERING FERN. Stipes 30–45cm, tufted, erect, firm, naked. Fronds 60–180×30cm+, bipinnate, fertile pinnae at apex, sterile pinnae 15–30×5–10cm, pinnules 2.5–5×1–2cm, oblong, blunt, often asymmetric at base, sessile or subpetiolate, margins finely minutely serrate; fertile pinnules cylindric, forming large panicle; rachis black-pubesc. Cosmopolitan. 'Crispa': 100–150cm; pinnules crisped. 'Cristata': 100–130cm; pinnules, pinnae and frond finely crested. 'Purpurascens': 120–180cm; growth purple when young, rachis purple throughout the season, possibly a form of *O. regalis* var. *spectabilis* from N America. var. ***spectabilis*** (Willd.) A. Gray. Rachis of fertile panicle sub-glabrous or glabrous. N & S America. Z2.

***O.cervina*** L. See *Olfersia cervina*.
***O.palustris*** Schräd. See *O.regalis*.
For further synonymy see *Nephrodium*.

**OSMUNDACEAE** Bercht. & Presl. *Leptopteris, Osmunda, Todea.*

**Osteomeles** Lindl. (From Gk *osteon*, bone, and *melon*, apple, referring to the fruit.) Rosaceae. 2 species of evergreen shrubs or trees. Leaves alternate, small, finely pinnate; stipules small, linear-lanceolate; leaflets small, entire, bristle-tipped. Flowers white, in small, terminal corymbs; calyx tube campanulate or turbinate, calyx teeth 5, acute, persistent; petals 5, oval-oblong, patent; stamens 15–20, inserted in the throat of the calyx; styles 5, distinct; stigmas thickened; ovules 1 per locule, erect. Fruit a small pome with a persistent calyx, 5-seeded. China to Hawaii and New Zealand. Z8.

CULTIVATION Native to hot dry river valleys, they are graceful small shrubs, grown for their clusters of white flowers with prominent stamens, carried in summer above evergreen leaves finely divided into deep green leaflets. Plants will bloom when still quite small. *O.subrotunda* makes a small slow-growing shrub; *O.schwerinae* can be induced to form a much taller plant when trained against a wall. In favourable climates, the red fruits eventually ripen to blue-black. *Osteomeles* spp. are hardy to temperatures between −5°C/23°F and −10°C/14°F, but should be given the shelter of a warm south- or southwest-facing wall where temperatures consistently fall to these levels. Alternatively, grow in large containers that can be moved into the cold greenhouse or conservatory during the winter months.

Grow in sun in fertile well-drained soils. For container-grown plants use a free-draining, medium-fertility, loam-based mix. Propagate by semi-ripe cuttings, or by layering. When seed is available, stratify over winter and sow in spring.

***O.schwerinae*** Schneid. To 3m. Branchlets slender, gracefully pendulous, short grey-pubesc. Lvs to 7cm, grey-pubesc., 15–31-foliolate; rachis slightly winged; petiole grey-pubesc.; leaflets sessile, elliptic to obovate-oblong, to 12×4mm, cuspidate. Fls to 1.5cm diam., in lax cymes to 6cm diam.; cal. teeth ovate-lanceolate, pubesc. outside, glabrous within; styles pubesc. Fr. oval-rounded, to 8mm, blue-black, glabrous. Spring–summer. S W China (Yunnan). var. ***microphylla*** Rehd. & Wils. Habit denser. Lvs smaller, less woolly; leaflets less numerous, to 5mm, elliptic to obovate, later glabrous. Infl. smaller, more dense; cal. glabrous. W China.

***O.subrotunda*** K. Koch. Resembles *O.schwerinae*, but smaller, slow-growing shrub, with branches tortuous, sericeous when young. Lvs 9–17-foliolate; leaflets to 8mm, rounded to obovate, ciliate, thinly adpressed-pubesc. beneath. Fls 1cm diam., in lax corymbs to 3cm diam.; style glabrous. Summer. E China.

***O.anthyllidifolia*** auct. See *O.schwerinae*.

**Osteospermum** L. (From Gk *osteon*, bone, and Lat. *spermum*, seed.) Compositae. About 70 species of shrubs, subshrubs or annual to perennial herbs, prostrate, ascending or erect. Stems often branched, glabrous or hairy. Leaves usually alternate, entire, toothed, pinnatifid or pinnatisect. Capitula radiate, few to many solitary terminal or in loose umbellate or corymbose panicles; receptacle nearly always naked, flat or convex; phyllaries in 1–5 series, margins scarious, outer smallest; ray florets female, usually yellow or orange, rarely white, pink or violet; disc florets tubular, male, yellow, white or violet. Fruit a usually dimorphic, cylindric, variously winged, angled cypsela; pappus absent. S to tropical Africa and Arabia.

CULTIVATION Although frequently treated as frost-tender annuals with most perennial species bearing their showy daisy flowers in their first year from seed, a number of *Osteospermum* spp. and hybrids show considerable resistance to frost. Given a warm sunny position with perfect drainage and shelter from cold winds, *O.ecklonis* and *O.barberiae* may overwinter where temperatures fall to between −5 and −10°C/23–14°F; *O.ecklonis* 'Weetwood' has survived occasional winter lows to −15°C/5°F. By raising a number of plants from seed and with the precaution of taking overwintering cuttings from valued specimens, *Osteospermum* provides the opportunity to experiment with cold tolerance. Otherwise, cultivate as for *Gazania*. Z9.

***O.amplectans*** (Harv.) Norl. Annual herb to 90cm. Stem simple. Lvs to 12cm, lower lvs elliptic to ovate to rhombic, base often auriculate, petiolate, more or less sinuate-dentate, upper lvs lanceolate or linear-lanceolate, dentate, sessile, often somewhat amplexicaul. Capitula in corymbose panicles; ray florets yellow to orange; disc florets yellow, purple at apex. S Africa.

***O.barberiae*** (Harv.) Norl. Spreading, rhizomatous perenn. to 50cm, glandular-pubesc. Stems decumbent, erect or ascending. Lvs to 15cm, oblong-lanceolate, linear-lanceolate to spathulate, sparsely and irregularly dentate, acute to sub-acute, base attenuate, amplexicaul. Capitula terminal, solitary, few; ray florets magenta above, usually light orange-brown beneath; disc florets deep purple or yellow. Autumn–early spring. S Africa. 'Compactum' ('Nanum'): to 10cm; fls deep pink with dark purple reverse.

***O.ecklonis*** (DC.) Norl. Robust shrub or subshrub to 1m. Stem branched above, branching at apex. Lvs to 10cm, linear-oblong, elliptic, or lanceolate, entire or remotely denticulate to coarsely serrate-dentate, glandular-pubesc. Capitula few to many, solitary or in loose corymbose panicles; ray florets white above, indigo, often with white margin beneath; disc florets bright blue. S Africa. 'Deep Pink Form': to 30cm; florets numerous, narrow, dark pink. Giant Mixed: to 35cm; fls in cream, orange and salmon pastels. 'Starshine': to 75cm; fls snow-white with blue eyes. 'Weetwood': to 25cm; fls white, olive green below.

***O.fruticosum*** (L.) Norl. Perenn. to 60cm. Stems decumbent, prostrate or ascending, woody below. Lvs to 10cm, often in basal rosettes, obovate, spathulate or oblanceolate, obtuse, mucronate, narrowed to a clasping base, margins entire or remotely callose-denticulate, slightly fleshy, glandular-pubesc., glabrescent. Capitula few, solitary; ray florets white above, violet to rose-lilac beneath; disc florets dull violet. All year. S Africa (SE coast).

***O.hyoseroides*** (DC.) Norl. Aromatic, glandular-pubesc. annual, to 60cm. Stems erect. Lvs glandular-pubesc. to nearly glabrous, lower to 10cm, oblong to oblanceolate, sinuate-dentate, semi-amplexicaul, upper oblong-linear to oblanceolate, sessile. Capitula few to many in loose corymbs; ray florets yellow to orange; disc florets yellow, dark violet at apex. S Africa.

***O.jucundum*** (E. Phillips) Norl. Perenn. herb, to 50cm. Stems many, rarely solitary, suberect-ascending, usually laxly branched from base. Lvs to 15cm, oblanceolate-elliptic to narrowly oblong-linear, coarsely and remotely dentate-denticulate, sessile or narrowly petiolate. Capitula few, solitary; ray florets red on both surfaces; disc florets black-purple at apex. S Africa.

***O.pinnatum*** (Thunb.) Norl. Annual to 30cm, viscid, downy. Stems much-branched. Lvs 1–2.5cm, pinnate, seg. linear, obtuse, usually entire. Capitula few, solitary; ray florets about 2.5cm, orange to yellow or buff-pink. S Africa.

***O.cultivars***. Many hybrids and cvs ranging in height from 25cm to 60cm and in a variety of bright colours; shorter cvs (to 25cm) include the white- and pink-backed 'Cannington Roy' and the pink 'Hopley's' and 'Langtrees'; taller cvs (to

60cm) include the white-fld variegated-lvd 'Silver Sparkler', the pink 'Pink Whirls' and 'Bodegas Pink' with variegated lvs, and 'Buttermilk' with pale yellow fls. 'Whirligig': foliage grey-green; ray florets powder-blue to chalky grey, strongly contracted with margins inrolled above mid-point, then expanded again at tip; disc florets dark blue-grey. The Cannington Hybrids include pink-, white- and purple-fld forms 15–30cm tall. Seed races such as the 25cm Dwarf Salmon and the 45cm Tetra Pole Star are also offered.

***O. jucundum*** hort. non (E. Phillips) Norl. See *O. barberiae*.
For further synonymy see *Calendula, Dimorphotheca* and *Tripteris*.

**Ostericum** Hoffm.
***O. florenti*** (Franch. & Savat.) Kitag. See *Angelica florenti*.

**Ostrowskia** Reg. (For Michael Nicolayevich von Ostrowsky, Minister of Imperial Domains and Russian patron of botany in the late 19th century.) Campanulaceae. 1 species, a perennial herb to 1.8m, erect, glabrous, unbranched, from a rhizoid stem. Close to *Campanula*, but distinguishable by its whorled leaves, more numerous calyx and corolla lobes, ovary locules and particularly by the pores of the capsules being twice the number of calyx lobes. Distinguished from *Michauxia* by lack of calyx appendages. Leaves 4–5 in distant whorls, narrowly ovate, dentate, to 15cm. Inflorescence a terminal raceme; flowers long-pedicellate; calyx lobes lanceolate; corolla campanulate, tube to 5cm, lobes broadly ovate, lilac suffused with white. Turkestan. Z7.

CULTIVATION Hardy to at least −15°C/5°F, with whorls of blue-green foliage arising from a thick deep taproot and large, beautifully textured, pale milk-blue, lilac-veined flowers. It dies back completely in midsummer and then requires a dry rest until late autumn, and so should be clearly marked with a cane or peg, and protected from wet with a frame light. Grow in a warm, sunny and sheltered position in deep, fertile, freely draining but moisture-retentive soil, enriched with leafmould or other well-rotted organic matter. Mulch in winter with leafmould, weathered ashes or bracken litter.

Rare in gardens because it is resentful of disturbance, slow and demanding to raise from seed, and although propagation is less demanding from root cuttings of larger sections of mature root, re-establishment is seldom rapid. Sow ripe seed in individual pots, plants may produce only seed leaves in their first year; the young roots are fragile and almost transparent and potting on, preferably into long toms, as their growth proceeds demands great care, as does planting out into their flowering position. Plants from seed may be expected to flower in their third or fourth year. Insert short sections (5–7.5cm/2–3in.) of thick roots vertically into a sandy propagating mix and keep just moist. William Robinson commented, 'It is worthy of any care to make it a success.'

***O. magnifica*** Reg. GIANT BELLFLOWER. As for the genus.

**Ostrya** Scop. (Gk shell, referring to the inflated husk.) Betulaceae (Carpinaceae). Some 9 species of deciduous, monoecious trees to 25m. Leaves alternate in 2 rows, veins parallel, margins dentate or serrate, often pubescent. Male inflorescence resembling *Carpinus*, but forming in autumn, flowers with 6–14 stamens. Female catkins terminal, bristly hirsute, with flowers in 3–12 pairs, each pair subtended by a caducous bract, each flower set in a sac-like husk, open at apex, becoming closed and inflated on fruiting, giving infructescence a hop-like appearance. Europe, Asia, America.

CULTIVATION Hop-hornbeams are slow to establish and therefore have not been as widely planted as they deserve; resembling the closely related hornbeams (*Carpinus* spp.), they bear clusters of hop-like fruits and have good autumn colour. Their cultural requirements are as for *Carpinus*. Fresh seed should be sown as soon as possible and germination will take place the following spring. If the seed has been allowed to dry out then it is best stratified, and even then germination will take up to 12 months. For the propagation of garden cultivars, graft on to *Carpinus betulus* stocks in winter.

***O. carpinifolia*** Scop. HOP HORNBEAM. To 20m. Crown rounded. Bark scaly, grey. Young shoots downy. Lvs ovate, rounded at base, acute at apex, to 10×5cm, lustrous dark green with adpressed hairs between veins above, paler below with sparse hairs on veins, veins in 15–20 pairs, margins double-dentate; petiole to 1cm, pubesc. Male catkins to 7.5×1cm; scales acute. Infructescence to 5cm; fr. 3–4mm; sac-like husk ovate, flat, to 1.5cm pubesc. Autumn. S Europe, Asia Minor. Z6.

***O. japonica*** Sarg. To 25m. Bole to 0.5m diam.; young shoots densely downy. Lvs ovate to ovate-oblong, long-acuminate, rounded to cordate at base, dark green pubesc. above, pale green, velvety downy below, margins irregularly sharp-toothed. Infructescence to 5×2cm; fr. to 0.5cm. Autumn. Japan, China, NE Asia. Z5.

***O. knowltonii*** Cov. To 10m. Young shoots downy, olive brown, becoming grey. Buds cylindric, hairy. Lvs ovate, cuneate to cordate at base, acute to obtuse at apex, to 6×3cm, irregularly biserrate, downy above and below, veins in 5–8 pairs; petiole to 5mm. Infructescence to 3×2cm; sac-like husk ovate, to 2cm; fr. ovoid, to 5mm, hairy at apex. Autumn. N America (Arizona, Utah). Z5.

***O. virginiana*** (Mill.) K. Koch. EASTERN HOP HORNBEAM; IRONWOOD. To 20m. Crown rounded. Young shoots glandular-pubesc., becoming glabrous. Lvs ovate-lanceolate, rounded to cordate at base, long-acuminate, 7×12×3–5cm; dark green, hairy on midrib and between veins above; pale green, pubesc. below, veins in 11–15 pairs; petiole to 5mm, glandular-hairy. Male catkins to 5cm. Infructescence to 6×3cm. Sac-like husk ovate, to 2.5cm, pubesc. in basal part; fr. spindle-shaped, to 1cm. Autumn. Eastern N America. var. ***glandulosa*** (Spach) Sarg. All parts more glandular-hairy than species type. Z4.

***O. italica*** Spach. See *O. carpinifolia*.
***O. vulgaris*** Willd. See *O. carpinifolia*.

**Ostryopsis** Decne. (*Ostrya* and Gk *opsis*, appearance.) Betulaceae (Carpinaceae). 2 species of deciduous, monoecious shrubs to 3m. Leaves alternate, ovate, double-dentate. Male flowers in cylindric catkins to 2cm; anthers hairy at tip. Female flowers in terminal, erect, short racemes; trifid involucral bract surrounding each flower. Fruit a nut, conic, surrounded by a trifid, leafy, tubular involucre to 2cm. China, Mongolia. Z6.

CULTIVATION As for *Corylus*.

***O. davidiana*** (Baill.) Decne. Shrub to 3m, densely branched; young shoots downy. Lvs broadly ovate, cordate at base, acute, 3–8×2–5cm, double-dentate, dark green, sparsely hairy above, downy below; petiole to 1cm. Male catkins to 2cm, on mature branches. Female infl. terminal. Fr. in clusters of 3–8, husks opening down one side to release nut. Spring. China (Kansu, Shansi, Hopei). Z4. var. ***cinerascens*** Franch. Lvs ovate, smaller than species type, with brown hairs. Male catkins to 3cm, purple. Fr. grey-hairy. China (Sichuan, Yunnan). Z6.

***O. nobilis*** Balf. f. & W.W. Sm. Shrub to 2m. Young shoots scabrous. Lvs rounded to ovate, to 4cm, tough, dull green above; olive-brown hairy below, double-serrate. Male floral bracts glaucous; male catkins to 2cm, rust-coloured. Spring. China (Sichuan, Yunnan). Z7.

**Osyris** L. (Name used by Dioscorides.) Santalaceae. 7 species of dioecious parasitic shrubs. Leaves alternate, short-petiolate. Male flowers in racemes borne at axils; sepals 3–4, pubescent at insertion of stamen; female flowers solitary or clustered 2–3 per axil, ovary tapering toward base. Fruit drupaceous. Mediterranean to E Asia, Africa. Z9.

CULTIVATION *O. alba* is a small, slender shrub found in dry rocky habitats in the Mediterranean, grown for its flowers in summer and the bright red, pea-sized berries which follow. In cool temperate zones, *O. alba* is grown in the cool glasshouse in a sandy, free-draining potting mix. Propagate by softwood cuttings in a closed case with bottom heat.

***O. alba*** L. Shrub to 1.2m. Branches diffuse, slender. Lvs narrow-lanceolate, coriaceous. Sep. 3, off-white. Fr. to 7mm, red. Mediterranean.

**Otanthus** Hoffm. & Link. (From Gk *ous*, ear, and *anthos*, flower, from the ear-shaped lobes of the florets.) Compositae. 1 species, a tufted, creeping, perennial, maritime herb to 50cm. Leaves to 1.5cm, alternate, numerous, imbricate oblong to oblong-lanceolate, entire to crenulate, sessile, fleshy, tomentose. Capitula discoid, few, in dense, umbellate clusters; receptacle conic, scaly; phyllaries numerous, 4–5mm, ovate, outer lanate, inner lanate only at apex; florets hermaphrodite yellow. Fruit a 4mm, compressed, curved cypsela; pappus absent. Summer. Coasts of W Europe to Near East. Z8.

CULTIVATION A rare wild flower of maritime shingle and stabilized dunes, *O. maritimus* is a densely white-felted creeping perennial useful as border edging and on rock gardens, especially in seaside gardens and in dry sandy soils. Cultivate as for *Andryala*.

***O. maritimus*** (L.) Hoffm. & Link. COTTON WEED. As for the genus.

**Otatea** (McClure & E.W. Sm.) Cald. & Söderstr. (A corruption of the Aztec name for these bamboos.) Gramineae. 2 species of delicate, tender bamboos forming open clumps. Culms medium-sized, nearly solid, sulcate above, glabrous; sheaths white-green, with few or no auricles or bristles; branches 3 at first, eventually many. Leaves long and narrow, obscurely tessellated, very variably hairy, margins slightly scaberulous on one margin; sheaths practically without auricles or bristles. Mexico to Nicaragua. Z10.

CULTIVATION As for *Bambusa*.

***O. acuminata*** (Munro) Cald. & Söderstr. Culms 2–8m×2–4cm, ultimately curving gracefully, with white powder below the nodes; sheaths glabrescent, the upper sheaths deciduous, the lower disintegrating *in situ*. Lvs 7–16×0.3–0.5cm, numerous, pendulous. Range as for the genus.

***O. acuminata*** ssp. ***aztecorum*** (McClure & E.W. Sm.) Guzman. See *O. acuminata*.
For further synonymy see *Arthrostylidium* and *Yushania*.

**Othera** Thunb.
***O. japonica*** Thunb. See *Ilex integra*.
***O. orixa*** (Thunb.) Lam. See *Orixa japonica*.

**Othonna** L. (From Gk *othone*, linen, in reference to the soft leaves. This name used by Dioscorides and Pliny for the same or similar plants.) Compositae. About 150 species of perennial herbs or small shrubs, usually glabrous and glaucous. Leaves entire to variously dissected, lobed or toothed, membranous, leathery or fleshy. Capitula radiate, rarely discoid, solitary or clustered in corymbs; receptacle convex or subconic; involucre more or less campanulate; phyllaries usually *c*8–10 in 1 series; ray florets yellow. Fruit an ovoid, hairy or glabrous cypsela; pappus of ray florets of very copious bristles in many series, pappus of disc florets uniseriate of few bristles. Mostly S Africa. Z9 unless specified.

CULTIVATION With the exception of *O. cheirifolia* – which given a position in full sun with the perfect drainage of the raised bed will tolerate temperatures as low as −15°C/5°F – most *Othonna* spp. need the protection of the cool to intermediate glasshouse in cool temperate zones. Many are grown in collections of cacti and succulents and are used in gardens in dry, essentially frost-free climates, especially in desert and semi-desert conditions. *O. capensis* has a trailing habit well suited to hanging baskets and dry stone walls and although not frost-hardy, small pieces of rooted stem may be overwintered as replacement stock in the cool glasshouse. Most are undemanding in cultivation, requiring only a very porous and moderately fertile sandy soil, with careful and moderate watering when in growth, allowing the medium to dry out between watering, and little or no water when dormant. Maintain a winter minimum of 5–10°C/45–50°F. Propagate by seed or cuttings. Propagate *O. cheirifolia* by softwood cuttings in early summer; aphids find the fleshy leaves of this species extremely attractive and may infest in such large numbers that they become disfiguring.

1 Capitula radiate — **2**
Capitula discoid — **13**

2 Rigid, more or less woody, branched and twiggy shrubs or subshrubs; flowering branches mostly terminal and 1-headed; capitula rarely subcorymbose — **3**
Trailing, decumbent or diffuse subshrubs, base woody, branches subsimple, ending in long, 1-few headed peduncles — **4**
Erect shrubs or herbs; stems virgate, simple and leafy below, more or less nude above, ending in a panicled or much-branched, corymbose inflorescence — **5**
More or less fleshy or succulent shrubs, half-shrubs, or sub herbaceous plants; stems irregularly branched, the older parts commonly nude and cicatricised; leaves often crowded at ends of branches, peduncles subterminal, 1 to several headed — **6**
Rootstock and caudex short, simple or multifid, woolly at the crown; leaves from crown, numerous, rosulate; peduncles scapose, simple, 1-headed, or sub-corymbose and several-headed — *O. retrorsa*
Root mostly tuberous; crown of root mostly woolly; radical leaves few, petiolate, or absent; stem simple or branched, alternately leafy; stem leaves sessile or petiolate; peduncle axillary and terminal, simple or branched — **11**

3 Evergreen, to 30cm; stems spreading; leaf apices obtusely rounded — *O. cheirifolia*
Deciduous, to 60cm; stems erect; leaf apices acuminate — *O. coronopifolia*

4 Leaves bluntly pinnatifid or subentire, copiously ciliate — *O. ciliata*
Leaves quite entire, or if lobed then sparsely ciliolate — *O. fructescens*

5 Inflorescence loosely panicled or subumbellate; phyllaries small and narrow; leaves semiamplexicaul — *O. quinquedentata*
Inflorescence densely corymbose; phyllaries broad; leaves cordate and auriculate-amplexicaul — *O. amplexicaulis*

6 Leaves linear or oblong, fleshy, semiterete or terete, nerves and veins absent — **7**
Leaves laterally lobed or pinnatifid — *O. quercifolia*
Leaves obovate or oblong, entire or toothed — **9**

7 Stems shrubby and fleshy; leaves crowded at end of branches; peduncles corymbose — **8**
Stems slender; leaves whorled at intervals, *c*25×6mm — *O. capensis*

8 Leaves linear-elongate, 3.5–8cm×2mm wide — *O. cylindrica*
Leaves cylindrical, 3.5–5cm long, 3–4mm diameter — *O. carnosa*

9 Peduncles corymbose, several-headed — **10**
Peduncles simple, 1-headed, or rarely forked — *O. arborescens*

10 Leaves attenuate to a slender petiole, entire, 3-nerved from middle — *O. triplinervia*
Leaves sessile, toothed or subentire, faintly nerved, thickish — *O. dentata*

11 Radical leaves linear-attenuate or linear-lanceolate, entire — *O. linifolia*
Radical leaves roundish, ovate or ovate-lanceolate, entire or crenate-lobulate, or absent — **12**
Radical leaves pinnatifid, pinnatipartite or lyrate — *O. pinnata*

12 Stem elongate, laxly leafy, branching, erect or climbing — *O. amplexifolia*
Stem short, flexuous, closely leafy, subsimple — *O. bulbosa*

13 Fleshy or succulent, small shrubs; branches mostly forked — **14**
Herbs, mostly with tuberous roots — *O. digitata*

14 Fruit glabrous; leaves toothed or lobed — **15**
Fruit silky; leaves entire — *O. furcata*

15 Euphorbia-resembling; leaves few- to many-toothed — *O. euphorbioides*
Subshrubs, only moderately succulent; leaves with 1 pair of teeth, or lobed — *O. retrofracta*

***O. amplexicaulis*** Thunb. Shrub, to 2m, glabrous. Stems erect, subsimple, terete, leafy. Lvs to 20×10cm, broadly obovate to oblong, mucronate, entire or minutely toothed, auriculate, amplexicaul, sessile to subdecurrent, gradually reduced above. Capitula radiate, in a terminal, much-branched, flat-topped corymb; phyllaries 8. Fr. silky-villous. Spring–summer. S Africa.

***O. amplexifolia*** DC. Somewhat ascending herb, glabrous and glaucous. Stem branched, woolly below. Lvs to 7×5cm, broadly ovate, cordate, acute or obtuse, amplexicaul, margin undulate or repand, mucronate, soft and slightly fleshy. Capitula radiate, solitary, terminal and axillary; phyllaries 9–10. Fr. dark brown, minutely hispid. S Africa.

***O. arborescens*** L. Succulent shrub, to 1m. Stem branched, flexuous, white-woolly on recent lf scars below. Lvs to 5×2cm, obovate-oblong, base attenuate, obtuse or subacute, margin entire or sinuate-toothed, fairly thick, axils hairy. Capitula radiate, usually solitary and terminal; phyllaries 5. Fr. villous. S Africa.

***O. bulbosa*** L. Glabrous to sparsely hairy herb. Stems short, flexuous, simple or branched, leafy below. Basal lvs to 12×5cm, ovate to oblong-lanceolate, acute, margin entire, membranous, petiolate, stem lvs oblong to obovate, margin occasionally repand, sessile, semiamplexicaul. Capitula radiate and solitary; phyllaries 7–10mm. Fr. silky-pubesc. Summer. S Africa.

***O. capensis*** L.H. Bail. LITTLE-PICKLES. Short herb. Stems trailing, branched, slender. Lvs to 2.5×1.5cm, scattered or often clustered, cylindric to cylindric-obovoid, acute, grooved, pale green, succulent, apex cartilaginous. Capitula radiate, solitary or paired, terminal, opening only in sun; phyllaries *c*9. Fr. glabrous or hairy. Summer. S Africa.

***O. carnosa*** Less. Shrub, to 30cm, fleshy, glabrous. Stem laxly branched, forked, terete, leafy at first, markedly scarred later. Lvs to 5×0.5cm, scattered, linear or somewhat fusiform, semiterete, spreading, base attenuate, acute, fairly thick, fleshy, glaucous. Capitula radiate, few, in a branched corymb; phyllaries 8–9. Fr. glabrous. S Africa.

***O. cheirifolia*** L. Evergreen shrub, to 40cm. Stem branched, branches spreading. Lvs to 8×2cm, lanceolate-spathulate, base attenuate, apex obtusely rounded, sessile, glaucous or tinged grey, thick. Capitula radiate, solitary and terminal; phyllaries *c*8–10. Fr. usually more or less hairy. Summer. Algeria and Tunisia. Z8.

***O. ciliata*** L. f. Shrub to 40cm. Stems several, decumbent, widely spreading, flowering branches ascending. Lvs to 5×1.5cm, oblong, obovate or spathulate, usually pinnatifid, lobes short, broad margin, ciliate-toothed, or occasionally entire, base attenuate. Capitula radiate, terminal, solitary; phyllaries *c*8. Fr. silky-pubesc. S Africa.

***O. coronopifolia*** L. non Thunb. Shrub, to 60cm. Stem erect, flexuous, often forked and bushy, glabrous. Lvs to 6×1cm, lanceolate or linear-lanceolate, entire or irregularly few-toothed, base attenuate, acuminate, leathery, thick. Capitula radiate, solitary or few, terminal; phyllaries 7–8. Fr. silky-villous. Summer–early autumn. S Africa.

***O. cylindrica*** (Lam.) DC. Shrub, to 1m, fleshy, glabrous. Stem laxly branched, forked, terete, leafy at first, markedly scarred later. Lvs to 8×0.2cm, scattered, linear-elongate, semiterete, spreading, base attenuate, acute, fleshy, glaucous. Capitula radiate, few to several, in a branched corymb; phyllaries 8–9, narrowly oblong, separate almost to base, margins membranous; ray florets to length of involucre. Fr. glabrous. S Africa.

***O. dentata*** L. Shrub to 90cm, succulent and glabrous. Stem branched, thick. Lvs to 5×3cm, subrosulate near branch apices, obovate, base cuneate, sessile, coarsely toothed to entire or subentire. Capitula radiate, few to several, in loose terminal corymbs; phyllaries *c*8. Fr. villous. S Africa.

***O. digitata*** L. Herb, to 45cm, glabrous, or pubesc. below. Stems simple or branched, lanate in axils, sparsely leafy. Lvs to 15×6cm, oblong to lanceolate, cuneate, entire, toothed, dentate or coarsely 3–5-lobed, lower, petiolate; stem lvs amplexicaul. Capitula discoid, solitary; phyllaries 8–10. Fr. adpressed silky-pubesc. Summer–early autumn. S Africa.

***O. euphorbioides*** Hutch. Shrub to 1m. Stems erect, very succulent, similar in habit to some succulent *Euphorbia* spp. Lvs to 1.5×0.5cm, reduced, narrowly oblanceolate or spathulate, fleshy, glabrous. Capitula discoid, solitary of few; phyllaries *c*9. Fr. glabrous. S Africa.

***O. fructescens*** L. Shrub, to 90cm. Stems decumbent, branched, leafy. Lvs to 10×4cm, obovate, base attenuate, mucronate, entire or ciliate, petiolate, upper stem lvs gradually reduced upwards to scales, oblong or linear, entire or toothed. Capitula radiate, in few to several clusters of 2–3; phyllaries *c*8. Fr. glabrous. Late summer. S Africa.

***O. furcata*** (Lindl.) Druce. Subshrub, to 1.2m. Stem branched, very pale grey or white. Lvs to 10×2cm, elongate-elliptic, entire, petiolate, gradually and progressively below. Capitula discoid, solitary or few to several in corymbose clusters; phyllaries 7–11. Fr. glabrous or often hairy. Namibia.

***O. linifolia*** L. f. Glabrous herb, to 40cm. Stems more or less nude, 2–3-forked, woolly at base. Lvs to 25×0.5cm, mostly basal, linear-attenuate or linear-lanceolate, tapered to both ends, entire, rigid, ribbed, veined or striate, lower axils woolly, stem lvs few, linear, sessile. Capitula radiate, solitary and terminal; phyllaries 9–10. Fr. silky-villous. Summer–early autumn. S Africa.

***O. pinnata*** L. f. Glabrous herb, to 50cm. Stems flexuous, laxly leafy, lower lf axils and base woolly. Lvs to 15×7cm, pinnatisect, seg. several, paired, to 25×8mm, oblong, ovate or subrotund, entire, decurrent. Capitula radiate, solitary and terminal; phyllaries 12–13. Fr. villous. Early summer. S Africa.

***O. quercifolia*** DC. Shrub, to 80cm. Stems erect, succulent, glabrous. Lvs to 10×2.5cm, pinnatifid, obtuse, base attenuate, lobes 3–4, 1 to 1.5cm, oblong, mucronate, petiolate. Capitula radiate, many, in a terminal compound corymb; phyllaries 5–6. Fr. glabrous. S Africa.

***O. quinquedentata*** Thunb. Shrub, to 1.3m. Stems erect, subsimple, loosely branched above robust, glabrous, leafy below. Lvs to 15×5cm, oblong, sessile, semi-amplexicaul, subdecurrent, coarsely or obscurely 5-toothed near apex, blunt, minutely mucronate, callous-margined, somewhat leathery. Capitula radiate, several, in a loosely umbellate panicle; phyllaries 7–8. Fr. silky-villous. S Africa.

***O. retrofracta*** Less. Subshrub, to 60cm. Stems branched, spreading or bent. Lvs to 8×3cm, oblong-lanceolate, base cuneate, 1-toothed or lobulate with a single tooth on each side. Capitula discoid, solitary, axillary; phyllaries *c*10–12. Fr. usually more or less glabrous. Summer. S Africa.

***O. retrorsa*** DC. Woody herb, to 40cm. Stems simple or branched, woolly and clad in dead leaf-bases below. Lvs to 8×1.5cm, rosulate at branch apices, oblong- to linear-spathulate, base attenuate, subacute, rigid, thin, reticulate-veined on both sides, margins ciliate. Capitula radiate, few to several in corymbs; phyllaries *c*8. Fr. silky-villous. S Africa.

***O. triplinervia*** DC. Succulent shrub, to 1m, glabrous. Stem subsimple or branched, thick and fleshy, leafy, becoming nude and markedly scarred below. Lvs to 8×2.5cm, crowded toward branch apices, obovate, obtuse, base attenuate, entire or repand, reticulate-veined, slightly fleshy. Capitula radiate, few to several, in a lax terminal corymb; phyllaries *c*5. Fr. villous. S Africa.

***O. aeonioides*** Dinter. See *O. furcata*.
***O. coronopifolia*** Thunb. non L. See *O. arborescens*.
***O. crassifolia*** Harv. See *O. capensis*.
***O. denticulata*** Dryand. in Ait. See *O. amplexicaulis*.
***O. integrifolia*** L. See *Tephroseris integrifolia*.
***O. palustris*** L. See *Tephroseris palustris*.
***O. tuberosa*** Thunb. See *O. bulbosa*.
For further synonymy see *Ceradia*, *Hertia* and *Othonnopsis*.

**Othonnopsis** Jaub. & Spach.
***O. cheirifolia*** Benth. & Hook. See *Othonna cheirifolia*.

**Otites** Adans. See *Silene*.

**Otochilus** Lindl. (From Gk *ous*, ear, and *cheilos*, lip; referring to the small ear-like appendages at the base of the lip.) Orchidaceae. Some 4–6 species of epiphytic or lithophytic orchids. Pseudobulbs arising near or from apex of previous season's pseudobulb, thus chain-like in habit, cylindric to tetragonal, and winged, apically bifoliate. Leaves linear to narrow-elliptic or ligulate, falling in second season. Inflorescence terminal, bracteate, slender; petals and sepals almost equal, narrow, free, spreading; lip sessile, basally saccate, midlobe entire, lateral lobes erect; column slender. Himalaya to SE Asia. Z9.

CULTIVATION As for *Bulbophyllum*, although the chain-like habit may necessitate some support or culture on long rafts.

***O. fuscus*** Lindl. Lvs to 12cm. Infl. to 10cm, a pendent spike or raceme; fls to 1.25cm diam.; sep. linear, spreading, white or pale pink; pet. similar, narrower; lip basally concave, midlobe linear, narrowing basally; column brown.

**Otoglossum** (Schltr.) Garay & Dunsterv. (From Gk *ous*, ear, and *glossa*, tongue, referring to the auriculate lateral lobes of the lip.) Orchidaceae. Some 7 species of epiphytic orchids; rhizomes thick, creeping. Pseudobulbs 1- or 2-leaved at apex and basally clothed by 1–2 leaf-bearing sheaths, well spaced on rhizome. Leaves fleshy. Raceme erect, large, long-stalked; flowers showy; sepals and petals subsimilar, spreading, obovate; lip pandurate, deflexed, basally replicate, adnate to foot of column; column small, base decurved, forming a blunt mentum with the ovary, apex cucullate, auriculate, stigma subquadrate to orbicular, anther operculate, incumbent, pollinia 2, fixed to a small viscidium by a subquadrate stipe. C & S America. Z10.

CULTIVATION As for *Odontoglossum*.

***O. brevifolium*** (Lindl.) Garay & Dunsterv. Pseudobulbs ovoid to ovoid-cylindrical, to 11cm, compressed, apically unifoliate with 1–2 leaf-bearing sheaths at base. Lvs to 30×9cm, ovate to elliptic-oblong, coriaceous, petiolate. Infl. to 60cm, erect, rarely pendent, stout, few- to many-fld; fls to 5cm diam.; sep. and pet. rich chestnut brown, margins yellow, dorsal sep. to 3×2cm, obovate or obovate-oblong, obtuse or retuse, undulate, lateral sep. oblique, obovate-oblong, undulate, pet. to 3×2cm, obovate or elliptic-oblong, obtuse or retuse, undulate; lip bright golden yellow with central transverse band, to 2.5cm, lateral lobes small, erect, semi-ovate or semi-triangular, apex rounded, midlobe cuneate to obovate, apex bilobed or retuse, disc with fleshy keel with a transverse frontal callus and a fleshy callus at base of each lateral lobe; column to 8mm, bialate, wings trilobed, dentate. Spring. Colombia, Ecuador, Peru.

***O. chiriquense*** (Rchb. f.) Garay & Dunsterv. Pseudobulbs to 11×6cm, unifoliate with 1–2 leaf-bearing basal sheaths, ovoid-oblong, compressed, often dull purple. Lvs to 30×9cm, elliptic-oblong, obtuse or retuse, coriaceous; petiole short. Infl. to 45cm, stout, erect, many-fld; fls to 7.5cm diam.; sep. and pet. bright yellow spotted and blotched rich chestnut brown, sep. free, to 3×2cm, widely spreading, obovate to elliptic-oblong, obtuse, strongly undulate, lateral sep. small, erect, auriculate, pet. subequal to sep.; lip to 2.5cm, subpandurate, 3-lobed, midlobe spreading or reflexed, obovate, obtuse or emarginate, disc tuberculate; column to 1cm, stout. Usually spring. Costa Rica, Panama, Colombia, Peru.

For synonymy see *Odontoglossum*.

**Otostylis** Schltr. (From Gk *ous*, ear, and *stylos*, style.) Orchidaceae. Some 3 species of terrestrial orchids allied to *Zygo-*

*petalum*. Pseudobulbs small, with several distichous, overlapping sheaths, apex 1- to several-leaved. Leaves narrowly lanceolate to narrowly elliptic. Inflorescence a lateral raceme, loosely to densely few to many-flowered; peduncle stout, slightly compressed; sepals and petals subsimilar, free, oblong to ovate-elliptic; lip often clawed, simple or trilobed, lateral lobes small, triangular or auriculate, midlobe large, ovate to obovate, disc with a raised callus, semicircular to reniform, dentate or undulate; column short, often with a short foot, wings 2, usually subquadrate or auriculate, clinandrium sometimes lobulate, anther terminal, operculate, incumbent, pollinia 4, compressed. Colombia, Venezuela, Trinidad, Guyanas to Brazil. Z9.

CULTIVATION As for *Odontoglossum*.

***O. brachystalix*** (Rchb. f.) Schltr. Pseudobulbs to 2cm, ovoid. Lvs to 70×5cm, linear-lanceolate, acute, plicate, apex recurved, strongly nerved. Infl. to 90cm, many-fld; sep. and pet. white, sep. to 18×12mm, ovate-elliptic to elliptic-lanceolate, acute to obtuse, lateral sep. oblique, pet. to 17×10mm, ovate or obovate, obtuse; lip white, to 12×12mm, lateral lobes erect, triangular, midlobe suborbicular or ovate to obovate, obtuse, callus pale yellow, irregularly dentate; column to 7mm, white marked purple at base, wings ovate to rectangular. Colombia, Venezuela, Trinidad, Guyana.

***O. lepida*** (Lind. & Rchb. f.) Schltr. Pseudobulbs to 6×1cm, fusiform to ovoid-fusiform, clustered. Lvs to 65×6cm, linear-lanceolate to linear-oblanceolate, acute or acuminate, plicate. Infl. to 70cm, several to many-fld; sep. and pet. white tipped pale rose, sep. to 20×10mm, elliptic-lanceolate to elliptic-oblong, acute, lateral sep. oblique, pet. similar to sep., oblique; lip to 18mm, white, simple, ovate-suborbicular, rounded or truncate, base cuneate, callus yellow, consisting of a W-shaped transverse ridge, dentate, crenulate; column to 8mm, white, wings subquadrate. Venezuela, Brazil, British Guyana.

For synonymy see *Aganisia, Koellensteinia* and *Zygopetalum*.

**Ottelia** Pers. (Latinized form of the Malabar name for these plants, *ottel-ambel*.) Hydrocharitaceae. 21 species of annual or perennial aquatics. Stems erect, occasionally creeping or rhizomatous. Leaves usually radical, heterophyllous, exstipulate; juvenile leaves linear to ellipsoidal or ovate, sessile; adult leaves petiolate, submerged or partially emersed, elliptic to orbicular, midrib prominent; petiole flexuous, often sheathing. Inflorescence subtended by a spathe of 2 fused bracts, submerged or emergent, pedunculate or subsessile; flowers unisexual or bisexual; sepals 3, free, narrowly triangular to ovate; petals 3, free, ovate to orbicular; usually clawed at base; stamens 3–15, often staminodal in female flowers; nectaries usually 3; ovary inferior; carpels and styles 3–20, a pistillodium in male flowers, stigmas 2 per style. Fruit a fleshy capsule; seeds ellipsoid or fusiform. Old World tropical and temperate regions, 1 New World species. Z9.

CULTIVATION Warm-water, floating aquatics with submerged or partially submerged foliage; cultivate as for *Egeria* in warm or tropical aquaria. Propagate from seed.

***O. alismoides*** (L.) Pers. Annual or perenn.; stems erect, contracted and corm-like. Lvs submerged, bases sheathing, adult lvs to 40×20cm, narrowly elliptic to widely ovate, cordate, translucent, midrib distinct with 2–10 longitudinal veins connected by numerous cross veins. Spathe membranaceous with 3 or more wings; fls usually bisexual; sep. 10–15×2–9mm, lanceolate to narrowly oblong; persistent; pet. to 30mm, obovate to orbicular, white, pink, pale blue to light purple, usually yellow at base. Fr. ovoid to ellipsoid; seeds 2000+ per fr., dehiscing with placentas as a pulpy mass, floating at first. N Africa, NE India to W China, SE Asia and Australia, introduced elsewhere, including N Italy, in association with irrigated crops.

***O. ovalifolia*** (R. Br.) Rich. Annual or perenn.; stem contracted, corm-like. Adult lvs partially emergent, elliptic to ovate, coriaceous, basally cuneate or cordate. Spathes shining when young, coriaceous; fls solitary, bisexual, sometimes cleistogamous, emergent; sep. to 27mm, persistent; pet. 3–6cm, clawed, cream with deep red base. Fr. to 7.5cm, beaked, disintegrating to release seeds; seeds to 3mm, many, narrowly ellipsoid, mucilaginous, pubesc. at first. Australia, New Zealand, New Caledonia.

***O. tenera*** Benth. See *O. ovalifolia*.
For further synonymy see *Damasonium*.

**Ougeinia** Benth.
***O. dalbergioides*** Benth. See *Desmodium ooieinense*.

**Ourisia** Comm. ex Juss. (For General Ouris of the Malvinas Islands (*d*1773).) Scrophulariaceae. Some 25 species hardy alpine perennial herbs or subshrubs, low-growing, rhizomatous. Leaves usually radical, crenate or entire, petiolate. Flowers often white, sometimes purple, scarlet or pink, axillary and solitary, in bracteate scapose corymbs or whorled racemes; calyx deeply 5-lobed; corolla slightly zygomorphic, tube short, slightly oblique, lobes 5, subequal, usually spreading; stamens 4 fertile, cohering, 1 rudimentary, minute. Fruit an ovoid capsule. Summer–autumn. Andes, Antarctic S America, New Zealand, Tasmania.

CULTIVATION An alpine genus, found in moist, open spaces and by streamsides in mountainous terrain, they are best cultivated on beds or rock gardens in soils which are cool and moisture-retentive but fast-draining and with a tendency to acidity. *O. sessiliflora*, as a fairly high altitude plant normally found on stony ground, is better suited to cultivation in the moraine. A dry continental climate is unsuitable (in the US they will do best in the Pacific Northwest) since although tolerant of all but the most severe winters, they require cool, moist atmospheres and soils during the summer months and drier conditions during the winter. *Ourisia* spp. are grown for their creeping, rhizomatous mats or tufts of leathery leaves, and for the graceful flowers in spring and early summer which individually resemble those of *Penstemon*. Moisture requirements and atmospheric conditions are sometimes more easily provided in the alpine house or a north-facing frame: grow in pans of a gritty alpine mix with added leafmould. In the open garden, plant out in spring into a north-facing or partially shaded position with shelter from scorching sun and drying winds. Propagate from fresh seed, which germinates well, or by division in spring.

***O. breviflora*** Benth. Lvs 7–10×5–12mm, all basal, clustered, hairy, ovate to orbicular, obtuse, basally truncate to cordate, somewhat crenate; petiole 1–3mm. Fls usually solitary, or in 2–4-fld racemes; peduncle 2–6mm, villous; bracts 6–10mm, broadly ovate, obtuse, dentate, hairy above; cal. 6–8mm, lobes oblong, obtuse, ciliate; cor. tube 10–14mm, violet with darker venation, lobes 3×2mm, linear to obovate, emarginate; stigma capitate. Fr. 4–6mm, subglobose, glabrous; seeds 1mm, oblong, reticulate, yellow-brown. Summer. Z8.

***O. caespitosa*** Hook. f. Stems to 12×0.2cm, much and closely branched, creeping, glabrous or variably hairy, rooting at nodes; branches very short, ascending. Lvs 4–8mm, usually close-set, spreading, recurved, often distichous, obovate-spathulate, obtuse, entire or more usually with 2–3 notches on each side, coriaceous; petiole very short, sheathing, with thin, fringed wings. Peduncle erect, 2–7cm, 1–5-fld, glabrous; bracts 1 or 2 pairs, opposite; cal. 6mm, lobes oblong, obtuse, glabrous; cor. white, to 16mm diam. Fr. 5mm, ovate-oblong. Spring–summer. New Zealand. var. ***gracilis*** Hook. f. Similar to species type but smaller in all its parts; lvs 4mm; peduncles 1–2-fld; fls 12mm; cal. lobes linear-oblong. New Zealand. Z7.

***O. coccinea*** Comm. ex Juss. Stems to 30cm. Lvs broadly elliptic or oblong, shallowly and irregularly dentate. Infl. a panicle, crowded, terminal; fls to 4cm, scarlet, drooping; stamens exserted, cream. Spring–autumn. Chile (Andes).

***O. macrocarpa*** Hook. f. Stems robust, erect, glabrescent, to 60cm, usually shorter from creeping rhiz. Lvs to 1.5cm, radical, persistent, petiolate, ovate-oblong to orbicular, 1–2cm, crenate, thick, leathery, dark green above, glabrous except margins ciliate. Peduncle stout; lower bracts paired, upper whorled; fls in several superposed whorls; pedicels robust, 2–7cm; cal. lobes 12mm, glabrous, linear-oblong, leathery; fls 15–25mm diam., white sometimes with yellow throat, tube broad, villous within, lobes obovate, retuse or cupped. Fr. 12mm, ovoid-oblong. Spring–summer. New Zealand. Z7.

***O. macrophylla*** Hook. f. Rhiz. short, robust; stems to 60cm, erect, downy or glabrescent. Radical lvs very variable, 2–22cm, ovate to orbicular-oblong, shallowly crenate, membranous, sparsely pubesc., midrib pubesc. beneath; petioles 2–15cm, basally sheathing. Peduncle erect; bracts subtended by a whorl of 2–4 lvs; each pedicel subtended by a bract, in 3–8 whorls, 1 to many per whorl, 3–5cm, glandular-pubesc.; cal. lobes narrow, entire, acute; cor. 20mm, white or white with purple streaks, lobes obovate, retuse. Fr. 8mm, ovoid. Summer. New Zealand. Z7.

***O. cultivars***. 'Loch Ewe' (*O. coccinea* × *O. macrophylla*): to 20cm, slowly spreading in tight rosettes; fls shell pink. 'Snowflake' (*O. macrocarpa* × *O. caespitosa* var. *gracilis*): to 10cm; lvs dark, glossy; fls white. Z7.

***O. uniflora*** Philippi. See *O. breviflora*.
For further synonymy see *Euphrasia*.

**Ovidia** Meissn. (For Ovid, the Latin poet who described the changing of the nymph Daphne into a laurel: *Ovidia* is closely related to *Daphne*.) Thymelaeaceae. 4 species of deciduous dioecious shrubs with supple shoots. Similar to *Daphne* but with a more slender style. S America. Z9.

CULTIVATION *Ovidia* spp. are found in montane and submontane zones to an altitude of 1500m/4875ft, in semi-shaded habitats, on moist humus-rich soils. They have supple and downy shoots bearing creamy white flowers, reminiscent of the closely related *Daphne*; those of *O. pillopillo* are conspicuously silky. They make attractive specimens for the woodland garden and sheltered shrub border. Cultivate as for *Daphne*.

***O. andina*** (Poepp. & Endl.) Meissn. Shrub to 2.25m. Young shoots downy. Lvs 5–13×1.5–3cm, oblanceolate to narrow-ovate, tips blunt or rounded, tapered to base, dull pale green and glabrous above, glaucous and hairy below, sessile. Male fls in dense, terminal umbels to 4cm diam.; peduncle stout, 2.5cm; pedicels slender, to 12mm; cal. 6mm diam., funnelform, 4-lobed, downy, cream-white; anth. red; female fls smaller with shorter peduncles. Fr. to 6mm, white, ovoid, stigma persistent. Summer. Chile.

***O. pillopillo*** (C. Gay) Meissn. Similar to *O. andina*, but shrub or small tree 3–9m. Shoots very downy. Lvs 2.5–8cm×6–8mm, sessile, oblanceolate, glabrous, somewhat glaucous. Cal. 1.5cm diam., tubular, 4-lobed, white exterior very downy. Fr. red-purple. Chile.

**OXALIDACEAE** R. Br. WOOD SORREL FAMILY. 8 genera and 575 species of small trees, shrubs and especially herbs with tubers or bulbs, usually accumulating oxalates. Leaves alternate, pinnate, palmate or 3-foliolate, rarely 1-foliolate, leaflets often folded at night denoting 'sleep movements', stipules usually absent. Flowers bisexual, regular, 5-merous, in axillary cymes on peduncles; calyx 5 free sepals, corolla 5 free petals, sometimes slightly connate at the base; stamens 10 in 2 whorls, outer usually with shorter filaments, all basally connate, sometimes 5 without anthers; ovary superior, of (3–)5 fused carpels, with free styles, 5-loculed, with axile placentas; ovules (1) 2-several in each locule. Fruit a loculicidal capsule or berry; seeds often with basal aril involved in explosion from capsule; embryo in copious oily endosperm. Some are troublesome weeds, e.g. *Oxalis* and *Biophytum*. Fruits of *Averrhoa* are edible, as star fruit, *A. carambola*. Some *Oxalis* spp. have edible leaves or tubers. Tropical, few temperate, especially S America and Cape. *Averrhoa, Biophytum, Oxalis*.

**Oxalis** L. (From Gk *oxys*, acid, referring to the sour taste of leaves.) SORREL; SHAMROCK. Oxalidaceae. 800 species of annual or perennial, stemmed or stemless herbs and shrubs, often with tuberous or bulbous underground parts; very rarely aquatic plants. Leaves radical or cauline, palmate; leaflets usually 3, sometimes more or phyllodic, often folding down at night; stipules adnate to petiole bases or absent. Flowers with a tristylic, heteromorphic arrangement of parts, on axillary peduncles; often in cymes or contractions of this to umbellate, 1- to many-flowered; bracteoles in pairs subtending pedicels and cyme branches, many and crowded in umbellate inflorescences; pedicels articulate below calyx and/or their base; petals usually partly fused at base, white, pink, red or yellow, stamens 10 in two whorls of 5, filaments fused in a tube; carpels 5, fused, styles 5, free. Fruit a dehiscent capsule; seed in a fleshy aril which ejects the seed from locule when ripe. Cosmopolitan but centres of diversity in S Africa and S America.

CULTIVATION Although a number of species are potential weeds (e.g. *O. articulata, O. corniculata, O. debilis, O. exilis, O. latifolia* and *O. pes-caprae*) that spread by means of seed and underground bulbils and may prove difficult to eradicate, *Oxalis* includes a number of beautiful ornamentals for a diversity of situations in the garden. Most species are low and spreading, the flowers and sometimes the leaves close up at night or in shade. Relatively few are reliably frost-hardy, but these include *O. adenophylla* and *O. enneaphylla* (particularly valued for their neatly pleated glaucous foliage, suited to the sunny raised bed and large trough or for well-drained, humus-rich, sandy niches on the rock garden), *O. magellanica* and *O. depressa* (for the well-drained interstices of paving or partially shaded bases of walls and rockwork), *O. acetosella, O. oregana* and *O. violacea* (for naturalizing in the wild and woodland garden in moisture-retentive, humus-rich soils with shade or dappled sunlight). *O. corniculata* var. *atropurpurea* is hardy and attractively bronzed but should be used only where self-sown seedlings will not cause nuisance.

Most of these will tolerate temperatures as low as −15°C/5°F, and thrive in temperate climates where summers are relatively cool, or where they can be given shade from the hottest sun in summer. Some of the annuals, including *O. rosea* and *O. valdiviensis*, are suitable for hanging baskets, window boxes and other containers, requiring a moderately fertile and retentive potting mix in sun or part shade. Some from the Cape and temperate South America may tolerate a few degrees of short-loved frost but are most safely grown in the alpine house in zones that experience severe or prolonged frosts; in positions where the root is protected from severe cold, as in rock or pavement crevices, they may re-emerge in spring. These include *O. bowiei, O. chrysantha, O. hirta, O. laciniata, O. latifolia, O. lobata, O. purpurata* and *O. tetraphylla*; all are easily grown in well-crocked pans or pots in a gritty, leafy alpine mix. Most other species from these regions are suitable for outdoor cultivation only in warm, essentially frost-free climates, otherwise requiring slightly warmer glasshouse conditions. The bulbous/tuberous species need a sunny position in pots of moderate fertility, loam-based mix with additional sharp sand and leafmould; maintain good ventilation, with a minimum temperature in the range 7–10°C/45–50°F. Liquid feed weekly and water moderately when in growth, allowing the medium to dry partially between waterings. Keep cool, dry and frost-free when dormant and repot annually as growth resumes, in late winter for spring-blooming bulbous types, in early spring for summer-flowerers and in late summer for those that bloom in autumn; repot herbaceous species in spring.

Tropical natives such as *O. alstonii, O. corymbosa, O. dispar, O. fruticosa* and *O. ortgiesii* thrive in a high-fertility, humus-rich potting mix, with plentiful water when in full growth, high humidity, bright filtered light with shade from the strongest sun, and a minimum temperature of 16°C/60°F. Given slightly lower temperatures and humidity, *O. hedysaroides, O. herrerae, O. megalorrhiza* and *O. peduncularis* thrive in similar conditions. *O. gigantea*, from semi-arid habitats, requires conditions that suit cacti and succulents.

Propagate by ripe seed, division, or offsets. Soft-stemmed species may be increased by cuttings in sand in a shaded closed case with gentle bottom heat, woody species by semi-ripe cuttings in similar conditions, rooting is enhanced by use of rooting hormone.

***O. acetosella*** L. WOOD-SORREL; CUCKOO BREAD; ALLELUIA. Creeping perenn., 3–12cm; rhiz. slender, scaly, pale green. Lvs trifoliate, petioles erect to 8cm; leaflets to 1.5×2cm, obcordate, pale green, sparsely hairy. Fls solitary, borne slightly above the lvs, 1.5–2cm across; pet. white, veined purple. Fr. 3–4mm, ovoid to spherical. Spring. N temperate America, Europe and Asia. var. ***purpurascens*** Mart. ('Rosea', 'Rubra'). Fls rose with purple veining. Z3.

***O. adenophylla*** Gillies. SAUER KLEE. Stemless perenn., 10–15cm, from a brown, scale-covered, tuberous base. Lvs numerous, erect to spreading; petioles 5–12cm, red-brown; leaflets *c*6×6mm, 9–22, obcordate, silver-grey, glabrous. Peduncles as long as lvs, 1–3-fld; fls *c*2.5cm across, lilac-pink to violet with darker veins and 5 purple spots in the white throat; sep. without orange calli. Late spring–early summer. Chile, W Argentina (Andes). 'Minima': lvs small. Z5.

***O. alstonii*** Lourteig. FIRE FERN; RED FLAME. Similar to *O. hedysaroides* but stems, petioles and flowering parts pubesc.; lvs maroon-red. Summer–autumn. Brazil. Z9.

***O. articulata*** Savigny. Stemless perenn. to 10–40cm; rhiz. to 14×2cm, little-branched, dark brown, tuberous, semi-woody, glabrous becoming cylindrical with articulations. Lvs 6–25cm, numerous, basal, petioles erect to sprawling, glabrous or with adpressed hairs; leaflets 3, 10–25×20–35mm, obcordate, green usually with punctate margin below, glabrous above, hairy beneath. Peduncles very numerous, to 40cm, erect to spreading; infl. a 5–10-fld umbellate cyme held well above the lvs; fls to 2cm across, bright mauve-pink; sep. with 2 orange apical calli. Summer–autumn. Paraguay. var. ***hirsuta*** Progel. Lvs hairy above. 'Alba': fls white. Z8.

***O. bifida*** Thunb. Perenn. with a weak, erect or procumbent, branched stem to 30cm; bulb scaly. Petioles slender, 1.5–4cm, congested at the stem apices; leaflets 3, 5–6×5–6mm, narrowly obcordate, divided to the middle or more, green, punctate with black marginal spots, glabrous above, sparsely hairy beneath. Fls solitary on peduncles 2.5–8cm long, *c*12mm across, purple-red with a yellow-green throat; sep. with purple-black apical calli. Spring–summer. S Africa (Cape Province). Z9.

***O. bowiei*** Lindl. Stemless perenn., 20–30cm with glandular hairs on the petioles, peduncles and cal. Bulb elongate with a smooth brown tunic covering pale brown flesh inside, and with a long, white, fleshy, contractile root. Petioles 5–15cm, stout, erect; leaflets 3, to 5×5cm, rounded to broadly obcordate, shallowly notched, rather thick and leathery, green, sometimes purple beneath, more or less glabrous above, more densely hairy beneath. Peduncles 10–30cm, erect, bearing 3–12-fld umbels, fls 3–4cm across, bright rose-red to pink, with a yellow-green throat; sep. with no calli. Summer–autumn. S Africa (Cape Province). Z8.

***O. bupleurifolia*** A. St.-Hil. Erect stemmed perenn., much-branched, to 40cm high; stem 3–5mm thick, woody, brown, naked below, leafy above. Lvs numerous, crowded at the stem apices, glabrous; petioles to 11cm and expanded into phyllodes 12mm wide; leaflets 3, 8×3mm, caducous, rarely present. Peduncles to 8cm, very variable in length, glabrous, flattened to 2mm wide; infl. a 2–4-fld umbel; fls to 1cm across, yellow; sep. pubesc., without calli. Summer–autumn. Brazil. Z9.

***O. caprina*** L. GOAT'S-FOOT; WOOD-SORREL. Nearly stemless, or very short-stemmed, almost hairless perenn., 15–20cm. Bulb scaly with a slender vertical rhiz. Lvs basal or at stem apex; petioles 2–5cm, erect to spreading; leaflets 3, 5–10×5–15mm, widely triangular in outline, deeply divided to about the middle, lobes obovate. Peduncles to 20cm, longer than petioles, weak, bearing 2–4-fld umbels; fls pale violet, rarely white, with pale green throat; sep. with 2 orange apical calli. Spring–early summer. S Africa (Cape Province). Z9.

***O. chrysantha*** Progel. Very hairy, mat-forming perenn. with slender, creeping aerial stem to 20cm, rather woody, rooting and producing leaf rosettes at basal nodes. Lvs numerous in clusters along stem, petioles 2–4cm, leaflets 3, 7×7mm, triangular-obcordate, green with white hairs. Peduncles 3.5cm; fls solitary, 1.5cm across, golden yellow with red markings at the mouth of the throat; sep. without calli. Fr. 11m, cylindrical, hairy. Summer–autumn. Brazil. Z8.

***O. corniculata*** L. PROCUMBENT YELLOW SORREL; CREEPING YELLOW OXALIS; CREEPING OXALIS. Creeping, much-branched, mat-forming, short-lived perenn., with many prostrate to ascending, slender stems 10–30cm long, from a short, vertical taproot. Lvs numerous along stem, petioles erect, 1–8cm, somewhat hairy, with fused rectangular stipules; leaflets 3, 5–15×8–20mm, obcordate, green, usually glabrous above and hairy beneath. Peduncles axillary, 1–10cm, bearing 2–6-fld umbels; flowers *c*1cm across, light yellow, sometimes with a red throat; sep. without calli. Fr. cylindrical, 12–15mm long, erect on deflexed pedicels. Spring–autumn. Cosmopolitan weed, origin unknown. var. ***atropurpurea*** Planch. Foliage purple-bronze and all parts suffused with purple. var. ***villosa*** (Bieb.) Hohen. Lvs hairy above and beneath. Z5.

***O. corymbosa*** DC. Stemless perenn., 15–40cm, with round bulb producing numerous loosely scaly, sessile bulbils with 3 nerves per bulb scale. Petioles 10–35cm, erect to spreading, with white patent hairs 0.5–2.5mm long; leaflets 3, 25–45×30–62mm, broadly obcordate, rounded, green, with dark spots beneath, sparsely hairy. Peduncles 15–40cm, erect, with white patent hairs as petioles; infl. a 8–15-fld, irregularly branched cyme; fls *c*1.5cm across, red to purple with darker veins and a white throat; sep. with 2 apical calli. Spring–early summer. S America (Brazil, Argentina). 'Aureo-reticulata': lvs with yellow veining, probably virus-induced. Z9.

***O. depressa*** Ecklon & Zeyh. Bulbous, nearly stemless perenn., 4–12cm, with an underground, slender, vertical rhiz. 5cm long or more, from bulb to soil surface. Petioles 8–20mm, glabrous, erect to spreading in a crown at soil surface; leaflets 3, 3–10×5–16mm, rounded to triangular-ovate, grey-green, sometimes dark-spotted, glabrous or sparsely hairy. Peduncles 1–10cm, erect; fls solitary held above the leaves, 1.5–2cm across, bright pink to rose-violet, with a yellow throat, purple and white forms are known; sep. without calli. Summer. S Africa (Cape Province). Z5.

***O. dillenii*** Jacq. Erect, stemmed annual to 40cm, branching freely from base; stem 5–40cm, pubesc., becoming caespitose with age, rooting freely at basal nodes. Lvs borne all over plant; petioles 3–8cm, tending to be grouped in whorls, pubesc., stipules narrow to rounded; leaflets 3, 4–20×7–25mm, obovate, green, glabrous above, pubesc. beneath. Peduncles 3–10cm, axillary, pubesc.; infl. usually a 2–3-fld umbel; fls *c*1cm across, yellow; sep. without calli. Fr. 13–25cm, cylindrical, strigose; seeds with white banding; pedicels deflexed in fruit. Autumn. Eastern N America.

***O. dispar*** N.E. Br. Small, softly pubesc. undershrub to about 60cm, woody at base with slender spreading branches. Lvs few; petioles 7–9cm, very slender, pubesc., petiolule to 2cm; leaflets 3, about 7×3cm, ovate-lanceolate, green, hairy both sides, laterals sessile, terminal petiolulate. Peduncles 7–9cm, slender; infl. a 7–10-fld contracted cyme; fls 2–3cm across, golden yellow, beautifully scented; sep. without calli. Spring–winter. Guyana. Z10.

***O. drummondii*** A. Gray. Bulbous, stemless perenn. to 20cm or more, bulb of open, papery, 3-nerved scales. Petioles 5–16cm, erect to spreading, glabrous; leaflets 3, V-shaped, deeply lobed to up to four-fifths of their length, lobes to 30×5mm. Infl. a 3–10-fld umbel held well above the lvs; fls *c*2cm across, purple; sep. with fused red apical calli. A variable species. Spring–summer. Mexico. Z9.

***O. enneaphylla*** Cav. SCURVY GRASS. Stemless perenn. to 14cm, with slender, creeping, horizontal rhiz. 5×2cm, covered in thick white scales with bulbils in their axils. Petioles 1.5–8cm, erect, occasionally hairy; leaflets 9–20, 4–12×2–8mm, obcordate, partially folded upwards, somewhat fleshy, glaucous blue, shortly hairy; fls solitary, held just above lvs, *c*2cm across, white to red, fragrant; sep. without calli. Spring–summer. Falkland Is., Patagonia. 'Alba': fls white. 'Ione Hecker' (*O. enneaphylla* × *O. laciniata*): lvs with rather narrower seg. and deeper green; fls large, to 3cm across, vivid blue at edge darkening to dark purple at centre. 'Minutifolia': dwarf form less than 5cm high. 'Rosea': to 6cm, fls rose-pink. 'Rubra': fls red. Z6.

***O. exilis*** A. Cunn. Very similar to a small form of *O. corniculata*, to 4cm tall and stems to 15cm long. Petioles 6–13mm; leaflets 3–5×3–7mm, green. Fls solitary. Fr. 5–8×3mm, globose-cylindrical, sparsely hairy. Spring–summer. Australia, New Zealand. Z8.

***O. fabaefolia*** Jacq. Glabrous, bulbous, stemless perenn. to 15cm tall; bulb to 4cm, ovoid; rhiz. long, brown, with membranous scales, the upper large and prominent. Petioles 1.5–10cm, with leaf-like wings orbicular to ligulate in outline; leaflets 2–5, 1.5–5cm, ovate to obovate or oblanceolate, rather thick with cartilaginous margin. Peduncles 1–7cm, erect; fls solitary, to 3cm across, yellow, white or mauve; sep. with brown apical calli. Summer–autumn. S Africa. Z9.

***O. flava*** L. Stemless perenn. to 25cm from a brown rhiz. 100×3mm covered in membranous scales. Petioles 2–6cm, erect to spreading; leaflets (2–)5–12, 7.5×20mm, narrow, digitate, oblong with an apical notch, green, glabrous. Fls solitary borne slightly above the lvs, *c*2.5cm across, bright yellow, white or very pale rose-violet with a yellow throat; sep. with several indistinct orange apical calli. A very variable species. Spring–early summer. S Africa (Cape Province). Z9.

***O. fruticosa*** Knuth. Shrubby perenn., irregularly branched and sprawling to 50cm high; stems red-brown, woody, densely leafy at apices. Lvs phyllodic, leaflets minute, occasionally present; petioles 11–13cm, expanded to a blade 3–4mm wide. Peduncles numerous, axillary, to 3cm; infl. 1–3-fld, cymose; fls to 1–1.5cm across, yellow; sep. without calli. Spring. Peru. Z9.

***O. gigantea*** Barnéoud. Erect shrub, 1–2.5m; stems long, wandering, little branched. Lvs numerous, fleshy; leaflets 3, small, *c*3.5mm, obcordate, hairy beneath. Peduncles *c*3mm, in leaf axils; fls solitary, or in 3–6-fld umbellate cymes; fls 1–2cm across, yellow; sep. without calli. Spring–summer. Chile. Z9.

***O. hedysaroides*** HBK. Erect subshrub to 1m, much branched, stem woody, leafy throughout. Petioles 3 to 6cm; leaflets 3, *c*25×20mm, widely ovate to rounded, green above, glaucous beneath, glabrous; terminal petiolule 6–10mm, laterals 1–2mm. Peduncles axillary, 3–7cm, erect, glabrous to minutely pubesc.; infl. a dichasial cyme of *c*6 fls; fls *c*1cm across, yellow; sep. glabrous, without calli. Spring–summer. C America (Venezuela, Colombia, Ecuador). 'Rubra': lvs maroon. Z9.

***O. herrerae*** Knuth. Branching, glabrous perenn. shrublet, 10–30cm, branches to 8mm thick, reddened, becoming brown with age. Petioles 2–5cm, spreading, fleshy, dilated in the centre to 3mm thick and tapering to the ends like a cigar; leaflets 3, 5–10×4–7mm, obcordate, fleshy, green, reddening with age, caducous, leaving petioles. Peduncles to 10cm, erect; infl. 5–7-fld unequally branched cymes; fls 1–1.5cm across, yellow with red veins; sep. edged red without calli. Summer. Peru. Z9.

***O. hirta*** L. Erect, decumbent or trailing, bulbous perenn.; stems to 30cm, branching above; bulbs to 15mm diam., small, round, each producing one deciduous stem; all parts of plant hairy. Lvs almost sessile; leaflets 3, 10–15×1.5–3mm, linear to oblong with an apical notch, green. Peduncles 1–5cm long, borne in upper leaf axils; fls solitary, *c*2.5cm across, variable in colour from red to violet and purple, or paler to white, rarely yellow, with a yellow throat; sep. without calli. A very variable species. Autumn. S Africa (Cape Province). 'Gothenburg': to 25cm; fls deep pink. var. ***fulgida*** (Lindl.) Knuth. Fls purple. var. ***rubella*** (Jacq.) Knuth. Fls deep red. Z9.

***O. incarnata*** L. Bulbous, glabrous, perenn. with erect to sprawling slender stems 10–50cm long; bulb to 2cm diam., rounded. Petioles 2–6cm in whorls up the stems; leaflets 3, 8–20×5–15mm, obcordate, translucent green with dark marginal spots beneath; leaf axils may bear red-brown bulbils. Peduncles 3–7cm, erect; fls solitary, 2cm across, white or very pale lilac, with darker veins and a yellow throat; sep. with several converging apical calli. Autumn. Namibia. Z9.

***O. laciniata*** Cav. Rhizomatous, stemless perenn., 5–10cm; rhiz. branching freely just below ground level forming an elongate chain of tiny, linked, scaly bulbils. Lvs arising from apex of rhiz.; petioles 2.5–7cm, erect, tinged pink; leaflets 8–12, to 2cm, obcordate, folded length-wise, glaucous green with purple, undulate margin, glabrous to softly hairy. Peduncles as long as lvs; fls solitary, *c*2.5cm across, very variable in colour, violet, crimson to lilac, blue and paler, all with darker veins and green throat, sweetly scented; sep. without calli, tips reddened. Late spring–summer. Patagonia. 'Ione Hecker': see *O. enneaphylla*. Z8.

***O. lasiandra*** Zucc. Bulbous, stemless perenn., 15–30cm or more, with a thick taproot densely covered in scaly bulbils at the apex; bulb scales 15–35-nerved. Petioles to 15cm, erect, stalks red-green with sparse to abundant patent hairs c2mm long; leaflets 5–10, to 5×2cm, narrowly wedge-shaped to strap-like, apex rounded, usually shallowly notched, green, glabrous. Peduncles twice as long as petioles, erect, succulent, with long, spreading hairs as the petioles; infl. a 9–26-fld umbel; fls c2cm across, crimson to violet, with a yellow throat; sep. and bracts with red apical calli. Summer–autumn. Mexico. Z9.

***O. latifolia*** HBK. Bulbous, stemless perenn., 7–25cm, producing numerous bulbils on short underground runners off the parental bulb; bulbils scaly, scales 5–11-nerved. Petioles 8–23cm, erect to spreading; leaflets 3, to 7×7cm, broadly deltoid to obcordate, dark green, glabrous. Peduncles to 23cm; infl. a 6–32-fld pseudo-umbel; fls 1.5–2cm across, violet-pink or paler, with a green throat; sep. with 2 orange-brown apical calli. Summer–autumn. Mexico to Peru; widely naturalized, can be a troublesome weed. Z9.

***O. lobata*** Sims. Stemless, bulbous perennial, 8–10cm, with tuberous roots; bulb to 2.5cm diam., round, densely covered in brown, woolly scales. Petioles 4–5cm, erect; leaflets 3, 5×6mm, obcordate, light green, glabrous, usually maculate, the lateral pair somewhat folded lengthwise. Peduncles almost twice the height of lvs; fls solitary, about 1.5cm across, golden-yellow, dotted and veined red; sep. with apical calli. Late summer–autumn. Chile. The lvs appear in spring then die down; they reappear with the flowers in the autumn. Z8.

***O. magellanica*** Forst. f. Reminiscent of a small *O. acetosella*; a prostrate, stoloniferous, carpet-forming perenn. to 4cm; rhiz. slender, scaly, bearing leaves and peduncles from the apex. Petioles 2–4cm, erect, sparsely hairy; leaflets 3, 5×5mm, obcordate, bronze-green, glabrous. Peduncles short, 1.5–3.5cm, erect; fls solitary, 1cm across, pure white; sep. without calli. Late spring-summer. S America, Australia; can become a garden pest. 'Nelson' ('Flore Pleno'): lvs tinged bronze; fls double, white. 'Old Man Range': lvs distinctive, grey tinged pink in summer; fls white, abundant. Z6.

***O. megalorrhiza*** Jacq. Glabrous perenn. with fleshy, erect to sprawling stems, 1–2cm thick, at first stemless but increasing to 30–40cm with age; stems little-branched, semi-woody at base and covered with leaf base scales, bearing lvs and peduncles toward the ends; rhiz. to 8cm, horizontal, woody, usually unbranched. Petioles to 8cm, erect, fleshy; leaflets 3, 11–18×10–20mm, obcordate, green, succulent, shiny above, with watery papillae appearing crystalline beneath. Peduncles as long as lvs, erect; infl. a 2–5-fld umbel; fls to 2.5cm across, bright yellow; sep. distinctly of two types, 3 outer broadly triangular with hastate bases and 2 inner smaller, linear-lanceolate, none have calli. Fr. 6×4mm, spherical; glabrous, enclosed within sep. until mature. Summer-autumn. S America (Bolivia, Chile, Galapagos Is., Peru); readily sets seed and can become a pest in glasshouses. Z10.

***O. melanosticta*** Sonder. Small, nearly stemless, bulbous perenn. to 2.5cm; bulbs 6.5–8.5mm, scaly. Petioles 1.5–2.5cm, erect to spreading, very hairy; leaflets 3, 7–11×5–9mm, obcordate to rounded, rather thick, green with orange spots (which blacken on drying), usually hairy on both surfaces, margins densely white ciliate. Peduncles as long as the petioles or shorter, erect, densely hairy; fls solitary, to 2cm across, yellow; sep. densely hairy, without calli. Late spring–summer. S Africa. Z9.

***O. nelsonii*** (Small) Knuth. Resembling *O. tetraphylla* but differing in bulb scales 5–12-nerved; plant with sparse to abundant hairs; leaflets 5 or 6, usually entire; fls larger, 1.5 to 2.5cm across, deep purple. Summer. Mexico. Z9.

***O. oregana*** Nutt. ex Torr. & A. Gray. REDWOOD SORREL. Perenn. reminiscent of a robust *O. acetosella*, rising to 6–20cm from a horizontal, creeping, brown, rhiz. Petioles 3–20cm, erect with patent hairs; leaflets 3, 2.5–3.5×2.7×4.5cm, widely obcordate, green, glabrous above, margins and undersurfaces with long hairs. Peduncles as long as or just longer than petioles, erect, hairy; fls solitary, 2–2.5cm across, pale lilac or darker, occasionally white; sep. hairy, without calli. Fr. 7–8mm, globose. Spring–autumn. Western N America. Z7.

***O. ortgiesii*** Reg. TREE OXALIS. Erect perenn. with persistent stems; to 45cm at flowering; rhiz. to 15–20cm×5mm, horizontal, brown-red, producing a single, sparsely branched stem; stems 20–40cm, hairy, green-purple. Lvs crowded at the stem apex; petioles 4–8cm, erect to spreading, densely hairy; leaflets 3, 6×3.5cm, obcordate, deeply divided into two large triangular lobes at the tips, olive-green above, red-purple beneath, hairy throughout. Peduncles to 30cm in upper lf axils; infl. a many-fld cyme; fls to 2.5cm across, lemon yellow with darker veins, caducous sequentially up the persistent main cyme branches leaving organs like octopus tentacles after flowering; sep. without calli, purple edged. Spring–winter. Peru (Andes). Z8.

***O. patagonica*** Speg. Stemless perenn. to 5cm with a semi-jointed, creeping rhiz.; rhiz. covered below with rounded orange scales, and above with narrow brown scales congested at the apex. Petioles 2–5cm, erect; leaflets 10–14, 7–8×3–5mm, obcordate, divided to base and folded lengthwise, glaucous grey, densely hairy. Peduncles 1.5–3.5cm, glaucous grey, hairy; fls solitary, 2.5cm across, red, pink to pink blue; sep. and pet. somewhat hairy, sep. without calli. Late spring–summer. Patagonia. Z8.

***O. peduncularis*** HBK. Erect to ascending, leafy stemmed perenn., flowering to 60cm; stems to 30cm, 5–7mm thick, succulent, red-green, glabrous. Lvs crowded toward the stem apex; petioles 4–15cm, somewhat fleshy, glabrous; leaflets 3, 12×9mm, obovate, fleshy, bright or pale green, usually with a purple margin, glabrous above, pubesc. beneath. Peduncles to 30cm, erect; infl. a 9–16-fld cyme held well above the lvs; fls 1.5cm across, yellow with red veins; sep. glabrous, green with purple margins, without calli. Spring–summer. Peru, Ecuador. Z9.

***O. pes-caprae*** L. BERMUDA BUTTERCUP; ENGLISH-WEED. Bulbous, stemless, glabrous, perenn., flowering to 20–40cm; bulbs with white, fleshy, contractile root and slender vertical stem to the soil surface, stem and crown bearing numerous sessile bulbils. Lvs numerous; petioles 3–12cm, erect to spreading, somewhat succulent; leaflets 3, 16–20×23–32mm, obcordate, bright green often maculate. Peduncles twice as long as petioles, erect; infl. a 3–20-fld umbellate cyme; pedicels somewhat nodding; fls 2–2.5cm across, deep golden yellow; sep. with 2 orange apical calli. Spring–early summer. S Africa (Cape Province). Widely naturalized in milder climates and can be a serious weed of cultivation. Seed is very rarely set in Europe but reproduces asexually by producing numerous bulbils. 'Flore Pleno': double-fld. Z9.

***O. polyphylla*** Jacq. Erect stemmed, bulbous perenn., 5–30cm; bulb to 2–3cm, ovoid, pale to dark brown; stem to 20cm, rather rigid. Lvs numerous, congested at the apices of the stems; petioles 1–5cm; leaflets 3–7, 1–3cm, linear, minutely emarginate, glabrous above, sparsely pubesc. or glabrous beneath, with 2 conspicuous orange-red apical calli. Peduncles 3–10cm, pubesc.; fls solitary, 1.5 to 3cm across, purple, rose-pink to rose-flesh colour or white, throat yellow; sep. with two orange apical calli. A very variable species. Summer. S Africa (Cape Province). Z8.

***O. purpurata*** Jacq. Bulbous perenn., 10–30cm high with no aerial stem; bulb without contractile root, rhizomatous with slender vertical stem to the soil surface and crown; fleshy underground stolons bear apical bulbils or occasionally further crowns. Lvs numerous; petioles to 30cm, erect to spreading, glabrous to pubesc.; leaflets 3, 1.5–5×2.7cm, obcordate, rounded, dark green and glabrous above, dark purple (variable) and hairy beneath, margins ciliate. Peduncles 10–30cm, erect sparsely hairy; infl. a 3–10-fld umbel; fls 2.5cm across, purple to violet with a yellow throat, sep. with 2 orange apical calli. A very variable species. Summer. S Africa (Cape Province). Z9.

***O. purpurea*** L. Bulbous perenn. to 15cm with no aerial stem; bulb to 17mm diam., smooth, rounded, black-brown; slender vertical stem from bulb to soil surface and crown. Petioles 2–8cm, usually spreading to prostrate, white-pubesc.; leaflets 3, 4–40×4–30mm, rhomboid to orbicular, or widely obovate, dark green above, maculate or deep purple beneath, glabrous except for a densely, long-ciliate margin. Peduncles erect, equal or shorter than lvs; fls solitary, 3–5cm across, rose-purple, deep rose to violet and pale violet, yellow, cream or white, all with a yellow throat; sep. without calli. Autumn–winter. S Africa (Cape Province). A very variable species particularly in leaf shape and flower size and colour. 'Bowles' White': fls white. 'Ken Aslet': to 7cm; lvs large, silky; fls yellow. Z8.

***O. regnellii*** Miq. Stemless, rhizomatous perenn. 10–25cm; rhiz. about 5cm long, simple or sparsely branched, vertical, densely covered in tubercle-like deltoid scales about 4mm diam. pressed against it. Lvs quite numerous; petioles 10–15cm, erect to spreading, glabrous; leaflets 3, to 25×50mm, broadly deltoid, emarginate, green suffused purple above, vivid purple beneath, sometimes with dark blotches. Peduncles few, 1–4, 10–20cm long, erect to spreading; infl. a 3–7-fld umbel; fls 1.5–2cm across, pale pink to white. Spring–summer. Peru, Brazil, Bolivia, Paraguay, Argentina. Z8.

***O. rosea*** Jacq. Erect stemmed annual flowering to 20–40cm, glabrous, often reddened at base, entirely herbaceous; stem 10–35cm, not thickened, much branched and leafy throughout. Petioles to 3cm, spreading; leaflets 3, to 11×11mm, obcordate, pale green, occasionally reddened beneath. Peduncles numerous, to 10cm, erect to spreading; infl. a lax bifurcating cyme of 1–3 fls; fls 1–1.5cm across, pink with darker veins and a white throat, rarely entirely white; sep. red-tipped but without calli. Fr. to 8mm, round, seed set readily. Spring. Chile.

***O. rubra*** A. St.-Hil. Clump-forming, stemless perenn. to 40cm, from a semi-woody, tuberous crown; tubers round to cylindrical, covered with red-brown scales, branched in tight clusters, in old plants this may rise above soil surface. Lvs numerous; petioles to 30cm, spreading to erect; leaflets 3, c18×15mm, obcordate, green, maculate, particularly around sinus, glabrous above, hairy beneath, ciliate. Peduncles to 40cm, erect; infl. a 6–12-fld umbellate cyme; fls 1–1.5cm across, red to pink; sep. with several apical calli. Summer. S Brazil to Argentina. 'Alba': fls white. 'Lilacana': fls lilac-purple. Z9.

***O. scandens*** HBK. Stem climbing to 1.5m, more or less herbaceous, glabrous, yellow-green, simple to sparsely branched, internodes 7–15cm. Petioles short, to 4cm; leaflets 3, to 18×13mm, obcordate, sharply toothed on front margin, thin, green, glabrous above, sparsely hairy beneath. Peduncles axillary, very short, 5–6mm, slender, sparsely hairy to glabrous; infl. a 3-fld cyme, cyme branches 2–3cm; fls 1–2cm across, yellow-green; sep. without calli. Spring. Colombia. Z9.

***O. smithiana*** Ecklon & Zeyh. Stemless, rather weak perenn., 10–20cm, glabrous; bulb to 2cm, round-ovate, red-brown with contractile root. Lvs 2–20; petioles 5–18cm, slender; leaflets 3, 1–4.5cm, polymorphous, sometimes heterophyllous, 2-lobed to middle or below almost to base, obcordate to obtriangular in outline, lobes linear, spreading, green, densely punctate above. Peduncles as long or longer than lvs; fls solitary, 2–3cm across, rose-lilac or white, throat yellow-green; sep. with 2 orange apical calli. Spring–summer. S Africa. Z9.

***O. stricta*** L. Annual, erect, single-stemmed when young, becoming branched basally and decumbent with age; stems 10–40cm, glabrous to pubesc., leafy throughout, not rooting at nodes but plant with underground stolons. Lvs tending to be in whorls; petioles 3–10cm, pubesc., stipules absent or very narrow; leaflets 3, 4–20×4–35mm, obcordate, green, glabrous above, somewhat pubesc. beneath. Peduncles 3–10cm, axillary, pubesc.; infl. a 2–5-fld dichotomous cyme; fls *c*1cm across, pale yellow; sep. without calli. Fr. 8–15mm, cylindrical, glabrous or sparsely hairy; seeds brown; pedicels erect in fruit. Summer–autumn. N America, E Asia.

***O. suksdorfii*** Trel. Closely allied and similar to *O. stricta*; differing in stems trailing or decumbent, infl. a 1–3-fld umbel or irregularly branched, fls somewhat larger. Summer–autumn. W US (S Washington to N California). Z7.

***O. tenuifolia*** Jacq. Slender stemmed bulbous perenn. 6–24cm, often caespitose; bulb to 3cm, ovoid, black-brown; stem erect, pubesc., with dense rosettes of lvs in upper parts and numerous short, abortive branches above. Lvs almost sessile, appearing fasciculate; leaflets 3, 4–9mm, linear, somewhat folded or with a rolled margin, emarginate, glabrous above, yellow-pubesc. beneath, maculate at apex and on margins. Peduncles numerous, 1–6cm, yellow pubesc., erect; fls solitary, 2–3cm across, purple to white with purple margin and yellow throat; sep. with apical calli. Winter. S Africa. Z9.

***O. tetraphylla*** Cav. LUCKY CLOVER; GOOD LUCK LEAF; GOOD LUCK PLANT. Bulbous, stemless perenn., flowering to 15–50cm; bulb large, 1.5–3.5cm, covered in hairy scales with fleshy contractile root. Petioles 10–40cm, erect to spreading, sparsely to moderately hairy; leaflets 4 (rarely 3), 2–6.5×2–3cm, strap-shaped to obtriangular, entire or shallowly emarginate, green, usually with a V-shaped purple band near the base pointing to the apex, usually glabrous above, hairy beneath. Peduncles 15–50cm, erect; infl. a 5–12-fld umbel; fls 1–2cm across, red to lilac-pink, rarely white, all with green-yellow throat; sep. with red apical calli. Summer. Mexico. 'Iron Cross': seg. formed by the coloured band on the leaflets entirely purple. Z8.

***O. trilliifolia*** Hook. Stemless perenn. flowering to 15–30cm from a stout, brown, vertical rhiz.; rhiz. 2–3mm thick, 4cm or more long, covered in leaf bases. Petioles 9–25cm, 1–1.5mm thick, rather succulent, erect; leaflets 3, 2.5–4cm, obcordate, glaucous green, glabrous above, hairy beneath, ciliate. Peduncles 10–25cm, erect; infl. a 2–8-fld umbellate cyme; fls *c*2cm across, white to pale violet; sep. without calli. Summer. Pacific N America. Z8.

***O. tuberosa*** Molina. OCA. Erect to decumbent, succulent-stemmed perenn. to 25cm; rhiz. greatly branched, tips swollen into fleshy tubers 4×3cm, covered in small triangular scales; stems fleshy, to 30×1cm, green-purple, densely pubesc., leafy in the upper part. Petioles 7–10cm, spreading, glabrous or sparsely hairy; leaflets 3, to 25×22mm, widely obcordate, green or suffused purple (particularly beneath), densely pubesc., rather thick. Peduncles 15–17cm, spreading, from upper leaf axils; infl. a 5–8-fld umbel; fls to 2cm across, yellow; sep. without calli. Summer. Colombia. Long cultivated as root crop oca of the high Andes, once grown in Europe as potato substitute. Three colours of tuber are grown: yellow, white and red; the red and yellow types have lost the ability to flower. Z7.

***O. valdiviensis*** Barnéoud. Compact, erect-stemmed annual, flowering to 10–25cm or more, glabrous with a thick fleshy taproot; stems (2–)5–10cm, densely leafy, unbranched. Petioles 4–14cm, erect; leaflets 3, 12–20×10–20mm, broadly obcordate with a narrow sinus, pale green, thin. Peduncles 8–18cm, from upper leaf axils; infl. a forked cyme of 4–14 fls; fls 1–1.5cm across, yellow, usually with brown veins; sep. often with a red margin, no calli. Fr. 6mm, globose, pendulous. Chile. Readily sets seed and may become a pest in glasshouses. Z9.

***O. versicolor*** L. Bulbous perenn. rising to 8–20cm high, or more shade, almost glabrous or sparsely pubesc.; bulbs 1.5–2.5cm, ovoid. black-brown; stems 3–15cm, erect to spreading, simple, somewhat woody. Lvs in apical clusters of 8 to 20; petioles 0.5–4cm; leaflets 3, to 12×2mm, cuneate-linear to linear, apex emarginate, glabrous to hairy, apex and margins maculate. Peduncles few, 1–4, to twice as long and thicker than petioles, more or less erect, glabrous to pubesc.; fls solitary, 2–3cm across, white to purple-white, throat yellow, margin purple-violet; sep. with apical calli. A variable species. Summer–autumn. S Africa (Cape Province). 'Candy Cane': compact; lvs small, round; fls white striped red. var. ***flaviflora*** Sonder. Fls yellow. Z9.

***O. violacea*** L. VIOLET WOOD SORREL. Stemless, bulbous perenn. flowering to 20cm or more, usually glabrous; bulb 1cm diam., brown, round, scaly, scales 3-nerved. Petioles 7–13cm, erect; leaflets 3, 8–20×10–28mm, obcordate, green, orange maculate around sinus. Peduncles 9–25cm, erect, much longer than petioles; infl. an umbel of 2–8(–16) fls; fls 1.5–2cm across, lavender, pink or paler (rarely white), all with green throat; sep. without calli. Spring–autumn. N America. Z5.

***O. vulcanicola*** J.D. Sm. Bushy perenn. with lax, succulent, persistent, red stems, 20–70cm tall, spreading with age, stems 2–3mm thick, much branched, hairy above. Lvs concentrated mid-stems upwards, very dense at apex; petioles 3–7cm; leaflets 3, to 4×2cm, obcordate, green flushed red and glabrous above, magenta and pubesc. beneath. Peduncles 4–8cm, almost equalling petioles; infl. 4–7-fld umbellate cyme; fls 1–1.5cm across, yellow with purple-red veins; sep. without calli. Summer–autumn. C America (El Salvador to Panama). Z9.

***O.*** **cultivars**. 'Beatrice Anderson': fls large, pink veined purple. 'Copper Glow': lvs thin, copper; fls yellow.

***O. amplifolia*** (Trel.) Knuth. See *O. drummondii.*
***O. asinina*** Jacq. See *O. fabaefolia.*
***O. binervis*** Reg. See *O. latifolia.*
***O. bipunctata*** Graham. See *O. corymbosa.*
***O. bowieana*** Lodd. See *O. bowiei.*
***O. carnosa*** Molina. See *O. megalorrhiza.*
***O. cathariensis*** N.E. Br. See *O. regnellii.*
***O. cernua*** Thunb. See *O. pes-caprae.*
***O. convexula*** Jacq. See *O. depressa.*
***O. corniculata*** L. (misapplied). See *O. dillenii.*
***O. corniculata*** var. ***microphylla*** Hook. See *O. exilis.*
***O. corniculata*** var. ***purpurata*** Parl. See *O. corniculata* var. *atropurpurea.*
***O. crenata*** Jacq. See *O. tuberosa.*
***O. cumingiana*** Turcz. See *Biophytum sensitivum.*
***O. cymosa*** Small. See *O. stricta.*
***O. debilis*** Kunth. See *O. corymbosa.*
***O. delicata*** Pohl. See *O. rosea.*
***O. dendroides*** HBK. See *Biophytum dendroides.*
***O. deppei*** Lodd. See *O. tetraphylla.*
***O. deppei*** Lodd. (misapplied). See *O. tuberosa.*
***O. elongata*** Jacq. See *O. versicolor.*
***O. enneaphylla*** var. ***patagonica*** (Speg.) Skottsb. See *O. patagonica.*
***O. europaea*** Jordan. See *O. stricta.*
***O. filicaulis*** Jacq. See *O. bifida.*
***O. flabellifolia*** Jacq. See *O. flava.*
***O. floribunda*** Lehm. See *O. articulata.*
***O. floribunda*** Lehm. (misapplied). See *O. bowiei.*
***O. floribunda*** Lehm. (misapplied). See *O. lasiandra.*
***O. floribunda*** Lehm. (misapplied). See *O. rosea.*
***O. floribunda*** Lehm. (misapplied). See *O. rubra.*
***O. floribunda*** var. ***alba*** Nichols. See *O. articulata* var. *hirsuta* 'Alba'.
***O. fontana*** Bunge. See *O. stricta.*
***O. fulgida*** Lindl. See *O. hirta* var. *fulgida.*
***O. grandiflora*** Jacq. See *O. purpurea.*
***O. herrerae*** Knuth (misapplied). See *O. peduncularis.*
***O. hirtella*** Jacq. See *O. hirta.*
***O. inops*** Ecklon & Zeyh. See *O. depressa.*
***O. intermedia*** Rich. (misapplied). See *O. latifolia.*
***O. lactea*** Hook. See *O. magellanica.*
***O. libyca*** Viv. See *O. pes-caprae.*
***O. lupinifolia*** Jacq. See *O. flava.*
***O. martiana*** Zucc. See *O. corymbosa.*
***O. multiflora*** Jacq. See *O. hirta.*
***O. navieri*** Jordan. See *O. dillenii.*
***O. pectinata*** Jacq. See *O. flava.*
***O. peduncularis*** HBK (misapplied). See *O. herrerae.*
***O. pentaphylla*** Sims. See *O. polyphylla.*
***O. punctulata*** Knuth. See *O. versicolor.*
***O. purpurata*** var. ***bowiei*** (Lindl.) Sonder. See *O. bowiei.*
***O. racemosa*** Savigny. See *O. rosea.*
***O. repens*** Thunb. See *O. corniculata.*
***O. rubella*** Jacq. See *O. hirta* var. *rubella.*
***O. rubra*** 'Delicata' (misapplied). See *O. rosea.*
***O. rubra*** Jacq. (misapplied). See *O. rubra.*
***O. sensitivum*** L. See *Biophytum sensitivum.*
***O. siliquosa*** hort. See *O. vulcanicola.*
***O. speciosa*** Jacq. See *O. purpurea.*
***O. squamoso-radicosa*** Steud. See *O. laciniata.*
***O. stricta*** L. (misapplied). See *O. dillenii.*
***O. succulenta*** Barnéoud (misapplied). See *O. herrerae.*
***O. tropaeoloides*** Schlachter. See *O. corniculata* var. *purpurata.*
***O. valdiviana*** hort. See *O. valdiviensis.*
***O. varabilis*** Jacq. See *O. purpurea.*
***O. versicolor*** Jacq., non L. See *O. polyphylla.*
***O. vespertilionis*** Torr. & A. Gray, non Zucc. See *O. drummondii.*
***O. vespertilionis*** Zucc. (misapplied). See *O. drummondii.*
***O. vespertilionis*** Zucc., non Torr. & A. Gray. See *O. latifolia.*

**Oxera** Labill. (From Gk *oxys*, sour, referring to the acrid sap.) ROYAL CLIMBER. Verbenaceae. Some 20 species of shrubs, often scandent, glabrous. Leaves opposite, coriaceous, simple, entire. Flowers white or yellow-white, in axillary, forked cymes, pedicellate, sometimes forming a panicle; calyx 4 or 5-lobed or dentate; corolla 4-lobed; stamens 2, long-exserted. Fruit a drupe. New Caledonia. Z10.

CULTIVATION As for *Petraea.*

***O. pulchella*** Labill. SNOWY OXERA. Scandent, evergreen shrub. Lvs to 12.5cm, entire or dentate, petiolate, upper lvs oblong, lower lvs oblong-lanceolate. Cymes many-fld; fls to 5cm, pendent, white or yellow-white; cal. conspicuous; cor. to 5cm, campanulate or infundibular, lobes broadly oblong. New Caledonia.

**Oxybaphus** L'Hérit. ex Willd. See *Mirabilis.*

**Oxycoccus** Hill.
***O. macrocarpos*** (Ait.) Pers. See *Vaccinium macrocarpon*.
***O. quadripetala*** Gilib. See *Vaccinium oxycoccos*.

**Oxydendrum** DC. (From Gk *oxys*, sharp, and *dendron* tree; the foliage tastes sour.) Ericaceae. 1 species, a tall deciduous shrub to 9m or small tree to 20m. Trunk slender, sometimes multi-stemmed, often curving or arched rather gracefully, bark rusty-red to grey, deeply fissured; branches ascending to horizontal forming a fine canopy in older specimens; branchlets glabrous. Leaves 8–20×3.8–9cm, alternate, oval, elliptic or oblong-lanceolate, acute, serrulate, thin textured, lustrous and glabrous above, glabrous beneath except for sparse down on basal half of midvein, pale to deep green colouring vivid red in autumn. Flowers in slender, terminal panicles 15–25cm long, panicle branches narrow, decurved then upswept, persisting in autumn, imparting a pale, rather ghostly appearance to the whole tree; calyx lobes 5, *c*5mm, pubescent, green-white, ovate or deltoid; corolla 6–9mm, white, cylindric to urceolate, finely downy, lobes 5, small, ovate, recurved; stamens 10, enclosed by corolla, anthers dehiscing through an apical slit. Fruit a 5-celled, woody capsule. Late summer–early autumn. E & SE US. Z5.

CULTIVATION Suitable as a lawn specimen or for growing in open woodland, where it will benefit from the shelter and protection of other trees. A slow-growing tree that rarely achieves its full stature at the northern limits of its hardiness, *Oxydendrum* is grown for its sprays of fragrant white flowers carried in mid- to late summer and for its glossy leaves which colour well in autumn, often in spectacular shades of plum-purple and red. It is slow growing in zones where temperatures drop to −20°C/−4°F. Grow in moist but well-drained soils, pH 4–6, in light dappled shade or in full sun for better flowering and autumn colour. Transplant with care, and maintain an organic mulch; specimens may take some time to re-establish themselves, and should be given careful attention until they do. Propagate from seed sown in autumn or spring, or by softwood cuttings in summer; treat with rooting hormone and root in a closed case with bottom heat.

***O. arboreum*** (L.) DC. SORREL TREE; SOURWOOD; TITI. As for the genus.
For synonymy see *Andromeda* and *Lyonia*.
For illustration see *Ericaceae*.

**Oxylobium** Andrews. (From Gk *oxys*, sharp, and *lobos*, pod; the seed pods are sharp-pointed.) Leguminosae (Papilionoideae). Over 30 species of evergreen shrubs or prostrate subshrubs. Leaves very short-stalked, simple, opposite, in pairs, whorls or, rarely, alternate stipules bristly or scarcely present. Flowers papilionaceous, in terminal, reduced axillary racemes; corolla usually yellow or pink-purple, standard suborbicular to reniform or transverse-elliptic, wings obliquely oblong, or elliptic, straight but incurved from claw, narrower than keel, auriculate, keel obliquely ovate-elliptic, incurved, auriculate or spurred; stamens diadelphous; ovary pilose, style incurved at 90°, stigma capitate, minute. Fruit a dehiscent, turgid legume, ovoid or oblong, usually just exceeding calyx, valves leathery, few- to many-seeded; seeds with or without strophiole. SW Australia. Z9.

CULTIVATION Found in coastal and riverside habitats, and on the higher ground of the tablelands; many species form the shrub layer in *Eucalyptus* forest. In warm temperate regions that are frost-free or almost so, they are grown for their leathery, dark, evergreen foliage and spikes of rich yellow flowers or pink, in shrub borders, in sun and in well-drained soils. In cooler regions they are suitable for tubs in the cool glasshouse or conservatory, cultivation otherwise as for *Brachysema*.

***O. ellipticum*** R. Br. Evergreen shrub to 3m. Stem prostrate or erect. Lvs *c*7.5cm, oval, dark green. Fls yellow. Fr. ovoid.

***O. lanceolatum*** (Vent.) Druce. Pubesc. shrub to 3m with slightly tawny young growth. Lvs *c*10×2cm, in irregular whorls or paired to alternate, lanceolate to ovate-lanceolate, mucronate, leathery; petioles to 5mm. Fls in spike-like terminal racemes to 15cm; pedicels to 4mm; cal. to 7mm, tube densely hairy, teeth lanceolate; cor. to 1.25cm, orange or yellow, standard red-patched, transversely elliptic; ovules 7–9. Fr. to 15×8mm, obliquely ellipsoid, acute or carinate, thickly leathery. Summer.

***O. linariifolium*** (G. Don) Domin. Shrub. Lvs *c*8×1cm, alternate or whorled, narrow-oblong or linear, mucronulate, strongly reticulate; petioles to 4mm; stipules with bristles to 2mm. Primary racemes terminal, often subtended by sub-opposite lvs, to 4cm with 5–20 spreading fls, secondary racemes axillary; pedicels 2mm; cor. yellow and red, standard suborbicular or subcordate to cuneate, yellow; ovary stalked, 16–18-ovulate. Fr. to 15×4mm, thickly downy. Spring. Australia.

***O. pulteneae*** A. DC. Bushy strigulose subshrub to 1m. Lvs *c*1×0.3cm, crowded 2–3 together, elliptic, elliptic-lanceolate, or subulate, coriaceous and thick with margins revolute; petioles some 1mm. Fls 2–4, in reduced terminal racemes; pedicels to 3mm; cal. strigulose or villous; cor. to 1cm, yellow or orange, standard emarginate; ovules 8–13. Fr. some 12×4mm, subsessile, ovoid-acuminate, turgid or compressed, dehiscent, valves thickly papery with long, soft hairs. Spring. Australia (NSW).

***O. callistachys*** hort. See *O. lanceolatum*.
For further synonymy see *Callistachys*.

**Oxypetalum** R. Br.
***O. caeruleum*** (D. Don) Decne. See *Tweedia caesulea*.

**Oxyria** Hill. (From Gk *oxys*, sour, referring to the acid flavour of the stems and leaves.) Polygonaceae. 2 species of glabrous perennial herbs, with stout rootstocks. Leaves nearly all basal, petiolate, stem leaves alternate, few. Flowers fertile, minute, in loose narrow panicles; sepals 4, inner pair enlarged in fruit; stamens 6; stigmas 2. Fruit an achene with 2 broad wings. Arctic, mts of N America, Europe, Asia.

CULTIVATION From arctic and northern temperate mountain habitats, on moist screes at 1700–2800m/2296–9180ft, *O. digyna* is locally common on enriched soils beneath bird roosts. Grown as a pot herb or sometimes as a scree and crevice plant on the rock garden, where it and will self-seed when conditions suit, to the detriment of other finer alpines. *O. digyna* is reliably hardy to −20°C/−4°F. Grow in full sun or partial shade in a moist but freely draining, lime-free soil enriched with leafmould. Propagate by seed or division.

***O. digyna*** (L.) Hill. MOUNTAIN SORREL. Glabrous perenn., 10–30cm, slightly succulent; roots stout. Lvs reniform to cordate, 1.5–2.5×2–4cm, entire, green to green-red in late summer; petiole long; stipules 2.5–5mm, membranous. Fls green, with red margin, in often congested panicles 4–10cm long; outer perianth seg. spreading, reflexed, 2mm; inner seg. 3–4mm in fr., adpressed, emarginate, green to red, ripening to form pale brown membranous wings, surrounding lens-shaped 3–4mm achene. Summer. Range as for the genus. Z2.

**Oxytropis** DC. (From Gk *oxys*, sharp, and *tropis*, keel; the keel petal is toothed at the apex.) POINT VETCH; LOCOWEED; CRAZY WEED. Leguminosae (Papilionoideae). Some 300 species of perennial, caulescent or acaulescent herbs. Lvs imparipinnate; stipules adnate to petiole, free or united; leaflets entire, estipulate. Fls in scapose axillary racemes or spikes; calyx tubular, with subequal teeth; corolla violet, purple, white, or pale yellow, standard erect, ovate or oblong, keel with an apical tooth; stamens 10, 9 united, 1 free. Fr. a legume, sometimes inflated, oblong to ovoid, dehiscent, unilocular or semi-bilocular; seeds several. N temperate regions. Closely related to *Astralagus*, but keel toothed at apex.

CULTIVATION Found in northern temperate, arctic and subarctic zones, in a range of generally impeccably drained habitats: in sandy and gravel soils surrounding glacial lakes, in mountain screes and moraines and in montane grassland. Like the closely related *Astragalus, Oxytropis* spp. are beautiful both in flower, bearing large rounded clusters on slender stems, and in foliage: the rosettes of fine, pinnate leaves are often very woolly or silky. They are grown in the rock garden, raised bed and alpine house, the last offering protection from winter wet – species with downy foliage will not tolerate low temperatures in combination with damp conditions. They resent root disturbance and some spp. fail to thrive in cultivation, probably in the absence of appropriate *Rhizobium*. Grow in full sun in deep, gritty and perfectly drained soils. Protect woolly-leaved species from winter wet with a propped pane of glass. Propagate from seed in early spring under glass, pricking out as cotyledons emerge to minimize damage to the tap root. Grow on in the cold frame, giving protection in the first winter, and plant out the following spring latter. Some species, notably *O. lambertii*, are toxic to stock (cattle, sheep and horses) possibly because they concentrate selenium from the soil, giving rise to a syndrome known as locoism.

***O. campestris*** (L.) DC. MEADOW MILKVETCH; YELLOW OXYTROPIS. Lvs to 15cm, in a basal rosette, 10–15-foliolate long-petioled, connate for about one half of their length, adnate to petiole for about one-third of their length; leaflets to 2.5cm, elliptic or lanceolate, acuminate, pilose-tomentose. Scapes to 20cm; racemes ovoid, 5–15-fld; cal. to 1cm, teeth to 3mm; cor. usually light yellow, standard to 2×1cm, slightly longer than wings, elliptic, broad-elliptic or obovate, emarginate, keel often violet or dark violet at apex, tooth to 2mm. Fr. to 18×8mm, ovoid, erect, long-pubesc. Summer–autumn. N Europe and mts of C & S Europe. ssp. ***sordida*** (Willd.) Hartm. Cal. teeth to 4mm; cor. yellow or light violet, standard slightly longer than wings, limb elliptic, broad elliptic or obovate. Scandinavia, Arctic Russia. ssp. ***tiroliensis*** (Sieber ex Fritsch) Leins & Merxm. Cal. to 8mm, teeth to 2mm; cor. usually light violet or white, standard narrow-elliptic, 2×1cm, wings 13mm. CE Alps. Z3.

***O. foetida*** (Vill.) DC. Acaulescent perenn. with sessile aromatic glands throughout. Stems glutinous. Leaflets 15–25 pairs, thick oblong-lanceolate or lanceolate, clammy, glabrous; stipules adnate to petiole for half their length. Scapes to 15cm, rather longer than lvs, lanate at apex; racemes ovoid, 3–7-fld; cor. yellow, standard to 22mm, limb elliptic. Fr. to 22×6mm, oblong-cylindric, often slightly curved, glandular, with a ventral septum only. Summer. SW Alps. Z6.

***O. halleri*** Bunge ex Koch. PURPLE OXYTROPIS. Acaulescent dwarf perenn. to 15cm, from stout rhiz., with adpressed to patent hairs. Lvs to 2.5cm; leaflets to 6mm, usually 10–14, to 18, in pairs, ovate-lanceolate to lanceolate, acute; stipules mostly free, shortly adnate to petiole. Scapes to 30cm, scapes and petioles with adpressed or erecto-patent hairs, sometimes only sparsely so; racemes 5–15-fld, ovoid, 2.5cm longer than lvs, elongate after flowering; cor. blue-purple, standard to 20mm, keel tooth to 1.5mm, dark purple. Fr. to 20×6mm, ovoid to narrow-ellipsoid, with short, dense, adpressed hairs, ventral and dorsal septa to equal diam., or ventral septum wider. Summer. Pyrenees, Alps, Carpathians, mts of Scotland. ssp. ***velutina*** (Sieber) Schwartz. Scapes usually 2–3mm diam., scapes and petioles densely downy; cor. pale purple. C Alps. Z6.

***O. jacquinii*** Bunge. Stout, caulescent herb to 40cm. Stipules united at base, adnate to petiole for up to one-third of their length; leaflets 14–20 pairs, ovate-lanceolate to lanceolate, sparsely hairy. Racemes subspherical, slightly elongate after flowering; cal. teeth about one quarter as long as tube; cor. purple-violet, standard to 13mm. Fr. to 30×8mm, unilocular, lanceolate-ovoid, acuminate, suberect, with hairs to 0.5mm. Alps. Z5.

***O. lambertii*** Pursh. PURPLE LOCO; LOCOWEED. Tufted, sometimes silky-pubesc. Lvs to 20cm; leaflets 7–15, linear to ovate, apex acute. Racemes 15cm, with 10–25 purple or pink to white fls; standard to 2.5cm. Fr. ovoid to ellipsoid, leathery, pubesc. SW US. Z3.

***O. lapponica*** (Wahlenb.) Gay. Resembles *O. jacquinii*, but stipules united for at least half their length and quite shortly adnate to petiole, fr. pendulous. Dwarf perenn. to 10cm, hairy. Leaflets to 14 pairs, oblong-lanceolate or lanceolate, with adpressed hairs throughout. Infl. short, 6–12-fld; racemes subspherical, scarcely elongate after flowering; cor. violet-blue, standard to 12mm suborbicular. Fr. narrow-oblong, to 1.5cm, pendulous, with short, adpressed hairs. Summer. Mts of Lapland, Pyrenees, Alps. Z3.

***O. lazica*** Boiss. Stemless, procumbent. Lvs 3–7cm; leaflets 0.3–1×0.4cm, in 6–15 pairs, oblong-ovate to elliptic, pilose. Scape 7–14cm suberect; infl. dense, with 4–10 white to purple-blue fls; cal. pubesc.; standard 1.7–2.2cm. Fr. 2cm, curved, oblong-ovate, adpressed pubesc. Asia Minor. Z5.

***O. megalantha*** H. Boissieu. Tufted. Stems procumbent to ascending, densely white or grey hairy. Lvs 5–8cm, radical; leaflets 2–3cm, 17–23, oblong-ovate to broadly lanceolate, slightly pubesc. above, densely so beneath. Scape 20cm; infl. with 7 purple-blue fls to 2cm; cal. silky-pubesc. outside. Japan. Z6.

***O. pilosa*** (L.) DC. WOOLLY MILKVETCH. Resembles *O. fetida*, but nearly or wholly eglandular. Perenn. to 50cm. Stem and petioles with patent hairs. Stipules narrow-triangular, very shortly adnate to the petiole; leaflets usually 9–13 pairs, occasionally to 15 pairs, linear-oblong or oblong, with adpressed hairs. Racemes ovoid to oblong, many-fld; cor. light yellow, standard to 14mm, broad-ovate. Fr. to 2cm, narrow-ovoid to cylindric, with long, dense, erecto-patent hairs and only a ventral septum. C & E Europe. Z6.

***O. pyrenaica*** Godron & Gren. Resembles *O. jacquinii*, with which it hybridizes. Dwarf perenn. to 15cm. Stipules free from each other but shortly adnate to petiole; leaflets to 20 pairs, oblong-elliptic or lanceolate, pointed, slightly concave, sericeous. Scape to 20cm, stout, lanate; racemes 8–20-fld, short, crowded, ovoid to spherical; cal. teeth usually more than half as long as tube; cor. purple or blue-violet, standard to 12mm. Fr. to 20×7mm, narrowly ovoid, acuminate, sparsely pubesc. Summer. Mts of S & SC Europe, especially Pyrenees. Z6.

***O. sericea*** Nutt. ex Torr. & A. Gray non (Lam.) Simonkai. Tufted herb. Lvs to 30cm, sericeous, canescent, rarely green, 9–25-foliolate; stipules to 3cm; leaflets to 4×1cm, opposite or somewhat scattered, ovate to lanceolate, obtuse or acute. Scapes to 30cm, usually stout, pilose; racemes to 18cm, 6–27-fld; pedicels to 3mm; cal. to 12.5mm, pubesc.; cor. usually white, standard to 2.5cm×12mm, oblong-obovate, deeply emarginate, wings to 2cm, keel to 2cm. Fr. to 25×8mm, narrow-oblong or ovoid-oblong, coriaceous. N America. Z3.

***O. shokanbetsuensis*** Miyabe & Tatew. Tufted, sparsely white-hairy. Stems to 15cm, procumbent. Lvs 6–10cm, lanceolate, white-pubesc.; leaflets 1–1.5×0.4cm, 19–26, glabrous above, pubesc. beneath. Scapes to 10cm, 5-fld; fls 2–2.3cm, purple-red. Japan. Z7.

***O. splendens*** Douglas. To 45cm, densely silky-pubesc. Lvs to 25cm, leaflets 2cm, in 7–15 clusters of 2–4, elliptic to lanceolate, acute. Fls pink to deep pink. Fr. 1.5cm, papery. W US. Z6.

***O. uralensis*** (L.) DC. Resembles *O. halleri*, but racemes do not elongate after flowering, and dorsal septum of fr. wider than the ventral septum. Summer. Ural Mts. Z6.

*O. albiflora* (Nels.) Schum. non Bunge. See *O. sericea*.
***O. montana*** ssp. ***jacquinii*** (Bunge) Hayek. See *O. jacquinii*.
***O. montana*** ssp. ***samnitica*** (Arcang.) Hayek. See *O. pyrenaica*.
***O. micans*** Freyn & Sint. See *O. lazica*.
***O. sericea*** (Lam.) Simonkai non Nutt. ex Torr. & A. Gray. See *O. halleri*.
***O. sordida*** (Willd.) Pers. See *O. campestris* ssp. *sordida*.
***O. tiroliensis*** Sieber ex Fritsch. See *O. campestris* ssp. *tiroliensis*.
For further synonymy see *Astragalus*.

**Ozothamnus** R. Br. (From Gk *ozos*, branch, and *thamnos*, shrub.) Compositae. About 50 species of evergreen shrubs and woody perennial herbs. Leaves alternate, simple, small and often heath-like. Capitula discoid, often in dense corymbs; involucre oblong-ovoid to turbinate-campanulate; phyllaries usually imbricate, with papery appendages, often conspicuously radiate, white, simulating ray florets; florets hermaphrodite, outer sometimes female. Fruit a glabrous to shortly villous cypsela; pappus of bristles. Australasia. Closely related to *Helichrysum*, in which it is usually included. Z9 unless specified.

CULTIVATION A diverse genus including smaller species with closely adpressed scale-like leaves suitable for the rock garden, trough and alpine house, such as *O. coralloides* and *O. selago*, and larger species for the shrub and mixed border; some, such as *O. secundiflorus*, the cascade everlasting, and *O. thyrsoideus* have flowers particularly well suited to drying. The shrubs are valued for their flowers and the dense, deep green foliage, a number of them, especially *O. hookeri*, *O. ledifolius* and *O. ericifolius*, with sweetly aromatic and volatile exudates that suit them well to sheltered situations where their perfume can permeate still air. *O. rosmarinifolius* is particularly attractive before flowering, when the close clusters of dark red buds contrast well with the white stems and dark green rosemary-like foliage.

*Ozothamnus* is frequently considered a tender genus although the neat and rounded *O. ledifolius* and the slender and upright *O. rosmarinifolius* will tolerate temperatures to −10°C/14°F, probably more with good drainage and shelter from cold drying winds; *O. antennaria* shows similar tolerance and *O. hookeri* and *O. thyrsoideus* have survived cold to −5°C/23°F without harm. Most species are found in dry or freely draining habitats and thrive in warm, sunny and sheltered situations with a sharply drained soil, especially so for alpine species *O. coralloides* and *O. selago*. *O. rosmarinifolia* occurs in the wild on moist and peaty heaths and by watercourses and more luxuriant growth may be had on moisture-retentive (but still well-drained) soils. Cut back leggy specimens in spring before growth commences. Propagate by semi-ripe cuttings in summer.

***O. antennaria*** (DC.) Hook. f. Shrub to 3m, young branches glutinous grey- to tawny-scurfy. Lvs to 3×1.5cm, oblanceolate to obovate, obtuse, glabrous, dark green above, grey or tawny scurf beneath; petioles very short. Capitula to 6mm diam., in dense clusters; phyllaries downy; florets over 20, dull white. Tasmania, especially mountains. Z8.

***O. coralloides*** Hook. f. Shrub to 50cm, branches spreading, densely tomentose. Lvs closely adpressed, imbricate, to 5×3mm, oblong, obtuse, margins revolute, thick and leathery toward apex, concave and densely woolly tomentose above, convex or obscurely keeled beneath, glabrous, lustrous. Capitula 6–8mm diam., solitary, surrounded by lvs; phyllaries in 3 series, linear-oblong, rigid, often recurved; florets 20–40, outer female. New Zealand. Z8.

***O. depressus*** Hook. f. Suberect or prostrate shrub to 1m, white- to grey-tomentose, branches spreading. Lvs closely adpressed, loosely imbricate, to 3mm, linear, concave, obtusely keeled, loosely woolly above, silky beneath. Capitula *c*4mm diam., solitary; phyllaries to 5mm, few, linear, acute glabrate or base densely tomentose; florets 8–12, outer 2–3 female. Summer. New Zealand.

***O. diosmifolius*** (Vent.) DC. Erect shrub to 3m, branches woolly to coarsely hairy. Lvs to 2cm, linear, closely revolute, usually tuberculate, rough above, woolly beneath. Capitula in terminal corymbs; phyllaries lacking radiating tips, spreading at length, stiff, white, outermost often tinged pink, opaque. SE Queensland, NSW.

***O. ericifolius*** Hook. f. Evergreen shrub, densely leafy, branching, to 3m; young stems downy. Lvs to 6×2mm, oblong-linear, obtuse, spreading, leathery, margins strongly revolute, glabrous or with few hairs above, downy with a sweetly aromatic, yellow exudate beneath. Capitula terminal on main and lateral branches, forming very long floral sprays; phyllaries light brown, inner with white, spreading tips; florets 5–6. Tasmania. Z8.

***O. glomeratus*** (Raoul) Hook. f. Shrub, to 3m, branches spreading, tomentose above. Lvs to 3×2cm, orbicular to broadly ovate or ovate-spathulate, obtuse to minutely apiculate, base abruptly attenuate, entire, glabrous, minutely reticulate above, tomentose beneath, petiole to 5mm. Capitula *c*3mm diam., sessile or in stalked, subglobose corymbs; phyllaries few, in 3 series, oblong, brown, base woolly; florets 8–15, outer 2–3 often female. New Zealand.

***O. gunnii*** Hook. f. Shrub, to 3m, branches densely woolly-tomentose. Lvs to 4cm, linear, mostly obtuse, margins revolute, tomentose above at first, becoming glabrous, woolly beneath. Capitula *c*5mm diam., in broad, dense, compound corymbs; phyllaries numerous, inner with white, radiating tips; florets 6–14, outer rarely female. Summer. Tasmania.

***O. hookeri*** Sonder. Erect shrub, to 2m. Lvs small, scale-like, erect, closely adpressed, margins reflexed, concave above, woolly beneath. Capitula small, in dense clusters; phyllaries few, inner with white, scarcely spreading tips; florets 2–4, all hermaphrodite. Summer. Victoria, Tasmania.

***O. ledifolius*** (DC.) Hook. f. KEROSENE WEED. Shrub to 1m, young shoots downy, older lvs and branches viscid, producing a sweetly aromatic yellow exudate. Lvs to 15×2mm, oblong to linear, obtuse, spreading, leathery, margins strongly revolute, glabrous or with few hairs above, downy beneath, rufescent at first. Capitula in dense terminal corymbs; phyllaries imbricate, tawny to yellow or red, innermost with white radiating tips, downy, viscid; florets 7–15, outer female. Tasmania. The aromatic secretion makes the plant highly inflammable, hence the popular name. Z8.

***O. purpurascens*** DC. Like *O. ericifolius* but lvs to 2cm and acute, with curry-like odour, and phyllaries usually pink to purple; florets 8–10. Tasmania.

***O. rosmarinifolius*** (Labill.) DC. Shrub to 3m, branches erect, more or less woolly at first. Lvs crowded, to 40×2mm, linear, mucronate, woolly beneath, margins revolute. Capitula to 4mm diam., many, in dense corymbs; phyllaries imbricate, sparsely hairy, light brown, usually crimson-tinged, inner with white radiating tips; florets *c*5–7. Summer. NSW, Victoria, Tasmania. Z8.

***O. scutellifolius*** Hook. f. Shrub to 2m, tomentose. Lvs minute, scale like, ovate, reflexed, margins revolute, glabrous to tomentose above, tomentose beneath. Capitula *c*4mm diam., in clusters of 3–5; phyllaries few, woolly pale brown, apices white, not spreading; florets 10–15, several outer florets female. Summer. Tasmania.

***O. secundiflorus*** (Wakef.) C. Jeffrey. Shrub to 2m, branches white-woolly. Lvs to 12mm, oblong-linear, sparsely downy above, densely woolly beneath. Capitula numerous, pendent, in clusters on short lateral branches forming long floral sprays, fragrant; phyllaries russet, inner with white radiating tips; florets *c*15. NSW, Victoria.

***O. selaginoides*** Sonder & F. Muell. Spreading perenn. herb or subshrub, to 30cm, glabrous. Lvs small, obtuse, spreading to almost recurved, base decurrent, fleshy, convex or flat beneath. Capitula *c*4mm diam., sessile in terminal clusters; phyllaries few, innermost with broad, white, spreading tips; florets 8, all hermaphrodite. Summer. Tasmania.

***O. selago*** Hook. f. Shrub to 40cm, young shoots arching or pendulous, tomentose. Lvs minute, densely imbricate, adpressed, ovate-deltoid, obtuse to subacute, thick and leathery in upper part, concave, woolly above, glabrous, lustrous, keeled beneath. Capitula *c*6mm diam., solitary; phyllaries to 5mm, in 3 series, linear-oblong, dull white or yellow-tinged, outer tomentose at base, inner leathery beneath, glabrous, tips spreading; florets 35–45, outer female. Summer. New Zealand (South Is.). Z8.

***O. thyrsoideus*** DC. SNOW IN SUMMER. Shrub to 3m, young shoots glutinous. Lvs to 5cm, narrowly linear, adpressed, dark green, resinous above, paler beneath with fine, adpressed down, except green midrib and narrowly recurved margins. Capitula *c*4mm diam., crowded in dense, rounded corymbs to 2cm; phyllaries pale brown, papery, inner with white, radiating tips. Summer. NSW, Victoria, Tasmania.

***O. vauvilliersii*** Hombron & Jacquinot ex Decne. See *Cassinia vauvilliersii*.
For further synonymy see *Helichrysum* and *Swammerdamia*.

# P

**Pabstia** Garay. (Named in honour of Dr. Guido Pabst, author of numerous articles on Brazilian orchids.) Orchidaceae. Some 5 species of epiphytic orchids allied to *Zygopetalum*. Pseudobulbs ovoid-cylindrical, with 2 leaves at apex and basally sheathed by leafy bracts. Leaves lanceolate, distichous, plicate. Inflorescence equalling leaves, few-flowered; flowers large, showy; sepals free, subequal; petals subsimilar to sepals, often with distinct coloration; lip shorter than sepals and petals, simple to trilobed, clawed, disc with a fleshy, basal, grooved callus; column curved, stout, dorsally pubesc., anther terminal, operculate, incumbent, pollinia 4, globose or subglobose, stipe obovate-oblong. Brazil. Z10.

CULTIVATION As for *Coelia*.

***P. jugosa*** (Lind.) Garay. Pseudobulbs 5.5–7×1.75–3cm, elongate-ovoid, clustered, compressed. Lvs 15–25×4.5–5cm, subcoriaceous, short-acuminate, dark lustrous green. Infl. 12–20cm, erect or arching 1-to few-fld; fls 5.5–7.5cm diam., fleshy, fragrant, long-lived; sep. to 3–3.25×1.5–1.7cm, white or cream, oblong or obovate-oblong, obtuse, spreading; pet. to 2.8×1.6cm, white or green-white, heavily blotched, spotted or broken-banded dark chocolate, maroon or rose-purple, narrowly obovate-oblong, obtuse or rounded, erect-spreading; lip to 2.5×1.3cm, white or cream, streaked and blotched violet-purple or rose purple, fleshy, deeply 3-lobed, lateral lobes small, erect, rounded, midlobe semicircular, rounded, disc 4-ridged, puberulent; column to 1.3cm, white spotted purple above. Summer. Brazil.

For synonymy see *Colax* and *Maxillaria*.

**Pachira** Aubl. (Name used in Guyana for these trees.) SHAVING-BRUSH TREE. Bombacaceae. 24 species of evergreen or deciduous shrubs or trees to 30m; trunk and branches sometimes spiny. Leaves to 30cm, alternate, digitate, leaflets 3–9, entire, elliptic to obovate-oblong, articulate at base. Flowers axillary, solitary or in few- to many-flowered cymes, subtended by 2–3 bracteoles, pedicel short; calyx cup-shaped, truncate or minutely dentate, or 3–5-lobed, persistent; petals to 35cm, 5, narrow, green- to yellow-white, or pink to red and purple, tomentose on external side; stamens very numerous, fused at base into long tube subequalling petals, free above, sometimes grouped in 5–15 fascicles; ovary 5-locular. Fruit a dehiscent woody capsule; seeds many, embedded in fleshy or fibrous pulp. Tropical America. Z10.

CULTIVATION As for *Ceiba*.

***P. aquatica*** Aubl. GUIANA CHESTNUT; WATER CHESTNUT; PROVISION TREE. Small tree, 5–20m. Leaflets to 30cm, 5–9, obovate to elliptic or elliptic-lanceolate, subsessile, glabrous. Fls short-lived; cal. campanulate to tubular, to 2cm, 5-glandular at base; pet. 35×2.5cm, green- to yellow-white, or pink to purple; stamens equalling pet., tube to 12.5cm, fil. white to red or scarlet, anth. red. Fr. subglobose to elliptic, to 30×12.5cm, brown. Estuaries, Mexico to northern S America.

***P. fendleri*** Seem. Tree to 30m; trunk with large buttresses, covered with stout spines as are branches. Leaflets 5, obovate, to 18cm, glabrous. Cal. truncate or undulate, to 1.5cm; pet. to 11cm×8mm, linear, white on inner side, brown externally; stamens in 5 fascicles, to 8.5cm. Fr. to 10cm, oblong-obovoid, 5-angled, densely packed with yellow-brown to brown fibres within; seeds many. Nicaragua to Colombia (lowland wet forest).

***P. insignis*** (Sw.) Savigny. WILD CHESTNUT. Tree to 30m, resembling *P. aquatica* but leaflets to 23×9cm, 5–7, obovate-oblong, entire. Cal. open-campanulate, often lacking glands; pet. to 23cm, erect, spreading above, brown-red to scarlet or purple, brown-tomentose externally; stamens very numerous, fil. purple above and sometimes at base, white below, anth. yellow. Fr. globose to ellipsoid, to 25cm. Brazil (dry forest).

***P. macrocarpa*** (Schldl. & Cham.) Walp. See *P. aquatica*.
***P. quinata*** hort. See *P. fendleri*.
For further synonymy see *Bombacopsis*.

**Pachycereus** (A. Berger) Britt. & Rose. (From Gk *pachys*, thick, and *Cereus*.) Cactaceae. 9 species of tree-like or shrubby cacti, often massive; stems stout, erect. Flowering areoles more or less different from the non-flowering, usually confluent, or connected by a groove, densely felted, spineless, or furnished with numerous long, setaceous spines; flowers small to medium-sized, diurnal or nocturnal, shortly tubular, funnelform or campanulate; tube with scales; floral areoles naked or woolly and/or bristly. Fruit subglobose, fleshy with red or purple pulp or soon dry, generally densely bristly, at least the apex, sometimes the bristles caducous; seeds broadly oval, 2.4–4.8×1.8–3.5mm, black-brown, shiny, not wrinkled or ridged, periphery keeled or not; relief flat or low-domed. Mexico.

CULTIVATION Grow in an intermediate greenhouse (min. 10–15°C/50–60°F); use 'standard' cactus compost: moderate to high inorganic content (more than 50% grit), pH 6–7.5; shade in hot weather; maintain low humidity; keep dry from mid-autumn until early spring, except for light misting on warm days in late winter.

***P. grandis*** Rose. Tree very similar to *P. pecten-aboriginum* and *P. pringlei*, but with a more fastigiate habit; trunk to 1m diam.; ribs 9–11; areoles discrete; central spines 3, lowest longest, to 6cm; radial spines 9–10, short. Fl. *c*4cm. Fr. as in *P. pecten-aboriginum*. S Mexico. Z9.

***P. hollianus*** (F.A.C. Weber ex J. Coult.) F. Buxb. Shrub to 4–5m, unbranched or sparsely branched from the base; stems 4–6cm diam., bark grey-green; ribs 8–14; areoles 1–3cm apart; central spines 3–5, 3–5(–10)cm, flattened in section, red-brown first, later grey or almost black; radial spines 12–14, unequal, 1–3.4cm. Fl. subapical, broadly tubular-campanulate, 7–10×3–3.5cm; scales of pericarpel and tube brown; floral areoles with wool, long hairs and bristles; outer tepals brown-green, inner white. Fr. ovoid, 6–8cm, brown-red; areoles with spines and bristles, deciduous at maturity; pulp purple. S Mexico (Puebla). Z9.

***P. marginatus*** (DC.) Britt. & Rose. Shrub 3–5(–7)m, unbranched or sparsely branched base; stems erect, 8–15(–20)cm diam., dark green; ribs 4–7; areoles adjacent or confluent; central spines 1–2, 10–15mm; radial spines *c*7, usually only 2–4mm. Flowering areoles with more numerous and bristly spines; fls 1–2 per areole, tubular, 3–5×3cm; floral areoles woolly and sometimes with small spines; inner tepals pale green-white or pink. Fr. 4cm diam., red, tinged yellow. C & S Mexico. Z9.

***P. militaris*** (Audot) D. Hunt. Tree to 5–6m; branches numerous, erect, *c*12cm diam., dark grey-green; ribs 5–7 on young branches, later up to 9–11; non-flowering areoles 5–10mm apart; spines 8–14, to 1cm, weak. Flowering zone an apical cephalium, 25–30×18–20cm overall; flowering areoles with numerous dense golden bristles, *c*5.5cm; fls 6–7×3.5–4cm; pericarpel and tube yellow-green; floral areoles with dense white, woolly hairs and a few bristles; inner tepals pale green. Fr. oblong, 3.5×2cm, red at first, soon dry, bristly at apex only. SW Mexico (Colima to Guerrero). In the 1970s, numerous top-cuts of stems with the remarkable 'Grenadier's Cap' cephalium were imported to Europe and rooted, but few have been coaxed into vegetative growth. Z9.

***P. pecten-aboriginum*** (Engelm.) Britt. & Rose. Resembling *P. pringlei*, but not glaucous when young and differing in having fewer (10–11) ribs and spines (8–12), and less woolly flowers. W Mexico. Z9.

***P. pringlei*** (S. Wats.) Britt. & Rose. Massive tree to 15m, with short trunk to 1m or more diam.; branches few to many, erect, 25–50cm diam., blue-green; ribs 11–15(–17); areoles discrete on young stems, 1–2cm apart and heavily spined, later becoming confluent or connected by a felted groove and less spiny; spines 20 or more on young stems, 1–3cm or sometimes the central longer, stout. Fl. 6–8cm; pericarpel and tube densely woolly in the axils of the scales; inner tepals white. Fr. 5–7cm diam., brown-felted and densely bristly, soon dry. NW Mexico (Baja California and Sonora). Z9.

***P. schottii*** (Engelm.) D. Hunt. Large shrub, 3–7m, branching at the base; stems numerous, erect, 10–15cm diam.; ribs usually 5–7; non-flowering areoles 2–2.5cm apart on lower part of stem, with *c*8–10 spines up to 12mm. Flowering areoles only 5–6mm apart, with very numerous weak, bristly spines, somewhat flattened and twisted, 3–7.5cm; fl. 1–several per areole, funnelform, nocturnal, *c*4×3cm with disagreeable smell; floral areoles sparsely woolly or naked; inner tepals pink or white. Fr. globose to ovoid 2.5–3×2–2.5cm, red, fleshy, spineless, splitting when ripe; pulp red. NW Mexico, SW US (S Arizona). *P. schottii* 'Monstrosus' is a peculiar spineless variant with irregular and distorted ribs. Z9.

***P. weberi*** (J. Coult.) Backeb. Massive candelabriform tree to 10m with short thick trunk and dense crown; branches numerous, vertical, *c*20cm diam., blue-green; ribs *c*10; areoles 2–3cm apart, grey-white felted, in adult stems connected by a narrow groove; central spine 1, to 10cm, stout, somewhat flattened; radial spines 6–12, 1–2cm. Fl. funnelform, 8–10cm; floral areoles with brown hairs and sparse bristles; inner tepals white. Fr. 6–7cm diam., densely covered with yellow bristly spines, splitting when ripe; pulp red. S Mexico. Z9.

***P. chrysomallus*** (Lem.) Schum. See *P. militaris*.
***P. columna-trajani*** (Karw. ex Pfeiff.) Britt. & Rose. See *Cephalocereus columna-trajani*.
***P. ruficeps*** (F.A. Weber ex Roland-Goss.) Britt. & Rose. See *Neobuxbaumia macrocephala*.
***P. tetetzo*** (F.A. Weber ex Schum.) Ochot. See *Neobuxbaumia tetetzo*.
For further synonymy see *Backebergia*, *Cephalocereus*, *Cereus*, *Lemaireocereus* and *Lophocereus*.

For illustration see CACTI and SUCCULENTS.

**Pachycymbium** Leach. (From Gk *pachys*, thick, and *kymbion*, a small cup, due to the thick, fleshy, campanulate flowers.) Asclepiadaceae. 32 species of succulent, leafless, perennial herbs, to about 20cm. Stems often rhizomatous, bluntly 4-angled, dark-mottled, teeth conical or flattened-deltoid, tapering, tuberculose, prominent, apices soft, subulate, formed by indistinct leaves. Inflorescence a 1- to few-flowered cyme, toward stem apex, sessile or pedicels short; corolla to 3cm diam., campanulate to flat, sometimes with a thickened annulus at tube mouth, lobed, corona variable, inner lobes lying almost on top of anthers. Fruit a spindle-shaped follicle, in pairs. Africa, Arabia. Z9.

CULTIVATION As for *Stapelia*, but with a winter minimum of 10°C/50°F; extra care should be taken with watering.

***P. baldratii*** (A. White & B.L. Sloane) M. Gilbert. Stems about 10cm, branched, 4-angled, not markedly grooved between angles, often tinged purple, teeth patent, apices pointing upwards. Fls sessile; cor. 2–8cm diam., pale mahogany brown or cream with tiny red spots, densely red-hispidulous, lobes dark mahogany brown, replicate toward apex; outer corona black-purple, cup-shaped, lobes 0.5mm, broadly rounded, inner corona with cerise lobes, each with 2 horns. Most material labelled as *P. baldratii* is *P. meintjesianum*. Eritrea, Kenya, N Tanzania.

***P. carnosum*** (Stent) Leach. Stems 6–15×4.5cm, 4-angled, grey-green spotted red, teeth 12mm, pointed, hard. Fls 1–3, 9–10mm diam., campanulate, exterior grey-mauve spotted red, interior deep cream with minute and dense tuberculate hairs, spotted dark red, 5-angled red-spotted ring around tube mouth. S Africa (Transvaal).

***P. decaisneanum*** (Lem.) M. Gilbert. Stems 10–40×1.5cm, erect, branching, tapering toward apex, green, mottled brown, distinctly grooved between rounded angles, teeth to 1.5cm, stout. Fls to 3; pedicels to 5mm; cor. 2.5cm diam., flat, dark purple, with pale papillae, tube short, campanulate, lobes 1–1.2cm, ovate-oblong, acute. Senegal, Mauritania, Morocco, Chad, Sudan.

***P. deflersianum*** (Lavranos) M. Gilbert. Stems to 7×1.5cm ascending, 4-angled, grey-green, with many oblong, brown blotches teeth to 12mm, stout, acute, patent. Fls solitary, toward stem apex; pedicels erect, to 1cm; cor. campanulate, grey-green with brown spots outside, tube cylindric, 1.3×1cm, base pink, glabrous, otherwise dark maroon, minutely warty, lobes 1.8cm, ovate-lanceolate, slightly ascending, dark purple-brown, with dense, hair-tipped papillae, margins revolute; outer corona pink, lobes fused, pouch-like, concave, margins dark purple-brown, inner corona dark purple-brown, lobes 4mm, linear. S Yemen.

***P. dummeri*** (N.E. Br.) M. Gilbert. Stems to 12×1cm, bluntly 4-angled, grey-green, striped dark red-brown, teeth to 10mm, spreading. Fls 1–4; pedicels erect, 1–1.5cm; cor. to 3.5cm diam., dark green, deeply lobed, tube 6mm, saucer-shaped, smooth, glabrous (mouth tuberculose), lobes 1.4cm, lanceolate or ovate-lanceolate, spreading, with dense, yellow-green, spindle-shaped papillae within, apical hairs 3mm; corona appearing 1-whorled, outer lobes cup-shaped, to 1mm, inner lobes to 2mm, apices irregularly 5-toothed. Uganda, Kenya, Tanzania.

***P. gemugofanum*** (M. Gilbert) M. Gilbert. Stems to 22cm, erect or procumbent, teeth tuberculose, to 2.2cm. Fls 1–3; pedicels to 5mm; cor. flat to shallowly campanulate, fleshy, deeply lobed, bright yellow or green-yellow to pale brown, often more brightly coloured toward centre, glabrous, smooth, tube 8mm diam., lobes to 12.5mm, ovate to deltoid, slightly revolute; outer corona dull pink, margin brown or shiny dark red, disc-like, about 5mm diam., inner corona dark red to umber, sometimes shiny. S Ethiopia.

***P. keithii*** (R.A. Dyer) Leach. Stems 7–9×3–4.5cm, branching at base, erect or spreading, glabrous, glaucous-green mottled red-brown, teeth to 1.5cm, alternate, acute. Fls 1–3, in clusters; pedicels to 2mm; cor. 1–2cm diam., dark maroon with sparse ivory spots, wrinkled, tube campanulate, warty, with a raised, 5-angled annulus, lobes 5mm, deltoid-acute, papillose, margins with clavate cilia; corona stalked, ochre, flushed red, outer whorl cup-shaped, lobes deeply bifid, inner corona lobes 0.5mm, spreading. S Africa (Natal, Transvaal), Swaziland, Zimbabwe, Mozambique.

***P. meintjesianum*** (Lavranos) M. Gilbert. Stems to 8×2cm, ascending, glaucous-green with darker or purple-brown spots, 4-angled, teeth to 5mm, stout. Fls solitary; pedicels 1cm; cor. to 3.5cm diam., flat, deeply lobed, glaucous-green blotched purple below, green-yellow with tiny blood-red spots above, minutely papillose, glabrous, lobes 1.5cm, deltoid, acute, with a central band of denser spots, edged blood-red, tipped olive green; outer corona 8mm diam., golden-yellow sparsely blotched red, lobes pouch-like, fused, inner corona golden-yellow with dense, tiny, blood-red spots, lobes 1mm. S Yemen.

***P. rogersii*** (L. Bol.) M. Gilbert. Stems to 10cm×8mm, ascending, prominently 4-angled, green, glabrous, teeth to 1.5cm, subulate. Fls in 3–4 dense clusters along stem; pedicels 1.3–1.5cm; cor. 3–3.5cm diam., pale yellow, tube 5mm diam. with dense, short, globose papillae, lobes slender, linear-acute, usually ascending to incurved, minutely papillose, margins replicate toward apex, ciliate toward base; outer corona lobes 3mm, oblong, spreading, apex, 3-toothed, inner corona lobes 8mm, erect, deeply bifid, twisted together at tips, fused at base to outer corona. Botswana, Zimbabwe, S Africa (Transvaal).

***P. schweinfurthii*** (A. Berger) M. Gilbert. Stems to 10×1.5cm, freely branching, bluntly 4-angled, pale green, with minute, pale red spots or stripes, glabrous, teeth to 1.5cm, apex small. Fls 2–5; pedicels erect, 3mm; cor. 1.5–2.5cm diam., flat, deeply lobed, pale green with pale brown blotches below, brown or yellow, spotted wine-red or purple, tuberculose and papillose above, tube flat, densely hairy, annulus at mouth, lobes deltoid-ovate, sparsely hairy; corona cream, outer whorl flat, star-shaped, margins lacerate. C and CE Africa.

***P. sprengeri*** (N.E. Br.) M. Gilbert. Stems to 15×1.5cm, erect to procumbent, branching freely, 4-angled, pale green with tiny red spots or stripes, teeth to 1.5cm. Fls in clusters of 5–6; pedicels stout, 3mm; cor. 2.3cm diam., flat, deeply lobed, pale green with small stripes and blotches below, light grey-brown to dark brown above, hairy, tube densely so, saucer-shaped, mouth slightly thickened, lobes 1–2cm, narrowly lanceolate to ovate, with hair-tipped papillae, slightly revolute, spreading; corona yellow to pink-brown or dark brown, outer whorl annular, truncate, inner corona lobes oblong. Ethiopia, Somalia, Sudan.

For synonymy see *Caralluma* and *Stapelia*.

**Pachylophus** Spach.
***P. macroglottis*** Rydb. See *Oenothera caespitosa* ssp. *macroglottis*.

**Pachyphragma** Rchb. (From Gk *pachys*, thick and *phragma*, fence, referring to the stout, ribbed septum of the pod.) Cruciferae. 1 species, a perennial, rhizomatous herb to 40cm. Rhizome to 8mm diam., coated in persistent old petiole bases. Leaves radical, 5–11×5–15cm, ovate-reniform or nearly round, cordate at base, crenate; petiole to 25cm. Stems leaves 4–5, smaller than basal leaves. Flowering stem to 40cm, simple; corymb dense, to 25-flowered; pedicels 9–20mm; flowers malodorous; sepals 4, ovate, 2mm; petals 4, to 9mm, white, veins pale green. Fruit a silicle 8–12×10–16mm, compressed, winged; seeds 2–3mm wide, brown, smooth. Caucasus, NE Turkey, naturalized GB. Z7.

CULTIVATION The glossy, dark green foliage of *P. macrophylla*, made up of almost circular, overlapping leaves, makes excellent weed-smothering groundcover in shade. It grows at a moderate pace and rarely becomes a nuisance. Masses of tiny white flowers emerge in late winter and early spring, often coincident with late snowdrops, followed by the re-growth of its winter-persistent rosettes, which achieve full cover and mid- to late spring. *Pachyphragma* withstands winter temperatures to at least −15°C/5°F, has high shade tolerance, and will thrive even in heavy clay soils. Grow in moist soil, in part or full shade. Propagate by seed in autumn, and by division or stem cuttings in late spring.

***P. macrophylla*** (Hoffm.) Busch. As for the genus.

For synonymy see *Pterolobium* and *Thlaspi*.

**Pachyphytum** Link, Klotzsch & Otto. Crassulaceae. 12 species of perennial herbs or subshrubs, succulent, glabrous; stems 1–3.5cm diam., becoming decumbent with age, occasionally branching. Leaves alternate, 10–60, 2.5–14×0.5–4cm, crowded, usually forming rosettes or more separate, turgid, fleshy, flattened to almost circular in cross-section, margin rounded, sometimes with small apical point, usually glaucous, tinged purple or pink-red. Flowering stems erect, axillary, covered with bracts; inflorescence a pendulous raceme; pedicels to 30mm; flowers campanulate or more cup-shaped; sepals 5, unequal or more regular, longer or shorter than petals; petals 5, overlapping toward and sometimes outcurved at tip, margin incurved below forming scale-like appendages to half the length of the petals, white, orange-red, pink, red, sometimes with broad marking across the whole width of the petal or with a differently coloured tip. Mexico Previously included in *Cotyledon*. Close to *Echeveria*, with which it hybridizes freely, forming × *Pachyveria* species. *Echeveria* lacks appendages on the petals. Z9.

CULTIVATION As for *Echeveria*.

***P. bracteosum*** Link, Klotzsch & Otto. Stems to 30cm high, 1–2.5cm diam. Lvs 15–30, 1–5×4–11×0.3–1.2cm, obovate to spathulate, glaucous or with white bloom. Flowering stems 15–60cm; fls 10–20; sep. 5, unequal, 12–24mm; pet. 5–9mm, white with broad red marking. Autumn–winter. Mexico (Hidalgo).

***P. compactum*** Rose. Stems to 12mm diam. Lvs 30–60, 18–30×12mm, fusiform, apex acute, glaucous, sometimes tinged red-purple. Flowering stems 30–40cm; fls 3–10; sep. 5, equal, to 7.5mm; pet. 5, to 9mm, orange-red with darker tips. Spring. Mexico.

***P. fittkaui*** Moran. Stems glutinous, to 15mm across. Lvs 20–35, 2.5–6.5×1.5–3×0.3–1.5cm, not forming rosettes, obovate, flattened, tip blunt to minutely pointed, glaucous or with grey-white bloom. Flowering stems 15–25; pedicels 15mm; fls 6–23; sep. 5, unequal, to 15mm; pet. outcurved, to 18mm, red. Mainly winter–early spring. Mexico (Hidalgo, Querétaro).

***P. hookeri*** (Salm-Dyck) A. Berger. Stems to 18mm across. Lvs 25–40, 24–50×6–15mm, scattered, circular in cross-section, apex minutely pointed, green with blue-grey to white bloom. Flowering stems 10–25cm; fls 3–15; sep. 5, 4–7.5mm, almost equal, pink toward base; pet. 5, 6–12mm, dark pink to light red. Year-round, especially spring. Mexico (San Luis Potosi).

***P. longifolium*** Rose. Stems 1–2.5cm diam. Lvs 20–60, 6–11×1.5–2.5×0.9cm, not forming rosettes, broader toward tip, mostly somewhat grooved beneath, apex blunt, obtuse or acute, purple-green with glaucous blue to white bloom. Infl. 10–50-fld; sep. 5, unequal, 12–15mm; pet. 5, 9mm, white, broadly marked with a red blotch. Summer–winter. Mexico (Hidalgo).

***P. oviferum*** Purpus. MOONSTONES. Stem to 12mm diam. Lvs 12–25, 30–50×18–30×16mm, crowded, obovate, oval, purple-glaucous, dense white bloom. Flowering stems 5–12, 5cm; infl. 7–15-fld; sep. 5, unequal, 12–25mm; pet. 5, to 9mm, pale green-white. Winter–spring. Mexico (San Luis Potosi).

***P. viride*** Walth. Stems 18–30mm diam. Lvs 12–40, 6–14×1.5–3×1.5cm, not forming rosettes, elliptic-oblong, apex blunt to obtuse, green to somewhat purple-red. Infl. 10–22-fld; sep. 5, uneven, 12–25mm; pet. 5, shorter than sep., white, broadly marked with a red blotch. Autumn–spring. Mexico (Querétaro).

***P. werdermanii*** Poelln. Stems decumbent, to 1m, 12mm diam. Lvs 10–35, 4–10×1.5–3.5×1.2cm, somewhat scattered, oblong or more elliptic, apex blunt to obtuse-rounded, blue-grey or whiter bloom. Flowering stems 15–25cm; infl. 10–22-fld; sep. 5, unequal, to 12mm; pet. 5, shorter than sep., pale pink with a broad darker pink blotch. Winter–spring. Mexico (Tamaulipas).

***P. aduncum*** (Bak.) Rose. See *P. hookeri*.
***P. amethystinum*** Rose. See *Graptopetalum amethystinum*.
***P. chloranthum*** Walth. See *Echeveria heterosepala*.
***P. heterosepalum*** Walth. See *Echeveria heterosepala*.
***P. roseum*** hort. ex Bak. See *P. hookeri*.
***P. sodalis*** (Berger Rose. See × *Pachyveria sodalis*.
***P. uniflorum*** Rose. See *P. hookeri*.
For further synonymy see *Cotyledon* and *Echeveria*.

**Pachypodium** Lindl. (From Gk *pachys*, thick, and *pous*, foot.) Apocynaceae. 17 species of highly stem-succulent, often cactus-like, spiny deciduous xerophytes ranging in habit from miniatures to shrubs and trees to 8m. Close to *Adenium*, but distinct by the armature and pappus at one end of the seed only. Bark tough and leathery. Leaf bases more or less elevated on tubercles arranged spirally round the stems; leaves deciduous, sometimes persisting in cultivation, simple, entire, leathery; spines in twos or threes, a pair of modified stipules, in some spp. with a third (or even fourth) smaller additional spine above the leaf bud. Flower white, yellow or red, tubular, with similar internal structure and pollination mechanism to *Adenium* but more diverse in size, colour and dimensions. Fruit 2 usually large follicles, sometimes the size of a banana, with abundant linear-oblong seeds plumed at one end. S and SW Africa, Madagascar. Z9.

CULTIVATION *Pachypodium* spp. require a winter minimum of 10°C/50°F. The four African spp. are less delicate than those from Madagascar, and *P. succulentum*, the southernmost, stands occasional frost. All require ample sun, a nutritious but porous medium, adequate ventilation and water whenever dry in summer, less when dormant or in winter. Leafless plants should be kept on the dry side or merely sprayed until growth is resumed. Seed will germinate easily. Cuttings, rarely available in quantity, can be rooted in a hot-box, with varying degrees of success. *P. succulentum* may be propagated by root cuttings. *P. lamerei* makes an ideal grafting stock for slower-growing or more delicate spp. Pest control as for succulents, see CACTI AND SUCCULENTS.

***P. baronii*** Costantin & H. Boissieu. Similar to *P. rosulatum*, with a massive shapeless caudex and crown of prickly branches to 3m. Fls brilliant red, salverform, c5.5×5cm. N Madagascar. var. ***windsori*** (Poiss.) Pichon. Smaller in stature, and with a white eye to the flower.

***P. bispinosum*** (L. f.) A. DC. Very similar to *P. succulentum*, distinguished by pink to dull purple flowers with a much broader cup-shaped tube and short, arching but not spreading lobes. E Cape.

***P. brevicaule*** Bak. Dwarf, rising only a few cm above soil level. The initially globose potato-like caudex broadens into a flat, irregularly lobed cake 30cm or more in diam. covered in tough brown skin and scattered with growing points. Lvs 2–4×1.2–1.6cm, in rosettes from amid a cluster of 3mm spines, dark green, subsessile and puberulent when young. Fls bright yellow, salverform, in a condensed cyme of 5×2–6cm; cor. to 1.5×2.5cm, tube narrow. Fr. to 10cm. C Madagascar. Early grafting on *P. lamerei* greatly accelerates development.

***P. decaryi*** Poiss. Identified by the reduced armature, similar to *Adenium* with almost smooth branches and tiny prickles up to 5mm. Fls 5–8cm×12cm, pure white, heavily perfumed. N Madagascar.

***P. densiflorum*** Bak. Similar to *P. rosulatum*, but the deep yellow fl. is differently formed, with the upper part of the tube opened out almost flat with the cone of stamens exposed in a shallow depression in the centre. C Madagascar. var. ***brevicalyx*** Perrier. Pedicels elongated; sepals minute, scale-like.

***P. geayi*** Costantin & H. Boissieu. Distinguished from the related *P. lamerei* by the longer, narrower lvs and overall covering of soft grey felt. Fls smaller, on much-branched cymes. SW Madagascar.

***P. horombense*** Pichon. Differs from *P. rosulatum* in having broad campanulate fls, 5-scalloped in cross section.

***P. lamerei*** Drake. Tree to 6m with a swollen, tapered or cigar-shaped cactus-like trunk covered in tough glossy bark and low spiralled tubercles; branching dichotomous, apical, following flowering; or, rarely, lateral; spines 3, lateral about 2.5cm, diverging, the central shorter, ascending. Lvs dark shining green, 25–35×2.5–11cm, variable in shape, short-petioled, with the margins and long pointed tip usually recurved. Fls 3–6×6–11cm, white, salverform, terminal on stout, branched 5–20cm peduncles. Fr. like 2 bananas, 15–20cm. S Madagascar. Cristate and variegated forms are known.

***P. lealii*** Welw. Caudex massive, irregularly branched, broader than tall or conically elongated to 6m, covered in tough silvery grey bark and tapering into thick tuberculate branches; spines 3, spreading, the laterals 2–4cm. Lvs scattered along new shoots and crowded at their tips, 2.5–8cm×12–40mm, fully deciduous, elliptic to obovate or oblanceolate, slightly wavy at the margins. Fls showy, white, salverform, 2.5–4cm, lobes asymmetric, 1.5–2.5cm long with curled margins. Fr. 7–10cm. S Angola, Namibia.

***P. namaquanum*** (Wyley ex Harv.) Welw. Solitary pachycaul trunk 1.5–2m×7–30cm, rarely with 1 or more erect branches, covered in spiralled tubercles armed with 3 straight spreading or declinate spines, the laterals 5–7cm, the central 1 (rarely 2) shorter. Lvs in an apical rosette, 8–12×2–6cm, oblong-elliptic to oblanceolate, pale green, downy, margins crisped. Fls in rings around the growing point, broadly cupped, sessile, 2.5–5×1cm, yellow-green outside, dull purple within. Fr. 2.5–4cm. NW Cape, S Namibia.

***P. rosulatum*** Bak. Stems pyriform when young, eventually forming a massive caudex wider than tall with a crown of thick, forked branches 1–1.5–3.5m high, smooth below but armed towards the tips with pairs of conical prickle-like, 6–11mm spines. New shoots lanate, later smooth and shining silvery green. Lvs 3–8cm, sessile, more or less elliptic. Fls held aloft on a 7–40cm forking peduncle, 4–10, yellow, tubular, 2–7cm×4–23mm, with 5 asymmetrical, rounded, 10–15mm lobes. Fr. 6–20cm. Madagascar. var. ***gracilius*** Perrier. Smaller, to 40cm diam. with fewer and slimmer branches and narrower red-brown spines.

***P. rutenbergianum*** Vatke. Tree to 8m with a tapered or pyriform trunk to 60cm diam. at the base and sparse crown of thick forking spiny branches; spines paired, brown, to 15mm. Lvs oblong-acuminate, to 16×4.5cm, short-petiolate. Fls large, white. C & S Cape.

***P. saundersii*** N.E. Br. Close to *P. lealii*, differing in its less hairy lvs. S Zimbabwe to N Natal.

***P. succulentum*** (L. f.) A. DC. Low, twiggy shrublet arising from a massive turnip-like underground caudex to 15cm diam. Stems 20–60×0.5–1.2cm, fleshy, sparingly branched. Lvs scattered along young shoots and clustered near the tips, to 6×1cm, oblong-lanceolate to oblanceolate, tomentose, with a pair of stipular spines to 25mm, rarely with 1–2 additional smaller spines above the lf bud. Fls few in short-stalked terminal cymes, 1–2cm long, with a narrow tube and flat, outspread limb 18–38mm diam., red, pink or particoloured to white. Fr. 4–6cm. C & S Cape to Orange Free State.

***P. giganteum*** Engl. See *P. lealii*.
***P. windsori*** Poiss. See *P. baronii* var. *windsori*.

**Pachyptera** DC. ex Meissn.
***P. alliacea*** (Lam.) A. Gentry. See *Mansoa alliacea*.
***P. hymenaea*** (DC.) A. Gentry. See *Mansoa hymenaea*.

**Pachyrhizus** Rich. ex DC. (From Gk *pachys*, thick, and *rhizon*, root.) Leguminosae (Papilionoideae). Some 6 species of tall, twining herbs with long, massive tuberous roots. Leaves trifoliolate, stipulate; leaflets often angular or sinuately lobed. Inflorescence an axillary raceme; cal. 4-lobed; standard broadly ovate, keel and wings curved; stamens 10, 9 united, 1 separate. Fruit flat, strigose, torulose. Summer. Tropical America, naturalized in Florida.

CULTIVATION *P. erosus* and *P. tuberosus* are cultivated for their edible tubers which when mature may reach 2m/6½ft. in length, weighing as much as 20kg/44lbs; the immature tubers are eaten either raw or cooked. The young pods of *P. erosus* are also used as a vegetable but must be thoroughly cooked to remove the toxic principle rotenone. *Pachyrhizus* spp. have potential as a natural insecticide. In temperate zones, *P. erosus* may be grown in the hot glasshouse in educational collections of tropical crops, and although unlikely to form tubers because of the photoperiod requirements, they make attractive and vigorous climbers and are very ornamental when carrying their long racemes of violet and purple flowers.

In tropical zones, *P. erosus* is tolerant of a wide range of climatic conditions but attains maximum growth in areas of moderate rainfall at elevations up to 1000m/3250ft. Tubers are not formed in daylengths of 14–15 hours and more, although vegetative growth is normal. Sow seed in sandy, well-drained soil on beds or ridges at intervals of 30–40cm/12–16in. in rows 60–75cm/24–30in. apart; closer spacings do not appear to affect the yield of pods but wider spacings are preferred for tuber production. Staking to a height of 2m/6½ft is necessary, although removal of the growing tip when plants reach 90cm/36in. is presumed to improve tuber quality. On marginally fertile soils, dressings of P and N may be beneficial. Immature pods are harvested 200–240 days from sowing and mature tubers at 150–180 days from sowing, before they become fibrous approximately 2kg/4.4lbs of tubers per plant may be expected. Propagate from pre-soaked seed; mature tubers may also be used as planting material to preserve trueness to type of some cvs.

***P. erosus*** (L.) Urban. YAM BEAN. Herbaceous twiner, 4.5m. Stem initially pubesc. Leaflets angular, rhomboid to ovate or subreniform, usually sharply dentate or lobed, lateral leaflets to 15cm, terminal leaflet to 19cm. Racemes dense; fls to 2.5cm, dark purple-violet to white, in axillary clusters. Fr. to 15cm; seeds red, brown or yellow, compressed, rounded or quadrate. C America.

***P. tuberosus*** (Lam.) A. Spreng. YAM BEAN; POTATO BEAN. Herbaceous twiner, to 7m. Leaflets ovate to ovate-rhomboid, usually entire or subentire, terminal leaflet to 25.5cm, lateral leaflets shorter. Racemes to 20cm, dense; fls to 22mm, crowded at axils, white to violet, with green spot at base of standard. Fr. to 30cm; seeds black or red, sometimes marked white, reniform. Amazon Basin.

***P. angulatus*** Rich. ex DC. See *P. erosus*.
***P. palmatilobus*** Benth. ex Hook. f. See *P. erosus*.

**Pachysandra** Michx. (From Gk *pachys*, thick, and *aner*, man, stamen.) Buxaceae. 4 species of evergreen or semi-evergreen, procumbent subshrubs or perennial herbs, with fleshy often rhizome-like stems and erect branches with leaves clustered at the branch tips. Leaves alternate, coarsely dentate or sometimes entire. Inflorescence a many-flowered erect, terminal or axillary spike; flowers white, small, apetalous, unisexual: 1–5 female flowers attached at the base of the peduncle, 5–40 sessile male flowers spirally arranged above; female flowers with 4–6 sepals, ovary trilocular; male flowers with 4 opposite sepals, 4 stamens. Fruit a capsule or drupe, with persistent styles; seeds dark brown to black, glossy. China, Japan, SE US.

CULTIVATION The most predominant use of *Pachysandra* spp. is as evergreen groundcover, and the most suitable subject for this purpose is *P. terminalis*. It is a vigorous grower, although not particularly invasive, and is best confined to inter- and under-planting of trees and shrubs where it can be allowed to form a dense evergreen carpet. *P. axillaris* and *P. procumbens* are less rampant growers and are more suitable for small-scale and specimen planting.

While the distribution of the genera is divided, the habitats are essentially similar. They occur in deciduous woodland, on gentle to steeply sloping sites, with moist soils which do not retain stagnant water. For successful cultivation these factors should ideally be duplicated. *Pachysandra* spp. will not thrive in dry soils or if exposed to strong sun or winds. They are tolerant of a range of pH and are ideally suited to dappled shade, where it may become necessary to contain and even to shear naturalized plantings of *P. terminalis* to sustain fresh green vigour and curb invasiveness. They are readily propagated by division in spring or from leafy shoot cuttings taken in late summer. *P. terminalis* is also reproduced by 8–25mm cuttings taken from the rhizomes in spring and inserted into a sandy mix. *P. procumbens* can be propagated by seed, although in the wild production of both fruit and seed is low.

***P. axillaris*** Franch. Woody, evergreen subshrub; stems less than 45cm, young shoots white. Lvs 5–10cm, 3–6 at the shoot apex, ovate, coarsely-toothed, base cuneate to round. Infl. to 2.5cm, axillary to lvs, white. Fr. a capsule. Spring. China. Z6.

***P. procumbens*** Michx. Semi-evergreen, perenn. herb, clump-forming to 30cm. Lvs 5–10cm, grey-green with mottled brown-green markings, ovate to round, coarsely toothed at the apex, narrowing below the middle to a long petiole, attached in very loose whorls to brown-pink-tinted stems. Infl. 5–10cm, arising from the base of the shoots; fls white; anth. pink, fragrant. Fr. a capsule. Spring. SE US. Z6.

***P. terminalis*** Sieb. & Zucc. Evergreen subshrub, to 20cm, glabrous. Stems somewhat fleshy, usually remaining green. Lvs 5–10cm, oblong-rhombic to oblong-obovate, apex strongly dentate, base cuneate, dark green, upper surface glossy. Infl. a 2–3cm, terminal raceme; fls white. Fr. an ovoid-globose drupe, white. Spring. Japan, NC China. Z5. 'Green Carpet': erect, low and compact; lvs small, finely toothed, deep green. 'Silver Edge': lvs light green, narrowly edged silver-white. 'Variegata': lvs variegated white; slow-growing.

**Pachystachys** Nees. (From Gk *pachys*, thick, and *stachys*, spike.) Acanthaceae. 12 species of evergreen perennial herbs and shrubs. Leaves opposite. Inflorescence a showy terminal spike; bracts large, overlapping; calyx lobes 5, equal or with the uppermost narrower; corolla tubular, showy, bilabiate; stamens 2, attached near base of corolla tube (cf. Justicia, to which this genus is closely related). Fruit a 4-seeded capsule. Tropical America. Z10.

CULTIVATION As for *Eranthemum*.

**Pachysandra** (×0.5) (a) *P. axillaris* (b) *P. procumbens* (c) *P. terminalis*

***P. coccinea*** (Aubl.) Nees. CARDINAL'S GUARD. Shrub to 2m. Lvs to 20cm, elliptic-ovate, entire, rugulose, short-stalked. Spike to 15cm, 4-sided owing to disposition of larger bracts in lower two-thirds; cor. to 5cm, scarlet. W Indies, northern S America.

***P. lutea*** Nees. Glabrous shrub to 1m. Lvs to 12cm, narrow-ovate to lanceolate, matt dark green with veins sunken above. Infl. to 10cm, rigidly erect, 4-sided; bracts to 2.5cm, golden to amber, cordate, papery, erect and closely overlapping; cor. to 4.75cm, white, curved. Peru.

For synonymy see *Beloperone, Jacobinia* and *Justicia*.

**Pachystegia** Cheesem.
***P. insignis*** (Hook. f.) Cheesem. See *Olearia insignis*.
***P. insignis*** var. ***minor*** Cheesem. See *Olearia insignis*.

× **Pachyveria** hort. Haage & Schmidt. *(Echeveria × Pachyphytum.)* Crassulaceae. 8 species of glabrous succulents. Leaves alternate, forming rosettes or more separate and scattered, fleshy, somewhat flattened or rounded below. Inflorescence usually of 1–3 cincinni; flowers bell-shaped, red to orange-red, usually with darker markings; petals sometimes showing the scales characteristic of *Pachyphytum*. Mexico. The characteristics of each hybrid depend on the parental species; thus it is difficult to delimit the hybrid genus. Z9.

CULTIVATION As for *Echeveria*.

× ***P. clavata*** Walth. *(Echeveria sp. × Pachyphytum bracteosum.)* Lvs *c*10×3cm, spathulate, grey-green. Infl. usually of 2 cincinni; sep. more or less equal length to pet.; scale-like appendages present.

× ***P. clevelandii*** Walth. *(Echeveria secunda × Pachyphytum bracteosum.)* Lvs 70, to 10×2.5cm, green-purple, tip fine-pointed. Sep. 4.5mm; pet. to 9mm, scale-like appendages absent.

× ***P. glauca*** Haage & Schmidt. *(Pachyphytum compactum × Echeveria* sp.*)* Lvs to 40, to 6×1.5cm, forming a dense rosette, almost circular or slightly flattened, semi-circular cross-section, to 1cm thick, glaucous, apex acute. Cincinnus solitary; sep. to 6mm; pet. to 12mm, yellow, tips red, outcurved, scales-like appendages present.

× ***P. mirabilis*** (Delile) Walth. *(Echeveria scheeri × Pachyphytum bracteosum.)* Lvs 60, to 6×2.6cm, apex acute, glaucous, broader toward tip. Cincinnus solitary; sep. equal length to pet.; scale-like appendages present.

× ***P. pachyphytoides*** (De Smet) Walth. *(Echeveria gibbiflora* 'Metalica' *× Pachyphytum bracteosum.)* Differs from *Pachyphytum bracteosum* in having lvs to 12×5cm, glaucous, tinged purple-red; infl. of 2–3 cincinni, pet. pink-red, scale-like appendages present.

× ***P. scheideckeri*** (De Smet) Walth. *(Echeveria secunda × Pachyphytum bracteosum.)* Lvs 50 6–7×1–2cm, forming a rosette, apex acute, blue-grey or whiter bloom, white striate surfaces. Cincinnus solitary; sep. 10mm; pet. 12mm, scale-like appendages absent.

× ***P. sobrina*** (A. Berger) Walth. *(Echeveria* sp. *× Pachyphytum bracteosum* or *Pachyphytum hookeri.)* Lvs 20, to 50×9×4.5mm, somewhat broader toward tip, apex acute. Infl. of 1–2 cincinni; sep. equal length to pet.; scale-like appendages present.

× ***P. sodalis*** (A. Berger) Walth. Lvs 15–25, to 8.5–3.5cm, apex acute, sharp-pointed, blue-grey, spathulate. Infl. trailing; sep. unequal; pet. equal length to sep., scale-like appendages present.

× *P. haagei* hort. See × *P. glauca*.
For further synonymy see *Diotostemon,* × *Echephytum, Echeveria, Pachyphytum,* and × *Urbiphytum*.

**Packera** Löve & D. Löve (For John G. Packer, botanist.) Compositae. About 60 species of perennial herbs, glabrous or tomentose with tufts of soft hairs. Leaves simple, entire to lyrate-pinnatifid, basal leaves petiolate, progressively reduced toward apex or uniform throughout. Capitula usually radiate, solitary to numerous; receptacle flat to convex, naked; phyllaries in 1 series; florets yellow to orange or red, ray florets female, disc florets hermaphrodite. Fruit a cylindric ribbed cypsela; pappus of bristles, soft, white. America, Eastern N Asia.

CULTIVATION A generous gardener might include the taller herbaceous species such as *P. bolanderi* and *P. aurea* in the wild garden or in collections of native plants, although the latter species, found in damp thickets and prairies, is invasive in habitat.

The lower-growing alpine spp. such as *P. cana* and *P. flettii*, from scree or other dry rocky habitats, are moderately pretty and are sometimes grown on the rock garden in sun in gritty, well-drained not too fertile soil. Propagate by seed, division or root cuttings.

***P. aurea*** (L.) Löve & D. Löve. GOLDEN GROUNDSEL; GOLDEN RAGWORT. To 80cm, sparsely tomentose at first, becoming glabrous. Basal lvs to 15cm, cordate-ovate, crenate or serrate, petiole long, apex broadly obtuse, sometimes tinged purple beneath; stem lvs pinnate, reduced above, uppermost sessile. Capitula radiate, 2cm diam., several or numerous, in corymbs; phyllaries often purple-tipped; florets yellow, ray florets rarely absent. Spring–summer. Eastern N America to Texas. Z3.

***P. bolanderi*** (A. Gray) W.A. Weber & Löve. To 60cm, more or less glabrous. Basal lvs to 7cm, orbicular-cordate, mostly shallowly palmately lobed, thick, persistent; stem lvs pinnatifid or lyrate-pinnatifid, much reduced. Capitula radiate, to 4cm diam., several in a compact cyme; phyllaries often loosely hairy with a few slender bracteoles; florets yellow. Summer. N California, SW Oregon. Z7.

***P. cana*** (Hook.) W.A. Weber & Löve. To 45cm, white-tomentose. Lvs mostly basal, to 5×2cm, narrowly oblanceolate to elliptic or ovate, entire or dentate, more or less glabrous above, petioles to 5cm; stem lvs few, reduced, often coarsely toothed or lobed, uppermost bract-like. Capitula radiate, to 4cm diam., several in a flat-topped terminal cluster; florets yellow, ray florets rarely absent. Summer. W N America. Z7.

***P. cymbalaria*** (Pursh) W.A. Weber & Löve. Dwarf, to 20cm, subglabrous. Lvs elliptic to obovate, entire to lyrate-pinnatifid; upper stem lvs pinnatifid, sessile, uppermost often reduced to lanceolate bracts. Capitula radiate, to *c*3cm diam., usually solitary; phyllaries lanceolate, bracteoles few, linear; florets yellow, ray florets often with violet stripes. Arctic E Asia and N America. Z3.

***P. flettii*** (Wiegand) W.A. Weber & Löve. WOOLLY BUTTERWEED. To 20cm, tawny tomentose at first, becoming glabrous. Basal lvs to 8×4cm, ovate to obovate, pinnatifid to lyrate-pinnatifid, lobes dentate; stem lvs few, linear, reduced above. Capitula radiate, to *c*3cm diam., 2–10 in a terminal, compact, cymose cluster; phyllaries glabrous, bracteoles few, well-developed, or absent; florets dark yellow. Summer. Washington State. Z6.

***P. obovata*** (Muhlenb. ex Willd.) W.A. Weber & Löve. To 70cm, stolons abundant. Basal lvs to 20×6cm, narrowly obovate to orbicular, obtuse, crenate-serrate, base sometimes deeply cut, petiole to 40cm; stem lvs often pinnatifid, reduced above, uppermost sessile. Capitula usually radiate, *c*3.5cm diam., 3–10 or more in a corymbose cyme; phyllaries often purple-tipped; florets yellow, ray florets sometimes absent. Spring–early summer. SE US. Z7.

***P. pauciflora*** (Pursh) Löve & D. Löve. RAYLESS ALPINE BUTTERWEED. To 40cm. Lvs somewhat succulent, basal lvs 5cm, elliptic-ovate to subrotund, crenate-dentate, petiole to 10cm; stem lvs toothed to pinnatifid, lobes obtuse, reduced above. Capitula usually discoid, to 1.5cm diam., 12, in a somewhat umbellate cyme; phyllaries generally suffused with maroon from tip; florets orange or tinged red, ray florets very short when present. Summer. E Canada to W N America. Z3.

***P. paupercula*** (Michx.) Löve & D. Löve. BALSAM GROUNDSEL. To 60cm. Basal lvs to 8cm, lanceolate to oblong or suborbicular, crenate-serrate to subentire, petiole to 8cm; stem lvs dissected, lower sometimes larger than basal lvs, upper reduced, sessile. Capitula radiate, to *c*3cm diam., 10–20 in a corymbose cyme; phyllaries carinate-thickened or thin, flat, often purple-tipped; florets yellow, ray florets sometimes absent. Summer. N America. Z3.

***P. werneriifolia*** (A. Gray) W.A. Weber & Löve. ALPINE ROCK BUTTERWEED. To 15cm, sparsely hairy. Lvs to 7×2cm, spathulate to oblanceolate, lanceolate-elliptic or orbicular-ovate, base attenuate, more or less entire, stem lvs few, reduced above, uppermost bract-like. Capitula radiate, to *c*3cm diam., 1–6, usually long-pedunculate; florets yellow. Summer. W N America. Z5.

For synonymy see *Senecio*.

**Paederota** L. (From Gk *paideros*, a word of various meanings – holm-oak chervil, acanthus.) Scrophulariaceae. 2 species of perennial alpine herbs. Leaves opposite, entire. Inflorescence a spike-like, bracteate, terminal raceme; calyx unequally 5-lobed; corolla blue or yellow, cylindrical tube with bilabiate limb usually shorter than tube, upper lip erect, entire, rarely 2-lobed, lower lip 3-lobed, more or less patent; stamens 2, usually exserted from corolla tube; stigma capitate. Fruit a capsule, loculicidal, uncompressed laterally, seeds numerous. S Europe. Z6.

CULTIVATION *Paederota* occurs in rock crevices and cliff face fissures, usually on limestone; *P. lutea*, the yellow veronica, is found at altitudes to 2200m/7150ft and is a protected species in its native regions. They are cultivated for their dense, terminal spikes of flowers, violet-blue in *P. bonarota*, and are grown on the moraine bed or in the alpine house as for the alpine species of *Veronica*.

***P. bonarota*** (L.) L. To 20cm; stems numerous, crispate-pubesc. Lvs 15–30×7–20mm, subsessile or shortly petiolate, hirsute to almost glabrous, 3–6 to 9 teeth per side, lower lvs broadly ovate-suborbicular, upper lvs oblong lanceolate. Infl. a dense raceme; peduncle 2–4cm, lengthening in fr., usually glabrescent; cor. 10–13mm, violet-blue, rarely pink, tube slightly exceeding limb; stamens equalling or slightly exceeding cor. tube. E Alps.

***P. lutea*** Scop. YELLOW VERONICA. Like *P. bonarota* but less hairy; lvs narrow-ovate to narrow-lanceolate, rarely broader, with 10 or more teeth per side. Cor. yellow, tube exceeding limb; stamens usually shorter than cor. E Alps, W Yugoslavia.

For synonymy see *Veronica*.

**Paeonia** L. PEONY. (From Gk *paionia*, possibly derived from Paion, the physician of the gods, who used the plant medicinally.) Paeoniaceae. Some 33 species of perennial herbs or shrubs ('Tree Peonies') to 2m. Rhizomatous, often with thick, tuberous roots. Leaves alternate, compound, often pinnate. Flowers solitary to many, terminal; sepals 5, green; petals 5–10, purple, red, pink, yellow or white; stamens numerous; carpels 2–8. Fruit composed of spreading, glabrous to pubescent follicles; seeds many, often with a fleshy, coloured outer layer. Europe, temperate Asia, NW America, China.

CULTIVATION Long-lived perennials divided into two distinct groups, the herbaceous perennials – which include the many garden forms and hybrids derived from *P. lactiflora*, the Chinese peony – and the shrubby perennials, the moutan or tree peonies largely derived from *P. suffruticosa*. Suitable for the herbaceous, mixed and shrub borders, they are grown for their splendid foliage, which in some cultivars assumes rich copper and red tints in spring and/or autumn, and beautiful to bowl-shaped flowers. Some have additional interest in their dehiscing fruits. Herbaceous peonies make good hosts for small early spring bulbs and narcissi, and for later bulbs such as *Gladiolus* spp. which will flower above the foliage. They are also excellent cut flowers if cut as they begin to open and laid flat in a cool dry place for 24 hours. Trim off 15mm/½in. from the stems before placing in water.

Herbaceous peonies will thrive in a wide range of temperatures, providing sufficiently low winter temperatures are achieved to ensure a dormancy period of approximately 60 days. Where winter temperatures fall below −10°C/14°F to −20°C/−4°F, especially in conjunction with little snowcover, protection with evergreen branches or bracken is advisable. Established plants are best left undisturbed, and because these gross feeders may live 25–50 years on one site, thorough pre-planting preparation is essential. Fork in generous amounts of well-rotted manure or garden compost, with bonemeal or super-phosphate, into the planting hole, ideally two weeks before planting to allow soil settlement. The crowns should be firmly set not lower than 25mm/1in. below the soil surface to ensure flowering, with care not to damage 'eyes' or roots. Where moving of established clumps becomes necessary, do so with a large root ball and keep well watered until re-established.

Peonies are lime-tolerant and may be grown in any moist fertile soil, with good drainage and a soil depth not less than 30cm/12in. Plant 60–90cm/24–36in. apart (depending on species), in early autumn for preference or in early spring, in sun or part shade, avoiding early morning sun on flowers in areas of late frosts. Hoe in bonemeal at 125g/m$^2$(4oz/yd$^2$) at planting time. Mulch annually in spring with well-rotted manure or garden compost, avoiding the immediate crown; lack of nutrition may result in failure to flower. Support clumps with galvanized wire hoop or grow through a plant support when foliage is half grown.

The tree peonies enjoy similar soil conditions with greater emphasis on good drainage, and a slight preference for lime. Because they start into growth earlier in spring they are slightly more tender than herbaceous types, and spring planting is preferred, spacing at two metres with the graft union of scion and rootstock 8–10cm/3–4in. below soil level. Their brittle stems may be damaged by strong wind, especially when young, and a sheltered position will also reduce frost damage to young shoots.

**Paeonia** (×0.33) (a) *P. delavayi* (b) *P. lutea* var. *ludlowii* (c) *P.*× *lemoinei*, flower (d) *P. suffruticosa* ssp. *rockii* (e) *P. potaninii* (f) *P. potaninii* var. *trollioides* (g) *P. lutea* × *P. potaninii*, flower

At winter temperatures between −10°C/14°F and −20°C/−4°F protect when young with a covering of bracken; if cut back by frost they may still shoot from the base. No pruning is necessary, except to remove dead wood in spring. Rejuvenation is possible, however, by cutting back to ground level in autumn.

Cultivars of herbaceous peonies are propagated by division in early autumn to allow establishment before heavy frosts, each division consisting of three stout shoots 10–15cm/4–6in. long, with 3–5 eyes; smaller pieces will take longer to flower. Lift roots and stand in shade for several hours so that roots become less brittle and cut with a sharp knife. Dust with fungicide before replanting.

All peonies can be raised from seed but named varieties and hybrids do not come true. Sow *firm* ripe seeds in autumn in a loam-based propagating medium, in pots in a shaded cold frame, transplanting to nursery bed 45cm/18in. apart when large enough to handle the following spring. Germination is slow if dormancy is allowed to develop; with fresh seed the root appears about six weeks after sowing, the shoot next spring. They will reach flowering size in 4–5 years, slightly longer with tree peonies.

Propagation of tree peonies is usually by grafting in summer using *P. lactiflora* or *P. officinalis* as rootstock. (Layering and hardwood cuttings (15–20cm/6–8in., in autumn) are possible but with low success rates.) A wedge-shaped scion, 4cm/1½in. long, bearing a single leaf with a vegetative bud, is pushed into a slit in the rootstock, which should be 10cm/4in. long, 1.2cm/½in. diameter. Plant in equal parts peat/sand, with the union covered, in a closed shaded frame, and leave to callus over. Admit air gradually to harden off. They should be ready to pot on by autumn, into 8cm/3in. pots; plunge pots in cold frame over winter, and spray against botrytis. As the pots fill with roots the following spring, plant out deeply in a frame to encourage scion rooting.

The major disease of peonies is *Botrytis paeoniae*, peony grey mould blight (sometimes called peony wilt.) Soft brown areas develop at leaf bases causing them to wilt. This is followed by a dark brown rot in both stem and leaf bases, and subsequently grey mould can be seen on stems at ground level. Young buds may blacken and wither, and grey mould develops on all damaged tissue. *B. cineria* causes similar symptoms later in the season. Both are best prevented by good hygiene, good drainage, and good air circulation. Cut plants down to ground level and destroy affected foliage in autumn, remove and replace top soil around plants. Spray on emergence of leaves, and twice at fortnightly intervals with specific fungicide. Peony ringspot virus (distinctive irregular yellow rings or mosaic on leaves) and peony blotch (*Septoria paeoniae*, grey-brown spots with reddish margins) are both generally tolerated, their effects being mainly cosmetic. *Armillaria melea* (honey fungus) may cause rapid death in tree peonies.

Subject to attack by the chrysanthemum eelworm (*Aphelenchoides ritzemabosi*), the leaf eelworm (*P. fragariae*) and, in warmer areas, by the root knot eelworm (*Meloidogyne* spp.). In Europe roots may be attacked by the larvae of swift moths (*Hepialus* spp.). In North America blooms and leaves may be damaged by the Japanese beetle (*Popillia japonica*), the rose chafer beetle (*Macrodactylus subspinosus*) and the small metallic blue-green beetles of the rose leaf beetle (*Nodonata puncticollis*). Good weed control and frequent cultivations discourage egg laying.

***P. anomala*** L. Herb to 50cm, glabrous. Lvs biternate, leaflets pinnatisect, seg. 2–3-lobed, narrow-oblong, acuminate, 5–9×0.5–1cm, dark green with bristly veins above, glabrous, glaucous beneath. Fls solitary, to 9cm diam.; pet. obovate, truncate at apex, bright red, undulate; stamens to 1.5cm, yellow; carpels 3–5, glabrous. Follicles to 2×1.5cm. Early summer. E USSR to C Asia. var. ***intermedia*** (Mey.) B. Fedtsch. & O. Fedtsch. Carpels tomentose. Z5.

***P. bakeri*** Lynch. Herb to 60cm. Stem villous. Lvs biternate, leaflets 7–10.5×3.5–6cm, ovate, base broadly cuneate to truncate, apex acute, dark green, glabrous above, glaucous, tomentose beneath. Fls solitary, to 11.5cm diam.; pet. obovate or suborbicular, cuneate at base, maroon-red; stamens many, fil. red, anth. yellow; carpels 3, densely hairy. Late spring–early summer. Origin unknown. Z5.

***P. broteri*** Boiss. & Reut. Herb to 40cm, glabrous. Lower lvs biternate, terminal leaflets deeply incised into 2–3 seg., upper lvs with leaflets entire, leaflets subsessile, apex acute, base cuneate. Fls solitary, to 10cm diam.; pet. broadly ovate, light pink; stamens to 2.5cm, yellow; carpels 2–4, with white, woolly hairs. Follicles to 4cm. Late spring–summer. Iberian peninsula. Z7.

***P. brownii*** Douglas ex Hook. Herb to 45cm. Stems glabrous. Lvs 5–8, biternate, dark green above, glaucous beneath; leaflets cut into 3 seg., seg. deeply divided, to 4-lobed, lobes entire or toothed, obtuse. Fls cup-shaped, to 3cm diam.; sep. ovate to orbicular, to 2×1cm, leathery; pet. to 1.5×1.5cm, broadly ovate to suborbicular, dark magenta; stamens to 1cm, yellow; carpels 5, glabrous, with a fleshy disc at base. Follicles erect to spreading, to 3×2cm; seeds cylindric. Summer. Western N America. Z7.

***P. californica*** Nutt. ex Torr. & A. Gray. Herb to 60cm. Stems glabrous. Lvs biternate, dark green above, pale green beneath, glabrous, leaflets sessile, papery, seg. narrowly oblong, lobed, lobes 2–3, acute to obtuse, occasionally incised. Fls cup-shaped, to 3cm diam.; sep. green, concave, outer sep. hemispherical, acuminate, to 1.5×1cm, inner sep. suborbicular, to 2cm diam., often marked red at base; pet. ovate to suborbicular, concave, to 2×2cm, purple-maroon; stamens to 1cm, yellow; carpels 3, to 1.5cm, glabrous, with a fleshy, lobed disc at base. Follicles to 3.5cm. Spring. S California. Z7.

***P. cambessedesii*** Willk. Herb to 45cm. Stems glabrous, tinged red. Lvs at regular intervals along stem, biternate, to 25cm, dark green, glabrous above with veins impressed, purple or pale green, marked purple, glabrous with raised veins beneath; leaflets lanceolate to elliptic, acute, to 10×5cm, entire; petioles to 10.5cm, tinged red. Fls solitary, to 10cm diam.; pet. broadly ovate, deep pink; stamens to 2cm, fil. red, anth. yellow; carpels 5–8, glabrous, purple. Follicles to 6cm. Late spring. Balearic Is. Z8.

***P. clusii*** Stern & Stearn. Herb to 30cm. Stems glabrous, pink. Lvs biternate, leaflets divided into seg., seg. 30+, narrow-oblong to elliptic, to 6×2cm, occasionally lobed or toothed, apex acute to acuminate, green above, glaucous, almost glabrous beneath. Fls to 10cm diam.; pet. 6–8, obovate, rounded at apex, white, rarely marked with pink; stamens to 2cm, fil. pink, anth. orange-yellow; carpels 2–4, hoary-tomentose, to 2cm. Fr. to 3cm. Spring. Aegean Is. (Crete, Karpathos). Z7.

***P. coriacea*** Boiss. Herb to 55cm. Stems glabrous, erect. Lower lvs biternate; leaflets to 9, some bifid, giving 14–16 seg., broadly elliptic, lanceolate to ovate, cuneate to rounded at base, acute, green, glabrous above, glaucous, glabrous beneath. Fls to 15cm diam.; pet. obovate, light pink; stamens to 2cm, fil. red, anth. yellow; carpels 2, glabrous. Follicles to 5cm. Late spring. S Spain, Morocco. var. ***atlantica*** (Coss.) Stern. Leaflets larger than type, hairy below; petioles hairy. Algeria (high altitude). Z8.

***P. delavayi*** Franch. Shrub to 1.6m, glabrous. Stems slender, hollow, cane-like, grey-brown, scarred with old petiole bases and sparsely branching near apex. Lvs biternate, to 27cm, held horizontally at top of stems, deeply and gracefully dissected; terminal set of 3 leaflets held 6cm away from laterals; leaflets ovate-lanceolate, to 10cm, dark green above, blue-green beneath, entire or toothed, occasionally lobed in lateral leaflets, terminal leaflets trifid. Fls to 9cm diam., sep. 5, suborbicular, 2–2.5cm diam., green, subtended by 8–10 leaf-like bracts, bracts ovate to lanceolate, abruptly acuminate, to 6×2cm; pet. obovate, cuneate at base, to 4×3cm, maroon; stamens to 2cm, fil. dark red, anth. yellow; carpels glabrous. Follicles 5, 3×1.5cm, with a fleshy, lobed disc at base. Summer. China (Yunnan, Likiang). 'Anne Rosse' (*P. delavayi* × *P. lutea* var. *ludlowii):* fls to 10cm diam., pet. lemon, exterior streaked red. Z6.

***P. emodi*** Wallich ex Royle. Herb to 75cm. Stems erect, light green, glabrous. Lvs biternate; leaflets 12–17×1.5–5.5cm, decurrent at base, elliptic, narrowing at base and apex, acuminate, entire or bilobed, dark green, glabrous throughout, terminal leaflets trifid. Fls to 12cm diam.; pet. obovate, to 4.5×2.5cm, white; stamens to 2cm, yellow; carpels 1–2, densely yellow-bristly. Follicles to 2.5cm. Spring. NW India. var. ***glabrata*** Hook. f. & Thoms. Carpels glabrous. Z8.

***P. japonica*** (Mak.) Miyabe & Tak. As for *P. obovata* except lvs villous below, fls opening less widely, pet. more concave, white. Early summer. Japan. Not easily cultivated. Plants offered under this name may be cvs of *P. suffruticosa* 'Japanese'. Z7.

***P. kesrouanensis*** Thiéb. As for *P. mascula* except carpels glabrous, stigma to 1cm, coiling only at the very tip. Spring. Syria. Z8.

***P. lactiflora*** Pall. Herb to 60cm. Stems erect, light green marked red. Lvs biternate, dark green, glabrous above, light green, glabrous except for sparse hairs on veins beneath; leaflets entire or lobed, elliptic to lanceolate, base cuneate, apex acuminate, margins rough-bumpy. Fls to 10cm diam., fragrant; pet. obovate, white, to 4.5×3cm; stamens to 1.5cm, yellow; carpels 4–5, glabrous; stigma pink. Follicles to 2cm. Summer. Tibet to China and Siberia. var. ***trichocarpa*** (Bunge) Stern. Carpels hairy. Old hybrids of *P. lactiflora* ('The Chinese Paeonies') vary in fl. colour from white to pink, deep red, crimson or maroon, and are single, double or semi-double in form. (white doubles) 'Festiva Maxima': a few pet. with basal blotch blood red. 'Kelway's Glorious': pet. base suffused cream, fls fragrant. (pink doubles) 'Auguste Dessert': salmon rose, margins silver. 'Carnival': outer pet. carmine pink, inner pet. cream and rose. 'Kelway's Lovely': bright rose-pink. 'Sarah Bernhardt': apple blossom pink. (red and purple doubles) 'Bunkers' Hill': semi-double, pet. pale crimson, stamens golden. 'Chocolate Soldier': rich black-red, inner pet. dotted yellow. 'Félix Crousse': deep carmine rose with a deeper red centre (1881). 'François Ortegat': fls fragrant, semi-double, fls crimson-purple (1850). 'Hidcote Purple': fls deep

**Paeonia** (×0.25) (a) *P. emodi* (b) *P. wittmanniana* (c) *P. mlokosewitschii* (d) *P. obovata* (e) *P. sterniana*, leaf (f) *P. peregrina* (g) *P. mascula* ssp. *russii* (leaf detail) (h) *P. mascula* ssp. *triternata* (leaf detail) (i) *P. mascula* (j) *P. bakeri*

maroon-purple. 'President Roosevelt': fls large, dark pink, richly fragrant. (single) 'Lord Kitchener', 'Poetic', 'Sir Edward Elgar': deep crimson. 'Pink Delight': blush pink. 'Whitleyi Major': pure white. (so-called Imperial varieties with petaloid stamens) 'Bowl of Beauty': fuschia-rose, petaloids pale yellow. 'Calypso': fls pale carmine, petaloids tipped gold. 'Instituteur Doriat': velvet carmine, edged white. 'Kelway's Majestic': cherry rose, petaloids lilac. 'Palermo': pale pink. Z6.

***P.*×*lemoinei*** Rehd. (*P. lutea* × *P. suffruticosa.*) Tree peony to 2m. Fls yellow or combinations of yellow and pink. Garden origin (France, 1909). 'Alice Harding': fls double, lemon yellow. 'Argosy': fls single, to 18cm diam., pet. primrose yellow, basal blotch carmine. 'Chromatella': fls double, sulphur yellow. 'La Lorraine': fls double, cream-yellow. 'L'Espérance': fls 15–20cm diam., pet. pale yellow, basal blotch crimson. 'Mme Louis Henry': fls 15–17.5cm diam., cream-yellow, suffused red. 'Souvenir de Maxime Cornu': fls double, pet. yellow, tinged brown, orange and red. 'Tria': fls in groups of 3, single; pet. 10–12, yellow; very early. Z7.

***P. lutea*** Delav. ex Franch. As for *P. delavayi* except involucre lacking from base of fl.; fls in groups of 2 or more, to 7.5cm diam.; bracts and sep. to 8; pet. yellow, carpels 3–4. Early summer. China. 'Superba': new growth bronze, later green; fls large, tinged pink at base. var. ***ludlowii*** Stern & Tayl. TIBETAN PEONY. To 2.5m. Fls to 12.5cm diam., earlier. Follicles 1–2. Spring. Tibet. Z6.

***P. macrophylla*** (Albov) Lom. Herb to 90cm. Lvs biternate, leaflets to 25×15cm, elliptic-lanceolate to almost orbicular, dark green, glabrous above, glaucous, sparsely hairy on veins beneath. Fls to 7.5cm diam.; pet. white, tinged yellow; carpels 2–4, glabrous. Spring. W Caucasus. Z7.

***P. mairei*** Lév. Herb to 90cm. Stems erect or spreading, glabrous. Lvs biternate; leaflets elliptic to obovate, cuneate at base, acuminate at apex, to 19×11cm, glabrous, dark green above, light green beneath, lateral leaflets occasionally bifid. Fls to 11cm diam.; pet. obovate to ovate-elliptic, obtuse, to 7×4cm, rose-pink; stamens to 2cm, fil. red, anth. yellow; carpels to 2.5cm, conic below, attenuate at apex, glabrous to yellow-brown-tomentose. Late spring. China (Yunnan). Z6.

***P. mascula*** (L.) Mill. Very variable herb, 25–60cm. Stems glabrous. Lvs biternate, leaflets 9–21, entire, often bifid or trifid, elliptic to broadly obovate, glabrous or pilose beneath. Fls to 13cm diam.; pet. 5–9, red, pink or white; fil. red, purple, pink or white; carpels 2–5; style to 1cm. ssp. ***mascula***. Herb to 60cm. Stems glabrous. Lvs biternate, green, glaucous above, glabrous below; leaflets 9–21, elliptic to obovate-elliptic, shortly acuminate, often deeply 2–3-lobed, terminal leaflets broadly elliptic, base cuneate, apex attenuate. Fls to 12cm diam.; pet. obovate, purple-red; fil. purple; carpels 2–5, tomentose; style to 1cm, coiled along the length. Summer. S Europe. ssp. ***arietina*** (Anderson) Cullen & Heyw. Lvs hairy below; leaflets 12–15, narrowly elliptic. E Europe, Asia Minor. 'Mother of Pearl': fls pale pink. 'Northern Glory': lvs grey-green; fls single, deep magenta-carmine. 'Purple Emperor': fls single, rose-purple. 'Rose Gem': fls single, bright blood-red. ssp. ***hellenica*** Tzanoudakis. Pet. white. SW Greece. ssp. ***russii*** (Biv.) Cullen & Heyw. Herb to 45cm. Lvs tinged purple, glabrous to sparsely hairy below. Follicles to 2.5m. Western C Greece, Ionian Is., Corsica, Sardinia, Sicily. ssp. ***triternata*** (Boiss.) Stearn & P.H. Davis. Leaflets 9–11, obtuse or subacute, concave above, undulate. Late spring. NW Yugoslavia to Asia Minor. Z8.

***P. mlokosewitschii*** Lom. Herb to 1m. Stems glabrous. Lvs biternate, leaflets to 10×6.5cm, broadly oblong to obovate, apex subacute to obtuse, dark to silvery green, glabrous above, glaucous, sparsely hairy beneath, hairs curved. Fls to 12cm diam.; pet. concave, broadly ovate, yellow; stamens to 2.5cm, yellow; carpels 2–4, densely hairy, stigma pale pink or yellow. Follicles to 5cm. Spring. EC Caucasus. Z6.

***P. mollis*** Anderson. Herb to 45cm. Stem villous to glabrous. Lvs biternate, leaflets to 10×4cm, sessile, bifid or trifid, lobes many, narrowly oblong to elliptic, base cuneate, apex acute, green, glabrous above, white-hairy beneath. Fls to 7cm diam.; pet. not spreading, obovate, red or white; stamens to 1.5cm, fil. red or pale yellow, anth. yellow; carpels 2–3, densely hairy. Fr. to 2.5cm. Summer. Origin unknown. Z6.

***P. obovata*** Maxim. Herb to 60cm. Stems erect, glabrous. Lvs biternate, leaflets to 14.5×18.5cm, unequal, base broadly oval or oblong, cuneate, apex abruptly acuminate, dark green, glabrous above, glaucous, sparsely hairy beneath, terminal leaflet obovate. Fls to 7cm diam.; pet. white to red-purple; stamens to 2cm, fil. white or pink, anth. yellow; carpels 2–3, to 2cm, glabrous, stigma coiled. Fr. to 3.5cm. Early summer. Siberia, China. var. ***willmottiae*** (Stapf) Stern. Leaflets to 6cm and over. Fls cup-shaped, to 10cm diam.; pet. obovate, white; fil. pink-red. Early summer. China. Z7.

***P. officinalis*** L. Herb to 60cm. Stems sparsely hairy, becoming glabrous. Lvs biternate, leaflets incised into several, narrowly elliptic to oblong, acute seg. to 11×2.5cm, green, glabrous above, sparsely hairy to glabrous beneath. Fls to 13cm diam., pet. obovate, widespread; stamens to 1.5cm, fil. red, anth. yellow; carpels 2–3, densely hairy. Fr. to 3cm. Summer. Europe. ssp. ***banatica*** (Rochel) Soó. Middle leaflet incised into seg., lateral leaflets entire. Carpels tomentose. Yugoslavia, Romania, Hungary. ssp. ***humilis*** (Retz.) Cullen & Heyw. Stems and petioles hairy. Leaflets incised into seg. to one-third of their length. Carpels glabrous. SW Europe. ssp. ***villosa*** (Huth) Cullen & Heyw. Stems and petioles somewhat floccose; leaflets as for ssp. *humilis*. Carpels tomentose. Summer. S France, Italy. Cvs include: 'Alba Plena': fls double, white. 'Anemoniflora Rosea': fls deep pink, petaloid stamens yellow, margins crimson. 'China Rose': fls single, salmon pink; stamens orange-yellow. 'Crimson Globe': fls single, garnet-red, petaloid stamens crimson and gold. 'James Crawford Weguelin': fls single, garnet-red, anth. yellow. 'Lize van Veen': fls double, white flushed pink. 'Mutabilis Plena': fls deep pink fading to blush pink. 'Rosea Plena': fls double, darker pink than 'Rosea Plena'. 'Rosea Superba': fls large double, pink. 'Rubra Plena': fls double, crimson. Z8.

***P. parnassica*** Tzanoudakis. Herb to 65cm. Stems hairy. Lvs biternate, leaflets 9–13-lobed, obovate to narrowly lanceolate, acute to short-acuminate, base cuneate, tinged purple above, becoming pure green, grey-green beneath, pilose, terminal leaflet usually entire, occasionally 2–3-lobed. Fls to 12cm diam.; pet. 9–12, obovate to orbicular, deep red; fil. tinged purple; carpels 2–3, tomentose; style spiralled. Early summer. SC Greece (mts). Z8.

***P. peregrina*** Mill. non Bornm. 1768. Herb to 50cm. Stems glabrous. Lvs biternate, rigid, seg. to 2cm, 15–17, occasionally divided 2–3-lobed, emarginate, lustrous green above, glaucous, glabrous or sparsely hairy beneath. Fls to 12cm diam., cup-shaped; pet. oblong-ovate to suborbicular, deep red; fil. pink or red; carpels 1–4, tomentose, stigma spiralling in upper part. Late spring–early summer. S Europe. 'Otto Froebel' ('Sunshine'): fls vermilion; early flowering. Z8.

***P. potaninii*** Komar. TREE PEONY. As for *P. delavayi* except stoloniferous, shorter (to 60cm), lf seg. narrower, fls to 6.5cm diam., not subtended by involucral bracts; pet. deep red to white. Early summer. China (Sichuan, Yunnan). 'Alba': fls and stigmas white, fil. green. var. ***trollioides*** (Stapf ex Stearn) Stearn. Lf seg. less ovate than type. Fls pale yellow; pet. curved inward giving flower the appearance of being only half open. W China, Tibet. Z7.

***P. rhodia*** Stearn. Herb to 35cm. Stems glabrous, tinged red. Lvs biternate; leaflets to 2.5×4cm, divided into 9–29 seg., ovate to oblong-elliptic or lanceolate, acute to shortly acuminate, glabrous, pale green beneath, central leaflet trifurcate, lateral leaflets bifurcate, entire or 3–4-lobed. Fls to 8cm diam.; pet. 6–8, obovate to orbicular, white; fil. red; carpels 2–5, tomentose. Fr. to 2.5cm. Spring. Rhodes. Z8.

***P.*×*smouthii*** Van Houtte. (*P. lactiflora* × *P. tenuifolia.*) Herb to 45cm. Lvs divided into many seg. Fls produced early in season, solitary, bright red, fragrant, sterile.

***P. sterniana*** Fletcher. Herb, 30–90cm, glabrous. Lvs to 30cm, alternate, seg. to 10×2cm, glabrous, elliptic or oblong-elliptic, acuminate or acute, dark green above, glabrous beneath. Fls solitary, white, to 8cm diam.; sep. ovate, apiculate, exterior sep. leaflike, lanceolate, to 1.5×1.5cm; pet. obovate, to 3.5×2cm; fil. white, anth. yellow; carpels pale green. Seeds 5, indigo. E Tibet. Z7.

***P. suffruticosa*** Andrews. MOUTAN PEONY. Shrub to 2m. Stems branching freely, erect. Lvs biternate deeply dissected; leaflets to 10cm, lanceolate to ovate, 3–5-lobed, terminal leaflet 3-lobed, terminal lobe to 9cm, lateral lobes to 5cm, lobes acute, pale green above, blue-green beneath, veins sparsely hairy. Fls to 15cm diam.; pet. many, to 8cm, concave, pink to white, with a deep purple, red-bordered basal patch, margins finely scalloped; fil. violet-red; carpels 5. Spring–summer. China, Tibet, Bhutan. A large number of cultivars, of which many originate in the Far East; fls single, semi-double and double, size variable, in range of colours from white and yellow through shades of pink and red to purple; 'Banksii': fls double, carmine. 'Godaishu': fls semi-double, large, clear white. 'Hana-daigin': fls double, large, violet. 'Kenreimon': fls purple with pink, petals turning inwards. 'Kintei': fls lemon streaked dark yellow. 'Koka-mon': fls large, red-brown striped white. 'Reine Elizabeth': fls fully double, large, salmon-pink tinged red, margins ruffled. 'Renkaku': fls double, dense, white, ruffled, anthers long, deep yellow. 'Yae-zakura': fls very large, double, soft cherry-pink. ssp. ***spontanea*** (Rehd.) S.G. Haw & L.A. Lauerier. Smaller. Leaflets with obtuse seg. Fls to 11cm diam.; fil. red, anth. yellow. China. Hybrids derived from *P. suffruticosa* × *P. lutea* include 'Cardinal Vaughn': fls ruby-purple. 'Duchess of Kent': fls rose-scarlet. 'Duchess of Marlborough' fls rose-pink. 'Lord Selborne': fls pale salmon pink. 'Montrose': fls pale lavender-lilac. 'Mrs William Kelway': fls white. 'Raphael' fls pale pink. 'Superba': fls cherry red. ssp. ***rockii*** S.G. Haw & L.A. Laucrier. ('Rock's Variety', 'Joseph Rock'): fls semi-double, spreading, white. Z7.

***P. tenuifolia*** L. Herb to 60cm. Lvs biternate; leaflets dissected and lobed in a tripinnate pattern to give many linear seg., obtuse glabrous, dark green above, glaucous beneath. Fls cup-shaped, to 8cm diam.; pet. oblanceolate to obovate, obtuse to emarginate, deep red; stamens to 1.5cm, yellow; carpels 2–3, roughly tomentose. Fr. to 2cm. Spring. SE Europe to Caucasus. 'Early Bird': fls single, deep red. 'Latifolia': habit tall; lf seg. broad. 'Plena': fls double, longer-lasting. 'Rosea': fls pale pink. Z8.

***P. veitchii*** Lynch. Herb to 50cm. Stems glabrous. Lvs biternate; leaflets incised into 2–4 seg.; seg. deeply cut into lobes or entire, oblong-elliptic, long-acuminate, dark green with hairy veins above glaucous pale green, glabrous beneath. Fls nodding to 9cm diam.; pet. obovate-cuneate, truncate to emarginate at apex, to 4.5×3cm, pale to deep magenta; stamens to 2cm, fil. pink, anth. yellow; carpels 2–4. Fr. to 1.5cm, strongly curved when ripe. Spring to early summer. China. 'Alba': fls cream-white. var. ***woodwardii*** (Stapf & Cox) Stern. To 30cm. Stems and petioles hairy. Lvs hairy beneath on veins and midrib. W China. Z8.

**Paeonia** (×0.25) (a) *P. lactiflora* (b) *P.*× *smouthii* (c) *P. tenuifolia* (d) *P. clusii*, flower (e) *P. coriacea* (f) *P. rhodia*, flower (g) *P. mollis*, flower, showing expanding carpels (h) *P. anomala*, leaf (i) *P. broteri* (j) *P. cambessedesii* (k) *P. veitchii* (l) *P. officinalis*

***P. wittmanniana*** Hartw. ex Lindl. To 120cm. Stems glabrous. Lvs biternate; leaflets to 16cm, broadly ovate to elliptic, acute, to 16cm, villous beneath, especially on veins. Fls to 12.5cm diam., pale yellow; carpels 2–4, tomentose; stigmas red. Spring to early summer. NW Caucasus. var. ***nudicarpa*** Schipcz. Carpels glabrous. Z7.

***P. cultivars.*** SAUNDERS HYBRIDS. A very wide range of hybrid herbaceous peonies which can largely be attributed to *P. officinalis, P. peregrina* and *P. lactiflora*, although many more species have been used. They include; 'Archangel (*P. lactiflora* × *P. wittmanniana* var. *macrophylla*): fls single, white. 'Daystar' (*P. mlokosewitschii* × *P. tenuifolia*): lvs pointed; fls yellow, early. 'Defender': fls red, early. 'Early Windflower' (*P. emodi* × *P. veitchii*): lvs narrow, fern-like; fls white, hanging. 'Golden Hind': lvs dark green; fls fully double, large, deep yellow. 'Renown': fls single, strawberry red suffused yellow. 'Savage Splendour': fls large, ivory splashed and edged purple, pet. twisted. 'Thunderbolt': fls single, black-crimson. 'Vesuvian': habit compact; lvs deep green, finely cut; fls fully double, black-red. 'White Innocence' (*P. lactiflora* × *P. emodi*): habit tall to 1.5m; fls white, centres green, late flowering. DAPHNIS HYBRIDS (Tree Peonies). Of recent development, these distinctive hybrids derive from the continuation of Prof. Saunders' work by Messrs Grantwich and Nassos Daphnis. They include; 'Artemis': habit tall, upright, stems and petioles tinged red; fls single, large, silky yellow. 'Gauguin': fls large, yellow veined red from bold red centre. 'Kronos': fls semi-double, dark red tinged blue. 'Marie Laurencin': lvs glossy; fls semi-double, lavender, centre of darker shade, symmetrical, pet. 10–12; very early.

***P. albiflora*** Pall. See *P. lactiflora*.
***P. arborea*** Donn. See *P. suffruticosa*.
***P. arietina*** Anderson. See *P. mascula* ssp. *arietina*.
***P. banatica*** Rochel. See *P. officinalis* ssp. *banatica*.
***P. brownii*** ssp. ***californica*** (Nutt. ex Torr. & A. Gray) Abrams. See *P. californica*.
***P. chinensis*** hort. See *P. lactiflora*.
***P. corallina*** Retz. See *P. mascula* ssp. *mascula*.
***P. corallina*** var. ***triternata*** Boiss. See *P. mascula* ssp. *triternata*.
***P. cretica*** Tausch. See *P. clusii*.
***P. daurica*** Andrews. See *P. mascula* ssp. *triternata*.
***P. decora*** Anderson. See *P. peregrina*.
***P. delavayi*** var. ***angustiloba*** Rehd. & G.H. Wils. See *P. potaninii*.
***P. delavayi*** var. ***lutea*** (Franch.) Finet & Gagnep. See *P. lutea*.
***P. edulis*** Salisb. See *P. lactiflora*.
***P. fragrans*** (Sab.) Redouté. See *P. lactiflora*.
***P. humilis*** Retz. See *P. officinalis* ssp. *humilis*.
***P. intermedia*** C. Mey. ex Ledeb. See *P. anomala* var. *intermedia*.
***P. laciniata*** Siev. See *P. anomala*.
***P. microcarpa*** Salm-Dyck. See *P. officinalis* ssp. *villosa*.
***P. moutan*** Sims. See *P. suffruticosa*.
***P. paradoxa*** Sab. See *P. officinalis* ssp. *humilis*.
***P. peregrina*** Bornm. non Mill. See *P. mascula* ssp. *arietina*.
***P. reevesiana*** (Paxt.) Loud. See *P. lactiflora*.
***P. russii*** Biv. See *P. mascula* ssp. *russii*.
***P. triternata*** Boiss. See *P. mascula* ssp. *triternata*.
***P. trollioides*** Stapf ex Stern. See *P. potaninii* var. *trollioides*.
***P. willmottiae*** Stapf. See *P. obovata* var. *willmottiae*.
***P. woodwardii*** Stapf. See *P. veitchii* var. *woodwardii*.

**PAEONIACEAE** Rudolphi. PEONY FAMILY. Dicot. 2 genera and 34 species of perennial rhizomatous herbs and subpachycaul shrubs. Leaves alternates, biternate; stipules absent. Flowers solitary, terminal, large, bisexual, sometimes beetle-pollinated, more or less regular; calyx (3–)5(–7) free sepals, rounded or subfoliaceous, much imbricate, persistent; corolla 5 (–13) free petals, large, imbricate; stamens numerous, with dichotomising vascular strands derived from 5 basal trunks; ovary superior, often surrounded by nectary-disc, (2)3–5(–15) free carpels, with expanded subsessile stigma; ovules several-numerous, with massive outer integument. Fruit a head of follicles; seeds mesotestal, large, with funicular aril (*Paeonia*) or compressed and winged (*Glaucidium*); endosperm copious, oily. Temperate Eurasia, Western North America. *Glaucidium, Paeonia.*

**Paesia** St.-Hil. (For Fernando Dias Paes Leme, a Portuguese administrator in Minas Geraës, *c*1660.) Dennstaedtiaceae. Some 12 species of terrestrial or, rarely, epilithic ferns. Rhizomes long-creeping, solenostelic, branched, covered with massed roots and chestnut to brown hairs or scales. Fronds stipitate, uniform, 2–4-pinnate-pinnatifid, usually glandular and rough, glabrous or pubescent, pinnae and pinnules oblique, margin of segments toothed to lobed, veins free, forked, rachis zigzag, costa fibrillose, pubescent; stipes erect and stiff. Sori marginal, continuous on vascular connective commisure, linear; indusia double, outer formed from modified margin of segments, rough, margin erose to undulate, inner more distinct and developed than in *Pteridium*, membranous; paraphyses absent; sporangia stalked; annulus 12–20-celled, incomplete, vertical; spores oblong to ellipsoid, monolete, bilateral, smooth to rugose. Malaysia to Polynesia, New Zealand. Z7.

CULTIVATION *P. scaberula* is native to high open habitats in the mountains of New Zealand, and is well suited to gardens in temperate and warm temperate regions, forming a mass of finely cut foliage offering potential as ground cover; it is a deciduous species. *P. scaberula* is hardy down to at least −15°C/5°F, and likes to grow in open sites in only part shade with up to six hours direct sun daily, less in hot dry regions. The soil should be acid with a pH of 4.0–6.0. Under glass, use a soilless propagating medium and keep in bright filtered light. Plant out in early summer and water plentifully until well established. Propagate by separation of sections of the creeping rhizome, or by spores.

***P. scaberula*** (A. Rich.) Kuhn. LACE FERN; SCENTED FERN. Terrestrial fern. Rhiz. to 2mm, wiry, stiff. Fronds to 45×25cm, 2–3- or, rarely, 4-pinnate, ovate to lanceolate, apex narrowly acute, leathery and stiff, more or less glandular-pubesc., pinnae to 25×5cm, short-petiolate, subopposite or alternate, distant, ovate to lanceolate or deltoid, apex narrowly acute, pinnules to 2.5×1cm, short-petiolate, lanceolate, seg. to 6×2mm, oblong, apex acute, margin entire to toothed or notched, or lobed at base, veins obscure, rachis rough; stipes to 30cm, rough, glandular-pubesc. and setose, yellow or chestnut to brown. Sori eventually covering surface of seg. except costa and apex and base. New Zealand.

For synonymy see *Allosorus*.

**Page, Russell** (1906–85). English garden designer. Page studied painting in Paris after education at Charterhouse and the Slade School of Art, University of London. His unusual boyhood interest in plants led to designing rock gardens, the first at the age of 17. He worked in a London landscape architect's office designing planting schemes for suburban blocks of flats. His work with Henry Bath at Longleat started his successful association with Geoffrey Jellicoe, landscape architect and authority on classical Italian gardens. Together, they designed the Caveman Restaurant project at Cheddar Gorge, the Royal Lodge, Windsor Great Park and the gardens at Ditchley. Their partnership ended at the outbreak of war in 1939. After wartime experience in Egypt and India, he rapidly established his own international practice.

Page acknowledged the early influence of Gertrude Jekyll. Like her, he was a painter first. His work was remarkable for its versatility combined with a strong sense of plant form. The Floralies de Paris (1957) was a massive short display set in a steel, concrete and glass framework and using rocks, water and over 14,000 plants. By contrast, he was involved with the long-term tree planting of the deer park and drive at Longleat. At La Leopolda, Villefranche, he met the challenge of including in the garden a small secluded swimming pool near to but hidden from the house, and delighted in the result. Other gardens include Palazzo Colonna, Rome, the Patino Gardens, Soto Grande and the Frick Gallery and William S. Paley Gardens, New York. In 1951, he created the Battersea Festival Gardens and received the OBE. His book, *The Education of a Gardener*, published in 1962, covers over 40 years experience and is a classic text for students of garden design.

**Paliavana** Vand. (From Palhava, a seat of the Prince of Braganza, a patron of botany.) Gesneriaceae. 3 species of evergreen shrubs; stem branching. Leaves opposite, fleshy, crenate, villous. Flowers axillary, solitary or in fascicles and a lax terminal raceme; calyx campanulate, adnate to ovary at base, lobes 5, subequal, acute, reflexed; corolla tube narrow to campanulate, limb oblique, lobes 5, rounded, somewhat reflexed; stamens 4, included, anthers connate into a cross; disc with 5 glands. Fruit an oblique, 2-valved capsule. Brazil. Z10.

CULTIVATION As for GESNERIADS.

***P. prasinata*** Benth. & Hook. f. Stem erect, prominently ringed at nodes, branching; branches roughly villous, becoming brown and woody. Lvs to 12×5cm, succulent, spreading, in opposite pairs, ovate-lanceolate, acuminate, acute at base, serrate, tomentose above, softly white-hairy beneath; petiole channelled. Fls 2 per axillary peduncle; cal. tomentose, seg. lanceolate, acuminate; cor. to 3cm, funnelform, green, spotted with black, inflated, limb revolute, seg. rotund. Brazil.

***P. schiffneri*** (Fritsch) Handro. See *Sinningia schiffneri*.

**Palicourea** Aubl. Rubiaceae. Some 125 species of shrubs or trees. Stems terete or 4-angled. Leaves sessile or petiolate, opposite or whorled; stipules persistent or deciduous, connate at base, 2-lobed or -cleft. Flowers sessile or short-pedicellate, in axillary or terminal panicles, cymes or corymbs; minutely bracteate; calyx tube turbinate or hemispheric, limb persistent, truncate or 5-toothed to lobed; corolla funnel-shaped to subcylindric, tube plane or curved, tube occasionally gibbous at base, pubescent at throat, lobes 5, valvate; stamens 5, inserted at throat, anthers linear, apex obtuse; ovary 2-celled, style 2-branched, stigma 2-lobed, ovules solitary in each cell, erect. Fruit a berry, globose to ellipsoid, 2-celled, pyrenes 2, 1-seeded, angular or crested. Tropical America. Z10.

CULTIVATION As for *Portlandia*.

***P. apicata*** HBK. Shrub, to 2m, or tree, to 10m. Stems terete. Lvs to 12×4cm, elliptic or lanceolate to oblong, apex attenuate to acute, base acute, lustrous and leathery to papery, glabrous, to pubesc. on veins, 12–14-veined; stipules to 4mm, lobed, glabrous; petioles to 11mm, glabrous; bracts to 3mm, ovate to deltoid or lanceolate, apex acute, glabrous. Fls in sessile, terminal, pyramidal panicles to 8×6cm, white or yellow to violet or purple; pedicels to 6mm, glabrous; cal. to 2mm, tube bell-shaped, teeth to 7mm, deltoid to suborbicular, glandular; cor. tube to 9mm, gibbous at base, tuberculose, exterior glabrous, lobes to 4×2mm, ovate or lanceolate to oblong, apex subacute or obtuse. Fr. to 8×7mm, subglobose to ovoid, 6–7-ribbed, glabrous. Venezuela.

***P. crocea*** (Sw.) Roem. & Schult. Shrub, to 5m. Stems terete or obsoletely 4-angled. Lvs to 20×6cm, ovate, lanceolate or elliptic to oblong, apex and base attenuate to acute, stiff and leathery, glabrous to sparsely and minutely pubesc. on veins beneath; stipules to 5mm, persistent, 2-lobed, linear, apex subulate to narrowly acute; petioles to 25mm. Fls in axillary or terminal, erect, branched, many-fld, pyramidal panicles or corymbs, yellow or orange to red; pedicels to 12mm, peduncles to 6cm; bracts to 1mm, deltoid, apex narrowly acute; cal. to 1mm, yellow, lobes deltoid; cor. to 1cm, tubular to cylindric, tube somewhat gibbous at base, glabrous, interior pubesc. at throat, lobes to 1mm, ovate. Fr. to 6mm, compressed ovoid to ellipsoid, crested, red to brown or black. Summer. W Indies and Cuba, C America, Northern S America.

***P. guianensis*** Aubl. Shrub or tree, to 3.5m. Stems 4-angled and robust, glabrous to minutely pubesc. Lvs to 25×13cm, ovate to elliptic, apex narrowly acute, base acute or obtuse and semi-decurrent, papery glabrous to minutely pubesc. on veins beneath; stipules to 15mm, persistent, 2-lobed, apex obtuse; petioles to 3cm. Fls in terminal, thyrsoid or corymbose panicles, yellow to orange; pedicels to 8mm, peduncles to 10cm, 4-angled; cal. lobes to 1mm, pubesc.; cor. to 15mm, tubular, tube distended above, exterior minutely pubesc. Fr. to 8mm, ovoid, succulent, minutely pubesc., purple to black. W Indies, C America, Northern S America. ssp. ***guianensis***. Ovary 3–4-celled. Guyana, Surinam, Brazil. ssp. ***barbinervia*** (DC.) Steyerm. Lvs densely pubesc. on veins. Cal. lobes ciliate; cor. tube pubesc. at throat. Venezuela, Brazil.

***P. nicotinaefolia*** Cham. & Schldl. Shrub or tree. Stems terete, initially pubesc. Lvs to 20×7cm, obovate to oblanceolate or elliptic, apex caudate, base acute or cuneate, 12–15-veined; stipules to 6mm, 2-lobed, apex acute; petioles to 2cm, glabrous. Fls in terminal, thyrsoid panicles to 18cm, yellow; peduncles to 7cm, 4-angled, pubesc.; cal. to 1mm, pubesc., lobes deltoid; cor. to 12mm, tubular, tube pubesc., lobes to 2mm, deltoid. Fr. to 6mm, compressed subglobose, ribbed, glabrous. S America.

***P. rigida*** HBK. Shrub, to 3m. Stems simple or sparsely branched, 4-angled and robust, glabrous. Lvs to 20×12cm, sessile or subsessile, ovate to elliptic, apex and base acute or obtuse, leathery, stiff and rugose, glabrous, 13–20-veined; stipules to 4mm, 2-lobed, apex subulate. Fls in many-fld, pyramidal, cymose panicles, yellow to orange; pedicels minutely pubesc., peduncles to 20cm, 4-angled; cal. lobes deltoid; cor. to 15mm, tube exterior. papillose, lobes to 5mm. Fr. to 5mm, compressed ovoid, grooved. Summer. Tropical S America.

***P. barbinervia*** DC. See *P. guianensis* ssp. *barbinervia*.
***P. brevithyrsa*** Britt. & Standl. See *P. crocea*.
***P. coccinea*** DC. See *P. crocea*.
For further synonymy see *Psychotria*.

**Palisota** Rchb. ex Endl., nom. cons. (For A.M.F.J. Palisot de Beauvois (1752–1820), French botanist and traveller.) Commelinaceae. 18 poorly differentiated species of rhizomatous, clump-forming, perennial herbs, some almost stemless with large, apparently radical leaves. Inflorescence thyrses sometimes borne low amid leaf stalks, often congested, cincinni elongate, not paired; flowers bisexual and male; sepals petaloid; petals free, not clawed, similar to sepals; pollen-bearing stamens 3, antepetalous, staminodes 2–3, antesepalous, lacking anthers, filaments bearded. Fruit an orange, pink or red, blue or black berry; seeds uni- or biseriate, exarillate, hilum punctiform, embryotega dorsal. Rainforests of tropical Africa. Z10.

CULTIVATION All species need a warm, humid and shaded greenhouse environment with a minimum temperature of 15°C/60°F, a well-drained potting mix and plentiful water when in full growth. Propagate by cuttings or seed.

***P. barteri*** Hook. Robust herb, usually almost stemless, but sometimes with a stem to 1m tall. Lvs 12–50×5–18cm, elliptic to somewhat ovate or obovate, held semi-erect or arching, thinly coriaceous, undulate, glossy light green, downy beneath, narrowed at base into a distinct petiole 2.5–25cm. Infl. ovoid, dense, 10–15cm, without conspicuous bracts; fls white. Fr. purple, usually ripening bright red. Spring. W & C Tropical Africa. Z9.

***P. bracteosa*** C.B. Clarke. Stemless herb or merely rhizomatous with a rosette of lvs arising at about ground level. Lvs 25–40×5.5–14cm, elliptic to oblanceolate or narrowly obovate, often with green-white stripe along midrib above, gradually cuneate to base, almost sessile or with petiole to 25cm. Infl. 4–18×1.5–4cm; bracts *c*5–10mm wide, conspicuous, ovate, long-ciliate; fls pink-white or white. Fr. red, pilose, beaked. Spring. W Tropical Africa. *P. elizabethae* Gent., in which the lvs are variegated with an attractive, feathery, white midstripe, is usually treated as *P. pynaertii* 'Elizabethae', but may be referable here. Z9.

***P. hirsuta*** (Thunb.) Schum. Robust herb to 6m, but flowering when 1.5m tall. Lvs *c*40×8cm, clustered towards apex of stems, elliptic, acuminate, short-petiolate, glossy green, subcoriaceous, petioles and sheaths with long dark brown hairs to 15mm. Infl. 10–30cm, lax, with numerous slender, stalked cincinni, off-white to pink-flushed; fls 1cm diam., opening late afternoon; pet. white, tipped maroon; anth. yellow. Fr. black-green or bruised purple-red, glossy. Winter–spring. W & C Tropical Africa. Z9.

***P. mannii*** C.B. Clarke. Usually stemless, sometimes with stems 30–100cm. Lvs 40–100×11–21cm; petiole to 30cm. Infl. elongate, 7–19×1.5–4cm, without conspicuous bracts; fls very numerous, small, white, later pale pink or lilac. Fr. green or white at first, turning yellow, orange-red or deep purple when mature. Spring. Tropical Africa. Z9.

***P. pynaertii*** De Wildeman. Virtually stemless. Lvs 35–90×10–25cm, clustered or in a rosette, narrowly ovate to obovate-lanceolate, acuminate, deep green and glabrous above, grey and velvety beneath, margins undulate, petiole thick, hairy, channelled, ciliate with long rufous hairs. Infl. ovoid, *c*10cm; fls white. Fr. red. Spring. Tropical Africa. A species of uncertain status. For the plant usually treated as *P. pynaertii* 'Elizabethae', see *P. bracteosa*. Z9.

***P. maclaudii*** Gand. See *P. hirsuta*.
***P. thyrsiflora*** Benth. See *P. hirsuta*.

**Paliurus** Mill. (Name for the genus used by Dioscorides.) Rhamnaceae. 8 species of spiny, deciduous or evergreen trees or shrubs to about 15m. Leaves alternate, 3-veined, ovate to cordate, entire to toothed, usually in 2 rows, with spinescent stipules. Inflorescence axillary, flowers small, 5-merous, yellow, styles 2–3. Fruit flat, dry, hemispherical, with a wide, membranous wing around the apex. S Europe to E Asia.

CULTIVATION From the dry sandy hills around the Mediterranean, where it ascends to altitudes of 3000m/97500ft. *P. spina-christi* is sometimes included in gardens with a biblical theme, thought to have been used for Jesus' Crown of Thorns. It has long been used in hedging, having a loose but bushy habit; the slender spiny stems emerge erect but later arch under the weight of side branches. The attractive flowers in summer are followed by unusual fruits and good clear yellow autumn colour. The young growth of *P. ramosissimus* is particularly attractive, being covered in rusty silky down. All species are suited to plantings at the base of a warm, south- or southwest-facing wall or for dry borders, especially on limy soils. *P. spina-christi* is hardy to −15°C/5°F, perhaps more, and although top growth will be cut down by frost, it re-emerges from the base provided that the roots are protected from damage. Other species are slightly less hardy.

Grow in full sun in any very well-drained fertile soil. Prune in winter to remove old and overcrowded growth, cutting back to the centre of the bush to conceal cuts and maintain shape. Cut overgrown specimens hard back to the base. Propagate by softwood cuttings in summer; by seed sown in the frame or under glass after a winter scarification. Also by root cuttings or simple layering.

**Palmae** (a) *Normanbya normanbyi* (×0.01) (b) *Jubaea chilensis* (×0.01), fruit (×0.75) (c) *Chrysalidocarpus lutescens* (×0.02) (d) *Licuala grandis* (×0.05), leaf margin, hermaphrodite flower (×4.5) (e) *Chamaerops humilis* (×0.02), leaf (×0.15) (inflorescence at base of petiole), part of inflorescence (×0.73)

***P. hemsleyanus*** Rehd. Tree to 10m or 15m, young growth slender, glabrous, with black thorns, rarely lacking spines. Lvs 6–10cm, 3-veined, obovate to oval-lanceolate, leathery, apex acute, base rounded, margins crenate, shiny dark green above, pale beneath. Fr. on short stalks, 3cm diam., with a russet-brown wing. S China. Z9.

***P. ramosissimus*** (Lour.) Poir. Shrub, 1.5–3m, branches flexuous, thorns sharp, young twigs with silky, rusty-brown pubescence. Lvs 3.5–5cm, on 3–4mm petioles, distinctly 3-veined, ovate to oblong, glabrous, base and apex blunt, margins with small teeth, dark glossy green above, paler beneath. Infl. an axillary cyme, tomentose; style 2-lobed at apex. Fr. to 12mm diam., woody, obconical, truncate, single-seeded. China, Korea, Japan, Taiwan. Z7.

***P. spina christi*** Mill. CHRIST'S THORN. Tree or shrub, 3–7m, twigs flexuous, hairy, thorns paired, 1 straight, 1 curved. Lvs 2–4cm, on short petioles, alternate, in 2 rows, entire to crenate-serrate, hairy on veins beneath. Infl. axillary, cymose, small, umbel-like, short-pedunculate, on current year's growth. Fr. 18–30mm diam., woody, 3-lobed, subglobose, wing undulate. Spring, summer. Spain to C Asia and N China. Long cultivated as a hedging plant. Z8.

***P. aculeatus*** Lam. See *P. spina-christi*.
***P. aubletii*** Benth. See *P. ramosissimus*.
***P. australis*** Gaertn. See *P. spina-christi*.
***P. orientalis*** Hemsl. See *P. hemsleyanus*.

**Palladio, Andrea** (1508–1580). Architect, born in Padua. Perhaps the most well known of 16th-century architects. Palladio's designs were disseminated with the publication of his *I Quattro Libri dell'Architettura* (1570) and the many republications and adaptations which followed. He directly addresses the design of villas and their gardens, stating that villas should ideally be situated near a river, both for reasons of transport and because 'it will render the prospect most agreeable' and 'ornament and water the fields, gardens and stalls'. The area around the villa should have the appearance of a 'great theatre', an opinion derived from Pliny the Younger and Vitruvius. This idea implied the notion of human activity and made cultivated land preferable to untamed nature; a prevalent Renaissance attitude.

The situation of the villa Capra (or the Rotunda) is described in detail: Palladio employed a site that was 'most agreeable ... because it is on a hillock with gentle approaches and is surrounded with other charming hills that give the effect of a huge theatre and they are all cultivated'. The villa consequently has a loggia on each of its four faces from which to view the different scenes. The Villa Barbaro at Maser displays Palladio's ability to integrate both villa and garden. In the garden is a nymphaeum, with olympian gods and wood-nymphs set in niches around a pool. Water travels from here to the kitchen, and, after irrigating the gardens, forms two fish ponds, from which the kitchen garden is watered. Palladio viewed the villa as an organism, stressing the importance of harmony between the house and its environment and consequently making exterior spaces reflect the proportions of the interior. Palladio's architecture has been enormously influential, leading, through Inigo Jones, to the Palladianism of 17th- and 18th-century England.

**Pallensis** (Cass.) Cass.
***P. spinosa*** (L.) Cass. See *Asteriscus spinosus*.

**Palma** Plum. ex Mill.
***P. elata*** Bartr. See *Roystonea elata*.

**PALMAE** Juss. (*Arecaceae* Schultz). PALM FAMILY. Monocots. 198 genera and 2650 species of evergreen monoecious or dioecious trees, shrubs and climbers, sometimes fiercely armed; stem woody, short to very tall, solitary or many by basal suckering, unbranched except at the base, few aerially branched. Leaves spirally arranged, usually very large and in terminal rosettes, with well-defined sheathing base; petiole absent, short or well-developed, variously armed or unarmed; lamina pinnate (feather palms), palmate (fan palms), less often entire or bipinnate, simple initially and often splitting during development into V-shaped (induplicate) or A-shaped (reduplicate) leaflets from the plicate condition; ligule a prolongation of the sheath, sometimes surrounding the stem or absent. Inflorescence usually axillary, simple or paniculate, with thick spadix-like branchlets; peduncle with prophyll and 1-several spathes. Flowers inconspicuous, sessile, usually insect pollinated, unisexual, 3-merous, almost regular; perianth usually 3+3, differentiated into calyx and corolla or undifferentiated, leathery or fleshy, green to yellow, red or white; stamens 3-many, free or united; staminodes frequently present in pistillate flowers; ovary usually 3-loculed, with 1 fertile and 2 abortive locules; stigmas erect or recurred. Fruit a berry or 2 fleshy or fibrous drupe, 1-seeded, rarely 2–10-seeded; endosperm usually very oily, with protein and hemicellulose, sometimes ruminate. Of great economic importance, producing an enormous range of foods, oils, fermented products, waxes, fibres, canes, etc. Moist tropics and subtropics, few in warm temperate and arid tropics. *Acanthophoenix, Acoelorraphe, Acrocomia, Aiphanes, Allagoptera, Archontophoenix, Areca, Arenga, Attalea, Bactris, Borassus, Brahea, Butia, Calamus, Carpentaria, Caryota, Ceroxylon, Chamaedorea, Chamaerops, Chambeyronia, Chrysalidocarpus, Coccothrinax, Cocos, Copernicia, Corypha, Cyrtostachys, Dictyosperma, Drymophloeus, Elaeis, Euterpe, Gaussia, Gronophyllum, Hedyscepe, Howea, Hydriastele, Hyophorbe, Hyphaene, Jubaea, Jubaeopsis, Laccospadix, Latania, Licuala, Linospadix, Livistona, Lodoicea, Maximiliana, Metroxylon, Nephrosperma, Normanbya, Nypa, Oncosperma, Orbignya, Parajubaea, Phoenicophorium, Phoenix, Pigafetta, Pinanga, Polyandrococos, Pritchardia, Ptychosperma, Raphia, Reinhardtia, Rhapidophyllum, Rhapis, Rhopalostylis, Roystonea, Sabal, Salacca, Schippia, Serenoa, Syagrus, Thrinax, Trachycarpus, Trithrinax, Veitchia, Verschaffeltia, Wallichia, Washingtonia.*

**Palms**. Palms are virtually unique in their habit of growth and hence have special potential as features in gardens and larger landscaped areas, where they can be grown outside. They are equally valuable as container-grown specimens in conservatories and dwellings. The dwarf species are naturally the most useful for containers. In most cases such plants are in their juvenile state, quite distinct from the adult, which they may not resemble in foliage, and they may be difficult to identify as young plants.

For outdoor cultivation frost-hardiness is the main limiting factor. Most need tropical or subtropical temperatures, but local climatic conditions and soils may affect the successful growth of palms even within the same climatic zone; local advice on suitable species should be sought.

Palms are most easily propagated from seed, although some can be increased by division or from suckers (*Chamaerops, Rhapis, Caryota, Ptychosperma, Chamaedorea* spp.). In most cases it is essential that seed be fresh, this being more important the more tropical the plant's origin; palms from temperate or arid zones have a considerably longer viability period (*Washingtonia, Trachycarpus, Chamaerops, Phoenix*). Some very tropical species have a viability of only a few days, or weeks (*Cyrtostachys, Rhopaloblaste*). It is worth enquiring the age of seed from importers or dealers, stale seed being a common cause of failure. An increasing number of specialist nurseries offer seedlings of rare and unusual species.

Seed can be collected from the parent tree when ripe, and that brought back from excursions in warmer climates is often successfully grown. All traces of flesh should be thoroughly cleaned off to discourage mould growth.

Seed should be planted, to its own depth, in any proprietary potting medium. The main requirements are an ability to hold moisture but to be free-draining. The potting medium should be moist but not wet. Small quantities of seed may be planted in pots or trays, buried 60–120mm/2½–5in. deep; the labelled containers are then placed in a seed propagator or a sealed plastic bag to retain humidity – an essential for successful germination. Large quantities of seed may be simply mixed with the moistened medium and placed directly in a clear plastic bag and removed individually on germination. No light is required. Large seeds such as the coconut and the rather smaller betel palm (*Areca catechu*) are half-buried in a seed-raising medium in individual pots.

The ideal temperature for successful germination varies with the species. Temperate-area palms will germinate well without addi-

**Palmae** (a) *Rhopalostylis baueri* flowering plant (male) (×0.014), male flowers (×1.2) (b) *Washingtonia robusta* mature plant with 'petticoat' of dead leaves (×0.014), leaf detached (×0.05) (c) *Pritchardia thurstonii* fruiting plant (×0.014), flower showing the deciduous corolla (×3.2) (d) *Livistona chinensis* habit (×0.014), leaf base with prominent ligule (e) *Copernicia prunifera* habit (×0.014); note leaf bases persistent on lower third of trunk (f) *Howea belmoreana* (×0.014)

**Palmae** (a) *Raphia farinifera* (×0.08) (b) *Arenga pinnata* (×0.01), male inflorescence, flower; female inflorescence, flower and fruit (×0.2) (c) *Hyphaene thebaica* (×0.01), leaf (d) *Rhapis excelsa* (×0.025) (e) *Aiphanes caryotifolia* (×0.01) (f) *Linospadix monostachya* (×0.025)

**Palmae** (a) *Verschaffeltia splendida* (×0.025) (b) *Phoenicophorium borsigianum* (×0.03) (c) *Hyophorbe lagenicaulis* (×0.025) (d) *Reinhardtia gracilis* (×0.025) (e) *Calamus caryotoides* (×0.04), fruit (×3) (f) *Nypa fruticans* (×0.015) inflorescence (×0.025), fruit (×0.08)

**Palmae** (a) *Areca catechu* (×0.02), fruit (×0.25) (b) *Butia capitata* (×0.02) (c) *Archontophoenix alexandrae* (×0.02) (d) *Acoelorraphe wrightii* (×0.02), portion of inflorescence (×0.75), flower and stamens enlarged (e) *Caryota mitis* (×0.02), and leaf

tional heat; tropical species may require 30–35°C/85–95°F. The time for germination also varies considerably. Fresh seed may sprout within a week or two, although this is not always the case. Most species will germinate within two or three months, but some may take up to two years. During this time the planting medium must not be allowed to dry out, and the temperature must be maintained. Techniques to hasten germination include filing or cracking the hard seed coat, soaking in warm or hot water for days or weeks, and soaking in acid, but opinions vary as to the success of these methods.

'Sprouts' should be potted up individually as soon as the first leaf appears. Some species grow an extensive root system before there is any top growth so this should not be delayed. 8cm/3in. pots are usually the best size to use and the young plants should be grown in a similar medium to that in which they germinated. More organic matter is appreciated by older plants. Most palms tolerate a wide range of soil types again origin should be used as a guide to possible preference, but the medium should be well-drained and moisture retaining. Place the newly potted palm in a warm and bright location but out of direct sunlight, and water well. The seed should not be removed from the seedling at any stage.

As the young plant grows it can be potted on into increasingly larger pots when in active growth. It used to be believed that palms grow best with restricted root space but this is not now thought to be the case, and potting on may be done as the roots fill the old pot. Watering must not be neglected, but should be carried out only when the surface of the potting medium feels dry to the touch. Keeping the potting medium continually moist may cause the roots to rot and the eventual death of the plant. Feeding with a balanced fertilizer suitable for potplants should be carried out regularly, especially if the plants cannot be potted on after reaching containers of largest possible size, but young plants should not be over-fed.

Most palms grown in pots under cover benefit from moisture in the air. Indeed, this is essential for many of the more tropical species. High air humidity can be provided in the greenhouse; in conservatories and in the home it is best achieved with an electric humidifier, which distributes minute water droplets into the air. The more expensive models switch off when a pre-set humidity level has been reached. Alternatively, the plants may be misted over, preferably with rainwater, but this needs to be done frequently to be of real benefit. Traditional methods such as grouping plants together, or growing them in pots standing on a tray of pebbles kept wet, may also help. A kitchen or bathroom is often a good place in which to grow a palm because of the higher humidity levels.

Bright indirect light is preferred by most species of palm. Many as seedlings grow on the jungle floor and consequently will tolerate rather low light levels (*Caryota, Phoenix roebelinii, Chamaedorea, Howea, Rhapis*). Sunlight filtered through net curtains is ideal as is a spot in a north-facing window. Direct sunlight through glass must be avoided as this will scorch the leaves.

In containers in the greenhouse, the conservatory or in the home, most palms grow slowly, generally as a result of dry air and insufficient levels of light. This can be an advantage as long as the plants remain healthy, for a palm can remain in the same container for a number of years, and will not grow too large for the space available. Conservatories are ideal places in which to grow palms, not least because of the increased light and temperature.

In warm and, in a few cases, in temperate areas, the young palm may be planted outside when considered sturdy enough, when two or three years old. Most require to be shaded from hot sun while young.

In the warmer parts of the world cultivated palms are an obvious and beautiful addition to the garden, but some care should be exercised as to species as many are extremely fast-growing and can dominate the landscape in a remarkably short space of time. Many do not like competition and look best as individual specimens, though others look good in twos or threes or larger groups of the same species. Mixed groups should usually be avoided. Palms are among the easiest of trees to care for, requiring virtually no maintenance apart perhaps from the removal of the occasional dead leaf.

The predictability of their mature size and shape makes garden design considerably easier than with most trees and shrubs, and the eventual size of the plant should be considered when choosing a site. Obstructions such as overhanging trees or wires should be taken into account, as much the individual species' preference for sunlight or shade. Most palms are not fussy as to soil type but any obvious deficiencies should be made up before planting.

In temperate areas the number of palms suitable for planting out is much diminished. However, there are several that thrive in favoured areas. These include the Chusan palm (*Trachycarpus fortunei*), its stiff-leaved variety 'Wagnerianus', the European or Mediterranean fan palm (*Chamaerops humilis*), the butia or jelly palm (*Butia capitata*) and the Chilean wine palm (*Jubaea chilensis*). Others that would undoubtedly be suitable but are difficult to obtain are the Andean wax palm (*Ceroxylon alpinum*) and *Parajubaea cocoides*, from Ecuador. The keen gardener who is prepared to go to some trouble to provide varying degrees of protection during the winter can grow several borderline species that are not strictly hardy in cool-temperature areas but grow reasonably well during the summer months. These include the Californian cotton palm (*Washingtonia filifera*), the feather duster palm (*Rhopalostylis sapida*) from New Zealand, and the Canary Island date palm (*Phoenix canariensis*). Finally, several species are worth mentioning as being extremely cold-resistant but requiring summer heat to grow well. These include the world's hardiest, the needle palm (*Rhapidophyllum hystrix*) which will withstand temperatures down to −20°C/−4°F, the palmetto palm (*Sabal minor*) and the blue hesper palm (*Brahea armata*).

In general, palms transplant readily, most having a fairly compact root system. Unlike most trees, palms move best when in active growth, generally in spring and early summer. Ideally, the palm should be prepared some months before being moved. A trench is dug all the way around the tree some two or three spade-widths from it and perhaps four or five deep, any roots that are encountered begin cut through. The trench is then filled in and the palm is left for at least three months, during which time new roots will grow from the base of the trunk; the cut roots do not re-grow. A few days before the move, the palm should be watered thoroughly to allow it to take up the maximum amount of water. The trench is then reopened and the root-ball is undercut. A crane or winch may be utilized at this stage to lift the tree from the ground. The weight of even a small tree with its root-ball is considerable, especially when wet, and should not be underestimated. The root-ball should be wrapped in hessian or black polythene to retain moisture, and the leaves should be tied in a bundle.

If the above method has been used it may not be necessary to remove any of the leaves. However, if the plant is to be transplanted immediately without the above preparation, approximately half the leaves should be cut back to reduce transpiration and the rest tied up as before.

A hole should be dug at the new site that is somewhat larger than the root-ball and a quantity of garden compost, good topsoil, well-rotted stable manure or lawn clippings, etc. should be used as a foundation for the palm. Lower the tree gently into place and back-fill the hole with more of the same mixture, firming it well down. Large trees should be staked or secured with guy wires. It is useful if soil is used to create a dished shape around the trunk to facilitate watering, which must be carried out regularly and often, perhaps once a day in dry areas, until the plant is well established. When it is in active growth – easily checked by marking the emerging leaf spear – the watering can be relaxed and the leaves untied. Many species are moved easily and successfully without the trenching method being employed, but if the time is available this is the safest method.

Generally speaking, palms are not especially prone to pests but ornamental palms may be become infested with a polyphagous aphid, the peach-potato aphid (*Myzus persicae*), mealybug (*Pseudococcus* spp.) and the oleander scale (*Aspidiotus nerii*). Currently, Lethal Yellowing Disease (LYD) is endemic in many parts of the US. It is caused by a virus, and rapidly results in the death of the palm. Many ornamental and commercial species are prone, most notably the coconut. It is thought to be spread by insects and the symptoms are a sudden yellowing of the foliage, followed by the death of the tree. As yet there is no cure.

**Palumbina** Rchb. f. Orchidaceae. 1 species, an epiphytic orchid. Pseudobulbs elliptic, narrow, compressed, sheathed, to 4.5×1.5–2cm. Leaves 1 per bulb, borne apically, linear-lanceolate, acute to acuminate, subcoriaceous. Inflorescence lateral, few-flowered; peduncle dark purple, slender; flowers white, petal base dotted violet, callus yellow, spotted red; dorsal sepal erect, elliptic to oblong-elliptic, broad, round to obtuse, to 1×0.5cm, lateral sepals fused; petals obovate, rounded or weakly notched, to 1×0.8cm; lip ovate-elliptic, sessile, obtuse to rounded, convex, callus warty; column fused to the lip, apex winged. Guatemala. Z10.

CULTIVATION As for the smaller *Oncidium* species.

***P. candida*** (Lindl.) Rchb. f. As for the genus.

For synonymy see *Oncidium*.

**Pamianthe** Stapf. (For Major Albert Pam (*d*1955), English horticulturist, and Gk *anthe*, flower.) Amaryllidaceae. 2 or 3 species of bulbous herbs. Bulbs globose, stoloniferous, tunicate, with a long stem-like neck of sheathing leaf-bases. Leaves evergreen or deciduous, linear with a rounded keel. Flowers 1–4 in a terminal umbel on a leafless, somewhat compressed peduncle; spathe valves linear; perianth white or ivory flushed green, with a long cylindrical tube; lobes 6, subequal, to 12×2.5cm with a yellow-green band down the centre, thickened basally; stamens 6, filaments short and incurved, fused at the base into a campanulate corona, to 8×5cm, with 6 short lobes; anthers versatile, exserted from the corona; style basally joined to perianth tube by 3 wings; ovary inferior, 3-celled. Fruit a capsule; seeds many, pale brown, winged at the apex. Northern S America. Z10.

CULTIVATION *P. peruviana* is an evergreen bulb grown for its arching, strap-shaped leaves and large, white and exquisitely fragrant flowers in early spring. *Pamianthe* is frost tender, but eminently suited to the glasshouse or conservatory, with a winter minimum temperature of 10°C/50°F. Plant in a fibrous, loam-based medium in late summer/early autumn with the neck of the bulb at soil level, and water sparingly until growth commences. Grow in bright indirect light and water moderately when in growth, reducing water after flowering to keep just moist enough to prevent wilting. Pot-grown plants may be moved outdoors for the summer, when danger of frost is passed. Top-dress in autumn, and re-pot every third or fourth year.

Propagate by offsets. Seeds take 12–15 months to mature on the plant, but germinate rapidly if sown when ripe in a warm and humid closed case.

***P. peruviana*** Stapf. Lvs to 50×4cm, 5–7, spreading. Peduncle exceeding lvs; fls 2–4, fragrant, perianth tube to 13cm, green, lobes to 13cm, white or flushed cream, the inner ones to 3cm wide, oblanceolate with a central green stripe; corona to 8cm, lobes bifid or mucronate, free portions of fil. to 12mm. Peru.

**Panax** L. (From Lat. *panax*, a cure-all, from Gk *panakes*, relating to the supposed marvellous virtues attributed by East Asians to ginseng.) GINSENG. Araliaceae. About 5 species of perennial, offsetting herbs with thickened or tuberous roots. Stems annual, scaly at base, to 0.8m, with a single whorl of 3 palmately 3–7-foliolate leaves and terminated by a solitary umbel (sometimes together with a subsidiary whorl of pedunculate umbels). Calyx 5-toothed; petals 5, overlapping in bud, spreading on opening; stamens 5; ovary 2–3-locular; styles free. Fruit drupaceous, 2–3-seeded. S & E Asia, Eastern N America.

CULTIVATION Moderately ornamental plants for woodland gardens in cool-temperate areas, grown as spreading groundcover, interesting for their delicate umbels of green-white flowers and the fruit which follows. Plant in moist, humus-rich soil and mulch annually with organic matter. Propagate from seed or by division of the tuberous rootstock.

Commercially, 'Manchurian Imperial' (*P. ginseng*) ranks as the highest quality crop followed by the 'Red Ginseng' (*P. ginseng*) of Korea, cultivated as a government monopoly crop and constituting one of the country's principle exports to China. The crop is grown under light shade in a rich, friable, moisture-retentive soil and the roots prepared by steaming for four hours in wicker baskets over boiling water. It is valued for its restorative powers as a tonic and stimulant, being sold at 250–500 times its weight in silver. *P. quinquefolius* is the North American substitute, classed as a third- or fourth-quality product, followed by Japanese ginseng, the least valuable.

***P. ginseng*** C.A. Mey. GINSENG; NIN-SIN. Rootstock somewhat carrot-shaped, branching when more fully developed, aromatic. Stems erect, the basal scales fleshy, persistent. Lvs 5-foliolate, leaflets elliptic to ovate, shortly stalked, gradually acuminate, the margins doubly toothed. Infl. axis above the leaf whorl elongate, with sometimes at least 1 subsidiary umbel in addition to the terminal cluster. Fr. red. Korea, NE China. The true ginseng. Z6.

***P. quinquefolius*** L. AMERICAN GINSENG; SANG. Rootstock to 2cm diam., cigar-shaped, often branching, aromatic. Stems to 1m; basal scales membranous, falling and disintegrating. Lvs 3–7-foliolate, the petioles to 10cm or so; leaflets to 16×8.5cm on stalks to 4.5cm, ovate to obovate, abruptly and slenderly acuminate, coarsely toothed. Infl. axis above the leaf whorl to 10cm, rarely to 30cm; fls green-white, mostly bisexual; styles 2. Fr. bright red, depressed-oblong, smooth, to 7×10mm. Early summer. Eastern N America. Z3.

***P. trifolius*** L. DWARF GINSENG; GROUNDNUT. Rootstock 12–13mm diam., nearly black, almost round. Stems to 20cm or so. Lvs 3–5-foliolate, the petioles to 4cm; leaflets to 8×1.5cm, sessile, oblanceolate or obovate, finely toothed. Infl. axis above the leaf whorl to 5cm; fls white, sometimes tinged pink, often male; styles 3. Fr. yellow, angled, to 4mm diam. Spring. Eastern N America. Z3.

***P. arboreus*** Forst. f. See *Pseudopanax arboreus*.
***P. balfourii*** Sander. See *Polyscias scutellaria* 'Balfourii'.
***P. crispatus*** Bull. See *Polyscias* 'Crispata'.
***P. davidii*** Franch. See *Metapanax davidii*.
***P. diffissus*** Bull. See *Polyscias* 'Diffissa'.
***P. discolor*** T. Kirk. See *Pseudopanax discolor*.
***P. dissectus*** Bull. See *Polyscias* 'Dissecta'.
***P. dumosus*** Bull. See *Polyscias* 'Dumosa'.
***P. elegans*** (Williams. See *Polyscias* 'Elegans'.
***P. excelsus*** hort. See *Polyscias* 'Excelsa'.
***P. fissus*** Bull. See *Polyscias* 'Fissa'.
***P. fruticosa*** L. See *Polyscias fruticosa*.
***P. fruticosus*** var. ***deleauanus*** (Lind.) N.E. Br.). See *Polyscias* 'Deleauana'.
***P. fruticosus*** var. ***multifida*** Veitch. See *Polyscias* 'Multifida'.
***P. fruticosus*** var. ***victoriae*** (Bull) N.E. Br. See *Polyscias guilfoylei* 'Victoriae'.
***P. laciniatus*** Williams). See *Polyscias guilfoylei* 'Laciniata'.
***P. lepidus*** Bull. See *Polyscias* 'Lepida'.
***P. lessonii*** DC. See *Pseudopanax lessonii*.
***P. nitidus*** Bull. See *Polyscias* 'Nitida'.
***P. ornatus*** Bull. See *Polyscias filicifolia* 'Ornata'.
***P. pinnatus*** Lam. See *Polyscias cumingiana*.
***P. plumatus*** Bull ex W. Richards. See *Polyscias* 'Plumata'.
***P. pseudoginseng*** auct., non Wallich. See *P. ginseng*.
***P. quinquefolius*** auct., non L. See *P. ginseng*.
***P. rotundatus*** Williams. See *Polyscias* 'Rotundata'.
***P. sambucifolius*** Sieb. See *Polyscias sambucifolia*.
***P. schinseng*** T. Nees. See *P. ginseng*.
***P. serratifolius*** Williams). See *Polyscias* 'Serratifolia'.
***P. splendens*** Kunth. See *Schefflera morototonii*.
***P. victoriae*** Bull. See *Polyscias guilfoylei* 'Victoriae'.

**Pancratium** L. (Name in Dioscorides for a bulbous plant.) Amaryllidaceae. About 16 species of bulbous perennial herbs. Leaves basal, 2-ranked, linear to lorate. Flowers 3–15 in a scapose umbel, or, rarely solitary, subtended by usually 2 scarious spathes, large, white, fragrant; perianth more or less funnelform, tube often enlarged at throat, lobes narrow, linear-lanceolate, spreading or almost erect; staminal corona conspicuous, basally united to base of filaments, anthers dorsifixed; ovary 3-celled, stigma capitate. Fruit a capsule; seeds numerous, black, angled. Canary Is., Mediterranean to Tropical Asia, W Africa to Namibia. Distinguished from *Hymenocallis* by its numerous seeds with thin, dry, black testa.

CULTIVATION The species most commonly grown in temperate gardens are those from warm Mediterranean habitats characterized chiefly by their impeccable drainage, where bulbs ripen fully in hot dry conditions in summer. Handsome plants grown for their strongly fragrant, white flowers in summer, they are suitable for the cool glasshouse or conservatory, or for outdoor cultivation given a warm sheltered position in full sun at the base of a south-facing wall. *P. illyricum* is hardy to −5°C/23°F; *P. maritimum* is almost as hardy although the foliage is susceptible to frost, and in temperate gardens, the necessary hot dry conditions for bulb ripening are seldom achieved. Plant outdoors 15–30cm/6–12in. deep on to a base of sharp sand, otherwise grow under glass as for *Amaryllis*. *P. zeylanicum* requires hothouse conditions, as for *Hippeastrum*. Propagate by offsets or from ripe seed.

***P. canariense*** Ker-Gawl. Resembles *P. illyricum* but lvs broader, pedicels much longer (to 3cm), corona teeth shorter, and free part of fil. scarcely as long as anth. Early autumn. Canary Is. Z9.

***P. illyricum*** L. Bulb large, covered with purple-black scales. Lvs 50×1.5–3cm, broad, ligulate, deciduous, glaucous, strongly veined. Scape to 40cm; pedicels 1–1.5cm; fls fragrant; perianth white, sometimes ivory or cream at base of seg. and on corona, tube c2cm, lobes 5cm, linear-oblong to narrowly elliptic; corona much longer than perianth, teeth paired, long and narrow, alternating with stamens; free part of fil. much longer than anth. Late spring-early summer. W Mediterranean Is. (Corsica, Sardinia). Z8.

***P. maritimum*** L. Resembles *P. illyricum* but bulb scales pale, bulb very long-necked; lvs longer and narrower, persistent; fls highly fragrant; perianth tube to 7.5cm, very slender; corona two-thirds length of perianth, with short triangular teeth alternating with stamens; free part of fil. about the same length as anth. Summer. Mediterranean, SW Europe. Z8.

***P. zeylanicum*** L. Lvs lorate-lanceolate, fresh green, not glaucous. Scape to 30cm; fls solitary; pedicels short; perianth lobes narrowly lanceolate longer than tube, fused at base, free and recurved toward apex; style exceeding stamens. Summer. Sri Lanka. Z10.

***P. amboinense*** L. See *Proiphys amboinensis*.
***P. aurantiacum*** HBK. See *Stenomesson aurantiacum*.
***P. australasicum*** Ker-Gawl. See *Proiphys amboinensis*.
***P. coccineum*** Ruiz & Pav. See *Stenomesson coccineum*.
***P. flavum*** Ruiz & Pav. See *Stenomesson flavum*.
***P. latifolium*** Ruiz & Pav. See *Urceolina latifolia*.
***P. mexicanum*** L. See *Hymenocallis concinna*.
***P. variegatum*** Ruiz & Pav. See *Stenomesson variegatum*.
***P. viridiflorum*** Ruiz & Pav. See *Stenomesson viridiflorum*.

**PANDANACEAE** R. Br. SCREW PINE FAMILY. Monocot. 3 genera and 675 species of dioecious (bisexual inflorescence or flowers in *Freycinetia*) pachycaul trees and shrubs or lianes with clasping aerial roots, sometimes epiphytic; prop-roots usually at base of stem; branching sympodial. Leaves simple, glabrous, parallel-veined, in 3 ranks (4 in *Sararanga*) appearing as spirals 'screw-pines' due to spiral growth of stem, bases sheathing, blades usually elongate (to 5 m), xeromorphic, with marginal spines, also on the midrib. Inflorescence terminal, with few bract-like leaves at the base, going gradually over into foliage leaves, usually a racemose spadix without bracts or bracteoles to the individual flowers which are very small and numerous. Male flowers in *Freycinetia* with rudimentary ovary but not in other genera; floral axis of the male inflorescence with a number of stamens, arranged in a racemose or umbel-like manner upon it; ovary in female flowers of numerous carpels in a ring, 1-loculed or numerous-loculed, the fusion almost complete, or reduced to 1 carpel or to a row of carpels transversally arranged; stigmas sessile; ovules 1 to few per locule. Fruit berries (*Freycinetia*) or drupes in heads, drupes with 12–80 pyrenes in *Sararanga*, mono-capillary with 1 seed or 'polydrupes' (connate carpels of phalanges) with united or separate endocarps; seeds small; endosperm copious, oily (starchy in *Freycinetia*). Many *Pandanus* species have edible fruits and the leaves are used for thatching and weaving. Old World tropics to New Zealand, mostly sea-coast or marsh plants. *Freycinetia, Pandanus*.

**Pandanus** R. Br. SCREW PINE. (From *pandang*, the Malayan name for these plants.) Pandanaceae. 600 species of dioecious, evergreen, woody trees or shrubs, usually erect, with conspicuous stilt roots, sometimes with prostrate, rooting stems. Trunk usually dichotomously branched, ringed by leaf scars. Leaves inserted in 3, twisted ranks, forming spirally arranged, terminal rosettes linear with acute, often long-acuminate tips, base an open sheath, margin and midrib beneath usually spiny-toothed, parallel veined; leaves just below inflorescences spathe-like, coloured, often white, sometimes scented. Flowers massed on terminal spadices, lacking calyx or corolla; male spadix a branched spike covered with stamens; female spadix solitary and simple, or racemose; ovary superior; staminodes lacking. Fruit an oblong-ellipsoid to globose syncarp of woody drupes, often pendulous. SE Asia, especially Malaysia, Australia. Z10.

CULTIVATION Grown for the sometimes thorny rosettes of sword- or strap-shaped foliage, disposed around the trunk or branch tips in spiralled fashion. *Pandanus* spp. frequently assume increasingly architectural outlines as they mature, especially as they develop aerial stilt roots for anchorage; in their native regions they are sometimes used in sand binding and erosion control. Flowers and fruit are carried only on large mature specimens, seldom seen in cultivation outdoors except in the tropics and subtropics. Juveniles of a number of species, notably *P. veitchii, P. pygmaeus* and *P. sanderi*, are handsome foliage plants for the home or conservatory. Grow in sun or light shade in any moderately fertile and well-drained soil. Under glass, admit full sun or bright filtered light and use a sandy loam-based medium with additional leafmould and some charcoal; maintain a minimum temperature of 13–16°C/55–60°F. Water plentifully and feed fortnightly with dilute liquid feed when in growth, allowing the surface of the medium to dry slightly between waterings; reduce water during winter to keep almost dry, carefully avoiding moisture on the foliage – an accumulation of water in the leaf axils will cause rot. The most luxuriant growth is achieved with buoyant high humidity, although, given access to sufficient moisture at the roots, the species described will tolerate slightly drier conditions in the home; stand pots on water-filled trays of gravel to maintain humidity. As pot-grown specimens mature they tend to heave themselves out of the pots; repot in late spring/early summer. If root pruning is necessary, keep plants in warm, lightly shaded humid conditions and water moderately until re-established. Propagate by offsets, suckers, by cuttings of lateral shoots in summer and by seed, pre-soaked for 24 hours before sowing.

***P. pygmaeus*** Thouars. Spreading shrub to 60cm, branched from base, with stilt roots. Lvs 30–60× to 1.5cm, apex narrowed to a fine point, glaucous beneath, spines on margin and midrib fine, slender, brown. Infl. on short erect peduncles hidden in upper lvs. Fr. oblong-ellipsoid, its drupes joined at base. Madagascar.

***P. sanderi*** Mast. Usually less than 60cm. Lvs 75×5cm, longitudinally striped yellow or golden and green, minutely spiny. Fr. unknown. Origin uncertain; possibly from Timor. 'Roehrsianus': robust; lvs to 1m, young lvs deep golden-yellow, later longitudinally striped pale yellow.

***P. utilis*** Bory. Branching tree to 20m. Lvs 0.5–2m×6–10cm, erect, somewhat rigid, glaucous, with red spines. Male fls scented; female fls borne on solitary, pendent, pedunculate infl. Fr. to 15cm or slightly more, made up of 100 drupes, each 3cm. Madagascar.

***P. veitchii*** Mast. & Moore. To 60cm. Lvs 50–100×75cm, narrowed to long point, slightly drooping, margin spiny, centre dark green bordered with pure or silvery-white. Fls and fr. unknown. Origin uncertain; possibly from Polynesia. 'Compactus' dwarf form.

**Pandorea** Spach. (For the Gk goddess *Pandora*.) Bignoniaceae. 6 species of lianes. Leaves pinnate; pinnae sparsely glandular below, opposite, in 1–7 pairs, oblong to ovate or elliptic. Inflorescences thyrsiform, mostly terminal; peduncle bractless; calyx cupular to campanulate, 5-lobed or truncate; corolla to 5cm, zygomorphic, tube cylindrical or funnelform, tube and lower side hairy; stamens hairy at base, unequal; ovary cells with many ovules. Capsule stalked, beaked, cylindrical to flat; valves cymbiform, leathery; seeds rounded, each in a thin wing. Australia, Papuasia, E Malesia, New Caledonia. Z9.

CULTIVATION *P. pandorana* is found in the fertile soils of coastal *Nothofagus moorei* woodlands of eastern Australia, in a climate that experiences high summer rainfall and an average winter minimum temperature of 0°C/32°F. Both *P. pandorana* and *P. jasminoides* have experienced short periods of frost, to −3 or −4°C, without appreciable damage and have proved very drought tolerant in cultivation. In warm temperate and subtropical gardens

**Pandorea and Tecomanthe** (×0.66) (a) *Pandorea jasminoides* (b) *P. pandorana* (c) *Tecomanthe speciosa* (d) *T. dendrophila*

*Pandorea* spp. make useful climbers for walls and pergolas, and are sometimes used as groundcover on banks. In cool temperate areas, they are handsome specimens for the back wall of a cool glasshouse or conservatory, especially when trained up along the rafters. They are grown for their beautiful glossy foliage and for their showy, frequently heavily scented blooms; those of *P. jasminoides* are carried from winter into early summer. The creamy flowers of *P. pandorana* are often very attractively marked with violet speckles and although small are carried in abundance. Cultivate as for *Bignonia*.

***P. jasminoides*** (Lindl.) Schum. BOWER PLANT. To 5m. Stem stout. Lvs pale green; pinnae 2.5–5×1–2cm, 4–9, ovate-lanceolate, apex obtuse. Cor. 4–5cm, white, streaked deep, rich pink within, short pubesc. Spring–summer. NE Australia. 'Alba': fls pure white. 'Lady Di': fls white, throat cream. 'Rosea': fls pink, throat darker. 'Rosea Superba': fls large, pink, throat darker, spotted purple.

***P. pandorana*** (Andrews) Steenis. WONGA-WONGA VINE. Evergreen to 6m (to 30m in habitat). Stem slender. Pinnae 3–10×1.5–6cm, usually in 6 pairs, ovate-lanceolate, glabrous, entire, sometimes crenate; petiolules to 1cm. Infl. terminal, lateral, or on old wood, 1–20cm; cal. 3mm, lobes short; cor. 1–3cm, tube twice length of lobes, tuberculate-puberulent, creamy yellow, streaked and splashed red or purple. Capsule 5–12×1.75–3×2.5cm, leathery; seeds to 3×2cm, including wing. Winter–spring. Australia, New Guinea, Pacific Is. 'Rosea': fls pale pink.

***P. amboinensis*** Boerl. See *Tecomanthe dendrophila*.
***P. australis*** Spach. See *P. pandorana*.
***P. brycei*** (N.E. Br.) Rehd. See *Podranea brycei*.
***P. dendrophila*** Boerl. See *Tecomanthe dendrophila*.
***P. ricasoliana*** (Tenf.) Baill. See *Podranea ricasoliana*.
For further synonymy see *Bignonia* and *Tecoma*.

**Panicum** L. PANIC GRASS; CRAB GRASS. (From a Lat. name for millet.) Gramineae. Some 470 species of annual or perennial grasses. Leaves threadlike to linear-ovate. Inflorescence paniculate to racemose, open to contracted; spikelets symmetric to laterally compressed, awnless, abscising at maturity, 2-flowered, lower flower male, upper flower hermaphrodite; lower glume truncate to awned, equal to or shorter than spikelet, upper glume as long as spikelet; lower lemma as for upper glume, leathery to rigid, margins involute, apex obtuse to acute or apiculate, upper lemma convex, becoming coriaceous; stamens 3. Pantropical to temperate N America. Z5.

CULTIVATION *Panicum* spp. are grown for the large intricately branched flowerheads which are used for drying; *P. virgatum*, a fairly hardy perennial species, is noted for its generosity of bloom and, in the form 'Rubrum', for the foxy russet colours in autumn which persist into winter. Grow in any moderately fertile well-drained soil in sun. Propagate annuals by seed sown in early spring under glass and set out after danger of frost is passed, perennials by division.

***P. boscii*** Poir. Culms to 70cm, glabrous or minutely puberulent. Lf sheaths glabrous; lvs to 12×3cm, spreading, sparsely ciliate at base, glabrous. Panicle to 12cm; spikelets papillose. E US.

***P. capillare*** L. OLD WITCH GRASS; WITCH GRASS. Annual, to 90cm. Stems clumped, upright to spreading, slender to robust. Lvs linear to narrow-lanceolate, to 30cm×1.4cm, stiffly pubesc.; sheaths stiffly pubesc. Panicles open, to 45cm+, green to purple; branches spreading; spikelets stipitate, to 3mm; lower glume to 2mm, upper glume, lower lemma acuminate, equal. Summer–autumn. S Canada, US. var. ***occidentale*** Rydb. Spikelets slightly larger than species type.

***P. maximum*** Jacq. Rhizomatous perenn. to 3m, densely tufted. Stems erect, 3–4-noded, simple or sparsely branched. Lf sheaths firm, lower compressed, otherwise terete; lvs linear, glabrous or softly pubesc. with scabrous margins; ligule membranous, very short, ciliolate. Panicle erect or nodding, to 45cm, occasionally glabrous, otherwise villous; spikelets to 5cm, oblong, subobtuse to acute, glabrous, pale green or tinged purple; glumes very dissimilar, obscurely nerved, lower rounded or slightly acute, hyaline, with 1–3 veins or unveined, upper membranous, 5-veined, same shape and size as spikelet; anth. to 1.5cm. Tropical Africa, naturalized US.

***P. miliaceum*** L. MILLET; BROOM CORN MILLET; HOG MILLET. Annual, to 120cm. Stems robust, erect, or decumbent at base. Lvs linear to linear-lanceolate, to 40×2cm; sheaths short, stiffly pubesc. Panicle open to contracted, to 30cm, branches rigid; spikelets stipitate, ovate to elliptic, to 6mm; upper fl. white or yellow to dark brown; lower glume to 4mm, apex sharp, acuminate to acute; upper glume, lower lemma long-acute. C, S & E Europe, Asia. 'Violaceum': infl. purple tinged.

***P. virgatum*** L. SWITCH GRASS. Perenn., to 180cm. Stems clumped, flimsy to robust, purple to glaucous green; rhizomes robust, creeping. Lvs linear, flat, erect, to 60cm×1.4cm, usually glabrous, green, becoming vivid yellow in autumn. Panicle open, to 50×25cm; branches spreading, stiff; spikelets short-stipitate, elliptic-ovate, to 6mm; lower glume to 5mm; upper glume slightly longer than lower lemma. Summer–autumn. C America to S Canada. 'Haense' ('Haense Herms'): habit weeping; lvs plum to rich burgundy in autumn, fls suffused red. 'Heavy Metal': lvs stiffly erect, pale metallic blue, yellow in autumn. 'Rotbraun' ('Red Bronze'): to 80cm; lvs light brown, flushed red at tips, rich autumn colour. 'Rotstrahlbusch': lvs vivid red in autumn. 'Rubrum': to 1m; lvs flushed red, bright red in autumn; seedheads rich brown, in clouds. 'Squaw': lvs tinted red in autumn. 'Strictum': narrowly upright, to 1.2m. 'Warrior': tall, strong-growing; lvs tinted red-brown in autumn.

***P. crus-galli*** L. See *Echinochloa crus-galli*.
***P. germanicum*** Mill. See *Setaria italica*.
***P. glaucum*** L. See *Setaria glauca*.
***P. italicum*** L. See *Setaria italica*.
***P. palmifolium*** Koenig. See *Setaria palmifolia*.
***P. plicatile*** Hochst. See *Setaria plicatilis*.
***P. plicatum*** Willd. non Lam. See *Setaria palmifolia*.
***P. plicatum*** hort. See *Setaria plicatilis*.
***P. plicatum*** Lam. non Willd. See *Setaria plicata*.
***P. polystachyum*** HBK. See *Echinochloa polystachya*.
***P. purpurascens*** Raddi. See *Brachiaria mutica*.
***P. ramosum*** L. See *Brachiaria ramosa*.
***P. sanguinale*** L. See *Digitaria sanguinalis*.
***P. spectabile*** Nees ex Trin. See *Echinochloa polystachya*.
***P. subquadriparum*** Trin. See *Brachiaria subquadripara*.
***P. sulcatum*** Aubl. See *Setaria sulcata*.
***P. teneriffae*** R. Br. See *Tricholaena teneriffae*.
***P. tonsum*** Steud. See *Rhynchelytrum repens*.
***P. variegatum*** hort. See *Oplismenus hirtellus* 'Variegatus'.
***P. viride*** L. See *Setaria viridis*.

For illustration see ORNAMENTAL GRASSES.

**Panisea** Lindl. (From Gk *panisos*, entirely like; referring to the uniformity of the segments.) Orchidaceae. Some 9 species of terrestrial orchids. Pseudobulbs small, clustered, each with 1–2, narrow-lanceolate to oblong-lanceolate, plicate leaves. Inflorescence a lateral raceme with few flowers and membranous bracts; sepals and petals subequal, lateral sepals basally saccate; lip fused to column base, claw sigmoid. NE India, SE Asia. Z10.

CULTIVATION See ORCHIDS.

***P. uniflora*** (Lindl.) Lindl. Pseudobulbs to 15mm, oblong, basally sheathed, bifoliate. Lvs 5–10cm, linear to linear-lanceolate, acuminate. Scape erect, usually shorter than pseudobulbs; fls solitary, yellow-brown; sep. and pet. to 20mm, oblong-lanceolate; lip trilobed, keeled, with 2 central ridges, margins undulate, midlobe ovate, entire, with 4 elongated dark brown spots, lateral lobes narrow, acute, longer. N India. Z10.

**Panterpa** Miers. See *Arrabidaea*.

**Papaver** L. (From Lat. *pappa*, food or milk, an allusion to the milky latex.) POPPY. Papaveraceae. 50 species of annual or perennial, glaucous, rarely glabrous herbs to 120cm. Latex white or yellow. Stems 1 to many, simple or branched, erect or ascending, usually minutely bristly. Leaves basal or cauline, pinnatifid to pinnatisect, toothed, serrate or, rarely, crenate, occasionally bristly, segments often pinnate or bipinnate, irregularly incised; basal leaves petiolate, stem leaves sessile with narrower lobes than in basal leaves. Flowers solitary; sepals 2, rarely 3, concave, overlapping, short-lived; petals 4, rarely 5 or 6, usually obovate, obtuse, creased in bud, often withering and falling early; stamens numerous; carpels numerous; stigmatic surface a disc, crenate to incised, convex to concave with 4–16 rays. Fruit a capsule, subcylindric to globose, glabrous to minutely bristly; seeds reniform. Europe, Asia, Australia, S Africa, Western N America.

CULTIVATION Poppies are easily grown in the mixed border, herbaceous border and in rock gardens. The annuals include *P. rhoeas*, the corn poppy, and its horticulturally developed descendants, the Shirley poppies, the opium poppy, *P. somniferum* and the *P. alpinum* complex, which benefits from some lime in the soil and is suitable for rock gardens, wall plantings and pavement crevices. Most will self-seed freely unless deadheaded. Sow annuals in situ, 5mm/1/5in. deep in spring or late summer in any well-drained soil, in a sunny position. Thin to 25–30cm/10–12in. apart and keep weed-free. Give late-sown plants cloche protection in winter. Support with twiggy brushwood if necessary. *P. nudicaule*, a short-lived perennial, can also be treated as an annual, but best results are obtained by growing as a biennial. The blooms, 10–12cm/4–5in. across on wiry stems, make good cut flowers lasting for up to a week, if cut in bud and the stems tips scalded in boiling water before arranging. Sow thinly in late spring/early summer in a cold frame or out doors. Transplant when big enough to handle, 15cm/6in. apart in rows 30cm/12in. apart, in a sunny well-drained bed. Transfer to flowering site in autumn or the following spring, in full sun and fertile soil.

The oriental poppies, *P. orientale*, are among the loveliest herbaceous perennials, although their flowering period is brief, and the leaves die back and leave gaps in the border. (This can be circumvented by placing them some distance from the front of the border, accompanied by later-growing tall plants, or by species which will sprawl into the gaps such as *Gypsophila paniculata* or *Limonium latifolium*.) The seed pods are attractive when dried. Plant in autumn for preference, or in spring, in any deep well-drained soil, in full sun. Staking will prevent storm damage. Propagate by division in early autumn or spring, or by root cuttings late summer/early autumn. Place 8–10cm/3–4in. pieces of thick roots, crown end up, in boxes of sandy medium in a cold frame. Keep moist, not wet, and protect from frost. Transfer to a nursery bed in spring for a season before planting out. Propagation from seed is possible, but named varieties do not come true.

Downy mildew (*Peronospora* spp.) causes yellow blotches on the leaves, with grey mould growth beneath, in damp conditions. It is rarely serious, but badly affected plants can act as source of infection for other plants of same genus and should be destroyed by burning. Poppies in both Europe and North America are prone to infestations by the black bean aphid (*Aphis tabae*) and by capsid bugs.

***P. aculeatum*** Thunb. Annual to 1m. Stems erect, few-branched, prickly, prickles yellow. Lvs to 30cm, sinuate-pinnate, tapering toward base, lobes 4–7, spreading, ovate, obtuse, dentate; stem lvs sessile with blunt teeth. Fls in a few-fld raceme; pet. to 1.5cm, obovate, orange-red without basal markings; stamens yellow; stigmatic disc 8–9-rayed. Fr. to 2×1cm ovoid or oblong. Summer. S Africa, Australia. Z8.

***P. alpinum*** L. Perenn. to 25cm. Stems scapose, often very short. Lvs basal, to 20cm, 2–3-pinnate, lobes 6–8, lanceolate, linear, ovate or ovate-lanceolate, acute, occasionally pinnatisect, to 1.5cm wide, glaucous grey-green to green, glabrous to sparsely bristly, toothed. Fls solitary on terete scapes to 25cm; pet. white, yellow or orange, rounded to obovate, to 2.5cm; stigmatic disc 4–5-rayed. Fr. to 1cm, oblong to obconic, with closely adpressed bristles. Summer. Alps, Carpathians, Pyrenees. Z5. A highly variable species of uncertain limitations. *Pp. burseri, kerneri, pyrenaicum* and *rhaeticum* are perhaps best treated as members of this complex.

***P. anomalum*** Fedde. Perenn. to 40cm. Stems very short. Lvs basal, to 10cm, pinnatifid to lobed, glaucous, subglabrous, lobes oblong, obtuse. Scapes erect to 40cm, orange-pubesc.; fls solitary; pet. orange, narrow, obtuse, to 2cm, margins slightly scalloped, fil. black; stigmatic disc 8-rayed. Fr. globose, to 1cm diam. Summer. C China. Z7.

***P. apokrinomenon*** Fedde. Perenn. to 60cm. Stems usually solitary, terete, densely hairy. Lvs basal and on stem, 12–25×4–6cm, pinnately lobed, oblong-ovate, lobes deeply incised, crenate to serrate; stem lvs sessile, clasping, cordate at base. Fl. buds pubesc.; fls solitary, red; stigmatic disc 6–7-rayed. Fr. clavate, to 2×0.5cm. Summer. C Asia (mts). Z7.

***P. apulum*** Ten. Annual to 40cm. Stems erect to ascending, branching. Lvs basal and on stem, bipinnatifid, lobes linear, obtuse, bristly hairy, basal lvs wider than stem lvs. Scapes pubesc.; fls solitary, to 5cm diam., purple; pet. to 2cm, obovate, with pale basal blotch; stamens dark purple; stigmatic disc 4–7-rayed. Fr. to 1cm ellipsoid. Summer. Mediterranean. Z8.

***P. arenarium*** Bieb. Annual to 50cm. Stems erect, branching. Lvs basal and on stem, bipinnate, seg. linear, obtuse, sometimes adpressed-pubesc. Scapes and sep. adpressed-pubesc.; fls to 6cm diam.; pet. purple with black basal blotch; anth. yellow; stigmatic disc 7–9-rayed. Fr. obovate-oblong, 1–2×0.5cm. Summer. Asia Minor. Z8.

***P. argemone*** L. PRICKLY POPPY. Annual to 50cm, hispid. Stems erect or ascending, simple or branching. Lvs pinnatisect, seg. linear to oblong-lanceolate, acute.

Fl. bud to 1cm, oblong to obovoid, sparsely hairy; fls orange-red; pet. to 2.5cm, not overlapping, obovate-oblong, tapering to base, occasionally with maroon basal spot; stamens pale mauve; stigmatic disc 4–6-rayed. Fr. to 2cm, oblong-cylindric to clavate, hispid. Summer. N Africa, S Europe. Z8.

***P. atlanticum*** (Ball) Coss. Perenn. to 45cm. Rhiz. woody, clothed in old lf bases. Lvs to 15cm, oblong-lanceolate, irregularly jagged-toothed or pinnatisect, pilose. Scape to 45cm, simple or forked, pilose in basal portion, adpressed-pubesc. toward fl.; pet. to 2.5cm, obovate, buff-orange to red; stigmatic disc 6-rayed. Fr. to 2.5cm, clavate, glabrous. Summer. Morocco. Z6.

***P. bracteatum*** Lindl. Perenn. to 1m. Stems erect, simple. Basal lvs to 45cm, pinnate, pinnatisect near apex, seg. lanceolate or oblong, serrate; stem lvs reduced. Scapes adpressed white hispid; floral bracts to 5cm, 2 at apex, below fls, deeply incised; fls to 10cm diam. or wider; sep. 2, imbricate, concave, white above, green beneath; pet. 4, obovate, red with purple spot at base; stigmatic disc 16–18-rayed. Fr. obovate-globose, glabrous, glaucous. Summer. Caucasus, Asia Minor. Z5.

***P. burseri*** Crantz. Perenn. to 25cm. Lvs basal, to 20cm, petiolate, 2–3-pinnate, glaucous, glabrous, seg. 6–8, linear-lanceolate to narrowly linear, acute. Scapes to 25cm, terete, with adpressed, setose hairs. Fls solitary; pet. to 2cm, rounded-obovate, usually white; stigmatic disc 4–5-rayed. Fr. oblong to subclavate, to 1cm. Summer. C Europe (mts). 'Alpinum': lvs fine, tinged grey; fls in range of pastel colours. Z5.

***P. californicum*** A. Gray. WESTERN POPPY. Annual to 60cm. Stems slender with erect, adpressed branches. Lvs to 7.5cm, pinnate, lobes obtuse to acute. Fl. bud to 1cm, obovoid, sparsely hairy. Scapes adpressed-pubesc.; pet. to 2.5cm, 4–6, 1 pair sometimes filiform, red with green or black, pink-rimmed basal spot; stigmatic disc 6–11-rayed. Fr. to 1.5cm, narrow-turbinate. Summer. US (California). Z8.

***P. commutatum*** Fisch. & Mey. Differs from *P. rhoeas* in its adpressed-pubesc. pedicels, blotched pet. and stalked ovary. Annual to 40cm. Stem erect, branching, sparsely hairy. Lvs to 15cm, pinnatifid adpressed-downy, seg. to 3cm, oblong to ovate, obtuse, dentate to entire. Pedicels long, adpressed-pubesc.; fls nodding at first, later erect; pet. obovate to ovate-orbicular, red with black basal spot. Fr. stalked, obovate, spotted black. Summer. Caucasus, Asia Minor. 'Lady Bird': to 45cm; fls crimson splashed with black. Z8.

***P. dubium*** L. Annual to 60cm. Stem robust, erect, branching, hairy. Lvs slightly glaucous, basal lvs pinnatisect or lobed, seg. ovate, obtuse; stem lvs bipinnate, seg. linear-lanceolate, acute. Sep. hispid; pet. to 2.5cm, suborbicular, red or white with black basal spot; anth. violet; stigmatic disc 4–10-rayed; peduncle adpressed-pubesc. Fr. obovoid, to 2×1cm. Summer. Europe, SW Asia. Z7.

***P. fauriei*** Fedde. Perenn. to 20cm. Lvs basal, pinnatifid, ovate, lobes oblong or oblong-ovate, broadly cuneate towards apex. Pet. to 2cm, yellow. Fr. to 1cm, ellipsoid, adpressed-pubesc. Summer. N Japan. Z8.

***P. fugax*** Poir. Biennial to 60cm, glaucous, sparsely hairy. Stems branched. Lvs to 20cm, lanceolate, pinnatifid, seg. distant, linear-lanceolate or oblong to ovate, serrate to dentate or entire; basal lvs to 15cm; stem lvs bract-like. Fl. buds to 1cm, ovoid-globose, glabrous to sparsely adpressed-pubesc.; fls to 3cm diam.; pet. rounded, short-lived, dull red, yellow toward base; stamens yellow; stigmatic disc 4–5-rayed; peduncles lax, glabrous. Fr. to 1cm, ovoid, glabrous. Summer. Asia Minor. Z8.

***P. glaucum*** Boiss. & Hausskn. To 50cm, branching at base. Stems erect. Lvs obovate-oblong, pinnatifid, glaucous, glabrous, seg. triangular-oblong, acute or obtuse, serrate to dentate; basal lvs to 15cm; stem lvs broadly cordate at base. Fls to 4cm diam; sep. glabrous; pet. suborbicular, red, with a black basal spot; stigmatic disc 12-rayed. Fr. to 2cm, globose. Summer. Syria, Iraq, Iran. Z8.

***P. heldreichii*** Boiss. Perenn. to 50cm. Stems erect, leafy, densely hoary-hispid. Lvs pilose; basal lvs to 20×5cm, oblong, cuneate towards base, stem lvs ovate-oblong, bract-like, wrinkled, serrate. Racemes few-fld, corymbose; fl. bud to 1cm, ellipsoid, white-hairy; peduncles erect, adpressed-pubesc.; pet. to 5cm, orange-red; stigmatic disc 4–6-rayed. Fr. to 1.5cm, narrowly oblong, glabrous, somewhat glaucous. Summer. C Mediterranean. Z8.

***P. hookeri*** Bak. ex Hook. f. Branching, annual herb, to 1.2m. Branches erect, ascending. Lvs to 12.5cm, sessile, ovate or lanceolate, coarsely toothed. Fls to 9cm diam., crenulate, pale rose to bright crimson, blotched blue-black at base, on long peduncles. Fr. 1.25cm diam., subglobose, glabrous. Scarcely distinct from *P. rhoeas*. Temperate Europe, Asia.

***P. ×hybridum*** L. ROUGH POPPY. Lvs twice or thrice pinnatipartite. Fls red, usually with purple spot at base of pet.; peduncles usually adpressed pubesc., stigmatic disc small, 6–8-rayed. Fr. ovoid, with stiff, curved bristles. Europe, W Asia. 'Fireball': to 25cm; fls double, orange-red.

***P. kerneri*** Hayek. As for *P. burseri* except pet. yellow. Fr. to 1cm, broadly clavate. Summer. C Europe (mts). Z5.

***P. laevigatum*** Bieb. Annual to 40cm, glabrous to sparsely setose. Stems simple or slightly branching. Lvs narrowly pinnate, glabrous or sparsely hairy, seg. of basal lvs ovate to oblong, obtuse, those of stem lvs 5–7, linear, acute. Sep. glabrous or slightly hairy; pet. obovate, red with black basal spot; anth. yellow; stigmatic disc 8–10-rayed. Fr. oblong-clavate. Summer. C Mediterranean Himalaya. Z8.

***P. lateritium*** K. Koch. Perenn. to 60cm, densely hairy. Stems many, branching. Lvs lanceolate, irregularly deeply serrate. Fls 1–3, to 5cm diam.; sep. pilose to hispidulous; pet. bright orange or red; stigmatic disc 5–6-rayed. Fr. oblong-clavate. Summer. Turkey. 'Flore Pleno': fls semi-double, orange. Z8.

***P. macrostomum*** Boiss. & Huet. Annual to 45cm. Stem erect, branching, sparsely hairy. Lvs pinnatisect, seg. of basal lvs oblong-lanceolate, those of stem lvs linear-lanceolate, sparsely to densely acute-dentate. Fls to 5cm diam.; pet. purple, sometimes with black basal spot which may be rimmed white; stigmatic disc 5–10-rayed. Fr. to 1.5cm, ellipsoid-oblong, glaucous. Summer. Armenia. Z8.

***P. monanthum*** Trautv. Perenn. to 45cm. Lvs basal, to 20×30cm, linear to oblong, pinnatifid, irregularly acute-dentate. Fls solitary; pet. 3–5cm, stigmatic disc 6–9-rayed. Fr. obovoid, glabrous. Summer. Caucasus. Z7.

***P. nordhagenianum*** Löve. Pubesc. perenn. to 35cm. Lvs long-petiolate, trifoliolate or pinnatisect. Scapes numerous; pet. yellow. Fr. to 2cm, broad-ellipsoid. Summer. Iceland, Faeroes, Scandinavia. Z4.

***P. nudicaule*** L. ICELANDIC POPPY; ARCTIC POPPY. Perenn. to 30cm. Stem very short. Lvs mostly basal, 3–15cm, pinnatifid to pinnatisect, somewhat glaucous, pubesc., seg. 3–4, oblong, acute, incised, occasionally mucronate. Fls to 7.5cm diam., solitary, sometimes double; pet. 4, obovate, outer pair larger, white with yellow basal patch, yellow, orange, peach or pale red, ruffled; anth. yellow; stigmatic disc 4–6-rayed. Fr. to 1.5cm, oblong or obovate-globose, usually hispid. Summer. Subarctic regions. 'Champagne Bubbles': to 40cm; fls to 12cm wide. 'Croceum': fls orange or orange-red. Garden Gnome Hybrids: dwarf, compact; fls in wide range including shades of yellow, orange and pink; seed race. 'Hamlet': fls large. Hybrid Matador: neat; stems firm; fls bright scarlet. Kelmscott Giant: stems long to 80cm; fls in pastel shades. Oregon Rainbows: to 55cm; fls delicate in pastel shades. 'Pacino': compact; fls abundant, pale yellow. Sparkling Bubbles Mixed: fls large, abundant, in range of rich and pastel colours; seed race. Unwins Giant Coonara: to 50cm; fls bright. Wonderland Hybrids: dwarf, hardy biennial to 25cm; fls large, in range of whites, oranges, yellows and reds. Z2.

***P. oreophilum*** Rupr. Perenn. to 15cm, forming dense mats. Stems numerous, branching above. Lvs hairy; basal lvs lanceolate-oblong and pinnatifid or acute and deeply incised; stem lvs sessile, narrow at base. Peduncles to 15cm, flexuous; fl. bud to 1.5cm diam., ovate-globose, densely hairy; fls 2 per stem; pet. to 4.5cm, deep red; stigmatic disc convex, 5–7-rayed. Fr. obovate-clavate, to 1cm. Summer. Caucasus. Z8.

***P. orientale*** L. ORIENTAL POPPY. Perenn. to 90cm. Stems erect, sparsely leafy. Lvs to 25cm, hispid; basal lvs pinnate, pinnatisect at apex, seg. distant, lanceolate or oblong; petioles sulcate; stem lvs reduced. Fl. bud to 3cm, ovate, canescent; fls solitary, to 10cm diam.; sep. 2, concave, white above; pet. to 6cm, 4–6, obovate, red, orange or pale pink usually with purple basal blotch; stigmatic disc 13–15-rayed. Fr. to 3cm diam., subglobose, glaucous, glabrous. Summer. SW Asia. Over 70 cvs, height 40–110cm, dwarf and compact to tall; stems nodding to erect; fls sometimes double, in a range of colour from white, pink and orange to deep red and purple, sometimes bicolour; pet. fringed or ruffled. 'Black and White': fls large, white with black centre. 'Cedric Morris' ('Cedric's Pink'): lvs grey-hirsute; pet. shell pink with a large violet-black basal spot. 'Fatima': compact; fls white with pink edges, dark spots. 'Glowing Embers': to 110cm, robust, erect; fls in 10cm diam., bright orange-red, pet. ruffled. 'Harvest Moon': to 1m; fls semi-double, deep orange. 'Indian Chief': fls maroon. 'Ladybird': fls very large, vermilion with black centre. 'May Queen': stems drooping; fls double, orange-vermilion. 'Mrs Perry': fls large, salmon-pink tinged apricot. 'Nana Flore Pleno': dwarf, to 45cm; fls double, orange-red, pet. ruffled. 'Perry's White': to 80cm; stems strong; fls grey-white with purple centre. 'Picotee': fls banded salmon and white. 'Redizelle': fls scarlet with black throat. 'Suleika': to 90cm; erect; fls deep red with blue gloss, spotted black, pet. fringed. Z3.

***P. pavoninum*** Fisch. & Mey. Annual to 25cm. Stems branching, hairy. Lvs to 10cm, pinnate or pinnatisect; basal lvs deeply incised; stem lvs oblong-linear, dentate, teeth mucronate. Pet. to 2.5cm, orbicular, red with black basal blotch; anth. purple; stigmatic disc 4–7-rayed. Fr. to 1cm, ovoid, yellow-pubesc. Summer. C Asia. Z8.

***P. persicum*** Lindl. Biennial to 45cm. Stems branching, leafy. Basal lvs to 25cm, oblong-lanceolate, pinnate, seg. dentate or entire, teeth mucronate; stem lvs much smaller. Fl. bud to 1.5×1cm, oblong, adpressed-pubesc.; fls to 5cm across, deep red with green basal blotch; stigmatic disc 5–6-rayed. Summer. SW Asia. Z9.

***P. pilosum*** Sibth. & Sm. Perenn. to 1m. Stems erect, leafy, hairy. Lvs adpressed-velutinous, basal lvs to 15cm, oblong, stem lvs to 3cm, bract-like, ovate-oblong, acute, irregularly toothed, lobed. Fls in a corymb, to 10cm across; sep. adpressed-pubesc; pet. rounded, scarlet or bright orange with white basal spot; anth. yellow; stigmatic disc 6–7-rayed. Fr. oblong-clavate, to 2cm, glaucous. Summer. Asia Minor. Z6.

***P. pseudocanescens*** Popov. As for *P. radicatum* except lf lobes broader, stamens more numerous, exceeding ovary. Summer. Siberia, Mongolia. Z3.

***P. pyrenaicum*** A. Kerner. Lvs pinnatipartite with oval, ovate-lanceolate or lanceolate seg., toothed or pinnately cut. Fls yellow, orange or white. Pyrenees. Material offered in cultivation under this name may be *P. rhaeticum*.

***P. radicatum*** Rottb. Densely tufted perenn. to 20cm. Lvs 5–10cm, pinnatifid or lobed, seg. lanceolate to obovate, entire or incised, acute. Scape to 20cm, rusty or black-pubesc.; fls to 5cm across; pet. white or yellow, rarely pink. Summer. N Europe, W Asia. Z3.

***P. rhaeticum*** Leresche. Perenn. to 10cm, tuft-forming. Lvs basal, to 7.5cm, pinnate, adpressed-pubesc.; seg. usually entire, rarely bipinnate, ovate to ovate-lanceolate, acute to rounded. Scape to 10cm; fls solitary; pet. to 2cm, rounded-obovate, somewhat truncate at apex, yellow or orange. Fr. to 1cm, oblong to obovate, hairy. Summer. Pyrenees. Z5.

***P. rhoeas*** L. CORN POPPY; FIELD POPPY; FLANDERS POPPY. Annual to 90cm. Stems erect, branching, hispid, rarely glabrous. Lvs pinnate or pinnatisect, seg. lanceolate, acuminate, to 15cm. Fls solitary, to 7.5cm across; sep. hispid; pet. orbicular or ovate, usually entire, occasionally crenate to emarginate, brilliant red sometimes with black basal spot; stigmatic disc 5–18-rayed. Fr. subglobose, to 2cm, glabrous. Summer. Temperate Old World. Shirley Poppies: fls medium-sized, single, white to scarlet (not mauve) or double, in a wide range of colours except yellow. 'Valerie Finnis': fls grey, mauve, pink and white; seed race. Z5.

***P. rupifragum*** Boiss. & Reut. Tufted perennial to 45cm. Lvs oblong or lanceolate, pinnately cut glabrous, pubesc. on veins. Fls to 7.5cm diam., pale brick-red. Spain. Z7.

***P. schinzianum*** Fedde. Hoary-pubesc. perenn. to 45cm. Lvs irregularly pinnatifid, obovate-lanceolate. Fls to 5cm diam; pet. obovoid, rusty to sealing-wax red. Origin unknown.

***P. sendtneri*** (Kerner) Fedde As for *P. rhaeticum* except lvs glaucescent, pet. white or yellow. Z4.

***P. somniferum*** L. OPIUM POPPY. Annual to 120cm, glaucous grey-green. Stems erect. Lvs basal and on stem, to 12.5cm, cordate, crenate-serrate or laciniate; stem lvs sessile, clasping. Fl. bud to 2cm, ovoid, glabrous; fls to 10cm across, pale white, light mauve, purple or variegated, frequently double; pet. suborbicular, erose, occasionally with dark basal spot; anth. yellow; stigmatic disc 5–18-rayed. Fr. 5–7×4–5cm, globose, glabrous. Summer. SE Europe, W Asia. ssp. ***setigerum*** (DC.) Corb. All parts pubesc. Lf lobes acute. Peony-flowered Hybrids: lvs grey-green; fls double; seed race. Z7.

***P. suaveolens*** Lapeyr. Tufted perenn. to 10cm. Lvs basal, to 7cm, pinnatifid, adpressed-pubesc., rarely near glabrous, seg. lanceolate or oblong, acute, entire, rarely pinnately lobed. Scape to 10cm, hispid; fl. bud ovoid, densely hairy; fls solitary, to 3cm diam.; pet. to 1.5×1cm, obovate, yellow or cream. Summer. Pyrenees, W Mediterranean. Z5.

***P. triniifolium*** Boiss. Bienn. to 30cm or more, glaucous, sparsely villous. Stems with spreading branches. Basal lvs to 7.5cm, ovate oblong, 2–3-pinnate, seg. narrow-linear, yellow-mucronate, stem lvs trifid. Fl. buds ovate to subglobose, glabrous; fls to 2.5cm across; pet. to 2cm, pale red; stigmatic disc 4–5-rayed. Fr. oblong to ovoid, glabrous, glaucous. Summer. Asia Minor. Z8.

***P. amurense*** hort. ex Karrer. See *P. nudicaule*.
***P. caucasicum*** Bieb. See *P. fugax*.
***P. croceum*** Ledeb. See *P. nudicaule* 'Croceum'.
***P. heterophyllum*** (Benth.) Greene. See *Stylomecon heterophyllum*.
***P. horridum*** DC. See *P. aculeatum*.
***P. macounii*** Greene. See *P. nudicaule*.
***P. mairei*** Battand. See *P. dubium*.
***P. miyabeanum*** Tatew. See *P. nudicaule*.
***P. setigerum*** DC. See *P. somniferum* ssp. *setigerum*.
***P. spicatum*** Boiss. & Bal. See *P. heldreichii*.
***P. umbrosum*** hort. See *P. commutatum*.

**PAPAVERACEAE** Juss. POPPY FAMILY. Dicot. 23 genera and 210 species of herbs, subshrubs or small pachycaul trees, with alkaloids and milky sap. Leaves spirally arranged, entire, lobed or dissected; stipules absent. Flowers usually large, bisexual, hypogynous (perigynous in *Eschscholzia*), solitary, less often in cymes or other types of inflorescences; calyx 2 free sepals (united in *Eschscholzia*), less often 4, enclosing bud, often caducous; corolla 4 free petals in 2 whorls, rarely absent or up to 16, crumpled in bud; stamens usually numerous (4–6 in *Meconella*), nectaries absent; ovary of 2 to numerous fused carpels, 1-loculed; ovules 1 to numerous; placentation parietal, sometimes meeting to form plurilocular ovary with axile placentation. Fruit a capsule with longitudinal valves or pores (follicle in *Platystemon*); seeds sometimes arillate; endosperm oily, copious. Dried latex of immature capsules of *Papaver somniferum* is the source of opium from which numerous alkaloids are derived, e.g. morphine, codeine and heroin. Poppy seeds also yield an edible drying oil, while oil from *Argemone* and *Glaucium* seeds is used in soap manufacture. Mostly North temperate. *Arctomecon, Argemone, Bocconia, Chelidonium, Corydalis, Dendromecon, Dicranostigma, Eomecon, Eschscholzia, Glaucium, Hunnemannia, Hylomecon, Macleaya, Meconella, Meconopsis, Papaver, Platystemon, Roemeria, Romneya, Sanguinaria, Stylomecon, Stylophorum.*

**Paphinia** Lindl. (Named after *Paphia*, the Cypriot name for Aphrodite.) Orchidaceae. Some 3 species of epiphytic orchids. Pseudobulbs small, ovoid to ovoid-oblong with several 2-ranked, overlapping sheaths, unifoliate to trifoliate. Leaves usually large, plicate, membranaceous, acute, lanceolate, prominently nerved. Inflorescence a basal raceme, short, erect to pendent, 1- to several-flowered, flowers large, showy; sepals subsimilar, lateral sepals articulated to column foot forming a short mentum; petals similar to sepals, smaller; lip articulate to column foot, smaller than tepals, unguiculate, trilobed, lateral lobes erect, falcate, oblong to ovate, midlobe obliquely triangular to sagittate, disc callose or variably crested with glandular hairs; column clavate, curved, with a short basal foot, apex often auriculate, anther terminal, operculate, incumbent, unilocular, pollinia 4, obovate or oblong, stipe elongate. Northern S America, Guatemala. Z10.

CULTIVATION Epiphytic orchids for semi-shaded positions in the intermediate house. See ORCHIDS.

***P. cristata*** (Lindl.) Lindl. Pseudobulbs to 5×2.5cm, becoming grooved, slightly compressed, light green. Lvs to 25×4.5cm, elliptic-lanceolate to linear-lanceolate, acute to acuminate, light green. Infl. to 15cm, pendent; sep. and pet. to 6×2cm, white to yellow, striped red or red-brown, linear-lanceolate to elliptic-lanceolate, acute to acuminate, concave; lip to 2×1.6cm, dark chocolate-purple with a white claw, fleshy, deeply 3-lobed, lateral lobes linear-falcate, acute, margins white, midlobe ovate-hastate to subsagitatte, acute or obtuse, cristate-fimbriate, disc with a fleshy white, laciniate callus; column to 3cm, yellow-green marked red-maroon at base, foot to 1cm, wings obliquely triangular. Venezuela, Colombia, Trinidad, Guyanas, Surinam.

***P. lindeniana*** Rchb. f. Pseudobulbs to 6.5×2.5cm. Lvs to 27×7cm, elliptic-oblong, acute to acuminate, petiole slender, terete. Infl. to 10cm, pendent, few to several-fld; sep. and pet. white variably marked dark red-purple, sep. to 5×2cm, fleshy, lanceolate, acuminate, concave; lateral sep. smaller than dorsal sep., apex reflexed, pet. to 4.5×1.5cm, similar to sep.; lip to 2.5×1.5cm, white, shaded dark red-purple at base, fleshy, slightly concave, lateral lobes obliquely ovate, acute, apically dentate, midlobe semi-hastate, densely fimbriate-papillose, disc with an elevated crest bearing numerous white fusiform hairs; column to 2.5cm, cream-green spotted light red at base, with a short fleshy foot. Venezuela, Brazil, Colombia, Peru, Guyana.

**Paphiopedilum** Pfitz. (From Gk *Paphos*, an Aegean island with a temple to Aphrodite, and *pedilon*, slipper, describing the saccate lip formed by the third petal of each flower.) VENUS' SLIPPER. SE Asia, India, Indonesia, SE China, New Guinea, Philippines, Solomon Is. Orchidaceae. About 60 species of sympodial orchids, mainly terrestrial, occasionally epiphytic or lithophytic. Roots thick, often ciliate, spreading from the base of each new growth and supporting the fans of leaves which cover an abbreviated stem. Pseudobulbs absent. Leaves 2 to several, leathery, conduplicate, oblong, ligulate or elliptic, persistent for more than one year, plain green or mottled with light or dark markings, in some species purple beneath. Flowers waxy, carried one to several on a slender terminal stalk; dorsal sepal large, erect, lateral sepals fused to form a synsepalum; petals horizontal or pendent; lip strongly saccate, forming a pouch; column short, bearing a fleshy staminode (a modified sterile stamen) at its apex, behind which the stigmatic surface is borne on a short stalk between 2 fertile anthers bearing the 2 pollinia; ovary inferior, 1-celled. Fruit a capsule, splits lengthwise when ripe; seeds fusiform or ellipsoid, wind-dispersed. SE Asia, India, Indonesia, SW China, New Guinea, Philippines, Solomon Is. Z10. A few natural hybrids occur within this horticulturally important genus and the past 120 years have seen artificial hybridization proceeding at a considerable pace; the trend towards breeding larger and rounder flowers with overlapping segments of heavier substance has recently shown a return to further use of primary and near primary crosses. The first artificial hybrid, registered by Veitch in 1869, was *P.* ×*harrisianum*, a cross between *P. barbatum* and *P. villosum*,

**Paphiopedilum** (×0.66) (a) *P. bellatulum* (b) *P. concolor* (c) *P. godefroyae* (d) *P. delenatii* (e) *P. armeniacum*

resulting in long-lasting, dark, glossy flowers. A few further notable examples are *P.×arthurianum* (*P.fairrieanum* × *P.spicerianum*), *P.×leeanum* (*P.insigne* × *P.spicerianum*), *P.×maudiae* (*P.callosum* × *P.lawrenceanum*) in both coloured and albino forms. Divisions of these and many other early hybrids are still in cultivation.

CULTIVATION A heated glasshouse or conservatory is desirable though plants can be grown satisfactorily under artificial lights in an indoor structure or on a windowsill providing certain needs are met. Relative humidity should be high, between 65–75% at all times. Shade from direct sunlight is essential on sunny days; light requirement 5000–10,000 lux. The temperature needed is 15–18°C/60–65°F night-minimum with a day lift of at least 5°C/9°F; species from cooler locations (e.g. *P.hirsutissimum, P.insigne, P.fairrieanum, P.spicerianum, P.venustum*) will tolerate a night-minimum of 7°C/45°F. With the exception of *P.venustum*, it can generally be assumed that other mottled-leaved species require warmer conditions, as do plain-leaved species with multiple-flowered inflorescences. A preferred day-maximum of 28°C/82°F should be aimed at, achieved by the use of shading and fans and by increasing moisture in the air around the plants rather than opening vents to allow escape of the humidity so vital to the well-being of these orchids.

Water throughout the year, aiming to drench the medium, which should be perfectly porous, once it begins to dry out. Plants should not be allowed to dry out completely, but waterlogged conditions are disastrous. Although foliar feeding and overhead misting are beneficial in optimum conditions, never allow water to stand on foliage or to settle for long periods in the centre of growths, as this encourages botrytis and is likely to result in the loss of flower buds and entire leads.

Compost can be composed of a variety of mixtures using conifer-bark, perlage, perlite and charcoal with possible additions of sphagnum moss and/or coarse peat; 4 grams of dolomite lime should be added to each litre of mix. *P.bellatulum* benefits from the addition of broken chalk to the crocks. When plants are in active growth fertilizer should be applied; in winter, when growth is slow, pot feeding should be at intervals of 3–4 weeks, increasing to fortnightly in the warmer, longer days of summer.

Fertilizer can be applied at shorter intervals if foliar feeding is practised. A fertilizer made specifically for orchids is preferable but a half-strength solution of any balanced fertilizer can be used, bearing in mind that high nitrogen content after flowering will aid new growth, followed by high potash to encourage optimum flower development. Annual repotting is desirable as they deteriorate rapidly when breakdown of compost impairs its free-draining qualities.

A number of rots and moulds can develop and spread fast if the affected part is not removed immediately. Insect pests can often be removed by hand as soon as these are noticed; aphids will sometimes infest the flowers and a lookout should be kept for ants which carry them into the glasshouse. Mealy bugs and scale insects occasionally attack the leaves and stems and mice can be a real problem, biting into flower buds to eat the immature pollens. An appropriate insecticide may be applied, paying scrupulous attention to the manufacturer's instructions.

Vegetative propagation is effected by division of plants, though this should be approached with caution as some species are notoriously shy-flowerers until multiple growths are achieved.

***P.acmodontum*** Schoser ex M.W. Wood. Closely allied to *P.argus* but differs in its smaller fls. Lvs oblong, elliptic, tessellated pale and dark green above, to 18×4cm. Infl. erect, 1-fld, to 25cm; bract ovate, to 3cm; dorsal sep. 4cm×31mm, white or pink, veined dark purple or purple-green; synsepalum 32×15mm, white tinged purple, veined purple and green; pet. spreading, 43×14mm, sparsely ciliate, green beneath, purple above, veined and spotted dark purple in basal half; lip deeply saccate, 10×23mm, bronze or olive green with darker veins; staminode ovate, 10×9mm. Spring. Philippines (Visayan Sea, Negros).

***P.adductum*** Asch. Closely related to *P.rothschildianum* but recognized by its decurved pet. and abbreviated staminode. Lvs about 6, to 26×4.2cm, oblong-ligulate to slightly lanceolate, dark green, margin hyaline. Infl. 2–3-fld, arching, to 29cm, pubesc.; bracts 4cm×13mm, green veined maroon; fls glabrous; sep. pale green-yellow or white, veined maroon; dorsal sep. arching, ovate, 6.5×3cm; synsepalum ovate, 6.5×3cm; pet. arcuate-dependent, linear-tapering, to 15cm×9mm; lip porrect, to 47×21mm, grooved on back; staminode rectangular, not covering stigma. Winter. Philippines.

***P.appletonianum*** (Gower) Rolfe. Lvs 6–8, narrowly elliptic to oblong-elliptic, to 25×4cm, obscurely tessellated pale and darker green with purple marking on lower base. Infl. 1–2-fld, to 48cm; bract green, lanceolate, to 2cm; fls 6–10cm across; sep. pale green, veined green, dorsal sep. ovate, cordate at base, apiculate above, 4.4×2.4cm, basal margins recurved; synsepalum elliptic-lanceolate, to 3×1.5cm; pet. spathulate, to 5.8×1.8cm, half-twisted in apical half, green, striped darker with maroon-black spots in basal half, purple above; lip 3–5cm, ochre to pale purple, veined darker; staminode transversely elliptic, to 1cm. Winter–spring. Philippines.

***P.argus*** (Rchb. f.) Stein. Lvs 3–5, narrowly elliptic, mottled pale and dark green above, purple at base beneath. Infl. 1-fld, to 45cm, purple or green, mottled purple, shortly pubesc.; bract elliptic, to 4.5cm×1.8cm; fls 6.5cm across; dorsal sep. to 4.5×3.5cm, white veined green, spotted purple toward base; synsepalum to 4.4×2cm, white veined green; pet. recurved, ligulate, to 6.5cm×1.8cm, white veined green, purple at apex, heavily spotted maroon, maroon hairs on margin long at base, shorter toward apex; lip green flushed pink, veined green, to 4.5×2.5cm; staminode lunate, to 0.9×1.1cm, pale brown-green, veined green. Spring. Philippines (Luzon).

***P.armeniacum*** S.C. Chen & Liu. Closely allied to *P.delenatii* but differs in growth habit, fl. colour and size of lip. Growths to 15cm apart on rhiz. Lvs 5–7, oblong, to 12cm×2.3cm, marbled dark and light blue-green above, densely spotted purple beneath, margins minutely serrulate. Infl. 1-fld, to 26cm, green spotted purple, brown-pubesc.; bract about 1.5cm, green spotted purple, brown-pubesc.; fls large, bright golden yellow; dorsal sep. ovate, to 5×2.5cm, pubesc. near base; synsepalum ovate, to 3.5×2cm; pet. ovate, rounded, to 5×3.5cm, ciliate, pubesc. at base; lip inflated, thin-textured, to 5×4cm, margins incurved, white pubesc. and dotted purple inside at base; staminode large, convex, cordate, acute, to 2×2cm. Spring–summer. China (Yunnan).

***P.barbatum*** (Lindl.) Pfitz. Very closely allied to *P.callosum*. Terrestrial or lithophytic. Lvs about 5, narrowly oblong-elliptic to elliptic, to 1.5×4cm, base sparsely ciliate, mottled pale and dark green above, pale green beneath. Infl. 1–2-fld, erect, to 36cm; bract ovate, to 2.5×1.5cm, green, pubesc.; fls about 8cm diam.; dorsal sep. ovate, to 5×5.5cm, white, green at base, veined purple; synsepalum narrowly ovate, to 3.5×1.5cm, pale yellow-green, veined green, flushed purple; pet. pale green beneath, purple above, veined darker, upper margin spotted dark maroon, deflexed, to 6×1.5cm, ciliate; lip to 4.5×2.5cm, incurved lateral lobes warty; staminode lunate, to 1×1cm, pale green, veined darker. Spring–summer. Peninsular Malaysia and Penang Is.

***P.barbigerum*** Tang & Wang. This relatively little known species related to *P.insigne* and *P.gratrixianum* differs in its small plant bearing small flowers, narrow leaves and differently shaped staminode. Lvs 4–6, suberect, linear, to 19×1.3cm, green. Infl. 1-fld, erect, about 16cm; bract elliptic, to 2cm; fls about 6cm diam.; dorsal sep. subcircular, up to 3.2×3cm, white with green base; synsepalum elliptic, to 3.5×1.5cm; pet. oblong-ligulate to ligulate-spathulate, to 3.4×0.9cm, fawn margined cream, base ciliate, margin undulate and sparsely ciliate; lip to 3×1.5cm, tan-brown, outer surface glabrous; staminode transversely elliptic, 0.6×0.8cm, pubesc., bearing a central boss. China (Guizhou, Yunnan).

***P.bellatulum*** (Rchb. f.) Stein. Calcicolous in limestone crevices with roots in a layer of leafmould and moss. Lvs 4–5, oblong-elliptic, to 14×5cm, dark green mottled pale green above, spotted purple below. Infl. 1-fld, rarely 2-fld, to 4.5cm; bract to 27×25mm, pubesc., pale green, spotted purple; fls round, 5.5–8cm diam., white or cream, heavily spotted maroon; dorsal sep. concave, to 3.5×4cm; synsepalum deeply concave, to 22×27mm; pet. somewhat concave, to 6×4.5cm; lip narrowly ovoid, to 4×2cm, margins strongly incurved; staminode 11×9mm. Summer. W Burma, Thailand.

***P.bougainvilleanum*** Fowlie. Most closely allied to *P.violascens* but differs in having longer, more strongly tessellated lvs and greener fls with smaller lips. Lvs 6–7, narrowly elliptic, to 22×4.2cm, pale green, tessellated darker. Infl. 1-fld, to 23cm; bract elliptic, 2.6cm, pale green; fls about 5cm across; sep. white, veined green, outer surface purple-pubesc., pet. white, veined green, apical margins flushed purple; lip and staminode green, veined darker; dorsal sep. ovate, to 3.8×4cm; synsepalum concave, ovate, to 2.7×1.7cm; pet. falcate, narrowly elliptic, to 5×2cm; lip to 5×2.6cm, narrowing to apex; staminode lunate, minutely pubesc., to 11×14mm. Autumn. Papua New Guinea.

***P.bullenianum*** (Rchb. f.) Pfitz. Closely allied to *P.appletonianum* and *P.hookerae*. Lvs 6–8, to 14×5.5cm, tessellated dark and light green above, sometimes flushed purple beneath. Infl. erect, 1-fld, to 25cm, pubesc.; bract 15–21mm, ciliate; fls to 9.5cm across; dorsal sep. usually concave, to 3×2cm, outer surface shortly pubesc., white, veined green, often marked purple at base; synsepalum lanceolate, to 2.5×1.5cm, white, veined green; pet. spathulate, to 5×1.5cm, ciliate, green at base, purple above, margins spotted maroon-black; lip to 4cm, emarginate at apex, ochre-green; staminode to 9×8mm, deeply incised at apex. Winter. Borneo, Sumatra, Peninsular Malaysia. var. ***celebesense*** (Fowlie & Birk) Cribb. Differs by having fewer spots on petal margins and lack of prominent emarginate apex to the lip.

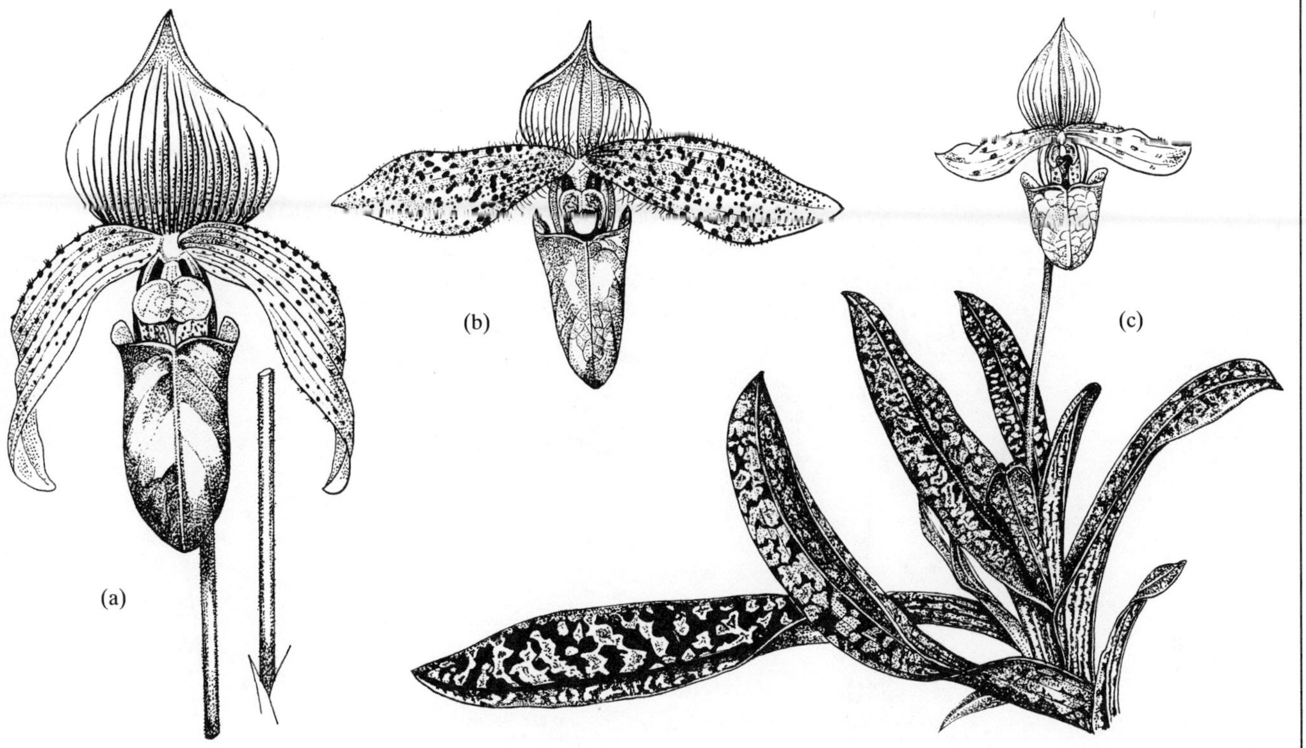


**Paphiopedilum** (×0.6) (a) *Paphiopedilum superbiens* (b) *P. sukhakulii* (c) *P. venustum*

***P. callosum*** (Rchb. f.) Stein. Very closely allied to *P. barbatum*. Lvs 3–5, narrowly elliptic, to 20×4.5cm, ciliate at base, tessellated pale and dark above, lower surface sometimes purple at base. Infl. 1-fld, rarely 2-fld, to 40cm; bract ovate to elliptic, to 28×20mm, green, sometimes marked purple, ciliate; fls 8–11cm across; sep. white flushed purple in lower half, veined purple and green, dorsal sep. broadly ovate, to 5.5×6cm, margins ciliate, recurved; synsepalum concave, to 3×2.5cm; pet. sometimes reflexed, sub-sigmoid, rounded at apex, to 6.5×2cm, white to yellow-green, apical third purple, maroon-spotted on upper margin and sometimes basal half; lip to 4.5×2.5cm, incurved lateral lobes warty, green, flushed maroon; staminode lunate, 11×7mm. Summer. Thailand, Cambodia, Laos. var. ***sublaeve*** (Rchb. f.) Cribb. Fls smaller than typical species; dorsal sep. smaller; pet. shorter, broader, less sigmoid, borne at 45° from horizontal, warty on upper margin. Peninsular Thailand, NW Malaysia.

***P. charlesworthii*** (Rolfe) Pfitz. Related to *P. spicerianum* and *P. druryi*, but differs in its pure white staminode and large, distinctively coloured and shaped dorsal sep. Lvs oblong-elliptic or linear-oblong, to 15cm×28mm, green above, spotted purple near base beneath. Infl. 1-fld, 8–15cm, pale green, pubesc.; bract obovate, to 32×20mm, pale green, spotted maroon, ciliate; fls to 8cm across; dorsal sep. transversely elliptic to circular, to 5.5×6.5cm, spreading or reflexed, outer surface finely pubesc., pink, veined darker; synsepalum elliptic, to 4cm×28mm, pale yellow, flecked and veined purple, finely pubesc. on outer surface; pet. horizontal, slightly incurved, ligulate-spathulate, to 4.5×1.5cm, slightly ciliate toward apex; lip wide-mouthed, to 43×27mm, pink-brown, veined darker, hairy within; staminode obovate, to 10×10mm, glabrous, white with central raised yellow boss. Autumn. Burma (Shan States only).

***P. ciliolare*** (Rchb. f.) Stein. Resembles *P. superbiens* but differs in the shape of the staminode and shorter lip. Lvs 4–6, oblong-elliptic to elliptic-oblanceolate, to 1.5×5cm, sparsely ciliate at base, mottled pale and darker green above, tinged purple at base beneath. Infl. 1-fld, erect, 20–32cm, purple, shortly pubesc.; bract ovate-lanceolate, 2–3cm, pubesc., ciliate; fls 7–9cm across; sep. white at base, pale purple and green above, veined purple, dorsal sep. ovate, to 5.5×5cm, ciliate; synsepalum elliptic-ovate, to 32×22mm; pet. slightly falcate, oblanceolate, to 7×2cm, ciliate, upper margins warty, white, spotted and veined dark purple; lip to 6×3.5cm, incurved lateral lobes warted, dark brown-purple; staminode transversely reniform, 3-lobed at apex, narrowly incised at base, to 14×7mm. Summer. Philippines.

***P. concolor*** (Batem.) Pfitz. Terrestrial or lithophytic on limestone hills often in dense shade. Lvs 4–6, oblong to elliptic-oblong, to 14×4cm, tessellated dark and pale green on upper surface, finely spotted purple beneath. Infl. 1–2-fld, rarely 3-fld, to 8cm, finely white-pubesc., purple or green spotted purple; bracts ovate, to 15×16mm, pubesc., green, spotted purple; fls to 7cm diam., yellow, rarely ivory or white, finely spotted all over with purple; dorsal sep. broadly ovate, to 35×33mm; synsepalum concave, elliptic to ovate, to 3×3cm; pet. elliptic, rounded at apex, to 4.5×2.5cm; lip ellipsoidal, fleshy, margins incurved, to 38×15mm; staminode shortly trullate to subtriangular, minutely ciliate, to 13×12mm. Summer–autumn. SE Burma, SW China (Yunnan), Thailand, Indochina.

***P. dayanum*** (Lindl.) Stein. Lvs oblong-lanceolate, to 21×5cm, tessellated dark and light yellow-green or blue-green, margins near apex minutely serrate. Infl. 1-fld, to 25cm, maroon, purple-pubesc.; bract lanceolate, to 2.5cm, pale green, pubesc.; fls to 14.5cm across; sep. white veined green, dorsal sep. ovate, to 6×3cm, ciliate; synsepalum ovate, to 5×2cm; pet. oblanceolate-spathulate, to 8×1.5cm, purple-pink, purple-ciliate; lip deep maroon, 5×2cm, apical margin ciliate, lateral lobes incurved, warted; staminode green, veined darker, transversely elliptic, reniform, 6×13mm. Summer. Borneo (Sabah only).

***P. delenatii*** Guill. Closely related to *P. armeniacum* and *P. micranthum*. Lvs 6–7, elliptic to oblong-elliptic, to 11×4cm, margins ciliate at base, mottled dark and pale green above, spotted purple below. Infl. 1-fld but commonly 2-fld, to 22cm, purple, white-hirsute; bract elliptic to ovate, to 15×10mm, green spotted purple, shortly pubesc.; fls to 8cm diam., pale pink with red and yellow markings on staminode, pubesc. within and without; dorsal sep. ovate, to 3.5×2.5cm; synsepalum similar, 3×2.9cm; pet. broadly elliptic, rounded at apex, 4.3×5cm; lip ellipsoidal to subglobose, 4×3cm, margins incurved, minutely pubesc.; staminode somewhat convex, ovate, to 17×16mm, ciliate. Spring. Vietnam.

***P. druryi*** (Bedd.) Stein. Stems short on a creeping rhiz. Lvs 5–7, suberect or spreading, narrowly oblong, to 20×3cm, coriaceous, light green with darker veins. Infl. 1-fld, erect, to 25cm; bract ovate, 12mm, green, purple-pubesc.; fls green-yellow or chartreuse, a central maroon-brown streak on dorsal sep. and pet., lip honey-yellow; dorsal sep. curved forward over lip, elliptic, to 4×3cm, pubesc., shortly ciliate on margins; synsepalum ovate, to 3.5×2.5cm, pubesc.; pet. incurved-porrect, narrowly oblong, slightly drooping, often dilated toward apex, to 43×18mm, pubesc., margins undulate and reflexed; lip slightly compressed, to 4.5×1.5cm; column short; staminode obcordate, 10–12mm long and wide with a small raised boss below centre. Summer. S India; perhaps extinct in the wild.

**Paphiopedilum** (a) *P. glaucophyllum* (b) *P. victoria-mariae* (c) *P. victoria-regina* (d) *P. insigne* (e) *P. villosum* (f) *P. hirsutissimum*

***P. emersonii*** Koopowitz & Cribb. Allied to *P. delenatii* and the Chinese *P. armeniacum*, *P. malipoense* and *P. micranthum*. Lvs about 4, coriaceous, ligulate, to 23cm×37mm, green, lower surface slightly keeled. Infl. erect, to 11.5cm, 1-or possibly 2-fld, subtended by a white, papery, basal, sterile sheath; bract elliptic, conduplicate, 28×22mm, white, papery; fls 8.5–9.5cm across, sub-campanulate, sep. white, campanulate, thick-textured, pet. white, flushed pink at base, lip creamy, rim flushed pink, spotted purple within, yellowing with age; staminode bright yellow marked with red; dorsal sep. elliptic-ovate, hooded over lip, margins recurved, 4.5cm×32mm, surfaces pubesc., outer side keeled; synsepalum elliptic subcircular, 3.5×3.5cm, both surfaces pubesc., outer side keeled; pet. broadly elliptic to subcircular, incurved, to 4.5×4.5cm, pubesc., villous at base; lip subporrect, 3.5×3cm, flared at base, apical margin incurved, grooved along veins; column short; staminode convex, trullate, 20×10mm; stigma spathulate, shortly papillose; anth. 2, with dry pollen. Spring. China (probably Guizhou).

***P. exul*** (Ridl.) Rolfe. Closely allied to *P. insigne* and *P. gratrixianum*. Terrestrial or lithophytic. Lvs 4–5, suberect, linear, to 35×3cm, yellow-green. Infl. 1-fld, to 18cm, slender, green, pubesc.; bract narrowly elliptic to elliptic, 44×24mm, green to yellow-green; fls about 6.5cm across; dorsal sep. ovate-elliptic, 4.5×3cm, outer surface pubesc., mainly white, centre yellow with raised maroon spots; synsepalum oblong-elliptic, 4.5×2.5cm, pale yellow-green, veined darker; pet. incurved, subhorizontal, narrowly oblong, 5cm×17mm, ciliate, pubesc. at base, margins undulate, glossy, buff-yellow, veined darker; lip 3.5cm×19mm, glossy, buff, veined darker; staminode obovate, 8×9mm. Summer. Peninsular Thailand.

***P. fairrieanum*** (Lindl.) Stein. Lvs 4–8, linear-ligulate, to 28×3cm, margins serrulate toward apex, mid to dark green, faintly mottled above, paler beneath. Infl. 1-fld, rarely 2-fld, to 45cm, green; bract elliptic, 14×8mm, white, purple-pubesc.; fls showy, sep. white, veined green and purple, somewhat purple suffusion on dorsal sep., pet. similar; dorsal sep. elliptic, to 8×7cm, ciliate, apical margins recurved, lateral margins undulate; synsepalum ovate, 3.5×2.5cm; pet. S-shaped, 5×1.5cm, ciliate, margins undulate; lip deep, outcurved at apex, 4cm×25mm, olive to yellow-green, veined darker; staminode elliptic, 9×7mm, yellow, centre veined green and purple. Autumn. Sikkim, Bhutan, NE India.

***P. glanduliferum*** (Bl.) Stein. Terrestrial, rarely epiphytic. Lvs 4–6, linear-oblong, to 40×5.5cm, basal margins sparsely ciliate, green, glabrous. Infl. 2–5-fld, to 50cm, purple to green-brown, shortly pubesc.; bract ovate, to 4.5cm, glabrous, pale yellow-green striped purple; fls to 16cm across, sep. and pet. yellow veined maroon, pet. margins maroon-warted on base, lip yellow, veined and flushed purple; dorsal sep. ovate to 5.5×3cm; synsepalum similar, to 5.5×3cm; pet. deflexed, linear-tapering, to 10×1cm, apical parts papillose, basal margins sparsely ciliate, usually twisted; lip subporrect, to 5.5×2cm, lateral lobes incurved; staminode convex, oblong to subquadrate, 17×12mm, sides hirsute. Summer. W New Guinea and adjacent islands.

***P. glaucophyllum*** J.J. Sm. Closely allied to *P. victoria-regina*; differs in its glaucous foliage; dorsal sep. lacking maroon stripes on veins; deflexed, long-ciliate white petals spotted purple, and obtuse staminode. Lvs 4–6, narrowly oblong-elliptic, to 28.5cm×53mm, glaucous, scarcely mottled when young, basal margins ciliate. Infl. to 20- or more-fld, green, mottled purple, pubesc.; rachis with internodes to 5cm; bracts elliptic, to 18mm, green, ciliate; fls in succession, never more than 2 open at a time, to 8.5cm across; dorsal sep. ovate to broad, to 33×32mm, shortly ciliate, outer surface pubesc., white or cream, centre yellow-green, veins flushed maroon; synsepalum ovate, to 32×18mm; pet. deflexed at 10–20° below horizontal, linear, to 5cm×9mm, apical half twisted, long-ciliate, pubesc. at base, white, spotted purple; lip to 4×2cm, pubesc. at base, pink-purple, finely spotted darker, margins pale yellow; staminode ovate, 15×9mm, green, apical half flushed purple. Summer. E Java. var. ***moquetteanum*** J.J. Sm. Differs from species type in its usually longer broader lvs, to 55×10cm, longer scape, few larger fls to 10cm across; dorsal sep. narrower, longer, yellow finely speckled purple. SW Java.

***P. godefroyae*** (Godef.-Leb.) Stein. Terrestrial or lithophytic. Lvs 4–6, oblong-elliptic, to 14cm×29mm, basal margins sparsely ciliate, tessellated dark and pale green above, usually spotted purple beneath. Infl. 1–2-fld, erect, to 8cm, purple, very shortly pubesc.; bract conduplicate, ovate, to 1.5cm, purple, shortly pubesc., fls about 5cm across, white or ivory-white, all seg. usually spotted purple; dorsal sep. concave, broadly ovate, to 33×37mm; synsepalum ovate, to 3×3cm; pet. oblong-elliptic, rounded, to 5.5×3cm, margins often undulate; lip ellipsoidal, to 3.5×1.5cm, margins strongly incurved; staminode transversely elliptic, to 9×11mm, apical margin 1-3-toothed, pubesc., ciliate. Summer. Peninsular Thailand, adjacent islands.

***P. gratrixianum*** (Mast.) Guill. Related to *P. villosum*; differs in its smaller and differently marked flowers. Lvs 4–7, suberect, linear, to 30×2.3cm, green, spotted purple near base beneath. Infl. 1-fld, to 25cm; bract narrowly oblong-lanceolate to obovate, to 4.5×1.5cm, green, spotted purple, glabrous; fls 7–8cm across; dorsal sep. ovate to obovate, to 5.2×4.6cm, white above, pale green below, purple-hairy; synsepalum ovate-elliptic, to 5×2.5cm, pale green, outer surface purple-pubesc.; pet. spathulate, to 5.2×2.5cm, glossy, yellow, flushed and veined purple-brown, minutely ciliate, reflexed side margins; lip to 4.2×2.8cm, tapering to apex, yellow flushed brown; staminode obcordate, 11×11mm, yellow, basal half purple-hairy, pustular with a central knob. Winter. Laos, possibly Vietnam.

***P. haynaldianum*** (Rchb. f.) Stein. Closely allied to *P. lowii*; differs in its villous peduncle; longer and narrower, heavily spotted dorsal sep., more tapering lip, and narrower staminode, simple excised at its apex. Terrestrial, lithophytic, or rarely epiphytic. Lvs 6–7, linear-ligulate, to 45×5cm, green. Infl. arching, 3–4-fld, to 51cm, purple, white-villous; bracts oblong-lanceolate, to 4.5cm; fls to 12.5cm across; dorsal sep. obovate-elliptic, apex cucullate, to 6×2.5cm, basal margin recurved, creamy white, sides flushed purple, centre green or yellow with basal half spotted maroon; synsepalum elliptic, 4.5×2.5cm, pale green, spotted maroon at base; pet. arcuate, spathulate, half-twisted, to 8cm×14mm, ciliolate, green or yellow, basal half spotted maroon, purple above; lip to 4.5cm×23mm, ochre-green, veined darker, purple-pubesc. within; staminode obovate, 12×8mm, apex incised, a short protuberance at base. Spring. Philippines (Luzon & Negros).

***P. hirsutissimum*** (Lindl. ex Hook.) Stein. Terrestrial or epiphytic. Lvs 5–6, linear-ligulate, to 45×2cm, green, spotted purple beneath. Infl. 1-fld, to 25cm, densely long-haired, subtended by 11cm sheath at base; bract elliptic, to 28mm, pubesc.; fls to 14cm across, sep. pale yellow to pale green with glossy dark brown suffusion almost to margins, pet. pale yellow, lower half spotted purple-brown, apical half flushed rose-purple; dorsal sep. ovate-elliptic, 4.5×4cm, margins undulate, ciliate; synsepalum similar, 36×22mm; pet. horizontal to deflexed, spathulate, 7cm×22mm, half-twisted toward apex, basal margins strongly undulate, pubesc., ciliate; lip 4.5×2cm; staminode subquadrate, convex, 10×8mm, pale yellow, spotted purple toward base, glossy dark brown toward middle. Spring–summer. NE India (Assam, Manipur, Lushai, Naga Hills). var. ***esquirolei*** (Schltr.) Cribb. Differs in its slightly larger fls, pet. to 8cm and shorter pubescence on peduncle and ovary. SW China (Yunnan and Guizhou) to N Thailand.

***P. hookerae*** (Rchb. f.) Stein. Lvs 5–6, oblong-elliptic, 23×5cm, boldly tessellated dark and light green above. Infl. 1-fld, to 50cm, purple, white-pubesc.; bract lanceolate, 30×14mm, pale brown, pubesc.; fls about 8cm across; dorsal sep. ovate, 4cm×29mm, basal margins reflexed, cream, centre flushed green; synsepalum elliptic, to 3×1.5cm, pale yellow; pet. deflexed, half-twisted in middle, spathulate, 5.5cm×22mm, ciliate, pale green, basal two-thirds spotted brown, apical third and margins purple; lip 42×17mm, brown, lateral lobes warted, apical margin ciliate, slightly reflexed; staminode circular, 10×10mm, apically excised, lateral lobes incurved-falcate at apex. Summer. Borneo (Sarawak and W Kalimantan). var. ***volonteanum*** (Sander ex Rolfe) Kerch. Differs in its narrower lvs, spotted purple below, pet. broader and more obtuse, lip slightly constricted below the horizontal mouth. Borneo (Sabah only).

***P. insigne*** (Wallich ex Lindl.) Pfitz. Very variable in fl. size and colour. Lvs 5–6, ligulate, to 32×3cm, green, spotted purple at base beneath. Infl. 1-fld, to 25cm, green, very shortly purple-pubesc.; bract elliptic or oblong-elliptic, to 5cm, glabrous, spotted purple at base; fls 7–10cm across; dorsal sep. ovate-elliptic to obovate-elliptic, 6.4×4cm, apical margins incurved, pale green, inner surface with raised maroon spots, margin white; synsepalum elliptic, 5×2.5cm, pale green, spotted brown; pet. slightly incurved, spathulate, 63×18mm, upper margin undulate in basal two-thirds, yellow-brown, veined red-brown; lip 5×3cm, yellow, marked purple-brown; staminode obovate, 10mm, yellow with purple hairs on surface, raised boss in centre. Autumn–winter. NE India (Meghalaya, Khasia Hills), E Nepal.

***P. javanicum*** (Reinw. ex Lindl.) Pfitz. Allied to *P. dayanum* but differs in its smaller, differently coloured flowers, reniform staminode lacking lateral teeth at apex, shorter dorsal sep., and shorter spotted pet. with margins only shortly ciliate. Lvs 4–5, narrowly elliptic, 23×4cm, pale green, veined and mottled darker. Infl. 1-fld, to 36cm, purple, shortly white-pubesc.; bract elliptic, to 25×14mm, pale green, lightly spotted purple, margins and midvein ciliate; fls to 9.5mm across; dorsal sep. ovate to elliptic, to 38×29mm, shortly ciliate, outer surface pubesc., pale green, veined darker, margin white-pink; synsepalum lanceolate, 26×13mm, outer surface pubesc., pale green; pet. usually deflexed at about 45° to horizontal, narrowly oblong, to 48×14mm, pale green, apical quarter pink-purple, basally spotted maroon; lip 4×2cm, outer surface shortly pubesc., lateral lobes verrucose, green, veined darker, often flushed brown; staminode reniform, 8×10mm, surface pubesc. Spring–summer. Java, Bali, Flores, possibly Sumatra. var. ***virens*** (Rchb. f.) Pfitz. Differs in pet. possibly less spotted. Lower slopes of Mount Kinabalu; Crocker Range in Sabah.

***P. kolopakingii*** Fowlie. Allied to *P. stonei* but differs in having many more, smaller fls. Terrestrial or lithophytic. Lvs 8–10, suberect, ligulate, to 60×8cm, green. Infl. to 14-fld, arching, to 70cm; bracts elliptic-lanceolate, to 5×1.5cm, green-ochre striped purple; fls to 10cm across; sep. white veined dark red-brown, pet. green, veined red, lip ochre, veined darker, staminode yellow; dorsal sep. ovate, 6.5×3.5cm, finely pubesc.; synsepalum ovate, 47×26mm, 2-keeled on back; pet. falcate, linear-tapering, to 7×8cm, minutely pubesc.; lip grooved behind, apex sharp, to 6cm×28mm; staminode convex, subquadrate, 15×10mm, sides pubesc. Borneo, central Kalimantan only.

***P. lawrenceanum*** (Rchb. f.) Pfitz. Closely related to *P. callosum* and *P. barbatum*; differs in having boldly tessellated lvs, very large dorsal sep., spreading pet. with upper and lower margins warted and differently shaped staminode. Lvs 5–6, elliptic to narrowly elliptic, to 19×6.5cm, dark green mottled yellow-green above, pale green beneath. Infl. 1-fld, to 31cm, pubesc., maroon; bract ovate, green, veined maroon; fls. to 11.5cm across; dorsal sep. broadly ovate-subcircular, to 62×62mm, lateral margins slightly reflexed, white,

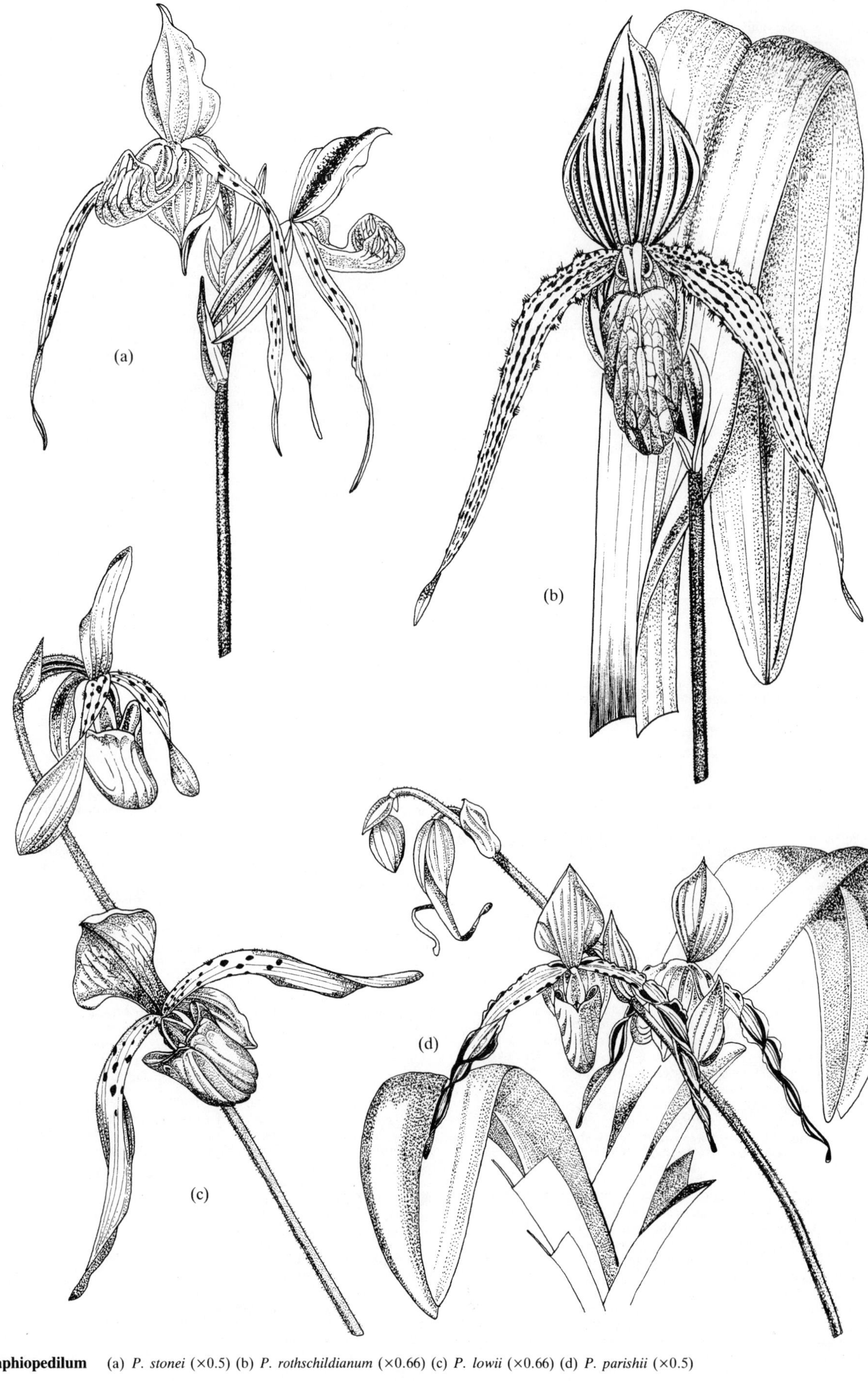


**Paphiopedilum** (a) *P. stonei* (×0.5) (b) *P. rothschildianum* (×0.66) (c) *P. lowii* (×0.66) (d) *P. parishii* (×0.5)

veined maroon above, green, below; synsepalum narrowly lanceolate, to 4×1.4cm, white flushed green, veined maroon; pet. at right angles to dorsal sep., ligulate, about 6cm×11mm, green with purple apex, margins purple-ciliate and maroon-warted; lip 65×32mm, lateral lobes incurved and maroon-warted, green overlaid dull maroon, spotted maroon within; staminode lunate, to 11×14mm, green veined darker, margin purple. Summer. Borneo (Sarawak and Sabah).

***P. lowii*** (Lindl.) Stein. Epiphytic or rarely lithophytic. Closely allied to *P. haynaldianum* but differs in lacking spotting on its more ovate elliptic dorsal sep., narrower pet. with more, smaller spotting basally, shorter broader lip and broader staminode, 3-toothed at its apex. Lvs 4–6, linear-ligulate, to 40×5cm, green. Infl. erect to arching, 3–7-fld, to 50cm, green mottled purple, shortly pubesc.; bracts elliptic, to 4.5×2cm, yellow, marked purple, pubesc.; fls to 14cm across; dorsal sep. elliptic-ovate, to 5.5cm×32mm, margins undulate and ciliate, pale green, basal half mottled purple, basal margins recurved; synsepalum elliptic, to 4cm, outer surface 2-keeled, pale green; pet. spathulate, often once-twisted in middle, to 9×2cm, ciliate, pale yellow, apical third purple, basal two-thirds spotted maroon; lip to 40×27mm, dull ochre brown; staminode obovate, apically 3-toothed, with a long erect hook at base, 10×7mm, pale ochre to brown-green. Spring–summer. Peninsular Malaysia, Sumatra, Java, Borneo, Sulawesi.

***P. malipoense*** S.C. Chen & Tsi. Allied to *P. armeniacum* but differs in fl. colour and its distinctive bicoloured staminode. Terrestrial on rocks in mixed montane forest. Growths occur on a more or less creeping, elongated rhiz. Lvs 7–8, leathery, oblong or narrowly elliptic, to 20×4cm, dark green, lower surface keeled and marked with purple. Infl. to 30cm, 1-fld; bract about 1.5cm; fls about 9cm across, sep. and pet. green with purple stripes and spots; dorsal sep. elliptic-lanceolate, to 45×22mm, 5-nerved, inner surface sparsely pubesc., villous without; synsepalum ovate-lanceolate, 7-nerved, 38×24mm; pet. obovate, about 40×34mm, villous at base, ciliolate, 9-veined, inner surface pubesc.; lip pale grey spotted purple within, deeply saccate, horizontal, 4.5cm, subglobose, margins inrolled, base villous within, outside finely pubesc.; staminode convex, broadly ovate-oblong, to 14×13mm, surface bearing 4 raised bosses in apical half. Spring. China (SE Yunnan).

***P. mastersianum*** (Rchb. f.) Stein. Lvs 4–6, to 30cm×43mm, oblong-elliptic, upper surface faintly tessellated dark and pale green. Infl. 1-fld, to 30cm, maroon, densely hairy; bract ovate-elliptic, green, ciliate, 29×20mm; fls to 9.5cm across; dorsal sep. broadly ovate, to 37×43mm, outer surface pubesc., cream with green centre; synsepalum ovate, to 29×20mm, green-yellow; pet. slightly reflexed, oblong-spathulate, to 5.5×2cm, very shortly ciliate, glossy, tinged green, spotted dark maroon near base, apical half flushed brown; lip to 52×30mm, pale rosy-brown spotted pale brown on lateral lobes; staminode lunate, to 11×10mm, base divided, apical margin excised, lateral lobes of apical margin incurved-falcate, pale green and brown. Summer. Moluccas (Ambon, Buru).

***P. micranthum*** Tang & Wang. Most closely related to *P. malipoense* but differs in fl. colour and its distinctive staminode. Growths clustered. Lvs 4–5, oblong-elliptic, to 15×2cm, upper surface mottled dark and pale green, spotted purple beneath. Infl. erect, 1-fld, to 20cm, purple, villous; fls large, thin-textured, sep. and pet. pale yellow, flushed pink above, veined red-purple; dorsal sep. ovate, to 2.5×3cm, outer surface villous; synsepalum elliptic, to 24×11mm; pet. elliptic-subcircular with rounded apex, to 33×34mm, ciliate, inner surface white-pubesc.; lip deeply inflated, elliptic-ovate, to 65×47mm, rose-pink, paler near base, spotted purple within; staminode convex, conduplicate longitudinally, circular to elliptic, 10×12.5mm, white flushed pink at base, yellow above, spotted red. Spring. SW China (Yunnan).

***P. niveum*** (Rchb. f.) Stein. Closely related to *P. concolor* (though nowhere overlapping in distribution) but differs in its taller infl., smaller fls, white in colour usually lightly spotted with purple, smaller ellipsoid lip and transversely elliptic staminode. Growths often clustered. Lvs 4–5, ligulate to narrowly elliptic, to 19×3.5cm, mottled very dark and pale green above, heavily dotted purple beneath, basal margins ciliate; infl. 1–2-fld, to 25cm, purple, shortly but densely white-pubesc.; bracts conduplicate, broadly ovate, to 14×12mm, white to pale green, spotted purple; fls about 6m diam., white, often dotted purple near base of seg. and front of lip, pubesc. on outside and base of pet. within, staminode yellow-centred; dorsal sep. very broadly ovate, to 3×5cm; synsepalum concave, ovate, to 28×22mm; pet. elliptic, rounded, to 39×26mm, margins shortly ciliate; lip ovoid to ellipsoidal, to 3×1.7cm, margins incurved; staminode broader than long, transversely elliptic, 1–3-toothed at apex, to 9×12mm. Summer. N Malaysia and S Thailand.

***P. papuanum*** (Ridl.) Ridl. Allied to *P. mastersianum* but differs in its smaller fls, dorsal sep. smaller with purple veins, pet. shorter and narrower, broader staminode and ovary with shorter hairs. Lvs 4–6, oblong to oblong-elliptic, to 22×4.2cm, tessellated dark and light green, veined dark green. Infl. 1-fld, to 28cm; bract ovate, to 1.5cm, pubesc.; fls to 9cm across; dorsal sep. ovate, to 25×26mm, ciliate, pubesc., outside, white with centre tinged yellow or green, veined purple; synsepalum elliptic-lanceolate, to 18×13mm; pet. oblong-lanceolate, to 42×17mm, ciliolate, dull maroon, basal half spotted black; lip to 3.7×1.4cm, dull crimson or brown-maroon; staminode 5×6mm, transversely lunate, notched above with short blunt apical teeth. Spring–summer. Highland New Guinea.

***P. parishii*** (Rchb. f.) Stein. Allied to *P. lowii* and *P. haynaldianum* but differs in its tapering green and black pet. with black warts on the margins and by its differently shaped staminode. Epiphytic or sometimes lithophytic. Lvs 5–8, ligulate, to 45×7.5cm, green. Infl. arching to suberect, to 50cm, to 9-fld; bracts large, conduplicate, broadly elliptic, to 4×3.5cm, margins undulate; fls to 13cm; sep. cream to green, veined darker, dorsal sep. elliptic, to 4.5×3cm, incurved on basal margins, recurved on apical margins; synsepalum ovate, to 4×2.9cm, margins recurved, outer surface 2-keeled; pet. decurved-pendent, linear-tapering, to 10.5×1.1cm, apical half spirally twisted, ciliate, basal margins undulate, green, spotted dark maroon below, margins and apical half dark maroon, maroon spots on lower basal margin; lip tapering to narrow apex, to 4.5×2cm, green, yellow-green or flushed purple; staminode obcordate, to 14×9mm, cream veined dark green. Summer. E & NE Burma, Thailand, SW China. var. ***dianthum*** (Tang & Wang) Cribb & Tang. Differs in having slightly larger fls, less spotted pet., papillose floral axis and bracts, glabrous, ovary and larger lip. SW China only.

***P. philippinense*** (Rchb. f.) Stein. Most closely allied to *P. randsii* and *P. sanderianum*; differs from the former in its longer tapering pet. and smaller narrower lip, and from the latter in its erect habit, much shorter pet., shorter dorsal sep., small blunt lip and smaller staminode. Terrestrial or lithophytic. Lvs to 9, ligulate, leathery, to 50×5cm. Infl. erect, 2–4-fld, to 50cm; bracts elliptic, pubesc., to 5×2cm; fls variable in size; sep. white, dorsal sep. ovate, to 5×2.5cm, striped maroon; synsepalum similar, to 5.5×3cm; pet. linear, tapering to apex, to 13cm×6mm, ciliate, white or yellow at base, maroon above, dark maroon warts on margin in basal half; lip small, rather ovoid, 3.8×1.4cm, yellow; staminode convex, yellow, veined green, purple-pubesc. on sides. Summer. Philippines and islands off N Borneo coast; on limestone, sea level to *c*500m. var. ***roebelenii*** (Veitch) Cribb Differs in its larger fls with longer pet. to 13cm. Philippines (Luzon only).

***P. primulinum*** M.W. Wood & Tayl. Lvs 4–7, narrowly oblong-elliptic, to 17×3.8cm, green, apex and lower margins ciliate. Infl. many-fld, opening in succession, lengthening to 35cm or more; bracts elliptic, 1.7cm, green; fls 6–7cm across, pale yellow with yellow-green sep.; dorsal sep. ovate, to 2.6×2.6cm, ciliate, pubesc. on reverse surface; synsepalum ovate, to 2.6×1.4cm; pet. linear-tapering, spreading; twisted in apical half, ciliate, 15° to horizontal, to 3.2×0.8cm; lip to 3.5×1.9cm, bulbous toward apex; staminode oblong-ovate, to 8×7mm. Summer. N Sumatra. var. ***purpurascens*** (M.W. Wood) Cribb. Differs in having fls flushed purple.

***P. purpuratum*** (Lindl.) Stein. Lvs 3–8, elliptic to oblong-elliptic, to 17×4.2cm, pale green below, tessellated light and darker green above, shortly ciliate toward base of margins. Infl. erect, 1-fld, to 20cm, slender, purple, purple-pubesc.; bracts narrowly ovate-elliptic; fls to 8cm across; dorsal sep. ovate-cordate, 3.5×3.6cm, white, veined purple-maroon; synsepalum lanceolate, to 2.7×1.5cm, green, veined darker; pet. more or less horizontal, narrowly elliptic to oblong, to 4.6×1.3mm, margin ciliate, glossy maroon, green-white near base, lower two-thirds spotted black-maroon; lip to 4×2cm, incurved, lateral lobes verrucose, brown-maroon; staminode lunate, to 8×11mm, pubesc. with acute apical teeth, pale ochre-purple, veined darker. Autumn. Hong Kong, adjacent parts of Guangdong Province of China, and Hainan Is.

***P. randsii*** Fowlie. Very closely allied to *P. philippinense* but differs in its thick fleshy lvs with yellowish border and shorter linear pet., not twisted and tapering only toward their apex. Growths clustered. Lvs 5–6, oblong, leathery, green, to 35×6cm. Infl. 3–5-fld, to 40cm, purple, densely hairy; bracts ovate, to 3×2cm, pubesc.; fls white, sep. and pet. veined maroon; dorsal sep. ovate, 4.2×2.2cm; synsepalum ovate, 3.2×2cm; pet. deflexed, arcuate, linear, 4.5×0.6cm; lip rounded and grooved at apex, 3.2×1.5cm, green-yellow; staminode convex, subquadrate, truncate, 5×4mm, pubesc. on sides, yellow. Summer. Philippines (Mindinau only).

***P. rothschildianum*** (Rchb. f.) Stein. Closest allies are *P. glanduliferum* and *P. adductum* but differs from them in its longer petals at an acute angle to the horizontal and a distinctive staminode. Terrestrial or lithophytic, often in large clumps. Lvs several, linear, to narrowly oblanceolate, to 60×5cm, sparsely ciliate at base, green; infl. 2–4-fld, erect, to 45cm, purple, shortly pubesc.; bracts ovate-elliptic, to 5.5cm, ciliate and hairy on midvein, pale green or yellow, striped purple; fls very large, to 30cm diam.; dorsal sep. ovate, to 6.6×4.1cm, ivory-white or yellow veined maroon; synsepalum similar but smaller, about 5.7×3.3cm; pet. to 12.4×1.4cm, narrowly tapering to rounded apex, yellow or ivory-white marked maroon; lip subporrect, grooved on back, about 5.7×2.2cm, golden, heavily suffused purple; staminode linear, bifid at apex, geniculate, to 16×5mm, margins and base densely glandular-pubesc., pale yellow-green. Spring–summer. Borneo.

***P. sanderianum*** (Rchb. f.) Stein. Lithophytic on vertical SE-facing limestone cliffs. Lvs 4–5, arcuate-pendent, linear, to 45×5.3cm, shiny, green. Infl. horizontal or slightly ascending, 2–5-fld; bracts elliptic-lanceolate, to 5cm, red-brown, margins and midvein ciliate. Fls about 7cm across, to 95cm; sep. yellow striped maroon; dorsal sep lanceolate, slightly concave, to 6.5×2.5cm; synsepalum similar, 2-keeled, to 6×2cm; pet. ribbon-like, pendent, undulate, twisted, tapering to apex, to 90×0.9cm, off-white to yellow, spotted maroon, maroon warts on basal margins, basal half ciliate, apex minutely pubesc.; lip subporrect, pointed at apex, to 5×2.5cm, lateral lobes incurved; staminode convex,

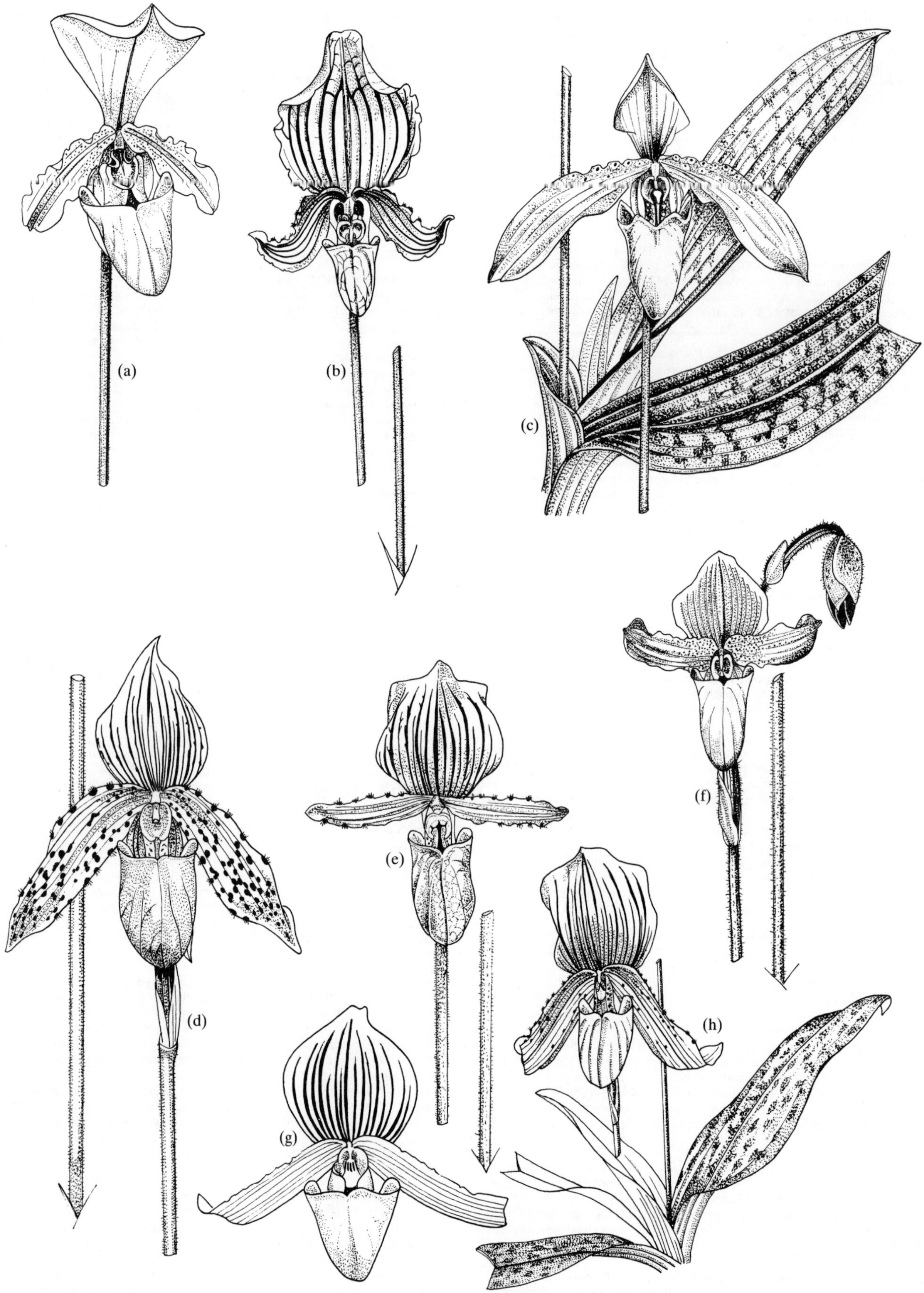


**Paphiopedilum** (×0.66) (a) *P. spicerianum* (b) *P. fairrieanum* (c) *P. appletonianum* (d) *P. argus* (e) *P. lawrenceanum* (f) *P. mastersianum* (g) *P.* Maudiae (h) *P. callosum*

oblong, to 13×11mm, basal and side margins pubesc. Winter. Borneo (Sarawak).

***P. spicerianum*** (Rchb. f. ex Mast. & T. Moore) Pfitz. Terrestrial or lithophytic. Lvs 4–5, spreading to pendent, narrowly oblong-elliptic to ligulate, to 30×6cm, basal margins undulate, glossy dark green, spotted purple toward base beneath. Infl. 1-, rarely 2-fld, to 35cm; bract elliptic, to 3cm; fls to 7cm across; dorsal sep. curving forward, obovate to transversely elliptic, to 4.2×5cm, sides recurved, both surfaces pubesc., white with central maroon vein and green-tinged base; synsepalum ovate, to 3.5×2.2cm, off-white; pet. falcate, linear-tapering, to 3.9×1.3cm, upper margin undulate, ciliate toward apex only, yellow-green with central brown-purple vein, flecking on other veins; lip to 4.3×3cm, glossy, pale green, flushed brown with darker veins; staminode obovate or transversely elliptic-obcordate, glabrous, 10×6mm. Winter. NE India, NW Burma.

***P. stonei*** (Hook.) Stein. Allied to *P. kolopakingii* but differs in its larger, more boldly marked fls. Lvs about 5, ligulate, to 70×4.5cm, green. Infl. 2–4-fld, to 70cm; bracts to 5.5×2.2cm; fls to 12cm across; sep. white, lined dark maroon, dorsal sep. ovate, to 5.7×4.4cm; synsepalum elliptic-ovate, to 5×3.4cm; pet. linear-tapering, dependent, to 15×0.75cm, sometimes twisted in apical half, yellow, lined and spotted maroon, sometimes flushed maroon in apical half; lip forward-pointing, grooved on back, to 5.7×2.8cm, pale yellow, strongly flushed pink and veined darker; staminode convex, subcircular, 14×11mm, coarsely hairy margined, yellow. Summer. Borneo (Sarawak only). var. ***platytaenium*** (Rchb. f.) Stein. Differs in having broader pet., to 2cm wide.

***P. sukhakulii*** Schoser & Sengh. Allied to *P. wardii* but differs in having greener fls, broader horizontal pet. marked with bold spots, shorter and broader sep., a longer staminode and lvs without purple spotting on their reverse. Roots thick, pubesc. Lvs 3–4, oblong-elliptic, 13×4.5cm, tessellated dark and yellow-green above. Infl. 1-fld; bracts 20×9mm, green; fls about 12cm across; sep. white veined green, spotted purple at base, outer surface pubesc., dorsal sep. concave, to 4×3cm, ciliate; synsepalum lanceolate, 3.4×1.6cm; pet. subhorizontal, to 6.2×2cm, green heavily spotted maroon, margins ciliate; lip saccate, 5×2.3cm, green, veined and flushed maroon, lateral lobes warty; staminode pubesc., 8×11mm, lower margin tridentate with lateral teeth incurved. Autumn. NE Thailand only.

***P. superbiens*** (Rchb. f.) Stein. Lvs 4–5, elliptic to oblong-elliptic, to 24×5cm, tessellated dark and light green above, flushed purple at base beneath. Infl. 1-fld, to 23cm, purple; bracts elliptic-lanceolate, to 3cm; fls to 8cm across; sep. white veined green and purple, marked green or purple-green at centre, pet. white, spotted maroon-purple, sometimes flushed purple, raised spots on upper margin and in basal half, lip dark maroon; dorsal sep. ovate, to 5.8×5.3cm, ciliate; synsepalum ovate, to 4×1.9cm; pet. somewhat recurved-falcate, to 7.5×1.9cm, ciliate, half-twisted in apical half; lip large, to 6.5×3cm, lateral lobes warted; staminode transversely reniform, to 12×20mm, apex bluntly 3-toothed. Summer. N & C Sumatra.

***P. tonsum*** (Rchb. f.) Stein. Variable in fl. size, pet. and staminode shape and pet. spotting. Lvs about 6, oblong-elliptic, to 20×4.5cm, veined green, upper surface mottled darker green. Infl. 1-fld, erect, to 35cm; bract elliptic-ovate, to 24×1.2cm; fls to 14cm across; sep. white, veined and tinged yellow-green, pet. olive to yellow-green, veined darker, black-warted on inner surface, lip olive-brown, flushed pink, veined darker; dorsal sep. obovate, about 4.5×4cm; synsepalum ovate, about 3.5×1.5cm; pet. slightly drooping, about 6.5×2cm; lip saccate, 5.5×3.3cm; staminode subreniform, dentate on lower margin, to 11×14mm. Autumn–winter. N & C Sumatra.

***P. urbanianum*** Fowlie. Related to *P. javanicum* and *P. argus*, differing from the former in its pet. markings, larger flat dorsal sep., brown-red lip and staminode; differs from the latter in its narrow, ciliate pet. and shape of staminode. Lvs 4–5, narrowly or oblong-elliptic, to 20×4cm, tessellated dark and light green above, basal margins ciliate. Infl. erect, 1-fld, rarely 2-fld, to 25cm; bract ovate, to 3×2cm, green veined maroon, pubesc.; fls to 10.5cm across; dorsal sep. ovate to broadly ovate, to 3.6×4.2cm, white veined green; synsepalum concave, ovate, to 3.1×1.9cm, green veined darker; pet. slightly recurved, oblanceolate, to 6×1.8cm, white lined green, basal two-thirds spotted maroon, apical half purple; lip to 4.5×3cm, dull purple, lateral lobes marked maroon, ciliate on apical margin; staminode subcircular to almost hexagonal, to 10×10mm, yellow-green lined green. Spring. Philippines.

***P. venustum*** (Wallich) Pfitz. ex Stein. Somewhat variable but recognized by its dark sea- or slate-green tessellated lvs, veined lip and recurved pet. with raised maroon spots. Lvs 4–5, elliptic to oblong-elliptic, to 25×5.5cm, surface dull to almost rough, ciliate near base, tessellated dark green and grey green above, densely spotted purple beneath. Infl. 1-fld (rarely 2-fld), to 23cm; bract elliptic-lanceolate, to 2.5cm; fls 8–9cm across, sep. white veined green, pet. white veined with green, warted maroon-black, flushed purple in apical half; dorsal sep. ovate, to 3.8×2.8cm, outer surface hirsute; synsepalum similar, to 3cm; pet. oblanceolate, recurved, ciliate, to 5.4×1.4cm; lip to 4.3×3.2cm, yellow tinged purple and veined green, lateral lobes verrucose; staminode reniform, to 9×11mm, minutely pubesc. with short, blunt, lateral apical teeth. Winter. NE India, E Nepal, Sikkim, Bhutan.

***P. victoria-mariae*** (Sander ex Mast.) Rolfe. Allied to *P. victoria-regina* but differs in certain floral characteristics. Lvs oblong-ligulate, ciliate near base, to 30×6.5cm, green mottled darker, flushed purple at base beneath. Infl. to 1m+, many-fld in succession showing 2 or 3 at a time; bracts elliptic-oblong, ciliate, green, to 3cm; fls 8–9cm across; dorsal sep. broadly ovate to obovate, to 2.9×3cm, ciliate, outer surface long-pubesc., pale yellow with centre bright green; synsepalum ovate, to 2.8×1.7cm, ciliate, outer surface long-pubesc.; pet. linear, horizontal-reflexed, to 4×1.1cm, shortly ciliate, twisted in apical half, green flushed brown to red-purple; lip tapers to apex, to 4×2.5cm, purple, margined yellow or green, lateral lobes finely spotted; staminode curved in apical half, to 10×7mm. Spring. S & CW Sumatra.

***P. victoria-regina*** (Sander) M.W. Wood. Lvs 4–6, narrowly oblong-elliptic, margins ciliate at base, to 28×6cm, green, flushed purple beneath. Infl. to 60cm, arching, rachis flexuous; bracts elliptic, ciliate, to 3.5×2.8cm, green; fls to 32 in succession, showing 1–2 at a time; dorsal sep. subcircular elliptic, to 3×3cm, yellow-green or white, lower half flushed green or yellow, veined dark purple, margins undulate, outer surface long-pubesc.; synsepalum elliptic, to 3×2.1cm, yellow-green, veined purple; pet. horizontal, ligulate, slightly recurved, to 4×0.8cm, yellow or pale yellow, spotted and streaked dark maroon, twice twisted, ciliate; lip to 4.1×2.1cm, pink with white rim, bulbously inflated, lateral lobes broadly rounded at apex; staminode convex, to 9×7.5mm, green, heavily flushed dark maroon, basal half pubesc. Autumn. Sumatra.

***P. villosum*** (Lindl.) Stein. This widespread and variable species is allied to *P. insigne* and *P. gratrixianum* but differs from both in having a shorter fl. stem, larger bract, larger fls with broader pet, longer lip and a villous ovary. Lvs 4–5, linear-ligulate, to 42×4cm, green, margins ciliate at base, spotted at base beneath. Infl. suberect to arching, 1-fld, to 24cm, densely hairy; bracts elliptic, to 6.5×3.8cm, glabrous, green, spotted maroon; fls to 11.5cm across; dorsal sep. obovate, to 6.5×3.5cm, basal margins reflexed, green, margined white, glossy maroon areas in centre; synsepalum ovate, adpressed to ovary, to 3.5×2.6cm, pale green; pet. incurved, obovate-spathulate, to 7×3cm, glossy, ciliate, red-brown with central maroon stripe; lip tapering to apex, to 6×3.8cm, ochre, flushed pink or red; staminode obcordate-obovate, about 16×14mm, verrucose, hirsute, a glossy knob in centre. Winter–spring. NE India, Burma, Thailand. var. ***boxallii*** Rchb. f. Differs in fl. colour with seg. narrower at base, dorsal sep. heavily spotted and purple marking on pet.

***P. violascens*** Schltr. Variable in lf and fl. size and shape of staminode. Terrestrial or, rarely, epiphytic. Lvs 4–6, elliptic to oblong-elliptic, to 22×4cm, grey-green, mottled darker above. Infl. 1-fld, to 30cm; bracts elliptic-lanceolate to elliptic-ovate, to 2.4cm, pubesc., ciliate; fls to 7.5cm, across; dorsal sep. broadly ovate, to 4.3×3cm, outer surface pubesc., white veined green; synsepalum ovate, to 2.6×1.6cm, pubesc. on outer surface, green veined darker; pet. deflexed 45°, obliquely oblong, to 4.4×1.8cm, minutely ciliate, white or green-white, apical three-quarters heavily flushed purple; lip to 5×2cm, deeply saccate, margin ciliate, green to ochre; staminode semicircular, to 7.5×14mm, green with purple pubescence. Spring. New Guinea and adjacent islands near coast.

***P. wardii*** Summerh. Allied to *P. sukhakulii* but differs in shape and colour of fls and in having dark green marbled lvs resembling those of *P. venustum*. Lvs 3–5, oblong-lanceolate, to 17cm, dark blue-green mottled paler above, mottled purple beneath. Infl. 1-fld, to 20cm; bracts lanceolate, ciliate, green flushed purple, 2–3cm; fls 8.5–10cm across; dorsal sep. ovate, to 5×3cm, outer surface pubesc., white veined green; synsepalum lanceolate, to 4.5×2.2cm; pet. oblong-lanceolate to oblong, to 6.5×1.7cm, spreading, somewhat pendulous to about 30° from horizontal, green-white flushed brown-purple, spotted dark maroon all over; lip to 5×2cm, lateral lobes warty, green-tinged or ochre, finely spotted brown; staminode lunate, to 10×14mm, finely pubesc., pale green veined darker. Winter. N Burma, SW China.

***P. wentworthianum*** Schoser. Related to *P. violascens* and *P. bougainvilleanum* but differs in its glossier more spreading pet., undulate on their upper margin. Lvs about 5, narrowly oblong to elliptic-oblong, to 25×4.5cm, tessellated light and dark green, shortly pubesc. Infl. 1-fld, to 35cm tall; bract elliptic-ovate, to 2.4cm; fls about 8cm across; dorsal sep. concave, broadly ovate, to 3.2×3.5cm, cream veined green with green centre; synsepalum ovate, to 2.5×2.6cm; pet. oblong-elliptic, spreading, about 20° below horizontal, to 4.5×2.5cm, glossy purple above, merging to brown and green toward base, ciliate, upper margin undulate; lip to 4.5×2.2cm, yellow-green flushed brown; staminode lunate, to 10×12mm, shortly pubesc., green. Spring. Bougainville and Guadalcanal.

Many of the above were originally combined in *Cypripedium*; these synonyms, now long defunct, have not been recorded here.

***P.* grexes and cultivars.**

*P.* A. de Lairesse: robust plants with beautiful mottled lvs; fls several on each stem, creamy yellow with maroon red striping.

*P.* Aladin: foliage medium green, somewhat mottled in some clones; fls strawberry pink.

*P.* Albion: dark green mottled lvs on small plants; fls white with bright green staminode.

*P.* Alma Gevaert: beautifully mottled lvs; fls lime green and white on tall stems, dorsal sep. striped.

*P.* Amanda 'Joyance': mid-green lvs; fls deep red.

*P.* Angela: grey-green-mottled lvs on small plants; fls white or pale pink spotted with pink-red.

*P.* Astarte: plain green lvs; fls pale yellow, fading to cream or white.

*P.* Berenice: strong plants with mid-green lvs; fls several on each tall stem, yellow-green with rose-pink pet. and brown-lined lip.

*P.* Betty Bracey 'Springtime': mid-green lvs; fls large, round, rich yellow-green with wide white border on dorsal sep.

*P.* Bingleyense: mid-green lvs; fls on tall stems, deep red.

*P.* Black Diamond: foliage very dark green and grey, attractively mottled; fls small, pale strawberry pink.

*P.* British Bulldog: medium green lvs; fls green-brown with heavily spotted white dorsal sep.

*P.* Caddiana: mid-green lvs; fls small but rich lime green.

*P.* Carat Gold: strong plants with mid-green lvs; fls round, golden yellow-green with white border on dorsal sep.

*P.* Cardinal Mercier: small plants with mid-green lvs; fls small but deep red.

*P.* Charles Sladden: small plants with densely mottled lvs; fls on short stems, rosy red with darker stripes.

*P.* Chianti 'Chilton': strong plants with mid-green lvs; fls large, round, golden yellow-green.

*P.* Christopher: strong plants with mid-green lvs; fls singly on tall stems, yellow-green with white border on dorsal, few spots.

*P.* Clair de Lune 'Edgard van Belle': the best of the 'Maudiae' types: large plants with distinctively mottled foliage; fls large on tall stems, lime green and white.

*P.* Cymatodes 'Beechense': large plants with beautifully mottled lvs; fls large, cream with wine red stripes and spots, the pet. with warts along the margin, lip brown.

*P.* Danaqueen: medium green lvs; fls rich chestnut brown with spotted dorsal sep.

*P.* Darling: attractively mottled dark green lvs; fls large on tall stems, attractive deep pink. Several fine clones have been awarded.

*P.* Delaina: attractively mottled, dark green lvs; several pink fls, usually borne consecutively.

*P.* Delophyllum: attractively mottled dark green lvs; several deep pink fls are borne consecutively.

*P.* Delrosi: attractively mottled foliage; very attractive fls on tall stems, deep pink with deeper pink striping.

*P.* Demura: small plants with mottled lvs; fls deep raspberry pink with white, heavily spotted dorsal sep.

*P.* Deperle: attractively mottled dark green lvs; fls cream or white. Some tetraploid clones with larger fls have been awarded.

*P.* Diana Broughton: plants with mid-green lvs: fls rather small, on tall stems, yellow-green with white margin to dorsal sep.

*P.* Dusty Miller: mid-green lvs on robust plants; white fls slightly freckled on dorsal sep., of fine form on tall stems.

*P.* Emerald: beautiful mottled foliage; attractive lime green and white fls.

*P.* Ernest Read: like an improved *P. callosum*; mottled foliage; fls on tall stems with large dorsal sep. shadow striped wine red and green on cream.

*P.* F.C. Puddle: mid-green lvs; white or pale lemon fls with few freckles on dorsal sep.

*P.* Faire-Maud: small plants with mottled lvs; fls small on tall slender stems, rich wine red with striped dorsal sep.

*P.* Frau Ida Brandt: robust plants with beautiful mottled lvs; fls large, several on each stem, white or cream and densely striped in wine red.

*P.* Freckles: robust plants with mid-green lvs; fls white or pale pink, well covered with rosy-red freckles.

*P.* Gorse: mid-green lvs; large round fls, rich yellow-green.

*P.* Goultenianum: similar to the above but fls wine red and white instead of green and white.

*P.* Goultenianaum 'Album': strong plants with beautifully mottled lvs; fls lime green and white with striped dorsal sep. and down-swept warted pet.

*P.* Gowerianum: strong plants with mottled foliage; fls lime-green and white or wine red and white, dorsal sep. boldly striped.

*P.* Harrisianum: strong plants with mottled lvs; red-brown glossy fls with striped dorsal on strong stems. The first *Paphiopedilum* hybrid made and flowered in 1859.

*P.* Hellas 'Westonbirt': well-known plant with mid-green lvs; fls lovely bright brown/golden with wide white margin on dorsal sep.

*P.* Henriette 'Fujiwara': mid-green lvs; several fls on tall slender stems, white and lime green resembling the *P. haynaldianum* parent but lacking spots.

*P.* Holdenii: attractive mottled foliage; fls lime green and white with striped dorsal sep.

*P.* Kay Rinaman 'Val': famous cross with mid-green lvs; large round fls, green-gold with white border on dorsal sep.

*P.* 'King of Sweden': famous cross with mid-green lvs; fls large, oval, lime green on tall stems.

*P.* Lawrebel 'Boynton': a beautiful primary hybrid with distinctive mottled lvs and large rosy fls with darker red stripes.

*P.* Leeanum: primary hybrid with light green lvs; fls small, yellow-brown dorsal edged white, with some small spots.

*P.* Leyburnense: lvs mid-green; fls deep strawberry pink with white staminode.

*P.* Madame Martinet: attractively mottled dark green lvs; very pretty pink fls on tall stems.

*P.* Makuli: attractive mottled foliage; fls small and distinctive, lime green and white or wine red and white, some forms very dark red with near black warts on pet.

*P.* Makuli 'Cat's Eyes': attractive mottled foliage; fls small and distinctive, lime green and white.

*P.* Maudiae: one of the best-known slipper orchids with attractive mottled lvs; fls distinctive, lime green and white with striped dorsal sep. Many slipper orchids similar to this in colour and shape are known as Maudiae types. Named clones include 'Magnificum' and 'The Queen'.

*P.* Maudiae 'Coloratum': attractive mottled lvs; fls on strong upright stems, large, wine red and white with striped dorsal sep. and green-brown lip.

*P.* Meadowsweet 'Purity': mid-green lvs; fls white or cream tinged with yellow.

*P.* Miller's Daughter: most famous of the white hybrid slipper orchids; lvs mid-green; fls white, good shape on tall stems; some clones slightly freckled.

*P.* Muriel Hollington: mid-green lvs; fls on tall stems, yellow or beige with few spots.

*P.* Nettie McMay: strong plants with attractive mottled foliage; fls on tall stems, large, wine red and white with large striped dorsal sep. and wart on pet.

*P.* Noche: lvs mid- to dark green; fls on short stems, deep wine red.

*P.* Olivia: a beautiful primary hybrid with dark mottled lvs; fls opening green and fading to a beautiful shell pink.

*P.* Onyx: attractively mottled lvs; fls green and white on tall stems.

*P.* Orchilla 'Chilton': famous red fls with narrow white margin to dorsal sep.

*P.* Paeony 'Regency': famous breeder; strong plants with medium green lvs; fls large, red and brown with white margin to dorsal sep.

*P.* Papa Rohl: an unusual primary hybrid with mottled lvs; fls green with a striped dorsal sep. and long, spotted pet.

*P.* Peter Black 'Emerald': strong plants with medium green lvs; fls green-brown with white, heavily spotted dorsal sep.

*P.* Primcolor: small plants with dark green lvs; fls clear yellow, several opening consecutively.

*P.* Psyche: primary hybrid; small plants with mottled lvs and white fls.

*P.* Red Maude: attractively mottled lvs; fls wine red with white margin to dorsal sep., pet. warted.

*P.* Redstart: medium green lvs; well-known wine-red fls.

*P.* Rosy Dawn: lvs mid-green, fls white, beige or pale pink with pink-red spots.

*P.* Royalet: medium green lvs; fls deep wine red, some with narrow white margin to dorsal sep.

*P.* Sheila Hanes 'Sweet Afton': mid-green lvs; lime green fls with white margin on dorsal sep.

*P.* Shillianum: large robust plants with mid-green lvs faintly mottled; several fls, cream base colour but heavily overlaid with stripes and spots in wine red.

*P.* Shireen: large robust plants with mid-green lvs; fls on tall stems, borne consecutively, dorsal sep. yellow and lip pink, pet. spirally twisted and hairy on the margins.

*P.* Silvara: lvs mid-green; fls on tall stems opening yellow green and fading to a glistening white.

*P.* Sir Redvers Buller: medium green, faintly mottled lvs; fls small but strong red-brown with lines of fine spots on white dorsal sep.

*P.* Small World: medium green lvs; rich chestnut brown to red with white dorsal, heavily spotted.

*P.* Song of Mississippi: strong robust plants with attractively mottled foliage; fls on tall strong stems, several appearing consecutively, dorsal sep. striped, lip pink, pet. twisted and spotted with darker colour.

*P.* St Alban: attractive mottled lvs in grey-green; fls small but deep wine red, early flowering.

*P.* St Swithin: large robust plants with mid-green lvs; fls large, several simultaneously, yellow-brown with dorsal and ventral sep. conspicuously striped in brown, lip large, brown.

*P.* Startler 'Glace': medium green lvs; fls on tall stems, deep wine red.

*P.* Sunset 'Alpha': medium green lvs; fls rich dark red.

*P.* Susan Tucker: robust plants with mid-green lvs; fls white on strong stems.

*P.* Swanilda: robust plants with mid-green lvs; fls white on strong stems.

*P.* Toby Strauss: mid-green lvs; very large fls, green or yellow and white, some with beige tones, clones variable.

*P.* Tommie Hanes 'Althea': well-known cross with mid-green lvs; fls lime green and white, fading to yellow.

*P.* Transvaal: large robust plants with dark green lvs; fls borne consecutively, yellow-pink with striped dorsal sep. and twisted pet.

*P.* Vanda M. Pearman: attractively mottled grey and dark green lvs; very pretty pink and white fls on short stems, sometimes scented.

*P.* Vintage Harvest 'Vinho Verde': strong growing plants with mid-green lvs; fls very large, round, medium green with white margin on dorsal sep.

*P.* Vintner's Treasure: foliage attractively mottled and flushed with purple beneath; fls on tall stems, wine red but very dark almost black in some clones.

*P.* Vodoo Magic: foliage attractively mottled; fls very dark wine red.

*P.* Whitemoor 'Norriton': large robust plants with mid-green lvs; fls white.

*P.* Wiertzianum: large robust plants with beautifully mottled lvs; fls several simultaneously, large, creamy base colour heavily overlaid with dark wine red stripes and spots.

*P.* Winston Churchill: strong plants with medium green foliage; large fls on strong stems, rich chestnut brown with heavily spotted white dorsal sep.

*P.* Yerba Buena: well-known cross with mid-green lvs; fls on strong stems, medium green and white.

***P. praestans*** Rchb. f. See *P. glanduliferum*.

**Papilionanthe** Schltr. (From Lat. *papilio*, moth and Gk *anthos*, flower.) Orchidaceae. Some 11 species of monopodial, epiphytic or terrestrial orchids. Stems slender, terete, erect or scrambling, often branching and rooting at nodes. Leaves in 2 ranks, alternate, terete, narrowly tapering, pungent or obtuse, obscurely grooved above, basally sheathing. Inflorescence usually a short, axillary raceme or panicle; sepals obovate, obtuse, weakly undulate, lateral sepals clawed; petals suborbicular, spreading, margins more undulate than in lateral sepals; lip trilobed, minutely pubescent, base saccate, midlobe bifid, broad, cuneate, lateral lobes large, often erect; spur saccate, conical. Himalaya to Malaysia.

CULTIVATION Vigorous scrambling epiphytes. *P. teres* and *P. hookeriana*, formerly included in *Vanda*, require sunny positions in the intermediate or warm house in baskets or beds of open bark mix. Syringe and water freely throughout the year. The former especially is an important garden plant and cut flower in the tropics and subtropics, notably in Singapore and Hawaii. Its offspring are listed under *Vanda*. *P. vandarum*, from cool hilly districts, requires lower temperatures (min. 7°C/45°F) and drier conditions in winter. Its stems are more slender than in the other two species listed here, a deep green and decked with short racemes of lace-like flowers. It is one of the most beautiful orchids for basket cultivation in the cool house. Propagate all by stem cuttings or division.

***P. hookeriana*** (Rchb. f.) Schltr. Stems scrambling, to 2.2m. Lvs 7–10×0.3cm. Infl. to 30cm; fls 2–12; dorsal sep. and pet. white or pale mauve, chequered deep mauve, faintly spotted, lateral sep. nearly white, lip deep purple, midlobe pale mauve marked purple; dorsal sep. obovate-oblong, obtuse, erect, undulate, crisped, to 2×1.5cm, lateral sep. spreading; pet. elliptic to orbicular, undulate, base twisted to reflexed; lip midlobe reniform to flabellate, to 3×4cm, weakly trilobed, lateral lobes triangular-falcate to oblong; spur short, to 0.2mm. Malaysia, China, Borneo, Vietnam. Z10.

***P. teres*** (Roxb.) Schltr. Stems to 1.75m but branching to form scrambling mats. Lvs erect and incurved, to 20×0.4cm. Infl. produced in continuous succession, 15–30cm; fls 3–6 per raceme, 5–10cm diam.; sep. and pet. white or ivory deepening to rose or magenta, lip buff to golden, banded or dotted blood-red or mauve; sep. ovate to subrhombic, undulate, obtuse, spreading, to 4×3cm; pet. orbicular, undulate, base twisted, to 4.5×4cm; lip midlobe flabellate to obcordate, deeply cleft, lateral lobes enveloping column; spur to 2.5cm, funnel-shaped. Thailand, Burma, Himalaya. Z9.

***P. vandarum*** (Rchb. f.) Garay. Stems to 2m, slender, terete, branching tangentially, sprawling, dark green, freely producing flattened grey roots and cascading or forming densely tangled clumps. Lvs to 10cm, borne at 45° to stem, slender, tapering, pungent, dark green often flushed purple. Infl. to 8cm, seldom branching, bearing flowers over several seasons; fls to 5 per infl., nocturnally fragrant, to 5cm diam., crystalline white, often tinted opal or basally flushed lilac to pink; sep. to 3.5×1.75cm, obovate, basally clawed, reflexed, undulate to crispate; pet. broader, more undulate, strongly reflexed and twisted; lip midlobe clawed, broadly obcordate, apically ruffed and deflexed, claw 3-ridged, lateral lobes falcate, erect, acuminate, apically denticulate with secondary, toothed lobe toward sinus of lateral and midlobes; spur cylindric, to 2cm. India, Burma. Z9.

For synonymy see *Aerides* and *Vanda*.

**Papperitzia** Rchb. f. (For William Papperitz, friend of Heinrich Reichenbach.) Orchidaceae. 1 species, an epiphytic orchid. Rhizome short, creeping. Pseudobulbs to 1cm, clustered, ancipitous, apex 1-leaved. Leaves to 7cm, linear, acuminate, coriaceous, glabrous, articulated. Inflorescence a basal raceme, erect to pendent, few- to several-flowered; fls to 1.5cm, green, yellow-pubesc.; dorsal sepal free, hood-like, subcaudate, conical-spurred, lateral sepals connate, navicular, subcaudate; petals free, similar to dorsal sepal; lip adnate to column base, fleshy, funnel-shaped at base forming a saccate pouch, pubescent within, callus trilobulate, slightly enveloping column; column short, apex alate-auriculate, footless, rostellum elongate, anther terminal, operculate, incumbent, pollinia 2, ceraceous. Mexico. Z10.

CULTIVATION As for *Encyclia*.

***P. lieboldii*** (Rchb. f.) Rchb. f. As for the genus.

For synonymy see *Leochilus*.

**Papuacedrus** Li. (From Papua, the native region of these plants, and Lat. *cedrus*, cedar, referring to the scented wood.) Cupressaceae. 2 species of monoecious evergreen trees closely allied to and often included in *Libocedrus*, to 50m. Crown conic, rusty-brown, exfoliating in scales. Juvenile leaves dimorphic: facial leaves small; lateral leaves lanceolate, flat, sharp acuminate, adnate to twig. Adult leaves smaller, dimorphic, decussate, scale-like, coriaceous: lateral leaves adpressed, incurved; facial leaves quadrilateral in cross section, keeled above, base decurrent. Male inflorescences with pollen sacs in whorls of 4. Female cones similar to *Libocedrus*, ovoid, scales 4, lanceolate or ovate, coriaceous, each scale with a short acute 1–2mm bract, placed centrally or towards the base; fertile scales larger than sterile scales, outer scales ovate, sterile. Seeds 4, two on each fertile scale, elliptic, 4mm, with two unequal wings to 6×3mm. New Guinea, Moluccas. Z10.

CULTIVATION Their native habitat is in cloud forest, with up to 350 rainy days per year; high humidity is essential. Usually only juvenile foliage produced under glass; adult foliage with fertile shoots can be induced by gibberellin treatments, or by prolonged overhead shading for many years followed by sudden exposure to fuller light on the upper crown; in wild, stage of development of adult foliage not known, probably not until sapling reaches canopy and full light. See also general notes on conifer cultivation under glass. Few areas where outdoor cultivation likely to succeed; New Zealand North Island and the wetter areas of E Australia should be suitable.

***P. arfakensis*** (Gibbs) Li. To 30m or more. Bark rust-brown; twigs segmented, flattened. Juvenile facial lvs in widely spaced pairs, rhombic to cuneate; lateral lvs flattened, 1–2cm, overlapping facial lvs. Adult lvs to 5mm, obtuse. All lvs glossy green above, marked glaucous bands beneath. Male cones to 16mm; scales to 20 per cone. Female cones to 8mm; fertile scales to twice length or more of infertile scales, bract nearer base of scale than on *P. papuana*. Seeds brown.

***P. papuana*** (F. Muell.) Li. Tree to 50m. Crown spreading, open; bark dark grey, grooved; twig apices curved. Lvs as for *P. arfakensis* when young. Lvs evenly formed; lateral lvs to 3×1–2mm, only partly obscuring facial lvs, to 2×2mm. Female cone to 13mm, glaucous brown; scales 4, reflexed at maturity.

***P. torricellensis*** (Schltr. ex Laut.) Li. See *P. papuana*.
For further synonymy see *Libocedrus*.

**Parabenzoin** Nak.
***P. praecox*** (Sieb. & Zucc.) Nak. See *Lindera praecox*.

**Paraboea** Ridl. (From Gk *para*, beside, and *Boea*.) Gesneriaceae. About 65 species of rosulate or caulescent perennial herbs and shrubs; young shoots woolly. Leaves opposite or whorled, arachnoid above, densely hairy beneath. Flowers paired in cymes; calyx segments 5, equal; corolla obliquely campanulate or with a short tube and flat limb, limb slightly bilabiate, white, blue or violet; stamens 2, inserted on corolla tube. Fruit a straight or spirally twisted, cylindric capsule. SE Asia. Z10.

CULTIVATION See GESNERIADS.

***P. rufescens*** B.L. Burtt. Caulescent perenn. herb. Lvs to 7×4.7cm, subcoriaceous, broadly ovate, rounded, crenate-serrate, olive-green above; petiole to 5cm, brown-tomentose. Peduncles to 13cm, flushed purple; cal. seg. to 3mm, linear-ovate, obtuse; cor. to 1×1.2cm, dark violet, broadly campanulate, limb oblique. Fr. sparsely pubesc. Thailand.

**Paracaryum** (DC.) Boiss. (From Gk *para*, beside, and *karyon*, nut, referring to the position of the nutlets.) Boraginaceae. Some 15 species of annual, biennial or perennial herbs, erect, prostrate or decumbent. Basal leaves numerous, usually long-petiolate; cauline lvs sessile or subsessile. Inflorescence becoming elongate, sometimes bracteate; calyx deeply lobed, elongate in fruit; corolla blue to purple-brown, cylindrical or infundibular to campanulate, usually with faucal appendages; anthers mostly included, linear to elliptic; stigma capitate. Nutlets 4, smooth glochidiate or aculeolate, often keeled, winged, wings entire to lacerate, inflexed, membranaceous. NE Africa to S Russia and Himalaya. Z8.

CULTIVATION As for *Anchusa angustissima*.

*P. himalayense* (Klotzsch) C.B. Clarke. Perenn. to bienn., to 60cm. Stems solitary to numerous, erect, long-branched, densely covered with white bristle hairs. Basal lvs to 9×1.5cm, oblong to oblong-lanceolate or spathulate-lanceolate, obtuse, sometimes slightly revolute, densely covered with white bristle hairs; cauline lvs small, lanceolate, sessile. Infl. terminal or axillary, lax; pedicel to 2mm in fr., usually erect; cal. to 2mm in fl., to 3mm in fr., lobes oblong to ovate, obtuse, pubesc.; cor. pink to white-blue, to 4mm, campanulate-cylindric, faucal appendages trapeziform; stigma to 1mm. Nutlets to 8mm diam., subrotund, wings with triangular teeth. Afghanistan, Pakistan, Kashmir, NW India.

*P. lithospermifolium* (Lam.) Grande. Perenn. Stems to 25cm, numerous, ascending or decumbent, grey or white sericeous-villous. Basal lvs to 4×1cm, mostly obovate. Cymes mostly simple; pedicels to 5mm in fl., to 11mm in fr.; cor. purple to red-violet, to 5.5mm, faucal scales emarginate, papillose; anth. to 1.5mm; style to 2mm. Nutlets to 9×8mm, subrotund, wings dentate. SE Europe.

*P. microcarpum* Boiss. Perenn. to 45cm, hirsute. Stems numerous, ascending to procumbent, sometimes slightly branched. Basal lvs to 10×2cm, oblong-spathulate, obtuse, long-petiolate; cauline lvs lanceolate, sessile. Infl. axillary or terminal, lax, bracteate; cal. to 3mm, lobes lanceolate; cor. bright blue, to 5mm, infundibular-campanulate, lobes ovate. Nutlets to 2.5mm. Kashmir, Afghanistan, Pakistan.

*P. racemosum* (Schreb.) Britten. Perenn., often tufted. Stems to 40cm, simple, ascending, villous or sometimes glabrescent. Basal lvs to 40×6mm, linear, tomentose, sericeous or pilose above, sparingly pilose beneath; cauline lvs, short-petiolate. Infl. a corymb or a panicle; cal. lobes to 10mm, sparingly pilose; cor. bright blue, to 15mm, infundibular; faucal scales to 6mm, narrowly linear, obtuse; anth. to 4mm; style to 15mm. Nutlets to 13mm diam., rotund, wings entire or sometimes denticulate. Turkey.

For synonymy see *Cynoglossum, Lepechiniella, Mattia* and *Mattiastrum*.

**Paraceterach** (F. Muell.) Copel. (From Gk *para*, similar to, and *Ceterach*, the name of another fern genus.) (Pteridaceae (Adiantaceae). 2 species of small terrestrial ferns. Stipes densely covered by chaffy scales. Fronds small, pinnate, densely clad with chaffy scales on lamina and rachis; veins free. Sori submarginal, confluent in continuous band round each pinna. Australia. Z10.

CULTIVATION As for *Cheilanthes*. Very tolerant of water loss; severe drought leaves the fronds curled up and shrivelled, but watering restores and straightens them.

*P. muelleri* (Hook.) Copel. Rhiz. short-creeping, to 6mm diam. Stipes 7.5–10cm, wiry, densely ferruginous-scaly. Fronds 10–25×2.5–9cm, erect to pendulous when growing on cliffs, pale green, thick and coriaceous; pinnae 4×1cm, oblong to ovate, entire, lower often auriculate; scales matted, pale brown; rachis wiry. NE Queensland.

*P. reynoldsii* (F. Muell.) Tind. Rhiz. creeping, densely scaly; scales with pale margins. Stipes short, dark brown to black, scaly. Fronds to 30cm, erect, crowded, linear-oblong, dark green, with flat pale scales beneath, becoming glabrous above; pinnae 8–15mm, generally opposite, suborbicular to oblong, entire, veins concealed; rachis dark brown to black, scaly. Australia, except in SE.

For synonymy see *Gymnogramma*.

**Paradisea** Mazz. (For Count Giovanni Paradisi of Modena (1760–1826.) Liliaceae (Asphodelaceae). 2 species of hardy perennials allied to *Anthericum*. Roots fleshy and fibrous; rhizomes short, clustered. Leaves basal. Scapes slender, bracteate; flowers to 20, showy, funneliform to campanulate, in lax racemes; tepals 6, free, clawed, white with apical spots, 3-veined; stamens and style upward-curving, anthers versatile. Capsule 3-valved; seeds small, numerous, ridged. Summer. S Europe (mts). Z7.

CULTIVATION Closely related to *Anthericum* and found in similar alpine meadow habitats, these are beautiful rhizomatous perennials grown for their grey-green, grasslike foliage and loose racemes of translucent, white, saucer-shaped flowers in early summer; they are fragrant and suitable for cutting. *P. liliastrum* makes an attractive clump-forming addition to the herbaceous border, leafing up in spring and dying back in autumn. *P. lusitanicum*, taller, tougher and with smaller flowers, will form dense spreading clumps and is useful for colonizing banks and open or partially shaded woodland. *Paradisea* is hardy to −15°C/5°F, probably more.

Grow in sun or dappled shade in fertile well-drained soils that do not become too dry in summer. Top-dress established clumps with garden compost or well-rotted manure in autumn. Propagate by division after flowering or in early spring, or by seed in spring in the cold frame.

*P. liliastrum* (L.) Bertol. ST BRUNO'S LILY; PARADISE LILY. Stem 30–60cm. Lvs 4–7, linear, 12–25×1cm. Raceme secund; fls 3–10; tepals 3–5cm, white with green apical spot; pedicels not articulated. Fr. 13–15mm. S Europe. 'Major': more robust, fls larger.

*P. lusitanicum* (Cout.) Samp. To 150cm, more robust than *P. liliastrum*. Lvs to 2cm wide. Fls white, to 2cm, in 2-ranked racemes; pedicels articulated. Portugal.

*P. liliastrum* var. *lusitanicum* Cout. See *P. lusitanicum*.
For further synonymy see *Anthericum*.

**Paragramma** (Bl. (as Sect.)) Moore. (From Gk *para*, beside, and *gramma*, letter.) Polypodiaceae. 1 species, an epiphytic fern. Rhizomes creeping, woody, dictyostelic, covered with roots as well as scales; roots massed, hairy; scales lanceolate, dentate, black. Fronds to 90×4cm, short-stipitate, uniform, simple, linear-lanceolate, apex acute or narrowly acute to obtuse, base long-attenuate, margin entire to somewhat revolute, fleshy to leathery, glabrous; veins markedly hidden and indistinct, reticulate, anastomosing into irregular, elongate areolae with free, divaricate, included veinlets; stipes to 8cm, approximate, jointed to rhizome. Sori sunken and cyst-forming, uniserial near margin, linear to oblong; paraphyses peltately attached to long-stalked; annulus 14-celled; spores glassy, more or less smooth. E Asia (Malaysia, Indonesia, Philippines). Z10.

CULTIVATION As for *Pyrrosia*.

*P. longifolia* (Bl.) Moore. As for the genus.

For synonymy see *Grammitis*.

**Parahebe** W. Oliv. Scrophulariaceae. (From Gk *para*, beside, and *Hebe*.) Some 30 species of prostrate or decumbent subshrubs, rarely herbs. Similar to *Hebe* but with laterally compressed capsules, suffruticose habit, flowers in axillary racemes. Stems woody at base, rooting, some forming low mats. Leaves opposite, mainly toothed or crenate, sessile or petioles very short. Flowers in axillary racemes, occasionally reduced to single bracteate flower, usually 4-partite; sepals 4, rarely a small fifth sepal; corolla size variable, tube length variable; petals usually unequal; stamens 2, staminodes absent; stigma capitate. Capsule usually to 4×5mm, laterally compressed, septum across narrowest diam., emarginate, 2-lobed, occasionally separating into 4 valves; seeds numerous, flattened, smooth. It is likely that *Parahebe* consists of many interbreeding hybrids and the species descriptions are at best rough groupings which can contain the genes for only one or all *Parahebe*; this is especially true of *P. catarractae*, *P. lyallii* and *P. hookeriana* (see also *P. catarractae*). New Zealand, New Guinea, Australia. Easily cultivated and offering good opportunities for artificial crossing.

CULTIVATION Neat-foliaged but sprawling, sun-loving small shrubs or herbaceous perennials, usually inhabiting the open, stony ground of river shingle or scree. In areas where winter temperatures do not fall below −5°C/23°F, they may be planted on sunny rock gardens and look particularly well if allowed to spill over the edges of dwarf walls and raised beds; the trailing stems of *P. lyallii* will root where they touch the ground. *P. perfoliata* makes an excellent foliage plant for grey borders, but should be given a spot sheltered from northeast winds and must be propagated regularly from cuttings, as plants older than about three years are less able to withstand severe winter conditions. *P. canescens* is best cultivated in the alpine house as it is so tiny when not in flower as to be easily lost in the open garden. Cultivation otherwise as for *Hebe*, but herbaceous types may also be propagated by division in spring.

*P. ×bidwillii* (Hook. f.) W. Oliv. (*P. decora* × *P. lyallii*.) Shrub to 15cm, mat-forming, procumbent. Lvs to 6mm, oblong to obovate, thick, coriaceous, entire or with 1 (occasionally 2) incision on either side. Fls in racemes to 20cm, narrow, axillary; cor. to 8mm diam., white, veins lilac. Summer. New Zealand. Plants grown under this name are often *P. decora* or *P. lyallii*. 'Kea': lvs small; stems long; fls white, veined crimson. 'Rosea': fls pink. Z8.

*P. birleyi* (N.E. Br.) W. Oliv. Subshrub, sprawling to 20cm. Branches to 3mm×15cm+, sparse, decumbent then ascending, fleshy when young, pubesc. at tips, glabrous with grey bark when mature. Lvs to 9×9mm, crowded, sessile or narrowed into short petiole, cuneate to obovate, densely pubesc. throughout, glandular-hairy, margin crenate, 5-lobed at apex. Fls single or paired, glandular-hairy; peduncles to 3mm; pedicels to 1.5mm; bracts to 5mm, obtuse; sep. to 6mm, oblong, obtuse; cor. to 20mm, white, tube short, pet. 5. Capsules obcordate, equalling cal., glabrous. New Zealand (South Is. in rocky clefts, 600–1000m, possibly to 3000m). Z8.

*P. canescens* (T. Kirk) W. Oliv. Minute prostrate herb, forming creeping rooted mats to 20cm. Stems to 10cm, filiform, much-branched, sparsely villous. Lvs to 2.5×1.5mm, subsessile or shortly petiolate, broad-ovate, sparsely pubesc., tinged brown, apex obtuse, margin entire. Fls single or rarely paired, subsessile; peduncles to 5mm, axillary, villous; pedicels to 5mm; sep. lanceolate-oblong, obtuse, small 5th sep. occasionally present; cor. to 6mm, blue, funnelform; pet. to 2.5×4mm, ovate-oblong, emarginate. Capsule to 1.5×2mm, exceeding cal., broad-obcordate, glabrous. Summer. New Zealand (South Is., on edges of lakes and ponds, coastal to lower montane). Z8.

*P. catarractae* (Forst. f.) W. Oliv. A polymorphic species, subshrubs with many intergrading forms; floral characters constant but of little taxonomic value, habit and size variable, lf shape is the main basis for identification, but is inadequate. Stems to 30cm, decumbent to ascending, woody when mature, usually bifariously pubesc., tinged purple when young. Lvs to 2×4cm, ovate to lanceolate, dark green above, paler beneath, glabrous, apex acute, margin sharply and closely serrate, subsessile or narrowed into petiole to 5mm, midrib and petiole pubesc. Fls very numerous, in racemes, glabrous to glandular-hairy; peduncles to 10cm; pedicels to 15mm; bracts to 5mm, glabrous; sep. to 3mm, ovate, acute to acuminate, ciliate; cor. to 1cm, white, veins pink or purple; pet. 4, obtuse. Capsule exceeds cal., obcordate, glabrous. Distinguished from *P. lyallii* by lvs larger, acute and serrate. Summer–autumn. New Zealand (lowland to montane streamsides and rocks). 'Alba': fls white. 'Delight': to 15cm, bushy; fls blue. 'Diffusa': to 20cm; lvs small, toothed; fls tiny, pink flushed, in sprays. 'Porlock': to 25cm; fls blue and white. 'Rosea': to 20cm; fls pink. Z8.

*P. decora* Ashwin. Subshrub, prostrate, mat-forming. Stems slender, woody, occasionally rooting at nodes; branches to 5cm, erect, leafy, uniformly pubesc. Lvs to 3×5cm, ovate to suborbicular, usually entire, fleshy, glabrous, often tinged red, apex rounded; petiole to 1.5mm, grooved, ciliate. Fls in racemes, to 15-fld, usually in whorls of 2 or 3; peduncles to 15cm, glabrous to sparsely pubesc.; pedicels to 10mm, glabrous; sep. to 3mm, ovate, acute, ciliate; cor. to 1cm, white to pink, venation often red, tube does not exceed cal.; pet. 4, obtuse, emarginate. Capsule broad-oblong, turgid, glabrous. New Zealand (wet montane screes and river-beds). Commonly grown in the UK under the name *P.* ×*bidwillii*. Z8.

*P. hookeriana* (Walp.) W. Oliv. Low subshrub, much-branched. Stems to 25cm, woody, prostrate to decumbent; branches to 15cm, bifariously or uniformly pubesc. Lvs to 8×12mm, close-set and imbricate, often erect or recurved, ovate to suborbicular, thick-coriaceous, pale green, margin deeply crenate or serrate; petiole to 3mm, pubesc. Fls in to 8-fld racemes, densely pubesc. or glandular-hairy throughout; peduncles to 6cm; bracts to 3mm, ciliate; sep. to 3mm, ovate-oblong, subacute; cor. to 1cm, white to pale blue; pet. 4, ovate-oblong, apex obtuse. Capsule much exceeding cal., broad-oblong, glabrous, turgid. Summer. New Zealand (North Is., 1200–1800m). The limits of this sp. are ill-defined, probably due to crossing with *P. catarractae*. var. ***hookeriana.*** Stems sparsely and uniformly pubesc. Lvs oval to ovate, pubesc. to glandular-hairy, apex usually obtuse, margin crenate, ciliate. Infl. densely glandular-hairy. Capsule to 6×5.5mm, valves acute to apiculate, not incurved. Z9.

*P. linifolia* (Hook. f.) W. Oliv. Subshrub to 12cm, much-branched, base woody, glabrous. Branches to 20cm, sprawling to erect, terete, occasionally rooting, slender. Lvs to 4×20mm, close-set, sessile, very shortly connate, linear to lanceolate, glabrous, apex subacute to acute, base ciliate, midrib depressed above, prominent beneath. Fls in distinctive racemes, to 4-fld, occasionally single bracteate fls, all parts glabrous; peduncles to 2cm; bracts to 8mm; sep. to 8mm, linear-oblong, obtuse; cor. to 15mm, white to pink; pet. 4, to 8×9mm, broad-ovate, veins red in 3 upper pet. Capsules to 5×6mm, exceeded by cal., obcordate, usually compressed, glabrous. Summer. New Zealand (South Is., wet rocky habitats, 700–1400m). 'Blue Skies': fls blue. Z8.

*P. lyallii* (Hook. f.) W. Oliv. Subshrub to 20cm, much-branched. Stems slender, usually woody, prostrate to decumbent, rooting at nodes, rarely erect; branches decumbent to ascending, bifarious or uniformly pubesc. Lvs to 8×10mm, suborbicular to linear-obovate, coriaceous, membranous, apex obtuse to rounded, margin crenate to bluntly serrate; petiole to 3mm. Fls numerous in racemes; peduncles to 12cm, occasionally glandular-hairy; pedicels to 15mm; bracts to 5mm, glabrous; sep. to 5mm, obovate, acute; cor. to 1cm, white to pink; pet. 4, to 8mm, spreading. Capsules obovate, turgid, glabrous, emarginate. Summer. New Zealand (South Is., lowland to subalpine streamsides and rocks). 'Rosea': fls pink. Z8.

*P. spathulata* (Benth.) W. Oliv. Subshrub, prostrate, forming mats to 25cm diam., main root very stout. Stems prostrate, woody; branches to 10cm, numerous, ascending or descending, pubesc. Lvs to 8×10mm, crowded, may form small rosettes, suborbicular, pubesc. or rarely glabrous, apex obtuse, margin crenate, narrowing abruptly to petiole to 5mm. Racemes numerous, to 7-fld, villous in all parts; peduncles to 15mm; pedicels to 3mm; bracts to 5mm, opposite, spathulate; cal. to 5mm; sep. to 3mm, oblong, obtuse; cor. to 8mm, white or occasionally lavender; pet. 4, rounded. Capsules equal to cal., broad-obcordate, compressed, hairy. Summer. New Zealand (North Is., scree slopes to 2000m). Z8.

***P. cultivars.*** 'Mervyn': to 8cm; lvs tinged purple; fls lilac blue. 'Miss Willmot': shrubby; fls rose-lilac.

*P. diffusa* (Hook. f.) W. Oliv. See *P. catarractae*.
For further synonymy see *Hebe*.

**Parajubaea** Burret. (Closely related to *Jubaea*.) Palmae. 2 species of unarmed, pleonanthic, monoecious palms. Stems solitary, erect, grey, faintly ringed. Crownshaft absent. Leaves pinnate, arching to pendent, sheath disintegrating into brown fibres; petiole short, flat above, convex beneath, glabrous; rachis exceeding petiole, slightly twisted, terete; pinnae single-fold, subopposite, linear, acuminate, apex shallowly divided or oblique, glabrous above, scaly beneath. Inflorescences interfoliar, erect to pendent, branched once, lower bract hidden among leaf sheaths, upper bract tubular, woody, deeply channelled, persistent; rachillae erect, closely adpressed to rachis; male flowers with sepals 3, overlapping, petals 3, exceeding sepals, stamens *c*15, pistillode 3-lobed; female flowers larger than males, with staminodes forming a shallow 3-lobed cup, pistil ovoid, 3-celled, stigma short, 3-lobed. Fruit to 5×4cm, ellipsoid to ovoid, with persistent perianth; epicarp smooth, mesocarp thin, fibrous, endocarp hard, irregularly sculptured, with 3 basal pores. Colombia, Ecuador, and Bolivia. Z10.

CULTIVATION *P. cocoides* experiences sub-zero temperatures in its native mountain habitat and should therefore be suitable for cultivation in warm temperate climates that suffer only occasional light frost. Propagate from fresh seed which germinates freely. For cultivation see PALMS.

*P. coccoides* Burret. Trunk to 15m×25cm, swollen at base, clean. Lvs to 5m, drooping; seg. regularly spaced, reduplicate, apex acuminate, yellow-green and shiny above, dull and scurfy beneath; rachis glabrous. Infl. nodding to pendent; male fls 10–12mm, purple in bud, yellow and lustrous when open, stamens *c*15. Fr. 4.5×3.5cm, ellipsoid, scurfy, dark green turning brown after falling; seed to 2cm. Ecuador, Colombia.

**Paramacrolobium** Léonard. (From Gk prefix *para*, like, alluding to the resemblance to *Macrolobium*.) Leguminosae (Caesalpinioideae). 1 species, a trees to 40m; branchlets black. Leaves alternate, paripinnate; leaflets to 15cm, 3–5 pairs, elliptic to oblong, base asymmetric, apex acuminate, subcoriaceous, glabrous, eglandular, golden-sericeous beneath; petiolules twisted; stipels absent; stipules intrapetiolar, united, oblong, semicylindric, bi-apiculate, persistent. Inflorescence to 8cm, compact, corymbose; buds enveloped by sepal-like bracts; sepals 4–5; petals 5, 2-lobed at apex, the largest spathulate and nearly 5cm long, blue-violet with green-blue basal spot; stamens 9, unequally united at base, 3 larger and fertile; ovary linear, long-stalked. Fruit flat, oblique-oblong, coriaceous, glabrous, winged along 1 suture, finely verrucose; seeds 3–8, rectangular. Sierra Leone to Congo, Kenya, Tanzania. Z10.

CULTIVATION *P. coeruleum*, from lowland rainforests, is an evergreen tree with smooth, grey-brown bark marked with very fine, long, straight striations, bearing blue-violet flowers in compact terminal panicles. Cultivate as for *Gliricidia*.

*P. coeruleum* (Taub.) Léonard. As for the genus.

**Paramansoa** Baill. See *Arrabidaea*.

**Paramongaia** Velarde. (From Paramonga, a locality in Peru where *P. weberbaueri* was collected.) Amaryllidaceae. 1 species, a deciduous bulbous herb. Bulbs to 6.5cm diam., tunicate, lacking a neck. Leaves to 75×5cm, 6–8, narrow-linear, bright green or glaucous, appearing with or after the flowers. Flowers solitary or sometimes 2, to 18cm diam., bright yellow, fragrant, on an erect leafless peduncle to 60cm; spathe valves linear, separate; perianth tube 10cm, cylindrical, lobes to 81×18mm, 6, spreading; anthers versatile, not exserted, from the large trumpet-like corona; style exserted from the perianth tube, not winged. Fruit to 3.6cm, a capsule; seeds many. Peru. Z10.

CULTIVATION From coastal zones and on the steep rocky hillsides of Peru to altitudes of 2700m/8775ft, the bulbs often pulling themselves down to depths of 30cm/12in. In autumn *P. weberbaueri* bears magnificent long-lasting blooms, strongly fragrant and of an intense deep yellow, on a stout stem which may reach 75cm/30in. in height. It is frost tender, but well suited to the warm glasshouse or conservatory. Plant deeply in well-crocked pots in a slightly acid medium comprising equal parts loam, leafmould and sharp sand, with added charcoal. Grow in full sun and water plentifully when in full growth, maintaining a minimum temperature of 18°C/65°F with high humidity and good circulation of air. Feed well-rooted specimens with dilute liquid feed when in growth. Reduce water as leaves begin to yellow and keep dry when dormant in summer, at a temperature of 21–24°C/70–75°F. Plants flower best when pot-bound; topdress annually in autumn as growth resumes. Propagate from offsets, or from seed.

***P. weberbaueri*** Velarde. COJOMARIA. As for the genus.

**Paranephelius** Poepp. (From Gk *para*, beyond, and *Nephelius*.) Compositae. About 7 species of perennial herbs or shrubs. Leaves opposite or basal, entire to pinnatifid, mostly white-tomentose beneath. Capitula radiate, few to numerous in cymose clusters, or solitary; receptacle scaly, flat; phyllaries in 3–8 series, lanceolate, rounded to acute or acuminate, outer shorter; ray florets numerous, yellow, female; disc florets funneliform, orange or yellow, hermaphrodite, 5-lobed. Fruit a cylindrical, ribbed, hispid or glabrous cypsela; pappus of scabrous bristles. N & S America. Z8.

CULTIVATION As for *Carlina*.

***P. ovatus*** Wedd. Dwarf, stemless perenn. herb, to 10cm. Lvs several in a basal rosette, to 4.5×3.5cm, elliptic to rhombic-ovate, base cuneate to nearly rounded, margin irregularly toothed, occasionally lyrate-pinnatifid, lobed at base, green and glabrous above, nerves impressed, flat and smooth or somewhat wrinkled-bullate, white cottony-tomentose beneath, midrib and lateral nerves prominent. Capitula to 9cm diam.; peduncle to 6mm, thick, white-cottony, with 2 narrowly lanceolate, scale-like purple-tinged bracts; receptacle scales deep red-purple; phyllaries more or less tinged purple especially at margins and apex, spathulate-oblong, apex usually rounded, outermost broadest, inner successively narrower and overtopping the outer, sharply acute with a short pungent tip; ray florets to 6cm, spreading-ascending and recurved; disc florets orange. Fr. glabrous; pappus bristles white, yellow below. Andes of Peru and Bolivia.

***P. uniflorus*** Poepp. & Endl. Dwarf, stemless perenn. herb, to 12cm. Lvs few to several in a basal rosette, to *c*10×5cm, obovate to obovate-lanceolate, deeply and irregularly acutely sinuate-toothed or pinnatifid, with acutely toothed lobes, dark green and rugose above, with sunken veins, snow-white adpressed-tomentose beneath. Capitula to 9cm diam.; peduncle to 10cm, stout, cylindrical, densely tomentose; receptacle scales shortly fimbriate; phyllaries linear-oblong, apex obtuse or acute, imbricate, inner narrowest; ray florets to 4cm, spreading; disc florets orange. Fr. glabrous; pappus bristles red. Andes of Peru and Bolivia.

For synonymy see *Liabum*.

**Paranomus** Salisb. (From Gk *para*, against, contrary to, and *nomos*, law, referring to the occurrence of two very different types of leaf on a single shoot.) Proteaceae. 18 species of small erect shrubs. Leaves evergreen, usually dimorphic, variously pinnate at base of shoot, entire and broadly spathulate to linear or oblanceolate on upper part, usually with incurved margins, rarely all leaves alike and fan-shaped and dissected into numerous obtuse linear segments, glabrous when mature or rarely persistently silky-tomentose. Inflorescence spike-like, terminal; capitula 4-flowered, subtended by a solitary bract; flowers bisexual, actinomorphic; floral bracts 4, imbricate; perianth cylindric in bud, limb elliptic, 4-partite to near base, tube short, usually cream to white or pink; stamens 4, anthers inserted at base of limb; stigma narrowly clavate on slender style. Fruit a nut, ivory-white, shining, smooth with basal ring of hairs, often apically beaked with remains of style; seed solitary. S Africa. Z9.

CULTIVATION As for *Protea*.

***P. reflexus*** (Phillips & Hutch.) N.E. Br. Bush 2.5×2m, densely bushy, branching from base; stems long. Lvs 7–8cm, crowded on stems, finely divided into slender lobes, channelled, acute, pale to mid green, red at apex, lvs on upper part of flowering stems distinctive, 3×2cm, entire, broad, reduced towards infl. Infl. terminal, 12×8cm, on velvety flowering stems to 60cm; perianth yellow-green to cream tinged pale green to buff, to 3cm in bud, seg. slender, separating after buds have turned downwards just before flowering. Autumn–winter. S Africa (SW Cape).

**Paraphalaenopsis** A.D. Hawkes. (From Gk *para*, beside, and *Phalaenopsis*.) Orchidaceae. Some 4 species of epiphytic, monopodial orchids resembling *Phalaenopsis* except in leaves few, cylindrical, canaliculate. Borneo. Z10.

CULTIVATION As for *Phalaenopsis*.

***P. denevei*** (Sm.) A.D. Hawkes. Lvs 3–6, fleshy, to 70×1cm. Infl. axillary to 13-fld, bracts triangular; tepals spreading, green-yellow to yellow-brown, lip white, spotted crimson; dorsal sep. ovate-elliptic to narrow-elliptic, to 2.5×1cm, lateral sep. ovate-elliptic, to 3×1.5cm; pet. ovate-lanceolate, basally cuneate, apically falcate, to 2.5×1cm; lip midlobe linear-spathulate, papillose, callus wrinkled, minutely toothed, lateral lobes oblong to triangular, falcate, to 1×5cm. W Borneo.

***P. labukensis*** (P.S. Shim) A. Lamb & C.L. Chan. Lvs to 1.6cm. Sep. and pet. raspberry pink, dotted and edged yellow, lip yellow, spotted purple, axe-shaped toward apex. Borneo.

***P. laycockii*** (M.R. Henderson) A.D. Hawkes. Fls to 5, to 1m. Infl. dense, to 15-fld; bracts ovate, to 1cm; fls magenta to lilac, lip blotched yellow and brown; dorsal sep. lanceolate-elliptic, narrow, to 4×1.5cm, lateral sep. ovate-lanceolate, oblique, to 4.5×1.5cm; pet. subfalcate, lanceolate, basally fleshy, cuneate, to 4×1.5cm; lip midlobe forward pointing, linear-spathulate, apical lobes triangular, disc pale yellow, striped brown, lateral lobes linear-oblong, erect, apex truncate to rounded; column white. SC Borneo.

***P. serpentilingua*** (Sm.) A.D. Hawkes. Lvs to 30cm. Infl. to 7-fld; fls scented, sep. and pet. white above, lip lemon yellow, banded purple; dorsal sep. elliptic to obovate-elliptic, to 1.5×1cm, lateral sep. elliptic to obovate-elliptic, to 2×1cm; pet. rhombic-lanceolate, basally fleshy, cuneate; lip midlobe recurved, linear, tip bifid, callus toothed, lateral lobes linear, falcate, to 1cm. W Borneo.

For synonymy see *Phalaenopsis*.

**Paraquilegia** J.R. Drumm. & Hutch. (From Gk *para*, near, and *Aquilegia*, to which it is closely related.) Ranunculaceae. 4 species of low, caespitose perennial herbs. Leaves alternate, petiolate, 2–3-ternate, lobed, glabrous or pubescent, sometimes glaucous. Flowers large, solitary on leafless stems, white to lilac; sepals 5, petaloid; petals form nectaries, sessile or subsessile, orbicular, elongate or tubular, concave below, apex emarginate; stamens numerous, anthers yellow; carpels 3–7, erect or declinate in fruit. Seeds keeled or narrow-winged, shiny glabrous or pubescent. Differs from *Isopyrum* in having several follicles and from *Semiaquilegia* in having no staminodes. C Asia mts to Himalaya. Z5.

CULTIVATION Delicate Himalayan natives with a preference for dry winters and cool climates, *Paraquilegia* spp. have lavender-blue buds, opening white to reveal the characteristic boss of golden stamens. They require careful cultivation, in full sun and in a well-drained alkaline soil, and may be difficult to establish; they are perhaps best cultivated in the alpine house, or in troughs in a gritty alpine mix. Sow fresh seed in autumn.

***P. anemonoides*** (Willd.) Ulbr. Densely caespitose glabrous perenn. to 18cm. Rootstock thick, with many crowns covered by remains of dead petioles. Lvs basal, long-petiolate, ternate, leaflets 1–2cm across, divided into many deeply lobed segments, glaucous; pedicels to 6cm. Bracts 2, linear or lanceolate; fls solitary, cup-shaped, 2–4cm across, white to lilac (W Himalayan plants have small white fls; in E Himalaya fls large, lilac); sepals 5, broad elliptic; nectaries 5, yellow, obovate. Carpels 3–7; follicles to 1cm, membranous with prominent veins; upper third forms beak; seeds grey-brown, pubesc. or glabrous. Summer. Himalaya (Pakistan to W China), C & N Asia.

***P. grandiflora*** (Fisch. ex DC.) Drumm. & Hutch. See *P. anemonoides*.
***P. microphylla*** (Royle) Drumm. & Hutch. See *P. anemonoides*.

**Parasitaxus** Laub. Podocarpaceae. 1 species, a monoecious, parasitic conifer, to 2m, specific to the host *Falcatifolium taxoides* (Podocarpaceae). It obtains nutrients by a process resembling root graftage and lacks haustoria. Leaves spirally arranged, loosely overlapping, succulent, tinged red, without chlorophyll; apex acute, incurved, entire. Male cones ovoid, to 4×2mm, scales to 1mm, tinged red, acuminate, microsporophyll triangular; peduncle to 6mm, scaly. Seed cones globose, 3–4mm, glaucous, produced on fertile, non-specialized twigs, subtended by 6 involucral bracts, ultimately shorter than seed; receptacle absent; seeds terminal, solitary, sessile, globose, 2mm, enclosed in purple to glaucous blue fleshy layer, wings absent. New Caledonia. Z10.

CULTIVATION Despite several attempts, no success has been achieved in bringing this unique parasitic conifer into cultivation; methods tried have included sowing of the seed (with various pre-treatments tried) next to the roots of the host species, rooting cuttings next to the host, and direct grafting of the shoots onto the host stem or roots. Although strictly protected in the wild, the species is rare and endangered. It occurs as an undershrub in dense tropical cloud forest with perpetual fog and rain (estimated 7–10 dry days per year), always in association with *Falcatifolium taxoides*; no other host species has been recorded.

***P. ustus*** (Vieill.) Laub. PARASITE YEW. As for the genus.

For synonymy see *Dacrydium* and *Podocarpus*.

**Parasyringa** W.W. Sm.
***P. sempervirens*** (Franch.) W.W. Sm. See *Ligustrum sempervirens*.

**Parathelypteris** (H. Itô) Ching. (From Gk *para*, beside, and *Thelypteris*.) Thelypteridaceae. 15 species of terrestrial ferns. Stipes generally castaneous or brown-castaneous at least near base, shining, glabrous or moderately densely clad with long, patent pale ash-grey hairs. Fronds oblong-lanceolate, always deeply bipinnatisect, firmly herbaceous to chartaceous; midrib of lateral pinnae not at all raised above level of lamina but always narrowly grooved, veins free, simple, all extending to margins. Warm & Tropical Asia, Malaysia, N America. Z10.

CULTIVATION As for *Thelypteris*.

***P. beddomei*** (Bak.) Ching. Rhiz. slender, wide-creeping. Stipes 15–22cm, slender, glossy. Fronds 15–30×7.5–10cm, oblong-lanceolate, firm; pinnae 4–5×1cm, central pinna largest, dissected to rachis into numerous entire, acute lobes to 2mm broad, margins recurved. Sri Lanka, Java.

***P. glanduligera*** (Kunze) Ching. Rhiz. long-creeping, slender, sparsely scaly. Stipes slender, lustrous, pale green tinged brown, pubesc., sparsely scaly near base. Fronds 15–45×5–15cm, narrowly deltoid to broadly lanceolate, acuminate at apex, not tapered to base, thinly pilose, densely so on veins above, yellow-glandular beneath; pinnae 2–8cm×7–15mm, spreading, linear-lanceolate, acuminate, sessile, regularly pinnatipartite, pinnules oblong-linear, obtuse, sub-entire, 2mm broad. E Asia (China to India, Japan, Korea, Indochina).

***P. nevadensis*** (Bak.) Ching. SIERRA WATER FERN. Rhiz. long-creeping, 2.5mm diam., scaly toward apex; scales 3–4mm, lanceolate, pale brown to ferruginous. Stipes 3–20cm, distant on rhiz., then clustered, stramineous above darkly ferruginous base, sparsely scaly. Fronds rhombic, often narrowly so, pinnate-pinnatifid, tapered both ends, acuminate and pinnatifid at apex, glabrous or very sparsely pilose on veins beneath; pinnae spreading to somewhat ascending or falcate, pinnatifid, seg. ascending. NW America (British Columbia to California).

***P. novae-boracensis*** (L.) Ching. NEW YORK FERN. Rhiz. slender, extensively creeping, 2mm diam., scaly particularly at apex; scales lanceolate, 3mm, golden brown. Stipes 5–30cm, brown at base, stramineous above, sparsely scaly. Fronds 30–60×10–15cm, distant then clustered, lanceolate, tapered to both ends, acuminate at apex, pinnate, membranous; pinnae 4–9cm, lanceolate, deeply pinnatifid, long acuminate, sessile, lower 2 pairs shorter and deflexed and often somewhat distant, ciliate and finely pubesc. beneath; seg. oblong, obtuse, flat, basal ones often enlarged. N America (Newfoundland to Ontario and Minnesota, South to N Carolina and Arkansas).

***P. simulata*** (Davenp.) Ching. Rhiz. slender, wide-creeping, tinged brown. Stipes 15–40cm, stramineous, brown at base, with deciduous scales. Fronds oblong-lanceolate, acuminate at apex, scarcely narrowed to base, rather thin and membranous, minutely pubesc., particularly near veins; pinnae to 12–20 pairs, lanceolate, pinnatifid; seg. obliquely oblong, obtuse, entire, margins slightly revolute on fertile fronds; veins simple, almost straight. NE US.

For synonymy see *Aspidium, Dryopteris, Lastrea, Nephrodium* and *Thelypteris*.

**Paratropia** DC.
***P. reinwardtii*** Decne. & Planch. See *Schefflera longifolia*.
***P. rotundifolia*** Ten. See *Schefflera rotundifolia*.

**Pardanthopsis** Lenz. (From *Pardanthus* (Gk *pardos*, panther and *anthos*, flower) and Gk *opsis* appearance.) Iridaceae. 1 species, a perennial herb closely resembling *Iris*, to 1m. Rhizomes slender producing many swollen roots. Leaves to 8 in fans, to 30×2.5cm. Inflorescence branching frequently, bearing thin spathes; flowers to 6 per spathe, ephemeral, to 4.5cm diam.; falls larger than standards, ivory spotted and striped maroon from base, flecked purple in centre; claw striped purple; style branches bilobed; perianth segments spiral tightly as they fade. Fruit cylindrical. Summer. Siberia, N China, Mongolia. Z7.

CULTIVATION A short-lived deciduous perennial grown for its beautifully marked and spotted ivory-white flowers, which are carried on branching stems in summer above a fan of blue-green, white-edged leaves. The individual blooms open during the afternoon, lasting for the day, the petals twisting spirally as they fade; *P. dichotoma* frequently flowers so freely over long periods that it exhausts itself and dies, but in favourable conditions will renew itself by self seeding. It is hardy in zones where temperatures fall to −15°C/5°F to −20°C/−4°F. Grow in a sunny border in any well-drained soil that remains adequately moist during the growing season but allows moderately dry conditions during dormancy. Propagate by seed sown ripe in the cold frame; plants flower at about a year old and represent an easily maintained supply of replacement stock.

***P. dichotoma*** (Pall.) Lenz. As for the genus.

For synonymy see *Iris*.

**Pardanthus** Ker-Gawl.
***P. chinensis*** (L.) Ker-Gawl. See *Belamcanda chinensis*.

**Paris** L. (From Lat. *par, paris*, equal, on account of the supposed regularity of its leaves and flowers.) Liliaceae (Trilliaceae). 4 species of deciduous herbaceous perennials. Rhizomes creeping. Stem erect, glabrous, to 40cm. Leaves 4–12 in a whorl near apex of stem. Flowers solitary, terminal; sepals 4–6, green; petals 4–6, yellow, linear; stamens 4–10, filaments flat, anthers basifixed; ovary superior; styles slender, 4, free. Fruit a fleshy, indehiscent, purple-black capsule. Spring–summer. Europe to E Asia. Many E Asian constituents of *Paris* have been removed to *Daiswa*.

CULTIVATION *Paris* spp. are found throughout temperate Europe and Asia, from Siberia to the Mediterranean. *P. quadrifolia*, herb paris, grows naturally on calcareous soils in damp, shaded woodland, often in natural association with *Polygonatum multiflorum*, Solomon's seal, and *Mercurialis perennis*, dog's mercury; in Britain, it is an indicator of ancient woodland.

Cultivated for its unusual yellow green flowers, borne in spring and early summer, and its symmetrically arranged foliage, *Paris* also bears poisonous blue-black berries in autumn. It is suited to the woodland or wild garden, or for shaded parts of the rock garden, and is hardy to at least −15°C/5°F. Plant rhizomes 12cm/4½in. deep in moisture-retentive, humus-soils enriched with leafmould, and in dappled shade. Propagate by division or by seed sown ripe in autumn.

***P. bashanensis*** Wang & Tang. Differs from *P. quadrifolia* in its narrower but longer lvs and reflexed sep. which are half as wide (3–4mm). China (Sichuan, Hubei). Z7.

***P. incompleta*** Bieb. Rhiz. slender, creeping. Stem weak, to 33cm. Lvs 6–12, oblong-lanceolate to obovate, prominently 3-veined, base narrowed into short petiole, 6–10cm, pale green. Pedicel shorter than lvs; sep. 4, pale green, sessile, lanceolate, 2.5–4cm, spreading; pet. absent; stamens 8, fil. 5–15mm, anth. 5–8mm, free portion of connective absent; ovary globose, dark purple; styles 4, much longer than stamens, 12–23mm. Turkey, Caucasus, Armenia. Z7.

***P. quadrifolia*** L. HERB PARIS. Stems glabrous, 15–40cm. Lvs usually 4, ovate with short petiole; if lvs more or less than 4, then other parts equal number of lvs. Fls erect, pedicel 2–8cm, yellow green; sep. 4, green, lanceolate, 2.5–3.5cm; pet. 4, equalling sep., very narrow, flattened, acute; stamens erect, fil. short, equal to anth., connective long; ovary globose, 4-celled; styles 4, shorter than stamens. Europe, Caucasus, Siberia, temperate E Asia. Z6.

***P. tetraphylla*** A. Gray Rhiz. slender, creeping. Stem erect, slender, to 40cm. Lvs 4–5, sessile, 3-nerved, oblong to elliptic, 4–10×1.5–4cm, acute. Pedicel 3–10cm; sep. similar in shape to lvs, green, 1–2cm×3–8mm, reflexed; pet.

absent; stamens 8, anth. 3–4mm, as long as fil., connective not extended beyond anth.; ovary ovoid, styles 4, slender, longer than stamens. Japan. Z8.

***P. verticillata*** Bieb. Rhiz. slender. Stem erect to 40cm. Lvs subsessile, 5–8, ovate to lanceolate. Pedicel 5–15cm, erect; sep. 4, ovate to lanceolate, 2–4×1–1.5cm, green; pet. 4, filiform, 1.5–2cm×11–27mm, reflexed, yellow; stamens 8–10, slightly longer than pet., fil. anth. and free portion of connective about same length, 5–8mm; ovary ovoid to quadrangular, dark purple brown; styles 4, short, recurved. Caucasus, Siberia, E Asia. Z7.

***P. apetala*** Hoffm. See *P. incompleta.*
***P. dahurica*** Fisch. ex Tersch. See *P. verticillata.*
***P. hexaphylla*** Cham. See *P. verticillata.*
***P. hexaphylla*** Cham. f. ***purpurea*** Miyabe & Tatew. See *P. verticillata.*
***P. japonica*** (Franch. & Savat.) Franch. See *Kinugasa japonica.*
***P. obovata*** Ledeb. See *P. verticillata.*
***P. octyphylla*** Hoffm. See *P. incompleta.*
***P. quadrifolia*** L. var. ***setchuanensis*** Franch. See *P. bashanensis.*
***P. quadrifolia*** Thunb. non L. See *P. tetraphylla.*
***P. verticillata*** Bieb. f. ***purpurea*** Miyabe & Tatew. See *P. verticillata.*
***P. yakusimensis*** Masam. See *P. tetraphylla.*

**Paritium** Juss.
***P. tiliaceum*** (L.) Juss. See *Hibiscus tiliaceus.*

**PARKERIACEAE** Hook. See *Ceratopteris.*

**Parkia** R. Br. (For Dr Mungo Park (1771–1806), Scottish surgeon, naturalist and explorer of the Niger River.) Leguminosae (Mimosoideae). Some 40 species of unarmed trees to 46m. Leaves bipinnate, alternate; petiole glandular; rachis usually glandular; pinnae to 25 pairs; leaflets sessile, to 70 pairs. Flowers in long-stalked, usually pendent, globose or pyriform heads, upper flowers yellow, tawny or red, lower flowers sterile, white or red; bracts obdeltate-spathulate, slightly exceeding calyx; petals slender, free or basally fused, 5, narrow-spathulate or ligulate, barely exceeding calyx; stamens 10, all fertile, shortly exserted, filaments connate below into a tube; ovary short-stipitate, style usually exserted, exceeding anthers. Fruit linear, ligulate or somewhat moniliform, sometimes falcate; seeds discoid to compressed-ellipsoid, embedded in an orange-pink mealy pulp. Tropics. Z10.

CULTIVATION *P. javanica*, occurring in rainforest, along low-lying riversides and on savannah, is a tall, spreading, evergreen tree grown in the tropics and subtropics as an ornamental for parks and large gardens. Cultivate as for *Inga*.

***P. javanica*** (Lam.) Merrill. Tree to 46m, with wide-spreading crown. Pinnae in 15–30 pairs, each with 50–70 pairs of leaflets, leaflets 6–13mm, acute. Peduncles 25–41cm; fl. heads 4cm diam., yellow-white. Fr. 38–51×4cm, stipitate, laterally compressed. Java.

**Parkinson, John** (1567–1650). Apothecary, gardener and herbalist. Parkinson was probably born in Nottinghamshire, and is known to have been practising as an apothecary at Long Acre, London, (where he had a garden) before 1616, later becoming apothecary to King James I. According to *Hortus Kewensis* (1810–13) Parkinson introduced seven species of plants to England, and also added 13 species to the recorded flora of Middlesex. He planted his large garden at Long Acre with a wide variety of plants (484 types are recorded), including many exotics sent to him by foreign correspondents.

In 1629 he wrote *Paradisi in Sole Paradisus Terrestris*, its punning title meaning 'Park-in-Sun's Paradise on Earth', dedicated to Queen Henrietta Maria, the wife of King Charles I, who subsequently awarded Parkinson the title of Botanicus Regius Primarius. The book was divided into three sections; the first dealt with the laying out of a garden and included a survey of garden plants, the second concerned kitchen gardens, and the third section dealt with orchards, vines and fruit trees. It described nearly 1000 plants, 780 illustrated with woodcuts, and includes the first account and picture of the Virginia spiderwort (*Tradescantia*) introduced by John Tradescant. A second edition was published in 1656.

Parkinson also published his *Theatrum Botanicum* in 1640; this describes nearly 3800 plants, divided into 17 tribes. Some of these divisions are pharmacological (for instance cathartic or narcotic) and others more systematic or environmental, although a miscellaneous category contains all plants falling outside these divisions. As such, the classification in the *Theatrum* is inferior to that of Mattias de L'Obel, whose botanical notes he used after his death, but the book is more original than Gerard's, and was for some time the most complete English treatise of its kind.

Parkinson died in London and was buried at St Martin's-in-the-Fields. His name is commemorated in the Central American genus of leguminous trees, *Parkinsonia*.

**Parkinson, Sydney** (*c*1745–1771). Botanical artist. Born in Edinburgh of Quaker parentage, he was initially apprenticed to a wool draper but from 1767 was engaged as an artist at Kew by the young Joseph Banks. In 1768 Cook's first voyage to the South Pacific was proposed by the Royal Society, primarily in order to observe the transit of the planet Venus. Banks invited Parkinson to accompany him on the expedition as botanical draughtsman. Early in 1769 the *Endeavour* reached Tierra del Fuego where, as throughout the expedition, many new plants were discovered. However, the crew suffered considerable deprivation as a result of the cold and lack of supplies. In mid-April they reached Tahiti, where Alexander Buchan, brought to paint the landscape, died. Consequently this task was added to Parkinson's painting of plants. In New Zealand over 400 new species of plants were collected and on arrival in Australia many new genera were noted in the area Cook named Botany Bay. Sailing to the Cape of Good Hope from Princes' Island in 1771, Parkinson contracted a fever and dysentery and died in January: he was buried at sea.

By the time of his death Parkinson had produced a considerable body of work (280 finished and botanically accurate paintings from around 900 drawings) and, after the return of the ship in July, a protracted struggle ensued between Banks and Parkinson's brother Stanfield over its ownership. Eventually Banks managed to secure them for £500 including unpaid salary and had the sketches finished by F.P. Nodder and four others. By 1778 over 500 plates had been engraved for publication but it was not until 1900 that they appeared through the efforts of James Britten as *Illustrations of the Botany of Captain Cook's Voyage Round the World in HMS Endeavour in 1768–1771 by Sir Joseph Banks and Daniel Solander: with a determination by James Britten*. Parkinson had sketched plants in Madeira, Brazil, Tierra del Fuego, the Society Islands, New Zealand, Australia and Java. However, neither the engravings nor the lithographic reproductions are of the best quality and it is in the original drawings that Parkinson's true ability is revealed. *Ficus parkinsonii* was named in his honour.

**Parkinsonia** L. (For John Parkinson (1567–1650), apothecary of London and author of *Paradisus* (1640).) Leguminosae (Caesalpinioideae). 12 or more species of shrubs or trees, usually armed; branches green. Leaves appearing 1-pinnate, but usually bipinnate with 1–3 pairs pinnae; leaflets very small. Flowers in numerous, short axillary racemes, occasionally crowded terminally; calyx lobes free almost to base; corolla yellow, standard white to yellow, blotched orange; stamens 10, subequal, about as long as perianth, filaments usually proximally pubescent. Fruit a legume, torulose and terete to oblong and flat, coriaceous to woody, 2–9-seeded. America, S & NE Africa. Z9.

CULTIVATION *Parkinsonia* spp. are found on semi-desert grassland and in canyons, although more luxuriant specimens are seen on moist, sandy or gravelly soils at altitudes of 900–1350m/2925–4385ft. They are graceful evergreens grown for their pleasing habit, green to silver boughs, fine foliage and attractive yellow orange flowers in spring; those of *P. aculeata* are sweetly scented. In dry, warm, frost-free zones, they are grown as lawn specimens, in the shrub border, and for hedging and screening. Their light, open nature allows turf to thrive in their shade. Grow in fertile, dry or perfectly drained soils in full sun.

In temperate zones, grow under glass in a porous, medium-fertility loam-based mix, in direct sunlight with low humidity and good ventilation when conditions permit. *P. aculeata* requires a minimum temperature of 15°C/60°F, *P. torreyana* tolerates slightly lower temperatures, 10–13°C/50–55°F. Water moderately when in full growth, and sparingly at other times. Prune lightly after flowering, and then only to remove obstructive or exhausted growth; by encouraging watershoots, pruning may spoil their natural weeping habit. Propagate from seed in spring.

***P. aculeata*** L. JERUSALEM THORN. Shrub or tree to 10m, armed; branchlets yellow-green to dark green smooth. Lvs bipinnate with 2–3 pinnae; leaflets to 0.5cm, many, reduced, opposite or scattered, ovate to oblong. Fls 2–15 in axillary racemes; pedicels to 1.5cm; cal. to 0.7cm, lobes reflexed and deciduous; cor. 2cm diam., yellow, seg. crispate to lacerate, standard villous-clawed, dotted orange. Fr. to 10×0.6cm, stipitate, irregularly torulose, terete, flat-beaked, 2- to few-seeded. Spring. Tropical America.

***P. florida*** (Benth. ex A. Gray) S. Wats. Tree to 8m, spreading, densely branched, usually armed, thorns to 6mm, solitary, rigid, slender; branches pendulous, blue- to grey-green. Lvs bipinnate with 1 pair of pinnae; petiole to 6mm; leaflets to 0.7×0.3cm, 1–4 pairs, ovate to obovate, somewhat pubesc. Fls 5–8 in intercalary racemes; pedicel 1cm; cal. 5mm; cor. yellow, 2.5cm diam., standard blotched red at base, suborbicular. Fr. to 8.5×1.2cm, irregularly oblong, flat, straight or curved, valves coriaceous, thick, 1- to few-seeded. Spring. SW US.

For synonymy see *Cercidium*.

**Parmentiera** DC. (For A. Parmentier (1737–1813), French apothecary who wrote on edible plants.) Bignoniaceae. 9 species of shrubs or trees. Lvs mostly opposite, palmately 3-foliolate; petiole often winged. Flowers solitary or in cauline groups of 2–3 on trunk or older branches; calyx spathe-like, split once to base; corolla white, sometimes tinted green, funnelform to campanulate, folded horizontally below; stamens subexserted; ovary cylindrical. Fr. linear to oblong, terete to ridged, outer layer firm, core fleshy; seeds held between core and cortex, in vestigial wing. C Mexico to Nw Colombia. Z10.

CULTIVATION *P. cereifera* is commonly found on limestone formations in its native Panama. Grown for its large flowers which give rise to the long, smooth and creamy white fruits (hence 'candle tree'), it is sometimes used as a lawn specimen in subtropical and tropical gardens. As *Parmentiera* does not flower until quite large, it is suitable only for a spacious glasshouse or conservatory. Cultivate as for *Jacaranda*.

***P. aculeata*** (HBK) Seem. COW OKRA; CAT; SAN LUIS POTOSI. To 10m. Branchlets terete, glabrous to puberulent. Lvs 3-foliolate, sometimes simple, rarely 4-foliolate; leaflets 1.5–5×0.6–2.5cm, obovate, terminal leaflet 1.5–6×0.6–3cm, apex acute to obtuse, base cuneate or attenuate, sessile or petiolules to 1cm; petiole 1.3–3.5cm, winged. Fls solitary or few-clustered; cal. 2.5–4cm, entire or split; cor. campanulate, 5–7×2–2.5cm at apex, white; stamens subexserted. Fr. 17×3cm+, curved, ribbed; seeds to 4×3mm. Mexico to Honduras, naturalized Queensland.

***P. cereifera*** Seem. PALO DE VELAS; CANDLE TREE. Small tree to 7m, branching from near base. Branches ascending; branchlets terete, lightly puberulent; stipules leafy, 6–10×3–4mm, or absent. Lvs opposite, 3-foliolate, leaflets 3–6.5×1.4–3.6cm, elliptic to rhombic, midrib puberulent above and beneath, apex acute to acuminate, base attenuate; petiole 2.4–6.2cm, winged, wing to 0.4cm wide. Fls solitary or in clusters of 2–3 on short shoots; pedicels 0.9–2.9cm; cal. 1.9–4.9×0.9–2.9cm, split once; cor. 3.7–6.4×1.8–2.9cm, white, tubular, horizontally folded below, tube 2.5–4.8cm, lobes basally connate, 1–1.1cm; stamens subexserted. Fr. to 54×2.4cm, linear, subterete, yellow, waxy, like large candle; seeds 3–4×3–4cm, wing narrow. Panama.

***P. alata*** (HBK) Miers. See *Crescentia elata*.
For further synonymy see *Crescentia*.

**Parnassia** L. (From Mount Parnassus, Greece.) GRASS OF PARNASSUS; BOG STAR. Saxifragaceae. 15 species of perennial, glabrous, usually evergreen herbs, to 60cm. Leaves in a basal rosette, reniform-ovate or oblong, 6cm, entire; petioles long, swollen at base. Flowering stem slender, erect, bearing a solitary terminal flower and a single, sessile bract; flowers white to pale yellow, large; sepals 5, fused at base to form a shallow cup; petals 5, spreading, clawed to sessile, occasionally fringed; staminode at the base of each petal; stamens 5; ovary superior, stigmas 3–4. Fruit a many-seeded, apically dehiscent capsule. Summer. N Temperate.

CULTIVATION Plants of ditches, marshy or boggy grassland and alpine pastures, *Parnassia* spp. bear buttercup-like flowers on long slender stems over basal rosettes of leathery, usually evergreen leaves. Plant on the rock or bog garden in constantly wet but well-drained soil and leave undisturbed. Add crushed limestone for calcicoles like *P. grandifolia*, *P. palustris* and *P. glauca*. *P. palustris* may be naturalized in marshy grass. In the alpine house, plant in pans of high-fertility loam-based medium with added grit and leafmould and ground limestone for calcicoles. Water plentifully. Propagate from seed in late autumn or divide clumps in spring.

***P. asarifolia*** Vent. To 50cm. Lvs reniform, 7.5cm broad. Bract orbicular, clasping flowering stem half way up; fls 2.5cm diam.; pet. white, clawed, entire; staminodes 3-lobed, just short of stamens. E US. Z6.

***P. caroliniana*** Michx. To 15cm. Lvs near orbicular, paler beneath to 6cm; petiole to 10cm. Bract sessile on lower half of scape; pet. white tinged green, 10–18mm; staminodes 3–4-lobed. C Canada to Carolina. Z4.

***P. fimbriata*** Banks in Koenig & Sims. To 30cm. Lvs reniform, 4cm; petiole 5–15cm. Bract at or above middle of scape, clasping; pet. white, clawed, margin fringed; staminode fleshy with several finger-like lobes. Alaska to California and Colorado. Z3.

***P. foliosa*** Hook. f. & Thoms. To 30cm. Flowering stem tetragonal, winged, bract sessile; sep. often reflexed; pet. white, fringed; staminode 3-lobed. India, W China, Japan. Z5.

***P. glauca*** Raf. To 60cm. Lvs ovate-orbicular, 5cm. Bract on or below mid-point of flowering stem, sometimes absent; fls 2–4cm; pet. entire; staminode 3-lobed, shorter than stamens. Newfoundland to Saskatchewan south to Indiana. Z3. Sometimes misidentified as *P. caroliniana*.

***P. grandifolia*** DC. To 60cm. Lvs orbicular, 3–10cm; petiole 3–15cm. Bract borne on or below mid point of scape, reniform; pet. 15–20mm; staminodes 3–5, lobes very narrow, joined only at base. Missouri to Virginia, S to Florida and Louisiana. Z6.

***P. nubicola*** Wallich. To 30cm. Lvs elliptic, 5–10cm. Flowering stem tetragonal; bract sessile; fls to 3.5cm diam., white; staminodes yellow. Himalayas. Z4.

***P. palustris*** L. To 15cm. Lvs ovate to 3cm; petiole 1–4 × blade length. Bract cordate, 3×2.5cm, clasping flowering stem; fls white, netted with green veins, 2.5cm diam; staminode divided into 5–11 fil., swollen at tips. N Temperate. var. ***californica*** A. Gray. Bract much reduced, above mid point of stem, not clasping; staminode fil. 17–27. Sierra Nevada. var. *montanensis* (Fern. & Rydb.) C. Hitchc. Bract rarely clasping, staminode fil. 5–9. W US. Z4.

***P. parviflora*** DC. To 30cm. Lvs oval-elliptic, narrowed at base, 1–3cm. Bract ovate, borne below mid point of flowering stem; pet. elliptic, 6–10mm; staminode fil. 5–10. Quebec to British Columbia, south to Idaho. Z2.

***P. wightiana*** Wallich. To 45cm. Lvs deeply cordate, 3cm. Fl. pale yellow; pet. obovate-oblong, fringed; staminodes 3–5-lobed, lobes swollen at apex. India, China. Z6.

***P. americana*** Muhlenb. See *P. caroliniana*.
***P. californica*** (A. Gray) Greene. See *P. palustris* var. *californica*.
***P. montanensis*** Fern. & Rydb. See *P. palustris* var. *montanensis*.
***P. multiseta*** Fern. See *P. palustris*.
***P. nudata*** Raf. See *P. asarifolia*.
***P. ovata*** Muhlenb. See *P. caroliniana*.
***P. repanda*** Raf. See *P. caroliniana*.
***P. rotundifolia*** Raf. See *P. caroliniana*.

**Parochetus** Buch.-Ham. ex D. Don). (From Gk *para*, near, and *ochetos*, brook, referring to the moist habitat.) Leguminosae (Papilionoideae). 1 species, a prostrate clover-like herb; stems slender, rooting at nodes. Leaves trifoliolate; leaflets to 2cm, obcordate. Flowers to 2.5cm, solitary or paired, pedunculate, deep blue; calyx campanulate, 5-lobed, brown-pubescent; standard erect, broad-obovate, stalked, much longer than wings and keel. Fruit a turgid legume to 2.5cm, straight, glabrous. Summer–autumn. Mts of tropical Africa, Asia to Java. Z9.

CULTIVATION *P. communis*, from moist grassy meadows and streamsides in tropical mountains to 1000m/3250ft, is a beautiful stem-rooting perennial grown for its cobalt-blue pea-flowers and neat, clover-like foliage. It is tolerant of temperate to −5°C/23°F and well suited to the rock garden, but in temperature zones is more commonly and safely grown in the cold glasshouse or alpine house, in pots and hanging baskets where the trailing stems can be encouraged to cascade or to root into a moss lining.

Grow in a moist but gritty, well-drained medium, and give a sheltered position in full sun outdoors or protect with an open cloche in winter. In zones at the limits of its hardiness, pot up and overwinter in frost-free but cold conditions. Propagate from seed or by removal of rooted runners.

***P. communis*** Buch.-Ham. ex D. Don. SHAMROCK PEA; BLUE OXALIS. As for the genus.

**Parodia** Speg. (For Dr Domingo Parodi (1823–90), pharmacist and student of the flora of Paraguay.) Cactaceae. Perhaps 35–50 species of low-growing cacti, simple or clustering; stems mostly small, globose to shortly cylindric, ribbed or tuberculate. Flowers subapical, diurnal, brightly coloured, shortly funnelform; scales narrow; floral areoles with hairs and bristles, or bristles restricted to the uppermost areoles. Fruit globose to clavate-cylindric, woolly and/or bristly, dry or nearly so, mostly thin-walled and disintegrating at or near base, or thick-walled and splitting laterally, or pink and fleshy at first, later hollow and dry; seeds diverse. S America (S Brazil, Uruguay, NE Argentina, S Paraguay and the E Andes of Bolivia and NW Argentina).

CULTIVATION Most *Parodia* ssp. are compact plants, often attractively spined and free-flowering, and the genus is accordingly popular with collectors. In nature they occur in a range of habitats, and some require rather higher minimum temperatures, and a shorter winter rest (2–4 months) than others. The following is only a general guide:

Parodia and Brasilicactus groups: grow in a cool frost-free greenhouse, min 2–7C/35–45°F; use 'standard' cactus compost: moderate to high inorganic content (more than 50% grit), pH 6–7.5; full sun; low air-humidity; keep dry from mid-autumn until early spring, except for light misting on warm days in late winter.

Eriocactus, Brasiliparodia, Notocactus and Wigginsia groups: grow in an intermediate heated greenhouse (min. 5–10C/40–50°F); use 'acid mineral' cactus compost: high inorganic content (more than 80%), below pH6; shade in hot weather; maintain low humidity; water or spray occasionally in winter.

There is no up-to-date treatment of the genus in either its present broad sense, or of its component species-groups, formerly credited with generic status. A great many ill-defined species have been described. The principal groups are distinguished as follows:

Parodia group (*Parodia* sensu stricto). Stems medium-sized, with tubercles or tuberculate ribs; spines hooked or straight. Seeds globose to ovoid, 0.4–1.25mm, brown or black-brown; relief flat or low-domed; strophiole present, large or small. Andes.

*Pp. ayopayana, chrysacanthion, comarapana, erythrantha, faustiana, formosa, gibbulosa, gracilis, heteracantha, maassii, mairanana, microsperma, miguillensis, mutabilis, nivosa, ocampoi, penicillata, procera, rigidispina, schuetziana, schwebsiana, stuemeri, tuberculata*

Eriocactus group. Stems medium-sized to large (to 1.8m), eventually cylindric, with numerous or very high, well-defined ribs bearing many closely placed areoles; spines never hooked. Flowers broad, yellow. Seeds broadly oval, expanded at the hilum or somewhat clavate, 0.7–1.2mm, brown; relief low-domed or par-convex (spinulate); strophiole absent. S Paraguay to S Brazil.

*Pp. claviceps, leninghausii, magnifica, schumanniana, warasii.*

Brasilicactus group. Stems tuberculate, tubercles small, hidden in dense straight spines. Flowers small; tube slender; floral areoles with conspicuous bristles but sparse wool. Seeds broadly oval, 0.8–1.2mm, black-brown; relief high-domed; strophiole absent. S Brazil.

*Pp. graessneri, haselbergii.*

Brasiliparodia group. Like *Parodia* sensu stricto, but seeds lacking a strophiole; spines sometimes hooked. S Brazil.

*Pp. alacriportana, brevihamata, buenekeri.*

Notocactus group (*Notocactus* (Schum.) Frič, sensu Backeb.). Stems medium-sized, weakly to strongly tuberculate-ribbed; spines usually straight (hooked in *P. caespitosa*). Flowers small to rather large (to 8cm); stigmas pink, red, purple or orange (rarely yellow). Seeds broadly oval, 0.8–1.4mm, brown; relief low- to high-domed, sometimes rugose; strophiole absent or the hilum conspicuous and corky. S Brazil, Uruguay, NE Argentina, S Paraguay.

*Pp. allosiphon, buiningii, caespitosa, concinna, herteri, horstii, mammulosa, mueller-melchersii, ottonis, rutilans, scopa, succinea, uebelmanniana, werdermanniana.*

Wigginsia group (*Malacocarpus* Salm-Dyck, non Fisch. & Mey.). Like the preceding group, but fruit partly immersed in the densely woolly stem-apex, fleshy at first, later drying and becoming hollow, often bright pink and partly naked. Seeds 0.9–1.2mm. S Brazil, Uruguay, NE Argentina.

*Pp. erinacea, neohorstii.*

***P. alacriportana*** Backeb. & Voll. Resembling *P. buenekeri* but stem usually smaller; ribs 17–31; central spines 5–25mm, one always hooked; radial spines whiter. Spring. S Brazil (E Rio Grande do Sul). Z9.

***P. allosiphon*** (Marchesi) N.P. Tayl. Simple; stem globose, 8–12×11–13cm, dark green; ribs *c*15–16, very high, straight and well-defined, with low tubercles below the areoles; central spines 4, 8–20mm, terete, stiff and sharp-pointed, dark red to black, then grey; radial spines *c*2 (more in young plants), thinner, laterally directed. Fl. 5.5×5cm, pale yellow; pericarpel and tube much shorter than the tepals. Fr. elongating below, to 3cm, not splitting, seeds escaping at base. Uruguay. Z9.

***P. aureicentra*** Backeb. Simple or clustering; stem globose to elongate, *c*15–40×8–15cm; ribs *c*13–20, more or less spiralled, tuberculate; central spines 4–12, to 7cm, some curved to hooked at apex, variously coloured; radial spines 20–40, to 12mm, setaceous to hairlike, white to pale yellow. Fl. 3.5–5cm, red. Fr. nearly globose, *c*1cm diam. Spring–summer. N Argentina (Salta). Z9.

***P. ayopayana*** Cárdenas. Simple or clustering; stems globose, 6–8×6–10cm (or in var. *elata* Ritter to 60×12cm); ribs *c*11, well-defined, *c*20mm high, vertical; areoles large, very woolly, *c*12mm apart; central spines to 4, 3–3.5cm, subulate, all straight, light brown to almost white; radial spines *c*6–11, 12–20mm, acicular, almost white. Fl. 3cm, orange-yellow; tube stout; floral areoles with dense white to orange wool, the uppermost with inconspicuous bristles. Fr. elongate, with seeds in the lower part only. Spring. C Bolivia (W Cochabamba). Z9.

***P. brevihamata*** W. Haage ex Backeb. Resembling *P. buenekeri*, but stem usually smaller (at least in cultivation); central spines only 2–10mm, 1 or more hooked. Fl. lemon-yellow. Spring. S Brazil (Rio Grande do Sul). Z9.

***P. buenekeri*** Buining. Simple or clustering; stem globose to elongate, to 8cm or more diam.; ribs *c*15–29, more or less vertical, tuberculate but well-defined; spines setaceous, glassy-white, brown or orange, later grey, often forming a brush-like tuft around the stem apex; central spines 4–6, 5–50mm, straight or one somewhat bent or hooked at apex; radial spines *c*14–20, 4–23mm, the lateral interlaced with those of adjacent ribs. Fl. 2.6–4×3.5–4cm, golden-yellow; floral areoles with tufts of brown wool and a few bristles. Fr. 8×8–10mm, thinly woolly. Spring. S Brazil (SE Santa Catarina, NE Rio Grande do Sul). Z9.

***P. buiningii*** (F. Buxb.) N.P. Tayl. Simple; stem depressed-globose to globose, to 8×12cm, pale grey- or glaucous-green; ribs *c*16, straight, thin and sharply acute, with narrow blade-like tubercles between the areoles; central spines 3–4, *c*2–3cm, straight, stiff, pale yellow, dark brown at base; radial spines *c*2–3, similar to the centrals but smaller. Fl. to 7×8cm, yellow; floral areoles with thick dark to light brown wool. Fr. elongating at base, to *c*3cm. Summer. N Uruguay, S Brazil (S Rio Grande do Sul). Requires very well-drained compost, a warm sunny position and watering throughout the year, except in mid-winter. Z9.

***P. caespitosa*** (Speg.) N.P. Tayl. Simple or branching by underground suckers; stem cylindric, 4–8×2–4cm; ribs 11–22, only 1–4mm high; areoles 1.5–4mm apart; central spines 1–4, 3–15mm, brown or red-brown, straight or some curved to hooked at apex; radial spines 9–17, 3–6mm, setaceous, white or pale yellow. Fl. rather large for the size of the plant, 2.7–4.2cm, sulphur- or lemon-yellow, only 1–4 produced together. Fr. ovoid, *c*1cm diam. Summer. S Brazil (Rio Grande do Sul), Uruguay. Z9.

***P. chrysacanthion*** (Schum.) Backeb. Simple; stem depressed-globose to eventually globose, to 12×10cm, rarely larger, apex depressed, very woolly and tufted with erect spines; ribs dissolved into spiralled tubercles; central and radial spines similar, 30–40, to 3cm, all straight, acicular to setaceous, golden-yellow or some paler. Fl. borne 1–9 together, rather small, *c*2cm, yellow; areoles of pericarpel more or less naked, those of the tube with wool and bristles throughout. Spring. N Argentina (Jujuy). Z9.

***P. claviceps*** (Ritter) Brandt. Simple or clustering; stem depressed-globose to shortly cylindric, 10–50×8–20cm or larger; ribs 23–30; spines to 2–5cm, acicular, pale yellow; central spines 1–3; radial spines 5–8. Fl. to 5.5×6cm; pericarpel and tube *c*32mm. Summer. S Brazil (Rio Grande do Sul). Z9.

***P. comarapana*** Cárdenas. Simple or clustering; stems 5–8×7–8cm; ribs 12–21, straight or spiralled, to 10mm high, tuberculate; central and radial spines poorly differentiated; central spines *c*4–8, 1–2cm, all straight, almost white to pale yellow, brown-tipped; radial spines *c*18–35, 3–10mm. Fl. to 2.5×3cm, yellow to orange; scales very narrow and hairlike at apex. Fr. globose, 8mm. Spring–summer. C Bolivia. Z9.

***P. concinna*** (Monv.) N.P. Tayl. Simple; stem depressed-globose, or somewhat elongate when old, 3–10×4–10cm, dark green, apex depressed; ribs 15–32, low, with conspicuous chin-like tubercles between the areoles; spines hairlike to setaceous, some more or less curved to twisted, brown, red-brown or partly white to pale yellow; central spines 4–6 or more, the longest *c*10–25mm, often poorly differentiated from the radials; radial spines 9–25, shorter, adpressed and interlaced. Fl. rather large, commonly 5–8×5–8cm, *c*1–5 produced together, lemon-yellow; pericarpel and tube elongate, equal to or longer than the tepals. Fr. ovoid to globose, *c*15mm, thin-walled, not elongating but splitting or disintegrating at maturity. Spring. S Brazil (Rio Grande do Sul), Uruguay. Z9.

**P. crassigibba** (Ritter) N.P. Tayl. Simple; stem depressed-globose 4–17cm diam., shining dark green; ribs 10–16, very low, rounded, with broad chin-like tubercles between the areoles; spines 5–30mm, all more or less adpressed, mostly curved, off-white to grey or pale brown; central spines 0–1; radial spines 6–14. Fl. rather variable in size, form and colour, 3.5–6×4.5–6cm, nearly white, yellow or red-purple. Fr. barrel-shaped, 5–10mm. Spring–summer. S Brazil (Rio Grande do Sul). Z9.

**P. erinacea** (Haw.) N.P. Tayl. Very variable, the young plants less woolly and more spiny than older specimens; simple; stem depressed-globose, globose, or short-cylindric when old, 6–30cm diam., light to dark green; apex very woolly in old plants; ribs 12–30, sharply acute, well-defined, areoles situated in notches; spines to 2cm, almost white, grey or brown, straight to strongly curved, subulate; central spine absent or 1; radial spines 2–12, mostly adpressed to stem. Fl. 3–5×4–7cm, glossy yellow, borne singly or 2–3 arising together from the stem-apex; pericarpel and tube short, often partly hidden in the wool of the stem apex; floral areoles with dense pale brown wool. Fr. elongating when ripe, clavate, to 4cm, pink or tinged red, partly naked, with sticky pulp at first, later drying and appearing hollow. Summer. S Brazil (Rio Grande do Sul), Uruguay, NE Argentina. Z9.

**P. erythrantha** (Speg.) Backeb. Resembling *P. microsperma*, but fl. slender, to 3cm diam., red or yellow; pericarpel more or less naked; floral areoles with wool and bristles throughout. Spring–summer. N Argentina (Salta). Z9.

**P. faustiana** Backeb. Resembling *P. stuemeri*. Stem globose, to 6cm diam.; ribs spiralled, tuberculate; central spines 4, stout, to more than 25mm, brown or darker; radial spines *c*20, to 10mm, glassy-white. Fl. yellow, red outside. N Argentina (Salta). Z9.

**P. formosa** Ritter. Resembling *P. microsperma*. Stem globose, rarely elongating in age, 3–8cm diam.; ribs 16–26 more or less dissolved into spiralled tubercles; central spines 1–12, 3–25mm, finely acicular, all straight, red-brown; radial spines 8–30, 3–12mm, like the centrals, all white or brown-tipped. Fl. few, 1.6–4×3.5–4.5cm, yellow. Fr. globose, 8mm diam. Spring–summer. S Bolivia (Tarija). Z9.

**P. gibbulosa** Ritter. Resembling *P. formosa*, but fl. numerous, 5 or more borne together, *c*1.8cm. Fr. only 2–2.5mm diam. Spring–summer. Bolivia (Chuquisaca). Z9.

**P. gracilis** Ritter. Simple; stem globose or somewhat elongate, 5–10cm diam.; ribs 13–19, more or less vertical, well-defined, 5–8mm high, tuberculate; central spines 4–10, 7–10mm, brown, red-brown or nearly white, all straight or rarely curved, not hooked except in very young plants; radial spines 14–20, like the centrals, 5–20mm, acicular to hairlike. Fl. 3–3.3cm, golden- to orange-yellow. Fr. almost globose, *c*5mm. Spring–summer. S Bolivia. Z9.

**P. graessneri** (Schum.) F. Brandt. Resembling *P. haselbergii*, but spines to 2cm or more, pale to golden-yellow, some pale brown or nearly all white. Fl. yellow-green, to *c*25mm, self-sterile; tepals half-erect or somewhat spreading but none closely surrounding style; stamens visible. Spring. S Brazil (E Rio Grande do Sul). White-spined variants of this sp. can be confused with *P. haselbergii* when not in flower. Z9.

**P. haselbergii** (Ruempl.) F. Brandt. Simple; stem depressed-globose to globose, 4–15cm diam., apex depressed and sometimes distorted or slanted in old plants; ribs 30–60 or more, very indistinct, dissolved into small tubercles; spines *c*25–60, to 1cm or more, densely covering the stem, setaceous to acicular, straight, glassy-white or the centrals tinged yellow. Fl. long-lived, clustered at the stem-apex, very numerous on large plants, rather variable in size and form, *c*15×9–11mm, brilliant orange-red or rarely orange-yellow; tube relatively long; floral areoles well-separated, with clusters of bristles but sparse wool; inner tepals remaining erect, closely surrounding style and hiding the stamens at first; outer tepals spreading. Fr. globose to short-oblong, *c*10mm, bristly, not woolly, pale yellow to almost white. Winter–spring. S Brazil (E Rio Grande do Sul), Z9.

**P. herteri** (Werderm.) N.P. Tayl. Simple; stem globose or slightly elongate, 10–15cm diam., dark green, becoming corky at base; ribs *c*20–30, high and straight, the areoles set in notches with chin-like tubercles between; central spines 4–6, to 2cm, subulate, brown; radial spines *c*8–17, to 12mm, acicular, entirely white or brown-tipped. Fl. *c*4×5cm, shocking pink or darker, pale to almost white in the throat, many produced together on large plants, in a ring around stem apex. Fr. globose. Summer. S Brazil (S Rio Grande do Sul), Uruguay. Z9.

**P. heteracantha** Ritter ex Weskamp. Resembling *P. rigidispina*, but central spines to 22mm; pericarpel nearly naked. N Argentina (Salta). Z9.

**P. horstii** (Ritter) N.P. Tayl. Simple or sparingly clustering; stem globose, later elongating, to 14cm diam., green but soon becoming corky from the base upwards; ribs 12–19, well-defined, 7–20mm high; areoles in shallow notches between low tubercles, 5–9mm apart; central spines 1–6, 8–30mm or more, acicular, yellow to brown, straight, curved or twisted; radial spines *c*10–15, 6–30mm, finer, white to pale brown. Fl. 3–4cm, yellow-orange, red or purple, arising very close to the stem-apex; stigmas orange-yellow, pink, purple or almost white. Fr. globose to barrel-shaped, 7–10×6–8mm. Summer–autumn, occasionally spring. S Brazil (Rio Grande do Sul). Z9.

**P. leninghausii** (Schum.) Brandt. Simple or more often clustering; stem cylindric, to 60×7–10cm or taller, green, apex usually slanted; ribs 30–35, straight; areoles close-set; spines pale to deep yellow or some pale brown, straight to slightly curved, finely setaceous; central spines *c*3–4, 20–50mm; radial spines 15–20 or more, 5–10mm. Fl. *c*5×6cm, lemon-yellow; floral areoles with dense brown wool and bristles throughout. Fr. globose, *c*20mm. Summer. S Brazil (Rio Grande do Sul). Z9.

**P. maassii** (Hesse) A. Berger. Very variable; simple, seldom clustering; stem 10–50×7–25cm; ribs *c*10–21, well-defined, straight or spiralled; central spines 1–6, 2–7cm, the lowermost longest and much stouter, strongly curved to hooked at apex, rarely almost straight, variously coloured; radial spines 6–18 (18–28 in f. *maxima* (Ritter) Krainz), mostly 1–4cm, straight or slightly curved, mostly acicular, paler than the centrals. Fl. *c*3–4.5cm, red to yellow; floral areoles woolly, only the uppermost with bristles. Fr. depressed-globose to slightly elongate, 5–10mm diam. (20–50mm in var. *commutans* (Ritter) Krainz). Spring–summer. S Bolivia, N Argentina (Jujuy). Z9.

**P. magnifica** (Ritter) F. Brandt. Simple, rarely clustering; stem globose or eventually elongate, 7–15cm diam., blue-green; ribs 11–15, straight, acute; areoles close-set or almost contiguous; spines 12–15 or more, 8–20mm, setaceous, golden-yellow. Fl. 4.5–5.5×4.5–5.5cm, sulphur-yellow. Fr. globose, 10mm. Summer. S Brazil (Rio Grande do Sul). Z9.

**P. mairanana** Cárdenas. Simple, later clustering; stem depressed-globose, *c*3–4×4–5.5cm, dark green, not very woolly at apex; ribs *c*13–14, somewhat spiralled, scarcely tuberculate; central spines 1–3, straight to hooked, light brown to nearly black, 8–20mm; radial spines *c*8–14, 3–12mm, acicular, almost white to pale yellow. Fl. 1–3.5×2–3.5cm, orange-red to golden-yellow; tube gradually flared above the pericarpel. Fr. ellipsoid, to 8mm. Spring. C Bolivia (Santa Cruz). Z9.

**P. mammulosa** (Lem.) N.P. Tayl. Simple; stem globose or somewhat elongate, 5–13cm diam., very dark green; ribs 13–21, rarely more, vertical, well-defined, with large, pointed, chin-like tubercles between the areoles; central spines 2–4, to *c*2cm or more, and then less easily distinguished from the radials, straight, rather stout and stiff, white to grey or pale brown, usually one strongly flattened; radial spines *c*6–25, 5–10mm, acicular or stouter, off-white to pale brown. Fl. *c*3.5–5.5cm, pale to golden-yellow; pericarpel and tube short and broad; floral areoles with very dense pale wool and few dark bristles. Fr. globose at first, later somewhat elongate, thin-walled, releasing seeds at base. Summer. S Brazil (Rio Grande do Sul), Uruguay, NE Argentina. Z9.

**P. microsperma** (F.A.C. Weber) Speg. Very variable; stem simple, rarely offsetting, depressed-globose to globose, sometimes elongate later, 5–20×5–10cm; ribs *c*15–21, more or less dissolved into spiralled tubercles; central spines 3–4, 5–20(–50)mm, red, brown or darker, the lowermost hooked at apex; radial spines 7–20, *c*4–8mm, setaceous, white. Fl. 3–3.5×4–5cm, yellow or red; floral areoles with wool and bristles throughout. Fr. nearly globose, *c*4–5mm diam. Spring–summer. N Argentina (Catamarca, Tucuman, Salta). Z9.

**P. miguillensis** Cárdenas. Resembling *P. ayopayana*, but more spiny; simple; stem depressed-globose to cylindric, 6–30×3–8cm; ribs 8–16, well-defined, 7–10mm high, vertical; areoles 1–5mm apart; central spines 4–9, 1–2.5cm, acicular or finer, all straight or somewhat curved, yellow-brown to dark brown; radial spines 12–18, 2–20mm, hairlike, nearly white to yellow-brown, intergrading with the centrals. Fl. 1.5–2.5×0.7–2cm, light to golden-yellow. Fr. elongate, 20–30×4–10mm. Summer. C Bolivia (La Paz). Z9.

**P. mueller-melchersii** (Backeb.) N.P. Tayl. Simple; stem globose, 5–8×5–6cm, dark green; ribs 21–24, low, with small rounded tubercles; central spines 1–3, 4–20mm, straight, not flattened, subulate to acicular, pale yellow, darker at base and apex; radials 14–18 or more, 2–8mm, slender-acicular, off-white. Fl. *c*3×4.5–5cm, pale golden-yellow. Fr. elongating at base, thin-walled, *c*7mm diam. Summer. Uruguay. Z9.

**P. mutabilis** Backeb. Resembling *P. microsperma*; central spines 4–10, yellow, red-brown or brown; radial spines 20–50 or more, very fine, white. Fl. 3–5cm diam., yellow. Spring–summer. N Argentina (Salta). Z9.

**P. neohorstii** (Theunissen) N.P. Tayl. Simple; stem globose, 3–9cm; ribs 18–26; central spines 1–6, 1–3cm, straight, pale below, dark brown to black at apex; radial spines 14–24, 3–7mm, adpressed, more slender, almost white. Fl. 2.5–4×2.5–3.5cm, shiny yellow. Fr. 8×4mm, hollow, hidden in the wool of the stem-apex. Summer. S Brazil (Rio Grande do Sul). Z9.

**P. nivosa** Backeb. Simple; stem globose or eventually somewhat elongate, to 15×8cm; ribs dissolved into spiralled tubercles; central spines 4, to 2cm, all straight, setaceous, white or one dark at base; radial spines *c*18, white, like the centrals but finer. Fl. *c*3×2.5–5cm, fiery red; floral areoles with wool and bristles throughout. Spring. N Argentina (Salta). Z9.

**P. ocampoi** Cárdenas. Clustering; stems shortly cylindric, 7–20×6–11cm; ribs 13–17, straight, well-defined, 5–10mm high; central spine 1, 5–25mm, straight, red-brown; radial spines 8–9, 10–25mm, red-brown. Fl. *c*3×5cm, yellow. Fr. obovoid, *c*5mm. Spring–summer. C Bolivia (Cochabamba). Z9.

**P. ottonis** (Lehm.) N.P. Tayl. Very variable; simple at first, later usually clustering; stem more or less globose, tapered at base, 3–15cm diam., variable in colour; ribs 6–15, rarely more, well-defined, rounded or acute; spines hairlike, straight, curved or twisted; centrals 1–6, 8–40mm, light to dark brown, red-brown or yellow; radials 4–15, 5–30mm, off-white to yellow or brown. Fl. 2.5–6cm, yellow or rarely orange-red; floral areoles with pale brown wool and bristles; stigmas usually red or purple, rarely orange to yellow. Fr. ovoid to short oblong, *c*9–12mm diam., not elongating at maturity, thick-walled, splitting lengthwise to expose the seeds and white pulp. Summer. S Brazil, Uruguay, NE Argentina, S Paraguay. Many regional forms have been described as species. The following varieties are recognized. var. ***ottonis***. Stems mostly 3–10cm diam.; ribs 6–12, rarely more. Fl. *c*4–6cm, few. S Brazil (Rio Grande do Sul), Uruguay, NE Argentina, S Paraguay. var. ***tortuosa*** (Link & Otto) N.P. Tayl. Stems to 15cm diam.; ribs 10 15, occasionally more. Fl. *c*2.5–4cm, many produced together. S Brazil (Paraná, Santa Catarina, Rio Grande do Sul). Z9.

***P. penicillata*** Fechser & Van Der Steeg. Stem globose, then cylindric, to 30(–70)×7–12cm; ribs 17–20, spiralled, tuberculate; spines developing early, forming a dense tuft at stem-apex, central and radial spines poorly differentiated; central spines to 10–20, to 5cm, straight, almost white, pale yellow or more rarely pale brown; radial spines to *c*40, shorter, glassy white. Fl. to 5×4cm, orange- to blood-red. Summer. N Argentina (Salta). Z9.

***P. procera*** Ritter. Simple; stem globose, clavate or cylindric, to 30×3–8cm; ribs *c*13, high, somewhat spiralled, scarcely tuberculate; central spines 4, 15–35mm, straight or one curved to hooked at apex, brown; radial spines 7–10, 7–15mm, hairlike, white to pale brown. Fl. to 3×2.5–4cm, yellow. Fr. globose, 5–8mm. Spring–summer. Bolivia (Chuquisaca). Z9.

***P. rigidispina*** Krainz. Resembling *P. microsperma*; central spines 4, to 7mm, stiff, all straight or one somewhat curved at apex (but not hooked), red to brown; radial spines 6–11, *c*5mm. Fl. slender, 3.7cm, yellow, smelling of iodine. N Argentina. Z9.

***P. rutilans*** (Daeniker & Krainz) N.P. Tayl. Simple; stem globose or somewhat elongate, *c*5cm diam., dark green; ribs 18–24, vertical or weakly spiralled, low, with chin-like tubercles between the areoles; central spines 2, the lower to 7mm, straight, stiff, red-brown; radial spines *c*14–16, to 5mm, slender-acicular, almost white, darker tipped. Fl. 3–4×6cm, pink, becoming paler to yellow-tinged in the throat. Fr. elongating at base, *c*15mm, thin-walled. Summer. N Uruguay. Z9.

***P. schuetziana*** Jajo. Simple; stem depressed-globose to somewhat elongate, to *c*11cm diam.; ribs *c*21, vertical or somewhat spiralled, tuberculate; central spines 1–4, the lowermost hooked, pale brown; radial spines *c*15, finely hairlike, interlaced, white. Fl. campanulate, *c*2cm, dark red. Spring–summer. N Argentina (Jujuy). Z9.

***P. schumanniana*** (Nicolai) F. Brandt. Usually simple; stem globose then cylindric, green, to 180×30cm (flowering when much smaller); ribs 21–48 (fewer in non-flowering juvenile plants), straight, acute, well-defined; spines golden-yellow, brown or red-brown, later grey, setaceous, straight or slightly curved; central spines 3–4, 10–30mm; radial spines *c*4, 7–50mm. Fl. 4–4.5×4.5–6.5cm, lemon- to golden-yellow; pericarpel and tube *c*20–25mm; floral areoles with dense wool and bristles throughout. Fr. globose to ovoid, 10–15mm. Summer. S Paraguay, NE Argentina. Z9.

***P. schwebsiana*** (Werderm.) Backeb. Usually simple; stem depressed-globose to shortly cylindric, 2.3–12×8cm, apex very woolly; ribs 13–20, low, somewhat spiralled, tuberculate; central spines 1–4, 1–2cm, the lowermost directed downwards, hooked, red-tinged to pale brown; radial spines *c*5–10, 5–12mm, tinged red or yellow at first. Fl. 2–3×2–2.5cm, dark red; tube abruptly constricted above the pericarpel; floral areoles woolly, only the uppermost with bristles. Fr. globose, very small, 3–4mm. Summer. C Bolivia (Cochabamba). Z9.

***P. scopa*** (Spreng.) N.P. Tayl. Simple or clustering; stem globose to cylindric, 5–50×6–10cm, dark green, but more or less obscured by spines; ribs 25–40, low, finely tuberculate; areoles only 3–8mm apart; central spines 3–4, 6–12mm, brown, red or white; radial spines *c*35–40 or more, 5–7mm, finely setaceous, glassy white or pale yellow. Fl. 2–4×3.5–4.5cm, bright yellow, many produced together in a ring around the stem apex. Fr. nearly globose, *c*7mm diam., base remaining attached to stem after dehiscence. Summer. S Brazil (Rio Grande do Sul), Uruguay. Z9.

***P. stuemeri*** (Werderm.) Backeb. Simple; stem globose at first, later cylindric, 15–25×7–12cm; ribs *c*15–22, straight, rarely spiralled, tuberculate; central spines 4–8, 11–25mm, all straight or one or more slightly to strongly curved (not hooked) at apex, pale yellow or brown; radial spines 9–35, to 20mm, off-white to pale brown. Fl. 2.5–4×2.5–5cm, red, orange or yellow. Spring–summer. N Argentina (Salta, Jujuy). Z9.

***P. succinea*** (Ritter) N.P. Tayl. Resembling *P. scopa*, but stem smaller, 2.5–7cm diam.; ribs 18–26; central spines 4–12, to 25mm, yellow, brown or violet-grey; radial spines 12–40, 3–10mm, off-white, pale yellow or brown. Fl. 3–3.6×3–4cm. Summer. S Brazil (Rio Grande do Sul). Z9.

***P. tuberculata*** Cárdenas. Simple, rarely clustering; stem depressed-globose, 7–11cm diam., apex not very woolly; ribs 13–20, spiralled, strongly tuberculate at first; central spines 1–4, 15–25mm, one hooked, brown to almost black or grey; radial spines 7–11, to 10mm. Fl. 1.8–2.7×3cm, yellow-red. Fr. globose, 6–7mm. Spring–summer. Bolivia (Potosi, Chuquisaca). Z9.

***P. warasii*** (Ritter) Brandt. Resembling *P. leninghausii* and *P. magnifica*; simple, rarely branched; stem to *c*50×10–15cm, green; ribs 15–16, areoles 4–6mm apart; spines *c*15–20, 1–4cm, acicular, yellow-brown to pale brown. Fl. 5–6cm diam., golden- to lemon-yellow. S Brazil (Rio Grande do Sul). Z9.

***P. werdermanniana*** (Herter) N.P. Tayl. Resembling *P. concinna*, but stem usually larger, to 13×10cm; ribs to 40; spines setaceous to acicular, straight, yellow to white, the radials not adpressed. Fl. *c*6×7cm, sulphur-yellow, 6 or more produced together in a ring around the stem apex. Spring. Uruguay. Z9.

***P. catamarcensis*** Backeb. See *P. microsperma*.
***P. gummifera*** Backeb. & Voll. See *Uebelmannia gummifera*.
***F. liliputana*** (Werderm.) N.P. Tayl. See *Blossfeldia liliputana*.
***P. sanagasta*** Weing. See *P. microsperma*.
***P. sanguiniflora*** Backeb. See *P. microsperma*.
***P. scopaoides*** Backeb. See *P. microsperma*.
***P. setifera*** Backeb. See *P. microsperma*.
***P. tilcarensis*** (Werderm. & Backeb.) Backeb. See *P. stuemeri*.
For further synonymy see *Echinocactus*, *Frailea*, *Notocactus* and *Wigginsia*.

**Paronychia** L. (From Gk *para*, beside, and *onyx*, nail, from the classical use of the plant for whitlows under the nails.) WHITLOW-WORT. Caryophyllaceae. About 40 species of low-growing annuals or perennials, sometimes woody at base. Leaves in pairs, linear-lanceolate to ovate, with silvery stipules. Flowers small, in dense axillary heads, more or less surrounded by conspicuous silvery bracts. Perianth segments 5 (rarely 4), sepaloid, often persistent and hardening with a strong terminal awn; stamens 5, (rarely 4); styles 2, free or partly joined. Capsule 1-seeded, irregularly dehiscent. Widespread throughout the tropical and warmer temperate regions in both the Old and the New World, common in the Mediterranean area.

CULTIVATION With the exception of *P. pulvinata* (cultivated in North America as an alpine), the species described are found in dry, rocky habitats around the Mediterranean. Algerian tea (*thé arab*), an infusion made with *P. capitata* and *P. argentea*, was used to treat tuberculosis and for its diuretic and aphrodisiac properties.

*P. argentea* is a silvery, carpeting species suitable for warm, dry, sandy soils, especially useful as groundcover after bulbs have flowered, and well suited to raised beds, wall and pavement plantings. *P. capitata* and *P. kapela*, of similar habit and use, are considered more attractive in flower: the conspicuous papery bracts which surround the tiny flowers are a translucent silver, but they are less tolerant of cold, winter wet in temperate gardens. All are hardy to between −5°C and −10°C/23–14°F, perhaps more with perfect drainage. Grow in a warm open position in full sun, in sharply drained, sandy or gritty soils; too rich a soil will reduce the attractive silvery qualities. Under glass, use well-crocked pots with a mix of equal parts loam, leafmould or equivalent, and coarse sharp sand. Water moderately when in growth and keep almost dry in winter. Propagate by division in spring or from cuttings rooted in a closed case with bottom heat.

***P. argentea*** Lam. Much-branched mat-forming perenn. Lvs small, ovate to lanceolate. Fls in dense axillary cymes partially covered by conspicuous, silvery, ovate bracts; perianth seg. *c*2mm, awned and with membranous margins. Summer. S Europe, N Africa, SW Asia. Z7.

***P. capitata*** (L.) Lam. Like *P. argentea* but with lvs linear-lanceolate to lanceolate and fls in distinct, very silvery heads; perianth seg. green, hooded, awnless and very unequal in length. Summer. Mediterranean area. Z5.

***P. kapela*** (Hacq.) Kerner. Like *P. argentea* but with fls in distinct, very silvery heads and perianth seg. green, hooded and awnless. Summer. Mediterranean area. Z7.

***P. pulvinata*** A. Gray. Densely pulvinate rock plant, woody at base. Lvs thick, 3–5mm; stipules silvery. Fls solitary, inconspicuous in lf axils. Summer. US (high 'tundra' of the Southern Rocky Mts). Z5.

***P. capitata*** auct. See *P. kapela*.
***P. chionaea*** Boiss. See *P. kapela*.
***P. nivea*** DC. See *P. capitata*.
***P. serpyllifolia*** Chaix. See *P. kapela*.

**Parrotia** C.A. Mey. (For F.W. Parrot (1792–1841), German naturalist, traveller and professor of medicine, who climbed Mt Ararat in 1829.) IRONWOOD; IRONTREE. Hamamelidaceae. 1 species, a deciduous, slow-growing, shrub or tree, to 10m. Bark smooth, grey, flaking. Branches spreading horizontally, young shoots stellate-pubescent. Leaves 6–10cm, alternate, entire, ovate

**Parrotia and allies** (a) *Parrotia persica* (×1), outline of tree in habitat, outline of spreading form typical of gardens (b) *Sycopsis sinensis* (×1) (c) × *Sycoparrotia semidecidua* (×1) (d) *Parrotiopsis jacquemontiana* (×1)

to obovate, strongly parallel-veined, margins unevenly, shallowly toothed at apex, sometimes tinged red on new growth, both surfaces stellate-hairy, deep green above, paler beneath, autumnal foliage richly coloured crimson, yellow and orange; petiole pubescent, 6mm. Flowers in dense clusters before leaves, 1cm diam., subtended by bracts; bract to 1cm, ovate, exterior dark brown and hairy, interior green; calyx 5–7-lobed; petals absent; stamens to 15, anthers prominent coral-pink to scarlet red, filaments white. Fruit a 2-parted capsule; seeds 1 per cell, 1cm, brown, apex acute. Early spring. N Iran. Most cultivated *Parrotia* is a broadly spreading to ascending selection; wild populations tend to be strongly upright in habit. Z5.

CULTIVATION A beautiful slow-growing tree with a distinctive low branching habit, *P. persica* becomes increasingly venerable and distinguished with age as it develops its characteristically overlapping and crossing network of branches. Suitable for use as a lawn specimen where its low domed shaped can be fully appreciated, it is grown for the deep, rich red clusters of anthers carried before leaf emergence in late winter/early spring, for its bark which flakes to give a mosaic of buff-pink and creamy yellow, and for its autumn colour, which in favourable seasons displays a spectrum of yellows, orange and deep crimson. Grow in sun or part shade in deep, fertile and well-drained loamy soils, preferably acid, although its shows good tolerance of alkaline and chalky soils. *Parrotia* usually requires no pruning but specimens will achieve a better shape if trained as standards when young to give a clear stem to about 1.8m/6ft. Propagate by seed in autumn (germination may take up to 18 months), softwood cuttings under mist in summer or by layering.

***P. persica*** (DC.) C.A. Mey. As for the genus. 'Pendula': branches pendulous, forming a dense, weeping dome.

***P. jacquemontiana*** Decne. See *Parrotiopsis jacquemontiana*.

**Parrotiopsis** (Niedenzu) C. Schneid. (From *Parrotia* and Gk *opsis*, appearance.) Hamamelidaceae. 1 species, a deciduous, erect tree, to 6m. Shoots stellate-pubescent. Leaves alternate, ovate to orbicular, 5–9cm, short-toothed with sharp tips, usually turning yellow in autumn, stellate-pubescent throughout; petioles to 13mm. Inflorescence made up of about 20 densely packed heads of yellow stamens, to 5cm diam., subtended by 4–6 ovate to orbicular, white, petal-like bracts; calyx of 5–7 sepals; petals absent; stamens 15–24; ovary superior, 2-celled. Fruit an ovoid, 2-beaked capsule. Spring–early summer. Himalaya. Z7.

CULTIVATION As for *Parrotia*.

***P. jacquemontiana*** (Decne.) Rehd. As for the genus.

***P. involucrata*** Decne. See *P. jacquemontiana*.
For further synonymy see *Parrotia*.

**Parrya** R. Br. (For Sir William Edward Parry (1790–1855), Arctic explorer.) Cruciferae. 25 species of perennial herbs. Leaves simple or pinnatifid, glandular-pubescent, rarely glabrous, tapering to a slender petiole; flowering stem often leafless. Inflorescence racemose; sepals 4, spreading, saccate at base, caducous; petals 4, white or purple, large, long-clawed; stamens 6, free, without appendages. Fruit a silique, linear or oblong, valves compressed with a single midvein; seeds compressed, winged or wingless. Summer. Arctic, Alpine regions, USSR, Alaska. Z3.

CULTIVATION Natives of rocky arctic habitats and of high mountain scree and moraine (to 4300–5300m/13,975–17,225ft in the Himalaya), *Parrya* spp. are low-growing specimens for the rock garden and alpine house, grown for their showy flowers; those of *P. nudicaulis*, violet with a darker centre, are fragrant. Although tolerant of very low temperatures, they may, as with other hairy-leaved alpine species, succumb to winter wet. Cultivate as for *Draba*.

***P. microcarpa*** Ledeb. 4–12cm. Lvs in rosettes, oblong to elliptic, stiffly white-hairy, tapering to a long petiole, entire; flowering stem lvs acute, narrow, sessile. Raceme short, dense; sep. 1–4×1–2mm, white-hairy; pet. 6–7×4–5mm, short-clawed. Fr. 8–20mm, linear-oblong, compressed, tapering above and below; seeds brown, wingless. Siberia, Mongolia.

***P. nudicaulis*** (L.) Reg. 5–30cm; base covered by the remains of old lf bases. Lvs 15–120×4–30mm, entire, lobed or pinnatisect. Sep. 5–8mm, often suffused pink; pet. 12–20mm. Fr. 15–50×3–8mm, constricted between seeds, style 1.5–4mm. Alaska, Yukon, Eurasia. Very variable and often divided into a number of subspecies.

***P. grandiflora*** Schischkin. See *P. microcarpa*.
***P. menziesii*** Greene. See *Phoenicaulis cheiranthoides*.
For further synonymy see *Draba*.

**Parsnip**. *Pastinaca sativa*. Umbelliferae. A biennial grown as an annual for its edible tapering root. It is a native of Siberia and Europe including Britain and has been cultivated at least since Roman times. It is widely grown in temperate regions, where it provides a valuable winter crop. The main harvesting period starts after roots have been first exposed to frost, which is considered to enhance their flavour. However, faster-maturing cultivars can be lifted during summer and storage of the later harvests provides continuity through until the following spring.

Parsnips require an open site and grow best on a deep, well-cultivated soil free of stones. Fresh manure should not be added as it may cause roots to fang. On poor or heavy soils, improved quality roots may be grown from seed sown directly into planting holes, about 90cm/35in. deep, 15cm/6in. across, made with a crowbar; care must be taken to avoid compaction of the surrounding oil. Fill the planting hole with fine earth or a fertile loam based propagating mix. This technique is also used for exhibition specimens. Parsnip seed rapidly loses viability and only fresh seed should be used in establishing the crop. Germination is slow and erratic under cold conditions and it is preferable to delay sowing until soil conditions improve during late spring, or alternatively raise young plants in peat blocks under protection using gentle heat. In open ground seeds should be sown 2cm/¾in. deep in groups of two or three seeds which can be singled following establishment. Plant spacing will depend on the choice of cultivar and the preferred size of root. For large roots (crown diameter in excess of 5cm/2in.), large-rooted cultivars spaced in rows 30cm/12in. apart with 15cm/6in. between plants within rows is recommended. For smaller cultivars this should be reduced to 20cm/8in. between rows and 8cm/3in. within rows.

Parsnips are relatively slow growing and are in the soil for a long period. The ground between widely spaced rows can therefore be usefully intercropped with faster-growing species such as radish or small lettuce. Parsnips develop a strong taproot and consequently watering is only required under dry conditions. However, if conditions become too dry, root splitting may take place following either rain or watering. Roots can be lifted when required from late summer onwards. They are hardy and will withstand exposure to frost, although harvesting during frosty conditions is easier if they are protected by a layer of straw or bracken. They may also be lifted and stored under cool conditions in boxes of sand. Pests and diseases include celery fly, carrot fly and canker.

Recommended cultivars include 'All America': smooth, slender, pure white flesh; 'Avonresister' small, bulbous, canker-resistant; 'Cobham Improved Marrow': long wedge-shaped, canker-resistant; 'Fullback Short Thick': stumpy; 'Gladiator Fl': uniform, medium to large, canker-resistant; 'Harris Model': uniform, tapered, very white; 'Hollow Crown': long, tapering; 'Tender and True': long, tapering; 'White Gem': wedge-shaped, canker-resistant.

**Parsonia** R. Br. (For John Parsons (1705–70), Scottish physician and naturalist.) Apocynaceae. 80 species of woody climbers. Leaves opposite. Inflorescence a terminal or axillary panicle; flowers small; corolla tubular, often inflated, limb 5-lobed. Asia, Australasia, Pacific. Some authors have taken up the name *Parsonia* for spp. now included in *Cuphea* (Lythraceae).

CULTIVATION Attractive climbers, suitable for the cool glasshouse or, in mild areas, for a sheltered situation outdoors, although *P. capsularis* has survived outside where winter temperatures occasionally fall to −10°C/14°F. They are tolerant of a range of soils, performing best in a well-drained but moisture-retentive soil in full sun. Water container-grown plants moderately when in growth and maintain good ventilation with a winter minimum of 5–7°C/40–45°F. Propagate by seed or by soft stem cuttings.

***P. capsularis*** R. Br. Evergreen climber to 5m. Stems slender, twining, glabrous or rough, buff tinted or marked chocolate or purple-green. Lvs highly variable in size and shape: 2–7.5cm, narrow-linear, simple or lobed, buff overlaid chocolate, pink or dark green in juvenile state, adult lvs 2.5–6×1.25–2cm, entire, seldom so beautifully marked as in juveniles. Infl. a terminal panicle, usually crowded; cor. to 3mm, white, campanulate, lobes recurved. New Zealand. Z9.

**Parthenium** L. (Ancient name, from Gk *parthenos*, virgin: only female florets produce fruit.) Compositae. About 15 species of aromatic herbs and shrubs. Leaves alternate, entire to pinnatisect. Capitula radiate, few to many solitary or in small corymbs; receptacle convex, scaly; involucre campanulate to hemispheric, phyllaries in 2–3 series, imbricate, dry, outer smaller; ray florets white or yellow-tinged, female, fertile, inconspicuous, disc florets many, hermaphrodite. Fruit of ray florets a compressed, keeled cypsela; pappus of 2–3 awns or scales, or absent. Summer. Tropical & subtropical America & W Indies.

CULTIVATION Found predominantly in semi arid and arid habitats, the aromatic *P. argentatum* on dry limestone soils, *Parthenium* spp. make interesting additions to native plant collections, if only by virtue of the latex that they produce. They have also been used in the restoration of prairie habitats and similar biotrope plantings. The fresh leaves of *P. integrifolium* have traditionally been used by the Catawaba Indians in the treatment of burns. Cultivate as for *Pittocaulon*.

***P. argentatum*** A. Gray. GUAYULE. Shrub to 1m, much-branched. Lvs to 5×1.5cm, oblanceolate, entire or sparsely dentate. Capitula many, 6mm diam., in a compact corymb. Texas, N Mexico. Z8.

***P. integrifolium*** L. WILD QUININE; AMERICAN FEVERFEW; PRAIRIE DOCK. Perenn. herb, 0.5–1m, simple or branched above. Lvs to 20×10cm, lanceolate-elliptic to broadly ovate, crenulate-serrate or sublyrate at base. Capitula to 10mm diam., several, in a broad, flat-topped corymb. E US to Wisconsin and Arkansas. Z3.

***P. argenteum*** hort. See *P. argentatum*.

**Parthenocissus** Planch. (From Gk *parthenos*, virgin, and *kissos*, ivy, a loose translation of 'virginia creeper'.) VIRGINIA CREEPER. Vitaceae. 10 species of generally deciduous woody vines, trailing or ascending with tendrils; tendrils branched, twining or with adhesive disks. Leaves alternate, palmately lobed or compound, occasionally simple and 3-lobed or unlobed. Inflorescence in terminal aggregated terminal clusters or in cymose panicles opposite leaves; flowers small, bisexual or unisexual; receptacle wanting; petals 4–5, separate, spreading at anthesis; stamens short, erect. Fruit a berry, dark blue or black, flesh thin; seeds 1–4. N America, E Asia, Himalaya.

CULTIVATION These attractive and vigorous climbers generally occupy moist soils in woodland or forest in the wild, climbing towards the light by means of tendrils, by their characteristic adhesive pads or, if conditions dictate, by twining and weaving. The most commonly cultivated spp. have escaped from gardens and naturalized; *P. quinquefolia* on walls and waste ground in Europe, *P. tricuspidata* is found in Yugoslavian forests to altitudes of 2100m/6825ft.

*Parthenocissus* spp. are invaluable for growing up and through sturdy trees, for growing over pergolas, walls and fences and for covering unsightly buildings. The twining or tendril-climbing spp., such as *P. inserta*, are very effective if allowed to weave through large shrubs, small trees and hedging; they need support if used to cover buildings, but are perhaps at their most beautiful given horizontal support so that they can form an elegant hanging curtain of foliage. The self-clinging spp. are unsurpassed for covering large areas of bare wall with the proviso that the more vigorous species, in particular *P. tricuspidata* and *P. quinquefolia*, need a structurally sound surface and must be prevented from reaching under house eaves and roof tiles and into window casements, since they will cause damage as their stems thicken. *P. tricuspidata* 'Beverley Brook' has smaller leaves and is less vigorous than the species.

All are grown for their handsome foliage, that of *P. henryana* is particularly striking, deep velvety green-bronze with contrasting silvery venation, much valued in floral arrangements. Most give a peerless display of transient autumnal brilliance in crimson and scarlet, complemented in good seasons by small, deep-blue fruits. Hardiness varies, ranging from tolerance of temperatures of −25°C/−13°F for *P. quinquefolia* and at least −15°C/5°F for *P. inserta*, *P. tricuspidata* and its cvs.; *P. henryana* withstands cold to between −5 and −10°C/23–14°F. *P. himalayana* is not reliably hardy in zones with prolonged low temperatures, and needs a sheltered position in zones at the limits of its hardiness.

Plant pot-grown specimens into a moisture retentive but well drained fertile soil, improving if necessary by the pre-planting incorporation of well rotted organic matter. *Parthenocissus* spp. require at least partial shade for good colour display; grow *P. quinquefolia*, *P. inserta* and *P. himalayana* in semi-shade on east or west facing walls, give *P. tricuspidata* and *P. henryana* a position in partial shade, or grow on a sunless wall. Give initial support until plants produce adhesive pads. Prune annually to keep growths away from the roof eaves etc., in autumn or early winter. For pergola trained specimens, cut the current season's growth back to one or two viable buds from the main framework, thus creating a spur system, from which the following season's growth can cascade.

Propagate species by seed, although some such as *P. inserta* and *P. tricuspidata* may hybridize and will not come true. Remove pulp and sow fresh out of doors or in the cold frame, or stratify for 6 weeks at or just below 5°C/40°F, and sow under glass in spring. The fruit pulp may cause skin irritation. Propagate cultivars by leaf bud cuttings in early to mid summer, taking care to avoid blind eyes, and root in a closed case with bottom heat. Also by 10–12cm/4–5in. basal hardwood cuttings of the current season's growth taken immediately after leaf fall; treat with rooting hormone, (0.8–1.0% I.B.A.) and root in individual pots with a bottom heat at 18–21°C/64–70°F. Pot on as soon as rooted to minimize root disturbance. Also by simple layering.

***P. henryana*** (Hemsl.) Diels. & Gilg. Vine, ascending, to 5m, deciduous; stems acutely 4-angled, glabrous; tendrils 5–7-forked, terminating in adhesive disks. Lvs compound; petiole 4–11cm; leaflets 4–12×1.5–6cm, 3–5, obovate to oblanceolate or narrowly ovate, acute at apex, tapered to base, coarsely dentate except near base, dark velvety green with pink and silvery variegations along main veins, green part of leaf turning red in autumn, slightly pubesc. on veins beneath, shortly petiolulate. Infl. terminal, leafy, a panicle of cymes to 18cm. Fr. dark blue; seeds 3. China. Z7.

***P. heptaphylla*** (Buckl.) Britt. & Small. Vine, climbing to 9m, deciduous; shoots terete to rather angular, ferruginous when young; tendrils long, forked. Lvs generally 7-parted, coarsely serrate, dark green above, paler beneath, glabrous; leaflets 3–6cm, oblong-obovate, cuneate at base. Infl. a lax cyme, 3–7cm diam.; fls tinged green. Fr. globose, 8–12mm, blue-black, inedible. Spring. Texas. Z9.

***P. heterophylla*** (Bl.) Merrill. Lvs compound, long-petiolate; leaflets 6–25×3–12cm, 3, or 1–2 on floral branches, coarsely crenate-serrate, lateral leaflets obliquely ovate-oblong, central one oblong, all shortly petiolulate, glabrous or pubesc. beneath. Infl. widely branched, glabrous; pet. patent, 4mm, green tinged yellow. Fr. red tinged black. China. Z8.

***P. himalayana*** (Royle) Planch. Vine, ascending, to 18m, deciduous; young stems partially woody, glabrous; tendrils with terminal adhesive disks. Lvs compound; petiole slender, 5–12cm; leaflets 5–15×4–10cm, 3, shortly petiolulate, central leaflet ovate, oval or obovate, lateral leaflets very obliquely ovate and often somewhat obliquely cordate at base, dentate, abruptly tapered to apex, dark green above, (becoming rich red in autumn), paler and somewhat glaucous beneath, glabrous above, very sparsely pubesc. on main vein beneath. Infl. laxly clustered, repeatedly forked; fls yellow tinged green. Fr. globose, 6mm, black. Late spring–summer. Himalaya. var. ***rubrifolia*** (Lév. & Vaniot) Gagnep. Leaflets smaller and relatively broader, tinged purple when young; infl. smaller. Taiwan, W China. Z9.

***P. inserta*** (A. Kerner) Fritsch. Vine, high-climbing, or shrubby; tendrils 3–5-branched, twining, without adhesive disks. Lvs palmately compound, glossy green (richly coloured in autumn), glabrous to thinly pubesc. beneath, long-petiolate; leaflets 5, elliptic to obovate, acutely serrate particularly in distal part, abruptly acuminate at apex, cuneate at base, sessile or petiolulate. Infl. forked at apex of peduncle, cymose with divergent branches forming a broadly rounded flower cluster. Fr. 6mm diam., almost black; seeds 3–4. Summer. N America (New England, Quebec west to Manitoba, south to Wyoming and Texas). 'Macrophylla': rough, hairy patches occasionally on young plants; lvs large, little autumn colour. Z3.

***P. laetevirens*** Rehd. Vine, high-climbing; tendrils thin, 5–8-branched. Lvs 5–10cm, elliptic to obovate, margins coarsely serrate, light green tinged yellow, glabrous, or sometimes pubesc. on veins beneath. Infl. paniculate, terminal, 15–25cm. Fr. 8mm diam., globose, dark blue; seeds 2–5. China (W Hupeh). Z9.

***P. quinquefolia*** (L.) Planch. VIRGINIA CREEPER; WOODBINE. Vine to 30m, glabrous throughout; stems slender, tinged red at first; tendrils 5–8-branched with numerous terminal adhesive disks with which the plant can attach itself to flat surfaces. Lvs or 3–5 radiating leaflets; petiole 2.5–10cm; leaflets 2.5–10cm×8–60mm, elliptic to obovate, acutely serrate particularly in distal part, abruptly acuminate at apex, cuneate at base, dull green above (rich crimson in autumn), paler and somewhat glaucous beneath, sessile or petiolulate. Infl. paniculate, terminal and from upper lf axils, fls in terminal umbellate clusters of 3–8; pet. deflexed, 3mm Fr. globose, 6mm diam., dark blue-black; seeds 2–3. Summer. E US (Maine west to Iowa & Kansas, south to Florida & Texas) to Mexico. 'Minor': 10–12 branchlets on tendrils; lvs broad, small, oval to elliptic. 'Murorum': tendrils short, abundant. var. ***engelmannii*** Rehd. Lvs smaller than species type. var. ***hirsuta*** Planch. Lvs and young stems softly white-pubesc. var. ***saint-paulii*** (Koehne & Gräbn.) Rehd. Tendrils 8–12-branched; lvs persistent in autumn, leaflets 12–15cm; infl. elongate. Z3.

***P. semicordata*** (Wallich) Planch. Similar to *P. himalayana* but young shoots setose; lvs smaller, setose beneath. Himalaya. Z9.

***P. tricuspidata*** (Sieb. & Zucc.) Planch. in DC. JAPANESE CREEPER; BOSTON IVY; VIRGINIA CREEPER. Vine, stems to 20m, climbing; young shoots glabrous; tendrils short, much-branched, with terminal adhesive disks. Lvs very variable, trifoliate, or suborbicular-deltoid, acuminately 3-lobed, or sometimes simple on young shoots, largest lvs to 20cm, green (rich crimson in autumn), glabrous above, pubesc. on veins beneath. Infl. on short shoots, in terminal thyrsoid panicles opposite lvs with several lateral branches; fls yellow tinged green; pet. deflexed, 3mm. Fr. somewhat flattened, 6–8mm diam., dull dark blue with bloom; seed 1–2. Summer. China, Japan. 'Atropurpurea': vigorous growth; lvs large, green tinged blue turning purple, red in spring and autumn. 'Aurata': lvs almost yellow, somewhat marbled green, red, rough margin. 'Beverley Brook': lvs exceptionally small, red in autumn. 'Green Spring': young lvs tinged red, later bright, glossy green above, dull beneath, to 25cm. 'Lowii'; MINIATURE JAPANESE IVY: smaller and more slender; lvs small, 2–3cm, 3–7-lobed, bright green tinged purple when young, colouring brilliant red in autumn; very elegant when young. 'Minutifolia': lvs large, glossy, later purple turning pink. 'Purpurea': lvs red tinged purple. 'Robusta': strong growth; lvs glossy, often trifoliate, red and orange in autumn. 'Veitchii' JAPANESE IVY: lvs small, simple or 3-foliate, coarsely crenate, with blistered variegation, purple when young. Z4.

***P. engelmannii*** Koehne & Gräbn. ex Gräbn. See *P. quinquefolia* var. *engelmannii*.
***P. henryi*** hort. See *P. henryana*.
***P. hirsuta*** Small. See *P. quinquefolia* var. *hirsuta*.
***P. inserens*** Hayek. See *P. inserta*.
***P. saint-paulii*** Koehne & Gräbn.. See *P. quinquefolia* var. *saint-paulii*.
***P. sinensis*** Diels & Gilg. See *P. himalayana* var. *rubrifolia*.
***P. spaethii*** Koehne & Gräbn. See *P. inserta*.
***P. thomsonii*** (Lawson) Planch. See *Cayratia thomsonii*.
***P. veitchii*** Gräbn. See *P. tricuspidata* 'Veitchii'.
***P. vitacea*** (Knerr) Hitchc. See *P. inserta*.
For further synonymy see *Ampelopsis, Cissus* and *Vitis*.

**Pasithea** D. Don. (For Pasithea (Aglaia), one of the three Graces.) Liliaceae (Asphodelaceae). 1 species, a rhizomatous perennial herb related to *Anthericum*. Leaves to 25cm, mostly basal, linear, grass-like, keeled. Scape slender, erect, exceeding leaves; flowers in loose, pyramidal panicles; perianth segments 6, basally united into a short tube, spreading, blue, inner segments paler than outer; stamens 6, 3 much shorter than the others. Fruit a small globose capsule. Chile. Z9.

CULTIVATION As for *Camassia*. Propagate from seed.

***P. caerulea*** (Ruiz & Pav.) D. Don. As for the genus.

**Paspalum** L. (From Gk *paspalos*, millet.) Gramineae. Some 330 species of glabrous to sparsely pubescent annual or perennial grasses. Stems flimsy to robust. Leaves narrow-linear to lanceolate or ovate, flat to rolled; ligules membranous. Inflorescence solitary, paired or clustered unilateral racemes; rachis winged; spikelets 2-flowered, solitary or paired, hemispherical to ovate, in 2–4 rows, awnless; lower flower sterile, upper flower hermaphrodite; lower glume absent or inconspicuous, upper glume and lower lemma equal spikelet, upper lemma usually obtuse, tough, involute. New World Tropics. Z8.

CULTIVATION Native to forest margins, savannahs and damp habitats, *Paspalum* spp. are valued as ornamentals for the branched spikes of flower, in which the individual florets are arranged in exceptionally neat and symmetrical formation along the raceme and, in *P. ceresia*, are clothed in long silver hairs. *P. ceresia* is tolerant of light, short-lived frost but may be grown in the cool glasshouse; *P. dilatatum* survives temperatures to −15°C/5°F. *P. notatum* is used as a coarse, low-maintenance, warm-season lawn grass. Grow in a sheltered position in a light, moderately fertile, porous soil in sun. Propagate by division or seed in early spring with gentle heat under glass.

***P. ceresia*** (Kuntze) Chase. Perenn., to 75cm. Stems flimsy, ascending. Lvs linear-lanceolate, to 20×1cm, flat, glabrous, glaucous. Racemes to 4 per infl., ascending, to 8cm; spikelets solitary, lanceolate to oblong, to 3mm, enveloped by silver hairs; ligules very short; anth. vivid yellow. Summer. Tropical S America.

***P. dilatatum*** Poir. DALLIS GRASS; PASPALUM. Perenn., to 180cm. Stems clumped, erect or ascending. Lvs linear, to 45cm×13mm. Racemes to 5, to 11cm; rachis winged; racemes borne on a central axis, to 20cm; spikelets elliptic to ovate, to 4mm, green tinged yellow; upper glume slightly pubesc.; lower lemma glabrous. Summer. S America, naturalized throughout US south of New Jersey.

***P. notatum*** Fluegge. BAHIA GRASS. Perenn. Stems to 50cm. Lvs flat or folded. Racemes to 7cm, recurved-ascending, mostly paired; spikelets to 2mm, ovate to obovate, smooth and glossy. Mexico, W Indies, S America; introduced US.

***P. racemosum*** Lam. Annual, to 90cm. Stems flimsy to robust, nodes dark brown. Lvs lanceolate to ovate, to 15×2.5cm glabrous; sheaths inflated. Infl. densely arranged; racemes to 80, beige to purple; spikelets solitary, elliptic, to 3cm. Autumn. Peru. Material under this name is often *P. elegans*.

***P. elegans*** Roem. & Schult. See *P. ceresia*.
***P. membranaceum*** Lam. See *P. ceresia*.
***P. stoloniferum*** Bosc. See *P. racemosum*.

**Passerina** L. (From Lat. *passer*, a sparrow; the beaked seed resembles the head of a sparrow.) Thymelaeaceae. 18 species of evergreen, heath-like shrubs. Leaves decussate, simple, entire. Flowers in spikes, 4-partite; calyx tubular with 4 lobes; petals absent; stamens 8, exserted. S Africa. Z9.

CULTIVATION Slow-growing, downy, heathlike shrubs, bearing conspicuously woolly flowers, *Passerina* spp. are frost tender, but suitable for cultivation in the alpine house or frame in temperate zones, where they can be protected from winter wet. Grow in a well-drained, gritty mix of equal parts loam, leafmould and coarse sharp sand. Water plentifully when in growth, and keep dry but not arid in winter. Topdress in early spring, and re-pot every other year. Propagate from semi-ripe cuttings as soon as suitable material becomes available.

***P. ericoides*** L. Branches short, slender, numerous, downy at first. Lvs closely adpressed to branches, 2mm, linear to ovate-oblong, tips blunt, thick, glabrous. Fls in short terminal spikes of about 8, borne on lateral twigs; bracts oblong, 2mm, interior white-woolly; cal. tube ovoid, 3mm, lobes elliptic, concave, obtuse, 2mm. S Africa.

***P. filiformis*** L. Tall, upright, lax shrub to 1.5m; stems grey-downy. Lvs many, erect, usually opposite, clothing stem, to 8mm, triangular in cross section, margins incurved, tips pointed and often incurved. Fls small, numerous, in dense spikes of about 12; bracts slightly wider than lvs, ovate, 5mm, exterior glabrous, interior woolly; cal. tube short, 5mm, ovoid toward base, cylindric and slender in upper part, lobes 3mm, spreading, elliptical, glabrous; stigma like a mop. Fr. dry, enclosed in base of cal. tube. S Africa.

***P. hirsuta*** Endl. See *Thymelaea hirsuta*.

**Passiflora** L. (From Lat. *passio*, passion and *flos*, flower, hence 'passion flower'. The name was given by the early Spanish missionaries in South America, in reference to a fancied representation in the flowers of the implements of the Crucifixion; the corona represented the crown of thorns, the five anthers the five wounds, the three styles the three nails, the five sepals and five petals the apostles, less Peter and Judas, and the hand-like leaves and flagellate tendrils the hands and scourges of Christ's persecutors.) PASSION FLOWER. Passifloraceae. Some 500 species of vines or scandent shrubs, sometimes erect herbs, shrubs or small trees. Shoots often angular, furnished with long, tightly spiralling tendrils arising at axils. Leaves alternate, extremely variable in shape, usually 3–5-lobed, sometimes bilobed or entire; petioles often with stalked glands. Flowers regular, bisexual, usually solitary, sometimes paired and axillary or in very short terminal cymes, usually subtended by 3 green bracts; calyx cupped to tubular, sepals 5, fleshy or membranous; petals 5, sometimes absent; filaments in several series, forming a showy corona, between petals and stamens; stamens 5 on a gynophore, anthers linear, ovate or oblong, 2-celled; stigma capitate; styles 3; ovary globose, ovoid or fusiform. Fruit usually a juicy, indehiscent, many-seeded berry; seeds compressed, reticulate, puncticulate or transversely furrowed. Tropical Americas, Asia, Australia, Polynesia.

CULTIVATION Grown as ornamentals for their exquisitely beautiful, intricately formed and often fragrant and nectar-rich flowers, and for their attractive, sometimes edible fruits; a number are grown commercially for their fruits in the subtropics and in tropical highlands. The fruits of many species are eaten raw, or in some cases used to prepare drinks, ice cream, pies, sauces and so on; some are canned in syrup or candied. *P. ligularis* is considered by many to be the best edible species, while *P. alata, P. laurifolia, P. mollissima* and *P. quadrangularis* are also widely cultivated for fruit.

Few species are sufficiently cold tolerant for outdoor cultivation in cool temperate zones. They include the more or less evergreen *P. caerulea*, which with the protection of a sheltered wall will survive occasional lows down to −15°C/5°F; in cooler conditions it may be regarded as a herbaceous perennial since with sufficient protection at the root it will resprout from the base in spring. *P. incarnata*, with a truly herbaceous habit, will resprout from the base if given deep mulch protection where temperatures fall to −20°C/−4°F. *P. lutea*, also herbaceous, is the hardiest species, occurring as far north as Pennsylvania, and surviving given similar treatment temperatures to −25°C/−13°F. They are fairly undemanding in their soil requirements, thriving in any moderately fertile, well-drained and adequately moisture-retentive soil, in sun or part-day shade. Provide the support of wire or trellis and, in less favoured areas, site with shelter from cold, drying winds, mulch with leafmould, bracken litter and a covering of evergreen branches, protecting top-growth with burlap or hessian if necessary. The remaining species need protected cultivation in cool temperate zones, making uniquely handsome and, under suitable conditions, productive specimens for the glasshouse or conservatory. *P. edulis, P. ×allardii, P. antioquiensis, P. caerulea-racemosa, P. ×exoniensis, P. ligularis, P. manicata* and *P. mollissima* will tolerate winter temperatures as low as 5°C/40°F, although they may defoliate in these conditions, and are better maintained with minima at 7–10°C/45–50°F. Most of the remaining species require a temperature range of 13–16°C/55–60°F.

When grown for fruit, warm conditions are necessary (*c*16°C/60°F) during flowering to ensure good pollination and fruit set, temperatures thereafter being less critical. Hand pollination using unrelated clones, or *P. caerulea*, and spraying with tomato setting hormone for seedless fruit, helps ensure good fruiting; *P. quadrangularis* is self sterile, and in *P. edulis* pollen is usually shed before the pistils are receptive. *P. coccinea* and *P. vitifolia*, amongst the most handsome of ornamentals, are also self sterile but will fruit if hand-pollinated.

Grow all species in a freely draining, fibrous loam-based mix with additional leafmould and sharp sand; *Passiflora* spp. are generally unfastidious as to soil type, given good drainage, but perform best on soils of only moderate fertility, especially with regard to nitrogen, which encourages foliar growth at the expense of flowering. They are best grown in large pots or tubs, or, if grown in the open border, with some root restriction. Provide full sun with shade from the hottest sun in summer, water plentifully when in growth, sparingly at other times. Prune to prevent overcrowding by removing the weakest shoots in spring, and again if necessary after flowering, pinching out unwanted growth regularly during the growing season; spur back to an established framework in spring. Propagate by heel or nodal cuttings rooted in individual pots in a sandy propagating medium in a closed case or by seed. Evidence suggests that a number of frost-tender species show greater tolerance to low soil temperatures when grafted on to *P. caerulea*, and it may be a worthwhile experiment to grow and fruit *P. edulis*, for example, on *P. caerulea* rootstock in more favoured temperate gardens. Provide a warm south- or southwest-facing wall and train as a single-stemmed specimen on support low enough to allow winter protection with straw and burlap/hessian or frame lights.

***P. actinia*** Hook. Stems vining, slender, subcylindric, glabrous. Lvs to 10×8cm, broad-oval or suborbicular, apex usually notched, base rounded or somewhat tapered, subpeltate, entire, glabrous, often glaucous beneath, subcoriaceous or membranous, 5–7-veined; stipules to 4×2cm, ovate; petioles slender, to 5cm, 4-glandular. Fls to 9cm diam., fragrant; pedicels slender, to 3cm; cal. campanulate, glabrous, white inside, green outside, sep. to 1.5cm diam., oblong-lanceolate, obtuse; pet. to 2×1cm, white; fil. 4–5-seriate the outermost to 3cm, banded blue, white and red. Fr. glabrous. Spring–summer. SE Brazil. Z10.

***P. adenopoda*** DC. Stems vining, angular, subglabrous or hispidulous. Lvs to 12×15cm, 3–5-lobed, lobes ovate, apex abruptly acuminate, base cordate, entire or denticulate, hispidulous, 3–5-veined; stipules 1×1.5cm, suborbicular; petioles to 5cm, pubesc., biglandular. Fls to 7cm diam.; pedicels to 2.5cm; sep. to 4×1cm, oblong-lanceolate, obtuse; pet. to 12×5mm, green-white to ivory, linear-lanceolate; fil. 1-seriate. Fr. to 2.5cm diam., globose, minutely-pubesc.; seeds 6×4mm, obcordate, reticulate. Mexico to Venezuela, E Peru. Z10.

***P. alata*** C. Curtis. Stems vining, stout, glabrous, with 4 winged angles. Lvs to 15×10cm, simple, ovate or ovate-oblong, apex acuminate, base rounded to subcuneate, entire or denticulate, membranous, glabrous, penninerved; stipules to 2×1cm, linear to ovate-lanceolate, entire or serrulate; petioles to 5cm, canaliculate, 2–4-glandular. Fls to 12cm diam., fragrant; pedicels to 2.5cm; sep. oblong, obtuse, glabrous green to white beneath, pale crimson above; pet. oblong, obtuse brilliant carmine; fil. 4-seriate to 3cm, banded purple red and white. Fr. to 10×6cm, obovoid or pyriform, glabrous, yellow. Spring–summer. NE Peru, E Brazil. 'Ruby Glow': fr. yellow, grapefruit-sized. Z10.

***P. ×alato-caerulea***. (*P. alata* × *P. caerulea*.) Stems angular, narrow-alate. Lvs trilobed, entire. Fls to 10cm diam., pink to purple, white outside; sep. white inside; fil. triseriate, blue-violet, white at apex. Garden origin. 'Imperatrice Eugénie': lvs 3-lobed; fls to 16cm diam., sep. white, pet. lilac-pink, fil. white and mauve. Z9.

***P. ×allardii*** Lynch. (*P. caerulea* 'Constance Elliot' × *P. quadrangularis*.) Vigorous. Lvs usually trilobed. Fls to 11.5cm diam., white, suffused pink; fil. deep cobalt-blue. Summer–autumn. Raised in 1907 by E.J. Allard in the University of Cambridge Botanic Garden. Z9.

***P. ×amabilis*** Lem. Stems vining, vigorous, slender, cylindric or subcylindric, glabrous. Lvs to 12×9cm, ovate-oblong or ovate-lanceolate, apex short-acute, base subcordate, entire, membranous, glabrous, penninerved or subtrinerved; stipules ovate-lanceolate, 1.5×0.3cm, acuminate, caducous; petioles to 4cm, slender, 2–4-glandular. Fls to 9cm diam.; pedicels to 4cm; cal. 1.5×1.5cm, short-tubular, glabrous, bright red inside, green outside, sep. 3.5×1cm, linear-oblong or linear-lanceolate; pet. similar to sep., bright red; fil. 4-seriate, white. Fr. glabrous. Spring. S Brazil. Z10. cf. *P. violacea*.

***P. amethystina*** Mikan. Stems vigorous, vining, slender, cylindric, glabrous or sparsely and weakly downy. Lvs to 6×10cm, trilobed, lobes oblong, apex obtuse, base cordate and often peltate, membranous, glabrous, somewhat glaucous beneath, 5-veined; stipules to 1×0.4cm, ovate-lanceolate, aristate; petioles to 4.5cm, 5–8-glandular. Fls to 8cm diam.; pedicels to 5cm; cal. campanulate, green, sep. to 6mm diam., oblong, carinate, sharp-tipped bright blue inside, green outside; pet. to 8mm diam., deeper in colour than sep., oblong, obtuse; fil. 4–5-seriate, to 2.5cm, dark purple; styles connate at base. Fr. ellipsoid, to 6×2.5cm, subglabrous. Autumn. E Brazil. Z10.

***P. antioquiensis*** Karst. BANANA PASSION FRUIT. Stems vining or sprawling, slender, cylindric, minutely rusty-pubesc. or tomentose. Lvs to 15×8cm, dimorphic, ovate to lanceolate, or trilobed, lobes lanceolate, subcordate or rounded at base, irregularly sharp-serrate, pubesc. or glabrous, lanuginose beneath; stipules to 7mm, subulate; petioles to 4cm, stout, glandular, lanuginose. Fls to 12.5cm diam.; pedicels to 50cm, lanuginose; cal. to 4cm, narrowly tubular, glabrous, rose-red or magenta, sep. to 6.5×2.5cm, oblong-lanceolate, obtuse; pet. oblong-lanceolate, obtuse, often of a deeper shade than sep.; fil. 3-seriate, corona small, violet. Fr. ellipsoid. Summer. Colombia. Z9.

***P. arborea*** Spreng. Tree or shrub to 10m. Branches alternate, cylindric, glabrous, initially rufous young. Lvs to 30×15cm, oblong or obovate-oblong, apex acute or briefly-acuminate, base rounded or subcuneate, membranous or subcoriaceous, bright green above, glaucous or with minute hairs on veins beneath, penninerved; petioles to 3cm. Fls to 7.5cm diam. clustered 3–6 on nodding axillary, peduncles to 6cm; cal. to 1×0.5cm, cylindric-campanulate, sep.

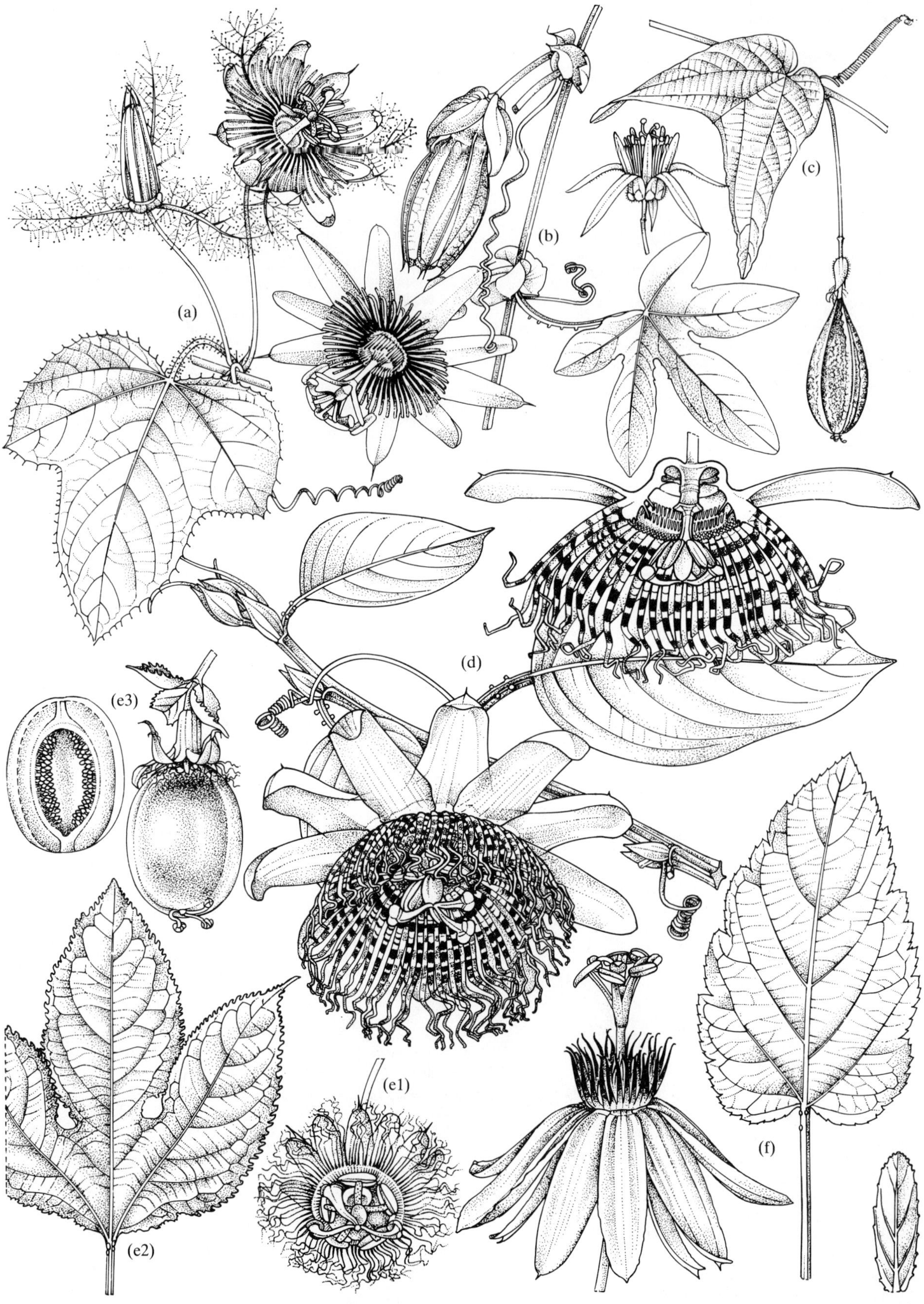


**Passiflora** (×0.66) (a) *P. foetida* (b) *P. caerulea* (c) *P. capsularis* fruiting branch, flower detached (d) *P. quadrangularis*, flowering branch, flower LS (e1) *P. edulis*, flower (e2) *P. edulis*, leaf (e3) *P. edulis* fruit and fruit LS (f) *P. coccinea* flower, leaf, bract to 3×1.2cm, green-white, linear-oblong, obtuse; pet. linear-oblong, obtuse close to sep. in colour, usually slightly less green; fil. triseriate, yellow. Fr. to 4×2.5cm, ovoid, somewhat yellow; seeds 6×3mm, ovate, punctate. Summer. Colombia. Z10.

***P.×atropurpurea*** Nichols. *(P. racemosa × P. kermesina.)* Fls dark blood-red, 7.5cm diam.; sep. purple inside; fil. violet, spotted white.

***P.aurantia*** Forst. f. Stems vining, angular, glabrous. Lvs to 7.5cm, shallowly trilobed, lobes ovate, blunt, acute sometimes lobulate. Fls to 10cm diam., bracts setiform; sep. pale pink deepening to orange-red, linear-oblong; pet. orange to brick red; fil. deep red, those of inner series forming a broad tube, those of outer to 2cm, united at base. Fr. 4cm, ovoid. Summer. Australia (Queensland). Z10.

***P.biflora*** Lam. Stems vining, 5-angled, furrowed, twisted, green or purple-green, subglabrous. Lvs to 10×10cm, narrowly suborbicular to reniform, sometimes bilobed, lobes lanceolate or ovate, apex usually acuminate, base truncate to cuneate, coriaceous, glabrous above, glabrous or minute-pubesc. beneath, reticulately 3-veined; stipules narrow linear-subulate or setiform, to 3mm; petioles to 3cm, eglandular. Fls to 3.5cm diam.; pedicels to 3cm; cal. patelliform or campanulate, white and glabrous inside, green and minute-pubesc. or subglabrous outside, sep. to 12×7mm, ovate-lanceolate, obtuse; pet. 8×5mm, white; corona 2.5cm diam., yellow, fil. biseriate; styles connate at base. Fr. to 2cm diam., globose, glabrous to dense minute-pubesc.; seeds to 3×2.5mm, obovoid, transverse-sulcate. Summer. Mexico to Colombia, Venezuela, Ecuador and Bahamas. Z10.

***P.bryonioides*** HBK. Stems vining, obtuse-angular or subcylindric, hispidulous. Lvs to 7×9cm, deeply trilobed, lobes oblong, lateral lobes themselves sometimes bilobed, apex acute or obtuse, base cordate, entire or dentate, hispidulous, 3–5-veined; stipules 5×2.5mm semi-ovate, cuspidate, ciliate; petioles to 5cm, biglandular, pubesc. Fls to 3cm diam.; pedicels to 3cm; cal. patelliform or campanulate, green-white, sep. to 13×5mm, ovate-lanceolate, obtuse or subacute; pet. 4×1mm, white, linear or linear-lanceolate; corona white, fil. 1-seriate; styles connate at base. Fr. to 3.5×2.5cm, ovoid; seeds 4×2.5mm, ovate, close-reticulate. SW US (Arizona), Mexico. Often confused with *P. morifolia*, which has purple fr. at maturity. Z8.

***P.caerulea*** L. PASSION FLOWER; BLUE PASSION FLOWER. Stems robust, subangular, striate, furrowed, glabrous, sometimes glaucous. Lvs to 10×2.5cm, palmately 5-, sometimes 3-, 7- or 9-, lobed, lobes oblong, apex obtuse or emarginate, base cordate, membranous, glabrous; stipules to 2×1cm, ovate; petioles to 4cm, 2–4-, rarely 6-, glandular. Fls to 10cm diam., faintly fragrant; pedicels to 7cm, usually stout; cal. cupulate, subcoriaceous, glabrous, white or pink-white inside, green outside, sep. to 2×1.5cm, oblong, obtuse; pet. to 2.5×1.5cm, oblong, obtuse, thin-textured, of a slightly clearer colour than sep. fil. 4-seriate, broadly banded, blue at apex, white at centre, purple at base. Fr. 6×4cm, ovoid or subglobose, glabrous, orange or yellow; seeds 5×4mm, obcordate or cuneate, coarse-reticulate. Summer–autumn. Brazil, Argentina. 'Constance Eliott': fls ivory white. 'Grandiflora': fls to 15cm diam. Z7.

***P.×caerulea-racemosa.*** *(P. caerulea × P. racemosa.)* Lvs deeply 5-lobed, glabrous. Fls dark violet, solitary; fil. deep purple-violet. 'Eynsford Gem': fls pink-mauve; fil. white. Z9.

***P.capsularis*** L. Stems vining, 3–5-angular, striate, subglabrous or pubesc. Lvs to 7×10cm, bilobed, lobes downward-pointing, lanceolate, apex acute, base cordate, subglabrous or pilosulous above, lighter and densely-pubesc. beneath, 3-veined; stipules linear-subulate, to 7mm; petioles to 3cm, eglandular. Fls to 6cm diam.; pedicels to 6cm, slender; cal. to 3cm×4mm, patelliform or campanulate, pilose, sep. linear-lanceolate, acute, green-white; pet. to 1.5×0.4cm, ivory, narrow oblong-lanceolate or subspathulate, obtuse; fil. yellow-white, 1–2-seriate; styles connate at base. Fr. to 6×2cm, ellipsoid or fusiform ridged and angled, ripening purple-red; seeds 3.5mm, ovate, transverse-sulcate. Summer. Nicaragua to C Brazil to Paraguay, Greater Antilles. Z10.

***P.×cardinalis*** hort. ex Mast. *(P. alata × P. racemosa (?).)* Intermediate between parents. Fls red, 7.5cm diam. Z10.

***P.cheilidonea*** Mast. Stems vining, angular, striate, lanuginose. Lvs to 14×8cm, oblong-lanceolate, bilobed or trilobed, lobes lanceolate, (the central lobe often reduced or merely a mucro in the apical sinus), apex acute, base subcordate or rounded, coriaceous, glabrous; stipules narrow-linear, acuminate; petioles to 2cm, somewhat purple. Fls to 5cm diam.; peduncles to 2cm; cal. glossy, sep. 2.5×1.2cm, yellow green, oblong-lanceolate; pet. 1.2×0.4cm, of a somewhat clearer colour; fil. biseriate, white, the outermost spotted violet. Fr. 1.5cm diam., globose, seeds 4×2.5mm, obovoid, transverse-sulcate. Summer. Colombia, Ecuador. Z10.

***P.cinnabarina*** Lindl. Stems slender, glabrous. Lvs to 10×10cm, usually trilobed, lobes ovate, cordate at base; petioles eglandular. Fls 6.5cm diam.; bracts setiform; sep. 2.5×1cm, bright scarlet, narrow-oblong; pet. vivid scarlet, to 1.25cm; fil. erect, corona yellow. Spring–summer. Australia. Z10.

***P.coccinea*** Aubl. RED PASSION FLOWER; RED GRANADILLA. Stems vining, subcylindric, obtuse-angular, deep-furrowed, finely rufous minutely-pubesc. to tomentose, somewhat purple. Lvs to 14×7cm, oblong, rarely suborbicular, apex acute to subobtuse, base subcordate, biserrate or crenate, membranous, subglabrous or minute-pubesc. above, tomentose beneath; stipules linear, to 6mm; petioles to 3.5cm, eglandular or biglandular at base. Fls to 12.5cm diam.; pedicels stout, to 8cm; cal. to 2×1.3cm, cylindric-campanulate, sep. to 5×1cm, exterior yellow, interior scarlet, linear-lanceolate, acute; pet. to 4×0.8cm, vivid scarlet, linear, acute; fil. triseriate, pale pink to white at base, deep purple toward apex. Fr. 5cm diam., ovoid or subglobose, finely tomentose, orange or yellow, green-striate and -mottled; seeds 6×4mm, narrow-obovate, minutely reticulate. Guianas, S Venezuela, Peru, Bolivia, Brazil. Z10.

***P.×colvillii*** Sweet. *(P. caerulea × P. incarnata.)* Lvs deep 3–5-lobed, dentate. Fls 9cm diam., white, rufous-spotted; fil. corona banded purple, white and blue. Z7.

***P.coriacea*** Juss. BAT-LEAF PASSION FLOWER. Stems vining, angular, densely and minutely when young. Lvs to 7×25cm, usually 2–3-lobed, lobes oblong-ovate, acute, rarely obtuse, broadly divergent, the whole lf. peltate, coriaceous, glabrous, reticulately 5-veined. Fls to 3.5cm diam., solitary and axillary, or in terminal racemes to 6cm; cal. patelliform or campanulate, yellow-green above, sep. to 1.5×0.5cm, oblong-lanceolate, obtuse; pet. absent; fil. ivory, biseriate; styles connate at base. Fr. to 2cm diam., globose, glabrous; seeds 4×2mm, obcordate to obovate, curved, beaked, coarsely reticulate. Mexico to N Peru and N Bolivia, Guyana. Z10.

***P.×decaisneana*** Planch. *(P. alata × P. quadrangularis.)* Fls 10cm diam., brilliant carmine; fil. purple and white. Also arising from this cross is the hybrid named as *P. ×innesii* Mast. (strictly a synonym) with fls off-white, speckled red; sep. white inside; corona fil. several-seriate, white, banded red at base, spotted violet above, apex white. Garden origin. Z10.

***P.edulis*** Sims. GRANADILLA; PURPLE GRANADILLA; PASSION FRUIT. Stems vining, bluntly angled, somewhat lanuginose or glabrous. Lvs to 10×20cm, deeply trilobed, lobes ovate, glandular-dentate, shiny above, glabrous; petioles biglandular. Fls to 7.5cm diam.; bracts 12.5mm+; sep. oblong, spreading, white above, green beneath; pet. somewhat narrower and paler than sep.; fil. white banded purple or indigo, strongly wavy towards tips. Fr. 5cm diam., ovoid, green-yellow to dull purple, speckled. Summer. Brazil. f. *edulis*. Fr. yellow. 'Alice': fls abundant; fr. egg-shaped, purple. 'Crackerjack': fr. large, deep purple to black, abundant. 'Purple Passion': fls purple. 'Supreme': fr. large, rounded. Additional purple-fruited cvs include 'Black Knight', 'Edgehill', 'Frederick', 'Purple Giant', 'Red Giant', 'Red Rover' and 'Sunnypash' (usually grafted on *P. caerulea*; very adaptable). f. *flavicarpa* Degen. Yellow-fruited cultivars include 'Brazilian Golden' and 'Golden Giant'. Z10.

***P.eichleriana*** Mast. Stems vining, slender, cylindric, glabrous, somewhat purple. Lvs to 8×10cm, trilobed, lobes oblong, apex mucronate, base cordate and subpeltate, entire, membranous, glabrous, 5-veined; stipules to 3×1.5cm, oblong-lanceolate, acuminate; petioles to 6cm, 6–8-glandular. Fls to 7cm diam.; pedicels to 6cm; cal. campanulate, glabrous, sep. 1cm diam., white-green, oblong, subcoriaceous; pet. white, oblong, membranous; fil. 6-seriate. Fr. 3.5cm diam., globose, coriaceous, glabrous. E Brazil, Paraguay. Sometimes confused with *P. subpeltata* or misnamed as its synonym *P. alba*. Z10.

***P.×exoniensis*** hort. ex L.H. Bail. *(P. antioquiensis × P. mollissima.)* Stems vining, initially lanuginose. Lvs to 10×12.5cm, base cordate, lanuginose, deeply trilobed; petioles 2.5cm, biglandular. Fls to 12.5cm diam., pendulous; cal. 6.5cm, tubular-cylindric, glabrous, exterior brick red, interior rosy pink, sep. oblong-lanceolate; pet. bright pink with a violet tint in the throat, oblong-lanceolate; corona small, somewhat white. Raised in 1870 by Veitch in Exeter. Z10.

***P.filamentosa*** Cav. Stems tall, vining, cylindric, lanuginose. Lvs to 8×12cm, usually palmately 5–7-lobed, lobes to 3cm diam., oblong-lanceolate, slightly toothed apex acuminate, base cordate, membranous, glossy above, glabrous or minutely villous; stipules to 4×1.5mm, aristate, asymmetrically serrulate, caducous; petioles to 4cm, biglandular. Fls to 8cm diam.; pedicels to 5cm; cal. campanulate, white, sep. to 1cm diam., narrow-oblong, obtuse; pet. similar in shape to sep., white tinted rose fil. several-seriate, white, the outermost banded blue. Fr. 4cm diam., globose; seeds 10×7mm, obcordate, broad-alate at margins, punctate. Autumn. C Brazil. Z10.

***P.foetida*** L. RUNNING POP; LOVE-IN-A-MIST; WILD WATER LEMON. Stems vining, malodorous when crushed. Shoots viscid, densely hairy. Lvs hastate, 3–5-lobed, thin-textured, adpressed-pubesc., glandular-ciliate; petioles to 6cm, eglandular. Fls to 5cm diam., subtended by 3 showy, deeply and finely glandular-fringed involucral bracts; pedicels to 6cm; cal. white to ivory streaked green, sep. ovate; pet. oblong, ivory; fil. several-striate white banded violet. Fr. to 2.5cm diam., globose or subglobose, sparsely, rarely densely, hirsute, yellow to bright red; seeds 5×2.5mm, ovate-cuneate, tridentate, coarse-reticulate. Summer–autumn. South America, Puerto Rico, Jamaica, Lesser Antilles. Z10.

***P.galbana*** Mast. Stems slender, vining, cylindric, somewhat flexuous, glabrous. Lvs to 13×6.5cm, oblong-lanceolate, entire, apex obtuse and mucronulate, base rounded or shallow-cordate, coriaceous, glabrous; stipules to 2×1cm, ovate-lanceolate, acute; petioles to 1.5cm, minutely-glandular. Fls on stout cylindric pedicels to 9cm, cal., fragrant, opening at night, broadly cylindric-campanulate, glabrous, sep. 4×0.7cm, narrow-oblong, white, horned; pet. 6.5mm diam., narrow-oblong, white to primrose yellow; fil. biseriate, to 12.5mm. Fr. to 7×2cm, narrow-ovoid, tapered at apex, glabrous; seeds to 5×3.5mm, obovate. Winter. E Brazil. Z10.

***P. garckei*** Mast. Stems vining, cylindric, or somewhat angular above, glabrous. Lvs to 15×25cm, trilobed, lobes oblong-lanceolate, apex acute to obtuse, base truncate or subcordate, subpeltate, entire or subentire, coriaceous, glabrous, reticulately 5–7-veined; stipules to 5×2cm, ovate or subreniform, mucronate; petioles to 10cm, 4–6-glandular. Fls to 8.5cm diam.; pedicels to 6cm; cal. campanulate, glabrous, sep. to 4×1cm, blue or purple above, oblong, cucullate; pet. to 3.5×1.2cm, lilac, oblong, obtuse; fil. several-seriate, white with a broad central violet band. Fr. subellipsoid, glabrous. Autumn. French Guiana, Guyana, Surinam. Z10.

***P. glandulosa*** Cav. Stems vining, cylindric or subangular, glabrous or minute-pubesc., purple-tinted. Lvs to 15×10cm, ovate-oblong to oblong-lanceolate, apex acute or acuminate and mucronulate, base cordulate to subacute, entire or somewhat undulate, glaucous, glabrous or minutely-pubesc. beneath, coriaceous; stipules linear-subulate or setiform, caducous; petioles to 2.5cm, biglandular. Fls red or scarlet; peduncles to 8cm; cal. to 2.5×1cm, cylindric, sep. to 5cm×13mm, oblong; fil. to 1.25cm, biseriate, pink. Fr. to 6×3cm, ovoid; seeds 8×4mm, obovate, finely reticulate. Spring. Guianas, Surinam, E Brazil. Z10.

***P. gracilis*** Jacq. ex Link. Stems vining, slender, subangular, glabrous. Lvs to 7×10cm, trilobed, lobes obtuse or rounded, cordate at base, entire, membranous, glabrous, glaucous beneath, 3-veined. Fls 2cm diam.; pedicels to 3cm; cal. patelliform or campanulate, sep. to 1×0.3cm, white to pale green, narrow-oblong, obtuse, concave; pet. absent; corona to 2cm diam., fil. biseriate; styles connate at base. Fr. 2.5×1.5cm, ellipsoid, glabrous, scarlet; seeds 4×3mm, subglobose. Summer. Venezuela. Z10.

***P. hahnii*** (Fourn.) Mast. Stems vining, slender, cylindric, angular, striate, glabrous. Lvs to 8×7cm, broadly ovate-lanceolate, entire, peltate at base, membranous, glabrous, 3–5-veined, minutely toothed, purple-tinted beneath; stipules to 4×2cm, crenate to entire, tinged purple; petioles to 3cm, eglandular. Fls to 6cm diam., white or cream; pedicels to 7cm; cal. patelliform or campanulate, glabrous, sep. and pet. to 3×1cm, oblong, obtuse; fil. biseriate, yellow; styles connate at base. Fr. to 3.5cm diam., globose, glabrous; seeds 5×4mm, ovate-oblong, somewhat curved, reticulate. Summer–autumn. C Mexico to Costa Rica, Colombia. Z10.

***P. herbertiana*** Ker-Gawl. Stems robust, vining or scandent, lanuginose. Lvs 9×9cm, trilobed, lobes triangular, truncate, lanuginose. Fls to 10cm diam., solitary or paired, white to pale orange-yellow, solitary or paired; sep. 4cm, linear-lanceolate; pet. to 2cm; corona broadly tubular, yellow, fil. to 1.25cm. Australia. Z10.

***P. holosericea*** L. Stems vining, cylindric, striate, corky below, usually lanuginose above. Lvs to 10×7cm, trilobed, lobes rounded, apex mucronulate, base cordate and bidentate, entire, velutinous-pubesc. above, dense soft-tomentose beneath, reticulately 3-veined; stipules 6mm; petioles to 2.5cm, biglandular. Fls to 4cm diam., fragrant, solitary or on 2–4-fld peduncles; cal. patelliform or campanulate, glabrous inside, densely-pubesc. outside, sep. to 1.5×0.5cm, white, ovate-lanceolate, obtuse; pet. to 1.3×0.6cm, white spotted red, oblanceolate or spathulate; fil. biseriate, yellow, purple at base; styles connate at base. Fr. 1.5cm diam., globose, glabrous or soft-pubesc.; seeds 3×2mm, obovate-obcordate, coarsely-reticulate. Mexico, Central America, C & W Cuba, N Colombia, N Venezuela. Z10.

***P. incarnata*** L. WILD PASSION FLOWER; MAY POPS; APRICOT VINE; MAY APPLE. Stems vining, cylindric, angular when young, glabrous or finely lanuginose. Lvs to 15×15cm, trilobed, lobes lanceolate, apex acute or acuminate, base cordate, finely serrate, membranous, deep green above, somewhat glaucous beneath, 3-veined; stipules to 3mm, setiform, caducous; petioles to 8cm, biglandular. Fls to 7.5cm diam.; sep. pale lavender with a horn-like apical projection; pet. white or pale lavender; fil. usually pink to purple. Fr. to 5cm, ovoid, yellow. E US. Z6.

***P. insignis*** (Mast.) Hook. Stems vining, cylindric, densely lanuginose. Lvs to 25×12cm, ovate-lanceolate, apex acute, base minutely cordate, denticulate, coriaceous, shiny, glabrous and rugulose above, densely rusty-woolly beneath, 3–5-veined; stipules 2×1cm, bipinnatisect; petioles to 2cm, 2–4-glandular. Fls pendulous; pedicels stout, to 20cm; cal. to 4cm×8mm, tubular-cylindric, tomentose, violet-crimson, sep. to 9×2cm, oblong, obtuse, concave; pet. to 7×1.5cm, rose-purple, oblong, obtuse; fil. 12.5mm, 1-seriate, white, mottled blue. Summer–autumn. Bolivia, Peru. Z10.

***P. jamesonii*** (Mast.) L.H. Bail. Stems vining, angular, glabrous. Lvs to 8×11cm, glabrous, trilobed, lobes subelliptic, apex acute or subobtuse and mucronate, base subcordate, spiny-dentate, subcoriaceous, glossy above; stipules to 2.5×0.8cm, oblong-lanceolate, deep-cleft. Fls to 10cm diam., pendulous; pedicels to 10cm; bracts deeply laciniate; cal. to 10cm, tubular-cylindric, bright rose glabrous, sep. to 5×2cm, oblong, obtuse; pet. rose to coral pink, oblong, obtuse; corona tinged purple. Fr. glabrous. Ecuador (Andes). Z9.

***P. jorullensis*** HBK. Stems vining, slender, subtriangular, dense-pubesc. Lvs to 8.5×8cm, bilobed or trilobed the third lobe often reduced to a mucro in the sinus, lobes rounded or subacute, apex mucronulate, base subcuneate or truncate, minutely pubesc. above, glabrous beneath, reticulately 3-veined; stipules setiform, to 3mm; petioles to 4cm, furrowed, eglandular. Fls to 4cm diam., orange turning pink; pedicels to 3cm; cal. patelliform or campanulate, glabrous, sep. 1.5cm×3mm, linear-lanceolate, acute; pet. to 4×1mm, slender, linear, obtuse; fil. 1-seriate, orange then pink almost equalling sep.; styles connate at base. Fr. 1cm diam., globose, glabrous, glossy black; seeds 3×2mm, obovate, transverse-sulcate. Autumn. C & S Mexico. Z10.

***P. kermesina*** Link & Otto. Stems vining, slender, cylindric, glabrous. Lvs to 8×10cm, trilobed, lobes oblong-ovate, apex rounded or subacute, base truncate or cordate, membranous, glabrous, deep green above, somewhat glaucous and purple-tinted beneath; stipules to 2.5×1.2cm, subreniform, rounded, glaucous beneath; petioles to 4cm, minutely 2–4-glandular. Fls to 8cm diam.; pedicels to 15cm, slender, tribracteate; cal. 1cm, cylindric-campanulate, glabrous, sep. to 4cm×7mm, linear-oblong, scarlet, obtuse, radiate, later reflexed; pet. similar to sep. fil. 3–4-seriate, violet-purple; styles connate at base. Fr. glabrous. E Brazil. Z10.

***P. ×kewensis*** hort. (*P. caerulea* × *P. kermesina*.) Fls 9cm diam., carmine, suffused-blue. Z8.

***P. laurifolia*** L. YELLOW GRANADILLA; WATER LEMON; JAMAICA HONEYSUCKLE; BELLE APPLE; VINEGAR PEAR; POMME-DE-LIANE. Stems vining, cylindric, glabrous. Lvs to 12×8cm, ovate-oblong or oblong, subacute to obtuse, apex usually mucronate, base rounded, entire, coriaceous, glossy, glabrous, strongly reticulately 1-veined; stipules to 4mm, narrow-linear, coriaceous; petioles to 1.5cm, stout, biglandular. Fls to 7cm diam.; pedicels to 3cm, rarely to 8cm; cal. to 1cm, cylindric-campanulate, glabrous, sep. to 2.5×1cm, green beneath, red above, oblong, obtuse; pet. similar to sep.; fil. 6-seriate, outermost purple banded red, blue and white. Fr. to 8×4cm, ovoid, glabrous, lemon-yellow or orange; seeds to 7×5mm, obcordate, finely reticulate. Summer. E Brazil, Peru, Venezuela, Guianas, W Indies, Trinidad. Z10.

***P. ×lawsoniana*** Mast. (*P. alata* × *P. racemosa*.) Lvs ovate-oblong, cordate at base. Fls to 10cm diam., somewhat red; sep. rufous. Z10.

***P. ligularis*** Juss. GRANADILLA; SWEET GRANADILLA. Stems vining, vigorous, cylindric, glabrous. Lvs to 15×13cm, broadly ovate, apex abruptly acuminate, base deeply cordate, entire, membranous, glabrous, blue-green beneath, penninerved; stipules to 2.5×1.2cm, lanceolate; petioles to 10cm, 4–6-glandular, with filiform glands. Fls to 9cm diam., pedicels to 4cm; cal. campanulate, glabrous, sep. to 3.5×1.5cm, green-white beneath, white or rosy above, ovate-oblong, acute; pet. similar to sep. but smaller; fil. 5–7-seriate, white banded, purple, the outer series equalling pet. Fr. to 8×5cm, ovoid, glabrous; seeds 6×4mm, narrow-obcordate, tridenticulate at apex, irregularly reticulate. Autumn. C Mexico, C America, Venezuela, Peru, W Bolivia. Z10.

***P. lutea*** L. Stems vining, slender, glabrous or sparsely downy. Lvs to 9×15cm, trilobed, lobes broadly triangular-ovate, apex rounded or obtuse, base rounded to subtruncate, usually membranous, reticulately 3-veined; stipules to 5mm, setiform; petioles to 5cm, eglandular. Fls to 2cm diam.; pedicels to 4cm, slender, ebracteate; cal. patelliform, light green, sep. to 1×0.3cm, linear-oblong, obtuse; pet. to 0.5×0.1cm, ivory, linear, subacute; fil. biseriate, white, pink at base. Fr. 1.5×1cm, globose-ovoid, purple; seeds to 5×3mm, broadly obcordate or suborbicular, transverse sulcate. Summer. E US (Pennsylvania to Texas). Z5.

***P. maliformis*** L. SWEET CALABASH; SWEETCUP; CONCH APPLE. Stems vining, cylindric, subangular when young. Lvs to 12×10cm, sometimes to 25×15cm, ovate, apex acute or abruptly-acuminate, base rounded to cordate, finely serrulate or undulate, membranous; stipules to 1.5×0.2cm, linear; petioles to 5cm, biglandular. Fls to 8cm diam., fragrant; pedicels to 5cm; cal. 1×1.2cm, campanulate, sep. 4×1.5cm, oblong, green; pet. 3×0.5cm, green-white spotted purple, linear-lanceolate; fil. several-seriate, the innermost to 3cm, purple-red banded white, the outermost shorter, banded white and violet. Fr. to 4cm diam., globose, green or orange-green; seeds to 6×4mm, oblong-obcordate, grey, fine-reticulate. Summer–autumn. Venezuela, Colombia, N Ecuador, W Indies. Z10.

***P. manicata*** (Juss.) Pers. RED PASSION-FLOWER. Stems vigorously vining, stout, angular, subglabrous or densely strigulose. Lvs to 8×9cm, lower lvs to 10×14cm, trilobed, lobes ovate, apex obtuse or subacute, base subcordate or rounded, serrate, glabrous or minutely downy above, tomentose beneath; stipules to 2×1cm, ovate; petioles to 5cm, 4–10-glandular. Fls vivid scarlet; pedicels to 7cm; cal. to 2×1cm, urceolate-campanulate, green-white inside, green outside, sep. to 3.5cm×7mm, oblong-lanceolate, obtuse; pet. oblong, obtuse; fil. 3–4-seriate, corona blue and white. Fr. to 5×3.5cm, ovoid or suborbicular, shiny deep green, glabrous; seeds 5×3mm, ovate, black, finely reticulate. Colombia to Peru. Z9.

***P. membranacea*** Benth. Stems vining, cylindric or subangular, striate, glabrous. Lvs to 10×10cm, orbicular, obscurely trilobed, base peltate, membranous, glabrous, 3-nerved; stipules to 1.5×3cm, cordate-reniform; petioles to 4cm, eglandular. Fls light green or cream; pedicels slender, to 15cm; cal. 2cm diam., broad-campanulate, glabrous, to 4×1cm, oblong-lanceolate, obtuse; pet. to 4×0.8cm, oblanceolate; fil. biseriate; styles connate at base. Fr. 4×3cm, ovoid, coriaceous, glabrous; seeds 4.5×3mm, oblong-ovate, finely reticulate. S Mexico to Costa Rica. Z10.

***P. mexicana*** Juss. Stems vining, obscurely 5-angled, furrowed, glabrous. Lvs to 8cm diam., glabrous, bilobed, lobes to 4cm, oblong, apex obtuse, base truncate or rounded, deep green and glabrous above, paler beneath, 3-veined; stipules to 2mm, setiform or narrow-linear; petioles to 2cm, eglandular. Fls to 4cm diam., maroon; pedicels to 3cm; cal. 1cm diam., patelliform, glabrous, interior white, exterior green to red, sep. to 1.5cm×5mm, narrow-lanceolate; pet. reflexed; fil. biseriate; styles connate at base. Fr. to 1.2cm diam., globose, glabrous; seeds 3×2mm, ovate, transverse-sulcate. SW US (S Arizona), C Mexico. Z9.

***P. miersii*** Mast. Stems vining, slender, cylindric, glabrous, often bright yellow. Lvs to 8×3cm, lanceolate, apex subacute or rounded, base subpeltate, truncate or rounded, subcoriaceous, glabrous, dark claret or maroon, netted with pale green veins beneath; stipules to 2.5×1.2cm, ovate, rounded; petioles to 1.5cm, slender, biglandular. Fls to 5cm diam.; pedicels to 5cm, slender, articulate; cal. campanulate, glabrous, sep. to 2.5×0.7cm, green, oblong, obtuse, aristate; pet. white tinted pink, obtuse; fil. 4-seriate, white, the outermost banded violet. Fr. to 4×2cm, obovoid or ellipsoid, glabrous; seeds obovate, reticulate. Summer. E Brazil. Z10.

***P. ×militaris*** hort. (*P. antioquiensis* × *P. manicata.*) Fls to 12.5cm diam., bright crimson. Z10.

***P. misera*** HBK. Stems vining, angular or flattened, striate, glabrous or subglabrous. Lvs to 13cm diam., bilobed, lobes to 2.5cm, apex rounded or subacute, base cordate or subtruncate, membranous, glabrous or pilosulous, flushed purple beneath reticulately 3-veined; stipules to 3.5mm, setiform to narrow-linear; petioles to 3.5cm, eglandular. Fls to 4cm diam.; pedicels to 10cm, slender; cal. patelliform or campanulate, interior white, exterior green and minutely-pubesc., sep. to 1.8×0.5cm, lanceolate-oblong to linear-oblong, obtuse; pet. to 1.3×0.4cm, white, linear-oblong, obtuse; fil. biseriate, tinted or marked purple; styles connate at base. Fr. to 13mm diam., globose or ovoid; seeds 3.5×2mm, narrow-ovate, transverse-sulcate. Autumn. Panama, northern & eastern America to N Argentina. Z9.

***P. mixta*** L. f. Stems vining, angular, glabrous or grey-pubesc. Lvs to 10×13cm, sometimes to 17cm, trilobed, lobes ovate-oblong, apex acute or abrupt-acuminate, base truncate or subcordate, serrate, glabrous and distinctly veined above, glabrous to velutinous beneath, coriaceous; stipules to 2×1cm, subreniform, cuspidate; petioles to 3cm, 4–8-glandular. Fls pendulous; pedicels to 6cm, stout; bracts sometimes woolly (var. *eriantha*) cal. to 11×1cm, tubular-cylindric, sep. to 4×1.5cm, pink to orange-red, oblong, obtuse; pet. same colour on sep. obtuse; corona a deep lavender or purple rim composed of 1 or 2 ranks of very short filaments. Fr. to 6×2.5cm, ovoid; seeds to 5×4mm, obovoid, reticulate. Summer–autumn. C Venezuela, Colombia, Ecuador, Peru, Bolivia. Z10.

***P. mollissima*** (HBK) L.H. Bail. CURUBA; BANANA PASSION FRUIT. Stems mining, cylindric, striate, with soft golden pubesc. Lvs to 10×12cm, trilobed, lobes ovate, apex acute, base subcordate, sharply serrate-dentate, soft-pubesc. above, tomentose beneath, membranous; stipules to 9×4mm, subreniform; petioles to 3cm. Fls pendulous; pedicels to 6cm; cal. to 8×1cm, olive-green, glabrous, long-tubular, sep. to 3.5×1.5cm, soft pink oblong, obtuse; pet. obtuse, same colour as sep.; corona reduced to a warty rim. Fr. to 7×3.5cm, oblong-ovoid, yellow-soft-pubesc.; seeds to 6×5cm, broad-obovate, reticulate. W Venezuela, Colombia, SE Peru, W Bolivia. Z6.

***P. mooreana*** Hook. f. Stems vining, subangular, stout, somewhat glaucous and scabrous, glabrous. Lvs to 12×10cm, glabrous, trilobed, lobes narrowly oblong-lanceolate, apex mucronate, base cuneate, coriaceous, glaucous beneath, distinctly reticulately 5-veined; stipules to 4×1cm, ovate-lanceolate, acuminate; petioles to 0.7cm, biglandular. Fls 6cm diam.; pedicels to 1.5cm; cal. campanulate, glabrous, white above, exterior green, sep. to 8mm diam., oblong, obtuse; pet. 1cm diam., white oblong, obtuse; fil. biseriate, blue, banded white and indigo. Fr. ovoid, glabrous, yellow; seeds 4×3mm, ovate, reticulate. Summer. S Bolivia, Paraguay, N Argentina. Z10.

***P. morifolia*** Mast. Stems vining, 4-angled, furrowed, subglabrous. Lvs to 11×15cm, trilobed, sometimes to 5-lobed, lobes ovate, apex acute, base cordate, dentate or subentire, membranous, deep green and uncinate-hispidulous above, lighter and pilosulous beneath; stipules 6×3mm, ovate; petioles to 6cm, biglandular. Fls to 3cm diam.; pedicels to 2cm; sep. to 1.5×0.4cm, either somewhat white and purple-mottled, or somewhat green uniformly, linear-oblong, obtuse; pet. to 0.8×0.4cm, inconspicuous, linear-lanceolate, obtuse; fil. 1-seriate. Fr. 2cm diam., purple, globose, glaucous, hispidulous; seeds 4mm, obcordate-obovoid, coarse-reticulate. Guatemala, Peru, Paraguay, Argentina. Very similar to *P. warmingii*. 'Scarlet Flame': fr. tasting of strawberries. Z10.

***P. oerstedii*** Mast. Stems vining, slender, subangular when young, later cylindric. Lvs to 13×9cm, lanceolate, apex acute or obtuse, only rarely bilobed or trilobed, base usually cordate, subpeltate, green and glabrous above, glaucous and glabrous to dense-tomentose beneath, 5–7-veined; stipules to 4×1.5cm, ovate; petioles to 4cm, (2-)4–6-glandular. Fls to 6cm diam.; pedicels to 4cm, glabrous; cal. to 8mm, campanulate, sep. to 3×1.2cm, white, ovate-lanceolate; pet. to 1.5×0.5cm white tinted pink, linear, obtuse; fil. several-seriate, purple. Fr. to 6×3cm, ovoid; seeds to 5×3mm, narrow-obovate, shallow-tridentate, coarse-reticulate. S Mexico to Colombia and C Venezuela. Z10.

***P. organensis*** Gardn. Stems vining, subangular, flattened, glabrous. Lvs dark green to chocolate brown with somewhat jagged-edged regions of silver, cream, pink or lime-green variegation, glabrous, bilobed, rarely trilobed, lobes to 3cm diam., divergent, broad-ovate to lanceolate, apex mucronulate, base rounded, membranous or subcoriaceous, 3–5-veined extrafloral nectaries conspicuous above as dark spots; stipules to 3mm, linear-subulate; petioles to 3cm, slender, eglandular. Fls to 5cm diam., cream to dull purple, usually solitary; peduncles to 4cm; cal. to 1.5cm diam., broad-patelliform, glabrous, sep. 1.5cm×5mm, oblong-lanceolate, obtuse, recurved; pet. to 7.5mm, ovate-lanceolate; fil. to three-quarters length of pet., 1-seriate, cream to dark violet to purple; styles connate at base. Fr. to 1.5cm diam., globose, glabrous; seeds 4.5×2.5mm, ovate, transverse 7–9-sulcate. E Brazil. Z10.

***P. penduliflora*** Bertero ex DC. Stems vining, strongly angular, striate, glabrous. Lvs to 7.5×8cm, suborbicular to triangular-obovate, shallowly trilobed with lobes acute or obtuse, sometimes subentire, rounded at base, trinerved, subcoriaceous or membranous; stipules to 4mm; petioles to 2cm, slender, eglandular. Fls to 4cm diam., pedicels to 10cm; cal. campanulate, sep. to 2×0.6cm, yellow green, oblong lanceolate, obtuse; pet. to 0.7cm, yellow green to ivory, oblanceolate, short-clawed at base; fil. 1-seriate; styles connate at base. Fr. to 1.5cm diam., globose or ovoid; seeds broad-ovate, transversely grooved. Spring–summer. E Cuba, Jamaica. Z10.

***P. perfoliata*** L. Stems vining, angular, striate, glabrous or lanuginose. Lvs to 6×2.5cm, oblong, bilobed, lobes widely divergent, rounded ovate, overlapping at base, perfoliate, subcoriaceous, 3-veined; stipules to 3mm, linear-subulate; petioles to 5mm, eglandular, glabrous or minute-pubesc. Fls maroon, solitary rarely paired; pedicels to 3cm; cal. to 1.3×0.8cm, turbinate-cylindric, sep. to 2×0.3cm, linear-subulate; pet. to 0.7cm diam., oblanceolate, acute; fil. 1-seriate, corona very short, yellow; styles connate at base. Fr. to 1.5cm diam., globose; seeds 3×2mm, ovate or somewhat obovate, transversely grooved. Summer. Jamaica. Z10.

***P. picturata*** Ker-Gawl. Stems vining, cylindric, glabrous. Lvs to 6×7cm, trilobed, lobes ovate, apex rounded or subacute, base subpeltate and usually rounded, glabrous, membranous, bright green above, somewhat purple beneath; stipules to 2.5×1cm, ovate; petioles to 3cm, slender, 2–6-glandular. Fls to 10cm diam.; pedicels to 12cm, stout; cal. 0.5×1.5cm, campanulate, glabrous, interior white, blue or violet, exterior green, sep. 2.5×1cm, linear-oblong, somewhat concave; pet. to 2.5×1.2cm, smaller than sep. pale rose or violet, oblong, obtuse; fil. biseriate the outermost white banded blue; styles connate at base. Fr. to 3.5cm diam., globose, glabrous; seeds to 5×3mm, obovate, coarsely-reticulate. Autumn. Surinam, Brazil. Z10.

***P. pinnatistipula*** Cav. Stems vining, long, angular, white-tomentose or lanate at first, later subglabrous. Lvs to 10×13cm, trilobed, lobes lanceolate, apex acute or acuminate and mucronate, base subcordate, sharp-serrate, rugose and glabrous above, densely grey-white-lanate beneath, coriaceous; stipules to 7×5mm, with pinnate, filiform lobes; petioles to 3.5cm, 4–6-glandular. Pedicels to 7cm, nodding; cal. to 5×1cm, tubular-cylindric, interior white tinged blue, exterior bright pink, densely-tomentose, sep. to 4×1cm, oblong, obtuse; pet. bright rosy pink, obtuse; fil. 2.5cm, biseriate, blue. Fr. 5cm diam., subglobose, somewhat tomentose or subglabrous, yellow-green; seeds 6×5mm, oblong, reticulate. Peru, Chile. Z10.

***P. psilantha*** (Sodiro) Killip. Stems vining, cylindric, striate, soft-pubesc. Lvs to 8×10cm, trilobed, lobes oblong-lanceolate, apex acuminate, base cordate, serrate-dentate, subglabrous or finely and minutely above, soft-pubesc., especially on veins, beneath; stipules to 1×0.5cm, subreniform; petioles to 2.5cm, 8–10-glandular. Fls pale red or white; pedicels to 2.5cm; cal. to 10×0.5cm, tubular-cylindric, glabrous, sep. to 3×0.5cm, narrow-oblong, obtuse; pet. obtuse. Fr. 5×2.5cm, ovoid, soft-pubesc.; seeds 6×4mm, obovate, reticulate. S Ecuador (mts). Z9.

***P. punctata*** L. Stems vining, subtriangular, flattened, striate, glabrous. Lvs to 5×12cm, oblong, glabrous, shallowly trilobed or bilobed, lobes rounded and emarginate, base truncate or subcordate, membranous, somewhat glaucous beneath, 3–5-veined; stipules to 5mm, linear-falcate; petioles to 6cm, slender, eglandular. Fls to 4cm diam., green-white; pedicels slender, to 8cm; cal. campanulate, glabrous, glossy light yellow-green, duller inside, sep. to 1.8×1cm, oblong-lanceolate, obtuse; pet. to 1.2×0.6cm, oblong-lanceolate, recurved; fil. biseriate; styles connate at base. Fr. 2cm, ellipsoid, glabrous; seeds 3×2.5mm, ovate, transverse-sulcate. Ecuador, N Peru. Sometimes confused with *P. misera*. Z10.

***P. quadrangularis*** L. GRANADILLA; GIANT GRANADILLA. Stems vining, stout, 4-angular, angles distinctly alate, glabrous. Lvs to 20×15cm, ovate-lanceolate, apex abruptly acuminate, base rounded, to cordate, entire, glabrous, penninerved; stipules to 3.5×2cm, ovate, acute; petioles to 5cm, stout, 6-glandular. Fls to 12cm diam.; pedicels to 3cm; cal. shallowly campanulate, glabrous, sep. to 4×2.5cm, green beneath, pearly grey-green tinted flesh pink above, ovate or ovate-oblong, concave; pet. to 4.5×2cm, fleshy, pale mauve-pink, oblong-ovate to oblong-lanceolate, obtuse; fil. 5-seriate, white, banded blue and red-purple, equalling sep. and strongly twisted. Fr. to 30×15cm, oblong-ovoid, glabrous; seeds to 1cm×8.5mm, broad-obcordate or suborbicular, reticulate. Tropical America. 'Variegata': lvs splotched yellow. Z10.

***P. racemosa*** Brot. RED PASSION FLOWER. Stems scandent or vining, almost 4-angled, striate, light green when young, glabrous. Lvs to 10×11cm, polymorphic, ovate and simple, or trilobed, lobes oblong, apex acute or subobtuse, base subpeltate, truncate or cordate, entire, coriaceous, glabrous, 5-veined; stipules to 1.5×1cm, broad-ovate; petioles to 4cm, slender, biglandular. Fls to 12cm diam., scarlet-red or white, in pendulous, 8–13-fld, racemes to 30cm; pedicels 1cm; cal. to 1.5×1.2cm, cylindric, glabrous, throat maroon, sep. to 4×1cm, oblong, with keel-like longitudinal wings; pet. oblong, obtuse; fil. triseriate, white banded dark purple, inner fil. red and very short. Fr. to 7×3cm, narrow-ovoid, obtuse, coriaceous, glabrous; seeds 5×3.5mm, obovate, reticulate. Brazil. Z10.

**Passifloraceae** (a) *Passiflora organensis* (b) *P. antioquiensis* (c) *P. aurantia* (d) *Malesherbia linearifolia* (e) *Adenia fruticosa* caudex (e1) flowers (e2) habit (f) *Passiflora coriacea* (g) *Adenia spinosa* habit

***P. rubra*** L. Stems vining, 3–5-angled, striate, densely grey-pubesc., rarely subglabrous. Lvs to 8×10cm, bilobed (rarely with a far smaller midlobe), cordate at base, membranous, downy; stipules to 8mm, setiform; petioles to 5cm, eglandular. Fls to 5cm diam.; pedicels ebracteate; cal. patelliform or campanulate, glabrous inside, pubesc. outside, distinctly 3-veined, sep. to 3×0.6cm, ivory to linear-lanceolate, subacute; pet. to 1.5×0.4cm, similar to colour to sep.; fil. 1–2-seriate, red-purple or lavender; styles connate at base. Fr. to 2.5×1.8cm, rarely to 5.5×2.5cm, ovoid or obovoid, hirsute, later subglabrous, seeds 4×2mm, ovate, mucronate, black, transversely grooved. Autumn. Colombia, Venezuela, Peru, Bolivia, E Brazil, W Indies. Z10.

***P. sanguinolenta*** Mast. & Lind. Stems vining, angular, dense villous-hirsute. Lvs densely villous-hirsute, lunate-bilobed, lobes to 2cm diam., lanceolate, apex mucronulate, base cordate, membranous; stipules setiform, to 5mm; petioles to 1.5cm, eglandular. Fls dull red or maroon; pedicels to 5cm, slender, ebracteate or bracts caducous; cal. to 2cm, cylindric, distinctly nerved, densely villous-hirsute, sep. to 2×0.5cm, linear-oblong; pet. to 1×0.3cm, linear; fil. biseriate. Fr. densely villous-hirsute. Ecuador (mts). Z9.

***P. seemannii*** Griseb. Stems vining, cylindric, striate, glaucous, glabrous. Lvs to 9×6cm, sometimes to 13×15cm, cordate-ovate, apex obtuse or abruptly acuminate and mucronate, base deeply-cordate, subentire, glaucous, glabrous, thin-textured; stipules to 1.5cm, linear, serrulate; petioles to 7cm, biglandular, sometimes 4-glandular. Fls to 10cm diam.; pedicels to 10cm; cal. 2cm, campanulate-funnelform, glabrous, white, tinged purple or violet, sep. to 4×1.5cm, ovate-lanceolate, obtuse, corniculate; pet. to 3.5×1.2cm, purple, oblong-lanceolate, obtuse; fil. biseriate. Fr. to 5×3.5cm, ovoid, glabrous; seeds 3×3mm, orbicular-ovate, reticulate. S Mexico to Panama, NW Colombia. Z10.

***P. serratifolia*** L. Stems vining, vigorous, cylindric, striate, minute-hirsute. Lvs to 12×7cm, ovate, apex acuminate, base rounded or cordate, serrulate, membranous or subcoriaceous, subglabrous above, minutely hirsute beneath; stipules 7mm, linear-subulate, serrulate; petioles to 12cm, densely and minutely hirsute, 6-glandular. Fls to 6cm diam., fragrant; pedicels to 7cm; cal. campanulate, sep. to 3×0.8cm, pink-purple, lanceolate, carinate; pet. to 2×0.6cm, oblong-lanceolate, obtuse, similar to sep. in colour; fil. several-seriate, the outermost to 3cm, blue, dark purple toward base. Fr. to 9×5cm, ovoid or subglobose, glabrous, yellow; seeds to 7×5mm, cuneate, tridentate toward apex, reticulate. Spring–autumn. E Mexico to Costa Rica. Z10.

***P. sicyoides*** Schltr. & Cham. Stems vining, slender, subglabrous or hispidulous. Lvs to 8×10cm, trilobed, lobes deltoid-acuminate, the midlobe much the longest, apex mucronate, base cordate, entire or denticulate, membranous, light green above, glaucous beneath, hispidulous, 3-veined; stipules to 7mm, ovate, cuspidate; petioles to 6cm, hispidulous, biglandular. Fls very fragrant, solitary or paired, to 4cm diam.; pedicels slender, to 3cm; cal. patelliform or campanulate, hispidulous, sep. to 2×1cm, yellow-green, oblong-lanceolate, acute downy beneath; pet. to 1.2cm, white, ovate-lanceolate; fil. 8.5mm, 1-seriate, white, banded red-purple; styles connate at base. Fr. obovoid, glabrous; seeds 5×4mm, obcordate, abruptly acute, coarsely reticulate. Summer. C & S Mexico. Z10.

***P. stipulata*** Aubl. Stems vining, cylindric, glabrous. Lvs to 8×10cm, trilobed, lobes broad-ovate, apex briefly acuminate or subacute, base subpeltate and cordate, membranous, glabrous, glaucous beneath, 5-veined; stipules ovate, to 3×1cm; petioles to 5cm, 2–5-glandular. Fls to 6cm diam., fragrant; pedicels to 5cm; cal. obconic-campanulate, glabrous, light green inside, darker outside, sep. to 3×1cm, green beneath, white-green above, oblong-lanceolate; pet. white to 3cm; fil. several-seriate, white, violet at base. Fr. glabrous. French Guiana. Z10.

***P. suberosa*** L. Stems slender, vining, becoming winged and corky below. Lvs entire to deeply trilobed, lobes linear-lanceolate to broad-ovate, apex acute or obtuse, base rounded sometimes peltate, membranous or subcoriaceous; stipules linear-subulate, to 8mm; petioles to 4cm, biglandular. Fls to 3cm diam., green-yellow to ivory, solitary or paired, axillary, sometimes in terminal, racemes; sep. ovate-lanceolate, subobtuse; pet. absent; fil. biseriate. Fr. to 1.5cm diam., globose or ovoid, dark purple or black, glaucous when young; seeds to 4×2mm, coarsely reticulate. Summer. Tropical America. Z10.

***P. subpeltata*** Ortega. GRANADINA. Stems vining, cylindric, striate, glabrous. Lvs to 9×12cm, trilobed, lobes oblong, apex rounded or obtuse, base often subpeltate or subcordate, glabrous; stipules to 4×2cm, oblong, mucronate; petioles to 6cm, slender, 2–4-glandular. Fls to 5cm diam.; pedicels to 6cm; cal. glabrous, sep. to 1cm diam., green beneath, green-white above, oblong, obtuse; pet. white, linear-oblong; fil. 5-seriate, white. Fr. to 4cm diam., ovoid or subglobose, glabrous, somewhat green; seeds 5×3mm, obovate, fine-reticulate. C Mexico, C America, Colombia, Venezuela. cf. *P. eichleriana*. Z10.

***P. trifasciata*** Lem. Stems vining, angular, striate, glabrous. Lvs to 10×10cm, glabrous, trilobed, lobes deltoid, apex acute or subobtuse, base cordate, membranous, dull dark green mottled pale green or yellow on either side of veins or above, maroon or violet beneath; stipules subulate, to 4mm; petioles to 5cm, eglandular. Fls to 3.5cm diam., fragrant; pedicels slender, to 3cm; bracts setiform; cal. broad-campanulate, glabrous, sep. 1.5×0.5cm, yellow-green, oblong, obtuse pet. 1×0.3cm, ivory-white, linear; fil. biseriate, yellow-green. Fr. to 2.5cm diam., globose, glabrous, glaucous; seeds 4×2mm, narrow oblong-ovoid, transverse-sulcate. Peru, Brazil. Z10.

***P. tuberosa*** Jacq. Tuberous-rooted. Stems vining, glabrous. Lvs to 6×12cm, oblong, deeply bilobed, lobes lanceolate, with a mucro in sinus, base rounded, subcoriaceous, glabrous, dark and glossy above, paler beneath, reticulately 3-veined; stipules to 5mm, narrow-linear, coriaceous; petioles to 2cm, eglandular. Fls to 5cm diam., white, solitary or paired; pedicels to 4cm; cal. patelliform or campanulate, glabrous, sep. to 2×0.6cm, oblong-lanceolate, obtuse; pet. to 1×0.4cm, ovate-lanceolate, obtuse; fil. white banded purple, biseriate; styles connate at base. Fr. glabrous. Summer–autumn. Caribbean (St. Thomas, Trinidad), Northern S America. Z10.

***P. tucumanensis*** Hook. Stems vining, angular, subcylindric below, glabrous, somewhat glaucous, sulcate. Lvs to 6×1.5cm, 3–5-lobed, lobes oblong-lanceolate, apex mucronate, base cordate and finely serrate, membranous, deep green above, somewhat glaucous beneath, glabrous, 3–5-veined; stipules ovate-lanceolate, to 3×1.5cm; petioles to 3cm, eglandular. Fls to 5cm diam., white, pedicels slender, to 2.5cm, eglandular; cal. campanulate, glabrous, white inside, green outside, sep. 5mm diam., oblong-lanceolate, cucullate; pet. white; fil. 12.5mm, several-seriate, white, banded violet. Fr. to 5×3.5cm, ovoid, glabrous; seeds 5mm, obovate, reticulate. Summer. NW Argentina. Z10.

***P. umbilicata*** (Griseb.) Harms. Stems vining, subcylindric, striate, glabrous. Lvs to 6×7.5cm, trilobed, lobes oblong-ovate, apex rounded or subacute and mucronate, base cordate, entire or somewhat undulate, subcoriaceous, 5–7-veined; stipules to 2×1cm, ovate, mucronate; petioles to 3.5cm, slender, eglandular or minutely biglandular. Fls more or less erect, maroon, violet or dark blue; pedicels to 9cm, stout, cylindric; cal. to 3.5×0.9cm, tubular-cylindric, glabrous, sep. to 3cm×6mm, linear-oblong; pet. linear-oblong, obtuse; fil. 5-seriate. Fr. to 7×4cm, ovoid, glabrous; seeds 5×4mm, oblong-obovate, tridentate, coarse-reticulate. C Bolivia, N Argentina. Z10.

***P. violacea*** Vell. Stems long, vining, cylindric or subangular, glabrous. Lvs to 12×15cm, trilobed, lobes oblong, base cordate and subpeltate, entire or subentire, membranous or subcoriaceous, glabrous, 5–7-veined, glaucous beneath; stipules ovate-oblong, to 3.5×1.5cm; petioles to 5cm, 3–8-glandular. Fls to 10cm diam., violet; peduncles somewhat stout, to 15cm; cal. campanulate, purple inside, pruinose outside, glabrous, sep. to 1cm diam., oblong or oblong-lanceolate, long-awned; pet. to 1cm diam., oblong-lanceolate, obtuse; fil. 6–7-seriate, to 4cm, violet, white at apex and base. Fr. glabrous. Autumn. Bolivia, E Brazil, Paraguay. Very similar to *P. amethystina*. Z10.

***P. viridiflora*** Cav. Stems vining, slender, angular, compressed, glabrous. Lvs to 7×9cm, lower lvs to 16×25cm, glabrous, deeply trilobed, lobes ovate to suborbicular, apex obtuse, entire, peltate, coriaceous, shiny deep green above, paler beneath, reticulately 3–7-veined; stipules 5mm, linear-lanceolate, acute; petioles to 6cm, biglandular. Fls green; pedicels to 2cm, ebracteate; cal. cylindric, gibbous, glabrous, sep. to 1.5×0.2cm, linear, acute; pet. absent; fil. 1-seriate. Fr. to 2cm diam., subglobose, glabrous; seeds to 5×3mm, obovate, reticulate. S Mexico. Z10.

***P. vitifolia*** HBK. Stems vining, cylindric, rusty tomentose. Lvs to 15×18cm, trilobed, vine-like, lobes acuminate, truncate to cordate at base, dentate or crenate, membranous, shiny above, densely minutely pubesc. or minutely tomentose, 3–5-veined; stipules setiform, to 5mm; petioles to 5cm, biglandular at base, densely rusty-tomentose. Fls to 9cm diam., scarlet, bright red or vermilion; pedicels stout, densely rusty-tomentose; cal. cylindric, subglabrous, sep. to 8×2cm, lanceolate, obtuse; pet. to 6×1.5cm, linear-lanceolate, obtuse; fil. 3-seriate, red to bright yellow. Fr. 5×3cm, ovoid, minutely pubesc.; seeds 5×3.5mm, obcordate, reticulate. Spring–summer. C America (Nicaragua), Venezuela, Colombia, Ecuador, N Peru. 'Scarlet Flame': fr. tasting of strawberries. Z10.

***P. warmingii*** Mast. Stems vining, slender, angular, furrowed. Lvs to 5×6cm, trilobed, lobes deltoid, acute, mucronulate, cordate at base, dentate, membranous, hispidulous above, minutely downy beneath, 3-veined; stipules semi-ovate, to 6×3mm; petioles to 5cm, slender, biglandular. Fls 2.5cm diam., white; peduncles to 1.5cm; cal. green-white, sep. to 1×0.5cm, lanceolate-oblong, obtuse; pet. to 7×3mm, lanceolate-oblong, obtuse; fil. biseriate, white at apex, purple-violet at base. Fr. ovoid, pilose; seeds 4×3mm, obcordate, coarsely reticulate. Colombia, Brazil, Paraguay. Perhaps not distinct from *P. morifolia*, and likely to be sunk into that species. Z10.

***P. watsoniana*** Mast. Stems vining, slender, cylindric, glabrous, purple-tinted. Lvs to 6×8cm, trilobed, lobes oblong, apex obtuse or subacute, base subpeltate and subtruncate, membranous, glabrous, green above, maroon beneath, 5-veined; stipules to 1.5×1cm, ovate or subreniform, subacute or rounded and aristulate; petioles to 3cm, slender, 2–5-glandular. Fls to 8cm diam.; pedicels slender, to 5cm; cal. 4mm, campanulate, glabrous, sep. 7mm diam., green beneath, white tinted violet above oblong-lanceolate; pet. 4mm diam., white-tinted violet to pale lilac, thin, linear-lanceolate, obtuse; fil. 5-seriate, erect, violet, banded white. Fr. glabrous. Summer–autumn. C & S Brazil. Z10.

***P. cultivars***. 'Amethyst': stems thin; lvs to 10cm diam., 3-lobed; pet. intense blue, corona fil. dark purple. 'Star of Bristol': slender vine; lvs 3–5 lobed; sep. to 5×1.5cm, green, purple above; pet. mauve, to 4.5×1.6cm, fil. 4–5-seriate, deep mauve at base, centrally banded of lilac, apex mauve; fr. ovoid, bright orange. 'Star of Clevedon': slender vine; sep. white, green and white outside, to 5×1.5cm; pet. white, to 5×1.5cm; corona fil. 4-seriate, purple at base, centrally banded white then blue-lilac. 'Star of Kingston' (*P.* 'Amethyst' × *P. caerulea*): as 'Star of Clevedon', but sep. tipped mauve inside, pet. light mauve, fil. deep mauve base, banded white, apex mauve.

***P. alba*** Link & Otto. See *P. subpeltata*.
***P. atomaria*** Planch. See *P. subpeltata*.
***P. banksii*** Benth. See *P. aurantia*.
***P. ×belottii*** Pépin. See *P. ×alato-caerulea*.
***P. fulgens*** Wallis ex Morr. See *P. coccinea*.
***P. grandiflora*** hort. See *P. caerulea* 'Grandiflora'.
***P. imthurnii*** Mast. See *P. glandulosa*.
***P. ×innesii*** Mast. See *P. ×decaisneana*.
***P. macrocarpa*** Mast. See *P. quadrangularis*.
***P. maculifolia*** Mast. See *P. organensis*.
***P. maximiliana*** Bory. See *P. misera*.
***P. medusae*** Lem. See *P. jorullensis*.
***P. onychina*** Lindl. See *P. amethystina*.
***P. peltata*** Cav. See *P. suberosa*.
***P. pfordtii*** Mast. See *P. ×alato-caerulea*.
***P. princeps*** Lodd. See *P. racemosa*.
***P. pruinosa*** Mast. See *P. garckei*.
***P. raddiana*** DC. See *P. kermesina*.
***P. tinifolia*** Juss. See *P. laurifolia*.
***P. van volxemii*** Triana & Planch. See *P. antioquiensis*.
For further synonymy see *Tacsonia*.

**PASSIFLORACEAE** Juss. ex Kunth. PASSION FLOWER FAMILY. Dicot. 18 genera and 600 species of lianes with axillary tendrils, shrubs and trees, often with unusual secondary growth and alkaloids. Leaves spirally arranged, entire or palmately lobed, usually with nectaries on the petiole; stipules usually small, deciduous, sometimes reduced. Flowers regular, usually bisexual, solitary or in cymes, with flat to tubular hypanthium, often with elongate androgynophore; calyx (3–) 5 (–8) free sepals, sometimes basally connate, persistent; corolla as many petals as and alternating with calyx, free or basally connate, with corona of 1 or more rows of filaments or scales; stamens 4–5 to numerous, usually alternate with petals, free or on gynophore; ovary superior,of 2–5 fused carpels, 1-loculed; styles usually connate only at the base; placentation parietal; ovules usually numerous. Fruit a berry or capsule; seeds with oily endosperm. Some *Passiflora* spp. have edible fruits, for example *P. maliformis* (sweet calabash), *P. edulis* (purple granadilla), *P. quadrangularis* (granadilla). Tropical and warm temperate, especially America. *Adenia, Malesherbia, Passiflora*.

**Pastinaca** L. (Lat. name for carrot, later used for parsnip.) Umbelliferae. 14 species of biennials or perennials, often with thick rootstock. Leaves simple or 1–2-pinnate, segments simple to pinnatisect; stem leaves reduced. Umbels compound, with 3–30 rays; involucre and involucel absent or composed of 1–2 short-lived bracts; flowers yellow; petals ovate, equal. Fruit elliptic, strongly compressed dorsally; mericarps with unwinged dorsal ridges, and narrowly winged lateral ridges; vittae commonly 1. Eurasia.

CULTIVATION *P. sativa*, the wild parsnip, occurs throughout northern Europe in dry grassland, often on calcareous soils. As with other members of the Apiaceae group (notably *Heracleum*), the sap contains phytotoxic chemicals which cause skin blistering in sunlight. For cultivation, see PARSNIP.

***P. sativa*** L. PARSNIP. Strong smelling bienn. to 1m, more or less hairy, from thick, white rootstock. Lvs 10–30cm, pinnate, seg. 5–11, ovate, base cuneate to rounded, *c*5cm; petiole of lower lvs only inflated at base, margins crenate-dentate. Umbels with 5–20 rays, to 10cm diam.; involucre occasionally 2 bracts, withering early; fls yellow. Fr. broadly elliptic, 5–7mm; mericarps with wing to 0.5mm, commissure broad. Summer. Europe, W Asia.

For synonymy see *Peucedanum*.

**Patersonia** R. Br. (For William Paterson (1755–1810), Lieutenant-Governor of New South Wales 1800–1810, an early botanical collector in Australia.) Iridaceae. About 20 species of perennial herbs; rootstock a short rhizome. Leaves clustered at base of stem, linear, distichous, usually forming a fan. Inflorescence few- to several-flowered sessile spikes enclosed in spathes; bracts scarious; flowers regular, short-lived, usually blue, occasionally yellow or white; perianth tube slender, outer 3 tepals broad, spreading, inner 3 erect, small, sometimes absent; filaments joined into tube; style filiform, longer than stamens, with 3 obovate, petaloid branches. Australia, Borneo, New Guinea. Z10.

CULTIVATION *Patersonia* spp. are considered frost tender in cool temperate zones, but are suited to cultivation in the cool glasshouse. Grow in a light, fertile and well-drained medium, in full light, watering plentifully when in growth. Propagate by careful division or, better, by seed in autumn.

***P. glabrata*** R. Br. Stem to 15cm. Lvs to 15–30cm long, less than 0.5mm wide, usually longer than stem. Fls purple. Australia (Victoria, NSW, Queensland).

***P. glauca*** R. Br. Stems very short, set close on rhiz. Lvs 15–50cm, less than 0.5mm wide, longer than stem, stiff, erect, narrowly linear. Spathes 2.5–3cm, glabrous, enclosing 2–4-fld spikes; fls blue, exserted from spathe; outer tepals *c*10mm, ovate. Australia (NSW to Tasmania).

***P. longiscapa*** Sweet. Lvs to 50cm, much shorter than stem. Spathes brown, spikelets 3–4-fld; fls blue-purple, the tube enclosed in spathe; outer tepals about 20mm, broadly ovate; tube velvet. Australia (Victoria, S Australia, Tasmania). Possibly synonymous with *P. occidentalis*.

***P. occidentalis*** R. Br. Stems usually 15–50cm, forming tufts. Lvs several to many, 15–55cm×2–11mm, somewhat ribbed, rigid, the margins hairy or scabrid. Spikelets few to several-fld; fls deep blue or purple; tube 25–35mm; outer tepals 15–35×10–20mm. Spring–summer. W Australia.

***P. sericea*** R. Br.. Stems to 30cm, covered with silky, woolly hairs. Lvs erect, stiff, *c*0.5mm diam., woolly at base when young. Spikelets several-fld; fls deep violet-blue; outer bracts woolly when young. Outer tepals broadly ovate, inner tepals lanceolate or ovate. Summer. Australia (Victoria, NSW, Queensland).

***P. umbrosa*** Endl. To 50cm. Lvs to 60cm, linear, rigid. Spathes 5–7cm long, keeled, glabrous; fls blue; outer tepals to 30mm, obovate. Summer. W Australia. 'Xanthina': fls yellow.

***P. media*** R. Br. See *P. glabrata*.

**Patrinia** Juss. (From E.L.M. Patrin (1742–1814), French traveller in Siberia.) Valerianaceae. Some 15 species of herbaceous perennials. Leaves opposite or basal, pinnately cut or lobed, basal leaves rarely entire. Flowers small, white or yellow, in corymbose panicles; calyx limb short, erect, somewhat toothed; corolla tube very short with 5 spreading lobes; stamens usually 4. Fruit a winged achene. Temperate Asia.

CULTIVATION Occurring predominantly in cool, shaded, montane habitats in moist, fertile and humus-rich soils, *Patrinia* spp. are suited to the herbaceous border, rock garden and woodland garden. Cultivate as for *Valeriana*.

***P. gibbosa*** Maxim. Stems to 22.5cm. Lvs to 15cm, more or less blistered, mostly basal, elliptic-ovate to broadly ovate, long-petioled, slender-pointed, pinnately cut and coarsely toothed. Fls in flat cymes to 10cm diam., yellow; cor. tube distinctly widened at base. Achenes broadly winged. Japan.

***P. triloba*** Miq. Stem to 60cm, erect, tinged red. Lvs to 5cm, mostly basal, deeply 3–5-pinnately lobed, upper lvs coarsely toothed. Fls golden-yellow, fragrant, in rather loose, 3-branched cymes, to 10cm diam. Japan. var. ***palmata*** (Maxim.) Hara. Fls with spurs to 3mm.

***P. villosa*** (Thunb.) Juss. Stem to 90cm. Lvs to 15cm, ovate, basal, simple to pinnatifid, white-pubesc., upper lvs sessile, toothed. Fls white in corymbose panicles. Japan.

**Paulownia** Sieb. & Zucc. (For Anna Paulowna, daughter of Paul I, Tsar of Russia (1795–1865).) Scrophulariaceae. About 17 species of deciduous trees to 20m or more. Shoots very thick when young, without terminal buds. Leaves opposite, usually large, cordate at the base, entire or 3–5-lobed, usually hairy at least beneath, hairs often stellate or dendroid (tree-like). Flowers numerous, in terminal panicles borne at the apices of the young shoots; the inflorescence-buds are laid down in the autumn and persist through the winter; calyx deeply 5-lobed, thick, usually hairy; corolla large, campanulate to foxglove-like, with 5 short, spreading lobes, white to violet, often yellow inside; stamens 4. Capsule leathery, containing numerous winged seeds. E Asia.

CULTIVATION *Paulownia* spp. occur in deciduous montane woodland at altitudes of 1500–1800m/4875–5850 ft. Mature specimens are exceptionally beautiful in full bloom with their low, rounded crowns and huge panicles of scented, foxglove-like flowers. The pollution-tolerant *P. tomentosa* is grown as a street and park tree in cities of continental Europe and has become widely naturalized in the eastern states of the US, from New York to Georgia, often as a roadside weed; those observed along the Pennsylvania highways flower even on very young plants, which suggests that some very hardy and potentially useful clones have established themselves there. *P. tomentosa* and its cv. 'Lilacina' are also grown in the mixed border, for their juvenile foliage. When grown as stooled specimens the downy heart-shaped leaves assume enormous proportions; with the necessary fertilizers and plentiful water they may reach 60–90cm/24–36in. in length, and almost one metre across. Such large leaves however, are susceptible to wind burn and need a sheltered position; they are particularly unattractive when damaged.

In temperate maritime climates such as those found in Britain, flowering may not occur annually. It is commonly supposed that flowering here is compromised by late spring frosts, since the light brown, almost spherical flower buds which form in late summer/ early autumn, begin to expand in mild spells of spring weather and may then be susceptible to damage. However, *P. tomentosa* flowers successfully in other regions with cool springs and evidence suggests that the flower buds can in fact tolerate 15°C of frost. It seem probable therefore that conditions in the previous season are more germane; and is, where sufficiently warm dry conditions prevail during flower initiation, and the season is long enough to allow wood to ripen, both flowering and frost tolerance are far more reliable. Once established, *P. fargesii* and *P. tomentosa* will tolerate temperatures to between −15 and −20°C/5 to −4°F; all species are frost tender when young, especially when grown on rich soils, but often resprout from the base if given a protective mulch at the roots in winter.

Grow in any deep, moderately fertile, moisture-retentive but well-drained soil, giving a site in full sun with shelter from strong winds, since branches tend to be brittle. For foliage effects stool back to the woody base in spring, and thin emerging shoots to a single stem; (the largest leaves are obtained on single-stemmed plants). Protect the roots with a bark mulch or evergreen prunings in very cold winters.

Propagate from seed sown at 15–20°C/60–68°F in spring, or when ripe; seed requires light for germination. Also from root cuttings in winter, or by 5–8cm semi-ripe heeled cuttings in summer, in the cold frame. *Paulownia* spp. are particularly susceptible to frost when young, and should be overwintered under glass in their first year. Susceptible to honey fungus, leaf spotting and occasionally to a virus causing witches brooms in the crown, whose effects are largely cosmetic.

***P. fargesii*** Franch. Tree to 12m; young shoots with stellate hairs, soon becoming glabrous. Lvs 15–21×12–14cm, long-ovate, cordate at base, entire, densely hairy beneath. Panicle-branches stalked, their stalks as long as the stalks of the individual fls; cor. foxglove-like, 5–7cm, usually violet or lilac, yellow within. Capsule ovoid, to 3.5cm. W China. Z7.

***P. fortunei*** Hemsl. Large tree to 20m, bark grey-brown. Lvs 14–21×7–12cm, long-ovate, cordate, glabrous and shining above, densely hairy beneath. Panicle-branches stalked, stalks as long as the flower-stalks; cor. foxglove-like, 8–10cm, cream flushed with lilac. Capsule long-ellipsoid, woody, 5–8cm. China, Japan. Z6.

***P. kawakamii*** Itô. Tree to 12m, with grey bark; twigs hairy at first, soon becoming glabrous. Lvs 11–30×8–27cm broadly cordate, 3–5-lobed, glandular-hairy above, densely so beneath. Panicle-branches not or scarcely stalked; cor. campanulate, 3–4.5cm, lilac. Capsule ovoid, 2–2.5cm. S China, Taiwan. Z6.

***P. tomentosa*** (Thunb.) Steud. Tree to 20m with a broad crown; young shoots thick, at first hairy, later glabrous. Lvs 17–30×12–27cm, broadly ovate, entire, hairy above, densely so beneath. Panicles large, the flower-bearing branches with stalks at least as long as the flower stalks; cor. foxglove-like, 5–6cm, violet with yellow stripes inside. Capsule ovoid, to 3cm. C & W China. 'Coreana': lvs tinted yellow, woolly beneath; fls violet, throat speckled yellow inside. 'Lilacina': young shoots glandular-hairy; cor. pale lilac. Z5.

***P. fargesii*** Osborn non Franch. See *P. tomentosa* 'Lilacina'.
***P. imperialis*** Sieb. & Zucc. See *P. tomentosa*.
***P. lilacina*** Sprague. See *P. tomentosa* 'Lilacina'.

**Pavetta** L. (From Malabar name for *P. indica*.) Rubiaceae. Some 400 species of shrubs or subshrubs, or trees. Stems terete. Leaves sessile or petiolate, opposite or 3-whorled, membranous, black and maculate; stipules interpetiolar, basally connate and sheath-forming, deltoid, apex truncate or aristate to mucronate. Flowers bisexual, in loose or dense, sessile or short-pedunculate, terminal or pseudoaxillary, few- to many-flowered cymes or corymbs; bracts connate, bracteoles (where present) free; calyx tube ovoid or turbinate to bell-shaped, limb persistent or deciduous, lobed or truncate, lobes 4, occasionally imbricate, ovate or deltoid to lanceolate; corolla cylindric to salver- or funnel-shaped, white or cream to green or, rarely, red, tube glabrous to pubescent at throat, lobes 4, spreading, twisted in bud, ovate, elliptic or lanceolate to oblong; stamens 4, exserted, anthers dorsifixed, linear to oblong; ovary 2-celled, style exserted, filiform to apiculate, glabrous to pubescent, stigma simple, club-shaped, ovules 1 or, rarely, 2, sunken and pendent. Fruit a berry, globose to ovoid, fleshy, lustrous, usually black, pyrenes 1–2, 1-seeded; seeds 2 or, occasionally, 1 abortively, hemispheric; endosperm horny. Tropical and subtropical Old World. Z10.

CULTIVATION As for *Cinchona*.

***P. abyssinica*** Fres. Shrub to 2.5m or tree to 9m. Stems erect to ascending, glabrous or pubesc. Lvs to 17×7cm, obovate or oblong to elliptic, apex narrowly acute or obtuse, base cuneate, thin-textured and papery, lustrous, glabrous to sparsely pubesc. or, initially, bristly; stipules to 1cm, deciduous, truncate, apex aristate; petioles to 2cm, glabrous or pubesc. Fls in loose, terminal corymbs to 12×6cm; pedicels to 1cm, glabrous or pubesc.; bracts to 7mm; cal. tube to 2mm, glabrous or pubesc., limb to 3mm, persistent, lobed, lobes to 5mm; cor. white, tube to 4cm, exterior glabrous, interior short-pubesc., lobes to 10×3mm, lanceolate or oblong, apex narrowly acute; style to 2cm. Fr. to 1cm, globose, crowned by persistent cal. limb, glabrous and lustrous, black. Tropical Africa.

***P. capensis*** (Houtt.) Bremek. Shrub to 2m. Stems terete, glabrous to minutely white-pubesc. Lvs to 5×2cm, obovate, apex narrowly acute, base cuneate, margin subfalcate, glabrous above, 4-veined; stipules apically cuspidate, pubesc.; petioles to 5mm. Fls in dense, terminal, subumbellate corymbs; bracts laciniate and ciliate; cal. tube to 15mm, interior pubesc., lobes to 4mm; cor. white, tube to 2cm, lobes to 7mm. Fr. lustrous and black. Summer. S Africa.

***P. gardeniifolia*** Hochst. ex A. Rich. COMMON BRIDE'S BUSH. Shrub or tree, to 7m. Stems glabrous or pubesc., bark smooth or fissured, grey to brown. Lvs to 12×6cm, elliptic to obovate or oblanceolate, apex acute or obtuse and hard-tipped, base attenuate to cuneate, margin entire, glabrous or pubesc.; stipules to 5mm, deltoid, apex narrowly acute, glabrous or pubesc.; petioles to 2cm, glabrous or pubesc. Fls in dense, short-pedunculate, terminal corymbs to 7cm wide; pedicels to 2cm, glabrous or pubesc.; bracts to 5mm, deciduous, membranous, pubesc., brown; cal. tube to 1mm, glabrous or pubesc., limb to 1mm, lobed or truncate, lobes to 1mm, ovate to deltoid, glabrous or pubesc.; cor. white to cream or pale yellow, tube to 2cm, exterior glabrous, lobes to 7×3mm, ovate to lanceolate, apex acute or obtuse. Fr. to 8×5mm, subglobose, lustrous and black. Tropical Africa.

***P. indica*** L. Shrub or tree to 3m. Stems glabrous or pubesc., bark grey to brown. Lvs to 25×8cm, elliptic or lanceolate to obovate or orbicular, apex acute or narrowly acute to caudate, base attenuate, thin-textured and membranous to leathery, 5–6-veined; stipules connate; petioles to 4cm. Fls short-pedicellate, in dense, sessile, terminal, corymbose cymes to 12cm wide; pedicels to 5mm; bracts membranous; cal. tube bell-shaped, limb truncate or obsoletely toothed or lobed, teeth or lobes ovate to deltoid; cor. white, tube to 2cm, lobes to 12mm, spreading, falcate, linear to oblong. Fr. to 7mm, globose, 2-pyrened and -seeded, black. Tropical Asia.

***P. montana*** Reinw. ex Bl. Shrub or tree, to 4m. Stems terete, glabrous. Lvs to 13×5cm, ovate or lanceolate to oblong, apex acute to caudate, base acute, herbaceous to leathery, glabrous to pubesc., 7-veined; stipules ovate, apex cuspidate, glabrous; petioles to 2cm, pubesc. Fls in loose, subsessile or short-pedunculate, terminal many-fld corymbs; cal. densely pubesc., limb toothed, teeth to 1mm; cor. white, tube to 2cm, exterior glabrous, teeth to 6mm. Malaysia, Indonesia.

***P. natalensis*** Sonder. NATAL BRIDE'S BUSH. Shrub or tree to 4m. Stems initially compressed, bark grey to brown. Lvs to 14×4cm, lanceolate or elliptic to oblong, apex and base attenuate, entire, glossy, glabrous; apex of stipules narrowly acute to cuspidate; petioles to 16mm. Fls in loose, pedunculate, axillary, cymose capitata to 11cm wide; peduncles to 10cm; cor. white, salver-shaped, tube to 2cm, lobes to 10×3mm. Fr. to 5mm, globose, black. S Africa.

***P. revoluta*** Hochst. DUNE BRIDE'S BUSH. Shrub or tree, to 6m. Bark white or grey to pale brown. Lvs to 8×4cm, obovate to elliptic, apex attenuate or obtuse, base attenuate, margin entire and falcate, lustrous and leathery, glabrous above and pubesc. on veins beneath; petioles to 1cm. Fls in dense, axillary or terminal, corymbose capitata to 4cm wide; cal. limb toothed, apex of teeth acute; cor. white, tube to 12mm, lobes to 8mm, spreading, lanceolate. Fr. to 1cm, globose, crowned by persistent cal. limb, black. S Africa

***P. assimilis*** Sonder. See *P. gardeniifolia*.

***P. caffra*** L. f. See *P. capensis*.
***P. javanica*** Bl. See *Ixora javanica*.
***P. obovata*** E. Mey. See *P. revoluta*.
***P. quinqueflora*** Sessé & Moq. See *Ixora ferrea*.
***P. rhodesiaca*** Bremek. See *P. gardeniifolia*.
***P. salicifolia*** Bl. See *Ixora salicifolia*.
***P. undulata*** Lehm. See *P. revoluta*.

**Pavonia** Cav. (For Jose Antonio Pavón (*d*1840), Spanish botanist and traveller.) Malvaceae. About 150 species of herbs, subshrubs and shrubs, hispid with simple and stellate hairs to nearly glabrous. Leaves simple, unlobed to palmately lobed, stipulate. Flowers axillary, solitary, in terminal globose clusters or paniculate inflorescences with reduced leaves; epicalyx segments 4 to many, free or connate; calyx campanulate or cup-shaped, 5-fid or 5-toothed; petals white, yellow or deep purple, often with basal spots; staminal column truncate or 5-toothed at apex; styles 10, stigmas capitate; ovary 5-celled. Fruit a schizocarp, mericarps 5, smooth, wrinkled, winged, prickly or awned, partly dehiscent, 1-seeded; seeds reniform-obovate. Tropics and Subtropics. Z10.

CULTIVATION Found in a diversity of habitats in the wild but frequently on sandy soils, *Pavonia* spp. are distinctive, frost-tender evergreens grown for their interesting flowers. Carried in summer or early autumn, these are distinguished by a whorl of markedly hairy bracts, often in contrasting colours to the petals and, at their centre, a prominent staminal tube, sometimes bearing attractive blue anthers. In tropical and subtropical zones, *Pavonia* is easily grown in any good garden soil in full sun; in cooler regions it is well suited to pot cultivation in the warm glasshouse or conservatory. Grow in a high-fertility loam-based mix with additional organic matter, in direct sun or in bright filtered light; maintain high humidity and a minimum temperature of 16–18°C/60–65°F. Water plentifully when in growth, and moderately and carefully during the shorter days of winter. Cut back hard in spring to remove long, straggling growth. Take greenwood cuttings in summer and root in sand in a closed case with gentle bottom heat. Also by seed.

***P.* ×*gledhillii*** Cheek. (*P. makoyana* × *P. multiflora*.) Evergreen shrub to 2m; branches few, pale brown, finely ridged, leafy branches green, terete. Lvs 10–16×2.5–4cm, elliptic-lanceolate, acute to acuminate, very obscurely serrate, glossy light green; petiole 2.5–5cm, stellate-hairy, dorsal ridge ciliate; stipules to 2.5cm, foliose, persistent, linear-lanceolate. Fls solitary, in upper lf axils; peduncles to 4cm at anthesis, shortly tomentose; pedicels 5mm, with longer indumentum; epicalyx seg. 9–10, 3×3–4.5mm, in one whorl, bright red, lanceolate, sparsely stellate-scabrid, margins ciliate; cal. 2cm, almost cylindric, densely stellate-tomentose, cal. teeth 1.5cm, triangular, grey-pink; cor. to 3cm, tubular, very dark purple; stamens with tube branching from within mouth of cor.; anth. entirely exserted, fil. bright red; pollen chalky lilac-blue; styles 9–10, red, stigmas capitate. Fr. shortly stellate-hairy. Widespread in horticulture in the US and Europe, apparently more so than one of its parents, *P. multiflora*, with which it has been confused. Two variants are known. 'Kermesina': dwarf; fls carmine. 'Rosea': fls rose.

***P. hastata*** Cav. Shrub or subshrub to 2m, with grey coarse indumentum. Lvs to 5cm, lanceolate to ovate, hastate to narrowly saggitate, dentate. Epicalyx seg. 5–6, to 5mm, shorter than cal. lanceolate to obovate; pet. to 3cm, pale red to white, with red spots at base. Mericarps to 4mm, brown, ribbed, reticulate, unarmed. Tropical S America, naturalized in S US (Georgia and Florida). Cvs to follow.

***P. makoyana*** E. Morr. Shrub to 80cm; stems covered with soft spreading hairs. Lvs 8–15cm, elliptic-lanceolate, acuminate, entire or obscurely sinuate, coriaceous dark green, glabrous, nerves red-brown beneath; petiole 1.5–3cm, hairy; stipules 1.2–2cm, elliptic or linear-lanceolate, acuminate, hairy, rose-red; sep. 8mm, campanulate, lobed to below the middle, acute; pet. 3cm, erect, dark brown-purple, linear-oblong, about 7-nerved, apex rounded; fil. and styles rose-red; anth. and stigmas blue-purple. Brazil.

***P. multiflora*** Juss. Shrub to 2m. Lvs to 25cm, lanceolate-ovate to oblong, almost entire to dentate. Fls solitary or in upper lf axils, sometimes terminal in leafless corymbs; epicalyx seg. 10–24, bright red, on 1 or 2 whorls, outer whorl to 4cm, sometimes early deciduous, ascending, linear, shorter than inner whorl; cal. shorter than epicalyx, red; pet. to 4cm, purple-red; staminal column exserted, slightly deflexed, red; anth. blue. Brazil.

***P. praemorsa*** (L. f.) Willd. Shrub to 3m; stems erect, rod-like; young branches tomentose. Lvs to 2.5×2.5cm, broadly obovate or fan-shaped, dentate-crenate, truncate, 3–5-nerved, scabrous above, canescent beneath; petioles much shorter than blades; stipules setaceous. Fls axillary, solitary; pedicels exceeding lvs; epicalyx seg. 12–14, very narrowly linear; cal. canescent, seg. ovate, acute; cor. bright yellow with a dark centre. Mericarps dorsally ridged. S Africa.

***P. semiserrata*** (Schräd.) Gürke. Tree to 7m; branches woody with white cortex, glabrous. Lvs 2–5×1–2cm, elliptic, 1-nerved, obscurely serrate, obtuse; petiole 0.5–1cm; stipules 6–8mm, erect, setaceous, glabrous. Fls 2–3cm, solitary, in axils of upper lvs, on long peduncles; epicalyx seg. 5–6, lanceolate, acute, glabrous, 3-nerved; cal. 1cm, campanulate, cal. teeth 4–5mm, acute after anthesis; pet. 1.5×0.6cm, purple; staminal column 2.5–3cm, striate, glabrous; fil. 5–7mm; styles 3–3.5cm; stigmas capitate. Mericarps 8–9mm, glabrous, reticulate-rugose on dorsal side, apex with 2 mucros, the inner cylindric, 1mm long, the outer conical and shorter; seeds 1.5mm. Brazil.

***P. sepium*** St.-Hil. Similar to *P. spinifex* but smaller, with narrower cuneate lvs; epicalyx and cal. about 6mm; pet. 1.2–2cm; mericarps with erect or ascending awns. S America.

***P. spinifex*** (L.) Cav. Shrub to 4.5m. Lvs 3–10×2–8cm, broadly ovate to ovate-lanceolate, serrate, obtuse; stipules subulate, 7–10mm. Fls solitary; epicalyx seg. 5–8, to 1.3cm, longer in fruit, narrowly oblanceolate, long-ciliate; cal. to 1cm; pet. 2–3.5cm, yellow. Mericarps 4–6mm, brown, reticulate, 3-awned, the 2 lateral awns to 1.2cm, strongly divergent. Bermuda, Mexico to Brazil and Peru, W Indies, Greater Antilles; naturalized SE US.

***P. intermedia*** hort. non St.-Hil. See *P.* ×*gledhillii*.
***P. mackoyana*** auct. See *P. makoyana*.
***P. semperflorens*** (Nees) Gürke. See *P. semiserrata*.
For further synonymy see *Goethea* and *Triplochlamys*.

For illustration see MALVACEAE.

**Paxistima** Raf. (From Gk *pachys*, thick, and *stigma*, stigma.) Celastraceae. 2 species of dwarf, evergreen, glabrous shrubs. Branches 4-angled, corky, warted. Leaves opposite, simple, serrulate, coriaceous, evergreen. Flowers solitary or clustered in axils, perfect, small; sepals 4; petals 4; stamens 4; ovary adherent to the disc; style very short; stigma shallowly 2-lobed. Fruit capsule, oblong, compressed, 2-valved, loculicidally dehiscent; seeds 1–2, with a white, many-lobed aril at base. N America.

CULTIVATION In the wild, *Paxistima* spp. grow in open coniferous woodland and rocky mountain terrain. In cultivation *P. myrtifolia* is best treated as peat garden shrub, where it thrives in a leafy, humus-rich soil in dappled shade and due to its suckering habit is ideally suited as a groundcover shrub. *P. canbyi* prefers a more exposed situation in freely drained soils associated with the rock garden, where it is tolerant of calcareous conditions. Both species are hardy enough to tolerate a minimum temperature of −20°C/−4°F, but frost damage may occur if the current year's wood has not been sufficiently ripened. Propagate by semi-ripe cuttings taken in late summer and given a little bottom heat.

***P. canbyi*** A. Gray. CLIFF GREEN; MOUNTAIN LOVER. Stems to 40cm. decumbent and rooting below, the distal portion erect or ascending, branched. Lvs to 2cm, numerous, sessile, linear-oblong, obtuse, revolute, entire or finely serrate. Pedicels solitary or few from some of upper axils, very slender, to 10mm; pet. green, to 2.5mm. Fr. to 4mm, white. Spring, summer. N America (mts of Virginia and N Carolina). 'Compacta': hardy, extra dwarf; lvs dark green later turning bronze. Z3.

***P. myrtifolia*** Wheeler. MOUNTAIN LOVER; OREGON BOXWOOD. Much-branched, very leafy shrub to 1m, sometimes spreading and almost prostrate; branches brown, glabrous. Lvs to 3cm, subsessile, ovate, oblong or oblanceolate, finely serrate, base cuneate, apex acute or obtuse, dark glossy green above, somewhat paler beneath. Peduncles to 3mm, 1–3-fld; sep. to 1mm; pet. to 1.5mm, rufescent. Fr. to 4mm, white. Spring, summer. Western N America (British Columbia to California, eastwards to Montana, Colorado, New Mexico). Z6.

***P. myrsinites*** (Pursh) Raf. See *P. myrtifolia*.

**Paxton,** Sir **Joseph** (1803–65). Gardener and architect. Following an apprenticeship in gardening, Paxton obtained work in the Horticultural Society's garden at Chiswick. He attracted the attention of the Duke of Devonshire, from whom the Society had leased the garden, and who, in 1826, appointed him head gardener at Chatsworth, his Derbyshire estate. Here Paxton made extensive alterations to the grounds, planting an arboretum, remodelling the estate village of Edensor, and designing fountains, most notably the Emperor Fountain, named in anticipation of a visit (which did not, in the event, take place) from the Emperor of Russia in 1844. This was the tallest gravity-driven fountain in the world, with a jet 267 feet high. Paxton travelled extensively with the Duke in Europe and Asia Minor.

Paxton quickly became famous as a designer of glasshouses, and an opponent of J.C. Loudon's ideas about the iron construction and curvilinear design. Paxton recommended instead a ridge-and-furrow roof that provided optimum light in both morning and afternoon, and which allowed a more cost-effective wooden construction. His first major glasshouse, the Great Stove at Chatsworth (1836–40), designed in collaboration with Decimus Burton, was a compromise between curvilinear style and ridge-and-furrow glazing, but throughout his career, Paxton relied more on wood than on iron for his glass buildings.

By the end of the 1830s, Paxton was accepting commissions for both glasshouses and landscape designs from private and corporate clients, For Richard Vaughan Yates he designed Prince's Park, Liverpool, followed by Upton Park, Slough. From 1843 to 1847 he laid out Birkenhead Park for the local corporation, with Edward Kemp as his foreman. In 1845–47 he designed the Coventry Cemetery; later he laid out parks in Glasgow (Kelvingrove, 1854; Queen's Park, 1860) and elsewhere.

In 1849 Paxton was the first in Europe to succeed in flowering the Amazonian waterlily, *Victoria amazonica*, and the following year built a special house to accommodate it. This building and, indeed, the leaf-ribbing of the lily itself, served as the prototype for his design for a building to house the Great Exhibition of 1851, for which he completed the plans at the last moment, in nine days, after 233 other plans had been rejected. The structure used cast-iron supporting columns, wrought-iron bars for the curved section of the roof, and wood for the glazing bars. The building (nicknamed the Crystal Palace by *Punch*) was erected in Hyde Park, using prefabricated sections that could be assembled by unskilled labour. Paxton was knighted for his achievement.

After the end of the Exhibition the Crystal Palace was dismantled, but Paxton formed a limited company to acquire the materials and re-erect it, in a much enlarged form, in a specially designed park on Sydenham Hill. Crystal Palace Park was laid out as a series of terraces with 'one great geometrical line' of cascades and steps forming a central axis from the Palace itself to the bottom of the hill; it boasted elaborate fountains and such educational features as a replica open-cast mine and a collection of models of prehistoric animals. Together with Edward Milner, who had been his assistant on the project, Paxton then went on to create People's Park, Halifax, as a reduced version of the same model, with a terrace and central axis.

Paxton's purely architectural work, largely done in collaboration with his son-in-law G.H. Stokes, included the country houses of Mentmore in Buckinghamshire, Ferrières near Paris, and Lismore Castle. From 1854 until his death he was the Liberal Member of Parliament for Coventry and was also very occupied with railway management.

Paxton edited *The Horticultural Register* (1831–36, edited by James Main from), and *The Magazine* (later *Paxton's Magazine*) *of Botany* (1834–49). With John Lindley, he collaborated on *A Pocket Botanical Dictionary* (1840) and *Paxton's Flower Garden* (1850–53); together they were founders of the *Gardeners' Chronicle* in 1841. Paxton's chief independent work was *A Practical Treatise on the Cultivation of the Dahlia* (1938). He became a Fellow of the Horticultural Society in 1826, and later served as a Council member and vice-president; he was elected a Fellow of the Linnean Society in 1833.

**Peaches and nectarines**. The peach (*Prunus persica*) originated from China. Its introduction westwards was probably via the old Silk Road through Kashmir and Afghanistan to Persia, and was doubtless assisted by the comparative ease with which worthwhile trees could be grown from seed. From Persia, distribution gradually proceeded through the Middle East and thence into Europe. The nectarine is a smooth-skinned form of the peach (the peach possessing a downy skin); it is common in parts of Turkestan. Distribution of both peach and nectarine to other continents was gradually extended from Europe – by the Spaniards to Central America and thence to North America, by the British to Australia. There are comparatively few records from ancient times but the peach was certainly cultivated by at least 2000BC and is mentioned in classical Greek and Latin texts.

There are numerous variations of the peach – cling-stone and free-stone (referring to the degree of adhesion of flesh to stone); red skin to almost white; yellow, green-white and white flesh; round or flattened fruits and with or without a point or 'nipple' at the apex.

In Britain, as with a number of hardy fruits, it was the influence of Henry VIII that heralded the marked advance of interest in peaches and nectarines, together with importation of new cultivars from the near Continent. John Rea in 1676 listed 35 named cultivars of peach and 11 of nectarine and it was already recognized that wall culture was necessary for any consistent success in the British climate. During the 18th century even more new cultivars were introduced, still with strong Continental, particularly French influence and with special attention to fine flavour. By the early 19th century, the Horticultural Society at Chiswick listed over 200 peaches and 70 nectarines in its established collections. Furthermore, peach breeding was now being practised, first by Thomas Andrew Knight and subsequently and into the 20th century by the famous nurserymen Rivers and Laxton. This activity was primed by the advances within the gardens of the large estates, where not only wall culture but also cultivation under glass was now becoming standard practice. Equally, increasingly fine quality and flavour were called for, resulting in the production of many new cultivars, a number of which are still in cultivation today (e.g. peach 'Peregrine' and nectarine 'Lord Napier').

The passing of the great estates has meant a marked reduction in peach-growing in Britain since World War I. Modern housing estates offer few suitable wall sites and peaches are now rarely grown in gardens. Successful seedlings are occasionally raised but when these are propagated for cultivation elsewhere good results are seldom obtained.

By contrast, peaches and nectarines are widely grown both domestically and commercially in many warmer climates, notably southern Europe, the US (except for the coldest areas), Australia, New Zealand, South Africa and China, and also on a smaller scale in many other countries where climatic conditions are favourable, including the Balkan countries, parts of Ontario in Canada, and Japan. The peach flowers early and so requires suitably warm springs, but any tendency towards a tropical climate will not provide adequate winter chilling.

For success the peach must have a site that is either not predisposed to early spring frosts or gives adequate protection from them. In Britain a warm wall of southerly aspect is generally necessary. Another severe limiting factor in the open garden is the widespread incidence of the disease peach leaf curl, which severely debilitates trees and frequently renders them worthless. This is less extensive on some favoured walls and almost non-existent where trees can be protected, for example by polythene, from winter and early spring rains. Examples of trees giving consistently successful results in the open garden are occasionally found in southern England where the microclimate of the site is favourable, and in most cases the cultivar is 'Rochester' or a chance seedling.

In the US colder slopes are sometimes used to delay flowering and reduce spring frost risk; in South Africa yellow-fleshed cling-stone cultivars are confined mainly to areas with cold winters and hot summers, such as the Transvaal High Veld, parts of the Orange Free State and the Cape, while in Australia cultivars with a low chilling requirement are now available for cultivation on the east and west coasts.

Peach and nectarine trees are not long-lived. This is partly due to the need for the tree to produce a constant supply of young shoots – it is only the young one-year-old wood that carries fruit, although a few fruiting spurs are also formed. It is therefore important to select a site with at least reasonably good soil and with good drainage. The pH level should be between 6.0 and 7.0, and on soils with higher readings problems from lime-induced chlorosis may well be encountered. Conversely, soils with pH 6.0

or less may well need a light application of lime worked in before planting; old mortar rubble or crushed lime grit is also useful on heavier soils.

Although seedlings often produce good crops of excellent fruit, it is essentially the selected, named cultivars that are propagated. In common with many hardy fruits, this requires the use of rootstocks for budding and these fall into two distinct categories – either seedling peach or selected clonal plum rootstocks that are known to be compatible with the peach and nectarine. The former will produce quite large trees although close planting in some commercial orchards (even as close as 2m/6½ft) will induce early fruiting and smaller tree dimensions. Of the plum rootstocks 'Brompton' (vigorous) and 'St. Julien A' (semi-vigorous) are widely used. In Australia, it is recognized that plum rootstocks are more tolerant of wet conditions and that root rot can be caused by soil nematodes, for which specially selected resistant rootstocks are now available. Clonal plum rootstocks are at risk from virus infection unless they are obtained from virus-tested stock.

A very wide range of cultivar is available. As they have different chilling requirements, local advice should be sought on which are best suited for individual localities. Breeding programmes are helping to widen the choice available and to make successful cultivation possible over a wider climatic range. The different types available may be classified approximately as follows: (i) Peaches: (a) white-fleshed and predominantly free-stoned, (b) yellow-fleshed, of firm texture and free-stoned, (c) yellow-fleshed and cling-stoned; (ii) Nectarines. For canning purposes cultivars in group (c) are the most widely grown. Cultivars common to several countries (e.g. Australia and the US) are 'Elberta', 'J.H. Hale' and 'Red Haven', all yellow-fleshed and with a free stone. A very large number of similar peaches is available in the US, including the hardy 'Canadian Harmony'. White-fleshed cultivars such as 'Babcock' and 'Carolina Belle' have finer flavour but with softer flesh which renders them less suitable for commercial production and marketing. Any commercial planting requires special attention to this and to the time of maturity and harvesting. Once ripe, the fruit will not hang on the tree for long and must be gathered extremely carefully to avoid bruising. A choice of cultivars to give a succession of ripening is desirable for continuity of picking and an even supply of fruit. In the US, genetic dwarf peaches are available, growing only to 1–2m/39–78in. and produced almost exclusively for garden cultivation. An example is 'Honey Babe'.

Nectarines have overtaken peaches in many places as commercial fruits for exporting. Of the many available in the US, 'Gold Mine' and 'Red Chief' are recommended white-fleshed cultivars. The more numerous yellow-fleshed include 'Fantasia', 'Flavortop', 'Garden State', 'Hardired' (very hardy), 'Independence', 'Mericrest' (very hardy), 'Panamint', 'Red Gold', 'Sun Glo' (hardy), 'Sunred' and 'Surecrop'. 'Necta Zee' and 'Nectar Baby' are genetic dwarfs.

In the UK, some cultivars are known to succeed under the right conditions but few are generally available. Those commonly listed are peaches 'Peregrine' (white-fleshed) and 'Rochester' (yellow-fleshed), both mid-season, and nectarines 'Lord Napier' (mid-season) and 'Pineapple' (late). A limited number of sources may offer additional choice, such as peaches 'Duke of York', white-fleshed, and 'Hales Early', pale yellow flesh, both early; 'Royal George' and 'Bellegarde', both late and with pale yellow flesh; and nectarines 'John Rivers' (early) and 'Elruge' (late), which was raised at Hoxton, London during the reign of Charles II. If a tree is to be tried in the open garden, the yellow-fleshed 'Rochester' is acknowledged as being the most likely to succeed, although it is of only moderate quality.

Predominantly, peaches and nectarines are satisfactorily self-fertile, although the peach 'J.H. Hale' is one of the exceptions. Some authorities maintain that in commercial plantations a mix of cultivars is preferable to allow cross-pollination. Self-fertility relies on satisfactory pollination, and the siting of trees, be it in garden or orchard, must encourage this by giving the most sheltered conditions possible. Suitable windbreaks should be established where called for.

Flowering is very early, even occurring in late winter if there has been prolonged mild weather, and in these circumstances in the garden situation hand-pollination may be essential to supplement any pollination by insects and so ensure a good set. Using a soft camel-hair brush or some cotton wool on a stick, the centres of flowers are gently brushed to transfer the pollen from anthers to stigma. This is done daily during flowering, preferably in the middle of the day when pollen will be dry and transfer more easily, but not under wet conditions. In the rare event of a cultivar requiring cross-pollination (e.g. 'J.H. Hale') it would be essential to obtain some flowering growths from another cultivar and transfer pollen from these or, failing this, to place the growths in jars of water and suspend these in the tree for which the pollen is required. Visiting bees and other insects will then effect cross-pollination as they work the tree.

Planting should be done by midwinter if possible. This ensures good establishment with some rooting possible before growth begins. Delay into late winter gives only a brief period before bud development begins and this can suffer if the root system has not yet taken hold. Since likeliest success in Britain will be on a wall site, the soil quality must be considered unless the ground is known to be fertile. Wall footings frequently take up some of the rooting area, and annual coverage of weeds and grass may have reduced drastically the availability of soil nutrients. Where such conditions exist it is essential first to eliminate pernicious weeds; if herbicides are used the necessary time clearance must be observed before planting. Subsequently, the planting site should be specially prepared by laying broken turves upside-down at the base, these being covered by good loam or garden soil. The turves should lie at least one spit down, and a little well-rotted manure can be added with the loam. Where such treatment has been required, it is vital to ensure thorough firming throughout.

Trees planted in the open ground are best supported by a stout bamboo cane or small stake for the first two seasons. Any possibility of bad drainage must be attended to before planting, and on heavy soils planting on a slightly raised bed may be advisable. In early spring a mulch of garden compost or rotted manure should be applied around the tree, mainly to conserve soil moisture so that growth is not impaired, and to smother weeds. Planting distances should be 5–7m/17–23ft for bush, 3.5–6m/11–20ft for fan, the larger distances for trees on peach seedlings and Brompton rootstocks.

Numerous tree forms are common in countries like Australia where peach and nectarine cultivation is easy and widespread. The vase- or goblet-shape bush is common but other types such as centre-leader, varying forms of palmette and other specialized systems are also used. In Britain, two tree forms predominate – the bush for open ground cultivation and the fan for wall-training. Whatever tree form is used, it is important to establish a distinct branch system which is subsequently used to produce an annual succession of young shoots for fruiting the following year. This is vital since, unlike apples and pears, the peach and nectarine shoots carry fruit only once, after which they are bare and unproductive.

TRAINING. Shaping for the desired form should be done in the spring following planting as growth is beginning, not in winter which encourages disease infection.

*Bush*. Maiden peach and nectarine trees normally carry plenty of laterals and four or five of these should be chosen, well-spaced, to form the basic branch system. Cut them back to one-third of their length and remove the centre leader immediately above the topmost lateral selected. One or two extra possible laterals may be left to carry the first few fruits the following year (subsequently to be removed), but the lowest should be pruned off completely to leave a clean stem of at least 0.5m/20in. In the following spring more shoots are then selected to expand and extend the branch system and these sub-branches are cut back to half their length. Other side-shoots may need shortening to 10–15cm/4–6in.

*Fan*. Where a maiden tree has good laterals, choose two of equal vigour 25–30cm/10–12in. above ground, one on the left and one on the right, and remove one-third of their length to a good bud. Tie the pruned shoots to a bamboo cane at a little less than 45° to the ground, the bamboo in turn being secured to horizontal support wires. That part of the tree above the selected laterals is pruned off immediately above them, together with any other unwanted laterals, the pruning cuts being coated immediately with a wound sealant. In the case of a maiden not possessing suitable laterals, cut the tree back to a good bud or lateral 50–60cm/20–24in. above ground; also cut out completely any excessively vigorous laterals but prune others back to one or two buds. As growth develops, keep shoots at the top of the central stem pinched back to one or two leaves. From the remainder select two of good and equal vigour as nearly opposite each other as possible and about 25–30cm/10–12in above ground level. These two shoots will form the initial main branches of the fan and are the equivalent of the two laterals selected on the well-feathered maiden at first, as described above. Once these shoots are well-developed and about 45cm/18in. long, they should be tied down carefully to bamboos (as described above). Meanwhile, all other shoots, although shortened by pinching, are retained in reserve in case a replacement shoot is needed following accident or disease.

Once the two main shoots are well-established and tied down, normally by mid-summer or soon after, the central stem is cut away immediately above them and the wound painted with a wound sealant. The following spring these shoots are reduced by one-third of their length. Thus the development of the initial stage from a maiden without laterals takes one year longer than that with laterals.

In the following season, four good shoots should be trained in on either side – one to extend the existing branch, one into the space below it and two above. Those above should be trained at a wide angle to avoid upright growth which may encourage excessive vigour and unbalance the tree shape. All other side shoots should be pinched back to one bud. The resulting bare centre of the fan will be filled in naturally within two or three years by less vigorous sub-branches and side shoots. The following spring the four branches on either side are pruned by about one-quarter of their length, adjusting this as necessary to obtain equal balance. More strong shoots should develop freely, the best placed of which are again chosen as further branches to fill in the remaining wall space; possibly a fourth season may be necessary to complete the fan but this will vary from tree to tree. Meanwhile, many side shoots will have formed and the treatment of these for cropping is covered below.

At all stages in the development of a fan, any shoots of excessive vigour must be cut out completely as soon as they become apparent. Where selected shoots vary unduly in vigour, the strong shoots should be depressed to a horizontal position, the weaker one more upright. Once vigour is evened out the shoots can be returned to their normal position.

PRUNING. In all cases, the need for pruning out older fruited shoots in favour of young shoots is the aim. Pruning is done while the tree is in active growth, not during the winter when the risk of disease infection is greater.

*Bush*. In spring each year, cut out a proportion of older shoots where possible to a visible wood but also after fruiting to a young shoot. Keep the centre of the tree open. Select strong new shoots to replace old branches that are too low and remove any that are crowded or crossing. By doing this annually, a maximum of young wood is maintained to aid fruiting capacity and the longevity of the tree.

Vase-shaped bushes in Australia, New Zealand, etc. receive much harder pruning, first by summer thinning, then by pruning back fruited shoots to replacements after harvesting, spacing these at 45cm/18in. to avoid over-cropping.

*Fan*. In spring select two new shoots arising from existing growths (the latter should carry both growth and fruit buds) one from the base and one half-way up. Remove any others near the base, together with any growing awkwardly between tree and wall, and shorten the remainder to one leaf to help feed developing fruits. Tie the new shoots in where possible. Where space allows, the terminal growth extending the fruit-bearing lateral can also be trained in immediately. After the fruit has been gathered, either cut the fruit-bearing lateral back to the replacement shoot(s) or, in younger trees, tie in all new shoots to fill existing space. On older trees good new shoots may replace older, weakened branches where necessary.

Balanced nutrition is important to ensure adequate production of young wood for fruiting. Starved trees can quickly deteriorate with attendant shortening of their useful life. Regular applications of a compound fertilizer, rather higher in nitrogen and potash than phosphate, should be given at about 75g/m$^2$/(2½oz/yd$^2$) in late winter, followed by a good mulch of well-rotted manure or compost when the soil is moist. After flowering, a liquid feed high in potash can also be given to induce quality and disease resistance, repeating the application every 2–3 weeks where desirable. Under British climatic conditions feeding must be adjusted in relation to tree performance – thus where little or no fruit is carried and growth is at least good, feeding should be withheld. A mulch is particularly valuable in conserving soil moisture in dry seasons, doubly so in countries with hot, dry summers.

Irrigation in summer may be essential for well-trained trees; apply approximately 5 litres (9 UK pt/11 US pt) around each tree every 10–14 days. In countries with hot, dry summers and with restricted water supplies, trickle irrigation is now widely used and is essential to successful growth and fruiting. Flood irrigation where practicable may cause problems connected with faulty drainage and water quality (see also IRRIGATION).

Following successful pollination and fertilization, fruitlets will begin to swell and the stones form. The number of fruitlets may have to be limited both for the well-being of the tree and to enable remaining fruits to attain a good size. Thinning should commence with fruitlets approximately the size of a hazel nut, reducing them to one per cluster and 8–12cm/3–5in. apart. Once of walnut size, fruits should be thinned further where necessary to about 22cm/9in. apart.

Propagation is by budding in late summer, grafting being possible but much more difficult.

Peaches and nectarines in gardens should not be picked until the flesh gives under gentle thumb pressure near the stalk end. White-fleshed cultivars in particular will mark easily if not handled with extreme care. The gathered fruit should be placed in a suitable container lined with soft paper or cotton wool and kept in a constantly cool dark place. Under commercial conditions, fruit is picked slightly under-ripe to enable it to withstand transport and marketing, for which the yellow-fleshed cultivars are preferred.

The use of fruit nets as bird protection may be necessary, the nets also being essential where damage to overwintering buds as from bullfinch is expected. Equally, double thickness netting is a considerable aid in frost protection but is a potential hazard if snow threatens, since the weight of any collapsing snow may cause branch breakage in the tree.

PEACHES AND NECTARINES UNDER GLASS. Where climatic conditions are not conducive to regular cropping in the open, cultivation under glass is a practical though laborious alternative. Where background heating is available to guarantee frost protection, trees can be started into growth and flowering very early, but even without heat the likelihood of success is high.

A border of good deep soil is essential and a fan-trained tree against a wall is the best method to adopt. A lean-to greenhouse is thus ideal: a minimum span of 2.75m/9ft is necessary for tree development. Suitably arranged horizontal support wires 7–8cm/2½–3in. away from the wall will be needed; in full-span houses greater difficulty will be encountered in negotiating the angle formed by the side and slanting roof and special fittings will be needed to carry the support wires 30–35cm/12–14in. from the glass. However, growths on the young tree are very flexible and can carefully be trained and tied into position to accommodate the angle. Initial training and subsequent pruning, disbudding, pinching and tying in are as already described for fan-trained trees.

Regular attention to detail is necessary because development under glass can be rapid.

Trees must be subject to full continuous ventilation once the crop has been cleared, through autumn and winter, to allow adequate chilling, without which abnormal and unsatisfactory tree performance is probable. Ventilation should be restricted from late winter to give a temperature of 8–10°C/46–50°F, raising this to approximately 20°C/68°F after ten days, with a night minimum of 4–8°C/39–46°F. The soil should never be allowed to dry out: skilful watering (coupled with the use of a soil auger) is therefore essential. Also the trees must be syringed on brighter days with tepid water mid-morning and early afternoon; ample ventilation may be necessary to prevent too high temperatures on sunny days but always with care if cold winds occur. This is particularly important during flowering, when the flowers should be lightly dusted with a camel-hair brush or cotton wool to ensure satisfactory pollination. Syringing should be withheld at this period and as fruits approach ripeness, subsequently restarting again following flowering and harvesting. Damping down of the ground should be practised as fruits develop but not during ripening. The syringing and damping down are major factors in keeping infestations of red spider mite at bay.

Fruit thinning will normally be necessary to a final spacing of 24–30cm/10–12in. The finer quality white-fleshed peaches (e.g. 'Peregrine') should be preferred, together with fine-flavoured nectarines such as 'Lord Napier'.

Feeding should consist of regular light top dressings of well-rotted manure in late winter. If this is lacking, a compound fertilizer high in nitrogen and potash should be applied at $100g/m^2$ followed by liquid feeds high in potash every 10–14 days during the summer, ceasing as ripening approaches. Peach leaf curl will not be a problem under glass, but mildew, aphids and red spider mite will require the necessary preventive measures to be taken.

PEACHES AND NECTARINES IN POTS AND CONTAINERS. Where neither suitable glasshouse nor garden space is available, cultivation in pots or other containers is a possibility. A major advantage is that trees can be moved to warmer frost-free sites (glasshouses, conservatories or patios), during the vulnerable periods of flowering, early fruitlet and ripening, particularly if genetic dwarf cultivars are used. However, skilled regular management is essential to success, particularly watering and feeding. A 30cm/12in. or 35cm/14in. pot is necessary, suitably crocked, and using a medium-fertility soil-based potting mix. It is best to start with a maiden tree, the roots of which can then develop within the pot. Firm planting is essential and a miniature bush type tree should be developed and managed accordingly. Regular repotting in autumn will be necessary, carefully teasing out some (not all) soil from the top and sides of the root-ball once the tree has been freed from the pot. The latter is washed and dried, crocked, and the tree then replaced with some fresh compost firmed around and over the root-ball. Young trees may require a slightly larger pot and any coarse roots should be removed in favour of fibrous ones. Suitable liquid feeds with high potash content should be given every 10–14 days in summer to supplement the nutrients in the compost, but stopping before fruits ripen. The trees should be kept in the open through autumn and winter to allow adequate chilling, nevertheless protecting the rootball against freezing by plunging the pot in the soil or wrapping it in hessian or other material. The plants may need protecting by netting to avoid bullfinch damage to buds.

PESTS AND DISEASES. Peaches and nectarines can be affected by many diseases which attack *Prunus* spp., including armillaria root rot (*Armillaria* spp.), bacterial canker (*Pseudomonas mors-prunorum*), brown rot (*Sclerotinia* spp.), crown gall (*Agrobacterium tumefaciens*), leaf curl (*Taphrina deformans*), powdery mildew (*Sphaerotheca pannosa*), rust (*Tranzschelia pruni-spinosae*), scab (*Fusicladium carpophilum*), shot-hole (*Stigmina carpophila*), silver leaf (*Chondrostereum purpureum*) and specific replant disease. Many viruses, the most important of which is plum pox, can affect trees in commercial production but are unlikely to be important in gardens.

Subject to infestation in Europe and North America by aphids, including the peach-potato aphid (*Myzus persicae*) and the black peach aphid (*Brachycaudus persicaecola*); various scale insects, including the oystershell scale (*Aspidiotus ostraeiformis*), brown scale (*Parthenolecanium corni*), woolly scales (*Pulvinaria* spp.); red spider mites (*Tetranychus* spp.); and earwigs and wasps which attack the fruits. In warmer regions may become infested with fruit flies including the Mediterranean fruit fly (*Ceratitis capitata*). Additional pests in North America include San Jose scale (*Quadraspidiotus perniciosus*); the oriental fruit moth (*Grapholitha molesta*) with pinkish white larvae that tunnel into tips of growing shoots and bore into fruits; the peach twig borer (*Anarsia lineatella*) with small reddish brown caterpillars which cause damage to shoots similar to that of the previous species; and clearwing moths including the peach tree borer (*Synanthedon exitiosa*) and lesser peach tree borer (*S. pictipes*).

**Pears**. *Pyrus* spp. (Rosaceae). The European pear has developed mainly from the species *Pyrus communis*, indigenous to Europe and much of Northern Asia, particularly in the Caucasus and Turkestan. It is occasionally found in Britain though whether it is native is open to question. Certain other species of *Pyrus* are thought to have contributed to the evolution of the European pear but without doubt *P. communis* is predominant. In Japan and the Far East, *P. pyrifolia* (syn. *P. serotina*) and *P. ussuriensis* have been the main source for the development of Asian pears. Crosses between *P. communis* and *P. pyrifolia* have occurred both naturally (in the case of 'Kieffer', a cultivar raised as a chance seedling in the US and at one time widely grown there and in South Africa, especially for canning) and through controlled breeding, but *P. pyrifolia* has played no part in the parentage of European cultivars.

The pear is often mentioned in classical Greek and Roman texts. In Britain, there is little evidence for its introduction but it is assumed that some pears must have come into the country during the Roman occupation. However, records show that after the Norman Conquest rather more importation of the latest cultivars from the near Continent occurred, particularly from France. This was further strengthened in the 16th century by the strong influence of Henry VIII, by which time seedlings of English origin were being produced, including numerous variations of the 'Warden' pear, a cultivar specifically for cooking. The cultivation of pears in England and Wales was now widespread both in the garden and in orchards; they are among the most long-lived of fruit trees.

Further introductions, particularly from Belgium and France, continued during the 18th and 19th centuries, one of the famous Belgian cultivars being 'Glou Morceau', raised in 1750 and still available today. In 1770, 'Williams Bon Chrétien' was raised at Aldermaston, Berkshire, a cultivar which is still grown worldwide (particularly for canning as 'Bartlett' pears; it was renamed 'Bartlett' when introduced to the US by a Lux Bartlett of Boston in 1799). European influence, especially Belgian, French and British, established the pear in those climates conducive to its successful cultivation – parts of North America and subsequently Australia and South Africa being specially favoured. 'Packham's Triumph' was raised in Australia *c*1896 and is still the most important cultivar there. It is also grown in South Africa and southern Europe.

During the 19th century, Thomas Andrew Knight and the Royal Horticultural Society played a prominent role in further developments in Britain and many new cultivars became available, both home-bred and from Belgium and France. Of major note from France was 'Doyenne du Comice' (1849), which is widely grown and generally accepted as the finest flavoured of all pears.

In England, the famous nurseries of Laxton and Rivers became major suppliers of pear trees, as of apples, for the large Victorian kitchen gardens of the great estates. 'Conference', the most widely grown and successful pear in Britain, was raised by Rivers in 1894. Their work continued through the first half of the 20th century, by which time controlled breeding programmes had developed at the John Innes and Long Ashton Research Stations. 'Merton Pride' from John Innes (1941) is still acknowledged as a particularly fine-flavoured fruit but is unreliable in cropping. From Long Ashton, 'Bristol Cross' (1921) was temporarily popular but 'Conference' remained more reliable.

Some initial breeding of pears also continued in other parts of the world, notably the US, and the one introduction from there of interest for garden culture in the UK was 'Gorham' for early to mid-season use. However, the incursion of the bacterial disease fireblight has severely restricted the successful cultivation of pears in the US, most of which is now concentrated in California and Oregon. Localized outbreaks of fireblight have also caused occasional problems in the UK since about 1960.

The shape of pears varies greatly with cultivar, markedly more so than with apples. The classification usually adopted (from Bunyard's *Handbook of Fruits – Apples and Pears*, 1920) includes six groups as follows: (1) Flat and round (e.g. 'Passe Crassanne'; (2) Bergamotte (flat, rounded/conical; e.g. 'Winter Nelis'); (3) Conical (e.g. 'Beurre Hardy); (4) Pyriform, or waisted (e.g. 'Doyenne du Comice'); (5) Oval (e.g. 'Emile d'Heyst'); (6) Calabash, longer than pyriform (e.g. 'Conference').

Pears flower comparatively early and freedom from frost and are good summer warmth is essential for consistent cropping. In Britain the possible ravages of bullfinch damage to the overwintering buds should be noted. Netting the trees is the only certain protection: without it severe damage can render a tree worthless, although this is localized and varies in intensity. Adequate shelter is essential to ensure warm conditions for cross-pollination and also to protect fruit and foliage from cold winds, which in severe cases can quickly blacken leaves and fruitlets. In many cases good results with late-maturing cultivars (e.g. 'Joséphine de Malines' and 'Glou Morceau') require the warmth of a south- or west-facing wall in cool-temperate regions for the production of quality, well-flavoured fruit. The incidence of scab is also reduced.

Choice of cultivar away from favoured southern counties of the UK becomes more restricted to early-ripening kinds. Similarly, in the northern states of the US there is a restriction in the range of cultivars that will withstand the harsher conditions, among the best being 'Calebasse Bosc'. By contrast, it is the cooler areas of Australia and South Africa that grow pears most successfully, the Asian pear being better suited to hotter districts. Of all countries historically associated with the development of the pear, however, it is France and Belgium that are in the forefront and, both in those countries and in parts of southern Europe such as Italy, the climate allows the successful growing of a wide range of cultivars covering a long period of ripening from midsummer to late winter. Fireblight however remains a serious problem.

The pear usually succeeds on most soil types although, as with apple, the highly calcareous areas may well induce deficiencies of iron and manganese through lime-induced chlorosis. Furthermore, the pear is more tolerant than apple of wet (not waterlogged) conditions but less so of drought, so that mulching and irrigation may be necessary where conditions dictate. This is particularly important for newly planted trees if they are to establish quickly and satisfactorily, and where mulching is undertaken regularly this will also eventually help to offset the deficiencies caused in calcareous soils. A well-drained, good medium loam is undoubtedly the best soil for pears, since it not only offers balanced food reserves but also moisture retention. The heavier soils will normally produce better-flavoured fruit than the hungry sands and gravels.

The availability of a suitable rootstock for pears has never been fully satisfied. Grown on pear seedling stock, trees can attain great stature and longevity but with attendant delay in cropping, and records show that over many centuries certain other species have been tried in an endeavour to reduce tree size and to quicken cropping. In the 16th and 17th centuries the hawthorn was recommended but with variable and inconclusive results. Some French writers at this time recommended the quince as the best alternative, many pear cultivars thriving on it with marked precocity of fruiting. Quince was slowly taken up by British growers, but with the same variability in material used as had occurred with the many selections of apple rootstocks. Early in the 20th century, Hatton at East Malling Research Station established two reliable selections of quince, A and C, that are still the standard rootstocks for pears in Europe today. 'Quince A' ('Angers Quince') is moderately vigorous and has been the most widely used; 'Quince C' is somewhat more dwarfing but only in recent years have virus-free strains become generally available. It is particularly useful for inducing early fruitfulness in naturally vigorous cultivars such as 'Doyenne du Comice'. A major disadvantage of quince rootstock is that it is not compatible with all cultivars of pear, among them 'Williams Bon Chrétien', 'Jargonelle', 'Marie Louise' and 'Packham's Triumph'.

Commercial orchards in other pear-growing areas of the world still tend to use rootstocks that produce larger trees. Quince rootstock is insufficiently vigorous to counter the hotter drier conditions often met with in the fruit-growing areas of Australia, South Africa and the US, although it is used to produce small trees for gardens. Seedling pear is still used in some cases and, in Australia, seedlings of the Asiatic species *Pyrus calleryana* are used, a selection known as D6 being considered best. Its use prevents the fruit disorder known as blackend developing in the scion cultivar.

The choice of cultivars for the garden in the UK is limited unless a suitable warm wall with a southerly or westerly aspect is available. 'Conference' is the most widely successful, 'Williams Bon Chrétien' and 'Doyenne du Comice' are also popular. Valuable new introductions from East Malling Research Station include 'Beth' (early September), 'Onward' (September–October) and, most recently, 'Concorde' (October). The later-ripening cultivars, even 'Doyenne du Comice', will require the warmth of a wall for the production of quality fruit where conditions are cooler. On south- or west-facing walls, 'Beurre d'Anjou', 'Beurre Hardy', 'Beurre Superfin', 'Doyenne du Comice', 'Emile d'Heyst' and 'Joséphine de Malines' can be grown; on south-facing walls, 'Le Lectier' and 'Passe Crassanne'. Purely culinary cultivars are now seldom grown but 'Catillac' is occasionally listed.

Until fireblight was reported in the UK around 1960, the early pear 'Laxton's Superb' was highly popular, particularly for garden culture. Ripening in August, it possessed fair eating quality and was reliable, but it proved to be particularly susceptible to fireblight, and was officially condemned and trees grubbed and burnt in an attempt to arrest the spread of this serious disease. Subsequent outbreaks when weather conditions favoured the disease have proved that it is now endemic and it has spread to a range of other rosaceous genera in gardens (e.g. *Cotoneaster, Pyracantha* and *Sorbus*) as well as to hawthorn in the wild.

Elsewhere, 'Williams Bon Chrétien' ('Bartlett') is probably the most widely distributed, being grown (largely for canning) in the US, Australia and South Africa as well as Europe. 'Packham's Triumph' is similarly popular, while 'Passe Crassanne', 'Glou Morceau' and 'Dr Jules Guyot' (among others) are also in commercial production. In North America all the pears of French origin are available as well as many of local raising like 'Harrow Delight' (Canadian), 'Luscious', 'Magness' and 'Moonglow'; 'Red Bartlett' and 'Sensation' are red-skinned. A US group called Southern-Cross Pears, or just 'hybrid pears' (sometimes named *Prunus* × *lecontei*) are crisp-fleshed and very long-keeping. They include 'Ayres', 'Kieffer', 'Orient' and 'Pineapple', and are usually grown for canning.

Most cultivars of European pear are not self-fertile and provision of suitable pollinator cultivars is imperative. 'Conference' is *not* self-fertile as often erroneously stated, although it sometimes does produce parthenocarpic (seedless) fruits under adverse conditions. Most cultivars are diploid, a few triploid or tetraploid. The high-quality 'Merton Pride' is also triploid. 'Bristol Cross', 'Beurre Bedford' and 'Marguerite Marillat' are male-sterile and therefore ineffective as pollinators. There are also two groups whose cultivars are incompatible, and detailed advice on pollination is therefore essential (see FRUIT FERTILITY RULES), introduced 'Onward' and 'Doyenne du Comice' are cross-incompatible. The time of flowering varies considerably and it is important to choose combinations within which flowering coincides as closely as possible. If a triploid is planted, the same pollinator provision is necessary as for apple.

Planting is best done in late autumn and early winter while the soil is still comparatively warm but can be delayed up to late winter if necessary. Later plantings may be slower in establishing and judicious mulching and watering may be necessary. Suitable staking is advisable in all cases for the first two years or so; trees on 'Quince C' rootstock may need staking permanently. Planting distances for the different tree forms closely follow those quoted for apple, the greater ones being selected for trees on 'Quince A' and the more vigorous cultivars, the lesser ones for 'Quince C'. Any trees on seedling pear will require at least 6m/19½ft spacing.

Soil management is predominantly the same as for apple but, since pears require rather more moisture, careful control of any grass sward is essential, particularly regular mowing and allowing the cut grass to lie. This is especially necessary for trees in lawns on quince stock. Irrigation must be given when called for.

Tree forms for garden trees closely follow those for apple, namely cordon and its variations, espalier, fan and dwarf pyramid. Commercial trees are more usually trained as goblet or vase shape, although in some cases (e.g. Australia) large centre-leader trees are grown. Trellis systems such as palmette are popular in southern Europe, also in Australia.

The training of pear trees closely follows that of apples. The cultivars vary considerably in their natural vigour: thus 'Conference' makes only moderate growth, whereas 'Doyenne du Comice' and 'Merton Pride' are more vigorous. In most cases, pears produce spur systems very readily and only a very few tip-bearers exist, 'Jargonelle' and 'Joséphine de Malines' being among them. Like apples, such cultivars are more difficult to manage in trained forms such as cordon or espalier. Where goblet- and vase-shaped trees are being trained, it is important that the initial branch angles with the main stem are wide; if too narrow, branches will break away from the trunk once heavy crops develop.

Established cropping pear trees frequently develop more intricate spur systems than do apples. The general build-up of trees is similar to apple and pruning is done at any time from leaf-fall to late winter. The degree of pruning will depend on the fruit bud to growth ratio – less pruning for vigorous trees than for those of more moderate or weak habit. Some laterals can be shortened to three or four buds to encourage spur formation, a few of the most vigorous removed completely if overcrowded. The spur systems on older trees will require shortening and even complete removal where overcrowded, otherwise too many small fruits may result. Branch shortening (dehorning) may be necessary when individual branches become too long, but in general tip-pruning should not be necessary. Where branches become too crowded, some branch thinning is essential but only a small proportion should be removed in any one season.

Pears require rather more nitrogen than do apples but only where growth is unsatisfactory. Potash is also important and rates to apply are generally as for apples. Under conditions of too high pH, iron and manganese deficiencies are common. Surface applications of rotted farmyard manure every two to three years will help, but in severe cases the deficiencies should be rectified by appropriate means. Trees that are neglected or starved will need extra applications of nitrogen, one in early spring and one in late spring.

Where heavy crops develop, some fruit thinning will be essential to enhance fruit size. Thin to one fruit per cluster, two if leafing is good and there is sufficient space. This should be done after the natural shedding of fruitlets about midsummer. Heavily laden branches will need support to prevent breakage.

The harvesting of pears requires careful monitoring, particularly for earlier cultivars, such as 'Williams Bon Chrétien'. The fruit may be picked while still green yet parting readily from the spur. If left too long the flesh will rapidly over-ripen and become 'woolly'. Later cultivars, on the other hand, must be allowed to mature fully; too-early picking will result in fruit shrivelling and loss of flavour especially under domestic storage conditions.

Domestically, pears are best stored either in polythene bags (as for apples) or in cool, dark, slightly moist conditions as found in cellars or outhouses. They should be conditioned in normal room temperature (18°C/65°F) for 2–3 days before consumption to ensure full flavour and good eating texture. Commercially, special cold storage conditions are called for with temperatures near freezing point.

Propagation of pears is normally by budding or grafting. The problem of incompatibility on quince involves special techniques, otherwise what at first appears to be a successful union between scion and the quince rootstock proves to be imperfect and weak and sooner or later the tree is likely to snap off at the union. The problem is overcome by double-working, which involves introducing a short piece of graftwood from a compatible cultivar which is grafted directly onto the quince, the incompatible cultivar then itself being grafted on top. An alternative is the placing of a small shield of the compatible variety in the budding operation, again to act as a bridge between the quince and the bud of the incompatible cultivar. The cultivar most commonly used as an intermediate stock in such situations is 'Beurre Hardy'; others include 'Doyenne du Comice', 'Pitmaston Duchess', 'Vicar of Winkfield' and 'Glou Morceau'.

ASIAN PEARS. The Asian pear, also known under a number of common names including Oriental, Chinese, Japanese and Nashi (the Japanese for pear), is derived from *P. pyrifolia* and *P. ussuriensis*. Japanese cultivars are selections of the former, while the Chinese are from hybrids between the two. *P. pyrifolia* is indigenous to Central and West China, where the fruits are eaten; *P. ussuriensis* is native to Northeast China and Eastern Siberia and is particularly hardy but with small unpalatable fruits. Until recently the Asian pears were generally restricted to the regions of or near to their origin – China and Japan – where they have been known and used since ancient times and where extensive commercial production progresses. Current cultivation is expanding world-wide, predominantly in Australian temperate zones, California and parts of Central America. The chilling requirement is less than that for European pears and so the potential for the Asian pear's extended cultivation is considerable.

In Britain the climate is not usually conducive to success, the fruit in poor seasons remaining small (golf-ball size or slightly larger) and bland in taste. Even in more favoured regions the flavour is less rich and the texture crisper and less melting than that of European cultivars; the fruit is also widely used in salads.

Cultivation is generally similar to that of European pears. Rootstocks include Asian pear seedlings, *P. betulifolia* and *P. calleryana*; in Japan, *P. pyrifolia* seedlings are favoured. Growth can be vigorous but trees tend to commence fruiting quite early. Fruit is borne on two-year and older wood, with some on one-year laterals.

Flowering occurs at the same time as with European pears (which are suitable as pollinators). Asian pears are partially self-fertile but a mixture of cultivars is advisable to assist adequate fertility. Heavy fruit set will require judicious thinning to encourage fruit size, reducing fruits to one per cluster one month after flowering and with an additional thinning around midsummer on naturally small-fruited cultivars.

Horizontal trellis systems as practised in Japan give excellent results but labour input is heavy. The ripening fruit predominantly turns from green to russet-brown but some Chinese cultivars turn paler green-yellow. Fruits are very delicate and mark easily. They will keep for about two weeks in normal room temperature but later-maturing cultivars can be stored for several months at freezing point. Numerous cultivars, mostly of Japanese origin, include 'A-Ri-Rang', 'Chojura', 'Hosui', 'Kikusui', 'Kosui' (highest-rated Japanese commercial cv), 'Niitaka', 'Nijiseiki' ('Twentieth Century'), 'Seigyoku', 'Shinko' and 'Shinseiki'; 'Tsu Li' and 'Ya Li' are of Chinese origin. Ripening of the earliest commences in late midsummer continuing through to early autumn for the latest.

The trees can also be decorative, with attractive white blossom, glossy green foliage and striking red autumn colouring.

DISEASES AND PESTS. Pears can be affected by armillaria root rot (*Armillaria* spp.), bacterial (blossom) blight (*Pseudomonas syringae*), bitter rot (*Glomerella cingulata*), blue mould and other storage rots (*Penicillium* spp. and other fungi), brown rot and blossom wilt (*Sclerotinia* spp.), canker (*Nectria galligena*), coral spot (*Nectria cinnabarina*), crown gall (*Agrobacterium tumefaciens*), fireblight (*Erwinia amylovora*), leaf curl (blister) (*Taphrina bullata*), powdery mildew (*Podosphaera leucotricha*), scab (*Venturia pirina*), silver leaf (*Chondrostereum purpureum*), sooty blotch (*Gloeodes pomigena*) and white root rot (*Rosellinia necatrix*). Pears can be the aecial host of several heteroecious rust fungi (*Gymnosporangium* spp.) and one of these *G. fuscum*, although rare in Britain, is common in Europe. Leaf fleck caused by *Mycosphaerella pyri* causes numerous small spots on the leaves and fruits but would be controlled by the routine fungicide sprays used for scab control. Pears can also be affected by several viruses and by the pear decline mycoplasma but these are unlikely to be of importance to the gardener, especially if certified virus-free plants can be obtained.

The more important pests include a gall midge, pear midge (*Contarinia pyrivora*); a gall mite, the pear leaf blister mite (*Eriophyes pyri*); the pear and cherry slugworm (*Caliroa cerasi*), often called pear sawfly in the US; pear psyllid or sucker (*Psylla pyricola*); pear thrips (*Taeniothrips inconsequens*) and the mussel scale (*Lepidosaphes ulmi*) referred to as the oystershell scale in the US. Several species of aphids attack pear; the most damaging in Europe is the pear-bedstraw aphid (*Dysaphis pyri*).

**Peas**. *Pisum sativum*. Leguminosae. Annuals grown for their edible seeds produced in pods; the wide range of cultivars includes some in which the entire immature pod may be eaten. The species is believed to have originated in Central or Southeast Asia but is no longer found in the wild. It was cultivated in Southwest Asia in early times, from where it was introduced to India and China. Although there are numerous references to the use of peas as a food in Europe during the 15th century, these relate to the ripe seeds and the habit of eating green peas probably did not spread from the European continent to Britain until well into the 16th century. Cultivation is now widespread in temperate regions and highland areas of the tropics.

Most cultivars thrive in a cool, humid climate with temperatures in the range 13–18°C/55–65°F. A minimum soil temperature of 10°C/50°F is required for germination. Peas are normally harvested from early summer until autumn but the season can be advanced by providing early protection with plastic or glass cloches. Garden peas can be boiled and served as a vegetable or used in the preparation of soups and stews. They may also be frozen or stored dry for later use. Mangetout cultivars are harvested and cooked entire when the peas are immature; some more recent cultivars can also be allowed to mature and are shelled in the normal way – these are the sugar peas which, as their name suggests, are exceptionally sweet. Mangetout peas can also be frozen. Peas require an open but sheltered site. Soils should be fertile and deeply cultivated, preferably incorporating manure or compost in the previous autumn to improve moisture retention. Light dressings of nitrogenous fertilizers will assist in establishing the crop but high levels will suppress the activity of the nitrogen-fixing *Rhizobium* nodules. A pH range of 6.0–7.5 is optimum and liming should be carried out if the soil is more acid. Overliming of organic soils can lead to the unavailability of manganese. Avoid growing peas on the same site for more than one year in five to avoid the build-up of soil-borne diseases.

Peas germinate poorly at temperatures below 10°C/50°F, when losses are liable to be high due to mice damage and fungal and bacterial diseases attacking the seed. Sowing should therefore be delayed until temperatures increase during late spring, or alternatively earlier sowings should be carried out under cloches. An early sowing should be followed by further sowings at about 3–4-week intervals until mid-summer to provide continuity of harvests. Alternatively, continuity can be achieved from a single sowing using a range of cultivars from different seasonal groups. Autumn harvests, when weather conditions permit, can be obtained from a summer sowing of an early dwarf cultivar. Im mild frost-free areas it may be possible to overwinter an autumn-sown crop to provide an early harvest the following spring although cloche protection may be advisable, depending on the local climate.

Seeds should be sown 4cm/1½in. deep at about 5cm/2in. apart, either in a 20cm/8in.-wide flat-bottomed drill or in a single row in a V-shaped drill. The distance between drills should be similar to the height of the peas at maturity, which may vary from 45cm to 115m/18–45in. depending on the cultivar. A number of alternative planting patterns is possible, including the use of 1m-wide beds in which peas are raised at a spacing of between 5–7cm/2–3in. between plants. Whichever system is used, peas should be provided with support from an early stage as soon as they produce tendrils, using traditional pea-sticks or wide mesh netting.

Young plants should be kept free of weeds and during flowering and pod set should be kept well-watered. Mulching during early development will help conserve moisture and keeps roots cool. Pods should be harvested regularly at a tender stage to ensure continued cropping. The pods of sugar and mangetout types should be harvested at an earlier stage, when the seeds first start to show signs of swelling. Fresh peas can be stored for up to 10 days at temperatures close to freezing point and in conditions of high humidity. Where dried peas are required for storage, pods should be left on the plants to full maturity, when the uprooted vines should be hung in a dry, well-ventilated place to complete drying.

A wide range of cultivars is available, which may be divided broadly into wrinkle-seeded and round-seeded types. The latter have a lower sugar content but, being hardier, are more suitable for cultivation during the colder months of the year, including overwintering. Cultivars also differ in their time to maturity. The earlier types are lower-yielding but depending on the temperatures will mature within 11–12 weeks, reaching a final height of about 45cm/18in. The higher-yielding maincrop selections require up to 14 weeks and may be over 1.5m/5ft tall. Near-leafless cultivars have been developed, primarily for commercial cultivation, but a few are available to gardeners. Mangetout or sugar peas are eaten pod and all; snap peas combine succulent pods with full-sized peas.

Recommended cultivars. *Early wrinkle-seeded*: 'Hurst Beagle', 'Early Onward', 'Kelvedon Wonder'. *Maincrop wrinkled-seeded*: 'Alderman', 'Hurst Green Shaft', 'Onward', 'Purple Podded', 'Waverex' (petit pois). *Early round-seeded*: 'Alaska', 'Douce Provence', 'Early Frosty', 'Feltham First' (dwarf), 'Meteor', 'Pilot'. *Maincrop round-seeded*: 'Freezonian', 'Green Arrow', 'Knight', 'Laxton's Progress A9' (dwarf), 'Nova' (self-supporting, good freezer), 'Makana' (self-supporting), 'Sparkle' (dwarf), 'Tall Telephone' (up to 2m tall), 'Thomas Laxton', 'Wando' (cold-resistant). *Semi-leafless*: 'Lacy Lady', 'Novella'. *Mangetout or sugar peas*: 'Carouby de Maussane', 'Dwarf Gray Sugar', 'Dwarf White Sugar', 'Edula', 'Mammoth Melting Sugar', 'Oregon Sugar Pod', 'Osaya Endo' (climbing: large pods), 'Snowflake', 'Tezieravenir'. *Snap peas*: 'Sugar Ann', 'Sugar Bon', 'Sugar Daddy', 'Sugar Mel', 'Sugar Rae', 'Sugar Snap'.

Pests that may attack peas include birds, mice, pea moth and pea thrips; common diseases include damping-off, downy mildew and black root rot. The most serious diseases of peas are downy mildew and fusarium wilt. Foot rot is a common disease encouraged by wet conditions, as are other fungal root rots. Powdery mildew can be damaging to late crops and there are several important virus diseases.

For asparagus pea and winged pea see *Psophocarpus*; for black-eyed pea, see *Vigna*.

**Pecluma** M. Price. Polypodiaceae. Some 35 species of usually epiphytic ferns. Rhizomes short- to long-creeping, simple; scales entire to dentate, glabrous or pubescent. Fronds stipitate, uniform, pinnate to pinnatifid, generally lanceolate or elliptic to deltoid or oblong, glabrous or pubescent below, involved when dry, segments approximate, adnate, linear to strap-shaped, usually decurrent at base, veins simple or forked, free or anastomosing, areolae with free, included veinlets; rachis occasionally scaly; stipes jointed to short phyllopodia, terete, glabrous or pubescent. Sori medial, at tips of veinlets, uniserial, circular; paraphyses absent or present; indusia absent; sporangia stalked; spores globose, bilateral, tuberculate or verrucose. Tropical America. Z10.

CULTIVATION As for *Polypodium*. The fronds of *P. pectinata* will curl up if the plant is dried out for short periods, resurrecting when re-watered.

***P. pectinata*** (L.) M. Price. Rhiz. to 1cm diam., short-creeping; scales to 6mm, dense, filiform, ciliate, dark brown. Fronds to 90×15cm, deeply pinnate-pinnatifid, lanceolate or elliptic to linear or oblong, attenuate and narrowly acute at apex, attenuate and lobed at base, glabrous or minutely pubesc., thin-textured, pinnae or lobes to 6×0.7cm, horizontal, apex obtuse, base dilated, entire or dentate, lowest reduced, veins forked, anastomosing; rachis pubesc.; stipes to 15cm, erect, glabrous or pubesc., scaly at base, purple to brown. W Indies, C to S America.

***P. plumala*** (Humb. & Bonpl. ex Willd.) M. Price. Rhiz. to 7mm diam., short-creeping, woody; scales to 4mm, lanceolate or deltoid to linear, apex narrowly acute, dark brown. Fronds to 45×10cm, deeply pinnate-pinnatifid, elliptic to linear or oblong, glabrous to pubesc. above, pubesc. and bullate-scaly below, pinnae or lobes to 3cm×3mm, to 100 pairs, apex obtuse, margin entire to ciliate, lowest reduced, veins obscure, forked, free; rachis minutely pubesc., scaly below; stipes to 8cm, glabrous or minutely pubesc. W Indies, C to S America.

For synonymy see *Goniophlebium*.

**Pecteilis** Raf. (From Lat. *pecten*, comb, referring to the form of the lip lateral lobes.) Orchidaceae. Some 4 species of terrestrial orchids. Stems erect. Leaves linear to ovate, cauline or, basal rosulate. Inflorescence erect; flowers few, white or white and yellow; sepals similar, spreading, free; petals narrower; lip trilobed, midlobe entire, lateral lobes fringed, spreading; spur slender. Tropical Asia. Z10.

CULTIVATION Beautiful terrestrial orchids for the cool and intermediate house. The most commonly grown is *P. susannae* with a strikingly fringed lip. Cultural requirements as for *Disa*.

***P. radiata*** (Thunb.) Raf. Stem to 45cm, erect, terete. Lvs 3–7, linear-lanceolate, acuminate, 2–10×0.3–0.7cm. Infl. terminal; bracts lanceolate, acuminate, to 1cm; fls 1–3; sep. ovate-lanceolate, acuminate, to 1×0.5cm, green; pet. white, ovate, subacute, margins white, jagged, minutely toothed; lip white, trilobed, to 2×3cm, midlobe linear-ligulate, acute, lateral lobes obovate, spreading, back and side margins deeply and irregularly divided; spur decurved, green. Japan, Korea.

***P. sagarikii*** Seidenf. Stem to 25cm. Lvs 2–3, ovate, 10–12×6–9cm, glossy, apex obtuse or rounded, in a basal rosette. Infl. erect, scape 2–4-sheathed; fls few, white or cream, fragrant; dorsal sep. ovate, acute, erect, to 2.5×1.5cm, lateral sep. lanceolate, acute, suberect, spreading; pet. similar, smaller; lip weakly decurved, convex, sometimes bright yellow, base obscurely trilobed, apex subobovate, rounded or obtuse, to 2–5×2cm, lateral lobes obscure, rounded; spur filiform, weakly incurved, 3–5cm. Thailand.

***P. susannae*** (L.) Raf. Stem to 1–20m, leafy. Lvs elliptic, to 12×5cm, concave, sessile. Raceme to 20cm; fls 4–6, white to green-white, fragrant; dorsal sep. subcircular, to 3cm diam., lateral sep. spreading linear, to 3.5×2.5cm, margins reflexed; pet. linear, falcate, to 1.5cm; lip trilobed, midlobe linear-spathulate, entire, to 3cm, lateral lobes deeply fringed; spur strongly decurved. China, Burma, Malaya.

For synonymy see *Habenaria*.

**Pectinaria** Haw. (From Lat. *pecten*, a comb, due to the finger-like projections on the inner corona.) Asclepiadaceae. 3 species of dwarf, succulent, clump-forming, leafless herbs closely related to *Stapeliopsis*, to 8cm. Stems 4–6-angled, subglobose, prostrate, apices sometimes burrowing, tuberculate, with small teeth. Flowers pedicellate, in clusters or solitary, from furrows between stem angles; calyx acutely 5-lobed; corolla tube short, broadly campanulate, lobes triangular, acute, joined at apices (like *Ceropegia*), producing a canopy with only narrow slits between lobes; corona 2-whorled, lobes of inner whorl recurved, often converging over the anthers, with dorsal projections divided into finger-like processes, forming a ring with lobes of outer whorl. Fruit a narrow, spindle-shaped, glabrous follicle, borne in pairs. S Africa (Cape Province). Z9.

CULTIVATION Found in the drier inland areas of the Cape Province on the eastern edge of the winter-rainfall area which often receives appreciable rain in summer as well, *Pectinaria* grow among rocks or, more usually, in the shelter of small shrubs such as *Ruschia spinescens*. Cultivate as for *Stapelia*, except that as these plants have burrowing prostrate stems, they should be grown in wide shallow pans and in a very open growing medium. In cool weather, care should be taken with watering.

***P. arcuata*** N.E. Br. Stems 5–10cm or more, prostrate, bluntly tetragonal in section, green, glabrous, to 1cm diam., apex burrowing. Fls to 3 per bundle, to 12mm, ovoid-acuminate; tube hemispherical, dark red; lobes 7mm, pale yellow, exterior flushed purple, interior dark purple at base, apex white spotted maroon; corona appearing 1-whorled, yellow.

***P. articulata*** (Ait.) Haw. Stems to 2cm diam., bluntly 5–8-angled, glabrous, with soft teeth. Fls 1–2; pedicel 2–15mm; cor. 5–8mm diam., purple, red-brown or pale yellow, exterior densely to sparsely papillose, interior with spiculate, crystalline papillae; lobes of outer corona bifid, lobes of inner whorl deltoid to truncate. ssp. ***articulata***. Stems to 6cm, 5–6-angled, grey-green, often flushed red, bracts numerous, spreading, seg. 3–5cm. Fls suberect; pedicel 5–15mm; cor., 5–8mm diam., flat-topped, more or less bowl-shaped, purple-brown, sometimes pale yellow, exterior papillose, interior purple-black, densely papillose; tube 2.5–3.5mm, bowl-shaped; lobes 2.5–3.5mm, tips recurved, fused inside tube; corona dark purple, sometimes pale yellow. ssp. ***asperiflora*** (N.E. Br.) P.V. Bruyns. Stems many, 2–8cm, curved, dark purple, 6–8-angled. Fls pendulous; pedicel decurved; cor. conical, 6–8mm diam., exterior densely papillose, interior papillose, dark purple, tube 2–3.5mm, lobes 3.5–6mm, fused outside tube; corona dark purple. ssp. ***borealis*** P.V. Bruyns. Fls facing upwards, 3.5mm long, 7mm diam., tube half the length, exterior covered in rounded glabrous papillae, interior with columnar papillae covered with round-topped spicules, dark purple brown, lobe tips joined, conical. Cape Province: Richtersveld. ssp. ***namaquensis*** (N.E. Br.) P.V. Bruyns. Fls usually facing horizontally or upwards; pedicels 2–10mm; cor. 5mm diam., shortly conical, pale grey-yellow or red-purple, interior densely covered with rounded dome-like papillae, covered in spinescent transparent spicules, tube just containing the staminal column, lobes with tips joining above the staminal column, their margins strongly folded back, conical in shape. Cape Province, nr. Springbok and Loeriesfontien.

***P. longipes*** (N.E. Br.) P.V. Bruyns. Mat-forming; stems 6×1–1.5cm, prostrate, brown-green, 6-angled, angles with pointed teeth. Fls solitary near apex of young growth; pedicel 1–3.5cm, erect but bent at 90° near the tip, fls held horizontally; cor. 8–12mm diam., yellow covered with translucent spicules, lobes spreading, deltoid to broadly ovate-deltoid, 2.5–3×2.5–3mm; corona yellow-orange, 2mm diam. Cape Province: Sutherland District.

***P. maughanii*** (R.A. Dyer) P.V. Bruyns. Mat-forming; stems 8×1–1.5, prostrate to semi-erect, 6-angled with pointed tooth on each tubercle, green to brown-green. Fls usually solitary; pedicels 5–25mm slender, erect, holding the fls erect; cor. 1.2–1.6mm diam., entire surface covered with fine transparent spicules, lobes 5–7×2.5mm, deep uniform dark purple-black, lobe margins replicate. Cape Province: Calvinia District.

***P. asperiflora*** N.E. Br. See *P. articulata* ssp. *asperiflora*.
***P. breviloba*** R.A. Dyer. See *Stapeliopsis breviloba*.
***P. saxatilis*** N.E. Br. See *Stapeliopsis saxatilis*.
***P. stayneri*** Bayer. See *Stapeliopsis saxatilis* ssp. *stayneri*.
***P. tulipiflora*** Luckh. See *Stapeliopsis saxatilis*.
For further synonymy see *Caralluma* and *Ophionella*.

**PEDALIACEAE** R. Br. SESAME FAMILY. Dicot. 18 genera and 95 species of herbs or shrubs, with indumentum of short-stalked hairs with head of 4 or more mucilage-filled cells. Leaves opposite, upper sometimes alternate, simple; stipules absent. Flowers bisexual, solitary or in dichasia with 1 or 2 extrafloral nectaries (abortive flowers) in axils of bracts at pedicel base; calyx (4) 5 sepals, usually forming lobed tube; corolla 5 fused petals, irregular, sometimes with basal spur, the limb often oblique or bilabiate; stamens 4, alternate with lobes and attached to tube, didynamous, with a posterior staminode; ovary superior, of 2 fused carpels, with terminal style, 2-loculed, placentation axile, sometimes subdivided by partitions or 1-loculed with intruded parietal placentas; ovules 1-numerous. Fruit a loculicidal capsule, drupe or nut, endocarp often armed with horns, hooks or prickles, or winged; seeds with straight embryo; endosperm absent or little, oily. Temperate and warm, especially coasts and arid regions. The hooked fruits of *Harpagophytum* and *Uncarina* are used as mousetraps in Madagascar. *Ceratotheca, Ibicella, Martynia, Proboscidea,*

*Pterodiscus, Sesamothamnus*. Sesame oil is obtained from the seeds of *Sesamum indicum*.

**Pedalium** Royen ex L.
***P. busseanus*** (Engl.) Stapf. See *Pterodiscus angustifolius*.

**Pedicularis** L. (Lat. word for this plant, from *pediculus*, louse, referring to the superstition that eating these plants caused lice infestation of livestock.) LOUSEWORT; WOOD BETONY. Scrophulariaceae. About 350 species of erect annual, biennial or perennial herbs. Leaves opposite, alternate or scattered, acutely dentate to bipinnatifid. Inflorescence a spikelike raceme; flowers yellow, pink, red or purple; calyx campanulate or tubular, variously lobed, usually longer on upper side; corolla bilabiate, upper lip helmet-shaped, frequently laterally compressed, often extended into a beak, lower lip shorter, with 2 longitudinal folds below sinuses, lobes obliquely spreading or adpressed; stamens 4, anthers glabrous. Capsule ovate to oblong, acute, flattened, often falcate or inequilateral, loculicidal, glabrous; seeds several, turgid, often somewhat winged. North Temperate regions, particularly Europe and Asia, in New World extending south to Ecuadorean Andes. Some species are partially parasitic on roots, and may not find correct hosts in cultivation.

CULTIVATION Semi-parasitic plants of cool-temperate regions, *Pedicularis* spp. are found in moist, shady places, on damp grassland, streamsides and alpine meadow or tundra: the attractive flowering spikes vary in brilliance from the crimsons of *P. densiflora* to the creams of *P. canadensis*. In the garden they are best established in semi-wild plantings, alpine lawns and partly shaded rock gardens where conditions approximate to those observed in the wild. Usually thriving in association with the roots of host grass spp., successful establishment, as with all semi-parasites, is often only the result of perseverance on behalf of the grower. Occasionally they may consent to cultivation in pans in a cold frame or alpine house. Plant in spring on partially shaded to sunny sites into well-drained, gritty but moist soils: *P. densiflora* will tolerate drier conditions. Propagate from seed sown in pans of turf collected from the proximity of wild colonies or directly onto the sites on which the plants are to remain. It may be possible to divide established plants in spring and to establish divisions near the mother plants.

***P. canadensis*** L. COMMON LOUSEWORT; WOOD BETONY. Perenn. herb. Stems 15–40cm, several, simple, erect, sparingly villous. Lvs to 13cm, mostly basal, lanceolate or oblanceolate to narrowly oblong, pinnately lobed more than half way to midrib, seg. oblong or ovate, crenate; petioles of lower lvs longer than lamina, reduced upwards, uppermost stem lvs subsessile. Fl. spikes solitary, 3–5cm; bracteoles oblanceolate, dentate towards apex; cal. very oblique, lateral halves entire, separated by a very short cleft above, deeply cleft below; cor. to 2cm, creamy yellow, purple or bicoloured, occasionally white, upper lip rounded, with 2 slender teeth. Fruiting spike to 20cm; capsule oblong, rather oblique, 15mm, 2–3× length of mature cal. Spring–summer. SE Canada to N Mexico, east to Florida. Z3.

***P. densiflora*** Benth. ex Hook. INDIAN WARRIOR. Perenn. herb. Stems 15–55cm, simple, clustered, finely to coarsely brown pubesc. Lvs 18–25×4–5cm, alternate, narrowly oblong to ovate, pinnatifid to pinnate, finely pubesc. to glabrescent; pinnules in 12–15 pairs, oblong-lanceolate, irregularly, often doubly, acutely dentate; petioles 4–10cm. Infl. dense, many-fld; bracteoles oblong-lanceolate, acutely dentate towards apex, equalling fls; pedicels 3mm; cal. 8mm, regularly 5-lobed, lobes triangular or acuminate-lanceolate, entire; cor. deflexed from cal. tube, 25mm, glabrous, upper lip cylindric, rounded at apex with obscurely protruding tip, 16mm, crimson to maroon, lower lip 2mm, lobes oblong-lanceolate, tinged yellow. Capsule somewhat decurved, 7mm; seeds 1–2 per cell, 4mm. Spring–early summer. SW US. Z6.

**Pedilanthus** Necker ex Poit. SLIPPER SPURGE; RED BIRD CACTUS; JEW BUSH. (From Gk *pedilon*, a sandal or shoe, and *anthos* flower, referring to the appearance of the flowers.) Euphorbiaceae. 14 species of monoecious, succulent shrubs. As for *Euphorbia* but involucre zygomorphic, spurred, glands 2, 4 or 6, concealed within involucre; inflorescence dichotomous or terminal cymes, female flower perianth rimlike. Southern N America to tropical America. Z9.

CULTIVATION Succulent shrubs for the dry subtropical garden, succulent house or home. *P.* 'Variegatus' is the most commonly grown and will withstand drought and dry soils.

***P. bracteatus*** (Jacq.) Boiss. CANDELLILA. Shrub, to 3m. Stems somewhat succulent, latex yellow. Lvs to 10×6cm, ovate to obovate, glabrous to puberulent. Infl. cyathia stipitate, green or pale green; involucre tubular, to 16mm, glands 2 or 4, crimson; spur not flattened or partitioned, apex rounded, lobes attenuate, thickened below. Fr. a dehiscent capsule. SE Sonora, N Sinaloa, NE Guerroi, Oaxaca.

***P. cymbiferus*** Schldl. Low shrub to 50cm. Stems to 3cm diam., grey-green. Lvs to 1.5cm, ovate to obovate, soon abscising. Infl. cyathia pink to vivid red, green at base; involucre tubular, to 16mm; spur oblique, to 13×6mm, apex truncate, 3-lobed, lobes attenuate, thickened below, lateral lobes small. Summer–early winter. Mexico.

***P. macrocarpus*** Benth. Shrub, to 1.5m. Stems cylindric, fleshy, waxy-bloomed, latex white. Lvs inconspicuous, caducous, to 10×0.4cm. Infl. terminal, bracts red, to 11×4mm; cyathia red, puberulent; involucre tubular, to 14mm, lobes deltoid-ovate to oblong; spur to 23mm, attenuate, flattened, 3-lobed, midlobe longest; glands 6; spur flattened, partitioned, lobes thickened beneath, truncate, lateral spur lobes inconspicuous. W Mexico.

***P. tithymaloides*** (L.) Poit. Evergreen or deciduous shrub, to 3m. Stems succulent or woody. Lvs to 6cm, ovate to elliptic, midrib keeled beneath; petiole to 12mm. Infl. bracts red, to 12×5mm; involucre tubular, to 15mm, red above, yellow-green at base; spur short, hooded, protruding to 3mm from involucral tube, medial lobes truncate, lateral lobes narrow; involucral bracts to 15mm. W Indies. 'Nana Compacta': branches upright; lvs dark green, dense. ssp. ***retusus*** Benth. Lvs retuse, ovate or obovate to elliptic, to 7.5×5cm. Lvs widest below middle. ssp. ***smallii*** (Millsp.) Dressler. JACOB'S LADDER; DEVIL'S BACKBONE; RIBBON CACTUS. Stems flexuous. 'Variegatus': lvs green, variegated white and red.

***P. aphyllus*** Boiss. ex Klotzsch & Garcke. See *P. cymbiferus*.
***P. smallii*** Millsp. See *P. tithymaloides* ssp. *smallii*.
For further synonymy see *Euphorbia*.

**Pediocactus** Britt. & Rose. (From Gk *pedion*, plain, and *cactus*, referring to the Great Plains habitat of the type species.) Cactaceae. Some 6 species of dwarf or low-growing cacti, simple or clustering; stems tuberculate. Flowers from near the stem-apex, campanulate; pericarpel more or less naked; tube very short, scaly. Fruit mostly top-shaped, nearly naked, dull-coloured, the dried perianth partly deciduous leaving a cap which opens like a lid as the pericarp splits vertically; seeds broadly oval, 2.3–2.9(–5.0)×1.0–2.1(–3.5)mm, black-brown, matt, rugose or not, keeled or not; relief low- to high-domed. W & SW US (Colorado Plateau, Columbia River and Great Basin, and the Rocky Mts).

CULTIVATION May be grown in an unheated greenhouse or out-of-doors with winter protection from rain; use 'standard' cactus compost: moderate to high inorganic content (more than 50% grit), pH 6–7.5; grow in full sun; keep dry from late autumn; if growing under glass, recommence light watering in late winter/early spring. With the exception of *P. simpsonii*, species of this genus are difficult to grow on their own roots and are usually grafted. Flowering is assisted by a cold winter rest (below 0°C/32°F), but failure can occur if water is not given once the buds have formed in early spring or late winter. *P. simpsonii* is hardy out of doors as far north as S England as long as it is protected from damp.

***P. bradyi*** L. Bens. Simple; stem 3.8–6.2×2.5–5cm, green, but obscured by spines; tubercles 3–4.5mm; areoles elliptic, 1.5–3mm; central spines 0 or rarely 1–2, 4mm, darker than the radials; radial spines 14–15, 3–6mm, subpectinate, white or yellow-brown. Fl. 1.5–2×1.5–3cm, pale yellow. Fr. broadly turbinate, 6×7.5mm, green; seeds 2.3×2mm. SW US (Arizona). Z9.

***P. knowltonii*** L. Bens. Simple or clustering; stem 0.7–5.5×1–3cm; tubercles tiny, only 2–4×1–2mm; central spines absent; radial spines 18–26, 1–1.5mm, adpressed, pale brown, pink or white. Fl. 1–3.5×1–2.5cm, pink. Fr. 4×3mm; seeds 1.5×1–1.2mm. Spring. SW US (Colorado, New Mexico). Z9.

***P. paradinei*** B.W. Bens. Simple; stem 3–7.5×2.5–3.8(–8)cm; tubercles to 5×3–5mm; central and radial spines weakly differentiated, hairlike, white to pale grey; central spines 3–6, 8–28mm; radial spines 13–22, 2–5mm. Fl. to 2.2×1.9–2.5cm, pale yellow or pink. Fr. 7–10×4.5–8mm; seeds 2.5×2mm. Spring. SW US (Arizona). Z9.

***P. peeblesianus*** (Croizat) L. Bens. Simple; stem obovoid, globose or depressed-globose, 2.2–6×2–5.5cm; tubercles 3–7×4–6mm; central spines absent or 1–2,

5–21mm, white to pale grey, corky; radial spines 3–7, 2–9mm, similar to the centrals. Fl. 1.5–2.5cm diam., cream, yellow or yellow-green. Fr. 7–11×6–11mm. Seeds 3×2mm. Spring. SW US (Arizona). Z9.

***P. sileri*** (Engelm. ex Coult.) L. Bens. Simple; stem depressed-ovoid to short-cylindric, 5–15(–25)×6–11.5cm; central spines 3–5, black-brown, becoming grey, 13–30mm; radial spines 11–15, 11–21mm, white. Fl. to 2.2×2.5cm, yellow; scales of tube and outer tepals conspicuously ciliate-fringed. Fr. 12–15×6–9mm. Seeds 3.5–5×3–3.5mm. Spring. US (Arizona). Z9.

***P. simpsonii*** (Engelm.) Britt. & Rose. Simple or clustering; stem globose to ovoid (2.5–)5–15×(3–)5–15cm, with spirally arranged tubercles; central spines 4–10, 5–28mm, red-brown, paler at base; radial spines (10–)15–28(–35), 3–19mm, white. Fl. 1.2–3×1.5–2.5cm, white, pink, magenta, yellow or yellow-green. Fr. 6–11×5–10mm. Seeds 2–3×1.5–2mm. Spring. W US. Z5.

***P. papyracanthus*** (Engelm.) L. Bens. See *Sclerocactus papyracanthus*.
For further synonymy see *Mammillaria*.

**Peersia** L. Bol.
***P. macradenia*** (L. Bol.) L. Bol. See *Rhinephyllum macradenium*.

**Peganum** L. (Name used by Theophrastus for the superficially similar 'rue'.) Zygophyllaceae. 5 or 6 species of erect herbs or subshrubs. Leaves pinnate, irregularly cleft; stipules minute, bristly. Flowers borne opposite a leaf; calyx 5-parted, persistent; petals 4–5, usually white, overlapping; stamens 12–15, inserted with petals at base of short disc, glabrous, dilated at base; ovary superior, globose, 3–4-celled; style triangular; ovules numerous. Fruit a capsule, trivalvate; seeds angular with spongy case. Mediterranean to Mongolia, Southern N America.

CULTIVATION Grown for its finely cut foliage and attractive white, green-veined flowers, *Peganum* suits the warm, sunny, herbaceous border. Grow in light, well-drained but retentive, fertile soil in full sun. Propagate by seed or division.

***P. harmala*** L. HARMAL. Herbaceous perenn., 50–100cm, glabrous, glaucous. Stem ascending, forking. Lvs 5–8×3–4cm, alternate, deeply pinnatisect, lobes narrow-linear, acute; stipules 3–4mm, acute. Fls 1–2cm, solitary, pedicellate; cal. seg. 12–18mm, exceeding or equalling pet., narrow-linear, acute; pet. white, oblong-elliptic; capsule 6–10mm, spherical, depressed. SE Europe to warm Asia. Z8.

**Pelargonium** L'Hérit. (From Gk *pelargos*, stork; the beak of the fruit resembles that of the stork.) Geraniaceae. About 250 species of subshrubs, herbaceous perennials and annuals; roots sometimes tuberous. Stems sometimes succulent or swollen. Leaves alternate, palmate or pinnate, simple or compound, usually lobed or toothed, often hairy, sometimes fleshy, sometimes aromatic; stipules present, sometimes persistent; petioles often long, sometimes persistent. Flowers bisexual, usually irregular, occasionally fragrant, often white, pink or purple, rarely yellow or brown, arranged in a pseudoumbel; calyx of 5 sepals with a spur formed at the base of the posterior sepal, the lower end of which is swollen with a nectiferous gland and joined to the pedicel; corolla of usually 5, free petals, sometimes 2 or 4, usually clawed, 2 upper petals usually larger than the lower 3; stamens 10, of which no more than 7 bear fertile anthers; stigmas 5. Fruit of 5, 1-seeded mericarps. Most from S Africa with a few from tropical Africa, Australia and Middle East. 7). *Pelargonium* includes many of the garden plants commonly known as 'Geraniums'. All cultivated species Zone 10 except *P. endlicherianum*.

CULTIVATION Species of the genus were first introduced to European gardens in the early 17th century; many others soon followed. Several have been used in hybridization, especially during the 19th century, to produce the hundreds of cultivars of complex and often uncertain parentage available today. With the exception of the hardy *P. endlicherianum*, pelargoniums succumb to wet cold and prolonged frost and are therefore tender in most temperate zones. They have nonetheless a long flowering season and are valued for greenhouse or house decoration, for summer bedding schemes, tubs, window boxes and hanging baskets. They may be divided into convenient groups and, with a few exceptions noted below, their cultural requirements are largely the same.

The tender pelargoniums are grown in a free-draining gritty potting medium, in a brightly lit, dry, well-ventilated position. Water carefully at all times to avoid waterlogging and keep nearly dry during periods of low temperatures and low light intensity. Deciduous and herbaceous subjects should not be watered, whatever the time of year, until growth recommences. Tuberous species, like *P. lobatum* and *P. triste*, die back entirely and should be kept dry while dormant. Gradually recommence watering when growth starts again. Avoid overwatering succulent species at any time, especially in cool and low light winter conditions. Repot when the plant outgrows its container or, in the case of slower-growing, tuberous species, when the medium sours. Do not use too large a container and, if possible avoid repotting during flowering.

Feed potted or containerized plants regularly during the growing season. Pinch out the tips of young plants to encourage branching and prune vigorous types like the scented-leaved to establish and maintain shape to avoid legginess. Many of the more robust hybrids benefit from severe pruning in autumn; it also encourages growth suitable for use as cuttings. Overwinter species and hybrids in frost-free conditions.

Zonal pelargoniums may be overwintered as cuttings taken in mid to late summer or old plants may be dug up and stored dry in a cool, frost-free place. Cut back, removing any dead growth, and repot in late winter when the plants show signs of regrowth.

Regal pelargoniums need a temperature slightly above 5°C/40°F in winter to continue growing and produce flowers for spring. Cuttings intended for bedding out should be hardened off before planting once late frosts are past. When planting out, choose a sunny site in a light, well-drained soil. Flowering will be poor if the soil is over-manured. Deadheading will encourage a succession of blooms.

Most species readily produce seed, which should be collected before it is explosively dispersed. Seed is best either sown fresh or in spring in a seed compost, thinly covered with compost or sand and kept at a minimum temperature of 13°C/55°F. Germination is usually within a few weeks but is occasionally delayed for several months. Avoid overwatering and pot on only when absolutely necessary. Seed is commercially available for bedding pelargoniums and it is possible to produce flowering plants for summer from seed sown in late winter or early spring. Many hybrids will produce seed but the progeny will not necessarily be identical to the parent.

Most species and hybrids may be propagated by stem cuttings. These root most successfully during the spring and summer. Use vigorous sturdy shoots about 5–10cm/2–4in. long, cut cleanly immediately below a node. Carefully remove leaves and stipules except those near the shoot apex and insert the cutting in sharp sand, 1:1 peat/sand, or the final potting medium. Keep the medium moist but avoid overwatering, which encourages blackleg, and humid conditions, which encourage grey mould. Roots will develop after 2–3 weeks in summer months. Root cuttings are useful for increasing stemless species. Use thick roots taken from near the base of the plant and cut into 5–8cm/2–3in. lengths. Place upright in a damp medium with apical end at soil level in a minimum temperature of 13°C/55°F. Small tubers of tuberous-rooted species may be detached and potted on under similar conditions.

Whitefly is a serious pest of pelargoniums in a greenhouse and difficult to eradicate unless dealt with at the first signs. They can be controlled with a systemic insecticide or by biological control. The leaves of some species, especially the succulent types, may be scorched by insecticides. Grey mould will attack both cuttings and mature foliage. It is encouraged by excess water in the soil, poor drainage, high humidity and cool temperatures. Control by hygiene (careful removal and disposal of dying leaves and flowers, etc.) and fungicides. Pelargonium cuttings may be destroyed by blackleg, a fungal disease which attacks the base of soft fleshy stems, blackening and rotting the tissue. It is encouraged by waterlogging and excess organic matter in the soil.

1 Leaves aromatic, not fleshy.

1.1 Leaves simple or deeply lobed.
*Pp. australe*, 'Blandfordianum', *capitatum*, *crispum*, *denticulatum*, *dichondrifolium*, 'Fragrans', *glutinosum*, *grossularioides*, *hispidum*, *odoratissimum*, *panduriforme*, *papilionaceum*, *quercifolium*, *radens*, *ribifolium*, *scabrum*, *tomentosum*, *vitifolium*.

1.2 Leaves more or less compound.
*Pp. abrotanifolium*, *crassipes*, *graveolens*, *hirtum*

2 Leaves fleshy, not aromatic.

2.1 Leaves simple or deeply lobed.
*Pp. acetosum*, ×*kewense*, *peltatum*, ×*salmoneum*, 'Saxifragoides', *tongaense*.

2.2 Leaves more or less compound.
*Pp. carnosum*, *ceratophyllum*, *crithmifolium*, *gibbosum*.

3 Leaves neither aromatic nor fleshy.

3.1 Tuberous or rhizomatous, stems usually short or succulent.
*Pp. echinatum*, *endlicherianum*, *incrassatum*, *lobatum*, *pinnatum*, *triste*.

3.2 Not forming tubers or rhizomes, stems succulent or swollen.
*Pp. cotyledonis*, ×*domesticum*, *fulgidum*, *hirtum*, ×*hortorum*, *scandens*, *tetragonum*.

3.3 Not forming tubers or rhizomes, stems not succulent or swollen.
*Pp. alchemilloides*, ×*ardens*, *betulinum*, *cordifolium*, *cucullatum*, ×*domesticum*, *elongatum*, *grandiflorum*, *inquinans*, *myrrhifolium*, *peltatum*, *quinquelobatum*, ×*schottii*, 'Splendide', *zonale*.

***P. abrotanifolium*** (L. f.) Jacq. SOUTHERNWOOD GERANIUM. Erect bushy plant to about 50cm, sometimes more, stems becoming woody with age and bearing remains of persistent petioles. Lvs aromatic, grey-green, variable but usually finely divided into 3–5 linear seg., to 15×20mm. Infl. 1–5-fld, unbranched. Fls usually white in cultivated plants but occasionally pink, 15mm diam.; pet. narrow-obovate, upper 2 marked maroon, pedicel very short, spur to 15mm. Spring–summer. S Africa.

***P. acetosum*** (L.) L'Hérit. Branching, somewhat straggling subshrub, subglabrous, to 60cm with rather brittle stems. Lvs glaucous with red margins, somewhat fleshy, obovate, coarsely toothed with wedge-shaped base, 2–6×1–3cm. Infl. 2–7-fld; fls salmon pink, 4cm diam.; pet. very narrow, upper 2 erect marked with darker veins; pedicel short but spur to 30mm; fertile stamens 5. Spring–summer. S Africa (E Cape).

***P. alchemilloides*** (L.) L'Hérit. Very variable, hairy herb, usually to about 30cm. Lvs to 10×12cm but often less, sometimes with dark red-brown circular zone, orbicular, with 5–7 irregularly toothed, shallow to deep lobes; petiole long, to 10cm; stipules ovate. Infl. about 5–fld; fls to 2cm diam., sometimes much smaller, white to cream to pink; pet. spathulate, sometimes with darker veins; spur to 8mm. Spring–summer. E & S Africa. This species has been divided into several varieties and should perhaps be split into 2 or more distinct species. Most plants grown as *P. grandiflorum* should be included here.

***P.* ×*ardens*** Lodd. (*P. fulgidum* × *P. lobatum*.) Similar to *P.* ×*schottii* but with lvs less deeply divided and fls smaller, bright but dark red marked with very dark purple-brown. Early summer. Garden origin.

***P. australe*** Willd. Straggling, softly hairy, herbaceous perennial to about 30cm. Lvs faintly aromatic, to 10cm diam., rounded, shallowly 5–7-lobed with deeply cordate base. Infl. compact, 5–10-fld; fls pale pink to white, almost regular, to 15mm diam.; 2 upper pet. veined deep pink, often emarginate; spur and pedicel short; fertile stamens usually 7. Spring–summer. SE Australia, Tasmania. A very variable species; plants collected in Tasmania under this name are smaller in all parts with dark green leaves and red petioles.

***P. betulinum*** (L.) L'Hérit. Erect or sprawling subshrub, woody at base, 30–60cm. Lvs glaucous, usually glabrous, broadly ovate, toothed, often edged red, to 3×2cm. Infl. usually 3–4-fld; fls large, to 2.5cm diam., pink or purple, sometimes white; upper pet. veined darker, broadly obovate, lower pet. narrower. Late spring. S Africa (SW & S Cape).

***P. 'Blandfordianum'***. (Parentage uncertain.) Spreading, branching, covered with short hairs. Lvs grey, aromatic, similar in shape to *P. graveolens*. Infl. 5–8-fld; fls white, sometimes tinged pink, to 2cm diam.; 2 upper pet. broadly obovate, rounded to emarginate at apex, marked red. Summer. Garden origin. A hybrid of obscure parentage, raised GB 1805.

***P. capitatum*** (L.) L'Hérit. ROSE-SCENTED GERANIUM. Decumbent or weakly erect, softly hairy, becoming woody at base with age, to 1m. Lvs rose-scented, velvety with crinkled margin, 3–5-lobed, 2–8cm diam. Infl. very compact, 10–20-fld; fls 15–20cm diam., usually mauve-pink; 2 upper pet. marked with darker veins; pedicel 1mm; spur to 3mm. Spring–summer. S Africa. The true species may not be often cultivated but appears to be represented in gardens by 'Attar of Roses'; which has a more upright habit and rougher, more strongly scented leaves This is probably a hybrid with *P. capitatum* as one parent.

***P. carnosum*** (L.) L'Hérit. To 50cm+; stems short, thick, succulent, branched, bearing remains of persistent petioles. Lvs variable to 15×5cm, more or less succulent, grey-green, usually deeply pinnately divided. Infl. branched with several 2–8-fld pseudoumbels; pedicels very short; fls under 1cm diam., white to pale yellow-green; pet. broadly ovate, 2 upper pet. marked with red lines; spur to 6mm. Summer–autumn. Southwest S Africa.

***P. ceratophyllum*** L'Hérit. Similar to *P. carnosum* but much smaller with stems less swollen, lvs more fleshy and infl. less branched. Summer. S Africa (W coast).

***P. cordifolium*** (Cav.) Curtis. Branched, spreading, hairy, woody at base, to 1m. Lvs 3–5-lobed, toothed, to 6×5cm, base deeply cordate, dull green above, paler and hairy below. Infl. branched, leafy, with 4–8-fld pseudoumbels; fls to 3cm diam., very irregular; 2 upper pet. to 2cm, obovate, purple with darker veins, lower pet. paler, unmarked, linear; spur to 8mm. Spring–summer. S Africa (S & E Cape).

***P. cotyledonis*** (L.) L'Hérit. About 30cm; stem thick, succulent, covered with rough scaly bark and persistent stipules. Lvs clustered at apices of stems, rounded, 2–5cm diam., dark glossy green with conspicuous veins above, densely grey-hairy below; petiole to 8cm. Infl. branched, each pseudoumbel 5–15-fld; fls regular, to 1cm diam.; pet. rounded, white, unmarked; spur very short. Late spring–early summer. S Atlantic (St Helena).

***P. crassipes*** Harv. Similar to *P. hirtum* but lvs less finely divided and petiole broad, persistent and reflexed with age; fls less regular, pet. oblong. Spring. Namaqualand.

***P. crispum*** (Bergius) L'Hérit. LEMON GERANIUM. Erect, branched, rather stiff subshrub, to 70cm. Lvs numerous, small, appearing 2-ranked, obscurely 3-lobed to reniform, to 10×15mm, rough, lemon-scented, margin coarsely and markedly crispate; stipules broad-ovate, to 4×5mm. Infl. 1–2-fld; fls to 2cm diam., usually pink; 2 upper pet. broadly spathulate, strongly marked with deep pink, lower pet. narrow; spur to 8mm. Spring–summer. S Africa (SW Cape). Probably a parent of many cvs with small scented lvs. 'Cinnamon': habit compact; lvs small, crisped, lemon scent with hint of cinnamon. 'Major': lvs larger. 'Minor': habit stiff, upright; lvs very small, crisped. 'Peach Cream': fls pink, peach scent. 'Prince Rupert: habit upright; lvs ruffled. 'Variegatum': lvs edged with cream.

***P. crithmifolium*** Sm. Similar to *P. carnosum* but lvs more fleshy; fls white and to 1.5cm diam., peduncles and pedicels longer, persistent, becoming hard and almost spiny. Spring. Namibia.

***P. cucullatum*** (L.) L'Hérit. Erect, hairy subshrub, to 2m+. Lvs to 5×6cm, rounded to triangular, with cordate base, toothed and sometimes lobed, but always hooded or cup-shaped, often with a red-tinted margin. Infl. with several 5-fld heads; fls large, usually about 3cm diam., bright purple-pink; pet. broad, 2 upper pet. with darker veins; spur 5–12mm. Spring–summer. Southwest S Africa. This variable species is the main parent of the regal pelargoniums. Semi-double fld plants are sometimes found.

***P. denticulatum*** Jacq. PINE GERANIUM; FERN-LEAF GERANIUM. Erect, branched subshrub to 1.5m. Lvs 6–8×7–9cm, strongly balsam-scented, very sticky, rough, triangular in shape and deeply bipinnatifid into narrow-toothed seg. Infl. 6-fld; fls 2cm diam., purple-pink; 2 upper pet. narrow-spathulate, emarginate, veined purple; pedicel to 2mm; spur to 9mm. Spring–summer. S Africa (S Cape). 'Filicifolium', 'Fernaefolium': lvs even more finely divided and upper 2 pet. very deeply bifid.

***P. dichondrifolium*** DC. Perenn.; stem short, becoming woody with age. Lvs crowded, dark grey-green, aromatic, reniform with crenate margin; petiole long, persistent, to 10cm. Infl. branched, 2–5-fld; fls white, to 2cm diam.; upper pet. oblong, marked with red lines; spur 2–3cm; fertile stamens 7. Summer. S Africa (E Cape).

***P.* ×*domesticum*** L.H. Bail. REGAL PELARGONIUMS. Name given to the hybrid group known as Regals; cultigens of complex ancestry, usually involving *P. grandiflorum*, *P. cucullatum* and others. Stems to 45cm, thick, branching, becoming woody at base if plants are allowed to grow beyond third year, otherwise fleshy, green, pubesc. Lvs to 10cm diam., reniform-orbicular to obscurely trilobed, undulate and coarsely denticulate, or more deeply divided. Fls usually large and showy in erect, long-peduncled umbels; pet. white, salmon, pink-purple or red, upper pair with dark veins and blotches. See cultivars below.

***P. echinatum*** Curtis. CACTUS GERANIUM; SWEETHEART GERANIUM. Erect subshrub, to 50cm with tuberous roots and succulent branched stems covered with persistent spiny stipules. Lvs ovate, lobed, to 6cm diam., grey-green above, paler and tomentose below. Infl. 3–8-fld; fls 15–20mm diam., usually white with dark red blotches on 2 upper pet.; spur 3–4cm; fertile stamens 6–7. Spring. Western S Africa. 'Miss Stapleton': fls bright purple-pink.

***P. elongatum*** (Cav.) Salisb. Straggling, decumbent, short-lived perennial with long and short glandular hairs. Lvs to 40×25mm, usually with a dark horseshoe-shaped mark, reniform with 5–7 crenate lobes; petiole long, to 7cm; stipules lanceolate. Infl. 1–5-fld; fls white to cream, 15mm diam.; 2 upper pet. veined red; spur 10–20mm. Spring–late summer. S Africa (SW Cape).

***P. endlicherianum*** Fenzl. Herbaceous rhizomatous perenn. Lvs mostly basal, rounded, with 5 shallow lobes and cordate base, to 6cm diam., hairy. Infl. 5–15-fld on peduncle to 20cm; fls bright purple-pink, fragrant; 2 upper pet. large, recurved, to 30×15mm, 3 lower pet. minute or absent; spur to 2cm. Summer. Turkey. Z7.

**Pelargonium** (×0.5) (a) *P. capitatum* (b) *P. acetosum* (c) *P. dichondrifolium* (d) *P. carnosum*

***P.*** Fragrans Group. Erect, much-branched subshrubs, 30–40cm. Lvs with strong spicy scent, grey-green with soft velvety texture, ovate with cordate base, 3-lobed and blunt-toothed. Infl. often with red-brown branched peduncle, each cluster 4–8-fld; fls to 15mm diam., white; 2 upper pet. erect, marked with red lines; spur to 6mm; fertile stamens 7. Spring–summer. S Africa. The status of this plant is uncertain and although considered to be a true species by some is perhaps best referred to as a group with the following cvs: 'Cody's Fragrans': similar to 'Old Spice' but with less crinkled lvs. 'Fragrans Variegatum': lvs edged with creamy yellow becoming almost green as they mature. 'Old Spice': compact form with grey-green crinkle-edged lvs. 'Snowy Nutmeg': habit low; lvs small, centre largely grey, broadly margined cream. 'Variegata': lvs edged with creamy yellow, becoming almost green as they mature.

***P. fulgidum*** (L.) L'Hérit. Scrambling or spreading to about 70cm with succulent stems becoming woody with age. Lvs pinnate or deeply pinnatifid, to 10×7cm, oblong with silvery sheen. Infl. branched with 4–9-fld pseudoumbels; fls scarlet, to 2cm diam.; pet. reflexed; spur to 2cm. Spring–early summer. S Africa (W Coast). *P. fulgidum* figures prominently in the ancestry of the Unique Pelargoniums; see cultivars below.

***P. gibbosum*** (L.) L'Hérit. GOUTY GERANIUM; KNOTTED GERANIUM. Scrambling, few-branched; stems succulent, becoming woody with swollen nodes on ageing. Lvs glaucous, slightly fleshy, pinnate with 1–2 pairs of leaflets, to 12×7cm. Infl. 5–15-fld; fls to 2cm diam., dull green-yellow, sweetly scented at night, pet. almost equal, obovate, reflexed; spur 2–3cm; fertile stamens 7. Summer. S Africa (W coast).

***P. glutinosum*** (Jacq.) L'Hérit. PHEASANT'S FOOT GERANIUM. Erect, branching subshrub to 1.5m. Lvs variable in shape but always strongly balsam-scented and very viscid, usually about 5×5.5cm, more or less triangular in outline, deeply lobed and coarsely toothed, glossy dark green. Infl. compact, 1–8-fld; fls pale to dark pink, 15mm diam.; pedicel 1mm; spur to 10mm. Spring. Southern S Africa.

***P. grandiflorum*** (Andrews) Willd. Erect or straggling to decumbent, glabrous, becoming woody at base. Lvs deeply palmately lobed ×5–7, each lobe coarsely toothed, to 8cm diam., glaucous, often with dark zone. Infl. usually 2–3-fld; fls cream to pink, large, to 4cm diam.; 2 upper pet. veined and sometimes blotched deeper purple; spur to 1cm. Spring–summer. S Africa (SW & W Cape). Not widely cultivated; many plants grown under this name are *P. alchemilloides*.

***P. graveolens*** L'Hérit. ROSE GERANIUM; SWEET-SCENTED GERANIUM. Erect, softly hairy subshrub, to 120cm. Lvs rose-scented, grey-green, to 4×6cm, more or less triangular in shape, deeply bipinnatifid, seg. slightly rolled under. Infl. 5-fld; fls white to very pale pink, 15mm diam.; upper pet. narrow-obovate, veined purple; spur 10–15mm. Spring–summer. S & NE South Africa. The plant described and illustrated by L'Héritier under this name appears to be a hybrid with rough, less hairy leaves and smaller, pale pink fls. Many similar cultivars have been widely used for the production of geranium oil and the parentage of many of the cultivars assigned to *P. graveolens* may not include the plant known under this name found wild in South Africa and described above, but probably *P. capitatum* and *P. radens*. The nomenclature of this group is therefore very confused and the name of species described should be reconsidered. 'Lady Plymouth': lvs margined with cream. 'Little Pet': habit compact; fls rose pink. 'Mint Rose': lvs edged pure white; peppermint scent. 'Radula': similar to *P. radens* but with less finely divided lvs and a less pungent scent. Flowers small purple pink. 'Red Flowered Rose': habit dwarf; lvs fingered; fls bright scarlet. 'Rober's Lemon Rose': habit vigorous; lvs soft grey-green, irregularly pinnate, lemon to rose scented; fls small, pink.

***P. grossularioides*** (L.) L'Hérit. Spreading to weakly erect, more or less hairless, short-lived; stems red, sparingly branched, internodes long. Lvs aromatic, rounded, lobed and toothed, to 4×5cm; petiole long, to 10cm. Infl. dense with many fls; fls deep magenta, about 8mm diam.; pet. almost equal, 2 upper pet. marked with darker blotches; fertile stamens 7; spur very short. Spring–summer. S & SE Africa.

***P. hirtum*** (Burm. f.) Jacq. Low-growing subshrub with short, thick stems bearing remains of persistent petioles. Lvs hairy, very finely divided, carrot-like, faintly aromatic, to 5m. Infl. with thin, leafy, branched peduncles, bearing 2–6-fld pseudoumbels; fls almost regular, bright pink, to 1.5cm diam.; pet. rounded; spur and pedicel to 5mm. Late winter–spring. S Africa (Cape peninsula).

***P. hispidum*** (L.) Willd. Erect, branching subshrub to, 2m+, covered with rough hairs and bristles. Lvs aromatic, deeply palmately lobed and irregularly toothed, to 9×10cm, veins conspicuous. Infl. leafy, with many 6–12-fld branches; fls very irregular, to 15mm diam., pale to dark pink; 2 upper pet. obovate, marked dark red, reflexed, lower pet. narrow, much smaller; spur to 4mm; stamens conspicuously exserted. Spring–summer. Southern S Africa.

***P. ×hortorum*** L.H. Bail. GERANIUM; BEDDING GERANIUM; ZONAL PELARGONIUM. Name given to the complex group of hybrids resulting from *P. inquinans* × *P. zonale*, which includes all the cvs known as Zonals. Members of this group are broadly characterized by succulent, glabrescent stems to 60cm, which become straggling in time, orbicular to reniform lvs to 10cm diam., which are sometimes basally cordate, undulate, crenate or sinuate and may be variegated or marked

**Pelargonium** garden forms (a) Zonal (a1) 'Cramden Red'. (b) Miniature Zonal (b1) 'Red Black Vesuvius' (b2) 'Mme Salleron' (b3) Mrs Henry Cox (b4) 'Chelsea Gem'. (c) Irene Zonal (c1) 'Electra'. (d) Cactus flower (d1) 'Spitfire' (e) Stellar hybrid (e1) 'White Starlet'. (f) Angel Miniature (f1) 'Catford Belle'. (g) Regal (g1) 'Carisbrooke' (g2) 'Glensheree' (g3) 'South American Bronze' (g4) 'Horace Parsons' (h) Ivy-leaved (h1) 'Roulette' (h2) 'Elegante' (h3) 'La France' (h4) 'Chocolate'

with dark, central, horseshoe-shaped zones, and erectly carried umbels of white, pink, red or freaked flowers with an elongated cal. spur and subequal pet. See cultivars below.

***P. incrassatum*** (Andrews) Sims Herb with large underground tuber. Lvs basal, narrowly ovate, 3–6×2–5cm, deeply pinnatifid, silver-pilose to canescent. Infl. a large pseudoumbel, 20–40-fld, on stem to 30cm; fls bright magenta, 2 upper pet. spathulate, to 20mm, 3 lower pet. much smaller with inrolled edges; spur to 4cm. Spring. S Africa (Western Cape).

***P. inquinans*** (L.) L'Hérit. Erect, branching, velutinous subshrub, to 2m. Lvs suborbicular, to 8cm diam., with 5–7 shallowly dentate lobes and deeply cordate base. Infl. 10–20-fld, sometimes to 30-fld; fls almost regular, usually bright scarlet; pet. rounded, to 20mm; fil. joined for most of their length; style and stamens barely exserted; pedicel very short; spur to 25mm. Spring–autumn. S Africa (E Cape). One of the main parents of the Zonal Pelargoniums.

***P.*** **×*kewense*** R.A. Dyer. (Probably *P. zonale* × *P. inquinans.*) Similar to *P.* ×*salmoneum* but lvs larger and greener, not thick, sometimes with dark circular zone when young, leaf base shallow, cordate; infl. to 27-fld, fls bright crimson-red with narrowly spathulate pet. Late spring–early autumn. Garden origin, 1929.

***P. lobatum*** (Burm. f.) L'Hérit. Herb with large underground tuber and very short stem. Lvs almost basal, softly hairy, to 30cm diam., usually less in cultivation, 3- or more lobed. Infl. branched with several clusters, each 5–20-fld; fls strongly scented at night, 2cm diam.; pet. rounded, very dark purple with yellow-green margin; spur to 3cm; fertile stamens 6. Spring. S Africa (S & SW Cape).

***P. myrrhifolium*** (L.) L'Hérit. Erect, hairy subshrub, to 30cm. Lvs to 5cm, oblong, pinnatifid or bipinnatifid. Infl. leafy, branched, 2–6-fld; fls white to pink; 2 upper pet. spathulate, veined deep red, to 15mm; fertile stamens 5, spur to 10mm. Spring–summer. S Africa (SW Cape). var. ***coriandrifolium*** (L.) Harv. Similar to the species type but sometimes decumbent. Lvs more finely divided, seg. width not exceeding 2mm. Fls larger; 2 upper pet. to 2cm, lower pet. much smaller; fertile stamens sometimes 7. Rather short-lived. Spring–summer. S Africa (W & SW Cape).

***P. odoratissimum*** (L.) L'Hérit. APPLE GERANIUM. Low-growing perenn. with short main stem but trailing flowering stems. Lvs light green, apple-scented, rounded, usually to 4cm diam., base cordate, margin crenate; petiole persistent, to 5cm. Infl. branched, each cluster 3–10-fld; fls small, to 12mm diam., white; 2 upper pet. oblong, marked with red veins; spur 5–7mm; fertile stamens 7. Spring–summer. S Africa (E & S Cape).

***P. panduriforme*** Ecklon & Zeyh. Erect subshrub to 1.5m, strongly balsam-scented, sometimes slightly viscid, with long hairs. Lvs soft, grey-green, panduriform, pinnate with rounded lobes, usually 35×25mm but sometimes much larger. Infl. 2–20-fld; fls 3cm diam., pale purple-pink; 2 upper pet. spathulate to 35mm, erect, marked with deep purple; spur to 10mm. Spring–summer. Southern S Africa.

***P. papilionaceum*** (L.) L'Hérit. Erect, hairy subshrub to 2m+, woody at base, with strong unpleasant scent. Lvs to 7×10cm, palmately veined, almost rounded, 3–5-lobed. Infl. with many 5–10-fld branches; fls to 2cm diam., light to dark pink; 2 upper pet. with dark purple central blotch and white basal area, obovate, 20×8mm, lower pet. very narrow, 7×2mm, pale; spur to 5mm. Spring–summer. Southern S Africa.

***P. peltatum*** (L.) L'Hérit. IVY GERANIUM; HANGING GERANIUM. More or less trailing or climbing plant. Lvs usually peltate, somewhat fleshy, bright green often with a darker circular zone, 3–7cm diam., with 5 triangular lobes. Infl. 2–9-fld; fls large, to 4cm diam., usually pale purple to pink; 2 upper pet. obovate, to 25mm, marked with darker pink veins; spur 3–4cm. Spring–summer. S Africa. This species is the main parent of the ivy-leaved pelargoniums of gardens. It shows considerable variation in the leaf characteristics in the wild. Plants known as *P. lateripes* have non-peltate leaves but should be assigned to *P. peltatum*. 'Saxifragoides': low-growing, prostrate, glabrous plant; lvs fleshy, to 2cm diam., with 3–5 acute lobes, dark green. Infl. 2–5-fld; fls 8–9mm diam., pink or white; 2 upper pet. reflexed with darker veins; spur 2mm; pedicel 4mm; spring–summer; of unknown origin, once thought to be a species but now considered to be a form or hybrid of *P. peltatum*.

***P. pinnatum*** (L.) L'Hérit. Herb bearing a cylindric, taproot-like, subterranean tuber to 25cm, usually shorter. Lvs to 30cm, slender, basal, erect, villous, pinnate, in a loose rosette; pinnae elliptic, to 2cm, borne in alternate whorls of 2–3. Peduncle slender, erect; infl. umbellate, open; fls to 3cm diam., delicate; upper pet. buff, veined rose and violet, apically blotched violet, lower pet. bronze suffused pink. Winter. S Africa.

***P. quercifolium*** (L.) L'Hérit. OAK-LEAVED GERANIUM; ALMOND GERANIUM; VILLAGE OAK GERANIUM. Erect, branching, viscid subshrub to 1.5m, strongly scented of balsam. Lvs rough with long glandular hairs, triangular in outline, deeply pinnately or palmately divided, each seg. deeply divided and irregularly toothed. Infl. 2–6-fld; fls 15mm diam., purple pink, 2 upper pet. emarginate, erect to reflexed, to 20mm, marked darker pink; spur 10mm. Spring–summer. Southern S Africa. Many plants in gardens assigned to this species may be geographical variants or hybrids of the species and are best referred to by the cultivar name only. 'Fair Ellen': low growing plant; lvs smaller more deeply cut but with more rounded lobes and a dark mark along midrib; fls pink; upper pet. toothed. 'Royal Oak': habit shrubby; lvs with rounded lobes, dark green with dark purple-brown blotch; fls purple pink with darker spots on upper petals. 'Giant Oak': lvs lobed, very large.

***P. quinquelobatum*** A. Rich. Straggling to prostrate, hairy, herbaceous plant. Lvs deeply 3–5-lobed with terminal lobe much longer, to 10×8cm, dull green; petiole long, to 12cm. Infl. to 5-fld; fls pale yellow-green to grey-blue-green, to 15mm diam.; upper pet. veined pink; spur to 3cm. Summer. E Africa.

***P. radens*** H.E. Moore. Somewhat similar to *P. graveolens*. Lvs rough, with strong pungent scent, margins of seg. strongly recurved. Infl. 5-fld; fls 15mm diam., pale or purple-pink; upper pet. to 17mm. Spring–summer. S Africa (S & E Cape). This plant is not the same as 'Radula' of gardens (see under *P. graveolens*) but may be a parent of it. 'Dr. Livingstone': habit tall, bushy; lvs deeply cut and lobed; lemon fragrance.

***P. reniforme*** Curtis. Erect subshrub with tuberous roots, becoming woody at base with age, sometimes reaching 1m. Lvs reniform, to 3cm diam., grey-green with velvety texture above, silvery grey below; petioles long, to 5cm+. Infl. branched, leafy, with 3–12-fld clusters; fls 1–2cm diam., deep magenta or deep pink; 2 upper pet. narrow-oblong, marked deep purple; spur 1–2cm; fertile stamens 6–7. Spring–summer. S Africa (E. Cape).

***P. ribifolium*** Jacq. Similar in habit to *P. scabrum* with rough aromatic lvs, but lvs with cordate base and rounded lobes. Fls white, upper pet. veined red; spur with very conspicuous nectiferous gland. Spring. S Africa (E Cape).

***P.*** **×*salmoneum*** R.A. Dyer. Erect branching subshrub, to about 1m. Lvs thick, more or less fleshy, green to somewhat glaucous, more or less rounded with 5 shallow-toothed lobes, base truncate to shallow cordate, to 5cm diam. Infl. 4–14-fld; fls salmon pink, to 4cm diam.; pet. obovate, subequal, about 25×15mm, 2 upper pet. veined deeper red; spur to 25mm; fertile stamens 5. Spring–summer. There is some confusion over the status of this plant which although known for many years as a species is now considered to be a hybrid, possibly with *P. acetosum* as one parent.

***P. scabrum*** (Burm. f.) L'Hérit. Erect subshrub to 1m, usually strongly lemon-scented, covered with rough stiff hairs. Lvs rough, rhomboidal, palmately veined, about 4×4cm, deeply 3-lobed with acute apices, toothed, lobes sometimes very narrow to linear. Infl. to 6-fld; fls white to pink to purple-pink, 15mm diam.; 2 upper pet. spathulate, to 15mm, veined deeper purple, lower pet. smaller; spur to 5mm. Early spring–summer. W & SW South Africa. 'M. Ninon': lvs dark, glossy; fls deep rose-pink; apricot scent.

***P. scandens*** hort. Very similar to *P.* ×*kewense* but the leaves have a very distinct and consistent, narrow, dark circular zone one-third from the outer margin. Late spring to autumn. The exact status and origin of this well-known plant is uncertain but it may be a hybrid of similar age and parentage to *P.* ×*kewense*. It is not equivalent to *P. scandens* Ehrh.

***P.*** **×*schottii*** Hook. f. (*P. fulgidum* × *P. lobatum.*) Subshrub with thick stems to 30cm. Many lvs basal, hairy, oblong, deeply but irregularly pinnately divided, with toothed margins. Infl. usually unbranched with 6–8-fld clusters; fls to 2cm diam., very dark crimson with distinct black blotches on pet.; pedicels short. Early summer. Garden origin, raised 1818 (Clifford).

***P.* 'Splendide'**. (Probably *P. tricolor* × *P. ovale.*) Often incorrectly grown as *P. tricolor* var. *arborea* or *P. violareum*. Stem short, erect, rather woody, bearing clusters of grey-green, hairy, ovate, sharply toothed lvs. Infl. branched with several 2–3-fld clusters; fls to 3cm diam.; 2 upper pet. rounded, dark red with base almost black, lower pet. white, sometimes becoming stained with pink.

***P. stenopetalum*** Ehrh. Similar to *P. zonale* but lvs only sometimes faintly zoned. Infl. to 10-fld; fls with very narrow red pet. Spring and summer. S Africa (Natal).

***P. tetragonum*** (L.) L'Hérit. SQUARE-STACK CRANESBILL. Succulent erect to sprawling plant; stems green, 3–4-sided, jointed at nodes and with long internodes. Lvs few, hairy, cordate, to 4cm diam., caducous. Infl. 2-fld; fls large, cream to pale pink; pet. normally 4, 2 upper pet. spathulate, to 40×15mm, marked with red lines, 2 lower pet. much smaller, fil. bent in centre; spur to 4cm. Spring. Southern S Africa.

***P. tomentosum*** Jacq. Low-growing but wide-spreading, to 50cm, strongly peppermint-scented. Lvs very soft, velvety, densely hairy, 4–6×5–7cm, palmate, with 3–5 rounded lobes, base cordate. Infl. with several 5–15-fld branches; fls 15mm diam., white; upper pet. obovate, to 9mm, marked with purple, lower pet. very narrow but longer; spur to 2mm. Spring–summer. S Africa (SW Cape). 'Variegatum': habit compact; lvs emerald edged with cream.

***P. tongaense*** Vorster. Semi-erect to decumbent perenn. Lvs 4–7cm diam., thick to fleshy, hairy, ivy-shaped, with 3–5 triangular lobes; petioles long, to 10cm. Infl. 3–10-fld; fls 25mm diam., bright scarlet; pet. almost equal, ovate with rounded apex; fil. joined for most of their length; style and stamens barely exserted; spur to 4cm. Summer. NE Natal.

***P. triste*** (L.) L'Hérit. Herb with turbinate to ovoid, woody, fissured, subterranean or exposed tuber. Stem very short, jointed, succulent. Lvs almost basal, variable but usually oblong in outline, to 45cm, finely 2–3-pinnate or pinnatifid, hairy. Infl. 5–20-fld with long peduncle; fls to 1.5cm diam., sweetly scented at night; pet. obovate, usually brown-purple with a dull yellow margin

**Pelargonium** (×0.5) (a) *P. triste* leaf, inflorescence, habit (b) *P. panduriforme* (c) *P. denticulatum* flowering branch, habit (d) *P. gibbosum* (e) *P. tetragonum*

but sometimes yellow or brown; spur to 3cm; fertile stamens 7. Spring–early summer. S Africa (NW to S Cape).

***P. vitifolium*** (L.) L'Hérit. Very similar to *P. capitatum*, strongly aromatic but more erect, to 1m; lvs less hairy and somewhat rough; infl. 5–10-fld, fls to 15mm diam., often paler pink. Spring–summer. S Africa (SW & S Cape).

***P. zonale*** (L.) L'Hérit. Erect or scrambling subshrub to 1m. Lvs almost orbicular, 5–8cm diam., lobed with irregularly crenate margins, often with a darker horseshoe-shaped zone. Infl. to 50-fld, usually less in cultivation; fls irregular, to 3cm diam., pale pink, sometimes red or white; pet. narrow, to 20×7mm, 2 upper pet. erect, marked with darker veins, lower 3 pet. spreading; spur 25mm. Spring–autumn. S Africa.

***P.* cultivars**. SCENTED-LEAVED PELARGONIUMS. This group contains plants with a wide range of habit and foliage. Often, however, the numerous fls are rather small. The scented-leaved pelargoniums are species, cultivars and hybrids scented of peppermint, rose, apple or nutmeg. 'Attar of Roses': lvs strongly scented of roses; 'Chocolate Peppermint': lvs large, lobed with central brown blotch, somewhat scented of peppermint; fls small, pink; 'Clorinda': strong-growing with large, pungent, rose-scented, lobed lvs and large rose-pink fls; 'Joy Lucille': grey-green, deeply cut, peppermint-scented lvs and white fls; 'Mabel Grey': robust, tall-growing, with rough, serrate, strongly lemon-scented lvs with pale purple fls; 'Lady Mary': a probable hybrid involving *P. crispum*. Lvs to 5-lobed, toothed, not undulate, coarse, strongly scented of lemons. Upper pair of pet. clear lilac, tinted mauve, veined and centrally marked darker purple, lower pet. unmarked; 'Peach Cream': habit similar to *P. crispum*; lvs splashed cream, peach-scented; fls pink; 'Prince of Orange' (derived from *P. crispum*): erect with orange-scented, light green lvs and large mauve fls; 'The Boar': scrambling plant with rounded lvs with dark brown central blotch; fls pale salmon pink. 'Viscosissimum': similar to *P. glutinosum* with very sticky, balsam-scented lvs sometimes with a darker streak along midrib; fls pink-purple.

UNIQUE PELARGONIUMS. Mostly plants raised in the early 19th century, probably from crosses involving *P. fulgidum*, the Unique Pelargoniums form a distinct if varied group. They are vigorous plants, woody at the base, often with scented lvs and fls larger than those of the species. They include: 'Aurore's Unique': lvs grey-green, hairy, fls bright red with very dark blotches and veins; 'Madam Nonin': fl. petals twisted to give the impression of a double fl., red with paler edges; 'Rollinson's Unique': lvs lobed, aromatic, fls magenta in a rather tight head; 'White Unique': bushy plants with white fls marked with purple-pink.

ZONAL PELARGONIUMS (see *P.* ×*hortorum*). These are the result of complex hybridization between several members of the Ciconium section and are a very important group, especially for bedding. They are long-flowering, vigorous plants with rather fleshy young stems becoming woody with age. Their lvs are rounded, shallow-lobed, sometimes with a darker, horseshoe-shaped zone. The single or double fls are in intense shades of scarlet and red, pink or orange. As yet, there are no real purple-flowered cvs in this group. Several distinctive strains beyond the typical forms have been developed of which the following are some of the more important.

Cactus-flowered pelargoniums have furled or quilled petals. Irenes, of American origin, are fast-growing, free-flowering and strong, with large flower-heads which may be used as cut fls. Stellar pelargoniums originating in Australia are small plants which have star-shaped, often zoned lvs. The upper petals of the fls are forked. Startel pelargoniums, an F1 selection, are similar to the older Stellar range, with pointed, tinted petals and comparable foliage. Miniature pelargoniums do not exceed 13cm in height but are very free-flowering and dwarf pelargoniums are 13–20cm. They are popular houseplants. Rosebud pelargoniums have fls with numerous small petals which are so tightly arranged that they look like half-opened roses.

*Foliage cultivars*. Some cultivars, sometimes known as fancy-leaved, are grown mainly for their foliage in shades of bronze or yellow, black or white. Humid conditions tend to reduce the intensity of the leaf coloration. The majority have single fls which may be removed if the foliage is important to a bedding scheme. Plants grown for bedding are propagated in summer and over-wintered as cuttings to be planted out when all danger of frost is past. Many cultivars may also be encouraged to flower indoors in winter by taking cuttings in spring and removing any fl. buds formed before early autumn. Cvs include: 'A.M. Mayne' (double): fls magenta flushed scarlet in centre; 'Appleblossom Rosebud' (rosebud): pet. white-edged pink with pale green centre; 'Caroline Schmidt' (coloured leaf): lvs with silver sheen, fls double, bright red; 'Dolly Vardon' (coloured leaf): lvs tricoloured, edged white, rose red and green, fls single, red; 'Fantasia' (dwarf): fls double, white; 'Gustav Emich' (semi-double): fls scarlet; 'Irene': the original Irene type with bright red semi-double fls; 'Miss Burdett-Coutts' (coloured leaf): lvs with carmine splashes, fls small, single vermilion; 'Mr Henry Cox' (coloured leaf): lvs variable with shades of green over red with yellow border, fls small, single, rose-pink; 'Mrs Pollock' (coloured leaf): lvs with green and dark red zones and yellow margin, fls small, single, vermilion; 'Mr Wren' (single): pet. orange-red, edged white; 'Mrs Quilter' (coloured leaf): leaf with bronze zone, fls single, pink; 'Party Dress' (Irene): fls pale rose-pink; 'Paul Crampel' (single): fls scarlet; 'Red Rambler' (rosebud): fls bright red; 'Santa Maria' (semi-double): fls salmon pink; 'Silver Kewense' (miniature): leaf edged white, fls single, red with narrow pet.; 'Spitfire' (cactus): fls scarlet, lvs variegated cream; 'Stellar White' (stellar): fls single, white; 'Stellar Grenadier' (stellar): fls double, crimson; 'Stellar Snowflake' (stellar): fls double, white; 'Tangerine' (cactus): fls double orange; 'Verona' (coloured leaf): lvs pale gold, fls small, single, pink.

REGAL PELARGONIUMS (See *P.* ×*domesticum*). Also known as Martha Washington, Lady Washington or Show pelargoniums, these have been raised mainly from *P. cucullatum*. They form bushy plants with five-lobed, toothed, often cupped lvs and large single, sometimes double, fls, predominantly in shades of purple, pink and white, usually streaked, striped or blotched. Flowering is mainly in mid- to late spring. This group is less suitable for bedding schemes. After propagation in summer, young plants are kept growing through the winter, potting on as necessary, pinching out the growing tip to produce bushy plants, and kept at a minimum of 5°C/40°F, to fl. the following spring. Feeding should commence with flowering. Cvs include 'Carisbrooke': fls large, pink, marked with maroon, pet. ruffled; 'Grand Slam': fls rose-red with darker markings; 'Pompeii': compact plant, pet. nearly black with very narrow pink-white margins; 'White Chiffon': fls pure white.

Angel pelargoniums show some resemblance to Regals but rarely exceed 30cm/12in. and the fls are single. Cvs include 'Catford Belle': fls rose-red with darker markings; 'Mrs G.H. Smith': fls off-white with pink markings.

IVY-LEAVED PELARGONIUMS. These have been developed mainly from *P. peltatum*. They have trailing, rather brittle stems and ivy-shaped, somewhat thick, aromatic lvs, sometimes with a small dark zone in the centre. The fls may be single, semi-double or double in a range of colours, sometimes striped, especially in shades of white, pink and purple. Their habit makes them ideal for hanging baskets or window boxes. With support and some means of attachment they may equally be encouraged to climb several metres. More recent developments are not so brittle as their forebears, having shorter internodes and a more bushy habit, or may even be dwarf with small lvs and fls. Cvs include: 'Crocodile': lvs cream-veined, fls single, rose-pink; 'Galilee': fls rose-pink, double; 'La France': fls semi-double, mauve veined white and purple; 'L'Elégante': off-white and green lvs shaded with pink when grown in light, fairly dry conditions, fls single, white, veined purple; 'Pink Gay Baby': miniature with pink single fls; 'Rouletta': semi-double white fls striped red.

***P. acerifolium*** L'Hérit. See *P. cucullatum*.
***P. angulosum*** (Mill.) L'Hérit. See *P. cucullatum*.
***P. burtoniae*** Bol. See *P. stenopetalum*.
***P. cordatum*** L'Hérit. See *P. cordifolium*.
***P. coriandrifolium*** (L.) Jacq. See *P. myrrhifolium* var. *coriandrifolium*.
***P. erodioides*** Hook. See *P. australe*.
***P. heracleifolium*** Lodd. See *P. lobatum*.
***P.* ×*limoneum*** Sweet. See *P.* 'Lady Mary'.
***P. malvaefolium*** Jacq. See *P. alchemilloides*.
***P. populifolium*** Ecklon & Zeyh. See *P. ribifolium*.
***P. relinquifolium*** N.E. Br. See *P. dichondrifolium*.
***P. roseum*** (Andrews) DC. See *P. incrassatum*.
***P. tabulare*** (L.) L'Hérit. See *P. elongatum*.
***P. terebinthaceum*** (Cav.) Desf. See *P. graveolens*.
***P. trilobatum*** Ecklon & Zeyh.. See *P. ribifolium*.

**Pelecyphora** Ehrenb. (From Gk *pelekys*, hatchet, *-phoros*, bearing; referring to the hatchet-shaped tubercles.) Cactaceae. 2 species of simple or clustering cacti, with globose or obconic tubercled stems; tubercles hatchet-shaped and laterally compressed, or scale-like and dorsiventrally compressed and then acute, keeled and somewhat incurved; areoles bipartite, the vegetative spine-bearing part abaxial, at the tubercle-apex, the woolly flowering part adaxial, in the tubercular 'axil', the two parts interconnected by a narrow groove or shallow corky ridge. Flowers subapical, shortly funnelform or campanulate; tube naked; perianth purple-pink. Fruit small, dry; seeds almost circular, *c*1.2×1.0mm, brown, matt; relief par-concave. NE Mexico.

CULTIVATION Grow in a cool frost-free greenhouse (min. 2–7°C/35–45°F); use 'standard' cactus compost: moderate to high inorganic content (more than 50% grit), pH 6–7.5; full sun; low air-humidity; keep dry from mid-autumn until early spring, except for light misting on warm days in late winter. Both ssp. are popular with collectors, but very slow-growing and difficult to raise from seed. Commercial extraction of wild plants has diminished natural populations, and is now prohibited.

***P. aselliformis*** Ehrenb. Simple or clustering; individual stems globose or obconic, to *c*10×5cm diam., dull grey-green or tinged purple-brown; tubercles hatchet-shaped, compressed laterally, *c*5mm high; areoles linear, elongate, to 8mm; tubercular groove at first marked by fine hairs, later corky; spines *c*40–60, to 4mm, fused at the base in two comb-like rows, white or grey. Fl. campanulate-funnelform, *c*2×3cm, purple-pink. Fr. spindle-shaped, soon dry after ripening and disintegrating in the stem apex. Summer. EC Mexico (San Luis Potosi). Z9.

***P. strobiliformis*** (Werderm.) Frič & Schelle ex Kreuzinger. Usually simple; stem depressed-globose to globose or ovoid, to 6cm diam., with thick taproot;

tubercles overlapping, scale-like, dorsiventrally compressed, acute, keeled and somewhat incurved; areoles apical; spines *c*9–12, to 5mm, off-white, deciduous. Fl. funnelform *c*3×4cm; tube slender; outer tepals fimbriate, pale, inner purple-pink. Fr. dry. Summer. NE Mexico (Tamaulipas). Z9.

***P. pectinata*** Stein. See *Mammillaria pectinifera*.
***P. pseudopectinata*** Backeb. See *Neolloydia pseudopectinata*.
***P. valdeziana*** H. Möller. See *Neolloydia valdeziana*.
For further synonymy see *Ariocarpus*.

For illustration see CACTI AND SUCCULENTS.

**Peliosanthes** Andrews. (From Gk *pelios*, livid, and *anthos*, flower.) Liliaceae (Convallariaceae). 1 species, a perennial herb. Rhizomes varying in length, erect or creeping. Leaves borne along rhizome and often in a terminal tuft, 10–50×1–12cm, linear to oblong-ovate or obovate; petioles 4–50cm. Inflorescence a 35(–75)cm several- to many-flowered raceme arising from rhizome; bracts scale-like; flowers 1–6 per bract; perianth lobes 6, to 8mm, erect or spreading, basally united into a tube, green, blue, violet or purple; stamens 6, at mouth of perianth tube, filaments united; ovary semi-inferior, 3-celled, styles columnar, often 3-lobed. Fruit a trilocular capsule; seeds blue. E Himalaya to SE Asia, China, Taiwan. Z9.

CULTIVATION Although not noted for the great tolerance shown by *Aspidistra*, *Peliosanthes* species can be grown in the warm glasshouse in conditions described as optimal for that genus. Propagate by division of rhizomes.

***P. teta*** Andrews. As for the genus. ssp. ***teta***. Fls 2–6 in the axils of bracts, usually green, rarely blue. ssp. ***humilis*** (Andrews) Jessop. Fls solitary in each bract axil, often white, blue, violet or purple, rarely green.

***P. albida*** Bak. See *P. teta* ssp. *humilis*.
***P. humilis*** Andrews. See *P. teta* ssp. *humilis*.
***P. violacea*** Bak. See *P. teta* ssp. *humilis*.

**Pellaea** Link. (From Gk *pellos*, dusky, referring to the dark stipes.) Pteridaceae (Adiantaceae). 80 species of ferns. Rhizomes solenostelic, creeping or abbreviated, scaly; stipes black. Fronds pinnate to variously compound; veins free. Sori submarginal, covering tips of veinlets; sporangia stalked, generally lacking paraphyses; annulus vertical, incomplete; indusia of reflexed margin of frond, continuous; spores tetrahedral, more or less globose, smooth to minutely spinose. Tropical and warm temperate regions.

CULTIVATION As for *Adiantum*. Fronds are brittle and, when broken, reveal a light green flexible core. Too much warmth and for too little light leads to weak, sappy growth. Particularly susceptible to hard scale.

***P. andromedifolia*** (Kaulf.) Fée. COFFEE FERN. Rhiz. slender, long-creeping, scales imbricate, narrow, bristly; stipes stramineous, glaucous. Fronds 15–70×5–20cm including stipe, distichous, tripinnate, pinnules remote, oblong, obtuse, sterile flat, fertile strongly revolute, 4–8mm wide, seg. 5–7; rachis slender, glabrous. California and Baja California. Z9.

***P. atropurpurea*** (L.) Link. PURPLE ROCK BRAKE. Rhiz. very short, shallowly creeping, scaly; stipes to 10–22cm, clothed with rough scales. Fronds 10–25×4–10cm, numerous, tufted, erect or ascending, narrowly ovate-triangular to oblong or oblong-lanceolate, bipinnate, pinnules to 1.5×1cm, ovate to elliptic-lanceolate, rounded and auriculate at base, obtusely attenuate at tip, fertile slightly narrower than sterile, dull or grey-green, often glaucous-rufescent when young, coriaceous, subglabrous to pilose; rachis hard, dark, glossy. N America. Z4.

***P. brachyptera*** (Moore) Bak. Rhiz. horizontal, elongate, nodose, rather stout, scales castaneous with pale margins, dentate, twisted; stipes channelled, at least as long as lamina, castaneous, glaucous, glabrous. Fronds to 40cm, including stipe, linear, bipinnate or occasionally tripinnate, grey-green, pinnae oblique to rachis, subequal, pinnate, subsessile or shortly stalked, pinnules 5–13, linear, margins strongly revolute, crenate, mucronate, subcoriaceous. Western N America (S Oregon, N California). Z8.

***P. breweri*** D.C. Eaton. Rhiz. short-creeping, scales twisted and tufted to 10mm; stipes bright glossy brown, transversely corrugate. Fronds 5–20×1.5–3.5cm including stipe, pinnate, linear-oblong, acute, pinnae in 6–12 pairs, mostly 2-lobed with upper lobe larger, or upper pinnae entire, seg. linear-ovate to deltoid. W US (Washington to California, Idaho and Utah). Z4.

***P. bridgesii*** Hook. Rhiz. short-creeping, scales tufted; stipes persistent, to length of lamina, dark, glossy chestnut. Fronds to 35cm including stipe, closely tufted, numerous, linear to linear-oblong, pinnate, grey-green, glabrous, coriaceous, pinnae opposite, broadly oval to cordate-oblong (sterile suborbicular), subsessile, generally conduplicate and falcate, margins narrowly revolute, soon reflexed (sterile flat), pale. Western N America (Oregon and Idaho to California). Z4.

***P. calomelanos*** Link. HARD FERN. Rhiz. tufted, hirsute, scaly; stipes 7–10cm, stout, slightly lanate-paleaceous below, glabrous above. Fronds 15–20×7–10cm, deltoid, 2–3-pinnate, pinnae erecto-patent, deltoid, pinnules 4–12×4–12mm, in 3–5 pairs, distinctly stalked, cordate, ovate-deltoid, hastate or ternate (particularly terminal pinnule of each pinna), or occasionally pinnate, rounded at apex, thick and coriaceous, glaucous, glabrous; rachis wiry, naked, shiny, black. Africa, India, China. Z9.

***P. falcata*** (R. Br.) Fée. SICKLE FERN. Rhiz. creeping, stout, scaly when young; stipes 5–15cm, erect to spreading, rather stout, wiry, very dark brown, clad with squarrose dark brown scales when young. Fronds 30–40×4–7cm, dull dark green above, paler below, more or less paleate below, pinnae 2–5×0.5–1cm, 40+ per side, subopposite to alternate, shortly stalked, lanceolate-oblong, cordate-truncate at base, apiculate at apex, upper pinnae smaller and sessile, veins concealed. India to Australasia. Z10.

***P. glabella*** Mett. Rhiz. short, stout, ascending, scales sinuate and bright castaneous; stipes dark castaneous, mostly glabrous. Fronds to 20cm including stipe, evergreen, densely caespitose, oblong to lanceolate, pinnate, occasionally bipinnate below, blue-green, coriaceous, seg. oblong-lanceolate, 3–5-lobed, often with at least 2 auricles, apex obtuse to submucronate, seg. of basal pinna soon withered, leaving persistent stipes. Indusia subentire, white, membranous. N America (British Columbia to Ontario and Vermont, south to Arizona and Texas). Z3.

***P. intramarginalis*** (Kaulf.) J. Sm. Stipes 8–15cm, tufted, erect, darkly castaneous. Fronds 15–30×5–10cm, broadly ovate-lanceolate, tripinnatifid, pinnae 5–8cm, opposite, lanceolate, cut nearly to rachis, pinnules linear-oblong. Mexico to Costa Rica. Z10.

***P. mucronata*** (D.C. Eaton) D.C. Eaton. BIRD'S FOOT FERN. Rhiz. thick, woody, scales tufted, castaneous; stipes 5–20cm, dull purple-brown. Fronds 10–30cm, 2–3-pinnate, stiff, mostly fertile, pinnae distant, subperpendicular to rachis, pinnules in 6–20 pairs, generally ternate, ultimate seg. 2–6mm, to 11, linear-oblong to elliptic, revolute to middle, glaucous, wrinkled. California and Baja California. Z9.

***P. ovata*** (Desv.) Weatherby. To 1m+; rhiz. short-creeping, slender, 3–5mm diam., scaly; stipes 10–35cm, arising at short interval, red tinged grey or darkly stramineous. Fronds 15–70×15cm, entangled, oblong, bipinnate to tripinnate, bright green, thickly herbaceous to subcoriaceous, glabrous, pinnae alternate, laxly spreading, ultimate, seg. 1–2.5cm, obliquely triangular-ovate to ovate-elliptic or suborbicular, obtuse to truncate at apex, truncate to cordate at base; rachis flexuous. America (Mexico S to Peru). Z10.

***P. paradoxa*** (R. Br.) Hook. Rhiz. medium- to long-creeping, generally deep underground; stipes to 15cm, stiffly erect-ascending, dark brown. Fronds 15–20×10–15cm, rather few, broadly ovate, pinnate, pinnae 4–10cm, alternate, 10 or fewer per side, lanceolate, broad at base, attenuate at apex, deep green; rachis dark and glossy. E Australia. Z10.

***P. rotundifolia*** (Forst. f.) Hook. Rhiz. creeping, rather stout, with brown scales when young; stipes 5–15cm, erect to procumbent, stout, densely ferruginous-scaly. Fronds 15–30×2–4cm, narrowly oblong, dull dark green above, paler below, coriaceous, glabrous or nearly so, pinnae 1–2×0.5–1.5cm, in 30+ pairs, patent, narrowly oblong to suborbicular, rounded to subcuneate at base, apiculate at apex, shortly stalked or upper often sessile, margins minutely crenate, veins concealed. New Zealand, Australia. Z10.

***P. sagittata*** (Cav.) Link. To 60cm; rhiz. compact, short-creeping, stout, densely scaly; stipes shorter than lamina, pale stramineous, sparsely deciduously scaly near base. Fronds ovate-oblong to triangular-ovate, pinnate to bipinnate, occasionally tripinnate, subcoriaceous, glabrous or occasionally minutely glandular-pubesc., pinnae to 5.5×3cm, patent, shortly stalked; pinnules ovate-triangular to sagittate, deeply cordate to sagittate at base, rounded to obtuse at apex, veins distinct, white-bordered; rachis usually minutely pubesc. Mexico to Guatemala; Colombia to Bolivia. var. ***cordata*** (Cav.) A. Tyron. Similar but with rotundate-cordate seg., glabrous rachis and tetrahedral-globose spores. Texas, Mexico. Z10.

***P. ternifolia*** (Cav.) Link. Rhiz. very short-creeping, branched; stipes 7–22cm, darkly castaneous to black. Fronds 15–45cm including stipe, rather few, linear, pinnate to pinnatisect in lower part at least, stiffly erect, pinnae generally ternately divided into basal pinnule pair and terminal seg., each 2–3cm, (in vigorous plants a second pinnule pair is sometimes present) or occasionally entire. C & S America, to Argentina and N Chile. Z10.

***P. viridis*** (Forssk.) Prantl. GREEN CLIFF BRAKE. Rhiz. short, shallowly creeping, scaly; stipes to 35cm, suberect or arching, generally much less. Fronds to 65cm+ including stipe, often almost as broad as long, numerous, broadly lanceolate to triangular, bipinnate or occasionally tripinnate, pinnules very variable, lanceolate to triangular or oblong, obtuse or acutely tapering, sometimes deeply lacerate, bright green, occasionally glaucous, often vivid green when young, softly herbaceous to coriaceous. Africa, particularly south and adjacent islands. Z10.

***P. wrightiana*** Hook. Rhiz. very short-creeping, branched; stipes 7–22cm, brown tinged purple. Fronds 15–45cm including stipe, rather few, narrowly triangular or occasionally linear, bipinnate at least in part, stiffly erect, pinnae to 2cm, lobed or divided into 3–11 seg. N America (Oklahoma to Texas and Arizona, N Mexico). Z6.

***P. atropurpurea*** var. ***simplex*** (Butters) Morton. See *P. glabella*.
***P. hastata*** (Thunb.) Prantl. See *P. calomelanos*.
***P. occidentalis*** (Nels.) Rydb. See *P. glabella*.
***P. ornithopus*** Hook. See *P. mucronata*.
***P. suksdorfiana*** Butters. See *P. glabella*.
For further synonymy see *Allosurus*.

**Pellionia** Gaudich. (For Alphonse Pellion, an officer who took part in Freycinet's voyage around the world.) Urticaceae. Some 50 species of herbs or subshrubs, sometimes from woody base, monoecious or dioecious; stems sometimes succulent. Leaves alternate, 2-ranked, asymmetric at base, subsessile, entire or dentate; stipules small or absent. Inflorescence a dense cyme; perianth segments over lapping, 4–5 in male flowers or 3–5 in female flowers; stamens 4–5; stigma penicillate. Fruit a compressed tubercled achene, enclosed by persistent perianth. Tropical & subtropical Asia, from India to Japan. Z10.

CULTIVATION Low-growing tropical perennials, grown for their attractively coloured foliage, often beautifully marked and veined with contrasting metallic colours in bronze and silver. Suitable for pot and pan cultivation, with trailing species well suited to hanging baskets, *Pellionia* spp. are particularly effective as groundcover in the tropical glasshouse. Grown in part shade to preserve flower colour, with high humidity, and a minimum winter temperature at 13–16°C/55–60°F, cultivation is otherwise as for *Pilea*.

***P. pulchra*** N.E. Br. RAINBOW VINE. Low spreading to creeping herb, glabrous except for sparse hairs on pedicels; stems fleshy, tinged purple. Lvs 2–5×1–3cm, obliquely oblong to elliptic, apex obtuse, base cuneate, marked dull black-green along midrib and veins above, purple below. Summer. Vietnam.

***P. repens*** (Lour.) Merrill. TRAILING WATERMELON BEGONIA. Creeping herb to 60cm; stems succulent, glabrous, tinged pink. Lvs 1–6cm, oblong to elliptic or orbicular, subsessile, scalloped, dark bronze-green above, often tinged violet with a broad central band of pale grey-green, tinged pink beneath, purple-edged. Summer. SE Asia (Vietnam to Malaysia and Burma). A clone of *P. repens* with silver-white marked pale green leaves is often grown as *P. argentea*.

***P. daveauana*** (Carr.) N.E. Br. See *P. repens*.
For further synonymy see *Elatostema*.

**Peltandra** Raf. (Name for Gk *pelte*, target or shield, and *aner*, stamen, referring to shape of stamens.) ARROW ARUM. Araceae. 3 species of aquatic perennial herbs. Rhizomes horizontal, with clusters of cataphylls. Lvs to 90cm, entire, sagittate or hastate, acute or acuminate, main lateral veins parallel, marginal veins 2–3, basal lobes with distinct midribs; petioles long, to 50cm. Peduncle equalling or exceeding petioles, sometimes recurved in fruit; spathes to 20cm, margins overlapping below, enclosing zone of female flowers, open above, margins undulate, green to white, limb decaying and deciduous after anthesis; spadix shorter than spathe, sometimes with short appendix; flowers unisexual, floral zones nearly adjacent or separated by zone of rudimentary sterile florets, female zone to half length of spadix; perianth absent; stamens 4–5, connate, poricidal; ovary unilocular, surrounded by cup-like structure of staminodal origin, ovules 1–3. Fruit a berry, green or red. N America.

CULTIVATION As for *Calla*.

***P. sagittifolia*** (Michx.) Morong. WHITE ARROW ARUM. Lvs to 15cm, sagittate to hastate, basal lobes spreading, acute or acuminate; petioles to 50cm. Peduncle subequal to or equalling petioles, erect in fruit; spathe to 10cm, tube green, limb acute, white, opening widely; spadix to 5cm, with female fls to half length, sterile florets present. Berries red. Early summer. SE US. Z7.

***P. virginica*** (L.) Kunth. GREEN ARROW ARUM. Lvs to 15–90×10–20cm, hastate, acute to acuminate, expanding after anthesis, bright green, veins distinct; petioles to 45cm. Peduncle recurved in fruit; spathe to 20cm, green, limb narrowly open, margins yellow to white, undulate; spadix with female fls one-fifth to one-third length, sterile fls few or absent; short appendix sometimes present. Berries green. Early summer. E & SE US. Z5.

***P. alba*** Raf. See *P. sagittifolia*.

**Peltapteris** Link. (From Gk *pelte*, shield, and *pteris*, fern.) Lomariopsidaceae. Some 4 species of small epiphytic ferns. Rhizomes wide-creeping, slender, scaly. Fronds erect, distant, dimorphic; stipes nonarticulate; sterile fronds flabellate, more or less finely dissected, the divisions dichotomous, glabrous or nearly so, veins free; fertile blades smaller than sterile, simple, orbicular, cordate, dentate or lobed. Sporangia cover the underside of the fertile fronds; indusia lacking. W Indies, C & S America. Z10.

CULTIVATION As for *Elaphoglossum crinitum*.

***P. peltata*** (Sw.) Morton. Rhiz. filiform and interlacing, tinged green, forming colonies; scales lanceolate, thin, pale brown. Sterile fronds to 15cm, blades reniform, 4–6× dichotomously divided, 2.5–5cm broad, ultimate seg. 0.5–1.5mm broad, stipes much longer than blades, sparsely scaly throughout; fertile fronds with blades 5–20mm broad, margin erose-dentate, translucent, glabrous, stipes longer than those of sterile fronds. Tropical America (West Indies, Mexico to Northern S America.)

For synonymy see *Acrostichum* and *Elaphoglossum*.

**Peltaria** Jacq. (From Lat. *peltatus*, armed with a shield, alluding to the shield-shaped, leaves.) Cruciferae. 7 species of glabrous perennial herbs. Leaves simple, mostly basal, entire, stem leaves cordate to hastate. Inflorescence corymbose; sepals 4, spreading; petals 4, white, short-clawed. Fruit a silicle, pendent, strongly compressed. Spring–summer. E Mediterranean to Iran and C Asia. Z6.

CULTIVATION Herbaceous perennials for the border and naturalistic plantings, bearing masses of flowers in early summer. Cultivate as for *Lunaria*.

***P. alliacea*** Jacq. 20–60cm. Lvs peltate, smelling strongly of garlic when crushed, stem lvs ovate-lanceolate, cordate, sessile. Pet. 3, 5–4.5mm. Fr. 6–10×5–9mm, round-ovate. E Europe.

***P. turkmena*** Lipsky. Shrubby herb, 50–70cm. Lvs oblong-ovate, entire to remotely toothed; petiole long; stem lvs short-petioled to sessile. Infl. branching; sep. 2.5mm, ovate, margin white; pet. 6mm, obovate; pedicel to 15mm, very thin. Fr. 13–18×8–10mm, 1-seeded. C Asia.

**Peltiphyllum** (Engl.) Engl.
***P. peltatum*** (Torr. ex Benth.) Engl. See *Darmera peltata*.

**Peltoboykinia** (Engl.) H. Hara. (From Gk *pelte*, shield, because of their shield-like leaves, plus *Boykinia*.) Saxifragaceae. 2 species of hardy, deciduous herbs with thick creeping rhizomes, to 85cm. Basal leaves peltate, shallowly lobed or deeply cleft with long petioles, becoming reduced, short-petiolate or sessile higher up the stem, toothed; stipules leaf-like or an expansion of the petiole base. Flowers borne in terminal cymes with floral parts in fives; sepals fused at base, campanulate, free sepal lobes erect, lanceolate or triangular; petals short-clawed, cream to pale yellow with glandular hairs, short-lived; stamens 10, in 2 whorls of 5 inserted on the rim of the floral cup; ovary semi-inferior. Fruit a capsule formed from the floral cup. S Japan (mts). Z7.

CULTIVATION Rare natives of mountain woodland in Japan, suitable for rich damp soils in shaded spaces. Cultivate as for *Heuchera*, but moist humus-rich soil is essential.

***P. tellimoides*** (Maxim.) H. Hara. 35–85cm. Basal lvs 15–30×10–30cm, orbicular to cordate, to 13-lobed, finely dentate; petiole 20–45cm, widened at base to form stipules, sometimes leaf-like. Cal. glandular, sep. lobes 3–6mm; pet. 2–3× longer than sep. lobes, cuneate at base; stamens shorter than sep. lobes. Early summer. Japan (C & N Honshu).

***P. watanabei*** (Yatabe) H. Hara. As *P. tellimoides* except lvs up to 10cm wider and longer, divided into 7–10 lobes for up to two-thirds of their length, acutely dentate. Japan (mts of Shikoku and Kyushu).

For synonymy see *Boykinia* and *Saxifraga*.

**Peltophorum** (Vogel) Benth. (From Gk *pelte*, a shield, and, *phoros*, bearing, referring to the shape of the stigma.) Leguminosae (Caesalpinioideae). Some 15 species of medium-sized evergreen trees. Leaves bipinnate; pinnae and leaflets usually numerous; stipules deciduous. Flowers yellow, in subterminal axillary racemes or terminal compound racemes; calyx lobes 5, unequal, overlapping; corolla segments 5, yellow, subequal, clawed, usually pubescent below; stamens 10, subequal; pistil substipitate, stigma broad or peltate. Fruit a short-stipitate, indehiscent legume, obovate to oblong-lanceolate, flat, winged. Pantropical.

CULTIVATION Vigorous tropical forest trees, eminently suited to their widespread use in tropical and subtropical regions as shade and ornamental park and avenue trees. *P. pterocarpum* is considered one of the finest, quickly forming a spreading, umbrella-shaped crown, robed in finely divided, deep green foliage. The large erect spikes of fragrant flowers, carried over long periods in summer, are exceptionally beautiful; tight, bronze-coloured buds open to reveal the crinkled, translucent, golden-yellow flowers with prominent deep-orange stamens. Their luminous qualities can be appreciated at close quarters as cut flowers. In warm temperate zones, mature specimens of *P. dubium* have been known to survive short-lived frosts to −5°C/23°F, but in temperate zones *Peltophorum* must be grown under glass as for *Delonix*.

***P. africanum*** Sonder. Petiole to 20cm; pinnae 4–10 pairs; leaflets to 8×3.5mm, sessile, 10–20 pairs, elliptic-oblong, obtuse, mucronate, pubesc., reticulate-veined. Fls in intercalary, terminally clustered racemes; pedicels to 11cm; cal. to 6mm; cor. to 2.5cm diam., yellow, pubesc. at base. Fr. to 9×2cm, oblong-lanceolate, tapering at both ends, flat, striped brown. Summer. S Africa.

***P. dubium*** (Spreng.) Taub. Petiole to 40cm, persistently rufous-tomentulose, usually glandular; pinnae 15–25 pairs; leaflets to 11×4.5mm, sessile, 10–25 pairs, short-oblong. Fls in terminal compound racemes to 30cm; bracts to 1cm, subulate, caducous; pedicels 1cm; cor. to 3.5cm diam., yellow; fil. villous at base; ovary villous. Fr. to 10×2.5cm, samaroid, elliptic to short-oblong, tapering both ends. Spring–summer. S America.

***P. pterocarpum*** (DC.) K. Heyne YELLOW FLAMBOYANT. Petiole to 40cm, rusty-tomentulose, rarely glandular; pinnae 7–15 pairs; leaflets to 2×1cm, sessile, 8–20 pairs, elliptic-oblong, rounded or emarginate at apex. Fls in terminal, ascending, compound racemes to 20cm; bracts to 1cm; pedicels to 1.5cm; cal. to 8mm; cor. to 4cm diam., yellow, with short-clawed obovate petals, margins frilled; pistil pilose. Fr. to 10×2.5cm, samaroid-elliptic to asymmetric-oblong, flat, narrow-winged, 2–3-seeded. Summer. Tropical Asia.

***P. brasiliense*** (L.) Urban. See *Caesalpinia brasiliense*.
***P. ferrugineum*** (Decne.) Benth. See *P. pterocarpum*.
***P. linnaei*** Benth. See *Caesalpinia violacea*.

**Peniocereus** (A. Berger) Britt. & Rose. (From Gk *penios*, a thread, and *Cereus*, alluding to the slender stems.) Cactaceae. About 20 species or prostrate or scandent shrubs; roots thickened, turnip-like or dahlia-like; stems slender, ribbed, sparingly-branched; epidermis hairless or papillose-downy, light green or rather dark; spines conspicuous, or adpressed and short. Flowers nocturnal or diurnal, occasionally terminating the stem; tube long and slender; floral areoles with bristles or spines. Fruit narrowly ovoid, tapered at apex, fleshy red, the spines or bristles more or less deciduous; seed broadly oval, 1.4–4.6×1.2–3.3mm, black-brown, shiny or matt, ruminate or not, periphery undifferentiated or crested with larger cells; relief flat to low-conical. C America to NW Mexico and SW US.

CULTIVATION Grow in an intermediate greenhouse (min. 10–15°C/50–60°F); use 'standard' cactus compost: moderate to high inorganic content (more than 50% grit), pH 6–7.5; shade in hot weather; maintain low humidity; keep dry from mid-autumn until early spring, except for light misting on warm days in later winter. Few of the species are seen in cultivation, and only *P. viperinus* and *P. serpentinus* flower at all readily.

***P. greggii*** (Engelm.) Britt. & Rose. Root large, turnip-like; stems mostly 30–60×1–2cm, dark grey-brown, papillose-downy; ribs 3–6, deep; areoles *c*4.5–6mm apart; spines 10–13, to 3mm. Fl. 15–21×7.5cm, white. C N & NW Mexico, SW US. Z9.

***P. johnstonii*** Britt. & Rose. Perhaps only a variety of *P. greggii*; rootstock tuberous, massive, 10–40×5–20cm; stems 1 or more, unbranched, clambering to 3m, 5–15mm diam.; ribs 3–5; central spines 1–3, to 8mm, subulate; radial spines 9–12, 1.5–9mm, brown to black. Fl. 15cm; tepals white, tinged pink outside. Fr. oblong-ovoid, 5–6cm, red, with black spines. NW Mexico (Baja California). Z9.

***P. maculatus*** (Weingart) Cutak. Shrub to 3m or more, sparsely branched; stems segmented, the seg. *c*50×3cm, olive-green, tinged purple, with small white spots; ribs 3–4; areoles 5–20mm apart; spines 6–9, 1–3mm. Fls 9–11cm, creamy white; outer tepals tinged purple red. Fr. pear-shaped, 5–3cm, red with red pulp. Spring–summer. Mexico (Guerrero). Z9.

***P. serpentinus*** (Lagasca & Rodriguez) N.P. Tayl. Rootstock thickened, more or less tuberous; stems 2–3m×3–5cm, green; ribs 10–17; areoles *c*10mm apart; spines 10–14, to 30mm long. Fl. 15–20×8cm, white, tinged red outside. Summer. Mexico, widely cultivated. Z9.

***P. striatus*** (Brandg.) F. Buxb. Stems to 1m×5–8mm, grey or blue-green; ribs 6–9; areoles 5–15mm apart; spines *c*9, to 3mm. Fl. 7.5–15×5–7.5cm, white to pink or purple-tinged. Fr. pear-shaped, 3–4cm, scarlet, with deciduous, bristly spines. NW Mexico, S Arizona. Z9.

***P. viperinus*** (F.A.C. Weber) Klusac ex Kreuzinger. Rootstock tuberous, dahlia-like; stems to 3m×1–1.5cm, dark grey-brown, papillose-downy; ribs 8–10, very low (stems almost terete); areoles 10–30mm apart; spines 9–12, to 5mm. Fl. to 3–9×4cm, bright pink to red. Summer. Central S Mexico. Perhaps referable here is *Wilcoxia papillosa* Britt. & Rose, a poorly understood species from W Mexico (Sinaloa), doubtfully reported as in cultivation. It has 3–5-ribbed stems and areoles with only 6–8 spines. Z9.

***P. diguetii*** (F.A.C. Weber) Backeb. See *P. striatus*.
***P. tomentosa*** Bravo. See *P. viperinus*.
For further synonymy see *Cereus*, *Neoevansia*, *Nyctocereus* and *Wilcoxia*.

For illustration see CACTI.

**Penjing**. Penjing is the description used in China to embrace two art forms – miniaturized plants in containers, and tray landscapes. It was practised in China as an art form over 2000 years ago – at least 800 years before the art was passed to Japan, where it became known as bonsai. The Chinese and Japanese forms of the art have subsequently developed on divergent paths, but the major general horticultural techniques used are common to both cultures and are described in outline in the entry for bonsai.

The two Chinese characters used by the Japanese to depict the concept of bonsai and given the meaning in Japanese of 'planting in a container', were in use in China by about 400 AD to mean 'pot plant'. In southern China these two characters are pronounced 'punsai' or sometimes 'pensai'. The earliest extant pictorial records of punsai in China are to be found in a T'ang dynasty royal tomb built in 706 AD. Two wall paintings in one of the corridors of the tomb show ladies of the court holding oval trays planted with miniature fruit trees in rocky landscapes. During the T'ang dynasty (618–907 AD) the growing of dwarfed trees became very popular at many levels in Chinese society and in many parts of that vast country. From this time onwards references to punsai occur regularly in Chinese poetry, prose and painting. The earliest surviving book on the subject was published in about 1170 AD. Over the centuries the art has had other names of which penjing has been current since the 13th century and is now the name most frequently used.

Through the centuries penjing has assumed a distinctive national character. But China is a vast country and local styles have waxed and waned to reflect local character, artistic concepts, climate and the range of plant material available. Master craftsmen and connoisseurs have developed personal styles. Penjing has thus long been accepted as an art form, referred to as 'solid painting' and as 'silent poem'. The title of one modern book by a Chinese master translates as 'Artistic Pot Plants', a common description in use since the 14th century. Penjing is an art which captures nature in a concentrated way, using stones and plants as raw materials: '...thus may ten thousand miles be illustrated in a foot, and one is free to wander and roam in a landscape without having to wax one's sandals or take up a bamboo staff.'

In China, as in Japan, most plants used in the art are those capable of being grown out of doors throughout the year – subtropical plants in southern China, frost-hardy plants in the north – but they would not necessarily be trees if planted in the open ground. Trees, shrubs and herbaceous material are all used. The training techniques keep the plants small, compact and healthy, as described for bonsai.

Penjing falls into two main categories: tree penjing and rock penjing. These categories are then further subdivided, but, as in other art forms, although categorization aids description it should not be regarded as a set of rigid rules.

Tree penjing may comprise one or more plants in a container and the individual compositions may be categorized further by the number and/or type of plant and/or by the overall design. Thus a tree penjing may, for example, consist of a simple specimen designed to awaken the memory of some ancient pine growing on a mountainside, or of a deciduous grove which will reflect the passage of the seasons, or of a flowering herb, shrub or tree to perfume the air in its season. Bamboo is frequently used in tree penjing.

Tree penjing are sometimes trained to represent concepts or to suggest objects somewhat in the manner of European topiary. Thus a suitable evergreen subject may have its trunk trained into the shape of an auspicious Chinese character or the branches on a suitably bulky trunk may be trained to create the impression of an elephant. Other styles which originated in different parts of the country included the Dancing Dragon Style from Anwhei, the Earthworm Style from Sichuan, the Five-tree Style from Kwangtung, the Flat-top Style of Hunan and Hupeh, the Pagoda Style of Yangchow, and the Three-winding Style practised in the north. These are, or were, legitimate designs in tree penjing which are not encountered in Japanese bonsai. However, in both tree penjing and bonsai such concepts as dragons may be depicted, usually without being identifiable as such to the untutored occidental eye.

Tree penjing, like bonsai, are grown in a wide variety of sizes from 'finger size', 2.5cm/1in. tall, to heights greater than that of a man. Composite groups may be in trays of great size, sometimes as long as 6–7 metres/20–25ft. Tree penjing may include rocks in the overall design, thus forming a continuum into the other category, namely rock penjing.

The category of rock penjing may be regarded as beginning with tree penjing compositions in which the rocks are slightly more important in the overall design than the plants and ending with designs in which there is no plant material at all. These last are categorized into two classes: 'stone and water' and 'stone and earth' penjing. In the former, stones – always very skilfully selected and often cunningly shaped and fixed together – are displayed in trays of water. In the latter, earth and stones form a mountain landscape with water sometimes symbolically represented by white gravel.

Rock penjing can be very small but often the compositions are as large as the big tree penjing. In contrast to tree penjing many of the smaller rock penjing compositions without plants are made for continuous indoor display. This aspect of the art was first introduced into Japan about 600 AD in the form of a present from the Chinese Emperor to the Japanese court. These scenery or landscape stones in Japan have become an art form known as *suiseki* – literally, water stones. In Japan it is unusual to adapt the natural shape of the rock and thus *suiseki* is a much more passive art form than rock penjing. In Japan tray landscapes incorporating both plants and rocks are called *saikei*, have become popular only since about 1950 and are regarded as separate from bonsai.

In China, both tree and rock penjing are displayed in gardens, and thus form part of them, whereas in Japan bonsai, *suiseki* and *saikei* are not normally incorporated into garden design but displayed separately.

In the formation of miniature landscapes – 'three-dimensional paintings' – the following simple guidelines apply to create perspective: for distance, lighter colours, smaller plants and stones, less detail; and for the foreground, darker colour, larger shapes and more detail. For foreground mountain summits, use deep and sharply fissured rock and for distant ranges, less clearly sculptured, more rounded stones.

Of the many influences of other arts of penjing two are worthy of special mention. Both relate to landscape painting.

In the T'ang period a style of painting known as 'literati' was developed in southern China. Although stylized it appears very free in form, in contrast to the northern school of painting which imposed strict rules. Scholars forsook the worldly life in order to spend time in the mountains where they could contemplate, write poetry, make simple gardens and grow pot plants which in due time included penjing. According to the aesthetic of the literati, the viewer is absorbed into a painting: he is transported into the scene and sits beside the waterfall or under the tree, and can see behind the rock to the view behind. So also with viewing penjing and thus the need to use some of the painterly techniques of the literati school in penjing design. '...If you aim to dispense with method, learn method. If you aim at facility, work hard. If you aim for simplicity, master complexity.' This is from a book called the 'Mustard Seed Garden Manual of Painting', which had a great influence in both China and in Japan in the 18th century. In Japan the *bunjin* free-form style of bonsai owes its origins principally to this work.

Late in the 19th century the penjing masters of Guangzhou (Canton) developed a training technique to assist in the production of very unstylized penjing. It is called *lingnan* – 'cut the trunk and let the branches grow'. It is a technique best suited to plants that respond to pruning by vigorous budding, such as elm, apricot and many of the subtropical species native to that part of China. First the trunk and branches are shortened, growth is then permitted until the new shoots are of the desired thickness, then they are cut in their turn. Each cutting back is planned so as to create a further forking of the branches. Harmonious proportions can be obtained, trees are usually natural-looking with very twiggy branches. But, as one Chinese master proudly claimed, *lingnan* penjing are 'created by human endeavour, but are free of artistic ideas regarding shape' – in strong contrast to the literati concept. The other Chinese schools of penjing use tying, wiring and carving to shape their plants as do Japanese bonsai masters, usually producing miniature trees which look like refined versions of full grown ones, but in Sichuan and Yangzhou penjing tend to be trained in quite artificial and sometimes grotesque shapes.

These different schools reflect in part the climatic variations in China and the different kinds of tree that can be used – growers in the south grow tropical and subtropical genera such as *Ehretia* (*Carmona*), elms (*Ulmus*) and *Sageretia*, while in the west and north box (*Buxus*), *Gingko*, plum (*Prunus*), *Pinus* and *Podocarpus* are among those cultivated. Chrysanthemum penjing is also practised. By whatever route, the highest skill in penjing is to show no trace of human touch and yet produce designs that are naturally beautiful.

**Pennisetum** Rich. ex Pers. (From Lat. *penna*, feather, and *seta*, bristle, referring to the plume-like bristles of some species.) Gramineae. Some 80 species of rhizomatous or stoloniferous annual or perennial grasses, to 340cm. Stems flimsy to robust, clumped. Leaves flat; ligule ciliate. Inflorescence terminal to axillary, spicate, cylindric to globose; spikelets clustered, to 4 per cluster, lanceolate to oblong, sessile to short-stipitate, 2-flowered, enclosed by an involucre of bristles; upper flower hermaphrodite, lower flower sterile or male; lower lemma absent or equal to spikelet, upper lemma blunt to acute, more robust than lower. Tropics, subtropics, warm temperate.

CULTIVATION Natives of woodland and savannah throughout the tropics *P. clandestinum* cultivated for fodder, used in erosion control, and as a lawn grass; *P. glaucum* a cereal crop, also used in beer-making; *P. purpureum* a forage grass, pulp used in paper production. Many spp. of the genus have decorative inflorescences; *P. pedicellatum* Trin. and *P. polystachyon* (L.) Schult. may be of interest for cultivation in a warm greenhouse. They are valued as ornamentals for their feathery and beautifully coloured panicles; in *P. alopecuroides* 'Burgundy Giant' the whole plant is richly coloured. Tender species are reliably perennial only in essentially frost-free zones but most are amenable to treatment as annuals or to pot or tub cultivation in the warm glasshouse in cool temperate zones. Grow in light porous soils in full sun. Propagate annuals by seed, perennials by division. *P.* 'Burgundy Giant' is propagated by stem cuttings under mist in late summer.

***P. alopecuroides*** (L.) Spreng. CHINESE PENNISETUM; SWAMP FOXTAIL GRASS; FOUNTAIN GRASS. Perenn., to 1.5m. Stems clumped, slender, upright. Lvs to 60cm×1.2cm, glabrous, scabrous; sheaths flattened. Infl. cylindric to narrow-oblong, to 20×5cm, yellow-green to dark purple; axis minutely warty, to 3cm, hispidulous; spikelets solitary or in pairs, lanceolate, to 8mm. Summer–autumn. E Asia to W Australia. 'Burgundy Giant': forming an upright clump to 1.2m; lvs broad, bronze tinted claret. 'Hameln': dwarf, to 50cm; lvs golden in autumn; fls white tinted green. 'Herbstzanber': small, to 50cm; early flowering. 'Moudry':

low; lvs wide, dark green, shiny; fl. heads dark purple to black. 'Weserbergland': somewhat dwarf. 'Woodside': robust; infl. dark purple; early flowering. var. ***purpurascens*** (Thunb.) Ohwi. CHIKARA-SHIBA. Spikelet bristles dark purple. var. ***viridescens*** (Miq.) Ohwi. Spikelet bristles pale green. Z7.

***P. latifolium*** Spreng. URUGUAY PENNISETUM. Perenn., to 270cm. Stems robust, erect, branched towards apex, branches bearing inflorescences, nodes pubesc. Lvs lanceolate, base attenuate, to 75×5cm, scabrous. Infl. compact, pendent, to 9cm×1.8cm, borne on threadlike pedicels, bristled; bristles as long as spikelet, 1–2× length of spikelets; spikelets lanceolate, to 5mm, solitary. Summer–autumn. Brazil, Peru, Argentina. Z9.

***P. macrostachyum*** (Brongn.) Trin. Resembles *P. setaceum* but lvs to 2.5cm wide, infl. more compact, tinged purple-brown; bristles not plumed.

***P. macrourum*** Trin. Perenn., to 180cm. Stems flimsy to robust, erect, clumped. Lvs linear, flat or rolled, to 60cm×1.3cm, scabrous. Infl. cylindric, compact, erect or inclined, to 30×2cm, pale brown to purple, with bristles equal to or longer than spikelet; axis covered with tiny warts; spikelets solitary, lanceolate, to 6mm. Summer–autumn. S Africa. Z7.

***P. orientale*** Rich. Rhizomatous perenn., to 90cm. Stems clumped, slender, decumbent, erect to spreading; nodes pubesc. Lvs narrow-linear, apices straight to flexuous, to 10cm×0.4cm, slightly rough. Infl. loose, to 14×2.5cm; axis pubesc. with bristles to twice length of spikelets; spikelets in fascicles of 2–5, lanceolate, to 6mm. Summer–autumn. C, SW Asia to NW India. Z7.

***P. setaceum*** (Forssk.) Chiov. FOUNTAIN GRASS. Perenn., to 90cm. Stems erect, stiff, slender, clumped, occasionally pubesc. beneath infl. Lvs narrow-elongate, erect, flat or rolled, to 30cm×0.3cm, rigid, very scabrous. Infl. erect to inclined, plumed, to 30×3cm, tinged pink to purple; axis scabrous; bristles unequal, loosely pubesc. near base, to 2.5cm, one to 3cm, more robust; spikelets to 0.6cm, solitary or in group to 3. Summer. Tropical Africa, SW Asia, Arabia. 'Purpureum' ('Atropurpureum'): lvs purple, infl. deep crimson. 'Rubrum' ('Cupreum'): tall; lvs maroon tinted bronze; plumes deep burgundy. A red-leaved form, never exceeding 60cm is also grown. Z9.

***P. villosum*** R. Br. ex Fries. FEATHERTOP. Perenn., to 60cm. Stems loosely clumped, erect to ascending, pubesc. below infl. Lvs flat or folded, to 15cm×0.6cm. Infl. cylindric to subglobose, compact, plumed, to 11×5cm, tinged tawny brown to purple; bristles spreading, variably pubesc. below middle, to 7.5cm; spikelets lanceolate, to 1.5cm; acute. Summer–autumn. NE Tropical Africa (mts). Z8.

***P. americanum*** (L.) Schum. See *P. glaucum*.
***P. asperifolium*** (Desf.) Kunth. See *P. setaceum*.
***P. atrosanguineum*** hort. See *P. setaceum*.
***P. caudatum*** hort. See *P. alopecuroides*.
***P. cenchroides*** hort. non Rich. See *Cenchrus ciliaris*.
***P. ciliare*** (L.) Link. See *Cenchrus ciliaris*.
***P. compressum*** R. Br. See *P. alopecuroides*.
***P. cupreum*** A. Hitchc. ex L.H. Bail. See *P. setaceum*.
***P. japonicum*** Trin. See *P. alopecuroides*.
***P. longistylum*** Vilm. non Hochst. See *P. villosum*.
***P. macrostachyum*** Freis. non (Brongn.) Trin. See *P. setaceum*.
***P. rueppelianum*** Hochst. See *P. setaceum*.
***P. ruppelii*** Steud. See *P. setaceum*.
***P. spicatum*** Roem. & Schult. See *P. glaucum*.
***P. typhoides*** (Burm.) Stapf & C. Hubb. See *P. glaucum*.
For further synonymy see *Gymnothrix*.

For illustration see ORNAMENTAL GRASSES.

**Penstemon** Schmidel. (From Gk *pente*, five, and *stemon*, stamen, referring to the prominent sterile fifth stamen.) Scrophulariaceae. About 250 species of subshrubs or perennial herbs, some grown as annuals. Leaves opposite, or occasionally ternate or upper alternate, lower generally petiolate, upper sessile. Infl. a racemose, cymose or thyrsoid panicle, showy; calyx 5-lobed; corolla tubular, almost regular to strongly bilabiate, upper lip 2-lobed, lower 3-cleft; stamens 4, paired, filaments arching, plus 1 staminode, elongate, often dorsally hirsute. Fruit a septicidal, cartilaginous capsule; seeds numerous, testa irregularly angled. Western N America (Alaska to Guatemala, mostly W US), 1 species in Kamchatka and N Japan.

CULTIVATION The warm colours of *Penstemon* spp. and cvs make a valuable contribution to the late summer and autumn flower garden. Diversity of natural habitat gives a variety of tolerance to differing garden sites. The majority of commonly cultivated spp. (e.g. *P. barbatus, P. isophyllus, P. hartwegii*) are found in dryish, sunny sites or in sub-alpine woodland, meadow and plains on light, often impoverished soils. Species such as *P. centranthifolius* are found in desert and semi-desert conditions. These spp. are (apart from the desert-natives) the least demanding in cultivation and are most frequently used in cold areas as annuals for seasonal colour or, where winter temperatures do not fall much below −5°C are planted out into herbaceous and mixed borders where they are usually found to be fairly drought tolerant: they are sometimes naturalized in an alpine flower lawn or wild garden. A few of the taller spp., such as *P. nemorosus*, inhabit moister woodland or meadowland soils. From the two parent spp. *P. hartwegii* and *P. cobaea*, have evolved the garden hybrids which are more frequently encountered in Great Britain than in North America: these will do best where summers are cool, but continue to perform moderately well in hot humid weather. A second group includes spp. such as *P. davidsonii, P. menziesii, P. scouleri, P. newberryi, P. acaulis* and *P. rupicola*, which are low-growing small shrubs or mat-formers of mountain areas and may be grown on rock gardens or as front of border plants. The greatest enemies of the genus in cultivation are frost and damp during the winter months.

Despite the extremely low temperatures that many species experience in habitat, prolonged low temperatures are usually accompanied by very dry conditions and/or snow cover, and many species do not thrive outside their native zones. The high alpine and montane species are in addition prone to sun scald in winter and need the airy protection of, for example, evergreen branches, in the absence of snow cover. The larger foliaged and flowered spp. tend to be the least winter-hardy and, as a precaution against losses, cuttings should always be taken in cold areas and the top growth of plants left to give some protection until spring. Planting on sharply drained, light soils may counteract the effects of winter wet in damp climates such as Britain. Species most resistant to frost and damp include *Pp. barbatus, ovatus, acuminatus, angustifolius, confertus, diffusus, digitalis, fruticosus, glaber, grandiflorus, hirsutus, laevigatus* and *menziesii*.

Many spp. that do not form basal tufts or rosettes of foliage tend to be short-lived and are inclined to behave as biennials (e.g. *Pp. ovatus, alpinus, angustifolius, azureus, glaber, glandulosus*); repropagate frequently. Plant out after last frosts in sunny, open sites with protection from cold east winds: those spp. naturally inhabiting open woodland will prefer part-day shade and other spp. may tolerate this. Soils should be fairly rich, light and free-draining: add grit or leafmould depending on soil types.

Grow alpines in good light, avoiding full exposure to hot sun (e.g. planted on a north-facing slope). A gritty moraine or scree bed, may be most suitable for the more difficult spp. requiring dry conditions around the neck and a continually cool and moist root run: alternatively, grow in pans of a gritty alpine medium in the alpine house or cold frame. Shear alpines back after flowering to maintain vigour and cut back taller plants almost to ground level, in spring after the last severe frosts. Propagate from seed (varieties do not come true) sown in spring at 13–18°C/55–65°F: if seed of the border hybrids is sown early enough, a reasonable show may be had in the autumn after sowing. Alternatively, take 5–10cm/2–4in. semi-ripe cuttings of non-flowering side-shoots in late summer, rooted in a sandy, free-draining medium in a closed frame: overwinter under frost-free conditions. Also from softwood cuttings in early summer. Perennial spp. forming basal tufts of foliage may be divided in spring.

Susceptible to chrysanthemum eel-worm (*Aphelenchoides ritzemabosi*) which is difficult to eradicate and usually produces symptoms of stunted growth and discoloured leaves. Take care not to introduce infected plant material, isolating new acquisitions before planting out: in spite of these precautions, the pest may be spread by wind-blown plant debris and on weeds. Destroy infested plants and maintain good garden hygiene.

***P. abietinus*** Pennell. Rootstock horizontal, forming mats to 1m diam.; stems ascending to erect, caespitose, 5–10cm tall. Lvs 1×0.1cm, crowded, linear, mucronate, sometimes folded along main vein, glabrous at least apically. Cal. lobes lanceolate-acuminate, sparingly glandular-pubesc., with broad scarious margin at base; cor. 14–18mm, deep blue or ultramarine with maroon tube, palate very sparsely hirsute, deeply bilabiate, lips subequal; staminode densely and shortly orange-yellow-hirsute throughout. Utah. Z3.

***P. acaulis*** L.O. Williams. Rootstock to 5cm, branched, subterranean. Lvs 1.5–2cm, in dense tufts, narrowly linear-spathulate, acute, green, glabrous or scabrous, more or less viscid. Fls solitary, sessile; cal. concealed amid foliage, lobes long-acuminate, glutinous; cor. 14–16mm, deep azure blue, moderately ampliate, limb prominent, to 10mm broad, throat strongly golden-hirsute within; staminode golden-brown-hirsute throughout. Fr. indehiscent, seeds being released by decay of buried capsule. Wyoming. In its natural habitat, *P. acaulis* appears stemless as the stems are buried each year by soil washed down over them: in garden conditions, this species may grow differently. Z3.

***P. acuminatus*** Douglas ex Lindl. SAND-DUNE PENSTEMON. To 60cm, glabrous and glaucous throughout or rarely minutely viscid; stems erect, rather stout. Lvs to 7cm, lanceolate to ovate, or uppermost suborbicular with acute tip, entire, lower stoutly petiolate, upper cordate-amplexicaul, coriaceous, veining conspicuous. Infl. thyrsoid, elongate, of 3–18 often congested clusters; cor. 12–18×4–5mm, throat gradually ampliate, limb obscurely bilabiate, blue-mauve; staminode apically dilated and golden-hirsute. Summer. Washington and Oregon to Idaho. Z5.

***P. alamosensis*** Pennell & Nisbet. Stems solitary or few, 70cm, glabrous. Lvs lanceolate to obovate, acute to obtuse at apex, stem lvs smaller than basal lvs, acute. Infl. narrow, somewhat secund, about half height of plant; pedicels sparsely glandular-pubesc.; cal. 3–5mm, lobes ovate to lanceolate, acute to acuminate, margins narrowly scarious, sparsely glandular; cor. almost regular, lobes 2–2.5cm, spreading bright red, glandular-pubesc. without; staminode glabrous. Summer. New Mexico (mts). Z9.

***P. albertinus*** Greene. To 40cm; stems clustered, more or less pubesc., often in lines, or glabrate. Lvs to 7cm, lanceolate, entire or shallowly remotely dentate, thin, glabrous. Infl. more or less glandular; cal. to 7mm; cor. to 2cm, light blue to violet or rarely pink, throat dilated, palate hirsute; staminode not exserted, golden-hirsute for less than one third of its length. Fr. to 9mm, glabrous; seeds to 2mm. British Columbia and Alberta to Idaho and Montana. Z3.

***P. albidus*** Nutt. Stems 15–40cm, generally 2–4 together, finely minutely pubesc. particularly below. Lvs 4–8×1–1.5cm, ascending, oblong-lanceolate, entire or remotely crenate, rounded at base, glabrous to very minutely pubesc. or scabrous. Infl. to 10cm, strict, glandular, axis pubesc.; cal. 6–7mm, lobes lanceolate, acuminate, densely glandular; cor. tube 1.5–2cm, gradually dilated, white or faintly flushed violet, minutely glandular-pubesc. within; staminode included, not dilated, sparsely hirsute at apex. Summer. S Canada to Oklahoma, Texas, Colorado and New Mexico. Z3.

***P. alpinus*** Torr. Very similar to *P. glaber* except stems and lvs glabrous to minutely pubesc.; sep. 4–7mm, long-acuminate; cor. glabrous to pubesc. or villous within. Wyoming and Colorado. Z4.

***P. ambiguus*** Torr. To 60cm, woody at base, glabrous; stems paniculately branched, shrubby, slender. Lvs 1.5–5×0.1cm, filiform or lowest linear, mucronate. Infl. laxly paniculate; peduncles slender, upper 1-fld; cor. rose-pink to flesh-pink becoming white, limb rotately expanded, obscurely bilabiate, lobes suborbicular, lower lobe somewhat hairy; staminode glabrous. Early summer–early autumn. Colorado and Utah to California and Texas, Mexico. Z3.

***P. anguineus*** Eastw. SISKIYOU PENSTEMON. Stems 30–80cm, glabrous below. Lvs 5–15×1–4cm including petiole, ovate to oblong, serrate or minutely dentate to subentire, upper amplexicaul, glabrous. Infl. thyrsoid, of 3–10 densely crowded clusters, or openly paniculate with divergent peduncles to 10cm; cal. 4–7mm, lobes lanceolate; cor. 13–18×4–6mm, deep lavender to blue-violet, abruptly ampliate, upper lip short, erect, lower lip longer, spreading, palate sparingly hirsute to glabrous; staminode exserted, glabrous or sparingly hirsute for half its length. Summer. Oregon to California. Z7.

***P. angustifolius*** Nutt. ex Pursh. To 30cm, strongly glaucous; stems erect, caespitose. Lvs to 7.5cm, linear to lanceolate, acuminate, rather thick, more or less fleshy. Infl. thyrsoid; cal. 4–8mm, lobes acute to acuminate; cor. 15–18mm, pink becoming sky-blue, glabrous within, bilabiate, lobes all spreading, to 12mm wide; staminode somewhat inflated toward apex, strongly hirsute. Summer. S Dakota and Wyoming to Colorado and Kansas. Z3.

***P. antirrhinoides*** Benth. CHAPARRAL BEARD-TONGUE. Shrub, 1–2.5m; stems spreading, much-branched, minutely pubesc. Lvs 1–2×0.2–0.7cm, crowded, elliptic, mostly entire, firm. Infl. a broad panicle, leafy; cal. 3–6mm, lobes ovate to suborbicular, obtuse to cuspidate-acute; cor. 16–20×8mm, throat abruptly dilated, upper lip broad, arching, lower lip reflexed, yellow tinged red-brown, viscid; staminode exserted, densely yellow-hirsute. Spring–summer. California and Baja California. ssp. ***microphyllus*** (A. Gray) Keck. As for type except twigs cinereous; lvs yellow-grey-green, canescent throughout; cal. 5–8mm, viscid, canescent, lobes oblong-lanceolate, acuminate. California to Baja California and Arizona. Z9.

***P. aridus*** Rydb. 10–50cm, densely caespitose, glabrous below infl. Lvs 2–4cm, linear to linear-subulate or narrowly oblanceolate, margins often involute, obscurely scabrid-denticulate, stem lvs smaller and erect, thick and stiff. Flowering stems to 10cm; infl. glandular-pubesc.; cal. 5mm, lobes linear-lanceolate; cor. 12mm, blue or tinged purple, tubular-funnelform, lower lip slightly exceeding upper; staminode slightly spathulate and yellow-villous at apex. Montana, Wyoming, Idaho. Z3.

***P. arkansanus*** Pennell. 30–90cm; stem caespitose, closely minutely cinereous-pubesc. Lvs 5–6×1–2cm, lanceolate to oblong-lanceolate, broadly rounded to cordate at base, entire or remotely dentate, lower petiolate, green, membranous, glabrous or subglabrous. Infl. paniculate, diffuse; fls very numerous, small; cal. 2–4mm; cor. 15–18mm, white without, purple or violet within with darker nectar-guides in throat, throat almost tubular with prominent ventral ridges, lower lobes projecting; staminode densely yellow-hirsute. Fr. 6–8mm. Late Spring–summer. Missouri and Arkansas to Texas. Z5.

***P. attenuatus*** Douglas Plant with well-developed basal rosette; stems slender, 30–60cm. Lvs 4–10×1–2cm including petiole, linear-lanceolate to oval, entire to very minutely dentate, reduced upwards, upper amplexicaul, deep green, glabrous. Infl. thyrsoid, strict, of 3–7 clusters, glandular-pubesc.; cal. 4–7mm, lobes lanceolate, entire, with narrow scarious margin; cor. ampliate, bilabiate, 14–20mm, pale yellow or blue-purple to violet, palate white-hirsute, staminode reaching orifice, apically golden-hirsute. Summer. Washington to Oregon and Idaho. ssp. ***pseudoprocerus*** (Rydb.) Keck Shorter; fls smaller, cor. blue-purple. Z4.

***P. auriberbis*** Pennell. Stems erect, to 35cm, minutely pubesc. Lvs to 7.5cm, linear to lanceolate, upper lvs broader than lower, entire or undulate-dentate, usually minutely pubesc. Infl. narrow, rather secund, densely glandular; cal. 7–9mm, lobes lanceolate, acuminate; cor. 18–25mm, lavender to purple, glandular without, lobes spreading, lower lobes bearded at base; staminode exserted, somewhat dilated, densely yellow-hirsute for most of its length. Summer. Colorado and Arizona. Z4.

***P. australis*** Small. Stems 40–80cm, finely pubesc. to minutely hirsute. Lvs narrowly lanceolate, basal oblanceolate to obovate, acuminate, minutely serrate, minutely pubesc. above and beneath. Infl. paniculate, slender, branches shorter than internodes; cal. 5–8mm; cor. 20–25mm, maroon, lower lobes creamy white within with purple lines; staminode densely hirsute. Summer. SE US. Z7.

***P. azureus*** Benth. Subshrub, 20–50cm. Lvs 1.5–6×0.5–1.5cm, blue-glaucous, glabrous, basal oblanceolate to obovate, shortly petiolate, stem lvs lanceolate to oblong, obtuse to acuminate, amplexicaul. Infl. thyrsoid, strict, subsecund; peduncles erect; cal. 4–6mm, lobes oblong to obovate, abruptly contracted to mucronate tip; cor. 20–30×7mm, tubular-campanulate, gaping, indigo, buds tinged yellow, glabrous; staminode dilated at apex, generally glabrous. Late summer. California. ssp. ***angustissimus*** (A. Gray) Keck. Lvs very narrow, pale yellow-green. Z8.

***P. barbatus*** (Cav.) Roth. Stems stout, 1m+, glabrous or minutely pubesc. at base. Basal lvs lanceolate to spathulate or ovate, stem lvs lanceolate to linear, glabrous or minutely pubesc. Cal. 6–10mm, lobes lanceolate, acute to shortly acuminate with scarious margins; cor. 3–4cm, red tinged pink to carmine, strongly bilabiate, throat gradually inflated, upper lobes projecting, lower lobes reflexed and yellow-hirsute at base; anth. exserted, staminode included, glabrous. Summer. New Mexico to Utah, Arizona and N Mexico. 'Albus': fls white. 'Carnea': fls pale pink. 'Coccineus': to 90cm; fls bright scarlet. 'Praecox': early-flowering. 'Praecox Nanus': habit dwarf; variety of colours. 'Roseus': fls pink. ssp. ***torreyi*** (Benth.) Keck. As for species type except stems more slender; stem lvs all linear; cal. 3–5mm, cor. scarlet, generally glabrous at base of lobes. Colorado to New Mexico and Arizona. Z3.

***P. barrettiae*** A. Gray. Forming dense, broad clumps, 20–40cm tall; stems shrubby below, much-branched. Lvs 4–6×2–2.5cm, ovate to elliptic-ovate, serrate, blue-glaucous, glabrous, basal lvs shortly petiolate, upper stem lvs amplexicaul. Infl. 7–25cm, thyrsoid, subracemose, dense; peduncles 1–3-fld; cal. 6–7mm, lobes ovate, acute to acuminate; cor. 35×8mm, lips projecting, short, lilac to rosy purple, ventral ridges very villous; anth. lanate, staminode half length of fertile fil., slender, subglabrous. Early summer. Washington and Oregon. Z7.

***P. berryi*** Eastw. Very similar to *P. newberryi* except cor. 27–33×8mm, with throat more ampliate, ventral ridges within bearded with longer, more supple hairs, stamens included. Oregon to California. Z7.

***P. bicolor*** (Brandg.) Clokey & Keck. 60–140cm, glaucous or glaucescent, glabrous to infl. Lvs 8cm, ovate, dentate, uppermost connate-perfoliate, thick, coriaceous. Infl. not leafy, rarely interrupted, glandular-pubesc. Cal. 4–6mm, lobes ovate; cor. to 2.5cm, white, yellow or pink, glandular without, gradually inflated, nearly regular, throat moderately ampliate, lower lip sparsely villous; staminode included or scarcely exserted, hirsute. Spring. Nevada and Arizona. Z5.

***P. brandegeei*** Porter. Stems stout, to 60cm, minutely pubesc. Lower lvs lanceolate to oblanceolate, glabrous, on short petioles, basal lvs often absent by anthesis, upper lvs lanceolate to elliptic, acute, sessile, sometimes cordate at base, to 10cm. Infl. spreading, many-fld, secund; peduncles minutely pubesc.; cal. 6–8mm, lobes ovate to orbicular, acuminate, margins broadly scarious; cor. 3–4cm, blue or tinged purple, glabrous or sparsely hairy, throat greatly expanded, lower lip deflexed or divergent; staminode exserted, dilated at apex, glabrous or very sparsely hairy at apex. Summer. Colorado and New Mexico. Z4.

***P. breviflorus*** Lindl. GAPING PENSTEMON. Shrub, 0.5–2m; stems numerous, virgate, rather lax, glaucous, glabrous. Lvs 1–1.5×0.3–1.2cm, lanceolate, minutely serrate to entire, subsessile, glabrous. Infl. 10–55×4–15cm, a pyramidal thyrsus, many-fld; pedicels glandular-pubesc.; cal. 5–10mm, lobes lanceolate; cor. 15–18mm, white flushed rose, with prominent purple guide-lines, buds tinged yellow, upper lip arching, helmet-shaped, more than half length of cor., lobes less than 2mm, lower lip strongly reflexed, parted almost to base into 3 oblong lobes, glandular-pubesc. without, more or less hirsute toward apex; staminode glabrous. Late summer–early autumn. California. Z7.

***P. brevifolius*** (A. Gray) Nels. 10–30cm, creeping, caespitose, with well-developed subaerial rhiz.-like stems, very minutely pubesc. Lvs 1.5–2.5×1–2cm, ovate to broadly ovate, or stem lvs elliptic-ovate, acute, thin. Infl. glandular-pubesc.; cal. lobes lanceolate; cor. 8–12mm, violet-blue, minutely glandular-pubesc. without, bilabiate, throat not inflated above, with weak ventral ridges, upper lobes abruptly spreading, slightly exceeded by lower lobes; staminode hirsute. Summer. Utah. Z3.

***P. bridgesii*** A. Gray. Subshrub, 30–100cm; stems erect, glabrous to minutely pubesc. Lvs linear to spathulate, basal obtuse and petiolate, upper acute and amplexicaul, 20–80×2–12mm, glabrous or subglabrous. Infl. a subsecund thyrsus, lax, rather narrow, glandular-pubesc.; cal. 4–8mm, lobes lanceolate, acuminate, with scarious margins; cor. tubular, strongly bilabiate, upper lip erect, lower sharply reflexed, 22–35×4mm, vermilion to scarlet, sparingly glandular; staminode glabrous. Summer. California and Baja California to Colorado and Arizona. Z4.

***P. buckleyi*** Pennell. Stems stout, to 40cm, glaucous and glabrous. Lvs oblanceolate to spathulate or lanceolate, obtuse to acute, glaucous, glabrous; petioles margined. Infl. narrow; cal. 4–5mm, lobes ovate, acuminate, margins scarious, glabrous; cor. 1.5–2cm, pale lavender to light blue with prominent guide-lines within throat, throat slightly expanded, lobes spreading; staminode yellow-hirsute. Spring–summer. Kansas to Texas and New Mexico. Z5.

***P. caelestinus*** Pennell. Stems erect, 25–40cm, minutely pubesc. to glabrate. Lvs 3–4×1–1.5cm, elliptic-ovate, dentate to entire, acute, stem lvs narrower, generally glabrous. Infl. thyrsoid, secund, to 5–8 fascicles, clusters 7–9-fld; cal. 3–4mm, lobes ovate; cor. 15–17mm, blue-violet with purple nectar-guides, glabrous or minutely glandular-pubesc. without, throat somewhat inflated, with 2 ventral ridges, base of lower lip villous, lobes bright violet-blue, upper lobes arched, lower lobes deflexed-spreading; staminode with tuft of stiff yellow hairs at apex. Montana. Z4.

***P. caesius*** A. Gray. CUSHION PENSTEMON. Plant with matted woody caudex, laxly caespitose; stems erect, 15–45cm, green tinged yellow or blue, glaucous, glabrous. Lvs 1–2cm, mostly basal, suborbicular, green tinged yellow or blue, glaucous, glabrous, coriaceous, stem lvs remote, reduced, becoming narrowly oblanceolate; petioles 1–2cm, slender. Infl. a thyrsoid panicle, lax, few-fld, glandular-pubesc.; cal. 4–7mm, lobes oblong; cor. gradually ampliate, lips 17–23×4mm, equal, small, blue tinged purple, throat glabrous within; anth. pale, staminode glabrous. Summer. California. Z8.

***P. caespitosus*** Nutt. ex A. Gray. Stems 15–40cm, decumbent to prostrate, widely creeping. Lvs to 1cm, linear to oblanceolate, more or less apiculate, minutely pubesc. or rarely glabrate. Infl. leafy; peduncles short, 1–3-fld; cal. lobes acuminate to attenuate, minutely pubesc., more or less scarious-margined, slightly glandular; cor. 14–18mm, light blue with purple throat, white or very pale within, throat sparingly hirsute within, tube scarcely inflated, upper lip erect, lower spreading, exceeding upper, lobes to 2mm; staminode shortly golden-hirsute throughout. Wyoming, Colorado and Utah. ssp. ***desertipicti*** (A. Nels.) Keck. Lvs densely minutely pubesc.; cor. tube abruptly inflated, pale blue without, staminode with dense, longer beard. Utah to Arizona. Z3.

***P. calcycosus*** Small. Stems to 1m, wholly glabrous to minutely hirsute. Lvs to 15×5cm, lanceolate to ovate-lanceolate, rounded at base, acutely serrate to subentire, glabrous below or very rarely minutely pubesc. on main vein. Cal. 6–8mm, lobes tapered regularly from base; cor. 2.5–3.5cm, sometimes smaller, violet-purple without, off-white within; anth. glabrous, staminode hirsute at apex. Summer. Maine to Michigan, south to Missouri, Alabama and Pennsylvania. Z4.

***P. californicus*** (Munz & I.M. Johnst.) Keck. Stems tufted, 5–15cm, densely leafy below, minutely adpressed cinereous-pubesc. Lvs 0.8–1.5cm, linear-oblanceolate, mucronate, rather thick, minutely adpressed cinereous-pubesc. Infl. a racemiform thyrsus, minutely glandular; cal. lobes ovate, acute to acuminate, margin scarious; cor. 14–18×4–6mm, narrowly tubular-funneliform, blue tinged purple; staminode yellow-hirsute at least apically. Summer. California and Baja California. Z8.

***P. campanulatus*** Willd. Stems 30–60cm, leafy, glabrous or minutely pubesc. Lvs linear to linear-lanceolate, acuminate, acutely serrate, lower very shortly petiolate, upper sessile and amplexicaul, to 7cm, smooth. Infl. elongate, lax, secund; peduncles generally 2-fld; cal. 8–10mm; cor. 2.5cm+, rosy purple or violet, glandular-pubesc. without, funnelform, bilabiate; staminode subglabrous to hirsute at apex. Early summer. Mexico and Guatemala. 'Pulchellus': fls violet or lilac. 'Purpureus': fls purple. Z9.

***P. canescens*** (Britt.) Britt. 30–90cm; stem closely minutely cinereous-pubesc. Lvs ovate to broadly lanceolate or oblong, broadly rounded to cordate at base, minutely serrate-dentate, lower petiolate, green, membranous, pubesc. Infl. laxly thyrsoid with ascending branches; cor. 2–3.5cm, purple or violet, with darker nectar-guides in throat, throat abruptly inflated, flattened, with prominent ventral ridges, lower lobes projecting; staminode densely hirsute. Fr. 6–8mm. Summer. E US. Z5.

***P. cardinalis*** Wooton & Standl. Stems erect, to 1m+, green or slightly glaucous, glabrous. Lvs to 12cm, elliptic to ovate or oblong, basal lvs obtuse at apex, stem lvs acute. Infl. narrow, secund; lower peduncles erect; cal. 3mm, lobes ovate, margins scarious; cor. 2–3cm, dull red to crimson, obscurely bilabiate, throat gradually dilated, constricted at orifice, lobes 2–3mm, upper erect, lower spreading or reflexed, yellow-hirsute at base; staminode not dilated, bearded at apex. Summer. Southern New Mexico. Z9.

***P. cardwellii*** T.J. Howell. Forming broad clumps 10–20cm tall, sometimes taller, glabrous below. Lvs 1.5–4×0.7–1.4cm, elliptic, remotely more or less minutely serrate. Infl. racemose, few- to several-fld, strict, sparingly minutely glandular-pubesc.; cal. 8–12mm, lobes lanceolate, acute to attenuate; cor. 25–38×7mm, brilliant purple, ventral ridges villous; staminode very slender, half length of fertile fil., yellow-hirsute. Summer. Washington and Oregon. 'Albus': fls white. 'Roseus': fls pink. Z8.

***P. caudatus*** Heller. Stems stout, to 50cm, glaucous, glabrous. Lvs lanceolate to spathulate, acuminate, stem lvs broader than basal, glaucous, glabrous. Infl. compact; peduncles short; cal. 4–7mm, lobes lanceolate to ovate, with broad scarious margins; cor. 1.5–2.5cm, blue to violet without prominent markings, throat gradually expanded, lobes subequal, spreading, lower lip sometimes sparsely pubesc. at base; staminode dilated, deep yellow-hairy. Summer. Kansas to Utah, New Mexico and Arizona. Z4.

***P. centranthifolius*** Benth. SCARLET BUGLER. Glabrous and glaucous throughout; stems 30–120cm, several, virgate. Lvs 4–10×1–3cm, lanceolate or basal spathulate, entire, lower lvs petiolate, upper lvs semiamplexicaul. Infl. thyrsoid, virgate, half height of plant; peduncles erect; cal. 3–6mm, lobes ovate to orbicular, abruptly acute, with broad scarious margins; cor. 25–33×4–6mm, tubular, lobes scarcely spreading, scarlet, glabrous; staminode glabrous. Early summer. California and Baja California. 'Pilatas Pink': fls pink. Z9.

***P. cinereus*** Piper. 10–50cm, with well-developed basal rosette, clump-forming; stems slender, grey, minutely cinereous-pubesc. Lvs of basal rosette to 5×0.8cm, lanceolate to narrowly ovate, usually entire, rather firm, minutely cinereous-pubesc., stem lvs abruptly reduced, almost linear. Infl. thyrsoid, of 3–9 rather lax, few-fld clusters, glandular-pubesc.; cal. 2–3mm, lobes ovate; cor. 9–13mm, subtubular to gradually ampliate, bright blue to indigo or blue-mauve; staminode reaching orifice, prominently bearded for one third of its length with short golden hairs. Summer. Oregon to Nevada. Z4.

***P. clevelandii*** A. Gray. Stems few to several, 30–70cm. Lvs ovate or upper deltoid-lanceolate to cordate, entire to serrate, deep green to glaucescent. Infl. a narrowly racemiform thyrsus, 10–30×3–6cm; pedicels usually glandular-pubesc.; cal. glandular-pubesc. or rarely glabrous, lobes ovate to suborbicular, flushed purple; cor. tubular-funnelform, tube shorter than throat, not contracted at orifice, lobes 17–24×5mm, quadrate, rotate-spreading, crimson or maroon, without distinct guide-lines, limb minutely glandular-pubesc. within; staminode 9–11mm, weakly hirsute or glabrous. Summer. California and Baja California. Z9.

***P. clutei*** A. Nels. 60–140cm, glaucous or glaucescent. Lvs to 5cm, lanceolate-ovate to ovate, acutely dentate, uppermost connate-perfoliate, somewhat coriaceous. Infl. leafy below, often interrupted; cal. 4–6mm, lobes ovate; cor. deep pink to rosy purple, glandular without, throat gradually inflated, ventricose, to 2.5cm, almost regular; staminode included or scarcely exserted, straight, glabrous or yellow-hirsute. Summer. Arizona. 'Albiflorus': fls white. Z7.

***P. cobaea*** Nutt. Stems 30–60cm, erect, stout, densely minutely pubesc. Lvs 10–20cm, oblong to lanceolate, acute at apex, obtuse at base, entire or usually minutely dentate, thinly pubesc. Infl. paniculate, short, lax; cal. 9–15mm, densely glandular; cor. tube 3.5–5cm, abruptly campanulate-ventricose above, pale to deep purple or white; staminode slender, sparsely hirsute. Late Summer. SC US (Nebraska to Missouri and Arkansas, south to Texas). Z4.

***P. comarrhenus*** A. Gray. Stems to 1m, minutely pubesc. to glabrate. Basal lvs 1–2.5cm, oblong-lanceolate, obtuse, tapered to winged petiole, stem lvs 3–6mm broad, linear-lanceolate, attenuate, sessile. Infl. elongate, lax, rather secund; cal. 4–5mm, lobes ovate, margins prominently erose-scarious; cor. 3–3.5cm, pale blue to blue-mauve, glabrous, strongly bilabiate, tube gibbous, upper lip projecting to erect, lower lip spreading to reflexed; staminode glabrous or very sparsely hairy at apex. Summer. Colorado to Utah, New Mexico and Arizona. Z4.

***P. concinnus*** Keck. ELEGANT PENSTEMON. 80–200cm; stems often flushed purple, minutely pubesc. Lvs 2–5×0.5–6cm, linear to oblanceolate, entire to dentate, somewhat glaucous, usually glabrous. Infl. narrowly thyrsoid, of 4–7 verticillasters, glandular-pubesc.; cal. 5–8mm, lobes narrowly lanceolate, flushed purple; cor. 8–10mm, blue-violet with dark purple nectar-guides, glandular-pubesc. without, palate white-pilose, moderately ampliate, lower lip reflexed; staminode exserted, pale yellow- to white-hirsute. Nevada and Utah (mts). Z3.

***P. confertus*** Douglas. YELLOW PENSTEMON. Glabrous throughout, with well-developed basal rosette; stems slender, 2–5cm. Lvs 3–7×2cm, lanceolate to oblanceolate, thin, stem lvs reduced; petioles short, slender. Infl. thyrsoid, strict, of 2–7 dense clusters; cal. 3–5mm, lobes lanceolate to broadly oblong, tips subulate to abruptly acuminate, very thin, very broadly scarious-margined; cor. 8–12mm, tubular, not strongly bilabiate, pale sulphur-yellow, palate brown-hirsute; staminode included, with short apical tuft of brown hairs. Summer. British Columbia to Alberta, Montana and Oregon. 'Violaceus': fls violet. Z3.

***P. cordifolius*** Benth. Scandent shrub, 1–3m. Lvs 2–5×1–3cm, lanceolate-ovate to cordate, remotely minutely serrate to dentate, lustrous dark green, glabrous to minutely pubesc.; veins conspicuous. Infl. a drooping pyramidal panicle, subsecund, compact; peduncles often reflexed, leafy; fls resupine; cal. 7–10mm; cor. 30–40×5mm, dull scarlet, upper lip helmet-shaped, lower lip broadly spreading; staminode included, densely yellow-brown-hirsute at apex. Early summer. California. Z8.

***P. corymbosus*** Benth. REDWOOD PENSTEMON. Shrub, 30–50cm. Lvs 1.5–4×0.5–1.5cm, elliptic, entire to remotely serrate, margin narrowly revolute, dark green, glabrous to canescent, coriaceous. Infl. corymbose, terminal, often many fld, densely glandular-pubesc.; cal. 6–10mm, lobes lanceolate; cor. narrowly tubular, upper lip helmet-shaped, lower lip spreading, 25–35×4mm, brick-red; staminode included, densely yellow-hirsute throughout. Summer. California. Z8.

***P. crandallii*** A. Nels. Occasionally somewhat shrubby at base; old stems prostrate and rooting, flowering stems decumbent to ascending, 30–120cm, minutely pubesc. Lvs 0.5–2.5×0.1–0.5cm, spathulate to oblanceolate, entire, minutely scabrous-pubesc. to subglabrous. Infl. elongate; cal. 4–6mm, lobes lanceolate, acute to acuminate, minutely scabrous-pubesc., obscurely glandular; cor. 15–20mm, blue to blue-lavender, glandular-pubesc. without, bilabiate, flattened with 2 ventral ridges, lobes spreading, palate sparsely hirsute; staminode included, densely golden-orange-hirsute for most of its length. Utah and Colorado. ssp. ***procumbens*** (Greene) Keck Stems decumbent, forming broad mats, to 10cm tall; lvs glabrous. Colorado. Z3.

***P. cusickii*** A. Gray. Stems clustered, 20–40cm, woody at base, hirtellous, grey-green. Lvs 3–6.5×0.3–0.8cm, linear to narrowly oblanceolate or lower spathulate, 30–65×3–8mm, grey-green, hirtellous. Infl. a narrow thyrsus; peduncles adpressed; cal. 4–7mm, lobes suborbicular, acuminate, glabrous or minutely pubesc.; cor. to 2.5cm, purple to blue, tube rapidly dilated into ample throat, limb gaping, clearly bilabiate, glabrous; anth. dark purple-black, staminode spathulate at apex, glabrous. Summer. Oregon to Idaho. Z4.

***P. cyananthus*** Hook. Stem erect, 30–60cm, slightly glaucous, glabrous throughout or minutely pubesc. near base. Lvs ovate, entire, stem lvs broadly rounded at base, to 6cm broad, glaucous. Infl. thyrsoid, not strongly secund, interrupted; cal. lobes attenuate, not or scarcely scarious-margined; cor. 2–2.5cm, bright blue, bilabiate, tube ventricose upwards; staminode hirsute to subglabrous. Late summer. Montana and Idaho to Colorado and Utah. Z4.

***P. cyaneus*** Pennell. Stems several, 40–80cm, glabrous. Lvs to 10×2cm, lanceolate, acute, basal on petioles to 5cm, stem lvs amplexicaul, light green. Infl. narrowly thyrsoid, secund, almost half height of plant, of 7–12 fascicles; cal. 5mm, lobes broadly ovate to suborbicular with white to pale blue scarious margin; cor. to 3cm, violet-pink when young, soon becoming deep sky-blue, violet in throat, glabrous, tube narrow, throat inflated, somewhat contracted at orifice, upper lip projecting, lower lip exceeding upper, lobes spreading to deflexed; staminode violet-blue, yellow-hirsute at apex. Summer. Idaho, Montana and Wyoming. Z3.

***P. dasyphyllus*** A. Gray. Stems to 70cm, minutely cinereous-pubesc. Lvs to 9cm, linear, tapered, acuminate, entire, minutely cinereous-pubesc. to glabrate. Infl. generally secund, glandular-pubesc.; peduncles erect, 1-fld; cal. 4–7mm, lobes ovate to lanceolate, acute to acuminate; cor. 2.5–3.5cm, blue or tinged purple, lower lip exceeding upper; staminode glabrous. Spring–summer. Texas to Arizona and Mexico. Z9.

***P. davidsonii*** Greene. Very similar to *P. menziesii* except lvs all entire; fls smaller, cor. 18–35mm. Washington to California. 'Albus': fls white. 'Broken Top': habit low and spreading to 40cm diam.; lvs neat-toothed; fls rich purple. ssp. ***thompsonii*** Pennell & Keck Larger in all parts. Z6.

***P. deustus*** Douglas. HOT-ROCK PENSTEMON. Stems erect, much-branched below, forming clumps 20–60cm high, glabrous or minutely glandular-pubesc. Lvs 1–5×0.5–2cm, linear-lanceolate to elliptic-ovate, coarsely serrate-dentate, acute to acuminate, shortly petiolate or those of fertile shoots sessile and amplexicaul, bright green. Infl. thyrsoid, strict, sparingly glandular; cal. lobes lanceolate; cor. 10–16mm, almost tubular, lower lip exceeding upper, yellow tinged brown with purple guide-lines, sparingly glandular; staminode reaching orifice, glabrous or rarely short-bearded toward apex. Summer. Washington to California, east to Wyoming. Z3.

***P. digitalis*** Nutt. Stems to 1.5m, often flushed purple, sometimes rather glaucous, usually glabrous and glossy. Lvs 10–15cm, oblong to oblong-lanceolate or narrowly triangular, entire to dentate, glabrous below. Infl. paniculate, branches erect to ascending, 10–30cm, glandular-pubesc.; cal. 6–7mm; cor. 2.5–3cm, white or flushed very pale violet, generally with purple nectar-guides within, tube dilated abruptly near middle; staminode hirsute. Summer. Maine to S Dakota, south to Texas, Alabama and Virginia. 'Albus': fls white. 'Nanus': habit dwarf. 'Woodville White': fls white. Z3.

***P. diphyllus*** Rydb. Very similar to *P. triphyllus*, except lvs more regularly arranged, nearly all opposite or subopposite. Montana to Idaho and Wyoming. Z3.

***P. dissectus*** Elliot. Stem to 50cm, minutely pubesc. Lvs pinnately parted, seg. 7–11, linear, 1–2mm broad, of variable length, obtuse, glabrous. Infl. paniculate, few-fld; peduncle long; cal. 4–5mm, lobes ovate-oblong; cor. to 2cm, purple, obscurely bilabiate; staminode exserted, yellow-hirsute at apex. Georgia. Z8.

***P. dolius*** M.E. Jones. Stems to 12cm, minutely cinereous-pubesc. Lvs entire, minutely cinereous-pubesc., lower 2–5cm, ovate-lanceolate, shortly petiolate, upper 1–4cm, oblanceolate, sessile. Infl. narrow; cal. 7–9mm, lobes linear-lanceolate, acuminate, not scarious, densely minutely pubesc; cor. 1.5–2cm, blue tinged purple, sparingly glandular-pubesc. without; staminode moderately yellow-hirsute. Summer. Utah to Nevada. Z4.

***P. eatonii*** A. Gray. EATON'S FIRECRACKER. Stems 60cm, few to several, virgate, glabrous or very minutely pubesc. Basal lvs to 18cm, oblanceolate, tapered to petiole-like base, stem lvs 4–10×1–3cm, lanceolate-oblong with amplexicaul base, green or glaucescent, coriaceous, glabrous. Infl. thyrsoid, strict, secund, many-fld, half height of plant, glabrous; cal. 4–6mm, lobes elliptic to broadly ovate, acute to shortly acuminate with narrow scarious margin; cor. subtubular, obscurely bilabiate, throat slightly expanded, lobes erect or spreading, 25–30×6–8mm, scarlet, glabrous; staminode glabrous or more or less bearded. Late summer. California to Nevada and Utah. Z4.

***P. ×edithae*** English. (*P. rupicola* × *P. barrettiae.*) To 25cm, mat-forming, glabrous. Lvs to 4.5cm, suborbicular to elliptic, dentate or entire, glaucous, glabrous. cor. to 4cm, pink; anth. lanate, staminode slightly hirsute at apex. A hybrid originated by Carl English in Seattle, US. Z7.

***P. ellipticus*** J. Coult. & E. Fisher. Forming lax mats; stems erect, 8–12cm. Lvs 2–3×1.5–2cm, broadly elliptic to suborbicular, obtuse, minutely serrate to entire, minutely black-punctate below. Infl. 3–4-fld, racemose, densely viscid-pubesc.; cal. 10–12mm, lobes lanceolate, attenuate; cor. 3.5cm, violet-purple, strongly bilabiate, ventricose, throat narrow, lobes erose; fertile stamens somewhat exserted, purple, staminode shorter, densely yellow-lanate above. Idaho. Z5.

***P. eriantherus*** Pursh CRESTED-TONGUED PENSTEMON; CRESTED BEARD-TONGUE. Stems 10–30cm, villous to canescent. Lvs 4–8cm, lanceolate to ovate, entire to remotely dentate, glandular-pubesc. to canescent. Infl. 4–13cm, thyrsoid, compact, densely glandular-pubesc.; cal. 7–12mm, lobes linear-lanceolate, accrescent; cor. 20–35×9–14mm, lilac-purple with deeper maroon-purple guide-lines, throat strongly ampliate, strongly bilabiate, palate conspicuously pilose; staminode prominently yellow-hirsute. Fr. 9–12mm. Summer. Washington to Alberta, Dakota and Nebraska. 'Nanus': habit dwarf. Z3.

***P. euglaucus*** English. Plant with well-developed basal rosette, glabrous and more or less glaucous throughout; stems 15–50cm, slender to rather stout. Lvs 4–10cm, elliptic, tapered to base, rather firm; petiole short. Infl. thyrsoid, strict, of 1–5 clusters, more or less remote, many-fld; cal. 4–5mm, lobes broadly oblong-obovate, with abrupt caudate tip half length of body; cor. 11–15mm, moderately ampliate, deep blue, palate lightly yellow-hirsute; staminode reaching orifice, with light to dense apical tuft of short golden hairs. Summer. Washington to Oregon (Cascade Mts). Z5.

***P. fendleri*** Torr. & A. Gray. Stems to 50cm, somewhat glaucous, glabrous. Lvs 2–9cm, lanceolate to ovate, obtuse, generally mucronate, shortly petiolate, somewhat glaucous, thick and firm, glabrous. Infl. narrow, 12–25cm; peduncles and pedicels erect; cal. 4–7mm, lobes ovate, acute to acuminate with broad scarious margins; cor. 1.5–2.5cm, blue with prominent deep violet guide-lines in throat, throat narrow, slightly expanded, lobes spreading; staminode dilated, densely yellow-hirsute at apex. Fr. 10–15mm. Spring–summer. Oklahoma and Texas to Arizona. Z6.

***P. flavescens*** Pennell. Stems 20–40cm, decumbent at base or erect, from well-developed basal rosette, minutely pubesc. or glabrous. Lvs 3–7×1–2cm, oblong-lanceolate, entire, obtuse to somewhat acute, upper amplexicaul, light green, glabrous. Infl. thyrsoid, of 2–6 fascicles, congested, glabrous; cal. 5–7mm, lobes ovate-attenuate, margins broadly scarious; cor. 12–15mm, yellow, glabrous without, villous at base of lower lip, throat semi-campanulate, with 2 ventral ridges, lobes light yellow, upper arched, lower deflexed-spreading; staminode reaching orifice, shortly yellow-hirsute in distal part. Montana and Idaho. Z3.

***P. floridus*** Brandg. ROSE PENSTEMON. Stems 60–120cm, several, erect, virgate, glabrous and blue-glaucous below infl. Lvs ovate, obtuse, irregularly spinose-dentate or uppermost subentire, sessile or semiamplexicaul, largest to 10×4cm, glabrous, blue-glaucous. Infl. thyrsoid, glandular-pubesc.; cal. lobes ovate; cor. abruptly inflated, gibbous, slipper-shaped with oblique orifice, base of lower lip projecting beyond base of upper lip, lobes reflexed, 22–30×12–15mm, rose-pink with yellow throat, often wholly tinged yellow in bud, with darker guide-lines; staminode glabrous. Summer. California and Nevada. Z5.

***P. fructicosus*** (Pursh) Greene. SHRUBBY PENSTEMON. Forming dense, broad clumps, to 40cm tall, glabrous or pruinose below infl.; stem shrubby at base. Lvs 1–5×0.5–1.5cm, narrowly lanceolate to oblanceolate or elliptic, entire or minutely serrate or dentate, greatly reduced upwards, green, often lustrous, coriaceous. Infl. strict, subsecund, rather dense, glandular-pubesc.; cal. 7–10mm, lobes lanceolate, acuminate to caudate; cor. 25–38×7mm, bright lavender-blue to pale purple, ventral ridges villous; staminode very slender, half length of fertile fil., yellow-hirsute. Spring–summer. Washington to Oregon, east to Montana and Wyoming. 'Albus': fls white. 'Major': fls large. ssp. ***serratus*** Keck. As for species except plant shorter and more shrubby; lvs prominently serrate-dentate. Z4.

***P. fruticiformis*** Coville. DEATH VALLEY PENSTEMON. Shrubby at base, 30–60cm; stems much-branched, glabrous and glaucous. Lvs narrowly linear-lanceolate, entire, margin more or less involute, to 6mm broad, glabrous and glaucous. Infl. thyrsoid, lax, short; cal. 5–7mm, lobes ovate to subrotund, abruptly short-acuminate; cor. tube short, throat strongly inflated, lobes reflexed, 20–27×10–13mm, white or flesh pink, limb pale lavender, with purple guide-lines, glabrous without; staminode exserted, densely yellow-hirsute. Summer. California (Death Valley). Z8.

***P. gairdneri*** Hook. Woody and spreading at base; stems erect, 10–30cm, densely leafy, minutely cinereous-pubesc. Lvs 1–3×0.1–0.3cm, alternate, linear, entire, generally recurved, margins revolute, minutely cinereous-pubesc. Infl. thyrsoid, strict, glandular-pubesc.; cal. lobes 5–8mm, lanceolate, acuminate to attenuate; cor. 15–20mm, throat 4–6mm broad, scarcely ampliate, limb 12–14mm diam., lobes more or less reflexed, lavender purple, limb deep blue, glandular within; staminode included or very slightly exserted, dorsally bearded for more than half its length with short yellow hairs. Summer. Oregon. ssp. ***oreganus*** (A. Gray) Keck. Lvs 2–7×0.3–0.5cm, apparently opposite; cor. pale blue or lavender to almost white. E Oregon and adjacent Idaho. Z4.

***P. garrettii*** Pennell. Subglabrous; stems several, 20–40cm. Lvs 6–10cm, lanceolate, acute, basal lvs shortly petiolate, stem lvs amplexicaul, stem lvs longer and narrower than basal, dull green, rather glaucous, glabrous. Infl. narrow, secund, sparingly glandular-pubesc.; cal. 4–6mm, lobes ovate, acuminate, margins pale, scarious, minutely dentate; cor. 2cm, blue, glabrous; staminode yellow-hirsute. Summer. Utah. Z4.

***P. gentianoides*** (HBK) Poir. Stem 60–120cm, erect, robust, glabrous. Lvs to 11cm, lanceolate, entire to dentate, acuminate, upper often in whorls of 3. Infl. a racemose thyrsus, leafy; peduncles short, several-fld; cor. 3cm, purple, tube very short, greatly enlarged above, somewhat bilabiate, lobes ovate; staminode recurved at apex, glabrous or sparsely hairy at apex. S Mexico and Guatemala. Z9.

***P. glaber*** Pursh. Plant with branched woody caudex; stems 50–65cm, solitary or many, assurgent, glabrous. Basal lvs lanceolate to obovate, smaller than stem lvs or wanting, stem lvs 3–12×1–3cm, linear-lanceolate to lanceolate, sessile to broadly amplexicaul. Infl. thyrsoid, congested, secund, 10–25cm; cal. 2–4mm, lobes ovate, broadly rounded to shortly acuminate at apex, margins broadly scarious and erose; cor. 2.5–3.5cm, posterior deep blue to indigo or rarely pink, anterior pale blue to white, with maroon nectar-guides within, glabrous without, throat moderately inflated, lobes of upper lip projecting, lobes of lower lip spreading to reflexed; staminode included or slightly exserted, apex glabrous or sparingly pale yellow-hirsute. Fr. 10–15mm. Late summer. Wyoming. 'Roseus': fls pink. Z3.

***P. glandulosus*** Douglas ex Lindl. Glandular-pubesc. throughout; stems stout, 50–100cm. Lower lvs 4–16×1.5–6cm, lanceolate, acutely serrate, on petioles half length of lamina, thin, soft, upper stem lvs lanceolate-ovate to cordate, amplexicaul, very gradually reduced upwards. Infl. of 2–5 congested remote clusters; cal. 10–15mm, lobes lanceolate, attenuate to acute; cor. 28–40×11–15mm, pale lilac to light violet, generally glabrous within; staminode glabrous. Summer. Washington and Oregon to Idaho. Z4.

***P. globosus*** (Piper) Pennell & Keck. Plant with well-developed basal rosette; stems 25–40cm, slender to stout, bright green, glabrous. Lvs 5–18cm including petiole, lanceolate to oblong, thin, stem lvs amplexicaul, bright green, glabrous. Infl. generally a single subcapitate cluster, dense, many-fld, sometimes 2–4 clusters; cal. 6–8mm, lobes oblong to obovate, abruptly narrowed to subulate tip, margin scarious, erose; cor. 15–20×7mm, gradually ampliate, bright blue to blue-purple, palate more or less prominently bearded; staminode included, densely golden-hirsute for half its length. Summer. Oregon to Idaho. Z4.

***P. gormanii*** Greene. Stems to 30cm, more or less pubesc., often in lines, or glabrate. Lvs lanceolate to spathulate, entire or sometimes shallowly minutely serrate toward apex, glabrous. Infl. more or less glandular; cal. to 7mm; cor. to 2.5cm, blue-purple, throat dilated, palate hirsute; staminode somewhat exserted, yellow-hirsute for more than half its length. Fr. to 8mm, glabrous; seeds to 2mm. Northwestern N America (Alaska through Yukon to Mackenzie district, south to British Columbia). Z3.

***P. gracilentus*** A. Gray. Crown compact; stems numerous, 20–70cm, bright green or sometimes glaucescent, glabrous below infl. Lvs 3–10×1–2cm, mostly basal, oblanceolate, stem lvs linear-lanceolate, entire, basal shortly petiolate, bright green or sometimes glaucescent, glabrous. Infl. a compact thyrsoid panicle, glandular-pubesc.; cal. 4–5mm, lobes lanceolate to ovate-oblong; cor. 1.5cm, purple tinged blue to maroon, slightly ampliate, somewhat bilabiate, lower lip villous within; anth. purple-black, staminode yellow-hirsute for 4–5mm. Summer. Oregon, California and Nevada. Z5.

***P. gracilis*** Nutt. SLENDER BEARD-TONGUE. Plant with well-developed basal rosette; stems 30–50cm, slender, glabrous to minutely pubesc. in lines. Lvs lanceolate to linear-lanceolate, serrate, basal petiolate, stem lvs 5–10cm, sessile, glabrous or finely pubesc. Infl. 5–15cm, slender, with short erect lateral branches, several-fld, glandular; cal. 6–9mm, lobes ovate; cor. 15–20mm, pale violet, bilabiate, throat narrow, flattened, strongly 2-ridged, lower lobes exceeding upper, hirsute at base; staminode yellow-bearded. Summer. Alberta to Manitoba, south to Wisconsin, Iowa, Nebraska and New Mexico. Z3.

***P. grandiflorus*** Nutt. LARGE BEARD-TONGUE. To 1m, glabrous throughout; stems erect, glaucous. Lvs 2–9×2–4cm, obovate-oblong becoming broadly ovate to suborbicular, subcordate and somewhat amplexicaul at base, reduced in length upwards, thick and firm, glaucous. Infl. 15–30cm, racemiform, interrupted; fls 2–4 per axil; pedicels short; cal. 9–11mm, lobes lanceolate; cor. 3.5–4.5cm, pink to blue-lavender or pale blue with magenta nectar-guides, tube abruptly dilated, lobes of upper lip spreading to reflexed, lobes of lower lip projecting or spreading. Fr. 1.5–2cm. Summer. N Dakota to Wyoming, Texas and Illinois. 'Albus': fls white. Z3.

***P. grinnellii*** Eastw. Small rounded bush, 30–100cm; stems branched below. Lvs ovate, coarsely to finely spinose-dentate or uppermost subentire, largest to 13×9cm, bright green or glaucescent. Infl. 4–8cm diam., thyrsoid, lax, cor. 20–30×10mm, tube short, throat strongly inflated, lobes reflexed, white or tinged pale purple or blue, paler without than within, with prominent guide-lines; staminode yellow-hirsute. Spring–summer. California. Z8.

***P. hallii*** A. Gray. Caespitose, glabrous or minutely pubesc.; stems erect, to 20cm. Lvs linear to ovate-lanceolate, entire, scarcely or not at all glaucous. Infl. thyrsoid, short, 5–15-fld, sparingly glandular-pubesc.; cal. minutely glandular-pubesc. without, lobe margins lacerate, broadly scarious; cor. 1.5–2cm, blue-violet, bilabiate, tube very short, throat abruptly inflated, decurved at base; staminode shortly hirsute or very rarely glabrous. Summer. Colorado (mts). Z3.

***P. harbourii*** A. Gray. Stems 5–10cm, caespitose, almost simple, minutely pubesc. Lvs 0.8–1.6×0.6–1cm, in about 3 pairs, obovate to oval, entire, upper sessile, rather thick, glabrous or minutely pruinose. Infl. thyrsoid, reduced to 2–3 crowded fls; pedicels short, viscid-pubesc.; cor. 14–18mm, purple, slightly bilabiate, throat rather broad, rather short, lobes rounded, lower lip hirsute within; staminode dilated at apex, hirsute. Colorado. Z4.

***P. hartwegii*** Benth. Stem 90–120cm, glabrous, sometimes slightly pubesc. above. Lvs to 10cm, lanceolate to ovate-lanceolate, entire, acuminate, glabrous. Infl. racemose-paniculate, glandular-pubesc.; peduncles elongate, 2–6-fld; cor. 5cm, deep scarlet, minutely viscid-pubesc. without, tubular-funnelform, gradually dilated above; staminode glabrous or minutely pubesc. at apex. Mexico. Z9.

***P. havardi*** A. Gray. To 60cm, glaucescent, smooth and glabrous. Lvs 5–10×2.5cm, obovate to elliptic or oblong, entire, lower long-petiolate, upper semiamplexicaul, smaller, coriaceous. Infl. a racemiform thyrsus, elongate, virgate; peduncles 3–5-fld; cor. 2.5cm, violet or blue, tubular, bilabiate, lips to 4mm, upper erect, lower spreading; staminode filiform, glabrous. SW Texas and adjacent Mexico. Z9.

***P. haydenii*** S. Wats. 20–45cm, clump-forming; stems decumbent to ascending, glabrous. Lvs to 11×1cm, linear to linear-lanceolate, entire, acuminate to acute, all sessile and amplexicaul, upper broader, somewhat glaucous, firm, glabrous. Infl. 6–16cm, thyrsoid, very compact, cylindric; fls fragrant; cal. 8–12mm, lobes subequal, linear-lanceolate, acuminate; cor. to 2.5cm, distinctly bilabiate, milky blue to milky lavender, with magenta nectar-guides in young fls, glabrous, throat inflated, lobes of upper lip arched-projecting, of lower lip projecting to spreading; staminode included, distally flattened, densely golden-hirsute near apex. Summer. Nevada. Z4.

***P. heterodoxus*** A. Gray. SIERRAN PENSTEMON. Plant with well-developed basal rosette; stems slender, 8–15cm. Lvs 5–20×4–8mm, linear-oblanceolate to spathulate, thin, glabrous, deep green; petiole 0.5–2cm, very slender. Infl. thyrsoid, generally reduced to a subcapitate cluster or 2–4 distinct clusters, dense, glandular; cal. 3–6mm, lobes oblong, abruptly narrowed to short, acuminate tip; cor. gradually ampliate, 10–16mm, indigo, palate prominently yellow-brown-hirsute; staminode included, apically bearded with short stiff yellow hairs, or glabrous. Summer. California and adjacent Nevada. Z5.

***P. heterophyllus*** Lindl. FOOTHILL PENSTEMON. Shrub, 30–50cm, glabrous throughout or rarely very minutely pubesc. at base of stems. Lvs 2–3×0.2–0.4cm, generally fasciculate, linear, tapered, green or glaucous. Infl. a subracemose thyrsus, strict; cal. 4–6mm, lobes oblanceolate with abruptly acuminate tip; cor. gaping, 25–35×9–12mm, rosy violet, lobes blue or lilac, buds tinged yellow; staminode somewhat dilated at apex, glabrous. Mid-summer. California. 'Blue Gem': habit dwarf. 'Heavenly Blue': fls blue to mauve. 'Zuriblau': to 50cm; fls bright blue. ssp. ***purdyi*** Keck. Plant mat-forming, minutely pubesc. throughout; lvs larger, 25–60×3–6mm, rarely fasciculate; cor. blue to light purple. California. Z8.

***P. hirsutus*** (L.) Willd. Plant with rhizome; stems several, erect, 40–80cm, glabrous or villous below, densely minutely glandular-pubesc. above. Lvs 5–12cm, lanceolate to oblong, subentire to dentate, acute at apex, rounded or truncate at base. Infl. rather lax, densely minutely glandular-pubesc.; cal. 5–6mm; cor. 2.5cm, dull purple with white lobes, tube not broadening toward mouth, orifice almost close by arched base of lower lip, tube pubesc. within. Fr. to 9mm. Late summer. Eastern N America (Quebec and Maine to Michigan and Wisconsin, south to Virginia and Kentucky). 'Caeruleus': fls blue-tinted. 'Purpureus': fls clear purple. 'Pygmeus': to 15cm high, floriferous; fls violet. 'Roseus': fls tinted pink. 'Rosinus': fls pink. Z3.

***P. humilis*** Nutt. ex A. Gray. Plant with well-developed basal rosette, densely tufted, forming clumps 10–30cm high, grey, minutely cinereous-pubesc. Lvs lanceolate to oblanceolate, tapered, entire, lower petiolate, 2–5cm, stem lvs reduced and amplexicaul, rather firm. Infl. thyrsoid, of 3–6 few-fld clusters, more or less confluent, glandular-pubesc.; cal. 3–5mm, lobes lanceolate to broadly oblong, obtuse to shortly acuminate; cor. nearly tubular, lower lip exceeding upper, 12–16mm, azure to lavender-blue, tube purple; staminode reaching orifice, with prominent apical tuft of golden hairs and sparse beard for one third of its length. Late summer. Oregon to Montana, south to Colorado and California. 'Albus': fls white. Z4.

***P. imberbis*** (HBK) Poir. Stems 30–60cm, shrubby at base, slender, glabrous or slightly minutely pubesc. Lvs 5–10cm, linear or lower linear-lanceolate, entire, acute, glabrous. Infl. laxly paniculate, elongate, few-fld; cal. 4–6mm, glandular-pubesc.; cor. 2.5cm, pink to red, slightly glandular without, somewhat bilabiate, elongate-funnelform, slightly gibbous below, lobes spreading; staminode glabrous. Mexico (mts). Z9.

***P. incertus*** Brandg. MOJAVE PENSTEMON. Forming shrubby clumps, 60–80cm; stems numerous, branched below, glabrous and glaucous. Lvs narrowly linear-lanceolate, glabrous and glaucous. Infl. thyrsoid, lax, somewhat glandular; cal. 5–7mm, lobes ovate-lanceolate to suborbicular; cor. 25–28×8mm, tube rather long, gradually expanded into ample throat, strongly bilabiate, lips reflexed, violet tinged red or purple, limb deep blue, without guide-lines, lower lip villous at base; staminode included, short, straight, densely hirsute for most of its length. Summer. California. Z8.

***P. isophyllus*** Robinson. Stems 70cm, somewhat decumbent at base, then erect, simple, stout, purple, minutely pubesc. Lvs 3–4×1cm, lanceolate, acute, sessile, margins entire, revolute, rather thick, glabrous. Infl. secund, 30cm, of opposite 3-fld clusters; cal. 8mm, purple; cor. 4cm, red, more or less white-pubesc., throat slightly dilated, limb 5-lobed, minutely crenate; staminode filiform, slightly dilated at apex, glabrous. Mexico. Z9.

***P. jamesii*** Benth. Stems to 50cm, erect, minutely pubesc. to glabrate. Lvs linear to lanceolate or spathulate, entire, undulate or irregularly serrate, tapered, minutely pubesc. to glabrate. Infl. narrow, secund, glandular-pubesc.; cal. 8–12mm, lobes ovate, acute to acuminate, sometimes with narrow scarious margin near base; cor. 2.5–3.5cm, pale lavender to blue with prominent guide-lines in throat, throat abruptly expanded, upper lobes erect, lower spreading or reflexed, glandular and prominently white-pilose at base; staminode exserted, not dilated, with apical tuft of long off-white to very pale yellow hairs, and shortly golden-bearded toward apex. Summer. W Texas to Colorado and New Mexico. Z4.

***P. keckii*** Clokey. Very similar to *P. speciosus* except infl. glandular, cor. glandular without and within, copiously hirsute at base of lower lip, staminode strongly bearded. S Nevada. Z6.

***P. labrosus*** (A. Gray) Hook. f. SAN GABRIEL PENSTEMON. Stems 30–70cm, single or few, erect, virgate, green or somewhat glaucescent, glabrous. Lvs 5–10×0.5–0.7cm, linear-oblanceolate, stem lvs linear, shortly petiolate, obtuse, rapidly reduced upwards, coriaceous. Infl. thyrsoid, strict, somewhat secund; cal. 4–5mm, lobes ovate, acuminate, with scarious margins; cor. 3–4cm, scarlet, glabrous, tubular, limb nearly half length of tube, upper lip erect, shallowly lobed, lower lip slit to base into reflexed linear lobes; staminode glabrous. Late summer. California and Baja California. Z9.

***P. laetus*** A. Gray. Subshrub, 20–80cm; stems often flushed purple, densely minutely pubesc. or canescent. Lvs linear to oblanceolate, upper stem lvs 2–10×0.2–1.2cm, lanceolate, grey-green to yellow-green, densely minutely pubesc. or canescent. Infl. thyrsoid, lax, narrow, glandular-pubesc.; cal. 4–8mm, lobes lanceolate, acuminate; cor. 2–3cm, blue-violet to blue-lavender, tubular-campanulate, limb bright blue, bilabiate, widely gaping, glabrous within; anth. purple, staminode glabrous, narrowly spathulate-tipped. Summer. California. ssp. ***roezlii*** (Reg.) Keck. Lvs much smaller, 2–7×2–12mm; cor. smaller, 1.5–2cm. Oregon to California and Nevada. Z5.

***P. laevigatus*** Sol. Stem 60–120cm, dull, glabrous or usually very minutely pubesc., often in stripes. Lvs to 15×4cm, lanceolate to narrowly oblong, dentate, glabrous, somewhat coriaceous. Infl. sparingly glandular; cal. 4–5mm; cor. to 2.5cm, tube abruptly dilated in distal half, pale violet without, white to very pale violet within; staminode sparsely shortly hirsute. Summer. Pennsylvania to Mississippi and Florida. Z4.

***P. laricifolius*** Hook. & Arn. Cushion-like, with much-branched, woody, subterranean caudex; flowering stems erect, 10–20cm, glabrous or minutely pubesc. Lvs 1.5–3.5cm, in dense, crowded rosettes, filiform. Cal. glabrous, lobes ovate-lanceolate, acuminate, with prominent scarious margin below; cor. 15–18mm, purple, tubular-campanulate, gradually ampliate, limb regular, spreading, prominent, lower lip bearded at base; staminode slightly exserted, shortly yellow-hirsute for distal third. Wyoming. ssp. ***exilifolius*** (A. Nels.) Keck Cor. 12–15mm, more abruptly ampliate, white with green-yellow tinge. Wyoming and adjacent Colorado. Z3.

***P. leiophyllus*** Pennell. Stems 15–60cm, slightly glaucous. Lvs 10–13×1–2cm, linear-lanceolate to narrowly lanceolate, basal lvs petiolate, stem lvs amplexicaul, dull green. Infl. narrow, secund; cal. 6–7mm, lobes lanceolate, acuminate, minutely glandular-pubesc.; cor. 2.5–3cm, blue, minutely glandular-pubesc. without, throat inflated; staminode scarcely dilated, slightly hirsute to glabrous. Summer. Utah. Z4.

***P. lemhiensis*** (Keck) Keck & Cronq. To 70cm, with compactly branched caudex, not creeping, sometimes glaucous, glabrous or minutely pubesc., not glandular. Lvs lanceolate to oblanceolate, entire or nearly so, rather narrow, to 2.5cm wide. Cal. to 1cm, lobes long-acuminate or subcaudate; cor. 2.5–3.5cm, blue-purple, palate glabrous; staminode glabrous. Idaho (Lemhi County) and Montana. Z4.

***P. lentus*** Pennell. Stems to 30cm, erect, glaucous, glabrous. Basal lvs to 4cm, ovate, abruptly contracted at base, on winged petioles to 2.5cm, stem lvs lanceolate to ovate, mucronate, amplexicaul at base, to 7cm. Infl. elongate, rather secund; cal. 3–6mm, lobes acute to acuminate, glabrous, with broad scarious margins; cor. 18–20mm, blue to purple, throat somewhat inflated, hirsute within on ventral side, lower lip greatly exceeding upper; staminode dilated, sparsely hirsute in distal half, densely so near apex. Summer. Colorado to Utah, New Mexico and Arizona. Z4.

***P. linarioides*** Gray. Stems to 50cm, erect to ascending, minutely pubesc. or glabrate. Lvs to 2.5×0.2cm, crowded on short sterile shoots and base of flowering stems, otherwise scattered, linear, mucronate. Infl. narrow, secund, glandular; cal. 4–7mm, lobes ovate with scarious margins; cor. 1.5–2cm, purple to violet with dark purple guide-lines, tube slender, throat gibbous, 2-ridged, lower lip densely yellow-hirsute at base; staminode bright yellow-hairy for most of its length, hairs tufted at apex. Summer. New Mexico and Arizona. ssp. ***coloradoensis*** (A. Nels.) Keck. Older stems decumbent at base, matted, rooting at lower nodes; cor. sparsely hirsute at base of lower lip, staminode sparsely white- or yellow-hairy below apical tuft. Colorado and Utah to New Mexico and Arizona. Z4.

***P. lyallii*** Gray. Stems to 80cm, glabrous below infl. or with lines of hairs. Basal lvs absent, stem lvs narrow, elongate, entire to remotely minutely serrate, to 10cm+, lower stem lvs reduced, glabrous or minutely rough-pubesc. Infl. somewhat paniculate, glandular; cor. to 4.5cm, lavender, glabrous without, conspicuously lanate-villous on prominent ventral ridges within, tube dilated; staminode glabrous. Alberta and British Columbia to Montana and Idaho. var. ***linearifolius*** (J. Coult. & E. Fisher) Krautter. Densely cinereous-pubesc. throughout; lvs smaller, 4–5cm. Idaho. Z4.

***P. menziesii*** Hook. Forming creeping mats; stems woody at base, flowering stems to 10cm, minutely pubesc. Lvs 0.5–1.5×0.4–0.7cm, elliptic to orbicular, more or less minutely serrate-dentate, green, glabrous, more or less glandular-punctate. Infl. racemose, few-fld, glandular-pubesc.; cal. 7–11mm, lobes lanceolate; cor. throat moderately dilated, 25–35×7mm, violet-purple, ventral ridges villous; anth. included, staminode very short, to half length of fertile fil., hirsute. Summer. British Columbia and Vancouver Is. to Washington. 'Microphyllus': habit compact, to 10cm; lvs small; fls lavender. Z7.

***P. miser*** A. Gray. GOLDEN-TONGUED PENSTEMON. Stems 10–25cm, minutely cinereous-pubesc. Lvs linear-lanceolate to elliptic, upper stem lvs linear to oblong, entire or rarely minutely remotely serrate or sinuate-dentate, densely minutely cinereous-pubesc. Infl. thyrsoid, compact, densely glandular-pubesc.; cal. 8–12mm, lobes lanceolate, acuminate; cor. 1.5–2.5cm, dull purple with purple guide-lines, tube long, abruptly dilating into ample throat, strongly bilabiate, palate pilose; staminode prominently exserted, hooked, strongly hirsute throughout with stiff, velutinous, deep orange hairs. Summer. Oregon, California and Nevada. Z5.

***P. montanus*** Greene. Forming loose clumps; stems to 15cm, arising annually from slender caudex, minutely cinereous-pubesc. Lvs evenly distributed to infl., oblong to ovate-lanceolate, dentate, lower obtuse, upper acute to acuminate, to 3cm, minutely cinereous-pubesc. Fls in 1–3 pairs; cor. 3cm, pink-purple, tube scarcely ventricose; anth. lanate, staminode glabrous. Idaho, Montana, Wyoming and Utah (mts). Z3.

***P. murrayanus*** Hook. To 90cm, glaucous and glabrous throughout; stem simple, erect. Lvs 15cm, spathulate to ovate, entire, stem lvs connate-amplexicaul, upper pairs united in oval disc. Infl. virgate, or few-fld clusters; pedicels slender; cor. to 2.5cm, deep scarlet, tubular, gradually widening upwards, lobes small; staminode glabrous. Late summer. Arkansas, Texas and adjacent Oklahoma and Mississippi. Z6.

***P. nemorosus*** (Douglas) Trautv. Plant with simple woody caudex; stems 30–80cm, few, erect, minutely pubesc. Lvs to 10×4cm, all cauline, lanceolate to ovate, serrate, rounded at base, lower lvs reduced, thin, glabrous or minutely pubesc. below. Infl. thyrsoid, few-fld or more open and extensive, glandular-pubesc.; cal. 6–13mm, lobes ovate; cor. strongly bilabiate, lower lip greatly exceeding upper, 25–35×8mm, rosy purple to light maroon, paler ventrally, strongly plicate, glabrous within; staminode around two thirds length of fertile fil., densely short-hirsute throughout. Summer. Vancouver Is. to California. Z8.

***P. neomexicanus*** Wooton & Standl. Stems to 70cm, glabrous. Basal lvs lanceolate to oblanceolate with margined petioles, sometimes absent by anthesis, stem lvs lanceolate to linear, 6–15mm broad, glabrous. Infl. elongate, secund; cal. 4–7mm, lobes obovate to oblong, obtuse to truncate, generally mucronate, margins scarious and erose; cor. 2.5–3.5cm, blue or tinged purple, throat broadly expanded, lobes spreading, lower lobes strongly hirsute at base; staminode strongly dilated, glabrous. Summer. S New Mexico (mts). Z9.

***P. newberryi*** A. Gray. MOUNTAIN PRIDE. Forming mats 15–30cm tall; stems decumbent to creeping, woody below, green or glaucescent, glabrous or very weakly pruinose. Lvs 1.5–4×1–1.5cm, elliptic to ovate, minutely serrate, shortly petiolate, much reduced on flowering stems, coriaceous. Infl. racemose, subsecund, short, dense, glandular-pubesc.; cal. 7–12mm, lobes lanceolate, acuminate to attenuate; cor. 22–30×5mm, throat slightly dilated, rosy red, ventral ridges bearded with short stiff hairs; stamens exserted, staminode very slender, three quarters length of fertile fil., yellow-hirsute. Summer. California and adjacent Nevada. f. ***humilior*** Sealy. Dwarf and bushy, to 15cm. Z8.

***P. nitidus*** Douglas. To 30cm; stems erect, very glaucous, glabrous. Lvs lanceolate to ovate, entire or very rarely remotely shallowly dentate, basal to 10×2.5cm, very glaucous, glabrous, thick and coriaceous. Infl. thyrsoid, compact to elongate, cylindric; cal. to 9mm; cor. to 2cm, bright blue, spreading-ascending, tube gradually dilated, palate glabrous; staminode bearded. Fr. to 12mm; seeds to 3mm. Summer. British Columbia to Saskatchewan, south to Washington, Wyoming and N Dakota. ssp. ***polyphyllus*** Pennell. Plants larger; lvs lanceolate to oblanceolate. Z3.

***P. oliganthus*** Wooton & Standl. Plant with well-developed basal rosette; stems to 60cm, erect, minutely pubesc. Basal lvs ovate to elliptic, stem lvs linear to lanceolate, mostly erect, glabrous or minutely pubesc. Infl. few-fld, glandular; peduncles erect; cal. 4–6mm, lobes lanceolate, acute to acuminate, margins scarious; cor. 1.5–2.5cm, blue to maroon, throat paler, strongly 2-ridged, lower lip exceeding upper, lower lobes bearded at base, glandular without; staminodes deep yellow-hairy for most of its length. Summer. Colorado to New Mexico and Arizona. Z4.

***P. ophianthus*** Pennell. Very similar to *P. jamesii* except fls smaller, cal. 6–9mm, cor. 18–22mm. Summer. Colorado and S Utah to New Mexico and Arizona. Z4.

***P. osterhoutii*** Pennell. Stems 40–80cm, pale green or glaucous, glabrous. Lvs conspicuously veined, rather glaucous, glabrous, basal lvs 10–15cm, ovate, acute, petiolate, stem lvs 5–9cm, lanceolate-ovate to ovate, acuminate, amplexicaul. Infl. narrow; cal. 7–8mm, lobes ovate, acuminate, glabrous, with broad scarious margin; cor. 2cm, blue to violet, glabrous without, pubesc. at base of lower lobes within; staminode densely golden-hirsute. Summer. Colorado. Z4.

***P. ovatus*** Douglas ex Hook. BROAD-LEAVED PENSTEMON. Stems 50–100cm, several, hirtellous or glabrous below. Lvs 5–15×1.5–4cm, ovate, acutely serrate-dentate, abruptly contracted below, shortly petiolate, bright green, sparingly hirtellous to glabrous. Infl. thyrsoid, of 4–10 rather lax clusters, lower on divergent peduncles, glandular-pubesc.; cal. 2–5mm, lobes lanceolate; cor. to 22×7mm, ampliate, bilabiate, lower lip exceeding upper, deep blue to indigo, palate villous or occasionally glabrous; staminode slightly exserted, glabrous or generally prominently bearded for one third of its length. Summer. British Columbia to Oregon. Z3.

***P. pachyphyllus*** A. Gray ex Rydb. Stems 30–60cm, several, pale or blue-glaucous, glabrous. Lvs ovate, pale green-glaucous, glabrous; basal lvs ovate, obtusely mucronate, 5–7cm, on margined petioles 3–5cm; stem lvs ovate-lanceolate, perfoliate, 3–5×2–4cm. Infl. thyrsoid, narrowly elongate, one third to half the height of plant, of 5–10 fascicles; cal. 5mm, lobes ovate with white to pale pink scarious margin; cor. 15–18mm, blue, mostly glabrous, throat inflated, ventrally rounded, upper lobes arched, lower lobes spreading, exceeding upper, lanate at base; staminode slightly exserted, densely yellow-hirsute toward apex. Summer. Utah. ssp. ***congestus*** (M.E. Jones) Keck Cor. subglabrous within, staminode pale yellow-hirsute. Z4.

***P. pallidus*** Small. Pubesc.; stem to 1m. Lvs to 10×2cm, lanceolate to oblong-lanceolate, entire or remotely dentate, pale green, firm and coriaceous, softly pubesc. Infl. somewhat paniculate, copiously glandular-pubesc.; cor. to 2.5cm, white with purple nectar-guides within, throat not strongly inflated; staminode densely yellow-hirsute in distal half. EC US (Michigan to Iowa, south to Kansas, Arkansas and Georgia). Z4.

***P. palmeri*** A. Gray. SCENTED PENSTEMON. Glaucous grey and glabrous below infl.; stems 50–140cm, erect. Lvs ovate-lanceolate, irregularly spinose-dentate or uppermost subentire, largest to 15×9cm, uppermost pairs connate-perfoliate. Infl. thyrsoid, virgate, secund; peduncles suberect, 2–3-fld; cal. 4–6mm, lobes broadly ovate; cor. 25–35×10–20mm, tube short, throat strongly inflated, lobes reflexed, white flushed pink or lilac with conspicuous rufescent guide-lines running from lower lip to throat, lower lip villous at base; staminode exserted, shaggy yellow-hirsute toward apex, glandular-pubesc. at base. Summer. California to Nevada, Utah and Arizona. Z5.

***P. parryi*** A. Gray. Stems 30–60cm, many, erect, glaucous, glabrous. Basal lvs oblanceolate to spathulate, stem lvs 5–8×1–2cm, oblong and auriculate-semiamplexicaul at base, glaucous. Infl. a racemiform thyrsus, lax, few-fld; fls very showy; cal. 2–6mm, glabrous or minutely pubesc.; cor. 1.5–2cm, rose magenta, glandular, funnelform, obscurely bilabiate, lobes large, orbicular; staminode hirsute or glabrous. Spring. S Arizona. Z8.

***P. payettensis*** Nels. & Macbr. Forming clumps 15–60cm high; stems several, arising from compact crown, bright green, glabrous. Lvs to 18×3cm, oblanceolate to narrowly obovate, entire, bright green, rather thick, glabrous; petioles slender, elongate, reduced upwards until upper lvs sessile. Infl. thyrsoid, of 3–7 many-fld clusters, often rather secund; cal. 5–8mm, lobes broadly lanceolate, abruptly narrowed to short attenuate tip; cor. 22–27mm, tube abruptly dilated into throat, limb ample, distinctly bilabiate, bright blue tinged purple, glabrous; staminode glabrous. Summer. Oregon to Idaho. Z4.

***P. peckii*** Pennell. Forming clumps; stems very slender, 25–50cm. Lvs 2–5cm, narrowly lanceolate to linear-lanceolate, tapered, deep green; petiole slender. Infl. thyrsoid, strict, virgate, of 2–5 somewhat crowded clusters, minutely glandular-pubesc.; cal. 2–3mm, lobes ovate, acute to acuminate, margins sub-entire, scarious; cor. 8–10mm, pale blue-mauve to white, limb expanded, palate low-ridged, rather pilose; staminode included, with few short apical hairs. Summer. Oregon. Z5.

***P. perpulcher*** A. Nels. Plant with compact caudex, eglandular. Lvs entire, upper linear-lanceolate to linear-oblong, to 1.5cm broad. Cal. 4–5mm, lobes broad, mucronate; cor. 2–2.5cm, palate glabrous; staminode hirsute. Idaho. Z4.

***P. pinifolius*** Greene. Stems to 40cm, numerous, woody at base, minutely pub-esc. to glabrate. Lvs crowded on lower part of stem, scattered above, filiform, rather thick, to 1mm wide, glabrous. Infl. secund; peduncles 1 per node, glandular-pubesc.; cal. 5–7mm, lobes lanceolate, acute, glandular-pubesc., margins scarious; cor. 2.5–3cm, scarlet, strongly bilabiate, throat narrow, 2-ridged, upper lobes projecting, lower spreading or reflexed, yellow-pilose at base; staminode included, bright yellow-hirsute for most of its length. Summer. New Mexico to Arizona and Mexico. 'Mersea Yellow': to 20cm, fls bright yellow. Z8.

***P. platyphyllus*** Rydb. 30–70cm, slightly glaucous; stems shrubby at base, minutely pubesc. particularly when young. Lvs 4–5cm, elliptic-ovate, generally acuminate. Cal. 5–8mm, lobes lanceolate; cor. 2–3cm, lavender-violet, glabrous, shallowly bilabiate, throat broadly inflated, lobes all spreading; anth. purple, staminode glabrous. Summer. Utah. Z3.

***P. pratensis*** Greene. WHITE-FLOWERED PENSTEMON. Plant with well-developed basal rosette; stems rather stout to slender, 25–50cm, light green, glabrous. Lvs linear-oblanceolate to elliptic, thin, 3–8cm including petiole, stem lvs slightly longer, upper amplexicaul, light green, glabrous. Infl. thyrsoid, strict, virgate, of 2–5 clusters; cal. 4–7mm, lobes lanceolate to oblong, entire to erose, with short acuminate tip; cor. 11–14mm, tubular to ampliate, white, buds tipped with yellow, palate hirsute with yellow hairs; staminode reaching orifice, with dense golden apical beard. Summer. Oregon to Idaho and Nevada. Z4.

***P. procerus*** Douglas. SMALL-FLOWERED PENSTEMON. Stems 10–40cm, slender, glabrous. Lvs 2–6cm including petiole, mostly cauline, lanceolate to oblanceolate or oblong, deep green, thin, mostly glabrous; petiole short, slender. Infl. thyrsoid, of 1–6 dense clusters, lower often remote; cal. lobes 3–6mm, elliptic to obovate, entire; cor. blue-purple, limb spreading, palate more or less bearded; staminode included, with few short, yellow, apical hairs. Summer. Northwestern N America (Alaska to Oregon, east to Wyoming and Colorado). Z3.

***P. pruinosus*** Douglas ex Lindl. CHELAN PENSTEMON. Stems 10–30cm, clustered, more or less minutely viscid-pubesc., sometimes densely cinereous below. Lvs 5–10×0.7–2cm, lanceolate to ovate, minutely serrate-dentate, more or less minutely viscid-pubesc.; petioles long, slender. Infl. thyrsoid, of 3–7 rather lax, many-fld clusters, distinctly glandular-pubesc.; cal. 3–5mm, lobes lanceolate to oblong, acute to acuminate; cor. 10–16×2–4mm, lower lip larger than upper, palate weakly hirsute to glabrous, indigo; staminode reaching orifice, with short apical tuft of yellow hairs. Summer. British Columbia to Washington. Z7.

***P. pseudospectabilis*** M.E. Jones. DESERT PENSTEMON. Stems 60–100cm, several, erect, virgate. Lvs ovate, prominently serrate, upper stem lvs connate-perfoliate forming discs to 12×6cm, rather thin, glaucous. Infl. thyrsoid, sparingly glandular; cal. lobes ovate, shortly acuminate; cor. rather ampliate, 20–26×6mm, rosy purple, often tinged yellow at throat, tinged yellow throughout in bud, with dark guide-lines within, minutely viscid-pubesc. but not at all villous at orifice; staminode glabrous. Spring–summer. California to Arizona. ssp. ***connatifolius*** (A. Nels.) Keck Lvs more finely serrate to subentire; infl. glabrous. Summer. New Mexico and Arizona. Z8.

***P. pulchellus*** Lindl. Stems rather woody at base, pubesc. Lvs lanceolate to oblong, serrate, acute, glabrous, with fascicles of smaller lvs in the axil of each main lf. Infl. lax, glandular; cor. 2–2.5cm, violet, paler below, slightly glandular without, throat dilated, lower lobes slightly pubesc. at base; staminode dilated, with short tuft of yellow hairs at apex. New Mexico. Z9.

***P. pumilus*** Nutt. Caespitose, grey-canescent throughout; stems 5cm, erect or ascending, very leafy. Lvs to 2.5cm, lanceolate or lower spathulate, attenuate at base. Fls in lf axils; peduncles short, 1–3-fld; cal. lobes lanceolate; cor. to 2cm, purple or blue, regularly funnelform, glabrous within; staminode sparsely yellow-hirsute, often more densely so at apex. Montana (mts). Z3.

***P. rattanii*** A. Gray. Stems 30–120cm, stout, glabrous below. Basal lvs 5–25×1–5cm including petiole, lanceolate to ovate, undulate-serrate to shallowly acutely dentate, stem lvs oblong, sessile, becoming cordate-amplexicaul above. Infl. thyrsoid, of 2–7 rather lax clusters, leafy below, densely glandular-pubesc.; lower peduncles 1–4cm, divergent; cal. 7–9mm, accrescent, lobes lanceolate, acute to attenuate, sometimes exceeding fr.; cor. 24–30mm, maroon to violet purple to blue-mauve, wide-pressed, abruptly ampliate, upper lip short, erect, lower lip longer, spreading, palate hirsute; staminode clearly exserted, moderately hirsute for half its length. Summer. Oregon to California. Z7.

***P. richardsonii*** Douglas. CUT-LEAVED PENSTEMON. Subshrub, 20–80cm, subglabrous to densely canescent. Lvs to 7×3cm, lanceolate, coarsely acutely serrate to pinnately parted with lobes again dentate or parted. Infl. a racemose to openly branched thyrsus, glandular-pubesc.; peduncles generally divergent; cal. 4–9mm, lobes ovate; cor. 18–30×7mm, pink to rosy lilac or bright lavender, with prominent white guide-lines, glandular-pubesc. without, lower lip occasionally sparsely hirsute within, throat dilated; staminode exserted, yellow-hirsute. Summer. British Columbia to Oregon. Z7.

***P. rotundifolius*** A. Gray. Glaucous and glabrous; stems arising from woody base. Lvs to 4cm, orbicular, entire, lowermost contracted to winged petiole, others sessile, thickly coriaceous. Infl. paniculate, many-fld; cal. 4mm; cor. 2.5cm, red, tubular, lobes 4mm, subequal, throat glabrous. Fr. 4–6mm, broadly ovate. N Mexico. Z9.

***P. rubicundus*** Keck. WASSUK PENSTEMON. Stems 50–120cm, few to several, erect, glaucous, glabrous. Lvs 2.5–10×1–3.5cm, oblanceolate or upper broadly lanceolate, dentate, lower petiolate, upper cordate-amplexicaul, glaucous, fleshy, glabrous. Infl. elongate, secund, clusters 2–3-fld; cal. 5–7mm, seg. ovate, acute, entire to undulate, glandular-pubesc. with narrow scarious margin; cor. 3–3.5cm, dark pink to deep rose with maroon nectar-guides, throat white within, minutely glandular-pubesc., palate hirsute, ventricose-ampliate, lobes short, those of lower lip reflexed; staminode exserted, yellow- to golden-hirsute, minutely glandular-pubesc. below. Summer. Nevada. Z5.

***P. rupicola*** (Piper) Howell. ROCK PENSTEMON. Forming flattened mats; stems woody below, flowering stems to 10cm, very glaucous, glabrous or more or less densely canescent. Lvs 0.8–2×0.6–1.2cm, elliptic to orbicular, minutely serrate-dentate, much reduced near infl., very glaucous, very thick, glabrous or canescent below; petioles glabrous or canescent. Infl. racemose, dense, few-fld, glandular-pubesc.; cal. 6–10mm, lobes lanceolate, acuminate to acute; cor. 27–35×8mm, throat moderately dilated, deep rose, ventral ridges sparsely villous; stamens slightly exserted, staminode half to three quarters length of fertile fil., filiform at apex, weakly to densely hirsute at apex. Late spring–summer. Washington to California. 'Albus': fls white. 'Diamond Lake': growth vigorous; lvs large; fls large, rich pink. 'Pink Dragon': habit compact; fls light salmon-pink. 'Roseus': fls pink. Z7.

***P. rydbergii*** A. Nels. Stems to 60cm, together with short vegetative shoots, glabrous or minutely pubesc., often in lines. Lvs oblong to elliptic, entire, obtuse to acute, tapered to base, basal very shortly petiolate, glabrous, lvs on flowering stems rather few, amplexicaul. Infl. interrupted, of 2 or more many-fld clusters; cal. 4–5mm, lobes linear, acuminate with broad scarious margins; cor. to 2cm, indigo, glabrous without, throat more or less expanded, densely yellow-hairy at base of lower lobes; staminode slender, yellow-hirsute at apex. Summer. Wyoming to Colorado and New Mexico. ssp. ***aggregatus*** (Pennell) Keck Cor. paler blue to purple. Z4.

***P. scouleri*** Lindl. Forming dense, broad clumps, 10–40cm tall, glabrous or pruinose below infl.; stem shrubby at base. Lvs linear-lanceolate, subentire to acutely serrate, mostly 2–5mm wide, greatly reduced upwards, green, often lustrous, coriaceous. Infl. strict, subsecund, rather dense, glandular-pubesc.; cal. 10–15mm, lobes linear-lanceolate, attenuate-caudate; cor. 3.5–5×1cm, bright lavender-blue to pale purple, ventral ridges villous; staminode very slender, half length of fertile fil., yellow-hirsute. Summer. N Washington to N Idaho and British Columbia. 'Albus': fls white. 'Purple Gem': to 10cm; fls violet-purple. 'Roseus': fls rose-pink. Z5.

***P. secundiflorus*** Benth. Stems to 50cm, erect, somewhat glaucous, glabrous. Lvs ovate to spathulate, stem lvs linear, obtuse or stem lvs acute, often mucronate, somewhat glaucous, glabrous. Infl. narrow, secund; cal. 4–7mm, lobes lanceolate, acute, margins often flushed pink or purple and scarious; cor. 1.5–2.5cm, blue or violet, unmarked, throat gradually inflated, lower lip hirsute; staminode dilated, conspicuously yellow-hirsute on upper side. Summer. Wyoming to Colorado and New Mexico. Z3.

***P. sepalulus*** A. Nels. 60–80cm, blue-glaucous, glabrous; stems shrubby at base. Lvs 6–9cm, linear-lanceolate, entire. Cal. 2mm, lobes rounded-ovate; cor. 2.5–3cm, pale lavender to pale violet, glabrous, shallowly bilabiate, throat broadly inflated, lobes all spreading; anth. dark grey, staminode glabrous. Summer. Utah. Z4.

***P. serrulatus*** Menz. CASCADE PENSTEMON. Subshrub, 30–70cm, glabrous below, minutely pubesc. above. Lvs 2–9×0.5–4.5cm, broadly lanceolate to spathulate, or stem lvs to cordate, subentire to irregularly dentate, serrate or shallowly laciniate, basal shortly petiolate. Infl. thyrsoid, of 1–5 dense clusters; peduncles erect; cal. 6–11mm, lobes lanceolate, broader ones laciniate; cor. 16–23×6mm, tubular-campanulate, deep blue to dark purple, sometimes sparsely pubesc. at base of lower lip; staminode yellow-hirsute. Late summer. S Alaska to Oregon. 'Albus': fls white. Z5.

**P. Six-Hills Hybrid.** *(P. davidsonii × P. eriantherus.)* To 15cm, bushy. Fls large; cor. violet. Late spring–early summer. Z5.

***P. smallii*** Heller. Stems to 120cm, simple, leafy throughout, glabrous below, sometimes slightly pubesc. above. Lvs 5–13×3–8cm, ovate to lanceolate, serrate, basal smaller, thin, smooth. Infl. thyrsoid, open, secund, more or less glandular-pubesc.; cal. to two-thirds length of cor. tube, lobes scarious-margined; cor. 3cm, bright pink-purple with white stripes within, abruptly tubular-campanulate, gibbous above, upper lip entire, lower exceeding upper, 3-lobed, densely yellow-hirsute. N Carolina and Tennessee. Z6.

***P. speciosus*** Douglas ex Lindl. Stems 20–80cm, caespitose, erect, glabrous to minutely pruinose-pubesc. or glaucescent. Lvs to 15cm, lanceolate to spathulate, entire, upper sessile, rather thick, glabrous to minutely pruinose-pubesc. or glaucescent. Infl. thyrsoid, elongate, of many obscurely interrupted clusters, more or less secund; cal. 4–8mm, lobes narrowly ovate to suborbicular with short tip; cor. 25–35×8–10mm, bright purple-blue, tube rather long, abruptly dilated into ample throat, limb large, strongly bilabiate; staminode glabrous or occasionally sparingly bearded at apex. Summer. Washington to California, to Idaho and Utah. Z3.

***P. spectabilis*** Thurber ex A. Gray non Wooton & Standl. Stems 80–120cm, several, erect, green or glaucescent, glabrous. Lvs 4–10×2–5cm, oblanceolate to ovate, upper stem lvs connate-perfoliate, coarsely serrate, green or glaucescent, glabrous. Infl. thyrsoid, lax, often half height of plant; cal. 4–7mm, lobes lanceolate-ovate to orbicular; cor. 25–33×8mm, tube abruptly expanded into ample throat, strongly bilabiate, upper lip almost erect, lower lip reflexed, lavender-purple, lobes blue, white within, lower lip sometimes weakly hirsute at base; staminode glabrous at apex. Early summer. California to N Baja California. Z7.

***P. strictus*** Benth. STIFF BEARD-TONGUE. Stems to 80cm, glabrous. Basal lvs spathulate, generally long-petiolate, stem lvs linear to broadly lanceolate, glabrous. Infl. narrow, secund; cal. 3–6mm, lobes ovate to lanceolate, acute, margins scarious; cor. 2–3cm, dark blue to violet, prominently bilabiate, throat moderately expanded, lower lobes exceeding upper, sometimes sparsely hairy at base; staminode dilated at tip, glabrous or very sparsely hairy at apex. Summer. Wyoming to Colorado, Utah, New Mexico and Arizona. Z3.

***P. subglaber*** Rydb. 30–100cm, glabrous or minutely pubesc.; stems erect. Lvs linear to broadly lanceolate, entire, not or scarcely glaucous. Infl. thyrsoid; cal. minutely obscurely glandular-pubesc. without, lobes ovate, shortly acuminate; cor. 22–30mm, blue bilabiate, tube narrow at base, then inflated, lower lobes spreading, glabrous at base; staminode shortly hirsute or glabrous. Summer. Wyoming and Utah. Z3.

***P. subulatus*** M.E. Jones. To 60cm, glabrous; stems erect, green or glaucescent. Lvs to 7.5cm, entire, green or glaucescent, basal lvs oblanceolate to elliptic, stem lvs linear-lanceolate to linear-subulate, amplexicaul. Cal. glabrous or minutely pubesc.; cor. to 2.5cm, scarlet, glabrous, narrowly tubular, obscurely bilabiate, limb very narrow; staminode subglabrous. Spring–summer. Arizona. Z6.

***P. superbus*** A. Nels. Very glaucous; stem to 180cm, stout, sparsely leafy. Lvs to 15cm, entire, acute, basal obovate, stem lvs ovate and sometimes connate-perfoliate, thick. Infl. thyrsoid, virgate, interrupted, many-fld; cor. 2.5cm, brilliant scarlet, almost funnelform, lobes spreading, to 6mm, rounded; anth. glabrous; staminode dilated at apex, hirsute. Mexico (Chihuahua and Sonora). Z9.

***P. ternatus*** Torr. ex A. Gray. BLUE-STEMMED PENSTEMON. Shrub, straggly, 0.5–1.5m; stems erect or scandent, wand-like, glaucous, glabrous. Lvs 2–5×0.2–0.9cm, in whorls of 3 or lowest opposite, lanceolate, tapered, remotely serrate-dentate, often folded along main vein, rather thick, glabrous. Infl. an elongated panicle, many-fld; cal. 3–5mm, lobes lanceolate, acuminate; cor. 23–30×4mm, narrowly tubular, upper lip helmet-shaped, lower lip spreading, scarlet, minutely glandular-pubesc.; staminode included, densely yellow-hirsute. Summer. California and Baja California. Z9.

***P. teucrioides*** Greene. Often mat-forming, to 10cm tall, with stout horizontal woodstock; stems erect or ascending, densely minutely cinereous-pubesc. Lvs to 1cm, crowded, linear, sharply mucronate, margins involute, densely minutely cinereous-pubesc.; cal. 5mm, lobes linear, minutely viscid-pubesc.; cor. 15–19mm, pale blue to blue-purple, throat somewhat ampliate with 2 ventral ridges, upper lip more or less erect, lower lip spreading, often exceeding upper; staminode golden-hirsute throughout. Colorado. Z4.

***P. thompsoniae*** (A. Gray) Rydb. Fibrous-rooted with woody caudex, forming mats or tufts 10–25cm diam., 2–5cm high; stems prostrate or ascending. Lvs 1–2cm, oblanceolate to spathulate-oblong, entire, mucronate, very pale grey, adpressed-pubesc. Infl. a racemiform thyrsus, leafy, obscurely viscid; cal. lobes acuminate to attenuate, sometimes with narrow scarious margin near base; cor. 13–18mm, to 5mm diam. at throat, subtubular, blue-violet, palate hirsute; staminode golden-hirsute for most of its length. Summer. California to Utah and Arizona. Z4.

***P. thurberi*** Torr. Bush, 30–60cm, woody below, intricately branched; stems many, erect, slender, glabrous. Lvs 1–3×0.1cm, narrowly linear, mucronate, entire, bright green, margins involute, more or less scabrid. Infl. a thyrsoid raceme; peduncles short, mostly 1-fld; cal. 2–3mm, lobes broadly ovate, abruptly acuminate; cor. obliquely salverform, lobes spreading, sparsely pubescence at base of lower lobes, with 2 ventral lines of pubesc. in throat, 12–15mm, blue to rosy lavender or maroon; staminode included, glabrous. Summer. California and Baja California to Arizona and New Mexico. Z9.

***P. tidestromii*** Pennell. Stem 30–50cm, minutely pubesc., glabrate above. Lvs 10–12×1–1.5cm, oblanceolate, obtuse, lower petiolate, upper amplexicaul, pale green, rather glaucous, minutely pubesc. Infl. narrow; cal. 3–5mm, lobes narrowly ovate, glabrous; cor. 1.5–2cm, blue, glabrous; staminode scarcely enlarged, yellow-hirsute. Summer. Utah. Z4.

***P. tolmiei*** Hook. ALPINE PENSTEMON. Plant with well-developed basal rosette, glabrous throughout; stems slender, 5–15cm. Lvs 1.5–5cm including petiole, lanceolate to elliptic, stem lvs amplexicaul; petiole short, slender. Infl. a single cluster; cal. 3–5mm, lobes very caudate-tipped; cor. somewhat ampliate, lower lip exceeding upper, 9–11mm, indigo or occasionally pale yellow, palate densely hirsute, limb spreading; staminode included, hirsute. Summer. Northwestern N America (British Columbia to Washington) Z7.

***P. triflorus*** Heller. Stems 60–90cm, erect, simple, glabrous to infl. Lvs to 10cm, spathulate or oblong, entire to dentate, lower on petioles to length of lamina. Infl. minutely glandular-pubesc. and viscid; peduncles to 2.5cm, slender, 3-fld; cor. 2.5cm+, bright rosy-purple, paler within with darker nectar-guides, gradually dilated, lobes spreading; staminode slightly dilated at apex, smooth. Texas. Z8.

***P. triphyllus*** Douglas. WHORLED PENSTEMON. Subshrub, 30–80cm, more or less minutely pubesc. Lvs 2–5×0.1–0.6cm, irregularly arranged, mostly ternate, some quaternate, alternate and scattered, linear to narrowly lanceolate, subentire to acutely pinnately dentate or cleft. Infl. thyrsoid, rather open, elongate; cal. 4–6mm, lobes lanceolate; cor. tube long, throat gradually ampliate, 13–17×3–4mm, pale lavender to bright blue-lilac with prominent guide-lines, lower lip sometimes sparsely hirsute within; staminode densely yellow-hirsute. Summer. Washington and Oregon to Idaho. Z5.

***P. tubaeflorus*** Nutt. Stems 50–100cm, glabrous. Lvs 8–12×2–5cm, elliptic or oblong-lanceolate, entire, rounded at base, obtuse to acute at apex. Infl. cylindric, slender, often interrupted; cal. 3–4mm, subglabrous or sparingly glandular; cor. tube gradually dilated from base, limb nearly regular, 2–2.5cm, white, throat minutely glandular-pubesc. within. Late spring–summer. EC US (Indiana to Wisconsin and Nebraska, south to Mississippi and Texas). Z4.

***P. unilateralis*** Rydb. 40–90cm, glabrous; stems erect. Lvs linear to ovate-lanceolate, entire, basal 6–12cm, not or scarcely glaucous. Infl. thyrsoid, of many several-fld fascicles; cal. lobes oblong-ovate, glabrous without, narrowly scarious-margined; cor. tube, bilabiate, tube gradually much inflated from base, glabrous or sparsely pubesc. within near front; staminode usually glabrous. Summer. Wyoming, Colorado. Z3.

***P. utahensis*** Eastw. UTAH BUGLER. Stems 30–60cm, several, virgate, glabrous. Lvs lanceolate, stem lvs tapered to petiole, stem lvs broadest at amplexicaul base, coriaceous, glabrous, glaucous, scabrid. Infl. a racemiform thyrsus, glabrous; cal. 3–5mm, lobes ovate to orbicular, abruptly acute, margin broadly scarious; cor. 18–24×4mm, subtubular, lobes rotately spreading or reflexed, carmine, glandular-pubesc. without, densely glandular within at orifice; staminode uncinate at apex, glabrous or slightly papillose at apex. Spring–summer. California to Nevada, Utah and Arizona. Z4.

***P. variabilis*** Suksd. Stems erect, much-branched below, forming clumps 20–60cm high. Lvs 1–5×0.2–0.8cm, in whorls of 3–4 or opposite, or becoming scattered, narrowly linear to lanceolate-oblong, entire to finely serrate. Infl. thyrsoid, branched or rarely strict; cal. glandular-pubesc. or occasionally glabrous; cor. 10–12mm, almost tubular, lower lip exceeding upper, yellow tinged brown with purple guide-lines, conspicuously glandular; staminode reaching orifice, generally bearded toward apex. Summer. Washington to Oregon. Z7.

***P. venustus*** Douglas. LOVELY PENSTEMON. Subshrub, 30–80cm, often glaucescent, mostly glabrous; stems with lines of minute pubescence. Lvs to 12cm, lanceolate to oblong, minutely serrate or dentate, often uncinate-toothed, scarcely petiolate, pungent. Infl. a spike-like panicle, continuous, subsecund; peduncles erect; cal. 3–6mm, lobes ovate; cor. 20–32×8mm, pale violet to violet-purple, lobes ample, ciliate; stamens somewhat exserted, staminode white-hirsute near apex. Early summer. Washington and Oregon to Idaho. Z5.

***P. virens*** Pennell. Forming mats; stems to 40cm, erect, slender, minutely pubesc. in lines. Lvs to 10×1.5cm, lanceolate, entire to minutely dentate, stem lvs smaller, bright green, glabrous. Infl. 6–18cm; cal. 2–4mm, lobes ovate, acute to acuminate; cor. to 1.5cm, pale to dark blue-violet, paler within with maroon to purple nectar-guides, glandular-pubesc. without, bilabiate, throat somewhat inflated, lobes of upper lip spreading to recurved, lower lip exceeding upper, lobes spreading, palate white-hirsute; staminode generally included, densely golden-hirsute at apex. Summer. Colorado. Z4.

***P. virgatus*** A. Gray. Stems to 80cm, often solitary, slender, minutely pubesc. to glabrate. Lvs linear to narrowly lanceolate, glabrous or minutely pubesc. Infl. narrow, secund; cal. 3–4mm, lobes elliptic to obovate, margins scarious and erose; cor. 1.5–2.5cm, blue or white, occasionally pink, usually with purple guide-lines, strongly bilabiate, throat broadly inflated, lobes of upper lip spreading or projecting, lobes of lower lip spreading or reflexed; staminode sometimes dilated, glabrous. Summer. New Mexico and Arizona. Z8.

***P. watsonii*** A. Gray. Clump-forming, glaucescent, glabrous or sometimes very minutely pubesc. in infl.; stems 30–60cm, weakly ascending. Lvs 2.5–5×1–2cm, oblong-lanceolate to ovate-lanceolate, acute to acuminate. Infl. thyrsus, rather lax; peduncles several-fld; cal. 2mm; cor. 12–16mm, violet-purple or white in part, narrowly funnelform, lower lip subglabrous at base; staminode densely golden-hirsute. Summer. Colorado, Utah and Nevada (mts). Z3.

***P. wherryi*** Pennell. To 60cm, minutely cinereous-pubesc. Lvs to 5cm, elliptic or stem lvs lanceolate and amplexicaul, entire to serrate, thin. Cor. to 2cm, pale lilac; staminode yellow-hirsute. Oklahoma and Arkansas. Z6.

***P. whippleanus*** A. Gray. Stems slender, to 60cm, glabrous or minutely pubesc. Basal lvs ovate to spathulate, stem lvs lanceolate to oblong-lanceolate, entire to minutely dentate, glabrous. Infl. elongate, glandular-pubesc.; cal. 7–10mm, lobes lanceolate, acute to acuminate, glandular, with narrow scarious margin near base; cor. 2–3cm, dull purple, glandular without, throat abruptly expanded, lobes of lower lip exceeding those of upper, villous; staminode not dilated, glabrous or sparsely hairy at apex. Summer. Wyoming and Idaho, south to Colorado, Utah, New Mexico and Arizona. Z4.

***P. whitedii*** Piper. Stems 10–40cm, pubesc. to glabrate. Lvs broadly linear to lanceolate or oblanceolate, entire to acutely dentate, upper stem lvs cordate amplexicaul, glabrous to densely minutely cinereous-pubesc. Infl. thyrsoid, of 3–6 remote dense clusters to 6cm diam., glandular-pubesc., leafy below; cal. 7–12mm, lobes lanceolate, acute to attenuate; cor. 18–23×6–9mm, maroon tinged blue with darker guide-lines, throat ample, limb rather small, palate somewhat pilose; staminode scarcely exserted, densely long-bearded for much of its length. Summer. Washington. Z7.

***P. wilcoxii*** Rydb. Stems 40–100cm, glabrous or sometimes minutely obscurely pubesc. below. Lvs 4–20×1–5cm including petiole, lanceolate to ovate, acutely minutely serrate-dentate to subentire, pale to bright green, rather thick, glabrous or rarely hirtellous below. Infl. thyrsoid, of several clusters or paniculate, sparingly glandular-pubesc.; cal. 3–5mm, lobes ovate, acute to acuminate; cor. 13–23×4–8mm, ampliate, lower lip greatly exceeding upper, bright blue to blue tinged purple; staminode slightly exserted, conspicuously yellow-bearded apically or in distal half. Summer. Oregon to Washington and Montana. Z4.

***P. wrightii*** Hook. Stem 40–60cm, erect, rather stout, pale, somewhat glaucous. Lvs 5–10×2.5cm, oblong or lowest obovate, upper stem lvs semiamplexicaul. Infl. thyrsoid, virgate, elongate, lax; cal. 5–6mm; cor. 18mm, bright rose-pink, slightly pubesc., throat ampliate, limb expanded to 18mm diam; staminode hirsute. Early summer. W Texas, New Mexico and Arizona. Z8.

***P. cultivars***. Over 130 cvs, from dwarf to 75cm high, fls in a wide variety of colours. 'Alice Hindley': lvs large; fls mauve and white trumpets. 'Amethyst': fls amethyst-blue. 'Apple Blossom': masses of small white, pink tipped fls. 'Barbara Barker': to 75cm; fls showy pink and white trumpets. 'Blue Spring': to 30cm; fls white. 'Burgundy': to 75cm; lvs large; fls deep wine-purple. 'Edithae': habit shrubby, prostrate; fls deep lilac. 'Evelyn': habit neat bush; lvs narrow; fls slim rose-pink spires with pale striped throats. 'Firebird': to 75cm; lvs narrow; fls clear red with honey guide-lines. 'Friedhelm Hahn': fls wine-red. 'Garnet': lvs narrow, dark green; fls garnet-red. 'Hidcote Pink': to 75cm, floriferous; fls pink. 'Hidcote Purple': to 75cm; fls purple. 'Hidcote White': to 75cm; fls white. 'Hopley's Variegated': variegated form of 'Alice Hindley'. 'Mother of Pearl': to 75cm; lvs narrow; fls white, flushed with purple. 'Old Candy Pink': fls vibrant pink. 'Pink Endurance': to 45cm; fls candy-pink, with honey guide-lines at throat. 'Prairie Fire': fls vivid orange-red, clustered around stem. 'Shoenholzeri' ('Firebird'): fls rich deep red, tubular. 'Snow Storm': to 60cm; fls white, turning pink tinted. 'Sour Grapes': to 60cm, fls tinted purple. 'Weald Beacon': fls tinted blue.

***P. acuminatus*** ssp. *congestus* Jones. See *P. pachyphyllus*.
***P. adamsianus*** Howell. See *P. fructicosus*.
***P. aggregatus*** Pennell. See *P. rydbergii* ssp. *aggregatus*.
***P. alpinus*** ssp. ***brandegeei*** (Porter) Harrington. See *P. brandegeei*.
***P. amabilis*** G.N. Jones. See *P. ovatus* and *P. pruinosus*.
***P. ambiguus*** var. ***thurberi*** A. Gray. See *P. thurberi*.
***P. amplexicaulis*** Buckley. See *P. buckleyi*.
***P. angustifolius*** ssp. ***caudatus*** (Heller) Keck. See *P. caudatus*.
***P. angustifolius*** var. ***caudatus*** (Heller) Rydb. See *P. caudatus*.
***P. angustifolius*** ssp. ***venosus*** Keck. See *P. caudatus*.
***P. arizonicus*** Heller. See *P. whippleanus*.
***P. azureus*** var. ***jeffreyanus*** A. Gray. See *P. azureus*.
***P. barbatus*** var. ***torreyi*** (Benth.) Gray. See *P. barbatus* ssp. *torreyi*.
***P. bradburii*** Pursh. See *P. grandiflorus*.
***P. caeruleus*** Nutt. See *P. angustifolius*.
***P. caeruleus*** hort. ex Vilm. non Nutt. See *P. hartwegii*.
***P. caespitosus*** A. Nels. See *P. caespitosus* var. *desertipicti*.
***P. canoso-barbatus*** Kellogg. See *P. breviflorus*.
***P. carinatus*** Kellogg. See *P. breviflorus*.
***P. cinerascens*** Greene. See *P. laetus* ssp. *roezlii*.
***P. coloradoensis*** A. Nels. See *P. linarioides* ssp. *coloradoensis*.
***P. confertus*** var. ***caeruleo-purpureus*** A. Gray. See *P. procerus*.
***P. congestus*** (M.E. Jones) Pennell. See *P. pachyphyllus* ssp. *congestus*.
***P. connatifolius*** A. Nels. See *P. pseudospectabilis* ssp. *connatifolius*.
***P. crassifolius*** Lindl. See *P. fructicosus*.
***P. cristatus*** Nutt. See *P. eriantherus*.
***P. cyananthus*** var. ***brandegeei*** Porter & Coult. See *P. brandegeei*.
***P. deserticola*** Piper. See *P. speciosus*.
***P. desertipicti*** A. Nels. See *P. caespitosus* var. *desertipicti*.
***P. diffusus*** Douglas ex Lindl. See *P. serrulatus*.
***P. douglasii*** Hook. See *P. fructicosus*.
***P. eastwoodiae*** Heller. See *P. utahensis*.
***P. eriantherus*** var. ***whitedii*** A. Nels. See *P. whitedii*.
***P. erosus*** Rydb. See *P. rydbergii*.

***P. exilifolius*** A. Nels. See *P. laricifolius* ssp. *exilifolius*.
***P. fructicosus*** ssp. ***cardwellii*** Piper. See *P. cardwellii*.
***P. fructicosus*** ssp. ***scouleri*** (Lindl.) Pennell & Keck. See *P. scouleri*.
***P. fructicosus*** var. ***crassifolius*** Krautter. See *P. fructicosus*.
***P. gairdneri*** var. ***oreganus*** A. Gray. See *P. gairdneri* ssp. *oreganus*.
***P. gentianoides*** Lindl. non (HBK) Poir. See *P. hartwegii*.
***P. glaber*** var. ***alpinus*** (Torr.) A. Gray. See *P. alpinus*.
***P. glaber*** var. ***cyananthus*** (Hook.) A. Gray. See *P. cyananthus*.
***P. glaber*** var. ***speciosus*** (Douglas ex Lindl.) Rydb. See *P. speciosus*.
***P. glaucus*** Graham. See *P. gracilis*.
***P. glaucus*** var. ***stenosepalus*** Gray. See *P. whippleanus*.
***P. gordoni*** Hook. See *P. glaber*.
***P. hians*** I.M. Johnston. See *P. grinnellii*.
***P. humilis*** ssp. *brevifolius* A. Gray. See *P. brevifolius*.
***P. intonsus*** Heller. See *P. corymbosus*.
***P. jamesii*** ssp. ***ophianthus*** (Pennell) Keck. See *P. ophianthus*.
***P. jeffreyanus*** Hook. See *P. azureus*.
***P. lacerellus*** Greene. See *P. rydbergii*.
***P. laevigatus*** var. ***digitalis*** (Nutt.) A. Gray. See *P. digitalis*.
***P. laricifolius*** var. ***exilifolius*** Pays. See *P. laricifolius* ssp. *exilifolius*.
***P. leptophyllus*** Rydb. See *P. wilcoxii*.
***P. lewisii*** Benth. See *P. fructicosus*.
***P. linearifolius*** J. Coult. & E. Fisher. See *P. lyallii* var. *linearifolius*.
***P. lobbii*** hort. ex Lem. See *P. antirrhinoides*.
***P. menziesii*** ssp. ***davidsonii*** (Greene) Piper. See *P. davidsonii*.
***P. menziesii*** var. ***crassifolius*** Schelle. See *P. fructicosus*.
***P. menziesii*** var. ***douglasii*** A. Gray. See *P. fructicosus*.
***P. menziesii*** var. ***lewisii*** A. Gray. See *P. fructicosus*.
***P. menziesii*** var. ***lyallii*** A. Gray. See *P. lyallii*.
***P. menziesii*** var. ***newberryi*** A. Gray. See *P. newberryi*.
***P. menziesii*** var. ***robinsonii*** Mast. See *P. newberryi*.
***P. menziesii*** var. ***scouleri*** A. Gray. See *P. scouleri*.
***P. metcalfei*** Wooton & Standl. See *P. whippleanus*.
***P. micranthus*** Nutt. non Torr. See *P. procerus*.
***P. micranthus*** Torr. non Nutt. See *P. strictus*.
***P. microphyllus*** A. Gray. See *P. antirrhinoides* ssp. *microphyllus*.
***P. missouliensis*** hort. See *P. albertinus*.
***P. nelsoniae*** Keck & J.W. Thomps. See *P. attenuatus*.
***P. newberryi*** ssp. ***berryi*** (Eastw.) Keck. See *P. berryi*.
***P. newberryi*** var. ***rupicola*** Piper. See *P. rupicola*.
***P. nitidus major*** Benth. in DC. See *P. pachyphyllus*.
***P. oreganus*** Howell. See *P. gairdneri* ssp. *oreganus*.
***P. palmeri*** var. ***bicolor*** Brandg. See *P. bicolor*.
***P. phlogifolius*** Greene. See *P. watsonii*.
***P. pickettii*** St. John. See *P. richardsonii*.
***P. pilifer*** Heller. See *P. speciosus*.
***P. pinetorum*** Piper. See *P. wilcoxii*.
***P. procumbens*** Greene. See *P. crandallii* ssp. *procumbens*.
***P. pseudoprocerus*** Rydb. See *P. attenuatus* ssp. *pseudoprocerus*.
***P. pubescens*** Sol. See *P. hirsutus*.
***P. pubescens*** var. ***gracilis*** A. Gray. See *P. gracilis*.
***P. puniceus*** Lilja non A. Gray. See *P. hartwegii*.
***P. puniceus*** A. Gray non Lilja. See *P. superbus*.
***P. puniceus*** var. ***parryi*** A. Gray. See *P. parryi*.
***P. purdyi*** hort. See *P. heterophyllus* ssp. *purdyi*.
***P. rattanii*** var. ***minor*** A. Gray. See *P. anguineus*.
***P. rex*** Nels. & Macbr. See *P. speciosus*.
***P. roezlii*** Reg. See *P. laetus* ssp. *roezlii*.
***P. saliens*** Rydb. See *P. eriantherus*.
***P. shantzii*** A. Nels. See *P. parryi*.
***P. similis*** A. Nels. See *P. jamesii*.
***P. speciosus*** ssp. ***lemhiensis*** Keck. See *P. lemhiensis*.
***P. staticifolius*** Lindl. See *P. glandulosus*.
***P. stenosepalus*** (A. Gray) T.J. Howell. See *P. whippleanus*.
***P. thompsonii*** hort. See *P. davidsonii* ssp. *thompsonii*.
***P. torreyi*** Benth. See *P. barbatus* ssp. *torreyi*.
***P. triphyllus*** ssp. ***diphyllus*** (Rydb.) Keck. See *P. diphyllus*.
***P. utahensis*** A. Nels. non Eastw. See *P. subglaber*.
***P. xylus*** A. Nels. See *P. crandallii*.
For further synonymy see *Chelone* and *Leiostemon*.

**Pentachondra** R. Br. (From Gk *pente*, five, and *chondros*, granule.) Epacridaceae. 3 species of small, spreading or prostrate shrubs. Leaves usually crowded, obovate to linear, striate. Flowers small, solitary, or a few clustered in upper leaf axils, shortly pedicellate; bracts many, minute, uppermost resembling a second flower; calyx 5-lobed; corolla tube short, 5-lobed, recurved, bearded inside; stamens 5, anthers exserted or included; ovary 5-celled. Fruit a fleshy drupe with 5–10 one-seeded nuts. Australia, New Zealand and Tasmania. Z8.

CULTIVATION *P. pumila*, found in boggy, peaty ground in alpine regions, is a low-growing, mat-forming evergreen, often clinging to moist rocks in its natural habitat. It is grown for its attractive, bronzed, heath-like foliage and tiny white flowers which open in early summer; they rarely bear the small orange-red fruits in cultivation. Grow in an open position in sun, in moisture-retentive, gritty, peaty pockets of lime-free soil in the rock garden. Hardy to about −5°C/23°F and intolerant of drought, *Pentachondra* may prove difficult in cultivation, and is most likely to succeed in climates with moderate winters and relatively cool, moist summers. Propagate by rooted offsets, by semi-ripe cuttings or by seed sown in autumn.

***P. pumila*** (Forst. & Forst. f.) R. Br. Procumbent, closely-branched, dwarf shrub to 15cm; branches ascending, glabrous to tomentose. Lvs to 0.5cm, numerous, crowded, oblong to obovate, tip pointed, callose, 3–7 veined beneath, margins ciliolate. Fls to 6mm, almost sessile, solitary, white, bracts many; sep. obtuse, ciliolate; cor. tube cylindric, lobes short, revolute, bearded inside. Fr. to 12mm diam., ellipsoid or pyriform, red. Winter. Australia, New Zealand.

**Pentactina** Nak. (From Gk *pente*, five, and *aktis*, ray.) Rosaceae. 1 species, a deciduous shrub to 70cm, close to *Spiraea*; young shoots angled, tinged red, glabrous. Leaves 2–3cm, alternate, short-stalked, oblanceolate to obovate, base cuneate, apex with 3–5 large teeth, glabrous above, silky pubesc. beneath, margins dentate; stipules absent. Inflorescence 6–8cm, slender, paniculate, arched sepals 5, triangular, persistent, becoming reflexed; petals 5, linear; stamens 20, white, exserted; pistils 5; ovules 2, follicles glabrous. Summer. Korea (Diamond Mts). Z5.

CULTIVATION *P. rupicola* grows in the rock crevices and cliffs of the remarkable geological formations in the Kumgang mountains of North Korea, also known as the Diamond mountains. It is grown for its graceful habit and clusters of small white flowers borne at the end of the shoots in summer, and is suitable for the rock garden. Cultivate as for *Petrophytum*.

***P. rupicola*** Nak. As for the genus.

**Pentadenia** Wiehler. (From Gk *pente*, five, and *aden*, gland.) Gesneriaceae. About 24 species of shrubs and climbers; stems ascending to pendent, sparsely to freely branching, to 3m. Leaves equal to unequal in opposite pairs. Flowers axillary, solitary or many in a cyme; calyx 5-lobed, lobes usually subequal; corolla erect in calyx, tubular, often spurred at base, limb 5-lobed, lobes subequal; stamens 4, anthers in coherent pairs at apex. Fruit a fleshy berry, often coloured. Tropical America. Z10.

CULTIVATION See GESNERIADS.

***P. angustata*** Wiehler. Stems ascending or descending, sparsely branching. Lvs in nearly equal pairs, to 10×3.5cm, elliptic, green and sparsely hirsute above, lighter green, often suffused with pink beneath. Fls 2–6 in a reduced cyme; cal. lobes lanceolate, dentate, pink to maroon, pubesc.; cor. to 2.7cm, orange, yellow or rarely pink, puberulent, lobes entire. Costa Rica.

***P. byrsina*** Wiehler. Stems woody, ascending, spreading or descending, sparsely branching, to 2m, maroon. Lvs in strongly unequal pairs, the larger lf to 8×3cm, leathery, lustrous, dark green, sparsely hairy above, light green or pink-flushed with white silky hairs beneath. Cor. to 2.4cm, white and constricted at base, inflated and magenta toward apex, limb pale yellow, puberulent outside. Fr. white, pubesc. Ecuador, Colombia.

***P. colombiana*** Wiehler. Stems to 3m, pendent, spreading, sparsely branched, finely white-hairy. Lvs in subequal pairs, to 4×2.4cm, ovate. Fls solitary; cal. fringed, pale green, sep. red at apex; cor. tubular, to 3cm, spur cream, tube deep pink, glandular-hairy, limb entire, pale green. Fr. globose, white, pubesc. Colombia.

***P. crassicaulis*** Wiehler. Stems to 3m, spreading, ascending or descending, branching, often marked with purple, sparsely pubesc. Lvs in equal pairs, to 7–9×3–5.5cm, ovate, acuminate, crenate. Fls solitary; sep. lanceolate, orange-green-pilose; cor. to 5.3cm, erect, tubular, spur cream, tube pale yellow, lobes yellow, glabrous. Colombia, Ecuador.

***P. ecuadorana*** Wiehler. Stems to 60cm, erect or spreading, sparsely branching, pubesc. Lvs in equal pairs, to 5–7.5×2–4cm, elliptic or oblanceolate, green. Fls few in reduced axillary cymes; cal. green; cor. to 4cm, erect, maroon, pink or yellow, silky hairy, limb lobes 2×2mm. Ecuador.

***P. microsepala*** (Morton) Wiehler Stems pendent, often prostrate, olive-brown, pubesc. Lvs densely arranged on stem, to 3.2×2.5cm, broadly elliptic, crenate, sparsely white-hairy. Cor. tubular, yellow, to 1.3cm. Fr. globose, white. Venezuela.

***P. orientandina*** Wiehler. Stems to 40cm, ascending or spreading, branching, pubesc. Lvs in strongly unequal pairs, the larger lf 6–9×2.5–3.5cm, elliptic to oblanceolate, acute or obtuse, entire, spotted with red beneath, apex translucent red; smaller lf often caducous. Fls 2–8 in a cyme; sep. subequal, to 10×1mm, lanceolate, tipped with red in fr.; cor. erect, to 2.5cm, tubular, entire, pale yellow. Fr. pink, pilose. Ecuador, Peru.

***P. spathulata*** (Mansf.) Wiehler. Finely hairy. Stems upright to spreading, olive-brown. Lvs in unequal pairs, elliptic, dark green, crenate, marked with red beneath. Fls many in cymes; cal. green, marked with red beneath; cor. arching, yellow. Fr. white. Ecuador.

***P. strigosa*** (Benth.) Hanst. Epiphyte. Stems woody, brown. Lvs to 7.5cm, oblanceolate to elliptic, marked with red beneath. Cal. green, often red-flushed; cor. to 6.3cm, ventricose, orange-yellow. Fr. mauve. Ecuador, Colombia, Venezuela.

***P. zapotalana*** Wiehler. Stems to 80cm, ascending, spreading or descending, sparsely branching, green-brown. Lvs in markedly unequal pairs, largest lf to 12×5cm, oblanceolate, acuminate, green, apices red beneath, smaller lf to 1.8cm. Fls 1–4 in a cyme; cal. yellow-green; cor. to 3.2cm, erect, tubular, pale yellow, constricted above spur. Fr. globose, white. Ecuador.

For synonym see *Alloplectus* and *Columnea*.

**Pentaglottis** Tausch. (From Gk *pente*, five, and *glotta*, tongue.) Boraginaceae. 1 species, a hispid perennial herb; stems to 1m branched, erect or ascending. Basal leaves to 40cm, ovate or ovate-oblong, acute, with reticulate venation, long-petiolate; cauline leaves acuminate, sessile. Inflorescence a dense cyme, axillary or terminal, bracteate, few to many-flowered; bracts conspicuous; calyx to 8mm in fruit, deeply 5-lobed, lobes linear-lanceolate; corolla blue, tube to 6mm, infundibular or cylindrical, limb to 10mm diam., rotate, with 5 elliptic, pubescent scales in throat; stamens 5, included, inserted above middle of corolla tube; style included, stigma capitate. Nutlets to 2mm, erect, ovoid, concave, black-brown, reticulate-rugose, with a collar-like ring at base. SW Europe. Z7.

CULTIVATION As for *Brunnera*. Propagate by seed.

***P. sempervirens*** (L.) Tausch ex L.H. Bail. As for the genus.

For synonymy see *Anchusa*.

**Pentapanax** Seem.
***P. henryi*** Harms. See *Aralia tomentella*.
***P. warmingianus*** (Marchal) Harms. See *Aralia warmingiana*.

**Pentaptera** Klotzsch.
***P. arjuna*** Roxb. ex DC. See *Terminalia arjuna*.

**Pentapterygium** Klotzsch.
***P. rugosum*** Hook. See *Agapetes rugosum*.

**Pentas** Benth. (From Gk *pente*, five, referring to the characteristic number of floral parts.) Rubiaceae. Some 30 or 40 species of perennial or, rarely, biennial herbs or shrubs. Stems erect to prostrate and scrambling, woody at base; branches subterete. Leaves petiolate, opposite or 3–5-whorled, typically ovate to lanceolate; stipules interpetiolar, divided into 2 or more setose segments, these filiform to subulate. Flowers bisexual, 1–3-morphous, crowded in terminal, much-branched cymes or flat-topped corymbs; calyx tube globose to ovoid, ribbed, limb tubular to campanulate, swollen, lobes 5, equal or unequal, persistent, 1–3 occasionally developed and foliaceous; corolla tubular to cylindric, tube often funnel-shaped and swollen above and pubescent at throat, lobes 5, unequal, valvate in bud, ovate to oblong; stamens 5, included or exserted, anthers included or exserted, linear to oblong, glabrous; ovary 2–3-celled, style included or exserted, 2-lobed, filiform, ovules many. Fruit a capsule, ovoid or obovoid to pyramidal or obconic, 2-celled or loculicidally 2–4-valved, ribbed and, occasionally, beaked, leathery to membranous; seeds globose to tetrahedral, brown, testa reticulate. Tropical Arabia and Africa, Madagascar. Z10.

CULTIVATION Woody-based herbs or shrubs with cymes or domed cymes of crowded flowers in a range of shades of red, pink or mauve. For the glasshouse (minimum temperature 7°C/45°F) or summer use outdoors in tubs and bedding schemes. Repropagate annually by soft stem-tip cuttings taken in late spring and inserted in a heated case.

***P. bussei*** K. Krause. Herb or shrub, to 4m. Stems erect or prostrate and scrambling, more or less pubesc. Lvs to 15×7cm, ovate or lanceolate to oblong, apex acute to narrowly acute, base cuneate, white-pubesc., especially beneath; stipule seg. to 15mm, 3–9, linear; petioles to 2cm. Fls dimorphous, in pedunculate, terminal and axillary, loose or dense, many-fld cymes to 8cm wide, scarlet; peduncles to 4cm; cal. tube to 2mm, glabrous to pubesc., lobes unequal, 1–3 developed and foliaceous, to 18×4mm, lanceolate, apex acute, pubesc., 3-veined, others to 6×2mm, linear to lanceolate; cor. tube to 18mm, exterior glabrous or pubesc., interior pubesc., lobes to 12×5mm, elliptic or lanceolate to oblong. Fr. to 6×4mm, obovoid. Tropical E Africa (Somalia to Kenya, Zambia).

***P. lanceolata*** (Forssk.) Deflers. STAR-CLUSTER; EGYPTIAN STAR-CLUSTER. Herb or subshrub, to 2m. Stems erect or prostrate, pubesc. Lvs to 15×5, ovate to elliptic or lanceolate, apex attenuate to acute, base acute or cuneate, pubesc.; stipule seg. to 1cm, 3–15, filiform, margin ciliate; petioles to 5cm. Fls subsessile, di- or trimorphous, in terminal and axillary, many-fld corymbs, pink or magenta to blue or lilac or, occasionally, white; cal. tube to 3mm, pubesc., lobes unequal, 1–3 developed and foliaceous, to 12×3mm, others to 3mm; cor. tube to 4cm, exterior glabrous or pubesc., lobes to 10×5mm, ovate or elliptic to oblong. Fr. to 6mm, obconic. Tropical Arabia (Yemen) to E Africa. ssp. ***quartiniana*** (A. Rich.) Verdc. Fls dimorphous, more or less pink to red; cor. tube to 22mm. Ethiopia. 'Avalanche': lvs streaked white; fls white. 'Kermesina': fls bright rose, throat violet. 'Quartiniana': fls rose, abundant.

***P. mussaendoides*** Bak. Shrub, to 4m. Stems erect, brown-pubesc. Lvs to 10cm, elliptic to oblong, apex acute. Fls 2-morphous, in terminal cymes or corymbs, pink or purple; cal. lobes unequal; cor. tube to 25mm. Madagascar.

***P. nobilis*** S. Moore. Herb or shrub, to 2m. Stems angular, pubesc., grey-black. Lvs to 20×9cm, ovate or elliptic to oblong, apex acute, base obtuse to cuneate, somewhat rough and bristly, especially above; stipule seg. to 2cm, 3–5, subequal, subulate; petioles to 10mm. Fls dimorphous, in pedunculate, loose, 6- or more-fld cymes or corymbs to 25×15cm, white and, occasionally, red-flushed, fragrant; peduncles to 12cm; cal. tube to 7mm, short-pubesc., lobes to 25×2mm, equal, spathulate to subulate, apex acute to apiculate; cor. tube to 15cm, pubesc., especially at throat, lobes to 20×7mm, ovate to oblong, apex acute. Fr. to 17×4mm, compressed globose to oblong, pubesc. Subtropical Africa (Zaire, Zambia, to Tanzania, Zimbabwe).

***P. parviflora*** Benth. Subshrub, to 60cm. Stems erect. Lvs to 8×3cm, ovate or elliptic to oblong or lanceolate, apex narrowly acute, base cuneate, minutely pubesc. on veins beneath; stipule seg. 2–3, filiform to subulate; petioles to 12mm. Fls subsessile, unimorphous, in pedunculate, dense, sparsely-branched cymes to 3cm wide, scarlet or blue to purple; cal. tube to 3mm, lobes to 3mm, equal, linear to oblong; cor. tube to 6mm, pubesc. at throat, lobes to 2mm, glabrous. Tropical W Africa.

***P. zanzibarica*** (Klotzsch) Vatke. Herb or, rarely, shrub, to 3m. Stems simple, more or less pubesc. Lvs to 15×6cm, ovate to lanceolate or elliptic, apex acute, base cuneate, pubesc.; stipule seg. to 14mm, 7. Fls dimorphous, in pedunculate, terminal and axillary, loose or dense cymes to 7cm wide, pink or red to lilac or mauve, or white; peduncles to 15cm; cal. tube to 1mm, pubesc., lobes to 9×2mm, unequal; cor. tube to 1cm, pubesc., lobes to 6×3mm, elliptic to oblong. Fr. to 5mm, globose, pubesc. Tropical E Africa (Uganda, Kenya, to Zaire, Tanzania). var. ***rubra*** Verdc. To 2.5m. Lvs to 17×7cm, bullate. Fls pink to red. Uganda, Kenya, Zaire.

***P. cultivars***. 'California Lavender': dwarf; fls pale lavender, in large umbels, profuse. 'California Pink': compact; fls pale pink, in broad umbels. 'Orchid Star': lvs light green; fls large, lilac. 'Tu-Tone': compact; fls pink, centre red, in large round umbels.

***P. coccinea*** Stapf. See *P. bussei*.
***P. coccinea*** sensu auct., non Stapf. See *P. zanzibarica* var. *rubra*.
***P. flammea*** Chiov. See *P. bussei*.
***P. klotzschii*** Vatke. See *P. bussei*.
***P. lanceolata*** Robyns, non (Forssk.) Deflers. See *P. zanzibarica* var. *rubra*.
***P. longituba*** De Wild. & T. Dur., non Schum. See *P. nobilis*.
***P. quartiniana*** (A. Rich.) Oliv. See *P. lanceolata* ssp. *quartiniana*.
***P. stolzii*** Schum. & K. Krause, pro parte. See *P. zanzibarica*.
***P. verruculosa*** Chiov. See *P. lanceolata* ssp. *quartiniana*.
***P. zanzibarica*** Robyns, non (Klotzsch) Vatke. See *P. zanzibarica* var. *rubra*.
For further synonymy see *Manettia, Ophiorrhiza, Pentanisia* and *Sacosperma*.

**Pentelesia** Raf. See *Arrabidaea*.

**Peperomia** Ruiz & Pav. RADIATOR PLANT. (From Gk *peperi*, pepper, and *homoios*, resembling, referring to its resemblance to the closely allied genus *Piper*, the source of peppercorns.) Piperaceae. About 1000 species of small, generally succulent, annual or perennial herbs. Leaves alternate, opposite or verticillate; stipules absent. Inflorescence of spikes, densely or laxly flowered; flowers minute, bracteate, sessile, sometimes sunk into axis; perianth wanting; stamens 2, filaments generally short, anthers globose or depressed-globose, bilocular, stigma often penicillate. Fruit a small berry, scarcely fleshy; seeds similar in shape to fruit. Flowers are produced erratically, but most species flower best in late summer. Pantropical. Z10.

CULTIVATION Grown primarily for their foliage foliage, in an extraordinary diversity of form, frequently fleshy or succulent, often attractively variegated or marbled, sometimes with distinctive metallic colouration or with deeply corrugated and quilted textures. The flowers are usually insignificant or take the form of long, slender wands of minute flowers, the notable exception is *P. fraseri*, with conspicuous spikes of white flowers much resembling those of the mignonettes (*Reseda* spp.). Grown in rockeries and as shade-tolerant groundcover in tropical and subtropical gardens, in cool temperate zones *Peperomia* spp. are suitable for the warm glasshouse or conservatory in pots, hanging baskets and as groundcover in the border; smaller species suit terraria and bottle gardens. The succulent-leaved species include many that are particularly suitable as houseplants, being tolerant of drier atmospheres. Grow in well-aerated, freely draining but retentive mediums that are rich in fibrous organic matter. Provide a moderately humid but buoyant atmosphere, with bright indirect light, ensuring shade from the strongest sun; green-leaved succulent species are tolerant of higher light levels, and succulent species generally require lower levels of humidity. Liquid-feed fortnightly and water moderately when in growth, drenching thoroughly and allowing the medium to dry partially between waterings; reduce water in winter to keep just moist. Most species require a minimum temperature of 10°C/50°F, performing better between 15–18°C/60–65°F. Propagate by division, leaf or stem cuttings, or by seed.

***P. acuminata*** Ruiz & Pav. Herb to 60cm+, glabrous; stem erect or ascending, sparingly branched. Lvs alternate, to 12×4cm, elliptic to lanceolate or oblanceolate, very sharply acuminate at apex, cuneate at base, veins pinnate; petiole short. Spikes terminal, solitary, erect, to 12cm; peduncles 38mm. Fr. dull red. Tropical America (Guatemala to Peru & Venezuela, W Indies).

***P. argyreia*** Morr. WATERMELON BEGONIA; WATERMELON PEPPER. Herb to 20cm; stem erect, rounded, dark red, fleshy, glabrous. Lvs alternate, 7×5.5cm, broadly ovate, concave, generally broadly acute at apex, rounded at base, peltate, margin flat or slightly reflexed, silver-grey above with dark green stripes along main veins, pale green beneath, coriaceous, glabrous; petiole 12×0.5cm, inserted 1.5cm from base of lamina, ungrooved, dark red with dark green flecks, minutely granular-glandular. Infl. terminal, appearing lateral, solitary or branched; peduncle 40×2mm, red, minutely glandular; spike 65×2.5mm, green. Northern S America to Brazil.

***P. arifolia*** Miq. Herb, medium-sized, glabrous; stem short, thick, internodes very short. Lvs alternate, 6×5cm, rounded-ovate, subacute to shortly acuminate at apex, rounded to subcordate at base, green with grey variegation; petiole 12cm. Infl. axillary; peduncle scape-like, 15cm; spikes 75×2.5mm. Fr. subglobose-ovoid. SE Brazil, Paraguay, Argentina.

***P. asperula*** P.C. Hutchison & Rauh. Erect herb, very succulent; stems with short internodes. Lvs 18×9mm, in dense rows, folded along main vein to expose lower surface, glossy and translucent above, dull green tinged grey and scabrous beneath. Spike short. Peru.

***P. berlandieri*** Miq. Creeping herb; stems branched, finely minutely pubesc., branches ascending, to 10cm. Lvs 0.7cm, verticillate, in whorls of 4, obovate, obtuse or emarginate at apex; petioles short. Spikes terminal, solitary, pedunculate, equal sized, to 2cm; fls embedded in spike, in pits with ciliate-hirtellous margins. Mexico to Costa Rica.

***P. bicolor*** Sodiro. Herb to 20cm, stoloniferous; stems branched, rooting at base then ascending, 2mm diam., sparingly pubesc. Lvs alternate, 3.5×3cm, elliptic or lower obovate, acute both ends, decurrent at base, reduced upwards, green above, tinged purple beneath, sometimes sparingly pubesc. along main vein above; petiole 7mm, grooved. Infl. terminal and axillary; peduncle 7mm, glabrous; spikes to 6cm, moderately densely fld. Fr. ovoid-globose, oblique at apex, to 1mm. Ecuador.

***P. blanda*** (Jacq.) HBK. Herb to 50cm, stems erect, rounded, rather fleshy below, soft above, pink to red. Lvs 3.8×1.8cm, mostly ternate, broadly elliptic to obovate, broadly acute and sometimes shortly acuminate at apex, broadly tapered to rounded at base, green above with paler pattern of veins, dark green beneath, thin, pubesc.; petiole 11mm, grooved, pink or green, hairy. Infl. terminal and from upper lf axils, paniculate, spikes 55×2mm, green; peduncle 1.5cm, pink hairy. S America, north to Florida, W Indies, S & C Africa & Sr Lanka. var. ***langsdorfii*** (Miq.) Hens. Lvs 7×3cm, elliptic to elliptic-obovate or subrhombic. W Indies, Venezuela, Colombia & Brazil.

***P. botteri*** C. DC. Stems sparingly branched, slender. Lvs 4×2.5cm, ternate to quaternate, ovate to elliptic-lanceolate or subrhombic, acuminate at apex, obtuse to rounded at base, minutely pilose-pubesc., particularly along veins; veins 5; petiole 1.5cm. Spikes terminal and axillary, filiform, ovary embedded in rachis. Mexico.

***P. camptotricha*** Miq. Rhizomatous herb to 45cm; stems branched above, densely hirsute. Lvs 2.5×1.5cm, verticillate below, in whorls of 4, rarely 3, opposite above, lower lvs suborbicular, 1cm diam., upper lvs obovate-rhombic, thick and succulent, green above, often flushed red beneath, densely pubesc.; veins 3; petioles short. Infl. terminal and axillary; peduncles short, hairy; spikes numerous, very slender, to 9cm. S Mexico.

***P. caperata*** Yunck. EMERALD-RIPPLE PEPPER; GREEN-RIPPLE PEPPER; LITTLE-FANTASY PEPPER. Herb to 20cm; stems erect, tough, rounded, to 1cm diam., dark green or tinged purple, glabrous. Lvs alternate, 3.2×2.5cm, cordate, broadly acute to rounded at apex, rounded or auriculate at base, often peltate, margins flat or minutely reflexed, entire or minutely dentate, dark glossy green, coriaceous and minutely pubesc. above, paler and glabrous beneath, veins deeply impressed, in V-shaped folds, prominent beneath; petiole 7.5cm, inserted 6mm from lamina base when peltate, green to dull red, shallowly grooved. Infl. solitary, lateral; spike bracts wanting; peduncle 6cm×2mm, glabrous; spike 38×2mm, pale green. Brazil (?). 'Emerald Ripple': lvs deep green. 'Little Fantasy': habit dwarf. 'Tricolor': lvs with deep green heart and wide cream edge and marked pink at lf base. 'Variegata' ('Variegated Ripple'): lvs deep green with wide cream edge.

***P. cerea*** Trel. Herb, succulent, glabrous; stems often pendent, 5mm diam. at base, more slender above. Lvs opposite below, often verticillate above, with 3–5 per whorl, 12×8mm, rounded-elliptic, margin minutely revolute; petiole 2mm. Spikes terminal, 10cm×3.5mm, dull dark red, fls somewhat remote; peduncle 1.5cm; bracts rounded-peltate. Peru.

***P. clusiifolia*** (Jacq.) Hook. Herb to 25cm; stems erect, rounded, tough, fleshy, to 1cm diam., green to purple, glabrous. Lvs alternate, 7.5×2.7cm, obovate to elliptic, broadly acute to rounded at apex, tapered to often clasping base, green or tinged purple, often flushed maroon on margin, succulent, minutely glandular-punctate above, main vein raised beneath and red at base; petiole 2.5×5mm, broadly grooved above, dark red, glabrous. Infl. terminal or lateral, solitary, sometimes on short lateral shoots; spike 30×3mm, pale green; peduncle 28×2mm, red, glabrous. W Indies, perhaps Venezuela. 'Jellie': lvs green and cream flushed pink, margin red. 'Variegata': lvs light green, variegated cream towards edge, margin red.

***P. columnella*** Rauh & P.C. Hutchison. Herb to 10cm, erect becoming sprawling; stems freely branched, to 6mm diam., concealed by lvs. Lvs in whorls of 5, downward-pointing, cordate, sessile, very succulent, to 8×6×5mm, green to dark green, with translucent shiny window above. Infl. simple or branched; spike to 15×4mm, green tinged yellow. N Peru.

***P. cordata*** Trel. & Yunck. Rather large herb, repent, glabrous; stems branched, branches 7.5cm, ascending. Lvs alternate, 7.5×5.5cm, rounded-ovate to elliptic-ovate, acuminate at apex, deeply cordate at base, slightly subpeltate, dark green above, paler and granular beneath; petiole 6.5cm. Spikes terminal, 70×3mm, fls close-set; peduncle 6cm; bracts round, peltate, glandular-punctate. Colombia (Cauca).

***P. crassifolia*** Bak. LEATHER PEPPER. Decumbent herb; stems to 30cm, glabrous. Lvs alternate, 12mm, orbicular, obtuse at apex, sparsely pubesc. below; petioles short. Peduncles short; spikes 6cm. Uganda.

***P. cubensis*** C. DC. Creeping or scandent herb, glabrous; stems with 9cm internodes. Lvs alternate, to 7.5cm, ovate, acuminate at apex, cordate at base, minutely ciliate along margins; 5–7-veined; petioles to 5cm. Infl. terminal or lateral; spikes in lateral pairs or terminal cluster of 3–4, to 2cm. Cuba.

***P. dahlstedtii*** C. DC. VINING PEPPER. Herb to 40cm, stems prostrate, square or conspicuously angled, rather tough, 4mm diam., rufescent, glossy, glabrous. Lvs generally ternate or quaternate, 4×2cm, elliptic, broadly acute to rounded at apex, tapered to base, green, glabrous, coriaceous, minutely glandular-punctate above, veins raised beneath; petiole 6.5×2mm, shallowly grooved, rufescent. Infl. terminal, a cluster of 1–4 spikes, spike bracts wanting; peduncle to 2.5cm, glabrous; spike 11cm×4mm, green tinged yellow. Brazil.

***P. dolabriformis*** HBK. PRAYER PEPPER. Herb to 25cm, stem erect, branched, rounded, to 2.5cm diam., green becoming silvery-patterned, glabrous. Lvs alternate, purse-shaped with the two halves folded together and fused, 28×13mm (folded), mucronate at apex, tapered to cuneate base, pale green, darker along line of fusion, succulent, glabrous; petiole 4mm, green. Infl. terminal, paniculate, of many spikes; spikes each 45×2mm, green; peduncles glandular-punctate. Peru.

***P. eburnea*** Sodiro. Herb, prostrate, 35cm; stems slender, laxly pilose becoming glabrous. Lvs alternate, 5×2.5cm, ovate, acuminate at apex, rounded or minutely cordate at base, scarcely peltate, brilliant green with emerald green veins, coriaceous, white pubesc. beneath, generally glabrous above; petiole 2.5cm, white, sparsely hairy. Infl. terminal; peduncle 4cm, laxly pilose; spike 50×2mm, close-fld. Fr. ellipsoid, 1mm. Ecuador.

***P. elongata*** HBK. Medium-sized herb, epiphytic, stoloniferous; stems 3mm diam., glabrous but for minutely hairy lines decurrent from nodes. Lvs alternate,

6×2cm, elliptic-lanceolate, acuminate at apex, acute at base, ciliate towards apex, glabrous; petiole 1.5cm, semi-amplexicaul, grooved above, ciliate. Infl. terminal or lf-opposed; peduncle 1.5cm; spikes solitary or in pairs, to 13cm×3mm, closely fld. Fr. ovoid-cylindric, 1mm. Northern S America (French Guiana, Surinam, Venezuela & Colombia).

***P. emarginella*** (Sw.) C. DC. Spreading herb, very delicate; stems filiform, branched, glabrous. Lvs alternate, rounded obovate to obcordate, obtuse to subtruncate and often emarginate at apex, rounded to subacute at base, often slightly peltate, 4mm wide, glabrous or very sparsely hairy, thin and membranous; petiole 3mm, glabrous. Infl. terminal, on fruiting branches to 2cm; peduncle filiform, to 1cm; spikes 1cm, laxly fld. Fr. ellipsoid, to 1mm. W Indies, C America & northern S America.

***P. fenzlei*** Reg. Erect herb, somewhat shrubby; stems very minutely pubesc. Lvs generally quaternate, obovate, obtusely rounded, entire, minutely pubesc., 3-veined; petiole very short. Spikes terminal, elongate, filiform, densely fld, pedunculate; bracts suborbicular, truncate at base, peltate. Origin unknown.

***P. flexicaulis*** Wawra. Erect herb, shortly stoloniferous; stems branched at base, rather zig-zag, dull red, fleshy. Lvs alternate, erect, oblanceolate, acute at apex, somewhat concave, succulent, 3×1.5cm, 1.5mm thick, dark green above, paler and flushed maroon beneath, 3 prominent veins above; petiole short. Peru ?.

***P. floridana*** Small. Similar to *P. obtusifolium* except lvs suborbicular to elliptic, to 9cm. S Florida.

***P. fraseri*** (C. DC. FLOWERING PEPPER. Herb to 40cm at anthesis, erect; stems rounded, longitudinally striate, to 1.5cm diam., dull red, minutely pubesc. Lvs 3.5×3.2cm, mostly basal, rosulate, basal lvs alternate, cauline lvs whorled, broadly ovate to suborbicular, broadly acute at apex, cordate at base, green above, tinged purple on veins with age, pale green beneath with bright red to pink veins and irregular pink spots, minutely glandular-punctate above, coriaceous; petiole 4.5cm, dull red to pink, ungrooved. Infl. terminal, paniculate, of numerous spikes, pleasantly fragrant; peduncle 7×1mm, shining white, glabrous; spike 2.5×1.5mm, white or tinged green. Colombia and Ecuador.

***P. galioides*** HBK. Herb to 40cm, stems erect, branched, rounded, tough, to 5mm diam., green, pubesc. Lvs verticillate, in whorls of 4–7, 18×6mm, elliptic, or obovate on young growth, broadly acute to rounded at apex, tapered at base, green, pubesc.; petiole 2mm, pubesc., finely grooved. Infl. terminal, solitary, spike 42×2mm, green; peduncle 9mm, minutely hairy at base. C & S America, W Indies.

***P. gardneriana*** Miq. Erect herb, rhizomatous, glabrous, succulent; stem short. Lvs alternate, 4cm, rounded-ovate to subreniform, obtuse at apex, cordate to truncate at base, bright green above, paler beneath, pellucid-glandular; petiole 7cm. Spikes terminal or axillary, solitary or paired, cylindric, 40×2mm; peduncles 1cm; bracts rounded-peltate. Brazil & Venezuela.

***P. glabella*** (Sw.) A. Dietr. Herb to 20cm; stems erect or sprawling, rounded, softly fleshy, glossy red, glabrous but for 2 lines of minute pubescence running up from each node. Lvs alternate, 3.8×3cm, broadly elliptic to somewhat obovate, rounded to obtusely acute at apex, broadly tapered to rounded at base, green, often black glandular-punctate, glabrous, fleshy; petiole 9×2mm, broadly grooved, red, glabrous. Infl. terminal and from upper lf axils, solitary; spike bracts scale-like; peduncle 6×3mm, green, glabrous; spike 8cm×3mm, green. C & S America, W Indies. Often with variegated foliate, but readily reverts to plain green. 'Variegata': lvs small, pale cream edged or variegated off-white.

***P. graveolens*** Rauh & Barthl. Erect shrubby herb to 15cm; stems 5mm diam., red. Lvs alternate or ternate, oblong, rounded or emarginate at apex, very succulent, to 6mm thick, somewhat boat-shaped, folded upwards along main vein, to 40×12mm, glossy bottle-green above, maroon beneath; petioles to 12mm, red. Spike axillary near shoot apex, to 13cm, green, with 'mousy' smell; peduncle to 12cm, red. Winter. Peru (Andes).

***P. griseo-argentea*** Yunck. IVY-LEAF PEPPER; SILVER-LEAF PEPPER; PLATINUM PEPPER. Herb to 20cm; stems erect, tough rounded, to 1cm diam., dark green, glabrous. Lvs alternate, 3.8×3cm, cordate, broadly acute to rounded at apex, auriculate or rounded at base, often peltate, margin flat or minutely reflexed, entire to minutely sinuate, grey-green above, paler green beneath, coriaceous, glabrous, veins deeply impressed above; petiole 50×3mm, inserted 5mm from lamina base, peltate, rounded or minutely grooved, pale green to pink, glabrous. Infl. solitary, lateral; spike bracts wanting; peduncle 80×2.5mm; spike 65×3mm, pale green. Brazil ?. 'Blackie': petioles dotted red; lvs thin, dark olive to black flushed bronze, somewhat gray beneath. 'Nigra': lvs corrugated, metallic black, somewhat gray beneath; catkins green.

***P. hirta*** C. DC. Rather straggling herb; stems somewhat ascending, freely branched, hirsute to pubesc. Lvs alternate, 4cm, ovate to obovate or rhombic-elliptic, acute, green, paler beneath, grey pubesc. above, ciliate, soft, satiny, palmately 5–7-veined, veins reticulate; petiole 2cm. Spikes 10cm, rachis minutely hirsute; peduncles 2.5cm. Cuba.

***P. hoffmannii*** C. DC. Herb, often epiphytic; stems spreading, branched, branches erect or ascending, 5cm. Lvs 6×4mm, generally quaternate, cuneate-obovate, pale to bright green, coriaceous-fleshy, glabrous; petiole 9mm, very minutely pubesc. Spike terminal, solitary, densely fld, 14×2mm, pale yellow-green; peduncle 9mm. Costa Rica to Colombia & Brazil.

***P. incana*** (Haw.) Hook. Herb to 30cm, somewhat shrubby; stems semi-erect to rather spreading, rounded, tough, to 2.5cm diam., green, white-lanate. Lvs alternate, 4.2×3.8cm, rounded to broadly ovate, often somewhat oblique, rounded to broadly acute or down-turned mucronate at apex, rounded to cordate at base, coriaceous, densely white-lanate. Infl. axillary and terminal, subtended by small; lanceolate, foliaceous bracts; spikes generally solitary, rarely 2+ per branch tip, 16×4mm, green; peduncles 18×4mm, white-lanate; anth. purple. SE Brazil.

***P. inquilina*** Hemsl. Herb, procumbent, succulent, very delicate; stems rooting at nodes, bright red. Lvs generally quaternate, orbicular to obovate, 5mm, green, fleshy; petiole very short. Spikes terminal on branches, 2.5cm, shortly pedunculate; bracts peltate. Fr. oblong, very small. Mexico & Guatemala.

***P. japonica*** Mak. Perenn. herb to to 30cm; stems erect, sparsely branched, terete, fleshy, densely minutely pubesc. Lvs verticillate, in whorls of 3–5, spreading, 18×11mm, elliptic to obovate, rounded to obtuse at apex, entire, slightly fleshy; petiole 5mm. Peduncle short, hairy; spike 3cm, many-fld, dense, glabrous; fls sessile, minute. Fr. globose, 4mm. Japan.

***P. lanceolata*** C. DC. Herb to 1m; stems branched; slender, 4mm diam., densely villous at nodes, sparingly villous to glabrate to between. Lvs verticillate, in whorls of 3–6, 32×12mm, elliptic-lanceolate to subrhombic, acute to acuminate at apex, acute at base, pubesc. on veins above, glabrous and more or less punctate beneath; petiole 8mm, narrowly winged, glabrous. Infl. terminal and axillary; bracts peltate; peduncles 8mm, glabrous, spikes 70×1mm, laxly-fld. Ecuador.

***P. leptostachya*** Hook. & Arn. Herb to 25cm; stems decumbent and rooting at base, soon ascending, densely hirtellous. Lvs opposite or ternate, 2.5×1.5cm, elliptic to obovate, shortly attenuate to obtuse at apex, acute to cuneate at base, hirtellous; petiole 7mm. Infl. terminal and axillary; peduncles 1.5cm, hirtellous; spikes numerous, slender, to 10cm. Fr. globose-ovoid, oblique at apex, to 1mm. Hawaii & other Pacific Is.

***P. liebmanii*** C. DC. Rhizomatous herb to 45cm; stems branched above, densely hirsute. Lvs verticillate, lower lvs generally in whorls of 5, those of branches in whorls of 2–4, obovate to rhombic-obovate, acute at apex, cuneate at base, thick and succulent, those of branches somewhat thinner and undulate, to 3cm, green above, those of main stem rufescent beneath, all densely pubesc., veins 3; petioles short. Infl. terminal and axillary; peduncles short, hairy; spikes numerous, very slender, to 9cm. S Mexico.

***P. maculosa*** (L.) Hook. Herb to 20cm, succulent, sparsely hairy; stems decumbent at base, then ascending, rooting from lower nodes, to 10mm diam., green with dark red spots. Lvs alternate, 8.5×14.5cm, elliptic-ovate, abruptly acuminate at apex, rounded to subcordate at base, peltate, more or less pubesc., or glabrate above; petiole 10cm, spotted, fleshy, pubesc. Spikes terminal, solitary or paired, to 250×6mm, rather laxly fld; peduncle to 5cm, pubesc. W Indies, Panama, northern S America.

***P. magnoliaefolia*** (Jacq.) Dietr. Very similar to *P. obtusifolia* except: generally of more upright habit and more leafy; lvs more contracted to rather acute apex; peduncles smooth and glabrous. Panama, northern S America & W Indies. 'Green & Gold': lvs irregularly spattered green and yellow. 'Golden Gates': lvs matt green and gold with bright green specks. 'USA': lvs edged yellow to cream. 'White Cloud': lvs wrinkled, edged white. 'Variegata': lvs variegated lime green.

***P. marmorata*** Hook. f. Herb to 30cm; stems erect, tough, rounded, short, to 1cm diam., glabrous. Lvs alternate, 10×5cm, ovate, obtuse to acute at apex, deeply cordate to auriculate at base with overlapping lobes, margin slightly reflexed, green above with silver-grey or white patterns between veins, minutely translucent-punctate, coriaceous, glabrous; petiole 6×4mm, very shallowly grooved near apex, glabrous. Infl. terminal or axillary, 1–3 together; spike bracts peltate; peduncle 5×0.5cm; spike 14×mm, green. S Brazil. 'Silver Heart': lvs dappled silver between veins.

***P. meridana*** Yunck. Herb to 50cm, succulent, glabrous; stems erect to ascending, maroon or rufescent, often more green above. Lvs alternate, 24×18mm, suborbicular-ovate to ovate-elliptic, subpeltate at base, dull to bright green above, paler below; petiole 25mm, pale green or flushed pink. Spike terminal, solitary or paired, 95×1.5mm, pale green or flushed rose or white; peduncle 12mm. Venezuela.

***P. metallica*** Lind. & Rodigas. Herb to 15cm; stems erect, rounded, to 4mm diam., pink or red, fleshy, glabrous. Lvs alternate, 2.5×1.2cm, elliptic, acute at apex, broadly tapered to rounded at base, green tinged brown with silvery-green band above, rufescent or tinged pink beneath, succulent, glabrous; petiole 6×2mm, red. Infl. terminal, solitary, spike bracts wanting; spike 40×3mm, pink; peduncle 1×2mm, red. Peru.

***P. microphylla*** HBK. Herb to 30cm, stems prostrate, rounded, tough, to 2mm diam., green, pubesc. Lvs verticillate, mostly quaternate, 1×0.6cm, broadly elliptic to obovate, rounded at apex, broadly tapered to rounded at base, green, glabrous, coriaceous becoming succulent with age; petiole 2mm, ungrooved green, minutely pubesc. Infl. terminal, solitary, with normal foliage lvs at base; peduncle 11mm, minutely pubesc.; spike 22×2.5mm, green. C & NW South America.

***P. moninii*** C. DC. Erect herb to 20cm; stems pubesc. Lvs opposite, 3.5cm, elliptic, tapered towards ends, subcoriaceous, pubesc. on veins below; veins 3; petiole 1cm. Spikes axillary, densely fld, rachis glabrous; bracts rounded, subsessile, peltate; peduncles 2.5cm, pubesc. Réunion Is.

***P. nivalis*** Miq. Herb to 20cm, stems erect or prostrate, rounded, rather thick below, glabrous. Lvs alternate, folded upwards into a wedge, but not as completely as in *P. dolabriformis*, 15×6mm, acute to acuminate at apex, cuneate at base, bright green above, white or flushed pink beneath, succulent; petiole 8×1mm, green. Infl. terminal, paniculate, on terminal stalk to 1.5cm; spikes numerous, 10×1mm; peduncle very short; bracts rounded, peltate. Fr. ovoid, stigma apical. Peru.

***P. obliqua*** Ruiz & Pav. Herb, rather large, glabrous; stems ascending. Lvs alternate, 5.5×2.5cm, oblanceolate-subrhombic, acuminate at apex, cuneate at base, veins pinnate; petiole 8mm. Spikes terminal or lateral, 3–4, each 50×2.5mm; peduncles 1cm. Peru.

***P. obtusifolia*** (L.) Dietr. BABY RUBBER PLANT; AMERICAN RUBBER PLANT; PEPPERFACE. Herb, sometimes epiphytic, stoloniferous; stem rooting at lower nodes, ascending, to 15cm, 5mm diam. below. Lvs alternate, 10×5cm, elliptic-obovate, rounded to emarginate at apex, cuneate at base; petiole 28mm, more or less winged. Spikes terminal or opposite lvs, solitary or rarely paired, to 150×3mm, closely fld; peduncle 7.5cm, red, minutely hirtellous; bracts small, rounded-peltate. Mexico to northern S America & W Indies. 'Alba': new growth cream, stem and petioles dotted red. 'Albo-marginata': lvs small, obovate, pale green irregularly edged cream. 'Gold Tip': lvs oblique, mottled pale yellow, heavily towards tip. 'Lougenii': lvs variegated cream. 'Minima': dwarf, dense; lvs shiny. 'Variegata': lvs more pointed, variegated pale green and marked cream towards margin; stems marked scarlet.

***P. orba*** Bunting. Herb to 15cm, bushy, stems erect, rounded, to 5mm diam., dull green flecked red, fleshy, hairy. Lvs alternate, ovate to elliptic, acute at apex, rounded at base, smooth, green, coriaceous, pubesc.; petiole 10×2mm, shallowly grooved, pale green, minutely red-punctate, hairy. Infl. terminal, solitary, generally with small, semi-sheathing lf at base; spike 85×3mm, red-punctate; peduncle 15×2mm, pink, hairy. Origin unknown. A juvenile form with numerous short stems and small lvs, which needs careful pruning to avoid progression to adult foliage, is offered as 'Pixie' or 'Teardrop'. 'Pixie' ('Teardrop'): miniature form.

***P. ornata*** Yunck. Herb to 20cm, erect; stems rounded, to 2cm diam., dark green, glabrous. Lvs alternate, crowded towards stem apex, 5×3.5cm, ovate to elliptic or suborbicular, broadly acute to rounded at apex, broadly tapered, rounded or cordate at base, margins clearly reflexed, green, often tinged red on veins below, fleshy, stiff, minutely glandular above; petiole 5×2.5mm, distinctly grooved above, pink to red. Infl. lateral, mostly compound, of 1–5 spikes; peduncle 1cm, minutely glandular; spike 28×2.5mm, fls rather remote, green tinged yellow. S Venezuela, N Brazil.

***P. peltifolia*** C. DC. Stems to 6mm diam., densely villous. Lvs alternate, to 27×17cm, ovate, acute to shortly acuminate at apex, rounded or notched at base, peltate, hairy; petioles to 11cm, villous. Spikes opposite upper lvs, 65×6mm, villous; bracts orbicular; peduncles 3cm, densely villous. W Bolivia.

***P. pereskiifolia*** (Jacq.) HBK. Herb to to 30cm, stems spreading, rounded to weakly angled or grooved, tough, to 5mm diam., green tinged dull red, sometimes minutely glandular-punctate. Lvs in whorls of 2–4, elliptic to broadly obovate, acute to somewhat acuminate at apex, tapered to base, 4×2.5cm, green, sometimes edged red, glabrous, succulent, veins slightly more translucent than lf; petiole 5×2mm, grooved, rufescent, minutely punctate. Infl. terminal, spikes 1–3, distinct spike-bracts wanting; peduncle 5cm, green, glabrous; spike 12×3mm, green. Colombia & Venezuela.

***P. perrottetiana*** Miq. Trailing or semi-trailing herb, succulent and fleshy, glabrous; stems branched, branches erect. Lvs opposite to quaternate, 2.2cm, broadly elliptic to obovate, dark green above, paler green beneath, glandular-punctate, 3 main veins visible above; petiole 4.5mm. Spike terminal, solitary, erect, 6cm, slender; peduncle 2cm. Mauritius.

***P. polybotrya*** HBK. Herb, rather large, glabrous, stem to 25cm, to 5mm diam. below, lf scars prominent. Lvs alternate, rounded-ovate, abruptly acute to acuminate at apex, truncate to somewhat cordate at base, peltate, to 9cm diam.; petiole 8cm, inserted 1.5cm from base of lamina. Infl. terminal, paniculate, to 30×15cm; spikes 3cm, sessile in umbellate clusters, densely fld. Fr. globose-ovoid, ridged. Colombia and Peru.

***P. prostrata*** hort. Decumbent herb, small, diffusely branched; stem filiform, trailing, white-pubesc. Lvs alternate, 1×1cm, rounded ovate, rounded at apex, obtuse to minutely subcordate at base, often subpeltate, glabrous or slightly pubesc. above, pubesc. beneath, veins white; petiole filiform, 2mm, pubesc. Infl. mostly terminal; peduncle 1cm; spikes solitary or multiple, 40×1mm. SE Brazil.

***P. pseudovariegata*** C. DC. Herb, rather succulent; stem erect or procumbent and rooting at lower nodes, short, 5mm diam. Lvs alternate, 12×5.5cm, oblong-lanceolate, acute at apex, subacute at base, glabrous above, pubesc. beneath, coriaceous; petiole 6.5cm. Peduncles 6cm; spikes solitary or paired, to 18cm, densely fld. Fr. ovoid, rostrate, 2.5mm. W Colombia. var. ***sarcophylla*** (Sodiro) Trel. & Yunck. As above except lvs glabrous throughout. SW Colombia & Ecuador.

***P. pubifolia*** hort. Perenn. herb, creeping, downy-pubesc. Lvs ovate, small, green with middle grey bar, fleshy.

***P. puteolata*** Trel. Herb to 40cm, stems prostrate, square or conspicuously angled, rather tough, rufescent, glossy. Lvs ternate or quaternate, 6.5×2.5cm, elliptic to narrowly elliptic, acute to rounded-acuminate at apex, tapered at base, green, with pale zones around veins, paler beneath, glabrous, stiff and coriaceous, minutely glandular-punctate above, veins sunken above, raised beneath; petiole 5×2mm, grooved, rufescent, minutely hairy on margins. Infl. a cluster of 1–4 spikes, terminal and lateral, each sometimes with minute spike bract; peduncle to 1.5cm, red, glabrous; spike 6×4mm, green. Colombia.

***P. quadrangularis*** (Thomps.) Dietr. Herb to 20cm, stems prostrate, square or angled, wiry and tough, rufescent, minutely pubesc. Lvs in whorls of 2–4, 2.1×1.6cm, broadly elliptic to orbicular, generally rounded at apex and base, green, sometimes flushed pale pink when young, coriaceous to succulent, veins very slightly or not at all raised beneath; petiole 3×1mm, shallowly grooved, minutely pubesc. Infl. axillary or terminal, axis with 2 scale-like bracts half-way up; peduncle to 2cm; spike 20×2mm, green. W Indies, Panama & northern S America.

***P. rotundifolia*** (L.) HBK. Herb to 25cm, creeping; stems rounded, to 1mm diam., green, glabrous or not. Lvs alternate, orbicular to broadly elliptic, rounded both ends or slightly cordate at base, 15mm, green, paler beneath, sparsely hairy, fleshy; petiole 3mm, grooved, hairy. Infl. terminal, solitary; flowering shoots short, erect, lvs 1–4; peduncle 5mm, sometimes swollen at base, generally hairy; spike 12×1mm, green or tinged pink. C & S America, W Indies, S Africa. var. ***pilosior*** (Miq.) DC. As above except more densely hairy; lvs with pale green reticulate pattern above; growth more vigorous. SE Brazil.

***P. rubella*** (Haw.) Hook. Herb to 15cm, stems erect, branched, rounded, to 3mm diam., dark red, sparsely villous. Lvs verticillate, in whorls of 4–5, 7×4mm, elliptic, broadly acute to rounded at apex, broadly tapered to rounded at base, convex below, light to dark green above, flushed pink below, glabrous above, sparsely hairy beneath; petiole to 2mm, red, minutely pubesc., main vein sometimes visible as pale, silvery line. Infl. terminal and solitary or a cluster with 2–3 lateral spikes from upper lf axils, spike 30×1mm, red; peduncle 3.5mm. W Indies.

***P. scandens*** hort. Herb, 60cm+; stems stout, swollen at nodes. Lvs alternate, to 7.5×6cm, ovate to suborbicular, long-acuminate at apex, truncate to subcordate at base; petioles to 3cm. Origin unknown. Perhaps synonymous with *P. serpens*.

***P. serpens*** (Sw.) Loud. Herb to 50cm, trailing; stems rounded, fleshy, pale green, sometimes flecked red. Lvs alternate, 4×2.5cm, lanceolate, acuminate at apex, rounded to cordate at base, margins reflexed, pale green, coriaceous, glabrous; petiole 14×2mm, pale green copiously flecked red. Infl. terminal, solitary; spike bracts generally filiform; peduncle 7×2.5mm, glabrous; spike 80×3mm, green; anthers purple. Panama to Brazil, Peru & W Indies. 'Variegata': lvs pale green roughly edged off-white.

***P. subpeltata*** C. DC. Small herb, perhaps scandent, glabrous; stems filiform. Lvs 2cm, rounded, acute at apex, cordate at base, peltate, pellucid, glabrous both sides; veins 5; petioles very long 4–8cm. Spikes axillary; fls rather remote; peduncle long, 32mmm, glabrous. Ecuador.

***P. trinervis*** Ruiz & Pav. Herb to 25cm, stoloniferous; stem ascending, 3mm diam., below, crisped-pubesc. Lvs alternate, 2.8×1.8cm, elliptic to elliptic-obovate, lower suborbicular, acute to acuminate at apex, acute to rounded at base, densely black-punctate, villous; petiole 8mm, grooved, pubesc. Infl. terminal and from upper lf axils; peduncle 8mm, pubesc.; spikes 8cm, slender, moderately densely fld. Fr. globose-ovoid, oblique, to 1mm. Western S America (Ecuador, Peru, Chile).

***P. trinervula*** C. DC. Herb to 15cm, stoloniferous; stem decumbent at base then ascending, 4mm diam. below, somewhat succulent, adpressed-villous to crisped-pubesc. Lvs alternate, rounded subrhombic-ovate, attenuate to somewhat acute apex, shortly acute at base, 18×15mm, green above, paler beneath, yellow glandular-punctate, succulent, crisped-pubesc.; petiole 6mm, crisped-pubesc. Infl. terminal and axillary; peduncle 8mm, pubesc.; spikes 4cm, moderately densely fld. Fr. globose-ovoid, oblique, to 1mm. Northern S America.

***P. tristachya*** HBK. Herb, medium-sized, glabrous; stem ascending, to 25cm, sparingly branched. Lvs alternate, 6.5×4.5cm, rounded-ovate, prolonged to acuminate apex, subsinuate-cordate at base, peltate, upper lvs scarcely so, membranous; petiole to 12cm, reduced upwards, inserted 1cm from base of lamina. Infl. terminal, of 3 spikes at end of bracted stalk; peduncle to 2cm; spike 60×1mm, close-fld, white when growing. Fr. globose-ovoid, 0.5mm. Colombia.

***P. urocarpa*** Fisch. & C.A. Mey. Spreading herb; stems rooting at nodes, ascending towards apex, 2.5mm diam., adpressed-pubesc. Lvs alternate, rounded-ovate, abruptly acuminate at apex, rounded or cordate at base, minutely ciliate toward apex, 3cm wide, thin and membranous; petiole 3cm, crisped-pubesc. Infl. axillary towards branch apex; peduncles 3.5cm, crisped-pubesc.; spikes 3.5cm, closely fld. Fr. rostrate, 1mm. Northern S America & W Indies.

***P. velutina*** Lind. & André. Herb to 20cm; stem erect, subsimple, 6mm diam. near base, succulent, densely hirtellous. Lvs alternate, 4.5×3.8cm, elliptic, acute, dull green above with shining silvery stripes along veins, bright red tinged pink beneath and white-punctate, margins often tinged pink or silver, coriaceous becoming succulent, glabrous or slightly hairy near base; petiole 8mm, grooved, pink, hirtellous. Infl. terminal and axillary; bracts peltate; peduncle 1cm; spike 70×3mm, green tinged pink or brown. Fr. globose, oblique at apex, stigma subapical. Ecuador.

***P. verticillata*** (L.) Dietr. Erect herb, branches to 50cm; stems rounded, to 8mm diam., pale green to pink, hirsute below, white-pubesc. above. Lvs verticillate, generally in whorls of 5, very variable, lowest lvs orbicular, 8mm, pale green above, rufescent or tinged pink beneath, thickly succulent, subsessile, upper lvs obovate, broadly acute at apex, broadly cuneate at base, to 3×3.5cm, pale green throughout, coriaceous, clearly veined; petiole to 3mm on upper lvs. Infl. terminal, paniculate, of numerous leafy-bracted spikes, spikes each 22×2mm, green; peduncle hairy, 14mm. W Indies.

***P. viridis*** hort. Stems decumbent, long, stout, swollen at nodes. Lvs ovate-lanceolate, acuminate at apex, truncate at base, petiolate, medium-sized, glossy green.

***P. angulata*** HBK. See *P. quadrangularis*.
***P. brevipes*** Benth. See *P. rotundifolia* var. *pilosior*.
***P. chachopoana*** Trel. See *P. microphylla*.
***P. fosteri*** hort. See *P. dahlstedtii*.
***P. haughtii*** Trel. & Yunck. See *P. puteolata*.
***P. hederaefolia*** hort. See *P. griseo-argentea*.
***P. langsdorfii*** Miq. See *P. blanda* var. *langsdorfii*.
***P. minima*** C. DC. See *P. emarginella*.
***P. nummularifolia*** HBK. See *P. rotundifolia*.
***P. pavasiana*** C. DC. See *P. pseudovariegata*.
***P. peltifolia*** hort. non C. DC. See *P. argyreia*.
***P. prostrata*** Mast. & Moore. See *P. rotundifolia* var. *pilosior*.
***P. pulchella*** Dietr. See *P. verticillata*.
***P. resedaeflora*** Lind. & André. See *P. fraseri*.
***P. sandersii*** DC. See *P. argyreia*.
***P. sarcophylla*** Sodiro. See *P. pseudovariegata* var. *sarcophylla*.
***P. scandens*** Ruiz & Pav. non hort. See *P. serpens*.
***P. tithymaloides*** Vahl. See *P. magnoliaefolia*.
***P. variegata*** Ruiz & Pav. See *P. maculosa*.
***P. verschaffeltii*** Lem. See *P. marmorata*.
For further synonymy see *Piper* and *Rhynchophorum*.

**Peranema** D. Don (From Gk *pera*, pouch, and *nema*, filament, an allusion to the pedicelled indusia.) Dryopteridaceae. 2 species of terrestrial ferns. Rhizomes short and erect, dictyostelic; scales dense, apex attenuate, chestnut to brown. Fronds stipitate, uniform, 3–4-pinnate or -pinnatifid, ovate to deltoid, rough, sparsely pubescent to scaly on veins; veins free; stipes approximate and clustered, scaly. Sori solitary on segments, on veins; indusia globose to, eventually, irregularly fractured and lobed with saucer-shaped base; paraphyses absent; sporangia stalked; annulus 14-celled, interrupted; spores bilateral. Tropical Asia. Z9.

CULTIVATION *P. cyatheoides* is found at altitudes up to 3000m/9750ft in the southern Himalaya. The yellow-green fronds may be up to 1.8m/6ft long, making the fern a striking addition to a woodland border. *Peranema* is hardy to at least −7°C/20°F and probably much colder. Until established some protection from extremes of cold is advisable, e.g. with dead vegetation or straw over the crown. Grow in a soil rich in leafmould with a pH of 5.0–7.0 and plant in a part-shaded site. Plant out in early summer. In the cold greenhouse, pot into a soilless potting medium and keep in bright indirect light; water moderately. Propagate by spores.

***P. cyatheoides*** D. Don. Rhiz. scales to 20×2mm, ovate to lanceolate, brown. Fronds to 90cm, 3–4-pinnate or -pinnatifid, pinnae petiolate, alternate, falcate, lanceolate, apex narrowly acute, pinnules to 4cm, sessile, oblong, apex of seg. obtuse, margin notched; veins free, forked; rachis and costa grooved above, pubesc., scaly beneath; stipes to 30cm, approximate and clustered, grooved above, scaly and pubesc. India, Nepal, China, Taiwan.

***P. formosana*** Hayata. See *P. cyatheoides*.
For further synonymy see *Sphaeropteris*.

**Peraphyllum** Nutt. (From Gk *pera*, very many, and *phyllum*, leaf.) Rosaceae. 1 species, an erect, deciduous shrub to 1.5–2m, differing from *Amelanchier* only in entire leaves and non-connate styles. Branches wide spreading, felted and glaucous only at first. Leaves 2–5×0.25–0.5cm, lanceolate, in clusters or spirally arranged along vigorous shoots, subsessile apex and base acuminate, leaves downy at first, becoming lustrous green, flowers sparse, margin sometimes sparsely toothed. Inflorescence a terminal, 2–5-flowered cluster; flowers 2cm diam., white often flushed pink; pedicels short, hairy; calyx lobes hairy; petals 5, circular, spreading; stamens 20 in a double row; styles 2–3. Fruit a pendent, 4-locular drupe, rounded, yellow, flushed red-brown, surrounded by persistent calyx. Late spring. NW US (Oregon to California and Colorado). Z5.

CULTIVATION From the dry hillsides of western North America, where long hot summers prevail, *P. ramosissimum* is grown for its clusters of white flowers, reminiscent of apple blossom, carried in spring. In favourable climates (rarely in the UK), flowers are followed by cherry-like fruits, yellow with a red cheek. In temperate climates grow in sheltered positions, with maximum sunlight and warmth. Grow in well-drained, neutral or lime free soils. Propagate by simple layering or by seed.

***P. ramosissimum*** Nutt. As for the genus.

**Pereskia** Mill. (For Nicholas Claude Fabry de Peiresc (1580–1637), councillor at Aix and patron of science.) Cactaceae. 16 species of trees, shrubs and woody climbers, some with tuberous roots; stems not conspicuously succulent, terete, unsegmented, not ribbed or tubercled. Leaves present, broad, flat, thin, not or only slightly succulent, deciduous or subpersistent; glochids absent; spines usually numerous. Inflorescence paniculate or corymbose, or flowers clustered or solitary; flowers diurnal, stalked or sessile; epigynal tube none; floral areoles with wool, often hairs, and rarely spines, perianth rotate, spreading or rarely erect, red, pink or white; ovary a cavity at the style-base or inferior. Fruit berry-like to pear-like, sometimes with persistent scales; pericarp juicy or tough, indehiscent; pulp present or absent; seeds more or less circular, 1.7–7.5mm, black-brown, shiny; relief flat. S Mexico, C America, North & West S America, Brazil.

CULTIVATION Grow in an intermediate greenhouse (min. 10–15°C/50–60°F); use 'standard' cactus compost: moderate to high inorganic content (more than 50% grit), pH 6–7.5; shade in hot weather; maintain low humidity; keep dry from mid-autumn until early spring, except for light misting on warm days in late winter.

***P. aculeata*** Mill. Woody climber, scrambling to 10m; main stems cane-like, 2–3cm thick; distal branches *c*4mm thick. Lvs lanceolate to elliptic or ovate, to 11×4cm, shortly petiolate, usually with a pair of small, persistent, claw-like spines, 4–8mm, resembling stipular spines, at the base; 'normal' spines developing at areoles on older growth only, numerous on trunk, straight. Fls numerous, in panicles, 2.5–5cm diam., scented; floral areoles with hairs and often small spines; perianth white or nearly so; ovary a hollow at the style-base. Fr. *c*2cm diam., pale yellow to orange, sometimes spiny, fleshy. Autumn. Tropical America. 'Godseffiana': lvs variegated yellow to peach-coloured, purple-tinted beneath; an attractive house-plant or conservatory subject, not easily recognized as a cactus. Z9.

***P. bleo*** (Kunth) DC. Shrub or small tree 2–8m; trunk to 15cm diam., spiny or not; branches 2–5cm diam. Lvs narrowly elliptic to oblong or lanceolate, acuminate, usually 6–20×2–7cm, fleshy, lateral veins 4–7, bifurcate, petiole equalling or longer than the spines; spines usually 1–5, 5–15mm, subulate, black with red base, later grey. Fls in a condensed raceme, 4–6cm diam.; pericarpel ebracteate except at rim; perianth bright red or orange-red; ovary inferior. Fr. turbinate, usually 4–5×4–5cm, naked or with 1–2 persistent bracts, yellow, thick-walled. Spring–summer. Panama, Colombia. Most plants illustrated as *P. bleo* are in fact *P. grandifolia*; eventually reintroduced in 1951 and renamed *P. corrugata* in ignorance of its real identity. Z9.

***P. grandifolia*** Haw. Shrub or small tree 2–5(–10)m; trunk to 20cm diam.; distal branches 5–8mm diam. Lvs narrowly elliptic, ovate or obovate-lanceolate, usually 9–23×4–6cm, rather thin, venation pinnate, lateral nerves *c*7–13; spines 0–8, 1–4cm, brown-black, straight, slender. Fls few to many, 3–5(–7)cm diam., proliferating from the pericarpels to form corymbs; floral areoles bracteate and shortly woolly; perianth pink to purple-pink; ovary inferior. Fr. pear-shaped, irregularly angled, 5–10×3–7cm, fleshy. Spring–autumn. Brazil; widely cultivated in tropical countries. Z9.

***P. lychnidiflora*** DC. Tree to 10(–15)m; trunk 30–40cm diam.; distal branches 4–5mm diam. Lvs unequal (anisophyllous) and very variable in shape and size, 2–8×1–4cm, oblanceolate or elliptic to obovate or nearly orbicular, acute, rounded or emarginate, cuneate, venation pseudopalmate, lateral veins 2–6, inconspicuous in fresh leaves; spines 0–3, 2–7cm, yellow- or red-tinged at first, later grey. Fls solitary, *c*6cm diam.; floral areoles with fleshy bracts and an occasional spine; perianth yellow-orange (darker in bud). Fr. globose or pear-shaped, 2.5–4cm diam., leathery, green-yellow, with fleshy pulp. Summer–autumn. S Mexico to Costa Rica. Z9.

***P. nemorosa*** Rojas Acosta. Similar to *P. sacharosa* but with narrower and larger lvs, larger fls and seeds, and tufts of hairs between the inner tepals and stamens. Spring–summer. S Brazil, Paraguay, Uruguay, Argentina. Z9.

***P. sacharosa*** Griseb. Shrub or small tree to 7m; distal branches 5–7mm diam. Lvs obovate to oblanceolate, 3–12(–20)×2–7(–10)cm, rather fleshy, venation pinnate, lateral veins 4–6(–9), indistinct; spines 1–8 (more on trunk), 1–6cm, stout, usually brown. Fls solitary or in clusters of 2–4, 3–7cm diam.; upper floral areoles with numerous silky to coarse, white or brown hairs; perianth pink, white at base; ovary half-inferior. Fr. pear-shaped, 4–5×4–5cm, tough fleshy, green or tinged yellow. Spring–autumn. NW Argentina, W Paraguay, Bolivia, W Brazil (Mako Grosso). Often confused with *P. grandifolia*, which is more widely cultivated. Many plants named *P. sacharosa* are in reality *P. nemorosa*. The true *P. sacharosa* is often cultivated under the synonym *P. sparsiflora*. Z9.

***P. weberiana*** Schum. Slender shrub, 1–3m, sometimes scandent; rootstock large, tuberous; canes 1cm thick; distal branches 2mm thick. Lvs 2.5–8×1–4cm, elliptic to narrowly elliptic-lanceolate, acute, cuneate, fleshy, venation pinnate, lateral veins 2–4, obscure; spines 3–5, 8–13mm, subulate, brown or yellow-brown. Fls solitary, 1.5–2.5cm diam., or proliferating from the pericarpel to form clusters; floral areoles few, spineless; perianth pink or white; ovary half-inferior. Fr. a nearly globose berry, 5–15mm diam., shiny black, juicy. Spring. Bolivia. Z9.

***P. amapola*** F.A.C. Weber. See *P. nemorosa*.
***P. antoniana*** (Backeb.) Rauh. See *P. weberiana*.
***P. conzattii*** Britt. & Rose. See *P. lychnidiflora*.
***P. corrugata*** Cutak. See *P. bleo*.
***P. godseffiana*** hort. See *P. aculeata* 'Godseffiana'.
***P. pereskia*** (L.) Karst. See *P. aculeata*.
***P. pititache*** Karw. ex Pfeiff. See *P. lychnidiflora*.
***P. sparsiflora*** Ritter. See *P. sacharosa*.
For further synonymy see *Pereskiopsis* and *Rhodocactus*.

For illustration see CACTI AND SUCCULENTS.

**Pereskiopsis** Britt. & Rose. (From *Pereskia* and Gk *-opsis*, appearance.) Cactaceae. About 9 species of sparsely branched or scrambling shrubs, to 4m; stems terete, unsegmented; leaves present, elliptic, obovate to spathulate or almost circular, more or less succulent, deciduous to persistent; glochids present; spines usually 1 to several, acicular. Flowers usually lateral, *Opuntia*-like, sessile, diurnal, rarely nocturnal; floral areoles with leaves, areoles and glochids; ovary inferior; tube none; perianth yellow, pink or red. Fruit fleshy, seeds few. Seeds broadly oval, 4–5mm; aril present, enclosing entire seed, light grey, surface trichomatous. Mexico and Guatemala. Closely allied to *Opuntia*, but with broad, flat, persistent leaves.

CULTIVATION Grow in an intermediate greenhouse (min. 10–15°C/50–60°F); use 'standard' cactus compost: moderate to high inorganic content (more than 50% grit), pH 6–7.5; shade in hot weather; maintain low humidity; keep dry from mid-autumn until early spring, except for light misting on warm days in late winter. All species are of tropical or subtropical origin, and require minimum temperature of about 10°C for successful cultivation. During the growing season they can be watered as frequently as non-succulent plants.

***P. aquosa*** (F.A.C. Weber) Britt. & Rose. Sparsely branched shrub, 1–2m, glabrous. Lvs elliptic, more or less acuminate, 6–8×2.5–3cm, margins often tinged red; glochids few, yellow; spines 1–2, 1–3cm, off-white. Fls subterminal, nocturnal (opening early evening, closing in the morning), golden-yellow, tinged red; pericarpel sometimes proliferating more flowers and fruits. Fr. pear-shaped, 4–5cm, green-yellow. Summer. Mexico The edible fruits are used in Mexico to make drinks and jam. Z9.

***P. diguetii*** (F.A.C. Weber) Britt. & Rose. Shrub to 1m or more; stems minutely pubesc. at first. Lvs 2–6×1.5–2.5cm, elliptic to ovate, abruptly acuminate, cuneate, minutely velvety-pubesc.; spines 1–4, usually short and weak in cultivated material, reported up to 7cm, almost black, in wild specimens. Fl. sessile on second year growth, *c*5cm diam., yellow, outer tepals tinged red. Fr. 3cm, red, minutely pubesc. Summer. Mexico. Frequently used as a grafting stock. Usually grown as *P. spathulata*, but the identity of *Pereskia spathulata* Otto ex Pfeiff., on which the name is based, is uncertain. Z9.

***P. gatesii*** Baxter. Scandent shrub to 2–3m, glabrous; main stem 15mm diam.; lateral branches numerous, short; leaves obovate, acute, up to 3.5×1.8cm, fleshy; glochids numerous, brown; spines 1– several, 5cm, with thin papery sheath, pale brown at first, eventually deciduous. Fl. rotate, 6.5cm diam., lemon-yellow. Fr. cylindric 2–2.7×0.7–1cm, pink, sterile, but producing vegetative shoots from the upper areoles. Summer. NW Mexico (Baja California). Apparently just a sterile clone of *P. porteri*. Instead of producing seeds, the plant propagates itself by the falling of ripened fruits which have developed branchlets at the upper areoles. Z9.

***P. porteri*** (Brandg. ex F.A.C. Weber) Britt. & Rose. Scandent shrub to 1.2m or more, glabrous; main stem to 3cm diam; leaves obovate, acute, 2–3cm, fleshy; glochids numerous, brown; spines 0–2 on young shoots, increasing to 3–8 or more, 3–5cm, on older growth, pale brown. Fl. *c*4cm diam., yellow. Fr. oblong, 4–7cm, orange, fertile. Summer. NW Mexico (Sinaloa and Baja California). Z9.

***P. rotundifolia*** (DC.) Britt. & Rose. Shrub, 3–4m; branches wide-spreading, *c*1cm diam., glabrous; leaves obovate or elliptic to orbicular and mucronate, 3–4cm, very fleshy, persistent, glochids off-white, spines 1, up to 6–10cm, stout, off-white. Fl. lateral, on second-year growth, 3cm diam.; perianth yellow, tinged pink. Fr. obovoid or clavate, 4×1.5cm, red. Summer. SW Mexico (Morelos to Chiapas). Z9.

***P. chapistle*** (F.A.C. Weber) Britt. & Rose. See *P. rotundifolia*.
***P. pititache*** (Karw. ex Pfeiff.) Britt. & Rose. See *Pereskia lychnidiflora*.
***P. spathulata*** hort. See *P. diguetii*.
***P. velutina*** Rose. See *P. diguetii*.

**Perezia** Lagasca. (For L. Perez, apothecary of Toledo, author of a history of drugs (1575).) Compositae. About 30 species of annual to perennial herbs or rarely shrubs, to 3m. Leaves basal or alternate, entire, toothed, pinnatifid or pinnatisect with toothed lobes, margins often spinulose, mostly sessile, often amplexicaul, glabrous to pubescent. Capitula bilabiate, solitary or many in a panicle or cyme; receptacle flat, naked; phyllaries imbricate, in 2 to many series, green to maroon, margins usually scarious; florets hermaphrodite, with a 3-toothed outer lip and shorter, 2-toothed inner lip, recurved, cream to yellow, pink, red, magenta, blue or purple. Fruit a subcylindrical to fusiform, glabrous to densely glandular-pubescent cypsela; pappus of white to brown bristles. S America. Z9.

CULTIVATION The low-growing *P. linearis* and *P. recurvata* are suitable for the rock garden, scree, raised bed or alpine house, which gives the necessary protection from winter wet; grow in a gritty, well-drained and moisture-retentive soil in sun or light, partial shade. Propagate by seed or division. Treat the annual species as frost-tender annuals and sow *in situ* in spring (or earlier under glass), in well-drained soil in sun.

***P. linearis*** Less. Tufted, often prostrate, perenn. herb to 30cm. Basal lvs lanceolate to spathulate, mucronate, mostly glabrous, stem lvs to 3×2.5cm, lanceolate, densely ciliate, amplexicaul. Capitula solitary, to 4cm diam., peduncles densely pubesc.; phyllaries in 3–6 series, outer lanceolate, acute, occasionally red-tipped, margins scarious, inner larger, apex glandular-hairy; florets blue or white. Fr. somewhat pubesc.; pappus beige or white, occasionally tinged pink. Winter–early spring. S Andes.

***P. multiflora*** (Humb. & Bonpl.) Less. Erect annual, to 50cm, glandular pubesc. Basal lvs to 9cm, oblong-lanceolate, stem lvs, ovate-lanceolate. Capitula few to many, to 2.5cm diam., in corymbose or paniculate clusters; phyllaries in 2–4 series, outer phyllaries ovate, mucronate, sometimes base scarious or rufescent, inner lanceolate; outer lip of outer florets blue or white, other lips and inner florets yellow. Fr. silky-hairy; pappus white or rufescent. Winter–summer. Andes (S Colombia to N Chile). ssp. ***sonchifolia*** (Bek.) Vuill. To 30cm. Basal lvs to 5cm, oblanceolate, stem lvs much smaller. Phyllaries ovate-oblong, with short apical spines. Pappus white. Uruguay.

***P. recurvata*** (Vahl) Less. Procumbent to erect, often mat-forming perenn. herb to 40cm. Lvs to 20×2mm, linear-lanceolate, imbricate, apex, spinose, base somewhat sheathing, recurved, rigid, margins revolute, ciliate, glabrous. Capitula terminal, to 3cm diam.; phyllaries in 3–9 series, outer ovate, mucronate, green, apex often red, margin scarious, inner longer, lanceolate; florets blue or white. Fr. subglabrous to puberulent; pappus pale brown, occasionally white. Late autumn–early spring. Southern S America.

***P. viscosa*** Less. Erect annual to 45cm often glandular. Lvs oblong-cuneate, obtuse, sinuate, somewhat glandular, basal lvs petiolate, stem lvs sessile. Phyllaries in 2 series, entire, mucronate, subequal; florets purple. Pappus rufescent. Summer. Chile.

***P. microcephala*** (DC.) A. Gray. See *Acourtia microcephala*.
***P. sonchifolia*** Bak. See *P. multiflora* ssp. *sonchifolia*.

**Periboea** Kunth. (For Periboea, one of the wives of Neptune.) Liliaceae (Hyacinthaceae). 2 species of perennial herbs. Bulbs tunicate. Leaves basal, linear, channelled, fleshy. Inflorescence a few-flowered raceme; perianth lobes 6, basally united into a tube, rose to lilac, falling early; stamens 6 in 2 series, arising from perianth tube. Fruit a 3-valved capsule; seeds globose, black, 1–2 per locule. S Africa. Z9.

CULTIVATION As for *Hyacinthus*.

***P. corymbosa*** (L.) Kunth. Lvs to 12cm, 3–6. Flowering stem to 7.5cm; fls to 1.5cm, in 4–8-fld corymbose raceme; perianth lilac-rose, tube to 0.75cm; stamens exserted.

For synonymy see *Hyacinthus*.

**Pericallis** D. Don. (From Gk *peri*, around and *kallos*, beauty.) Compositae. About 14 species of perennial herbs or shrubs. Leaves alternate or in a basal rosette, simple, palmately veined, petiolate. Capitula radiate, solitary or in a corymb or panicle, involucre campanulate; phyllaries many, equal; florets white, pink, mauve or purple, usually hermaphrodite. Fruit a ribbed cypsela, somewhat compressed; disc fruit smaller, densely hirsute with caducous pappus; ray fruit sparsely hirsute, pappus absent. Macronesia. Z9.

CULTIVATION The florists' cineraria, *P. ×hybrida*, is the most frequently seen in cultivation, flowering within about six months from seed, and valued for the exceptional profusion of bloom which sometimes covers the plant so densely as to almost obscure the foliage. In warmer climates with frost-free winters and warm dry springs they are sometimes used as bedding but are more usually grown as winter flowering house plants or cool conservatory specimens and are discarded after blooming. Available in a wide range of cultivars and seed races, from compact Grandiflora and Multiflora types to the more graceful, branching 'Stellata' forms which carry the bloom clear of the mound of foliage. Surface sow seed in early to late summer in a sandy, soilless propagating medium and germinate in light shade at 13°C/55°F. Prick out individually into small pots with a low-fertility loam based mix, and pot on successionally into a medium-fertility potting mix. Ensure excellent drainage, water freely but carefully and liquid feed fortnightly when roots have filled the pots; plants collapse rapidly if overwatered. Admit bright filtered and provide shade in summer, maintaining cool, humid and well-ventilated conditions at temperatures no more than 16°C/60°F. Overwinter at 7–10°C/45–50°F, increasing temperatures to about 16°C/60°F if necessary to hasten flowering once buds have formed.

Subject to attack by chrysanthemum leaf miner, thrips, whitefly, red spider mite and aphid. Also to fungal crown and root rots, causing rapid collapse, rust, powdery mildew and various leafspot and leaf mottling viruses, including tomato spotted wilt virus.

***P. appendiculata*** (L. f.) R. Nordenstam. Shrub to 1m; stems ascending, white-lanate. Lvs ovate, pinnatifid, lobes 7–9, base cordate, toothed, glabrous and glossy above, white-lanate beneath; petiole white-lanate. Capitula 1–1.5cm, clustered in a corymb or panicle; ray florets white, disc florets yellow, tinged purple. Fr. glabrous. Canary Is.

***P. cruenta*** (L'Hérit.) R. Nordenstam. Perenn. herb to 1m; stems lanate. Lvs ovate to ovate-lanceolate or triangular-cordate, 5–15cm wide, margins crenate-ciliate to sinuate-dentate, base attenuate, petiole, winged, pubesc. above, carmine pink- to purple-tomentose beneath. Capitula 2.5–4cm diam., in open, cymosely-branched, rather flat panicles; ray florets pink to maroon or purple; disc florets dark purple. Spring–summer. Tenerife.

***P. ×hybrida*** R. Nordenstam. FLORIST'S CINERARIA. A variable complex of forms appearing to have originated in England as hybrids between *P. lanata* and *P. cruenta* and possibly other spp. Perenn. herb, often grown as annual, variable, forming compact cushions or openly branched plants to 1m. Lvs variable, ovate to suborbicular, often light green. Capitula to 5cm diam., clustered in corymbs; floret colour very variable, from white to pink, red, maroon, deep purple, violet and blue, ray florets sometimes bicoloured, with white base and coloured apex. Naturalized in damp places in areas of mild climate, e.g. coastal California. Compact and tufted to branched forms are widely cultivated, in a range of colours, some doubles; habit dwarf, compact, low to medium height; lf size variable; fls single or double, small to very large, with variously coloured rays from white to shades of pink, red, purple and blue, often with contrasting eye, centre cushion purple. Amigo Hybrids: very compact, to 20cm; lvs small; fls long-lasting, to 5cm diam., several bright colours; seed race. California Super Giant: habit compact, basal branching to 45cm high; fls large to 15cm across in range of colours from red to purple and blue. Cindy Mixture: very compact; fls in blue, carmine, dark red and copper, several bicolours; seed race. Dwarf British Beauty Mixed: compact, to 30cm; fls in several bright colours, some with contrasting white centres; early; seed race. Elite Hybrids: compact; fls to 41cm diam., in formula blend of pink, rose, carmine, bright red and blue shades, some bicolours; early; seed race. Erfurt Dwarf Mixture: compact, dense, to 20cm; fls, to 4cm diam., several bright colours; seed race. 'Grandiflora': medium height; fls large, blue with white eye. 'Grandiflora nana Zwerg' ('Gmunder Zwerg'): habit dwarf; lvs small; fls medium in range of colours including rose, deep red, entirely blue or with white eye, and white. Jubilee Dwarf Mixture: dwarf, to 25cm; lvs small, compact; fls to 5cm diam., in formula blend of blue, red, pink and white solids and bicolours; seed race. Mini-Starlet Mixed: very dwarf and compact, to 20cm; fls in tight clusters, to 4.5cm diam., wide range of bright colours; seed race. Mini Starlet Series: to 15cm; fls single, small. Moll Improved Hybrids: spreading, to 60cm; fls to 5cm diam., range of 9 bright colours, including bright scarlet, blue with eye, strawberry red, light blue and white; seed race. Multiflora nana Goldcentre: fls small, in solid colours with centre cushion formed by protruding yellow anthers. Saucer Series: to 4cm; fls single, exceptionally large. 'Siter's Rainbow Purple': habit compact; lvs small; very large heads of magenta-purple fls with white eye. Starlet Mixture: compact, to 20cm; lvs small; fls to 4cm diam., wide colour range, solids and bicolours; seed race. 'Stellata nana': habit compact to 45cm; fls somewhat small, petals narrow, star-like, white with blue centre, also in blue and shades of pink. Superb Series: to 40cm; fls large, single. Tosca Hybrids: dwarf, to 25cm; lvs compact; fls large, in wide colour range, few bicolours; early; seed race. Tourette Mixture: to 26cm; fls to 4cm diam., wide colour range; early; seed race.

***P. lanata*** (L'Hérit.) R. Nordenstam. Subshrub to 1m; stems ascending to procumbent, flexuous, densely pubesc. Lvs to 15cm, broadly ovate-cordate to suborbicular, sparsely dentate or pinnatifid, lobes 5–7, densely pubesc. beneath, petiolate. Capitula 3–5cm diam., usually solitary, occasionally clustered in loose terminal corymbs, violet-scented; ray florets mauve, disc florets purple. S Tenerife.

***P. multiflora*** (L'Hérit.) R. Nordenstam. Perenn. herb to 1m; stems erect, hairy below, glabrous and glaucous above. Lvs broadly ovate to suborbicular, base cordate, glabrous above, wispy-hairy beneath; petioles auriculate, winged above. Capitula large, showy, clustered in an open, much-branched panicle; ray florets lilac; disc florets dark purple. Canary Is.

For synonymy see *Cacalia, Cineraria* and *Senecio*.

**Perilla** L. Labiatae. Some 6 species of annual herbs. Leaves opposite, often variegated or coloured. Flowers paired in verticillasters along lateral and terminal spikes; calyx campanulate, 10-nerved, 5-toothed, bilabiate; corolla limb bilabiate, 5-lobed, tube shorter than calyx; stamens 4 in 2 pairs, subequal. Fruit 4 nutlets, reticulate. India to Japan. Z8.

CULTIVATION Moderately fast-growing annuals grown for their ornamental and often aromatic foliage, used as a foil for other plants in the border. Grow in rich, well-drained but moisture-retentive soils in full sun. The incorporation of compost or well-rotted manure before planting will encourage quick and vigorous growth. Propagate from seed sown under glass in early spring, to plant out in early summer. Pinch out young plants to encourage bushiness.

***P. frutescens*** (L.) Britt. To 1m, erect, pubesc. Lvs 4.5–12×3–7cm, broadly ovate, acuminate, deeply serrate, green sometimes speckled purple; petioles 1.5–3.5cm. Infl. to 10cm, bracts prominent, equalling cal.; cal. 3–3.5mm, gibbous at base; cor. 3.5–4mm, white, ringed with hairs within. Summer. Himalaya to E Asia; naturalized Ukraine. 'Atropurpurea' lvs deep red-purple. var. ***nankinensis*** (Lour.) Britt. Lvs laciniate-dentate, dark bronze or purple, margins crisped, fringed. China; naturalized E US. f.f. *rosea* L.H. Bail. Lvs variegated red pink, light green and crenate.

***P. crispa*** (Thunb.) Tan. See *P. frutescens* var. *nankinensis*.
***P. fruticosa*** D. Don. See *Elsholtzia fruticosa*.
***P. laciniata*** W. Mill. & L.H. Bail. See *P. frutescens* var. *nankinensis*.
***P. ocimoides*** L. See *P. frutescens*.
For further synonymy see *Ocimum*.

**Periploca** L. (From Gk *peri*, around, and *ploke*, referring to the twining habit of some species.) Asclepiadaceae. 11 species of glabrous shrubs, sometimes twining. Leaves opposite. Flowers in loose cymes or corymbs. Fruit composed of 2 follicles. Mediterranean to E Asia, Tropical Africa. Z6.

CULTIVATION A strongly growing climber for arches, fences and pergolas, *P. graeca* is grown for its dark shining foliage, which remains green until leaf fall, and for the interesting if ill-scented flowers; the yellow fruits and sap are poisonous. It is occasionally grown as a wall climber, but requires wire or other support. Easily grown in a warm position in full sun in any moderately fertile and well-drained soil. Little pruning is needed other than to remove weak and overcrowded growth in spring. Propagate by seed, division, layers or by semi-ripe cuttings in summer.

***P. graeca*** L. SILK VINE. Deciduous twiner to 10m. Lvs 2.5–5cm, ovate to lanceolate, glossy dark green. Fls 8–12 in long-stalked corymbs, malodorous, exterior yellow-green, interior maroon to chocolate, limb to 2.5cm diam., lobes 5, spreading, downy. Follicles to 12cm, narrowly cylindrical. SE Europe to Asia Minor.

**Peristeria** Hook. (From the Gk *peristerion*, dove, referring to the dove-like appearance of the column.) Orchidaceae. Some 7 species of epiphytic or terrestrial orchids allied to *Acineta*, from which it can be distinguished by the articulated lip. Rhizome short. Pseudobulbs fleshy, oblong-ovoid to subconical, dull green, 1- to several-leaved. Leaves often elongate, plicate, conspicuously petiolate. Inflorescence a basal raceme, erect to pendent, short or elongate; peduncle stout, terete; flowers numerous, opening in succession, showy, thickly fleshy, cupped, subglobose, highly fragrant; sepals subequal, suborbicular, dorsal sepal free; lateral sepals united at base; petals similar to sepals, smaller; lip fleshy, hypochile articulate or continuous with column base, concave, 3-lobed, lateral lobes erect, spreading, clasping column epichile rounded, simple, articulated to hypochile, disc often callose; column short, stout, footless, erect to slightly arcuate, apex often bialate or biauriculate, anther terminal, operculate, incumbent, bilocular, pollinia 2, waxy, pyriform or oblong. Panama to Colombia, Venezuela, Guyanas, Brazil, Peru. Z10.

CULTIVATION See ORCHIDS.

***P. aspersa*** Rolfe. Epiphytic or terrestrial. Pseudobulbs to 11×6cm. Lvs to 75×12cm, 1–4 per pseudobulb, elliptic-lanceolate. Infl. to 15cm, arching, densely several-fld; fls to 3cm diam., heavily scented; sep. and pet. red-yellow or orange-yellow spotted red-maroon, sep. to 3.5×3.5cm, concave, elliptic, obtuse, lateral sep. wider than dorsal sep.; pet. to 2.8×1.8cm, elliptic-lanceolate, concave, obtuse; lip orange spotted dark maroon, clawed, hypochile to 2×1.7cm, continuous with column foot, 3-lobed, lateral lobes elliptic to subrhombic, separated by 2 elevated calli, midlobe elliptic-oblong, epichile to 17mm, elliptic-oblong, slightly recurved, with an apical V-shaped callus; column to 15mm, usually biauriculate. Venezuela, Brazil, Colombia.

***P. elata*** Hook. Terrestrial. Pseudobulbs to 12×8cm. Lvs to 100×12cm, 3–5 per pseudobulb, broadly lanceolate or oblanceolate, acuminate, clear green. Infl. to 130cm, erect, many-fld; fls waxy, very strongly scented, white; sep. to 3×2.5cm, broadly concave, ovate to suborbicular, acute to obtuse; pet. to 25×18mm, elliptic-obovate, obtuse; lip to 3cm, hypochile continuous with column base, 3-lobed, lateral lobes white spotted red-rose, obovate to elliptic-obovate, separated by a transverse, oblong callus, midlobe ovate to elliptic, concave, epichile white, subquadrate, retuse, with a central, fleshy, sulcate callus; column to 11mm, white, subconic. Costa Rica, Panama, Venezuela, Colombia.

***P. pendula*** Hook. Epiphytic. Pseudobulbs to 15×5cm. Lvs to 80×12cm, 2–4 per bulb, elliptic-lanceolate to oblong-lanceolate, acute to acuminate. Infl. to 20cm, several-fld, pendulous; fls pale green or yellow-green, tinged and spotted red-purple; sep. to 3.5×2.5cm, ovate-subrotund to ovate-elliptic, obtuse; pet. slightly smaller than sep., ovate-elliptic; lip enclosed by lateral sep., hypochile to 2.5cm, 3-lobed, lateral lobes erect, elliptic to subquadrate, separated by a lunate callus, midlobe oblong, epichile ovate-rhombic or ligulate, recurved, obtuse, with a large, sulcate, V-shaped callus; column to 15mm, wings 2, porrect, oblong, obtuse. Venezuela, Peru, Brazil, Guyanas, Surinam.

***P. barkeri*** Batem. See *Acineta barkeri*.

**Peristrophe** Nees. (From Gk *peri*, around, and *strophos*, girdle, referring to the involucre.) Acanthaceae. Some 15 species of usually evergreen perennial herbs and subshrubs. Leaves opposite, entire. Flowers solitary or clustered in axils surrounded by an involucre or narrow bracts; calyx lobes 5, free, thin, dry or transparent; corolla long-tubular, limb 2-lipped; stamens 2, included. Old World Tropics. Z10.

CULTIVATION As for *Eranthemum*.

***P. hyssopifolia*** (Burm. f.) Bremek. Shrubby perenn. to 60cm. Stems low, spreading, densely branched, initially pubesc. Lvs 2–8cm, ovate-lanceolate, finely acuminate, dark green, subcoriaceous. Fls deep rose pink to magenta, in small clusters. Java. 'Aureo-variegata' (MARBLE LEAF): lvs centrally zoned ivory to yellow, the variegation extending and bleeding outwards along veins.

***P. speciosa*** (Roxb.) Nees. Subshrub to 1m. Stems grey. Lvs to 12cm, ovate-elliptic, glossy dark green. Fls paired or in threes arising from leafy bracts on short side branches or on stalks from upper leaf axils; cor. to 5cm, magenta to violet, blotched crimson, tube twisted, deeply split. India.

***P. angustifolia*** Nees. See *P. hyssopifolia*.
***P. salicifolia*** (Bl.) Hassk. See *P. hyssopifolia*.

**Pernettya** Gaudich.
***P. angustifolia*** Lindl. See *Gaultheria mucronata* var. *angustifolia*.
***P. ciliaris*** G. Don. See *Gaultheria myrsinoides*.
***P. ciliata*** Small. See *Gaultheria myrsinoides*.
***P. furens*** auct. See *Gaultheria insana*.
***P. furiens*** (Hook. & Arn.) Klotzsch. See *Gaultheria insana*.
***P. insana*** (Molina) Gunckel. See *Gaultheria insana*.
***P. lanceolata*** (Hook. f.) B.L. Burtt & Hilliard. See *Gaultheria lanceolata*.
***P. mucronata*** (L. f.) Gaudich. ex Spreng. See *Gaultheria mucronata*.
***P. mucronata*** var. ***angustifolia*** (Lindl.) Reiche. See *Gaultheria mucronata* var. *angustifolia*.
***P. mucronata*** var. ***rupicola*** (Phillips) Reiche. See *Gaultheria mucronata* var. *rupicola*.
***P. macrostigma*** Colenso. See *Gaultheria macrostigma*.
***P. nana*** Colenso. See *Gaultheria parvula*.
***P. pentlandii*** DC. See *Gaultheria myrsinoides*.
***P. prostrata*** (Cav.) DC. See *Gaultheria myrsinoides*.
***P. prostrata*** ssp. ***pentlandii*** (DC.) B.L. Burtt. See *Gaultheria myrsinoides*.
***P. pumila*** (L. f.) Hook. See *Gaultheria pumila*.
***P. pumila*** var. ***leucocarpa*** (DC.) Kausel. See *Gaultheria pumila* var. *leucocarpa*.
***P. rupicola*** Phillips. See *Gaultheria mucronata* var. *rupicola*.
***P. tasmanica*** Hook. f. See *Gaultheria tasmanica*.
***P. tasmanica*** var. ***neozelandica*** T. Kirk. See *Gaultheria parvula*.

**Perovskia** Karel. (For the 19th-century Turkestani statesman, B.A. Perovskii.) Labiatae. 7 species of late-flowering, deciduous, perennial, aromatic shrubs or semishrubs. Stem woody or woody at base, pubescent, with sparse golden glands. Leaves deeply toothed or laciniate, grey-green, petiolate. Flowers numerous, paniculate, tubular, zygomorphic, 2-lipped; stamens 4; carpels 2, deeply divided; calyx densely pubescent with sparse gold-coloured glands, lower lip 2-toothed, upper lip entire or 3-toothed. Asia Minor, Iran, C Asia, Himalaya. Z6.

CULTIVATION From the freely draining screes and gravels of Asia and the Himalaya, *Perovskia* spp. are cultivated for their deeply cut grey-green aromatic foliage and tall, erect spires of lavender or violet-blue flowers. Their stems, which provide a strong vertical element in the herbaceous border, are pale grey or white when leafless and provide useful contrast to other, more strongly coloured, winter stems.

*Perovskia* spp. are tolerant of dry chalk soils; they are suited to maritime situations and are hardy to −15°C/5°F, although stems above ground may be killed by frost. However, the best foliage effects are obtained on new growth and plants are best cut back almost to the base in spring. Grow in perfectly drained soils, in full sun. *Perovskia* will tolerate some shade, although in these circumstances they lose their firm and upright habit and may need staking. Propagate by softwood cuttings in late spring, or from 7.5cm/3in. cuttings of lateral shoots with a heel in the cold frame in summer.

***P. abrotanoides*** Karel. Subshrub to 1m. Stem pubesc. with gold glands, woody at base. Lvs to 70×25mm, oval to oblong, deeply divided, the lobes subdivided, bipinnatisect, grey-green; petioles to 8mm. Fls numerous, subsessile, in many whorls of 4, sometimes 6, forming panicles to 40cm; cor. pink, to 11mm; cal. campanulate, violet. Fr. a nutlet. Late summer. Afghanistan, W Himalaya. Z5.

***P. artemesioides*** Boiss. Closely resembles *P. abrotanoides* but differs in persistent pubescence; possibly a geographical race of *P. abrotanoides*. Baluchistan. Z6.

***P. atriplicifolia*** Benth. Subshrub or herb to 150cm. Lvs variable, to 6×3.5cm, lanceolate to cuneate, petiolate, grey-green crenate or coarsely toothed, upper lvs linear. Infl. a narrow panicle of soft blue fls; cal. and cor. resembling *P. abrotanoides*. Late summer. Afghanistan, Pakistan. 'Blue Mist': fls light blue, flowers earlier; 'Blue Spire': infl. larger. Z6.

***P.* 'Hybrida'.** (*P. abrotanoides* × *P. atriplicifolia*.) Lvs to 5cm, ovate, pinnatisect-bipinnatisect, grey-green. Infl. a long panicle of lavender-blue fls. Garden origin. Z5.

***P. scrophulariaefolia*** Bunge. Subshrub to 1m. Stems woody at base, pubesc. with gold-coloured glands. Lvs to 7×3.5cm, ovate, obtuse or cordate at base, glandular throughout, prominent veins beneath; petiole to 1cm. Infl. a leafless pyramidal panicle to 30cm, consisting of whorls of up to 6 fls; pet. violet or white, twice length of cal.; cal. purple; bracts to 2.5mm, lanceolate, pubesc. Fr. a smooth, brown, obovate nutlet. Late spring–early summer. C Asia. Z6.

**Perry, Frances** (born 1907). Horticulturist and writer. Educated at Enfield County School, Middlesex, Frances Everett was interested in wild flowers and horticulture from an early age. Her near neighbour, E.A. Bowles of Myddelton House, Enfield, fostered her early interest in gardening and suggested she attend the horticultural college, then for women, at Swanley. On graduation in 1925 she worked briefly in Bowles' garden before he recommended her to Amos Perry of the Hardy Plant Farm, Enfield. She gained valuable experience there with aquatic plants, water lilies, ferns, perennials and hardy bulbs. She married Amos Perry's eldest son, Gerald A. Perry, in 1930, and her first book, *Water Gardening* (1938), became a standard treatment. She published several other works on this topic, including *The Garden Pool* (1951), *Water Gardens* (1962) and *The Water Garden* (1981). She was gardening editor of the *Observer* for many years, and produced *The Observer Book of Gardening* in 1982, as well as a broadcaster and lecturer, touring the US, Australia, New Zealand, Canada and South America. In 1943 she became horticultural advisor to Middlesex County Council and in 1951 was appointed its Organizer of Agricultural and Horticultural Education. She was also Principal of Norwood Hall College of Horticultural and Agricultural Education from 1953–67, and received an MBE for her services in this field in 1962. Her close links with the Royal Horticultural Society culminated in her becoming its vice-president and the first woman elected to the Council (1968). The Society awarded her the Veitch memorial Medal in 1964 and the Victoria Medal of Honour in 1971.

Gerald Perry died in 1964, and in 1977 Frances Perry married the gardener and horticultural journalist Roy Hay (1910–1989). She was elected Fellow of the Linnean Society in 1945. Her other books include *The Herbaceous Border* (1948), *The Woman Gardener* (1955), *The Collins Guide to Border Plants* (1957), *Flowers of the World* (1972), *Plants and Flowers* (1974) and, with Roy Hay, *Tropical and Subtropical Plants* (1982).

**Persea** Mill. (Name used by Theophrastus for an Egyptian tree.) Lauraceae. 150 species of evergreen trees or shrubs. Leaves entire, alternate and pinnately veined. Flowers bisexual or unisexual, inconspicuous, yellow-green, in axillary or terminal panicles; perianth tube short, lobes 6, subequal or with outer 3 smaller; stamens 9 in male or perfect flowers; ovary sessile; style slender; stigma small, flattened. Fruit a berry or drupe, ellipsoid to pyriform. Tropical and subtropical America, Macaronesia, SE Asia.

CULTIVATION *P. americana*, the avocado, is widely cultivated for its fruit. The three races, Mexican (M), Guatemalan (G) and West Indian (W), correspond to the subtropical, semitropical and tropical climate respectively. Similarly, the oil content of the fruit declines from high (over 20%) to low (under 10%). The fruit contains 3–30% oil of the same consistency as olive oil. The sugar content is low, but there is much vitamin A and moderate amounts of vitamins B and C. The oil can also be used for cosmetic purposes. The major avocado producers are Mexico and the US; the fruit is also exported to Europe from Israel, South Africa and Kenya.

Each avocado flower opens twice: the pistil (female part) ripens first; it then closes to open many hours later in the male stage. The duration of closing also differs: in group A it takes more than 24 hours, from morning to next afternoon; in group B it closes for less than 24 hours, from afternoon to the following morning. This renders self-pollination unlikely, but not impossible; cold or rain may upset the rhythm. However, single trees – with no pollinator nearby – seldom bear fruit. In every orchard are least two clones should be planted.

The tree is large and the branches are elongated from terminal buds. There are two flushes per season. Lateral buds are easily shed, and pruning must therefore be handled carefully. A seed can germinate in about a month, but it take only 17 days with the seed coat removed. Seedling trees bloom after 5–7 years; grafted trees start flowering in the third year. Depending on the race, avocado thrives best in climates ranging from subtropical to fully tropical. Avocado grows on all kinds of soils, if well-drained to at least 1m below the surface. The tree suffers from saline conditions, but West Indian rootstocks are fairly tolerant. As the branches are brittle, shelterbelts may be needed as protection against strong winds.

'Fuerte', a Mexican × Guatemalan (M×G) hybrid, is the most popular cultivar. Its fruit is shiny green and pear-shaped, weighs around 300g and contains about 22% oil; the flower type is B. The tree is fairly cold-resistant and has a horizontal habit of growth. 'Hass' (G), group A, is self-fertile and has warty fruit that turns dark purple when mature. Other cultivars grown in the subtropics are 'Zutano' (M×G, group A), 'Bacon' (M×G, group B) and 'Nabal' (G, group A). Florida cultivars are better suited to warmer climates. The most important cultivars, ranked from early to late, are: 'Pollock' (W, group B), 'Simmonds' (W, group A), 'Tonnage' (G, group B), 'Monroe' (G×W, group A), 'Taylor' (G, group A) and 'Choquette' (G×W, group A). 'Lula' (late, G×W, group A) produces well in Texas. There are many others.

A good avocado cultivar must have a good and regular yield of high-quality fruit of medium weight (about 400g) and small seeds in a well-filled cavity. The fruit should hold well on the tree and have a good storage life. A small- or medium-sized tree with spreading habit is preferred. At least 3 cultivars with successive harvesting seasons are desirable. The West Indian cultivar 'Waldin' is commonly used as a rootstock in Florida. Two 'Duke' (M) selections were found to be good rootstocks. Their rooted cuttings performed better than the seedlings. Later selections are G6 and G22.

Seedling trees are commonly grown in the tropics, but cultivars grafted on seedling rootstock are preferable. To avoid root rot in the nursery, seed must not be gathered from fallen fruit. Instead, picked fruit of selected trees, free from sunblotch virus, should be used. The seeds are disinfected in water of 50°C for 30 minutes, cooled and air-dried. Seedcoats, tops and bottom are cut away and the seeds are sown, broad side down, at 30×60cm; a layer of sand, no more than 1cm thick, should cover the top. If good seed is scarce, it may be split lengthwise in 4–6 parts; they will germinate if a piece of the embryo is present. Alternatively, seeds are sown in polythene bags filled with perlite. It takes about four weeks for a seed to germinate. Two weeks later terminal scions of healthy trees are cleft- or side-grafted on to the seedling stocks. Some five weeks later, transplantation to bigger containers takes place. However, in most tropical countries 4-month-old seedlings are used for side- or veneer-grafting. It is important to protect the roots of bagged plants against excessive heat.

Plant in holes deep and wide enough to accommodate the roots, spaced from 5×5 to 12×12m. A cover crop or vegetables may be grown between the trees, but tomato, eggplant and other Solanaceae must be excluded because of the fungus disease they carry. To ensure adequate pollination, 2–4 rows of a group A cultivar should alternate with 2–4 rows of a group B cultivar. Beehives must be placed in the orchard when the trees are in bloom. Dead trees must be replaced immediately.

As mechanical cultivation is harmful to the shallow root system of avocado, it is better to plant to cover crop in the humid tropics and to use herbicides in drier areas. Where rainfall falls below $E_p$ for more than two months, the trees must be irrigated. Flooding is the cheapest method but it promotes root rot; sprinkling or drip irrigation are preferred. Experiments in Israel show that 60% of class A pan evaporation is sufficient. Feeding requirements resemble citrus. 1.4kg N per tree is sufficient in Florida; young trees in Brazil get 100g NPK. Zinc deficiency has to be corrected, but the spray must be directed toward the underside of the leaves.

Trees with a spreading habit, such as 'Fuerte', need little pruning. In cultivars with erect habit, e.g. 'Bacon', 'Zutano', 'Reed', the terminal buds are pinched out after each flush. To keep picking costs low, trees should not grow higher than 5m; this reduces wind damage and spraying costs as well. Older trees are pruned selectively. In thinning, every other diagonal row is removed after ten years and the other diagonal must go six years later. Thus a

6×6m orchard is changed to 6×8.5m and then to 12×12m. Naturally, weak and unproductive trees are the first to go.

Insects and mites can generally be controlled biologically, but in cases of heavy infestation by scales and mites spraying with a suitable insecticide is recommended. Root rot, caused by a *Phytophthora* fungus, is the worst threat to avocado culture. Copper sprays, a metalaxyl soil drench and a trunk injection of fosetyl-A1 are used to cure the disease, but prevention is better. The nursery must be kept absolutely free from the fungus by disinfection of tools and others measures. Scab and anthracnose are also caused by fungi. Sunblotch virus is transmitted by pollen, grafting or seed.

Yields of 15 tonnes per hectare have been reported, but the average is only half that figure. Mature fruit may be left hanging on the tree for weeks, without damage. Fruit size, oil content and an assigned date are used as maturity standards. The fruit is picked by means of long poles with a bag and a knife, operated by a rope. It is then cleaned, graded, sized and packed in flat trays. In the tropics, avocado fruit will suffer chilling damage if stored below 13°C/55°F; in the subtropics, a temperature of 10°C/65°F is recommended for storage. At destination, the fruit is ripened by retailers for 1–2 weeks at 20°C/70°F.

In cool temperate zones, *P. americana* is occasionally grown for interest. Plants are prone to leaf spotting, take up to seven years to fruit, and if grown from seed are likely to produce fruit of inferior quality. Grow in a well-drained, medium-fertility, loam-based mix, syringe daily in summer and water moderately when in growth, less in winter. Maintain a minimum temperature of 13–16°C/55–60°F. Place the seed (pointed end up) with the top about 1cm/½in. above the surface of the potting mix, keep moist and shaded at 15–20°C/60–70°F and move into full light following germination which may take up to 5–6 months. Alternatively, suspend seed by means of toothpicks just above water level in a jar or vase. Propagate also by greenwood cuttings in a closed case with bottom heat.

***P. americana*** Mill. AVOCADO PEAR; AGUACATE; ALLIGATOR PEAR; PALTA. Tree or shrub to 20m. Lvs 10–25cm, ovate-elliptic, acuminate or abruptly acute, sometimes near aristate, subcoriaceous to papery, dull dark-green above, paler beneath, appearing slightly glaucous. Panicles terminal, rufous; fls green, finely downy. Fr. to 12cm, oblong-ovoid to pyriform, skin thick, leathery, glossy dark green, pale punctate, to dark purple-green, tuberculate, flesh lime-green to yellow, firm; smooth and oily seed ovoid, 4cm, solitary. C America, widely cultivated throughout warm temperate and tropical regions. Cultivated avocados will usually conform to one of three types, Guatemalan, W Indian, Mexican. Guatemalan and West Indian avocados fall within the circumscription of the typical variety var. *americana*. The Mexican avocados belong to var. *drymifolia* (Schldl. and Cham.) S.F. Blake, with lvs aromatic, fr. small, narrow, thin-skinned. *Guatemalan*: mostly winter and spring ripening; rich-flavoured, high oil content. 'Gwen': fruits small to medium; long-season. 'Nabal': medium to large, nearly round. 'Pinkerton': medium size, round to pear-shaped. 'Reed': medium to large, late summer. 'Whitsell': medium-sized, pear-shaped, spring-summer. 'Wurtz': small to medium, pear-shaped; tree small, suitable for containers and greenhouses. *Mexican*: Similar to Guatemalan but somewhat hardier; thin-skinned, high oil content. 'Brogdon': medium to large, pear-shaped. 'Mexicola': small, heat- and cold-resistant; used as a parent. 'Zutano': small to medium, pear-shaped. *West Indian*: mostly summer and autumn ripening, low oil content. 'Pollock': very large (to 2½/2kg). 'Simmonds': large. *Guatemalan × Mexican*: fairly high oil content; include some of the most important commercial cultivars. 'Bacon': ovoid, crops well, some frost tolerance. 'Ettinger': medium size, pear-shaped, heavy copper. 'Fuerte': medium to large, pear-shaped, possibly most popular cultivar worldwide. 'Hass': medium size, pear-shaped to ovoid, purple to black skinned, heavy cropper. 'Jim': small to medium, good frost tolerance. 'Lula': medium size, pear-shaped, heavy cropper, good frost tolerance. 'Sharwil': medium size, oval, important Australian cultivar. *Guatemalan × West Indian*: important commercially in Florida; winter ripening. 'Booth 8': medium size, oblong prolific. 'Choquette': large, oval, tree size suitable for in gardens. 'Hall': large, pear-shaped. 'Monroe': large; heavy cropper. *Others*: Several very large-fruited cultivars are grown, mostly in Hawaii: 'Fujikawa', 'Ota' and 'Yamagata' are more or less pear-shaped, with high oil content; 'Marcus Pumpkin' has extremely large fruit, low oil content. A miniature cultivar, known as cocktail avocado, rather resembling a small gherkin in appearance, has recently been introduced. Z10.

***P. indica*** (L.) Spreng. Tree to 20m. Crown domed, broad, branchlets thick, shots initially sericeous. Lvs 8–20×3–8cm, lanceolate, obtuse or acute, glabrous. Fls to 1cm diam., inconspicuous, cream to green-yellow in a crowded, terminal, corymbose panicle to 15cm. Fr. to 26cm, ovoid-ellipsoid, ripening blue-black. Azores and Canary Is. Z9.

***P. caustica*** Spreng. See *Lithrea caustica*.
***P. gratissima*** Gaertn. See *P. americana*.
***P. leiogyna*** S.F. Blate. See *P. americana*.

**Persicaria** L.
***P. affinis*** (D. Don) Ronse Decraene. See *Polygonum affine*.
***P. alata*** (D. Don) Gross. See *Polygonum alatum*.
***P. amphibia*** (L.) S.F. Gray. See *Polygonum amphibium*.
***P. amplexicaulis*** (D. Don) Ronse Decraene. See *Polygonum amplexicaule*.
***P. bistorta*** (L.) A. Samp. See *Polygonum bistorta*.
***P. campanulata*** (Hook. f.) Ronse Decraene. See *Polygonum campanulatum*.
***P. capitata*** (Buch.-Ham.) Gross. See *Polygonum capitatum*.
***P. filiformis*** (Thunb.) Nak. See *Polygonum virginianum*.
***P. orientalis*** (L.) Vilm. See *Polygonum orientale*.
***P. polystachya*** (Wallich ex Meissn.) H. Gross. See *Polygonum polystachyum*.
***P. runcinata*** (Buch.-Ham. ex D. Don) H. Gross. See *Polygonum runcinatum*.
***P. sericea*** (Pall. non hort.) H. Gross. See *Polygonum sericeum*.
***P. vacciniifolia*** (Wallich ex Meissn.) Ronse Decraene. See *Polygonum vacciniifolium*.
***P. virginiana*** (L.) Gaertn. See *Polygonum virginianum*.
***P. vivipara*** (L.) Ronse Decraene. See *Polygonum viviparum*.
***P. weyrichii*** (F. Schmidt) Ronse Decraene. See *Polygonum weyrichii*.

**Persoonia** Sm. (For C.H. Persoon (1755–1837), author of *Synopsis Plantarum*.) GEEBUNG. Proteaceae. Some 75 species of undershrubs, shrubs or small trees. Leaves usually alternate, simple, entire. Flowers small, solitary or few to many in a raceme, yellow to white or sometimes green; perianth segments usually free, sometimes coherent near base, recurved; anthers inserted within perianth tube; nectary glands 2 or 4; ovary sessile or short-stipitate, with 1 or 2 ovules, style and stigma terminal. Fruit a 1- or 2-seeded drupe. Australia. Z9.

CULTIVATION *Persoonia* spp. are not easy to propagate. *P. comata* and *P. saccata* have been successfully raised from one-year-old treated seed; remove the flesh and scarify seed by removing a small portion of the seed coat. Sow in autumn, stand seed tray in sun over the following summer, germination rates of about 46% may then be expected in the following autumn. The seedlings produce many cotyledons, and it is imperative to prick out as soon after emergence as possible (1–2 days), since the taproot is brittle and easily damaged. Some species have been successfully raised from semi-ripe cuttings, and *P. pinifolia* from softwood cuttings. Otherwise as for *Banksia*. Lignotuberous species may be increased by etiolated cuttings.

***P. chamaepeuce*** Lhotsky ex Meissn. DWARF GEEBUNG. Prostrate shrub, 30cm high and 1m wide. Lvs 2cm, narrow-linear. Fls dull yellow, solitary in lf axils. Summer. E Australia.

***P. comata*** Meissn. Erect, many-stemmed shrub to 1.5m. Lvs 6–15cm, narrow-cuneate, glabrous and flat, 1-nerved, margins recurved. Fls dull yellow in subapical racemes; perianth hairy and saccate. Spring–early summer. W Australia.

***P. cornifolia*** Cunn. ex R. Br. BROAD-LEAVED GEEBUNG. Shrub to small tree to 6m; young growth covered in grey or red-brown hairs. Lvs 4–12cm, narrow-elliptic to broadly ovate, on a short hairy petiole. Fls dull yellow, solitary or in terminal racemes to 3cm long; perianth hairy, to 15cm. Summer. E Australia.

***P. hirsuta*** Pers. Hairy, medium shrub to 1m. Lvs to 12mm, linear to oblong, margins recurved. Fls yellow, axillary, almost sessile; perianth 10mm, hairy. Summer. E Australia.

***P. lanceolata*** Andrews. Erect rounded shrub to 2m high and wide. Lvs 3–7cm, lanceolate to elliptic, apex short and abrupt. Fls yellow, solitary, axillary; perianth 1cm. Summer.

***P. laurina*** Pers. Erect shrub to 1.5m. Leaves 4–9cm, ovate to elliptic. Fls yellow, solitary, axillary or in clusters of 4–6; perianth rusty hairy, 12mm. Young fr. hairy. Early summer. E Australia.

***P. levis*** (Cav.) Domin. BROAD LEAVED GEEBUNG. Medium to tall shrub to 5m with flaky red bark. Lvs 8(5)–10(20)cm, thick, lanceolate to narrow-ovate. Fls yellow, solitary, axillary or short terminal racemes. Summer. E Australia.

***P. linearis*** Andrews. Tall, open shrub to 5m with black flaky bark. Lvs 3–8cm, narrow to broad-linear. Fls yellow, solitary, axillary; pedicels 2–8mm; perianth hairy. Summer. E Australia.

***P. longifolia*** R. Br. SNOTTYGOBBLE. Shrub to small tree, 3–6m, with red-brown, flaky bark. Lvs 12–20cm, falcate. Fls yellow, axillary or in terminal racemes;

perianth ferruginous, with minute, silky hairs. Mid-spring and summer. W Australia.

***P. myrtilloides*** Sieb. ex Schult. and Schult. f. Small to medium shrub to 1.5m with hairy branches. Lvs 2–4cm, lanceolate to ovate. Fls yellow, rarely green, solitary, axillary and pendulous; pedicels to 10mm; perianth 10mm, hairy. Late spring–summer. E Australia.

***P. nutans*** R. Br. Variable from low, spreading shrub to 1.5m wide, to erect and 1m high. Lvs 7–30mm, narrow-linear to broadly ovate. Fls yellow, axillary; pedicels to 10mm; perianth smooth, tube 8mm. Summer. E Australia.

***P. pinifolia*** R. Br. PINE LEAF GEEBUNG. Tall, spreading shrub 3m high and wide. Lvs 6.5cm, linear-terete. Fls yellow, solitary, axillary towards last 10cm of branches; perianth 10mm, hairy. Summer. E Australia.

***P. saccata*** R. Br. SNOTTYGOBBLE. Erect shrub, 0.5–2m. Lvs 5–15cm, almost terete, slender, grooved. Fls yellow or green-yellow, solitary, axillary in a sub-terminal, raceme-like arrangement; perianth 1–1.4cm, saccate, pubesc. Spring–early summer. W Australia.

**Pescatorea** Rchb. f. (For V. Pescatore of Château Celle St. Cloud near Paris, orchid collector.) Orchidaceae. Some 15 species of epiphytic orchids allied to *Huntleya* and *Bollea*. Rhizome short. Pseudobulbs absent. Leaves distichous, arranged in a fan, thin-textured, membranaceous to subcoriaceous, conduplicate. Fls. showy, solitary, on short, slender, erect or arching stalks; sepals fleshy, concave, dorsal sepal free, lateral sepals shortly connate; petals subsimilar to sepals, narrower; lip fleshy, articulated with column foot, base contracted into a ligulate claw, continuous with column foot, trilobed, lateral lobes small, midlobe rounded, convex or ventricose, revolute, disc with a prominent, fleshy, semicircular, pluricarinate callus; column stout, erect, subterete, pilose, base produced into a short foot, anther terminal, operculate, incumbent, bilocular, pollinia 4, waxy. Costa Rica to Colombia. Z10.

CULTIVATION As for *Huntleya*.

***P. bella*** Rchb. f. Resembles *P. cerina* except fls larger, to 9cm diam.; tepals white-violet or pale violet, tips banded deep purple-violet; lip yellow-white, apex blotched purple-violet, hooded, callus large, marked purple, pluricarinate; column purple, base blotched yellow-white, spotted purple. Colombia.

***P. cerina*** (Lindl.) Rchb. f. Lvs to 60×5cm, erect or arching, elliptic-lanceolate to linear-lanceolate, acute or acuminate. Infl. to 10cm, erect to horizontal; fls to 7.5cm diam., highly fragrant; sep. white to pale yellow, blotched yellow-green at base of lateral sep., dorsal sep. to 32×18mm, obovate to elliptic-linear, obtuse, lateral sep. to 35×20mm, elliptic-lanceolate, obtuse; pet. white, similar to dorsal sep.; lip to 30×25mm, yellow, lateral lobes subfalcate, callus large, often marked red-brown; column to 15mm, white, anth. violet. Costa Rica, Panama.

***P. dayana*** Rchb. f. Lvs to 60×5cm, oblong-oblanceolate, acuminate. Infl. to 11cm; fls to 7.5cm diam., highly fragrant, long-lived; tepals milk-white, often tipped rose-purple; sep. to 45×25mm, oblong-obovate, obtuse; pet. smaller, suborbicular-rhomboid; lip to 30×23mm, white flushed purple-violet, ovate or elliptic to oblong, convex, retuse, callus purple-violet, large, lunate, several keeled; column white, anth. purple. Colombia.

***P. lehmannii*** Rchb. f. Lvs to 45×1.5cm, linear-lorate, acute. Infl. to 15cm, often horizontal; fls to 8.5cm diam., waxy, fragrant, long-lived; sep. and pet. white, densely marked red-purple, oblong-cuneate, slightly concave, acute; lip dark purple, front portion oblong, retuse, revolute, with numerous, long, purple papillae, callus with many chestnut-brown keels. Colombia, Ecuador.

For synonymy see *Huntleya* and *Zygopetalum*.

**Pests and pest control**. See Appendix, PESTS, DISEASES AND DISORDERS.

**Petalostemon** Michx.
***P. candidum*** Michx. See *Dalea candida*.
***P. gattingeri*** (A.A. Heller) A.A. Heller. See *Dalea gattingeri*.
***P. oligophyllum*** Torr. See *Dalea candida* var. *oligophylla*.
***P. purpureum*** (Vent.) Rydb. See *Dalea gattingeri*.
***P. villosum*** Nutt. See *Dalea villosa*.
***P. violaceum*** Michx. See *Dalea purpurea*.

**Petamenes** Salisb. ex J.W. London.
***P. abbreviatus*** (Andrews) N.E. Br. See *Gladiolus abbreviatus*.
***P. schweinfurthii*** (Bak.) N.E. Br. See *Gladiolus schweinfurthii*.

**Petasites** Mill. (From Gk *petasos*, a broad-brimmed hat, referring to the shape of the leaves.) BUTTERBUR; SWEET COLTSFOOT. Compositae. Some 15 species of dioecious, perennial herbs, with rhizomes. Leaves mostly basal, often lobed; stem leaves spathe or scale-like. Capitula discoid or radiate, solitary to many, in a panicle produced usually before basal leaves, stems greatly elongated in fruit; involucre campanulate; phyllaries in 1–3 series; male capitula usually with 1–10 peripheral, tubular or ligulate florets, sterile disc florets tubular, male, fertile; female capitula with numerous fertile, tubular or ligulate florets, and a few central, sterile, tubular florets. Fruit a cylindrical, glabrous cypsela; pappus of simple, rough, hairs. N temperate regions.

CULTIVATION *Petasites* spp. generally occur in permanently damp, often shaded habitats at streamsides, in water meadow and moist, open woodland; *P. spurius* is found on dunes and in other sandy habitats with plenty of readily available moisture. *P. paradoxus* occurs in gravel beds by streamsides on limestone.

Despite being extremely rampant and dangerously invasive, some *Petasites* spp. are not without value in the garden if sited with due regard to their habits; like the closely related coltsfoot (*Tussilago*), most species flower in spring before the emergence of the leaves. *P. fragrans* (not reliably hardy where temperatures fall below −15°C/5°F) has strongly vanilla-scented flowers carried in mid winter, with or just before the leaves; they are useful for cutting or may be pot grown, although some individuals find the scent overpoweringly sweet especially in confined spaces. Suitable for naturalizing on rough banks or in hedge bottoms, *P. fragrans*, with other low-growing species like *P. albus*, *P. paradoxus* and *P. frigidus*, makes very effective groundcover in wilder areas of the garden; it tolerates drier conditions than other species.

Where larger, moist and shady areas of the wild or woodland garden are unlikely to be intensively cultivated (the deep and extensive root system will prove difficult to eradicate), *P. japonicus* and its var. *giganteus* make stately and impressive colonies, especially at the waterside, out-competing all other species that may grow in similar situations. They are of interest in early spring, when the milk-white flowers appear at ground level, cupped in a symmetrical rosette of pale green bracts, and later as the enormous leaves emerge, sometimes reaching 1.5m (60in.) in diameter, on stout stems to 2m (80in.) in height. *P. hybridus* and *P. spurius* are smaller plants having similar although less ornamental effects, the first at least makes a valuable early nectar source for honey bees. Where *P. hybridus* is used, select the male-flowered (staminate) plant. All may be confined by plantings in sunken tubs or barrels, although best effects are obtained by massed plantings. Grow in deep, fertile and humus-rich soils that are permanently moist but not stagnant, in shade, semi-shade or sun. Propagate by division or seed.

***P. albus*** (L.) Gaertn. Lvs 14–40cm diam., orbicular-cordate, regularly lobed, lobes dentate, basal lobes usually divergent, glabrous above, lanate beneath, stem lvs to *c*5cm, 5–26, occasionally sheathing at base, sometimes with a rudimentary lamina. Infl. 15–30cm; capitula discoid; male capitula 5–40; female capitula 13–45; involucre to 12mm; phyllaries pale green, entire, glandular-pubesc.; florets yellow-white. Spring. N & C Europe to W Asia. Z5.

***P. fragans*** (Vill.) Presl. WINTER HELIOTROPE. To 30cm. Lvs reniform-cordate, lobed, basal lobes convergent to divergent, glabrous above, pubesc. beneath, margins regularly dentate, lower stem lvs to 7cm, 2–7, lower usually sheathing at base, many with a rudimentary lamina. Capitula radiate, 6–20; involucre to 11mm; phyllaries pale green or tinged purple, sparsely long-hairy; florets white-pink, vanilla-scented; ligules to 6mm. Winter. C Mediterranean. Z7.

***P. frigidus*** (L.) Fries. Lvs deltoid-cordate, coarsely dentate or sparsely lobed, basal lobes divergent, glabrous above, pubesc. below, stem lvs to 6cm, 4–11, lower usually with a sheathing base, sometimes with a rudimentary lamina. Capitula radiate, male capitula 5–9, female capitula 8–12; involucre to 1cm; phyllaries green or purple, pubesc.; florets white-yellow or red; ligules to 4mm. N Europe. Z5.

***P. hybridus*** (L.) P. Gaertn., Mey. & Scherb. BOG RHUBARB; BUTTERBUR. To 1m. Lvs to 60cm diam., orbicular-cordate, somewhat angular, lobed, basal lobes convergent, sparsely tomentose beneath, margin irregularly dentate, stem lvs to 6cm, 5–20 in male plants, 17–35 in female, lower lvs not sheathing at base, sometimes with rudimentary lamina. Capitula discoid; male capitula 16–55; female capitula 25–130; male involucre to 9mm, female smaller; phyllaries entire, tinged purple, sparsely hairy at base; florets lilac-pink or yellow. Spring–summer. Europe, N & W Asia. Z4.

***P. japonicus*** (Sieb. & Zucc.) Maxim. To 1m. Lvs to 80cm diam., reniform-cordate, lobed, basal lobes convergent, glabrous above, pubesc. beneath, margin irregularly dentate, stem lvs to 7cm, 15–25, subcordate, lower almost cordate, rarely with a rudimentary lamina. Capitula discoid; involucre to 1cm high; phyllaries entire, rarely emarginate, green, sparsely pubesc.; florets tubular, pale mauve to almost white. Fr. to 4mm, glabrous; pappus to 12mm. Spring. Korea, China, Japan, naturalized in Europe. var. ***giganteus*** (F. Schmidt) Nichols. Lvs 0.9–1.5m across; petioles to 2m. Japan. Z5.

***P.paradoxus*** (Retz.) Baumg. Lvs deltoid-cordate to hastate, rarely bilobed at base, basal lobes usually divergent, densely white-tomentose beneath, margin usually regularly dentate, stem lvs to 6cm, 5–22, sheathing at base, sometimes with a rudimentary lamina. Capitula discoid, male capitula 5–26, female capitula 10–32, male involucre to 10mm, female slightly smaller; phyllaries entire, rufescent, minutely glandular-pubesc.; florets red-pink to white. Spring. European mts. Z5.

***P.spurius*** (Retz.) Rchb. Lvs deltoid-hastate, lobed, lobes 2–5 at each side of the base, glabrous above, pubesc. beneath, margins regularly dentate, stem lvs to 10cm, 2–12, lower sheathing at base, very rarely with a rudimentary lamina. Capitula radiate, 10–45; male involucre to 8mm, female smaller; phyllaries pale green, glabrous, apex ciliate or fimbriate; florets yellow. USSR, E Romania.

***P.giganteus*** F. Schmidt. See *P.japonicus* var. *giganteus*.
***P.niveus*** (Vill.) Baumg. See *P.paradoxus*.
***P.vulgaris*** L. See *P.hybridus*.
For further synonymy see *Tussilago*.

**Petastoma** Miers.
***P.langlasseanum*** Kränzl. See *Mansoa hymenaea*.
***P.tonduzianum*** Kränzl. See *Mansoa hymenaea*.

**Petrea** L. (For Lord Robert James Petrie (1714–43) of Thorndon, Essex, owner of one of the best private collections of exotics in Europe, supervised by Phillip Miller.) BLUE BIRD VINE; PURPLE WREATH; QUEEN'S WREATH; SANDPAPER VINE. Verbenaceae. 30 species of lianes, shrubs, or small trees. Leaves opposite or whorled, simple, entire, exstipulate, deciduous, often semi-deciduous or evergreen in cultivation, rough, venation prominent. Inflorescence indeterminate, racemose, axillary or terminal, elongate, many-flowered; bracts small or absent; flowers hypogenous, bisexual, regular or occasionally zygomorphic, each subtended by 1 to many caducous bracteoles; torus distinct and ring-like, swollen; calyx inferior, gamosepalous, tube campanulate, mostly ribbed, lobes 5, blue, purple, violet or white; corolla inferior, gamosepalous, hypercrateriform, darker than calyx, slightly zygomorphic, lobes 5, subequal, rounded; stamens 4, included in corolla at or near middle of tube, filaments short, slender, anthers medifixed, oblong or ovate; ovary subglobose or obovoid, bilocular, each locule uniovulate, stigma small, capitate. Fruit drupaceous, enclosed by accrescent fruiting calyx, containing 2 1-seeded stones. Tropical America and Mexico; *P. volubilis* naturalized in India. Z10.

CULTIVATION *Petrea* spp. (particularly *P.volubilis*) are widely cultivated in the Tropics, where the dark green foliage and showy blue racemes account for their popularity both as vigorous climbers and as weeping standards. Plant outside in full sunlight to light shade on freely draining soils tending to low pH. Water and spray copiously during the growing season. Prune hard after flowering (spring in the Tropics) to maintain a simple branch pattern, avoiding congestion and the accumulation of fallen leaves, which are slow to decompose.

In cool-temperate zones, under glass, grow in direct sun or bright filtered light with medium to high humidity and a winter minimum temperature of 10°C/50°F, 18°C/65°F in summer. Mist frequently in warm sunny weather. Plant in large tubs, open beds or under and through staging in a freely draining, lime-free medium enriched with leafmould. Propagate by layering (both simple and air) or semi-hardened nodal cuttings inserted in sand with bottom heat and misted regularly. *Petrea* is afflicted by scale and mealybug. The coarse, tough, upper leaf surfaces and granular-fissured bark favour the secondary problem of sooty mould. Regular hosing down of well-established vines should hold such infection in check.

***P.arborea*** HBK. BLUE PETREA; TREE PETREA. Subscandent shrub or small tree. Branches slender, grey, conspicuously lenticellate, glabrate; twigs short-pubesc. Lvs to 16×8cm, decussate-opposite, sessile or subsessile, thin-textured, grey-green above, brighter green beneath, elliptic, obtuse or slightly retuse, base cordate or subcordate, slightly asperous on both surfaces. Infl. to 16cm, ascending or nodding, densely pubesc.; cal. to 17mm, blue, lobes longer than tube, to 12×4mm, obtuse; cor. to 7mm, lobes rounded, cambridge blue; fil. glabrous, staminode obsolete; ovary obovoid; fruiting cal. tough, accrescent. Colombia and Venezuela to Guyana and Trinidad. Commonly confused in hort. with *P. volubilis*. 'Broadway': fls white.

***P.kohautiana*** Presl. FLEUR DE DIEU. Liane to 20m. Branches stout, light grey or ashy-white, obtusely tetragonal, glabrate, conspicuously lenticellate; lf scars prominent. Lvs to 20×11cm, decussate-opposite, petiolate, coriaceous, dark green, broadly elliptic, apex and base variable, glabrate. Infl. to 60cm, erect or nodding, scabrous; bracts to 5mm, narrowly ovate, ciliate, scabrous outside; cal to 2cm, violet or blue, lobes exceeding tube, acute or obtuse, sometimes emarginate; cor. to 2cm, lobes rounded, violet or blue; fil. pilose, staminode minute; ovary obovoid, glabrous. Fr. obovoid-oblong, to 6mm, glabrous. W Indies, Antilles. var. ***anomala*** Mold. Fls white.

***P.racemosa*** Nees. PURPLE WREATH. Woody vine or shrub, branches grey or brown, densely puberulent. Lvs to 18×8cm, chartaceous, becoming membranous, elliptic, obtuse to subacute, base attenuate or acute, bright green, serrate or denticulate, glabrous. Infl. to 31cm, axillary, erect or nutant, loosely many-fld; peduncles to 2cm, densely puberulent; pedicels to 2cm, glabrous; cal. tube to 6×2mm, obconic, adpressed-puberulent, lobes to 14×5mm, narrowly obovate, subglabrous or slightly puberulent; cor. hypocrateriform, tube to 9mm, infundibular, exterior slightly pubesc. towards apex, interior densely long-pubesc., lobes to 7.5×6mm, broadly ovate, densely short-pubesc. Northern S America.

***P.volubilis*** L. PURPLE WREATH; SAND PAPER. Woody vine to undershrub, to 12m. Branches and branchlets twining, pale brown to ashy grey, slender, shortly pubesc., conspicuously lenticellate, lf scars conspicuous. Lvs to 21×11cm, decussate-opposite, oblong-elliptic, apex acute or shortly acuminate, base cuneate, petiolate, subcoriaceous, scurfy, deep green above, lighter green and densely or sparsely pubesc. beneath, somewhat viscid. Infl. to 22–36cm, an erect, arching or pendent crowded, cylindrical raceme; bracts to 8mm, narrow, caducous; cal. lilac, lobes longer than tube, to 18×6mm, oblong, apex round; cor. to 8mm, tube densely pubesc. in upper quarter, lobes broadly elliptic, puberulent, indigo to amethyst; fil. glabrous, staminode obsolete; ovary oblong-obovoid, glabrous; fruiting cal. accrescent, stiff, densely pubesc. C America and Lesser Antilles, introduced elsewhere. 'Albiflora': fls white.

**Petrocallis** R. Br. (From Gk *petros*, rock, and *kallos*, beauty, from its habitat.) Cruciferae. 1 species, an alpine perennial herb to 5cm. Foliage cushion-forming, much like many species in *Draba* or *Saxifraga*. Leaves to 6mm, digitately 3-lobed, in tight rosettes. Flowering stems leafless, hairy, bearing a few-flowered corymb; flowers small; sepals 4; petals 4, to 5mm, pink-lilac, sometimes blue. Fruit a silique, inflated, obovate, few-seeded. Pyrenees, Alps, Carpathians. Z4.

CULTIVATION *P.pyrenaica* grows on rocks and screes, often, but not exclusively, on limestone at 1700–2900m/5525–9425ft. It forms dense, neat cushions of fine grey-green foliage, with pale lilac-pink, vanilla-scented flowers in spring, and is grown on scree or in the alpine house, where the scent is best appreciated. Cultivate as for *Draba*.

***P.pyrenaica*** (L.) R. Br. As for the genus.

***P.fenestrata*** Boiss. See *Elburzia fenestrata*.
For further synonymy see *Draba*.

**Petrocoptis** A. Braun. (From Gk *petra*, rock, and *kopto*, to cut or break: the Gk equivalent of *Saxifraga*.) Caryophyllaceae. 7 closely related species of perennial, tussock-forming rock plants resembling species of *Lychnis* and *Silene*, and differing technically only in the seeds, which have a tuft of hairs at the hilum. The capsule, developing from an ovary with 5 styles, opens with 5 teeth, like *Lychnis*. Endemic to the Pyrenees and mts of N Spain. Z7.

CULTIVATION Found in the wild in calcareous rocky, mountain habitats, *Petrocoptis* spp. are suitable for the rock garden. *P.glaucifolia* forms tussocks of grey-green foliage, covered in summer by masses of starry carmine flowers with a white eye. Those of *P.pyrenaica* are paler pink or white. *Petrocoptis* is also suitable for the alpine house. Grow in moderately fertile, sharply drained soil; with protection from excessive winter wet, *Petrocoptis* spp. are hardy to between −10°C to −15°C/14–5°F. Cultivate under glass as for *Paronychia*. Propagate from seed in early spring in a sandy propagating medium; they can be expected to flower in their first year from seed and are sometimes grown as annuals.

***P. glaucifolia*** (Lagasca) Boiss. Loosely caespitose, glabrous perenn. with thin, fragile, flowering stems to 15cm. Basal lvs not in a rosette, ovate to lanceolate. Infl. a lax, few-fld cyme with scarious bracts; cal. 5–8mm; pet. limb 12–15mm, entire or shallowly indented, pink-purple. Summer. N Spain (mts).

***P. pyrenaica*** (Bergeret) A. Braun. Like *P. glaucifolia* but lvs in a basal rosette; bracts green with a scarious margin, and pet. limb c10mm, white or pale pink. Summer. W Pyrenees.

***P. lagascae*** (Willk.) Willk. See *P. glaucifolia*.
For further synonymy see *Lychnis*.

**Petrocosmea** Oliv. (From Gk *petros*, rock, and *kosmos*, decoration, referring to the natural habitat.) Gesneriaceae. Some 29 species of perennial, pubescent, rhizomatous herbs. Leaves rosulate, petiolate, pubescent. Flowers 1 to several in an axillary, scapose inflorescence; calyx 5-partite, or the segments united into 2 lips; corolla tubular or campanulate, limb 2-lipped, upper lip 2-lobed, lobes oblong-elliptic, obtuse, often shorter than lobes of lower lip, lower lip 3-lobed, lobes equal to subequal; stamens 2; disc absent. Fruit a many-seeded capsule. Asia (mts).

CULTIVATION Resembling an African violet, *P. nervosa* is near-hardy in Zone 8 and should certainly stand alpine house conditions, provided it is not overwet, in a fibrous, gritty, acid mix. See GESNERIADS.

***P. kerrii*** Craib. Lvs to 10×6cm, ovate-lanceolate to oblong, irregularly dentate; petiole to 10cm, pilose. Fls 1–3 on scapes to 5cm; cal. 2-lipped, pilose below, glabrous above, 5-lobed, upper 2 lobes to 0.4cm; cor. white, tube to 0.3cm, upper lip to 0.7cm, shorter than lower lip, lobes to 0.4cm, blotched yellow at base; ovary pubesc., style glandular. Thailand. Z10.

***P. nervosa*** Craib. Lvs to 5.5×5.5cm, erect to suberect, obovate to elliptic-obovate or orbicular, obtuse, cuneate to cordate at base, sparsely pilose on veins beneath. Fls solitary or 2–3 on scapes to 6cm; cal. 5-lobed, lobes to 4mm, lanceolate, obtuse; cor. blue, tube to 3mm, limb to 1cm across, upper lobes to 6mm, ciliate, lower lobes to 7mm. Fr. to 5mm. Yunnan. Z9.

***P. parryorum*** C. Fisch. Rhiz. very swollen, densely tomentose at apex. Lvs to 10×3cm, tufted, orbicular or elliptic-ovate or oblong, peltate, obtuse, bullate, margin undulate; petiole to 3.5cm, white-hairy. Fls 1–12 in axillary cymes on scapes to 7.5cm; cor. violet, tube to 0.9cm, obliquely campanulate, lobes to 0.3cm. India. Z10.

**Petromarula** Vent. ex Hedw. f. Campanulaceae. 1 species, a robust perennial herb to 50cm. Leaves to 30cm, pinnately lobed, lobes dentate to serrate. Flowers clustered in a long, unbranched spike; calyx deeply 5-lobed; corolla divided nearly to base in to 5 linear lobes, lobes to 1cm; stamens 5 with filaments swollen at base, anthers free; styles much longer than corolla lobes; stigma knob-like. Fruit a capsule with 3 pores opening at the middle. Crete. Z8.

CULTIVATION As for the alpine species of *Phyteuma*.

***P. pinnata*** (L.) A. DC. As for the genus.

**Petronymphe** H.E. Moore. (From Gk *petros*, rock, and *nymphe*, nymph.) Liliaceae (Alliaceae). 1 species, a perennial herb. Corm tunic membranous. Leaves to 60cm, linear, 5–7-keeled. Scape to 60cm, arched toward summit; inflorescence an umbel, to 14-flowered, subtended by 3–4 spreading bracts; pedicels to 7.5cm, slender; perianth to 5cm, tubular, pale yellow lined green, lobes 6, 0.5cm, spreading; stamens 6, inserted at throat of tube, filaments pale yellow, anthers blue-violet; ovary superior, 3-celled, on a short stalk united to the perianth tube at 3 angles. Mexico. Z9.

CULTIVATION As for *Allium*.

***P. decora*** H.E. Moore. As for the genus.

**Petrophila** R. Br. (From Gk *petros*, rock, and *-philos*, loving, referring to the habit of the species.) Proteaceae. Some 40 species of shrubs. Leaves rigid, coriaceous, often divided. Inflorescence a dense spike or cone, usually terminal, subtended by an involucre of bracts; flowers usually white or yellow; perianth tube slender, usually separating into 4 segments; nectary scales absent; anthers sessile; ovary sessile; with 1 or 2 pendent ovules, style filiform, apex often pubescent, stigma small. Fruit a small, dry indehiscent nut. Australia. Z9.

CULTIVATION Propagate by seed or semi-ripe cuttings, otherwise as for *Hakea*.

***P. biloba*** R. Br. Erect prickly shrub to 2m. Lvs to 1.5cm, rigid, 3-lobed or pinnately 4-lobed. Fls grey to pink, in small, ovoid, sessile, axillary heads; perianth 2cm, villous. Late winter–spring. W Australia.

***P. brevifolia*** Lindl. Erect, spreading shrub to 2m. Lvs 2.5–2.8cm, terete, with long spiny tips. Fls cream-yellow in terminal, sessile, ovate heads; perianth 1.6cm, silky hairy. Mid-winter–late spring. W Australia.

***P. carduacea*** Meissn. Erect shrub to 2cm. Lvs 3–5cm, oblong-lanceolate, sessile, pinnatifid, prickly toothed. Fls yellow, in a globular, later ovoid, axillary, pedunculate head to 3cm. Spring.

***P. circinata*** Kipp. ex Meissn. Dense shrub to 60cm. Lvs 7–12cm, terete, twice pinnate, young growth red; petiole 4–6cm. Fls white to yellow, in large terminal heads. Spring. W Australia.

***P. divaricata*** R. Br. Prickly shrub 1–1.5m. Lvs 3–8cm, divaricate, twice-pinnate, seg. terete. Fls yellow-cream in sessile, ovoid heads in upper lf axils; cone scales villous. Late winter–spring. W Australia.

***P. diversifolia*** R. Br. Erect shrub to 2m. Lvs 3–7cm, doubly compound, trifid, flat lvs. Fls pale-pink to white on axillary, pedunculate heads; perianth tube 12mm. Late winter–spring. W Australia.

***P. drummondii*** Meissn. Erect, rigid, dwarf shrub to 50cm. Lvs 3–6cm, terete, twice or thrice ternately divided; early season lvs shorter than late season. Fls yellow in sessile, terminal, ovoid to globular heads. Spring. W Australia.

***P. ericifolia*** R. Br. Erect, rounded shrub to 1m. Lvs to 1.2cm, glandular or glabrous, terete, blunt, adpressed. Fls yellow in terminal, sessile heads; outer bracts and perianth glutinous, perianth hairy. Late winter–spring. W Australia.

***P. fastigiata*** R. Br. Erect, rounded shrub to 90cm. Lvs to 7cm, erect, obtuse, twice or thrice ternately divided. Fls yellow in terminal, sessile, ovoid heads; perianth 1cm, glabrous. Spring. W Australia.

***P. heterophylla*** Lindl. Straggly erect shrub, to 1–2.5m. Lvs 5–10cm, linear to linear-lanceolate, flattened with prominent veins, 2–3-fid. Fls yellow in axillary, sessile, ovoid-oblong heads; perianth to 2cm long. Late winter–spring. W Australia. Not as attractive as most species and becomes straggly when old. Light pruning makes it bushier.

***P. linearis*** R. Br. PIXIE MOPS. Low, semi-sparse shrub to 1m. Lvs 4–8cm, flat, thick, rigid with rounded margins, falcate. Fls pink, very hairy, in sessile, globular to ovoid, terminal heads; perianth 2.5cm. Spring. W Australia.

***P. longifolia*** R. Br. More or less prostrate shrub, 30–45cm. Lvs 16–30cm, terete, entire. Fls cream to yellow in terminal, sessile heads, 8–10mm long; perianth hairy. Spring. W Australia.

***P. macrostachya*** R. Br. Erect shrub to 1m high. Lvs to 7cm, flat, deeply divided into 3-lobes each lobe often divided into 3 shorter lobes. Fls yellow in a sessile, axillary or terminal, 5cm cone; perianth smooth, 12mm. Fr. with long marginal hairs. Spring. W Australia.

***P. media*** R. Br. Erect, open shrub to 45cm. Lvs 4–10cm, rigid, thick, terete. Fls yellow, sweetly scented, in terminal, sessile, oval heads; perianth villous. Winter–spring. W Australia.

***P. pulchella*** (Schräd.) R. Br. CONESTICKS. Tall, sparse shrub to 3m, sometimes dwarfed to 50cm. Lvs to 9cm, terete, 2–3× pinnate. Fls creamy-yellow, in terminal clusters of 2–3 heads; perianth silky hairy, 14mm. Late spring–summer. E Australia.

***P. rigida*** R. Br. Intensely divaricate, rigid shrub, 60cm–1m. Lvs to 2.5cm, trichotomously divided into terete seg. Fls yellow-white in terminal, sessile, ovoid-oblong, 12mm-diam. heads. Spring. W Australia.

***P. serruriae*** R. Br. Erect, medium, prickly-leaved shrub, 1–2m. Lvs to 3cm, intricately divided, 2–3× pinnate. Fls white-yellow to pink in sessile, solitary, ovoid-globular, 10mm-diam. heads. Late winter–spring. W Australia.

***P. shuttleworthiana*** Meissn. Rigid, rounded, shrub, 60cm–2m. Lvs 7cm, cuneate, deeply 3-fid, seg. linear and sharply pointed; petiole 3.5cm. Fls cream-white in sessile terminal or axillary oblong to cylindrical heads. Late winter–spring. W Australia. Similar to *P. macrostachya*, but the infl. is better displayed and larger.

***P. squamata*** R. Br. Erect shrub, 60cm–1m. Lvs 4cm, long-petioled, once or twice ternately divided in 5–10mm, flat, pungent-pointed lobes. Fls creamy-white in 10mm diam. ovoid, sessile, axillary heads. Late winter–spring. W Australia.

**Petrophytum** Rydb. (From Gk *petra*, rock, and *phyton*, plant, referring to the plant's habitat in rocky crags high in the mountains.) ROCK SPIRAEA. Rosaceae. 3 species of evergreen, caespitose subshrubs; shoots prostrate, very short. Leaves crowded, oblanceolate to spathulate, coriaceous, entire. Flowers bisexual, in short, dense racemes; calyx teeth 5, valvate, calyx cup hemispheric; petals white, 5, overlapping; stamens 20–40, filaments much longer than sepals; carpels 3–7; style filiform; ovary pubescent. Fruit a group of coriaceous follicles, dehiscent on both sutures. N America (mts). Related to *Spiraea*, but leaves evergreen and entire, and follicles dehiscent down both sides.

CULTIVATION They are grown for their neat habit of growth and short spikes of white flowers in summer. *P. hendersonii* forms compact mounds of congested branches with deep green, sometimes bronzed, foliage. The small leaves of *P. caespitosum* form a dense silky carpet, rarely more than 10–15cm/4–6in. across. *Petrophytum* spp. are suitable for growing in tufa, on scree, or in crevices on the rock garden. They may flower more prolifically when grown in the alpine house but are reliably hardy outdoors, *P. hendersonii* as low as −20°C/−4°F, *P. caespitosum* and *P. cinerascens* down to −15°C/5°F. Grow in full sun in perfectly drained, calcareous soils. Grow under glass in a gritty alpine mix and water freely when in growth, keeping dry but not arid in winter. Propagate *P. hendersonii* by softwood cuttings in early summer, in a closed case: cuttings root easily within 6–8 weeks. Other species germinate freely from seed, if sown as soon as it becomes ripe. Sometimes attacked by polyphagous aphids, and in hot dry summers occasionally infested with red spider mite.

***P. caespitosum*** (Nutt.) Rydb. Depressed subshrub forming dense mats to 80cm diam.; branches prostate, densely sericeous-pubesc. Lvs to 12×4mm, spathulate, blue-green, 1-nerved, in rosettes, cauline lvs linear, densely sericeous-pubesc. Peduncles bracteate, to 10cm; spike to 4cm, usually simple; cal. teeth oval-lanceolate, 1.5mm, acute, canescent; pet. 1.5mm, usually obtuse; ovules 2–3. Follicles 3–5, 2mm, 1–2-seeded; seeds linear-obovoid, 1.5mm, smooth, brown. Summer. US (Rocky Mts). Z3.

***P. cinerascens*** (Piper) Rydb. Dense subshrub; shoots short, stout. Lvs oblanceolate, to 2.5cm, obtuse or subacute, thick, coriaceous, 3-veined, ash-grey, sparsely pubesc. Peduncle to 15cm, cinereous; pedicels to 4mm, with linear-subulate bracteoles near base; cal. teeth lanceolate, to 2mm, acuminate, cinereous; pet. spathulate or oblanceolate, 2mm, obtuse. Follicles 4–7, 3mm, sparsely pilose; seed usually solitary, acute at each end. Summer–autumn. N America (Columbia River, Washington). Z5.

***P. elatius*** (S. Wats.) Heller. Dense subshrub. Lvs to 2×0.4cm, oblanceolate, acute, sericeous-pubesc.; petiole usually distinct. Infl. to 10cm, often branched; pedicels to 4mm; cal. slightly turbinate; cal. teeth lanceolate, 2mm, acute or acuminate; pet. oblanceolate, to 3mm. Summer–autumn. Mts of W US (Utah to Arizona).

***P. hendersonii*** (Canby) Rydb. Dense grass-like subshrub; shoots short, stout. Lvs spathulate, to 2×0.6cm, thick, usually 3-veined, sparsely villous. Peduncle to 8cm, sparsely sericeous; pedicels to 5mm, with a small, linear-subulate bracteole at centre; cal. teeth oblong, 1.5mm, obtuse; pet. obovate or oval, 2.5mm. Follicles 2mm, glabrate except for the strigose ciliate upper suture. Summer–autumn. N America (Olympic Mts, Washington). Z5.

For synonymy see *Eriogynia, Luetkea* and *Spiraea*.

**Petrorhagia** (DC.) Link. (From Gk *petra*, rock and *rhagas*, fissure; cf. *Petrocoptis*.) Caryophyllaceae. 25–30 species of annual or perennial herbs, with a general resemblance to species of *Gypsophila*. Technically the genus occupies an intermediate position between *Gypsophila* and *Dianthus*; the epicalyx, if present, is usually not clearly differentiated (but see description of *P. saxifraga* below). Eurasia, especially in the E Mediterranean. Only one species is cultivated to any extent.

CULTIVATION *P. saxifraga*, found in the wild in rocky and sandy habitats to 1300m/4225ft and sometimes naturalized on walls, is tolerant of low-fertility soils and will self-seed freely. Suitable for rock gardens, dry walls, raised beds and for border edging, it is undemanding in cultivation, valued for its dainty habit, delicate texture and for the profusion of pink flowers carried on slender stems in summer; double-flowered forms such as the darker flowered *P. s.* 'Pleniflora Rosea', and the more compact *P. s.* 'Rosette' are particularly attractive. It is hardy to −15°C/5°F. Grow in sun in a well-drained, sandy soil. Propagate species by seed sown in late winter, cultivars by soft stem cuttings of non-flowering shoots in early summer.

***P. saxifraga*** (L.) Link. Subglabrous, mat-forming perenn. to 40cm. Lvs linear, keeled. Infl. a loose-fld cyme; epicalyx bracts 4, membranous, half as long as cal.; cal. 3–6mm, with 5 green angles; pet. 5–10mm, pale pink with deeper pink veins, indented limb and short claw. Summer. S & C Europe. 'Alba': fls white. 'Alba Plena': fls double, white. 'Lady Mary': to 8cm tall; fls double, soft pink. 'Pleniflora Rosea': low; fls double, pink. 'Rosea': fls light pink. 'Rosette': more compact; fls double, pink. Z6.

For synonymy see *Dianthus, Kohlrauschia* and *Tunica*.

**Petroselinum** Hill. (From *petros*, a rock, and *Selinum*.) PARSLEY. Umbelliferae. 3 species of biennials, from thick rootstock. Leaves 1–3-pinnate. Umbels compound; involucre and involucels present; calyx teeth minute; flowers white, green-yellow or tinged red; petals emarginate, apex inflexed. Fruit ovoid, slightly compressed laterally; mericarps with filiform ridges; vittae solitary. Europe.

CULTIVATION A biennial herb, usually cultivated as an annual for its leaves, which are used for flavouring and garnishing. A dual-purpose form of the species, known as Hamburg or turnip-rooted parsley, is also cultivated for its parsnip-shaped roots which provide an excellent winter vegetable. The leaves of Hamburg parsley are hardier than those of the common parsley.

The species is a native of southern Europe and has become naturalized in many temperate countries. It is widely cultivated throughout the world including tropical regions. Parsley is thus tolerant to a fairly wide range of environmental conditions. The natural season of availability is from summer through to early winter but can be readily extended by protecting plants with, for example, cloches or a layer of straw.

Both the stems and leaves can be used as a flavouring and the curly-leaved forms provide an attractive garnish. The broad-leaved forms are said to have a better flavour. Parsley is difficult to dry satisfactorily but may be readily frozen.

A fertile, moisture-retentive soil in either a sunny or partially shaded situation is preferable. The crop grows poorly on light acid soils and plants cannot tolerate poorly drained conditions. Parsley is propagated from seed which is usually sown direct in drills 2cm/¾in. deep to achieve a final spacing of about 10cm/4in. between plants. Hamburg parsley should be spaced at twice this distance to permit full development of the roots. Germination is often slow and may take as long as four to six weeks. It is important to keep the soil moist during this period. Alternatively, plants may be raised under protection in modular trays for transplanting when soil conditions are favourable.

Plants should be kept well watered and free of weeds throughout the growing season. For continuity an early sowing should be made in the spring to provide the main summer supply. A summer sowing will ensure fresh leaves for the autumn and early winter period. The latter can be extended by providing protection to the plants *in situ* or potting up a few for transfer to a cold glasshouse when they will provide a supply through the winter until the following spring. Harvest by cutting fresh leaves as required. Cutting plants back to ground level from time to time will ensure regrowth of fresh leaves. The roots of the Hamburg form may be lifted during the winter and used in a similar way to parsnips. The main pest and disease problems are carrot fly and aphids, which can transmit the carrot motley dwarf virus.

***P. crispum*** (Mill.) A.W. Hill. PARSLEY. Glabrous bienn. to 80cm; stem striate, solid. Lvs triangular in outline, 3-pinnate, seg. ovate, base cuneate, to 3cm, petiole sheathing at base, margins toothed, 3-fid (often crispate in cvs); upper stem lvs with entirely sheathing petiole. Umbels with 8–20 rays, to 3cm, flat-topped, terminal umbel with bisexual fls, lateral umbels with male and bisexual fls; involucral bracts 1–3, entire to 3-fid; involucel of 5–8 bracteoles, small; fls yellow. Fr. to 3mm; mericarps with low ridges, commissure narrow. Summer. Europe. Over 20 cvs; very dwarf and compact to tall and upright, some exceptionally hardy; lvs lightly curled to flat, deeply to finely cut, very dark green to bright emerald. 'Afro' (tall, upright; lvs tightly curled, dark green), 'Clivi' (dwarf, neat; base lvs remain green), 'New Dark Green' (very dwarf, compact, hardy; lvs bright emerald green), 'Paramount' (hardy, vigorous growth; lvs very dark green, dense, closely curled), 'Italian Plain Leaf' (lvs flat, plain, deeply cut, dark green), 'Darki' (very tolerant of cold; lvs very dark green, tightly curled), 'Crispum' (lvs plain, strong flavour), 'Champion Moss

Curled' (lvs curled, finely cut, deep green). var. ***neapolitanum*** Danert. ITALIAN PARSLEY. Lvs not curled. var. ***tuberosum*** (Bernh.) Crov. TURNIP-ROOTED PARSLEY; HAMBURG PARSLEY. Root thick, fleshy, white, edible with nutty flavour.

**Petteria** C. Presl. (For Franz Petter (1798–1853), Professor at Spalata, who wrote on the botany of Dalmatia.) DALMATIAN LABURNUM. Leguminosae (Papilionoideae). 1 species, a shrub, erect, to 2m, allied to *Genista* but leaves trifoliolate, calyx tubular, and upper part of calyx broad, falcate. Leaves to 7cm, long-stalked, trifoliolate; leaflets unequal, elliptic to rounded, glabrous above. Flowers to 2cm, yellow, in upright, dense, terminal clusters; calyx adpressed-pubescent; standard emarginate. Fruit to 5cm, light brown, glabrous. Spring. Yugoslavia (Dalmatia, Montenegro). Z6.

CULTIVATION Occurring in mountain scrub, *Petteria* has an open, upright habit and much resembles *Laburnum* in leaf, although the scented yellow flowers in late spring or early summer are carried in erect racemes at the ends of the current season's growth. As with *Laburnum*, the seeds are poisonous. Hardy to −15°C/5°F and tolerant of poor, dry soils. Grow in moderately fertile, well-drained soil in sun. Pruning is usually unnecessary. Propagate by softwood cuttings in summer or from ripe seed in autumn.

***P. ramentacea*** (Sieber) C. Presl. As for the genus.

For synonymy see *Cytisus*.

**Petunia** Juss. (From Brazilian *Petum*, a name applied to the closely related tobacco plant, *Nicotiana*.) Solanaceae. Some 35 species of annual or perennial herbs or shrubs. Stems branched, pubescent, viscid. Leaves alternate, entire, small; upper leaves subopposite. Flowers solitary, borne in upper leaf axils, violet or white or pale yellow, blue or red to pink; disc fleshy, hypogynous; calyx deeply 5-lobed; corolla salverform to funneliform, tube cylindric, limb lobes equal, overlapping, or spreading; stamens 4, staminode 1, attached to corolla; ovary 2-chambered, style filiform, stigma truncate, capitate. Fruit a 2-chambered capsule; seeds numerous, globose to reniform. Tropical S America. Z7.

CULTIVATION Although many species of *Petunia* are frost-tender herbaceous perennials, the hybrid selections (derived largely from *P. axillaris*, *P. violacea* and *P. integrifolia*) are most commonly grown annually from seed. Their fluted, funnel-shaped flowers provide reliable summer colour over a wide spectrum, encompassing rich violets and crimsons, bicolors and picotees, pale yellows and other pastel shades; modern varieties have added variation in flower shape with doubles and frilled petals. They are used for bedding in borders, tubs and window boxes or cultivated in pots under glass for winter and early spring flowering. The dwarf types make particularly good edging plants and trailing varieties (*e.g.* 'Cloud Mixed' and 'Balcony Blended Mixed') are suitable for hanging baskets, and as summer groundcover in borders; a single plant may cover up to a metre of soil. Grandiflora Hybrids generally have fewer and larger flowers than the Multiflora types, but are less weather resistant, spotting badly after rain: F1 hybrids of both types show increased vigour and uniformity. Extremely tolerant of poorer soils and maritime exposure.

Petunias require plenty of sunshine and settled, dry summer weather to make a good display, although recent developments such as the 'Resisto' and 'Plum Crazy' mixtures show greatly improved performance in windy, rainy conditions. The species, such as large, white-flowered *P. axillaris* and the more prostrate *P. integrifolia*, are less spectacular plants with sparser flowering, but have the natural charm of the wild plant; in temperate areas grow in the cool to intermediate glasshouse. Plant out in the open garden in late spring, early summer into a light, well-drained soil in a sunny position; excessively rich soils and shade cause plants to produce lush foliage at the expense of flowering. Dead-head regularly. Taller plants may require a little support with fine brushwood, especially on exposed sites.

Pot plants should be grown in low-fertility, loam-based medium and given a dilute liquid feed fortnightly when the roots have filled the pots; grow on in a cool, well-ventilated greenhouse or in cold frames and water plentifully during the summer. Give minimum temperatures of 10–13°C/50–55°F in winter and stake lightly.

Propagate from seed pressed lightly on to the surface of a finely sieved seed mix: sow from late summer to autumn for winter- to early spring-flowering pot plants, from late winter to early spring for summer bedding. Germinate at 15–20°C/60–68°F and keep evenly moist, watering from below when necessary. Prick out both large and small seedlings in seed mixtures to retain the balance of colour. Harden off in the cold frame for planting out after the last frosts. Also from softwood cuttings in late summer or early autumn, or in spring from stock plants, cut back and top-dressed in late winter and then forced under gentle heat. Cuttings were the most common method of increasing named varieties until reliable seed strains became available and are still useful for the double-flowered and ruffle-edge sorts which do not always come true from seed.

Susceptible to aphid attack (particularly under glass), beetles, flea-hoppers, tarnished plant bug, scale insect, caterpillars and root knot nematode. A range of viruses which cause leaf mosaic, mottling and failure to flower, include those common to many of the Solanaceae such as cucumber mosaic, tobacco mosaic and, if planted in close proximity to potatoes and tomatoes, potato viruses X and Y: these are transmitted by hands (especially those of smokers), propagating knives and aphids; cuttings may not produce disease-free plants. Virus is not seed-borne. Aphid control, good hygiene and the destruction of affected specimens will limit transmission of the diseases; do not plant near other susceptible subjects or into soil in which infected plants were previously grown. In North America 'Curly Top' and 'Aster Yellows' (a mycoplasma-induced disease) affect cultivated plants. Other disease include foot and root rots induced by a variety of soil-borne fungi (including spp. of *Rhizoctonia*, *Phytopthera* and *Pythium*); heavy, wet and badly aerated soils and planting too deeply will encourage infection. Pot-grown plants and in particular the double-flowered selections are susceptible to conditions of poor soil drainage which may cause yellowing of the foliage.

***P. axillaris*** (Lam.) BSP. LARGE WHITE PETUNIA. Annual herb, to 60cm. Stems decumbent to erect, sticky-pubesc. Lvs ovate to lanceolate-ovate, alternate, sessile, to 5×1.5cm, decurrent. Fls nocturnally fragrant; pedicels to 4cm; cal. to 2cm, lobed, lobes oblong; cor. tube obconic, to 5cm, buff-white, salverform, limb to 5cm diam.; fil. to 3cm, attached to middle of tube. Fr. conic. S Brazil, Uruguay, Argentina.

***P. ×hybrida*** hort. Vilm.-Andr. PETUNIA. A complex group of hybrids, thought to be *P. axillaris* × *P. integrifolia*. Resembles *P. integrifolia*, but habit stouter, fls larger, to 10cm, to 13cm diam., cor. tube funneliform, slightly inflated below throat; stamens attached below middle of cor. tube; limb to 3cm+. Cvs include forms varying in all aspects of flower structure and colour, single or double fls available, many colour-marking patterns. Over 200 cultivars to which new varieties are regularly added, displaying a wide range of flower type, colour and markings; habit from dwarf, compact to tall, occasionally pendulous; fls single or double, striped, prominently veined or picotee, colour ranges from white to blue, mauve and vivid pink. *Fls single.* 'Appleblossom': fls soft flesh-pink, fringed. 'Blue Frost': fls large, violet blue edged white. 'Chiffon Cascade': fls light pastel mauve. 'Burgundy Star': hardy; fls wine red with white star, long-lasting. Daddy Hybrids: well-branched; fls large to 10cm, attractive veining, in range of colours from pastel pink to deep orchid purple. Dazzler Hybrids: to 20cm, compact, neat; fls large, abundant, in range of colours including white, shades of pink, orange, red and violet. 'Fluffy Ruffles': fls 15cm across, often tricoloured with contrasting veining and throat colour, ruffled; seed race. 'Flamenco': fls magenta rose. 'Lacy Sails': fls true blue, veined. 'Sheer Madness': dense to 30cm; fls pink with darker veins, large, prolific. 'Super Cascade Lilac': dwarf, compact; fls rose-lilac; early flowering. 'Super Cascade Blush Improved': dwarf, compact habit, hardy; fls large. 'White Carpet': tall, compact, uniform, hardy; fls white, early flowering. Yellow Magic': vigorous; fls large, lightly ruffled, pale yellow, abundant. *Fls double.* 'Apple Tart': hardy; fls rich scarlet red, fragrant, abundant. 'Blue Danube': fls lavender blue veined dark violet. 'Purple Pirouette': bushy, well-branched; fls bicoloured, purple edged white. 'Red Bouquet': fls large, fringed, bright scarlet. 'Snowberry Tart': fls medium, pure white, fragrant. *Picotee.* 'Blue Picotee': fls large, deep violet with white ruffled edge. 'Hoolahoop': fls intense scarlet edged white. 'Velvet Picotee': fls rich red ringed white, edged ruffled.

***P. integrifolia*** (Hook.) Schinz & Thell. VIOLET-FLOWERED PETUNIA. Annual herb or small, short-lived shrublet, to 60cm. Stems branched, viscid-pubesc.; branches spreading, glandular-pubesc., tips erect. Lvs elliptic to lanceolate, to

5×2cm, entire; petiole to 2.5cm. Fls solitary, axillary, interior violet, exterior violet to rose red; peduncle to 3cm; cor. tube to 4cm, striate; throat to 13mm diam., limb 2-lipped, to 3cm, violet, lobed, lobes 5, obtuse; stamens 4; staminode 1. Argentina.

***P.fimbriata*** hort. See *P.* ×*hybrida*.
***P.grandiflora*** hort. See *P.* ×*hybrida*.
***P.inflata*** R.E. Fries. See *P. axillaris*.
***P.multiflora*** hort. See *P.* ×*hybrida*.
***P.nana*** hort. See *P.* ×*hybrida*.
***P.nyctaginiflora*** Juss. See *P. axillaris*.
***P.superbissima*** hort. See *P.* ×*hybrida*.
***P.violacea*** hort. non Lindl. See *P. integrifolia*.
***P.violacea*** Lindl. See *P. integrifolia*.
For further synonymy see *Nicotiana* and *Salpiglossis*.

**Peucedanum** L. (Name used by Hippocrates.) Umbelliferae. Some 170 species of perennial and biennial herbs or shrubs. Leaves 1- to many times pinnate or ternate. Capitula compound; calyx teeth conspicuous or absent; flowers white to yellow, occasionally pink; petals ovate, with long, inflexed apex. Fruit dorsally compressed; mericarps with winged lateral ridges, and prominent dorsal ridges; vittae 1–3. Eurasia, Tropical & S Africa.

CULTIVATION Widely naturalized in rough grassland habitats. *P.palustre*, milk parsley, occurs in wet habitats on calcareous soils. *P.ostruthium*, masterwort, is native to mountains in central and southern Europe, usually in damp meadows and at streamsides. They are suitable for group planting in the wild garden or in other naturalistic landscapes. Most bear loose umbels of flowers and have finely divided foliage; *P.ostruthium*, was once cultivated as a pot herb and for medicinal use. Grow in any moisture-retentive soil in sun. Propagate by seed.

***P.austriacum*** (Jacq.) Koch. Glabrous perenn. to 120cm; stem solid, branching above. Lvs 3–4-pinnate, seg. pinnately lobed, lobes oblong; upper stem lvs less divided; petioles auriculate. Umbels 15–40-rayed; involucral bracts numerous, deflexed; involucel similar; cal. teeth ovate-lanceolate; fls white. Fr. 6–9mm; mericarps with thin lateral wings 1.5–2.5mm. Summer. C & S Europe. Z6.

***P.cervaria*** (L.) Lapeyr. Subglabrous perenn. to 1.5m; stem terete, striate. Lvs to 50cm, 2–3-pinnate, seg. ovate to ovate-oblong, to 5cm, lower seg. 1–4-lobed, margins sharply dentate. Umbels with 15–30 puberulent rays; involucral bracts numerous, deflexed, some pinnatisect; involucel of numerous, deflexed bracteoles; cal. teeth ovate; fls white. Fr. 5–9mm; mericarps with thick lateral wings to 1mm. C Europe to Asia. Z6.

***P.ostruthium*** (L.) Koch. MASTERWORT. Subglabrous perenn. to 1m; stems hollow, striate. Lvs triangular in outline, 1–2-ternate, seg. 5–10cm, lanceolate to ovate, irregularly toothed, middle seg. occasionally 3-lobed, petiole long, base slightly inflated, sheathing; upper lvs small, seg. often pinnatifid, petiole entirely sheathing, inflated. Umbels with 30–60 rays, to 5cm; involucral bracts few or absent; involucels few; fls white or tinged pink. Fr. *c*4mm; mericarps broad winged. Summer. Mts of C & S Europe. var. ***angustifolium*** (Bellardi) Alef. Lvs narrow. Z5.

***P.palustre*** (L.) Moench. MILK PARSLEY. Subglabrous or glabrescent bienn. to 1.5m; stem hollow, often tinged purple. Lvs to 50cm, 2–4-pinnate, seg. 0.5–2cm, lanceolate to ovate in outline, serrulate, pinnatifid, petiole long, canaliculate above, base sheathing; upper lvs reduced, petiole entirely sheathing. Umbels with 15–40 puberulent rays, to 5cm; involucral bracts usually 4, linear-lanceolate, deflexed; involucels similar; cal. teeth ovate; fls white. Fr. 4–5mm; mericarps with thick wing *c*0.5mm. Summer. Europe to C Asia. Z6.

***P.verticillare*** (L.) Koch ex DC. Monocarpic after 4 or 5 years, 1–3.5m; stems hollow, striate. Lvs to 50cm, triangular in outline, ternately 2–3-pinnate, seg. 2.5–8cm, ovate to ovate-oblong, 3-lobed or irregularly toothed, petiole puberulent; upper lvs reduced, with sheathing petiole. Lateral umbels smaller than terminal umbels and bearing male fls; rays 10–30; involucral bract 1 or absent; involucels few, slender; fls pale green-yellow. Fr. *c*8mm; mericarps with wings to 2.5mm. E & EC Alps, to Hungary and Italy. Z7.

***P.angustifolium*** Rchb. f. See *P. ostruthium* var. *angustifolium*.
***P.graveolens*** (L.) C.B. Clarke. See *Anethum graveolens*.
***P.sativum*** Benth. & Hook. See *Pastinaca sativa*.

**Peumus** Molina. (Latinized form of Chilean vernacular name.) Monimaceae. 1 species, a tree or shrub, 3–6m, rarely much more, dioecious, aromatic. Leaves 3–7×1–5cm, ovate-elliptic or oblong, acute, entire, somewhat coriaceous, rough, dark green above, paler and yellow-pubescent beneath. Inflorescence a short terminal or axillary raceme; flowers 5–10mm across, male larger than female; perianth 10–12 lobed in two series, stellate-pubescent, bearing 5–10 petiolate scales; stamens 40 or more, reduced to nectaries in female, filaments flattened, anthers dehiscing longitudinally; ovary superior, carpels 2–9, free, uniloculate, each with single ovule. Fruit a drupe, 5–7mm long, 2–9 on receptacle, ovoid, fleshy, 1-seeded. Chile. Z9.

CULTIVATION Sometimes grown as an ornamental in warm, frost-free climates such as that of California, otherwise requiring the protection of the cool to intermediate glasshouse, grown in a freely draining, sandy soilless potting mix. Propagate by seed or semi-ripe cuttings in sand in a closed case with bottom heat.

***P.boldus*** Molina. BOLDO. As for the genus.

***P.fragans*** Pers. See *P. boldus*.
For further synonymy see *Boldoa* and *Ruiza*.

**Pfeiffera** Salm-Dyck.
***P.cereiformis*** Salm-Dyck. See *Lepismium ianthothele*.
***P.ianthothele*** (Monv.) F.A. Weber. See *Lepismium ianthothele*.

**Phacelia** Juss. (From Gk *phakelos*, a cluster, referring to the arrangement of the flowers.) SCORPION WEED. Hydrophyllaceae. 150 species of annual, biennial and perennial downy to glandular-pubescent herbs. Leaves largely alternate, pinnatifid, pinnatisect or entire. Flowers blue, violet or white in terminal cymes or racemes; calyx lobes 5, narrow; corolla tubular at base, spreading as a 5-lobed limb, the lobes usually shorter than the tube; stamens 5, anthers inverting at maturity; style bifid, often deeply so. Fruit a 1–2-celled capsule. Western N America, E US, S America.

CULTIVATION Grown in the annual border for their nectar-rich flowers, those of the aromatic *P.campanularia* are of a particularly intense gentian blue, whilst the softer lavender blooms of *P.tanacetifolia* are particularly useful for attracting pollinating bees into the garden. *P.campanularia* thrives in poor sandy soils, and is also useful in pots overwintered in the cool glasshouse, (5–7°C/40–45°F) for early spring flowers. Sow seed under glass in early spring or *in situ* in spring in any moderately fertile well-drained soil in sun. Provide unobtrusive support for taller species.

***P.bipinnatifida*** Michx. Bienn. to 40cm, often smaller, downy throughout, glandular toward apex. Lower lvs large, long-petioled, pinnate, leaflets 3–5, ovate, subsessile, deeply biserrate to pinnatifid. Racemes terminal, loosely many-fld; peduncle glandular-pubesc.; cor. to 1.5cm diam., violet-blue, broadly campanulate, margins ciliate; fil. bearded. Eastern N America. Z5.

***P.campanularia*** A. Gray. CALIFORNIA BLUEBELL. Glandular-hispid annual, 15–40cm. Stems intricately branched. Lvs elliptic to ovate, angular-toothed to irregularly crenate; petiole exceeding lf blade. Cymes lax; cor. to 2.5cm, dark blue spotted white at the base of each cor. lobe sinus, sometimes wholly white, showy, broadly campanulate-funnelform, cor. tube exceeding lobes. S California. Z9.

***P.congesta*** Hook. BLUE CURLS. Hirsute to sericeous annual to 60cm. Stems usually erect. Lvs petiolate toward apex of stems, pinnatifid to finely pinnatisect, lobes irregular, ovate, obtuse. Corymb dense, terminal; cor. to 0.75cm, blue, campanulate; fil. glabrous. Texas, New Mexico.

***P.divaricata*** (Benth.) A. Gray. Downy annual to 30cm. Stems branching freely and spreading at base. Lvs 2.5–7.5cm, oblong or obovate, entire, sparsely toothed near base or, occasionally, 3-lobed. Cymes densely fld; cor. to 1.25cm, blue-violet, campanulate; fil. shorter than cor. N California.

***P.grandiflora*** (Benth.) A. Gray. Robust, glandular-pubesc. annual to 90cm. Lvs to 20cm (petiole included), broadly elliptic to ovate-orbicular, irregularly biserrate, base rounded to truncate; petiole equalling or exceeding blade. Cymes erect, crowded; cor. to 3.25cm, lilac or white. S California.

***P.linearis*** (Pursh) Holzing. Erect pubesc. annual to 32cm, pubescence soft, grey, not glandular. Lvs to 7cm, linear to narrowly lanceolate, usually entire, more rarely pinnatifid or palmatifid, sessile. Infl. short, crowded; cor. to 1.25cm, broadly campanulate, violet or white. Western N America.

***P.minor*** (Harv.) Thell. ex F. Zimm. WHITLAVIA. Erect, viscid, shortly pubesc. annual, 15–60cm. Lvs to 10cm, oblong to ovate, coarsely biserrate, petiolate. Racemes many-fld, terminal; cor. to 2cm, lilac-blue, violet or, rarely, white, tubular-campanulate, base of tube swollen, lobes short, spreading; fil. glabrous. S California. 'Gloxinioides': fls white at centre.

***P.parryi*** Torr. Viscid, downy annual, 15–60cm. Lvs to 10cm, ovate, coarsely biserrate or lobed. Cymes terminal, lax, many-fld; cor. to 2.5cm diam., purple-blue marked or spotted yellow or white at centre, campanulate-rotate, cor. tube equalling or shorter than lobes; fil. bearded. S California to Mexico.

***P. purshii*** Buckley. MIAMI MIST. Downy annual to 75cm. Lvs to 5cm, oblong to elliptic, pinnatifid to pinnate, seg. lanceolate to elliptic, petiolate or sessile, amplexicaul. Cor. light blue, centre white, lobes fringed. E US.

***P. sericea*** (Graham) A. Gray. Bienn. or rather woody-based, short-lived perenn. to 60cm, normally shorter, in some cases dwarf, tufted. Lvs to 10cm, those near base oblong to oblong-elliptic, deeply and, typically, narrowly pinnatifid, sericeous, long-stalked, upper lvs usually entire, sessile. Cymes short, arranged in a dense, spike-like, narrow panicle; cor. deep blue, indigo or mauve, rarely white, campanulate, persistent; stamens long-exserted, fil. 2–3× length of cor. Western N America. ssp. ***ciliosa*** (Rydb.) G. Gillett. Lvs more broadly lobed and less silky. Cor. urceolate-campanulate, half length of fil. Oregon to NE California, Arizona to Wyoming. Z3.

***P. tanacetifolia*** Benth. FIDDLENECK. Erect, hispidulous annual, 15–120cm. Lvs to 24cm, oblong-elliptic to ovate, 1–2× pinnatifid to pinnate, seg. oblong to lanceolate, adpressed short-pubesc.; petiole short. Cymes terminal, crowded, corymbose; cor. to 1.5cm, deeply campanulate, blue to lilac or mauve. California to Mexico.

***P. viscida*** (Benth. ex Lindl.) Torr. Densely glandular-pubesc. annual, 7–55cm. Lvs to 7.25cm, ovate to orbicular, bidentate; petioles short or absent in upper lvs. Cymes lax, borne opposite lvs; cor. to 1.25cm, broadly campanulate, pale blue to lilac, the centre and base of tube flushed rose to purple, rarely pure white; fil. bearded. California.

***P. ciliosa*** Rydb. See *P. sericea* ssp. *ciliosa*.
***P. whitlavia*** A. Gray. See *P. minor*.
For further synonymy see *Eutoca* and *Whitlavia*.

**Phaedranassa** Herb. (From Gk *phaidros*, bright, and *anassa*, lady, referring to the beauty of the flowers.) QUEEN LILY. Amaryllidaceae. About 6 species of bulbous, herbaceous perennials, 25–60cm. Leaves 1–4, petiolar, narrow to broadly oblong, appearing at same time as or after flowers; blades 15–30×3–7cm; petioles 5–18cm. Flowers 4–11, showy, drooping, borne in umbels on scapes to 70cm; perianth narrow funnel-shaped or nearly cylindric, with narrow, spreading lobes at apex, red marked with green or bi-coloured; flowers similar to those of *Urceolina* but differ in having corona of hyaline teeth between the 6 anther filaments; stamens exserted. Fruit a globose, deeply furrowed, 3-valved capsule containing many small black seeds. S America; native to Andes but cultivated in Costa Rica. Z8.

CULTIVATION Widely cultivated in their native regions, *Phaedranassa* spp. are rarely grown in Europe, although in temperate zones they make beautiful plants for the cool glasshouse or conservatory or, in mild-winter areas in a well-drained border, at the base of a south wall. In spring or early summer *Phaedranassa* spp. bear umbels of brilliantly coloured, narrowly tubular flowers with anthers protruding from the rim of the bell; in *P. carmioli* they are bright red, flushed green at the base and marked with green and yellow at the lips. The leaves appear with or slightly later than the flowers.

Plant in autumn, with the bulb neck at soil level, in a mix of equal parts loam, leafmould, and sharp sand; keep cool and just moist until growth begins, then water moderately and grow in full light at a minimum temperature of 7°C/45°F. Dry off as foliage dies down in late summer or autumn, and keep cool and dry over winter until growth resumes in early spring. Propagate by offsets and seed.

***P. carmioli*** Bak. To 60cm. Bulb to 5cm diam. Lvs 1–3, ovate, to 60cm including 20cm-long petiole. Fls 6–10, to 5cm, straight, glaucous crimson, tipped green with yellow fringe; perianth seg. largely united; stamens shortly exserted, fil. white; scape to 60cm. Fr. 1.5×0.5cm. Spring–summer. S America.

***P. cinerea*** Ravenna. Bulb 3.7–6×2–6cm, neck to 8cm. Lvs 2, elliptic-lanceolate, to elliptic, 29–51×7–15cm, short-acuminate, tapering to base, olive-green or grey above, somewhat glaucous; petiole 11–17cm. Scape 25–80cm; fls 7–17, 3.2–5.5cm long, coral-pink, green at apex, separated by narrow white band, perianth tubular; stamens exserted, fil. white, anth. green with yellow pollen. Ecuador.

***P. dubia*** HBK. Fls 5cm long or more, purple-pink, tipped green; perianth lobes revolute; stamens exserted by 7mm; scape to 45cm. Spring–summer. Peru. var. ***obtusa*** Herb. Perianth lobes obtuse. Peru.

***P. lehmannii*** Reg. Lvs solitary, elliptic-lanceolate, acute, dark green above, glaucous green below. Fls in 3-fld umbel, to 2.5cm, scarlet, lobes shortly spreading; stamens exserted by 1.5–2cm. Spring–summer. Colombia.

***P. schizantha*** Bak. Fls with very short green tube; perianth lobes convergent at tips, to 3cm, bright red, fading to pink at apices. Late autumn. Ecuador.

***P. tunguraguae*** Ravenna. Bulb ovoid, 5.5×4.5–5cm, neck short, brown. Lvs 3 or less, hysteranthous, lanceolate or oblanceolate, 29–40×5.3–8cm, glossy dark green; petiole 6–9cm. Scape terete, solid, to 54cm; fls 6–8, to 3.2cm long, coral-red, apex green; perianth seg. connate at base to 3.5mm. Ecuador.

***P. viridiflora*** Bak. Bulb 4–5×3–4cm, neck 6cm, brown. Lvs 2–3, hysteranthous, narrow-lanceolate, 25–40×4–5cm, bright green above; petiole 6–9cm. Scape to 66cm; fls 5, yellow-green, campanulate-tubular; perianth tube 1cm, tepals oblanceolate, to 2.4cm. Ecuador and possibly Peru.

***P. chloracra*** Herb. See *P. dubia*.
***P. eucrosioides*** (Bak.) Benth. & Hook See *Eucrosia stricklandii*.
***P. rubro-viridis*** Bak. See *Eustephia coccinea*.
***P. ventricosa*** Roezl. ex Wallace. See *P. dubia*.

**Phaedranthus** Miers.
***P. buccinatorium*** (DC.) Miers. See *Distictis buccinatoria*.

**Phaenocoma** D. Don (From Gk *phainos*, shining, and *kome*, hair; from the nature of the involucre.) Compositae. 1 species, a leafy, monoecious, evergreen shrub, to 60cm, lanate at first. Leaves very small, ovate, acuminate, often scale-like, imbricate. Capitula discoid, solitary, to 4cm diam.; phyllaries in several rows, red-purple, outer shortest, adpressed, inner recurved; florets numerous, bright yellow, outer female, inner male. Fruit a cypsela; pappus of scabrous bristles. Winter. S Africa (SW Cape). Z9.

CULTIVATION Grown on sunny rockeries and borders in warm, mediterranean-type climates, otherwise in the cool glasshouse; the flowers are useful for drying. Grow in full sun, with good ventilation, in well-crocked pots with a medium comprising equal parts sieved leafmould and silver sand; water moderately and carefully when in full growth, keeping almost dry in winter. Repot if necessary as growth resumes in spring. Propagate by seed or by semi-ripe cuttings in sand over a layer of peat in a closed case with gentle bottom heat.

***P. prolifera*** (L.) D. Don. As for the genus.

**Phaeomeria** Lindl. ex Schum.
***P. magnifica*** (Roscoe) Schum. See *Etlingera elatior*.
***P. speciosa*** (Bl.) Merrill. See *Etlingera elatior*.

**Phaius** Lour. (*Phajus*) (From Gk *phaios*, grey, referring to the flowers which darken with age or damage.) Orchidaceae. Some 30 species of terrestrial orchids. Stems with or without pseudobulbs, sometimes cylindric. Leaves few, large, plicate. Inflorescence an axillary, erect raceme; flowers showy; sepals and petals similar, spreading; lip entire or lobed, sessile, erect, fused to the column; base spurred or inflated. Indomalaya, S China, Tropical Australia. Z10.

CULTIVATION Striking terrestrial orchids for shaded, humid positions in the intermediate or warm greenhouse. The most commonly grown is *P. tankervilliae* with broad leaves overtopped by erect racemes of topaz to chocolate and rose-pink flowers. *P. flavus* is valued for its yellow-spotted leaves. Pot in well-crocked clay long-toms in a mix of bark, leafmould, charcoal, garden compost and a little dried FYM. Water throughout the year, allowing a slight drying between applications and avoiding wetting of foliage. Repot every third year and increase by division.

***P. australis*** F. Muell. Pseudobulbs ovoid, clustered, 4–7-leaved, to 7×7cm. Lvs lanceolate, plicate, dark green, to 125×10cm. Infl. to 2m; fls 4–10, to 10cm diam., maroon, veined yellow above, white below; sep. elliptic, acuminate; pet. oblong-ovate, to 6cm; lip midlobe crisped, lateral lobes entire, enveloping the column and callus plate, from lip base to apex; spur to 10mm, narrow. Australia.

***P. callosus*** (Bl.) Lindl. Pseudobulbs 6–12cm. Lvs elliptic to oblong-lanceolate, acuminate 60–110×16–26cm; petiole to 40cm. Sep. and pet. yellow-brown above, red-brown beneath, lip long-pubesc., white often golden yellow, blotched violet or yellow, streaked red-brown, spur yellow; sep. and pet. oblong, obtuse, to 5cm; lip trilobed, crenate, plicate, midlobe rectangular, forward-pointing, lateral lobes round; spur conic. Malaysia.

***P. flavus*** (Bl.) Lindl. Pseudobulbs ovoid-cylindric, to 10–15×5–6cm. Lvs elliptic-lanceolate, acuminate, spotted pale yellow, 40–48×10–11cm. Infl. 30–45cm; fls 6–8cm diam., yellow, rarely white, lip streaked brown, spur white;

sep. oblong, to 4cm; pet. similar, smaller; lip remotely trilobed, rhombic-orbicular, interior hirsute, midlobe trapezoid, lateral lobes rounded; spur conic. India, Malaysia, Java.

***P. francoisii*** (Schltr.) Summerh. Similar to *P. humblotii* except lip laterals yellow, dotted red, apical point of midlobe deeper red, tepals narrower. Madagascar.

***P. humblotii*** Rchb. f. 45–80cm. Pseudobulbs spheric. Lvs elliptic-lanceolate, plicate, acute, 25–40×6–10cm. Infl. 60–90cm; fls 7–10, rose, blotched white and red, lip midlobe deeper; sep. ovate, 3–3.5×2cm; pet. similar, smaller; lip to 3×3cm, trilobed, base hirsute, lateral lobes rounded, erect, apex teeth 2, yellow. Madagascar.

***P. mishmensis*** (Lindl.) Rchb. f. To 140cm, usually shorter. Pseudobulbs obscure. Stems fleshy, sheathed below, leafy above. Lvs 6–8, elliptic-lanceolate to oblong-ovate, plicate, 15–30×8–12.5cm. Infl. lax, to 30cm; fls erect, 5–6cm diam., pale rose, purple-brown or dark red, lip pink or white, speckled purple; sep. linear-oblong, erect, spreading concave, to 3.5×1cm; pet. linear-oblanceolate, narrow, acute, to 3×0.6cm; lip cuneate at base, midlobe subquadrate or oblong, entire, notched, lateral lobes rounded, embracing column, disc ridge central, pubesc.; spur conical, arched, narrow, to 1.5cm. India, Burma, Thailand to Philippines.

***P. tankervilliae*** (Banks) Bl. 60–200cm. Pseudobulbs ovoid-conic, 2.5–6cm. Lvs elliptic-lanceolate, acuminate, 30–100×20cm; petiole 15–25cm. Infl. erect; fls 10–20, 10–12.5cm diam.; white, green or rose beneath, red yellow-brown, or white above, edged gold, lip interior pink to burgundy, base yellow, exterior white, midlobe red-orange or white and pink; sep. and pet. lanceolate or oblanceolate, spreading, acuminate; lip tubular becoming trilobed, ovate-lanceolate, acuminate, acute or truncate, apex crisped, recurved; spur slender, apex forked. Himalaya to Australia.

***P. tetragonus*** Rchb. f. Stems to 30cm+, 4-angled, subalate. Lvs ovate-lanceolate, plicate, long-acuminate. Infl. lax; fls large, 8–10, maroon, tinted green above, green below, lip orange-red, streaked yellow; sep. and pet. similar oblong, acute; lip midlobe crisped, apex broad-pointed, central lamellae, 3, lateral lobes embracing column. Mauritius, Sri Lanka.

***P. tuberculosus*** (Thouars) Bl. Rhiz. short, ascending. Pseudobulbs along rhiz., small, obscured by lf sheaths, 5–6-leaved. Lvs lanceolate, narrow, plicate, 30–60×2–3cm; petiole long, sheathing. Infl. 40–65cm; fls white, lip midlobe white, margins spotted lilac or violet, lateral lobes yellow, dotted red, disc and callus yellow; sep. elliptic-lanceolate, 3.2–4.4cm; pet. similar, slightly smaller, to 2.4cm; lip spreading, obscurely trilobed, midlobe deflexed, spreading, undulate, lateral lobes semi-orbicular, glabrous, erect, spreading; disc base glandular-pubesc., ridges 3, warty. Madagascar.

***P. grandifolius*** Lour. See *P. tankervilliae*.
***P. maculatus*** Lindl. See *P. flavus*.
***P. roseus*** Rolfe. See *P. mishmensis*.
***P. wallichii*** Hook. f. See *P. tankervilliae*.

**Phalacraea** DC. (From Gk *phalakros*, bald, referring to the lack of a pappus on the achene.) Compositae. 4 species of perennial herbs; stems decumbent at base. Leaves opposite, ovate to oblong or triangular, crenate to serrate, glandular-punctate beneath. Capitula discoid, in loose cymes; phyllaries in 2–4-series, subequal, gland-dotted; florets white. Fruit a prismatic, ribbed cypsela; pappus absent. Colombia, Ecuador, Peru. Z10.

CULTIVATION As for *Piqueria*.

***P. latifolia*** DC. To 50cm. Lvs broadly ovate to deltoid, base truncate to cordate. Capitula 5–6mm diam.; florets tinged purple. Peru.

For synonymy see *Piqueria*.

**Phalacrocarpum** (DC.) Willk. (From Gk *phalakros*, bold-headed, and *karpos*, fruit.) Compositae. 2 species of perennial herbs. Stems woody at base. Leaves opposite, toothed to deeply divided. Capitula radiate, solitary; receptacle convex, naked; phyllaries in 3 series; ray florets female, white or purple; disc florets tubular-campanulate, 5-lobed, yellow, outer hermaphrodite, fertile, inner male or sterile and petaloid. Fruit an obconical-cylindrical, slightly compressed cypsela with 6–7-ribs, white. SW Europe. Z9.

CULTIVATION As for *Andryala*.

***P. oppositifolium*** (Brot.) Willk. Grey-white tomentose or silky. Stems simple or branched at base, ascending. Lvs obovate, pinnatipartite to pinnatisect, seg. lanceolate or 2-pinnatisect with linear lobes. Capitula 3–5.5cm diam., on peduncles to 20cm. N & C Portugal, N Spain.

**Phalaenopsis** Bl. (From Gk *phalaina*, moth and *opsis*, appearance.) MOTH ORCHID. Orchidaceae. 40 species of epiphytic, monopodial orchids. Stems short, usually simple, composed of overlapping leaf bases, freely producing adventitious roots. Leaves 2–6, distichous, alternate, broad-obovate or oval, often drooping, glabrous, glossy or coarsely papillose, dark green flushed purple or mottled grey, green and silver, midvein sometimes sunken, base conduplicate with a distinct abscission line above short, fleshy sheath. Inflorescence axillary, appearing basal, erect to arching, a simple or branched raceme; flowers one to many; sepals almost equal, free, spreading, elliptic to broadly spathulate, usually smaller than petals; lip 3-lobed, fused to column foot or at right angles, midlobe fleshy with complex basal calli, apex often lobed, the lobes terminating in horn-like projections or filaments, highly coloured, lateral lobes erect. Asia, Australasia. Z10.

CULTIVATION Epiphytes for the intermediate or warm greenhouse, growing cases (especially *P. cornu-cervi* and *P. violacea*) and warm shaded and humid positions in the home. Grown for their beautiful moth-like flowers matched, in some species, by superbly marked foliage (*P. schilleriana* and *P. stuartiana*). Many grexes are now offered. Grow in pots, baskets or on rafts. The medium should consist of coarse bark, perlag and charcoal. Rooting is freely adventitious and should be encouraged by frequent mistings (periodically with a dilute feed), but never when temperatures are below 18°C/65°F, at which point rots will be encouraged by an accumulation of moisture in the vulnerable growth axis. A humid, buoyant atmosphere is essential, as is shade. Drench pots throughout the year whenever the medium begins to dry out. Propagate by meristem culture or by plantlets sometimes produced on old inflorescences.

***P. amabilis*** (L.) Bl. Lvs to 5, elliptic, to obovate, coriaceous or fleshy, glossy green above, to 50×10cm. Infl. arching, to 1m; fls to 10cm diam., fragrant, sep. and pet. white, often pink below, sep. elliptic-ovate, to 4×2.5cm, pet. larger, almost circular; lip white, base red, margins yellow, midlobe cruciform, side projections triangular, with 2 yellow-tipped appendages, callus almost square, yellow, dotted red, ridges 2, lateral lobes oblanceolate. E Indies, Australia.

***P. amboinensis*** J.J. Sm. Lvs to 4, elliptic to oblong-elliptic or oblanceolate, to 25×10cm. Infl. 1 or several, arching; fls few, cream to orange-yellow, striped cinnamon; dorsal sep. elliptic to ovate-elliptic, lateral sep. broadly ovate or ovate-elliptic, keeled near apex; pet. ovate or rhombic-ovate; lip clawed, midlobe ovate or oblong-ovate, central keel margins serrate, apex merging with spherical callus, lateral lobes oblong-ligulate, apex falcate. Indonesia.

***P. aphrodite*** Rchb. f. Resembles *P. amabilis* except in fls to 7cm diam.; lip midlobe subtriangular, not cruciform, callus with deeper red markings. Philippines to Taiwan.

***P. cochlearis*** Holtt. Lvs 2–4, oblong-ovate to oblong-elliptic, prominently veined above, to 20×10cm. Infl. branched, to 50cm; fls few, white to pale green or yellow, sep. and pet. with 2 light to orange-brown basal stripes, dorsal sep. narrow to lanceolate-elliptic, to 20×10mm, somewhat revolute, lateral sep. ovate, pet. narrow-elliptic or lanceolate-elliptic; lip fleshy, midlobe primrose, striped red to orange-brown, orbicular, apex rounded or notched, disc ridged, central calli lamellate, lateral lobes oblong-linear, centrally grooved. Sarawak.

***P. corningiana*** Rchb. f. As *P. sumatrana* except fls few, to 5cm diam.; sep. and pet. pale yellow, apex vertically or horizontally barred mahogany red to crimson, dorsal sep. obovate to oblanceolate, lateral sep. ovate, apex channelled, pet. lanceolate; lip midlobe and column base deep magenta to carmine, midlobe elliptic-oblong, narrow, convex, central keel apex callused, pubesc., callus forked, orange-yellow, lateral lobes oblong-ligulate. Borneo, Sarawak.

***P. cornu-cervi*** (Breda) Bl. & Rchb. f. Lvs oblong to ligulate, apex often shallowly bilobed, to 25×4cm, olive green. Infl. to 40cm, branching, floral axis flattened, broad with 2 rows of alternate bracts; fls waxy yellow to yellow-green; sep. marked red-brown, blotches stripes and spots cinnamon, apices keeled, dorsal sep. obovate-elliptic, margins weakly recurved, lateral sep. elliptic to elliptic-lanceolate; pet. lanceolate; lip fleshy, white, midlobe anchor-shaped, projections hooked, lateral lobes almost square, red-brown or striped cinnamon. SE Asia.

***P. equestris*** (Schauer) Rchb. f. Lvs to 5, oblong, apex channelled, base tapering, to 20×6.5cm, somewhat coriaceous, dark green above, often flushed rose-purple beneath. Infl. 1 to many, arched, simple or branched, to 30cm; fls to 4cm diam.; sep. and pet. rose or white suffused rose, sep. oblong-elliptic, margins slightly recurved, pet. elliptic; lip deep pink to purple, midlobe ovate, concave, apex fleshy, callus 6–8-sided, peltate, yellow, spotted red, lateral lobes oblong, marked yellow. Philippines, Taiwan.

***P.fasciata*** Rchb. f. Stem short. Lvs elliptic to obovate, to 20cm. Infl. erect or arched; fls fleshy, waxy, pale to deep yellow, to 4cm diam., sep. and pet. striped or banded red-brown to cinnamon; dorsal sep. elliptic, lateral sep. ovate-elliptic; pet. similar, oblique; lip midlobe oblong-ovate, convex, apex magenta, base orange-yellow, central keels terminal, callus ovate, orange, central disc orange, papillose, projecting appendage forked, lateral lobes ligulate, dotted orange. Philippines.

***P.fimbriata*** J.J. Sm. Lvs oblong-elliptic, arched 15–25cm. Infl. to 30cm, pendent; fls many, opening simultaneously, white to cream, basal bars magenta; sep. and pet. ovate-elliptic, to 2cm; lip midlobe ovate, convex, fleshy, fringed, upcurved, central keel dentate, terminal callus white-pubesc., callus at lateral lobe junction with 3 plates, lateral lobes oblong, convex. Java, Sumatra.

***P.gigantea*** J.J. Sm. Lvs 5–6, oblong-ovate, pendent, coriaceous, glossy, to 50×20cm. Infl. to 40cm; fls scented, cream to yellow, sep. and pet. blotched and lined maroon to dark purple, sep. spreading, elliptic, base fused to the column foot, pet. elliptic; lip fleshy, white, striped, or lined magenta, midlobe ovate, apical callus ovoid, bidentate, lateral lobes triangular, centrally callused. Borneo, Sabah.

***P.hieroglyphica*** (Rchb. f.) H. Sweet. Lvs broadly ligulate, coriaceous, to 30×10cm. Infl. pendent or arched; sep. and pet. white lined red-purple, apex tinted green, ovate-elliptic, apex keeled; lip to 2cm, midlobe truncate, apex jagged, central keel pubesc., fleshy, terminal callus ovoid, lateral lobes oblong, apex notched, callus between lateral lobes papillose, appendages 2, forked. Philippines.

***P.*×*intermedia*** Lindl. (*P.aphrodite* × *P.equestris.*) Lvs elliptic, fleshy, arched, green above, purple beneath, to 30×8cm. Fls white to deep rose; dorsal sep. elliptic, lateral sep. ovate, to 4cm; pet. elliptic; lip midlobe obovate, apex tapering, bidentate, central callus almost square, lateral lobes obovate. Philippines.

***P.*×*leucorrhoda*** Rchb. f. (*P.aphrodite* × *P.schilleriana.*) Lvs green above, spotted silver-grey, purple beneath. Infl. arching, pendent, to 70cm. Fl. variable, pure white to deep rose, margins rose; sep. elliptic to ovate; pet. reniform to circular; lip white, dotted or lined yellow and purple (rarely entirely purple), midlobe variable, apex tapering, filamentous or anchor-shaped, appendages 2, callus irregularly dentate, deep yellow, rarely paler, spotted deep red, lateral lobes spathulate. Philippines.

***P.lindenii*** Loher. Lvs oblong-lanceolate, dappled silver-white, to 25×4cm. Infl. dense, fls tinged white, dotted rose at centre; dorsal sep. oblong-elliptic, lateral sep. oblong-ovate; pet. elliptic-rhombic; lip to 1.5cm, midlobe circular, centrally concave, tipped purple-pink, lined rose, apex pointed, central callus 6–8-sided, lateral lobes obovate to ligulate, white, basally dotted red or orange, with 3 purple lines at apex. Philippines.

***P.lobbii*** (Rchb. f.) H. Sweet. Lvs broad, elliptic, to 13×5cm. Sep. and pet. cream, dorsal sep. oblong-elliptic, lateral sep. ovate, pet. obovate, to 8×5mm; lip with 2 vertical red-brown stripes, fused to column foot, midlobe mobile, triangular, apex rounded, basal plate margins irregular, minutely dentate, central callus fil. 4. India, Himalaya.

***P.lueddemanniana*** Rchb. f. Lvs oblong-elliptic, arched, spreading or pendent, dull olive green, to 30×10cm, usually shorter. Infl. erect or pendent, to 30cm, branched or simple, flexuous, becoming horizontal; fls to 6cm diam.; sep. and pet. white, laterally or horizontally striped brown-purple, dorsal sep. elliptic to oblong-elliptic, lateral sep. ovate-elliptic, to 3cm, pet. smaller; lip to 2.5cm, carmine, base yellow, midlobe oblong to ovate, apical callus white, pubesc., papillose at lobe junction, projection bifid, lateral lobes oblong. Philippines.

***P.maculata*** Rchb. f. Lvs 2–3, oblong-ligulate, to 20×4cm. Infl. arched, simple; fls few; sep. and pet. white or pale rose, banded purple, dorsal sep. oblong-elliptic, lateral sep. ovate-elliptic, shorter than sep.; lip white, midlobe oblong, convex, base keeled, apex purple, callused, central callus appendage bifid, lateral lobes oblong, apex notched. Borneo, Sulawesi.

***P.mannii*** Rchb. f. Lvs 4–5, oblong, to 40×7cm. Infl. pendent, usually simple; fls fragrant, to 4.25cm, many, opening in succession; sep. and pet. green or yellow, blotched cinnamon, sep. ovate-lanceolate, apex keeled beneath, pet. lanceolate, margins revolute, to 2cm; lip to 10mm, white and purple, midlobe anchor-shaped, callus often hirsute, basally continuing into midlobe, forming a central, semicircular callus, lateral lobes almost square, toothed, papillose. Himalaya, Vietnam.

***P.mariae*** Warner & Williams. Lvs fleshy, ligulate, to 30×7cm. Infl. pendent, branched or simple; fls to 5cm diam.; sep. and pet. oblong-elliptic, white or cream, horizontally striped and blotched brown-red, base rarely spotted purple; lip pale mauve to purple, midlobe expanded, apex dentate, central keel and apical callus pubesc., central callus projections several, bifid, lateral lobes broadly ligulate, apices toothed. Philippines.

***P.micholitzii*** Rolfe. Lvs obovate, arching to pendent, to 16×6cm. Infl. arching; fls successional, white to pale green; dorsal sep. elliptic, lateral sep. ovate; pet. ovate-elliptic, to 3×2cm; lip fleshy, midlobe rhombic, central patch villous, apical swelling tapering to a basal keel, central callus bifid, lateral lobes falcate, calli orange-yellow. Philippines.

***P.pallens*** (Lindl.) Rchb. f. Lvs elliptic to obovate, fleshy, pendent, to 20cm. Infl. arching or erect; fls solitary or few, to 5cm diam., sep. and pet. pale lemon to yellow-green, horizontal lines and dashes brown, oblong-elliptic, to 2cm; lip to 2cm, midlobe white, ovate, narrow, apex margins dilated, dentate, base keeled, apical callus pubesc., callus appendages at lobe junction 2, bifid, lateral lobes oblong, yellow. Philippines.

***P.parishii*** Rchb. f. Lvs elliptic to obovate, fleshy, arching or pendent, to 12×5cm, dark green. Infl. erect or arching, to 15cm; fls open simultaneously; sep. and pet. white, sep. elliptic to circular, dorsal sep. to 8mm, lateral sep. to 10mm, pet. elliptic to obovate; lip to 1.5cm, midlobe purple, triangular, callus semicircular, margins fringed, central disc projections bristle-like, lateral lobes vestigial, triangular, white or yellow, spotted brown or purple. Himalaya, Vietnam.

***P.pulchra*** (Rchb. f.) H. Sweet. Lvs oblong-elliptic, arched, fleshy, to 15×5cm. Fls few, deep magenta-purple, with faint stripes or bars; dorsal sep. erect, elliptic, lateral sep. ovate; pet. elliptic or ovate-elliptic; lip midlobe ovate to flabellate, keel irregularly dentate, disc papillose, apex callused, midlobe callus fleshy, bifid, lateral lobes oblong-linear, erect. Philippines.

***P.reichenbachiana*** Rchb. f. & Sander. Lvs elliptic to obovate, to 35×7cm. Infl. erect or arched, to 45cm; fls to 4cm diam.; sep. and pet. green-white to yellow, barred red-brown and cinnamon, dorsal sep. elliptic or elliptic-ovate, lateral sep. ovate to ovate-lanceolate, pet. ovate to ovate-elliptic; lip base orange-yellow, midlobe ovate, angular, tipped magenta and pale violet, apex margins with minute irregular dentations, callus yellow, bifid, lateral lobes white, oblong-linear to circular, becoming papillose. Philippines.

***P.sanderiana*** Rchb. f. Lvs 1–3, elliptic or oblong-elliptic, dark green above, marked silver-grey beneath. Infl. to 80cm, axis purple, branched or simple; fls to 7.5cm diam., colour and marking variable, sep. and pet. ovate-elliptic, pink, dappled white, or wholly white; lip to 3cm, midlobe triangular, white or yellow, striped purple or brown, apex with 2 filiform projections, callus horseshoe-shaped, yellow or white, spotted red, brown, or purple, lateral lobes ovate, white, spotted pink. Philippines.

***P.schilleriana*** Rchb. f. Lvs elliptic, dark green, mottled silver-grey above, purple beneath, to 45×11cm. Infl. branching, pendent; fls to 250+, fragrant, white to pink, mauve and rose-purple; sep. and pet. edged white, dorsal sep. elliptic, to 3.5cm, lateral sep. similar, ovate, basally spotted carmine-purple, pet. rhombic, undulate; lip midlobe circular, white to magenta, appendages 2, anchor-shaped, central callus base truncate, lateral lobes elliptic, spreading, basally yellow, dotted red-brown. Philippines.

***P.speciosa*** Rchb. f. Lvs elliptic, arched or recurved, to 20×8cm. Infl. arched or pendent, to 30cm; fls fleshy; sep. and pet. oblong-elliptic, white-rose, blotched purple, pet. bases striped white; lip midlobe ovate, white, marked purple, central keel serrate, apical callus pubesc., central callus appendage bifid, lateral lobes triangular, yellow at base, tips white. Nicobar Is.

***P.stuartiana*** Rchb. f. Lvs fewer, narrower and shorter than in *P.schilleriana*, elliptic-oblong, green blotched grey above, purple beneath, to 35×8cm. Infl. branched, pendent, to 60cm; fls to 6cm diam., fragrant; sep. white, lateral sep. elliptic to ovate-elliptic, yellow, dotted red-brown at base; pet. almost square to circular, lacking yellow base; lip to 2.5cm, almost circular, apex anchor-shaped, callus spotted orange, almost square, apical projections on lateral lobes similar to lateral sep. in colour, obovate, basal appendages white, horn-like. Philippines.

***P.sumatrana*** Korth. & Rchb. f. Lvs oblong to obovate, to 30×11cm. Infl. erect or slightly arched, rarely branched, to 30cm; fls to 5cm diam.; sep. and pet. oblong-lanceolate, white to pale yellow, banded cinnamon; lip midlobe oblong-elliptic, white, with red or purple stripes flanking a central keel, apex hirsute, callus of several forked plates, lateral lobes linear-oblong, cream, often spotted orange, margin brown or yellow, apices bidentate. Malaysia, Sumatra, Borneo, Java.

***P.violacea*** Witte. Habit diminutive. Lvs elliptic to obovate, to 25×12cm, glossy light green. Infl. ascending or arched, thick, jointed, to 12.5cm; fls few (usually only one opening at the time), to 4.5cm diam.; sep. and pet. broadly elliptic, sharply acute, obscurely keeled beneath, often slightly incurved, amethyst fading to white or lime green at apex; lip midlobe oblong, convex, apiculate, with central keel, violet tipped with white pubescence, central crest yellow, forked toward midlobe, lateral lobes short, erect, oblong, yellow; column white or amethyst. Colour highly variable; forms from Borneo are of the deepest mauve and often fragrant. Sumatra, Borneo.

***P.*grexes and cultivars.**

*P.* Abendrot: large plants with dark green lvs and tall spikes; fls deep pink, up to 10cm diam.

*P.* Allegria: large plants with arching and branching sprays of nearly pure white fls.

*P.* Barbara Moler: compact plants with long, branching fl. spikes; fls star-shaped, 5–7.5cm diam., white heavily overlaid with pink spots and solid pink near the centre; some forms are yellow-green with light brown blotches, lip purple and orange.

*P.* Cabrillo Star 'Santa Cruz': strong growing plants with long arching spikes;

fls of good shape, 10–10.5cm diam., white, generously dotted with magenta freckles, lip very dark magenta.

*P.* Capitola 'Moonlight': large robust plants with very strong arching spikes of many fls; fls white, 10–10.5cm diam.

*P.* Caribbean Sunset: compact plants; fls star-shaped, yellow, striped and spotted with chestnut.

*P.* Carmen Coll: compact plants; strong spikes of deep pink fls, darker in the centre, lip brilliant orange and petunia purple.

*P.* Cassandra: small but compact and strong plants; fls white with spotted sep., miniature.

*P.* Cast Iron Monarch 'The King': very large plants with tall arching sprays; a famous hexaploid clone with large white fls to 12.5cm diam.

*P.* Doris: one of the first of the large white-fld hybrids, large plants with long arching sprays; also a few pale pink clones.

*P.* Elise de Valec 'Boissy': strong plants with branching spikes; fls good shape, white or cream, heavily overlaid with red spots, lip outlined with yellow.

*P.* Esme Hennessy: compact plants; well-shaped white fls, red lip.

*P.* Gladys Read 'Snow Queen': large robust plants with arching sprays of many fls; fls pure white; 10–12.5cm diam.

*P.* Golden Amboin: strong growing plants with tall spikes; fls star-shaped, primrose yellow, evenly dusted with fine chestnut freckles, lip orange red, 7.5–9cm diam.

*P.* Golden Emperor: compact plants with few-fld sprays of lemon yellow fls, orange lip.

*P.* Golden Sands: medium-sized plants with branching spikes; fls lemon yellow with dense covering of fine light brown spots, orange at the lip base.

*P.* Gorey 'Trinity': strong plants with tall spikes; fls large and good shape, deep yellow which does not fade, white towards the centre and with darker yellow on the lip.

*P.* Hennessy: compact plants with branching fl. spikes blooming throughout the year; fls well-shaped, 7.5–11cm diam., white to light pink with red or pink stripes, lip purple and orange.

*P.* Henriette Lecoufle 'Boule de Neige': very large plants with branching sprays of exquisite, large, pure white fls.

*P.* Hilo Lip: robust plants with dark green lvs and tall spikes; fls various shades of pink with contrasting white lip, up to 7.5cm diam.

*P.* Joey: small plants; fls green-yellow barred with light brown, lip lilac, orange at the base.

*P.* Line Renaud 'Casino de Paris': robust plants with tall arching spikes; fls white or pale pink with deep red purple lip, good shape.

*P.* Lippeglut: large plants with dark green lvs and tall arching spikes; fls deep pink with darker lip of excellent shape and size. Lipperose, Lippstadt and Lippexauber are rather similar.

*P.* Little Mary: compact but strong plants with large arching and branching sprays; 3.8cm diam., excellent shape, deep pink with dark magenta lip, long-lasting.

*P.* Lundy 'Mont Millais': robust plants with tall arching spikes; fls of good shape, creamy yellow with pink stripes, lip deeper yellow and rose pink.

*P.* Mistinguett: large robust plants with tall spikes; fls 7.5–10cm diam., deep pink throughout and finely dotted with a deeper pink especially on the lip.

*P.* Nero Wolfe: strong plants; fls pink, striped with darker pink, lip red.

*P.* Ondinette: compact plants, branching sprays; fls round, large petals, deep pink with white lip.

*P.* Opaline: large plants with dark green lvs and robust fl. spikes; very large white fls of excellent shape and substance.

*P.* Orchid World: compact plants; fls bright yellow, spotted darker yellow but paler in centre, lip orange at base

*P.* Orglade's Clever Face: strong compact plants with short spikes, often branching; fls strong yellow background with heavy chestnut striping, orange red lip.

*P.* Orglade's Lemon Dew: vigorous, compact plants with branching spikes; fls pale lemon yellow, white towards the centre and with darker yellow on lip, very floriferous.

*P.* Party Dress: compact plants with large branching sprays of many fls, small, up to 5cm diam., round and pink.

*P.* Party Poppers: small but strong plants with branching sprays; fls variable, miniature whites, pastel pinks and stripes.

*P.* Pink Leopard: compact plants with large sprays; fls of good shape, white, heavily freckled with red, lip marked with chestnut.

*P.* Redfan: large robust plants with tall spikes; fls *c*7.5cm diam., white with ruby red lip.

*P.* Sierra Gold 'Suzanne': compact plants; lovely golden yellow fls with white lip.

*P.* Sophie Hausermann: small plants with few, rich brick-red fls.

*P.* Sourire: large plants with attractive silvery mottled lvs; fls pale to deep pink, good shape, 7.5–10cm diam.

*P.* Temple Cloud: large plants with long arching spikes; fls 10–14cm diam., pure white and heavy textured, long-lasting.

*P.* Zauberrose: large, robust plants with tall arching spikes; fls deep pink with very large pet., lip darker, excellent shape and size.

*P.* Zuma Chorus: compact plants with branching spikes; fls white striped magenta, lip attractively marked in orange and bright rose pink, column pink.

***P. delicosa*** Rchb. f. See *Kingidium delicosum*.
***P. denevei*** Sm. See *Paraphalaenopsis denevei*.
***P. grandiflora*** Lindl. See *P. amabilis*.
***P. lueddemanniana*** var. ***hieroglyphica*** (Rchb. f.) Veitch. See *P. hieroglyphica*.
***P. lueddemanniana*** var. ***purpurea*** (Rchb. f.) Veitch. See *P. pulchra*.
***P. pulcherrima*** (Lindl.) J.J. Sm. See *Doritis pulcherrima*.

**Phalaris** L. (Classical Gk name for a kind of grass.) Gramineae. Some 15 species of annual or perennial grasses. Stems flimsy to robust. Leaves flat, often long-acute; ligules thin. Inflorescence a compact panicle; spikelets ovate, to 3-flowered, short-stipitate, laterally compressed, awnless, flowers 1–3, 1 flower hermaphrodite, fertile, the others sterile, reduced to subulate lemmas; glumes equal, conspicuously keeled; fertile lemma keeled, leathery, shiny, acute. N Temperate (Mediterranean, S America, California). *P. arundinacea* used for hay, fodder; *P. canariensis* cultivated for bird seed; *P. aquatica* a fodder grass.

CULTIVATION Valued for their tolerance of a range of soil situations, dry and wet, and grown for attractive seed heads for drying (*P. canariensis*) and for the brightly variegated foliage (*P. arundinacea* and cvs), most perennial species are also cold-tolerant to between −15 and −20°C/5 to −4°F. *P. arundinacea* and *P. a.* 'Picta' are noted for their invasive tendencies (of great value in making impenetrable groundcover), providing useful colour contrast in the foliage border and in wet soils at stream and pond-side; they can be confined where necessary to planting in a sunken, bottomless half barrel. *P. a.* 'Mervyn Feesey' has brighter colour and is less invasive, as is *P. a.* 'Dwarf's Garters'. Propagate perennials and cultivars by division, annuals from seed sown *in situ* in spring, or earlier under glass.

***P. aquatica*** L. TOOWOMBA CANARY GRASS; HARDING GRASS. Perenn., to 1.5m. Stem loosely or densely clumped, slender to robust, internodes swollen near base of stem. Lvs to 30×1cm, glabrous, rough to smooth, green sometimes tinged blue, narrow-acuminate; ligules to 8mm. Panicles cylindric to ovoid-cylindric, compact, to 11×1cm, pale green or tinged purple; spikelets elliptic-oblong, to 8mm; glumes lanceolate, winged above; wing entire; fertile lemma ovate, to 6mm, tough, downy. Summer–autumn. S Europe, Mediterranean. Z8.

***P. arundinacea*** L. REED CANARY GRASS; GARDENER'S GARTERS; RIBBON GRASS. Rhizomatous perenn., to 1.5m. Stems robust, erect, or bent at base, glaucous. Lvs to 35×1.8cm, glabrous; ligule to 1cm; sheaths smooth. Infl. narrow, to 17cm; spikelets oblong, to 4mm; glumes narrow-lanceolate, to 6mm; fertile lemma narrow-oblong, sterile lemmas villous, to 2mm. Summer–autumn. Eurasia, N America, S Africa. 'Dwarf's Garters': as 'Picta' but dwarf, to 30cm. 'Luteo-Picta': small; lvs striped golden-yellow. 'Mervyn Feesey': small; lvs light green, boldly striped white; fl. stalked tinted pink. 'Picta' ('Tricolor'): lvs striped white, usually predominantly on one side of leaf. 'Streamlined': lvs mainly green, edged white. Z4.

***P. canariensis*** L. CANARY GRASS; BIRDSEED GRASS. Annual, to 120cm. Stems flimsy to robust, solitary to clumped. Lvs linear to linear-lanceolate, to 25×1.3cm, glabrous, scabrous. Infl. ovoid to ovoid-cylindric, compact, erect, to 6×2cm; spikelets obovate, to 1cm×0.4cm; glumes oblanceolate, winged above, abruptly acute; fertile lemma narrow-ovate, to 6mm, pubesc., shiny yellow when mature, sterile lemmas to 5mm+. Summer–autumn. W Mediterranean. Z6.

***P. minor*** Retz. Annual, to 120cm. Stems flimsy, solitary or clumped, erect or ascending. Lvs to 15×0.6cm, glabrous; ligule to 6mm. Infl. ovoid to cylindric, compact, to 7cm×1.6cm, pale green; spikelets to 6mm; glumes narrow oblong, with a toothed wing; fertile lemma narrow-ovate, to 3mm, grey, downy. Summer. Mediterranean to NW France. Z6.

***P. nodosa*** Murray. See *P. aquatica*.
***P. stenoptera*** Hackel. See *P. aquatica*.
***P. tuberosa*** L. See *P. aquatica*.
For further synonymy see *Digraphes* and *Typhoides*.

**Phanerophlebia** Presl. (From Gk *phaneros*, clear, visible, and *phlebion*, vein.) Dryopteridaceae. Some 8 species of terrestrial ferns. Rhizomes short-creeping to suberect, scaly; stipes with a few persistent scales at base and sometimes distally. Fronds imparipinnate, chartaceous to subcoriaceous, glabrous or with a few minute scales; pinnae entire to minutely spinose, proximal ones short-stalked; veins forking, free to anastomosing. Sori round, usually in several series; indusia peltate, persistent or caducous, absent in a few species. N America (Arizona to Texas, Mexico), C America, S America (to Venezuela).

CULTIVATION Attractive ferns from medium to high altitudes in tropical regions, particularly in Central America. Full hardiness is not proven but *P. macrosora*, from 2500–3000m/8125–9750ft in the mountains of Mexico, can tolerate temperatures at least as low as −15°C/5°F. Survival in extremely cold temperatures will be enhanced in a protected woodland environment where the crown can also be insulated from the cold by dead vegetation or straw. Plant in a woodland site in a soil rich in organic matter with a pH in the range 5.0–7.0. In the cool greenhouse, pot into a soilless potting medium and keep in bright indirect light. Water moderately and plant out in early summer. Propagate by spores.

***P. juglandifolia*** (Humb. & Bonpl. ex Willd.) J. Sm. Rhiz. suberect, short; stipes to 45cm, with a few ovate, brown scales. Fronds to 90cm, glabrous or with a few minute scattered scales; pinnae 20×5cm, 1–6 pairs, subfalcate, elliptic to ovate, base rounded to cuneate, entire to minutely spinose only at tip, terminal conform, often the largest. Mexico to Venezuela. Z10.

***P. macrosora*** (Bak.) Underw. Rhiz. stout; stipes to 60cm, densely scaly, scales spreading, ovate, to 15mm, stramineous to light tan. Fronds to 1.35cm, scaly below with narrowly lanceolate, minute scales; pinnae 15–25×2–4cm, narrowly oblong-lanceolate from a somewhat inequilateral base, upper base rounded to broadly cuneate, lower base excavate, margins cartilaginous, entire to minutely spinose. Mexico to Panama. Z9.

***P. fortunei*** (J. Sm.) Copel. See *Cyrtomium fortunei*.
***P. macrophylla*** (Mak.) Okuy. See *Cyrtomium macrophyllum*.
For further synonymy see *Cyrtomium*.

**Pharbitis** Choisy.
***P. hederacea*** (L.) Choisy. See *Ipomoea hederacea*.
***P. imperialis*** hort. See *Ipomoea × imperialis*.
***P. nil*** (L.) Choisy. See *Ipomoea nil*.
***P. purpurea*** (L.) Choisy. See *Ipomoea purpurea*.

**Pharus** P. Browne. (From Gk *pharos*, a wide cloth or covering, referring to the broad leaf blades.) Gramineae. Some 5 species of perennial grasses. Leaves linear to oblong, sometimes ciliate, petiole twisted; ligule papery, glabrous. Inflorescence a delicate panicle; spikelets awnless; male spikelet terminal; female spikelet 1-flowered; glumes 2, membranous, sometimes abscising, shorter than flower, entire; palea 2-ribbed; lemma cylindric, chalky, becoming leathery, to 5-ribbed or more, minutely pubescent, margins inrolled; male spikelets smaller than female. Summer. Tropical America. Z9.

CULTIVATION As for *Hyparrhenia*.

***P. latifolius*** L. To 90cm. Lvs oblanceolate to narrowly-obovate, to 25×10cm; petiole to 10cm. Panicle to 30cm, loose; female spikelets to 18mm; glumes tinged brown or purple; lemma tinged pink; male spikelets to 4mm, glabrous. 'Vittatus': lvs striped white, tinged pink.

**Phaseolus** L. (Lat. diminutive of Gk *phaselos*, name used by Dioscorides for a kind of bean.) BEAN. Leguminosae (Papilionoideae). Over 20 species of annual or perennial, usually climbing herbs. Leaves trifoliolate; stipules small, not decurrent; leaflets stipellate. Flowers in axillary racemes; calyx campanulate, bilabiate; standard orbicular, symmetric, keel with a spirally coiled beak; stamens diadelphous, uppermost distinct; style pubescent inside, the thickened part twisted more than 360°; stigma oblique. Fruit a linear-oblong, dehiscent legume, usually many-seeded. New World. Closely allied to *Vigna*, which differs from *Phaseolus* in having stipules often basally appendaged, the thickened part of the style less strongly twisted, the keel beak recurved, not spirally coiled, and in several technical characteristics related to pollen and biochemistry.

CULTIVATION For *P. coccineus* and *P. vulgaris*, see BEANS. Lima beans or butter beans, *P. lunatus*, are vigorous plants usually grown as annuals. They are grown for their edible seeds which must be boiled before eating to destroy hydrocyanic acid. They are available in both bush and climbing forms, the latter generally being more productive. Lima beans are very frost tender, prone to drop their flowers on very nitrogen-rich soils, and are even less tolerant of cold and wet than the scarlet runner bean, *P. coccineus*, although their cultivation requirements are otherwise similar. They are usually grown on ridges, raised beds or mounds to ensure the necessary good drainage, and seed should not be planted until the soil has warmed up; where frosts occur late into the season, they are sometimes started under glass, to be set out when danger of frost is passed. In warm temperate climates, lima beans mature about 12–16 weeks from sowing. In the tropics cultivation is restricted to elevations between 300–1200m/1000–4000ft; temperatures above 27°C/80°F adversely affect fertilization and pod formation is reduced in very hot weather. In cooler maritime climates such as those in the UK, the growing season is usually too short and too cool for the beans to mature and crops are seldom worthwhile.

***P. acutifolius*** A. Gray. Annual. Stems short, twining. Leaflets to 6×4cm, thin, linear-lanceolate or lanceolate-ovate, attenuate-acuminate. Fls white to pale purple, few, on very short peduncles. Fr. to 9×1.5cm, 2–10-seeded; seeds 8.5×5.5mm, round, variable in colour. SW US, Mexico. var. ***latifolius*** G. Freeman. TEPARY BEAN. Terminal leaflets to 9.9×5cm, lateral leaflets to 8×5cm. Fr. linear. 'Blue Speckles': blue-specked white seeds, not suitable for desert conditions. 'Brown Speckles': brown-speckled grey seeds, needs cool conditions. 'Golden': yellow-seeded, very prolific, tolerates heat and drought. 'Mitla Black': black-seeded, best for soup, two crops a year. 'Sonoran Brown': brown-seeded, early-maturing, grows well in drought and heat. Z10.

***P. coccineus*** L. SCARLET RUNNER BEAN; DUTCH CASE-KNIFE BEAN. Resembles *P. vulgaris*, but perenn. (albeit usually treated as an annual), racemes many-fld and longer than lvs, cor. to 3cm, scarlet, sometimes with white wings and keel, keel beak forms 1–1½ turns of a spiral. Leaflets to 13cm, ovate-cordate. Fr. to 30.5cm; seeds broad, to 2.5cm, black, mottled buff to red. Tropical America. 'Albus' WHITE DUTCH RUNNER: fls and seeds white. For further cvs see BEANS. Z10.

***P. lunatus*** L. LIMA BEAN. Twining or erect, grown as an annual. Lvs long-petiolate; rachis to 2.5cm; stipules to 4cm, narrow-triangular; leaflets to 10cm, ovate to rhombic or deltoid, obtuse to acute or subacute; stipels inconspicuous, ovate to linear. Infl. to 20cm, axillary; pedicels to 7mm; cal. to 0.3cm, broad-campanulate, pilose; cor. yellow-green or white to lilac, standard 1cm diam., wings 1cm, keel narrow, 1cm. Fr. to 10×1.5cm, oblong-lunate, 2–4-seeded; seeds to 1×0.5cm, red-brown, reniform. Winter–spring. Tropical S America. *Bush*: 'Baby Fordhook' (very dwarf); 'Burpee Improved' (large seeds in large clustered pods); 'Dixie Speckled Butterpea' (seeds red, speckled darker); 'Dixie White Butterpea' (vigorous, white-seeded, succeeds in dry conditions); 'Fordhook 242' (improved 'Fordhook', large creamy green seeds, heat-tolerant); 'Henderson' (very dwarf, small-creamy white seeds); 'Jackson Wonder' (small seeds, buff mottled dark purple, low but spreading, heat- and drought-tolerant); 'Thorogreen' (small green seeds, upright plant easily picked, long-bearing). *Pole or Climbing*: 'Burpee's Best' (long pods, few large green seeds, vigorous); 'Florida Butter' (small seeds, buff spotted red-brown, heavy cropping); 'King of the Garden' (large creamy seeds, heavy cropper); 'Prizetaker' (very large green seeds, pods in clusters); 'Sieva' (small green seeds, useful as fresh pods, shelled or dried seeds). Z10.

***P. vulgaris*** L. KIDNEY BEAN; GREEN BEAN; SNAP BEAN; HARICOT; COMMON BEAN; FRENCH BEAN; FRIJOL; RUNNER BEAN; STRING BEAN; SALAD BEAN; WAX BEAN. Erect or climbing annual to 4m. Leaflets to 10×6cm, ovate or ovate-orbicular, acuminate. Racemes shorter than lvs, to 6-fld; cor. to 1.8cm, white, pink or purple, keel beak forms 2 turns of a spiral. Fr. to 50×2.5cm, narrow, flat or subcylindric, brown; seeds 1.3cm, elongate or globose, red, brown, black, white, or mottled. Summer. Tropical America. For cultivars, see BEANS. var. ***humilis*** Alef. The widely grown 'bush' bean. Z10.

***P. aconitifolius*** Jacq. See *Vigna aconitifolius*.
***P. angularis*** W. Wight. See *Vigna angularis*.
***P. aureus*** Roxb. See *Vigna radiata*.
***P. bipunctatus*** Jacq. See *P. lunatus*.
***P. calcaratus*** Roxb. See *Vigna umbellata*.
***P. caracalla*** L. See *Vigna caracalla*.
***P. giganteus*** hort. See *Vigna caracalla*.
***P. inamuenus*** L. See *P. lunatus*.
***P. limensis*** Macfad. See *P. lunatus*.
***P. lobatus*** Hook. See *Vigna hookeri*.
***P. multiflorus*** Lam. See *P. coccineus*.
***P. mungo*** L. See *Vigna mungo*.
***P. puberulus*** HBK. See *P. lunatus*.
***P. pubescens*** Bl. See *Vigna umbellata*.
***P. radiatus*** L. See *Vigna radiata*.
***P. saccharatus*** Macfad. See *P. lunatus*.
***P. sublobatus*** Roxb. See *Vigna radiata*.
***P. xuaresii*** Zucc. See *P. lunatus*.

**Phegopteris** Fée. BEECH FERN. (From Gk *phegos*, acorn, and *pteris*, fern.) Thelypteridaceae. 3 species of terrestrial ferns. Rhizomes erect or ascending to creeping, branched. Fronds stipitate, uniform, 1–2-pinnate or -pinnatisect; pinnae basally attached to stipes by winged rachillae, veins free, often forked; rachis and costa covered with scales and cellular hairs; stipes scaly, pubescent. Sori marginal or nearly so, on segments, dispersed over veins, circular to oblong, indusia absent, sporangia spiny; spores reniform, ridged. N temperate & SE Asia.

CULTIVATION The delicate yellow-green foliage of *Phegopteris* spp. is produced in slowly spreading colonies. All species are fully hardy (i.e. to −30°C/−22°F). They thrive in moist woodland gardens and shady borders but *P. connectilis* will readily colonize a shady rock garden if the soil and rock is acid (pH 4.0–6.0). Ideally, these ferns prefer a sunless position. Under glass, keep in a cold house in a soilless potting medium and water moderately, particularly in summer. Plant out in early summer. Propagation is normally by division but it is also possible by spores, which ripen from early to late summer.

***P. connectilis*** (Michx.) Watt. BEECH FERN; LONG BEECH FERN; NARROW BEECH FERN; NORTHERN BEECH FERN. Rhiz. long-creeping, to 2mm wide; scales few, lanceolate, to 5mm long, pubesc., brown. Lamina to 15×20cm, thin-textured, emerald green, horizontal to decumbent, sagittate or deltoid to ovate, apex attenuate, pubesc.; pinnae opposite, lowest pair free, down-curved, oblong or linear to lanceolate, narrowly acute at apex, deeply pinnatifid, to 8×2cm, seg. approximate, oblong, obtuse at apex, entire to notched or dentate at margin, to 5mm wide; stipes erect, 1cm distant, to 15cm long, straw-coloured, brown at base. N America, Europe, W Asia. Z5.

***P. decursive-pinnata*** (Van Hall) Fée. Rhiz. erect or suberect to short-creeping. Lamina to 60cm, arcuate to ascending, pinnate or 2-pinnatifid, attenuate at apex and base; pinnae linear, occasionally pinnatifid at margin; stipes to 20cm, their scales lanceolate to linear, pubesc. China, Taiwan, Japan, Korea, Himalaya. Z6.

***P. hexagonoptera*** (Michx.) Fée. BROAD BEECH FERN. SOUTHERN BEECH FERN. Distinguished from *P. connectilis* by its broader fronds with basal pinnae not decurved but spreading. Rhiz. wide-creeping. Lamina 1–2-pinnate, deltoid, to 35×35cm, glandular-pubesc.; pinnae to 15×5cm, pinnatifid, pinnules pinnatifid, to 3cm, seg. obtuse, dentate at margin. Eastern N America. Z5.

***P. dryopteris*** (L.) Fée. See *Gymnocarpium dryopteris*.
***P. effusa*** (Sw.) Fée. See *Lastreopsis effusa*.
***P. munita*** Mett. See *Lastreopsis munita*.
For further synonymy see *Dryopteris* and *Thelypteris*.

**Phellodendron** Rupr. (From Gk *phellos*, cork, and *dendron*, tree, referring to the corky bark of some species.) Rutaceae. 10 species of deciduous tall trees, aromatic. Bark often thick and corky; winter buds concealed below petiole. Leaves opposite, pinnate, handsome; leaflets crenate to subentire, translucent-punctate. Inflorescence terminal, paniculate, small; flowers dioecious, small, yellow tinged green; sepals and petals 5–8, ovate-lanceolate; stamens 5–6, exceeding petals. Fruit a drupe, globose, pea-sized, black, with 5 single seed-pits. Temperate and subtropical E Asia.

CULTIVATION Fine lawn specimens for large open areas, their open branching habit becoming increasingly picturesque with maturity, as the bark becomes deeply furrowed. Performing best in zones where summers are long and hot, the pungently aromatic foliage gives fine, clear yellow autumn tints, and on female trees the black fruits often persist well into winter. Grow in deep, fertile, moisture-retentive but well-drained soils in an open position in full sun. Although hardy to at least −20°C/−4°F, the young growth is sometimes damaged by late spring frosts, usually resulting in a more closely branching bushy habit. Propagate species by seed in autumn or spring desirable forms by softwood or heeled semi-ripe cuttings in summer rooted in a closed case with bottom heat. Alternatively, take root cuttings in late winter.

***P. amurense*** Rupr. Tree to 15m; crown broad; bark pale grey, thick, corky, deeply grooved; twigs yellow tinged grey to yellow tinged orange. Lvs to 35cm; leaflets 5–10×3–5cm, 9–13, broadly ovate to ovate-lanceolate, elongate acuminate, dark glossy green above, glaucous beneath; rachis tomentose; midvein pubesc.; lvs turning yellow in autumn and early-deciduous, in late summer. Infl. 6–8cm, pubesc.; fls 6mm. Fr. 1cm diam., with strong turpentine scent. Early summer. N China, Manchuria. Z3.

***P. chinense*** Schneid. Tree to 10m; bark thin, dark grey-brown; shoots ferruginous when young. Leaflets 7–14cm, 7–13, oblong-lanceolate, elongate acuminate at apex, broadly cuneate at base, dull dark yellow tinged green above, light green and tomentose beneath. Infl. 5–6cm, short, conical, dense, tomentose; ovaries pubesc. Fr. 9mm. C China. Z5.

***P. japonicum*** Maxim. Tree, 5–10m; bark thin, with plates, finely grooved, deep brown; shoots ferruginous when young. Lvs 25–35cm; leaflets 6–10cm, 9–13, ovate to ovate-oblong, oblique and somewhat cordate or truncate at base, dull green above, light green and grey tomentose beneath, particularly on veins. Infl. erect, male 10×5cm, female more slender, tomentose; fls 6mm; ovaries glabrous. Fr. 1cm. C Japan. Z6.

***P. lavallei*** Dode. Tree, 7–10m+; bark thick and corky; shoots ferruginous when young. Lvs 20–35cm; leaflets 5–10cm, 5–13, ovate-elliptic to oblong-lanceolate, acuminate at apex, cuneate at base, dull yellow tinged green above, light green and pubesc. at least when young beneath; rachis softly pubesc.; petiole 3–4mm. Infl. 6–8cm, lax, many-fld, pubesc.; ovaries glabrous. Fr. copiously produced. Early summer. C Japan. Z6.

***P. sachalinense*** (F. Schmidt) Sarg. Tree, 7m+, with broad crown; trunk straight, bark thin, dark brown, finely channelled, becoming platelike with age, not at all corky; twigs ferruginous. Lvs 22–30cm; leaflets 6–12cm, 7–11+, ovate to ovate-oblong, acuminate at apex, rounded at base, dull green above, glaucous beneath, glabrous or subglabrous, margins sometimes somewhat ciliate. Infl. 6–8cm, subglabrous. Fr. 1cm. SAkhalin, N Japan, Korea, W China. Z3.

***P. wilsonii*** Hayata & Kanehira. Branchlets glabrous. Lvs 27×15cm, including petioles; leaflets 8–8×3–4cm, *c*9, opposite or alternate, ovate-oblong, acuminate at apex, obliquely truncate at base, chartaceous, glabrous above, pubesc. on veins beneath; petiolules 2–5mm. Infl. terminal or axillary, 8cm; style short, stigma 5-lobed, hairy; fil. hairy. Fr. 7–8mm, globose. Taiwan (mts).

***P. amurense*** var. ***japonicum*** (Maxim.) Ohwi. See *P. japonicum*.
***P. amurense*** var. ***lavallei*** (Dode) Sprague. See *P. lavallei*.
***P. amurense*** var. ***sachalinense*** F. Schmidt. See *P. sachalinense*.

**Phellosperma** Britt. & Rose.
***P. tetrancistra*** (Engelm.) Britt. & Rose. See *Mammillaria tetrancistra*.

**Phenakospermum** Endl. Strelitziaceae. 1 species, a giant herb to 10m, closely resembling *Ravenala* except stems less prominent, leaves to 1.25m, dark glossy green, midrib often tinted coral-red, more elliptic ovate than oblong lanceolate. Inflorescence terminal with 7 bracts, carinate, deflexed, 30–45cm; flowers borne in axils of bracts, white; stamens 5. Capsule 3-celled; seed with orange aril. Brazil, Guyana. Z10.

CULTIVATION As for *Strelitzia nicolai*.

***P. guyannense*** (Rich.) Endl. ex Miq. As for the genus.

For synonymy see *Ravenala*.

**Pherosphaera** Archer.
***P. hookeriana*** Hook. non Archer. See *Microstrobos niphophilus*.
***P. fitzgeraldii*** F. Muell. ex Hook. See *Microstrobos fitzgeraldii*.

**PHILADELPHACEAE** D. Don. See *Hydrangeaceae*.

**Philadelphus** L. (Probably for Ptolemy Philadelphus (ruled 285–246 BC), patron of the arts and sciences.) MOCK ORANGE. Hydrangeaceae (Philadelphaceae). 60 species of shrubs with mainly peeling bark. Axillary buds exposed or hidden within the bases of the petioles. Leaves usually deciduous, opposite, simple. Flowers in racemes, panicles or cymes, or solitary, often strongly scented; sepals 4; petals 4; stamens numerous; ovary inferior, surmounted by a nectar-secreting disc; carpels 4, united; styles 4, partially or wholly united. Fruit a many-seeded capsule, generally with the persistent sepals at the top; seeds usually with tails. C & N America, Caucasus, Himalaya, China and eastern Asia. Numerous hybrids have been raised and cultivated, and these blur the distinctions between the species.

CULTIVATION Suited to shrub and mixed borders; the larger spp. such as *P. delavayi, P. pubescens, P. purpurascens* and the fastigiate *P. ×virginalis* 'Burfordiensis' are valuable in screens or informal hedging. *Philadelphus* spp. are also useful at woodland edge or, better, in open glades or other sheltered positions, where cool still air can be permeated by fragrance; blooms last well indoors in water. Those with a particularly heady scent include *P. coronarius, P. delavayi, P. microphyllus* and cvs, *P. ×lemoinei* 'Avalanche' and *P. ×purpureo-maculatus* 'Belle Etoile'; fragrance in *P. ×purpureo-maculatus* is particularly strong and may be overpowering in confined situations. Fragrance in double-flowered forms is almost invariably less intense, although some *P. ×virginalis* and *P. ×purpureo-maculatus* cvs retain a delicate scent. In *P. delavayi* 'Nymans Variety' and *P. purpurascens* the strongly scented flowers are exceptionally beautiful, pure white in contrast with the conspicuous purple calyces. Some species, such

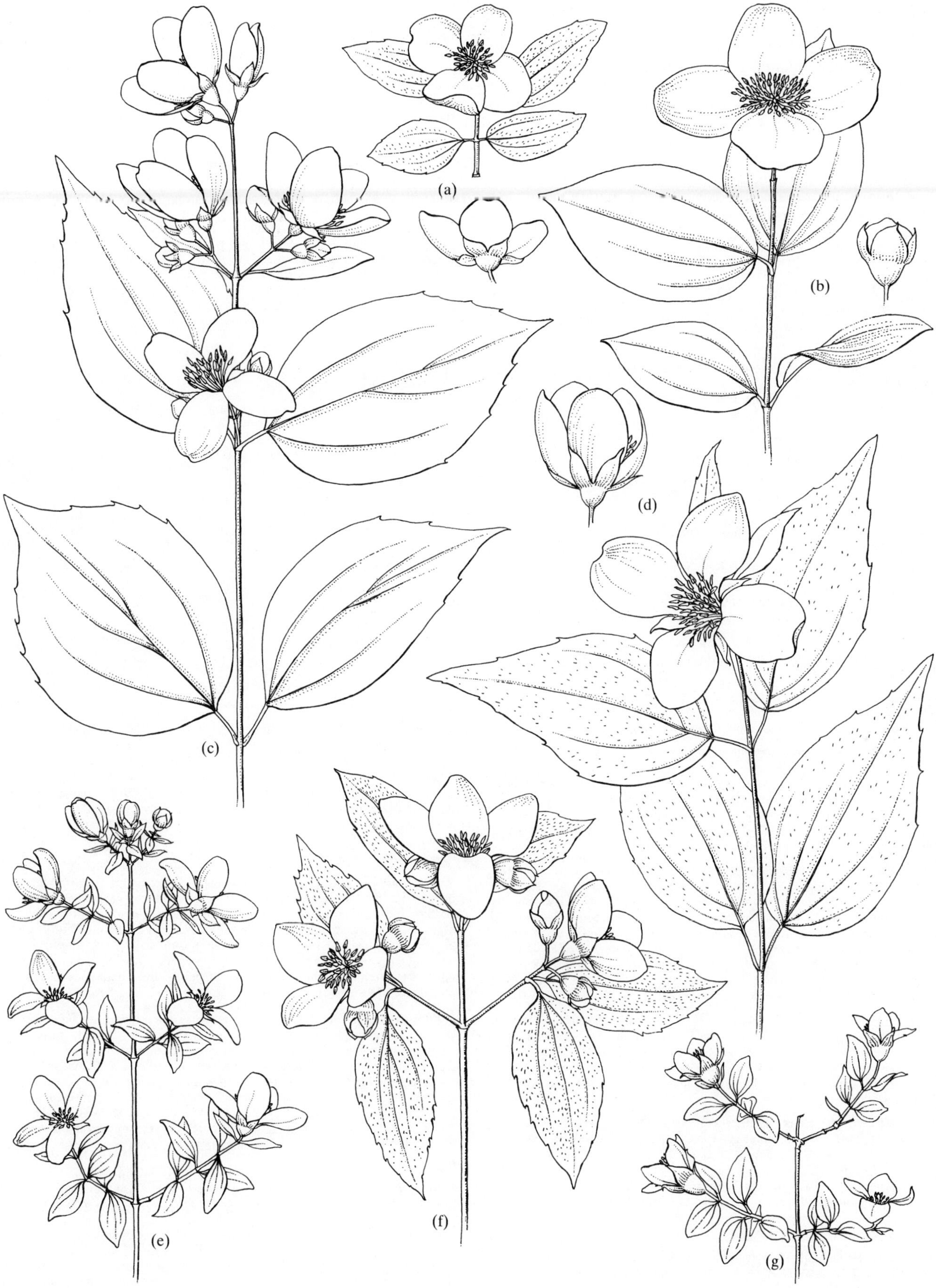


**Philadelphus** (×0.5) (a) *P. coulteri* (b) *P. inodorus* (c) *P. californicus* (d) *P. mexicanus* (e) *P. microphyllus* (f) *P. hirsutus* (g) *P. serpyllifolius*

as *P. hirsutus, P. inodorus* and *P. sericanthus*, are beautiful in flower but are scentless or almost so.

Although *Philadelphus* spp. sometimes exhibit a coarseness in habit, this is frequently a result of exploitation of their tolerance of poor soils, and/or neglect of regular pruning. *Philadelphus*, with few exceptions, is a sturdy and undemanding genus, easily grown in any moderately fertile soil, including thin, chalky soils. Most will tolerate winter temperatures of at least −15°C/5°F, *P. coronarius, P. incanus* and *P. microphyllus* to −20°C/−4°F. *P. mexicanus* and *P. karwinskyanus* need wall or other protection in cool temperate zones. Most spp. tolerate partial shade, but flower better in sun, especially *P. argyrocalyx* and *P. microphyllus*. Treat as for *Deutzia*.

1 Axillary buds hidden within the bases of the petioles.

1.1. Flowers in racemes.
*Pp. brachybotrys, caucasicus, coronarius, dasycalyx, delavayi, incanus, intectus, kansuensis, laxiflorus, pekinensis, pubescens, purpurascens, satsumanus, satsumi, schrenkii, sericanthus, shikokianus, subcanus, tenuifolius.*

1.2 Flowers solitary, in threes or in dichasial cymes.

1.2.1. Large shrubs, leaves 4–10cm long; stamens 60–90.
*Pp. floridus, inodorus.*

1.2.2. Small, compact shrubs, leaves at most 3cm long; stamens 35–50.
*Pp. argenteus, argyrocalyx, microphyllus.*

2 Axillary buds exposed.

2.1. Stigmas united into a column; seeds without tails.

2.1.1. Leaves hairy on both surfaces, all the hairs straight.

2.1.2. Leaves hairy on both surfaces, hairs on the lower curled and woolly.
*P. serpyllifolius.*

2.2. Stigmas mostly free, not united into a column; seeds with short or long tails.

2.2.1. Flowers in dense panicles; calyx persisting almost at the top of the fruit.
*Pp. californicus, cordifolius, insignis.*

2.2.2. Flowers solitary, in threes, or in depauperate panicles; calyx persisting around the circumference of the fruit.

2.2.2.1. Leaves acuminate; stigma crested.
*Pp. karwinskyanus, mexicanus.*

2.2.2.2. Leaves acute or obtuse; stigma not crested.
*P. coulteri.*

***P. argenteus*** Rydb. Similar to *P. argyrocalyx* but lvs ovate-oblong, strigose to hispid above, ovary with straight, adpressed hairs. US (California), Mexico (Baja California). Tender, and uncommon in cultivation. Z9.

***P. argyrocalyx*** Wooton. Erect shrub to 2m; twigs grey-brown, the second-year bark usually intact; current growth with rusty, shaggy hairs. Axillary buds hidden. Lvs 1–3.5×0.4–1.5cm, ovate, ovate-lanceolate or elliptic, base obtuse, apex acute or obtuse, dark green, glabrous or becoming so above, sparsely shaggy-bristly and paler green beneath. Fls solitary on short stalks (1–2mm), cross-shaped, to 3.5cm wide, white and slightly fragrant; cal. densely white-woolly. Seeds long-tailed. Summer–late summer. US (New Mexico). Z7.

***P. brachybotrys*** (Koehne) Koehne. Shrub to 3m; bark of the second year brown-grey, not peeling; current growth shaggy-hairy, becoming glabrous. Axillary buds hidden. Lvs 2–6×1–3cm, ovate, base rounded, apex shortly acuminate, finely toothed or almost entire, sparsely adpressed-bristly above and on the veins beneath. Fls 5–7 in short racemes, cream, disc-shaped, *c*3cm across; ovary, cal., disc and style hairless; stamens 30–40; style about as long as stamens, stigmas spathulate, inner surface 1mm long, outer 2mm. Seeds short-tailed. Summer. SE China. There is some doubt as to whether the plants in cultivation under this name are genuine or of hybrid origin. Z7.

***P. ×burkwoodii*** Burkw. & Skipw. *(P. mexicanus × ?.)* Dwarf shrub with prominent winter buds, bark very dark brown in the second year and eventually peeling; current growth adpressed stiffly-hairy. Lvs 3.5–6.6×1.5–3cm, oval-elliptic, glabrous above, sparsely hairy beneath. Fls 1–5, in panicles, cross-shaped, 5–6cm across, fragrant; sep. short-hairy or partially so; disc and style hairless. Garden origin. Z7.

***P. californicus*** Benth. Erect shrubs to 3m; second-year bark dark brown; current year's growth soon becoming glabrous. Axillary buds exposed. Lvs ovate or ovate-elliptic, those on non-flowering shoots 4.5–8×3–5cm, those on flowering shoots 3–5×2–3cm (rarely to 8cm long), all glabrous except for tufts in the vein angles beneath, base acute, obtuse or sometimes rounded, apex acute, entire or obscurely toothed. Fls 3–5 in a panicle, to 2.5cm across, cross-shaped, fragrant; sep. ovate, hairless; stamens 25–37; disc and style hairless. Seed short-tailed. Summer. US (California). Z7.

***P. caucasicus*** Koehne. Like *P. coronarius*, but disc and style pubesc. Summer. USSR (Caucasus). var. ***aureus*** Rehd. Smaller; lvs tinged yellow. Z6.

***P. cordifolius*** Lange. Very similar to *P. californicus*, but lvs often larger, and fls numerous, in dense panicles. US (California). Z7.

***P. coronarius*** L. Shrubs to 3m; bark dark brown, slowly peeling in the second year; current growth sparsely downy, becoming glabrous. Axillary buds hidden. Lvs 4.5–9×2–4.5cm, ovate, mostly glabrous but downy on the major veins and in the vein-angles beneath, margins irregularly and shallowly toothed, base obtuse or acute, apex acuminate. Fls 5–9 in short terminal racemes, creamy white, strongly fragrant, 2.5–3cm across; sep. triangular, acute, glabrous; stamens *c*25; disc and style glabrous. Seeds with long tails. Early summer. S Europe (Austria, Italy, Romania), USSR (Caucasus). 'Aureus' ('Foliisaureis'): habit compact; lvs golden yellow to lime green; fls fragrant; requires shade. 'Bowles's var': lvs edged white. 'Deutziiflorus' ('Multiflorus Plenus'): dwarf; fls double, more freely produced than 'Duplex'; pet. pointed, narrow. 'Dianthiflorus' dwarf; fls double; pet. narrow. 'Duplex' ('Nanus', 'Pumilus'): dwarf to 1m; lvs small 3–5cm, oval; fls double, solitary to groups of 5, sparse, produced only with age; pedicels hairy. 'Gracieux': fls double, creamy white; pet. sometimes fimbriate. 'Maculiformis': fls 3cm; pet. red at base; considered to be a bud mutation. 'Primuliflorus' ('Rosiflorus Plenus'): like 'Dianthiflorus', but taller to 2m; lvs to 7cm; pedicel hairy; fls solitary to groups of 5. 'Salicifolius': lvs narrower; tips of pet. bear a few hairs; may be of hybrid origin. 'Speciosissimus': dwarf, lvs small. 'Zeyheri': vigorous, to 2.5m, greater in width; lvs 6–10cm; fls 2.5cm diam. unscented, poorly produced; prone to winter dieback; considered by some to be a hybrid, *P. coronarius × P. inodorus* var. *grandiflorus*. Z5.

***P. coulteri*** Wats. Shrub to 1.3m; current year's growth hairy. Axillary buds exposed. Lvs 1.5–3×1–1.5cm, ovate to ovate-elliptic, more or less entire, apex obtuse, acute or apiculate, strigose on both surfaces. Fls solitary or rarely in threes; cor. disc-like, 2.5–3.5cm across; ovary and sep. densely white-hairy outside; disc pubesc. at the centre; pet. white; stamens 34–38; styles united in the lower half. Summer. Mexico. Z9.

***P. ×cymosus*** Rehd. (Parentage unknown.) Erect shrub to 2.5m; bark brown, not peeling. Lvs ovate, sparsely toothed, hairy below especially on the veins. Fls in cymes of 1–5; sep. and disc hairless; some stamens may be petal-like. Garden origin. Cvs compact to vigorous, 1–8m, upright to arching; lvs 4 to 10cm in length, ovate to more narrow, hairy to glossy green; fls single to double, 4–10cm diam., cupped to wide opening, fragrant to very fragrant, white to creamy white; pet. in one case each pink stained and reflexed. 'Amalthée': lvs glossy green above; fls 4cm, pink at base, slightly fragrant. 'Bannière': upright to 2m; fls abundant, semi-double. 'Bouquet Blanc': fls semi-double, milky white, fragrant borne in great profusion. 'Conquette': branches arching; lvs long, to 10cm; fls single to double very fragrant, in cymes of 3–5; the type of the cross. 'Dresden': low growing. 'Mer de Glace' fls double, fragrance slight. 'Monster': very vigorous 3–8m; lvs to 15cm; fls 5cm, in racemes of 9. 'Nuée Blanche': fls single to semi-double, creamy, fragrant, profuse. 'Perle Blanche': habit compact; fls single to semi-double, fragrant. 'Rosace': fls wide opening, semi-double. 'Velleda': fls rounded with rose fragrance. 'Voie Lactée': vigorous, lvs large, fls to 5cm, freely produced; pet. reflexed. Z5.

***P. delavayi*** Henry. Shrub to 4m; bark of second year grey-brown, grey or chestnut-brown, not peeling; current growth hairless, glaucous. Lvs ovate-lanceolate or ovate-oblong, base rounded, apex acuminate, 2–8×2–5cm on flowering shoots, much larger on non-flowering shoots, usually with forward-pointing teeth but sometimes entire, all sparsely bristly above, densely adpressed shaggy-hairy beneath. Fls in racemes of 5–9 (rarely more), 2.5–3.5cm across, disc-shaped, pure white, fragrant; cal. glabrous, glaucous, tinged with purple; stamens *c*35; disc and style glabrous. Early summer. SW China. 'Nymans Variety': cal. plum-coloured. Z6.

***P. ×falconeri*** Nichols. (Parentage unknown.) Shrub to 3m, bark brown, peeling in the second year; branches slender and pendulous; current growth hairless. Axillary buds hidden. Lvs 3–6.5×1–2.5cm, ovate or ovate-elliptic, rounded or obtuse at the base, faintly toothed, veins with adpressed bristles beneath. Fls 3–5 in cymes, abundant, to 3cm wide, pure white, star-shaped; pet. elliptic, pointed; styles much longer than stamens, sterile. Summer. Garden origin. A hybrid of unknown parentage which is shy at flowering but sometimes produces an abundance of fls. Z5.

***P. floridus*** Beadle. Shrub to 3m; current year's growth hairless, brown, second-year growth chestnut. Axillary buds hidden. Lvs 4–10×2–6cm, mostly ovate-elliptic, base rounded or obtuse, apex sharply acuminate, almost entire or inconspicuously and remotely toothed, evenly adpressed-bristly beneath, hairless above except for a few adpressed bristles on the veins. Fls in threes or rarely solitary or in racemes, ovary and cal. shaggy-hairy; fls disc-shaped, 4–5cm across; pet. almost circular, *c*2.5cm, pure white; stamens 80–90, to 1.5cm; stigma oar-shaped. Seeds long-tailed. Early summer. US (Georgia). var. ***faxonii*** Rehd. Fls smaller, in the shape of a cross; sometimes regarded as a cultivar. Origin unknown. Z6.

***P. hirsutus*** Nutt. Low, spreading shrub with slender, slightly twisted arching branches, to 2.5m; shoots widely divergent, second-year bark dark brown, peeling, current year's growth with shaggy hairs. Axillary buds exposed. Lvs 2.5–7×1–5cm, ovate-elliptic or ovate-lanceolate, base rounded, apex acuminate, sharply toothed, uniformly covered with hairs with swollen bases above and densely shaggy beneath. Fls 1–5 on very short shoots with 1–2 pairs of lvs, disc-shaped, *c*2.5cm across; sep. broadly triangular, shaggy-hairy; style and disc hairless. Seeds without tails. Early summer. SE US (North Carolina to Georgia). Z6.

**Philadelphus** (×0.5) (a) *P. coronarius* (b) *P. incanus* (c) *P. pubescens* (d) *P. intectus* (e) *P. delavayi* (f) *P. tomentosus* (g) *P.* × *lemoinei* 'Avalanche' (h) *P.* × *virginalis* (i) *P.* × *cymosus* 'Conquête'

***P. incanus*** Koehne. Erect shrub to 3.5m, bark grey and smooth to the second year, later peeling; current growth hairy. Axillary buds hidden. Lvs oval-elliptic, 4–8.5×2–4cm on flowering shoots, to 10×6cm on non-flowering shoots, all tapered to rounded at the base, slender-pointed, sparsely bristly above, adpressed-bristly beneath. Fls 7–11 in racemes, white, *c*2.5cm across; cal. and fl stalk adpressed-bristly like the lvs; stamens 35. Seeds very short-tailed. Later summer. China (Hubei, Shaanxi). Z5.

***P. inodorus*** L. Arching shrub to 2–3m, bark of the second year chestnut-brown, peeling; current year's growth hairless. Axillary buds hidden. Lvs 5–9×2–3.5cm, ovate-elliptic or elliptic, more or less entire or faintly toothed, sparsely adpressed-hairy or almost glabrous above, hairy on main veins and vein angles beneath. Fls 4–5cm across, in cymes of 1, 3 or rarely 9; fl stalk, ovary and cal. all hairless; stamens 60–90; style equal to the longest stamens, hairless, stigmas swollen. Seeds long-tailed. Summer. SE US. var. ***grandiflorus*** (Willd.) Gray. Pet. almost orbicular at first, later oblong; the half-open fl is campanulate. E US. Z5.

***P. insignis*** Carr. Erect shrub to 4m, second-year bark grey (rarely brown), smooth. Axillary buds exposed. Lvs 3.5–8×1.5–6cm, ovate or ovate-elliptic, base obtuse, acute or rounded, apex acute or strongly acuminate, more or less entire or faintly toothed, coarsely adpressed-hairy beneath. Fls in threes in panicles, 2.5–3.5cm across; sep. ovate, usually adpressed-hairy; stamens *c*30; disc and style hairless. Seeds short-tailed. Summer. W US (California, Oregon). Considered by some authors to be a hybrid (*P. californicus* × *P. pubescens*). Z7.

***P. intectus*** Beadle. Erect shrub to 5m, bark silvery, not peeling; current growth glabrous. Axillary buds hidden. Lvs on non-flowering shoots ovate to oblong-elliptic, 6–10×4–6cm, on flowering shoots 3–6×1.5–3.5cm, all with base rounded to obtuse, apex acuminate, glabrous or rarely hairy beneath, with a few forward-pointing teeth on the margins. Fls in racemes of 5–9, disc-shaped, *c*3cm across; sep. ovate, tailed; ovary glabrous; stamens 38; disc and style hairless. Seeds long-tailed. Summer. SE US. Z5.

***P. kansuensis*** (Rehd.) S.Y. Hu Upright shrub to 7m; current year's growth with curly hairs, eventually becoming hairless, second-year bark grey-brown, peeling. Axillary buds hidden. Lvs ovate or ovate-lanceolate, to 11×6.5cm on non-flowering shoots, 3–5×1–2cm on flowering shoots, all more or less entire or faintly toothed, base obtuse or rounded, apex pointed, uniformly bristly-hairy above, hairs on the veins beneath with swollen bases. Fls 5–7 in racemes, disc-shaped, *c*2.5cm across; flower stalks bristly-hairy; pet. oblong-rounded; stamens *c*30, disc bristly at its rim; style hairless. Seeds short-tailed. Summer. NW China. Z7.

***P. karwinskyanus*** Koehne. Like *P. mexicanus*, but fls in a several-fld panicle, cor. 2.5–3cm across, pet. hairless outside. Mexico. Tender and very uncommon in cultivation. Z9.

***P. laxiflorus*** Rehd. Like *P. brachybotrys*, but lvs uniformly bristly above, styles club-shaped, bark of second-year shoots chestnut-brown. Summer. China (Shaanxi, Gansu, Hubei). Z6.

***P. ×lemoinei*** Lemoine. (*P. coronarius* × *P. microphyllus*.) Low compact shrub as wide as high, with peeling bark. Lvs 1.5–2.5×0.7–1.2cm, ovate, glabrous above, sparsely bristly below, base rounded or obtuse, apex acuminate, with about 6 teeth. Fls usually in threes, more rarely solitary or in fives, cross-shaped, *c*3cm across; sep. ovate, hairless; pet. notched; stamens *c*25. Summer. Garden origin. Cvs with habit arching to upright; lvs 2.5–15cm, mottled and variegated to smooth dark green; fls 2.5–6cm, white to creamy, fragrant to very fragrant; pet. sometimes waved, dentate or cut. 'Avalanche': upright, fls very fragrant. 'Candelabre': slow, compact; fls 3.5cm in dense heads; pet. waved and dentate. 'Coupe d'Argent': branches arching; fls to 3cm, flat, rose-scented. 'Dame Blanche': small, lvs to 15cm, dark smooth green; fls semi-double, creamy, 'Erectus': upright, fls very fragrant. 'Fimbriatus': to 80cm, fls double; pet. cut. 'Innocence': lvs mottled yellow; fls single to semi-double, very fragrant. 'Innocence Variegatus': lvs edged cream. 'Lemoinei': spreading, fls pure white, very fragrant; the type of the cross. fragrant; pet. fimbriate. 'Manteau d'Hermine': lvs small to 2.5cm; fls creamy, double, fragrant; buds red. 'Silver Showers' ('Silberregen'): fls solitary, wide-opening, scented of strawberry. Z5.

***P. lewisii*** Pursh. Erect shrub to 3m; second-year growth brown-yellow to chestnut-brown, bark not peeling but with transverse cracks; current year's growth glabrous but ciliate at the nodes. Axillary buds hidden. Lvs 4–5.5×2–3.5cm, base rounded, apex acute, obtuse or shortly acuminate, more or less entire or inconspicuously finely toothed, very sparsely covered with long, rough hairs on the veins above and with tufts of hair in the vein angles beneath, margins ciliate. Fls in racemes of 5–11, cross-shaped, 3–4.5cm across; sep. ovate, 5–6×3mm, wide at the base; stamens 28–35, the longest being half the length of the pet.; anth. and disc hairless; style shorter than the longest stamens, hairless, undivided or slightly divided above. Seeds long-tailed. Early summer. Western N America (British Columbia to California). var. ***gordonianus*** (Lindl.) Koehne. Lvs more densely hairy and more strongly toothed, fls disc-shaped. Summer. Western US (Washington to California). 'Waterton': young shoots red-brown, fls creamy, star-like. Z5.

***P. mexicanus*** Schldl. Tender, climbing, evergreen shrub to 5m with long, drooping branches; bark dark brown wrinkled; current growth long-bristly. Axillary buds exposed, prominent. Lvs 5–11.5×2–5cm, ovate, adpressed-bristly on both surfaces, base rounded to cordate, apex long-acuminate, more or less entire or with a few tiny teeth. Fls solitary or in threes, yellow-white, rose-scented, 3–4cm across; pet. hairy on both surfaces. Summer. Mexico, Guatemala. 'Rose Syringa': pet. with pink-purple basal marking. Z9.

***P. microphyllus*** A. Gray. Low, erect, graceful shrub to 1m; current growth adpressed-pubesc., second-year bark chestnut-brown, shiny, soon flaking off. Axillary buds hidden. Lvs 1–1.5×0.5–0.7cm, oval-elliptic or sometimes lanceolate, entire and ciliate, hairless or becoming so above, softly shaggy-hairy beneath, base obtuse, apex acute or obtuse. Flowering shoots 1.5–4cm long, with 1 or rarely 2 pure white, very fragrant fls which are cross-shaped and *c*3cm wide; sep. lanceolate; stamens *c*32. Seeds with very short tails. Early summer. SW US. Z6.

***P. ×nivalis*** Jacques. (Probably *P. coronarius* × *P. pubescens*.) Arching shrub to 2.5m, bark dark brown, peeling; current growth hairless. Lvs 5–10×2.5–6cm, ovate or ovate-elliptic, base rounded or obtuse, apex acuminate, faintly toothed, hairless above, uniformly shaggy-hairy beneath. Racemes with 5–7 double fls; sep. with dense, long, rough hairs; cor. disc-shaped, 2.5–3.5cm across; disc and style hairless. Early summer. Garden origin. 'Plenus': fls double. Z5.

***P. pekinensis*** Rupr. Low compact shrub to 2m; bark of the second year dark brown, peeling; current year's growth hairless. Axillary buds hidden. Lvs on non-flowering shoots ovate, 6–9×2.5–4.6cm, those of flowering shoots 3–7×1.5–2.5cm, all rounded or obtuse at the base, long-pointed at the apex, toothed, hairless on both surfaces or sometimes with tufts of hairs in the vein angles nearest the stalk beneath. Racemes with 3–9 yellow-white, fragrant, disc-shaped fls, 2–3cm across; cal. and disc hairless, sep. ovate, *c*4mm; stamens 25. Seeds with short tails. Early summer. N & W China. Z4.

***P. ×polyanthus*** Rehd. (Thought to be *P. insignis* × *P. ×lemoinei*.) Erect shrub, bark dark brown, eventually peeling; current year's growth with a few shaggy hairs. Lvs 3.5–5×1.5–2.5cm, ovate, base rounded or obtuse, apex acuminate, entire or with a few sharp teeth, hairless above, sparsely hairy with short, adpressed bristles beneath. Fls 3–5 in cymes or corymbs, cross-shaped, *c*3cm across; ovary and cal. pubesc., sep. tailed at apex; stamens *c*30. Summer. Garden origin. 'Atlas': to 2m; lvs to 6cm, often mottled; fls 5–6cm in racemes of 5–7, wide opening, milky-white, slightly fragrant. 'Boule d'Argent': habit compact, fls 4cm in cymes of 5–7, semi-double, scarcely fragrant. 'Favourite': to 2m, fls large, cross shaped, cupped; pet. serrate; stamens yellow. 'Gerbe de Neige': very free flowering. The type of the cross. 'Mont Blanc': to 1m, fls cross shaped, pure white, fragrance strong. 'Norma': to 1.5m, branches arching; fls 4cm cupped, freely borne, fragrance slight. 'Pavillon Blanc': low bush, branches arching; fls creamy-white, fragrant. Z5.

***P. pubescens*** Lois. Shrub to 5m; second-year bark grey, first-year bark not peeling; current growth hairless. Axillary buds hidden. Lvs 4–8×3–5.5cm on flowering shoots, ovate, base rounded, apex abruptly acuminate, remotely toothed or entire, glabrous above except for rough, short, stiff hairs on the veins, shaggy-bristly-hairy beneath. Fls 5–11 in racemes, white, scentless, *c*3.5cm across; stamens *c*35; disc and style hairless. Seeds large, with short tails. Early summer. SE US. Z6.

***P. purpurascens*** (Koehne) Rehd. Shrub to 4m; bark of second year brown or grey, smooth; current growth hairless. Axillary buds hidden. Lvs ovate to ovate-lanceolate, 1.5–6×0.5–3cm on flowering shoots, much longer on non-flowering shoots, usually uniformly adpressed-bristly above and on the veins beneath, finely toothed. Racemes usually with 5–9 bell-shaped fls 3–4cm wide and very fragrant; cal. green tinged with purple, glaucous; stamens 25–30; style and disc hairless. Summer. S China. var. ***venustus*** (Koehne) S.Y. Hu. Young growth with shaggy hairs. SW China. Z6.

***P. ×purpureo-maculatus*** Lemoine. (*P. ×lemoinei* × *P. coulteri*.) Shrub to 1.5m, bark black-brown, eventually peeling in the second year; current growth hairy. Lvs 1–3.5×0.6–2.5cm, broadly ovate, base rounded, tip acute, entire or almost so, with a few scattered hairs beneath. Fls solitary or in threes or fives, fragrant, epigynous zone with short, rough hairs; cor. disc-shaped, 2.5–3cm across, pet. almost circular, white, purple at base; stamens *c*30. Summer. Garden origin. Habit dwarf to vigorous, 80cm–1m, arching to upright and narrow; lvs 3–9cm; fls 4–8cm, fragrance slight to strong. 'Beauclerk' ('Sybille' × 'Burfordiensis'): to 2m, fls to 8cm, centre pink; pet. broad. 'Belle Etoile': to 2m, fls to 8cm, centre purple; pet. broad; pineapple-scented. 'Bicolore': dwarf; lvs 3cm, fls creamy, centre purple. 'Etoile Rose': fls carmine at centre fading to apex, scarcely fragrant. 'Fantasie': to 80cm, fls rounded. 'Galathée': branches arching, fl solitary, centre pink. 'Nuage Rose': fls far opening, centre pink. 'Oeil de Pourpre': habit upright and narrow; lvs small; cupped, centre dark. 'Ophelie': free-flowering, fl. centre purple, fragrance mild. 'Purpureo-Maculatus': fls solitary, centre pink-purple; the type of the cross. 'Romeo': free-flowering, fl. centre wine-red. 'Sirene': fls flat, centre pale pink. 'Suprise': fls large, centre dark pink-purple. 'Sybille': free-flowering, fl. centre pink. 'Sylvanie': free-flowering, fls large, centre pink. Z5.

***P. satsumanus*** Miq. Similar to *P. satsumi* but with uniformly downy lvs. Summer. Japan. Seldom found in cultivation. Z6.

***P. satsumi*** (Sieb.) S.Y. Hu. Upright shrub to 3m; second-year twigs brown, bark eventually peeling; current growth becoming hairless. Axillary buds hidden. Lvs on non-flowering shoots ovate or broadly elliptic, 6–9×3–5cm, with coarse, forward-pointing teeth, base obtuse or rounded, apex long-acuminate, those on flowering shoots ovate or ovate-lanceolate, 4.5–7×1.5–4.5cm, base tapered, obtuse or sometimes rounded, apex long-acuminate, all with sparse bristles or hairless above, with stiff hairs on the veins beneath and in the vein angles. Fls 5–7 in a raceme, cross-shaped, slightly fragrant, *c*3cm wide; pet. oblong-ovate; stamens 30; style hairless, shortly divided at the apex. Seeds with medium tails. Summer. Japan. Z6.

***P. schrenkii*** Rupr. Upright shrub to 4m, two-year-old bark grey or rarely brown, with transverse cracks, rough-hairy at first. Axillary buds hidden. Lvs ovate, occasionally ovate-elliptic, 7–13×4–7cm on non-flowering shoots, 4.5–7.5×1.5–4cm on flowering shoots, all with base acute or obtuse, tip acuminate, remotely finely toothed or almost entire, sparsely shaggy-hairy on the main veins beneath, usually glabrous above. Fls 3–7 in racemes, cross-shaped, very fragrant, 2.5–3.5cm wide; sep. ovate, 3–7mm; stamens 25–30; disc hairless; style hairy. Seeds short tailed. Summer. Korea to USSR (E Siberia). var. ***jackii*** Koehne. Lvs more obviously toothed, the veins hairy below. Summer. N China, Korea. Z5.

***P. sericanthus*** Koehne. Shrub to 3m; current growth glabrous or soon becoming so, second-year bark grey or grey-brown, slowly peeling. Axillary buds hidden. Lvs 4–11×1.5–5cm, oval-elliptic or elliptic-lanceolate, apex acuminate, base obtuse or rounded, usually coarsely toothed, sparsely adpressed-bristly above and on the veins beneath. Fls 7–15 in racemes, pure white, unscented, *c*2.5cm across; cal. and flower stalk densely adpressed-bristly; disc and style hairless. Seeds short-tailed. Summer. China (Sichuan, Hubei). Z6.

***P. serpyllifolius*** Gray. Somewhat spiny shrub to 1.5m; current year's growth hairy. Lvs ovate to ovate-lanceolate, entire, pubesc. throughout, lanate beneath. Fls solitary, 1–1.5cm diam. Ovary and sep. white-hairy; stamens *c*20; styles united. Summer. Southern US and Mexico.

***P.* ×*splendens*** Rehd. (Thought to be *P. inodorus* var. *grandiflorus* × *P. lewisii* var. *gordonianus*.) Upright shrub; bark of the second year dark brown, peeling; current growth glabrous. Lvs 6–11.5×2.5–5cm, oblong-elliptic, base rounded, apex acuminate, inconspicuously and finely toothed or almost entire, hairless or rough, shaggy-hairy on the veins and vein angles beneath. Fls in crowded racemes of 5–9, disc-shaped, *c*4cm wide, slightly scented; pet. rounded, pure white; ovary, cal., disc and style hairless; stamens 30. Summer. Garden origin. Z5.

***P. subcanus*** Koehne. Erect shrub to 6m; current growth brown, glabrous or soon becoming so, older bark grey-brown, smooth, peeling late. Axillary buds hidden. Lvs 4–14×1.5–7.5cm, ovate or ovate-lanceolate, base rounded or obtuse, apex acuminate, obscurely finely toothed on flowering shoots but with forward-pointing teeth on non-flowering shoots, all sparsely covered with upright hairs above, shaggy-hairy on the veins beneath. Fls 5–29 in racemes 2.5–22cm long; fls disc-shaped, 2.5–3cm across, pure white, slightly fragrant; cal. curly-hairy; pet. circular to obovate, long curly-hairy at base; stamens *c*30; disc downy, lower style hairy. Seeds with very short tails. Early summer. W China. Rare in cultivation; most commonly seen is var. *magdalenae* (Koehne) S.Y. Hu, which is somewhat smaller in all its parts and has the flower stalks and cal. only slightly downy with curly hairs. Early summer. SW China. Z6.

***P. tenuifolius*** Rupr. ex Maxim. Upright shrub to 3m; current year's shoots pubesc. Axillary buds hidden. Lvs to 11×6cm, ovate, distantly toothed, glabrous except for sparse hairs on the veins and in the vein angles beneath. Fls 5–9 in a raceme, slightly fragrant, 2.5–3.5cm across; sep. and ovary hairy; stamens 25–30; styles fused for half their length. Capsule obconical. Summer. E USSR, Korea. Z5.

***P. tomentosus*** Royle. Shrub to 3m, similar to *P. coronarius* apart from the downy undersides of the lvs; second-year bark cinnamon, eventually peeling off; current growth hairless or becoming so. Lvs 4–10×2–5cm, ovate or rarely lanceolate, base rounded or obtuse, apex acuminate (often strikingly so), becoming hairless above, uniformly shaggy-hairy beneath or rarely almost hairless. Fls 5–7 in a raceme, *c*3cm across, cross-shaped, fragrant; pet. obovate-oblong, cream; disc and styles glabrous, stigmas club-shaped. Early summer. N India, Himalaya. Z6.

***P. triflorus*** Wallich. Like *P. tomentosus* but lvs hairless beneath, ovary hairless, seeds with short tails. Summer. Indian Himalaya. The name *P. nepalensis* Koehne has been applied to specimens of both this species and *P. tomentosus*; it is, however, in the strict sense, a synonym of *P. triflorus*. Z6.

***P.* ×*virginalis*** Rehd. Of doubtful origin but with strong characteristics of *P. pubescens*. A stiffly upright shrub to 2.5m; second-year bark grey, peeling only when old; current growth with shaggy hairs. Lvs 4–7×2.5–4.5cm, ovate, base rounded, apex shortly acuminate, becoming glabrous above, uniformly rough-shaggy hairy beneath. Fls in racemes, usually double, pure white, very fragrant, 4–5cm wide; cal. densely hairy; style hairless. Summer. Garden origin. Habit dwarf to tall; lvs 3–11cm; fls 4–7cm, white to cream, fragrance light to strong. 'Albâtre': fls pure white, profuse. 'Argentine': fls large, double. 'Burfordiensis': to 3m; lvs 11×5cm; fls 7cm in racemes of 5–9, stamens yellow, conspicuous; similar to 'Monster' in *P.* ×*cymosus*. 'Dwarf Minnesota Snowflake': very dwarf; fls double, profuse, very fragrant. 'Fleur de Neige': to 1m, fls 4cm, semi-double; stamens yellow. 'Fraicheur': fls large, very double, creamy, profuse. 'Glacier': fls creamy, very double, late. 'Le Roy': to 1m, fls cream. 'Minnesota Snowflake': to 1.5m; lvs well retained; fls double. 'Natchez' fls single, to 5cm. 'Purity': fls single, to 5cm, profuse. 'Pyramidal': vigorous, fls semi-double. 'Savilos': to 5cm, single to semi-double. 'Schneestrum': fast growing, pure white double. 'Virginal': fls double in loose heads; the type of the cross. Z5.

***P.* cultivars and hybrids**. 'Buckley's Quill' ('Frosty Morn' × 'Bouquet Blanc'): semi dwarf; fls double, fragrant; pet. long. 'Faxonii': habit arching; fls cross-shaped. 'Frosty Morn': fls 3cm, double; noted for its frost tolerance. 'Mrs E.L. Robinson': fls large fragrant. 'Patricia' (resembles *P. lewisii*): lvs leathery, dark green; fls in racemes of 3–7, very fragrant. 'Slavinii': rounded bush to 3m; lvs 6.5–9.5cm; fls 6cm, cross shaped, abundant. 'Splendens' (possibly *P. inodorus* var. *grandiflorus* × *P. lewisii* var. *gordonianus*): habit full, rounded; fls single, wide opening, fragrance slight; pet. rounded. 'Stenopetalus' (possibly a form of *P. pubescens*): fls campanulate. 'Thelma' (origin unknown, possibly *P. purpurascens*): habit low, graceful, lvs 2.3cm; fls 1.5cm, campanulate.

***P. billiardii*** Koehne. See *P. insignis*.
***P. brachybotrys*** var. ***purpurascens*** Koehne. See *P. purpurascens*.
***P. columbianus*** hort. See *P. inodorus* var. *grandiflorus*.
***P. coronarius*** var. ***tomentosus*** (Royle) Hook. & Thoms. See *P. tomentosus*.
***P. floribundus*** Schräd. See *P.* ×*cymosus*.
***P. gloriosus*** Beadle. See *P. inodorus* var. *grandiflorus*.
***P. godohokeri*** Kirchn. See *P. hirsutus*.
***P.* ×*insignis*** Carr. See *P. insignis*.
***P. lasiogynus*** Nak. See *P. schrenkii* var. *jackii*.
***P. lewisii*** var. ***californicus*** (Benth.) Torr. See *P. californicus*.
***P. nepalensis*** Koehne. See *P. triflorus*.
***P. pallidus*** Hayek ex Schneid. See *P. coronarius*.
***P. pekinensis*** var. ***brachybotrys*** Koehne. See *P. brachybotrys*.
***P. pekinensis*** var. ***kansuensis*** Rehd. See *P. kansuensis*.
***P. pubescens*** var. ***intectus*** (Beadle) Moore. See *P. intectus*.
***P. rubricaulis*** Carr. See *P. pekinensis*.
***P. salicifolius*** hort. See *P. coronarius* 'Salicifolius.
***P. speciosus*** Schräd. ex DC. See *P. inodorus* var. *grandiflorus*.
***P. speciosus*** misapplied. See *P. satsumi*.
***P. venustus*** Koehne. See *P. purpurascens* var. *venustus*.
***P. verrucosus*** Schräd. ex DC. See *P. pubescens*.
***P. viksnei*** Zam. See *P. tenuifolius*.

**×Philageria** Mast. *(Philesia × Lapageria.)* Liliaceae (Philesiaceae). Scrambling shrub, habit similar to *Lapageria* but less vigorous. Leaves 4.5×1–1.5cm, lanceolate, leathery, 3-veined; petioles 0.5–0.7cm. Flowers solitary or few at ends of branches (as in *Philesia*), drooping, but outer tepals 3.8×1.6cm, not more than two-thirds length of inner, fleshy, dull red deep or magenta with a blue bloom, inner tepals 6×3cm, bright rose, more faintly bloomed; filaments spotted pink. Summer. Garden origin (Veitch, 1872). Z9.

CULTIVATION As for *Lapageria*. Propagate by simple layering.

**×*P. veitchii*** Mast. *(Lapageria rosea × Philesia magellanica.)* As for the genus.

**Philagonia** Bl.
***P. fraxinifolia*** Hook. See *Tetradium fraxinifolium*.

**Philesia** Juss. (From Gk *phileo*, to love, from the beauty of the flower.) Liliaceae (Philesiaceae). 1 species, a branching, erect shrubby evergreen monocot of dense, rather box-like habit with subterranean stolons, 15–30cm in cultivation, to 120cm in the wild. Stems somewhat woody at base, slender, rather flexuous, purple-green, glabrous, bearing scale-like leaves; branches angled with scale leaves at base. True leaves 1.5–3.5×0.3–0.8cm, short-stalked, crowded on upper branches, oblong-lanceolate, pinnately veined, leathery, deep glossy green above, paler, glaucescent beneath, margins somewhat revolute. Flowers solitary or few at the ends of branches, slender-campanulate, pendent, subtended by overlapping, pale green, subulate bracts; tepals 6, the outer 3 1.5–2.2cm, narrowly ovate, obtuse, tinged green or pink, the inner 3 4.5–6.5cm, oblong-obovate, purple-red, sometimes faintly flecked orange-pink, slightly united at base, spreading above, each with a basal nectarial pouch; stamens 6, filaments united into a tube for two-thirds of their length, anthers basifixed; style clavate, slightly exceeding stamens, apex slightly lobed. Fruit a rounded berry. Summer. Chile. Z9.

CULTIVATION As for *Lapageria*. Propagate by removal of suckers or by greenwood or semi-ripe cuttings in summer in a closed shaded case.

***P. magellanica*** Gmel. As for the genus.

***P. buxifolia*** Willd. See *P. magellanica*.

**Philippicereus** Backeb.
***P. castaneus*** (Philippi) Backeb. See *Eulychnia castanea*.

**Phillyrea** L. (Gk name for the genus.) MOCK PRIVET. Oleaceae. 4 species of evergreen shrubs, to 6×3m. Leaves opposite, entire or toothed, short-petioled, glossy green, glabrous. Flowers small, clustered in axils of previous year's growth, green-white, fragrant. Calyx and corolla 4-lobed; calyx short, broad; corolla with short tube; stamens 2. Fruit an ovoid, single-seeded drupe. Mediterranean to Asia Minor. Z7.

CULTIVATION As for *Osmanthus*.

***P. angustifolia*** L. Shrub to 3m, densely branching. Shoots minutely pubesc., slightly warty; lvs linear-lanceolate, coriaceous, to 6×1cm, olive green, entire, rarely dentate, glabrous. Fr. blue-black. Summer. Mediterranean. 'Rosmarinifolia': lvs narrower, smaller, to 6×4cm, grey-green, somewhat glaucous.

***P. latifolia*** L. Shrub or small trees to 9m, branching densely. Young shoots and pedicels minutely downy. Lvs to 6cm, ovate to elliptic-lanceolate, dentate or entire in smaller lvs, broad-acuminate, basally cordate, glossy, dark green, glabrous, paler below, veins 5–12 pairs. Fls off-white, basally flushed green in short-stemmed axillary clusters. Fr. blue-black, ovoid to globose, to 6mm diam. Late spring. Mediterranean. 'Buxifolia': lvs small, obovate, usually entire. 'Spinosa': lvs markedly dentate, ovate.

***P. decora*** Boiss. & Bal. See *Osmanthus decorus*.
***P. media*** L. See *P. latifolia*.
***P. spinosa*** Mill. See *P. latifolia* 'Spinosa'.
***P. vilmoriniana*** Boiss. & Bal. See *Osmanthus decorus*.

**Philodendron** Schott. (From Gk *phileo*, to love, and *dendron*, tree, alluding to the climbing or epiphytic habit.) Araceae. 350+ species of epiphytic or terrestrial evergreen climbing shrubs, small trees or stemless herbs; juvenile phase often distinct from adult. Stems stout bearing adventitious roots; internodes very short (less than 1mm) to elongate. Leaves often large, to 1m+, entire or lobed to pinnatifid to pedate, oblong or ovate, cordate to sagittate, coriaceous, usually dark green, venation pinnate with primary and secondary veins parallel; petiole to 1.5m, stout, often equalling or sometimes exceeding lamina, sheathed, often with groove above between longitudinal marginal ridges, occasionally geniculate above or swollen and forming pseudobulbs at base, leaf scars very distinct on stem; leaves subtended by membranous cataphylls which sometimes persist, covering stem. Peduncles axillary, 1–11, to 45cm, but often short; spathe to 30cm, fleshy, forming tube around spadix below, expanded above, hooded to cymbiform, persistent, often with resinous ducts, white to green and yellow, often marked with red and purple; spadix shorter than or subequal to spathe, sometimes shortly stipitate, usually white, densely covered by unisexual flowers, male and female zones adjacent, sometimes fragrant; perianth absent; stamens 2–5, lowest male flowers sterile; ovary 2- to many-locular, ovules 1 to many. Fruit a berry, white to orange or red. Some myrmecophytes. Tropical America.

CULTIVATION In subtropical climates, the self-supporting, self-heading spp. (forming strong stems with a crown of leaves) make spectacular lawn specimens and in cooler regions all are suitable for the intermediate to hot glasshouse and as house or conservatory plants. *P. imbe, P. cannifolium* and *P. verrucosum* are suited to cool windowsills and *P. scandens, P. erubescens* and *P. cordatum* are useful for hanging baskets. Those with a 'bird's nest' habit (often epiphytes from the exposed high canopy) are the most compact. *P. wendlandii* has made important contributions in the breeding of compact and upright hybrids. *P.* 'Wend-imbe' and *P.* 'Lynette' are particularly attractive.

Grow in an open, fertile, moisture retentive mix of loam, peat or bark, coarse leafmould and coarse sand. Maintain a day temperature of 21–27°C/70–80°F, falling to 15–21°C/60–70°F at night when in growth, with a winter minimum of 15°C/60°F. Site in part shade or in filtered light, ensuring protection from bright summer sun; provide good air circulation but avoid draughts of both cold and warm air (as in central heating vents). Mist frequently when in growth and water moderately, reducing as temperatures fall in winter. When plants are in full growth and roots have filled the pots, feed regularly with 10:10:5 NPK liquid fertilizer. Provide the support of a moss pole for vining types, and keep the pole moist. Encourage branching in *P. scandens* by pinching out the tip. Self-heading types may also need the support of canes. Propagate by air layering, stem tip or leaf bud cuttings rooted in individual small pots in a closed case with bottom heat at 21–25°C/70–77°F. Seed when available will germinate at 20°C/68°F, grow seedlings on at 18–21°C/65–70°F. *Pythium* spp. may cause root rots of mature specimens if overwatered.

***P. angustisectum*** Engl. Stems climbing; internodes to 5cm. Lvs to 60×45cm, reflexed, ovate in outline, basal sinus triangular, pinnatisect, seg. to 2.5cm across, 16 per side, linear, acute, with 1 vein, glossy dark green above; petiole terete, subequal to lamina. Peduncles short; spathe to 15cm, green externally with pink margins, yellow within. Colombia.

***P. auriculatum*** Standl. & L.O. Williams. Stems stout, climbing; internodes short. Lvs to 90×35cm, erect, narrow-elliptic-oblong, basally auriculate, veins paler than lamina; petiole shorter than lamina, subcylindric. Peduncle 12.5cm; spathe to 28cm, green-white. Costa Rica.

***P. bahiense*** Engl. Close to *P. ruizii*, differing in smaller lvs. Lamina to 35×12.5cm, main lateral veins 5–6 paired; petiole to 15cm, sheathed in basal half. Brazil (Bahia).

***P. barrosoanum*** Bunting. Stems climbing, internodes 3–6×4cm. Lvs 40×25cm, reflexed, hastate, 3-lobed, median lobe ovate, apex acuminate or mucronate, lateral lobes 30×17.5cm, elliptic-ovate, very unequal, base rounded, sinus very broad, veins broad; petiole to 75cm, cylindric. Peduncles 4–5, to 10cm; spathe to 20cm, green, tinged red, tube red within; spadix equaling spathe, shortly stipitate. S America.

***P. bipennifolium*** Schott. HORSEHEAD PHILODENDRON; FIDDLE-LEAF PHILODENDRON. Stems climbing, tall, internodes long. Lvs 45–15cm, reflexed, 5-lobed, glossy dark green, terminal lobe long, to 25×10cm, obovate, lateral lobes angular, obtuse, basal lobes broadly oblong-triangular, sinus open; petiole terete, shorter than lamina. Peduncle short; spathe 11cm, green-cream. SE Brazil.

***P. bipinnatifidum*** Endl. Large, arborescent, stems to 2m×10cm, becoming decumbent with age; internodes short; leaf scars prominent; aerial roots stout. Lvs to 1m, reflexed, ovate in outline, sagittate, pinnatisect, seg. many, overlapping, obtuse, again pinnatifid or sinuate, flat or undulate, bright green; petioles equalling lamina, flat between marginal ridges above. Peduncle to 10cm, solitary; spathe 30×7cm, green to dark purple-red externally, cream with red margin within. SE Brazil. The name *P.* 'Barryi' refers to hybrids between the formerly distinct species. 'California type': arborescent; lvs very deeply cut, scoop-shaped, dark green. 'German Selloum': graceful; lvs finely cut, segments undulate. 'Johnsii': lvs somewhat lobed and in rosette form when young. 'Miniature Selloum': dwarf; lvs small, heavy, petioles thick. 'Uruguay': lvs large, thick, lobes frilled. 'Variegatum': lvs marbled light green to yellow, petioles streaked cream; self-heading.

***P. brenesii*** Standl. Stems climbing. Lvs to 50×25cm, lanceolate- to ovate-oblong, deeply cordate, coriaceous, midrib broad, prominent, main lateral veins to 8+ pairs; petiole subequal to lamina. Spathe to 15cm, tube inflated, green externally, dark-red within. Costa Rica.

***P. cannifolium*** Kunth. Stem prostrate, internodes short. Lvs 45×15–20cm, erect, lanceolate to ovate, acute to acuminate, base obtuse to truncate, coriaceous, glossy, midrib broad, main lateral veins many; petioles to 40cm, swollen and spongy, widely channelled above, margins angular. Peduncles to 17cm; spathe 17cm, nearly cylindric, green, becoming cream above, base cherry-red within. SE Brazil.

***P. cordatum*** (Vell. Conc.) Kunth. HEART-LEAF PHILODENDRON. Stems tall, climbing, internodes short. Lvs 45×25cm, reflexed, ovate-triangular, sagittate, basal lobes round-angular, overlapping or with narrow sinus to 15cm, margins undulate; petioles shorter than or exceeding lamina. Spathe to 15cm, green. SE Brazil.

***P. ×corsinianum*** Senoner. (Parents unrecorded, probably including *P. verrucosum*.) Stems climbing, tall, internodes short, fibrous remains of cataphylls persistent at nodes. Lvs 75×60cm, reflexed, ovate, base cordate, shallowly pinnate-lobed, marked metallic red-purple between green veins beneath when young, becoming green; petioles subequal to lamina. Peduncle short, with white lines; spathe 18cm, tube purple externally, limb green-white, spotted red.

***P. crassinervium*** Lindl. Stems climbing, tall, internodes to 10cm. Lvs to 60×10cm, narrow-elliptic-oblong, long-acuminate, cuneate at base, coriaceous, midrib convex, inflated, to 1.5cm across, lateral veins many; petioles to 18cm, subcylindric. Peduncle exceeding petioles; spathe to 15cm, constricted above tube, green beneath, dull white above, base cherry-red within. SE Brazil.

***P. cruentum*** Poepp. REDLEAF. Close to *P. ruizii* differing to lamina less broad, to 40×10cm, basal lobes acute; petioles to 18cm. Spathe to 15cm, white externally, red within. Peru.

***P. devansayeanum*** Lind. Stem prostrate or climbing; internodes 3–4×8cm. Lvs to 100cm, ovate, cordate, glossy, orange-brown when young, midrib and main lateral veins purple-red beneath; petioles to 150cm, erect, winged below, purple-red. Peduncle to 10cm; spathe to 15cm, white above, light red beneath. Peru, W Ecuador.

***P. distantilobum*** K. Krause. Stems climbing. Lvs to 40×35cm, erect, ovate-oblong in outline, pinnatifid nearly to midrib, seg. 5–6 per side, oblanceolate to linear, acuminate, to 5cm across, entire or basal seg. bifid, interstitial sinuses wide, angular; petiole subequal to lamina. Peduncles several, to 12.5cm; spathe to 8.5cm, green-white. Brazil (Amazonia).

***P. domesticum*** Bunting. SPADE-LEAF PHILODENDRON. Stems climbing. Lvs 60–30cm, reflexed, elongate triangular, sagittate, undulate, glossy bright green, basal lobes round-oblong to triangular, main lateral veins in 5–6 pairs; petiole equalling lamina, flattened above toward apex, centrally longitudinally ridged. Peduncle to 15cm; spathe to 18cm, green externally, deep pink-red within with green border. Origin unknown. 'Variegatum': lvs splashed yellow, cream and acid green.

***P. erubescens*** K. Koch & Augustin. RED-LEAF PHILODENDRON; BLUSHING PHILODENDRON. Stems tall, climbing, purple or red-purple when young, with deep pink to pink-brown cataphylls. Lvs to 40cm, reflexed, ovate-triangular, base short sagittate-cordate, somewhat coriaceous, glossy dark green above, coppery-purple beneath; petiole equalling lamina, flattened towards apex, tinged purple. Peduncle purple-red; spathe 15cm, cymbiform, dark purple externally, crimson within, scented; spadix white, equalling spathe. Colombia. 'Burgundy' (hybrid): lvs leathery, to 30cm, base cordate to hastate, flushed red, veins burgundy, stem claret. 'Golden Erubescens': vigorous climber; stems thin, round; lvs gold, tinted pink beneath and when young. 'Imperial Red': lvs dark purple to red. 'Red Emerald': vigorous; stems claret; lvs long-cordate, to 40cm, dark green with red ribs beneath, shiny, petioles long and rich red.

***P. fendleri*** K. Krause. Stems climbing to 5m, internodes to 2–6×5–6cm, cataphylls becoming scarious, deciduous. Lvs 60cm, reflexed, triangular-ovate in outline, pinnatifid, marginal seg. 11–23×3–8cm, 6–9 per side, oblong, obtuse, with 1 main lateral vein per seg., sinus wide, midrib convex; petioles to 90cm, terete, shortly sheathed at base. Peduncles 4, to 18cm; spathe 18cm, green externally, rich dark maroon within, tube 5cm, inflated; spadix shorter than spathe. Colombia, Venezuela, Trinidad.

***P. fibrillosum*** Poepp. Stems climbing, fibrous remains of cataphylls persistent. Lvs 40×18cm, erect, oblong-elliptic, tapering to each end, membranous, main lateral veins many, prominent; petiole 18cm, apex geniculate. Spathe to 7.5cm, purple below. Peru.

***P. fragrantissimum*** (Hook.) Kunth. Stems climbing when young, branching above when adult. Adult lvs 45–60cm, oblong-cordate to sagittate, petioles deeply grooved above, juvenile lvs ovate, small, with winged petioles. Spathe to 23cm, convolute and hooded, tube bright red, limb pale cream, very fragrant; spadix subequal to spathe, acute, tapering upwards. Northern S America.

***P. giganteum*** Schott. Large, stems climbing, to 10cm diam., internodes short, remains of cataphylls persistent. Lvs to 100×60cm, reflexed, ovate, cordate or sagittate, basal lobes rounded, overlapping; petioles stout, equalling or much exceeding lamina. Peduncle short, stout; spathe to 23cm, tube inflated, cherry-red, limb oblong, white within, dull red externally; spadix stout, sessile. Caribbean Is. to Trinidad.

***P. gloriosum*** André. Stems prostrate, internodes short, with persistent scarious remains of cataphylls. Lvs 40×33cm, reflexed, broad-ovate, cordate-sagittate, basal lobes rounded, dark velvety green above, midrib and main veins ivory-white; petioles to 75cm, flattened above, streaked white. Peduncle to 16.5cm, white-lined; spathe 16.5cm, tube pale green, tinged pink, limb pink. Colombia. 'Terciopelo Redondo': lvs sage green with pale green venation, tinted pink beneath.

***P. grandifolium*** (Jacq.) Schott. Stems climbing, dull green with purple spots, internodes to 5×3cm. Lvs 50×35cm, entire, lanceolate, cordate, acuminate to cuspidate, subcoriaceous, basal lobes ovate to quadrangular, obtuse; midrib prominent, main lateral veins 7–8 per side; petiole to 45cm, terete, shortly grooved at base. Peduncles 1–2, to 10cm; spathe to 11cm, tube somewhat inflated, yellow-green externally, purple within, limb ovate, cream within. Venezuela, French Guiana, Martinique.

***P. grazielae*** Bunting. Stems climbing, internodes to 5cm, Lvs 8.5×10.5cm, reflexed, subreniform, cordate, acuminate, coriaceous, main lateral veins numerous; petioles to 7.5cm, terete, sheathed below in juvenile phase. Peduncle 2cm, spathe 4–5cm, slender, green-white; spadix to 4cm. Amazonian Peru, Brazil.

***P. ilsemannii*** Sander. Variegated juvenile phase of undetermined sp., possibly allied to *P. cordatum*. Stems climbing. Lvs reflexed, narrow-ovate, cordate-sagittate, heavily marked white with green and grey-green patches. Origin unknown.

***P. imbe*** Endl. Stem climbing, red-purple. Lvs 33×18cm, reflexed, ovate-oblong, cordate to sagittate, glossy above, basal lobes rounded, sinus narrow, 7.5cm, main lateral veins in 3 pairs, widely spreading; petiole terete, equalling lamina. Peduncle short; spathe 15cm, tube green externally, red within, limb broad-ovate, cream; spadix slender. SE Brazil. 'Goldiana': dense; lvs long-ovate, rich green with gold speckles, red beneath, yellow when young, petioles short. 'Variegatum': lvs irregularly blotched green, dark green and cream. 'Weber's Selfheading': climber; lvs thick, very shiny, oblique oblanceolate, midrib light green, ribs red beneath, petioles red spotted yellow-green.

***P. inaequilaterum*** Liebm. Stems slender, woody, climbing. Lvs to 30×15cm, spreading to erect, membranous, ovate to elliptic-oblong, acuminate, base obtuse or truncate, main lateral veins numerous, widely spreading; petioles to 20cm, winged to geniculum. Spathe 15cm, green-white. Mexico to Colombia.

***P. inconcinnum*** Schott. Stems climbing, internodes 5cm. Lvs 20×8.5cm, oblong to narrow-obovate, acuminate, base emarginate, midrib broad, main lateral veins in 5–7 pairs; petioles to 20cm+, flattened above, sometimes winged in basal half. Spathe to 14cm, green-yellow externally, cream within, red at base. Venezuela.

***P. insigne*** Schott. Stems short, erect. Lvs 100×22cm, erect, oblanceolate-spathulate, acuminate, base cuneate, obtuse or acute, coriaceous; midrib to 2.5cm at base, main lateral veins 2.5cm apart, spreading; petioles to 12.5cm, thick, sheathed below. Peduncle to 38cm; spathe 18cm, green externally becoming yellow or tinged purple, cherry-red within. Northern S America.

***P. krebsii*** Schott. Stems climbing, internodes 2.5–10cm. Lvs 35×20cm, spreading, ovate to oblong-elliptic or elongate-triangular, cordate, subcoriaceous, glossy dark green, midrib broad, lateral veins numerous; petioles 12.5cm, terete. Peduncle equalling petiole; spathe 10cm, green. Caribbean Is.

***P. lacerum*** (Jacq.) Schott. Stems climbing, to 30m, internodes long. Lvs 75cm, reflexed, ovate to round in outline, cordate, pinnatisect to less than halfway to midrib, lobes cuneate, obtuse, midrib and main lateral veins prominent; petioles terete, to 90cm. Peduncles several, 20cm+; spathe 12.5cm, tube inflated, dull red-purple externally, purple within, limb green-yellow. Cuba, Jamaica, Hispaniola.

***P. latilobum*** Schott. Stems climbing. Juvenile lvs entire; adult lvs 30×25cm, ovate-triangular in outline, base obtuse to sub-truncate, 3-lobed toward apex, median lobe to 15cm across, broad-ovate, acute, lateral lobes rounded, with upper margin shorter and somewhat curved, obtuse, main lateral veins 6. Peru.

***P. lingulatum*** (L.) K. Koch. Stems slender, climbing. Lvs to 40cm, membranous, oblong-elliptic to ovate, acuminate, truncate to emarginate at base, glossy dark green above; petioles slightly exceeding lamina, widely winged except for apical 1.5–6.5cm. Spathe 15cm, cream, becoming green with age. W Indies.

***P. linnaei*** Kunth. Epiphyte, stem to 10cm. Lvs 50–70×8–11cm, forming a rosette, elongate, oblanceolate to spathulate, coriaceous, midrib prominent, 1cm across, main lateral veins numerous, 3mm apart; petioles stout, semi-terete, sheathed to apex. Peduncle to 22cm; spathe tube red-purple, limb white or green externally, sometimes red-spotted; spadix stipitate. Amazonian Brazil.

***P. mamei*** André. Stem prostrate, internodes very short, cataphylls becoming scarious, red-brown, persistent. Lvs 60×45cm, reflexed, ovate, sagittate, basal lobes angular, irregularly spotted grey-green between main veins, veins impressed; petioles subequal to lamina, flattened above with short winged section near apex, red at base and apex. Peduncle 5cm, red-purple; spathe 15cm, maroon or brown-red externally. Ecuador.

***P. maximum*** K. Krause. Stems climbing, 5cm diam., internodes short, remains of cataphylls persistent. Lvs 135×73cm, reflexed, long-ovate, sagittate, undulate to sinuate, dark green above, midrib and main lateral veins pale; petiole to 105cm, flattened above. Peduncle to 30cm; spathe 20cm, green. Brazil (Acre).

***P. melanochrysum*** Lind. & André. BLACK-GOLD PHILODENDRON. Stems climbing, internodes long. Lvs 100×30cm, reflexed to pendent, oblong-lanceolate or narrow-ovate, sagittate, acuminate, basal lobes overlapping or sinus narrow, velvety black-green above, veins pale green, copper-coloured when young; petioles to 50cm, scabrous; juvenile lvs smaller, ovate-cordate, basal lobes sometimes connate; petioles sheathing below. Spathe 20cm, tube green, limb acuminate, white. Colombia.

***P. melinonii*** Brongn. ex Reg. Stems erect, covered by persistent fibrous remains of cataphylls. Lvs 100×40cm, erect, ovate-triangular, emarginate, midrib concave, pale green, main lateral veins in 8–9 pairs; petioles stout, flattened above, rounded beneath, margins narrowly winged; juvenile lvs oblong, base truncate, rose-purple below. Spathe 16.5cm, tube inflated, olive-green tinged red externally, rose-purple within, limb cream. Northern S America.

***P. mexicanum*** Engl. Stems climbing, internodes long. Lvs reflexed, long-triangular, more or less hastate, median lobe 38×18cm, lateral lobes 23×8.5cm, lanceolate to oblong, curved; petioles 60cm. Spathe to 15cm, green externally, ruby-red within. Mexico.

***P. microstictum*** Standl. & L.O. Williams. Stems climbing. Lvs to 23×20cm, broad-triangular to nearly reniform, long-acuminate, emarginate or truncate in juvenile phase, coriaceous, main lateral veins numerous; petioles equalling lamina, broadly sheathed at base. Peduncle exceeding petiole; spathe 15cm, green externally, tube dark red within at base. Costa Rica.

***P. myrmecophilum*** Engl. Stems climbing, internodes short. Lvs 25–50×17.5–30cm, erect, entire, ovate, cordate to hastate, coriaceous, basal lobes obtuse to rounded, to 17cm, separated by deep sinus; petioles to 50cm, grooved, sheathed beneath, inhabited by ants. Peduncle to 20cm; spathe to 15cm, lanceolate-ovate, white and purple, or purple with margin white. Amazon basin.

***P. ochrostemon*** Schott. Stems climbing, slender, internodes long. Lvs 28×11.5cm, spreading or erect, oblong-elliptic to oblong, base truncate, midrib narrow, main lateral veins in 10–12 pairs; petioles shorter than laminae, narrowly winged, auriculate at apex. Spathe 15cm, tube green externally, yellow-green within, limb yellow. SE Brazil.

***P. ornatum*** Schott. Stems climbing, internodes to 10cm when juvenile, 2.5cm when adult, fibrous remains of cataphylls persistent. Lvs 60cm, reflexed, ovate, deeply cordate, glossy dark green, sometimes spotted with grey, veins red beneath; petiole equalling lamina, flattened above toward apex, somewhat scabrous, purple when young. Peduncle short, red with white streaks; spathe 14cm, apex 2cm, long-subulate, cream within, tube green externally, limb white, tinged red externally. Venezuela to Peru & SE Brazil.

***P. pedatum*** (Hook.) Kunth. Stems tall, climbing, internodes long. Lvs reflexed, ovate in outline, irregularly pinnatifid, terminal lobe 45×30cm, median seg. elliptic, obovate or rhombic, lateral seg. to 5 per side, oblong, obtuse, with 2 or more main lateral veins each, basal lobes 27×17cm, widely spreading; petioles exceeding lamina, terete, sometimes verrucose toward apex; juvenile lvs with 5 lobes. Spathe 12.5cm, green externally, becoming white toward apex, cream within, red-purple at base of tube. S Venezuela, Surinam to SE Brazil.

***P. pinnatifidum*** (Jacq.) Schott. Stems erect, short and stout, covered by persistent remains of cataphylls and petiole bases, internodes long. Lvs to 60cm, triangular-ovate, acuminate, pinnatifid, lateral lobes to 20×5cm, 5–6 per side, oblong, obtuse, basal lobes with 2–4 divisions, separated by broad sinus, glossy above; petioles equalling or exceeding lamina, swollen at base, deeply grooved above, spotted purple-brown. Spathe to 23cm, tube fusiform, green to dull purple, limb cymbiform, white; spadix equalling spathe, dull yellow. Venezuela, Trinidad.

***P. pinnatilobum*** Engl. Stems climbing, angular, internodes to 3.5cm or to 10cm when juvenile. Lvs to 50cm across, erect, ovate-orbicular, pinnatifid, lateral seg. 1.5cm across, to 13 per side, narrow, acuminate, basal lobes bifid; juvenile lvs with fewer seg. and basal lobes reduced; petioles equalling lamina, grooved above. Peduncles clustered, 22cm; spathe 10cm, green, tinged pink at base externally. Brazil (Amazonia).

***P. radiatum*** Schott. DUBIA PHILODENDRON. Stems climbing. Lvs to 90×70cm, reflexed, ovate in outline, cordate-sagittate, deeply pinnatifid, terminal lobe with 8 pairs oblong or further 3-parted seg., interstitial sinuses narrow, basal lobes 5-parted, lateral veins fused at sinus; petioles exceeding lamina, terete. Peduncles clustered; spathe to 25cm, tube inflated, dull red-purple externally, cherry-red within, limb green externally, white within. C America.

***P. rubens*** Schott. Stems erect or climbing, stout, internodes long. Lvs 50×28cm, reflexed, ovate, sagittate-cordate, acuminate, basal lobes rounded; petioles to 60cm, subterete, somewhat scabrous towards apex. Peduncle red with white streaks; spathe 15cm, green, spotted white externally, red-purple within. Venezuela.

***P. rugosum*** Bogner & Bunting. Stems climbing, internodes 1.5–3×4cm. Lvs to 35×30cm, ovate, cordate, apex cuspidate, coriaceous, bright green, markedly rugose above, smooth beneath, midrib convex, main lateral veins 7–10, inconspicuous; petioles to 40cm, terete, grooved toward base. Peduncles 1–4, to 5cm, red; spathe to 10cm, dark red below, paler red above, apex green; spadix to 9cm, sessile, cream. Ecuador.

***P. ruizii*** Schott. Stems climbing. Lvs 60×23cm, narrowly elliptic- to oblanceolate-oblong, base obtuse, truncate or auriculate, coriaceous, main lateral veins in 10 pairs, scarcely distinct from secondary veins; petioles much shorter than lamina, 25cm. Peduncles clustered; spathe to 10cm, pale green. Peru.

***P. sagittifolium*** Liebm. Stems climbing, internodes short. Lvs to 60×30cm, long triangular-oblong, sagittate, subcoriaceous, glossy bright green, basal lobes to 12.5cm, triangular, obtuse, midrib broad, main lateral veins to 6–7-pairs, spreading; petioles subequal to lamina, flattened to convex above. Spathe to 18cm, green, purple at base within. SE Mexico.

***P. scandens*** K. Koch & Sello. HEART-LEAF PHILODENDRON. ssp. ***scandens*** f. *scandens*. Stems slender, climbing, but becoming pendent, internodes long. Lvs 30×23cm, reflexed, ovate-cordate, acuminate, glossy green above, green or red-purple beneath, main lateral veins in 2–3 pairs; petioles slender, shorter than lamina, subterete, channelled above. Infl. borne on pendent shoots; peduncle short; spathe to 19cm, green externally, limb white within, sometimes tinged red at base. Mexico and W Indies to SE Brazil. f. ***micans*** (K. Koch) Bunting. Lvs bronze above, red to red brown beneath, basal lobes larger, slightly overlapping. ssp. ***oxycardium*** (Schott) Bunting. Juvenile lvs glossy, brown when immature, green when mature. E Mexico. 'Variegatum': lvs dark green marbled off-white and green-grey.

***P. schottianum*** H. Wendl. ex Schott. Stems climbing, internodes short. Lvs 60×40cm, broad-ovate, cordate, main lateral veins in 5–6 pairs; petioles exceeding lamina, subcylindric. Peduncle red; spathe 12.5cm, green externally, red-purple within. Costa Rica.

***P. speciosum*** Schott. ex Endl. Close to *P. williamsii*. Stems erect and decumbent, branching from horizontal part, erect to 100cm, internodes very short. Lvs 60–95×45–60cm, reflexed, sagittate, glossy dark green, median seg. to 60cm, basal lobes smaller, main lateral veins 5–6 per side, pink to purple beneath; petiole to 100cm, grooved, with winged margins. Peduncle 13cm; spathe 30cm, cylindric, dull dark green, margin maroon externally, carmine-magenta within; spadix to 30cm. Brazil. 'Ballenger's Exotica' (*P. speciosum* × *P. eichleri*): lvs very large, to 1.5m long, thick, deep green, hastate, deeply lobed, edges cut.

***P. squamiferum*** Poepp. Close to *P. pedatum*. Stems climbing. Lvs 60×45cm, pinnatifid, 5-lobed, lobes entire, median lobe elliptic to rhombic, lateral lobes oblong-triangular, falcate, basal lobes elliptic, separated by broad sinuses; juvenile lvs entire or 3-lobed; petioles 15–30cm, red, terete, densely covered by fleshy bristles. Peduncles 7.5cm, paired, verrucose, red; spathe to 10cm, tube red-purple, limb green-yellow and red-purple externally, cream within. Eastern S America (Surinam, French Guiana, Brazil). 'Florida' (*P. pedatum* or *P. laciniatum* × *P. squamiferum*): climber; lvs in 5 lobes, midrib pale, ribs indented, brown to red beneath; petioles thin, round, somewhat warty. 'Florida Compacta' (*P. pedatum* var. *palmisectum* or *P. quercifolium* × *P. squamiferum*): non-climbing; lvs thick, deep green; petioles round, marked plum. 'Florida Variegata': lvs irregularly blotched pale cream, often covering half the leaf.

***P. teretipes*** Sprague. Epiphyte; stems pendent. Lvs 28×6.5cm, 5–7, lanceolate-oblong, acuminate, green with red margin; petioles red, to 20cm. Spathe to 18cm, tube narrow, limb obovate-oblong, cream, red at base; spadix cylindric, equalling spathe. Colombia.

***P. tripartitum*** (Jacq.) Schott. Stems climbing, internodes long. Lvs more or less reflexed, 3-lobed nearly to base, lobes to 25×7.5cm, elongate ovate-elliptic, median sometimes oblanceolate, lateral lobes 25cm, inequilateral, sides rounded; petioles slightly exceeding lamina, terete. Peduncle short, solitary; spathe 15cm, tube green, purple at base within, limb white. S America.

***P. trisectum*** Standl. Close to *P. tripartitum*, but smaller in all parts. Lf lobes 19×3.5cm, nearly equal, united at base, lateral lobes equilateral, curved; petioles to 33cm. Peduncle 11.5cm; spathe 10cm, green-white. Costa Rica.

***P. tweedianum*** Schott. Stems erect, 50–100cm, or subterranean, appearing acaulous, internodes very short. Lvs 30–50×25–40cm, reflexed, broad ovate-triangular, sagittate, apex obtuse, apiculate, basal lobes obtuse, separated by oblong sinus to 10cm, somewhat glaucous, margins weakly undulate, main lateral veins 3–5 per side; petioles 40–90cm, exceeding lamina, flattened to broadly sulcate above. Peduncle to 45cm; spathe to 20cm, green externally, cream within. S Brazil, Uruguay.

***P. undulatum*** Engl. Stems erect or decumbent, to 200×20cm, internodes very short. Lvs 40×80×30–65cm, 8–10, reflexed, ovate, sagittate, median lobe to 55×65cm, lateral seg. 4–7 per side, acute, subtriangular to rounded, basal lobe to 25×35cm, margin sinuate; petiole 90cm. Peduncle 22cm; spathe 20cm, green externally, purple within. Brazil (Mato Grosso), Paraguay.

***P. verrucosum*** Schott. Stems climbing, internodes to 15cm. Lvs 60×40cm, reflexed, ovate, sagittate-cordate, margins shallowly sinuate, shimmering dark green above with pale green zones along midrib and main lateral veins, red-violet beneath; petioles equalling lamina, flattened above, covered by fleshy red, green or white scales (also covering peduncle, spathe and cataphylls). Peduncle to 20cm; spathe 21cm, red-brown, becoming lime-green above externally, pink-red within, white above. Costa Rica to Ecuador.

***P. warscewiczii*** K. Koch. Stems very large, climbing. Lvs semideciduous, reflexed, membranous, triangular, bipinnatifid, primary lobes few, deeply lobed, ultimate seg. occasionally dentate, basal sinus very broad, with lateral veins united. Peduncle 5cm; spathe to 15cm, green externally, cream within; spadix sessile. Guatemala.

***P. wendlandii*** Schott. Stems erect to prostrate. Lvs 75–90×20cm, forming a rosette, erect, narrow-obovate, truncate or with small auricles at base, midrib 2.5cm broad, convex, main lateral veins impressed; petioles 30×3.5cm, flattened above, spongy. Spathe 18cm, tube pale olive-green tinged purple externally, dark red within, limb cream. C America (Nicaragua to Panama). 'Lynette' (*P. wendlandii* × *P. elephoglossoides*): 'bird-nest' form; lvs thick, vivid green, ribs indented. 'Tricolor' (*P. hastatum* 'Variegatum' × *P. wendlandii*): lvs long, lanceolate, splashed cream and white.

***P. williamsii*** Hook. f. Stems erect, arborescent, 5–7.5cm diam. Lvs to 90cm, reflexed, oblong-triangular, sagittate, median lobe to 35cm across, basal lobes to 22cm, oblong-ovate, obtuse, coriaceous, main lateral veins united at sinus, veins dull purple beneath; petioles to 90cm. Peduncle 30cm; spathe 30cm, green outside, cream within. Brazil (Bahia).

***P.*** cultivars. 'Angra dos Reis': lvs thick, broad-sagittate, very glossy; stalks marked red. 'Beleza do Acre': climber; lvs broad sagittate, to 1m, shiny, margin wavy, ribs lighter. 'Brazilian Arrow': rosette, later tree-like; lvs lanceolate, hastate, to 80cm, lobed, vivid green, thick, veins paler, petioles thin. 'Choco': climber, dense; lvs heavy, to 30cm, dark lush green, veins white. 'Edmundo Barroso': creeping; lvs thick, upright, ovate-oblong, midrib raised. 'Emerald King': lvs to 30cm long, spade-shaped, pointed. 'Emerald Queen': lvs bright green, hastate, shiny, petioles short; Fl hybrid. 'Jungle Gardens' ('São Paulo' × *P. selloum*): tree-like with age; lvs large, bright green, pinnately cut, segments somewhat lobed, slightly wavy. 'Jungle Gardens Variegated': lvs blotched white to yellow. 'Majesty': dense; stems thick; lvs large, lanceolate, dark green flushed copper, red petioles and beneath. 'Minas Gerais': small epiphyte; lvs like fine arrows, edges wavy, petioles thin; self-heading. 'New Red': non-climbing; lvs arrow-shaped, deep metal red. 'New Yorker': climber; lvs sagittate, dipped, thick, dark green, veins lighter, tinted red when young, petioles dotted maroon. 'Painted Lady': lvs sagittate, gold when young, later mottled green; petioles tinted red. 'Queremal': rosette; lvs cordate, erect, firm, shiny. 'Red Duchess': climber; lvs to 25cm long, cordate, dark green, shiny, tinted red beneath, petioles red. 'Santa Leopoldana': climbing; lvs long sagittate, thick, to 1m, dark green, shiny, ribs white, edges red; petioles and stems red; spathe tinted red. 'São Paulo': lvs cupped, vivid green. 'Seaside': vigorous, arborescent; lvs large, thick, heavily cut, lobes frilled; disease-resistant. 'Silver Cloud': vigorous, climbing; lvs thick, waved, splattered silver towards edge, pale beneath, petioles broad and flat, finely striped white. 'Venezuela': 'bird-nest' form; lvs thick, oblanceolate, corrugated.

***P. andreanum*** Devansaye. See *P. melanochrysum*.
***P. asperatum*** K. Koch. See *P. ornatum*.
***P.*** 'Barryi'. See *P. bipinnatifidum*.
***P.*** 'British Guiana'. See *P. pinnatifidum*.
***P. calophyllum*** Brongn. ex Lind. & André. See *P. insigne*.
***P. coerulescens*** Engl. See *P. inaequilaterum*.
***P. cordatum*** misapplied. See *P. scandens*.
***P. deflexum*** Poepp. ex Schott. See *P. myrmecophilum*.
***P. deflexum*** hort. non Poepp. ex Schott. See *P. barrosoanum*.
***P. dubium*** Chodat & Visch. See *P. tweedianum*.
***P. dubium*** hort. non Chodat & Visch. See *P. radiatum*.
***P. duisbergii*** Epple ex Bunting. See *P. fendleri*.
***P. eichleri*** Engl. See *P. undulatum*.
***P. elegans*** K. Krause. See *P. angustisectum*.
***P.*** 'Fernleaf'. See *P. pinnatilobum*.
***P. fibrillosum*** hort. non Poepp. See *P. grazielae*.
***P. guatemalense*** Engl. See *P. inaequilaterum*.
***P. guttiferum*** hort. non Kunth. See *Monstera standleyana*.
***P. hastatum*** hort. non K. Koch & Sello. See *P. domesticum*.
***P. imperiale*** Schott. See *P. ornatum*.
***P. laciniatum*** (Vell. Conc.) Engl. See *P. pedatum*.
***P. laciniosum*** Schott. See *P. pedatum*.
***P. martianum*** Engl. See *P. cannifolium*.
***P. micans*** K. Koch. See *P. scandens* ssp. *scandens* f. *micans*.
***P. nobile*** Bull. See *P. linnaei*.
***P. oxycardium*** Schott. See *P. scandens* ssp. *oxycardium*.
***P. panduraeforme*** misapplied. See *P. bipennifolium*.
***P. pertusum*** Kunth & Bouché. See *Monstera deliciosa*.
***P. pittieri*** Engl. See *P. scandens* ssp. *scandens* f. *scandens*.
***P. sagittatum*** hort. See *P. sagittifolium*.
***P. sagittifolium*** misapplied. See *P. ilsemannii*.
***P. selloum*** K. Koch. See *P. bipinnatifidum*.
***P. sellowianum*** Kunth. See *P. imbe*.
***P. sodiroi*** hort. ex Bellair & St. Leger (invalid). See *P. ornatum*.
***P. triumphans*** hort. See *P. verrucosum*.

**Phinaea** Benth. (Anagram of the related genus *Niphaea*.) Gesneriaceae. 9 species of rhizomatous perennial herbs; stems simple, short, erect or ascending. Leaves opposite, often clustered near stem apex, dentate to crenate, petiolate, thin and soft. Inflorescence axillary; pedicels 2 to many in upper leaf axils; calyx turbinate-campanulate, lobes spreading, equal or subequal; corolla subrotate, tube very short, limb spreading, broadly 5-lobed, white or pale lilac; stamens 4, generally with a staminode; ovary more than half inferior, style stout, stigma slightly dilated. Fruit a capsule, 2-valved; seeds numerous. Mexico to northern S America. Z10.

CULTIVATION See GESNERIADS.

***P. albo-lineata*** Benth. ex Hemsl. Stems erect, 22cm, hairy. Lvs remote below, crowded above, ovate, acute, crenate-serrate, long-petiolate, rich velvety green above with white veins, flushed purple beneath. Pedicels crowded, arising from upper lf axils, 1-fld, hispid; cal. tube short, lobes broadly rounded, hispid; cor. rotate or subrotate, lobes subequal, rounded, crenate, concave, snowy white; stamens 4, staminode present. Early autumn. D America.

***P. multiflora*** C. Morton. Stem 13cm, pilose. Lvs few, to 8×5cm, ovate to rhombic, acute at apex, obtuse to rounded at base, dentate, green with paler veins, green or tinged red below, thinly membranous, pilose. Fls 1 to numerous, in clusters towards stem apex; pedicels 1.5cm, white-villous; cal. tube very short, villous, lobes oblong, 6mm; cor. rotate, to 1cm, tube to 6mm, white, pilose without, lobes equal, suberect, glandular without; stamens 4; ovary villous. Mexico.

***P. rubida*** Fritsch. See *Niphaea oblonga*.

**Phlebodium** (R. Br.) J. Sm. (Diminutive of Gk *phlebion*, vein.) Polypodiaceae. Some 10 species of epiphytic ferns. Rhizomes creeping, dictyostelic, branching, fleshy and thick; scales dense, lanceolate, ciliate, golden-brown. Fronds uniform, ovate, pinnatifid or subpinnate, glabrous, leathery, membranous, or papery, occasionally glaucous; veins pinnate, reticulate, anastomosing into costal and minor areolae, usually sterile, and major areolae with 2–3 excurrent, included veinlets terminating at apex; stipes remote, jointed. Sori superficial, median in major areolae, circular; paraphyses absent; sporangia hairless; annulus 12-celled; spores kidney-shaped to oblong, glassy. Tropical America. Z10.

CULTIVATION As for *Polypodium*. Vigorous cultivars of *P. aureum* are effective when planted out in the glasshouse border if provided with good drainage, but are especially effective grown in hanging baskets. So easily raised from spores that they may become a nuisance where conditions are favourable.

***P. aureum*** (L.) J. Sm. GOLDEN POLYPODY; RABBIT'S-FOOT FERN; HARE'S-FOOT FERN. Epiphytic or epilithic fern. Rhiz. surface-creeping, to 15mm wide; scales dense, linear to lanceolate or ovate-triangular, apex narrowly acute, base obtuse, margin toothed, golden-brown to russet. Fronds to 1m×50cm, grey-green erect, arching, or pendent, deeply pinnatifid, ovate to oblong or deltoid, seg. to 30×5cm, to 35, narrowly linear to lanceolate, oblong or strap-shaped, apex acute or obtuse, margin wavy, main terminal lobe like these lateral seg. but longer; veins anastomosing into costal areolae, oblong, major areolae with or without free, included veinlets, and minor, marginal areolae; stipes to 50cm, scaly at base to glabrous, lustrous red-brown. Tropical America (Florida to Argentina, W Indies). var. ***areolatum*** (Humb. & Bonpl. ex Willd.) Sota. Fronds erect, smaller, leathery, glaucous. 'Cristatum': fronds erect or arching, glaucous, spreading and crested at apex of fronds and their seg. 'Mandaianum' BLUE FERN: fronds and their seg. curved and wavy at margin. 'Undulatum': fronds and their seg. notched and very wavy at margin, grey to silver.

***P. decumanum*** (Willd.) J. Sm. Epiphytic fern. Rhiz. to 2cm wide; scales dense, linear to filiform, toothed and ciliate at margin, soft, light red-brown. Fronds to 120×60cm, few, deeply pinnatifid, arching or spreading, oblong, leathery, glaucous, seg. to 30×7cm, strap-shaped to oblong or lanceolate, margin wavy and cartilaginous, toothed in sinuses, terminal lobe larger; included veinlets prominent, parallel; stipes to 60cm, glabrous, lustrous. Tropical America (Mexico to Argentina, W Indies).

***P. nitidum*** J. Sm. ex Hook., non Kaulf. See *Microgramma nitida*.
For further synonymy see *Chrysopteris, Goniophlebium* and *Polypodium*.

**Phleum** L. (From Gk *phleos*, a type of reed with a compact inflorescence.) Gramineae. Some 15 species of annual or perennial grasses. Leaves flat. Inflorescence paniculate, spicate, cylindric to subglobose; spikelets axis elongated, laterally flattened, abscising; glumes equal, longer than flower, membranous, conspicuously keeled, mucronate to awned; lemma to 7-ribbed, keeled, shorter than glumes; apex awnless or mucronate. N, S temperate regions, S America. Z5.

CULTIVATION Occasionally grown for the soft, densely flowered cylindrical inflorescence which dries and dyes well, *P. pratense* is an attractive addition to the wild flower meadow. Grow in any ordinary soil in sun. It is grown for pasture and is a common cause of hayfever. *P. bertolinii* is a pasture and turf grass. In addition to those described below, *P. paniculatum* Huds. and *P. subulatum* Asch. & Gräbn. may be worthy of cultivation. Sow seed of *P. subulatum* in spring *in situ*, perennials also by division.

***P. phleoides*** (L.) Karst. Perenn. to 60cm. Stems clumped, slender, erect. Lvs flat or rolled, to 13×0.4cm. Infl. narrow cylindric, to 10×0.6cm, tinged green to purple; spikelets narrow oblong, mucronate, with rough and bristly keel. Summer. NW Africa, Europe, N Asia.

***P. pratense*** L. TIMOTHY; CAT'S TAIL; MEADOW CAT'S TAIL. Perenn. to 1.5m. Stems clumped, robust, ascending, swollen at base. Lvs to 45×1cm, glabrous; ligules papery, blunt, to 0.6cm. Infl. compact, cylindric, to 30×1cm; spikelets oblong, compact, to 0.4cm, 1-fld; glumes narrow oblong, keel ciliate, awned; awn to 0.2cm; palea equalling lemma. Summer. C, N, W Europe.

***P. boehmeri*** Wibel. See *P. phleoides*.
***P. nodosum*** L. See *P. pratense*.
***P. phlaroides*** K. Koch. See *P. phleoides*.
***P. pratense*** var. ***nodosum*** (L.) Huds. See *P. pratense*.

**Phlogacanthus** Nees (From Gk *phlox*, flame, and *Acanthus*, alluding to the brilliant flowers of some species.) Acanthaceae. Some 15 species of perennial herbs and subshrubs. Leaves usually large, entire or toothed. Flowers in long, thyrse-like, terminal or short, axillary spikes; corolla tubular, showy, curved, limb bilabiate; stamens 2. Asia. Z10.

CULTIVATION As for *Crossandra*.

***P. thyrsiformis*** (Hardw.) Mabb. Shrub to 2.25m. Lvs to 22cm, elliptic-lanceolate. Infl. to 30cm, thyrse-like, terminal; fls orange. N India.

***P. thyrsiflorus*** Nees. See *P. thyrsiformis*.

**Phlomis** L. (From Gk *phlomos*, mullein, alluding to the woolly stems and leaves of some species.) Labiatae. About 100 species of pubescent or woolly herbs, subshrubs or evergreen shrubs to 1.8m. Stems floccose at first. Leaves opposite, narrow to ovate, rugose; bracts similar or reduced. Flowers in axillary verticillasters; bracteoles often numerous, narrow to ovate usually subulate; calyx tubular, 5-toothed; corolla yellow, white, purple or pink, 2-lipped, upper lip hooded, lower 3-lobed, spreading; stamens 4; style branches unequal. Fruit a 3-sided nut. Mediterranean to C Asia and China.

CULTIVATION A large genus including shrubs native to dry and rocky habitats in Europe and herbaceous perennials which occur in grassland in Europe and Asia, *Phlomis* spp. are grown primarily for their dense whorls of lipped flowers, in butter yellow or shades of lilac, carried above the foliage on tall and erect stems. Many spp. also have attractive foliage; that of *P. fruticosa* is soft grey-green and aromatic. *P. samia* and *P. russeliana* have large heart-shaped leaves that overlap to make extremely effective weed-smothering groundcover. The herbaceous species make attractive and undemanding additions to the herbaceous or mixed border; they may need staking in exposed and windy positions. *P. russeliana, P. samia* and *P. tuberosa* are reliably hardy to −15°C/5°F, the last re-emerging from tuberous roots even when top-growth is killed. With a sheltered position and perfect drainage, *P. fruticosa* will tolerate temperatures almost as low. Most other species, with the exception of the tender *P. purpurea*, will tolerate temperatures of −5°C/23°F.

Grow in full sun in well-drained soils, with shelter from cold winds. Large-leaved species such as *P. samia* and *P. russeliana* will tolerate light shade. For shrubby species with downy leaves good drainage is particularly important; these plants are tolerant of the poor gravelly soils that approximate to those of their natural habitat. Cut back shrubby spp. after flowering to maintain shape. Perennial spp. may be cut down in autumn, although the dead flowering stems are sometimes left on for winter interest. Propagate shrubby species by softwood cuttings in summer, or by semi-ripe cuttings in a sandy propagating mix in the cold frame in autumn; also by simple layering. Divide herbaceous species in autumn or spring, taking care with *P. tuberosa* not to damage the tubers. Sow seed in spring at 15–18°C/60–65°F.

**1** Corolla yellow or yellow-brown.

1.1 Petiole usually more than 2cm long.
*Pp. armeniaca, chrysophylla, ferruginea, fruticosa, longifolia, russeliana, viscosa.*

1.2 Petiole absent or less than 2cm long.
*Pp. grandiflora, lanata, lychnitis, lycia.*

**2** Corolla purple or pink.

2.1 Leaves usually less than 13cm long, verticillasters less than 10-flowered.
*Pp. italica, pungens, purpurea, rotata.*

2.2 Leaves usually greater than 13cm long, verticillasters more than 10-flowered.
*Pp. alpina, bovei, bracteosa, cashmeriana, herba-venti, pratensis, rotata, samia, setigera, tuberosa, umbrosa.*

***P. alpina*** Pall. To 45cm, white-pubesc. throughout. Lvs 20cm, ovate-lanceolate to cordate. Verticillasters 20–30-fld; bracteoles subulate; cal. teeth bristly; cor. tinted purple. Altai Mts, Mongolia. Z8.

***P. armeniaca*** Willd. To 60cm. Lvs 2–10×1–2cm, ovate-oblong to linear-lanceolate, obtuse, tapering towards base, crenulate to shallow-lobed, short stellate-pubesc. above, canescent beneath; petioles to 7cm; bracts linear-lanceolate, short-petiolate or sessile. Verticillasters 2–5, distant or crowded toward apex, 4–10-fld, bracteoles subulate, 3–10mm, tomentose; cal. 13–17mm, stellate-tomentose; cor. 25–35mm, yellow. Summer. Turkey, Caucasia, N Iran. Z7.

***P. bovei*** Noë. Erect perenn. herb to 1m. Stems covered in branching, eglandular, stellate hairs with a few glandular stellate hairs. Basal lvs largest, 6–8×2–4cm, broadly cordate-oblong, margins coarsely crenate, apex obtuse to acute, upper surface green, bullate, pubesc., lower densely pubesc.; petiole to 6cm, pubesc. Infl. an interrupted spike of dense distant verticillasters; cal. 16–18mm, subtubulose, teeth short, distinctly mucronulate at apex; cor. to 3.5cm, purple-pink, upper lip porrect, lower lip purple-spotted within, lateral lobes revolute, subentire, middle lobe broadest, to 9mm, outside of cor. more or less yellow-tomentose. Algeria, Tunisia. ssp. ***maroccana*** Maire. To 1.5m. Stems covered in glandular hairs, viscose, with a few eglandular hairs. Cal. to 2cm, fusiform, glandular pubesc., teeth subulate; cor. 4–4.5cm, purple-pink, upper lip slightly shorter than lower, spotted purple within but not all sides, lobes spreading not revolute, lateral 3 lobes rounded, middle lobe broadest, to 23mm, outside of cor. white-tomentose. Morocco. Z9.

***P. bracteosa*** Royle. Robust, to 1m, little branched. Lvs 5–10cm, ovate, cordate, coarsely serrate, rugose above, downy beneath, short-petiolate. Verticillasters many-fld; bracteoles equal cal.; cor. blue-purple. W temperate Himalaya. Z8.

***P. cashmeriana*** Royle. Robust, to 90cm. Stems densely woolly. Lvs 13–23×5–10cm, ovate-lanceolate, obtuse, entire in lower part, broadly rounded at base, downy above, white beneath; petiole 10–15cm. Verticillasters many-fld; bracteoles subulate, exceeding cal.; cal. 10–15mm; cor. pale lilac. Summer. Kashmir, W Himalaya. Z8.

***P. chrysophylla*** Boiss. Low evergreen subshrub. Lvs to 6×4cm, broadly elliptic to oblong-elliptic or oblong-ovate, obtuse, mostly truncate to cordate at base, densely yellow pubesc., golden, downy when young; petioles 2–3cm; bracts subulate, spine-tipped. Fls in distant, many-fld verticillasters or paired; cal. teeth minutely spine-tipped; cor. golden yellow. Summer. Lebanon. Z9.

***P. ferruginea*** Ten. Shrub to 90cm. Branches rusty-tomentose. Lvs oblong-lanceolate, crenate, obtuse, cordate at base, white beneath; petiole to 4cm; bracts lanceolate, acute or acuminate, petiolate. Verticillasters 12–30-fld; bracteoles linear to narrow-lanceolate, 12–19mm; cal. 13–19mm; cor. 25–27mm, yellow. Summer. Italy, Crete. Z9.

***P. fruticosa*** L. JERUSALEM SAGE. Spreading subshrub to 130cm, tawny-pubesc. to floccose throughout. Lvs 3–9×2–3cm, ovate-lanceolate, truncate or cuneate at base, dull green, markedly rugose above, hoary stellate-tomentose beneath, entire or crenulate; petiole to 4cm; bracts mostly lanceolate, obtuse, sessile or petiolate. Verticillasters cymose, 1–2, 20–30-fld; bracteoles obovate or broadly lanceolate, 10–20×3–7mm, pilose, stellate-pubesc. to lanate; cal. 10–20mm, stellate-lanate; cor. 30mm, golden yellow. Summer. Mediterranean W to Sardinia. 'Edward Bowles' (possibly *P. russeliana* × *P. fruticosa*): robust; lvs to 15×7cm; petiole to 14cm; fls pale yellow. Z7.

***P. grandiflora*** H.S. Thomps. To 2m, woody at base. Lvs 3–8×2–4cm, ovate to oblong, abruptly cuneate, rounded-truncate or cordate at base, entire or crenulate, dull green, short-pubesc. above, hoary stellate-tomentose beneath; petiole to 3cm; bracts oblong, sessile or short-petiolate. Verticillasters single, many-fld; bracteoles numerous, glabrous above, sparsely pubesc. below, broadly ovate to ovate-lanceolate, acuminate, 12–18×3–10mm; cal. 13–17mm, felty and pilose; cor. 30–40mm, yellow. Spring–summer. E Mediterranean. Z8.

***P. herba-venti*** L. Perenn. herb to 70cm. Stems green, eglandular, stellate-hirsute with hairs 2–4mm long. Stem lvs 9–18cm, ovate or lanceolate, base truncate, rounded or cordate, margins crenate or serrate, surfaces glabrous or shortly hirsute above. Verticillasters (6) 10–14-fld; bracteoles 11–15mm, subulate, stellate tomentose; cal. 8–15mm, stellate-tomentose, teeth 2–7mm, subulate, cor. 15–20mm, purple or pink upper lip galeate, nutlets smooth. Mediterranean Region, Balkans, SW & Central Asia. This is a very variable species and had previously included *P. pungens*, which differs largely in leaf shape and in the indumentum. Z7.

***P. italica*** L. Subshrub to 30cm. Lvs to 5×2cm, oblong to oblong-lanceolate, obtuse, white-tomentose, shallow-crenate, petiolate; bracts lanceolate, acute, petiolate. Verticillasters distant, 6-fld; bracteoles subulate to linear-lanceolate, 12–20mm; cal. 15–20mm, densely canescent, hairs concealing short, rounded teeth; cor. 20mm, pink or pale lilac. Summer–autumn. Balearic Is (not native to Italy). Z8.

***P. lanata*** Willd. Shrub to 50cm. Young stems golden-floccose. Lvs 1.5–2.5cm, oblong to rounded, woolly; petiole to 1cm; bracts rounded, subsessile. Verticillasters 1 to several, 2–10-fld; bracteoles broad-elliptic or obovate, mucronate, 6–10mm; cal. woolly, 10–12mm, teeth to 1mm; cor. orange-yellow, 2cm. Summer. Crete. Z8.

***P. longifolia*** Boiss. & Bl. Eglandular shrub to 130cm. Stems more or less pubesc. Lvs 3–7×1.5–4cm, lanceolate to oblong or ovate, cordate or subcordate at base, margins crenulate or crenate-serrate, upper surface green-tomentose, lower grey to yellow stellate-tomentose, petioles to 5cm; floral lvs ovate-deltoid to lanceolate. Verticillasters 1–3, distant, (6) 12–20-fld; bracteoles numerous, 8–20mm, linear-lanceolate, densely hispid; cal. 15–20mm, sessile, stellate-tomentose, teeth subulate; cor. 3–4cm, yellow. var. ***longifolia.*** Basal lvs lanceolate. Cal. teeth 1–3mm. S Anatolia, Lebanon, Syria. var. ***bailanica.*** (Vierh.) Huber-Morath). Basal lvs oblong or ovate. Cal. teeth 3–6mm. Anatolia, Syria, Lebanon, Cyprus. Z9.

***P. lychnitis*** L. LAMPWICK PLANT. Subshrub to 70cm, white-pubesc. throughout. Lvs 5–11×1cm, oblong-linear, entire, clasping, sessile; bracts dilated at base. Verticillasters 4–40-fld; bracteoles linear, 12–20mm, cal. 15–20mm; cor. 20–30mm, yellow. Summer. SW Europe. Z8.

***P. lycia*** D. Don. Much-branched eglandular shrub to 150cm. Lvs more or less densely yellow- or golden stellate-tomentose, especially when young; lower stem lvs 2–5×1–2cm, small, oblong-lanceolate, subcordate or cordate at base, margin crenulate, short-petiolate; floral lvs short-petiolate, often larger and broader. Verticillasters 1–2, 6–12-fld, bracteoles 8–11×1–2mm, linear-lanceolate, white lanate; cal. densely white lanate, sep. 8–11×1–2mm; cor. 25–30mm, yellow. SW Anatolia. Z9.

***P. pratensis*** Karel. & Kir. Stem simple, densely pubesc. Lvs oblong, cordate, crenate, petiolate. Verticillasters many-fld; cor. tinted purple. Siberia. Z5.

***P. pungens*** Willd. Perenn. herb to 70cm, clothed in very short white stellate-tomentose hairs, sometimes with a secondary indumentum of longer hairs 1–3mm, rarely glabrous, eglandular. Stem lvs 5–13×1–6cm, lanceolate to ovate-lanceolate, margins denticulate or serrate, rarely entire, stellate-hispidulous; petiole to 10cm. Verticillasters 2–7, 2–6(–15)-fld; bracteoles subulate, 11–17mm, stellate-tomentose sometimes with hispid hairs; cal. 8–15mm, stellate-tomentose sometimes with hispid hairs, teeth subulate 2–7mm; cor. 15–25mm, purple or pink, upper lip galeate. Nutlets smooth. Spain, eastwards to C Russia, including Caucasus, N Iran, Turkey and Syria. 4 varieties are recognized. Z7.

***P. purpurea*** L. To 60cm. Stems woolly. Lvs 5–10×2–5cm, broadly lanceolate, coriaceous, undulate, stellate-pubesc. above, floccose beneath; petiole to 5cm; bracts numerous, imbricate, petiolate, acuminate. Verticillasters to 12-fld; cal. sharply toothed; cor. 25mm, rose to mauve, rarely white, downy. Summer. Spain, Portugal. Z8.

***P. rotata*** Benth. Lvs suborbicular, thick, leathery, crenate, deeply rugose, woolly beneath; petiole dilated. Verticillasters in a dense subsessile head; bracteoles narrow; cal. 8mm, funnel-shaped, teeth spiny; cor. small, purple-blue. Alpine Himalaya, W China. Z7.

***P. russeliana*** (Sims) Benth. To 1m. Lvs 6–20×6–12cm, broadly ovate, obtuse, create, cordate at base, grey-green, thinly stellate-tomentose above, more densely so and hoary beneath; petiole to 28cm. Verticillasters 2–5, distant, 12–20-fld; bracteoles subulate, tomentose, tip curved upwards, to 20×2mm; cal. to 25mm, slightly 2-lipped; cor. 25–35mm, upper lip hooded, ciliate. Summer. W Syria. cf. *P. viscosa*. Often confused in cult. with *P. samia*, which has pink fls. 'Lloyd's Variety': upright and bushy, to 1m; lvs grey; fls absent. 'Nova': fls golden yellow. Z7.

***P. samia*** L. To 1m. Lvs 8–23×5–15cm, subcordate, crenate or serrate, stellate-tomentose above, tomentose and glandular-pubesc. beneath; petiole to 18cm; bracts ovate or lanceolate, acuminate, short-petiolate. Verticillasters 3–5, 10–20-fld; bracteoles subulate, 20–26mm; cal. 18–25mm, stellate to glandular-pubesc., teeth bristle-tipped, to 12mm; cor. 30–35mm, purple, upper lip subglabrous. Spring–summer. N Africa, Yugoslavia, Greece. Z7.

***P. setigera*** Falc. Tall, subglabrous herb. Lvs ovate, acuminate, rounded or cordate at base, crenate; petioles short. Verticillasters many-fld; cal. 7–12mm; cor. purple. Temperate Himalaya. Z8.

***P. tuberosa*** L. To 150cm. Roots producing small tubers. Lvs oblong-ovate, obtuse, sagittate, subauriculate or cordate at base, simple-pubesc. above, stellate-pubesc. beneath; petiole to 30cm; bracts sessile or subsessile, lanceolate-ovate to triangular. Verticillasters numerous, upper crowded, lower distant, 14–40-fld; bracteoles subulate; cal. 8–13mm, teeth spiny; cor. purple or pink, upper lip straight, 15–20mm, ciliate. Summer. C & SE Europe to C Asia. Z6.

***P. umbrosa*** Turcz. Coarsely pubesc. herb. Lvs suborbicular to cordate. Verticillasters many-fld; cor. purple. N China. Z7.

***P. viscosa*** Poir. Much-branched shrub to 130cm. Lvs glandular puberulent, sometimes with a loose indumentum of stellate hairs above, densely stellate tomentose below, lower lvs 4–15×1.5–7cm, broadly ovate to oblong-lanceolate, base cordate, margin crenate, petiole to 4cm; floral lvs oblong to lanceolate. Verticillasters 1–4, (6) 12–20-fld; bracteoles 15–22×2–4mm, subulate, linear or narrowly lanceolate, hispid, viscid; cal. 18–25mm, shortly pedicillate, densely hispid, viscid, teeth 5–8mm, subulate; cor. 25–35mm, yellow. Nutlets smooth. Anatolia, SW Asia. *P. viscosa* of gardens is *P. russeliana* (Sims) Benth. Z8.

***P. glandulosa*** Schenk. See *P. viscosa*.
***P. herba-venti*** ssp. ***pungens*** (Willd.) Maire ex DeFilipps. See *P. pungens*.
***P. latifolia*** Royle ex Benth. See *P. bracteosa*.
***P. leonorus*** L. See *Leonotis leonorus*.
***P. lunariifolia Sm.*** var. ***russeliana*** Sims. See *P. russeliana*.
***P. nepetifolia*** L. See *Leonotis nepetifolia*.
***P. ocymifolia*** Burm. f. See *Leonotis ocymifolia*.
***P. superba*** K. Koch. See *P. russeliana*.
***P. taurica*** Bunge. See *P. pungens*.

**Phlox** L. (From Gk *phlox*, the name used for *Lychnis* L. by Theophrastus.) PHLOX. Polemoniaceae. 67 species of herbaceous to shrubby, evergreen or deciduous annuals or perennials to 2m; habit erect, diffuse or caespitose. Leaves entire, usually opposite, upper sometimes alternate. Inflorescence a terminal, paniculate or corymb-like cyme; flowers showy, 5-merous, rarely solitary, white, pink, maroon to crimson, blue or purple; calyx narrow-campanulate or tubular, ribbed, lobes acuminate or acute, margins and region below sinuses membranaceous-scarious; corolla hypocrateriform, throat narrowed, tube slender; stamens included, short unequal. Fruit a capsule, ovoid to oblong, rupturing calyx at maturity, 3-locular; seeds 1 to few per locule, not mucilaginous when wet. US (Alaska) and W Canada to N Mexico.

CULTIVATION Grown for their tall, stately habit and generous masses of flowers, the taller herbaceous types, such as *P. paniculata*, *P. maculata* and *P. glaberrima*, have long been mainstays of the herbaceous and mixed border in summer, valued for their often intensely fragrant blooms in a wide range of colour from pure white through shades of pink to crimson and purple. They are also suitable for less formal situations, in the light dappled shade of the woodland edge. Grow in full sun or part shade in deep, moisture retentive fertile soils that are rich in organic matter; *P. glaberrima* prefers lime free soil. Top-dress with a balanced fertilizer and mulch with well rotted organic matter in spring and take out weaker shoots when the clump reaches 15cm/6in. tall. Divide every third or fourth year to maintain vigour and flower quality. Staking is usually necessary only in exposed situations; deadhead to prevent self sown seedlings which are usually of inferior quality. Divide cultivars in early spring. Alternatively take 5cm/2in. soft stem cuttings in spring from forced rootstocks; lift clumps in late autumn, overwinter in the frost-free frame, and force into growth at 10°C/50°F in late winter. Also by root cuttings in late winter. Species may be increased by seed but hybridize freely and may not come true.

Most of the lower-growing types and their cvs are eminently suited to rock garden and peat terrace, forming mats of foliage which become dense carpets of often brilliant colour when in flower; the more vigorous species such as *P. subulata* and the slightly less rampant *P. douglasii* make good ground cover on the rock garden or at path edges, especially useful for softening hard lines at the border front. The smaller cushion-forming species such as *P. caespitosa* and *P. missoulensis* are suitable in scale for sink and trough plantings; tiny and demanding types such as *P. nana* are more safely grown in the alpine house.

Grow in fertile, well-drained soils enriched with leafmould; *P. stolonifera*, *P. adsurgens* and *P.* ×*procumbens* are calcifuge. Most species grow in full sun or in light shade in drier soils; *P. divaricata* prefers some shade. Clip over after flowering to remove dead flower heads. In the alpine house grow in pans in a mix of equal parts loam, leafmould and sharp sand; more demanding species such as *P. bryoides* are best introduced as seedlings into a very lean mix comprising three parts silver sand with one part leafmould. Propagate trailing species by removal of rooted sections in spring or early autumn, cushion types by cuttings of non-flowering shoots in spring. Also by seed.

The annual species such as *P. drummondii* and its cvs are useful as seasonal fillers in the border or for bedding. Sow under glass in spring and harden off before planting out after danger of frost is passed.

*P. maculata* and *P. paniculata* are susceptible to stem eelworm which causes swollen shoots and narrow distorted leaves; destroy infected plants and do not replant in infested soil, ensure propagating material is taken from clean stock on clean soil. Leafy gall disease, *Corynebacterium fascians*, causes fasciation of young shoots and leaves; destroy affected stock. Phlox are also susceptible to powdery mildew, grey mould and fungal leaf spots; the last usually cause only cosmetic damage. The risk of spreading golden nematode limits the import and export of *Phlox* cvs and most countries have developed their own range of recommended cultivars.

***P. adsurgens*** Torr. ex A. Gray Slender perenn. with underground rootstocks; stems prostrate to ascending, to 30cm. Lvs 1–2.5cm, sessile, rounded to narrowly ovate, glabrous. Infl. lax, few-fld, glandular-hairy to villous; fls on slender, 0.5–2cm long peduncles; cal. 1–1.3mm, lobes spreading, subulate; cor. to 2.5cm diam., pale to bright pink or purple, tube, 1.2–2cm, sometimes white inside, lobes 7–12mm, obovate, rounded to emarginate. Fr. *c*5mm. Summer. US (Oregon, N California). 'Black Buttes': habit creeping; lvs grey-green; fls lavender, abundant. 'Red Buttes': fls large, deep pink, lobes overlapping. 'Wagon Wheel': stems woody; lvs oval; fls pink, lobes narrow. Z6.

***P. alyssifolia*** E. Greene Compact, branching, subshrubby perenn., 3–10cm tall. Lvs to 1.2×0.2–0.5cm, elliptic-lanceolate to oblong, often glandular-hairy, margins with white, cartilaginous thickening, ciliate toward base, apex cuspidate. Infl. 1–5-fld; fls fragrant, on 2.5–25mm peduncles; cal. lobes narrowly triangular, cuspidate, with thickened margins; cor. 1–1.8cm, pink or purple, rarely white; styles 6–12mm. ssp. ***alyssifolia.*** Infl. (1–)3(–5)-fld, densely glandular-hairy; cal. 0.8–1.1cm; cor. 1.1–1.5cm, lobes *c*1×0.7cm, obovate, blunt, tube paler inside, with 1–3 striae. Late spring–early summer. US (Montana to Wyoming and NW Nebraska), Canada (Saskatchewan). ssp. ***abdita*** (Nels.) Wherry. Infl. 3–5-fld, glandular-hairy; cal. 1–1.3cm; cor. 1.2–1.8cm, lobes *c*1.3×0.8cm, narrowly to broadly obovate, blunt to subacute. Late spring–early summer. US (Western S Dakota, N Wyoming). Z5. ssp. ***collina*** (Rydb.) Wherry. Infl. 1–3-fld, hairy but not glandular; cal. (0.7–)0.8–1cm; cor. 1–1.2cm, lobes *c*0.7×0.5cm, obovate, blunt. Late spring. US (W Montana). Z3.

***P. andicola*** Nutt. Erect perenn., 5–12cm tall, spreading via rhiz. Lvs to 1.5–2×0.1–0.2cm, linear-subulate, subacerose, glabrescent to pilose. Infl. 1–5-fld, with kinky hairs; fls on 2–5mm long peduncles; cal. 7–11mm, lobes subulate, cuspidate; cor. (0.9–)1.2–1.5(–1.7)cm, white, rarely pale yellow or purple, lobes *c*8×6mm, obovate; styles 6–9mm. Spring–early summer. US (N Dakota to Nebraska and NE Colorado). Z5.

***P. ×arendsii*** hort. *(P. divaricata × ? P. paniculata.)* To 60cm. Lvs to 10cm, lanceolate-ovate to linear-lanceolate. Fls lavender or mauve, 2.5cm diam., in clusters to 15cm diam. Garden origin. 'Anja': fls purple tinged red. 'Hilda': fls lavender centred pink. 'Lisbeth': fls lavender-blue. 'Susanne': fls white centred red. Z3.

***P. austromontana*** Cov. Woody-based, caespitose perenn., 5–10(–15)cm tall. Lvs 1–1.5cm, pungent to acerose, glabrous beneath, white-hairy above. Fls solitary at branchlet apices, on short peduncles; cal. 6–10mm, lobes acerose, sinuses folded; cor. lavender or pink to white, tube 1.1–1.4cm, lobes 5–7mm, obovate. Fr. 4–5mm. Late spring–summer. US (S California to Arizona and Utah), Mexico (Baja California). Z6.

***P. bifida*** (L.) Beck. SAND PHLOX. Caespitose perenn., to 20cm tall. Lvs to 3–6×0.2–0.4cm, distant, linear to lanceolate or narrowly elliptic, ciliate, upper pilose. Infl. glandular-hairy, lax, (3–)6–9(–12)-fld; fls sweet-scented; cal. 6.5–9.5mm, lobes linear-subulate, cuspidate; cor. 0.9–1.4cm, lavender (rarely lilac) to white, lobes *c*1×0.75cm, apex deeply emarginate, notch (1.5–)3–5.5mm deep; styles 6–12mm. Spring–early summer. US (SW Michigan to Kansas and Arkansas). 'Alba': fls white. 'Colvin's White': mound-forming; fls white, fragrant. 'Starbright': habit low, compact, mat-forming; fls deeply divided, pale blue. Z6.

***P. borealis*** Wherry Caespitose perenn., 6–9cm tall. Lvs 8–15×1.5–2.5mm, linear, ciliate, glabrescent. Infl. 1–3-fld, 2.5–7.5cm, with glandular and simple hairs; fls on (4–)8–25mm long peduncles; cal. 9–12mm, lobes linear, cuspidate; cor. 8–12mm, lavender, lilac or white, tube broadening toward apex, lobes 8×7–14×13mm, broadly obovate, emarginate or entire. Summer. US (Alaska). Z2.

***P. bryoides*** Nutt. Cushion-forming perenn.; clumps 2–5cm tall. Lvs 3–5×1–1.5mm, broadly subulate to oblong, densely overlapping, apex cuspidate, arachnoid-pubesc. Fls solitary, sessile, green parts tomentose; cal. 4–7mm, lobes linear-subulate, cuspidate; cor. 4–8mm, 7–9mm diam., white or pale lilac, tube sometimes exceeded by cal., lobes *c*4.5×2.5mm, elliptic; styles 2–6mm long. Spring–early summer. US (Oregon and W Montana to Nevada and W Nebraska). Z3.

***P. buckleyi*** Wherry. SWORD-LEAF PHLOX. Evergreen perenn., 15–45cm tall, spreading via slender rhiz. Lvs 5–10(–12.5)cm, linear-ensiform, long-acuminate, thick, glabrescent. Infl. dense at first, lax later, glandular-hairy, 6–25-fld; fls on 3–9mm long peduncles; cal. 7–13mm, lobes linear-subulate, short-aristate to cuspidate; cor. 1.7–2.3cm, pink to bright purple, glandular-hairy, lobes *c*10×8mm, broadly to narrowly obovate, apex blunt to truncate or erose-emarginate; styles 1.4–2cm, sometimes exserted with 1 anth. Early summer. US (Virginia, W Virginia). Z6.

***P. caespitosa*** Nutt. CUSHION PHLOX. Cushion-forming perenn.; stems branching, erect to spreading. Lvs 4–8(–12)mm, linear overlapping, rigid, 3-veined, glandular-hairy to glabrous, apex apiculate, margins thickened, villous-ciliate. Fls terminal, solitary, (sub)sessile; cal. 6–8mm, hispid-ciliate, lobes subulate-pungent; cor. 1–1.5cm, white to pale blue, lobes 4–7mm. ssp. ***caespitosa.*** Mounds 15–25cm tall. Summer. US (Oregon and Montana to California and New Mexico). ssp. ***condensata*** (A. Gray) Wherry. Mounds to 4cm tall. Lvs adpressed. Summer. US (Colorado). ssp. ***pulvinata*** Wherry. Mounds 3–7cm tall. Lvs spreading. Summer. US (Idaho to California and Colorado). Z5.

***P. carolina*** L. THICK-LEAF PHLOX. Perenn. to 1.2m, glabrescent. Lvs to 15(–17.5)×0.3–1cm at base, narrowly oblong-lanceolate to linear, smaller and sparse above, thick, veins indistinct. Infl. a compound cyme; fls on short peduncles; cal. 6–8mm, lobes broadly linear, with indistinct apical awns, veins prominent; cor. to 2(–2.4)cm, pink to purple, rarely white; anth. subexserted; styles almost completely fused. Late spring. US (N Carolina and NW Florida to NE Texas and Illinois). 'Bill Baker': to 45cm; fls large, pink. 'Gloriosa': fls salmon-pink. Z5.

***P. cuspidata*** Scheele. Delicate annual, 5–55cm tall, sparsely hairy, simple or branched. Lvs to 3.5×0.8cm, opposite and oblanceolate beneath, alternate and linear to elliptic above. Infl. a spiral cyme of glomerules; fls on peduncles to 6mm; cal. 7–10mm, with fine glandular pubescence, apex with a 1–1.5mm long awn; cor. 0.8–1.5cm, purple to pink, tube paler inside, faintly striate. Spring. US (E Texas, S Oklahoma). Z6.

***P. diffusa*** Benth. Perenn. subshrub, 10–30cm tall, prostrate to decumbent, base stout, branching. Lvs 1–1.5cm, linear-subulate, yellow-green, acerose, sparsely tomentose to subglabrous. Fls usually solitary, terminal on short leafy branches; peduncles very short; cal. 8–10, lobes subulate, villous; cor. to 1.2cm diam., white or lilac to pink, tube 9–13mm, lobes 6–7mm, broadly to narrowly obovate; stigma 3-lobes. Fr. 4–5mm. Late spring–summer. US (Washington and S Dakota to California and Utah). Z7.

***P. divaricata*** L. WILD SWEET WILLIAM; BLUE PHLOX. Perenn. to 45cm, spreading, with decumbent to prostrate sterile shoots rooting at nodes. Lvs to 5×2.5cm, oblong to ovate or elliptic on sterile shoots, on fertile ones smaller, broadly to narrowly lanceolate. Infl. a compound cyme, minutely glandular-pubesc.; cal. 7–11mm, lobes with an indistinct apical awn; cor. 1.2–1.8cm, to 4cm diam. lavender to pale violet or white, tube sometimes darker inside, lobes *c*1.3×0.8cm, emarginate to erose. Spring. US (E Texas and N Alaska to Eastern S Dakota and Wisconsin), Canada (Quebec). 'Alba': fls white. 'Dirigo Ice': to 30cm; fls clear blue. 'Grandiflora': fls large. Z4.

***P. douglasii*** Hook. Perenn. to 20cm tall, usually less, laxly caespitose, glandular-hairy. Lvs 1–1.2×0.075–0.15cm, stiff, subulate to linear-subulate, pungent, dark green. Infl. 2.5–7.5cm, 1–3-fld; fls on 1–6mm long peduncles; cal. 7.5–9.5mm, lobes linear-subulate, cuspidate, with a prominent rib; cor. 1–1.3cm, lobes *c*7.5×5mm, obovate; styles 4–7mm. ssp. ***douglasii.*** 10–20cm tall. Infl. 1–3-fld; fls strongly fragrant; cal. fused for around three-quarters of its length; cor. white, lavender or pink. Spring–early summer. US (NW Montana to Washington and NE Oregon). Z5. Over 20 cultivars, many of which are derived from hybrids with other species, distinguished largely by flower colour; height 6–15cm, habit mat forming, neat and compact to vigorous; lvs narrow to lanceolate; fls in range of colours including shades of pink, mauve, purple and red, often with contrasting centres. 'Boothman's Variety': to 6cm; fls lavender marked blue around centre. 'Concorde': fls crimson-violet with dark grey eye. 'Crackerjack': habit compact; fls saucer-shaped, magenta, abundant. 'Eva': habit neat; fls lavender. 'Holden Variety': fls lilac with dark purple eye. 'Iceberg': fls white tinged blue. 'Red Admiral': habit vigorous, compact; fls crimson. 'Rose Queen': fls pink tinged silver. 'Tycoon': fls red, abundant. 'Waterloo': fls rich crimson-red. ssp. ***rigida*** (Benth.) Wherry. 2.5–7.5cm tall. Fls solitary, slightly fragrant; cal. fused for around half of its length; cor. white or pink. Spring–early summer. US (NW Montana to E Washington and NE Oregon). Z5

***P. drummondii*** Hook. ANNUAL PHLOX; DRUMMOND PHLOX. Annual, 10–50cm tall, hairy, sometimes glandular, simple to branched. Lvs variable, narrowly oblanceolate to ovate to lanceolate, subsessile, sessile or clasping, opposite at base, alternate and broader above. Infl. somewhat spiral, a group of 2–6 glomerules; fls on peduncles to 1.5cm; cal. 7–12mm, lobes fused for one-third of their length; cor. 1–2.2cm, pubesc., rarely glabrous, purple, violet, pink, lavender, red or white, rarely pale yellow, often paler inside tube with markings around throat; styles 2–3mm, 1 ovule per locule. Spring. US (E Texas). 'Brilliant': to 50cm; fls in dense heads, white centred rose. 'Carnival': fls large with contrasting centres. Dwarf Beauty Hybrids: habit dwarf; fls abundant in range of colours, early flowering. 'Gigantea': fls large in wide range of colours. Globe Hybrids: habit dwarf, hemispherical; fls in range of pastel and dark shades. 'Grandiflora': fls purple above, white beneath. Palona Hybrids: habit dwarf, compact, bushy, globe-shaped; fls in range of colours including bicolors. 'Petticoat': habit dwarf to 10cm; fls in range of colours including shades of white, pink and purple, bicolors. 'Rotundata': corolla lobes broad. 'Twinkle' ('Sternenzauber'): corolla lobes cuspidate, narrow, often cut and fringed. Z6.

***P. floridana*** Benth. Erect or ascending perenn., 20–50(–80)cm tall, glabrous except infl. Lvs to 4–8(–9)×0.3–0.6(–0.7)cm, oblong to linear or lanceolate, smaller above mid-stem. Infl. dense, glandular-pubesc. (6–)12–24(–36)-fld; fls on peduncles to 8(–12)mm; cal. 7–11mm, lobes subulate, subaristate to cuspidate, sinus membrane often folded; cor. 1.5–2(–2.2)cm, pink to purple, tube paler inside, with 1 or 2 (rarely 3) dark striae at each lobe base, lobes *c*1.1×0.8cm, obovate, obtuse. ssp. ***floridana.*** Lvs matt. Cor. pink to purple. Summer. US (Georgia, Florida, Alabama). ssp. ***bella*** Wherry. Lvs glossy. Cor. pastel pink. Summer. US (W Florida). Z7.

***P. glaberrima*** L. SMOOTH PHLOX. Rhizomatous perenn. to 1.5m. Lvs to 5–15×0.5–1cm, linear at base, linear-lanceolate or broadly linear above, usually glabrous, rarely sparsely hairy. Infl. a panicle of small cymes; fls on 3–12(–25)mm long peduncles; cal. 7–12mm, subcampanulate, lobes broadly subulate, with prominent ribs, cuspidate; cor. 1.8–2.3cm, pink to purple, rarely white, lobes 7×5–13×10mm, orbicular to obovate. 'Interior': to 35cm; fls rose to red-purple. ssp. ***glaberrima*** Infl. 15–*c*125-fld; cymes few-fld; cal. 7–9mm. Late spring. US (Virginia to S Carolina). Z4. ssp. ***triflora*** (Michx.) Wherry. Infl. 12–25(–50)-fld; cymes 3-fld; cal. 8–12mm. Late spring-summer. US (Maryland Indiana to Georgia and Alabama). Z4.

***P.×henryae*** Wherry. *(P. bifida × P. nivalis.)* Vigorous perenn. to 15cm tall. Lvs to 1.5cm, narrowly linear to lanceolate. Fls to 2.5cm diam.; cor. lilac-purple, lobes deeply emarginate. Spring–early summer. Garden origin. Z6. 'Blanda': plant small; lvs blue-grey.

***P.idahonis*** Wherry. Perenn. 50–100cm tall, with a slender rhiz., fine-hairy. Lvs to 6–8×1.5–2.5cm, sessile, oblong at base, ovate-cordate above. Infl. a 9–50(–100) fld compound cyme; fls on 8–15mm long peduncles; cal. 9–14mm, lobes broadly subulate, short-aristate, sinus-membranes folded; cor. 1.5–2cm, lavender to lilac, rarely white, lobes *c*9×7mm, obovate; styles 1.4–1.8cm. Early summer. US (C Idaho). Z6.

***P.kelseyi*** Britt. Perenn. dwarf shrub, 7–15cm tall, somewhat succulent. Lvs to 1.2–2.5×0.2–0.35cm, linear-lanceolate, acuminate, quite thick, glabrous or hairy. Infl. usually glandular-hairy, 1.5–fld; fls pungently scented, on 3–10(–20)mm long peduncles; cal. 8–12mm, lobes linear-subulate, cuspidate; cor. 1–1.5cm, white to lilac or lavender, somewhat blue-hued, lobes *c*7.5×5mm, obovate; styles (4–)6–8mm. Late spring. US (E Idaho, SW Montana, S Wyoming). 'Rosette': habit compact, circular; fls pink, abundant. Z5.

***P.maculata*** L. WILD SWEET WILLIAM; MEADOW PHLOX. Rhizomatous perenn., 35–70(–125)cm tall, glabrous to minutely hairy; stem often red-streaked or spotted. Lvs to (4.5–)6.5–13×1–2.5cm, linear at base, lanceolate or ovate above, cordate and clasping near infl. Infl a 75–150-fld panicle, formed by small cymes; fls on 3–5(–7)mm long peduncles; cal. 5.5–7.5mm, lobes triangular-subulate, cuspidate; cor. 1.8–2.5cm, pink, purple or white, sometimes with a dark purple ring in throat, lobes *c*9×8mm, orbicular to ovate. 'Alpha': fls lilac-pink, fragrant. 'Miss Lingard': to 80cm, hardy; fls salverform, white, sometimes with pale pink ring near centre, fragrant. 'Omega': fls white centred lilac, fragrant. ssp. ***maculata.*** Lvs glabrous above, pilose beneath. Infl. cylindric; fls often sweet-scented; cor. 1.8–2.5cm; styles 1.5–2cm. Late spring. US (Connecticut to N Carolina). ssp. ***pyramidalis*** (Sm.) Wherry. Lvs glabrous or glabrescent throughout. Infl. cylindric to narrowly conical; fls usually not scented, cor. 2–2.5cm; styles 1.4–1.8(–2.3)cm. Summer. US (Ohio to N Carolina and Missouri). Z5.

***P.missoulensis*** Wherry Mound-forming perenn., 5–10cm high. Lvs to 1.5–2.5×0.15–0.25cm, linear-lanceolate to linear, apex subacerose, glandular-pilose, margins ciliate. Infl. with herbaceous parts densely glandular-hairy; fls solitary, fragrant; peduncle 2–8cm, cal. 1–1.3cm, bright pink to lavender, lobes *c*8×6mm, obovate to orbicular; styles 5–7mm. Spring. US (Montana to Nevada and Colorado). Z4.

***P.multiflora*** Nels. Caespitose perenn.; habit decumbent, 8–15cm tall. Lvs 1.5–2.5×0.15–0.2cm, linear, usually glabrous. Infl. 1–3-fld, glabrous to sparsely hairy or glandular; cal. 9–13mm, lobes linear-subulate, cuspidate; cor. 1–1.6cm, white or lilac to pink, lobes obovate; styles 6–12mm. ssp. ***multiflora.*** Fls solitary, on 0.75–1.5cm long peduncles; cal. lobes with a rib; cor. 1–1.5cm, lobes *c*8×6mm, never emarginate. Late spring–early summer. US (Colorado to Montana). ssp. ***patula*** (Nels.) Wherry. Infl. 1–3-fld; fls on 1.8–3.5cm long peduncles; cal. lobes lacking a rib; cor. 1.2–1.6cm, lobes *c*10×7mm, sometimes emarginate. Late spring–summer. US (Colorado to S Montana). Z3.

***P.nana*** Nutt. SANTA FE PHLOX. Erect or ascending perenn., 10–25cm tall, often much-branched, glandular-pubesc., often densely so (especially stem apex and herbaceous parts of infl.). Lvs 1.2–4×0.2–0.5cm, linear-lanceolate, usually deciduous. Fls few, solitary, usually terminal; cal. 1–1.5cm; cor. pink, hypocrateriform, tube 1.3–1.7cm, lobes 1.2–2cm, obovate, margins erose. Late spring–summer. US (W Texas to Arizona), New Mexico. 'Arroya': fls carmine-rose. 'Chameleon': fls cream turning pink. 'Manjana': fls rose-pink. 'Mary Maslin': fls scarlet with yellow eye. 'Paul Maslin': fls lemon-yellow with chocolate eye. 'Tangelo': fls rich orange. 'Vanilla Cream': fls large, cream with dark eye. Z7.

***P.nivalis*** Lodd. ex Sweet. TRAILING PHLOX. Subshrub to 30cm tall, forming mats or cushions; sterile shoots long, decumbent, evergreen, fertile ones erect, deciduous. Lvs of sterile shoots subulate, fertile shoot lvs to 2.5cm, lanceolate, with multicellular hairs. Infl. a terminal, bracteate cyme, 3–6-fld, glandular to pubesc.; fls on 3–25mm long peduncles; cal. 6–10mm, lobes lanceolate-attenuate, cuspidate; cor. 1.1–1.7cm, purple, pink or white, lobes *c*1.2×0.7cm, emarginate to erose, rarely entire; styles 3–4mm, included. Spring US (Virginia to W Florida and E Texas); introduced elsewhere in US. 'Azurea': fls light blue. 'Camla': fls salmon-pink. 'Jill Alexander': fls pink. 'Nivea': habit compact; fls white. 'Sylvestris': fls to 1.5cm across, pale pink. Z6.

***P.ovata*** L. MOUNTAIN PHLOX. Perenn.; sterile shoots decumbent, evergreen, fertile shoots erect, 25–50(-65)cm tall. Lvs variable, glabrous, to 5–15×1.2–5cm, elliptic to oblong and long-petiolate on sterile shoots, and at bases of fertile ones, otherwise ovate to oblong, sessile. Infl. usually 15–30-fld, subglabrous to densely short-hairy; cal. (7–)9–11(–13)mm, lobes elongate-triangular, apex cuspidate; cor. (1.2–)1.6–2.4cm, dull magenta, pink, purple, or rarely white, lobes 8×7–14×12mm, obovate; styles sometimes exserted with 1 or 2 anth. Late spring. US (Pennsylvania and NE Indiana to Alabama). Z5.

***P.paniculata*** L. PERENNIAL PHLOX; SUMMER PHLOX; AUTUMN PHLOX; FALL PHLOX. Erect perenn. 60–100cm tall, subglabrous to puberulent. Lvs 1.2–12×0.8–5cm, on short petioles, subsessile, ovate or lanceolate to elliptic, apex acuminate, venation reticulate, raised, margins toothed, ciliate. Infl. a terminal, compound, corymbiform cyme, many-fld, often dense; fls on short peduncles or subsessile; cal. 6–9mm, lobes linear-lanceolate; cor. 2–2.8cm, blue, lavender, pink or white, tube hairy, lobes 8–12mm; stamens included. Summer. US (New York and Georgia to Arkansas and Illinois); introduced elsewhere in US. Over 100 cultivars and seed races are offered, largely distinguished by flower colour; height to 100cm, habit dwarf, neat and compact to full, vigorous and free-branching; lvs variegated in a few cvs; fls in wide range of colours including white, shades of pink, lilac, orange and red, often with contrasting eye. 'Amethyst': fls violet. 'Balmoral': growth strong to 100cm; fls in large heads, pale pink. 'Brigadier': lvs dark green; fls deep pink suffused orange. 'Blue Ice': fl. buds pink opening white, occasionally tinged blue, in large trusses. 'Eventide': fls light mauve blue. 'Fairy's Petticoat': to 75cm; fls pale mulberry with dark eye. 'Fujiyama': to 75cm; cylindrical heads of pure white fls. 'Harlequin': lvs variegated, fls purple. 'Mother of Pearl': to 75cm; fls white suffused pink. 'Nora Leigh': to 90cm; lvs variegated; fls pale lilac. 'Prince of Orange': to 80cm; habit strong; fls orange-pink. 'Prospero': hardy, to 90cm; fls pale lilac. 'Starfire': to 90cm; fls deep red. 'White Admiral': to 90cm; fls pure white. Z4.

***P.pilosa*** L. PRAIRIE PHLOX. Perenn., to 60cm tall. Lvs to 12.5×1cm, linear at base, smaller and lanceolate above. Infl. a large panicle formed by small cymes; fls on 3–20mm long peduncles; cal. 8–15mm, lobes with a 3mm long apical awn; cor. 1–2cm, glabrous to pubesc. or glandular, lobes 8–16mm, lavender, purple, white or pink apex blunt to apiculate; styles 1.5–5mm. ssp. ***pilosa.*** Glandular-pubesc. at least above. Cor. 1–1.6cm. Spring. US (E Texas). ssp. ***pulcherrima*** Lundell. Coarsely pubesc. but not glandular. Cor. 1.2–2cm, lobes 1–1.5cm. Spring. US (E Texas). Z5.

***P.×procumbens*** Lehm. *(P. stolonifera × P. subulata.)* Clump-forming perenn., 15–25cm tall; habit decumbent. Lvs to 2.5×0.5cm, oblanceolate to elliptic. Infl. lax, a flat panicle; fls on peduncles to 2cm; cal. 8–9mm, lobes broadly subulate, cuspidate; cor. bright purple; anth. golden; styles 9–15mm. Spring. Garden origin. 'Variegata': lvs variegated cream; fls deep pink. 'Millstream': habit dense; lvs dark, narrow; fls rich lilac-pink. 'Rosea': fls pale pink. Z4.

***P.pulchra*** (Wherry) Wherry. Perenn., 25–50cm tall, spreading via branching rhiz., glabrous to pilose. Lvs to 3–6×1–2cm, narrowly elliptic and short-petiolate at base, broadly elliptic and sessile above, margins with fine cilia. Infl. 12–36-fld, glabrous to sparsely pilose; cal. 8.5–12.5mm, lobes broadly subulate, cuspidate, sinus-membranes folded; cor. 2–2.4cm, pink, lilac, lavender or white, lobes 1.2–1.5×1–1.4cm, orbicular to obovate, blunt or rarely erose; styles 2–2.5cm, sometimes exserted with 1 or 2 stamens. Late spring–early summer. US (Alabama). Z5.

***P.sibirica*** L. SIBERIAN PHLOX. Caespitose perenn., base woody, 8–15cm tall. Lvs to 3–6×0.15×0.3cm, linear, long-acuminate, sometimes falcate, sparsely pilose, margins with fine cilia. Infl. (1–)3–6-fld, pubesc., sometimes glandular; fls on 2–4cm long peduncles; 8–13mm, lobes linear, subaristate; cor. 1–1.2cm, tube widening toward apex, lobes *c*9×6mm, obovate, erose-emarginate to entire; styles 7–10mm, ovules 2 per locule. Spring–early summer. USSR (Siberia). Z3.

***P.speciosa*** Pursh. BUSH PHLOX. Shrub to 60(–120)cm. Lvs to 3–7.5×0.2–0.7cm, linear to lanceolate, pilose and basally ciliate towards infl. Infl. a 3–18-fld corymb, glandular-hairy; fls on 1–4cm long peduncles; cal. 8–14mm, lobes linear, cuspidate; cor. 0.9–1.5cm, to 2.5cm in diam., pink to purple or white, tube paler inside, often with conspicuous striae, lobes *c*10×7mm, obtuse or emarginate. Spring. US (Washington and Idaho to Arizona and New Mexico). Z4.

***P.stolonifera*** Sims. CREEPING PHLOX. Creeping, stoloniferous perenn., forming 15–25cm talls mats. Lvs on sterile shoots to 4.5×1.8cm, on a long, coarsely ciliate petiole, obovate (rarely oblanceolate), on fertile shoots to *c*2×2cm, oblong to ovate, sessile. Infl. lax, *c*6-fld, glandular-hairy; fls on 0.5–3cm long peduncles; cal. 9–11, lobes linear-subulate, subcuspidate; cor. 2.1–2.5cm, pilose, some hairs glandular, violet to lavender or purple to lilac, lobes *c*1.4×0.9cm, obovate; anth. 1 or more usually exserted, golden. Spring. US (Pennsylvania Georgia). 'Ariane': to 20cm; lvs pale green; fls in large, loose heads, white with yellow eye. 'Blue Ridge': lvs glossy; fls blue. 'Bruce's White': habit creeping, dense; fls white with yellow centres. 'Home Fires': fls rich pink. 'Mary Belle Frey': fls pink. 'Pink Ridge': fls soft pink, petals broad. 'Rosea': fls pale pink. 'violacea': fls mauve-blue. 'Violet Vere': fls violet. Z4.

***P.subulata*** L. MOSS PHLOX; MOUNTAIN PHLOX; MOSS PINK. Perenn. forming dense mats or cushions to at least 50cm, villous to hirtellous, hairs multicellular. Lvs 6–20×1–1.5mm, elliptic to linear, ciliate towards base, apex apiculate. Infl. a few-fld, terminal, bracteate cyme; fls on 3–15mm long peduncle; cal. 6–8mm, spinulose, lobes lanceolate-attenuate; cor. 1–1.3cm, pink to lavender or white, lobes 7–10mm, apices emarginate; stamens subexserted to included. Spring. US (New York to Maryland and Michigan); introduced elsewhere in US. Over 30 cultivars distinguished largely by flower colour; height 5cm to 20cm, habit trailing, neat, often vigorous; lvs needle-like; fls in range of colours from white through shades of pink, lavender, and blue to carmine red, often with contrasting centres. 'Apple Blossom': fls pale lilac with dark eye. 'Fort Hill': fls deep pink, fragrant. 'G.F. Wilson': to 15cm; fls large, blue with pearl hue. 'Greencourt Purple': fls mauve with dark eye. 'Maiden Blush': fls pink with red eye.

'McDaniel's Cushion': fls bright pink, numerous. 'Marjorie': fls bright rose-pink. 'May Snow' ('Maischnee'): fls pure white. 'Red Wings': fls carmine-red with dark centre. 'Samson': fls large, deep rose-pink. 'White Delight': lvs pale green; fls pure white. Z3.

***P.* hybrids and cultivars**. 'Chatahoochee' *(P. divaricata* ssp. *laphamii* × *P. pilosa)*: stems arching to 20cm; fls bright blue with cerise eye. 'Charles Ricardo' *(P. divaricata* × *P. pilosa)*: to 15cm; fls pale blue, fragrant. 'Kelly's Eye' *(P. douglasii* × *P. subulata)*: fls shell pink with crimson eye. 'Laura': habit low, compact; fls pastel pink.

***P. abdita*** Nels. See *P. alyssifolia*.
***P. alba*** Moench. See *P. maculata*.
***P. canadensis*** Sweet. See *P. divaricata*.
***P. condensata*** (A. Gray) E.E. Nels. See *P. caespitosa* ssp. *condensata*.
***P. decussata*** Lyon ex Pursh. See *P. paniculata*.
***P. douglasii*** Hook. var. ***austromontana*** Jeps. & H.L. Mason. See *P. austromontana*.
***P. mesoleuca*** E. Greene. See *P. nana*.
***P. ovata*** var. ***pulchra*** Wherry. See *P. pulchra*.
***P. pyramidalis*** Sm. See *P. maculata* ssp. *pyramidalis*.
***P. reptans*** Michx. See *P. stolonifera*.
***P. rigida*** Benth. See *P. douglasii* ssp. *rigida*.
***P. stellaria*** A. Gray. See *P. bifida*.
***P. suffruticosa*** Vent. See *P. carolina*.

**Phoberos** Lour. See *Scolopia*.

**Phoebe** Nees. (Gk female name, equivalent of Lat. Luna, moon.) Lauraceae. 70 species of evergreen trees and shrubs. Wood aromatic. Leaves simple, alternate, pinnately veined. Flowers bisexual, fragrant, in panicles or corymbs; perianth 6-parted, the lobes regular, sepal-like, persistent, becoming hard and enclosing base of fruit; stamens 12, fertile stamens in 3 rings, those of the third ring each with 2 basal glands; sterile stamens forming innermost ring. Fruit a berry, enclosed in persistent calyx. E Asia. Z10.

CULTIVATION As for *Cinnamomum*.

***P. formosana*** (Hayata) Hayata. Tree to 15m, usually shorter. Bark smooth, brown. Branchlets dark brown, initially tomentose. Lvs 16×3.5cm, elliptic-oblong to lanceolate-ovate, apex acute, base cuneate, subcoriaceous, lustrous deep green above, tomentulose beneath with prominent, reticulate venation; petioles 2cm. Panicles to 12cm, small, axillary; fls to 0.4cm diam., white, sericeous. Fr. to 1cm, purple to blue-black, embedded in brown perianth remnants. China, Taiwan.

***P. sheareri*** Gamble. See *P. formosana*.

**Phoenicaulis** Nutt. (From Gk *phoinix*, purple-red, and *kaulos*, stem.) Cruciferae. 1 species, a tufted, perennial herb to 20cm. Caudex simple or branched, covered in the remains of old petiole bases. Leaves in a dense basal rosette, 3–10cm, broadly lanceolate-spathulate, stellate-pubescent, entire. Inflorescence a showy raceme, flowers small, pink-purple, occasionally white; sepals 4, 4mm; petals 4, long-clawed, to 10mm. Fruit a silique, to 4cm, compressed, oblong-lanceolate, glabrous, dehiscent, spreading horizontally; seeds 2–4, brown. Spring. Western N America. Z5.

CULTIVATION *P. cheiranthoides* occurs at high altitudes in the Rockies in Nevada, Idaho and Washington, sometimes on alkaline soils. In its natural range, winter temperatures may fall to −25°C/ −13°F and below, although as with many alpine species it dislikes winter wet. It is best for sunny, well-drained pockets of gritty soil on the rock garden, where it will bear bright racemes of rose-pink or purple flowers in spring. Propagate from seed, as for *Draba*.

***P. cheiranthoides*** Nutt. As for the genus.

For synonymy see *Parrya*.

**Phoenicophorium** H.A. Wendl. (Named after the genus *Phoenix*.) LATANIER PALM. Palmae. 1 species, a pleonanthic, monoecious palm, to 16m. Stem solitary, clothed with black spines when juvenile, markedly ringed, to 10cm diam. Crownshaft absent. Leaves arching to 2×1m, pinnately ribbed but undivided, emarginate, neatly abscising; sheath tomentose, with large black spines at first, becoming bare, margin tattering; petiole channelled above, convex beneath, with scattered scales, with large black spines beneath on young plants; blade bright green or tinged red, margins divided along ribs to one-third depth of leaf, each lobe further shallowly divided at apex, acute to acuminate, glabrous above, scaly below. Inflorescences interfoliar, erect, to 1m, branched to ×2, amid 2 bracts, lower bract persistent, tubular, leathery, tomentose, unarmed or black spiny, upper bract within lower bract, woody, deciduous, unarmed; peduncle slender, glabrous, much longer than rachis; rachillae pendent, flexuous, bearing spirally arranged floral triads (2 male, 1 female), with solitary or paired male flowers at apex: male flowers asymmetrical, sepals 3, overlapping, petals far exceeding sepals, 3, valvate, stamens 15–18, pistillode absent; female flowers with 3 overlapping sepals and 3 overlapping petals, 6 staminodes, pistil 1-celled, stigmas 3. Fruit ellipsoid to ovoid, to 1cm, red, with basal stigmatic remains and persistent perianth; epicarp shiny, mesocarp thin, fleshy, endocarp thin; seed ovoid. Mahé and Silhouette Is. in the Seychelles. Z9.

CULTIVATION A tall, slender and very attractive feather palm occurring predominantly in humid and sheltered habitats; suitable for outdoor cultivation in the humid tropics or in the hot glasshouse, it requires constant high humidity and shelter from wind to avoid scorching of the foliage. Propagate by seed. For cultivation see PALMS.

***P. borsigianum*** (K. Koch) Stuntz. As for the genus.

For synonymy see *Stevensonia*.

For illustration see PALMS.

**Phoenix** L. DATE PALM. (Gk word for the date palm.) Palmae. Some 17 species of pleonanthic, dioecious palms. Stems solitary or clustered, clothed with persistent leaf bases or bare and obliquely scarred, sometimes absent. Leaves pinnate, induplicate, marcescent, sheath fibrous; petiole channelled above, convex beneath; pinnae single-fold, regularly spaced or clustered along rachis, emerging brown-floccose or waxy, becoming scaly, lowermost pinnae reduced to spines. Inflorescences interfoliar, erect to arching, branched once; lower bracts glabrous or floccose, occasionally bivalved, upper bract inconspicuous; rachillae pendent, bearing solitary, cream-yellow or pale orange flowers; male flowers with petals 3, valvate, exceeding calyx, stamens 6, pistillode usually absent; female flowers globose, petals overlapping, to 2×length calyx, staminodes 6, carpels 3. Fruit oblong-ellipsoid to ovoid, 1-seeded, yellow, orange, green, brown or red to blue-black; epicarp shiny, mesocarp fleshy or pasty; seeds 1, with longitudinal groove. Africa, Asia. Z9.

CULTIVATION *P. dactylifera*, the date palm, has been cultivated for at least 5000 years. Although its origins are obscure, it seems likely that it occurred naturally in North Africa and Western Asia, and it now grows in arid zones from Morocco to Pakistan. The date is an enormously important crop in arid zones – the fruit is a staple food for long periods of the year. The wood and leaves are used in construction. Fibre from leaf and bark is used in rope- and basket-making, and when woven with camel hair it provides strong cloth for tent making. Dates are grown commercially in Saudi Arabia, Iran, Egypt, and Iraq, the latter being a major exporter, and in the US, in Arizona and California. The capacity of *P. dactylifera* to subsist with little care, on saline subsurface water, and in very hot locations, has led to its being replanted in Israel and the Jordan valley, where other crops would be difficult. Commercial fruit production relies on long hot summers with low humidity but little rain and copious irrigation, since rain may spoil pollination and cause rot in young fruit. Fruit set is ensured by hand or mechanical pollination and the quality of the fruit by limiting yield to about 50kg/110lbs per plant. Pollen can remain viable for several years. Fruits are hand-picked and ripened by incubator. Large yields are not obtained until plants are 5–8 years of age, and can range from 20–100kg/44–220lbs per annum.

In tropical, subtropical and warm temperate zones such as California, Florida and the south of France, *P. dactylifera* is a valuable ornamental, an admirable subject for avenue plantings. *P. rupicola*, a slender and graceful palm, and *P. canariensis* are

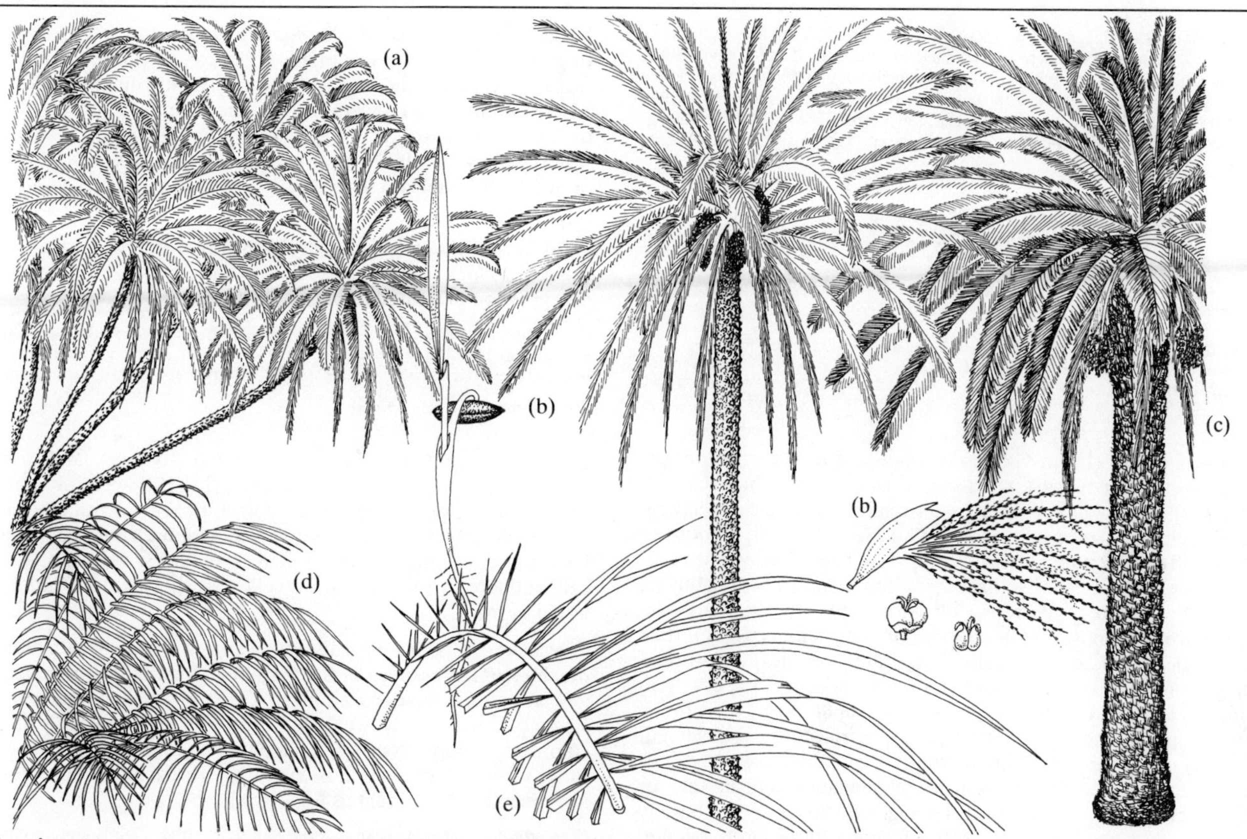


**Phoenix** (a) *P. reclinata* suckering habit (×0.075) (b) *P. dactylifera* palm with fruit (suckers removed) (×0.075), female inflorescence (×0.125), flower showing separate carpels (×0.75), seedling (×0.4) (c) *P. canariensis* palm with fruit (×0.075) (d) *P. roebelinii* crown (×0.04) (e) *P. loureirii* portion of leaf showing pinnae arranged in two planes (×0.25), cf. closely related *P. roebelinii*

also decorative ornamentals. Alongside *P. sylvestris*, the wild date (grown in India as a source of sugar and molasses), these are the most frost-hardy of the genus. They withstand full sun, dry atmospheres, and are tolerant of a wide range of soil types.

In cooler temperate zones, grow these species in a glasshouse with a minimum temperature of 10–13°C/50–55°F, and other more tropical species with minimum of 17°C/63°F; use a well-drained, fibrous, loam-based mix, and water plentifully in the growing season. A dilute liquid feed at fortnightly intervals is beneficial. Remove basal suckers to create taller single-stemmed specimens. Large specimens are often used for interior decoration. *P. rupicola* is the most commonly grown, but the small stature of the rather more tender *P. roebelinii* makes it a desirable container specimen.

Propagate from seed, after soaking for 24 hours, with a bottom heat of 21–27°C/70–80°F. *P. dactylifera* may be sown outdoors in mild areas, but seedlings will require winter protection. Propagate suckering species by offsets. See also PALMS.

***P. abyssinica*** Drude. Differs from *P. reclinata* only in the urceolate female cal. and hard endocarp. Ethiopia.

***P. acaulis*** Roxb. Trunk to 30cm diam. squat, ovoid, usually buried or obscured. Lvs to 90cm, waxy; pinnae to 45×1cm, few, in clusters of 2–4 along rachis, marginal veins conspicuous. Infl. to 30cm, subsessile; male fls with pet. obtuse; female with fls cal. to half length of cor. Fr. to 2×1cm, ovoid, red to blue-black, edible. Assam to Burma.

***P. canariensis*** hort. ex Chabaud. CANARY ISLAND DATE; CANARY DATE PALM. Trunk to 15×0.9m, solitary with oblong scars wider than long. Lvs to 6m, rachis sometimes twisted; pinnae crowded, regularly spaced along rachis, held almost in one plane. Male fls 1cm; female fls with cal. equalling cor. Fr. 2×1cm, oblong-ellipsoid, yellow tinged red. Canary Is.

***P. dactylifera*** L.. DATE; DATE PALM. Trunk to 30m, slender, suckering; petiole scars as long as wide or longer. Lvs to 3m; rachis rigid; petiole 20–100cm, with leaf-spines to 15cm; pinnae 30×2cm, to 80 on each side of rachis, regularly spaced or clustered, rigid, dull green. Female rachillae to 40cm, cal. half as long as pet., pet. 4×4cm; male peduncle to 60cm, bracts brown-scurfy when young, pet. 0.8×0.3cm. Fr. 4–7×2–3cm, oblong-ellipsoid, yellow to brown; mesocarp thick, sweet, edible. A cultigen, probably originating in W Asia and N Africa. 'Abbada': medium size, cures to black; 'Barhi' ('Barhee'), small to medium, syrupy, very high sugar content; 'Dayri' ('Dairee', 'Dairi'), medium to large, ripens to black, sweet, adapted to heavy soils; 'Deglet Noor', medium to large, semi-dry, sweet, late ripening, needing much heat to ripen, originated in Saharan oasis nearly 400 years ago; 'Halawi', medium to large, honey-flavoured, keeps well; 'Khadrawi', medium to large, meaty, rich-flavoured; 'Medjool', large to very large, needing thinning, very sweet; 'Saidy', large and broad, semi-dry, very sweet; 'Thoory', medium to large, dry, sweet nutty flavour, keeps a year of more; 'Zahidi', medium size, used as either soft or dry date, meaty and syrupy.

***P. lourierii*** Kunth. Stems 1.8–4.5m, often clustered. Lvs twisted and reflexed; pinnae clustered in groups along rachis, waxy, rachis with brown persistent and pale deciduous scales. Male fls to 0.5cm, pet. obtuse; female fls cal. half length of cor. Fr. red, 1–2×1cm. India to China.

***P. paludosa*** Roxb. Stems to 9m, slender, clustered. Lvs spreading; pinnae paired, clustered or in 2 rows, green above, white-waxy beneath, secondary veins 4–8 each side of central rib, prominent, brown-scaly. Infl. orange; male fls to 1cm; female fls cal. half length of cor. Fr. 1×0.5–1cm, orange, becoming black. Bengal to Malay Peninsula, Andaman Is.

***P. pusilla*** Gaertn. Stems to 3m, usually shorter, stout, covered in lf bases. Lvs to 2m, crowded; pinnae rigid, held in differing planes along rachis. Infl. interfoliar; fls cream. Fr. to 1.2cm, purple-black. S India, Sri Lanka.

***P. reclinata*** Jacq. SENEGAL DATE PALM. Stems to 10m, slender, clustered, clothed with red-brown woven sheaths. Lvs to 2.5m, arching to decurved, often twisted; petiole 15cm, tinted orange, apparent petiole 50cm, armed with 6mm spines; pinnae to 25×2cm, to 120 each side, clustered in fanned groups, tattering, green, not glaucous. Infl. to 1.5m; fls cream becoming brown, musty; male fls 0.6cm; female fls with ring-like cal., half length of cor. Fr. 1.3–1.7×0.9–1.3cm, pale yellow to red. Tropical Africa.

***P. roebelinii*** O'Brien. MINIATURE DATE PALM; PYGMY DATE PALM; ROEBELIN PALM. Stems to 2m, slender, especially at base, expanding toward crown, often leaning, clothed above with old petiole bases, roots forming a basal mass. Lvs to 1.2m; pinnae to 25×1cm, *c*50 each side, grey-green, regularly spaced along rachis and held in one plane, drooping, silver-scurfy, especially beneath. Infl. to 45cm; fls cream; male fls 1cm; female fls 0.5cm, cal. less than half length of pet. Fr. 1×0.5cm, ellipsoid, black. Laos.

***P. rupicola*** Anderson. CLIFF DATE; WILD DATE PALM; INDIA DATE PALM; EAST INDIAN WINE PALM. Stem to 7m×20cm, not clothed in persistent lf bases. Lvs to 3m, often twisted about rachis; pinnae 80 or more each side, held in one plane along rachis, grey peltate-scaly on ribs beneath. Infl. to 1.2m, much branched, pendent; male fls 1cm; female fls with cal. half length of cor. Fr. 2cm, oblong-ellipsoid, glossy yellow ripening deep purple-red. Himalayan India, Sikkim, Assam.

***P. sylvestris*** (L.) Roxb. WILD DATE; INDIA DATE. Stem to 15m×30cm, scarred. Lvs to 4.5m, grey-green; pinnae to 45×2.5cm, arranged in clusters in 2–4 planes along rachis. Infl. to 90cm; male fls to 1cm; female fls cal. half length of cor. Fr. to 3cm, oblong-ellipsoid, orange-yellow, to purple red. India

***P. cycadifolia*** hort. ex Reg. See *P. canariensis*.
***P. hanceana*** Naudin. See *P. loureirii*.
***P. humilis*** Royle. See *P. loureirii*.
***P. pumila*** Reg. See *P. reclinata*.
***P. spinosa*** Schum. & Thonn. See *P. reclinata*.
***P. tenuis*** hort. See *P. canariensis*.
***P. zeylanica*** Trimen. See *P. pusilla*.

**Pholidota** Lindl. (From Gk *pholis*, scale and *ous*, ear; the bracts are scaly and ear-like.) RATTLESNAKE ORCHID. Orchidaceae. 29 species of epiphytic or terrestrial orchids. Rhizomes creeping. Pseudobulbs clustered or remote, cylindric or conical, smooth or ribbed, often becoming laterally compressed and 4-sided with age, basally sheathed. Leaves solitary or paired, apical, linear, obovate or elliptic, acute, glabrous, obscurely plicate, stalked. Inflorescence racemose, from centre of new shoots, erect then sharply decurved and pendulous, spiralling or flexuous; bracts conspicuous overlapping, closely 2-ranked, concave, papery, subtending each flower; flowers numerous, small, white to brown; dorsal sepal ovate to elliptic, broad, coriaceous, few-veined, lateral sepals ovate to ovate-oblong, often basally grooved, or with prominent midrib; petals ovate or obovate to linear, few- or many-nerved, flat to concave; lip sigmoid to straight, basally saccate, lateral margins erect, often forming lobes, apex bilobed or entire often with keels and calli. Indomalaya, W Pacific. Z9.

CULTIVATION Intriguing epiphytic orchids for the intermediate house. The wand-like, spiralling racemes are clothed in slightly inflated bracts, resembling a rattlesnake's tail. See ORCHIDS.

***P. articulata*** Lindl. Pseudobulbs slender or swollen, wrinkled, to 15cm, borne at apex of previous year's pseudobulb. Lvs ovate to linear-lanceolate, to 20×5cm, venation prominent. Infl. to 6.5cm; bracts brown, to 1cm, falling as fls open; fls to 65, fragrant; sep. and pet. cream, green-white to pink, tips rarely darker, lip similar, keels buff, central constriction green-yellow to yellow-brown. India, China, Burma, Thailand to Celebes.

***P. chinensis*** Lindl. Pseudobulbs ovoid, wrinkled, to 11cm. Lvs to 20cm, ovate-oblong to linear-lanceolate. Infl. axis strongly flexuous, to 30cm; fls to 35, green-white to white, lip cream-white, column pale buff, tinged pink; dorsal sep. to 1×1cm, ovate to elliptic, obtuse to acute, 5–9 veined, midrib prominent, lateral sep. ovate to ovate-oblong, apical point often broad, midrib with a rounded to flattened keel; pet. ovate-lanceolate to linear-lanceolate, midrib sometimes swollen; lip basal lobes erect, rounded, basal nerves keeled, apically recurved to reflexed, entire, tip obtuse to acute, sometimes with swollen venation or minutely papillose. Burma, China.

***P. convallariae*** (Rchb. f.) Hook. f. Pseudobulbs slender to swollen, wrinkled when dry, to 7cm. Lvs linear-lanceolate, to 21×2.5cm, midrib prominent beneath. Infl. axis flexuous, to 10cm; fls 3–28; dorsal sep. to 10×5mm, ovate to ovate-oblong, midrib prominent, lateral sep. similar, midrib often prominently keeled; pet. to 7×5mm, ovate, venation sometimes branched; lip to 6.5mm, base deeply concave, lateral margins rounded, basal depression shallow, basally fused, apical lobes semi-elliptic, overlapping, keels 3–5, prominent. India, Burma.

***P. imbricata*** (Roxb.) Lindl. Pseudobulbs clustered, cylindric, swollen, longitudinally wrinkled or sunken, appearing translucent olive green, to 10cm. Lvs ovate-oblong to linear-lanceolate to 50×10cm, coriaceous, underside light green, often tinted red, venation prominent. Infl. to 15cm, spiralling; bracts papery, light brown, imbricate, persistent, concealing fls; fls to 130, white to cream, tinted yellow to pink; dorsal sep. ovate, forming a hood to 7×5mm, lateral sep. ovate-oblong, to 8×5mm; pet. falcate, apex truncate or rounded; lip basally concave, with 1–2 orange spots, lateral lobes erect, triangular to semi-orbicular, central nerves forming orange to yellow, wing-like keels, apex bilobed, lobes semi-elliptic, tip rounded, often acute. Vietnam, Solomon Is., Australia to Fiji.

***P. khasiyana*** Rchb. f. See *P. articulata*.

**Pholistoma** Lilja. (From Gk *pholis*, scale, and *stoma*, mouth.) Hydrophyllaceae. 3 species of prostrate or weakly climbing annual herbs closely related to *Nemophila*, from which it can be distinguished by the retrorse bristly spikes on the upper stems. Stems rather succulent and easily broken, usually angled and spiny. Leaves pinnatifid. Flowers white, blue or mauve, borne in cymes or, more rarely, solitary; calyx lobes 5; corolla lobes 5; stamens 5; style shallowly cleft. Fruit a capsule, 1-celled, setose or prickly. Southwest N America.

CULTIVATION A useful climber for temporary cover on fences and tree stumps etc., especially in informal situations. Cultivate as for *Nemophila*. Prick out seedlings when large enough to handle and grow on in individual pots until set out.

***P. auritum*** (Lindl.) Lilja. FIESTA FLOWER. To 1.2m. Lvs oblong in outline, hirsute, expanded and clasping at base, lobes 7–11. Fls to 2.75cm diam., blue, lilac or violet marked with deeper streaks, grouped 2–5 at shoot tips. California.

For synonymy see *Nemophila*.

**Phoradendron** Nutt. (From Gk *phoreo*, to bear, and *dendron*, tree.) FALSE MISTLETOE. Viscaceae (Loranthaceae). Some 200 species of bisexual or unisexual, parasitic shrubs, with chlorophyll. Leaves opposite, simple, entire, sometimes reduced to scales. Flowers small; male calyx 3-lobed, stamens 3, very short; female calyx adnate to ovary, ovary 1-celled, with 1 ovule. Fruit a small viscid berry. US. Z6.

CULTIVATION The translucent white berries of *P. serotinum*, much resembling those of the European mistletoe, *Viscum album*, and also used for decoration at Christmas, is seldom cultivated since it can severely weaken its host plant, especially in large colonies. It may occur spontaneously in gardens and has a wide range of hosts, although it is commonly restricted to one species in any given locality. Treat as for *Viscum*.

***P. serotinum*** (Raf.) M. Johnst. AMERICAN MISTLETOE. Habit densely bunching, to 1m diam.; twigs glabrous, terete, woody, brittle. Lvs to 5cm, obovate or oblanceolate, evergreen, opposite, tinged yellow. Fls borne in spikes. Fr. small, globose, off-white, translucent. New Jersey to Florida, West to S Illinois and Texas.

***P. flavescens*** (Pursh) Nutt. See *P. serotinum*.

**Phormium** Forst. & Forst. f. (From Gk *phormos*, basket, a plaited referring to the use made of the fibre.) FLAX LILY. Agavaceae. 2 species of large, rhizomatous, evergreen, perennial herbs, to 4.5m, becoming woody at base; roots fleshy, fibrous. Leaves basal, persistent, sword-shaped, folded towards the base and keeled, equitant, 2-ranked, stiff, with many fine close longitudinal stripes. Inflorescence an erect panicle on a leafless branched scape, with alternate deciduous papery bracts, upper bracts subtending and entirely enclosing the alternately branched flowering stems, 1.5–4.5m; flowers dull olive to red-yellow, bisexual, bilaterally symmetrical; perianth, more or less erect, tubular at base, segments 6, inner reflexed at tips; stamens 6, protruding; ovary superior, elongate, locules 3; flower stalks jointed near the apex. Fruit a long capsule, to 10cm; seeds many, black, shiny, flattened, ridged. New Zealand. Z8.

CULTIVATION These handsome perennials provide a striking contrast of form in the large flower border, carrying their stiff, leathery, sword-shaped leaves in crowded fans that emerge from the fat rhizomes; a number of cvs have finely coloured foliage, striped red, yellow and green in *P. c.* 'Tricolor' and with creamy yellow stripes in *P. c.* 'Variegatum'; this last is remarkable in flower, the dark plum-coloured flowering spikes making an extraordinary contrast with the foliage. Several cvs have beautifully bronzed or dark coppery leaves, sometimes richly striped with salmon pinks and rich reds as in *P. t.* 'Dazzler' and *P. t.* 'Aurora'; they last well when cut for floral arrangements. In summer, the statuesque plum-coloured flowering stem of the mature *P. tenax*, bearing deep red, tubular flowers, may reach heights of almost 5m/16ft in favourable conditions; those of *P. colensoi* are less impressive in stature, no less attractive and better suited to smaller gardens. *Phormium* spp. thrive in the equable climates of coastal gardens; inland, they can be grown where winter temperatures do not fall much below −10°C, especially if given a deep mulch of bracken litter or leafmould to protect the rhizomes. Grow in full sun in any moderately fertile, moisture retentive but well drained soil. Propagate by division or by seed.

***P. colensoi*** Hook. f. MOUNTAIN FLAX. To 2.1m. Lvs to 150×6cm, flexible, drooping, base usually pink. Infl. to 2m, often inclined. Fls 2.5–4cm, green tinged orange or yellow; per. tube lobed, tips strongly recurved. Fr. a pendulous, cylindric capsule to 20cm, gradually narrowed to apex, twisted and becoming pale fibrous and spirally curved with age; seeds 8–10mm, elliptic, plate-like. Summer. Many hybrids and cultivars available, some of obscure parentage. 'Apricot Queen': to 1m; lvs recurved, arching, dark green and apricot edged bronze. 'Cream Delight': to 1m, compact; lvs arching, green with wide central cream patch and several narrow stripes. 'Dark Delight': lvs to 1.2m, broad, strongly ascending but drooping at tips, dark plum. 'Duet': lvs to 30cm, narrow, stiff, bright green variegated cream. 'Jack Spratt': dwarf, compact and upright; lvs pale bronze. 'Maori Chief': vigorous; lvs to 1.2m, ascending, pink, red and buff. 'Maori Maiden': upright; lvs to 90cm, tinted bronze and striped red. 'Maori Queen': lvs deep pink, edged purple. 'Maori Sunrise': small, to 70cm; lvs arching, slender, apricot and pink edged bronze. 'Sundowner': vigorous, to 1.8m; lvs broad, erect, cream with dull purple centre, broadly edged pink fading to cream. 'Sunset': dwarf, to 30cm; lvs narrow, waved and twisted, soft bronze. 'Tricolor': lvs drooping, green striped cream and edged red; fls yellow. 'Variegatum': lvs with margins striped cream to lime.

***P. tenax*** Forst. & Forst. f. NEW ZEALAND FLAX; NEW ZEALAND HEMP. To 4.5m. Lvs to 3m×5–12cm, stiff, erect, tough, leathery, acuminate, margin red or orange; base of plant usually pale. Infl. to 5m, usually erect. Fls dull red, to 6cm, ovary erect. Fr. a capsule 5–10cm, erect, 3-angled, straight, abruptly contracted at apex; seeds 10×5mm, plate-like, sometimes twisted. Summer. 'Aurora': lvs, striped red, bronze salmon pink and yellow. 'Bronze Baby': dwarf; lvs red tinted bronze, outer lvs arching. 'Burgundy': lvs deep claret. 'Dazzler': habit pendulous, to 75cm; lvs narrow, lax, red, edged maroon. 'Goliath': growth vigorous. 'Nana Purpureum' ('Alpinum Purpureum'): dwarf, to 45cm; lvs purple tinted bronze. 'Purpureum': lvs maroon; 'Radiance': lvs variegated bright yellow. 'Tom Thumb': dwarf, to 40cm; lvs narrow, upright, bright green edged bronze. 'Variegatum': lvs striped with creamy yellow and white; 'Veitchii': creamy-white stripes on middle of lvs. 'Williamsii Variegated': vigorous; lvs large with thin marginal lines and central yellow stripe. 'Yellow Wave': to 1m; lvs broad, arching, brilliant yellow variegated green with age.

***P.* cultivars.** 'Pink Panther': lvs bright pink, edged red. 'Thumbellina': dwarf; lvs red tinted bronze.

***P. cookianum*** Le Jolis. See *P. colensoi*.
***P. hookeri*** Hook. f. See *P. colensoi*.

**Photinia** Lindl. (From Gk *photeinos*, shining, referring to the leaves.) CHRISTMAS BERRY. Rosaceae. To 60 species of deciduous and evergreen trees and shrubs. Leaves alternate, simple, entire to small-toothed; petiole short; stipule leaflike. Inflorescence a terminal corymb or short panicle; sepals 5, persistent; petals 5, white; stamens about 20; styles 2. Fruit a globose pome, carpels 3–5, fused with calyx tube, red. E & SE Asia, north to Himalaya, W US.

CULTIVATION *Photinia* spp. are used in the shrub border, woodland garden, as wall shrubs and as lawn specimens. *P. davidiana* and *P.* ×*fraseri* are useful informal hedge or screening plants. The evergreen species are grown primarily for their attractive, glossy foliage, sometimes maintaining the bright coloration of the young foliage into early summer. Young foliage is particularly effective in *P.* ×*fraseri* 'Rubens', which has glossy scarlet young leaves, and in clones such as *P.* ×f. 'Robusta', with strong coppery red young growth, and *P.* ×f. 'Red Robin', a brilliant red-bronze; the young leaves of *P. serrulata* hold their copper-red colour throughout the growing season. *P. davidiana* is a vigorous pollution-tolerant evergreen; the older leaves turn crimson in autumn, and the abundant bright red fruits persist well into winter, being apparently unattractive to birds. With the above exception, deciduous species are usually more reliable in the production of flowers and fruit in cool temperate climates than are the evergreens, and often colour well in autumn; the elegant *P. villosa* and *P. v.* var. *sinica*, give rich scarlet and gold autumn colour, the latter being amongst the most decorative in fruit.

*P. benthamiana*, *P. davidsoniae*, *P. glomerata*, *P. integrifolia* and *P. prionophylla* are the most tender species, and where temperatures fall regularly below −5°C/23°F, should be given the protection of a wall or a sheltered woodland position. Other spp. will tolerate temperatures to −7 to −12°C/19–10°F, *P. villosa*, and *P. davidiana* are reliably hardy to −15°C/5°F. Grow in well-drained fertile soils in sun or light shade, giving evergreen subjects protection from cold winds which will scorch the foliage. Evergreens are tolerant of calcareous soils; *P. davidiana* will grow in a range of soils including heavy clay, and will tolerate a degree of drought. Deciduous species have calcifuge tendencies. Propagate deciduous species from seed sown in autumn; desirable cvs and evergreen spp. by semi-ripe basal cuttings, rooted with bottom heat (18°C/64°F) in a closed case. Susceptible to fireblight, particularly *P. davidiana*.

***P. beauverdiana*** Schneid. Deciduous shrub to narrow tree to 10m, resembling *P. villosa* but with all parts glabrous; shoots purple-brown with pale lenticels when young. Lvs 5–13×2–5cm, narrow-obovate to lanceolate, long narrow-pointed, base cuneate, small-toothed, teeth dark glandular-tipped, vein pairs 8–14, conspicuous; petiole 1cm. Infl. 5×2.5cm, terminal on leafy shoots on 1-year-old wood; fls 1cm diam.; pet. round, clawed. Fr. 6m, ovoid, purple. Late spring. W China. var. ***notabilis*** (Schneid.) Rehd. & Wils. Lvs to 12.5cm, broader and larger than species type, vein pairs 12. Infl. 7.5–10cm wide. Fr. 7–8mm, orange red. China (W Hupeh). Z6.

***P. benthamiana*** Hance. Lvs oblong, entire, hairless. Infl. a much-branched corymb, hairy. N India. Z9.

***P. davidiana*** (Decne.) Cordot. Large shrub or small tree. Habit extremely vigorous. Branches erect, dark green. Lvs lanceolate or oblanceolate, leathery, entire. Fr. globose, vivid crimson, borne in conspicuous pendent bunches along the branches. W China. Salicifolia group: lvs narrow-lanceolate, veins more conspicuous. Infl. densely pubesc. Undulata group: medium-sized shrub, less vigorous than species type; branches widely spreading; lvs to 7.5cm, margins wavy. 'Fructu Luteo': fr. bright yellow. 'Prostrata': low-growing. Z8.

***P. davidsoniae*** Rehd. & Wils. Evergreen shrub to tree to 15m, shoots downy, red when young, becoming partly spiny. Lvs 7.5–15mm oblanceolate to narrow elliptic, tapered to base and apex, thick, dark shiny green above, paler beneath, veins beneath downy at first. Infl. 7–10cm, downy; fls 1cm diam. Fr. 8mm, globose, orange-red, glabrous. Late spring. C China. Z9.

***P.* ×*fraseri*** Dress *(P. glabra × P. serrulata.)* Vigorous evergreen shrub. Lvs 7–9cm, elliptic-ovate to elliptic, small-toothed, apex tapered, base wedge-shaped, coppery at first, becoming shiny dark green above, paler beneath; petiole 1.2–2.3cm, downy. Infl. 10–12cm diam. Garden origin. 'Birmingham': lvs obovate, thick, leathery, coppery at first becoming dark green; the type of the cross. 'Indian Princess': dwarf compact form; lvs to 4.5cm, coppery-orange when young. 'Red Robin': lvs sharply toothed, dark red at first becoming dark shiny green. 'Robusta': young lvs coppery-red. 'Rubens': to 1.5m, habit dense; lvs bright sealing-wax red when young. Z8.

***P. glabra*** (Thunb.) Maxim. JAPANESE PHOTINIA. Evergreen, entirely glabrous shrub, 3–6m. Lvs 5–8×1.5–4cm, elliptic to narrow obovate, base cuneate, red at first, becoming dark shining green; petiole 1–1.5cm. Infl. 5–10cm diam., a loose terminal panicle; fls 1cm; pet. white, sometimes flushed pink, hairy at base. Fr. 5mm, globose, red becoming black. Late spring. Japan. 'Rosea Marginata': lvs variegated green, white, grey and pink. 'Variegata' ('Pink Lady'): lvs pink at first, becoming green edged white. Z7.

***P. glomerata*** Rehd. & Wils. Deciduous shrub, 6–10m, shoots long-hairy, red. Lvs 12–18cm, narrow oblong-oblanceolate, shortly tapered, margins somewhat rolled, finely toothed, these glandular tipped, red at first, becoming yellow green above, paler beneath, vein pairs 6–9, long-haired at first. Infl. 6–10cm, closely long-haired; fls fragrant; pedicel short. Fr. 5–7mm, ovate, red. China (Yunnan). Z9.

***P. integrifolia*** Lindl. Small tree, all parts hairless. Lvs 7.5–12.5cm, oblanceolate, tapered, entire. Fls to 1cm diam. Fr., 5mm, globose, glaucous blue. Himalaya. Z8.

***P. nussia*** (D. Don) Kalkman. Large shrub or small tree to 6m. Lvs to 10cm, oblanceolate to obovate, leathery, dark glossy green, finely toothed. Fls in flattened tomentose clusters. Fr. downy, orange. Himalaya, SE Asia. Z9.

***P.* 'Palette'.** Slow-growing. Lvs conspicuously marked with cream-white blotches, tinged pink when young. Z9.

***P. parvifolia*** (Pritz.) Schneid. Deciduous shrub, 2–3m; young shoots glabrous, dark red. Lvs 3–6×1–3cm, oval to obovate, slender-pointed, base cuneate, small-toothed, teeth glandular tipped, dark green above, paler beneath, quickly becoming glabrous. Infl. 3cm, an umbellate panicle of 5–9 fls, on short leafy twigs; fls 1cm diam.; pet. rounded, sparsely hairy inside. Fr. 1cm, oval, orange red to bright red. Late spring. China (Hupeh). Z6.

***P. prionophylla*** (Franch.) Schneid. Evergreen stiffly branched shrub to 2m; young shoots grey downy. Lvs 2.5–7.5×1.5–5cm obovate to oval, base tapered, leathery, margins sharply serrate, upper surface dark green, downy only at first, lower surface downy, veins prominent; petiole 1cm. Infl. 7.5cm, corymbose, erect; fls 5mm diam. Fr. 0.5cm, globose, crimson, downy around cal. Summer. China. Z9.

**P. 'Redstart'**. (*P. davidiana* 'Fructu Luteo' × *P.* ×*fraseri* 'Robusta'.) Large shrub or small tree. Lvs to 11cm, bright red at first, becoming dark green, finely and sparsely toothed above the middle. Fls white in dense hemispherical corymbs; cal. and pedicels red-purple. Fr. orange-red, tinged yellow. Z7.

***P. serrulata*** Lindl. Evergreen shrub to tree 5–12m; young shoots red, glabrous. Lvs 10–10×3–8cm, ovate to obovate, base round to acuminate, shallow-toothed, glabrous, leathery, red at first, becoming shiny dark green above, paler yellow-green beneath; petiole 2–4cm, hairy. Infl. 10–15cm in width, a terminal corymbose panicle; fls 1cm diam.; pet. glabrous. Fr. 5mm, globose to ovoid, red. Spring. China. 'Aculeata' ('Lineata'): stems red at first; lvs with larger teeth. 'Rotundifolia': smaller than species type; lvs smaller and more rounded; cor subglobose. Z7.

***P. villosa*** (Thunb.) DC. Deciduous shrub or small tree to 5m; young shoots downy at first. Lvs 3–8×2–3cm, obovate to lanceolate-ovate, apex long tapered, leathery, margins toothed, teeth glandular-tipped, deep green above, paler, yellow-green and hairy beneath, becoming bright orange-red in autumn. Infl. 5cm diam., corymbose; stalk warted, downy; fls 1cm diam. Fr. 8mm, ellipsoid, red. Late spring. Japan, Korea, China. var. ***laevis*** (Thunb.) Dipp. Lvs smaller, narrower, long-pointed, all parts very soon glabrous. Japan. f. ***maximowicziana*** (Lév.) Rehd. Lvs obovate, apex rounded, base cuneate, turning yellow in autumn, veins indented above. Korea. var. ***sinica*** Rehd. & Wils. Narrow tree to 8m; young shoots downy. Lvs 2–8×1–3cm, oval to oblong, acuminate, finely toothed, quickly glabrous, bright green above, paler beneath, turning red in autumn. Infl. 1–2cm diam., downy. Fr. 12mm ovate, orange-red, stalk warty. C and W China. Z4.

***P. arbutifolia*** (Ait.) Lindl. See *Heteromeles arbutifolia*.
***P. crenatoserrata*** Hance. See *Pyracantha crenatoserrata*.
***P. deflexa*** Hemsl. See *Eriobotrya deflexa*.
***P. eugeniifolia*** Lindl. See *P. benthamiana*.
***P. glabra*** 'Red Robin'. See *P.* ×*fraseri* 'Red Robin'.
***P. japonica*** (Thunb.) Franch. & Savat. See *Eriobotrya japonica*.
***P. maximowicziana*** (Lév.) Nak. non. Decne. See *P. villosa* var. *laevis* f. *maximowicziana*.
***P. notabilis*** Schneid. See *P. beauverdiana* var. *notabilis*.
***P. serrulata*** 'Robusta'. See *P.* ×*fraseri* 'Robusta'.
***P. subumbellata*** Rehd. & Wils. See *P. parvifolia*.
***P. variabilis*** Hemsl. See *P. villosa*.
For further synonymy see *Eriobotrya, Pyrus, Pourthiaea* and *Sorbus*.

**Photinopteris** J. Sm. (From Gk *photeinos*, bright, shining, and *pteris*, fern.) Polypodiaceae. 1 species, an epiphytic and terrestrial fern. Rhizomes long-creeping, 1cm wide or more, green to frosted and glaucous, dictyostelic; scales to 8mm, ciliate, peltate, deciduous, chestnut brown. Fronds to 70cm, pinnate, short-petiolate, joined to rachis, auriculate, sterile (lower) pinnae to 25×10cm, to 10 pairs, ovate, apex narrowly acute, base obtuse to cuneate, falcate, glabrous, thick-textured, leathery, fertile (upper) pinnae to 25×1cm, more numerous, linear, veins prominent below; stipes to 30cm. Sori continuous each side of midrib, dorsal, sporangia glabrous, annulus 12-celled, spores ellipsoid, smooth, glassy. SE Asia. Z10.

CULTIVATION As for *Polypodium*.

***P. speciosa*** (Bl.) Presl. As for the genus.

For synonymy see *Lomaria*.

**Photoperiodism**. Photoperiodism is the phenomenon whereby plants are capable of measuring the relative lengths of day and night. By this means they are able to sense seasonal time and synchronise their life cycles and development with it. The responses of plants to daylength frequently concern aspects of reproduction, especially flowering, and it is presumed that these responses have a strong adaptive value; thus in angiosperms the opportunities for cross-pollination and the production of viable seeds are maximized, if all the members of a species-population flower at the same time. It is probably no coincidence that many animal pollinators, for instance insects, exhibit photoperiodic responses and there is likely to have been co-evolution between seed plants and their insect pollinators. Many other phases of plant development are timed to take place during certain seasons. These are often related to the avoidance of seasonally occurring environmental stresses, such as drought and cold (see PLANTS AND STRESS); these include leaf growth, dormancy, formation of storage organs, leaf fall and the onset of frost-hardiness. As well as responding to seasonal temperature changes, all these aspects of the plant's development and life cycle are frequently found to the photoperiodically controlled. Unfortunately, scientific knowledge of the detailed mechanism(s) of photoperiodism is incomplete. Most of what is known, as well as its application, concerns the effects of daylength on flowering.

Of the approximately 300,000 species of plants on earth, only a few hundred have been subjected to controlled artificial photoperiods; and it seems there may ultimately be almost as many variations on the general response to photoperiod as there are species. It is hardly surprising that, in general, plants growing far from the equator respond to longer daylengths than those growing closer to the equator. While for some tropical plants subtle changes in water relations or temperature may trigger flowering, many others do respond to daylength and are capable of detecting the small changes in daylength which occur at around 5–15° from the equator. Latitudinal variation in response can occur within a species, with ecotypes and varieties being matched to latitude. This matching is sometimes quite precise, as in the case of soybean varieties grown in the United States, which will only achieve optimum performance within an approximately 50-mile range of latitude.

In the photoperiodic control of flowering, the apparently wide variety of response-types has been conveniently divided into several categories. True day-neutral plants in which flowering is unaffected by day-length are probably comparatively rare, but cucumber (*Cucumis sativa*) and kidney bean (*Phaseolus vulgaris*) are two examples.

Short-day plants (SDPs) flower in response to short days; or more precisely, to days shorter than a certain critical length, which may, however, be greater than 12 hours. This concept can be a little confusing at first, when the classic SDP cocklebur (*Xanthium strumarium*) requires days which are less than about 15½ hours (a relatively long day); while the equally classic long-day plant (LDP) henbane (*Hyoscyamus niger*) requires days which are longer than about 11 hours (a relatively short day). Cocklebur is an example of an SDP which will flower after just one short day, while spinach (*Spinacia oleracea*) is an LDP responding to a single inductive long day. Much more common are species requiring several cycles of the appropriate photoperiod for floral induction. Among SDPs are those such as *Kalanchoë blossfeldiana*, which have an absolute or qualitative requirement for days shorter than the critical length; along with others such as sunflower (*Helianthus annuus*), which will eventually flower in days longer than the critical length, known as quantitative SDPs. Similarly, an example of an absolute LDP is hibiscus (e.g. *Hibiscus syriacus*), while spring wheat (*Triticum aestivum*) is a quantitative LDP. These response types can be further modified in some species by exposure to cool temperatures or less commonly to warm temperatures. In addition there are several species which respond to various combinations of daylengths, for instance long days followed by short days promote flowering in *Kalanchoë laxiflora*, while short days followed by long days are required by white clover (*Triflorum repens*).

The great majority of plants need to have reached a certain stage of development before they are capable of responding to daylength (i.e. they become ripe enough to flower); thus henbane must be 10–30 days old before it can respond to long days, while many trees will not flower until they are tens of years old; and the required number of inductive cycles often decreases with age. Ripeness to flower is associated with loss of juvenility and plant physiologists quantify it by 'physiological time', that is the possession of a minimum number of leaves, rather than simply by the passage of chronological time.

Much remains to be discovered about the precise physiological and molecular mechanisms of photoperiodism, but it is clear that for all the response types it is the length of night or darkness, rather than daylength, which is the critical factor. It appears that the photoreversible plant pigment phytochrome is involved, reverting from its active form during the dark period. The presence of a high proportion of phytochrome in its active form somehow inhibits flowering in SDPs, while promoting it in LDPs. This simple 'hour-glass' hypothesis of time measurement is not the whole answer to the mechanism of photoperiodism, as there is ample evidence for the simultaneous involvement of plants' endogenous rhythms (oscillatory time). However, it does go a long way towards explaining the possibility for artificial manipulation of flowering-time in practical horticulture. The best known example of this in Britain is the supply of all-year-round chrysanthemums. Chrysanthemums are SDPs, which are naturally induced to flower by the shortening days of late summer. However, when grown under controlled conditions under glass, they can be prevented from flowering until required, right through the autumn and winter, by using artificial lights to extend daylengths or, more efficiently, to provide one or several brief night-breaks. The success of night-breaks in preventing flowering is thought to be due at least in part to the fact that at the end of the day a high proportion of the phytochrome in the plant's leaves is in the active form, thus inhibitory to flowering in an SDP. During a long night, dark reversion of phytochrome to its inactive form means that by the end of the night phytochrome is incapable of inhibiting flowering. Night-breaks with a white or red light allow a rapid photoconversion of phytochrome to its active (presumably inhibitory to flowering in SDPs) form, and the vegetative state can thus be maintained. When flowering is required the night breaks are suspended and a few long nights allow flowering to be induced. In the long days (short nights) of summer flowering can be induced by artificially lengthening the nights by applying black-outs to the glasshouse. The flowering of some SDPs as with carnations, can be manipulated in analogous ways. Flowering in these species is promoted by daylength extensions or night breaks but they are generally less sensitive to short night breaks than SDPs.

*Thermoperiodism* describes the generally beneficial effects on the growth of plants of an environment in which the temperature fluctuates diurnally, rather than remaining constant. It seems that the effect is closely linked to photoperiodism in many cases, operating via phytochrome balances and interactions with the plant's circadian rhythms. Many plants grow just as well at an optimum constant temperature as they do when day and night temperatures vary. Perhaps the best example of an obligate requirement for temperature fluctuations is in the removal of seed dormancy in some species (see SEEDS: PHYSIOLOGY AND GERMINATION).

**Phragmipedium** Rolfe. (From Gk *phragma*, partition, and *pedilon*, slipper, referring to the trilocular ovary and the slipper-shaped lip.) LADY-SLIPPER. Orchidaceae. Some 20 species of terrestrial, lithophytic or epiphytic orchids. Stems short, clustered, clothed with leaves; roots fibrous. Leaves distichous, overlapping in fans, coriaceous, sulcate, conduplicate, usually ligulate, arching. Inflorescence a raceme or panicle, terminal, erect, usually several-flowered; peduncle usually terete, pubescent, sheathed; ovary shortly pedicellate, trilocular; flowers large, showy, short-lived; dorsal sepal free, slightly concave, lateral sepals fused as a synsepalum; petals free, spreading or pendent, similar to sepals or long-caudate; lip sessile, inflated, slipper-shaped, margins involute; column short, stout; fertile stamens 2, laterally adnate, anther 2-celled; staminode peltate-scutate, triangular, rhombic or rounded; pollen granular. C & S America. Z10. Formerly included variously in *Cypripedium*, *Paphiopedilum*, and *Selenipedium*. *Selenipedium* now refers strictly to species of reed-like habit with ephemeral, slipper-shaped flowers and is probably not cultivated.

CULTIVATION As for warm-growing *Paphiopedilum* spp.

***P. besseae*** Dodson & J. Kuhn. Fls small, scarlet, strongly pouched; sep. and pet. short, broad.

***P. boissierianum*** (Rchb. f.) Rolfe. Lvs 6–8, to 80×5cm, acute. Raceme subequal to lvs, erect, loosely 3–15-fld; tepals bronze or olive green veined dark green, edged white or brown, dorsal sep. to 6×1.5cm, lanceolate or oblong-lanceolate, acuminate, undulate-crisped, synsepalum to 6×3cm, ovate-oblong, pet. to 10cm, widely spreading, linear-lanceolate, twisted, undulate-crisped; lip unguiculate, pendent, obovate-saccate, brown in front, lateral lobes strongly incurved, heavily spotted green-brown; staminode transversely elliptic-reniform. Ecuador, Peru.

***P. caricinum*** (Lindl. & Paxt.) Rolfe. Terrestrial. Lvs 3–7, rigid, suberect, to 50×1.5cm, narrowly linear. Raceme or panicle to 40cm, several-fld; fls borne in succession; tepals bronze to olive edged purple-green, dorsal sep. to 2.5×1.5cm, ovate-lanceolate to lanceolate, acute to obtuse, undulate, synsepalum broadly ovate-oblong, acute, to 2.5×1.5cm, pet. to 8×4mm, linear-lanceolate, acute, pendent, twisted, undulate; lip yellow-green, to 3.5cm, lateral lobes spotted dark green and purple, strongly incurved. Peru, Bolivia, Brazil.

***P. caudatum*** (Lindl.) Rolfe. Lvs 5–9, to 60×6cm. Raceme to 80cm, 2–4-fld; fls largest of the genus, to 125cm across; sep. white to yellow-green with dark green venation, dorsal sep. to 15×3cm, lanceolate, acute, arched over lip, strongly undulate to spiralled, synsepalum to 10×4.5cm, lanceolate to ovate-lanceolate, long-acuminate, strongly undulate, pet. purple-brown to green-brown, to 60×1cm, linear-lanceolate, pendulous, spiralling; lip yellow near base, apex tinted pink or maroon, veined green, to 7×2cm, calceolate, 3-lobed, lateral lobes strongly incurved, spotted green. Mexico to Peru, Venezuela, Colombia, Ecuador.

***P. ×dominianum*** hort. (*P. caricinum* × *P. caudatum*.) Stem erect. Lvs linear-elongate. Infl. 3-fld; fls yellow-green, tinged with copper-brown; lip deep red-brown in front, with sharper reticulations, yellow-green behind, mouth incurved, yellow spotted dark purple.

***P. grande*** hort. Stems to 1m. Lvs to 65cm, salverform. Infl. many-fld.; fls large; dorsal sep. yellow-white, with yellow-green venation, elongated, incurved; pet. to 30cm, ribbon-like, pendent, yellow-white and pubesc. toward base, crimson toward apex; lip large, basal lobes white, unfolded, spotted crimson, yellow-green in front, paler beneath; staminode yellow flushed crimson.

***P. hartwegii*** (Rchb. f.) L.O. Williams. Lvs to 60cm. Raceme to 90cm, loosely several-fld, with several basal, red-brown sheaths; fls green-yellow; dorsal sep. to 5×2cm, ovate-oblong, attenuate above, undulate, synsepalum ovate-elliptic, to 5×4cm, undulate; pet. to 9cm, linear-ligulate or linear-lanceolate, pendent, twisted, slightly undulate-crisped; lip unguiculate, slightly slipper-shaped, lateral lobes retuse, subquadrate. Ecuador, Peru.

***P. klotzschianum*** (Rchb. f. ex Schomb.) Rolfe. Lvs to 35×1cm. Raceme to 60cm, erect, 2–3-fld; fls opening singly; sep. pink-brown veined maroon, dorsal sep. to 3×1cm, lanceolate, subacute, synsepalum to 3×2cm, ovate, obtuse; pet. pale brown veined green or maroon, to 5×1cm, pendent, linear, obtuse, twisted; lip to 3×1.5cm, slipper-shaped, lateral lobes strongly incurved, minutely pubesc., yellow spotted brown, midlobe white. Venezuela, Guyana.

***P. lindenii*** (Lindl.) Dressler & N. Williams. Resembles *P. caudatum* except lip simple, unpouched, similar to pet., wider at base. Colombia, Peru, Ecuador.

***P. lindleyanum*** (Schomb. ex Lindl.) Rolfe. Lvs 4–7, to 50×6cm. Raceme or lightly branched panicle to 1m, 3–7-fld; sep. pale green or yellow-green, veined red-brown, pubesc. below, dorsal sep. to 3.5×2cm, elliptic, obtuse, concave, synsepalum to 3×2.5cm, elliptic, obtuse; pet. yellow-green at base, white-green toward apex, margins and veins flushed purple toward apex, to 5.5×1cm, linear-oblong, rounded, undulate; lip pale yellow-green with yellow-brown venation, to 3×1.5cm, 3-lobed, lateral lobes spotted light purple, incurved, midlobe inflated, margins incurved. Venezuela, Guyana.

***P. longifolium*** (Warsc. & Rchb. f.) Rolfe. Lvs to 60×4cm. Infl. to 40cm, several-fld, erect; fls produced singly, long-lived; dorsal sep. pale yellow-green, veined dark green or rose, edged white, to 6×2cm, lanceolate, acute, erect or curved forward, sometimes undulate, synsepalum to 6×4cm, pale yellow-green, veined dark green, ovate, acute; pet. pale yellow-green, margins rose-purple, to 12×1cm, spreading, linear or linear-lanceolate, twisted; lip yellow-green, to 6×1.5cm, slipper-shaped, 3-lobed, margins strongly incurved and spotted pale rose to magenta. Costa Rica, Panama, Colombia, Ecuador.

***P. sargentianum*** (Rolfe) Rolfe. Lvs to 50×6cm. Raceme or panicle to 40cm, 2–4-fld; tepals green or yellow-green veined purple-green, dorsal sep. to 3×1.5cm, ovate-elliptic, acute, concave, ciliate, synsepalum to 3×2cm, ciliate, pet. to 6×1.5cm, oblong-ligulate, acute, spreading, slightly twisted, ciliate, margins tinged purple; lip yellow or yellow-green veined purple, slipper-shaped, lateral lobes spotted purple, with 2 small, white tubercles on inner margin. Brazil.

***P. schlimii*** (Lind. & Rchb. f.) Rolfe. Lvs to 35×3cm. Raceme or panicle to 50cm, 5–10-fld; tepals white flushed rose-pink, dorsal sep. to 2×1cm, ovate-oblong, obtuse, concave, synsepalum broader than dorsal sep., pet. slightly longer than sep., spreading, spotted pink at base, elliptic; lip rose-pink, inflated, ellipsoid, lateral lobes incurved, streaked white and rose-carmine. Colombia.

***P. ×sedenii*** (Rchb. f.) Pfitz. (*P. longifolium* × *P. schlimii*.) Sep. ivory white, flushed pale rose, exterior rose-pink; pet. white, margins tinged rose-pink, twisted; lip rose-pink, lobes white spotted rose; staminode white, slightly dotted pink.

***P.*** grexes.

*P.* Ainsworthii: strong growing plants; fls consecutively, white and pale pink, larger than in *P. ×sedenii*.

*P.* Grande: very large plants; tall infl. with several large fls simultaneously, green-brown with very long pet.

*P.* Nitidissimum: large plants with several fls simultaneously; fls yellow-green with pink margins and brown lip.

*P. warscewiczianum* (Rchb. f.) Schltr. See *P. caudatum*.

**Phragmites** Adans. (From Gk *phragma*, fence or screen, referring to the screening effect of many plants growing together along streams.) REED. Gramineae. Some 4 species of rhizomatous perennial reed grasses, to 3m or more. Stems robust. Leaves linear, flat, attached to stem, blades deciduous; ligules papery, ciliate. Inflorescence terminal a large, plumed panicle; spikelets stipitate, to 13 flowered rachis laterally compressed sericaceous; lowest flower male or sterile; callus plumed; glumes shorter than lowest lemma, to 5-ribbed; palea longer than lemma; lemma membranous, to 3-ribbed, glabrous, entire. Cosmopolitan, Tropics to temperate regions.

CULTIVATION Occurring in marsh, fen and riverside habitats in temperate and tropical zones, *P. australis* is an elegant perennial, valued for the soft and showy flowering panicles, which retain their beautiful metallic sheen even on drying, and for the golden russet autumn colours. The species is notable for its aggressive invasiveness and tolerance of extremely low winter temperatures to −20°/−4°F and below (*P. a.* ssp. *altissimus* is slightly less hardy). *Phragmites* thrives in deep, moisture-retentive soils, but is generally suitable only for the larger landscape unless confined in containers, or as a marginal or submerged aquatic. Propagate by division.

***P. australis*** (Cav.) Trin. ex Steud. COMMON REED; CARRIZO. Stems robust, to 3.5m. Lvs to 60×5cm+, attenuate, flexuous to curved, margins scabrous. Infl. oblong to ovoid, erect to pendent, loose to compact, sericeous, tinged brown to purple, to 45cm; spikelets lanceolate, to 17mm, 2–10-fld; glumes lanceolate, persistent, papery, to 6mm; fertile lemmas enveloped in white hairs, to 8mm. Summer–autumn. Cosmopolitan. 'Humilis': dwarf. 'Rubra': infl. tinted crimson. 'Striatopictus': less vigorous, lvs striped pale yellow. 'Variegatus': lvs striped bright yellow, fading to white. ssp. ***altissimus*** W. Clayton. To 6m; panicles to 40cm; glumes tridentate. Z5.

***P.*** 'Giganteus'. See *P. australis* ssp. *altissimus*.
***P. communis*** Trin. See *P. australia*.
***P. communis*** var. ***giganteus*** (Gay) Husnot. See *P. australis* ssp. *altissimus*.
***P. flavescens*** hort. See *P. australia*.
***P. maxima*** Chiov. See *P. australia*.
***P. vulgaris*** (Lam.) Crépin. See *P. australis*.
For further synonymy see *Arundo*.

**Phryganocydia** Mart. ex Bur. Bignoniaceae. (From Gk *phryganon*, undershrub, and *kydion*, greater.) 3 species of lianes; pseudostipules absent. Stem without glandular patches. Leaves 2-foliolate, often with simple tendril. Flowers solitary or in lax panicles; calyx spathe-like, split; corolla tubular-funnelform, lilac to magenta, lepidote outside; stamens didynamous; ovary conical to terete, lepidote; disc absent. Capsule linear, flattened, median nerve not prominent, lepidote; seeds with 2 brown wings. Costa Rica to Brazil. Z10.

CULTIVATION A rampant climber found in open, low-lying habitats, often at the roadsides, *P. corymbosa* is one of Trinidad's most beautiful climbers, bearing a profusion of fragrant pink or purple trumpet-shaped blooms, in several flushes over the season. Cultivate as for *Tecoma*.

***P. corymbosa*** (Vent.) Bur. ex Schum. Stem 5cm diam. Lvs 2-foliolate, usually with tendril; leaflets elliptic to ovate-elliptic, apex obtuse, base rounded, 4–20×2–11cm with 3 nerves, principal nerve red-brown beneath; tendrils simple, 7–16cm. Fls magenta, throat white; cal. 1cm; cor. funnelform, 4–9×1–2.5cm. Fr. 12–53×1–3cm, linear-oblong, pilose; seeds 1–2×4–7cm. Panama to Brazil and Bolivia.

For synonymy see *Spathodea*.

**Phrynium** Willd. emend Schum. (From Gk *phrynion*, toad; these are marsh-dwelling plants.) Marantaceae. About 15 species of herbaceous perennials, rarely branching. Lvs basal; petioles long, sheathed at base, pulvinate at apex. Inflorescence a spike or capitulum; prophylls 1–3 per flower pair; bracteoles absent; sepals unequal, subovate-oblong; corolla tube rarely exceeding calyx, lobes oblong; outer staminodes 2, petaloid, callose staminodes short, often many, cucullate staminode short; ovary trilocular. Fruit a 3-seeded capsule, 1–2 often aborted, exocarp hard; seeds grooved, aril thin. India, SE Asia. Z10.

CULTIVATION As for *Thalia*, but in temperatures no lower than 10°C/14°F.

***P. villosulum*** Miq. To 2m. Lvs to 35×15cm, basal, ovate-oblong, acute, leathery, light green with dark bands over prominent lateral veins above, midrib pubesc. beneath; petiole short; pulvinus callose; sheath pubesc. Infl. basal or cauline, to 4.5cm; bracts ovate, villous. Malaysia.

***P. allouia*** (Aubl.) Roscoe. See *Calathea allouia*.
***P. basiflorum*** Ridl. See *P. villosulum*.
***P. coloratum*** Hook. See *Calathea colorata*.
***P. compressum*** (A. Dietr.) K. Koch. See *Ctenanthe compressa*.
***P. cylindrica*** Roscoe. See *Calathea cylindrica*.
***P. daniellii*** Benn. See *Thaumatococcus daniellii*.
***P. flavescens*** (Lind.) Sweet. See *Calathea flavescens*.
***P. flexuosum*** Benth. See *Marantochloa cuspidata*.
***P. houtteanum*** K. Koch. See *P. villosulum*.
***P. jagorianum*** K. Koch. See *Stachyphrynium jagorianum*.
***P. lubbersiana*** hort. See *Ctenanthe lubbersiana*.
***P. macrostachyum*** Benth. See *Megaphrynium macrostachyum*.
***P. metallicum*** K. Koch. See *Calathea metallica*.
***P. picturatum*** Lind. See *Calathea picturata*.
***P. propinquum*** Poepp. & Endl. See *Calathea propinqua*.
***P. sanguineum*** Hook. See *Stromanthe sanguinea*.
***P. setosum*** Roscoe. See *Ctenanthe setosa*.
***P. textile*** Ridl. See *Ataenidia conferta*.
***P. varians*** K. Koch & Mathieu. See *Calathea varians*.
***P. variegatum*** K. Koch. See *Calathea variegata*.
***P. villosum*** Lodd. See *Calathea villosa*.
***P. zebrinum*** (Sims) Roscoe. See *Calathea zebrina*.
For further synonymy see *Heliconia*.

**Phuopsis** Benth. & Hook. Rubiaceae. 1 species, a slender perennial herb to 30cm; stems slender. Leaves in whorls of 6–8, narrow-lanceolate, slender-pointed, spiny-ciliate, sessile. Flowers small, pink, hermaphrodite, clustered; calyx with an obovoid tube, limb obsolete; corolla tubular-funnel-shaped with 5 oblong-ovate, obtuse, valvate lobes; style simple, tip capitate. USSR (Caucasus). Z7.

CULTIVATION *Phuopsis*, closely related to *Crucianella*, is a mat-forming perennial grown for the profusion of scented flowers borne at the tips of the creeping stems, and suitable for ground cover on the rock garden, and on banks. Hardy to −20°C/−4°F. Grow in moist, gritty but well-drained soils in full sun, or light shade. Propagate by removal of rooted stems, by semi-ripe cuttings or from seed sown in autumn.

***P. stylosa*** Benth. & Hook. As for the genus.

**Phycella** Lindl. Amaryllidaceae. About 7 species of bulbous herbs. Leaves narrow-linear. Flowers 2–12, in drooping umbels, borne terminally on leafless hollow peduncles; perianth declinate, funnel-shaped with a short tube, red, purple, red and yellow, or yellow-green, gaping, convolute to closed, with 6 lobes, stamens 6, in 2 rows, inserted into the bases of the lobes, declinate, subequal, each with 2 subulate processes at the base; stigma obscurely 3-fid or capitate. Fruit a capsule with many flat black seeds. S America. Z9.

CULTIVATION Frost-tender bulbs, grown for their brightly coloured umbels of drooping, funnel-shaped flowers. Cultivate as for *Hippeastrum*.

***P. bicolor*** Herb. Bulb globose, 5cm diam., neck 2.5–5cm, dark brown. Lvs 4, synanthous, linear, 46–60×1.3cm, obtuse, tapering to base. Scape 30–45cm, terete, slender; spathe valves lanceolate, to 3.8cm, equalling pedicels; fls 4–9, ascending, to 5cm long, bright red, green-yellow at base, perianth tube short, with 6 minute teeth at base, lobes oblanceolate, connivent; stamens unequal, declinate, not exserted, style exserted. Autumn. Chile.

***P. phycelloides*** (Herb.) Traub. Lvs to 30cm, 3–4, linear, narrow, glaucous, appearing with the fls. Scape to 25cm; spathe valves linear, exceeding pedicels; fls to 7cm, 3–6, erect, brilliant red, yellow in the centre, perianth tube to 2cm, lobes ovate-lanceolate, connivent except for the apex; stamens equalling perianth, with ciliate processes; style exserted; stigma obscurely trifid. Chilean Andes.

For synonymy see *Amaryllis, Habranthus* and *Hippeastrum*.

**Phygelius** E. Mey. ex Benth. Scrophulariaceae. A genus of 2 species and many hybrids; evergreen or semi-evergreen shrubs and subshrubs to 1–1.5m. Stems woody at base, soft above; shoots erect, glabrous, angular. Lower leaves opposite, upper alternate, ovate-lanceolate, bluntly serrate. Inflorescence often one-sided; flowers pendulous; corolla tubular, pink to orange-red, narrowing towards base, 5-lobed, margins sharply recurved; sepals 5, overlapping lobes; stamens 4 (occasionally 5), filament thick; ovary 2-chambered, ovules many; stigma short. Mid summer–late autumn. S Africa. Z8.

CULTIVATION Tender shrubs, tolerating temperatures of –5°C/23°F, usually treated as herbaceous perennials in areas where temperatures fall much below freezing in winter. Although dying back to ground level in severe weather, on well-drained soils *Phygelius* spp. will sprout from the base. Spring growth is rapid and plants will give useful front to mid-border height, proving remarkably drought-tolerant and freely producing their warmly coloured panicles of fuchsia-like flowers from summer until late in the season. In warm-temperate regions or in colder areas when given the protection of a warm south- or west-facing wall, *P. capensis* will thrive in its naturally shrubby form, reaching heights of up to 1.8m/6ft: it may also be trained as a wall shrub and tied into trellis supports.

Plant out in spring in a sunny site (part-day shade will be tolerated) with a moderately fertile, light soil. Where the ground freezes, give the running rootstock a heavy winter mulch to provide frost protection and cut back the previous season's dead top growth to ground level in spring. Clear shrubby specimens of dead wood in spring. Plants may also be grown in large pots or tubs in the cool greenhouse or conservatory. Seed is abundantly produced and germinates freely: sow in spring at 15–18°C/60–65°F and overwinter young stock in frost free conditions. Alternatively, take semi-ripe cuttings of spp. and named cvs in late summer.

***P. aequalis*** Harv. ex Hiern. Lvs to 10×5cm. Pedicels 1.5cm; fls dusky pink, orange near mouth, lobes crimson; tube curving inwards below, with spreading lobes as in *P. capensis*, but internodes shorter, infl. denser. 'Yellow Trumpet' ('Aurea', 'Cream Trumpet'): dense bushy habit; lvs broader than species type; infl. 1-sided, fls pale cream-yellow, lobes deeper.

***P. capensis*** E. Mey. ex Benth. CAPE FUSCHIA. Sometimes a weak shrub to 3m in cult. Lvs 7.5×3.3cm. Pedicels to 4cm; fls loosely spaced, pale orange to deep red, pendulous, tube somewhat bowed, limb oblique, mouth irregular, lobes becoming strongly recurved. 'Coccineus': lvs 8.6×3.6cm; fls rich orange, lobed orange-red.

***P. ×rectus*** Coombes. (*P. aequalis* × *P. capensis*.) Fls pendulous, pale red; lobes deeper, sharply recurved, revolute; tube straight; pedicel to 3cm. Garden origin. 'African Queen' (*P. aequalis* × *P. capensis* 'Coccineus'): fl. buds pendulous, tips inclined to stem when open; cor. tube almost straight, upturned towards mouth, pale red; lobes orange-red. 'Devil's Tears' (*P. ×rectus* 'Winchester Fanfare' × *P. capensis* 'Coccineus'): lf margins undulate, infl. regular; fls pendulous, inclined to stem when open, cor. upturned towards irregular mouth, deep red-pink, deeper in bud; lobes orange-red, throat yellow. 'Moonraker' (*P. aequalis* 'Yellow Trumpet' × *P. ×rectus* 'Winchester Fanfare'): lvs lanceolate, serrate; fls pendulous, pale yellow; lobes deeper; tube concave above, straight below, upturned towards irregular mouth; lobe margins sharply recurved. 'Pink Elf' (*P. aequalis* 'Yellow Trumpet' × *P. ×rectus* 'Winchester Fanfare'): dwarf selection to 75×90cm; lvs lanceolate; infl. paniculate, sparsely flowered but recurrent flowering; fls held at 45° from stem; cor. pale pink straight, down-curved when open; lobes deep crimson, margins sharply recurved, throat yellow. 'Salmon Leap' (*P. ×rectus* 'Winchester Fanfare' × *P. capensis* 'Coccineus'): fl. buds pendulous, at 45° to stem; cor. orange, lobes deeper, margins sharply recurved. 'Winchester Fanfare' (*P. aequalis* 'Yellow Trumpet' × *P. capensis* 'Coccineus'): close to 'African Queen' but with broader lvs and pendulous, straight-tubed fls dusky red-pink with scarlet lobes.

**Phyla** Lour. (From Gk *phyle*, clan or tribe, an allusion to the many florets in a tight head.) FROGFRUIT. Verbenaceae. Some 15 species of perennial herbs, creeping or procumbent, sometimes woody at base, subglabrous to densely adpressed-strigose. Leaves opposite, usually serrate-dentate. Inflorescence an axillary spike, solitary or paired in leaf-axils, pedunculate, usually elongate in fruit; bractlets small; flowers small, numerous, dense, sessile, borne in axils of bractlets; calyx thinly membranous; corolla tube straight or slightly curved, limb 4-lobed, lobes rounded or emarginate; stamens 4, included, didynamous, inserted near middle of corolla tube, filaments short; ovary bilocular, with 1 ovule per locule, style short. Fruit ellipsoid, compressed, enclosed by calyx. Warmer regions of the Americas. Z10.

CULTIVATION A low-growing, stem-rooting plant, forming dense foliage mats studded with small nectar-rich flowers throughout summer in warm, dry essentially frost-free climates, *P. nodiflora* is useful as drought-tolerant groundcover on sunny banks. Although it performs better on moderately fertile soils it also tolerates soils of low fertility in California and is sometimes used as a substitute for lawn-grass: it withstands treading and mowing, although this inevitably reduces flowering. Grow in any freely draining soil in sun. Propagate by division or seed. For dense cover, set plugs at 30–60cm/12–24in. spacings and water until established.

***P. canescens*** (HBK) Greene. Branches white, strigose-pubesc., rugose. Lvs to 2.5×1cm, elliptic, ovate or obovate to oblanceolate, obtuse, base cuneate, dentate, densely pubesc. above, subglabrous beneath. Infl. solitary; peduncle to 8cm; bracts to 3mm, obovate, acuminate, purple, pubesc. to subglabrous; cal. tube to 2mm, densely villous; cor. to 4mm, white to lilac, exterior puberulent. Fr. to 2×1mm, oblong. S America.

***P. lanceolata*** (Michx.) Greene. Stem to 60cm, simple or slightly branched, glabrous or strigulose, with white adpressed hairs. Lvs to 7.5×3cm, chartaceous, ovate, oblong or oblong-lanceolate, acute, base cuneate, sharply serrate, sparsely adpressed-strigulose above and beneath; petiole to 1cm. Infl. to 3.5cm in fr., becoming cylindric with age, densely fld; bracts to 3mm, obovate, acute, adpressed-strigulose; cal. compressed; cor. pale blue, purple or white. Fr. globose. Central and southern US, Mexico.

***P. nodifera*** (L.) Greene. Stems to 90cm, creeping, much-branched; branches ascending or procumbent, glabrescent to adpressed-strigulose. Lvs to 7×2.5cm, obovate, oblanceolate or spathulate, obtuse or rounded to subacute, serrate-dentate, glabrous to strigulose. Infl. to 2.5cm, cylindrical with age; peduncle to 11cm, adpressed-puberulent to glabrous; bracts green or violet, obovate or ovate-oblong, long-acuminate; cal. minute; cor. white or lilac with a yellow eye, exterior slightly strigulose. Fr. to 1.5mm, obovoid, puberulent. Tropics and subtropics.

***P. dulcis*** (Trev.) Mold. See *Lippia dulcis*.
For further synonymy see *Lippia* and *Verbena*.

**Phylica** L. (From Gk *phylikos*, leafy, referring to the densely leafy stems of plants in this genus.) CAPE MYRTLE. Rhamnaceae. About 150 species of low, evergreen, ericoid shrubs, to about 3m. Leaves alternate, margins revolute, densely hairy. Inflorescence a spike, head or raceme, usually terminal. Flowers with 5 sepals; petals usually absent, if not bristle-like or filamentous and pubescent; stamens 5, style not divided. S Africa, Madagascar, Tristan da Cunha.

CULTIVATION A frost-tender genus grown for the heads of soft flowers (those of *P. plumosa* are particularly valued by flower arrangers) and for the dark lustrous foliage. Grow in a moisture-retentive but freely draining, humus-rich and preferably lime-free soil, in sun or light dappled shade. *P. superba* tolerates some lime. Maintain good ventilation under glass, water plentifully as flower buds develop, moderately at other periods, reducing to keep almost dry in winter with a minimum temperature of 5–7°C/40–45°F. Propagate by seed or greenwood cuttings in a closed case with bottom heat.

***P. ericoides*** L. Dense shrub, 30–90cm, shoots evenly erect, with tufts of soft hairs. Lvs 6–12mm, very dense, linear. Fls solitary or in fascicles, axillary and terminal, 6mm diam., globose; cal. surrounded by dense, white, woolly pubescence. S Africa (Cape Province). Z9.

***P. plumosa*** L. Shrub to 2m, all parts long-pubesc., of upright habit, shoots densely leafy. Lvs 2–3cm, linear-lanceolate, finely glandular-punctuate, glabrous above, woolly-hairy beneath. Infl. 2–3cm, spicate, surrounded by many pale brown, feathery bracts. S Africa. Z10.

***P. aethiopica*** Hill. See *P. ericoides*.
***P. microcephala*** Willd. See *P. ericoides*.
***P. pubescens*** Lodd. See *P. plumosa*.

**Phyllanthus** L. (From Gk *phyllon*, leaf, and *anthos* flower, in allusion to the flowers of some species being apparently borne on the edge of the leaves.) Euphorbiaceae. 650 species of monoecious or rarely dioecious trees, shrubs and herbs, of very diverse habit, often with flattened leaf-like organs (cladophylls). Leaves vary greatly in size, simple, alternate, sometimes 2-ranked on lateral branches giving the appearance of pinnately compound leaves, entire, usually glabrous; petioles always shorter than the blades. Inflorescences axillary, or more-or-less greatly reduced cymes; flowers without petals, pedicelled or sessile, disc usually evident; sepals 4–6, imbricate; stamens usually 3–5 but may be 2–12; ovary usually 3-celled. Fruit usually a capsule, sometimes a berry or drupe, each cell 2-seeded. Tropics and warm temperate regions. Z10.

CULTIVATION A large genus of non-succulent herbs, trees and shrubs, some of which are grown for their fruit, timber or medicinal uses. *P. emblica* 'Aonla' or 'Myrobalan', first introduced to Florida as a possible source of tannin, is an evergreen tree cultivated for its very acid, pectin-rich fruit, a good source of carbohydrates, vitamin C and minerals. It is an attractive ornamental in the humid and semi-arid tropics, with light elegant foliage, flushed pink when young. *P. acidus* is less ornamental, also grown for its acid fruit used in relishes or sweetened for desserts. Young specimens of *P. arbuscula* are attractive pot plants.

All species are undemanding in their soil requirements, given a sunny site or part-day shade. In temperate areas, they make graceful glasshouse specimens, with an interesting flowering display. Grow in a high-fertility loam-based medium, with added farmyard manure and a small quantity of broken brick, with strong filtered light, a humid atmosphere, and a minimum night temperature of 15°C/60°F. Propagate from seed, by budding or by root sprouts. Also by greenwood cuttings with bottom heat in a closed case or under mist.

***P. acidus*** (L.) Skeels. OTAHEITE GOOSEBERRY; GOOSEBERRY TREE. Small shrub or tree to 10m. Lvs 6–7.5cm, 2-ranked, ovate-lanceolate to broadly ovate. Cymes many-fld, small; fls tiny, red. Fr. angled, yellow-green, to 2cm diam. S Asia; naturalized tropical America.

***P. angustifolius*** (Sw.) Sw. FOLIAGE FLOWER. Shrub to *c*3m; branches 2.5–5mm thick, red-brown or grey-brown. Cladophylls to 10cm, ovate to lanceolate, primary axis ending abruptly or with a very short tip. Cymules male or bisexual, of mostly 1 or 2 (rarely 3) female and *c*2–5 male fls; fls red, cream, or yellow-green. Jamaica, Swan Is., Cayman Is., naturalized US.

***P. arbuscula*** (Sw.) J.F. Gmel. FOLIAGE FLOWER. Shrub or small tree to 7m. Cladophylls (2.5)4–11cm, elliptic to lanceolate, acute or acuminate, often paler yellow beneath. Cymules bisexual, of 1 female and *c*3 or 4 males, or proximal cymules male; fls cream coloured, green or scarlet. Jamaica. Sometimes confused with *P. angustifolius* in cult.

***P. ×elongatus*** (Jacq.) Steud. *(P. arbuscula × P. epiphyllanthus.)* Shrub. Cladophylls to 25cm, 2-ranked, lanceolate, primary axis ending in a floriferous cladophyll 10–13cm long. Fls pink. W Indies.

***P. emblica*** L. EMBLIC; MYROBALAN. Much-branched deciduous shrub or tree to 15m. Bark grey, flaking. Lvs 1–2cm, 2-ranked, linear-oblong, obtuse, nearly sessile. Fls small, yellow, clustered in axils of lvs. Fr. somewhat lobed, yellow, to 2.5cm diam. Tropical Asia.

***P. epiphyllanthes*** L. Shrub or small tree, generally 1–3m. Branches deciduous, cylindrical. Cladophylls (3–)5–25(–32)cm, falcate or linear-falcate, toothed toward tip, striately veined. Cymules usually bisexual, each with 1–3 female and several to many male fls; fls red. Widespread in the W Indies.

***P. juglandifolius*** Willd. Symmetrical tree; branches 30–60cm, resembling pinnate lvs, deciduous, leaving large scars when they fall. Lvs *c*10×2.5cm, oblong-lanceolate, acute to acuminate, rounded or cordate at base. Fls yellow-green. Fr. large, green, 3-celled. Tropical S America.

***P. mimosoides*** Sw. Shrub *c*1–5m, with a slender usually unbranched trunk and a terminal crown of leafy branchlets, younger parts hairy. Lvs pinnate, distichous, rachis filiform; leaflets *c*5–11(–13)×2–4(–6)mm, asymmetrically oblong or oblong-obovate and often falcate, nearly sessile, distichous. Cymules axillary; fls off-white. Fr. minute, yellow-green. Lesser Antilles.

***P. montanus*** Sw. Shrub or tree *c*2–5m; branches 2–8mm thick, terete, smooth, grey-brown. Scale lvs minute, deciduous. Flowering branches leaf-like, in 2 vertical rows, lanceolate to oblong or elliptic, 5–15cm, outline wavy, with shallow notches; normal lvs occasional, to 1cm. Cymules usually bisexual, pulviniform, each with a single (rarely 2) female and *c*3–12 male fls; male fls pale red, female fls dark purple. Jamaica.

***P. niruri*** L. Annual herb. Stem simple or considerably ramified, 15–50cm, olivaceous, smooth, terete. Lvs mostly 7–15(–17)×(3–)4–8(–9)mm, 2-ranked on branchlets, asymmetrically ovate or elliptic. Proximal cymules of 3–7 successively maturing male fls, the distal nodes with solitary female fls, fls minute, yellow-white, sometimes slightly red at the base. Flowering and fruiting throughout the year. W Indies.

***P. proctoris*** Webster. Shrub to 3m. Branches of current year's growth *c*1.5–2.5mm thick, terete, grey-brown; branchlets crowded, 3.5–5cm, 2-ranked. Cladophylls *c*4–11cm, linear-lanceolate, toothed from base. Cymules male or bisexual, of 1–3 male fls and/or 1 female; fls green-white. Jamaica.

***P. pulcher*** Wallich. Small shrub. Lvs broadly ovate, apiculate, glabrous, glaucous beneath, stalks very short. Fls yellow, red at base; peduncles bright red; male fls in lower lf-axils, solitary or in few-fld clusters; female fls in upper lf-axils, solitary, stouter. Java, Sumatra, Borneo.

***P. pulchroides*** Beille. Symmetrical shrub with branches at right angles to stem. Lvs apparently pinnate, glossy-green. Male fls in clusters of 2 or 3, sometimes solitary, brick-red, fringed with pale yellow hairs; female fls larger than males, solitary toward tips of branches. C & S Vietnam.

***P. reticulatus*** Poir. Shrub or small tree, 2–3.5m. Lvs well-developed, elliptic or oblong-elliptic, 1–4cm, glabrous; petiole short. Fls in axillary clusters of 2–5, of which 1 is female, red-yellow; pedicels slender. Old World Tropics.

***P. salviaefolius*** HBK. Similar to *P. pulcher*. Shrub with spreading branches and close set lvs. Lvs 2-ranked, ovate-oblong, acute, downy above, hairy beneath. Male fls green, small, on long filiform pedicels; female fls tinted red, larger, on short pedicels. Colombia, Ecuador, Venezuela.

***P. verrucosus*** Thunb. Much-branched shrub, 1.5–3m. Branches grey, warty. Fl-branches with 3–5 lvs. Lvs to 1.5cm, obovate to elliptic, rounded, often retuse, thin, glabrous; petiole 1.5cm. Fls monoecious, 1 female fl. to several male fls in clusters; sep. usually 6 (occasionally 4 or 5); stamens usually 6. S Africa.

***P. chantrieri*** André. See *P. pulchroides*.
***P. discoideus*** (Baill.) Muell. Arg. See *Margaritaria discoidea*.
***P. distichus*** (L.) Muell. Arg. See *P. acidus*.
***P. grandifolius*** auct. See *P. juglandifolius*.
***P. linearis*** sensu Griseb. See *P. proctoris*.
***P. nivosus*** W.G. Sm. See *Breynia nivosa*.
***P. speciosus*** Jacq. See *P. arbuscula*.

**× Phylliopsis** Cullen & Lancaster. *(Phyllodoce × Kalmiopsis.)* Ericaceae. 1 species, an evergreen subshrub, usually to 30cm. Bark shiny brown, with a short-hirsute indumentum. Leaves 1.5–2×0.6–0.8cm, alternate, almost flat, oblong-obovate, apex rounded, base cuneate, margins somewhat revolute, pale green beneath with brown-yellow glands, lustrous and dark green above; petiole *c*1mm. Flowers numerous in elongated racemes; pedicels red, 10–13mm, to 25mm at anthesis; bracts similar to leaves, bracteoles 2, enclosing pedicel base; sepals 5, blunt, ciliate; corolla *c*10mm diam., bell-shaped, red-purple, 5-lobed; stamens 6–8, falling early, not projecting from corolla, filaments 5–6mm, hairless, thread-like, anthers pale brown; ovary subspherical, thickly glandular, inconspicuously 5-carinate, short-downy at base; style *c*5mm, red; stigma capitate, inconspicuously 5-lobed. Mature fruit not known. Spring. Garden origin.

CULTIVATION Suitable for the rock garden, peat terrace or alpine house, × *Phylliopsis* is a small evergreen shrub grown for its clusters of deep pink, bell-shaped flowers borne in spring, and sporadically throughout summer. It shows a greater tolerance of warm dry summers than most ericaceous species. Propagate by semi-ripe cuttings in late summer, in a closed case with bottom heat, pinching out shoot tips at first, potting on to encourage a bushy and compact habit. Otherwise, cultivate as for *Phyllodoce*.

***P. ×hillieri*** Cullen & Lancaster. *(Phyllodoce breweri* (Gray) Heller × *Kalmiopsis leachiana* Rehd.) As for the genus. 'Coppelia': fls large, cup-shaped, pink-lilac. 'Pinocchio': compact, hardy; lvs small, glossy; fls small, rich pink, in spikes. Z6.

**Phyllitis** Ludw.
***P. sagittata*** (DC.) Guinea & Heyw. See *Asplenium sagittatum*.
***P. scolopendrium*** (L.) Newman. See *Asplenium scolopendrium*.

**Phyllobolus** N.E. Br.
***P. resurgens*** (Kensit) Schwantes. See *Sphalmanthus resurgens*.

**Phyllocalyx** O. Berg. See *Eugenia*.

**Phyllocarpus** Riedel ex Endl. (From Gk *phyllon*, leaf, and *karpos*, fruit.) Leguminosae (Caesalpinioideae). 2 species of thornless trees. Leaves alternate, paripinnate, eglandular; stipules semi-persistent, erect; leaflets in sparse pairs. Flowers flamboyant, in crowded, short racemes clustered at bare nodes, appearing fascicled; hypanthium short; calyx lobes 4, free, subequal, overlapping; corolla lobes 3, obovate; stamens 10, connate below in a dorsally cleft sheath, separate above, anthers unequal; pistil stipitate. Fruit an oblong-falcate, flat, indehiscent legume, winged along upper suture, 1–2-seeded. Tropical America. Z10.

CULTIVATION *P. septentrionalis* is found on thinly wooded, dry, rocky hillsides to altitudes of 300–600m/975–1950ft in Guatemala and Honduras. In its native regions, it is a tall, widespreading tree noted for its prolific displays of exuberant scarlet flowers, and it was for these decorative qualities that it was introduced to Florida. *Phyllocarpus* spp. grew rapidly in Florida, but showed marked tendencies to form weak crotches that were prone to split in storms; they also failed to bloom reliably. Cultivate as for *Delonix*.

***P. septentrionalis*** J.D. Sm. To 10m, or 30m in tropics. Lvs markedly distichous; petiole to 15cm, eglandular; stipules to 1.5cm, semi-lanceolate, acuminate; leaflets to 8×4.5cm, 4–8 pairs, elliptic, reticulate-nerved, glossy above. Fls scarlet; pedicels to 1.5cm, bracteate-jointed near base; cal. and cor. to 10mm; stamens exserted beyond cor., fil. irregularly separating from basal sheath; ovary stipitate. Fr. to 15×5cm, scale-like, flat, somewhat lunate, wing to 1cm diam. Spring. C & S America.

**PHYLLOCLADACEAE** (Pilger) H. Keng. See *Phyllocladus*.

**Phyllocladus** Rich. & A. Rich. CELERY PINE. (From Gk *phyllon*, leaf, and *klados*, young branch or shoot, referring to the leaf-like shoots.) Phyllocladaceae. 5 species of evergreen, monoecious or dioecious coniferous trees or shrubs to 30m. Shoots dimorphic; normal shoots with a terminal bud and heavily modified leaf-like shoots (*phylloclades*), variable in shape, leathery, cuneate at base, narrowed into a petiole-like region, basal half entire; apical half of phylloclades incised, often deeply or shallowly toothed, simple or pinnate, 2–30×1–5cm. Leaves radial on normal shoots, subtending the phylloclades, and also in phylloclade margins, much reduced, scale-like; juvenile leaves, on seedlings only, acicular, 6–20mm. Male 'cones' catkin-like, grouped terminally; female cones borne singly in scale-leaf axils or on margins of phylloclades. Cones berry-like, composed of 1 to several scales with arils surrounding nut-like seeds at base; seeds 1 per scale. Malaysia, Indonesia, New Guinea, Tasmania, New Zealand.

CULTIVATION All require high rainfall and humidity; frost tolerance varies from about −20°C/−4°F in *P. alpinus*, to −5°C/23°F or lower still in *P. hypophyllus*.

***P. alpinus*** Hook. f. ALPINE CELERY PINE. To 9m, sometimes shrubby. Phylloclades spirally arranged to sub-opposite, subsessile to sessile, simple, irregular to rhombic, lacerate, lobes linear, coriaceous, 2–4×1–2cm, rarely to 6cm, glaucous grey-green. Juvenile lvs linear, to 1.5cm, soon falling; adult lvs scale-like, 0.2–1mm long. Male fls to 5mm, red. Cones arranged in tight clusters on irregular phylloclades, red; seeds 2–5, elliptic, to 2–3mm, dark green to black; aril white, 5mm. New Zealand (mts). 'Silver Blades': phylloclades silvery blue-green. Z8.

***P. asplenifolius*** (Labill.) Hook. f. CELERY TOP PINE. To 20m; bark thick, scaly. Branches irregularly arranged. Phylloclades simple, rhombic to deltoid, lobed, 2–5×2–3cm; lobes obtuse. Juvenile lvs subulate, to 15mm. Cones as in *P. alpinus*, but more often terminal on phylloclades; 8mm. Tasmania. Z9.

***P. glaucus*** Carr. TOATOA. To 15m; bole to 60cm diam., branches whorled. Phylloclades spirally arranged, clustered at apex of normal shoot with a few smaller phylloclades along rest of shoot, pinnate, 10–40cm; pinnae 9–17, rhombic in outline, cuneate to broad-ovate basally, 3–6×2–4cm, glaucous below, rugose above, lobed, shallow-serrate. Juvenile lvs linear, to 1.5cm; adult lvs scale-like, minute. Male fls to 20 in terminal groups, to 2.5cm. Cones at base of rachis of phylloclades, to 15mm, deep pink, 8–20 fertile scales; seeds exserted, to 5mm, black; aril white. New Zealand (North Island). Z10.

***P. hypophyllus*** Hook. f. Shrub or tree to 30m. Phylloclades arranged as in *P. glaucus*, pinnate, to 15cm; pinnae 5–12, in whorls, ovate to cuneate, obtusely or sharply shallow-toothed, apex occasionally bilobed, 2–8×1–4cm. Male fls in clusters, cylindric; peduncles to 2.5cm. Cones as in *P. glaucus* but terminal on phylloclades; scales to 15, mostly sterile; seeds 2–3, to 5mm. Philippines, Indonesia, Papua New Guinea. Z10.

***P. trichomanoides*** D. Don. TANEKAHA. Monoecious tree to 20m. Bark black on outer surface, red beneath. Branches whorled. Phylloclades 2-ranked, alternate, pinnate, to 30cm, glaucous; pinnae 7–15, roughly rhombic, to 2.5cm, shallow-crenate; apical segment cuneate, broader than laterals. Juvenile lvs linear, to 2cm, falling; adult lvs much smaller. Male fls in clusters. Cones borne laterally toward base of phylloclades; scales to 15, mostly sterile; seeds 1–3, to 3mm. New Zealand. Z9.

**Phyllodoce** Salisb. (For a sea nymph of Greek mythology, one of Cyrene's attendants, mentioned by Virgil.) Ericaceae. 8 species of small, scandent to erect, evergreen shrubs. Leaves alternate, numerous, linear, imbricate, texture leathery, margins dentate, strongly revolute, soft-downy beneath; petioles short. Flowers pendulous or suberect in terminal racemes, subumbellate clusters or, more rarely, solitary; pedicels glandular; bracts 2; calyx lobes 4–6, usually 5, tapering to acute apex; corolla pitcher- or bell-shaped, lobes 5, short; stamens 8–12, filaments slender, anthers lacking appendages, dehiscing through oblique, apical pores; ovary subglobose, 5-locular, ovules numerous; style slender, thread-like. Fruit dry, subglobose or ovoid, 4–6 valved; seeds many, narrowly winged. Arctic & Alpine regions of N hemisphere.

CULTIVATION Suitable for the peat terrace and for cool, damp, peaty niches on the rock garden, *Phyllodoce* are neat and dainty evergreens with heath-like foliage and terminal clusters of flowers, often carried over long periods in spring or early summer. All except *P. nipponica* will tolerate temperatures as low as −15°C/5°F. Grow in moist but well-drained, peaty, acid soils, in partial shade or in good light (but not direct sun) and maintain a mulch of acidic organic matter. *P.* ×*intermedia* is the most tolerant of warm dry summers, although in general the genus thrives only in regions with cool summers. Protect *P. nipponica* with a covering of twiggy branches in areas that experience prolonged frosts without the benefit of snow cover. Trim over after blooming to maintain compact habit.

Propagate by semi-ripe heel cuttings or softwood tip cuttings in late summer, treat with hormone-rooting preparations and root in a closed case with bottom heat. Also by seed in spring, or by layering.

***P. aleutica*** (Spreng.) A.A. Heller. Small, decumbent or scandent, evergreen shrub 10–30cm, forming thick mats; branches very leafy, somewhat downy. Lvs 8–14×1.5mm, linear, apex blunt, margins finely toothed, hairless, tapering to base, flattened, vivid green above, olive-green beneath with white lines; petiole short or absent. Fls 6–12 in drooping, terminal heads; pedicels 12–40mm, glandular soft-hirsute; cal. lobes 5, 4–5mm, oval-lanceolate, thickly glandular soft-hirsute; cor. 7–8mm, pale yellow-green, pitcher-shaped, hairless; fil. white, anth. pink. Spring–summer. Japan. 'Flora Slack': fls white. Z2.

***P. breweri*** (A. Gray) A.A. Heller. PURPLE HEATHER; BREWER'S MOUNTAIN HEATHER. Semi-prostrate, evergreen shrub 10–40cm; young shoots erect, very leafy. Lvs 6–20×0.15–0.2mm, linear, apex obtuse, dark and glossy green; petiole small or absent. Fls many in erect, terminal racemes 5–10cm long; pedicels to 20mm, downy and sparsely glandular; cal. lobes 5, 3.5–4.5mm, oblong, apex blunt, hairless on dorsal surface, ciliate on margins; cor. bell-shaped, dark roseate, *c*8mm diam., lobes equalling or exceeding tube; stamens exserted; style exserted. Fr. a globose capsule, 3–3.5mm diam., shorter than or equal to cal. lobes. Late spring–summer. W US (California). Z3.

***P. caerulea*** (L.) Bab. Stems 10–35cm, erect or scandent. Lvs 6–12×*c*0.15mm, linear to linear-oblong, texture leathery, apex blunt, margins revolute, dark and glossy green. Fls solitary or 3–4 in drooping umbels; pedicels to 38mm, slender, glandular-downy; cal. lobes 5, lanceolate, pubesc.-ferruginous; cor. 7–12mm, lilac to purple-pink, pitcher-shaped, lobes 5, short; stamens 10, included. Fr. *c*4mm, a glandular-downy capsule. Spring–summer Alpine summits and high ground Asia, Europe & US (sparse in Scotland & Pyrenees). Z2.

***P. empetriformis*** (Sm.) D. Don. PINK MOUNTAIN HEATHER. Low, diffuse, mat-forming shrub, 10–38cm. Stems ascending, pubesc. when young. Lvs 6–15mm, linear or linear-oblong, apex blunt to somewhat sharp-tipped, margins glandular-dentate, glossy green above. Fls few to numerous, in umbellate clusters; pedicels 12–28mm, thin and glandular-downy; cal. lobes 2.5mm, hairless except for cilia on margins, apex blunt; cor. 5–9mm, bell-shaped, rose-pink, hairless, lobes 5, *c*2mm, recurved; fil. glabrous, somewhat exceeding anth., anth. brown-purple. Fr. a glandular-downy, globose capsule, 2.5–3.5×3–4mm. Spring–summer. Western N America (British Columbia to California). Z3.

***P. glanduliflora*** (Hook.) Cov. YELLOW MOUNTAIN HEATHER. 20–40cm, branches stiff and erect. Lvs 4–12mm, linear, numerous, crowded, margins exiguously glandular-dentate, apex rounded, dark green. Fls fragrant, solitary or 3–8 in clusters; pedicels 10–30mm, thickly glandular-hirsute; cal. lobes *c*3mm, persistent, green, broadly lanceolate, glandular-downy, glandular-ciliate on margins; cor. lutescent or olive-coloured, 5–9mm, tube downy, lobes 5, minute, hairless, reflexed; fil. downy, anth. purple; ovary pubesc., style exceeding anth. Fr. a glandular-downy, globose capsule, 4–5×*c*3mm. Spring–summer. Western N America (Alaska to S Oregon, east to Rocky Mts). Z3.

***P.*×*intermedia*** (Hook.) Rydb. (*P. empetriformis* × *P. glanduliflora.*) Dense, bushy subshrub, 15–23cm. Lvs 6–16×1.5–2mm, linear, apex blunt or subacute, dark and glossy green, minutely dentate at margins; petioles very short. Fls solitary; pedicels 12–18mm, glandular-hirsute, slender; cal. *c*3mm, lanceolate, acute or blunt at apex, ferruginous, glandular-downy at base; cor. *c*6mm, mauve to purple-red or yellow-pink, ovate-campanulate to pitcher-shaped, hairless, lobes 5, rounded. Spring. Western N America. 'Drummondii': habit flat; fls dark purple. 'Fred Stoker': fls light purple. Z3.

***P. nipponica*** Mak. Small, branched, sub-erect shrub, 7–23cm. Branches angular. Young stems exiguously downy, glandular-setose. Lvs 5–12×*c*1.5mm, numerous, diffuse, sessile, broadly linear, conspicuously revolute, apex blunt or subacute, margins minutely glandular-dentate, deep green and hairless above when young, white-downy beneath. Fls 3–7 in pendulous, terminal, subumbellate infl.; pedicels 20–25mm, erect, often red-tinged, glandular soft-hirsute and white downy throughout; cal. lobes 1.5–3mm, green, ovate, hairless, acute at apex, minutely ciliolate; cor. 6–7×*c*6mm, rose to white, bell-shaped, hairless, lobes rounded at apex; stamens and style enclosed; fil. hairless, anth. brown. Fr. a globose capsule. Spring–summer. N Japan (Alpine parts of Honshu and Shikoku). var. ***amabilis*** (Stapf) Stoker. Cal. lobes red; tip of cor. limb red or pink; anth. short, crimson. var. ***oblongo-ovata*** (Tatew.) Toyok. Larger. Lvs 8–12×*c*2mm. Summer. Z3.

***P. tsugifolia*** Nak. Small shrub to 15cm. Lvs to 12mm, linear, apex blunt or subacute. Fls in terminal, subumbellate infl.; pedicels glandular-hirsute on upper half, otherwise glabrous; cal. lobes ovate, hairless, apex sharp-tipped, about one third of cor. length; cor. white, pitcher-shaped. N Japan. Z3.

For synonymy see *Bryanthus*.

**Phyllostachys** Sieb. & Zucc. (From Gk *phyllon*, leaf, and *stachys*, spike, for the 'leafy' inflorescence.) Gramineae. Some 80 species of medium and large bamboos, readily recognized by their grooved culms and branching habit. Rhizomes running, but in colder climes and less favourable conditions the culms stay in close clumps appearing pachymorph. Culms hollow and grooved, or at least flattened on alternate sides where the branches emerged; lower down they may be terete or, when young, flexuous, zigzagging from node to node; sheaths caducous, except sometimes at the base, with or without auricles or scabrous bristles; nodes with varying amounts of white powder below; branches typically two, unequal, often with a third runt between which may soon drop off, branchlets soon numerous. Leaves medium-sized or small, narrow-lanceolate, tessellate, one third green, two thirds glaucous beneath, glabrous above but often with a few hairs beside the midrib beneath, margins varyingly scaberulous; sheaths soon caducous, with or without auricles and bristles. China, India, Burma.

CULTIVATION Spectacular bamboos suited to specimen and grove planting on rich damp soils, sheltered from harsh winds and prolonged exposure to hard frosts. All require heavy feeding when active. Propagate by large divisions in spring, transferring straight to the desired site and misting or drenching frequently until established. See BAMBOOS.

***P. angusta*** McClure. Resembles *P. flexuosa*, but with culms straight, not flexuous, little white powder, yellow-green not black; sheaths much paler, striped and hardly dotted, with paler ligules. Z8.

***P. arcana*** McClure. Culms somewhat ribbed, sometimes curved at base, with white powder, sometimes blackening with age; sheaths striped with no or few dots, no auricles or bristles, ligule broad, convex; nodes prominent. Z8.

***P. aurea*** (Carr.) A. & C. Riv. FISHPOLE BAMBOO; GOSAN-CHIKU; HOTEI-CHIKU. Culms 2–10m×2–5cm, thick-walled, glabrous, green later brown-yellow with a little waxy powder below the nodes where, on most culms, are markedly cup-shaped swellings, the lowest internodes very short and asymmetrical; sheaths lightly spotted and streaked, glabrous except for a narrow fringe of white hairs at the base, lacking auricles and bristles, blades long and narrow, ligule very short, ciliate; sheath scars with short white hairs; branches rather erect. Lvs 5–15×0.5–2cm; sheaths usually with small auricles and bristles, ligule downy. SE China, naturalized Japan. 'Albo-variegata': culms slender; lvs striped white. 'Holochrysa': culms yellow, sometimes striped green; lvs occasionally striped. 'Violascens': culms to 6m, gouty, swollen, green thinly striped purple or yellow in time, ultimately violet; nodes prominent; branches short, dense; lvs to 12cm, glossy above, glaucous beneath. Z6.

***P. aureosulcata*** McClure. YELLOW-GROOVE BAMBOO. Culms 3–10m×1–4cm, sometimes markedly geniculate below, somewhat rough below the prominent nodes with white waxy powder at first, yellow-green, the grooves fading to yellow; sheaths striped, with few or no spots, sometimes hairy at base with bristles and auricles, ligule broad, blades rather broad; branches erect. Lvs 5–17×1–2.5cm; sheaths with or without auricles and bristles. NE China. 'Spectabilis': culms yellow with a green groove. Z6.

***P. bambusoides*** Sieb. & Zucc. GIANT TIMBER BAMBOO; MADAKE; KU-CHIKU. Culms 3–30m×1.5–20cm, arising late, noticeably erect, stout, fairly thick-walled, green, glabrous with no or very little white powder; sheaths large, thick, rough and rather heavily marked, glabrescent, mostly with 1–2 small auricles and kinked bristles, ligule narrow, ciliate, blades mostly short and rather narrow. Lvs noticeably large and broad, 9–20×2–4.5cm, their stalks longer than in other species, (to 8mm), sheaths usually with auricles and prominent bristles to 1.2cm, ligule medium-sized, hairless. Native in China and perhaps Japan, widely grown elsewhere. 'Castillonis': differs from 'Holochrysa' in having green grooves to the culms. 'Castillonis Inversa': a sport from 'Castillonis' with green culms and yellow grooves. 'Holochrysa' ('Allgold'): smaller and more open, with golden-yellow culms, sometimes with green stripes. Z7.

***P. bissetti*** McClure. Culms medium-sized, slightly scabrous, powdery at first; sheaths lightly striped, unspotted, mostly with auricles and bristles, blades narrow. Leaves large, sheaths in auricles. Z5.

***P. dulcis*** McClure. Culms tall, thick, strongly tapered, ribbed, striped, hairless, with abundant powder; sheaths smooth, pale, striped, with a few spots, auricles and bristles, ligule broad, rounded, blade crinkled, narrow; nodes prominent. Lvs sometimes pubesc. beneath; sheath with auricles and bristles. Z8.

***P. edulis*** (Carr.) Houz. MOSO BAMBOO; MOUSOU-CHIKU. Culms 3–27m×4–30cm, very thick, strongly tapered, grey-velvety when young, ultimately green or almost orange, with white powder below the nodes, curved near the base, where the nodes are much closer together; sheaths thick with much brown mottling, ciliate and strewn with erect hairs, ligule long, ciliate, blades small, glabrous, auricles large, sometimes absent, bristles prominent. Lvs 5–12×0.5–2cm, numerous; sheaths with no or poorly developed auricles and bristles. China, introduced Japan. f. ***heterocycla*** (Carr.) Muroi TORTOISESHELL BAMBOO; KIKKOUCHIKU. A distortion with lowest internodes of some culms short, bulging on alternate sides. Z7.

***P. flexuosa*** (Carr.) A. & C. Riv. Culms 2–10m×2–7cm, slender, often flexuous to the top, the outermost spreading, green-yellow, finally almost black, glabrous with white powder below the nodes; sheaths acuminate, smooth with some dark markings, lacking auricles and bristles, ligule dark, ciliate, blades narrow. Lvs 5–15×1.5–2cm, sheaths lacking auricles except in first young shoots, medium-sized, downy. China. Z6.

***P. humilis*** Munro. Culms small, 3–5m, rough, dark at first, later pale green; sheaths papery, grey-white, striped, ciliate with white hairs, auricles and, sometimes, bristles, ligule long. Mature lvs small, glabrous, with or without bristles. Z8.

***P. makinoi*** Hayata. Tall to vigorous; culms rough, glaucous for some time, with white powder; sheaths spotted, glabrous, ligule long, dark, lacking auricles or bristles. Lf sheaths with auricles and bristles. Z8.

***P. meyeri*** McClure. Strong grower; culms with little white powder; sheaths spotted and blotched with white hairs at the base, without auricles or bristles, blade long and narrow. Lf sheaths with few or no auricles or bristles. Z8.

***P. nidularia*** Munro. Culms 3–5–10m×0.5–4cm, somewhat flexuous to arching, nearly solid below, slightly ribbed, yellow-brown, glabrescent, with white powder below the nodes; sheaths streaked, ciliate, with brown hairs near the base, ligule short, ciliate, blades often flared at the base and merging into the broad smooth clasping auricles, bristles absent or few and small, nodal ridges prominent, sheath scars fringed with brown hairs. Lvs 6–14×0.9–2cm, rather broad and stubby, sheaths with small or no auricles or bristles. N & C China. Z7.

***P. nigra*** (Lodd. ex Lindl.) Munro. BLACK BAMBOO; KURO-CHIKU. Culms 3–10m×1–4cm, rather thin with white waxy powder below the nodes, green at first, typically turning shining black in the second or third year; sheaths glabrescent, unspotted except toward the apex, auricles and bristles prominent, ligule tall, blades broad, crinkled; nodes prominent; branches rather erect. Lvs 4–13×0.8–1.8cm, thin, glabrous with poor or no auricles or bristles, ligule small, downy. E & C China, widely cultivated elsewhere. 'Boryana': culms green blotched brown. var. ***henonis*** (Mitford) Stapf ex Rendle. The condition most often encountered in the wild: culms all green, later yellow-green, downy and rough when young, foliage abundant. f. ***punctata*** (Bean) Mak. Culms variously marked dark purple-brown, often mistaken for the species type. Z7.

***P. nuda*** McClure. Robust; culms thick-walled, ribbed, glabrous, sometimes geniculate below, with much white powder at first; sheaths rough, striped, the lower blotched, ligule prominent, rounded, without auricles or bristles; nodes rather prominent. Lf sheaths without auricles or bristles. Z8.

***P. propinqua*** McClure. Differs from *P. meyeri* in lacking the white hairs at the base of the shining culm sheath. Z8.

***P. rubromarginata*** McClure. Culms slender, hairless, habit rather open, sheaths unspotted and unstriped, the lower edged above with red when fresh, ligules fringed red, without auricles or bristles, blades narrow. Lvs rather broad; sheaths with red ligules. Z8.

***P. sulphurea*** (Carr.) A. & C. Riv. OUGON-KOU CHIKU; ROBERT OUGON-CHIKU. Culms 4–12m×0.5–9cm, increasingly yellow with age, sometimes striped green, lower nodes usually minutely pitted, hairless, with a little white powder below them; sheaths thick, ultimately spotted and blotched brown, glabrous, usually lacking auricles or bristles; branches erect. Lvs 6–16×1.5–2.5cm, rather narrow, sometimes striped; sheaths on young culms with auricles and bristles. E China. var. ***viridis*** R.A. Young. KOU-CHIKU. The larger and more usual wild plant with green culms which never reach a good size in cooler climes. Z7.

***P. viridi-glaucescens*** (Carr.) A. & C. Riv. Culms 4–12m×1–5cm, arising early, often curved at the base, smooth, glabrous, with white waxy powder below the nodes; sheaths rough, well marked with dark spots and blotches, glabrescent with 0–2 auricles and bristles, ligule long, blades narrow; nodes fairly prominent; branches spreading. Lvs 4–20×0.6–2cm, sheaths usually with auricles and bristles. E China. Z7.

***P. vivax*** McClure. A vigorous species of open habit. Culms 3–25m×2.3–12.5cm, ribbed, pale grey, glabrous, with white waxy powder below the nodes; sheaths with many spots and blotches, glabrous, lacking auricles or bristles, ligule small, blades narrow, crinkled; nodes prominent, somewhat asymmetrical. Lvs 7–20×1–2.5cm, sheaths lacking auricles or bristles. E China. Z8.

*P.* 'Allgold' (sensu Chao). See *P. sulphurea*.
***P. elegans*** McClure. See *P. viridi-glaucescens*.
***P. fastuosa*** (Marliac ex Mitford) Nichols. See *Semiarundinaria fastuosa*.
***P. heterocycla*** (Carr.) Matsum. See *P. edulis*.
***P. heterocycla*** f. ***pubescens*** (Mazel ex Houz.) Muroi. See *P. edulis*.
***P. henonis*** Mitford. See *P. nigra* var. *henonis*.
***P. kumasasa*** (Zoll. ex Steud.) Munro. See *Shibataea kumasasa*.
***P. mazellii*** A. & C. Riv. See *P. bambusoides*.
***P. mitis*** sensu A. & C. Riv. See *P. sulphurea* var. *viridis*.
***P. mitis*** auctt. non A. & C. Riv. See *P. edulis*.
***P. nevinii*** Hance. See *P. nigra* var. *henonis*.
***P. puberula*** (Miq.) Nak. See *P. nigra* var. *henonis*.
***P. pubescens*** Mazel ex Houz. See *P. edulis*.
***P. quilioi*** (Carr.) A. & C. Riv. See *P. bambusoides*.
***P. reticulata*** sensu K. Koch. See *P. bambusoides*.
***P. ruscifolia*** (Sieb. ex Munro) Satow. See *Shibataea kumasasa*.
***P. tranquillans*** (Koidz.) Muroi. See *Hibanobambusa tranquillans*.
***P. viridis*** (R.A. Young) McClure. See *P. sulphurea* var. *viridis*.
***P. viridis*** var. ***robertii*** Chao & Renvoize. See *P. sulphurea* var. *viridis*.
***P. viridis*** 'Robert Young'. See *P. sulphurea* var. *viridis*.

**Phyllota** Benth. (DC.) (From Gk *phyllon*, leaf, and *ous*, ear, referring to the leaf shape.) Leguminosae (Papilionoideae). 10 species of shrubs; stems terete. Leaves simple, entire, linear, margins revolute; stipules minute or absent. Flowers solitary, axillary; pedicels to 5mm; bracts foliaceous; bracteoles inserted at base or on base of calyx, scarious or herbaceous; calyx pubescent, 2 upper lobes broader, occasionally connate into an upper lip; petals all clawed, standard ovate to orbicular, equal to or longer than wings and keel, wings oblong, keel much incurved; stamens all, or at least the outermost, adnate to petals at base; ovary sessile, pubescent; style dilated or thickened at base, incurved or subulate above, stigma small, terminal. Fruit a 1–2-seeded ovate, turgid legume, bivalved. SW & E Australia. Z10.

CULTIVATION *P. phylicoides* is a small, upright health-like shrub bearing bright yellow flowers in summer. Culture as for *Dillwynia*.

***P. phylicoides*** Benth. Some 60cm. Lvs to 2cm, many, narrow-linear, blunt or with a recurved point, tuberculate, occasionally sparsely pubesc. Fls yellow, in upper axils forming terminal, leafy heads or spikes, or becoming lateral by elongation of the terminal shoot; cal. 6.5mm, glabrous or villous, lobes about equal to tube; standard to 13mm, wings and keel somewhat shorter. Summer. S Australia.

***P. aspera*** Benth. See *P. phylicoides*.
***P. comosa*** Benth. See *P. phylicoides*.
***P. squarrosa*** Benth. See *P. phylicoides*.

**Phymatodes** (Willd.) Pichi-Serm.
***P. bifrons*** Hook. See *Solanopteris bifrons*.
***P. billardieri*** (R. Br.) Presl. See *Microsorium diversifolium*.
***P. crustacea*** (Copel.) Holtt. See *Lecanopteris crustacea*.
***P. diversifolium*** (Willd.) Pichi-Serm. See *Microsorium diversifolium*.
***P. novae-zelandiae*** Pichi-Serm. See *Microsorium novae-zelandiae*.
***P. punctatum*** (L.) Presl. See *Microsorium punctatum*.
***P. scandens*** (Forst. f.) Presl. See *Microsorium scandens*.
***P. scolopendria*** (Burm. f.) Ching. See *Microsorium scolopendrium*.
***P. sinuosa*** (Wallich) J. Sm. See *Lecanopteris sinuosa*.
***P. vulgaris*** Presl. See *Microsorium scolopendrium*.

**Phymatosorus** Pichi-Serm.
***P. diversifolia*** (Willd.) Pichi-Serm. See *Microsorium diversifolium*.
***P. nigrescens*** (Bl.) Pichi-Serm. See *Microsorium nigrescens*.
***P. parksii*** (Copel.) Brownlie. See *Microsorium parksii*.

**Phymosia** Desv. Malvaceae. 8 species of shrubs or small trees. Leaves simple, palmately lobed. Flowers in open naked cymes in upper leaf axils; epicalyx of 3 segments, free or united at base; petals rose to red; stamens united in a tubular glabrous column; styles as many as mericarps, stigmas terminal or slightly lateral. Fruit a schizocarp, mericarps to 60, large, thin-walled, reniform, stellate-hairy on dorsal side, 2–3-seeded, splitting at maturity into 2 valves; seeds glabrous. Mexico, Guatemala, W Indies. Z10.

CULTIVATION In warm, frost-free zones, they are easily grown in the mixed or shrub border and as specimens, in any moderately fertile, well-drained soil. They do not tolerate wet soils and have long taproots, so should be planted out from their containers when young. In temperate zones, they require the protection of the cool to intermediate glasshouse, cultivated as for *Malvaviscus*. Propagate by seed or softwood cuttings in sand in a shaded propagating case.

***P. abutiloides*** (L.) Desv. BAHAMAS PHYMOSIA. Shrub to 3m, densely stellate-hairy. Lower lvs to 20cm, sharply 5- or 7-lobed, lobes serrate; upper lvs much smaller. Fls in corymbose infl. in axils of upper lvs, or in terminal panicles; epicalyx seg. 3, shorter than cal., linear, deciduous; cal. to 8mm, 5-lobed, lobes triangular-ovate, acute; pet. 1–1.5cm, pink or rose, white-veined, apex notched, red-streaked at base. Mericarps 20, 1cm long, reniform, stellate-hairy above; seeds black. Bahamas.

***P. rosea*** (DC.) Kearney. Shrub or small tree to 5m. Lvs to 25cm, deeply 3-, 5- or 7-lobed, lobes acute to acuminate, crenate-dentate. Fls to 6.5cm long, showy; epicalyx seg. slightly shorter than sep. thin, connate and enclosing the flower bud, splitting at anthesis; cal. 2–4cm; cor. subcampanulate, rose to dark red. Mericarps 1.8cm. Mexico, Guatemala.

***P. umbellata*** (Cav.) Kearney Shrub or small tree to 6m. Lvs to 20cm, shallowly 3-, 5- or 7-lobed, sinuate-dentate. Fls to 4cm; epicalyx seg. free, spathulate, narrowed at base into a claw; cal. to 2.5cm; cor. campanulate, rose-red. Mericarps 1.5cm. Mexico.

For synonymy see *Sphaeralcea*.

**Phyodina** Raf.
***P. navicularis*** (Ortgies) Rohw. See *Callisia navicularis*.
***P. rosea*** (Vent.) Rohw. see *Callisia rosea*.

**Physalis** L. GROUND CHERRY; HUSK TOMATO. (From Gk *physa*, bladder or bellows, referring to the inflated calyx.) Solanaceae. Some 80 species of annual or perennial herbs, to 3m. Stems glabrous to pubescent, to 3cm diam. Leaves linear to ovate, stipitate, alternate, opposite or in whorls of 3, entire, margin undulate to pinnatifid. Flowers solitary, sessile, axillary, white tinged violet or yellow, often purple at maturity; calyx campanulate, 5-lobed, accrescent, becoming inflated in fruit; corolla campanulate to rotate, tube short, limb 5-lobed, plicate; stamens 5, attached to corolla tube; style filiform, stigma capitate. Fruit a sessile, globose berry, yellow to green, enclosed by calyx. Cosmopolitan, especially Americas.

CULTIVATION Grown for their fruit or for flowering display. *P. alkekengi* is used extensively for decoration, with inflated calyces that provide a vivid orange display in the autumn garden; these are also used for drying (cut stems when the calyces begin to colour, and air dry.) This and other species of similar habit tends to be rather invasive, and can be checked by spading out underground runners in autumn. *P. peruviana* yields the dessert fruit known as the Cape gooseberry. It is not reliably hardy beyond areas that are frost-free or almost so, but in temperate zones can be grown for fruit in a cool glasshouse. *P. ixocarpa*, or tomatillo, an annual cultivated for its fairly large fruits, may be grown as for outdoor tomato. The husk tomato, *P. pubescens*, described by Parkinson in 1640 and grown by Philip Miller in the 1730s, yields small, yellow, tomato-like fruits with a thin husk. All species are easily cultivated on any well-drained soil, in sun or light shade. Propagate annuals from seed, surface-sow in the cold frame in autumn, or *in situ* in spring. Divide perennials, or increase from seed.

***P. alkekengi*** L. CHINESE LANTERN; WINTER CHERRY; BLADDER CHERRY. Perenn., to 60cm. Rhiz. creeping, branched. Stem solitary, simple or branched. Lvs deltoid-ovate to rhombic, to 12×9cm, apex acuminate, base truncate to cuneate; petiole to 6cm. Fls pendent, white; pedicel equalling fls, glabrous; cal. to 2cm, becoming inflated to 5cm, orange, surrounding fr. in autumn and winter, sparsely pubesc. to glabrous, lobed, lobes lanceolate; cor. to 1.5×2.5cm, 5-lobed, yellow to cream, sometimes tinged green, shallow sinuses between lobes; anth. yellow. Fr. to 17mm, red to scarlet; seeds yellow. Summer. C & S Europe, W Asia to Japan. 'Gigantea' ('Monstrosa'): fr. large. 'Pygmaea': dwarf. 'Variegata': lvs deeply bordered cream and yellow-green. Z6.

***P. heterophylla*** Nees. CLAMMY GROUND CHERRY. Rhizomatous perenn., densely glandular-pubesc., to 90cm. Stems and lvs sticky-pubesc. Lvs ovate, to 10cm, sinuate to dentate, base rounded to oblique; cor. to 2×2.5cm, yellow, frequently spotted purple; anth. blue, to 5mm. Fr. small, yellow, edible, surrounded by a green-brown cal. Summer–autumn. SE US. Z8.

***P. ixocarpa*** Brot. ex Hornem. TOMATILLO; JAMBERRY; MEXICAN HUSK TOMATO. Annual, subglabrous to glabrous, to 120cm. Stems branched, erect to spreading. Lvs lanceolate to ovate, entire or dentate, apex acuminate, base cuneate. Fls to 18mm diam.; pedicels shorter than fls, to 5mm; cal. yellow, veined purple, lobes lanceolate to deltoid-ovate; cor. tube yellow, with 5 dark brown patches, to 1.5cm, throat brown to purple; limb to 2.5cm diam.; anth. purple, to 3mm, ovate. Fr. to 2.5cm+, viscid, violet, almost filling cal. when mature. Mexico, S US. 'Golden Nugget': fr. yellow. 'Large Green': fr. large. 'Purple': medium-sized, fr. purple. 'Purple Husk': fr. small, husks purple. 'Rendidore': fr. large, yellow-green. 'Verde Puebla': fr. large, yellow. Z8.

***P. lobata*** Torr. Perenn. Lvs ovate to lanceolate to linear-lanceolate, pinnatifid, to 10×3cm, base cuneate; petiole winged, to 10×3cm. Fls pedunculate; peduncles to 3cm; cor. rotate, to 18mm diam., blue to purple, sometimes yellow to white; anth. to 2mm. Seeds crenate. SW US, Mexico. Z8.

***P. peruviana*** L. CAPE GOOSEBERRY; PURPLE GROUND CHERRY. Perenn. Stems erect, pubesc., stout, to 1m. Lvs ovate to cordate, to 10×7cm, entire or undulate, dentate, apex acuminate, base cordate; petiole to 4cm. Fls white; cal. to 1cm, becoming ovoid, pubesc., to 4cm, 5-lobed, persistent; cor. to 14×5mm, yellow, blotched brown or purple, 5-lobed, lobes blue-green; anth. 5, violet. Fr. globose, purple, to 2cm diam. Summer. Tropical S America. 'Giallo Grosso' ('Large Golden Italian'): fr. large. 'Goldenberry': fr. large, sweet. Z8.

***P. philadelphica*** Lam. TOMATILLO; MILTOMATE; PURPLE GROUND CHERRY; JAMBERRY. Annual, subglabrous, to 60cm. Stems erect, branched. Lvs ovate to broadly lanceolate, 10×4cm, apex acuminate, base cuneate, margins entire or dentate at base; petiole to 5cm. Cal. to 1cm, lobes to 5mm, ovate, enlarging to 5cm, green, veined violet, occasionally splitting; cor. to 3cm diam., yellow, marked purple-brown; fil. violet. Fr. yellow to purple, edible. Mexico, naturalized eastern N America. 'Purple de Milpa': fr. small, purple-tinged, sharp-flavoured, keeps well. Z7.

***P. pruinosa*** L. STRAWBERRY TOMATO; DWARF CAPE GOOSEBERRY. Resembles *P. peruviana* but stems branching at base, lvs cordate, oblique, pinnately toothed. Annual, to 45cm. Stems viscid, bluntly angled. Lvs to 8cm, coarsely dentate. Fls dull yellow, to 13mm. Fr. yellow, edible. Eastern N America. Z5.

***P. pubescens*** L. GROUND CHERRY; HUSK TOMATO; STRAWBERRY TOMATO; DOWNY GROUND CHERRY. Annual, villous. Stems erect, to 90cm, branched, ridged. Lvs ovate, to 11×7cm, dentate, teeth unequal, acute, apex acute, base cordate to truncate; petiole to 7cm. Cal. to 1cm, enlarging to 3cm, teeth to 5mm, narrow-lanceolate, green; cor. to 12mm diam., yellow, blotched purple at throat; anth. purple, to 2mm. Fr. to 1.5cm, yellow. Summer–autumn. Americas. 'Cossack Pineapple': fr. small, yellow, pineapple-flavoured. 'Goldie': fr. medium-sized; plants well branched, decorative, prolific. Z7.

***P. subglabrata*** Mackenzie & Bush. Subglabrous to glabrous perenn., to 120cm. Lvs ovate to lanceolate, to 10cm, entire to dentate. Fls stipitate, yellow; pedicel equals fls; cal. lobes lanceolate; cor. tube to 2.5cm diam., tipped purple; anth. to 3mm. Fr. red to purple. Summer–autumn. Eastern N America. Z5.

***P. bunyardii*** Mak. See *P. alkekengi*.
***P. edulis*** Sims. See *P. peruviana*.
***P. franchetii*** Mast. See *P. alkekengi*.
For further synonymy see *Quincula*.

**Physaria** (Nutt.) A. Gray. (From Gk *physa*, bellows, alluding to the fruits.) BLADDERPOD. Cruciferae. 14 species of perennial herbs. Rootstock elongated. Leaves numerous, often in terminal rosettes, obovate to lanceolate, round or lobed, petiolate, entire or toothed. Flowering stems simple, few-leaved. Inflorescence racemose, elongating in fruit; flowers small; sepals 4, oblong to linear, hairy; petals 4, spathulate, glabrous, yellow, rarely purple. Fruit a silicle, bilobed at apex, inflated, style persistent; seeds brown, wingless. Western N America. Similar to *Lesquerella* but with larger, less papery, 2-lobed fruit. Z6 unless specified.

CULTIVATION Montane or alpine species of western North America, *Physaria* spp. are found in dry, open and sunny habitats on scree or rocky terrain. They are grown for their neat rosettes of grey or silver foliage and for the flower spikes, which are followed by the attractive bladder-like seed heads. In their native zones, temperatures drop to −20°C/−4°F and below, but they will not tolerate such low temperatures in combination with winter damp. Grow in perfectly drained soils on the rock garden, or on scree, in full sun. Propagate by seed or division in spring.

***P. alpestris*** Suksd. To 15cm. Rootstock simple or sparsely branched. Lvs 3–5×1–2cm, obovate, rarely acute, silvery stellate-pubesc. Flowering stems 5–15cm, several, erect to horizontal, lvs few, 5–15×3–5mm, oblanceolate; raceme corymbose; sep. 8–10×1.5–2mm, oblong; pet. 12–14×2–3mm, clawed, spathulate. Fr. much inflated, 10–15×7–10mm, hairy; style 5–7mm.

***P. didymocarpa*** (Hook.) A. Gray. To 10cm. Lvs 15–40×8–16mm, numerous, obovate, crenate to toothed, sometimes entire; petiole long. Flowering stems numerous, somewhat prostrate, lvs 10–20×4–8mm, entire; raceme congested at first; sep. 6–8×1.5–2mm, pubesc., keeled; pet. 10–12×3–4mm, yellow. Fr. strongly inflated, erect, sparsely hairy; style to 9mm. Z3.

***P. geyeri*** (Hook.) A. Gray. Rootstock usually simple. To 30cm. Lvs 30–70×8–12mm, obovate, entire, rarely sparsely broad-toothed; petiole winged. Flowering stems 10–30cm, numerous, somewhat prostrate, lvs entire, 15–30×3–5mm; sep. oblong, 5–7×1–2mm; pet. spathulate, 8–12×3–4mm. Fr. moderately inflated, 6–9×5–7mm, shallow-emarginate, style 5–7mm. Z3.

***P. oregana*** Wats. To 35cm. Rootstock simple. Lvs 40–60×8–15mm, obovate, broadly toothed; petiole slender. Flowering stems 1–35cm, several to many, lvs 15–25×3–5mm, broad-oblanceolate, entire to sparsely toothed; sep. 5–7×1mm, oblong; pet. 9–12×2–3mm, spathulate, lemon yellow. Fr. 18–25×10–12mm, moderately inflated to slightly compressed; style 1–2mm.

**Physianthus** Mart.
***P. albens*** Mart. See *Araujia sericofera*.
***P. auricarius*** Graham. See *Araujia graveolens*.
***P. megapotamicus*** Mart. See *Araujia angustifolia*.

**Physocarpus** Maxim. (From Gk *physa*, bladder, and *karpos*, fruit, referring to the inflated follicles.) NINEBARK. Rosaceae. 10 species of deciduous shrubs; bark exfoliating. Leaves alternate, simple, large, palmately lobed, often coarsely veined; petioles present; stipules soon abscising, conspicuous. Flowers in terminal corymbs; calyx tube campanulate, stellate-pubescent; sepals 5, valvate, persistent; petals white to light pink, 5, rounded, patent; stamens 20–40, inserted on a disc in the throat of the calyx tube; carpels 1–5, connate at base or for more than half their length; styles filiform; stigmas capitate. Fruit a group of inflated follicles, splitting open at both seams, 2–4-seeded; seeds ovoid, shiny, bony. N America, NE Asia.

CULTIVATION Suited to the shrub border and used in urban massed plantings, *Physocarpus* spp. are grown for their clusters of white, sometimes pink-tinted flowers, carried in early summer. *P. opulifolius*, a vigorous, widespreading shrub, has attractive peeling bark (hence the popular name, ninebark); cv. Luteus has bright young foliage of a good clear yellow. *P. malvaceus*, with an elegant and upright habit of growth, is more tolerant than other species of dry soils. All prefer acid soils and will quickly become chlorotic on shallow chalk; they are hardy to −25°C/−13°F. Grow in moist, moderately fertile soils in full sun. Prune when necessary after flowering, thinning out old and overcrowded shoots by cutting back to ground level. Propagate by removal of suckers, by seed, or from softwood cuttings in a closed case with bottom heat.

***P. alternans*** (Jones) J.T. Howell To 1.5m, densely branched; bark tawny or grey-white. Young branchlets stellate-pubesc. and often glandular. Lvs rounded to rhombic, to 18mm diam., cordate, 3–7-lobed, lobes double-crenate, stellate-pubesc.; petioles to 1cm. Fls 3–12 in terminal corymbs; cal. tube to 4mm diam., stellate-hairy outside, glabrous within; cal. teeth stellate-hairy, ovate, 3mm; pet. to 4mm diam.; stamens 20. Follicle solitary, 5mm, stellate-pubesc. Summer. Mts of W US (California to Nevada).

***P. amurensis*** (Maxim.) Maxim. To 3m. Branchlets glabrous to somewhat grey-pubesc. Lvs to 10×9cm, ovate, 3–5-lobed, lobes pointed, green and subglabrous above, white-green and somewhat lanuginose beneath, finely and doubly serrate-incised, teeth acute. Fls 1.5cm diam., in lax corymbs to 5cm; cal. densely stellate-tomentose, lobes triangular; pet. lanuginose outside; stamens 40, anth. purple. Follicles 3–4 together, lanuginose. Summer. Manchuria, Korea. Z5.

***P. bracteatus*** (Rydb.) Rehd. To 180cm+; bark chartaceous, exfoliating. Young shoots yellow, glabrous. Lvs to 7cm, broad-ovate, often cordate at base, usually 3-lobed, lobes double-crenate. Fls 12mm diam., in several-fld, hemispheric, 50mm diam. cymes; bracts spathulate to obovate, foliaceous; pedicels and cal. densely stellate-pubesc. Follicles in pairs, connate for half their length. Summer. US (Colorado). Z6.

***P. capitatus*** (Pursh) Greene. Erect shrub to 3m. Lvs to 7×4cm, broad-ovate, glabrous above, stellate-tomentose beneath, irregularly double-serrate, larger, more deeply lobed and with sharper teeth on long shoots. Fls white to light pink, numerous, in dense, hemispheric corymbs to 7cm diam.; pedicel 13mm, lanuginose; cal. very lanuginose; cal. teeth ovate, to 3mm; pet. to 3mm. Fr. 3–5 together, to 7mm, glabrous, red, usually 2-seeded; seeds obliquely pyriform, to 2mm, straw-coloured. Spring–summer. Western N America. Z6.

***P. glabratus*** (Rydb.) Rehd. Resembles *P. monogynus*, but lvs not as deeply lobed, lobes double-crenate, pedicels and cal. glabrous or subglabrous, and fls slightly larger. US (Colorado). Z4.

***P. malvaceus*** (Greene) Kuntze. To 2m, of erect habit. Stems erect, stellate-lanuginose; shoots densely stellate-tomentose. Lvs to 6×6cm, rounded to broad-ovate, round to cordate at base, double-crenate, stellate-pubesc., often glabrous above, 3-lobed, occasionally 5-lobed on non-flowering shoots, lobes broad-rounded. Fls white, 1cm diam., in few-fld, 3cm diam. corymbs; pedicel and cal. lanuginose. Fr. in pairs, slightly keeled and flat, with erect beaks, 1–2-seeded. Summer. Western N America. Z6.

***P. monogynus*** (Torr.) Coult. MOUNTAIN NINEBARK. To 1m, usually with decumbent stems. Branches brown, glabrous to sparsely stellate-pubesc. Lvs suborbicular-ovate to reniform, to 4cm, glabrous or subglabrous, green, usually deeply 3–5-lobed, incised; petioles to 1.5cm. Fls showy, in corymbs; bracts lanceolate, caducous; pedicels to 1.5cm, usually sparsely stellate-pubesc.; cal. hemispheric, 3mm diam., stellate-pubesc.; cal. teeth ovate-lanceolate to elliptic, usually obtuse, densely stellate-pubesc.; pet. orbicular, 3mm; fil. slender, filiform, anth. didymous; carpels 2–3; styles terminal. Follicles 2–3, connate above middle, 5mm, densely stellate-pubesc., with ascending-patent beaks, usually 2-seeded; seeds obliquely pyriform, 1.5mm+, shiny. Spring–summer. C US. Z5.

***P. opulifolius*** (L.) Maxim. NINEBARK. To 3m; bark glabrous, brown, shredded. Branchlets glabrous. Lvs to 7.5×7.5cm, oval to rounded, cordate at base, glabrous, double-toothed, usually 3-lobed, lobes crenate or also acute; petiole to 2cm. Fls often pale pink, or white tinged with rose, to 1cm diam., in many-fld, 5mm diam. corymbs; pedicel slender, lanuginose or glabrous; stamens 30, purple. Follicles 3–5, 6.5mm, connate at base, completely glabrous, red, usually 2-seeded; seeds ovate. Summer. Central & Eastern N America. 'Dart's Gold': low-growing, to 1.2m; lvs bright gold in summer; fls white, washed pink. 'Luteus': lvs golden on young growth, later olive green or tinted bronze. 'Nanus': low-growing, to 1.8m, bushy, dense; lvs small, dark green, sparsely and shallowly lobed. var. ***intermedius*** Rydb. To 1.5m. Young shoots glabrous or subglabrous. Lvs oval-rounded, to 6cm, slightly stellate-pubesc. beneath to subglabrous, shallowly 3-lobed, lobes obtuse double-crenate. Fls 12mm diam. in dense cymes; pedicels and cal. stellate-pubesc. to subglabrous. Follicles stellate-pubesc. US. Z2.

***P. alabamensis*** Rydb. See *P. opulifolius*.
***P. intermedius*** (Rydb.) Schneid. See *P. opulifolius* var. *intermedius*.
***P. missouriensis*** Daniels. See *P. opulifolius* var. *intermedius*.
***P. pauciflorus*** Piper. See *P. malvaceus*.
***P. ramaleyi*** Nels. See *P. opulifolius* var. *intermedius*.
***P. stellatus*** (Rydb.) Rehd. See *P. opulifolius*.
***P. torreyi*** (S. Wats.) Maxim. See *P. monogynus*.
For further synonymy see *Neillia*, *Opulaster* and *Spiraea*.

**Physochlaina** G. Don. (From Gk *physa*, bladder, and *chlaina*, cloak, in reference to the inflated calyx.) Solanaceae. 6 species of erect, glabrous, perennial herbs; stems simple, many, from the same root. Leaves membranaceous, entire or with undulate margins, petiolate. Flowers erect in a terminal corymb; calyx tubular to campanulate, slightly 5-lobed, persistent; corolla funnelform to campanulate, with 5 broad, short, obtuse, overlapping lobes; filaments inserted into the bottom of the corolla, hairy at the base; stigma dilated. Fruit a 2-celled capsule, included in the calyx. C Asia. Z8.

CULTIVATION Occurring in rock fissures, caves and on stony slopes, *Physochlaina* will grow easily in any fairly dry soil in part shade; *P. orientalis* is particularly valuable for its early lilac flowers. Plant autumn to spring. Propagate from seed or by division in spring.

***P. orientalis*** (Bieb.) G. Don. To 45cm. Lvs deltoid-ovoid, repand or entire, acute, downy, pale green, petiolate. Fls pale purple-blue, in an erect-capitate raceme; cal. nearly twice as long as the capsule; cor. gradually widening toward the top. Iberia, around Narzana.

***P. praealta*** (Decne.) Miers. Glandular, downy, to 120cm, branched above. Lvs to 15cm, ovate or cuneate, margins entire or undulate; petiolate. Fls in terminal branched clusters, to 10cm diam.; cal. bell-shaped, 5-lobed, to 6mm, reaching 2.5cm in fruit; cor. to 3cm, funnelform, with 5 spreading lobes, green-yellow with purple veins; stamens and style exserted. Fr. enclosed in the tubular calyx. Pakistan to C Nepal.

***P. grandiflora*** Hook. See *P. praealta*.
***P. physaloides*** G. Don. See *Scopolia physaloides*.
For further synonymy see *Hyoscyamus*.

**Physostegia** Benth. (From Gk *physa*, a bladder, and *stege*, a covering.) OBEDIENT PLANT; FALSE DRAGON HEAD. Labiatae. 12 species of erect perennial herbs to 2m. Stems normally unbranched below the inflorescence, glabrous. Stem leaves all sessile or lower pairs petiolate, petioles to 6.5cm, blade glabrous, broadly elliptical, ovate, obovate or linear, margins entire or serrate. Inflorescence of 1–20 racemes; floral bracts lanceolate to ovate; calyx regular, 5-lobed, obscurely 10-nerved, campanulate, throat glabrous; corolla bilabiate, white to deep red-violet, upper lip flat to galeate, lower lip 3-lobed; stamens 4, ascending under upper lip of corolla, barely exserted. Nutlets triangular. N America. The popular name 'obedient plant' arises because the flowers and calyces remain put if re-positioned.

CULTIVATION All species inhabit damp places in the wild: their white running rhizomes spread rapidly in rich fertile loamy soil when there is abundant water present. Most species can survive on drier poorer soils but their spread and stature will be considerably diminished. Long periods of drought will prove fatal. *Physostegia* spp. are ideal central or rear herbaceous border plants, standing tall and elegant in large spreading clumps in well-mulched soil; watch must be kept on the running rhizomes of more vigorous clones of *P. virginiana*.

Propagate from removal of rhizomes when dormant or before the winter rosette starts growing upwards becoming the flower stem. Seed may be sown in the autumn placed outside in a cold frame to germinate either before or after winter. Fungal rots and bacterial rot may attack the fleshy rhizomes, which must be removed and the healthy pieces isolated in severe cases.

***P. digitalis*** Small. Erect, robust perenn. to 2m. Lvs 5–17×1.5–7cm, oblanceolate, obovate to elliptical, apex acute to acuminate, margin subentire to bluntly serrate, upper and middle stem lvs sessile, lowest 1–4 pairs petiolate, upper stem lvs much reduced. Fls borne in racemes, raceme axis densely pubesc. to tomentose; floral bracts 3–9mm, lanceolate to ovate; fls tightly packed, adjacent calyces overlapping; cal. 4–8mm, enlarging to 13mm in fruit; cor. pale lavender to off-white, usually spotted inside with purple. Nutlets trigonal, smooth. Midsummer. S US (Louisiana, Texas). Z8.

***P. parviflora*** Nutt. ex A. Gray. Erect perenn. to 70cm. Lvs to 12×3cm, lanceolate, narrowly ovate to elliptical, margins serrate, lower lvs occasionally subentire, upper stem lvs scarcely reduced, all lvs usually having 1–3 pairs of primary veins, middle stem lvs sessile, lowest pairs petiolate. Fls borne in racemes, raceme axis densely puberulent, stalked glands scattered throughout; floral bracts 2–4mm, ovate to lanceolate; fls tightly packed, adjacent calyces overlapping; cal. bearing stalked glands, tube 3–5mm, enlarging to 7.5mm, lobes acute; cor. lavender to red-violet, spotted and streaked inside with purple, densely puberulent to finely tomentose. Nutlets smooth, trigonal. Mid–late summer. C & W Canada and US. Z2.

***P. purpurea*** (Walter) Blake. Erect perenn. to 140cm. Lvs very variable, 1–6×0.2–4.5cm, linear, spathulate, obovate, oblong, elliptical or pandurate, apex obtuse to rounded, margins blunt to sharply serrate, upper stem lvs greatly reduced; lowest 1–6(–10) pairs of lvs petiolate or all lvs sessile; petioles to 6cm. Fls borne in racemes, raceme axis more or less densely pubesc.; floral bracts 2–4mm, ovate to lanceolate; fls tightly packed or fairly loose; cal. glandular to punctate, but not bearing stalked glands, tube 3–8mm enlarging to 10mm, lobes acute; cor. white to lavender-purple, usually spotted and streaked with purple inside, finely tomentose. Nutlets trigonal, smooth. Early–mid summer. E US. Z5.

***P. virginiana*** (L.) Benth. ssp. ***virginiana***. Erect perenn. to 180cm; primary rhiz. usually much-branched, forming creeping clumps. Lower middle stem lvs sessile or lowest 1–7 pairs petiolate, sessile lvs 2–18×3–5cm, very variable, elliptic, lanceolate, oblanceolate or spathulate, margins sharply serrate, rarely entire. Fls borne in 1–20 racemes, raceme axis pubesc.; floral bracts usually not present; fls tightly or loosely spaced, calyces overlapping or free; cal. tube 2.5–6mm enlarging to 10mm, lobes acute to attenuate; cor. red-violet, lavender or white usually spotted and streaked purple. Nutlets trigonal, smooth. Summer–autumn. Canada, N US. ssp. ***praemorsa*** (Shinn.) Cantino. Erect perenn. herb, 100–180cm; rhiz. usually short, unbranched or if branched shortly so. Lvs very variable, middle stem lvs usually 2–30mm wide, elliptic-oblanceolate, obovate, ovate or spathulate, margin sharply serrate. Fls in 1–8 racemes, raceme axis pubesc.; sterile floral bracts present to 40 pairs; fls usually tightly packed, calyces usually overlapping; cal. tube 3.5–8mm enlarging to 10–11mm. Nutlets trigonal, smooth. Midsummer–late autumn. C & S US and NE Mexico. 'Alba': fls white. 'Bouquet Rose' ('Rose Bouquet'): to 1.2m; fls lilac-pink. 'Galadriel': dwarf, to 45cm; fls pale lilac-pink. 'Gigantea': to 2.2m, fls pink. 'Morden Beauty': lvs willow-like; fls pink. 'Pink Bouquet': to 90cm; fls rose pink, in dense terminal clusters. 'Rosea': fls large, pink, in spikes. 'Snow Crown': fls large, white, in dense spikes. 'Summer Snow': short, to 1m; fls white. 'Summer Spire': to 60cm; fls rose pink. 'Variegata': to 1m; lvs tinted grey, boldly edged cream; fls pale lavender-pink. 'Vivid': fls claret-pink. Z4.

***P. denticulata*** (Ait.) Britt. See *P. virginiana* ssp. *virginiana*.
***P. latidens*** House. See *P. virginiana* ssp. *virginiana*.
***P. nivea*** Lund. See *P. virginiana* ssp. *virginiana*.
***P. nuttallii*** (Britt.) Fassett. See *P. parviflora*.
***P. obovata*** (Elliott) Godfrey. See *P. purpurea*.
***P. praemorsa*** Shinn. See *P. virginiana* ssp. *praemorsa*.
***P. serotina*** Shinn. See *P. virginiana* ssp. *praemorsa*.
***P. speciosa*** (Sweet) Sweet. See *P. virginiana* ssp. *virginiana*.
***P. variegata*** (Vent.) Benth. See *P. virginiana* ssp. *praemorsa*.

**Phyteuma** L. (Name used by Dioscorides for an obscure aphrodisiac plant, meaning simply 'the plant'.) HORNED RAMPION. Campanulaceae. Some 40 species of perennial herbs. Leaves alternate, the lower leaves conspicuous, the upper leaves sometimes few and small. Flowers in terminal spikes or heads, usually sessile, sometimes shortly pedicellate; bracts small or involucrate; calyx tube adnate to ovary, limb 5-merous; corolla 5-merous nearly to base, lobes linear, spreading to recurved, sometimes connate at tip; stamens free from corolla; filaments broadened at base; anthers free. Fruit a capsule, laterally dehiscent. Europe, Asia. Z6 unless specified.

CULTIVATION A diverse genus including undemanding perennials such as *P. betonicifolium* and *P. spicatum* for the border and woodland garden, in sun or part shade in any fertile, well-drained soil; *P. nigrum, P. ovatum* and *P. orbiculare* are sometimes grown amongst thin meadow grasses in approximation of their natural habitat. With the exception of the very small, high-altitude alpines, the lower-growing species are easily grown in neutral or slightly alkaline soils on the rock garden. More demanding species include *P. hemisphaericum* and *P. humile*, which occur on freely draining acid substrates, and the more challenging, but distinctively beautiful *P. comosum*, which inhabits deep crevices on limestone in the wild. The smaller alpines need the impeccable drainage of scree or raised bed and are susceptible both to slugs and winter wet; all suit pan cultivation in the alpine house in a lean and gritty alpine mix. Propagate by division in spring or after flowering or by seed in autumn; prick out seedlings into individual pots and pot on successionally until planting out, avoiding root disturbance.

***P. balbisii*** A. DC. Erect, to 10cm. Lower lvs cordate to broadly ovate, petiolate, upper lvs lanceolate, entire to irregularly denticulate. Infl. globose to obovoid; cor. white tinged with blue. Summer. N Italy. Z7.

***P. betonicifolium*** Vill. Stem erect, glabrous, to 70cm. Lower lvs to 5cm, ovate to lanceolate, base cordate or obtuse, serrate, long-petiolate, upper lvs narrower. Infl. a cylindric spike; bracts few; cor. violet-blue; stigma 3-lobed. Summer. Pyrenees.

***P. charmelii*** Vill. Glabrous, erect, to 30cm. Lower lvs ovate-cordate, serrate, long-petiolate, upper lvs lanceolate irregularly dentate. Fls in ovoid to globose heads; cor. curved in bud, blue. Summer. Apennines.

***P. comosum*** L. Tufted, to 10cm, glabrous. Lower lvs ovate-cordate, serrate, long-petiolate, upper lvs lanceolate to acuminate. Fls in umbellate clusters, short-pedicellate to sessile; cor. tubular, inflated at base, violet. Summer. Alps.

***P. hemisphaericum*** L. Erect or ascending, to 10cm. Lower lvs to 8cm, linear-lanceolate, acuminate, upper lvs narrower, entire to serrulate. Infl. ovoid to spherical; bracts lanceolate, short; cor. blue, occasionally tinged with white. Alps to Austria.

***P. humile*** Schleich. ex Gaudin. Tufted, erect, to 15cm, glabrous. Lower lvs crowded, linear-oblanceolate, glabrous, upper lvs few, narrow-linear. Infl. globose; bracts lanceolate, usually serrate; cor. deep blue to violet. Summer. Switzerland.

***P. michelii*** All. To 60cm. Lvs ovate to linear-lanceolate, serrate, petiolate. Fls in ovoid spikes; bracts abruptly recurved; cor. pale to deep blue. Summer. S Europe.

***P. nigrum*** F.W. Schmidt. Erect, to 25cm, glabrous. Lower lvs to 5cm, cordate, blunt to obtuse, long-petiolate, upper lvs smaller, oblong-ovate. Infl. ovoid; bracts linear, acuminate; cor. curved in bud, dark violet, tinged with black. Summer. C Europe.

***P. orbiculare*** L. ROUNDHEADED RAMPION. Usually erect, to 50cm, glabrous. Lower lvs to 10cm, lanceolate to elliptic, cordate, irregularly serrate, petiolate, upper lvs similar, but sessile. Infl. dense, spherical; bracts lanceolate to acuminate; cor. dark blue to violet. Summer. Europe. var. ***austriacum*** (G. Beck) G. Beck. Upper lvs narrow ovate; bracts erect.

***P. ovatum*** Honck. Erect, to 60cm, glabrous. Lower lvs ovate to deeply cordate, acuminate, dentate, long-petiolate, upper lvs narrower. Infl. dense, obovoid; bracts ovate, spreading to abruptly recurved; cor. dark violet. Alps.

***P. pauciflorum*** L. Tufted, to 8cm. Lvs to 3cm, oblanceolate to ovate, entire or apically toothed. Infl. spherical, fls few; bracts elliptic-acuminate, serrulate; cor. blue. Alps.

***P. pedemontanum*** R. Schulz. Habit erect. Lvs rosulate, prolific, ligulate-acuminate, apically denticulate, stem lvs few, small. Infl. spherical, dark, blue. Summer. Alps.

***P. scheuchzeri*** All. To 40cm, habit loose. Lower lvs linear to oblong-lanceolate, cuneate, bluntly dentate, long-petiolate, upper lvs linear, entire, almost sessile. Infl. spherical; bracts linear, leafy; cor. dark blue. Summer. Alps.

***P. sieberi*** Spreng. Erect, or ascending, to 10cm. Lower lvs ovate to narrow elliptic, sinuate, upper lvs ovate, sessile. Infl. globose; bracts lanceolate, serrate; cor. deep blue. Summer. Alps.

***P. spicatum*** L. SPIKED RAMPION. Erect, to 80cm, glabrous. Lower lvs ovate-cordate, serrate, upper lvs sessile. Infl. dense, spicate; bracts linear; cor. white, cream or blue. Summer. Temperate Europe.

***P. tenerum*** R. Schulz. To 45cm. Lower lvs lanceolate, upper lvs linear-lanceolate, sessile or short-petiolate. Fls dark blue. W Europe.

***P. vagneri*** A. Kerner. Erect, to 30cm. Lower lvs deeply cordate, crenate to serrate, long-petiolate, upper lvs lanceolate, subsessile. Infl. a dense ellipsoid to spherical head; bracts narrow lanceolate; cor. dark violet, tinged with black. Hungary.

***P. zahlbruckneri*** Vest. Erect, to 90cm, glabrous. Lower lvs narrow-ovate, base cordate, crenate, long-petiolate, upper lvs basally cuneate. Infl. in obovoid spikes, lax; cor. dark blue. E Europe, Yugoslavia.

***P. austriacum*** G. Beck. See *P. orbiculare* var. *austriacum*.
***P. campanuloides*** Bieb. See *Asyneuma campanuloides*.
***P. canescens*** Waldst. & Kit. See *Asyneuma canescens*.
***P. halleri*** All. See *P. ovatum*.
***P. limoniifolium*** (L.) Sibth. & Sm. See *Asyneuma limoniifolium*.
***P. lobelioides*** Willd. See *Asyneuma lobelioides*.
***P. scorzonerifolium*** Vill. See *P. michelii*.

**Phytolacca** L. POKEWEED. (From Gk *phyton*, plant, and Fr. *lac*, lake, a red pigment, from the crimson juice of the berries.) Phytolaccaceae. 35 species of herbs, shrubs and trees, glabrous or nearly so. Leaves ovate, elliptic or lanceolate, simple, entire, usually petiolate. Flowers small, apetalous, in erect or drooping spike-like racemes, terminal and axillary; pedicels with basal bracts; calyx 4- or 5-lobed, white, pink or red; stamens 6–33, in 1 or 2 rows; pistils and styles 5–16. Fruit a fleshy berry, with 5–16 free or connate carpels; juice red-purple. Temperate and warm regions.

CULTIVATION *P. americana*, with other herbaceous and shrubby species, is suitable for the open woodland garden, in massed plantings or as a specimen in the shrub and mixed border, although most spp. have ill-scented foliage and due consideration must be given to the poisonous nature of the attractive berries in gardens where children have access. *Phytolacca* spp. are usually tall and sturdy specimens valued for their flowers, the spikes of shining berries which follow and for autumn colour. The most commonly seen in temperate gardens, *P. americana* and *P. clavigera* are hardy to about −15°C/5°F, the first almost certainly more.

In warm, frost-free climates, the arborescent *P. dioica*, with its wide-spreading crown, is grown as a shade tree in parks and large gardens, the swollen and buttressed basal portion of the trunk often providing integral seating. In cooler climates, *P. dioica* is semi-evergreen and may develop as a large shrub given a warm, sheltered position. Grow in moisture-retentive, fertile soils in full sun or light shade and provide support for taller species in exposed situations. Herbaceous species will self seed freely under favourable conditions, often to the point of nuisance. Propagate by seed sown in autumn or spring or by division of perennial species (the roots in some spp. are also poisonous). Also by cuttings. *P. americana* is an alternative host of a number of viral diseases, including mosaics, ringspots and virus yellows that affect members of the Amaryllidaceae, Liliaceae and Solanaceae.

***P. acinosa*** Roxb. INDIAN POKE. Subglabrous herbaceous perenn., to 150cm; stems succulent, stout. Lvs to 25cm, lanceolate, long-pointed, tapering to a short petiole, green, thinly succulent. Racemes to 15cm, suberect, extending to 20cm in fruit; pedicels glabrous; cor. 7mm diam. with 5 obovate, acute, spreading perianth seg., green with a white margin; stamens 8–10 anthers rose-coloured. Fr. fleshy, 8 per fl. Kashmir to SW China, SE Asia. Z8.

***P. americana*** L. POKE; POKEWEED; SCOKE; GARGET; PIGEON BERRY. Foetid herbaceous perenn., to 4m. Stems often purple, regularly divided above. Lvs to 30cm, oblong or ovate-lanceolate, acute or acuminate, green, becoming purple in autumn. Fls 6mm diam., white, in racemes to 20cm, erect, but drooping in fruit. Berries 1.2cm diam., glossy, green becoming red then purple-black. N & C America. Z4.

***P. clavigera*** W.W. Sm. Branched deciduous subshrub, to 1.5m. Lvs to 15×8cm, ovate-elliptic or ovate-lanceolate, slightly undulate; petiole to 2.5cm. Racemes erect, dense, shorter than the lvs at flowering but to 30cm in fruit; pedicels to 4mm; cal. lobes to 4×3mm, ovate, obtuse, white becoming purple; stamens 12. Fr. markedly depressed, 10mm diam., black with dark red juice, forming a dense mass on the raceme axis; seeds to 33mm, black. China (Yunnan). Z6.

***P. dioica*** (L.) Moq. OMBU; BELLA SOMBRA. Fast-growing, evergreen, dioecious tree, to 20m; trunk broad, with a high water content, and large outgrowths at the base, forming a circle to 2m diam.; crown broader than the tree is high. Lvs 10cm+, elliptic or ovate, glabrous, leathery, with a prominent midrib, turning yellow then purple. Fls white, in erect or drooping racemes equalling the lvs; male fls with 20–30 stamens much exceeding the cal.; female fls with 10 staminodes and 7–10 carpels. Fr. black, pistils joined at the base. S America. Z9.

***P. esculenta*** Van Houtte. Branched herb, to 1m, base woody. Lvs to 15cm, suborbicular to ovate-elliptic, acuminate; petioles to 2.5cm. Racemes to 12cm; pedicels to 12mm, scabrous, fls to 8mm diam., white; stamens 8, anth. white. Fr. depressed-globose, purple-black; seeds black, shiny, to 3mm. China, Japan. Z6.

***P. heterotepala*** H. Walter. Glabrous shrub, with suberect branches. Lvs to 1.3×0.5mm, ovate-elliptic or elliptic, papery or leathery, entire, with a narrow yellow zone around the margin; petiole to 2cm. Infl. to 250×13mm, suberect, lax, much exceeding the lvs, cylindrical; pedicels 4mm with linear membranous bracts; cal. seg. unequal, to 3mm, white, becoming green in fr.; stamens shorter than cal. Fr. red, to 11mm diam.; seeds subreniform, 2.5mm. Mexico. Z9.

***P. icosandra*** L. Herb, to 2m. Lvs to 20×9.5cm, elliptic, acuminate, mucronate, thick; petioles to 6cm. Racemes to 15cm, erect, pedunculate, many, axillary or terminal; fls subsessile or on pedicels to 5mm; sep. to 3.2×3mm, elliptic to ovate, green, white or red-tinged, persistent; stamens 8–20. Fr. to 8mm diam., fleshy, green ripening dark red, then black; seeds to 2.5mm, black and shiny. Mexico, S America. Z9.

***P. octandra*** L. Spreading or erect subshrub to 2m. Stems often red-tinged. Lvs to 20×5cm, elliptic to ovate-lanceolate, acute or mucronate. Racemes erect, to 11cm in fruit; fls to 7mm diam., densely packed; cal. seg. broad ovate, to 3mm, white or pale green, becoming pink or crimson at fruiting; stamens 8–10. Fr. to 8mm diam., shiny black with dark red juice; seeds to 2.5mm diam., subglobose, glossy black. New Zealand. Z9.

***P. acinosa*** var. ***esculenta*** Maxim. See *P. esculenta*.
***P. acinosa*** var. ***kaempferi*** (A. Gray) Mak. See *P. esculenta*.
***P. decandra*** L. See *P. americana*.
***P. kaempferi*** A. Gray. See *P. esculenta*.
***P. mexicana*** Gaertn. See *P. icosandra*.
***P. volubilis*** Heimerl. See *Ercilla spicata*.

**PHYTOLACCACEAE** R. Br. POKEWEED FAMILY. Dicot. 18 genera and 65 species of herbs, shrubs, trees or lianes, often glabrous and somewhat succulent; secondary growth with concentric rings of vascular bundles. Leaves simple, alternate, stipules minute or absent. Flowers usually regular, bisexual, small, in spikes or panicles, rarely in cymes or solitary; calyx 4 or 5 (–10) free sepals, sometimes basally connate; corolla usually absent or small and alternate with calyx (e.g. *Stegnosperma*); stamens 4(-numerous), often in 2 alternate whorls, filaments sometimes basally connate; ovary (1)2-numerous carpels, more or less connate but styles distinct, locules as many as carpels; receptacular nectary sometimes around ovary or stamens; each locule with 1 basal ovule. Fruit a drupe or nut, rarely a capsule, carpels often separating; seeds with curved embryo around copious hard or starchy perisperm and sometimes an aril; endosperm absent. Tropical and warm, especially America. *Agdestis, Ercilla, Phytolacca, Rivina, Trichostigma*.

**Piaranthus** R. Br. (From Gk *piaros*, fat, and *anthos*, flower, due to the broad, flat corolla.) Asclepiadaceae. Some 16 species of very dwarf, succulent, leafless, perennial herbs, to 5cm. Stems short, erect to prostrate, in small sections said to resemble potatoes, 4–5-angled, ridges blunt, toothed, teeth sharp, in threes, uppermost largest. Flowers small, clustered near apex; pedicels erect; corolla flat, tube absent or campanulate, lobes lanceolate to ovate or triangular, softly hairy inside; corona a whorl of 5 lobes with dorsal, truncate crests with tiny teeth or warts. Fruit a spindle-shaped follicle, in pairs. S Africa, Namibia. Z9.

CULTIVATION As for *Duvalia*.

***P. comptus*** N.E. Br. Stems dense, to 3×1.4cm, dull grey-green, teeth short, acute. Fls to 4 per cluster; pedicel 4–12mm; cor. to 2cm diam., deeply lobed, less flat, glabrous, green-brown below, white, covered in dense, short, soft hairs above, lobes 5–9mm, ovate-lanceolate, blotched red-brown, slightly recurved, sometimes ciliate; corona lobes to 2mm, linear-lanceolate, yellow, sometimes spotted maroon. Cape Province, Namaqualand.

***P. cornutus*** N.E. Br. Stems to 3.5×1.6cm, globose or oblong, grey-green, very bluntly angled, teeth 3–5, tuberculate. Fls paired; pedicels 6–18mm; cor. to 3cm diam., deeply lobed, glabrous below, primrose-yellow blotched red above, lobes to 1.5cm, lanceolate, acuminate; corona lobes 2mm, narrow linear-lanceolate to subulate, yellow. Cape Province, Namaqualand.

***P. disparilis*** N.E. Br. Stems stout, near-cylindric, dull grey-green, with short, acute teeth. Fls solitary, near stem apex; pedicel erect, to 8mm; cor. to 2.5cm diam., flat, pale pink with fine, pale yellow transverse stripes, downy, lobes to 8mm, lanceolate, acuminate, slightly recurved; corona lobes 1.5mm, lanceolate or linear-oblong, entire or 3-toothed at apex, yellow. Cape Province.

***P. foetidus*** N.E. Br. Stems to 4cm, indistinctly 4–5-angled or globose to oblong, green to grey-green, teeth tuberculate. Fls 1–6, malodorous, usually paired near stem apex; pedicels erect, to 1.8cm; cor. 1.5–2cm diam., flat, glabrous, green or flushed purple below, yellow, blotched and banded crimson to maroon, downy above; lobes to 9mm, ovate-lanceolate, acute, margins revolute; corona dark orange-yellow, lobes to 2.5mm, linear-lanceolate to oblanceolate, margins and crest dark purple-brown. Cape Province, Namibia.

***P. geminatus*** (Masson) N.E. Br. Stems to 4.5×2cm, subovoid, bluntly angled, teeth few, tiny, projecting. Fls paired near stem apex; pedicels 6–12mm; cor. to 3cm diam., flat, deeply lobed, outside green, flushed red below, ochre to buff, flecked red, pubesc. above; lobes to 1.4cm, spreading, lanceolate, attenuate, margins revolute; corona yellow, star-like, lobes 2mm, narrow-oblong or linear-lanceolate, crest flat, smooth. Cape Province.

***P. globosus*** A. White & B.L. Sloane. Stems to 2×1.2cm, ovoid to globose, glabrous, pale green, with 2–4 minute teeth per angle. Fls 1–2, near stem apex; cor. to 1.3cm diam., flat, glabrous below, pale green-yellow, dappled pale red or lavender, downy below, lobes 7mm, ovate-lanceolate, acute, margins slightly revolute, apex recurved; corona yellow, with a lavender or red-spotted crest, lobes 1mm, lanceolate or ovate. Known only in cult.

***P. pallidus*** Lückh. Stems globose to oblong, angles rounded, green, glabrous. Fls 2–4, near stem apex; pedicels 6–12mm; cor. flat, glabrous below, pale yellow above, lobes to 1.3cm, attenuate; corona lobes yellow, 2mm, lanceolate or linear-lanceolate, apex toothed or bifid, crest 3–5-toothed. Cape Province.

***P. parvulus*** N.E. Br. Stems to 4.5×1.4cm, ovoid to ovoid-oblong, grey-green, blotched pale red, teeth 3–5, tuberculose, 3mm. Fls to 12 per cluster, from midway on stem to apex; pedicels erect, slender, 6–12mm; cor. to 1.2cm diam., flat, glabrous below, straw-yellow above, lobes 4–5mm, deltoid-lanceolate, spreading, acute; corona lobes yellow, 1.5–2mm, acute or irregularly 2–3-toothed, crest minutely tuberculose at apex. Cape Province.

***P. pillansii*** N.E. Br. Stems to 4×1.6cm, creeping, subclavate, obtusely angled to semi-terete, pale green flushed red, teeth small, tuberculose. Fls in pairs near stem apex; pedicel to 16mm; cor. to 3.5cm diam., flat, lobed almost to base, glabrous below, wholly yellow to olive above, or heavily marked red, sometimes dark red, finely banded lime, downy above, lobes to 1.6cm, narrow-lanceolate, spreading, acute, margins recurved; corona lobes yellow, over 2mm, lanceolate, entire or 3-toothed, crest blunt, ridged or minutely tuberculose. Cape Province.

***P. pulcher*** N.E. Br. Stems to 2.5×1.2cm, globose or oblong, grey-green, teeth small, tuberculose. Fls paired or solitary near stem apex; pedicels stout, erect, 6–12mm; cor. to 2cm diam. dark green or brown, glabrous below, pale green-yellow with dark red-brown blotches, densely covered in soft, white and purple hairs above, lobes to 11mm, attenuate, narrow, spreading or ascending; corona dark yellow, lobes to over 2mm, linear-subulate, crest flat-topped, papillose. Cape Province.

***P. ruschii*** Nel. Stems to 1.8×1.2cm, erect or prostrate, oblong to globose, grey-green, angles rounded, teeth tuberculose. Fls fragrant, 2–3 per cluster; pedicel 5mm; cor. to 1.8cm diam., flat, green-yellow, heavily blotched dark brown above, lobes 11mm, ovate-lanceolate, acute, with dense, conspicuous, short white hairs; corona yellow, lobes linear, with many-toothed crest. Namibia.

**Picea** A. Dietr. (From Lat. *pix*, pitch, obtained from the resin of *P. abies*.) SPRUCE. Pinaceae. Some 35 species of evergreen monoecious, coniferous trees, to 20–60m or more. Crown conical in outline, often domed or columnar in older specimens. Bole columnar, mostly to 1.5m diam., to 5m in *P. sitchensis*, with scaly bark, often exfoliating in flakes, becoming furrowed in some mature trees, usually red-brown, purple-brown or grey. Branches in whorls, usually only a few metres long, more or less horizontal. Young produced on the branches from buds subtended by a leaf base, rough and weakly furrowed. Buds to 1cm, occasionally resinous. Leaves in spirals, usually pressed forward onto stem, not petiolate, but borne on a pulvinus (projecting part of the shoot), acicular, entire, never emarginate, 5–50mm, with basal pulvini remaining after leaf fall, 4-sided, usually with stomata on all faces and occasionally flattened. Young trees up to 2–5 years old have much finer, more slender leaves than older trees; leaves in the upper crown of mature trees are stouter and more radial and assurgent (less pectinate or forward-pointing) and with denser stomata than on low branches. The difference between leaves from upper and lower crown branches of one tree is often greater than the difference between leaves from equally positioned branches of different species. Monoecious; male cones produced on the previous year's shoots from buds in the axils of leaves mostly near the apex, pollen sacs numerous; female cones solitary, from or at buds near the apices of the previous year's shoots, erect, green or red. Cones sessile, 2–20×1–5cm, becoming pendulous after pollination, ripening in 4–8 months and falling 1–3 years later, ovoid to cylindric with large, usually thin scales obscuring the very short bracts, green to purple, ripening pale to dark brown; seeds 2 per scale, winged, black-brown when fertile, infertile seeds paler. Most of Northern Hemisphere except Africa.

CULTIVATION A genus adapted mainly to cold, wet northern plains or in mountains, at increasing altitude with distance south. Only one is invariably coastal, *P. sitchensis*, which stretches in a 2000km/1200 mile arc from Alaska to mid-California from the high water mark to 400m/1300ft, rarely to 900m/2925ft in S Alaska. Most are hardy to −30°C/−22°F or lower, except for those from Taiwan, Yunnan, the Himalaya, Mexico, and Californian origins of *P. sitchensis*, these are hardy to −15°C/5°F to −20°C/−4°F. All thrive on acidic soils of pH 4–6; several also tolerate limestone and a few, notably *P. omorika*, chalk. All resist exposure to some degree, although *P. torano* is much better well-sheltered from drying winds. All do well in high rainfall and on damp but well-drained soil, except for *P. pungens* and the *P. asperata* complex, which prefer cold, dry, high mountain sites. *P. sitchensis* makes an enormous specimen tree where rainfall is over 1200mm/48in., to over 60m/195ft tall and 2.5m/26ft diam. in Scotland, but demands cool wet summers and will not grow in the E US. *P. smithiana* makes a handsome specimen to 37m/120ft high and *P. abies* can be 45m/145ft, but is often dull and less impressive. Many others, like *P. orientalis, P. omorika* and *P. likiangensis*, are attractive individually for shape or colour. *P. pungens* and its glaucous cvs are very popular blue trees, but are very susceptible to *Elatobium* damage (see below) in mild areas where winter temperatures do not regularly fall below −8°C/18°F (much of lowland Britain included); blue cvs of *Pseudotsuga menziesii* ssp. *glauca, Abies concolor* and *Pinus monophylla* are considerably better under these conditions. *P. breweriana* is one of the finest of all weeping trees, though it is very slow growing for the first 20 years. In forestry, *P. sitchensis* is unsurpassed for rapid-volume production in cool wet mountains on blanket peat in Western Britain, and *P. abies* (and to a lesser extent *P. omorika*) are widely planted for timber and shelter in regions too dry or liable to late frosts for good specimens of *P. sitchensis*, as also in Eastern N America. In some upland areas, notably over granitic or other base-poor soils, growth rate and health have been seriously affected by aluminium toxicity induced by 'acid rain' pollution.

Cultivate as for *Abies*, except that they are most tolerant of exposure and less tolerant of shade; they should therefore be planted in the open and not under the cover of other trees. They are also more tolerant of poor, peaty soils. As with other conifers, propagation is better from seed than grafts; in *Picea breweriana* this is especially important, grafted plants never making good trees. Seed should preferably be wild collected or from extensive single-species plantings as most species hybridize freely when planted together in cultivation. Propagate dwarf cvs by cuttings; if grafted on normal rootstocks they grow too vigorously.

Several rust fungi, mostly species of *Chrysomyxa*, affect spruce, especially *P. abies*, but none are serious problems. Those occurring in Britain are *Chrysomyxa abietis* and *C. ledi* var. *rhododendri*, both of which cause yellow transverse bands on the needles. *C. abietis* is only known to infect spruce on which it produces the teliospore stage, whereas *C. ledi* var. *rhododendri* produces uredio- and teliospores on rhododendron and aeciospores on spruce. Spruces can also be affected by armillaria root rot (*Armillaria* spp.) and phytophthora root rot (*Phytophthora cinnamomi*). In Britain the most serious disease of plantation conifers, including spruce, is fomes root and butt rot caused by the fungus *Heterobasidion annosum* (syn. *Fomes annosus*); this and many of the other diseases to which the trees are susceptible are unlikely to be a problem on isolated garden trees.

The most important pests of spruce are common to Europe and North America. These include the green spruce aphid (*Elatobium abietinum*), the most serious pest on spruce in gardens, which can cause complete defoliation of several species, particularly in warmer areas and following mild winters; a red spider mite, the conifer spinning mite (*Oligonychus ununguis*), can also be responsible for premature fall of needles; the spruce gall adelgids (*Adelges abietis, A. cooleyi* and *A. viridis*) induce 1–3cm pineapple-shaped galls to develop. The European spruce sawfly (*Diprion hercyniae*) and the spruce budworm (*Choristoneura fumiferana*) are destructive pests of opening buds and young shoots in North America.

Young specimens of *Picea* in areas with public access should be given special protection in December; theft for the christmas tree trade can be a serious problem.

**1** Cones with very thin, papery scales, mostly pale buff.

1.1 Leaves strongly flattened, much bluer beneath than above.
*Pp. sitchensis, jezoensis*.

1.2 Leaves not flattened, equally blue all round.
*Pp. glauca, engelmannii, pungens*.

**2** Cones with moderately thin brown or purple scales, leaves moderately flattened with stomata on both sides but more beneath than above.

2.1 Scales toothed, waved or acute.
*Pp. balfouriana, likiangensis, purpurea, spinulosa*.

2.2 Scales rounded, very finely toothed.
*Pp. alcoquiana, glehnii, mariana, rubens*.

**3** Cones brown, purple, with thicker scales, and leaves strongly flattened, green with no stomata above and white beneath with many.
*Pp. breweriana, omorika, farreri, brachytyla*.

**4** Leaves not flattened, stomata equally all round; cones with thicker scales.

4.1 Cones scales not smoothly rounded, usually striated and/or acute and notched at apex.
*Pp. abies, asperata, koyamai, meyeri*.

4.2 Cone scales smoothly rounded, mostly glossy brown, not striated; leaves very short, under 1cm.
*P. orientalis*.

4.3 Cones scales as 4.2, leaves longer, acute, sharp but not fiercely, mostly more or less pectinate, with leaves subtending side-buds pointing out at a different angle to rest of leaves.
*Pp. alpestris, morrisonicola, obovata, schrenkiana, smithiana, wilsonii*.

4.4 Cones scales as 4.2 but relatively thicker; leaves viciously sharp, easily drawing blood, radial all round shoot.
*Pp. chihuahuana, crassifolia, martinezii, maximowiczii, neoveitchii, torano*.

Note: spruces are very variable, and individuals may key into the wrong groups on occasion, particularly between groups 4.1 and 4.3. The groups above generally reflect real botanic relationships, but are not wholly in accord with published taxonomic accounts. Most spruces hybridize readily in cultivation, and specimens grown from garden collected seed are often unidentifiable.

***P. abies*** (L.) Karst. NORWAY SPRUCE. To 55m; bole to 1.5m diam.; bark red-brown, becoming grey or purple, flaking in thin plates. Crown conical, columnar with age, branches level or drooping with more or less upward-growing apices, branchlets variably pendulous. Young shoots usually glabrous, sometimes pubesc., rust to red-brown. Buds not resinous, to 7mm, ovoid, brown. Lvs 1–2.5cm, dark green, apically obtuse, slightly flattened in young trees. Cones cylindric, green or purplish, ripening brown, 8–18×3–4cm, to ×5–6cm open; scales rhombic, woody, usually emarginate or truncate at tip. Seeds brown-black, 4–5mm with a pale brown 10–15mm wing. N & C Europe. 'Over 100 cvs in Europe and N America, categorized primarily by height and habit. Of the upright selections of normal habit, conical forms include the slender, to 20m 'Cupressina' and 'Viminalis' and the broadly conical 'Pyramidata'; sparse forms include the irregularly branched 'Virgata' (SNAKE-BRANCH SPRUCE) and 'Cranstonii'. Weeping forms include the upright, very pendulous 'Frohburg' and 'Inversa' and the semi-prostrate 'Lorely'; notable low-growers (to 5m) include the narrow-conic 'Concinna', the broad-conic 'Conica' and the profusely coning 'Acrocona'. Of several dwarfs (to 3m), notable selections include the very slow-growing 'Clanbrassiliana' (3m in 180 years), the irregular 'Pachyphylla' and 'Pygmaea', and the more regular 'Elegans' and 'Humilis'; globose dwarfs include the stoutly branched 'Nana Compacta' and 'Pyramidalis Gracilis' and the finer 'Gregoryana' and 'Hystrix'; flat-topped dwarfs include the slow-growing 'Little Gem' (2cm p.a.) and the mat-forming 'Repens'. Cvs noted for needle colour include the yellow to gold 'Aurea' and 'Aurescens', the steel-blue 'Coerulea' and the dwarf gold-variegated 'Callensis' and 'Helen Cordes'. Z4.

***P. alcoquiana*** (Veitch ex Lindl.) Carr. ALCOCK'S SPRUCE. To 25m; bark grey, deeply furrowed, flaking in square scales. Crown broad conical, with long level to ascending branches. Shoots pubesc., white or buff, becoming red-brown, rarely slightly glabrous. Buds slightly resinous, conic, brown. Lvs 1–2cm, dark green with some stomata above, blue-green with distinct white lines of stomata beneath, imbricate, upward-curving, slightly flattened. Cones sessile, purple, becoming brown, ovoid, 6–12×3.5cm; seed scales obovate, apically obtuse, toothed; seeds dark brown. C Japan. 'Howell's Tigertail': broad-growing dwarf, branches upturned at tips. 'Prostrata': dwarf, completely prostrate. var. ***acicularis*** (Shiras. & Koyama) Fitschen. Shoots pubesc. Lvs curved, glaucous. Probably natural hybrid with *P. koyami*. var. ***reflexa*** (Shiras. & Koyama) Fitschen. Shoots pubesc. Seed scales entire, apex reflexed. Z5.

***P. alpestris*** Brügger ex Stein. To 30m; mostly considered as a syn. or var. of *P. abies* but more distinct than many widely accepted Chinese species, and probably more related to *P. smithiana* or *P. obovata*. Bark grey-white; shoots densely pubesc. Lvs 1–2cm, at right angles to shoot, stout, glaucous blue-green with many stomatal lines. Cones similar to *P. smithiana*, 7–14×3–4cm, open to 6cm, stout, heavy, with smoothly rounded scales shaped as *P. obovata* but 15–20mm wide. SE Switzerland (Graubünden, high mts.). Z4.

***P. asperata*** Mast. DRAGON SPRUCE. To 40m, 25m in cult.; bark purple-grey to grey-brown, exfoliating in thick plates. Branches sagging on older trees, apices upward-growing. Shoots pale yellow-brown, glabrous or slightly pubescent, with swollen pulvini. Buds ovoid-conic, to 1.5cm, slightly resinous, buff; bud scales often reflexed at apex. Lvs glaucous blue or blue-green, becoming dark green, 1–2cm×1mm, stiff, somewhat curved, obtuse, slightly imbricate. Cones 5–16cm, cylindrical, brown; scales obovate, obtuse, striated; seeds brown-black. W China. 'Pendula': pyramidal to 2m, convexly weeping; lvs tinged blue. var. ***aurantiaca*** (Mast.) Boom. ORANGE SPRUCE. Shoots deep orange, becoming grey. Cones shining brown; seed scales rhombic-ovoid, striated. China (W Sichuan). var. ***retroflexa*** (Mast.) Cheng. TAPAO SHAN SPRUCE. Bark greyer than species type. Shoots orange-yellow, becoming grey, glabrous. Lvs acute, spreading. Cones 8–13×2.5–4cm; seed scales finely striate. China (SW Sichuan). Z6.

***P. balfouriana*** Rehd. & Wils. To 40m, similar to *P. purpurea*. Crown dense, but less so than *P. purpurea*; upper shoots level not erect; bark orange, finely flaky. Shoots densely pubesc., orange or pink-brown. Lvs 1–1.5cm×1.5–2mm, moderately flattened, green-grey above with some stomata, greyer beneath with more stomata. Cones larger than *P. purpurea*, 5–9×2–2.5cm, with broader, flatter scales, purple with violet brown. SW China (W Sichuan, E Tibet). var. ***hirtella*** (Rehd. & Wils.) Cheng ex Y.L. Chen. Branchlets densely hairy. Lvs longer, to 2cm, much brighter blue than species type. Cones slightly larger, to 10cm, purple-green. SW China (NW Sichuan). Z6.

***P. brachytyla*** (Franch.) Pritz. SARGENT SPRUCE. To 40m; trunk to 1.5m diam. Bark grey or purple-grey, becoming scaly. Crown conic, becoming domed. Branches horizontal with upward-growing apices; branchlets variably pendulous. Shoots beige to yellow-brown, glabrous or slightly downy, pulvini small. Buds conic-ovoid, pale brown, slightly resinous, to 5mm. Lvs 10–12.5×1.5mm, slightly imbricate above, spreading to sides and below shoot, flattened, lustrous green above, vivid white beneath with 2 broad stomatal bands, apex acute or obtuse. Cones 6–12cm, cylindric, green or purple, ripening dark brown; scales broadly obovate, often with an acute or wavy apex. SW China, E Assam. var. ***complanata*** (Mast.) Rehd. Bark light grey. Cones to 14cm; seed scales truncate or obtuse. SW China. Z8.

***P. breweriana*** Wats. BREWER'S SPRUCE. To 35m, to 20m in cult., slow growing. Bark smooth, grey or purple-grey, becoming scaly. Crown ovoid-conic. Branches horizontal, apices upward-pointing, branchlets vertically pendulous, to 2.5m long. Young trees sparse, open, not pendulous. Shoot pubesc. ridged, red-brown to buff, becoming grey. Buds conic, obtuse, red-brown, to 6mm, resinous. Lvs flattened, obtuse, 2.5–3.5cm, 1–5–2cm on young trees, glossy deep green above, 2 white stomatal bands beneath, somewhat curved, radial on hanging shoots and imbricate above, spreading below on level branch leaders. Cones 8–14×2–2.5cm, opening to 3–4cm, cylindric, purple then red-brown, resinous; seed scales large, well spaced, obovate, apex smoothly rounded; seeds black, 3mm. N California and S Oregon (Siskiyou Mts). Z6.

***P. chihuahuana*** Martinez. To 30m. Bark silver-grey, flaking in large scales. Branches horizontal; shoots very stout, densely branched, variably pendulous, pale yellow-brown. Buds to 8mm; bud scales acute. Lvs blue-green, to 20×1.7mm, stout, 3–6 stomatal lines above and beneath, curved, acuminate, with a hard, very sharp apex, spreading radially. Cones 7–14×3cm, fusiform-cylindric, glossy yellow-brown; scales numerous, densely packed, stiff, thick, obovate, apically obtuse, margin smoothly rounded. NW Mexico (Chihuahua, Durango, scattered and rare). Z8.

***P. crassifolia*** Komar. To 25m, crown conic-columnar, branches level or ascending. Shoots pale orange-yellow, often bloomed; buds ovoid, 9mm. Lvs stout, 12–22×1.5–2.5mm, rigid, more or less radial, straight or somewhat curved forwards, green with stomata on all faces. Cones 7–11×2–3cm; scales rounded, broad. NW China (Nei Monggol, Qinghai, Gansu; mts). Not certain in cult., young trees from seed imported from China since 1970 as this species have lvs to 35mm, and may be wrongly identified. Z5.

***P. engelmannii*** Parry ex Engelm. ENGELMANN SPRUCE. To 45m. Bark thin, buff, splitting into small plates, resinous. Crown conic to narrowly acute. Branches in dense whorls, often slightly upward-pointing, branchlets variably pendulous. Shoots yellow-brown becoming red-brown, finely glandular-pubesc. Buds ovoid-conic, to 6mm. Lvs straight or curved, blue-green or glaucous blue, soft, flexible, apex acute or obtuse, 1.5–3cm, forward-pointing, mostly radial. Cones 3–8×2–2.5cm, ovoid to cylindric, pale yellow-brown, to red-brown; scales very thin, oblong, irregularly toothed; seeds black, 2mm, wings 10mm. Western N America (mts). 'Argentea': lvs grey, tinged silver. 'Fendleri': branches pendulous; lvs to 3cm. 'Glauca': attractive upright; lvs with vivid blue sheen. 'Microphylla': dwarf, bushy, compact. 'Snake': highly irregular upright; tinged blue. f.f. *glauca* hort. ex Beissn. Lvs intense glaucous blue; most cvs selected from this form. ssp. ***mexicana*** (Martinez) P. Schmidt. Lvs longer, 2–4cm, stiffer and sharper; cone scales slightly thicker. Mexico (rare in Nuevo Leon & Chihuahua). Z3.

***P. farreri*** Page & Rushforth. BURMESE SPRUCE; FARRER SPRUCE. Related to *P. brachytyla*; to 35m, branches level, branchlets arched-drooping with pendulous pale brown shoots slightly pubescent at first. Lvs forward pointing over top of shoot and depressed below, 17–24×1mm, flattened, glossy green above without stomata, vivid white stomatal bands below. Cones 6–12×2cm, scales more rounded than *P. brachytyla*, margin wavy. Upper Burma, Yunnan border. Z8.

***P. ×fennica*** (Reg.) Komar. *(P. abies × P. obovata.)* Natural hybrid intermediate between parent species. NE Sweden E to Ural Mts. Z3.

***P. glauca*** (Moench) Voss. WHITE SPRUCE. To 25m; trunk to 2m diam. Bark light grey becoming darker with white cracks. Crown conic. Branches level or descending, rarely pendulous, with upward-growing tips; branchlets dense, bunched. Shoots off-white, becoming buff then brown, glabrous, lustrous. Buds ovate, brown, to 6mm; bud scales keeled, mucronate. Lvs stiff, dull blue-green, 10–18mm, sharply acute, imbricate to assurgent above shoot, spreading at sides and below. Cones 3–5×1cm; ovoid-cylindric, tapering at ends, green becoming light brown; scales very thin obtuse, margin rounded, flexible. Canada, far NE US. Several more or less globose dwarf cvs (e.g. 'Echiniformis', 'Lilliput', 'Little Globe', 'Nana'). 'Aureospicata': young shoots yellow, later green. 'Coerulea' ('Caerulea'): to 2m, densely pyramidal, lvs tinged silver-blue. 'Hendersonii': similar to 'Coerulea', young shoots lateral, later pendulous. 'Parva': prostrate, dense, laterally flat crowned; lvs tinged blue. 'Pendula': weeping, upright leader with very pendulous red branches; lvs tinged blue. 'Pinsapoides': upright strong-grower; lvs tinged blue. 'Sander's Fastigiate': dwarf, tight, narrow upright; 'Laurin' is similar. var. ***albertiana*** (S. Br.) Sarg. To 45m. Shoots pubesc. Buds slightly resinous. Lvs longer, to 2.5cm. Cones ovoid, to 4cm. Northwest N America (Canadian Rocky Mts.). 'Alberta Globe': mutation of 'Conica', globose. 'Conica': to 4m, dense, conical; lvs permanently juvenile, 11–15×0.5mm, very slender, curved. 'Elegans Compacta': mutation of 'Conica', more conical, twigs tinged yellow. 'Gnom': slow-growing mutation of 'Conica' (to 5cm p.a.). 'Laurin': small, dense, mutation of 'Conica'. var. ***porsildii*** Raup. Short lvs; pubesc. shoots. Alaska & Yukon. Z2.

***P. glehnii*** (F. Schmidt) Mast. SAKHALIN SPRUCE. To 30m. Bark dark brown, flaking in thin plates. Crown narrowly conic, very dense. Shoots red, becoming purple-brown, deeply furrowed, bristly pubesc. Buds ovoid, red-brown, resinous, to 6mm. Lvs densely arranged, green to blue-green above, with 2 white stomatal bands beneath, obtuse, 0.5–1.5cm, imbricate above shoot, spreading to sides and below. Cones 4–8cm, cylindric, purple, bloomed violet, ripening brown; scales densely arranged, obtuse, waved, sometimes irregularly toothed. Japan (Hokkaido), Sakhalin. Z4.

***P. jezoensis*** (Sieb. & Zucc.) Carr. YEZO SPRUCE. To 35m, rarely 45m. Bark brown, becoming purple-brown, flaking in round plates. Crown conic. Branches level, branchlets more or less pendulous. Shoots white to light yellow, glabrous, lustrous, darkening with age. Buds ovoid-conic, glossy brown, resinous. Lvs glossy, 1–2cm, flattened, 1.5mm broad, dark green above, duller beneath with 2 white to blue-white stomatal bands, acute, imbricate above stem, spreading below, and to sides, pointing forward toward shoot apex. Cones 4–7cm, cylindric, yellowish-brown; scales oblong, thin, stiff, margins fine-toothed. NE Manchuria, E Siberia, N Korea, Japan (Hokkaido), Sakhalin. 'Yatsubusa': dense and rounded; lvs vivid blue and green bicolor. 'Yosawa': dwarf, upright and regular. ssp. ***hondoensis*** (Mayr) P. Schmidt To 50m. Shoots darker, orange, to red-brown with age; buds bright purple, very resinous. Lvs silver-white below. Cones darker red-brown, with stiffer scales than type. Japan (Honshu). 'Aurea': young lvs gold, later brown, then green. Z2.

***P. koyamai*** Shiras. To 25m; trunk to 50cm diam. Bark grey-brown, flaking in thin, oblong scales. Crown conic. Branches dense, apices growing upwards. Shoots buff, becoming purple-brown, glabrous or glandular-pubesc. Buds conic-ovoid, obtuse, brown, to 4mm, very resinous; bud scales acuminate. Lvs densely arranged, assurgent, blue-green or grey-green mostly curved, acute or obtuse, not sharp-pointed, 7–15mm, stomatal lines distinct above. Cones 4–9cm, ovoid-cylindric to cylindric, light green, becoming brown; scales thin, ovate, obtuse, striated, finely small-toothed. Japan (C Honshu). Z6. *P. koraiensis Nak.* has slightly longer, more spreading lvs and broader cones, but is only doubtfully distinct. To 30m. N Korea, NE Manchuria, SE USSR. Z5.

***P. likiangensis*** (Franch.) Pritz. To 50m. Bark grey, smooth, becoming scaly or shallow-fissured. Crown open, broad conic. Branches level to ascending. Shoots buff or yellow-brown, glabrous or slightly downy; pulvini twisted. Buds conic, purple-brown, 4–6mm, resinous; bud scales short, acuminate. Lvs 8–15mm, acuminate, sharp, dark green to blue-green, flattened, though keeled above and beneath, 2 blue-white stomatal lines beneath, 2 faint bands above, forward-growing, loosely imbricate above shoot, spreading below. Cones oval-cylindric, 7–13×3cm, red to purple; scales thin, soft, obtuse, obovate, margins finely toothed, truncate-acuminate to acute. SW China (S Sichuan, W Yunnan), SE Tibet, E Assam). var. ***montigena*** (Mast.) Cheng ex Chen. Lvs short, 6–15mm; cones intermediate between species type and *P. balfouriana*; may be hybrid between these. Most cultivated trees named as this are *P. asperata* wrongly labelled. SW China (W Sichuan). Z8.

***P. ×lutzii*** Little. (*P. sitchensis* × *P. glauca.*) Natural hybrid, intermediate between parents; very hardy in cold wet sites, used for forestry in Iceland. Alaska (Kenai Peninsula). Z3.

***P. mariana*** (Mill.) BSP. BLACK SPRUCE. To 20m, rarely more. Bark red-brown to grey-brown, exfoliating in thin flakes. Crown conic, often untidy in cult. Branches usually downswept; lower branches often layering normally. Shoots red-brown, red glandular-pubesc.; pulvini flattened. Buds purple-brown, acute, 6mm, not resinous. Lvs densely arranged, 0.5–1.5cm, blue-green above, off-white stomatal stripes beneath, stiff, obtuse. Cones 2–4×1.5cm, fusiform, mauve, becoming grey-brown, persisting on parent for several years; scales woody, rounded apically, margins finely toothed; seeds dark brown. Northern N America. 'Argenteovariegata': some lvs almost completely white. 'Aurea': lvs tinged gold. 'Beissneri': dwarf, slow-growing to 5m, similar to 'Doumettii', broader, lvs tinged blue. 'Beissneri Compacta': dwarf to 2m. 'Doumettii': dwarf to 6m, globose-conic when young, becoming irregular; crown dense; lvs bright blue-green. 'Empetroides': dwarf, procumbent, branches sparse. 'Ericoides': dwarf, procumbent, lvs tinged blue. 'Fastigiata': conical dwarf, branches slender, ascending. 'Nana': very dwarf and globose to 50cm, slow-growing to 3cm p.a., more than one clone in cult. 'Pendula': upright leader, branches weeping. 'Semiprostrata': short-stemmed, semi-prostrate dwarf. Z2.

***P. mariorika*** hort. (*P. mariana* × *P. omorika.*) 'Kobold': dense and globose to 1×1m in 20 years, shoots stiff, tinged red. 'Machala': spreading dwarf to 50cm×1m, middle branches semi-erect, lvs with blue tint.

***P. martinezii*** Patterson. Related to *P. chihuahuana*; to 30m, crown open, irregular cylindric with age, similar to *P. smithiana*; bark thin, scaly, grey. Shoots glabrous, yellow; buds to 1cm. Lvs all round shoot, directed forward, 16–27×1.5mm, bright glossy green, apex sharply acuminate. Cones 9–16×3cm, scales thick, rigid, larger and less numerous and congested than in *P. chihuahuana*, to 2cm wide, orange-brown. NE Mexico (Nuevo Leon, very rare and endangered, only two small groves known). Z8.

***P. maximowiczii*** Reg. ex Mast. To 25m. Bark red-brown, rough, becoming fissured, flaking in thin scales. Crown dense, conic. Branches with upward-growing tips. Shoots glabrous, yellow-brown, becoming greyer and lighter. Buds ovoid, obtuse, red-brown, to 5mm, not or slightly resinous. Lvs sparse, to 15mm, lustrous dark green, acute, straight, radial above shoot, spreading below. Cones to 7cm, cylindric-oblong, light green, becoming brown; seeds scales entire, obtuse. Japan (Honshu). Z7. Most trees in GB labelled as this species are hybrids.

***P. meyeri*** Rehd. & Wils. Very similar to *P. asperata*; to 30m. Shoots yellow-brown; lvs 1.5–3cm, slightly flattened, acute, blue- or grey-green. Cones 6–9×3cm, pale brown, scales rounded, matt, striated. NW China (Hebei, Shanxi, N Shaanxi, E Nei Monggol.)

***P. morrisonicola*** Hayata. TAIWAN SPRUCE. To 40m. Similar to *P. wilsonii*, but shoots sparse, pendulous only 2–3mm diam., pale yellow-grey, glabrous. Buds to 3–4mm, subtending leaf projecting widely. Lvs 10–20×0.8mm, slender, sharply acuminate, glossy dark green, adpressed to shoot above, spreading below. Cones 5–8×1.5–2cm, oblong-cylindric; scales obovate, obtuse, apex smoothly rounded. Taiwan. Z8.

***P. neoveitchii*** Mast. To 30m, crown conic to ovoid-columnar with age; bark grey-brown, scaly. Shoots stout, glabrous or slightly pubescent, yellow-brown. Lvs similar to *P. torano*, stout, 15–20×2mm, spreading radially, curved forwards, dark yellow-green, very sharp pointed. Cones 8–14×4cm, green ripening yellow-brown, very stout, with few, very large, thick heavy scales to 3cm wide, margin rounded, wavy. Seed 7×4.5mm. Largest cone scales and seeds of any spruce. C China (NW Hubei, Shaanxi, NE Sichuan, Shanxi; rare). Trees from Chinese seed sent under this name since 1970 are *P. wilsonii*. Z5.

***P. obovata*** Ledeb. SIBERIAN SPRUCE. To 35m. Bark purple-grey, exfoliating in fine plates. Branches level to downswept; branchlets mostly pendulous. Shoots buff to orange-brown, thinly to densely glandular-hairy. Buds ovoid or conic, orange-brown, to 5mm, resinous, the subtending leaf projecting widely. Lvs shiny green, to 2cm, acuminate, adpressed to shoot above, slightly spreading to sides and below shoot. Cones 5–8×2cm, ovoid-cylindric, green or purple, ripening mid-brown; scales obovate, broadly obtuse, glossy apex smoothly rounded, 10–15mm wide. N Europe (E Finland) to E Siberia. Z1.

***P. omorika*** (Pančić) Purkyne. SERBIAN SPRUCE. To 35m. Bark orange-brown to purple-brown, becoming cracked and flaking in fine plates. Crown conic to narrowly spire-like. Branches downswept near bole, bowing upwards at tips; branchlets dense, moderately pendulous. Shoots buff to red-brown, becoming darker, with dark brown to black glandular hairs. Buds globose to ovate, pale brown, to 5mm. Lvs 10–20×1.5–2mm, flattened, keeled on midrib, dark green to blue-green, with 2 silver-grey stomatal bands beneath, upper lvs adpressed to stem, side and lower lvs spreading. Cones 3–7×2cm, fusiform, purple, ripening red-brown, often persistent for more than one year, closely adpressed, broadly obtuse, finely irregularly toothed. Yugoslavia. 'Expansa': vigorous procumbent dwarf, branch ends slightly ascending. 'Frohnleiten': irregular, loose dwarf, to 40cm after 10 years. 'Gnom': broadly conical dwarf, slow-growing to 3cm p.a. 'Minima': short-branched dwarf. 'Nana': globose to broadly conic-pyramidal dwarf. 'Pendula': slender and upright, branches pendulous. 'Pendula Bruns': similar to 'Pendula', branches more pendulous. 'Pimoko': dense, irregular and low-growing to 30×40cm. Z5.

***P. orientalis*** (L.) Link. ORIENTAL SPRUCE; CAUCASIAN SPRUCE. To 50m; bole to 1.5m diam. Bark smooth, pink-grey, becoming cracked, forming small raised plates. Crown conic, dense, becoming ovoid-columnar with age; branches slightly ascending. Shoots pubesc., red-brown, becoming greyer. Buds red-brown, ovoid-conic, to 5mm, not resinous. Lvs 0.5–0.8cm, the shortest of any spruce, slightly flattened, apex blunt, bevelled, dark green, obtuse, adpressed to stem above, slightly spreading to sides and below. Male fls deep red, female fls purple. Cones 5×9–1.5cm, purple, ripening, brown, cylindric-conic to fusiform; scales obovate, broadly obtuse, entire, to 15mm wide. Caucasus, NE Turkey. 'Atrovirens': lvs very dark green. 'Aurea': young lvs gold, later dark green, with gold tint. 'Aurea Compacta': broadly pyramidal and compact semi-dwarf; upper lvs gold, lower lvs green. 'Compacta': broadly conical dwarf. 'Early Gold': mutation of 'Aurea', lvs also green-gold in winter. 'Gowdy': narrowly conical to 3.5m; lvs small, rich green. 'Gracilis': very dense dwarf, oval in growth, to 6m, slow-growing (to 7cm p.a.). 'Nana': globose dwarf to 1m, very slow-growing (to 2.5cm p.a.). 'Nigra Compacta': narrow and compact to 2m, lvs glossy dark green. 'Nutans': spreading, weeping and irregular in growth, lvs very dark green. 'Pendula': compact and slow-growing; twigs nodding. Z5.

***P. pungens*** Engelm. BLUE SPRUCE; COLORADO SPRUCE. To 40m+; to 25m in cult. Bark purple-grey, deeply grooved, forming thick scales. Crown dense, conic, becoming columnar-conic. Lower branches downswept in older trees. Shoots light brown to orange, glabrous, ridged. Buds ovoid-conic, acute, buff, to 5mm; bud scales paper-thin, reflexed, forming a rosette at bud base. Lvs 2–2.5cm, radial, assurgent, grey-green to bright pale blue, thickly glaucous, stiff, sharply acuminate. Cones 6–12×2.5–3cm, oblong-cylindric, green bloomed violet, ripening light brown; scales thick based with thin tips, flexible, emarginate, finely toothed and undulate. US (S Rocky Mts). Over 40 cvs in Europe and America, mostly with blue-tinted needles, some with green or yellow; of the blue upright selections, notable example include the short-needled 'Microphylla', 'Endtz', 'Oldenburg', the very blue 'Koster' and 'Moerheim' and the compact 'Fat Albert'; notable blue-tinted dwarfs include the globose 'Glauca Globosa' and 'Pumila' and the slow-growing 'Montgomery'. 'Glauca Procumbens' is almost recumbent and 'Glauca Pendula' an irregular, graceful weeping form; notable yellow and green selections include the sulphur 'Aurea', 'Lucky Strike' (also with profuse cones) and the dark green 'Viridis'. f. ***glauca*** (Reg.) Beissn. The group name for all plants with lvs very glaucous to blue-grey. Z3.

***P. purpurea*** Mast. PURPLE-CONED SPRUCE. To 45m, less in cult. Bark orange-brown, flaking; scaly in old trees. Crown dense, columnar to conic; apices of upper branches forming competing leaders at crown apex. Shoots pale brown, dense, long pubesc. Buds conic. Lvs deep green above, blue-white beneath, moderately flattened, acute or obtuse, to 1.5cm, adpressed above shoot, parted below. Cones 3–6×2cm, ovoid, purple, bloomed violet ripening purple-brown; scales rhombic, strongly undulate. China (NW Sichuan, S Gansu). Z5.

***P. rubens*** Sarg. RED SPRUCE. To 30m; bole to 1m diam. Bark purple-brown, becoming red-brown, flaking in fine, concave plates. Crown dense, narrowly conic. Lower branches bowed, ascending at tips. Shoots buff, pubesc., becoming glabrous. Buds ovoid, acute, red-brown, to 5mm, slightly resinous; bud scales to 5mm, papery, acuminate. Lvs grass-green, becoming darker, glossy, 10–15×1.5mm, crowded on upper part of stem, parted below. Cones 2–5cm, ovoid-oblong, lustrous red-brown, soon falling or occasionally persistent 2–4 years; seed scales convex, broadly obtuse, stiff and woody, irregularly finely toothed. Northern N America. 'Nana': broadly conic dwarf; young shoots spreading, very short, tinged red. 'Virgata': similar to *P. abies* 'Virgata', sparse and slender. Z3.

***P. schrenkiana*** Fisch. & Mey. Similar to *P. smithiana*. To 45m. Bark grey. Crown dense, conic to columnar. Branches level, rarely downswept or pendulous. Shoots stout, beige, glabrous, occasionally pubesc. Buds ovoid, light brown, to 10mm, not resinous; basal bud scales loosely adpressed, acuminate to obtuse; the leaf subtending the bud projecting widely. Lvs stiff, straight or bowed, grass-green, acute or obtuse, 2–3cm, more numerous above shoot. Cones 6–11×2–3cm, ovoid-cylindric, often slightly curved, purple-brown, resinous; seed scales obovate, 12–15mm broad, margins smoothly rounded. C Asia (E Tien Shan). ssp. ***tianschanica*** (Rupr.) Bykov. Lvs 1–2cm. Cones less than 7cm; seed scales obovate. C Asia (W Tien Shan). Z4.

***P. sitchensis*** (Bong.) Carr. SITKA SPRUCE. To 90m, bole to 5m diam., in wild; already to 60×2.5m in cult. Bark red-grey, exfoliating in coarse scales. Crown broad, conic, branches straight, slightly ascending, branchlets moderately pendulous. Shoots light yellow-brown, becoming darker, grooved, glabrous. Buds ovoid, obtuse, brown, to 5mm, resinous; bud scales adpressed to bud. Lvs 15–25mm, dark green, with 2 blue-white stomatal bands beneath and none or few fine lines above, stiff, acuminate, sharply pointed, flattened, slightly keeled, imbricate above stem, spreading to sides and below. Cones 3–10×1.5cm when closed, opening to 3.5cm broad, cylindric-oblong, pale green, ripening beige; scales very thin oblong-rhombic, undulate, margin serrate; bracts to 8mm long, the longest of any spruce, very occasionally slightly exserted. N America (Pacific Coast, Alaska to California). 'Compacta': broadly conic, dense dwarf to 2m, branches spreading, young shoots tinted yellow. 'Microphylla': dwarf, very slow-growing to 25cm after 10 years, upright and narrowly conic. 'Nana': slow-growing dwarf, habit open; lvs tinted blue. 'Speciosa': branches dense and ascending; lvs tinted blue, weak in growth. 'Strypemonde': compact and very slow-growing dwarf; lvs tinted blue. 'Tenas' ('Papoose'): broadly conical, compact dwarf to 75cm, blue striation below. Z7.

***P. smithiana*** (Wallich) Boiss. MORINDA SPRUCE; HIMALAYAN SPRUCE. To 55m, to 37m in cult. Bole 2m diam. Bark dull grey-purple, grooved, splitting into round scales. Crown conic, becoming columnar with age. Branches horizontal, ascending at apices. Shoots stout, pendulous, pale brown, becoming greyer, glabrous. Buds ovoid to ovoid-conic, lustrous purple-brown, to 1cm, resinous, the leaf subtending the bud spreading widely. Lvs loosely radial, 3–4(–5)cm, dark green, apex acuminate. Cones 10–16cm, rarely 20cm, cylindric, curved, tapered at ends, shiny pale green, ripening brown, resinous; scales semi-circular, stiff and woody, entire, to 2.5cm wide. Seeds large, 6mm. W Himalaya (Afghanistan to C Nepal). Zone 8, selected clones hardy to Z7.

***P. spinulosa*** (Griff.) Henry. SIKKIM SPRUCE. To 65m, to 35m in cult. Bark pale grey, rough, flaking in square plates, fissured. Crown open, broadly conic, becoming domed-columnar in old trees. Shoots arching down, then pendulous, off-white to grey-pink, glabrous. Buds ovoid, obtuse, brown, to 5mm, slightly resinous. Lvs 1.5–3.5cm, flattened, 1mm broad, flexible, shiny, dark green above with few or no stomatal lines, 2 bright blue-white stomatal bands beneath, acute, growing forward above stem, widely spreading to sides and below; radial on pendulous shoots. Cones 6–12×2.5cm, cylindric-conic, curved, green, ripening shiny red- or orange-brown; seed scales leathery, flexible, rhombic, margins finely toothed, 10–15mm wide. E Himalaya (Sikkim, Bhutan to W/C Assam, grading into *P. likiangensis*). Z8.

***P. torano*** (K. Koch) Koehne. TIGER-TAIL SPRUCE. To 45m, to 25m in cult. Bole to 1m diam. Bark grey-brown, rough, flaking in scales. Crown dense, conic. Branches more or less ascending, becoming pendulous in very old trees. Shoots stout, beige, glabrous. Buds conic, acute, 5–10mm long, not resinous. Lvs 12–25×2mm, very stout, radial, very stiff, extremely sharp, shiny yellow-green, not flattened. Cones 6–12×4cm, oblong-ovoid, sessile, yellow-green, ripening red- to orange-brown; scales elliptic, leathery, broadly obtuse, margins finely toothed or entire. S Japan. Z6.

***P. wilsonii*** Mast. WILSON'S SPRUCE. To 45m to 20m in cult. Bark red-brown, flaky, later greyer, exfoliating in large, thin scales. Crown conic, becoming columnar. Shoots moderately slender, off-white or pale grey-buff, glabrous; pulvini minute. Buds ovoid, obtuse, shiny brown, to 5mm, slightly resinous, the leaf subtending the bud spreading widely. Lvs grass-green, acute, pointed, straight or slightly curved, 10–18mm, imbricate above stem, spreading at sides, parted below. Cones 4–7×2m, oblong-cylindric, green, often tinged purple, ripening, light brown; scales nearly circular, occasionally obtuse-rhombic, entire, margins sometimes finely toothed. China (NW Hubei, NW Sichuan, S Gansu, Shanxi). Z5.

***P. abies*** var. ***alpestris*** (Brügger) P. Schmidt. See *P. alpestris*.
***P. albertiana*** S. Br. See *P. glauca* var. *albertiana*.
***P. ascendens*** Patschke. See *P. brachytyla*.
***P. aurantiaca*** Mast. See *P. asperata* var. *aurantiaca*.
***P. bicolor*** (Maxim.) Mayr. See *P. alcoquiana*.
***P. complanata*** Mast. See *P. brachytyla* var. *complanata*.
***P. excelsa*** (Lam.) Link. See *P. abies*.
***P. heterolepsis*** Rehd. & Wils. See *P. asperata*.
***P. hondoensis*** Mayr. See *P. jezoensis* ssp. *hondoensis*.
***P. koraiensis*** Nak.See *P. koyamai*.
***P. likiangensis*** var. ***balfouriana*** (Rehd. & Wils.) Hillier. See *P. balfouriana*.
***P. likiangensis*** var. ***hirtella*** (Rehd. & Wils.) Cheng ex Y. Chen. See *P. balfouriana*.
***P. likiangensis*** var. ***purpurea*** (Mast.) Dallim. & Jackson. See *P. purpurea*.
***P. likiangensis*** var. ***rubescens*** Rehd. & Wils. See *P. balfouriana*.
***P. mexicana*** Martinez. See *P. engelmanii* ssp. *mexicana*.
***P. montigena*** Mast. See *P. likiangensis* var. *montigena*.
***P. obovata*** var. ***alpestris*** (Brügger) Henry. See *P. alpestris*.
***P. polita*** (Sieb. & Zucc.) Carr. See *P. torano*.
***P. retroflexa*** Mast. See *P. asperata* var. *retroflexa*.
***P. shirasawae*** Hayashi. See *P. alcoquiana* var. *acicularis*.
***P. tianschanica*** Rupr. See *P. schrenkiana* ssp. *tianschanica*.
***P. watsoniana*** Mast. See *P. wilsonii*.

**Pickeringia** Nutt. ex Torr. & A. Gray (For C. Pickering (1805–1878), American botanist, zoologist and anthropologist.) CHAPARRAL PEA; STINGAREE-BUSH. Leguminosae (Papilionoideae). 1 species, a spiny, evergreen shrub, 1–3m. Branches spreading widely, sparsely puberulent or glabrous, olive green. Leaves alternate, trifoliolate, crowded, subsessile; leaflets 0.8–1.5cm, glabrous or nearly so, bright green above, blue-green beneath, oblanceolate to obovate, entire, tough. Flowers axillary, solitary; calyx about 0.6cm; cor. 1.5–2cm, crimson, red-purple or rose, with a triangle of mustard-yellow at base of standard; stamens 10, separate. Fr. to 5cm, flat, linear. Late spring–summer. Southwest N America (California, Baja California, New Mexico). Z9.

CULTIVATION Found on dry, rocky, mountain slopes and ridges, *P. montana* is a xerophytic shrub, spreading by means of an extensive network of underground stems. It is often one of the first species to reestablish itself after bush fires. In cultivation it requires conditions that approximate to those of its natural habitat, i.e. a dry, sunny site on gritty soils with only brief exposure to a few degrees of frost, if any. Propagate by seed and division.

***P. montana*** Nutt. ex Torr. & A. Gray. As for the genus.

**Picrasma** Bl. Simaroubaceae. 8 species of deciduous trees; buds naked and pubescent. Leaves alternate, odd-pinnate, estipulate, crowded at end of branchlets. Flowers small, unisexual and bisexual on the same plant, in loose axillary cymes; sepals ovate, imbricate, persistent; petals 4–5, oblong, valvate; stamens 4–5, inserted at base of the 4–5-lobed disc, longer than petals with ovate anthers; carpels free, united by the slender style at the apex into slender stigmas. Fruit obovoid or subglobose berries, endocarp thin. Tropical America, Indomalesia. Z10.

CULTIVATION As for *Quassia*.

***P. ailanthoides*** (Bunge) Planch. Slender tree to 12m; young shoots red-brown with yellow spots. Lvs to 38cm, alternate, pinnate, glabrous, leaflets to 10cm, 9–13, glossy green, ovate, oblique at base, rounded or acute at apex, margins sharp-toothed, short-stalked. Fls 1cm across, green, in loose clusters 15–20cm long and wide. Fr. 6–7mm, globose-ovoid, with persistent cal. Spring. Japan, N China, Korea.

***P. excelsa*** Roxb. Tree to 24m. Lvs 30cm+, glandular-hairy, leaflets many, coarsely toothed. Fls in much-branched panicles. Samara 5×1.3cm, twisted at base, copper-red, strongly veined. India.

***P. quassioides*** (Hamilt.) Benn. See *P. ailanthoides*.

**Picridium** Desf.
***P. tingitanum*** (L.) Desf. See *Reichardia tingitana*.

**Picris** L. BITTERWEED; OX-TONGUE. (Name used by Theophrastus and Dioscorides for a bitter herb.) Compositae. Some 45 species of annual to perennial herbs with milky sap. Leaves alternate, simple, entire, toothed or pinnatisect. Capitula ligulate, solitary or several in corymbs; receptacle more or less flat, naked; phyllaries in several series, imbricate, outer shorter, spreading; florets hermaphrodite, yellow, outer usually with red stripe beneath. Fruit a curved, ribbed cypsela; pappus of 2 rows of plumose, deciduous hairs. Mediterranean, Asia, African nuts. Z6.

CULTIVATION The European species are amongst those legions of little yellow composites found as widespread weeds in dry grassland, wasteland, rubbish tips and railway embankments, and in vineyards; they are sometimes offered as wild flowers and are possibly useful in habitat as an indicator of calcareous soils. Sow *in situ* in any soil.

***P.echioides*** L. BRISTLY OX-TONGUE. Spiny annual or bienn., to 1m. Lvs to 25×10cm, elliptic to lanceolate or oblanceolate, petiole winged, margin, upper lvs amplexicaul, sessile. Phyllaries linear-lanceolate to ovate, bristly hairy, inner longer. Fr. 5–7mm. Summer. S Europe.

***P.hieracioides*** L. Bienn. or perenn., to 1m. Lvs to 14×5cm, lanceolate to oblanceolate, tapering to petiole, entire or toothed, upper lvs sessile, amplexicaul, toothed. Phyllaries lanceolate to narrowly elliptic, outer shorter. Fr. 3–6mm; pappus cream. Summer. Europe, Asia, naturalized elsewhere.

***P.kamtschatica*** Ledeb. Stout annual, to 105m, with hooked hairs. Lvs to 20×9cm, lanceolate to oblanceolate, bristly, serrate. Phyllaries linear to lanceolate, with black hairs. Fr. red-brown; pappus light-grey. Summer. Transcaucasia.

**Pieris** D. Don (Named for the *Pierides*, (Muses).) Ericaceae. Some 7 species of evergreen trees, shrubs or ligneous vines. Branches often terete; bark usually grey or brown, longitudinally striate. New growth often tinged red or bronze; leaves alternate, persistent, entire or serrated, texture leathery, sparsely hirsute, the hairs gland-tipped, often glaucous, petiolate. Flowers often scented, in erect or drooping, terminal or axillary racemes or panicles; bract usually 1, bracteoles usually 2; calyx lobes 5, valvate; corolla white, pitcher-shaped; lobes 5, overlapping, short, usually glabrous on both surfaces; stamens 10, filaments flat, papillose, anthers ovoid, dehiscing through large, elliptic pores; ovary subspherical, glabrous to thickly hirsute, locules 5, ovules numerous; style pillar-shaped; stigma truncate to capitate. Fruit subspherical, erect, sutures 5; seeds numerous; brown, small, testa loose, thin. E Asia, Himalaya, E US, W Indies.

CULTIVATION Decorative evergreens for the shrub border, peat terrace and especially for the stable and sheltered environment of the woodland garden; smaller and slow-growing species such as *P.japonica* and its cultivars are amenable to cultivation in pots or tubs, especially useful for those who garden on alkaline soils. Grown for their dense panicles of firm textured, waxy flowers, reminiscent of those of lily-of-the-valley (*Convallaria*) and usually white, although a number of pink flowered forms of *P.japonica* are available. In some species, the flowers are sweetly scented, as in *P.japonica*; in others, their subtle fragrance deserves investigation at close quarters. The young spring foliage however, is their primary attraction, being strikingly coloured in brilliant shades of red, red-bronze, and copper-red. The hybrid *P.*'Forest Flame' is exceptionally beautiful, emerging a glossy bright red and fading through pink and cream before becoming dark green at maturity. *P.formosa* is the most frost tender of the genus, tolerating temperatures to −10°C/14°F. The remaining species are hardy at least to −15°C/5°F, with *P.japonica* tolerating temperatures to −20°C/−4°F, and *P.floribunda* to −25°C/−13°F.

Grow in moisture-retentive, well-drained soils that are lime-free and humus-rich, in dappled shade or in sun (where flowers are carried in great abundance). Give a position with protection to the north and east, sheltered from strong winds and frost; the young foliage is particularly vulnerable to frost, although damaged specimens will usually regenerate giving a second, less spectacular display of coloured foliage. Maintain a mulch of organic matter such as leafmould to conserve water and to protect the roots from frost; flower panicles formed in autumn may drop prematurely due to frost or insufficient soil moisture. Remove frost-damaged growth as soon as possible. Deadheading after flowering is beneficial where practicable. Old overgrown specimens may be slowly rejuvenated by annual removal of one or two branches over a period of several years.

Propagate species by seed sown in spring on fine moss peat; keep moist and shaded in the cool glasshouse: progeny may not come true. Take semi-ripe or softwood basal cuttings in summer and treat with 0.8% IBA, root in a closed case with bottom heat. Softwood cuttings from forced plants give better rooting. Also by layering. *Pieris* spp. sometimes succumb to an incurable fungus infection, and fungal leafspots may be disfiguring in wet seasons. Treat the latter with a systemic fungicide. Also susceptible to *Phytophthora* root rot.

***P.floribunda*** (Pursh ex Sims) Benth. & Hook. FETTER BUSH. Shrub to *c*2m. Bark grey to grey-brown. Twigs terete to somewhat angled, thinly to thickly downy and stiff hirsute. Lvs 30–80×10–28mm, alternate, elliptic to ovate, margins serrate and ciliate, apex sharp-tipped, base rounded to broadly wedge-shaped; dull green above, sparsely glandular-hirsute above and beneath; petiole 4–11mm. Fls in dense terminal panicles 5–10cm long; pedicels 2–4.5mm, thickly downy and sparsely glandular-hirsute; bracts 2–9mm, bracteoles 0.9–2.3mm, linear to narrow deltoid; cal. off-white, lobes ovate; cor. 4–7×3–5.5mm, pitcher-shaped, white; fil. 2–3mm long. Fr. 4–6×4–6mm, subglobose to ovoid; seeds 2.5–3.5mm, with 2 inconspicuous wings. Spring. SE US. 'Elongata': hardy; fls in long terminal panicles, later-flowering. 'Karemona': hardy; fls white. 'Spring Snow': growth compact; fls white, early flowering. Z5.

***P.formosa*** (Wallich) D. Don. Shrub or small tree, 2.5–5m exceptionally to *c*7.5m. Young wood glabrous, bark grey to grey-brown. Lvs 25–100×8–35mm, elliptic or obovate, margins finely serrate, apex sharp-tipped or blunt to acuminate or mucronate, base narrowly cuneate to rounded, coriaceous, dark and lustrous green, sparsely glandular-hirsute; petioles 2–16mm. Fls many, in erect to drooping, axillary panicles or racemes or, more rarely, terminal panicles to 15mm; pedicels 2–9mm; bracts 2–5.5mm, bracteoles 0.8–1.8mm; cal. lobes 2–4.5×1–2mm, deltoid, apices sharp-tipped; cor. 4–9×3.5–5.5mm, white, rarely pink-tinged, urceolate to cylindric, long-hairy; fil. 2–4.5mm. Fr. 3–6×4–7mm, globose or subglobose, ovoid, glabrous; seeds 2–3mm. Spring. SW China, Vietnam, Himalaya, Nepal. 'Charles Michael': young growth red; fls large. 'Charles Williams': fls white in large panicles. 'Henry Price': lvs broad, dark green, deep red when young, deeply veined. 'Jermyns': buds red in winter, opening white. 'Wakehurst': to 5.4m, hardy, vigorous; lvs bright red fading to pink before turning deep green, oblong-elliptic to oblanceolate, margins serrated; fls in large clusters. var. ***forrestii*** (Harrow) Airy Shaw. To 3m. New growth glabrous, scarlet. Lvs 6–10cm, elliptic-lanceolate, apex acuminate, margins finely serrate. Fls in drooping, terminal panicles, fragrant; cal. white, lobes lanceolate; cor. 9mm, dull white, scented. Spring. W China (Yunnan), Burma. Z7.

***P.japonica*** (Thunb.) D. Don ex G. Don. LILY OF THE VALLEY BUSH. Shrub or small tree, 2.7–4m. Bark grey to brown; twigs terete or somewhat angled, usually glabrous when young. Lvs 25–100×8–30mm, obovate to lanceolate, margins serrate, coriaceous, apex sharp-tipped to blunt or acuminate, base tapering to narrowly cuneate, emerging pink to red or bronze, hardening dark and lustrous green, sparsely glandular-hirsute. Fls in erect to drooping, axillary racemes or panicles 6–12cm long; pedicels 2–8mm; bracts 1.5–6mm, bracteoles 0.5–2.5mm; cal. often red-brown, lobes deltoid, finely downy on outside; apices sharp-tipped; cor. 5–8×3–4.5mm, urceolate to cylindrical, white, rarely tinged pink; fil. 2.5–4.5mm. Fr. 3–5×4–7mm, subglobose to ovoid, glabrous; seeds 2–3mm. Late winter–spring. Japan, Taiwan, E China. Over 40 cultivars; habit occasionally compact, dense, from slow-growing, low, to tall; young growth often shaded red or bronze, lvs sometimes margined or variegated; fl. colour ranges from white through shades of pink to deep red. Cultivars include: 'Bert Chandler': young lvs pale pink turning glossy yellow, white then dark green. 'Blush': fl. buds pink opening to white tinged rose. 'Brouwer's Beauty': hardy, dense; lvs glossy, dark, margins slightly serrated; fls indigo-purple. 'Cavatine': hardy; fls white, long-lasting, late flowering. 'Compacta': compact, dense, to 1.8m; lvs small. 'Christmas Cheer': fls bicolored white and deep rose-red, early flowering. 'Daisen': vigorous; lvs abundant; buds dark pink, fls red fading to pink. 'Debutante': habit compact; fls large, pure white. 'Firecrest': young growth bright red. 'Flamingo': young growth bronze-red; fls deep pink. 'Flaming Silver' ('Havila'): young lvs bright red, margin pink at first, soon silver-white; sport of 'Forest Flame'. 'Forest Flame': *(P.formosa* 'Wakehurst' × *P.japonica)*: habit compact, symmetrical when young; lvs oblanceolate or oblong-oblanceolate, margins finely serrated; young growth red changing to pink, ivory, then pale green; fls in large spreading panicles. 'Pygmaea': dwarf, slow-growing; lvs blade-like; fls white. 'Scarlett O'Hara': young lvs red; fls off-white splashed red. 'Snow Drift': young growth bronze-red; fls large on long, upright panicles, abundant. 'Valley Valentine': buds crimson, fls deep purple-red. 'Variegata': lvs small, margined silver; fls white. 'White Caps': infl. exceptionally long, white. Z6.

***P.phillyreifolia*** (Hook.) DC. Shrub 50cm–1m or, more commonly, lianes, climbing by means of flattened rhiz. Bark brown or grey; twigs subterete. Lvs 20–60×5–20mm, elliptic, ovate or somewhat inversely so, margin revolute, apex serrate, base narrow cuneate to round, apex sharp-tipped, very sparsely glandular-hirsute; petioles 1.5–6.5mm. Fls 4–12 in axillary racemes; pedicels 2–7.5mm; bracts 1–2mm; bracteoles 0.7–2mm, linear to narrowly deltoid; cor. 6–8×4–5mm, white, cylindrical-urceolate, fil. 4–6mm, glabrous. Fr. 2.5–4×3.5–5.3mm, subglobose, glabrous; seeds 0.9–1.3mm. Winter–spring. E US. Z7.

***P.bodinieri*** Lév. See *P.formosa*.
***P.elliptica*** (Sieb. & Zucc.) Nak. See *Lyonia ovalifolia* var. *elliptica*.
***P.forrestii*** Harrow. See *P.formosa* var. *forrestii*.

***P. macrocalyx*** Anthony. See *Lyonia macrocalyx*.
***P. mariana*** (L.) Benth. & Hook. f. See *Lyonia mariana*.
***P. nana*** (Maxim.) Mak. See *Arcterica nana*.
***P. nitida*** (Bartr.) Benth. & Hook. f. See *Lyonia lucida*.
***P. ovalifolia*** (Wallich) D. Don. See *Lyonia ovalifolia*.
***P. taiwanensis*** Hayata. See *P. japonica*.

**Pigafetta** (Bl.) Becc. Palmae. 1 species, a pleonanthic, dioecious palm to 50m. Stem erect, to 40cm diam., conspicuously ringed, green, becoming grey-brown, base with mass of spine-like roots. Crownshaft absent. Leaves pinnate, arching, to 6m, neatly abscising; sheath densely tomentose, distally armed with soft spines; petioles to 2m, channelled and unarmed above, convex beneath, rachis and petiole armed with soft spines beneath; pinnae crowded, regularly spaced along rachis, linear, acuminate, margins and main veins bristly, midrib prominent. Inflorescences to 2m, axillary, horizontal, included clockwise around trunk, branched ×2, sheathed in 1–9 imbricate bracts; rachillae pendent, bearing minute bracts subtending white flowers: male flowers with calyx campanulate, petals 3, basally connate and valvate, stamens 6, pistillode minute; female flowers calyx cupular, splitting, corolla 3-lobed, staminodes fused into 6-lobed ring, pistil globose, 3-celled, stigmas 3, reflexed. Fruit to 1.2cm, ovoid, cream to yellow, epicarp scaly, mesocarp thin. Sulawesi, Moluccas, Papua New Guinea. Z10.

CULTIVATION A robust and rapidly growing feather palm which in habitat quickly colonizes forest clearings and other situations in full light; it occurs in high rainfall, humid tropical regions and is much valued there for its timber and as a specimen ornamental. In cooler regions it requires warm glasshouse conditions. Propagate by fresh seed which will usually germinate within a month. For cultivation see PALMS.

***P. filaris*** (Giseke) Becc. As for the genus.

**Pilea** Lindl. (From the Gk *pilos*, cap, referring to the shape of the larger sepal, which in some species covers the achene.) Urticaceae. Some 600 species of annual or perennial herbs, monoecious or dioecious, repent, decumbent or erect, sometimes woody at base. Stems simple or branched. Leaves usually opposite, often unequal, entire to serrate, sometimes conspicuously 3-veined, with many linear to stellate cystoliths giving the appearance of opalescent spots; stipules intra-axillary, deciduous or persistent. Inflorescence solitary, axillary, a cyme or a loose panicle, sometimes sessile; flowers minute; perianth segments 4 in males or 3 in females; ovary erect, stigma sessile, penicillate. Fruit an achene, enclosed in persistent perianth, compressed, ovate to orbicular; seeds ovoid to spherical. Tropics (except Australia). Z10.

CULTIVATION A genus of low-growing or prostrate and trailing tropical perennials grown for their beautiful foliage, *Pilea* spp. exhibit a diversity of leaf form ranging from the neat, tiny, round leaves of *P. nummularifolia* through the ferny succulent leaves of *P. microphylla* and *P. serpyllacea*, to those perhaps most commonly seen in cultivation, such as *P. cadierei*, *P. involucrata* and the many named cvs, with their deeply quilted and richly coloured foliage, often with fine bronzed and silvered markings. In tropical and subtropical gardens *Pilea* spp. are used as edging, in the rockery and larger species as groundcover in the shade of shrubs and trees. In cooler climates, they are attractive pot plants for the home or warm conservatory, the trailing species being especially suited to small hanging baskets and as groundcover in the glasshouse; many of the smaller species are especially suited to the close conditions of the terrarium and bottle garden. Grow in an open, porous and freely draining soilless medium, rich in organic matter, or in a medium-fertility loam-based mix with additional sharp sand, in bright indirect light or part shade. *P. microphylla* and *P. serpyllacea* will tolerate greater exposure to sunlight. High humidity is the ideal (most will tolerate less than ideal). Water to keep evenly moist (not wet) when in full growth, and liquid feed every two or three weeks. Reduce water to more moderate and careful applications in winter, when a minimum temperature of 10–13°C/50–55°F is appropriate. Do not allow plants to dry out and site away from draughts. Repot annually in spring; plants often degenerate in their third or fourth year and should then be replaced. Propagate by stem cuttings in spring which root readily in a sandy propagating mix in a closed case with bottom heat, increase creeping species by division. Also by seed.

***P. cadierei*** Gagnep. & Guillaum. Spreading to erect perennial herb or subshrub to 50cm. Branches becoming rigid and rather woody at base; branchlets slender, soft, terete, green tinted pink. Lvs to 8.5×5cm, in opposite pairs, obovate to oblong-oblanceolate, apex acute to broadly tapering, dentate, silver on a dark green ground or wholly metallic. Vietnam. 'Minima': dwarf, freely branching; stems pink; lvs small, elliptic, deep olive green, raised patches of silver, margins crenate.

***P. crassifolia*** (Willd.) Bl. Bushy herb to 120cm, monoecious or dioecious. Stems ascending, glabrous. Lvs to 13×4cm, ovate or elliptic to lanceolate, acuminate, rounded at base, lustrous green above, veins often red-pink beneath, serrate; stipules large, deciduous, oblong-lanceolate; petiole to 4cm. Infl. a paniculate cyme; female fls red, sessile; male fls pedicellate. fr. to 1mm, obliquely ovate, rounded. Jamaica.

***P. grandifolia*** (L.) Bl. Suffrutescent herb to 2m, usually dioecious, glabrous. Lvs to 22×16cm, broadly ovate to elliptic, acuminate, base obtuse or rounded, dentate-serrate, lustrous dark green with red venation; stipules to 2cm, persistent, ovate-oblong. Infl. a cyme, to 12cm, loosely many-fld; fls purple, red, white or sometimes green. Fr. minute, elliptic. Jamaica.

***P. involucrata*** (Sims) Urban. FRIENDSHIP PLANT; PANAMICA. Trailing to erect herb, hairy to pilose; stems branched, branches 20–30cm. Lvs to 6×3cm, ovate to obovate, hairy, coarsely toothed, 3-nerved, marked bronze, silver or red. Infl. a long-stalked, corymbose or paniculate cyme, 7–8cm across; male fls few at the base of the many-fld female cymes. Summer. C & S America. 'Liebmannii': lvs tinged silver. 'Moon Valley': lvs ovate, quilted, crenate, tinged bronze, broad silver band along middle, edges dotted silver; resembling a cv. of *Coleus*, sometimes placed under *P. crassifolia* but more likely to belong in *P. involucrata* because lvs and hairy. 'Norfolk': habit small, dense; lvs broad, oval, bronze to black-green, raised silver bands; fls small, rose. 'Silver Panamiga': stems brown, hairy; lvs ovate or rhombic, blue-silver, deeply toothed towards apex.

***P. microphylla*** (L.) Liebm. ARTILLERY PLANT; GUNPOWDER PLANT; PISTOL PLANT. Annual or short-lived perennial to 30cm, dioecious or monoecious, succulent, glabrous, densely branched. Lvs to 10×3mm, usually smaller, in unequal pairs, crowded, obovate to orbicular, pale green, obtuse or subacute, entire, succulent, petiolate. Fls minute, white tinged red, in dense cymes; female fls sessile; male fls short-pedicellate; anth. dehiscing abruptly. Fr. minute, ovoid, brown, compressed. Mexico to Brazil. 'Variegata' ('Confetti'): lvs blotched white and pink.

***P. nummularifolia*** (Sw.) Wedd. Dioecious or sometimes monoecious herb. Stem repent or trailing, pilose-villosulous; to 2.5mm, ovate to ovate-rounded, persistent. Lvs to 2cm, in similar pairs, broadly ovate to suborbicular, crenate, pale green, usually strigillose, cystoliths linear, inconspicuous. Fls minute, green, axillary, in dense, short-peduncled cymes. Fr. minute, ovoid. Summer. Tropical S America, W Indies.

***P. peperomioides*** Diels. Erect herb, somewhat succulent (superficially resembling *Peperomia* spp.), monoecious or dioecious. Stems elongate, glabrous. Lvs to 9×9cm, succulent, elliptic to suborbicular, entire, pale green, prominently veined, cystoliths minute, fusiform; stipules to 18mm, persistent, brown, ovate to lanceolate, acute or acuminate, scarious; petioles to 6cm. Infl. to 14cm, a panicle, subflexuose; fls cream to pale green. Summer. W Indies.

***P. repens*** (Sw.) Wedd. BLACK-LEAF PANAMICA. Creeping herb to 30cm. Stems pilose, becoming glabrous, branches erect or ascending. Lvs to 3.5×3cm, often unequal, obovate or ovate to suborbicular, obtuse or rounded, base rounded or truncate, glabrous or pilose, crenate or crenate-serrate, cystoliths prominent, linear; petioles to 2.5cm. Infl. long-pedunculate. Fr. minute, ovate. Summer. W Indies.

***P. serpyllacea*** (Knuth) Liebm. Resembles *P. microphylla* except herb tinged red throughout. Lvs to 15×5mm, entire to crenate. Fls inconspicuous. Summer. Tropical northern S America.

***P.* cultivars**. 'Black Magic': dense, mat-forming; lvs small, round, margins wavy, somewhat crenate, green shaded bronze. 'Coral': stems tinged red; lvs long, ovate, glossy, margins crenate, copper above, tinged purple beneath. 'Silver Tree': stalks white, hairy; lvs ovate, quilted, margins crenate, tinged bronze, broad silver band along middle, dotted silver on sides.

***P. callitrichoides*** (Knuth) Knuth. See *P. microphylla*.
***P. muscosa*** Lindl. See *P. microphylla*.
***P. pubescens*** misapplied. See *P. involucrata*.
***P. serpyllifolia*** misapplied. See *P. serpyllacea*.
***P. spruceana*** misapplied. See *P. involucrata*.

**Pileanthus** Labill. (From Gk *pilos*, cap, and *anthos*, flower; the flower is enclosed in a 1-leaved involucre.) Myrtaceae. 3 species of evergreen shrubs. Stem branching. Leaves entire, narrow. Flowers pink, red, orange to white, occurring in the upper leaf axils. W Australia. Z10.

CULTIVATION As for *Leptospermum*.

***P. filifolius*** Meissn. SUMMER COPPER CUPS. Shrub to 1m with a spread of 1m. Stem slender, erect, branching and hairy. Lvs 1.2cm, narrow, terete, opposite, thick, cylindrical and blunt, scattered along the stems. Fls pink-red, in clusters from the upper leaf axils to 2cm diam. on a 2cm-thick flower stalk; sep. 10; pet. 5, large, sometimes frilled.

**Pileostegia** Hook. f. & Thoms. (From Gk *pilos*, felt, and *stege*, roof, referring to the form of the corolla.) Hydrangeaceae. 4 species of climbing or prostrate evergreen shrubs related to *Hydrangea* and *Schizophragma*, distinguished in having flowers all alike in terminal, corymbose panicles. Calyx cup-shaped, 4–5-lobed; petals 4–5; stamens to 0.5cm, inserted in calyx cup with petals; ovary semi-inferior, 5-celled, ovules many, style stout, 5–6-lobed at apex. E Asia.

CULTIVATION *Pileostegia* is a useful subject for a north or east facing wall, although it flowers more profusely in sun. Propagate by nodal stem and tip cuttings taken from young growth as the foliage expands, treat with rooting hormone and root in a closed case with bottom heat; also by seed and layers. Otherwise, cultivate as for *Decumaria*.

***P. viburnoides*** Hook. f. & Thoms. 6–10m. Stems self-clinging; branchlets initially scurfy, later glabrous. Lvs 5–18cm, narrow-oblong to ovate-lanceolate, opposite, entire, coriaceous, glossy dark green, pitted above, prominently and closely veined beneath. Panicles to 15cm, crowded, borne profusely; fls 0.8cm diam., white; stamens conspicuous, slender. India, China, Taiwan. Z9.

For synonymy see *Schizophragma*.

**Pilgerodendron** Florin.
***P. uviferum*** (D. Don) Florin. See *Libocedrus uvifera*.

**Pilocereus** Lem.
***P. arrabidae*** Lem. See *Pilosocereus arrabidae*.
***P. chrysacanthus*** F.A.C. Weber. See *Pilosocereus chrysacanthus*.
***P. coerulescens*** Lem. See *Pilosocereus coerulescens*.
***P. glaucescens*** Lem. See *Pilosocereus piauhyensis*.
***P. glaucochrous*** Werderm. See *Pilosocereus glaucochrous*.
***P. hapalacanthus*** Werderm. See *Pilosocereus hapalacanthus*.
***P. leucocephalus*** Poselger. See *Pilosocereus leucocephalus*.

**Pilosella** Hill. (Diminutive of Lat. *pilosus*, hairy.) Compositae. Some 18 species of hairy, perennial herbs with horizontal rhizomes and leafy or underground scaly stolons, with simple and stellate hairs. Stems few to numerous. Leaves in basal rosettes, entire or slightly denticulate, stem leaves, if present, small. Capitula ligulate, one to several per stem; receptacle flat, pitted; involucre campanulate; phyllaries imbricate in many series; florets yellow to red, outer sometimes striped red below. Fruit a cylindrical, 10-ribbed cypsela, to 3mm; pappus of white to pale brown hairs. Eurasia and N W Africa. The species are sexual or partially apomictic; most species hybridize freely. Z5.

CULTIVATION Ranging through grassland, sand dunes, waste and cultivated ground to altitudes of 300m/975ft, *Pilosella* spp. are strongly stoloniferous and invasive but are well suited to the tops of dry walls and other situations that approximate to habitat; the deep coppery orange to brick-red flowers are carried throughout summer, useful in the wild garden as a nectar source for bees and butterflies. Grow in sun in any well-drained soil. Propagate by seed and division.

***P. aurantiaca*** (L.) F.W. Schultz & Schultz-Bip. Stolons leafy. Lvs above or below ground, numerous, to 20cm, oblanceolate to elliptic, obtuse to acute, base attenuate, pale green or glaucous, with simple, eglandular hairs, stem lvs 1–4. Capitula 2–25, to 2.5cm diam. in a terminal corymb, scape to 65cm, with long dark hairs; phyllaries to 3mm wide, lanceolate, obtuse to acute; florets orange to orange-red. Summer. Europe (a weed in N US and Pacific Coast).

***P. officinarum*** F.W. Schultz & Schultz-Bip. Stolons usually numerous, long, slender, leafy. Lvs 1–12×0.5–2cm, oblong to lanceolate or spathulate, obtuse or acute, narrowed to base, with simple eglandular hairs, densely stellate-hairy at least below. Capitula solitary, on 5–50cm scape with glandular, simple and stellate hairs; phyllaries 6–15×1–2mm, linear-lanceolate, acute; florets lemon, commonly striped red below. Summer. Temperate Eurasia.

For synonymy see *Hieracium*.

**Pilosocereus** Byles & Rowley. (From Lat. *pilosus*, hairy, and *Cereus*.) Cactaceae. About 45 spp. of shrubs and trees, shrubby or arborescent, base or trunk to 10m; ribs (3–)4–30, often cross-furrowed; areoles, at least the flowering, with more or less abundant woolly hairs (but lacking in a few well-known spp.), sometimes as long as 5cm and forming skeins covering the ribs. Flowers tubular-campanulate, 4–10cm, nocturnal; pericarpel and tube fleshy, naked (or with minute scales), often tinged brown or purple; limb rather narrow, usually white or pale pink; stamens very numerous. Fruit ovoid to depressed-globose, smooth, fig-like, splitting open when ripe, usually with red pulp, the perianth persistent, blackened; seeds broadly oval, 1.7–2.0×1.1–1.4mm, black-brown, shiny; relief flat. US (Florida), Mexico, Caribbean region, and trop. S America (especially E Brazil). Formerly known under the misapplied name *Pilocereus* (i.e. *Pilocereus* sensu Schum. et al., non Lem.) or included in *Cephalocereus* Pfeiff.

CULTIVATION Grow in a heated greenhouse (min. 10–15°C/50–60°F); use 'acid standard' cactus compost: moderate to high inorganic content (more than 50% grit), below pH 6; grow in full sun; maintain low humidity; water very sparingly in winter (to avoid shrivelling).

***P. alensis*** (F.A.C. Weber ex Roland-Goss.) Byles & Rowley. Shrub, 2–5m; stems to 12cm diam.; ribs 10–14; areoles *c*1cm apart, with few white hairs; spines *c*10, to 2cm, brown then grey. Flowering areoles producing very long tufts of dense, off-white hair; fl. described as green-purple. W Mexico (Sonora to Michoacan). See *P. leucocephalus*. Z9.

***P. arrabidae*** (Lem.) Byles & Rowley. Shrub to 3(–4)m, mostly branched near base; stems 4.5–9.5cm diam., dark to yellow-green; ribs (5–)6–8; areoles to *c*3cm apart, 6–8mm diam., with a few long hairs and 9–14 pale brown to pale yellow spines to 4cm. Flowering areoles like the non-flowering; fls rather broad, *c*7×5cm, creamy white. Fr. *c*5×6cm, green with magenta pulp. Summer. E Brazil (coastal). Z9.

***P. catingicola*** (Gürke) Byles & Rowley. Tree to 7m, very woody and with branches arising in whorls from the trunk; stems 8–12cm diam., grey-green to light waxy blue; ribs (3–)4–6; areoles *c*1.5cm apart, 7–10mm, with dense tufts of hairs to 1.5cm; spines 15–18, to 4cm, stout, opaque, grey to pale brown. Flowering areoles developing dense, off-white wool to 3cm; fl. very stout, usually flattened, to *c*7×7cm, white. Fr. to 6cm diam., purple. E Brazil (Bahia). Z9.

***P. chrysacanthus*** (F.A.C. Weber) Byles & Rowley. Shrub or tree to 5m or more, with many branches; stems to 9cm diam. or more, blue-green; ribs 9–12; areoles *c*1cm apart; spines 12–15, to 4cm, golden. Flowering areoles with dense tufts of hair and spines; fl. very stout, to 8cm, pale pink. Fr. to 4cm diam., red or purple. Summer. S Mexico. Z9.

***P. chrysostele*** (Vaup.) Byles & Rowley. Shrub, usually not exceeding 3m, branched near base; stems green; ribs 20–30; densely clothed in short yellow spines, areolar hairs inconspicuous; spines numerous, short, yellow. Flowering areoles developing dense tufts of wool and bristles; fl. short and broad, to 5cm; tube pale pink; tepals white. NE Brazil. Z9.

***P. coerulescens*** (Lem.) Ritter. Shrub to *c*1.5m, branching from the base; stems 4–6cm diam., green; ribs 13–17 (sometimes more in flowering zone), 4mm high; areoles 3–6mm apart, copiously white-hairy and with bristles 1–3cm; spines finely acicular, pale golden-yellow, darker at base; central spines 4–15, 5–30mm; radial spines 8–16, 4–15mm. Fl. 3.5–6cm; pericarpel and tube green or red-green; inner tepals white. Fr. 1.2–4×2.5–5cm, red, with white or red pulp. E Brazil (Minas Gerais). Z9.

***P. collinsii*** (Britt. & Rose) Byles & Rowley. Shrub to 2.5m; stems 4–5cm diam., blue-green; ribs 7–10, narrow; areoles to 1.5cm apart, *c*1cm diam., with long hairs; spines *c*10, to 2.5cm, almost black or grey. Flowering areoles more hairy; fl. slender, to 7cm, tinged green or purple. Fr. 3–4cm diam., blue, later dull red. S Mexico. Vegetatively similar to the Caribbean *P. royenii*. Z9.

***P. glaucochrous*** (Werderm.) Byles & Rowley. Resembling *P. pentaedrophorus*; narrow tree or shrub to 4m, with few slender branches; stems to 7cm diam., light blue; ribs 5–10; areoles with white, grey or almost black felt at first, usually bearing long hairs to 4cm; spines 12–16, to 5cm, translucent yellow or some pale brown. Fl. slender, to *c*5.5cm, dirty pink, some tepals pale to almost white. E Brazil (Bahia). Z9.

***P. gounellei*** (F.A.C. Weber) Byles & Rowley. Shrubby, but often with a very short trunk, branching, repeatedly near the apex of each stem and forming a low broad mass of stems to 2(–3)m high; stems green or glaucous; ribs 8–13, strongly tuberculate, the valleys between sinuate; areoles large and well-separated; central spines *c*4, 4–12cm, vary variable in length and colour; radial spines *c*12 or more, much shorter, adpressed. Fl. tubular, immersed in wool, to 9cm, white to pale pink; tube brown or tinged green. Fr. to 6cm diam., usually depressed-globose, green to dull purple. NE Brazil. Z9.

***P. hapalacanthus*** (Werderm.) Byles & Rowley. Resembling *P. catingicola*, but ribs 6–12, much lower; areoles scarcely woolly; spines shorter and weaker. Fl. less massive. NE Brazil (coastal). Z9.

***P. lanuginosus*** (L.) Byles & Rowley. Tree to 10m or more, variably branched; stems to 12cm diam., blue at first; ribs to 13; areoles rather woolly at first; spines 7–25 or more, pale yellow to pale brown. Flowering areoles bearing large tufts of wool, flowers to 7cm, white. Fr. depressed-globose, red. N South America. Z9.

***P. leucocephalus*** (Poselger) Byles & Rowley. Eventually a tree to 6m, more or less branched; stems 5–10cm diam., dark green or glaucous and blue-green at first; ribs 6–9; areoles *c*1–1.5cm apart, the upper densely clothed with white hairs 2–6cm; spines pale brown or yellow at first; central spines 1–2, 2–3cm; radial spines 7–12, *c*1cm. Fl. 6–8cm; outer tepals purple-brown; inner tepals pale pink. Fr. depressed-globose, to 6cm diam., blue-purple. Summer. E Mexico, C America. The name *P. leucocephalus* was misapplied by Britton and Rose to a plant from western Mexico (*P. alensis*) and, as a consequence, the present species is usually encountered under the name *P. palmeri*. Z9.

***P. moritzianus*** (Otto ex Pfeiff.) Byles & Rowley. Resembling *P. lanuginosus*; stems to 10cm or more diam., green to blue-tinged; ribs 7–10; areoles to *c*1.2cm apart, woolly at first; spines 9–11, to 3.5cm, pale brown. Flowering areoles with small tufts of wool to 1cm; fl. *c*5cm diam., red. N Venezuela. Z9.

***P. pentaedrophorus*** (Labouret) Byles & Rowley. Stem simple, or few-branched at base, erect or decumbent, slender, 2–5m or more tall, only *c*3–7cm diam., vivid blue-green; ribs 4–6(–10), notched above the areoles; areoles with short hairs; spines to *c*12, unequal, the longest 4cm, yellow. Fl. 4–6cm, curved; pericarpel and tube glabrous, green; inner tepals white. Fr. depressed-globose, 3×5cm, blue-green with purple-red pulp. E Brazil. Z9.

***P. piauhyensis*** (Gürke) Byles & Rowley. Tree to 10m, more or less branched; stems to 10cm diam., vivid pale blue to green; ribs 7–16; areoles *c*1.5cm apart, the non-flowering with spines and a few off-white hairs; spines *c*18–25, 5–15mm, golden-yellow. Flowering areoles densely tufted with white hairs; fl. 6–7cm; pericarpel and tube naked, blue- or brown-green; inner tepals white to pink. Fr. depressed-globose, *c*6cm, tinged blue. E Brazil. Z9.

***P. purpusii*** (Britt. & Rose) Byles & Rowley. Simple or somewhat branched, to 3m; stems slender, to 4cm diam., green; ribs 12, narrow; areoles close-set, at most 1cm apart, bearing long white hairs when young; spines to 3cm, pale yellow. Flowering areoles more crowded, with silky white hair; fl. *c*7cm, pale pink. Fr. 2.5–4cm, red. N Caribbean (Florida to Cuba). Z9.

***P. royenii*** (L.) Byles & Rowley. Tree, to 8m or more; stem stout, dark green to blue-green; ribs 7–11; spines variable, often only 1cm, sometimes much longer. Fl. 5cm; tube yellow-green or tinged purple; inner tepals white. Fr. 5cm diam., red-green. Caribbean. Z9.

***P. backebergii*** (Weingart) Byles & Rowley. See *P. lanuginosus*.
***P. nobilis*** (Haw.) Byles & Rowley. See *P. royenii*.
***P. palmeri*** (Rose) Byles & Rowley. See *P. leucocephalus*.
***P. werdermannianus*** (Buining & Brederoo) Ritter. See *P. coerulescens*.
For further synonymy see *Cactus*, *Cephalocereus*, *Cereus* and *Pilocereus*.

**Pilularia** L. PILLWORT. (From Lat. *pilula*, diminutive of *pila*, ball, referring to the sporocarps.) Marsileaceae. About 6 species of semi-aquatic ferns, fully submerged or terrestrial forms usually sterile. Rhizomes long-creeping, very slender, submerged. Fronds erect, reduced to a thin, tapered, filiform or subulate stipe. Sporocarps usually hidden in mud, globular, black, 2–4-chambered, each chamber with a sorus producing many sporangia; pedicels short. Temperate regions except Africa. Z8.

CULTIVATION As for *Marsilea*. Hardy to −10°C/14°F, plants tend to grow emerse at the margins of ponds and lakes, the edges becoming free floating. Habit and appearance is very much like a sedge or grass, and can be grown for curiosity in a container of loamy medium and kept moist by submerging the base in water.

***P. americana*** A. Br. Rhiz. filiform, widely creeping. Fronds setiform, sometimes solitary, nodes beneath the lvs rooting. Sporocarps to 2mm diam., 2–4-chambered, usually 3-chambered, laterally attached to pedicel; pedicels short, descending, arcuate; megaspores 10–17 per chamber, not at all constricted medially. W US (Oregon to S California and Arkansas).

***P. globulifera*** L. Rhiz. caespitose or creeping, slender, nodes to 4cm apart, rooting at every node. Fronds 2.5–10cm, bright green. Sporocarps 4-chambered, erect, sub-sessile at base of plant, 3–4mm, diam., pubesc.; megaspore ovoid, 15–20 per chamber, constricted above middle. W Europe.

**Pimelea** Banks & Sol. ex Gaertn. (From Gk *pimele*, fat, referring to the oily seeds.) RICE FLOWER. Thymelaeaceae. 80 species of compact evergreen shrubs or herbs. Leaves alternate or opposite, often decussate, sessile or nearly so, usually small, simple, entire. Flowers polygamous or dioecious, in terminal heads to 5cm across surrounded by involucre of leaf-like coloured bracts; perianth tubular, lobes 4, spreading, petal-like, pink, red, yellow or white, often silky villous; petals absent; stamens 2, usually longer than tube; style glabrous, stigma capitate; ovary superior, carpels 2, each containing a single ovule (one carpel constricted). Fruit a 1 seeded drupe or nut, green, red or black. Australasia (New Zealand, Australia, Timor, Lord Howe Is.). Z9.

CULTIVATION Compact and slow growing plants, best suited to cultivation in the cool glasshouse (winter minimum 5–7°C/40–45°F) in cool temperate zones. Many spp. have beautiful young growth clothed in characteristic silky white down, a feature which also appears on the flowers. *P. prostrata* forms carpets of interlaced black stems with grey-green foliage, and bears fragrant downy white flowers, followed by small white fruits. Given a neutral to slightly acid soil with perfect drainage, a cool root run, full sun and shelter from cold and drying winds, *P. prostrata* will tolerate temperatures to −5°C/23°F, and is suited to cultivation on the rock garden, or on scree. The additional protection of an open cloche in severe winter weather is advisable. *P. gnidia*, *P. rosea* and *P. spectabilis* may also be worth trying in these conditions, in favoured areas.

Grow glasshouse specimens in a mix of lime-free loam with sharp sand, or in a mix of equal parts of rubbed leafmould and sharp sand. Water moderately when in growth and allow to become dry, but not arid when temperatures drop. Good direct light and ventilation is essential in winter. Flowers are borne on the tips of shoots made in the previous season; deadhead and prune after flowering, pinching out tips to maintain compact growth. Repot when fresh growth appears after pruning.

Propagate by semi-ripe cuttings taken with a heel in summer, or by softwood cuttings in spring, in a closed case. Keep young plants moist and slightly shaded, at about 10–13°C/50–55°F, and spray with a fine mist until established. In dry atmospheres, red spider mites may infest plants; apply suitable biological control or systemic insecticide. Some species may suffer sudden dieback, as in the closely related *Daphne*.

***P. arenaria*** A. Cunn. Much-branched shrub, 30–60cm, main stems creeping; shoots white with silky hairs. Lvs decussate, often crowded at first, later distant, short-petiolate or sessile, 6–12×3–5mm, ovate to oblong or orbicular, tips rounded to acute, shiny-silky beneath. Fls 6mm diam., pure white in heads of to 152cm diam.; involucral bracts 7×5mm; perianth exterior silky, lobes broadly ovate. Fr. berry-like, white or red, 3mm. Early summer. New Zealand.

***P. drupacea*** Labill. Erect shrub to 2m; young shoots silky-hairy. Lvs opposite, 2.5–7cm, ovate or narrow-elliptic to elliptic, tips acute to obtuse, dark green and glabrous above, paler with often short hairs beneath, margins lightly ciliate. Fls white, bisexual, in terminal clusters of 4–7, or in upper lf axils; involucral bracts 2–4, narrow-elliptic to elliptic, to 17×7mm; tube 5mm, silky-hairy, lobes ovate, acute, to 3.5×2mm; fil. shorter than perianth tube, to 1.25mm. Fr. succulent, ovoid, black. Summer. S & E Australia, Tasmania.

***P. ferruginea*** Labill. Erect shrub to 2m. Lvs opposite, crowded, to 12mm, ovate or oblong, shiny green, glabrous above, often hairy beneath, margins revolute. Fls rose-pink in almost spherical heads 2.5–4cm diam. at ends of branchlets; involucral bracts pink or red; tube to 12mm, slender, hairy, 4mm, lobes oblong, 4mm, exterior adpressed-downy. Late spring–early summer. W Australia.

***P. glauca*** R. Br. Erect, much-branched shrub, to 1m, all parts except infl. glabrous. Lvs opposite, to 20×5mm, narrow-elliptic to narrow-ovate, blue-green, midrib prominent, usually somewhat concave; petioles to 1mm. Fls bisexual, in terminal clusters of to 35 per head; involucral bracts 4, to 16×7.5mm, narrow-elliptic to narrow-ovate, acute to acuminate; perianth cream-white, tube to 15mm, interior glabrous, exterior short-hairy, lobes elliptic, to 3×1.75mm; fil. shorter than lobes, anth. pale orange. Fr. green, ovoid, to 4.5×1.75mm. Summer. Australia, Tasmania.

***P. gnidia*** (Forst. & Forst. f.) Willd. Erect, much-branched, glabrous shrub to 1.5m; branches stout. Lvs crowded, to 20×6mm, oblong to oblong-lanceolate, light green, leathery, shiny above; petioles to 1mm. Fls to 5mm diam., in heads of to 30, pale rose, silky; involucral bracts ovate, nearly acute, 12×6mm; peduncles to 23mm; tube 8–12mm, lobes 4mm, narrow-ovate to oblong. Fr. dry, 3mm. New Zealand.

***P. hispida*** R. Br. Erect, much-branched shrub, 60–120cm; shoots glabrous. Lvs 12–25×3–6mm, oblong-lanceolate. Fls to 6mm diam., crowded in heads to 4cm diam.; perianth pale rose, tube slender, hairy, 12mm, lobes hairy below. Summer. W Australia.

***P. imbricata*** R. Br. Shrub to 50cm; shoots slender, erect, often covered with soft spreading hairs. Lvs alternate or opposite, 6–12×2mm, oblanceolate to narrow-oblong. Fls 4mm diam., white, in heads 25–30mm diam.; perianth tube slender, exterior long-hairy, interior short-downy; anth. brown. Spring–summer. W Australia.

***P. linifolia*** Sm. Upright or prostrate shrub 30–90cm, all parts except infl. glabrous; shoots slender. Lvs opposite, 10–35×1–7mm, linear to oblong or linear-obovate, tips acute, green or blue-green, paler beneath, midrib prominent; petioles to 2mm. Fls bisexual or female, 6–9mm diam., white tinged pink, in erect, terminal, globose heads of to 60, heads 3cm diam.; involucre of 4–8 bracts, narrow-elliptic to ovate, to 19×10mm, tinged blue, green or red-purple; tube 1.5mm, silky-hairy, lobes 3mm. Fr. green, ovoid, to 5.5×2mm. Early summer, most of the year in the wild. Australia, Tasmania.

***P. longiflora*** R. Br. Upright shrub to 120cm. Shoots very slender, hairy. Lvs 6–15×2mm, alternate and opposite, linear, hairy. Fls 8mm diam., white, in terminal, globose heads 3cm diam.; perianth silky, tube to 1.5cm, lobes linear. Summer. W Australia.

***P. lyallii*** Hook. f. Small, prostrate or partly erect shrub; branches short and erect or trailing to 50cm, usually white silky-hairy. Lvs closely set and overlapping, 4–8mm, shape variable, narrow-oblong to ovate-elliptic to lanceolate, tips acute, concave, sparsely silky-hairy beneath; petioles short and thick. Fls white, silky-hairy, 4–6mm diam., in heads of 3–4; involucral bracts broad-ovate; perianth 8mm, lobes ovate, tips blunt, 3–4mm. Fr. berry-like or dry. New Zealand.

***P. nivea*** Labill. Erect, straggly or bushy shrub to 2m, all parts except upper surface of lvs white with thick layer of woolly or cotton-like hairs. Lvs opposite, almost sessile, to 15mm, round-ovate to orbicular, thick, margins recurved, white-downy beneath, glabrous and shiny above. Fls hermaphrodite, white, cream or pink, 6mm diam., in many-fld globose heads 18–24mm diam.; involucral bracts similar to lvs; tube 2mm, hairy, lobes oblong. Fr. dry, 3mm. Summer. Tasmania.

***P. pauciflora*** R. Br. Erect, much-branched, dioecious shrub, to 3m. Lvs opposite, to 20×3.5mm, narrow-elliptic to oblong, midrib prominent beneath; petioles 1mm. Fls white to green-yellow, terminal, 2–4 per head in male plants, 3–7 in female plants, in upper lf pair; involucre of 2–4 bracts, ovate to elliptic, to 11mm. Fr. to 5mm, narrow-ovoid, red, enclosed by persistent base of perianth. Early summer. Australia, Tasmania.

***P. prostrata*** (Forst. & Forst. f.) Willd. Variable, low shrub; branches wide-spreading or forming tufted habit; shoots adpressed-silky, lf scars on stems obvious. Lvs opposite, in ranks of 4, crowded, sessile or nearly so, 2–12mm, ovate to elliptic-oblong, often recurved, glabrous, dull green above, margins often red, somewhat leathery. Fls 3–6mm diam., hermaphrodite or unisexual, fragrant, white, in small crowded heads of 3–10, 18mm diam., on short side-shoots near the ends of branches, silky-downy; tube swollen at base, exterior hairy, to 3mm. Fr. 2mm, white or red, fleshy or dry. New Zealand.

***P. rosea*** R. Br. Erect shrub, 30–60cm. Lvs scattered, linear-lanceolate, tips pointed, margins recurved. Fls 6mm diam. rose to white, in crowded hemispheric heads to 4cm diam.; tube 8mm, hairy, lobes hairy below. Summer. Australia.

***P. sericea*** R. Br. Much-branched shrub 60–120cm; shoots densely silvery silky-hairy. Lvs mostly opposite, almost sessile, usually crowded, 6–15mm, round-ovate to ovate, densely silvery silky-hairy beneath, glabrous above. Fls many, hermaphrodite, 5–9mm diam., white tinged pink, in terminal heads 3cm diam.; involucral bracts similar to lvs; perianth downy, tube to 10mm, lobes 3mm. Fr. dry, 3.5mm. Early summer. Tasmania.

***P. spectabilis*** (Fisch. & C.A. Mey.) Lindl. Erect shrub, 1–1.25m; shoots glabrous. Lvs opposite, crowded, to 4cm, linear to lanceolate, glabrous, glaucous beneath. Fls 1.5cm diam., pale to rich pink or yellow, in crowded, globose heads to 7cm; tube and lobes hairy; involucral bracts about 6, ovate, margins tinged pink. Early summer. W Australia.

***P. suaveolens*** Meissn. Shrub, 30–60cm; shoots glabrous. Lvs ovate-lanceolate, 12–35×4.5–6mm, twisted, concave, thick, glabrous, leathery. Fls 12mm diam., yellow in bud, opening to pale rose, hemispherical heads, 5cm diam.; bracts 4–8, large; tube slender, downy, 2cm, in lobes ciliate. Summer. W Australia.

***P. sylvestris*** R. Br. Freely branched, glabrous shrub, 60–90cm. Lvs 12–25×3–6mm, opposite, oblong to lanceolate. Fls 5–9mm diam., pale rose, in heads 4–5cm diam.; tube slender, 6–12mm. Summer. W Australia.

***P. traversii*** Hook. f. Dwarf shrub to 60cm; shoots stout, glabrous, often twisted. Lvs sessile, thickly set, overlapping, in tiers of 4, to 9×6mm, obovate-oblong to orbicular, tips blunt, thick, margins often tinged red. Fls in heads of to 20, white to pink, very silky; involucral bracts broad-ovate, to 7×6mm, tube 6–9mm; lobes 3–4mm, ovate-oblong. Fr. ovoid to oval, 3–4mm, brown, dry. New Zealand.

***P. virgata*** Vahl. Slender, upright shrub to 50cm; stems with grey to white hairs with obvious lf scars. Lvs to 20×5mm, sessile or petioles narrow, to 1mm, linear to lanceolate to oblong-lanceolate, tips acute to acuminate, smooth above, hairy beneath. Fls small, in heads of 6–12; involucral bracts 7mm wide; perianth 6–10mm, villous, lobes blunt, ovate. Fr. berry-like, white or deep red, ovoid, to 6mm, apex hairy. New Zealand.

***P. graciliflora*** Hook. See *P. sylvestris*.
***P. intermedia*** Lindl. See *P. glauca*.
***P. linoides*** Cunn. See *P. linifolia*.
***P. macrocephala*** Hook. See *P. suaveolens*.
***P. nana*** Graham. See *P. imbricata*.
***P. petraea*** Meissn. See *P. imbricata*.
***P. tomentosa*** (Forst. & Forst. f.) Druce. See *P. virgata*.

**Pimpinella** L. (A corruption of the medieval Latin *pipinella* (=*bipinella*), from the Lat. *bipennis*, two-winged; an allusion to the pinnate or bipinnatifid leaves.) Umbelliferae. 150 species of annuals, biennials and perennials. Leaves simple, ternate or 1–3-pinnate; stem leaves commonly 2-pinnate. Umbels compound; involucre and involucel sometimes absent; calyx teeth minute or absent; flowers white or yellow, to deep pink or purple; petals slightly emarginate, with inflexed apex, glabrous or pubescent below. Fruit ovoid-oblong to subglobose, slightly laterally compressed, glabrous to hairy; mericarps with filiform ridges; vittae 2–3. Eurasia, N Africa.

CULTIVATION *P. saxifraga*, found in dry grassland, usually on lime, and *P. major*, from similar but usually more shaded habitats, are grown as medicinal herbs and occasionally in the wild flower meadow. *P. anisum*, anise, is a strongly aromatic annual which also has medicinal properties, but it is better known for its culinary uses. It requires long warm summer to ripen seed, but is nevertheless useful in the herb garden, grown for its foliage. Grow in a warm sheltered position in full sun, in light, well-drained soil. In cooler areas, sow seed under glass in early spring, planting out after hardening off in late spring; otherwise sow *in situ* in spring.

***P. anisum*** L. ANISE; ANISEED. Aromatic annual to 50cm, finely pubesc., branching above. Lower lvs 2–5cm, simple, reniform to ovate, dentate or shallowly lobed; lower stem lvs pinnate, seg. 3–5, ovate or obovate, dentate; upper stem lvs 2–3-pinnate, seg. linear; petiole sheathing. Umbels 7–15-rayed; involucral bracts 1 or absent; involucel of few bracteoles or absent; fls white or yellow-white. Fr. 3–5mm, adpressed-hairy. Summer. C & S Europe, USSR, Cyprus, Syria, Egypt.

***P. major*** (L.) Huds. GREATER BURNET SAXIFRAGE. Perenn. to 1m, glabrous to slightly pubesc.; stem sulcate, hollow. Lower lvs pinnate, seg. 3–9, coarsely serrate to lobed, ovate or oblong, *c*6cm, petioles long; stem lvs 3-lobed, smaller, petiole short and sheathing, with membranous margin. Umbels with 10–25 rays, to 4cm, lateral umbels with mostly or all male fls; involucre and involucels commonly absent; fls white to pink. Fr. 3–4mm; mericarps with prominent, slender ridges. Summer. Europe. 'Rosea': to 60×30cm; lvs fern-like; fls pale pink, delicate. Z5.

***P. peregrina*** L. Bienn. to 1m, finely pubesc. Lower lvs *c*15cm, pinnate, seg. 5–9, suborbicular, base cordate, margin crenate; stem lvs 1–2-pinnate with linear, often recurved seg. Umbels with 8–50 filiform rays; involucre and involucels absent; fls white; pet. glabrous. Fr. *c*2mm, with spreading hairs. Early summer. S Europe, Caucasia, Crimea, C Asia. Z6.

***P. saxifraga*** L. BURNET SAXIFRAGE. Perenn. to 1m, scarcely pubesc.; stem terete, branched. Lower lvs pinnate, seg. in 4–6 pairs, ovate to lanceolate in outline, serrate to pinnatifid, to 2.5cm; stem lvs with 3 pairs of narrow lobes; petiole inflated, tinged purple. Umbels with 6–25 rays, *c*3cm; involucre and involucels absent; fls mostly bisexual, white, occasionally tinged pink or purple. Fr. to 2.5mm; mericarps with slender ridges. Summer. Europe, including GB. Z4.

***P. tragium*** Vill. Perenn. to 60cm, pubesc. to glabrous; stem solid. Lower lvs oblong in outline, pinnate, seg. obovate or lanceolate, crenate to dentate, or lobed; stem lvs few, often reduced to sheath. Umbels 6–15-rayed, lacking involucre and involucels; fls white, occasionally tinged pink; pet. hairy below. Fr. 2–3mm, shortly tomentose. Summer. S & E Europe. Z7.

***P. magna*** L. See *P. major*.
For further synonymy see *Anisum*.

**PINACEAE** Lindl. PINE FAMILY. Gymnosperms. 9 genera and 194 species of usually evergreen, resinous, monoecious trees and a few prostrate shrubs; branches opposite or whorled; shoots either long only or long and short. Leaves acicular, spirally arranged. Male cones small, herbaceous, stamens many; female cones usually woody, with spirally arranged scales, closed until ripe, each scale with 2 ovules on the upper surface, subtended by a united bract; seeds usually 2 per scale, usually winged; embryo with

**Pinanga** (a) *P. coronata* clumping palms (×0.03) (a1) details of unisexual flowers (ranks of triads showing protogynous female in centre with male on either side) (×1.5), (a2) enlargement of female flower (×4), (a3) details of fruit (×0.25) (b) *P. javana* flowering solitary palm (×0.03) (c) *P. malaiana* clumping palms in fruit (×0.03) (c1) young seedling showing two-lobed leaves and germination directly from seed (×0.5) (d) *P. densiflora* clumping palms in fruit (×0.03) (e) *P. disticha* small clumping palms in fruit (×0.05)

several cotyledons. Some species are an important source of timber and wood pulp, producing resins, including turpentine; some produce edible seeds. North temperate, South to Central America, West Indies, Somalia and Java. *Abies, Cathaya, Cedrus, Keteleeria, Larix, Nothotsuga, Picea, Pinus, Pseudolarix, Pseudotsuga, Tsuga*.

**Pinanga** Bl. (From the Malay name for these palms, *pinina*.) PINANG, BUNGA. Palmae. Some 120 species unarmed, pleonanthic, monoecious palms. Stems solitary or clustered, ringed, sometimes stilt-rooted, sometimes absent. Crownshaft distinct. Leaves entire and pinnately ribbed, or pinnate; petiole terete or channelled above, sometimes lacking; pinnae regularly spaced or irregularly clustered on rachis, 1 to several-fold, varying in shape on the same tree, apices acute, acuminate or truncate and notched, sometimes mottled, pale beneath, scaly and hairy. Spike simple or once-branched infrafoliar, erect at first, usually becoming pendent, bud enclosed in a deciduous or persistent papery bract; flowers in triads (2 male, 1 female) in spiralling or opposed ranks: male flowers asymmetrical with sepals 3, petals 3, acute, stamens (6)12–30, pistillode present; female flowers with sepals 3, united or free, overlapping, petals 3, overlapping, staminodes absent, pistil 1-celled. Fruit globose to fusiform, red, orange or black, occasionally brown or green, with apical stigmatic remains; mesocarp thinly fleshy. Himalaya and S China to Papua New Guinea. Z10.

CULTIVATION Occurring in the shady understorey of tropical forest, sometimes on river banks which are occasionally inundated, *Pinanga* spp. are small feather palms well suited to shaded niches in humid, tropical gardens. Many are suitable for tub cultivation in the warm, humid glasshouse; their distinctive foliage is often beautifully marked and coloured when young. They are not generally tolerant of dry conditions, which limits their use in the home. Propagate by fresh seed; division of established clumps may also be possible. For cultivation see PALMS.

***P. coronata*** (Bl. ex Mart.) Bl. Stems 3–5(6)m×4cm, clumped. Pinnae crowded, several-fold, linear-lanceolate, slightly falcate, slender-pointed, upper pinnae truncately toothed at tip; rachis glabrous. Infl. erect, becoming nodding; rachillae 7–15. Fr. to 1cm, ellipsoid, black. Java, Sumatra.

***P. dicksonii*** (Roxb.) Bl. ex H.A. Wendl. Trunk 5–6m×5cm. Lvs 1.25m; pinnae 30–60cm, crowded, sessile, broadly linear, upper pinnae confluent. Infl. branches robust, densely flowered. Fr. 2cm, red. India.

***P. disticha*** (Roxb.) Bl. ex H.A. Wendl. Trunk 0.6–1.8m, usually clustered. Lvs 30–40cm; pinnae obovate-cuneate, simple and deeply forked, or just a few broad based pinnae. Infl. to 7.5cm, simple. Fr. elliptic, small, red. Malaya.

***P. insignis*** Becc. Trunk tall, woody. Pinnae subulate, regularly spaced along rachis, semi-rigid to rigid, apices acuminate, deeply notched. Fr. 2.5cm, red. Philippines.

***P. maculata*** Porto ex Lem. TAMY'S PALM; TIGER PALM. Stem slender, smooth. Lvs entire or with 1–2 seg. each side, or pinnate with wide, sessile, pendent pinnae, bright green, mottled with dark green, purple or yellow above. Fr. large, bright red. Philippines.

***P. malaiana*** (Mart.) R. Scheff. Stems to 3m×4cm, clustered. Lvs to 1.8m or more; pinnae to 70cm, subalternate, 18–20, several-fold, linear-lanceolate, slender-pointed, glaucous beneath. Infl. 3–5-branched, reflexed. Fr. 2.5×1cm, ovoid, purple-red. Malay Peninsula, Sumatra, Borneo.

***P. paradoxa*** (Griff.) R. Scheff. Trunk 0.5–2m×0.6cm. Lvs 30cm, oblong, entire or with 3–6 pairs of linear-lanceolate, sigmoid seg. 10–15cm long. Malacca.

***P. patula*** Bl. Stems to 2.5m×2.5cm, clustered, erect, smooth, ringed, swollen at base. Lvs to 1.5m, oblong, irregularly pinnate; pinnae 1–5 fold, sigmoid, acuminate. Infl. green becoming red, recurved; rachillae 2–5. Fr. 1.5×0.6cm, orange-yellow, ovoid-oblong. Sumatra, Borneo.

***P. pectinata*** Becc. Stems to 5m×9cm, clustered. Lvs to 1.25m, pinnate, pinnae to 40×4.5cm, 1–5 fold, blue-green beneath. Infl. bears 3–5 rachillae to 12.5cm. Fr. 1.5×0.5cm, oblong-ovoid. Malay Peninsula.

***P. philippinensis*** Becc. Stems to 3cm diam., stepped. Crownshaft conspicuous, swollen, pale. Pinnae held erect, broad, apices, pointed, deep green. Fr. 1.5cm. Philippines.

***P. scortechinii*** Becc. Trunk to 3m, solitary. Pinnae crowded, lanceolate, acuminate, 2–5-fold. Infl. with rachillae 5–6, ascending to erect; fls arranged in 4 longitudinal ranks. Fr. 1.5×0.9cm, ovoid-ellipsoid. Malay Peninsula.

***P. ternatensis*** R. Scheff. Stem solitary. Lvs 3.5m; pinnae to 1m, lanceolate, falcate, 2-fold. Infl. rachillae spiralling. Ternate Is.

***P. bifida*** Bl. See *P. disticha*.
***P. kuhlii*** Bl. See *P. coronata*.

**Pinckneya** Michx. (Named for Charles Cotesworth Pinckney (1746–1825), Revolutionary politician and general from South Carolina.) Rubiaceae. 1 or 2 species of shrubs or trees. Branches terete. Leaves petiolate, opposite, membranous, deciduous; stipules interpetiolar, caducous. Flowers several in terminal and axillary corymbs; calyx irregularly 5-lobed: 3–4 lanceolate to subulate, 1–2 occasionally developed into enlarged, petiolate, leaflike, deciduous, rose-coloured limb; corolla salverform, tube elongate, spreading at throat, interior hairy, lobes 5, recurved; stamens 5, exserted; ovary 2-celled, style exserted, filiform, 2-lobed, ovules many. Fruit a capsule, subglobose, 2-celled, 2-lobed, 2-valved from top, valves 2-parted to middle, persistent through winter; seeds many, compressed, horizontal, with winged and reticulate-veined testa; embryo elongate, albumen fleshy. SE US, Northern S America. Z9.

CULTIVATION *P. pubens*, from swampy habitats in the South-eastern US, is grown for its colourful enlarged pink or white sepals. Grow in the cool glasshouse or conservatory (min. 7°C/45°F), in a soilless leafmould or peat-based medium, and water plentifully when in growth; reduce water in the winter, but do not allow the potting medium to dry out. Propagate from ripewood cuttings in autumn, and keep cool but frost free over winter.

***P. pubens*** Michx. GEORGIA BARK; FEVER TREE; BITTER-BARK. Shrub or tree to 9m. Lvs to 20×10cm, elliptic to oblong, ovate or oval, apex acute, base narrowed and tapering, hairy to minutely pubesc., dark green above, paler beneath, 6–8-veined; petioles to 3cm; stipules triangular to oblong, acute, to 1cm; light brown. Fls in corymbs to 20cm wide; bracts linear to lanceolate or subulate; peduncles pubesc.; enlarged cal. lobe to 7×5cm, oval or ovate, acute or obtuse at apex and base, membranous, minutely pubesc., on petiole to 1cm, other cal. lobes to 1cm cor. to 4cm, yellow-green, lobes oblong to linear, acute or obtuse, marked brown or purple. Fr. to 2cm; seeds with wings to 10×8mm. S Carolina to Florida.

**Pinellia** Ten. (For Giovanni Vincenzo Pinelli (1535–1601), of the Botanic Garden, Naples.) Araceae. 6 species of low, cormous, perennial herbs. Tuber globose to depressed globose, 2–4cm diam. Leaves basal, synanthous, simple to compound with 3–7-segments, segments to 18cm; petioles to 35cm, slender, bulbils sometimes borne by leaves at junction of veins and petiole or on the lower part of the petiole. Peduncle 3–50cm, shorter than or exceeding petioles, solitary and not forming part of the same shoot as the leaves; spathe persistent, margins overlapping below to form a tube, limb expanded above, oblong, concave, flat or channelled, green, sometimes striped purple; spadix with zone of female flowers adnate to base of spathe tube, male zone free, not adjacent to female; perianth absent; stamens 1–2; ovary unilocular, ovules solitary; sterile appendix present, slender, elongate, sigmoid, long-exserted from spathe, ascending. Fruit a single-seeded berry. China, Japan. Z6.

CULTIVATION As for the hardy species of *Arum*.

***P. cordata*** N.E. Br. To 10cm. Lvs 3–5cm, lanceolate, cordate, green with veins marked in cream; petioles short, purple, bulbiliferous at junction of lamina and petiole. Spathes to 3cm, strongly incurved, green with purple veins; spadix long-exserted, erect, to 7cm above the spathe, pleasantly fragrant of fruit. Summer. China.

***P. integrifolia*** N.E. Br. Corm small, depressed-globose. Lvs 3.5–7.5cm, 1–3, ovate to oblong, acute; petiole to 15cm. Spathe to 3.5cm, limb lanceolate; spadix sigmoid, appendix exserted to 3.5cm. Summer. China, Japan.

***P. pedatisecta*** Schott. Corm to 4cm diam. Lvs pedate, seg. 7–11, median seg. to 18cm, ovate-lanceolate to lanceolate. Peduncle shorter than petioles; spathe to 19cm, limb to 15cm; appendix shorter than spathe, yellow-green. Summer. N & W China.

***P. ternata*** (Thunb.) Breitenb. Corm to 2cm diam. Lvs simple when young, compound with 3 leaflets when adult; leaflets 3–12×1–5cm, sessile, ovate-elliptic to oblong; petiole bulbiliferous. Peduncle to 40cm; spathe to 7cm, green, tube 1.5–2cm, limb lanceolate, curved at apex, glabrous externally, puberulent with-

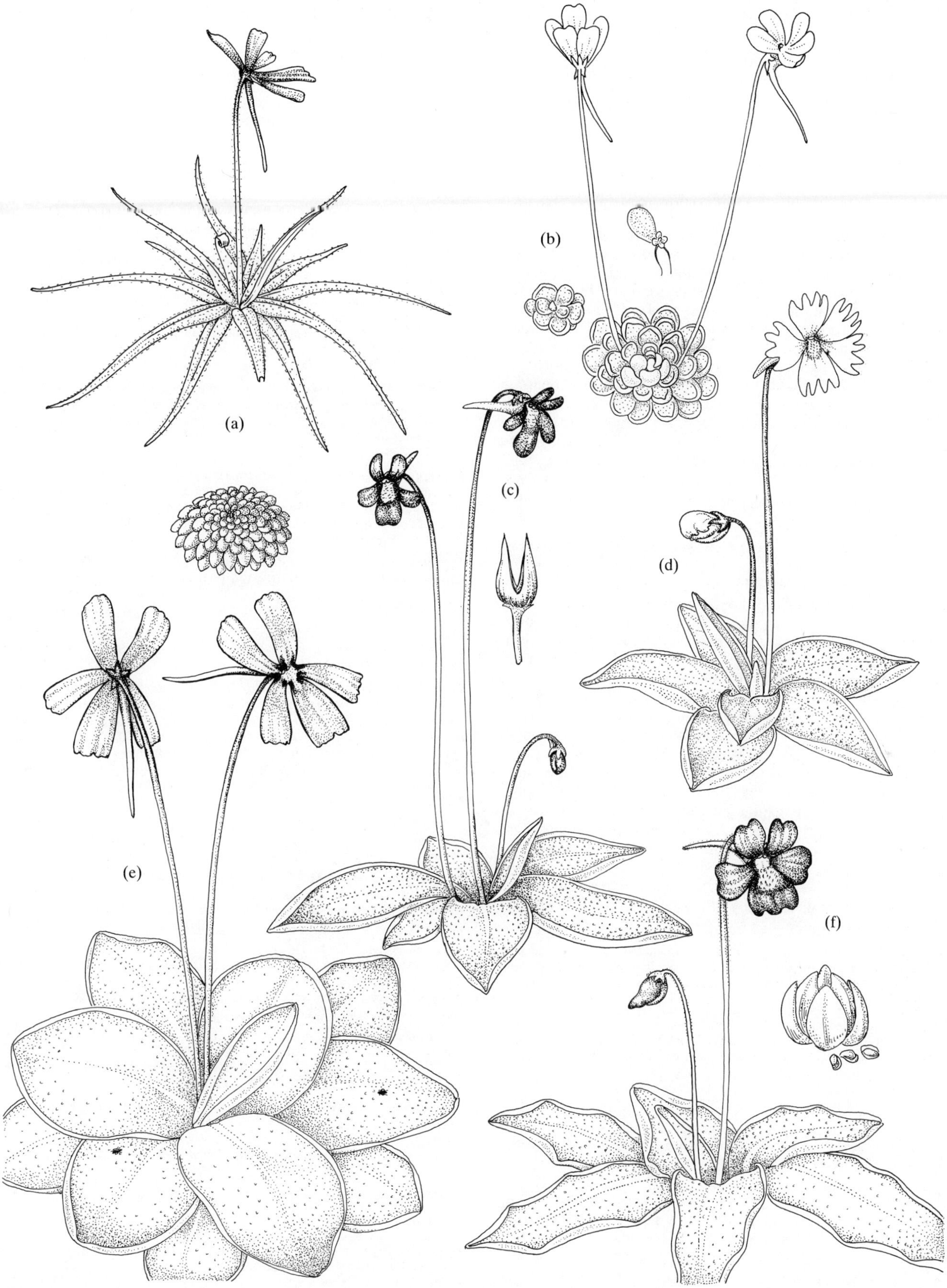


**Pinguicula** (a) *P. gypsicola* flowering plant, winter rosette (×0.75) (b) *P. esseriana* flowering plant, small rosette, proliferating leaf (×0.75) (c) *P. vulgaris* flowering plant (×0.75), fruit (×1.5) (d) *P. lutea* (×0.75) (e) *P. moranensis* (×0.75) (f) *P. longifolia* flowering plant (×0.75) with hibernaculum and gemmae (×2)

in; spadix appendix to 10cm, slender, erect, clasping with apex of spathe, green, purple below. Summer. Japan, Korea, China.

***P. tripartita*** (Bl.) Schott. Corm to 3cm diam., brown-fibrous. Lvs pedatisect, seg. 8–20×2–12cm, 3, ovate, abruptly short-caudate. Peduncle to 50cm; spathe 6–10cm, green externally, purple within, tube to 3cm, limb lanceolate, obtuse, apex slightly curved, papillose within; appendix 15–25cm. Summer. S Japan.

***P. tuberifera*** Ten. See *P. ternata*.

**Pinguicula** L. (From Lat. *pinguis*, fat, from the greasy appearance of leaves.) BUTTERWORT. Lentibulariaceae. 46 species of acaulescent carnivorous perennial herbs, 2.5–30cm. Leaves radical, in rosettes, often with distinct forms in winter and summer, usually congested in winter, or sometimes forming rootless resting buds, hibernacula, larger and expanded in summer; leaves entire, orbicular to ovate to oblong, sometimes linear often with margin somewhat involute, covered by glands sessile or shortly stipitate glands secreting sticky mucilage and digestive enzymes. Flowers axillary, borne on elongate naked scape, usually solitary, occasionally 2–3 on branched scapes; calyx bilabiate, upper lip 3-lobed, lower lip 2-lobed; corolla to 2.5cm, bilabiate with lobes spreading, spurred, open at throat with palate raised, often spotted or streaked, usually hairy, upper lip 2-lobed shorter than lower, lower 3-lobed, purple to pink, white or yellow, throat and palate often contrasting; stamens 2, filaments curved; ovary unilocular, ovules numerous. Fruit a capsule opening by 2 valves; seeds numerous, small. Late spring to summer. Europe, Circumboreal, Americas to Antarctic.

CULTIVATION Most species will grow well in a peat/sand mixture, although some of the tropical species thrive in compost which also includes some loam. Shallow pots are necessary as the root system is weak. Most desire light shade. Hardy species require cold winter conditions which they survive in the form of tight winter-resting buds with practically no roots. If grown outside it is important to prevent birds or other animals disturbing them. They may be propagated by dividing the resting buds, or by seed. Other northern species retain their leaf rosette throughout the winter and are best kept in the cool greenhouse. Central American species require warm greenhouse conditions with a winter minimum of 13°C/55°F, or they will tolerate a house windowsill. Some produce distinct winter and summer types of foliage and require much less water in winter than in summer when they should remain very moist. Propagation is by division in spring, surface-sown seed or leaf cuttings in spring. The latter should be placed on the compost surface, with the wounded petiole just covered by compost. Warmth and high humidity are necessary.

Species from the southeastern US require a position out of direct sunlight and high humidity in a peat/sand compost, and in cool temperate areas should be grown in the cool greenhouse.

***P. agnata*** Casper. Lvs 3.3–5.5×1–1.5cm, 8–12, spathulate or obovate-oblong, apex rounded, thick and succulent. Scapes 1–3, 5–12cm; cor. 1.8–2.2cm, with lobes subequal, white or pale mauve-blue, darker towards margins, throat green. Mexico. Z10.

***P. alpina*** L. Hibernaculum-forming. Lvs 2.5–4.5×0.8–1.4cm, 5–8, elliptic-oblong to lanceolate-oblong, yellow-green, margin involute. Scapes 1–8, 5–11cm; cor. 1–16cm, white with yellow spots on palate, lobes of upper lip triangular, of lower obovate; spur curved, 2–3mm, pale yellow. Capsule ovoid-oblong. Arctic, mountains of Europe, extinct in Scotland. Z3.

***P. caerulea*** Walter. Overwintering as rosette. Lvs 1–6×1–2cm, ovate-oblong, dull pale green, margin involute. Scapes 1–6, 10–30cm; cor. 2.5–4cm, pale violet veined darker violet, lobes to 1cm; spur subulate, 4–10mm. E US (N & S Carolina, Georgia, Florida). Z8.

***P. colimensis*** McVaugh & Michel. Winter rosette lvs 1–2cm, numerous, spathulate, obtuse, summer rosette lvs 1.5–4cm before flowering, 6–10, obovate-oblong, rounded, later enlarging to 6–12×3–6.5cm. Scapes 1–3, 6–14cm; cor. 3.5–5cm, deep rose-pink, throat wide; spur long, curved, pale pink. Mexico. Z10.

***P. corsica*** Bernard & Gren. Hibernaculum-forming. Lvs 2.5–3.5×1–1.6cm, 5–9, ovate to obovate-oblong, yellow-green, petiolate. Scapes 4–9cm; cor. 1.6–2.5cm, pale blue to pink, veined purple in throat, lobes of upper lip narrowly oblong-lanceolate, lobes of lower lip not divergent; spur 4–6mm, cylindric-subulate. Corsica. Z9.

***P. cyclosecta*** Casper. Lvs *c*25 in dense rosette, obovate-spathulate, winter lvs to 1cm, summer lvs to 3×1.2cm. Scapes 1–3, 3–5cm; cor. with wide-open throat, deeply bilabiate, lobes rounded, to 2cm, mallow-purple, throat white; stigma rust-red. Mexico. Z10.

***P. ehlersiae*** Speta & Fuchs. Winter lvs *c*60 in a dense rosette, spathulate, summer rosette to 3.5cm across, lvs *c*25, rounded-spathulate, pale copper-pink, margins involute. Scapes 9–11cm; cor. to 2.5cm, with wide-open throat, lilac to mallow-purple, throat white; spur to 2.2cm. Mexico. Z10.

***P. filifolia*** Wright ex Griseb. Lvs 8–15×0.3cm, 7–20, erect, lanceolate, narrowing to apex. Scapes 2–3, 12–19cm; cor. 14–16mm, white or pink or blue or purple or pale-lilac, lobes subequal. Cuba & Isle of Pines. Z10.

***P. grandiflora*** Lam. Hibernaculum-forming. Lvs 3–4.5×2.5cm, 5–8, oblong to obovate-oblong, yellow-green, margins slightly involute. Scapes 1–5, 6–15cm; cor. 2.5cm, purple to pink or white, white at throat, lobes often overlapping; spur to 12mm, straight. Capsule subglobose. W Europe (SW Ireland, Spain to France). Z7.

***P. gypsicola*** Brandg. Lvs of winter rosettes 1–0.35cm, many, overlapping, sessile, oblong-cuneate or spathulate, obtuse, non-carnivorous, summer lvs 4–7×0.25cm, 10–30, erect, lanceolate-linear, carnivorous. Scapes 3–7, 7.5–12.5cm; cor. 2–4cm, violet-purple or purple-pink, veined darker purple, lobes narrow. Mexico. Z10.

***P. hirtiflora*** Ten. Overwintering as rosette. Lvs 2–6×1–2.5cm, 6–9, elliptic-oblong to ovate-oblong, apex truncate or emarginate, pale green. Scapes 1–3, 5–11cm; cor. to 2.5cm, pink to blue, white and yellow in throat, lobes emarginate; spur 6–10mm, subulate. C & S Italy, Balkans (Albania, Yugoslavia, Greece). Z6.

***P. longifolia*** Ramond ex DC. Hibernaculum-forming. Lvs 6–13×1–2cm, 5–11, lowermost elliptic, rest linear-lanceolate, obtuse, suberect, somewhat undulate, petiolate. Scapes 1–8, 10–15cm; cor. 2.2–4cm, lilac to pale blue, spotted white at base of lower lip, lobes of lower lip overlapping; spur 10–16mm, cylindric-subulate. S Europe Mts (French Alps, Pyrenees, Apennines). Z6.

***P. lusitanica*** L. Overwintering as rosette. Lvs 1–2.5×1cm, 5–12, oblong-ovate, strongly involute, very pale green suffused pink. Scapes 1–8, 2.5–15cm, very slender; cor. 7–9mm, pale pink to pale-lilac, throat yellow, lobes rounded, emarginate; spur 2–4mm, subcylindric, deflexed. W Europe (including GB). Z7.

***P. lutea*** Walter. Lvs 1–6.5×0.8–2cm, oblong-obovate, yellow-green, margin weakly involute. Scapes 1–8, 10–50cm; cor. 2–3.5cm, bright chrome-yellow, lobes subequal, to 1cm; spur 4–10mm, subulate. SE US. Z8.

***P. moranensis*** HBK. Winter rosette lvs 1–3×1cm, 25–40, caespitose or subsessile or subpetiolate, spathulate or oblong-obtuse or cochleariform, summer rosette lvs 6–11.5×3–6cm, 6–9, petiolate, round-ovate or obovate-obtuse, margin revolute or flat. Scapes 3–5, 13–18cm; cor. 3.5–5cm, violet-purple to pink, lobes of upper lip divergent, linear-oblong or rounded-obovate, 1.5–2.5cm, lobes of lower lip subcuneate or obtuse or sublinear, spreading, 1–2.5cm, throat white with contrasting darker purple or crimson markings at base of lobes. Variable. Mexico. Z10.

***P. planifolia*** Chapm. Lvs 3–10cm, elliptic, acute, suffused dull red to purple, or occasionally self green. Scapes several, 20–40cm; cor. 2–3cm, purple to pink or white, throat dark pink; spur 3mm, sac-like, obtuse. SE US. Z8.

***P. primuliflora*** Wood & Godfrey. Lvs 4–8×1–2cm, 8–16, oblong, base-spathulate, apex rounded, margins involute, pale green. Scapes 2–4, 9–17cm; cor. to 2.5cm, rose-pink or violet-blue, white at base of lobes, yellow in throat, lobes subequal, obovate or suborbicular, emarginate. SE US. Z8.

***P. vallisneriifolia*** Webb. Hibernaculum-forming. Lvs in spring 3–4×1.5–2cm, elliptic-ovate, sessile, margin not involute, in summer lvs 10–20×0.8–2cm, suberect, ligulate, acute, margin undulate, petiolate. Scapes 1–8, 10–15cm; cor. 2.5–3.5cm, violet, throat white, hairy, lips unequal, lobes obovate, overlapping; spur 10–14mm, cylindric-subulate. S Spain. Z8.

***P. vulgaris*** L. Hibernaculum-forming. Lvs 2–4.5×1.5–2cm, 5–11, prostrate, oblong to obovate-oblong, margin involute, yellow-green. Scapes 1–6, 7.5–18cm; cor. 1.5–2cm, violet, throat white, lips very unequal, lobes oblong, divergent; spur 3–6mm, cylindric-subulate. NW & C Europe. Z3.

***P. zecheri*** Speta & Fuchs. Winter rosette lvs 2–2.5×0.5cm, 40–50, narrow-spathulate, summer rosette lvs 6–7.5×3.5–4.5cm, 10–15, narrow-elliptic, margin involute, bright green, short-petiolate. Scapes 1–4, 8–10cm; cor. 3.5cm, mallow-purple, darker at centre, throat white, lobes subequal; spur 3.5–4cm. Mexico. Z10.

***P. bakeriana*** Sander. See *P. moranensis*.
***P. caudata*** Schldl. See *P. moranensis*.
***P. ehlersae*** auct. See *P. ehlersiae*.
***P. flos-mulionis*** Morr. See *P. moranensis*.
***P. macrophylla*** McVaugh & Michel. See *P. moranensis*.
***P. orchidioides*** DC. See *P. moranensis*.
***P. rosei*** Wats. See *P. moranensis*.

**Pinus** L. (Lat. name for this tree.) Pinaceae. About 110 species of evergreen, monoecious conifers. Trees or (rarely) shrubs, mostly ovoid-conic in habit when young, crowns spreading and irregular when mature. Bark furrowed or scaly, usually thick. Winter buds scaly, often resinous, a single central bud surrounded by a pseudowhorl of smaller buds, in some species often also a second pseudowhorl of buds part way along the annual shoot (multinodal). Shoots dimorphic: (a) long shoots, appearing like the normal shoots of other trees; (b) dwarf shoots, only 1mm or less long, spirally arranged on the long shoots, and usually falling with the leaves. Leaves trimorphic: (a) needles, slender, stiff, green or glaucous green, triangular or semi-circular (rarely terete) in section, grouped (1)2–5(6) on dwarf lateral shoots in fascicles with a basal sheath of 8–12 scales, these either persistent, or deciduous within the first season; needle margins finely serrate or sometimes entire; stomatal lines visible on all or 1–2 surfaces; (b) small brown (non-photosynthetic), triangular scale leaves, subtending the needle fascicles, spirally arranged, on the long shoots, similar to the bud scales and often most conspicuous on the lower parts of young shoots; (c) juvenile foliage, shorter, single glaucous leaves borne only in the first 1–2(–10) years of life, spirally arranged, thin, flattened (significant and described separately only for the few species where it is retained for much more than 2 years). Male cones (strobili) cylindric, catkin-like, yellow, red or orange, produced in spirally arranged clusters, axillary at the base of long shoots; fertile scales spirally arranged, each with 2 pollen sacs below. Female cones axillary or subterminal, either solitary or in pseudowhorls of 2–10 (rarely more), ovoid or cylindric to subglobose, sometimes resinous, usually spreading or pendulous when mature; scales spirally arranged, persistent, slightly to very woody, imbricate, each subtended by a partially united smaller bract; exposed part of scale with a rhombic woody scale shield (apophysis), often with a crossridged keel, with a central or terminal protuberance, or umbo. Cones mature in 18–24 months, in 3 species 36 months; growth in first 12 months restricted to umbo, apophysis develops in 13th month onwards. In 36 month ripening species umbo is double, with a concentric ring round the central umbo. Cones either opening at maturity, or remaining closed for many years, the seed being stored until the parent trees are killed by forest fires, the heat of the fire also opening the cones. Cone dimensions cited are for closed cones unless otherwise specified. Seeds 2, above each fertile scale, with a hard testa, winged, with a long, or in some spp., short or vestigial wing. N hemisphere, from the Arctic Circe S to C America, N Africa and SE Asia, just crossing the equator in Sumatra.

CULTIVATION Pines are amongst the most important timbers in temperate and tropical regions, cultivated for timber and for their resins, used for products such as turpentine, wood tar and pitch, or for their edible seeds. All of the large species are important timber trees; *P. sylvestris, nigra, contorta* and *ponderosa* are extensively used in cool temperate plantation forestry, as are *P. radiata, patula, elliottii, massoniana* and *canariensis* in warm temperate areas and *P. caribaea* var. *hondurensis, patula* ssp. *tecunumannii, merkusii* and *kesiya* in subtropical zones. *P. pinaster* and *P. palustris* are the most important for resin production, but many others are also extensively tapped. Large edible seeds are produced by about 30 species; the most important in commerce are of *P. pinea* (S Europe, as pine nuts, pignons, pignola, etc according to language), *P. gerardiana* (Pakistan & Afghanistan, the 'chilgoza' nuts often seen in Indian food shops), *P. koraiensis* (exported from N China), and in Mexico and the American SW, the pinyons *P. edulis* and *P. cembroides*. Another edible product is Greek retsina wine, flavoured with resin of *P. halepensis*, and commercial supplies of vanillin flavouring are a by-product of other resins released from pine pulpwood. In US, pines are popular as Christmas trees, mostly *P. sylvestris* var. *hamata* but also even *P. ponderosa*; they are generally too long-leaved and open branched for British tastes, though *P. sylvestris* and *P. contorta* are becoming more frequent; they are better than *Picea abies* as the needles do not fall, but not as well shaped as *Abies* species and riskier, being more inflammable than *Abies* (to either candles or faulty electric lights) if allowed to dry out. The cones are also popular as Christmas decorations; the commonest in recent trade are *P. kesiya* from the Philippines, and *P. massoniana* and *P. elliottii* from China, but *P. pinaster* and occasionally others are also sold, while in California the impressive 60cm/24in. cones of *P. lambertiana* are used but sadly not exported to Britain.

Pines are excellent trees for parks and gardens, having good foliage, cones and crown shape; most are long lived and many are large trees. The large number of species means that at least some are well adapted to almost every climate and soil condition in the world, from arctic Siberia to the tropics, from coastal saltmarsh to 4000m/13000ft altitude, and from dry chalk to deep wet acid peat; even many individual species will tolerate a wide range of these. In comparison with most other genera in Pinaceae, most are drought tolerant and warmth loving; their best growth in Britain is in the centre and east, where genera like *Abies* and *Picea* do not thrive. All the northern species and a few high altitude southern species are hardy to zone 7 or less, but those from lower altitudes in the south are tender, only in zones 8–10. Those from continental climates require considerable summer heat for good growth; in Britain they are slow-growing, sinuous-boled and half or less of their size in the wild, and often fail to produce any cones.

Pines provide the best trees of any for coastal shelter, many resisting salt-laden gales with impunity. On the Atlantic coast of Britain, as on the Pacific coast of US, the best are the very fast-growing *P. muricata* and *P. radiata*; coasts too cold for these; such as E US, N Europe and Japan, rely on *P. nigra* and *P. thunbergii*.

There are many excellent pines for garden planting. For small gardens, the slow-growing pinyon and lace-bark pines are beautifully shaped; they are best on freely drained sites, and are highly drought tolerant. Among these, *P. monophylla* is a very neat conic bright blue tree, while *P. bungeana* has marvellous smooth bark in a patchwork of white, green and pink. Further north or at high altitudes, the foxtail pines are similarly valuable, at their best in cold dry summers which defeat most plants; *P. aristata* grows well in Iceland. Their long-held needles make a dense, rich show of good health and vigour, yet so slow growing that the smallest garden can accommodate them. Also for cold sites is *P. pumila*, with fine blue-green foliage and not over 3m/10ft tall. For slightly larger garden, *P. pungens* makes a small tree on the poorest sands, with thick needles and fascinating spiny cones ripening salmon-pink.

For large gardens and parks, the range of good pines is enormous; the boldest foliage is on *P. engelmannii*; in cold areas *P. jeffreyi* and *P. ponderosa* replace it. *P. coulteri* is also grown for its bold foliage, but more for its massive cones. Many of the white pines have delicate silky foliage; the Eurasian species are better as they resist blister rust (see below). *P. peuce* is very resilient, happy in all soils and exposures; *P. wallichiana* has longer cones and needles, but *P. armandii* is better, with a degree of grace not shown by either of these. Of the American ones, *P. ayacahuite* is slightly more rust-resistant than most, and has the unique distinction of being the only tropical tree (natural range 14–20°N) hardy in central Scotland (57°N); it also has the longest cones of any conifer to grow well in Britain.

In warm-temperate areas like S Africa and Australia, the recently described *P. praetermissa* is a fine, glossy-leaved small tree with interesting round cones, while *P. patula* and *P. lumholtzii* have excellent pendulous foliage. *P. maximartinezii* is grown for its cones, similar to a mediaeval mace in shape and size.

All pines are light-demanding, and should be planted in full sun; even side shade can adversely affect growth if it lasts for long each day. The majority benefit from good drainage. For propagation see CONIFERS.

Many different rust fungi can affect pines and several are widespread. The white pine blister rust, *Cronartium ribicola*, causes a devastating disease of the American white pines, especially *Pinus strobus* and *P. lambertiana*. The mycelium is perennial in the bark and results in large cankers which kill the branches and after a few years, the whole tree. Orange aeciospores are produced on these cankers and infect the alternate hosts, currants, especially the

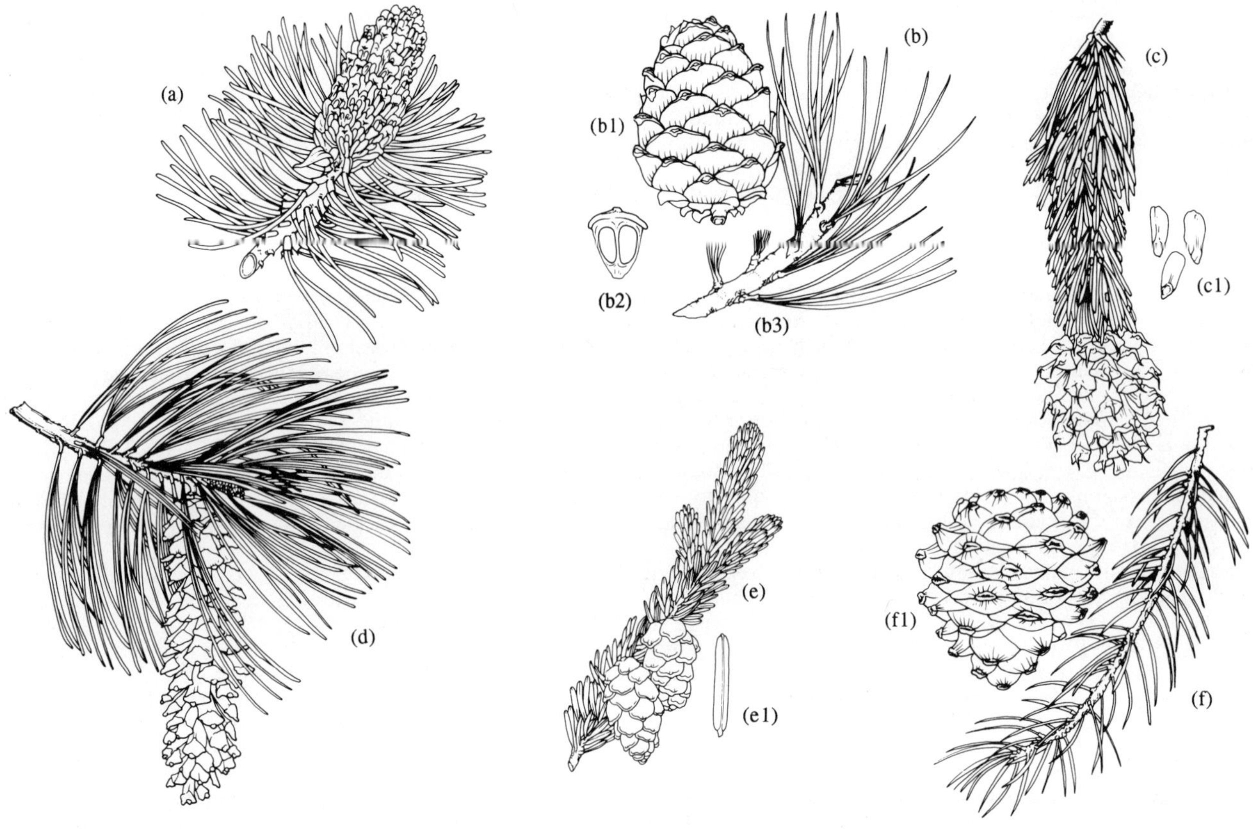


**Pinus** (not to scale) (a) *P. pumila* (b) *P. cembra* (b1) cone (b2) cone scale (b3) stem (c) *P. aristata* (c1) seeds (d) *P.wallichiana* (e) *P. nigra* (e1) needle (f) *P. monophylla* (f1) cone

blackcurrant (*Ribes nigrum*) on which the uredio- and teliospores are produced. The related fusiform rust *Cronartium fusiforme* causes a similar serious disease in the SE US on *P.tarda* and related species; strict plant health regulations have kept it out of Britain and Europe to date. Other less serious rusts include the pine twisting rust, *Melampsora populnea*, which mainly affects *Pinus sylvestris*; the pine resin-top rust, *Endocronartium pini*, also on *P.sylvestris*, may girdle and kill the branches. A needle rust is caused by *Coleosporium tussilaginis*, and needle cast by the fungus *Lophodermium* spp.; the latter is worst in cool, damp areas on species adapted to drier conditions. *Pinus* can also be affected by armillaria root rot (*Armillaria* spp.) and phytophthora root rot (*Phytophthora cinnamomi*). In Britain the most serious disease of plantation conifers, including pines, is fomes root and butt rot caused by the fungus *Heterobasidion annosum* (syn. *Fomes annosus*); this and many of the other diseases to which the trees are susceptible are unlikely to be a problem on isolated garden trees.

Important pests common to Europe and North America include the pine shoot moth (*Rhyacionia buoliana*) with brown caterpillars up to 18mm long, which can be a serious pest of young trees though boring into and killing shoots, including the terminal shoot; pine adelgids (*Pineus* spp.); several species of sawflies including the fox-coloured or European pine sawfly (*Neodiprion sertifer*) and *Diprion* spp., which are defoliating pests; and a red spider mite, the conifer spinning mite (*Oligonychus ununguis*).

Although often useful for identification of species, the length and number of leaves per fascicles are not good phylogenetic markers, being related mainly to climatic conditions. *Pinus* is divided into 3 distinctive subgenera, which recent research suggests may deserve full generic recognition in the future, outlined below with keys:

Subgenus *Strobus* Lemmon (Genus *Strobus* Opiz). WHITE OR SOFT PINES. Cone cylindrical, rarely ovoid, umbo terminal, apophysis without a sealing band where scales meet on closed cone; seeds with a strongly adnate wing. Leaves with a single vascular bundle. Fascicles always of 5 slender leaves, serrulate or entire, stomata all or most on inner faces, with early deciduous sheath. Shoot smooth, not ridged, scale leaves early deciduous and not decurrent along shoot. Bark smooth grey on trees up to about 30cm diameter, becoming coarsely cracked but never scaly.

Subgenus *Ducampopinus* (A. Chev.) de Ferré ex Critchf. & Little (genera *Caryopitys* Small; *Ducampopinus* A. Chev.) PINYON & FOXTAIL PINES. Cone ovoid, globular or rarely cylindrical, umbo dorsal, apophysis without a sealing band; seeds with an articulate wing. Leaves with a single vascular bundle. Fascicles with 1–5 leaves, serrulate or entire, stomata often all or most on inner faces, rarely equally on all faces, sheath early deciduous or variably partly persistent. Shoot smooth, not or a little ridged, but not scaly or flaking, scale leaves very small and deciduous. Bark smooth for many years, remaining smooth and exfoliating or becoming rough plated or fissured, but not thickly scaly.

Subgenus *Pinus* typical or hard pines. Cone conic or ovoid, umbo dorsal, apophysis with a sealing band. Leaves with a double vascular bundle. Fascicles with 2–6(–8) leaves, always serrulate and with stomata equally on all surfaces, sheath persistent (deciduous in 2 spp.). Shoot rough, ridged, with persistent scale leaves (occasionally deciduous, when mostly scaly after 2–3 years with exfoliating thin layers or bark). Bark either rough, thickly scaly, or thin, finely scaly with flaking papery layers exfoliating.

For further information on the classification of *Pinus*, see Rushforth (1987). Many pines cannot be reliably identified without cones.

Key to subgenus *Strobus*

**1** Shoots densely pubescent, cones soft, not very woody, not opening when ripe, seeds large with wing reduced to a narrow rim.
*Pp. cembra, koraiensis.*

**2** Shoots thinly pubescent, cones hard, slightly opening when ripe but not releasing seeds, scales slightly reflexed; seeds large, with wing reduced to a narrow rim.
*Pp. albicaulis, pumila.*

**3** Shoots thinly pubescent or glabrous, cones opening when ripe to release seeds, scales not reflexed; seeds small or large, with a long to very short wing.
*Pp. amamiana, armandii, bhutanica, dalatensis, fenzeliana, lambertiana morrisonicola, parviflora, peuce, wallichiana, wangii.*

**4** Shoots thinly pubescent or glabrous, cones opening when ripe to release seeds, scales reflexed at least at tips; seeds small or large, with a long to very short wing.
*Pp. ayacahuite, chiapensis, flexilis, monticola, strobiformis, strobus, veitchii.*

Key to subgenus *Ducampopinus*

**1** Leaf sheath fully deciduous.

1.1 Leaves slender, 1.5mm, in 3s; seeds large, with a very short wing; bark smooth, white and shedding in small plates. Temperate.
*Pp. bungeana, gerardiana.*

1.2 Leaves flat and broad, 3–5mm, in 2s; seeds small, with a long wing; bark not as above. Tropical.
*P. krempfii.*

**2** Leaf sheath semi-persistent to fully persistent.

2.1 Leaves in 5s, short, 2–4cm; seeds small with a long wing.
*Pp. aristata, balfouriana, longaeva.*

2.2 Leaves in 3–4s, longer, 6–10cm; seeds small with a long wing.
*P. rzedowskii.*

2.3 Leaves in 1–5s, short or long; seeds large with a very short wing.
*Pp. californiarum, cembroides, culminicola, discolor, edulis, johannis, maximartinezii, monophylla, nelsonii, pinceana, quadrifolia, remota.*

Key to subgenus *Pinus*

(Note: leaf sheath persistent in all except group 1. The groups in set 4 are artificial and do not represent real relationships; also species with variable needle number appear more than once.)

**1** Leaf sheath fully deciduous, shoot rough, exfoliating after 2 years.
*Pp. leiophylla, lumholtzii.*

**2** Shoot buds ovoid-conic to cylindric, resin free and with fringed, revolute scale tips; leaves in 2–3s; cones glossy red-brown, 5–23cm, heavy, hard, woody. 1–2 whorls of branches produced each year. [Wood with small (pinoid) ray-cell pits.]
*Pp. brutia, canariensis, halepensis, merkusii, pinaster, pinea, roxburghii.*

**3** Shoot buds mostly acute-conic, scale tips loosely adpressed; leaves in 2–3s, 4–30cm, if over 20cm, fine, not stout; shoot variously buff to brown, not bloomed nor green after first winter, prominent narrow grooves between decurrent scale leaves on first year shoot; cones small, 3–11cm, mostly matt, grey, yellow-brown or chestnut, not tinged red, light to moderately heavy; small to very small spine on umbo, placed slightly off centre. Only 1 whorl of branches produced each year. [Wood with large (fenestriform) ray-cell pits.]
*Pp. densata, densiflora, heldreichii, henryi, kesiya, luchuensis, massoniana, mugo, nigra, sylvestris, resinosa, tabulaeformis, taiwanensis, thunbergii, tropicalis, yunnanensis.*

**4** Shoot buds mostly blunt-cylindric or cylindric-conic, scales tips mostly adpressed, resinous or not; leaves in 2–5(–8)s, 4–35cm, fine or stout; grooves between decurrent scale leaves less well defined. Cones small to very large, 3–35cm, spine on umbo (small to very large) centrally placed. 1–3 whorls of branches produced each year. [Wood with small (pinoid) ray-cell pits.]

4.1 Shoots stout, 1.5–2cm thick, bloomed, buds with scale tips free; leaves in 3s or 5s, long, 20–30cm, blue-grey; cones massive, 10–35×10–18cm closed, scales stoutly spiked, seeds large, over 1cm.
*Pp. coulteri, sabiniana, torreyana.*

4.2 Shoots stout or not, bloomed or not, buds as 4 generally; leaves short to long, coarse or fine, blue or green. Cones small to large, 4–25×2–8cm, not massively heavy; matt or glossy; seeds small, 3–8mm.

4.2a Leaves mostly in 2s or 2s and 3s mixed; generally short, 3–18cm.
*Pp. banksiana, clausa, contorta, densa, echinata, elliottii, glabra, muricata, ponderosa* var. *scopulorum, pungens, radiata* var. *binata, virginiana.*

4.2b Leaves mostly in 3s or rarely 4s; generally medium 7–25cm.
*Pp. attenuata, caribaea, elliottii, engelmannii, greggii, hartwegii, herrerai, jeffreyi, lawsonii, occidentalis, palustris, patula, ponderosa, radiata, rigida, serotina, taeda, teocote.*

4.2c Leaves mostly in 5s or rarely 6–8; generally long 10–40cm.
*Pp. apulcensis, arizonica, cooperi, devoniana, durangensis, engelmannii, gordoniana, hartwegii, maximinoi, montezumae, oaxacana, occidentalis, oocarpa, praetermissa, pringlei, pseudostrobus, rudis.*

***P. albicaulis*** Engelm. WHITEBARK PINE. To 20m. Crown spreading, shrubby at higher altitudes with 1–10 main stems; bark grey-white, smooth, exfoliating; branches horizontal, upcurved at tips; twigs red-yellow or orange to brown, becoming grey; smooth-pubesc., flexible; buds resinous, broadly ovoid, acuminate, scales yellow-brown or red-brown, long-acuminate, loosely adpressed. Needles 5 per fascicle, 4–7cm×1mm, short-acuminate, stiff, flexible, dark green, entire, persisting for 6–8 years, stomatal lines on all 3 surfaces; sheath to 15mm, deciduous in first year. Cones 4–7×4–5cm, ovoid, indehiscent, matt purple when young, turning brown; scales short, thick, not opening when mature, apophysis with a sharp-pointed umbo. Seeds 7–9×7mm, sweet, edible, dispersed by birds. N America (British Columbia to California). Similar to *P. flexilis*, distinguished by its non-opening cones and smaller seeds. 'Flinck': dwarf form. 'Noble's Dwarf': shrubby, of compact habit. Z2.

***P. amamiana*** Koidz. Related to *P. parviflora* and *P. fenzeliana*, not to *P. armandii*; to 25m; bark smooth, grey, becoming thick-scaled on old trees. Shoots dark brown with scattered black pubescence. Needles in 5's, sheath deciduous; straight, 6–11cm, glossy dark green with indistinct stomatal lines on inner faces. Cones 4.5–7×2.5cm, glossy orange-brown; scales moderately thick; seed 10mm with a 1mm rudimentary wing. S Japan (Yakushima, Tanegashima). Z9.

***P. apulcensis*** Lindl. Tree to 22m, crown domed when mature; bark very rough, deeply fissured. Needles 5 per fascicle, 15–30cm, stout, grey-green; sheath persistent. Cones ovoid, 10–15×5cm, opening to ×9cm, buff, symmetrical scales stiff, thick; umbo protuberant, with a sharp 2mm mucro. E Mexico. *P. estevezii* (Martinez) Perry (*P. pseudostrobus* var. *estevezii* Martinez) probably synonymous, has cones smaller, to 13cm, slightly asymmetric. NE Mexico. GB 1984. Z9.

***P. aristata*** Engelm. ROCKY MOUNTAINS BRISTLECONE PINE. To 18m. Crown with ascending, whorled, dense branches, occasionally procumbent; bark dark grey, smooth and green when young, becoming fissured, rust-brown; shoots rust-brown or orange-brown, brighter beneath, with short pale hairs, becoming darker with age; buds to 7mm, ovoid, dark rust-brown, acuminate, outer scale loosely adpressed. Needles 5 per fascicle, 2.5–4cm×1mm, persisting to 15 years, sulcate, with flecks of white resin, bright green, blue-white on inner surface in first year of growth, darker later, densely arranged on shoot, curved along the shoot in the first year, more spreading later; sheath split in first year, but persisting, revolute, to 4 years at leaf bases. Young female cones to 1cm, sessile, dark purple, maturing cylindric-ovoid, brown, 5–10cm, apophysis convex, cross-keeled, umbo a narrow, bristle-like thorn, to 8mm. Seeds to 6mm, ovate, light grey-brown, wing articulate, to 1.5cm. US (Rocky Mts). Easily distinguished by the resin flecks. 'Cecilia': dwarf form. Z3.

***P. arizonica*** Engelm. ARIZONA PINE. Tree to 35m, similar to *P. ponderosa* ssp. *scopulorum* but shoots slender, yellow-brown bloomed white or pink; needles in fascicles of 5, rarely 4 or 3, 13–20cm. Cones 5–8cm, scales 15–20mm wide, thin, shiny, flexible, umbo with a sharp spine, opening when ripe and falling soon after but leaving basal scales on branch. US (SE Arizona, SW New Mexico), NW Mexico. var. ***stormiae*** Martinez. Lvs 3–5 per fascicle, longer and coarser, 20–28cm; cones 6–12cm, scales stiffer, less shiny, umbo with a small prickle. US (W Texas), NE Mexico. Z8.

***P. armandii*** Franch. CHINESE WHITE PINE. To 40m, usually shorter. Branches horizontal, spreading widely; bark thin, grey to green-grey, smooth, becoming cracked into plates when mature; shoots yellow-green to olive green, often slightly bloomed; minutely pubesc. to glabrous, becoming olive brown at maturity; winter buds cylindric, or ovoid, obtuse, pale brown, slightly resinous, bud scales long-acuminate, spreading near apex. Needles in fascicles of 5, 10–18cm, bright glossy green, acute, thin, flexible, spreading or pendulous, often kinked near the base, persisting 2, rarely 3 years, outer face with no stomata, inner face white-green to glaucous blue, dentate; sheath abscising in the first year. Cones cylindric to oblong-conic, in groups of 1–3, short-stalked, 8–20×4–11cm, erect, becoming pendulous in the second year; seed scales matt yellow-brown, incurved, thick, woody, terminally acutely tapered or rounded, umbo small, obtuse. Seeds brown-red, to 13×11mm, wing less than 1mm, scabrous. C & W China. var. ***dabeshanensis*** (Cheng & Law) Silba. Lvs shorter, 8–15cm; seeds to 16mm. E China (Anhui, Dabieshan mts). var. ***marstersiana*** Hayata. To 25m. Trunk to 1m diam. Needles to 15cm, lime green. Cones broader, to 20×8cm; scales yellow- to red-brown, apex often slightly reflexed. Seeds to 13mm. Taiwan. Z7.

***P. attenuata*** Lemmon. KNOBCONE PINE. To 24m, often multistemmed in cult.; crown slender-conic, branches ascending to erect; bark dark brown at base of bole, splitting to form loose scales, upper bole light brown, smooth; shoots glabrous, orange-brown; buds spindle-shaped, long-acuminate, to 24mm, slightly resinous, scales tightly adpressed. Needles 3 per fascicle, slender, 11–18cm, sharply acuminate, erect, yellow-green, falling after 3–4 years, serrate, stomatal lines on all faces; sheath to 12mm, persistent. Cones reflexed down branches, subsessile, in groups of 2–4, slender-conic, 9–17×4–5cm, distinctly asymmetrical, remaining closed for many years, dorsal scales conically enlarged, umbo thick, bowed, thorned, shaded scales flatter, thorns shorter. Seeds oval, black, to 7mm, wings to 3cm. W US (Coastal mts and Sierra Nevada, California, S Oregon). Z7.

***P. ×attenuradiata*** Stockw. & Righter. (*P. attenuata* × *P. radiata.*) Resembles *P. radiata* more than *P. attenuata* in habit, but hardier than *P. radiata*, branches more frequently. Z7.

***P. ayacahuite*** Ehrenb. ex Schldl. MEXICAN WHITE PINE. To 55m in wild, usually shorter in cult. Resembles *P. monticola* in habit. Bole to 1.5m diam.; bark smooth, light grey when young, rust-brown, rough, fissured and shallowly ridged on older trees; shoots grey to light brown, rusty red pubesc., rarely glabrous; buds brown, resinous, conical, to 15mm, bud scales with long, distinct tips. Needles 5 per fascicle, 9–18cm×1mm, thin, pendulous, 3-sided, falling after 3–4 years, silver to blue-green ventrally due to stomatal lines, shiny green on outer face without stomata, margins finely toothed; sheath to 1.5cm, deciduous. Cones short-stalked, sub-terminal, pendulous, solitary or grouped, very resinous, often slightly curved cylindric, 16–35×4–5cm closed, opening to ×8–11cm; scales thin, flexible, elliptic-oblong, 4–6×2.5–3cm, apex usually recurved with a small, blunt umbo, basal scales falcate. Seeds ovate, 6–8mm, dark grey with brown spots, wings narrow, 30–40mm, obliquely truncate. C America (Guatemala to S Mexico). Z7.

***P. balfouriana*** A. Murray. FOXTAIL PINE. To 25m in wild, very slow growing. Crown slender-conic; bark grey, ridged; twigs with white patches of resin; shoots orange-brown, pubesc.; winter buds resinous, ovoid, short-acuminate, to 7mm. Needles 5 per fascicle, curved, 20–50×1mm, glossy dark green; stomatal lines white, on inner surface only; falling after 10–20 years. Cone 7–13×2.5–3cm, opening to ×5–7cm, oblong-cylindric, purple-brown to red-brown; scales fragile, narrow, elongate, apophysis with a central umbo, bearing a short spine to 1mm. Seed 9×4mm, patterned light brown on dark brown, wing pale brown, articulate. US (N California, Klamath mts). var. ***austrina*** (R.J. Mastr. & J.D. Mastr.) Silba. Very similar; cones smaller 6–10cm. US (California, S Sierra Nevada). Z5.

***P. banksiana*** Lamb. JACK PINE. To 23m, often less. Crown irregular, ovoid-conic; bark scaly, fissured, orange-grey to red-brown; branches irregularly arranged, annual growth usually with 2 whorls; shoots flexible, green to brown, glabrous; buds very resinous, light brown, cylindric, to 10mm, scales tightly adpressed. Needles 2 per fascicle, twisted, spreading, 2–5cm×1.5mm, light green to yellow green, obscurely serrate, falling after 2–4 years; sheaths to 4mm, persistent. Cones 3–6.5×2cm, ovoid-conic, often in pairs, yellow-buff fading to grey, small, often curved, pointing forward along shoot, umbo unarmed or with a very small spine, remaining closed for many years on the tree. Seeds 2–3mm, black-brown, wings to 12mm. N America (Nova Scotia to Yukon, Minneapolis to New Hampshire). 'Annae': needles tinted yellow. 'Compacta': dense and fast-growing dwarf. 'Tucker's Dwarf': denser than 'Compacta'. 'Uncle Fogy': prostrate, fast-growing. Z2.

***P. bhutanica*** Grierson, Long & Page. EAST BHUTAN PINE. To 25+m, trunk and branches sinuous. Shoots grey-green bloomed white, thinly glandular pubesc. Needles 5 per fascicle, 15–28cm, pendulous, glossy green with white stomatal band on inner faces, sheath deciduous. Cone similar to *P. wallichiana* but scales red-brown not buff, and usually smaller, 17–20mm wide and flatter. E Himalaya (C Bhutan to Assam, wet outer ranges). Z9.

***P. brutia*** Ten. TURKISH PINE; CALABRIAN PINE. To 30m, crown conic becoming irregular with age; bark on bole thick, orange with black fissures; in upper crown thin, flaking, orange-red. Shoots grey, glabrous; buds ovoid, with fringed scales with revolute tips. Needles sparse, yellow-green, 10–15cm, spreading, on some trees to 25–29cm and pendulous, slender, 1mm, 2 per fascicle, rarely 3, indistinct stomatal lines on both sides; sheath 1.5cm, persistent. Cones spreading, not reflexed, on a 1–10×10mm thick peduncle; stouter than *P. halepensis*, 5–11×3.5–4.5cm closed, red-brown, scales 20mm wide, very hard and stiff. Seeds 7–8×5mm, with a broad, auricled, 15–20×10mm wing. NE Greece & Turkey to Lebanon, Crimea & E Black Sea coast; naturalised in S Italy (Brutium) from where described. ssp. ***eldarica*** (Medv.) Nahal. ELDAR PINE. Lvs slightly shorter, 8–13cm, cones shorter, 5–8cm. Azerbaijan, N Iraq, very rare in wild but also extensively naturalized or ?wild Iran to Pakistan; extremely drought tolerant. Z7.

***P. bungeana*** Zucc. ex Endl. LACEBARK PINE. To 25m, often multi-stemmed, slow growing. Crown columnar or bushy; bark white to grey-green, smooth, exfoliating in small, round flakes to reveal cream or pale yellow, darkening through green, olive-brown to red-purple; shoots olive green, becoming grey-green, glabrous; winter buds resin-free, ovoid to ellipsoid, to 13mm, acuminate. Fascicles scattered; needles 3 per fascicle, 5–9cm×2mm, hard, shiny, sharply acuminate, dark yellow-green on outer face, pale grey-green on inner face, smelling of turpentine when crushed, finely serrate, stomatal lines visible on all surfaces; leaf sheaths short, abscising in 1st year. Cones sub-terminal, solitary or in pairs, short pedunculate, bluntly ovate, 4–6.5×3–5cm, apophysis wide, with a transverse ridge, wrinkled; umbo with a 2mm reflexed spike. Seeds ovate, 10×8mm, dark brown, wings short, easily separated. C & N China. Z5.

***P. californiarum*** D. Bail. CALIFORNIA SINGLE-LEAF PINYON. Closely similar to *P. monophylla* in single needles but otherwise more like *P. edulis*. Small tree to 10m. Needles 1 per fascicle, 4–6cm×1.5–2mm thick, dark grey-green (not glaucous blue), 9–16 resin ducts in leaf; sheath semi-persistent, 5–7mm, reflexed but not revolute. Cones globular, 3–4cm, opening to ×4–5cm; seed 12mm, edible, oily, with very short 2mm wing. US (SE California), Mexico (N Baja California). ssp. ***fallax*** (Little) D. Bail. ARIZONA SINGLE-LEAF PINYON. Has only 2–7 resin ducts in the 1.2–1.7mm broad lvs. US (SW Arizona). Z9.

***P. canariensis*** C. Sm. CANARY ISLANDS PINE. To 60m, usually less, narrowly conical when young, domed when mature; crown broad, branches regularly whorled, lower branches often persistent; bark thick, dark to rust brown, scaly and deep-fissured. Shoots glabrous, yellow-brown; buds not resinous, large, ovate, acute, scales lanceolate, margins fringed, tips revolute. Needles 3 per fascicle, pendulous or spreading, falling after 2–3 years, 15–30cm×1mm, acute, bright green, stomatal lines on all sides; sheaths to 2cm, persistent. Juvenile foliage blue-green, 3–6cm, often produced on trees up to 10 years old, occasionally longer. Cones brown, ovoid-conic, subterminal, solitary or grouped 2–4, subsessile, spreading to pendulous, 8–20×5–6cm, opening to ×7–13cm; scales thick, apophysis bluntly cross-keeled, with a flattish umbo. Seeds 13mm, dark grey, wing adnate, to 3cm. Canary Is. (La Palma, Tenerife, Grand Canary). Z9.

***P. caribaea*** Morelet. CARIBBEAN PINE. To 30m; closely related to *P. occidentalis* and perhaps better treated as a variety of it. Crown open, broad, round, or irregular; bark grey to brown, ridged, exfoliating in large flat plates; shoots orange-brown; buds cylindric, acuminate, red-brown, bud scales narrow, apex acute, margin fringed. Needles usually 3, sometimes 4 per fascicle, crowded at their bases, dropping after 2 years, 15–25cm, olive green to dark glossy green, stomatal lines on all sides; sheaths persistent, to 12mm, pale brown when young, dark grey-brown when mature. Cones glossy rust-brown, subterminal, reflexed, 5–10×2.5–3.5cm, opening to ×5–7cm, deciduous; scales flat to slightly swollen with a weak transverse ridge, umbo with a small thorn, to 1mm. Seeds triangular, narrowly ovate, 6mm, wings to 3cm, moderately adnate. W Cuba. var. ***bahamensis*** (Griseb. Barrett & Golfari BAHAMAS PINE. To 22m. Needles often 2 as well as 3 per fascicle, cones narrower when open, to ×4–5cm, umbo more prominent, 2mm; seeds 5mm with an articulate wing. Bahama & Caicos Is. var. ***hondurensis*** (Loock) Barrett & Golfari HONDURAN PINE. To 44m, very fast growing. Needles 3 to 4, occasionally 5 per fascicle, longer, to 33cm; cones larger, to 13cm, darker brown, apophysis less swollen but with a strong transverse ridge and stout, sharp, spinal 4–5mm umbo; seed 6.5mm with an articulate wing. C America (extreme SE Mexico to Nicaragua), very important in tropical forestry. Z10.

***P. cembra*** L. SWISS PINE; AROLLA PINE. To 25m. Crown dense, narrow-columnar to acute-ovate, often branched from the ground; bark smooth, grey-green, becoming brown suffused grey, furrowed, scaly when mature; branches short, densely twiggy; shoots tomentose, yellow-brown, turning dark-grey in the second year; buds resinous, ovate, to 11mm, apex acute, scales long-acuminate. Needles stiff, in dense fascicles of 5, 6–11cm, obtuse-acuminate, falling after 3–5 years, margin 6–finely serrate, dark green on the exterior surface, stomatal lines on 2 blue-white interior surfaces; sheaths deciduous after 1 year. Cones resinous, obtuse-ovate, 4–7.5×4cm, purple when young, brown when mature, only on trees over 30 years old, subterminal, subsessile, broken up by birds or rodents when ripe years and the seeds dispersed by them; scales thick, obtuse, to 2cm wide, umbo small, grey. Seeds in pairs, brown, 10×8mm, edible, wing reduced to a thin rim. C Europe (Alps, Carpathians). 'Aurea': lvs yellow. 'Aureovariegata': lvs yellow. Compacta Glauca': compact and conic with ascending branches; needles tinted blue. 'Jermyns': compact and conic, very slow-growing. 'Kairamo': needles profuse, dense at branch tips. 'Monophylla': slow-growing, irregular dwarf. 'Nana': tightly pyramidal dwarf; needles tinted blue. 'Pendula': branches pendulous. 'Pygmaea': dwarf form, to 40cm. 'Stricta': narrowly columnar, branches ascending. 'Variegata': needles stippled yellow, sometimes entirely yellow. Z4. ssp. *sibirica* (Du Tour) Rupr. SIBERIAN PINE. Needles with 3 resin canals, not 1; cones larger 6–9×5cm. Siberia. Z1.

***P. cembroides*** Zucc. PINYON PINE; MEXICAN NUT PINE. To 15m. Crown domed; bark of older trees thick, deeply rectangular fissured, black-brown, branches outspread; shoots dark orange, glabrous or pubesc.; buds resin-free, elliptic, to 12mm, scales densely imbricate, pale brown with darker tips. Needles 2–3 per fascicle, clustered on shoot tips, 3–6cm; apex sharp-acuminate, entire, olive green, falling after 4–5 years, stomatal lines on all 3 surfaces; sheaths semi-persistent, revolute. Cones sessile or subsessile, globose, 3–4cm, bright green when young, opening to ×5cm, orange- or buff-brown, about 10–12 fertile scales, apophysis pyramidal with a transverse ridge, 12–16mm wide, umbo 5mm broad, slightly protruding; seed 15mm, golden brown, edible, flesh pink (other pinyons white); with a 2mm wing remaining on the scale when seed falls. Mexico (mts in NW, NE & C), US (W Texas, rare). 'Blandsfortiana': very slow-growing dwarf, to 25cm in 15 years, irregular in growth. ssp. ***lagunae*** (Pass.) D. Bail. To 21m. Needles longer, 5–7.5cm, 2–3 per fascicle; cones on 6mm peduncles, ovoid 4.5×3.5cm opening to ×5cm; scales longer and narrower, 8–12mm wide. Seeds 15mm, with pink flesh. S Baja California. ssp. ***orizabensis*** D. Bail. Bark as for *P. discolor*. Needles 3–4 per fascicle, 3.5–5.5cm, with stomata mostly on inner faces. Cones subsessile, larger, 5–6×5cm, opening to ×7.5cm, scales flatter, 18–20mm wide; seed larger, 18–20mm, flesh pink. Mexico (Puebla, SE of type). Z8.

***P. chiapensis*** (Martinez) Andresen. CHIAPAS WHITE PINE. To 35m+, crown ovoid-conic, becoming broad with long level branches; bark smooth grey; rectangular-fissured on old trees. Shoots slender, smooth, green-brown, scattered pubescence soon lost; buds ovoid-cylindrical, brown, resinous. Needles 5 per fascicle, 8–13cm, slender, bright green, with glaucous stomatal bands on inner surfaces only, sheath soon lost. Cones on 2–3cm long slender peduncles, 10–17×2.5cm, orange-brown; scales similar to *P. strobus* but not reflexed at tips, stiffer and broader, to 19mm wide. Seed 5mm with 25mm adnate wing. S Mexico, Guatemala. Z10.

***P. clausa*** (Chapm.) Vasey. SAND PINE. Shrub or small tree to 10m; crown irregular, bark scaly. Branches smooth; shoots, rust-brown. Needles 2 per fascicle, 5–9cm, slender, dark green; sheaths persistent. Cones ovoid-conic, 5–8cm; scales thin, lightly ridged, umbo curved or straight. Most cones remain closed for many years, rusty brown fading to grey. US (Florida). Z9.

***P. contorta*** Douglas ex Loud. SHORE PINE. To 25m, shrubby on poor sites. Crown domed, columnar or ovoid; young trees conical, bushy at base; bark red to yellow-brown, fissured into small squares; shoots green-brown, orange-brown when mature; buds cylindric, erect. Needles 2 per fascicle, densely arranged, twisted, yellow to dark green, persistent 3–6 years, 4–5cm×1.5mm; sheaths to 6mm. Cones ovoid, 3–7cm, usually opening when mature; scales narrow, yellow-brown, umbo with a sharp thorn. Seeds black, to 4mm, wing to 2cm. Coastal NW US (S Alaska to Oregon). 'Compacta': upright, dense; needles dark green. 'Frisian Gold': needles with conspicuous gold tint, even in summer. 'Pendula': rare weeping form. 'Spaan's Dwarf': irregular, pyramidal dwarf to 1.5m; needles dark green. ssp. ***bolanderi*** (Parl.) Critchf. MENDOCINO SHORE PINE. Shrub; lvs slender, 1mm, cones remaining closed for 2–3 years, with thicker scales, bark very dark brown. US (N California coast). ssp. ***latifolia*** (Engelm.) Critchf. LODGEPOLE PINE. To 30m. Bark thick, ridged, rarely thin and scaly. Needles 8cm×2mm, more spreading, brighter green than species type, cones remaining closed when mature, except in the event of a forest fire. Canada (Brit. Columbia) to US (Rocky Mts). ssp. ***murrayana*** (Grev. & Balf.) Critchf. SIERRA LODGEPOLE PINE. To 50m. Bark thin, pink-brown. Needles olive green, to 8cm×2mm, cones paler, buff, open when ripe and falling soon after, 4–6cm. US (California, Sierra Nevada Mts). Z7.

***P. cooperi*** Blanco. To 33m; similar to *P. rudis* and *P. arizonica* but with shorter needles and larger cone scales. Crown ovoid-conic, becoming domed; bark rough, thick, plated and deeply fissured on old trees, dark red-brown. Shoots stout, red-brown bloomed glaucous; buds cylindric, some scales free at tips, brown. Needles stout, 7–11cm, 5 per fascicle, grey-green, sheath persistent, 12mm. Cone short pedunculate, 5–9cm ovoid-conic, slightly oblique, opening when ripe but persistent on tree for several years before falling complete; scales stiff, nearly flat, buff to brown with brown lines radiating from umbo, to 20mm wide, with a small prickle on umbo; seed 5mm with a 20mm wing. NW Mexico (high mts). Z7.

***P. coulteri*** D. Don. BIG-CONE PINE. To 30m. Crown broad conic, becoming ovoid; stem erect; branches spreading; bark brown to black with scaly ridges; shoots thick, green-brown, bloomed pale purple in first year, becoming brown suffused grey in second year; buds resinous, cylindric to ovoid, long-acuminate. Needles 3 per fascicle, 20–32cm×2mm, grey or blue-green, stiff, finely serrate, sharp-acuminate, falling after 2–3 years, stomatal lines on all surfaces, sheaths to 3cm. Cones yellow-brown, ovoid-conic, reflexed down stem, short-pedunculate, 20–40×15cm, wider when open, massively woody, to 3kg fresh weight, the largest cone of any conifer, scales with a stout sharp, hook-like 2–4cm umbo. Seeds black, oval, 15×8mm, wings to 3cm. Coastal mts of NW Mexico, California. Z8.

***P. culminicola*** Andresen & Beaman. CERRO POTOSI PINYON. Shrub, to 5m. Crown compact, widely branching; bark green-grey, scaly. Needles 5 per fascicle, stomatal lines bright white on 2 inner surfaces, outer face glossy-green, apex obtuse-acuminate; sheaths semi-persistent, to 6mm, revolute when mature, forming a rosette at the needle base. Plants often sub-dioecious. Cones subglobose, 2.5–4×2–3.5cm, opening to ×4.5cm; fertile scales to 14, similar to those of *P. cembroides*. Mexico (Nuevo Leon and Coahuila). Z7.

***P. dalatensis*** De Ferré. To 40m. Shoots slender, grey-grey, finely pubesc., soon glabrous. Needles 5 per fascicle, 5–10cm, glossy green, with glaucous stomatal bands on inner faces; sheath early deciduous. Cones similar to *P. peuce*, 6–11cm, yellow-brown bloomed glaucous; seed 9mm with a 25mm wing. S Vietnam (mts). Z10.

***P. densa*** (Little & Dorman) Laub. & Silba. SOUTH FLORIDA SLASH PINE. Similar to *P. elliottii*, but smaller cones and seedlings with a fire-resistant 'grass' stage. To 30m, crown narrow conic becoming rounded irregular on long clear stem; bark thick, rough, deeply fissured. Needles mostly 2, some 3 per fascicle, 18–25cm, stiff, dark green, sheath persistent, 15mm. Cones 6–11×2.5cm, slender conic opening ovoid to ×7cm, glossy chestnut, scales 8–12mm wide, with a 1.5mm spine on umbo. S Florida. Z10.

***P. densata*** Mast. To 30m. Crown ovoid-conic, becoming rounded and irregular with age; bark thick, fissured, grey-brown at base, thinner and red-grey on upper stem. Shoots grey-brown, glabrous, stout; buds conic or ovoid-conic, brown. Needles 2, occasionally 3 per fascicle, 8–15, occasionally to 20cm, stout, dark green with indistinct stomata lines on both sides, sheath persistent, 12mm. Cones 4–7×2.5–3.5cm, ovoid, often oblique with dorsal scales very thickened and pyramidal, or more symmetrical and flatter; thick, hard, woody, sub-shiny, buff- or orange-brown, opening when ripe but often persistent 3–4 years. Umbo with a 1.5mm prickle. Seed 6mm with a 12mm wing. SW China (S Gansu, Sichuan, N Yunnan, mts). Many trees in cult. in GB as *P. tabulaeformis* are this species. Z6.

***P. densiflora*** Sieb. & Zucc. JAPANESE RED PINE. To 35m, much less in GB cult. Crown conic in young trees, wide-spreading, irregular rounded when mature; bark rust-brown, scaly, fissured and grey at base; shoots green tinged white, becoming pink-brown; buds slightly resinous, ovoid, brown, to 13mm, bud scales slightly reflexed. Needles 2 per fascicle, 7–10cm×1mm, slender, bright green; sheaths persistent, to 15mm. Cones buff to pale brown, ovoid, solitary or in clustered whorls, subsessile 4–6cm; scales thin; umbo with a short thorn or obtuse point. Seeds ovate, to 4mm, black, wings to 18mm. Japan, Korea. Over 90 cvs have been listed, mostly rare in cult.; the following are still grown. 'Alice Verkade': dwarf to 70×70cm in 10 years, tightly globose. 'Aurea': needles with gold tint or spots. 'Globosa': slow-growing, hardy and hemispherical to 1m. 'Jane Kluis': broadly globose dwarf to 75cm; needles compact. 'Oculus-draconis': irregular, alternate, yellow and green variegated needles. 'Pendula': vigorous, semi-prostrate. 'Rezek WB Seedling': rounded, mushroom-like head. 'Umbraculifera': very slow-growing umbrella form to 4×6m; needles bright green. Z5.

***P. devoniana*** Lindl. MICHOACAN PINE. To 35m, crown conic becoming ovoid or rounded and domed with age; bark thick, deeply fissured, very rough even in upper crown. Shoots very stout, 2.5cm thick, scaly, rough, brown; buds large, to 3cm, red-brown, resinous. Needles 5 per fascicle, rarely 6, very long 25–45mm; stout, 2.5mm, light to dark green, sheath persistent, 25–35mm; scale lvs 15mm, persistent. Cones large, 15–35×5–6cm closed, long cylindric-conic, opening to ×11cm ovoid-cylindric, buff to brown, matt; scales very variable, apophysis mostly longer than wide and much thickened with a weak transverse ridge, umbo 8mm wide, with weak forward-pointing spine easily lost. Seed 7–8mm with 3cm wing. Listed in most texts as *P. michoacaënsis*; widely hybridizing in wild, and much confused with, *P. montezumae*, which normally less stout shoots and lvs, smaller cones, apophyses mostly wider than long and with a strong transverse ridge, and umbo with stouter reflexed spine. C & S Mexico, Guatemala. Z9.

***P. discolor*** Bail. & Hawksw. BORDER PINYON. Small tree to 15m, crown rounded; bark thin, becoming black with shallow fissures bright orange at centre. Shoots slender, pale grey, glabrous; buds cylindric, acute, slightly resinous, scales long acuminate, pale brown with red tips. Needles 3 per fascicle, 2.5–6cm, slender, 0.9mm, glossy green outer surface with no stomata, bright white stomatal bands on inner faces, margin entire; sheath semi-persistent, revolute. Trees often dioecious, especially at N end of range. Cones on 5mm peduncle, small, ovoid-globular, 2–3×2–2.5cm, opening to ×4cm, orange-buff; up to 12 fertile scales, apophysis lightly keeled, umbo flat; seeds 12mm, edible, flesh white, oily; 2mm wing remaining on the scale at seed release. US (SE Arizona, SW New Mexico), NW Mexico. Z8.

***P. durangensis*** Martinez. DURANGO PINE. To 40m, crown conic becoming rounded and domed; bark rough, deeply fissured; dark grey-brown. Shoots stout, rough, brown bloomed blue at first; buds conical, light brown, not resinous. Needles mostly in fascicles of 6 (only pine with this number regular), occasionally 5, 7 or 8 (some trees with all 5), 12–20cm, 1.5–2mm thick, dark green to grey-green, sub-shiny with indistinct stomata on all 3 surfaces; sheath 16mm, persistent. Cones 6–10×3cm, ovoid-conic opening ovoid to ×6cm, mid brown; scales hard, thin edged with a pyramidal, strongly transverse ridged apophysis, umbo with a sharp 2mm persistent spine. Seed 7mm with 2.5cm wing. W Mexico (Durango, scattered S to Michoacan). Z8.

***P. echinata*** Mill. SHORT-LEAF PINE. To 35m, much less in GB cult. Crown conic, open; bole and larger branches often with epicormic shoots; bark dark grey, red-brown when mature; branches whorled, thin, horizontal or ascending; shoots orange brown bloomed pale green, becoming dark brown, bark exfoliating after 3 years; winter buds resinous, bud scales rust-brown, tightly adpressed, brown, ovoid, apex acute, to 6mm. Needles 2–3 per fascicle, 8–13cm×1mm, soft, flexible, yellow-green, short-acuminate, falling after 2–5 years, finely serrate, stomatal lines visible on both sides; sheath about 1cm. Cones single or clustered, pale brown, subsessile, ovoid-conic, obtuse, 4–7×2cm, opening to ×3–4cm, usually persistent, apophysis thickened, nearly diamond-shaped, crossridge sharp, thorn incurved, often deciduous. Seeds small, ovate, to 5mm, wing to 13mm. SE US. Z6.

***P. edulis*** Engelm. ROCKY MOUNTAIN PINYON. To 15m. Crown compact, domed; bark silvery grey, scaly, ridged red-brown; shoots stiff, orange, bloomed glaucous blue, tinged red; buds ovoid, scales densely imbricate. Needles 2 per fascicle, 3–6cm×2mm, outer face dark green, inner glaucous, falling after 3–9 years; sheaths revolute, as in *P. cembroides*. Cones subglobose, pale brown or green-brown, 3–4.5×3–4cm; scales 4–8, umbo with a central depression and minute spine. Seeds to 11×15mm, dark red-brown. SW US (Colorado, Arizona, New Mexico). Z5.

***P. elliottii*** Engelm. SLASH PINE. To 35m, bole to 90cm diam. Crown dense, domed; bark grey, fissured, purple-brown when mature, exfoliating in large plates; shoots brown when young, becoming grey-brown when mature, rough, scaly; winter buds white-fringed. Needles 2–3 per fascicle, crowded at branch apices, 20–30cm×1mm, falling after 2–3 years, stiff, dark green, glossy, finely serrate, stomatal lines visible on all surfaces; sheaths persistent, pale brown, grey when old. Cones shiny chestnut brown, subterminal, short stalked or subsessile, spreading or reflexed, narrow conic, 9–15×3–4cm closed, ovoid to ×8–10cm when open, soon deciduous, apophysis raised, to 20mm wide, terminating in a thick, grey thorn to 3mm. Seeds ovate to triangular, to 6mm, black or grey, wings to 30mm. SE US (South Carolina to Louisiana, coastal plains). Z9.

***P. engelmannii*** Carr. APACHE PINE. To 35m, bole to 80cm diam.; bark dark brown to very dark grey, rough, deeply fissured, forming plates; shoots stout, 2cm thick. Needles 3, rarely 4 per fascicle, dense, 30–40cm, bright green or olive green, falling after 2 years, finely toothed, stomatal lines 12 on the outer face, 6 on the inner; sheaths brown, 3–4cm, persistent. Cones hard, heavy, ovoid to oblong-conical, asymmetric, 10–18×5–6cm, opening to ×10cm, yellow-brown, apophysis protuberant, subconic, reflexed, with a recurved, woody umbo. Seeds ovate, 8mm, wing brown, to 30mm. SW US, Mexico. Z8.

***P. fenzeliana*** Hand.-Mazz. Similar to *P. amamiana* and *P. morrisonicola*. To 35m. Shoots slender, red-brown, glabrous or pubesc.; buds resinous, scales acute triangular, 2.5mm, ciliate fringed. Needles 5 per fascicle, 7–12cm (to 18cm?), slender, 0.6mm, glossy green on outer surface, 4–5 green-white rows of stomata on inner faces; sheath early deciduous. Cones with a 2cm peduncle,

6–10×2.5cm, opening to ×4–5cm, glossy yellow-brown; scales about 50 in number, 14–18mm wide; seeds about 10mm long with an adnate 4mm wing. China (Hainan), Vietnam, rare and endangered in wild; little known. Z9.

***P. flexilis*** James. LIMBER PINE. To 25m, bole to 1.5m diam. Crown open broad conic when young, broadly rounded when mature; bark smooth, thin, light grey when young, later dark grey when mature, furrowed; branches candelabra-like, horizontal with upswept ends; shoots yellow-green when young, later grey-brown, glabrous, or pubesc., very flexible; buds broadly cylindric to ovate, apex acute, to 1cm. Needles 5 per fascicle, pointing toward shoot apex, 4–8cm×1mm, sharply acuminate, entire, densely crowded, falling after 5–6 years, sometimes dentate in south of range, stomatal lines faintly visible on all sides, blue-green; sheaths abscising. Male strob. red, female purple; cones 6–14×5–6cm, subsessile, subterminal, erect, yellow ochre, glossy; fertile scales thick, woody, perpendicular to axis when mature, apex rounded, umbo dark, obtuse. Seeds oval, to 11×9mm, wing to 1mm. SW Canada to US (Rocky Mts, N Arizona, California and Colorado). 'Extra Blue': irregular and erect to 2.5m; branches dense, tufted. 'Firmament': needles tinted blue; resistant to blister rust. 'Glauca Pendula': vigorous, prostrate; needles long, thick, blue. 'Glenmore': needles long, to 11.5cm, tinted silver. 'Nana': bushy dwarf; needles short, to 3cm. 'Pendula': stems and branches weeping. 'Tiny Temple': slow-growing dwarf to 10cm p.a.; needles to 7cm, tinted blue. 'Vanderwolf's Pyramid': erect; needles tinted blue. Z3.

***P. gerardiana*** Wallich ex D. Don. CHILGOZA PINE. To 21m. Crown compact, rounded; branches short, thick, spreading horizontally; bark thin, silver grey, exfoliating in plates (as for *P. bungeana*); shoots olive green when young, yellow-brown when mature; buds ovoid, apex acute. Needles 3 per fascicle, erect, spreading, 7–10cm×2mm, green, falling after 3 years; sheaths deciduous, abscising after 1 year. Cones very resinous, 10–18×8–12cm, bluntly ovoid, scales pyramidal, with a sharp crossridge, usually reflexed, umbo triangular, short-acuminate. Seeds cylindric, to 25×5mm, edible, wing very short, remaining in cone. NW Himalaya, Kashmir, NW Pakistan, N Afghanistan. Z7.

***P. glabra*** H. Walter. SPRUCE PINE. To 35m, bole to 75cm diam. Bark rust-brown, smooth, grey, thin on upper trunk, branches horizontal; buds brown, ovoid, apex acute. Needles 2 per fascicle, 5–9cm×1mm, short-acuminate, dark green, falling after 2–3 years, thin, twisted, stomatal lines on all surfaces; sheaths short. Cones solitary, short-stalked, ovoid, 5–6cm, buff-brown, reflexed; scales soft, pliable, apophysis slightly thickened, with a small deciduous thorn. Seeds triangular, 4mm, wing to 13mm. US (S Carolina, Louisiana, Florida). Z8.

***P. gordoniana*** Hartw. ex Gordon. GORDON'S PINE. Tree to 35m, crown rounded, dense; bark thick, fissured at base, thin and exfoliating above, orange-red. Shoots dark green turning brown, buds large, cylindric-conic, not resinous. Needles 5 per fascicle, 23–38cm×1.5mm, bright green with stomata on all sides but more on inner faces; sheath persistent, 2cm. Cones on a stout 10mm peduncle, conic 8–12×3–4cm, apophyses very rugose with numerous grooves radiating from the umbo, rhombic, red-brown, low pyramidal with a blunt umbo of same colour. Seeds 5mm, brown with a 20–25mm wing. SW Mexico. Z9.

***P. greggii*** Engelm. ex Parl. To 20m, sometimes to 30m. Crown broadly conic, becoming domed when mature; young bark grey, smooth, basal bark rough, ridged; shoots thin, yellow-brown, strongly bloomed white in first year; buds cylindric, sharply acuminate occasionally resinous. Needles 3 per fascicle, 7–13cm×1mm, short-acuminate, spreading, pale green, falling after 3 years, stomatal lines visible on all surfaces; sheath to 13mm. Cones yellow-brown, 6–13cm, ovoid to conical, sessile, irregular, asymmetric, recurved, often in groups of up to 8, persisting closed for many years until opened by forest fires. Seeds ovate, to 5mm, wing to 20mm. Mexico. Z8.

***P. ×hakkodensis*** Mak. (*P. parviflora* × *P. pumila*.) Low, 6m, slow-growing. Needles longer, more twisted, rougher than *P. pumila*. Cone as *P. pumila*, or slightly larger and rougher scaled. Japan (N Honshu). Z4.

***P. halepensis*** Mill. ALEPPO PINE. To 20m. Crown conic when young, arching, umbrella-shaped, becoming globose, stems often bowed or twisted; bark smooth, silver-grey, becoming red-brown, fissured and scaly when mature; shoots glabrous; buds resin-free, ovate to 1cm, scales with revolute tips, margins fringed. Needles 2 per fascicle, rarely 3, spreading, 6–10cm, stiff, very slender, 0.8mm, persistent 2 years, indistinct stomatal lines on all sides; sheaths to 1cm, persistent. Cones 5–12×2.5–3.5cm, oblong-conic, in groups of 1–3, reflexed down shoot, red-brown, persisting for many years after ripening, often unopened, scales slender, 15mm wide, moderately flexible, apophysis smooth, flat, umbo flat or rarely raised. Seeds black to dark brown, 6×3mm, wing slender, 2.5cm. Mediterranean (Morocco and Spain to Libya, Greece and Israel). Z8.

***P. hartwegii*** Lindl. To 25m, rarely 35m. Crown columnar, domed; bark grey, thick, scaly; buds resinous, apex acute, long-ovoid, rust-brown. Needles 3–5 per fascicle, to 15cm, stiff, dark to glaucous green; sheath to 17mm. Cone very dark purple to black, cylindric-ovoid, acute, asymmetric, to 16cm; scales thin, flexible, apophysis bulbous, umbo prominent, thorn minute, forward-pointed. Seeds very dark brown, to 5mm, wing to 13×6mm. High mountains in C & S Mexico to Honduras and NW El Salvador. Z8.

***P. heldreichii*** Christ. BOSNIAN PINE. Tree to 25m, bole erect or ascending. Crown ovoid conic; bark ash grey, splitting into furrows, exposing yellow-grey patches; buds ovoid, brown to grey-white. Needles 2 per fascicle, 6–9cm×2mm, acuminate, spiny-tipped, falling after 5–6 years, stiff, curved forward, glossy dark green, dentate, stomatal lines on all surfaces; sheaths to 13mm. Cones solitary or 3-whorled, ovoid; scales soft, brittle; apophysis to 5–10×4mm wide, 12cm, yellow-brown, umbo short, acute. Seeds elliptic, to 6mm, wings to 2cm. W Balkan Peninsula, SE Italy, Greece (Thessalian mts). 'Aureospicata': broadly conic, slow-growing; needles tips yellow. 'Compact Gem': compact and slow-growing dwarf to 25 by 30cm after 10 years; needles dark green. 'Pygmy': slow-growing, mound-forming dwarf; needles dark green. 'Satellit': conic, very narrow; needles dark green. 'Schmidtii': compact, dense and slow-growing dwarf; needles rich green. Z5.

***P. henryi*** Mast. To 25m. Similar to *P. densiflora*. Shoots glabrous, prominently grooved; buds ovoid-conic, red-brown. Needles 2 per fascicle, 7–12cm, slender, 1mm, dark green, sheath persistent. Cones small, 2.5–5cm, conic opening ovoid to ×4.3cm, scales yellow-buff, shiny, to 11mm wide, apophysis stiff with smooth margin, moderately thickened, umbo very small, slightly raised to sunken, mucronate. Seed 4–5mm with 2cm wing. C China (W Hubei, NE Sichuan, S Shaanxi). Z7.

***P. herrerai*** Martinez. To 30m, crown conic becoming rounded; bark as in *P. teocote*. Shoots slender, red-brown, often bloomed glaucous, buds cylindrical, yellow-brown, not resinous. Needles 3 per fascicle, 11–20cm, very slender, soft and drooping, glossy light green; sheath persistent, 13mm. Cones on a slender 5–10mm peduncle, ovoid-conic, very small, 2.5–5×2cm, opening to ×3.5cm when ripe and falling up to a year later, buff, shiny; scales hard and stiff, apophysis slightly swollen, umbo slightly raised, grey-brown. W & SW Mexico. Z10.

***P. ×holfordiana*** A.B. Jackson. (*P. veitchii* × *P. wallichiana*.) To 30m. As for *P. wallichiana*, but with young shoots finely pubesc., cones wider, scale end broad, acute, not reflexed. Z8.

***P. ×hunnewelli*** A.G. Johnson. (*P. strobus* × *P. parviflora*.) Crown open; young shoots pubesc. Needles to 9cm, arched, twisting, green tinged blue. Cones subsessile. Seeds to 1cm, brown, tinged purple. Z6.

***P. hwangshanensis*** Hsia ex C.H. Tsoong. Similar to *P. thunbergii*. To 25m. Shoots glabrous, grey-brown, grooved; buds cylindric with abrupt conic tip, brown. Needles 2 per fascicle, 5–8cm, 1mm broad, fresh green, sheath persistent. Cones small, 4–5cm, conic opening ovoid to ×5cm, scales pale buff, matt, to 11mm wide, not stiff, apophysis with rounded wrinkled margin, umbo sunken, minute mucronate. Seed 4mm. E China (Anhui, Jiangxi, Zhejiang; mts). Z7.

***P. jeffreyi*** Balf. ex A. Murray. JEFFREY'S PINE. To 55m, bole to 1.5m diam. Crown dome-shaped, top conic; bark black-brown, splitting, forming large plates on mature trees; branches stout, spreading, low branches often pendulous; shoots blue-white with a violet bloom, becoming grey-brown in the second year; buds resin-free, large, oblong-conical or ovoid-cylindric, red-brown, scales with tips free. Needles 3 per fascicle, 14–27cm×2mm, matt grey-green, sharp-acuminate, finely serrate, falling after 2 years, stomatal lines, 10–12 on outer face, 4–6 on inner, sheaths to 16mm, persisting. Cones short-stalked or subsessile, ovoid-conical, spreading, 10–24×6–8cm, open ×10–15cm, scales to 4–6×2.5cm, apophysis pyramidal, pale buff-brown, crossridge stout, umbo with a sharp, reflexed 4mm thorn. Seeds oval-oblong to triangular, 10mm, wings to 3cm. US (S Oregon) to Mexico (N Baja California). Z8.

***P. johannis*** Pass. Multistemmed shrub or small tree to 10m, very similar to *P. discolor* and possibly not distinct; crown rounded. Shoots slender, pale grey, glabrous; buds cylindric, acute. Needles 3 per fascicle, 3–5cm, slender, 1mm, dark green outer surface with no stomata, white stomatal bands on inner faces, margin entire; sheath semi-persistent, revolute. Plants normally monoecious. Cones on 3–4mm peduncles, small, ovoid-globular, 3–4×2.5–3cm, opening to ×4cm, orange-buff; up to 12 fertile scales, apophysis lightly keeled, umbo flat; seeds 12mm, edible, flesh white, oily; 2mm wing remaining on the scale at seed release. NE Mexico. Z8.

***P. kesiya*** Royle ex Gordon. To 40m, bole to 1m diam. Bark thick, deeply fissured; shoots brown; buds conical, apex acute, scales brown, tips distinct. Needles 3 per fascicle, 15–24cm×0.5mm, grey-green, falling after 2 years, stomatal lines visible on all sides; sheath to 2cm. Cones 5–11×3cm, dark brown, symmetrical, subsessile, solitary or in groups of 3; scales to 2cm, apophysis thick, cross-keeled in centre. Seeds about 1cm, wing rounded at apex. Assam (Khasi mts) to SE Yunnan, Indochina & N Philippines, at higher altitudes than *P. merkusii*. Z9.

***P. koraiensis*** Sieb. & Zucc. KOREAN PINE. To 50m in wild, less in cult. Habit as for *P. cembra* but looser; young bark smooth, brown suffused grey, becoming furrowed, with scaly ridges when mature; branches horizontal to erect; shoots green; buds to 2cm, ovoid to cylindric, scales lanceolate, adpressed except at apices. Needles 5 per fascicle, loosely arranged, 6–12cm×1mm, falling after 3 years, outer face blue green, apex obtuse, margins serrulate, stomatal lines blue-white, on inner faces only; sheaths soon deciduous. Young male and female strobili red; cones terminal, subsessile, erect, conical-cylindric, 8–16×5–7cm, bright green or purple; scales leathery, margin undulate, tips elongated, umbo acute. Seeds obovate, to 16×12mm, brown suffused grey, edible, wing reduced to a 0.5mm ridge on seed. NE Asia (Amur region), Manchuria, Korea, to Japan (Honshu). 'Silveray': needles thick, tinted blue. 'Tortuosa': needles spirally twisted, especially at branch tips. 'Variegata': needles tinged yellow to entirely yellow. 'Winton': bushy dwarf, to 2×4.5m after 30 years. Z3.

***P. krempfii*** Lecomte. To 40m. Bark rust-brown, smooth. Needles 2 per fascicle, 4–7cm×4mm; up to 11cm×6mm on young trees; flattened, lanceolate, sharply pointed. Cones 4–7×2–3cm, ovoid, red-brown, opening at maturity, apophysis pyramidal, similar to *P. balfouriana* and *P. rzedowskii*, but smaller. Easily distinguished from other spp. of *Pinus* by its needles to 5mm wide. S Vietnam, rare & endangered. Z10.

***P. lambertiana*** Douglas. SUGAR PINE. To 70m in wild, to 35m+ in cult., bole to 3m diam., seldom branched below 30m in mature wild trees. Bark smooth, pale brown to grey-green, becoming thick, splitting and ridged in mature trees; branches long, whorled, horizontal; shoots rust-brown, pubesc., becoming orange-brown, smooth; buds resinous, ovoid to cylindric, to 8mm, scales red-brown, tightly adpressed. Needles 5 per fascicle, 6–11cm×1.5mm, sharp-acuminate, rigid, twisted, dark green, falling after 2–3 years, stomatal lines all surfaces, though most numerous on blue-white inner surfaces; deep green above; sheaths to about 2cm, deciduous. Cones the longest of any conifer, 20–64×6–7cm closed, opening ×9–16cm, sub-terminal, pendulous, long pedunculate, on 5–15cm stalk, glossy yellow or orange-brown, falling after 2 years; scales leathery, apophysis slightly thickened, convex, apex blunt, reflexed, spreading when open. Seeds brown, oval-oblong, to 1.5×1cm, wings to 2cm. US (Oregon, California) to Mexico (N Baja California). Highly susceptible to blister rust disease. Z7.

***P. lawsonii*** Roezl ex Gordon To 25m, crown conic becoming rounded; bark as in *P. teocote*. Shoots slender, yellow, often bloomed glaucous, buds cylindrical, light brown, not resinous. Needles 3 or 4, occasionally 5 per fascicle, 13–23cm, coarse and stiff, glaucous or blue-green; sheath persistent, 13mm. Cones on a slender 10–15mm peduncle, ovoid, 5–8cm, opening when ripe and falling 1–2 years later, yellow to brown, shiny; apophysis swollen or pyramidal, umbo slightly raised. SW & S Mexico. Z10.

***P. leiophylla*** Schiede ex Schldl. & Cham. SMOOTH-LEAF PINE. To 30m. Crown irregular, open; bark dark brown; bole with epicormic shoots and clustered needles; young shoots yellow to blue-green, bloomed pale. Needles 5 per fascicle, to 15cm, grey-green, falling after 2 years, thin, finely serrate, short-acuminate; sheath to 2cm, orange, quickly deciduous. Cones maturing in 3 years, solitary or grouped, lateral or subterminal, smooth, ovate to ovate-conic, persistent, 3–6cm, long stalked, peduncle to 2cm; scales to 2cm, apophysis brown, swollen or flat, umbo 4mm. Seed 5mm, wing to 13mm. Central Mexico (mts). ssp. ***chihuahana*** (Engelm.) E. Murray. Needles thicker and stiffer than species type, mostly 3, sometimes 4 or 5, per fascicle. NW Mexico. Z9.

***P. longaeva*** Bail. ANCIENT PINE. To 20m, very similar to *P. balfouriana*, but cone scales aristate. Crown conic, becoming rough, twisted. Bark chocolate brown, in plates; branches erect to pendulous; shoots rust-brown, pubesc. Needles 5 per fascicle, 2–4cm×1mm, acute, green with white stomatal bands on inner faces, pointing towards shoot apex, later spreading, resin canals visible above as 2 grooves. Cone ovoid-cylindric, red brown, 5–11cm; umbo thornlike, 2–5mm, easily broken. US (White Mts, E California, Nevada and Utah). Often confused with *P. aristata*, but resin drops absent in *P. longaeva*. The oldest plant in the world, growing to 5000 years in cold semi-desert mountain tops. 'Sherwood Compact': tight and conic, branches ascending. Z4.

***P. luchuensis*** Mayr. OKINAWA PINE. To 25m, similar to *P. thunbergii*. Crown irregular; bark thin, grey, exfoliating in scales when mature; winter buds resinous, red, bud scales compactly arranged. Needles 2 per fascicle, 12–16cm. Cones ovoid-conic, 4–6cm, brown. S Japan (Ryuku Is., Okinawa). Z9.

***P. lumholtzii*** Robinson & Fern. To 25m, bole to 40cm diam. Crown open; branches level, lower branches pendulous; shoots level, chestnut-brown, bloomed blue; buds ovoid, red-brown. Needles 3 per fascicle, rarely 2 or 4, hanging vertically, 20–30cm, bright green to olive green, finely serrate; sheaths to 3cm, deciduous. Cones maturing in 2–3 years, 3–6cm, ovate, symmetrical, pendulous, deciduous, apophysis thickened, centre thickened, brown, centre very dark brown; peduncles curved, 10–20mm. W & NW Mexico. Z8.

***P. massoniana*** Lamb. To 25m, occasionally to 40m. Crown spreading, ovate or flattened; bark grey at base, splitting, forming thick, irregular plates; red-grey in upper crown, exfoliating in thin flakes; branches horizontal; shoots brown, not bloomed; buds resinous, oblong, pale brown, apex acute, scales loose, tips reflexed. Needles 2 per fascicle, 13–20cm×0.5–1mm, dark green. Cones 4–7×4cm, ovoid-oblong, chestnut brown, deciduous, apophysis red-brown; umbo smooth, thorn absent, adpressed to the lower scale. Seeds dark brown, to 5mm, wing to 15mm. C & SE China, Taiwan, N Vietnam. Z7.

***P. maximartinezii*** Rzed. MARTINEZ PINYON. To 11m. Crown open; bole branching from base; winter buds conic, to 12mm. Needles 5 per fascicle, 9–13cm in wild, up to 20cm on glasshouse-cultivated plants; pale glossy-green above, white beneath, entire or dentate, apex acute or obtuse. Cone 15–23×10–15cm, ovoid to oblong-ovoid, apophysis thick, heavy, pyramidal-ovoid, spreading; fertile scales 30–60, yellow-buff. Seed dark brown, to 3cm×13mm; the largest of any pine. Seedlings with up to 24 cotyledons, more than any other plant in the world. Mexico (SW Zacatecas). Z10.

***P. maximinoi*** H.E. Moore. THINLEAF PINE. Trees to 35m, crown rounded; bark thick, fissured at base, very thin, smooth and flaking above, orange-red. Shoots dark green turning brown, slender, bloomed glaucous when young; buds cylindric-conic, not resinous. Needles 5 per fascicle, very slender, 20–30cm×0.8mm, bright green with stomata on all sides; sheath persistent, 1.5cm. Cones on a thin 5mm peduncle, conic 7–10×3cm, rarely to 14cm, scales very thin though stiff, flat, rhombic, red-brown, umbo flat or slightly raised, of same colour. Seeds 5mm, brown, with a 20–25mm wing. S Mexico to Honduras. Z10.

***P. merkusii*** Jungh. & De Vries. SUMATRAN PINE. Tree to 45m, crown open, similar to *P. brutia*, trunk often sinuous; bark thick, deeply fissured, scaly, black-brown. Shoots grey-brown, moderately stout; buds ovoid-conic, scale margins fringed, tips revolute. Needles 2 per fascicle, rarely 3, 15–20cm, slender pale green with indistinct stomatal bands on both faces; sheath persistent. Cones with 1cm peduncle, ovoid-cylindric, 5–7.5×2.5cm, opening ovoid to ×5cm, glossy red-brown, not heavy; scales thin except outer half of apophysis, which thickened and slightly reflexed, with transverse ridge, umbo flat. Seed 5×3mm, with 2–2.5cm wing. Philippines, Sumatra, the only pine to cross the equator. ssp. ***latteri*** F. Mason. TENASSERIM PINE. Very similar and best treated as a subspecies of above; differs in longer stouter needles, 18–27cm; cones larger and heavier, cylindric-conic, 6–12×2.5cm, scales flatter, regularly rhombic with transverse and vertical ridges; seeds 6×4mm, with 2.5cm wing. Burma to Indochina and extreme SW China. Z10.

***P. monophylla*** Torr. & Frém. SINGLE-LEAF PINYON. To 15m, often with many stems. Crown domed; bark smooth when young, becoming ridged with age; winter buds dark brown, bud scales obtuse. Needles solitary, vary rarely in fascicles of 2, circular in section, 4–6cm, 1.7–2.3mm thick, stiff, glaucous blue-green, 2–7 resin ducts in leaf, usually bowed, sharp-acuminate, falling after 4–12 years; sheaths semi-persistent, revolute. Cones 5–9×3–5cm, ovoid-conic, yellow buff, opening to ×4.5–8.5cm; fertile scales to 16, apophysis woody, thickened pyramidally, umbo obtuse, seed 20mm, flesh floury (not oily), edible; 2mm wing remaining on scale after seed release. SW US (W Utah, N Arizona to S California). 'Tioga Pass': branches ascending; needles blue. Z6.

***P. montezumae*** hort. non Lamb. MONTEZUMA PINE; ROUGH-BARKED MEXICAN PINE. To 35m. Crown columnar to conic, becoming rounded when mature; bark rust-brown, rough, fissured irregularly; shoots buff to red-brown; buds resin-free, ovate-acute, to 2cm, scales red-brown, fringed with hairs. Needles 5 per fascicle, rarely 4–6, erect, spreading or pendent, compactly arranged on shoots, 15–30cm×2mm, falling after 3 years, green, acute, stomatal lines on all surfaces; sheaths to 3cm, persistent. Cones solitary or grouped, 12–25cm, broadly cylindric-conical to ovoid-conical, yellow to rust-brown, slightly asymmetric, short stalked, apophysis buff to glossy brown, flat to slightly convex, crossridged, umbo with a deciduous, spreading or reflexed thorn. Seeds brown, spotted black, ovate, about 6mm, wings to 2cm. W & NE Mexico to Guatemala. Most of the trees in GB cultivated as this species are actually *P. rudis*. var. ***lindleyi*** Loud. Cone more cylindric than species type, scales more numerous, smaller. Z9.

***P. monticola*** Douglas ex D. Don. WESTERN WHITE PINE. To 45m in cult., 60m in the wild, bole to 2m diam. Crown conical; bark smooth, pale brown when young, grey-brown, fissuring to square to rectangular plates when mature; shoots rust-brown, pubesc.; buds resinous, cylindric to globose, about 13mm, scales adpressed. Needles 5 per fascicle, 7–10cm, falling after 3–4 years, glossy bright green on outer face, blue-white stomatal bands on inner faces, apex blunt, densely serrate; sheaths deciduous, to 2cm. Cones with 1–2cm stalks, solitary or in groups, sub-terminal, becoming pendulous, 12–22, rarely to 28×5cm, narrowly conic to cylindric, gently curved, green to purple-green when young, yellow-brown when mature; apophysis thin, matt or sub-shiny, exterior convex, rounded-rhombic, margin sharp, basal scales reflexed, umbo dark brown. Seeds ovate, dark grey or grey-brown, to 5mm, wings about 2.5cm. Canada and W US (British Columbia to Oregon, east to Montana). 'Ammerland': vigorous clone, fast-growing to 50cm p.a; needles tinted blue. 'Minima': dwarf, needles short, tinted blue; witches' broom. 'Pendula': stem bowed; branches weeping. 'Skyline': slender upright; needles conspicuously blue. var. ***minima*** Lemmon. Cones shorter, 9–15cm, glossy yellow-ochre with rounded apophysis. US (California, Sierra Nevada Mts). Z4.

***P. morrisonicola*** Hayata. TAIWAN WHITE PINE. Resembles *P. parviflora*, distinguished by its larger lvs, larger, paler cones and smaller seeds. To 25m, bole to 1.2m diam. Bark brown, suffused grey, smooth, becoming furrowed when mature; winter buds ovoid. Needles 5 per fascicle, 6–10cm×1mm, glossy yellow-green, stomatal lines only on inner faces. Cones ovoid to oblong-ovoid, glossy yellow ochre, to 10×5cm; seed scales oblong-ovate, tips rounded, apophysis rounded, umbo small. Seeds ovate, about 9mm, wings about 16mm. Taiwan. Z8.

***P. mugo*** Turra. MOUNTAIN PINE; DWARF MOUNTAIN PINE. Shrub, to 6m. Crown conic; stem ascending, short or procumbent, branches erect or decumbent; bark grey-brown, scaly, splitting into irregularly shaped plates; shoots green when young, becoming very dark brown when mature, glabrous; buds very resinous, ovoid-oblong, about 7mm, acuminate. Needles 2 per fascicle, often bowed, twisted, 3–7cm×2–3mm, dark green, apex acute, stomatal lines faint on both sides. Cones subterminal, sessile or subsessile, spreading, in groups of 1–3, 2–6×3cm, ovoid to conic, symmetrical, apophysis dark brown, umbo grey-brown, flattened with a slight point, surrounded by a dark ring. Seeds ovate, about 4mm, buff to brown suffused grey, wings to 1.5cm. C Europe, Balkan Peninsula (mts). 'Allgau': very flat in growth; shoots and needles short. 'Aurea': semi-dwarf to 1m; needles turning gold in winter. 'Compacta': dense and globose with ascending shoots. 'Frisia': dense irregular upright, to 2×1.5m. 'Glendale': habit depressed globose; leaders erect. 'Gnom': broad pyramidal semi-dwarf to 2×2m. 'Hesse': low, compact, cushion-forming dwarf; needles slightly tortuous. 'Humpy': very compact, globose dwarf, slow-growing to 4cm p.a. 'Kissen': dense and flattened to 80×30cm. 'Knappenburg': irregular, broad, dense dwarf; winter buds tinted red. 'Kobold': broadly globose dwarf; branches stiff and thick. 'Kokarde': needles speckled gold; appearing in gold rings from above. 'Mops': broadly upright dwarf to 1.5m, slow-growing, dense. 'Ophir': flattened globose to 60cm, attractively yellow in winter. 'Pal Maleter': needle tips conspicuously yellow in winter. 'Prostrata': prostrate. 'Rigi': narrow-conic. 'Slavinii': broadly dwarf, mat-forming, prostrate with ascending tips; needles dense, tinted blue. 'Trompenburg': broadly globose; needles bright green. 'Variegata': needles stippled yellow. 'Winter Gold': open, wide and low in growth to 1m; needles spreading, tortuous, tinted gold in winter. ssp. ***uncinata*** (Ramond) Domin. Resembles *P. mugo*, but to 25m. Stem usually single and erect. Cones asymmetric, 2.5–6cm, apophysis recurved pyramidal, umbo protruding. Switzerland to W Alps, Cevennes, Pyrenees. 'Grune Welle': compact globose dwarf; needles bright green, coarse. 'Leuco-Like': upright conical dwarf to 50×35cm after 10 years; needles coarse, ascending, dark green. 'Paradekissen': very compact, flattened, mat-forming dwarf to 10×3cm after 10 years; needles lateral, coarse, dark green. Z3.

***P. muricata*** D. Don. BISHOP PINE. To 25m in wild, 40m in cult.; bole to 1.2m diam. Crown broad-conic, becoming rounded when mature; bark red-brown, deeply splitting to thick long plates; branches spreading; shoots green, becoming orange-brown; buds very resinous, to 2.5cm, dark rust-brown, conic to cylindric, apex acute. Needles 2 per fascicle, rarely 3, 12–15cm×2mm, twisted, green after 3–4 years, falling; sheaths to 13mm, persistent. Cones glossy, nut-brown, 4–9×3–7cm, ovoid, sessile, asymmetric, solitary or whorled, spreading or reflexed, remaining closed for up to 70 years; scales facing away from stem, with a triangular umbo, widely protruding, thorn sharp, thick, recurved. Seeds triangular, about 5mm, black, wings to 2.5cm. Western N America (California, N Baja California). var. ***borealis*** Axelrod. Crown slender, conic to old age; lvs tinged blue; cones with more numerous, smaller scales. NW California coast. Z8.

***P. nelsonii*** G.R. Shaw. Shrub to small tree, to 9m. Branches long, thin, open; bark smooth, grey; shoots thin, grey. Needles to 3 per fascicle, tightly adpressed and appearing single, 4–10cm×1mm, regularly dentate; sheaths persistent. Cones arranged in diverging pairs, cylindric, 9–14×5cm, on stout stems, falling after 3 years; peduncles bowed, to 5cm, persistent; fertile scales to 45, red-brown, tips red, umbo large but indistinct. Seeds large, about 10×8mm, wing remaining in cone, 1mm. NE Mexico. Z8.

***P. nigra*** Arn. BLACK PINE. To 40m+. Crown ovoid-conic., becoming flat topped or rounded with age, very dense, tips upswept; bole straight; bark grey to dark grey-brown, deeply fissured; young branches whorled, becoming irregular when mature; shoots glabrous, pale to orange-brown; buds resinous, ovoid to cylindric. Needles 2 per fascicle, dark green, stiff, falling after 4 years, occasionally to 8 years, 8–14cm×2mm, straight or bowed, finely toothed; sheaths to 12mm, persistent. Cones 5–8×2.5cm, opening to ×5cm, in groups of 1–4, sessile to subsessile, spreading, yellow-grey to buff, glossy, mature and opening after 2 years, apophysis slightly to bluntly keeled, umbo dark brown, usually with a small thorn. Seeds about 6–7mm, grey, wings to 25mm. SE Europe (S Austria to Romania & C Italy, N Yugoslavia). 'Aurea': young shoots with gold needles, later green tinted grey. 'Balcanica': irregular, contorted, cushion-forming dwarf. 'Bujotii': dense, globose dwarf; needles dark green, slightly tortuous. 'Columnaris': columnar; branches short; needles long. 'Geant de Suisse': columnar-fastigiate; needles very long, to 18cm. 'Globosa': semi-dwarf, slow-growing; branches short; needles to 16cm. 'Hornibrookiana': compact, globose, mound-forming dwarf. 'Jeddeloh': dense and compact; twigs and needles short. 'Nana': broadly upright and shrubby to 3m, slow-growing to 5cm p.a. 'Pyramidalis': narrowly conic; branches bowed and ascending; needles tinted blue. 'Strypemonde': vigorous, ascending; needles bright green; witches' broom. 'Variegata': needles stippled gold. 'Wurstle': compactly globose; needles long, vivid green; witches' broom. 'Zlatiborica': needles tinted gold. ssp. ***nigra*** var. ***nigra*** AUSTRIAN PINE is described above, other varieties and sspp. are: var. ***caramanica*** (Loud.) Rehd. TURKISH BLACK PINE. Single trunk. Bark pink-grey to yellow buff on old trees; lvs 8–16cm; cones 5–10cm, yellower, apophysis thicker. Turkey, Cyprus, Greece, S Yugoslavia. var. ***pallasiana*** (Lamb.) Schneid. CRIMEAN PINE. Often 2–3 main trunks in cult. Bark as above var., lvs 12–18cm, cones 6–11cm, buff (not yellower), apophysis thicker. Crimea. ssp. ***monspeliensis*** (Salzm. ex Koehne) E. Murray. CEVENNES BLACK PINE. Crown more open, branches regular, level. Lvs 14–18cm, slender, 1–1.5mm, cone with flatter apophyses. S France, Pyrenees, NE Spain. This ssp. also includes these western, thin-leaved populations: var. ***maritima*** (Ait.) Melville. CORSICAN PINE. To 55m in wild, 45m in cult. Lvs 12–18cm, slender, 1.5mm. Cone 5–9cm, apophysis flattish. Corsica. var. ***mauretanica*** Maire & Peyerimh. SPANISH BLACK PINE; ALGERIAN BLACK PINE. Lvs 12–18cm, 1.7mm thick, cones 5–7cm. SE Spain, N Algeria, N Morocco. Z5.

***P. oaxacana*** Mirov. To 30m, crown tall, rounded, bark thick and fissured at base, thin, flaking, pale brown in crown. Shoots brown bloomed glaucous at first. Needles 5 per fascicle, 20–30cm, drooping, pale grey-green, sheath persistent. Cones 7–15×6cm, opening to ×10cm, ovoid, dark brown, somewhat asymmetric, apophysis greatly thickened, pyramidal, umbo greyer, stout. SE Mexico to Honduras. Z9.

***P. occidentalis*** Sw. To 40m, crown, bark, shoot and buds as for *P. caribea*. Needles 3–5 per fascicle, occasionally 2, 15–23cm. Cones erect when young, short stalked, ovoid-conic when mature, 4–8cm, glossy nut-brown, deciduous, apophysis with a small-thorned umbo. E Cuba, Dominican Republic, Haiti. Z10.

***P. oocarpa*** Schiede ex Schldl. Tree to 25m; crown conic, becoming rounded in old trees; bark thick, rough, grey, fissured on bole, thinner in upper crown, orange-red. Shoots stout, stiff, red-brown with the bark scaly in broad flakes by third year; buds ovate-conic, red, resinous. Needles dense, 5 per fascicle, 20–28cm, coarse, stiff, 1.5–2mm wide, mid-green with indistinct stomatal lines on all faces, margins serrate; sheath 2–3cm, persistent. Cones on a strong 2–3cm long peduncle, ovoid-globular, 5–8×4–6cm, sub-shiny brown or orange-buff, often remaining closed for several years; on opening, to ×6–9cm, with basal scales never being shed and other scales reflexing at base, not curving; inner face of scales dull; apophysis with up to 5 radiating lines from the umbo, umbo same colour, 3mm, slightly raised and weakly mucronate. Seed rounded at end, 5mm, sooty black with 1.5–2cm wing. S & W Mexico to N Nicaragua. var. ***trifoliata*** Martinez. Lvs 3 per fascicle, otherwise same. NW Mexico. var. ***manzanoi*** Martinez. Probably a natural hybrid with *P. patula*; cones conic, lvs 4–5 per fascicle, less stout and stiff. C Mexico. Z9.

***P. palustris*** Mill. PITCH PINE; LONGLEAF PINE; SOUTHERN YELLOW PINE. To 40m, much less in GB cult., bole to 90cm diam. Crown ovoid-conic; bark red-brown, deeply ridged, exfoliating in thin plates; shoots orange-brown, ridged, stout; buds resin-free, cylindric, very large, 2–6cm, bud scales metallic-white, fringed. Needles 3 per fascicle, to 45cm on young plants, 18–30cm on mature trees, finely toothed, acute, bright green, falling after 2 years, densely arranged, stomatal lines visible on all surfaces; sheaths to 25mm. Cones subterminal, spreading, cylindric to oblong-conic, 15–25cm; fertile scales thin, apophysis dull brown, umbo with a short, reflexed thorn. Seeds 10–12mm, wings about 3.5cm. SE US (Virginia to Florida). Z8.

***P. parviflora*** Sieb. & Zucc. JAPANESE WHITE PINE. To 20m, sometimes to 30m. Crown ovoid-conic in wild, compact, usually irregular and spreading in cult.; bark grey-black, smooth, exfoliating in small plates when mature; shoots pale green-brown, becoming light grey when mature, pubesc.; buds resin-free, ovoid, about 5mm, yellow-brown. Needles 5 per fascicle, 3–6cm×1mm, blunt, falling after 3–4 years, curved, twisted, stiff, finely toothed, exterior surface glossy dark green, stomatal lines blue-white, on 2 interior surfaces. Cones solitary or clustered, subsessile, spreading, symmetrical, ovoid to cylindric, 4–8, rarely to 10×3cm, persistent, or falling after 3–7 years; scales leathery-woody, rugose, matt, incurved, rust-brown, apophysis often twisted or irregular, convex, tips rounded, umbo flat. Seeds elliptic, brown-black, about 10mm long, wings short. S & C Japan (mts). 'Adcock's Dwarf': diminutive and slow-growing, to 75cm, forms a congested bun. 'Blue Giant': vigorous and regular to 15m; branches ascending; needles tinted blue. 'Brevifolia': narrow, upright and sparse; needles dense, short, stiff, tinted blue. 'Fukusumi': asymmetrical dwarf to 75cm; needles curving, conspicuously blue. 'Gimborn's Ideal': slender, upright to 8m; needles tinted blue. 'Gimborn's Pyramid': dense, broadly compact to 3×2m; needles vivid blue in spring. 'Glauca': irregular, sparse pyramidal upright to 12m; usually less, needles blue, coarse and twisted; cones profuse; frequently used for bonsai. 'Glauca Brevifolia': sparse, narrow upright; branches ascending; needles tinted blue; cones profuse. 'Glauca Nana': semi-dwarf, to 1m; needles short, strongly tinted blue. 'Goykukasen': slow-growing; needles vividly tinted bright blue. 'Hagoromo': globose dwarf; needles coarse, bright green. 'Negeshi': slender and regular pyramidal form, dark green. 'Saentis': wide and compact in growth with long needles. 'Saphir': irregular and slow in growth; needles sapphire-blue. 'Schoon's Bonsai': rare dwarf; branches irregular, ascending. 'Tempelhof': vigorous and fast-growing; trunk thick. 'Variegata': needles speckled or bordered light yellow. var. ***pentaphylla*** (Mayr) Henry. Cones broader than species type, apophysis not twisted, only slightly convex, seed wings as long as seed. Occurs further north, in N Honsiu. Z5.

***P. patula*** Schiede ex Schldl. & Cham. PATULA PINE; MEXICAN WEEPING PINE. To 45m. Crown open, ovoid, conic or open, spreading; in GB cult, owing to frost damage, stems often many, branching at base; bark scaly at base, exfoliating, papery above, rust-brown, as for *P. sylvestris*; shoots blue-green, bloomed, becoming glabrous, red-brown; winter buds resin-free, cylindric, acuminate, to 2.5cm, bud scales narrow-lanceolate, margin fringed, apex acute. Needles 3 per fascicle, 15–28cm, pendulous, thin, bright green to yellow-green, falling after 2–3 years, serrate, stomatal lines on all sides; sheaths to 1.5cm, persistent. Cones in groups of 2–5, remaining closed for up to 20 years, subsessile, 5–10cm, ovoid to conic, asymmetric, apophysis often slightly convex, umbo indented with a very small deciduous thorn. Seeds triangular, grey, spotted black. C & E Mexico. ssp. ***tecunumanii*** (Eguiluz & Perry) Styles. To 55m. Needles 3–4 per fascicle, cones long stalked, peduncle to 20mm, bowed; cones opening at maturity. SE Mexico to Nicaragua. Z8.

***P. peuce*** Griseb. MACEDONIAN PINE; BALKAN PINE. To 35m. Crown ovoid-conic; bole often branched from base; bark smooth, grey, thick, later grey-brown, deeply ridged, scaly at base; branches slightly ascending when young, level when mature; shoots green, glossy, becoming grey-brown; buds resinous, brown, ovate-acute, about 1cm. Needles 5 per fascicle, 7–10cm×1mm, pendulous, blue-green, sharp-acuminate, finely serrate, stomatal lines on all sides, more conspicuous on inner face; sheaths to about 2cm, rapidly deciduous. Cones resinous, subterminal, solitary or in groups of 2–4, pendulous, short stalked,

7–15×3cm, ×6–7cm open, cylindric, symmetric, pale brown; scales obovate, ridged longitudinally; peduncle about 1cm. Seeds ovate, 8mm, wing 2cm. S Yugoslavia, Greece, Albania. 'Aurea': needles soft yellow, brighter in winter. 'Aureovariegata': needles bright yellow on young shoots, later green. 'Glauca Compacta': tight in growth; needles blue. Z5.

***P.pinaster*** Ait. MARITIME PINE. To 35m. Crown ovoid-conic when young, becoming broad rounded or irregular, bark thick, rust-brown, deeply fissured; bole sinuous, very rarely straight, branches level to pendulous; shoots red-brown, glabrous, becoming rough, furrowed; buds resin-free, large, spindle-shaped, to 3.5cm×12mm, red-brown, margin fringed with white hairs, scale apices revolute. Needles 2 per fascicle, stout, 2.5mm broad, yellow- or grey-green, stiff, shiny, sharp-acuminate, falling after 2–3 years, finely dentate, stomatal lines on all surfaces; sheaths to 2.5cm, very dark brown. Cones 8–18×4–5cm, opening ×7–11cm, ovoid-conic, single or in groups of 2–5, sub-sessile, red-brown and shiny when mature, often remaining closed for 3–5 years, apophysis pyramidal, 1.5–2.5cm wide, crosskeel sharp, umbo dark grey, prominent, stout, 3mm, acute, straight. Seeds oval-oblong, 1cm, wings to 3cm. Atlantic Europe to Greece, Mediterranean. 'Aberdoniae': tall with stout, spreading branches; needles rich green. 'Lemoniana': small, to 10m with broad crown; branches spreading. 'Nana': dense, globose, flat-topped dwarf; needles light green. 'Variegata': needles gold, short, to 7cm, interspersed with green needles, occasionally entire shoot gold. Z8.

***P.pinceana*** Gordon. WEEPING PINYON. To 12m, often branched from base. Crown many-branched; bark smooth, grey; shoots hanging, blue-bloomed, glabrous; buds cylindric. Needles 3 per fascicle, 5–10cm, straight, bright green or glaucous green, stomatal lines only on inner faces, grey-green; sheaths to 5mm, semi-deciduous with 1–2mm persistent. Cones solitary, cylindric, 6–9cm, symmetric, peduncles slender, 1.5–2.5cm, scales few, large, orange, umbo dark, concave. Seeds to 13×8mm, wing short, remaining in cone. Mexico (SW Coahuila to Hidalgo, rare & scattered). Z9.

***P.pinea*** L. STONE PINE; To 25m. Crown domed, umbrella-shaped; mature bark scaly, orange, red to yellow-brown, with deep longitudinal furrows; branches horizontal, upswept at ends; shoots yellow-brown, glabrous; buds to 2cm, resin-free, rust-brown, ovate, apex acute, thin, scale margin fringed silver, tips revolute. Needles 2 per fascicle, 12–18cm×2mm, rarely to 28cm, twisted, glossy green, falling after 2–3 years, apex acuminate, stomatal lines visible on all surfaces; sheaths to 12mm, grey-brown. Juvenile foliage blue-grey, single flattened lvs 3–4cm long, retained for 4–6 years (much longer than most pines). Cones sub-terminal, solitary, occasionally in groups of 2–3, ovoid to subglobose, 8–15×6–10cm, maturing in 3 years; fertile scales thick, with spreading ridges, apophysis rhombic at cone apex, hexagonal at base, umbo flat, to dark brown, grey-white. Seeds to 2×1cm, buff brown with black, powdery coating, wings rudimentary, occasionally to 1cm. Mediterranean. 'Correvoniana': prostrate dwarf, very small, to 30cm wide after 20 years. 'Fragilis': seeds thin-shelled; widely cultivated for edible seed in S Europe. Z8.

***P.ponderosa*** Douglas ex Lawson. PONDEROSA PINE; WESTERN YELLOW PINE. To 50m, bole to 1.5m diam. Bark to 15cm thick, yellow-brown, deeply fissured, exfoliating in large yellow to rust brown, scaly plates when mature; darker brown on young trees; branches stout, whorled, spreading, hanging in lower crown, tips upturned. Shoots green-brown, not bloomed, buds resinous, oblong to cylindric, apex acute, red-brown, scales adpressed. Needles 3 per fascicle, falling after 2–4 years, spreading, straight or gently curved, 11–22cm×1.5–2mm, dull green with 8–12 stomatal lines on the outer face and 4–5 on the inner faces; sheath persistent, to 25mm. Cones solitary or 2–4 together, subsessile, spreading, symmetrical or slightly oblique, green or purple, 6–10×4cm, opening to ×5–8cm, mid to red-brown, sub-shiny, largest scales on cone 15–20mm wide, apophysis nearly flat or raised across transverse ridge, umbo with a 1.5–2mm straight mucro. Seeds 8–9mm, dark brown with a 15–18mm wing. W US & SW Canada (S British Columbia to NE California). ssp. ***washoensis*** (Mason & Stockw.) E. Murray. Very similar to type; needles shorter, 11–17cm×2mm, stout. Cones small, 5–8cm, with numerous scales always purple before ripening, seed 8–10mm. US (W Nevada, NE California, SE Oregon). ssp. ***scopulorum*** (Engelm.) E. Murray. More compact than species type, to 35m. Needles frequently mixed 2 and 3 per fascicle and shorter, 7–15cm, rarely 20cm×1.5–1.8mm. Cones ovate, fewer scaled, green ripening buff to brown, 6–9cm, rarely 12cm; seeds 6–8mm, with 20–25mm wing. US (Rocky Mts, E Montana to Arizona & New Mexico). *P.benthamiana* Hartweg. (PACIFIC PONDEROSA PINE) is similar and best treated as a ssp. Larger tree to 65m×2.5m diam. Needles 3 per fascicle, longer, 15–27cm, less stout, 1.3–1.7mm, green. Cones larger, 8–13×4cm green, opening to ×7–9cm, buff-brown, scales to 23mm wide; seeds 7–8mm with 25–30mm wing. US (Pacific coast & Sierra Nevada, Washington to California). Z4.

***P.praetermissa*** Styles & McVaugh. Small tree to 20m; crown rounded or irregular in old trees. Shoots flexible, slender, only 2–4.5mm thick, red-brown with the bark shredding in narrow flakes by third year; buds ovate, small, red, not resinous. Needles sparse, 5 per fascicle, 8–16cm, slender, 0.5–0.7mm, wide, light green, glossy with indistinct stomatal lines on all faces, margins finely serrate; sheath 12mm, persistent. Cones on a slender 2–4cm long peduncle, ovoid-globular, 4.5–6.5×3.5–4cm, glossy green-tinged buff, often remaining closed for several years; on opening, to ×6.5–8cm, with basal scales invariably being shed and other scales recurving; inner face of scales with a pearly lustre found only in this species and *P. halepensis*; apophysis with a fine transverse line, umbo mid brown, 3mm, slightly raised and weakly mucronate. Seed pointed at end, 4mm, freckled, with 2cm wing. SW Mexico. Z9.

***P.pringlei*** G.R. Shaw. Tree to 25m; crown conic, becoming rounded in old trees; bark rough, scaly, plated on bole, thin in upper crown, dark red-brown to grey. Shoots stout, stiff, yellow-brown; buds large, red, not or slightly resinous. Needles 3 per fascicle, 17–26cm, coarse, stiff, 1.5–2mm wide, yellow-green with indistinct stomatal lines on all faces, margins serrate; sheath persistent, 1.5–2cm. Cones on a strong 1cm long peduncle, ovoid-conic, 5–9×3–5cm, sub-shiny brown or yellow ochre, often remaining closed for several years; on opening, to ×5–7cm, basal scales not shed; apophysis swollen or raised, with up to 5 radiating lines from the umbo, umbo grey-brown, 3mm, slightly raised and weakly mucronate. Seed rounded at end, 5mm, sooty black, with 1.5–2cm wing. S Mexico to N Nicaragua. Z9.

***P.pseudostrobus*** Lindl. SMOOTH-BARK MEXICAN PINE. To 40m. Crown dense, rounded; branches whorled; bark yellow and smooth in upper crown, rough, grey and fissured on lower bole; shoots yellow-green, becoming rust-brown, pruinose; buds slightly resinous, oblong to oblong-conic, yellow to light brown. Needles 5 per fascicle, bright or blue-green, 15–25cm×1mm, flexible, finely dentate; sheaths brown, to 1.5cm, persistent. Cones 6–12cm, rarely 16cm, singly or in pairs, ovoid to oblong-ovoid, peduncles to 5mm; apophysis 4-sided, cross-ridge only slightly developed, with a small, deciduous thorn. SW Mexico to Honduras. Z9.

***P.pumila*** (Pall.) Reg. DWARF SIBERIAN PINE. Prostrate shrub, to 3m, trunk absent, or rarely small tree, to 6m. Branches prostrate to ascending; shoots green when young, becoming grey-brown, short-pubesc.; buds very resinous, to 1cm, scales adpressed, lanceolate, apical scales filamentous. Needles 5 per fascicle, 4–8cm×1mm, twisted densely arranged, glossy, green outer face, blue-white stomatal lines visible on interior surfaces, finely toothed or entire; sheaths abscising in 1st year. Male strob. dark red; cones grouped, subterminal, short-stalked, spreading, ovoid, 3–6×3cm, violet-black when young, red to yellow-brown when mature; scales 15–20mm wide, umbo triangular, spreading. Seeds to 1cm×7mm, wing reduced to a thin rim round the seed. NE Asia (E Siberia, Kamchatka, S to N Japan, mts), tolerates –70°C in NE Siberia). 'Blue Dwarf': irregular in growth, branches vigorously ascending; needles tortuous, tinted blue. 'Chlorocarpa': cones yellow-green. 'Draijer's Dwarf': flat-growing, compact; needles tinted light silver. 'Glauca' ('Dwarf Blue'): variable, broad, bushy, slow-growing; needles light grey-blue. 'Globe': very dense globose form to 2×2m; needles tinted silver. 'Jeddeloh': vigorous, broadly horizontal, centre depressed. 'Jermyns': compact, conic, slow-growing dwarf. 'Nana': dense and globose semi-dwarf to 3×3m; male fls claret; needles tortuous, bright grey-green. 'Saentis': upright and ascending. Z1.

***P.pungens*** Lamb. TABLE MOUNTAIN PINE; HICKORY PINE. To 15m, rarely 25m in cult. Crown rounded, broad, bole short; bark dark brown, exfoliating in irregular sheets; shoots green, becoming red-brown, shiny, glabrous; buds resinous, cylindric, dark brown, apex blunt, to 2cm. Needles 2 per fascicle, occasionally 3, 4–8cm×2mm, stiff, twisted, yellow-green, apex sharp-acuminate, smelling of lemon when crushed, stomatal lines on all surfaces; sheaths persistent, about 5mm. Cones ovoid, axillary, solitary or in groups of 2–5, sub-sessile, often symmetrical, 5–9×4–6cm, open ×6–8cm, pink to pale brown, mostly long persistent; scales 15mm wide, apophysis pyramidal, crossridges sharp, umbo oblong-conical, thorn stout, 4–7mm, spreading, very sharp. Seeds 5mm, brown to black, wings to 2.5cm. Eastern N US (New Jersey to Georgia, Appalachian mts). Z6.

***P.quadrifolia*** Parl. ex Sudw. PARRY'S PINYON. Small tree to 15m; crown rounded. Shoots light grey, densely pubesc.; buds light brown, slightly resinous. Needles 5 per fascicle, or in frequent trees showing hybrid introgression from *P.californiarum*, 4 or 3; 2–4cm×1mm, slightly curved forwards, outer surface glossy green without stomata, or in hybrids, duller with some stomata, inner surfaces with dense white stomatal bands; sheath semi-persistent, revolute. Cones subsessile, subglobose, 3.5–5cm, opening to ×5.5–7cm, red-brown, in hybrids to ×4–6cm, and orange-brown, 6–11 fertile scales, apophysis with a central raised area with a flat umbo at top, hybrids with a pyramidal apophysis; seeds 16mm. US (extreme S California), Mexico (N Baja California), extensively hybridizing with *P. californiarum* in most of range. Z8.

***P.radiata*** D. Don. MONTEREY PINE. To 25m in wild; in cult. on better soil 30–45m, rarely 65m in New Zealand; bole to 2.5m diam. Crown ovoid-conic, becoming rounded, dense; young bark purple-grey, becoming grey to dark brown, deeply fissured when mature; shoots yellow-brown, glabrous; winter buds slightly resinous, glabrous, cylindric, to 2cm, short-acuminate, scales chestnut brown, shiny. Needles 3 per fascicle, 10–16cm×1mm, thin, sharp-acuminate, bright green, stomatal lines not clearly visible; sheaths to 13mm, persistent. Male strob. yellow; cones sessile or subsessile, solitary or in groups of 2–6, conspicuously asymmetric, reflexed down stem, ovoid-conic, very variable in size, 6×4cm to 16×11cm, sometimes 16×6cm like *P. attenuata* when closed, glossy yellow-brown, becoming grey, remaining closed for up to 35 years; exposed scales thick, swollen, umbo with a tiny deciduous thorn. Seeds ovate, 5–7mm, wing 2.3cm. US (California: Monterey peninsula). 'Aurea': needles vivid gold when young. 'Isca': regular, globose; needles deep green. var. ***binata*** (Engelm.) Lemmon. Needles to 13cm×2mm, 2 per fascicle, occasionally 3 cones often symmetric, 6–9cm. Guadelupe I., Baja California. var. ***cedrosensis*** (Howell) Silba.

Needles 2 per fascicle; cones often symmetric, 5–7cm. Cedros I., Baja California. Z8.

***P.*×*reflexa*** (Engelm.) Engelm. *(P. flexilis* × *P. strobiformis.)* Natural hybrid intermediate between parents; very variable. SW US (Arizona, New Mexico). Z7.

***P. remota*** (Little) D. Bail. & Hawksw. PAPER-SHELL PINYON. Small tree or shrub to 7m; crown irregular. Shoots light grey, slender, glabrous; bud scales light brown with red tips, slightly resinous. Needles 2, occasionally 3 per fascicle, 3–5.5cm×1.5mm, both surfaces with stomata, grey-green; sheath semi-persistent, recurved but not revolute. Cones on a 5mm peduncle, subsessile, subglobose, 2–4×2–3.5cm, opening to ×3–6cm, glossy yellow, 5–7 fertile scales, apophysis slightly swollen, flattish, with a recessed umbo; seeds 13–16mm. US (W Texas), NE Mexico. Z8.

***P. resinosa*** Ait. RED PINE. To 35m. Bole slender, branches horizontal, ascending at tips, basal bark thick, fissured, bark above rust-brown, shallowly grooved; shoots orange to purple-brown, glabrous, not bloomed; buds resinous, ovoid to narrow-conic, long-acuminate, to 2cm, red-brown. Needles 2 per fascicle, 10–17cm×1mm, brittle, densely covering twigs, twisted, bright olive green, sharp-acuminate; sheaths to 2cm, falling after 2–4 years. Male strob. purple; cones very similar to *P. massoniana*, sub-terminal, solitary or in pairs, sessile, spreading, symmetric, 3–6×2–3cm, open ×3.5–5cm, ovoid-conic, nut-brown, apophysis crossridge not clearly defined, umbo obtuse, darker brown. Seeds to 4–5mm, oval, wing to 15mm. Eastern N America (Newfoundland to New York and Ontario). 'Globosa': dense, globose dwarf; shoots pale yellow. Z3.

***P.*×*rhaetica*** Brügger. *(P. mugo* × *P. sylvestris.)* To 20m. Bark brown suffused grey. Needles 3–5cm, dark green suffused, grey acute. Cones 3–4cm, ovoid, short-stalked, yellow-brown when mature, umbo pointed. Garden origin; also sometimes found wild in C Europe, from where described. Z4.

***P. rigida*** Mill. PITCH PINE; NORTHERN PITCH PINE. Tree to 25m. Crown irregular, rounded, open; bole often with adventitious shoots; bark dark grey or red-brown, deeply furrowed, scales plate-like; branches level; shoots pale green, orange-brown when mature, glabrous, grooved; buds resinous, brown, cylindric to ovoid-oblong, to 1.5cm, apex sharply pointed. Needles 3 per fascicle, yellow to pale green, stout, twisted, becoming dark grey-green, 7–10×2–2.5mm, occasionally to 14cm, falling after 3 years, stomatal lines visible on both sides; sheaths rust-brown, to 13mm, persistent. Cones lateral, in groups of 1–4, rarely to 30, sessile or peduncle to 7mm, ovoid-conic, 4–7×3–4cm, symmetric, pale brown, opening ×5–6cm when mature, persistent, apophysis flat to convex, umbo flat or raised, thorn slender, sharp, 1–4mm, persistent. Seeds triangular, grey, about 5mm, wings brown, about 1.5cm. NE US (N Georgia to Maine), extreme SE Canada. Z4.

***P. roxburghii*** Sarg. CHIR PINE; LONG LEAVED INDIAN PINE. Closely resembles *P. canariensis*, but with more conspicuous umbos. To 50m. Crown broad when mature; bark grey to rust-brown, fissured, exfoliating in broad, scaly plates; shoots, yellow-grey to light brown; buds not resinous, scales as *P. canariensis*. Needles 3 per fascicle, 20–40cm×1mm, pale to yellow-green, pendulous, flexible, long-acuminate, finely serrate, persistent 1–2 years, stomatal lines indistinct, on all faces; sheaths to 2.5cm. Cones subsessile or short-stalked, ovoid-conic, 9–24×6–8cm, apophysis 1–2cm thick, woody, cross-keeled, apex tapered, recurved, umbo thickened, reflexed. Seeds to 11mm, wings to 2.5cm. Himalaya (Afghanistan to Bhutan). Drought tolerant; in driest areas lvs shed after 10–11 months, thus occasionally deciduous. Z9.

***P. rudis*** Endl. ENDLICHER'S PINE. Tree to 24m. Crown high, rounded, umbrella-shaped; bark dark grey, rough, deeply fissured; shoots stout, variably bloomed; buds cylindric, apex round-conic, light brown, often resinous. Needles 5 per fascicle, rarely 4 or 6, 10–25, occasionally 30cm×2mm, radiating like a chimney sweep's brush, blue-green to grey-green; sheaths to 2.5cm. Cones solitary or in pairs, long-ovoid, 6–12cm, symmetrical, apex tapered, dark brown, peduncle to 1cm, apophysis keel transverse, umbo raised, thorn recurved, conical, persistent. C & N Mexico (mts). Most of the cultivated plants in GB of *P. montezumae* are in fact a long-foliaged form of this species. Z8.

***P. rzedowskii*** Madrigal & Caball. To 30m. Crown open, irregular; bark grey, wrinkled, fissured; shoots grey-brown, pubesc.; buds conical. Needles 3–4 per fascicle, flexible, 6–10cm×1mm, stomatal lines absent on exterior, dense on glaucous inner face. Cone bright rust-brown, oblong-cylindric, pendulous, 10–15×6–8cm; scale flexible, apophysis pyramidal, thick, umbo pointed, small, peduncle to 4cm. Seeds to 1cm×5mm, wing to 3.5cm×13mm. Mexico (SW Michoacan). Z10.

***P. sabiniana*** Douglas ex D. Don. DIGGER PINE. To 25m. Crown open, rounded; bark deeply furrowed, brown suffused grey, exfoliating in irregular scales, red-brown below; branches undulate, irregular; shoots bloomed glaucous blue-green, ridged, glabrous; buds slightly resinous, light brown, narrow-cylindric, apex acute, to 2.5cm, scales adpressed, margin fringed. Needles 3 per fascicle, outspread or pendulous, 18–30cm×1–2mm, glaucous, pale grey-green, sharp-acuminate, finely serrate, stomatal lines on all surfaces; sheaths to 2.5cm, silky, grey-brown. Cones 12–25×9cm, ovoid, solitary, or in pairs, short stalked, falling after 3–7 years, nut-brown, peduncle curved, pendulous; scales to 5cm, apophysis pyramidal, tapering, umbo stout, 1–3cm, sharp, deflexed or S-shaped. Seeds to 2–2.5cm, wing short, thick-based. W US (California: Sierra Nevada). Z8.

***P.*×*schwerinii*** Fitschen. *(P. wallichiana* × *P. strobus.)* As for *P. wallichiana*, but crown wider. To 25m or more. Young shoots green, bloomed, scattered short-pubesc. Needles 5 per fascicle, thin, pendulous, 8–14cm. Cones subterminal, grouped, 10–20×4cm, cylindric, resinous, peduncle to 2.5cm. Garden origin. Raised several times to introduce genes for resistance to white pine blister rust into *P. strobus*, from the resistant *P. wallichiana*. Z6.

***P. serotina*** Michx. POND PINE. Tree to 30m. Bark furrowed, scaly, often with epicormic growths; buds very resinous. Foliage similar to *P. taeda*, except for broader, yellower lvs, 2mm, and resinous buds. Needles 3 per fascicle, yellow-green, longer than those of *P. rigida*, to 20cm. Cones buff yellow, subglobose, variable, 6×5–9×7cm, often persisting for many years. SE US (N Carolina, Florida). Z8.

***P.*×*sondereggeri*** Chapm. *(P. palustris* × *P. taeda.)* Natural hybrid. Bark rust-brown; young shoots beige; buds conic. Needles 3 per fascicle, sharp-acuminate; sheath to 2cm. SE US. Z8.

***P. strobiformis*** Engelm. SOUTHWESTERN WHITE PINE. To 35m. Crown ovid-conic, becoming rounded; bole to 1m diam. Bark grey-white, smooth when young, dark brown, furrowed when mature; shoots grey-brown, finely pubesc.; winter buds resinous, brown, oblong-ovate to cylindric. Needles 5 per fascicle, dark blue-green, 8–14cm, sheath to 2cm, soon deciduous, stomatal lines visible on inner surfaces, finely serrated. Cones short-stalked, pendulous, cylindric, 18–35cm, yellow-brown to red-brown, opening when mature; scales thick, rounded, apophysis shiny, reflexed, umbo obtuse, thornless. Seeds ovate, 11–12×10mm, grey-brown, spotted black, wings to 8mm, or shorter. NW Mexico. var. ***carvajalii*** Silba. Longer cones, 25–50cm, with strongly revolute apophyses. SW Mexico (Jalisco). Z8.

***P. strobus*** L. WEYMOUTH PINE; EASTERN WHITE PINE. To 50m. Crown broad-conic; bole smooth, grey-green, later longitudinally fissured, brown when mature; branches horizontal; shoots pale green-brown, finely pubesc. or glabrous; buds slightly resinous, ovoid-oblong, apex acute, to 8mm, scales adpressed. Needles 5 per fascicle, not bowed, blue-green, 7–13cm, apex obtuse, abscising after 2 years, serrate, stomatal lines on inner faces only. Cones pink-brown, subterminal, in groups of 1–3, pendulous, narrow-cylindric, 8–16×2cm, rarely to 20cm, peduncles to 2.5cm, apophysis thin, slightly convex, umbo obtuse. Seeds ovate, to 6mm, wing to 2cm, brown. SE Canada to Allegheny Mts, E US. Over 30 cvs, ranging from dwarf to narrow upright forms; of the dwarfs, notable selections include the blue-tinted 'Billaw', 'Blue Shag' and 'Pumila' and the 'nana' group ('Nana', 'Pygmaea', 'Radiata', 'Umbraculifera') with light green needles; several dwarfs such as 'Macopin' and 'Sea Urchin' are developed from witches' brooms; larger globose forms include 'Oliver Dwarf' and 'Unconn'; upright pyramidal cultivars include the tortuous 'Fastigiata' and the gold-needled 'Hillside Winter Gold'; weeping cultivars include 'Inversa' and 'Pendula'; 'Alba' is notable for its pure white new growth. Z3.

***P. sylvestris*** L. SCOTS PINE. To 30m, rarely 40m. Crown ovoid-conic, becoming rounded with age. Bark thin, red-brown, exfoliating to show rust-brown beneath, thick and fissuring at base of bole with purple ridges, flaking in stout scales; shoots green-brown when young, becoming pale pink-brown when mature; winter buds resinous, occasionally resin-free, oblong-ovate, 1–2cm, rust-brown. Needles 2 per fascicle, 4–6cm×2mm, rarely to 10cm on vigorous trees, twisted, blue to pale grey-green, often yellow-green in cold winters (below −10°C for long periods), persisting 2–4 years, finely serrate, stomatal lines on both sides; sheaths to about 8mm, orange-brown, becoming grey-brown when old. Male strob. bright yellow, globose; cones solitary or in groups of 2–6, ovoid-conic, subsessile, 3–7×2–4cm, buff grey-brown, apophysis to about 8mm across, flat or pyramidal, crossridge protruding; umbo with a very small thorn or thornless, shiny, beige. Seeds to 4mm, oval-oblong, wing to 2cm. Siberia to E Asia, Europe, including Scotland, and previously England, Wales & Ireland, where native populations extinct *c*1750. Over 60 cvs, differentiated by growth and needle habit; notable dwarfs include the blue-tinted conic 'Beuvronensis', 'Glauca Nana', and 'Compressa', and the vivid blue 'Doone Valley' and the 3m 'Watereri'. 'Globosa Viridis' and the yellow-needled 'Moseri' are attractive pyramidal dwarf forms; prostrate, creeping dwarfs include the blue-tinted 'Hillside Creeper' and 'Albyns' and the very dark green of 'Repens' and 'Saxatilis'; 'Lodge Hill' and 'Oppdal' are irregular dwarfs derived from witches brooms, 'Gold Coin' and 'Gold Medal' are richly gold in winter; notable cvs of normal growth include the pyramidal 'Fastigiata', 'Pyramidalis Glauca' and the vivid blue of 'Mt. Vernon Blue'; weeping forms include 'Mitsch Weeping' and 'Pendula'. Other cvs notable for needle colour are the silver tinted 'Argentea Compacta' and 'Alba', the gold-tinted 'Aurea', 'Beissneriana' and 'Nisbet's Gem', the soft white 'Nivea' and the stippled white 'Variegata'. var. ***hamata*** Steven. Remains blue-green even in cold winters, hence better as a Christmas tree. SE Europe, Turkey, Crimea, Caucasus. Z2. var. ***lapponica*** Fries ex Hartmann. Lvs shorter, 2.5–4.5cm, dark green; cones smaller, 2.5–5cm. N Scandinavia, N Siberia. Z1. var. ***mongolica*** Litvi. Shoots smooth, grey-green, lvs to 9cm. NE Mongolia, NE China, SC Siberia. Z2.

***P. tabulaeformis*** Carr. CHINESE RED PINE. Tree to 25m+, crown ovoid-conic, becoming irregular and flat-topped with age. Bark fissured, dark grey at base, red, scaly and thin in upper crown. Shoots yellow-brown, grooved, darkening with age; buds ovoid-conic. Needles 2 per fascicle, 9–15cm, mid-green, 1.3mm thick, indistinct lines of stomata on both sides; sheath persistent, 10mm. Cones ovoid-conic, 3.5–7×3cm closed, opening to ×4–7cm, matt buff; apophysis finely wrinkled, to 15mm wide, umbo with a small 2–3mm forward-pointing spine. Seeds pale, 5–7mm with a 12mm wing. N & NW China (Beijing to Gansu). var. ***mukdensis*** (Uyeki ex Nak.) Uyeki. Cones with broader scales, to 20mm, with unusual stiff card-like texture, not woody; umbo larger, 5mm wide with a 3–4mm forward-pointing spine, and larger seeds to 9mm. NE China (S Manchuria), N Korea. Many trees cult. in GB as *P. tabulaeformis* are *P. densata* from Sichuan, e.g. Wilson 1369; Wilson 8815 is *P. tabulaeformis* var. *mukdensis*. Z5.

***P. taeda*** L. LOBLOLLY PINE. To 40m, trunk to 1m diam. Crown domed, branches spreading; bark very dark brown, scaly when young, becoming grey to red-brown, furrowed when mature; young shoots glabrous, bloomed; winter buds resinous, sharp conic to cylindric, to 13mm, bud scales rust-brown, margins fringed. Needles 3 per fascicle, occasionally 2, pale green, slender, twisted, 15–25cm×1–2mm, long-acuminate, finely dentate, stomatal lines on all sides; sheath to 2.5cm. Cones lateral, in groups of 2–5, sessile, ovoid-conic, 6–14cm, buff rust-brown, apophysis pale brown, pyramidal, crosskeel sharp, umbo a stout recurved thorn. Seeds triangular, 5–7mm, black-brown, wing to 2.5cm. SE US (S New Jersey to Florida, E Texas, Oklahoma). Z7.

***P. taiwanensis*** Hayata TAIWAN PINE. Tree to 35m (12m in cult.), allied to *P. densiflora* (not *P. thunbergii* as often stated); crown conic, flatter in old trees; bark fissured and scaly. Shoot green-brown, bud scales with long free tips. Needles 2 per fascicle, 8–12cm, slender, mid-green, sheath persistent. Cones 4.5–7×2–3cm, to ×4–6cm open, orange-brown, scales numerous, small, smoothly rounded, umbo small, flat, with a minute mucro. Taiwan (mts). Z8.

***P. teocote*** Schiede ex Schldl. & Cham. TWISTED LEAF PINE. To 30m. Bark on bole thick, furrowed, in plates, on upper trunk, thin, scaly, exfoliating, red-orange to brown; young shoots glabrous, bloomed blue-white over brown; buds resinous, cylindric to conic, to about 2cm; scales with margins fringed. Needles 3 per fascicle, occasionally 2–5, spreading, stiff, 10–15cm×1.5mm, dark green, sharp-acuminate, finely dentate, stomatal lines on all sides; sheaths to 25mm, persistent. Cones subterminal, sometimes lateral, solitary or in pairs, spreading or reflexing, 4–6cm, rarely to 9cm, oblong-ovoid, buff-brown to chestnut-brown; scales to 2cm×9mm. Seeds small, wing narrow. Mexico (mts). Z8.

***P. thunbergii*** Parl. JAPANESE BLACK PINE. To 30m. Crown open, with few, long, level or sinuous branches; irregular; bark black-grey, furrowed; young shoots orange-yellow, becoming grey to grey-black, glabrous; buds resin-free, ovoid, acute, scales white, margins fringed. Needles 2 per fascicle, 7–14cm×2mm, densely arranged, spreading, twisted, dark green, sharp-acuminate, falling after 3 years, stomatal lines on all surfaces; sheaths to 13mm. Cones solitary stalked, spreading, short, in small groups, or in dense clusters of up to 50+ on some cultivated forms, 3–7×3cm, ovoid-conic, scales relatively large and few, apophysis pink-buff, matt, rhombic, flat or compressed-pyramidal, blunt, cross-ridge sharp, not raised, umbo with a small deciduous spine. Seeds oval, 5mm, buff grey-brown, wing to 2.5cm, pale, striped dark brown. Coastal Japan, S Korea. 'Kotobuki': small and pyramidal in growth, needles short, bright green. 'Majestic Beauty': dense and compact; resistant to salt and smog damage. 'Mt Hood Prostrate': low-growing to 2.5×4m; needles very dark green. 'Pygmaea': compact dwarf to 1.5m; needles long, rich green 'Shioguro': compact and globose; needles long, bright green. Z6.

***P. torreyana*** Parry ex Carr. SOLEDAD PINE. To 16m, often taller in cult. to 35m, trunk to 60cm diam. Crown conic, becoming domed; bark deeply fissured, in large scales, brown suffused grey; young shoots pale green, bloomed white, becoming purple brown or red-brown, finally dark brown; buds large, to 6cm, resin-free, cylindric, long-acuminate, scale margin fringed. Needles 5 per fascicle, very stout, densely arranged, 20–32cm×2mm, dark green, persisting 2–4 years, stomatal lines on all surfaces; sheath about 2cm, persistent. Cones 10–15cm, ovoid, symmetrical, short stalked, shiny, nut-brown when mature, opening up to a year after ripening, peduncle reflexed, to 3cm, apophysis thickened, umbo short, occasionally incurved. Seeds 2cm, elliptic, buff speckled brown, very short, thick wing encircling seed. SW US (by San Diego, & Santa Rosa Island, Calif.). Z8.

***P. tropicalis*** Morelet. Tree to 30m, crown ovoid-conic. Needles 2 per fascicle, 20–30cm, stiff, erect, bright green, with numerous very large resin ducts. Cones 5–8cm, similar to *P. yunnanensis*, rufous-brown, apophyses low pyramidal, umbo with a minute blunt mucro. W Cuba, Isle of Pines. Z10.

***P. veitchii*** Roezl. As *P. strobiformis*, of which best treated as a ssp., but cones larger; 22–45×6–7cm opening to ×10–13cm, scales hard and woody, 3–4cm wide with long recurved or S-shaped apophysis. Seed 11–12×9mm, wing broad, 11–16×12–14mm. Distinguished from *P. ayacahuite* by the much stouter cones and larger seeds. C Mexico. Z8.

***P. virginiana*** Mill. SCRUB PINE; VIRGINIA PINE. Tree to 15m or shrub, trunk to 50cm diam. Bark thin, furrowed; branches irregular, spreading, often twisted; young shoots yellow-brown tinged red, glabrous, bloomed pale pink; buds very resinous, spindle-shaped, apex acute. Needles 2 per fascicle, 4–7cm, yellow-green to dark green, twisted, stiff, apex sharp, finely serrated, falling after 3–4 years. Cones in groups of 2–4 or solitary, oblong-conic, 3–7cm, symmetric, subsessile, spreading to pendulous, yellow-buff to rust-brown, apophysis diamond-shaped, umbo with a short, sharp, thorn. Seeds ovate, to 4mm, wing to 1cm. E US (New York to Alabama and Georgia). Z6.

***P. wallichiana*** A.B. Jackson. HIMALAYAN PINE; BLUE PINE; BHUTAN PINE. To 50m, usually less in cult. Crown conic, or irregular with age. Bark grey-brown, becoming fissured; upper branches whorled, ascending, straight, not sinuous, lower branches horizontal, often branching to base in open-grown trees. Shoots glabrous, olive green bloomed lilac, becoming grey; buds resinous, cylindric-conic, pale brown, to 8mm. Needles 5 per fascicle, persisting 2–3 years, hanging, flexible, grey-green to waxy blue, 11–17, occasionally 20cm×1mm, acute, stomatal lines on inner faces only; sheaths to 2cm, soon deciduous. Male strob. to 1cm; cones subterminal, solitary or in groups of 2–3, erect, becoming pendulous, cylindric, 14–28×4cm closed, opening to ×10cm, green, ripening buff or yellow-brown; scales keeled, apophysis thin, broad, 20–30mm wide; cone peduncle to 6cm. Seeds ovate, 7mm, wings to 2.5cm. Himalaya (Afghanistan to Assam). 'Densa': dense and conic; needles short. 'Glauca': needles conspicuously blue. 'Nana': globose dwarf with attractive long, pendulous silver needles. 'Silverstar': slow growing, globose to conic; needles notably blue, short. 'Umbraculifera': low-growing, mushroom-headed dwarf; needles pendulous, light green. 'Vernisson': branches ascending; needles long; hardy to zone 7. 'Zebrina': vigorous conic upright; branches ascending; needles variegated yellow. Z8.

***P. wangii*** Hu & Cheng. Tree to 30m, closely related to *P. parviflora*; bark smooth grey, becoming dark brown, hard and cracked into square plates. Shoots pale grey, with rufous pubescence; buds acute, 3mm, brown. Needles 3–7cm×1mm, rigid, twisted and curved as in *P. parviflora*, glossy dark green on outer face, blue-white stomatal bands on inner faces; sheath early deciduous. Cones similar to *P. parviflora* but pedunculate, on 0.5–2.5cm stems, 5–9cm, scales few, rugose red-brown becoming grey-brown, persistent several years after seeds fall. Seeds smaller, 9–11×5mm, with a longer 2cm wing. S China (Yunnan to Guangdong). Z8.

***P. yunnanensis*** Franch. To 35m. Crown conic, becoming flat; bark thin, red-brown, exfoliating on upper trunk, thick, furrowed and scaly at base. Needles bright green to dark green, 3 per fascicle, occasionally 2; 15–30cm×1mm, pendulous; sheath persistent. Cones in groups of 1–3, 5–11cm, orange to yellow-brown, glossy, becoming dark brown; apophysis slightly raised, umbo raised, with a small spine. Scales hard, stiff. Seeds 6mm, wing 15–20mm. China (SW Sichuan to W Yunnan). Z8.

***P. apachea*** Lemmon. See *P. engelmannii*.
***P. aristata*** var. ***longaeva*** (Bail.) Little. See *P. longaeva*.
***P. armandii*** var. ***amamiana*** (Koidz.) Hatsusima. See *P. amamiana*.
***P. australis*** Michx. See *P. palustris*.
***P. ayacahuite*** var. ***brachyptera*** G.R. Shaw. See *P. strobiformis*.
***P. ayacahuite*** var. ***veitchii*** (Roezl) G.R. Shaw. See *P. veitchii*.
***P. bahamensis*** Griseb. See *P. caribea*.
***P. benthamiana*** Hartweg. See *P. ponderosa*.
***P. bonapartea*** Roezl ex Gordon. See *P. veitchii*.
***P. brachyptera*** Engelm. See *P. ponderosa* ssp. *scopulorum*.
***P. cembra*** var. ***pumila*** Pall. See *P. pumila*.
***P. cembroides*** var. ***bicolor*** Little. See *P. discolor*.
***P. cembroides*** var. ***edulis*** (Engelm.) Voss. See *P. edulis*.
***P. cembroides*** var. ***monophylla*** (Torr. & Frém.) Voss. See *P. monophylla*.
***P. cembroides*** var. ***parryana*** (Engelm.) Voss. See *P. quadrifolia*.
***P. cembroides*** var. ***remota*** Little. See *P. remota*.
***P. chihuahana*** Engelm. See *P. leiophylla* ssp. *chihuahana*.
***P. chylla*** Lodd. See *P. wallichiana*.
***P. clusiana*** Clem. ex Arias. See *P. nigra* ssp. *monspeliensis*.
***P. cubensis*** Griseb. See *P. occidentalis*.
***P. divaricata*** (Ait.) Dum.-Cours. See *P. banksiana*.
***P. douglasiana*** Martinez. See *P. gordoniana*.
***P. eldarica*** Medv. See *P. brutia* ssp. *eldarica*.
***P. elliottii*** var. ***densa*** Little & Dorman. See *P. densa*.
***P. estevezii*** Perry. See *P. apulcensis*.
***P. excelsa*** Wallich ex D. Don. See *P. wallichiana*.
***P. fenzlii*** Anton & Kotschy. See *P. leiophylla*.
***P. formosana*** Hayata. See *P. morrisonicola*.
***P. funebris*** Komar. See *P. densiflora*.
***P. griffithii*** McClell. See *P. wallichiana*.
***P. halepensis*** var. ***brutia*** (Ten.) Henry. See *P. brutia*.
***P. hamiltonii*** Ten. See *P. pinaster*.
***P. heterophylla*** Sudw. non Koch non Presl. See *P. elliotii*.
***P. himekomatsu*** Miyabe & Kudô. See *P. parviflora*.
***P. inops*** Sol. See *P. virginiana*.
***P. insignis*** Douglas ex Loud. See *P. radiata*.
***P. insularis*** Endl. See *P. kesiya*.
***P. jaliscana*** Pérez. See *P. pringlei*.
***P. khasya*** Royle. See *P. kesiya*.
***P. khasyana*** Griff. See *P. kesiya*.
***P. kochiana*** Klotzsch ex Koch. See *P. sylvestris* var. *hamata*.
***P. laricio*** Poir. See *P. nigra* var. *maritima*.
***P. latisquama*** Engelm. See *P. pinceana*.
***P. latteri*** Mason. See *P. merkusii*.
***P. leucodermis*** Antoine. See *P. heldreichii*.
***P. leucosperma*** Maxim. See *P. tabulaeformis*.
***P. lindleyana*** Gordon. See *P. montezumae* var. *lindleyi*.
***P. longifolia*** Salisb. See *P. palustris*.
***P. longifolia*** Roxb. non Salisb. See *P. roxburghii*.
***P. lutea*** Walter. See *P. taeda*.
***P. lutea*** Martinez, non Walter. See *P. cooperi*.
***P. macrophylla*** Engelm. See *P. engelmannii*.
***P. maritima*** Mill. See *P. pinaster*.

***P. martinezii*** Larsen. See *P. durangensis*.
***P. michoacaënsis*** Martinez. See *P. devoniana*.
***P. mitis*** Michx. See *P. echinata*.
***P. montana*** Mill. See *P. mugo*.
***P. montana*** var. ***uncinata*** (DC.) Heering. See *P. mugo* ssp. *uncinata*.
***P. montezumae*** hort. See *P. rudis*.
***P. montezumae*** var. ***hartwegii*** (Lindl.) Engelm. See *P. hartwegii*.
***P. montezumae*** var. ***rudis*** (Endl.) G.R. Shaw. See *P. rudis*.
***P. mughus*** Scop. See *P. mugo*.
***P. murrayana*** Balf. See *P. contorta* ssp. *murrayana*.
***P. oocarpa*** var. ***microphylla*** G.R. Shaw. See *P. praetermissa*.
***P. oocarpa*** var. ***ochoterenai*** Martinez. See *P. patula* ssp. *tecunumannii*.
***P. oocarpoides*** Lindl. ex Loud. See *P. oocarpa*.
***P. parryana*** Engelm. See *P. quadrifolia*.
***P. parviflora*** var. ***morrisonicola*** (Hayata) Wu. See *P. morrisonicola*.
***P. patula*** var. ***macrocarpa*** Mast. See *P. greggii*.
***P. pentaphylla*** Mayr. See *P. parviflora* var. *pentaphylla*.
***P. ponderosa*** var. ***arizonica*** (Engelm.) G.R. Shaw. See *P. arizonica*.
***P. ponderosa*** var. ***jeffreyi*** (Murray) Vasey. See *P. jeffreyi*.
***P. ponderosa*** var. ***macrophylla*** (Engelm.) G.R. Shaw. See *P. engelmannii*.
***P. pseudostrobus*** ssp. ***apulcensis*** (Lindl.) Stead. See *P. apulcensis*.
***P. pseudostrobus*** var. ***apulcensis*** (Lindl.) G.R. Shaw. See *P. apulcensis*.
***P. pseudostrobus*** var. ***coatepecensis*** Martinez. See *P. apulcensis*.
***P. pseudostrobus*** var. ***estevezii*** Martinez. See *P. apulcensis*.
***P. remorata*** Mason. See *P. muricata*.
***P. rigida*** ssp. ***serotina*** (Michx.) Clausen. See *P. serotina*.
***P. rigida*** var. ***serotina*** (Michx.) Loud. ex Hoopes. See *P. serotina*.
***P. russelliana*** Lindl. See *P. montezumae*.
***P. scopulorum*** Lemmon. See *P. ponderosa* ssp. *scopulorum*.
***P. sibirica*** Du Tour. See *P. cembra* ssp. *sibirica*.
***P. sinensis*** Lamb. See *P. massoniana*.
***P. sinensis*** auct. non Lamb. See *P. tabulaeformis*.
***P. sinensis*** var. ***yunnanensis*** G.R. Shaw. See *P. yunnanensis*.
***P. strobiformis*** Sudw. non Engelm. See *P.* ×*reflexa*.
***P. strobus*** var. ***chiapensis*** Martinez. See *P. chiapensis*.
***P. subpatula*** Royle. See *P. patula*.
***P. tabulaeformis*** var. ***densata*** (Mast.) Rehd. See *P. densata*.
***P. tabulaeformis*** var. ***yunnanensis*** (Franch. hort. See *P. yunnanensis*.
***P. taeda*** var. ***heterophylla*** Elliott. See *P. elliotii*.
***P. tecunumanii*** Eguiluz & Perry. See *P. patula* ssp. *tecunumanii*.
***P. tenuifolia*** Benth. non Salisb. See *P. maximinoi*.
***P. tuberculata*** D. Don. See *P. radiata*.
***P. tuberculata*** Gordon (non D. Don). See *P. attenuata*.
***P. uncinata*** Ramond ex DC. See *P. mugo*.
***P. uyematsui*** Hayata. See *P. morrisonicola*.
***P. wilsonii*** G.R. Shaw. See *P. densata*.
***P. wrightii*** Engelm. See *P. occidentalis*.

**Piper** L. PEPPER. (Classical Lat. name.) Piperaceae. More than 1000 species of erect shrubs, tough woody climbers and small trees, rarely more herb-like, often with pungent odour; stems often swollen at nodes. Leaves alternate, lamina often attached asymmetrically to petiole, one side lower than other; stipules absent or attached to petiole. Inflorescence axillary or opposite leaf, a cylindric spike, or rarely compounded of several spikes; flowers of New World species bisexual, of Old World species unisexual, subtended by often concave floral bract; perianth wanting; stamens 2–10; stigmas 2–4, generally 3. Fruit a drupe with this mesocarp; seed 1. Pantropical. Z10.

CULTIVATION *P. nigrum* is cultivated commercially in the rich alluvial soils of the low altitude, wet tropics, either as a second or subsidiary crop in the shade of tree crops or with other species cultivated to provide shade; other than the cultivation of *P. nigrum* and *P. betle* in botanic collections of economically important plants, in temperate zones *Piper* spp. are more commonly grown as ornamentals. With the exception of *P. kadsura* which will tolerate short-lived light frost in sheltered woodland sites in humus rich soils that approximate to those in habitat, *Piper* spp. are suitable for the warm glasshouse or conservatory, valued for their often very attractively marbled foliage, notably so in *P. crocatum*, and *P. ornatum*. Given the support of trellis or wires for climbing species, they require soils and conditions similar to those described for the related *Peperomia*. Pruning to remove weak growth and thin congested growth is best done in late winter/early spring before growth commences. Propagate by seed or by semi-ripe cuttings in sand in a closed case.

***P. angustifolium*** Lam. Shrub, small, branched; twigs slender, pubesc. Lvs 9×2cm, narrowly lanceolate, tapered to acuminate apex, acute to subcuneate at base, margins narrowly revolute, glabrous, glossy, glandular-punctate beneath; petiole pubesc. Spikes small; peduncle pubesc. French Guiana.

***P. auritum*** HBK. Tree, 4.5m, soft-wooded, often rather aromatic. Lvs 25×16cm, ovate to elliptic-ovate, acute to acuminate at apex, deeply cordate at base, clearly asymmetric with one side 1–2cm longer than other at petiole, thinly pubesc. above, more densely so beneath; petiole 7cm, winged. Spikes 18×0.4cm; peduncles slender, 5cm; bracts triangular-subpeltate; fls creamy. Fr. obpyramidal-trigonous, small, glabrate. Mexico.

***P. betle*** L. BETEL; BETLE PEPPER. Climber to 5m; stem rounded, woody, nodes scarcely swollen, frequently producing adventitious roots, glabrous. Lvs 13.5×7.5cm, broadly ovate to cordate, acute to acuminate at apex, rounded to cordate at base, green, smooth and glabrous, somewhat coriaceous, petiole 13×2mm, glabrous, with stipules extending to half its length. Infl. lf-opposed, solitary, male spike 115×5mm, female 55×8mm, pale green glaucous; peduncle 2cm×1.5mm. Fr. to 12cm, embedded in rachis and coalescing into a fleshy red mass. Indian to Malay Peninsula. Extensively grown in SE Asia for its leaves ('*pan*') and spikes which are chewed with betel nut (fruit of the palm *Areca catechu*) and lime.

***P. borneense*** N.E. Br. Dwarf herb, 22–30cm; stems stout, green, densely pilose, internodes short. Lvs elliptic to elliptic-oblong, acute at apex, auriculate-cordate at base, rather large, deep green above with broad, pale silver-grey stripes between principal veins, paler green beneath, rugose, glabrous above, pubesc. beneath; veins 11; petiole stout, 2.5cm, green, hairy. Spikes axillary, cylindric, 7×0.5cm; peduncles stout, 3cm, pale green, hairy; stigmas 3–5. Borneo.

***P. cubeba*** L. f. CUBEB; CUBEB PEPPER. Climber to 3m; stems round, smooth, somewhat swollen at nodes, glabrous. Lvs 14×6cm, elliptic to lanceolate, acute to acuminate at apex, broadly tapered, rounded or somewhat cordate at base, and often asymmetric, green above, paler beneath, smooth; petiole 11×2mm, grooved above. Infl. lf-opposed, solitary, erect becoming pendulous, spikes unisexual, male 85×4.5mm, female 75×18mm; peduncles 30×2.5mm, glabrous. Fr. loosely arranged, red-brown, long-pedicellate. Indonesia.

***P. decurrens*** DC. Shrub, stem stout, pale green with white spots and black lines, branches glabrous. Lvs rather remote, 12×4.5cm, lanceolate, acuminate to minutely mucronate at apex, cuneate to acute at base, slightly decurrent on petiole, green with metallic iridescence; petiole 8mm. Bracts oblong-obovate, cucullate, rather fleshy, margins ciliate; stigmas 3, style wanting; stamens 4, anth. articulate. Costa Rica to Colombia.

***P. guineense*** Schum. & Thonn. GUINEA CUBEB; ASHANTI PEPPER; BENIN PEPPER. Vine, stems climbing over trees to 23m. Lvs alternate, very variable, 10×7cm, suborbicular to oval on main stem, oval to lanceolate on lateral branches, acuminate at apex, cordate or rounded at base; petioles 3cm on main stem lvs, 12mm on those of lateral branches. Spikes erect in fl., pendent in fr., 3cm; peduncle 7mm, glabrous; bracts ciliate; stamens 2, perhaps rarely 3; stigmas 3–5, sessile. Fruiting spikes 7cm, tomentose; fr. 4.5mm diam., red, dry; pedicel 7mm. Tropical Africa (Guinea to Uganda and Angola).

***P. kadzura*** (Choisy) Ohwi. JAPANESE PEPPER. Scandent shrub, clambering over rocks and trees; branches slender, with aerial roots. Lvs 6.5×3.5cm, ovate, or rounded-cordate on young plants, long-acuminate at apex, rounded at base, entire, dark green, paler beneath, rather stiff and thick, often sparsely pubesc. Spikes 3–8cm, female shorter than male; peduncles pendulous; bracts peltate. Fr. globose, 3.5mm diam., red. Japan, S Korea, Ryukyus.

***P. longum*** L. Slender climber, 3m; stems angled or fluted, not or scarcely swollen at nodes, rather hairy. Lvs 7.5×4cm, broadly lanceolate to lanceolate-elliptic, broadly acute to obtuse at apex, rarely somewhat acuminate, deeply auriculate at base, very slightly asymmetric, green above, paler beneath, smooth, minutely hairy below, densely glandular-punctate; petiole 12×1mm, grooved. Infl. lf-opposed, solitary, erect, male spikes 6cm×2.5mm, female spikes 2cm×6.5mm; peduncle of male spikes 3cm, of female 11mm, minutely pubesc. Fr. very densely arranged. Tropical E Himalaya.

***P. macrophyllum*** HBK. Large shrub, stems striate, branches erect, glabrous. Lvs alternate, oblong, large, obtusely acuminate at apex, oblique at base, entire, glabrous; veins 10–12; petiole short, broad, grooved. Spikes opposite lvs, erect; peduncles long; stamens 4–6; style wanting, stigmas 3. E Indies.

***P. magnificum*** Trel. LACQUERED PEPPER. Shrub, erect, to 1m; stem winged. Lvs 15×11.5cm, ovate to broadly elliptic or suborbicular, rounded or broadly acute at apex, cordate to auriculate at base with sinus to 3cm deep, glossy deep green, bright maroon beneath with white margin and veins, quilted, glabrous above, hairy beneath; petiole 3.5cm, longitudinally ridged, broadly winged, wings clasping stem at base. Infl. lf-opposed, terminal, solitary, pendulous, spike bisexual, 3.5×0.5cm; peduncle winged, 12mm, flushed maroon. Peru.

***P. metallicum*** Hallier f. Scandent herb to more than 1m; stems 2.5mm diam., red when young, becoming dull deep green with age, glabrous, with adventitious roots from nodes. Lvs alternate, to 15×11cm, ovate, apex acuminate and mucronate, scarcely contracted to petiole at base, tinged red when young, beautiful metallic deep green when mature, rufescent with silvery sheen beneath, thick; veins reticulate, dark red; petioles to 4×0.4cm. Fls and fr. unknown. Borneo.

***P. methysticum*** Forst. KAVA; KAVA-KAVA. Shrub, erect, to 4m; stem rounded, glabrous, nodes swollen. Lvs 17×13cm, cordate to suborbicular, rounded, obtuse or broadly acute at apex, rarely somewhat mucronate, deeply auriculate at base with sinus to 5cm deep, deep green above, paler beneath, smooth, minutely granular-pubesc. above, pubesc. beneath; petiole 3cm, broadly winged for to half its length, wings membranous at edge, more or less glabrous. Infl. terminal or lf-opposed, solitary or several together, spikes unisexual, 12×0.4cm; peduncles 15×2mm, sparsely hairy. S Pacific.

***P. nigrum*** L. COMMON PEPPER; PEPPER PLANT; BLACK PEPPER; WHITE PEPPER; MADAGASCAR PEPPER. Climber to 4m, monoecious or dioecious; stems rounded, swollen at nodes, glabrous. Lvs 9×6cm, broadly ovate to cordate, broadly tapered, rounded or weakly cordate at base, acute to obtuse, often shortly acuminate at apex, green, glabrous; petiole 22×2mm, deeply grooved. Infl. lf-opposed, solitary, pendulous, spikes mostly bisexual, 7.5cm×0.6cm; peduncle 15×1.5mm, glabrous. Fr. loosely arranged, 5mm diam., dark red when fully ripe. S India & Sri Lanka, naturalised in N Burma and Assam.

***P. officinarum*** DC. Lvs oblong-elliptic, attenuate to acuminate apex, tapered to rather unequal acute to cordate base, glabrous, coriaceous; veins rather prominent beneath, feathered; petiole glabrous. Infl. cylindric, densely fld; peduncle longer than petiole, glabrous; stamens 2–3; stigmas 3, style wanting, ovary embedded in and coalescing with rachis. Fr. crowded in dense spikes, subglobose, coalescing. India, Malaysia.

***P. ornatum*** N.E. Br. CELEBES PEPPER. Shrub, extensively spreading, creeping or weakly climbing, to 5m; stem rounded, wiry, dark green or rufescent, glabrous. Lvs 9.5×7.5cm, broadly cordate to suborbicular, peltate with petiole attached 1–2cm from lower margin, obtuse and rounded or acute and attenuate at apex, rounded to somewhat cordate at base, finely mottled dark green, pink and silver above, flushed maroon beneath; petiole 7.5×0.3cm, grooved above, with stipules to 12mm when young. Infl. unknown, probably rarely produced. Sulawesi. Sometimes erroneously offered as *P. crocatum*.

***P. porphyrophyllum*** (Lindl.) N.E. Br. Shrub very extensively spreading, creeping or sometimes weakly climbing, to 8m; stem rounded with longitudinal grooves, wiry, rufescent, often with lines of hairs. Lvs 12.5×10.5cm, broadly cordate to suborbicular, generally obtuse and shortly mucronate at apex, cordate to auriculate at base, thin, dark green above with red and white spots, flushed purple beneath; petiole 33×3mm, grooved. Infl. lf-opposed, male spikes 12×0.4cm, female 3×0.8cm; peduncles 2.5cm, hairy. Malay Peninsula, Borneo.

***P. rubronodosum*** Nichols. Shrub; stems fleshy, scabrous, red at nodes. Lvs deep sea green frosted with silver-grey, especially when young; petioles tomentose-pubesc. Colombia.

***P. rubrovenosum*** hort. ex Rodigas. Vine; stems flexuous, woody. Lvs obliquely elliptic to cordate, acute to acuminate at apex, entire, bright deep green above, paler beneath, glabrous, rather coriaceous; veins 5, marked by irregular rose lines above; stipules adnate to petiole, pink. Infl. and fr. unknown. New Guinea.

***P. sylvaticum*** Roxb. MOUNTAIN LONG PEPPER. Climber to 4m; stem rounded, becoming woody, with longitudinal lines, nodes somewhat swollen. Lvs 9×5cm, ovate to cordate, acute to acuminate at apex, broadly tapered, rounded or cordate at base, often somewhat asymmetric, dark green above, paler beneath, rough, glandular-pubesc. on main veins beneath, glandular-punctate on minor veins; petiole 10×1mm, grooved. Infl. lf-opposed, solitary, erect, male spikes 55×3mm, female 19×6mm; peduncles 9×1.5mm, minutely glandular-pubesc. Fr. densely arranged but individuals distinct. Subtropical E Himalaya.

***P. unguiculatum*** Ruiz & Pav. Shrub, 3m+, essentially glabrous; twigs slender. Lvs 7×2.5cm, lanceolate-oblong to oblong-ovate, acuminate at apex, rounded at base, glabrous or minutely pubesc. above near base; petiole 7mm, minutely pubesc. Spikes 45×2mm, fls close-set; peduncle 1cm, slender, glabrous; stamens 5–6, rarely 4. Fr. crowded, rather pointed ovoid, minutely velvety-pubesc. Peru.

***P. bicolor*** Yunck. See *P. magnificum*.
***P. celtidifolium*** Desf. See *P. unguiculatum*.
***P. elongatum*** Poir. See *Peperomia elongata*.
***P. emarginellum*** Sw. ex Wikstr. See *Peperomia emarginella*.
***P. futokadsura*** Sieb. See *P. kadzura*.
***P. maculosum*** L. See *Peperomia maculosa*.
***P. magnoliaefolium*** Jacq. See *P. Peperomia magnoliaefolia*.
***P. trinerve*** Vahl. See *Peperomia trinervis*.
For further synonymy see *Artanthe*.

**PIPERACEAE** Agardh. PEPPER FAMILY. (Including Peperomiaceae (Miq.) Wettst.) Dicot. 14 genera and 1940 species of shrubs, lianes, epiphytes or small trees, rarely herbs; aromatic, usually with spherical ethereal oil cells, often with alkaloids; vascular bundles usually scattered (as in monocots) but with intrafascicular cambium, the outermost often becoming continuous by cambial growth. Leaves simple, alternate; stipules adnate to petiole or absent. Flowers small, naked, unisexual or bisexual, in axils of small peltate bracts on dense fleshy spikes; perianth absent; stamens 1–10, often 3+3, filaments free; ovary superior, of (1–)4 fused carpels, 1-loculed, with 1 ovules. Fruit a berry or drupe, 1-seeded; endosperm scanty; perisperm copious, starchy; embryo minute, hardly differentiated when seeds ripen. Tropical. *Piper nigrum* fruits are the source of both black and white pepper; *P. betle* leaves are used to wrap betel nuts, *Areca catechu*, used for chewing; the roots of *P. methysticum* provide kava, a narcotic, sedative and ceremonial drink in Fiji and other Pacific Islands. Tropical. *Macropiper, Peperomia, Piper*.

**Piptadenia** Benth.
***P. macrocarpa*** Benth. See *Anadenanthera colubrina* var. *cebil*.

**Piptanthus** D. Don ex Sweet. (From Gk *piptein*, to fall, and *anthos*, flower; the calyx, corolla and stamens fall off together, leaving the young pod without a calyx at base.) Leguminosae (Papilionoideae). 2 species of shrubs or small trees. Leaves trifoliolate, stalked; stipules opposite the petiole, basally connate, the bifid apices acute. Flowers yellow, in loose or congested, axillary or terminal racemes, arising 3 per node, each from the base of a conspicuous bract; calyx 5-lobed, 2 uppermost lobes connate for most of their length, villous; standard broad, emarginate, wings and keel auriculate; stamens 10, separate, anthers uniform; pistil stipitate; ovary oblong, 3–10-ovulate, glabrous to pubescent, style confluent, filiform, incurved, stigma minute, terminal. Fruit a legume, oblong, compressed 2–10-seeded; seeds compressed, obliquely elliptic, strophiolate. Himalaya.

CULTIVATION Both species occur in montane habitats, *P. nepalensis* as high as 3600m/11700ft, *P. tomentosus* in open woodland and scrub at around 3000m/9750ft. The close silver down of the emerging leaves contrasts with the deep glossy green of the upright stems. As the foliage of *P. nepalensis* matures it becomes a dark, shining blue-green. The leaves of *P. tomentosus* retain their silvery pubescence, an attractive feature which also appears markedly on the lemon yellow flowers and to a lesser degree on the pods.

Both species will tolerate temperatures to −15°C/5°F; where such low temperatures are prolonged they become deciduous and may suffer some damage to their rather tender hollow branches, although given adequate protection at the roots, their natural stooling habit allows them to re-sprout from the base. In zones at these limits, *Piptanthus* should be given the protection of a south- or southwest-facing wall.

Grow in full sun in any moderately fertile, well-drained soil, including calcareous and dry soils. In spring, cut back damaged growth to sound wood; prune after flowering to remove old and overcrowded growth at ground level. Propagation is easiest from seed sown under glass when ripe or in early spring; germination usually occurs within 7–10 days. Pot on until final planting out to minimize root disturbance. Take semi-ripe basal cuttings, cut through the solid part of the stem at the node, and root in a sandy propagating mix in a closed case. Also by layering.

***P. nepalensis*** (Hook.) D. Don ex Sweet. Shrub or small tree to 4m. Leaflets to 15×4cm, lanceolate to linear-ovate, subglabrous to puberulent beneath, not tomentose. Fls bright yellow, in axillary or terminal racemes to 15cm, standard occasionally with purple-brown or with grey markings; cal. to 1.6cm, pubesc.; standard 2.5×2cm, broad-cordate, emarginate, wings slightly shorter than keel, keel to 32mm, keel blade to 2.5cm; stamens to 2.8m; ovary glabrous or villous-ciliate on dorsal margin. Fr. to 22×2cm, puberulent to subglabrous; seeds to 6×5mm. Summer. Himalaya. Z8.

***P. tomentosus*** Franch. Shrub or small tree to 4m. Leaflets to 12×5cm, ovate to somewhat elliptic-oval, thickly silky-tomentose and prominently veined, particularly beneath. Fls lemon-yellow, in axillary or terminal racemes to 15cm; cal. to 1.5cm, densely pubesc.; standard 2.5×2cm, broad-cordate, emarginate, wings equal keel, keel blade to 1.6cm; stamens to 2cm; ovary densely tawny-tomentose. Fr. to 7×1.2cm, puberulent; seeds 4.5×4mm. Spring–summer. China (NW Yunnan, S Sichuan). Z8.

***P. bicolor*** Craib. See *P. nepalensis*.
***P. concolor*** Craib. See *P. nepalensis*.
***P. forrestii*** Craib. See *P. nepalensis*.
***P. laburnifolius*** (D. Don) Stapf. See *P. nepalensis*.
***P. leiocarpus*** Stapf. See *P. nepalensis*.
For further synonymy see *Baptisia*.

**Piptatherum** Palib.
***P. multiflorum*** (Cav.) Palib. See *Oryzopsis miliacea*.

**Piqueria** Cav. (For Andres Piquer, Spanish physician, who published a translation of Hippocrates in 1757.) Compositae. 7 species of erect, annual to perennial herbs or subshrubs. Leaves mostly opposite, lanceolate or ovate, entire, toothed or serrate, petiolate or sessile. Capitula discoid, small, few in compound, loose panicles; receptacle flat, naked; phyllaries in one series, obovate to oblong; florets white to pale yellow, occasionally tinged lavender. Fruit a glabrous cypsela; pappus absent. Tropical America. Z10.

CULTIVATION Reliably perennial in zones that are frost-free or almost so, *P. trinervia* is easily grown in a sunny position in any moderately fertile soil. Grown for the light sprays of small flowers, *Piqueria* lasts well in water and has commonly been grown in the cool glasshouse as a cut flower for autumn and winter use. For this purpose, take basal cuttings from overwintered stock in spring, and root in a closed case. Pinching frequently for bushy plants, grow on in a medium-fertility loam-based mix, with full light and good ventilation, watering to keep evenly moist when in full growth, reducing as temperatures fall in autumn and winter. Provide a winter temperature of 5–7°C/40–45°F. Alternatively, lift plants grown in the open border and pot up in autumn. Propagate also by seed and division. Prone to aster virus yellows and to basal rots.

***P. trinervia*** Cav. Perenn. herb, to 1m. Lvs to 7×1.5cm, narrowly ovate to lanceolate, base rounded to cuneate, serrate. Involucre to 3mm high; phyllaries 4, pale green; florets cream-white. Fr. to 2mm. Autumn–winter. Mexico, C America, Haiti.

***P. latifolia*** DC. See *Phalacraea latifolia*.
For further synonymy see *Stevia*.

**Piquetia** N.E. Br.
***P. pillansii*** (Kensit) N.E. Br. See *Kensitia pillansii*.

**Piriadacus** Pichon.
***P. hibiscifolius*** (Cham.) Pichon. See *Arrabidaea corallina*.

**Pirigara** Aubl.
***P. speciosa*** Kunth. See *Gustavia speciosa*.
***P. superba*** Kunth. See *Gustavia superba*.

**Pisaura** Bonato. See *Lopezia*.

**Piscidia** L. (From Lat. *piscis*, fish, and *caedere*, to kill or destroy; the bruised leaves, powdered bark and twigs yield fish-poisons.) JAMAICA DOGWOOD. Leguminosae (Papilionoideae). Some 8 species of trees. Leaves alternate, imparipinnate. Flowers in congested lateral panicles; calyx lobes subequal, upper lip short-notched; petals clawed; stamens 10, all united, but uppermost free at base. Fruit a linear, indehiscent legume, with 4 broad, longitudinal wings. C America to W Indies and Florida. Z10.

CULTIVATION *Piscidia* spp. are generally found in dry thickets and woodland in their native regions; they are grown for their flowers, which appear before the new leaves, and for their decorative seed pods. Cultivate as for *Gliricidia*.

***P. piscipula*** (L.) Sarg. JAMAICA DOGWOOD; WEST INDIAN DOGWOOD; FISH FUDDLE. To 15m. Lvs to 25cm; leaflets to 10cm, in 3–4 pairs, elliptic-ovate, estipellate, acute, glabrous above, puberulent beneath, undulate or weakly dentate; petiolules 5mm. Pedicel to 5mm; cal. to 0.5cm, campanulate, densely grey-puberulent; cor. to 1.5cm, blue-purple to white striped red, standard suborbicular, emarginate, keel and wings auriculate. Fr. to 7cm, wings thin, lobed and crispate. S Florida, W Indies.

***P. erythrina*** L.. See *P. piscipula*.
For further synonymy see *Icthyomethia*.

**Pisonia** L. (For Wilhelm Pison (*d.* 1678), Dutch naturalist.) Nyctaginaceae. Some 35 species of trees and shrubs, climbing or erect to 18m. Leaves to 40×7.5cm, opposite, simple, entire, usually petiolate. Inflorescence a subsessile or pedunculate panicle or cyme, usually unisexual, rarely bisexual or with hermaphrodite flowers; calyx corolla-like, 2–3-lobed; male perianth funnel-shaped, lobes short, spreading, deltoid, stamens to 40, exserted, filaments unequal, basally united; female flowers with longer and narrower perianth tube, swollen at base, stamens rudimentary; ovary elongate, style exserted, usually lateral. Fruit an achene, to 3.5cm, glabrous or glandular-tuberculate, 5-ridged, subtended by persistent calyx. Tropics, mainly America. Z10.

CULTIVATION Attractive foliage specimens for tropical and subtropical gardens; in temperate areas grow under intermediate glasshouse conditions in borders or large containers. The variegated cv. of *P. umbellifera* (with pink or red-flushed young foliage) could make a good houseplant. Plant in spring into any well-drained soil in full sun or part shade. Grow in containers of a medium-fertility, loam-based mix with the addition of bark chippings, giving strong filtered light and medium humidity; water moderately during the growing season, sparingly in winter. Repot or top-dress in late winter or spring, pruning to shape or to restrict growth at the same time. Propagate by greenwood cuttings rooted with bottom heat of 20°C/68°F in summer in a humid, warm atmosphere: alternatively by air-layering.

***P. umbellifera*** (Forst. & Forst. f.) Seem. BIRD-CATCHER TREE; PARA-PARA. Tree to 18m+, glabrous. Lvs to 40cm, oblong. Fls to 8cm, pink or yellow; cal. 5-lobed; stamens 6–14. Fr. to 3.5cm, 5-ribbed, ribs viscid. Mauritius, Australia, New Zealand. 'Variegata': lvs marbled pale green, margins creamy white, flushed pink especially when young.

***P. zapallo*** Griseb. Lvs to 12.5×7.5cm, broadly elliptic. Fls in small clusters, cymes pedunculate; stamens 5. Fr. 2cm. Argentina.

**Pistacia** L. (From Gk *pistake*, pistachio.) PISTACHIO. Anacardiaceae. About 9 species of dioecious trees and shrubs. Leaves alternate, deciduous or persistent, pinnate, rarely simple or trifoliate, membranous or leathery. Inflorescence a panicle or raceme, unisexual; bracts 1–3, herbaceous or membranous; petals absent; male flowers with stamens 3–8, usually 4–5, anthers ovate or oblong, filaments short, inserted on disc, pistillode reduced or absent; female flowers with ovary superior, globose or ovoid, unilocular, style 1, short, stigmas 3, occasionally 2, papillose, staminodes absent. Fruit an obovoid to globular drupe, often laterally compressed, fleshy; seeds 1, laterally compressed. Mediterranean, C Asia to Japan, Malesia, Mexico, S US. Z9 unless specified.

CULTIVATION *P. vera* has long been cultivated in its native regions, Western Asia and the Mediterranean; it is grown in Iran, Turkey and Syria, the major exporters of the nut, and in California, Arizona and Texas. It occurs in hilly and mountainous regions, to 1500m/4875ft, with a temperature range between −10°C/14°F in winter and 40°C/104°F in summer, largely on sandstone formations, although it also enjoys a light calcareous soil in cultivation. It flourishes in conditions with long hot summers, low humidity and on poor soils. To set fruit, male and female plants must be grown, at a ratio of 1:5.

In cool temperate climates, the genus is represented mainly by the ornamental *P. chinensis*, the Chinese pistachio. Reaching upwards of 20m/65ft, it is a popular shade tree in the southern US, but it is grown chiefly for its elegant and glossy foliage, which has fine autumn colour. It survives in Washington DC. *P. chinensis* is sometimes used as graft stock for *P. vera*. The slow-growing Mediterranean native, *P. terebinthus*, the source of China turpentine, can also be grown in cool temperate regions; it has handsome and aromatic glossy leaves. *P. lentiscus*, also aromatic, the source of mastic, makes an evergreen shrub to 4m/13ft, requiring wall protection in cool regions. Plant hardy species in spring, in a sunny position, and in well drained deep light soil.

Grow tender species in intermediate to hot glasshouse conditions, minimum 13–16°C/55–60°F, in low humidity and direct light, in a well-drained loam-based medium. Water by drenching thoroughly and allow to dry moderately between waterings. Sow seed in late winter–early spring in loam-based seed propagating medium at 25°C/77°F. Germination is variable. Sound fresh nuts must be soaked overnight in water before sowing; if the drupe is entire, soak overnight in alkalized water, and rub through a sieve or with coarse sand to remove the pulp. In commercial cultivation, choice varieties of *P. vera* such as 'Minnularia', and 'Fimminedda' are propagated by budding or grafting. Dormant buds from old wood are budded on to year-old understocks of *P. vera*, *P. terebinthus* or *P. atlantica* in spring, when the bark lifts freely. Selected female varieties are also grafted onto 2–3-year-old seedling understock of *P. terebinthus* or *P. atlantica*. Grafts bear fruit in their third or fourth year, and in alternate years thereafter. Since the plants are dioecious, a male branch is often grafted on simultaneously, or male branches may be gathered and preserved until the female flowers open, for pollination by hand; if pollination does not occur, shells continue to grow empty to normal size.

*Pistacia* are more prone to fungal root rots than other members of the Anacardiaceae.

***P. atlantica*** Desf. BETOUM; MOUNT ATLAS MASTIC. Tree to 20m. Branches brown to grey. Lvs imparipinnate; leaflets 7–11, to 6×1.5cm, lanceolate, obtuse not mucronate; rachis winged. Male panicle to 10×4cm, compact, later loosening, bracts linear-lanceolate; stamens 5–7, anth. oblong-ovate; female panicle erect or ascending, 8–15cm, bracts 2–4, oblong-ovate, 1 bract lanceolate; ovary globose. Fr. obovoid, to 8×6mm. N Africa. var. ***latifolia*** DC. Tree to 15m. Lvs larger; leaflets 6–8, occasionally 9, lanceolate to oblong to broadly ovate. E Mediterranean.

***P. chinensis*** Bunge. Tree to 15m, occasionally taller. Lvs deciduous, paripinnate; leaflets 10–20, about 8×2cm, lanceolate, strongly oblique at base, acute or acuminate, mucronate to cuspidate, terminal leaflet shorter; petiole 3–10cm. Male panicle puberulent, to 5×3cm; female panicle 8–18cm. Fr. scarlet becoming purple-blue, thinly fleshy. China, Taiwan, Philippines. ssp. ***integerrima*** (Stewart) Rech. f. Lvs paripinnate or imparipinnate, 15–25cm; leaflets broadly lanceolate to oblong, slightly oblique at base, to 10×3.5cm. Afghanistan to Kashmir. Z8.

***P. lentiscus*** L. (sensu lato). MASTIC; LENTISCO; CHIOS MASTIC. Tree or shrub to 4m, evergreen. Lvs coriaceous, paripinnate; leaflets 4–6, rarely more, 15–45×6–16mm, glabrous, ovate, oblong-lanceolate or elliptic, obtuse to mucronate. Male infl. a raceme, sometimes branched, compact, 1–2.5cm, bracts pubesc., ovate to oblong, concave, stamens 4–5, pistil rudimentary; female infl. a raceme, sometimes branched, in clusters of 1–4, bracts triangular, ovate or oval, ovary ovoid. Fr. red becoming black, globose to lenticular, 4–5mm, fleshy. Mediterranean except NE Africa.

***P. mexicana*** HBK. COPALL. Tree to 6m. Branches angular, pubesc., later glabrous. Buds coriaceous. Lvs imparipinnate, to 15cm; leaflets 16–36, 10–26×6–9mm, thin, often alternate, oblong, acute, mucronate, oblique, margins occasionally revolute, terminal leaflet smaller; petiole glabrous, 1–3cm. Male panicle compact, 5–8cm; bracts densely pubesc.; stamens 4–5; female panicle 5–11cm. Fr. sessile, globose to lenticular, 4–6mm, red to black. Mexico, Guatemala.

***P. terebinthus*** L. CYPRUS TURPENTINE; TEREBINTE; TEREBINTHO. Tree or shrub, 2–6m, deciduous. Lvs imparipinnate, 10–20cm; petiole to 8cm; leaflets 6–12, 3–5cm, ovate-lanceolate to oblong, obtuse or acute, mucronate, glabrous, veins pubesc. Male panicle 6–10×2–4cm, bracts brown, pubesc., oblong; female panicle diffusely branched, 15–20×8–15cm, bracts to 3.5mm, oblong-lanceolate. Fr. obovoid, to 7×6mm, slightly oblique, purple, wrinkled, thinly fleshy. Iberia to Turkey, Morocco to Egypt. var. ***macrocarpa*** Zoh. Fr. 7–9×7–9mm, more fleshy than species type. var. ***oxycarpa*** Zoh. Fr. attenuate, obovoid, acute, mucronate, 8×6mm.

***P. texana*** Swingle. AMERICAN PISTACHIO; LENTISCO. Tree branching from base. Lvs 9–17, 5–10cm, imparipinnate, sessile, alternate, oblong, acute, mucronate, strongly oblique, membranous; leaflets 10–22×5–9mm, terminal leaflet smallest, midrib pubesc. Female panicle crowned, 4–7cm. Fr. dark brown, lenticular, 5–6mm broad, obliquely tipped, fleshy. S US, Mexico.

***P. vera*** L. PISTACHIO; GREEN ALMOND; FUSTUQ. Tree to 10m, deciduous. Lvs 10–20cm, coriaceous, imparipinnate; petiole to 10cm; leaflets 3 or 5, 5–12×3.7cm, glabrous or sparsely puberulent along midrib, broadly lanceolate to ovate, acuminate or acute, shining above, dull beneath. Male panicle compact, 5–8×2–3cm; female panicle looser and longer than male. Fr. long-pedicelled, oblong-linear to ovate, laterally compressed, variously coloured, often with red. W Asia. 'Kerman': vigorous, female, large easily opened nuts. 'Peters': recommended pollinator. 'Sfax': female, small nuts in large easily harvested clusters.

***P. formosana*** Matsum. See *P. chinensis*.
***P. narbonensis*** L. See *P. vera*.
***P. reticulata*** Willd. See *P. vera*.

**Pistia** L. WATER LETTUCE; SHELL FLOWER. Araceae. 1 species, an evergreen, floating aquatic, forming dense rosettes linked by fragile, scaly stolons. Roots fine, feathery, in spreading bunches from undersides of rosettes. Leaves to 20×7cm, broadly wedge-shaped, apex rounded, truncate or retuse, spreading to semi-erect, fluted above, prominently 7–15-ribbed below with aerenchyma toward base and a fine covering of water-repellent depressed hairs throughout, blue-green above, pearly beneath. Spathe 0.8–1.25cm, leaf-like, inconspicuous, part-hidden among leaf axils, downy, sessile, sheathing at base; spadix minute, largely fused to spathe; flowers unisexual, lacking perianth, males several, yellow in a short-stalked apical cluster, female solitary. Pantropical, now a widespread weed of rivers and lakes, first recorded on the Nile, possibly having originated from Lake Victoria. Z10.

CULTIVATION *P. stratoites* occurs in a wide range of aquatic habitats, in India from sea level to altitudes of 1000m/3250ft, often in natural association with *Pontederia cordata* or *Salvinia auriculata* in tropical America. Forming lustrous floating cups of foliage, which lie flat on the water's surface given room or which rise out of the water when in dense colonies. *Pistia* may also produce dwarf land forms if stranded in wet soil.

Grown as a marginal in pools in the tropical glasshouse or as a free floating aquarium specimen, where it provides useful cover for spawning fish. Grow in lime-free water, pH.6.5–7.0, with a minimum temperature of 10–15°C/50–60°F, but an optimal temperature of 19–22°C/66–72°F to keep evergreen and in growth. Provide full light but with protection from strong summer sun and maintain a humid aerial environment and fertile bottom medium rich in decaying organic matter. During pool cleaning, or where a rest period is necessary, grow on in a mix of moist loam and sand. Propagate by removal of plantlets in summer or by seed sown in spring at 28°C/82°F, cover with sand and keep almost submerged in bright light.

***P. stratoites*** L. As for the genus.

**Pisum** L. (Name used by Virgil.) PEA. Leguminosae (Papilionoideae). 5 species of annual herbs, often climbing by means of tendrils. Stems glabrous, terete. Stipules leafy, oblong-orbicular, often black-blotched; leaflets 1–3 pairs, oval, smaller than stipules. Flowers solitary or 2–3; calyx teeth large, leafy; wings adnate to keel. Fruit a flattened to cylindric, inflated, oblong-linear legume, obliquely acute, bivalved; seeds sub-globose. Mediterranean, W Asia.

CULTIVATION See PEAS.

***P. sativum*** L. GARDEN PEA. Glaucous annual to 2m; tendrils branched. Stipules to 10×6cm, obliquely ovate, dentate, rounded and semi-amplexicaul at base; leaflets to 7×4cm, 1–4 pairs, suborbicular to elliptic or oblong, entire or dentate. Peduncle 1–3-fld; fls to 3cm; cal. to 2cm, teeth subequal, ovate-lanceolate; standard white sometimes suffused lilac, broad, wings white, sometimes stained dark red-purple. Fr. to 15×3cm, oblong-linear or linear, 3–10-seeded; seeds 5mm+ diam. S Europe. var. ***arvense*** (L.) Poir. FIELD PEA; DUN PEA; GREY PEA; MUTTER PEA; PARTRIDGE PEA; PELUSKINS. Stipules spotted red. Fls bicoloured. Seeds to 8mm, frequently angled and blotched. var. ***macrocarpon*** Ser. EDIBLE-PODDED PEA; SUGAR PEA; SNOW PEA. Fr. to 18cm, soft, thick, fibrous inner lining absent, indehiscent. ssp. ***elatius*** (Bieb.) Asch. & Gräbn. Leaflets 2–4 pairs, ovate-elliptic, entire or subdentate. Peduncles 1–3-fld; fls to 3cm, bicoloured. Fr. to 7×1.2cm; seeds densely papillose.

***P. arvense*** L. See *P. sativum* var. *arvense*.
***P. elatius*** Bieb. See *P. sativum* ssp. *elatius*.
***P. graecum*** Quézel & Contandr. See *Lathyrus grandiflorus*.

**Pitcairnia** L'Hérit. (For Dr William Pitcairn (1711–91), London doctor.) Bromeliaceae. 260 species of terrestrial perennial herbs, occasionally lithophytic or epiphytic; most stemless, but a few species with long stems or even underground runners sheathed with old leaf bases. Leaves in a bundle or dense spiral along the stem, in two to many rows, sheath small, sometimes thickened and bulbous, blade linear to broadly lanceolate, toothed or entire, sometimes di- or trimorphic. Inflorescence simple or compound; flowers bisexual, showy, ephemeral, sessile to long-pedicellate; sepals free and rolled, unequally overlapping; petals free, long and narrow, zygomorphic, variable in colour. Floral bracts large and conspicuous to minute. Fruit a capsule, narrow, with two tail-like appendages, or broad and winged; a few species have naked seeds. C & S America, W Africa. Z9.

CULTIVATION See BROMELIADS.

***P. andreana*** Lind. To 20cm to flower. Lvs to 35cm, linear-lanceolate and petiolate, acute, densely white-scaly beneath, sparsely so above. Infl. laxly branched, slightly scaly; fls few, in racemes; floral bracts narrowly ovate; pedicel 10mm, slender; sep. lanceolate, acute; pet. zygomorphic, orange, yellow near apex, acute, naked. Colombia.

***P. ×darblayana*** André. *(P. corallina × P. paniculata.)* Large, vigorous. Lvs to 1.7m, petiolate, entire, base and apex acute. Infl. and panicle ascending, lax; fls many; pedicel 2cm; floral bracts oval, acute; sep. brick-red, acute, slightly overlapping; pet. red, narrowly lanceolate, forming a tube to 7cm. Garden origin.

***P. heterophylla*** (Lindl.) Beer. 10–20cm in flower. Lf bases suborbicular-ovate, dark brown, spinose, forming a bulb-like base; blades sometimes dimorphic: outer lvs absent or reduced to sharp-toothed, dark brown spines, inner lvs to 70cm, green, linear, attenuate and filiform, glabrous, abscising at base before flowers mature, pet. vestiges spiny; new lvs emerge after the fr. is mature. Infl. subspicate or a compound head, 3–12-fld; floral bracts ovate; pedicel 3mm, obconical; sep. 3cm, narrowly triangular, thin, attenuate, winged or keeled; pet. to 5.5cm, pink-red, linear, with a sac-like scale above the base. Mexico to Venezuela and Peru. var. ***exscapa*** Mez. Lvs homomorphic. Pet. red. Guatemala, Colombia.

***P. maidifolia*** (Morr.) Decne. To 1.3m in flower. Lvs dimorphic, in a loose rosette; outer lvs reduced to black sheaths; inner lvs with narrowly ovate, brown-scaly sheaths; petiole unarmed, to 20cm; blades lanceolate, acute, glabrous, 50–100cm. Infl. simple, one-sided, becoming loose, subcylindrical; floral bracts broadly ovate, acute, green or yellow, often tinged red, papery; pedicel 1cm; sep. glabrous, broadly elliptic, blunt, keelless; pet. 5–6cm, linear, unequal, white or white-green, often recurved. Late spring. Honduras to Colombia and Surinam.

***P. spicata*** (Lam.) Mez. To 1m in flower, often taller. Lvs dimorphic, in sterile offsets reduced to dark, serrate spines to 15cm, in fertile plants to 1.4m; sheaths toothed, narrowly triangular-ovate, brown-scaly; blades linear, white-scaly beneath. Infl. 15–28cm, densely racemose, on a white-scaly, straight scape with leaflike to triangular-ovate bracts; floral bracts narrowly lanceolate-triangular; pedicels 6–11mm, slender; sep. 1.6–2.3cm, lanceolate, apex rounded with a short mucro; pet. to 4.8cm, red, with an ovate basal scale. Martinique.

***P. xanthocalyx*** Mart. To 130cm in flower. Lvs entire or sparsely and minutely spinose; sheaths suborbicular, small, brown, veins prominent, covered with a scale membrane; blades linear to linear-lanceolate, apex filiform, glabrous above, covered by a white scale-membrane beneath. Infl. crowded, simple, glabrous, 30–60cm; floral bracts linear-lanceolate; pedicel 15–20mm, slender, nodding; sep. 15–20mm, subtriangular, orange, often with tufts of hairs and scales at the apex; pet. 45–50mm, primrose yellow, with apical appendages. C Mexico.

***P. cernua*** Kunth & Bouché. See *P. heterophylla* var. *exscapa*.
***P. exscapa*** Hook. See *P. heterophylla* var. *exscapa*.
***P. flavescens*** Bak. See *P. xanthocalyx*.
***P. funckiana*** A. Dietr. See *P. maidifolia*.
***P. lepidota*** Reg. See *P. andreana*.
***P. macrocalyx*** Hook. See *P. maidifolia*.
***P. maydifolia*** Decne. See *P. maidifolia*.
***P. mazaifolia*** hort. ex Beer. See *P. maidifolia*.
***P. mirabilis*** Mez. See *Puya mirabilis*.
***P. morrenii*** Lem. See *P. heterophylla*.
***P. sulphurea*** K. Koch. See *P. xanthocalyx*.
***P. zeifolia*** K. Koch. See *P. maidifolia*.

**Pithecellobium** Mart. (From Gk *pithekos*, ape or monkey, and *ellobion*, earring, a translation of the Brazilian name, *brincos de sahoy*.) Leguminosae (Mimosoideae). Some 20 species of shrubs or trees, armed with stipular thorns. Leaves bipinnate; petiole usually glandular; leaflets opposite. Flowers in axillary heads or spikes arranged in terminal or axillary panicles; calyx short-lobed; corolla 5-lobed; stamens 10 to numerous, filaments showy, basally united into a tube; ovary sessile or stipitate, glabrous or puberulous. Fruit a straight to coiled, dehiscent or indehiscent legume, valves chartaceous. Subtropical & tropical America, introduced to Asia. Z10.

CULTIVATION Grown for their pleasing habit, neat foliage and nectar-rich flowers, often scented and usually globose, resembling those of the related *Mimosa*. *P. dulce* is an excellent shade tree for warm temperate regions and, if pruned hard, also an attractive if rather fierce hedge. Cultivate as for *Inga*.

***P. dulce*** (Roxb.) Benth. MANILA TAMARIND; HUAMUCHIL; OPIUMA; MADRAS THORN. Shrub or tree, usually armed with nodal spines to 1.2cm. Pinnae 2, each with 2 leaflets, initially pilose, later glabrous; leaflets to 5×2cm, elliptic. Fls green to light yellow, in terminal racemes; peduncles solitary to clustered, villous; cal. and cor. minutely pubesc. to villous; cal. 1mm; cor. 2.5mm. Fr. to 10×1.5cm, oblong-falcate to circinate, torulose, dehiscent, valves red and coriaceous; seeds black, aril white. Spring. Mexico, C America, introduced Philippines.

***P. flexicaule*** (Benth.) Coult. TEXAS EBONY. Tree to 20m, spreading, large-crowned, armed with black, stipular spines to 0.5cm; branches stout, flexuous. Leaflets 1cm, 3–6 pairs, elliptic-oblong, thick, subglabrous, somewhat shiny. Fls in yellow spikes; cal. sticky-puberulent; stamen sheath often exserted from cor. Fr. to 15×3cm, oblong, straight to falcate, indehiscent; seeds red. Summer. SE US (Texas), N Mexico.

***P. junghuhnianum*** Benth. Tree. Lvs 20cm+, pinnae 2–4, terminal pinna with 3–4 pairs leaflets, leaflets variable, to 7.5cm, oblong or rhomboidal. Fls orange-yellow, heads stalked, 2–3 together in axils or shortly racemose. Fr. flat, contorted. W Indies.

***P. keyense*** Britt. ex Britt. & Rose. BLACK BEAD. Spreading shrub or small tree, unarmed. Pinnae 2, each with 2 leaflets; petioles to 1.5cm; leaflets to 5×4cm, obovate to narrow-elliptic, coriaceous, reticulate-veined. Fls to 2.5cm diam., white to yellow often flushed pink, in terminal or intercalary racemes; peduncles to 3.5cm; cal. and cor. adpressed-puberulent to glabrous; cal. 1.5mm; cor. to 5mm. Fr. to 20×1cm, narrow-oblong, curved to circinnate, turgid, dehiscent valves coriaceous and dark brown; seeds black, shiny. Winter–spring. Florida, W Indies, NS America.

***P. unguis-cati*** (L.) Benth. CAT'S-CLAW; BLACKBEARD; BLACK JESSIE. Shrub or small tree, unarmed or armed with spines to 5mm. Pinnae 2, each with 2 leaflets; petioles to 2.5cm; leaflets 6×3.5cm, obovate to elliptic. Fls white to yellow-green, in axillary racemes; peduncles to 2.5cm; cal. and cor. subglabrous to finely strigose-puberulent; cal. 1.5mm; cor. to 6mm. Fr. to 15×1cm, oblong to linear, initially curved, later circinnate, turgid, dehiscent, irregularly constricted, valves coriaceous and red to dark brown; seeds black. W Indies, S Florida.

***P. guadalupense*** (Pers.) Chapm. See *P. keyense*.
***P. saman*** (Jacq.) Benth. See *Albizia saman*.
For further synonymy see *Ebenopsis, Inga* and *Siderocarpus*.

**Pithecoctenium** Mart. ex Meissn. (From Gk *pithekos*, ape or monkey, and *ktenion*, comb, referring to the spiny fruits.) Bignoniaceae. 12 species of lianes. Branches hexagonal; pseudostipules falling early. Leaves 2–3-foliolate, terminal leaflet often replaced by trifid tendril, tendril often further divided to 15-fid, some tendril tips form swollen rings. Inflorescence a terminal raceme or panicle; calyx cupular, truncate, thick, 5-denticulate, lepidote, puberulent; corolla white, tubular-campanulate, thick and fleshy, puberulent outside; anthers glabrous; ovary ellipsoid or cylindrical, densely pubescent; ovules multi-seriate; disc annular, pulvinate. Fruit a capsule, flattened-elliptic, woody, valves parallel, densely spiny; seeds winged, surrounded by hyaline membranous wing. Americas, Mexico, to Brazil and Argentina. Z10.

CULTIVATION Slender climbers, attractive in foliage and flower and interesting in fruit; *P. cyanchoides* has felted young growth and large panicles of showy white flowers which produce small, flat seed pods covered in yellow bristles. Cultivate as for *Anemopaegma*.

***P. carolinae*** Nichols. To *c*3m. Lvs jugate; leaflets apex acuminate, base cordate, lightly pubesc. Fls white, tube tinted yellow, fragrant; cal. campanulate, truncate, faintly 5-dentate; cor. tube arcuate, tomentose, lobes slightly recurved, laciniate, crispate, spreading. Brazil.

***P. crucigerum*** (L.) A. Gentry. Stem 10cm diam. Leaflets 3.3–18×2–14.7cm, ovate to suborbicular, apex acuminate, base cordate, membranous, lepidote, venation pubesc.; petioles 2.9–7.2cm; petiolules 1.6cm, lepidote and pubesc. Infl. to 15-fld; rachis pubesc.; cal. 8–12×9–11mm, leathery, lepidote and pubesc.; cor. 3.6–6.1×1–1.8cm, often bent 90° in middle of tube, densely pubesc., yellow in throat, otherwise white. Fr. 12–31×5.2–7.5cm, oblong to elliptic, tuberculate. Mexico to N Argentina and Uruguay.

***P. cynanchoides*** DC. Leaflets 2.5–4×2–4cm, ovate, reniform or triangular, apex acuminate, margin ciliate. Cal. 7–8mm, 5-denticulate, pubesc.; cor. 3–6cm, white streaked yellow in throat. Fr. oblong, to 8mm. Brazil to Argentina.

***P. buccinatorium*** DC. See *Distictis buccinatoria*.
***P. cinereum*** DC. See *Distictis laxiflora*.
***P. clematideum*** Griseb. See *P. cynanchoides*.
***P. echinatum*** (Jacq.) Baill. See *Pithecoctenium crucigerum*.
***P. laxiflorum*** DC. See *Distictis laxiflora*.
For further synonymy see *Bignonia*.

**Pittocaulon** H. Robinson & Brettell. (From Gk *pitta*, pitch, and *kaulos*, stem.) Compositae. 5 species of shrubs or small trees. Leaves alternate, palmate, petiolate, falling before anthesis. Capitula radiate, clustered at branch apices in corymbs or umbels;

florets yellow. Fruit a glabrous cypsela; pappus of bristles. Mexico, C America. Z10.

CULTIVATION Occurring in desert and semi-desert habitats, *P. praecox* is suitable for outdoor cultivation only in dry, frost-free zones but is sometimes included in collections of cacti and succulents in cooler climates. Grow in full sun in a gritty freely draining medium with additional limestone chippings, maintain low humidity, good ventilation and water moderately when in growth, keeping dry but not arid in winter. Provide a minimum temperature of 7–10°C/45–50°F. Propagate by seed, division or offsets.

***P. praecox*** (Cav.) H. Robinson & Brettell. Shrub or small tree, to 5m. Lvs clustered at branch apices, to 15cm, 5–7-lobed, lobes acuminate, glabrous, petiole to 12cm. Phyllaries in 1 series, apex pubesc.; ray florets few, to 105cm. Fr. 4–6mm; pappus 5–8mm. Mexico.

For synonymy see *Cineraria* and *Senecio*.

**PITTOSPORACEAE** R. Br. PITTOSPORUM FAMILY. 9 genera and 240 species of trees, shrubs, lianes, sometimes spiny. Leaves evergreen, simple, leathery, alternate, usually entire; stipules absent. Flowers bisexual, regular, solitary or in corymbs or thyrses, each with 2 bracteoles; calyx 5 free sepals, sometimes basally connate; corolla 5 petals, usually basally connate forming a distinct tube, lobes imbricate; stamens 5, alternate with corolla, sometimes weakly connate basally; ovary superior, of 2 (3–5) fused carpels, usually 1-loculed with simple style; ovules several-numerous on parietal or axile placentas. Fruit a capsule or berry; seeds often in viscid pulp and with 2–5 cotyledons at base of copious oily proteinaceous endosperm. Tropical and warm Old World, especially Australia to Malesia. *Billardiera, Bursaria, Hymenosporum, Marianthus, Pittosporum, Sollya*.

**Pittosporum** Banks ex Gaertn. (From Gk *pitta*, pitch, and *sporos*, seed, referring to the sticky, resinous coating found on the seeds.) Pittosporaceae. About 200 species of evergreen trees and shrubs, to 10m, rarely to 30m. Leaves alternate to somewhat whorled, entire or rarely with sinuate teeth or lobes. Inflorescence a corymb, umbel or cluster, axillary or terminal, 1- to several-flowered; flowers often sweetly scented, pink to very dark red or yellow, white or green-hued; sepals 5, free or fused at the base; petals 5, cup-shaped at base or reflexed; stamens 5; ovary 2–4-locular. Fruit a dry, woody capsule, 2–3(–4)-valved, usually globose or ovate, seeds with a sticky resinous coating, many, not winged. Australasia and S Africa to S & E Asia and Hawaii. Z9.

CULTIVATION Grown for their beautiful, glossy foliage and often honey-scented flowers, *Pittosporum* spp. are suited to a variety of situations in cultivation, from border and tub in the cool glasshouse or conservatory, as shrub border specimens in mild, coastal climates or for warm, sunny walls in regions at the limits of hardiness. *P. tenuifolium, P. crassifolium* and *P. ralphii* can provide attractive, wind-resistant hedging in coastal gardens, either as informal screens or clipped in more formal situations. Some spp. such as *P. tenuifolium*, whose leaves have neatly waved margins, are much valued by flower arrangers; its cvs range from the variegated cultivars such as 'Garnetii' with cream-edged leaves spotted pink, to dark-leaved cultivars such as 'Purpureum', the bronzed mature leaves contrasting well with the pale green of the young growth, and dwarf types, such as 'Tom Thumb', low, compact and rich mahogany red. *P. tenuifolium* and *P. tobira* are amongst the hardiest species, tolerating temperatures as low as −10°C/14°F, more with wall shelter; *P. ralphii, P. eugenioides* and *P. dallii* are hardy to about −5°C/23°F. The variegated cvs are usually less hardy than the species.

Grow in well-drained soils, with *P. ralphii, P. crassifolium* and variegated cvs in full sun; other species will tolerate light part day shade, but wood will ripen better in an open sunny position. All need shelter from cold, drying winds and will benefit from the protection of a deep dry mulch of bracken litter at the root. Under glass, water moderately, maintain good ventilation and provide a winter minimum temperature at about 5–7°C/40–45°F. Most will benefit from spending the summer out of doors once danger of frost is passed. They regenerate freely from old wood and if necessary can be cut quite hard back in spring to remove frost-damaged growth.

Propagate by seed sown in autumn or spring, progeny may not come true to type. Increase cvs by 7.5cm/3in. long semi-ripe basal cuttings in summer and root in a closed case with bottom heat at 16°18°C/60–65°F or by basal ripewood cuttings in late autumn in the cold frame. *P. dallii* also by budding.

***P. bicolor*** Hook. f. Shrub or small tree, 5–10m, young twigs densely tomentose, pale brown, bark pale grey, smooth. Lvs 3–6×0.4–0.8cm, linear, entire, leathery, dark green and glabrous above, white-tomentose beneath at first, later brown, margins somewhat inrolled. Infl. 1- to several-fld, axillary; fls *c*1cm diam., yellow with dark red-brown markings, fragrant; sep. small; anth. yellow. Fr. 6–8mm diam., subglobose, 2-valved; seeds red-yellow. Spring. SE Australia, (Tasmania).

***P. cornifolium*** A. Cunn. Shrub to 2m, young twigs slender, glabrous, rarely downy when young. Lvs 3.5–8×0.5–3cm, subsessile, in clusters at twig apices, narrowly obovate or oval-lanceolate, apex acute, entire, glabrous, leathery. Infl. 2–5-fld, terminal; fls unisexual, *c*8mm diam., dark red, musk-scented, males on 1.2–1.8cm long, slender, pubesc. peduncles, females on shorter, thicker ones; pet. and sep. subulate, sep. small; anth. yellow. Fr. 1–1.2cm diam., ovoid, 2–3-valved, vermilion inside. Early spring. New Zealand (North Is.).

***P. crassifolium*** Banks & Sol. ex A. Cunn. CARO; KARO; EVERGREEN PITTOSPORUM. Shrub or small tree to 5(–10)m, densely branching, with a narrow, almost columnar crown, bark dark grey, smooth, young twigs tomentose. Lvs 5–7(–10)×2–2.5cm, alternate, oblong to elliptic or obovate, extremely leathery, dark green and glabrous above, white- or buff-tomentose beneath when young, pale brown at maturity, margins slightly inrolled and thickened. Infl. a terminal cluster, with 1–5 female or 5–10 male fls; pet. ligulate, recurved, dark crimson to purple. Fr. 2–3cm, globose to elliptic, usually 3-valved; seeds black. New Zealand (North Is.). 'Compactum': habit dwarf, densely branched; lvs in tight whorls, grey-green; fls small, maroon, in clusters. 'Variegatum': to 2.5m; lvs variegated with white.

***P. dallii*** Cheesem. Small tree, 4–6m, with a rounded crown, young twigs red-hued, bark pale grey. Lvs 5–11×*c*2.5cm, on 6–18mm long, red-hued petioles, in clusters at twig apices, base and apex acuminate, dark green above, sharply and coarsely toothed. Infl. a dense, terminal cluster, 2.5–5cm diam.; fls 12mm diam., white, fragrant, on pubesc. peduncles; sep. subulate; pet. narrowly obovate, anth. bright yellow. Fr. *c*1.2cm, ovoid, with a short, spine-like apex. Summer. New Zealand (South Is.).

***P. divaricatum*** Ckn. Shrub to 1(–4)m, densely branched, with stiff, much divided and tangled young twigs, pubesc. when young. Lvs dimorphic, 1.2–2×*c*3mm, linear to obovate and pinnatisect or dentate when young, 6–12mm and linear-obovate to ovate at maturity, tough and leathery, deeply toothed, lobed or entire. Fls terminal, solitary, 4mm; pet. spathulate, very dark maroon. Fr. *c*6mm diam., subglobose. Late spring. New Zealand.

***P. eriocarpum*** Royle. Small tree to 3–4m, young twigs, lvs and infl. covered in pale brown tomentum. Lvs to 15cm, oblanceolate-oblong, obovate or broadly obovate-oblong, leathery. Infl. a terminal panicle, 1- to few-fld; fls to 9mm, yellow, fragrant. Fr. to 6mm diam., globose, laterally compressed, 2-valved, pubesc. Late spring. New Zealand.

***P. erioloma*** C. Moore & F. Muell. Shrub to 5m. Lvs to 5cm, in whorls, obovate to oblanceolate, leathery, glabrous, margins revolute. Infl. terminal, 2–7-fld, fls cream-white with red markings. Fr. to 2cm diam., 3-valved, glabrous. Solomon Is.

***P. eugenioides*** A. Cunn. TARATA; LEMONWOOD. Tree to at least 10m, densely branched, bark pale grey, twigs dark, glabrous. Lvs 5–10×1–3cm, fragrant when crushed, narrowly ovate to oblong, base and apex acuminate, thin, glossy pale green, glabrous, margins recurved, not wavy. Infl. terminal, a cluster of corymbs, dense, many-fld, on a short peduncle; fls 1.5mm diam., yellow-green, honey-scented, on hairy peduncles; sep. small, pet. *c*3mm, ligulate. Fr. 6mm, ovoid, 2–3-valved. Summer. New Zealand. 'Platinum': habit neat, compact, pyramidal; stems brown-purple; lvs light green margined silver. 'Variegatum': lf margins cream shaded yellow. 'Zita Robinson': habit erect; lf margins wavy.

***P. floribundum*** Wight & Arn. Small tree, bark pale grey. Lvs to 20cm, lanceolate, glabrous, margins wavy. Infl. a many-fld terminal panicle; fls to 6mm, yellow-green. Fr. to 6mm diam., globose, 2-valved, with few seeds. N India, Nepal.

***P. glabratum*** Lindl. Shrub, 1–1.5m, twigs glabrous. Lvs 5–12×2–3.5cm, on petioles to 1cm, in clusters at twig apices, narrowly ovate, apex long-acuminate, base cuneate, glossy-green above, paler beneath, margins entire, membranaceous, uneven. Infl. a 6–10-fld terminal or axillary cluster; fls 8–12mm, fragrant, on peduncles to 2cm; pet. dull pale yellow, fused into a tube at base, cor. lobes 5, recurved, oblong. Fr. to 2.5cm, 3-valved, glabrous, woody. Late spring. S China.

***P. hawaiiense*** Hillebrand. Small tree to 6m, bark smooth, white. Lvs to 20cm, obovate-oblong, glabrous, chartaceous, veins deeply impressed above. Infl. an axillary, few-fld cluster; fls cream-white Fr. to 2.5cm diam., globose, woody, rugose. Hawaii.

***P. heterophyllum*** Franch. Shrub, 1–1.5(–3)m, densely branched and leafy, twigs glabrous. Lvs to 3.8×1–2.5cm, ovate or obovate to lanceolate, apex obtuse, base cuneate. Infl. terminal or axillary, to 7-fld; fls often clustered into panicles, pale yellow, fragrant, on slender, 1cm long peduncles. Fr. to 9mm diam., globose, 2-valved. Late spring–early summer. W China.

***P. hosmeri*** Rock. Tree to 10m. Lvs to 60cm, oblong, more or less leathery, brown-hairy beneath, margins revolute. Infl. axillary, to 10-fld, racemose; fls to 12mm, cream-white. Fr. to *c*5cm diam., globose, 2–4-valved, orange at maturity. Hawaii.

***P. napaulense*** (DC.) Rehd. & Wils. Shrub or small tree to 6m, occasionally scandent. Lvs 7–20×2.5–5.5cm, on *c*2cm petioles in clusters at twig apices, elliptic, coriaceous, glabrous, apex acuminate, base attenuate. Infl. 2–5cm diam., a cluster of few to many panicles, white-hairy; fls sweetly scented; sep. *c*2mm, ovate, fused at base; pet. *c*6×2mm, yellow, ovate-oblong, free. Fr. *c*5×7mm, ovoid, compressed at base and apex, 2-valved, striate inside; seeds 4–6, red. Late spring–summer. India (Sikkim), Bhutan, Nepal.

***P. patulum*** Hook. f. Shrub or small tree, 2–5m, crown conical, sparsely branched, twigs and peduncles pubesc., otherwise glabrous. Lvs dimorphic, when young 3–5×0.5cm, linear, margins lobed, at maturity 4–5×1–1.5cm, on short, thick petioles, lanceolate, entire or shallowly toothed, leathery. Infl. a terminal cluster, 4–8-fld; fls to 1cm, campanulate, dark crimson, strongly fragrant, on slender peduncles to 1.2cm. Fr. 8mm diam., globose, woody. Late spring. New Zealand (South Is.).

***P. phillyreoides*** DC. NARROW-LEAVED PITTOSPORUM; WEEPING PITTOSPORUM; DESERT WILLOW. Shrub or small tree to 10m, young twigs pubesc., otherwise glabrous, twigs pendulous. Lvs 2–10×0.2–1cm, linear-lanceolate or linear-oblong, flat, apex acute, with a small, runciform mucro. Infl. axillary, a cymose cluster, rarely 1-fld; sep. 2mm, ovate, spreading; pet. 7–15mm, cream-yellow, narrowly oblong, apices recurved. Fr. 1–2cm, ovate or ovate-cordate, 2(–3)-valved, dark yellow or orange, apex acute to obtuse; seeds several, red. Australia.

***P. ralphii*** T. Kirk Shrub, 2.5–5m, young twigs tomentose. Lvs to 15cm, on slender, 1–2cm petioles, oblong to oblong-obovate, leathery, white- or pale brown-tomentose beneath, vein pairs 9–12, margins flat or revolute, not thickened. Infl. terminal, 3-10-fld, an umbellate cluster; fls small, dark crimson; anth. yellow. Fr. *c*2cm, globose to elliptic, 3-valved. New Zealand (North Is.).

***P. revolutum*** Ait. Shrub, 2–3m, young twigs brown-tomentose. Lvs 3–11×0.8–2cm, narrowly elliptic to lanceolate, pale brown-tomentose beneath, especially on midrib, dark green above, acuminate at base and apex. Infl. terminal, a 1- to few-fld umbel; fls 8–12mm; peduncle woolly; sep. subulate; pet. yellow, recurved. Spring. Australia (NSW).

***P. rhombifolium*** A. Cunn. ex Hook. QUEENSLAND PITTOSPORUM; DIAMOND LEAF PITTOSPORUM. Tree to at least 30m, glabrous. Lvs 7.5–10cm, long-petiolate, rhomboid to rhombic-ovate or narrowly oval, glossy green, leathery, apical half with coarse and irregular teeth. Infl. compound, 4–7.5cm diam., axillary or terminal, many-fld; fls 8–12mm diam., white. Fr. to 9mm, subglobose, 3-valved. Late autumn. E Australia.

***P. tenuifolium*** Banks & Sol. ex Gaertn. TAWHIWHI; KOHUHU. Tree to 10m, trunk slender, densely branching, with very dark grey or almost black young shoots. Lvs 2.5–10cm, elliptic, obovate or oblong, glabrous, margins flat, revolute or undulate, pale green but glossy. Infl. axillary, 1- to few-fld; fls with a honey-like fragrance; pet. 6–12mm. Fr. 1–1.2cm diam., (2–)3(–4)-valved, subglobose, wrinkled at maturity, walls thin. New Zealand. Over 25 cvs, 90cm–3m, occasionally dwarf; young growth colour variable, white through grey to black tinged red; lvs variegated grey to shades of purple to dark green and black. 'Abbotsbury Gold': lvs 2–3cm, rounded-obovate, yellow with an irregular, green wavy margin. 'Deborah': lvs small, variegated white and cream. 'Elia Keightley' ('Sunburst'): 3–5m, habit slender; lvs 2–4cm, rounded-ovate, very slightly wavy. 'Garnetii' (*P. tenuifolium* × *P. ralphii*): to 4m, twigs grey; lvs 4–6cm, ovate-elliptic, grey-green, margin white with pink spots, slightly wavy. 'Golden King': habit upright, to 3m; lvs 3–5cm, ovate to broadly ovate, pale golden-green, margins wavy. 'Irene Paterson': to 1.2m; lvs 2.5–4cm, ovate-elliptic, white with green spots, margin very wavy. 'James Stirling': habit open; twigs black tinged red; lvs 1–2cm, silver-green, ovate-rounded, margins wavy. 'Limelight': lvs 2–5.5cm, elliptic, lime-green with dark green, very slightly wavy margins. 'Margaret Turnbull': to 1.8m; lvs dark green, heavily variegated with gold centre. 'Nigricans': twigs black; lvs 2.6–6cm, oblong-elliptic, margins wavy. 'Purpureum': habit open; lvs green at first, when mature 3–6cm, oblong-elliptic, dark purple-bronze, margins very wavy. 'Saundersii' (*P. tenuifolium* × *P. ralphii*): twigs dark grey; lvs 4–7cm, obovate to ovate, grey-green, margins white with pink spots, slightly wavy. 'Silver Magic': lvs small, silver turning pink. 'Sterling Gold': habit erect; lvs small, mottled gold. 'Tom Thumb': 1–2m, habit compact; lvs 3–6cm, oblong-elliptic, dark purple-bronze, with very wavy margins. 'Tresederi' ('Silver Queen'): 1–4m, habit compact; lvs 3–5cm, elliptic, silver-grey. 'Variegatum': 3–4, twigs grey; lvs 3–5cm, elliptic, green with a flat, cream margin; possibly of hybrid origin. 'Warnham Gold': lvs 3–5cm, elliptic-ovate, golden-green at first, golden-yellow when mature; especially colourful in autumn. ssp. ***tenuifolium.*** Lvs 2.5–7cm, oblong to elliptic-ovate. Fls dark purple-black. ssp. ***colensoi*** (Hook. f.) T. Kirk. Young twigs finely hairy. Lvs 5–10cm, oblong-lanceolate to ovate-oblong, thick, dark green. Fl. usually solitary, purple. New Zealand.

***P. tobira*** Ait. TOBIRA; MOCK ORANGE; JAPANESE PITTOSPORUM. Bushy, erect shrub or small tree to 5m. Lvs 3–10×2–4cm, short-petiolate, obovate, apex rounded, base cuneate, tough and leathery, dark green and glossy above, midrib pale, margins revolute. Infl. a terminal, umbellate cluster, 5–7.5cm diam., usually several-fld; fls orange-blossom-scented, 2.5cm diam.; pet. broadly oblong, cream-white to lemon-yellow, darker with age. Fr. to 1.2cm diam., globose to pyriform, 3-valved, tomentose. Spring–early summer. China, Japan. 'Compacta': habit compact, dense, spreading; lvs glossy, thick, margins curled under. 'Variegata': lvs variegated with ragged white margin; fls small, fragrant. 'Wheeler's Dwarf': habit miniature, compact, dense; lvs small, glossy, dark green, mound-forming.

***P. turneri*** Petrie. Tree, 4–9m, conical, twigs glabrous, erect. Lvs 2.5–3×1–1.2cm, obovate or linear-oblong, thin but leathery, sparsely hairy and entire, toothed or lobed when young, glabrous and entire or with few teeth at maturity. Infl. terminal, usually on lateral shoots, a 6–12-fld cluster; fls pink to purple; pet. ligulate, reflexed. Late spring–early summer. New Zealand.

***P. umbellatum*** Banks & Sol. ex Gaertn. Tree to 10m. Lvs to 10cm, oblong-lanceolate to elliptic, leathery, margins revolute. Infl. a terminal, 4–15-fld umbel; fls 1.5cm, orange-red, fragrant. Fr. to 1.25cm diam., 2-valved, 4-lobed. New Zealand.

***P. undulatum*** Vent. VICTORIAN BOX; ORANGE BERRY PITTOSPORUM; CHEESEWOOD. Tree, 9–14m. Lvs 7–15×2.5–5cm, acuminate at base and apex, laurel-like, membranaceous, shiny dark green above, pale beneath, margins wavy, entire. Infl. 5–7.5cm diam., a terminal cluster of 1 to several umbels, 4–15-fld; fls 1.2–1.8cm diam., fragrant, cream-white. Fr. to 1.2cm diam., 2-valved, subglobose, yellow, brown or orange. Wood used in manufacture of golf clubs. Late spring–summer. E Australia. 'Variegatum': lvs with white margins.

***P. viridiflorum*** Sims CAPE PITTOSPORUM. Shrub to 3(–6)m, twigs hairy. Lvs 2.5–10×1.2–3cm, obovate, apex rounded, glossy dark green above, leathery, margins flat or revolute. Infl. 2.5–5cm diam., a many-fld terminal panicle; fls to 6mm, jasmine-scented; pet. yellow-green, acute, reflexed. Fr. to 6mm diam., subglobose, 2-valved. Late spring. S Africa.

***P. flavum*** Hook. See *Hymenosporum flavum*.
***P. mayi*** hort. See *P. tenuifolium*.
***P. nigricans*** hort. See *P. tenuifolium*.

**Pityopsis** Nutt. (From Gk *pitys*, pine, and *opsis*, appearance.) Compositae. 8 species of erect perennial herbs, usually stoloniferous and silky hairy. Leaves alternate, linear to lanceolate or ovate, often grass-like, entire, veins parallel. Capitula radiate, few to many in a corymb; involucre turbinate; phyllaries in several series, lanceolate, glabrous to glandular or silky; ray florets, female, yellow; disc florets numerous, hermaphrodite, yellow, lobes erect or spreading. Fruit a linear or fusiform cypsela; pappus a double row of fine bristles. E US to C America.

CULTIVATION Suited to the wild garden, native plant collections and other naturalistic plantings; grow in sun in well-drained acid soils. Propagate by seed or division.

***P. falcata*** (Pursh) Nutt. To 30cm. Stems erect, occasionally branching above, silky white-pubesc. Lvs to 9×0.5cm, broadly linear, acuminate, falcate, lower sparsely pubesc. to glabrous, sessile, upper lvs smaller, glabrous. Capitula 1–5 on white-hairy peduncles to 4cm; involucre 5–8mm; phyllaries glabrous to silky-villous; ray florets to 8mm. New Jersey to S New York State. Z6.

***P. graminifolia*** (Michx.) Nutt. SILK GRASS. To 50cm. Stems erect, branched above, silky white-hairy. Lvs to 25×2cm, linear, grasslike, silky hairy, stem lvs smaller, upper lvs often bract-like. Capitula to 15mm diam., solitary to numerous on peduncles to 10cm; involucre 7–12mm; outer phyllaries later reflexed, hairy, inner glandular; ray florets to 14mm. SE US (Florida, Louisiana). var. ***latifolia*** (Fern.) Semple & Bowers. Variable. Lvs commonly grasslike, often wider than species type. Phyllaries silky-hairy. Late summer–autumn. SE US to Honduras. var. ***tenuifolia*** (Torr.) Semple & Bowers. Upper lvs much reduced. Involucre 5–8mm; ray florets to 7mm. Late summer. Texas to N Carolina. Z8.

***P. pinifolia*** (Elliott) Nutt. To 50cm, nearly glabrous. Stems often clumped, leafy. Basal lvs in a rosette, to 40×4mm, linear, acute, silky-villous, sessile; stem lvs crowded, to 8cm, light green, sparsely pubesc. to glabrous. Capitula to 2cm diam., few to several; peduncles to 4cm; involucre 5–8mm; phyllaries scarious; ray florets to 7mm. Autumn. Georgia, N & S Carolina. Z8.

***P. microcephala*** (Small) Small. See *P. graminifolia* var. *tenuifolia*.
***P. nervosa*** (Willd.) Dress. See *P. graminifolia* var. *latifolia*.
For further synonymy see *Chrysopsis* and *Heterotheca*.

**Pityrogramma** Link. (From Gk *pityron*, bran, and *gramma*, line, referring to scaly linear sori.) Pteridaceae (Adiantaceae). About 40 species of fairly small terrestrial ferns. Rhizome short-creeping, clad to stiff, dark scales; stipes rather wiry, dark, glossy. Fronds tufted, erect or drooping, linear to deltoid-pentagonal, pinnate to tripinnate, sometimes glandular above, conspicuously silvery to golden farinaceous beneath; veins free. Sori along veins, often confluent; indusium wanting; spores globose-tetrahedral, dark, perine irregularly reticulate-ribbed. Americas and Africa. Z10.

CULTIVATION As for *Adiantum*. A genus especially beautiful for the gold or silver dusting of farina on the underside of the pinnae and on the stipes. *P. calomelanos*, the silver fern, is a frequently grown species, but *P. c.* var. *aureoflava*, the golden fern, is more commonly encountered still, being of greater vigour than the type. Useful in containers, they are best elevated to reveal the undersides of the fronds, and can be cultivated in the home in a position of good light but out of direct sunlight. Propagation can be by division of older crowns, which rarely branch, or from spores which germinate readily and develop rapidly, almost to the point of becoming a weed in the glasshouse. Underpotting suits them best, and watering should be undertaken with care during the winter months.

***P. argentea*** (Willd.) Domin. Rhiz. erect to procumbent, short, 2mm diam.; scales linear attenuate, brown. Stipe to 30cm, grooved above, castaneous, glabrous. Fronds tufted, arching, fragile, herbaceous, lamina to 30×20cm, deltoid-ovate, 3–4-pinnatifid, white, pink or yellow-farinaceous beneath; pinnae narrowly deltoid-ovate, petiolate, pinnules to 5×2.5cm, well spaced, alternate, deltoid, secondary pinnules cuneate to broadly oblong-ovate, deeply pinnatifid, lobes entire, obtuse or emarginate at apex, 1mm broad; secondary rachis often winged. Southern Tropical Africa.

***P. calomelanos*** (L.) Link. SILVER FERN. Rhiz. short, erect, scales narrow, brown; stipes 20–55cm, dark purple, scaly towards base, farinaceous when young. Fronds to 60×30cm, ovate, bipinnate or tripinnatifid at base, papyraceous, silver-white farinaceous beneath; pinnae to 17×5cm, deeply lobed, acuminate at apex, pinnules narrowly deltoid, oblique, lobed, largest to 3cm; rachis grooved above. Tropical America, now pantropical. var. ***aureoflava*** (Hook.) Weatherby ex L.H. Bail. GOLDEN FERN. More vigorous, farina golden beneath.

***P. chrysophylla*** (Sw.) Link. GOLD FERN. Stipes to 2×length of lamina, dark brown, tinged ferruginous or black. Fronds 20–60cm, ovate to ovate-triangular, bipinnate or more compound, bright golden-yellow or rarely white-farinaceous beneath; rachis dark. W Indies (Lesser Antilles & Puerto Rico) and S America, widely naturalized as a subtropical weed.

***P. ×hybrida*** Domin. (*P. chrysophylla* × *P. calomelanos.*) A vigorously growing, luxuriant fern. Fronds larger than *P. chrysophylla* margins doubly dentate, scarcely revolute under.

***P. pallida*** (Weatherby) Alt. & Grant. Rhiz. multicipital, 2mm diam.; scales narrowly lanceolate, brown with broad black central stripe. Stipes 5–25cm, black, sometimes tinged purple, glabrous or sparsely white-farinaceous. Fronds 2–9×2–9cm, pentagonal to broadly ovate-lanceolate, pinnate-pinnatifid, bipinnate-pinnatifid toward base on large plants, pinnae entire to pinnate-pinnatifid, white glandular above, more or less densely white farinaceous beneath. California.

***P. pearcei*** (Moore) Domin. Vigorously growing. Stipes 15–30cm. Fronds to 30×45×30cm, ovate-lanceolate to elongate-deltoid, to 4-pinnate, copiously dissected, glabrous, white or bright yellow farinaceous beneath; pinnae equilateral or almost so, lowest 10–15cm, pinnules imbricate; ultimate seg. slender. C & S America (Panama, Costa Rica, Colombia).

***P. pulchella*** (Moore) Domin. Growth erect. Stipes 15–22cm, farinaceous. Fronds 15–30×10–15cm, tufted, tripinnatifid, dark green above, pure white-farinaceous beneath; pinnae inequilateral, lowest largest, pinnules imbricate; seg. flabellate-cuneate, strongly dentate. Venezuela.

***P. schizophylla*** (Bak. ex Jenman) Maxon. Rhiz. decumbent, 3–5mm, diam.; scales few, mostly toward apex, deltate. Stipes 4–7cm, dark brown tinged purple, shining, sparsely white farinaceous near base. Fronds 30–60cm, closely tufted, erect, scarcely or not at all farinaceous, with proliferous buds in axil; lamina linear lanceolate to narrowly oblong, 4-pinnate, generally bifurcate below apex, bright green, membranous; pinnae 3–6×1.5–2.5cm, numerous, alternate, oblique or spreading, ovate-lanceolate, delicately dissected, ultimate pinnules cuneate-bifurcate, to 0.5mm, across; rachis grooved above, dark brown tinged purple. W Indies (Jamaica and Hispaniola).

***P. sulphurea*** (Sw.) Maxon. JAMAICA GOLD FERN. Rhiz. decumbent to ascending, short-lived, 10×5mm; scales few, towards apex, linear-lanceolate, brown; stipes 2–10cm, glossy brown tinged purple. Fronds 15–40cm, laxly ascending, tufted, lamina 12–30×3–12cm, linear-lanceolate to ovate-lanceolate, acuminate at apex, narrowed abruptly to base, bipinnate-pinnatifid or tripinnate, light green, membranous, sparsely to heavily lemon-yellow farinaceous beneath; pinnae to 6×2.5cm, narrowly deltoid, short-stalked, pinnules trapeziform to obliquely broadly oblong-ovate, larger ones pinnatifid to pinnate at base; ultimate seg. flabellate-cuneate; rachis weak, brown near base, green and narrowly winged toward apex. W Indies (Greater Antilles).

***P. tartarea*** (Cav.) Maxon. Rhiz. 3–8×1–2cm, decumbent to erect, woody; scales to 10cm, present towards apex, lanceolate, attenuate, deep yellow tinged brown, lustrous. Stipes almost to length of lamina, dark brown tinged purple, glossy, very stiff; fronds 40–150cm, rigidly spreading, lamina 20–80×7–35cm, elongate deltoid, acuminate at apex, pinnate-pinnatifid to bipinnate, dark green, lustrous above, densely white farinaceous beneath, coriaceous; pinnae sometimes remote, narrowly deltoid, lowest to 20×8cm, pinnules remote, spreading, oblong to linear-oblong, entire to crenate at base, or on large plants pinnatifid. Tropical America.

***P. triangularis*** (Kaulf.) Maxon. CALIFORNIAN GOLD FERN. Rhiz. short-creeping or somewhat ascending, fairly thick, scales narrow; stipes stiff, about 2× length of lamina, round and ungrooved, very dark brown, sometimes with red tinge, glabrous but for base. Fronds numerous erect, to 35cm including stipe, deltoid-pentagonal, pinnate; pinnae linear-oblong, pinnately lobed, basal pinnae largest, pinnate, obliquely deltoid with largest pinnules on lower side; seg. rounded to obtuse, generally decurrent, coriaceous, subglabrous above, white or rather yellow to deep orange farinaceous beneath; veins branched. N America (British Columbia to Baja California, east to Idaho, Nevada and Arizona). In dry weather fronds curl up, displaying characteristic pale underside.

***P. viscosa*** (D.C. Eaton) Maxon. SILVERBACK FERN. Rhiz. short-creeping or ascending, 2mm diam.; scales linear-lanceolate, brown with broad black central stripe; stipes 5–20cm, brown or somewhat ferruginous, glabrous. Fronds 3–12×1.5–8cm, broadly lanceolate to pentagonal, pinnate-pinnatifid or pinnate-bipinnatifid at base, pinnatifid toward apex, pinnae entire to bipinnatifid, viscid glandular above, more or less densely white to pale yellow farinaceous beneath. California.

***P. decomposita*** (Bak.) Domin. See *P. pearcei*.
***P. ebenea*** (L.) Proctor. See *P. tartarea*.
***P. triangularis*** var. ***pallida*** Weatherby. See *P. pallida*.
For further synonymy see *Acrostichum*, *Anogramma* and *Gymnogramma*.

**Placospermum** C.T. White & Francis. (From Gk *plax*, a flat body, and *sperma*, seed, alluding to the flattened seeds.) Proteaceae. Tall tree to 30m. Leaves small, oblanceolate to lobed, to 9cm in juvenile stage, adult leaves to 17cm, spathulate to oblanceolate. Flowers in terminal branching racemes, pink-red; pedicel 13mm long; perianth cylindrical, 13mm, with 1 fertile and 3 sterile stamens. Fruit a globular, woody follicle to 38mm with to 20 flat seeds. Spring. E Australia. Z10.

CULTIVATION Occurring in high altitude tropical rainforest, *Placospermum* is seldom cultivated although it makes an attractive foliage specimen when young. It is suitable for the intermediate to warm glasshouse in cool temperate zones. Grow in a freely draining, low-fertility, loam-based mix with slow-release fertilizers that are low in phosphates, maintain high humidity and water plentifully when in growth, less at other times with a winter minimum temperature at 10–13°C/50–55°F. *P. coriaceum* is tolerant of full sun and deep shade when established, best foliage effects may be obtained in bright filtered light. Propagate by fresh seed.

***P. coriaceum*** C.T. White and Francis. ROSE SILKY OAK. As for the genus.

**Plagianthus** Forst. & Forst. f. (From Gk *plagios*, oblique, and *anthos*, flower, in allusion to the asymmetric petals.) RIBBON WOOD. Malvaceae. 2 species of shrubs or trees. Leaves simple; stipules early caducous. Flowers unisexual or bisexual, small, in terminal or axillary panicles, or solitary; epicalyx absent; petals yellow or white; stamens united in a tubular column, anthers 8–20; style branches 2, rarely 3; stigmas decurrent. Fruit asymmetric, splitting irregularly at maturity, 1–2-loculed, each 1-seeded; seeds pendulous. New Zealand. Z8.

CULTIVATION As for *Hoheria*.

***P. divaricatus*** Forst. & Forst. f. Shrub to 2.5m; stems divaricately and densely branched, sparsely stellate-pubesc.; bark dark brown. Lvs 2–3×0.3–0.5cm, alternate or in small fascicles, linear-spathulate to narrow-obovate, entire; petioles 3mm. Fls bisexual, solitary or few in short lateral cymes; cal. 2mm, campanulate, teeth irregular; cor. 5mm diam., yellow; anth. 8–12, sessile on the staminal column; stigma clavate or flattened. Fr. 5mm, globose, occasionally 2-lobed, densely stellate-pubesc., dehiscent irregularly from the apex; seeds 1, rarely 2 or 3. New Zealand.

***P. regius*** (Poit.) Hochr. RIBBON WOOD. Deciduous polygamodioecious tree to 15m; trunk to 1m diam. Young plants shrubs to 2m, densely branched, indumentum stellate; lvs distant, petioles 0.5cm, blades 0.5–2×0.3–1.5cm, broadly ovate to ovate-lanceolate, crenate-serrate; plant gradually changing to adult flowering stage with larger lvs. Adult plants with membranous lvs, 1–7.5×0.5–5cm, ovate to ovate-lanceolate, acuminate, coarsely crenate-serrate; subfloral lvs 0.3–1×0.1–0.5cm. Fls 3–4mm diam., mostly unisexual, occasionally perfect, in paniculate cymes to 25cm; pedicels 5mm, slender; cal. 2mm, campanulate, with 5 narrow-triangular teeth; pet. white, spathulate-oblong, clawed; male fls with exserted staminal column; stamens numerous, subsessile on the column; anth. about 12, red; styles aborted, included in the column. Seeds solitary. New Zealand.

***P. betulinus*** A. Cunn. See *P. regius*.
***P. lyallii*** (Hook. f.) A. Gray ex Hook. f. See *Hoheria lyallii*.
***P. pulchellus*** (Willd.) Hook. f. See *Gynatrix pulchella*.
***P. sidoides*** Hook. See *Asterotrichion discolor*.

**Plagiobothrys** Fisch. & C.A. Mey. (From Gk *plagios*, oblique, and *bothros*, hollow, referring to the hollows on the sides of the nutlets.) Boraginaceae. Some 50 species of annual or perennial herbs, usually adpressed-pubescent. Basal leaves clustered, opposite or sometimes rosulate, oblong to linear. Inflorescence a slender spike or a raceme, often bracteate; calyx mostly persistent, deeply lobed, lobes oblong or lanceolate; corolla white, tube short, lobes overlapping, rounded, spreading; style short, slender, ovules 4. Fruit of 1–4 nutlets, nutlets ovoid, smooth or angled, incurved or erect, areola median to basal. W America, Australia.

CULTIVATION Treated as a hardy annual, for any well-drained soil, in sun.

***P. nothofulvus*** (A. Gray) A. Gray. POPCORN FLOWERS. Annual herb to 50cm. Stems erect, branched above, hispidulous or villous. Basal lvs to 10cm, rosulate, oblanceolate, slightly villous; cauline lvs few, linear-lanceolate. Infl. a slender forked spike; bracts usually absent; cal. to 3mm, densely villous; lobes to 3mm, erect; cor. to 8mm wide. Nutlets ovoid-rounded, acute, areola median, annular. N America (Washington to California).

For synonymy see *Eritrichium*.

**Plagiolirion** Bak. (From Gk *plagios*, oblique, and *lirion*, lily, from the form of the flower.) Amaryllidaceae. 1 species, a perennial herb. Bulb round, long-necked. Leaves to 15×7.5–10cm, 2–3, basal, apex obtuse, bright green above, darker beneath, petiolate. Flowers to 12, in an umbel, white, small, zygomorphic, with 1 segment pointed downwards, 5 ascending. Summer. Colombia. Z9.

CULTIVATION As for *Eucharis*.

***P. horsmannii*** Bak. As for the genus.

**Plagiospermum** Oliv.
***P. sinense*** Oliv. See *Prinsepia sinensis*.

**Plagius** L'Hérit. ex DC. Compositae. 1 species, a perennial herb, to 1m. Stems much branched, glabrous, woody below. Leaves alternate, obovate to ovate-oblong, dentate, base auriculate. Capitula discoid, 1–2cm diam., in terminal, 4–10-headed corymbs; receptacle convex, naked; phyllaries in 2–3 series, keeled dorsally; florets hermaphrodite, tubular, yellow. Fruit an obconical, white-ribbed cypsela, *c*2mm; pappus an auricle. Corsica, Sardinia. Z8.

CULTIVATION As for *Chrysanthemum*.

***P. flosculosus*** (L.) Alava & Heyw. As for the genus.

For synonymy see *Chrysanthemum*.

**Planchonella** Pierre. (For Jules Émile Planchon (1823–88), French botanist.) Sapotaceae. About 60 species of woody, perennial, evergreen trees or shrubs, to at least 15m. Leaves alternate, leathery, simple. Inflorescence a small, axillary cluster, flowers small, white, sepals 4(–5), small, petals stamens and staminodes 4(–5). Fruit a berry, seeds with a long, narrow ventral scar. E Asia to W Polynesia and New Zealand. Z10.

CULTIVATION A moderately ornamental evergreen, bearing small, inconspicuous flowers and clusters of small fruit, *P. costata* is suitable for outdoor cultivation in mild, frost-free, warm temperate climates. Easily grown in any moderately fertile, well-drained soil in sun. Propagate by seed or semi-ripe cuttings.

***P. costata*** (Endl. Pierre. Tree to 15m, with latex. Lvs elliptic to obovate-oblong, glossy, pubesc. only on midrib beneath. Infl. 1(–2)-fld, fls (3–)4(–6)mm diam., on stout, curved peduncles to 1.2cm; cal. lobes ovate, hairy; cor. lobes 4mm, obovate-oblong; stamens 5, staminodes 5, subulate. Fr. to 2.5cm, ellipsoid to ovoid; seeds (1–)2–3(–4), hard, curved, almost as long as fr. New Zealand. There is some debate over whether the plants of mainland New Zealand and Norfolk Is. are separate species.

For synonymy see *Sideroxylon*.

**Planera** Gmel. (For Johann Jacob Planer (1743–89), German physician and botanist.) WATER ELM; PLANER TREE. Ulmaceae. 1 species, a deciduous tree or shrub to 14m, polygamo-dioecious, latex absent; crown broad; branchlets pubescent, lenticulate. Leaves 3–7cm, 2 ranked, ovate-oblong, acuminate, serrate, base oblique, rough, pilose and dark green above, puberulous and paler beneath, midrib yellow, venation conspicuous, yellow, straight then bifurcating near margin; petiole 3–6mm, slender, terete; stipules lateral, free, red. Inflorescence in fascicles, mostly unisexual, sometimes bisexual on same tree; calyx 4–5 lobed, divided almost to base, campanulate; corolla absent; stamens 4–5, inserted below ovary; ovary superior, ovoid, bicarpellate, stipulate, tuberculate, absent in male, style 1, persistent, stigmas 2. Fruit a nut-like drupe, 8–12mm, dry, ovoid, narrowed at short peduncle, prickly-tuberculate, light brown; seed ovoid, oblique, lacking endosperm, 1 per fruit. SE US. Z6.

CULTIVATION As for *Celtis*; prefers wet swampy sites and requires hot summers for good growth.

***P. aquatica*** (Walter) Gmel. As for the genus.

***P. abelicea*** (Lam.) Schultz. See *Zelkova abelicea*.
***P. acuminata*** Lindl. See *Zelkova serrata*.
***P. davidii*** Hance. See *Hemiptelea davidii*.
***P. ulmifolia*** Michx. See *P. aquatica*.

**PLANTAGINACEAE** Juss. PLANTAIN FAMILY. Dicot. 3 genera and 255 species of herbs, few shrubs, sometimes with alkaloids. Leaves simple, usually alternate, with parallel venation; stipules absent. Flowers usually small, regular, bisexual (*Littorella* monoecious and *Bougueria* gynomonoecious), usually in pedunculate bracteate heads or spikes without bracteoles; calyx (3)4 fused sepals; corolla (3)4 fused membranous petals; stamens (1–)4, alternate with corolla and attached to it, anthers versatile; ovary superior, of 2 fused carpels, with 2-lobed stigma, 2-loculed, with 1–40 ovules on axile placentas in each locule (1-loculed with 1 basal ovule in *Littorella* and *Bougueria*). Fruit a circumscissile membranous capsule or achene in persistent calyx; seeds with copious translucent endosperm. Some species are troublesome weeds, seeds of some *Plantago* species are used as laxatives. Cosmopolitan. *Plantago*.

**Plantago** (Tourn.) L. (Lat. name for this plant.) PLANTAIN. Plantaginaceae. 200+ species of herbs. Stemless or rarely with leafy stems, scapes arising from leaf axils. Leaves often all basal, otherwise opposite or alternate. Flowers in small spikes, bisexual, regular, generally 4-merous; calyx tubular, lobes equal or 2 larger than others; corolla salverform, tube constricted at throat or cylindric, limb spreading, papery. Fruit a pyxis, generally 2-celled, partitions falling away with seeds; seeds generally flattened-concave, dark brown or black. Cosmopolitan.

CULTIVATION A genus better known to most gardeners for the common and persistent lawn weeds that it includes, some *Plantago* spp. are attractive alpines in which the familiar basal rosettes are notable for their dense covering of fine silvery down; these are suitable for the rock garden, in crevice, scree or warm, gritty soil in full sun. *P. nivalis* needs some protection from winter wet and is sometimes grown in the alpine house; unlike other species it needs lime-free soil. *P. major* and its cvs are sometimes grown in the herbaceous border, in any moderately fertile soil in sun. Propagate by seed or division.

***P. affra*** L. Like *P. arenaria* except strongly glandular-pubesc. at least above; bracts all similar, 4–8mm; sep. oblanceolate, equal, 3–4.5mm; seeds narrowly oblong. S Europe.

***P. alpina*** L. Perenn., stock laxly branched. Lvs in several rosettes, dimorphic, 3–10cm×2–5mm, those subtending scapes broadly deltoid, others linear, abruptly attenuate, flat, generally glabrous. Scapes numerous, erect, stout, exceeding lvs; spikes 10–30×3mm, dense; bracts ovate, narrowly keeled, broadly margined, green tinged purple without; cor. white. Capsule 2-locular; seeds 2–4. Summer. C & S Europe (mts). Z3.

***P. arborescens*** Poir. Dwarf shrub to 60cm; stems woody, much-branched, branches ascending, copiously leafy. Lvs 2–4cm, fasciculate or opposite, patent or ascending, densely crowded toward stem tips, linear, more or less filiform, dark green, finely pubesc., margins ciliate. Peduncles 3–5cm; spikes ovoid, few-fld. Canary Is. Z9.

***P. arenaria*** Waldst. & Kit. Annual; stems to 50cm, erect, branched, pubesc. above, glandular below. Lvs 3–8×0.1–0.3cm, linear or linear-lanceolate. Peduncles 1–6cm, spikes 5–15mm; lowest 2 bracts to 1cm, others to 0.4cm; sep. unequal, anterior obovate-spathulate, 0.4cm, posterior ovate-lanceolate, 0.3cm; cor. tube 0.4cm, lobes 0.2cm. Capsule 0.2cm; seeds oblong-elliptic, cymbiform, 0.2.5cm. Europe, except W & N.

***P. argentea*** Chaix in Vill. Perenn., 20–50cm. Lvs in 1 or few rosettes, generally erect, 10–30×0.5–1.5cm including petiole, linear-lanceolate, acute to acuminate, entire, sometimes sericeous, particularly beneath, veins 3–5; petiole winged. Scape slender, striate, 10–60cm; spike ovoid becoming cylindric, 0.5–2cm; bracts to 0.4cm, margins hyaline; cor. brown or white; stamens white. Capsule oblong, 0.3cm; seeds 2, concave. Summer. S & C Europe. Z6.

***P. coronopus*** L. CUT-LEAVED PLANTAIN; BUCK'S-HORN PLANTAIN. Annual or short-lived perenn., with taproot with rootcrown 2.5cm diam. in older plants producing several tufts of lvs. Lvs 2.5–12cm, spreading, pinnately divided or bipinnatifid in robust plants, seg. linear, acute to acuminate, often remote. Scapes more or less decumbent, 5–35cm including spikes; spikes slender, 3–9cm; bracts ovate with hyaline margins; fls crowded, more or less imbricate, perfect; sep. 3mm, pubesc., margins white; cor. lobes lanceolate, reflexed. Capsule 2–4-seeded, seeds winged all round. Summer. Europe. Z6.

***P. cynops*** L. 1753 non 1762. SHRUBBY PLANTAIN. Dwarf shrub to 45cm, evergreen; branches erect, downy when young. Lvs 2.5–6.5×0.1cm, narrowly linear, grooved above, trigonous, margins scarious. Peduncle 4–9cm, erect, slender, downy; spikes ovoid, dense, 1cm; bracts broadly ovate with hyaline margins, cor. 3mm diam., lobes lanceolate, white tinged yellow. Summer. C & S Europe; has appeared in SE England. Z6.

***P. lanceolata*** L. ENGLISH PLANTAIN; NARROW-LEAVED PLANTAIN; RIBWORT; RIB-GRASS; RIPPLE-GRASS; BUCKHORN. Perenn. or bienn.; rootstock with long tufts of brown hair at lf bases. Lvs in several rosettes, generally erect, 4–40×0.5–3.5cm including petioles, narrowly oblong-lanceolate, acute to acuminate, entire or remotely minutely dentate, glabrous above, pubesc. beneath; petiole winged; veins 3–5, parallel, rib-like. Scapes slender, strongly 5-sulcate, 10–60cm; spike 1.5–6×0.5–1cm, ovoid becoming cylindric; bracts elongate, margins hyaline; cor. brown; fil. white, anth. yellow. Capsule 3–4mm, oblong, seeds 2, concave. Europe. 'Marginata': lvs edged and blotched with white. Z6.

***P. major*** L. COMMON PLANTAIN; WHITE-MAN'S FOOT; CART-TRACK-PLANT. Perenn., sparingly pubesc. Lvs 5–20cm, horizontally spreading, ovate, subcordate at base, entire or irregularly dentate; petiole broad, winged at apex. Scapes curved, often decumbent, 8–40cm including spike; cor. lobes to 1.5mm, reflexed. Capsule ovoid, 3mm; seeds 8–18, angled, reticulate. Summer. Eurasia, naturalized worldwide; a troublesome weed of lawns and cultivated ground. 'Atropurpurea': lvs purple tinged bronze above, green tinged bronze below. 'Nana': lvs prostrate, green, scapes reclining. 'Rosularis' (ROSE PLANTAIN): monstrous form, scape stout, with apical coma of green lvs to 9cm diam. replacing flowering spike. 'Rubrifolia': groundcover; lvs large, dark maroon. 'Variegata': lvs variegated cream and green. Z5.

***P. maxima*** Juss. ex Jacq. Perenn. Lvs generally in several rosettes, ovate-elliptic, entire or remotely minutely dentate, narrowed to base, more or less hairy, veins 9; petiole longer than lamina. Scapes exceeding lvs; spikes 5–20cm, dense; sepals almost free, to 3mm, dark brown; cor. tube 2mm, lobes 2mm; stamens 10–12mm. Capsule 3mm; seeds 4, 2mm. E Europe (S USSR, Romania, Hungary). Z6.

***P. media*** L. HOARY PLANTAIN. Perenn. Lvs in single or few rosettes, 5–15×3–8cm including petiole, ovate-elliptic, entire or remotely crenate, narrowed to base, more or less crispate-hairy; petiole to length of lamina. Scapes greatly exceeding lvs; spikes dense, 2–6cm, to 15cm in fr.; sep. green or flushed purple; cor. lobes to 2mm; stamens exserted, 8–13mm, fil. lilac, anth. lilac or white. Capsule 3–4mm; seeds 2–4, 2mm, plano-convex. Europe. Z6.

***P. nivalis*** Boiss. Perenn. Lvs in basal rosette, to 1cm, linear-lanceolate, contracted at base, mucronate at apex, white-sericeous both sides. Scapes terete, to length of lvs; spikes globose, to 1cm; bracts prominently keeled, somewhat bilobed, margins brown; sep. free, membranous, with brown margins; cor. 2mm, green; anth. yellow. Capsule globose, 2-locular; seeds 2, rugose. S Spain (mts). Z6.

***P. psyllium*** L. 1753 non 1762. FLEAWORT; SPANISH PSYLLIUM. Annual to 60cm, glandular-pubesc.; stem erect, simple or branched. Lvs narrowly linear-lanceolate to linear, entire to remotely minutely dentate. Peduncles arising from upper lf axils; spikes ovoid-globose, dense, glandular-hairy; bracts ovate-lanceolate, acute to acuminate; sep. oblong, attenuate; cor. lobes lanceolate acute. Mediterranean.

***P. reniformis*** G. Beck. Perenn. Lvs generally in 1 rosette, 5–17×2.5–10cm including petiole, ovate-cordate to suborbicular, irregularly dentate to subdigitate near base, more or less crispate-hairy; petiole to 2× length of lamina. Scapes exceeding lax, striate; spikes dense; sep. to 2.5mm, brown tinged green or flushed purple; cor. tube 2mm, lobes to 1.5mm; stamens exserted, 4–8mm. Capsule 3mm; seeds 2, 2mm. SW Yugoslavia, N Albania. Z6.

***P. sempervirens*** Crantz. Dwarf shrub to 40cm; stems freely branched, minutely pubesc. Lvs 1–6×0.1cm, linear to linear-subulate, entire to remotely minutely dentate, minutely scabrid-pubesc. Peduncles 2–10cm; spikes 5–15mm, 5–12-fld; bracts ovate, lower broader, 5–10mm; sep. unequal; cor. tube 4–5mm, lobes 3mm. Capsule 3–5mm; seeds 3–4, ovate, cymbiform. SW Europe to Italy. Z7.

***P. subulata*** L. Perenn., stock densely branched. Lvs in many rosettes, 3–25×0.1–0.2cm, linear, trigonous for most of their length, apiculate at apex, rigid, sometimes hairy. Scapes erect, generally not exceeding lvs; spike 2–5cm×2–3mm; bracts acuminate; cal. lobes with membranous margins. Capsule 2-locular; seeds 2–4. S Europe. Z6.

***P. cynops*** L. 1762 non L. 1753. See *P. sempervirens*.
***P. psyllium*** L. 1762 non L. 1753. See *P. affra*.
***P. ramosa*** Asch. See *P. arenaria*.

**Plant anatomy**. All green plants are made up of cells. The simplest plants are composed of single cells that have to carry out all essential life processes. Among these are some of the algae. They have to manufacture their own structural materials from the resources of air, water and minerals, using the energy of the sunlight in the process known as photosynthesis. They are enclosed in a rigid but frequently flexible casing, the cell wall, which contains cellulose as one of its major components. They contain all the enzymes needed for respiration and the vital processes of food storage, growth and reproduction by cell division.

Each cell contains genetic material that produces day-to-day instructions for life itself within the cell, and regulates all the processes that go on in the life history of the cell. When the cell divides to become two new individuals, the genetic material replicates itself, so that both cells can have a set.

During the course of evolution, some groups of plants became more complex. There are filaments of cells, for example, as in the bubbling blanket weeds of our ponds. Cells of other microscopic algae are arranged in balls, or in nets. Some are arranged in sheets, as in the familiar green seaweed. As more complex plants evolved, it was not possible for all cells to remain the same. Some became specialized to perform particular functions. For example, the cells of the holdfast in seaweeds are different from those in the fronds. In multicelluar algae, reproduction is often the special task of some cells only – the whole body does not divide into two. Very early on in the evolution of plants, special processes of cell division appeared, enabling sexual reproduction to take place.

Unlike the algae, the plants we grow in gardening are complex, composed of many millions of cells of specialized types, each type with its own particular functions. Plant anatomy is the study of these cell types, and their grouping into tissues. Each species has its own particular arrangement of tissues, but these are composed of a basic set of cell types. Tissue arrangements in closely related species are usually very similar. Closely related species within a genus often share many characteristics of their tissues and can be recognized as belonging together.

The cell types and their arrangements are subject to a terminology of their own. Here we aim to explain this, and show how plants are constructed. We can often tell from the particular anatomy of a species what sort of growing conditions it will thrive in; for example, if it is specialized for growth in a wet or a dry environment. When we know what the tissues of the healthy plant look like, we can detect disease, or symptoms of inadequate growing conditions. Knowledge of anatomy also helps a great deal in choosing the best methods for preparing cuttings, selecting parts for tissue culture, in grafting and in repairing a wound, or cutting or pruning to produce the best wound healing.

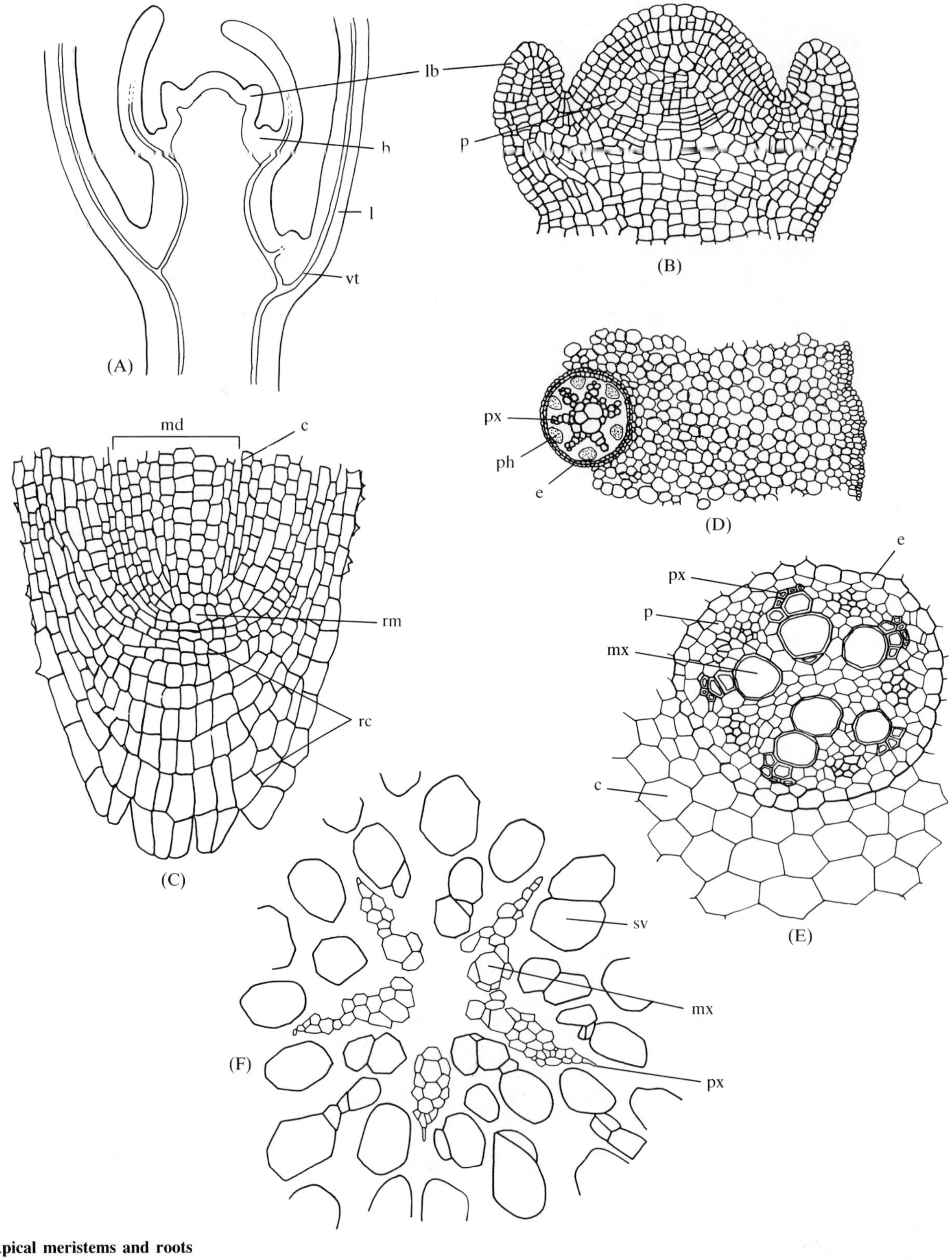


**1 Apical meristems and roots**

(A) *Plectranthus* sp. apical meristem, LS, diagram (×12). (B) *Plectranthus* apical meristem, LS, showing arrangement of cells; divisions in the outer layer are mainly at right angles to the surface, and in the inner layers, both at right angles and perpendicular to the surface (×40). (C) LS with cell detail of root apex; at this level the root cap is firmly attached to the apical meristem of the root itself. (D) *Ranunculus* sp. root, low-power TS, with a wide cortex of rounded cells and a central vascular system to the inner side of the endodermis (×100). (E) *Trillium*, detail of centre of root, TS, with pentarch xylem, and phloem poles, surrounded by a one-layered pericycle and endodermis (×160). (F) *Populus* sp. root, centre, showing pentarch primary xylem of narrower elements (star-like) and wider vessels of the secondary xylem (cells drawn only in part) (×160); b = bud,
c = cortex, e = endodermis, l = leaf, lb = leaf buttress, md = medullary region, mx = metaxylem, p = pericycle, ph = phloem,
px = protoxylem, rc = root cap, rm = root meristem, sv = secondary xylem vessel, vt = vascular trace.

THE MAIN TISSUE SYSTEMS. Each organ of the plant – for example, leaf, stem, root – will be described in its own section. Here we consider the main tissue systems common to them. There are several problems that the land plant has to overcome:

(1) *Mechanical*. It must support itself one way or another so that the parts that contain the chloroplasts responsible for photosynthesis can be held so that sunlight falls on them.

(2) *Protection*. The plant must have an outer covering that is able to regulate water loss, preventing excess drying but allowing for water movement to the air in special areas in the leaves, for example, so that transpiration can occur. The skin must also form a barrier to the entry of pathogens. In addition, it must be strong enough to contain the internal pressures built up in the plant, without rupturing. It must allow light to penetrate, where it covers photosynthetic tissue. If the plant grows in thickness, there must be a means of increasing the area of the covering.

(3) *Movement of water and food materials within the plant*. In a large and complex plant there has to be a specialized plumbing system so that water and minerals taken up by the roots can reach the leaves and other green areas of photosynthesis. The products of photosynthesis have to be carried from their sites of manufacture to the growing points, or into storage for later use.

(4) *Reproduction*. The flowers or other reproductive structures need to be placed where pollination can function efficiently or, in the case of ferns, the male gamete can reach the egg cell, and so that the seed or spores can be dispersed effectively.

(5) In plants with long lives, there is the need either to grow and increase in size from year to year (the formation of wood, as secondary thickening, for example) or develop some form of perennial organ from which annual shoots can arise (e.g. a bulb, storage root or tuber).

MECHANICAL SUPPORT SYSTEMS. Plants that are submerged in water or partly submerged and floating obtain considerable support from the water itself. If they are removed from the water, they collapse. Clearly, land plants must have something which is lacking or poorly developed in such water plants. Two principal methods of support are used. The simpler depends on water pressure in the cells (turgor), and a tough, slightly elastic outer covering to the plant. Most seedlings rely on this method, as do the tender growing tips. In water shortage, these readily wilt. Some succulent plants rely almost entirely on water pressure and tough skins for support. Take for example the leaves of aloes (Fig. 2N, O). If these lack water, they shrivel and collapse to thin, papery structures. An aloe plant deprived of water protects the growing point. The older leaves dry first, and the youngest leaves remain turgid the longest.

The more complex and most widespread method of mechanical support is to provide special strengthening tissues which act like reinforcing rods in concrete, or girders in buildings and bridges. There is economical and efficient use of the thick-walled specialized cells. Their wall materials is expensive in resources to the plant. The main cell types, which will be described below, are collenchyma, sclerenchyma and xylem.

Many plants use a combination of both hydraulic pressure (turgor), and mechanical stiffening. Growing points and immature leaves, for example, rely largely on turgor pressure, whereas the stems that have undergone secondary growth in thickness have thick-walled cells supporting them.

Thin-walled cells in the growing tips of plants (apical meristems) are termed parenchyma (Fig. 1B, C). They are the basic cell type from which all other sorts develop. In the meristem their cytoplasm is dense, with few vacuoles. As they mature, they enlarge, and the vacuoles which contain watery sap increase in volume. This is the first stage of growth. Such enlarged cells may remain parenchymatous throughout the life of the plant. The earliest of the strengthening tissues to develop, particularly in dicotyledons, is collenchyma. These cells are often much more elongated than the parenchyma and their walls become thickened with cellulose, particularly at the angles (Fig. 7A, C). They remain alive, with an active cytoplasm. In stems they are usually found just below the epidermis (skin), in several layers. If the stem is ridged or perhaps square in section as in mint (*Mentha* spp.), then the strands of collenchyma are found in the ridges, or at the stem angles (Fig. 7B). In leaves, the collenchyma is often found close to the epidermis in relation to the midrib, main veins and around the outer part of the leaf stalk (petiole) to the inner side of the epidermis.

One of the special properties of collenchyma is that the cells form in elongating organs (stems and leaves) and grow in length with the organ itself. When growth in length has ceased, sometimes the walls of collenchyma cells become further thickened, adding extra layers to the inner side. At first, these are composed mainly of cellulose; later they may become impregnated with another strengthening material, lignin.

Sclerenchyma cells form strengthening tissues that generally develop fully after growth of the leaf, or a particular part of a stem, has ceased. When they are mature, they lose their cell contents and die. Their thickened cell walls are a mixture of cellulose and lignin, and walls are of even thickness (Fig. 6A–D). They are of two main sorts, very elongated fibres, with pointed ends, or variously shaped sclereids (Fig. 3J).

Fibres are found in bark, giving it a stringy texture; fibres and fibre-like cells often form strengthening cylinders to the inner side of the epidermis in grass and other stems – bamboo canes provide a familiar example. Fibres may form strands inside the outer surface of stems, rather like those of collenchyma. In leaves, it is common for the veins to be strengthened with strands, girders or sheaths of fibres (Fig. 2K, L, M; 3C; 7D, E, F). A good example can be found in the older leaves of *Montbretia*, where the veins appear very tough because of the sclerenchyma. Fibres also strengthen the walls of many fruits – for example, the pods of runner beans which become 'stringy' with age. Plant breeders have developed stringless varieties to overcome this.

Many commercial fibres come from strands in the outer (cortical) parts of stems; flax (*Linum*) is an example. Sisal, from *Agave*, is made up of the fibre strands and fibre caps associated with the veins of the leaves of these monocotyledons. Coir fibre comes from the outer part of the coconut fruit.

Sclereids are often blunt-ended, thick-walled cells (Fig. 6A–D). They vary greatly in shape: small, more or less cubic or rounded sclereids give the gritty texture to pear fruits; similar sclereids in multiple layers form the shells of hazel nuts, and the stones of cherries, plums and apricots; somewhat longer sclereids are a common feature of bark. In leaves with a tough texture (sclerophyllous), one frequently finds sclereids acting rather like pit-props, extending between the surfaces through the thickness of the leaf. Olive and *Osmanthus* leaves have these; they are often branched or forked or have bent ends. In *Camellia* leaves they are branched in three dimensions and rather star-like (astrosclereids). Sclereids often cluster round the vein endings in such leaves. They are also frequently found strengthening leaf margins (edges).

When dicotyledons and gymnosperms have stems that grow in thickness (secondary thickening), most of the mechanical tissue formed is secondary xylem (wood). This is a complex tissue, itself composed of many cell types, and is described later. Secondary growth in thickness also takes place in some monocotyledonous stems (e.g. *Dracaena*) but no secondary xylem is formed, just new veins (vascular bundles) and parenchyma around them, from the outer portion of the stem. The stems in palms are made up of primary growth only. They reach their maximum width shortly below the growing tip of the shoot. Some do expand near the base, but not by forming secondary wood. The strengthening tissue in these stems is made up of fibres and parenchyma cells whose cell walls are thickened and lignified. Most of the vascular bundles have strong fibre strands accompanying them.

THE OUTER SKIN. The skin covering the leaves, young stems, flowers and fruits is called the epidermis (Fig. 2N, O; 3E, H); that covering the young roots, the rhizodermis. It is frequently only one cell layer thick, but on the serial parts of some plants, particularly those subjected to very drying conditions in their

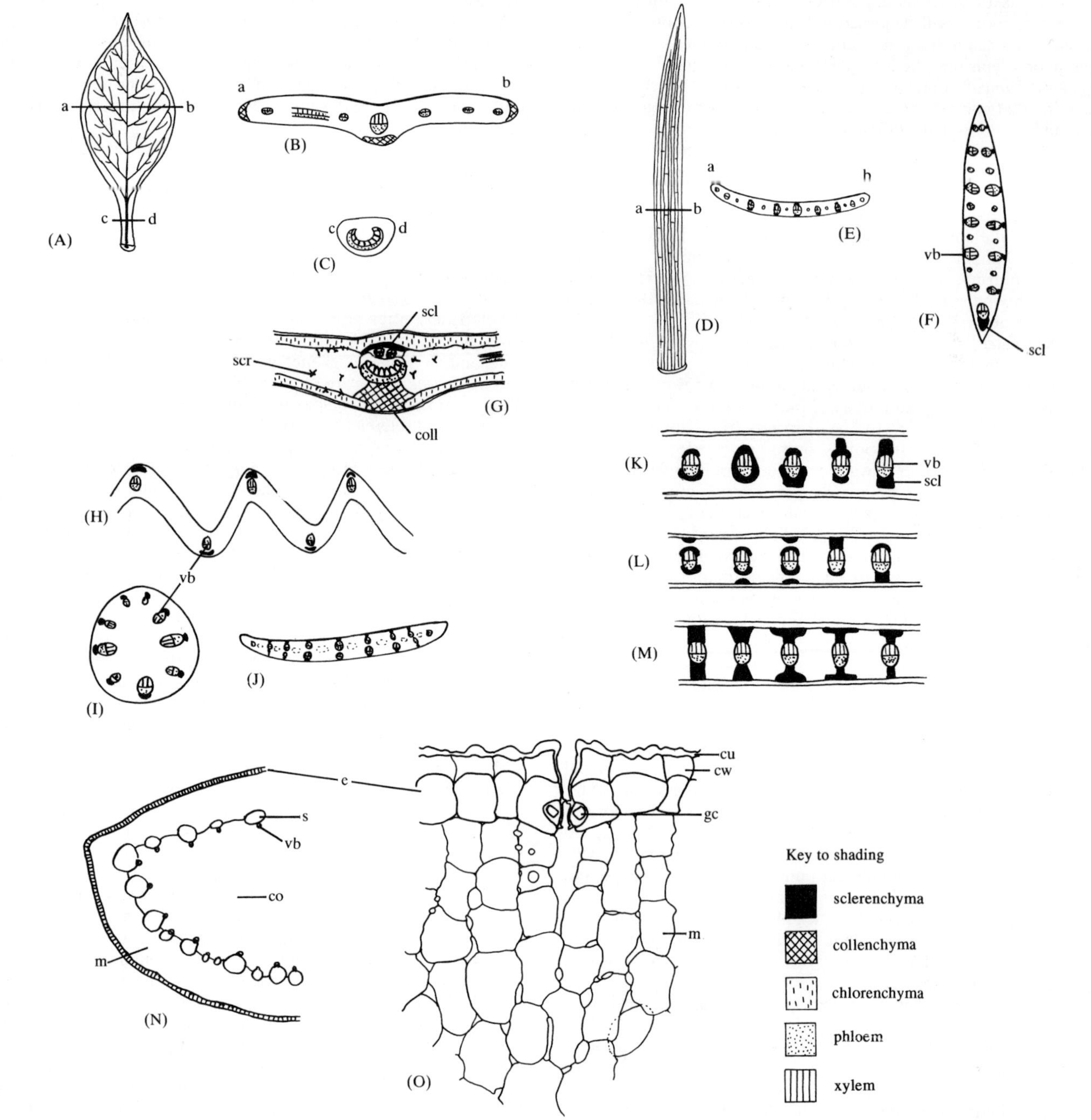


**2 Leaf structure**

(A)–(C), diagrams of dicot leaf vasculature (A) venation in surface view, with levels of section indicated for (B) and (C). (B) TS, lamina, with large midrib bundle and smaller veins, some cut obliquely; note collenchyma strengthening at margins and abaxial to midrib. (D)–(F), diagrams of strap shaped monocot leaf vasculature. (D) venation in surface view, with level of section of fig. (E) indicated. (E) TS lamina, with single row of vascular bundles in this dorsiventrally flattened leaf; sclerenchyma strengthening is indicated at the phloem poles of larger bundles. (F) TS diagram of a unifacial leaf (as in many *Gladiolus* spp.), with only the abaxial epidermis present, a large keel bundle and pairs of vascular bundles facing one another along the blade. (G) diagram of the midrib region in *Sonneratia*; the midrib bundles are composed of a large, abaxial arc and two small, inverted strands adaxially. Both collenchyma and sclerenchyma are present, and there are sclereids in the mesophyll. (H)–(J) diagrams of a range of forms of monocot leaves in TS. In (H) the plicate (folded) leaf has alternate vascular bundles inverted; in (I) the leaf is unifacial, cylindrical and the bundles are in a ring (e.g. some *Juncus* spp.). (J) shows a leaf that is secondarily dorsiventral and might be imagined as the product of compressing a leaf like that in (I); it lacks a true adaxial surface. A number of *Iris* spp. are like this. (K)–(M) diagrams showing some of the range of shapes of sclerenchyma strengthening that can occur in monocot leaves. Caps are confined to the bundle poles, strands are often near the epidermis and do not connect with bundle caps, girders connect bundle caps to the epidermis. The shape of the strengthening is usually characteristic for a species. (N),(O) *Aloe ramosissima* leaf TS. (N) margin, showing wide mesophyll, vascular bundles with enlarged, secretory parenchyma caps at phloem poles and central colourless, water-storing cells (×12.5). (O) detail of (N); the cuticle is thick, as is the outer epidermal wall; stomata are sunken; the mesophyll is of sub-palisade cells in many layers. This is a water storing xerophyte (×160).

a–b, c–d = levels of section; co = colourless cells; coll = collenchyma; cu = cuticle; cw = cell wall; e = epidermis; gc = guard cell of stoma; m = mesophyll; s = secretory cells; scl = sclerenchyma; scr = sclereid; vb = vascular bundle.

natural habitats, it may be two- or more layered. Epidermal cells commonly have outer cell walls that are thicker than the others; generally the walls are composed largely of cellulose. Most plants have a cuticle covering the outer wall; this is thinnest in water plants, where it can be difficult to detect, and frequently thickest in plants adapted for growth in dry habitats (xerophytes). In plants from 'moderate' habitats, (mesophytes), the cuticle is often only slightly thickened. Some rainforest trees with leaves that persist on the plant for several years also have thick cuticles. The cuticle is composed of cutin, a fatty, water-impermeable material. It provides part of the 'waterproofing' of the plant, and may help to prevent the entry of pathogens. Frequently there is a layer of wax to the outer side of the cuticle. When this is thick, it appears as a 'bloom', for example on the fruit of plums, or the leaves of *Sedum*. When giving a white appearance to the surface, the wax is reflecting light and heat; it can play a part in reducing heat gain from the sun. Flowers as well as fruits have cuticles and sometimes wax or other substances on their epidermises. The cuticle is often thin on the rhizodermis.

The leaf epidermis, and to varying degrees the epidermis of stems and floral parts, has not only the unmodified epidermal cells, but also stomata, composed of cells that can regulate the size of a pore or hole in the epidermis, and hence control the rate of water loss through transpiration (Fig. 3E, G, H; 4A–J). The simplest stomata consist of two cells, one on either side of the pore, called guard cells. These change shape with changes in hydraulic pressure, and thereby open or close the pore. The walls of guard cells are unevenly thickened and this assists the shape changes with pressure. In many plants the guard cells are associated with subsidiary cells. These can be distinguished from other epidermal cells because they are of distinctive shapes, or have thinner walls. Stomata may be present on upper and lower leaf surfaces (e.g. aloes) the lower surface only (e.g. oak and most temperate-region deciduous trees) and on only the upper surface, as in some aquatic plants with floating leaves (e.g. *Victoria*).

Other epidermal cells may develop to form papillae, hairs or scales (collectively called trichomes) (Fig. 5A–N). Scales and many sorts of hair are large enough to see with the naked eye. Hairs are very varied indeed, from the soft hairs on *Verbascum* to the water-absorbent hairs on bromeliads, to glandular hairs on mints and stinging hairs on nettles. They show a wide range of size, colour and complexity. Hairs are responsible for the characteristic, diagnostic appearance of the lower surface of *Rhododendron* leaves. The hairs on some species are thick-walled and have thick cuticles. By slowing the wind speed over the leaf surface, they help reduce its drying effect. In plants of the high tropical mountains, hairs on the tree lobelias and *Senecios* help to act like an insulating blanket. The air trapped between them prevents excessive cooling at night, and excessive heating (and damage by high ultraviolet light intensity) by day. Mention must also be made of the sticky hairs and the glandular hairs which produce digestive enzymes in carnivorous plants like *Drosera* and *Pinguicula*.

Roots of the majority of species have specialized root hairs near their growing tips. These are thin walled and function in the absorption of water and salts from the soil, greatly increasing the root surface area available for this operation.

The original epidermal layer becomes split in most species that show secondary growth in thickness of stem or root. It is normally replaced by a secondary protective 'skin', the cork, which makes up part of the bark. Cork cells are produced from an actively dividing layer of unspecialized cells, the cork cambium or phellogen (Fig. 7G). The phellogen normally develops in the cortex, or outer part of the stem or root. It can form just to the inner side of the epidermis, or at varying depths towards the phloem. It produces layer after layer of cork cells to its outer side. Most of these have a waterproof substance, suberin, in their walls. Some, like those of the lenticels or 'breathing pores', may be thin-walled and unsuberized.

Barks of different appearance and texture develop on particular species because cork cambia are diverse in their activity and position. Some cork cambia form complete cylinders ensheathing the stem. If they produce even cork layers, a smooth bark results. In birches, for example, several layers of suberized cells are often followed by some layers of thin-walled, weak cells. The bands alternate, and a peeling bark results. The scale-like bark on pines is developed from a cork cambium made up of lens-like structures. Barks that are fibrous, like the stringy-bark *Eucalyptus* species, contain fibres, elongated, thick-walled cells forming part of the phloem.

THE TRANSPORT SYSTEMS. Mention has already been made of the veins in stems and leaves (vascular bundles) in the section on mechanical systems. This is because the two are frequently intimately associated.

The plant has two main long-distance transport systems. The xylem facilitates the movement of water and dissolved salts taken up by the roots from the soil (or hydroponic solution) to the leaves and growing points of the shoots.

The phloem channels soluble materials synthesized by photosynthetic chlorenchyma (most frequently in the leaves, but also in green stems and other green parts of the plant) to points of demand, like the growing tips, expanding leaves, growing roots, stems, flowers or fruits, or to storage organs for later use. Phloem also conducts mobilized food reserves from storage organs when these are needed elsewhere in the plant.

In general, water and salts move in one direction in the xylem, and sugars and other synthesized substances in either direction in the phloem, depending on demand. In certain circumstances of water stress, reverse flow can take place in xylem, when for example, water may leave hydrated leaves and flow to the vital apical meristems. Sugar solutions may also be found in the xylem from time to time, as in the syrup of maple syrup.

The cells of xylem lie parallel with the cells of the phloem in the vascular bundles of the stem and leaves. In the primary root, the xylem and phloem strands alternate, in a ring. As they pass into the stem, they become reorganized to take up an arrangement with the phloem strand in each vascular bundle facing the outside, and the xylem strand the inside of the stem. In most dicotyledons, there is one ring of vascular bundles in the primary stem. In monocotyledons, the vascular bundles can be in several rings, or they may even appear to be scattered in a stem cross-section. Even when they are present in very large numbers (thousands) in palm stems, they are arranged in an orderly way, but this is seldom apparent from a single section (Fig. 7A, D, E, F).

The cells of the functional phloem remain alive. In the angiosperms, phloem is composed of several sorts of cell: thin-walled sieve-tube elements, elongated cells with special sieve-like areas on their end walls (sieve plates), or on overlapping side walls are modified to transport most of the synthesized materials. They do not have a nucleus, but receive their instructions for life processes from the narrower but also elongated companion cells that run along side them, each with a nucleus. If a companion cell is killed, the sieve-tube element adjacent to it cannot function. Phloem also often contains small parenchyma cells and thick-walled, dead fibres (Fig. 7H).

In contrast, the cells of the functional xylem die shortly after they have matured. They are elongated cells, with specialized wall thickenings that help prevent them collapsing inwards when the water they contain is put under tension by the evaporating forces of the transpiration stream. The first-formed xylem cells, the protoxylem, have strengthening in the form of hoops or annuli, or of helices. These cells form in parts of the root, stem or leaf that are still expanding or growing in length. The special thickening allows the cells to stretch considerably before they break. When growth in length of a particular part is complete, the next-formed xylem cells, the metaxylem, have much more rigid walls. These tend to be of more or less even thickness, except for certain areas termed pits, that remain thin. The water conducting xylem cells are of two basic types, tracheids and vessel elements. In tracheids, pits form the areas in the walls of adjacent tracheids through which the water can pass most freely. The pits may be arranged in

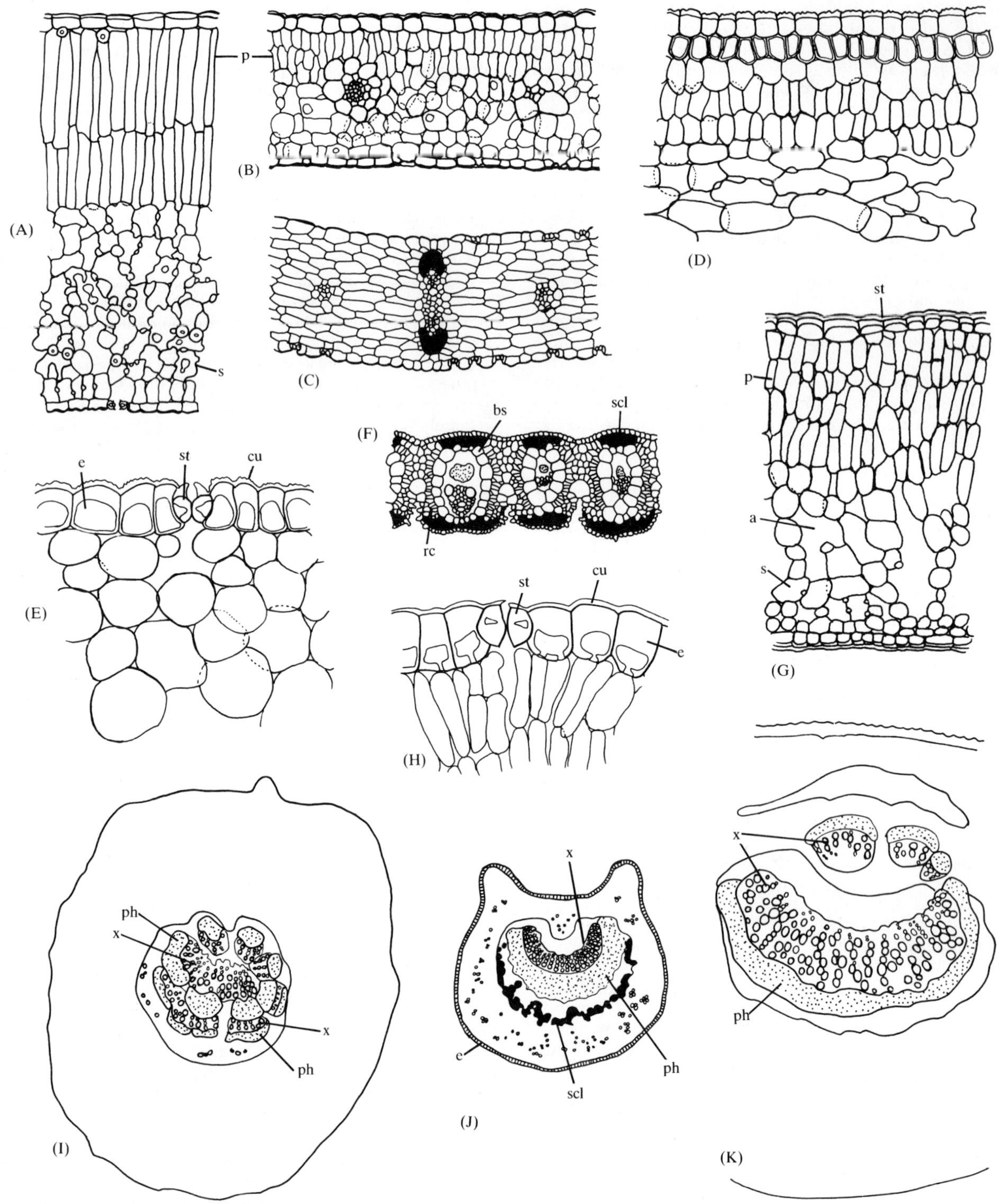


**3 Details of leaf transverse sections**

(A) *Olea europaea*; mesophyll of two adaxial palisade cell layers and several layers of spongy cells abaxially; note scattered sclereids (×160). (B) *Prunus* sp., similar to (A), but palisade cells shorter and spongy cells less lobed; note minor vein with parenchyma bundle sheath (×80). (C) *Gladiolus* sp. with little-differentiated mesophyll; note strong sclerenchyma caps to larger vascular bundle (shown solid black) (×80). (D) *Eryngium* sp., adaxial epidermis with a single layered hypodermis beneath it; short palisade cells in 2–3 layers and transversely elongated spongy cells (×390). (E) *Eulophia* sp. showing thick cuticle and outer walls of epidermal cells, stoma with pronounced outer cuticular flanges to guard cells and mesophyll of rounded cells. (F) *Eleusine jaegeri*, a $C_4$ grass, which has chloroplasts in the parenchyma cells of the outer bundle sheath, as well as in the radiating palisade chlorenchyma; the vascular bundles are also close together (×80). (G) *Osmanthus* sp. with 4–5 layers of palisade cells followed by spongy mesophyll with large air spaces. (H) *Boscia*, detail of epidemis showing very thick walled cells, with pits to palisade chlorenchyma cells beneath (×90). (I)–(J) petioles showing a range of vascular bundle arrangement. (I) *Salvadora persica*, (J) *Prunus* sp., (K) *Sonneratia* sp. midrib.

a = air space; bs = bundle sheath; ch = chlorenchyma; cu = cuticle; e = epidermis; h = hypodermis; p = palisade cells; ph = phloem; rc = radiating palisade chlorenchyma; scl = sclerenchyma; scr = sclereids; st = stoma; x = xylem.

single, long rows, as in the tracheids of many conifers or, as in angiosperm tracheids and vessel elements, where they may be smaller, and arranged in several rows in which they may be opposite or alternate. They do not often cover the whole wall (Fig. 8A, B).

Pit pairs between gymnosperm tracheids have a complex structure. They are more or less circular; the thin area has a thickened central part, called the torus. The thickened wall around the pit overarches the thin area, on both sides; it stands proud of the thin membrane, and forms a reduced aperture. This pit border, its pore and the torus, give the pit the appearance of a bull's eye in face view (see Fig. 8F, G, H, I). If there is a change in pressure in a tracheid, due to damage, for example, the thin pit membrane allows the torus to move to one side, effectively plugging the pore.

The bordered pits in angiosperms are not so complicated; they in the vast majority of species lack a torus, and simply have overarching borders. If the tracheid is next to a fibre or parenchyma cell, the pit pairs become modified. They are bordered on the side facing the inner part (lumen) of the tracheid, but are not bordered where facing the lumen of the other cell. They are called half-bordered pits. Pits in fibres and parenchyma cells are 'simple' and not bordered.

The vessel elements mentioned above are joined one end on to the next, in a single file, to form a vessel (Fig. 8A). Vessels can be several centimetres long, and composed of numerous vessel elements. The feature vessel elements are perforated at one or both ends. This distinguishes them from tracheids and enables water to flow relatively freely along the axis of a vessel. The perforations have well defined forms. The simplest (and thought to be the most advanced) is a perforation with only a rim of thickening. These simple perforation plates are usually transverse, that is, at right angles to the long axis of the cell. Among other types of perforation are scalariform (ladder-like) plates, which are usually oblique, and divided by several to many transverse bars. Vessels are considered to have been derived from tracheids during the course of evolution. The length and width of vessel element, their type of perforation plates and wall pitting, are thought to relate to the normal ecological conditions in which plants grow. The first-formed xylem of vascular bundles in stem, leaf and root is called the primary xylem. In addition to the conducting cells, parenchyma is often present. Secondary xylem, (wood) which develops in gymnosperms and most dicotyledons, but not monocotyledons, is more complex; it is described later.

PHOTOSYNTHETIC TISSUES. Mention has already been made of one of the functions of the mechanical tissues, to hold the photosynthetic tissues to the light, and of the vascular tissues to supply water and salts, and to carry away the synthesized food materials. The cells that constitute the photosynthetic tissue itself are a specialized form of parenchyma, called chlorenchyma. They appear green since they contain chloroplasts, cell organelles that contain the pigment, chlorophyll.

In the leaf, the chlorenchyma constitutes part or all of the mesophyll. Stems in which photosynthesis takes place usually have the chlorenchyma concentrated in layers near the surface; chlorenchyma also frequently occurs in immature flowers and fruits. The term mesophyll refers strictly to the chlorenchyma of leaves. The yellow or white with green variegation of leaves or stems is due to abnormal areas in the green tissue where chloroplasts are not fully developed, and remain as leucoplasts. This is a frequently a genetically controlled condition, but can be caused by viruses. It may be a chimeral condition. The simplest chlorenchyma consists of rounded cells of relatively little differentiated parenchyma (Fig. 3E). The cells may be slightly taller than wide, with the long axis at right angles to the leaf surface (Fig. 3C). In many leaves, the chlorenchyma is more specialized. Two main types of cell are recognized: palisade-like cells, which are tall, narrow cylinders and spongy cells, which are wider and irregularly lobed (Fig. 3A). Palisade cells are normally arranged so that the long axes of the cylinders are at right angles to the surface. The spongy cells may have no preferred orientation.

Palisade cells may form one or more layers (Fig. 3B, D). If present on only one side of the leaf, that side tends to be the adaxial (upper) surface, with spongy cells to the other side. In some species, palisade is present next to the adaxial and the abaxial (lower) epidermises. These are numerous, narrow air spaces (intercellular spaces) between palisade cells. Some palisade cells have short, peg-like projections arranged in 4–6 longitudinal rows. These join on to projections on neighbouring cells, forming a resilient tissue with a very high volume of intercellular spaces. Such cells are common in xerophytes.

In many monocotyledons, particularly in Liliaceae and Iridaceae, the chlorenchyma cells appear rounded in transverse sections of the leaf, but in longitudinal sections can be seen to be axially elongated. They may be regularly or irregularly lobed.

The arrangement of palisade cells and other leaf tissues is very characteristic in leaves of plants that have a form of photosynthesis involving molecules with four carbon atoms, rather than the more frequent three carbon molecules, in their biochemical pathways. The cluster of anatomical characters, called the 'kranz' syndrome in $C_4$ plants, is illustrated in Fig. 3F. It is more frequent in tropical than temperate plants, and involves more efficient use of the $CO_2$ in photosynthesis. The palisade cells radiate from the parenchyma sheath to the vascular bundle. The sheath itself contains chloroplasts that differ in their fine structure from those of the palisade cells. Vascular bundles are closely spaced, rarely with more than three chlorenchyma cells between them.

Chloroplasts are commonly more densely arranged in palisade cells, and less densely packed in spongy cells, probably because lower light intensity reaches the cells nearer the lower surface of the leaf. In many species, the palisade layers are separated from the spongy tissue by larger, colourless parenchyma cells. The colourless cells may function in water storage (Fig. 2N).

Well-developed chlorenchyma may be present in young stems. It is particularly well developed in leafless plants, in which the stems assume the function of leaves, as for example, most Cactaceae. Green floral parts and immature fruits also contain chlorenchyma. Chloroplasts have even been found in the roots of some floating water plants. A range of types of chlorenchyma is illustrated in Fig. 3A–H.

In addition to storage products, such as starch granules, oil droplets and aleurone, for example, other substances may be found in the lumina of cells, particularly parenchymatous cells. These have in the past been called waste products, but not it is recognized that many of them have functions. Tannins, dark substances, are common in many parts of the plant in a large number of species. They have a bitter taste, and may deter animal feeding. Crystals are also common; these are normally of calcium oxalate. They have many forms, from prisms, rhombs to needles. They may be solitary or in clusters, as in druses (prisms) or raphides (needle-like, in parallel bundles, enclosed in mucilaginous 'sacs'); Fig. 6E–I. If tannin or crystals are contained in special cells, distinct from those in which they are set, these are called idioblasts – hence tannin idioblasts. Silica bodies consist of opaline material; they are found in relatively few families, and occur mainly in stem, leaf or secondary xylem. They are present in specialized epidermal cells of the leaves of many grasses, for example, where their shapes (saddle-shaped, cross-shaped, oblong etc.) are often diagnostic. They are very hard, and wear down the teeth of herbivores (which have evolved continuously growing teeth that compensate); Fig. 6J–M.

Other fairly common cell contents include mucilage and resins. Mucilage is found, for example, in the bark of elm, and resins are found in many conifer genera. Latex occurs in a number of families, e.g. Euphorbiaceae, Papaveraceae, Asclepiadaceae and Compositae. It is present either in individual latex cells, or in laticifers, that may be very extensive and branched. Latex is frequently irritant; that from a number of Euphorbiaceae is poisonous. Rubber is made from the latex of *Hevea* bark.

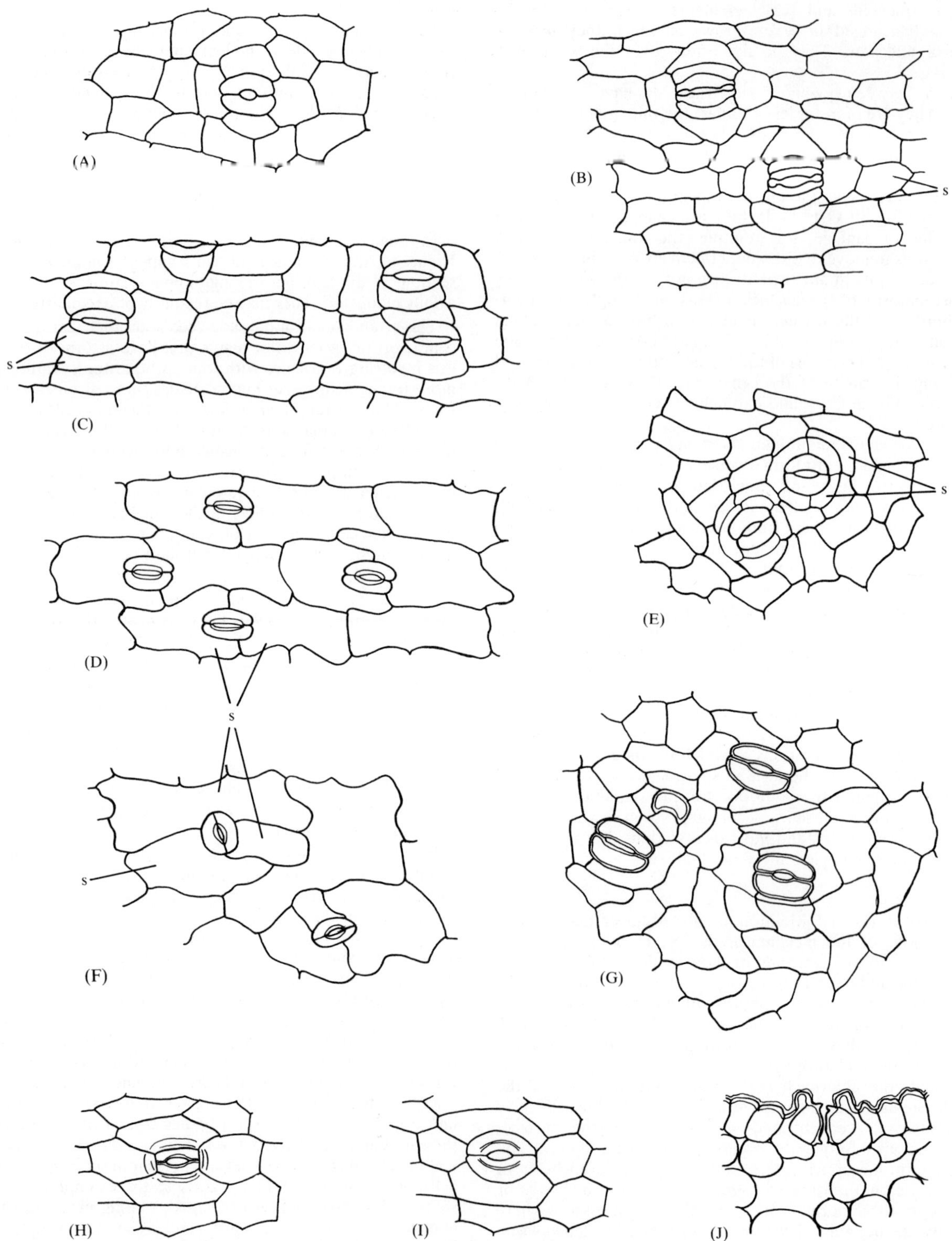


**4 Leaf epidermis in surface view** (except (J) TS).

(A) *Ranunculus acris* anomocytic stoma, with no discernible subsidiary cells (×220). (B) *Washingtonia filifera*, stomata tetracytic, with a pair of terminal and a pair of lateral subsidiary cells (×600). (C) *Eryngium* sp. with paracytic stomata; sometimes more than one lateral subsidiary cell is present (×390). (D) *Dianthus* sp. with diacytic stomata, a large subsidiary cell is present at either pole (×160). (E) *Piper betle*, cyclocytic stomata, with concentric rings of subsidiary cells (×390). (F) *Brassica campestris*, anisocytic stomata, each with three unequal subsidiary cells (×390). (G) *Rosa* sp., anomocytic stomata; note base of broken glandular hair (×390). (H)–(J) *Cordyline baueri*, anomocytic stoma (×390); (H) high focus, with papillae overarching guard cells, (I) low focus, showing guard cell outline, (J) TS, showing details of the papillae above the guard cells.

s = subsidiary cells.

THE LEAF. Leaves have very varied morphology. Their anatomy is also very varied; leaves with very different outlines may share similar anatomy, and leaves with similar outlines can have quite different internal tissue arrangements. This is because (i) leaves of closely related species or genera often have similar structure and (ii) the anatomy of the leaf is frequently strongly correlated with the environment preferred by the plant. In the first instance, this is a great help to people who wish to identify small leaf fragments, in for example forensic work. In the second case, the morphological and anatomical adaptations of leaves give a good indication to the horticulturist of the type of growing conditions normally encountered by the plant.

A 'model' leaf of a dicotyledonous plant is shown in Fig. 2A–C. It consists of a lamina and petiole. In surface view the veins (vascular bundles) can be seen; there is a prominent central vein, the midrib, and from this, to either side branch secondary veins. Between these are finer tertiary or third-order veins, and frequently very fine quaternary veins which may join with others to form a closed or net-like system, or terminate freely in the mesophyll, to form an open system. The venation is often more prominent on the lower (abaxial) surface. By holding a leaf to a bright light, the veins are often seen more readily. The 'model' monocotyledonous leaf shown in Fig. 2D,E lacks a petiole. The lamina is narrow and strap-shaped. The veins run more or less parallel with one another, along the leaf axis. Wide veins alternate with narrower second and third-order veins. There are fine transverse veins at intervals. This distinction between dicotyledon and monocotyledon leaves is only partial: there are linear dicotyledon leaves, e.g. some *Plantago* species, whereas the leaves of *Smilax, Strelitzia* and *Arum*, for example, in the monocotyledons are not strap-shaped.

The arrangement of the veins is very characteristic of a species. Details in dicotyledons such as whether the secondary veins reach the margin or not, or whether they enter marginal teeth, as well as the angle at which they leave the midrib, are just some of the factors to be taken into consideration. When the main vein pattern is particularly typical of a plant it is mentioned in the Dictionary descriptions.

Transverse sections of the 'model' dicotyledon and monocotyledon leaves are shown in Fig. 2A,C,E. The relationship of the midrib or primary veins to the mesophyll can be seen. In most dicotyledons, the xylem in each vein faces the upper (adaxial) surface, and the phloem the lower (abaxial) surface. This is frequently not so in monocotyledons. Although many species have dorsiventrally flattened leaves, like the majority of dicotyledons (e.g. the grasses), cylindrical, unifacial, flanged and other types are very common. A wide range of leaf sections occurs for example in the Iridaceae. Here the veins show diverse orientations: diagrammatic examples are shown in Fig. 2H,J.

In Figs. 2B, some of the veins appear cut obliquely; this is because they run at an angle to the midrib.

In Fig. 3B and 3G the epidermal cells are arranged in a single layer. Those on the adaxial surface are larger than the abaxial cells. Stomata are confined to the abaxial surface in some examples, but they can occur on both surfaces or the adaxial surface only. The margins may have papillae, there are often hairs over the veins.

The collenchyma in the dicotyledon leaf (Fig. 2G) strengthens the margins, and the veins. It is close to the epidermis. Lignified parenchyma and sclerenchyma are shown performing a similar function in the monocotyledon (Fig. 2K). Parenchyma bundle sheaths are shown in both examples, but the monocotyledon also has sclerenchyma sheaths to the large bundles.

The petiole in dicotyledons consists of epidermis, an outer region of parenchyma (often chlorenchyma), frequently with collenchyma in the periphery, and in the centre, vascular tissue. The appearance of vascular tissue in cross section can be varied, but several distinct types are frequent. Commonly the individual vascular bundles are very closely arranged, and appear as a continuous arc. This may be shallow, U-shaped, or with the ends nearly meeting to the adaxial side. The xylem is to the inner and the phloem to the outer side of the arc. The upper margins of the arc may be recurved. Sometimes the vascular strands are separated from one another by a few layers of narrow parenchyma cells. This type of arrangement gives flexibility to the petiole, allowing it to twist without damage, but resisting the downward loading of the lamina. There may be additional vascular strands; one common type has a strand inverted either at the top of the arc, or partly enclosed by it. The cross-sectional appearance of the petiole is often different at different levels. Near the base, close to its insertion on the stem, the strands may be more distinctly separated from one another. Common numbers of strands (leaf traces) leaving the stem are one, three or five. Some plants have many more than this, for example cycads; in monocotyledons (that lack true petioles) there are also numerous strands at the leaf base. Towards the end of the petiole, where the lamina begins to be apparent, strands (single bundles, or groups of bundles) commonly become detached from the end of the arc, to form part of the lamina vasculature. Examples of petioles in cross section are shown in Fig. 3I,J, and a series of named examples of leaf cross sections is shown in Fig. 3A–D,F,G. Leaves vary in the different arrangements of chlorenchyma, the presence or absence of sclereids, tannin ideoblasts, crystals or silica bodies, and the range of arrangements of mechanical tissue.

THE STEM. Stems in their primary, unthickened state, whether monocot or dicot, frequently share a similar arrangement of tissues in the internodal region. The epidermis may be one or more layers thick; to its inner side is the cortex. In some species there is a further layer or layers of cells between the epidermis and cortex, the hypodermis, the cells of which have thickened walls. Hypodermal cells arise from the cortex and are not usually arranged in line with cells of the epidermis, whereas in a multiple epidermis commonly the lines of cells can be seen, since they arise from cell divisions of the epidermis itself.

The cortex may consist in part or entirely of chlorenchyma, or its inner layers may be colourless parenchyma. There is often a defined boundary between the cortex and the centre ('medullary') region. This is usually made up of one or several layers of parenchymatous cells that may be rich in starch granules. It is sometimes referred to as an endodermis, but this is an incorrect use of the term unless a clear casparian thickening can be seen. These are suberised layers in the anticlinal walls of the cells (see root endodermis). It may be called a starch sheath, if starch rich, or an endodermoid sheath.

The next structures to be seen are the vascular bundles. As mentioned earlier, in most dicots they occur in one ring; in monocots, they are more commonly in several rings, or appear scattered. The bundles are usually arranged with the phloem pole facing outwards, and the xylem inwards. In some dicots, commonly in climbers, for example in the Cucurbitaceae, an inner phloem pole may also be present.

The vascular bundles are set in a parenchymatous ground tissue, which in the stem centre forms the pith. As mentioned in the section on mechanical tissues, the stem in some plants has considerable strengthening sclerenchyma, collenchyma or lignified parenchyma. This is particularly the case in species adapted to grow in dry conditions, and in many monocots. Two primary stems are illustrated in Fig. 7A,E, but even in these, the dicots show the first stages of secondary growth in thickness.

Stems often have sclereids in the cortex and pith, and the parenchymatous cells may contain a range of substances, e.g. crystals, tannin or silica bodies.

ROOTS. Primary roots have a distinctly different arrangement of vascular tissue from primary stems; the proportion of cortex to vascular cylinder is much greater, and a true endodermis is present. In secondarily thickened roots of dicots and conifers (monocot roots are all primary) the distinction is less evident, but there are features like the higher proportion of parenchyma in dicots that make roots distinctive. Generally examination of the central part of root or stem will reveal the remains of the primary xylem,

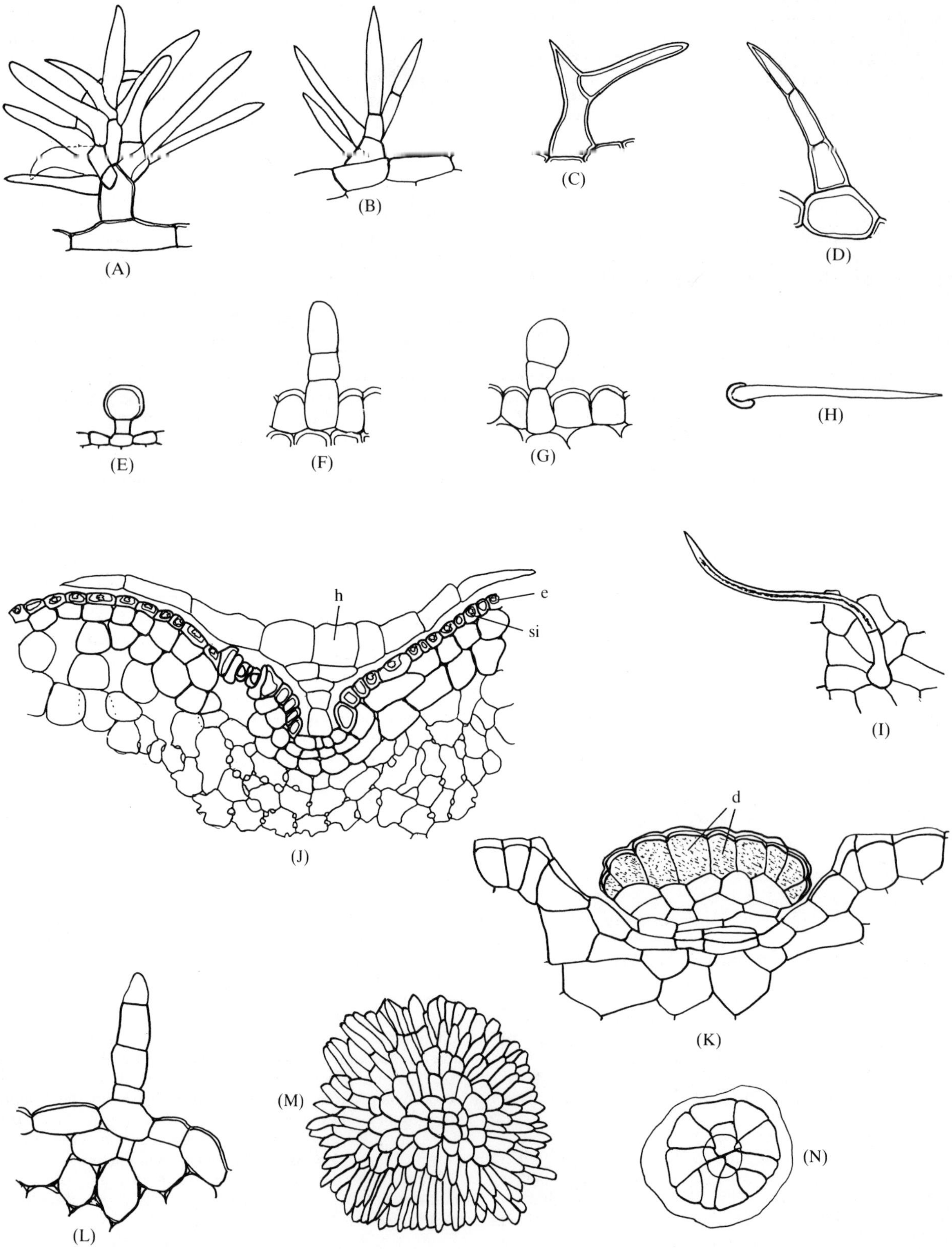


**5 A selection of hair types from leaves**

(A)–(C), (E) *Hyptis arborea* (×390), (A), (B), (C) various degrees of branching; (E) glandular, with a single short stalk cell and terminal glandular cell. (D) *Eriope* sp., simple uniseriate filamentous hair with thick walls. (F), (G) *Mentha × piperita* (×630), thin walled, uniseriate, hairs; (G) is glandular. (H) *Triticum dicoccum*, sharp, thick walled unicellular hair (×390). (I)–(N) *Myrica gale* (×390); (I) bicellular filamentous hair with dark contents. (N), surface view of peltate, glandular hair. (J), (M) *Puya chilensis*, non-glandular, peltate hair; (J) in TS, (M) in surface view (×160). (K) sunken multicellular glandular (enzyme producing) hair of the carnivorous *Nepenthes ampullaria*. (L) simple filamentous hair in *Cucurbita pepo* (×390).

d = dark cell contents; e = epidermis; h = hair; si = silica body.

which is very distinctive in roots. Although roots lack nodes and internodes, they can in some species develop adventitious buds, a feature made use of in propagation, so the presence or absence of buds is not an absolute guide in distinguishing roots from shoots.

The apical meristem is protected from damage as the root pushes through soil by a root cap. This is a thimble-like structure, developed by the meristem to its outer side. The edges of the root cap wear away as the root grows, but its tip is constantly renewed. Root caps can be seen readily on the tips of aerial roots in epiphytes. The apical meristem of the root produces no lateral organs, unlike the stem apex, in which leaf buttresses are formed, and a little distance from the apex, bud initials, in the axils of the forming leaves. Fig. 1C shows a diagram of a root apical meristem.

Working from the outside, inwards, the root epidermis (rhizodermis) forms the covering of the primary root; a cuticle is very thin or absent. The rhizodermis usually bears root hairs a short distance from the tip, but some, for example in apples, do not. In some epiphytes, the aerial roots have a multiple epidermis, or velamen. This is a common feature in orchids and is thought to aid water absorption and retention. The cortex may be composed entirely of parenchyma, or there may be a distinct layer (or layers) of exodermal cells, with lignified cell walls some way into the cortex.

In water plants and those usually growing in waterlogged soils, the cortex can have very large air spaces, joined to some in the stem, and allowing gas exchange to take place. In plants that are normally adapted to growth in dryer, better aerated soils, the cortex is 'solid', and lacking large air spaces, although it is a feature of cortical parenchyma cells that they usually have well-developed intercellular spaces. The inner boundary of the cortex is formed by the endodermis. This is composed of one or more layers of specialized cells, most of which have a band of suberised thickening in their anticlinal walls called the casparian strip, band or thickening. This effectively waterproofs the walls, and means that any water being taken up by the root has to pass through the cell cytoplasm, via membranes that can control which minerals are passed into the plant. Potentially harmful elements, usually metals, can thus be confined to the cortex.

Some of the grasses that can colonize spoil heaps which contain heavy metals do so by virtue of their exceptional ability to control their uptake of the metals.

At regular intervals round the endodermis are passage cells. These remain relatively thin walled, when as in the normal course of development, the other endodermal cells have thickening layers on their inner periclinal and anticlinal walls, the U-shaped thickenings.

Inside the endodermis is the one- to several- layered pericycle; parenchymatous tissue, unspecialized, and thin walled. It is from this that root branches develop in dicots and conifers, and since it is next to the vascular system, it enables the newly developing roots to be directly 'plumbed in'. The primary vascular system consists of xylem strands alternating with phloem strands. The protoxylem poles of the xylem strands are oriented outwards (exarch), with the metaxylem to their inner side. This is the opposite of stems, where the protoxylem points to the stem centre (endarch). Passage cells of the endodermis are opposite the protoxylem poles. The centre of the root may be thin-walled parenchyma, but often the cell walls become thickened and lignified (Fig. 1D–F).

Usually in dicots there are three, four or five protoxylem poles, and the roots are called triarch, tetrarch or pentarch, respectively (Fig. 1D–F). Conifers are commonly diarch or triarch. Monocots, in which roots remain primary, frequently have a large number of protoxylem poles, and are termed polyarch.

There are several specialized root forms. In monocots with bulbs or corms, some roots are often contractile and adjust the depth of the storage organ in the soil. It is often the central vascular system which contracts, and the cortex becomes distorted, like a concertina. Other monocot roots may develop an especially wide cortex, and may store water. The roots themselves may become thickened for food storage. Common examples are *Dahlia*, carrot, parsnip and celandine. Food storage is often associated with secondary thickening.

SECONDARY GROWTH IN THICKNESS. *The vascular cambium.* Stems in monocots, dicots and gymnosperms, and roots in dicots and gymnosperms, may grow in thickness by secondary growth. Growth in stem thickness is far more common in dicots and gymnosperms than in monocots, and the method of thickening in monocots is very different from that in the others. In dicots and gymnosperms the vascular bundles have parenchymatous cells between the phloem and xylem that have retained their juvenile, unspecialized condition. They are able to divide, like the meristem cells of the growing shoot and root tips. They constitute the vascular cambium and form by cell division additional phloem cells to the outside, and xylem cells to the inside (Fig. 7H). Generally about seven times more xylem than phloem cells are formed, so the xylem develops at a much more rapid rate. In most dicots and all gymnosperms the cells in the parenchyma between the vascular bundles also become meristematic, forming a cambium (called the interfascicular cambium, a term that harks back to the time when the vascular bundles themselves were called 'fascicles' and had 'fascicular cambium') and join in a ring with the cambium of the vascular bundles. The interfascicular cambium cells also divide to form phloem to the outside and xylem to the inside. In this way a complete vascular cylinder is formed.

In some climbing dicot species, the cambium between the vascular bundles, or the parenchyma cells between the bundles, divides to form additional parenchyma only, not phloem and xylem. This seems to be an adaptation that provides parts of the stem which can be compressed during twining, without loss of the conducting function of the vascular system, which remains as individual strands, each strand growing mainly in radial and only very slightly in tangential thickness (Fig. 7D). In the dicots, the cambium can in some species periodically produce layers of phloem to the inner side, and then revert to xylem formation. This is found in some mangrove species, for example.

As the stem increases in thickness, the cambium is pushed further and further from the stem centre by newly formed xylem. It would split if it were not for the fact that it adds to its circumference by cell divisions at right angles (anticlinal divisions) to those forming the layers of phloem and xylem. The phloem is squashed against the cortex by the outward movement of the cambium. Its outer cells become compressed, and eventually reabsorbed. Increase in the circumference of the phloem is often effected by cell expansion, particularly in the outer parts of the rays. Growth in root thickness is described above.

Monocots' stems cannot increase in thickness in the same way as dicots because the vascular bundles do not develop a cambium. They are termed 'closed' as opposed to 'open'. Indeed, the bundles in the stem are frequently ensheathed by fibres. As mentioned above, the thickness of palm stems is established in the apex of the shoot, which becomes very wide in some species by cell divisions in the primary thickening meristem. This produces large amounts of parenchyma, in which are embedded the very numerous vascular bundles developing to supply the large leaves.

The stems of some monocots increase in width by the cell divisions in a secondary thickening meristem that develops in the parenchyma of the outer cortex. This produces entire, new vascular bundles, set in a parenchymatous ground tissue. *Dracaena* and some *Aloe* species show this type of thickening.

*The cork cambium.* When the stem thickens, in monocots, dicots or gymnosperms, it is clear that the epidermis will soon be subject to considerable stress, and unless its cells divide anticlinally, it will rupture, and it usually does. The protective function is replaced by the development of a new system, a peripheral meristem call the phellogen, or cork cambium. This forms phellem or cork cells by division to the outer side, and parenchymatous phelloderm cells to the inner side (Fig. 7G). The walls of some or all of the cork cells become impregnated with a waterproof substance, suberin. The phellogen can develop from cell layers any-

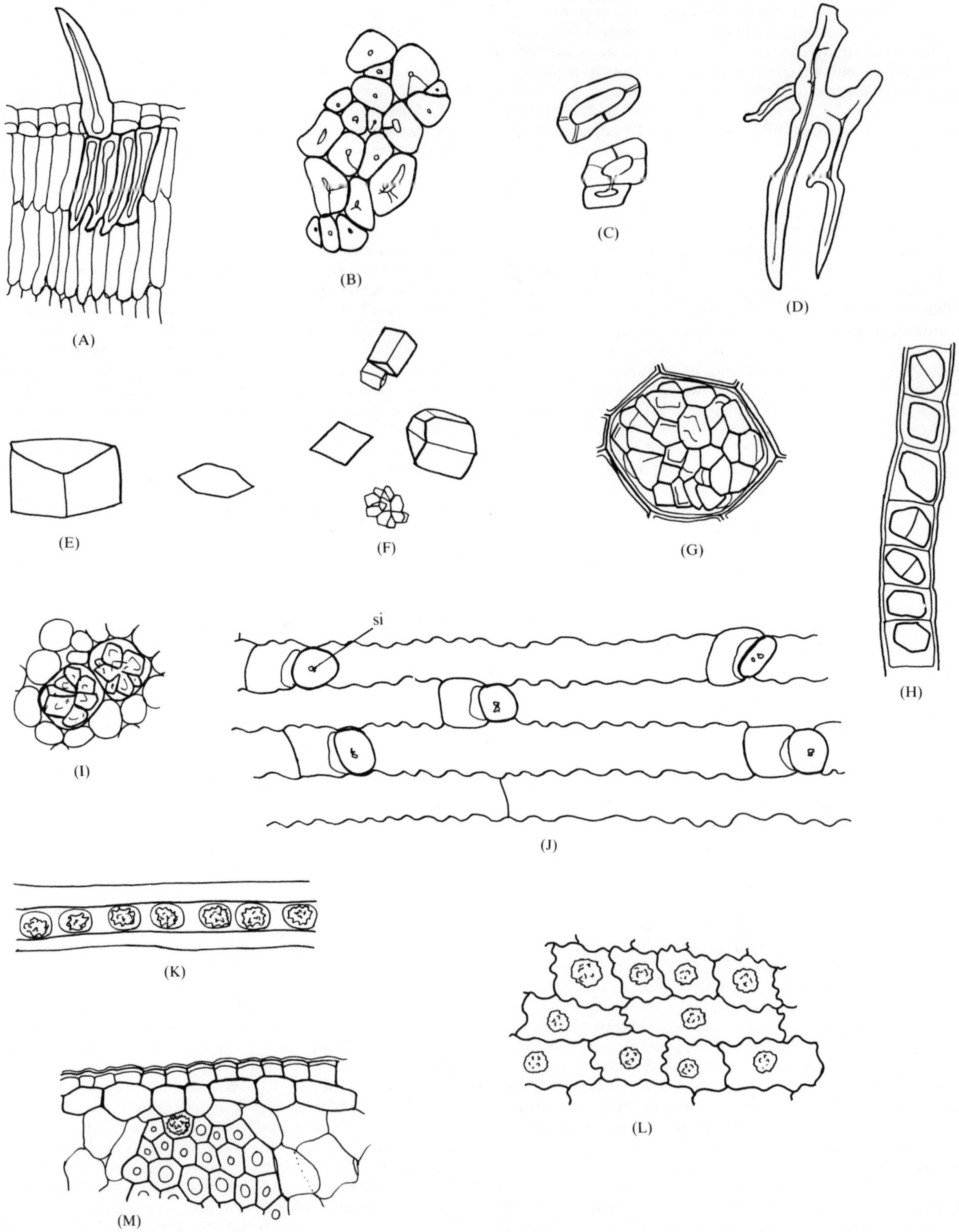


**6 Sclereids, crystals and silica bodies**

(A) *Boscia* sp., with short, columnar sclereids in outer palisade mesophyll of leaf; note unicellular, thick walled hair (×160). (B) group of more or less isodiametric sclereids from bark of *Fraxinus excelsior* (×630). (C) similar sclereids from bark of *Calluna vulgaris* (×630). (D) *Osmanthus* sp., branched astrosclereid from leaf (×160). (E) *Vaccinium vitis-idaea*, rhombic crystals from bark (×630). (F) *Calluna vulgaris*, rhombic and cluster crystals (druses) from bark (×630). (G), (I) *Parottia persica*, large cluster crystal from petiole and smaller ones from mesophyll (×630). (H) chambered crystals from wood of *Prosopis chilensis* (×630). (J) Silica bodies in short epidermal cells of *Triticum dicoccum* leaf (×630). (K)–(L) *Washingtonia filifera*, row of spheroidal nodular silica bodies in cell adjacent to sclerenchyma bundle cap (×630); (K) as seen in LS, (L) in TS. (M) *Puya chilensis* leaf epidermis with silica bodies (×630).

si = silica body.

where in the cortex, and its position – near the surface, further in or deep seated – is a feature of the species concerned.

*Bark*. The outer appearance of the bark is dependent on the nature of the cork layers and the cortex. Lenticels are areas of unsuberised cells, often forming beneath the original epidermal stomata. They can be very conspicuous, for example in *Prunus*. If the cork cells are laid down in bands of suberised and unsuberised layers, the bark will peel, as in *Betula*. If there is a succession of new cork cambia, each new one deeper in than the others, the bark may fissure and fall in flakes or plates, as in *Platanus*. Barks with high fibre contents may become stringy, for example some *Eucalyptus* species. Commercial cork comes from harvesting of the outer bark layers of *Quercus suber*. Several years of growth (about seven) are allowed to accrue, and the bark carefully peeled. There is only one, persistent cork cambium in this species.

*Wound healing and grafts*. When plants are injured, the cells in the damaged area that are relatively unspecialized, such as parenchyma, are capable of reorganizing themselves and becoming meristematic. They can then divide and form cells that start to heal the wound. If the vascular or cork cambia are exposed, they often respond quickly. The cells produced are at first parenchymatous, and form a callus. Later they may be influenced by undamaged cells close to them, and become corky, or become organized to form a new extension of the cambium which then divides to produce new xylem and phloem. The wound can thus heal over. In horticulture, removal of branches is a common practice. If the branch is sawn off slightly proud of the surface, the cells in the 'collar' of the branch stand a chance of dividing to form the wound healing callus, and wound healing is much more rapid than if the branch is sawn off flush, removing the collar.

The closed nature of monocot vascular bundles, lacking cambium, means that grafting cannot take place in monocots. Grafting relies on the presence of a cambium and its ability to influence the wound callus parenchyma cells which develop when grafts are attempted. In dicots and gymnosperms, when the stock and scion are cut, a wound response occurs, leading to a proliferation of parenchymatous callus tissue. If the two parts were not brought together, so that the vascular cambium of each was as close as possible, wound healing would normally occur. However, in the graft, part of the callus is induced by the cambium to become cambium itself (rather as the tissue between the dicot primary vascular bundles is induced to form interfascicular cambium at the onset of secondary growth in thickness). This new cambium bridges the gap between the stock and scion, and in time, with the development of successive growth increments of new phloem and xylem, the union becomes strong. Since the cambium is a very delicate tissue, there must be no movement between stock and scion, or bud and stem in bud grafting, until the new bond is formed. This is why grafts are held securely with grafting tape or other materials when they are made.

*Secondary xylem*. Of the products of the vascular cambium, the secondary xylem forms a much larger proportion of the stem than does the secondary phloem. There is often annual periodicity in the formation of growth increments, particularly in plants from temperate climates, but trees from the tropics may have no clear boundaries between the growth from one year and that of the next. The increments, when clearly defined, are called annual rings; however, it is possible for a late frost, or severe defoliation mid-season, to result in an additional growth ring being formed in a year. Dendrochronology, the science of dating wood from a study of growth ring width, depends on the fact that there is variation in width from year to year, in response to the differing weather conditions. Trees of the same species, from the same region, can be expedited to respond similarly. So a very old tree of known age can act as an index for the age of woods of trees of the same species that grew for part of their lives during the same period. In fact a chronology of growth ring widths is built up from the evidence provided by thousands of trees.

The growth rings in some species are easy to see in cross section (TS), often with the unaided eye, but certainly with a ×10 lens, because the first formed vessels of each year are much wider than the later formed vessels. Oak, ash and elm are all examples of these 'ring porous' woods (Fig. 8A). It is less easy to see the rings in woods where the early vessels are similar in widths to those formed later (diffuse porous) unless a lens is used; beech, holly lime and apple are examples of these woods.

In primary xylem, all the cells are elongated in the direction of the long axis of the stem (some more than other, fibres are longer than parenchyma cells for example). In secondary xylem, there is an additional tissue system that is orientated at right angles to the long axis of the stem, and is composed of structures that radiate from the cambium towards the stem centre, called rays. Rays are formed by the division of short cells in the vascular cambium called ray initials. They extend into both phloem and xylem (Fig. 7H). The height of a ray can be seen in a section cut at a tangent to the stem axis (a tangential, longitudinal section, TLS.); Fig. 8C, G. When the wood is cut along a radius, in a longitudinal direction (RLS), the side view of a ray can be seen. Fig. 8A, D, H shows the three-dimensional structure of secondary wood. Wood anatomists need to study the TWS, TLS, and RLS of a sample, so that they can see all the features of the axial and radial systems.

The rays are composed largely of parenchyma, which in many woods acts as a storage region for starch reserves, and a place where tannins, crystals, silica bodies and other substances can be held without affecting the flow of the sap. In gymnosperms it is common for tracheids to be present in the rays, orientated with their long axis radial, (Fig. 8H) and in some dicots there are radially orientated vessel elements and tracheids. However, parenchyma cells are usually the most conspicuous tissue type. Rays can be one cell layer wide (as seen in TLS), when they are termed uniseriate (Fig. 8G). Biseriate rays are two cells wide at their widest part, and multiseriate rays several to many cells wide. In TLS, it can be seen that the widest part of the ray is usually mid way between top and bottom, frequently giving a lens-shaped outline (Fig. 8A). Ray width and height are important diagnostic characters, more or less typical of a species. Rays are present in most species with secondary xylem. *Hebe* is an interesting exception.

Ray parenchyma cells may be procumbent, that is longer than high, or they may be square or upright as seen in RLS. They can all be similar in shape and size, when the ray is termed homocellular, or they may be of two or more shapes or sizes, forming a heterocellular ray. Sometimes those in the outer layer are conspicuously different from the rest, and are called sheath cells. So there is a very wide range of permutations and combinations possible, each of which is characteristic of the species, but many are shared by a wide range of species, often in different families.

The axial system of the wood of gymnosperms consists mainly of the multi-purpose tracheids (Fig. 8F, G), but may also have axial parenchyma cells. Dicot wood is more complex, with more evident division of labour between the cells types. Vessels are present in all but the more primitive families, for example, *Drimys* of the Winteraceae. They may be solitary, that is separate from one another, as seen in TS, or variously grouped into radial chains, multiples, tangentially or obliquely oriented chains and so on. Their outline in TS may be rounded or angular (Fig. 8B, E). They show the range of perforation plates described above, usually with only one type predominating in a species. In many species where the vessels have coarse wall pitting, the older vessels develop tyloses that block them. These are formed by the intrusion of the cell walls of parenchyma next to the vessel element into the lumen, where they extend to fill the space. Tyloses may remain thin-walled, or the walls may become thickened. Tylosis can be a response to wounding, or the ingress of a pathogen. The overproduction of tyloses in elms, in response to invasion by the fungus responsible for Dutch elm disease, causes the premature death of branches that thereby had their water supply cut off. Tracheids may or may not be present. They are usually narrower than vessels, and are often adjacent to them.

Fibres are usually present to a greater or lesser extent (Fig. 8B, E). Their walls are usually of even thickness, ranging from very thick, with little or no lumen to thin. (The lumen is the

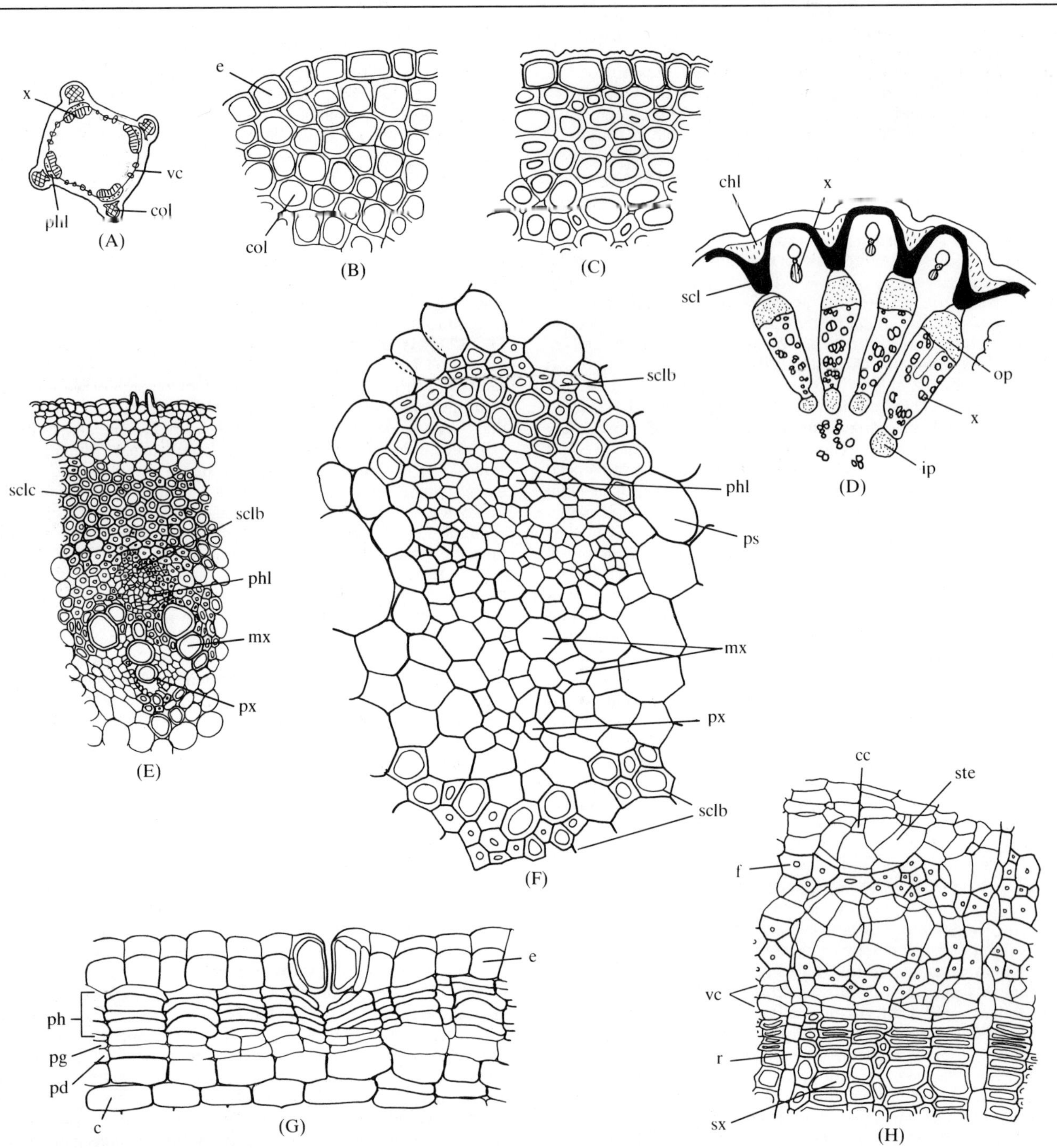


**7 Details of primary and secondary stem** TS (C, leaf)

(A), (B) *Mentha* × *piperita*; (A) low magnification diagram of 'square' section, with collenchyma in angles, opposite major vascular bundles; smaller bundles becoming joined together and to larger bundles by vascular cambium (×12.5). (B) collenchyma from stem angle (×390). (C) *Sonneratia alba* leaf, collenchyma beneath adaxial epidermis, at midrib. (D) *Acanthosicyos horridus*; vascular bundles remain separate during secondary growth in thickness, and are bicollateral, with phloem adjacent to both metaxylem and protoxylem. A ring of smaller outer bundles is found next to the ribbed sclerenchyma cylinder (×12.5). (E) *Stipa* sp. has a well developed sclerenchyma cylinder to the inner side of the chlorenchyma; in it are embedded the closed vascular bundles (lacking vascular cambium), one of which is shown. The sclerenchyma bundle cap at the phloem pole is distinct, since its fibres are much narrower than those of the sclerenchyma cylinder (×160). (F) *Eulophia petersii*; this vascular bundle is also closed; in addition to the sclerenchyma bundle caps it shows a partly encircling parenchyma sheath. The metaxylem tracheids are thin walled (×390). (G) *Tilia* 'Petiolaris', early stage in development of periderm; the epidermis is still intact and a phellogen has developed by division of cortical cells close to the epidermis. Several layers of phellem (cork) and a layer of phelloderm have been formed by divisions in the phellogen (×400). (H) *Tilia tomentosa*, sector of vascular cambium. The cambial zone is 2–3-layered; newly formed secondary xylem has become thick walled; rays and cells of the axial system can be seen. Rays are present but less distinct in the secondary phloem, where sieve tube elements and companion cells, and phloem fibres can be seen (×400).

c = cortex; cc = companion cell; chl = chlorenchyma; col = collenchyma; e = epidermis; f = fibre; ip = inner phloem; mx = metaxylem; op = outer phloem; pd = periderm; pg = phellogen, ph = phellem; phl = phloem; ps = parenchyma sheath; px = protoxylem; r = ray; scl = sclerenchyma; sclb = sclerenchyma bundle cap; sclc = sclerenchyma cylinder; ste = sieve tube element; sx = secondary xylem vessel; vc = vascular cambium; x = xylem.

cell cavity, which in living cells contains the cytoplasm and nucleus, and in dead cells may be empty.) Their proportion and degree of wall thickening have a marked effect on wood density. In many species they are the main cell type between the vessels; the other is axial parenchyma. In conifers axial (and radial) resin canals may be present. These are lined by a layer of secretory, epithelial parenchyma. Secretory canals, secreting a range of substances, are also found in some dicot woods.

Axial parenchyma cells may be scattered in between the vessels and fibres, or grouped into tangential bands, sometimes marking the beginning or end of a growth boundary. They may be centred on or closely related to the vessel distribution, where they are termed paratracheal, or not related to vessels and apotracheal. Paratracheal arrangements, with lateral wing-like extensions (aliform) are common in legume woods. In LS, axial parenchyma cells often appear in chains of two to eight; they are derived from the same elongated (fusiform) cambial initials that produce vessel elements, fibres and tracheids. If no subsequent division occurs, the parenchyma cells remain fusiform.

In some families, the cambium is arranged in a regularly storeyed way, like levels in a building. This can result in their products also being storeyed. This is particularly striking when rays are storeyed and appear in regular rows as seen in TLS. Axial parenchyma and fibres also often retain the storeyed arrangement, as do the narrower vessel elements, but often fibres grow in length after they have been formed, and wider vessel elements tend to lose the regular appearance.

Crystals are common in ray cells and axial parenchyma or fibres; in the latter two, the cells may become subdivided or chambered, each unit with a crystal. The crystals can show a wide range of forms, but are mostly composed of calcium oxalate. Silica bodies when present in wood give it very poor working properties, since they are hard, and will blunt tools. Wood containing silica bodies, however, can often last well under water. The various animals that bore into wood similarly suffer from a blunting of their cutting parts. Tannins and other substances are commonly deposited in the inner growth rings, contributing to the darker colour of the heartwood. The outer sapwood generally lacks the dark coloured deposits, and hence is lighter in colour.

Wood, then is a very complex material, each species with its own characteristic combination of features which usually enables one to identify it (or to a group of closely related species) by microscopic examination. The wide range of different character combinations that exist in different species accounts for the range of their different properties and so their uses.

*Secondary thickening in roots*. Dicot and conifer roots (but not monocot roots) commonly have the ability to become secondarily thickened. They develop a vascular cambium between the phloem and xylem; at first this follows the star-like outline of the primary xylem, but after several growth increments, assumes a circular or oval outline in TS. As mentioned above, root wood is softer and more parenchymatous than trunk wood (Fig. 1F).

As in the stems, the epidermis (rhizodermis) splits as the root grows in diameter, and a cork cambium develops in the cortex, providing a root bark, in combination with cortex and secondary phloem tissues.

Secondarily thickened roots of pencil thickness and above can often be identified by careful analysis of their xylem and bark characters. This is particularly valuable when it is necessary to find which of a number of trees of different species close to a root-blocked drain is the culprit, or is the possible cause of damage to the foundations of a building. The owner of a tree is responsible for its roots!

VEGETATIVE PROPAGATION. Mention has been made of the ability of relatively undifferentiated cells to become meristematic again under certain circumstances, for example wounding. This is the basis for several common horticultural methods of propagation.

In stem and root cuttings the damaged cambium at the lower end of the cutting develops a wound callus, which in time produces new root apex initials, and hence new roots, in suitable material. These are called adventitious roots, since they form in places where roots would not normally be expected. Sometimes roots develop adventitiously from the nodal region in cuttings. There is usually a lot of parenchyma in nodes. Where layering of shoots is successful, adventitious roots arise from nodes of stems bent and held down below soil level. *Erica* and *Rhododendron* are commonly propagated by layering; it may not be necessary to bruise the nodal tissue to stimulate rooting although it often helps. Air layering of plants like *Ficus* also depends on the rooting response to a moist environment. Some plants spread naturally by rooting at the nodes, for example couch grass; this helps to make it such a difficult weed to remove by mechanical means. Even small stem (rhizome) fragments will root. *Rubus* also spreads by rooting at nodes or tips of scrambling stems.

In some species, stem cuttings will not root unless they are 'soft'. This is often because when 'ripe' or hard, they develop fibres and sclereids in the cortex that act as a mechanical barrier to the roots that arise from deep in the tissue, preventing them from emerging. Taking cuttings young, before the barrier develops, can be a help. Misting, shade and bottom heat help such softwood cuttings to root before they wilt and die. If neither soft nor hardwood cuttings from stems succeed, it is worth trying root cuttings. These often need to be collected in the autumn, stored in a cool, dark, frost-free place, in bundles. The ends callus over, and in the spring, the cuttings can be put in trays, in rooting compost. They often do best if inserted upright and lightly covered; they need to be the right way up. If a sloping cut is used to mark the lower end, and the upper end trimmed straight on collection, there is no problem in knowing which way up they are.

In leaf cuttings, prepared with or without damaging the veins, new root and shoot initials may form, and whole new plantlets develop either from vein ends (e.g. *Bryophyllum*) or along the veins (e.g. *Gloxinia*). In leaf cuttings where new plantlets develop from the cut end of the petiole (e.g. African violets), it is usually as a result of a wound callus forming first, leading to the development of root and shoot initials.

Tissue culture and meristem culture both depend on the development of a callus from small fragments of plant material placed in or on a suitable sterile culture medium. It is from the callus, again, that the development of new plantlets is induced. The process is rarely straightforward, and experiments have to be done to produce the correct balance of nutrients and hormones in the medium to stimulate the growth of both shoots and roots.

FLOWER ANATOMY IN ANGIOSPERMS. Flowers are specialized structures that in evolution have become efficient in sexual reproduction. This type of reproduction involves fusion of male and female gametes and leads to fruit and seed production. A flower consists of an axis bearing floral organs. There is great diversity in flower form and arrangement, and number of parts. Here a generalized flower will be described, and the basic anatomy of the reproductive parts discussed.

Some floral organs are sterile, the sepals and petals (often indistinguishable in monocots, and called tepals). Others are fertile, the stamens (male) in the androecium, composed of the anther and filament, and the carpels (female) in the gynoecium, with stigma, style and ovary. One or more carpels may form the ovary.

The sterile petals or tepals are often little developed in flowers that are wind pollinated, but showy in animal pollinated flowers, with morphological adaptations that suit particular pollinators to particular flowers. Where they are insect pollinated in particular, there are often also anatomical features of the petal epidermis adapted to the attraction and comfort of the pollinator. Some petal colour is optical; the shape of the epidermal cells can cause interference colours to be seen. Special footholds may be developed, giving purchase to the feet of the pollinator. In the petal cells there may be pigments, either as solid inclusions, or as part of the cell sap. Some pigments are visible only in the ultraviolet part of the spectrum, which can be seen by insects. Nectaries are a further attractant, provided in many species.

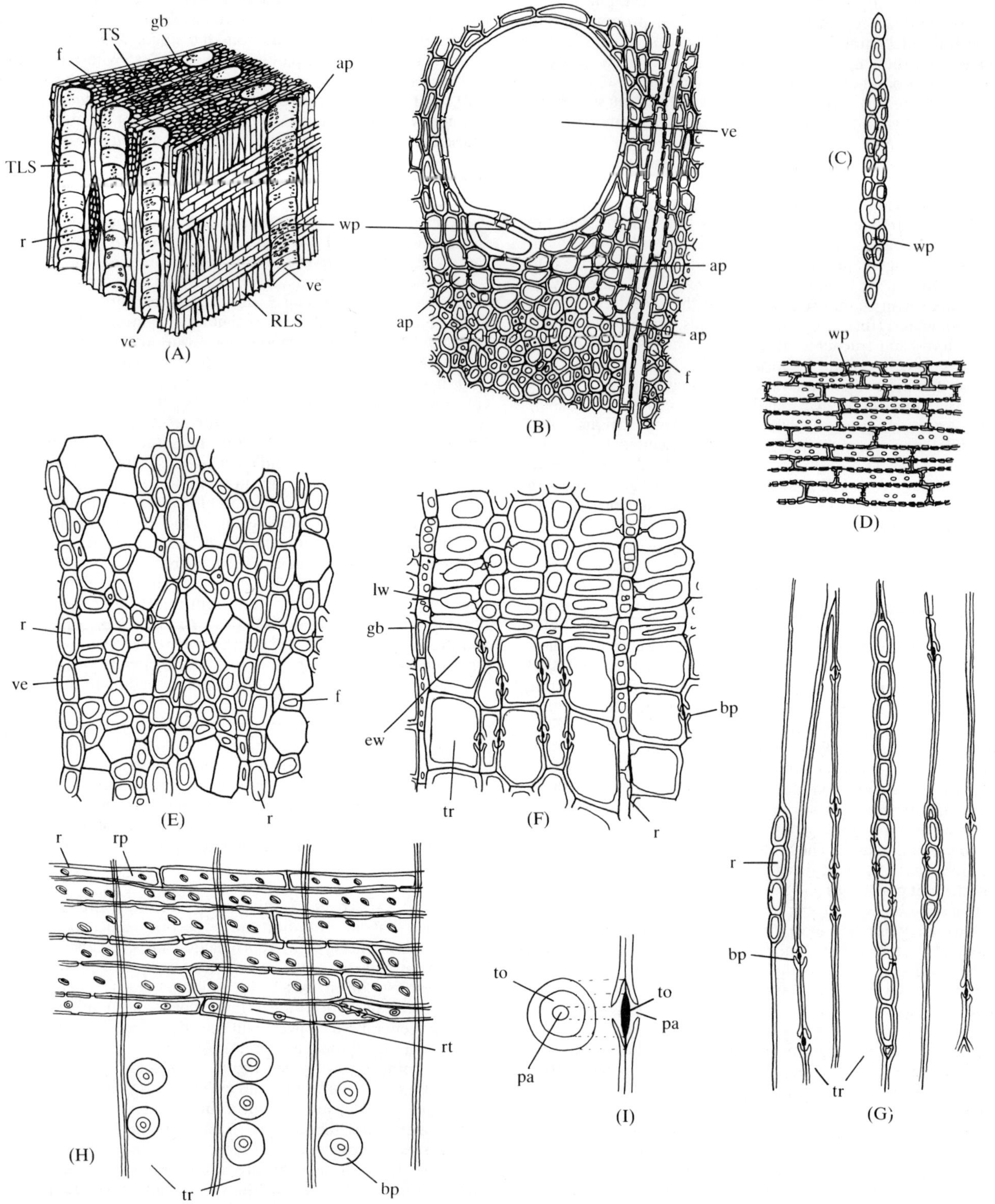


**8** (A) diagram of cube of secondary xylem, showing the planes from which sections are made: TS = transverse section; TLS = tangential longitudinal section; RLS = radial longitudinal section. Note the wide vessels of early wood and the narrower ones of late wood, the rays, fibres and axial parenchyma. (B)–(D) *Prosopis chilensis* secondary xylem (×320). (B) TS; note wide vessel with bordered pits in the thick wall, thick walled axial fibres, thin walled axial parenchyma and a ray. (C) ray in TLS, (D) ray in RLS; note wall pitting. (E) *Empetrum nigrum*, TS secondary xylem showing narrow, thin walled vessels in multiples, fibres and rays (×350). (F)–(I) *Larix decidua* secondary xylem: (F) TS, tracheids and rays; note distinct growth ring boundary, with narrower tracheids of late wood bordering wide, early wood tracheids; bordered pit pairs can be seen (×320). (G) TLS and (H) RLS, with rays and tracheids. The rays are composed of ray parenchyma and ray tracheids, each with distinct wall pitting (×320). (I) diagram of bordered pit pair in surface view and section; note the torus, a thickening of the pit membrane, the overaching pit borders and the narrow pit aperture.

ap = axial arpenchyma; bp = bordered pit; cp = cross field pit; ew = early wood; f = fibre; gb = growth boundary; lw = late wood; pa = pit aperture; r = ray; rp = ray parenchyma; rt = ray tracheid; to = torus; tr = tracheid; ve = vessel; wp = wall pitting.

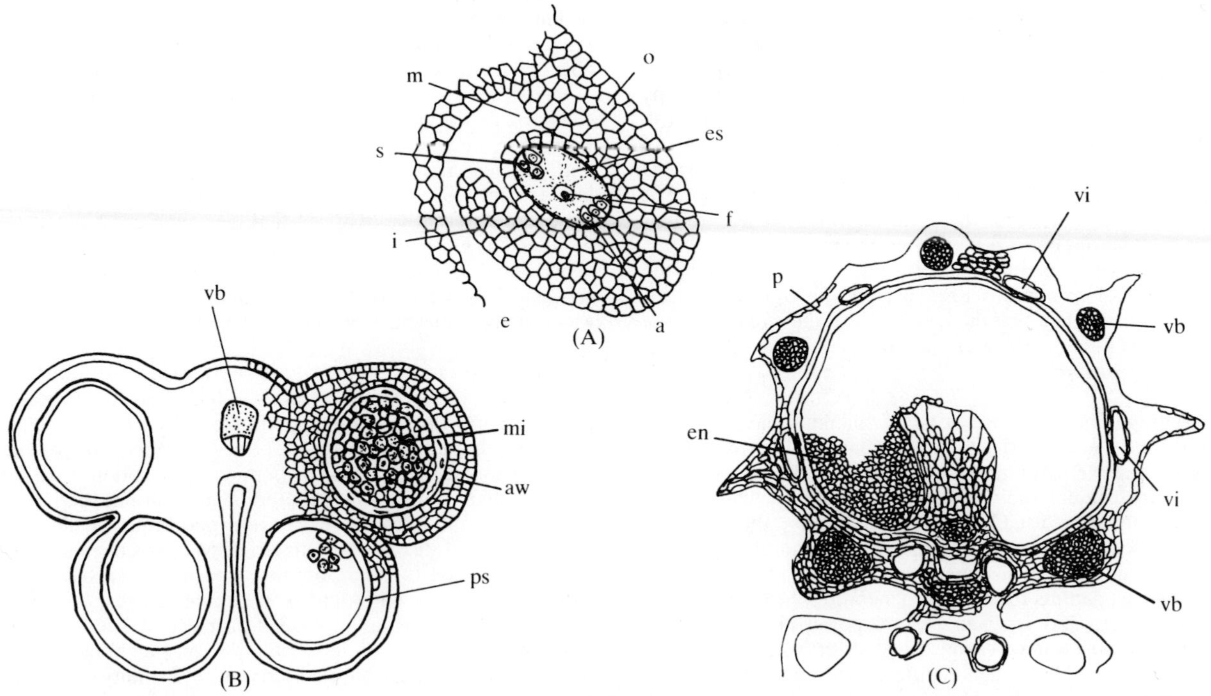


**9** (A) Diagram of immature ovule, LS, showing embryo sac with central fusion nucleus, antipodal cells, egg cell and synergids. The micropyle becomes narrow at maturity (×60). (B) *Lilium* immature anther, TS, with pollen sacs containing microsporocytes which divide to form pollen grains. Cell detail drawn only in part (×35). (C) diagram of half of a mericarp (fruit) of *Foeniculum* sp., showing vittae (secretory canals) in fruit wall (pericarp), vascular bundles and storage tissue. Cell detail drawn only in part (×35).

a = antipodal cells; aw = anther wall; e = egg cell; es = embryo sac; en = endosperm; f = fusion nucleus; i = integument; m = micropyle; mi = microsporocytes; p = pericarp; ps = pollen sacs; vb = vascular bundle; vi = vitta.

The anthers usually have two pollen sacs, in which numerous pollen mother cells (microsporocytes) are formed (Fig. 9A). These cells are diploid (with $2n$ chromosomes) and each divides by meiosis, a reduction division, halving the chromosome number in the resultant four cells, to form four haploid pollen grains (each with $n$ chromosomes). Ovules develop on the carpels; each is attached to the ovary wall by a short stalk, the funicle. There are two longitudinal files of ovules in the carpel of the pea, for example, and three carpels make up the syncarpous ovary of *Iris*. The ovules have a covering of one or two integuments; there is a small hole in them, the micropyle. At maturity, each ovule contains a very large cell, the embryo sac. This is the product of meiosis; it has the haploid ($n$) number of chromosomes. It is the survivor of four cells resulting from a meiotic division.

Further mitotic cell divisions (which retain the same number of chromosomes in each daughter cell) follow in both the pollen grain and the embryo sac. In the pollen grain, one $n$ nucleus is the male gamete, and in the embryo sac, one n nucleus is the female gamete (egg cell). Pollination brings the pollen to the stigma. The pollen germinates, and a pollen tube which grows down the style to allow the male gamete to reach the micropyle of the ovule, close to the embryo sac, which it enters, fusing with the egg cell to form the zygote (fertilization).

This means that the diploid number of chromosomes ($2n$) is restored. The zygote become the embryo of the seed. The diploid number is maintained in cell divisions (mitoses) in the meristems throughout the life of the new plant, from germination to maturity. Only in the pollen sacs and ovules do reduction divisions occur.

The fertilization process in angiosperms is complicated by the fact that in the embryo sac, two of the haploid nuclei other than the egg cell fuse and become $2n$; and in the pollen tube, a second haploid nucleus, in addition to the male gamete, enters the embryo sac and fuses with the $2n$ nucleus, forming a triploid, $3n$ cell. In seeds which develop an endosperm, it forms from this triploid cell. The outcome is a 'double fertilization', one of the characters that separates the angiosperms from the gymnosperms, in which only a single fertilization, to produce the zygote, takes place. The anatomy of the cross section of an anther is shown in Fig. 9A, and an LS of an ovule is shown in Fig. 9B.

See also GENETICS.

SEED ANATOMY. In angiosperms the seed develops from an ovule, usually following fertilization. It has a seed coat, or testa, developed from the integuments, an embryo from the zygote and sometimes an endosperm from the triploid nucleus (see above). In some species the tissue around the embryo, the perisperm, may form food reserve (e.g. nutmeg) and in others, the seed leaves or cotyledons may store food (e.g. pea). Food reserve materials include starch granules, fats, oils and protein.

The micropyle may be visible, and if the stalk or funicle becomes detached, it can form a scar or ridge, the raphe. Other appendages can develop, like a caruncle or an aril; these can have quite diverse origins.

The testa cells may become thick-walled; hairs or projections may form, or some cells might become mucilaginous. The adaptations are often related to the mains of dispersal and the length of time the seed might remain dormant. A range of different pigments may develop. Seed coat appearance is characteristic of a species, and can be used in identification.

The embryo has an axis called the hypocotyl-root axis. The shoot meristem forms at one end, and gives rise to the shoot bud, with cotyledon(s) and the stem apical meristem. At the other end is the root meristem, often with a root cap.

FRUIT ANATOMY. In true fruits, the ovary wall develops into the fruit wall or pericarp. When closely surrounding a single seed, it can itself appear seed-like; the caryopses of grasses and the achenes of buttercups are such fruits. Often several to many seeds are contained in a single ovary (carpel), as in legumes, and several carpels may become fused into a complex fruit, as in *Lilium*.

The pericarp normally consists of three distinct tissue layers, the exocarp, mesocarp and endocarp. The plum is a wet or fleshy fruit; it displays the three layers. The skin is the exocarp, the flesh the mesocarp and the stone the endocarp, enclosing the seed. In dry fruits, the layers of the pericarp may be less distinct. Fig. 9C shows the dry fruit of *Foeniculum*, fennel. The legume pod is often fleshy when immature, the state in which we eat runner beams and mangetout peas; as it matures, the mesocarp dries up.

False fruits develop in a number of ways; the fleshy part of the apple or pear, for example is formed from the top of the fruit stalk, or receptacle enclosing the true fruit. In the strawberry the receptacle swells and becomes succulent, bearing the fruits (achenes) on its surface.

**Plant breeding**. For thousands of years, mankind has cultivated plants for food, fuel, clothing and ornament. The process of cultivation creates environments which differ from the wild. In order to flourish under their new living conditions, wild species taken into cultivation usually change genetically, that is, they evolve under domestication. This is distinct from another process, surely of great antiquity, where certain plants within the cultivated crop are saved as parents for the next generation. Selection by the new environment, and by man, exerts powerful evolutionary pressures: crops which have been cultivated for a short time usually show appreciable genetic differences from their wild progenitors; those that have been cultivated for millennia may have evolved so far that their wild parents are a matter of speculation.

The sciences of botany and, more recently, genetics have been responsible for further genetic change in crop plants. A series of techniques derived from these sciences have greatly increased man's ability to breed plants that comply with precise requirements. This new technology – plant breeding – can be defined as the fixation of a desirable combination of genes in a cultivar.

There are broadly two types of cultivars: those where a good genetic combination is maintained by avoiding the genetic mixing associated with sexual reproduction – these are clonal cultivars, propagated vegetatively; and those where genetic recombination is manipulated to produce the desired genetic mix in seed-propagated cultivars. Both types are of great importance in horticultural crops. With a few exceptions, clonal cultivars are derived from perennial species (trees, shrubs, divisible herbaceous plants, or species with perennating organs such as bulbs, runners, stolons or tubers), while seed-propagated cultivars derive from annual or biennial species.

TRADITIONAL HORTICULTURAL BREEDING. The basic technique with clonal breeding is to generate a genetically variable population by hybridizing two or more cultivars, or related species, or even genera. The hybrid plants are grown and the best individuals are identified. These are propagated clonally by any of several methods, including dividing (as for herbaceous ornamentals), striking cuttings (soft fruit and tropical fruits like breadfruit), or grafting on to stock plants (top fruit, tropicals like mango, avocado and citrus).

Most bedding plants and vegetables are produced from seed. Until about the 1940s, seed-propagated cultivars were open-pollinated (OP), that is, each new generation of a cultivar came from seed produced by allowing plants of the preceding generation to flower together. Breeding consisted of saving the best plants so that their genes could contribute to the next generation. An increasing knowledge of genetics meant that the identification of the best parents became less haphazard. For example, statistical analysis of the good and bad aspects of the progeny from known parents gave better information about which parents contained the best genes, or could contribute to the best genetic combinations in their offspring.

It was common for seedsmen to advertise their stocks of well-established clonal or seed-based cultivars as 'improved', 'reselected' or 'so-and-so's strain', reflecting attempts to maintain or improve the cultivar. Modern marketing and legislation have rendered these terms redundant (or even illegal) for most vegetable and fruit species, but they persist in ornamental species.

There were clear differences in the kinds of open-pollinated cultivars, depending on the natural breeding system of the species. Inbreeders (e.g. lettuce, tomato, peas) consisted of genetically uniform cultivars which tended to give uniform crops. In order to breed improved cultivars of inbreeders it was necessary to hybridize different cultivars so that new gene combinations could be selected. Outbreeders – the majority of species – consisted of genetically variable cultivars, often referred to as land-races, or strains. These gave variable crops, and selection within a cultivar was usually sufficient to achieve a genetic improvement in these species.

MODERN HORTICULTURAL BREEDING. The recent advent of micropropagation (tissue culture) has helped increase the efficiency of propagating clonal cultivars. The cost per plant has decreased dramatically in some species, notably some orchids. In other cases (such as potatoes), micropropagation may not be cheaper than conventional methods of multiplication but may allow faster multiplication, easier transport of propagules, and the maintenance of disease-free material. Micropropagation has also led to the clonal breeding of some species which had otherwise been restricted to seed propagation (e.g. asparagus).

Much of the breeding of seed-propagated species since the 1940s has depended on manipulation of the breeding system, particularly to give F1 hybrid cultivars. The ability of breeders to exploit the breeding system of plants to produce F1 cultivars has been a deciding factor in determining which vegetable and ornamental species have become or remained important since the 1940s. Several 'cottage garden' species have slipped into obscurity because F1 breeding has been impractical or too expensive. Apart from the biological advantages of F1s – they are more uniform than OPs and can have higher yields – their main commercial advantage to the breeder is that seed saved from the crop will not breed true to the type, that is, the only source of seed of that cultivar is its breeder, who has, therefore, some protection over the investment he has made in breeding the cultivar.

F1 hybrid breeding uses two processes: the production of true breeding, inbred lines, and the hybridization of two of these lines to give the F1 cultivar. Generally, one of these processes exploits a 'natural' aspect of the species, and the other has to be manipulated artificially. Thus, some species (such as tomato and geranium) will naturally self-pollinate and produce inbred lines, but these must be hybridized by hand or with the help of 'artificial' male sterility, to produce F1 cultivars. Others (e.g. brassicas, primula) must be self-pollinated by hand or some other artificial method (e.g. by using high levels of carbon dioxide) to produce the inbred lines. Inbred lines can also be produced by repeatedly hybridizing closely related plants through several generations. 'Natural' systems which ensure cross-pollination are then exploited by the breeder to ensure that inbred lines hybridize to give the F1 cultivar.

Recent advances in genetics – particularly in knowledge of the chemistry of genes – are leading to several new techniques being adopted by breeders. These techniques, loosely referred to as 'genetic engineering', are likely during the 1990s to result in new colour forms in ornamentals, and perhaps resistance to pests and diseases in several horticultural species.

LEGISLATION. Most horticultural cultivars sold to the general public are subject to legislation designed to protect the buyer and the breeder.

Many countries, including those in the European Community, specify the levels of germination and trueness to type of seed of vegetable cultivars. It is likely that future legislation will extend such consumer protection to young plants and other propagules, and perhaps other horticultural species.

The seed buyer in European Community countries is also protected by the National Listing of vegetable cultivars. Broadly, each new cultivar has to be tested officially to show distinctness from existing cultivars, uniformity of type, and stability across different samples (referred to as DUS tests). Another set of tests – VCU (value for cultivation and use) – is also necessary for National Listing, but is currently restricted to agricultural crops, although this includes potatoes. Until a cultivar is accepted onto the National List, it cannot legally be sold. It is then entered on to the EC Common Catalogue of Varieties, and can be sold in any EC country. The current EC legislation is restricted to sales of seed, but in future is likely to include young plants.

An international convention, coordinated by the Union for Protection of New Varieties of Plants (UPOV), allows breeders to register their cultivars for Plant Breeders Rights (PBR), using DUS or similar tests. They can then license the further propagation of their cultivars, collect royalties, and generally protect their investment. Theoretically, a breeder can apply for PBR for a cultivar of any horticultural species; however, in practice it is usually restricted to clonal or OP cultivars, which could otherwise be multiplied without any control by the breeder. F1 hybrid cultivars, which do not breed true from seed saved from the crop, confer an automatic protection for the breeder, and breeders seldom seek PBR for such cultivars. Another voluntary scheme, Fleuroselect, operates in European countries, whereby ornamental cultivars can be registered and gain similar protection to PBR.

New international legislation is imminent which is likely to confer the equivalent of patent rights over some of the products of genetic engineering. At present, the release of genetically engineered cultivars is rigidly licensed by national legislation and agreements, as a precaution against potential environmental and health problems.

The advent of PBR has increased the investment in commercial breeding over the last two decades, and many new cultivars have appeared in consequence. A patenting arrangement for the products of genetic engineering is likely to have the same effect. In contrast, National Listing has resulted in many old cultivars disappearing, because the amounts of seed sold of such cultivars cannot cover the costs of registration. For the same reason, investment in the breeding of minor types of vegetables, and of cultivars with restricted sales, has almost disappeared.

See also PLANT VARIETY PROTECTION LAWS.

BREEDING AND THE HOME GARDENER. It is illegal to multiply and sell, or advertise for sale, cultivars which are protected by the legislation described above. However, the amateur gardener is free to save seed, or multiply clonal cultivars for his own use. He can also combine this operation with his own breeding, in order to improve an existing strain, or even to breed a completely new one.

There is one overriding principle when saving seed or multiplying clones, for whatever purpose: only the best plants should be used, as these are less likely to harbour disease, and may possess the best genes. The broad outlines of the exercise are given below; more detail can be found in Watts (1980).

*Seed-propagated vegetables*. The majority of vegetable cultivars now grown by market and amateur gardeners have been bred by commercial companies; a few have been bred by state-owned research organizations; a very small number have been bred by private individuals – usually people with an academic or commercial plant-breeding background. Breeding a vegetable cultivar for sale (even assuming that a commercial partner handles the legislation, marketing, etc.), requires not only a sound knowledge of breeding, but perhaps heated greenhouses (individual plants are often isolated in insect-proof structures), a large area of suitable land, and a laboratory, which are likely to be well beyond the facilities available to most gardeners.

The home gardener can save the seed of several species which naturally inbreed. For example, swedes will set their own seed, which will be true to type if cross-pollination is avoided: before the flowers open, the flowering head should be enclosed in a paper or perforated cellophane bag. Lettuce, french beans (dwarf or climbing) and peas are facultative inbreeders, and will breed true to type without the necessity of bagging the flowers. The same applies to non-F1 hybrid cultivars of tomatoes.

With the exception of swede, nearly all the brassicas are obligate outbreeders, that is, they are particularly prone to being cross-pollinated by any other brassicas which are flowering at the same time within several hundred metres, depending on insect movements. Although the idea of a hybrid of cauliflower/brussels sprout or turnip/chinese cabbage appeals, because of the idea of getting both crops on the same plant, in practice such hybrids only combine the non-crop characteristics of their parents. It is probably not worth the trouble of growing plants from seed saved from home-grown brassicas.

Seed saved from outbreeding species where the crop is the flowers, fruit or seeds – such as cucurbits (cucumbers, courgettes, squashes, etc.) aubergines, peppers, sweetcorn, runner beans and broad beans – generally give crops which are sufficiently true to the type. Again, seed from F1 hybrid cultivars will give disappointing results, and if more than one cultivar is being grown within, say, 50 metres of the seed crop, then an unacceptable number of off-types may result, due to cross-pollination.

It is probably a waste of time to save seed from outbreeding species where the crop is a non-floral organ, as in celery, carrot, onion, leek and beetroot. This is because seed is often only successfully saved from those plants within a crop which have prematurely bolted up to flowering. Seed saved from these will tend to show the same characteristics in the next generation, giving high proportions of useless, bolted plants.

Indeed, this illustrates one of the paradoxes of most vegetable breeding: because we are usually interested in a part of the plant which detracts from its ability to produce seed, the plants giving the best seed yields often have the worst genetic potential to give good crops. Large bulbs, roots, heads, curds, etc. are particularly prone to rotting during the flowering phase.

*Seed-propagated ornamentals*. Many ornamental species possess one great advantage to the breeder over most vegetables: they have been selected to produce flowers. In some cases, floriferousness is a consequence of the failure to set seed, often due to male sterility, and sometimes to triploidy. Generally, however, 'earliness' (which is physiologically similar to bolting) and the production of large numbers of well-formed flowers are desirable characteristics in an ornamental species, and are not detrimental to seed production.

Many common ornamentals are inbreeders, and can be treated in the same way as the inbreeding vegetables. They include wallflower, salvia, delphinium, salpiglossis, nicotiana, pansy, geranium, impatiens, antirrhinum and marigold. Some can easily be self-pollinated, including cyclamen, petunia and alyssum, but may show inbreeding depression. A few need to be cross-pollinated, and can be treated like the cucurbits, as described above; daisy and sunflower possess a self-incompatibility system; primula is dioecious; and others, like *Begonia rex*, are monoecious. As with the vegetables, seed saved from F1 hybrid ornamental cultivars is likely to give poor results, particularly in terms of dull and insipid flower colours.

*Clonal fruit, vegetables and ornamentals*. The amateur has a much better chance of breeding improved cultivars in clonally multiplied species than in those propagated by seed. With a few notable exceptions (e.g. roses, chrysanthemums), commercial breeders have tended to neglect clonally propagated species because of the greater rewards from breeding seed-propagated cultivars. Where species have been bred as clonal cultivars, far less is known of the genetic controls involved, and the breeding has been proportionately less precise, leaving more scope for the amateur.

Virtually all clonal cultivars are heterozygous, that is, their progeny, whether from self- or cross-pollination, will be genetically diverse. The likelihood is that if a clonal cultivar (e.g. of apple, gooseberry, artichoke, potato or daffodil) is self-pollinated, then a high proportion of the offspring will suffer from inbreeding depression or will be defective in some obvious way; some will be acceptable, and a very small proportion (probably none) will be equal to or better than the parent variety. Generally, it will not be worth growing less than 100 plants, because of the likelihood of a very low proportion of good individuals. The proportion of good progeny will be slightly greater if two (or more) good cultivars are crossed together and, because the greatest effort in the exercise is in the growing of the progeny, it is probably best for the amateur to cross-pollinate rather than self-pollinate the parental cultivars.

There are many different types of clonal species, each with its particular attributes, but for an 'ordinary' species with hermaphrodite flowers, the basic procedure for cross-pollination is as follows. The flower being used as the female parent must be emasculated in order to prevent selfing. The flower bud is carefully slit open with a small blade a day or two before it would normally open. All the immature anthers are removed, using a needle or forceps. All other flowers and the growing point are then removed from the branch bearing the emasculated flower, in order to prevent self-pollination. The branch is covered with a paper or cellophane bag to prevent unintentional cross-pollination. Two days later, pollen from the other cultivar is transferred with an artist's brush to the stigma of the emasculated flower, or dehiscing anthers can be held in forceps and dusted over the stigma. The branch is then labelled and re-bagged. The bag should be removed a week or two later to prevent excess humidity, and the fruit is left to develop normally.

GENETIC RESOURCES. All plant breeding programmes involve the selection of new genetic combinations from a 'pool' of genetic variation. The breeder has to generate this variation in order to start his programme. Most breeding programmes start with current or recently obsolete cultivars which are either themselves genetically variable, or which are crossed together to give variable populations. Occasionally the breeder may only be able to generate the variation required by using uncultivated forms of the crop or related species, which he will cross with a current cultivar, so that he can eventually recombine the generally good characteristics of the cultivar with a particular character (e.g. disease resistance) from the exotic parent. It is relatively common in such programmes for unpredictable recombinants to appear, and these may themselves be useful. Some recent developments in genetics (including genetic engineering) have the effect of greatly expanding the range of species which can be used to donate genetic material to the recipient cultivar.

The genetic resources used by the breeder, therefore, fall into three categories. (1) Current and recently obsolete cultivars, which are the product of considerable breeding effort towards current growing conditions, market requirements, etc. Virtually all breeding programmes use such material. (2) Old and fully obsolete cultivars, uncultivated and wild forms, and related species, which may possess many genes which could be useful in a new cultivar, either as discrete, recognizable characters, or in unexpected ways. (3) Potentially, any life form which through genetic engineering might contribute one or a few genes with relatively predictable effects.

GENE BANKS. Many international and national efforts have sought to conserve genetic resources for use by breeders in the future. Much of this work has been prompted by the genetic erosion of such resources, mainly as traditional farming practices have changed. The major coordinated efforts have been by the United States Department of Agriculture and the International Board for Plant Genetic Resources. These and other bodies support an international network of gene banks where seed samples, particularly from the category 2 above, are stored in low temperature and humidity, which should ensure the longevity of the seed.

Clonal crops, and those with 'recalcitrant' seeds (which cannot be stored in low temperature or humidity) cannot be accommodated in conventional gene banks. The cost of maintaining such crops in the field can be exorbitant, and much recent work has been concerned with the feasibility of storing such material as tissue cultures, or in extremely low temperatures, protected from the effects of freezing by cryopreservative chemicals.

For a detailed account of the physiological processes involved in plant breeding, see PLANT REPRODUCTION. See also GENETICS AND GENETIC ENGINEERING

**Plant health and quarantine**. Every grower of any specialized collection of plants understands the need to check the condition of new plants obtained for inclusion in the collection. Most gardeners would not buy or accept a plant which seemed to be seriously diseased or infested, but it is not always easy to see signs of potential trouble. Insect pests and mites can be well hidden, for example, in dormant plant material; diseases may not become apparent for some time after new growth has started. Many kinds of damaging organisms can be hidden in soil and on or in roots, and some kinds of seeds can carry pests and diseases on surfaces, in debris, or even inside the seed. Wherever possible, the specialist grower will isolate new material until it is found to be healthy and clean. In some situations the introduction of a new plant can also involve problems of weed infestation.

Just as individual growers try to avoid the difficulties of pest control by preventing development of a problem, so countries and continents set up regulations to prevent entry of harmful organisms which are not already in their areas. The authorities also have special isolation methods, sometimes including quarantine stations, mainly to protect important crops from potential damage or destruction.

The UK, for example, has special research centres licensed to receive material of some important crop plants, and does not allow any other imports of these protected groups for growing. In the US there are plant quarantine stations associated with all the main ports of entry, and Canada, Australia, New Zealand and South Africa have somewhat similar arrangements. Almost every country has phytosanitary regulations controlling entry of plant material; the degree of control depends on the potential risk of bringing in pests or diseases of importance to agriculture, horticulture or forestry.

Some kinds of high-risk plants are prohibited entry, others will be allowed in only if certified to have come from a pest- or disease-free area, and some sorts of material will be allowed free entry. Most countries also have lists of particular organisms which are not established within their borders, and which must not be present in consignments. In some important cases, diseases in particular must not be present in the area from which the plant material comes.

Seeds generally present the best means of introducing clean new material because they can be thoroughly cleaned of debris and any pests they might carry. Some seeds may, however, carry pests inside them, a few groups can carry important virus diseases, and various sorts can have pathological fungi or bacteria on their surfaces.

Dormant cuttings usually present less of a hazard than those in full growth or with leaves. Rooted plants in general present the greatest range of potential problems because of the very large numbers of minute organisms which can exist in and around their surfaces. Even washing off all the soil cannot guarantee that the roots are free of such problems as nematode infestations in tiny areas of damaged tissue, or fungal and bacterial spores. Many of these organisms are harmless but some are potentially serious, either for the plant carrying them or for other plants once introduced to a new environment. Most countries prohibit the entry of any kind of compost or soil because of the risks involved.

Bulbs, corms and tubers might carry virus infections, bacteria or fungi within their tissues, and various pests can live inside them or remain hidden among dry scales and root bases.

The danger of introducing potential weed species is also sometimes a very real hazard (see PLANT INTRODUCTIONS; WEEDS). Weeds, including plant parasites, can cause tremendous damage to agricultural crops and forestry areas, they can make areas of land totally unusable for particular crops, or they can infest and seriously damage areas of wild countryside.

The degree of risk of introducing pests and diseases varies with geographical origin. The greatest threats to British agriculture and horticulture, for example, usually come from quite distant areas of the world with somewhat similar climates, although the deadly Dutch Elm disease merely travelled across the Channel. Pests from such regions are likely to be able to survive elsewhere and are also likely to find suitable host plants both in cultivated and wild areas. Organisms coming in from tropical regions, on the other hand, are less likely to find a suitable environment in which to flourish, but could still present serious threats to indoor plant collections.

In an area such as Europe and the Mediterranean region many pests and diseases will be common to neighbouring countries, and the risks of introducing problems with plants are relatively small. Some countries, therefore, allow travellers to carry small amounts of plant material from place to place, but there are restrictions on certain important crop groups and it is still necessary to avoid carrying diseased or infested material.

The current British plant health regulations are set out in the Plant Health (Great Britain) Order 1987 and the Import and Export of Trees, Wood and Bark (Health) (Great Britain) Order 1980.

Cleaned seeds of most kinds can be brought or sent in freely, but some crop kinds have to be accompanied by plant health (phytosanitary) certificates. These include beet, lettuce, lucerne, pea and tomato. Seeds of all kinds of *Rubus* and *Prunus* spp. are capable of carrying important virus diseases of other crops and must not be imported without special certificates. Grass and crucifer seeds are restricted entry from Australia, New Zealand and parts of South America.

Potatoes (both tubers and true seeds) are prohibited entry except to special research centres, and all imports, even for consumption, are directly controlled by the Ministry of Agriculture.

Dormant bulbs and corms can be brought in, in limited quantities, from the Continent, and a few plants or cuttings are allowed under a baggage concession. Many kinds of plants, and most trees, are prohibited entry from outside the European and Mediterranean region, and others have to be certified free of pests and diseases before they will be allowed in. Generally speaking, if plants or other vegetative material is to be imported, it is essential to ask the advice of the Plant Health Division of the Ministry of Agriculture, Fisheries and Food; material arriving without the necessary import clearance and plant health papers will be subject to customs seizure and subsequent destruction. The Ministry will issue import licences when necessary.

The United States requires all potential importers of living plant material to obtain prior approval, and issues numbered permit labels for packages. These ensure that the consignments go straight to plant inspection stations for examination prior to quarantine treatment or release. Clean seeds of many herbaceous species are allowed in, but all woody plant seeds go through plant inspection. Bulbs of most kinds can go straight to importers, but must have health certificates from the countries of origin.

Canadian, Australian and South African regulations are somewhat similar, with stricter controls on issue of import permits and treatment on arrival.

The authorities responsible for plant health are usually part of departments of agriculture and/or forestry, and will provide detailed advice on application. Most such centres also hold summaries of other countries' regulations and can advise on both imports and exports.

The transport of plant material involves risks to horticulture and agriculture in all parts of the world. Careful examination of plants on arrival is sensible, and it is irresponsible to send someone a diseased specimen. A plant which presents no plant health hazard in Britain could be a noxious weed or a potential source of serious infection in some other part of the world.

Nematodes are prime examples of often very damaging pests which are very easily brought in on imported plant material. They are minute, difficult to identify, and can occur in enormous numbers. The South American leafminer, *Lirioneyza liridobrensis*, has become well-established in horticultural centres in the Netherlands and is such a serious threat to British horticulture that the law relating to imports was changed in 1989 to restrict the entry of a wide range of potential hosts. It attacks a very wide range of horticulturally important flowers and vegetables with serious results.

The Western flower thrip, *Frankliniella occidentalis*, originating in the US, is now established as a pest in Britain, causing severe damage to flowers and foliage of a wide range of plants, and is very difficult to control. Furthermore, the pest is capable of carrying the extremely damaging virus disease, tomato spotted-leaf virus, affecting many plants including ornamentals.

Juniper pear rust, *Gymnosporangium asiaticum*, occurs naturally in Japan, where it is common to grow juniper hedges around orchards, *Juniperus chinensis* and the pear *Pyrus pyrifolia* being the main hosts of the fungus. The disease was first discovered in the UK on bonsai junipers imported from Japan, an important reason for the strict controls that exist on bonsai imports.

It is better to avoid the risk of infestation than to try to control it after introduction. Chemical controls are not always effective as many pests and diseases have resistance to some treatments. Introduced plants often seem to acquire extra vigour in new environments, perhaps due to the absence of their natural predators, and are seldom amenable to control (see PLANT INTRODUCTIONS).

In addition to the plant health regulations and the rules concerning international movement of endangered plants (see CONSERVATION and CITES), there are also rules in most countries controlling the collecting of any plant material, including seeds, from wild areas. In most places, the landowner's or national or local approval has to be given for any specimens to be removed.

Seeds present fewer plant health risks than other kinds of material. The careful collection of small seed samples also causes much less disturbance to wild populations of plants, and less damage to the environment than removal of plants or even cuttings. In addition, a small sample of seeds presents the grower with a much better representation of the natural variability of the species than a single plant or a bunch of cuttings. Seedlings also provide a better chance of selecting good forms, and hardier individuals.

**Planting and transplanting**. Planting is the operation of setting plants into the garden, whether they have been grown at home or bought, and whether small seedlings, bulbs, or nursery stock such as trees and shrubs. Transplanting is a form of planting, the term being more often used to refer to young plants grown from seed or cuttings being moved either into permanent quarters or to a larger container or to a nursery bed. Transplanting is also carried out in nurseries to keep plant roots compact, so that when sent to the customer there will be the minimum check to growth. Such nursery transplanting, which is usually done annually for trees and shrubs, prevents any long straggling roots from developing. The use of container-grown plants in recent years has reduced the amount of nursery transplanting.

*Nursery stock*. Young trees and shrubs will generally overtake older and larger specimens within a few years; they are also less expensive. Except where a sense of maturity is required quickly, the less expensive small plants are the preferred choice, though very small plants may need additional care, especially with weeding, watering and feeding, during the first season.

Special planting schemes may require large specimens to give height to a flat site within a limited time-span, and for public places more mature specimens may be required to reduce the risk of losses through vandalism.

Semi-mature trees, the largest nursery trees normally available, 6–9m: immediate impact or screening, areas where smaller trees might be vandalized. Semi-mature trees must be lifted with a specially prepared and protected root-ball, which can be done with various types of mechanical tree diggers and tree spades. Some of these can be used to carry the tree to its prepared planting site. Planting can only be undertaken by specialist firms with suitable equipment.

Seedlings and young rooted cuttings are not normally planted in final positions, as they will not have formed an adequate root system and may also be unable to compete with weeds. They are usually transplanted to produce sturdier plants with a compact root system, or in nurseries may also be undercut (mechanically with a blade beneath the soil) to achieve a similar effect. The gardener can deal with a few such plants by planting them in suitably sized pots.

*Field-grown plants*. Field-grown trees and shrubs are often larger and have a more extensive root system than container-grown plants of a similar age, but the sale and planting of these is confined to a limited period, their lifting is labour-intensive and restricted by soil conditions. Large nurseries use mechanized field production from planting to lifting but most stock grown for sale in garden centres is container-grown from cuttings or seed through to sale; sometimes field-grown plants are potted up (containerized) prior to sale.

If a large number of plants is required, for hedging for instance, field-grown bare-root stock is usually more cost effective. Trees and shrubs that do not transplant well bare-root are usually sold as root-balled plants if lifted from the field – that is, with their roots and some field soil carefully removed from the line and wrapped in hessian (burlap) – a kind of sub-containerization which allows some mobility of stock even at hostile times of the year, for some continuing fibrous root development within the ball itself, and for heeling-in without effective planting. These are generally cheaper than container-grown plants of similar size, and it may be possible to buy larger plants than is normal with container-grown equivalents.

If bare-root plants are moved at the correct time, they should establish as successfully as root-balled plants, and may be less expensive. Many trees and shrubs are unsuitable for balling (roses for instance) because they lack a substantial fibrous root system; plants that do not normally transplant well bare-root, but which have a root system suitable for root-balling, such as hollies and daphnes, are usually sold either container-grown or balled; the balled plants are likely to be less expensive because they will have been field grown, and should establish successfully; many garden centres prefer to stock container-grown plants, however, as these are easier to maintain in good condition for a longer period.

*Container-grown plants*. Most nursery stock is now sold containerized. This greatly extends the planting period over that for bare-root and root-balled (balled and burlapped) plants. Plants grown in containers can be planted at any time of year provided the ground is not frozen or waterlogged, and the plants are watered in thoroughly until established if the weather is dry.

Container-grown plants are generally more expensive than bare-root or balled plants, but failures should be fewer if they are properly planted and cared for afterwards, and provided they have not become starved or pot-bound.

Some genera resentful of root disturbance do not transplant well if field grown. These include *Magnolia, Cytisus, Elaeagnus* and *Cistus*. Shrubs that produce a good fibrous root system, such as *Rhododendron*, transplant well as balled field-grown plants.

*When to plant*. In temperate regions liable to frost, bare-root plants and root-balled (balled and burlapped) plants should be planted at the appropriate season. Mid and late autumn is a good time for most, as the soil is still warm and there is usually sufficient moisture to encourage the formation of new roots. Dormant plants can be planted through until early spring, but if they are received when the ground is frozen or waterlogged they should be heeled in or otherwise protected until the soil is suitable. Heeling-in is temporary planting: a trench is dug in a convenient place that will not become waterlogged, and the plant roots placed close together in this, covered with soil and firmed in. They should be safe for several weeks, but if the delay before final planting is likely to be only short, it may be better to keep the bare-rooted plants in a cool shed, ensuring that the roots do not dry out (pack moist peat or sacking around them). In large-scale production, bare-root plants are often kept for long periods in cold storage.

Many herbaceous subjects are planted in the autumn, but some are best planted in spring, including any plant likely to be lost in winter through cold or wet. A few exceptions are best planted at other times: bearded irises are best lifted and replanted in mid to late summer. Some woodland plants, including many primulas, are best divided and replanted in early or midsummer, immediately after flowering.

Bare-root or balled evergreens are best planted in mid or late spring, to reduce the risk of losses through desiccation (see *Aftercare* below).

*Transplanting*. Trees and shrubs transplanted within the garden should be treated like root-balled plants except that they can usually be moved directly to their new positions without the need for root-wrapping, unless the soil-ball is too large and heavy to carry without wrapping.

Moderately large shrubs (up to about 2m/6½ft) can sometimes be moved successfully within the garden if well prepared beforehand. If possible, six to twelve months before moving the plant, remove a trench around half of the root system and undercut it with a spade. This encourages the production of additional fibrous roots. The ground must be moist when the shrub is finally undercut from both sides, prior to moving. A piece of hessian or thick plastic sheet should be pushed beneath one half of the root-ball and the plant gradually eased on to this so that the material can be pulled tightly around the soil-ball before it is lifted.

Renovations of established herbaceous borders should be done in autumn – if possible during mid or late autumn. The work may also be done during early and mid-spring, but autumn is to be preferred. Plants that are to be retained should be lifted and their roots covered with soil while the border is being prepared. They should then be divided and replanted to a previously prepared plan as for a new border.

Frost-tender plants, such as most summer bedding plants, should not be planted until all reasonable risk of frost has passed. This will depend on location; if in doubt about your district, be guided by when the local parks departments plant theirs. Always ensure the plants have been thoroughly hardened off (gradually acclimatized to outdoor conditions), and do not be guided by calendar alone; delay planting if the weather is cold, or there are strong drying winds.

*Preparation*. Ground preparation should be very thorough for all plants, though annuals (frost-tender or hardy) do not normally require rich soil. If the ground is too well manured and fertilized, some plants may produce a lot of leaf at the expense of flower; in the case of plants like nasturtiums (*Tropaeolum majus*), lush leaves may grow over and hide the flowers. A light dressing of a balanced fertilizer is all that is usually required, with an application of bulky organic matter (such as farmyard manure or garden compost) every couple of years on light or impoverished soil.

For perennials of all kinds, and especially trees and shrubs, every effort must be made to improve the soil structure. Dig deeply; if on shallow, chalky soil try to break up the ground with a pickaxe if possible, and add a generous quantity of a bulky organic material, such as garden compost, well-rotted manure, pulverized bart, coir, peat or spent mushroom compost (the last contains chalk or limestone, which is unlikely to make an already alkaline soil even more alkaline, but it would be better to use something that would lower the pH slightly, such as leafmould or well-rotted manure). It is better to incorporate the organic material throughout the depth of cultivation, rather than in the bottom spit (spade depth) alone, which might be unavailable to newly planted plants. If the ground is already fertile and well cultivated, it will be sufficient to fork over the ground, incorporating some organic material at the same time. It is not a good idea to import soil to fill the planting hole unless it has a similar structure to that of the surrounding ground, otherwise tree or shrub roots may tend to grow mainly within the 'plug' of better soil and fail to root adequately into the surrounding area.

*Planting*. The root-ball should always be moist before planting (bare-root plants can be soaked for an hour or two before planting). Roots and root-balls should not be left exposed to hot sun or drying winds while the ground is being prepared.

The planting hole is best made with a trowel for small plants and with a spade for larger ones. Plants with long vertical roots must have holes of sufficient depth to accommodate them without bending them, but in general planting holes should be wider than deep, so that the roots can be spread sideways, not bunched together. A dibber should be used only for very small seedlings and small taprooted plants such as brassicas, and for special cases like leeks.

The planting hole for bare-root plants should generally be wider than for container-grown plants, but even for these it should be much wider than the actual container, to allow for a few of the larger roots to be teased out from the root-ball and laid out in the hole. This will encourage rapid rooting out into the surrounding soil.

Always remove the container from container-grown plants. The plants can usually be knocked out easily; if large roots have grown through the drainage holes (a sign of neglect), slit the container to avoid damaging the roots. Plants with thick roots that have spiralled around the inside of the container may fail to grow satisfactorily, because such roots are usually impossible to tease out and never grow out into the soil.

Add bulky organic material such as pulverized bark, and a slow-acting fertilizer such as bonemeal or hoof-and-horn meal to the heap of soil removed, and use this to refill the hole. The soil around small plants should be firmed with the hand as filling proceeds. With large plants of most sorts, the foot can be used both at the filling and at the final stages: although the soil must not be too compacted, it must be firm for shrubs and trees. Heavy soils will need less firming than light ones. Shake the tree to settle the soil between the roots before firming.

'Notch' planting is a useful technique where a large number of transplants have to be planted (for woodland planting, for instance, or for growing on in a nursery). The blade of a spade is inserted into the ground and rocked to and fro to make a slit. The transplant roots are inserted into the slit to the correct depth, and the soil pushed around them by inserting the spade blade into the soil again a few centimetres away to push the soil back. The heel is then used to firm the ground adequately.

Trees will usually require staking unless they are small. In rural areas, or where animals are a problem, a tree guard to protect the stem can be as important as the stake. (See also SUPPORT.)

Do not plant too deeply. This is especially important with plants grafted near soil level. In the case of bare-root plants, use the old soil mark as a guide to planting depth; with container-grown plants aim to just cover the root-ball.

Container-grown plants raised in soilless mediums should always have the root-ball fully planted and its upper surface covered, albeit shallowly, with the soil of the planting site. An exposed collar of old substrate, no matter if exposed by only a few centimetres, will act as a wick, either absorbing too much water or drying out too quickly – a common cause of mysterious planting deaths.

*Aftercare*. Unless planting in a rainy period, always water-in thoroughly, and continue to water in dry weather until the roots have grown into the surrounding soil and the plant has begun to establish.

Newly planted evergreens may need shelter-protection if planted in the autumn or winter, or in very exposed and windy sites. Unlike deciduous trees and shrubs, they will continue to lose water through their foliage, which the roots may not be able to replace if the ground is frozen and a good root system has not yet been developed. Strong winds increase the amount of moisture lost, and evergreens planted from early autumn onwards (even if container-grown) will generally benefit from temporary wind protection until the spring. A sheet of hessian or plastic sheeting or even a fine-mesh net, fixed to canes around the plant, is all that is required. Leave the top exposed for good ventilation.

Mulching or hoeing to eliminate competition from weeds will greatly increase the chances of successful establishment. Mulching has the dual benefit of conserving moisture and suppressing weeds, but organic mulches need to be thick to be effective. Proprietary sheet tree and border mulches – or homemade ones from thick polythene or pieces of roofing felt – are very effective for trees and shrubs. Always make sure the ground is moist before applying a mulch. At all costs, avoid smothering the base of the plant. Weed control is important because weeds compete for available water and nutrients (and for light if the tree or shrub is small and the weeds tall). Grass also competes for moisture, and especially for the element nitrogen; for that reason it is better to leave an area around the base of a specimen tree or shrub free of grass.

**Plant introductions**. The introduction of plants into gardens from the wild has been a continuous process from the first cultivation of cereals in the Fertile Crescent to the enthusiastic collection of exotic ornamentals in the 19th century. Many new plants are still coming into cultivation today, although there are now controls designed to protect the environment of their origin.

The type of plants being introduced in any one period has been largely a consequence of the exploration and settlement of new areas of the world, but has also depended upon successful transportation and preservation techniques. Collectors have been spurred on by different commercial and scientific interests and affected by changing tastes in gardening and cookery. Even though only a fraction of the plants that have been introduced remain in cultivation, most gardens now contain a blend of the world's plants, and discovering how they got there is a fascinating historical exercise.

EARLY INTRODUCTIONS. The first record of a deliberate plant introduction dates from 1495BC, when Queen Hatshepsut had 32 frankincense trees brought to Egypt from 'the land of Punt' (Somalia), packed in wicker baskets. All but one of the trees survived the journey and they were planted in front of the great temple at Dehr-el-Bahri, Luxor. Some 275 plants which her successor, Thutmose III, brought back from Syria are depicted in his temple at Karnak, but these have not been identified. It can be assumed that the majority of introductions right up to the 16th century were plants for food, flavouring or use in herbal medicine rather than for ornament, but there is some evidence that roses and lilies were prized before Classical times and as early as 1100BC King Tiglath-Pileser boasted, 'Cedars and box ... I have carried off from the countries I conquered; trees that none of the kings my forefathers possessed. These trees I have taken and planted in my own country, in the parks of Assyria.'

Theophrastus's botanical treatises around 280BC describe a number of flowers grown for garlands but, with the exception of double roses, these were native plants; his list of vegetables, on the other hand, includes many plants from western Asia (specified three centuries later by Pliny as from Syria), which seems to have been the main centre for vegetable breeding. Moreover, Theophrastus's list demonstrates the cultivation of fruit and vegetable varieties, as it includes three different cabbages, four lettuces and a large number of fruit cultivars. It is clear from the writings of Pliny that the number of cultivars had grown enormously by AD70, and he describes most of the modern herbs (including *Nigella sativa* and celery for use as a flavouring, but excluding sage). Among the relatively few new species listed are peaches, cherries, possibly the apricot, the carrot and other vegetables. The description of the Lacuturnian cabbages sounds like an early hearting cabbage, and the Arician seems to resemble the modern Brussels sprout.

Around AD800 the Emperor Charlemagne issued a list of the plants to be cultivated on his estates, the *Capitulare de villis*. This reveals that most of the vegetables grown by the Romans had survived the northern invasions, and that a few additional flavouring herbs had been introduced. Many of the names used, such as *Pisos mauriscos*, moorish peas, are difficult to identify or relate to modern vegetables, but the Franks were also instructed to grow many familiar fruits and nuts such as apples, cherries, peaches, walnuts and pine nuts.

While gardening in Europe was for many centuries confined to economic plants, in China the distinction between plants grown for medicinal rather than ornamental use became blurred before the Christian era and flower cultivation seems to have reached a peak at about the same time as Charlemagne issued his *Capitulare*. In the Near and Middle East the original horticultural emphasis seems to have been on the creation of parks, in which trees were the principal feature, but during the 1st millennium AD plants were being brought from China along the Silk Route, while some Asian and European plants (including henna and *Narcissus tazetta*) travelled to China.

The ornamental gardening tradition of the East was introduced to Europe by the Moors when they settled in Spain in the 8th century; they brought with them a number of new plants from the Near East and were responsible for bringing a number of indigenous plants into cultivation. Ibn al'Awwam listed the plants in cultivation in Andalusia in about 1200; these included the apricot, banana, carob, date palm, watermelon, lemon and bitter orange among new fruits, and among new vegetables some such as colocasia that were only suited to the Mediterranean climate as well as cauliflower, aubergine, gherkin and spinach, plants which were not to reach northern Europe for a century or more. Among the new ornamentals were the Indian bead tree, *Melia azederach*, and jasmines from Asia, hibiscus from China, and many plants from the Spanish flora including the Judas tree, iris, hellebore, lavender, two sorts of violet, various narcissi and a number of colour forms of stock, wallflower, mallow and waterlily.

The Spanish conquest of South America in the 16th century brought the next wave of plant introductions to Europe. The most significant of these seems today to have been the potato but in fact, partly because the original cultivars did not thrive in northern Europe and partly because the inhabitants of northern Europe were wary of eating any solanaceous plants, it took 200 years for the potato to become productive and accepted. Despite the reluctance to eat solanaceous plants, capsicums quickly became popular, any peppery flavour being appreciated. The tomato was soon eaten around the Mediterranean but was treated as an ornamental plant in Britain and the US until the 19th century. French beans were immediately popular and ousted the cowpea in a very short time, but the scarlet runner bean was long grown only for its decorative qualities.

North America only produced the Jerusalem artichoke, which never had more than novelty value in Europe, and even taking into account the possibility that many of the squashes from Central America had their origins further north, the traffic of vegetables here seems to have been very much from Old World to New. A bill of 1631 of the seeds obtained in New England by John Winthrop from Robert Hill of London survives to show that among the vegetables and herbs were those that had been more or less discontinued in Britain, such as bloodwort, lang-de-boeuf (*Picris echioides*) and lovage. By far the most expensive seeds listed are that of the fairly newly introduced cauliflower (seed of which was probably imported from Genoa) and 'hartichockes', newly introduced from the wild. The 17th century was to see an enormously increased number of ornamental plants in cultivation in Europe and it is noteworthy that flower seeds too appear in the Winthrop bill, among them columbine, monkshood, stock, wallflower and violet.

COMMERCIAL IMPORTS. Some newly discovered plants were of such commercial importance that they came to play a role in political struggles. Ironically, the very value of some tropical plants inhibited their wider introduction as traders sought to control supply and thus keep prices high. Spices such as pepper, nutmeg, ginger and cloves were in great demand in the Middle Ages, both to enliven and preserve food, and originally these arrived in Europe via Saudi Arabia. Traders attempted to keep secret where the spices grew and it was not until Vasco da Gama rounded the Cape of Good Hope at the end of the 15th century that their true habitats were discovered.

Early in the 16th century the Portuguese occupied many of the Moluccas and Ceylon, thus securing a monopoly on nutmeg, cloves and cinnamon. Pepper and ginger were more widely planted but, owing to the long journeys involved, remained very expensive. A century later the Dutch seized the monopoly from the Portuguese and further raised the price of nutmeg and cloves by restricting their growth to the islands of Amboina and Banda respectively, destroying all other stocks in neighbouring islands. Although they were unable to eradicate all the cinnamon trees in Sri Lanka, they suppressed any attempt by the Singalese to export bark from their wild trees. The Dutch held on to their monopoly until around 1770, when various Frenchmen, of whom Pierre Poivre is the best known, succeeded in smuggling material to the islands of Mauritius and Réunion. Early in the 19th century Christopher Smith, one of Sir Joseph Bank's protégés, introduced large numbers of nutmegs to Malaysia; their offspring were introduced to the West Indies in 1824, arriving in Grenada, still one of the main centres of production, in 1843. Needless to say, once the spices were readily available, the price rapidly dropped.

The cultivation of another great European desideratum of the Middle Ages, sugar, had even more profound consequences. Sugar cane was well known and had been grown by the Moors in Andalusia from 714AD; by 1150 they had some 75,000 acres under the crop but, for reasons which remain unclear, trade subsequently ceased. Like the spices, sugar cane required a tropical climate and by the early 16th century sugar was also being manufactured in the West Indies. By the middle of the 17th century Bermuda, St Kitts, Barbados and Jamaica all had sugar cane plantations and the need for a workforce to tend them resulted in the creation of a large-scale slave trade. Between 1640 and 1651 the number of slaves in Barbados rose from a few hundred to over 20,000, and their presence led to the introduction of tropical crops from Africa and elsewhere.

The first of these would seem to have been the Lisbon yam, *Dioscorea alata*, which was taken from the Portuguese island of San Tomé to Lisbon to supply the slave ships bound for the West Indies, where the crop later became established. The Spaniards took the cowpea, *Vigna unguiculata*, to the New World in the late 16th century and in about 1700 it was taken to the Carolinas, where it is now much cultivated under the name of blackeyed bean.

The first attempt to introduce breadfruit from Tahiti for the slave trade ended with the famous mutiny on HMS *Bounty* in 1789, but three years later HMS *Providence* was successful, although the sugar barons were disappointed to find that breadfruit never became a staple food. The one important food to have been taken in the opposite direction in this period was the groundnut, *Arachis hypogaea*, which the Spaniards took to the Philippines, whence it spread over much of eastern Asia.

Coffee, which had been brewed in Arabia in the 15th century, was introduced to Indonesia by the Dutch in the late 17th century and to the West Indies and Brazil in the early 18th century. It was not until 1840 that Brazil became the leader in world production while Colombia, which is now the second-largest producer, did not start exporting until 1935.

An expedition to Ecuador in 1858, financed by Kew and led by Richard Spruce, collected seeds of *Cinchona pubescens* 'Succirubra' in the belief that the plant would be a good source of quinine. Eventually plants and seeds were sent to India and Sri Lanka but in the early 1860s an Australian obtained seeds of a Peruvian plant, *C. officinalis* 'Ledgeriana', which were purchased by the Dutch and raised in Indonesia. This proved to be far richer in the drug than any other species of *Chinchona* and is now the only one employed.

Attempts were made in the 1870s to introduce the rubber plant, *Hevea brasiliensis*, from South America, but met with little success until 1876, when Henry Wickham sent a large quantity of seed to Kew. In 1877 Kew sent 22 plants to the Singapore Botanic Garden where they languished until 1898, when the failure of the coffee crop at last persuaded planters to try the new crop. Malaya and Indonesia subsequently became the world's largest producers of rubber.

In the Far East the soya bean, *Glycine max*, has been cultivated for many centuries but this has only recently become an important crop in the US, where a number of new cultivars has been raised.

THE SEARCH FOR ORNAMENTALS. While nations battled over the lucrative crops, ordinary citizens were showing great enthusiasm for new garden plants. From Mexico the Spaniards had brought back the fragrant tuberose and the oddly shaped sprekelia, as well as tagetes, parent of 'French' and 'African' marigolds, while hyacinths, tulips, anemones and ranunculus were being imported from Turkey. Plants from North America grew well in northern Europe and were in great demand: the French brought over *Lilium canadense, Thuja occidentalis* and *Robinia psuedoacacia*, while John Tradescant the Younger made at least three expeditions to Virginia in the early 17th century, bringing back a number of plants including the deciduous swamp cypress (*Taxodium*) and the tulip tree (*Liriodendron*). There was a demand from gardeners for any plant that was not native, irrespective of its ornamental value. The Tradescants, for example, were just as delighted with their nettles and docks as they were with their cyclamen and North American asters, and this attitude persisted in botanic gardens well into the 19th century.

PLANT COLLECTION AND DISTRIBUTION. Tradescant's visits to Virginia in the 17th century arose from a commission from the Virginia Company to explore sources of naval timber and plant-collecting expeditions abroad for botanical purposes alone appear to date from the 18th century. Nevertheless, travellers with botanical interests would not only bring back plants or seeds themselves, but might also arrange for correspondents in foreign places to send them material.

The earliest introductions seem to have been distributed on a personal basis; the interested parties knew each other and exchanged plants. There were chandlers who sold economic seeds, but the establishment of nurseries for the sale of ornamentals seems to have started in the latter half of the 17th century. While the French firm of Morin may have started earlier, the first British nursery whose catalogue has survived is that of Lucas in 1677. Early in the 18th century the first plant collectors were employed, generally by syndicates of two or three rich men. For example, Mark Catesby was hired by a syndicate headed by William Sherard and including Sir Hans Sloane, Dr Mead and the Duke of Chandos, for an expedition in 1722–6 to collect plants and other items of natural history in Carolina. Catesby had previously sent seeds from Virginia, where he lived from 1712 to 1719, and some of these were acquired by the nurserymen Robert Furber and Thomas Fairchild, who also seem to have obtained material from the second voyage.

The largest nursery at the turn of the century was that eventually known as London & Wise, although there had been three other partners when the Brompton Park Nursery was first established in 1681. George London would seem to have been the leading spirit in collecting and introducing new plants, and the nursery not only supplied these, often in very large quantities, but also designed gardens where the new plants were included. Nevertheless, the novelties were mainly in demand from keen gardeners or from other nurserymen (including customers from as far afield as Genoa) and it was mainly the private gardener who first obtained new plants from abroad.

Around 1733 a syndicate led by the Quaker linendraper, Peter Collinson, first employed John Bartram of Philadelphia to collect plants, seeds and items of natural history. Originally there were only four subscribers, but in time they increased to 20, each of whom paid Bartram £5 per year, while in 1765 Bartram was appointed King's Botanist with a salary of £50 per year. Bartram may therefore be seen as one of the earliest professional collectors; he sent seeds and plants to Collinson for 30 years, so that the number of plants he introduced to cultivation was considerable. Collinson shared the large quantities of seed sent over by Bartram with the nurserymen James Gordon and Christopher Gray; he also obtained seed from correspondents in China and Siberia. His friend Dr Fothergill, jointly with Dr Pitcairn, employed Thomas Blaikie in 1775 to collect plants in the Alps and succeeded in introducing a large number of alpines to British gardens. The prices paid for new plants were so attractive that other 18th-century collectors either started a nursery business in America like William Young, or, like John Fraser and William Lyon, brought their plants back to England and established them in their own nursery or offered them for sale by auction.

Collectors were sent out by other countries too: André Michaux collected for a small syndicate in Carolina, while Peter Kalm was sent by the Swedish government to collect principally plants of economic value, but, being a pupil of Linnaeus, his botanical interests were wide. Some Americans started nurseries on their own account with a view to exporting plants to Europe. Among these was Humphry Marshall, who wrote the first description of American trees, and John Bartram's descendants established a nursery in Philadelphia with a thriving export trade, particularly to the Loddiges nursery in London.

By the 18th century it became worthwhile for nurseries such as Hugh Low and Veitch to pay the considerable cost of a private collector themselves. Owing to the increasing cheapness and efficiency of heating glasshouses, many of these expeditions were to the tropics – the introduction of the Wardian Case, a sort of portable, tightly-sealed glass box, made the import of plants by sea less hazardous (see WARDIAN CASE). The Belgian government sent Jules Linden to collect in Cuba and Mexico in 1837, and in 1841 he went to Venezuela. Linden subsequently opened a nursery in Belgium and dispatched collectors himself to many parts of South America. Another Belgian nurseryman who employed many collectors was Henry Sander, who eventually settled in Britain and concentrated on tropical orchids.

From the mid-18th century onwards there were numerous bodies, collecting ornamental plants. Under the aegis of Sir Joseph Banks, Kew sent collectors to many parts of the world; the Emperor of Austria also sent out collectors, while Tournefort's extensive voyages in the Near East were financed by the French government. John Gibson was sent to India by the Duke of Devonshire, and there were freelance collectors who explored remote areas and sent back plants either to nurserymen or for sale at auction. Once the interest in novel plants became established, sea captains might load up with a few specimens to sell to collectors at home. Thus *Camellia reticulata* 'Captain Rawes' is named after Richard Dawes, captain of an East Indiaman, who passed it to a gardener friend in 1820.

Botanic gardens have been less influential in plant introduction than might be expected. When Kew was sending out collectors to all parts of the globe, it was the private garden of the King. The Crown was forbidden to engage in trade, so the Kew acquisitions could only be distributed if plants were exchanged with nurserymen. Leading nurserymen such as Malcolm, Lee and Loddiges sponsored their own collectors and were therefore able to offer plants to exchange with Kew. In the colonies, exchange was easier: Telford in Mauritius and Wallich in Calcutta shared plants between their botanic gardens, and Wallich sent back numerous plants to Britain, usually to private individuals rather than to commercial establishments. Other British botanic gardens in the 19th century also had dealings with independent collectors: the Dublin Botanic Garden received Indian plants from Major Madden and Argentine plants from James Tweedie (who also supplied other botanic gardens) while the Glasgow garden obtained Australian plants from Charles Fraser.

Once Kew was taken over by the Office of Works in 1841 it would have been free to take part in syndicated collect, but seems to have done little in this way. Although Sir William Hooker sent out collectors, their main remit was to obtain herbarium specimens and Kew collectors such as Wilford and Oldham have very few live introductions assigned to them.

METHODS OF COLLECTION AND TRANSPORTATION. While the exploration of completely new habitats brought with it moments of wonder, plant collectors faced many kinds of practical problems, not least of which was the danger to themselves from hostile terrains and tropical diseases. Of 22 Veitch collectors, for example, five made only a single trip; of the remaining 17, seven died in the field as a result of disease and Thomas Lobb had to have a leg amputated. David Douglas, who collected for the Horticultural Society, ended his life in Hawaii, mangled by a wild bull after falling into a pit trap.

From the end of the 17th century the collector would usually supply the recipient of his plants with field notes, a herbarium specimen and a watercolour painting, but the early records were often too vague for the botanists at home to make a scientific identification. By the 19th century the tradition that exists today had become well established: the collector provides herbarium specimens and numbers them in sequence, be they seeds, bulbs or living plants, and describes such plants in his field notes. Botanists' diagnoses depend on good herbarium specimens and collectors are not encouraged to name their plants with any accuracy, so that a loose description such as 'evergreen tree, 40 feet high, white flowers' often suffices. In the last century even making the herbarium could be a problem; it was not usually possible for the collector to provide all aspects of the plant from leaves to flowers and fruits and possibly even the roots; in districts with a prolonged rainy season it was extremely difficult to dry the plants adequately (when Gibson was collecting in the Khasia hills in 1836 he had to light fires although the temperature was in the 90s) and James Drummond in Western Australia complained that he could not even get any paper in which to press his specimens.

Collectors making a long stay would often establish a small plot where plants could be preserved either until they set seed or until the collector was ready to pack them for the voyage home; many plants would not survive the ordeal. Seeds or bulbs, corms and tubers in a dormant state were the most resilient to the long sea journeys and damaging effects of salt spray. However, in some tropical districts where rains were frequent, it was often difficult to dry the seeds or bulbs before they became mouldy or were attacked by insects. Packing seeds in sugar seemed to be effective, although these had then to be stored in glass bottles to discourage vermin. Desiccated plants were put in wooden chests with broken glass to protect them from rats on board.

Early in the 19th century, Indian azaleas, *Rhododendron simsii*, were greatly prized, but Dr Ellis maintained that only one plant per thousand ever arrived safely in Britain. Since the plants had to go from China through the Tropics, around the Cape and back to the Tropics again, it is not surprising that losses were high. This was not always the case – in 1818 John Reeves, the tea inspector for the East India Company, came home on leave with 100 plants, of which 90 arrived safely – but as late as 1833 Loudon reported as particularly successful a shipment in which out of 25 plants seven survived the voyage. Since azaleas were cultivars, it was essential to provide plants, and the same applied to chrysanthemums and camellias. It was not until the invention in the 1830s of the sealed Wardian Case that living plants could be transported satisfactorily, although in violent storms it was usually the plants that would be jettisoned first to lighten the ballast.

By no means all of the vast number of plants introduced remain in cultivation, while quite often plants have been reintroduced, having been allowed to die out. For example Parkinson, in his *Paradisus* of 1629, lists *Ramonda myconi* and *Rhododendron hirsutum* as garden plants, although the usually accepted introduction dates are 1731 and 1656. In the 19th century Paxton complained that good introductions were being lost, because their initial treatment was wrong, usually being grown too hot. Others prove too difficult to cultivate and some plants seem to drop out of general cultivation for no clear reason. In the late 19th century, the climbing fern *Lygodium microphyllum* was an essential plant to flower arrangers, but most modern arrangers have probably never seen it. Bouvardias were favourite greenhouse subjects but seem largely to have disappeared and, since most were hybrids, are unlikely to be seen again.

THE INFLUENCE OF FASHION. With the spread of commercial horticulture, the emphasis for collectors was on ornamentals rather than just on novelties such as those collected by the Tradescants in the 17th century, but the demand for them would depend, to a certain extent, on prevailing fashions. Until Gertrude Jekyll and her followers, no one would have thought of cultivating euphorbias and even now they do not command universal appreciation. On occasion collectors were told by their financiers to concentrate on specific plants. Thus Ernest Wilson's first trip for Veitch was principally to obtain *Davidia involucrata* (the handkerchief tree), while the main object of his second expeditions was *Meconopsis integrifolia*. George Forrest was collecting all the ornamentals he could, but he was paid a bonus for every new species of rhododendron he introduced and so would tend to concentrate on that genus. Nevertheless, the collector would usually send back a variety of plants, besides those he had been asked to look out for, and it would be up to his patrons to decide which plants to cultivate commercially.

IMPORTING PLANT HYBRIDS. Hybridization, both of esculents and ornamentals, provided another source of plants which might be imported. Perhaps the most significant of these was the crossing of the large-fruited but dioecious strawberry, *Fragaria chiloensis*, with the North American *F. virginiana*, which occurred in France around 1766 but does not seem to have reached other countries before the 19th century. Many of the early pears and plums seem to have originated in France, while Britain was noted for its apples. However, the nurseryman Richard Williams bred the 'Williams' pear in the 18th century and Laxton bred 'Conference' in the late 19th century.

Before the science of genetics was understood most cultivars were the result of selection and the resultant plants showed a certain amount of variation. The introduction of F1 crosses produced plants of reliable consistency, which tend to mature simultaneously, an advantage to the commercial grower but perhaps less attractive for the amateur.

POLITICAL RESTRICTIONS. Politics have continued to affect the type of plants available to collectors. Both the Portuguese and the Spaniards were very reluctant to admit collectors to their South American possessions and it was not until these secured independence in the 1820s that much could be done there. Earlier the Spanish government had given Humboldt and Bonpland permission to travel in South America and they amassed a huge herbarium, but did little in the way of plant introduction apart from a number of dahlia cultivars which form the basis of our modern dahlia. Quite early in the 18th century William Houston had been botanizing in Mexico from the ports of Vera Cruz and Campeche, but his movements were restricted. Banks was able to get permission for two Kew collectors to collect in the vicinity of Rio de Janeiro and in 1814 to travel to São Paulo, but otherwise horticultural exploration had to wait until the 1820s, when plants became available from Chile, and until the 1840s and 1850s for the rest of the continent.

Access to the Far East was even more restricted. The British East India Company was confined to Macao, with permission to visit Canton during the tea sales; at Canton were the famous Fa-Fee nurseries whence cultivated Chinese plants could be obtained. It was, however, very difficult to get plants back alive and even seeds were liable to become mouldy. In the early years of the 18th century the Emperor of China had employed Jesuits as scientific advisers and several growers, including Peter Collinson, received seeds of Chinese plants from d'Incarville and Père Héberstein, but from 1755 no foreigners other than tea traders were allowed. After the infamous opium war of 1840–42, limited travel was possible and Robert Fortune was sent by the Horticultural Society to collect plants in those parts of China to which foreigners were not allowed; since he travelled with Wardian cases the majority of his plants arrived back safely. On his second voyage in 1848 Fortune disguised himself as a Chinese and travelled to the tea-growing district, 200 miles from Shanghai, where he obtained both seeds and young plants of the tea tree, which were destined for India. After 1860 the whole of China was notionally open to foreigners, although most of the information about the flora of western China came from missionaries, most of them French, such as Délavay, Soulié and Farges.

Japan was closed to foreigners until the mid-19th century. The Dutch East India Company was allowed to trade in Japanese products, but they were confined to the island of Deshima, off Nagasaki. They were obliged to send an embassy to Tokyo once a year, but they were confined to their carriages while making the journey. In 1826 Siebold managed to make some quite extensive excursions and to send back a number of plants but was unfortunately caught in possession of map of Japan two years later and first imprisoned and later banished. He returned in 1859, by which time most of Japan was available to plant collectors.

THE 20TH CENTURY. After 1914 plant collecting reverted to the tradition of syndicates, but the modern collector has tended to have a much larger number of patrons than his 18th-century counterpart. Some botanic gardens, such as Kew, still sponsor expeditions, but these are more generally an affair of numerous subscribers.

The introduction of plants from the wild is now being curtailed, albeit not rapidly enough, by concern for the environment (see CONSERVATION). In the 19th century Roezl was collecting orchids in Central America by the ton and no one protested. Nowadays it is realized not only that the number of plants of any one species is finite, but also that all nature is interdependent and reducing the number of plants may have effects on the chain of animal life from insects to mankind. The introduction of living plants is now only a last resort; where possible, introductions are effected by means of seeds, which nature necessarily overproduces, and if seeds are not available propagating material can be rapidly moved by air freight.

By no means all plant introductions are beneficial. The classic example is the prickly pear, *Opuntia* spp., introduced to Australia as a garden curiosity in the late 19th century. By 1900 these plants had spread over four million hectares; by 1925 over 24 million. Biological control by an Argentinian moth in the 1930s succeeded in decimating the prickly pear. Less success has been obtained against the blackberry, introduced into Australia and New Zealand. They have spread excessively in both countries; it is said in New Zealand there is one plant in North Island and one in South Island.

Other introductions which have enjoyed the conditions of their country of introduction to devastating effect include Australian *Metrosideros* spp. in Florida; tropical American *Lantana camara*, which in the late 20th century was swamping the native flora in Hawaii and was also intrusive in Australia; the South African 'Bermuda buttercup', *Oxalis pes-caprae*, so-called because it was first introduced to the Bermudas and thence via Malta to the Mediterranean, where it fills olive groves and similar terrain; Australian *Crassula helmsii*, introduced to Britain and the US as an aquarium plant and now spreading relentlessly in many wetlands; and the South American water hyacinth, *Eichhornia crassipes*), and tropical American water ferns (*Salvinia* spp.), which have choked waterways and lakes throughout the tropics and subtropics. The spread of the feral *Rhododendron ponticum* in Wales and Scotland has resulted in the extinction of many native herbs and a corresponding diminution of insect life.

Introductions also carry the risk of infection – sometimes with terrible results. In the 1860s, the introduction of North American vines to France resulted in the devastation caused by the aphid *Phylloxera vitifoliae*, which wiped out most of the French vineyards and was only curbed by grafting European *Vitis vinifera* on to stock of the American *V. labrusca*, which is resistant to the pest. The introduction of Japanese *Castanea crenata* into the US resulted in the native American *C. dentata* being infected by the chestnut blight, *Endothia parasitica*, which killed many trees and seems likely to cause the extinction of the species in its native country. It will still survive in cultivation outside America, but that is small comfort. The necessity of health certificates may well prevent the future introduction of pests like phylloxera and chestnut blight, but the spread of foreign plants, with their attendant problems, is not easily anticipated. (See also PHYTOSANITATION.)

**Plant life forms**. Plants have diversified into many different growth forms. Perhaps the commonest classification of these different habits is into trees, herbs, shrubs and climbers, but these rather simplistic terms often mask different sub-types and intermediate forms. For example, every gardener knows that the distinction between trees and shrubs is frequently vague. Trees are generally tall and woody and with a central main trunk, whereas shrubs are smaller, often with several stems which may not be entirely woody – but these are simplifications. The term herb is still cruder, as it includes woody evergreen perennial herbs such as thyme (*Thymus* spp.) and some soft-leaved perennials that, despite the wholly deciduous connotations of 'herb' and 'herbaceous', remain evergreen, for example *Liriope* and *Euphorbia* spp. Short-lived annuals such as shepherd's purse (*Capsella bursa-pastoris*), bulbous or cormous plants such as *Crocus* and *Colchicum* that die back completely during unfavourable seasons are also herbs. Subshrubs (suffrutices) are intermediate forms that do not fit easily into either of the herb or shrub categories. They have a partially woody (lignified) basal portion that is either short-lived or forms slowly over time. This great diversity of growth forms can be explained partly as the result of the demands and limitations of the natural environment of a given plant, and partly the nature of its own growth, both at the apex and in stem thickening. It is, then, habitat and habit.

Plants growing close together in favourable conditions, such as often exist in tropical rainforests, have to compete with each other for sunlight, and thus are evergreen, and generally trees, climbers or epiphytes. Of course, trees also occur in temperate areas with an unfavourable (cold, dry) winter season, but they are often deciduous (especially among dicotyledons), losing their leaves during the winter months to reduce water loss during that time. In places where conditions are less favourable, such as high alpine regions, where there are daily extremes of temperature and high light intensity, plants are often small, with their growing points close to the ground surface, and sometimes have an underground storage organ.

*Stem-thickening growth.* Increase in stem thickness is achieved by various different means in different plant groups, and this has a bearing on the growth habit. Most conifers and dicotyledons have a vascular cambium which is normally productive throughout the life cycle, resulting in a more or less conical structure, tapering at the apex, according to the degree of apical dominance. Monocotyledons, on the other hand, lack a vascular cambium but have a lateral meristem (primary thickening meristem) near the apex which establishes a broad, sometimes sunken, apical region. Arborescent monocotyledons achieve further stem thickening either by means of a secondary thickening meristem (as in *Yucca* and *Dracaena*), or by diffuse cell divisions (in palms). The broad apical region establishes the characteristic pachycaul (thick-stemmed) habit, with stems of more or less even thickness. Indeed, pachycauly is to some extent correlated with the primary thickening meristem, which also occurs in cycads and some tree ferns, both similar in habit to arborescent monocotyledons. A similar meristem also occurs in a few dicotyledons with short thick stems, such as some Cactaceae.

*Monopodial and sympodial growth.* In plants with a monopodial habit, growth is maintained at the terminal (apical) bud, whereas in sympodial shoots the terminal bud dies back, usually after flowering, and is replaced by the lateral (axillary) buds. Many monocotyledons are sympodial, particularly those with a creeping rhizome, such as *Iris*. Indeed, the lack of a vascular cambium in monocotyledons may also have led to sympodial growth, which itself resulted in the production of underground resting organs such as corms and bulbs, which are much more common among monocotyledons than dicotyledons. In some bamboos, the whole shoot dies back after flowering, and in some cases growth then continues from an axillary bud on the rhizome. In woody dicotyledons, branching may follow a monopodial or sympodial pattern, or a mixture of the two, and this has a bearing on the ultimate shape of the branches. For example, mistletoe (*Viscum album*) has a characteristic dichasial (forked) branching pattern,

**Climbers and roots** (a) Rattan (climbing palm) with hooked spines on leaf extension (b) *Clematis* with clasping petioles (c) Virginia creeper with adhesive pads on branched tendrils (d) Rose with hooked thorns (e) Twining tendrils *(Passiflora)* (f) Cirrhous leaves (*Gloriosa*) (g) Adventitious roots (ivy) (h) Prop or stilt roots (mangrove) (i) Buttress roots (j) Aerial roots (epiphytic orchid) (k) Liane (*Monstera*) with main stem and descending aerial roots (l) Strangler fig with anastomosing roots where the terminal bud usually dies after flowering, and two lateral buds (rather than just one, as in many other cases) grow out to replace it. In the same way, artificial pruning also strongly influences the ultimate shape of a tree or shrub, by causing dormant lateral buds to grow out.

*Raunkier's classification.* Raunkier (1934) devised a novel classification of five basic types of plant life form. The first four types (phanerophytes, chamaephytes, hemicryptophytes and cryptophytes) are based mainly on the position of the buds and apical meristems in relation to the soil surface. The fifth type (therophytes: annual plants) is based on the duration of life.

Phanerophytes are plants where the buds that will survive the unfavourable season (resting buds) are borne well above the soil surface. Plants of this type may be deciduous or evergreen, and include most trees and shrubs, many climbers, and also some larger woody herbs such as species of *Erica*. Raunkier recognized several sub-types of phanerophytes, based largely on the degree of protection of the buds (either with or without bud scales). Plants that grow in continuously warm, moist environments without distinct seasons are included in this category. He also noted that in most phanerophytes (except certain weeping trees), the shoots are more or less negatively geotrophic, that is, they grow upwards away from the ground.

Most of the so-called alpines, which include many of the most attractive small garden plants, are either chamaephytes or hemicryptophytes. In chamaephytes, the resting buds that survive the winter are just above the soil surface, the inflorescences and other aerial parts dying back to about this level. Chamaephytes include many trailing plants, such as *Lysimachia*, and also cushion plants, such as some *Saxifraga* spp. The winter buds are protected by withered leaves. Hemicryptophytes have the resting buds more or less at or just in the soil surface, protected by the surrounding remains of old leaves, as in rosette plants such as the daisy (*Bellis perennis*). They often spread by means of horizontal stolons or rhizomes, and may have underground storage organs, but do not die back entirely beneath the soil. *Alchemilla vulgaris* and *Hepatica nobilis* are examples of hemicryptophytes, with green leaves throughout the winter, and also the dandelion (*Taraxacum vulgare*), with underground root tubers.

The resting buds of cryptophytes occur below the soil surface. This category therefore includes water plants (helophytes and hydrophytes), and also geophytes, which are perennial plants whose aerial parts die back completely each year to an underground storage organ, such as a rhizome (e.g. some species of *Iris*), bulb (e.g. *Tulipa*, and other species of *Iris*) or corm (e.g. *Crocus*).

*Underground storage organs and vegetative reproduction.* Rhizomes are underground stems that last for more than one growing season, and are usually horizontally oriented. Many plants have rhizomes, and these serve a dual role both as food storage organs (in cases where they are somewhat swollen, such as ginger, and species of *Iris*), and organs for vegetative reproduction, ensuring the lateral (often sympodial) growth of the plant. If a branch of a rhizome is broken off, it can be replanted and grown elsewhere, thus ensuring an efficient means of vegetative propagation. Sometimes an underground stem or rhizome turns upwards and forms new aerial plants (suckers), that eventually become disconnected from the parent plant. This is especially characteristic of certain trees, such as poplar (*Populus*) and elm (*Ulmus*), and can be a nuisance in a small garden. Horizontal above-ground stems for vegetative growth, such as occur in the strawberry (*Fragaria*), are called runners or stolons, and these also produce plantlets that are eventually independent of the parent.

Many underground storage organs have thickened contractile roots, which serve to pull them deeper into the soil. Corms are a modified form of swollen underground stem, usually vertically oriented in the soil and representing a single year's growth, although they may be composed of several internodes (e.g. in *Crocus*). Most corms have an outer 'tunic' of dry protective leaf bases. In rare cases, such as *Crocosmia*, the corms from previous years do not wither away, resulting in a string of persistent corms, of which the basal ones sometimes put out axillary branches to form new corms.

Stem-tubers are swollen underground stems that bear the resting buds, the other parts of the shoot system dying back during the unfavourable season. When used in its broadest sense, this term can also include corms and also many rhizomes, but it is most commonly applied to those plants where the tubers are swollen pieces of subterranean stolons, such as in the potato (*Solanum tuberosum*), where the 'eyes' are axillary buds at the nodes. If a potato is left in the ground, the eyes will develop into shoot systems, including rhizomes which will bear more tubers, and the food reserves in the original tuber will eventually be used up. On the other hand, root tubers (such as in *Dahlia*) cannot be used for vegetative propagation, as they are simply swollen or tuberous storage roots, and therefore lack axillary buds. In such cases growth occurs from buds formed on a central crown, which can be divided accordingly.

In bulbs, of which the onion (*Allium*) is a well-known example, the stem is reduced to a flat disc-like structure, with swollen fleshy leaf bases or scale leaves. In *Hippeastrum* bulbs the fleshy storage leaves are composed of the bases of the previous year's foliage leaves, whereas tulip bulbs are composed entirely of fleshy non-photosynthetic scale leaves. *Narcissus* and *Iris* bulbs have a mixture of the two types. New bulbs form from axillary buds in the old bulb, and may be split off for re-planting. (See also BULBS).

*Duration of life and seasonality.* Plant life cycles vary greatly in duration. In annual plants (therophytes) the entire life cycle takes place during one growing season, and the next generation survives in the form of seeds. Annuals are particularly numerous in deserts and other places where unfavourable growth conditions are typically severe and prolonged, sometimes for many years. Ephemerals such as shepherd's purse (*Capsella bursa-pastoris*) live only a few weeks and can have several generations in one summer, rapidly colonizing new ground. In temperate climates, summer annuals such as petty spurge (*Euphorbia peplus*) germinate in the spring and die in the autumn. Winter annuals such as annual buttercup (*Ranunculus* spp.) germinate in the autumn and are dead by the following summer, thereby avoiding the competition of spring plants. Some plants, the biennials, such as foxglove (*Digitalis*) and mullein (*Verbascum*) take two years to grow, flower, fruit and die. The first year is vegetative, to build up food reserves, and they overwinter in the form of a rosette of leaves with an underground storage organ; flowering and fruiting occur in the second year. Biennial plants, with a longer growing time, thus tend to be larger than annuals. Some plants live for several years, then flower and die: these, which include *Saxifraga longifolia* and most agaves, are termed monocarpic.

Plants that survive for several years are perennials, although in some cases the aerial parts die down at the end of each season (as in *Galanthus*, the snowdrop, or *Crocus*), whereas in many others they persist from year to year. Perennials can be herbaceous or woody. Many tropical rainforest plants, which are less affected by adverse seasons, are evergreen, and may grow more or less continuously for several hundred years. Deciduous trees may also grow for a very long period, but shed their leaves before the seasonal dormant period, when there is almost no growth or water uptake, and the next season's leaves are enclosed in resting buds.

*Climbers.* Some plants raise their leaves high above the ground by climbing up surrounding structures (such as other plants). These are called climbers or vines or, in the case of tropical woody creeping vines, lianes (lianas). Vines may spiral tightly around the supporting structure, in the case of twiners, such as bindweed (*Convolvulus*), and the runner bean (*Phaseolus*). In *Clematis* the petioles tend to hook themselves round adjacent shoots; and other plants have certain organs modified into grasping tendrils. Most tendrils are modified leaves or leaflets of compound leaves, for example, in the sweet pea (*Lathyrus odoratus*), but in the passion flower (*Passiflora*) tendrils are modified axillary shoots, and similarly in Virginia creeper (*Parthenocissus*), where individual tendrils have short adhesive discs at the ends, which develop when the growing tip comes into contact with a firm surface. In ivy (*He-*

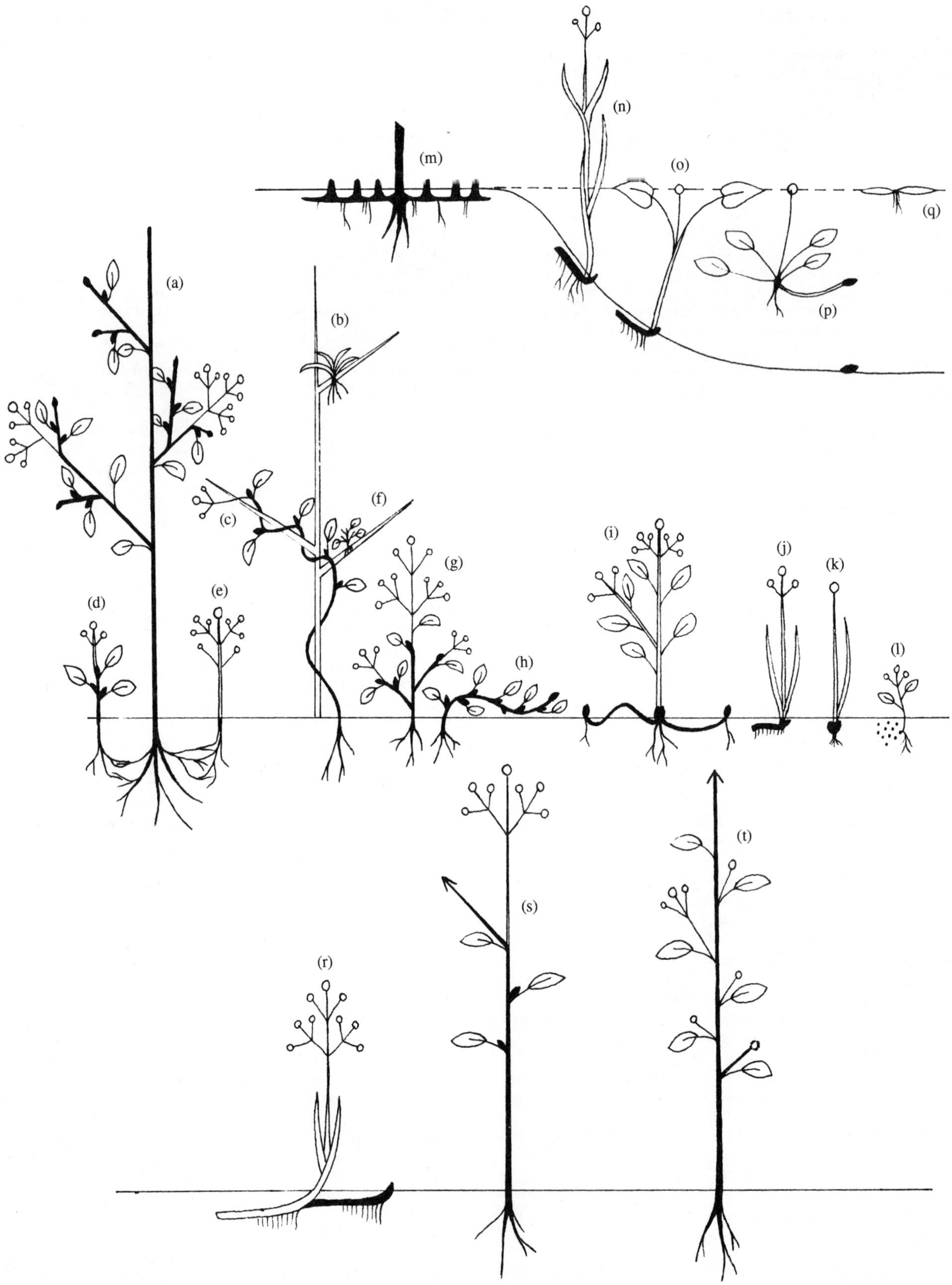


**Life forms and growth habits** (Open circles indicate flowers. Thick black regions indicate perennial parts, except in (r), where black indicates subsequent season's growth). (a) Phanerophyte. (b) Epiphyte. (c) Climber (liane). (d) Partial parasite. (e) Obligate parasite. (f) Epiphytic partial parasite. (g,h) Chamaephytes. (i) Hemicryptophyte. (j) Cryptophyte-geophyte (rhizomatous). (k) Cryptophyte-geophyte (cormous or bulbous). (l) therophyte (annual). (m) Mangrove with pneumatophores. (n) Cryptophyte-helophyte. (o) Cryptophyte-hydrophte. (p) Cryptophyte-hydrophte (submerged). (q) Cryptophyte-hydrophte (surface floating). (r) Cryptophyte with sympodial growth. (s) Phanerophyte with sympodial growth. (t) Phanerophyte with monopodial growth.

*dera helix*), the twining stems produce groups of short adventitious roots at the nodes which penetrate cracks in surrounding bark or masonry, sometimes causing damage to buildings. Many tropical climbers, such as *Monstera* or *Philodendron*, also adopt this strategy; the adventitious aerial roots – often as long as the main stem of the plant itself – serve a double function, by attaching the plant when they adhere to the surface of the supporting tree and by seeking water. Perhaps the simplest type of climber is the scrambler, such as bramble (*Rubus*), where the stems grow vertically for a while, then bend under their own weight, and lean on surrounding vegetation. This habit is described as sprawling or scandent, and many such plants are assisted by thorns or prickles which lodge the stems of the supporting plants.

*Epiphytes.* Broadly, epiphytes are plants that grow on branches of trees or rock faces (or even telegraph poles and wires and lamp-posts). More usually, however, the term is restricted to plants growing upon others without parasitism, a condition common in orchids, aroids, bromeliads and ferns in warm regions and in mosses elsewhere. Plants found on rocks and buildings are termed lithophytes. Since their roots are never in deep substrates, epiphytes tend to live in moist conditions such as wet tropical forests, although relatively short-lived epiphytes also grow in temperate regions and some orchids, bromeliads and cacti grow epiphytically in arid places. Many epiphytes have developed special methods of obtaining nutrients from their surroundings, some epiphytic bromeliads collect and absorb water and other nutrients in a rigid cup-shaped rosette of leaves, and others trap water in special hairs. Most epiphytic tropical orchids have aerial roots that absorb surrounding moisture.

*Buttress and stilt roots.* Although buttress or stilt roots can sometimes be seen in temperate regions, they are found most often on tropical rain forest plants. Buttresses occur on kapok (*Ceiba pentandra*) and many *Ficus* spp., which are competitive for greater height and sunlight, and achieve more support at their bases by this means. Stilt roots are found in many forest trees and are also a feature of tidal mangrove vegetation, such as in *Rhizophora*, where branched looping roots grow from the trunk and lower branches, and are exposed for at least part of the day, although often covered at high tide. *Rhizophora* also produces negatively geotrophic, spongy, specialized breathing roots or pneumatophores. In temperate zones, this strategy may also be observed in the swamp cypress *Taxodium distichum* (alongside trunk buttressing), particularly if found in waterlogged conditions.

*Water plants.* Some plants, such as ground ivy (*Glechoma hederacea*), are apparently equally at ease either submerged in the water or on (relatively) dry land, without obvious modifications for an aquatic life. Others may have floating or aerial leaves depending on their habitat, or at different stages in their life cycle. In general, plants that grow in and around the water's edge (helophytes), such as the bulrush (*Typha* spp.), project their aerial parts above the surface of the water. The leaves of true aquatics (hydrophytes) are more often either floating or submerged. A rheophyte is a plant that inhabits running water.

Submerged leaves may be long, trailing and ribbon-like, as in some species of *Potamogeton*, or narrow, forming feathery shoots, as in Canadian waterweed (*Elodea canadensis*). The blades of floating leaves, such as in the waterlilies (e.g. *Nymphaea* spp.), are usually large and entire, with a long petiole. Heterophylly is common among water plants; for example, some waterlilies may have aerial, floating or submerged leaves, each somewhat different in form. Submerged leaves are generally produced in the winter and spring, and when the water is fast flowing, and floating leaves during the flowering season. In *Eichhornia crassipes*, a very common and attractive water weed, the petioles are swollen into bladder-like organs, enabling the plant to float and disperse easily; however, the bladders are reduced in a plant rooted on a muddy shore. The air-filled tissue that forms the floating vessels of the water hyacinth is known as aerenchyma. It can be found as a woody excrescence in marginals like the tropical legume, *Neptunia*. Many water plants are rooted in the soil below, but some, such as duckweed (*Lemna*), are free floating, with their roots hanging down into the water. *Elodea canadensis* is capable of living unattached for considerable periods of time. It disperses by parts breaking off and rooting elsewhere downstream, as well as by seed (sometimes rarely produced: it never reproduces sexually in Britain). In most cases flowers are raised above the water surface, although a few aquatics, such as the hornwort (*Ceratophyllum*) and some water starworts (*Callitriche*) and *Vallisneria*, even flower underwater.

Most water plants occur in freshwater, although some prefer brackish water, but there are a few species of submerged marine flowering plants, the eel-grasses (Zosteraceae) and *Posidonia* (Posidoniaceae), and of course the seaweeds represent a specialized group of marine algae.

*Xerophytes and succulent plants.* Many groups of plants have become modified for life in a dry (xeric) environment, and these are sometimes called xerophytes, or xeromorphic plants. For example, succulent plants, which normally grow in areas with a scarce or unpredictable water supply, are able to store water in enlarged cells in swollen leaves (in *Sedum, Crassula*, etc.) and in Aizoaceae, where leaves may be reduced to more or less separated 'plant bodies', or swollen stems (as in cacti, and succulent euphorbias). Some cacti can survive for several years with very little extra moisture, and can sustain up to a 70% water loss with little apparent ill effect. Other xeromorphic adaptations protect against high light intensity (such as needle-like leaves, or densely hairy leaves), or against excessive water loss (such as rolled leaves). Some xeromorphic features, such as thick, leathery leaves and swollen stems, may also occur in plants from relatively wet areas, for example the pseudobulbous orchids, but these environments are usually nutrient-deficient in some other respect or 'locally' xeric, either by virtue of the seasons or the site of the plant in question if it be – say – an orchid growing in the exposed crown of a tree.

*Protective structures.* Some plants have structural modifications, such as thorns, spines and prickles which protect them against being eaten by animals, though some occur as adaptations or for climbing. Thorns are modified shoots with very sharp points, as on hawthorn (*Crataegus*), which can become matted together to form dense impenetrable hedges. Spines are modified leaves, as in many cacti, such as *Opuntia*, or parts of leaves, such as the sharp marginal spines of holly (*Ilex*) leaves, or even stipules (e.g. in *Robinia*). In gorse (*Ulex*), both leaves and stems are spiny. The sharp, pointed 'thorns' of roses are correctly called prickles, as they are outgrowths of the epidermis. Many spiny or thorny plants make good hedges; for example, *Berberis, Pyracantha* and *Ilex*, and, in the tropics, prickly cacti and euphorbias. Other protective structures include the hairs of the stinging nettle, *Urtica dioica*, trees like *Laportea*, and are typical of a family like the Loasaceae.

*Abnormal modes of reproduction.* Certain plants from environments that are deficient in particular essential nutrients, especially nitrates, have special methods of obtaining these nutrients from other sources, often involving specialized morphological structures.

Parasites, which obtain their nutrients directly from other plants, may be wholly dependent on their hosts (obligate parasites), or only partially so (partial parasites). Obligate parasites are often more or less colourless, because they are devoid of green chlorophyll for photosynthesis, and their leaves are frequently reduced or even lacking altogether. Dodder (*Cuscuta*) is an annual plant that is parasitic on the stems and leaves of hosts such as clover and heather. It lacks roots except in the seedling stage. The seedling survives alone for a brief period with its tip circling to locate a host, and when it finds one it twines around it and produces suckers. Obligate root parasites such as toothwort (*Lathraea squamaria*) are less obvious because, although the inflorescence is aerial, for most of the time the plant is entirely subterranean, with a branched rhizome that extracts nutrients from roots of other plants (usually hazel and elm). The roots attach themselves to those of the hosts by tiny suckers, and small processes penetrate the host roots and absorb food and water. Occasionally, as in *Rafflesia*, a genus including the biggest flowers in the vegetable kingdom, the parasite inhabits the roots and occasionally the climbing stems of its liane hosts.

Partial parasites retain their green leaves, as they obtain some of their food by photosynthesis, and can sometimes survive independently, although they are far less vigorous under these circumstances. Many Scrophulariaceae, such as the eyebrights (*Euphrasia* spp.) are root partial parasites, for example on grasses.

Mistletoe (*Viscum album*) is a well-known parasite on the branches of trees such as apple and hawthorn, sending processes (haustoria) deep into the wood of the host. It has photosynthesizing leaves but cannot survive without a host.

Saprophytes, which are typically devoid of chlorophyll, live on dead, rotting organic matter. Mushrooms and toadstools are saprophytes, and examples among the flowering plants include *Neottia* and *Corallorhiza* (both Orchidaceae) and *Monotropa*, the Indian pipe. *Neottia nidus-avis* (bird's-nest orchid) grows in dense beech woods with very little sunlight, and lives on decaying leaves. It has an aerial inflorescence and subterranean branching shoots like a bird's nest. These higher plant saprophytes depend on certain beneficial soil fungi which actually invade the root tissues. This symbiotic association is called the mycorrhizal habit and is not confined to plants that are normally called saprophytes. It is important to many conifers, and a milder form of the association occurs in such common garden subjects as beech, oak, rhododendron, apple, and most terrestrial orchids, especially in conditions where humus is plentiful. In the typical plant/fungus association tree roots become short and stocky and are surrounded by a layer of fungal cells; the roots have no root hairs and the fungus strands (mycelium) permeate them; in herbaceous plants the fungus actually penetrates the root cells. The mycorrhizal roots receive their nourishment from the soil entirely via the fungus.

Root nodules, which occur on certain types of plant (often from nitrate-deficient habitats such as moorlands), are small swellings containing symbiotic bacteria. The bacteria convert free nitrogen in the air to nitrates, which are essential to the life of the plant. Root nodules are especially characteristic of the pea family (Leguminosae), and can be important in crop rotation; farmers often grow clover in a field that has previously grown cereal crops, then plough the clover back into the ground to replenish the nitrates.

Some plants have developed varying degrees of symbiosis in order to obtain vital nutrients – most notably the obligate myrmecophiles, which attract and house colonies of ants (see MYRMECOPHILOUS PLANTS). Some plants that grow in nitrate-deficient environments, such as marshes, obtain extra nitrogen by catching and digesting insects. Indeed, it is likely that many plants with sticky surfaces, such as stems of *Silene* and leaves of horse chestnut (*Aesculus*), are able to digest enzymatically the insect carcasses that become attached to them. However, true carnivorous or insectivorous plants have developed special methods of trapping insects (see CARNIVOROUS PLANTS).

See also ALPINES; CACTI AND SUCCULENTS; PLANT ANATOMY; ROOTS.

**Plant pathology**. See Appendix, PESTS, DISEASES AND DISORDERS.

**Plant physiology**. The life of a plant is made up of a large number of interconnecting processes, finely adjusted and coordinated to give the objects we see in our gardens. Animals also carry out similar processes but the fact that they are alive is made more obvious because of their movement. The evidences of life in a plant are more subtle. All living things, plants and animals, share certain fundamental processes without which life would stop. Plants, like animals, need to feed (nutrition) and rid themselves of waste products (excretion). Some of this food they burn to produce energy (respiration) used for movement and growth. Some of the food is used to provide raw materials for this growth. A growing organism eventually produces more of its own kind (reproduction). Living creatures react and respond to their environment (sensitivity). Plant physiology deals with the ways plants carry out these processes and the changes that take place in the substances that make up a plant. These changes are referred to as metabolism.

All living things are made up of interconnected units called cells. Every cell contains protoplasm, a complex syrupy mixture of substances in a watery matrix. Protoplasm is divided up into a clear cytoplasm and a denser nucleus which contains the 'messages' which make the life processes work (Figure 1). In addition, plant cells have two things that animal cells lack – a rigid cell wall made of cellulose and a sac full of watery sap, the vacuole. Plant cells often have little bodies called chloroplasts, as described later. Cells can grow to different shapes and sizes and have different functions. They usually occur together in large numbers called tissues. Different kinds of tissue are put together in a definite pattern called an organ (e.g. a leaf). A whole living plant consists of several of these organs coordinated together.

PLANT CHEMISTRY

Plants are very clever chemists. They can manufacture (synthesize) a huge variety of chemicals, many of which can be made by human chemists only with great difficulty or not at all. Some are obvious like starch, oil, protein and wood, while others are more subtle like pigments, scents and drugs. All play some part in a plant's life and many are used by humans to their advantage. The major chemicals used in a plant's day-to-day life are carbohydrates, oils and proteins. Many plants produce large amounts of eventually non-living material, such as wood, which is part of their mechanical support system.

CARBOHYDRATES. These are chemicals containing the elements carbon, hydrogen and oxygen. The atoms of these elements are joined together to make simple groups or units called sugars. These simple sugar units can be strung together into complicated arrangements called polysaccharides. Whenever a large number of simple chemical units are joined together to make a complex structure the result is called a polymer. Plastics are examples of artificial polymers. There are several kinds of polymer made in nature which are of prime importance to life.

*Sugars*. Glucose and fructose are two sugars found in all living things. We taste them in sweet fruit and honey. Galactose, mannose, ribose, xylose and arabinose are other sugars which play a major part in metabolism. Sucrose is made of two simple sugar units, glucose and fructose, and in some plants such as sugar cane and sugar beet it accumulates in large quantities.

*Polysaccharides*. Starch is one important example, made of long chains of dozens of glucose units and in fact used by the plant as a glucose store. Most plants could not store a syrupy sugar solution but can easily cope with a white, inert powder. Gums and mucilages produced by plants are also polysaccharides. Cellulose is the other main example; cotton wool is almost pure cellulose. Plant cell walls are made of cellulose fibres laid down to form sheets. Like starch it is also made of glucose units but they are joined together in a different way to make the hard fibres.

OILS AND FATS (Lipids). These also contain carbon, hydrogen and oxygen but in different proportions than in carbohydrates. At ordinary temperatures they are either liquid (oils) or solid (fats). 'Unsaturated' oils and fats will take up more hydrogen and are thus chemically reactive. 'Saturated' oils and fats will not and so are inert. They are all made up of two parts, glycerine and an acid fraction. These so-called 'fatty' acids are selected from a whole list of substances, which is the reason why there are many kinds of fats and oils. They can be burnt to give energy and are often stored by plants, especially in certain seeds, as energy stores.

PROTEINS. These are made from nitrogen as well as carbon, hydrogen and oxygen. Some of them also contain sulphur. They are another example of a natural polymer, giant structures made up of thousands of individual units called amino acids. There are hundreds of different amino acids found in the plant kingdom but only 22 are found in proteins, plant or animal. It is the different number and arrangement of these amino acids which leads to the enormous variety of living things. Every type of plant or animal

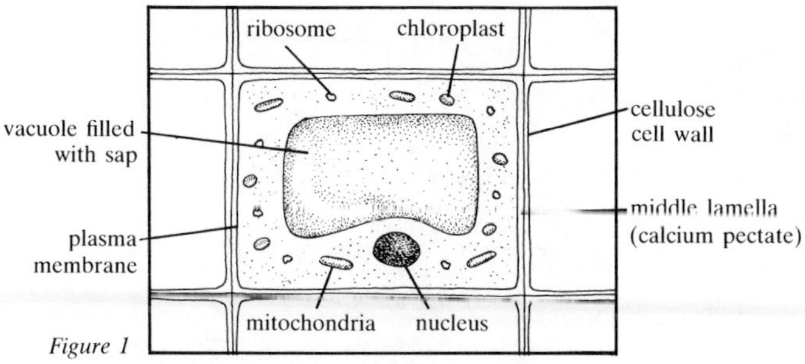


*Figure 1*

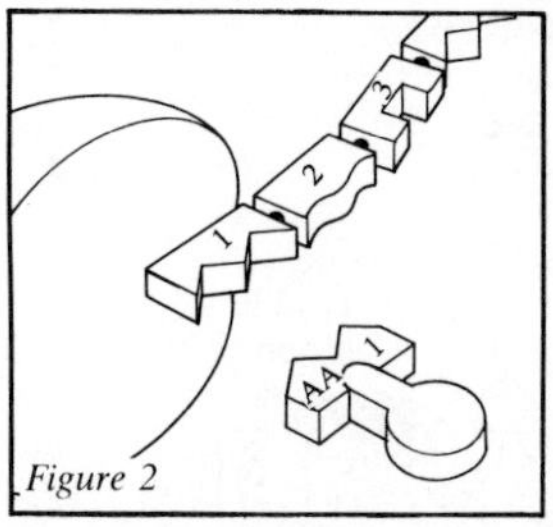
*Figure 2*

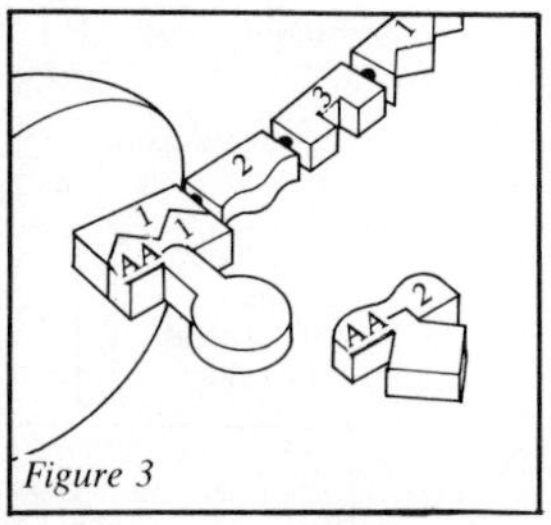
*Figure 3*

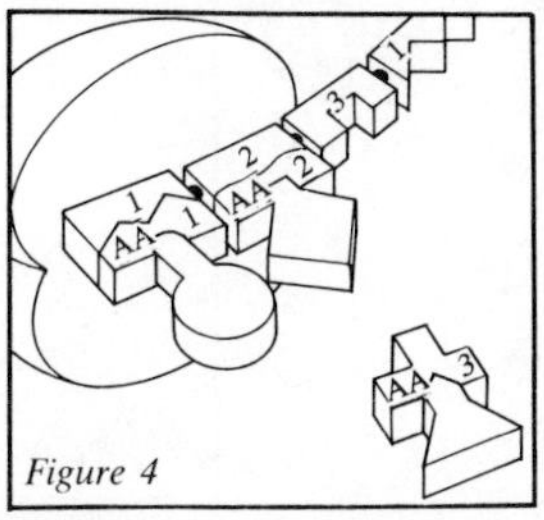
*Figure 4*

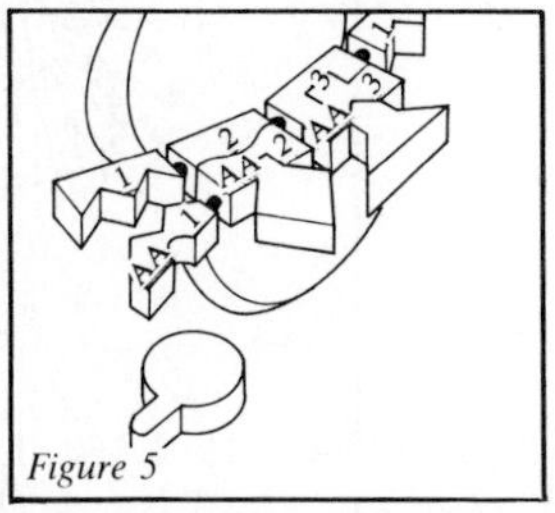
*Figure 5*

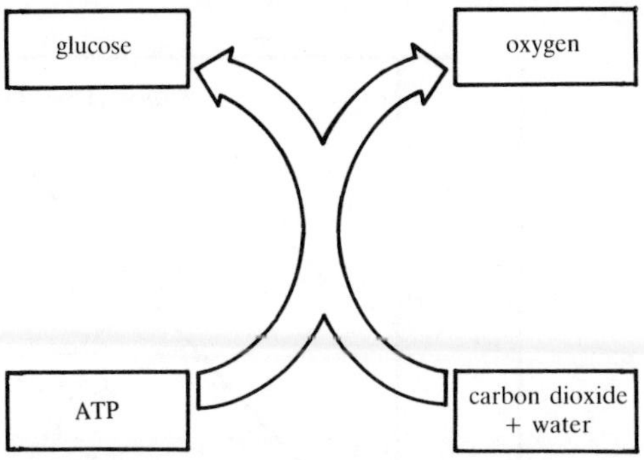


*Figure 6*

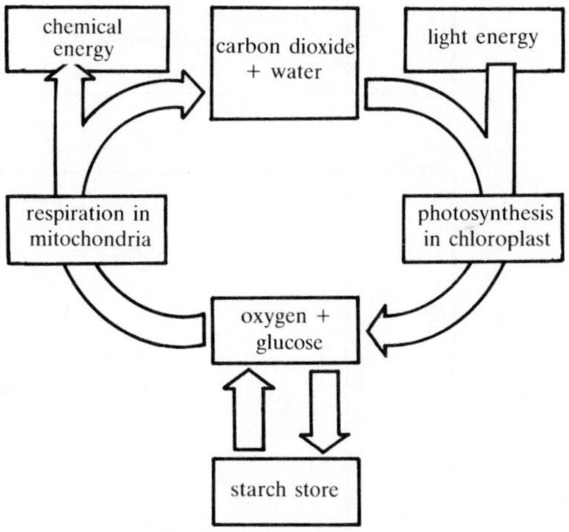


*Figure 7*

**Plant physiology** (1) Diagram of layout of a typical photosynthetic plant cell with its major organelles (2-5) Building the Proteins (see text) (6) Creation of ATP (7) Diagram of carbon cycle in a green plant, showing the conversion of light energy into chemical energy

has its own distinct set of protein patterns, and the proteins within each set are different from each other.

*Protein patterns – the nucleic acids*. There must be some sort of master pattern or code to make sure that when new protein is made in a cell it has exactly the same protein as the old, so that buttercup grows more buttercup and cow grows more cow. These patterns are held in the nucleus by another type of biological polymer, DNA (deoxyribonucleic acid). They make up the chromosomes. When more protein of a particular type needs to be made, its own particular pattern is copied from the master DNA pattern into another nucleic acid, RNA (ribonucleic acid), which travels out from the nucleus to the cytoplasm. Only part of the DNA pattern is copied by this so-called messenger RNA (mRNA) according to the kind of protein needed by the organism at that particular moment. The amino acids are then prepared for joining up by each one being attached to another kind of RNA, transfer RNA (tRNA) of which each acid has its own individual type.

*Building the proteins*. Amino acids are built up into proteins on tiny bodies called ribosomes in the cytoplasm. Each ribosome is a double structure. One end of the messenger RNA strand joins to it. The first amino acid in the protein sequence, together with its own transfer RNA, attaches to the ribosome guided by the code on the RNA (Figure 2). The second amino acid and its tRNA join it (Figure 3). The two are then joined to each other. A third amino acid with its tRNA attaches to the ribosome and is joined to the first two (Figure 4). The tRNA of the first amino acid is then shed and goes back into the cytoplasm to become attached to another detached amino acid of the right sort (Figure 5). A fourth amino acid joins the chain and so it goes on until a complete protein with the right number and sequence of amino acids is formed. This moves away from the ribosome and mRNA which then can be used again.

ENZYMES. Many chemical processes proceed very slowly if left to themselves. Some ordinary starch mixed with water will just stay the same indefinitely. Spit into the mixture and very rapidly the starch will be turned into sugar: saliva contains an agent which greatly speeds up the chemical reaction. Such agents are called catalysts and are much used in industrial processes. The kind found in living tissues are referred to as enzymes and are always proteins. Enzymes in our mouth, stomach and intestine break down the food (digestion). Other enzymes in the tissues carry out (catalyse) all the processes of life.

Enzymes are very specific as to the process they will catalyse, so that each reaction has its particular enzyme. Being proteins they are easily destroyed (denatured) by heating, just like an egg white coagulating. They have an optimum temperature at which they work best and also an optimum acidity or alkalinity.

'SECONDARY' COMPOUNDS. As well as the major biochemicals members of the plant kingdom between them contain thousands of chemical substances. Their role in a plant's life is usually not known so they have been regarded as 'secondary' in contrast to the main 'primary' substances. They may well have very important functions. Many are highly biologically active and have been used as medicines and poisons. Others are used as flavourings, colourings and scents.

*Alkaloids*. These substances are highly active, often poisonous, and certain plant families (e.g. Solanaceae, Ranunculaceae) are particularly rich in them. Chemically the group is very varied but one thing they have in common is the presence of nitrogen. Nicotine is a well-known alkaloid from tobacco which is useful as an insecticide. Some poppies contain the all-too-notorious opium alkaloids. Quinine and caffeine are two alkaloids in common use. The curare blow-pipe poisons are alkaloids of use in surgery as temporary paralysis agents.

*Terpenoids*. Many of the strong scents associated with plants are terpenes, sometimes called 'essential oils', although not chemically oils. Examples are menthone from mint, lavendulol from lavender and geraniol from scented pelargonium. Also in the

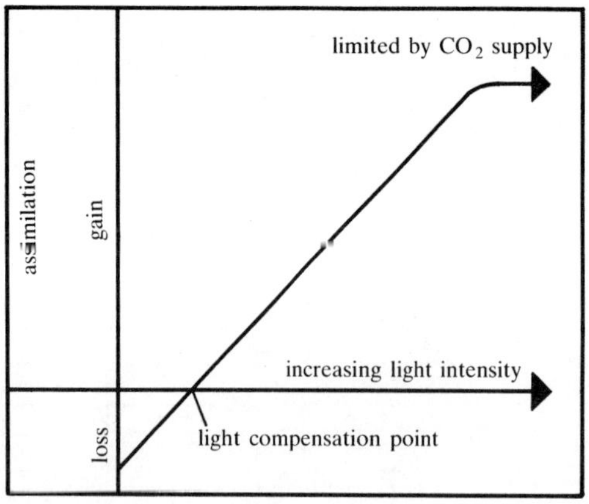


*Figure 8*

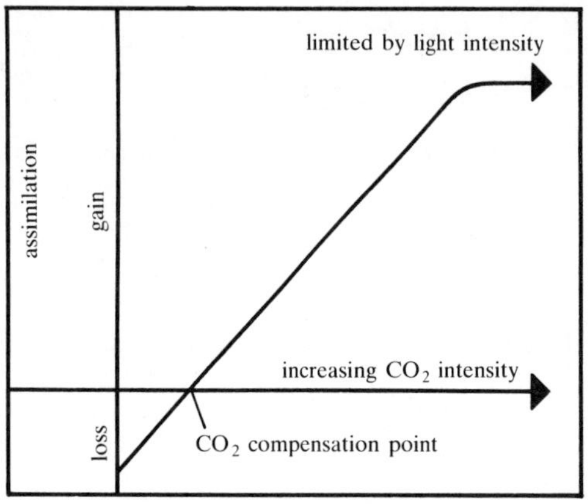


*Figure 9*

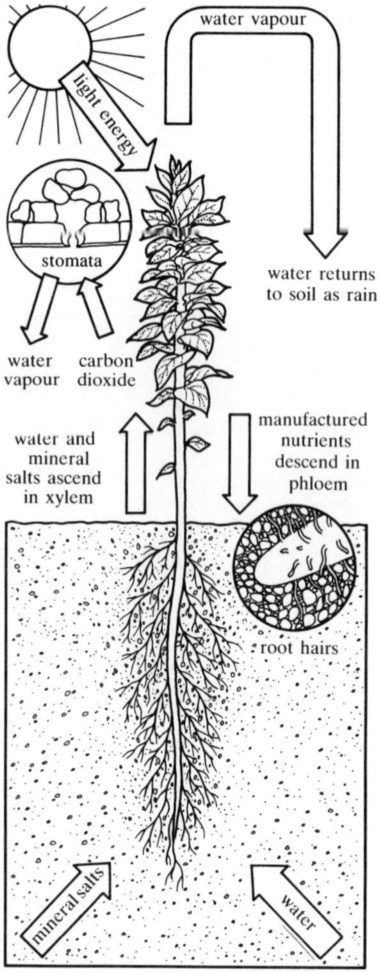


*Figure 11*

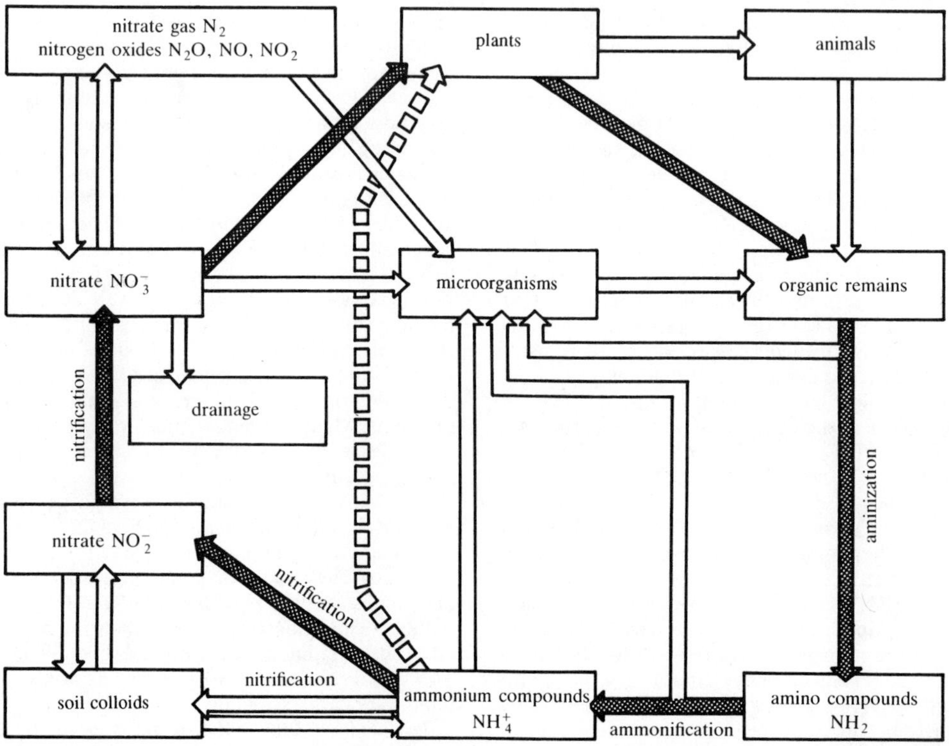


*Figure 10*

**Plant physiology** (8) Relation between assimilation (carbohydrate synthesis) in a leaf, and light intensity (9) Relation between assimilation (carbohydrate synthesis) in a leaf, and $CO_2$ concentration (10) The Nitrogen Cycle: diagram showing the circulation of nitrogen in nature (11) Diagram showing the movements of water and nutrients in a typical plant category are carotenoids which give orange, red and yellow colours to plants, such as carotene in carrots, lycopene in tomatoes and xanthophyll in leaves. Rubber, which occurs as globules in many kinds of plant latex, is a complex polymer of a simple terpenoid called isoprene.

*Phenolics*. Other types of plant flavour and scent, such as vanillin from vanilla orchid pods and eugenol from cloves, are phenolic in nature. A useful phenol is salicylic acid from willow bark which has been developed to give a synthetic derivative, aspirin, one of the world's most useful drugs. Other examples are the humulenes from hops which give the flavour to beer and the cannabinoids from hashish. Lignin, which makes up the substance of wood, is a complex phenolic polymer. Most red, blue and purple flower colours are produced by anthocyanins which are phenolic materials also containing sugars and sometimes metal atoms.

pH – ACIDS AND BASES. All watery solutions are either acidic, alkaline (basic) or neutral (in between). Special dyes called indicators will change to a different colour in each of the three conditions so that you can tell which is prevailing. A scale of acidity or alkalinity can be worked out mathematically with values which correspond to shades of the different colours of the indicator dye. On this scale, called the pH scale, neutral solutions always have the value of 7. Acidic solutions have values below 7 and alkaline solutions values above 7. The further away from 7 the value, the more acidic or alkaline the solution, and the indicator dye changes to an appropriate shade of colour.

Living cells are mostly water and therefore have a characteristic pH. This applies to all biological fluids such as plant sap and animal blood. If for any reason the pH of a cell is forced away from its normal pH, perhaps by some abnormal metabolic event, then the health of the organism is threatened. This rarely happens because of the cell buffer system. A buffer is a mixture of certain mineral salts in such proportions that addition of acids or bases will be automatically compensated for so that the pH rapidly returns to normal. Different buffer mixtures regulate different pH's. Of course, a large excess of added acid or base can override a buffer and then lasting harm can be done.

COLLOIDS. Substances that are insoluble in water can nevertheless, if ground very finely, produce a 'colloidal suspension' which does not settle out and cannot be filtered. The clay part of soil is such a colloid. Living protoplasm is a colloid suspension containing those proteins not soluble in water. Particles of a colloid are electrically charged which helps to keep them from settling. The charge on clay particles can be neutralized by liming, which results in the formation of aggregates giving the soil a coarser, less sticky tilth. Charged soil colloids attract the mineral salts which become absorbed on their surfaces (ion exchange), from which they can subsequently be released. This acts as a reservoir for mineral salts.

## RESPIRATION

All living things, plants, animals and micro-organisms respire. Breathing is a separate process, sometimes called 'external respiration', by which oxygen in the air is carried from the outside to the living cells where true respiration, 'internal respiration', takes place. Waste carbon dioxide goes the other way. Breathing in animals is usually quite complex, involving lungs and a blood system. In plants it is rather simpler.

Respiration is quite simply the release of energy from a fuel, comparable in many ways to the burning of a fuel in a steam or petrol engine. If respiration stops, life stops, irreversibly, so that even a resting seed in a seed packet should be respiring, although at a very slow rate.

In living things the fuel to be burnt is a carbohydrate, glucose. This burning needs oxygen to sustain it and just as in a fire or the carburettor of a motor car if the air is cut off respiration stops. Two waste products are produced from respiration, carbon dioxide and water.

ENERGY. Different kinds of energy are produced as a result of respiration. Animals require a lot of mechanical energy for movement. Plants use more chemical energy for growing – increasing their bulk and adding different organs. If glucose were burnt on a fire the energy produced so rapidly would be mainly heat energy. In living things the burning is more gradual and at a lower temperature through a series of a great many biochemical reactions. The product from these reactions is a substance called adenosine triphosphate (ATP) and it is this that contains the energy in a chemical form (Figure 6). ATP can then be used by different biological systems to liberate different kings of energy. For instance, ATP in a muscle gives mechanical energy for movement: ATP in a poppy capsule gives chemical energy for opium manufacture.

Chemical reactions are speeded up if the temperature is raised and respiration, which consists of many dozens of reactions, is similarly accelerated. Above about 35°C/95°F, however, enzymes start to be denatured and if this process is allowed to go on for any length of time then the rate of respiration will inevitably slow down. Although a high rate of respiration produces much energy it also uses up the food reserves of the plant which need to be replaced by a correspondingly high rate of photosynthesis if healthy growth is to continue.

The ratio of oxygen to carbon dioxide in the atmosphere and the absolute concentrations of both gases all have effects on respiration. Excess carbon dioxide slows respiration partly by its narcotic effect and partly by causing the stomata to close, thus impeding oxygen uptake. A lack of oxygen reduces respiration, although many living cells can adapt to respiring at very low oxygen concentrations. This occurs at the centre of fruits, in yeast cells immersed in a liquid, or in silage bacteria in a silo. It is called anaerobic respiration or fermentation and instead of carbon dioxide produces alcohol or lactic acid as a waste product. Also, of course, less energy is produced.

## PLANT NUTRITION AND GROWTH

All living things grow, that is, add to their body substance, perhaps at different rates at different times. Growth can be observed by making measurements of length and breadth or by weighing. As living things contain a high proportion of water, which can vary according to the outside conditions, it is more accurate to measure increase in body substance by weighing the dry material left after the water has been driven off by heating. This of course kills the plant or animal.

In the previous section we have seen that all living things respire, burning carbohydrate in oxygen to release energy. Animals take in foodstuffs to provide the substances they need for growth and respiration. Plants do not take in complex foodstuffs, except the unusual carnivorous plants, but just use simple substances from the air and from the soil. Carbon dioxide from the air goes into a plant and is combined with water to form glucose. The energy to carry this out comes from light and the process is called photosynthesis. Water and mineral salts flow in from the soil and are used in a variety of ways.

PHOTOSYNTHESIS. Joining carbon dioxide and water together chemically to form a more complex substance like glucose requires a considerable amount of chemical energy. This is almost impossible to achieve in an ordinary laboratory. However, green plants can trap light energy, which in nature would be from sunlight, and transform it into chemical energy which is then used to accomplish the synthesis. Enzymes make all the various reactions happen. Light energy is trapped by the green pigment chlorophyll, which occurs in chloroplasts where the synthesis takes place (Figure 7).

This appears to be respiration in reverse but the two processes take place by different mechanisms, in different places and using different enzymes. Notice that respiration goes on all the time, in light and darkness, and produces carbon dioxide, but that during light periods photosynthesis occurs as well, using up the carbon dioxide and producing oxygen. The stronger the light then the more photosynthesis occurs, within limits. If on the other hand illumination is decreased, then photosynthesis falls until a point is reached at which glucose formation is just balanced by breakdown during respiration. This degree of light intensity is called the Light Compensation Point (Figure 8).

Plants adapted for growing in the shade have a low compensation point so that they can still achieve a net gain of glucose when the light intensity is low.

Research has shown that photosynthesis is made up of two processes, the so-called Light Reaction and the Dark Reaction. During the light reaction, light trapped by chlorophyll brings about the splitting of water ($H_2O$) into oxygen which is the waste product and a special form of hydrogen, not the free gas. Hydrogen is a fuel; it can be burnt in oxygen to give energy. This energy is transferred into ATP (see above) and then this compound is used to drive a complex series of reactions turning carbon dioxide into glucose. It it this latter part that is called the dark reaction because no extra light is needed for it. The dark reaction is sometimes called dark fixation of carbon dioxide. The glucose produced is of course a soluble sugar and if formed in large quantities would soon become a sticky syrup in the plant and disturb its activities. A few plants such as sugar maple and sugar cane can tolerate these high levels of sugar but most plants cannot. Nonetheless, plants need to accumulate reserves of sugar to be used for respiration (a necessity for life) during darkness or very dull weather when photosynthesis is nil or very low. They do this by turning the glucose into starch which is insoluble in water and so does not form a syrup but is stored in starch grains. When needed these stores break down and release glucose (Figure 6).

If the amount of carbon dioxide supplied to a plant is gradually increased from nothing there comes a concentration at which the amount used in photosynthesis exactly balances that lost in respiration so that no net gain or loss of glucose occurs. This concentration is called the carbon dioxide compensation point and photosynthesis can only be effective above this (Figure 9).

An increase in light intensity, carbon dioxide concentration or temperature can result in increased photosynthesis but this increase is limited in two ways. Firstly there is a level at which each of these harm the living tissue of the plant and would eventually kill it. Light harms by radiation damage, carbon dioxide by a narcotic effect and temperature by degrading (denaturing) the enzyme proteins. Secondly, at lower levels, their effect on photosynthesis is limited by each other. Thus an increase in photosynthesis produced by a moderate increase in light intensity is brought to a stop when the carbon dioxide runs out. In the same way increases following an increased concentration of carbon dioxide stop if there is insufficient light energy to fuel the reactions. An increase in temperature speeds up both respiration and photosynthesis, the former more quickly, so that soon respiration burns up the glucose faster than photosynthesis can replace it. These balances are referred to as the Principle of Limiting Factors and must be taken into account if plants are grown in unnatural conditions in attempts to enhance growth. Thus in glasshouses plants may be given extra light, artificially, but this will only be successful if enough carbon dioxide is available. On the other hand addition of extra carbon dioxide to that already in the atmosphere is again only successful if the light intensity is strong enough to allow sufficient photosynthesis. A high temperature in a glasshouse, especially during dull weather, can cause the plants to respire their glucose away and actually decrease in weight.

Chlorophyll itself can be a limiting factor because it is needed in sufficient quantities to trap sufficient light energy for the greatest photosynthesis allowed by the other limiting factors. Chlorophyll contains carbon, hydrogen, oxygen, nitrogen and magnesium and if any of these are deficient then the full possible degree of photosynthesis cannot be achieved. The carbon, hydrogen and oxygen come from glucose produced by photosynthesis itself, while the nitrogen and magnesium come from mineral salts originating in the soil. If the soil is deficient in these salts or conditions are too cold for them to be taken up adequately then there will be a deficiency in chlorophyll and its concentration becomes limiting to photosynthesis. Other internal factors controlling photosynthesis depend upon the concentration of mineral nutrients from the soil, so any deficiency of these can affect the process. In plants, chlorophyll is enclosed in discrete bodies called chloroplasts and the number and arrangement of these can govern the efficiency of light-trapping. Chloroplasts are embedded in the cytoplasm of rows of oblong cells (known as palisade mesophyll) just underneath the leaf epidermis. Even the arrangement of the leaves themselves can have an effect. Thus in very sunny climates some plants align their leaf edge on to the direction of the sun, to avoid heat and ultra violet radiation damage. However, by doing this they also fail to take full advantage of the available light energy. In more temperate climates leaves are often aligned facing the sun so that the broad leaf blade absorbs all the light possible.

Plants growing close together will shade each others' leaves. There is a certain density of planting at which the plants do not affect each other like this but are yet not so thinly planted as to waste space. Also of course the leaves of one plant can shade each other, as can other organs. It is thus important to remove redundant parts which are having this effect, giving particular attention to ageing leaves which are senescing, losing chlorophyll, and therefore not photosynthesizing themselves at maximum efficiency but impeding the photosynthesis of younger leaves by such shading.

*Alternative methods of photosynthesis*. Some plants have been found to have their chloroplasts in two locations. Some are in the palisade mesophyll as already described. Others are found in a layer of cells forming a sheath around the leaf's vascular bundles (Kranz tissue). Moreover, they differ in that the mesophyll chloroplasts do not form starch but the sheath ones do. What happens is that illuminated mesophyll chloroplasts fix carbon dioxide into compounds with four carbon atoms, either malic acid or aspartic acid. These are transported to the sheath cells where they are broken down to form carbon dioxide again. This is then photosynthesized in the normal way with glucose and the starch as products. The process has a low carbon dioxide compensation point and is efficient in scavenging all available carbon dioxide in the atmosphere, especially at high temperatures. The system ('C4 photosynthesis', referring to the four carbon acids above) is found in many tropical grasses and has been much studied in sugar cane. It also occurs in temperate families, notably Chenopodiaceae and Amaranthaceae.

Another variation occurs in succulent plants living in hot, dry habitats. Because of the extreme drying conditions of the atmosphere and lack of water in the soil, the transpiration stream must be reduced to a very low level so that desiccation is avoided, in spite of succulence. To do this, the stomata are closed during the day. However, this means that carbon dioxide in the air cannot be taken up during the day, when photosynthesis should be taking place. During the cooler nights the stomata are open and carbon dioxide can then enter the plant. Succulent plants can fix this carbon dioxide in the dark, into malic acid which is stored until daylight. It is then broken down to release carbon dioxide which is made into glucose by the normal process of photosynthesis. This process ('Crassulacean Acid Metabolism', CAM) separates carbon dioxide fixation from photosynthesis in time, whereas C4 photosynthesis separates them in space.

## MINERAL NUTRITION

We have seen that the elements carbon, hydrogen and oxygen are obtained by a green plant from carbon dioxide in the air and water in the soil. Carbohydrates and fats particularly are made from these elements. Proteins which make up the living structure of the cell contain the element nitrogen also, which is obtained from mineral nitrates in the soil. Most proteins contain sulphur and this is also derived from the soil. Phosphorus in phosphates plays a central part in energy production. There is a small number of metallic elements which culture tests have shown to be essential for normal healthy plant growth and all these are also derived from the soil. All these substances are dissolved in the soil water and are taken up by plant roots and are then carried to other parts of the plant where they are used.

*Anthocyanin pigmentation*. Weedy species which are able to survive, even if in a stunted condition in inhospitable environments such as gravel paths, are usually observed to have abnormal red or purple colourations in their leaves and stems. This is due to the formation of anthocyanins, the same pigments that occur normally in many flowers and in the leaves of species such as the copper beech. This is a typical starvation symptom, an indication of a deficiency of nitrogen and phosphorus, although the reasons for it are not known.

NITROGEN. Air contains a large amount of nitrogen gas which is invisible, odourless and cannot support life or burning.

**Composition of air**

| | *By weight* | *By volume* |
|---|---|---|
| Nitrogen | 76% | 78% |
| Oxygen | 23% | 21% |
| Carbon dioxide | 0.04% | 0.03% |
| Others | 1.30% | 0.95% |

Although there is so much nitrogen available in this form, plants cannot make use of it but rely entirely on the combined nitrogen in soil nitrates. A few micro-organisms can use atmospheric gaseous nitrogen and incorporate it in their own protein, which on their death decomposes and puts nitrate into the soil. Nitrates are very soluble so that they are easily leached out of soil by water. A light sandy soil leaches more easily than a heavy soil where the clay and humus hold on to the nitrates.

A great part of the nitrogen taken up by the plant is incorporated in protein as already mentioned. Nucleic acids, which carry the genetic information, contain nitrogen, as does the green pigment chlorophyll, on which photosynthesis depends. The other important pigment metabolite, which occurs in the cytochromes, also contains nitrogen.

The most obvious sign of a deficiency of nitrogen in a plant is the lack of production of chlorophyll, which gives a yellowing (chlorosis) of the leaves. Senescent leaves also yellow as the chlorophyll is broken down at a faster rate than it is formed. The older leaves of a deficient plant yellow before the younger leaves because what nitrogen there is is transported from older to younger. Because of the lack of protein there is a lack of growth and especially a lack of production of organs such as fruits and seeds.

Nitrogen deficiency can be corrected by supplying the soil with either organic nitrogen, such as some form of manure or with nitrate salts, such as potassium, calcium or ammonium nitrate. The former needs to decompose and thus release the nitrogen, as nitrate, slowly. The latter are soluble and have an immediate effect.

Nitrogen stimulates growth, and is often applied to plants at this start of their growing season. Plants which have received an excess of nitrogenous fertilizer have abundant lush vegetative growth with deep green leaves and flowering often delayed. This abundant soft growth is often susceptible to fungus infection.

THE NITROGEN CYCLE. A normal soil can quite quickly become depleted of nitrates both through loss in drainage and uptake by growing plants. In natural vegetation there is a cyclic process by which the nitrogen in plants and animals is returned to the soil ready to be taken up again (Figure 10).

*Stage 1*. Plants, or parts of them, can be eaten by animals or if not they will eventually die and fall on the soil. The animals excrete copiously and also themselves die and fall on, or remain on, the soil. This dead and waste organic material is attacked by all sorts of scavengers and rotted down. During this process in a normal soil, putrefying bacteria break down the proteins so that the nitrogen in them is released as ammonia. Free ammonia is an evil-smelling poisonous gas which you can sometimes smell on heavily contaminated wet soils. It is toxic to plants. In its combined form, ammonium salts, the ammonia is odourless and harmless but very soluble in water and easily turned into toxic ammonia gas.

*Stage 2*. Ammonium salts can be taken up by plants but tend to cause the starch reserves to be rapidly used up. Normally ammonium salts are converted by a group of nitrifying soil bacteria (*Nitrosomonas*) into compounds called nitrites. These substances are quite toxic but fortunately are rapidly converted by another group of nitrifying soil bacteria (*Nitrobacter*) to nitrates. Nitrifying bacteria flourish in a well-aerated soil at moderate temperatures with sufficient soil nutrients to maintain their own growth.

*Stage 3*. The usual form of nitrogen taken up by plant roots is nitrate nitrogen. By a long series of biochemical processes it is then incorporated into protein and the other nitrogenous substances of the plant body. The first step is attack on nitrate by an enzyme, nitrate reductase, which exists in the roots of most plants. A few unusual plants lack this enzyme and so cannot make use of nitrates but must take up their nitrogen in the form of ammonium salts or possibly urea, a soluble organic nitrogenous substance.

*Other routes*. As already described, nitrate nitrogen can be lost from the soil by being easily washed out. In heavy, waterlogged soils nitrate nitrogen can be turned into nitrogen gas by the activity of certain bacteria which only operate under these conditions. They are termed anaerobic bacteria and can only be active in the absence of gaseous oxygen. In order to respire they are able to use the oxygen in nitrate and release the nitrogen as the free gas (Figure 10).

*Nitrogen fixation*. Although atmospheric nitrogen gas cannot be used by plants there are soil bacteria which can do so and by their activity ('fixation') return nitrogen to the nitrogen cycle. *Azotobacter* lives in most soils and can readily fix nitrogen into its own protein which eventually will be returned to the soil as nitrate. A very important group of soil bacteria (*Rhizobium*) live not free in the soil but enclosed in bulbous structures (nodules) on the roots of certain plants, mostly those belonging to the pea, bean, and clover family, Leguminosae. Although these are the best-known ones there are others living on a number of other plants, for example *Actinomyces* in nodules on alder roots.

These nodule bacteria fix nitrogen gas into protein which eventually goes to soil nitrate when the nodule rots. Some leguminous plants are better at fixing nitrogen through their nodule bacteria than others. If much of the plant of some species is removed, either by cropping or by being eaten by animals, the net nitrogen content of the soil where they grow can actually decrease in spite of nitrogen fixation. Peas are a good example of this. Alfalfa, on the other hand, is so efficient at fixing nitrogen that it contributes nitrogen to the soil even when the tops are cropped.

PHOSPHORUS. This element occurs in the soil in the combined form of phosphate salts and also in undecomposed organic forms. Some kinds such as potassium or ammonium phosphates are soluble in water and can be taken up by plants. There are several types of calcium phosphates, some of which are very insoluble and occur for instance in gallstones or the tartar on teeth. The types occurring in minerals can be slowly broken down by weathering and release soluble phosphate into the soil which then becomes available for plant use. Soluble phosphate can be strongly adsorbed to soil colloids. For various reasons phosphorus in the soil is unavailable to the plant in either extreme acid or alkaline conditions. Metals such as aluminium, iron or calcium can combine with phosphate to form insoluble residues under these extreme conditions. Soil micro-organisms can compete with plant roots for soil phosphate.

Phosphorus plays a part in many biochemical events in the living plant, particularly those which involve the generation and transfer of energy. It is also part of important membranes in living cells, contained in substances called phospholipids. Phosphorus is a component of nucleic acids, both RNA and DNA.

Phosphorus is important in forwarding the formation of flowers and fruit, hardens vegetative growth and strengthens plant stems. Symptoms of phosphorus deficiency in plants are similar to those of nitrogen deficiency except that there is more tendency to develop necrotic areas. Leaves often have a dark blue-green coloration.

POTASSIUM. This element is a very reactive metal which is always found in nature joined with other elements forming mineral salts. These are soluble in water and occur in all normal soils, often adsorbed on clay or humus particles. There are also insoluble forms in soil minerals from which the soluble salts can be slowly released by weathering.

Potassium salts are part of the salt balance of the plant cell. Their passage in and out of guard cells controls turgor and hence opening and closing of the stoma. Potassium is also involved in nutrient transport so that its deficiency indirectly reduces photosynthesis; conversely, it can enhance photosynthesis in periods of low light. It is most needed in the latter part of the growing season, when young wood ripens. It is itself mobile so that if there is a short supply young leaves deprive older ones. Such plants are stunted and the leaves age prematurely. Plants take up potassium from the soil in excess of their requirements in 'luxury uptake', and for this reason it is preferable to supply potassium-containing fertilizer in frequent small doses rather than a large treatment, most of which would be wasted.

CALCIUM. This is another reactive metallic element, found in nature always joined up in mineral salts. These are often only slightly soluble in water. The most widespread calcium mineral in nature is calcium carbonate which makes up the chalk and limestone rocks and also most shells. Soluble calcium salts are dissolved in the soil water and taken up by roots. They are also strongly adsorbed to soil colloids. Calcium salts form part of the salt balance in plant cells. Calcium is much involved in cell division, in the organization of the chromosomes during mitosis. It accumulates along the plane of division between the two new cells in the position where the cellulose cell wall will form. It remains located here, combined to make calcium pectate, the substance of the middle lamella. Calcium is an activator for several enzyme systems. Because of the part played in cell division, a deficiency of calcium results in damage to the growing tips of stem and root and chlorosis occurs along the margins of younger leaves.

Liming can increase the amount of available calcium and also have a beneficial effect on a soil by decreasing the acidity and in a heavy clay soil by causing the fine sticky clay particles to aggregate. It can be overdone, however, especially in sandy soils and can result in the turning of soluble phosphates into insoluble forms. Iron, manganese, zinc, copper and boron tend to be less available after overliming.

MAGNESIUM. This metallic element is similar to calcium in its chemistry but is less abundant; it is found in magnesium limestones and dolomite as magnesium carbonate. Magnesium is part of the chlorophyll molecule and so is centrally involved in photosynthesis. It also plays a part in binding parts of the ribosome together to form the protein-synthesizing unit. It is also an enzyme activator. A deficiency of the elements shows up of course as an extensive interveinal chlorosis starting in the older leaves and spreading to the younger leaves in extreme cases. Anthocyanin pigmentation often occurs.

SULPHUR. This occurs commonly in nature as sulphate salts. Calcium sulphate (gypsum) is very insoluble but can be slowly weathered. Other sulphates are dissolved in the soil solution and are usually adequate in normal soils. All proteins contain sulphur. It also occurs in several important biochemicals and in membranes. Members of some plant families characteristically contain odoriferous sulphur compounds often appreciated for their pungent taste, examples being mustard, radish, onion and garlic. Sulphur deficiency, like nitrogen deficiency, is indicated by a general chlorosis which is shown however by the young leaves first.

### TRACE ELEMENTS

IRON. Iron occurs in soils as soluble iron (ferrous and ferric) salts in the soil solutions and also as insoluble forms in rocks. It is part of the molecules of a series of proteins (cytochromes) important to all living things for respiration. Iron is not part of chlorophyll but takes part in its synthesis so that a deficiency is shown up by an extensive chlorosis starting in the younger leaves, a reflection of the relative immobility of iron in the plant. This is also indicated by the chlorosis taking place between the leaf veins which are often left as a distinct green network.

MANGANESE. This is a metallic element which occurs in soils in several forms, soluble and insoluble. The soluble forms available for plant uptake are favoured in acid, poorly aerated soils and therefore are at risk from over-liming. Manganese is a cofactor of several enzymes and is especially implicated in photosynthesis. Deficiency results in an interveined chlorosis attacking either the younger or older leaves according to plant species and turning soon to necrosis.

COPPER. This metallic element is present in soils combined in the mineral salts as two chemically different forms, cuprous and cupric, of which the second is that taken up by plant roots. Although traces are essential for healthy plant growth an excess is toxic, and the difference between the two levels is not very great. Soils heavily contaminated with copper, perhaps from industrial pollution, can support a sparse flora which have become adapted to the element largely by restricting its uptake. Also, much of the copper content of soils is in a form unavailable to plants. Copper is an enzyme cofactor, especially in systems concerned with respiration and photosynthesis. Deficiency is shown by necrosis of the tips of young leaves extending along the margins until the whole leaf withers.

ZINC. Zinc occurs in soils as zinc salts. These are more available to plants in acid soils and can be depleted by overliming or use of excess phosphate fertilizer which forms an insoluble complex. The difference between a sufficiency and toxic excess is not great. Zinc is an enzyme cofactor and is particularly involved in the synthesis of auxin. Because of this a deficiency is often shown by a lack of growth of internodes producing a rosetting effect. This is accompanied by an interveinal mottled chlorosis, becoming necrotic, of the older leaves.

MOLYBDENUM. This metal is found in soils in a series of oxides and also as soluble molybdic acid or molybdate salts which are the forms available to plants, although needed at only very low concentrations. As the soil becomes more alkaline uptake increases; it can therefore be enhanced by liming. Molybdenum is a cofactor in enzymes concerned with nitrogen metabolism, nitrate reductase which acts on nitrates taken up by the root, and nitrogenase which the nodule bacteria use to fix atmospheric nitrogen. A deficiency of molybdenum therefore has the appearance of a deficiency of nitrogen, starting in the older leaves. The chlorotic leaf blades soon become necrotic and wither, leaving the midrib, giving a characteristic 'whiptail' effect.

BORON. Boron is a non-metallic element present in soils as boric acid and is more available in acid conditions. Its normal concentration is low and higher levels quickly become toxic. Boron seems to be concerned with sugar transport and perhaps many other activities but its rôle is obscure. Deficiency results in breakdown at the growing points of root and shoot leading to spectacular 'heart rots'. This is accompanied by malformation of the leaves and suppression of flower formation.

CHLORINE. This poisonous gas occurs in nature in mineral salts, chlorides, which are relatively harmless unless they contain a poisonous metal. Sodium chloride, common table salt, is one example and makes the sea saline. Most soils contain adequate chlorides and indeed an excess can be toxic to plants. Chlorine is involved in the light reaction of photosynthesis, its deficiency leading to a chlorosis and wilting of the plant.

BENEFICIAL ELEMENTS. A number of elements present in soils have been shown to be not absolutely essential for all plant growth but to be beneficial to many. Sodium, for instance, can partially replace potassium as a nutrient and is essential for growth of plants which have a seaside origin, such as sugar beet. Silicon is widespread in nature in clays and also in sand and flints, which are silicon dioxide (silica). Grass leaves are strengthened with hard, sharp ridges of silica. If the grass gets insufficient silicon to make these, the plant grows normally but is more susceptible to disease and damage. Horsetails (*Equisetum*) also contain a great deal of silica. The metal cobalt is not essential for plant growth but is essential to the growth of *Rhizobium*, the root nodule, nitrogen-fixing bacterium, so that indirectly a leguminous crop can suffer nitrogen deficiency from a lack of cobalt.

### WATER IN PLANT LIFE

All living tissues are mostly water, up to about 80 or 90 percent. Although normal to us, water is an unusual substance chemically, with some unique features.

(1) Water dissolves more substances than any other solvent, even if in many cases the amounts dissolved are so small as to be unnoticeable, for instance iron or lead in tap water. This makes water a very good medium for the host of biochemical reactions that make up life.

(2) Water has a high specific gravity compared with substances of a similar chemical nature. Also it has the peculiar property of contracting when cooled, down to a minimum at a temperature 4°C/39°F above its freezing point. This means that ice at freezing point is lighter than water a few degrees warmer and therefore floats. All other liquids sink when they freeze. This has the inconvenient consequence that water in a container expands at the freezing point and may well burst the container. However in nature, ponds and lakes freeze from the top so that liquid water is often left below in which life can survive unharmed by stresses which can take place during freezing and thawing.

(3) Water has a very high specific heat capacity. This means that it takes a lot of heat to warm water up, compared with other liquids, and it is also slower to cool down. As a result of this, a world containing water does not get overheated during the day or overcooled at night. The temperature changes are more gradual, more even, less extreme.

(4) Water has a high heat of vaporization and a high heat of fusion. This means that a great deal of heat is needed to turn liquid water into vapour and a lot of heat needs to be removed to turn liquid water into ice. The consequence of this is also stability, so that very great amounts of heat gain or loss are needed to change water from one state to another.

Many of the functions of water in plants are understandable in the light of these special properties. Water is the main constituent of cytoplasm and is imbibed by the protein matrix. It is a major biochemical reagent and also is the medium for biochemical transformations. Water provides the transport system for the plant. Water enters cells and gives them turgor which provides size and shape. Water is a major climatic force in the environment.

*Diffusion*. This is the movement of molecules of a substance from a region of high concentration to a region of low concentration (Diffusion Gradient). If no other substance is there then diffusion proceeds unhindered. Usually other molecules *are* present so the molecules of one substance must diffuse past molecules of the other. If the molecules of the second substance are close together and relatively stationary then they may form some sort of barrier. If two different kinds of molecules are diffusing together then they independently diffuse down their own diffusion gradients. Water is the medium for diffusion in living cells. The cell membranes can form barriers for some substances.

*Osmosis*. This is a kind of diffusion where there is a barrier across a concentration gradient which will only allow molecules of a certain size to go through (semi-permeable). In living cells such a barrier is a cell membrane which lets water through but not many of the substances dissolved in the water. If two regions are separated by such a membrane and one of them contains a more concentrated solution than the other, then water will flow into it from the more dilute solution.

*Turgor*. Water will flow into a plant cell by osmosis, creating a pressure against the outer cell membrane, as if it were air in a balloon. The rigidity so produced is called turgor and gives form to the living tissue.

*Imbibition*. Water as either vapour or liquid can diffuse into the pores of a solid so that the solid swells due to an attraction between the liquid and the surfaces. Passage of water along the pores is increased by capillary action.

*Capillary action*. A liquid is said to have a high surface tension when the molecules at the surface have a strong pull into the body of the liquid. Such a liquid in a narrow tube clings to the inside surface of the tube so that it rises round the edges and forms a curved surface to the liquid, the meniscus. The narrower the bore of the tube, the stronger the pull is in relation to the bulk of liquid and the higher the level rises. This is capillary action.

*The transpiration stream*. In all plants there is a movement of water, in through the roots, up the stem and out through the leaves. This stream is maintained partly by *root pressure* from below and partly by a pull from above caused by evaporation from the leaves. Water is taken in through the fine *root hairs* which very much enlarge the absorbtive surface and passes into the xylem vessels. In these it passes up the stem. To prevent undue water loss leading to desiccation, leaves are covered by a more or less impermeable cuticle. This is pierced by holes (stomata) whose aperture is controlled by the change in shape of two *guard cells*. Thus the passage of water vapour through each stoma is also controlled (Figure 11). Evapotranspiration is the sum of transpiration from leaves of plants in a given area plus the rate of evaporation from the bare soil surface.

In hot dry weather evaporation is more rapid. Rapid air movement also causes greater evaporation. So long as adequate water comes in from the soil the transpiration stream increases under these conditions, but if there is not enough water wilting rapidly occurs. Plants avoid wilting to varying degrees by closing their stomata and thereby reducing the transpiration stream. However if the stomata close then carbon dioxide for photosynthesis cannot be taken in. Plants adapted for living in very dry situations avoid this by adopting an alternative form of photosynthesis, such as CAM. A decreased rate of transpiration means that less mineral salts are transported to the leaves.

*Physiological drought*. It may happen that a plant is living in a soil with perfectly adequate moisture but at so low a temperature that the roots cannot take it up. These plants are under drought conditions and, if water loss through the leaves continues unabated, will wilt. To overcome this many such plants have adopted a deciduous habit, shedding their leaves and thus removing the evaporative surfaces. They also lose their photosynthetic mechanism of course, and so go into a state of reduced metabolism subsisting on stored nutrients. This is totally appropriate to a cold period of reduced metabolic activity. Evergreen plants which retain their leaves in winter develop xeromorphic characters to control water loss. These characters are also possessed by plants successfully enduring true drought. They include thick cuticles with waterproof wax coverings, stomata sunk in pits and protected by hairs, and small, rolled leaves, with the stomata on the inner surface.

### CONTROL OF PLANT GROWTH AND DEVELOPMENT

There is more to the growth of a plant than just increase in size. After all, a plant put in the dark grows taller, if more spindly (etiolation) but can hardly be said to be growing successfully. For continued healthy growth a plant must acquire more cells which arise by division of existing cells. These new cells then enlarge to full size. All this involves more plant material being formed; protein, carbohydrate and many other substances. This growth of plant substance is measured not by an increase in size but by an increase in dry weight (assimilation). Growth involves more than just this, however, because the multiplying plant cells also become specialized and assume a characteristic shape, size and function (differentiation). The specialized cells then become grouped into organs and finally all these growth events are coordinated both in space and time.

*Senescence*. Plant parts have only a limited life. As a leaf ages it becomes yellow and loses its ability to photosynthesize. In fact chlorophyll and the leaf protein are being broken down all the time but in a young leaf are rebuilt at a faster rate. As the leaf ages this rebuilding slows down and finally stops. Often the leaf is shed by a definite zone of weakness (the abscission zone) being formed at the base of the petiole where the break then occurs.

*Growth regulation*. All these events in a plant's life are under a variety of controls. Sometimes control comes from the availability of nutrients from the soil or light for photosynthesis. Many of a plant's reactions are controlled by substances produced in very small quantity in the plant but exerting a great effect on its growth and development. Such substances are called growth regulators or sometimes plant hormones. One of these is a very simple chemical, the gas ethylene, which is often given off during burning. In the past large doses of this substance from the vapour of gas or paraffin lamps produced gross effects such as defoliation on adjoining plants. The smoke from burning newspapers has been used to ripen pineapples. An over-ripe apple in a box produces ethylene which will cause unripe fruit to hasten their ripening. The presence of ripe apples can cause flowers such as carnations to wilt.

Other more complex chemicals have profound effects on plant growth. Auxins will cause stems to elongate and roots to form on cuttings. Gibberellins will cause a dramatic increase in height, although often without sufficient strength. They will also break the dormancy of buds and seeds and can induce flowering in plants needing long day-lengths or cold overwintering periods. Cytokinins stimulate cell division and can cause differentiation of organs. They also delay senescence and thus lengthen the shelf-life of leaf vegetables. Abscisic acid is a regulator which inhibits growth and in nature probably governs the exuberant activity of some of the growth promoters.

In the healthy plant growth is controlled by a balance of these various natural chemicals. An imbalance leads to lethal effects. Advantage is taken of this in the use of hormone weedkillers where a growth promoter is used in excess to produce abnormal, unhealthy and ultimately fatal growth. These substances are usually synthetic imitations of plant chemicals because they are easier to manufacture, distribute and apply.

AFTERWORD. A world without plants would be aesthetically unthinkable to most of us. It would also be uninhabitable. Plants do not give the same impression of activity as animals with their active movement. However plants are active and ingenious organic chemists and all of the life chemicals on earth come from photosynthesis and following events. Fossil minerals such as oil and chalk have also come the same way in the past. This is why the efforts of the conservation movement are not just fanciful but of urgent necessity. The increasingly abused tropical rainforests are not just luxury reserves but gigantic chemical factories supplying the substance of life for other plants and for animals. A gardener cultivating a small space is contributing towards life even if the immediate object is personal rather than altruistic. Gardeners can indeed often grow plants with success in ignorance and blind to the science involved, but what greater satisfaction does a knowledge, even slight, of the workings of these plants give to the sensitive, perceptive grower. The science of the workings of plants is called plant physiology.

See also NUTRITION; PLANT ANATOMY; SOILS.

**Plant reproduction.** The practice and potential of plant breeding, both commercial and amateur, is based on the manipulation of the natural reproductive capacity of plants.

### SEXUAL REPRODUCTION

*Pollen, stigma, style and ovary*. Pollen grains develop in the anther following meiosis in the sporogenous cells. When mature, pollen is either two- or three-celled. The bicelled form is more common and comprises a vegetative cell in which floats a generative cell. The tricelled form comprises a vegetative cell in which float two sperm cells. Both types of pollen grains are enclosed by two cell walls. The inner wall (intine) is primarily made of pectin and cellulose; it is variable in thickness, particularly at the sites of pores or apertures, and is similar to the cell wall found in the plant meristem. The outer wall (exine) is specialized, comprising a complex carotenoid polymer called sporopollenin which is highly non-biodegradable and often found fossilized in rock. This wall is morphologically highly variable, and characteristic features are used in taxonomic analysis.

Both walls are receptacles for wall-held materials. The intine holds proteins, predominantly found at the pore or apertural sites. Exines may hold a variety of chemicals including carbohydrates and lipids and in some cases small amounts of protein. These chemicals have been named tryphine and pollenkitt.

The stigma is usually found at the apex of the style and is the site which receives pollen. Morphology and anatomy is remarkably variable and this character can be used in classification. Stigmas can broadly be classified into two types based on presence or absence of a surface secretion – wet and dry. Each of these types can be further subdivided on the basis of the cells which comprise the surface. These cells are called papillae.

In wet stigmas, the surface of the stigma may be non-papillate to papillate and secretion can be limited to the basal spaces between papillae (a small amount) or may flood the surface and obscure any papillae present. Examples are Rosaceae and Liliaceae. In dry stigmas all surfaces examined so far are papillate. Examples are Gramineae, Compositae and Cruciferae.

Styles comprise an epidermis, ground tissue, vascular bundles and a pollen-tube-transmitting tissue, which may be positioned more or less centrally among other tissues. The transmitting tissue may be an open canal (e.g. Liliaceae), a solid cylindrical core of cells (e.g. Solanaceae), or a suspension of cells and stylar secretion (e.g. Leguminosae).

Both stigma and stylar secretions comprise a complex cocktail of chemicals including proteins, lipids and carbohydrates. Some of the proteins appear to have enzymatic activity, some act to enhance the adhesion of pollen on to the stigma, and some are involved in the recognition of the pollen touching down on the stigma. The latter group are thought to be glycoproteins, compound molecules comprising a combination of proteins and carbohydrates.

The ovary comprises variable numbers of ovules, from one to numerous. Each ovule is the location for the embryo sac. The embryo sac is positioned close to the micropyle, a small hole which itself is formed by the inner and outer integuments, and is often surrounded by a single- to multi-layer of cells called the nucellus. Each ovule is provided with a vascular strand which enters the ovule through the funiculus. Some ovules develop a specialized structure called a hypostase at the chalazal end of the embryo sac. The function of the hypostase is believed to be one of transport of solutes to the embryo sac and developing seed.

The embryo sac is a product of meiosis in the archesporial cell, which itself develops from the nucellus. The embryo sac generally comprises seven cells and eight nuclei. At the micropylar end are the two synergid cells and the egg cell, a structure referred to as the egg apparatus. In the middle is the central cell which is the only binucleate cell in the embryo sac. At the chalazal end are the three antipodal cells. Only one synergid cell may be present, or synergids may rarely be entirely absent, as in *Plumbago zeylanica*. The antipodal cells are the most variable, being ephemeral in many species (to give a five-celled embryo sac) or may multiply sometimes dramatically to give hundreds of cells as in Gramineae. In Gramineae, antipodal cells may persist following fertilization and their DNA amount may increase dramatically, and their chromosomes may become polytene.

POLLINATION AND FERTILIZATION. When pollen touches down on the stigma, exine- and intine-held chemicals are released on to the stigma surface. Some of these chemicals are involved in literally sticking the pollen grain to the stigma surface or papillae. In dry stigmas such an adhesion is of considerable significance in relation to subsequent events. Pollen is released from the anther in a state of dehydration and when grains land on the stigma they must take up water either from the surrounding atmosphere or from the stigma surface or secretion (hydration).

Some of the released chemicals are believed to be involved in stigmas and pollen recognizing each other. This is particularly true of self-incompatibility.

Pollen grains produce a pollen tube which carries the gametes to the ovary. Pollen germination is the initiation and early development of that tube. The tube forms at one of the germinal apertures and extends by tip growth. The pollen tube may find easy access to the style in plants with a stylar canal. In other plants the pollen tube may be required to penetrate a stigmatic cuticle and the outer layer of the papilla cell wall in order to be directed towards the stylar-transmitting tissue where the tube grows in the middle lamella.

The pathway of the pollen tube to the ovary is through the stylar-transmitting tissue zone. In those plants where there is a stylar canal, the pollen tubes grow within that canal generally in the secretion which fills the canal. They may grow under the cuticle which, if present intact, has been detached from the canal cell walls by the accumulating secretion. Pollen tubes extend and grow by tip growth, and it is believed that they absorb nutrition from the secretion in order to achieve rapid rates of growth.

In solid styles, the pollen tube grows intercellularly in the area of the middle lamella which is considered to be the zone of least resistance. The tip of the pollen tube appears to secrete enzymes, and these will aid breakdown of the middle lamella as well as providing the tube with potential energy-rich compounds and wall components.

The ovary is hollow, but the transmitting zone cells of the style are continuous with cells which guide the pollen tubes to the ovules and micropyles. The tubes appear to grow over the surface of these pathway cells.

Single pollen tubes enter the micropyle (a canal formed from the inner and outer integuments) and traverse the nucellus, if present. Pollen tubes grow intercellularly as in the solid style. The pollen tube enters one of the synergid cells, through the filiform apparatus, and discharges the sperm cells via a pore in the tube wall – this may be analagous to a controlled bursting of the pollen tube. The synergid cell which is entered is often apparently degenerate, degeneration having been stimulated by pollination and having progressed during the process of pollen touch-down and pollen tube growth to the ovary. The sperm cells, released into the base of the synergid cell, then migrate to the walls of the egg and central cells. The delivery of sperms ensures that the sperm cells are placed towards the basal part of the synergid cell and, at this position, the synergid, the egg and the central cells are separated only by their respective plasma membranes. The transfer of sperms, a mystery at present, is not restricted by a cellulose wall.

The egg nucleus is the target of one sperm nucleus. The central cell (polar) nuclei are the target of the second sperm nucleus. Polar nuclei may or may not fuse prior to entry of the sperm nucleus into the central cell. All three nuclei fuse eventually. Egg-sperm fusion forms the zygote which will divide to produce the young embryo. Polar nuclei-sperm fusion will develop into endosperm.

In dicotyledons, the endosperm is short-lived, and its role is taken by the cotyledons.

BREEDING SYSTEMS: INBREEDERS. Cleistogamy (literally 'closed gametes') is a most extreme form of inbreeding where self-pollination and self-fertilization take place within closed flowers. There appear to be few species known which are obligately cleistogamous; the majority of species develop cleistogamous flowers after normal allogamous flowers set no seed (e.g. *Viola riviniana, Hordeum murinum*). The efficiency of cleistogamy is also often affected by the environment.

Seed is set predominantly as a result of self-pollination. This occurs when pollen from the same flower, or a different flower in the same inflorescence or on the same plant, alights on the stigma. Few plant species are totally inbreeding or totally outbreeding. If a wholly genetically heterozygous plant is self-pollinated, the resulting progeny from that plant will be 50% homozygous and 50% heterozygous in one generation. Within seven generations of selfing, the progeny from the originally fully heterozygous plant will be virtually fully homozygous – indeed they will have developed into a number of lines, each of which will breed true.

BREEDING SYSTEMS: OUTBREEDERS. Seed is set predominantly as a result of cross-pollination. Pollen arrives from a flower of a different plant and may be transferred by wind (anemophily), by insects, or, more rarely, by larger animals. Flowers which require pollination by animals are usually larger and more colourful or odoriferous than inbreeding counterparts. A number of devices have been evolved which enhance outbreeding.

*Protandry/protogyny*. A common means of increasing the efficiency of outbreeding is the separation of sex in time. Protandry is the dehiscence of anthers and shedding of pollen in an open flower before the stigma is receptive. Protogyny is the development of a receptive stigma before the pollen is shed from the anthers.

*Dioecy*. Male and female plants are found which ensures separation of sex in space. Flowers on male plants may well possess reduced and non-functional female parts and flowers on female plants may possess the same form of male parts. Some dioecious plants have sex chromosomes, and generally but not exclusively the male is heterogametic (e.g. *Asparagus officinalis, Humulus lupulus, Spinacia oleracea*). The occurrence of unisexual flowers may be modified by the environment.

Dioecy is rare but most plant families do have dioecious species. The Salicaceae (willows and poplars) are a family of entirely dioecious species. Dioecy enforces outbreeding although it cannot preclude sib mating, i.e. crossing of males and females in the progeny from one female plant.

*Monoecy*. In monoecious species, male and female flowers are found on the same plant but in separate inflorescences (Begoniaceae, Cucurbitaceae, *Zea mays*). The system is made more efficient since most monoecious species are dichogamous, usually protandrous.

*Androdioecy and gynodioecy*. Androdioecious species are very rare and comprise populations of male plants and hermaphrodite plants. Gynodioecious species are more common and comprise plants with female flowers exclusively and plants with hermaphrodite flowers. In order to set seed the females must receive pollen from an hermaphrodite flower. Most gynodioecious species are self-compatible (*Origanum vulgare*), but there are self-incompatible exceptions (*Plantago lanceolata*).

*Subandroecy, subgynoecy and polygamy*. These are conditions which are manifested by occasional seed set in apparently male inflorescences, or a lack of seed in apparently normal female inflorescences. They may result from unstable sex expression in dioecious species.

SELF-INCOMPATIBILITY. Self-incompatibility (SI) enforces outbreeding with variable degrees of efficiency, depending on species and environment. It is the inability of perfectly fertile functional gametes to fuse to form a zygote. The principle means by which SI is effected is the inhibition of pollen tube growth so that there is no delivery of the male gametes to the embryo sac.

There are two common forms of self-incompatibility, sporophytic and gametophytic. Sporophytic SI is found in dicotyledons only, e.g. Compositae, Cruciferae and Primulaceae. It is characterized generally by plants with dry stigmas, tricellular pollen and inhibition of pollen tubes on the stigma surface. A single multi-allelic genetic control is found with dominance of alleles in stigma and/or pollen. The Primulaceae provide a special case of sporophytic incompatibility. The incompatibility gene has only two alleles (one dominant form and one recessive) which are linked to a complex of genes controlling flower morphology. Pin plants are homozygous/recessive, thrum plants are heterozygous.

Gametophytic SI is more abundant, being found in species of Gramineae, Liliaceae, Rosaceae and Solanaceae. It is characterized by wet stigmas, bicelled pollen grains, and pollen tube inhibition in the style, ovary or micropyle (with a significant exception being species in Gramineae which are similar in characteristics to sporophytic self-incompatibility). Genetic control is by a single multi-allelic gene with independent action of all alleles.

HYBRIDIZATION. As previously outlined, hybridization includes any form of crossing which may occur in the wild or be made under controlled conditions by man. Generally, hybridization is further described by the level at which it takes place – intraspecific (between inbred lines and cultivars), interspecific, and intergeneric. In general, the fertility of the hybrid is reduced at the higher levels. Reduction in fertility may be so pronounced as to render the hybrid sterile.

Hybridization has played a major part in both horticulture and agriculture in the improvement of the main crop species, particularly wheat and maize. Major characters which have been improved are yield and disease-resistance but a host of other characters have been selected for, including frost hardiness, uniform maturity and dwarfing, or selected against, for instance brittle rachis.

Some F1 hybrids can be propagated asexually and these may be the new cultivar themselves. Others require the production of F2 and succeeding generations and are subjected to selection by plant breeders who produce them. More recently, the production of F1 hybrid seed for growers by crossing selected inbred lines has become popular. The F1 hybrid exploits hybrid vigour (see below). The grex hybrids in orchids are F1 hybrids often at the intergeneric level.

*Inbreeding depression*. Severely reduced seed sets are frequently found when outbreeding plants are selfed. The siblings may exhibit a variety of abnormal characteristics from chlorotic seedlings to reduced size and fecundity. These characters are avoided by plant breeders.

*Male sterility*. Occasionally in plant populations, male-sterile plants appear. In these plants, the sporogenous tissue in the anther fails to undergo meiosis, or fails in pollen development, and the tissue degenerates. There are three types of male sterility, namely genetic (determined by a recessive male-sterile allele), cytoplasmic, and genetic-cytoplasmic (determined by a recessive allele in the nucleus and by an alteration in the DNA in the mitochondrion). Male sterility is not a breeding system. It has been employed by plant breeders as a means of making controlled crosses in a breeding programme by emasculating large numbers of plants genetically and cheaply. Plant breeders have to maintain male-sterile lines and may also need restorer lines to bring back and improve male fertility.

*Barriers to seed set*. Following fertilization, a number of potential barriers greet the young embryo and endosperm. In wide hybrids, the mitotic divisions which follow fertilization can become abnormal, the chromosomes of the male parent getting out of phase with the chromosomes of the female parent. Within a few divisions the chromosomes of the male parent are lost and the embryo dies unless it is rescued using tissue culture techniques. The resultant embryo will be haploid but can be useful to the plant breeder. By doubling the chromosome number, a homozygous line can be produced immediately.

A number of post-zygotic difficulties, primarily related to cell differentiation, have also come to light. Their significance depends on species and on the level at which a cross is made.

*The F1 hybrid*. The term F1 (first filial generation) hybrid is used for the product following a cross between two parent inbred lines, cultivars, species or genera. F1 hybrids are highly genetically heterozygous but morphologically (phenotypically) uniform. The F2 generation, produced by selfing or intercrossing F1 individuals, will be less heterozygous but morphologically (phenotypically) very variable. After several generations of selfing, the population from an original F1 will segregate into morphologically distinct lines or families.

*Heterosis*. F1 hybrids often exhibit a phenomenon known as hybrid vigour, or heterosis. This characteristic is manifested in increased yield and fecundity of the F1 progeny. Some of the improvements are very large, and this is one characteristic upon which the F1 seed trade has developed.

ASEXUAL REPRODUCTION

APOMIXIS. *Vegetative reproduction*. In many herbaceous perennials, clones are developed and multiplied by stolons (*Fragaria vesca, Ranunculus repens*), rhizomes (*Elymus repens, Iris* spp.), and bulbils, either around the root (*Oxalis* spp.) or on stems (*Lilium* spp.). Most plants that exhibit this form of reproduction also have a phase of flowering and sexual reproduction. It may therefore be considered to be facultative apomixis.

*Vivipary and pseudovivipary*. These include the development of plantlets on the margins of leaves, which then drop to the ground and root, as in *Bryophyllum pinnatum*, and the formation of plantlets on the apex of an inflorescence in the place of flowers, as in *Agave* spp. and *Poa alpina*.

AGAMOSPERMY. *Seed apomixis* is the development of seed but without the fusion of gametes; however, pollination may be required to trigger seed development.

*Adventitious embryony*. Normal sexual reproduction is necessary for the development of apomictic embryos. Once double fertilization has occurred and the embryo and endosperm begin to develop, stimulation of apomictic embryos in the nucellus begins. The final outcome may now be variable, from the development of an apomictic embryo outcompeting all other embryos to a mixture of apomictic and sexually produced embryos in the seed. The sexually produced endosperm survives and is either used by the apomictic embryo or shared between apomictically derived and sexually derived embryos, for instance in *Citrus* spp.

*Apospory*. Pseudogamy is required: there must be pollination, pollen tube growth and delivery of sperm cells into the embryo sac. One sperm nucleus must fuse with the polar nuclei to form the endosperm. Development of an apomictic embryo, though it almost always starts prior to pollination, can only proceed successfully with the additional development of the endosperm.

Embryo sacs develop from nucellar cells. One or some embryo sacs can be produced following a conventional meiosis, as well as apomictically. Unreduced embryo sacs will have unreached egg cells and unreduced polar nuclei. Sexually produced embryo sacs can be fertilized in this system, therefore this form of apomixis is facultative.

*Diplospory*. The embryo sac is developed either following a failure and non-reduction of chromosome number in female meiosis or by mitotic division of the archesporial cells. There is no requirement of pollination or fertilization for embryos to develop into seeds. This form of apomixis is usually obligate.

*See also* GENETICS AND GENETIC ENGINEERING; MICROPROPAGATION; PLANT BREEDING; SEEDS; VEGETATIVE PROPAGATION.

**Plant variety protection laws**. Plant breeding is an ancient agricultural practice. Plant variety protection law is rooted firmly in the 20th century. Depending on the country where protection is required, different forms of legal protection may be open to the breeder of a new variety, on application to the appropriate authority. At the international level, legal protection for plant varieties is extremely complicated. No one national law or system on plant breeders rights or patents can claim properly to be representative of the rest, since each differs from every other, substantively or procedurally, in certain respects. The sum of these various legal regimes is an intricate web of rules and procedures, and the reader who wishes to penetrate this web should consult the specialist works on the subject. It would ill-serve the aim of introducing the reader to the general principles of plant variety protection law if the discussion sought to embrace the rather dull intricacies of the law. This introduction is addressed to the plant breeder, gardener, horticulturalist, farmer, agricultural economist, and non-specialist lawyer. It gives a broad outline of the law, and indicates some of the legal issues.

Plant varieties may be protectable under either the UPOV system of plant breeders, rights or the industrial patent system, or under both in some countries (e.g. Australia, the US). Most developed countries are members of UPOV (International Union for the Protection of New Varieties of Plants) and these countries adhere, with variations, to the UPOV model. The countries of Western Europe are signatories to the European Patent Convention (EPC). The system established by the EPC shares a common set of principles with the patent systems of the world's main industrialized countries outside of Europe; and, though it differs importantly from these systems by prohibiting the patenting of plant varieties *as such*, the EPC will serve nonetheless as a model for the task in hand.

UPOV SYSTEM OF PLANT BREEDERS' RIGHTS. The UPOV Convention or, to give it its proper title, the International Convention for the Protection of New Varieties of Plants, was revised in March 1991. This convention is an international legal code (or model law) that forms the basis of the existing national laws on plant breeders' rights in the countries that are members of the UPOV. The original text, the convention of 1961, was amended twice (in 1972 and 1978), before the major 1991 revision. Prior to the 1961 Convention, several countries had either introduced a system of monopoly rights for certain plant varieties (e.g. the US, Germany, the Netherlands, Spain), imposed statutory levies on arable land or crop production (e.g. the Netherlands) or supported voluntary measures for compensating breeders (e.g. France, Belgium). These various forms of protection or compensation were of limited success.

The earliest known law on the protection of new plant varieties is a decree by Pope Gregory in 1833 which gave the breeder or finder of a new plant limited protection in respect of the plant within the precincts of Saint Peter's Patrimony. This decree predates by about one hundred years a United States law, the Plant Patent Act 1930, which is widely regarded as the first real attempt by any country to protect the work of plant breeders. Under the 1930 Act (still in force) the breeder of any new and distinct variety of asexually reproduced plant (for example, rose, apple) can apply for a plant patent in respect of the variety. The 1930 Act influenced plant breeders in other developed countries to seek similar protection. But the measures that their efforts secured approached the problem from different directions and with different philosophies. There was no single uniform solution at an international level until the advent of UPOV.

The post-war years from the late-1940s to mid-1950s saw a renewed debate at various international conferences on the question of patent protection for plant varieties, but in the main plant breeders were hostile to the industrial patent system and they sought an international alternative to it. A crucial move in that direction was made in 1956, when the French Government took the initiative suggested by ASSINSEL (an international association of plant breeders and seed firms) and invited the governments of the countries of Western Europe to send representatives to an international conference on the protection of new plant products. This was held in Paris in 1957, and nearly all the governments that were invited sent representatives. The Paris Conference of 1957 led, through the work of expert committees (where the interests of plant breeders were fully represented), to the UPOV Convention 1961.

The 1978 text of the UPOV Convention reflects essentially the thinking of a quite different era in plant breeding, that of the 1950s and 1960s. It could not have foreseen the major advances that have occurred in the plant breeding sciences since the mid-1970s. When the 1961 Convention was drawn up, recombinant DNA technology (or genetic engineering) was scarcely conceivable beyond the annals of science fiction. Now it is a technique applied by plant breeders. The 1978 text had to be revised in a major way if the UPOV system was to continue to play a significant role in the promotion of plant breeding and address the problems and challenges inherent in the 'new biology'. In March 1991, the Convention underwent 'root and branch' revision during a Diplomatic Conference held in Geneva. The 1991 text provides broader and deeper protection for plant varieties than its predecessors.

The 1991 text of the UPOV Convention is the new model law for the 1990s and beyond, and national laws on breeder's rights in the countries that ratify this Convention will have to be brought into conformity with the new text. But that does not mean that national laws will be exactly the same, or worded in identical terms. While the basic principles in the 1991 text must be given legal force in each country that is a 'Contracting Party' to the 1991 Convention, the examination of varieties submitted for protection and the scope of the protection afforded by breeders' rights (to take just two examples) are likely to vary between UPOV countries.

*Protectable subject matter*. The UPOV Convention is concerned only with the protection of plant varieties. Plant breeding methods and propagation techniques are outside the scope of the Convention, and these are protectable, if at all, under the industrial patent system. The cultivated plant variety (or cultivar) is a group of plants which, by reasons of its characteristics, is distinct from other known varieties in cultivation and which, when reproduced or propagated in the appropriate manner, is stable in its essential features.

As well as varieties bred by crossing parental plants and selecting among the offspring, other cultivars may be eligible for protection. A cultivar developed from a variety found growing in the wild or arising as a natural sport or mutation (e.g. the Golden Delicious apple) or a cultivar resulting from the controlled irradiation of plant material is protectable subject matter. UPOV countries bound by the 1991 text are required to provide protection for varieties of all plant genera and species (Article 3).

*Conditions for grant of breeders' rights*. The 1991 Convention, in Article 5, gives the conditions that a variety must satisfy in order to qualify for a grant of legal protection. The variety must be new, distinct, uniform and stable, and it must have an acceptable name (or other designation). Assessing whether a variety satisfies the distinctness, uniformity and stability (DUS) criteria usually involves growing the variety over at least two growing seasons.

Novelty is a basic requirement of legal systems that grant any form of monopoly right. Plant breeders' rights, or indeed an industrial patent of invention, may not be granted for what is old, or publicly known or available when such rights are applied for.

The novelty rule in Article 6 deems a variety to be new if, when breeders' rights are applied for, the breeder has not sold or otherwise disposed of varietal material of the applied for cultivar, for the purposes of exploiting the variety, outside certain time limits. If the breeder, for example, sells, or consents to the sale of, propagating material in a UPOV country more than one year before applying there for breeders' rights on the variety from which the material comes, he is apt to disqualify the variety from a grant of breeders' rights unless it is determined that the sale was not for the purposes of exploiting the variety.

The distinctness rule (Article 7) requires the applied for variety to be clearly distinguishable from any other variety whose existence is a matter of common knowledge at the time when the rights are applied for. Usually more than one characteristic lends distinctness to a variety. Morphological or physiological traits, such as shape or length of leaves, flower colour, resistance to chemical sprays, but not some indefinable taste or smell, may differentiate an applied for variety clearly from other commonly known cultivars. The characteristics that distinguish a protected variety need not be of any commercial value in its cultivation or use.

The distinctness rule is concerned with *inter*varietal differences. The uniformity rule (Article 8) looks at *intra*varietal differences. Thus the question whether a variety is distinct is asking whether a group of plants differs clearly by one or more characteristics from prior, commonly known types. If within the group under examination some individuals differ noticeably from the rest, this may call into question whether the applied for variety is sufficiently uniform and stable to qualify for a grant of breeders' rights.

Intravarietal variation is tolerated within limits that depend on the variety's reproductive system (vegetatively propagated, self-fertilized, or cross-fertilized). Very few, if any, off-types (plants which differ in their expression from that of the variety) are tolerated in vegetatively propagated cultivars (e.g. strawberries, apples, chrysanthemums) and fully 'selfing' types (e.g. the garden pea). The stability rule (Article 9) requires that the variety must remain true to its description after repeated reproduction of the variety, for example, between one seed generation and the next.

Finally, the 1991 Convention has complex rules on the naming of varieties (Article 20). Every variety submitted for a grant of breeders' rights must be given a name or other designation. A protected variety can have one name only, its officially registered, generic name. The name must not be liable to mislead or cause confusion concerning the characteristics, value or identity of the variety. When these rules are translated into national law, in most UPOV countries the legal position is likely to be much as it was under the 1978 text of the Convention. That is, a person who markets reproductive material of a different variety in the same class as the protected variety and under that variety's registered name, or a name so nearly resembling it as to be likely to deceive or cause confusion, will commit an actionable wrong against the owner of the protected variety for which the name is registered.

*Applications and examination*. The person entitled to apply for and be granted breeders' rights for a new variety is, primarily, the person who bred, or discovered and developed, the variety, that is to say, the breeder (Article 1). If the breeder is an employee, or if he has been commissioned to breed the variety, the employer or the commissioner, as the case may be, is the person entitled.

The breeder is free to choose when and where to file his first application (Article 10), and thereafter to file applications in respect of the same variety in other UPOV countries and to enjoy a right of priority there provided he applies within 12 months of the filing date of his first application (Article 11). The filing date is a crucial date not only for priority purposes but also when examining a variety under the rules on novelty and distinctness. An application must be 'duly filed', that is, in accordance with relevant rules, before it can be given a 'date of filing'. An application filed out of time may be rejected.

The authority empowered under national law to grant breeders' rights must examine the applied for variety to determine whether it is novel, distinct, uniform and stable (Article 12). The DUS examination may involve an official growing trial of the variety under appropriate conditions in the country of application, or it may be done on the basis of growing tests or other trials which have already been carried out.

*Scope of protection*. The 1991 Convention affords the holder of breeders' rights far greater protection than is given in the 1978 text. Under Article 14 of the 1991 text, the holder may prohibit, or authorise subject to conditions, various commercial acts. These acts, which constitute the minimum legal protection that a UPOV Member State must provide, include multiplying, selling, exporting or importing propagating material (e.g. seed for sowing, vegetative cuttings) or harvested material (e.g. wheat seed for milling, cut flowers, fruit) of the protected variety. Breeders' rights may be extended to products made directly from harvested material (e.g. wine from grapes, flour from wheat seed). Acts that contravene these exclusive rights may be proceeded against by way of a legal action for infringement. The minimum period of breeders' rights is 20 years (25 years for trees and vines) from the date of grant (Article 19), although the rights may be nullified or cancelled before this period expires (Articles 21 and 22).

An important provision in the 1991 Convention is that in Article 14(5), dealing with so-called 'dependent' varieties. A dependent variety is any variety that is not clearly distinguishable from the protected variety, any variety the production of which (as in the case of an F1 hybrid) requires the repeated use of the protected variety, or (most importantly) any variety that is essentially derived from the protected variety. If a variety (B) is essentially derived from a protected variety (A), then variety B may not be commercialized without authorization from the owner of variety A. This provision catches the piratical practice of 'cosmetic breeding', in which a rival breeder 'repackages' the economically valuable features of variety A in a distinctive garb (variety B), in order to avoid paying tribute or royalty to the owner of the protected variety. The 1978 text of the UPOV Convention does not prohibit that practice.

The 1991 Convention has several exceptions to plant breeders' rights (Article 15). Breeders' rights do not extend to acts done privately and for non commercial purposes, acts done for experimental purposes, and acts done for the purposes of breeding other varieties and commercializing them (except where they are dependent varieties). Thus, a home gardener could multiply a protected variety for home use or consumption without infringing the exclusive rights, but a market gardener or a farmer who multiplied a protected variety would be likely to infringe.

When varietal material of a protected variety is sold or otherwise commercialized by or with the consent of the holder of the exclusive rights, the purchaser can do as he or she wants with the material (e.g. sow the seed, mill the wheat seed, plant the apple tree), except that, save with permission, he cannot use it for further propagation of the protected variety (e.g. take or graft cuttings to create a commercial orchard) (Article 16).

*Nullity and cancellation*. If, after breeders' rights have been granted, it should transpire that, when the rights were applied for, the variety lacked the requisite novelty or distinctness, or that the rights were granted to a person not entitled to them, then the grant must be declared null and void *ab initio* (Article 21). The rights may be cancelled for the future if the holder does not maintain his variety or if his efforts in that regard are unsuccessful and he cannot therefore provide the granting authority with reproductive material bearing the traits that merited the grant of breeders' rights (Article 22). Finally, the rights may be cancelled if the holder fails to pay such fees as may be payable to keep the grant of rights in force.

*National seed regulations*. The 1991 Convention (Article 18) recognizes that UPOV countries may wish to regulate the production, certification and marketing of seeds and propagating material. But the system for granting plant breeders' rights is regarded as quite separate from any system of seed control.

In the European Communities there are regulatory systems at national level that implement the Community's much-amended Directives on the marketing of seed (potato, beet, fodder plant, cereal, oil and fibre plant, vegetable). The main objective of these Directives is to ensure that seed can move freely throughout the community, and towards that end they establish a regime of minimum quality and labelling standards and uniform category descriptions.

Where a variety is not protected by a grant of breeders' rights, any person who wishes to can reproduce the variety as long as he complies with the requirements in the seed laws (where these apply to the particular plant species). It is a criminal offence, plant breeders' rights or no, to market seed or reproductive material of a plant which does not comply with the seed laws.

Varieties that comply with national regulatory systems in Community countries qualify for entry on the National List and the Community's Common Catalogue (comprising the national lists of the Member States).

EUROPEAN COMMUNITY SYSTEM. A proposal to establish a system for granting a Community plant variety right was published in August 1990. The proposed system is designed to adapt the current situation, determined by various national plant variety protection regimes, to the circumstances of the Single European Market, and to strengthen, in the light of the development of new breeding techniques, the protection available to plant breeders. It will allow the plant breeder to acquire, upon a single application, direct and uniform protection throughout the Community for varieties of all botanical taxa and hybrids of taxa. But it will not replace national systems: these will continue to grant national rights to a breeder or variety owner who decides to 'take the local route' to legal protection.

EUROPEAN PATENTS OF INVENTION

The European Patent Convention (EPC) was signed in Munich in October 1973 by a number of Western European countries, including the United Kingdom. The EPC establishes a system of law common to the Contracting States for granting European patents of invention, or Europatents for short. In each of the Contracting States for which a Europatent is granted by the European Patent Office (EPO), the patent is to have the same effect, and be subject to the same conditions, as a national patent. A Europatent can be seen as a bundle of national patents.

*Historical background*. The roots of the patent system go back in time at least as far as, and possibly well beyond, 1474, when the Venetian Republic passed a law giving every inventor who disclosed 'any new and ingenious device' to the Venetian authorities a ten-year legal monopoly over the device. The aim of this law was to encourage inventors 'to apply their genius' and 'build devices of great utility and benefit to our commonwealth'. A similar objective lay behind the British *Statute of Monopolies* 1623 which both condemned as a vexatious interference with trade the granting of monopolies over common merchandise and affirmed (in Section VI) that a patent could be granted 'to the true and first inventor' in respect of 'any manner of new manufacture' for a period of fourteen years.

Of these two enactments, the Statute of 1623 is widely regarded as the true progenitor of the modern system; and such phrases in Section VI as 'manner of new manufacture' and 'true and first inventory' serve in the patent laws of several countries with a legal heritage that stems from the Common Law of England (though, since the Patents Act 1977, these phrases are no longer to be found in British patent law).

But, prior to the 1960s, there was really little or nothing in the way of an international patent system in Europe, let alone in the wider world. True, there were shared or common principles, but these did not go to make an organized, integrated whole at the international level. Each country pursued its own economic ends through its national patent system, and the devil could take the hindmost. There were considerable differences between these national systems. Some countries (e.g. Germany, The Netherlands, and Switzerland) examined patent applications far more thoroughly than others (e.g. Britain) before granting patents; some barely examined them (e.g. Belgium, Italy). Moves towards creating a European patent system began in the late-1950s, yet for various political reasons the discussions lingered until the late 1960s, when under a fresh impetus they revived, to culminate in the European Patent Convention 1973.

*National patent systems*. It was thought by many that the advent of the EPC would, within a few decades, spell the end of national patent systems in Europe. That is not yet in sight, though some national patent offices may not be thriving concerns. Alongside the EPC system, each member country of the EPC continues to run its own national patent office. In the United Kingdom, for example, the Patents Act 1977 brings the British patent system broadly into line with the system established by the EPC and provides a national route to the grant of a British patent which is essentially similar to the system for the grant of a Europatent. It is a matter for professional advice whether an inventor should apply for a Europatent or for separate national patents. While the EPC is not a part of national law directly, it nonetheless exerts a most persuasive influence on the development of national patent systems in EPC countries.

*Patentable subject matter*. A Europatent may be granted only for a technical invention, as opposed to a literary or an artistic 'invention' or a mere discovery. That said, certain technical matter is excluded by Article 53 EPC from the grant of a patent: (a) inventions the publication or exploitation of which would be contrary to 'ordre public' or morality, and (b) plant or animal varieties or essentially biological processes for the production of plants or animals, not being microbiological processes or the products thereof.

The European Patent Office, in interpreting paragraph (b), takes the strict and narrow line that, while a plant *variety* cannot be patented as such, plants in general are not excluded by Article 53(b). This distinction is quite important because it opens a door to a European patent for the plant breeder, particularly the breeder of hybrids, the seed of which, though it can produce a uniform crop, is not stable in the conventional sense (see the EPO decision on LUBRIZOL's Application [1990] Official Journal of the European Patent Office, page 71).

The exclusion in paragraph (b) does not embrace technical methods of breeding, cultivating, or conditioning plants (including plant varieties). Thus, in one case, a Europatent was granted for a method of treating plant material (including seed of known varieties of wheat, millet and barley) in a specified way with chemicals in order to make it resistant to agricultural chemicals (see the EPO decision on CIBA-GEIGY's Application [1984] Official Journal of the European Patent Office, page 112). Nor does paragraph (b) prevent the patenting of genes.

There is also an opening for the plant breeder in the phrase 'microbiological processes or the products thereof'. If a plant variety is the product of a microbiological process, as for example a variety produced by 'gene-splicing' (or recombinant DNA) technology arguably is, then it avoids the ban in Article 53(b). The reason why a plant breeder would strive to circumvent paragraph (b) is that an industrial patent may afford him wider and stronger protection for his work than plant breeders' rights; and the grant of a patent for a variety as the product of a microbiological process would not preclude the breeder from seeking plant breeders' rights on the variety. The two forms of protection would cover different aspects of the breeder's work.

*Conditions for grant of Europatent*. Where there is proper subject matter in a European patent application, the EPO must be satisfied that the invention described therein is new, involves an inventive step and is industrially applicable before granting the patent applied for. An invention is considered to be new if, at the date of filing the application, it is not publicly available (Article 54 EPC); it is considered to involve an inventive step if, having regard to what is publicly available, it is not obvious to a person skilled in the art (Article 56 EPC). The patent applicant must describe the invention fully and completely so that it can be performed by a skilled person in the art to which the invention pertains or contributes. This fictitious person is seen as a somewhat dull, unimaginative know-all, a relative of the better-known man on the Clapham omnibus.

Several decades before the advent of the European Patent Convention, it was this legal requirement for a full and complete description that convinced most plant breeders that the patent system was not suited for the protection of plant varieties. It was seen as a nigh-impossible standard for the plant breeder to meet. It led plant breeders to press for a separate system of legal protection, and their efforts led to the UPOV system. The existence of the UPOV system goes most of the way to explaining the exclusion in Article 53(b) EPC. The UPOV system avoids, obviously, what was seen in the 1950s as the main obstacle to the protection of a plant variety by means of an industrial patent: it does not require the plant breeder to give a detailed taxonomic description, let alone a full and complete description in the industrial patent sense, of the plant variety that he wants to protect. Other differences between the two systems are that the UPOV rule on novelty is less strict (or more tolerant) and inventive step and industrial applicability are not conditions for a grant of plant breeders' rights.

But the legal requirement for a full and complete description is not seen nowadays as the obstacle that in former times it was perceived to be. There is a well-developed system for depositing biological material for patent purposes, to supplement the description in a patent specification. Moreover, advances in the biological sciences may allow the plant breeder, within a few decades, to give a full and complete description of a new plant as easily as the industrial chemist can describe a new compound. Pressure is increasing in Europe to delete the exclusion both in Article 53(b)

EPC and from national patent laws.

*Applying for patents.* Whether to apply for a patent, or plant breeders' rights, should be a commercial decision. Obtaining rights under the patent system or the UPOV system, and maintaining them in several countries, can require a considerable financial outlay. If a would-be applicant cannot envisage any economic gain or tactical advantage from owning such exclusive rights, or if he or she lacks the resources or cannot obtain the backing needed to maintain the rights in force and to police them against infringers, or if only weak rights would be granted on an application, an application would make little commercial sense. However, commercial sense is often in short supply with inventors.

If, possibly after taking professional advice, the decision is taken to apply for a patent, the would-be but inexperienced applicant is best advised to employ a patent agent or attorney to prosecute the application through to grant. Indeed, applicants with experience of the ways of patent systems invariably employ a patent agent to act for them. Both the European Patent Office and national patent offices supply guides on how to apply for a patent; and they may give an applicant very limited practical assistance with his application. But it remains for the applicant to get his application into proper and timely order, and to ensure that his invention gets the maximum protection allowed by the law. If he under-protects it, a rival can circumvent his patent; and if he over-protects it, a patent granted on the application can be invalidated or revoked. By comparison, applying for breeders' rights under the UPOV system is fairly straightforward. The UPOV system is 'user-friendly' for applicants, and an applicant does not usually need to employ a professional adviser.

*Examination of applications.* Eighteen months after a European patent application is filed, it is published (unless it has been withdrawn beforehand). This gives the public access to the application, and of course to details of the invention described therein. If the application decides to proceed with his application, the EPO must be asked to examine the application. An examination fee, additional to the application fee, must be paid, otherwise the application will be lost. The examination is carried out by a technically qualified examiner, who may need to be convinced, by a reasoned legal or technical argument, that a patent should be granted. Even if a patent is granted on the application, there is no guarantee that it will withstand an attack by a determined opponent. Unlike an examiner under the UPOV system, who examines the applied for variety by growing it from propagating material, the patent examiner does not examine a physical embodiment of the invention but relies on the written description of it.

*Scope of protection.* The scope of protection (or what constitutes infringement) of a European patent is determined by national patent laws in the EPC countries for which the Europatent was granted. In other words, after grant a Europatent is treated as a national patent. The life of a patent is 20 years from the date of filing for the patent, subject to payment of renewal fees. However, the life of a patent may be brought to an early end by an infringer successfully challenging its validity and getting it revoked.

Broadly, it is an infringement of a national patent under, for example, the UK Patents Act 1977 for any unauthorized person (a) where the invention is a product, to manufacture or market the patented product in the United Kingdom; (b) where the invention is a process, to use the patented process there or to market there any product obtained directly by means of that process (section 60). It is also a patent infringement to supply, knowingly and without the consent of the patent owner, any means, relating to an essential element of the invention (e.g. a particular chemical), for putting the invention into effect.

There is no infringement where an act, that otherwise would infringe, is done privately and for purposes that are not commercial, or is done for experimental purposes relating to the subject matter of the invention. These exceptions (or defences) are to be read quite strictly, otherwise they could be used to undermine patent protection. If, for example, a plant variety is patented, its use to breed other plant varieties for commercial purposes would be unlikely to be regarded as 'experimental'.

*European Community harmonization.* Measures intended to harmonize national laws within the European Community on the protection of biotechnological inventions were proposed by the Community's Council of Ministers in October 1988, but progress on these measures awaited the outcome of the deliberations on a new UPOV Convention, now the 1991 Convention. The Community proposal reiterates the availability of patent protection for (i) biological materials (including animals, plants, plant or animal parts, and non-varietal classifications), (ii) biotechnical processes for the production of animals and plants, and (iii) microbiological processes (i.e. processes carried out with the use of or performed upon or resulting in microbiological material), outside the present constraints in Article 53(b) EPC. It seeks, among other things, to bring harmony where in Europe there is discord: at the interface of the patent system and the plant variety rights system.

**Platanthera** Rich. (From Gk *platys*, wide, and Lat. *anthera*, anther.) Orchidaceae. Some 85 species of herbaceous, terrestrial orchids. Tubers 2, ovoid to ellipsoid, tapering. Stem erect. Basal leaves 1–3, ovate, reduced to sheaths on stem. Spike cylindric; flowers green or white; dorsal sepal and petals incurved, forming a hood, lateral sepals spreading, recurved; lip linear-oblong to lanceolate, entire or, rarely, 3-lobed; spur cylindric, long. Summer. Temperate N and S hemisphere.

CULTIVATION See ORCHIDS, The Hardy Species.

***P. bifolia*** (L.) Rich. LESSER BUTTERFLY ORCHID. To 50cm. Basal lvs almost opposite, oblong-lanceolate, broadly elliptic or obovate. Spike to 20cm; bracts equal ovary; fls fragrant, white, tinted green; lateral sep. lanceolate, spreading, recurved; lip 8–12mm, decurved, white, rarely lime-green, spur to 40mm, slender, almost horizontal, exceeding ovary. Late spring–summer. Mediterranean, USSR. Z6.

***P. blephariglottis*** (Willd.) Lindl. To 50cm, erect, leafy. Basal lvs 2–4, elliptic to lanceolate. Spike 15–25-fld; fls white; sep. oblong-ovate, lateral sep. reflexed; pet. oblong, finely dentate or entire; lip ovate, fringed, spur to 20mm. Mid–late summer. N America. Z7.

***P. chlorantha*** (Custer) Rchb. GREATER BUTTERFLY ORCHID. As *P. bifolia* except spike lax, lateral sep. ovate-lanceolate; fls earlier, larger, darker green, less fragrant, spur 18–40mm, apex slightly dilated. Late spring–summer. Europe, Mediterranean. Z7.

***P. ciliaris*** (L.) Lindl. To 100cm. Basal lvs 5–30×1–5cm, 2–4, lanceolate, ridged. Spike 30–60-fld; fls orange; bracts lanceolate; sep. ovate, lateral sep. spreading; pet. linear, fringed at apex; lip to 25mm, oblong, fimbriate, spur 25–35mm. Mid summer–early autumn. Eastern N America. Z7.

***P. grandiflora*** (Bigelow) Lindl. Stem to 120cm, erect, glabrous. Lvs elliptic to lanceolate, basally sheathing stem. Spike to 25cm, 30–60-fld; sep. elliptic, lateral sep. spreading; pet. oblong, margins finely dentate; lip to 25cm, narrowing toward base, fimbriate, spur to 25mm, slender. Summer. Eastern N America. Z7.

***P. integra*** (Nutt.) Gray. Stem to 60cm, leafy, erect. Basal lvs lanceolate. Spike cylindric, dense; fls golden-yellow; dorsal sep. obovate, concave, lateral sep. orbicular, obtuse; lip oblong, rounded, finely denticulate, spur to 6mm, slender. Summer. C and eastern N America. Z8.

***P. japonica*** (Thunb.) Lindl. To 60cm. Basal lvs oblong, sheathing stem. Fls golden to lime-green; sep. oblong-lanceolate, spreading, dorsal sep. smaller forming hood with pet.; lip ligulate, spur to 15mm downward-pointing. Summer. SW and eastern N America. Z8.

***P. nivea*** (Nutt.) Luer. To 60cm. Lvs lanceolate, sheathing stem below, bract-like on stems. Spike cylindric; fls white; dorsal sep. ovate, lateral sep. oblong, falcate, upper edge obscurely lobed near base; pet. oblong, falcate, basally dilated; lip linear-elliptic, recurved from centre, spur 15mm, almost horizontal. Summer–early autumn. Southwest & N eastern America. Z8.

***P. orbiculata*** (Pursh) Lindl. To 60cm. Basal lvs 2, almost opposite, elliptic-oblong to orbicular, fleshy. Spike lax; fls green-white; sep. ovate to ovate-lanceolate, reflexed, dorsal sep. orbicular, erect; pet. ovate to ovate-lanceolate, reflexed; lip to 24mm, linear-oblong, pendent, slightly recurved, spur to 50mm, slender, cylindric. Summer–early autumn. Northern N America. Z7.

***P. psycodes*** (L.) Lindl. To 90cm. Lvs elliptic to lanceolate, sheathing base of stem, reduced toward apex. Spike 8–12cm; fls purple; bracts lanceolate, sometimes edged purple; dorsal sep. elliptic, concave, lateral sep. elliptic-ovate, spreading; pet. obovate, denticulate; lip 3-lobed, fimbriate, spur 12–18mm slender. Eastern N America. Z6.

***P. montana*** Rchb. f. See *P. chlorantha*.

**Platanus** L. (Gk name for *P. orientalis* from *platys*, broad, in allusion to the broad, flat leaves.) SYCAMORE; BUTTONWOOD; PLANE; PLANE TREE. Platanaceae. 6–7 species of monoecious, mostly deciduous trees to 50m. Bark thin, pale, scaling off in small plates, rarely rough and persistent on old trees. Shoots rather stout; buds conic, with one exposed scale, enclosed within leaf petiole in summer, terminal bud absent. Leaves alternate, mostly palmately 3–7-lobed, pubescent at first but mostly soon glabrous and glossy, long-petiolate; stipules caducous. Flowers in dense globular clusters on a long peduncle in leaf axil; 3–8 sepals and petals. Fruit an obovoid achene 2mm long with a basal spur with a ring of hairs, packed tightly into the 2–3cm globose fruit-ball; fruit balls 1–7 on a long fibrous peduncle. Mostly N America; one in each of SE Europe to SW Asia, and Indochina.

CULTIVATION Large, fast-growing and long-lived trees with decorative bark and remarkable tolerance of air pollution and compacted soil. *P.* ×*acerifolia* is much planted as a street tree, dominant in numerous cities around the world; it withstands pollution because of its glossy, easily rain-cleaned leaves and rapidly flaking bark. One parent, *P. orientalis*, is a finer tree, with a more rugged crown and deeply cut leaves, but is slower-growing, while the other parent, *P. occidentalis*, is large and fast-growing but susceptible to disease. All planes require warm to hot summers; they are slow-growing and poorly shaped in Scotland and N England, and *P. occidentalis* does not grow well north of Central France. *P. orientalis* and *P. occidentalis* and their hybrid are hardy to zone 5–6, but the others are much less so. The natural habitat of all planes is on river gravels and silt with ready access to water, but given access to ground water, they tolerate drought well, making large trees in dry Southern Europe and California. The short, fine, stiff hairs shed from the leaves in spring and the fruit in autumn have been implicated in bronchial problems; these are worst in dry climates where they are blown around more readily.

Propagate by seed, cuttings or layers; pre-treat moistened seed of the species at 2°C/35.6°F for two months, sow in early spring in a cold frame for frost protection. Seed can be stored if cold and dry; that of *P.* ×*acerifolia* is often infertile. Heeled hardwood cuttings taken in autumn at leaf-fall are easily rooted in a cold frame. For commercial propagation, layers are pegged down from a coppiced stool. Plant when 30–250cm/1–8ft tall; larger plants to 5m/16ft can be moved more successfully than most trees. Full sun is essential.

Plane anthracnose, caused by the fungus *Gnomonia veneta* (syn. *G. platani*), causes sporadic dieback of shoots, occasionally spreading to make large cankers on branches. It is worst in cool, damp summers and on those species less adapted to such conditions; hence *P. occidentalis* is the most likely to be attacked, and often killed by it in Britain, while *P. orientalis* is virtually immune. *P.* ×*acerifolia* varies in susceptibility between clones.

***P.* ×*acerifolia*** (Ait.) Willd. LONDON PLANE. *(P. occidentalis* × *P. orientalis.)* Large, deciduous tree to 50m with a smooth, erect trunk; bark peeling off in flakes, cream weathering to grey. Lvs variable in shape, usually truncate to shallowly cordate at the base, 3- or 5-lobed, 12–25cm wide, the lobes triangular to broad triangular, margins sinuately toothed to entire; stipules medium-sized; petiole 3–10cm. Fr. globose *c*2.5cm thick, usually in groups of 2 together, occasionally in threes or solitary, bristly, nutlets ovoid or globose with the remnant of the style at the apex. Origin unknown. 'Augustine Henry': lower branches pendulous; lvs 25–35cm wide, 5-lobed, slightly blue-green, tomentose beneath at first, veins remaining so. 'Cantabrigiensis': lvs smaller than species type, more deeply lobed, more slender, more delicate in all respects, base truncate with a small, cuneate central portion. 'Hispanica': Lvs often to 30cm wide, normally 5-lobed, the lobes toothed, base truncate to slightly cordate, venation beneath and leaf petiole with a persistent tomentum; fr. grouped 1–2. 'Kelseyana': lvs yellow variegated. 'Mirkovec': lvs becoming red-tinged in summer, colouring purple-red in autumn. 'Pyramidalis': habit upright, lower branches not drooping, bark rougher; lvs mostly 3-lobed, lobes only slightly toothed; close to *P. occidentalis*, possibly a back-cross. 'Sutternii': lvs white-blotched speckled over the entire surface. 'Tremonia' ('Dortmund'): habit quite narrow, conical, very fast growing. Z7.

***P. mexicana*** Moric. Tree to 20m. Lvs to 20cm wide, mostly 5-lobed, lobes entire, acuminate, lower surfaces off-white-tomentose. Fr. heads 1 or 2 on a peduncle, rough, tawny-hairy, 3.5cm diam. NE Mexico. Z9.

***P. occidentalis*** L. AMERICAN SYCAMORE; BUTTONWOOD; AMERICAN PLANE. Tree to 50m, bole to 4m diam. Trunk not continuous to the peak, branches directed upward, usually straight; bark exfoliating in small plates. Lvs generally 3-lobed, 10–18cm wide, middle lobe shorter than its basal width, margins coarsely sinuate, occasionally entire, base obtuse to cuneate, glabrous above, tomentose beneath at first, remaining hairy in veins. Stipules very large, often conical to tubular. Fr. clusters usually solitary, occasionally in pairs, nutlets rounded at the apex. SE US. Before 1990 *P.* ×*acerifolia* was often grown and sold under this name. var. ***glabrata*** (Fern.) Sarg. Lvs smaller, tougher, more deeply lobed, usually truncate at base, sinuses about one third into the leaf blade, the lobes long acuminate and often entire or also coarsely and sparsely dentate. Iowa to NE Mexico. Z5.

***P. orientalis*** L. ORIENTAL PLANE. Tree to 30m. Trunk usually continuous to the peak; bark exfoliating in large plates; twigs usually more horizontally spreading. Lvs deeply 5–7 lobed, occasionally 3-lobed on the younger shoots, 10–20cm wide, lobes much longer than wide, the sinuses reaching nearly to the middle of the blade, base usually long cuneate, occasionally truncate. Stipules small. Fr. clusters in groups of 3–4 or more, occasionally in pairs, nutlets conical, apex becoming the style. SE Europe to Asia Minor. var. ***insularis*** A. DC. CYPRIAN PLANE. Lvs 5-lobed, the sinuses very deep, the lobes further lobed with ascending teeth, lobes very long acuminate at the apex, base more or less cordate. Fr. heads only *c*1.5cm thick, usually 2–3 together, occasionally to 4, nutlets with acute, pubesc. heads and a persisting, elongated style. Crete. Plants cult. under this name are usually erroneously labelled. 'Cuneata' lvs deeply incised, lobes entire to lobulate. Z7.

***P. racemosa*** Nutt. CALIFORNIA SYCAMORE; ALISO. Tree 30(40)m. Lvs usually cordate to truncate, 15–30cm wide, deeply 3–5-lobed, thick and tough, deep green above, lighter and tomentose beneath, the lobes narrow and entire or sparsely dentate. Fr. clusters grouped 3–7 together, nutlets tomentose when young, with a conical or globose apex. W US (California), NW Baja California. Z8.

***P. wrightii*** S. Wats. ARIZONA SYCAMORE. Tree to 25m. Lvs deeply 5–7-lobed, tomentose beneath, often eventually nearly glabrous, the lobes lanceolate, entire to sparsely dentate. Fr. clusters grouped 2–4, the individual heads usually stalked, normally glabrous, nutlets truncate to hemispherical, styles usually abscising. N America; Arizona to NW Mexico. Z8.

***P.* ×*acerifolia*** var. ***hispanica*** (Münchh.) Bean. See *P.* ×*acerifolia* 'Hispanica'.
***P.* ×*acerifolia*** f. ***argenteovariegata*** hort. See *P.* ×*acerifolia* 'Sutternii'.
***P.* ×*acerifolia*** f. ***pyramidalis*** (Jankó) C. Schneid. See *P.* ×*acerifolia* 'Pyramidalis'.
***P.* ×*aureovariegata*** hort. See *P.* ×*acerifolia* 'Kelseyana'.
***P. californica*** Benth. See *P. racemosa*.
***P. californica*** hort. non Benth. See *P. racemosa*.
***P. cantabrigiensis*** Henry. See *P.* ×*acerifolia* 'Cantabrigiensis'.
***P. cretica*** Dode. See *P. orientalis* var. *insularis*.
***P. cuneata*** Willd. See *P. orientalis* var. *cuneata*.
***P. cyprius*** hort. See *P. orientale* var. *insularis*.
***P. densicoma*** Dode pro parte. See *P. occidentalis* var. *glabrata*.
***P. glabrata*** Fern. See *P. occidentalis* var. *glabrata*.
***P.* ×*hispanica*** Mill. ex Münchh. See *P.* ×*acerifolia*.
***P.* ×*hybrida*** Brot. See *P.* ×*acerifolia*.
***P. orientalis*** var. ***cretica*** Dode. See *P. orientalis* var. *insularis*.

**Platycarya** Sieb. & Zucc. (From Gk *platys*, broad, and *karya*, nut.) Juglandaceae. 1 species, a monoecious tree or shrub to 12m; pith solid. Branches pubescent, later glabrous, yellow-brown to chestnut. Leaves alternate, odd-pinnate, exstipulate, 15–30cm; leaflets 7–15, sessile, ovate to oblong-lanceolate, acuminate, biserrate, 4–10cm, slightly pubescent, later glabrous. Male inflorescence a slender, erect catkin, 5–8cm, in clusters of 4–8; perianth absent; stamens 8–10; female inflorescence a solitary, cone-like catkins, terminal, ovoid-oblong, about 3cm; bract adnate to ovary; styles 5. Fruit a nutlet, small-winged, to 5mm. Summer. C & S China.

CULTIVATION Small to medium-sized trees which prefer warm dry continental climates where temperatures do not drop below about −12°C/10°F in winter. *P. strobilacea* makes a good specimen tree or large shrub with elegant, pinnate foliage. Propagate from ripe or stratified seed, by layering or by splice/veneer grafting on to *Carya* stock. Cultivation otherwise as for *Carya*.

***P. strobilacea*** Sieb. & Zucc. As for the genus.

For synonymy see *Fortunaea*.

**Platycerium** Desv. STAGHORN FERN; ELKHORN FERN; ANTELOPE EARS. (From Gk *platys*, broad, and *keras*, a horn, referring to the fronds.) Polypodiaceae. Perhaps 18 species of epiphytic or, occasionally, epilithic ferns. Rhizomes spreading or short-creeping, often branched, dictyostelic, hidden by fronds; scales dense, variously shaped, entire at margin, papery to leathery. Fronds in 2 rows, distinctly dimorphous: sterile fronds 'nest'- or 'basket-leaves' few, sessile or, rarely, short-stipitate, persistent, erect, adpressed at base, circular to oblong, peltate, cordate at base, entire to shallowly 2-lobed at upper margin, thick, fleshy or leathery, and grey to green, to thin, dry, papery, brown, enclosing massed roots and humus; fertile fronds short-stipitate, deciduous, erect to arching or pendent, wedge-shaped to dichotomously branched from base into few to many deep lobes, antler-like, leathery, green; all fronds densely stellate-pubescent to glabrous; main veins dichotomously branched to parallel, secondary reticulate, anastomosing into areoles with, occasionally, few free, included veinlets; stipes jointed. Sporangia and paraphyses in large, variously placed soral patches on lower surface of fertile fronds, acrostichoid; paraphyses stellate-pubescent, flat to spine- or club-like; annulus 20–34-celled; spores bean-shaped, glabrous, glassy. Tropics. Z10.

CULTIVATION Epiphytic ferns of temperate to tropical rainforest requiring glasshouse cultivation. *P. bifurcatum* from southernmost areas of Australia may be subjected to light frosts. Grown for foliage effect mounted on walls of glasshouse or conservatory; on the trunks of trees or tree ferns in tropical and temperate areas, and look best when grown to specimen size. *P. bifurcatum* will grow indoors with frequent syringing. The strongly epiphytic habit of this genus does not lend them well to container cultivation; they perform better mounted on slabs of tree fern, bark, or (for larger specimens) on hardwood slabs furnished with moss and/or epiphytic fern potting mix retained with wire mesh. Clumping species (e.g. *P. hillii*) can be grown in hanging baskets. All rely on atmospheric moisture rather than water directly at the roots – daily syringing with soft water during the summer growing season is beneficial, water being applied moderately to the roots. Established specimens will envelop their mount; they are best watered by immersing in tepid water. Water should be applied sparingly when growth slows through the winter months. They enjoy bright filtered light, and will tolerate a little direct sun for part of the day. Feed is best applied as a monthly foliar spray on actively growing plants. Plants should only need remounting as they outgrow their existing supports, or if it starts to decay. Specimen plants can be very heavy, and need to be securely attached with wire; smaller plants are secured with nylon fishing line.

Vegetative propagation of clumping species (e.g. *P. hillii*) is by division of larger offsets (above 25cm/10in. diam.) taken as growth commences in spring. The rhizome is buried beneath layers of many dead, closely packed, sterile fronds or 'pads': it is a matter of severing through the layers of pads until the rhizome is cut through, and the division remounted onto a fresh support. Close attention should be given to watering until the division has become established. Unbranching species (e.g. *P. grande*) can only be propagated from spores: these usually germinate readily, but can be difficult to establish.

***P. andinum*** Bak. SOUTH AMERICAN STAGHORN. Sterile fronds 60×30cm+, sessile, erect, cuneate and 2–3-lobed at upper margin, entire at lower margin; fertile fronds to 3m, pendent, cuneate to linear, narrowly and dichotomously forking into 3 or more branches, pale grey to green. Soral patches to 4, medial, linear, to 50×8cm. S America (Peru, Bolivia).

***P. bifurcatum*** (Cav.) C. Chr. COMMON STAGHORN FERN; ELKHORN FERN. Sterile fronds to 60×45cm, sessile, erect or adpressed, rounded to heart- or kidney-shaped, entire, wavy, or shallowly and irregularly lobed at upper margin, papery; fertile fronds to 90cm, erect, spreading, or pendent, base cuneate to spathulate, 2 or 3 (occasionally to 5) times dichotomously forked, leathery, seg. to 20×3cm, strap-shaped, apex obtuse, all fronds more or less stellate-pubesc.; stipes of fertile fronds to 10cm, sulcate and winged, stellate-pubesc., red-brown. Soral patches to 10, to 22×7cm, linear, superficial, more or less covering lower surface of fertile seg.; sporangia pear-shaped; annulus 23–32-celled; paraphyses stalked, stellate-pubesc., 8–15-armed. SE Asia, Polynesia, subtropical Australia.

***P. coronarium*** (J.G. Koenig ex Muell.) Desv. Sterile fronds to 100×50cm, sessile, erect to recurved, entire at lower margin, elliptic, deeply and irregularly lobed at upper margin (to 5 times), basally thick and fleshy, bright green; fertile fronds to 3m, pendent, spreading at base, narrowly elliptic to obovate, to 7 times narrowly and dichotomously forked, pendent, sterile central lobe, 2 spreading, sterile strap-like and forking divisions at base, fertile lobe to 35×25cm, horizontal, semicircular to heart-, shell- or kidney-shaped, fleshy, on stalk to 7cm. Soral patches in dense mass on lower surface of fertile lobe; sporangia stellate-pubesc.; annulus 20–24-celled; paraphyses stalked, 12–20-armed. SE Asia (Malaysia to Philippines).

***P. elephantotis*** Schweinf. CABBAGE FERN; ELEPHANT'S EAR FERN. Sterile fronds to 90×45cm, sessile, erect, rounded to oblong, cuneate in upper part and truncate at apex, entire to markedly wavy at upper margin, entire at lower margin, stellate-pubesc. to glabrous, membranous and prominently veined in upper part; fertile fronds to 75×55cm, pendent, obovate to obcuneate, apex rounded, base cuneate, undivided and margin more or less entire, leathery, densely stellate-pubesc. and russet below, more or less glabrous above. Soral patch 1, to 40cm wide, apical on lower surface of fertile frond, rounded to oval or obovate; sporangia stellate-pubesc.; annulus 26–31-celled; paraphyses short-stalked, 7–9-armed. Tropical Africa (Sudan to Mozambique).

***P. ellisii*** Bak. Sterile fronds to 30×20cm, sessile, adpressed, rounded, entire to very shallowly lobed; fertile fronds to 60cm, erect, obovate to cuneate, entire or 2-lobed at upper margin, light green. Soral patches 1 or, occasionally, 2, apical on lobes or below sinus, to 20cm, oblong or narrowly and acutely 2-lobed; annulus 20–22-celled; paraphyses short-stalked, 10–14-armed. Madagascar.

***P. grande*** (Fée) Kunze. STAGHORN FERN. Sterile fronds to 110×180cm, sessile, spreading to adpressed, suborbicular to heart- or kidney-shaped, cuneate in upper part and truncate at apex, upper margin to 5 times deeply and irregularly dichotomously lobed, lower margin entire to wavy, papery, bronze to green, stellate-pubesc., strongly ribbed and veined; fertile fronds to 180cm, stipitate, pendent, cuneate, dichotomously forked, leathery, main forks cuneate, dividing into strap-shaped seg. to 30cm long. Soral patch 1, to 50×30cm, superficial below sinus of first fork, semi-circular; sporangia pear-shaped; annulus 25–33-celled; paraphyses short-stalked, 7–14-armed. Malaysia, Australia, Philippines.

***P. hillii*** T. Moore. NORTHERN ELKHORN FERN. Sterile fronds to 40×24cm, sessile, adpressed, rounded and shallowly lobed at upper margin, otherwise entire; fertile fronds to 70cm+ long, to 20cm wide or more below divisions, short-stipitate, erect or suberect, broadly cuneate to spathulate in lower part, irregularly and dichotomously forked or, occasionally, palmately lobed in upper third, sparsely stellate-pubesc., dark green, seg. to 20×6cm, narrowly elliptic to obovate. Soral patches on lower surface of ultimate seg., rounded to oblong; annulus 26–31-celled. Australia (Queensland), New Guinea. Cvs include 'Bloomei', 'Drummond', 'Drummond Diversifolium', 'Pumilum'. 'Drummond': fertile fronds to 30cm, pendent, broadly fan-shaped, to 10 or more times dichotomously divided.

***P. holttumii*** De Joncheere & Hennipman. Sterile fronds to 115×135cm, sessile, spreading, cuneate and truncate in upper part, to 6 times regularly and dichotomously lobed at upper margin, wavy at lower margin, green; fertile fronds to 125cm, spreading, cuneate, 2-lobed, and to 5 times laterally forked at upper margin, pale grey to green, lobes cuneate, forks pendent. Soral patches superficial, 1 in sinus of each lobe, semi-circular, to 45×35cm; annulus 26–31-celled. SE Asia (Thailand to Malaysia).

***P. madagascariense*** Bak. Sterile fronds to 35×22cm, subsessile, adpressed, rounded, minutely toothed at margin, prominently veined with intermittent sunken areas, forming distinctive 'waffle-pattern'; fertile fronds to 30cm, erect to pendent, cuneate to fan-shaped, to 3 times dichotomously forked at upper margin. Soral patches 1 or 2 on seg., to 16×39cm; annulus 23–25-celled. Madagascar.

***P. quadridichotomum*** (Bonap.) Tard. Sterile fronds to 40×17cm, sessile, erect to adpressed, cuneate and truncate in upper part, entire or toothed or wavy at upper margin, entire at lower margin; fertile fronds to 40cm, pendent, cuneate, to 4 times dichotomously forked at upper margin, densely stellate-pubesc. beneath. Soral patches to 4, medial between sinuses, to 9×3cm; annulus 21–28-celled. Madagascar.

***P. ridleyi*** Christ. Sterile fronds to 50×40cm, stipitate, adpressed, rounded and shallowly lobed, entire at margin, veins prominent; fertile fronds to 17×15cm, erect, kidney-shaped, to 8 times dichotomously forked, with 1 sterile and 1 fertile, or 2 sterile, branches, to 7 times dichotomously forked, and fertile central lobe, rounded to obovate, elliptic, or shell-shaped, horizontal, stalked, stalk to 10cm. Otherwise largely as *P. coronarium*. SE Asia (Thailand, Malaysia to Indonesia).

***P. stemaria*** (Beauv.) Desv. TRIANGULAR STAGHORN FERN. Sterile fronds to 60×3cm, sessile, erect, cuneate, apex truncate, entire or irregularly toothed or wavy, occasionally more or less shallowly lobed at upper margin; fertile fronds to 90cm, spreading or, in var. *laurentii*, pendent, broadly cuneate to triangular, once or twice dichotomously forked, stellate-pubesc. below. Soral patches superficial, around sinuses (at apex on var. *laurentii*), broadly triangular to crescent- or V-shaped, to 30×22cm; annulus 24–29-celled. Tropical Africa.

***P. superbum*** De Joncheere & Hennipman. STAGHORN FERN. Sterile fronds to 160×150cm, sessile, spreading to falcate, cuneate, apex truncate, to 4 times dichotomously forked or lobed, entire or waxy, stellate-pubesc. to glabrous, grey to green; fertile fronds to 2m, spreading to pendent, cuneate, to 5 times narrowly and dichotomously forked, seg. often twisted. Soral patch 1, superficial, central near sinus, semi-circular, to 42×68cm, dark brown; annulus 26–34-celled. Australia.

***P. veitchii*** (Underw.) C. Chr. SILVER ELKHORN FERN. Sterile fronds to 45×18cm, sessile, adpressed, elliptic in upper part, twice deeply and irregularly forked or lobed, stellate-pubesc., seg. linear to strap-like; fertile fronds to 70cm, erect or suberect to spreading, narrowly cuneate, to 3 times dichotomously forked, stellate-pubesc., seg. triangular to linear, to 4cm wide, densely stellate-pubesc., pubescence on fronds 5-rayed, distinctively silver-white. Soral patches apical on seg.; annulus 26–32-celled. Australia (Queensland).

***P. wallichii*** Hook. Sterile fronds to 65×50cm, sessile, erect or falcate, cuneate, truncate at apex, to 5 times deeply (as much as upper half) and irregularly lobed, entire at lower margin; fertile fronds to 70cm, pendent, cuneate, 3-lobed (2 fertile, 1 sterile), to 3 times laterally forked, leathery, densely yellow to green stellate-pubesc. below. Soral patches superficial, 2 in ultimate sinuses, semi-circular, to 20×15cm; sporangia stellate-pubesc.; annulus 27–32-celled. E India, China, Malaysia.

***P. wandae*** Racib. Sterile fronds to 125×135cm, sessile, spreading to falcate, cuneate, truncate at apex, to 6 times dichotomously forked at upper margin, wavy at lower margin and distinctively laciniate or dentate near base; fertile fronds to 2m, spreading, 2-lobed, lobes cuneate, one to 4 times laterally forked, the other not, seg. pendent. Soral patches superficial, 1 in sinus of each lobe, semi-circular to narrowly elliptic, to 33×60cm; annulus 26–30-celled. New Guinea.

***P. willinckii*** T. Moore. JAVA STAGHORN FERN. Sterile fronds to 70×50cm, sessile, erect, rounded, to elliptic in upper part, to 4 times deeply and dichotomously forked at upper margin; fertile fronds to 90cm, short-stipitate, pendent, cuneate to spathulate in lower part, to 5 times dichotomously forked at upper margin, pale grey to green, segments narrowly triangular to strap-shaped, densely stellate-pubesc. below; stipes to 1cm. Soral patches around sinuses of, and onto, terminal seg.; annulus 25–31-celled. Indonesia, New Guinea. 'Lemoinei': fronds initially with white and woolly stellate pubescence, and more rigid. 'Payton': fertile fronds to 38cm with to 8 seg., rigid. 'Scofield': fertile fronds wider than species type, more widely forked, seg. to 3cm wide.

***P. aethiopicum*** Hook. See *P. stemaria*.
***P. alcicorne*** Auct., Hook. non Desv. See *P. andinum*.
***P. alcicorne*** hort. non Desv. See *P. bifurcatum*.
***P. angolense*** Welw. ex Bak. See *P. elephantotis*.
***P. biforme*** (Sw.) Bl. See *P. coronarium*.
***P. biforme*** var. ***erecta*** Ridl. See *P. ridleyi*.
***P. bifurcatum*** var. ***hillii*** (T. Moore) Domin. See *P. hillii*.
***P. bifurcatum*** var. ***quadridichotomum*** Bonap. See *P. quadridichotomum*.
***P. bifurcatum*** var. ***veitchii*** (Underw.) Hennipman & Roos. See *P. veitchii*.
***P. bifurcatum*** var. ***willinckii*** Hennipman & Roos. See *P. willinckii*.
***P. coronarium*** var. ***cucullatum*** v.A.v.R. See *P. ridleyi*.
***P. diversifolium*** Bonap. See *P. ellisii*.
***P. ellisii*** var. ***diversifolium*** C. Chr. See *P. ellisii*.
***P. grande*** var. ***bambourinense*** Domin. See *P. superbum*.
***P. madagascariense*** var. ***humblotii*** Poiss. See *P. madagascariense*.
***P. sumbawense*** Christ. See *P. willinckii*.
***P. velutinum*** C. Chr. See *P. elephantotis*.
***P. wilhelminae-reginae*** v.A.v.R. See *P. wandae*.
For further synonymy see *Alcicornium*.

**Platycladus** Spach. (From Gk *platys*, broad, and *klados*, a young branch, referring to the spreading branches.) ORIENTAL THUJA; BIOTA. Cupressaceae. 1 species, an evergreen, monoecious conifer to 15m. Bark rust-brown, fibrous. Crown conic to broadly ovate or irregular. Stems often numerous; branches many, ascending; shoots outspread in a single longitudinal plane, light green. Lvs closely adpressed, 2mm, arranged in lateral and facial pairs, grooved, obtuse, light or dull green, becoming bronze tinged in winter, the facial pairs smaller, unscented when crushed. Cones erect, oblong, 10–20mm, fleshy, becoming woody, blue-green, with a waxy bloom; scales 4–8, usually 6, in pairs, apices with a recurved thick, fleshy bract; apical pair sterile, fertile scales bearing 2 ovate seeds 3–6×2–3mm, brown, without wings. W China (E Inner Mongolia to Yunnan), N Korea; also a small wild population in NE Iran. Z6.

CULTIVATION As for *Cupressus* (not *Thuja*), but much more cold tolerant. By far best growth on dry, freely drained sites, often alkaline in reaction, particularly over old building rubble in villages and towns. In GB, best specimens, to 15m/49ft, in Midlands. Also widely planted in E Asia; E & C US, SW to California, and S Europe. In wild, grows mainly on steep rocky valley sides, often on cliffs, in dry areas of W China. Propagate by seed, freely produced in cult., or by cuttings.

***P. orientalis*** (L. f.) Franco. As for the genus. Numerous cvs., ranging from dwarf forms to small trees; some with juvenile, needle-like lvs., others green, golden, slightly variegated, or with filamentous branches. 'Elegantissima', slow-growing, dense, yellow green, the commonest form in cult.

For synonymy see *Biota* and *Thuja*.

**Platyclinis** Benth. See *Dendrochilum*.

**Platycodon** A. DC. (From Gk *platys*, broad, and *kodon*, bell, alluding to the form of the flower.) BALLOON FLOWER; CHINESE BELLFLOWER. Campanulaceae. 1 species, a perennial herb. Stem glabrous, branched above, to 70cm. Leaves whorled below, alternate above, lanceolate to elliptic-lanceolate, dentate, green tinged with blue. Flowers terminal, in few-flowered corymbs or solitary; corolla broadly campanulate, with abruptly acuminate lobes, much inflated in bud, exterior grey to slate blue deepening on opening, interior sky blue, azure or white rarely opal-pink; filaments dilated at base, anthers free; stigmata 5. Fruit a capsule, dehiscing apically between stamens and sepals. Summer. D China, Manchuria, Japan. Z4.

CULTIVATION For the herbaceous border and rock garden, *P. grandiflorus* is valued primarily for its flowers, opening from large, balloon-shaped buds to wide bell-shaped flowers, with a range of rich or pale blues or, in 'Mother of Pearl', pale pink; all have a satisfactorily substantial texture and last well when cut. Plants are beautiful from emergence in spring throughout summer, first producing study, purple flushed stems, gradually unfolding whorls of fresh green leaves, the toothed edges outlined with dark chocolate-maroon. Hardy to between −15 and −20°C/5 to −4°F; mulch with bracken or leafmould where low temperatures are prolonged.

*P. grandiflorus* is tolerant of a range of soils but fares best in deep, well-drained, light loamy soil in sun of light dappled shade. It emerges late in spring and its position should be clearly marked to avoid damage when hoeing, etc. Propagate by seed sown in spring which germinates freely and quickly; plants flower in their second year from seed. Since the compact clumps of this plant spread slowly, they are best left undisturbed although increase is possible by basal cuttings with a piece of root attached and by careful division.

***P. grandiflorus*** (Jacq.) A. DC. As for the genus. Some 40 cvs: fls single or double, white, pink, and light blue to dark purple-blue. 'Album': fls white, often veined blue. 'Apoyama': habit dwarf; fls large, deep mauve. 'Baby Blue': habit dwarf, bushy; fls blue. Balloon Series: habit dwarf, compact; fls blue. 'Hakone Double Blue': fls double, deep violet-blue. 'Komachi': fls remaining balloon-shaped, blue. 'Perlmutterschale' ('Mother of Pearl'): fls large, pale pink. 'Plenum': fls semi-double, pale blue. 'Shell Pink': fls delicate pink.

***P. glaucus*** (Thunb.) Nak. See *P. grandiflorus*.
For further synonymy see *Campanula* and *Wahlenbergia*.

**Platycrater** Sieb. & Zucc. (From Gk *platys*, broad, and *krater*, bowl, referring to the shape of the calyx in the sterile flower.) Hydrangeaceae. 1 species, a low, procumbent, deciduous shrub to 1m. Branchlets glabrous; branches ultimately covered in thin, exfoliating, dark brown bark. Leaves 10–20cm, opposite, oblong to lanceolate, apex narrow-acuminate, base cuneate, margins finely sinuate-serrate, thin-textured, sparsely pubescent above, more so beneath, especially on veins. Inflorescence a loose terminal cyme; flowers small, white, 5–10 per cyme, the outer, sterile flowers showy, disc-like, formed of 3–4 fused sepals; stamens many. Seeds abundant, narrow, winged at each end. Japan. Z8. *Platycrater* is broadly similar to *Hydrangea* (particularly to *H. angustipetala*), from which it is readily distinguished by the form of the outer sterile flowers.

CULTIVATION Suitable for cool, lightly shaded positions on the rock garden or, where winter temperatures fall much below −5 to

−10°C/23–14°F, in the cold glasshouse, with treatment as for *Deinanthe*. Propagate by greenwood cuttings, by seed and by layers.

***P. arguta*** Sieb. & Zucc. As for the genus. 'Hortensis': infl. reduced to 3–5 fertile fls.

**Platykeleba** N.E. Br.
***P. insigne*** N.E. Br. See *Sarcostemma insigna*.

**Platylobium** Sm. (From Gk *platys*, broad or flat, and *lobion*, pod, referring to the shape of the fruit.) Leguminosae (Papilionoideae). 4 species of shrubs or subshrubs; stems prostrate, slender, unarmed. Leaves opposite, rarely alternate, 1-foliolate, ovate to cordate; stipules ovate or narrow-ovate, persistent. Flowers 1 to several, axillary; pedicels bibracteolate, often scaly; calyx pubescent; standard orbicular or reniform, much longer than the other petals; stamens 10, connate by their filaments in a sheath split open on the adaxial side, anthers uniform, dorsifixed, with a broad connective. Fruit an oblong, flat legume, with a conspicuous, flat wing to 5mm deep, valves thin, several-seeded; seeds ellipsoid or ovate-ellipsoid, arillate. E Australia. Z9.

CULTIVATION *Platylobium* spp. occur predominantly on low-fertility soils in dry forest and heath. They are grown for their conspicuous, brightly coloured flowers and evergreen, almost heart-shaped foliage, while the prostrate habit renders a number of species useful for erosion control in their native regions and in other regions with a warm, essentially frost-free climate. In cool temperate zones, grow in the cool glasshouse. Cultivate as for *Dillwynia*.

***P. formosum*** Sm. FLAT PEA. Shrub to 1.5m; shoots subglabrous. Lvs to 5×4cm, very short-stalked, cordate or ovate, cuspidate, base rounded or cordate. Fls solitary, axillary and terminal; pedicel hairy; cal. to 1cm, pubesc.; standard 2.5cm diam., deeply notched, bright yellow, blotched dark red at base. Fr. to 4×2cm, stipitate. Summer. Australia, Tasmania.

***P. obtusangulum*** Hook. COMMON FLAT-PEA; NATIVE HOLLY. Low, spreading shrub. Lvs to 3×3cm, opposite, broadly triangular to ovate-cordate, mostly glabrous above, glabrous to downy beneath. Fls 1–3 per axil; pedicels very short, concealed by imbricate scales and bracts; cal. to 1.2cm, long-adpressed white-pubesc.; standard 1.4–2cm, oblong or reniform, pink-red or brown beneath, orange-yellow above, wings narrow-obovate, shorter than standard, keel obovate, shorter than wings. Fr. to 3×1.5cm, subsessile. Autumn. S Australia.

***P. triangulare*** R. Br. IVY FLAT-PEA. Readily distinguished from the closely related *P. obtusangulum* by the pedicels to 1.5cm. Summer. Australia (Victoria, Tasmania).

***P. angulare*** hort. See *P. triangulare*.
***P. murrayanum*** Hook. See *P. triangulare*.
***P. parviflorum*** Sm. See *P. formosum*.

**Platylophus** D. Don. (From Gk *platys*, broad, and *lophos*, crest, referring to the compressed apex of the fruit which appears as a crest.) Cunoniaceae. 1 species, an evergreen tree to 18m. Leaves opposite, trifoliate, leaflets to 7.5×2cm, sessile, usually serrate, sometimes entire; stipules small. Flowers loosely clustered, axillary, small, white or cream, strongly sweet-fragrant; pedicels elongate; calyx 4- or 5-lobed; petals 4 or 5; stamens 8 to 10; ovary bilocular. Fruit a capsule, bilocular, minute, russet-coloured; seeds 2, oblong, curved. S Africa. Z9.

CULTIVATION As for *Caldcluvia*.

***P. trifoliatus*** (Thunb.) D. Don. WHITE ALDER. As for the genus.

For synonymy see *Weinmannia*.

**Platymiscium** Vogel (From Gk *platys*, broad or flat and, *mischos*, stem.) Leguminosae (Papilionoideae). Some 20 species of trees and shrubs. Leaves opposite or 3–4-verticillate, imparipinnate; stipules interpetiolar, caducous; leaflets opposite, estipellate. Flowers in clustered axillary racemes; bracts and bracteoles small; calyx obconic at the base or rarely obtuse, teeth short, unequal; standard orbicular or ovate, wings obliquely oblong, keel straight or somewhat incurved, obtuse; stamens 10, all united in a sheath split above or, rarely, with vexillary stamen separate, anthers versatile; ovary long-stipitate, 1-ovulate, style filiform, incurved, stigma small, terminal. Fruit a stipitate, oblong, flat, membranous, indehiscent legume, 1-seeded; seeds large, reniform, compressed. Tropical America. Z10.

CULTIVATION In their native zones, *Platymiscium* spp. occur on moist soils in forests and grassy savannahs where they commonly act as hosts to colonies of ants. *P. trinitatis* is an ornamental tree grown as a specimen in large gardens and parks in frost-free warm-temperate and subtropical regions. The flowers, carried on year-old wood before the new foliage emerges, have a sweet, violet fragrance that often carries for long distances. Cultivate as for *Gliricidia*.

***P. floribundum*** Vogel. Tree. Lvs imparipinnate, leaflets 6×2.5cm, 5, opposite, oblong, acuminate. Racemes to 10cm, simple, *c*30-fld; cor. 12.5cm, yellow, wings and standard erect, oblong. Fr. 5–6.5cm, oblong, base attenuate, apex rounded, flattened. Brazil.

***P. pinnatum*** (Jacq.) Dugand. Erect shrub to 4m. Lvs to 15cm; leaflets to 7.5cm, ovate, apex acuminate. Fls in racemes to 10cm, yellow, fragrant, standard reflexed. Colombia.

***P. trinitatis*** Benth. ROBLE. Tree to 30m. Leaflets to 12×7cm, 3–5, elliptic, obtuse; petiolules to 8mm; petioles to 9cm. Racemes yellow-pubesc.; pedicel to 5mm; cal. fine-pubesc., 6mm; cor. 16mm, yellow, clawed, standard minutely puberulous, keel and wings basally auriculate; stamens all connate. Fr. to 8×3cm, glabrous. Trinidad, Guyana.

**Platyopuntia** Engelm.
***P. corrugata*** (Salm-Dyck) Ritter. See *Opuntia corrugata*.

**Platyosprion** Maxim.
***P. platycarpum*** (Maxim.) Maxim. See *Cladrastis platycarpa*.

**Platystele** Schltr. (From Gk *platys*, broad, and *stele*, column, referring to the short, broad column characteristic of the genus.) Orchidaceae. Some 12 species of small epiphytic orchids, closely allied to *Pleurothallis*. Rhizome short; secondary stems small, tufted, apically unifoliate. Leaves conduplicate at base forming a conspicuous petiole. Inflorescence a raceme or a fascicle, terminal or lateral, slender, short or elongate, usually many-flowered; flowers small, opening in succession, pedicellate; sepals similar, subequal, somewhat spreading, lateral sepals shortly connate; petals subsimilar to sepals; lip minute, fleshy, simple, ovate to suborbicular, disc with an inconspicuous or prominent callus; column short, broad, apex dilated, anther terminal, operculate, incumbent, unilocular, pollinia 2, waxy, obpyriform. C & S America. Z10.

CULTIVATION As for *Pleurothallis*.

***P. compacta*** (Ames) Ames. Secondary stems inconspicuous, concealed by white scarious sheaths. Lvs to 55×35mm, linear-oblanceolate, obtuse, apex minutely tridentate, coriaceous. Infl. to 10cm, densely many-fld; fls minute, yellow-green, usually spotted purple; sep. to 3×1mm, elliptic-oblong, subacute or rounded, lateral sep. almost free, oblique; pet. to 3×1.5mm, obliquely oblong-elliptic to oblanceolate, rounded; lip to 1mm, ovate-cordate or ovate-suborbicular, acute or acuminate. Guatemala, Honduras, Costa Rica.

***P. johnstonii*** (Ames) Garay. Secondary stems to 2mm. Lvs to 6×4mm, oblong-lanceolate to oblong-elliptic, rounded, apex minutely tridentate. Infl. to 22mm, 1 to few-fld, erect or arching; fls minute, cream-white; sep. narrowly lanceolate or ovate-lanceolate, attenuate-acuminate; lateral sep. smaller than dorsal sep., free; pet. similar to dorsal sep., oblique; lip to 1mm, ovate, acute, papillose; disc with an elevated, transverse callus, emarginate. Venezuela, Colombia, Ecuador.

***P. misera*** (Lindl.) Garay. Secondary stems to 20mm. Lvs to 60×10mm, oblanceolate or oblong-spathulate, acute or subobtuse. Infl. to 17cm, filiform, few to many-fld; fls small, tan or green suffused purple; sep. to 3mm, ovate, acute; pet. to 3mm, ovate-lanceolate, acuminate; lip to 2mm, velvety, ovate-oblong or ovate-lanceolate, acute or acuminate; column minute, anth. white. Colombia.

***P. ornata*** Garay. Secondary stems to 5mm. Lvs to 22×3mm, light green, ovate-spathulate or oblanceolate, rounded or obtuse, apex minutely tridentate. Infl. usually shorter than lvs, erect or ascending, densely many-fld; fls minute, purple; sep. to 1mm, ovate or ovate-elliptic, acute or obtuse; pet. oblong-oblanceolate, acute; lip dark purple, ovate, acute or acuminate, concave, finely glandular; column to 0.5mm, pale purple. Venezuela.

***P. ovalifolia*** (Focke) Garay & Dunsterv. Secondary stems small or absent. Lvs to 8×4mm, elliptic to obovate, somewhat fleshy, acute or apiculate. Infl. to 15mm, erect or ascending, 1 to few-fld; fls minute, pale cream or pale yellow; sep. to 2×1mm, membranaceous, elliptic to ovate, acute or obtuse, shortly connate; pet. smaller than sep., oblong-oblanceolate, subacute; lip subequal to pet., ovate-triangular to ovate-lanceolate, acute or acuminate. W Indies, Trinidad, Venezuela, Surinam, Guyana, Brazil.

***P. stenostachya*** (Rchb. f.) Garay. Secondary stems to 3.5cm, enclosed within several tubular, white sheaths. Lvs to 35×5mm, suberect-spreading, coriaceous, obovate to linear-spathulate, obtuse. Infl. to 1.5cm, axillary, few to several-fld; fls minute; tepals yellow-green or yellow-brown, sep. to 1.5×1mm, elliptic, acute, pet. similar; lip dark maroon edged white, fleshy, elliptic, densely papillose; column dark maroon, anth. white. Mexico to Panama, Venezuela & Colombia.

For synonymy see *Humboldtia, Pleurothallis* and *Stelis*.

**Platystemon** Benth. (From Gk *platys*, broad, and *stemon*, stamen, referring to the expanded filaments.) CREAMCUPS; CALIFORNIAN POPPY. Papaveraceae. 1 species, an annual, very variable herb. Stems to 30cm, erect or decumbent, branching at base; branches loose, spreading, glabrous. Leaves to 7.5cm, subsessile, opposite to clustered, linear to oblong-lanceolate, entire, clasping stem at base, densely pubescent, veins parallel. Flowers terminal, solitary, to 2.5cm diam., yellow or yellow and white; peduncles to 7.5cm, axillary, stiff; sepals 3, ovate; petals 6, short-lived; stamens many, unequal. Fruit 6–25-carpellate, splitting into 1-seeded segments. Summer. N America (California). Z8.

CULTIVATION An annual native to grassy places of western N America, from California to Arizona, *Platystemon* covers great areas of open country in spring with its pale yellow or cream flowers. In gardens it is suitable for edging borders or for sowing in drifts in the rock garden. Cultivation as for *Papaver rhoeas*, but thin seedlings to 10cm/4in. for best effect.

***P. californicus*** Benth. As for the genus.

***P. leiocarpus*** Fisch. & Mey. See *P. californicus*.

**Platythyra** N.E. Br.
***P. barklyi*** (N.E. Br.) Schwantes. See *Mesembryanthemum barklyi*.

**Plectocephalus** D. Don. (From Gk *pleko*, to twist, and *kephale*, head.) Compositae. About 6 species of erect, annual to perennial herbs. Leaves alternate, simple, entire to pinnatifid. Capitula discoid, solitary or few, terminal on thickened peduncles; involucre cylindrical to globose; phyllaries numerous, with scarious appendages, outer pectinate fringed, inner laciniate fringed; outer disc florets larger, ligulate, sterile, central florets tubular, hermaphrodite. Fruit a cypsela; pappus of numerous bristles. C & S America. Z9.

CULTIVATION As for *Centaurea*.

***P. chilensis*** G. Don ex Loud. Perenn. to 1.2m, slightly woody at base. Lvs to 7cm, pinnatifid, lobes linear, acute, entire to slightly dentate. Involucre *c*2cm diam.; florets red. Fr. to 6mm, cylindric-prismatic. Autumn. Chile.

For synonymy see *Centaurea*.

**Plectorrhiza** Dockr. (From Gk *plektos*, twisted, and *rhiza*, root.) Orchidaceae. 3 species of epiphytic orchids. Roots tangled. Stems long, wiry. Leaves persistent, many, central veins prominent. Inflorescence a raceme; flowers small, fragrant; sepals and petals almost equal; lip attached to column base, trilobed, saccate, lateral lobes small, midlobe small, hollow or fleshy, spur horizontal or at right angles to column, pubescent projection near opening. Australia, Lord Howe Is. Z9.

CULTIVATION Epiphytes for brightly illuminated positions in the intermediate house. See ORCHIDS.

***P. tridentata*** (Lind.) Dockr. TANGLE ORCHID. To 30cm. Roots from internodes, tangled. Lvs to 10cm, 4–20, linear-oblong, falcate, acute. Racemes to 12cm, lax, 3–15-fld; fls fragrant, green, sometimes marked red-brown; dorsal sep. forms a hood; lip shorter than sep., trilobed, appendage hirsute, spur to 3cm, narrow, white with pale green basal blotch. Late summer–mid winter. E Australia.

**Plectostachys** Hilliard & B.L. Burtt. (From Gk *plectos*, braided, and *stachys*, spike referring to the delicately branched habit.) Compositae. 2 species of more or less white-tomentose subshrubs. Leaves to 30mm, elliptic to orbicular, cobwebby to glabrous above, white-tomentose beneath, sessile to shortly petiolate. Capitula radiate, in small, rounded, corymbose clusters; phyllaries in 3–4 series, apices white; ray florets female, yellow, disc florets hermaphrodite. Fruit a cypsela; pappus of partly scabrid bristles. Natal and Cape Provinces. Z9.

CULTIVATION As for *Helichrysum*.

***P. serphyllifolia*** (A. Berger) Hilliard & B.L. Burtt. Straggling, to 1.5m, young branches sparsely white-tomentose. Lvs to 10mm, broadly elliptic to suborbicular, glabrous above, sparsely tomentose beneath, subsessile. Phyllaries in 3 series. Fr. *c*1mm. Spring. Cape Peninsula.

For synonymy see *Helichrysum*.

**Plectranthus** L'Hérit. (From Gk *plektron*, spur, and *anthos*, flower: the corolla often has a basal spur.) Labiatae. 350 species of annuals, perennial herbs or shrubs. Stems and leaves herbaceous, semi-succulent or succulent. Inflorescence paniculate, racemose or spicate, usually terminal, flowers in verticils, occasionally solitary more often cymes; bracts small; calyx 2-lipped, subequally 5-toothed, upper lip of one single tooth, lower lip of 4 lanceolate deltoid to subulate teeth; corolla tube variously gibbous, bilabiate, upper lip usually 4-lobed, lower longer than upper, navicular; stamens 4, 2 rarely abortive, attached at the corolla mouth, free or rarely united in a sheath at the base, lying in the lower corolla lip. Nutlets ovoid or oblong, smooth. Africa, Asia & Australia. Z10.

CULTIVATION This large genus provides many attractive ornamental flowering plants for conservatory or bedding outside in summer. There are some attractive foliage plants, such as *P. forsteri* 'Marginatus', and also a wide range of attractive foliage trailing plants useful in hanging baskets, such as *P. madagascariensis* 'Variegated Mintleaf' and *P. verticillatus* 'Variegatus'. Most species grow rapidly, making handsome specimens in a few months. The shrubby species (e.g. *P. saccatus*) make excellent pot plants for the cool or intermediate glasshouse provided they are given plentiful watering during the growing season. They prefer a dry regime with sparing watering during winter. A medium-fertility loam-based potting medium suits all. The trailing species are easily grown in large hanging baskets or planted as groundcover under glass. These species require less light than the upright shrubby ones, which should be given as much light as possible during winter. The shrubby species can become excessively large. Growth can be restrained by keeping the plant in a medium-sized pot and by pruning to shape the plant. The hairy-leaved succulent species require more light through the year than those with less hairy green leaves.

Propagate by cuttings of new growth taken at any time of year, or by removal of rooted branches of the trailing species or from seed sown under glass in spring.

***P. amboinicus*** (Lour.) Spreng. SOUP MINT; MEXICAN MINT; INDIAN MINT; COUNTRY BORAGE; FRENCH THYME; SPANISH THYME. Decumbent, many-stemmed, aromatic, perenn. herb. Stems to 1.5m with ascending infl. Lvs 4.5×4cm, petiolate, ovate to ovate deltoid, densely pubesc. on both surfaces and gland-dotted, apex obtuse or rounded, margin crenulate; petiole 4–11mm. Infl. spicate, fls in dense glomerate verticils, bracts persistent; cal. 4–6mm, glandular-villous, uppermost tooth longest, apiculate; cor. 7–9mm, lilac, mauve or white tube slightly bent at middle expanding to throat, upper lip 1.5–2mm, lower lip 4mm; stamens united at base. Tropical to S Africa; widely cultivated. A form with white margined leaves is in cultivation.

***P. argentatus*** S.T. Blake. Spreading more or less hairy shrub to 1m. Branches ascending, covered in silvery hairs. Lvs 5–11×3–6cm, canescent, (especially when young), ovate, apex acute or acuminate, margin evenly crenate, dentate, both surfaces glandular; petioles 1–5cm. Infl. racemose to 30cm, verticillasters 9–11-fld, bracts 2–3mm, ovate, not glandular; fls pale blue-white; cal. 1.6–2.5mm; cor. 9–11mm, tube only slightly decurved, oblique at mouth, glabrous, upper lobes and lower lip sparsely pubesc., lower lip equal in length to tube. Nutlets circular. Australia. 'Green Silver' is a widely cultivated clone.

***P. forsteri*** Benth. Decumbent, aromatic, perenn. herb. Stems straggling, to 1m, upper part pubesc., lower sparsely so. Lvs 1.5–3.5cm, ovate to broad-ovate, pubesc. on both surfaces, glandular beneath. Margins crenate or crenate serrate; petioles 1–3cm. Infl. racemose, solitary, pedunculate; bracts broadly ovate, to 1.8mm; verticillasters 6–10-fld, fls pale to mid-blue or mauve; cal. 1.5 to 2.5mm, pubesc., glandular; cor. 3–8mm, 2-lobed, both lobes pubesc., often glandular, lateral lobes ovate, lower lip shorter than the tube. Nutlets circular, smooth. New Caledonia, Fiji, E Australia Is. 'Marginatus' ('Variegatus'): bushy, vigorous; lvs scalloped, variegated cream; fls small, white, in sprays. A golden-variegated form is widely cultivated under the name *P. coleoides*; this name however applies to another Asian species which is little known.

***P. fruticosus*** L'Hérit. Erect, free-branching shrub to 2m, usually tinted purple, sparingly pubesc. or glandular. Lvs 4–14×3–11cm, petiolate, broadly ovate to ovate-elliptic, apex obtuse or acute, margin crenate-dentate, sparsely pubesc., underside gland-dotted and suffused with purple; petiole 2.5cm. Infl. paniculate, fls in 1–3-fld cymes forming 2–6-fld verticillasters; cal. 7–8mm, glandular-hispid; cor. 5–13mm, blue-mauve or pink or pale blue speckled with purple on the upper lip, tube deflexed, narrowing slightly, upper lip 2–6mm, lower lip 2–5mm, boat-shaped. S Africa.

***P. madagascariensis*** (Pers.) Benth. Procumbent or decumbent semi-succulent herb. Stems to 1m, rooting at nodes or erect to 45cm, sparingly to densely tomentose often glandular. Lvs 1.5–4.5×1–2.5cm, petiolate, slightly succulent, ovate to subrotund, upper surface strigose, undersurface medium to densely tomentose, gland-dotted, apex obtuse to rounded, margin crenate to crenate dentate; petioles 5–35mm. Infl. terminal and on laterals, simple or with 2 branchlets near base; fls in 3–8-fld cymes, forming 6–16-fld verticillasters; bracts to 3mm, early deciduous; cal. 4–5mm, gibbous at base, glandular-scabrid; cor. 5–18mm, white or mauve to purple, lips often dotted with red-tinged glands, tube bent at middle, lower lip boat-shaped, longer than the tube. S Africa, Mozambique & Madagascar. A fragrant-lvd variegated form of this species is commonly grown as a trailing plant under the name 'Variegated Mintleaf' or incorrectly as *P. coleoides* 'Variegata'.

***P. oertendahlii*** T.C.E. Fries. Freely branching, semi-succulent, perenn. herb. Stems decumbent, to 1m long, rooting at nodes, to 20cm tall, glandular-tomentose. Lvs 3–4×2.5–4cm, petiolate, semi-succulent, ovate to suborbicular, sparingly villous, lower surface purple, apex acute to obtuse, margin crenate dentate, ciliate; petiole to 4cm. Infl. simple or branched, fls in sessile 3-fld cymes forming 6-fld verticils; cal. to 8mm, glandular-hispidulous; cor. white or suffused with mauve, tube 8–13mm, expanding to saccate base narrowing gradually, upper lip 5mm, lower lip 4–5mm, concave; stamens short, 2–3mm. S Africa (Natal). 'Variegatus': lvs to 4cm, green-bronze, variegated silver and off-white, particularly at edges.

***P. saccatus*** Benth. Erect, soft-stemmed, shrub to 1.2m, freely branched. Stems tinged purple, glandular-puberulous. Lvs 2–7×1.5–5cm, petiolate, blade, semi-succulent, ovate to ovate-deltoid, subglabrous to glandular-puberulous, apex acute, margin dentate with few large teeth; petiole to 5cm. Infl. simple or rarely branched near base; racemes to 12cm with few but large fls in sessile 1–3-fld cymes forming 2–6-fld verticils; cal. to 8mm, subglabrous, cor. mauve, pale blue rarely white, tube deflexed, enlarged and markedly saccate at base narrowing slightly to the throat, lower lip navicular; stamens 5–10mm. Eastern S Africa. var. ***longitubus*** Codd. Similar to type in habit but leaves larger and cor. tube longer, 2–2.6cm, but narrower at the base, cor. lips usually smaller.

***P. verticillatus*** (L.f.) Druce. Semi-succulent, procumbent, perenn. herb. Stems glabrous or slightly pubesc., more than 1m long rising to 25cm high. Lvs 1.5–4×1.2–4cm, petiolate, succulent, ovate to rotund, glabrous to pubesc., undersurface red, gland-dotted, apex acute to rounded, margin crenate-dentate with 3–6 pairs of teeth; petiole to 3cm. Infl. simple or with a pair of branches near the base; fls in sessile 1–3-fld cymes forming 2–6-fld verticils; cal. to 7mm, not gibbous, uppermost tooth erect, lower 4 spreading; cor. 1–2.5cm, white to pale mauve with a few mauve spots on upper lip or speckled with purple, tube deflexed, expanded to saccate base, lower lip shallowly boat-shaped; stamens 5–7mm. Eastern S Africa, Swaziland, Mozambique. This species yield some attractive variegated forms.

***P. arthropodus*** Briq. See *P. fruticosus*.
***P. behrii*** Compton. See *P. fruticosus*.
***P. charianthus*** Briq. See *P. fruticosus*.
***P. coleoides*** hort. non Benth. See *P. forsteri*.
***P. galpinii*** Schltr. See *P. fruticosus*.
***P. nummularius*** Briq. See *P. verticillatus*.
***P. peglerae*** Cooke. See *P. fruticosus*.
***P. scutellarioides*** (L.) R. Br. See *Solenostemon scutellarioides*.
***P. thunbergii*** Benth. See *P. verticillatus*.
***P. urticaefolius*** (Lam.) Salisb. See *P. fruticosus*.
For further synonymy see *Coleus* and *Ocimum*.

**Plectrelminthus** Raf. (From Gk *plektron*, spur, and *helmins*, worm.) Orchidaceae. 1 species, an epiphytic orchid. Roots stout, arising from base of stem. Stem short, leafy. Leaves numerous, 10–35×1.5–3.5cm, ligulate, unequally bilobed at apex, light yellow-green. Racemes arising from axils of lower leaves, pendent, to 60cm, rachis flexuous, 4–12-fld; flowers scented, fleshy, pale green, usually tinged with bronze, lip ivory-white, tipped green; ovary and pedicel twisted so that the lip lies parallel to the rachis: in a pendent inflorescence it therefore points upwards; sepals 3.5–5cm, lanceolate, acute, petals slightly shorter, lower edges of lateral sepals project backwards behind spur and are joined at base; lip 6cm including a basal claw 12–15mm long and an acuminate tip around 15mm long, the intermediate part fan-shaped, the edge undulate; basal claw with 2 projections meeting in middle and forming a V-shape; spur 17–25cm, cylindric, coiled; column large; anther-cap with beak-like projection. W Africa, from French Guinea to Zaire. Z10.

CULTIVATION As for *Angraecum*.

***P. caudatus*** (Lindl.) Summerh. As for the genus.
For synonymy see *Angraecum*

**Plectritis** DC. Valerianaceae. 4 species of annual herbs. Leaves simple, opposite, mostly entire. Flowers white, pink or rose in headlike or dense interrupted spikes; calyx obsolete; corolla with a basal spur and 5 lobes; stamens 3, ovary inferior, 1-celled. Fruit a winged or wingless achene. Western N America.

CULTIVATION As for *Fedia*.

***P. congesta*** (Lindl.) DC. Stem to 45cm. Lvs to 5cm, obovate to oblong-ovate. Fls to 8mm, pink to rose, in headlike clusters; cor. spurred, 2-lipped. Achenes winged. British Columbia to N California.

**Pleioblastus** Nak. (From Gk *pleios*, many, and *blastos*, buds, alluding to the branches which are borne several per node.) Gramineae. Some 20 species of dwarf to medium-sized bamboos rhizomes with short or far-running. Culms erect, almost always hollow, typically with 3–7 branches spreading from the upper nodes, in some species with 1–2 branches from low down, all leafing from the top downwards; sheaths fairly persistent. Leaves scaberulous, tessellate, with smooth white bristles or none, the apex horizontal in all those here except *P. simonii*. China, Japan.

CULTIVATION See BAMBOOS.

***P. akebono*** (Mak.) Nak. Culms slender, 20–50×1–2cm, glabrous throughout; branches erect, 1–2 from low down. Lvs 5–7cm×1–1.5mm in 2 rows, mostly suffused white or yellow. Not yet traced in the wild, but comes true from seed. Z7.

***P. argenteostriatus*** (Reg.) Nak. Differs from the more frequently encountered *P. variegatus* in being sturdier and more upstanding with culms to 1m. Lvs 1.4–2.2×1.0–2.1cm, hairless; sheaths hairless except at the base, nodes pubesc. at first. Unknown in the wild; cultivated in Japan. Z7.

***P. auricoma*** (Mitford) D. McClintock. KAMURO-ZASA. Culms 1–3m×2–4mm, sometimes purple-lined, softly hairy; sheaths rather persistent, shorter than the internodes, ciliate and markedly downy when young; nodes prominent with white waxy powder below; branches usually 1–2 from low down. Lvs 12–22×1.5–3.5cm, softly hairy throughout, especially when young, brilliant yellow with green stripes of various breadths; sheaths downy, ciliate, purple, bristles few or none. *P. kongosanensis*, a later name, probably describes the wild original. Cultivated and naturalized in Japan. f. ***chrysophyllus*** Mak. Lvs entirely golden-yellow. Z7.

***P. chino*** (Franch. & Savat.) Mak. Rhiz. sometimes invasive. Culms 2–4m×0.5–1cm, sometimes purple, glabrous with white wax below nodes; sheaths glabrescent, lacking bristles; nodes hairless; branches 3 or more, spreading. Lvs 12–25×1–3cm, green throughout, sometimes slightly downy beneath, or ciliate; sheaths often tinted purple above, ciliate with bristles. C Japan. f. ***angustifolius*** (Mitford) Muroi & H. Okamura in Sugimoto. Lvs to 1.3cm across, often downy beneath, striped white in varying degrees, occasionally entirely green. f. ***gracilis*** (Mak.) Nak. Lvs to 0.6cm across, glabrous, usually variegated white. Z6.

***P. gramineus*** (Bean) Nak. Differs from *P. linearis* in its glabrous culm sheaths; culms 2–5m×0.5–2cm, glabrous with white waxy powder below the nodes; sheaths glabrescent, lacking bristles; branches many, from the upper parts of the culms. Lvs 15–30×0.8–2cm, numerous, narrow, long-acuminate, glabrous, pendulous, somewhat twisted toward apex, sheaths glabrous, often lacking bristles, ligule long, rounded. Japan, E China. Z7.

***P. humilis*** (Mitford) Nak. Culms 1–2m×2–3mm, glabrous; sheaths glabrous, purple when young; nodes glabrous with white waxy powder below; branches 1–3, low down. Lvs 10–25×1.5–2.3cm, glabrescent; sheaths slightly downy, with or without bristles, ligule minute, downy. C Japan. var. ***pumilus*** (Mitford) D. McClintock. More robust and compact, differs most clearly in the nearly always conspicuously bearded scars of the upper culm sheaths. Lvs a fresher green.

***P. linearis*** (Hackel) Nak. Differs from *P. gramineus* in its hairy culm sheaths with a truncate ligule and flatter, rather shorter lvs. C Japan. Z7.

***P. pygmaeus*** (Miq.) Nak. DWARF FERN-LEAF BAMBOO; KE-OROSHIMA-CHIKU. Stems very small and slender, 10–20cm×1mm, typically solid and flattened above, glabrous with white powder. Sheaths sometimes hairy or ciliate; nodes sometimes pubesc.; branches 1–2, low down. Lvs 2–4cm×0.2–0.5cm, in 2 close ranks, usually slightly downy, especially beneath; margins sometimes withering papery white in hard winters. Unknown in the wild; cultivated in Japan. var. ***distichus*** (Mitford) Nak. Much more frequently grown than species type, often misnamed *P. pygmaeus*, and sometimes under cultivar names such as 'Minezuzme' 'Orishimazasa' or 'Tsuyuzasa'. All selections have taller stems, to 1m; sheaths, nodes and lvs usually hairless; lvs 3–7×0.3–1cm, to 8 pairs arranged in 2 close ranks atop the stems. A vigorous runner with very sharp, pointed rhizomes. Z6.

***P. simonii*** (Carr.) Nak. SIMON BAMBOO; MEDAKE. Rhiz. usually not far-running. Culms 3–8m×1.2–3cm, stout, thin-walled, glabrous; sheaths rather persistent, eventually standing away as the branches develop, sometimes slightly hairy toward the base, ligule prominent, ciliate; nodes with white waxy powder below; branches finally numerous from higher up the culm. Lvs 13–27×1.2–2.5cm, often half-green, half-glaucous beneath, some of the earliest white-striped at first; sheaths glabrous, usually with a sloping apex, ligule downy. C & S Japan. f. ***variegatus*** (Hook. f.) Muroi. Less robust than species type with lvs variable, some broad, some narrow, some white-striped. Z6.

***P. variegatus*** (Sieb. ex Miq.) Mak. DWARF WHITE-STRIPED BAMBOO; CHIGO-ZASA. Culms 20–75×0.5–2cm; sheaths minutely downy, ciliate, lacking bristles; nodes glabrous with white waxy powder below; branches 1–2, erect, mostly from low down. Lvs 10–20×0.7–1.8cm, downy chiefly below, dark green with cream stripes of varying breadth; sheaths purple-lined, minutely downy, ciliate, bristles few or none. Probably a selection of the green-leaved var. viridis (Mak.) D. McClintock (*P. shibuyanus* Nak.). Widely cultivated in Japan; unknown in the wild. Z7.

***P. angustifolius*** (Mitford) Nak. See *P. chino* f. *angustifolius*.
***P. argenteostriatus*** f. ***akebono*** (Mak.) Muroi. See *P. akebono*.
***P. argenteostriatus*** f. ***pumilus*** (Mitford) Muroi. See *P. humilis* var. *pumilus*.
***P. chino*** var. ***argenteostriatus*** (Reg.) Mak. See *P. argenteostriatus*.
***P. chino*** var. ***viridis*** f. ***pumilus*** (Mitford) S. Suzuki. See *P. humilis* var. *pumilus*.
***P. distichus*** (Mitford) Muroi & H. Okamura. See *P. pygmaeus* var. *distichus*.
***P. fortunei*** (Van Houtte) Nak. See *P. variegatus*.
***P. kongosanensis*** 'Auricoma'. See *P. auricoma*.
***P. maximowiczii*** (A. & C. Riv.) Nak. See *P. chino*.
***P. pygmaeus*** var. ***distichus*** 'Akebono'. See *P. akebono*.
***P. shibuyanus*** 'Variegatus'. See *P. variegatus*.
***P. simonii*** var. ***heterophyllus*** (Mak. & Shirasawa) Nak. See *P. simonii* f. *variegatus*.
***P. vaginatus*** (Hackel) Nak. See *P. chino* f. *gracilis*.
***P. viridistriatus*** (Reg.) Mak. See *P. auricoma*.
For further synonymy see *Arundinaria, Nippocalamus, Sasa* and *Yushania*.

**Pleiogynium** Engl. (From Gk *pleios*, many and *gune*, woman, referring to the many-seeded fruit.) Anacardiaceae. Some 3 species of trees. Leaves pinnate usually imparipinnate; leaflets opposite, entire. Inflorescence a panicle, sometimes racemose or spiciform, axillary; calyx 4- to 6-lobed; petals 4–6, imbricate; stamens 8–12 twice as many as petals, filaments filiform to subulate, glabrous, anthers oblong or obovoid, aborted or sterile in female flowers; disc annular, pulvinate, slightly crenulate; ovary 5–12-loculate, rudimentary in male flowers; styles 5–12; stigmas spathulate. Fruit a drupe, endocarp hard, free from testa; seeds 5–12. Pacific Is., Malaysia, NE Australia. Z10.

CULTIVATION Native to Australia, New Guinea, and the Pacific Islands, *Pleiogynium* is cultivated in California, Florida, Hawaii and other areas that are frost-free or almost so. It has a thick trunk and irregular shape and bears edible tomato-shaped fruits used in jams and jellies. Cultivation as for *Anacardium occidentale* (cashew).

***P. timoriense*** (DC.) Leenh. To 48m, sometimes buttressed. Bark peeling, fissured. Leaflets 3.5–13.5×2–6cm, 6–12, elliptic-oblong to elliptic-lanceolate, sometimes ovate, basally unequal, cuneate or decurrent, apically acute or acuminate; terminal petiolule to 4cm, others shorter. Male infl. to 30cm; female infl. to 3cm, rarely to 15cm; bracts triangular; pet. ovate-oblong, to 3mm. Fr. broadly obovoid, about 1.5×2cm, red to dark brown, smooth, glabrous. Pacific Is., Malaysia, NE Australia.

***P. cerasiferum*** (F.J. Muell.) Parker. See *P. timoriense*.
***P. pleiogyna*** F. Muell. See *P. timoriense*.
***P. popuanum*** C.T. White. See *P. timoriense*.
***P. solandri*** (Benth.) Engl. See *P. timoriense*.
For further synonymy see *Spondias*.

**Pleione** D. Don. (For Pleione, mother of the Pleiades.) INDIAN CROCUS. Orchidaceae. Some 16 species of dwarf, deciduous, epiphytic or terrestrial orchids. Pseudobulbs clustered, usually only 2 seasons' growth persisting, ovoid to conic, globose, ellipsoid or pyriform. Leaves emerging rolled, among bracts, thin-textured, erect to arched, plicate, petioles short. Inflorescence solitary, terminal in emerging growth, bracteate; flowers 1–2, slender-stalked, occasionally fragrant, white, pink to magenta, rarely yellow; sepals and petals free, spreading, lanceolate; lip marked brown, yellow or red, rolled-tubular, entire to obscurely trilobed, sometimes fused to column base, apical margins irregularly toothed, laciniate or fimbriate, callus forming few or many hirsute lines or lamellae on upper surface. India to Taiwan, Thailand. Z8.

CULTIVATION See ORCHIDS. They require annual repotting at the end of a cool dry rest, preferably several pseudobulbs to a pan in a fairly dense bark-based medium. Commence watering to promote flower, then leaf development. Following flowering in spring, keep moist and well fed in bright airy conditions to ensure full leaf and pseudobulb formation. As the leaves wither, reduce water and temperatures. These small and beautiful orchids will thrive in the alpine and cold greenhouse. *P. formosana* has been grown successfully outdoors in Zone 7, in pockets of leafy, perfectly drained soil on the rockery and given minimal winter protection.

***P. aurita*** Cribb & Pfennig. Pseudobulbs conical, to 4.5cm. Lf solitary. Infl. erect, to 16cm; fl. solitary, pale pink to rose or purple, paler at base; bract pale pink, venation darker; dorsal sep. elliptic to oblong-elliptic, to 4cm, concave, incurved, lateral sep. elliptic, to 4.5cm; pet. ligulate or spathulate, rounded or obtuse, to 4.5cm, sharply reflexed, like a hare's ears; lip to 4cm, obscurely trilobed at apex, undulate, margins irregularly toothed, callus 5-ridged, orange-yellow, pubesc. China (Yunnan).

***P. bulbocodioides*** (Franch.) Rolfe. Pseudobulbs pyramidal or conical, to 3cm. Lf solitary, elliptic-lanceolate, narrow, to 14cm+, acute. Infl. erect, to 20cm; fl. solitary, pink to rose-purple or magenta, lip marked dark purple; dorsal sep. oblanceolate, to 4.5cm, lateral sep. narrow, elliptic, to 4.4cm; pet. oblanceolate, to 5cm; lip obovate, obscurely trilobed, to 4.5cm, apical margins irregular, notched, callus lamellae 4–5, irregularly toothed. China.

***P. formosana*** Hay. Pseudobulbs globose to ovoid, often slightly flattened, to 3cm, green to dull dark purple. Lf solitary, elliptic to oblanceolate, to 25×5cm. Infl. to 25cm; fls 1–2, white, lilac or magenta, lip white, typically stained or marked yellow; dorsal sep. elliptic-oblanceolate, narrow, to 6cm, acute, lateral sep. elliptic, narrow, oblique, subacute; pet. linear to oblanceolate; lip entire or trilobed, tip notched, apical margin undulate, fimbriate, lamellae 2–5, entire or jagged. E China.

***P. forrestii*** Schltr. Pseudobulbs narrow-ovoid or conical, to 3×1.5cm, dark green flushed purple at base, old pseudobulbs with a collar-like lf base at the apex. Lf solitary, elliptic-lanceolate, to 15×4cm. Infl. precedes lf; fl. solitary, pale golden yellow or white, lip spotted brown or crimson; sep. oblanceolate, lateral sep. oblique, to 40×10mm; pet. oblanceolate, falcate; lip elliptic-obovate, fimbriate, apex notched, lamellae 5–7, entire. China.

***P. hookeriana*** (Lindl.) Williams. Pseudobulbs ovoid or conical, to 3×1.5cm, purple or green, often in clusters and stoloniferous. Lf solitary, elliptic-lanceolate to oblanceolate, to 20×4.5cm; petiole to 4cm. Infl. to 15cm, appearing with the lf; fl. solitary; sep. and pet. lilac-pink to rose, sometimes dotted pale violet, rarely white, lip white, dotted yellow-brown or purple, lamellae and disc yellow, dorsal sep. oblanceolate or oblong-lanceolate, lateral sep. lanceolate, falcate, pet. oblanceolate, spreading; lip cordate, obscurely trilobed, apex notched, margin fringed, callus lamellae 7, barbed. C Nepal to S China.

***P. humilis*** (Sm.) D. Don. Pseudobulbs olive green, pyriform, to 6×2cm. Lf solitary, oblanceolate, to elliptic, to 2.5×3.5cm, acute. Infl. emerging before lf; fls 1–2, nodding or spreading, white, lip spotted and streaked bronze or blood red, central zone pale yellow; dorsal sep. linear-oblanceolate, almost acute, to 5cm, lateral sep. oblanceolate, oblique, to 5.5×9cm; pet. linear to oblanceolate, oblique, almost acute; lip oblong-elliptic, base saccate, apex notched, obscurely trilobed, apical margins jagged, lamellae 5–7, barbed, lateral lobes incurved, erect. Burma, NE India.

***P. ×lagenaria*** Lindl. (*P. maculata* × *P. praecox*.) Pseudobulbs squat-ellipsoid, to 25×25mm. Lvs 1–2, oblanceolate, acute, to 32×5cm. Fls. 1–2 per pseudobulb, almost erect, spreading; pet. and sep. pink to rose-purple, lip white, central patch yellow, margins blotched purple, sep. linear-lanceolate, to 5×1cm, acute, pet. linear, acute; lip obscurely trilobed, to 4×3cm, midlobe almost rectangular, toothed, lateral lobes erect, callus of 5 longitudinal, papillose lines along centre, extending to apex. Asia, SW China.

***P. limprichtii*** Schltr. Pseudobulbs conical to ovoid, pale to deep green or purple, to 4×2.5cm. Lf solitary, lanceolate, appearing after fls, to 1.5×0.5cm. Fls 1–2, rose-pink to magenta, lip paler, spotted ochre or crimson, lamellae white; dorsal sep. elliptic, to 3.5×1cm, lateral sep. narrow-elliptic, acute; pet. oblanceolate, falcate, acute; lip almost orbicular, apex obscurely trilobed, to 4×3.5cm, apical margins deeply and irregularly laciniate, callus lamellae 4, minutely toothed or jagged. SW China, N Burma.

***P. maculata*** (Lindl.) Lindl. Pseudobulbs turbinate, beaked, covered in the netted, fibrous remnants of sheaths. Lvs 2, elliptic-lanceolate to oblanceolate, acute, to 25×3.5cm. Fls erect, fragrant, cream, rarely streaked pink, lip white, central blotch yellow, apical margins blotched purple, lamellae white; dorsal sep. oblong-lanceolate, lateral sep. lanceolate, falcate, to 4×1cm; lip oblong, obscurely trilobed, midlobe notched, margin undulate, jagged, callus extending to apex, comprising 5–7 papillose lines. India, Bhutan, Burma, SW China, Thailand.

***P.praecox*** (Sm.) D. Don. Pseudobulbs turbinate, beaked, green, dappled or spotted red-brown or purple. Lvs usually 2, elliptic-lanceolate, acuminate, to 2.5×1cm; petiole to 6cm. Infl. appearing at lf fall, to 13cm; fls. 1–2, white to rose-purple, lamellae yellow; sep. oblong-lanceolate, 7×1cm; pet. linear-lanceolate, falcate, to 7cm; lip midlobe cleft, toothed or deeply and irregularly fringed, callus forming 3–5 papillose lines. Indochina, Burma.

***P.speciosa*** Ames & Schltr. Pseudobulbs ovoid to conical, to 3×1.5cm. Lf elliptic-lanceolate, to 15cm+, partially developed at flowering. Infl. to 22cm; fls 1–2, bright magenta, lip blotched peach, lamellae yellow; dorsal sep. elliptic, narrow, acute, lateral sep. narrow, elliptic, oblique, to 7cm; pet. oblanceolate, falcate; lip almost rhombic to obovate, appearing whole and truncate, apical margins minutely toothed, callus comprising 2–4 minutely toothed keels. China.

***P.yunnanensis*** (Rolfe) Rolfe. Pseudobulbs squat, conical, to 2×1.5cm. Lf lanceolate to elliptic, narrow-acuminate; petiole to 5.5cm. Infl. erect, appearing before lvs; fls 1–2, pale lavender to rose pink, rarely white; lip flecked red or purple; dorsal sep. oblong-oblanceolate, obtuse, to 4×1cm; pet. oblanceolate, obtuse; lip obscurely trilobed, midlobe subrectangular, undulate, lacerate, callus 5-ridged, entire, lateral lobes erect or incurved. N Burma, China.

***P.* grexes and cultivars.**

*P.* Alishan: pseudobulbs large and dark; fls 2 per stem, pale to dark pink with variable lip markings; 'Sparrowhawk', 'Goldfinch' and 'Merlin' are the best clones.

*P.* Barcema: pseudobulbs flattened and wrinkled, green; fls January (cross between autumn- and spring-flowering species), mid-lavender-pink with frilled lip.

*P.* Brigadoon: large purple-hued pseudobulbs: fls 2 per stem, pale mauve shading to violet, lip marked with red and yellow. 'Stonechat' and 'Woodcock' are good cvs.

*P.* Eiger: pseudobulbs large, green; fls 2 per stem in January and February, mostly white shaded with pink.

*P.* El Pico: pseudobulbs rather flat, dark green; fls late, pale mauve pink to dark rosy purple. 'Goldcrest', 'Kestrel' and 'Pheasant' are the best clones.

*P.* Erebus: pseudobulbs variable from squat to pyriform; fls pale violet purple, lip white spotted with dark red and with yellow lamellae. 'Redshank' and 'Willow Warbler' are good clones.

*P.* Fuego: pseudobulbs small, dark green; flowers prolifically, rather variable.

*P.* Hekla: pseudobulbs tall, pyriform, dark green to purple; fls elegant, petunia purple with a frilled lip. 'Partridge' is a particularly fine dark clone.

*P.* Irazu: pseudobulbs rather small, dark green: fls mallow purple or strawberry purple with a white lip. 'Mallard' is a particularly dark form.

*P.* Shantung: pseudobulbs very large, green to dark purple; fls deep yellow or white flushed with pink. The best-known and most vigorous clone is 'Muriel Harberd' and is the largest apricot-coloured cv.; 'Fieldfare' has large pale yellow fls.

*P. Stromboli*: pseudobulbs large, rather flat, dark green to purple-black; fls on tall stems, mostly dark red-pink. 'Fireball' is one of the most intensely coloured of all *Pleione* cultivars.

*P.* Tongariro: pseudobulbs green; fls 2 per stem, long-lasting, various shades of imperial purple, the lip marked with red and yellow. 'Jackdaw' has the darkest fls.

*P.* Versailles: the first hybrid *Pleione* raised; fls 2 per stem, very pale mauve-pink to deep rose pink. The clone 'Bucklebury' is particularly fine and very floriferous.

***P.pogonioides*** (Rolfe) Rolfe. See *P. bulbocodioides*.
***P.pricei*** Rolfe. See *P. formosana*.

**Pleiospilos** N.E. Br. (From Gk *pleios*, full, and *spilos*, dot, referring to the leaf surface, which is often covered in dots.) LIVING GRANITE; LIVING ROCK; STONE MIMICRY PLANT. Aizoaceae. 4 species of highly succulent, stemless, clump-forming perennials. Leaves solid and similar in texture to lumps of granite (hence popular name), usually 1–2 pairs per shoot, sometimes 3–4 pairs, opposite and decussate, very thick, flat above, apex obtuse to acute, united at base and more or less rugosely inflated, grey-green or dark green with translucent dots. Flowers sessile or shortly pedicellate, solitary or several together, large, yellow to orange, often scented of coconut. Late summer. S Africa (Cape Province: Little and Great Karroo). Z9.

CULTIVATION Highly succulent plants native to summer-rainfall regions, these are attractive and easily grown additions to the succulent plant collection. Grow in greenhouses in temperate regions or outside in warmer areas with no winter rainfall. They require full sun at all times with low humidity and only frost protection over winter if dry. Pot up in spring in any well-drained, low moisture-retaining medium. Water infrequently and only during warm sunny spells for spring to autumn. No water at all should be given from late autumn to early spring. Care must be taken during the growing season to avoid the plants' remaining wet for too long, as this can cause the leaves to rupture. Feeding is best achieved by repotting plants into fresh soil-based potting mix every 2–3 years or, if grown in soilless potting mix, use a weak, liquid, low N fertilizer once a month from midsummer to mid-autumn. Propagation and pest and disease control as for *Conophytum*.

***P.bolusii*** (Hook. f.) N.E. Br. MIMICRY PLANT; LIVING ROCK CACTUS. Usually solitary with 1 pair of lvs, the old lvs shrivelling as new ones grow; lvs 4–7cm long, 3–3.5cm thick, upper surface often broader than long, lower surface rounded, clavately thickened at apex and often drawn chin-like over the upper surface for 2–3cm, red-green or brown-green with numerous dots. Fls 1–4 together, more or less sessile, 6–8cm diam., golden-yellow. Cape: Karroo.

***P.compactus*** (Ait.) Schwantes. Stemless, clump-forming. Lvs 4–6 per shoot, 22–44×5–7×6–8mm, very rounded (convex) below, blunt-carinate below the tip, brown-green or red-green with a purple to blue tinge, densely spotted. Fls solitary, 2.5–3cm diam., light yellow. Cape: Oudtshoorn District. ssp. ***canus*** (Haw.) Hartm. & Liede. Lvs 4–8 per shoot, 3–9×1–3.5×0.7–2.5cm, acute, triquetrous, apical portion acutely carinate below, grey-green to purple-tinged. Fls 3.5–8cm diam., usually solitary, golden yellow to pale yellow. Cape: Karroo. ssp. ***minor*** (L. Bol.) Hartm. & Liede. Lvs 4–6 per shoot, 2.5–8×0.7–2×0.5–1cm, acute, underside keeled above, expanded toward the tip, green to grey-green with prominent dots, keel and margins sometimes reddened. Fls 4.5–7cm diam., glossy yellow. Cape: Little Karroo.

***P.nelii*** Schwantes. SPLITROCK; CLEFTSTONE; MIMICRY PLANT. Stems usually solitary. Resembling *P. bolusii* in stature. Lvs 2–4, flat above, rounded below and drawn chin-like over the upper surface so that the lf is hemispherical, fissure deep and widely gaping, dark grey-green with numerous dots. Fls solitary, 7cm diam., salmon pink to yellow to orange. Cape: Willowmore District.

***P.simulans*** (Marloth) N.E. Br. Lvs 6–8×5–7×1–1.5cm, usually paired, spreading, ovate-triangular, upper surface flat or trough-like, lower surface often thickened toward the tip, never pulled forward or chin-like, red-, yellow-, or brown-green, conspicuously spotted, slightly undulating and tuberculate. Fls 1–4 together, yellow, light yellow, sometimes orange, fragrant. Cape: Graaff Reinet and Aberdeen Districts.

***P.archeri*** L. Bol. See *Tanquana archeri*.
***P.borealis*** L. Bol. See *P. compactus* ssp. *canus*.
***P.clavatus*** L. Bol. See *Tanquana archeri*.
***P.dekenahii*** (N.E. Br.) Schwantes. See *P. compactus* ssp. *canus*.
***P.dimidiatus*** L. Bol. See *P. compactus* ssp. *minor*.
***P.hilmarii*** L. Bol. See *Tanquana hilmarii*.
***P.kingiae*** L. Bol. See *P. compactus* ssp. *canus*.
***P.latipetalus*** L. Bol. See *P. compactus* ssp. *canus*.
***P.loganii*** L. Bol. See *Tanquana archeri*.
***P.minor*** L. Bol. See *P. compactus* ssp. *minor*.
***P.multipunctatus*** hort. See *P. compactus* ssp. *canus*.
***P.nobilis*** (Haw.) Schwantes. See *P. compactus* ssp. *canus*.
***P.optatus*** (N.E. Br.) Schwantes. See *P. compactus*.
***P.pedunculata*** L. Bol. See *P. nelii*.
***P.prismaticus*** (Schwantes) Schwantes. See *Tanquana prismatica*.
***P.roodiae*** (N.E. Br.) Schwantes. See *Tanquana prismatica*.
***P.sororius*** (N.E. Br.) Schwantes. See *P. compactus* ssp. *minor*.
***P.tricolor*** N.E. Br. See *P. nelii*.
***P.willowmorensis*** L. Bol. See *P. compactus* ssp. *canus*.
For further synonymy see *Punctillaria*.

For illustration see AIZOACEAE.

**Pleiostachya** Schum. (From Gk *pleion*, many and *stachys*, spike.) Marantaceae. 3 species of caulescent, rhizomatous herbs, 1–3m. Leaves distichous, homotropic, 1–2 at base, otherwise cauline, ovate to oblong, apex eccentric; pulvinus with basal annulus; petiole often rigid at junction with sheath. Inflorescence 1–12 panicles, branched, laterally compressed; bracts distichous, conduplicate, strongly overlapping, fibrous, persistent; bracteoles membranous, 1–3-keeled, flowers 2 per cymule; sepals fibrous, linear, acute; corolla tube white, 2.5–5cm; outer staminode, 1, purple, callose staminode yellow, tipped purple, fleshy; stigmatic surface with a protruding orifice; ovary inferior trilocular. Fruit a 1-seeded dehiscent capsule, seed black with a white aril. Tropical America from Mexico to Ecuador. Z10.

CULTIVATION As for *Calathea*.

***P. pruinosa*** (Reg.) Schum. Erect. to 2m. Rhiz. short. Lvs to 45cm, oblong to lanceolate, dark green above, purple beneath; petiole long, pubesc. Infl. a short spike, to 10cm, bracteolate; fls white and purple. C America.

For synonymy see *Maranta*.

**Pleomele** Salisb.
***P. deremensis*** (Engl.) N.E. Br. See *Dracaena deremensis*.
***P. gracilis*** hort. See *Dracaena cincta*.
***P. reflexa*** (Lam.) N.E. Br. See *Dracaena reflexa*.
***P. thalioides*** (hort. Makoy ex E. Morr.) N.E. Br. See *Dracaena thalioides*.

**Pleonotoma** Miers. (From Gk *pleios*, many, and *temno*, to cut; the leaves are much divided.) Bignoniaceae. 14 species of scrambling lianes. Branches tetragonal, angles sharp. Leaves once or twice pinnate with trifid tendrils. Flowers in racemes, usually terminal on branchlets; calyx cylindrical, split one side; corolla tubular-campanulate, ventricose, bilabiate, 5-lobed; stamens 4, didynamous, incurved, included, with fifth rudimentary staminode; ovary cylindrical, glabrous, rugose; disc pulvinate. Fruit a capsule, linear, compressed; seeds flat, in hyaline wings. Americas. Z10.

CULTIVATION As for *Anemopaegma*.

***P. variabilis*** (Jacq.) Miers. Trunk to 3cm diam. Lower lvs twice trifoliate, upper lvs ternate, with trifid tendril; leaflets 2–16×0.8–1cm, elliptic to ovate-elliptic, apex acute to acuminate, base truncate to cuneate; petioles 2–7cm. Fls in short racemes; cal. to 9mm, truncate; cor. 6–10×1–3cm at mouth, tubular-funnelform, tube pale yellow, limb white to cream. Fr. 15–30×1.5–3cm, linear to oblong, acute, flattened, verrucose-tuberculate. Guatemala to Venezuela and Trinidad.

For synonymy see *Bignonia*.

**Pleopeltis** Humb. & Bonpl. ex Willd. (From Gk *pleos*, full, and *pelte*, shield.) Polypodiaceae. Some 40 species of epiphytic ferns. Rhizomes creeping, elongate, dictyostelic, occasionally branching; scales clathrate. Fronds sessile and basally jointed, or stipitate, uniform, simple or, rarely, pinnatifid, oblong to lanceolate, entire or undulate at margin, membranous or leathery to rigid, glabrous or scaly; veins anastomosing arcuately, with free, included veinlets. Sori at apices of 2 or more confluent, excurrent veinlets, uniserial, median, usually circular, occasionally elongate-oblong to linear; initially with conspicuous, peltate paraphyses; annulus 14-celled; spores more or less smooth, glassy, yellow to orange. Tropical America to Africa, Asia, Japan, Hawaii. Z10.

CULTIVATION As for *Pyrrosia*.

***P. macrocarpa*** (Bory ex Willd.) Kaulf. Rhiz. long-creeping to 2mm wide; scales to 3×1mm, adpressed, lanceolate or ovate, apex narrowly acute, margin toothed or torn, occasionally hairy, pale to dark brown, often with central black stripe. Fronds to 30×1cm, stipitate, simple, linear to lanceolate or elliptic, apex and base attenuate, entire, margin undulate, leathery to rigid, more or less glabrous above, scaly beneath; scales many, to 1mm wide, peltate, circular to lanceolate, stipes to 15cm, scaly to glabrous, green to grey or black. Tropical America, Africa, Asia.

***P. percussa*** (Cav.) Hook. & Grev. Rhiz. long-creeping, wiry; scales adpressed, lanceolate. Fronds to 30×3cm, lanceolate, apex narrowly acute, base narrowed, margin entire, leathery, sparsely scaly beneath; stipes remote, to 7cm. Tropical S America.

***P. accedens*** (Bl.) Moore. See *Lemmaphyllum accedens*.
***P. alternifolia*** (Willd.) Moore. See *Microsorium nigrescens*.
***P. diversifolia*** (Willd.) Melvaine. See *Microsorium diversifolium*.
***P. hemionitidea*** (Presl) Moore. See *Colysis hemionitidea*.
***P. iridoides*** (Poir.) Moore. See *Microsorium punctatum*.
***P. lima*** v.A.v.R. See *Selliguea lima*.
***P. lycopodioides*** (L.) Presl. See *Microgramma lycopodioides*.
***P. musifolia*** (Bl.) Moore. See *Microsorium musifolium*.
***P. nigrescens*** (Bl.) Carr. ex Seem. See *Microsorium nigrescens*.
***P. normalis*** (D. Don) Moore. See *Microsorium normale*.
***P. phyllitidis*** (L.) Alston. See *Campyloneurum phyllitidis*.
***P. phymatodes*** (L.) Moore. See *Microsorium scolopendrium*.
***P. pteropus*** (Bl.) Moore. See *Microsorium pteropus*.
***P. punctata*** (L.) Bedd. See *Microsorium punctatum*.
***P. subnormalis*** (D. Don) v.A.v.R. See *Microsorium normale*.

**Pleurosorus** Fée. (From Gk *pleuron*, rib, vein, and *sorus*.) Aspleniaceae. Some 3 species of terrestrial ferns. Rhizomes short and erect; scales clathrate, aciculate. Fronds stipitate, uniform, pinnate to pinnatifid, herbaceous, pubescent; veins free, forked; stipes approximate and clustered to tufted, pubescent to scaly. Sori elongate on veins, eventually confluent and covering lower surface; indusia absent; sporangia stalked; annulus 18–22-celled, vertical, incomplete; spores globose to oblong, bilateral, reticulate to tuberculose, black. Chile; Spain and Morocco; Australia and New Zealand. Z9.

CULTIVATION As for *Asplenium*.

***P. rutifolius*** (R. Br.) Fée. Rhiz. short and erect; scales lanceolate, brown. Fronds to 10×3cm, oblong, apex obtuse, membranous, occasionally glandular, white- to rusty-pubesc., pinnae to 15×10mm, to 4 pairs, subopposite to alternate, approximate, obovate to flabellate, base obliquely cuneate, margin subentire to lobed or somewhat incised; veins flabellate, rachis pubesc.; stipes to 5cm, occasionally glandular, rusty-pubesc. Australia, Tasmania, New Zealand.

For synonymy see *Ceterach*, *Grammitis* and *Gymnogramma*.

**Pleurospermum** Hoffm. (From Gk *pleuron*, rib and *sperma*, seed.) Umbelliferae. 3 species of biennial or perennial herbs. Leaves 2–3-pinnate. Umbels compound; involucral bracts few to many, often compound; involucel of many bracteoles, margins entire to toothed or pinnatifid, often white; calyx teeth small or absent; flowers white; petals suborbicular, short-clawed. Fruit ovoid-oblong, compressed laterally; mericarps with spongy mesocarp, prominently 5-ribbed, often slightly winged; vittae solitary. E Europe, Asia. Z7.

CULTIVATION *P. brunonis* is an undemanding and moderately ornamental umbellifer sometimes grown in the herbaceous border for its flowers and foliage. Grow in any moderately fertile, well-drained soil in sun. Propagate by seed or division.

***P. brunonis*** (DC.) C.B. Clarke. Perenn. to 170cm. Lvs pinnate, seg. lanceolate, 3-lobed, toothed. Umbels with 10–25 rays, in infl. to 20cm diam.; involucre of several, lobed bracts; involucel of 5–8 oblong bracteoles, large, with white, toothed margins; fls white-pink. Fr. ellipsoid, *c*5mm; mericarps with narrower dorsal and intermediate wings. Summer. Pakistan to W Nepal.

**Pleurothallis** R. Br. (From Gk *pleuron*, rib, and *thallos*, stem, referring to the rib-like stems of many species.) Orchidaceae. Some 900 species of epiphytic or lithophytic orchids allied to *Restrepia*, *Stelis* and *Masdevallia*. Rhizome short or protracted, creeping. Secondary stems not pseudobulbous, small to elongate, usually tufted, erect, thinly sheathed, usually unifoliate. Leaves terminal, coriaceous to fleshy, often flushed purple-red with age, sessile or petiolate, erect to spreading, often basally sulcate or conduplicate, linear-lanceolate to ovate, sagittate or spathulate. Inflorescence a raceme, terminal or, rarely, lateral, 1- to many-flowered, short to elongate; flowers small, sometimes secund, subtended by inconspicuous bracts; sepals subequal, erect or spreading, dorsal sepal free or briefly connate with lateral sepals, lateral sepals slightly to entirely connate, concave or gibbous at base; petals smaller than sepals, sometimes clavate at apex; lip usually shorter than petals, entire or 3-lobed, usually unguiculate; column shorter than or equal to lip, often alate, footless or with short foot, anther terminal, operculate, incumbent, 1- or 2-celled, pollinia 2, waxy, ovoid or pyriform, lacking a stipe. Tropical America. Many of the larger species described here will be considerably smaller in cultivation. Z10.

CULTIVATION Small tufted orchids suited to growing cases or buoyant, shady conditions in the cool to intermediate house. Pot tightly in pans containing a fine-grade bark-based orchid mix. Keep damp at all times and syringe during warm weather. Propagate by division.

***P. brighamii*** S. Wats. Secondary stems to 6mm. Lvs to 9×1cm, oblanceolate to elliptic-oblong, obtuse or acute, coriaceous, bright lustrous green. Infl. to 10cm, 1- to several-fld, filiform; fls yellow striped red-brown or with green and brown markings; dorsal sep. to 10×3mm, elliptic to oblong-lanceolate, acute to acuminate, lateral sep. connate to middle or more, oblong to ovate-oblong, obtuse; pet. to 4×2mm, obovate or spathulate, acute or acuminate; lip to 4×2mm, oblong-ligulate, obtuse, ciliate, with an auriculate lateral lobe at each side near base, disc with 2 intramarginal keels, base fleshy. Guatemala and British Honduras to Panama.

***P. cardiostola*** Rchb. f. Secondary stems to 20cm. Lvs to 14×4cm, fleshy-coriaceous, lanceolate to narrowly ovate, acuminate, light green; petiole to

18cm, terete. Fls usually solitary, successive, brown or pale green-brown, to 3cm diam., interior downy; pedicel to 1cm; dorsal sep. to 1.5×1cm, broadly ovate, obtuse or acute, 7-nerved, lateral sep. fused, fleshy, broadly ovate or cordate; pet. to 9×3mm, fleshy, lanceolate to oblanceolate; lip to 3×4mm, fleshy, ovate to subrhombic, light green-yellow, with central depression; column fleshy, white, to 2mm. Venezuela, Colombia, Ecuador.

***P.fulgens*** Rchb. f. Secondary stems minute. Lvs to 8.5×2cm, elliptic to obovate-spathulate, attenuate. Infl. a few-fld fascicle; peduncle subequal to lvs; fls bright cinnabar-red; dorsal sep. to 9×4mm, ovate-lanceolate, acuminate, lateral sep. to 12×3mm, connate to middle, gibbous at base; pet. to 4×2mm lanceolate, acute; lip to 5×3mm, elliptic, obtuse, lateral lobes small, erect, with 2 calli near middle. Costa Rica, Panama.

***P.gelida*** Lindl. Secondary stems to 35cm, unifoliate; sheaths to 8cm, brown. Lvs to 25×7cm, ovate-elliptic to oblong-elliptic, subacute to obtuse, coriaceous. Infl. 1- to several-fld, to 30cm, erect; fls secund, pale yellow to green-yellow, downy above; dorsal sep. to 8×3mm, oblong-lanceolate to oblong-elliptic, strongly concave, lateral sep. connate almost to middle, to 7×3mm, narrowly oblong to elliptic; pet. to 4×2mm, oblong to spathulate, obtuse or truncate, often emarginate; lip to 3×1mm, oblong-cuneate, rounded or truncate, with 2 lamellate calli near middle; column to 2mm. Florida, Mexico to Panama, W Indies, S America.

***P.grobyi*** Batem. ex Lindl. Secondary stems to 1cm. Lvs to 7×1cm, obovate, spathulate or oblanceolate, purple-green below, coriaceous, short-petiolate. Infl. to 15cm, loosely few- to several-fld; fls small, membranous, green, white or yellow-orange, marked red-purple; dorsal sep. to 10×3mm, ovate to ovate-lanceolate, acute to acuminate, concave, lateral sep. connate, forming a bidentate lamina to 12×3mm; pet. to 3×1mm, obliquely obovate to lanceolate, acute or obtuse; lip to 3×1mm, oblong, rounded or obtuse, canaliculate; column to 3mm, clavate, alate, apex tridentate. Mexico and W Indies to Peru and Brazil.

***P.immersa*** Lind. & Rchb. f. Secondary stems to 7cm, stout, enveloped by 2 brown tubular sheaths. Lvs to 19×4cm, coriaceous, oblong-oblanceolate, lustrous bright green, apex obtuse and retuse. Infl. to 40cm, erect, loosely many-fld; peduncle slightly compressed; fls usually pendent, yellow-green or purple-brown with dark venation; dorsal sep. to 14×4mm, elliptic-lanceolate, acute, dorsally keeled below middle, densely pubesc. above, lateral sep. connate almost to apex, to 13×7mm, elliptic-oblong; pet. to 4×3mm, obovate-spathulate; lip to 5×2mm, triangular-hastate, arcuate-decurved, disc 3-nerved, with an intramarginal linear callus on each side; column to 4mm with short foot, slender, arcuate, apex trilobed, wings irregularly dentate. Mexico, Guatemala, Honduras, Costa Rica, Venezuela, Colombia, Panama.

***P.lanceana*** Lodd. Stems short, unifoliate. Lvs to 9×3cm, erect to pendent, elliptic-oblong, obtuse, fleshy. Infl. 1–3, produced in succession, exceeding lvs, many-fld; fls small; dorsal sep. yellow flecked purple-crimson, to 10×2mm, linear, acute, apex swollen, lateral sep. yellow, connate almost to apex, to 10×5mm, linear-lanceolate, acute, concave, pubesc.; pet. golden-yellow tinged pink, to 3mm, ovate, lacerate, acuminate; lip yellow-brown spotted maroon, to 3×2mm, fleshy, elliptic, rounded, papillose; column to 2mm, dark maroon, apex yellow, arcuate, alate. Guatemala, Costa Rica, Trinidad, tropical S America.

***P.loranthophylla*** Rchb. f. Stems to 10cm, erect. Lvs to 10×3.5cm, suberect, coriaceous, elliptic-oblong, apex tridentate, lustrous bright green; petiole to 7cm, terete, glabrous. Infl. 1 to few racemes, loosely several-fld; fls light brown tinged maroon, variously spotted maroon; dorsal sep. to 11×2mm, lanceolate, acute, lateral sep. entirely connate, to 10×4mm, slightly bifid; pet. to 8×2mm, lanceolate, apex attenuate; lip to 6×3mm, ovate, acute; column short, pale brown-green, terete, curved. Venezuela, Colombia, Ecuador, Peru, Bolivia.

***P.octomerioides*** Lindl. Secondary stems to 15cm, borne at frequent intervals on creeping rhiz. Lvs to 12×2cm, narrowly elliptic to oblong-lanceolate. Fls borne in clusters, fleshy, small; sep. pale yellow, to 7×2mm, spreading, narrowly obovate, obtuse, lateral sep. shortly connate, slightly oblique; pet. pale yellow, slightly smaller than sep., narrowly elliptic-oblong, acute or subacute; lip to 3×1mm, fleshy, oblong, papillose; column to 2mm, alate, apex dentate, with minute foot; anth. red or yellow. Mexico to Panama.

***P.phalangifera*** (Presl) Rchb. f. Secondary stems to 34cm. Lvs to 17×8cm, erect, sessile, ovate to ovate-elliptic. Infl. 1–3, to 30cm, loosely few- to many-fld; fls large, spreading, yellow-green to purple; dorsal sep. to 40×7mm, base lanceolate, long-attenuate above, lateral sep. connate to apex, lanceolate, long-acuminate; pet. to 35×3mm, linear-lanceolate, caudate, erose; lip to 5×3mm, deflexed in middle, 3-lobed, lateral lobes erect, orbicular, midlobe oblong, apiculate; column to 4mm, dilated above, foot short. Venezuela and Colombia to Peru.

***P.platyrachis*** (Rolfe) Rolfe. Secondary stems to 2cm, stout. Lvs to 20×3cm, oblanceolate-ligulate, acute to obtuse, fleshy, apex minutely tridentate, petiolate. Infl. to 35cm, erect, few- to many-fld; fls fleshy, opening in succession; sep. bright red or orange-red, white toward base, spreading, inner surfaces verrucose except at bases, dorsal sep. to 20×6mm, ovate-lanceolate, subacute, cucullate, lateral sep. to 20×4mm, connate below middle, lanceolate, acute; pet. bright red, to 5×1mm, ligulate, rounded, verruculose; lip to 6×2mm, fleshy, curved, callused at margins; column dilated, alate, foot short. Mexico to Panama, Colombia, Venezuela.

***P.prolifera*** Herb. ex Lindl. Secondary stems to 20cm. Lvs to 8×4cm, fleshy-coriaceous, ovate to ovate-lanceolate. Infl. shorter than lvs, few- to many-fld; fls small, deep purple or red-brown; sep. to 9×3mm, oblong or oblong-lanceolate to triangular-lanceolate, acute, 3-nerved, lateral sep. connate in basal half; pet. to 5×1mm, oblanceolate to spathulate, acuminate to acute, pale purple, dentate; lip to 5×2.5mm, elliptic to ovate, obtuse or rounded, base fimbriate, apex denticulate, papillose within; column to 3mm, papillose. Venezuela, Brazil.

***P.pruinosa*** Lindl. Secondary stems to 8cm. Lvs to 5×1cm, coriaceous or sub-coriaceous, elliptic-oblong or lanceolate. Infl. 1–3, few-fld, usually exceeding lvs; fls pale yellow or white-green; dorsal sep. to 4×2mm, lanceolate to ovate-lanceolate, concave, 1–3-nerved, lateral sep. entirely connate, to 4×3mm, ovate to suborbicular, concave, 2- or 4-nerved; pet. minute, slender, 1-nerved; lip to 2×1mm, fleshy, triangular-lanceolate to ovate, acute or acuminate, disc obscurely 3-keeled; column to 1mm, stout. Honduras, Costa Rica, Panama, Venezuela, Colombia, Ecuador, Peru, Guianas, W Indies.

***P.quadrifida*** (La Ll. & Lex.) Lindl. Secondary stems to 17cm, usually shorter. Lvs to 16×3cm, oblanceolate to elliptic-oblong, obtuse, glossy grey-green. Infl. to 40cm, many-fld; fls fragrant, pendent, yellow or pale yellow-green; dorsal sep. to 10×4mm, ovate-oblong to elliptic-lanceolate, subacute, concave, lateral sep. almost entirely connate, elliptic-oblong to ovate, cucullate, subacute; pet. to 10×4mm, short-clawed, narrow-ovate to elliptic-lanceolate; lip to 6×3mm, basal portion fleshy, orbicular, crenulate, apical portion ovate; column to 4mm, slender, apex dentate. Mexico to Panama, W Indies, Venezuela, Colombia.

***P.ruscifolia*** (Jacq.) R. Br. Secondary stems to 40cm, slender, rigid. Lvs to 20×6cm, elliptic-oblong to lanceolate, coriaceous, short-stalked. Fls clustered, slightly fragrant, to 2cm, pale green to pale yellow; dorsal sep. to 10×3mm, ovate-lanceolate, concave near base, lateral sep. connate to apex, to 10×3mm, lanceolate; pet. to 8×1mm, slender; lip to 2×1.5mm, fleshy, ovate to sub-quadrate, acute, disc 3-nerved; column to 2mm, with a prominent foot. W Indies, Guatemala, Costa Rica, Panama, northern S America.

***P.secunda*** Poepp. & Endl. Secondary stems to 40cm. Lvs to 30×6cm, erect, elliptic or oblong, sessile or shortly petiolate, bright green above, glaucous green below. Infl. to 20cm, pendent, few-fld; sep. translucent yellow-green, dorsal sep. to 15×6mm, ovate-oblong to lanceolate, lateral sep. entirely connate, to 15×12mm, suborbicular-ovate, acuminate, concave, striped purple; pet. red or yellow, to 15×3mm, lanceolate or elliptic, acuminate, porrect; lip yellow, minute, suborbicular-ovate; column white-yellow, minute. Venezuela, Colombia, Ecuador, Peru.

***P.segoviensis*** Rchb. f. Secondary stems densely caespitose, to 6cm. Lvs to 13×1.5cm, oblanceolate to ligulate, retuse. Infl. to 17cm, few- to several-fld, slender-stalked; fls variable in colour, yellow-green blotched brown to dark red-purple; dorsal sep. shortly connate with lateral sep., to 11×4mm, lanceolate to oblong-lanceolate, acute or acuminate, interior pilose to glabrous, margins slightly revolute, lateral sep. connate almost to apex, narrowly elliptic, apex bidentate, interior pilose to glabrous; pet. to 4×2mm, obliquely oblong, glabrous; lip to 4×2mm, lateral lobes basal, erect, oblong to lanceolate-falcate, midlobe oblong, obtuse or rounded, disc 2-ridged; column to 3mm, curved, foot short. Mexico to Panama.

***P.sertularioides*** (Sw.) Spreng. Rhiz. slender, creeping. Secondary stems to 5mm. Lvs to 40×4mm, linear-oblanceolate to linear-spathulate, obtuse. Infl. filiform, usually shorter than lvs, 1- or 2-fld; fls straw-yellow; sep. to 5×1mm, lanceolate, acute or acuminate, lateral sep. shortly connate, slightly gibbous; pet. to 4×1mm, linear-lanceolate, acuminate, 1-nerved; lip to 3×1mm, fleshy, sessile, linear-lanceolate, obtuse, minutely auricled; column to 2mm, with short foot, apex slightly trilobulate. Mexico, Guatemala, Honduras, Nicaragua.

***P.stenopetala*** Lodd. ex Lindl. Secondary stems to 14cm. Lvs to 10×3cm, elliptic-oblong or oblanceolate, obtuse; petiole to 2cm. Infl. to 27cm, many-fld; fls yellow-white or green-white; sep. to 2cm, narrow-lanceolate or linear, acute, interior pubesc., lateral sep. free, oblique at base; pet. to 6mm, obliquely oblong, rounded, apiculate, with a fleshy mid-nerve; lip to 6mm, ovate to rhombic, recurved, base cuneate, anterior portion papillose; column to 5mm, clavate, alate, wing triangular, concave. Brazil.

***P.tribuloides*** (Sw.) Lindl. Secondary stems to 1cm. Lvs to 7×1.5cm, obovate to oblanceolate, retuse, subcoriaceous. Infl. a fascicle of 1–3 fls; peduncle to 1cm; fls minute, to 8mm, brick-red or dark maroon; sep. to 8×4mm, papillose, dorsal sep. oblong-lanceolate or oblanceolate, acute, concave below middle, lateral sep. often entirely connate, oblong or oblong-lanceolate, acute, cucullate; pet. to 3×1mm, obliquely oblong-oblanceolate, acute, fleshy; lip to 3×2mm, linear or oblong-lanceolate, bidentate below middle, ciliate, disc fleshy; column to 3mm, alate above. C America, W Indies.

***P.tuerckheimii*** Schltr. Secondary stems to 35cm. Lvs to 25×7cm, elliptic to oval or lanceolate, obtuse, coriaceous. Infl. to 35cm, erect, solitary, loosely many-fld; fls large, purple-maroon and white or cream, papillose-puberulent; dorsal sep. to 25×6mm, lanceolate, acuminate, cucullate, lateral sep. connate almost to apex, to 25×9mm, elliptic to oblong-lanceolate; pet. white, to 8×4mm, ovate to oblong-obovate, apex rounded and cucullate; lip to 10×3mm, linear-lanceolate, reflexed, base auriculate, callus 2-keeled, papillose; column to 4mm, apex 4-toothed. Mexico to Panama.

***P. velaticaulis*** Rchb. f. Secondary stems to 30cm. Lvs to 22×9cm, oblanceolate-ligulate, petiolate. Racemes shorter than lvs, many-fld; fls fragrant, pale green or yellow-green; dorsal sep. to 6×2mm, ovate or oblong-lanceolate, subacute, 3-nerved, lateral sep. to 5×2mm, almost free, lanceolate, acute, 3-nerved; pet. to 3mm, oblong to oblong-lanceolate, obtuse, 1-nerved; lip to 2mm, ovate-oblong, obtuse, 3-lobed, lateral lobes fleshy, auriculate; column to 1mm. Costa Rica, Panama, W Indies, Venezuela to Peru.

***P. acrisepala*** Ames & Schweinf. See *P. brighamii*.
***P. amethystina*** Ames. See *P. segoviensis*.
***P. angustisegmenta*** Schweinf. See *Barbosella cucullata*.
***P. araguensis*** Ames. See *P. secunda*.
***P. astrophora*** Rchb. f. ex Kränzl. See *Lepanthopsis astrophora*.
***P. atropurpurea*** (Lindl.) Lindl. See *Zootrophion atropurpureum*.
***P. barboselloides*** Schltr. See *P. brighamii*.
***P. calerae*** Schltr. See *P. immersa*.
***P. cerea*** Ames. See *P. octomerioides*.
***P. ciliaris*** (Lindl.) L.O. Williams. See *Trichosalpinx ciliaris*.
***P. ciliata*** Knowles & Westc. See *P. lanceana*.
***P. compacta*** (Ames) Ames & Schweinf. See *Platystele compacta*.
***P. dura*** Lindl. See *Trichosalpinx dura*.
***P. endotrachys*** Rchb. f. See *P. platyrachis*.
***P. floripectin*** Rchb. f. See *Lepanthopsis floripectin*.
***P. ghiesbreghtiana*** Rich. & Gal. See *P. quadrifida*.
***P. glomerata*** Ames. See *P. ruscifolia*.
***P. intermedia*** Schltr. See *P. loranthophylla*.
***P. johnstonii*** Ames. See *Platystele johnstonii*.
***P. krameriana*** Rchb. f. See *P. immersa*.
***P. lasiosepala*** Schltr. See *P. immersa*.
***P. lindenii*** Lindl. See *P. secunda*.
***P. longissima*** Lindl. See *P. quadrifida*.
***P. marginata*** Lindl. See *P. grobyi*.
***P. mathewsii*** Lindl. See *P. phalangifera*.
***P. megachlamys*** Schltr. See *P. tuerckheimii*.
***P. miersii*** Lindl. See *Barbrodria miersii*.
***P. misera*** Lindl. See *Platystele misera*.
***P. octomeriae*** Schltr. See *P. octomerioides*.
***P. ophiocephala*** Lindl. See *Restrepiella ophiocephala*.
***P. ornata*** (Garay) Foldats. See *Platystele ornata*.
***P. ospinae*** R.E. Schult. See *Restrepia antennifera*.
***P. ovalifolia*** (Focke) Rchb. f. See *Platystele ovalifolia*.
***P. pauciflora*** Schltr. See *P. pruinosa*.
***P. periodica*** Ames. See *P. brighamii*.
***P. pfavii*** Rchb. f. See *P. platyrachis*.
***P. picta*** Lindl. See *P. grobyi*.
***P. pittieri*** Schltr. See *P. velaticaulis*.
***P. plumosa*** Lindl. See *P. lanceana*.
***P. punctata*** (Karst.) Schltr. See *P. loranthophylla*.
***P. stenostachya*** Rchb. f. See *Platystele stenostachya*.
***P. verrucosa*** (Rchb. f.) Rchb. f. See *Scaphosepalum verrucosum*.
***P. wercklei*** Schltr. See *P. segoviensis*.

**Plumbagella** Spach. (A diminutive form of *Plumbago*, a closely related genus.) Plumbaginaceae. 1 species, an annual herb. Stem to 50cm, erect or ascending, 3- or 4-angled, tinged red, branching from base, spinose at base. Leaves 3–15×1–3cm, alternate, sessile, ovate-lanceolate, acuminate, entire, base cordate, slightly decurrent, smooth, blotched or spotted beneath. Inflorescence compact, spiciform, 3–5-flowered, borne in axil of bracts; bracts 2, ovate-lanceolate, unequal; flowers hermaphrodite, pedicellate; calyx about 4mm, tubular-conical, partially 5-ribbed, not glandular, segments 5, triangular, equalling tube, glandular; corolla gamopetalous, 5-lobed, narrowly campanulate, slightly exceeding the calyx, blue-violet; stamens 5, inserted at corolla base; ovary superior, uniloculate; style filiform. Fruit a capsule, dark brown; seed about 3mm, ovoid, rust-brown. Summer. C Asia.

CULTIVATION As for *Ceratostigma*.

***P. micrantha*** (Ledeb.) Spach. As for the genus.

For synonymy see *Plumbago*.

**PLUMBAGINACEAE** Juss. LEADWORT FAMILY. Dicot. 22 genera and 440 species of perennial herbs, shrubs or lianes; stems often with cortical and/or medullary bundles or alternate rings of concentric xylem and phloem, anthocyanins present. Leaves simple, entire to lobed, alternate; stipules usually absent; foliage usually with scattered glands exuding water and calcium salts. Flowers regular, bisexual, 5-merous, in panicles, cymose heads or racemes; calyx 5 fused sepals, forming 5- or 10-ribbed tube, often petaloid and membranous; corolla usually 5 fused petals, often persistent; stamens 5, opposite corolla and sometimes adherent to it; ovary superior, of 5 fused carpels, 1-loculed, with distinct styles or 1 apically lobed, ovule 1, basal on a slender funicle. Fruit usually an achene, sometimes capsule with apical valves or circumscissile, enclosed in persistent calyx; seed with straight embryo; endosperm copious starchy or absent. Cosmopolitan, especially maritime. Extracts of some *Limonium* and *Plumbago* species are used medicinally. *Acantholimon, Armeria, Ceratostigma, Goniolimon, Limoniastrum, Limonium, Plumbagella, Plumbago, Psylliostachys.*

**Plumbago** L. (From Lat. *plumbum*, lead; the plant was thought to be a cure for lead poisoning.) LEADWORT. Plumbaginaceae. 15 species of shrubs, perennial or annual herbs. Leaves alternate, simple, entire, often auriculate at base. Inflorescence a spicate terminal raceme, 2–3-bracteate; spikelets usually 1-flowered; calyx tubular, 5-parted, often conical after anthesis, 5-ribbed, scarious between ribs; corolla gamopetalous, tube slender far exceeding calyx, limb 5 lobed, spreading; stamens 5 rarely 4, free, filaments 5, usually dilated at base; ovary superior, oblong, style 1, pubescent below, usually long and slender stigmatic lobes 5. Fruit a capsule, splitting into 5 valves; valves 1-seeded. Warm and tropical regions.

CULTIVATION *P. auriculata*, the species most commonly seen in cultivation, makes a beautiful specimen for warm temperate, frost-free gardens, as cover for fence, trellis and pergola, as a free-standing informal hedge or as a container plant; in cooler climates it is suitable for the cool to intermediate glasshouse or conservatory, treated as a climber with support, in the border or as a tub specimen. It is valued for the profusion of sky blue flowers borne on the current season's growth throughout summer into late autumn or, in warm conditions, into early winter. Flowering usually occurs in the second year from seed; since *P. auriculata* is tolerant of a range of environmental conditions and flowers when young, it is sometimes used as a short-term houseplant. *P. scandens* requires similar conditions to *P. auriculata*; the remaining species, including the handsome winter-flowering climber *P. indica*, need warm or tropical glasshouse conditions in temperate zones. Annual species are easily grown in the sunny flower border from seed sown *in situ* in spring or earlier under glass. *P. europaea* requires treatment as for perennial species of *Limonium*.

Grow *P. auriculata* in a well-drained, high-fertility, loam-based mix in direct sunlight, with a winter minimum of 7°C/45°F, ventilating freely when conditions allow at temperatures above 10°C/50°F. Water plentifully and liquid-feed fortnightly when in full growth, reducing water after flowering to keep just moist in winter. Tie to supports as growth proceeds. Prune hard in late winter, either to the base or by cutting lateral growth hard back to a more permanent framework of branches. Grow tender species such as *P. indica* in bright filtered light or in sun, with some shade in summer, maintaining moderate to high humidity, with a minimum temperature 16–18°C/60–65°F. Cut back to within 10–15cm/4–6in. of the base in spring, for flowers in summer; unpruned specimens will bloom in later winter in warmth.

Propagate *P. auriculata* by semi-ripe cuttings of non-flowering lateral growth with a heel, rooted in sand in a closed case with gentle bottom heat. Propagate *P. indica* by basal cuttings and root cuttings. Also by seed in spring.

***P. aphylla*** Bojer ex Boiss. Herb, sparingly branched. Lvs 5–25mm, on young stems only, oblong-ovate, auricles absent. Racemes to 6cm; cal. about 8mm, green; cor. white; tube about 15mm; lobes emarginate, edged red; style densely long pubesc. at base. Madagascar. Z10.

***P. auriculata*** Lam. CAPE LEADWORT. Shrub, evergreen; stems long-arching, somewhat scandent. Lvs to 7×4mm, oblong to oblong-spathulate, tapering into petiole. Spikes short; cal. lobes triangular; cor. 2.5cm across and 4cm long, pale blue. S Africa, naturalized S Europe. Z9.

***P. caerulea*** HBK. Annual, 30–50cm, erect; stems branching, terete, arching. Lvs ovate-oblong, more or less rhomboidal, acuminate, glabrous, entire, attenuate at base; petiole winged, auricled. Spikelets 1- to few-fld; cal. to 1cm;

cor. to 1.5cm; tube rich purple; lobes acute, deep blue with central dark line; fil. not dilated. Peru.

***P. europaea*** L. Perenn. herb to 1m; stems erect, slender, much branching. Lower lvs to 8×5cm, broadly elliptic to broadly lanceolate, glaucescent, glabrous, auriculate, short-petioled; upper lvs sessile, much shorter. Fls subsessile; cal. to 7mm, teeth triangular; cor. to 12mm, lobes obovate, violet to deep pink. Fr. 5–8mm, oblong-ovoid. W Mediterranean to Balkans and Soviet C Asia. Z6.

***P. indica*** L. Herb or subshrub, semiscandent or erect, glabrous; petiole usually somewhat clasping. Lvs 5–11×2–5cm; spikes 10–30cm, lax; cal. 8–9mm, glandular-pubesc., tinged red; cor. deep rosy pink to pale red or purple; tube to 2.5cm; style often fringed below. SE Asia. Z10.

***P. pulchella*** Boiss. Subshrub, slender, erect, much-branched; stem to 1m. Lvs ovate-oblong, acuminate, mucronate; petiole reduced, clasping; spikes lax; fls about 1.5cm; cal. not glandular; cor. blue-violet, tube half as long again as cal. Mexico. Z10.

***P. scandens*** L. DEVIL'S HERB; TOOTHWORT. Shrub, decumbent to scandent; branches grooved, glabrous. Lvs to 10cm, oblong to oblong-lanceolate, mucronate, tapering to short petiole. Infl. paniculate; cal. tube glandular pubesc.; cor. to 2cm, white or blue, lobes mucronulate; stamens 4. Summer. S US to Tropical S America. Z10.

***P. zeylanica*** L. Shrub to 1m, somewhat scandent; branches many-angled. Lvs 3–12×2–5cm, ovate to oblong, acute or obtuse, tapering to petiole; petiole to 1cm, bearing basal auricles. Spikes dense, glandular pubesc.; cal. to 12mm; cor. to 25mm, white, lobes ovate; anth. blue to violet; style glabrous. Fr. 5-angled. SE Asia to Australia. Z10.

***P. auriculata*** Bl. non Lam. See *P. zeylanica*.
***P. capensis*** Thunb. See *P. auriculata*.
***P. coccinea*** Salisb. See *P. indica*.
***P. flaccida*** Moench. See *P. zeylanica*.
***P. floridana*** Nutt. See *P. scandens*.
***P. glandulosa*** Willd. ex Roem. & Schult. See *P. caerulea*.
***P. humboldtiana*** Roem. & Schult. See *P. caerulea*.
***P. lactea*** Salisb. See *P. zeylanica*.
***P. larpentiae*** Lindl. See *Ceratostigma plumbaginoides*.
***P. mexicana*** HBK. See *P. scandens*.
***P. micrantha*** Ledeb. See *Plumbagella micrantha*.
***P. occidentalis*** Sweet. See *P. scandens*.
***P. rhomboidea*** Hook. non Lodd. See *P. caerulea*.
***P. rhomboidea*** Lodd. non Hook. See *P. pulchella*.
***P. rosea*** L. See *P. indica*.
***P. virginica*** Hook. f. See *P. zeylanica*.
***P. viscosa*** Blanco. See *P. zeylanica*.

**Plumeria** L. (For Charles Plumier (1646–1706), French traveller and writer on the flora of Tropical America.) FRANGIPANGI; TEMPLE TREE; NOSEGAY; WEST INDIAN JASMINE; PAGODA TREE. Apocynaceae. 8 species of deciduous shrubs and small trees trees to 8m. Branches candelabriform, cylindrical, swollen, glabrous, grey-green, with petiole scars and plentiful milky sap. Leaves alternate, entire, petiolate, oblong or lanceolate-elliptic, pinnately veined, the emerging foliage scattered on the club-like branch tips and glossy, dark red-green, claw-shaped. Flowers white, yellow, pink or mixtures of these colours, showy, bisexual, fragrant, borne usually on bare branches in terminal thyrses; calyx lobes 5, tipped with glands; corolla slaverform or funnelform, the limb of 5 spreading, ovate-elliptic lobes; stamens on corolla; style 1, fusiform; ovaries 2, semi-inferior. Fruit twinned tough follicles. Tropical America. Z10.

CULTIVATION Widely planted as lawn specimens in subtropical and tropical zones, and valued for their tolerance of coastal conditions, *Plumeria* spp. bloom on bare branches in climates with a pronounced dry season, but will remain evergreen in more humid conditions. The soft thick branches will bleed profusely if broken. Although mature specimens may tolerate occasional drops of temperature to just below freezing, in temperate zones, *Plumeria* spp. succeed best as pot specimens for the cool glasshouse, conservatory or sunny windowsill, grown for their beautiful, sometimes scented flowers.

Grow in a well-drained medium with full sun or part-dry shade. Water moderately when in growth, keep almost dry in winter, with a minimum temperature of 10–13°C/50–55°F. Established plants may be successfully transplanted with care. Propagate species by seed (they may not come true), or cultivars by stem tip cuttings before leaves emerge in spring. Allow to dry for several days before rooting in a cool, shaded position in a well-drained medium kept on the dry side until rooting takes place. Red spider mite may be a problem under glass.

***P. alba*** L. WEST INDIAN JASMINE. Sparingly branched tree to 6m tall, with a spread to 4m. Lvs to 30cm, lanceolate, often rather bullate, usually finely pubesc. beneath, with a conspicuous marginal vein above. Fls to 6cm diam., yellow with white centres, cor. tube to 2.25cm. Fr. to 14cm. Puerto Rico, Lesser Antilles.

***P. obtusa*** L. To 8m. Lvs to 20cm, obovate to oblong, tip obtuse, often emarginate, sometimes tapering shortly, largely glabrous, marginal connecting vein conspicuous; petiole to 5cm, glossy. Fls white, yellow at centre; cor. salver form, limb to 7cm diam., tube to 2.5cm. Fr. to 22cm. Bahamas, Greater Antilles. var. ***sericifolia*** (C.H. Wright) Woodson. Lf undersurfaces, petioles and infl. pubesc. Hispaniola, Cuba, Yucatan.

***P. pudica*** Jacq. To 4m. Lvs to 30cm, oblong-spathulate, apex blunt or briefly tapering, base cuneate, very short-stalked. Cor. near-funnelform, white or ivory marked yellow, limb to 1.8cm diam., tube to 2.5cm. Fr. to 17cm. Colombia, Venezuela.

***P. rubra*** L. To 7m. Branches very stout. Lvs to 40cm, obovate, broadly elliptic or oblong-lanceolate, bright green with a paler midrib and conspicuous marginal connecting vein, sometimes sparsely pubesc. beneath. Infl. an open, spreading, thyrsiform cluster on a stout peduncle; fls typically rose-pink with a yellow throat, but highly variable in colour – white, yellow, golden, bronze, rose or combinations thereof, fragrant; cor. to 10cm diam., salverform, tube to 2.5cm. Fr. to 30cm. Mexico to Panama. f. ***acutifolia*** (Poir.) Woodson. Cor. white, throat golden. f. ***lutea*** (Ruiz & Pav.) Woodson. Cor. yellow, exterior often suffused pale red. f. ***tricolor*** (Ruiz & Pav.) Woodson. Cor. white, edged rose, throat yellow.

***P. emarginata*** Griseb. See *P. obtusa*.

**Plums** *Prunus* spp. (Rosaceae). The plums of today have derived from a number of species over thousands of years. In Europe, including Britain, the sloe or blackthorn (*Prunus spinosa*) and the bullace (*P. institia*) are widespread, while the cherry or plum myrobalan (*P. cerasifera*) is native of southwest Russia bordering on the Caspian Sea. The plum as grown in Britain and Europe today is now classified as *P. domestica* and is considered to have arisen, in its many forms (both shape and colour) from hybridization between *P. cerasifera* and *P. spinosa* in southwest Asia/southeast Europe, whence the various selections were gradually spread and introduced over many centuries in a westerly and northwesterly direction.

The main groups of plums are as follows.

(1) *P. domestica*, with wide variations in shape, size and colour. Several distinct types are distinguishable, including Reine Claude or Greengage types, with round fruits, green with cerise marblings and with a rich, sweet flavour; Transparent Gage type with partially transparent skins through which the outline of the stone is visible; Prune types, purple-skinned and usually with a high sugar content and an affinity to successful drying. Many *P. domestica* cultivars are grown in Europe, the US, Australia, New Zealand and South Africa, especially in the cooler areas.

(2) Damson. Selections from *P. institia* with small purple-black, oval, often necked fruits, initially astringent and acid but often with a richer, sweeter flavour when fully ripe. Typically listed as 'Damson'; 'Merryweather' is a widely grown cultivar; see DAMSONS.

(3) Cherry plums. Selections from *P. cerasifera* both red and yellow fruited (and black in Southwest Asia) of more indifferent cooking quality. The trees flower very early (late winter–early spring) and selections are grown more widely in Britain for foliage effect (e.g. *P. c.* 'Pissardii') and as rootstocks (e.g. 'Myrobalan B') than for fruiting, since cropping is minimal because of frost.

(4) The Salicine or triflora plum. Selections from *P. triflora* or Japanese plum, these are widely grown in Japan, southern Europe, South Africa and California but, like cherry plums, flower too early for successful fruiting in northern Europe. Fruits are round and, among modern cultivars, large; in colour they are red, yellow and purple.

Other minor groups are identifiable, for instance the Mirabelle plums of France, which are selections of bullace (*P. institia*) with black or green-red fruits. They mostly have cultivar names prefixed with 'Mirabelle', as in 'Mirabelle de Metz'. Another group is also known among horticulturists as gage-type plums – cultivars that are not greengages but which have particularly rich-flavoured flesh, e.g. 'Jefferson' and 'Denniston's Superb'.

In North America the native species *P. americana, P. angustifolia, P. munsoniana, P. nigra* and *P. subcordata* have given rise to a number of cultivars that are particularly suited to harsher (cold and heat) conditions. They also impart disease resistance. These include: 'Dandy' and 'South Dakota' (green-skinned), and 'Grenville', 'Patterson's Pride' and 'Pembina' (red/purple skinned). However, they are of indifferent quality and the European and Japanese plums offer a far greater range of quality. Some cultivars have resulted from crosses between the American and Japanese plums to give increased hardiness and disease-resistance.

The Romans were responsible for introducing different types of plum into Britain. From these, seedlings arose in the wild increasing the potential for further development, with time, in association with the indigenous populations of *P. institia* and *P. spinosa*. However, until the 16th century plums were dried and preserved rather than eaten as fresh fruit. With the enthusiasm for fruit-growing that flourished during the reign of Henry VIII, new and sometimes richly flavoured cultivars were introduced from the Continent, particularly France, with some fine prune types from the Balkans. By the early 1700s many varieties were being propagated by nurserymen and the famous 'Coe's Golden Drop' was bred towards the end of the century. It arose from a stone of 'Green Gage', a cultivar that had reputedly originated in Armenia and had been introduced to Italy, then to France and so to Britain. In France it was known as 'Reine Claude' (hence the Reine Claude type in the classification) and is still widely grown there. The name 'Green Gage' arose because a consignment of trees sent by John Gage, a priest living near Paris early in the century, was received by his brother in Suffolk with the label missing from the 'Reine Claude' trees. He then proceeded to name the cultivar 'Green Gage' after his brother.

By the early 19th century many excellent cultivars existed in Britain and the Horticultural Society listed 281 in its collection, though many were synonyms and more still were worthless. No major or organized progress in the introduction of new cultivars occurred until, under the influence of the Horticultural Society and of Thomas Andrew Knight, the leading nurserymen Thomas Rivers and Thomas Laxton embarked on what was to become a long and famous association with fruit and fruit-breeding. Their ascendancy coincided with the period of the Victorian kitchen garden, for which new cultivars were constantly sought, and this situation continued until the final decline of the large estates after World War II. Numerous fine cultivars were introduced during this period, some of which are still widely listed today, and concurrently cultivars reached other parts of the world.

Plums are widely grown in gardens and some cultivars (e.g. 'Victoria') will usually succeed in all but the harshest areas. Commercial orchards have long been in steady decline due largely to greatly reduced interest in preserved and canned plums, these being replaced by home-frozen or imported samples of many other fruits. The commercial production of high-quality dessert plums is difficult because of Britain's uncertain climate and equally because the choicest varieties were bred for the Victorian walled gardens, not for open orchards. There is, however, an awakening interest in home production of choicer plums, aided by a major breeding programme which began at Long Ashton Research Station in 1968 and was transferred to East Malling Research Station in 1985.

The potential for plums depends on a sunny but sheltered site and reasonable freedom from spring frosts to encourage good pollination and fruit-set. In Britain, southern and particularly the drier southeast counties give success with a wider range of cultivars including gages, but humidity and rain during the ripening period often causes premature skin splitting and rotting in choicer kinds. Wall culture is advisable for consistently good results with the best gages and gage types, which naturally flourish best in rather warmer climates.

Most soils are suitable but highly calcareous and badly drained conditions are to be avoided. Longevity is often reduced on very dry, sandy soils unless consistently good husbandry is effected. A pH of 6.0–6.5 should be aimed for; readings on the alkaline side may give rise to lime-induced chlorosis.

Rootstocks currently used are predominantly 'St. Julien A' (moderately vigorous) and 'Pixy' (moderately dwarfing). The former is a selection from the many forms of 'St. Julien' grown from seed in France; 'Pixy' is a recent introduction and is a selection from seedlings of 'St. Julien d'Orleans'. Other older rootstocks still occasionally used are 'Myrobalan B' and 'Brompton' (both vigorous) while others of long standing, such as 'Mussel', 'Common Plum' and 'Pershore' (moderately vigorous) have lapsed for various reasons, e.g. difficulty with suckering ('Mussel'), with propagation and with compatibility. 'St. Julien A' and 'Pixy' have the advantages of giving moderate and small-sized trees respectively that quickly commence cropping, and universal compatibility. The production of rootstocks is either by layering or by hardwood cuttings in protected bins with periods of controlled temperature at the cutting base. A few varieties, such as 'Pershore', will root readily from hardwood cuttings and thrive successfully on their own roots. In the US, seedling 'Myrobalan' is the normal rootstock but where incompatibility occurs (e.g. with 'Stanley') alternative clonal rootstocks are called for, for instance 'Brompton' or 'St. Julien'. Peach stocks are sometimes used for the Japanese plums. In Australia the 'Buck' plum rootstock is recommended for European plums and 'Myrobalan' or 'Marianne' for Japanese types.

There is a reasonable range of cultivars available and where conditions are conducive to regular cropping, a succession of fruiting would be possible from mid-summer through to mid-autumn, varying according to weather pattern. However, the number of cultivars that will reliably set and sustain good crops on a regular basis in the UK is limited; the majority of fine-flavoured cultivars (e.g. 'Green Gage', 'Jefferson', 'Coe's Golden Drop') are generally uncertain in cropping unless given suitable wall space.

In the US, the European plums are suited especially to New York State and East Coast regions, while the Japanese types are preferred on the West Coast. Similarly, in Australia and South Africa the European cultivars are favoured in the cooler areas. The Japanese types flower earlier and need warmer, frost-free early spring conditions.

Damsons and cherry plums are found only on a limited scale in the UK but prunes are grown in quantity in certain areas of France, the Balkans, California and Australia, where dry, sunny conditions aid the harvesting and drying of this fruit.

Besides the cultivars already mentioned the following are recommended: *European plums* (green/yellow-skinned) 'Alabaster', 'Reine Claude de Bavay', 'Yellow Egg'; (red/purple-skinned) 'Empress', 'Mount Royal', 'Peach', 'Seneca'. *Japanese plums* (green/yellow-skinned). 'Early Golden', 'Howard Miracle', 'Kelsey', 'La Crescent', 'Ptitsin', 'Shiro', 'Wickson'; (red/purple skinned) 'Abundance', 'Beauty', 'Bruce', 'Burbank', 'Elephant's Heart', 'Friar', 'Mariposa', 'Morris', 'Ozark Premier', 'Pipestone', 'Santa Rosa', 'Satsuma', 'Superior', 'Toka', 'Waneta'. *Prune cultivars* 'Brooks', 'Early Italian', 'Italian', 'Prune d'Agen', 'Stanley'. *Cherry plums* 'Compass', 'Manor', 'Opata', 'Sapa', 'Sapata'.

Source of supply is important to ensure that trees are healthy and true to name. In the UK, where EMLA status material is specified, this is the best guarantee with both rootstock and scion having originated from virus-tested stock under a scheme initiated by East Malling and Long Ashton (hence EMLA).

Fertility in European plums (*P. domestica*) falls into three distinct categories. Class A: cultivars entirely failing to set with their own pollen; Class B: cultivars setting a poor crop (2–5%) with their own pollen; Class C: cultivars setting a full crop with their own pollen. Cultivars in Classes A and B require at least one other suitable cultivar close by as a pollen source for cross-pollination. There are isolated cases of unsuitable combinations because of incompatibility but usually, provided flowering of the two or more cultivars overlaps adequately, and given fair weather, then cross-pollination and subsequent crop-set should result. The necessity for the presence of bees and other pollinating insects is paramount and sheltered conditions are greatly conducive to their activity, particularly as plums flower early in spring when cold winds can predominate. The Japanese plums (*P. salicina*) mostly require suitable combinations for cross-pollination; they will not cross-pollinate with European plums or vice versa. Hand-pollination with a soft camel-hair brush or cotton wool is advantageous if good weather conditions are lacking.

The introduction of less vigorous rootstocks producing smaller trees has greatly increased the possibility of the successful garden cultivation of the plum. The standard and half-standard trees with their need for space and the difficulties they present for pruning, spraying and picking should no longer be a choice unless for some special circumstance. Tree types best suited for open garden culture are the bush and the pyramid. A variation on the latter is the spindle and for wall culture the fan is the best option (plums do not respond readily to other forms such as the cordon or espalier employed for apples and pears). Equally, the smaller tree is particularly attractive for the commercial orchard and modern plantings reflect this with the use of small bush or spindle-type trees. In all cases, steady production of young growth is essential since this bears the finest fruit, although a good proportion is also produced on older wood. In the US and South Africa large vase-shaped bushes are favoured, sometimes also centre-leader trees. In Australia the vase is also popular, and the espalier and intensive systems such as Bouché Thomas are also used.

Planting is best done in late autumn to early winter and no later than late winter if possible, as growth commences early. The ground must be weed-free. All newly planted trees should be suitably staked and tied, permanently if on dwarfing 'Pixy' rootstock. Planting distances in gardens should be approximately 3.5m/11ft for bushes, 2.75m/9ft for spindles, 3m/10ft for pyramids; in orchards 3.5m–5.25m/11–18ft should be allowed between rows (the greater distance for the more vigorous stocks and cultivars) and machinery requirements also need consideration. Fan-trained trees require a wall or fence height of at least 1.75m/6ft and a span of 3m/10ft minimum with at least 3m/10ft between trees, rather more if on 'St. Julien' rootstock.

Plums are best grown in clean, cultivated ground, although commercially a permanent grass sward as for apples is often established. In town gardens special attention to feeding and irrigation is essential, especially to trees on more dwarfing rootstocks. Irrigation is always essential in hot dry regions.

The formative pruning of trees is most important to ensure an even distribution of well-angled branches. This reduces the risk of serious breakages under the weight of crop or windy conditions. The plum is very prone (particularly in certain cultivars) to two serious diseases – silver leaf and bacterial canker – that gain entry predominantly through injuries and pruning wounds. Thus branch formation should be as strong as possible; also pruning of young trees should be delayed until late spring when the risk of infection through pruning wounds is less than in winter.

The bush is developed ideally from a feathered maiden cut to 76cm/30in. Feathers are removed from the basal 45cm/18in. of stem. Between about 45cm/18in. and 75cm/30in. three or four well-spaced laterals should be selected and shortened by two-thirds of their length, these radiating out like the spokes of a wheel. It is important that the main branches should originate over a length of the trunk rather than close together to minimize damage from any major breakage. In subsequent years, further suitably placed branch leaders are selected and shortened by about one-third, any badly placed strong growths being removed completely.

The pyramid is also built from a feathered maiden which is cut to a good bud at 1.5m/5ft. Any feathers below 45cm/18in. are removed; those remaining under 30cm/12in. in length are left untouched, while any longer ones are reduced by half. Subsequently young growth is summer-pruned once shoots have hardened in their lower half (pruning too early will only result in the formation of unwanted secondary growths) by cutting all maiden lateral and branch leaders to 20cm/8in. and sub-laterals to 15cm/6in. The central leader is not summer-pruned, but is shortened by two-thirds the following April. This treatment is repeated annually, but with the adjustment that once tree height has reached about 2.5m/8ft the shortening of the central stem is delayed until early May, when it should be reduced to 2.5m/8ft or to any other predetermined height.

The formation of the spindle closely follows that of the pyramid initially but with some important differences. Retained laterals are left unpruned and summer pruning of new growth is not practised. The tree is in effect left to develop freely with branches radiating out from the trunk. For pruning of mature pyramids and spindles see FRUIT PRUNING AND TRAINING.

The fan-trained tree is preferably built up from two specially selected shoots, one on either side of the main stem and about 25cm/10in. from ground level. To accomplish this the maiden tree, if feathers are available at the level required, is cut back to them and the feathers themselves shortened by two-thirds. All other feathers are removed. Maidens not suitably feathered are cut at about 40cm/16in. above ground. From the ensuing growths, two suitably placed strong shoots are selected, one on either side, and are trained to supporting bamboos at approximately 30° to the ground. All other growths are cut back to two buds, any very strong ones being removed completely; once the two chosen shoots are safely established, the remainder too can be pruned off. The following spring the two established shoots must be shortened to one-third of their length and from each should be trained an extension shoot, one shoot underneath and two above, all being trained out fan-wise. Any surplus shoots are again initially shortened and then removed once the selected shoots have been safely trained in. The latter are all shortened by one-third in early spring and further new shoots developed from them later. In this way the initially empty centre of the fan is gradually filled in. This method of training the fan is to be preferred to using a central stem with shoots radiating from it, because unless training is meticulous, vigorous growth at the top of this central stem will begin to overshadow lower portions of the tree.

Pruning established trees should always be done during the summer when the risk of infection from silver leaf is less. Early summer is ideal, while fruitlets are still small, and all wounds over 2.5cm/1in. in diameter should be sealed immediately with a suitable paint. On bush trees and spindles pruning consists of removing any low, crowded, crossing or damaged growths or branches keeping the number of cuts to a minimum. On pyramids and fans, shortening of all new shoots once hardened at the base should be done annually. On the pyramid, summer-pruning continues as outlined under formative pruning, while for fans shoots are shortened to three leaves from their base, with any excessively vigorous or surplus growths pinched out as soon as noticed.

Plums require adequate levels of nitrogen and potash and occasional applications of phosphate. Sulphate of ammonia at 25g/m$^2$ in spring (or nitro-chalk at the same rate where pH is below 6.0) and sulphate of potash in late winter at the same rate every other year are typical requirements. However, where growth is strong, nitrogen should be withheld. Applications of superphosphate at 75g/m$^2$ every 3–4 years are also desirable. Occasional mulching in early spring with farmyard manure is also beneficial where practicable.

Watering is advantageous, coupled with adequate mulching, and may be essential in drier, hotter regions of Australia, South Africa and the US.

Fruit-thinning is essential when a good set has occurred, but should be delayed until stoning has taken place – the development of the embryo stone confirms that pollination has been successful. (It should be noted that an apparently good set manifested by a mass of small fruitlets can abort within 2–3 days following unsuccessful pollination; the minute fruitlets turn yellow and drop.) Thin the fruitlets in late summer to 10–15cm/4–6in. apart with a pair of scissors. Remaining fruits will attain excellent size and branch breakages will be reduced to a minimum. Spraying the flowers or fruitlets with certain chemicals for fruit thinning in commercial orchards has so far met with mixed success due to varying conditions from one year to the next.

Fruit should be gathered firm ripe, preferably picking a tree over two or three times for dessert samples rather than clearing the whole crop. Any broken branches should be pruned off as soon as seen and the wound painted.

Propagation is normally by budding in late summer/early autumn. Grafting is an alternative and is favoured in Japan, but is not usually as acceptable or easy as for apple due to possible infection with silver leaf disease.

*Diseases*. Plums and damsons can be affected by several diseases which attack *Prunus* spp. and other trees including armillaria root rot (*Armillaria* spp.), bacterial canker and shot hole (*Pseudomonas morsprunorum*), brown rot and blossom wilt (*Sclerotinia fructigena* and *S. laxa*), crown gall (*Agrobacterium tumefaciens*), fly speck (*Schizothyrium pomi*), powdery mildew (*Podosphaera tridactyla*), scab (*Fusicladium carpophilum*), sooty blotch (*Gloeodes pomigena*) and silver leaf (*Chondrostereum purpureum*). Plum rust, *Tranzschelia pruni-spindsae* var. *discolor*, causes yellow spots on the upper leaf surfaces; the orange-brown urediospores and later the darker coloured teliospores are produced underneath the leaves. Victoria plums are particularly prone to infection. *Anemone* species are an alternate host for this fungus and aeciospores are produced on the lower surfaces of their leaves. Pocket plums is a disease caused by the fungus *Taphrina pruni* in which the fruit is malformed and lacks a stone; *Taphrina institiae* causes witches' brooms. Several virus diseases affect plums, the most important being Sharka disease caused by the plum pox virus: this produces pale spots and blotches on the leaves while the fruit, which is useless, shows uneven ripening and dark bands and rings in the flesh. To avoid the disease, certified virus-free plants should be obtained and the aphid vector, *Myzus persicae*, needs to be controlled.

*Pests*. The most important European pest of plums and damsons are aphids including the leaf-curling plum aphid (*Brachycaudus helichrysi*), the damson-hop aphid (*Phorodon humuli*) and the mealy plum aphid (*Hyalopterus pruni*), which also occurs in North America; larvae of the plum sawfly (*Hoplocampa flava*) which tunnel into fruits at the fruitlet stage; caterpillars of the plum fruit moth (*Cydia funebrana*), which are pink and red and up to 15mm/⅝in. long, bore into ripening fruits; the defoliating caterpillars of various spp. of winter moths; the magpie moth (*Abraxus grossulariata*); and the fruit tree red spider mite (*Panonychus ulmi*). Both winter moth and the fruit tree red spider mite also occur in North America. Plums may also be attacked by capsid bugs, some scale insects, and wasps and birds which damage the fruits. In North America the trees may become infested with the rusty plum aphid (*Hysteroneura setarcae*); by the plum curculio (*Conotrachelus nenuphar*), a weevil with spring and autumn foliage-feeding adults and white legless larvae that feed on ripening fruits; and by caterpillars of the oriental fruit moth (*Grapholitha molesta*), which tunnel into shoot tips and later invade the fruits.

**Pneumatopteris** Nak. (From Gk *pneuma*, wind, breath, and *pteris*, fern.) Thelypteridaceae. Some 80 or more species of terrestrial or, occasionally rupestral ferns. Rhizomes short and erect or suberect, rarely long-creeping; scales attenuate, often ciliate at margin. Scales broad, often with marginal hairs. Fronds usually large, attenuate at base, sparsely short-pubescent or glabrous and pustular beneath, but not glandular, pinnae many, lobed at margin, basal pinnae reduced, the reduction abrupt or gradual, lobes often cartilaginous at margin, veins free or anastomosing at sinus membrane, areolae with excurrent veinlet running to, or short of, margin; rachis and costa sparsely pubescent below; stipes barely pubescent, scaly at base. Sori circular; indusia usually present; sporangia with glandular hairs; spores winged, light brown. Old World Tropics to Hawaii. Z10.

CULTIVATION As for *Christella*. When conditions are optimum, the crown and emerging fronds of this fern become covered in a thick layer of mucus (thought to be as a protection against pests).

***P. pennigera*** (Forst. f.) Holtt. Rhiz. short, erect and arborescent, to 10cm wide, covered with roots and scales. Stipes to 50cm. Fronds to 1m×30cm, pinnae to 20×3cm, distant, subopposite, oblong, acute or narrowly acute at apex, lobed at margin, about 4 pairs of basal pinnae gradually reduced and auricled, lobes to 20×6mm, subfalcate, oblong, apex obtuse, margin entire to notched or undulate, veins simple or forked, basal veins anastomosing; rachis and costa bearing ovate scales on lower surface when young. New Zealand, Australia.

For synonymy see *Dryopteris* and *Thelypteris*.

**Poa** L. (Classical Gk name for pasture grass.) MEADOWGRASS; BLUE GRASS; SPEAR GRASS. Gramineae. Some 500 species of mostly perennial, sometimes dioecious grasses, of variable habit. Stems slender to robust. Leaves narrow, folded to flat or bristled, basal sheaths occasionally thickened or flattened, apex blunt to hooded, ligules membranous. Inflorescence paniculate, open to compact; spikelets stipitate, 2- to several flowered, upper flower rudimentary; rachilla glabrous; glumes acute, persistent, upper glume 3-ribbed; palea keeled, rough to ciliate or smooth; lemmas protruding from glumes, awnless, herbaceous to papery, keeled, keels to 7-ribbed, base glabrous to ciliate; stamens 3; ovary glabrous; hilum round. Cool temperate regions.

CULTIVATION *P. annua* L. is a weed, found in turf; *P. arachnerifera* Torr. a fodder and lawn grass in S US; *P. compressa* L. a pasture grass; *P. nemoralis* L. grown for pasture and hay; *P. pratensis* L. (Kentucky blue grass) grown for forage and valued throughout the northern US as a lawn grass on damp limy soils; *P. trivialis* L. a meadow and pasture grass, a turf grass on wet soils; *P. alpina* L., *P. bulbosa* L., *P. bulbosa* var. *vivipara* Koeler (which bears live plantlets in the upper parts of the spikelet), *P. flexuosa* Sm. and *P.* ×*jemtlandica*, a rare hybrid of *P. alpina* × *P. flexuosa* Sm., may also be of some horticultural value.

*Poa* includes a number of species valued for their blue foliage, especially bright in *P. colensoi* and *P. labillardieri*. *P. pratensis* and *P. nemoralis*, the blue grasses or meadow grasses, are amongst the most commonly used of cool-season turf grasses. Grow in sun in any porous moderately fertile garden soil, with good moisture retention for the New Zealand species. Propagate by division or seed.

***P. abbreviata*** R. Br. Habit very dwarf, to 2cm. Lvs dark green. Spikelets minute, soft.

***P. alpina*** L. ALPINE MEADOW GRASS; BLUE GRASS. Perenn., tufted. Stems to 50cm, glabrous, smooth, somewhat thickened at base. Lvs to 5×0.3cm, linear, short-acuminate, thick, flattened; ligules to 4mm. Panicles to 7cm, ovoid, dense, shortly branched; spikelets to 1cm, with 3–7 fls; glumes broad, almost equal; lemmas glabrous, downy on keel and marginal veins. C Asia, USSR. var. ***vivipera*** (L.) Tzvelev. Spikelets replaced by numerous plantlets.

***P. annua*** L. Annual or bienn. Stems to 30cm, smooth, creeping or erect. Lvs to 3.5mm diam., narrowly linear, flat, smooth; ligules to 2mm. Panicles to 7cm, pyramidal, loose; spikelets to 5.5mm, closely spaced, with 3–7 fls; glumes unequal, the lower 1-veined, the upper 3-veined; lemmas subobtuse, sparsely pubesc. on keel and marginal veins. Europe, US.

***P. bulbosa*** L. BULBOUS MEADOW GRASS. Perenn., densely tufted. Basal sheaths swollen, forming a bulb. Culms to 55cm, erect, glabrous, terete. Lvs to 1.5mm diam., narrow-linear, tightly involute; ligules to 2mm, acute to rounded, hyaline. Panicles to 6cm, oblong, compact; branches scabrous, short; spikelets to 6mm, green or on keel and marginal veins, obscurely veined. Eurasia, N Africa; naturalized US.

***P. chaixii*** Vill. BROAD-LEAVED MEADOWGRASS; FOREST BLUEGRASS. Perenn., to 120cm. Stems clumped, erect, robust. Lvs to 45×1cm, flat or folded, bright green; sheaths flattened, keeled. Panicles ovoid to ovoid-oblong, open, to 25×11cm; spikelets ovate to oblong, to 6mm, to 4-fld; lemmas lanceolate-oblong, to 4mm, glabrous. Spring–summer. Europe, SW Asia. Z5.

***P. colensoi*** Hook. f. Perenn., to 25cm. Stems erect or arching, flimsy, smooth, ridged, blue-green. Lvs to 16cm×0.2cm, threadlike, intensely blue-green, margins involute. Infl. paniculate, panicle lax, to 5cm; spikelets blue, becoming brown-tinged; glumes oblong-ovate. New Zealand. Z7.

***P. glauca*** Vahl. GLAUCOUS MEADOWGRASS. Glaucous perenn., to 40cm. Stems upright, stiff. Lvs to 8cm×0.4cm, glabrous; ligules to 3mm. Infl. erect, stiff, to 10×4cm, sometimes variegated purple; spikelets ovate to oblong, to 6mm, to 6-fld; glumes 3-ribbed; lemma oblong, obtuse, to 4mm, keeled, keels downy. Summer–autumn. N Eurasia, northern N America. Z5.

***P. iridifolia*** Hauman. Perenn., to 90cm. Stems clumped, robust. Lvs flat or folded, erect, to 50cm×1.8cm, glabrous; lower sheaths conspicuously keeled, flattened; ligules to 3mm. Panicles ovoid, erect to pendent, to 30×7cm, green; spikelets densely arranged, oblong to oblong-lanceolate, to 1cm, to 5-fld; lemmas lanceolate to oblong, to 4mm, base pubesc., keeled, keels margins partially short-pubesc. Summer. Uruguay, Argentina. Z8.

***P. labillardieri*** Steud. Perenn. to 1m. Lvs to 30cm or more, slender, grey-green; lvs and sheaths loose on flowering stems; spikelets tinged purple or green, with hairlike stalklets; outer husks short with slender tips, inner husks 4–6. Australia.

***P. nemoralis*** L. WOOD MEADOWGRASS Perenn., to 90cm. Stems clumped, erect to spreading. Lvs to 12cm×0.3cm, glabrous; ligules very short, membranous. Panicles ovoid to cylindric, to 20cm; branches spreading; spikelets lanceolate to ovate, laterally flattened, to 5-fld; glumes persistent, subequal, 3-ribbed, keeled, to 4mm; lemmas narrow-oblong, to 4mm, keeled; palea equal to lemma, keeled. Summer. Europe, temperate Asia, NE America. Grown for ornament and cover, will not tolerate mowing. Z5.

***P. palustris*** L. SWAMP MEADOWGRASS. Perenn., to 1.5m. Stems clumped, flimsy to robust. Lvs to 20cm×0.4cm, scabrous; ligules to 5mm. Panicles ovoid to oblong, to 30×15cm, tinged yellow-green or purple; spikelets ovoid to oblong, to 5mm, to 5-fld; lemmas narrow-oblong, keeled, keels short pubesc., tipped brown-yellow. Summer. N temperate. Z5.

***P. pratensis*** L. KENTUCKY BLUE GRASS; JUNE GRASS. Perenn., loosely tufted. Stems to 90cm, ascending, smooth, terete. Lvs to 4mm diam., narrow-linear, flattened, smooth or scabrous; ligule to 1.5mm, rounded to truncate. Panicles to 20cm, pyramidal; branches scabrous, lowest in whorls of 3–5; spikelets to 6mm, ovate, green, with 2–5 fls; lanceolate, pubesc. on keel and marginal veins. Eurasia, N Africa. Z3.

***P. caesia*** Sm. See *P. glauca*.
***P. curvula*** Schräd. See *Eragrostis curvula*.
***P. fertilis*** Host. See *P. palustris*.
***P. mexicana*** Hornem. See *Eragrostis mexicana*.
***P. pilosa*** L. See *Eragrostis pilosa*.
***P. plumosa*** Retz. See *Eragrostis tenella*.
***P. serotina*** Ehrenb. See *P. palustris*.
***P. sudetica*** Haenke. See *P. chaixii*.
***P. trichodes*** Nutt. See *Eragrostis trichodes*.
For further synonymy see *Agrostis*.

**Podachaenium** Benth. ex Ørst. (From Gk *pous*, a foot, and *achene*, referring to the narrow, 2-winged stalk at the base of the fruit.) Compositae. 2 species of trees or shrubs. Leaves opposite, occasionally alternate above, pinnatifid or dentate, petiolate. Capitula radiate, in corymbose panicles; receptacle convex to conical, scaly; involucre globose; phyllaries in 2–3 series, narrow, herbaceous; ray florets female, fertile, white; disc florets hermaphrodite, fertile, yellow. Fruit a 3-angled, compressed cypsela, often with narrow basal wings contracted into a basal stalk; pappus of scales. C America. Z10.

CULTIVATION A vigorous and showy specimen for the shrub border in zones that are essentially frost free, and for the intermediate to hot glasshouse in cool temperate climates. Cultivate as for *Bartlettina*.

***P. eminens*** (Lagasca) Schultz-Bip. Shrub or small tree, to 8m, with softly tomentose branches. Lvs to 30cm, broadly ovate to suborbicular, lobes angular, nearly glabrous above, pale grey- to brown-tomentose beneath, upper lvs nearly entire. Capitula to 2.5cm diam.; phyllaries elliptic-oblanceolate. Fr. to 2.5cm including basal stalk; pappus 1mm. Spring–summer. Mexico to Costa Rica.

For synonymy see *Ferdinanda*.

**Podalyria** Willd. (Named for Podalyrius, son of Aesculapius, celebrated in Greek mythology as a skilful physician.) Leguminosae (Papilionoideae). 25 species of shrubs. Leaves simple, linear to elliptic or suborbicular, usually subcordate at base, margins revolute, densely tomentose; stipules subulate, often caducous. Flowers 1–2, on axillary peduncles; bracts and bracteoles small; calyx campanulate, villous, lobes subequal; standard suborbicular or oblate, wings broad, oblique, keel shorter than wings, broad-obovate, truncate; stamens 10, free or united at base, filaments usually flattened and smooth at the base; ovary sessile, densely villous, ovules many in 2 rows; style slender, filiform, stigma minute, terminal, capitate. Fruit a turgid, ovoid or oblong, dehiscent legume, valves coriaceous; seeds few, strophiolate. S Africa (E Cape to Natal). Z9.

CULTIVATION *Podalyria* spp. usually occur in woodland habitats. In warm temperate, essentially frost-free climates, they make attractive ornamentals for the shrub border and specimen plantings. Although they will tolerate several degrees of frost in their native regions, in cool temperate zones all species are best grown in the cool glasshouse. They are grown for their downy foliage and masses of strongly fragrant flowers. *P. sericea* is perhaps the most attractive of the genus, having silver-downy foliage which becomes golden with maturity; the small seed pods which follow the lavender-pink, sweetly scented flowers are also downy, and persistent.

Plant in well-drained, humus-rich soils in sunny positions. *Podalyria* spp. become increasingly drought-tolerant as they mature, although flowering is better on moisture-retentive soils. Under glass, grow in a medium-fertility loam-based mix with additional leafmould and water moderately, giving a dilute liquid feed fortnightly when in growth. Maintain a winter minimum of 7–10°C/45–50°F, with good ventilation when conditions allow. Propagate from seed, or by cuttings of short lateral shoots with a heel, in a sandy propagating mix in a closed case with bottom heat.

***P. calyptrata*** (Retz.) Willd. To 3m. Lvs to 5×4cm, elliptic or obovate, grey-green, thinly pubesc.; petiole to 5mm; stipules inconspicuous, caducous. Fls to 3cm; buds large, spherical, enveloped by fused, caducous bracts; pedicels to 4mm; hypanthium to 14mm; standard to 4cm diam., light pink to lavender-purple, purple at base, emarginate, wings lavender, keel white, obtuse, striate; ovary to 8mm, oblong-lanceolate, hairs to 2mm, ovules 8–11, style 5mm. Fr. to 3×1cm, ascending, flat, valves tawny-villous; seeds few. Spring–summer.

***P. sericea*** (Andrews) R. Br. To 1m. Lvs to 2×2cm, obovate, submucronate, initially silvery-, later golden-sericeous, venation obscure; petiole 2mm; stipules, to 3mm, rigid, usually persisting. Fls solitary, to 10mm; buds not enveloped by bracts; bract narrow, caducous, occasionally with basal stipular appendages; hypanthium to 8mm; cor. lavender, standard emarginate, wings obliquely ovate, subauriculate, keel auriculate; ovary oblong. Fr. to 3×0.9cm, valves tawny-villous; seeds many. Winter.

***P. styracifolia*** Sims. See *P. calyptrata*.
For further synonymy see *Sophora*.

**Podangis** Schltr. (From Gk *pous*, foot, and *angos*, vessel.) Orchidaceae. 1 species, an epiphytic orchid. Stem 2–3cm, rarely to 11cm, 3–4-leaved at apex. Leaves 4–16cm×5–12mm, fleshy, bilaterally flattened. Inflorescence a raceme, shorter than leaves, densely-flowered, subcapitate; flowers white; anthers green; pedicel and ovary 8–12mm; sepals and petals free, 3.5–5mm, elliptic, obtuse; lip 6mm, more or less orbicular, entire, crenulate; spur 11–14mm, wide-mouthed, constricted in middle, swollen and often bifid at apex; column stout, 1.5mm; pollinia and stipites 2. Tropical Africa. Z10.

CULTIVATION As for *Angraecum*.

***P. dactyloceras*** (Rchb. f.) Schltr. As for the genus.

**Podanthes** Haw.
***P. pulchellus*** Haw. See *Orbea pulchella*.

**PODOCARPACEAE** Endl. PODOCARPUS FAMILY. Gymnosperms. 12 genera and 155 species of evergreen usually dioecious resinous trees (one root parasite, *Parasitaxus*, only parasitic gymnosperm known.) Leaves spirally arranged, decussate in *Microcachrys*, acicular, lanceolate, ovate or scale-like. Male cones catkin-like, with many bracts, male flowers usually with many stamens; female cones with few to many bracts, fertile bracts with 1 seed at maturity; seed seated on or enveloped by an aril-like fleshy structure, attractive to bird-dispersers; cotyledons 2. Some are used for timber. Southern hemisphere to Japan and Central America, tropical African mountains. *Acmopyle, Afrocarpus, Dacrycarpus, Dacrydium, Falcatifolium, Halocarpus, Lagarostrobus, Lepidothamnus, Microcachrys, Microstrobos, Nageia, Parasitaxus, Podocarpus, Prumnopitys, Retrophyllum, Saxegothaea, Sundacarpus*.

**Podocarpus** L'Hérit. ex Pers. (From Gk *pous*, foot and *karpos*, fruit, referring to the fleshy receptacle at the base of the seed.) PODOCARPS; YELLOW-WOOD. Podocarpaceae. About 100 species of evergreen, monoecious or dioecious trees or shrubs. Bole straight in tree sized species; bark exfoliating in strips; branches irregular to decussate or whorled. Buds ovoid to globose; bud scales few, overlapping. Leaves densely or loosely spirally arranged, often twisted at base to be apparently opposite in 2 ranks, or in dense clusters, overlapping to a certain extent, bilaterally flattened, broad acicular, linear, sometimes falcate, 1–26×0.2–3cm or more, thin, flexible or rigid, coriaceous, margin entire, base decurrent, remaining green for 1–3 years, then becoming the same colour as the bark. Male flowers solitary or in groups to 5, axillary, or many in narrow elongate spicate inflorescences, in leaf axils subtended by basal scales, yellow, peduncle naked. Female cones carried on a 1–30mm naked peduncle, with 1–2 fertile scales, their receptacles connate, at first green and like a thick continuation of the peduncle, ripening into a soft red fleshy bead-like aril 5–8×3–6mm, on some species to 15×15mm, with the 1–2 erect seeds apical on the receptacles. Seeds ovate, mostly 5–20mm, with a pointed or blunt apex, green ripening brown, with a thin leathery layer derived from the scale and a thick woody layer protecting the endosperm. Mexico, C & S America, C & S Africa, Asia (Himalaya to Japan), Australasia.

CULTIVATION With about 100 species, wide variation is found in the requirements, but all are shade tolerant at least when young and prefer shelter at all stages; most demand high humidity and rainfall, and few are very frost tolerant; in Britain good growth is generally only seen in the mild winters of the SW and Ireland. The hardiest are the high altitude shrubs *P. nivalis* and *P. alpinus* from New Zealand and Tasmania, and two tree species, *P. nubigenus* from Chile and *P. macrophyllus* from China & Japan, all hardy to about −25°C/−13°F. However, *P. macrophyllus* requires hot humid summers and is poor in Britain, though extensively grown and sometimes naturalized in SE US and California; its erect cv. Maki is a very popular garden and hedge plant in S China and Japan, and is also the commonest form in the US; more than one clone is involved, but it does not appear to be a botanical variety. Conversely, *P. nubigenus* requires cool summers, but more than most demands humidity and incessant rain, so again only grows in Ireland and the west, not for the warm winters but for the rain. *P. salignus* is the best in Britain, making a very attractive tree in the Southwest and Ireland (where it seeds freely and is naturalized in some gardens), and a shrub elsewhere, with long glossy green leaves. *P. alpinus* and *P. nivalis* are hardy as far northeast as S Sweden and coastal Norway, and are good plants for the rock garden; plantings should comprise several female and one or two male clones for the benefit of the very attractive red fruit, often densely borne. Greater drought tolerance is shown by *P. spinulosus*, but this is not hardy in Britain; it is valued in its native SE Australia and also California. *P. elongatus* is also tolerant of hot dry summers, and probably the best species for Mediterranean climates. The 80 species not described are largely confined to tropical mid-altitude cool wet cloud forest with little seasonal variation, and are not amenable to cultivation in most inhabited regions; new species are still being discovered with further botanical exploration, and many are rare with very limited ranges.

Propagation is generally similar to *Taxus*, by seeds or cuttings; seed may need to be stratified for up to a year, and it is often easier to use bird-sown seedlings if available (cf. *P. salignus*, above). Cuttings should include an erect lead shoot if good shape is wanted; side shoots give prostrate plants. Plant in mid-spring, after risk of hard frost has passed, using small plants 30–70cm/12–28in. Little pruning is required, mainly removal of low branches where tree form is desired; many species make good hedge plants, and like *Taxus* many re-grow from hard pruning. They differ from *Taxus* in not being poisonous, and are more suitable for gardens with young children. There are no diseases or pests outside of their native regions.

The following key to the species described below is based only on leaf size and shape, and does not represent true relationships.

1 Leaves small, under 4cm long.
*Pp. alpinus, cunninghamii, hallii, lambertii, lawrencii, nivalis, nubigenus, totara.*

2 Leaves medium to long, 4–25cm, broad in relation to length, mostly less than 10 times longer than broad, mostly straight, rarely falcate.
*Pp. coriaceus, dispermus, elatus, elongatus, latifolius, macrophyllus, matudae, oleifolius, neriifolius.*

3 Leaves long and slender, 4–14cm, mostly more than 10 times longer than broad, commonly falcate.
*Pp. drouynianus, henkelii, longifoliolatus, salignus, spinulosus,* also some (especially juvenile) *hallii, neriifolius.*

***P. alpinus*** R. Br. ex Hook. f. TASMANIAN PODOCARP. Shrub, to 3m. Stems densely branched; branches level or upswept. Buds ovoid to globose, 1mm. Lvs densely arranged, moderately upswept, linear-oblong, 6–12×1.5–2mm, dark buff green above, pale green tinged blue beneath, obtuse to apiculate; midrib keeled. Male cones solitary in lf axils, sessile, to 6mm. Receptacle fleshy, to 6×5mm, vivid red. Seeds 1, occasionally 2, ovoid, 5×2mm. SE Australia (NSW, Victoria, Tasmania). Z7.

***P. coriaceus*** Rich. YACCA PODOCARP. Tree, to 20m, bole to 1m diam. Lvs densely spirally arranged, linear-lanceolate, straight to bowed, 8–18×1–2cm, coriaceous; apex long acuminate; midrib conspicuous below; petiole to 6mm. Male cones to 60×6mm. Fr. on 7–10mm peduncle, receptacle red, often tinged blue, fleshy; seeds ovoid, 9×7mm, apex obtusely crested. West Indies (Puerto Rico to Trinidad). Z10.

***P. cunninghamii*** Colenso. Name of uncertain application; Colenso's description suggests the hybrid *P. totara* × *P. hallii*, occasionally found wild in New Zealand, but may be just a syn. of *P. totara*. Lvs and shoots as *P. totara*; bark as *P. hallii*. New Zealand (S Island).

***P. dispermus*** C.T. White. Tree, to 18m; bark pale brown tinged grey, scaly. Lvs spirally arranged, linear to narrow-lanceolate, 10–20×2–3cm, apex acuminate, base attenuate to a short petiole, dark green, shiny above, midrib clearly visible. Male cones sessile, in groups of 1–3, to 30×3mm; receptacle very fleshy, scarlet. Seeds elliptic, to 25×15mm, usually 2 per fr. Australia (N Queensland). Z11.

***P. drouynianus*** F. Muell. Shrub, resembles *P. spinulosus* in habit, to 2m. Buds to 5mm. Lvs subsessile, spirally arranged, linear, 5–8cm×2–3mm, green above, green tinged blue beneath, apex sharp-acuminate, margin involute, midrib conspicuous. Male cones solitary or in small clusters, 6–12×4mm. Fr. on peduncle to 25mm; receptacle fleshy, 12–25cm, purple, glaucous; seeds to 2cm. W Australia (extreme SW, 250km S of Perth). Z10.

***P. elatus*** R. Br. ex Mirb. ROCKINGHAM PODOCARP; BROWN PINE. Tree, to 30m in wild, bole to 1m diam., often fluted at base; branches solitary or in whorls. Lvs variable, oblong to lanceolate, straight or bowed, 5–15cm×7–12mm, occasionally to 21cm on young trees, pale green above, midrib clearly visible above, apex obtuse, occasionally mucronate, lf base attenuate. Male cones in clusters of 2–3, to 5cm. Fr. on peduncle to 10mm; receptacle globose, to 12mm, blue-black; edible; seeds sessile, solitary, ovoid, 6–8mm. E Australia (SE Queensland, NSW). Sometimes mislabelled as *P. macrophyllus, P. neriifolius* or other species. Z10.

***P. elongatus*** (Ait.) L'Hérit. ex Pers. CAPE YELLOWWOOD; AFRICAN YELLOWWOOD. Tree to 30m, or shrub. Crown rounded; bark thin, grey or grey suffused green; branchlets brown; shoots green suffused yellow, ridged. Lvs spirally arranged to opposite, densely toward shoot apex, spreading to erect, narrow-oblong or elliptic, 3–6cm×3–5mm on mature trees, to 12cm×12mm on young trees, green tinged blue above, some stomata above as well as beneath. Male cones sessile, solitary or in clusters of 2–5. Fr. on peduncle to 9mm; receptacle 10–15mm, fleshy, red to purple, apex bifid. Seeds elliptic to ovoid, 7–10mm. S Africa (W Cape). Some material cultivated as *P. elongatus* is *Afrocarpus falcata*. Z10.

***P. hallii*** T. Kirk. Resembles *P. totara*, but bark differs; young trees also differ in lvs, and less strictly branched in habit. Tree to 20m; bole to 120cm diam., bark thin, papery, exfoliating in large thin sheets; shoots nodding in young specimens. Lvs on mature trees spirally arranged, 25–40×4–5mm, linear-lanceolate, stiff, coriaceous, glaucous beneath, midrib conspicuous beneath; on young trees to 7cm, rarely 9cm, long acuminate, apex sharp, arranged more pectinately. Fr. as *P. totara,* except seed narrow ovoid with acute apex. New Zealand (South Island, Stewart Island). Z8.

***P. henkelii*** Stapf. FALCATE YELLOWWOOD. Tree, to 35m; bole to 2m diam.; bark charcoal grey, exfoliating in long strips; branches pendent; shoots pale green, ridged. Lvs similar to *P. salignus*, spirally arranged, grouped at branch apices, drooping, attenuate, falcate, often bowed, 5–15cm×4–91mm, tapering to apex, base glaucous green, midrib distinct beneath. Fr. pedunculate; receptacle green tinged glaucous blue, fleshy. Seeds sessile, ovoid to globose, 10–12mm diam., yellow-green, seed coat coriaceous, hard. S Africa (SW Tanzania to Natal & E Cape). Z10.

***P. lambertii*** Klotzsch. Tree to 25m, branches whorled, numerous. Lvs spirally arranged, erect, crowded, narrow oblong to linear-lanceolate, 25–35×2–4mm, sub-sessile. Male cones clustered 3–6 on a 5–15mm peduncle. Fr. on a 5–10mm peduncle, receptacle fleshy, 4mm, seed subglobose. NE Argentina, SE Brazil. Z10.

***P. latifolius*** (Thunb.) R. Br. ex Mirb. YELLOWWOOD. Tree to 30m, or shrubby; bole to 3m diam.; bark dark grey, smooth, becoming ridged, exfoliating in long strips; branches spreading to erect. Shoots angular, grooved. Lvs spirally arranged to subopposite, linear-elliptic, 4–10cm×6–10mm on mature trees, to 20cm×18mm on young trees, spreading, usually grouped at branch apices, straight or falcate, rigid, dark glossy green to green tinged blue without stomata above, midrib distinct beneath. Fr. on a 5mm peduncle; receptacle red tinged purple, fleshy, sweet-tasting, 8–14mm; seeds 6–10mm, obovate to subglobose, green tinged blue, or violet, apex curved. Africa (S Sudan to S Natal). Z10.

***P. lawrencii*** Hook. f. Spreading shrub to small tree, to 10m. Bark thin; branches slender. Lvs spirally arranged, narrow-linear, 15–25×1.5–3mm, green suffused bronze, apex mucronate. Male cones solitary or in groups of 2–4; peduncle to 8mm; receptacle, seed solitary, rarely in pairs, 4×2.5mm, narrow acute ovoid. Fr. 6×5mm, bright red. New Zealand (South Island, mts.). Z7.

***P. longifoliolatus*** Pilger. Tree, to 12m. Bark furrowed, red or grey-brown; bud scales long-acuminate, to 1cm×3mm, reflexed. Lvs densely arranged, erect or spreading, lanceolate, 5–10cm×6–10mm coriaceous on mature trees, to 14×11mm on young trees, midrib prominent above. Male cones solitary, sessile, to 15mm. Fr. on slender 10–18mm peduncle; receptacle to 8mm, fleshy; seeds in groups of 1–2, rarely 3, ovoid to obovoid, 9–10×5mm, green tinged blue, apex slightly crested. New Caledonia. Z10.

***P. macrophyllus*** (Thunb.) D. Don. BIGLEAF PODOCARP; KUSAMAKI. Tree to 15m, or shrub to 2m. Branches level; shoots densely arranged. Lvs densely spirally arranged, erect to spreading, broad linear-lanceolate, 8–10cm×9–11mm on mature trees, to 18cm×14mm on young trees, dive-green above, green tinged yellow beneath, soft-coriaceous, flexible, midrib distinct, apex bluntly acute. Male cones cylindric to 35mm in clusters of 1–4. Fr. short pedunculate, receptacle 12–15mm, fleshy, red; seed elliptic, to 1cm, green-brown. S China (Yunnan to Jiangsu), Japan. 'Maki': fastigiate, lvs radially arranged, often shorter, 5–9cm; several clones involved. var. ***nakai*** (Hayata) Li & Keng. Lvs 6–8cm×8–12mm on mature trees, lanceolate, apex bluntly acuminate, more tapered than in type. Taiwan. Z7.

***P. matudae*** Lundell. Tree to 30m, bole to 1.5m diam. Buds with 3mm acuminate-aristate outer scales. Lvs 4–9cm×10–15mm, to 15cm×18mm on vigorous shoots; lanceolate, sometimes falcate, coriaceous; midrib raised above and beneath. Male cones solitary or paired, cylindrical, 3–5cm, sessile with scales at base as shoot buds. Fr. on 5–20mm peduncles, receptacle 6×6mm, red-brown, seed broad ovoid, 10–15×8–12mm, slightly crested. NE Mexico (Tamaulipas) south to Costa Rica, wet mts. Z9.

***P. neriifolius*** D. Don. OLEANDER PODOCARP; THITMIN. Tree, to 40m+. Bark brown, suffused grey or red, exfoliating in strips; branches horizontal, spreading, whorled. Buds conic, 2mm; scales ovoid to triangular. Lvs narrow-lanceolate, very variable, 4cm×5mm to 24cm×28mm, coriaceous, flexible, glossy green above, paler beneath, midrib slightly raised above and beneath, apex acute; petiole to 6mm. Male cones sessile, short, in groups of 1–4, to 8cm×3mm. Fr. on 1–2cm peduncle, receptacle 8mm; seeds elliptic to globose, 10mm. SE Asia to W Pacific (E Himalaya to extreme SW China and Malaysia, Philippines, Melanesia E to Fiji). Some populations treated as varieties or separate species, e.g. var. *degeneri* Gray, on Fiji. Z10.

***P. nivalis*** Hook. ALPINE TOTARA. Resembles *P. alpinus*, but lvs elliptical, wider. Shrub, erect to prostrate or procumbent, to 2m×3m wide. Terminal buds globose, 1mm, green. Lvs densely spirally arranged, elliptical to oblong-ovate, 6–18×3mm, obtuse, stiff, coriaceous, margin thickened. Male cones pedunculate, lateral, in groups of 1–4, to 15mm; peduncles to 5mm; seed cones solitary; peduncles to 3mm; receptacle red, to 7mm. Seeds ovoid, to 6mm. S New Zealand (mts). Z7.

***P. nubigenus*** Lindl. CLOUD PODOCARP; CHILEAN PODOCARP. Tree to 20m, resembles *P. totara*. Bole to 1m diam., bark brown tinged purple; branches short. Buds ovoid-conic, scales lanceolate. Lvs spirally arranged to moderately pectinate, lanceolate to slightly falcate, 2–4cm×3–4mm, stiff, coriaceous, bright green above, 2 blue-white stomatal bands beneath; apex sharp-spined. Male cones short pedunculate, occasionally bunched, to 6mm. Fr. fleshy red receptacle with 1(–2) ovoid seeds 8mm long. S America (S Chile, SW Argentina). Z7.

***P. oleifolius*** D. Don. Tree to 20m, bark yellow-brown; branching dense. Buds ovoid, small, scales obtuse. Lvs spirally arranged but appearing sub-opposite, sparse, broad lanceolate, 3–8cm×6–12mm, apex acuminate midrib marked by a groove above and ridge beneath. Male cones 2.5cm, sessile, solitary. Fr. on a 5–15mm peduncle, receptacle fleshy, bright red-purple, 6–9×4mm, seed 1(–2), ovoid, 8mm, with acute crested apex. C & S America (S Mexico to Venezuela & Bolivia). Z10.

***P. salignus*** D. Don. WILLOWLEAF PODOCARP; WILLOW PODOCARP; MAÑIO. Tree, to 20m, or shrub in cold areas. Crown columnar or conic; branches irregular, slightly pendulous; bark brown tinged red, fibrous, exfoliating in strips. Buds ovoid 2mm. Adult lvs narrow-lanceolate, mostly somewhat falcate, 8–12cm×5–7mm, short-acuminate or obtuse, shiny green above, paler beneath, abscising after 2–3 years; juvenile lvs straighter, 5–10cm, long-acuminate, apex spined; on young trees to 2–3m tall, grading into adult lvs. Male cones narrow-cylindric, to 35mm, pendulous, narrow. Fr. on 20–25mm peduncle, receptacle fleshy, 8mm, dark red to violet; seeds solitary or paired, elliptic to oblong, 8×10×3–4mm, dark green to brown, apex crested. Central S Chile. Z8.

***P. spinulosus*** (Sm.) R. Br. ex Mirb. SPINY LEAF PODOCARP. Shrub, to 1.5m. Stems densely branched. Lvs sub-sessile, spirally arranged, 4–8cm×2–4mm, some only 2cm long; lanceolate, long acuminate, sharply spined, dark yellow-green. Male cones axillary, to 1cm. Fr. with receptacle violet, bloomed waxy blue, edible, 10×8mm, pruinose. Seeds 1 or 2, to 13×8mm; apex beaked. Australia (New South Wales). Z10.

***P. totara*** G. Benn ex D. Don TOTARA. Tree, to 30m. Crown ovoid; bole to 2m diam.; bark dark brown, to silver-grey, thick, becoming deeply fissured, exfoliating in stringy strips; branches spreading; terminal buds 1mm, globose or ovoid. Lvs pectinate beneath, spreading above around shoot, a few recurved; 15–25×3–4mm, linear-lanceolate, straight or slightly falcate, acute, sharply spined, coriaceous, stiff, green tinged yellow-grey ridged above, midrib conspicuous beneath; on young trees larger, to 30mm. Male cones short-pedunculate, in groups of 1–3. Fr. on short pedicel; receptacle fleshy, orange red to bright red, 5–6mm; seed 1–2 on receptacle, subglobose to ovoid, 4–5mm, apex rounded, not acute as in *P. hallii*. New Zealand. Z9.

***P. acicularis*** Van Houtte ex Gordon. See *P. elatus*.
***P. acutifolius*** T. Kirk. See *P. lawrencii*.
***P. amarus*** Bl. See *Sundacarpus amarus*.
***P. andinus*** Poepp. ex Endl. See *Prumnopitys andina*.
***P. antillarum*** R. Br. See *P. coriaceus*.
***P. appressus*** Maxim. See *P. macrophyllus*.
***P. bidwillii*** Hooibr. See *P. spinulosus*.
***P. bracteata*** Bl. See *P. neriifolius*.
***P. chilinus*** Rich. See *P. salignus*.
***P. chinensis*** Wallich ex Parl. See *P. macrophyllus*.
***P. cunninghamii*** sensu Laub., non Colenso. See *P. hallii*.
***P. cupressina*** R. Br. ex Mirb. See *Dacrycarpus imbricatus*.
***P. dacrydioides*** A. Rich. See *Dacrycarpus dacrydioides*.
***P. discolor*** Bl. See *P. neriifolius*.
***P. elongatus*** Carr. non L'Hérit. See *Afrocarpus falcata*.
***P. ensifolius*** R. Br. See *P. elatus*.
***P. ensisculus*** Melville. See *P. henkelii*.
***P. eurhyncha*** Miq. See *Sundacarpus amarus*.
***P. falcatus*** (Thunb.) R. Br. ex Mirb. See *Afrocarpus falcata*.
***P. falcatus*** Engl. non (Thunb.) R. Br. ex Mirb. See *Afrocarpus gracilior*.
***P. falciformis*** Parl. See *Falcatifolium falciforme*.
***P. ferruginoides*** Compton See *Prumnopitys ferruginoides*.
***P. ferrugineus*** D. Don ex Laub. See *Prumnopitys ferruginea*.
***P. fleuryi*** Hickel. See *Nageia fleuryi*.
***P. forrestii*** Craib & W.W. Sm. See *P. macrophyllus*.
***P. gracillimus*** Stapf. See *Afrocarpus falcata*.
***P. horsfieldii*** Wallich. See *Dacrycarpus imbricatus*.
***P. imbricatus*** Bl. See *Dacrycarpus imbricatus*.
***P. ladei*** Bail. See *Prumnopitys ladei*.
***P. lawrencii*** auct. non Hook. f. See *P. alpinus*.
***P. leptostachya*** Bl. See *P. neriifolius*.
***P. longifolius*** Parl. See *P. macrophyllus*.
***P. mannii*** Hook. f. See *Afrocarpus mannii*.
***P. meyerianus*** Endl. See *Afrocarpus falcata*.
***P. milanjianus*** Rendle. See *P. latifolius*.
***P. minor*** (Carr.) Parl. See *Retrophyllum minor*.
***P. montanus*** (Willd.) Lodd.See *Prumnopitys montana*.
***P. nageia*** R. Br. ex Mirb. See *Nageia nagi*.
***P. nagi*** (Thunb.) Mak. See *Nageia nagi*.
***P. pedunculata*** Bail. See *Sundacarpus amarus*.
***P. pungens*** D. Don. See *P. spinulosus*.
***P. richei*** Buchholz & Gray. See *P. matudae*.
***P. rospigliosi*** Pilger. See *Retrophyllum rospigliosi*.
***P. sect. Polypodiopsis*** Bertr. See *Retrophyllum*.
***P. spicatus*** R. Br. ex Mirb. See *Prumnopitys taxifolia*.
***P. taxifolius*** Kunth. See *Prumnopitys montana*.
***P. taxifolius*** Sol. ex D. Don non Kunth. See *Prumnopitys taxifolia*.
***P. taxodioides*** Carr. See *Falcatifolium taxoides*.
***P. thunbergii*** Hook. See *P. latifolius*.
***P. totara*** var. ***alpina*** Carr. See *P. alpinus*.
***P. totara*** var. ***hallii*** (T. Kirk) Pilger. See *P. hallii*.
***P. ulgurensis*** Pilger. See *P. latifolius*.
***P. usambarensis*** Pilger. See *Afrocarpus usambarensis*.
***P. ustus*** (Vieill.) Brongn. & Griseb. See *Parasitaxus ustus*.
***P. vitiensis*** Seem. See *Retrophyllum vitiense*.
***P. wallichiana*** Presl. See *Nageia wallichiana*.

**Podocytisus** Boiss. & Heldr. (From Gk *pous*, foot, and *Cytisus*.) Leguminosae (Papilionoideae). 1 species, an unarmed shrub to 2m; branchlets glaucous, terete when young. Leaves trifoliolate crowded; petioles 3–10mm; leaflets 5–15mm, obovate, mucronulate, sessile, grey-green; stipules absent. Flowers 5–10 in terminal, erect, often pyramidal racemes, to 15cm long; pedicels 5–8mm; bracteoles 1–2, minute, borne at midpoint of pedicel; calyx shortly campanulate, bilabiate, the upper lip lightly cleft, the lower lip longer than the upper, shortly 3-toothed; corolla 15–20mm, yellow, standard orbicular, wings and keel equalling standard, keel beaked; stamens monadelphous; style involute, stigma capitate. Fruit to 1cm, ovate to oblong, compressed, winged. Late summer. Balkans, Turkey, Greece. Z8.

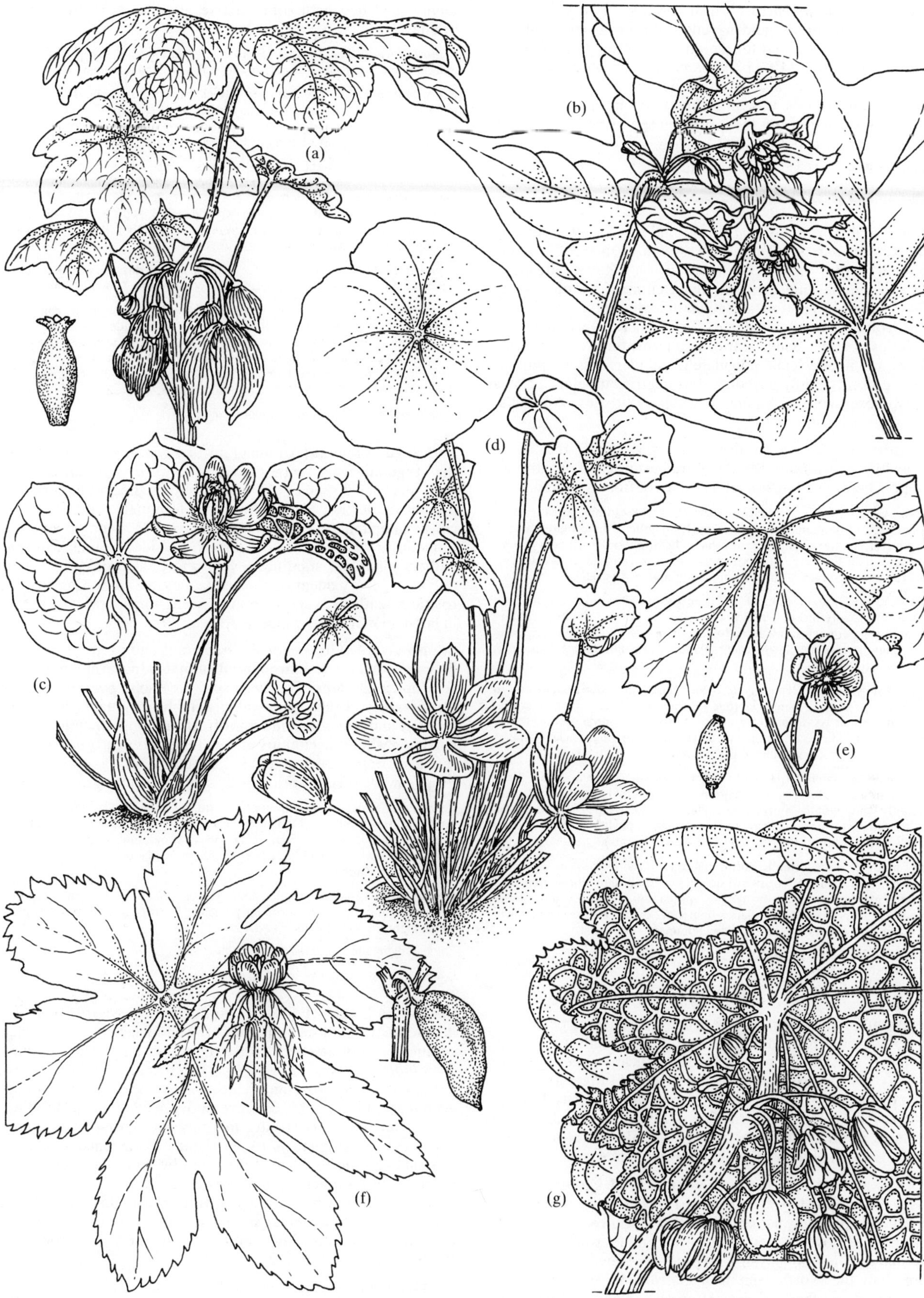


**Podophyllum and allies** (a) *Podophyllum pleianthum* (×0.66) (b) *Ranzania japonica* (×0.66) (c) *Jeffersonia ladiphylla* (×0.33) (d) *Jeffersonia dubia*(×0.66) (e) *Podophyllum hexandrum* (×0.5) (g) *Podophyllum versipelle* (×0.5)

CULTIVATION *P. caramanicus*, which occurs in dry scrubby habitats, is grown for its golden yellow flowers carried on the current season's growth, and for the attractive grey-green foliage. Hardy to about −10°C/14°F, *P. caramanicus* may be cut back by frosts in winter but, given good drainage and protection at the roots, will sprout from the base in spring. Grow in full sun in well-drained soil. Propagate from seed, or from semi-ripe cuttings in a closed case with gentle bottom heat.

***P. caramanicus*** Boiss. & Heldr. As for the genus.

For synonymy see *Cytisus* and *Laburnum*.

**Podolepis** Labill. (From Gk *pous*, foot, and *lepis*, scale, referring to the stalked phyllaries.) Compositae. About 18 species of annual to perennial herbs, usually cobwebby-hairy. Leaves alternate, rosulate and cauline, linear to lanceolate, entire. Capitula discoid or radiate, solitary, numerous, terminal or axillary; receptacle flat, naked; involucre campanulate to hemispheric, phyllaries in several series, outer sessile, scarious, intermediate with herbaceous claws; ray florets female, ligulate or tubular, yellow, pink or purple; disc florets hermaphrodite, asymmetric, tubular. Fruit a terete, papillose cypsela; pappus of capillary bristles. Australia. Z9.

CULTIVATION Useful for air drying as everlastings, treated as annuals as for *Acroclinium*. Seedlings are best pricked out into individual pots before setting out after danger of frost is passed.

***P. canescens*** Cunn. ex DC. Annual, to 80cm. Lvs to 8×15mm, mostly basal, oblanceolate, base attenuate, petiolate; stem lvs elliptic to lanceolate, sessile. Capitula several, in loose panicles; involucre hemispheric, to 2.5cm diam.; phyllaries lanceolate to ovate, light brown to red-brown, rugose, claws slender, glandular; ray florets to 1cm, yellow. Summer–autumn. S Australia.

***P. gracilis*** (Lehm.) Graham. Annual, to 50cm. Lvs usually cauline, to 8×1cm, oblanceolate to broadly linear, white-woolly beneath, sessile. Capitula solitary to many on flimsy peduncles; involucre to 2cm diam.; phyllaries light brown to red-brown, smooth, shining, claws slender, glandular; ray florets to 1.5cm, pink. Summer. W Australia.

***P. jaceoides*** (Sims) Voss. Perenn., to 70cm. Basal and lower stem lvs to 20×2cm, linear to oblanceolate, glabrous to scabrous above, sparsely white-woolly beneath, upper lvs linear to lanceolate, clasping. Capitula solitary to few in a loose cyme; involucre; to 3cm diam.; phyllaries ovate, acute, claws linear, glandular; ray florets to 2.5cm, yellow. E & SE Australia, Tasmania.

***P. robusta*** (Maid. & Betche) J.H. Willis. Robust perenn., to 60cm. Basal lvs to 20×4.5cm, spathulate, glabrous, amplexicaul, margins crinkled; stem lvs broad-linear, densely white-woolly above, sessile, clasping, decurrent. Capitula few in a dense, terminal cluster; involucre to 2.5cm diam.; phyllaries broad-ovate, smooth, scarious; ray florets to 2cm, yellow. E Australia (mts).

***P. rugata*** Labill. Perenn., often to 60cm, glabrous. Basal lvs to 8cm, narrowly lanceolate to oblanceolate, often absent; stem lvs to 10×1.5cm, elliptic, linear or oblanceolate, glabrous or sparsely hairy. Capitula solitary to few in a loose cyme; involucre to 3cm diam.; phyllaries imbricate, ovate, obtuse, red-brown, claws glandular; ray florets to 1.5cm, yellow. Summer. S Australia.

***P. acuminata*** R. Br. See *P. jaceoides*.
***P. aristata*** Benth. See *P. canescens*.
***P. rosea*** Steetz. See *P. gracilis*.

**Podophyllum** L. Berberidaceae. Around 5 species of perennial, rhizomatous herbs. Rhizome horizontal, occasionally tuber-like. Leaves large, peltate, palmately lobed, radical; flowering stem leaves 1 to several, similar to basal leaves. Flowers terminal, solitary or several; sepals usually 6, deciduous; petals 6–9, to 25mm, red-yellow or white; stamens 6–18; ovary ovoid; stigma sessile, large. Fruit a plum-like berry, large, fleshy, ovoid; seeds numerous. Eastern N America to E Asia and Himalaya.

CULTIVATION Plants for the woodland or wild garden, or for moist and shaded borders. The fruit of *P. peltatum* is edible when ripe but may be painfully cathartic; the rhizomes, leaves and seeds are poisonous. Grow in deep, humus-rich, moist soil, in filtered light or shade. The Himalayan *P. hexandrum* benefits from more moisture than the North American *P. peltatum*, so incorporate garden compost or other organic matter when planting. Propagate by division, from cuttings of the rhizome, or from fresh ripe seed, in a sandy propagating medium in the cold frame, or outdoors in a loamy seed bed with some coarse grit incorporated to improve drainage.

***P. aurantiocaule*** Hand.-Mazz. Similar to *P. hexandrum* except lvs 4–7-lobed, margin fine toothed, fls 2–4, pet. cream-yellow. China (Yunnan). Z7.

***P. hexandrum*** Royle. 25–30cm. Rhiz. thick. Stem fleshy, around 8mm diam. Lvs to 25cm across, 3–5-lobed, each lobe further 3-lobed at tip. Fls solitary, terminal, appearing before lvs mature; sep. 3; pet. 6, 25–40mm, white-rose pink; stamens 6, 16mm, fil. curved. Fr. 2–5cm, red, edible. W China, Himalaya. Z6.

***P. peltatum*** L. MAY APPLE; WILD MANDRAKE. Rhiz. creeping. Lvs 30cm across deeply palmately lobed ×5–9, lobes 2-lobed at apex, sometimes finely hairy on lower surface. Flowering stem with 2–3 lvs or leafless. Fls nodding, 3–5cm wide, borne in axils of upper lf or between two highest lvs; pet. large, 25–40mm, white, apex toothed; stamens 12–18. Fr. green, ripening to yellow, 2–5mm, edible. Spring. Eastern N America south to Texas. Z4.

***P. pleianthum*** Hance. Similar to *P. versipelle* except rhiz. very thick to tuberous, lf lobes shallow, blunt, fls 5–8, pet. 6–9, to 60mm diam. C & SE China. Z7.

***P. versipelle*** Hance. Rhiz. not creeping, thick. Stems pale green, annual, erect. Lvs peltate, 40cm across, irregularly very deeply divided, 5–8 lobed, margin finely toothed; flowering stem lvs 2. Infl. an umbel, 8-fld, terminal, exceeded and concealed by highest lf; pedicel pendulous, to 5cm; fls deep crimson, malodorous; sep. 6, 12×6mm, hairy on the back; pet. 6, 18–35×6–8mm, glabrous; stamens 6, 18mm. Fr. less than 4cm, fleshy. China, Tibet. Z7.

***P. japonicum*** Itô. See *Ranzania japonica*.

**Podranea** Sprague. (An anagram of *Pandorea*, another genus in the Bignoniaceae, with which *Podranea* was once united.) Bignoniaceae. 2 species of climbing shrubs. Leaves imparipinnate; pseudostipules not leafy. Flowers in terminal, pyramidal thyrses; calyx campanulate, lobes regular; corolla 5cm, showy, pink, funnelform-campanulate, glabrous outside; stamens included; anthers glabrous; staminode very short, glabrous; disc cupular-pulvinate; ovary linear, glabrous; ovules in 8 rows. Capsule linear, rostrate, leathery, valves smooth; seeds small, transverse-oblong, in large membranous wings. S Africa. Z9.

CULTIVATION Grown for their fragrant and pretty, foxglove-like flowers, often carried throughout summer. In warm temperate and subtropical gardens, *Podranea* spp. are useful evergreen climbers for pergolas, trellis and walls; established plants are drought tolerant and will withstand light frosts although they may become partly or wholly deciduous at low temperatures. *Podranea* requires less water but otherwise is cultivated as for *Bignonia*. Propagate by seed in spring or by semi-ripe cuttings.

***P. brycei*** (N.E. Br.) Sprague. QUEEN OF SHEBA; ZIMBABWE CLIMBER. Stem quadrangulate, nodes pubesc. Leaflets 9–11, *c*2–4×0.6–1.3cm, margin serrulate. Infl. to 10cm, lax; cal. to 1.3×1.3cm, scaly, lobes deltoid, mucronate; cor. 3.8×1.8cm at throat, lobes 1.3–2.3cm, pale purple, villous inside tube, lobes ciliate. Capsule to 30×1.5cm. Zimbabwe.

***P. ricasoliana*** (Tanf.) Sprague. PINK TRUMPET VINE. Woody climber. Leaflets 5–11, margin entire. Infl. terminal panicles; fls to 6cm, pale pink striped red, throat glabrous; cal. inflated. S Africa.

For synonymy see *Pandorea* and *Tecoma*.

For illustration see HERBS.

**Poellnitzia** Uitew. (For Karl von Poellnitz (1896–1945), specialist in succulent plants.) Liliaceae (Asphodelaceae). 1 species, a succulent perennial herb, offsetting from base, closely allied to *Astroloba*. Leaves 2.5–4×2× to 0.4cm, 4-ranked, ovoid-triangular, squarrose-imbricate, apex triquetrous, pungent-acuminate, thick, hard, concave above, yellow-green to glaucous green, longitudinally striate, margins and apex of keel minutely scabrid. Flowering stems to 30×7cm; inflorescence a subsecund, terminal raceme to 12cm, subtended by lanceolate, 6mm, fertile bracts; pedicels erect, 6–7mm; flowers 2–2.5×0.5–0.6cm, narrowly tubular, tube pale red, segments with brown midveins, connivent, margins minutely crenate; stamens scarcely exceeded tube; ovary cylindric; style equalling anthers. Summer. S Africa (Cape Province; Bonnie Vale). Z9.

CULTIVATION As for *Haworthia*.

***P. rubrifolia*** (L. Bol.) Uitew. As for the genus.

For synonymy see *Aloe* and *Apicra*.

**Pogonia** Juss. (From Gk *pogon*, beard, referring to the bearded or fringed crest of the lip typical of the genus.) Orchidaceae. Some 10 species of erect, terrestrial orchids. Roots fibrous, slender. Tubers globose, usually producing a single leaf. Inflorescence 1 to 3-flowered; flowers terminal; sepals subequal, free or slightly ringent, usually erect; petals similar to sepals, held over lip, shorter and wider than sepals; lip sessile or clawed, erect, simple or 3-lobed, inrolled round column, smooth or lammellate, bearded or fringed; column free, elongate, subterete, wingless, footless, clinandrium denticulate, anther terminal, operculate, incumbent, pollinia 2, granular. Widely distributed, mostly temperate Asia and N America. Z3.

CULTIVATION Hardy orchids suitable for bog gardens, streamsides and damp acid pockets in the rock garden. See ORCHIDS, The Hardy Species.

***P. ophioglossoides*** (L.) Juss. Roots fleshy, pubesc. Stems to 40cm, slender, terete, green or brown-green. Lvs to 12×3cm, ovate to elliptic or ovate-lanceolate, obtuse to subacute. Fls rose to white, fragrant; dorsal sep. to 23×6mm, elliptic-oblong to linear-oblong, subobtuse, lateral sep. to 27×6mm, linear-oblong to linear-lanceolate, acute to obtuse; pet. to 25×11mm, obovate-elliptic to oblong-elliptic, rounded; lip to 25×10mm, narrowly oblong-spathulate, apex lacerate-dentate, disc bearded, with short, fleshy, yellow-white bristles; column to 10mm. US.

***P. divaricata*** (L.) R. Br. See *Cleistes divaricata*.
***P. rosea*** (Lindl.) Rchb. f. See *Cleistes rosea*.
For further synonymy see *Arethusa*.

**Pogonopus** Klotzsch. (From Gk *pogon*, beard, and *pous*, foot, referring to shape of flower.) Rubiaceae. Some 5 species of shrubs or trees. Leaves petiolate, opposite, thin-textured; stipules interpetiolar, deciduous. Flowers in loose terminal, cymose panicles, showy; calyx turbinate, 5-toothed, deciduous, one tooth developed into enlarged, petiolate, leaflike, brightly coloured limb; corolla tubular, pubescent at throat, limb short, lobes 5; stamens 5, inserted in corolla tube, anthers versatile, exserted, linear; ovary 2-celled, style branches 2, oblong or linear, obtuse, ovules many. Fruit a capsule, somewhat woody, apically areolate, 2-celled, 2-valved from top; seeds numerous, endosperm fleshy. Tropical America. Z10.

CULTIVATION As for *Bouvardia*.

***P. speciosus*** (Jacq.) Schum. Shrub or tree, to 10m. Branches russet or grey, lenticellate; branchlets pubesc. to almost glabrous. Lvs to 22×10cm, obovate to oval- or elliptic-obovate, apex narrowly acute, base cuneate, pubesc. beneath, 8–13-veined; petioles subterete, to 2cm, sulcate, minutely pubesc.; stipules to 5mm, triangular, short-pointed, minutely pubesc. Pedicels to 1cm, minutely pubesc.; bracts linear or leaf-like; cal. to 5mm, minutely pubesc., teeth triangular, short-pointed, enlarged lobe ovate, to 5×4cm, obtuse at apex and base, crimson to purple, on petiole to 2.5cm; cor. to 3cm, pubesc., purple or pink, lobes triangular-ovate, acute at apex. Fr. to 7×6mm. Summer. C to Northern S America.

***P. exsertus*** Ørst. See *P. speciosus*.
For further synonymy see *Macrocnemum*.

**Poinciana** L.
***P. gilliesii*** Wallich ex Hook. See *Caesalpinia gilliesii*.
***P. pulcherrima*** L. See *Caesalpinia pulcherrima*.
***P. regia*** Bojer. See *Delonix regia*.

**Poincianella** Britt. & Rose.
***P. mexicana*** (Gray) Britt. & Rose. See *Caesalpinia mexicana*.

**Poinsettia** Graham. See *Euphorbia*.

**Poisonous plants**. Many plants contain chemicals which are poisonous to humans, livestock and game animals. A great many plant families contain some poisonous species, the Euphorbiaceae (spurge family), Ranunculaceae (buttercup family) and Solanaceae (nightshades, angel's trumpets, tobaccos etc.) having many more poisonous species than most. In some plants every part is poisonous, in others, poison may be restricted to one kind of organ – rhizome or rootstock as in *Convallaria* and *Iris*, fruit as in *Daphne*, or foliage as in *Rheum*. In the latter – which includes rhubarb – the blade of the leaf is poisonous, whereas the fleshy petiole or stem which we eat is not. In some cases parts of the plant which are poisonous can be rendered innocuous by cooking, the most widespread example used as a staple food being cassava or manioc (*Manihot esculenta*), where cooking is combined with crushing the starchy roots to expel the prussic acid within them. In the distant past, painful experiment must have led to the building up of a corpus of knowledge of what was poisonous, what edible, and what could be transformed from one to the other (as with cassava), and this knowledge was passed down through the generations. This basic knowledge is certainly shared in part with primates. Equally the uses of poisonous plants were developed, including such well-known examples as the curare and wourate arrow-poisons from *Strychnos toxicaria* in South America (*S. nux-vomica* is the source of strychnine), *Antiaris toxicaria* – the upas tree of fable, to sleep under which meant death – in tropical Asia, and other tropical plants in different continents, used primarily against game animals. Later, plant poisons were administered more subtly, for instance in food, to kill fellow human beings, like hemlock (*Conium*) with which Socrates met his end, and the angel's trumpets (*Brugmansia*) widely used in the tropics. Such plants are, or were, the stock-in-trade of medicine men and shamans the world over. Some of the poisons, like the morphine of *Papaver somniferum*, and equally curare, became transformed into useful drugs and anaesthetics (see also ETHNOBOTANY).

It should perhaps be observed that the notion that plants are poisonous to deter predators is certainly not universally true. Although many plants poisonous to man are equally so to mammals, they are not poisonous to small harmful predators and parasites including slugs and snails, sap-sucking insects and nematodes (eelworms).

A great many garden plants are poisonous, but deaths resulting from ingestion of these plants by humans are low in comparison to the total number of reported plant poisonings and in comparison to other accidental poisonings. This is partly because the few dangerous plants are well known and therefore avoided, and partly because the less dangerous ones are toxic only if eaten in large amounts. Humans are unlikely to eat these plants in large quantity as they are usually unpalatable. While it can be stated with certainty that a particular plant is poisonous, because of the frequency or severity of incidents reported because of it, it is difficult to state that a plant is definitely not poisonous just because there are no documented incidents. There are also differences in susceptibility to toxins between individuals and differences in toxicity within some plant species dependent on genetics, environment and maturity. The toxicity of many cultivated species and varieties of plants is often not known. In instances where poisonous properties are known, these are mentioned in the descriptions of species in this work, though some of the better-known poisonous species are mentioned below as illustrative examples.

Young children are most at risk from plant poisoning because they frequently put things into their mouths and colourful flowers or berries may be especially attractive to them. In addition, their small body size means a higher proportion of substance taken in comparison to the same amount being taken by adults. Although relatively few plants are likely to be fatal if eaten, the effects are often disagreeable and so young children should be kept away from any poisonous plants, and older children taught to recognise them and be warned of the dangers. Medical advice must always be sought if poisoning is suspected. A representative portion of the plant which was ingested will be helpful for its identification and to determine the extent of poisoning.

In some species all parts of the plant are very poisonous even when eaten in small quantities, for instance monkshood (*Aconitum napellus*), yew (*Taxus baccata*), where only the fleshy aril round the seed is not poisonous, oleander (*Nerium oleander*), where deaths have even followed the use of the twigs for skewering meat in kebabs, hemlock (*Conium maculatum*), where children have died simply by using the hollow stems as blowpipes, and castor-oil plant (*Ricinus communis*), where the highest concentrations of toxins are present in the seed, one or two or which can kill a child. Another deadly seed is the red and black precatory bean (*Abrus precatoria*), often made into necklaces, one of which can be lethal to a child.

As already noted, toxins are often concentrated in a specific part of the plant; thus *Amaryllis* and other monocots like *Colchicum*, *Galanthus*, *Hyacinthus* and *Ornithogalum* have toxins concentrated in their bulbs (forms of sea squill, *Urginea maritima*, are used for rat poison). The less palatable green parts of plants, including unripe berries, are often more toxic than the colourful ripe fruits (probably a device to prevent the fruits being eaten by animals until the seed is mature). This is the case with the *Solanum* species of nightshade, whereas deadly nightshade (*Atropa*) concentrates toxins in the ripe berries. Seeds of *Laburnum*, *Wisteria*, *Malus* (apple) and *Prunus* (peaches, plums, etc.) are poisonous. Foliage is poisonous in a wide range of ornamental garden shrubs and herbaceous plants, and in *Dieffenbachia*, widely grown as a house plant, where eating a leaf or stem causes severe inflammation of the mouth and throat (hence the name 'dumb cane'). Toxicity may decrease as the plant matures, for example larkspurs (*Delphinium* spp.) are most toxic when young.

Mistaken identification can lead to poisonous plants being eaten instead of edible ones. Various poisonous bulbs, for instance those of bluebells and daffodils, have been eaten in mistake for onions, and deadly nightshade berries have been mistaken for blueberries. People making herbal teas have mistakenly included plants containing toxins in sufficient quantities to produce harmful effects.

Young pets such as puppies and kittens are, like children, inclined to eat anything that they encounter, including plant material, and should be kept away from potentially hazardous plants. Veterinary advice should be sought if poisoning is suspected. Poisoning of livestock by plants is often more serious than in other animal groups, as a result of the large quantities taken and the longer time spent on digestion. Thoughtless disposal of garden rubbish such as hedge trimmings from plants like box (*Buxus sempervirens*), laburnum (*Laburnum anagyroides*), cherry laurel (*Prunus laurocerasus*), privet (*Ligustrum* species), *Rhododendron* spp. and yew, into fields where it may be accessible to livestock, is an important cause of sporadic poisoning. Even dried material of many poisonous plants (as in hay) can have the same level of toxicity as fresh material.

It should be added that a number of fungi are toxic, some, like the aptly named death-caps (*Amanite phalloides* and *A. verna*) being deadly. Mushrooms and 'toadstools' should never be eaten unless identification is totally positive.

It is important that gardeners should be aware of the risk of poisoning by certain plants or products made from plants, due to physical contact with them. This type of poisoning rarely results in death, but may produce a skin reaction known as contact dermatitis, ranging from mild irritation to chronic blistering. The mechanisms used by plants to cause this dermatitis can be divided into five groups: (a) mechanical irritants such as cactus spines; (b) stings, such as those produced by stinging nettles (*Urticaceae*), where a toxin is mechanically injected. (c) phototoxins, which are chemicals activated by sunlight, such as those produced by rue (*Ruta graveolens*) and giant hogweed (*Heracleum mantegazzianum*); sap of the latter can raise huge blisters on unprotected skin and cause permanent scarring; (d) allergens, which cause the majority of contact dermatitis. They induce sensitization almost immediately or sometime later and sensitivity to them may change with continued exposure. Susceptibility to allergens varies greatly between individual people, as does the degree of symptoms experienced. Delay in reaction time, and the fact that in some cases symptoms may not be restricted to the part of the body which came into contact with the plant, can make it difficult to pinpoint the offending plant species. Allergy to a particular group of chemicals in one plant species can infer allergy to similar chemicals in others. Examples of allergenic plants producing contact dermatitis are: *Dendranthema* (*Chrysanthemum*), *Primula obconica*, ivy (*Hedera helix*) and poison ivy (*Rhus radicans*). A few people suffer skin rashes from fruits like mango (*Mangifera*) and cashew (*Anacardium*) which belong to the same family as poison ivy. Some apparently harmless gardener's pursuits like removing seeds from the seed-cases of *Helleborus* spp. can produce unpleasant skin reactions (the whole plant is highly toxic). Hayfever falls into the allergen-producing groups of symptoms and is the result of allergy to wind borne pollen. (e) The fifth type of mechanism is direct irritant, where everyone will have a reaction on their first and every contact if the concentration of toxin is sufficient. Many plants are capable of evoking this type of dermatitis, for instance irritation from the sap of *Daphne*, *Euphorbia* and *Ranunculus* spp. Other examples of direct irritant action are plants producing irritation of the gut, such as hot peppers (*Capsicum* species). Contact with potentially dermatitic plants can be avoided by wearing protective clothing. If the symptoms are severe or persistent medical advice should be sought.

**Polanisia** Raf. (From Gk *polys*, many, and *anisos*, unequal, referring to the numerous stamens which are unequal.) Capparidaceae. Some 6 species of annual or perennial herbs. Stems simple or branched, erect. Leaves trifoliate, petiolate; leaflets entire; stipules linear, small. Inflorescence an elongate, terminal raceme; sepals free, deciduous; petals clawed to subsessile, dimorphic, white-cream or pink to magenta, truncate or emarginate, erose or laciniate; stamens 8–27, unequal; style slender, stigma inconspicuous. Fruit a silique, elongate, usually sessile; seeds numerous, subspherical. N America, Mexico.

CULTIVATION As for *Cleome*.

***P. dodecandra*** (L.) DC. To 1m, sparsely branched at base, pubesc. Lf petioles to 6cm; leaflets to 6×2cm, narrowly lanceolate to ovate or obovate, acute to rounded. Infl. to 4cm, densely many-fld; bracts suborbicular to lanceolate; sep. to 9mm, ovate, or lanceolate, obtuse to acuminate; pet. to 27×6mm, white to deep pink, obcordate to spathulate, deeply emarginate to truncate; stamens 10–27, fil. to 5cm, purple, anth. to 2mm; style to 4cm. Fr. to 9.5×1cm, oblong to fusiform; seeds red to dark brown. Central and Eastern N America. Z5.

***P. tenuifolia*** Torr. & A. Gray. To 90cm, closely branched. Lf petioles to 2cm; leaflets to 50×2mm, linear or filiform, mucronate, fleshy. Infl. to 15cm, few-fld; sep. to 2.5mm, triangular-lanceolate, acute, reflexed; pet. to 7.5×5mm, white, sometimes tinged purple, broadly ovate to spathulate, emarginate or truncate, strongly dimorphic; stamens 8–13, fil. to 6mm, subclavate, white, anth. to 2mm; style to 4mm, stigma strongly capitate. Fr. to 70×2mm, narrowly linear-fusiform; seeds orange-brown to grey-brown. Southeastern N America. Z9.

***P. graveolens*** Raf. See *P. dodecandra*.

**Polaskia** Backeb. (For C. Polaski, of Oklahoma.) Cactaceae. 2 species of small, broad-crowned trees resembling *Myrtillocactus* but with somewhat larger flowers. Fls small, urceolate or campanulate, diurnal, creamy white or pale pink. Fr. globose, 2–4cm, red, juicy, edible. Seeds broadly oval, 1–1.6×0.8–1.3mm, black-brown, shiny, ruminate, keeled or not; relief low-domed. S Mexico.

CULTIVATION Grow in an intermediate greenhouse, min. 10–15°C/50–60°F; use 'standard' cactus compost: moderate to high inorganic content (more than 50% grit), pH 6–7.5; shade in hot weather; maintain low humidity; keep dry from mid-autumn until early spring, except for light misting on warm days in late winter.

***P. chende*** (Roland-Goss.) Gibson & Horak. Tree to 7m, with trunk 50–80×25–30cm and broad crown; stems erect or upcurved, 5–7cm diam., yellow-green; ribs 7–9, 2–3cm high, fairly acute; areoles *c*2cm apart, 5mm diam., almost black; central spines 0 or 1, rudimentary; radial spines 5(–6), 5–15(–30)mm, pale brown at first. Fl. campanulate, to 5×5cm, delicately scented; pericarpel and tube 1.5cm diam; scales and areoles numerous, small, the latter with 2–3 bristles to 1cm or more; outer tepals tinged purple-red, inner pale pink; stigmas 12, pale yellow. Fr. globose, 3.5–4cm diam., purple with numerous spines to 8mm; pulp purple. S Mexico (Puebla, Oaxaca). Z9.

***P. chichipe*** (Roland-Goss.) Backeb. Small tree to 5m, with short trunk to 1m diam. and dense candelabriform crown; juvenile stems pruinose; adult stems to 7cm diam., clear green; ribs 9–12, 2cm high, sinuate; areoles in the sinuses, 1–1.5cm apart; central spine 1, somewhat longer than the radials; radial spines 6–9, 3–10mm, grey with almost black tip. Fl. subapical, 1 per areole, urceolate-rotate, *c*3×3cm; pericarpel and tube with imbricate apiculate scales, tube very short; tepals creamy white, soon revolute. Fr. globose, 2–3cm diam.; pericarp red, with caducous areoles and small spines 3–4mm; pulp juicy, red. S Mexico (S Puebla, N Oaxaca). Z9.

For further synonymy see *Heliabravoa* and *Lemaireocereus*.

**POLEMONIACEAE** Juss. PHLOX FAMILY. Dicot. 20 genera and 275 species of herbs, shrubs, lianes (*Cobaea*) or small trees (*Cantua*). Leaves simple, pinnate or palmate, alternate, less often opposite or whorled; stipules absent. Flowers bisexual, usually in head-like cymes, rarely solitary; calyx (4)5(6) fused sepals, lobes sometimes unequal; corolla (4)5 (6) fused petals, often bilabiate, lobes convolute in bud; stamens attached to corolla tube and alternate with lobes, sometimes at different levels; annular nectary-disc usually around ovary; ovary superior, (2)3(4) fused carpels, with as many locules; placentation axile, style terminal with as many stigma-lobes; ovules 1-numerous per locule. Fruit a capsule, usually loculicidal, sometimes indehiscent; seeds 1-numerous, often mucilaginous when wetted, endosperm scanty or copious, oily. America, especially West and North, Eurasia. *Cantua, Cobaea, Collomia, Eriastrum, Gilia, Ipomopsis, Langloisia, Leptodactylon, Linanthus, Navarretia, Phlox, Polemonium.*

**Polemonium** L. (Name used by Dioscorides, possibly for the early Athenian philosopher Polemon, or perhaps from *polemos* war.) JACOB'S LADDER; SKY PILOT. Polemoniaceae. 25 species of erect, decumbent or spreading annuals or more commonly rhizomatous and caespitose perennials, often foul-smelling, to 5m. Leaves usually alternate, pinnate compound or very deeply pinnatifid, leaflets entire or divided. Inflorescence a lax or dense, axillary or terminal cyme; flowers sometimes solitary; calyx 5-lobes, (sub)campanulate, herbaceous, enlarging with fruit but not rupturing, lobes acuminate to deltoid; corolla narrowly funnelform to rotate-campanulate, usually blue or white, rarely purple, yellow or pink, lobes rounded to spathulate; stamens and style included to exserted, filaments equally inserted. Fruit ovoid to subglobose, 3-locular; seeds 1 to many per locule, elongate, sometimes mucilaginous when wet. Temperate to Arctic regions, N Hemisphere, southern S America, especially montane areas.

CULTIVATION *P. caeruleum* is native to damp grassland and rocky habitats, frequently on limestone soils; *P. boreale* occurs in stony and sandy soils in arctic Europe, *P. viscosum* occupies similar niches in alpine and arctic habitats in western North America. *P. reptans* is found in damp woodland and meadow. Sometimes short lived but often seeding to the point of nuisance, the taller *Polemonium* spp. are valued for the loose clusters of flowers carried on slender but sturdy stems above the basal rosettes of fine pinnate foliage. Grown in the herbaceous and mixed border and in the wild garden; *P. caeruleum* is a tolerant cottage garden favourite and is occasionally grown in the herb garden, recommended by Culpeper in the treatment of 'malignant fevers and pestilential distempers'. *P. reptans* is useful in moist shaded borders. Low-growing alpine species such as *P. viscosum, P. brandegei* and *P. pulcherrimum* are suited to the rock garden; *P. boreale* is more safely grown with protection from winter wet in the alpine house.

Grow in sun or part shade in moist, well drained and fertile soil; *P. viscosum* in lime-free soil. Dead head to prevent self seeding. Grow alpines in a gritty, well-drained soil enriched with leafmould with shade from the hottest sun in summer. In pots use a mix of equal parts loam, leafmould and sharp sand over good drainage. Water moderately when in growth and keep almost dry in winter. Propagate species by seed in autumn, named and desirable varieties by division in spring.

***P. boreale*** Adams. NORTHERN JACOB'S LADDER. Perenn. 8–30cm tall; habit erect or ascending, pubesc. or glandular. Lvs mostly basal, with 13–23 pubesc. leaflets, usually 4–12×1–5mm, oval or elliptic to oblong, apex obtuse or acute. Infl. capitate; cal. 5–10mm, campanulate, lobes oblong to lanceolate; cor. 1.5–2cm, campanulate, blue to violet, lobes slightly longer than tube. Summer. Circumboreal. Z3 'Album': fls white.

***P. brandegei*** (A. Gray) E. Greene. Erect perenn. 10–30cm tall, densely glandular-pubesc., viscid. Lvs mostly basal, pinnate at base, leaflets many, appearing whorled, oval to narrowly oblong, entire or divided. Infl. a short raceme-like cluster; cal. to 8mm; cor. 2–2.5cm, funnelform with a very narrow tube. ssp. ***brandegei.*** Lvs aromatic. Cor. yellow or golden-yellow. Late spring–summer. US (Montana to Colorado and New Mexico). Z4. ssp. ***mellitum*** (A. Gray) Wherry. Lvs musky-scented. Fls pleasantly scented; cor. white to ochroleucous. Summer–early autumn. US (Wyoming and Nevada to Colorado and New Mexico). Z3.

***P. caeruleum*** L. JACOB'S LADDER; GREEK VALERIAN; CHARITY. Perenn., 30–90cm tall, glabrous at base, glandular-pubesc. towards infl. Lvs to 40ccm, imparipinnate, leaflets usually 17–27, lanceolate to elliptic or oblong-lanceolate, subsessile and smaller toward apex. Infl. terminal or axillary, lax; fls on short ped.; cal. 3–7mm, campanulate, lobes lanceolate, acute; cor. 8–15mm, 10–25mm diam., rotate-campanulate, blue, rarely white, lobes ovate, subacute to rounded. Fr. subglobose; seeds rugose, not mucilaginous when wet. 'Album': fls white. ssp. ***caeruleum.*** Basal lvs with 17–27 leaflets. Infl. many-fld; cor. 8–15mm, blue; stamens exserted. Late Spring–summer. N & C Europe, N Asia. ssp. ***amygdalinum*** (Wherry) Munz. Basal lvs with 19–27 leaflets. Infl. strict; cor. 13–15mm, blue; stamens included; style exserted. Summer. US (Alaska to California and Colorado), Canada (Yukon and British Columbia). Z2. ssp. ***himalayanum*** (Bak.) Hara. Cal. very densely glandular-hairy; cor. to 4cm diam., lilac-blue, lobes to 2cm, ovate. Spring–summer. Pakistan to W Nepal. var. ***lacteum*** (Lehm.) Benth. Cor. white. N & C Europe, N Asia. ssp. ***van-bruntiae*** (Britt.) J.F. Davidson. Stamens and style long-exserted. Summer. NW US. ssp. ***villosum*** (J.D. Rudolph ex Georgi) Brand. Basal lvs with to 17 leaflets. Infl few-fld; cor. 18–22mm. Summer. US (Alaska) and Canada (British Columbia) to Arctic and Subarctic Europe and N Asia. Z2.

***P. californicum*** Eastw. Perenn., 10–20(–30)cm tall, glandular-hairy; stems solitary to subcaespitose. Lvs reduced above base, leaflets 11–23, 5–20m, ovate to lanceolate, usually acute, glandular-pilose to subglabrous. Infl. cymose, with entire to pinnatifid bracts; cal. *c*5–8mm, narrowly campanulate; corolla 8–15mm diam., rotate-campanulate, tube white, lobes blue. Fr. *c*3mm; seeds *c*1.5mm, dark. Summer. NW US. Z6.

***P. carneum*** A. Gray. Erect perenn., 10–40(–100) cm tall; rhiz. horizontal, woody. Lvs with 11–19 elliptic or lanceolate to ovate leaflets, usually 1.5–4.5×0.6–2.3cm, long-petiolate at base, shorter on stem. Infl. lax, terminal; fls few; cal. 7.5–14mm; cor. (1.5–)1.8–2.8cm, campanulate, usually pink or yellow, sometimes dark purple to lavender, rarely pink or blue. Late spring–summer. US (W Washington to N California). Z6. 'Album': fls white. 'Rose Queen': fls deeper pink.

***P. delicatum*** Rydb. SKUNKLEAF JACOB'S LADDER. Small, slender perenn., 10–20cm tall, spreading via a slender rootstock, glandular-hairy. Lvs 3–8cm, with 5–11 leaflets, 3–20mm, oblong, ovate or ovate-lanceolate, acute, very thin. Infl. compound, with 3–4 fls per branch; pedicels 5–15mm, cal. 4–5, lobes lanceolate, acute; cor. *c*7×8mm, campanulate, blue to violet; stamens usually included. Summer. US (Idaho to New Mexico and Arizona). Z6.

***P. elegans*** E. Greene. Dwarf, caespitose perenn., to 15cm tall, densely glandular-pubesc. Lvs mostly basal, base expanded and papery, on short petioles, leaflets usually 13–27, 2.5–6×1–3.5mm, entire. Infl. capitate-cymose; cal. 5.5–8.5mm, lobes (sub)acute; cor. 1.2–1.5cm, tubular-funnelform or funnelform, blue, lobes shorter than tube, spreading; stamens exserted. Summer. Washington to British Columbia. Z5.

***P. foliosissimum*** A. Gray. LEAFY JACOB'S LADDER. Erect perenn., 40–120cm tall, sparsely villous to puberulent, often glandular toward infl. Lvs 3–15cm, leaflets (3–)5–25, 0.8–5×0.2–1.2cm, narrowly oblong or lanceolate to elliptic, in ranks, terminal largest. Infl. terminal and axillary, corymbiform, dense; fls sessile or subsessile; cal. 4.5–9mm; cor. 1–1.8cm, campanulate, blue-violet, cream or white; stamens included or exserted. US (Utah, Nevada and Wyoming). var. ***foliosissimum.*** Mainly 50–90cm tall. Cor. blue to violet, rarely white. Seeds mucilaginous when wet. Summer–early autumn. Z4. US (Idaho and Wyoming to Arizona and New Mexico). var. ***alpinum*** Brand. Mainly 80–120cm tall. Cor. white, lobes triangular-attenuate. Summer. Z5. var. ***flavum*** (E. Greene) Davidson. Stout, 40–70cm tall. Cor. yellow, tawny-red outside, lobes acute or acuminate. Summer–early autumn. US (New Mexico, S Arizona). Z3.

***P. mexicanum*** Cerv. ex Lagasca. Erect perenn., 30–40cm tall, glandular-hairy, viscid. Lvs pinnate, mostly on stem, leaflets 23–27, subsessile, ovate to elliptic or lanceolate, 1–1.2cm acute. Infl. corymb-like, axillary, few-fld; cal. to 1cm; corolla 1–1.2cm diam., broadly campanulate, violet-blue. Summer early autumn. Mexico. Z7.

***P. pauciflorum*** S. Wats. Perenn. to 50cm. Lvs to 15cm, mostly on stem, leaflets 11–25, to 25×6mm, elliptic or lanceolate, glandular-pubesc. toward infl. Infl. at branch apices, 1–2-fld; pedicels to 4.5cm; cal. *c*1.5cm, lobes acuminate, sharp; cor. to 3(–4)cm, funnelform, yellow or yellow-green, often purple-hued, held horizontally, lobes to 1cm; stamens equalling tube. Summer. US (W Texas to S Arizona), Mexico (Chihuahua). Z7.

***P. pulcherrimum*** Hook. Perenn., 0.5–3(–5)m tall; stems more or less erect, subglabrous except glandular infl. Lvs with 11–25(–37) leaflets, to 3.5×1.5cm, opposite or offset, cauline lvs reduced. Infl. dense; cal. 4–6mm, lobes lanceolate-oblong, (sub)acute; cor. 7–13mm, (sub)campanulate, blue to violet or white, tube yellow inside, lobes 8–25mm. Late spring–summer. US (Alaska) and Canada (Yukon) to US (W Utah and California). Z4.

***P. reptans*** L. GREEK VALERIAN. Erect or spreading perenn., 30–70cm tall, glabrous, spreading via a creeping rhiz. Lvs pinnate, leaflets 7–19, (sub)sessile, elliptic, oblong or oblong-lanceolate, apiculate or acute. Infl. lax; pedicels 5–10mm; cal. 5–10mm, lobes triangular to triangular-ovate; cor. 1.5–2cm diam., blue, lobes cuneate or spathulate. Fr. 5–6.5mm, oval or ovoid-oval. Spring–early summer. E US. Z4. 'Album': fls white. 'Blue Pearl': to 25cm; fls blue. 'Lambrook Manor': mound-forming to 45cm; fls lilac-blue.

***P.×richardsonii*** hort. (*?P. caeruleum × P. reptans.*) Perenn. to 50cm, with a somewhat creeping rhizome. Fls to 4cm diam., sky-blue. Late spring–summer. Garden origin. Z6. 'Album': fls white.

***P. viscosum*** Nutt. Perenn., to 20(–40)cm tall, densely glandular. Lvs to 15(–20)cm, mostly basal, short-petiolate, base papery, leaflets many, usually 2–5-lobed almost to base, seg. 1.5–6×3mm. Infl. densely cymose-capitate; cal. 7–12mm, lobes narrow, acute; cor. (1.3–)1.7–2.5(–3)cm, tubular-funnelform to subfunnelform, blue to violet, lobes shorter than tube. Summer. Canada (British Columbia) to US (Arizona, New Mexico and Montana). Z5.

***P. yezoense*** (Miyabe & Kudô) Kitam. Perenn. 35–45cm tall, spreading via short rhiz. Lvs at base 13–16cm, on 3.5cm long petioles, leaflets 19–23, ovate-lanceolate, apex mucronate, smaller above. Infl. lax, corymb-like, glandular-hairy; pedicels 8–12mm; cal. 9–10mm, lobes lanceolate; cor 2.2–2.5cm, blue, lobes elliptic, apex emarginate. Late spring–summer. Japan (Hokkaido). Z5.

***P.*** **cultivars**. 'Hopley's': fls pale pink. 'Sapphire': fls small, light blue. 'Pink Beauty': fls tinged purple.

***P. acutiflorum*** Willd. ex Roem. & Schult. See *P. caeruleum* ssp. *villosum*.
***P. amoenum*** Piper. See *P. carneum*.
***P. caeruleum*** var. ***grandiflorum*** Manning. See *P. caeruleum* ssp. *himalayanum*.
***P. caeruleum L.*** var. ***album*** hort. See *P. caeruleum* ssp. *himalayanum* var. *lacteum*.
***P. caeruleum L.*** var. ***yezoense*** Miyabe & Kudô. See *P. yezoense*.
***P. confertum*** A. Gray. See *Polemonium viscosum*.
***P. filicinum*** E. Greene. See *P. foliosissimum*.
***P. flavum*** E. Greene. See *P. foliosissimum* var. *flavum*.
***P. haydenii*** Nels. See *P. pulcherrimum*.
***P. himalaiacum*** hort. See *P. caeruleum* ssp. *himalayanum*.
***P. himalayanum*** hort. See *P. caeruleum* ssp. *himalayanum*.
***P. humile*** Salisb. See *P. reptans*.
***P. lindleyi*** Wherry. See *P. pulcherrimum*.
***P. mellitum*** A. Gray. See *P. brandegei* ssp. *mellitum*.
***P. occidentale*** E. Greene. See *P. caeruleum* ssp. *amygdalinum*.
***P. sibiricum*** D. Don. See *P. caeruleum*.
***P. van-bruntiae*** Britt. See *P. caeruleum* ssp. *van-bruntiae*.
***P. villosum*** J.D. Rudolph ex Georgi. See *P. caeruleum* ssp. *villosum*.
***P. viscosum*** ssp. ***mellitum*** (A. Gray) Davidson. See *P. brandegei* ssp. *mellitum*.

**Polianthes** L. (From Gk *polios*, bright, and *anthos*, flower.) Agavaceae. 13 species of perennial herbs to 1m with thick, elongate, bulb-like bases, often from a short rhizome with thickened roots. Leaves few, succulent, lanceolate or linear, thin, entire; stem leaves much reduced. Inflorescence terminal, bracteate, a spike-like raceme; flowers orange-red or white, mostly in pairs; perianth tube long, cylindrical to narrowly, funnel-shaped, bent near base, segments 6, short, unequal; stamens 6, filaments thread-like, short, anthers linear, erect, dorsifixed; style thread-like, stigmas 3-lobed, ovate, sickle-shaped; ovary inferior, 3-chambered. Fruit a capsule, crowned by persistent perianth; seeds flat, with a loose testa. Mexico. Z9.

CULTIVATION Tuberose has long been valued for its spikes of very strongly scented, waxen-white flowers, traditionally grown on in English hothouses and hotbeds for a long succession of bloom in the pleasure grounds in summer; their fragrance is sometimes considered too overpowering for use in confined spaces, although they were traditionally used as cut flowers to decorate churches in Italy, the cooler temperatures prolonging the life of the bloom and, no doubt, dissipating the intense fragrance. The essential oil of tuberose is extracted by cold enfleurage from the flowers and used extensively in perfumery; 1150g of flowers yields 1gm of oil.

A frost-tender tuberous perennial, *Polianthes* usually flowers in midsummer. Given protection and a minimum temperature of 15°C/60°F, with successional plantings they may be forced to flower almost throughout the year. In cool temperate climates, *Polianthes* is grown in the warm, sheltered flower border, to be lifted and dried off in autumn and stored in sand to overwinter in frost free-conditions. Otherwise, grow in bright direct sunlight in the glasshouse or conservatory. Plant singly into a 15cm/6in. pot, into a mix of fibrous loam with additional well-rotted manure and leafmould or equivalent; give bottom heat at about 15–18°C/60–65°F, keeping the potting mix just moist until the leaves appear. Water plentifully when in full growth, and feed fortnightly with liquid fertilizer. Dry off after leaves fade in winter. Propagate by seed or offsets in spring.

***P. geminiflora*** (La Ll. & Lex.) Rose. To 60cm; rhiz. bulbous, 2.5–3cm diam. Basal lvs 5–6, 30–40×1.5cm, linear, stem lvs 4, shorter, lanceolate, erect, adpressed to stem. Infl. 30–50cm; raceme 8–30cm; bracts thin, dry; perianth bright red-orange, to 2.5cm, seg. ovate, green, to 2cm; anth. reaching tube of throat; each fl. subtended by 1 bract, 2 bracteoles. Fr globose. Summer.

***P. tuberosa*** L. TUBEROSE. To 1m; rhiz. tuberous. Basal lvs to 45×1.5cm, in rosettes, thin, linear, bright green, deeply grooved in lower half, frequently spotted brown beneath, stem lvs 8–12, reduced, clasping. Fls very fragrant, in a lax spike; bracts green, lanceolate; perianth pure waxy white, 3–6cm, seg. oblong-lanceolate, spreading, showy. Only known as a cultigen; cultivated in pre-Columbian Mexico, added to chocolate as a flavouring. 'Excelsior Double Pearl': an improved form of 'The Pearl'. 'Single Mexican': fls single, to 5 spikes, long-lasting; possibly typical. 'The Pearl': fls double, highly fragrant. var. ***gracilis*** Link & Otto. Habit more slender, lvs narrower, perianth with long slender tube, seg. linear.

***P. maculosa*** (Hook.) Shinn. See *Manfreda maculosa*.
***P. runyonii*** Shinn. See *Manfreda longiflora*.
***P. variegata*** (Jacobi) Shinn. See *Manfreda variegata*.
***P. virginica*** (L.) Shinn. See *Manfreda virginica*.
For further synonymy see *Bravoa* and *Coetocapnia*.

**Poliothyrsis** Oliv. (From Gk *polios*, grey-white, and *thyrsos*, panicle.) Flacourtiaceae. 1 species, a deciduous tree, to 15m. Leaves alternate, broadly ovate, to 15cm, dentate, hairy beneath; petiole to 3.5cm. Inflorescence a loose terminal panicle, to 20cm, white-hairy with small deciduous bracts; flowers 8mm diam., long-pedicelled, white becoming yellow, unisexual; sepals 5; petals absent; stamens many; styles 3. Fruit a 3–4-valved capsule, to 2cm, with many winged seeds. C China. Z7.

CULTIVATION A slender small tree with a bushy crown, bearing fragrant creamy flowers in late summer. On older specimens the deeply furrowed bark is also attractive. The flowers are carried on the current season's growth; prune when necessary in early spring. Hardy to −15°C/5°F. Cultivate as for *Idesia*.

***P. sinensis*** Oliv. As for the genus.

**Polyandrococos** Barb. Rodr. (From Gk *polys*, many, *aner*, man, stamen and *Cocos*, the coconut palm, referring to the many stamens which cover the inflorescences at anthesis.) BURI PALM. Palmae. 1 species, a pleonanthic, protandrous, monoecious palm. Stems closely ringed, roughened. Crownshaft absent. Leaves pinnate, erect, marcescent, sheaths clothed with rust-coloured mat of hair; petiole channelled above, convex beneath; rachis curved or straight; pinnae single-fold, regularly spaced or clustered on rachis, held in one or differing planes along rachis, glabrous above, waxy-tomentose beneath, apex emarginate to praemorse or acuminate. Flowers borne on simple, interfoliar spikes, to 1m, amid 2 bracts, upper bracts larger, woody, club-shaped, channelled, apex acute; flowers arranged proximally in triads (2 male, 1 female), with only male flowers above: male flowers with sepals 3, basally connate, petals 3, exceeding sepals, stamens *c*60–100; female flowers smaller than male flowers, with sepals 3, overlapping, petals 3, exceeding sepals, overlapping, staminodes forming a cup, pistil 3-celled. Fruit spherical to ovoid, green to yellow, with apical stigmatic remains and persistent basal calyx, *c*3cm diam.; mesocarp fleshy, fibrous. Brazil. Z10.

CULTIVATION Occurring in a variety of habitats, coastal and inland, in the open and in woodland, usually on poor, dry and sandy soils, *P. caudescens* is valuable for its tolerance of poor soils and dry conditions. Propagate by seed which may be slow to germinate. For cultivation see PALMS.

***P. caudescens*** (Mart.) Barb. Rodr. As for the genus.

**Polyarrhena** (L.) Cass. (From Gk *polys*, much, and *arrhen*, male.) Compositae. About 4 species of perennial herbs and subshrubs. Capitula radiate, solitary; ray florets female, white or tinged purple above, purple to red beneath; disc florets hermaphrodite or male. Fruit a rounded, elliptical, pale brown to yellow cypsela; pappus fragile, deciduous. S and W Cape Province.

CULTIVATION As for tender spp. of *Euryops*.

***P. reflexa*** (L.) Grau. Straggling subshrub, to 1m. Lvs oblong to lanceolate, reflexed, sessile, serrate. Phyllaries in several series, inner with reflexed apices; ray florets white, tinged red beneath. Summer. SW Cape Province.

For synonymy see *Aster* and *Felicia*.

**Polybotrya** Willd. (From Gk *polys*, many, and *botrys*, grape-cluster, referring to the massed sori.) Dryopteridaceae. Some 25–35 species of terrestrial, epilithic or epiphytic ferns. Rhizomes short- to long-creeping or ascending, dictyostelic, occasionally branched, covered with massed roots as well as scales; scales dense, spreading or adpressed, apex attenuate. Fronds stipitate, dimorphous, anadromous, lanceolate or deltoid to oblong, leathery to papery, firm-textured, glabrous to pubescent or scaly, sterile fronds 1–3-pinnate or -pinnatifid, fertile fronds smaller than sterile, 1–4-pinnate or -pinnatifid, ephemeral, pinnae and segments often modified to much-reduced, narrow laminar material, veins free or anastomosing, in which case areolae without free, included veinlets; rachis and costa grooved above; stipes distant, scaly, grey or straw-coloured to brown. Sori covering lower and, occasionally, upper surface of segments, discrete or confluent, circular or linear to oblong; indusia absent; paraphyses present or absent; sporangia stalked; annulus 15–22-celled; spores ellipsoid, bilateral, monolete, echinate to somewhat tuberculate, orange to brown. Tropical America. Z10.

CULTIVATION Ferns of tropical and subtropical forest, growing terrestrially when young but climbing later to become scandent (see *Bolbitis*). The creeping rhizomes are stout and hairy, plants being fairly tolerant of short periods of drought, but watering should be copious during the growing season, moderate as growth slows during the winter months. Needing the protection of a warm glasshouse in cold climates, where high humidity combined with good air circulation can be provided. Best accommodated in broad containers, or in baskets, and given a support such as a moss pole or piece of tree fern fibre up which to scramble. Plants are robust, but growth may be slow, and benefit from bright filtered sunlight and a monthly feed with high-N fertilizer during the summer months. Repot annually in spring, just before growth recommences into a medium suitable for terrestrial ferns. Propagate by division of rooted pieces of rhizome, or from spores.

***P. osmundacea*** Willd. Epiphytic. Rhiz. to 3cm, ascending, woody; scales to 2×1cm, lanceolate, apex twisted and hair-like, margin subentire to toothed, lustrous, pale brown. Fronds arched, sterile fronds to 1.8×1m, 3-pinnate or -pinnatifid, ovate to deltoid or lanceolate, papery, glabrous to, rarely, glandular beneath, pinnae to 40×30cm, 13–18 pairs, lanceolate to deltoid, base unequal, pinnules to 14×4cm, petiolate, lanceolate, apex narrowly acute, seg. approximate, subfalcate, ovate or lanceolate to rhomboid or oblong, apex acute, base unequal, margin subentire to toothed, fertile fronds shorter, 3-pinnate or -pinnatifid, deltoid, seg. to 12mm, falcate, linear, veins free, forked; rachis and costa glabrous or pubesc. beneath; stipes to 50cm, erect and stiff, scaly at base. Mexico, W Indies, to Brazil.

***P. apiifolia*** J. Sm. See *Psomiocarpa apiifolia*.
***P. aristeguietae*** Brade. See *P. osmundacea*.
***P. cervina*** (L.) Kaulf. See *Olfersia cervina*.
***P. cyathifolia*** Fée & L'Hermin. See *P. osmundacea*.
***P. latifolia*** Meyen. See *Hemigramma latifolia*.
For further synonymy see *Acrostichum* and *Dorcapteris*.

**Polycarpa** Lind. ex Carr.
***P. maximowiczii*** Lind. ex Carr. See *Idesia polycarpa*.

**Polycycnis** Rchb. f. (From Gk *polys*, many, and *kyknos*, swan, in allusion to the resemblance of the flowers to swans.) Orchidaceae. Some 7 species of epiphytic orchids closely allied to *Cycnoches*. Rhizome short. Pseudobulbs short, ovoid to subcylindrical, bases enveloped by coriaceous, leafy sheathing bracts, 1–3-leaved at apex. Leaves large, plicate, conduplicate, petiolate. Inflorescence a basal raceme, erect to pendent, few- to many-flowered; flowers showy, pedicellate; sepals free, subequal, spreading or reflexed, carinate; petals subsimilar to sepals, sometimes with an elongate, stalked base; lip usually with a trilobed hypochile, adnate to column base, lateral lobes erect or spreading, apex usually pubesc., epichile inserted on the under-surface of hypochile, simple or obscurely 3-lobed, subcordate to obovate-lanceolate, acute or acuminate, disc often with a pubesc. callus; column elongate, terete, slender, arched, apex dilated, footless, sometimes winged, anther terminal, operculate, incumbent, unilocular, pollinia 2, waxy, cylindrical, with a prominent stipe. Panama and Costa Rica to Colombia, Guyana and Peru. Z10.

CULTIVATION As for *Catasetum*.

***P. barbata*** (Lindl.) Rchb. f. Pseudobulbs to 4.5×2.5cm, clustered, ovoid, grooved. Lvs to 40×10cm, elliptic-lanceolate, acute or acuminate. Infl. to 32cm, usually pendent, loosely many-fld; fls thin-textured, short-lived, pale, clear yellow spotted red, the lip white spotted red or purple; pedicel elongate, pubesc.; sep. to 25×8mm, lanceolate, acuminate, concave; pet. to 24×3mm, narrowly oblanceolate; lip with hypochile to 9mm, lateral lobes auriculate, erect, epichile obscurely 3-lobed, ovate, acuminate, lateral lobes subauriculate, disc with a densely pubesc. callus; column to 22mm. Costa Rica, Panama, Colombia, Venezuela, Brazil.

***P. muscifera*** (Lindl. & Paxt.) Rchb. f. Pseudobulbs to 6cm, subcylindrical. Lvs to 37×12cm, elliptic, acute; petiole to 11cm. Infl. to 60cm, erect to arching; peduncle pubesc.; fls small, thin-textured, pale brown marked light maroon, the lip light brown-green spotted maroon; sep. to 20×5mm, oblong-lanceolate or linear-lanceolate, acute, slightly concave; pet. to 22×3mm, linear or linear-oblanceolate, slightly sigmoid, acute; lip to 20mm, hypochile with 2 basal, linear-falcate horns, lateral lobes erect, obliquely lanceolate, acuminate, epichile simple or obscurely 3-lobed, ovate-hastate, acute or acuminate, disc with a fleshy, subelliptic, pubesc. keel; column to 2cm, winged at apex. Panama, Venezuela, Colombia, Ecuador, Peru, Bolivia.

***P. vittata*** (Lindl.) Rchb. f. Pseudobulbs to 7cm, lustrous pale green-brown, ovoid-subconical to subcylindrical. Lvs to 54×15cm, elliptic to oblong-lanceolate, acute; petiole to 9cm, slender. Infl. to 20cm, erect or suberect, loosely many-fld; fls to 5cm diam., spreading, white or cream, densely striped deep red-maroon or chocolate; sep. to 30×5mm, lanceolate to linear-lanceolate, acute to acuminate, concave; pet. to 25×5mm, obliquely lanceolate or elliptic-lanceolate, acuminate; lip to 18mm, fleshy, hypochile clawed, 3-lobed, with a small, linear, pubesc. horn at base, fleshy keel separating lateral lobes, lateral lobes small, porrect, ovate-oblong, obtuse, epichile rhombic or ovate-rhombic, acute or rounded, glabrous, disc with a longitudinal, sulcate callus; column to 1.5cm. Colombia, Venezuela, Guianas, Brazil, Peru.

For synonymy see *Cycnoches* and *Houlletia*.

**Polygala** L. (Name used by Dioscorides, from Gk *polys*, much, and *gala*, milk, from a reputation for promoting secretion of milk.) MILKWORT; SENECA; SNAKEROOT. Polygalaceae. 500 species of annual or perennial shrubs and herbs, rarely trees. Leaves usually alternate, may be opposite or whorled, simple, entire. Flowers in terminal or axillary racemes, irregular, sometimes showy, ranging in colour sometimes on the same plant; sepals 5, the inner 2 petal-like (wings); petals 3–5, often united, the lower petal (keel) often crested; stamens 8, rarely 6, filaments united into a sheath split on upper side. Fruit a capsule; seeds usually pubescent or with an aril. Subcosmopolitan.

CULTIVATION Grown for the slender spikes of pea-like flowers in summer, the hardy species, *P. lutea*, *P. calcarea*, *P. chamaebuxus*, and *P. paucifolia* var. *grandiflora* are suitable for the rock garden. A number of the alpine species, such as *P. chamaebuxus* and *P. vayredae*, often do not thrive in mild damp winters and may be more successfully grown with protection from winter wet in the alpine house. Tender species, *P. balansa*, *P. galpinii* and *P. myrtifolia* need the protection of the cool glasshouse in cool temperate zones.

Grow in part shade or in sun where soils remain moist throughout the growing season in moderately fertile, moisture-retentive but well-drained soil. Under glass, grow in bright filtered light, provide shade from the hottest summer sun and maintain good ventilation. Pot firmly into a medium-fertility potting mix with additional sharp sand and leafmould or equivalent, water plentifully and feed fortnightly with dilute liquid feed when in full growth. Reduce water to keep just moist in winter with a minimum temperature of 5–7°C/40–45°F. Cut leggy specimens hard back in late winter. Propagate by seed in spring or by softwood or semi-ripe cuttings in a sandy propagating mix in a closed case with gentle bottom heat. Whitefly may be a problem pest under glass.

***P. alba*** Nutt. Stem many, to 30cm, from a perenn. root. Lvs to 2.5cm, alternate, mostly linear. Fls white with green centres, crest often purple, wings elliptic. Capsule elliptic. N America. Z4.

***P. alpestris*** Rchb. f. Stems 7–15cm, few, decumbent or ascending. Lvs increasing in size upwards, the upper broadly lanceolate. Racemes 1.5–3.5cm, 5–20-fld, dense; fls blue or white. S & SC Europe, from the Alps to the Pyrennees and Greece. Z6.

***P. amara*** L. Stems 5–20cm, numerous, arising from the centre of a basal rosettes. Basal lvs 15–35×6–10mm, elliptical to obovate, the upper lanceolate to oblong, widest near the middle, acute. Racemes 8–25-fld; fls blue, violet, pink or white; cor. 3.5–6.5mm, distinctly articulated between tube and keel and between keel and crest. Capsule. 3.5–5.5mm. Mts of EC Europe and N Yugoslavia. Z6.

***P. amarella*** Crantz. Similar to *P. amara* but cauline lvs obtuse, widest near apex. Cor. 2–4mm, scarcely articulated. Much of Europe, but absent from most of the south. Z6.

***P. apopetala*** Brandg. Shrub or small tree, to 5m. Lvs to 8cm, alternate, lanceolate to ovate, obtuse. Fls pink-purple, wings nearly orbicular. Capsule elliptic. N America. Z4.

***P. arillata*** Buch.-Ham. ex D. Don). Shrub, 1–3m. Lvs 10–15cm, lanceolate, ovate-lanceolate, or elliptic-oblong. Fls in drooping, usually panicled racemes, the wings ovate, red-purple, keel yellow, amply crested. Capsule broadly reniform. India, Sri Lanka, SE Asia. Z10.

***P. calcarea*** F.W. Schultz. Stems 10–20cm, with decumbent, usually leafless stolons terminating in leaf-rosettes, from which arise a number of almost erect flowering stems. Lvs glabrous or sparsely hairy, rosette lvs spathulate to obovate, lvs of flowering stems smaller, linear-lanceolate, obtuse. Racemes 6–20-fl; fls usually blue or white. Capsule 4–6mm. W Europe, including S England. 'Lillet': fls bright blue. Z7.

***P. chamaebuxus*** L. Evergreen shrub, procumbent and creeping, 5–15cm, shoots 4-sided, yellow-green to red-green. Lvs 1.5–3×0.5–1cm, elliptic to obovate, entire, margins slightly recurved, leathery, tough, somewhat glossy above. Fls solitary or in pairs in leaf-axils, 10–14mm, wings cream-white, keel yellow, with a 2- to 6-lobed crest. Fr. 6–8mm, flat-globose, sessile. C Europe to Italy. 'Kamniski': to 20cm, strong; fls in wide range of colour including white, pink, purple and yellow, occasionally with second flush of fls. 'Loibe': lvs mat-forming, dark green; fls deep purple and yellow, abundant. var. ***grandiflora*** Neilr. wings purple, pet. yellow. Z6.

***P. cowellii*** (Britt.) S.F. Blake. VIOLETA; VIOLET TREE; TORTUGUERO. Small to medium-sized, deciduous tree, 5–13m. Lvs 5–13×2.5–6cm, alternate, elliptic, slightly thickened and leathery, yellow-green, lateral veins many, nearly parallel, slightly raised, thin. Fls in short, lateral racemes, violet, showy, *c*2cm diam.; sep. 5, wings elliptic; pet. 1.2cm. Capsules 3–4cm, flattened, unequally 2-winged. Puerto Rico. Z10.

***P. ×dalmaisiana*** hort. (*P. oppositifolia* × *P. myrtifolia.*) Shrub, 1–3m. Lvs to 2.5cm, alternate or opposite on same plant, elliptic, lanceolate to ovate. Fls purple-red or rosy red, flowering almost continuously. Garden origin.

***P. lutea*** L. YELLOW MILKWORT; CANDYWEED; YELLOW BACHELOR'S-BUTTON. Bienn., to 30cm. Lvs 2.5–5cm, in a rosette, lanceolate, oblanceolate, obovate or spathulate. Fls in dense spikelike racemes to 4cm long, orange-yellow, wings obliquely elliptic. Capsules cuneate-obovate. N America. Z6.

***P. myrtifolia*** L. Erect, much-branched shrub, 1–2.5m. Lvs 2.5–5cm, alternate, elliptic-oblong or obovate. Fls in short, terminal racemes, closing at night, green-white veined purple, wings obliquely ovate, keel crested, cor. 13–18mm. Capsule obovate, emarginate, narrowly winged. S Africa. var. ***grandiflora*** Hook. Fls large, rich purple. Z9.

***P. paucifolia*** Willd. FLOWERING WINTERGREEN; BIRD-ON-THE-WING; FRINGED POLYGALA; GAY-WINGS. Perenn., to 15 or 18cm, rhizomatous, stoloniferous. Upper lvs to 4cm, clustered, ovate to oblong, lower lvs distant and scale-like. Fls 1–4 together, rose-purple or rarely white, wings obovate, keel fringed; stamens 6. Capsule nearly orbicular. N America. Z2.

***P. senega*** L. SENGA ROOT. Stems several, to 45cm, from a thick perenn. root. Lvs to 5cm, alternate, linear-lanceolate. Fl. in terminal racemes, white or green-white, very small, wing suborbicular. Capsule subglobose. N America. The root and minutely glandular-puberulent stem readily distinguish this species. Z2.

***P. vayredae*** Costa. Perenn., normally only to 5cm. Lvs 2–2.5cm, alternate, linear-lanceolate to linear. Fls axillary, solitary or paired, wings and upper pet. pink-purple, keel tinged yellow, with 5–9-lobed, fimbriate crests. Capsule 9–13mm, obcordate-orbicular. E Pyrenees. Z6.

***P. virgata*** Thunb. Nearly deciduous shrub or small tree (most of the lvs abscise in winter), 1.5–2m; branches straight and erect, reed-like. Lvs 2–2.5cm, alternate, linear to lanceolate. Fls in terminal racemes, purple or pink, wings nearly orbicular, keel crested. Capsule obcordate. S Africa. var. ***speciosa*** Harv. Basal lvs more obovate to cuneate, the apical lvs more linear, all obtuse. Flowers in racemes, *c*15cm long, purple-violet; fl. stalks outspread, bracts quickly abscising. S Africa. Z9.

***P. vulgaris*** L. GAND FLOWER; MILKWORT. Small perenn. with tufted base, and numerous spreading or ascending branches; stems 7–35cm, glabrous or sparsely hairy. Lvs alternate, the lower obovate to elliptic, the upper linear-lanceolate. Racemes 10–40-fld, rather dense, conical at first, elongating in fr.; fls blue, pink or white; sep. obovate; cor. tube usually longer than the upper pet. Fr. compressed, broadly obovate. Europe and Mediterranean. Extremely variable. Z6.

***P. alpestris*** Spach. See *P. chamaebuxus*.
***P. amarella*** Coss. & Germain. See *P. calcarea*.
***P. chamaebuxus*** var. ***purpurea*** Neilr. See *P. chamaebuxus* var. *grandiflora*.
***P. diversifolia*** L. See *Securidaca diversifolia*.
***P. speciosa*** Sims. See *P. virgata* var. *speciosa*.

**POLYGALACEAE** R. Br. MILKWORT FAMILY. Dicot. 18 genera and 950 species of trees, shrubs, lianes and herbs, sometimes parasitic and often with extra-floral nectaries. Leaves alternate, simple and entire; stipules usually absent, sometimes a pair of glands or spines. Flowers bisexual, 2-bracteolate, usually strongly irregular, hypogynous, in spikes, racemes or panicles; calyx 5 free sepals, rarely basally connate, the 2 inner often petaloid; corolla 3 or 5, often adnate to stamens to form a tube; stamens 4+4 or 10 or 3–7, usually basally connate with anthers, annular disc sometimes around ovary; ovary superior, 2–5 (–8) fused carpels, 2-loculed, with 1 pendulous ovule in each locule, rarely 1-loculed with numerous ovules. Fruit a loculicidal capsule, nut, samara or drupe; seeds arillate or hairy; endosperm absent to copious, oily. Subcosmopolitan, except New Zealand, W Pacific and arctic zones. *Polygala, Securidaca*.

**POLYGONACEAE** Juss. BUCKWHEAT FAMILY. Dicot. 51 genera and 1150 species of trees, shrubs, lianes or herbs, often with unusual vascular structure and apparent swollen nodes. Leaves simple, usually entire, alternate; stipules conspicuous and often united as a scarious sheath 'ocrea' around the stem. Flowers bisexual (plants rarely dioecious), regular, small, often with pseudopedicel above articulation with pedicel, often in involucrate fascicles subtended by persistent ocreola in simple or branched inflorescences; perianth 2–6 fused segments with minute tube, green or more or less petaloid, often 3+3 free segments but not differentiated into calyx and corolla, or 5 arising spirally, persistent and often accrescent in fruit; stamens (2)3+3, 8(9 or more), filaments sometimes basally connate, often of 2 lengths; annular nectary-disc around ovary or nectaries between stamens; ovary of (2)3(4) fused carpels; 1-loculed; styles more or less united; ovule 1 basal. Fruit often trigonous achene or nut, sometimes enclosed in persistent perianth, often forming a wing or fleshy hypanthium; seeds with starchy and oily endosperm, sometimes ruminate. Some provide edible products such as *Fagopyrum esculentum* (buckwheat), *Rheum rhaponticum* (rhubarb), *Rumex acetosa* (sorrel). *Polygonum* (knotweeds) and *Rumex* (docks) can be troublesome weeds. Cosmopolitan, especially N temperate. *Antigonon, Atraphaxis, Coccoloba, Eriogonum, Homalocladium, Muehlenbeckia, Oxyria, Polygonum, Rheum, Rumex, Ruprechtia, Triplaris*.

**Polygonatum** Mill. (From Gk *polys*, many, and *gonu*, joint, referring to the many-jointed rhizome; name used by Dioscorides.) Liliaceae (Convallariaceae). Some 30 species of mostly hardly, rhizomatous, perennial herbs. Rhizome horizontal, jointed, with many scars. Stems erect to arching. Leaves alternate, opposite, or whorled, ovate, lanceolate, or linear. Flowers green to yellow, nodding or pendulous, axillary, solitary or emerging frequently in loose racemes or subumbels; perianth terete, marcescent, deciduous, with 6 erecto-patent lobes; stamens 6. Fruit a blue-black, or red, several-seeded berry. N US, Europe, Asia.

CULTIVATION Occurring predominantly in woodland habitats, frequently on calcareous soils, *Polygonatum* spp. are valued for their graceful, usually arching habit, fine foliage and for the small pendant waxy flowers which are often faintly scented, more noticeably so in *P. odoratum*. The flowers last fairly well when cut and *P. multiflorum* is sometimes forced under glass for this purpose. Ranging in size from the small, densely rhizomatous

*P. hookeri*, for the peat terrace and alpine house, through low growing types such as *P.* ×*hybridum* 'Striatum' (less vigorous than the species), to *P. biflorum*, which on rich moist soils may reach heights of 1.8m/6ft and more.

Most are valued for form and textural contrasts in the foliage garden and shaded herbaceous or mixed border, and are eminently suited to naturalizing in the woodland garden. With the possible exceptions of *P. falcatum* and *P. stenanthum*, which need deep mulch protection where temperatures fall to between −5 and −10°C/23–14°F, most are tolerant of temperatures to at least −15°C/5°F; the hardiest species, the whorled Solomon's seal, *P. verticillatum*, *P. sibiricum*, *P. multiflorum*, *P. odoratum* and *P. pubescens* are reliable down to −20°C/−4°F. All benefit from a deep mulch of leafmould or bracken litter where low temperatures are prolonged to protect the shallowly rooting rhizomes.

*Polygonatum* spp. are tolerant of a range of conditions except heat and drought but are best grown in fertile humus rich, moisture retentive but well drained soil in cool semi-shade or shade. Leave undisturbed once planted and allow to establish large clumps for best effects. Propagate by division or by seed in autumn, germination may be slow and offspring may not come true. Larvae of the saw fly will strip foliage in summer, and slugs may also be a problem.

***P. biflorum*** (Walter) Elliott. Stem 40cm–2m, erect or arched, slender, glabrous. Lvs 4–18cm, alternate, sessile, narrow-lanceolate to broadly elliptic, glabrous or minutely puberulent and glaucous beneath. Fls drooping, solitary or clustered 1–4 per peduncle; perianth 1.1–2.3cm, green-white, terete, tepals 3–4mm; stamens borne about half-way up the tube, fil. filiform, glabrous, occasionally minutely warty. E US, SC Canada. Z3.

***P. falcatum*** Gray. Stem to 85cm. Lvs to 23cm, narrow-lanceolate to ovate-elliptic, alternate, sickle-shaped, sometimes minutely rough on veins beneath. Fls 2–5, drooping; perianth 1.1–2.2cm, white, terete; stamens borne about half-way up the tube, fil. usually glabrous, occasionally puberulent or warty, 5–7mm. Japan, Korea. Often cultivated as *P. pumilum*. Z6.

***P. hirtum*** (Poir.) Pursh. Stem 20–120cm, erect, angular, sparsely puberulent above. Lvs 10–15, 7–15cm, alternate, lanceolate to ovate, puberulent beneath. Fls to 2cm long, white, drooping from axils, solitary or borne in axillary peduncles of 1–5; tepals with green tips, forming cylindric tube, 1–2.5cm; fil. glabrous or glandular. EC and SE Europe, W USSR, NW Turkey. Z5.

***P. hookeri*** Bak. Stem to 10cm, glabrous. Lvs alternate, 1.5–2cm, linear to narrow-elliptic, glabrous beneath, emerging on stem in apical clusters. Fls solitary in leaf-axils, erect, *c*2cm, purple or lilac; perianth 1.1–1.2cm, pink to purple, occasionally green-yellow, tepals free, 4–5mm, spreading; stamens borne about half-way up to the tube, fil. glabrous. E Himalaya, China. Z6.

***P. humile*** (Maxim.). Close to *P. hirtum*, differs in its solitary or paired infl. Z5.

***P.* ×*hybridum*** hort. (*P. multiflorum* × *P. odoratum.*) Intermediate between the parents; the most common sp. in cult. 'Flore Pleno': fls double. 'Striatum' ('Variegatum'): lvs striped creamy white, somewhat undulating. Z6.

***P. multiflorum*** (L.) All. Stem to 90cm, terete, arched, glabrous. Lvs 5–15cm, alternate, elliptic-oblong to ovate, amplexicaul, glabrous beneath; petioles very short. Fls white, drooping, borne on peduncles of 2–5; perianth 9mm–2cm, constricted in the middle, with green tip; stamens borne near mouth of tube, fil. sparsely puberulent. Europe, Asia. Z4.

***P. odoratum*** (Mill.) Druce. Stem to 85cm, glabrous, angular, arched. Lvs 10–12, lanceolate to ovate, alternate, ascending, glabrous beneath. Fls 2–4 per peduncle, drooping, fragrant; perianth white, 8–20mm with green tip, terete or spreading at mouth of tube; stamens borne near mouth of tube, fil. glabrous, occasionally minutely warty. Europe, Asia. 'Gilt Edge': lvs edged yellow. 'Grace Barker': lvs striped creamy white. 'Variegatum': stems red when young; lvs narrowly edged creamy white. var. ***thunbergii*** (C. Morris & Decne.) Hara Stems to 1.1m. Lvs to 15cm. Z4.

***P. pubescens*** (Willd.) Pursh. Close to *P. odoratum*, differs in fls yellow-green, tepals contracted at base and spreading, minutely warty inside; fil. densely warty. E to SC Canada, South to Georgia and North Carolina. Z3.

***P. roseum*** (Ledeb.) Kunth. Stem to 70cm, glabrous, terete, sulcate. Lvs 7–15cm, ascending, linear to narrow-lanceolate, acuminate, sub-petiolate, upper opposite or ternate, whorled in clusters of 3 at tips of stems, often minutely rough on veins beneath. Fls erect, rose, solitary or in pairs, borne in lf axils; perianth 1–1.2cm, tube terete, finely toothed, tepals narrowly reflexed; stamens borne about half-way up the tube, fil. papillose. W Siberia, C Soviet Asia. Z3.

***P. sibiricum*** Delaroche. Close to *P. verticillatum*. Stems to 1m. Infl. solitary or clustered to 30 per peduncle. W Siberia, Soviet C Asia. Z3.

***P. stenanthum*** Nak. Stem to 120cm, glabrous, terete. Lvs 8.5–17.5cm, lanceolate to ovate, alternate, glabrous beneath. Fls drooping, solitary or clustered in peduncles of 2–4; perianth 2.1–3.6cm, white, cylindric, tepals free, 4–7mm; stamens borne near mouth of tube, fil. warty. Japan, Korea. Z7.

***P. stewartianum*** Diels. Close to *P. verticillatum*. Lvs always whorled, 5–10cm and apically tendrilous. Tepals purple-pink; stamens borne near the mouth of the tube. Europe, temperate Asia. Z6.

***P. verticillatum*** (L.) All. Stem 20–100cm, erect, angular, glabrous or occasionally sparsely puberulent. Lvs 6.5–15cm, opposite or whorled, alternate lower down, sessile, linear-lanceolate to narrow-ovate, minutely rough on veins beneath. Fls to 1.5cm, green, campanulate, drooping, solitary, or in clusters of 2–3; perianth 5–10mm, white, constricted in the middle; stamens borne about half-way up tube, fil. glabrous. Europe, temperate Asia, Afghanistan. Z5.

***P. canaliculatum*** (Muhlenb.) Pursh. See *P. biflorum*.
***P. commutatum*** (Schult.) Dietr. See *P. biflorum*.
***P. giganteum*** Dietr. See *P. biflorum*.
***P. japonicum*** Morr. & Decne. See *P. odoratum*.
***P. latifolium*** (Jacq.) Desf. See *P. hirtum*.
***P. macranthum*** (Maxim.) Koidz. See *P. stenanthum*.
***P. macrophyllum*** Sweet. See *P. verticillatum*.
***P. officinale*** All. See *P. odoratum*.
***P. vulgare*** Desf. See *P. odoratum*.

**Polygonum** L. (From Gk *polys* many, and *gonu*, joint; the stems have conspicuously swollen nodes.) KNOTWEED; SMARTWEED; FLEECE VINE; SILVER LACE VINE. Polygonaceae. Some 150 species of mostly annual or perennial herbs, occasionally aquatic or scramblers, or woody subshrubs, stems appearing jointed. Leaves alternate, various shapes but not cordate, simple, entire; stipules (ochreae) sheathing. Flowers small, sometimes showy, fertile, clustered in axils of leaves or bracts, or in terminal panicles or spikes; perianth funnel- or bell-shaped, segments 3–6, commonly 5, usually equal, petal-like, white, pink or red; stamens 3–9; stigmas 2–3. Fruit a 2–3-angled achene, enclosed by persistent perianth, or protruding to half its length. N temperate regions.

CULTIVATION A diverse genus with species suited to a number of situations in the garden. Although most have invasive potential which must be taken account of when siting, this tendency can often be used to advantage in larger landscape plantings. *P. japonicum*, introduced as an ornamental, has become widely naturalised as a pernicious and serious weed pest in Britain, proving extremely difficult to eradicate and sufficiently strong to penetrate tarmac; only the less invasive forms like 'Spectabile', with leaves marbled in white green and red, and *P. japonicum* var. *compactum* should be accommodated in (larger) gardens, with due care to prevent escape into the wider landscape. The climbing species such as *P. baldschuanicum* and *P. aubertii* make vigorous and rapidly climbing cover for large tree stumps, and are particularly useful for clothing unsightly garden structures, especially on poorer soils; they are perhaps better suited to less well-manicured areas, although both species are very handsome when in full flower. The dense foliage of well-established plants provides excellent cover and nest sites for garden birds. They may be difficult to eradicate once established and will out compete most other common climbers, even robust species such as *Lonicera periclymenum. The Russian vines may be confined by the most severe pruning in lat winter, sprouting freely from older wood.*

*Aquatic and semi-aquatic species such as P. amphibium* and *P. coccineum* are suitable for larger ponds as submerged plants or for the bog garden and other naturalistic sites with permanently moist soils; both root at the nodes wherever they come into contact with the soil. In cool, moist situations in semi shade, *P. campanulatum* makes a beautiful and robust perennial, bearing small elegant bell shaped blooms over long periods in summer. In the herbaceous border, the vigorous clump-forming *P. bistorta* is valued for large, weed-smothering foliage and dense spikes of soft pink bloom, 'Superbum' is a superior colour form; *P. milletii* is similar, but more compact, the deep crimson spikes. The creamy flowered *P. alpinum* may be invasive but excess growth is easily controlled by uprooting the edges of the clump periodically. These border species flower for longer periods on moist soils. *P. molle* and *P. amplexicaule* are stout, clumping perennials extending their period of interest from the first flush of bloom in midsummer often through until first frosts, the form *P. amplexicaule* 'Atrosanguineum' has particularly fine crimson flowers. *P. scoparium* has unusual wiry stems, and closely resembles *Ephedra* or the horsetails, *Equisetum* spp.; it is suitable for the foreground of borders and is sometimes grown in the rock garden. Lower mat-forming species such as *P. affine* and *P. vacciniifolium* make good ground cover for the front of herbaceous borders but in the rock garden are more safely placed at the foot of rockwork where their spread does not threaten less robust alpines. These two last are extremely valuable for their late flowers, which dry to rich chestnut shades and persist into winter, forming fine contrast to the rusty autumn and winter tints of the fading foliage. The well-marked foliage of the invasive *P. capitatum* also provides good cover; it is also grown in tubs and hanging baskets, where it may be given winter protection in zones experiencing winter temperatures below about −5°C/23°F. Most species are reliable to between −15 and −20°C/5 to −4°F, with the possible exception of *P. scoparium*, hardy to about −15°C/5°F, needing a warm sheltered position with well-drained soil to thrive in cool temperate gardens.

The flowers of a number of species dry well, often assuming rich chestnuts or golden brown coloration on air drying; these include the long stems of *P. baldschuanicum* and *P. aubertii*, used in swags and garlands, and the typical bistort spikes of *P. bistorta*, and *P. affine* for smaller-scale arrangements.

Grow in moisture-retentive, not too fertile soils in sun or part shade. Propagate perennials by division. Propagate climbers by hardwood nodal cuttings of stem pieces with two nodes in late winter; root in close case with gentle bottom heat at 10–12°C/50–55°F; top growth may resume before rooting has occurred. Increase *P. multiflorum* by soft tip cuttings in summer rooted in a closed case with bottom heat. Also by seed. Perennial weed species may eventually succumb to the systematic application of translocated herbicide or by digging out although each piece of root left *in situ* will regenerate freely.

***P. affine*** D. Don. Low, creeping, mat-forming perenn. to 25cm. Lvs 3–10cm, mostly basal, elliptic to oblanceolate, acute, narrowed to short petiole, dark green becoming red-bronze in autumn, margin entire or finely toothed; stipules conspicuous, to 3cm, papery, brown. Fls in dense, erect spikes, 5–7.5cm, pink or red; perianth seg. 4–5mm, broadly elliptic. Late summer–autumn. Himalaya. 'Border Jewel': low, spreading; lvs dark, glossy; fls pink. 'Darjeeling Red': lvs elongated, tapering and leathery; fls pink turning dark red, long-lasting. 'Dimity': spreading, to 25cm tall; lvs red in autumn; fls white. 'Donald Lowndes': spreading, compact; fls salmon pink ageing to dark pink. 'Himalayan Border Jewel': low-creeping, to 10cm; fls small, light pink. 'Superbum': vigorous growth; lvs rich browns in autumn; fls pale pink ageing to crimson, cal. red. Z3.

***P. alatum*** D. Don. Perenn. to 1m, glabrous to sparsely hairy; stems erect or low and procumbent, leafy. Lvs 3–7×2–4cm, ovate to deltoid-ovate, base cordate; petiole winged, 2–3cm; stipules tubular, pale brown. Fls in heads, to 1.5cm diam., pale pink; peduncles glandular, hispid towards tip. Summer. Himalayan China (NW Yunnan). Z8.

***P. alpinum*** All. ALPINE KNOTWEED. Perenn. to 1m; rhiz. short, creeping; stems glabrous or with adpressed or spreading hairs. Lvs 3–8×1–3cm, ovate to lanceolate, acute, hairy; stipules pale brown, soon falling. Fls in loose panicles, white; perianth seg. 2–3mm, ovate-oblong. Fr. 4–5mm, pale brown, exceeding perianth. Summer. Alps to SW Asia. Z5.

***P. amphibium*** L. WILLOW GRASS. Perenn. with creeping rhiz., semi-aquatic. Aquatic plants floating, stems 30–100cm, glabrous, with adventitious roots from nodes. Lvs 7–10×2–4cm, oblong or lanceolate, truncate to slightly cordate at base; petiole 2–4cm. Terrestrial plants with few-branched stems, glabrous to slightly pubesc.; lvs 7–12×1–1.5cm, oblong to lanceolate, strigose hairs, margin ciliate, sessile or short petiolate; stipules hispid. Fls in dense spikes, 2–5cm, pink or red; perianth seg. about 3.5mm; stamens 5; styles 2. Fr. 2mm, biconvex. Summer. N temperate regions. Z5.

***P. amplexicaule*** D. Don. Perenn. to 1m; rootstock woody. Lvs 8–25×4–10cm, ovate to lanceolate, acuminate, cordate at base, downy beneath; petiole long; stem lvs many, clasping; stipules to 6cm. Fls in loose spikes to 8cm, often paired, rose-red to purple or white; perianth seg. about 3–5mm. Fr. 4–5mm. Summer–early autumn. Himalaya. 'Alba': fls white. 'Arun Gem': low, to 30cm; fls curving downward, dark pink, with bronze tips. 'Atrosanguineum': bushy; fls deep rich crimson. 'Fire Tail': low; fls bright crimson. 'Inverleith': habit dwarf; fls on short spikes, dark crimson. 'Roseum': vigorous growth; fls pale pink. 'Rubrum': fls red. Z5.

***P. aubertii*** L. Henry. RUSSIAN VINE; CHINA FLEECE VINE; SILVER LACE VINE. Vigorous, twining, woody vine to 15m; stems glabrous. Lvs 3–10cm, ovate to ovate-oblong, acute, slightly cordate at base, bronze-red on opening, margins wavy; petioles long. Fls in branched axillary and terminal panicles, white or green-white to pink in fr., fragrant; perianth seg. 4–6mm in fr., outer seg. winged. Fr. 4mm. Late summer–autumn. W China, Tibet, Russia (Tadzhikistan). Z4.

***P. baldschuanicum*** Reg. MILE-A-MINUTE VINE; RUSSIAN VINE. Climber resembling *P. aubertii* but more woody; fls in broader, drooping panicles, white tinged pink; perianth 6–8mm across in fr. Late summer–autumn. Iran (Bukhara). Z4.

***P. bistorta*** L. BISTORT; SNAKEWEED; EASTER LEDGES. Glabrous perenn., to 60cm; rootstock stout. Lvs 10–20cm, ovate to oblong, obtuse, truncate at base, margins wavy; petiole long, winged in upper half; stem lvs triangular, acuminate, sessile; stipules to 6cm, brown. Fls in dense, cylindrical spikes, sessile, 2–5cm, rose or white; perianth seg. 4–5mm. Fr. 5mm. Summer. Europe, N & W Asia. ssp. ***carneum*** (Koch) Coode & Cullen. Fls in conical to spherical spikes, 2–3cm, pedunculate. Russia (Caucasus), Turkey. 'Superbum': over 75cm; fls in dense spikes, cyclamen pink. Z4.

***P. bistortoides*** Pursh. Perenn. to 70cm, resembling *P. bistorta* but basal lvs 10–25×0.5–3cm, lanceolate to oblong, tapering to petioles, not winged. Fls in dense racemes, white. Summer. NW US (British Columbia to California, Rocky Mts). Z5.

***P. campanulatum*** Hook. f. LESSER KNOTWEED. Creeping, stoloniferous perenn. to 1m; stems branched, pubesc. or tomentose. Lvs 3.5–12×2–2.5cm, lanceolate to ovate or elliptic, cuneate at base, white- to pink-brown hairy beneath; petiole short; stipules papery. Fls in loosely branched, nodding panicles, pink-red or white, fragrant; perianth campanulate, 4–5mm. Fr. 2mm. Summer–early autumn. Himalaya. Z8. var. ***lichiangense*** (W.W. Sm.) Steward. Lvs grey-white hairy beneath; fls white. W China. Z5. 'Album': spreading; fls white, in loose panicles. 'Rosenrot' ('Roseum'): habit upright; fls dark rose. 'Southcombe White': fls white.

***P. capitatum*** Buch.-Ham. ex D. Don. Perenn. to 7.5cm with slender, creeping stems to 30cm, rooting at nodes, glandular-hairy. Lvs 2–5×1–2.5cm, ovate to elliptic, green with purple V-shaped band; short petiole; stipules papery brown, about 5mm. Fls pink in dense, spherical heads to 15mm diam. on 1–3cm stalks. Fr. 2mm. Summer. Himalaya. 'Magic Carpet': creeping, compact, to 10cm high, fast growing; fls pink. Z8.

***P. coccineum*** Muhlenb. WATER SMARTWEED. Semi-aquatic perenn.; stems glabrous 50–500cm, rooting at nodes, shoots slightly pubesc. Lvs 3–10cm, oblong or elliptic, obtuse or acute. Infl. a dense, cylindrical spike, 1–3cm; fls pale rose; perianth 4–5mm. Fr. lenticular, 2.5–3mm. Summer. N US. Z5.

***P. dibotrys*** D. Don. Pubesc. perenn. to 1m; resembling *P. fagopyrum* but stems more robust. Lvs 6–15cm, broadly triangular, acute or obtuse, cordate, sparsely pubesc.; petiole long; upper lvs narrower and clasping. Fls clustered at tips of open branched panicles, white; perianth about 5mm. Fr. a 3-angled achene, 6–8mm. Late summer. Pakistan to SW China. 'Variegata': vigorous growth early shoots bright red; lvs pink and yellow when young, later marbled green and butter yellow; large.

***P. emodi*** Meissn. Low trailing perenn. resembling *P. affine* but lvs 3–8cm×2–4mm, narrower, linear-lanceolate, entire. Fls in loose, slender spikes, 2.5–3.5cm, red. Summer. Kashmir to SW China. Z7.

***P. fagopyrum*** L. BUCKWHEAT. Erect annual to 60cm; stem glabrous to slightly hairy, hollow, few-branched. Lvs to 7cm, triangular-ovate, base cordate, often as long as broad, dark green; petiole grooved, upper lvs sessile. Fls in terminal and axillary panicles, white, fragrant; perianth 3–5mm. Fr. 3-angled, about 6mm, smooth. Late summer to early autumn. C & N Asia.

***P. griffithii*** Hook. f. Tufted perenn. from woody rootstock, to 45cm, resembling *P. macrophyllum*. Basal lvs 10–15cm, oblong or elliptic, acute, hairy below, margins undulate; stem lvs small, oblong-ovate, slightly clasping. Fls in simple or branched, drooping spikes to 10cm, rich crimson; perianth seg. 5–8mm; styles bright purple. Summer. N India, W China. Z7.

***P. japonicum*** Meissn. JAPANESE KNOTWEED; MEXICAN BAMBOO. Dioecious, rhizomatous perenn. to 2m; stems stout, branched above, occasionally red-brown, glabrous to adpressed-pilose. Lvs broad-ovate, acuminate, base truncate, 6–12×5–10cm, glabrous; petioles short; stipules 8–15mm. Infl. axillary, branched panicles, branches 5–9cm; fls cream-white. Fr. lenticular to compressed, 3-angled, 2–4mm. Late summer–early autumn. Japan. var. ***compactum*** (Hook. f.) Bail. Compact form to 70cm, lvs nearly circular, dark green, margins crimped; fls in denser, erect panicles, to 6cm, red-brown. E Asia. 'Spectabilis': lvs red later marbled with yellow. Z4.

***P. lanigerum*** R. Br. Perenn. to 2m, resembling *P. orientale* but lvs 10–15cm, narrower, ovate-lanceolate, acuminate, silvery, white-hairy, rarely glabrous above. Fls in panicles to 5cm, pink or white. Summer–early autumn. Tropics. Z9.

***P. macrophyllum*** D. Don. Perenn., 5–15cm, occasionally to 30cm, rootcrown stout. Lvs 3–12×2–6cm, mostly basal, oblong acute to broadly linear, rounded at base; petiole long; stem lvs small, acute, cordate at base, clasping; stipules 1–5cm, brown. Fls about 2mm, in dense spikes to 8cm, pink or red. Summer. Himalaya to W China. Z5.

***P. milletii*** (Lév.) Lév. Resembles *P. macrophyllum*. Stem to 50cm. Lvs to 30×2–4cm, linear-lanceolate to oblong, cuneate at base; petiole winged; upper lvs clasping at base. Fls in dense broad-cylindrical to rounded heads, 1.5–4cm, crimson; perianth seg. 4–5mm. Summer–early autumn. Himalaya to SW China. Z5.

***P. molle*** D. Don. Shrubby perenn. to 2.5m, softly tomentose. Lvs 10–20×4–12cm, lanceolate to elliptic-lanceolate, acuminate, densely hairy above, long-hairy beneath; stipules truncate, entire. Fls in dense, branched, tomentose panicles to 30cm, white or cream, slightly fragrant; perianth seg. 1.5–2mm. Fr. berry-like, perianth enclosing achene, 2.5–4mm, purple-black. Late summer. Himalaya. Z7.

***P. multiflorum*** Thunb. Climbing perenn., 1–2m+; root tuberous; stems slender, branched, red. Lvs 3–6×2.5–4.5cm, ovate-cordate, short-acuminate, green, shiny; petiole long; stipules short. Infl. loose, branched tomentose panicles; fls white; perianth 1.5–2mm, 7–8mm in fr. Fr. a 3-angled achene, enclosed in perianth, 2.5mm. Autumn. China. Z7.

***P. orientale*** L. PRINCE'S FEATHER; PRINCESS FEATHER; KISS-ME-OVER-THE-GARDEN-GATE. Pilose-hairy annual, 1–1.5m; stems stout, branching. Lvs 10–20×7–15cm, broadly ovate, short acuminate, base slightly cordate; stipules 7–30mm, brown. Fls in dense, branched, drooping spikes, 5–12cm, pink to rose-purple or white. Fr. 3mm. Late summer–autumn. E & SE Asia, Australia, naturalized N America.

***P. polystachyum*** Wallich. HIMALAYAN KNOTWEED. Shrubby perenn. to 2m, glabrous to softly hairy. Lvs 10–25×3–10cm, lanceolate to oblong-lanceolate, acuminate, slightly cordate or truncate at base, veins tinged red, softly hairy beneath; petiole 1–3cm, often red; stipules entire, persistent, hairy beneath. Fls in much-branched, leafy, axillary or terminal panicles, 15–45cm, white or pale pink, fragrant; perianth c3mm, outer 2 seg. narrower than 3 inner seg. Fr. 3-angled, 3mm, exceeding perianth. Late summer. Himalaya. Z6.

***P. sachalinense*** Schmidt. GIANT KNOTWEED; SACALINE. Perenn. resembling *P. japonica* but 2–4m; stems more robust, red-brown, forming a coarse thicket. Lvs 15–30×10–20cm, ovate-oblong, base slightly cordate, glabrous. Fls in shorter, denser panicles, to 10cm, white-green. Fr. 4–5mm. Late summer-autumn. USSR (Sakhalin Is.). Z4.

***P. scoparium*** Req. ex Lois. Perenn., 50–120cm; rootstock branched, woody; stems erect, little-branched. Lvs to 1.5cm, narrow, caducous; stipules short, red-brown. Fls solitary or paired in loose terminal spikes, white-pink; perianth seg. elliptic, 2–3mm. Fr. scarcely exceeding perianth, rare. Late summer. Corsica, Sardinia. Z7.

***P. tenuicaule*** Bisset & Moore. Glabrous perenn. with short, thick rhiz. Lvs mostly basal, 3–8×2–3cm, ovate-elliptic, slightly cordate or cuneate at base; petiole long, narrowly winged; stipules to 5mm, brown; stem lvs few, small, sessile. Fls in loose spike, some 3.5cm, on flowering stem 7–15cm, white, fragrant; perianth some 3mm. Fr. exceeding perianth. Spring–summer. Japan. Z6.

***P. tinctorium*** Ait. Annual to 80cm; stems erect, sparingly branched. Lvs to 8×6cm, oval or ovate, glabrous; petiolate; stipules narrow, tinged red. Fls in compact spikes, forming a leafy panicle, red or pink. Fr. glossy, 2–3mm. Summer. USSR.

***P. vacciniifolium*** Wallich ex Meissn. Low, trailing perenn.; stems woody, much-branched, to 30cm. Lvs 1–2.5×0.5–1cm, ovate or elliptic, acute, glaucous beneath; petiole short; stipules brown, finely toothed, some 1cm. Fls in loose, erect spikes, 3–8cm, pink; flowering stem 10–20cm; perianth about 4mm, elliptic. Early autumn. Himalaya. Z7.

***P. virginianum*** L. Perenn. to 120cm, glabrous to roughly hairy. Lvs 8–15×4–9cm, ovate to elliptic, acuminate, acute to rounded, glabrous to roughly pubesc.; petiole to 3cm; stipules 5–10mm, pubesc. Fls in slender, terminal and axillary spikes 20–40cm, green-white or tinged pink; perianth seg. 4, elliptic, 2.5mm; styles 2. Fr. 2-angled, ovate, to 4mm. Late summer–early autumn. Japan, Himalaya, NE US. 'Painter's Palette': lvs variegated with gold, overlaid by area of pink brown. 'Variegata': lvs broad, variegated ivory and primrose yellow. Z5.

***P. viviparum*** L. ALPINE BISTORT; SERPENT GRASS. Perenn. to 30cm, with thick bulb-like rootstock covered in fibrous old lf bases; stems erect. Lvs 2–10×0.8–2.5cm, linear-lanceolate to oblong, acute or obtuse, margins inrolled, lower lvs long-petioled, upper lvs sessile; stipules papery, to 4cm. Fls in slender terminal spikes, 2–10cm, pink to rose-white, lower fls replaced with numerous purple-brown bulbils, 2–4mm; perianth c3mm; stamens exserted. Fr. 2.5–3mm. Summer. N US, Europe, Arctic to temperate Asia. Z3.

***P. weyrichii*** Schmidt ex Maxim. Robust perenn. to 1.5m; stems sparsely branching, roughly hairy below hairy above, green. Lvs 8–17cm, ovate, acuminate, dull, green above, white-tomentose beneath, margins of upper lvs revolute; petioles becoming successively shorter. Infl. dense, pubesc., terminal panicles, resembling *P. molle* but fls pale green-white; perianth 2–2.5mm. Fr. 6–8mm, exceeding perianth. Summer. USSR (Sakhalin Is.). Z5.

***P. brunonis*** Meissn. See *P. affine*.
***P. carneum*** Koch. See *P. bistorta* ssp. *carneum*.
***P. chinense*** misapplied. See *P. dibotrys*.
***P. compactum*** Hook. f. See *P. japonicum* var. *compactum*.
***P. cuspidatum*** Sieb. & Zucc. See *P. japonicum*.
***P. cymosum*** Trev. See *P. dibotrys*.
***P. equisetiforme*** hort. non Sm. See *P. scoparium*.
***P. filiforme*** Thunb. See *P. virginianum*.
***P. hayachinensis*** Mak. See *P. macrophyllum*.
***P. lichiangensis*** W.W. Sm. See *P. campanulatum* var. *lichiangense*.
***P. muhlenbergii*** (Meissn.) S. Wats. See *P. coccineum*.
***P. oxyphyllum*** Wallich ex Meissn. See *P. amplexicaule*.
***P. paniculatum*** Bl. See *P. molle*.
***P. regelianum*** Komar. See *P. bistorta*.
***P. reynoutria*** hort. non Mak. See *P. japonicum* var. *compactum*.
***P. rude*** Meissn. See *P. molle*.
***P. sphaerostachyum*** Meissn. See *P. macrophyllum*.
***P. sphaerostachyum*** auct. non Meissn. See *P. milletii*.
***P. senegalense*** misapplied. See *P. lanigerum*.
***P. sericeum*** hort. non Pall. See *P. alpinum*.
***P. sieboldii*** De Vriese. See *P. japonicum*.
***P. spaethii*** Dammer. See *P. orientale*.
***P. speciosum*** Meissn. See *P. amplexicaule*.
***P. undulatum*** Murray. See *P. alpinum*.
For further synonymy see *Bilderdykia, Bistorta, Fagopyrum, Fallopia, Persicaria, Reynoutria* and *Tovara*.

**Polypodium** L. POLYPODY. (From Gk *polys*, much, and *pous*, foot.) Polypodiaceae. Some 75 species of epiphytic, lithophytic or terrestrial ferns. Rhizomes creeping, branched, dictyostelic; scales often deciduous, basally peltate, entire, dentate or ciliate, more or less clathrate. Fronds stipitate, uniform to, occasionally, slightly dimorphous, entire to pinnate or pinnatifid, membranous to papery, glabrous, pubescent, or scaly, veins free, forked, or reticulate and anastomosing, areolae 1-rowed or more, with or without free, often excurrent, included veinlets; stipes closely clustered or remote, jointed to phyllopodia. Sori superficial or sunken, uniserial or more on each side of costa or, rarely, discrete and irregularly scattered, dorsal, terminating lowest anterior veinlet or acroscopic fork of divaricate veinlet, circular or oval to elongate-linear; paraphyses absent or, where present, filamentous, branched, or clathrate; annulus 12–18-celled; spores ellipsoid to oblong or reniform, bilateral, monolete, smooth to reticulate, tuberculate, or papillose. Mainly temperate N hemisphere.

CULTIVATION Usually epiphytic, sometimes terrestrial, ferns of cosmopolitan distribution. Grown for their foliage, some also for their distinctive rhizomes (e.g. *P. formosanum*). Tropical/warm temperate species need glasshouse protection in cold climates; hardy species (e.g. *P. vulgare*) grow well in the fern border, mixed border, or will colonize drystone walls. Epiphytic species can be mounted on bark or tree fern (where they require frequent syringing), but are more easily maintained in shallow pans of epiphytic fern medium. Watering should be moderate, and plants are tolerant of short periods of drought and direct sunlight, although bright filtered sunlight is preferred. Propagation is by division, or from spores. See also FERNS.

***P. adnatum*** Klotzsch. Epiphytic. Fronds to 75×30cm, pinnate, ovate, narrowly acute at apex, membranous, hoary-pubesc., opaque and dark grey or green, pinnae to 20×5cm, spreading, distant, opposite, elliptic to lanceolate, apex narrowly acute, base attenuate and decurrent, margin notched to dentate, main veins approximate, areolae each with solitary free, included veinlet; stipes to 30cm, glabrous, lustrous brown. C to S America. Z10.

***P. brasiliense*** Poir. Epiphytic or lithophytic. Rhiz. to 8mm wide; scales to 5mm, adpressed or spreading, lanceolate, apex attenuate to narrowly acute, margin membranous and undulate, brown. Fronds to 80×40cm, erect or arching, pinnate, lanceolate or ovate, leathery, glabrous, pinnae to 22×3cm, to 18 pairs, entire, short-petiolate to adnate, erect to spreading, approximate or distant, lanceolate or oblong, long-acuminate, base cuneate or obtuse, areolae 3–6-rowed, each with 2 or more free, excurrent veinlets; rachis glabrous; stipes to 55cm, remote, terete, glabrous. S America. Z10.

***P. californicum*** Kaulf. Lithophytic or terrestrial. Rhiz. to 1cm wide; scales to 7mm, adpressed or spreading, ovate to deltoid, narrowly acute, russet. Fronds to 30×15cm, ascending, deeply pinnatifid, oblong or ovate to deltoid, acute or narrowly acute, herbaceous to membranous, seg. to 6×1cm, spreading, oblong to linear, apex acute or obtuse, base decurrent, entire to notched or dentate, veins free or anastomosing, areolae with free, included veinlets; stipes to 20cm, glabrous, straw-coloured. N America (California). Z9.

***P. cambricum*** L. WELSH POLYPODY. Close to *P. vulgare*, from which it may be distinguished by its broader, softer fronds. Epiphytic. Rhiz. long-creeping, to 5mm wide; scales to 12mm, lanceolate, dentate at margin, red-brown. Fronds 13–50×7–10cm, pinnatifid, deltoid or oblong, apex acute, base truncate, seg. to 9mm wide, acute or obtuse; stipes to 20cm, erect, brown. Europe. 'Cambricum': plumose form first discovered in 1668 in South Wales; pinnae lacerated, sterile, rare, 30–40cm; there are several forms differing slightly from the original form:

'Barrowii': frond more leathery than 'Cambricum', pinnae seg. crisped and elongated, rare, 25–35cm; 'Hadwinii': frond narrow, not greatly congested, very rare, 15–25cm; 'Prestonii': frond narrow, congested, pinnae seg. overlapping, vary rare, 15–25cm; 'Oakleyae': similar to 'Cristatum' but lamina short with stipe normal length hence a dwarf form, 20cm; 'Whilharris': tall, leathery, frond narrow with pinnae deeply lacerated, 30–40cm. 'Cristatum': pinnae and frond tip crested, 20–30cm. 'Grandiceps': pinnae crested, crest at frond tip large, three named forms: 'Foster': small terminal crest, frond narrow, rare, 20–30cm; 'Fox': large curled crest, frond broader, rare, 20–30cm; 'Parker': entire frond absorbed into enormous crest, probably extinct, 10–20cm. 'Macrostachyon': tip of frond elongated, 20–35cm. 'Omnilacerum' ('Oxford Superbum'): pinnae irregularly pinnatifid throughout the frond, 20–40cm. 'Pulcherrimum': pinnae broad, nearly and regularly pinnatifid, 20–35cm. 'Semilacerum': pinnae irregularly pinnatifid along part of frond, usually the basal half, 20–30cm; there are several named forms: 'Falcatum O'Kelly': narrow form with pinnae curving toward apex, rare, 30cm; 'Jubilee': pinnae seg. broad and even, 25cm; Robustum': pinnae seg. irregularly pointed or rounded, twisted and dark green, 30cm. Z6.

***P. catharinae*** Langsd. & Fisch. Rhiz. wide-creeping; scales spreading, subulate, attenuate, russet to dark brown. Fronds to 30×10cm, deeply pinnatifid, ovate, narrowly acute at apex, glabrous, membranous to leathery, seg. to 8×1cm, spreading, approximate, oblong, apex obtuse, base somewhat decurrent, margin entire to undulate, veins anastomosing, areolae 1–2-rowed; stipes to 15cm, lustrous, straw-coloured. C to S America. Z10.

***P. fauriei*** Christ. Resembles *P. formosanum* but with slender, more scaly rhiz. Epiphytic. Rhiz. to 3mm wide, long-creeping, scales to 3mm, dense, spreading, ovate, membranous, brown. Fronds to 20×8cm, arching to pendent, pinnate, lanceolate to ovate, attenuate at base, grass-like to papery in texture, glabrous above, pubesc. below, pinnae to 5mm wide, to 25 pairs, spreading, lanceolate to linear, acute or obtuse at apex, somewhat notched at apical margin, veins indistinct; rachis prominent; stipes to 6cm, glabrous to scaly at base, straw-coloured. Japan, Korea. Z9.

***P. formosanum*** Bak. GRUB FERN; CATERPILLAR FERN. Rhiz. long-creeping, to 6mm wide, green to chalky white, frosted and glaucous, eventually glabrous; scales sparse, caducous. Fronds to 50×15cm, arching to pendulous, pinnate, ovate to oblong, thin, pale green, sparsely and minutely pubesc., pinnae to 7×2cm, to 30 pairs, jointed to midrib, spreading, horizontal, lanceolate to linear, acute or narrowly acute at apex, entire or subentire, veins anastomosing; rachis pubesc. above; stipes to 30cm, remote, terete, rigid, glabrous, lustrous, straw-coloured to brown. E Asia (China, Taiwan, Japan). Z9.

***P. glycyrrhiza*** D.C. Eaton. LICORICE FERN. Epiphytic or terrestrial. Rhiz. creeping, compressed, to 5mm wide, sweetly licorice-flavoured but inedible; scales to 9mm, dense, deciduous, ovate to oblong or deltoid, narrowly acute at apex, red-brown. Fronds to 35×15cm, pinnate to pinnatifid, lanceolate to elliptic or oblong, caudate or attenuate, thin-textured, seg. to 6×1cm, alternate, falcate, linear, apex attenuate, base dilated, irregularly notched at margin, basal seg. reduced, veins oblique, forked, free; stipes to 15cm, remote, glabrous straw-coloured. N America (Alaska to California). 'Grandiceps': large bunched crests, rarely, if ever, fertile, 30cm. 'Malahatense': pinnae lacerated; two forms: one sterile, one fertile, 30cm. 'Longicaudatum': frond as species type apart from a greatly elongated frond terminal, 30cm. Z7.

***P. hesperium*** Maxon. WESTERN POLYPODY. Terrestrial. Rhiz. to 5mm wide, sweet-flavoured; scales to 5mm, crowded, ovate, narrowly acute, dentate, red-brown. Fronds to 20×5cm, ascending, deeply pinnatifid, deltoid or lanceolate to linear or oblong, apex attenuate to narrowly acute, herbaceous to membranous, pale green to somewhat glaucous, seg. to 30×8mm, spreading, alternate, spathulate or oblong to elliptic or ovate, apex obtuse, margin entire to notched or dentate, veins forked; stipes to 10cm, close, glabrous, straw-coloured. N America. Z5.

***P. interjectum*** Shivas. Distinguished from the allied *P. cambricum* by its tough lvs and from *P. vulgare* in having broad lf seg. Terrestrial or epiphytic. Rhiz. creeping. Fronds to 25cm, pinnatifid, deltoid or lanceolate to linear or strap-shaped, subcoriaceous, grey to green, seg. obtuse, margin entire or notched. W Europe. Z5.

***P. kuhnii*** Fourn. Epiphytic, lithophytic or terrestrial. Fronds 65×30cm or more, pinnatifid, lanceolate to ovate, scaly below, membranous, seg. to 23×1cm, plane to falcate, attenuate at apex, veins forked, free or anastomosing. Sori uniserial. C to Northern S America. Z10.

***P. lepidopteris*** (Langsd. & Fisch.) Kunze. Rhiz. long-creeping; scales adpressed, subulate, sometimes ciliate, red-brown. Fronds to 45×8cm, pinnate or pinnatifid, linear to lanceolate, apex caudate or narrowly acute, base attenuate, pubesc.-scaly, subcoriaceous, seg. spreading, horizontal, close, ovate or oblong to linear or spathulate, decurrent at base, margins entire or undulate, basal seg. abruptly reduced; stipes to 8cm, erect, remote, scaly. S America. Z10.

***P. lepidotrichum*** (Fée) Maxon. Epiphytic. Rhiz. to 7mm across; scales to 4mm, dense, lanceolate to linear, attenuate at apex, lustrous straw-coloured to chestnut. Fronds to 65×23cm, pinnate to pinnatifid, ovate or obovate to deltoid, scaly, seg. to 12×1cm, to 18 pairs, adnate, deltoid to linear, apex acute or narrowly acute, base decurrent, veins obscure, costa prominent; stipes to 20cm, sulcate, scaly, straw-coloured. C & S America. Z10.

***P. loriceum*** L. Epiphytic. Rhiz. creeping, to 5mm wide, green to frosted and glaucous, often curling; scales to 4×1mm, adpressed, deciduous, oblong to lanceolate, attenuate, dark brown. Fronds to 50×25cm, erect, pinnatifid, oblong to deltoid, elliptic, or lanceolate, apex caudate or narrowly acute, base truncate or attenuate, thin-textured, glabrous, seg. to 10×2cm, adnate, borne close together, falcate, horizontal, oblong or strap-shaped, apex narrowly acute, base dilated, entire or subentire, veins forked; rachis prominent, sulcate, scaly at base; stipes to 20cm, remote, terete, glabrous. W Indies, C to S America. Confused in cult. with *P. formosanum*, from which it differs in larger, erect fronds and smaller sori close to midrib. Z10.

***P. maritinum*** Hieron. Terrestrial or epiphytic. Rhiz. creeping. Fronds to 60cm, pinnate, oblong to deltoid, pinnae spreading, oblong, obtuse at apex, dilated at margin; stipes remote. C to S America. Z10.

***P. menisciifolium*** Langsd. & Fisch. Epiphytic. Rhiz. scandent or creeping, to 8mm wide; scales to 5×3mm, ovate, chestnut to dark brown. Fronds to 70×30cm, arching, pinnate to pinnatifid, ovate or obovate to lanceolate, dark green, leathery or membranous to papery, seg. to 20×3cm, to 25 pairs, sessile, spreading, horizontal, subfalcate, close to overlapping, oblong or lanceolate, apex acute or obtuse, base attenuate; stipes to 40cm, erect, glabrous. S America (Brazil). Cultivated plants are frequently more compact than typical specimens, with shorter fronds. Z10.

***P. mosenii*** C. Chr. Rhiz. creeping. Fronds to 90cm, pinnatifid, seg. to 20×2cm, plane or falcate, linear or oblong to lanceolate, apex acute, base attenuate and dilated; stipes to 30cm, remote. S America. Z10.

***P. plebeium*** Schltr. & Cham. Rhiz. creeping; scales grey to red-brown. Fronds to 30×15cm, deeply pinnate or pinnatifid, ovate or oblong to deltoid, acute at apex, somewhat fleshy, leathery to membranous, scaly below, seg. to 9mm wide, spreading, horizontal, linear to oblong or spathulate, apex acute or obtuse, margin entire or notched, veins obscure, sunken, forked, free; rachis scaly; stipes to 20cm, remote, erect, red-brown. C to S America. Z10.

***P. polypodioides*** (L.) Watt. RESURRECTION FERN. Highly variable. Epiphytic or terrestrial. Rhiz. long-creeping, to 3mm wide; scales to 4mm, dense, adpressed, lanceolate or ovate, narrowly acute, entire to ciliate or erose, dark brown. Fronds to 15×6cm, erect, deeply pinnatifid, deltoid or oblong, apex attenuate to acute, margin truncate, involved when dry and extended in rain (hence common name), somewhat leathery, seg. to 25cm×5mm, to 17 pairs, distant, spreading, linear or oblong, apex obtuse, base dilated, entire or irregularly notched, scaly, veins indistinct, forked, free or anastomosing; stipes to 10cm, remote, erect, scaly. Americas, S Africa. Z7.

***P. ptilorhizon*** Christ. Rhiz. creeping, to 3mm wide, frosted and glaucous. Fronds to 24×12cm, pinnatifid, deltoid to lanceolate, scaly, seg. to 22 pairs, plane, apex acute or obtuse, base dilated, veins forked, free or anastomosing; stipes remote. C America (Costa Rica). Z10.

***P. pyrrholepis*** (Fée) Maxon. Epiphytic. Rhiz. creeping, to 7mm wide; scales to 3mm, spreading, attenuate, ciliate at margin, red-brown. Fronds to 50×7cm, pinnatifid, lanceolate to linear or oblong, apex attenuate, seg. to 35cm×6mm, to 40 pairs, adnate, oblong to linear, obtuse at apex, scaly; rachis and costa prominent; stipes to 20cm, 2cm apart, sulcate, scaly, chestnut. Mexico. Z10.

***P. rhodopleuron*** Kunze. Epiphytic. Rhiz. long-creeping, to 5mm wide; scales to 5mm, lanceolate to ovate, brown. Fronds to 32×13cm, deeply pinnatifid, deltoid or lanceolate to linear or ovate, scaly below, seg. to 33 pairs, lanceolate or oblong, apex acute or obtuse, red, veins forked, free or anastomosing, red; rachis and costa red; stipes to 15cm, remote, red. C America. Z10.

***P. scouleri*** Hook. & Grev. COAST POLYPODY; LEATHERY POLYPODY. Epiphytic or lithophytic. Rhiz. to 1cm wide, frosted and glaucous; scales to 1cm, deciduous, deltoid to ovate, dentate at margin, red-brown. Fronds to 40×15cm, pinnate to pinnatifid, ovate to deltoid, thick-textured and rigid, leathery, seg. to 14 pairs, adnate, spreading, linear to oblong, obtuse, entire to notched or undulate and cartilaginous at margin; rachis prominent, scaly at base; stipes to 10cm, erect, rigid, glabrous. N America (W coast). Z9.

***P. subpetiolatum*** Hook. Epiphytic. Rhiz. long-creeping, to 5mm wide; scales to 7mm, overlapping, lanceolate or deltoid to ovate, entire, red to brown. Fronds to 45×30cm, pinnate to pinnatifid, lanceolate or deltoid to ovate or oblong, leathery or membranous, seg. to 10×1cm, sessile and adnate or decurrent to short-petiolate, remote, alternate, lanceolate, apex acute or obtuse, base truncate or cuneate and attenuate, margin notched, glabrous or sparsely pubesc., veins forked, free; stipes to 30cm, remote, sulcate, glabrous. C America. Z10.

***P. thyssanolepis*** A. Braun ex Klotzsch. SCALY POLYPODY. Epiphytic or terrestrial. Rhiz. to 4mm wide, long-creeping; scales to 4mm, dense, adpressed, imbricate, lanceolate to ovate, apex acute, margin erose, brown to black. Fronds to 25×10cm, erect, deeply pinnate, deltoid or oblong, apex attenuate, base truncate, thick-textured, leathery, pinnae to 4×11cm, to 11 pairs, distant, ascending, oblong to lanceolate or elliptic, apex acute or obtuse, base dilated, entire, pubesc. above, scaly below, veins free or anastomosing; rachis scaly; stipes to 30cm, erect, rigid, scaly. W Indies, Texas to Peru. Z9.

***P. triseriale*** Sw. Rupestral or terrestrial. Rhiz. creeping, to 12mm wide; scales to 6mm, adpressed to spreading, ovate, attenuate to narrowly acute, erose, grey to dark brown. Fronds to 60×40cm, arching or pendent, pinnate, ovate to oblong, herbaceous to leathery, pinnae to 15×2cm, to 12 pairs, sessile, distant, erect to spreading, linear or strap-shaped to lanceolate or elliptic, apex acute or obtuse, base dilated and obtuse or cuneate, entire, veins anastomosing; stipes to 35cm, erect, glabrous, lustrous straw-coloured to red-brown. W Indies, C to S America. Z10.

***P. virginianum*** L. ROCK POLYPODY; AMERICAN WALL FERN. Lithophytic, epiphytic, or terrestrial. Rhiz. long-creeping, to 7mm wide, bitterly flavoured; scales to 5mm, dense, lanceolate, attenuate at apex, dark brown. Fronds to 25×7cm, arching or pendent, deeply pinnatifid, lanceolate or deltoid to oblong, leathery to thin-textured, glabrous, seg. to 4×1cm, to 25 pairs, alternate to subopposite, lanceolate to linear or oblong, apex attenuate, base obtuse, margin entire to notched and undulate, veins obscure; stipes to 15cm, glabrous, straw-coloured. N America, E Asia. 'Bipinnatifidum' pinnae regularly and deeply lacerated; probably sterile, a plumose form, 20cm. Z5.

***P. vulgare*** L. COMMON POLYPODY; ADDER'S FERN; WALL FERN; GOLDEN MAIDENHAIR. Epiphytic, lithophytic or terrestrial. Rhiz. relatively thick, creeping and mat-forming, sweetly flavoured; scales to 5mm, lanceolate, attenuate at apex, membranous, red to brown or blonde. Fronds to 30×15cm, ascending to erect (usually held at 45° to rhiz.), deeply pinnatifid, lanceolate to ovate or oblong or linear, attenuate at apex, glabrous, thin-textured to drily subcoriaceous, seg. to 6cm×7mm, to 15 pairs, close, spreading, horizontal to ascending, oblong to linear, obtuse, entire to notched or dentate at apex; rachis prominent; stipes to 10cm, erect, straw-coloured. N America, Europe, Africa, E Asia. 'Bifidograndiceps': a fine, regularly crested form with each pinna tip bi- or trifid, 30–40cm. 'Bifidum': basal seg. cleft. 'Cornubiense': pinnae broad, neatly and regularly pinnatifid (as with *P. australe* 'Pulcherrimum'), but some fronds, or parts of fronds, always revert to normal, species form, very common, 30–40cm. 'Cornubiense multifidum': form with pinnae and frond tip slightly crested, 30cm. 'Cornubiense Grandiceps': terminal crests large, 25–30cm. 'Cristatum': seg. crested at tip. 'Elegantissimum': a refined form of 'Cornubiense', pinnae divisions finer, rare, this variety can become coarse and revert to normal 'Cornubiense', 30cm. 'Glomeratum': fronds branched and pinnae crested, no two fronds alike; a curiosity, 20–30cm. 'Jean Taylor' ('Congestum Cristatum'): a superb finely cut dwarf grandiceps form; like 'Cornubiense', some fronds or parts of fronds revert to normal; sections of rhiz. which produce coarse fronds should be removed; rare, 10–20cm. 'Ramosum': rachis branched many times, 20–30cm. 'Ramosum Hillman': seg. forking and crested. 'Trichomanoides Backhouse': a finely cut form, a non-crested form of 'Jean Taylor', very rare, 20cm. Z3.

***P. accedens*** Bl. See *Lemmaphyllum accedens*.
***P. areolatum*** Humb. & Bonpl. ex Willd. See *Phlebodium aureum* var. *areolatum*.
***P. arisanense*** Hayata. See *Goniophlebium amoenum*.
***P. aspidistrifrons*** Hayata. See *Microsorium steerei*.
***P. aureum*** L. See *Phlebodium aureum*.
***P. aureum*** var. ***reductum*** (Humb. & Bonpl. ex Willd.) Jennean. See *Phlebodium aureum* var. *areolatum*.
***P. australe*** Fée. See *P. cambricum*.
***P. brownii*** Wikstr. See *Dictymia brownii*.
***P. capitellatum*** Wallich. See *Arthromeris wallichiana*.
***P. carnosum*** Kellogg. See *P. scouleri*.
***P. coronans*** Wallich ex Mett. See *Pseudodrynaria coronans*.
***P. ensato-sessilifrons*** Hayata. See *Colysis hemionitidea*.
***P. feei*** (Bory) Mett. See *Selliguea feei*.
***P. fortunei*** Kunze. See *Drynaria fortunei*.
***P. fraxinifolium*** hort. See *P. menisciifolium*.
***P. hemionitideum*** (Presl) Mett. See *Colysis hemionitidea*.
***P. intermedium*** Hook. & Arn. See *P. californicum*.
***P. iridoides*** Poir. See *Microsorium punctatum*.
***P. japonicum*** (Franch. & Savat.) Maxon, non Houtt. See *P. fauriei*.
***P. juglandifolium*** D. Don. See *Arthromeris wallichiana*.
***P. latipes*** Langsd. & Fisch. See *P. mosenii*.
***P. linguaeforme*** Mett. See *Microsorium linguaeforme*.
***P. liukiuense*** Christ. See *P. formosana*.
***P. membranaceum*** D. Don. See *Microsorium membranaceum*.
***P. meyenianum*** (Schott) Hook. See *Aglaomorpha meyeniana*.
***P. neriifolium*** Schkuhr. See *P. triseriale*.
***P. normale*** D. Don. See *Microsorium normale*.
***P. normale*** var. ***madagascariense*** Bak. See *Microsorium pappei*.
***P. novae-zelandiae*** Bak. See *Microsorium novae-zelandiae*.
***P. occidentale*** (Hook.) Maxon. See *P. glycyrrhiza*.
***P. owariense*** Desv. See *Microgramma owariensis*.
***P. pachyphyllum*** D.C. Eaton. See *P. scouleri*.
***P. palmeri*** Maxon. See *Microgramma nitida*.
***P. pappei*** Mett. ex Kuhn. See *Microsorium pappei*.
***P. parksii*** Copel. See *Microsorium parksii*.
***P. persicifolium*** Desv. See *Goniophlebium persicifolium*.
***P. piloselloides*** L. See *Microgramma piloselloides*.
***P. propinquum*** Wallich. See *Drynaria propinqua*.
***P. pteropus*** Bl. See *Microsorium pteropus*.
***P. punctatum*** (L.) Sw. See *Microsorium punctatum*.
***P. rubidum*** Kunze. See *Microsorium rubidum*.
***P. sparsisora*** Desv. See *Drynaria sparsisora*.
***P. splendens*** (J. Sm.) Hook. See *Aglaomorpha splendens*.
***P. squamulosum*** Kaulf. See *Microgramma squamulosa*.
***P. steerei*** Harr. See *Microsorium steerei*.
***P. subauriculatum*** Bl. See *Goniophlebium subauriculatum*.
***P. vacciniifolium*** Langsd. & Fisch. See *Microgramma vacciniifolia*.
***P. vulgare*** var. ***columbianum*** Gilbert. See *P. hesperium*.
***P. vulgare*** var. ***japonicum*** Franch. & Savat. See *P. fauriei*.
***P. vulgare*** var. ***occidentale*** Hook. See *P. glycyrrhiza*.
***P. wrightii*** (Hook.) Mett. ex Diels. See *Colysis wrightii*.
For further synonymy see *Goniophlebium*, *Marginaria* and *Synammia*.

**Polypogon** Desf. (From Gk *polys*, many, and *pogon*, beard, referring to the setaceous panicles.) Gramineae. Some 18 species of annual or perennial grasses. Stems often decumbent, slender, upright or ascending. Leaves flat, scabrous. Inflorescence paniculate, contracted to spicate, bristled; spikelets short stipitate, 1-flowered, abscising; glumes narrow, equal, enclosing flower, papery to leathery, scabrous, 1-ribbed, entire to 2 lobed, awned; lodicules absent; palea inconspicuous; lemma membranous, truncate to acute, 5-ribbed; awn straight to sharply bent or absent, shorter than those of the glumes. Summer–autumn. Warm Temperate. Z8.

CULTIVATION Inhabitants of damp pasture and salt marshes, *Polypogon* spp. are grown for their compact silky inflorescence, used in fresh and dried arrangements, and particularly effective where space allows drift plantings. Sow seed *in situ* in spring in any moderately fertile, well-drained soil in sun.

***P. fugax*** Nees ex Steud. Annual to 60cm. Stems loosely clumped, upright or ascending. Lvs to 20×1cm, glabrous, scabrous above; ligules to 0.5cm. Infl. cylindric, compact, to 15×3cm, silky; spikelets oblong, to 0.3cm, tinged green to purple; glumes emarginate, rough, awns to 0.3cm. Warm temperate Asia, NE Africa.

***P. monspeliensis*** (L.) Desf. ANNUAL BEARD GRASS; BEARD GRASS; RABBIT'S FOOT GRASS. Annual to 60cm. Stems solitary or clumped, slender. Lvs to 15×0.8cm, glabrous; ligules to 1.5cm. Infl. narrow-ovoid to cylindric, to 15×3cm, tinged light green to yellow green, silky; spikelets narrow oblong, to 0.3cm; glumes obtuse, emarginate, short-ciliate, rough below, awns to 0.8cm, glumes to twice length of lemmas; lemmas shiny, awned. Cosmopolitan in Europe, naturalized N America.

***P. littoralis*** hort. See *P. fugax*.

**Polyscias** Forst. & Forst. f. (From Gk *polys*, many, and *skias*, shade, canopy, referring to the sometimes large, many-branched, spreading inflorescences reminiscent of some Umbelliferae.) Araliaceae. About 100 species of unarmed evergreen shrubs or trees to 25m or so but mostly rather smaller, some with a strong anise-like odour; well-grown tree species with an umbellifer-like crown, the leaves aggregated towards branch ends. Leaves simple, trifoliolate or once to twice or more times compound and then odd-pinnate. Inflorescences terminal, pseudolateral or on short shoots, paniculate, sometimes umbelliform or racemiform, once or more times compound; flowers solitary or more commonly in umbels or heads, racemosely or, when solitary, sometimes spicately arranged along inflorescence branches; pedicels, when present, jointed just below the ovary; petals 4–15, abutting one another in bud; ovary 2–13-locular, the locules equal to or more or less than the number of petals; styles usually united at base, becoming recurved above. Fruit drupaceous, remaining wholly inferior at maturity, surmounted by the persistent, indurated styles. Africa, Madagascar, Mascarene Is., S Asia, Ceylon, Malesia, Micronesia, Pacific Is. (except Hawaii and Marquesas), and Australia; particularly well represented in Madagascar (37 or more species), Mascarene Is. (13 species), New Guinea (17 species) and New Caledonia. The classification of the Polyscias group and its cultivars is in need of further study; most of the 'fancy' forms are here listed under *Polyscias* cultivars.

CULTIVATION In humid tropical and subtropical gardens, the larger forms of *Polyscias* make handsome shade trees with broad, umbrella-shaped crowns. As shrubs, older specimens generally make rather leggy, ungainly individuals, although some, including *P. sambucifolia*, are more elegant in shape and show good wind resistance. A better use for most of the shrubby sorts, with their rapid growth, dense branch system and tolerance of shearing, is as hedging or screening plants giving a soft, feathery foliage effect:

*P.guilfoylei, P.filicifolia* and *P.fruticosa* with spp. of *Codiaeum* are among the most commonly used hedging plants in many tropical lowlands. In temperate regions the marvellous variation in foliage form and colour, including a wealth of leaf dissection and serration as well as variegation/blotching/spotting of foliage, petioles and stems, make them beautiful foliage specimens for hot glasshouse conditions where minimum night temperatures of 16°C/60°F (rising by 3–6°C/−10°F by day) and high humidity are maintained: most of the listed cvs are more compact than the typical plants and will therefore make adaptable plants for containers. Also as houseplants where adequate warmth and humidity are available: arrange in groups or in shallow trays of damp pebbles to create a humid microclimate. In the open, plant into any well-drained but moisture-retentive, reasonably fertile soil in sun or part shade: hedge plants benefit from regular feeding. Under glass, grow in a medium fertility, loam-based mix in strong, filtered or indirect light: good light conditions (but not direct sunlight) are likely to give stronger leaf colourings. Damp down regularly in hot weather and spray over foliage: avoid draughts or fluctuations in temperature which cause foliage drop. Water plentifully during the growing season, sparingly in winter and feed mature container-grown plants monthly. Cut away straggly growth in spring.

Propagate easily by softwood cuttings or leafless stem sections in summer, rooted in a closed case with bottom heat; alternatively by air-layering or, less frequently, from seed. Susceptible to red spider mite and mealybug (especially under dry, hot conditions), scale insect and root nematode.

1 Flowers spicately or racemosely arranged, not in umbels. Main axis of inflorescence without terminal umbel. Leaves twice compound, blades always entire. Ovary 2-locular. Plants without strong odour.
*P. elegans.*

2 Flowers umbellate on short peduncles; umbels numerous, more or less uniformly arranged along inflorescence branches, flowering in a single cycle. Main axis of inflorescence without terminal umbel. Leaves once compound, 13–51-foliolate. Ovary 2–5-locular. Plants without strong odour.
*Pp. murrayi, nodosa.*

3 Flowers umbellate on short peduncles; umbels more or less numerous, irregularly arranged along inflorescence branches, flowering in 2 or more cycles. Main axis of inflorescence without terminal umbel. Leaves simple, trifoliolate, or once or twice pinnately compound, the segments or leaflets often highly dissected; stipular sheaths elongate. Ovary 2–5-locular. Plants with strong anise odour.
*Pp. cumingiana, quilfoylei, filicifolia, fruticosa, scutellaria* and nearly all variegated and other 'fancy' cultivars usually referable to *Polyscias*.

4 Flowers umbellate on short or variously elongate, sometimes branch-like peduncles; umbels relatively few, flowering in 2–3 cycles. Main axis of inflorescence with a terminal umbel. Leaves once-compound and to 11-foliolate or more highly dissected. Ovary 2-locular. Plants without strong odour.
*P. sambucifolius.*

***P. cumingiana*** (C. Presl) Fernandez-Villar. Coarse-looking, glabrous shrub or tree to 4m, not branched or but little-branched. Lvs crowded towards branch ends, once-pinnate, to 100cm, 5–9-foliolate, arising from a sheathing base 5–6cm, blades ovate-oblong or elliptic, shortly stalked, plane, to 30×13cm, apex narrowed, base obtuse to rotund or truncate or slightly cordate, often oblique, margin entire or minutely and distantly toothed. Infl. large, terminal, paniculate, sometimes partly leafy, the main axis to 140cm with primary branches to 120cm, radiating from the apex and also spreading from pseudowhorls along its length; fls in small umbels or irregularly distributed, bracteate peduncles; pet. 4–5, rarely 6; ovary 2–5-locular. Fr. purple to black towards maturity, to *c*5mm diam. C & E Malesia, mainly near coasts. Widely cultivated in settled areas in E Malesia and eastwards. *P. filicifolia* and *P. guilfoylei* are probably derivatives. Z10.

***P. elegans*** (C. Moore ex Muell.) Harms. CELERY WOOD; MOWBULAN WHITEWOOD; SILVER BASSWOOD. Somewhat pachycaul tree to 20m, at first unbranched, in time branching and forming a spreading, somewhat rounded crown; young parts pale brown to grey-hairy. Lvs twice pinnate, glabrescent, to 110×50cm or more; petiole sheath small; leaflets ovate or elliptic, entire, to 6×3cm. Infl. terminal, paniculate, twice compound, spreading, some hairiness persisting; main axis stout, to 30cm, the primary branches diverging along its length, reaching 30cm; secondary or peduncular branches similarly arrayed, to 10m, bearing racemosely arranged flowers; pet. 5; ovary 2-locular. Fr. dark purple, round, somewhat compressed, 5×5mm. E Australia (Kiama northwards), S & SE New Guinea. Z10.

***P. filicifolia*** (C. Moore ex Fourn.) L.H. Bail. ANGELICA; CHOTITO; FERN-LEAF ARALIA. Large erect glabrous shrub, the bark when young olive or tinged purple with white spots. Lvs in younger plants 9–17-foliolate, sometimes drooping, blades narrowly elliptic, fairly closely spaced, stalked, more or less deeply cut or pinnatifid, to 10cm or more long, bright green, the midribs tinted purple, apex and base attenuate, margins distantly and shallowly toothed; succeeding lvs with similarly divided but longer leaflets, followed by lvs more as in *P. cumingiana*. Infl. as *P. cumingiana* but less well developed, infrequently produced and abortive. A probable cultigen originating in E Malesia or the W Pacific, now widespread in warmer regions. Widely grown in the tropics as a specimen or hedge plant. Sometimes treated as a form of *P. cumingiana*. 'Ornata': juvenile lvs similar to typical form, but fairly soon passing into adult lvs; these oblong, entire, fairly closely spaced along rachis. GB 1888. 'Marginata' and 'Variegata': leaflets white-margined. Z10.

***P. fruticosa*** (L.) Harms. MING ARALIA. Glabrous erect shrub or small tree to 5–8m; young shoots with prominent lenticels. Lvs 1–3-pinnate, variable in size, to 75cm, the base clasping the stem, the petiole and rachis spotted; seg. shortly stalked, variable in size and shape but most often linear-lanceolate, narrow-ovate or oblong, to 20×5cm but commonly smaller, apices markedly acute, margins toothed or, particularly in more proximal seg., lobed or irregularly pinnatisect, the teeth spiny, surfaces most often olive green with a red tinge, the purple-red more evident below. Infl. paniculate, diffuse, to 15cm; fls in small umbels; ovary 2–3-locular. Fr. round, compressed, to 5×6mm. A possible cultigen originating in E Malesia or the W Pacific, now widespread in warmer regions. Widely grown in warm regions as a specimen or hedge plant. See cultivars. Z10.

***P. guilfoylei*** (Bull) L.H. Bail. GERANIUM ARALIA; WILD COFFEE; COFFEE TREE. Erect glabrous shrub or treelet to 6m or so, usually little-branched, in time forming narrow, spindly clusters of vertical stems; young parts brown-olivaceous green, with many light stripes. Lvs 5–9-foliolate, to 60cm but usually somewhat less, the sheathing base to 4cm, blades stalked, rotund to broadly ovate or oblong-elliptic, often oblique, plane, the terminal blade to 15×12.5cm, the lateral blades smaller, margins irregularly but sharply spiny-toothed and often obscurely lobed, surfaces mostly green but marginal areas white or cream. Infl., when produced, terminal, paniculate, somewhat umbelliform and diffuse; main axis to 4cm, the primary branches mostly radiating from the apex, the 50cm; secondary branches mainly in verticilliform clusters along the primary branches or radiating from their ends, to 8cm; fls in small umbels at ends of secondary branches or on peduncles along them, brown in bud, yellow-green when open; pet. 5; ovary usually 3-locular. Fr. round, to 5mm diam. A probable cultigen originating in E Malesia or the W Pacific, now widespread in warmer regions. Widely grown in the tropics as a specimen or hedge plant. 'Crispa': slow growth, compact; lvs glossy, tinged bronze, sharply toothed. 'Laciniata': shrub; lvs twice-pinnate, drooping; primary pinnae 5, the seg. of various shapes and sizes but mainly lanceolate with white margins, the margins also variously toothed and cut. 'Monstrosa': shrub; lvs once-pinnate, 3–7-foliolate, the blades elliptic with grey-blotched surfaces and creamy-white margins, the margins irregularly cut. 'Variegata': leaflets with irregular white or cream patches. 'Victoriae' LACE ARALIA: relatively compact; lvs 3–5-foliolate, the primary pinnae deeply divided and redivided, the terminal portion larger; seg. elliptic, tapering at base, the margins with a pure white border and irregularly toothed or cut. Z10.

***P. murrayi*** (F. Muell.) Harms. PENCIL CEDAR; UMBRELLA TREE. Straight-trunked pachycaul tree to 20m, in basic form and growth much as *P. elegans*. Lvs once-pinnate, 13–51-foliolate, to 122cm, the rachis jointed; blades shortly stalked, oblong to narrowly oblong, to 20cm, softly textured, almost glabrous, finely toothed to almost entire, green on both sides, turning black on drying. Infl. terminal, paniculate, pyramidal; fls in umbels 2.5cm diam., racemosely arranged along the primary infl. branches; pet. 5; ovary 2-locular. Fr. almost blue, somewhat compressed. E Australia (extreme NE Victoria to NE Queensland). The usual inclusion here of *Aralia splendidissima* Bull ex W. Richards (GB 1876, originally imported from the 'South Sea Islands'), a juvenile form, is doubtful, particularly as some authorities suggest an origin in New Caledonia. Z10.

***P. nodosa*** (Bl.) Seem. BINGLIU; RANGIT; WILD PAPAYA. Similar to *P. murrayi*, but attaining 25m and with lvs to 3m, sessile leaflets to 15×4cm, fls in heads and a 5-locular ovary. Fr. round. Malesia, Solomon Is. (Bougainville). In New Guinea at higher altitudes replaced by *P. ledermannii* Harms, a celery-tree to 15m or more with fls in umbels and a 3–4-locular ovary. Z10.

***P. paniculata*** auct., non (DC.) Bak. The plants initially recognized as *Terminalia elegans* Bull ex Hibb. (GB 1866; Belgium 1867; originally imported from 'Madagascar'), a juvenile form with coloured, trifoliolate lvs, have been placed here since 1887. They belong, however, to a recently described species of *Gastonia* from Mauritius. See also *P. guilfoylei*.

***P. sambucifolia*** (Sieb.) Harms. ELDERBERRY PANAX. Glabrous shrub or small tree to 6m, spindly when arborescent. Lvs very variable, once or twice compound; undifferentiated lvs to 40cm, 9–11-foliolate; blades stalked or sessile, broadly elliptic to linear-lanceolate, to 8×2cm, stalked or sessile; upper surface green above, paler beneath, margins entire or remotely toothed, midrib forming a ridge above; more differentiated lvs once- or twice-compound, seg. sessile, variously pinnatifid, the upper part of the rachis winged, the whole sometimes markedly glaucous. Infl. terminal or on short shoots, paniculate, 1–3 times compound, columnar to pyramidal; pet. 5, yellow to green; ovary 2-locular. Fr.

almost blue and translucent, later purple, round, to 9mm across, somewhat compressed. Spring and early summer. E Australia (Victoria to S Queensland). The pattern of forms and variation, to which several names have been applied, remains imperfectly understood. Z9.

***P. scutellaria*** (Burm. f.) Fosb. Shrub or small narrow tree to 6m; twigs stout. Lvs 1–3-foliolate, rarely to 5-foliolate, to 30cm; sheathing base to 6cm; blades broadly elliptic or orbicular, often shield-like, to 28cm wide though commonly smaller, the apex rounded, the base obtuse to cordate, margins entire or obscurely and minutely spine-toothed or sometimes more or less lobed, surfaces uniformly green or, in some forms, with white margins or points. Infl. terminal, paniculate, somewhat umbelliform, to 60cm; main axis much reduced, to 3cm; primary branches several, radiating, to 40cm; secondary branches mostly more or less verticillately arranged along primary branches or radiating from the apex, to 3cm; fls yellow-green, in small umbels at ends of secondary branches or on short peduncles along them or also at their ends; pet. 5–9; ovary usually 3–5-locular. Fr. round, to 5mm diam. A possible cultigen originating in E Malesia or the W Pacific, now widespread in warmer regions. The few obviously associated cultivars are treated below. Many other 'fancy' forms, derived from chimeras or hybrids and seldom or never flowering, exist. 'Balfourii' BALFOUR ARALIA: tree to 7m, usually rather smaller in cult.; stems erect, green, speckled grey; lvs 1–3-foliolate, blades broadly ovate to orbicular, to 10cm wide, margins toothed or cut, often white. 'Cochleata': lvs unifoliolate, shield-like. 'Pennockii': lvs 1–3-foliolate, blades yellow green with white along midrib and main veins, the margins upturned. 'Tricochleata': lvs 3-foliolate; similar to and possibly not distinct from 'Balfourii'. Z10.

***P.*** cultivars. Mostly dwarf. 'Balfourii': see *P. scutellaria*. 'Crispa': similar to 'Crispata', but more crinkly. 'Crispata' CHICKEN GIZZARD: compact; lvs odd-pinnate, 3-foliolate, the leaflets overlapping, blades triangular-rotund in outline, the lateral more or less bifid, margins toothed and sometimes incised. GB 1888. 'Deleauana': lvs pinnately 3–5-divided, the primary divisions again and again split into smaller seg., especially below; seg. linear to wedge-shaped or, outwardly, oblique-subelliptic, these latter variously serrate and lobate; marginal teeth white-apiculate. 'Diffissa': lvs bipinnate, crisped, bright green; leaflets linear-oblong, lobed and spiny-toothed. 'Dissecta': erect, branching; lvs drooping, bipinnate; leaflets wedge-shaped, obovate, often bilobed, the margins long-toothed. GB 1882. 'Dumosa': to 50cm, with short, densely foliaged stems; lvs pinnately divided, green, the outline round-ovate, primary divisions closely spaced, ultimate seg. very variable in form, their margins spiny-toothed; petiole brown or olive-green, mottled brighter green. 'Elegans': dense; lvs leathery, finely divided; resembles 'Deleauana'. 'Excelsa': see 'Plumata'. 'Fissa': stems erect, branching, with pallid spots; lvs tripinnate, blades linear-lanceolate, white-toothed, the teeth few, incurved. 'Laciniata': see *P. guilfoylei*. 'Lepida': dense; lvs twice-ternately divided, the terminal seg. largest, lateral pinnules of secondary seg. obliquely obovate, but central one much reduced and distinctly covered by the lateral pinnules; margins deeply incised and spinosely toothed. 'Marginata' DINNER-PLATE ARALIA: shrub; lvs 1–3-foliolate; blades more or less rotund, green with margins white-bordered or pointed, the venation somewhat palmate. 'Monstrosa': see *P. quilfoylei*. 'Multifida': compact, with feathery crown of tripinnatisect lvs, the seg. to 1cm or so, linear or linear-lanceolate, tipped with a short white bristle; margins often also with bristly teeth. GB 1887. 'Nitida': compact shrub; lvs round-obovate, margins with slightly spinulose teeth and 1–2 incisions towards the base. 'Ornata': see *P. filicifolia*. 'Plumata': shrub; lvs bipinnate, the pinnules pinnatisect, sharply toothed; ultimate seg. small, narrow, very fine; more finely cut than *P. guilfoylei* and possibly like 'Elegans'. 'Quercifolia': compact; lvs 5-foliolate; blades large, dark coppery green, pinnatifid, oblong or rotund in outline. 'Rotundata': lvs closely set; 3–5-pinnate, the main divisions further divided, ultimate pinnules more or less variegated, somewhat round, serrated at the edge, the teeth extending into minute spines. 'Serratifolia': stem and petioles marked with brown; lvs compound, leaflets serrated at edge. 'Spinulosa': stem and petioles spotted and suffused with crimson; lvs odd-pinnate, 5–7-foliolate, blades dark green, oblong, acute; margins spinulose, the teeth tinged red. 'Victoriae': see *P. guilfoylei*.

***P. balfouriana*** (Sander ex André) L.H. Bail. See *P. scutellaria* 'Balfourii'.
***P. fruticosa*** 'Elegans'. See *P.* 'Elegans'.
***P. paniculata*** hort., non (DC.) Bak. See *P. guilfoylei*.
***P. pinnata*** Forst. & Forst. f. See *P. scutellaria*.
***P. tricochleata*** (Miq.) Fosb. See *P. scutellaria* 'Tricochleata'.
For further synonymy see *Aralia*, *Nothopanax*, *Panax* and *Tieghemopanax*.

**Polystachya** Hook. (From Gk *polys*, many, and *stachys*, spike.) Orchidaceae. About 200 species of epiphytic, occasionally lithophytic or terrestrial, orchids. Stems usually pseudobulbous at base, clustered on a woody rhizome, the pseudobulbs 1- to several-noded, bearing 1 to several leaves. Inflorescence terminal on pseudobulb, racemose, paniculate or more or less spicate, 1- to many-flowered. Flowers non-resupinate, usually not opening wide, often pubescent on outside, white, green, brown, yellow, orange, pink or purple, rarely red; lateral sepals oblique, forming mentum with column foot; lip entire or trilobed, with or without a callus, often fleshy and recurved; column short and stout with more or less elongated foot; pollinia 2, stipes 1. Africa, Madagascar, east to Philippines, Indonesia and New Guinea, S US, Caribbean, C & S America. Z10.

CULTIVATION Epiphytes usually of compact habit and small stature, suitable for pans, baskets and rafts in brightly lit, humid, intermediate conditions. A brief dry rest should be imposed in winter. See ORCHIDS.

***P. adansoniae*** Rchb. f. Epiphytic, occasionally lithophytic, 10–30cm. Pseudobulbs 2.5–9×1cm, oblong, conical or cylindrical, ribbed, green or yellow-green, 2–3-lvd at apex. Lvs to 20×1.5cm, linear or ligulate, slightly lobed at apex. Spike 5–12cm, densely many-fld; fls yellow-green or almost white, anth. and tip of lip purple or brown; bract 4–8mm, hair-like; median sep. 3.5×1.5mm, ovate, acuminate, lateral sep. 4–5.5×2.5–3mm, obliquely ovate, acuminate; mentum narrow, 7mm high; pet. 2×1mm, linear-oblong; lip to 4×3mm, trilobed in apical half, recurved, with fleshy, pubesc. callus between lobes, lateral lobes rounded, midlobe lanceolate, acuminate; column 1.5mm; ovary 3–5mm. Widespread, Tropical Africa.

***P. affinis*** Lindl. Epiphytic, erect or pendent, to 50cm. Pseudobulbs almost orbicular but dorso-ventrally flattened, 1–5cm wide, 2–3-lvd. Lvs 9–28×2.5–6cm, including 5–14cm petiole; lamina oblanceolate or oblong. Infl. racemose or paniculate, erect or pendent, to 40cm, laxly many-fld; peduncle covered with overlapping scarious sheaths; fls fragrant, white or yellow with red-brown markings, outside pubesc.; sep. 6.5–8×3–6mm, median sep. lanceolate, lateral sep. obliquely triangular-ovate, forming mentum 4.5–6mm high; pet. 5.5–6.5×1.5–2mm, oblanceolate, truncate; lip 6.5–7.5×4.5–5.5mm, recurved, obscurely trilobed, lateral lobes erect, midlobe 2–3×2.5–3.5mm, ovate to suborbicular, subacute or rounded; disc with fleshy, puberulent ridge; column 1mm. W Africa, Central African Republic, Zaire, Uganda, Angola.

***P. bella*** Summerh. Epiphytic, 15–20cm. Pseudobulbs to 4×2cm, oval, compressed, 1–2-lvd. Lvs 5–16×2–3cm, elliptic or ligulate, leathery, petiolate. Infl. racemose or paniculate, erect, pubesc., to 25cm, fairly densely many-fld; fls yellow or golden yellow, the lip with deep orange central streak; pedicel and ovary arched, 9–10mm; median sep. 12–14×3–3.5mm, lateral sep. 15–17×5–5.5mm, obliquely lanceolate, acute; pet. 8–11×1.5mm, linear-oblanceolate; lip 9.5–11.5×5–5.5mm, obscurely trilobed, lateral lobes erect, 1mm, midlobe 4.5–5×2.5mm, triangular-lanceolate, acuminate, fleshy, recurved, with low callus at base; column 2.5–3.5mm. Kenya.

***P. campyloglossa*** Rolfe. Dwarf, epiphytic, to 12cm. Pseudobulbs 1–2×0.5–1cm, ovoid or globose, 2–3-lvd. Lvs 5–10×1–2cm, oblanceolate or linear, minutely bilobed at apex, dark green sometimes edged with purple. Raceme slightly longer than lvs, 2–6-fld; peduncle pubesc.; sep. and pet. green, yellow-green or yellow, lip white, lateral lobes purple-veined; pedicel and ovary 5mm, pubesc.; median sep. 8–13×4–7mm, ovate, acute, lateral sep. to 14×10mm, obliquely triangular, acute, forming mentum 6.5–9.5mm high; pet. 6.5–9.5×2–3mm, oblanceolate; lip 8–11×6–9.5mm, trilobed, recurved, with pubesc. disc and conical callus at junction of lobes, lateral lobes erect, rounded, pubesc., midlobe 4–5×2–5mm, ovate, fleshy, glabrous; column 3mm, stout. E Africa, Malawi.

***P. concreta*** (Jacq.) Garay & Sweet. Large, epiphytic, sometimes lithophytic, rarely terrestrial. Pseudobulbs 1–5×1cm, ovoid or conical, sometimes ribbed, 3–5-lvd. Lvs to 30×5.5cm, oblanceolate or elliptic, minutely bilobed at apex, dark green, sometimes purple-tinged. Panicle to 50cm, many-fld; peduncle covered with scarious sheaths; fls rather fleshy, small, yellow, pale green, pink or dull red-purple with white or cream lip; pedicel and ovary 6mm; median sep. 2–3×2–2.5mm, ovate, acute, lateral sep. 3–5.5×3–3.5mm, obliquely ovate, apiculate, forming mentum 3–4mm high; pet. 2–3.5×1mm, oblanceolate; lip 3.5–5×2.5–4mm, trilobed about halfway, recurved, with fleshy longitudinal callus running from base to junction of lobes, lateral lobes 1mm, triangular or oblong, midlobe 1.5–2.5×2–3mm, suborbicular; column 1–2mm, foot to 3mm. Widespread in tropical Africa; Florida, C & S America.

***P. cultriformis*** (Thouars) Spreng. Epiphytic or lithophytic, to 25cm. Pseudobulbs 2–18cm, 2–12mm wide at base, conical or cylindrical, clustered on rhiz., 1-lvd. Lf 3–36×1–5.5cm, elliptic, acute or obtuse, auriculate at base, articulated 2–6mm above apex of pseudobulb. Infl. racemose or paniculate, to 30cm, several- to many-fld; fls white, green, yellow, pink or purple; pedicel and ovary 6mm; bracts 4–5mm; median sep. 4–8×2–4.5mm, ovate, apiculate, lateral sep. 5–8×3–6mm, obliquely triangular, apiculate, mentum to 7mm; pet. 3.5–7.5×1–2.5mm, linear to spathulate; lip 4–8×3–6mm, recurved, trilobed in apical half, with fleshy yellow central callus, lateral lobes rounded, midlobe 1.5–4.5×1.5–3.5mm, oblong, apiculate; column 0.5–3.5mm. Widespread in tropical Africa; S Africa, Madagascar, Mascarene Is., Seychelles.

***P. dendrobiiflora*** Rchb. f. Epiphytic on *Xerophyta* spp., lithophytic or terrestrial. Pseudobulbs 1.5–5×0.5–1cm, conical, ribbed, clustered, 5–10-lvd. Lvs 8–25×0.5–1.5cm, linear, grass-like, deciduous. Infl. paniculate, borne on old pseudobulbs when plants leafless, to 80cm; peduncle covered with brown, scarious sheaths; branches few to many; fls in clusters of 1–3, well spaced out, opening over a long period, opening wide, pale to deep lilac-pink or white, lip sometimes with red or lilac spots; pedicel and ovary 10–12mm; dorsal sep. 6.5–12×3–4mm, oblong, obtuse, lateral sep. similar but oblique, mentum conical, 3–5mm high; pet. 6–12×2.5–4.5mm, oblong, rounded; lip 7–11×4–5.5mm, entire, with yellow, slightly pubesc. longitudinal callus toward base, ovate-oblong, recurved, rounded at apex, the edge often undulate; column 2.5–4mm, winged; anth. cap deep lilac. Burundi, Kenya, Tanzania, Malawi, Zambia, Zimbabwe, Mozambique, Angola.

***P. foliosa*** (Hook. f.) Rchb. f. Erect epiphyte to 45cm. Pseudobulbs to 2cm, ovoid. Lvs 2–5, to 20×3cm, narrowly elliptic, obtuse. Peduncle covered with scarious sheaths; panicle with several branches, rather laxly many-fld; fls fleshy, green or yellow-green; median sep. 3×2mm, ovate, acute, lateral sep. 4×2.5mm, obliquely triangular, acuminate; pet. to 2.5mm long, less than 1mm wide, linear or narrowly oblanceolate; lip to 4×3mm, trilobed, with farinose disc and ovoid callus, midlobe oblong, apex recurved, emarginate, lateral lobes triangular-falcate, acute; column to 1mm, column foot less than 1mm. Tropical C & S America, Grenada.

***P. galeata*** (Sw.) Rchb. f. Epiphytic, to 40cm. Pseudobulbs 6–14cm×2–5mm, cylindrical, clustered, 1-lvd. Lf 8–27×1–3.5cm, oblanceolate or ligulate, acute or obtuse, coriaceous, articulated 1–5mm above apex of pseudobulb. Raceme shorter than lf, pubesc., to 6-fld; fls white, green, yellow-green, yellow or pink, with some purple spots; dorsal sep. 7–14×3–7mm, ovate, apiculate, pubesc., lateral sep. 10–22×6–18mm, obliquely triangular, pubesc., with recurved apiculus, mentum 13–22mm high; pet. 4.5–11×1–3.5mm, spreading, linear or spathulate; lip 10–21.5×4–14mm, fleshy, trilobed, recurved, lateral lobes erect, midlobe 3–7×2–8mm, pubesc. in centre, quadrate to orbicular, apiculate, the apiculus reflexed; column 1–3mm. W Africa, Zaire, Angola.

***P. goetzeana*** Kränzl. Erect or pendent epiphyte. Pseudobulbs 5–15×5–7mm, obliquely conical, 3–4-lvd. Lvs 8–22cm×4–8mm, linear, grass-like, usually deciduous. Raceme erect, shorter than lvs, 3–5-fld; peduncle covered with scarious sheaths; sep. lime green or yellow-green, purple-veined, pet. and lip white, the lip with yellow central line; pedicel and ovary 6mm, arched, pubesc.; dorsal sep. 9–14×3.5–5.5mm, lanceolate, lateral sep. 13–15×7–9mm, obliquely triangular, acute, mentum 5–8mm high, broadly conical; lip 11–15×9–10mm, recurved, pubesc., trilobed at about the middle, with a yellow, pubesc. keel running from the base to junction of lobes, lateral lobes erect, rounded, midlobe 5.5–8×6–9mm, subquadrate, apiculate, the edge undulate; column 4–5mm. Tanzania, Malawi.

***P. kermesina*** Kränzl. Epiphyte, to 11cm. Pseudobulbs to 2cm×1–1.5mm, arising from middle of previous growth, 2-lvd. Lvs 2–4cm×1.5–2.5mm, linear, acute. Raceme shorter than lvs, 1–3-fld; fls rather fleshy, orange or scarlet, opening almost flat, with sep. and pet. recurved near apex; dorsal sep. 4×4mm, ovate or orbicular, obtuse, lateral sep. 5×6.5mm, obliquely ovate-orbicular, obtuse, forming mentum 3mm high; pet. 4×1.5mm, oblong; lip 8–9×4mm, fleshy, with long, hairy claw, obscurely trilobed, lateral lobes rounded, midlobe 3.5×3.5mm, orbicular, with a tooth-like callus at junction of lobes; column 1mm. Zaire, Uganda.

***P. lawrenceana*** Kränzl. Lithophytic, forming clumps. Pseudobulbs 2.5–5.5×1–1.5cm, conic-elliptic, glossy green with 2–3 nodes, 3–4-lvd. Lvs to 15×2cm, lax, ligulate, slightly bilobed at apex. Raceme to 16cm, laxly 6–8-fld; peduncle pubesc.; fls fleshy, pubesc. on outside; sep. and pet. yellow-green flushed with maroon, lip bright pink, occasionally pale pink, with white callus; dorsal sep. 9×4.5mm, ovate, acute, lateral sep. 11×6.5mm, obliquely ovate-triangular, acuminate, forming subconical, incurved mentum 5.5mm high; pet. 8×2.5mm, oblanceolate, obtuse; lip 9×8mm, recurved, trilobed, lateral lobes erect, oblong, midlobe 7×6mm, broadly ovate, obtuse, with central groove and smooth, fleshy callus; column 2mm. Malawi.

***P. leonensis*** Rchb. f. Pseudobulbs subglobose, 1cm diam., set closely on rhiz., 3–6-lvd. Lvs 7–20×1–2.5cm, lanceolate, acuminate. Raceme to 20cm, laxly several-fld; sep. and pet. pale green, usually flushed with purple-brown, lip white, lateral lobes tinged purple; median sep. 3–4mm, ovate, obtuse, lateral sep. 4–5mm, obliquely triangular, obtuse, forming narrow, cylindrical mentum 5–6mm high; pet. 4mm, oblong, obtuse; lip 6mm, trilobed, lateral lobes triangular-oblong, obtuse, midlobe ovate, obtuse; disc pubesc.; column 2mm, stout. W Africa.

***P. melliodora*** Cribb. Epiphytic, forming large clumps; pseudobulbs about 3×2cm, oblong, bilaterally flattened, 1-lvd. Lf 15×3cm, erect, narrowly oblong-elliptic, rounded at apex. Raceme to 10cm, to 8-fld; fls honey-scented, waxy, white, the lip purple-edged with yellow callus, anth. cap pink; median sep. 12×7mm, ovate, acuminate, lateral sep. 15×10mm, obliquely triangular, acuminate, with wide median keel on outside, mentum 8mm high, conical, bilobed at apex; pet. 11×4.5mm, oblong, acute; lip 11×9mm, recurved, obscurely trilobed; column 4mm long. Tanzania.

***P. modesta*** Rchb. f. Small epiphyte, rarely lithophyte. Pseudobulbs 8–25×3–15mm, conic or ovoid, yellow or purple, clustered on rhiz., 3–5-lvd. Lvs to 8×1.5mm, lanceolate, edged purple. Infl. racemose or with a few short branches, densely several- to many-fld; fls glabrous, fleshy, pale yellow tinged with purple, lip usually darker yellow; pedicel and ovary 3–4mm; bracts 2–3mm, triangular, acute; median sep. 3×2mm, ovate, acute, lateral sep. 5×3mm, obliquely triangular, forming rounded mentum 3mm high; pet. 3×1mm, oblanceolate; lip 4×3mm, trilobed, recurved, with no callus but with a pubesc. cushion, lateral lobes erect, 1mm, rounded or acute, midlobe 1–2mm, suborbicular, bullate, obtuse or emarginate; column 1.5mm. Resembling *P. concreta* and sometimes considered conspecific, but differing mainly in lack of callus and much smaller size. Widespread, tropical Africa.

***P. mystacidioides*** De Wildeman. Creeping or pendent epiphyte with dimorphic stems; pseudobulbs either narrowly cylindrical and stem-like with many distichous lvs, or swollen with 1 terminal lf, in either case arising some distance above base of previous growth. Lvs fleshy, bilaterally compressed, 2–15cm×5–10mm. Infl. single-fld; fls relatively large, white with red or purple marks, or pale brown; sep. 8–9mm, pubesc.; lip 10–11×5–6mm, trilobed, lateral lobes small, midlobe oblong, slightly emarginate. Ivory Coast, Cameroun, Zaire.

***P. odorata*** Lindl. Epiphytic, rarely lithophytic, 20–40cm. Pseudobulbs 2–4.5×0.5–1.5cm, almost globose to narrowly conical, 4–8-lvd. Lvs 13–26×3–4cm, oblanceolate to elliptic, minutely bilobed at apex. Panicle 10–30cm, including peduncle to 15cm; branches 6–15, many-fld; fls scented, pubesc. outside, white, pale green or dull red-brown; sep. flushed with red or purple, lip white, midlobe pink-tinged, callus yellow; median sep. 5×2.5–3mm, ovate, acuminate, lateral sep. 8–9×4–5.5mm, obliquely ovate, apiculate, forming mentum 4–5.5mm high; pet. 4.5–5×1–1.5mm, oblanceolate; lip 7–8×5–7.5mm, recurved, trilobed about halfway, lateral lobes erect, 4×2.5mm, midlobe 2.5–3×3.5mm, suborbicular, emarginate, the edge crenulate; callus fleshy, 2×1mm, lying between lateral lobes; column 2–2.5mm. W Africa, Zaire, Uganda, Tanzania, Angola.

***P. ottoniana*** Rchb. f. Dwarf epiphyte. Pseudobulbs 10–20×8–12mm, obliquely conical, in chains or clustered. Lvs 2–3, 7–12cm×6–9mm, linear or linear-lanceolate. Raceme erect, 1–6-fld; fls white tinged with pink or lilac, lip with yellow central stripe; pedicel and ovary 10mm; median sep. 10–11×2–3mm, lanceolate, acute, lateral sep. 12–14×7mm, obliquely lanceolate; pet. 10×2mm, oblanceolate; lip obscurely trilobed in basal half, 10–11mm, reflexed toward apex; column 5mm, slender; anth. cap violet. S Africa, Swaziland.

***P. paniculata*** (Sw.) Rolfe. Erect epiphyte, 22–40cm. Pseudobulbs 5–18cm×13–22mm, cylindric, clustered, with 3–4 nodes, 3–4-lvd. Lvs 10–30×2–3.5cm, distichous, ligulate, unequally bilobed at apex. Panicle to 21cm, many-fld; peduncle glabrous, 5–13cm; fls small, orange or vermilion, the lip marked with darker red; median sep. 3×1mm, lanceolate, acute, lateral sep. 3–4×1.5–2mm, obliquely lanceolate, acute, forming conical mentum to 1.5mm high; pet. 2.5–3×0.5mm, oblanceolate; lip 2.5–3×1.5–2mm, entire, ovate or elliptic; column 1mm. W Africa to Zaire.

***P. pubescens*** (Lindl.) Rchb. f. Epiphytic or lithophytic. Pseudobulbs conical, 2–3-lvd. Lvs 6–7×1.5–2cm, broadly lanceolate or elliptic. Raceme erect, several- to many-fld; peduncle and rachis pubesc.; fls opening fairly widely, golden yellow, lateral sep. and lip with red lines; pedicel and ovary 10–15mm; median sep. 10–12×4mm, lanceolate, acute, lateral sep. obliquely ovate, 14×7mm; pet. 11–12×4mm, oblanceolate; lip 9–12mm, trilobed about halfway, lateral lobes 1–2mm, covered with white, silky hairs, midlobe 5–6mm; column very short. S Africa, Swaziland.

***P. villosa*** Rolfe. Epiphytic, rarely lithophytic. Pseudobulbs to 4×1.5cm, oblong or conical, sometimes slightly bilaterally flattened, ribbed, yellow-green with 2–3 nodes, 3–4-lvd. Lvs to 18×3cm, oblanceolate or ligulate, rounded or minutely bilobed at apex. Raceme 15–20cm, including pubesc., 10–13cm peduncle, densely many-fld; fls densely hairy on outside, primrose-scented, pale green, white or cream, the lip white with purple spots on side lobes and at base of midlobe; pedicel and ovary 9–10mm; bracts to 15×7mm, broadly ovate, acuminate; median sep. 7–10×3–4mm, ovate, acute, lateral sep. 9–13×4–7mm, obliquely lanceolate, acuminate, slightly keeled on outside, mentum 4mm high, rounded; pet. 6–7×1.5–2mm, oblanceolate, acute; lip 5–8×3–4mm, rather fleshy, recurved, trilobed, with glabrous yellow callus at junction of lobes, lateral lobes erect, rounded, midlobe 2.5×2.5mm, bullate, ovate, acute or acuminate; column 1.5mm. Tanzania, Zambia, Malawi.

***P. virginea*** Summerh. Epiphytic. Pseudobulbs 5–11cm, cylindrical or conical, loosely clustered on short, creeping rhiz., 1-lvd. Lf 12–26×1–3cm, lanceolate, obtuse, articulated 1mm above apex of pseudobulb. Raceme 4–9cm, shorter than lf, to 10-fld, the fls opening in succession; fls white, scented; median sep. 8.5–12×4.5–7.5mm, ovate, apiculate, lateral sep. 8.5–12×4.5–9.5mm, obliquely triangular, forming conical mentum 9–10mm high; pet. 8–13×3–4.5mm, elliptic to ovate; lip 11.5–15.5×8–11mm, recurved, trilobed, with central fleshy callus, lateral lobes erect, rounded, midlobe 4–6×4–6.5mm, triangular to subquadrate, apiculate; column 1–3mm. Zaire, Burundi, Rwanda, Uganda.

***P. vulcanica*** Kränzl. Epiphytic or lithophytic. Pseudobulbs 1–9cm×5–15mm, narrowly cylindrical, tightly clustered on short, creeping rhiz., 1-lvd. Lf 2.5–11cm×1–4mm, linear, articulated 3–4mm above apex of pseudobulb. Raceme 2–9cm, shorter than lf, to 5-fld, the fls borne in succession; sep. creamy white flushed with rose-pink, pet. and lip wine red or purple; median sep. 3–6.5×1.5–3.5mm, ovate, apiculate, lateral sep. 4–8×3.5–9mm, obliquely triangular, apiculate, forming conical mentum 7–8mm high; pet. 3–6×1–2.5mm, spathulate, obtuse; lip 5–10×4–7mm, fleshy, recurved, trilobed, with or without a somewhat pubesc., fleshy callus in middle, lateral lobes erect, midlobe 1–4×1.5–6mm, suborbicular, apiculate; column 1–2mm; anth. cap rose-purple. Zaire, Uganda.

***P. zambesiaca*** Rolfe. Small, epiphytic, often lithophytic. Pseudobulbs 1–2×1cm, ovoid, slightly bilaterally flattened, often wrinkled, forming clumps or chains,

2–3-lvd. Lvs 3–8×1–1.5cm, lanceolate or oblanceolate, pale glaucous green, often purple-edged. Raceme 5–7.5cm, usually shorter than lvs, pubesc., 3–20-fld; fls pubesc. on outside, yellow or yellow-green, lip white or pale yellow, purple-veined on lateral lobes; pedicel and ovary 6–9mm; bracts 4–6mm, white tinged green, ovate, acuminate; median sep. 8–10×3.5–4.5mm, ovate, acute, lateral sep. 9–12×4–6mm, obliquely triangular, acuminate, keeled on outside; pet. 6–7×1.5–2mm, oblanceolate; lip 6–7×4–5mm, fleshy, recurved, with brown, pubesc. callus at base, lateral lobes erect, rounded, midlobe bullate, ovate, acute; column 1.5mm. Tanzania, Malawi, Zambia.

***P. adiantiforme*** (Forst. f..) J. Sm. See *Rumohra adiantiformis*.
***P. bracteosa*** Lindl. See *P. affinis*.
***P. buchananii*** Rolfe. See *P. concreta*.
***P. capense*** (Willd.) J. Sm. See *Rumohra adiantiformis*.
***P. coriaceum*** (Sw.) Schott. See *Rumohra adiantiformis*.
***P. cultrata*** Lindl. See *P. cultriformis*.
***P. flavescens*** (Lindl.) J.J. Sm. See *P. concreta*.
***P. gerrardii*** Harv. See *P. cultriformis*.
***P. luteola*** (Sw.) Hook. See *P. concreta*.
***P. minuta*** (Aubl.) Frappier ex Cordm. See *P. concreta*.
***P. rufinula*** Rchb. f. See *P. concreta*.
***P. tayloriana*** Rendle. See *P. dendrobiiflora*.
***P. tessellata*** Lindl. See *P. concreta*.

**Polystichopsis** (J. Sm.) Holtt.
***P. mutica*** (Franch. & Savat.) Tag. See *Arachniodes mutica*.
***P. nipponica*** (Rosenst.) Tag. See *Arachniodes nipponica*.

**Polystichum** Roth. (From Gk *polys*, many, and *stix*, a row, referring to the regular rows of sori seen on many species.) HOLLY FERN. Dryopteridaceae. More than 175 species of small to medium-sized terrestrial ferns. Rhizomes erect or decumbent, woody, densely paleate at apex; stipes not articulate to rhizome, generally paleate. Fronds erect, arching, or occasionally recurved, mostly 1–3-pinnate, rarely almost simple, uniform or more or less dimorphic, generally coriaceous, more or less paleate; ultimate divisions more or less auriculate, generally serrate to minutely spinose; rachis grooved; veins always free. Sori dorsal to subterminal on veins, round; indusium orbicular, centrally peltate, rarely wanting; spores bilateral. Cosmopolitan.

CULTIVATION A large genus widely distributed from alpine cliffs to tropical forests. Many species and cultivars are of immense value as plants of the rock garden or herbaceous border; other more tender species are suitable for pot culture in the greenhouse. The commonest species in cultivation (*P. setiferum*) is hardy to −30°C/−22°F or more, but many other species are equally hardy, notably those from montane habitats in Asia (e.g. *P. prescottianum*) or North America (e.g. *P. munitum*). Some protection of favourite exotic species in cold periods is advisable; a bundle of dead fern fronds (not *Polystichum*) resting loosely over the crown is efficient protection.

*Polystichum* spp. like a well-drained site: in the wild they usually grow among rocks or on moderately dry banks. They are susceptible to winter damp and it is therefore advisable to plant crowns at an angle of 60–70° from the vertical with the roots and side of the crown protected by a rock. This technique is particularly valuable when establishing *P. lonchitis*. *Polystichum* will tolerate part sun for up to six hours a day in moist soil. In full shade under trees in a water-retentive soil they can tolerate quite dry conditions. Preferred pH is 6.5 to 7.5; in very acid soils some species, such as *P. setiferum*, gradually lose vigour.

Plant out in late spring or throughout summer in cool spells, watering well until established. In spring it is wise to remove the previous season's fronds as they might harbour the fungal disease *Taphrina wettsteiniana*. Related to peach leaf curl, once established it can only be controlled by using a systemic fungicide in late winter or early spring. In severe cases subsequent sprays in summer may be necessary. Aim to protect the crown of the plant. *T. wettsteiniana* is native or naturalized in southern and western Europe, occurring on *P. lonchitis* and *P. setiferum*, particularly in wet summers. Symptoms are black lesions on the upper surface of the pinnae with a fine granular layer of white sporing bodies on the underside.

Under glass, there is a *Polystichum* species suited for all ranges of temperatures. In all cases shade will be needed in high summer and good drainage in the pot is essential. Use a low-fertility loam-based mix with grit added; water moderately. Propagate by spores or division in spring. Also by bulbils in late summer/early autumn, where appropriate.

***P. acrostichoides*** (Michx.) Schott. CHRISTMAS FERN. Rhiz. creeping, scaly at apex; stipes 10–25cm, green, scaly. Fronds 20–50×5–12cm, linear-lanceolate, pinnate, acuminate, not reduced at base, pinnae alternate, 20–35 each side, spreading, linear-oblong, acute, acutely auriculate at base, minutely spinose-dentate, dark green and glabrous above, clad in hair-like scales below, fertile upper pinnae abruptly reduced. N America (Nova Scotia to Wisconsin, south to Florida, Texas and Mexico). Z4.

***P. aculeatum*** (L.) Roth. Rhiz. thick, ligneous; stipe short, brown scaly. Fronds 30–90×5–22cm, lanceolate, pinnate or bipinnate, generally persistent, rigid, pinnae to 50 per side, pinnate or pinnatifid; pinnules serrate, obliquely decurrent, sessile or subsessile. Indusium thick, persistent. Europe. Z5.

***P. andersonii*** L.S. Hopk. Rhiz. stout, decumbent, scales large, thin, palely castaneous; stipes 5–25cm, paleaceous. Fronds 40–80×8–20cm, in a close crown, narrowly lanceolate-oblong to lanceolate-elliptic, sub-bipinnate, long-acuminate, pinnae numerous, slightly ascending, narrowly deltoid, subpinnate, at base, basal seg. enlarged, seg. oblique, elliptic, more or less adnate, decurrent, strongly serrate; rachis sulcate, paleaceous. NW America (British Columbia, Montana, Washington). Z4.

***P. australiense*** Tind. Rhiz. clad in dull papery brown scales; stipes likewise scaly. Fronds to 120×20cm, 2–3-pinnate, dark green, harsh and coriaceous, with a proliferous bud near apex of main rachis, pinnules serrate, with short apical spine longer than serrations. Australia (NSW). Z10.

***P. braunii*** (Spenn.) Fée. Rhiz. erect; stipes thick, 13–18cm, densely scaly. Fronds to 80×20cm, oblong-lanceolate, generally bipinnate, acuminate, soft, usually dying in autumn, pinnae 30–40 per side, alternate above, subopposite below, pinnate to pinnatifid, pinnules 9–15 per side, ovate-deltoid to ovate-oblong, acute, serrate, obliquely decurrent, scarcely or not at all auriculate, sessile or subsessile, minutely spinose-dentate with incurved teeth, softly pubesc. above, veins scaly on both sides. N America, Eurasia. Z5.

***P. californicum*** (D.C. Eaton) Underw. Rhiz. stout, suberect; stipes to 35cm, sulcate, copiously paleaceous below, nearly naked above, scales darkly castaneous. Fronds 20–75×5–20cm, linear-oblong to narrowly linear-lanceolate, attenuate, subcoriaceous, becoming coriaceous with age, pinnae numerous, ascending or spreading, linear, broadened at base, obliquely pinnatifid to incised, seg. elliptic, decurrent, distinctly aristate; rachis minutely paleaceous. W US (Washington to California). Z8.

***P. craspedosorum*** (Maxim.) Diels. Rhiz. short; stipes few, short, spreading, 0.5–5cm, densely clad in rusty brown scales. Fronds 5–18×1.5–3.5cm, lanceolate, pinnate, pinnae 1–1.5cm, in 15–35 pairs, spreading, narrowly oblong, obtuse at apex, broadly cuneate and auriculate at base, sessile, dentate, rachis often much prolonged, proliferous and rooting at apex. NE Asia (Japan, Korea, China, Manchuria to E Siberia). Z4.

***P. cystostegia*** (Hook.) Cheesem. Rhiz. stout, erect, branched, scales to 15mm, pale brown; stipes 5–15cm, rather stout, densely scaly at rhiz. Fronds 8–15×3–5cm, lanceolate to oblong-lanceolate, pale green, softly membranous, pubesc. particularly when young, pinnae to 4×1.5cm, numerous, rather distant, ovate, pinnate to pinnatifid, pinnules ovate to lanceolate, crenate, to 1cm; rachis winged. New Zealand. Z7.

***P. dudleyi*** Maxon. Rhiz. decumbent, densely paleaceous, scales brown to grey, large, thin; stipes 15–45cm, ascending, sulcate, paleaceous. Fronds 25–75×8–25cm, oblong-lanceolate to narrowly ovate, acuminate to attenuate, pinnae contiguous, oblique, linear to narrowly oblong-lanceolate, attenuate, filiform-paleaceous particularly below, pinnules obliquely ovate or ovate-oblong, auriculate, serrate to incised. California. Z8.

***P. falcinellum*** Moore. Rhiz. short, stout, ascending; stipes 10–30cm, generally clad in copious glossy brown scales. Fronds 30–150cm, evergreen, lanceolate, pinnate, tapered at base, pinnae 2.5–10cm, very numerous, linear, acuminate, acutely biserrate, subsessile, auriculate on upper side at base, subtruncate on lower side, generally paleate below; rachis generally paleaceous as stipes; veins free, once or twice forked. N America. Z5.

***P. fallax*** Tind. Rhiz. clad in dark brown or black papery scales and fine, downy scales; stipe similarly scaly on lower part. Fronds to 70×20cm, 2–3-pinnate, with no proliferous buds, pinnules ovate, margins irregularly serrate, apical spine longer than marginal ones. Australia (NSW, Queensland). Z10.

***P. imbricans*** (D.C. Eaton) Wagner. Stipes 5–20cm, scales elongate, concolourous, darkly castaneous. Fronds 20–45×4–9cm, linear, pinnate, subtruncate at base, tapered to acute to acuminate at apex, pinnae 2–4.5cm, entire, shortly minutely spinose, auriculate at upper base, excavate at lower; rachis scaly as stipes. NW America (British Columbia to California). Z7.

***P.*×*kruckebergii*** Wagner. (*P. lonchitis* × *P. lemmoni.*) Stipes 2–10cm, clad in long, pale scales. Fronds 8–20×1.5–3cm, linear-lanceolate, scarcely tapered to truncate base, acute at apex, pinnate to pinnatifid, pinnae oblong, short, lobulate with larger basal auricle on upper side, lower pinnae rather distant from median ones. N America (British Columbia to California, east to Montana, Idaho and Utah). Z4.

***P.*×*kurokawae*** Tag. Stipes rather stout, 25–30cm, scaly. Fronds 40–80×20–25cm, broadly lanceolate to oblong-ovate, slightly narrowed towards base, pinnae 2–2.5cm wide, pinnules oblong-ovate to ovate, oblique, obtuse to subacute, mucronate, spinose-dentate, scaly below, sparsely so above; rachis with pale chestnut to dull brown spreading scales. Japan. Z8.

***P. lachenense*** (Hook.) Bedd. Rhiz. rather stout; stipes erect, 3–10cm, densely brown-scaly at base, sparsely so above. Fronds 8–20×1.5–2.5cm, linear-lanceolate, pinnate, acute, pinnae to 15–25 pairs, spreading, ovate, sessile, coarsely awned-dentate or occasionally lobed, sparsely scaly beneath. NE Asia (Japan, China to Himalaya). Z8.

***P. lemmoni*** Underw. Rhiz. tufted, ascending, stout, beset with old stipe bases; stipes 3–15cm, stramineous, very paleaceous at base. Fronds 10–30×1.5–5cm, linear to narrowly lanceolate-oblong, pinnate to pinnatifid, succulent, pinnae numerous, generally imbricate, deltoid-oblong to deltoid-ovate, pinnae at base, pinnatifid nearer apex, seg. close, spreading, trapeziform-ovate to obliquely ovate, obtuse, crenate. NW America (Washington to California). Z7.

***P. lentum*** (D. Don) T. Moore. Very similar to *P. proliferum*, but fronds bipinnate, never tripinnate. Himalaya. Z8.

***P. lepidocaulon*** (Hook.) J. Sm. Rhiz. short, ascending; stipes few, 10–40cm, with dull brown scales. Fronds 15–40×6–15cm, narrowly ovate, pinnate, broadest at base, often rooting and proliferous at apex of prolonged rachis, pinnae 3–10×0.5–2cm, 10–20 per side, lanceolate, spreading, acuminate, subentire to undulate-dentate, sessile, scaly below; rachis with adpressed scales to 4mm; veinlets occasionally somewhat anastomosing. NE Asia (Japan, Taiwan, China, Korea). Z8.

***P. lonchitis*** (L.) Roth. NORTHERN HOLLY FERN. Rhiz. short, erect or ascending; stipes very short or almost wanting. Fronds 20–60×3–7cm, linear-lanceolate, pinnate, tapered to both ends, persistent, rigid, coriaceous, pinnae 25–40 each side, spreading at 90° to rachis, lanceolate, occasionally overlapping, slightly curved, auriculate on upper side at base, margins serrate, acuminate, dark green and glabrous above, scaly beneath, very shortly stipitate; rachis densely deciduously scaly. Europe. Z4.

***P. macleaii*** (Bak.) Diels. Rhiz. erect, densely clad with thin brown scales; stipes 30–55cm, pale brown or tinged green, clad with ferruginous to brown scales, particularly near base and when young. Fronds 40–60×20–24cm, numerous, clustered, erect or arching, narrowly oblong, pinnate, with triangular terminal seg. to 4cm, coriaceous, rigid; pinnae in 25–40 pairs, alternate, linear-lanceolate, attenuate, serrate, dark green and glabrous above, minutely brown-scaly below, veins prominent, repeatedly forked; rachis pale brown, scaly to subglabrous. S Africa. Z9.

***P. makinoi*** (Tag.) Tag. Stipes tufted, 20–40cm, stramineous, with chestnut to brown scales. Fronds 30–60×10–20cm, pinnae acute to acuminate, pinnules 7–15×3–6mm, obliquely ovate, obtuse to subacute, with short apical spine, adpressed spinose-dentate, coriaceous-herbaceous, scaly beneath; rachis with dense, spreading to deflexed scales. Japan. Z8.

***P. mayebarae*** Tag. Rhiz. stout, short, densely clad in old stipe stumps; stipes stramineous, densely clad in brown to black scales. Fronds 30–40×10–18cm, ovate-lanceolate, bipinnate, pinnae lanceolate, 1.5–3cm wide, pinnules 8–15×5–8mm, rhombic-ovate, spinose-dentate in distal portion, with short apical spine; rachis with prominent black to brown scales. Japan. Z8.

***P. mohrioides*** (Bory ex Urv.) C. Presl. Stipes to 18cm, densely scaly, scales ovate, acuminate, dark brown with paler margins. Fronds 20–60×6–15cm, elliptic-lanceolate to ovate-lanceolate, bipinnate, pinnate 3–8×1–2cm, lanceolate to oblong-lanceolate, pinnae, pinnules 8–12×4–7mm, ovate to sub-rhomboid, acute, obtusely lobed to shallowly pinnatifid. Tierra del Fuego, Falkland Is. Z5.

***P. munitum*** (Kaulf.) Presl. Rhiz. short, erect to procumbent, densely covered in mid-brown scales on young parts, or by persistent old frond bases on older parts; stipes to 18cm, densely scaly near base. Fronds to 90cm, evergreen, linear, pinnate, rigid, coriaceous, harsh; pinnae to 40 per side, linear, acuminate, serrate to biserrate; rachis green, flattened, sulcate. N America. Z4.

***P. neolobatum*** Nak. Stipes rather stout, stramineous, brown below, densely scaly. Fronds 20–80cm, broadly lanceolate, gradually acuminate, bipinnate, pinnae in 15–40 pairs, spreading, lanceolate to ovate, acuminate, subsessile, coriaceous, sparsely scaly above, more densely so below, pinnules 7–15×3–7mm, obliquely ovate, acute, mucronate, remotely spinose-dentate, lustrous both sides, veins slender; rachis densely scaly. NE Asia (Japan, China, India, Taiwan). Z8.

***P. polyblepharum*** (Roem.) Presl. Rhiz. erect to ascending, densely clothed in old stipe stumps; stipes tufted, stout, 20–30cm, stramineous, densely clad with membranous brown scales to 2.5cm. Fronds 30–80×15–25cm, narrowly oblong-ovate, bipinnate, short-acuminate, slightly narrowed at base, deep green and slightly lustrous above, pinnae 15–25mm wide, pinnules 8–15×4–6mm, oblong-ovate, oblique, mucronate, adpressed spinose-dentate, scaly below; rachis densely scaly. Japan, S Korea. Z5.

***P. prescottianum*** (Wallich) Moore. Stipes 2–7cm, clad in soft, pale scales. Fronds 15–30×3–3.5cm, deeply pinnatifid to subpinnate, acute at apex, pinnae 1–2×0.5–1cm, ovate-oblong to elongate-lanceolate, truncate at base, uniformly serrate, soft and membranous, scaly beneath. Himalaya. Z5.

***P. proliferum*** (R. Br.) Presl. MOTHER SHIELD FERN. Rhiz. thick, massive and trunk-like with age, densely clad in dark brown, glossy scales often with paler margins; stipes densely similarly clad at base. Fronds to 100×30cm, bipinnate to tripinnate, dull, pale green when young, dark green when mature, with proliferous buds near apex of main rachis, pinnules serrate, apical spine as long as marginal ones. Australia (NSW, Victoria, Tasmania). Proliferates freely, forming plantlets near frond apices which root as the frond ages, giving rise to large colonies. Z10.

***P. retrorsopalaeceum*** (Kodama) Tag. Rhiz. short, stout; stipes tufted, 20–40cm, clad in membranous brown scales. Fronds 40–100×15–30cm, abruptly acuminate, slightly narrowed to base, pinnules oblique, ovate to ovate-oblong, obtuse, mucronate, ascending- to adpressed-dentate; rachis scaly with adpressed scales beneath, spreading scales above. Japan. Z8.

***P. richardii*** (Hook.) J. Sm. Rhiz. stout, erect, scales subulate, very dark brown with pale margins; stipes stout, 15–30cm, paleaceous below, hairy above. Fronds 25–30×10–15cm, lanceolate to deltoid-oblong, bipinnate, acuminate, very dark green and glabrous above, paler and somewhat scurfy beneath, coriaceous, pinnae 5–10×2–4cm, lanceolate, acuminate, pinnules to 15×5mm, lanceolate- to ovate-oblong, sharply serrate to crenate or subentire, lower very shortly stalked, upper decurrent-confluent. New Zealand, Fiji. Z9.

***P. rigens*** Tag. Stipes 20–40cm, stramineous above, darker brown below, with long-acuminate brown to black scales. Fronds 30–45×10–20cm, narrowly ovate-oblong, bipinnate, acuminate, firmly coriaceous, pinnae 15–25mm broad, lanceolate, lowest very shortly stipitate, pinnules 10–12×4–7mm, obliquely ovate, mucronate, spinose-dentate to subentire, decurrent on very narrowly winged rachis, glabrous above, with scattered scales beneath; rachis scaly. Japan. Z7.

***P. scopulinum*** (D.C. Eaton) Maxon. WESTERN HOLLY FERN. Rhiz. erect; stipes clustered, 2–12cm, densely scaly. Fronds 10–30×2.5–4cm, linear-lanceolate, pinnate, acute, somewhat reduced at base, glabrous above, paleaceous below; pinnae 30–40 per side, alternate, spreading at 90° to rachis, obtuse to somewhat acute, larger auriculate. N America (Quebec, W US). Z2.

***P. setiferum*** (Forssk.) Woyn. SOFT-SHIELD FERN. Rhiz. thick, ligneous; stipes to 12cm, thickly clad in broad pale orange-brown scales. Fronds 30–120×10–25cm, often prostrate, lanceolate, bipinnate, generally not persistent, soft, pinnae to 11×2.5cm, to 40 per side, pinnate, pinnules serrate, not decurrent, distinctly stipitate; rachis bearing bulbils at junctions with primary pinnae. S, W & C Europe. 'Acutilobum': 50–70cm; pinnules narrowed and pointed, completely undivided except for a 'thumb' on some basal pinnules; frond texture hard. 'Congestum': 30–50cm; frond congested, often combined with cresting. 'Cristatogracile Moly': 30–50cm; pinnae and frond lightly crested, dark green; an old variety, rare. 'Cristato-pinnulum': 70–80cm; pinnules fan-shaped and notched along margin; frond slightly depauperate along rachis, bulbiferous; very striking variety. 'Divisilobum': 50–70cm; texture hard, bulbiferous; pinnules narrowed and pointed (as with 'Acutilobum') but pinnules clearly divided at least near base of frond. There are many named forms of which the following are distinct: 'Divisilobum Bland': the best wild find of 'Divisilobum', 50–70cm; bottom half of frond feathery with pinnae overlapping, bulbiferous. (Divisilobum grandiceps group): forms of 'Divisilobum', 30–60cm, with enormous terminal ramose heads, some pinnae branched at tips, bulbiferous. 'Divisilobum Inveryanum': 50cm; a crested form of 'Divisilobum', frond spreading, bulbiferous. 'Divisilobum laxum': 50–60cm; pinnae and pinnules well separated, an airy form of 'Divisilobum'. 'Foliosum Walton': 30–50cm; a fine foliose form. 'Gracillimum': raised form 'Plumosum Bevis', 30–50cm; pinnules greatly elongated with some tasselling at tips in well-developed specimens, frond spreading and very open; very rare. 'Lineare' ('Confluens'): 30–80cm; pinnules narrow, pinnules at base of pinnae often missing. 'Multilobum': 60–80cm; akin to 'Divisilobum' but pinnules divide into segments which are not narrowed, frond not glossy. 'Plumosum Bevis': 60–90cm; pinnules elongated into fine points, toward tip of frond pinnae curve toward apex, dark green with a glossy surface; usually sterile but when spores are produced wonderful progeny have resulted, e.g. 'Plumosum Drueryi', 'Plumosum Green' and 'Gracillimum'. 'Plumosum Drueryi': raised from 'Plumosum Bevis', 60–70cm; pinnules divided, dark green, completely sterile; very rare. 'Plumosum Green': 60–70cm; raised from 'Plumosum Bevis'; pinnules deeply divided into narrow segments, frond quadri-pinnate and completely sterile; very rare. 'Plumosum Moly': wild find, 100–120cm, tall feathery fronds with broad pinnules, tri-pinnate completely sterile; rare. 'Rotundatum': 50cm; pinnules rounded. 'Wakeleyanum': 50–90cm; pinnae cruciate in mid section of frond, frond narrow. Z7.

***P. setigerum*** (Presl) Presl. *(P. braunii × P. munitum.)* ALASKAN HOLLY FERN. Stipes 6–20cm, scales on lower part broad, pale brown, on upper part slender, stramineous. Fronds 25–90×8–20cm, rhombic, pinnate-pinnatifid to sub-bipinnate, tapered to base, acute to acuminate at apex, pinnae oblong, distal lanceolate, deeply lobed to subpinnate at base; rachis scaly as stipes. NW America (Alaska to British Columbia). Z3.

***P. silvaticum*** (Colenso) Diels. Stipes 5–25cm, densely clad with broad, shiny, dark brown scales with pale margins. Fronds 15–40×5–18cm, elliptic to narrowly so, bipinnate, dark green above, pale green below, pinnae 3–10×1–3cm, main veins winged, pinnules elliptic to ovate, deeply dissected, with long, fine apical points; rachis densely scaly as stipes. New Zealand. Z8.

***P. tripteron*** (Kunze) Presl. Rhiz. erect to ascending, clad with old stipe stumps; stipes erect, 10–40cm, pale green, laxly scaly, scales to 15mm, brown. Fronds 20–45×5–10cm, lanceolate, pinnate, acuminate, pinnae 2.5–5×0.5–1cm, 20–35 per side, lanceolate, strongly oblique on anterior side at base, acuminate, often falcate, ascending-dentate, occasionally lobulate, with slender, soft apical awn, glabrous above, sparsely scaly beneath, pinnules in 8–15 pairs; rachis pale green, sparsely scaly. NE Asia (Japan, Korea, China to E Siberia). Z6.

***P. tsussimense*** (Hook.) J. Sm. Rhiz. rather stout, short, clad in old stipe stumps; stipes tufted, pale green to stramineous, browner at base, with black to brown scales to 5mm. Fronds 25–40×10–20cm, broadly lanceolate to oblong-ovate, acuminate, pinnules 7–15×3–7mm, ovate to oblong-ovate, oblique, mucronate, spinose-dentate, sessile, glabrous and glaucous above; rachis prominently scaly as stipes. NE Asia (Japan, China, Korea, Taiwan). Z7.

***P. vestitum*** (Forst. f.) Presl. Rhiz. stout, ascending, branched, to 15cm diam., densely paleaceous with scales to 2cm; stipes to 45cm, stout, usually densely paleate, brown. Fronds 30–75×10–25cm, oblong-lanceolate, bipinnate, dark green above, paler below, rather harsh; pinnae to 12×2.5cm, lanceolate-oblong, acute to acuminate, pinnules to 15mm, generally very close-set, ovate-oblong to subrhombic, variously dentate, very shortly stalked; rachis grooved, paleate and hairy. S Atlantic (New Zealand, Tasmania, Tierra del Fuego). Z7.

***P. adiantiforme*** (Forst. f..) J. Sm. See *Rumohra adiantiformis*.
***P. angulare*** (Kit. ex Willd.) C. Presl. See *P. setiferum*.
***P. aristatum*** Hook. non (Forst.) Presl. See *P. richardii*.
***P. aristatum*** (Forst.) Presl. See *Arachniodes aristata*.
***P. aristatum*** var. ***simplicium*** (Mak.) Matsum. See *Arachniodes simplicior*.
***P. auriculatum*** (L.) Presl. See *P. harpophyllum*.
***P. capense*** (Willd.) J. Sm. See *Rumohra adiantiformis*.
***P. caryotideum*** (Wallich) Diels. See *Cyrtomium caryotideum*.
***P. coriaceum*** (Sw.) Schott. See *Rumohra adiantiformis*.
***P. falcatum*** (L. f.) Diels. See *Cyrtomium falcatum*.
***P. fortunei*** (J. Sm.) Nak. See *Cyrtomium fortunei*.
***P. hispidum*** (Sw.) J. Sm. See *Lastreopsis hispida*.
***P. lobatum*** (Huds.) Chevall. See *P. aculeatum*.
***P. lobatum*** var. ***chinense*** Christ. See *P. neolobatum*.
***P. macrophyllum*** (Mak.) Tag. See *Cyrtomium macrophyllum*.
***P. monotis*** Christ. See *P. tsussimense*.
***P. nipponicum*** Rosenst. See *Arachniodes nipponica*.
***P. plicatum*** (Poepp. ex Kunze) Hicken. See *P. mohrioides*.
***P. rhomboideum*** Schott. See *Arachniodes amabilis*.
***P. schkuhrii*** Presl. See *Lastreopsis hispida*.
***P. simplicius*** (Mak.) Tag. See *Arachniodes simplicior*.
***P. standishii*** (Moore) C. Chr. See *Arachniodes standishii*.
***P. tsussimense*** var. ***mayebarae*** (Tag.) Kurata. See *P. mayebarae*.
For further synonymy see *Aspidium*.

**Polyxena** Kunth. (For Polyxenus (Priam), King of Troy.) Liliaceae (Hyacinthaceae). 5–6 species of dwarf perennial herbs, seldom exceeding 15cm. Bulbs with a dense mat of soft branching roots and tubular, membranous, truncate tunics extending into a neck. Leaves 10–15×cm, 2, basal, opposite, ovate to linear, canaliculate, spreading above, sheathing below, glabrous. Flowers fragrant in a terminal corymb; peduncle concealed by sheathing leaf bases; bracts small, membranous; pedicels short; tepals 6, salverform, marcescent, fused into a long narrow tube, lobes spreading; stamens 6, in 2 series, filaments fused to base of tube; ovary trilocular, style terete, stigma apical. Fruit a rounded, 3-valved, capsule; seeds globose, black, shiny. Early spring. S Africa. Z9.

CULTIVATION As for *Massonia*.

***P. angustifolia*** Bak. Lvs 10×2.5cm, erect. Fls 6 or more in a spike; tepals 7.5–16cm, white, reflexed for half their length. Cape Province.

***P. corymbosa*** (L.) Jessop. Lvs 2–3, narrow, linear, erect. Flowering stem to 5cm; tepals carmine, outside paler. Cape Peninsula.

***P. odorata*** Nichols. Lvs 10–12.5×0.6cm. Flowering stem 1.5–2.5cm; fls subsessile, held between lvs, white. Cape Province. Closely resembles *Massonia*.

***P. pygmaea*** Kunth. Lvs to 10×2.5cm. Flowering stems 10–15cm; fls to 2cm diam.; tepals lilac, recurved. Cape Province.

For synonymy see *Massonia* and *Neobakeria*.

**Pomaderris** Labill. (From Lat, *poma*, a lid, and *derris*, skin, referring to the membrane surrounding the capsular fruit.) Rhamnaceae. About 40 species of evergreen, woody, perennial shrubs or small trees (always shrubs in cultivation), 2–4m. Leaves alternate, oblong to aciform, large to small, more or less covered in rusty to white stellate pubescence. Inflorescence cymose, often terminal and paniculate, corymbose; flowers small; calyx 5-lobed, tube fused to ovary; petals absent or 5; stamens 5. Fruit a small, 3-valved, dry capsule. Spring–summer. Australia, New Zealand. Z9.

CULTIVATION *P. rugosa* occurs in poor coastal clays; *P. apetala* is found in *Nothofagus* forest in Tasmania and in eucalypt woodland in Australia, as is *P. elliptica*, which has also naturalized on the coast of North Island, New Zealand. Grown for the fluffy heads of yellow flowers and often felted foliage, *Pomaderris* spp. are suited to warm borders or rock gardens (select according to size) in essentially frost-free zones; otherwise for the cool glasshouse. *P. kumeraho* flowers in early spring; the buds of the following year's flowers are produced concurrently and require a full year to develop fully. *Pomaderris* spp. are unsuitable for shallow soils over chalk; cultivation otherwise as for *Colletia*. Propagate also by seed; *P. kumeraho* produces seed in abundance, but this may take three years to germinate.

***P. apetala*** Labill. Shrub or small tree to 4m. Lvs 5–7cm, oval or oval-oblong, apex subacute to obtuse, markedly rugose and glabrous above, margins with small, irregular, rounded teeth, densely clothed in stellate hairs beneath; petioles 1cm. Infl. 7–25cm, axillary or terminal, paniculate, subpyramidal; fls many, *c*6mm diam., apetalous, pale yellow; cal. tube stellate-hairy. Fr. half concealed by cal. tube; seeds *c*1.5×1mm, dark. Australia.

***P. elliptica*** Labill. Shrub to 2m, with young growth, lower lf surfaces and cal. covered in white stellate hairs. Lvs 5–10×2–5cm, ovate to elliptic-lanceolate, glabrous above. Infl. a 5–7cm-wide flat cluster; fls pale yellow; pet. broad. Australia, New Zealand.

***P. kumeraho*** A. Cunn. Rounded shrub, 2–3m, with slender branches. Lvs to 6×3cm, oval or elliptic, glaucous above, stellate-pubesc. beneath. Infl. to 10cm diam., dense; fls yellow; cal. with both stellate and simple hairs on tube 2.5mm long. Fr. one-third concealed by cal. tube; seeds 1.6×1mm, glossy dark brown. New Zealand.

***P. phylicifolia*** Lodd. Shrub to 1m, habit ericoid, young growth densely lanate. Lvs 4–12×1–2mm, larger on younger plants, oblong to linear, with inrolled margins concealing stellate pubescence beneath. Infl. groups of axillary, lax cymes forming large, leafy panicles; fls small, apetalous, pale yellow; cal. tube 4.5mm. Fr. *c*3mm, one-third covered by cal. tube; seeds to 1.6–2mm, glossy dark brown. Spring. Australia, New Zealand.

***P. rugosa*** Cheesem. Erect, much-branched shrub to 3m. Lvs 1–5.5cm on petioles to 5mm, oblong-lanceolate to elliptic, stellate-hairy beneath, rusty-brown near veins. Infl. axillary or terminal, cymose; fls *c*4mm diam., apetalous, cal. covered in stellate hairs. Fr. *c*3.5mm, three-quarters concealed in cal. tube; seeds 2×1mm, dark brown. New Zealand.

**Pomatocalpa** Breda. (From Gk *pomatos*, flask or cup, and *kalpe*, pitcher, referring to the lip shape.) Orchidaceae. Some 60 species of epiphytic, monopodial orchids. Stems short or long, rarely climbing. Leaves oblong or lorate. Racemes nodal, erect or decurved, often branched, dense; flowers many, small; sepals and petals free, spreading, almost equal; lip trilobed, base fused to column foot, midlobe forward-pointing or recurved, fleshy, ovate-triangular or semi-orbicular, lateral lobes triangular, broad, posterior margin fused to column foot; spur round, saccate, a ligulate projection from the back wall often extends to the mouth. China, Malaysia, Australia, Polynesia. Z9.

CULTIVATION As for *Sobralia*.

***P. latifolia*** (Lindl.) J.J. Sm. Stems 5–30cm, stout. Lvs oblong, glossy, coriaceous, often yellow-green, to 20×4cm. Infl. erect, 15–40cm; sep. and pet. green-yellow, speckled or edged maroon; dorsal sep. to 0.5×0.2cm, concave, lateral sep. shorter; pet. to 0.5×0.2cm; lip yellow, midlobe ovate-triangular, lamellae on interior wall crenate, truncate, white, weakly suffused violet, interior of lateral lobes spotted red; spur yellow-green, speckled brown. Malaya, Sumatra, Java.

***P. siamensis*** (Rolfe ex Downie) Summerh. Stems to 35cm, leafy. Lvs linear-oblong, to 17×2cm. Infl. branched, 40–50cm; fls minutely pubesc; dorsal sep. ovate, obtuse, apex notched, exterior minutely pubesc., lateral sep. fleshy, ovate, acute, to 0.4–0.2cm; pet. spathulate, apex irregular, slightly oblique, to 0.4–0.2cm; lip trilobed, to 0.4cm, midlobe cordate, base broad, lateral lobes truncate; spur stout, cylindric, fleshy; callus oblong, erect, irregularly truncate, thick near aperture, with 2 backward-pointing lamellae. Thailand.

***P. spicata*** Breda. Stem short, stout. Lvs oblong-lorate, coriaceous, undulate, to 28×2cm. Infl. dense, simple or branched, decurved, to 15cm; fls pale yellow, sep. and pet. blotched maroon, spur lamellae violet, tipped white; sep. and pet. ovate-oblong, obtuse, to 0.5cm, lateral sep. incurved, obovate, pet. narrow at base, lip midlobe ovate-triangular, obtuse, spur interior with dentate, 2-ridged lamellae on dorsal surface. India to Vietnam, Philippines.

For synonymy see *Cleisostoma*.

**Poncirus** Raf. Rutaceae. (Latinized form of French *poncire*, a type of citrus (possibly derived from *pomsire*/*pomsiri* = *pomme de Syrie*).) 1 species, a fast-growing, small, deciduous tree, much-branched, armed with stout green axillary spines to 6cm. Twigs dimorphic, normal twigs with internodes 1–5cm, and spineless foliage spurs developing from buds on year-old twigs, with internodes less than 0.5mm, with 1–5-leaves. Leaves trifoliolate; terminal leaflet 3–6×1.5–2.5cm, minutely crenate, cuneate at base, with prominent main vein, lateral leaflets slightly smaller, sessile; petioles 1–2.5cm, winged. Flower buds subglobose, scale-covered, formed in early summer then overwintering before opening before or with leaves the following spring; flowers axillary, solitary, scented, subsessile, generally 5-merous; sepals almost free, ovate, persistent, to 10×4mm; petals subspathulate, narrowed to claw at base, soon deciduous, 2–3×1–1.5cm, white; stamens 20+ (–60), filaments free, unequal; ovary pubescent, generally 7-locular, ovules numerous, in 2 rows in each locule; style short, stigma rather large. Fruit globose to somewhat pyriform, sessile, 3–5cm diam., dull lemon-yellow, fragrant when ripe, densely pubescent; peel 0.5–1cm thick, rough, with copious oil glands; pulp sparse, of narrow pulp vesicles with very acid juice; seeds ovoid, very numerous. Spring. C & N China. Z5.

CULTIVATION Grown for the interlacing network of stiff thorny branches which are extremely attractive in winter and most useful in forming impenetrable barriers and hedges, *P. trifoliata* also bears sweetly scented flowers in late spring/early summer on the previous year's wood, followed by decorative but inedible fruits. Hardy to −15°C/5°F, it is sometimes used as a frost resistant rootstock for *Citrus*. Grow in any well-drained fertile soil in sun. Prune if necessary to remove any dead or damaged wood in spring; clip hedging in early summer. Propagate by seed, removed from flesh when ripe and sow in the cold frame in autumn; also by semi-ripe cuttings in summer.

***P. trifoliata*** (L.) Raf. TRIFOLIATE ORANGE; BITTER ORANGE. As for the genus.

For synonymy see *Citrus*.

**Ponerorchis** Rchb. f. (From Gk *poneros*, worthless, and *orchis*.) Orchidaceae. Some 24 species of terrestrial orchids. China, Japan.

CULTIVATION As for the hardier *Calanthe* spp.

***P. graminifolia*** Rchb. f. Roots tuberous, ovoid. Stems slender, 8–15cm. Lvs linear, to 12×0.8cm, acute to acuminate, arching. Racemes secund; fls few, rose-purple; sep. oblong, obtuse, 1-nerved, lateral sep. oblique; pet. ovate, oblique, erect, forming a hood with the dorsal sep.; lip ascending, deeply trilobed, lobes ovate; spur to 2cm. China, Japan. Z8.

**Pongamia** Vent. (From the Malabar name, *pongam*, for this plant.) Leguminosae (Papilionoideae). 1 species, an evergreen tree to 25m. Stems erect, short, with widely spreading branches. Leaves alternate, imparipinnate, bright green, glossy; leaflets 5–9, ovate, estipellate. Flowers in axillary racemes to 12.5cm; bracts caducous; bracteoles 2, small, subtending the calyx, often caducous; calyx campanulate or cupuliform, truncate, short-dentate; corolla pink-mauve or cream, standard suborbicular, broad, usually inflexed, biauriculate basally, thinly sericeous-pubescent beneath, wings oblique, slightly adnate to keel, keel obtuse; stamens united into a tube, anthers dorsifixed, connective pubescent; ovary 2-, rarely 3-ovulate; style filiform, glabrous; stigma small, terminal. Fruit legume, oblique-oblong, flat, smooth, 1-seeded; seed reniform. Summer–autumn. Indomalaysia, Australia. Treated by some authors as a species of *Millettia* Wight & Arn. Z10.

CULTIVATION Occurring in coastal forest and at streamsides, *P. pinnata* is a most ornamental tropical tree, widely used in street and avenue plantings and as a shade tree in large gardens, parks and on tea plantations. Rich in nitrogen, its leaves and flowers can be composted to provide a highly fertile litter. It has a good tolerance of maritime conditions and is well adapted to lakeside plantings. Since it has a deep root system, the ground under its spreading canopy remains sufficiently moist and fertile for underplantings. The foliage is highly aromatic when bruised, attractively coloured in shades of pink and red on emergence and glossy bright green with maturity; the pendent racemes of fragrant flowers are also beautiful. Cultivate as for *Gliricidia*.

***P. pinnata*** Pierre. INDIAN BEECH; KARANJA; THINWIN; KARUM TREE; POONGA OIL TREE. As for the genus.

**Pongelia** Raf. See *Dolichandrone*.

**Pontederia** L. (For Giulio Pontedera (1688–1757), Professor of Botany at Padua.) PICKEREL WEED; WAMPEE. Pontederiaceae. 5 species of perennial, aquatic or semi-aquatic, marginal herbs. Rhizomes branched, often submerged, floating or creeping; aerial stems erect or prostrate. Leaves lanceolate or sagittate to hastate or cordate to ovate or reniform, entire, dark green or somewhat glaucous, venation parallel, curving outwards; petioles long, sheathing and clasping at base, except leaf below inflorescence. Inflorescence spicate, with few to many flowers, enclosed by spathe when young; peduncle extending in fruit; solitary leaf below spathe; flowers small, zygomorphic, with bilabiate tubular perianth, each lip with 3 basally connate lobes, blue to purple or white to green-white, largest lobe spotted yellow; stamens 6, unequal, in 2 groups of 3, anthers introrse, versatile, filaments and perianth tube covered with glandular hairs; stigmas 3-lobed, each lobe bifid, tristylous or homostylous; carpels 3, 2 aborted, 1 fertile, unilocular, forming a 1-seeded nutlet surrounded by hardened base of perianth tube. Seeds reniform or ovoid. N & S America, mostly eastern.

CULTIVATION Marginal aquatics grown in full sun for their bold foliage and spikes of blue flowers; also in tubs to 30cm/1ft depth. Remove dead foliage after frosts. Propagate by division in spring, by cuttings in summer or from moist green seed sown with a covering of silver sand and submersed in 2cm/1in of water after seedling emergence.

***P. cordata*** L. PICKEREL WEED; WAMPEE. Variable aquatic perenn. to 1.3m. Lvs erect in 2 loose ranks cordate, sagittate, ovate or lanceolate, to 18×21cm; petioles to 60cm, except lf below infl. where to 30cm. Infl. 2–16cm, on peduncle to 35cm; fls many, to 17mm across, blue to white; anth. blue; styles 3. Fr. and seeds reniform, surrounded by toothed and ridged, hardened perianth base. Summer. Eastern N America to Caribbean. Z3.

***P. azurea*** Roem. & Schult. non Sw. See *Eichhornia crassipes*.
***P. azurea*** Hook. non Sw. nec Roem. & Schult. See *Eichhornia crassipes*.

**PONTEDERIACEAE** Kunth. PICKEREL WEED FAMILY. Monocot. 7 genera and 31 species of hydrophytes, sometimes free-floating, occasionally annual, branching sympodial, glabrous. Leaves usually with sheath, distinct petiole (sometimes inflated with aerenchyma) and expanded lamina with parallel curved-convergent veins (filiform in *Hydrothrix*), in basal rosettes, distichous or alternate along stem; roots with vessel-elements (often in stems also). Flowers bisexual, regular or irregular, often tristylous, solitary or in terminal racemes, spikes or panicles, subtended by a sheath, usually insect-pollinated; perianth 3+3(4 in *Scholleropsis*), petaloid, more or less basally connate; stamens 3+3 or 3+staminodes or 1+2 staminodes, adnate to perianth-tube; ovary superior, of 3 fused carpels; 3-loculed with axile placentas, or 1-loculed with intruded parietal placentas, usually with septal nectaries and 1 style; ovules numerous (1 pendulous in *Pontederia*). Fruit a loculicidal capsule (nut in *Pontederia*), maturing under water; seeds longitudinally ribbed with red tegmen; endosperm copious, starchy with outer aleurone layer. Several are serious weeds of waterways and rice fields, such as *Eichhornia crassipes* (water hyacinth) and *Pontederia cordata* (pickerel weed).

Some have edible parts as *Monochoria* and *Pontederia*. Tropical and warm, especially America, extending to N temperate. *Eichhornia, Heteranthera, Monochoria, Pontederia*.

**Pope, Alexander** (1688–1744). Poet and gardener. The son of a linen-draper, Pope was born in London. He suffered a severe illness at the age of twelve, after which the family moved to Binfield in Windsor Forest. His earliest writings were 'Pastorals', produced at the age of sixteen, and this genre could be said to encapsulate Pope's greatest preoccupations: classical forms and the world of the garden. His artistic aims are elucidated in the *Essay on Criticism* (1711) in which he praises 'Unerring NATURE ... At once the source, and end, and test of Art'. After establishing himself financially with the publication of his translation of the *Iliad* (1715–20), he and his mother moved to a villa at Twickenham in 1719 and there Pope spent the rest of his life, devoting the time when he was not writing to his own garden and grotto and the practice of landscape gardening. He spent his summers 'rambling', as he put it, on the estates of friends and acquaintances in southern England, thus providing himself with the opportunity to observe and criticize current gardening fashions.

His garden at Twickenham, unfortunately no longer extant, has been considered a compendium of his opinions on landscape gardening, and a description of its 'pleasing intricacy' was published in 1745 by Pope's gardener, John Searle. The five-acre garden alongside the Thames boasted what its author called a 'maze of fancy'; a complex of thickets and lawns, interwoven trees, alleys and walks, banks and hillocks, an obelisk dedicated to Pope's mother, a bowling green, a shell temple designed by William Kent, an amphitheatre, a wilderness and the famous grotto or subterranean passage – with its inset stones, shells, pieces of glass and the sound of a 'perpetual rill' – leading from the house, under the lawn and the public Hampton Road, and up into the landscape garden proper.

Pope described his ideal in an early essay in the *Guardian* in 1713 as 'the amiable Simplicity of unadorned Nature'. His principles were not altogether original; similar opinions were voiced by William Kent, Charles Bridgeman, Sir Henry Wotton, Stephen Switzer, Lord Shaftesbury and Joseph Addison. However, Pope did much to popularize and publicize the new styles in garden design.

Perhaps the most celebrated public statement of his principles of gardening – which included attention to topography and the artful negligence of regularity – were published in his verse 'Epistle to Lord Burlington' (1731):

> In all, let Nature never be forgot, ...
> Consult the Genius of the Place in all,
> That tells the Waters or to rise or fall, ...
> Now breaks, or now directs, th'intending Lines;
> Paints as you plant, and as you work, Designs.

The epistle received a highly critical reception, in response to which Pope wrote his last public defence of the new style of gardening, *A Master Key to Popery or a True and Perfect Key to Pope's Epistle to the Earl of Burlington*. His more casual remarks on gardens were recorded by Spence and in 1737 the publication of his letters permitted the public to discover many of Pope's private insights and observations regarding specific landscapes and gardens. In addition to his writings on the subject, Pope also gave encouragement and practical advice to his gardening friends at Marble Hill, Lord Burlington at Chiswick and to Lord Bathurst at Richings Park and Cirencester Park. He was also highly influential in the redesigning of the gardens at Bevois Mount near Southampton, and Wimpole Hall in Cambridgeshire.

**Populus** L. (Lat. vernacular name for the genus.) POPLAR; COTTONWOOD; ASPEN. Salicaceae. Some 35 species of deciduous, dioecious trees, to about 40m. Buds with several unequal scales, often resinous. Twigs angular to cylindrical in section. Leaves alternate, usually ovate to lanceolate or triangular, entire, toothed or lobed, on a long, terete, cylindrical or flattened petiole, often with glands at junction with leaf lamina. Inflorescence a pendulous catkin, borne before leaves; male catkins denser than female, from axil of a fimbriate or toothed scale, each flower with a toothed or laciniate bract and a stalked, cupulate disc, stamens many, anthers red or purple; female catkins longer, ovary ovoid or rounded, in a cupulate disc, stigmas 2–4, styles short or absent. Fruit a 2–4-valved capsule; seeds minute, with a apical tuft of white hairs, released in late spring or early summer. Europe, Asia, N Africa, N America.

CULTIVATION A large genus of northern hemisphere natives, from a wide variety of habitats, *Populus* spp. share many characteristics with the closely related *Salix*, and require careful selection and siting. Most species produce debris in the form of seed 'cotton', twigs and leaves, and most have greedy and extensive root systems. They are best suited to forestry and to the broader landscape, where they are undeniably useful as windbreaks and visual screens. (One commonly used fastigiate poplar for this purpose, *P. nigra* 'Italica', is probably the least suitable, having fragile branches, and being particularly prone to basal rots which may cause sudden collapse; *P. nigra* 'Plantierensis' has stronger and lower branches, and a denser head.) While selected cultivars may be suitable for large gardens, they should be sited at least 40 metres/130ft from buildings, drains, walls and roads, especially on clay soils, since they are known to cause extensive damage to foundations and drainage systems.

Many *Populus* spp. are useful on difficult sites. *P. alba* and its cvs and *P.* ×*canescens* are tolerant of salt-laden winds (but not of saline conditions at the roots). *P. fremontii* and *P. tremula* var. *davidiana* are tolerant of extremely alkaline soils. *P. canadensis* 'Regenerata' is tolerant of urban pollution (and is often pollarded, where it has outgrown its allotted space). *P. tremula*, the British native aspen, is sometimes used to improve heavy soils in neglected woodland.

The young foliage of some spp., notably *P. balsamifera*, *P.* ×*jackii* 'Gileadensis' and *P. trichocarpa*, emit a pleasant, light balsam scent, especially after rain. Others colour well in autumn, amongst them *P.* ×*canadensis, P.* ×*generosa, P. maximowiczii* and *P. tremuloides*. Some of the hardier species have a positive requirement for low temperatures to thrive, although *P.* ×*berolinensis, P. alba* and *P. deltoides* tolerate both extremes.

Grow on deep, fertile and well-drained, near neutral soil. Mound planting is advised on wet sites. All *Populus* spp. are intolerant of root and branch competition; space at 8m/26ft or more. *P. lasiocarpa* should be sheltered from wind. Propagate *P.* ×*canescens, P. grandidentata, P. tremula* and *P. tremuloides* by suckers, layers or root cuttings. All other species root easily from hardwood cuttings except *P. wilsonii*, which must be grafted. They can also be grown from seed, surface sown within three days of ripening, on moist silt. All species hybridize readily.

The most serious disease is bacterial canker, caused by *Aplanobacter populi*, where a cream-coloured bacterial slime may ooze from cracks in the young shoots in the spring and large cankers may develop on the branches and stems. Selected clones are resistant to the disease. Another disease which can girdle the young shoots and cause dieback is the fungus *Cryptodiaporthe populae*. Small black pycnidia, from which cream-coloured conidia are exuded during wet weather, are present on the bark lesions. Black spots which can cause the leaves to fall prematurely and are associated with a shoot dieback by fungi in the genera *Marssonina* and *Venturia*. *Taphrina populina* (syn. *T. aurea*) distorts the leaves and causes large yellow blisters on their lower surfaces. Several rust fungi of the genus *Melampsora* affect poplars and produce yellow urediospore and dark teliospore pustules on the lower leaf surfaces. Spraying with a copper-based fungicide can give some control of all the above-mentioned diseases but is not likely to be practicable on large trees. Poplars can also be affected by armillaria root rot (*Armillaria* spp.) and silver leaf (*Chondrostereum purpureum*). A yellow leaf-mosaic can be caused by the poplar mosaic virus, but is only likely to be of importance where trees are grown for timber production.

In Europe, galls may be formed on the leaf petioles by aphids (*Pemphigus* spp.) The foliage may also be attacked by defoliating insects such as willow leaf beetles (*Phyllodecta* spp.) with small, metallic blue, red or green beetles up to 5mm, long; the hazel sawfly (*Croesus septentrionalis*), with green-blue larvae up to 25mm long that feed in groups on the leaf edges; caterpillars of the eyed hawk-moth (*Smerinthus ocellata*) and leaf weevils (*Phyllobius* spp.). Wood-boring insects on poplars include caterpillars of the goat moth (*Cossus cossus*) and larvae of the poplar longhorn beetle (*Saperda carcharias*). In North America, petiole galls are caused by the aphid *Pemphigus populitransverus* and foliage may be attacked by a leaf beetle, the imported willow beetle (*Plagiodera versicola*), and by red-humped caterpillars (*Schizura concinna*), which are strikingly coloured with a red head, the body marked with black and yellow lines and a red hump on the first abdominal segment. The poplar borer (*Saperda calcarata*), a longhorn beetle, may bore into the wood.

***P.*** **×*acuminata*** Rydb. (*P. angustifolia* × *P. deltoides*.) To 20m, 20–50cm diam. at breast height, crowns spreading, flat-topped, bark pale brown. Young twigs slender, glabrous, orange-brown, grey-brown by third year, cylindrical; buds red-brown, acuminate, very resinous, sparsely bristled. Lvs to 13.5cm, lanceolate to rhombic-lanceolate, long-acuminate, base broadly cuneate, sometimes with 1 or 2 inconspicuous glands, minutely to coarsely crenate-serrate, pale green throughout; petioles 2–4.5cm, slightly flattened toward apex, shallow-channelled above. Male catkins 5–9cm, lax, 25–50-fld; fls with 25–40 stamens; pedicels 1–2mm. Female fls with broad, compact stigmas. Infruct. to 16.5cm; pedicels to 5mm; fr. 2-3-valved, 5–7mm, broadly ovoid. Spring. Canada (Alberta) to US (W Texas). Z3.

***P. alba*** L. WHITE POPLAR; SILVER-LEAVED POPLAR; ABELE. To 30m, usually less, crown broad, bark smooth, grey, suckering. Young twigs and base of buds densely white-tomentose; buds 5mm, ovoid. Lvs 6–12cm, ovate, base subcordate, long shoots lobed ×3–5, lobes coarsely toothed, short shoots serrate, usually ovate to elliptic-oblong, dark green and glabrous above, densely white-woolly beneath (grey-woolly on shorter shoots); petioles 1.2–3.7cm, subterete. Male catkins 4–7cm, stamens 5–10, anth. purple. Infruct. 8–10cm, fr. 2-valved. Late winter. S, C & E Europe, N Africa to C Asia. 'Globosa': tall shrub with a broadly rounded habit and young lvs pink, grey-woolly beneath. 'Intertexta': young lvs dull white, becoming yellow-speckled (GB 1789). 'Nivea': juvenile form; young twigs, lf underside and petiole chalk white; lvs deeply lobed; characters less obvious with age. 'Paletzkyana': lvs deeply lobed. 'Pendula': branches pendent. 'Pyramidalis': tall tree, bark grey-green, narrowly conical in habit; lvs large, very deeply lobed, often glabrous and more or less green beneath. 'Raket' ('Rocket'): slender, columnar; stems grey; lvs glossy green above, silver-grey beneath. 'Richardii': lvs golden-yellow above, white-woolly beneath. var. ***subintegerrima*** Lange. Lvs coriaceous, almost entire. Z3.

***P. angustifolia*** James. NARROWLEAF COTTONWOOD; WILLOW-LEAVED POPLAR. To 20m, crown narrowly conical. Young twigs glabrous, slender, cylindrical, later orange-brown; buds small, glabrous, sharply acuminate. Lvs 8–10cm, lanceolate to oval-lanceolate, base cuneate, margins inrolled, round glandular-toothed, pale green beneath, willow-like; petioles *c*1cm. Male catkins 4–6cm; female catkins 5–10cm. Fr. 2-valved. W US, N Mexico. Z3.

***P. balsamifera*** L. BALSAM POPLAR; HACKMATACK; TACAMAHAC. To 30m; branches ascending, suckering from base. Young twigs glabrous; buds to 2.5cm, long-acuminate, thickly covered in a fragrant, viscid resin. Lvs subcoriaceous, crenate, glabrous, margins ciliate, venation conspicuously reticulate. Male catkins 5–7.5cm; female catkins 12–14cm. Fr. 2-valved. var. ***balsamifera.*** Young twigs always cylindrical; buds glossy yellow. Lvs 7–12cm, oval to ovate-lanceolate, acute, base rounded or broadly cuneate, dark glossy green above, white or pale green beneath; petioles 3–5cm, cylindrical. N US, Canada, USSR. 'Aurora': lvs yellow white, pale and spotted dark green toward plant centre. var. ***michauxii*** (Dode) Henry. Lvs ovate, base rounded or subcordate, midrib and venation slightly hairy below; petioles and twigs slightly pubesc. N US. var. ***subcordata*** Hylander. Crown rounded. Young twigs red-brown to olive-brown, sometimes slightly angular. Lvs 12–16cm, broadly ovate to triangular, acuminate, base cordate, dark green and glossy above, metallic white below, especially on veins; petioles 2–6cm, channelled above, very hairy, tinged red. Capsules stalked. NE US, Canada. Z2.

***P.*** **×*berolinensis*** K. Koch. (*P. laurifolia* × *P. nigra* 'Italica'.) BERLIN POPLAR. To 25m, slenderly columnar, branches ascending. Young twigs somewhat angular, downy, yellow-brown, later yellow-grey; buds green, sticky. Lvs 7–12cm, broadly ovate or rhombic-ovate, long-acuminate, base rounded or cuneate, crenate to serrate, bright glossy green above, paler beneath, more or less glabrous, margins thin, translucent; petioles 2–4cm, hairy, cylindrical. Male catkins 4–7cm; fls with 15 stamens. Z2.

***P.*** **×*canadensis*** Moench. (*P. deltoides* × *P. nigra.*) CANADIAN POPLAR. Tall, fast-growing tree to 30m, crown broad. Young twigs glabrous or slightly hairy, cylindrical to somewhat angular, lenticels round or linear; buds resinous. Lvs 7–10cm, triangular to ovate, long-acuminate, base truncate, with teeth less dense and sometimes with 1 or 2 glands, margins crenate, initially ciliate but soon glabrous; petioles tinged red. Male catkins to 7cm; fls with 15–25 stamens. Spring. 'Aurea': lvs golden yellow, becoming yellow-green, petiole red. 'Eugenei': to 50m, columnar, bark of crown pale; twigs glabrous, ascending, somewhat angular; buds small; lvs coppery-brown when young, 5–8cm, triangular to rhombic, short-acuminate; petioles green; male catkins only, 3–3.5cm. 'Gelrica': trunk slightly crooked, bark white with pale spots and rings, crowns dense; young twigs glabrous; lvs red-brown when young, later pale green, broadly deltoid, base shallowly cordate, on short shoots rounded to broadly cuneate, glabrous, coarsely dentate; petioles tinged red; male. 'Marilandica' (MAY POPLAR): trunk short, crown broad, rounded, branches spreading, often crooked, basal branches often growing downwards; young lvs brown, soon pale green, to 10cm, rhombic to triangular-ovate, apex slenderly acute, entire; petioles green, flattened; female. 'Regenerata': trunk straight, branches whorled, spreading, bark pale grey; young twigs brown, base grey, slender, pendulous, buds short, acute, glabrous; young lvs pale brown, soon pale green, lvs triangular; petioles tinged red; female. 'Robusta': columnar, branches ascending, almost whorled; young twigs green, becoming red, finely hairy; buds glabrous, red-brown; lvs red-brown when young, 10–12cm, glossy, tough, triangular, with to 2 basal glands, teeth rounded, regular, apex entire, glabrous; petioles becoming red; male catkins, 7–9cm; fls with 20 stamens. 'Serotina' (LATE POPLAR; BLACK ITALIAN POPLAR): to 40m, crown broadly conical, later rounded, open; young twigs brown, grey at base, flexible, smooth, glabrous; buds acute; young lvs not borne until late spring, 7–10cm, red-brown, ovate-triangular to equilaterally triangular, base truncate, matt dark green when mature; petioles tinged red; male. Z4.

***P.*** **×*canescens*** (Ait.) Sm. (*P. alba* × *P. tremula.*) GREY POPLAR. To 45m; crown rounded, bark yellow-grey, with horizontal, angular scars. Young twigs grey-woolly below, soon glabrous, later dark grey-brown; buds woolly at base. Lvs 6–12cm, triangular-ovate, base cordate, dark green above, grey-woolly beneath, ciliate, teeth glandular, rounded, lvs on short shoots oval-suborbicular, soon glabrous; petioles 1–7.5cm, flattened to subterete, woolly to glabrous. Male catkins 6–10cm, stamens 8–15 per fl.; female catkins 2–10cm, bracts lońg-ciliate, laciniate to about half bract length, stigmas yellow or purple, 2 or 4-lobed. Early spring. Spontaneous natural hybrid, USSR (Georgia), Iran to C Europe. 'Aureo-variegata': lvs marbled yellow; slow growing. 'Macrophylla' PICKART'S POPLAR: fast-growing; lvs on long shoots to 15cm. 'Pyramidalis': crown broadly conical, bark grey-green, upper branches steeply ascending, lower branches spreading. Z4.

***P. cathayana*** Rehd. tree to 30m. Young shoots cylindrical, olive-green, becoming orange-yellow to grey-yellow. Lvs on short shoots ovate, often narrow, 6–10×3.5–7cm, acuminate, base rounded, rarely cordate, glossy green above, white beneath; lvs on long shoots 10–20cm, slightly cordate, petiole 2–6cm, glabrous. Male catkins 5–6cm, female catkins 10–20cm. NW China to Korea. Z4.

***P. deltoides*** Bartr. ex Marshall EASTERN COTTONWOOD; NECKLACE POPLAR. To 30m; crown broad, bark pale green-yellow. Young twigs cylindrical, longer shoots angular, ribbed, glabrous, green lightly tinted red, lenticels linear, white; buds ovate, sharply acuminate, brown, sticky, balsam-scented. Lvs 7–18cm, deltoid-ovate to rhombic, base cordate to truncate, often with 2–5 glands, apex acute, entire, margins densely ciliate, teeth coarse, incurved, glandular; petioles tinged; red. Male catkins 7–10cm; fls with 40–60 stamens. Fr. 3–4-valved. E & C US. 'Carolin': long branches conspicuously angled; lvs thick, cordate at base. 'Cordata': lf base cordate; petioles yellow-green. ssp. ***monilifera*** (Ait.) Eckenw. Branches pale yellow, glossy. Buds downy-hairy. Lvs deltoid-ovate, often wider than long, with 2 basal glands, abruptly acuminate, apex broadly triangular, teeth few, large, especially toward base, more or less glabrous, yellow-green. Pedicels all short in infruct. Canada (Ontario, Saskatchewan) to US (Texas). ssp. ***wislizenii*** (S. Wats.) Eckenw. Lvs 5–10cm, triangular to broadly ovate, short-acuminate, base slightly cuneate or rounded, lacking glands, coarsely crenate, teeth few, more or less glabrous (even when young). Female catkins 5–15cm, slender; peduncles 1–1.5cm, elongate in infruct. Early spring. Colorado to N Mexico. Z2.

***P. fremontii*** S. Wats. COTTONWOOD. To 30m, to 120cm diam. at breast height, trunk short, straight or dividing near base into 2 or 3 branches, crown more or less conical. Young twigs thick, smooth, round, glabrous, brown-grey, base grey; buds resinous, smooth, ovate, blunt, yellow-brown, with short, stiff hairs. Lvs 4–14cm, broadly deltoid-ovate to rhombic, sharply acuminate, apex entire, base slightly cordate or cuneate, lacking glands, yellow-green, teeth coarse, rounded, upward-curving, margins translucent, slightly ciliate or glabrous; petiole 4–7cm, flattened. Male catkins 4–13cm, lax, 10–30-fld; male fls with 10–30 stamens. Fr. 6–10mm, broadly ovate to globular, 3–4 valved; peduncle 1–3mm. Late winter–spring. California to Arizona, N Mexico. Z7.

***P.*** **×*generosa*** Henry. (*P. deltoides* × *P. trichocarpa.*) To 35m, crown narrowly cylindrical, branches ascending. Young twigs dark red, brown by third year, densely hairy to glabrous; buds narrowly ovoid, tinted red, softly hairy, with much yellow resin. Lvs 7–15cm, rhombic-ovate to broadly deltoid-ovate, base broadly cuneate or truncate, margins finely crenate-serrate, translucent, basal glands 2 in late lvs, rounded, prominent, sometimes 1 or 2 inconspicuous glands in first lvs; petioles 3–6.5cm, subterete, apically channelled. Male catkins 2.5–5cm, laxly 40–50-fld, pedicels 1–2mm; fls with 30–40 stamens; floral disc

2–3mm wide; female catkins to 15cm, glabrous, with 3 styles. Spring. US (Idaho, Wyoming, Montana). Z6.

***P. glauca*** Haines. Lvs broad, ovate, to 18×20.5cm, base weakly cordate, finely serrate, glaucous, finely pubesc. below; petiole to 14cm. Fr. ovoid to oblong, white-lanate. Nepal. Z7.

***P. grandidentata*** Michx. BIG-TOOTHED ASPEN; CANADIAN ASPEN. To 20m; crown narrow, rounded, bark smooth. Young twigs grey woolly, later brown, shiny; buds coated with grey wool. Lvs 7–10cm, ovate, coarsely sinuate on long shoots, elliptic with sharper teeth on shorter shoots, apex acute, pale grey-woolly at first, soon glabrous above, midrib yellow; petioles 2.5–6cm, slender, slightly flattened toward apex. Male catkins 3–6cm. Infruct. 6–12cm, fr. 3–4-valved. Eastern N America. Z3.

***P. ×jackii*** Sarg. (*P. balsamifera* × *P. deltoides.*) 10–30m, 20–100cm diam. at breast height, crown obovoid, bark grey-brown, tinted orange. Young twigs red-brown, hairy or glabrous, pale brown-orange by third year; buds ovoid, tinged red, very resinous, glabrous or with a few small bristles. Lvs 2.5–11.5cm, deltoid-ovate, acuminate, base subcordate with 2–3 prominent glands, blue-green above, pale green lightly tinged blue beneath, margins finely crenate-serrate; petioles 2–5.5cm, glabrous, slightly compressed toward apex. Male catkins 5–15cm, lax; fls on 1–3mm pedicels, stamens 25–40, floral discs 2.5–4cm wide; female fls with reflexed, platelike stigmas. Fr. 2–3-valved, ovoid. Spring. Central and Eastern N America. 'Aurora': lvs boldly variegated pale pink, especially on strong shoots. 'Gileadensis' BALM OF GILEAD: lvs to 17cm, deltoid-ovate, base cordate, petioles covered in stiff, dense hairs, also lf veins below; only female fls known, infruct. 7–16cm. Z2.

***P. lasiocarpa*** Oliv. CHINESE NECKLACE POPLAR. To 25m, crown rounded. Young twigs angular, thick, densely woolly at first, later glabrous, yellow-brown; buds resinous, coarse, basal scales hairy. Lvs to 15–35×10–23cm, ovate, acute, base cordate, margins glandular-crenate, teeth incurved, glossy grey-green above, paler and downy beneath, veins red; petioles 5–10cm, red. Male catkins 8–9cm, thick, many stamens per flower. Infruct. 15–20cm; some catkins polygamous, male at base, bisexual or female towards apex. SW China. Z5.

***P. laurifolia*** Ledeb. LAUREL POPLAR. To 20m, crown spreading. New growth prominently angled, grey-yellow, apex somewhat pubesc. when young, winter buds erect, glutinous. Lvs on long shoots ovate-lanceolate to lanceolate, acuminate, base rounded, minutely glandular-serrate, glossy green above, white-pubesc. beneath (often only on the midrib); lvs on short shoots elliptic-ovate, base rounded. Fr. sparsely pubesc. NW India to NE Siberia, Japan. f. ***lindleyana*** (Carr.) Rehd. Lvs narrower, often lanceolate on the long shoots, narrow-elliptic on the shorter, base round to broad-cuneate. Z6.

***P. maximowiczii*** Henry. DORONOKI; JAPANESE POPLAR. To 40m, crown broad, bark grey, deeply fissured. Young twigs red, cylindrical, densely hairy, later glabrous, grey; buds 1.5–2cm, resinous, acute. Lvs 6–12cm, elliptic to oval-elliptic, apex abruptly acuminate to a twisted, plicate cusp, base slightly cordate to rounded, matt dark green and wrinkled above, pale green beneath, margins glandular-serrate and ciliate, veins hairy above and beneath, somewhat leathery; petioles 2–4cm. Male catkins 5–10cm; fls with 30–40 stamens. Infruct. to 25cm, fr. capsules subsessile, glabrous, 3–4-valved, not ripening until early autumn. NE China, Japan, Korea. Z4.

***P. nigra*** L. BLACK POPLAR. To 30m; crown broad, rounded, trunk often thickly knotted, bark deeply fissured with age. Young twigs cylindrical; buds to 1cm, red-brown, resinous, narrowly ovate-acuminate. Lvs 5–10cm, rhombic, triangular or ovate, sometimes wider than long, apex slenderly acuminate, base cuneate or truncate, green, paler beneath, margins translucent, finely crenate, eciliate, glands always absent; petioles 3–7cm, slender, flattened. Male catkins 3–5cm; fls with 12–20 stamens, anth. crimson. Female fls with 2 stigmas. Infruct. 10–15cm; fr. 5–6mm, broadly ovoid, 2-valved. Spring. W Europe, N Africa, USSR (Siberia). 'Afghanica': columnar; bark almost white with age; young twigs grey, initially hairy; lvs triangular-ovate, base broadly cuneate. var. ***betulifolia*** (Pursh) Torr. DOWNY BLACK POPLAR; MANCHESTER POPLAR. Young twigs initially hairy, brown-orange; bud apices blunt. Lvs hairy when young, smaller, tapering gently to acute apex; petioles yellow-green, hairy. Spring. W Europe. 'Charkowensis': crown oblong, broad, pyramidal, branches ascending; young branches sparsely pubesc. 'Italica' LOMBARDY POPLAR; ITALIAN POPLAR; PYRAMIDAL POPLAR: columnar, branches steeply ascending; young twigs brown at apex, later grey; lvs small, rounded-rhombic; petioles tinged red; male. 'Gigantea': as 'Italica' but broader; winter twigs orange; female. 'Lombardy Gold': lvs golden. 'Plantierensis': habit columnar (less so than 'Italica'); young twigs hairy; lvs small; petioles tinged red, hairy. 'Vereeken': crown columnar-conic. 'Vert de Garonne': as 'Italica' but broader and densely leafy. Z2.

***P. sieboldii*** Miq. JAPANESE ASPEN. Tree to 20m, suckering. Young twigs thick, buds and twigs initially white-downy. Lvs 5–8cm, apex short-triangular, base short, cuneate, with 2 prominent glands, dark green and glabrous above, white-hairy beneath, subglabrous with age, margins finely glandular-serrate; petioles 1–4cm, hairy. Japan. Z4.

***P. simonii*** Carr. Tree to 30m, slender, crown narrow, bark grey-green, branchlets pendulous. Young twigs red-brown, glabrous, angular; buds acute, resinous. Lvs 6–12cm, rhombic-elliptic, acute, crenate, bright green above, pale green beneath; petioles 1–2cm, red. Male catkins 2–3cm; fls with 8 stamens. N & WC China. 'Fastigiata': columnar; young twigs subangular, thin, dark brown, very steeply ascending; lvs small, obovate, base long-cuneate; petioles 1cm. 'Pendula': branches weeping. Z2.

***P. suavolens*** Fisch. non C. Schneid. To 30m in wild. Young twigs yellow-brown, cylindrical, hairy above nodes; buds acute, brown, fragrantly resinous. Lvs 5–12cm, oblong-elliptic, apex short, abruptly acuminate, often twisted, leathery, thick, crenate, very pale green and hairy beneath; petioles 1–4cm. Male catkins to 5cm. Infruct. thick, to 15cm. N China, N Japan, Korea, USSR (E Siberia). Z3.

***P. szechuanica*** C. Schneid. To 40m in wild. Young twigs red-brown, angular, later yellow-brown and subcylindrical; buds resinous, purple, glabrous. Lvs 7–20cm, tinged red at first, ovate-oblong on long shoots, broadly ovate on short shoots, crenate, teeth with apical glands, apex acuminate, base rounded or slightly cordate, bright green above, white-silver beneath, veins red; petioles 2–7cm. Fr. subsessile, 3–4-valved. W China. Z4.

***P. ×tomentosa*** Carr. (*P. alba* × *P. adenopoda.*) CHINESE WHITE POPLAR. To 40m. Young twigs grey-woolly, buds less so. Lvs to 15m, smaller on shorter shoots, triangular-ovate, acuminate, biserrate, grey-woolly beneath, later glabrous, lacking lobes. Generally resembling *P. alba*. N China. Z4.

***P. tremula*** L. ASPEN; QUAKING ASPEN. To 20m; crown broad, much-branched, bark yellow-grey, smooth, fissured and dark grey with age, suckering. Buds about 5mm, ovate, glabrous, dark brown, resinous. Lvs 3–12cm, oval to sub-orbicular, acute, base with 2 glands, truncate or cordate, margins undulate, crenate, grey-green above, pale green beneath, seeming to be in permanent motion; petioles 4–7cm, slender, glabrous, strongly flattened. Male catkins 5–8cm, scales densely white-hairy, fls with 6–15 stamens, anth. maroon. Fr. to 4mm. Late winter. NW Europe to N Africa, USSR (Siberia). 'Erecta': narrow, upright; branches dense. 'Pendula': small tree, twigs pendulous; catkins purple. 'Purpurea': lvs tinged red. 'Tapiau': very vigorous, growing by to 2m per season. var. ***davidiana*** (Dode) Schneid. Habit lax. Lvs shallowly dentate. var. ***villosa*** (Láng) Wesm. Young twigs hairy in first year. Lvs persistently hairy. Z2.

***P. tremuloides*** Michx. AMERICAN ASPEN. To 20m in cult., trunk slender, bark very pale yellow-grey, suckering. Young twigs red-brown, buds slightly resinous. Lvs 3–7cm, broadly oval to suborbicular, short-acuminate, base truncate to broadly cuneate, margins finely serrate, ciliate, dark glossy green above, blue-green and glabrous beneath, pale yellow in autumn; petioles 3–9cm, flattened. Male catkins 5–8cm, more slender than *P. tremula*. Canada to Mexico. Z1.

***P. trichocarpa*** Torr. & A. Gray. BLACK COTTONWOOD; WESTERN BALSAM POPLAR. To 35m, slenderly pyramidal, crown open, broadly ascending, bark smooth, yellow-grey. Young twigs olive-brown, glabrous to hairy, slightly angular, becoming ochre-grey, cylindrical; buds 1–1.5cm, narrowly ovoid-acuminate, resinous, glabrous, slender. Lvs 8–25cm, ovate to rhombic-oblong, slenderly acuminate, base rounded or truncate, leathery, venation reticulate, shallowly toothed, dark green and glabrous or subglabrous above, white or pale brown beneath; petioles 3–6cm. Male catkins 3.5–6cm, subsessile, fls with 30–60 stamens, anth. crimson. Female catkins 6–15cm, ovaries woolly. Fr. 3-valved, hairy. Spring. Western N America. 'Fritz Pauley': a female clone. 'Pendula': branches weeping. 'Scott Pauley': a male clone. Z5.

***P. tristis*** Fisch. Shrubby. Twigs cylindric, dark red-brown, pubesc., winter buds to 3cm, glutinous. Lvs oblong-ovate, acuminate, crenate and ciliate, 7–12cm, base round to cordate, black-green above, white and finely-pubesc. beneath; dead lvs persistent. USSR. Z1.

***P. violascens*** Dode. Similar to *P. lasiocarpa* but shoots thinner, buds smaller. Lvs ovate on lateral shoots, 10–22cm, violet-red when young, becoming dull green, venation red, pubesc. beneath; petiole violet. China. Z6.

***P. wilsonii*** C. Schneid. To 25m, crown regularly conical. Young shoots red at first, later green or grey-brown, glabrous, thick, stiff, cylindrical; buds large, glossy-resinous, glabrous. Lvs 8–18cm, broadly cordate, apex truncate, margins crenate, more or less glabrous, dull green above, blue or tinged grey beneath; petioles to 15cm. Infruct. 7.5–15cm, slender, woolly at first, capsules more or less glabrous with age, 3-valved. C & W China. Z5.

***P. yunnanensis*** Dode. To 25m or more. Young twigs glabrous, strongly angular, at first pale green or tinged red, later brown; buds glabrous, resinous. Lvs 6–15cm, ovate to obovate-lanceolate, acute, base broadly cuneate, red when young, margins crenate, teeth glandular, bright green above, pale green beneath, midrib red, on fertile shoots midrib longer, more markedly cuneate, apex blunter; petioles 6–12mm, red. Infruct. 10–15cm, fr. 3–4-valved, glabrous. China (Yunnan). Z5.

***P. angulata*** Ait. See *P. deltoides*.
***P. balsamifera*** var. ***viminalis*** Loud. See *P. laurifolia*.
***P. balsamifera*** var. ***candicans*** (Ait.) A. Gray. See *P. ×jackii* 'Gileadensis'.
***P. bolleana*** Lauche. See *P. alba* 'Pyramidalis'.
***P. candicans*** Ait. See *P. ×jackii* 'Gileadensis'.
***P. carolinensis*** hort. See *P. deltoides* 'Carolin'.
***P. davidiana*** Dode. See *P. tremula* var. *davidiana*.
***P. eugenei*** hort. (Simon-Louis). See *P. ×canadensis* 'Eugenei'.
***P. ×euroamericana*** (Dode) Guinier. See *P. ×canadensis*.
***P. gelrica*** (Houtz.) Houtz. See *P. ×canadensis* 'Gelrica'.
***P. ×gileadensis*** Roul. See *P. ×jackii* 'Gileadensis'.
***P. hickeliana*** Dode. See *P. alba* var. *subintegerrima*.

***P. jacquemontiana*** var. ***glauca*** (Haines) Kimura. See *P. glauca*.
***P. koreana*** Rehd. See *P. maximowiczii*.
***P. lindleyana*** Carr. See *P. laurifolia* f. *lindleyana*.
***P. marilandica*** Bosc ex Poir. See *P.* ×*canadensis* 'Marilandica'.
***P. michauxii*** Dode. See *P. balsamifera* var. *michauxii*.
***P. monilifera*** Ait. See *P. deltoides* ssp. *monilifera*.
***P. nigra*** var. ***thevistina*** Dode Bean. See *P. nigra* 'Afghanica'.
***P. picardii*** hort. See *P.* ×*canescens* 'Macrophylla'.
***P. plantierensis*** Simon-Louis. See *P. nigra* 'Plantierensis'.
***P. pyramidalis*** Salisb. See *P. nigra* 'Italica'.
***P. regenerata*** hort. ex C. Schneid. See *P.* ×*canadensis* 'Regenerata'.
***P. robusta*** C. Schneid. See *P.* ×*canadensis* 'Robusta'.
***P. sargentii*** Dode. See *P. deltoides* ssp. *monilifera*.
***P. serotina*** Hartig. See *P.* ×*canadensis* 'Serotina'.
***P. suaveolens*** C. Schneid. non Fisch. See *P. cathayana*.
***P. tacamahaca*** Mill. See *P. balsamifera*.
***P. vernirubens*** Henry. See *P.* ×*canadensis* 'Robusta'.
***P. villosa*** Láng. See *P. tremula* var. *villosa*.
***P. wislizenii*** (S. Wats.) Sarg. See *P. deltoides* ssp. *wislizenii*.

**Porana** Burm. f. (Derivation obscure; native name in E Indies.) Convolvulaceae. Some 20 species of slender, twining herbs or shrubs. Leaves alternate, cordate-ovate, many-nerved, entire. Flowers small, in terminal panicles or cymes, sometimes solitary and axillary, white, blue or purple; sepals subequal, spreading to starry, some or all becoming enlarged, scarious, prominently veined and falling with the fruit; corolla campanulate or funnelform, lobes broad, spreading, plicate. Tropical Asia, Australia. Z10.

CULTIVATION As for *Ipomoea*.

***P. paniculata*** Roxb. BRIDAL-BOUQUET; CHRIST VINE; SNOW CREEPER; SNOW-IN-THE-JUNGLE; WHITE CORALLITA. Liane to 9m. Lvs cordate, to 15×4cm, slender-acuminate, glabrous above, white-pubesc. beneath. Fls in large, many-fld, terminal, pendulous, much-branched panicles; 3 sepals enlarged; cor. to 8mm, white, tubular-campanulate, obscurely lobed. Summer. N India, Upper Burma.

**Porlieria** Ruiz & Pav. (For Andrew de Porlier, Spanish benefactor of botany.) Zygophyllaceae. 6 species of shrubs or small trees; branches rigid, spreading; branchlets stout. Leaves opposite, pinnate; leaflets subopposite, linear to linear-oblong, entire, with spiny basal stipules and sleep movements in darkness. Flowers axillary, sometimes clustered, short-stalked, hermaphrodite; sepals 4–5, overlapping, sometimes joined at base; petals 4–5, slightly exceeding calyx; stamens 8–10, exceeded by petals, anthers biloculate, filaments bearing truncate scale at base; ovary superior on a disc; carpels 4, each with 4 ovules; styles 4. Fruit a globose capsule, somewhat fleshy, 4-angled; seeds 4 per fruit at maturity. Texas to S America. Z10.

CULTIVATION As for *Guaiacum*.

***P. angustifolia*** Gray. TEXAS PORLIERIA; SOAP BUSH. Shrub or small tree, to 7m, compact; bark grey to black. Leaflets about 12×3mm, 4–8 pairs, linear, subsessile, coriaceous, lustrous dark green, oblique at base; petiole pubesc. Fls solitary or in clusters; sep. 5, concave; pet. 5, clawed, violet to purple; stamens 10; ovary densely downy. Fr. 1–2cm across, yellow to red. Texas, Mexico.

***P. hygrometra*** Ruiz & Pav. Shrub to 2m, much-branched. Lvs subsessile; leaflets about 8×2mm, 9–10 pairs, linear to linear-oblong, obtuse, sometimes mucronate, subcoriaceous, margins ciliate. Fls to 8mm, solitary; pedicel downy; sep. 5, downy; pet. 5; stamens 8; ovary glabrous. Fr. brown. Peru.

**Porpax** Lindl. (From Lat. *porpax*, shield-handle, a reference to the shape of the flowers.) Orchidaceae. Some 10 species of minute epiphytic orchids. Pseudobulbs turbinate or spherical, flattened, clustered along rhizomes. Leaves 2, sessile. Flowers 1–3, at apex of pseudobulb; sepals forming a tube with the small, free petals, dorsal sepal forming a hood, lateral sepals basally oblique, fused to the column foot. Tropical Asia. Z10.

CULTIVATION As for *Polystachya*.

***P. meirax*** King & Pantl. Pseudobulbs turbinate, to 10mm diam., dry sheaths reticulate. Lvs 2, elliptic-oblong, to 2.5cm, emerging after fls. Fls solitary, dull brown; bract erect, concave; sep. fused, tubular, bilobed, lobes ovate; pet. shorter than tube, oblong-lanceolate; lip ovate-orbicular, notched, midlobe oblong, apex tapering, entire, lateral lobes rounded. Autumn. Sikkim.

For synonymy see *Eria*.

**Porroglossum** Schltr. (From the Gk *porro*, forward, and *glossa*, tongue, referring to the porrect lip.) Orchidaceae. Some 25 species of epiphytic or terrestrial orchids closely allied to *Masdevallia*. Rhizome short to elongate. Pseudobulbs absent. Secondary stems erect or ascending, stout to slender, shorter than leaves, enveloped by 2 or 3 overlapping sheaths, bearing a single apical leaf. Leaves erect, fleshy or coriaceous, elliptic to obovate, sometimes tinged purple, smooth to verrucose. Inflorescence a lateral raceme, few to several-flowered, erect; flowers produced in succession often resupinate; sepals fleshy to membranaceous, fused at base forming a campanulate tube, glabrous or pubesc., apices contracted into short to elongate tails; petals smaller than sepals, linear or oblong, obtuse or rounded; lip adnate to apex of column-foot, fleshy, obtriangular or obovate, glabrous to pubesc., with a long linear claw curved around apex of column-foot, callus basal, longitudinal or transverse; column short, erect, semiterete, usually broadly winged, foot elongate, porrect, with a free apex, pollinia 2, obliquely pyriform. Venezuela, Colombia, Ecuador, Peru to Bolivia. Z9.

CULTIVATION As for *Masdevallia*.

***P. amethystinum*** (Rchb. f.) Garay. Secondary stems to 15mm, erect, slender. Lvs to 100×14mm, narrowly obovate, acute, long-petiolate. Infl. to 25cm, few-fld; peduncle filiform, glabrous; sep. bright rose, dorsal sep. to 5×7mm, transversely obovate, acuminate, apex reflexed, tail to 2mm, lateral sep. to 9×7mm, obliquely oblong, obtuse, tails to 14mm, orange, slender; pet. to 4×2mm, translucent, ovate, rounded; lip to 4×4mm, white tinged and spotted dark purple, cuneate, broadly obtuse, base deflexed; column to 2mm, stout, foot to 5mm. Ecuador.

***P. echidnum*** (Rchb. f.) Garay. Secondary stems to 7cm, erect, stout. Lvs to 14×1.5cm, elliptic-oblong to narrowly obovate, verrucose, petiolate, acute, dull green tinged purple. Infl. to 20cm, few-fld; peduncle downy; sep. brown or green with brown venation, exterior slightly verrucose, dorsal sep. to 7×6mm, obovate or triangular-oblong, obtuse, tail to 25mm, erect to reflexed, lateral sep. to 8×8mm, broadly oblong or triangular-oblong, obtuse, tails to 25mm, slender, reflexed; pet. to 4×1.5mm, translucent brown, linear-oblong, rounded; lip to 8×4mm, light brown flecked red, or dark brown, obovate-spathulate, obtuse, apex ciliate, disc with a cushion-like longitudinal callus; column to 3mm, stout, foot to 8mm. Colombia.

***P. meridionale*** Ortiz. Secondary stems to 1cm, slender. Lvs to 4.5cm, green mottled purple below, elliptic, obtuse to subacute, verrucose, long-petiolate. Infl. to 10cm; peduncle slender, glabrous; sep. clear pale purple spotted purple, dorsal sep. to 7×5mm, ovate, subacute, exterior subverrucose, tail to 9mm, erect, lateral sep. to 7×6mm, transversely ovate, obtuse, tails to 8mm, orange-brown; pet. translucent, to 4×1mm, ovate-oblong, rounded; lip to 4×4mm, purple, cuneate-obtriangular, truncate, pubesc., apiculate, disc with a transverse basal callus; column to 2.5mm, stout, foot to 4mm. Peru.

***P. mordax*** (Rchb. f.) Sweet. Secondary stems to 2cm, slender, erect, dark brown-black. Lvs to 8cm, narrowly elliptic to narrowly obovate, subacute, subverrucose, long-petiolate. Infl. to 15cm; peduncle glabrous, slender; sep. pale green tinged purple, erose, subverrucose, dorsal sep. to 20×8mm, ovate, obtuse, concave, tail absent, lateral sep. to 18×4mm, obliquely ovate, obtuse; pet. to 5×2mm, translucent, ovate, rounded; lip to 5×5mm, pale green, cuneate-obtriangular, obtuse, ciliate, disc with a deep purple, longitudinal callus; column to 2.5mm, stout, foot to 5mm. Colombia.

***P. muscosum*** (Rchb. f.) Schltr. Secondary stems to 4cm, slender, erect. Lvs to 15×2cm, green tinged purple, elliptic to narrowly ovate, acute or obtuse, petiolate or subpetiolate. Infl. to 26cm, few-fld; peduncle erect, densely pubesc.; sep. light brown to brown or green, exterior glabrous to subverrucose, dorsal sep. to 8×6mm, obovate, subacute to obtuse, tail to 30mm, slender, erect or reflexed, lateral sep. to 10×6mm, obliquely ovate, acute to obtuse, tails to 30mm, slender; pet. to 5×1.5mm, clear yellow-white to brown, ovate-oblong, rounded; lip to 5.5×4mm, white tinged rose or purple, cuneate to obovate-spathulate, obtuse, apex ciliate, disc with a low, longitudinal callus; column to 2.5mm, stout, foot to 6mm. Colombia, Ecuador, Venezuela.

***P. olivaceum*** Sweet. Secondary stems to 1.5cm, slender, erect. Lvs to 10×1.5cm, narrowly elliptic, acute, slender-petiolate, subverrucose to prominently verrucose. Infl. to 27cm, several-fld; peduncle slender, erect; sep. light brown to light yellow-brown, veined dark brown, dorsal sep. to 5×6mm, obovate, obtuse, tail to 3mm, slender, reflexed, lateral sep. to 4×7mm, obliquely oblong, broadly obtuse, tails to 13mm, slender; pet. to 5×2mm, clear pale yellow or pale brown, ovate-oblong, rounded; lip to 5×4mm, yellow, distal portion purple, short-pubesc., obtuse, apex ciliate, disc with a raised, longitudinal callus, rounded; column to 2mm, stout, foot to 5mm. Ecuador, Colombia.

***P. portillae*** Luer & Andreetta. Secondary stems to 1.5cm, erect, slender, dark brown-black. Lvs to 6×1.5cm, elliptic, obtuse; petiole elongate, slender, dark-brown-black. Infl. to 11cm, few-fld; peduncle erect, slender, glabrous, fls non-resupinate; sep. yellow tinged rose-pink, minutely spotted purple, dorsal sep. to 7×6mm, oblong, obtuse, concave, tail to 5mm, reflexed, lateral sep. to 6×8mm, transversely oblong, obtuse, tails to 7mm, reflexed; pet. to 5×1mm, rose-pink, ovate-oblong; lip to 5×5mm, rose flecked purple, obtriangular, truncate, apex ciliate, obscurely 3-lobed, disc with a low basal callus; column to 2.5mm, stout, foot to 4mm. Ecuador.

***P. rodrigoi*** Sweet. Secondary stems to 0.5cm, slender, erect. Lvs to 4.5cm, elliptic, obtuse to subacute, petiolate. Infl. to 7cm; peduncle slender, glabrous; sep. purple, dorsal sep. to 5×6mm, transversely ovate, obtuse, concave, tail to 1.5mm, recurved, slender, lateral sep. to 4×5mm, obliquely ovate, obtuse, tails to 5mm, light yellow; pet. to 3×1.5mm, clear red-purple, ovate-oblong, rounded; lip to 3×3mm, white tinged rose-pink, cuneate, obtuse, retrorse, apiculate, disc with a low basal callus; column to 2mm, stout, red-purple, foot to 3mm. Colombia.

***P. xipheres*** (Rchb. f.) Garay. See *P. muscosum*.
For further synonymy see *Masdevallia* and *Scaphosepalum*.

**Portea** Brongn. ex K. Koch. (Named for Dr M. Porte (*fl.* 1845), French tropical plant collector.) Bromeliaceae (Bromelioideae). 7 species of perennial, terrestrial herbs, to 2m in flower. Leaves in a rosette, dark green, stiff, scaly, spinose. Inflorescence erect, compound, much-branched, on a slender, central scape with brightly coloured bracts; flowers on slender pedicels, perfect, blue or violet; sepals fused, pungent, highly asymmetric; petals free, symmetric, with 2 fimbriate basal scales; stamens shorter than petals, strongly fused to inner whorl. Fruit a fleshy berry. E Brazil. Distinguished from the *Aechmea* by its fused sepals. Z9.

CULTIVATION See BROMELIADS.

***P. petropolitana*** (Wawra) Mez. To 1m in flower, stemless. Lvs to 80cm, in a dense rosette; sheaths large, subelliptic, densely brown-scaly, apex toothed; blades acute, toothed, spines straight or upward-curving, 4mm, black, apex with coarse, brown spines. Infl. to 50cm, subcylindric, laxly 3-pinnate, branches to 12cm; scape stout, red-brown, elliptic, overlapping bracts; lower infl. bracts broadly lanceolate, others reduced; floral bracts 5mm, narrowly triangular; pedicel 10–40mm; sep. 15mm, fused for half their length, pink-orange, with a lateral wing; pet. 30mm, lavender-blue, claw linear, blade narrowly elliptic, with 2 fimbriate basal scales.

***P. tillandsioides*** (Reg.) Nichols. See *Aechmea recurvata* var. *ortgiesii*.

**Portenschlagia** Vis.
***P. australis*** (Vent.) Tratt. See *Cassine australis*.

**Portlandia** P. Browne. (For Margaret Cavendish Bentinck, Duchess of Portland (1715–85), a correspondent of Rousseau.) Rubiaceae. Some 20 or more species of shrubs or small trees, usually glabrous throughout. Leaves petiolate or sessile, opposite, leathery; stipules intrapetiolar, often connate at base or with petioles, deciduous or persistent. Flowers peduncled, axillary or terminal, solitary or few, white or scarlet or purple; calyx tube obovoid or campanulate, 4–7-lobed; corolla campanulate or funnelform to tubular, lobes usually 5, valvate and triangular; stamens usually 5, inserted at base of throat or tube, filaments slender, connate, pubescent, anthers dorsifixed or basifixed, exserted or included, linear; ovary 2-celled; style filiform, cleft to 2-branched; ovules many. Fruit a capsule, oblong to ovoid or obovoid, loculicidally 2-valved, leathery; seeds many, adnate at base, compressed; endosperm fleshy. W Indies, Mexico, C America.

CULTIVATION *Portlandia* spp. are beautiful, glossy leaved evergreen shrubs and small tress from tropical regions of central America, grown for their flowers. The solitary bell-shaped flowers of *P. grandiflora*, as large as those of the trumpet lilies, are white with reddish throats and are heavily fragrant on summer evenings. Those of *P. coccinea*, though smaller, are scarlet with yellow anthers. Grow in the hot glasshouse (min. 16–18°C/60–65°F) in a high-fertility loam-based mix, with high humidity. Water plentifully. Propagate from semi-ripe cuttings, in a closed case with bottom heat at 18–21°C/65–70°F.

***P. coccinea*** Sw. Shrub to 3m, often less; branches compressed, grey. Lvs to 12×7cm, ovate or ovate-oblong to elliptic, acute at apex, acute or obtuse at base, lustrous, pale beneath, veins 5–7, conspicuous; petioles to 5mm; stipules deltoid, pointed, to 8mm. Fls axillary, solitary or paired; peduncles to 15mm; cal. tube oblong, lobes to 18mm; cor. funnel-shaped, to 7×5cm, scarlet or crimson, interior lined white, lobes to 15mm, obtuse or subacute. Fr. subglobose to obovoid, to 17×15mm, ribbed. Jamaica.

***P. grandiflora*** L. Shrub to 3m. Lvs to 16×10cm, ovate to oblong or elliptic, sharp-pointed at apex, obtuse to subacute at base, 7–10-veined; petioles to 1cm; stipules deltoid, acute to obtuse, to 1cm. Fls axillary, solitary; peduncles to 1.5cm; cal. tube obconic, 1cm, lobes elliptic or lanceolate or ovate, acute, to 3.5cm; cor. funnel-shaped to tubular, to 20×6cm, white and pink-flushed to cream, lobes triangular, obtuse or acute. 3cm. Fr. obovoid, to 2.5cm. Summer. W Indies.

***P. platantha*** Hook. Similar to *P. grandiflora*, but only 1m high. Lvs ovate to elliptic, lustrous, dark green. Cor. to 3cm. Summer. America.

***P. coriacea*** Sw. See *P. coccinea*.
***P. grandiflora*** var. ***latifolia*** DC. See *P. grandiflora*.
***P. hexandra*** Jacq. See *Coutarea hexandra*.

**Portulaca** L. (From *portilaca*, Lat. name used by Pliny.) PURSLANE; MOSS ROSE. Portulacaceae. 40 species of fleshy or trailing, mostly annual herbs. Leaves alternate or nearly opposite, flat or sometimes cylindrical, often with tufts of bristles in the axils, the upper forming a leafy involucre subtending the often showy and variously coloured flowers. Flowers purple, yellow, or pink; sepals 2; petals 4–6, usually 5; stamens 8 to many. Fruit a small conical many-seeded capsule, opening by the tops falling as a lid. Widely distributed in warm and tropical regions. The flowers open in direct sunshine, close in shadow.

CULTIVATION *P. grandiflora* is grown for its fleshy, moss-like foliage and for the profusion of individually short-lived, brightly coloured flowers carried over long periods in summer. Ideally suited as a low-growing seasonal filler in flower beds and borders, as edging and in window boxes and other containers, it is easily grown from seed sown *in situ* in spring, in any low-nutrient, freely draining, sandy soil in full sun. *P. oleracea* is cultivated for its fleshy leaves, rich in iron with a mild acid flavour, eaten raw in salads, cooked with spinach in *soupe bonne femme*, and widely used in Indian, Greek and Middle Eastern cuisine. Grow in freely draining, light-textured soil in a sunny but sheltered position. Successional sowings *in situ*, from early summer onwards, will ensure succulent leaves throughout the summer; earlier harvests can be obtained by sowing under glass, setting out at 15cm/6in. spacings after danger of frost has passed. Leaves may be harvested within two months of sowing, cutting results in a fresh crop until flowering occurs; remove flowerheads before seeding to avoid undesirable self-seeding.

***P. grandiflora*** Hook. ROSE MOSS; SUN PLANT; ELEVEN-O'CLOCK. Stems prostrate or ascending, to 30cm high but usually lower. Lvs cylindrical, to 2.5cm, thick, fleshy, mostly alternate but sometimes paired or clustered. Fls single to double, rose, red, yellow, white, often striped, 2.5cm diam. or more. Brazil, Argentina, Uruguay. 'Afternoon Delight': dwarf, spreading; fls large, double, in wide range of colours including pink, orange, scarlet and white; seed race. 'Aztec Double': fls double, bicolored gold and fuschia. Calypso Hybrids: fls mainly double. Cloudbeater Hybrids: fls double, gold, carmine, scarlet, apricot, white and pink; seed race. Dwarf Double Minilacea Hybrids: compact; fls large in shades of scarlet, rose pink, apricot, cream and gold, abundant. Extra Double Hybrids: spreading; fls double, small, rose shaped in range of bright colours; seed race. 'Jewel': branches tinged red; lvs small and narrow; fls large, double, rose-pink with darker centre. Magic Carpet Hybrids: fls double, in range of colours including white, pink, orange, red and yellow, occasionally striped. Peppermint Candy: fls single, bicolored red and white. Sundance Hybrids: neat, spreading; fls double in range of bright colours. Sunny Boy Hybrids: dwarf, spreading; fls mainly double. 'Swanlake': fls large, double, white. Wildfire Hybrids: low-lying; fls in bright colours; seed race.

***P. oleracea*** L. PURSLANE; PUSSLEY. Stems thick and soft, prostrate or trailing, forming mats. Lvs to 3cm, spathulate to obovate. Fls bright yellow, to 1cm diam.; stamens sensitive, move when touched. Cosmopolitan and weedy, but probably originally from India. The wild, weedy form may be eaten as greens or salad, but is not cultivated. Many selfing lines formerly described as species now refer to *P. oleracea*. 'Giganthes': prostrate; fls double, yellow, 2.5cm diam. var. ***sativa*** DC. KITCHEN-GARDEN PURSLANE. Stems to 45cm, erect, thicker, very succulent. Lvs obovate. Fls 1.2cm diam.

***P. pilosa*** L. Stems thick, red, with tufts of white shaggy hairs. Lvs 1.2cm, cylindrical, red-margined. Fls yellow, to 1.2cm diam. SE US and Mexico. 'Hortualis': SHAGGY GARDEN PURSLANE. fls red-purple, larger than species type, to 2cm diam.

***P. arachnoides*** Haw. See *Anacampseros arachnoides*.
***P. filamentosa*** Haw. See *Anacampseros filamentosa*.

***P. lanceolata*** Haw. See *Anacampseros lanceolata*.
***P. oleracea*** var. ***giganthes*** L.H. Bail. See *P. oleracea* 'Giganthes'.
***P. pilosa*** var. ***hortualis*** L.H. Bail. See *P. pilosa* 'Hortualis'.

**PORTULACACEAE** Juss. PURSLANE FAMILY. Dicot. 21 genera and 400 species of shrubs or herbs, often succulents. Leaves alternate or opposite, simple; stipules scarious, tufts of hairs or absent. Flowers usually regular and bisexual, solitary or in heads or other inflorescences; calyx 2 free sepals (or probably bracteoles), up to 9 in *Lewisia*, usually persistent; corolla (2–)4–6(–18 in *Lewisia*) free petals, sometimes basally connate, often caducous; stamens as many as and opposite the petals, or 1, or numerous and in bundles, sometimes basally adnate to petals; nectary ring or nectaries around stamens; ovary superior, of 2–3(–9) fused carpels, with distinct styles or lobed style, half-inferior in *Portulaca*, 1-loculed with free-central placenta; ovules 1-numerous. Fruit a capsule, rarely indehiscent; seeds often shiny, with abundant starchy perisperm; endosperm absent. The common purslane, *Portulaca oleracea* is used as a pot herb. Cosmopolitan, especially America. *Anacampseros, Ceraria, Claytonia, Lewisia, Montia, Portulaca, Portulacaria, Spraguea, Talinum.*

**Portulacaria** Jacq. (From Lat. *portulaca*, purslane.) Portulacaceae. 1 species of much-branched fleshy shrubs to 3m; branches often projecting horizontally, nodally segmented, cylindric, succulent. Leaves 12×10–21×2mm, opposite, sessile, smooth glossy green, obovate, with or without a small pointed tip, upper surface flat, lower surface slightly convex. Flowers in small clusters, 1mm diam., pale pink, inconspicuous. Late spring–early summer. S Africa. Z9.

CULTIVATION Forming dense thickets in habitat, providing an important food source for elephants and other herbivores, hence the common name, the slow-growing *P. afra* is sometimes used for hedging in dry, mediterranean-type climates. The soft-grey brown stems, studded with small succulent leaves, become intricately interwoven as plants mature. In cool temperate climates *P. afra* and its cultivars need protected cultivation in the cool glasshouse, where they are grown in pots and hanging baskets. Propagate by cuttings of young stems, allow to dry for 12–24 hours in a shaded, well-ventilated place before inserting in damp sand or perlite. Otherwise, treat as for *Crassula*.

***P. afra*** Jacq. ELEPHANT BUSH. As for the genus. 'Tricolor': branches pendulous with age; lvs small, obovate, variegated with cream, edges marked rose; fls pale pink. 'Variegata': dense; stems tinged red; lvs pale green broadly margined cream with thin pale-red edge. var. ***foliis-variegatis*** Jacobsen. Lvs mottled yellow. var. ***macrophylla*** Jacobsen. Lvs larger, 25×17mm. var. ***microphylla*** Jacobsen. Lvs circular, 6mm diam.

***P. namaquensis*** Sonder. See *Ceraria namaquensis*.
***P. pygmaea*** Pill. See *Ceraria pygmaea*.
For further synonymy see *Crassula*.

**Posadaea** Cogn. Cucurbitaceae. 1 species, a climbing, pubescent herb. Tendrils simple to bifid. Leaves ovate to orbicular, entire or shallowly 3–7-lobed, occasionally remotely denticulate, cordate, membranous, to 18×19cm. Male inflorescence a raceme, short, few-flowered; calyx tube campanulate, lobulate, to 1cm; corolla yellow, rotate, exterior pubescent, lobes 5, rounded, sparsely dentate, to 1cm; stamens 3, anthers white. Female inflorescence to 5cm; flowers similar to male except staminodes 5; ovary inferior, elliptic-ovoid, pubescent; stigmas 3. Fruit a berry, globose, rugose, to 10cm diam.; stalk stout; seeds many, compressed, obovate, to 15×10×2mm. Guatemala to Ecuador and Brazil. Z10.

CULTIVATION As for *Trichosanthes* except that multiple planting and cross-pollination are not required.

***P. sphaerocarpa*** Cogn. As for the genus.

**Posoqueria** Aubl. (From *Aymara posoqueri*, Guyanan name for *P. longiflora*.) Rubiaceae. Some 16 species of shrubs or trees. Stems branched, glabrous or pubescent, branches terete. Leaves petiolate, opposite, margin entire, leathery; stipules interpetiolar, deciduous. Flowers pedicellate, in terminal, many-flowered corymbs, white or red, fragrant; calyx tube obovoid, limb persistent, lobes 5; corolla salver-shaped, tube pendent, gibbous in bud, glabrous or pubescent, lobes 5, oblique, twisted in bud, apex obtuse; stamens 5, inserted at throat, anthers exserted, basifixed, linear to oblong, apex acute, pubescent; ovary 1–2-celled, style filiform, stigma 2-lobed, included, ovules many, peltate. Fruit a berry, globose to ovoid, 1–2-celled, fleshy; seeds angular, testa membranous, endosperm fleshy. Tropical America. Z10.

CULTIVATION *Posoqueria* are grown for their remarkable and very fragrant blooms, often carried in profusion and known colloquially as 'needle flowers', this referring to the exceptionally long corolla tube which sometimes reaches 30cm/12in. in length. In some species, the pollen is ejected explosively. Cultivate as for *Bouvardia*.

***P. coriacea*** Mart. & Gal. Tree, to 20m. Stems glabrous. Lvs to 27×16cm, ovate or obovate to suborbicular or, rarely oblong, apex obtuse or subacute, base obtuse or truncate, leathery to fleshy, glabrous, 5–8-veined; stipules to 28mm, ovate, lanceolate, suborbicular, or oblong, apex acute or obtuse, glabrous; petioles to 2cm, glabrous. Fls in 10–25-fld cymes or corymbs; pedicels to 23mm, glabrous; cal. to 8mm, tube to 4×4mm, turbinate to bell-shaped, glabrous, lobes to 5×5mm, orbicular; cor. salver-shaped, tube to 25cm, lobes to 25×10mm, strap-shaped to oblong, apex obtuse. Fr. to 8×5mm, obovoid. Mexico and C America to Colombia and Venezuela. ssp. ***formosa*** (Karst.) Steyerm. Cal. lobes to 4×5mm, ciliate. Colombia, Venezuela.

***P. latifolia*** (Rudge) Roem. & Schult. Shrub to 2m or tree to 6m. Stems glabrous. Lvs to 25×13cm, ovate or oblong to elliptic or lanceolate, apex acute or narrowly acute to cuspidate, base obtuse, margin falcate, leathery, prominently 6–8-veined; stipules to 6mm, deltoid, apex acute; petioles to 2cm. Fls in dense, few- to many-fld, terminal, pedunculate corymbs, white; pedicels to 1cm; cal. to 5mm, limb somewhat lobed, lobes deltoid to orbicular, ciliate; cor. tube to 17cm, pubesc. at throat, lobes to 3cm, oblong, apex obtuse; anth. to 6mm. Fr. to 5cm, globose, bossed, yellow. Spring. W Indies, Mexico to Brazil. ssp. ***gracilis*** (Rudge) Steyerm. Lvs prominently veined beneath. Cal. lobes more orbicular than species type; cor. shorter.

***P. longiflora*** Aubl. Shrub, to 2.5m. Stems glabrous. Lvs to 14×6cm, lanceolate to oblong, apex narrowly acute, base attenuate to acute, margin undulate and subfalcate, thick-textured and lustrous, 8-veined; stipules to 8mm, ovate to deltoid or lanceolate, apex acute to narrowly acute, glabrous; petioles to 1cm. Fls in 6–12-fld, terminal, umbellate corymbs, white; pedicels to 15mm; cal. tube to 1mm, lobes to 2mm, ovate to deltoid, apex acute; cor. tube to 15cm, curved and pendent, interior smooth to papillose, pubesc. at throat, lobes to 3cm, linear, apex acute. Fr. to 5×3cm, orange. Summer. Guyana to Brazil.

***P. trinitatis*** DC. Tree, to 6m. Lvs to 26×12cm, ovate or elliptic to oblong, apex narrowly acute, base obtuse, lustrous and glabrous, veins prominent beneath; stipules to 23mm, lanceolate to oblong, apex acute or obtuse; petioles to 15mm. Fls inn pedunculate corymbs; pedicels to 12mm, peduncles to 3cm, pubesc.; bracteoles subulate; cal. tube to 4mm, apex of lobes obtuse; cor. tube to 17cm, pubesc. at throat, lobes to 3cm, oblong. Fr. to 5cm, yellow. W Indies.

***P. acuminata*** Mart. See *P. longiflora*.
***P. formosa*** (Karst.) Planch. See *P. coriacea* ssp. *formosa*.
***P. gracilis*** (Rudge) Roem. & Schult. See *P. latifolia* ssp. *gracilis*.
For further synonymy see *Solena*.

**Potamogeton** L. (From Gk *potamos*, river, and *geiton*, neighbour, referring to the natural habitat.) Potamogetonaceae. About 90 species of freshwater, perennial, glabrous pondweeds. Shoots upright, usually arising from creeping rhizomes rooted in the bottom of the pond, stream or river; occasionally the rhizomes survive very dry conditions by remaining underground, with the leaves becoming aerial rather than floating. Leaves submerged and/or floating, alternate, variable in shape and size depending on flow and depth of the water, sheathing or stipulate at base, veins parallel. Flowers produced either above the water or submerged, hermaphrodite, small, green, in pedunculate, interrupted or continuous fleshy spikes; bracts absent; petals absent; perianth of 4 sepaloid unguiculate segments; anthers sessile; styles short, carpels 1–4, free or united at base. Fruit a head of drupelets. Cosmopolitan. Hybridization occurs naturally, forming mostly sterile, vigorous clones in waterways; these spread by broken-off fragments or winter buds. In cultivation, these are fast-growing plants in need of constant checking.

CULTIVATION Many *Potamogeton* spp. produce only submerged leaves and are frequently grown in aquaria for their foliage effect;

cool temperate natives are generally less amenable to cultivation in for indoor tanks, having high light requirements and low tolerance of the relative warmth in winter. *P. crispus, P. filiformis* and *P. perfoliatus*, all with entirely submersed leaves, are the most suited to aquaria; those that produce floating leaves, for example *P. gramineus*, may be inhibited from doing so by pinching the stems. When selecting species for outdoor pools, *P. coloratus*, and *P. gramineus* will prove less invasive. *P. natans* and *P. lucens* are more suitable for larger stretches of water, in more confined spaces, their rapid spread needs constant checking. Grow all spp. in a loam-based medium or sand with a proportion of loam. Give full sun or strong light: *P. coloratus, P. crispus, P. filiformis, P. gayi* and *P. perfoliatus* prefer alkaline water. Remove fading foliage and thin colonies when necessary. Propagate by stem cuttings in spring/summer or scaly resting buds in spring where produced.

***P. acutifolius*** Link. SHARP-LEAVED PONDWEED. Rhiz. absent. Stems flat, branched, to 1m. Lvs to 7cm, all underwater, sessile, linear, sharp-pointed to mucronate, main veins with many smaller vein-like strands, 2–4mm wide; stipules open. Spikes of 2–4-few fld heads, about the same length as peduncle. Fr. 3–4mm. Summer. Europe (GB, S Sweden and NW Russia south to C Italy and Greece), Asia and Australia.

***P. coloratus*** Hornem. FEN PONDWEED. Stems cylindric, to 1m. Floating lvs to 10×5cm, ovate to lanceolate, base cuneate to subcordate, translucent, veins net worked and often tinged red; petiole no longer than lamina; submerged lvs to 18cm, petiolate, narrower and thinner than floating lvs, tips obtuse, often tinged red; stipules membranous, veins well spaced. Spikes densely fld. Fr. to 1.75mm, green. Summer. W & C Europe, N Africa.

***P. crispus*** L. CURLED PONDWEED. Stems terete, scaly resting buds produced at stem ends. Lvs all underwater, to 10cm×3–15mm, sessile, narrow-oblong, margins crisped or undulate at maturity, young lvs flat, lightly toothed, tips blunt to acute, veins 3–5; stipules small, membranous, quickly fading. Spikes 12mm on peduncles to 5cm. Fr. 4–5mm, beaked. Summer. Europe, naturalized E US and California.

***P. filiformis*** Pers. Stems thread-like, to 40cm. Lvs all underwater, to 20cm, slender, to 1–1.5mm wide, tubular at base at first, 1-veined; stipules closed. Peduncles long; fls in whorls of 2–5, widely spaced especially in fruit. Fr. to 2.75mm, beak short, central. N Europe, N US, Asia, Egypt, Australia.

***P. gayii*** A. Bennett. Stems thread-like, much-branched especially in upper parts. Floating lvs to 7cm, oval; stipules obvious; underwater lvs to 8cm, sessile, light green to red-brown. Spikes few-fld; peduncles thickened at top. Summer. S America.

***P. gramineus*** L. VARIOUS-LEAVED PONDWEED. Stems to 1m+. Floating lvs to 7×3cm, elliptic or elliptic-ovate, base round or cuneate, not transparent, petiole often longer than lamina; underwater lvs to 8×3cm, sessile, usually narrow-elliptic, base cuneate, margins finely denticulate when very young, undulate, tips acuminate or acute; stipules obvious. Spikes cylindrical, many-fld; peduncles thickened near the top. Fr. 2–3mm. Summer. Widespread in Europe except Mediterranean, N US.

***P. lucens*** L. SHINING PONDWEED. Stems stout, to 2m+. Lvs all underwater, to 20×6cm, narrow-elliptic to obovate-elliptic, base cuneate, tips acuminate, acute or cuspidate, pale green, translucent, margins undulate; stipules large; petioles short or long. Spikes densely fld; peduncle thickened at top. Fr. to 4mm. Summer. Europe, W Africa.

***P. malaianus*** Miq. Stems unbranched to slightly branched. Lvs all underwater, to 12cm, linear-oblong to lanceolate, margins wavy and indistinctly toothed; petioles 3cm. Spikes many-fld. Japan, China to India, Malaysia.

***P. natans*** L. BROAD-LEAVED PONDWEED. Stems unbranched or slightly so. Floating lvs to 12.5×7cm, broad-oval, base cuneate to subcordate with flexible joint at base; petioles often longer than blade; submerged lvs reduced to linear phyllodes, to 3mm wide, obtuse, not transparent; stipules large. Fr. to 4mm. Summer. Europe, N US.

***P. nodosus*** Poir. LODDON PONDWEED. Floating lvs to 15×6cm, elliptic to broad-elliptic, opaque; petiole longer or shorter than blade; submerged lvs to 20×4cm, petiolate, narrower, longer, lanceolate, tips obtuse, margins finely denticulate at first, net-veined; stipules conspicuous, large. Spikes many-fld; peduncle long, to 15cm. Fr. 3–4mm. Summer. Europe, N US.

***P. pectinatus*** L. FENNEL PONDWEED. Stems and lvs filiform. Lvs all underwater, to 2mm wide, deep green, linear, margins often inrolled giving bootlace appearance, tips acute to acuminate to mucronate; stipules open, margins edged white. Fl. spikes short, flexuous, cylindrical at first. Fr. 3–5mm, short-beaked. Summer. Europe, E US to S America, Africa.

***P. perfoliatus*** L. PERFOLIATE PONDWEED. Stems branched. Lvs all submerged, to 10×6cm, sessile, deep green, translucent, ovate to lanceolate, base cordate and stem clasping, tips rounded or blunt, margins finely denticulate when young; stipules membranous, small, quickly fading. Spikes 15–25mm; peduncle stout. Fr. to 3.5mm. Summer. Europe, N US.

***P. rutilus*** Wolfg. SHETLAND PONDWEED. Rhiz. absent. Winter buds produced on ends of side branches. Lvs all submerged, to 1.5mm wide, stiff, tips finely pointed, veins 3–5, lateral ones conspicuous; stipules closed, tubular towards base when young, veined. Fr. 1.5–2mm. Summer. N, C & E Europe.

***P. americanus*** Cham. & Schldl. See *P. nodosus*.
***P. densus*** L. See *Groenlandia densa*.

**POTAMOGETONACEAE** Dumort. PONDWEED FAMILY. Monocot. 2 genera and 90 species of freshwater perennial glabrous herbs, rooted in substrate, with creeping sympodial rhizomes and erect leafy shoots; roots with vessel-elements. Leaves alternate, with basal open sheath, ligule and parallel-veined lamina, linear or expanded atop a petiole in floating species. Flowers bisexual, small, wind-pollinated, regular, in bractless spikes arising above water; perianth 4 free segments, valvate, fleshy, with short claws; stamens 4, opposite and adnate to claws, anthers sessile; ovary of 4 free carpels, alternate with stamens, each with terminal style or sessile stigma and 1 ovule. Fruit a head of 1–4 drupelets (achene in *Groenlandia*), usually floating with help of aerenchymatous pericarp; endosperm absent. Cosmopolitan. *Groenlandia, Potamogeton*.

**Potato**. *Solanum tuberosum*. Solanaceae. A short-lived herbaceous perennial which is cultivated as an annual for its swollen, underground stem tubers. After flowering, the plant produces small green or purple-green berries which are poisonous.

The potato originated in the Andean highlands (Peru, Colombia, Ecuador, Bolivia), where it had been cultivated by the Incas for over 2000 years before the arrival of the Spanish in the 16th century. It was first recorded in Europe in 1587 and rapidly became a staple crop in Ireland and much of Northern Europe. It was taken to North America by immigrants from Scotland and Ireland in the early 18th century. The European crop suffered from an epidemic of late blight (*Phytophthora infestans*) that caused widespread famine in Ireland during 1845 and 1846, when an estimated million persons died of starvation and a further million emigrated, mainly to the United States. Potato cultivation is now widely distributed throughout the world in temperate and tropical regions both for human consumption and as a stock feed.

There is a very large genetic variability within the species, and cultivars now exist for a wide range of environmental conditions; ancient Andean cultivars are being used to increase this range. Tuber formation proceeds better under cooler conditions; there are cultivars adapted to warmer tropical areas although the potato is a difficult crop to grow in the hot humid lowlands compared to the cooler highland areas. Temperatures in the region of 22°C/72°F favour early growth, but during later development lower temperatures of around 18°C/65°F are more optimal. High soil temperatures can retard stolon initiation and tuberization, which is generally best in the range 16–20°C/60–68°F, although cultivars have been selected for cultivation at higher temperatures in the tropics. Potato foliage is very susceptible to damage by frost.

The standard technique for propagating potatoes is through the use of tubers, provided the health of the so-called 'seed' tubers can be maintained, to guarantee quality characteristics and rapid establishment of the crop, a factor which is particularly beneficial where the growing season is short. Research continues on the development of true seed for potatoes but at its present stage this produces unacceptable levels of variability in the resulting tubers. An alternative approach under investigation is the use of microtubers produced *in vitro* by tissue culture. These have the potential for combining the advantages of normal tubers with the convenience of true seed. However, although the technology may eventually be available to the gardener, at present the standard method of propagation will continue to be via traditional seed tubers.

In temperate regions the potato can be harvested throughout the summer months and tubers can be stored to extend the season of availability throughout most of the year. It is also possible to obtain earlier harvests of immature or 'new' potatoes which have a superior flavour to the later crop.

The potato is a versatile vegetable which can be cooked and served in a variety of ways. Potatoes are industrially processed by drying, canning and frying as crisps. If developing tubers are exposed to light they become green and poisonous and must not be eaten even after cooking.

Potatoes require an open, frost-free site, preferably with a slightly acid soil (pH 5.0–6.0). The most suitable soils are deep, fertile, well drained and moisture retentive, although cultivation can be carried out on a wider range of soil types. They should always be grown on at least a three-year rotation to avoid the build-up of eelworm. The soil should be deeply cultivated in the autumn prior to planting, incorporating heavy dressings of farmyard manure or compost. Potatoes have a fairly high demand for nitrogen but excessive applications, particularly to the early crop, can lead to excessive leaf production and increased risk of disease.

The crop should be propagated from healthy, virus-free tubers and wherever possible the best quality, certified seed potatoes should be purchased. These should not be planted outside until the risk of frost has passed but initial growth can be started indoors by a process known as 'sprouting' or 'chitting'. This is particularly useful for advancing development of the early cultivars.

Chitting is carried out during the latter part of winter by standing tubers in shallow trays in a light position (but out of direct sunlight) in a cool but frost-free environment. The dormant buds ('eyes') on the surface of the tuber are concentrated at what is often referred to as its 'rose' end. This should be placed uppermost in the trays to allow a number of buds to develop into strong shoots about 2.5cm/1in. long prior to planting. Depending on conditions, the process of chitting will take about six weeks. Longer shoots are liable to damage during planting and it may be necessary to provide cooler, lighter conditions if early growth is too rapid. For early potatoes the number of sprouts per tuber should be restricted to two or three by rubbing off the excess at planting, thus ensuring a harvest of larger-sized new potatoes. In the case of later maincrop potatoes all shoots should be retained for higher yield.

Planting can commence in early spring starting with early cultivars. The chitted tubers should be planted rose end uppermost either in drills 10–12cm/4–5in. deep or in individual planting holes before covering with 2–3cm/¾–1¼in. of soil, taking care not to damage the developing sprouts.

Recommended planting distances vary with cultivars and tuber size but the earlier ones should be planted closer together than the later maincrop. Typically, early potatoes are planted approximately 35cm/14in. apart in rows 35–45cm/14–18in. apart, whereas the row spacing for later cultivars should be increased to 75cm/30in. Seed tuber size can significantly affect final yields and tuber size and ideally seed tubers should be approximately the size of a hen's egg. The practice of cutting large tubers in half is not recommended as is can encourage disease.

Planting can be advanced by either planting under cloches or by covering with perforated clear plastic film or non-woven polypropylene 'fleece', all of which contribute to soil warming during early growth. An uncovered early crop can be protected from the occasional late frost by covering exposed shoots with straw or by drawing a thin layer of soil over them.

Potatoes should be earthed up during growth to prevent the greening of those tubers produced at the soil surface. The process of earthing up also serves to kill off weed seedlings. In practice, a single operation when plants are about 20cm/8in. high is often sufficient, drawing soil to approximately 10cm/4in. depth around the stems. Very small tubers (*c*10g) planted close together in bed systems tend not to produce stolons at soil level and may therefore not need earthing-up. A more time-consuming way of preventing tubers from greening and at the same time eliminating weed competition is to cover the newly planted area with black polythene anchored firmly at the edges by a covering of soil. When the leaves start to push up the plastic, slits should be cut and the developing shoots pulled through. A crop produced in this way is easily harvested following removal of the plastic.

Once tubers begin to develop they should be kept well supplied with water to ensure maximum growth. Depending on growing conditions, tubers are ready to harvest 90–120 days from planting. Potatoes may be lifted as required, removing the entire crop including the smallest tubers, which may otherwise contribute to a weed and disease problem in following seasons. Potatoes required for storage should be left in the ground for a couple of weeks after the haulm has been removed to allow the skins to harden. They should be allowed to dry thoroughly before storing in a cool dark environment, when they will provide a supply until the following season. Optimum conditions for storage are between 4–10°C/39–50°F with high humidity. At lower temperatures starches are converted to sugars, giving the tubers an unpleasant sweet taste.

Pests include wireworm, cutworms, slugs, potato cyst and eelworm. The most important diseases in garden cultivation include gangrene, blackleg, blight (late blight), early blight, common scab, powdery scab and various virus diseases, in particular leaf roll and mosaic.

A number of serious diseases require rigorous official quarantine measures if found in the UK. These are wart disease (which has a limited distribution) and ring rot and spindle tuber, which are not established in the UK. Because these diseases are easily carried over by tubers it is important to obtain fresh 'certified' seed each year and not to save one's own. For the same reason, damaged, diseased or undersized tubers should not be put on garden rubbish heaps, where they may sprout in the following season, and volunteer potatoes should also be dug up and destroyed.

Cultivars vary in time of maturity, disease resistance, flavour and skin colour. The following are recommended in the UK. *Earlies*. 'Accent': pale cream, firm waxy flesh; excellent flavour; moderate drought resistance. 'Arran Comet': waxy texture; excellent flavour, especially good for salad use. 'Arran Pilot': late first early; white skin and flesh; firm and waxy; excellent flavour; heavy cropper; good resistance to drought and frost; some susceptibility to blight. 'Charlotte': very early; smooth skinned; firm, creamy yellow flesh; excellent flavour, especially good for salads. 'Concorde': pale yellow, firm, waxy flesh of fine flavour; good cropper; performs well on a range of soil types. 'Dunluce': very early; white-skin; creamy, slightly floury flesh; good flavour; also suitable for forcing in pots. 'Epicure': old variety; moderate yields of white skinned tubers; white, floury-textured flesh; good flavour; recovers well from frosting. 'Estima': second early; smooth, pale yellow skin and flesh; good cooking and keeping quality; high yielding; good drought and blight resistance. 'Foremost': firm white flesh of excellent flavour; good storage and moderate yields. 'Kondor', ('Condor'): second early; red skin; firm, creamy yellow flesh; stores well and heavy cropping; good resistance to blight. 'Lola': first early; pale yellow, floury-textured flesh of good flavour; heavy cropping.

'Marfona': second early; pale yellow skin; creamy flesh; cooks well without discoloration; heavy crops of large tubers; good for poor, dry soils. 'Maris Bard': very early; white skin; creamy flesh with good cooking qualities; heavy cropper. 'Maris Peer': slightly dry, creamy flesh of waxy texture and good flavour; especially good for salads. 'Nadine': second early; smooth skin; moist, firm flesh; good cropper; also for exhibition; some resistance to potato cyst nematode. 'Pentland Javelin': white skin; very white, fairly waxy flesh; especially good for boiling and salads; stores well; some resistance to potato cyst nematode; good for exhibition. 'Ratte': second early; long tubers with firm, waxy yellow flesh; retains its excellent flavour, (similar to that of Pink Fir Apple) throughout season; excellent for boiling and salads. 'Red Craig's Royal': second early; very attractive pink skin; good flavour; especially good for salad use; good cropper. 'Ulster Prince': not prolific but fine-flavoured white flesh; good storage; performs best on warm soils. 'Ulster Sceptre': among the earliest of commercially cultivated varieties; soft, waxy white flesh; rarely discolours on cooking. 'Wilja': second early pale yellow skin and flesh; dry waxy texture; good cooking qualities; high yielding but needs deep ridging to prevent greening.

*Main crop*. 'Cara': smooth white skin, pink eyes; firm flesh; stores well; heavy cropping; good for exhibition. 'Desirée': pink skin; pale yellow, moist, soft-textured flesh; rarely discolours on cooking; high yielding; drought-resistant; some susceptibility to common scab. 'Kirsty': large round tubers; white skin; soft creamy flesh; stores well. 'King Edward': pink-flushed skin; dry, floury texture; high quality tubers; rarely discolours; heavy cropper. 'Maris Piper': white skin; creamy white flesh; good cooking quality especially for frying; dry, floury texture; high yielding; some resistance to potato cyst nematode. 'Pink Fir Apple': very old variety; small,often knobbly tubers with pink skin; yellow waxy flesh; excellent flavour which is retained into New Year; good for boiling (with skin), and especially for salads; low yielding. 'Pentland Dell': soft, dry, creamy-white flesh; tends to disintegrate on cooking. 'Pentland Squire': early maincrop; soft, dry texture; good all-round cooker; high yielding; susceptible to hollow heart. 'Romano': very attractive deep rose skin; creamy, firm-textured flesh; high yielding; good blight resistance; good for exhibition.

The following are recommended in the US. *Earlies*. 'Caribe': early; large tubers with blue-purple skin; soft creamy flesh; performs well across Canada and US; high yielding; (65 days). 'Irish Cobbler': early; white skin and flesh; adaptable to range of US conditions and for heavy soils; some discoloration on cooking; reliable high yields; some resistance to rots in storage; (65 days). 'Norland Russet': netted russet skin; white flesh; good range of cooking qualities; high yielding; resistant to scab; (65 days). 'Red Norland': very early; red skin; white flesh; especially good boiler without discoloration; some scab resistance; (65 days). 'Superior': medium early; white skinned, uniform tuber; good storage; some resistance to scab; (65 days). 'White Rose': early; long tubers with smooth white skin; firm, white flesh; good flavour, especially for salads; does not store well. 'Yukon Gold': medium-early; large tubers; pale yellow-brown skin; yellow flesh of excellent texture and flavour; stores very well; moderate yields; (65 days).

*Main crop*. 'All Blue': midseason; deep blue skin; firm, moist lavender blue flesh; smoky flavour; good storage; high yields; (80 days). 'Brigus': midseason; blue purple skin; creamy yellow flesh; especially good for baking and boiling; high yielding; some blight and wart resistance; (80 days). 'Cherokee': white skin and flesh; excellent flavour retained well during long storage; good resistance to scab and late blight; (90 days). 'Chieftain': attractive red skin; white flesh; good yields; some resistance to scab and late blight in the field; (90 days). 'Kennebec': mid to late season; white skin and flesh; cooks without discoloration; good cooking qualities; high yield; susceptible to scab and sunburn; (80 days). 'Pink Pearl': pink skin; white flesh of good flavour; vigorous; late maturing; some wart and blight resistance; (90 days). 'Red Pontiac': mid to late season; smooth dark red skin; some darkening on boiling; high yielding; drought tolerant; some susceptibility to scab; (80 days). 'Ruby Crescent': long tubers; attractive rose-pink skin; yellow, firm, waxy flesh of excellent flavour; good range of cooking qualities; heavy yields. 'Russet Burbank' ('Netted Gem'): strongly netted, russet skin; good range of cooking qualities; widely grown throughout US; (80 days). 'Saginaw Gold': midseason; tan skin; yellow, waxy flesh of excellent flavour; good cooking qualities; good resistance to hollow heart and virus; (80 days). 'Urgenta': midseason; orange-pink skin; pale yellow flesh of excellent flavour; light fluffy texture on cooking; high yields; some resistance to drought and wart; (80 days).

*Late season*. 'Bintje': late maturing; yellow-brown skin; yellow waxy flesh of excellent flavour; especially good for boiling, baking; high yielding; good storage; (90 days). 'Explorer': thin-skinned tubers with creamy white flesh; one of the first true potato seed available to the home gardener; does not carry tuber-borne diseases; (120 days). 'Green Mountain': late maturing; oblong, white-skinned tuber; good flavour but tendency to discolour on cooking; heavy yields but best suited to light soils and cool growing season; (90 days). 'McNeilly Everbearing': large red-skinned tubers; soft white flesh; especially good for baking; excellent storage; harvests well into autumn. 'Russian Banana': late maturing; yellow skin; yellow waxy flesh of excellent flavour; heavy yields; good resistance to a range of diseases. 'Yellow Finn': late maturing; yellow-brown skin, some russetting; bright yellow, smooth-textured moist flesh; very sweet flavour; (90 days).

For sweet potato, see *Ipomoea*.

**Potentilla** L. CINQUEFOIL; FIVE-FINGER. (From Lat. *potens*, powerful, referring to the plant's alleged medicinal properties.) Rosaceae. About 500 species of mostly perennial but some annual and biennial herbs and shrubs. Leaves stipulate, alternate, palmate, pinnate or trifoliate, leaflets entire, margins often toothed, basal leaves longer than cauline leaves in all but the shrubby species. Flowers usually saucer-shaped, solitary or in terminal or axillary clusters, 4-, 5-, or 6-parted; epicalyx of 5 green bractlets alternate with calyx; sepals 5 or 4, often flushed yellow or red; petals 5 (or more in double varieties), yellow, white, yellow suffused with red, red, crimson or purple; receptacle hairy; stamens 10–30. Carpels 4–80; styles almost basal, lateral or terminal. Fruit a group of achenes. N hemisphere.

CULTIVATION A large genus grown for its flowers, often carried over long periods from early summer into autumn, that includes a number of small shrubs for the shrub or mixed border, herbaceous perennials for the flower border, and alpine species for the rock garden. *Potentilla* spp. often occur on calcerous soils, but most will also thrive in slightly acid soils. *P. recta, P. visianii* and *P. coriandrifolia* prefer acid soils; *P. nivea* has a marked preference for lime. With the possible exception of *P. coriandrifolia*, which is more successful in the alpine house, the commonly grown species are hardy to −25°C/−13°F.

The shrubby *P. fruticosa* and its numerous varieties and cultivars, some of which have attractive silvery foliage, form loose and floriferous mounds suitable for the front of the shrub border, for mass planting as groundcover, and also as low informal hedging. The summer and autumn blooms of the border perennials, largely derived from *P. nepalensis, P. atrosanguinea, P. a.* var. *argyrophylla* and *P. recta*, are held on slender stems well above the foliage; these are selected for their warm and brilliant shades of yellow, terracotta, vermilion, mahogany and deep crimson, well suited to strong colour schemes and to cottage gardens.

The alpine species are suitable for crevice and scree on the rock garden, or for growing on walls; some species, such as *P. cinerea, P. eriocarpa* and *P. clusiana*, form low mats of grey or silver foliage, carrying their flowers on short stems (the leaves are reminiscent of, but far less invasive than the British native *P. anserina*, silverweed). *P. nitida* is small and neat and well suited to sink or trough plantings.

Grow in well-drained soils in full sun to part shade; too rich a soil will produce soft foliar growth at the expense of flowers. Strong, bright light will bleach flower colour (for good or ill), although flowering is most prolific in sun. Grow *P. nitida* in poor gritty soil or on scree in full sun. In the alpine house, use a low-fertility loam-based mix, with added grit. Prune shrubby species in early spring, removing weak growth at ground level, and cutting back strong growth by half or one third. Old neglected plants may be rejuvenated by cutting hard back, although this may be more safely done in two or more stages. Trim hedges in spring. Propagate perennial species by seed sown in autumn or early spring, cultivars and hybrids will not come true, so divide in spring or autumn. Remove rooted runners from alpine species. Propagate shrubby species by softwood cuttings in summer and, except for cultivars, by seed in autumn.

***P. alba*** L. Low-growing, vigorous, spreading perenn. herb to 10cm. Basal lvs palmate, leaflets 5, 2–6cm, oblong to obovate-lanceolate, apex toothed, green and hairless above; stipules linear, acute, leathery; stem lvs simple or divided into leaflets, silvery silky beneath at first. Fls to 2.5cm diam., in groups of to 5, peduncles upright; sep. lanceolate, silky, apex slender; pet. obovate, to 10mm, longer than sep., white; fil. glabrous. Fr. smooth. Spring–summer. C, S & E Europe. Z5.

***P. alchimilloides*** Lapeyr. Perenn. herb to 30cm. Stems woody below, clothed in old stipule remains. Basal lvs palmate, long-petioled, leaflets 5–7, narrow-obovate or oblong, hairless and deep green above, white silky beneath, apex lightly toothed; stipules acute, linear-lanceolate; stem lvs with fewer leaflets. Fls many, to 4cm diam. in compact corymbs; bractlets linear; sep. lanceolate; pet. white, obovate, notched, twice length of sep. Pyrenees. Z6.

***P. andicola*** Benth. Tufted, silky hairy perenn. Lvs few; basal lvs pinnate, leaflets 3–5, ovate, toothed. Fls many; sep. half as long as pet.; pet. yellow, obcordate. Colombia. Z8.

***P. ×anglica*** Laich. (*P. erecta* × *P. reptans.*) Similar to *P. erecta* but stems trailing, to 80cm, nodes rooting; lvs not falling early, leaflets obovate, margins coarsely toothed; fls 4- or 5-parted, 1 to few in cymes; pet. 8mm, to twice length of sep., yellow to apricot, blotched brown at base; stamens to 20. W Europe. Z5.

***P. anserina*** L. SILVERWEED; GOOSE-GRASS; GOOSE-TANSY. Low-growing, stoloniferous perenn. Stems procumbent, to 80cm. Lvs to 10–20cm, rosulate, pinnate, leaflets to 25, to 5cm, oblong to ovate, tips obtuse, margins deeply serrate, green above, silver silky beneath. Fls to 2.5cm diam., solitary, axillary; bractlets usually longer than sep., triangular lanceolate; sep. ovate or broad elliptic, half as long as pet.; pet. to 1cm, yellow. Achenes many, abaxial surface grooved. N US, Europe, Asia. Z5.

***P. apennina*** Ten. Perenn. to 20cm, white-tomentose. Lvs ternate, leaflets to 1.5×0.6cm, obovate, apex toothed, silvery downy, sometimes hairless above. Fls to 7.2cm diam.; bractlets linear, as long as or just shorter than sep.; sep. ovate; pet. to 12mm, longer than sep. Achenes pubesc. Balkans. Z6.

***P. argentea*** L. HOARY CINQUEFOIL; SILVERY CINQUEFOIL. Much-branched, somewhat tomentose perenn. to 50cm. Stems woody at base, leafy. Basal lvs petiolate, palmate, leaflets 5, rarely 7, to 2.5cm, upper lvs sessile or almost so, leaflets 3, 5, or 7, obcordate, recurved, deeply toothed, green and glabrous above, white hairy beneath. Fls 12mm diam., terminal in leafy cymes; sep. ovate, just longer than bractlets; pet. sulphur-yellow, obovate, slightly notched, as long as sep. Early summer. Europe, Asia Minor, Siberia. Z4.

***P. arguta*** Pursh. TALL CINQUEFOIL. Perenn. herb, 30–100cm, stems woody at base, upright, thickly glandular-hairy. Basal lvs petiolate, pinnate, leaflets 7–11, ovate to obovate, hairy, margins serrate, upper lvs palmate, leaflets 3, lanceolate. Fls 2cm diam., in narrow capitate cymes; bractlets lanceolate, much smaller than sep; sep. oblong-obovate, tips acute or mucronate, same size as pet.; pet. broadly rounded, white or cream. Summer. N America. Z3.

***P. atrosanguinea*** Lodd. ex D. Don. Hairy perenn. to 90cm; stems few-branched. Lvs long-petioled, leaflets 3, to 7.5cm, palmate, elliptic-ovate to obovate, margins sharp toothed, silky above, white hairy beneath. Fls to 3cm diam. in paniculate cymes on slender pedicels to 5cm; sep. slender-pointed; bractlets elliptic-oblong; pet. deep purple-red, obcordate. Late summer. Himalaya. var. ***argyrophylla*** (Lehm.) A.J.C. Grierson & D.G. Long. Fls yellow or yellow-orange. Hybrids derived from these and (in some cases) *P. nepalensis* include: 'Etna': to 45cm; lvs tinted silver; fls deep crimson. 'Firedance': habit small, to 30cm; fls deep coral; long flowering. 'Gibson's Scarlet': habit tall, to 45cm; lvs soft green; fls bright scarlet. 'Mons. Rouillard': to 45cm; fls double, dark copper. Z5.

***P. aurea*** L. Mat-forming perenn. to 30cm; upper stem silvery hairy. Lvs digitate, leaflets 5, silver hairy on margins and veins beneath, oblong, margins with 5 sharp teeth at tip; stipules lanceolate, blunt; stem lvs smaller with shorter petioles. Fls few in lax clusters, to 2cm diam.; sep. silky, lanceolate; bractlets linear lanceolate, smaller than sep.; pet. to 11mm, golden yellow, base deeper, obcordate, 1.5× length of sep. Summer. Alps, Pyrenees. 'Aurantiaca': to 15cm; fls sunset yellow. 'Flore Pleno': habit small, to 10cm; fls double, light gold. 'Goldklumpen' ('Gold Clogs'): to 15cm; fls bright gold with orange ring. 'Rahboneana': fls semidouble, golden yellow. ssp. ***chrysocraspeda*** (Lehm.) Nyman. Leaflets 3, teeth often obtuse. Fls to 12, yellow. Upper Carpathians. Z5.

***P. ×bicolor*** Lindl. (*P. atrosanguinea* var. *argyrophylla* × *P. atrosanguinea.*) Fls yellow with orange and red. Z6.

***P. brauniana*** Hoppe in Sturm. Dwarf perenn.; stems to 5cm, slender, spreading, slightly hairy. Lvs ternate, leaflets to 1.5×1cm, obovate, margins shallow toothed at apex, hairless above, lightly hairy beneath; basal lf stipules broad ovate, blunt. Fls solitary, to 5, to 2.5cm diam., sep. lanceolate; bractlets oval, obtuse; pet. 5mm, yellow, wedge-shaped, to 1.5× as long as sep.; style base swollen. Summer. E Pyrenees, Alps. Z6.

***P. ×brennia*** Huter ex A. Kerner (*P. crantzii* × *P. nivea.*) Intermediate between parents. Basal lvs with 4–5 leaflets. Z5.

***P. breweri*** Wats. Similar to *P. drummondii* but lamina not as wide, thickly white hairy when young, leaflets to 2.5cm, 8–12, paired. US. Z7.

***P. buccoana*** Clementi. Ascending perenn. to 60cm. Leaflets 3, margins coarsely toothed, 5cm. Fls numerous in cymes, 12mm diam.; pet. obcordate, yellow. W Asia. Z6.

***P. calabra*** Ten. Similar to *P. argentea*; lvs smaller, silvery, leaflets narrower. Sicily. Z6.

***P. canadensis*** L. Silky-hairy, small, creeping perenn.; stems prostrate. Lvs not completely opened at flowering; leaflets 5, cuneate-obovate, margins toothed toward apex. Fls 12mm diam., yellow. N America. Z3.

***P. caulescens*** L. Silky perenn. to 30cm. Lvs digitate, leaflets 5–7, to 3cm, oblong, apex few-toothed, silver silky beneath. Fls to 2cm diam., many, in loose cymes; sep. lanceolate, as long or just shorter than bractlets; bractlets narrower than sep.; pet. to 1×0.5cm, white to light pink, just longer than sep., tips with tiny point; fil. swollen at base; style light yellow. Alps. Z5.

***P. chrysantha*** Trev. Perenn. Lvs digitate, leaflets 5–9, to 10×5cm, obovate to elliptic, margins serrate. Fls 2.5cm diam., in terminal cymes on lateral hairy stems to 50cmm; sep. shorter than pet., ovate; bractlets linear to lanceolate, same length as sep.; pet. 8mm, golden yellow. C & S Europe. Z6.

***P. cinerea*** Chaix ex Vill. Dwarf clump-forming perenn. to 10cm; stems procumbent, rooting, densely stellate and simple hairy. Lvs digitate or ternate, leaflets 3–5, to 2×0.9cm, narrow obovate, margins dentate, grey-green above, grey beneath; basal lf stipules linear. Fls to 6, 2cm diam., in cymes; sep. ovate to lanceolate; bractlets lanceolate or elliptic, mostly just shorter than sep.; pet. to 7mm, pale yellow, longer than sep. Summer. C, E & S Europe. Z3.

***P. clusiana*** Jacq. Pubesc. perenn. to 15cm; stems hairy, base somewhat woody, slender. Lvs digitate, leaflets 5 or 3, to 12mm, obovate, apex rounded 3–5-toothed, glabrous above, silky beneath; stipules lanceolate, acute. Fls 1–3, 2.5cm diam.; sep. lanceolate; bractlets linear, just shorter than sep.; pet. to 10×8mm, white broad-obovate, notched, longer than sep., fil. glabrous. Summer. Alps. Z6.

***P. concolor*** Rolfe. Perenn. to 30cm, upright, hairy. Basal lvs pinnate, upper lvs trifoliate, leaflets 2.5–5cm, obovate-elliptic. Fls 5cm diam. in few-fld cymes; bractlets ovate-oblong; pet. dark yellow, base orange. Summer. W China (Yunnan). Z6.

***P. coriandrifolia*** D. Don. Perenn. to 15cm, slightly hairy to glabrous. Basal lvs to 10cm, many, short-petioled, pinnate, leaflets many, sessile, 5mm wide, deeply cut into linear hair-pointed lobes, lobes again divided, giving leaves fern-like appearance; stipules awl-shaped; stem lvs smaller. Fls to 2cm diam., in terminal, few-fld loose clusters; sep. triangular; bractlets linear-oblong; pet. twice as long as sep., obcordate, acute, white, sometimes yellow, base red. Summer. Himalaya. Z7.

***P. crantzii*** (Crantz) G. Beck. ALPINE CINQUEFOIL. Perenn. herb, to 20cm, not mat-forming; rootstock woody. Lvs digitate, leaflets 3 or 5, 2×1.5cm, obovate to cuneate, margins obtuse, toothed at apex, green, hairless or almost so above, sparsely to densely hairy beneath; stipules ovate, often persistent. Fls 1–12, to 2.5cm diam., flattened; sep. triangular-ovate; bractlets elliptic or oblong, acute, as long or shorter than sep.; pet. to 1cm, yellow, often orange spotted at base, broad obovate, emarginate, larger than cal. seg. Spring. N US, N, C & S Europe. Z5.

***P. crassinervia*** Vis. Perenn. to 40cm; stems ascending, covered in spreading hairs. Basal lvs palmate, petioles long, leaflets 5, broad-obovate, tips rounded, deeply bluntly-toothed in upper half, velvety, veins prominent beneath; stipules linear. Fls in many-fld cymes; sep. lanceolate; bractlets linear, longer than sep.; pet. obovate, white. Summer. Corsica, Sardinia. Z7.

***P. crinita*** A. Gray. Perenn. to 30cm, silky hairy. Lvs many, pinnate; leaflets to 17, to 2cm, oblong, margins toothed at apex, silky hairy beneath. Fls many, 1cm diam., pet. yellow. C & S US. Z4.

***P. cuneata*** (Wallich) Lehm. Tufted perenn., woody at base; stems upright or creeping, silky to hairless. Lvs 6–15cm, short-petioled, trifoliate, obovate or rounded-cuneate, tips broad, 3-toothed, leathery, green above, glaucous beneath. Fls solitary, to 2.5cm diam.; peduncles short, naked; bractlets elliptic, obtuse; sep. triangular pointed, much shorter than pet.; pet. yellow, rounded. Summer. Himalaya. Z5.

***P. delphinensis*** Gren. & Godron. Perenn. to 45cm. Lvs digitate, leaflets 5, to 2×3cm, obovate, green, margins roughly toothed except near base. Fls 2.5cm diam., many, on laterally hairy peduncles to 50cm; sep. triangular, acute; bractlets lanceolate; tips acute, nearly as long as sep.; pet. to 12mm, yellow, twice length of sep., emarginate. SW Alps. Z6.

***P. diversifolia*** Lehm. Perenn. to 30cm; rootstock woody. Lvs usually digitate, leaflets 5 or 7, to 5cm, oblanceolate, margins toothed toward apex, hairless to strigose beneath. Fls 12mm diam.; pet. oblanceolate, yellow. W US. Z3.

***P. dombeyi*** Nestl. Tufted perenn. to 15cm, green-brown, scantily soft-hairy. Lvs to 1.2×0.5cm, orbicular, leaflets 3 or lvs divided into 3 lobes, margins deeply toothed. Fls few; pet. 5mm, yellow. Peru. Z8.

***P. drummondii*** Lehm. Perenn. to 45cm, lightly hairy. Lvs ovate-oblong, leaflets paired, 4–10, 6cm, cuneate-obovate, margins serrate. Fls few, 2cm diam. US. Z3.

***P. egedii*** Wormsk. Similar to *P. anserina* but petioles, peduncles and stolons almost hairless. Lvs 50cm, leaflets to 30, to 5cm, oblong to obovate, white-tomentose to glabrous beneath. Fls 3–4cm diam.; pet. yellow. Coastal W US, E Asia. Z4.

***P. erecta*** (L.) Räusch. Perenn. to 50cm. Lvs in terminal rosettes, often dying early, ternate or sometimes digitate, leaflets 3–5, to 3×1cm, wedge shaped to lanceolate, apex dentate, hairless or lightly hairy above. Fls 1cm diam., in terminal cymes; sep. 4, broad lanceolate; bractlets narrow-oblong; pet. 4, just longer than sep. Summer. Europe except Mediterranean. Z5.

***P.eriocarpa*** Wallich ex Lehm. Perenn.; rhiz. to 25cm, ascending, covered in sheathing stipules; stems to 45cm. Lvs few, long-petioled, leaflets 3, to 4cm, cuneate, margins toothed and incised toward apex. Fls to 4cm diam., yellow. Himalaya. Z7.

***P.fissa*** Nutt. To 30cm, glandular-hairy. Lvs pinnate, leaflets to 13, rounded, margins deeply cut. Fls numerous in cymes, to 2cm diam; pet. cream-white, larger than sep. US. Z4.

***P.flabellifolia*** Hook. ex Torr. & A. Gray. Stems narrow, to 30cm. Lvs mostly basal, few, leaflets 3, to 4cm, subsessile, cuneate, margins deeply saw-toothed. Fls in cymes, 2cm diam., few; pet. yellow. Western N America (British Columbia to California). Z7.

***P.flagellaris*** Willd. ex Schldl. Diffuse perenn.; branches prostrate, slender, downy, rooting. Lvs palmate, leaflets 5, lanceolate, margins sharp-toothed, tips acute, smooth. Fls solitary on axillary peduncles; pet. obovate, yellow, shorter than sep., entire. Siberia. Z2.

***P.fruticosa*** L. SHRUBBY CINQUEFOIL; GOLDEN HARDHACK; WIDDY. Deciduous, rounded, much-branched, leafy shrub, to 60–150cm; stems upright; bark brown, peeling. Lvs pinnate or trifoliate, leaflets 3 or 5, to 2.5cm, sessile, ovate to lanceolate, apex acute, light to mid-green, silky hairy, margins revolute. Fls to 4cm diam., solitary or in groups of 2–3; bractlets narrow-lanceolate, often 2-parted; sep. lanceolate, blunt; pet. bright yellow or white, rounded. Late spring–summer. N hemisphere. Extremely variable polymorphic species; many regional variants have been described as distinct species, but in this account they are treated as varieties of *P.fruticosa*. In cultivation the botanical situation has been obscured by the presence of many hybrids between different varieties that have been given Latin names, and the existence of approximately 130 cultivars. In this account the wild varieties are described first, followed by the principal cultivars without attribution to variety or hybrid group. var. ***albicans*** Rehd. & Wils. Leaflets 5, elliptic-oblong, grey-green and pubesc. above, white-tomentose beneath. Fls to 2cm diam., medium yellow. W China (Sichuan). var. ***arbuscula*** (D. Don) Maxim. Low shrub to 60×100cm. Stems ascending or procumbent; stipules large, brown, leaflets usually 5 occasionally 3, 1cm+, lobed, light to mid-green, thick, white hairy beneath, veins reticulate beneath. Fls 3cm diam., in lax clusters, rich yellow. Summer–autumn. Himalaya, N China. f. ***rigida*** (D. Don) Hand-Mazz. To 60cm. Lvs 3cm, leaflet 3, elliptic, to 2.5×1cm, green above, blue-green beneath. Fls to 3cm diam., deep yellow. Himalaya. var. ***davurica*** (Nestl.) Ser. To 50cm; stems; upright, twigs red, pendulous. If stipules brown; lvs pinnate, hairless, leaflets 5, to 2.5cm, obovate, without stalks, light to mid-green. Fls abundant, solitary to few, 2.5cm diam.; peduncles 2.5cm, hairy, pedicels hairy; bractlets usually wider than sep.; pet. white to pale yellow. Summer–autumn. China, E Siberia. var. ***mandschurica*** (Maxim.) Wolf. Low-growing, to 45cm; lvs grey silky hairy; fls to 2.5cm diam., white. Manchuria. A clone in cultivation is sometimes named 'Manchu'. var. ***subalbicans*** Hand-Mazz. Close to var. *davurica*. To 1.5m; stems stiffly hairy. Lvs sparsely white hairy above, more thickly hairy beneath. Fls many in compact cymes, large, white, on short pedicels. W China (Gansu, Shanxi). var. ***tenuiloba*** Ser. Slow-growing; to 45×90cm. Lvs small, leaflets 5, linear. Fls to 2.5cm, diam., golden-yellow. WN America. var. ***unifoliolata*** Ludl. To 1m; stems densely leafy. Lvs simple, or occasionally with 2 leaflets, 0.7–1.5cm. Fls solitary, 2–3cm diam., golden-yellow. Bhutan.

The numerous cultivars range in form from low creeping mats to large erect bushes, with foliage of different shades and degrees of hairiness, and flowers ranging from white, through yellow to copper, vermilion and pink. Many of those at the red end of the spectrum are prone to fading in strong sunlight and should therefore be sited in a more shady place. Many cultivars have several names and this can cause confusion.

'Abbottswood': lvs blue-green; fls pure white. 'Abbottswood Silver': unstable sport: lvs edged cream-white. 'Beanii': stems upright; lvs deep green; fls to 2.5cm diam., white. 'Beesii': slow-growing, compact, to 60cm; leaflets 3–5, to 1cm, elliptic, silvery silky above, veins hairy beneath; fls 2.5cm diam., in a conical cluster, golden-yellow. 'Daydawn': fls salmon pink; sport from 'Tangerine'. 'Donard Gold': prostrate, to 50cm tall, but much wider; lvs green; fls golden-yellow. 'Elizabeth' ('Arbuscula'; 'Sutter's Gold'): to 1×1m; fls to 3.5cm diam., golden-yellow. 'Farreri' ('Gold Drop'): to 60×90cm; lvs small, leaflets 7, 0.5–0.8cm; fls 2–3cm, golden-yellow; 'Farrer's White' is a derivative of this, with lvs yellow-green and fls white. 'Farrer's Red Form': refers to a collection of seed made by Farrer in W China from red-flowered plants, but at first the seedlings flowered yellow; eventually the gene for redness surfaced in *P.* 'Tangerine'; red-flowered cvs are now common. 'Friedrichsenii' ('Berlin Beauty') *(P.f.* var. *fruticosa* × *P.f.* var. *davurica)*: a grex of several clones of which this is the nominate plant): upright, to 1.5m. Lvs pinnate, ovate to oblong, large, leaflets 5–7, to 3cm, pale green above, paler beneath; fls 3cm diam., light yellow to white. 'Goldstar': semi-erect, to 80cm, spreading; fls 4–5cm diam., golden-yellow, abundant. 'Jackman': stems erect, to 1.2m; lvs to 6cm, leaflets 7, lanceolate to elliptic, deep green above, blue green beneath; fls 3.5–4cm diam., golden-yellow, abundant. 'Katherine Dykes': to 1.5m, spreading widely; lvs 3cm, leaflets 5, grey-green, densely pubescent beneath; fls 3cm diam., primrose yellow. 'Klondike': resembling 'Farreri' but leaflets larger, 1–1.8cm; fls 3.5–4cm diam., bright yellow.

'Lady Daresbury': to 90cm; leaflets 5, blue-green, densely pubesc. beneath; fls to 3.5cm, mid-yellow. 'Longacre': low-growing, spreading widely; leaflets 5, blue-green; fls 3cm diam., sulphur-yellow. 'Maanelys' ('Moonlight'): to 1.2m; lvs 4cm, leaflets 5, blue-green; fls 2.5–3cm diam., soft yellow, paler beneath. 'Mount Everest': stems upright, to 1m; leaflets 5, narrow, yellow-green; fls 3–3.5cm diam., white. 'Ochroleuca': to 1.2×1.8m, stems spreading; lvs 3cm, leaflets 5–7, oblong-elliptic, narrow, green above, blue green beneath; fls 3cm diam., pale yellow, white beneath. 'Parvifolia': to 80cm; leaflets 7, very small, green above, blue-green beneath; fls 2cm diam., yellow. 'Primrose Beauty': branches spreading or drooping; leaflets to 1.5cm, grey-hairy; fls deep cream with darker centre. 'Princess': lvs green; fls clear pink. 'Pyrenaica' ('Farreri Prostrata'): procumbent, to 20cm; lvs 2cm, leaflets 3, oblong-elliptic, green above blue-green beneath; fls 2.5cm diam., golden-yellow. 'Red Ace': to 75×120cm; fls bright vermilion above, pale yellow beneath; colour fades in bright sunlight. 'Rhodocalyx': a selection from var. *davurica*; low growing; fls nodding; pedicels and cal. crimson; cor. white. 'Royal Flush': resembling 'Red Ace' but fls deep pink. 'Snowflake': lvs large, deep green; fls white single to double. Sulphurascens Group (*P.f.* var. *arbuscula* × *P.f.* var. *davurica*): variable; fls usually pale yellow; some of the best cvs are derived from this parentage; originally found wild in W China (Yunnan). 'Sunset': low-growing, resembling 'Tangerine'; fls orange-yellow to brick-red, depending on age and climatic conditions. 'Tangerine': low-growing, lax habit; lvs small, leaflets 7, green; fls 3cm diam., orange to copper- to golden-yellow. 'Veitchii': to 1.5m; lvs 2.5cm, leaflets 5, 1cm, pale green; fls 2.5cm, white with stamens dull red. 'Vilmoriniana': to 90–120×150cm; lvs grey-hairy above, white-tomentose beneath; fls ivory-white to pale yellow. 'Walton Park': to 60cm, spreading; lvs to 4cm, deep green above, blue-green beneath; fls in clusters of 1–5, 3.5–4cm diam., golden-yellow. 'William Purdom' ('Purdomii'): to 1m; lvs 3cm, leaflets 7, oblong-elliptic, pale green above, grey-green beneath; fls 2–2.5cm diam., pale yellow.

***P.fulgens*** Wallich ex D. Don. To 60cm. Lvs 5–15cm, leaflets in unequal pairs, many, to 4cm, margins acutely toothed, spreading hairs beneath. Fls silvery pubesc. in panicles or corymbs, 1cm diam., yellow. Himalaya. Z7.

***P.glandulosa*** Lindl. Perenn. to 60cm; stems and petioles glandular. Lvs pinnate, petiolate, basal lvs large, leaflets 5–7, downy, toothed, round-ovate or obovate, tips nearly acute or obtuse; stipules ovate-lanceolate, acute; stem lvs smaller, leaflets usually 3. Fls 1.5cm diam., in open leafy cymes; sep. oblong or ovate-lanceolate; bractlets narrow, longer than sep.; pet. broad-ovate to obovate, light yellow or crimson, same size as sep. Summer. W US. Z7.

***P.gracilis*** Douglas ex Hook. Upright perenn. to 60cm; stems slender, downy. Basal lvs long-stalked, palmate, leaflets 5–7, to 5cm, obovate or oblanceolate, margins deeply sharply toothed, green and smooth, or nearly so above, white-hairy beneath; stipules large, lanceolate, hairy; stem lvs few, subsessile. Fls many, to 2cm diam. in panicles; sep. ovate, slender-pointed; bractlets lanceolate; pet. obcordate, yellow, longer than sep. Late summer. W US. Z4.

***P.grandiflora*** L. Pubesc. perenn. herb, to 45cm; stems upright, branching, velvety. Lvs of 3 leaflets, leaflets 1.2–3.5cm, obovate, apex toothed; stipules ovate-lanceolate, almost free. Fls few, 2.5cm diam., in upright few-fld cymes; sep. lanceolate, half length of pet.; bractlets narrower and shorter than sep.; pet. gold-yellow, obcordate. Summer. C Europe, S France to Austria. Z6.

***P.haematochroa*** Lehm. Softly hairy upright tufted perenn. to 60cm; rootstock thick and woody. Lvs palmate, basal lvs long-petioled; leaflets 3–7, to 9cm, elliptic-oblong, margins crenate. Fls to 20, 3.5cm diam., brown-red; sep. ovate, slender-pointed; pet. brown-red, larger than sep. Mexico. Z8.

***P.heptaphylla*** L. Perenn.; stems short, ascending. Lvs digitate, leaflets 5–7, to 2.5×1.1cm, ovate-lanceolate, margins dentate; basal lf stipules ovate-lanceolate, acute. Fls 1–10 on lateral, slender peduncles often with red glandular hairs; sep. ovate-lanceolate; bractlets linear lanceolate, shorter than or as long as sep.; pet. 7mm, yellow. C & E Europe. Z6.

***P.hippiana*** Lehm. Perenn.; stems 30–60cm, upright, silky. Basal lvs petiolate, pinnate; leaflets 7–10, upper three 1–4cm, joined, oblong or oblong-lanceolate, margin obtusely and deeply toothed, silky-hairy; stipules entire or almost so. Fls 1–3cm diam., in loose terminal cymes; sep. nearly as long as pet., ovate-lanceolate; bractlets similar to sep., acute; pet. wedge-shaped, sometimes emarginate, bright yellow. Summer. W US. Z6.

***P.hirta*** L. Similar to *P.recta* but without glandular hairs on stems and lvs, only long eglandular hairs. Leaflets linear to oblanceolate, margins toothed at apex with 3–7 obtuse teeth. Fls large, yellow, in terminal panicles. Summer. C & S Europe, Asia Minor, N Africa. Z6.

***P.×hopwoodiana*** Sweet. (*P.nepalensis* × *P.recta.*) Perenn. herb to 45cm. Lvs palmate, leaflets 5. Fls rose-red at base with pink zone, edges white. Z5.

***P.longifolia*** Willd. Perenn., stems to 50cm, thickly bristly hairy and glandular. Lvs pinnate, leaflets to 13, to 2×1.2cm, lanceolate, margins toothed. Fls abundant in terminal panicles, almost pin-headed; pedicels to 1cm; sep. ovate, tips acuminate; bractlets linear to oblong, as long as sep.; pet. 8mm, obcordate, just longer than sep., yellow. Summer. C Asia. Z6.

***P. matsumurae*** T. Wolf. Perenn.; stems to 15cm, ascending. Leaflets 3, to 1.2cm, obovate or rounded, margins toothed, lightly hairy. Fls 12mm diam., yellow. Japan. Z7.

***P. megalantha*** Tak. Softly hairy tufted perenn. to 30cm. Basal lvs to 8cm wide, leaflets 3, broad obovate, margins coarsely crenate, lightly hairy beneath. Fls solitary, to 4cm diam., bright yellow. Summer. Japan. Z5.

***P. micrantha*** Ramond ex DC. Dwarf tufted perenn.; stems to 15cm, thickly pubesc. Basal lvs ternate, leaflets to 5cm, obovate, margins serrate, green and pubesc. above, grey-downy beneath; stem lvs simple; stipules brown, oval, acute, short. Fls 8mm diam., 1–3, interior white, exterior flushed rose; sep. ovate-lanceolate, deep red above at base; bractlets ovate-lanceolate; pet. to 5mm, white or pink, as long or just shorter than sep.; fil. ciliate. Achenes wrinkled. Spring. S & C Europe to Iran. Z6.

***P. montana*** Brot. Perenn., usually stoloniferous. Stems to 20cm, pubesc. Basal lvs of 3–5 leaflets, stem lvs with 1–3 leaflets, leaflets to 3cm, obovate or oblong, margins crenate-dentate at tip, green and pubesc. above, grey-silky beneath and on margins; stipules lanceolate. Fls 1–4, 2.5cm diam.; sep. ovate or obovate; bractlets linear or lanceolate, as long or just shorter than sep.; pet. 6–9mm, white, obcordate, longer than sep. Achenes smooth. Summer. W & C France. Z6.

***P. multifida*** L. Perenn. herb; stems to 30cm, upright, tomentose. Lvs pinnate to almost digitate, tomentose, leaflets to 9, to 4×2cm, pinnatisect, lobes to 5, narrow, green above, silvery beneath. Fls many, 12mm diam. in terminal corymbs; bractlets oblong-linear; sep. ovate-lanceolate, as long as, or just longer than bractlets; pet. yellow, 6mm, just longer than sep., obcordate. Summer. SE France, Lapland, USSR to Tibet and Korea. Z3.

***P. nepalensis*** Hook. Perenn. herb; stems leafy, erect, to 60cm+, hairy. Basal lvs with petioles to 30cm, leaflets 5, 3–8cm, obovate or elliptic-obovate, coarsely toothed, hairy; stipules ovate or oblong, to 2.5cm, lower entire, upper lobed. Fls 2.5cm diam. in long branching panicles; pedicels long; sep. purple above, acute; bractlets blunt; pet. purple-red or crimson, base deeper, obcordate, somewhat undulate, twice as long as sep. Summer. W Himalaya. 'Flammenspiel': to 40cm; fls red narrowly edged yellow. 'Miss Willmott' ('Willmottae'): to 40cm; fls cherry red; name often misapplied. 'Roxana': to 40cm; buds red, fls salmon pink. Z5.

***P. neumanniana*** Rchb. Mat-forming evergreen perenn. to 10cm; stems woody, procumbent, nodes rooting. Lvs digitate, leaflets 5–7, to 4×1.5cm, obovate, margins dentate, basal lvs narrow. Fls to 12, 2.5cm diam., on axillary peduncles; sep. ovate; bractlets lanceolate, blunt, shorter than sep.; pet. 10mm, yellow, longer than sep. Spring onwards. N, W & C Europe. 'Goldrausch': to 10cm; fls bright gold. 'Nana': to 7.5cm; lvs vivid green; fls gold. Z5.

***P. nevadensis*** Boiss. Tufted silky perenn.; stems to 30cm, procumbent. Basal lvs digitate, leaflets 5, to 2×1.5cm, margins roughly round-toothed, green and almost smooth above, silky hairy beneath, stipules sheathing, narrow-lanceolate; upper lvs trifoliate, stipules ovate-lanceolate. Fls to 4, terminal or axillary, 2.5cm diam.; sep. ovate; bractlets oblong, just shorter than sep.; pet. longer than sep., to 7mm, yellow, obcordate. Summer. S Spain (Sierra Nevada). Z7.

***P. nitida*** L. Tufted, silver-grey, downy perenn. to 5cm; stems to 10cm. Lvs ternate; leaflets to 1cm, oblanceolate to obovate, apex usually 3-toothed, silvery-silky; stipules lanceolate. Fls 2.5cm+ diam., 1–2, terminal; sep. narrow-triangular, longer than bractlets; bractlets linear; pet. to 1.2×1cm, white or pink, base deeper, apex notched, longer than sep. Summer. SW & SE Alps. 'Alannah': fls pale pink. 'Alba': fls white. 'Compacta': very dwarf, to 5cm; fls large, gold. 'Lissadel': fls vivid pink. 'Rubra': fls deep rose, free-flowering. Z5.

***P. nivalis*** Lapeyr. Perenn. herb to 30cm, thickly pubesc. Lvs digitate, leaflets 5–7, to 2cm, obovate, margins toothed in upper third, velvety pubesc., grey-green to green. Fls many, to 2.5cm diam.; sep. triangular lanceolate; bractlets narrow lanceolate, longer than sep.; pet. 7mm, white, shorter than sep.; fil. glabrous. Summer. N & E Spain, Pyrenees, SW Alps. Z6.

***P. nivea*** L. Perenn. to 20cm, subglabrous to silky hairy. Basal lvs palmate, leaflets 3, to 2.5×0.5cm, ovate, margins toothed, green and slightly hairy above, stem lvs smaller; stipules brown, awl-shaped, pubesc. above., thickly white-tomentose beneath. Fls to 12 in terminal cymes; sep. lanceolate; bractlets linear, shorter than or as long as sep.; pet. 9mm, obcordate, yellow, just longer than sep. Summer. N hemisphere. Z2.

***P. norvegica*** L. Annual or perenn. to 45cm. Lvs in threes or pinnate, leaflets to 7×4cm, elliptic, oblong or obovate, green, margins serrate. Fls 6–12mm diam., roughly hairy, in clusters in upper lf axils; cal. increasing with age, sep. 5mm in flower, to 10mm in fruit, ovate; bractlets oblong, almost blunt, longer than sep. in fruit; pet. 5mm, yellow, shorter or as long as sep. Late spring–summer. N & C Europe, N US. Z3.

***P. palustris*** (L.) Scop. Rhiz. long and creeping. Lvs pinnate, leaflets 3, 5 or 7, to 6×2cm, oblong, margins roughly serrate, subglabrous beneath. Fls to 3.5cm diam., on stem to 45cm in loose terminal cyme; sep. to 15mm, ovate, tip acuminate, purple tinged; epicalyx linear, much smaller than sep.; pet. dark purple, half as long as sep. Europe, N US. Z3.

***P. peduncularis*** D. Don. Perenn. with long ascending rootstock; stems 10–20cm, erect or ascending. Lvs 10–20cm, leaflets 1–4cm, numerous, oblong, margins serrate, smooth or silky above, silky beneath. Fls 2cm diam., few, in corymbs, yellow. Himalaya. Z7.

***P. pensylvanica*** L. Perenn. herb, grey-hairy; stems to 80cm, upright. Lvs pinnate, leaflets 5–19, to 7×2cm, lanceolate, margins roughly toothed, green or grey, short bristly hairy above, grey-hairy beneath. Fls 12mm diam., abundant, in terminal panicles; bractlets linear-lanceolate, same length as sep.; pet. 10mm, obovate, yellow, long or longer than sep. Summer. Spain, N US. Z4.

***P. quinquefolia*** Rydb. Ascending or spreading somewhat pubesc. perenn. to 20cm. Basal lvs numerous, digitate, leaflets 3 or 5, to 2.5cm, oblanceolate or obovate, deeply cut into lanceolate or oblong lobes, silky green above, white-tomentose beneath. Fls to 12mm diam., few to many, yellow. NW & C US. Z4.

***P. recta*** L. Perenn.; stems to 45cm, velvety hairy, with long hairs and glandular hairs. Lvs digitate, leaflets 5–7, to 3.5cm, oblong-lanceolate, green, margins serrate to pinnatisect. Fls many, to 2.5cm diam., in corymbs; sep. triangular lanceolate; bractlets linear, as long or just longer than sep.; pet. to 12mm, yellow, as long or just longer than sep., obcordate. Summer. 'Macrantha' ('Warrenii'): fls bright yellow, in loose clusters. Z4.

***P. reptans*** L. Rampant pubesc. perenn.; stems to 100cm, trailing, nodes rooting. Lvs in rosette, glandular hairy, leaflets 5 or 7, to 7×2.5cm, obovate, margins toothed. Fls 25mm diam., 5-parted, solitary, axillary; pedicels glandular-hairy; cal. glandular-hairy, sep. variable; bractlets variable; pet. to 12mm, to twice length of sep., yellow, notched; stamens 20. Europe, Asia. Z5.

***P. rupestris*** L. Pubesc. perenn. to 45cm. Lvs pinnate, leaflets 5–7, to 4×3.5cm, ovate to nearly rounded, margins doubly crenate, green, pubesc. above and beneath. Fls to 2.5cm diam., 1 to many on stem to 60cm; sep. triangular, epicalyx seg. lanceolate, shorter than sep.; pet. white, to 14mm, longer than sep. N US, W & C Europe. 'Alba': fls white. 'Nana ('Pygmaea'): habit dwarf, stems erect; fls in clusters, white. Z5.

***P. salesoviana*** Stephan. Few-branched, deciduous, upright, narrow shrub to 1m. Leaflets 7–13, to 4cm, linear-oblong, sessile except apical leaflet with short stalk, margins serrate, deep green above, white-tomentose beneath; stipules silvery. Fls 3cm diam., nodding, to 7 in cymes; sep. lanceolate, as long as pet.; bractlets linear, half as long as sep.; pet. obovate, white flushed red. Summer. Turkestan, SE Siberia, Himalaya, W China. Z4.

***P. saxifraga*** Ardoino ex De Not. Tufted perenn. herb. Lvs ternate or digitate; leaflets 3–5, to 3cm, linear to obovate, apex usually 3-toothed, margin rolled back, leathery, almost glabrous and green above, silver downy beneath, stem lvs smaller toward apex; stipules linear-lanceolate, apex slender-pointed. Fls to 20 in loose terminal cymes; sep. ovate to lanceolate; bractlets linear, shorter than sep.; pet. 6mm, white, longer than sep., entire to emarginate. Early summer. SE France, Alps. Z6.

***P. simplex*** Michx. OLD FIELD CINQUEFOIL. Similar to *P. canadensis* but with tuberous swellings on ends of stolons at end of season. Lvs usually fully developed at flowering. Fl. stem arching. E & C US. Z3.

***P. speciosa*** Willd. Perenn. Lvs ternate; leaflets 3cm, broad to elliptic obovate, margins crenate-dentate in basal third, white-tomentose beneath. Fls to 8m, on short pedicels, 15–25mm diam., sep. broad ovate; bractlets linear, as long or longer than sep.; pet. 10mm, white, just longer than sep. W & S Balkans. Z6.

***P. thurberi*** A. Gray. Perenn. to 75cm, pubesc. and glandular-hairy. Lvs palmate; leaflets 5–7, 2.5–5cm, broadly oblanceolate, tips rounded, margin roughly toothed. Fls 2cm diam. in lax clusters. S US and Mexico.

***P. ×tonguei*** hort. ex Baxt. (*P. anglica* × *P. nepalensis*.) Stems procumbent, not rooting. Leaflets 3–5, obovate, dark green. Fls apricot with carmine-red eye. Garden origin. Z5.

***P. valderia*** L. Perenn. to 40cm, shortly grey-tomentose; stem weak. Lvs digitate, leaflets 5–7, to 3cm, unequal, linear-obovate, margins dentate in upper half, velvety beneath, sometimes smooth above. Fls many, 1cm diam., in dense corymbs; sep. triangular-lanceolate; bractlets linear-lanceolate, as long or shorter than sep., slightly notched. Summer. Maritime Alps, Balkans. Z6.

***P. visianii*** Pančić. Perenn. herb.; stems to 40cm, pubesc., glandular. Lvs pinnate, leaflets 5–17, to 2.5×1.5cm, obovate to cuneate to ovate, hairy, margins 2–7-toothed. Fls 5cm diam., mostly abundant in loose terminal cymes; pedicels 10mm+; sep. lanceolate; pet. 10mm, yellow, longer than sep., obcordate. NW Balkans, Serbia. Z5.

***P. alpestris*** Haller. f. See *P. crantzii*.
***P. ambigua*** Cambess. See *P. cuneata*.
***P. arbuscula*** D. Don. See *P. fruticosa* var. *arbuscula*.
***P. argyrophylla*** Wallich ex Lehm. See *P. atrosanguinea* var. *argyrophylla*.
***P. argentea*** var. ***calabra*** (Ten.) Fiori & Paol. See *P. calabra*.
***P. beanii*** hort. See *P. fruticosa* 'Beanii'.
***P. blaschkeana*** Turcz. ex Lehm. See *P. gracilis*.
***P. coccinea*** Hoffmeister. See *P. nepalensis*.
***P. comarum*** Nestl. See *P. palustris*.
***P. corsica*** Sieber ex Lehm. See *P. rupestris*.
***P. dahurica*** hort. See *P. fruticosa* var. *davurica*.
***P. davurica*** Nestl. See *P. fruticosa* var. *davurica*.
***P. dubia*** (Crantz) Zimmeter. See *P. brauniana*.
***P. formosa*** D. Don. See *P. nepalensis*.

***P. fragiformis*** Willd. ex Schldl. See *P. megalantha*.
***P. frondosa*** Greene. See *Horkelia frondosa*.
***P. glabra*** Lodd. See *P. fruticosa* var. *davurica*.
***P. glabrata*** Willd. ex Schldl. See *fruticosa* var. *P. davurica*.
***P. gordonii*** (Hook.) E. Greene. See *Ivesia gordonii*.
***P. meifolia*** Wallich. See *P. coriandrifolia*.
***P. menziesii*** Paxt. See *P. ×bicolor*.
***P. minima*** Hallier f. See *P. brauniana*.
***P. nuttallii*** Lehm. See *P. gracilis* var. *glabrata*.
***P. opaca*** L. See *P. heptaphylla*.
***P. pacifica*** T.J. Howell. See *P. egedei*.
***P. pyrenaica*** Willd. See *P. fruticosa* 'Pyrenaica'.
***P. splendens*** Buch.-Ham. ex Trev. See *P. fulgens*.
***P. splendens*** Ramond ex DC. See *P. montana*.
***P. ×sulphurascens*** Hand-Mazz. See *P. fruticosa* Sulphurascens Group.
***P. sulphurea*** Lam. See *P. recta*.
***P. tabernaemontani*** Asch. See *P. neumanniana*.
***P. ternata*** Lehm. See *P. aurea* ssp. *chrysocraspeda*.
***P. tommasiniana*** F.W. Schultz. See *P. cinerea*.
***P. tormentilla*** Stokes. See *P. erecta*.
***P. tormentilla-formosa*** hort. See *P. ×tonguei*.
***P. transcaspia*** T. Wolf. See *P. recta*.
***P. veitchii*** Wils. See *P. fruticosa* 'Veitchii'.
***P. villosa*** Dulac. See *P. crantzii*.
***P. vilmoriniana*** hort. See *P. fruticosa* 'Vilmoriniana'.
***P. viscosa*** Donn ex Lehm. See *P. longifolia*.

**Poterium** L.
***P. canadense*** (L.) A. Gray. See *Sanguisorba canadensis*.
***P. caudatum*** Ait. See *Bencomia caudata*.
***P. sanguisorba*** L. See *Sanguisorba minor*.
***P. tenuifolium*** Franch. & Savat. See *Sanguisorba tenuifolia*.

**Pothos** L.
***P. aureus*** Lind. & André. See *Epipremnum aureum*.
***P. celatocaulis*** N.E. Br. See *Rhaphidophora celatocaulis*.
***P. tricolor*** hort. See *Epipremnum aureum* 'Tricolor'.
***P. wilcoxii*** hort. See *Epipremnum aureum* 'Wilcoxii'.

**×Potinara**. *(Brassavola × Cattleya × Laelia × Sophronitis.)* Orchidaceae. Quadrigeneric hybrids made from species and hybrids of these genera and named after a french orchid grower, Monsieur Potin. The plants are mostly smaller and more compact in growth than the brassolaeliocattleyas, cattleyas and laeliocattleyas and have smaller flowers than those hybrids. The best red and orange colours, as well as some very fine yellows, are found in this group of intergeneric hybrids. A selection of the finest is listed below.

× *P.* Alyce: strong plants; fls large, excellent shape, solid red with darker red lip.

× *P.* Amangi: vigorous plants of medium size; fls true crimson red of excellent shape; several awarded clones.

× *P.* Carrousel 'Crimson Triumph': strong plants; fls clear burgundy red with full red lip, fine form, one of the best of the early red cattleyas.

× *P.* Fortune Peak: typical cattleya-type plant of medium size; fls pale green-pink with brilliant raspberry red lip with yellow flash in the centre.

× *P.* Fortune Teller: strong plants, sometimes tall; rich shades of orange and yellow orange, sometimes veined red, with darker orange lip; many fine awarded clones.

× *P.* Gordon Siu 'Red Radiance': compact plants; striking red fls of excellent form; one of the best of the large flowered red cattleyas.

× *P.* Sao Paulo: strong plants, one of the best semi-yellows; fine large blooms with yellow sep. and pet. contrasting with rich purple lip.

× *P.* Tapestry Peak: strong plants; fls lovely pink with deep purple and yellow in the throat of the ruffled lip, excellent shape; several awarded clones.

× *P.* Twenty Four Carat: small plants with fls of excellent shape; fls bright golden yellow throughout.

**Pots and potting**. Plants were grown in pots by the early Egyptians, Greeks and Chinese and were traditionally made from baked clay: old hand-made pots can be identified by the uneven finish and rather ridged surface inside the pots. Moulds were used Italy for the manufacture of terracotta pots and since the late 1940s pots have been produced by mechanized manufacturing methods using hydraulic presses. Various plastics have replaced clay or terracotta, except for decorative tubs and containers. Most plants grow equally well in clay or plastic, but some show a preference for one or the other.

Conventionally shaped pots are usually classified by the internal diameter at the rim, sometimes the external diameter, but clay pots used to be graded according to the number that could be made from a certain quantity of clay (known as a 'cast'). The largest size made from one cast was an 18-inch (45cm), and was called a 'number one'; 32 pots measuring 6¼ inches (16cm) could be produced from the same amount of clay and these would be called '32s'. In the very small sizes, the number from a cast did not vary much (usually there were 72), and the very small ones were often referred to as 'thumbs' (2½in.) and 'thimbles' (2in.). Even smaller sizes were made.

The proportions of most pots are similar, with a tapering shape to allow easy removal of the root-ball for repotting. Most pots have a rim which strengthens the pot and makes stacking easier. Special sizes and shapes are produced for particular uses. The pan (often referred to as a seed pan or mini-pot) is less than half the depth of a normal pot; it is usually used for seed-sowing, but also for shallow-rooting plants such as many bromeliads, cacti and alpines. The larger sizes, usually of clay, can be round or square. Three-quarter pots are intermediate in depth between pan and normal pots; they are used on the European continent more than in the UK or US. Half-pots, which as the name implies are half the depth of a normal pot, are often used for plants such as azaleas. Long toms are much deeper in proportion to width, and are used for plants with tap roots that would be too restricted by a normal pot, or which produce deep roots which resent restriction or disturbance.

The use of plastics has enabled the easy production of rectangular pots, which make better use of bench space because they can be packed together more with no wasted space. A square pot of the same diameter will hold more potting medium than a circular one, and it may be possible to use a slightly smaller size for a given plant. But packing pots close together at maximum density may lead to cultural problems if the leaves touch each other and there is poor circulation of air around the pots.

Pots must have drainage holes; there is usually a large central one in a clay pot, several smaller ones around the base in a plastic pot. Plastic pots are not normally crocked (see below), and are generally more suited to capillary watering. Pots for orchids have additional holes in their sides to ensure that the compost is aerated and the root-run free; some plastic orchid containers have meshed sides.

Plastic pots are light, clean, and easy to handle; they will become brittle and may be split or cracked with rough handling or age, but there are equally breakages and losses with brittle clay pots. Plastic pots are the best choice if you are using capillary watering, as there is no necessity for a wick to be inserted through the drainage holes. The potting medium will dry out less quickly in a plastic pot, but it is more difficult to know when water is needed. One can tell when the medium in a clay pot is becoming dry by tapping the pot: a dry pot will give a ringing note, a wet one a dull note.

Clay pots are aesthetically pleasing, are useful where the weight is an advantage for stability (for large palms or tall plants like sansevierias for instance), and for low-growing plants, such as alpines, where a plastic pot may detract from the appearance. Plants that need good drainage, such as alpines and many orchids, will also benefit from the container's porosity. The porosity of clay also means that roots are likely to be better oxygenated, there is less risk of overwatering, and excess fertilizer is less likely to build up in the potting medium. Clay pots vary in their resistance to frost, which will be determined by the nature of the clay, the method of purifying and processing the clay, the method of manufacture (pressing is stronger than slip-casting) and the temperature of the kiln.

Polythene (polyethylene) is used for collapsible, fold-flat pots. These are inexpensive and useful for growing on cuttings and young plants outdoors or in the greenhouse. They are best discarded after a single use. Polypropylene is the plastic widely used, but for container pots (the large black pots used for container-grown hardy plants), a proportion of polythene (polyethylene) is used to ensure they do not become too brittle while standing outdoors in cold weather.

**Pots and containers** (a) Standard flower pots (b) Long Tom (c) Dwarf or half pot (d) Deep half pot (e) Alpine pan (f) Plastic and wooden seed trays (g) Pots ranging in size from 3.5–40cm diameter; larger sizes (planters) are in clay or thick plastic (h) Clay and plastic pots with drainage holes (i) Clay orchid pots (j) Plastic mesh pot (k) Peat pots, individual and strips, with seedling (l) 'Whalehide' cropping pot (m) Compressed expandable peat pellet, with growing seedling (n) Strawberry pot (o) Plastic window box, with drip tray (p), (q), (r) Hanging baskets: plastic, wire, and slatted wood orchid basket (s) Self-watering containers with canvas wick (left) and soil 'wick' (right)

Peat pots can be used in the greenhouse, or where the appearance does not matter, for plants that are eventually to be transplanted. These are generally made of a mixture of sphagnum moss peat and wood fibre (sometimes impregnated with plant food). Both round and square peat pots are made. Those intended for small seedlings are sometimes sold in strips to fit into seed trays.

Roots will eventually grow through the walls of a peat pot, which will in time disintegrate when planted out in the garden. They are useful for young plants that resent root disturbance, such as salvias, and there are longer versions for deep-rooted plants like sweet peas and runner beans. Care must be taken to keep the potting medium damp: peat potting mediums in peat pots can dry out and be difficult to rewet if neglected.

Expandable peat pellets (fertilized compressed peat held in a net) are only suitable for rooting cuttings and direct sowing of seeds. They are later planted into conventional pots intact. A peat-based potting medium should be used when potting up plants in expandable peat pellets, otherwise it may be difficult to keep the initial root-ball moist.

'Whalehide' (bitumenized cardboard) is used for ring-culture pots, which are bottomless tubes, with an approximately 23cm (9in.) top and a slighter taper, used to hold the potting medium when stood on the aggregate for the ring culture of tomatoes, cucumbers, peppers, etc. They are discarded at the end of the season. Similar pots, but with a bottom to hold the compost, are available: described as 'cropping pots' they are used for plants like greenhouse chrysanthemums, which are moved into the greenhouse in the autumn.

Glazed pots, which are often large and decorative, need special care with watering, but can be attractive in a patio or conservatory setting.

There is no standardization of pot sizes. They vary not only from one country to another, but also between manufacturers. In the UK, some pots sold in metric sizes may be manufactured to Imperial sizes and described in rounded conversions; pots manufactured to a true metric size may be sold as the nearest equivalent Imperial size in garden centres. Pot diameter is not an indication of standard capacity: apart from full pots and half pots, there may be intermediate sizes.

Container pots (those used by commercial growers for hardy plant stock) are often described by capacity rather than dimension (1 litre, 2 litre, ½ gallon, 1 gallon, etc). This enables the grower to estimate accurately his use of potting medium and has for many buyers of container-grown plants because a gauge of the size and maturity of the purchase, as were formerly the inch/diameter pot sizes.

Pot saucers are shallow containers with a near vertical rim, made to accommodate pots of various sizes. They prevent water that has passed through the potting medium escaping further.

All pots should always be cleaned thoroughly before being reused. It improves the appearance of clay pots, which often acquire a white scaly deposit (efflorescence) which is toxic, unsightly and reduces porosity, and growth of green algae; it also reduces likelihood of contagion.

POTTING. The initial placing of plants in pots from seed trays (sometimes called potting off or potting up), or the operation of moving already potted plants to bigger pots from smaller ones (the latter also being called potting on or repotting). All container-grown species will have differing potting requirements. Some, notably orchids, bromeliads, succulents and alpines, will be especially idiosyncratic. What follows is an outline of the common principles of potting.

Young and rapidly growing plants need potting-on fairly frequently to avoid a check to growth, especially plants grown from seed or cuttings that reach their maturity within a season.

Slower-growing plants need repotting less often; eventually, larger plants cannot be moved on any further because there is a limit to the size of container that can be handled or obtained. Plants that have reached this stage can often be maintained by replacing the top and bottom layers of the potting medium by 5cm/2in. each year, and by regular feeding.

Plants should be potted up or repotted when they are about to start growth or are growing actively. Winter-flowering subjects may require repotting in autumn. Repot young plants when the roots begin to cover the exterior of the root-ball, and before they start to spiral round densely at the base of the pot. Cuttings should be potted up as soon as they are well rooted. Repot larger plants as soon as there is excessive root growth through the drainage hole (plants grown on capillary benches or mats will tend to do this anyway), if roots appear on the surface, and if growth is poor and the compost is packed with roots that are beginning to spiral round the pot (it may be necessary to knock the plant out of the pot to check this). Equally, repot if roots have failed to establish themselves due to overpotting or poor cultivation. Some plants with fleshy roots (such as chlorophytums) may push part of the root-ball out of the pot if neglected. Although a pot-bound plant is often at optimum condition, this is not sustainable; most plants should be repotted once they become pot-bound, in the ways described above.

A few plants succeed best if the roots are restricted. These should be potted on only when the top growth is out of proportion to the pot. Sansevierias are best repotted only when the roots fill the pot and start to emerge from the compost (restraining the growth keeps the plant compact); aspidistras are not repotted frequently, and the variegated form is usually better if slightly starved and pot-bound. Cacti can be repotted less frequently than most plants, although annual repotting means healthier plants. Bromeliads, cacti, orchids and other groups that are epiphytic or partly epiphytic require relatively small pots for their size.

Overpotting (using a pot that is too large) should be avoided: the potting medium may not be explored fully by the roots, and therefore remain too wet, stagnate, and affect growth. Normally, choose a pot only one or two sizes larger than the existing pot.

Soak clay pots for at least an hour before use (so that they do not draw too much moisture from the compost). Clay pots also require a crock (piece of broken pot, often called shard in US, or other material such as scraps of broken expanded polystyrene) over the drainage hole to retain the compost yet allow free drainage. Crocking for epiphytic and xerophytic subjects may often be more complex and involve a complete covering of the floor of the pot with packed, vertical shards with an additional layer of grit, sharp sand, pea-gravel or charcoal. A layer of the potting medium is then inserted, sufficient to bring the level of the old pot to a suitable height below the rim of the new pot. This may be around 12mm/½in. for small sizes and 25mm/1in. for large ones, to allow space for water when watering.

A plant is most easily removed from its old pot by turning it upside down and placing the fingers of one hand across the surface of the rooting medium with the growths protruding between the fingers. The pot rim is then brought down fairly sharply on a hard surface like a potting bench, when the root-ball should come free. If the roots are binding it to the pot, run a knife round the inside of the pot, then repeat as above. It may be necessary to place a large plant on its side and tap the pot with a wood mallet or other tool while the base of the plant is pulled on.

When the plant has been removed from its old pot, it is placed on the layer of new potting medium in the new pot; fresh medium, which should be moist but not wet (it should hold together when squeezed into a ball, but fall to pieces when placed on the bench), is trickled in round the root-ball, being gently pushed down with the fingers or a potting stick (a short thick cane) or a soil rammer (a narrow wedge of wood) to ensure no air pockets are left. Banging the pot down lightly on a hard surface should help to settle the rooting medium.

An alternative method, suitable for peat-based potting mediums and plastic pots, is to pack the rooting medium around the old pot, making sure it comes to the right level in the new pot, then withdraw it to leave a mould of the right size. Knock the plant out of the old pot, insert the root-ball in the mould, and firm gently. This method is only suitable for thin-walled plastic pots.

In general, large woody plants should be firmed more solidly than those with soft growth, while soil-based potting mediums can be firmed much more than peat-based ones. Newly potted plants will appreciate moister and shadier conditions than usual for a few days while they recover from the trauma.

It is best to repot into a similar rooting medium – if a peat-based, rooting, medium root-ball is put into a loam-based medium, watering may be difficult and the plant may not root into the new compost satisfactorily. If the old root-ball is a mass of roots tightly wound around the wall of the pot, loosen some of these to encourage easier rooting into the fresh rooting medium. If a valuable plant has formed a mass of rots through the drainage holes of the old pot, it may be better to break the old pot than to damage the roots, to avoid a check to growth (plastic pots can be cut away with heavy-duty scissors or cutters).

ORNAMENTAL CONTAINERS. Decorated pots have been used for plants for thousands of years by many civilizations. Ancient Egyptian paintings and decorations show ornate vases being used as containers, and the Greeks and Chinese also produced attractive as well as functional pots. By Roman times terracotta pots were often decorated with swags of fruit and flowers, and in late Medieval and Renaissance times simple pot shapes were often decorated with handles, bands of clay and scoring. Decorative containers are currently produced in classical styles, as well as simpler modern styles such as shallow dish-shaped and plain rectangular containers.

Terracotta is still one of the most useful materials for large traditional pots and urns or vases, but glazed ceramic pots are also popular, perhaps planted with bamboos and other Oriental plants. Traditional and classical containers, such as Elizabethan *jardinières*, Venetian troughs, Gothic urns and Versailles vases, available in reconstituted stone, are useful for creating a period garden. Traditional Versailles tubs, especially suitable for large shrubs or small trees because of their generous capacity, are available in timber and plastic.

Plants grown in decorative containers outdoors need regular watering and feeding for much of the year; the larger the container and the more potting medium it contains, the less rapidly it is likely to dry out and the greater the reserve of nutrients.

Windowboxes are particularly useful for small gardens. Plastic boxes are popular on grounds of cost and weight (especially important if the containers have to be carried on brackets below the window) and can be made less obtrusive by false fronts across the sill. Windowboxes should be at least 20cm/8in. (preferably 25cm/10in.) deep if they are not to dry out rapidly. Allowing for 2.5cm/1in. of drainage material and 2.5cm/1in. of space between potting medium and the top of the box for watering, the 15–20cm/6–8in. of compost is barely adequate for shrubby plants and other perennials. For seasonal bedding, width is important: 15cm/6in. is the minimum practical width, but if the sill or bracket is large enough for a 20cm/8in.-wide box, an extra row of plants can be added. The additional width also enables pots to be plunged more easily into the box for transient displays.

Tubs, troughs and urns should hold an adequate volume of potting medium, especially those to be planted with shrubs and small trees. Shape can be deceptive (especially those that taper towards top and bottom), so check the capacity. A 20-litre/4½ UK gallon/5¼ US gallon capacity is the minimum for permanent plantings, though the number of plants used must depend on the shape of the container.

Inward-tapering tops, as in some classically shaped vase-like containers, are unsuitable for shrubs and similar perennials which form a large root system and may eventually require moving to a larger container, as it may be impossible to remove the plant with the root-ball intact. A substantial rim or ridge that can be used to lift the container will be useful if it has to be moved.

A variety of materials is commonly used for tubs, troughs and windowboxes.

*Concrete* is easily cast into a variety of shapes, which range from rectangular planters to classical urns and vases; the finish is generally much coarser than reconstituted stone, and inferior when viewed closely. From a distance, however, they are just as effective as the more expensive reconstituted stone containers. Weight is a major handicap with concrete, but this can be an advantage for the stability of large shrubs and small trees. The heavy weight makes this an unsuitable material for windowboxes. Newly cast concrete should be allowed to weather before use so that any free lime will not affect the plants; usually this will have dissipated while the containers have been on display.

*Glass-reinforced cement* is used to produce thin-profile troughs and other containers, often with fine, elegant detailing. Cement is used to bind glass fibres, producing strength in a thin profile. The capacity is usually generous, but weight may make the material unsuitable for window-boxes.

*Glass-reinforced plastic* (glass-fibre) containers are expensive but have a long life. The material is sometimes used where a modern but very light container is required, but it is also much used to create reproduction lead cisterns and other 'antiqued' containers. It is sometimes possible to have containers specially made to a particular colour. Glass-reinforced plastic windowboxes are generally light and elegant, and usually hold a generous amount of potting mix.

*Glazed ceramic* containers are widely available, and often ornately decorated. Many are produced in traditional Chinese and Japanese styles, and are particularly useful for creating an oriental atmosphere, perhaps planted with bamboos or other suitable plants. Check that they are suitable for outdoors if likely to be used in an area subject to frosts.

*Plastics* are widely used, polypropylene being a popular choice. Being relatively cheap and easily moulded, a wide range of plastic containers is available, from windowboxes to tubs, urns, and other planters, in many colours, including an 'antiqued' or weathered finish that resembles stone or concrete from a distance. The plastics used for containers will become brittle after a few years, and may break or split if knocked, but many will give years of use and are not expensive to replace. Cheap plastic windowboxes can be used as 'liner' boxes for more expensive or more decorative outer casings, or given false fronts that are visually more attractive.

*Recycled cellulose fibre* is used for planters and troughs intended for seasonal displays. These peat-coloured containers may last for a couple of seasons. Although not visually attractive they are inexpensive and acceptable for massed planting with bright and colourful flowers.

*Reconstituted stone* is used mainly for reproducing traditional urns, vases, and other containers that would originally have been curved from stone. The material is more expensive than concrete but aesthetically more pleasing, with fine detail convincingly reproduced. Once it has weathered it is difficult to tell from real stone except on close examination.

*Stone* is rarely used for new containers, but antique stone containers are available from specialists. Stone sinks and troughs, popular for alpines in the UK, are sometimes available, but imitation stone is more often used and alpine troughs are made from 'hypertufa' (see ROCK GARDENS).

*Terracotta*, high-fired clay, is one of the oldest materials used for containers, but it must be frost-proof if used in areas subject to freezing temperatures. This can be aided by providing a good depth of drainage material. Terracotta is naturally porous and should be soaked on first use or it will absorb water from the potting medium. Algal growth may appear, or white efflorescence from salts in the clay: these can normally be scrubbed off with water. Large decorative shrub-pots and attractive urns and vases are often ornately decorated; terracotta windowboxes are also generally well ornamented, but their weight demands a strong, secure position on a wide sill.

*Wood* is traditionally used for large shrub or small tree containers such as Versailles tubs (usually painted white), though there are plastic versions made to look like wood. Wooden window boxes and troughs may be available locally, but the main advantage of wood is the ability to make the box to a non-standard size to fit a particular sill.

Hardwoods such as oak and elm, and naturally rot-resisting timbers such as cedar, are more durable than the less expensive softwoods. These can be used, however, if thoroughly treated with a wood preservative suitable for use near plants. Although even treated softwood will rot, it should last for many years.

FIXING AND SECURING WINDOWBOXES. Windowboxes must be secured safely. Sash-type windows with broad sills generally have adequate space to secure the box safely; raising it on small blocks will prevent water collecting beneath it and protect woodwork. As most sills slope, wedge-shaped pieces of wood can be used to level the box while also raising it off the sill to allow air to circulate.

Casement windows, which open outwards, usually have narrow sills and boxes would in any case prevent the windows being opened effectively. Boxes are best fixed *below* the window, using specially designed brackets which are sufficiently strong and have a 'lip' to prevent the box sliding off the bracket. The brackets must be firmly secured to the masonry with wall plugs (usually supplied); position them sufficiently far beneath the window so that plant growth does not obstruct opening.

Where the boxes could be a hazard if they were to fall, secure them with safety chains, fixed to hooks screwed into the box (if timber) or threaded through drilled holes, and secured to strong hooks fixed to the masonry with wall plugs.

HANGING CONTAINERS. Traditional hanging baskets are made from stout galvanized wire, roughly hemispherical in shape. Hanging baskets are now widely used outdoors, suspended from low eaves or porches or from stout brackets fixed to a wall, but in the heyday of the greenhouse they were generally regarded as indoor containers. They are often at their best in the protected environment of a greenhouse or conservatory, where wind is unlikely to damage them.

Outdoors, half-baskets (wall-baskets) may be as effective as a full basket. Full baskets usually have to be turned regularly to obtain even growth (special swivel hooks are available to facilitate this), and they are likely to dry out very quickly if suspended in an exposed position. Terracotta is used for wall pots (similar to wall-baskets, but usually ornate and more attractive when not filled with plants). Mangers are sometimes used as large wall baskets (modern versions are sold for this purpose).

Hanging pots are widely used to display a single plant as an attractive specimen, usually one with a trailing or cascading habit. These are generally suspended by three or more plastic rods extending from a hook, the ends being clipped in to the specially designed plastic pot. A drip tray is often clipped to the base.

In commerce, large baskets of 35cm/14in. or more are used: these hold a generous amount of potting medium to support the plants, and are less likely to dry out rapidly. They require very substantial supports, however, and for domestic use of 30cm/12in. basket is more suitable. Baskets smaller than 25cm/10in. are likely to be difficult to manage, and the display is often less satisfactory. Hanging pots containing a single well-grown mature plant may be more attractive than a very small mixed basket.

Some baskets, especially those designed to take pre-formed liners, are relatively shallow. A basket that is deep in proportion to its width will hold more mixture, and therefore a better reservoir of nutrients and moisture.

Hanging containers used by local authorities for street decoration are made of glass-reinforced plastic and include a large reservoir for water, but these are designed specifically for use on very strong supports such as lamp posts.

*Galvanized wire* is the traditional material for baskets. The wire is generally protected with paint or a plastic coating; although often coloured green or white, this makes no difference to the appearance of a well-grown basket, which will be completely covered with plants.

The size of the mesh is important if planting is required in the sides. Small plants can be inserted through a small mesh by rolling up the leaves in a small piece of plastic or paper and threading the 'tube' through from the inside, or by planting very small plants in 'plugs' (see SEED SOWING). A larger mesh makes planting through the sides relatively easy.

*Plastic mesh baskets* resemble ordinary wire baskets in shape. They are generally more obtrusive visually until covered with plants, but the mesh is often large enough to make side planting relatively easy. Some are designed for use with proprietary liners.

*Recycled cellulose fibre* hanging containers are intended for seasonal plants. The peat-coloured material is not visually attractive, but the compost capacity is generally satisfactory and when planted with suitable trailing or cascading plants is barely visible. These are only intended to last a season or two, and come with their own special hanger.

*Plastic hanging containers* are available in many forms. Some are simple hanging pots, suspended with plastic rods and complete with a simple drip tray. Others are more decorative, contain a small reservoir to hold water and may be fitted with chains. This type of container is particularly suitable for use indoors because watering is less of a problem and the drip tray offers some protection to floors, but they are also widely used outdoors.

*Wooden baskets* are very suitable for orchids and other epiphytic plants, but by lining them with a fine-mesh wire-netting or inserting a plastic pond-planting basket, they can be treated like an ordinary wire basket and lined with sphagnum moss to contain a normal potting medium.

This kind of basket can be made from lengths of wood about 30cm/12in. long, the exact number depending on the depth of the container. Having reserved enough pieces to produce an evenly spaced out base, excluding the end pieces, drill a hole at each end of the others, to take a small-link chain (available from hardware shops). Treat all the pieces with a wood preservative safe near plants, and screw the base lengths in position, spacing them with even gaps. Thread a length of chain through the holes on one side (so the chain runs beneath the base between the two holes), then do the same with another length of chain on the opposite side. Thread the chains through the alternative 'rungs' until the desired depth is reached. Fix the chains to a hook.

BASKET LINERS FOR MESH BASKETS. *Sphagnum moss* is the traditional basket liner, but will turn brown if not kept moist. *Polythene* is cheap and readily available: scrap pieces are adequate. Transparent polythene is acceptable, but black is usually chosen on aesthetic grounds. To avoid excessive puckering, make a series of slits up the sides, from near the base, and overlap as necessary. These will ensure drainage also. Trim surplus material as necessary, to produce a neat finish. Plants can be inserted in the sides by making slits with a knife.

*Coir fibre* liners are made from jute and coconut fibre (the coconut-fibre side faces outwards). With care these liners will last for more than a season, but planting in the sides is difficult. *Polyurethane foam* liners are available in a range of sizes to suit baskets of various sizes. They can be trimmed to size if necessary, and it is relatively easy to plant in the sides where the slits overlap. They may last for more than one season, but will disintegrate with time.

*Recycled cellulose fibre* liners are rigid and designed to fit specific baskets. It is not practical to plant in the sides, and they are visually less attractive than moss unless covered by cascading plants. *Whale-hide* (bitumenized cardboard) liners are available in sizes to fit most popular baskets. Plants can be set in the sides where the 'petals' of the disc overlap. Some have a capillary mat in the base to help retain moisture.

PLANTING A BASKET. Most modern basket designs have a flat base that makes them stable to work on. Traditional wire baskets have a curved base and it is necessary to stand these on a bucket or similar container for stability.

When using moss, place a layer about 2.5cm/1in. thick in the base and up the sides to the level of the first row of plants. Insert plants in the sides as required, then add more moss and compost, building up the basket in tiers. Less damage is usually caused to the plants if the foliage is threaded carefully through the mesh from the inside, rather than trying to push the roots through from the outside. For better cover, stagger the rows in the sides.

When using one of the other liners, add compost to the required level of the first row of plants in the side, insert them through slits or overlaps in the liner, then add more compost to the level of the next row of plants.

For planting a mixed basket, insert a large plant in the centre (perhaps a fuchsia or pelargonium in a mixed summer-bedding basket). This is likely to be a pot-grown plant and the root-ball should be left as intact as possible. Set other plants, which are more likely to be seedlings, around the edge at the top. Cascading plants set around the rim, such as trailing pelargoniums of cascading fuchsias, should be planted at a slight angle to encourage as much growth as possible to tumble over the edge of the basket. Mixed plantings work best in large baskets. A small container is likely to be more effective planted with a single subject, creating a ball of flowers or foliage.

Whether using moss or an alternative liner, a thick layer of moss placed over the top of the basket after planting will help to reduce the speed at which the compost dries out, and by breaking its force will reduce the chance of compost being washed away when water is applied.

Loam-based potting mixtures are recommended for long-term plants, such as large shrubs and small trees, in tubs and troughs. The additional weight is useful for stability and plants will benefit from the better supply of nutrients. Annual topdressing is advisable and feeding will still be necessary.

Soilless mixtures are generally used for windowboxes and hanging baskets because of their lighter weight; since these containers are more often used for seasonal displays the lack of long-term nutrients is less important, especially if supplementary feeds are given. They have the shortcoming of drying out easily and being difficult to rewet thoroughly with ordinary watering.

Proprietary potting mixtures are available specifically for containers such as hanging baskets and windowboxes. These generally contain loam with a higher proportion of peat or other substrate than normal to reduced the weight, combining the benefits of a loam-based mixture with some of those of soilless ones. Moisture-holding additives, such as superabsorbent polymers, vermiculite and others, are also used in container composts. See also POTTING MEDIUMS.

**Potting mediums**. Several terms are used to describe the growing mediums used in containers. The word 'compost' is widely used in the UK as a general term for potting mediums but in other countries the term only refers to the product of a compost heap. However, 'compost' can conveniently be used to describe traditional potting mediums such as the John Innes composts. The more recent lightweight mediums which are primarily based on peat are often referred to as mixes, particularly in the US. The term 'medium' (pl. sometimes media) is a general one which includes both the traditional potting composts and the soilless mixes. In some European countries the word substrate is synonymous with medium.

Generally, potting mediums are classified as being either soil- or loam-based if they contain mineral soil, and soil- or loam-less media if they are based on lightweight ingredients such as peat or bark. However this division is not exclusive since some growers incorporate a small proportion of soil in a basic lightweight mix.

A good-quality potting medium is essential for successfully raising and growing plants in containers. Ordinary garden soil is unsuitable for growing plants in pots because of its poor texture and problems with pests and diseases. In the past, gardeners used their own, often secret, recipes for making potting composts. These were based on a wide range of materials such as leafmould, animal manures, mortar, wood ashes, sand and grit, which were added to soil. These composts were very variable in their results and research in the 1930s by Lawrence and Newell at the John Innes Horticultural Research Institute led to the development of standardized composts based on sterilized loam. The John Innes composts were found to be suitable for growing a wide range of plants and are still in use today. Since the 1950s there has been a considerable increase in the development and use of lightweight soilless mixes, often based on peat. This is mainly due to the difficulties in obtaining supplies of good-quality loam and also because the loam has to be heat-sterilized.

In spite of the large increase in the use of soilless mediums in recent years, soil-based composts such as John Innes still have some advantages. Soil-based composts are heavier than peat-based mixes so pots will be more stable, although the extra weight may be a disadvantage in certain circumstances. Good quality John Innes composts are considered to be more tolerant to over- and under-watering and the addition of loam ensures that micro-element deficiencies are not a common problem. The loam and organic nitrogen in these composts makes them less susceptible to the fluctuations in the levels of available nutrients that can occur in a soilless medium. However the use of materials like peat in soilless mixes ensures a greater degree of standardization of materials with less variability between batches than for soil-based composts. Soilless mediums are lighter to handle and do not have to be sterilized before use. Mixes with different physical properties, such as increased aeration, can be made by selecting appropriate grades of materials. However, the reserves of mineral nutrients can be limited in soilless mediums and this necessitates frequent feeding or the use of slow-release fertilizers.

An ideal potting medium should have good physical and chemical properties. The physical structure of a potting medium consists of particles of solid matter interspersed with pores or voids which are filled with either air or water. A medium with a high total pore space (TPS) has the potential for good water retention and aeration. An ideal medium should drain well after irrigation and so have an optimum air-filled porosity (AFP – the proportion of the volume of the medium that contains air after drainage following saturation with water), and at the same time it should hold adequate reserves of water which are available for plant growth. The degree of acidity (pH) should be appropriate for particular groups of plants and the medium should contain reserves of plant nutrients. Potting mediums should also be free from harmful insects, diseases and weeds. The ideal is to match the physical and nutritional conditions of the medium to different plants or purposes.

SOIL-BASED MEDIUMS. The John Innes composts are perhaps the best known soil-based potting mediums. There are two basic formulations – the John Innes seed compost for germinating seeds and rooting cuttings, and the John Innes potting composts for growing on plants. The potting composts are available in three grades referred to as JIP-1, JIP-2 and JIP-3, which contain increasing amounts of base fertilizers to accommodate varying degrees of plant vigour and seasonal changes in growth rate.

**Composition of Potting Mediums**

| | *Bulk ingredients (by volume)* | *Fertilizers* | *Weight ($kg\ m^{-3}$ or $g\ l^{-1}$)* |
|---|---|---|---|
| Seed | 2 loam | ground limestone | 0.6 |
| | 1 peat | superphosphate | 1.19 |
| | 1 sand | | |
| Cuttings | 1 loam | | |
| | 2 peat | | |
| | 1 sand | | |
| JIP-1 | 7 loam | ground limestone | 0.6 |
| | 3 peat | hoof and horn | 1.19 |
| | 2 sand | superphosphate | 1.19 |
| | | potassium sulphate | 0.6 |

The formulations are based on mixtures of sterilized loam, peat and sand together with additions of ground limestone and fertilizers. The quantities and proportions of these ingredients used in the seed compost and JIP-1 are shown in the Table. The quantities of fertilizer added for JIP-1 are doubled or tripled to produce the higher fertility JIP-2 and JIP-3 respectively. The hoof and horn, superphosphate and potassium sulphate can be obtained ready mixed as 'John Innes Base' fertilizer.

The sterilized loam supplies clay which retains plant nutrients, and it also contains microelements and organic matter. Loam is the most important ingredient in these composts since it affects the physical, nutritional and biological properties of the compost. However loam is also the most variable of the ingredients and so has to be carefully selected and prepared. Its texture or composition should be a clay loam which can be identified by its ability to produce a smear or polished surface when a moist sample is rubbed between the fingers. The loam should consist of many small aggregates which do not disintegrate when wet. The size of these particles affects the ability of the compost to supply air and water to the roots. The loam should also contain fibrous organic matter such as undecomposed grass roots as well as more decomposed humus.

Loams suitable for John Innes should have a pH between 5.5–6.5. High pH loams (pH>7.0) are not suitable, but the pH of more acidic loams can be adjusted with the addition of lime when the loam is prepared. Any deficiency in elements such as phosphorus and potassium can also be corrected by adding suitable fertilizers. It is essential that the loam is heat sterilized to remove harmful insects and diseases. However pasteurization has to be carefully controlled since it can, with certain loams, lead to the production of substances which are toxic to plants.

The peat and sand act as physical conditioners in the compost. Peat increases the total pore space of the media and improves the ability of the compost to retain water and provides aeration. Sphagnum peats are suitable and it is important that fine, dusty peats are not used. The sand improves the drainage of the compost and should be a coarse grade and lime-free.

Different batches of John Innes compost will always be variable because of differences in the quality of the materials used as bulk ingredients. It is impossible to judge the quality of John Innes composts from appearances alone; quality can only be gauged by laboratory analysis. In the UK many of the manufacturers of John Innes composts belong to the John Innes Manufacturers Association (JIMA) which maintains standards.

Ideally, the John Innes composts should be used within a short time of being made, perhaps within as little as four weeks, since changes in the forms and amounts of available nitrogen and the pH can occur and these can affect seedlings' growth. The length of time which the compost can be stored depends on the moisture content of the compost, the temperature and the amounts of organic nitrogen which have been added. The John Innes seed and JIP-1 composts, having a low fertilizer content, can be stored for longer than JIP-2 and JIP-3. It is important to avoid purchasing compost that is too wet and it should be stored off the ground in a cool dry place which is protected from rain and direct sunlight. Mixing the fertilizers into the compost shortly before use will also help to minimize storage problems.

Under average growing conditions, the low-fertility seed compost is used for seed sowing and pricking out and the JIP-1 for potting into 9cm pots. Seeds of strong-growing plants may, during spring and early summer, be sown into JIP-1. This can be considered as a medium fertility compost suitable for many plants such as house plants. JIP-2 and JIP-3 are used for growing more vigorous plants and for potting on into larger pot sizes such as 13 and 25cm pots. These grades are also suitable for large tubs and window boxes.

Lime-hating (calcifuge) plants such as *Erica* and *Rhododendron* spp. require a more acidic (lower pH) compost. A non-standard, acid compost suitable for these plants has been developed and, termed JIS-A, it consists of John Innes seed compost in which the normal addition of 0.6kg/m$^{-3}$ of ground limestone is replaced by 0.6 kg/m$^{-3}$ of sulphur. (Results from JI potting compost treated similarly were not so satisfactory.)

When using John Innes composts it is important not to over-compact them when filling pots and trays as this will increase the risks of waterlogging through poor drainage. Plants grown in these composts will still need feeding once the nutrients in the compost are used up.

SOILLESS MEDIUMS. Throughout the world a wide range of materials has been used in formulations of soilless mediums. Mixes are usually based on peat amended with materials such as sand, perlite and vermiculite. The use of peat is, however, neither universal nor universally acceptable. Alternatives are being sought, for example composted bark or coir. Materials such as pine needles and leafmould have been used for many years for growing azaleas.

More recently there has been interest in developing new growing mediums by composting several waste materials such as straw, sewage sludge, municipal refuse, and animal wastes. However the quality of different batches of mediums derived from these types of organic materials can be variable and they can deteriorate during storage. In addition there are potential health risks if contaminated residues persist in the medium and it is advisable to handle any organic material with care; always wear gloves or wash hands when handling mixes containing these materials, and avoid dusty conditions by working in a well-ventilated area.

Coir is a material derived from the outer husks of coconuts. Its physical and chemical properties are similar in many ways to peat and, after more research and evaluation, this material may form a useful alternative to peat in growing mediums.

Where peats have been used (i.e. in almost all soilless mixtures prior to its association with ecological destruction), they have tended to be undecomposed medium-grade sphagnum (moss) peats are suitable for soilless mixes; the more decomposed sedge peats are usually too fine and acidic and break down quickly. Some formulations of soilless mediums are made from a blend of different grades of peat. Peat is deficient in the principal plant nutrients and so these have to be added as fertilizers, and lime is also included to neutralize the natural acidity of peat.

Where peat is undesirable or not readily available it is replaced as the main component of a soilless mix by bark. In other instances bark is added to peat to improve the aeration of the mix. Bark is a naturally variable material and cannot be used fresh because of the presence of toxins, while the biological decomposition of cellulose in the bark can cause nitrogen deficiency. Pine bark is often stacked and aged before use to reduce the toxicity of the bark. Other barks, particularly those derived from hardwood species, are composted under controlled conditions before use.

Coarse sands or grits can be added to peat to change the physical properties of the mix. One of their main functions is to increase the weight of a mix to improve the stability of tall plants growing in pots. Fine sands should not be used since they can fill the pores in peat and so reduce aeration and drainage. Suitable sands should also be lime-free to prevent the occurrence of nutritional disorders.

Perlite and vermiculite can be used as a lightweight substitute for sand in soilless mixes. Perlite consists of white, lightweight aggregates produced by heating a crushed, volcanic mineral to about 1000°C. Horticultural perlite is available in several grades and the particles are stable and do not break down over time. Perlite holds water mainly in the cavities on the surface of the particles, and so mixes containing perlite are well aerated and have a lower water content. Mixes containing 50% or more perlite are used for rooting cuttings under mist. Perlite does not contain any plant nutrients nor does it absorb them from added fertilizers.

Vermiculite consists of amber-coloured particles of a sponge-like mineral. It is produced by heating particles of a micaceous mineral to 1000°C for about 60 seconds. This causes the layers of the mineral to expand due to trapped water being converted to steam. The resulting lattice structure has a high porosity and so can hold water and air. Unlike perlite, vermiculite contains some potassium and magnesium and can absorb mineral elements such as calcium, magnesium, potassium and ammonium nitrogen from added fertilizers, and this can reduce losses of these nutrients by leaching. Several grades of vermiculite are available; however, industrial grades made for insulation should not be used in potting media since they are too alkaline and contain a water-repellant.

Particles of vermiculite are more unstable than perlite, but they should last long enough for use with plants which are regularly repotted.

There are several other materials that are sometimes found in peat mixes. These include plastic such as polystyrene granules; expanded aggregates made from clays, shales and pulverized fuel ash; and flocks of rockwool. These materials, like perlite and grit, are added primarily to modify the physical properties of the potting mix, although some may also influence the nutritional properties as well.

Lime is added to peat mixes as a mixture of ground chalk or limestone (calcium carbonate) and ground magnesium limestone, to reduce the acidity of the mix and to provide a source of calcium and magnesium for plant growth. The quantities required depend on the type of peat and the other ingredients in the mix and reduced amounts are added to ericaceous mixes which are intended for growing lime-hating species.

The essential major nutrients – nitrogen, phosphorus and potassium – are applied as either soluble inorganic fertilizers such as potassium nitrate and superphosphate or in a slow-release form which will release nutrients over a period of time. Soilless mediums containing soluble fertilizers usually require early and frequent liquid feeding because the addition of large amounts of soluble fertilizers can impair germination and cause salt damage to seedlings; also the water-soluble nutrients are not readily retained by soilless mediums and so can be lost by leaching if pots are overwatered. In slow-release fertilizers the nutrients either dissolve very slowly or granules of soluble fertilizer are coated with a resin or plastic which controls the rate at which the nutrients are released into the mediums; these coated fertilizers are often added to mixes used in the commercial production of container-grown trees and shrubs. Trace elements such as iron, which are required by plants in only very small quantities, have also to be added to peat-based mixes and these are usually applied in a slow-release form as powdered glass frits or as soluble chemicals.

Manufacturers produce several types of soilless mediums for different purposes. Mixes which are designed for germinating seeds and for rooting cuttings contain low amounts of fertilizer to avoid potential problems of high salt levels. Seedlings and rooted cuttings have to be moved on to a suitable potting medium which contains higher levels of plant nutrients for plant growth. All-purpose mixes are a compromise between these two types of mix. General potting mixes are designed for growing a wide range of species but these mixes will eventually require liquid feeding to sustain growth. The timing and regularity of feeding will depend on the vigour of the plants, the size of the pots and the amount of nutrient leaching, and most manufacturers recommend feeding after four to six weeks.

Other mixes are made for use with specific groups of plants or growing techniques. As already noted, the quantity of lime is reduced in ericaceous mixes which are used for growing lime-hating plants. Coarse mixes are available for orchids and epiphytic plants and these mixes may also contain charcoal to keep the mediums sweet. Mixes for alpines and cacti and succulents often include a proportion of loam-based (John Innes) medium mixed with the peat and grit. Mediums for producing blocks contain more humified sphagnum and sedge peats, and are mechanically compressed into cubes into which seeds or cuttings are inserted. Soilless mediums are also exclusively used in modules or grow-bags for tomatoes and other crops and flowers.

Gardeners can make their own soilless mediums, but this only becomes economical if large quantities are required regularly. A general potting mix can be made from three parts sphagnum peat plus one part of either coarse sand or a lightweight amendment such as perlite. A fertilizer kit is the most convenient way of adding all the required nutrients. Soilless mediums must not be over-firmed into pots and trays as this will reduce the aeration of the mix after watering. Peat can be difficult to remoisten if it is allowed to become too dry and some manufacturers include a wetting agent in the mix to aid rewetting. Soilless mediums should be watered when drops of water cannot be readily squeezed from a sample of peat taken from a few centimeters below the surface of the medium in a pot.

See also AMELIORANTS; STERILIZATION; SUBSTRATES AND SOIL AMELIORANTS.

**Poupartia** Comm. ex Juss. ('Called '*Bois de Poupart*' in Isle of Bourbon' (Nicholson).) Anacardiaceae. 12 species of monoecious or dioecious, medium-sized trees or shrubs; bark thick, clinging, secreting a fluid. Leaves imparipinnate, caducous, alternate, crowded at ends of branches. Male inflorescence a cluster, female a raceme; sepals 4–5, rarely 6, free, imbricate; petals exceeding sepals, alternate, 4–5, rarely 6; stamens 8–20, staminodes in female, filaments free, disc shallow, entire or lobulate; ovary 2–5-locular, unilocular by abortion, pistillode in male; locules uni-ovular; styles 2–5. Fruit a drupe, more or less fleshy; seeds sub-reniform, somewhat compressed; testa papery. Tropical Africa to Tropical Asia. Z10.

CULTIVATION As for *Spondias*.

***P. borbonica*** Lam. HOG PLUM. Tree or shrub to 15m. Lvs glabrous; leaflets 7–9, sessile, elliptic to ovate, acuminate, basally oblique, juvenile lvs pubesc. with red venation, to 19-foliate; petiole 5–10cm. Infl. many, terminal, paniculate; fls small; stamens 10. Fr. deep purple, plum-like. Madagascar.

***P. caffra*** (Sonder) H. Perrier. See *Sclerocarya birrea* ssp. *caffra*.
***P. pinnata*** Blanco. See *Spondias pinnata*.
For further synonymy see *Spondias*.

**Pourouma** Aubl. (From S American vernacular name.) Cecropiaceae. Around 23 species of dioecious, lactiferous trees, often with stilt roots. Leaves spiral, entire, palmate; stipules fully amplexicaul, connate. Inflorescence solitary or in pairs, axillary, 1–3-branched; bracts often linear. Male flowers densely glomerate or partly solitary, perianth segments 3–4, free or fused and lobed, stamens 4, occasionally fewer, filaments straight; female flowers solitary or clustered, usually pedicellate, perianth tubular, 3–4-lobed; ovary free; stigma discoid, 2-lobed. Fruit with fleshy perianth, endocarp crustaceous. C & Tropical S America. Z10.

CULTIVATION As for *Artocarpus*.

***P. cecropiifolia*** Mart. TANARIBE; UVA DEL MONTE; To 20m. Branchlets short, stout, sharply annulate, heavily wrinkled. Lvs digitate; petiole to 20cm, terete; leaflets 9–11, oblanceolate, acuminate, sometimes shortly confluent at base, 10–20×2.5–4cm, pubesc. and slightly rough above, white-tomentellous beneath. Infl. to 10cm; peduncle stout, recurved. Fr. velutinous, ovoid when young, shortly and stoutly pedicellate, basally slightly umbilicate, glabrous, yellow-green, about 2cm, mucilaginous. Upper Amazon Basin.

**Pourthiaea** Decne.
***P. arguta*** Lav. non Decne. See *Photinia villosa* var. *laevis*.
***P. parvifolia*** Pritz. See *Photinia parvifolia*.
***P. villosa*** (Thunb.) Decne. See *Photinia villosa*.

**Pouteria** Aubl. (From an indigenous name.) Sapotaceae. 50 species of evergreen, woody shrubs and trees, to at least 30m. Leaves alternate, usually oblong-lanceolate, entire, on short petioles. Inflorescence an axillary cluster or solitary; sepals 4–11, imbricate (4–6), spirally arranged (6–11) or in pairs (4); corolla cyathiform to tubular, tube shorter than or equal to lobes, green or white to yellow, lobes usually erect, 4–6(–9); stamens 4–6(–9), alternate with staminodes, usually included, partially fused to corolla, staminodes equal in number to corolla lobes, ovary superior. Fruit a berry, usually fleshy; seeds 1 to several, broadly ellipsoid, with a long scar. Pantropical. Z10.

CULTIVATION *P. sapota*, widely grown in the lowland tropics in Central America for its large, carbohydrate-rich fruit, and *P. campechiana*, with smaller, sweeter fruit of mealy texture, are handsome and productive ornamentals in tropical and warm subtropical gardens. On perfectly drained soils in maritime areas, they show good wind resistance, but will tolerate a range of soil types (pH 5–7), including sandy and clay soils (provided subsoil drainage is good). Both species are susceptible to waterlogging and will defoliate if subjected to even short periods of drought; when mature, *P. campechiana* will survive short-lived light frost.

They are sometimes grown in cool temperate areas in collections of economic plants, with treatment as for *Chrysophyllum*, although they are unlikely to fruit in any but the largest glasshouse. Propagate by seed removed from their husk before sowing, or by side-grafting on to seedling understocks. Air-layering may also be possible.

***P. campechiana*** (HBK) Baehni. CANISTEL; EGGFRUIT; SAPOTE BORRACHO/AMARILLO. Tree to 17m, usually shorter, especially in cult. Lvs in spirals, 7.9–25(–33)×10cm, on 1.2–2.5(–4.5)cm petioles, narrowly elliptic to oblanceolate, apex acute to rounded, glabrous, vein pairs 9–18, chartaceous. Infl. a 2–3-fld axillary fascicle, fls green-white, probably unisexual; sep. 0.45–1.1cm, 5(–6), broadly ovate to suborbicular, with short hairs outside; cor. 0.75–1.35cm, cylindrical, lobes 5–7, rounded or truncate, stamens and staminodes 5–7. Fr. 2.5–7cm, ellipsoid to subglobose, yellow to green or brown with a smooth, membranaceous skin, pulp mealy, orange or yellow, sweet, edible; seeds 1–6, 2–3.8cm, ellipsoid or crescent-shaped. Mexico to Panama.

***P. sapota*** (Jacq.) H.E. Moore & Stearn. SAPOTE; MAMMEE SAPOTE; MARMALADE PLUM. Tree to at least 30m. Lvs (10–)18–35(–60)cm, on 1.3–4.7cm petioles, spirally arranged, oblanceolate, chartaceous, glabrous above, sparsely pubesc. on midrib or glabrous beneath, vein pairs 20–25. Fls 1.2cm diam., in 3–6-fld fascicles; sep. 8–10mm, with adpressed hairs outside, outer 1.5–2mm, inner 5–6mm; cor. broadly tubular, 0.7–1cm, lobes 5, 2.5–4mm, broadly oblong or spathulate, stamens and staminodes 5. Fr. 9–12cm, broadly ovoid to ellipsoid, skin roughened, brown to grey-brown, pulp bright orange, buttery, very sweet; seeds 1, 6–7cm, ellipsoid, glossy dark brown. Mexico to Nicaragua. Most cvs have medium-sized fruit (0.5–1kg) e.g. 'Mayapan', 'Pantin', 'Tazumal'; 'Magana' has fruit to 2.5kg.

***P. mammosa*** Jacq. See *P. sapota*.
For further synonymy see *Lucuma*.

**Praecitrullus** Pang. (From Lat. *prae*, before, and *Citrullus*.) Cucurbitaceae. 1 species, a climbing or trailing monoecious herb. Stem strongly villous or hispid. Tendrils slender, 2–3-fid. Petiole pubescent. Leaves sparingly pinnately lobed, hispid, slightly denticulate to entire, veins densely hispid venation beneath; probract spathulate. Male flowers solitary, yellow; calyx campanulate, pubescent, lobes obconic, to 1cm; stamens 3, 2 connate; pedicel about 1mm; female flowers solitary, yellow; calyx broadly campanulate, lobes about 0.5mm, lanceolate; ovary villous or softly pubescent. Fruit a subspherical berry, to 6cm diam., light or dark green; seeds ovate-oblong, to 8mm, smooth, pale yellow. Early spring–autumn. India, Pakistan. Distinguished from *Citrullus* by echinate pollen grains, sparingly pinnatifid lobes and chromosome number. Z10.

CULTIVATION As for *Citrullus*.

***P. fistulosus*** (Stocks) Pang. As for the genus.

For synonymy see *Citrullus*.

**Prasophyllum** R. Br. (From Gk *prason*, leek, and *phyllon*, leaf.) Orchidaceae. Some 70 species of terrestrial orchids. Leaf sheathed, solitary, terete, sometimes bract-like. Flowers in a slender-stalked spike or raceme, resupinate, green, white or purple, sometimes fragrant; dorsal sepal lanceolate, erect, recurved or forming a hood, lateral sep. free or partially fused; lip sessile or attached to a projection at the column base, lanceolate oblong or ovate, fimbriate, entire or denticulate, base concave, apex recurved, callus broad or reduced to a central ridge. Winter–summer. Australia, New Zealand. Z9.

CULTIVATION Terrestrial orchids for the alpine or cool house. See ORCHIDS.

***P. australe*** R. Br. To 75cm. Fls sessile, white tinted green or brown; dorsal sep. to 8mm, ovate-lanceolate, recurved or erect, concave, lateral sep. fused, or free; pet. centrally striped red-brown, smaller than lateral sep., yellow-green; lip white, basally convex, undulate, callus abruptly terminating in two mounds. Australia.

***P. despectans*** Hook. f. SHARP MIDGE ORCHID. To 40cm. Lvs reduced to narrow sheaths. Raceme dense, pyramidal; fls small, to 45, pale yellow-green, brown or purple; dorsal sep. to 2mm, ovate, concave, acuminate, lateral sep. 2.5–4.5mm, lanceolate-falcate, cylindric, basally fused; pet. to 3mm, ovate-lanceolate, acute; lip to 3.5mm, mobile, lanceolate, recurved, callus raised, minutely serrate or entire. SE Australia, Tasmania.

***P. rufum*** R. Br. RED MIDGE ORCHID. To 40cm. Lvs reduced to narrow sheaths. Spike dense 2–6cm, fls few to many, green or red-brown to dark maroon, rarely grey-green and red; dorsal sep. to 3mm, broad-ovate, hooded, lateral sep. diverging, exceeding dorsal sep., often gland-tipped; pet. lanceolate to triangular; lip obovate, crenate, deep purple, denticulate at tip; callus raised, dark. SE Australia.

**Pratia** Gaudich. (For M.C.L. Prat-Bernon of the French navy who accompanied Freycinet but died in 1817, a few days after the expedition set sail.) Campanulaceae. About 20 species of mostly prostrate, small, perennial herbs. Stems slender, wiry, usually branching and creeping, rooting freely. Leaves alternate, dentate, often sessile. Flowers small, solitary, dioecious, often aborted; calyx tube adnate, ellipsoid; corolla bilabiate, oblique, lobes involute. Fruit a berry. Closely related to *Lobelia*. Australia, New Zealand, tropical Africa, S America.

CULTIVATION *Pratia* spp. occur predominantly in damp, shady and sheltered niches, and in cultivation provide dense low groundcover for the rock garden or peat terrace, covered for long periods in summer by small starry flowers followed in favourable conditions by tiny, globose berries. The more robust species such as *P. pedunculata* also thrive in boggy substrates, although all are less cold tolerant and more prone to slug damage when grown in very moist conditions. Given good drainage on gritty soils, *P. pedunculata* is hardy to at least −13°C/9°F and may prove invasive, but it is generally so low growing as to be unobtrusive; other New Zealand natives are almost as hardy: *P. angulata* has at times become a weed of lawns in gardens where temperatures fall to −10°C/14°F and below. *Pratia* spp. do not thrive where summers are long and hot, and in the US are likely to be most successful in the Pacific Northwest.

Grow in a sheltered position in sun or light part day shade in gritty, moist but freely draining soil. In the alpine house grow in pans in a mix of equal parts loam, leafmould and sharp sand, water plentifully when in growth and keep just moist in winter. Repot if necessary in spring. In zones that experience prolonged low temperatures, pot up divisions as insurance and overwinter in the well-ventilated cold glasshouse of frame. Propagate by seed in autumn in a sandy propagating mix or by division.

***P. angulata*** (Forst. f.) Hook. f. Creeping, slender, glabrous perenn. Lvs suborbicular, truncate or obtuse at base, succulent, serrate, short-petiolate. Fls to 1cm, virtually sessile; cor. white with purple veins, tubular, limb oblong. Fr. crimson. Summer. New Zealand. 'Ohau': fls large, white; fr bright red. Z7.

***P. arenaria*** Hook. f. Habit like *P. angulata* but lvs larger, denticulate and fls pure white, short-pedicellate. Summer. New Zealand. Z8.

***P. macrodon*** Hook. f. Prostrate, glabrous perenn. Lvs to 0.8cm, ovate to elliptic, base cuneate, irregularly serrate. Fls shortly petiolate to sessile; cor. to 1cm, white-cream. Fr. tinged with purple. New Zealand. Z7.

***P. nummularia*** (Lam.) A. Braun & Asch. Creeping, stems slender, finely pubesc. Lvs orbicular to cordate, coarsely dentate. Fls small; cor. to 1cm, mauve, pale pink, to yellow or green, throat golden, lower lip marked purple. Fr. purple to purple-black. Summer. Tropical and subtropical Asia. Z9.

***P. pedunculata*** (R. Br.) F. Muell. ex Benth. Slender, slightly pubesc. perenn., stems creeping or prostrate, with short ascending flowering branches. Lvs to 9mm diam., ovate or orbicular, with few prominent teeth, subsessile. Fls small, on slender axillary pedicels longer than lvs; cal. lobes narrowly lanceolate, obtuse; cor. to 7mm, lobes subequal, oblique. Fr. small, pubesc., globular. Australia. 'County Park': fls blue. 'Jack's Pass': habit creeping; fr a deep red berry. 'Tom Stone': habit trailing; fls pale blue. Z7.

***P. perpusilla*** (Hook. f.) Hook. f. Minute perenn. herb, creeping. Stems branched, wiry. Lvs minute, oblong or ovate-oblong, acute or obtuse, fleshy, deeply dentate, glabrous or short-pubesc., sessile or subsessile. Fls to 6mm, on short axillary peduncles or subsessile; cal. tube short, usually pubesc., lobes lanceolate, recurved; cor. lobes narrow, acute. New Zealand. 'Fragrant Carpet': fls white, fragrant. 'Summer Meadows': lvs bronze-coloured; fls fragrant, white. Z8.

***P. physaloides*** (A. Cunn.) Hemsl. Stem to 130cm, flexuous, slightly branched. Lvs to 17cm, ovate, acute, serrate, glabrous or sparsely pubesc. Infl. a raceme, terminal, shorter than lvs, 5–15-fld; cor. to 5cm, pale blue, pubesc. Fr. to 12mm diam., coriaceous, blue. New Zealand. Z8.

***P. repens*** Gaudich. Habit prostrate, creeping. Lvs reniform, sinuate, petiolate. Fls 1cm+, long-pedicellate; cor. funnelform, split at back, white suffused with violet. Summer. Falkland Is. Z7.

***P. begoniifolia*** (Wallich ex Roxb.) Lindl. See *P. nummularia*.
***P. linnaeoides*** Hook. f. See *Lobelia linnaeoides*.

***P. littoralis*** R. Cunn. See *P. angulata*.
For further synonymy see *Lobelia*.

**Prenanthes** L. (From Gk *prenes*, drooping, and *anthos*, a flower, referring to the drooping capitula.) Compositae. About 15 species of erect, much branched, perennial herbs, with latex. Leaves alternate, pinnatisect, base sagittate-cordate, petiolate beneath, sessile above. Capitula ligulate, numerous nodding, in racemes or panicles; involucre cylindrical; phyllaries in 2–3 series; florets yellow white to purple. Fruit a compressed cypsela; pappus of fine bristles. N temperate to African mts. Z5.

CULTIVATION As for *Cicerbita*.

***P. purpurea*** L. RATTLESNAKE ROOT. To 1.5m. Lvs to 18×4cm, elliptical to oblong, rarely pinnatisect, entire to dentate. Capitula in a panicle; involucre to 15×5mm; florets purple, rarely white. Summer. C & S Europe.

***P. alba*** L. See *Nabalus albus*.
***P. aspera*** Michx. See *Nabalus asper*.
***P. autumnalis*** Walter. See *Nabalus autumnalis*.
***P. serpentaria*** Pursh. See *Nabalus serpentarius*.
***P. virgata*** Michx. See *Nabalus autumnalis*.

**Prepodesma** N.E. Br.
***P. orpenii*** (N.E. Br.) N.E. Br. See *Aloinopsis orpenii*.
***P. uncipetala*** N.E. Br. See *Hereroa uncipetala*.

**Prestonia** R. Br. (For Charles Preston (*d*1711), Professor of Botany at Edinburgh.) Apocynaceae. 65 species of tall, climbing, woody vines with milky sap. Leaves opposite, stipulate, entire, pinnately-veined. Flowers bisexual, in dense lateral corymbose cymes or umbels, sessile or shortly stalked; corolla funnelform, limb 5-lobed, flaring, with a crown of 5 scale-like segments included in throat; stamens carried on corolla, anthers surrounding and in contact with stigma. Fruit a pair of many-seeded follicles; seeds comose. Tropical America. Z10.

CULTIVATION As for *Allamanda*.

***P. quinquangularis*** (Jacq.) Spreng. Lvs to 15cm, oval to oval-ovate, apex pointed, base rounded to obtuse, thin-textured, veins red or purple, ultimately white, glabrous or subglabrous; petioles 2cm. Fls in clusters of 6–20; cal. lobes abruptly reflexed; cor. 1.2–1.5cm long, 1.8cm across, yellow-green, lobes obovate, abruptly reflexed. Fr. to 35cm, robust, follicles fused at apex; seed hairs yellow-brown. Summer. Lesser Antilles to Guyana, Venezuela.

**Primula** L. (From the diminutive of Lat. *primus*, first; the mediaeval Lat. name *Primula veris* (from which the generic name is taken) means 'firstling of spring'.) Primulaceae. 400 species of perennial, mostly alpine herbs with short rhizomes. Leaves in basal rosettes, radical, simple, entire, toothed or lobed, many species with farina, a wax secreted from glands on surfaces of leaves. Peduncles often conspicuous, sometimes reduced and hidden in rosette, the flower 'stalk' being an elongated pedicel. Inflorescence terminal, verticillate or umbellate with involucral bracts, or a simple raceme, green parts often farinose; bracteoles absent; calyx tubular or campanulate, often angular or ridged, persistent, 5-lobed; flowers 5-merous, often fragrant; corolla tube usually exceeding calyx, limb regular, flat or incurved, sometimes slightly oblique, lobes 5, usually overlapping, emarginate; most species heterostylous, either bearing flowers with short styles and anthers at mouth of flower (thrum-eyed), or with long styles and anthers down inside flower (pin-eyed). Stamens 5; style filiform; stigma capitate. Fruit a capsule contained by or exceeding calyx, splitting apically at maturity into 5 or 10 lobes, or breaking irregularly. Northern Hemisphere, Ethiopia, Tropical mts to Java and New Guinea, southern S America.

CULTIVATION The genus *Primula* is one of the largest and most important in cultivation in temperate gardens, ranging from the most amenable and undemanding of plants, to those which present an irresistible challenge to the most skilled of growers and it is impossible in a work of this concise nature to give so large and beautiful a genus the comprehensive treatment that they deserve. A number of sections, although botanically interesting, are not represented in general cultivation, either because they are difficult, unavailable or of little horticultural value, these include: *Amethystina* (obdurate, beautiful and difficult to flower), *Carolinella*, *Chartacea*, *Cordifolia*, *Davidii*, *Dryadifolia*, *Fedtschenkoana*, *Malvacea*, *Minutissimae*, *Pinnatae*, *Pycnoloba*, *Souliei* and *Troglodyta*. With the exceptions of the *Auganthus*, (*Sinenses*), *Monocarpicae* (*Malacoides*), *Obconicolisteri* (*Obconica*) and *Sphondylia* (*Floribundae*) groups, which are grown primarily as annuals for winter and spring display as pot plants in the cool glasshouse, and the legion, large-flowered hybrids of the polyanthus type which can be used as bedding biennials, most primulas are treated as (more or less) hardy perennials, indeed many of the European primulas seem to perform noticeably better following sub-zero temperatures in winter. The most valuable sections for outdoor cultivation include *Aleuritia*, *Armerina*, *Auricula*, *Capitatae*, *Denticulata*, *Oreophlomis*, *Parryi*, *Petiolares*, *Primula*, *Proliferae*, and *Sikkimensis*; the following sections are represented in general cultivation by at least one species: *Bullata*, *Capitatae*, *Chrystallophlomis*, *Cortusoides*, *Cuneifolia*, *Julia*, *Megaseifolia*, *Muscarioides*, *Reinii*, *Soldanelloides*.

Selections from these groups can be made to suit an enormous diversity of garden situations. In general, the members of each section within the group share not only physical and genetic characteristics, but frequently also cultural and management requirements. Whilst these are usually based on conditions in habitat, blanket recommendations deny the adaptability and tolerance of many commonly grown species to a range of soil types, light and moisture levels – generalizations are nearly always open to modification in the light of experience. Almost without exception, however, primulas demand relatively cool summers with adequate levels of atmospheric humidity, a ready supply of soil moisture when in growth with a well-drained and well-aerated soil that allows excess moisture to drain freely away during the winter months to avoid risk of root rots. A fertile medium loam with additional organic matter and coarse sand, with ground limestone on acid soils, is the ideal starting point for most primulas and can be adapted to suit individual requirements. The majority of European and American species thrive in or will tolerate sun whilst the Asiatics generally need cool, light shade unless the soil remains constantly moist, when some will need shade only during the warmest part of the day. Propagation is by seed, division, cuttings, root cuttings, leafbud cuttings and increasingly by micropropagation. With the possible exceptions of *P. viali* and *P. denticulata*, seed germination in primulas is inhibited at temperatures above 20°C/70°F, and seed of most of the alpine primulas and members of the sections Primula and Petiolares needs stratification. Primulas are relatively free from pests and diseases. The most damaging are vine weevil, red spider mite and aphid, particularly root aphid, and slugs; the main diseases, generally avoided by good hygiene and suitable cultural conditions are botrytis, root rots and viruses. Their particular cultivation requirements will be considered by section.

Section *Aleuritia* (Bird's eye primulas). Characterized by basal rosettes of farinose leaves and the heads of small, usually pink or pale mauve blooms with the distinctive yellow eye, carried clear of the foliage on a more or less mealy stem. Native to a range of alpine habitats from the relatively low altitude, moist, sedgy pasture of the tiny, fragrant jewel-like *P. scotica*, in humus deposits in rocky crevices in and above woodland for *P. frondosa* and in high altitude damp and stony pasture for *P. farinosa* and *P. halleri*, most are suitable for the rock garden in a sunny position with shade from the hottest sun at midday, in a gritty and freely draining soil that does not dry out during the growing season; *P. scotica* is well suited to trough or raised bed, protected from competition from more vigorous neighbours. All suit pan cultivation in the alpine house, shaded from spring onwards, in a gritty, medium fertility loam-based mix with additional leafmould; water plentifully when in full growth, avoiding the foliage and keep almost, but not completely dry in winter. Most die back in winter to a tight, densely farinose resting bud; under glass, dead foliage is best remove to avoid risk of botrytis and when grown outdoors *P. scotica* may be best given the protection of a propped pane of glass. With the possible exception of *P. frondosa*, which may be increased by careful division, they are usually short-lived in cultivation, but usually set abundant seed which generally germinates well without stratification. Hybrids are unknown in this section.

Section *Armerina*. Only *P. involucrata* from this group is in general cultivation. Native throughout the Himalaya and Western China, between 4000–5000m/13000–16250ft, it occurs in abundance in moist meadows flushed with melt water and is much valued for its sweetly scented heads of creamy, crystalline flowers on long slender stems above a loose rosette of green leaves. Given a moist situation in partial shade, such as by streamside or in the woodland garden, it usually proves long-lived. In too dry conditions it may become dormant by late summer. Propagate by seed, which is often produced in abundance or by division.

Section *Auricula*. Perhaps one of the most important sections for cultivation in the rock garden and alpine house, represented most commonly by the beautiful hybrids and cultivars derived from *P. auricula* and *P. hirsuta* (*P.* ×*pubescens*) and the many cultivars of *P. marginata* which have lent some of the loveliest blues to the group. Given an open site on the rock garden, in a freely draining, moderately fertile, humus rich sandy loam, that does not dry out during the growing season, many of the more robust hybrids will prove floriferous and undemanding; most will require some protection from the strongest summer sun. *P. carniolica* and the calcifuge *P. latifolia*, native to rocky pasture and shady cliff crevices, prefer cooler, north facing or otherwise shaded niches. The early flowering *P. palinuri*, unusual in having nodding golden-yellow flowers, is native to sandy pockets in tufa cliffs and is one of the most tolerant of the genus to dry conditions; it is suitable for the sunny scree bed. *P. deorum*, from damp pasture requires a more reliable and equable moisture supply. Although very hardy, *P. marginata* and its cvs flower relatively early and are very attractively farinose; both features may suffer from exposure to the weather in the open garden. As with other members of the section, they may be grown to perfection in the alpine house in a medium-fertility, loam-based mix with one part grit and additional leafmould, top-dressed with limestone chips. Water carefully and moderately when in growth, liquid feed occasionally; reduce water as plants enter dormancy in late summer and autumn and water very sparingly during winter, to avoid dessication. The removal of dead foliage will help avoid botrytis. *P. allionii* and its cultivars are more demanding, almost invariably requiring alpine house or plunge frame protection. Occurring naturally in limestone cliff crevices. *P. allionii* is positively calcicole and requires perfect drainage and ventilation, with shade from early spring until autumn; grow in leaner mixes, with higher proportions of grit, (up to one third by volume) and a top dressing of the same. They are best watered from below and are often double-potted to allow more careful regulation of moisture which should be fresh, clean and plentiful when in full growth; reduce gradually and keep plants almost dry when dormant. The regular removal of dead foliage throughout winter is imperative, with a fungicidal spray at any sign of infection. Propagate by seed, division and cuttings.

Section *Denticulata*. The only member of the section in general cultivation, *P. denticulata*, is one of the most amenable and reliably hardy of primulas in cultivation. One of the most abundant of Himalayan primulas in habitat, forming sheets of colour on open slopes, in shrubberies and in moist shady gullies, it is easily grown in any moisture retentive soil in sun or part shade. Suitable for beds and borders, and sometimes used in spring bedding, in the rock garden it is best confined to the foot of rockwork where its coarse foliage will not swamp more choice alpines. Cultivars are available in a colour range from pure white through to rich glowing red-purple. Propagate by seed, cuttings or root cuttings. Seed-raised plants, unless from selected strains, have a tendency to revert to mauve.

Section *Oreophlomis*. Although it occurs naturally in wet meadows, marsh and by streamsides and in damp rocky habitats flushed by snow melt water, often flowering precociously in habitat, *P. rosea*, the best-known species of its group, is tolerant of the drier conditions that may be expected in cultivation. Hardy and amenable, this species and other members of the section such as *P. clarkei* and *P. warshenewskiana* will thrive in moist, peaty soils in part shade, but will grow in sun in soils that do not dry out during the growing season. *P. rosea* may self sow where condition suit. Propagate by fresh seed, or division of selected forms.

Section *Parryi*. From damp, shaded, rocky mountain habitats, in cliff crevice and often by alpine streams, *P. parryi*, the good-natured *P. ellisiae* and *P. rusbyi* are the most commonly seen in cultivation. *P. parryi* is a handsome and robust American, sometimes overpoweringly fragrant, and of suitable scale for larger peat terraces or shaded borders, in moist but well drained humus-rich soils in part of full shade. Members of this group are herbaceous and often long-lived once established. The elegant *P. ellisiae* and *P. rusbyi* are also grown in the alpine house, with treatment as for the Auricula section. *P. augustifolia*, which occurs near the line of perpetual snows in the Colorado Rockies, requires similar but careful cultivation. *P. cusickiana* is more challenging but exquisitely beautiful, its deep violet, yellow-eyed flowers with a fragrance reminiscent of sweet violets. It blooms in very moist conditions at snow melt in the Wallowa mountains, thereafter experiencing increasingly dry conditions, almost to the point of baking in summer. Propagate by seed, which usually germinates freely, or by careful division after flowering.

Section *Petiolares*. The beautiful and challenging Petiolarid Primulas, predominantly mid to high altitude Himalayan and Western Chinese species in cultivation, occur in acidic humus soils in forest (evergreen species), or above the tree line (deciduous); they grow in conditions characterized by cool and constant high humidity, experiencing abundant rainfall in summer, usually protected with a snow blanket in winter when dormant. Outdoor cultivation is generally restricted to damp, shady microclimates in the gardens of the cooler north and north west of Britain, parts of New Zealand, Australia and western Canada; here they may even self seed. The most amenable for outdoor cultivation include *P. edgeworthii*, *P. gracilipes*, *P. sonchifolia* and *P.* 'Linnet', they are best given protection of a propped pane of glass in winter. Grow in a rich, fertile, lime-free, loam-based mix with plentiful leafmould and some granitic grit over perfect drainage; the shallow fibrous roots should never dry out, water plentifully and regularly, misting over in the evenings in warm weather. Provide shade, ensuring no direct sun at all throughout the summer, and maintain perfect ventilation with buoyant high humidity; temperatures above 25°C/77°F lead to rapid collapse. The petiolarids are gross feeders: give liquid foliar feed at fortnightly intervals when in full growth and repot annually in spring or late summer. Propagate by division, or by fresh seed, in a cool shaded frame (plants usually require hand-pollinated crosses between pin-eyed and thrum-eyed plants); germination may occur in autumn or following stratification the following spring. Pot on regularly; plants sometimes flower in their first year from seed. Micropropagation is increasingly used to raise virus-free stock. Vine weevil and aphids, which carry viruses, are the most serious pests.

Section *Primula*. Members of this section grow best in a medium to heavy moisture retentive loam with the addition of plentiful organic matter, in a cool position with light to medium shade, or with part day sun. All benefit from regular division (every other year) and a mulch of well rotted and graded organic matter. The wild species, *P. vulgaris* of shady woodland, coppice and hedgebank, *P. elatior* and *P. veris*, also found in moist meadow and pasture, are eminently suited to the wild garden in conditions approximately to those in habitat. The legion cultivars in this group which include singles, doubles, polyanthus types (probably derived originally from crosses between *P. veris* × *P. vulgaris* ssp. *sibthorpii*), and the beautiful Gold Lace polyanthuses, are often grown in the cold glasshouse, as short season houseplants, and for exhibition, under similar conditions to those described for the florist's auriculas (see AURICULAS). In general, the large leaved polyanthus types, and double flowered cultivars are more prone to sun scorch and perform best in dappled shade.

**Primula** (× 1) (a) *P.verticillata* (b) *P.denticulata* (c) *P. sinopurpurea* (d) *P. malacoides* (e) *P. rosea* (f) *P. vialii,* habit (f1) inflorescence

The productive crosses of *P. vulgaris* with *P. juliae* (Pruhonicensis Hybrids) have given rise to an enormous range of cultivars, valued not only for their beauty, but also for their cold hardiness, reliably perennial nature and for the profusion of bloom carried over long periods, commencing in early spring, sometimes in mild winters blooming shortly after New Year.

Some of the Pruhonicensis Hybrids have been selected for colour and form and are widely grown commercially as spring season houseplants (they undoubtedly achieve perfection under glass) and although these plants may later be accommodated in suitable situation in the garden, they may not prove as hardy as the more robust cultivars grown primarily as garden plants. One of the earliest of this group to attract attention, *P.* 'Wanda', is notable for its tolerance of a range of soil types, thriving in dappled shade and sun.

The bedding Polyanthus are available in a number of named series with an extensive colour range, to be raised from seed and treated as biennials. They include the exceptionally large flowered Regal series; the Pacific series, both dwarf and giant, with fragrant, brilliant, velvety flowers, and the low growing Posy series, predominantly pastel with contrasting centres. Surface sow seed in late spring, keep constantly moist and germinate at temperatures no higher than 20°C/68°F; prick out and grow on to set out in late autumn.

Section *Proliferae* (candelabra primulas). Mostly easy and rewarding, these robust perennials, with their distinctive tiered whorls of bloom on long sturdy stems, are often the spring and early summer mainstays of the streamside and bog garden, seen at their best *en masse*; for sun or part shade, they require deep, fertile, humus-rich soils, that remain moist throughout the year although not waterlogged in winter. A number of vigorous hybrid series, chiefly derived from the Western Chinese spp. such as *P. bulleyana*, *P. beesiana* and *P. burmanica*, are available with a range of exuberant colours, including 'Harlow Carr' and 'Sunset Shades'; *P. japonica* and *pulverulenta* are the most commonly grown species. *P. aurantiaca*, *P. cockburniana* and *P. chungensis* are more delicate in form, the two last of less outrageous colour. Propagate by seed or division.

Section *Sikkimensis*. The most commonly grown species in this section. *P. sikkimensis*, *P. florindae* and *P. alpicola*, are elegant perennials of wet montane meadow and pasture, valued for their tall, slender scapes of nodding, fragrant bell shaped flower, often carried over relatively long periods in summer. Less commonly seen is the delicate, scented and exquisitely beautiful *P. ioessa*, especially so in the white-flowered form, for the peat terrace or moist well-drained border; the winter-resting buds of spp. in this section retreat below soil level and a marker is recommended to avoid damage when cultivating. All require deep moist humus-rich soils, in sun where soils remain reliably moist, or in shade. Suitable for the shady herbaceous border, streamside, bog and woodland garden. Propagate by division or seed, which is often set in abundance and will self sow where conditions suit.

Section *Capitatae*. Often short-lived species for moist, leafy soil in part shade, suitable for the peat terrace and woodland garden. *P. capitata* forms a neat rosette of leaves, densely farinose below, and bears a dense head of bell-shaped flowers, which emerge from tight, farinose bud. Often blooming late in the season, it is useful for autumn colour. Propagate by seed, which is usually set in abundance.

Section *Crystallophlomis*. High alpines usually experiencing wet summers, relatively dry autumns and long winters under a snow blanket which protects the bulb-like resting bud; they are usually demanding in cultivation, although *P. chionantha* is widely grown. Give a deep, well drained soil in a sunny position with the protection of a propped pane of glass.

Section *Cortusoides*. Herbaceous plants requiring conditions similar to the *Capitatae* section, for the woodland garden. *P. sieboldii* has long been cultivated in Japan for its large and richly coloured flowers and many selections have been made. It thrives in fertile, well drained soil or may be grown in pots in the cool greenhouse. The plants become dormant in midsummer and will not reappear before spring. Propagate by seed or division of mature clumps.

Section *Muscarioides*. Often short-lived plants, the most commonly grown species, *P. viali* is a distinctive plant, notable for the spikes of rich red buds which open to blue-purple flowers; for the damp garden, often planted by stream and pondside, requiring a rich, humus soil in sun or part shade. Propagate by seed.

Section *Reinii*. Japanese species native of cool humid woodland, high pasture, and shaded rocky habitats, often experiencing mist and cloud under natural conditions. Grow in moist but perfectly drained soils, or north facing screes, with cool, high humidity, and dappled shade. Propagate by fresh seed or careful division.

Section *Soldanelloides*. Beautiful and delicate plants, the exquisitely scented *P. flaccida*, with large, soft lavender, bell-shaped flowers, and *P. residii*, with white or pale blue flowers above a low rosette of hairy leaves, are the most common in cultivation. Grow in a moist soil in partial shade, in the sheltered woodland garden or peat terrace, with a propped pane of glass in wet winter conditions, or in the alpine house in a peaty gritty medium. Propagate by seed.

Cultivation under glass. The most important as decorative pot plants for winter and spring flowering are *P. malacoides*, *P. sinensis* and *P. obconica*, the two last bearing leaf hairs which cause allergic reaction in sensitized individuals. Sow seed between early summer into early autumn for a succession of bloom; use a soilless propagating mix and germinate at 15°C/60°F. Grow on in the shaded frame in a medium-fertility loam-based mix with additional leafmould or equivalent and grit. Bring under glass in late autumn, or before first frost and maintain good light and ventilation with a minimum temperature of 5–7°C/40–45°F. The section *Sphondylia*, which includes the fertile hybrid *P.* 'Kewensis', is less commonly grown but requires similar treatment.

The great diversity of form displayed by the genus *Primula* has lead to the creation of numerous supraspecific subdivisions at the subgeneric, sectional and subsectional levels in which related species are placed on taxonomic grounds. As this division is also an important feature when cultivation requirements are under consideration a synopsis of the characters of each section is presented here. The system followed is that presented by Fenderson (1986), which represents a synthesis of modern views on *Primula* taxonomy and largely replaces the system of Smith and Fletcher (1941–49). This has lead to the submergence of many sectional names familiar to horticulturists – these are indicated as synonyms. The numbering system provides a cross-reference between subdivision and species descriptions.

**1** Subgenus *Sphondylia* (Duby) Rupr.

Section *Sphondylia* Duby (*Floribundae* sensu W.W. Sm. & Fletcher)

Type species: *P. verticillata* Forssk.

Plants farinose or efarinose; leaves involute, with lamina membranous. Peduncles well developed, usually with several superimposed umbels with several flowers in each; bracts well developed, resembling leaves; flowers yellow; capsule globose, persistent. W Himalaya to coastal mountains of Arabian peninsula and mountains of Ethiopia and Somalia.

Subgenus *Auriculastrum* Schott

**2** Section *Auricula* Duby

Type species: *P. auricula* L.

Leaves involute, more or less coriaceous, often with thickened margins, farinose or efarinose, glandular or eglandular. Inflorescence a simple umbel, long-pedunculate to subsessile, sometimes farinose or glandular; flowers many or few to solitary, pink, lavender or yellow (occasionally white). Capsule globose, persistent. European mountains.

**I** Subsection *Arthritica* Schott

Leaves coriaceous, glabrous or with stalked glands only at margins, margins entire, cartilaginous. Flowers pink.

**II** Subsection *Auricula*

Plants farinose. Leaves cartililaginous, entire or dentate. Flowers yellow.

**III** Subsection *Brevibracteata* Widmer

Plans with colourless glands, or glabrous, usually farinose; leaves dentate or subentire; inflorescence distinctly pedunculate; bracts 1–4mm, ovate, often scarious; fls lavender to violet or pink.

**IV** Subsection *Chamaecallis* Schott

Leaves cuneate, broadest in upper part, margin deeply serrate in upper portion only; peduncle short (0.2–3cm); flowers 1–2; bracts 0.4–3cm, leaf-like; corolla lobes very deeply bifid.

**V** Subsection *Cyanopsis* Schott

Plants efarinose; leaves much longer than broad, fleshy, glabrous with punctate glands, margins cartilaginous; inflorescence pedunculate; bracts 0.4–3cm; flowers blue or violet-rose.

**VI** Subsection *Erythrodosum* Schott

Plants efarinose; leaves fleshy, with coloured glands, margins dentate; inflorescence pedunculate; bracts 1–4mm, ovate, often scarious; flowers rose to violet.

**VII** Subsection *Rhopsidium* Schott

Plants efarinose; leaves fleshy, colourless-glandular-pubescent above and below; inflorescence pedunculate or subsessile; bracts 0.4–3cm, narrowly lanceolate to oblong, usually leaf-like, occasionally scarious; flowers rose to violet.

**3** Section *Cuneifolia* Balf. f.

Type species: *P. cuneifolia* Ledeb.

Plants efarinose; leaves cuneate, usually coarsely but sparsely dentate, lacking conspicuous glands and cartilaginous margins; inflorescence a pedunculate simple umbel; flowers pink to or white. Japan, NE Asia, Alaska, California.

**4** Section *Parryi* (W.W. Sm. & Fletcher) Wendelbo

Type species: *P. parryi* A. Gray

Plants usually somewhat farinose; leaves elongate-elliptic, margins crenate or shallowly serrate; inflorescence a pedunculate simple umbel; flowers pink to purple. W US (mountains).

**5** Subgenus *Primula*

Section *Primula* (*Vernales* sensu W.W. Sm. & Fletcher in part)

Type species: *P. veris* L.

Plants efarinose; leaves revolute with flattened, broad petioles, lamina often decurrent, membranous, not lobed, pubescent to subglabrous, eglandular, margins sometimes pubescent but never cartilaginous, remotely denticulate; inflorescence a simple umbel, pedunculate or peduncle absent; flowers yellow, pink or purple, occasionally white, calyx often strongly ribbed, sometimes inflated; capsule ellipsoid, persistent. Europe to E Asia.

**6** Section *Megaseifolia* Balf. f. (*Vernales* sensu W.W. Sm. & Fletcher in part)

Type species: *P. megaseifolia* Boiss.

Leaves reniform, glandular beneath, petioles slender; inflorescence pedunculate, peduncle, bracts and pedicels glandular; flowers purple. Caucasus.

**7** Section *Julia* Fedsch. & Los.-Losinsk (*Vernales* sensu W.W. Sm. & Fletcher in part)

Type species: *P. juliae* Kuzn.

Plants glabrous; leaves reniform, lamina not decurrent to slender petiole; peduncle absent, flowers long-pedicellate, purple. Caucasus.

**8** Subgenus *Auganthus* (Link) Wendelbo

Section *Auganthus* (Link) Pax ex Balf. f. (*Sinenses* sensu W.W. Sm. & Fletcher)

Type species: *P. sinensis* Sab. ex Lindl.

Plants efarinose, glandular-pubescent; leaves revolute, lobed, long-petiolate; inflorescence pedunculate with solitary or several superposed umbels; flowers white, pink or lilac; capsules ovoid-globose, persistent. China.

**9** Section *Monocarpicae* Franch. ex Pax (*Malacoides* sensu W.W. Sm. & Fletcher)

Type species: *P. malacoides* Franch.

Plants often annuals, farinose and glandular-pubescent; leaves revolute, lobed, petioles long, slender; inflorescence pedunculate, with several superposed umbels; capsule globose. E Asia.

**10** Section *Cortusoides* Balf. f.

Type species: *P. cortusoides* L.

Plants efarinose, usually glandular-pubescent; leaves lobed, petioles long, slender; inflorescence a pedunculate simple umbel; flowers pedicellate, corolla funnel-shaped, pink or white, occasionally yellow, calyx slender, ribbed, not enlarging significantly in fruit; capsule ovoid-ellipsoid, equalling calyx. C & E Asia, Japan.

**I** Subsection *Cortusoides*

Leaves with lateral veins pinnate; calyx many-veined.

**II** Subsection *Geranioides* (Balf. f.) W.W. Sm. & Fletcher

Type species: *P. geraniifolia* Hook. f.

Leaves with lateral veins chiefly basal; calyx few-veined.

**11** Section *Malvacea* Balf. f.

Type species: *P. malvacea* Franch.

Plants efarinose; lamina and petiole glandular-pubescent; inflorescence a raceme, long-pedunculate; flowers rose, lilac, white or yellow to orange, calyx much enlarged and disc-like when mature; capsule globose. SW China.

**12** Section *Pycnoloba* Balf. f.

Type species: *P. pycnoloba* Bureau & Franch.

Plants efarinose; lamina and petiole glandular-pubescent; inflorescence a contracted raceme; corolla to 1cm, wine-red, calyx very large, 2.5–3cm broad. China.

**13** Section *Obconicolisteri* Balf. f. (*Obconica* sensu W.W. Sm. & Fletcher)

Type species: *P. obconica* Hance.

Plants efarinose, with well developed rhizome; leaves revolute, lamina and petiole glandular-pubescent, often irritant; inflorescence a pedunculate simple umbel; flowers pink or white, calyces cupular, enlarging after flowering; capsule globose, dehiscing by irregular crumbling. E Himalaya to W China.

**14** Section *Reinii* Balf. f.

Type species: *P. reinii* Franch.

Plants less than 18cm, efarinose; leaves revolute, rounded, dentate or lobed, petioles slender; peduncle slender; flowers few, pink or white, calyx small; capsule ellipsoid, sometimes oblique, much exceeding calyx. Japan.

**15** Section *Pinnatae* Knuth

Type species: *P. filchnerae* Knuth

Plants efarinose, with articulated hairs; leaves pinnate or nearly so, lamina membranous; inflorescence a simple umbel on a slender peduncle; flowers pink. E China.

**16** Section *Bullatae* Pax

Type species: *P. bullata* Franch.

Plants farinose or efarinose, with woody stems forming compact sub-shrubby cushions; leaves revolute, entire, rigid or leathery, with surface conspicuously rugose or bullate, glandular-pilose; inflorescence a simple pedunculate or subsessile umbel; flowers yellow, white, pink or lilac; capsule subglobose to obovoid, included in calyx. W China.

Subgenus *Carolinella* (Hemsl.) Wendelbo

**17** Section *Carolinella* (Hemsl.) Pax

Type species: *P. partschiana* (Hemsl.) Pax

Plants efarinose; leaves revolute, more or less cordate, not or very shallowly lobed, finely covered by articulated hairs, petiole usually long and slender; inflorescence a short raceme; flowers pink or violet. SW China, N Vietnam.

Subgenus *Craibia* Wendelbo

Type species: *P. petiolaris* Wallich

**18** Section *Chartacea* Balf. f. (*Petiolares* Pax sensu W.W. Sm. & Fletcher in part)

Type species: *P. chartacea* Franch.

Plants efarinose; leaves revolute, ovate-elliptic, chartaceous, glabrous, long-petiolate; inflorescence with simple pedunculate umbel; flowers pink, lavender, blue or purple. E Himalaya, SE Asia.

**19** Section *Davidii* Balf. f. (*Petiolares* Pax sensu W.W. Sm. & Fletcher in part)

Type species: *P. davidii* Franch.

Plants efarinose, hairy; basal bud covered by chaffy brown scales; leaves revolute, coriaceous, strongly reticulate-veined beneath, hairy on veins below; inflorescence a simple pedunculate umbel; flowers blue, violet or purple. W & S China.

**20** Section *Petiolares* Pax

Type species: *P. petiolaris* Wallich

Plants farinose or efarinose, usually overwintering as basal bud covered by reduced scale leaves; lamina usually unlobed, membranous, base decurrent or rounded, with broad midrib and petiole; inflorescence an umbel, peduncle usually shorter than leaves at anthesis, expanding later; flowers pink, violet, white, blue or yellow. Himalaya to W & S China.

**I** Subsection *Edgeworthii* (W.W. Sm. & Fletcher) A. Richards

Plants farinose; resting bud at or above soil level, always somewhat expanded; scale leaves fleshy, persistent; leaves dimorphic, subentire at flowering, dentate later, membranous to fleshy, glabrous; peduncle to 2cm at anthesis, exannulate. W Himalaya.

**II** Subsection *Griffithii* W.W. Sm. & Fletcher

Plants farinose; resting bud small, tightly imbricate, at or below soil level; bud scales fleshy, farinose, persistent; leaves entire or crenate at flowering; peduncle elongated at anthesis, equalling leaves; flowers annulate. E Himalaya.

**III** Subsection *Petiolares*

Plants more or less evergreen, not forming resting buds; leaves erose-denticulate; peduncle absent or very short at anthesis; flowers pink to magenta or yellow, more or less annulate. Himalaya.

**IV** Subsection *Sonchifolia* (W.W. Sm. & Fletcher) A. Richards

Plants farinose; resting bud loosely imbricate, large, ovoid, at or above soil surface; bud scales fleshy, persistent; leaves membranous to fleshy, dentate at flowering; peduncle very short at 5cm at anthesis, elongating later; flowers blue. E Himalaya, W China.

**V** Subsection *Tongolensis* W.W. Sm. & Fletcher

Plants efarinose; bud scales conspicuous, persistent; leaves monomorphic, membranous to fleshy, glabrous; peduncle absent; flowers long-pedicellate, annulate. E Himalaya, W China.

Subgenus *Aleuritia* (Duby) Wendelbo

**21** Section *Proliferae* Pax (*Candelabra* W.W. Sm. & Fletcher)

Type species: *P. prolifera* Wallich emend Bentv.

Plants usually robust, farinose or efarinose; leaves in basal rosettes, revolute, lamina merging with petiole; inflorescence of several superimposed whorls on long peduncles; flowers pink, red, purple, yellow or orange, occasionally white, calyces ribbed; capsule globose. E Himalaya, SE Asia, W China.

**22** Section *Sikkimensis* Balf. f.

Type species: *P. sikkimensis* Hook.

Leaves efarinose, revolute, with distinct petioles; inflorescence usually farinose, long pedunculate, with single umbel, or occasionally 2–3 superimposed umbels; flowers pendent on long pedicels, corolla campanulate, usually heavily farinose within; capsule cylindric. E Himalaya, W China.

**23** Section *Troglodyta* Wendelbo

Type species: *P. afghanica* Wendelbo

Plants farinose, glandular; leaves revolute, reniform to orbicular, base cordate, membranous margin coarsely dentate, venation palmate, petiole distinct, slender; inflorescence an umbel; flowers yellow; capsule subglobose, included in calyx. Afghanistan.

**24** Section *Crystallophlomis* Rupr. (*Nivalis* W.W. Sm. & Fletcher)

Type species: *P. nivalis* Pall.

Plants usually with farinose scales surrounding resting bud; leaves revolute, usually lanceolate or oblanceolate, decurrent to imbricate, sheathing petioles, fleshy or membranous, glabrous, usually farinose below, margins entire or very finely denticulate or crenulate; inflorescence usually a single umbel, pedunculate; bracts not saccate; flowers purple, yellow or white, corolla lobes usually entire; capsule large, ellipsoid-cylindric. Caucasus, C Asia to Himalaya & China.

**I** Subsection *Agleniana* W.W. Sm. & Fletcher

As for the section but leaf-bases often swollen; corolla campanulate, exannulate; capsule subglobose, disintegrating when ripe.

**II** Subsection *Calliantha* (Pax.) W.W. Sm & Fletcher

As for the section but corolla annulate, lobes deeply emarginate.

**III** Subsection *Crystallophlomis*

As for the section but species with yellow flowers may have corolla lobes erose or emarginate.

**IV** Subsection *Maximowiczii* (Balf. f.) W.W. Sm. & Fletcher

As for the section but plants efarinose; corolla lobes narrow, oblong to linear, often reflexed.

**25** Section *Cordifoliae* Pax. (*Rotundifolia* sensu W.W. Sm. & Fletcher)

Type species: *P. roxburghii* Balakr.

Plants farinose; leaves revolute, rounded or cordate at base; peduncle slender, with single umbel; flowers pink, violet, lavender, white or yellow; capsule globose-ovoid to ellipsoid-cylindric. E Himalaya to W China.

**26** Section *Amethystina* Balf. f.

Type species: *P. amethystina* Franch.

Plants efarinose; leaves revolute, with many small sunken glands, glabrous, margin cartilaginous, remotely dentate; flowers violet, blue, wine-red, white or yellow, corolla campanulate; capsule ovoid, equalling calyx. E Himalaya, W China.

**27** Section *Fedtschenkoana* Wendelbo (*Farinosae* sensu W.W. Sm. & Fletcher in part)

Type species: *P. fedschenkoi* Reg.

Plants glabrous, nearly efarinose; leaves revolute, obovate-elliptic to spathulate, attenuate to broad petiole; inflorescence a few-flowered umbel, pedunculate; flowers pink-purple, corolla annulate, lobes subentire; capsule broadly ovoid-globose. Afghanistan, Soviet C Asia.

**28** Section *Oreophlomis* Rupr. (*Farinosae* sensu W.W. Sm. & Fletcher in part)

Type species: *P. auriculata* H.J. Lam.

Plants often efarinose, usually with well developed rhizome; leaves revolute, regularly serrate; inflorescence a pedunculate simple umbel; bracts saccate, flowers long-pedicellate, rose-pink or purple, occasionally yellow or white, corolla tube exceeding calyx; capsule short-ovoid. W Asia, Caucasus to Himalaya to W China, Japan.

**29** Section *Aleuritia* Duby (*Farinosae* sensu W.W. Sm. & Fletcher in part)

Type species: *P. farinosa* L.

Plants usually farinose, sometimes efarinose, rhizome poorly developed; leaves revolute, lanceolate to spathulate, seldom with acute apex, margins subentire, occasionally finely serrate or crenulate, decurrent to broad and indistinct petiole; inflorescence a pedunculate simple umbel, pedicels well developed; flowers lilac, pink or purple, very rarely yellow or white, corolla lobes deeply emarginate. Widely distributed in temperate climates.

**I** section *Aleuritia*

Plants white- or yellow-farinose, or efarinose; capsule cylindric, much exceeding calyx. Europe, Arctic Eurasia and N America, Asia, N America, southern S America.

**II** Subsection *Gemmifera* W.W. Sm. & Fletcher

Plants with basal bud scales; leaves efarinose, somewhat glandular; inflorescence white-farinose; corolla sometimes oblique, tube twice length of calyx. E Himalaya, W China.

**III** Subsection *Glabra* W.W. Sm. & Fletcher

Plants very dwarf, more or less efarinose; leaves spathulate; pedicels shorter than calyx; flowers less than 1cm diam., corolla tube equalling calyx. E Himalaya, W China.

**IV** Subsection *Inayatii* W.W. Sm. & Fletcher

Leaves densely yellow-farinose, strap-shaped, very much longer than broad; capsule more or less equalling calyx. NW Himalaya.

**V** Subsection *Pulchella* W.W. Sm. & Fletcher

Leaves densely yellow-farinose, fleshy; bracts not auriculate; corolla tube much exceeding calyx; capsule exceeding calyx. SW China.

**VI** Subsection *Pulchella* W.W. Sm. & Fletcher

Leaves densely yellow-farinose, fleshy; bracts not auriculate; corolla tube much exceeding calyx; capsule exceeding calyx. SW China.

**VI** Subsection *Yunnanensis* (Balf. f.) W.W. Sm. & Fletcher

Leaves densely yellow-farinose, oblong to elliptic, distinctly longer than broad; bracts leaf-like, conspicuous; capsule shorter than or equal to calyx. SW China, N Burma.

**30** Section *Armerina* Lindl. (*Farinosae* sensu W.W. Sm. & Fletcher in part)

Type species: *P. involucrata* Wallich

Plants efarinose; leaves revolute, usually entire, petioles elongate, slender; inflorescence a simple pedunculate umbel; bracts saccate or auriculate; pedicels long, curved; flowers white or pink, corolla tube much exceeding calyx; capsule exceeding calyx. N America, Arctic Eurasia, C Asia, Himalaya, W China.

**I** Subsection *Armerina*

Rhizome of annual duration.

**II** Subsection *Chamaecome* O. Schwarz

Rhizome persistent.

**31** Section *Souliei* Balf. f. ex W.W. Sm. & Fletcher

Type species: *P. souliei* Franch.

Plants dwarf, farinose; leaves serrate or somewhat pinnatifid, membranous, scabrid above, petioles long; inflorescence a secund umbel; bracts not saccate; flowers pendent, lavender, blue or pink; capsule ovoid or ellipsoid-cylindric, equalling calyx. W China.

**32** Section *Minutissimae* Pax.

Type species: *P. minutissima* Jacq. ex Duby

Plants very dwarf (to 2–3cm), often stoloniferous, forming congested mats; leaves dentate; inflorescence subsessile; bracts not saccate or auriculate, sometimes absent; flowers usually solitary, blue, violet or pink, corolla lobes deeply emarginate, tube much exceeding calyx; capsule narrowly cylindric. Himalaya, W China.

**I** Subsection *Bella* (Balf. f.) W.W. Sm. & Fletcher

Corolla throat closed by tufts of hairs.

**II** Subsection *Minutissimae*

Corolla throat glabrous or sparsely hairy.

**33** Section *Dryadifolia* Balf. f.

Type species: *P. dryadifolia* Franch.

Plants sub-shrubby, with thick woody rhizomes, farinose; leaves marcescent, ovate to orbicular, surface bullate, margins crenulate, revolute, petiole distinct; inflorescence with short peduncle; bracts conspicuous, hooded; flowers few, more or less sessile, wine-red to pink and purple or yellow, annulate; capsule ellipsoid-ovoid to cylindric, equalling calyx. W China.

**34** Section *Denticulata* Watt

Type species: *P. denticulata* J.E. Sm.

Plants pubescent or subglabrous, farinose to efarinose; leaves forming basal rosette, lamina decurrent to broad petiole, margins usually denticulate; inflorescence a dense, spherical capitulum on a long peduncle; flowers sessile or subsessile, erect, pink to purple, sometimes white; capsule subglobose, included in calyx. Afghanistan to W China.

**35** Section *Capitatae* Pax.

Type species: *P. capitata* Hook.

Plants farinose; leaves oblong, decurrent to petiole, surface rugose, margins denticulate; inflorescence a dense, disc-like capitulum, long-pedunculate; flowers subsessile, horizontal or pendent, purple; capsule subglobose, included in calyx. E Himalaya, W China.

**36** Section *Muscarioides* Balf. f.

Type species: *P. muscarioides* Hemsl.

Plants usually efarinose; leaves decurrent, with long articulated hairs; inflorescence a long-pedunculate condensed spike or capitulum; flowers slightly zygomorphic, with posterior lobes of corolla and calyx somewhat enlarged, corolla tube longer than limb; capsule short-ellipsoid, slightly exceeding calyx. E Himalaya, W China.

**37** Section *Soldanelloides* Pax.

Type species: *P. soldanelloides* Watt

Leaves pubescent, not farinose, decurrent to petiole; inflorescence a pedunculate capitulum or condensed spike, or flowers solitary or few; flowers sessile, reflexed or pendent, blue, white or purple, corolla usually exannulate, farinose within, tube short, limb broadly campanulate or funnel-shaped; capsule globose, more or less included in calyx. E Himalaya, W China.

***P. algida*** Adams. (29-I) Variable, farinose or efarinose. Lvs oblong or oblanceolate, denticulate, rarely entire, 1.5–7×0.5–2.5cm, apex obtuse to rounded, gradually tapering to winged petiole, upper surface efarinose, lower surface with white or yellow farina or efarinose. Peduncle 3–20cm, 35cm in fr., farinose or efarinose. Infl. a 3–12-fld symmetrical umbel; bracts linear-lanceolate, 3–11mm, becoming reflexed in late flowering on fr.; pedicels unequal, shorter than bracts, doubling in fr.; cal. campanulate, 5–10mm, lobes oblong or lanceolate, often stained purple; cor. to 1.5cm diam., annulate, homomorphic or heteromorphic, flat, violet to violet-pink, sometimes white, tube white or yellow, equalling cal. Capsule as long as cal.; seeds rounded or ovoid, brown, surface vesicular, to 0.5mm. Spring. Caucasus, mts of E & NE Turkey, N Iran. Z5.

***P. allionii*** Lois. (2-VII) Viscid. Lvs 1.5–4.5×0.7–1.2cm, oblanceolate to suborbicular, entire, crenulate or finely serrate, fleshy, very viscid, densely pubesc., withered lvs often persistent for some years, tips of glandular hairs pale, to 0.4mm; petiole narrow to winged. Scapes very short, to 8mm in fr., 1- to 5-fld; bracts 1–3mm, broadly ovate; pedicels 1–5mm; cal. 3–6mm; cor. 1.5–3cm diam., pale pink to red-purple with white eye, sometimes white, lobes obovate, emarginate, overlapping; tube 1–1.5cm. Early spring. French and Italian Maritime Alps. 'Anna Griffith': lvs bright green, dentate; fls very pale pink, lobes with several notches. 'Alba': white fls. 'Apple Blossom': lvs mid-green, crenate; fls relatively large, rose-pink, shading to white; pet. edges wavy; thrum-eyed. 'Avalanche': lvs crenate; large flowered albino, pin-eyed. 'Celia': pet. 7–8, overlapping, cor. deep lilac-pink, thrum-eyed. 'Crowsley Variety': lvs small, grey-green, very slightly toothed; cor. deep crimson with white eye. 'Margaret Earle': fls to 3cm diam.; pet. wavy; similar to seed parent, except thrum-eyed. 'Mary Berry': lvs light green, slightly crenate; fls to 3cm diam., cor. dark red-purple, thrum-eyed. 'Pinkie': dwarf, forming a tight cushion, early-flowering; fls pink, thrum-eyed. 'Praecox': autumn-flowering; fls lilac-pink, thrum-eyed. 'Snowflake': fls white, crystalline, flushed with pink, thrum-eyed; pet. overlapping, undulate, lip emarginate. 'Superba': parent of 'Margaret Earle', which it resembles; fls relatively large, rose with white eye, pin-eyed; pet. broad, overlapping. 'Viscountess Byng': lvs grey-green, subentire; fls purple-pink, with white eye, thrum-eyed; pet. broad, wavy. 'William Earle': fls to 3cm diam., lilac-pink, with white eye, thrum-eyed; pet. very broad (5 may form complete disc), wavy.

Many hybrids produced in cultivation but only that with *P. marginata* found wild. In most cases the hybrid offspring are intermediate between the parents to varying degrees. The following are the most frequently encountered:

*P. allionii* × *P. auricula*. See *P.* ×*loiseleurii*.

*P. allionii* × *P. hirsuta*. Lvs glandular-hairy. Peduncle short or absent. 'Ethel Barker': Lvs long-petiolate, pubesc.; peduncle very short; fls 3–5, bright carmine with white eye.

*P. allionii* × *P. marginata*. Both wild and artificially produced clones are grown; most resemble a compact, few-fld *P. marginata*. 'Miniera': was a clone collected in the wild; the name was not published as a grex-name but has been widely so used. 'Sunrise': lvs serrate, glossy green, efarinose; peduncle short; fls to 20, pale lilac-pink with centre white, lobes irregularly toothed.

The most important hybrids of *P. allionii* are those derived from hybrids of *P. marginata*, especially 'Linda Pope' (qv), a parent of the following. 'Beatrice Wooster': lvs larger than *P. allionii*, less glandular; peduncle shortly exceeding lvs; fls clear pink with white centre. 'Clarence Elliott' (*P. allionii* × 'White Linda Pope'): lvs resembling those of *P. allionii*; peduncle 5–7cm; fls to 7, 2.5–4cm diam., bright lilac with small white eye and yellow throat, lobes 5, overlapping. 'Fairy Rose': lvs deeply and irregularly serrate; peduncle very short; fls large, rose-pink, with very narrow white eye. 'Joan Hughes': lvs resembling those of *P. marginata*, regularly toothed; peduncle short, glandular; fls to 20, to 1.5cm diam., deep magenta-pink, darker at lobe-margins, with white centre.

*P. allionii* × *P.* ×*pubescens*. Offspring very variable. 'Margaret': rosettes compact; lvs ovate to broadly lanceolate, grey-green, margins finely dentate and ciliate; peduncle 2cm; fls to 20, to 2.5cm diam., lilac-pink, centre white, lobes overlapping. Z7.

***P. alpicola*** Stapf. (22) Lvs to 10×7.5cm, elliptic, apex rounded, base cuneate or cordate, denticulate or crenulate, petiole to 15cm, winged, sheathing at base. Peduncle 15–50cm, farinose above; bracts lanceolate to ovate, to 2cm; pedicels 2–5cm, farinose; cal. to 1cm, campanulate, tinged purple, farinose, lobes triangular, recurved at tip; cor. white, yellow, purple or violet, to 2.5cm diam., broadly funnel-shaped, eye farinose, fragrant, lobes round, emarginate. Summer. SE Tibet. The colour forms of *P. alpicola* have been named var. *alba* W.W. Sm.: fls white; var. *luna* (Stapf) W.W. Sm.: fls soft yellow; var. *violacea* (Stapf) W.W. Sm.: fls violet, variable in shade. Z6.

***P. amoena*** Bieb. (5) Rosette upright when young, becoming rosulate. Lvs 5–16×2–4cm, petioles membranously winged, shape very variable, elliptic, ovate, obovate, spathulate, irregularly crenate or denticulate, bright green above, usually densely pubesc. beneath, sometimes subglabrous, apex round or obtuse, base usually tapering to petiole, sometimes cordate or truncate. Peduncle 5–15cm, hirsute; infl. usually secund, 2–18-fld, usually 6–10-fld; bracts 2–8mm, linear-lanceolate, pubesc.; pedicels 5–40mm, more or less erect; cal. tubular, strongly ridged, 8–12mm, lobes ovate to lanceolate, ciliate; cor. 1.5–2.5cm diam., flat to shallowly funnel-shaped, exannulate, violet-blue to lavender-blue to purple with yellow eye (albinos are known), lobes obovate, deeply emarginate. Capsules longer than cal. Early spring. Caucasus, NE Turkey (mts). Z5.

***P. angustifolia*** Torr. (4) Lvs upright, entire or denticulate, oblanceolate to lanceolate, lamina 0.5–7×0.3–1cm, usually curled inwards along longitudinal axis, apex round, base tapering to narrowly winged petiole, petiole usually shorter than lamina, sheathing at base. Peduncle 0.5–10cm; infl. usually solitary, sometimes 2–4-fld; bracts linear to lanceolate, 1–6mm; pedicels very slender, 3–10mm; cal. tubular, 5–8mm, lobes lanceolate; cor. 0.7–2cm diam., exannulate, flat to funnel-shaped, rose-lilac to purple-pink, eye clear yellow, surrounded by white margin, albinos known, lobes obovate, emarginate, slightly overlapping. Capsule ovoid to cylindrical, 3–5mm, long, smaller than cal.; seed to 1mm, irregularly quadrate and angled. Spring. Rocky Mts. Z6.

***P. anisodora*** Balf. f. & Forr. (21) Aromatic. Lvs to 25×18cm, obovate, apex obtuse, denticulate; petiole broad, winged. Peduncle stout, to 60cm; infl. 3–5 superposed, 8–10-fld whorls; bracts linear-lanceolate, to 15mm; pedicels pendulate, to 15mm; cal. cup-shaped, to 5mm, lobes ovate; cor. brown-purple, to 15mm diam., eye green, lobes crenulate. Summer. SW China (Yunnan, Sichuan). Z6.

***P. appenina*** Widm. (2-VI) Rosette openly rosulate. Lvs 2.5–6.5×1–2.5cm, subentire, upper half shallowly denticulate, obovate or broadly oblanceolate, apex rounded or obtuse, base narrowly or abruptly tapering into petiole, lvs covered with very short glandular hairs, glands fairly large, yellow in young lvs, orange-brown later. Peduncles 1–9cm; infl. covered in tiny glandular hairs, symmetrical, 1–8-fld, sometimes 12-fld; bracts 1–4mm, rotundate to ovate-oblanceolate, apex obtuse, with wide translucent margin; pedicels 3–10mm; cal. 4–7mm, conical to campanulate, lobes broadly ovate to triangular, obtuse, adpressed in fl., spreading slightly in fr.; cor. to 2.5cm diam., exannulate, lilac to magenta-pink, eye white, lobes, obovate, emarginate, sometimes overlapping, tube 20–23mm, 2–3× longer than cal. Capsule shorter than cal. Spring. Italy (mts). Z7.

***P. atrodentata*** W.W. Sm. (34) Very close to *P. denticulate* but smaller in all parts. Lvs 1–4cm, spathulate, densely white- or yellow-farinose beneath. Peduncle to 10cm; calyx lobes nearly black in colour; cor. to 2cm diam., lavender, with a yellow eye, fragrant, lobes emarginate. Himalaya.

***P. aurantiaca*** W.W. Sm. & Forr. (21) Lvs oblanceolate to obovate, to 20×8cm, denticulate, apex rounded. Peduncle to 30cm, tinged red; infl. 2–6 whorls, superposed, 6–12-fld; bracts linear-lanceolate, to 19mm; pedicels to 17mm; cal. narrowly campanulate, dark red, to 17mm; cor. red-orange, 15mm diam., lobes narrowly obovate, emarginate. Summer. SW China (Yunnan). Z6.

***P. aureata*** Fletcher. (20-III) Lvs broad-spathulate to oblong, to 10×37cm long, irregularly toothed, apex obtuse, both surfaces white-farinose, base tapering to short, winged, red-tinged petiole. Peduncle very short; infl. 10-fld; bracts linear-lanceolate, to 15mm; pedicels to 15mm, densely farinose; cal. 15mm, lobes ovate, acute, recurved; cor. cream to yellow, to 4cm diam., eye dark yellow, lobes broad-obovate, toothed, recurved. Spring. Nepal. ssp. ***fimbriata*** A. Richards ex Gould. Lvs finely dentate. Corolla to 3cm diam., uniform pale cream-yellow, with narrower orange eye, lobes deeply toothed. Nepal.

***P. auricula*** L. (2-II) Lvs 1.5–12×1–6cm, suborbicular to lanceolate, usually obovate, margins and surface with or without farina, entire to dentate, fleshy, glabrous or with scattered, short glandular hairs, margins pale, narrowly cartilaginous, glandular-pubesc. Peduncle 1–16cm, often farinose; infl. 2–30-fld; bracts 1–8mm, ovate to transversely ovate, more or less scarious; pedicels 2–20mm; cal. 3–7.5mm, usually farinose; cor. 1.5–2.5cm diam., deep yellow, lobes obovate, emarginate, throat white-farinose, fragrant. Spring. Alps, Carpathians, Apennines. Wild forms of *P. auricula* have in the past been given subspecific or varietal rank based on the presence or absence or degree of characters such as farina, lf ciliation, and fragrance. Amongst these are: ssp. *bauhinii* (Beck) Ludi. (Short cilia on lf margin, fls lemon-yellow, scented, farinose or efarinose.) var. *albocincta* Widmer. (Heavily farinose in cor. and on lf-margins.) ssp. *ciliata* (Moretti) Ludi. (Efarinose, lf-margins long-ciliate, fls deep yellow, unscented, Italy.) Natural variation in individual wild populations is such that these distinctions cannot be maintained although the names may be a

**Primula** (× 1) (a) *P. juliae* (b) *P. edgeworthii* (c) *P. sikkimensis* (d) *P. elatior* (e) *P. reidii* (f) *P. sherriffae* (g) *P. nutans*

useful guide to the appearance of plants in cultivation, especially the more distinct heavily farinose plants that would fall under var. *albocincta*. However, these names should not be applied as if they referred to cultivars.

Some true cvs of *P. auricula* have been selected, including 'Blairside Yellow': plant compact, 5–10cm, efarinose; lvs to 5×2cm, shallowly dentate; fls to 1.5cm diam., yellow. 'Broadwell Gold': vigorous, farinose; peduncles to 10cm; fls deep golden-yellow with farinose centre, lobes undulate. *P. auricula* hybridizes with many species in cultivation but few of these hybrids are widely grown. They are usually intermediate between the parents in appearance. The exception is the hybrid with *P. hirsuta*, *P.* ×*pubescens* and the immense complex of Show, Border and Alpine Auriculas (see AURICULAS). *P.* ×*venusta* Host. is the wild hybrid with *P. carniolica*; formerly commonly grown it is now apparently extinct in cultivation and extremely scarce in the wild due to overcollecting. Z3.

***P. auriculata*** H.J. Lam. (28) Rosettes scantily farinose, over-wintering as ovoid bud, enveloped by scales. Lvs 12–30×2.5–4cm, broadly oblanceolate to lanceolate, very sharply serrate-dentate, apex rounded or obtuse, base narrowing to a broad, flat petiole. Peduncles 8–60cm. Infl. compact, symmetrical, or globose, 8–20-fld; bracts lanceolate, base swollen; pedicels 2–6mm; cal. campanulate, 5–7mm; cor. 1.5–2.5cm diam., lilac, 9–12mm, tube 2–3× cal., throat pale green. Capsule ovate to globose, as long as cal. Spring. S Caucasus, Turkey (mts). Z5.

***P. beesiana*** Forr. (21) Lvs to 22×6cm, oblanceolate to obovate, attenuate to base, irregularly dentate, slightly farinose below. Peduncle to 40cm, farinose above; infl. of 2–8 superimposed whorls of 8–16 fls; pedicels 1–3cm, farinose; calyx 0.5–0.75cm, tubular-campanulate; cor. to 2cm diam., rose-carmine with yellow eye, lobes obovate, emarginate, tube to 1.5cm, yellow. W China (Yunnan, Sichuan).

***P. bellidifolia*** King ex Hook. f. (36) Lvs 5–15×2.5cm, oblanceolate to spathulate, obscurely toothed, apex obtuse, base narrowed to winged petiole. Peduncle 10–30cm, farinose toward apex; infl. 10–15-fld; bracts small, obtuse; pedicels 10–15mm, farinose; cal. to 5mm, campanulate, farinose, lobes rounded; cor. mauve to blue-violet, to 16mm diam., eye farinose, lobes obovate, emarginate. Spring. Tibet, Bhutan, Sikkim. Z5.

***P.* ×*berninae*** Kerner. (*P. latifolia* × *P. hirsuta*.) (2) Fertile hybrid, displaying a wide range of forms between parents. 'Windrush': fls large, red-purple.

***P. boothii*** Craib. (20-III) Lvs 3–15cm, broadly spathulate to elliptic, coarsely toothed, short-petiolate. Peduncle very short or absent; infl. many-flowered; pedicels farinose, to 5cm; cal. to 6mm, lobes triangular, acute, farinose; cor. pink, 3cm diam., eye brown-yellow, lobes obovate, often 3-toothed. Spring. E Himalaya. 'Alba': fls white. 'Edrom': fls pale pink with white eye, lobes finely toothed. Z6.

***P. bracteosa*** Craib. (20-III) Lvs 5–16×2–6cm, spathulate to obovate-spathulate, apex rounded, tapering to broad-winged petiole at base, dentate, farinose throughout. Peduncle very short; infl. many-fld; pedicels 45mm, slender, farinose; cal. short, lobes ovate; cor. pale lilac, to 2.5cm diam., eye yellow, lobes obovate, 2–3-toothed tube 1.5–3cm. Spring. Bhutan. Z6.

***P.* ×*bulleesiana*** Janson. (*P. bulleyana* × *beesiana*.) (21) Plants intermediate between parents: fls orange-yellow to mauve. 'Asthore Hybrids' were a selected seed strain of this. Hybrids of the Section Proliferae (Candelabra) are now likely to be of very complex parentage, with parents also including *P. aurantiaca*, *P. chungensis*, *P. cockburniana*, *P. burmanica* and *P. pulverulenta*. Selected seed strains have been named, such as Sunset Shades and Harlow Carr, often with very vivid fls.

***P. bulleyana*** Forr. (21) Lvs 12–35×3–10cm, ovate to ovate-lanceolate, dentate, apex rounded, base narrowed. Peduncle stout, to 60cm; infl. 5–7-whorls, superposed, many-fld; bracts to 2.5cm, linear, farinose; pedicels to 2.5cm, farinose; cal. cup-shaped, to 8mm, lobes awl-shaped, inner surface farinose; cor. deep orange, to 2cm diam., lobes broad obovate, emarginate. Summer. SW China (Yunnan). Z6.

***P. burmanica*** Balf. f. & Kingdon-Ward. (21) Lvs to 30×8cm, oblanceolate, dentate, apex obtuse, base tapering to winged petiole. Peduncle stout, to 60cm; infl. 3–6 whorls superposed, 10–18-fld; bracts to 2.5cm; pedicels to 2cm; cal. to 1cm, lobes linear; cor. red-purple, 2cm diam., eye yellow, lobes obcordate, entire or shallowly emarginate. Summer. Upper Burma, China. Z6.

***P. calderiana*** Balf. f. & R. Cooper. (20-III) Lvs 5–30×1–6cm, oblanceolate to spathulate, irregularly denticulate. Peduncle 5–30cm, brown-purple, pubesc. Infl. 5–10-fld; pedicels curved; cal. campanulate, to 6mm; cor. maroon to purple, to 3cm diam., eye yellow, lobes broad, irregularly indented. Spring. Himalaya. ssp. ***strumosa*** (Balf. f. & Cooper) A. Rich. Lvs to 10cm, lanceolate or oblanceolate, irregularly serrate, apex obtuse, base tapering to short, winged petiole. Peduncle to 20cm, farinose above; infl. 15-fld; pedicels 1–1.5cm, farinose; cal. erect, lobes oblong; cor. yellow, to 2.5cm diam., eye golden yellow, lobes oblong. Summer. Bhutan, Nepal, SE Tibet. Z6.

***P. Candelabra Hybrids***. (21) Named cvs of unknown parentage. See also *P.* ×*bulleesiana*. 'Bonfire': to 35cm; peduncle deep brown; fls apricot-red. 'Inverewe' ('Ravengalss Vermilion'): to 45cm; peduncles very numerous; fls bright orange-scarlet, sterile. 'Red Hugh': fls bright orange-red, fertile.

***P. capitata*** Hook. (35) Lvs to 12.5–15×2cm, oblong, denticulate, oblanceolate or oblong-spathulate, apex acute or rounded, sometimes slightly farinose above, white-farinose beneath. Peduncle 15–30cm, farinose; infl. crowded, somewhat flattened; bracts lanceolate, outer deflexed; cal. to 5mm, campanulate, farinose, lobes ovate, acuminate; cor. violet, to 12mm diam., lobes obcordate, spreading. Summer. SE Tibet, Bhutan. ssp. ***crispata*** (Balf. f. & W.W. Sm.) W.W. Sm. & Forr. Lvs efarinose throughout. Fls open, in a flattened head. ssp. ***mooreana*** (Balf. f. & W.W. Sm.) W.W. Sm. & Forr. Lvs efarinose above, densely white-farinose beneath, apex rounded. Sikkim. Z5.

***P. capitellata*** Boiss. (29-I) Plant with short, thick rhiz. bearing persistent scale-lvs. Lvs 1.5–10×0.5–1.5cm, oblong-lanceolate to spathulate, apex obtuse to acute, tapering to short, broad petiole, subentire to dentate, glabrous above, white-farinose beneath. Peduncle 2.5–25cm. Infl. a dense 5–12-fld umbel; pedicels absent or very short, to 1mm; calyx campanulate, 3–4mm; cor. to 0.7cm diam., rose-pink, weakly annulate, lobes obcordate, shallowly emarginate, tube to 8mm. Iran, Afghanistan.

***P. carniolica*** Jacq. (2-III) Lvs efarinose, 2–15×1–4cm, obovate to oblanceolate, subentire or shallowly toothed towards apex, shining, fleshy, margin narrowly cartilaginous, glabrous, tapering to winged petiole. Peduncle 5–20cm; infl. 2–15-fld; bracts 1–7mm, ovate to transversely ovate, more or less scarious; pedicels 2–20mm; cal. 3.5–7mm, campanulate, lobes triangular, obtuse; cor. purple-pink, to 2cm diam., throat white-farinose, lobes obcordate. Yugoslavia (mts). Z6.

***P.* ×*carueli*** Porta. (*P. glaucescens* × *spectabilis*.) (2) Intermediate between parents and difficult to distinguish; fertile. Italian Alps.

***P. cawdoriana*** Kingdon-Ward. (37) Lvs forming flat rosette, to 4×1.5cm, obovate to spathulate, dentate, pubesc., apex tapering to broad petiole. Peduncle 7.5–15cm, farinose toward apex; infl. 3–6-fld; bracts to 6mm, ovate, tinged purple; cal. to 8mm, cup-shaped, lobes oblong, acute; cor. pale mauve, to 3cm long, 3cm diam., funnel-shaped, eye white, lobes oblong, 2–3-notched. Spring. SE Tibet. Z6.

***P. chionantha*** Balf. f. & Forr. (24-III) Lvs 15–25×2–5cm, lanceolate, toothed or subentire, white farinose beneath, especially when young, apex obtuse, base tapering to broadly winged petiole. Peduncle stout, 35–70cm, farinose toward apex; infl. of 1–4 superposed, many-fld whorls; bracts to 12mm, subulate, farinose; pedicels to 25mm, farinose; cal. campanulate, to 1cm, lobes oblong, farinose; cor. 2.5cm diam., white, fragrant, lobes elliptic, entire. Early summer. SW China (Yunnan). Z6.

***P. chungensis*** Balf. f. & Kingdon-Ward. (21) Lvs to 30cm, elliptic to oblong-obovate, irregularly toothed and shallowly lobed, glabrous, apex obtuse, base narrowed. Peduncle to 60cm; infl. 2–5 superposed whorls, 10-fld; bracts to 8mm, lanceolate, farinose; pedicels to 2cm; cal. campanulate, farinose, lobes triangular, acute; cor. pale orange, to 18mm diam., tube red, fragrant, lobes broadly obovate. Summer. China, Bhutan, Assam. Z6.

***P. clarkei*** G. Watt. (28) Lvs scattered, not in rosettes, to 5×2cm, including petiole, orbicular to broadly ovate, finely dentate, base cordate or truncate. Peduncle usually absent; infl. 1–6-fld; pedicels 4–6cm; cal. to 6mm, tubular, lobes lanceolate, acute; cor. rose-pink, to 2cm diam., eye yellow, lobes obovate, deeply emarginate. Spring. Kashmir. 'Johanna' (*P. clarkei* × *P. warshenewskiana*): lvs to 3cm, ovate, margin serrate; petiole relatively long, red; peduncle to 20cm; fls to 15, 1cm diam., clear pink with yellow eye, lobes emarginate. 'Peter Klein' (*P. clarkei* × *rosea*): 10–15cm; lvs resembling *P. clarkei*; peduncle stout; fls deep pink. Z7.

***P. clusiana*** Tausch. (2-I) Rosettes tightly rosulate. Lvs 1–9×0.5–3cm, oblong to elliptic, ovate or obovate, stiff, leathery, entire, margins narrowly cartilaginous, ciliate, dark green, glabrous, shiny above, grey-green beneath, apex acute, obtuse or rounded, base tapering gradually into short, winged petiole. Peduncle 1–5cm, rarely to 11cm; infl. green parts short-glandular-hairy; umbel symmetrical, 1–4-fld; bracts 4–18cm, narrowly linear, oblong or lanceolate, acute or obtuse, base thickened, frequently stained purple; pedicels 2–15mm, stiff, erect; cal. 8–17mm, tubular, sometimes tinged red, lobes ovate; cor. 1.5–4cm diam., exannulate, bright rose, fading to lilac, throat glandular-pubesc., eye white, lobes obcordate, deeply cleft. Capsule 4–7mm diam. Spring. W Austrian Alps. Z6.

***P. cockburniana*** Hemsl. (21) Lvs to 15×4cm, oblong to oblong-obovate, obscurely lobulate and denticulate, apex obtuse. Peduncle to 30cm, slender. Infl. of 1–3, superposed, few-fld whorls; bracts to 5mm, lanceolate, farinose; pedicels to 2.5cm, farinose; cal. campanulate, to 6mm, farinose, ovate, acute; cor. dark orange-red, to 15mm diam., lobes oblong-obovate. Summer. China. Z5.

***P. concholoba*** Stapf & Sealy. (36) Lvs to 2–8×1.2cm, oblanceolate-oblong to oblong, pubesc. above and below, base tapering to winged petiole. Peduncle to 18cm; infl. 10- to 20-fld; cor. bright violet, exterior white-farinose, to 12mm, lobes concave and connivent. Late spring–early summer. Himalaya. Z5.

***P. cortusoides*** L. (10-I) Lvs 5–10×2–3cm, ovate, lobulate, irregularly dentate, pubesc., base cordate, petioles 7.5–10cm, slender narrowly winged, covered with long hairs. Peduncle 15–30cm, pubesc.; infl. 2–15-fld; bracts lanceolate, acute, shorter than pedicels; pedicels 5–15mm, glabrous or slightly pubesc.; cal. tubular, pubesc., lobes lanceolate, acute, ciliate; cor. pink to red-violet, rarely white, to 2cm diam., lobes obcordate, deeply emarginate. Capsule oblong, about 2× length of cal. Early summer. W Siberia. Z3.

***P. cuneifolia*** Ledeb. (3) Glabrous, with open rosette. Lvs 1–3×0.5–2.5cm, fleshy, upper half coarsely dentate, oblanceolate, obovate or cuneate, apex rounded, base tapering to membranously winged petiole. Peduncle 4–30cm; infl. discoid, 1–9-fld; bracts awl-shaped, 1.5–5mm; pedicels 4–20mm; cal. campanulate, 3–6mm, lobes acute or obtuse; cor. to 2cm diam., annulate, heteromorphic, rose red to magenta, eye yellow, occasionally with white margin, albinos known. Capsule globose to ovoid, slightly smaller than cal.; seed 1–1.5mm diam., irregularly quadrate, angled. Spring–early summer. E Siberia, N Japan, Aleutian Is., W & S Alaska to British Columbia. Z3.

***P. cusickiana*** A. Gray. (4) Lvs upright to rosulate or prostrate, 2–5×0.3–1cm, oblanceolate to oblong, obtuse, entire or sparsely dentate, somewhat succulent, petiole broad winged, sheathing to base. Peduncle 3–9cm; fls 1–4 in umbel; bracts lanceolate to ovate, 0.3–1cm; pedicels unequal, to 0.8cm, sometimes slightly farinose; cal. to 0.9cm, deeply lobed, green to maroon; cor. to 1.5cm diam., deep violet or occasionally white, exannulate, fragrant, eye yellow, lobes obovate, undulate or emarginate, tube to 1.5× cal. Oregon, Idaho (Wallowa mts).

***P. daonensis*** Leyb. (2-VI) Efarinose. Lvs 1.8×0.5–2cm, narrowly cuneate-obovate, rarely ovate, dentate toward apex, fleshy, viscid, covered with glandular hairs producing an orange secretion. Peduncle 1.5–9cm, usually longer than lvs in fr.; infl. 2–8-fld; bracts 1–3mm, ovate to obovate, more or less scarious; pedicels 1–6mm; cal. 2.5–6mm, tubular to campanulate, lobes broad-ovate; cor. pink to lilac, throat usually white, 1–2cm diam., lobes obovate, emarginate. Capsule about as long as cal. Spring. E Alps. Z5.

***P. darialica*** Rupr. (29-I) Lvs 2–8×1–3cm, obovate, oblong or spathulate, apex rounded to obtuse, gradually attenuate to base, margins sharply denticulate, efarinose above, cream-white-farinose or efarinose beneath, petiole broadly winged. Peduncle 2.5–10cm, sometimes farinose towards apex; fls 2–15 in erect, symmetric umbel; bracts 0.3–0.4cm, linear, not swollen below, becoming reflexed; pedicels to 0.8cm; calyx cup-shaped, to 0.5cm, divided to halfway into lanceolate lobes; cor. to 1.4cm diam., annulate, pink to carmine-red, with yellow eye, lobes obovate, deeply emarginate, overlapping, tube to twice length calyx. Capsule cylindric, 2× calyx. Caucasus. Plants in cultivation as *P. darialica* are almost always *P. frondosa*.

***P. denticulata*** Sm. DRUMSTICK PRIMULA. (34) Lvs to 10cm, oblong-obovate or spathulate in fl., later to 30cm, when oblong to oblanceolate, sharply denticulate, more or less farinose beneath, apex obtuse, base narrowing to broadly winged petiole. Peduncle 10–30cm; infl. head crowded, subglobose; bracts short, leafy; cal. tubular to campanulate, lobes linear, obtuse, brown-green; cor. pale purple to red-purple, sometimes white, to 17mm, eye yellow, lobes obcordate, emarginate. Spring–early summer. Afghanistan to SE Tibet and Burma. 'Alba': fls white with yellow eye. 'Cashmeriana': lvs and peduncles farinose. 'Karryann': lvs with cream-variegated margins. 'Rubra': fls red-purple; many red-flowered forms have been selected and named; they are not always so vigorous as the mauve or white plants. Z5.

***P. deorum*** Velen. (2-V) Lvs 2–15×0.4–2cm, narrowly oblanceolate to oblong, erect or erecto-patent, coriaceous, shining, with very short pale glandular hairs above, margin cartilaginous, entire. Peduncle 5–20cm, fragrant, viscid, more or less dark violet toward apex; infl. 3–18-fld; bracts 3–10mm, narrowly triangular-lanceolate; pedicels 3–10mm; cal. 3–6mm, tubular, tinged purple, lobes obtuse; cor. deep red to violet-purple, to 2cm diam., lobes obovate, emarginate. April. SW Bulgaria (mts). Z5.

***P. deuteronana*** Craib. (20-III) Plant more or less efarinose. Lvs 1.5–5×1–2cm, oblong-obovate to oblong-ovate, tapering to short petiole. Margin irregularly denticulate. Peduncle absent; pedicels 1–2cm; fls numerous; cor. to 3cm diam., pale purple with annulus yellow, lobes obovate, toothed or lobed on margin or at apex, tube to 2cm, hairy within. Himalaya (C Nepal to Sikkim).

***P. ×digenea*** Kerner. *(P. elatior × P. vulgaris.)* (5) Frequent and fertile hybrid, displaying a wide range of forms between parents. Z5.

***P. ×discolor*** Leyb. *(P. auricula × P. daonensis.)* (2) Fertile hybrid, very variable. Fls purple to pale yellow. Those resembling *P. auricula* may be distinguished as hybrids by lvs having red glandular hairs. Those resembling *P. daonensis* distinguished by lvs subentire, or farinose. Z6.

***P. edgeworthii*** (Hook. f.) Pax. (20-I) Young lvs 5–7.5cm, spathulate, irregularly serrate or lobulate, undulate; mature lvs to 15cm, ovate, base truncate or cordate, petiolate. Peduncle very short or absent; pedicels 2.5–8cm; cal. tubular, lobes broad, acute or obtuse, farinose; cor. blue, lilac, pink or white, to 3cm diam., eye orange-yellow edged white, lobes obovate, acute, entire to deeply emarginate. Spring. W Himalaya. 'Ghose's': lvs light green, farinose; fls pale mauve or blue, with yellow eye. Z4.

***P. elatior*** (L.) Hill. OXLIP. (5) Rosettes upright at flowering, becoming openly rosulate. Lvs 5–20×2–7cm, ovate to oblong or elliptic, crenate, often erose, pubesc. to subglabrous above, pubesc. beneath, apex rounded, base usually contracting abruptly into petiole; petiole long, broad, winged, hirsute, basally sheathing. Peduncle 10–30cm, stiff, upright, pubesc.; infl. secund, many-fld; bracts 3–6mm, linear to ovate, papery; cal. 6–15mm, narrowly tubular; cor. yellow, 2–2.5cm, odourless, throat green-yellow to orange, lobes obcordate, emarginate. Capsule longer than cal., cylindrical, sometimes tapering to apex; seeds 1–1.5mm diam., ovoid to subspherical to cuboid, dark brown to black. Spring–early summer. Europe to Near East. ssp. ***leucophylla*** (Pax.) H. Harrison ex W.W. Smith & Forr. Lvs gradually attenuate to petiole, grey-tomentose below when young, margins entire to crenulate. Calyx lobes short. Romania. ssp. ***pallasii*** W.W. Sm. & Forr. Lvs gradually attenuate to petiole, glabrous, margin dentate. Fls few. N Asia, south to N Iran. ssp. ***ruprechtii*** (Kusn.) H. Harrison. Close to ssp. *leucophylla*, differing in lvs persistently tomentose. Caucasus, Armenia. Z5.

***P. erythrocarpa*** Craib. (34) Close to *P. denticulata*. Lvs oblanceolate, somewhat farinose beneath. Peduncles 10–35cm, farinose above; fls mauve, eye yellow. E Himalaya (Bhutan, S Tibet).

***P. ×facchinii*** Schott *(P. minima × P. spectabilis.)* (2) Possibly fertile. Very variable. Z6.

***P. farinosa*** L. (29-I) Farinose or occasionally efarinose, heterostylous. Lvs 1–10×0.3–2cm, oblanceolate to elliptic, obtuse, entire or finely denticulate, white farinose beneath; petiole variable in length, winged. Peduncle 3–20cm; infl. 2-many-fld; bracts 2–8mm, linear-lanceolate to subulate, base gibbous; pedicels to twice as long as bracts, lengthening in fr.; cal. 3–6mm, cylindrical or urceolate, often tinged black or purple, lobes obtuse, rarely acute; cor. 8–16mm diam., lilac-pink, rarely purple or white, throat yellow, lobes obcordate, deeply emarginate, tube 5–8mm. Capsule 5–9mm, equal to or to twice as long as cal. Scotland and C Sweden to C Spain to Bulgaria, N Asia and N Pacific. ssp. ***exigua*** Velen. Similar to *P. farinosa* but usually smaller. Lvs efarinose or sparingly farinose. Peduncles, bracts and cal. efarinose; fls 2–6 on longer pedicels than species type. Bulgaria (mts). Z4.

***P. fedschenkoi*** Reg. (27) Plants glabrous, nearly efarinose; roots somewhat tuberous, becoming dormant in summer. Lvs obovate-elliptic to spathulate, to 6cm, attenuate to broad petioles, margins dentate. Peduncle 4–12cm; infl. a few-fld umbel; cor. purple-pink, with darker eye, annulate, lobes entire or very shallowly emarginate. Capsule broadly ovoid-globose. Afghanistan, Soviet C Asia.

***P. firmipes*** Balf. f. & Forr. (22) Lvs 2.5–7.5cm, ovate or rounded, apex obtuse, base cordate, margins deeply crenate-dentate, petiole to 20cm, winged, sheathing at base. Peduncle 10–40cm, yellow-farinose above; infl. a 2–10-fld umbel; pedicels 1.5–3.5cm, slender; bracts lanceolate; 1.5cm; cal. 0.8cm, broad-campanulate, farinose, lobes lanceolate, somewhat recurved; cor. 2cm diam., soft yellow, nodding, farinose within, lobes obovate, emarginate. E Himalaya to W China, N Burma.

***P. flaccida*** Balakr. (37) Lvs 10–20×2–5cm, elliptic or obovate, denticulate, soft-pubesc., apex acute, base narrowed to winged petiole. Peduncle 20–40cm, efarinose; infl. densely 5–15-fld; bracts minute, lanceolate; cal. broadly campanulate, to 5mm, lobes ovate, acute; cor. lavender to violet, to 2.5cm diam., broadly funnel-shaped, farinose, downward-pointing. Summer. China.

***P. ×floerkeana*** Schröd. *(P. glutinosa × P. minima.)* (2) Fertile, very variable. Fls deep purple to bright pinks. Very common in Alps. Z5.

***P. floribunda*** Wallich. (1) Plants pubesc. Lvs ovate to elliptic, margin coarsely dentate, petiole broadly winged. Peduncle 5–25cm; infl. of 2–6 superposed umbels of 3–6 fls in each; pedicels unequal, to 2cm; calyx 6mm, hairy, lobes ovate, acute, enlarging in fr.; cor. to 1cm diam., yellow, lobes entire or very shallowly emarginate, tube long, slender, hairy. Capsule included in calyx. W Himalaya (Afghanistan to W Nepal).

***P. florindae*** Kingdon-Ward. (22) Lvs 5–20cm, broadly-ovate, dentate, shining, apex rounded, base deeply cordate; petiole 4–20cm, stout, winged, often tinged red. Peduncle stout, to 90cm; infl. 40+-fld; bracts to 2.5cm, oblong or broad-lanceolate, apex often toothed, base swollen; pedicels 2.5–10cm, slender, spreading; cal. campanulate, yellow-farinose, to 1.5cm, lobes triangular, often recurved; cor. yellow, densely creamy-farinose within, to 2cm diam., strongly fragrant, pendent, funnel-shaped, lobes broad-ovate. Summer. SE Tibet. 'Rubra': fls orange to crimson; often sold as *P. florindae* Orange or Red Hybrids: probably of hybrid origin, possibly with *P. waltonii* as the other parent; usually smaller than *P. florindae*. Z6.

***P. forrestii*** Balf. f. (16) Subshrub with long woody rhiz., glandular-hairy throughout. Lvs 3–8×2–5cm, ovate-elliptic, crenate to serrate, apex obtuse, base rounded or subcordate, distinctly rugose above, white- or yellow farinose beneath when young, becoming efarinose; petiole to 10cm. Peduncle stout, 15–22cm; infl. 10–25-fld; bracts to 2cm, ovate, leafy; pedicels 2–3cm; cal. to 1cm, campanulate, lobes ovate, obtuse; cor. yellow, to 2cm diam., eye orange, lobes broad-obcordate, deeply emarginate. Summer. China. Z6.

***P. ×forsteri*** Stein. *(P. hirsuta × P. minima.)* (2) Usually sterile, very variable. Widely grown. f. ***bilekii*** (Sunderm.) Widm. Differs from *P. minima* in lvs glandular-pubesc., more teeth with shorter cartilaginous tips. Infl. to 3-fld; fls brighter red, lobes broader than in *P. minima*. f. ***kelleri*** (Widm.) Widm. Similar to *P. hirsuta* but lvs with cartilaginous tips, bracts longer, shortly glandular-pubesc. f. ***steinii*** (Obrist) Widm. Intermediate between *P. hirsuta* and *P. minima*. 'Dianne' (selected seedling from *P. ×forsteri* possibly with another parent): lvs broadly spathulate, with 6–7 sharp teeth at apex; peduncle to 4cm; fls 1–3, deep magenta-crimson. Z5.

***P. frondosa*** Janka. (29-I) Lvs to 10×2.5cm, spathulate or obovate, denticulate or crenulate, densely farinose beneath, apex rounded, base tapering to winged petiole of variable length. Peduncle 5–12.5cm, slightly farinose toward apex; infl. 1–30-fld; bracts to 5mm, linear, not swollen at base; pedicels to 2.5cm; cal. tubular-campanulate, to 1.5cm, farinose, lobes lanceolate, acute; cor. rose-lilac to red-purple, to 1.5cm diam., eye yellow, lobes obcordate, deeply emarginate, tube yellow, just exceeding cal. to twice as long. Late spring. Balkans. Z5.

***P. gambeliana*** Watt. (25) Rhiz. very short, with few farinose bud scales. Lvs 2–30×0.5–6cm, including petiole, lamina ovate to orbicular, apex rounded, obtuse or acute, base deeply cordate or occasionally truncate, efarinose, margin crenate, petiole long, slender. Peduncle 3–25cm; infl. a solitary umbel, or 2 superimposed umbels of 1–8 fls; pedicels to 1cm at anthesis, 2.5cm in fruit; cal. 0.5–0.8cm; cor. to 2.5cm diam., purple-pink to violet-pink, throat yellow, lobes broadly obcordate, deeply emarginate, tube 1–2.5cm. E Himalaya.

***P. geraniifolia*** Hook. f. (10-II) Lvs 5–20×3–8cm, orbicular, pubesc., lobes 7–9, rounded, crenate, apex acute, base cordate; petiole 5–7.5cm long, pubesc. Peduncle 10–30cm, pubesc.; infl. 2–12-fld, lax; bracts to 1.5cm, lanceolate; pedicels 5–12mm, pubesc.; cal. tubular to campanulate, to 6mm, lobes ovate, acute, spreading; cor. pink to pale purple, 1–2cm diam., semi-pendent, lobes obcordate. Summer. E Himalaya, Yunnan. Z5.

***P. glaucescens*** Moretti. (2-I) Lvs 1–10×0.5–2.5cm, broadly lanceolate to oblong, patent when mature, coriaceous, stiff, shining, glabrous, margin cartilaginous, minutely crenulate, apex acute, base narrowed. Peduncle 3–12cm; infl. 2–6-fld; bracts 4–30mm, triangular-lanceolate to linear; pedicels 3–20mm; cal. 6–18mm, tubular, tinged red, lobes linear or lanceolate; cor. pink-red to lilac, to 2.5cm diam., lobes obcordate, deeply notched. Spring. Italian Alps. Z6.

***P. glomerata*** Pax. (35) Lvs 3–15×1–3cm (including petiole), oblong, oblanceolate or obovate-spathulate, erose to denticulate, white-farinose when young, base tapering to winged petiole which is usually tinged red at base. Peduncles 10–30cm, with a rosette of oblong to oblanceolate, raggedly toothed lvs. Infl. in compact, globose heads; pedicels short; cal. farinose; cor. purple-blue, to 1.5cm diam., pendent, erect, funnel-shaped, tube 8–15mm, lobes 6–10mm, obcordate, spreading, deeply emarginate. Late summer–early autumn. Himalaya. Z6.

***P. glutinosa*** Wulf. (2-V) Viscid, secretion rarely drying to white crust. Lvs 1.5–6×0.3–0.8cm, usually erect, narrowly oblanceolate to oblong, coriaceous, with minute, pale glandular hairs above, margin somewhat cartilaginous, apex more or less rounded. Peduncle 1.5–9cm; infl. 2–8-fld; bracts 4–12mm, broadly ovate to oblong, viscid; pedicels to 3mm; cal. 5–9mm, lobes obovate, obtuse; cor. deep violet, rarely white, to 2cm diam., fragrant, lobes ovate, emarginate. Early summer. E Alps, C Yugoslavia. Z4.

***P. gracilipes*** Craib. (20-III) Lvs 4–15×1–5cm, oblong-spathulate to elliptic, irregularly toothed, efarinose, rounded at apex, tapering to broad-winged petiole at base. Peduncle absent; infl. many fld; bracts to 6mm, lanceolate; pedicels 1–6cm; cal. about one-third as long as cor. tube, lobes triangular, acute, farinose; cor. bright pink-purple, eye small, orange-yellow with narrow white border, lobes 2–4cm, obovate, irregularly toothed, spreading. Late spring–early summer. C Nepal, SE Tibet. 'Winter Jewel': to 15cm; lvs with margin finely dentate; fls bright rose-pink. Z5.

***P. griffithii*** (Watt) Pax. (20-II) Lvs 6–30×2–6cm, ovate to nearly sagitate, base attenuate to broad petiole, or rounded to cordate, sparsely farinose below, margin irregularly dentate. Peduncle 10–20cm at anthesis, enlarging later, to 45cm in fruit; infl. a single umbel of 5–12 fls; pedicels 1–2cm; cal. 0.5–0.8cm; cor. to 2.5cm diam., deep purple with yellow eye, lobes obcordate, shallowly emarginate, tube 1–2cm. E Himalaya (Bhutan, S Tibet).

***P. halleri*** J.F. Gmel. (29-II) Farinose, homostylous. Lvs 2–8×0.5–3cm, elliptic to obovate, subentire or minutely denticulate, usually beneath densely yellow-farinose. Peduncle 8–18cm, stout, farinose; infl. 2–12-fld; bracts 5–10mm, narrowly lanceolate, base subsaccate or slightly auriculate; pedicels 5–10mm; cal. 8–12mm, farinose; cor. 15–20mm diam., lilac, tube 20–30mm; stamens inserted at tube apex; style exserted. Capsule cylindrical, equalling or exceeding cal. Spring. Alps, Carpathians, Balkan Peninsula (mts). Z5.

***P. ×heerii*** Brügger. *(P. hirsuta × P. integrifolia.)* (2) Uncommon sterile hybrid. Distinct from *P. hirsuta* by absence of white eye to cor.; distinct from *P. integrifolia* by presence of teeth on lf margins. From the rivers Bernina and Upper Engadine, headwaters of the Rhine, and wherever parents meet. Z5.

***P. heucherifolia*** Franch. (10-II) Lvs to 6–15×3–8cm, orbicular, with 7–11, broadly triangular lobes, slightly pubesc., somewhat pilose, base cordate; petiole red-villous. Peduncles 15–30cm; infl. 3–9-fld; bracts to 1cm, linear-lanceolate; pedicels 1–3cm; cal. to 5mm, red, lobes triangular, acute; cor. mauve-pink to deep purple, to 2.5cm diam., pendent, lobes obovate, emarginate. Early summer. Tibet, China. Z5.

***P. hirsuta*** All. (2-VI) Efarinose. Lvs 2–9×1–3.5cm, ovate, obovate or sub-orbicular, finely or coarsely dentate, fleshy, viscid, glandular-pubesc., producing a pale or red-brown secretion, base abruptly narrowed into winged petiole. Peduncle 1–7cm, usually shorter than lvs; infl. 1–15-fld; bracts 1–8mm, ovate to obovate, more or less scarious; pedicels 2–16mm; cal. 3.5–9mm; cor. to 2.5cm diam., pale lilac to deep purple-red, usually with white centre, lobes obovate, emarginate. Spring. C Alps, Pyrenees. Z5.

***P. hyacinthina*** W.W. Sm. (36) Lvs 16–18×2–2.5cm, oblanceolate to oblong, apex obtuse or rounded, base attenuate to broad, winged, hairy petiole, margins irregularly dentate, white-farinose beneath. Peduncle 20–45cm; infl. a compact spike or capitulum of numerous deflexed fls; cal. to 0.5cm; cor. to 1.7cm, violet, strongly hyacinth-scented, lobes obcordate, 4×5mm, tube 1cm. SE Tibet.

***P. ianthina*** Balf. f. & Cave. (21) Lvs to 25×5cm, oblong-oblanceolate, apex rounded, base sharply attenuate to winged petiole, glandular-punctate above and beneath, margin finely denticulate. Peduncle to 60cm, yellow-farinose at nodes; infl. of 3 superposed many-fld whorls; pedicels 1cm, somewhat farinose; cal. to 0.5cm; cor. to 2cm diam., violet, lobes obcordate, rounded, shallowly emarginate, tube 1cm. Sikkim.

***P. incana*** M.E. Jones. (29-I) Rosettes rosulate. Lvs 1.5–8×0.5–2cm, elliptic to spathulate, usually denticulate, rarely entire, farinose beneath, apex obtuse or rounded; petiole winged, to length of lamina or absent. Peduncle stout, erect, 5–45cm, farinose toward apex; infl. capitate, 2–14-fld; bracts 5–10mm, linear-lanceolate to linear-oblong, base swollen, pedicels stiff, erect, farinose, shorter than or equal to bracts; cal. farinose, campanulate, 7–10mm, lobes oblong or triangular; cor. to 1cm diam., annulate, homomorphic, lilac fading toward centre, eye yellow, tube equalling or slightly exceeding cal. Capsule oblong, slightly longer than cal. Spring–early summer. E Alaska to E Colorado, locally on SW and SE shores of Hudson Bay. Z4.

***P. integrifolia*** L. (2-VII) Slightly viscid, secretion sometimes drying to form white crust. Lvs 1–4×0.6–1.2cm, often not reaching full length until after anthesis, elliptic to spathulate, entire or subentire, fleshy to coriaceous, slightly viscid, glandular hairs pale-tipped, margin ciliate, the cilia variously deflexed, patent or more or less erecto-patent. Peduncle 0.5–5cm; infl. 1–3-fld; bracts 2–10mm, lanceolate to oblong; pedicels to 3.5mm at anthesis; cal. 6–12mm, tubular, lobes oval, obtuse, glandular; cor. red-purple or pink-lilac, to 2cm diam., lobes obovate, deeply cleft. Early summer. C Alps, E and C Pyrenees. Z5.

***P. ×intermedia*** Porta. *(P. clusiana × P. minima.)* (2) With *P. clusiana* as seed parent sterile, with *P. minima* fertile. Fls can be very large, rose. Distributed in most of area covered by *P. clusiana*. Z5.

***P. involucrata*** Wallich. (30-I) Lvs 3–15×0.5–2cm, ovate to oblong, entire or obscurely denticulate, glabrous, long-petiolate, apex rounded, base rounded. Peduncle 10–30cm; infl. 2–6-fld; bracts 4–5mm, oblong to lanceolate; pedicels shorter than bracts, erect to nodding; cal. tubular, 5-ribbed, glabrous, lobes lanceolate, acute, tips often recurved; cor. white, 1–2cm diam., eye yellow, tube purple, 1–1.5cm, lobes obcordate, notched. Summer. Pakistan to SW China. Z5.

***P. ioessa*** W.W. Sm. (22) Lvs to 6–20×1–2.5, narrowly oblong or oblanceolate to spathulate, sharply and deeply toothed, apex rounded, base narrowed to petiole of equal length to lamina. Peduncle 10–30cm; infl. 2–8-fld; bracts to 1.5cm, linear; pedicels 1.5–4cm, yellow-farinose; cal. campanulate 5–10mm, almost black, farinose, lobes triangular, often recurved; cor. pink-mauve to violet or white, fragrant, to 2.5cm diam., funnel-shaped, lobes broad-obcordate, farinose inside. Spring–early summer. SE Tibet. Z6.

***P. irregularis*** Craib. (20-III) Lvs to 8–12×3cm at anthesis, when densely yellow-farinose, to 18×6cm in fruit, more or less efarinose, oblong-elliptic to elliptic-obovate, apex rounded, base cuneate or attenuate, margin deeply dentate, sometimes shallowly lobed and dentate. Peduncle 1–2cm at anthesis, farinose, to 13cm later; infl. an umbel of 12–20 fls; pedicels 1.5–3cm, glandular; cal. lobes obtuse, farinose, glandular cor. to 2.5cm diam., pink with yellow eye surrounded by white zone, lobes broadly oblong-ovate, regularly toothed, tube 1.5–2.5cm. Himalaya (Nepal to Sikkim).

***P. japonica*** A. Gray. (21) Lvs to 25×8cm, obovate, oblong or broad-spathulate, finely and irregularly crenate-dentate, apex obtuse, base tapering to winged petiole. Peduncle to 45cm; infl. of 1–6 superposed, many-fld whorls; bracts to 1.5cm, linear-lanceolate; pedicels to 2cm; cal. tubular, to 1.5cm, farinose within, lobes triangular; cor. purple-red, crimson, pink to white, to 2cm diam., lobes obcordate. Early summer. Japan. 'Fuji': fls white. 'Millers Crimson': to 45cm; abundant crimson fls; breeds true from seed. 'Postford White': to 45cm; fls white with yellow eye. 'Valley Red': to 50cm; fls bright red. Z5.

***P. jesoana*** Miq. (10-II) Lvs to 35×10cm, erect, orbicular-cordate, 7–9-lobed, tinged purple, base tapering to winged petiole. Peduncle 10–30cm; infl. 2–6-fld; pedicels 30–10mm at anthesis, expanding later; cor. pink or pink-purple, rarely white, to 2cm diam., eye yellow, lobes obcordate, emarginate. Spring. Japan. Z6.

***P. juliae*** Kuzn. (7) Plant efarinose, stoloniferous. Rosettes open. Lvs round, 2–10×0.5–3cm, coarsely crenate, base deeply cordate; petioles narrow, sheathing at base, marked red. Peduncle absent; infl. borne on tip of rhiz. branches; bracts 3–4mm, linear to lanceolate; pedicels equal to or longer than petioles; cal. narrowly tubular, 5–8, strongly ridged, lobes lanceolate; cor. 2–3cm diam., exannulate, deep blue-magenta, darker red around yellow eye. Spring. Caucasus. Z5.

***P. ×juribella*** Sunderm. *(P. minima × tyrolensis.)* (2) Infrequent hybrid resembling *P. minima* but lvs incurved and calyx tinged purple, features of *P. tyrolensis*. Dolomites.

**Primula** (× 1) (a) *P. marginata* (b) *P. suffrutescens* (c) *P.capitata* (d) *P. polyneura* (e) *P. allionii* (f) *P. forrestii*

***P.* 'Kewensis'.** (1) An alleged allopolyploid, said to have been derived from hybrid, *P. floribunda* × *P. verticillata*, at RBG Kew, in 1898, which had thrum-eyed fls. The fertile *P.* 'Kewensis' was reported to have arisen as a cross between a shoot bearing pin-eyed fls, and the normal fl., however the chances of such a somatic mutation occurring are tiny and the story is probably more complex. Lvs 15–20cm, obovate to spathulate, denticulate, sparingly farinose, apex acute, base tapering to winged petiole with sheathing base. Peduncles several, to 30cm; infl. of 2–5 superposed, 6- to 10-fld whorls; bracts 2.5–5cm, ovate-lanceolate, serrate, leafy; pedicels slender, 1–2.5cm; cal. 1–1.5cm, campanulate, lobes lanceolate, entire; cor. yellow, fragrant, to 2cm diam., lobes broad-obcordate. Early spring. Z9.

***P. kisoana*** Miq. (10-II) Plant covered with short red hairs. Lvs to 15cm, orbicular-cordate, with 6 pairs of broad-crenate lobes; petiole 7.5–10cm. Peduncle 5–20cm; infl. 2–6-fld; bracts 0.5–1cm; pedicels to 1cm; cal. campanulate, to 1cm, lobes linear-lanceolate; cor. 2.5–3cm diam., deep rose or rose-mauve, lobes obcordate, deeply emarginate. Spring. Japan. Z6.

***P. kitaibeliana*** Schott. (2-VII) Viscid. Lvs 2–9×1–4cm, not reaching full length until after anthesis, elliptic to obovate, mostly with shallow, distant teeth, sometimes entire, fleshy, malodorous, densely covered with hairs. Scape 2–5cm; infl. 1–3-fld; bracts 2–10mm, linear; pedicels 2–12mm; cal. 7–13mm, tubular, lobes acute to obtuse; cor. pink to lilac, to 2.5cm, diam., lobes obcordate, emarginate. Late spring. W and C Yugoslavia. Z7.

***P. latifolia*** Lapeyr. (2-III) Lvs efarinose, 3–15×1–4.5cm, oblanceolate to obovate, rarely dentate, usually with wide teeth near apex or subentire, fleshy, fragrant, viscid, glandular-pubesc. Peduncle 3–18cm; infl. 2–20-fld, secund; bracts 2–9mm, ovate to obovate, more or less scarious; pedicels 2–20mm; cal. 2–6mm; cor. 1–2cm diam., purple or dark violet, fragrant, lobes oblong to obovate, emarginate, throat more or less farinose. Late spring-early summer. S, W and C Alps. Z5.

***P.* ×*loiseleurii*** Sunderm. *(P. allionii* × *auricula.)* (2) Variable, usually compact plants intermediate between parents; fls pink or yellow. Garden origin. 'Lismore Yellow' *(P. allionii* 'Alba' × *P. auricula)*: lvs dentate, glossy dark green, glandular-pubesc.; peduncle 0.5–2cm; pedicels 0.5–2cm; fls to 11, 2.5cm diam., cream-yellow with darker yellow eye, lobes not overlapping, emarginate.

***P. luteola*** Rupr. (28) Rosette openly rosulate. Lvs 10–30×2–5cm, lanceolate to elliptic to oblanceolate, efarinose, sharply denticulate, recurved, apex obtuse or rounded, base tapering gradually to winged petiole. Peduncle robust, 15–35cm, white-farinose toward apex; infl. symmetrical to globose, 10 to 25-fld; bracts linear to lanceolate, 5–7mm, base swollen; pedicels farinose, 10–20mm; cal. campanulate, 5–6mm, lobes farinose within and on edges, lanceolate; cor. to 1.5cm diam., exannulate, yellow. Capsule round, included in cal. Spring. E Caucasus. Z5.

***P. macrophylla*** D. Don. (24-III) Lvs 15–25×1.5–3cm, erect, lanceolate to oblanceolate, entire or crenulate, white-farinose beneath, apex acute or obtuse, base tapering gradually to sheathing petiole. Peduncle 12.5–25cm, farinose above; infl. 5–25-fld; bracts to 2cm, awl-shaped; pedicels to 2.5cm, farinose; cal. to 1.5cm, cylindrical, farinose within, lobes linear to lanceolate; cor. purple, violet or lilac, eye usually darker or tinged yellow, to 2cm diam., tube 1–3cm, lobes obovate, entire. Summer. Himalaya. Z6.

***P. magellanica*** Lehm. (29-I) Rosette openly rosulate. Lvs 1–10×0.7×2.5cm, rhombic to obovate to lanceolate or spathulate, serrulate-dentate, apex obtuse or rounded, base tapering gradually to petiole, efarinose or more frequently white- or yellow-farinose beneath. Peduncles 5–15cm, rarely 3–50cm, farinose above; infl. tight, symmetrical, few- to many-fld; bracts 5–10cm, lanceolate, base swollen; pedicels 1–3mm, farinose, lengthening in fr.; cal. campanulate, 8–10mm, lobes oblong to lanceolate; cor. 1–2cm diam., annulate, usually white, cream or lilac to purple, homomorphic, sometimes heteromorphic, fragrant, eye yellow, lobes obovate, deeply emarginate. Capsule ellipsoid, longer than cal. Spring. Southern S America, Falklands. Z7.

***P. malacoides*** Franch. FAIRY PRIMROSE; BABY PRIMROSE. (9) Lvs 2–4cm, broad-oblong to ovate, with 6–8 pairs of shallow, dentate lobes, pubesc., apex acute, base cordate; petiole 5–7.5cm. Peduncle slender, 20–30cm; infl. of 2–6, distant, superposed, 4–6-fld whorls; bracts very short, acute, farinose; pedicels to 2.5cm; farinose; cal. to 1.5cm, campanulate, base swollen, farinose, lobes short, acute, spreading, cor. mauve to pink, red, or white, to 1.5cm diam., lobes obcordate. Winter. China. Z8.

***P. marginata*** Curtis. (2-III) Rosette openly rosulate. Lvs 1.5–10×1–4cm, obovate to oblong, regularly and deeply serrate-dentate, leathery, fleshy, apex obtuse or rounded, base tapering to a winged petiole, young lvs white or yellow-farinose, mature lvs farinose on margins, surfaces with small, sessile glands. Peduncle erect, 2–12cm, farinose above; infl. symmetrical, 2–20-fld; bracts 2–5mm, broadly ovate to lanceolate, sometimes leafy; pedicels 3–20mm, farinose; cal. campanulate, 3–5mm, densely farinose within, less so outside, often flushed red, lobes broadly ovate or triangular, obtuse, cor. lilac to lavender or blue, sometimes violet or pink, shallow funnel-shaped, 1.5–3cm diam., faintly fragrant, eye white-farinose, lobes obcordate. Capsule subglobose, equal to or longer than cal. Spring. Maritime, Cottian Alps. 'Alba': cor. usually small, pale pink, fading to white. 'Barbara Clough': lvs to 9×3cm, broad-lanceolate, often yellow-farinose, denticulate; cor. pink to lilac, eye white, lobes rounded. 'Beamish Variety': lvs to 7×2cm, broad-lanceolate, white-farinose, denticulate; fls blue, eye white-farinose. 'Beatrice Lascaris': possibly a hybrid; compact, slow-growing; lvs to 3×1.5cm, broad spathulate, yellow-farinose, denticulate; cor. blue, eye white-farinose, flat. 'Caerulea': lvs 6×1.5cm, spathulate, white-farinose, denticulate; cor. blue, funnel-shaped. 'Clear's Variety': lvs to 6×2cm, spathulate, yellow-farinose, dentate; peduncle and pedicels short; cor. small, lilac, eye white. 'Correvon's Variety': vigorous, lvs to 5×3cm, deeply incised, dentate, yellow-farinose; cor. large, lavender. 'Drake's Form': larger than species type, resembles 'Pritchard's Variety'; cor. pale lilac to lavender. 'Elizabeth Fry': lvs to 5×2cm, spathulate, yellow-farinose, denticulate; peduncles 4- to 5-fld, cor. large, silvery lavender. 'Highland Twilight': lvs broad, 4.5×3cm, denticulate; cor. rich purple to blue. 'Holden's Variety': compact; lvs narrow, 5×1.5cm, farinose, regularly serrate; fls small; cor. blue, funnel-shaped. 'Inschriach Form': lvs 5×2.5cm, spathulate, farinose, denticulate; fls blue. 'Ivy Agee': lvs densely farinose; fls large; cor. lilac to blue, eye cream. 'Kesselring's Variety': similar to 'Pritchard's Variety' but fls smaller, appearing 2–3 weeks later; white-farinose throughout; fls deep lavender. 'Pritchard's Variety': lvs to 9×4cm, broadly spathulate, grey-green, dentate to serrate, farinose chiefly on margins, laminae sparingly farinose; peduncle 5–8cm, slightly farinose; infl. to 8-fld; cor. lilac to purple, eye white-farinose. 'Rosea': lvs to 5×1.5cm, narrow-elliptic, denticulate, base narrowing to short petiole; fls lilac to pink. 'Rubra': lvs to 7×2.5cm, broad-ovate to lanceolate, denticulate, very pale yellow-farinose; fls deep rose to lilac. 'Waithman's Variety': lvs to 5×2cm, spathulate, dentate, white-farinose; fls pale blue.

Several excellent garden plants have *P. marginata* as one parent and largely resemble it in habit. Amongst them are: 'Barbara Barker' ('Linda Pope' × *P.* ×*pubescens* 'Zuleika Dobson'*)*: lvs green with white-farinose dentate margins. Fls to 2cm diam., lavender-blue with white eye; *P.* ×*pubescens* 'Zuleika Dobson' has been lost from cultivation. 'Hyacinthia' (derived from *P. marginata* 'Beamish Variety'): robust; lvs serrate, light green, slightly farinose at margins, fls to 3cm diam., hyacinth blue, lobes 6, overlapping. 'Linda Pope' *(P. marginata* × *?)*: lvs large, dentate, heavily white-farinose; fls rounded, mauve-blue with white-farinose eye. 'Marven' *(P. marginata* × *P.* ×*venusta)*: lvs light green, farinose, short-petiolate; peduncle stout, farinose; fls to 15, deep violet-blue with dark eye bordered by white-farinose zone. 'White Linda Pope' ('White Lady') (seedling of 'Linda Pope'): lvs obovate, dentate, peduncles 10cm; fls to 10, to 2.5cm, pale-green when young, becoming white with pale yellow-green eye. Z7.

***P. megaseifolia*** Boiss. (6) Lvs 2.5–15×2.5–12cm, in loose rosettes, ovate to round, crenate-dentate to subentire, teeth slightly mucronate, apex obtuse or rounded, base cordate, dark green, glabrous above, paler beneath, pubesc.; petiole 1–10cm, pubesc., stained red. Peduncle 1–10cm, pubesc., stained red; infl. secund, 2–9 fld; bracts 5–10mm, lanceolate; cal. tubular, 10–15mm, strongly ridged, lobes lanceolate; cor. 1.5–2.5cm diam., exannulate, magenta-rose to rose-pink, eye white, throat yellow, tube yellow, lobes obovate, deeply emarginate. Capsule oblong, slightly larger than cal. Early spring. Black Sea Coast, N Turkey. 'John Fielding' *(P. megaseifolia* × *P. juliae)*: lvs 4.5×4cm, elliptic, margin dentate; peduncle 10cm; fls to 5, 2.3cm diam., orchid-purple. Z7.

***P. melanops*** W.W. Sm. & Kingdon-Ward. (24-III) Lvs to 25cm, lanceolate, irregularly crenate-serrate, white- or yellow-farinose beneath, margin often recurved, base tapering to a broad, winged petiole. Peduncle 20–35cm, farinose above; infl. of 1–2 superimposed umbels 6–12-fld; bracts to 0.5cm, awl-shaped; pedicels absent at flowering, to 5mm in fruit; cal. tubular, 5-ribbed, farinose within, lobes awl-shaped; cor. purple, eye black, to 2cm diam., fragrant, lobes ovate. Early summer. China. Z5.

***P. minima*** L. (2-IV) Lvs 0.5–3×0.3–1cm, cuneate, shining, coriaceous, entire, apex truncate or rounded, deeply and densely dentate, teeth apices cartilaginous, glandular-pubesc., hairs pale, scattered or few. Peduncle 0.2–4cm; infl. 1–2-fld; bracts 3–8mm, linear to lanceolate; pedicels to 3mm; cal. 5–9mm, lobes obtuse; cor. 1.5–3cm diam., exannulate, bright pink, lilac or white, lobes very deeply emarginate, appearing Y-shaped, throat glandular pubesc. Late spring. S Europe (mts). Z5.

***P. mistassinica*** Michx. (29-I) Plant efarinose to slightly farinose, producing offsets by budding from roots. Rosette openly rosulate. Lvs 0.5–7×0.2–1.6cm, narrow, oblanceolate to spathulate, upper half dentate or denticulate, some subentire, apex obtuse or rounded; petiole obsolete to half length of blade. Peduncle slender, 3–21cm; infl. symmetrical, upright, 1–10-fld; bracts 2–6mm, linear, base thickened; pedicels slender, 0.5–3.5cm; cal. tubular, 3–6mm, sometimes farinose, lobes lanceolate to oblong; cor. annulate, pale pink, lilac, blue-purple, rarely white, tube yellow, to 2cm diam., eye yellow to orange, lobes obovate, notched. Capsule slightly larger than cal.; seeds 0.5mm, smooth, irregularly rounded. Spring–early summer. Canada, NE US. var. ***macropoda*** (Fern.) Boiv. Farinose, very rarely efarinose, hetero- or homomorphic. Rosettes openly rosulate. Lvs 1–23×0.3–3cm, oblanceolate to spathulate, denticulate, apex subacute to obtuse to rounded, efarinose or slightly farinose above, white-farinose beneath. Peduncle stout, erect, 1–45cm, farinose near apex; infl. symmetrical, 1–17-fld; bracts 5–14mm, lanceolate to awl-shaped, base swollen; pedicels erect, to 5cm or absent; cal. campanulate, 5–11×3.6mm, lobes variable; cor. to 1.5cm diam., annulate, lilac to purple-pink, eye orange-yellow fading to orange, tube yellow, lobes obcordate, cleft. Spring. E Canada, N US (mts). Z3.

***P. modesta*** Bisset & S. Moore. (29-I) Lvs 2.5–7.5×1–1.5cm, elliptic to spathulate, undulate-crenate or serrate, yellow-farinose beneath, apex obtuse, base tapering to winged petiole of equal length. Peduncle 2.5–12.5cm; infl. 2–15-fld; bracts 0.5–1cm, linear to lanceolate, acute, base slightly swollen; pedicels to 2.5cm, farinose; cal. to 5mm, lobes triangular; cor. pink-purple, to 1.5cm diam., lobes obcordate, deeply emarginate. Spring. Japan. var. ***fauriae*** (Franch.) Tak. Smaller in all parts. Lvs broadly ovate, scarcely dentate, margin revolute, narrowed and long-decurrent to petiole. Pedicels 1–2cm. Hokkaido, Honshu. var. ***matsumurae*** (Petitm.) Takeda. Plants stout. Lvs oblanceolate, obscurely dentate, gradually attenuate to base. Peduncle robust; fls to 10 per umbel. Hokkaido. Z6.

***P. mollis*** Nutt. ex Hook. (10-I) Softly pubesc. Lvs to 7.5cm, broad-ovate, obscurely lobed, crenate, apex rounded, base cordate; petiole 7.5–10cm. Peduncle 10–60cm; infl. of 2–10 superimposed, 4–9-fld umbels; bracts 1–1.5cm, linear; pedicels 1–1.5cm; cal. to 1cm, funnel-shaped, red, lobes triangular, green; cor. rose to crimson, to 2cm diam., eye yellow, lobes obovate, emarginate. April. Himalaya. Z7.

***P. ×muretiana*** Moritzi *(P. integrifolia × P. latifolia.)* (2-III) Reputedly sterile; very variable. Fls more brilliantly coloured than parents. Z5.

***P. muscarioides*** Hemsl. (36) Lvs 10–20×3–5cm, obovate or elliptic, crenate or dentate, slightly pubesc. above, apex obtuse, base tapering gradually to winged petiole. Peduncle to 40cm, farinose above; infl. compact heads or short spikes, many-fld; bracts linear to 1cm; cor. deep purple-blue, to 10mm diam., fragrant, tubular, deflexed, pendent. Early summer. China. Z5.

***P. nipponica*** Yatabe. (3) Lvs 2–4×0.5–1.5cm, cuneate or obovate-cuneate, apex obtuse, coarsely dentate towards apex, rather fleshy. Peduncle 7–15cm; infl. a 1–8-fld umbel; bracts linear, small; pedicels 1–2cm, sparsely farinose; cal. 0.4cm, narrowly cup-shaped, deeply lobed; cor. to 1.5cm diam., white with yellow eye, lobes obliquely spreading, emarginate, tube 5mm; capsule ovoid-ellipsoid, equalling or exceeding calyx. Japan (Honshu).

***P. nivalis*** Pall. (24-III) Lvs to 15–25×1–4cm, lanceolate or narrowly elliptic, initially somewhat revolute, later becoming flat, crenate or dentate, glabrous, efarinose or slightly farinose beneath, apex subacute or obtuse; petiole short, broadly winged. Peduncle 15–20cm in fl., to 35cm in fr.; infl. 8–12-fld; bracts to 2cm, lanceolate, acute, base connate; pedicels to 2cm, outer pedicels pendent; cal. cup-shaped, 0.5–1cm, lobes lanceolate; cor. purple 2–2.5cm diam., lobes oblong, entire. Spring. C Asia. Z4.

***P. nutans*** Georgi. (30-I) Efarinose throughout. Rosettes upright, rosulate. Lvs 1–12×0.5–1.5cm, oblong to ovate to orbicular, entire or obscurely denticulate, fleshy, apex rounded, base tapering gradually or contracting abruptly to narrowly winged petiole. Peduncle 2–30cm; infl. upright, 1–10-fld; bracts 5–12mm, oblong, tinged yellow, base auriculate; pedicels upright, 0.5–4.5cm; cal. tubular, 5–8mm, prominently ribbed, sometimes tinged red, lobes ovate, acute, ciliate; cor. 1–2cm diam., annulate, lilac to pink-purple, eye yellow, lobes obovate to cuneate, deeply emarginate; styles 'pin-eyed' and 'thrum-eyed', exserted. Capsule 1.5× larger than cal. Early summer. Mts of N Asia, N USSR, N Scandinavia, Alaska, SW Yukon. Z5.

***P. obconica*** Hance. GERMAN PRIMROSE; POISON PRIMROSE. (13) Lvs to 15cm, ovate or elliptic to oblong, coarsely dentate or lobulate, apex obtuse, base cordate; petiole 5–10cm, soft-haired. Peduncles several, 15–17.5cm, softly pubesc.; infl. 10–15-fld; bracts 0.5–1cm, linear; pedicels to 2.5cm; cal. 1–1.5cm, funnel-shaped, lobes very short, acute; cor. pale-lilac or purple, to 2.5cm diam., eye yellow, lobes obovate, deeply emarginate. Winter. China. Z8.

***P. palinuri*** Petagna. (2-II) Lvs efarinose, 3–20×2–7cm, broadly spathulate to oblong-ovate, more or less dentate, fleshy, viscid, fragrant, pubesc. or glabrous, margin slightly cartilaginous, glandular-hairy, hairs colourless. Peduncles 8–20cm; infl. 5–25-fld; bracts 5–25m, farinose, outer bracts broadly ovate, acute, inner bracts lanceolate; pedicels 5–20mm, farinose; cal. 6–10mm, tubular-campanulate, densely farinose, lobes short, acute; cor. to 3cm diam., deep yellow, throat with white, farinose ring, lobes obovate, not spreading. Spring. S Italy. Z5.

***P. parryi*** A. Gray. (4) Plant emits strong odour said to resemble carrion. Rosettes flat to upright. Lvs 6–33×1–6cm, obovate to oblong to oblanceolate, usually erect, recurved, leathery, frequently contorted, entire or finely denticulate, surfaces covered in short capitate glands, apex acute to obtuse; petiole obsolete to very short, winged. Peduncle stout, erect, 8–40cm; infl. usually secund, 3–20-fld; bracts 5–15mm, glandular, ovate to oblong-lanceolate, overlapping at base, sometimes denticulate; pedicels of varying length, to 10cm, erect, sometimes pendent; cal. 8–15mm, tubular, glandular, often tinged purple, lobes narrow linear, acute; cor. to 3cm diam., exannulate, purple-red to magenta, eye yellow with dark halo, tube yellow, to 2.5cm diam., lobes obovate to orbicular. Early summer. W US (mts). Z4.

***P. pedemontana*** Thom. ex Gaudin. (2-VI) Usually efarinose. Rosettes openly rosulate. Lvs 1.5–10×1–3cm, obovate, oblong-lanceolate to spathulate, upper half entire to shallowly denticulate, upper surface nearly glabrous, margins densely covered with brick-red to dark red glandular hairs, apex obtuse or rounded, base tapering to petiole; petiole winged, obsolete or to 10cm long. Peduncle 2.5–12cm, rarely 15cm; infl. symmetrical, 1–16-fld; bracts 1–3mm, glandular, broad-ovate, papery; pedicels 2–15mm, glandular; cal. campanulate, 3–8mm, glandular, lobes triangular, acute or obtuse, adpressed to tube in young fls; cor. pink, eye white, tube white inside, slightly glandular, lobes obovate, emarginate. Capsule subglobose, usually as long as cal. Early summer. Alps, Pyrenees. Z6.

***P. petiolaris*** Wallich. (20-III) Efarinose. Rosette tight, contracted in flower, later expanded. Lvs to 15cm, spathulate, denticulate, apex obtuse, base tapering to distinct petiole. Peduncle 3–5×1.5cm at flowering; infl. many-fld; pedicels 2–5cm, later absent; cal. tubular, lobes distinctively ribbed; cor. 1.5cm diam., pink, eye yellow with thin white border, lobes deep obovate, irregularly 3-toothed. Early summer. Himalaya (Uttar Pradesh to Sikkim).

***P. Petiolares Hybrids***. (20) Cultivars unattributable to individual spp. 'Linnet': close to *P. petiolaris* and *P. gracilipes*; lvs finely dentate; fls very numerous, farinose in bud, deep pink with white zone surrounding yellow markings at base of each lobe. 'Soup Plate (*P. sonchifolia × P. whitei*): overwintering buds very large; fls numerous, ice-blue. 'Tantallon' *(P. whitei × P. edgeworthii)*: lvs 5×1.5cm at anthesis, lanceolate, acute, sharply dentate, sparsely farinose above and beneath; peduncle 1cm, pedicels to 2cm, both farinose, as is calyx; fls 14–18, to 3cm diam., violet-blue, with yellow-green eye surrounded by narrow white zone. 'Tinney's Appleblossom' *(P. boothii × P. aureata)*: lvs oblong, finely dentate, deep green, stained red beneath; fls numerous, white with yellow eye, pink-tinged toward end of lobes, lobes dentate at apex. 'Tinney's Dairymaid': *(P. boothii × P. aureata)*: lvs mid-green; fls numerous, to 3.5cm diam., milk-white with yellow eye, throat green, lobes overlapping, finely dentate. Z5.

***P. poissonii*** Franch. (21) Lvs to 18×4cm, oblong-obovate, denticulate, usually revolute, glaucous, apex obtuse, base tapering to winged petiole. Peduncle to 45cm; infl. of 2–6 superposed whorls; bracts to 1cm, linear; pedicels to 2cm, erect; cal. cup-shaped, to 5mm, lobes triangular; cor. purple to crimson, to 2.5cm diam., eye yellow, lobes obcordate, deeply notched. Summer. China. Z6.

***P. polyneura*** Franch. (10-I) Softly pubesc. or subglabrous. Lvs 4–30×2–10cm, including petiole, ovate to orbicular, 7–11-lobulate, apex obtuse; petiole 2.5–20cm. Peduncle to 23cm; infl. of 1 or 2–3, superimposed 10–50-fld umbels; bracts to 1.5cm, lanceolate; pedicels to 2.5cm; cal. to 1.5cm, tubular, lobes lanceolate, acute; cor. pale rose to rich rose-red to crimson or purple, to 2.5cm diam., eye yellow, lobes obcordate, shallowly emarginate. Early summer. China. Z5.

***P. prolifera*** Wallich emend Benth. (21) Lvs to 35×7cm, oblanceolate, oblong-obovate or lanceolate, denticulate, glabrous, apex acute, base tapering to winged petiole. Peduncle to 90cm. Infl. of 4–6, superposed, 12–20-fld whorls; bracts 1–2cm, linear-lanceolate, farinose; pedicels to 1cm, farinose; cal. campanulate, 5–10mm, exterior densely creamy-farinose, lobes triangular, slightly recurved; cor. to 2.5cm diam., golden-yellow, fragrant, lobes obovate, deeply emarginate. Early summer. E Himalaya to Indonesia.

***P. Pruhonicensis Hybrids***. (5×7). Name covers many hybrids between *P. juliae* and members of the Vernales section of *Primula*, including *P. ×pruhoniciana* (*P. juliae × P. vulgaris*), with fls blue, and *P. ×helenae* (*P. juliae × P. vulgaris*), fls many colours. There are many cvs, the main ones listed below. 'Betty Green': fls crimson, eye clear yellow. 'Blue Cushion': vigorous; fls blue. 'Blue Horizon': vigorous, free-flowering, fls bright grey-blue, eye yellow. 'Blue Riband': vigorous, fls deep blue, centre shade red. 'Bunty': free-flowering; fls purple to blue, eye yellow. 'Craddock White': fls white, eye yellow. 'Crimson Cushion': fls blood red. 'Crimson Queen': fls large, red. 'Crispii': fls mauve-pink. 'Dinah': fls burgundy red, eye olive green. 'E.R. Jones': fls salmon pink, flushed orange. 'Gloria': fls scarlet, eye yellow, lobes with white marks on inside. 'Groenekens Glory': fls bright mauve-pink, eye green. 'Icombe Hybrid': fls large, rose to mauve, eye white 'Iris Mainwaring': compact; fls pale blue, flushed pink. 'Jill': compact; fls mauve-purple, eye white tinged green. 'Lilac Time': fls on short polyanthus-like stems, pale rose-lilac. 'Lingwood Beauty': fls red, eye deep orange. 'Morton Hybrid': very dwarf; fls red, eye yellow, large. 'Mrs Frank Neave': fls small, red. 'Mrs Macgillavry': fls rich violet-mauve. 'Pam': fls small, long, red-purple. 'Perle Von Bottrop': fls vivid red-purple. 'Purple Cushion': similar to 'Wanda', lvs tinged red. 'Purple Splendour': fls large, purple-red, eye pale yellow. 'Queens of the Whites': fls large, clear white. 'Romeo': vigorous, prolific; fls very large, violet. 'Snow Cushion': fls small, pure white. 'Snow White': vigorous; fls white. 'Wendy': fls pale pink, flushed mauve, lobes frilled. 'Wanda': most popular variety, fls purple-red. *Cvs of polyanthus habit* 'Beamish Foam': fls pink, splashed pale yellow. 'Ideal': fls purple, eye yellow. 'Kinlough Beauty': fls salmon-pink, lobes with cream stripe. 'Lady Greer': fls small, pale yellow. 'McWatts Cream': fls small, cream. 'Tawny Port': dwarf, long-flowering, lvs tinged red; fls wine-red. 'The Bride': fls pure white. *Double primroses* Plants with double fls. Early forms derived from *P. vulgaris*. *P. juliae* used since 1900. They include 'Alba Plena': fls white. 'Arthur du Moulin': fls very deep violet; one of few doubles to produce pollen in quantity. 'Bon Accord Gem': vigorous; fls rose-red, shaded with mauve. 'Bon Accord Lilac': fls lilac, lobes yellow at base. 'Bon Accord Purple': fls large, creamy-white tinged green, lobes frilled. 'Castlederg': fls deep yellow, splashed pink and brown. 'Chevithorne Pink': pedicels short; cor. pink. 'Cloth of Gold': lvs large pale green; fls yellow. 'Crimson King': fls large, deep red. 'Double Sulphur': fls sulphur-yellow. 'Double White': vigorous, with primrose habit; fls white. 'Lady Isobel': fls deep yellow. 'Marie Crousse': fls violet, splashed and edged white. 'Mrs A.M. Wilson': vigorous; fls large, red. 'Our Pat': lvs tinged crimson-bronze; fls sapphire blue. 'Quakers Bonnet': vigorous; fls pink-lilac. 'Red Paddy': fls small, red, flushed pink, edged silver.

***P.*** ×***pubescens*** Jacq. (*P. auricula* × *P. hirsuta.*) (2) Fertile hybrid, very variable. Can be distinguished from *P. hirsuta* by lvs sometimes entire, farinose. Cal. slightly farinose. Cor. white, yellow, pink, red, purple, brown, often appears faded. 'Alba': all white forms, usually compact with globular heads of up to 15 fls. 'Bewerly White': vigorous; fls many heads, creamy-white. 'Boothmans Variety' ('Carmen'): fast-growing, floriferous; fls crimson red, eye white, lobes overlapping, notched. 'Christine': rosettes compact; lvs green-yellow, nearly sessile, shallowly crenate; peduncles 7–10cm; infl. 2- to 8-fld, cor. deep rose, eye white. 'Faldonside': peduncles 7–10cm; fls red-pink, eye white. 'Freedom' ('Belluensis'): vigorous; lvs dark green, denticulate, petioles elongating in maturity; fls deep lilac. 'The General': vigorous, lvs lanceolate, shallowly denticulate, pale green, peduncle 7–10cm, infl. few-fld, cor. rich red, eye yellow. 'Harlow Car': lvs mid-green, shallowly denticulate; peduncles 7–10cm; fls large, creamy white. 'Mary Curle': lvs pale green, broad-lanceolate, denticulate; peduncles 5–7cm; infl. to 18-fld; pedicels farinose; cal. farinose; cor. trumpet-shaped, eye white-farinose, long narrow tube. 'Mrs J.H. Wilson': rosette-forming; lvs grey-green, broad-lanceolate to obovate, young lvs sharply serrate at tip; peduncle to 7cm; infl. many-fld, cor. purple, centre white, fragrant. 'Ruby': fls small, wine-red, centre white. 'Rufus': lvs to 7×5cm, pale green, shallowly denticulate; peduncles to 9cm; infl. 16-fld, cor. brick-red, to 3cm diam., eye golden yellow, lobes overlapping, notched. 'Wharfedale Buttercup': lvs 6–10×4–5cm, obovate, irregularly serrate, farinose when young; peduncle 10–12.5cm; fls 15–20, to 3cm diam., sulphur-yellow, throat darker yellow. Z5.

***P. pulverulenta*** Duthie. (21) Lvs to 30×10cm, obovate or oblanceolate, dentate, apex obtuse, base tapering to winged petiole. Peduncle slender, to 90cm, farinose; infl. with many superposed, many-fld whorls; bracts subulate, farinose; pedicels to 2cm, spreading, farinose; cal. to 1cm, farinose, lobes triangular; cor. deep red, to 2.5cm diam., eye darker red or purple, lobes obcordate, deeply notched. Summer. China. Bartley Hybrids: fls pink and pastel. Z6.

***P. redolens*** Balf. f. & Ward. (16) Low subshrub; rhiz. short, woody, covered by marcescent lvs. Lvs 6–12×1.5–3cm, elliptic to oblong, apex rounded, base attenuate to distinct petiole, rugose to bullate above, somewhat farinose beneath. Peduncle 10–20cm; infl. a single 5–12-fld umbel; pedicels 1.5–2cm; cal. to 0.8cm; cor. to 2.5cm diam., pale purple-pink or lilac-pink to pinkish-cream, or white, fading pale violet, eye yellow, lobes obcordate or rounded, deeply emarginate at apex, tube 1–1.5cm. China (W Yunnan).

***P. reidii*** Duthie. (37) Rosettes lax. Lvs 3–20×2–3cm, oblong or lanceolate, crenate or lobulate, apex obtuse, base narrowing to winged petiole with long hairs. Peduncles slender, 6–15cm, farinose above; infl. 3–10-fld, compact, fragrant; bracts 1–3mm, often lobed; cal. cup-shaped, 6–8mm, lobes ovate, farinose; cor. white, 2–2.5cm diam., tube 2–2.5cm, globular, pendent, lobes broad-ovate, emarginate. Early summer. Himalaya (Kashmir to C Nepal). var. ***williamsii*** Ludlow. More robust. Fls pale blue to white. W & C Nepal. Z6.

***P. reinii*** Franch. (14) Lvs 2–26cm, orbicular to reniform, shallowly 7–9-lobed, crenate to dentate, villous beneath, apex obtuse, base cordate. Peduncle 2–10cm; infl. 1–3-fld; bracts 1.5–2cm, adpressed; pedicels to 2.5cm; cal. to 2cm, tubular to campanulate, lobes ovate; cor. rose to purple, 1.5–3cm diam., eye yellow, lobes obcordate, deeply emarginate. Early summer. Japan. Z7.

***P. renifolia*** Volg. (6) Lvs 3–5cm diam., rounded to reniform, base cordate, dull green and rugose above, densely white-tomentose beneath, margins unevenly crenate-dentate to subentire, petiole slender, narrowly winged. Peduncle short or equalling lvs; fls 2–3 in umbel; bracts 1–3, lanceolate; pedicels 2cm, finely hairy; calyx campanulate to tubular-campanulate, lobes triangular, acute; cor. to cm, blue-violet with yellow eye, exannulate, lobes obovate, emarginate, tube much exceeding cal., yellow-green. Caucasus.

***P. reptans*** Hook. f. ex Watt. (32-II) Forming mats of prostrate rosettes. Lvs 0.4–0.6cm, ovate to rounded, margin revolute, deeply dentate, petiole short. Fls sessile, solitary; cor. to 1.5cm diam., pale purple to pink, eye white, lobes obcordate, deeply emarginate, tube 4× cal. Himalaya (Pakistan to C Nepal).

***P. reticulata*** Wallich. (22) Lvs to 4–40×2–10cm, long-petiolate, oblong to ovate, dentate, apex obtuse, base cordate, petiole to 30cm. Peduncle 20–40cm; infl. lax, few- to many-fld; bracts to 2.5cm, lanceolate; pedicels 1–5cm, farinose, outer bracts pendent, inner bracts erect; cal. 5–10mm, campanulate, farinose, lobes lanceolate, recurved; cor. yellow or white, 1–2cm diam., funnel-shaped, farinose within, lobes obovate, slightly emarginate. Summer. C Nepal to SE Tibet. Z6.

***P. rosea*** Royle. (28) Lvs partially developed in flower, enlarging to 20×4cm in fruit, obovate to oblanceolate, crenate or denticulate, apex obtuse, base narrowed to winged petiole. Peduncle 3–10cm at flowering, 20–50cm in fruit; infl. lax, 4–12-fld; bracts to 1cm, lanceolate, long-acuminate, base pouched; pedicels to 1cm; cal. to 8mm, campanulate, lobes broad-lanceolate, acute or acuminate; cor. rose-pink to red, 1–2cm diam., eye yellow, lobes obcordate, deeply cleft. Summer. NW Himalaya. 'Gigas': to 10cm; fls large, bright pink. 'Grandiflora': to 20cm; fls large, rich pink. 'Micia Visser de Geer' ('Delight'): fls clear soft pink. Z6.

***P. roxburghii*** Balakr. (25) Lvs 5–20×2–12cm including petiole, ovate to orbicular, crenate, sometimes yellow-farinose below, apex obtuse or rounded, base cordate; petiole thick, as long or longer than lamina. Peduncle 10–30cm; infl. 2–16-fld, lax; bracts to 1cm, linear to awl-shaped, glandular; pedicels to 2cm, farinose; cal. 1–1.5cm, campanulate, farinose, lobes oblong to oblanceolate, acute or obtuse; cor. pink to purple, 1.5–2cm diam., eye golden-yellow, lobes obcordate, entire or slightly crenate. Early summer. W Nepal to Sikkim.

***P. rusbyi*** Greene. (4) Lvs 3–8×1–2.5cm, elliptic to spathulate, erect, efarinose, entire or denticulate, glandular especially beneath, apex acute, obtuse or rounded; petiole winged, very short, to 2× length of lamina, sheathing at base. Peduncle 6–20cm, often white-farinose above; infl. frequently secund, 4–12-fld; bracts ovate to lanceolate, 3–8mm, farinose, base overlapping; peduncle 1–3.5cm, white-farinose; cal. tubular to subcampanulate, lobes lanceolate, acute, tinged purple; cor. annulate or exannulate, rose-red to magenta to deep purple, to 2cm diam., eye yellow bordered crimson, tube pale green, lobes obcordate, somewhat incurved. Spring. SE Arizona, SW New Mexico. Z7.

***P. sapphirina*** Hook. f. & Thoms. (17) Lvs 0.5–1×0.2–0.5cm, oblanceolate to obovate, attenuate to short, broad petiole, white-hairy above, margin coarsely dentate. Peduncle to 5cm, very slender; fls 1–4, nodding; cal. to 2.5cm; cor. to 0.5×0.6cm, violet-purple to blue, lobes ovate, deeply emarginate, tube very short. E Himalaya.

***P. saxatilis*** Komar. (10-I) Lvs 6–20×3–6cm, oblong to ovate-oblong, shallowly dissected into irregular, rounded, entire or dentate lobes, crisped, covered with long hairs, apex obtuse or rounded, base cordate; petiole narrowly winged. Peduncles to 30cm; infl. 3–15-fld; bracts shorter than pedicels, lanceolate, acute; pedicels 2–4cm, glabrous or slightly pubesc.; cal. subglabrous, conically enlarged, lobes lanceolate, acute; cor. rose-lilac, to 2.5cm diam., lobes obovate, deeply emarginate. Summer. NE Asia. Z4.

***P. scandinavica*** Bruun. (29-I) Lvs 2–3×0.5–0.8cm, narrowly obovate to spathulate, apex obtuse or rounded, base attenuate to winged petiole, margins denticulate to subentire, lightly or not farinose above, densely white-farinose beneath. Peduncle 4–10(–18)cm; infl. a symmetrical 2–10-fld umbel; bracts to 0.8cm, linear-lanceolate to subulate, somewhat bulbous at base; pedicels to 1.5cm; cal. to 7mm, tubular, ridged, dark-tinged, deeply lobed, farinose, glandular; cor. 0.9–1.5cm, purple-violet, eye yellow, annulate, lobes obovate, deeply emarginate, tube to 0.9cm. Norway, W Sweden.

***P. scapigera*** Craib. (20-III) Lvs to 15×4cm, oblong to spathulate, to elliptic or obovate, sharply and irregularly dentate or lobulate, apex obtuse, base narrowed to short petiole, later lvs enlarged, with longer petiole. Peduncle less than 4cm at flowering, elongating later; infl. few-fld; pedicels slender, 2.5–5cm; cal. narrow-campanulate, farinose, lobes ovate, obtuse; cor. pink to purple, to 3cm diam., yellow eye bordered white, lobes broad-obovate, toothed. Spring. W Himalaya. Z5.

***P. scotica*** Hook. (29-I) Farinose, homostylous. Lvs 1–5×0.4–1.5cm, elliptic, oblong or spathulate, entirely or remotely crenulate-denticulate, usually abundantly farinose beneath. Peduncles 1–2, 0.5–6cm; infl. 1- to 6-fld; bracts 2–5mm, lanceolate, base subsaccate; pedicels 1–5mm; cal. 4–6mm, campanulate, lobes ovate, obtuse; cor. 5–8mm diam., dark purple with yellow throat, rarely white, lobes obcordate, deeply notched. Spring–autumn. N Scotland. Z4.

***P. secundiflora*** Franch. (22) Lvs 25–30×1–4cm, oblong to obovate or oblanceolate, finely crenate to coarsely serrate, farinose beneath when young, apex acute or obtuse, base narrowed to short petiole. Peduncle 30–60cm, farinose above. Infl. 10–20-fld, more or less secund; bracts 1–1.5cm, farinose, lanceolate; pedicels to 5cm; cal. to 1cm, campanulate, farinose within, lobes lanceolate, acute; cor. red-purple or deep rose-red, 1.5–2.5cm diam., pendent, lobes obovate to oblong, rounded. Summer. W China. Z6.

***P. serratifolia*** Franch. (21) Lvs to 20×5cm, oblong-ovate to obovate, apex rounded, base attenuate to petiole, margin coarsely and irregularly dentate. Peduncle to 45cm; infl. a single umbel or 2 superposed umbels, with 5–10 fls in each; pedicels 1–2cm; cal. to 0.7cm; cor. to 2.5cm diam., yellow, with streaks of orange running between throat and apex of lobes, lobes obovate, entire or shallowly emarginate, tube 1–1.5cm. W China (Yunnan, SE Tibet), N Burma.

***P. sieboldii*** E. Morr. (10-I) Lvs 10–40×2–7cm, ovate to oblong including petiole-ovate with numerous dentate lobes, base cordate; petiole 5–10cm. Peduncle 30cm; infl. 6–10-fld; bracts to 2cm, linear to lanceolate; pedicels to 3.5cm; cal. to 2cm, funnel-shaped, spreading, enlarging in fr., lobes lanceolate, acute; cor. white, pink or purple, 2.5–3cm diam., eye white, lobes broad-obcordate, cleft. Early summer. Japan, NE Asia. 'Alba': fls white, petals entire. 'Fimbriated Red': fls bright cerise, petals deeply cut and notched. 'Istaka': fls white edged and backed purple-pink, deeply fimbriate. 'Kuisakigarri': fls white, very finely cut, resembling a snowflake. 'Musashino': fls large, pale rose above, darker beneath. 'Shi-un': fls finely fimbriate, red-lavender fading to lavender blue. 'Snowflake': fls scarcely cut, wide-petalled, snow white. 'Sumina': fls deep nisteria blue, petals slender-clawed and retuse. 'Yubisugata': fls broad, jaggedly cut, undersurface white, upper surface lavender with a white 'eye'. Z5.

***P. sikkimensis*** Hook. f. (22) Lvs 10–40×2–7cm, elliptic or oblong to oblanceolate, shining, serrate or dentate, apex rounded or acute, base tapering to an attenuate or short, winged petiole. Peduncle 15–90cm; infl. many-fld, single or sometimes superposed; bracts to 2cm, lanceolate, farinose, base swollen; pedicels 5–10cm, farinose, pendulous, becoming erect in fr.; cal. campanulate, to 1–1.5cm, densely yellow-farinose, lobes lanceolate, acute, recurved; cor. yellow or occasionally cream-white, to 2.5cm diam., pendent, funnel-shaded, lobes oblong to obcordate, entire or emarginate, lightly farinose within. Early summer. W Nepal to SW China. 'Tilman no. 2': 45–60cm; fls rich yellow, strongly scented. var. ***pudibunda*** (Balf. f. & Cooper) W.W. Sm. & Fletcher. A high altitude extreme; in cultivation practically indistinguishable from the species itself. var. ***hopeana*** (Balf. f. & Cooper) W.W. Sm. & Fletcher. Plants smaller, reduced in all parts. Fls white or pale yellow becoming white. Bhutan, Tibet, 4500–5000m. Z6.

***P. sinensis*** Sab. ex Lindl. (8) Softly pubesc. Lvs 7.5–10cm, broad-ovate to orbicular, with 4–5 pairs of dentate lobes, often red beneath, base cordate; petiole to 18cm. Peduncles several, 10–15cm; infl. of 1 or more 6–10 fld whorls; bracts to 2cm, lanceolate, entire or serrate; pedicels 5–8cm; cal. 1–1.5cm, conic, base more or less concave, lobes short, triangular to ovate; cor. in many colours, usually purple to pink, 2–5cm diam., eye yellow, lobes obcordate, entire or incised. Winter–spring. China. 'Filicifolia': lvs crisped. 'Fimbriata': fls fringed or crested. 'Stellata': fls in superposed umbels. Z8.

***P. sinopurpurea*** Balf. f. (24-III) Lvs to 5–35×1.5–5cm, oblong-lanceolate, finely and evenly serrate, yellow-farinose beneath, apex acute or obtuse, base narrowed to petiole; petiole broad, winged, to 20cm. Peduncle 30–45cm, farinose above; infl. 6–12-fld; bracts to 1cm, ovate to lanceolate; pedicels to 2.5cm, pendent; cal. tubular, purple, farinose within, lobes lanceolate; cor. violet, to 3cm diam., eye pale, lobes round, overlapping. Summer. China. Z5.

***P. soldanelloides*** Watt. (37) Minute, mat-forming, glabrous and efarinose. Lvs 0.8–1.5cm, deeply pinnately lobed, apex rounded, tapering to relatively long petiole. Peduncle 2.5–4cm; fls solitary; cal. campanulate, dull black-green, lobes deeply incised, triangular-ovate; cor. 1–1.5cm long, white, broadly campanulate, nodding, lobes oblong-ovate, emarginate or dentate at apex. E Himalaya (C Nepal to SE Tibet).

***P. sonchifolia*** Franch. (20-IV) Lvs to 20×5cm, oblong to obovate, usually glabrous, serrate, lobulate, apex obtuse, base narrowed to short, broad-winged petiole. Peduncle robust, elongating during flowering, from very short, obscured by lvs, to 30cm in fruit; infl. 3–20-fld; bracts very short, ovate; pedicels 1–1.5cm, stiff, farinose; cal. campanulate, 5–10mm, lobes blunt, entire or toothed, farinose; cor. variable blue to purple, to 2.5cm diam., eye yellow, edged white, lobes obovate to suborbicular, entire or slightly toothed. Early spring. W China. Z6.

***P. spectabilis*** Tratt. (2-I) Lvs 1.5–10×1–4cm, outermost pressed to ground, broad oval-rhomboid to obovate to elliptic or oblong, apex obtuse to acute, shining, with scattered, minute depressions above appearing as black dots, margin cartilaginous. Peduncle 2–15cm; infl. 2–5-fld; bracts 2–15mm, linear-lanceolate, red-tinged; pedicels 3–20mm, erect; cal. 3–15mm, tubular, lobes ovate or lanceolate, stained purple; cor. 2–4cm diam., pink-red to lilac, lobes obovate, deeply emarginate, glandular beneath. Early summer. Italian Alps. Z6.

***P. specuicola*** Rydb. (29-I) Rosettes upright. Lvs 4–13×7–20cm, spathulate, sinuate-dentate, crisped, apex obtuse to rounded, densely white-farinose beneath, less so above, base narrowing gradually to short petiole. Peduncles 10–16cm, farinose above; infl. 2–10-fld; bracts 4–10mm, lanceolate, base thickened; pedicels farinose, 5–10mm, lengthening in fr.; cal. campanulate, farinose, 6–9mm, lobes lanceolate, acute; cor. exannulate, violet, to 1cm diam., eye yellow, tube yellow. Capsule larger than cal. Spring. SE US. Z7.

***P. suffrutescens*** A. Gray. (3) Glabrous, glandular throughout. Rhiz. and stem long, branching, woody, bearing rosettes at branch apices and persistent lvs some way down from apices. Rosettes openly rosulate. Lvs 1.5–3×0.5–1cm, broadest near apex, cuneate to spathulate, thick, fleshy, upper half of lamina crenate to dentate or serrate, or deeply dentate with 3–8 teeth, dusky green above, pale green to yellow-green below, apex rounded, base tapering gradually to a broad, short, winged petiole. Peduncles 3–13cm; infl. symmetrical to upright, 2–10-fld; bracts 2–6mm, lanceolate to linear; pedicels 5–15mm; cal. campanulate, 5–7mm, lobes lanceolate to acute; cor. annulate to exannulate, rose pink to red or purple, to 2cm diam., eye and tube yellow, lobes obovate, emarginate. Capsule 4mm diam., globose. Spring. SW US (California). Z8.

***P. takedana*** Tatew. (14) Lvs 8–16×3–6cm, orbicular to reniform, deeply cordate at base, 5–7-lobed, widely dentate, softly hairy, petiole long. Peduncle 8–15cm, slender; infl. an umbel of 2–3 fls, occasionally 2 superimposed umbels; pedicels 8–12cm; cor. to 1.5cm diam., white, campanulate to funnel-shaped, lobes obovate-oblong, semi-erect. Japan (Hokkaido).

***P. tanneri*** King ssp. ***tanneri***. (20-III) Not in cult. ssp. ***tsariensis*** (W.W. Sm.) A. Richards. Lvs 8–13×1.5–2cm, elliptic to ovate-lanceolate, crenate, apex obtuse, base broad-cuneate, rounded or subcordate. Peduncle to 15cm; infl. 1–8-fld; pedicels to 2cm; cal. 5–10mm, lobes ovate or lanceolate, spreading; cor. blue to purple, to 3cm diam., eye yellow, lobes broad-ovate, emarginate. Spring. SE Tibet.

***P. tibetica*** Watt. (30-II) Lvs 1–5×0.2–1cm, ovate, elliptic or spathulate, entire, fleshy, apex obtuse, base tapering to winged petiole, to 5cm. Peduncles several, 3–15cm; infl. 1–10-fld; bracts to 1cm, narrow-oblong, obtuse or acute, base short-auriculate; pedicels to 8cm; cal. to 5mm, narrow-campanulate, 5-ribbed, lobes lanceolate, acute; cor. pink, 5–10mm diam., eye yellow, tube less than 1cm, lobes obcordate, deeply notched. Mid summer. Tibet, Nepal, Sikkim. Z6.

***P. tschuktschorum*** Kjellmann. (24-III) Usually efarinose. Lvs lanceolate to spathulate, 3–8×0.5–1.5cm, irregularly dentate or entire, apex acute to subacute, base tapering gradually to winged petiole shorter than to equal length of lamina. Peduncles glabrous, to 15cm, rarely 20cm; infl. usually 3–5-fld, rarely more than 10-fld; bracts narrow lanceolate to acute; pedicels slender, 1–1.5cm, commonly white-farinose; cal. campanulate, 4–6mm, lobes lanceolate, occasionally black, usually white-farinose within; cor. pink, to 2cm diam., tube 6–10mm, lobes entire, subspathulate. Capsule cylindric, exceeding cal. Summer. N Asia, Alaska. Z5.

***P. tyrolensis*** Schott. (2-VII) Viscid. Lvs 1–3×0.5–1.5cm, suborbicular to broadly obovate, finely dentate, ciliate, cartilaginous, fleshy, densely pubesc., glandular hairs pale, withered lvs persistent. Peduncle 0.5–2cm; infl. 1–2-fld; bracts 2mm, linear to oblong; pedicels to 2.5mm; cal. 5–8mm, campanulate, lobes ovate, obtuse; cor. rose, 1–2.5cm diam., lobes obovate, emarginate. Summer. S Tyrol. Z5.

***P. ×variabilis*** Goupil. *(P. veris × P. variabilis.)* (5) Fertile, very variable between parents.

***P. ×venusta*** Host. *(P. auricula × P. carniolica.)* (2) Rare, fertile. Fls red with white centre, to rose, to crimson, to purple or brown. Otherwise very variable. Z6.

***P. veris*** L. COWSLIP. (5) Rosettes upright in fl., becoming open in fruit. Lvs 5–20×2–6cm at fl., larger when mature, ovate to oblong-ovate, crenate to erose-crenate, sometimes entire, recurved when young, apex rounded, base narrowing abruptly to winged petiole, sheathing at base, pubesc. above, subglabrous to white-tomentose beneath. Peduncles 6–30cm, pubesc.; infl. 2–16-fld, fragrant; bracts 2–7mm, pubesc., linear to lanceolate; pedicels 3–20mm, unequal, pubesc.; cal. broadly tubular to campanulate, baggy, 8–15mm, lobes triangular to rounded, 5-ridged, pubesc. especially ridges, mucrons 1 to several; cor. exannulate, yellow, 1–1.5cm diam., orange mark at base of each lobe, lobes obcordate. Capsule ovoid, 6–10mm diam., included in cal. Late spring–early summer. Europe, W Asia. ssp. ***canescens*** (Opiz) Hayek. Lamina grey-tomentose beneath, gradually attenuate to petiole. Cal. to 1.6–2cm; cor. 0.8–2cm diam., only slightly concave. SC Europe, S France, N Spain. ssp. ***columnae*** (Ten.) Ludi. Lamina ovate, cordate at base, white-tomentose beneath. Cal. 1.6–2cm; cor. 1–2.2cm diam., flat, tube longer than calyx. S Europe, N Turkey. ssp. ***macrocalyx*** (Bunge) Ludi. Lamina elliptic, more or less grey-tomentose beneath, often hairless, gradually attenuate to long petiole. Cal. 1.5–2cm, often very hairy; cor. 1.8–2.8cm diam., tube exceeding calyx. SE Russia, N Asia, E Turkey. Z5.

***P. verticillata*** Forssk. (1) Lvs 10–30cm, lanceolate to ovate-lanceolate, acute, attenuate to short broad-winged petiole, margin irregularly sharp-serrulate, white-farinose beneath. Peduncle 10–60cm; infl. of 2–4 superposed many-fld whorls; bracts leaf-like, to 3.5cm, ovate-lanceolate, serrulate; pedicels to 2cm; cal. 0.8cm, campanulate, farinose, lobes ovate-lanceolate, entire or irregularly serrate; cor. to 2cm diam., yellow, fragrant, lobes broad-ovate, emarginate. SW Arabian Peninsula (Saudi Arabia, Yemen, Aden), NE Africa (Ethiopia, Somalia).

***P. vialii*** Delav. ex Franch. (36) Lvs 10–30×4–7cm, broad-lanceolate to oblong, pubesc., irregularly dentate, apex obtuse, base tapering to winged petiole. Peduncle stout, 30–40cm, farinose above. Infl. in dense spikes; bracts linear; cal. globose-campanulate, 5mm, red in bud, later pink; cor. blue to violet, to 1cm diam., deflexed, lobes ovate, acute. Summer. China. Z7.

***P. villosa*** Wulf. (2-VI) Efarinose. Lvs 2–15×1–4cm, broadly to narrowly obovate or spathulate to oblong, dentate toward apex, sometimes entire, fleshy, viscid, glandular-pubesc., producing red to black or brown secretion. Peduncle 2–15cm, usually longer than lvs in fruit, red-glandular-pubesc.; infl. 4–12-fld; bracts 1–5mm, ovate to obovate, more or less scarious; pedicels 2–15mm; cal. 3–6.5cm, campanulate, lobes triangular, obtuse; cor. pink to lilac, to 2.5cm diam., centre white, lobes obovate, emarginate. Capsule as long or slightly longer than cal. Early summer. Tyrol, Switzerland. Z5.

***P. ×vochinensis*** Gusmus. *(P. minima × P. wulfeniana.)* (2) Probably fertile. Very wide range of forms, all small, 1–2-fld. Those resembling *P. wulfeniana* with brilliantly coloured fls. E Dolomites. Z6.

***P. vulgaris*** Huds. PRIMROSE. (5) Rosette openly rosulate. Lvs 5–25×2–6cm, oblanceolate to obovate, irregularly dentate to crenate, often erose, glabrous above, pubesc. beneath, apex rounded, base gradually tapering into a short, winged, sheathing petiole. Peduncle absent; infl. to 25-fld, sometimes fragrant; bracts 10–15mm, linear; pedicels 6–20cm, pubesc., semi-pendent in fl., decumbent in fr.; cal. tubular, 10–22mm, prominently 5-ridged, ridges pubesc., lobes lanceolate, acute; cor. exannulate or annulate, pale yellow, 2.5–4cm diam., lobes ovate, emarginate, base orange. Capsule ovoid, 2–2.5cm diam., brown, sticky. Spring. W & S Europe. ssp. ***balearica*** (Willk.) W.W. Sm. & Forr. Similar to *P. vulgaris*. Petiole longer than lamina, narrowly winged, lvs glaucescent beneath. Fls white, very fragrant. ssp. ***sibthorpii*** (Hoffsgg.) W.W. Sm. & Forr. Lvs contracted more or less abruptly into petiole, slightly pubesc. below. Fls usually red or purple. E Balkan Peninsula. Cvs include forms with single or double fls, in a wide range of colours. 'Hose in Hose': an abnormality with one cor. within another. 'Jack in the Green': abnormality with cal. leafy. Z6.

***P. waltonii*** G. Watt ex Balf. f. (22) Lvs 8–30×2–7cm, elliptic-oblong to oblanceolate, sharply toothed, apex rounded, base cuneate, petiole winged, equal to lamina. Peduncle to 60cm; infl. few to many-fld; bracts to 2cm, lanceolate, tinged purple, farinose; pedicels 1.5–7cm, cal. campanulate, to 1cm, tinged purple, farinose, lobes triangular, often recurved; cor. pink to deep wine-purple, to 2cm diam., pendent, funnel-shaped, with farinose bands within. Early summer. SE Tibet, Bhutan. Z6.

***P. warshenewskiana*** B. Fedtsch. (28) Lvs 1.5–7×1.5–1.8cm, oblong or obovate to oblanceolate, apex rounded or obtuse, base attenuate to short winged petiole, margin finely denticulate. Peduncle very short, or 2–5cm; infl. a 1–8-fld umbel; pedicels to 1cm, increasing to 2.5cm in fruit; cal. to 0.5cm; cor. to 1.2cm diam., bright rose or pink, with yellow eye surrounded by narrow white zone, lobes obcordate, deeply emarginate, tube to 1.5cm. C Asia to N Himalaya.

***P. whitei*** W.E. Sm. (20-IV) Lvs 2–10cm in flower, later to 30×1–3cm, spathulate to oblong-spathulate, denticulate, slightly farinose above and beneath, apex obtuse, base tapering to winged petiole. Peduncle very short, later elongating; infl. 5–10-fld; pedicels 3–5cm; cal. to 1cm, lobes oblong, fringed; cor. blue to violet, to 2.5cm diam., eye white or yellow-green, lobes obovate, regularly toothed. Spring. E Himalaya. *P. bhutanica* Fletcher (*P. whitei* 'Sherriff's Variety') was distinguished by its more conspicuously dentate perianth lobes; botanically it is no more than a form of *P. whitei*, but the name persists in horticulture. 'Arduaine': vigorous, sterile; lvs narrow, serrate; fls ice-blue, with pale yellow eye. Z6.

***P. wilsonii*** Dunn. (21) Lvs to 20×5cm, evergreen, oblanceolate, denticulate, glaucous, apex rounded, base narrowing to winged petiole. Peduncle to 70cm; infl. of 3–6, superposed whorls; bracts linear, to 1cm; pedicels to 2cm; cor. purple, to 2cm diam., concave, lobes round, entire to shallowly emarginate. Summer. China.

***P. wollastonii*** Balf. (37) Rosettes compact. Lvs 2.5–5×1.25–2.5cm, oblanceolate to obovate, dentate, crenate or subentire, densely pubesc., farinose or efarinose beneath, apex obtuse, base tapering to short, winged petiole. Peduncle 12–20cm; infl. 2–6-fld; bracts lanceolate, cal. cup-shaped, to 5mm, lobes triangular-pointed, purple or green; cor. light or dark purple, or blue, to 2.5cm diam., bell-shaped, very fragrant, tube 1.5–2cm, farinose. Spring. C to E Nepal, Tibet. Z6.

***P. wulfeniana*** Schott. (2-I) Lvs 1.5–4×0.5–1.2cm, lanceolate or elliptic to oblanceolate to obovate, patent when mature, shining, coriaceous, entire, densely glandular-pubesc., glands concealed by non-farinose secretions. Peduncle 0.5–7cm; infl. 1–2-fld; bracts 3–15mm, lanceolate to linear; pedicels 2–8mm; cal. 6–12mm, tubular, lobes ovate, obtuse; cor. rose-red to lilac, to 2.5cm diam., lobes obovate, deeply cleft. Spring. Austrian Alps to S Carpathians. Z5.

***P. yuparensis*** Tak. (29-I) Lvs 1.5–3×0.5–1cm, oblanceolate to elliptic, apex obtuse or rounded, gradually attenuate to short, winged petiole, efarinose above, sparsely white-farinose beneath when young, margins finely denticulate. Peduncle 4.5–6cm; fls 2–3 in umbel; pedicels to 1.3cm; cal. to 0.7cm; cor. to 1.5cm diam., purple, lobes obcordate, shallowly emarginate, tube to 1.4cm. Japan. Z6.

***P. acaulis*** (L.) Hill. See *P. vulgaris*.
***P. albo-cincta*** Widm. See *P. auricula*.
***P. balbisii*** Lehm. See *P. auricula*.
***P. bhutanica*** Fletcher. See *P. whitei*.
***P. biflora*** Huter. See *P. ×floerkeana*.
***P. ×bilekii*** Sunderm. See *P. ×forsteri* f. *bilekii*.
***P. carpathica*** (Griseb. & Schenk) Fuss. See *P. elatior*.
***P. ciliata*** Moretti. See *P. auricula*.
***P. comberi*** W.W. Sm. See *P. magellanica*.
***P. commutata*** Schott. See *P. villosa* ssp. *commutata*.
***P. crispa*** Balf. f. & W.W. Sm. See *P. glomerata*.
***P. crispata*** Balf. f. & W.W. Sm. See *P. capitata* ssp. *crispata*.
***P. decipiens*** Duby. See *P. magellanica*.
***P. ×deschmannii*** Gusmus. See *P. ×vochinensis*.
***P. elatior*** ssp. ***meyeri*** (Rupr.) Valent. & Lamond. See *P. amoena*.
***P. exigua*** L. See *P. farinosa* ssp. *exigua*.
***P. fauriae*** Franch. See *P. modesta* var. *fauriae*.
***P. fauriae*** var. ***samanimontana*** Tatew. See *P. modesta* var. *fauriae*.
***P. finnmarchica*** Jacq. See *P. nutans*.
***P. grandis*** Trautv. See *Sredinskya grandis*.
***P. ×helenae*** Arends. See *P.* Pruhonicensis Hybrids.
***P. helodoxa*** Balf. f. See *P. prolifera*.
***P. imperialis*** Jungh. See *P. prolifera*.
***P. ×juliana*** Rosenheim & May. See *P.* Pruhonicensis Hybrids.
***P. ×kelleri*** Widm. See *P. ×forsteri* f. *kelleri*.
***P. laurentiana*** Fern. See *P. mistassinica* var. *macropoda*.
***P. lichiangensis*** Forr. See *P. polyneura*.
***P. longiflora*** All. See *P. halleri*.
***P. macrocalyx*** Schur. See *P. veris*.
***P. matsumurae*** Petitm. See *P. modesta* var. *matsumurae*.
***P. moorcroftiana*** Wallich. See *P. macrophylla*.
***P. mooreana*** Balf. f. & W.W. Sm. See *P. capitata* ssp. *mooreana*.
***P. nivalis*** var. ***macrophylla*** (D. Don) Pax. See *P. macrophylla*.
***P. nutans*** Delavay ex Franch. non Georgi. See *P. flaccida*.
***P. oenensis*** Thomas ex Gremli. See *P. daonensis*.
***P. officinalis*** (L.) Hill. See *P. veris*.
***P. ×pruhoniciana*** Zeeman. See *P.* Pruhonicensis Hybrids.
***P. pruhonicensis*** Zeeman ex Bergmans. See *P.* Pruhonicensis Hybrids.
***P. ×pruhonitziana*** Zeeman. See *P.* Pruhonicensis Hybrids.
***P. rotundifolia*** Wallich. See *P. roxburghii*.
***P. rubra*** J.F. Gmel. See *P. hirsuta*.
***P. sibirica*** Jacq. See *P. nutans*.
***P. sibthorpii*** Koch non Hoffsgg.. See *P. vulgaris*.
***P. sibthorpii*** Hoffsgg. non Koch. See *P. vulgaris* ssp. *sibthorpii*.
***P. smithiana*** Craib. See *P. prolifera*.
***P. ×steinii*** Obrist. See *P. forsteri* f. *steinii*.
***P. strumosa*** Balf. f. & Cooper. See *P. calderiana* ssp. *strumosa*.
***P. stuartii*** var. ***purpurea*** (Royle) Watt. See *P. macrophylla*.
***P. tsariensis*** W.W. Sm. See *P. tanneri* ssp. *tsariensis*.
***P. uralensis*** Fisch. See *P. veris*.
***P. veitchii*** Duthie. See *P. polyneura*.
***P. viscosa*** Vill. non All. See *P. hirsuta*.
***P. viscosa*** All. non Vill. See *P. latifolia*.
***P. vittata*** Franch. See *P. secundiflora*.
***P. wettsteinii*** Wiem. See *P. ×intermedia*.
***P. winteri*** Will. Wats. See *P. edgeworthii*.

**PRIMULACEAE** Vent. PRIMROSE FAMILY Dicot. 22 genera and 800 species of herbs, rarely shrubby. Leaves spirally arranged, opposite or whorled, usually simple and toothed (pinnatisect in *Hottonia*) often forming a basal rosette; stipules absent. Flowers bisexual, regular (irregular in *Coris*), often heterostylous, in umbels, panicles, heads or solitary; calyx 5 united petals into a short or long tube, with spreading or reflexed lobes; stamens 5, opposite corolla lobes and attached to the tube, anthers introrse; staminodes sometimes present and alternate with stamens; ovary superior, of 5 fused carpels (half inferior in *Samolus*), 1-loculed, with rudimentary partitions at the base; style 1; ovules 5 to numerous, on free central placenta. Fruit a capsule, rarely indehiscent; seeds 1 to numerous; endosperm copious, starchless, with reserves of oil, protein and amylose. Subcosmopolitan, but especially N hemisphere. *Anagallis, Androsace, Ardisiandra, Coris, Cortusa, Cyclamen, Dionysia, Dodecatheon, Douglasia, Hottonia, Lysimachia, Omphalogramma, Primula, Samolus, Soldanella, Sredinskya, Trientalis, Vitaliana.*

## Prinos L.

***P. ambiguus*** Michx. See *Ilex ambigua*.
***P. dubia*** G. Don. See *Ilex amelanchier*.
***P. lucidus*** Ait. See *Ilex coriacea*.
***P. glaber*** L. See *Ilex glabra*.
***P. laevigatus*** Pursh. See *Ilex laevigata*.
***P. verticillatus*** L. See *Ilex verticillata*.

**Prinsepia** Royle (For James Prinsep (1799–1840), Secretary of the Asiatic Society of Bengal.) Rosaceae. 3–4 species of deciduous spiny shrubs. Leaves alternate, simple, entire or serrulate, usually clustered; stipules minute, lanceolate, deciduous or persistent. Flowers in short, 1–4-flowered, axillary racemes; calyx cup-shaped, persistent, lobes 5, broad, short, concave; petals 5, rounded, spreading; stamens 10–30, filaments short; carpels 1, stigma capitate, style subterminal, inserted near base, ovules 2. Fruit an ellipsoid, thin-fleshy drupe; stone somewhat sculptured. Himalaya to N China and Taiwan.

CULTIVATION *Prinsepia* spp. are grown for their distinctive arching habit, which displays to advantage the fragrant spring flowers, carried in the leaf axils. The flowers, carried on the previous season's wood in *P. uniflora* and *P. sinensis*, are most plentiful on plants grown in full sun, and in long hot summers may be followed by attractive, juicy and edible fruits. Larger branches often show decorative peeling bark. They are hardy to −15°C/5°F. Grow in well-drained moderately fertile soil, in full sun or light shade. In temperate climates, better fruiting and flowering is achieved on a south- or southwest-facing wall. Prune only to remove dead wood. Propagate by softwood cuttings in a closed case with bottom heat, or by seed stratified overwinter and sown in spring.

***P. sinensis*** (Oliv.) Oliv. To 2m+, rather loose, spreading. Branches light grey-brown, with spines to 1cm. Lvs to 8×1.3cm, ovate-lanceolate to lanceolate, acuminate, bright green, fine-ciliate, entire or slightly serrulate; petioles slender. Fls bright yellow, 1.5cm diam., clustered along 1-year-old branches; pedicels 1cm; stamens 10. Fr. ovoid or subglobose, 1.5cm, red to purple; stone ovoid, flattened. Spring. Manchuria. Z4.

***P. uniflora*** Batal. To 1.5m, lax, spreading. Young shoots glabrous; branches ashy grey, with spines to 1cm. Lvs to 6×0.8cm, linear-oblong to narrow-oblong, somewhat acute or rounded, dark glossy green above, lighter beneath, glabrous, entire or remotely serrulate; petioles short. Fls white, 1.5cm diam., 1–3-fasciculate; pedicels to 5mm; pet. 5mm diam.; stamens 10, anth. yellow. Fr. cherry-like, to 1.5cm diam., dark red to maroon, short-stalked; stone ovoid, flattened. Spring. NW China. Z5.

For synonymy see *Plagiospermum*.

**Prionopsis** Nutt. (From Gk *prion*, saw, and *opsis*, appearance.) Compositae. 1 species, an erect, annual or biennial herb, to 1.5m. Leaves alternate, to 8×4cm, ovate, serrate-ciliate, sessile. Capitula radiate, to 4cm diam., solitary or few in a loose cyme; receptacle flat; phyllaries in 3–4 series, imbricate, linear-lanceolate, outer shorter; ray florets female, fertile, yellow; disc florets numerous, sterile or fertile, yellow. Fruit a cylindrical-ovoid cypsela to 4mm; pappus of bristles. Texas, New Mexico. Z9.

CULTIVATION A drought-resistant species found on prairies, waste ground and similar open, freely draining terrain throughout its range, *P. ciliata* is infrequently cultivated outside its native regions, but is well suited to naturalistic plantings in any deep, gritty and nutritionally poor soils in full sun. Propagate by seed, sown *in situ* or in paper pots to minimize disturbance to the deep taproot.

***P. ciliata*** (Nutt.) Nutt. As for the genus.

For synonymy see *Donia* and *Haplopappus*.

**Prionotes** R. Br. (From Gk *prionion*, a small saw, alluding to the serrated leaves.) Epacridaceae. 1 species, a small prostrate or scandent shrub, in habitat a climbing epiphyte, growing on trunks of dead and decaying trees. Branches glabrous, erect, slender, intertwining. Leaves to 2cm, elliptic or oblong, blunt, dark green, thick-textured, short-petiolate, margins minutely callose-serrate. Flowers solitary in upper leaf axils, pendulous on slender glandular pedicels to 1.25cm, rose pink to scarlet; corolla to 2.5cm, inflated-tubular, subventricose at base, constricted at throat. Summer. Tasmania. Z9.

CULTIVATION Occurring as an understorey epiphyte scrambling over dead or decaying trunks and on rocks on sheltered banks in temperate montane forest or woodland, *Prionotes* is a calcifuge grown for its richly coloured flowers carried in profusion. Suitable for outdoor cultivation in regions that are frost-free or almost so, in a sheltered situation that approximates to its habitat; otherwise, grow in a moist, acid, medium to heavy soil with additional composted bark, in the cool glasshouse in part shade. Propagate by tip cuttings in autumn.

***P. cerinthoides*** R. Br. CLIMBING HEATH. As for the genus.

**Pritchardia** Seem. & H.A. Wendl. (For W.T. Pritchard, 19th-century British official in Polynesia and author of *Polynesian Reminiscences*.) LOULU PALMS. Palmae. Some 37 species of pleonanthic, hermaphrodite palms to *c*20m. Stem solitary, erect, ringed and vertically grooved. Crownshaft absent. Leaves costapalmate, induplicate, marcescent to neatly abscising; sheath tomentose, disintegrating into a mass of fibres; petiole to *c*1m, unarmed, flat or grooved above, convex beneath, tomentose, adaxial hastula a ridge, abaxial hastula absent; blade to *c*1m diam., divided to half radius into segments, segments single-fold, shallowly divided at apex, rigid and held in one plane along rachis, or pendent, scaly beneath, ribs tomentose. Inflorescences interfoliar, solitary or in groups of 2–4, amid several sheathing, tomentose bracts, branched ×3; rachis shorter than peduncle; rachillae straight, curved or flexuous, bearing cream to yellow or orange solitary flowers; calyx shallowly 3-lobed, coriaceous; corolla exceeding calyx, with 3 lobes forming a deciduous cap; stamens 6, filaments basally connate, tubular; pistil 3-celled; stigmas 3-lobed. Fruit spherical, red, green, or dark brown to black, to *c*3.5cm, with apical stigmatic remains. Fiji, Hawaii, Pacific Is. Z10.

CULTIVATION Extremely handsome fan palms, with neat and elegant crowns, occurring predominantly in high rainfall areas, sometimes on volcanic soils. They are suitable for outdoor cultivation in wind-sheltered gardens in the humid tropics and subtropics and require some shade from sun to avoid foliage scorch. They are also attractive as juveniles in the warm glasshouse in cooler regions. Propagate by seed. For cultivation see PALMS.

***P. pacifica*** Seem. & H.A. Wendl. FIJI FAN PALM. Trunk to 10m×30cm. Petioles exceed 1m; lf blades 1m diam., seg. *c*90, acuminate, apices acute, rigid. Infl. to *c*1m, equalling or shorter than lvs; fls yellow. Fr. 1.2cm, black, spherical. Tonga, introduced to Fiji before European colonization.

For illustration see PALMS.

**Pritzelago** Kuntze. (For Georg August Pritzel (1815–1874), German botanist and botanical bibliographer.) Cruciferae. 1 species, a tufted, perennial herb, to 10cm. Stock often woody, branched. Leaves pinnately cut, lobes to 2.5cm, entire, simple hairy or glabrous, petioled. Flowering stems straight, usually leafless. Flowers very small; sepals 4, equal at base; petals 4, equal, entire, abruptly clawed, 3–5×3mm; stamens 6, entire. Fruit a silicle, oblong or ovoid, compressed, 2 seeds per cell, style 1mm. Spring–summer. C & S Europe (mts). Z7.

CULTIVATION Suitable for sinks, troughs and raised beds, and for fine screes on the rock garden (where they will self-seed once established), they are tolerant of part shade and so are well adapted to cooler north-facing banks and pockets. Grown for their dark green mats of pinnatifid foliage and abundant spikes of pure white flowers, carried over long period in spring, and relatively undemanding in their requirements. Cultivate as for *Draba*.

***P. alpina*** (L.) Kuntze. CHAMOIS CRESS. As for the genus. ssp. ***auerswaldii*** (Willk.) Greuter & Burdet. To 15cm. Flowering stems flexuous, leafy. ssp. ***brevicualis*** (Spreng.) Greuter & Burdet. To 5cm. Pet. gradually tapering to claw, 1–2mm wide. Stigma sessile.

For synonymy see *Lepidium* and *Noccaea*.

**Proboscidea** Keller in Schmidel. UNICORN PLANT; DEVIL'S-CLAW; ELEPHANT-TUSK; PROBOSCIS FLOWER. (From Gk *proboskis*, snout, referring to the beaked fruit.) Pedaliaceae. About 9 species of stout annual or perennial herbs, viscid-pubescent or glandular, strongly scented. Leaves opposite or upper sometimes alternate, broad, long-petiolate. Infl. terminal, open, lax; calyx 'spathe-like' 4–5-dentate, split to base on lower side, deciduous; corolla funneliform-campanulate, declined, limb oblique, lobes 5, subequal, spreading. Fruit a 2-valved capsule, falsely 4-locular, crested at least below with prominent incurved apical beak, endocarp woody, sculptured, exocarp fleshy, with age separating from endocarp; seeds numerous, tuberculate. S America north to C US. Z10.

CULTIVATION As for *Martynia*.

***P. arenaria*** (Engelm.) Decne. SAND DEVIL'S CLAW. Stems spreading, 30–50cm. Lvs 3–6cm, suborbicular to reniform, distinctly lobed. Floral bracts broadly oblong to elliptic; cal. to 1cm; cor. tube swollen; limb 3–4cm diam., yellow or copper, often with purple spots. Fr. body 5–6cm, horns 10–12cm, crested both sides. S US (W Texas to S Arizona) to Mexico.

***P. fragrans*** (Lindl.) Decne. SWEET UNICORN PLANT. Similar to *P. louisianica* except lvs generally distinctly 5-lobed; fls fragrant; cor. violet-purple to red-purple, upper lobes often blotched with darker purple, lower lobe with bright yellow band extending into throat. Mexico.

***P. louisianica*** (Mill.) Thell. COMMON UNICORN PLANT; COMMON DEVIL'S CLAW; RAM'S HORN. Annual, minutely glandular-viscid throughout; stems 30–100cm, branched, prostrate or ascending. Lvs 6–20cm, broadly ovate to suborbicular, oblique, deeply cordate, entire to very shallowly sinuate; petioles stout, 5–15cm. Infl. racemose, several-fld; cal. 1.5–2cm, lobes rather acute to obtuse; cor. 3.5–5cm, dingy white to cream to purple, throat always yellow, pale flowers blotched or flecked with rose-purple. Fr. body 4–6cm, crested on upper side, horns 1–3× length of body, pubesc. S US to Mexico; naturalized Australia.

***P. petiolaris*** hort. A listed name of no botanical standing.

***P. jussieui*** Keller in Schmidel. See *P. louisianica*.
***P. louisiana*** Wooton & Standl. See *P. louisianica*.
***P. lutea*** Stapf. See *Ibicella lutea*.
For further synonymy see *Martynia*.

**Proiphys** Herb. (From Gk, *proi*, early, and *phyo*, to bring forth, referring to the premature germination of the seed.)

Amaryllidaceae. 3 species of perennial herbs; bulbs subglobose, tunicated. Leaves basal, elliptic to ovate, expanding after flowering, midvein prominent, primary veins looped; petiole channelled above. Inflorescence umbellate; involucral bracts 2–4, ovate; perianth funnel-shaped, white, lobes 6, elliptic to obovate, apiculate, spreading, fused at base; stamens 6, inserted at throat of perianth tube, filaments united and expanded in basal half into a distinct corona, anthers versatile; ovary inferior, globose, 1- or 3-locular; stigma small. Fruit subglobose, 1–3-seeded; seeds globose, smooth, green. NE Australia. Z10.

CULTIVATION *Proiphys* spp., grown primarily for their umbels of pure white flowers, also have attractively arching evergreen leaves on long footstalks. Although frost tender they are well suited to pot cultivation in temperate zones; the more slender *P. cunninghamii* needs a minimum temperature of 12°C/54°F while *P. alba*, from more tropical climates, needs minimum temperatures of 16–18°C/60–64°F. Pot singly in autumn, with the nose of the bulb at soil level, in a well-drained mix of fibrous loam, leafmould and well-rotted manure. Water plentifully when in growth, reducing after flowering so that plants are just moist enough to prevent flagging, when at rest in winter. Propagate by seed or offsets. Pests and diseases as for *Amaryllis*.

***P. alba*** (R. Br.) Mabb. Bulb 2–4cm diam. Lvs 10–35×2–10cm, elliptic to ovate, apex acute to acuminate, base cuneate; petiole 7–35cm. Flowering stem to 60cm; umbel 10–30-fld; bracts 2–3cm, 3–4; perianth tube 8–15mm, lobes 6–24mm; fil. united for 3–12mm. Queensland.

***P. amboinensis*** (L.) Herb. Bulb to 8cm diam. Lvs 20–30×15–35cm, reniform or broadly ovate, apex emarginate to short-acuminate, base cordate, margin undulate; petiole 15–60cm. Flowering stem 15–90cm; umbel 5–25-fld; bracts 3–10cm, 3–4; perianth tube 2.5–3cm, lobes 2.5–4cm; fil. united for 2–3mm. W Australia.

***P. cunninghamii*** (Ait. ex Lindl.) Mabb. BRISBANE LILY. Bulb to 5cm diam. Lvs 10–25×8–13cm, ovate, apex acute or shortly acuminate, base rounded; petiole 10–25cm. Flowering stem 25–80cm; umbel 5–12-fld; bracts 1.5–5cm, 2–3; pedicels to 4.5cm; perianth tube 8–12mm, lobes 15–18mm; fil. united for 12–16mm. SE Queensland, NSW.

For synonymy see *Eurycles* and *Pancratium*.

**Promenaea** Lindl. (For Promeneia, the prophetess of Dodona mentioned by Herodotus.) Orchidaceae. Some 15 species of diminutive epiphytic orchids. Rhizome short. Pseudobulbs small, clustered, fleshy, ovoid to circular, laterally compressed, bearing to 5 leaves, 1–3 at apex, the others basally sheathing. Leaves ovate-lanceolate, short-petioled or sheathing, sometimes conspicuously veined, plicate or undulate, olive to sea-green, obscurely conduplicate. Inflorescence axillary, from base of pseudobulb, shorter or equalling leaves, horizontal to pendent, 1–2-flowered; flowers often showy, fleshy, pure primrose yellow to cream spotted and streaked maroon; sepals and petals subsimilar, free; lateral sepals adnate to column foot forming a short mentum; lip articulated to apex of column foot, trilobed, lateral lobes enveloping column, narrow, erect, midlobe spreading, disc with a lobed or tuberculate callus; column produced into a short foot at base, fleshy, subterete, wingless, anther terminal, operculate, incumbent, pollinia 4, waxy, obovoid, compressed. Brazil. Z10.

CULTIVATION Diminutive orchids for the cool or intermediate house. Grow in pans of a fine-grade bark mixing semi-shade. Water carefully throughout the year. See ORCHIDS.

***P. rollissonii*** (Lindl.) Lindl. Pseudobulbs to 2.5cm. Lvs to 9×2.5cm, thin-textured, oblong to lanceolate, acute or acuminate. Infl. to 6cm; sep. and pet. pale yellow, recurved: sep. to 22×8mm, ovate-oblong, acuminate, concave; pet. to 18×10mm, ovate-spathulate, acuminate, concave; lip shorter than lateral sep., yellow spotted red-purple, lateral lobes small, oblong-subfalcate, acute or obtuse, denticulate-undulate, midlobe ovate or obovate, short-acuminate, disc with a transverse callus; column to 8mm, clear yellow-green, subclavate. Brazil.

***P. stapelioides*** (Lindl.) Lindl. Pseudobulbs to 2.5cm. Lvs 3–10×0.75–2.5cm, ovate-lanceolate to oblong-ligulate, grey-green, papillose. Infl. to 5cm; fls to 5cm diam.; sep. and pet. cream to buff with broken, concentric bands of maroon, ovate, acute, spreading; lip dark purple, lateral lobes paler than midlobe, linear-falcate, midlobe ovate-oblong or ovate-suborbicular; column pale yellow-green. Brazil.

***P. xanthina*** (Lindl.) Lindl. Pseudobulbs to 2×1.5cm. Lvs 2.5–7×0.75–1.5cm, ovate-lanceolate to oblong, acute, grey-green. Infl. 2.5–10cm horizontal to nodding; fls to 5cm diam., strongly fragrant, long-lived; sep. and pet. primrose yellow, sep. to 20×10mm, ovate-lanceolate to oblong-lanceolate, acute, pet. subequal to sep., narrowly ovate, acute; lip to 15×12mm, bright yellow, lateral lobes slightly spotted brick red, oblong-subfalcate, obtuse, midlobe obovate or obovate-suborbicular, obtuse or rounded, apex denticulate, disc with a fleshy 3-lobed crest; column to 17mm, arcuate, clavate, spotted red. Brazil.

***P. citrina*** D. Don. See *P. xanthina*.
For further synonymy see *Maxillaria*.

**Pronephrium** Presl. (From Gk. *pro*, before, and *nephrion*, kidney.) Thelypteridaceae. Some 65 species of terrestrial or, rarely, rupestral ferns. Rhizomes suberect to long creeping. Lamina uniform or dimorphous, simply pinnate or simple, glabrous to pubescent, pustular, or glandular below (glands sessile, yellow), pinnae crenate to entire, rarely conspicuously lobed, basal pinnae not or little reduced, but often with narrowed bases; surfaces usually pustular when dry, veins anastomosing, areolae with (occasionally free) excurrent veinlet. Sori scattered over veins, occasionally confluent; sporangia often glandular or short-setose; indusia present or absent, often hairy, spores winged. India & Ceylon, S China to Queensland, east to Fiji. Z10.

CULTIVATION As for *Christella*.

***P. asperum*** (Presl) Holtt. Rhiz. short-creeping. Stipes to 70cm, glabrous. Lamina simply pinnate, ovate, 60cm+, glabrous to short-pubesc., occasionally glandular beneath, pinnae to 35×6cm, 6–16 lateral and 1 terminal, sessile, elliptic to oblong and parallel-sided, apex narrowly acute, base cuneate, margin crenate or slightly toothed, veins 12–15-paired, excurrent veinlets free or meeting next vein above; costa pubesc. Sori medial to submarginal and confluent; indusia glabrous or pubesc.; sporangia not setose. Philippines & Malay Peninsula south to Queensland.

***P. triphyllum*** (Sw.) Holtt. Rhiz. long-creeping, to 3mm wide, short-pubesc.; scales to 3mm. Stipes to 2cm apart, to 10cm (sterile) or 20cm (fertile), scaly at base, straw-coloured. Lamina pinnately trifoliate, to 25cm, pinnae to 10×3cm, 2 lateral and 1 terminal, lateral pinnae short-petiolate, opposite, lanceolate or oblong, apex narrowly acute, unequal at base, margin sinuate, terminal pinna similar but oblong, obtuse or cuneate at base, margin occasionally entire, longer, veins 10–12-paired (sterile) or 7-paired (fertile), prominent below, excurrent veinlet free or not. India & Ceylon & SE Asia to Japan & Queensland.

For synonymy see *Meniscium* and *Thelypteris*.

**Proserpinaca** L. (Possibly derived from the Lat. *proserpo*, to creep, referring to the creeping stems of most species.) MERMAID WEED. Haloragidaceae. Some 5 species of aquatic herbs, glabrous. Stems usually simple, creeping. Leaves alternate, often dimorphic; submerged leaves pinnatifid; emersed leaves serrate to pinnatifid. Flowers minute, axillary, solitary or clustered, white to green; sepals 3 or 4; petals 3 or absent; stamens 3 or 4; ovary 3 or 4-locular; stigmas 3 or 4, terete to conical-subulate, ovules 1 in each locule. Fruit a nut, 3 or 4-locular, angular; seeds 3 or 4, cylindrical. N & C America, W Indies. Z10.

CULTIVATION Native to shallow ponds and bogs, *P. palustris* is a slow growing species for cool water aquaria and ponds in frost-free zones. Grow in coarse sand with additional clay, in water at pH 7.0–8.0, at a temperature between 14 and 20°C/57–68°F. Propagate by stem cuttings.

***P. palustris*** L. Stems to 1m, ascending or suberect, sometimes branched. Lvs dimorphic, submerged lvs to 6cm, sessile, pinnatifid, seg. 8–14, to 3cm, linear-filiform, emersed lvs to 8.5×1.5cm, lanceolate to oblanceolate, entire to serrate. Fls solitary or in small clusters; sep. ovate to triangular, acute to obtuse, ascending or converging. Fr. to 3mm, pyramidal or ovate-pyramidal, slightly tuberculate. N & C America, W Indies.

***P. pectinata*** Lam. Stems to 40cm, decumbent, simple or branched. Lvs similar, to 3cm, pectinate or pinnatifid, seg. linear to filiform, acute, entire to slightly serrate. Fls sessile or subsessile; sep. ovate, obtuse, persistent; pet. absent. Fr. to 4mm, ovoid to pyramidal, slightly tuberculate. N & C America, W Indies.

**Prosopis** L. (From the Gk name for the burdock.) MESQUITE. Leguminosae (Mimosoideae). Some 44 species of trees, shrubs and subshrubs. Branches usually spiny. Leaves bipinnate; petiole with sessile, circular, apical gland; stipules small or modified into spines; leaflets many, mostly opposite, linear, oblong, small, entire, obscurely pinnately veined. Flowers in axillary, spike-like racemes, green-white, rarely red; calyx campanulate; petals linear, mostly connate; stamens 10, separate, anthers elliptic, dorsifixed, introrse, with an apical gland; ovary stipitate, villous or glabrous; style filiform. Fruit a loment, linear, straight or falcate; seeds ovoid, compressed, hard, brown. Warm America, SW Asia, Africa. Z10.

CULTIVATION *Prosopis* spp. are often found as dominant species in desert and semi-desert conditions where rainfall may be less than 80mm/3in. per annum, growing in light, sandy or gravel soils along watercourses and other sites with subterranean moisture; they commonly occur on over-grazed land. In arid climates, they are used in erosion control, to stabilize dunes, in shelterbelts and living fences. All species have fragrant, nectar-rich flowers from which bees make a fine-flavoured clear honey. The sugar-rich pods are fed to cattle and used in the brewing of mesquite.

*Prosopis* spp. are also occasionally grown as ornamentals, and native stands make an impressive landscape feature in arid locations. They are extremely drought-resistant, often thorny, have finely divided foliage, and bear green to cream-yellow flowers in clusters of spherical heads or elongated spikes. With deep and extensive root systems, they do not transplant well and should be grown on in pots until their final planting out. Grow in full sun in conditions that approximate to those of their natural habitat, or, in temperate zones, in a glasshouse with a minimum winter temperature of 5°C/40°F in a sandy potting medium; water moderately when in growth and keep dry in winter. Propagate by seed, by removal of suckers, or from semi-ripe cuttings in sand in a closed case with gentle bottom heat.

***P. alba*** Griseb. Tree to 15m. Branchlets pendulous; spines few, only on strong shoots, to 4cm. Petiole to 8cm; pinnae to 14cm; leaflets to 17×2mm, 25–50 pairs, linear, acute or subacute, faintly nerved beneath. Racemes to 11cm; fls green-white to yellow; cal. 1mm, puberulous; cor. 3mm; stamens 4.5mm; pistil 5mm. Fr. to 25×2cm, stipitate, falcate, annular or straight, fleshy, acuminate, compressed, yellow. Subtropical Argentina to Peru.

***P. glandulosa*** Torr. HONEY MESQUITE. Shrub or tree to 9m; spines to 4.5cm, axillary, mainly solitary. Petiole to 15cm; pinnae to 17cm; leaflets to 6.5×0.5cm, 6–17 pairs, linear or oblong, obtuse, glabrous, subcoriaceous, prominently veined beneath. Racemes to 14cm, crowded; fls many; cor. to 3.5mm; ovary stipitate, villous. Fr. to 20×1.3cm, short-stipitate, straight or subfalcate, compressed to subterete, submoniliform, yellow or violet-tinged, glabrous, 5–18-seeded; seeds oblique to longitudinal. SW US, Mexico.

***P. juliiflora*** (Sw.) DC. Tree to 12m, occasionally shrub-like with spreading branches; spines to 5cm, axillary, sometimes absent. Petiole to 7.5cm; pinnae to 11cm; leaflets to 23×5.5mm, 6–29, elliptic-oblong, glabrous or ciliate, rarely pubesc., emarginate or obtuse, mucronulate, pinnately to reticulately nerved. Racemes to 15cm; fls green-white, turning light yellow. Fr. to 30×1.7cm, stipitate, straight or falcate, apex incurved, compressed, yellow to brown; seeds oval, brown. Northern S America, C America. (Often misnamed *P. glandulosa*.) var. ***horrida*** (Kunth) Burkart. To 8m; spines to 7.5cm. Petiole to 7cm; pinnae to 10cm; leaflets 1.5×0.4cm, 10–15 pairs per pinna, elliptic, ovate to oblong, obtuse, pubesc., pale, reticulate-nerved. Racemes to 12cm; fls green-white. Fr. to 24cm×12mm, straight or subfalcate, compressed, submoniliform, subglabrous, brown; seeds to 26. Peru. var. ***inermis*** (HBK) Burkart. Spines absent. Leaflets finely pubesc. Ecuador.

***P. pubescens*** Benth. SCREWBEAN. Shrub or tree to 10m. Spines to 8cm. Leaflets to 12×4mm, 5–9 pairs per pinna, elliptic-oblong, subacute. Fls sessile, pubesc., yellow; cal. to 1mm; cor. to 3mm, finely pubesc. and on inner apex; stamens to 5mm, anth. 1mm; ovary white-villous, style glabrous. Fr. to 5.5×0.6cm, cylindric, puberulous or glabrescent, yellow; seeds to 3.5mm reniform-ovoid. SW US, NW Mexico.

***P. atacamensis*** Philippi. See *P. alba*.
***P. chilensis*** auct. non (Molina) Stuntz. See *P. glandulosa*.
***P. chilensis*** var. ***glandulosa*** (Torr.) Standl. See *P. glandulosa*.
***P. horrida*** Kunth. See *P. juliiflora* var. *horrida*.
***P. juliiflora*** var. ***constricta*** Sarg. See *P. glandulosa*.
***P. juliiflora*** var. ***glandulosa*** (Torr.) Cockerell. See *P. glandulosa*.
***P. odorata*** Torr. See *P. pubescens*.
***P. siliquastrum*** var. ***longisiliqua*** Philippi. See *P. alba*.
For further synonymy see *Algarobia, Mimosa, Neltuma* and *Strombocarpa*.

**Prosopostelma** Baill.
***P. aculeatum*** Descoings. See *Folotsia aculeatum*.
***P. grandiflorum*** Choux. See *Folotsia floribundum*.

**Prostanthera** Labill. (From Gk *prostheke*, appendage, and Lat. *anthera*, anther, from the spur-like projections on the anthers.) AUSTRALIAN MINT BUSH. Labiatae. About 50 species of evergreen shrubs or small trees, viscid, usually strongly aromatic. Leaves opposite, simple. Flowers in leafy racemes or terminal panicles; calyx bilabiate, campanulate, 10-nerved, lips entire or notched; corolla bilabiate, tube short, upper lip 2-lobed, erect, hooded, lower lip 3-lobed, patent, middle lobe largest; stamens 4, in pairs, anthers usually with 1–2 spurs. Fruit 4 reticulate-rugose nutlets, enclosed by persistent calyx. SE Australia, Tasmania. Z9.

CULTIVATION With the exception of *P. cuneata* which tolerates temperatures of −15°C/5°F, predominantly frost-tender evergreen shrubs, grown for their conspicuous flowers and aromatic foliage which yields a strong, sweet, minty scent when brushed (*P. nivea* has little or no scent on the foliage.) They make excellent specimens for the glasshouse or large conservatory, in pots or planted directly into the border. The large-leaved *P. lasianthos*, which can reach a height of 5m/16ft in the stream gullies of Tasmania, can be judiciously pruned in cultivation to keep within bounds and to reveal the attractive smooth red bark on the stems.

Grow *P. cuneata* outdoors in full sun, on fast-draining soils, pH 5–7, with access to plentiful water in summer. Grow the other species under glass in well-crocked clay pots of a medium-fertility loam-based mix; mature specimens are particularly attractive when grown in ornamental clay pots (up to 60cm/24in. diam.). Give direct light, maintain low humidity and water plentifully when in full growth, sparingly at other times. The pruning of *Prostanthera* must be careful and judicious; the majority of growth is at the extremities of each branch, and whole branches are removed to shape the plant. It is most important to retain sufficient growth to sustain the plant or it will not regenerate properly. Prune immediately after flowering. Propagate from seed in spring or by semi-ripe cuttings in late summer.

***P. baxteri*** A.M. Cunn. ex Benth. Erect shrub to 2m. Lvs 1–2cm, linear, terete, erect, sessile, lvs silvery-pubesc. Fls large, axillary; cal. lavender, prominent, densely pubesc.

***P. cuneata*** Benth. Dense, divaricate shrub, to 1m. Shoots downy. Lvs to 6mm, ovate to orbicular, cuneate at base, bright shiny-green, margins revolute, entire or subentire, sessile or short-petioled, very fragrant when crushed. Fls numerous, terminal in leafy racemes; cal. equals or exceeds lvs, lips subequal; cor. 12mm diam., white with purple or violet blotches in throat. Summer. SE Australia, Tasmania.

***P. denticulata*** R. Br. Shrub, prostrate or erect to 1m. Shoots glandular-pubesc. Lvs to 2cm, acute, sessile or subsessile, shiny green, margins and upper surfaces setose. Fls in distant pairs forming interrupted terminal racemes; buds usually sheathed with deciduous bracts; cor. mauve-violet. Summer. E Australia.

***P. lasianthos*** Labill. VICTORIA DOGWOOD; VICTORIA CHRISTMAS BUSH. Variable sp., woody, to 8m. Shoots glabrous. tetragonal. Lvs 5–8cm, lanceolate, serrate, paler below, petiolate. Fls fragrant, paired in short leafless racemes forming branched terminal panicle to 15cm; cor. pubesc., white or cream, rarely tinted violet or lilac, spotted brown or yellow in throat, lobes broad, to 25mm wide. Summer. SE Australia, Tasmania.

***P. linearis*** R. Br. Erect shrub to 3m. Branchlets glabrous. Lvs to 2.5cm, linear, obtuse, entire, subsessile, margins somewhat revolute. Fls in leafy terminal racemes; cor. 5mm, white to mauve, pubesc., throat sometimes spotted brown. SE Australia.

***P. melissifolia*** F. Muell. BALM MINT BUSH. Slender shrub to 2m. Lvs 2.5cm, ovate-elliptic, dentate, rarely entire, lobes obtuse, highly fragrant when crushed. Fls in terminal racemes; cal. lips equal; cor. mauve, purple or pink. SE Australia.

***P. nivea*** A.M. Cunn. ex Benth. Tall bushy shrub to 3m. Stems tetragonal, subglabrous. Lvs to 4cm, linear, acute, sessile, margins involute. Fls solitary in axils of upper lvs, forming leafy racemes to 15cm; cal. to 5mm, prominent; cor. snow-white or tinted blue, to 15mm diam., twice length of cal., pubesc., lower lip with 3 large lobes. Spring. SE Australia, Tasmania.

***P. ovalifolia*** R. Br. Erect shrub, to 4m. Lvs to 1.5cm, oval to ovate-lanceolate, entire, dull glaucous. Fls numerous in short terminal racemes; infl. lvs bracteate, deciduous; cal. lips sub-equal, entire, subglabrous; cal. purple, rarely mauve or white tinted lilac. E Australia.

***P. rotundifolia*** R. Br. MINT BUSH. Shrub to 3m. Shoots canescent. Lvs very variable according to climate, orbicular to ovate, cuneate at base, entire, obscurely dentate or crenate, dark green above, paler below, petiolate. Fls in short, loose, terminal or axillary racemes; subtending lvs reduced; cal. to 3mm in flower, lips

2, subequal, entire; cor. to 12×8mm, violet or lilac, lower lobes projecting. Spring. SE & S Australia. 'Chelsea Pink': lvs aromatic, grey-green, cuneate at base; fls pale rose, anth. mauve.

***P. scutellarioides*** (R. Br.) Briq. Spreading, divaricate shrub, 60–100cm. Shoots sparsely pubesc. Lvs to 1.5cm, linear, acute, sessile, rough, short-setose, paler below, margins revolute. Fls solitary, axillary, violet or mauve; cal. campanulate, 2-lipped, lips often retuse or emarginate, acute; cor. 7mm diam., lobes rounded. Autumn. E. Australia.

***P. sieberi*** Benth. Shrub, spreading or erect to 2m. Lvs to 2.5cm, ovate to oblong, obtuse, cuneate at base, coarsely dentate, strongly fragrant when crushed. Fls 4–8 in short, terminal racemes; cal. lips broad, subequal, cor. 12mm diam., pale mauve to violet, lower lip deeply 3-lobed. Spring. SE Australia.

***P. striatiflora*** F. Muell. Erect to 2m. Lvs 1.5–2.5×0.5cm, rigid, lanceolate to linear-lanceolate, obtuse, entire, sessile or short-petiolate. Fls axillary, upper fls crowded in a leafy terminal raceme; cor. large, cream, conspicuously streaked crimson within.

***P. violacea*** R. Br. Slender shrub, to 2m. Shoots rough, pubesc. Lvs to 5mm, ovate to orbicular, crenate, short-petioled, margins slightly recurved, short-setose. Fls 4–6, in small racemose heads, violet or lavender; cal. glandular-hairy; cor. campanulate at base, lobes 5, unequal. Spring. SE Australia.

***P. empetrifolia*** Sieb. ex Spreng. See *P. scutellarioides*.

**Protea** L. (For Proteus, the ancient Gk sea-god, famed for an ability to change shape, in reference to the diversity of species.) Proteaceae. 115 species of shrubs or occasionally small trees, some with woody subterranean lignotubers. Branches erect or prostrate. Leaves entire, tough, coriaceous. Inflorescence terminal, solitary, or rarely axillary and clustered, subtended by coloured involucral bracts; bracts often hirsute at apex; receptacle flat; flowers bisexual, bilaterally symmetric; perianth segments 4, tubular in bud, 3 upper segments remaining fused to form a sheath, the other separating as the flower opens, and soon deciduous; anthers 4, sessile, attached to perianth limb, all fertile or 1 sterile and reduced to a linear staminode; style straight or curved, tapered to apex. Fruit an achene. Africa (mostly South Africa, some in Tropical Africa). Z9.

CULTIVATION *Protea* spp. occur in a range of habitats, in sandy soils at the coast and only on limestone soils for *P. obtusifolia*; most are found in hilly areas and on mountain slopes, to 1300m/4265ft for *P. neriifolia* and to 1700m/5575ft for *P. grandiceps*. Grown primarily for their flowers, attractive in bud and spectacular when open, often cupped in glossy waxen bracts, and sometimes conspicuously fringed, *Protea* flowers are invaluable for cutting and drying. Many species also have handsome foliage and make impressive specimens for the border in frost-free Mediterranean type climates, or in tubs, large pots and borders in the cool glasshouse or conservatory in cool temperate zones; pot-grown specimens may be moved outdoors during the summer months.

Grow in full light with low humidity and good air circulation day and night throughout the year; the extension of day length by supplementary lighting is beneficial with young plants although they are best shaded from the hottest summer sun. Use a perfectly drained, low-nutrient potting mix comprising equal parts peat and grit, with additional charcoal, ensuring pH is 6.5 or below; *Pp. cynaroides, neriifolia, obtusifolia* and *susannae* will tolerate slightly more alkaline conditions. Proteas are extremely sensitive to nitrates and phosphates, which may be toxic even at moderate levels, although they may suffer from magnesium deficiencies; apply dilute liquid feed of magnesium sulphate and urea in spring and autumn and water plentifully but judiciously when in flower and full growth. Maintain a winter minimum temperature of 5–7°C/40–45°F with a summer maximum at about 27°C/80°F. Prune if necessary in spring. Outdoors, grow in nutritionally poor well drained neutral or acid soil, in full sun but in a situation shaded from early morning sun in winter and protected from dessicating winds, leave undisturbed once planted; exposure to frosts is usually fatal although *Pp. aristata, eximia, nana, repens* and *neriifolia* will tolerate light short-lived frosts once established. At Tresco Abbey in the Scilly Isles during the winter of 1987, frosts to −9°C/16°F over a period of 10 days were recorded and although 70% of *Protea* spp. were lost, *P. longiflora* and *P. cynaroides* were among the survivors. Propagate species by seed sown fresh in autumn in a 2:3 mix of peat and grit in individual small pots in the frost free cold frame or cool glasshouse. Keep seedlings moist but not waterlogged and ensure full ventilation. Pot on as soon as roots begin to fill pots to avoid root disturbance and feed occasionally with a dilute solution of magnesium sulphate. Propagate desirable forms by semi-ripe cuttings in summer.

***P. aurea*** (Burm.) Rourke. Shrub to 5m. Lvs 15–40×4–9mm, ovate to oblong, glabrous or glabrescent. Infl. to 12cm, terminal, cylindric in bud, obconical when open; inner involucral bracts to 9×1.5cm, reflexed when mature, cream with green tinged to crimson, margins pubesc.; stamens all fertile; styles straight, to 10cm, cream to crimson. Spring–summer. S Africa (Cape Province).

***P. burchellii*** Stapf. Stems subterranean, branched, branches rising slightly above the ground, pubesc. above when young. Lvs 15–22×1.5–2.5cm, linear-oblanceolate, acute, attenuate beneath, glossy green, glabrous or minutely pubesc. near base, veins prominent. Infl. subglobose, to 6.5×4cm; involucral bracts ovate to oblong, obtuse to subobtuse, dark chestnut-brown, glabrescent; stamens all fertile; style strongly curved, 4.5cm. Spring–summer. S Africa.

***P. compacta*** R. Br. Erect shrub to 3.5m. Lvs 5–13×2–2.5cm, oblong to elliptic, obtuse at apex, sessile, coriaceous, glabrescent, margins horny. Infl. oblong in bud, obovoid when open, 7–10cm diam.; involucral bracts 8-seriate, outer ovate, acute, inner to 10×1.5cm, narrowly oblong, rounded, longer than outer, bright pink or occasionally white, margins ciliate; stamens all fertile; styles slightly incurved, to 7cm, pink. Spring–summer. S Africa (Cape Province).

***P. cynaroides*** (L.) L. KING PROTEA. Shrub to 2m with lignotuber. Stems few, massive, glabrous. Lvs 8–14×2–13cm, orbicular to elliptic, cuneate, coriaceous, glabrous; petiole 4–18cm. Infl. 12–30×12–20cm, cupulate to goblet-shaped when open (resembling globe artichoke); involucral bracts to 12cm, 12–13-seriate, lanceolate, deep crimson to pink or cream with green tinge, silky-downy; stamens all fertile; style straight, 8–9.5cm. Late spring–summer. S Africa (Cape Province).

***P. eximia*** (Knight) Fourc. Shrub or small tree to 5m, sparingly branched; stems erect. Lvs 6–10×3–6.5cm, ovate, cordate at base, glaucous to green tinged purple, coriaceous, glabrous. Infl. oblong to obconic, to 14×12cm; involucral bracts 4–10cm×8–15mm, in 2 clearly defined series, margins ciliate, inner bracts spathulate, splayed at flowering, pink tinted red; 3 stamens fertile; style 6–7.5cm, pink. Spring–summer. S Africa (Cape Province).

***P. grandiceps*** Tratt. Shrub to 2m. Lvs 8–13×3–8.5cm, erect, ovate to obovate, rounded at apex, sometimes somewhat cordate at base, sessile, green, often with red, ciliate margins, coriaceous, glabrous. Infl. oblong to goblet-shaped, to 14×8cm; involucral bracts to 8×2cm, 8-seriate, spathulate, inner larger than outer, coral pink, tips incurved and conspicuously hirsute with white or purple hairs (or both); stamens all fertile; style curved, to 7.5cm. Summer. S Africa (Cape Province). Flower colour apparently dependant on light intensity, indoor-grown plants having green bracts. Summer.

***P. lacticolor*** Salisb. Shrub or small tree to 6m. Lvs 7–11×2.5–5cm, ascending, lanceolate, truncate at base, more or less acute at apex, blue-green. Infl. oblong, to 8×6cm; involucral bracts to 5×1.5cm, incurved at apex, ivory, cream or rich pink, pubesc. without, margins pilose, particularly at apex; stamens all fertile; style straight, to 7cm. Spring–summer. S Africa (Cape Province).

***P. magnifica*** Link. Small shrub; stems stout, villous. Lvs to 10×5cm, oblong or lanceolate, acute at apex, narrowed or subcordate at base, margins undulate, subglaucous, coriaceous, hairy along margins, veins distinct. Infl. turbinate-obovoid, to 15×12cm; involucral bracts clearly differentiated into 7–8 series, creamy pubesc. to tomentose, outermost ovate to ovate-lanceolate, densely white-ciliate, innermost linear-lanceolate, elongate, acute, densely ciliate on margins; stamens all fertile, anth. yellow; style rather stout, white. Spring–summer. S Africa (Cape Province).

***P. mundi*** Klotzsch in Otto & Dietr. Small shrub; branches minutely tomentose above. Lvs 4–10.5×1–3cm, lanceolate or elliptic-lanceolate, subobtuse, narrowed to base, sometimes loosely pilose when very young, otherwise glabrous, veins distinct. Infl. 7–7.5×5cm; involucral bracts 11–12 seriate, outer ovate, obtuse, green, ciliate, pubesc. on back, inner oblong or oblong-spathulate, white pubesc. to tomentose, white ciliate on margins; stamens all fertile; style almost straight, 5cm. Spring–summer. S Africa.

***P. nana*** (Bergius) Thunb. MOUNTAIN ROSE. Small compact shrub, 60–120cm, glabrous; branches slender, smooth. Lvs 12–24×1–2mm, linear, mucronate at apex, soft, light to mid-green, occasionally flushed red. Infl. pendulous, cupulate, 4cm diam., on slender curved branches; bracts 25×8mm, smooth, brilliant rose to crimson, to wine or mahogany, buff in centre, or occasionally tinged green, exceeding fls; fls crowded in cone-shape; perianth red, hirsute with red hairs. Late spring. S Africa (SW Cape).

***P. neriifolia*** R. Br. Shrub to 3m, erect. Lvs 10–18×1.5–3cm, ascending, narrowly oblong with parallel sides, acute to obtuse at apex, sessile, dark to bright green, glabrescent. Infl. goblet-shaped when fully open, to 13×8cm; involucral bracts to 14×1.5cm, oblong to spathulate, incurved at tip, white to dark pink, very densely black (occasionally white), hirsute at apex; 3 stamens fertile; style straight, to 7cm. Spring–summer. S Africa (Cape Province).

***P.obtusifolia*** Meissn. Shrub or small tree to 4m. Lvs 10–15×2–4cm, ascending, oblanceolate to elliptic, coriaceous, glabrescent. Infl. goblet-shaped when open; involucral bracts to 10cm×12mm, deep pink to creamy green, margins fringed; fertile stamens 3; style straight, to 7cm. Spring–summer. S Africa (Cape Province).

***P.pudens*** Rourke. GROUND ROSE. Procumbent, spreading plant, to 40×100cm. Stems trailing. Lvs 6–10×0.2–0.5cm, crowded, linear, secund, grey-green. Infl. terminal, resting on ground, campanulate, 5–8×4–6cm; involucral bracts red-brown to deep dusky rose; flowering stems 12–20cm; fls white, hairy, tipped with purple-black awns. Winter. S Africa (S Cape).

***P.repens*** (L.) L. Shrub or small tree to 4m; stems erect. Lvs 5–15×0.5–2cm, erect, linear to lanceolate, acute to rounded at apex, glabrous. Infl. to 6cm, obovoid in bud, goblet-shaped when fully open, to 9cm diam.; involucral bracts to 11×2cm, acute, creamy white, sometimes tinged dark red or pink at apex, glabrous, resinous and sticky; fertile stamens 3; style slightly curved, to 9cm. Spring–summer. S Africa (Cape Province).

***P.scolymocephala*** (L.) Reichard. Shrub to 1.5m; stems erect, branched. Lvs 3.5–9cm×3–6mm, linear to spathulate, acuminate at apex, glabrous. Infl. spheric in bud, to 3cm diam., bowl-shaped when fully open, to 4.5cm diam.; involucral bracts to 25×7mm, rounded and concave at apex, slightly reflexed with age, creamy green, pink at apex, ciliate; stamens all fertile; style strongly incurved, to 2.5cm. Late spring–summer. S Africa (Cape Province).

***P.susannae*** Phillips. Shrub to 4m, of loose habit. Lvs 8–16×1.5–3cm, oblong, acute at apex, glabrescent, coriaceous, margins horny. Infl. goblet-shaped when fully open, to 10×11cm; involucral bracts to 8×2cm, spathulate, rounded and somewhat concave at apex, pink tinged brown, sticky brown resinous without; fertile stamens 3; style straight, to 7cm. Spring–summer. S Africa (Cape Province). Lvs have an offensive sulphurous odour when bruised.

***P.longiflora*** Lam. See *P.aurea*.
***P.minor*** Compton. See *P.pudens*.

**PROTEACEAE** Juss. PROTEA FAMILY. Dicot. 75 genera and 1350 species of evergreen shrubs, trees, often accumulating aluminium; roots without mycorrhizae but often with short lateral 'proteoid' roots. Leaves alternate, usually simple to pinnate or bipinnate, often xeromorphic; stipules absent. Flowers bisexual or unisexual (plants monoecious or dioecious), regular or irregular, protandrous, pollination by insects, birds or marsupials, 4-merous, solitary or paired in axile of bract, in racemes, umbels or involucrate heads, or 2-flowered inflorescence in secondary racemes; calyx 4 fused sepals, valvate, often petaloid, usually with basal tube sometimes cleft on 1 side or 3 connate and 2 free; corolla a 4-lobed annular nectary disc or (2–)4 scales or glands, alternate with corolla, or absent; stamens opposite calyx, filaments broad and usually adnate to calyx, anthers with 1 fertile theca (1 often sterile); ovary superior, of 1 carpel, sometimes not closed, style elongate; ovules 1 or 2 (to many); placentation marginal. Fruit a follicle, nut, achene or drupe, often 1-seeded when indehiscent; seeds often winged; embryo straight, oily, with 2(–8) cotyledons; endosperm usually absent. Some provide timber, e.g. *Grevillea*; macadamia nuts are from *Macadamia integrifolia*. Tropical and subtropical, especially S hemisphere, mostly Australia and S Africa. *Adenanthos, Agastachys, Banksia, Bellendena, Buckinghamia, Conospermum, Dryandra, Embothrium, Franklandia, Gevuina, Grevillea, Hakea, Hicksbeachia, Isopogon, Knightia, Lambertia, Leucadendron, Leucospermum, Lomatia, Macadamia, Mimetes, Oreocallis, Orites, Paranomus, Persoonia, Petrophila, Placospermum, Protea, Roupala, Serruria, Stenocarpus, Stirlingia, Synaphea, Telopea, Xylomelum.*

**Protected cultivation**. This may be defined as any system or technique of growing plants in which the adverse effects of the natural aerial environment are mitigated or eliminated. The degree of protection can vary from simple devices which protect from wind or frost to complex environmental control systems such as those used in heated greenhouses. The earliest forms of protection were provided by the fenced and walled gardens of the Middle Ages. These led to the progressive development of a wide range of protecting devices which may be classified as 'high' or 'low level'.

HIGH LEVEL. High-level protection is characterized by having a covering structure of sufficient height to allow all the cultural operations to be done from within. Such systems afford protection to the operator as well as the plants and include greenhouses and film plastic structures. Walk-in plastic film structures have a supporting structure of galvanized steel tubes anchored to concrete foundation blocks and connected by a continuous ridge. They are available in single- and multi-span form in spans ranging from 4.3m/14ft to 8.5m/27½ft. The cladding may be of long-life polythene film, plastic netting, woven polythene or a mixture of film and netting, depending on use and requirements. Some structures may be designed primarily to provide shade (e.g. lath houses covered with spaced wooden laths or trellis-work, which allow air to enter but are sufficient to curtail the full force of the sun and to provide some protection against light frost and wind). Plastic tunnels are normally ventilated by side and end ventilators or by fans. The majority of plastic structures are unheated but where heating is required it is normally a simple warm air system.

LOW LEVEL. In low-level protection the covering is close to crop level and does not permit working access. Low-level protection includes cloches, frames, low-level plastic tunnels and plastic ground covers.

*Cloches*. The cloche or bell glass is the oldest protecting device recorded. It originated in Italy in the late 16th century, being noted by de Serre in his *Théâtre d'Agriculture* of 1600 as being widely used by French gardeners. Bell cloches were made in a large range of shapes and sizes, but the standard type were 425mm/17in. across the mouth and 380mm/15in. high. They are best known for their use by the *maraîchères* of the Paris region in the 19th century for forcing early vegetables and salads in the system of 'French' gardening. They were used in gardens generally for protecting tender plants but in Britain they were seldom used commercially except in a few 'French' gardens established in the early 1900s, for the growing of violets. Bell glasses were highly labour-intensive and awkward to handle. Specimens may still be found but they are now only of historic interest.

*Lantern cloches* or hand glasses have been known since the 17th century. They were similar to bell glasses but differed in being made up from small panes held together in a lead, copper or iron framework. Models varied in shape and size, but all had straight sides, a square, hexagonal or octagonal section and a pointed top with a carrying ring at the apex. They were used only in private gardens and have been replaced by less expensive alternatives.

*Continuous cloches* were introduced shortly after the end of World War II. They consisted of two or four panes of glass held together by a wire frame and clips. The two most popular types were the 'tent', consisting of two panes, and the 'barn', with four panes. Depending on the height of the bottom panes, barn cloches were designated 'high' or 'low'. Units were 45–60cm/18–24in. long and placed end to end in rows to form a range. They were widely used in small market gardens and by amateurs to produce early strawberries, salads and vegetables, with cropping sequences devised to obtain maximum use over the year. Use declined from the early 1960s and they have been replaced almost entirely by low plastic tunnels.

*Low plastic tunnels* consist of 38mu (150 gauge) clear polythene film supported at 750mm intervals by 6swg or 8swg wire hoops with eyes at ground level. The film is secured by a loop of baler twine fixed through the eye of each loop. Film is available in widths from 1.22m/4ft to 3.7m/12ft, giving tunnels 0.75m/30in. to 2m/6½ft wide, 1m/39in. being the most usual. On a field scale the film can be laid mechanically from a tractor-mounted dispenser. Low plastic tunnels are widely used in commercial and private horticulture, particularly for the production of early strawberries and salads. Ventilation is given by raising the sides.

*Frames* are structures usually with a low timber, brick or blockwork base covered with timber-framed glass lights. In some instances the whole frame may be fabricated in steel or aluminium with the sides as well as the top glazed. The first recorded use of frames is in André Mollet's *Jardin de Plaisir*, published in 1651, with the first illustration in van der Groen's *Den Nederlandtsen*

*Hovenier* of 1670. The earliest lights were made up from small panes mounted in leaded lights supported by a timber frame. Such a light is illustrated by de la Quintinye in *Instructions pour les jardins fruitiers et potagers*, dated 1697.

The invention of putty in 1737 led to the glass being supported by wooden or iron sashes and to the development of the traditional 'English' and 'French' framelights. The standard English light was 6′×4′ and the French light 4′2″×4′2″ each with three intermediate sashes. The Dutch light was introduced in 1880 and, in contrast to the earlier lights, had a single sheet of glass 1.42×0.73m/4ft 9in.×30in. fitted loose and retained by grooves in the sides of the frame, giving a light 1.5×0.8m/5ft×31in. overall. All three types of light have been widely used in gardens for the propagation, forwarding and protecting of a wide range of plants.

The French and Dutch lights were used in specific systems for producing early vegetables and salads. French lights were used in association with bell glasses on hotbeds. The bases of the frames were usually 20cm/8in. deep, with a 5cm/2in. slope from back to front and made up in units, each taking three lights. Dutch lights were used in a modification of French gardening but without the use of hotbeds. The frame bases were similar but they were set up as long continuous runs instead of separate units. In Dutch gardening the lights were used in both single- and double-span arrangement.

Crop production in frames is highly labour-intensive. Their use has declined rapidly since the 1960s and they have been replaced commercially by walk-in plastic tunnels but are still widely used by amateurs and in parks and botanic gardens.

*Film plastic covers* are the simplest and least costly system of protected cultivation. They may be used in three main ways: first, as a floating cover placed over a drilled or transplanted crop (potatoes, carrot, lettuce, courgette); second, as a surface mulch covering the soil with crops drilled or planted through the film (sweet corn, runner beans); third, as a cover to provide a system of field storage for crops *in situ* through the autumn and winter (celery, carrot, leek, cabbage). The effect of the film cover is to provide soil warming, protection from frost and to prevent damage and desiccation by wind.

If used as a floating cover, the film may be clear and perforated or slit, or white spun-bonded. It is applied immediately after drilling or planting, or as part of a single operation, and is removed before the crop matures. For a surface mulch, the film may be clear or black and is applied before drilling. For field storage, the film may be black and applied over a layer of straw (carrot, swede, celery) or white spun-bonded and applied directly over the crop (leek, cabbage). The covers may be applied by hand or by machine. It is essential to ensure that the edges are securely anchored by covering with soil. Suitable films are available in widths ranging from 2m to 10m.

See also GREENHOUSE.

**Protowoodsia** Ching.
***P. manchuriensis*** (Hook.) Ching. See *Woodsia manchuriensis*.

**Prumnopitys** Philippi. (From Gk *prumne*, stern and *pitys*, pine.) Podocarpaceae. Some 10 species of dioecious, occasionally monoecious, evergreen, coniferous trees. Buds small, globose or ovoid, green, few-scaled. Leaves similar to those of *Taxus*, spirally arranged, petiole often twisted to give 2-ranked effect, linear, bilaterally flattened. Male cones solitary or in groups of 2–20, on specialized lateral shoots, cylindric to ovoid, 1–3cm×2–3mm, scales numerous, acuminate. Fruit 1–8 on a 2–4cm racemose peduncle, mature in 6–8 months, drupe-like, 8–25mm, with soft edible pulp wholly enclosing the hard seed; no swollen receptacle. Dispersed by birds. S America (Andes mts from Costa Rica to Bolivia & also S Chile), New Zealand, E Australia, New Caledonia. *Prumnopitys* has been separated from the genus *Podocarpus* on the basis of internal leaf morphology and the absence of an enlarged basal receptacle in the fruit. The leaves are also softer and less sharp than those of *Podocarpus*.

CULTIVATION *P. andina* is the hardiest species, making an attractive, soft-foliage yew-like tree or shrub with similar requirements to *Podocarpus salignus*. The other species are similar but less cold tolerant; the two New Zealand spp. grow in S Ireland but others require glasshouse treatment. Apart from their native areas, they can also be grown in W Europe and the Pacific coast of N America. All tolerate clipping well, and make excellent hedge plants, without the toxicity problems of *Taxus*. Propagation is as for *Podocarpus*.

***P. andina*** (Poepp. ex Endl.) Laub. PLUM-FRUITED YEW. Tree to 25m or shrub, usually dioecious; bark smooth, grey-brown tinged red. Crown dense, rounded to irregular. Shoots green, becoming dark brown suffused grey after 3 years. Lvs linear, 10–25×2mm, to 30mm on vigorous shoots; soft, flexible, often curved or twisted, bright green above, 2 pale green stomatal bands beneath, midrib inconspicuous, apex bluntly acute; petiole very short. Male cones in racemes of 5–20, sessile, spreading, 10–25mm, white tinged yellow. Fr. 1–4 on a 2–3cm curved peduncle, drupe-like, ovoid, 15–20×10–15mm, pale green ripening dark purple, apex mucronate. S Chile, SW Argentina. Z8.

***P. ferruginea*** (D. Don) Laub. MIRO. Tree to 25m, bole to 1m diam.; bark brown suffused grey, exfoliating in scales. Lvs 13–25×2.5mm, to 30mm on young trees, 2-ranked in a flattened spray, linear-falcate, dark green above, yellow green beneath, becoming rust-brown when dried, midrib narrow, margin slightly revolute, apex bluntly acute; petiole to 3mm. Male cones sessile, solitary or paired, to 12×3mm, erect, cylindric, on a short peduncle. Fr. solitary, drupe-like, ovoid-acute, 15–20mm, bright red bloomed pink, on a 1cm scaly peduncle. New Zealand. Z9.

***P. ferruginoides*** (Compton) Laub. Tree to 15m or more, similar to *P. ladei*. Lvs spirally arranged, 15–20×3mm, leathery, apex blunt acute. Fr. rounded or ovoid, not acute or mucronate at apex, 10–12mm. New Caledonia. Z10.

***P. ladei*** (Bail.) Laub. Tree to 30m, bole to 2m diam., bark smooth, brown tinged red. Lvs spirally arranged, sessile, green, 12–16×3mm, obtuse. Male cones solitary, sessile, terminal. Fr. solitary, ellipsoid, 18–25×12–15mm, purple, pruinose; apex acute. Australia (NE Queensland). Z10.

***P. montana*** Willd.) Laub. Tree to 25m. Lvs spirally arranged but petioles twisted to give pectinate layout; linear to falcate, 10–20×2.5–3mm, green above, 2 pale stomatal bands beneath; apex acute. Male cones 20–25 on a 4–5cm raceme, 1cm. Fr. solitary, 15mm, apiculate; peduncle leafy. N Andes (N Peru to Costa Rica). Z10.

***P. standleyi*** (Buchholz & Gray) Laub. Tree to 25m, branches pendent or spreading; twigs green to brown, tinged red. Lvs 12–25×2.5–3mm, ridged above, glaucous beneath, acute or mucronate. Male cones spirally arranged, on panicles of 15–25, to 13mm; panicles 4–8cm. Fr. 10–15mm, on 25mm scaly peduncle; seed 10×6mm, apex mucronate, testa striated. C Costa Rica. Z10.

***P. taxifolia*** (Sol. ex D. Don) Laub. MATAI. Tree to 25m. Crown rounded; branches erect to drooping. Bark blue-black or brown tinged purple, exfoliating in large plates. Twigs pendulous in young specimens. Lvs linear to falcate, 7–15×1.5–2mm, dark green above, glaucous green tinged bronze beneath, midrib prominent, apex obtuse, or apiculate. Male cones in racemes of 15–30, sessile, cylindric, 3–5×1–2mm; raceme to 25mm. Fr. globose, 8–10mm, black, pruinose, apex mucronate, with 5–8 on a 3–4cm raceme. New Zealand. Z9.

***P. amara*** Bl. Laub. See *Sundacarpus amara*.
***P. elegans*** Philippi. See *P. andina*.
***P. spicata*** (R. Br. ex Mirb.) Mast. See *P. taxifolia*.
For further synonymy see *Podocarpus*.

**Prunella** L. (From *Brunella*, pre-Linnean name for the genus; the origin is obscure but may stem from *Die Breaune*, German for quinsy, a throat infection which these plants allegedly cured.) SELF HEAL; HEAL ALL. Labiatae. 7 species of soft, decumbent perennial herbs. Stems erect, simple. Leaves petiolate, entire, opposite. Inflorescence of dense spikelets or subcapitate; verticillasters 4–6-flowered; bracts leaflike, differing from the leaves, ovate to orbicular; flowers short-pedicellate; calyx tubular-campanulate, 10-nerved, bilabiate, upper lip broad shortly 3 toothed, lower lip narrow with two long subulate teeth; corolla tube shortly exserted from the calyx, 2-lipped, upper lip erect, somewhat hooded, lower lip shorter, deflexed, 3-lobed; stamens 4, didymous, 2 long and 2 short, lower pair longest; style bifid, lobes subulate. Fruit of 4 nutlets, ovoid or oblong, smooth, keeled. Eurasia, N Africa, N America.

CULTIVATION Hardy herbaceous perennials useful for fully exposed areas or areas of partial shade, *Prunella* spp. can be grown in pockets on the rock garden but care is necessary on account of their running stems. *P. grandiflora* has several colour variants: 'Alba', white; 'Rosea', pink, and 'Rubra', red. *Prunella* is also useful as groundcover in similar situations as *Ajuga*, and for meadow and rough grassland and other naturalistic plantings. Propagate from seed sown into a pan and placed outside in spring or from removal of sections of rooted stem.

***P. grandiflora*** (L.) Scholler. Sparsely pubesc. perenn. to 60cm. Lvs to 10×4cm, ovate to ovate-lanceolate, margins entire or crenulate; petioles to 9cm. Infl. not subtended by lvs; bracts to 2×2cm; cal. 15mm, teeth of upper lip subequal, teeth of lower lip 3–4mm, lanceolate, ciliate; cor. more than 18mm (to 30mm), lips deep violet, tube off-white. Europe. ssp. ***grandiflora***. Lvs cuneate at base, not lobed. Infl. not more than 5cm. Europe except Portugal and SW Spain (calcicole). ssp. ***pyrenaica*** (Gren. & Godron) Bolós & O. Bolós. Lvs hastate. Infl. to 8cm. SW Europe (calcifuge). 'Alba': fls pale to white. 'Rosea': fls pink. 'Rotkäppchen' ('Red Cap'): fls carmine. 'Loveliness': fls pale lilac. 'Loveliness White': fls white. 'Loveliness Pink': fls pink. Z5.

***P. hyssopifolia*** L. Glabrous or sparsely pubesc. perenn. to 40cm. Lvs 3–8×0.3–1.8cm, linear-lanceolate to elliptic-lanceolate, entire, usually sessile, lower lvs sometimes shortly petiolate. Infl. subtended by lvs; bracts 10×10mm; cal. 8mm, teeth of upper lip subequal, teeth of lower lip 3mm, lanceolate, ciliate; cor. 15–18mm, violet, rarely off-white. SW Europe. Z6.

***P. laciniata*** (L.) L. Densely pubesc. perenn. Stems to 30cm. Lvs to 7×3cm, upper lvs pinnatifid, lower lvs lobed or pinnatifid; petiole absent or to 4cm. Infl. subtended by a pair of lvs; bracts 10×15mm; cal. 10mm, upper lip truncate, teeth scarcely apparent, teeth of lower lip linear-lanceolate, to 2.5mm, ciliate; cor. to 18mm, yellow-white, rarely rose-pink or purple. SW & C Europe. Z6.

***P. vulgaris*** L. Glabrous or sparingly pubesc. perenn. Stems to 50cm. Lvs 5×2cm, ovate to broadly ovate, margins usually entire; petioles 1–4cm. Infl. subtended by a pair of lvs; bracts 5–15×7–13mm; cal. 8mm, teeth mucronate, middle tooth of upper lip wider than laterals, teeth of lower lip 2mm, lanceolate, ciliate; cor. 10–15mm, tube as long as cal., upper lip sparingly pubesc., dark blue, purple, rarely white. Europe. Z3.

***P. alba*** Pall. ex Bieb. See *P. laciniata*.
***P. latifolia*** Brot. See *P. grandiflora*. ssp. *pyrenaica*.

**Pruning**. Pruning is the practice of cutting out parts of plants and is carried out by gardeners for specific purposes: it applies almost entirely to woody plants. In the wild, plants may be naturally pruned when weak or dying branches are torn off by wind, browsed by animals or reduced by fire. The main reasons for pruning in the garden are to rid plants of dead, diseased or unsightly growth, to maintain a manageable and attractive shape, to prevent overcrowding of other plants, to improve the size or quality of flowers and fruits, and to enhance vigour. Considerations of space and personal taste may also have influence, and woody plants in general are remarkably tolerant of various pruning activity.

Pruning differs according to subject, and specific guidance for woody plants is given throughout the Dictionary. In healthy plants, pruning stimulates regrowth and a primary aim is to develop and maintain a good framework and the continual production of young growth for foliage, flower and fruit production. Pruning to remove dead or diseased growth should be done as soon as possible after infection occurs, and cuts should be made right back into healthy wood. Prunings should be carefully disposed of, so that they cannot form a source of reinfection. Excessively hard pruning can promote over-regeneration in the form of long leafy 'water shoots', which according to species may be undesirable in causing delay in flowering and fruiting, the loss of good structure and possible disease encouragement through excessively dense growth. In the majority of instances a balanced pruning regime is called for.

The timing of pruning requires special consideration and reference. In general it is advisable to avoid the operation when risk of disease infection, for instance silver leaf (*Chondrostereum purpureum*), is high; or, when choice is possible, when there is risk of new resultant growth being damaged by cold, heat or sun scorch.

EVERGREENS. Cutting evergreens is often necessary or beneficial for rejuvenation, shaping and the removal of dead or diseased parts. Young growth is often more readily damaged by extremes of temperature and by strong sunlight than is mature growth and pruning should therefore be undertaken in late spring. *Elaeagnus* spp., *Laurus nobilis, Rosmarinus officinalis* and evergreen *Cotoneaster* spp. are examples of plants treated in this way. Rhododendrons and camellias can be suitably pruned by the removal of flowering branches, which may be used for decoration. Where more drastic restriction becomes essential, it may mean sacrificing much or all of the following year's flower display, and these evergreens should not be forced into new growth too early. Special care should be taken to cut back to buds or shoots because there may be no regrowth from old bare wood. In this respect much depends on species, age and locality.

Conifers have a natural tendency to lose their lower branches as they age. The kind of clutter that accumulates within the tree can best be appreciated by looking up through it. Good tree surgery will remove dead or dying growth and greatly improve both the appearance and health of the tree. Conifers of narrow erect habit may be pulled apart by snow, wind or heavy rain. It is difficult to rectify this solely by pruning and there is always a risk in shortening such displaced branches, especially if this means cutting back into bare wood from which there may be no regeneration. This is mainly a matter for tying and training, which may be helped by the complete removal of some branches. For more detailed information, see CONIFERS.

DECIDUOUS PLANTS. Many deciduous woody ornamentals which bear flowers on short shoots and spurs of an established framework, require no more than occasional pruning. It is done for shaping, tidying and renovation purposes rather than the encouragement of replacement flowering shoots. *Amelanchier lamarckii, Hamamelis mollis, Potentilla fruticosa, Viburnum carlesii, Hibiscus syriacus*, and *Chaenomeles speciosa* are examples of this group, and the work is best carried out in late winter or spring outside of the specific flowering period. As a general guide to the principles of pruning the majority of deciduous shrubs which benefit from regular attention, especially in order to encourage a good supply of flowering shoots, two main groups may be considered.

First, plants blooming from midsummer onwards on wood produced in the current season should have their flowered shoots pruned in early spring. Subjects in this group, such as *Buddleia davidii, Caryopteris ×clandonensis, Eccremocarpus scaber, Hydrangea paniculata* and *Spiraea japonica* benefit from cutting back to within one or two buds of the previous season's growth. Those which may not form a woody framework, depending on locality, such as *Ceratostigma willmottianum, Perovskia atriplicifolia, Leycesteria formosa* and hardy fuchsias should have all stems cut back to a few inches from ground level – the procedure known as stooling. Plants in this group grown for stem or foliage effect, such as *Rubus cockburnianus* and *Cotinus coggygria* should be stooled. Bright-stemmed *Salix* and *Cornus* spp. may be stooled, or 'headed' back on an upright stem or 'leg' – the procedure known as pollarding. A particularly striking example is *Paulownia tomentosa*, which produces leaves many times normal size if stooled or pollarded.

These procedures allow for new growth to be made and become sufficiently mature to produce flowers in the same year. Some young growth is likely to follow quickly and will almost certainly be more tender than mature growth. Pruning should therefore be delayed until the danger of frost is past.

The second general group for consideration covers the large number of summer flowering woody plants which bear bloom or shoots produced in the previous seasons, such as *Philadelphus coronarius, Deutzia scabra, Buddleja alternifolia, Kerria japonica, Hydrangea × macrophylla* and *Weigela florida*. These respond to the thinning out of old branches and crowded shoots, and the removal of faded flower trusses, immediately after blooming. This ensures minimum interference with flowering and allows the plant time to produce and mature new growth for flower production in the following year.

Earlier-flowering subjects in this group, such as *Jasminum nudiflorum, Forsythia ×intermedia* and *Prunus triloba*, should have flowered shoots cut out soon after blooming to encourage vigorous replacement growth in the longest possible growing season.

Some shrubs native to warm regions, or hybrids specially produced in gardens for long flowering, have such an extended season that they cannot be classified either early or late flowering. These benefit from an initial fairly hard pruning in spring, followed by regular removal of the faded flowers. Most deciduous trees and shrubs grown for foliage characteristics can be pruned at almost any time of the year, though summer pruning is advantageous since the effect required is best judged when the plants are carrying leaves.

Deadheading is a useful method of pruning heathers and lavender. With these, removing dead flower stems as soon as they cease to provide a decorative feature is beneficial in stimulating new growth and prevents plants from becoming straggly and bare. Deadheading of larger plants, such as lilacs and rhododendron, avoids the plant's energies being channelled into seed production and also improves the appearance of the plant. In some cases, such as *Koelreuteria paniculata*, the seed pods are decorative and can be left to add to the plant's display.

PRUNING IN WARM CLIMATES. The timing of pruning in the tropics and subtropics is affected by the existence or otherwise of a well-defined resting period. Many trees and shrubs can be pruned at almost any time, though preferably soon after flowering or fruiting and never in long periods of dryness. Pruning principles are the same as for temperate areas, with special consideration of removing dead, weak, diseased and badly placed growth. Pruning may be particularly necessary because of extra vigour in plants and also to rejuvenate old shrubs which become straggly; these can be cut down to around 30–50cm, preferably at the start of a rainy season.

ROSES. Roses are pruned in varying ways according to their type. Shrub roses, for example, should have old, diseased or dead wood removed with some trimming to maintain shape; but the highly bred modern bush roses like hybrid teas and floribundas need cutting back moderately hard, or sometimes severely, if they are to produce good growth and flowers the next season and not to end up as an unsightly, disease-prone mass of long twiggy shoots. Pruning for all the different groups is dealt with under ROSE.

CLIMBERS. Detailed pruning of woody climbers can be difficult because of their often tangled growth. With wisterias, ornamental vines and some others that make stout permanent stems it may be possible to use similar pruning methods to those used in the cultivation of grape vines, namely to spread out a permanent framework of growth over the available space and shorten all side growths to this. As a rule, it is convenient to spread the work over summer and autumn or winter, shortening young shoots little by little at the earlier period and then cutting them back more severely when they are dormant.

Climbers which produce weaker stems (e.g. some *Clematis, Jasminum* and *Lonicera* spp.) may require more drastic pruning to remove the exhausted mass of the previous season's flowered growth. Tangles of old bare stems are not only unsightly, but also provide an unstable framework for new growth. Such cases may require severe thinning or pruning of a few selected leads to near ground level. If grown on a system of wires and wall-nails, a congested climber may be detached from the wall as if it were a blanket, gently laid out on the ground and the dead and dying material (usually that next to the wall) 'fleeced' off before reattaching.

FRUIT. For fruit trees and bushes the objective is to build a strong framework in the formative years, and to ensure a regular supply of replacement shoots or spurs capable of producing sufficient blossom for a full crop of good quality fruit. The removal of diseased parts and the maintenance of controlled growth with branches open to air and sunlight are also important reasons for pruning.

Pome and stone fruits flower on wood usually one or more years old. Pruning of branches, shoots and spurs of established trees should aim at producing a balance of old and new wood. Gooseberries and currants bear flowers mainly on shoots of the previous year but also on older wood and spurs. In pruning established blackcurrants, about one third of the total number of branches is removed annually to encourage the production of young wood which fruits best. Other currants and gooseberries should have leaders reduced to about half their length, and laterals cut back short. Summer-fruiting raspberries bear fruit on laterals arising on canes produced in the previous year, and these are cut to ground level after cropping. Autumn-fruiting raspberries bear fruit on canes of the current year, and are pruned to ground level in the late winter. Blackberries and hybrid berries, although their canes are perennial, are pruned on the replacement system in the same way as summer-fruiting raspberries.

The pruning of apples, pears, gooseberries and currants is carried out during dormancy. Stone fruits are pruned in spring and summer in order to avoid exposure to the active stages of silver leaf disease and bacterial canker. Additional summer pruning is an essential means of restricting vigorous growth with intensive tree forms, and of developing and maintaining food structure in gooseberries and red and white currants. For further details, see FRUIT TREE PRUNING and the entries on individual fruits.

TECHNIQUES. All pruning cuts should be made cleanly with sharp tools directly above a growth bud or at a point where another stem or branch joins that being removed, or close to it. It is good practice to make pruning cuts to shoots and small branches sloping at an angle of 45° down from a bud. Buds so selected should of course be pointing in the direction in which the resulting shoot is desired. The aim in every case is to avoid leaving any length of stem or branch without the ability to produce leaves (to draw sap) which might otherwise give rise to dieback. The wounds left by the removal of large branches are likely to heal over most rapidly if the cut is made just a little removed from the trunk, beyond the slight swelling which encircles its base.

There is difference of opinion about the value of wound dressing with proprietary paints intended to protect wounds from infection and hasten healing. Arboriculturists accept that untreated wounds heal faster and that large wounds are only briefly protected since paint cover cracks and soon ceases to give any protection. There is strong evidence to suggest that wound-dressing actually inhibits the natural healing process. Undoubtedly many gardeners still feel reassured to see wounds covered with something claimed to be both antiseptic and sealant and in some countries wholly cosmetic dressings are sold to answer this need.

Care must be taken that branches which are being removed with a saw do not break and tear bark from the main limb. The branch should first be cut off a short distance from the trunk and two further cuts then made: a shallow undercut from the lower surface of the branch and a second complete cut from above just a little nearer the trunk or limb. The branch will snap off cleanly and the short remaining stub can be removed without fear of damage since it will have insufficient weight to cause tearing.

See also ARBORICULTURE.

**Prunus** L. (Lat. name for these plants.) PLUM; CHERRY; PEACH; ALMOND; APRICOT. Rosaceae. 430 species of deciduous, sometimes evergreen, shrubs or trees. Leaves alternate, serrate, sometimes entire; stipules present. Flowers usually white, often pink to red, solitary or in clusters or racemes; calyx 5-lobed; petals 5; stamens many; pistil solitary; style elongate; ovary superior. Fruit a fleshy, usually 1-seeded, pruinose drupe; stone compressed. N Temperate regions, S America.

CULTIVATION *Prunus* ssp. occur mainly in the temperate zones of the northern hemisphere, but with some representatives in the Andes. Many are found in woodland, at the woodland edge, or in hedgerows. *P. pensylvanica* plays a vital role in the natural regeneration of its native forests, acting as a nurse to the seedlings of other, longer-lived species, which eventually grow to shade it out. *P. maritima*, a coastal native, and *P. besseyi*, from the hot dry plains east of the Rockies, both occur in sandy habitats; and a number of the Asian species are found on inhospitable rock ledges and cliffs.

*Prunus* is probably unsurpassed in its combination of use with beauty; its fruiting species yield peach and nectarine, plums, almond, apricots, including the delicious wild Hunza apricot from Kashmir, cherries, cherry-plums or mirabelle, damsons and greengages. *P. spinosa* yields sloes, an addition to gin; its wood used for blackthorn walking sticks and, in Eire, for shillalahs.

In ornamental terms, *Prunus's* range of virtues is almost as diverse, with species suitable as lawn or border specimens, for formal training as wall-grown specimens, or in naturalistic plantings at the woodland edge or in the woodland garden. *Prunus* spp. are grown for their attractive habit and form, their decorative bark, their fine autumn colours and for their unrivalled display of blossom which, with judicious selection of spp. and cvs, can be extended almost throughout the year, from the late autumn and winter blooms of *P. subhirtella* 'Autumnalis', through late spring/ early summer with the late-flowering Japanese cherries such as 'Fugenzo' and 'Shirofugen', and into summer with the intermittent flushes of blossom on *P. cerasus* 'Semperflorens'. The majority flower during the spring, *P. cerasifera* and its cvs, and *P. davidiana* being amongst the earliest; in a mild season the latter will flower shortly after New Year. The British natives *P. avium* and *P. padus* have long been valued for their blossom; Moses Cook, in 1676, observed that 'their blossoms are a great relief to the industrious bees at that season'.

The shrubby species, *P. incisa, P. ×cistena* and *P. spinosa*, are used for hedging, the last especially useful in cold, exposed and maritime areas. *P. cerasifera* and its dark-leaved cvs, when grown as shrubs also make excellent hedging plants. The evergreens, *P. laurocerasus* and *P. lusitanica*, are often used as screens, being most attractive when allowed to develop their natural form without clipping, or in more formal hedging; both make good game cover, and so are often planted as understorey in woodland. *P. laurocerasus* is extremely tolerant of shade and tree drip, growing in conditions with almost no direct light, although it will not thrive in shallow chalk soils; in these conditions *P. lusitanica* makes an admirable substitute. Species grown primarily for their beautiful peeling bark include *P. serrula*, a glossy deep mahogany-red, and *P. maackii*, a shining foxy-russet. The bark of both species has a tactile quality, useful in preventing the build-up of algal growth which obscures their beauty; otherwise, this can be removed with a soft brush and water in summer.

The Japanese cherries (the Sato-zakura group), most notable for their often fragrant blossom, contribute a range of form and habit, from the upright narrow columns of 'Amanogawa' and stiffly ascending branches of 'Sekiyama', to the small weeping domes of 'Kiku-shidare'. This group includes many small trees for the confined spaces of urban gardens, where their tolerance of pollution is especially useful. Most colour well in autumn, in shades of yellow and tawny orange, and many also have attractively bronzed leaves in spring, in beautiful contrast to the emergent blossom.

Grow in well-drained moisture-retentive soils, siting deciduous species in full sun to ensure good flowering and autumn colour. *P. glandulosa* and *P. triloba* thrive when trained against a sheltered south- or southwest-facing wall. Plant evergreens in sun to semi-shade; *P. lusitanica, P. lyonii* and *P. ilicifolia* are tolerant of full sun. Stake standard specimen trees until established, especially in areas exposed to wind, and protect stems from rabbits and hares, who will ring-bark young trees. In very rich soils, some species may make rank growth, reducing flowering potential and increasing susceptibility to disease. With the exception of *P. laurocerasus*, which becomes chlorotic on shallow chalk, most *Prunus* spp. grow particularly well on calcareous soils.

Prune when necessary in late summer, ensuring a long enough period for wounds to heal before the onset of winter. Cut back the flowered shoots of *P. glandulosa* and *P. triloba* to 2–3 buds from the base, especially when grown as wall shrubs. If grown as a flowering hedge, trim after flowering. Cut back *P. laurocerasus* and *P. lusitanica* with secateurs in spring or late summer; neglected specimens can be rejuvenated by cutting hard back into old wood in spring.

Propagate species from seed; they may hybridize and not come true, although seed-raised specimens are generally longer-lived. Collect seed when ripe, remove flesh and stratify in damp peat for 10–14 weeks (3–4 weeks for *P. dulcis* and *P. armeniaca*) prior to sowing. Alternatively sow outdoors in the cold frame in autumn and protect from rodents. Propagate shrubby species such as *P. glandulosa, P. laurocerasus, P. pumila, P. tenella* and *P. triloba* by simple layering in early spring. Cultivars are propagated commercially by budding or grafting; the Japanese and large-flowered cherries on to *P. avium*; bird cherry types, such as *P. cornuta, P. serotina* and *P. virginiana*, on to *P. padus*. Species such as *P. cerasifera, P. conradinae, P. incisa, P. spinosa* and *P. subhirtella*, can be propagated by semi-ripe heel cuttings in summer, in a closed case with bottom heat at 16–18°C/60–65°F. Most tree and shrub species can be propagated by softwood cuttings taken when plants are growing strongly, in spring and early summer, treated with hormone-rooting preparations, and rooted with mist and bottom heat.

*Prunus* is susceptible to a number of pest and disease problems: dieback and disease susceptibility is increased on poorly drained soils. Aphids such as mealy plum aphid (*Hyalopterus pruni*) causes sooty mould on *P. domestica*. Cherry black fly (*Myzus cerasi*) mainly on *P. avium, P. cerasus* but also on *P. serrulata* and *P. ×yedoensis*, causes sooty mould and distortion of young leaves and shoots with a subsequent check on growth. Spray heavy infestations with a specific aphicide. *Prunus* spp., particularly plums and blackthorn, are sometimes the winter host for the waterlily aphid *Rhopalosiphum nymphaeae*, a persistent source of re-infection when these genera are grown in close proximity.

Silver leaf (*Chondrostereum purpureum*) is the most damaging disease of *P. domestica* but others, including *P. dulcis, P. armeniaca, P. cerasus, P. avium* and *P. lusitanica*, are also susceptible. The disease causes a silvery sheen to the leaves which later split, and dark staining of the wood accompanies branch die back. Plants may recover spontaneously; remove affected deadwood and burn. In severe cases where the whole tree is affected, uproot and burn. *Taphrina deformans*, peach leaf curl, is most prevalent on *Prunus persica, P. dulcis* and *P. armeniaca*, especially in cold damp springs and in moist soils, causing reddened blistered and distorted leaves soon after bud burst; fruit may later show similar symptoms. If practicable remove and burn affected parts, spray with a sulphur-based fungicide in late winter and before bud burst. *Taphrina cerasi* is sometimes the causal agent of witches' brooms, the effects are largely cosmetic.

Several leaf spot diseases affect *Prunus*. *Blumeriella jaapii*, common in Northern Europe but not found in Britain, is most damaging and prevalent in wet seasons and causes extensive defoliation. *Prunus laurocerasus* sometimes develops shot hole, caused by *Trochila laurocersi* or *Stigmina carpophila*; yellow-brown spots darkening as conidia mature finally drop out. Shot hole is more prevalent on plants grown on waterlogged soils, and also when pruning is done in summer, wounding leaves that are then open to invasion. Prune in autumn. Also affected by honey fungus, *Armillaria mellea*.

See also ALMONDS, APRICOTS, CHERRIES, PEACHES AND NECTARINES, PLUMS.

***P. alleghaniensis*** Porter. NORTHERN SLOE; ALLEGHANY PLUM; SLOE. Shrub or, less often, small tree to 3.5m. Branches smooth, dark grey; young branchlets rufous, lustrous. Lvs to 9×3cm, lanceolate to oval-lanceolate, apex acute or acuminate, finely and sharply serrate, green and glabrous or sparse-pubesc. above, pale green and pubesc. beneath, midvein prominent; petiole to 12mm, pubesc.; stipules linear, with bright red glands at margin. Fls to 12mm diam., in sessile, 2–4-fld umbels; pedicels to 1cm, slender; cal. narrow-obconic, tube 3mm, lobes 2mm, narrow oblong-ovate, erect; pet. 5mm, white, round-obovate, abruptly narrowed to a short claw. Fr. 1cm diam., subglobose, somewhat oval or obovoid, dark purple, blue-pruinose, flesh yellow; stone 12×8mm, obovoid, obtuse at apex, turgid. Spring. NE US. Z5.

***P. americana*** Marsh. WILD PLUM; AMERICAN RED PLUM; AUGUST PLUM; GOOSE PLUM; HOG PLUM. Tree to 10.5m. Bark dark brown, exfoliating; branches spiny; young branchlets chestnut, later dark brown. Lvs to 10×5cm, oval, sometimes oval-oblong to narrow-obovate, apex acuminate, base gradually narrowed, green and glabrous above, pale and glabrous beneath, sharply and sometimes double-serrate; petiole to 14mm, pubesc. above; stipules linear. Fls to 2.5cm diam., in subsessile, 3–4-fld umbels; pedicels to 1.5cm, slender, glabrous; cal. tube 3mm, obconic, glabrous, lobes 3mm+, lanceolate or oblong-lanceolate, obtuse or sometimes acute; pet. to 1×0.6cm, oblong-oval or obovate. Fr. to 2.5cm, usually subglobose, red-orange to red, minutely white-punctate, blue-pruinose, flesh yellow; stone to 16×14mm, oval, apex pointed or rounded, turgid. Spring. E & C North America. Edible cvs, known as 'American plums', include hybrids (usually with *P. salicina*): 'Grenville', red mottled yellow, large, dessert quality; 'South Dakota', yellow, dessert quality, cold-hardy. Z3.

***P.*** **×*amygdalo-persica*** (Weston) Rehd. *(P. dulcis* × *P. persica.)* Tree or shrub. Lvs similar to *P. dulcis*, scabrous-serrate. Fls to 5cm diam., light pink. Fr. peach-like, dry. 'Pollardii': fls large, rich pink, March; type of the cross. Z4.

***P. angustifolia*** Marsh. CHICASA PLUM; CHICKASAW PLUM. Shrub or small tree to 3m. Bark dark rufous, somewhat smooth. Lvs to 5×2cm, lanceolate or oval-lanceolate, usually strong conduplicate, acute, usually narrowed at base, margin fine glandular-serrate, glabrous and lustrous green above, pale beneath; petiole to 1cm, usually red and pubesc.; stipules linear-lanceolate, glandular, serrate. Fls to 9mm diam., in 2–4-fld umbels; pedicels to 6mm, glabrous; cal. tube to 2.5mm, obconic, glabrous, lobes ovate, obtuse, shorter than tube, glabrous, ciliate at margin, eglandular; pet. 4mm, ovate-orbicular or obovate-orbicular. Fr. subglobose, small, flesh yellow; stone to 12mm×1cm, oval, obtuse or pointed, obtuse at base. Winter–spring. S US. var. ***watsonii*** (Sarg.) Waugh. SAND PLUM. Shrub to 2m. Branches stiff; branchlets spiny. Lvs to 4.5×2cm, oval or oblong-oval; petiole slender, to 18mm, glabrous. Fls with anth. sometimes red. Fr. stone 14×9mm, oval, rarely obovoid, apex rounded or pointed, base truncate or oblique. Spring. US (Kansas to New Mexico). Z6.

***P. apetala*** Franch. & Savat. CLOVE CHERRY. Deciduous small tree to 7mm. Bark grey-brown or dark purple; branchlets grey-brown. Lvs to 9.5×4.5cm, obovate or obovate-elliptic, apex acuminate, base obtuse, acute or truncate, margins incised, green and adpressed pubesc. above, lighter and patent-pilose beneath; petiole to 11mm, patent-pilose. Fls to 2cm diam., flat, in 1–3-fld umbels; peduncles short; pedicels to 16mm, patent-pilose; cal. tube tubular, to 1cm, pale brown, sep. to 4mm; stamens 27; pistil to 16mm. Fr. 8mm diam., round-ovoid, black. Spring. Japan (N to C Honshu). Z6.

***P. armeniaca*** L. APRICOT. Tree to 10m, with spherical-flat or somewhat elongate, patent crown. Bark rufous; branches glabrous. Lvs to 12×11cm, orbicular or ovate, glabrous, irregularly serrate to subcrenate; petioles to 5.5cm, canaliculate, dark red, glandular at base. Fls to 4cm diam., white or, rarely, pink, usually solitary; cal. tube cylindric, thinly pubesc. proximally, dark red-green; pet. orbicular, oval or obovate; stamens 25–45, fil. white, anth. yellow. Fr. to 5.5×5cm, globose, ovoid or, rarely, obovoid, white to orange-red or yellow, pubesc.; stone globose to ovoid or obovoid. Spring–summer. N China. var. ***ansu*** Maxim. Small tree. Shoots flushed purple. Lvs rounded. Fls pink; sep. strongly reflexed. Often confused with *P. mume*. 'Flora Pleno': shoots flushed purple in spring; fls semi-double, buds carmine opening pink, in dense clusters. 'Pendula': branches weeping. 'Variegata': lvs variegated white. For edible cvs see APRICOTS. Z5.

***P.*** **×*arnoldiana*** Rehd. *(P. cerasifera* × *P. triloba.)* Closely resembles *P. triloba*, but lvs more elliptic, larger, thicker, less coarsely serrate, and less pubesc.; fls white, appearing with lvs; pedicels longer; sep. reflexed and pubesc. inside. First grown at the Arnold Arboretum from the *P. triloba* wild form pollinated by *P. cerasifera*; of interest as a plum–almond hybrid. Z4.

***P. avium*** L. BIRD CHERRY; SWEET CHERRY; GEAN; WILD CHERRY; MAZZARD. Tree to 20m, occasionally to 30m, with broadly conical crown. Young shoots glabrous. Lvs 10.5×5cm, oblong-ovate, acuminate, coarsely and irregularly crenate-serrate, pubesc. on sides of midrib and veins beneath; petiole 3cm, glabrous, glandular. Fls 2.5cm diam., white, in sessile, several-fld umbels; cal. tube 6mm, broadly-urceolate, glabrous, sep. reflexed. Fr. 2cm, cordate-ovoid, dark maroon. Spring. Europe to Asia Minor, Caucasus, W Siberia. 'Asplenifolia': lvs deeply cut, narrow. 'Decumana': lvs very large, stretched convex, to 30cm long, to 18cm wide; fls large, to 25mm diam. 'Fastigiata': habit narrowly upright to conic. 'Nana': habit dwarf; branches short; fls solitary. 'Pendula': branches semi-pendulous, somewhat stiff. 'Plena' ('Multiplex', 'Grandiflora'): habit tall, to 17m high, to 10m wide; branches wide-sweeping with age; bark brown, shiny, peeling horizontally, silver and rough with age; lvs bright green, orange and red in autumn; fls double, to ×4cm, rosette form, pure white in hanging clusters, early May. 'Premorsa' ('Praemorsa'); lvs notched at apex, deformed. 'Rubrifolia': lvs purple flushed red. 'Salicifolia': lvs deeply cut, very narrow. For edible cvs see CHERRIES. Z3.

***P. besseyi*** Bail. WESTERN SAND CHERRY; ROCKY MOUNTAINS CHERRY. Bushy subshrub to 120cm, erect or often prostrate. Lvs to 4.5×1.5cm, oval-elliptic or oblong-obovate, apex acute, rarely obtuse, base cuneate, lower half sharp-serrate, glabrous; petiole to 6mm; stipules linear, glandular-serrate. Fls to 12mm diam., 3–4-clustered; pedicels to 7mm, glabrous, glandular; cal. glabrous; pet. 6mm, oblong-oval, narrowed to a claw. Fr. to 18mm diam., globular or slightly oblong, black to red and yellow; stone to 1×0.8cm, subglobose to ovoid, apex obtuse or pointed, base rounded or slightly truncate. Spring. 'Black Beauty': small, black, sweet, crops well. 'Hansen's': large, purple-black, good flavour. Z3.

***P. bifrons*** Fritsch. Low shrub to 2m, semi-erect. Young shoots pubesc. Lvs dimorphic, dark sage-green above, silver-tomentose beneath, lvs on young branches to 3.5×2cm, broad-ovate to obovate, acute, lvs on previous year's shoots 22×9mm, nearly oblanceolate, conspicuously more blunt at apex; petiole 3mm. Fls 2cm diam., pink, solitary or paired; pedicel very short; cal. tube 7mm, campanulate, somewhat ventricose at base; pet. subrotund, sparse long-pubesc. dorsally near the base; style shorter than stamens, villous below. Fr. 8mm diam., cordate-rotund, amber-crimson, pubesc., later glabrous; stone almost smooth. Himalaya (SW Afghanistan, Kashmir). Z5.

***P.*** **×*blireana*** André. *(P. cerasifera* 'Atropurpurea' or 'Pissordii' × double form of *P. mume*.) Shrub or small tree to 4.5m, of rounded habit. Branchlets somewhat cernuous. Young lvs to 6cm, oval, bronze-red, green by summer; petiole to 1.5cm. Fls 3cm diam., bright rose, double, solitary; sep. glandular; ovaries pubesc. Spring. Garden origin (Lemoine, 1906). 'Moseri': lvs light red flushed brown; fls small, pale pink, sep. without glands; vigorous. Z5.

***P. brigantina*** Vill. BRIANÇON APRICOT. Deciduous shrub or small bushy tree to 6m. Stem short. Lvs to 7.5×6.5cm, ovate or oval, short-acuminate, often slightly cordate at base, biserrate, pubesc. beneath, especially on midrib and veins; petiole to 17mm. Fls 2cm diam., 2–5-clustered, white or pale pink. Fr. a small, clear yellow, smooth apricot. SE France (Briançon). Z7.

***P. buergeriana*** Miq. Tree to 9m. Young shoots pubesc. or glabrescent. Lvs to 11cm, elliptic to oblong-elliptic, apex acuminate, base cuneate, light green and almost completely glabrous beneath; petioles to 12mm. Fls 7mm diam., white, in thin, puberulous racemes to 8cm; cal. tube cup-shaped, sep. short, denticulate; stamens slightly exceeding pet.; style short. Fr. subglobose, black. Japan, Korea. Z5.

***P. campanulata*** Maxim. TAIWAN CHERRY; FORMOSAN CHERRY; BELL-FLOWERED CHERRY. Deciduous small tree. Bark purple-brown; young branches brown, glabrous. Lvs to 11×8cm, elliptic, apex acuminate, base rounded, double-serrate, teeth acute, deep green above, green beneath, glabrous; petioles to 12mm, glabrous, glandular; stipules long, much-divided. Fls to 3cm diam., campanulate, cernuous, in 5–6-fld umbels; peduncles glabrous; pedicels to 1.5cm, glabrous; cal. tube campanulate, glabrous, lobes broad ovate-triangular, entire; pet. round, retuse, claret; stamens 30–40; style and ovary glabrous. Fr. 11mm diam., subglobose, black-purple. Spring. S Japan, Taiwan. 'Okame' *(P. campanulata* × *P. incisa)*: habit broadly ovate, to 8m high, to 7m wide; lvs small, dark green, light green when young, flaming orange in autumn; fls shocking pink, in clusters to 3, profuse, long-lasting. 'Plena': fls double, small, carmine. 'Shosar' *(P. campanulata* × *P. sargentia)*: habit tall, broadly columnar; stalks deep red; lvs grass green, later yellow flushed copper; fls single, large, to 4cm across, dark pink. Z7.

***P. canescens*** Bois. HOARY CHERRY; GREYLEAF CHERRY. Shrub to 3m. Bark later exfoliating, leaving a shiny brown, mirror-like reflecting trunk; branchlets stiffly ascending; young shoots grey-fawn, pubesc. Lvs 6×3cm, ovate to ovate-lanceolate, acuminate, rounded at base, coarse-serrate, pubesc. above, densely pubesc., beneath, often stalked glandular near base; petioles 1cm; stipules dentate. Fls 12mm diam., tinted pink, in 2–5-fld, compact corymbs; bracts foliaceous; pedicels 5.5mm, pilose; cal. tube red, campanulate to urceolate, glabrous above, pubesc. at base, sep. narrow-triangular, patent, often ciliate; pet. oblong-ovate; style lax-pilose below. Fr. 1cm, subspherical, cherry-red. Spring. China (Hupei, Sichuan). Z6.

***P. caroliniana*** (Mill.) Ait. CHERRY LAUREL; LAUREL CHERRY; WILD ORANGE; MOCK ORANGE. Evergreen tree to 12m. Branchlets thin, glabrous. Lvs to 12×3.5cm, oblong-elliptic to elliptic-lanceolate, apex acute to acuminate, mucronate, glabrous, coriaceous, dark green and lustrous above, paler beneath; petioles thick, broad, glabrous. Fls to 5mm diam., in congested racemes; pedicels to 4mm; cal. tube obconic, lobes small, thin, rounded; pet. cream, minute; stamens orange, exserted. Fr. to 13mm, ovoid to subglobose, short-pointed, lustrous, black. Spring. S US (Florida to Texas and North Carolina). Z7.

***P. cerasifera*** Ehrh. CHERRY PLUM; MYROBALAN. Deciduous tree-like shrub to round-headed tree to 9m, often spiny. Young bark glabrous. Lvs to 6.5×3cm, ovate, oval or obovate, dentate, bright green, lanuginose on midrib and veins beneath. Fls to 2.5cm, pure white, solitary. Fr. to 3cm diam., round, smooth, red to yellow, somewhat pruinose, indented at the junction with the stalk. Spring. Asia Minor, Caucasus. 'Diversifolia' ('Asplenifolia'): lvs ovate to lanceolate, irregularly lobed or toothed, purple tinted bronze; fls white; a sport of 'Pissardii'. 'Festeri': lvs large; fls large, pink; related to 'Pissardii'. 'Hessii' ('Hessei'): habit small, shrubby; shoots purple; lvs narrow, pale green, later purple tinted bronze, toothed and mottled cream; fls pure white; slow-growing. 'Hollywood' ('Trailblazer') ('Nigra' × 'Shiro'): lvs green, later red-brown, to 9cm long; fls pale pink, appearing before lvs; fr. large red. 'Frankthrees': broadly globe-shaped, to 7m high, to 7m wide; trunk sturdy; lvs large, dark purple, flushed green when young; fls pink; vigorous; a sport of 'Newport'. 'Lindsayae': habit slender; shoots nearly black when young; lvs red-brown, later green; fls to 2cm across, solitary or paired, light almond pink. 'Louis Asselin': habit small, shrubby, lvs green speckled white; slow-growing. 'Mount St. Helens': sport and improved form of 'Newport'. 'Newport' ('Newportii'): habit shrubby, to 3m high; lvs brown tinged bronze; fls small, white to light pink. 'Pendula': habit weeping; stems interlacing; lvs green; fls white. 'Pissardii': lvs large, dark red, later purple; fls white, buds pink, profuse, appearing before foliage; fr. maroon, globose, to 3cm diam. 'Purpusii': lvs green, turning red-brown, later pink and yellow along midrib. 'Rosea' *(P. cerasifera* 'Vesuvius' × *P. spinosa)*: lvs fading from purple flushed bronze, to green flushed bronze, to green; twigs and shoots almost thornless; stems purple; fls dense, clear salmon pink, later fading. 'Spencer Thundercloud': habit compact, dwarf; fls pink, fragrant; fr. large, edible. 'Thundercloud': habit tall, broadly ovate, to 10m; lvs rusty brown, dull bronze in autumn; fls pink. 'Vesuvius' ('Krauter's Vesuvius'): habit broadly globe-shaped, to 5m; stems red-black; lvs large, red-black; fls pink fading to blush; tolerant to hot and sunny conditions. 'Woodii': lvs small, deep red-black; fls pink. ssp. ***divaricata*** (Ledeb.) Schneid. More slender than species type and looser habit. Lvs rounded at base. Fls smaller. Fr. globose, 2cm diam., yellow, not indented at the junction with the stalk. Balkans, Asia Minor, Caucasus, C Asia. Z4.

***P. cerasoides*** D. Don. Semi-pendulous tree. Bark grey-brown, glossy. Lvs to 12×5cm, obovate-elliptic or obovate, apex acuminate, base rounded, double-serrate, deep green above, light green beneath; petioles to 1.5cm, light green-brown, sparse-pubesc., pale green-glandular above; stipules short, viscid. Fls 4cm diam., in 2–3-fld umbels; peduncles glabrous; pedicels to 2.5cm, glabrous; cal. tube cylindric, sep. lanceolate, glabrous; pet. to 18×14mm, round, obovate, retuse, pale red; stamens 40–50; style and ovary glabrous. Fr. 13mm×1.5cm, flattened, broad-ellipsoid, yellow-brown, rugose. Autumn–winter. Himalaya, China (Yunnan), N Burma. var. ***rubea*** F.B. Ingram. To 30m. Shoots glabrous. Lvs to 11×5cm, broad oval-oblong to obovate, caudately acuminate, finely and densely serrate, teeth uneven, gland-tipped, bright green above, paler beneath, glabrous except for pubesc. on veins beneath. Fls in 2–4-fld, pendulous umbels; cal. to 9mm, tubular-campanulate, crimson, brown at base, sep. 5mm, ascending, ovate, obtuse, carmine; cor. 14mm, campanulate, pink-red, pet. not patent. Fr. 1.5cm, ellipsoid, red. Spring N Bengal, Bhutan, Assam, Upper Burma, China (W Yunnan). Z8.

***P. cerasus*** L. SOUR CHERRY. Bushy shrub or small round-headed tree to 6m. Young shoots glabrous. Lvs 6.5×3.5cm, narrow-ovate to elliptic-obovate, acute, finely and doubly serrate, dark glossy green, glabrous, occasionally slightly pubesc. beneath when young; petioles 1.5cm, glabrous, often glandular. Fls 23mm diam., white, in sessile, several-fld umbels; pedicels to 3cm; cal. tube broadly urn-shaped. Fr. 18mm diam., subglobose, dark red; stone 8×7mm, broad-ellipsoid. Spring. SE Europe to N India, Iran, Kurdistan. var. ***austera*** L. MORELLO CHERRY. Tree to 9m, usually of somewhat pendulous habit. Branches stout. Fls to 6cm; pedicels longer. Fr. dark or black-red, with dark-coloured juice; stone globose. 'Bunyardii': lvs small, obtuse; flower stalks to 5cm. 'Cucullata': lvs convex. 'Laciniata': lvs deeply cut. 'Persiciflora': fls double, soft pink. 'Plena': fls semi-double, white. 'Polygyna': habit spreading, semi-pendulous; fls and fr. profuse. 'Pulverulenta': lvs regularly variegated yellow and white. 'Rhexii': habit round-headed, to 10m high, to 8m wide; branched and twigs thin; lvs dark green, glossy; fls large, to 4cm diam., tight rosette form, white, early May. 'Salicifolia': lvs narrow lanceolate, to 12cm×3cm, doubly serrate. 'Semperflorens': habit dense to pendulous; fls loosely grouped to 4, white, April and June; fr. small, dark red, sour. 'Umbraculifera': habit dwarf, dense, rounded; lvs narrow. 'Variegata': lvs blotched white. var. ***caproniana*** L. AMARELLE CHERRY; KENTISH RED CHERRY. Tree to 9m, round-headed. Branches stout, usually erect. Lvs to 12×5.5cm, broad-elliptic, apex acuminate or short-mucronate, base cuneate, crenate-serrate, dark or bright green above, lighter beneath, shiny, glabrous; petioles to 3cm. Fls in 2–4-fld umbels; pedicels shorter; pet. to 13mm, white. Fr. globose, light red, juice colourless; stone usually globose, smooth. var. ***frutescens*** Neilr. BUSH SOUR CHERRY. Shrub to 1m, of suckering habit with flexuous crown. Branchlets slender, cernuous, stoloniferous. Lvs to 7.5×4.5cm, ascending, wide or elongate-elliptic or obovate, acute, glabrous. Fls in 2–3-fld umbels; pet. 1cm, entire. Fr. 1cm, globose, dark red, juice colourless; stones ovate. C Europe. var. ***marasca*** (Host) Viv. MARASCHINO CHERRY. Tree, strongly branched. Branches cernuous, frequently hanging to the ground. Stipules larger. Fls in compact infl. Fr. black-red, very small. For edible cvs, see CHERRIES. Z3.

***P. changyangensis*** (F.B. Ingram) F.B. Ingram. CHINESE SPRING CHERRY. Small tree to 10.5m. Young shoots pilose. Lvs 5×2.5cm, ovate to oblong-obovate, abruptly acuminate, dense-pilose beneath, later pilose on venation only; petioles to 9mm, eglandular, clearly pilose; stipules to 1cm, linear-lanceolate, fine-serrate. Fls 23mm diam., pink-white, in 3–5-fld corymbs; pedicels to 3cm, villous; cal. tube to 5×4.5mm, urn-shaped, tumid at base, pubesc., sep. tapering, serrulate, pubesc.; pet. incised; stamens 18; style 9.5mm, villous at base. Fr. 9.5mm diam., subglobose, purple-black. China (W Hupei). Z6.

***P. ×cistena*** (Hansen) Koehne. *(P. cerasifera* 'Atropurpurea' × *P. pumila.)* Shrub to 2.5m, weakly growing. Lvs to 6cm, obovate-lanceolate, acuminate, red-brown, serrate, lustrous above; petiole to 1.5cm. Fls 1 or 2, white; cal. and pedicel red-brown. Fr. black-purple. Garden origin. 'Crimson Dwarf': habit dense, upright, to 1.2m high, to 1.2m wide; lvs pointed, red tinted bronze, crimson when young; shoot tips brilliant red; fls single, shell pink, calyces dark red, spring. 'Schmidteis': habit broadly globe-shaped, to 5m high, to 4m wide; lvs large, purple, flushed green when young; fls single, pink; vigorous; a sport of *P. ×cistena*. Z3.

***P. cocomilia*** Ten. Shrub or small tree to 5m, usually without spines. Branchlets glabrous or sparsely adpressed-pubesc. Lvs to 4×2cm, elliptic to obovate-elliptic, glandular-crenulate, glabrous or adpressed-pubesc.; petiole 1cm. Fls to 1.5cm diam., white, 2–4-clustered; pedicels to 4mm. Fr. 2cm, ovoid-globose, yellow, flushed red, pendent. N Italy. Z6.

***P. conadenia*** Koehne. Tree to 10m. Young shoots glabrous. Lvs to 9cm, obovate, caudately acuminate, rounded to slightly cordate at base, glabrous or subglabrous beneath, double-serrate, teeth glandular, glands conical, large. Fls in 5–8-fld racemes; pedicels to 1.5cm; styles pubesc. Fr. ovate, red; stone punctate. W China. Z5.

***P. concinna*** Koehne. Shrub or small tree, 2–4m. Young shoots glabrous. Lvs to 7×3cm, oval-oblong to obovate-oblong, long-acuminate, base round to cuneate, scabrous, simple to biserrate, dark green above with scattered pubescence, venation pubesc. beneath; petioles 6mm, usually tinged red, somewhat pubesc., biglandular; stipules linear, small. Fls 2.5cm diam., white or occasionally tinted soft pink, solitary or grouped in sessile clusters of 2, sometimes 4; pedicel 1cm, subtended by leafy bracts; cal. 7mm, glabrous, purple, narrowly campanulate; sep. entire, narrowly campanulate; sep. entire, narrowly triangular, pet. 12mm, incised, obovate. Fr. ovate, purple-black. April. C China. Z6.

***P. consociiflora*** Schneid. Small deciduous tree. Young shoots brown, glabrous. Lvs to 7.5×3cm, conduplicate in the bud state, oblanceolate to obovate, apex acuminate, base tapered, denticulate, teeth glandular, axillary-lanuginose on venation beneath. Fls 13mm diam., white, 2–3-clustered in 2.5cm diam. fascicles; pedicels 6.5mm, slender, glabrous; cal. funneliform, glabrous, lobes narrow-triangular; ovary glabrous. Fr. globose. Spring. China. Z6.

***P. cornuta*** (Royle) Steud. HIMALAYAN BIRD CHERRY; BIRD CHERRY. Tree to 15m. Lvs to 15×6cm, elliptic, acuminate, cuneate to subcordate at base, finely serrate, glabrous or pubesc. beneath, axillary pubesc. on the lateral venation beneath; petioles to 2.5cm, usually with 1–2 glands toward apex; stipules to 1.5cm, linear-lanceolate. Fls in terminal racemes to 25cm; pedicels to 5mm; cal. cup to 3mm, glabrous, lobes broad-triangular, 1mm, short-ciliate with stout, glandular pubesc.; pet. to 3.5mm, white, suborbicular; stamens to 3mm. Fr. ellipsoid to subglobose; stone to 8mm. Spring–summer. Himalaya (Bhutan, Sikkim). Z5.

***P. cyclamina*** Koehne. Tree to 9m. Young shoots glabrous. Lvs 10×4.5cm, oblong-obovate to oblong, apex abruptly acuminate, base broad-cuneate or rounded, glabrous, serrations often gland-tipped, strongly ribbed and slightly rugose; petioles 1cm, glandular, grooved; stipules occasionally fimbriate, stalked-glandular. Fls 3.5cm diam., rose-pink, in usually 4-fld corymbs; pedicels 17.5mm, glabrous or sparse-villous; cal. tube 4mm, broad-campanulate, glabrous, sep. longer than cal. tube, sparsely ciliate, strongly reflexed; pet. narrow-ovate, deeply incised. Fr. ovoid, red; stone small, smooth. Spring. C China (Mts of Hupeh). Z6.

***P. ×dasycarpa*** Ehrh. *(P. armeniaca × P. cerasifera.)* BLACK APRICOT. Small tree to 6m. Young shoots numerous, slender, glabrous, olive red. Lvs to 6cm, oval to orbicular-ovate, short-acuminate, finely and narrowly irregular-crenate, pubesc. on veins beneath, somewhat rugose; petiole to 2.5cm, often glandular. Fls white, pink-tinged; pedicels to 7mm, slender, thin-pubesc.; cal. teeth orbicular, small. Fr. 3cm diam., subglobose, magenta to violet-black, velutinous-pubesc., purple-pruinose. Spring. C Asia, Asia Minor. Z5.

***P. davidiana*** (Carr.) Franch. DAVID'S PEACH. Deciduous tree to 9m. Branchlets erect, rod-like, glabrous, Lvs to 13×4cm, lanceolate, long-acuminate, dark green and shiny above, paler beneath, fine- and sharp-toothed; petiole to 2cm, glandular. Fls 2.5cm diam., white or pale pink, solitary; cal. glabrous, lobes oblong, rounded. Fr. 3cm diam., spherical, yellow, lanuginose; stone punctate. Winter–spring. China. 'Alba': branches upright; lvs and shoots light green; fls white. 'Rubra': fls pink tinted red. Z4.

***P. ×dawyckensis*** Sealy *(P. canescens × P. dielsiana.)* Tree to 9m, young shoots downy; bark dark brown, shining. Lvs to 9cm, elliptic or narrowly ovate, coarsely serrate, pubesc. above and beneath; petiole to 1.5cm. Fls 2–4 in short corymbs, to 2cm diam., pale pink; cal. tube pubesc. at base, to 6mm. Fr. ellipsoid, to 1.5cm, amber-red. China. 'Dawsar': habit upright, small; shoots; lvs, fl. stalks, cal. pubesc.; fls large, pink-purple, fading later, cal. tinted red, pet. incised at apex. Z6.

***P. dielsiana*** Schneid. Tree to 6m. Bark tawny brown; young shoots pubesc. Lvs 10×4cm, oblong-obovate to oblong, abruptly acuminate, broad-cuneate at base, glabrous above, pubesc. beneath, especially on veins; petioles 1.5cm, grooved, glandular, clearly pilose; stipules branched, gland-tipped, fimbriate. Fls 3.5cm diam., white or pale pink, in corymbose racemes; peduncle long, with foliaceous bracts; pedicels with round gland-fimbriate bracts at base; cal. tube 4cm, broad-campanulate, pubesc. at base, sep. longer than tube, strongly reflexed; pet. incised. Fr. 8mm diam., broad-ovate; stone smooth. China (W Hupei, E Sichuan). Z6.

***P. ×domestica*** L. *(P. spinosa × P. cerasifera* ssp. *divaricata.)* PLUM; COMMON PLUM. Deciduous tree to 12m, without spines or somewhat spiny. Lvs to 10×6cm, elliptic or oblong, pubesc., later glabrous or sparsely pilose beneath, especially on veins; petioles to 2cm. Fls to 2.5cm diam., white, 2–4-clustered; pedicels to 2cm. Fr. to 8cm, pendent, ovoid or subglobose, yellow or red to violet and dark blue, flesh green or yellow; stone almost smooth. Spring. S Europe, Eurasia. 'Plantierensis': fls semi-double, white; fr. violet. ssp. ***insititia*** (L.) Schneid. BULLACE. Branches brown, often spiny; branchlets lanuginose. Lvs pubesc. Fr. usually rounded or broad-ellipsoid, smaller, usually dark purple; stone less compressed than species type, edges blunt. See also BULLACE; DAMSON; PLUMS. Z5.

***P. dulcis*** (Mill.) D.A. Webb. ALMOND; ALMOND TREE. Deciduous trees to 9m, of bushy habit when old. Branchlets glabrous. Lvs to 13×4cm, lanceolate, apex long-acuminate, base broad-cuneate to round, light green above, glabrous, fine-toothed; petiole to 2.5cm, glandular. Fls to 5cm, solitary or paired; pedicel short; cal. tube campanulate, lobes 4mm, oblong, rounded, lanuginose near edges; pet. rose or almost white. Fr. to 6.5cm, ovoid, velutinous-lanuginose, flesh dry; stone smooth, punctate. Syria to N Africa. 'Alba': fls single, white. 'Alba Plena': fls double, white. 'Erecta': to 6m, habit broadly columnar; branches erect; fls pink. 'Macrocarpa': fls to 5cm diam., palest pink; fr. to 8cm long, large, edible. 'Pendula': branches pendulous. 'Praecox': fls pale pink, 2 weeks earlier than type. 'Purpurea': lvs red flushed purple. 'Roseoplena' ('Rosea Plena'): fls double and dense, to 4cm diam., dark pink. For fruiting cvs, see ALMONDS. Z7.

***P.*×*dunbarii*** Rehd. *(P. americana × P. maritima.)* Resembles *P. maritima*, but shoots later glabrous, lvs larger, more acuminate, less pubesc. beneath, and serrations more scabrous; pedicel and cal. later glabrous. Fr. purple, larger; stone flatter. US. Z3.

***P.*×*eminens*** Beck. *(P. cerasus × P. fruticosa.)* Erect shrub to 3m. Intermediate between parents, but lvs and fls larger, and petioles and pedicels longer than those of *P. fruticosa*. Z4.

***P. fasciculata*** (Torr.) A. Gray. DESERT ALMOND. Divaricately much-branched deciduous shrub to 3m. Branchlets short, stiff. Lvs to 1.5cm, fascicled on short branchlets, oblanceolate-spathulate, entire, pale green, minutely pubesc. Fls 6mm diam., subsessile, 2–3-clustered; cal. tube 2mm; pet. 3mm, oblanceolate. Fr. to 12mm, ovoid, dry, brown-tomentose; stone smooth. Spring. N America (California to Arizona). Z7.

***P. fenzliana*** Fritsch. Shrub or tree to 1.5m. Branches divaricate, very long, purple. Lvs to 8×2cm, elliptic-lanceolate, orbicular, often cuneate at base, subcoriaceous, smooth, green above, paler beneath, crenate-serrate, adjacent teeth unequal; petiole 1.5cm. Fls 1–5-clustered; cal. tube campanulate, red, lobes somewhat short, obtuse or acuminate; pet. pink, broad-oval or almost rounded, incised. Fr. sessile, rounded, velutinous; stone to 2.5×1.5cm, ovoid, compressed, acuminate or obtuse. Spring–summe. Caucasus. Z4.

***P. fremontii*** S. Wats. DESERT APRICOT. Deciduous shrub or small tree to 4m, rigidly branched. Branchlets often spine-tipped, rufous, glabrous. Lvs to 2cm, round to broad-ovate, serrate; petioles to 4mm. Fls solitary or few-clustered; pedicels to 12mm, thin; cal. tube 2.5mm, campanulate, sep. 1.5mm, ciliate; pet. to 6mm, white. Fr. to 14mm, elliptic-ovoid, yellow, puberulent, dry. Spring. US (California.) Z7.

***P. fruticosa*** Pall. STEPPE CHERRY. Shrub to 1m, rarely to 2m, with dense crown. Branches erect or cernuous, producing root suckers. Shoots virgate, later glabrous. Lvs to 5cm, oblong-elliptic, obovate or lanceolate, apex acute or obtuse, base cuneate, glabrous, shiny dark green above, much paler beneath; petiole to 1.5cm; stipules narrow, linear, dentate. Fls in 3–4-fld umbels; pedicels to 2.5cm, glabrous, recurved, cal. tube campanulate; pet. to 7mm, white, obovate, usually incised. Fr. to 1.5cm, subglobose, usually mucronate, dark red; stone acute at both ends. Spring. C & E Europe to Siberia. 'Pendula': branches slender, pendulous. 'Variegata': branches slender, pendulous; lvs green speckled cream. Z4.

***P.*×*gigantea*** (Späth) Koehne. *(P. dulcis × P. persica × P. cerasifera.)* Closely resembles *P. cerasifera*. Lvs to 12cm, elliptic-oblong to elliptic-lanceolate; petiole usually biglandular. Fls light pink, subsessile, sterile; cal. tube hemispheric, lobes rounded, subglabrous or slightly long-pubesc.; pet. obovate, convex. Z4.

***P. glandulosa*** Thunb. DWARF FLOWERING ALMOND. Shrub to 90cm, rarely to 2m. Terminal shoots strict, virgate, smooth. Lvs to 7×3cm, oblong-oval or lanceolate, thin-mucronate, glabrous or sparsely pubesc. above, pubesc. only on midrib beneath, irregularly fine-serrate; petioles to 7mm; bracts to 1cm, subulate, with glandular margins. Fls usually 2-clustered, rarely solitary or 3-clustered; pedicels to 2cm, glabrous or sparse-glandular; cal. tube broad-campanulate, sep. recurved, often glandular-dentate; cor. to 2cm diam., pet. 1cm, obovate or ovate-elliptic, red, becoming pink or white. Fr. 1cm, globose, dark red; stone obovate, mucronate. Spring. C & N China, Japan. 'Alba': fls single, pure white. 'Alba Plena' ('Alboplena'): shoots pendulous; lvs large, to 12cm length, to 2cm width; fls double, large, to 2.5cm across, white, profuse. 'Sinensis' ('Rosea Plena'): shoots large, pendulous, dark green; lvs large, to 12×2cm, dark green; fls large, to 2.5cm diam., double, bright pink, profuse. Z4.

***P.*×*gondouinii*** (Poit. & Turpin) Rehd. *(P. avium × P. cerasus.)* DUKE CHERRY. Lvs like *P. avium*. Branchlets usually slender. Fr. large, resembling a heart cherry. Garden origin. 'Schnee': small tree or shrub, globose, to 3cm wide, densely branched; lvs to 7cm, elliptic, dark green; fls single, dazzling white, in clusters, very profuse. For edible cvs see CHERRIES. Z4.

***P. gracilis*** Engelm. & A. Gray. Straggling shrub to 120cm. Bark grey; young branchlets pubesc., initially dull rufous. Lvs to 5×2.5cm, oval, rarely ovate, pointed at each end, finely pubesc. above, pale and strongly pubesc. beneath, fine-serrate, teeth usually acute, gland-tipped when young; petiole to 8mm, pubesc., usually eglandular. Fls to 1cm diam., in 2–4-fld umbels; pedicels to 1cm, fine-pubesc.; cal. tube 2.5mm, campanulate, fine-pubesc., lobes to 2mm, ovate, acute, entire or denticulate near apex, eglandular, pubesc.; pet. 5×3mm, obovate to obovate-orbicular. Fr. to 18mm diam., globose or somewhat oval, usually red, light pruinose; stone 13×9mm, oval, obtuse, stout-alate ventrally, smooth. Spring. SW US (N Oklahoma and W Arkansas south to Texas). Z6.

***P. gravesii*** Small. Unarmed shrub to 1m. Bark dark, somewhat rough; branchlets usually puberulent. Lvs to 3×2.5cm, orbicular to oblong-orbicular, sharp-serrate, green and subglabrous above, paler and pubesc., at least on veins, beneath; petioles 3mm, pubesc.; stipules linear, glandular, pubesc. Fls to 1.5cm diam., sometimes solitary, or in 2–3-fld umbels; pedicels 6mm, pubesc.; cal. pubesc., tube to 3mm, lobes to 2.5mm, ovate, obtuse, eglandular; pet. orbicular, 5mm. Fr. to 1.5cm diam., globose, deep purple, light blue-pruinose; stone 8×6.5mm, subglobose or broad-oval. US (Connecticut). Z5.

***P. grayana*** Maxim. JAPANESE BIRD CHERRY. Small, rather compact tree to 9m. Young shoots glabrous or somewhat pubesc. Lvs 9×4.5cm, oblong ovate to oblong-obovate, acuminate, somewhat pubesc. on midrib, serrations fine-aristate; petioles 1cm, eglandular. Fls 1cm diam., white, in many-fld racemes; sep. very small; pet. reflexed. Fr. 8mm diam., black; stone smooth. Japan. Z6.

***P.*×*hillieri*** hort. *(P. incisa × P. sargentii.)* Small, densely branched tree to 9m. Lvs bronze-coloured, double-serrate, pubesc. on venation beneath. Fls 3cm diam., blue-pink, single, 1–4-grouped; pedicels long, thin, somewhat pubesc.; cal. tube narrow cylindric-funnelform, bronze-red, glabrous, lobes narrow ovate-lanceolate, irregularly dentate, pubesc. on margins. Spring. Garden origin (Hillier, *c*1928). 'Hilling's Weeping': small tree; branches slender, almost perpendicularly weeping; fls pure white, profuse in early April. 'Kornicensis': tree to 5m; shoots glabrous, red-brown; lvs to 12cm, elliptic-acuminate, biserrate; fls clustered to 4, light pink; fr. dark red. 'Spire': tree to 8m, basal width to 3m, conical, upright; lvs richly tinted in autumn; fls single, almond pink; early-flowering. Z6.

***P. hirtipes*** Hemsl. Loosely branched tree to 12m+. Young shoots glabrous. Lvs 7.5×4.5cm, usually obovate to obovate-oblong, abrupt-acuminate, glabrous, occasionally pubesc. on veins at first, serrations small; petiole 11mm, glabrous. Fls 2cm diam., 3–4-clusters; cal. tube 4mm, campanulate-urceolate, glabrous; pet. white, occasionally pink, narrow-ovate, deeply incised; style usually glabrous. Fr. 1cm, ovoid, red; stone almost smooth. Spring. C China. 'Malifolia': fls large, to 4cm wide, late-flowering. 'Semiplena': fls semi-double, milky pink, fading to white, long-lasting. Z8.

***P. hortulana*** Bail. Tree to 9m. Bark thin, exfoliating in plate-like scales, dark brown; branchlets dark rufous or chestnut, occasionally with grey blotches. Lvs to 11×4.5cm, ovate-lanceolate, acuminate, abruptly rounded at base, yellow-green, glabrous and slightly lustrous above, pale green and pubesc., at least on venation, beneath, serrations rounded or subcrenate, glandular; petioles to 2.5cm, pubesc. above, glandular toward apex; stipules linear, glandular-serrate. Fls to 1.5cm diam., in 2–5-fld umbels; pedicels thin, to 14mm, glabrous; cal. campanulate, tube 3mm, glabrous, lobes oblong-ovate, mostly glabrous, glandular at margin; pet. to 8mm, oval or oblong-orbicular. Fr. to 2.5cm diam. globose, red to yellow, usually with white dots; stone to 17×11mm, globose to oblong. C US. 'Mineri': lvs thick, coarsely toothed; fr. firm, produced late. Z6.

***P. humilis*** Bunge. HUMBLE BUSH CHERRY. Shrub to 1.5m. Young shoots puberulous. Lvs 4×2cm, obovate to elliptic, cuneate at base, fine-serrate. Fls 14mm diam., pink-white, solitary or paired; style glabrous. Fr. 13mm diam., subglobose, red. N China. Z5.

***P. ilicifolia*** (Nutt.) Walp. HOLLY-LEAVED CHERRY; ISLAY. Dense evergreen shrub or small tree to 8m. Branchlets soon grey or rufous. Lvs to 5cm, ovate to round, coarsely spiny-toothed, coriaceous; petioles to 12mm. Fls in few- to many-fld racemes to 6cm; sep. to 1mm, deltoid; pet. to 3mm, white, round-oblong. Fr. to 1.5cm, ovoid-ellipsoid, red, rarely yellow; stone ovate, smooth, apiculate. US (California). Z9.

***P. incana*** (Pall.) Batsch Erect shrub to 2m. Branchlets slender, straight, lanuginose, later glabrous. Lvs to 4×1.5cm, elliptic to narrow-oblanceolate, serrate to incised-serrate, glabrous or puberulent above, later glabrous, white-tomentose beneath, sometimes later glabrous beneath; stipules subulate, persistent. Fls 1–2; pedicels 2mm; cal. tube to 8mm, cylindric; pet. to 7mm, pink. Fr. to 7mm diam., subglobose, dark red; stone somewhat reticulate-grooved. Spring. SE Europe, Asia Minor. Z6.

***P. incisa*** Thunb. FUJI CHERRY. Small tree to 5m. Young branchlets sometimes pubesc. Lvs to 5×3cm, obovate or ovate, short-acuminate, pubesc. above and on veins beneath, double-serrate, teeth acute; petioles to 1cm. Fls white to rose, in sessile, 1–3-fld umbels; pedicels to 2.5cm, glabrous to thin-pubesc.; cal. tube to 6mm, usually glabrous, lobes to 3mm; pet. 1cm, retuse. Fr. to 8mm, ovoid, purple-black. Spring–summer. Japan (mts of SC Hondo). 'February Pink': fls light pink flowering by February. 'Moerheimii': habit small, weeping, wide-spreading, dome-shaped; fls pink in bud, fading to blush-white; flowers in late March. 'Okame' *(P. incisa × P. campanulata)*: habit neat; fls carmine, cal. and stalks red tinted; flowers in March. 'Praecox': fls pale pink, flowers in January. Z6.

***P. jacquemontii*** Hook. f. Straggling shrub to 3m+. Stem slender; young shoots glabrous. Lvs to 6×3cm, dimorphic, ovate-elliptic to obovate-oblong, pointed at both ends, or to 3cm, oblanceolate, regularly and sharp-serrate, glabrous, dark green above, paler beneath; stipules branched filiform on young shoots, minute on old stems, caducous. Fls 19mm diam., rose-pink, sometimes solitary, usually paired; pedicels 5mm; cal. tube 7mm, tubular-campanulate, gibbous at base, sep. 2mm; style shorter than stamens, glabrous. Fr. 1.5cm diam., subglobose, red. NW Himalaya. Z7.

***P.japonica*** Thunb. ORIENTAL BUSH CHERRY. Shrub to 1.5m. Branches thin, elongate, often puberulent when young. Lvs to 7cm, ovate, rarely ovate-lanceolate, acuminate, rounded or occasionally cuneate at base, double-serrate, teeth acute, completely glabrous or short-pubesc. on veins beneath; petioles to 3mm; stipules longer than petioles, laciniate, denticulate. Fls white or pale pink, single, small, 2–3-clustered; pedicels to 1cm. Fr. 14mm, subglobose, dark red; stone pointed at both ends. C China to Korea, Japan. 'Alba': fls white. 'Engleri': lvs long-acuminate; stalks long; fls long, pale pink, fr. to 1.5cm diam. 'Thunbergii': lvs long-acuminate, fls light pink. var. ***nakaii*** (Lév.) Rehd. Small shrub, to 50cm. Lvs very broadly ovate, usually pubesc. beneath. Fls few, light pink. Fr. large, plum-like. Manchuria. Z4

***P.×juddii*** E. Anderson. *(P.sargentii × P.yedoensis.)* Tree, similar to *P.sargentii* but lvs copper-tinted when young, deep crimson in autumn. Fls larger, abundant, pale to intense pink. Z6.

***P.kansuensis*** Rehd. Deciduous shrub or small tree to 6m. Bark smooth, brown; shoots rod-like. Lvs to 10×3cm, lanceolate, thin-acute, fine-serrate, pubesc. on midrib; petiole to 5mm. Fls 2cm diam., white, mostly paired, in infl. to 4.5cm; cal. grey, pubesc. outside, ciliate, lobes 3mm, oblong-ovate, pet. 9.5mm, round-ovate; stamens 9.5mm, fil. white, anth. yellow; style yellow. Fr. globose, velutinous-pubesc., flesh white; stone furrowed, not punctate. Winter–spring. NW China. Z4.

***P.lannesiana*** (Carr.) Wils. Name used by Wilson to describe a Japanese cherry of garden origin; the wild type with fragrant white fls, now known as *P.speciosa*, he named *P.lannesiana* f. *albida*. Japanese botanists use the name *P.lannesiana* to cover the numerous flowering garden cherries, many of which are thought to be either *P.speciosa* or *P.serrulata* var. *spontanea*, or hybrids of the two. See *P.*Sato-Zakura Group.

***P.×laucheana*** Bolle ex Lauche. *(P.padus × P.virginiana.)* Tree to 15m. Young shoots light brown, pitted; branchlets slightly pendulous. Lvs almost round, short-acuminate, round at base, fine adpressed-scabrous serrate, paler beneath, axillary-pubesc. on veins; petiole usually glandular. Fls longer than lvs, in short, upright racemes; pet. round. Fr. 12mm, diam., black-red. Garden origin. Z3.

***P.laurocerasus*** L. CHERRY LAUREL; LAUREL CHERRY. Shrub or tree to 3m, rarely to 6m, often strongly branching. Branches glabrous. Lvs to 25cm, oblong-elliptic, acuminate, glossy and dark green above, paler beneath, glabrous or glabrescent, coriaceous, with 2–4 glands at midrib base beneath. Fls white, small, in dense racemes to 10cm; pet. 3mm, obovate; stamens 20; style not divided; stigma capitate. Fr. 8mm, globose-ovoid, black; stone ovoid, smooth. Spring. SE Europe, Asia Minor. Over 40 cvs: 1–4m high, habit wide and broad to tall and upright, open to dense; lvs 6–25cm long, 2–10cm wide, entire to slightly dentate, light to dark green, or variegated; flowering spring, and sometimes autumn. 'Aureovariegata': shrub-like, to 4m; lvs striped yellow. 'Camelliifolia': lvs curled and margins involuted. 'Caucasica': vigorous, upright shrub; lvs large, light green, glossy. 'Castlewellan': narrow, dense, to 2m; lvs slightly contorted, densely speckled white; slow-growing. 'Herbergii': habit pyramidal, to 2m; lvs narrow, bright green above. 'Magnifolia' ('Latifolia'): tall, wide-spreading, vigorous; lvs very large, deep green, shiny. 'Marbled White': habit broadly conical; lvs strikingly marbled grey or white; slow-growing. 'Mischeana': growth flat and low; lvs dark green, glossy, margins undulate; fls on long racemes in autumn. 'Otto Luyken': compact and broad-growing shrub, erect stems to 1m high; lvs narrow glossy dark green; fls abundant, free-flowering. 'Reynvaanii': dense, erect, to 2m; lvs dull green; fls sparsely on older plants. 'Schipkaensis': broad, cup-shaped, to 2m; lvs large; fls abundant, on erect racemes; very hardy. 'Zabeliana': growth almost horizontal, wide; lvs light green; fls on long, erect racemes; very hardy. Z7.

***P.litigiosa*** Schneid. TASSEL CHERRY. Small tree to 7.5m+, of rather ascending habit. Young shoots glabrous. Lvs 7×3.5cm, narrow-obovate to oblong-ovate, acuminate, finely and sharply serrate, glabrous above, axillary-pubesc. on veins beneath. Fls white, 22.5mm diam., in 2–3-fld, subsessile umbels; peduncle to 7mm; cal. tube broad-campanulate, sep. triangular, reflexed; pet. broad-oval, entire; stamens long, wide-spreading; style long, sericeous below. Fr. 11×7mm, ellipsoid, semi-translucent, scarlet-red; stone smooth. China (Hupei). Z6.

***P.lobulata*** Koehne. RIBBED CHERRY. Tree to 9m, with broad crown. Young shoots pilose. Lvs 7×3.5cm, narrow-ovate to narrow-obovate, apex acuminate, base broad-cuneate, double-serrate, initially short setose-pubesc. above, pilose on veins beneath, later glabrous; petioles 9mm, sparse-pilose, mostly eglandular; stipules 4mm, small glandular-fimbriate, caducous. Fls 1.5cm diam., white, cernuous, solitary or paired; pedicels 13mm, pilose, with small bracts at base; bracts broad-ovate, with gland-tipped teeth at margin; cal. tube 6.5mm, campanulate, gibbous at base, slightly wrinkled, pubesc., sep. 3mm, blunt-triangular, serrate, ciliate; pet. broad-oblong, entire; stamens 34; style glabrous, somewhat longer than stamens. Fr. 12mm, round-cordate, dark crimson. China (W Hupei, Sichuan, N Yunnan). Z6.

***P.lusitanica*** L. PORTUGUESE LAUREL CHERRY; PORTUGAL LAUREL. Evergreen shrub of wide, bushy habit, or tree to 20m. Branchlets red, glabrous. Lvs to 12cm, oblong-ovate, acuminate, somewhat serrate, dark green and shiny above, paler beneath. Fls to 13mm diam., white, erect, in racemes to 15cm; pedicel to 8.5mm; cal. cup-shaped, lobes shallow, rounded; cor. 1cm diam. Fr. 8mm, ovoid, pointed, dark purple. Summer. Iberian Peninsula. ssp. ***azorica*** (Mouill.) Franco. AZORES LAUREL CHERRY. Shrub or small tree to 4m. Lvs to 10×6.5cm, large, ovate-elliptic. Fls in shorter, fewer-fld racemes. Fr. to 13mm, longer than pedicels. Azores. 'Angustifolia': lvs to 8cm, oblong-lanceolate. 'Myrtifolia': habit rounded, neat; lvs to 6cm, nearly ovate. 'Ormistonensis': habit compact; lvs dark green, leathery. 'Variegata': lvs small, margined white, sometimes flushed pink in winter. Z7.

***P.lyonii*** (Eastw.) Sarg. CATALINA CHERRY. Resembles *P.ilicifolia*, but lvs much larger. Evergreen shrub or tree to 15m. Lvs to 10cm, narrow ovate, dark green, glabrous, mostly entire. Fls in many-fld racemes to 12cm. Fr. to 2.5cm, globose, nearly black. Spring. US (California.) Z8.

***P.maackii*** Rupr. MANCHURIAN CHERRY; AMUR CHERRY. Tree to 16m, with patent crown. Bark dark-grey, covered with slender, pellucid paper-bark, like the bark of birch. Young branches pubesc. Lvs 10×5cm, elliptic or oblong, mucronate, orbicular at base; stipules to 7mm, linear, dark purple, with oblong glands. Fls in 10–30-fld racemes; pedicels somewhat cernuous; cal. tube ovoid, lobes acute, oval, with glandular teeth; pet. white, oblong; stamens longer than pet.; style slender, pubesc. Fr. 5×4mm, ovoid-globose, dry, black. Spring. Korea, Manchuria. 'Amber Beauty': habit uniform; branches slightly ascending. Z2.

***P.macradenia*** Koehne. Small tree, to 10m, closely related to *P.maximowiczii*. Young shoots glabrous. Lvs 4.5–6.5cm, ovate to oval-elliptic, base cuneate to rounded, entire to biserrate, pubesc. beneath. Fls in 3- to 4-fld, pubesc., corymbose racemes; cal. very densely pubesc. Fr. globose, dark red; stone ribbed. W China. Z5.

***P.mahaleb*** L. ST. LUCIE CHERRY. Patent tree to 9m+. Young shoots grey-pubesc. Lvs 4.5×3cm, broad-ovate to round-obovate, glabrous, occasionally pubesc. on midrib beneath, serrations small, crenate; petiole 12.5mm, eglandular. Fls 14mm diam., white, in 5–7-fld, corymbose racemes; cal. tube 3.5×3.5mm, cup-shaped, sep. 3mm, entire. Fr. 6mm, round-ovoid, black. Europe, Asia Minor. 'Albomarginata': lvs broadly margined off-white. 'Aurea': lvs heavily splashed yellow. 'Bommii': habit very pendulous. 'Monstrosa' ('Globosa'): dwarf, habit rounded and bushy; slow-growing. 'Pendula': branches nodding. 'Xanthocarpa': fr. yellow. Z5.

***P.mandshurica*** (Maxim.) Koehne. Tree to 15m, with divaricate and wide crown. Branchlets cernuous, dark rufous. Lvs to 12×6cm, oval-lanceolate to broad-oval, abruptly acuminate, wide-rounded or somewhat tapering, rarely cordate, at base, scabrous-serrate, deep green above, paler beneath, glabrous except axillary-pubesc. on veins. Fls 3cm diam., pale pink, solitary; pedicels to 5mm; ovaries pubesc. Fr. 2.5cm diam., globose, yellow; stone small, obtuse, smooth. Spring. Manchuria, Korea. Z6.

***P.maritima*** Marsh BEACH PLUM. Straggling shrub to 180cm, rarely to 2.5m. Bark very dark grey or brown; lower branches decumbent or often prostrate; young branchlets usually pubesc. Lvs to 6.5×4cm, usually ovate or elliptic, acute, narrowed at base, evenly and sharp-serrate, dull green and glabrous above, paler and soft-pubesc. beneath; petioles to 6mm, pubesc. Fls to 14mm diam., in 2–3-fld umbels; pedicels 7mm, strongly pubesc.; cal. tube 2mm, campanulate, strongly pubesc., lobes 2mm, oblong, obtuse, short-pubesc.; pet. 7×4mm, oblong or oblong-ovate. Fr. 1.5cm diam., globose, dull purple, sometimes crimson or yellow; stone 10×9mm, ovate, turgid. Spring–summer. E US. 'Eastham': large well-flavoured fruit, heavy cropper; 'Hancock': sweet, juicy, early ripening; 'Squibnocket': selected for high quality, also ornamental and a good soil binder. Z3.

***P.maximowiczii*** Rupr. MIYAMA CHERRY. Tree to 7.5m, sometimes to 12m+. Branches patent. Lvs 4.5×3.5cm, obovate, abrupt-acuminate, cuneate at base, coarse-serrate, single- or double-incised, clearly pubesc. on venation beneath; petioles 1cm, dense-pubesc. Fls 1.5cm diam., cream-white, in erect, 5–10-fld, corymbose racemes; pedicel 1.5cm, pubesc., with large, foliaceous bract at base; cal. tube 4mm, conical-cup-shaped, sep. pointed, serrate; stamens often 30+. Fr. 5mm diam., globose, black. Spring. Japan (C Hondo to Sakhalin), Korea, Manchuria (Amur). Z4.

***P.mexicana*** Wats. BIG-TREE PLUM. Tree to 12m. Bark exfoliating in platelike scales. Lvs to 10.5×6.5cm, oblong-obovate or obovate, acute or abruptly acuminate, rounded or subcordate at base, sharp- or double-serrate, yellow-green above, paler beneath, short-adpressed pubesc. above, stronger pubesc. beneath; petioles to 12mm, velutinous, glandular; stipules usually lobed. Fls to 18mm diam., in subsessile, 2–4-fld umbels; pedicels to 1.5cm; cal. campanulate, tube to 3mm, lobes oblong or ovate-oblong; pet. 6mm. Fr. to 3cm diam., globose, magenta, blue-pruinose; stone to 16×12mm, obovoid to subrotund. SW US to Mexico. Z6.

***P.mira*** Koehne. Shrub or tree to 10m. Shoots slender, smooth, green. Lvs to 10cm, lanceolate, apex acuminate, base round, sparse-crenate, entire toward apex, long-pubesc. on midrib beneath; petiole 2–4-glandular. Fls to 2.5cm diam., white-pink, solitary or paired, subsessile; cal. red, sep. ovate, pubesc. at margins; pet. obovate-rotund. Fr. 3cm diam., globose, dense-tomentose, with white flesh; stone smooth. China (mts of W Sichuan). Z5.

***P.mugus*** Hand.-Mazz. TIBETAN CHERRY. Shrub to 90cm. Young shoots buff-lanuginose. Lvs 4×2.5cm, broad-ovate, apex bluntly acuminate or round, base broad-cuneate, dark green, sparsely setose-pubesc. above, glabrescent or sparse-pubesc. on midrib beneath, doubly serrate; petiole 6mm, glabrous; stipules 1cm, linear-subulate, dentate. Fls 1.5cm diam., shell-pink, solitary or paired; pedicel 2cm, glabrous; cal. tube 9.5mm, tubular-campanulate, glabrous, sep. blunt-triangular, teeth gland-tipped. Fr. 9mm, ellipsoid, dark red. SE Tibet. Z5.

***P. mume*** Sieb. & Zucc. JAPANESE APRICOT; MEI. Deciduous tree to 9m, of rounded habit. Branchlets lustrous, glabrous, green. Lvs to 10cm, rounded or broadly ovate, broad-cuneate at base, sharp- and often double-serrate, sparse-pubesc., later glabrous except midrib beneath; petiole to 2cm. Fls to 3cm, pale rose, solitary or paired, subsessile; cal. 13mm diam., lobes oblong-rotund; pet. broad-obovate. Fr. to 3cm diam., globose, somewhat pubesc., yellow; stone perforated. Spring. S Japan. 'Alba': fls single, pure white, abundant; strong growing. 'Alboplena' ('Alba Plena'): fls semi-double, white; early-flowering. 'Alphandii': fls double, clear pink; flowers in March. 'Benishidori' ('Benishidon'): fls double, to 1cm diam., intense pink, fading later, fragrant. 'Bonita': to 6m; fls semi-double, rose red. 'Dawn': fls large, double, pale pink, ruffled; late-flowering. 'Kobai': fls double, light pink, profuse. 'O-moi-no-wac': fls semi-double, cup-shaped, white, occasional pet. or even whole flower pink; flowers late March. 'Peggy Clarke': fls double, deep rose, cal. red. 'Pendula': habit small, weeping; fls single or semi-double, light pink; flowers late February. 'Rosemary Clarke': fls semi-double, white, cal. red, fragrant; early-flowering. 'W.B. Clarke': habit weeping in maturity; fls double, pink. Z6.

***P. munsoniana*** Wight & Hedr. Tree to 8m. Young shoots glabrous, later dark rufous. Lvs to 10×4cm, lanceolate to oblong-lanceolate, usually acute, rounded at base, finely glandular-serrate, bright green and lustrous above, paler and axillary sparse-pubesc. on venation beneath; petioles to 2cm, bi-glandular; stipules linear, glandular-serrate. Fls to 1.5cm diam., 2–4-clustered; pedicels to 12mm; cal. tube 3mm, campanulate, lobes ovate-oblong to oblong; pet. to 7mm. obovate or oblong-obovate. Fr. globose or oval, bright red, white-punctate, light-pruinose; stone to 1.5×2cm, oval. C US. Z6.

***P. myrtifolia*** (L.) Urban. Little information available. Lvs small. Fr. small, spherical. Jamaica, Greater Antilles. Z10.

***P. napaulensis*** (Ser.) Steud. Tree to 20m. Lvs 18×5cm, narrow elliptic-lanceolate, acuminate, cuneate, rotund or subcordate at base, fine-serrate; petiole to 1cm, bi-glandular. Fls in racemes to 25cm; cal. cup pubesc., lobes eglandular; pet. to 5mm, obovate. Fr. to 1.5cm×13mm, ovoid, stone to 8mm. Himalaya (Bhutan, Sikkim). Z7.

***P. nigra*** Ait. CANADIAN PLUM; CANADA PLUM. Small tree to 9m. Bark grey, exfoliating in platelike scales. Lvs to 13×7cm, oval or obovate, abruptly acuminate, rounded at base, green and glabrous above, paler and pubesc. on veins beneath, coarsely and unevenly serrate; petiole to 18mm; stipules linear or lobed, margins glandular. Fls to 3cm diam., in subsessile, 2–3-fld umbels; pedicels to 2cm, usually glabrous; cal. red, tube to 5mm, narrow-obconic, lobes to 5mm; pet. to 12mm×1cm, white, sometimes tinged pink, oblong-ovate to sub-orbicular, erose. Fr. to 3×2.5cm, oblong-ovoid, orange-red to deep crimson to orange-yellow; stone 2×1.5cm, oblong-oval. NE America. 'Princess Kay': habit upright; bark black; fls double, white; fr. red; flowers in early May. Z2.

***P. ×nigrella*** W.A. Cumming. *(P. nigra × P. tenella.)* Shrub to 3m, of globose habit. Lvs to 4cm diam., oblanceolate to oblong, sometimes lanceolate, apex acute, base cuneate. Fls 3.5cm diam., lilac, sterile. Spring. Garden origin. 'Muckle': type of the cross. Z3.

***P. nipponica*** Matsum. JAPANESE ALPINE CHERRY; NIPPONESE CHERRY. Shrub to small tree to 5m. Lvs to 8×4.5cm, obovate, caudate-acuminate, thin-pilose and pale green beneath, occasionally adpressed-pilose above, incised and double acute-serrate; petioles to 1.5cm, glabrous. Fls pink, in 1–3-fld, sessile umbels or in umbellate corymbs; pedicels to 3cm, glabrous; cal. tube 6mm, glabrous, lobes 4mm; pet. 12mm, retuse. Fr. 8mm diam., globose, purple-black. Spring–summer. Japan. var. ***kurilensis*** (Miyabe) Wils. KURILE CHERRY. Petioles or pedicels or both pilose. Japan (Kurile, Sachalin, Hokkaido). 'Kursar' *(P. nipponica* var. *kurilensis × P. sargentii)*: habit upright, spreading, to 6m high, to 5m wide, vigorous; lvs rich orange tints in autumn; fls single, pet. somewhat rounded, deep cerise pink. 'Ruby': lvs carmine in autumn; fls lilac-pink, later fading. Z5.

***P. padus*** L. BIRD CHERRY; COMMON BIRD CHERRY. Deciduous tree to 15m. Bark dark brown; branches cernuous; young branchlets fine-pubesc., later glabrous. Lvs to 9×6cm, obovate to elliptic or narrow-obovate, apex abruptly acuminate, base obtuse to rotund, acutely serrate, glabrous except axillary pubesc. on veins beneath; petioles to 1.5cm, glabrous, glandular. Fls to 1.5cm diam., white, in many-fld, glabrous to puberulent racemes to 12cm; pedicels to 12mm; cal. tube broad-obconic, lobes ovate, glandular-dentate; pet. to 6mm, orbicular, loose-dentate; stamens short. Fr. globose, pea-sized, black; stone oval, rugose. Europe, W Asia to Korea and Japan. 'Albertii': habit broadly conical, dense; fls profuse, on long racemes; free-flowering. 'Aucubifolia': lvs speckled yellow. 'Aurea': lvs flushed yellow when young, foliage robust; fls large. 'Bracteosa': floral bracts exceeding pet., later abscising. 'Chlorocarpos': fr. green tinted yellow. 'Colorata': stems deep purple; lvs purple flushed copper, later dark green, tinted purple beneath; fls pink, carmine in bud; fr. dark maroon. 'Heterophylla': lvs sometimes deeply incised. 'Leucocarpos': twigs somewhat pubesc.; fr. off-white. 'Nana': habit almost hemispherical, to 3m high, densely branched. 'Pendula': branches drooping. 'Plena': fls semi-double, large, long-lasting. 'Purple Queen': habit small, to 7m; lvs purple flushed copper when young, on dark shoots, later with purple tinted veins and underside; fls pale pink. 'Spaethii': habit broad; flowers to 2cm wide, on elongated racemes, not profuse. 'Stricta': fls in erect racemes. 'Waterii' ('Grandiflora'): habit broadly conical at first, later rounded, to 10m; lvs oval, light green; fls white, in pendulous, elongated racemes, almond-scented; fr. small, black; flowers late May. var. ***commutata*** Dipp. Medium-sized tree; habit vigorous, spreading. Lvs and fls 3 weeks earlier; lvs coarser, crenate; fls in long racemes to 15cm. Z3.

***P. pedunculata*** (Pall.) Maxim. Shrub to 2m. Branches divaricate. Lvs to 5×1cm, oblong-obovate or oblong-oval, apex acuminate, base cuneate, acute-serrate, ciliate-pubesc.; petioles to 5mm; stipules narrow, to 4mm. Fls pink, solitary; pedicels to 8mm, ciliate; cal. tube to 5×4mm, campanulate-calyciform, glabrous, lobes broad-triangular, recurved; pet. to 1cm diam., broad-orbicular; style glabrous; ovary dense-pubesc. Fr. 1cm, ovoid or oblong-ovoid, pubesc.; stone ovate, very pale brown, scabrous but not pitted. Spring–summer. Siberia. Z4.

***P. pendula*** Maxim. Deciduous tree to 15m. Bark grey; young branches glabrous or erect-pubesc.; branchlets pendulous. Lvs to 10×5.5cm, elliptic, short caudate-acuminate, obtuse at base, deep green above, green beneath, pubesc., shallow and simple-serrate; petioles to 18mm, densely adpressed-pubesc., bi-glandular; stipules short. Fls 3cm diam., single, in umbels; pedicels to 3cm, erect-pubesc.; cal. tube urceolate, adpressed-pubesc., lobes lanceolate, serrate; pet. white, elliptic, retuse; stamens 19–24; style pubesc. beneath; ovary glabrous. Fr. 1cm diam., subglobose, black-purple. Spring. Japan. var. ***adscendens*** Mak. Branches elongate, somewhat slender, light grey-brown, ascending-pilose when young. Japan (Mts of Honshu, Shikoku, Kyushu). Z6.

***P. pensylvanica*** L. f. BIRD CHERRY; PIN CHERRY; RED CHERRY. Tree to 9m. Young shoots glabrous. Lvs 9×1.5cm, narrow-ovate, acuminate, narrowed or rotund at base, glabrous, fine-serrate with glandular, incurved teeth. Fls 1.5cm, white, in 4–8-fld umbellate clusters. Fr. 6mm diam., globose, red. N America (Canada to N Carolina and Colorado). Z2.

***P. persica*** (L.) Batsch. PEACH. Small tree to 8m. Branches elongate, glabrous, red on the sunny side, reverse side often green. Lvs to 15×3.5cm, lanceolate to broad-oblanceolate, long-acuminate, glabrescent, serrulate; petioles to 1cm, glandular above. Fls pink to white, to 3.5cm diam., in groups of 1–2; pedicels very short; cal. campanulate, short-pubesc. Fr. to 7cm diam., globose, flesh white or yellow, very juicy; stone elliptic, oval or orbicular, acuminate, compressed, hard, with deep furrows and pits. Spring–autumn. China. Ornamental number over 40 cvs: habit ranges from dwarf to weeping to erect; lvs range from light green to green tinted red; fls vary from single to double, to ×4cm, pure white to deepest red, occasionally striped. Among the cvs notable for habit are 'Nana' (dwarf, to 1m; lvs large, pendulous; fls light pink, profuse), 'Alboplena Pendula' (weeping; fls double, white, abundant), 'Crimson Cascade' (weeping; fls carmine), 'Windle Weeping' (umbrella-forming; fls cup-shaped, semi-double, pink; vigorous); cvs notable for foliage include 'Royal Redleaf' (lvs brilliant red, later green tinted red); among cvs notable for fls are 'Alba' (wood green; lvs light green; fls single, white), 'Alboplena' (fls double, white, profuse), 'Iceberg' (fls semi-double large, pure white), 'Helen Borchers' (fls semi-double, clear pink; vigorous), 'Cardinal' (fls semi-double, rosette, deep burgundy), 'Klara Mayer' (shrub-like; fls double, to ×4cm, strong red-pink; fr. pale green, tinted red), 'Russel's Red' (habit dense; fls double, striking red), 'Palace Peach' (fls double, small, deepest red), 'Peppermint Stick' (fls double, white, striped red), 'Dianthifolia' (fls very large, semi-double, pet. narrow, striped deep red), 'Versicolor' (lvs light green; fls double, white usually striped rust red, profuse; slow-growing). For edible cvs, see PEACHES and NECTARINES. Z5.

***P. pilosiuscula*** Koehne. Semi-erect tree to 9m, sparsely branched. Young shoots thin-pubesc. Lvs 6.5×3.5cm, oval to oblong-obovate, apex acuminate, base rotund or cuneate, short setose-pubesc. above, occasionally conspicuously pubesc. beneath, usually only on veins, single-serrate, aristate-pointed. Fls white or tinted pink, in 2–3-fld, rarely 5-fld, corymbose umbels; cal. tube 4.5mm, broad-campanulate, sep. triangular, becoming slightly reflexed; stamens 25, wide-spreading, exserted; style long, lax-pilose below. Fr. 1cm, ellipsoid, red. Spring. C & W China. Z5.

***P. pseudocerasus*** Lindl. YING TAO CHERRY. Small tree to 5.5m. Young shoots sparse-pubesc., later glabrous. Lvs 9×5.5cm, broad-obovate to obovate-ovate, abruptly acuminate, irregularly coarse-serrate. Fls 2cm diam., white, in elongated racemose corymbs; pedicels pubesc.; cal. tube 4mm, broad-campanulate, gibbous, pubesc. at base; pet. rotund. Fr. 1.5×1.5cm, cordate-globose to ellipsoid, amber-red. Spring. China. 'Wadai' *(P. pseudocerasus × P. subhirtella)*: habit shrub-like, tall, multistemmed; twigs may have aerial roots at nodes; lvs elliptic-acuminate, to 8cm; fls small, pale pink, darker in bud. Z6.

***P. pubigera*** Koehne. Medium-sized tree. Fls small, creamy white, in pendulous racemes to 18×2.5cm. W China.

***P. pumila*** L. SAND CHERRY. Shrub to 180cm, occasionally semi-prostrate. Young shoots glabrous. Lvs 4×1.2cm, oblanceolate to narrow-obovate, shallow-serrate toward apex, grey-green above, glaucescent beneath; petioles 8mm; stipules linear-lanceolate, irregularly short-pinnatifid. Fls white, 2–4-clustered; pedicels 12mm; cal. tube cup-shaped, lobes serrulate; pet. 12.5mm diam., narrow-obovate, widely spaced. Fr. 1cm diam., subglobose, dark red. Spring. NE US. var. ***depressa*** (Pursh) Bean. Prostrate, growing flat on the ground, to 30.5cm. Lvs more slender, broadest toward apex, usually rounded or obtuse, tapered to the base, blue-white beneath. Fr. rounded-ellipsoid. var. ***susquehanae*** (Willd.)

Jaeger To 90cm. Lvs obovate, blunt-serrate toward apex, white-green beneath. Fr. smaller, astringent. Z2.

***P. rivularis*** Scheele. CREEK PLUM. Shrub to 2.5m. Stems slender. Lvs to 7.5×4cm, ovate to oblong-ovate, apex short-acuminate, base rounded, glandular-serrate, glabrous and green above, pale green and pubesc. beneath; petioles to 12mm; stipules linear or lobed, glandular. Fls 1cm diam., in 2–5-fld umbels; pedicels to 8mm, slender, glabrous; cal. campanulate, tube 2mm, glabrous, lobes 2mm, ovate or oblong-ovate; pet. to 5mm, obovate-orbicular. Fr. 1.5cm diam., subglobose, red. Spring. US (Texas). Z8.

***P. rufa*** Hook. f. HIMALAYAN CHERRY. Patent tree to 6m+. Shoots rusty-fawn lanuginose when young. Lvs to 7×2.5cm, narrow-oval to obovate-lanceolate, glabrous above, pubesc. on venation beneath, finely serrate, each tooth terminating in a pear-shaped gland; petiole 1cm. Fls 16mm diam., white or pink-white, mostly solitary, sometimes 2–3 together; cal. tube 9×4mm, tubular-campanulate, gibbous, wrinkled and red above, sep. broad-triangular, fine-serrate; pet. subrotund, entire. Fr. 1mm, ellipsoid, dark red; stone clearly grooved. Himalaya. var. ***tricantha*** (Koehne) Hara. Lvs more elongate. Pedicels and cal. tube pubesc.; pet. dorsally adpressed-pubesc. Z8.

***P. salasii*** Standl. Tree. Lvs to 14×4.5cm, oblong-lanceolate, apex broad-acuminate, base rounded, sharp-serrate, pale and eglandular beneath; petiole to 18mm, with 2 glands at apex. Fls in racemes to 18cm; pedicels to 4.5mm; cal. cup 2.5×3.5mm, glabrous inside, sep. 1.5mm, broad ovate-triangular, obtuse, pet. to 4.5mm, broad-rounded, white. Fr. 13mm, globose, broad-rounded. C Guatemala (mts). Z7.

***P. salicifolia*** Kunth. MEXICAN BIRD CHERRY. Tree to 12m. Young shoots glabrous, sometimes pubesc. Lvs 8.5×3cm, lanceolate, acuminate, cuneate at base, coriaceous, often completely glabrous, very finely serrate; petioles 6mm, usually glabrous. Fls 1cm diam., white, in loose, cernuous, 20–30-fld racemes; pedicels 9mm. Fr. 17.5mm diam., subglobose, shallow-sulcate. S America (Mexico to Peru). 'Ecuadorian': large sweet fruit, tree drooping, heavy cropper; 'Fausto': large sweet fruit, good cropper; 'Harriet': large fruit, tree dwarf; 'Huachi Grande': large mild-flavoured fruit, very heavy cropper. Z6.

***P. salicina*** Lindl. JAPANESE PLUM. Small tree to 10m. Shoots rufous, glabrous. Lvs to 12cm, oval-obovate to broad-oval, apex abruptly acuminate, base cuneate, finely and obtusely double-crenate, bright green, glossy above, dull beneath, glabrous, rarely pubesc. beneath; petioles to 2cm. Fls to 2cm diam., 2–4-clustered, white, pedicels to 1.5cm, glabrous; cal. lobes oval-ovate, glabrous, slightly crenate. Fr. to 7cm diam., globose to ovoid, yellow or red, sometimes green or violet. Spring. China, Japan. Z6.

***P. sargentii*** Rehd. Tree to 18m+. Stems erect-patent. Lvs 10.5×5cm, broad oblong-elliptic to obovate-oblong, acuminate, simple- or double-serrate, serrations coarse, sharp-pointed, rufous, later green and glaucescent-glossy beneath; petiole 22.5mm. Fls to 4cm diam., blue-pink, in 2–4-fld, sessile umbels; pedicel stout, to 2cm; cal. tube 7×3mm, narrowly tubular-campanulate; pet. broad ovate-oblong to obovate, incised. Fr. 11×8mm, elongate-ovoid, deep glossy crimson. Japan. 'Columnaris' ('Rancho'): habit columnar, to 10m high, to 5m wide; bark mahogany; lvs dark green, glossy, flaming red and gold in autumn; fls single, pink, early-flowering. 'Accolade' *(P. sargentii × P. subhirtella)*: habit open-topped, to 6m high, to 6m wide, older plants somewhat pendulous, vigorous; lvs to 10×5cm, elliptic-oblong, long acuminate, serrate, bright green; fls semi-double, to 4cm diam., shocking pink in pendulous groups to 3, early April. Z4.

***P.* Sato-zakura Group**. The Japanese flowering cherries will be dealt with in this section. They are currently taken together under the collective name 'The Sato-zakura Group'. These trees are often of complex parentage, but are most probably derived from *P. serrulata*. This collective name encompasses the species *P. donarium* Sieb., *P. lannesiana* Wils. (this name was sometimes used by Japanese botanists for the many hybrids of *P. serrulata* var. *spontanea* × *P. speciosa*) and *P. pseudocerasus* Lindl. See USDA pamphlet, 'The Nomenclature of Cultivated Japanese Flowering Cherries (*Prunus*): The Sato-zakura Group'.

'Amanogawa' ('milky way' or 'celestial river') ('Erecta'): narrowly fastigiate, to 6m high, to 120cm wide; lvs tinted yellow when young, yellow marked red in autumn; fls densely clustered, single, occasionally semi-double, pale pink, fragrant, freely produced, early to mid May; fr. small, black, infrequently produced. 'Ariake' ('dawn') ('Candida'): to 6m; lvs tinted bronze when young; fls single, to 6cm diam., pink in bud, opening blush. 'Asagi': strong-growing; lvs flushed red when young; fls abundant, single, to 4.5cm diam., pale yellow; mid-April to early May. 'Benden': narrowly upright, strong-growing; branches ascending; lvs pale copper when young, coral red in autumn; fls single, pink-lilac; mid-April. 'Botanzakura' ('Botan-sakura', 'Moutan'): habit broadly upright, small, weak-growing; lvs serrate, pale bronze when young, flame orange in autumn; fls grouped to 4 in loose corymbs, single, to over 5cm diam., blush pink fading to white. 'Daikoku': habit small, branches sharply ascending; lvs bright green, with awned teeth, flushed yellow when young; stalks long, rigid; fls in pendulous, loose corymbs, double, to 5cm diam., bright lilac pink, cluster of leafy carpels at centre; late spring. 'Edozakura' ('Yedo Zakura', 'Yedo-sakura', 'Nobilis'): habit small, broadly upright; lvs broadly oblong to obovate, short-acuminate, golden brown when young; fld semi-double, to 5cm diam., cal. lobes short, pet. to 12, carmine in bud opening almond pink; early April. 'Fudansakura' ('Fudan Zakura'): habit small; fls single, to 4cm diam., cal. red, buds soft pink, opening white, in sessile clusters; November to April, precocious fls smaller. 'Fugenzo' ('goddess on a white elephant') ('Benifugen', 'James H. Veitch'): habit spreading, crown rounded; lvs finely toothed, copper when young; fls in long pendent clusters to 3, double, large, rose pink, 2 leafy carpels at centre; mid-May, profuse. 'Fukurokuju': habit spreading, to 6m high, to 10m wide, weak-grower; lvs bronze when young, later dark green; fls in loose corymbs to 4, single with a few extra pet., soft pink fading to white; late April.

'Geraldinae' ('Asano'): habit small, narrowly upright; branches ascending; lvs narrow lanceolate, green flushed bronze when young; fls double, to 5cm diam., freely produced in short-stemmed clusters; pet. to 100, pointed, deep pink flushed mauve. 'Gyoiko' ('Tricolor'): inverted cone-shaped; fls semi-double, to 4cm diam., cream slashed green; pet. tips burgundy; free-flowering, early May. 'Hatazakura' ('Hatasakura'): fls single, small, white with ragged edges. 'Hizakura' ('Hisakura', 'Ichiyo'): to 6m, habit open, branches wide spreading; fls single to semi-double, wreathed along main growths in corymbs to 4, large, deep rose pink; cal. purple; mid-April. 'Horinji': to 5m, erect, sparsely branched; lvs lanceolate, ochre when young; fls clustered at shoot tips, semi-double, to 4.5cm diam., cal. purple, pet. to 14, pale pink; late April. 'Imose': to 9m, strong and free-growing; lvs pale copper when young, to lobster red, gold by leaf drop; fls in long, loose clusters, abundant, double, to 4.5cm diam., pet. to 30, mauve pink. 'Itokukuri': habit erect, bushy; lvs flushed bronze when young; fls in loose clusters at branch tips, semi-double, light pink. 'Jo-nioi' ('Affinis', 'Elegant Fragrance'): habit tall, to 11m, branches widely ascending; lvs golden-brown when young; fls grouped to 5, single, small, pure white, almond-scented, profuse; late April. 'Kaba': fls double, white strongly flushed green. 'Kiku-shidare' ('weeping chrysanthemum cherry') ('Kiku-shidare-sakura', 'Cheal's Weeping', 'Rosea'): small tree, to 3cm diam., branches steeply pendulous; lvs lanceolate, dark green, pale green at first; fls densely clustered, double, to 3cm diam., clear deep pink, pet. pointed; April. 'Kikuzakura': shrub-like, erect; lvs flushed bronze when young; fls double, globose, pet. to 200, soft pink; weak grower. 'Kirigayatsu' ('Mikuruma-gaeshi', 'Diversifolia'): habit open, small tree to 7m, with long ascending branches; lvs short-toothed, pale brown when very young, copper red with yellow markings in autumn; fls densely packed in clusters, mainly on main stems, single or semi-double, to 5cm, pale pink edged in deeper pink. 'Kirin': fls densely double, pet. thin, buds carmine later deep pink; late flowering. 'Kokonoe' ('Kokonoye-sakura'): small tree; lvs flushed bronze when young; fls semi-double, large, to 4.5cm diam., soft pink, profuse; early-flowering.

'Ojochin' ('large lantern') ('Senriko'): habit stiff, stout, to 7m; lvs large, broadly elliptic, leathery, bronze at first; fls in long-stalked clusters to 8, single, to 5cm diam., pink in bud, opening blush; late May. 'Okiku-sakura' ('Okiku'): habit stiff and upright; lvs flushed bronze when young; fls in dense and hanging clusters, double, to 5cm diam., pale pink, carpel leaf-like. 'Okumiyaku' ('Shimidsu', 'Shimidsu-sakura'): habit small, wide-spreading, flattened crown; fls grouped to 6 in pendulous corymbs to 20cm long, double, large, to 5cm diam., buds flushed pink opening white, pet. fringed at margin, with 2 leafy carpels in centre; mid-May. 'Oshokun' ('Conspicua'): habit broad and flat, to 3m; branches twisted; lvs tinted bronze when young; fls in short-stalked clusters, double, carmine in bud, opening malmaison pink, profuse. 'Pink Perfection': habit vase-shaped; lvs pale bronze when young; fls in long pendulous clusters, double, to 4.5cm diam., bright rose in bud, opening clear pink (sometimes fls show 2 shades); mid-April; from a seed of 'Okumiyako' and possibly 'Sekiyama'.

'Sekiyama' ('Kanzan', 'Kwanzan', 'Purpurascens'): branches stiffly ascending, eventually spreading, to 12m, vigorous; lvs large, short-toothed serrations, lightly tinted red, yellow copper in autumn; fls grouped to 5 in pendulous clusters, fully double, very large, buds maroon opening cyclamen pink, sometimes tinged blue, often with 2 leaf-like carpels. 'Shiro-fugen' ('white god') ('Albo-rosea'): habit wide and spreading, flat-topped, to 10m high; bark dark brown; lvs brown, crimson flushed bronze when young; fls in loose hanging clusters, double, pink in bud, opening white, fading to pink-mauve with darker centre, bracts often leaf-like; mid May. 'Shirotae' ('snow white' or 'double white') ('Hosokawa', 'Mount Fuji', 'Kojima'): small tree, branches spreading horizontally, occasionally pendulous; lvs deeply serrate, teeth with long tips, pale green, tinted bronze with young, golden in autumn; fls grouped to 3 in pendulous corymbs, freely produced before lvs, single (sometimes semi-double on older plants), large, to 5.5cm diam., snow white, hawthorn fragrance; early April. 'Shogun': lvs richly tinted in autumn; fls semi-double, deep pink, profuse on older plants; vigorous. 'Shosar' *(P. campanulata × P. sargentii)*: habit broadly fastigiate, strong growing; lvs bright green, yellow tinted copper in autumn; fls single, large, to 4cm diam., clear cerise pink, flower stalks and cal. dark red; late March. 'Shujaku' ('a southern constellation') ('Campanuloides'): to 5m; lvs small, short-aristate teeth, stipules and bracts small, bronze when young; fls grouped to 6, semi-double, profuse, somewhat bell-shaped, to 4cm diam., pet. to 15, pale pink; late April. 'Sumizome' ('ink dye', referring to shadow pattern): lvs tinted bronze when young; fls semi-double, to 4.7cm diam., pet. to 14, gentle pink.

'Taguiarashi' ('Ruiran'): habit broadly upright; lvs 1-toothed, tinted brown when young, stipules and bracts small and incised; fls grouped to 4 on long stalks, single, plate-shaped, to 4.7cm diam., soft pink fading later. 'Taihaku' ('great white cherry') ('Tai-haku'): habit tall and spreading, to 12m; bark with prominent brown tinted lenticels; lvs large when mature, to 20×12cm, with pronounced 'drop-tips', bright green, red flushed bronze when young, gold by leaf fall; fls to 6cm diam., single, saucer-shaped, pet. tips distinctly notched, pure white, blush pink in bud; mid-April; tetraploid. 'Taizanfukan': habit shrub-like, tightly erect and well-branched; shoot's bark rough when older; lvs small, leathery, dark green, bronze when young; stalks of lvs and fls downy; fls densely clustered, very double, pale pink, many buds but few bloom. 'Taki-nioi' ('fragrant cloud', 'fragrance of a waterfall') ('Cataract'; 'Gozanoma-nioi'): habit widely spreading, to 7×7m; lvs red tinted bronzed when young, appearing with fls; fls single, loosely arranged, very abundant, small, snow white, hawthorn fragrance. 'Taoyame' ('Tao-yoma', 'Taoyame Zakura'): habit low and spreading; lvs brown flushed red or copper when young; fls semi-double, fragrant, shell pink fading to blush, cal. and pedicels purple-brown. 'Temari': fls single or semi-double, to 4.5cm diam., light pink, in rounded infl. at shoot tips.

'Ukon' ('yellowish') ('Grandiflora'): funnel-shaped, horizontally spreading, to 7m high, to 10m wide, vigorous; lvs pale bronze when young, flame red and plum in autumn; fls semi-double, large, to 4.5cm diam., primrose or sulphur tinted green; late April. 'Umineko' ('seagull') (*P. incisa* × *P. speciosa*): habit narrow and upright, to 8m high, to 3m wide; lvs large, bright green, orange and red in autumn; fls abundant, single, to 2.5cm, cup-shaped, pure white, stamens gold; April. 'Uzuzakura' ('Hokusai', 'Roseaplena' 'Spiralis'): habit wide-spreading, vigorous, to 8m high, to 10m wide; lvs dark green, leathery, tinted brown when young, rich autumn shades; fls in long-stalked corymbs, semi-double, to 4.7cm diam., pet. to 12, shell pink, dark spot developing at centre with age; mid-April. 'Washinoo' ('eagle's tail') ('Washi-no-o'): habit vigorous, stout branched, wide open head; fls single, to 4cm diam., clustered on short peduncles to 5, buds shell pink opening pure white, scented; freely produced; early April. 'Yae-akebono': habit open, small; fls profuse, semi-double, pink; late April. 'Yae-marasakizakura' ('Purpurea', 'Yae Murasakai Zakura'): habit small, to 3m, slow growing; lvs deep green, copper red when young, brilliant orange in autumn; fls semi-double, with to 10 pet., buds red in winter, opening pink-purple, very abundant; late April, free flowering. 'Yokihi': medium tree, branches spreading or widely ascending; lvs green flushed bronze when young; fls freely produced in loose clusters, semi-double, large, to 4.5cm diam., pale pink with outer ring of pet. slightly darker; late April.

***P. ×schmittii*** Rehd. (*P. avium* × *P. canescens.*) Resembles *P. canescens* in narrow habit and bark, and *P. avium* in taller growth, and shapes of lvs and cal. tube. Vigorous small tree of narrow, erect habit with a vase-shaped crown. Bark shiny, mahogany-coloured. Lvs to 8cm, elliptic-oblong, acuminate, soon glabrous above, pubesc. on veins beneath; petiole to 2.5m. Fls pale pink; pedicels to 1.5cm, with large bracts at base; cal. tube campanulate; pet. 1cm, broad-ovate. Garden origin. Z5.

***P. scoparia*** (Spach) Schneid. Large shrub or small tree to 6m. Branches slender, broom-like; twigs rod-like with few lvs. Lvs 2–4cm, narrowly linear, sparsely fine-dentate to subentire, red-bronze when young becoming bronze-green and then green. Fls 2.5cm diam., pale-pink; pet. almost circular. Fr. 2cm, oval, pubesc. Iran.

***P. scopulorum*** Koehne. Tree of upright habit, 11–12m. Fls very small, fragrant, white flushed pink in spring. China.

***P. sericea*** (Batal.) Koehne. Tree to 18m. Young shoots glabrous. Lvs 9×3.5cm, narrow elliptic-obovate to narrow-oblong, cuneate or rounded at base, glabrous above, usually brown-tomentose beneath, small-serrate. Fls 8mm diam., white, in congested, many-fld, long-cylindric racemes. Fr. 12.5mm, ovoid, black. China (Sichuan). Z6.

***P. serotina*** Ehrh. BLACK CHERRY; RUM CHERRY. Tree to 30m. Branches glabrous when young. Lvs 8.5×3.5cm, lanceolate-oblong to narrow-ovate, cuneate at base, vivid shiny green, glabrous, often pubesc. on midrib beneath, fine- and incurved-serrate; petioles 1.5cm, glandular, glabrous. Fls 8mm diam., white, in cylindric, 12cm racemes. Fr. 9mm diam., round, black. N America. 'Asplenifolia': Lvs narrow, margins deeply and irregularly cut. 'Cartilaginia': branches more erect; lvs large, to 15×6cm, vibrant green, glossy. 'Pendula': branches drooping, twigs delicate; slow-growing. 'Pyramidalis': habit conical. 'Phelloides': lvs narrow-lanceolate, pendulous. Z3.

***P. serrula*** Franch. BIRCH-BARK TREE. Tree to 15m. Young shoots fine-pubesc. Bark shiny mahogany-brown. Lvs 7.5cm×9mm, lanceolate, rounded at base, fine-serrate, pubesc. on venation beneath, later glabrous; petioles 1cm, sometimes glandular; stipules linear. Fls 2cm diam., white, in subsessile, 1–4-fld umbels; pedicels 12mm, sparse-pubesc.; cal. tube 6mm, campanulate, gibbous, lobes triangular; style spare-pubesc. at base; stamens longer than pet., slightly patent. Fr. 12mm×1cm, ovoid, bright red; stone grooved. Spring. China (mts of N Yunnan, Sichuan). Z5.

***P. serrulata*** Lindl. ORIENTAL CHERRY. Deciduous tree to 3m, sparsely branched. Branchlets stiffly outspread; shoots glabrous. Lvs to 13×6.5cm, ovate, long-acuminate, smooth, shiny, serrulate. Fls 3.5cm diam., pure white, double, 3–5-clustered; pedicels to 4cm. Fr. a small, black cherry. Spring. China. var. ***spontanea*** (Maxim.) Wils. HILL CHERRY; JAPANESE MOUNTAIN CHERRY; YAMAZAKURA. To 18m. Bark brown or grey with conspicuous persistent lenticels. Lvs to 11.5×4.5cm, elliptic-ovate to obovate-oblong, apex acuminate, base cuneate, deep green above, somewhat glaucous beneath, double-serrate, teeth shortly setose-tipped; petiole to 2cm, glandular. Fls to 2.5cm, diam., white or pink, in few-fld corymbs; cal. tube narrow tubular-campanulate, sep. 6mm, narrow, entire; pet. incised. Fr. 6.5mm, subglobose, magenta. Japan (S Hondo). Z5.

***P. sibirica*** L. Shrub or small tre to 3m. Branches patent, grey-brown or rufous, glabrous. Lvs to 10×7cm, ovate to orbicular, long-acuminate, cordate or rounded at base, simple and fine-serrate; petiole to 3cm, slender, with small glands or eglandular. Fls solitary; pedicels to 2mm; cal. tube cylindric-conical, red, sep. elongate-oval, acuminate, recurved; pet. white and pink-veined or pale pink. Fr. to 2.5×2.5cm, globose, pubesc., yellow or orange; stone to 2×2cm. Spring. E Siberia, Manchuria, N China. Z5.

***P. ×sieboldii*** (Carr.) Wittm. (*P. speciosa* × *P. apetala.*) Slow-growing small tree. Shoots glossy; branches dark grey-brown, rather stout, patent-pubesc. when young. Lvs to 10cm, obovate, long slender-pointed, dark green and adpressed-pubesc. above, lanuginose beneath, usually double-serrate; petiole to 2cm, lanuginose. Fls to 4.5cm diam., pink, semi-double, in 3–4-fld corymbs; peduncles to 4cm; pedicels to 2.5cm, pubesc. Spring. Japan. 'Caepitosa' ('Naden', 'Water-er's Cherry', *P.* 'Takasago' (Sato-zakura Group)): habit round-topped, to 8m high, to 7m wide; lvs covered in short hairs, tinted bronze or red when young, mid green, deep red in autumn; fls semi-double, to 4.5cm diam., pale pink, profuse, mid-April. Z6.

***P. simonii*** Carr. Shrub or small tree with pyramidal crown. Shoots glabrous. Lvs to 10cm, ovate-lanceolate, strong-acuminate, fine-crenate, glabrous, dark green, veins branched at very acute angles; petioles short, 2–4-glandular. Fls to 2.5cm diam., white, 3-clustered; pedicels to 4mm. Fr. to 6cm diam., globose, red, flesh bright yellow; stone small, suborbicular, rough. Spring. N China. Z6.

***P. ×skinneri*** Rehd. (*P. japonica* × *P. tenella.*) Subshrub to 1m. Lvs to 5cm, ovate-oblong, acuminate, lightly double-serrate, pubesc. on midrib beneath. Fls many, bright pink, small; pedicels pubesc.; cal. tube narrow-campanulate pubesc. Garden origin. 'Baton Rouge': fls profuse. Z6.

***P.* 'Snofozam' ('Wayside White Weeper', 'Snow Fountains').** Habit dwarf, moderately weeping, to 4m high, to 3m wide. Lvs dark green, orange and gold in autumn. Fls single, white, profuse. Fr. small, black.

***P. speciosa*** (Koidz.) Ingram. OSHIMA CHERRY. Loosely branched tree to 12m+. Bark pale grey-fawn. Lvs 10×6cm, elliptic-ovate to narrow-obovate, abruptly acuminate, sparse-pubesc. on midrib when young, later glabrous, bronze-green; petioles occasionally pubesc., later glabrous. Fls white, in lax, 3.5cm diam. corymbs; cal. tube 5.5mm, narrowly tubular-campanulate. Spring. Japan. Z6.

***P. spinosa*** L. SLOE; BLACKTHORN. Very spiny shrub or small tree to 8m. Young shoots short, rufous, short-pubesc., rarely glabrous; branches divaricately patent. Lvs to 5cm, elliptic to oblong-obovate, apex obtuse, base cuneate, fine-serrate to crenate, pubesc., later glabrous. Fls to 2cm diam., white, solitary, rarely paired; pedicels to 1.5cm, strict, glabrous or sparse-pubesc., grey. Fr. to 1.5cm, globose to globose-conoid, black, glaucous-pruinose, aril green. Spring. Europe, N Africa, Asia Minor. 'Plena': branches spiny, black; fls double, small, white, profuse; slow-growing. 'Purpurea': habit compact, neat; lvs red when young, later green tinted purple; fls pale pink. 'Variegata': lvs irregularly variegated white. Z4.

***P. ssiori*** F. Schmidt. JAPANESE BIRD CHERRY. Tree to 23m+. Young shoots glabrous. Lvs 9.5×4cm, oblong to oblong-obovate, acuminate, rounded to cordate at base, glabrous above, axillary-pubesc. beneath, serrulate, serrations fine-aristate; petioles 22.5mm, glandular. Fls 9mm diam., white, in many-fld racemes. Fr. black; stone somewhat rugose. C Japan. Z5.

***P. subcordata*** Benth. PACIFIC PLUM; WESTERN WILD PLUM; OREGON PLUM. Shrub to 3m, sometimes to 8m. Bark grey-brown, furrowed, somewhat scaly. Lvs to 5×4cm, orbicular to ovate, apex rounded and obtuse, base usually rounded or subcordate, incised-serrate or -biserrate, pubesc., later glabrous; petioles to 12mm, glabrous or pubesc., glandular; stipules lanceolate, with glandular margins. Fls to 18mm diam., in 2–4-fld, umbellate clusters; pedicels to 13mm; cal. tube 3mm, campanulate, lobes 3mm+, oblong or oblong-obovate; pet. to 9mm, oblong or obovate, entire. Fr. to 3cm, oblong, maroon or rarely yellow; stone to 18×17mm, oblong to orbicular. Spring. Western N America. Z7.

***P. subhirtella*** Miq. WINTER FLOWERING CHERRY; SPRING CHERRY; HIGAN CHERRY; ROSEBUD CHERRY. Deciduous, broad-crowned tree to 18m. Bark grey, branches spreading to arching; branchlets slender, long rather cascading, young shoots slender, pubesc. Lvs to 8cm, ovate to lanceolate, acuminate, serrate, bright green above, with slightly pubesc. venation beneath. Fls in groups of 2–5, appearing before lvs, to 18mm diam.; cal. tube to 6mm, red-purple, slightly pubesc., bulging at base; sep. to 3mm, triangular; pet. pale pink to white, incised. Fr. to 9mm, ovoid, purple-black. Autumn, winter and early spring, often remontant with warm spells. Japan.

'Ascendens Rosea': branches widely ascending; fls clear shell pink, cal. tinted red. 'Autumnalis' ('Jugatsu Sakura'): habit spreading, to 5m; lvs deeply serrate, red and orange in autumn; fls semi-double, pet. somewhat frilled, opening white, pink in bud, stamens dark pink, almond-scented, November to April, winter fls in sessile clusters, spring fls on stalks to 4cm. 'Autumnalis Rosea': as white form but fls soft pink centre. 'Elfenreigen' (*P. subhirtella* × *P. concinna ?)*: habit narrow, open branched; lvs brown tinted when young, intense autumnal colouring; fls white, pet. narrow, loose stellate form; flowers late April. 'Floreplen0': habit dome-shaped; fls fully double, to 3cm diam., opening palest pink, pink in bud. 'Fukubana': branches broadly ascending, to 8m; fls semi-double, 12–14 pet., deeply notched, striking deep pink, darker in bud, mid-May; fertile. 'Grandiflora' ('Dai Higan Sakura'): branches widely ascending; fls large, to 5cm, palest pink, not profuse, late March. 'Hally Jolivette' (*P. subhirtella* × *P. yedoensis*) × *P. subhirtella*): habit rounded, to 4m, densely branched; shoots slender, tinted red; lvs to 4.5cm, narrow-ovate, sharply toothed, hairy above and more so beneath; fls double, small, buds pink, opening white with pink centre; flowers for 3 weeks.

'Pandora' (*P. subhirtella* 'Rosea' × *P. yedoensis*): habit shrub-like, broadly fastigiate, to 7m high, to 4m wide; shoots loose, nodding; lvs ovate-elliptic, to 7cm long, pubesc. beneath; fls single, pale pink with darker edge; very abundant. 'Pendula' ('Ito Sakura', 'Shidare Higan'): habit weeping; branches slender; lvs wide; fls small, faded pink; abundant, freely produced, early April. 'Pendula Plena Rosea' ('Sendai Ito Sakura', 'Pendula Flore Pleno'): habit weeping; fls double, rosette form, strong pink. 'Pendula Rosea': habit weeping, dome-shaped; fls rich pink in bud, fading later, profuse. 'Pendula Rubra' ('Ibara Ito Sakura'): habit weeping; branches slender; lvs lanceolate, red and yellow in autumn; fls deep pink, ruby in bud, early April. 'Plena': fls double, flat, pink in bud, opening paler, profuse. 'Rosea' ('Beni Higan Sakura'): habit upright; fls cup-shaped, pedicels short, bracts serrated, rose pink, in umbels to 4. 'Rosy Cloud': habit spreading, upright, to 6m; fls double, soft pink, fragrant, long-lasting. 'Stellata' ('Pink Star'): habit erect, slightly spreading, to 7m high, to 7m wide; fls single, 3.5cm across, pet. narrows oblong, clear shell pink, clustered to 5 at end 15cm of shoots so appears to form single panicle. 'Whitcombii': habit broadly globe-shaped, to 10m high, to 12m wide; lvs green, opening light green; fls single, pink fading to white. Z5.

***P. ×sultana*** Voss. (*P. salicina* × *P. simonii.*) WICKSON PLUM. Tree of narrow, erect habit. Lvs elongate-lanceolate. Fr. very large, maroon, flesh yellow. Garden origin. 'Wickson': habit narrow and upright; lvs lanceolate; fr. large, maroon, fleshy yellow. Z6.

***P. sweginzowii*** Koehne. Shrub to 1.5m. Lvs to 7.5×3.5cm, linear-lanceolate or lanceolate, acuminate, glabrous, biserrate, scabrous; petioles to 7mm; stipules to 1cm×2mm, linear or linear-lanceolate, leaflike. Fls dark pink; cal. tube to 8mm, subcylindric, glabrous, teeth to 4mm, glandular-fimbriate; pet. to 17mm, obovate or oblong-oval, cuneate at base. Fr. to 2.5cm, ovoid or orbicular-ovoid. Spring–summer. Turkestan. Z6.

***P. szechuanica*** Batal. Resembles *P. maximowiczii*. Small tree. Lvs to 4cm, with disc-shaped, compressed bracts; petiole black-purple. Fl. bracts to 8mm, disc-shaped, compressed. Fr. stone completely smooth. China (Sichuan). Z6.

***P. tangutica*** (Batal.) Koehne. Dense, spiny shrub to 4m. Branchlets brown, fine-pubesc., later glabrous. Lvs to 3cm, oblanceolate to oblong, acute, cuneate at base, dark green, paler beneath, fine-crenate. Fls 2.5cm diam., pink-red, solitary; cal. lobes elliptic, inconspicuously dentate, glabrous; pet. obovate; stamens 30. Fr. 2cm diam., subsessile, dense-tomentose, dehiscent; stone rotund, scabrous. W China (Sichuan). Z5.

***P. tatsienensis*** Batal. Closely resembles *P. litigiosa*, but lvs caudately acuminate, glabrous, teeth with large, conical glands at tips, floral bracts glandular-toothed, glands disc-shaped, rotund, and fr. 1cm diam., rufous. W China. Z6.

***P. tenella*** Batsch DWARF RUSSIAN ALMOND. Low, deciduous shrub to 1.5m, of bushy habit. Branchlets glabrous. Lvs to 9×2.5cm, obovate or oblong, somewhat thick, acute, scabrous-serrate, dark shiny green above, paler beneath, glabrous. Fls 13mm+ diam., rose-red, sessile, very many, 1–3-clustered. Fr. 2.5cm, ovoid, grey-yellow, velutinous-lanuginose; stone broad-ovate, scabrous. Spring. C Europe to E Siberia. 'Alba': lvs light green; fls pure white. 'Fire Hill': habit dwarf, to 75cm high, forms thickets of thin erect stems; fls intense red, profuse; a selection of *f. gessleriana*. 'Speciosa': shrub, to 0.8m, fls large dark pink in bud, opening lighter. Z2.

***P. texana*** Dietr. TEXAS ALMOND; PEACH BUSH. Subshrub, or bushy habit. Bark grey; branches very irregular; branchlets light grey, strong-pubesc. Lvs to 3×1.5cm, ovate to oblong-elliptic, obtuse, green and pubesc. above, grey-tomentose beneath, distinctly glandular-serrulate; petioles to 4mm, pubesc.; stipules linear, glandular. Fls to 12mm diam., solitary or paired; pedicels to 4mm, grey-pubesc.; cal. tube 2mm, lobes 2mm, ovate-oblong, glandular-serrulate; pet. to 6mm, white, oblong, obtuse. Fr. small, dense velutinous-pubesc.; stone to 1.5×1cm, ovoid, rounded at base. Summer. US (Texas). Z6.

***P. tomentosa*** Thunb. DOWNY CHERRY. Shrub of bushy habit, to 2.5m, occasionally to 5m. Young shoots dense-tomentose. Lvs 5.5×2.5cm, obovate to oblong, rounded or abruptly acuminate, cuneate at base, slightly rugose, green, pubesc. above, dense-lanuginose beneath, coarse-serrate; petioles 3mm; stipules linear-subulate, often branched. Fls 23mm diam., white or pink-white, solitary or paired; cal. tube 5mm, broad-campanulate, sometimes glabrous, lobes 3mm, triangular, serrulate; style white sericeous-pubesc. towards base. Fr. 12.5mm, subglobose, shallow-sulcate, usually somewhat pubesc. red. N & W China, Tibet, Kashmir. 'Leucocarpa': fr. white. Z2.

***P. triloba*** Lindl. FLOWERING ALMOND. Deciduous shrub or small tree to 4.5m. Young shoots usually glabrous; branchlets dark brown, dense velutinous-pubesc. Lvs to 6.5×3cm, ovate or obovate, often trilobed, tapering at both ends, irregularly and coarsely biserrate, somewhat pubesc. beneath. Fls to 2.5cm diam., pink-white, solitary or paired; cal. 5mm, glabrous, lobes shallow, rotund. Fr. 13mm diam., globose, red, lanuginose. Spring. China. 'Petzoldii': twigs glabrous; lvs elliptic to ovate; fls single, to 2cm diam., pet. pink. var. ***simplex*** (Bunge) Rehd. The wild form. Fls single, small, pink. Fr. red tinted, pubesc., somewhat globose. Z5.

***P. umbellata*** Elliott. SLOE. Tree to 6m. Bark dark brown. Lvs to 7×3cm, lanceolate to oval, apex usually acute, narrowed or rarely rounded at base, fine-serrate, glabrous above, usually pubesc. on venation beneath, sometimes on margin towards base; petioles to 7mm, pubesc. Fls to 18mm diam., in 2–4-fld umbels; pedicels to 1cm, thin, glabrous; cal. tube 3mm, narrow-obconic, lobes to 2mm, ovate; pet. to 6mm, oblong-ovate to suborbicular. Fr. to 2cm diam., globose, red, yellow or dark purple, glaucous-pruinose. Spring. E US. Z8.

***P. undulata*** D. Don, non sensu F.B. Ingram. Evergreen shrub or tree to 12m. Lvs to 15×6cm, elliptic or oblong, apex long-acuminate, cuneate at base, entire or shallow-serrate; petioles to 1cm; stipules 5×1mm, entire, caducous. Fls white or cream, in racemes; pedicels to 7mm; sep. 1mm, broad-triangular, minute-pubesc. at apex; pet. to 4mm, elliptic, glabrous; fil. 3mm, glabrous. Fr. ovoid; stone to 2cm×12mm. Himalaya (Bhutan, Sikkim). Z6.

***P. ×utahensis*** Koehne. (*P. angustifolia* var. *watsonii* × *P. besseyi.*) Closely resembles *P. besseyi*, but lvs to 6cm, elliptic to elliptic-oblong or oblong-obovate, fine-serrate, shiny above, and fr. dark, rufous, somewhat pruinose. Western N America. Z4.

***P. vaniotii*** Lév. Deciduous tree to 15m. Lvs to 11×6cm, oblong to ovate-oblong, short-acuminate, cuneate to rotund at base, glabrous, serrulate; petioles to 2.5cm, glabrous or subglabrous, with 1–2 glands. Fls many, in racemes to 14cm; cal. tube broad-cupulate, buff; cor. 8mm diam., white. Fr. to 6×5mm, ovoid. W China to Taiwan. Z5.

***P. verecunda*** Koehne. Tree to 20m. Bark grey-brown or purple-brown. Lvs to 12×5.5cm, obovate or obovate-elliptic, caudate-acuminate, rounded or somewhat cordate at base, biserrate, green above, lighter beneath, shiny, soft-pubesc.; petioles to 2cm, red, patent-pubesc. Fls to 3cm diam., in 2–4-fld corymbs; peduncles 12mm; pedicels to 2cm, patent-pubesc.; cal. tube 6mm, elongate-campanulate, rufous, lobes 5mm, oblong, entire, glabrous; pet. to 2cm, white or light red, obovate or elliptic, incised; stamens 40; pistil to 14mm, glabrous. Fr. to 1cm diam., purple-black. Spring. Japan, Korea. Z8.

***P. virginiana*** L. Shrub to 3.5m, or rarely small tree. Young shoots glabrous. Lvs 8×4.5cm, broad-obovate or broad-elliptic, abrupt-acuminate, glabrous, axillary sandy-pubesc. on venation, very fine-serrate. Fls 1cm diam., white, in somewhat dense, 30-fld racemes. Fr. round, dark red to black; stone smooth. Western N America. 'Canada Red': habit broadly pyramidal, well-branched, to 8m; lvs opening green, later purple. 'Duerinckii': lvs broadly elliptic. 'Leucocarpa': fr. pale amber. 'Nana': habit dwarf. 'Pendula': branches drooping. 'Schubert': habit dense, spreading, to 6m high, to 7m diam; lvs green, later brown tinted maroon, eventually dark brown. var. ***demissa*** (Torr. & A. Gray) Torr. WESTERN CHOKEBERRY. Erect shrub or small tree to 3m, of more bush-like habit. Branchlets glabrous or pubesc. Lvs to 9cm, ovate to obovate, shorter acuminate, round to slightly cordate at base, sometimes lanuginose beneath; petiole bi-glandular. Fr. dark red. US (Washington to California). var. ***melanocarpa*** (A. Nels.) Sarg. Shrub or small tree. Branchlets smooth. Lvs smaller, stouter than species type, glabrous beneath; petiole eglandular. Fls white, in compact, erect to ascending racemes. Fr. almost black. US (Rocky Mts from California to British Columbia). 'Xanthocarpa': fr. yellow. Z2.

***P. webbii*** (Spach) Vierh. Shrub or small tree to 6m, densely branched. Short shoots spiny, young shoots red. Lvs to 4.5×0.9cm, oblong-linear, acute, cuneate at base, shallow glandular-crenate, light green above, paler beneath, glabrous; petiole to 12mm. Fls 2cm diam., white, solitary, sometimes clustered; cal. short-cylindric, glabrous, lobes 3mm, short-elliptic; stamens 26, fil. becoming pink, pet. broad-obovate, somewhat bilabiate. Fr. 2cm, conical, dense velutinous-pubesc. Sicily to Asia Minor. Z6.

***P. wilsonii*** (Schneid.) Koehne. Tree to 10m. Lvs to 13×6cm, obovate, acuminate, rotund at base, fine-serrate, sericeous-pubesc. beneath; petioles to 1.5cm, 1–4-glandular. Fls in pubesc. racemes. C China. Z6.

***P. ×yedoensis*** Matsum. (*P. ×subhirtella* × *P. speciosa.*) TOKYO CHERRY. Small tree to 15m, broadly upright. Bark smooth; young branchlets ascending-pubesc. Lvs to 12cm, elliptic, acuminate, biserrate, vivid green above, paler and ascending-pubesc. beneath; petiole golden-yellow with brick-red pubesc. Fls to 3.5cm diam., pure white, single, precocious, in 5–6-fld, ascending-pubesc. racemes; pedicel, cal. and style pubesc. Fr. globose, pea-sized, black. Spring. Japan. 'Akebono': fls single, pure pink. 'Erecta': habit stiffly fastigiate, compact, twiggy; fls single, to 4cm diam., somewhat cup-shaped, pale rose, faintly scented; late March. 'Ivensii': main branches arch horizontally, branchlets slender and nodding; fls to 2cm diam., pink in bud, opening white, fragrant; March. 'Moerheimii': shrub-like, to 3m, weeping; twigs pendulous, grey; lvs elliptic; fls pink fading to white; to 2cm diam., pedicel pubesc., cal. purple; late-flowering. 'Shidare Yoshino' ('Pendula'): habit weeping; annual growth to 1.5m; fls snow white, profuse on older plants. Z5.

***P. acida*** Ehrh. See *P. cerasus* var. *caproniana*.
***P. acida*** sensu K. Koch, non Ehrh. See *P. cerasus* var. *frutescens*.
***P. acuminata*** Michx. See *P. maritima*.
*P.* 'Affinis'. See *P.* 'Jo-nioi' (Sato-Zakura Group).
*P.* 'Albo-rosea'. See *P.* 'Shiro-fugen' (Sato-Zakura Group).
***P. americana*** var. ***nigra*** Waugh. See *P. nigra*.
***P. amygdalus*** Batsch. See *P. dulcis*.
***P. ansu*** (Maxim.) Komar. See *P. armeniaca* var. *ansu*.
***P. armeniaca*** ssp. ***brigantiaca*** (Vill.) Dipp. See *P. brigantina*.
***P. armeniaca*** var. ***mandshurica*** Maxim. See *P. mandshurica*.
***P. armeniaca*** var. ***sibirica*** K. Koch. See *P. sibirica*.

***P.*** 'Asano'. See *P.* 'Geraldinae' (Sato-zakura Group).
***P.*** 'Benifugen'. See *P.* 'Fugenzo' (Sato-zakura Group).
***P. borealis*** Poir. See *P. nigra.*
***P. bracteata*** Franch. & Savat. See *P. maximowiczii.*
***P. brigantiaca*** Vill. See *P. brigantina.*
***P. bungei*** Walp. See *P. humilis.*
***P.*** 'Campanuloides'. See *P.* 'Shujaku' (Sato-zakura Group).
***P.*** 'Candida'. See *P.* 'Ariake' (Sato-zakura Group).
***P. capollin*** Zucc. See *P. salicifolia.*
***P. caproniana*** (L.) Gaudin. See *P. cerasus* var. *caproniana.*
***P. capuli*** Cav. ex Spreng. See *P. salicifolia.*
***P.*** 'Cataracta'. See *P.* 'Taki-nioi' (Sato-zakura Group).
***P. ceraseidos*** Maxim. See *P. apetala.*
***P. ceraseidos*** var. ***kurilensis*** Miyabe. See *P. nipponica* var. *kurilensis.*
***P. cerasifera*** var. ***blireana*** (André) Bean. See *P.* ×*blireana.*
***P. cerasifera*** var. ***gigantea*** Späth. See *P.* ×*gigantea.*
***P. cerasoides*** var. ***campanulata*** Koidz. See *P. campanulata.*
***P. cerasus*** var. ***humilis*** Bean. See *P. cerasus* var. *frutescens.*
***P.*** 'Cheal's Weeping'. See *P.* 'Kiku-shidare' (Sato-zakura Group).
***P. chicasa*** Michx. See *P. angustifolia.*
***P. communis*** (L.) Arcang. non Huds. See *P. dulcis.*
***P. conradinae*** Koehne. See *P. hirtipes.*
***P. crassipes*** Koidz. See *P. apetala.*
***P. crenata*** Koehne. See *P. apetala.*
***P. cuneata*** Raf. See *P. pumila* var. *susquehanae.*
***P. damascena*** Ehrh. See *P.* ×*domestica.*
***P. dehiscens*** Koehne. See *P. tangutica.*
***P. demissa*** Nutt. ex Dietr. See *P. virginiana* var. *demissa.*
***P. depressa*** Pursh. See *P. pumila* var. *depressa.*
***P. divaricata*** Ledeb. See *P. cerasifera* ssp. *divaricata.*
***P.*** 'Diversifolia'. See *P.* 'Kirigayatsu' (Sato-zakura Group).
***P. domestica*** var. ***cerasifera*** Ser. See *P. cerasifera.*
***P. domestica*** var. ***myrobalan*** L. See *P. cerasifera.*
***P.*** ×***effusa*** (Host) Schneid. See *P.* ×*gondouinii.*
***P. emarginata*** Walp. See *P. nigra.*
***P.*** 'Erecta'. See *P.* 'Amanogawa' (Sato-zakura Group).
***P. eriogyna*** C. Mason. See *P. fremontii.*
***P. glandulosa*** (Hook.) Torr. & A. Gray non Thunb.. See *P. texana.*
***P. glauciphylla*** Ghora & Panigr. See *P. cornuta.*
***P.*** 'Grandiflora'. See *P.* 'Ukon' (Sato-zakura Group).
***P. haussknechtii*** Schneid. See *P. webbii.*
***P. helenae*** Koehne. See *P. hirtipes.*
***P. himalaica*** Kit. See *P. rufa.*
***P.*** 'Hokusai'. See *P.* 'Uzuzakura' (Sato-zakura Group).
***P.*** 'Hosokawa'. See *P.* 'Shirotae' (Sato-zakura Group).
***P. hosseusii*** Diels. See *P. cerasoides* var. *rubea.*
***P.*** 'Ichiyo'. See *P.* 'Hizakura' (Sato-zakura Group).
***P. insititia*** L. See *P.* ×*domestica* ssp. *insititia.*
***P. integrifolia*** Sarg. non Walp. See *P. lyonii.*
***P. intermedia*** Host non Poir. See *P.* ×*eminens.*
***P. involucrata*** Koehne. See *P. pseudocerasus.*
***P. iwagiensis*** Koehne. See *P. nipponica.*
***P. jacquemontii*** var. ***bifrons*** Ingram. See *P. bifrons.*
***P. jamasakura*** Sieb. ex Koidz. See *P. serrulata* var. *spontanea.*
***P. jamasakura*** var. ***speciosa*** Koidz. See *P. speciosa.*
***P.*** 'James H. Veitch'. See *P.* 'Fugenzo' (Sato-zakura Group).
***P.*** 'Kajima'. See *P.* 'Shirotae' (Sato-zakura Group).
***P.*** 'Kanzan'. See *P.* 'Sekiyama' (Sato-zakura Group).
***P. kurilensis*** Miyabe ex Tak. See *P. nipponica* var. *kurilensis.*
***P.*** 'Kwanzan'. See *P.* 'Sekiyama' (Sato-zakura Group).
***P. lanata*** Mackenzie & Bush. See *P. americana.*
***P. latidentata*** Koehne. See *P. mugus.*
***P. melanocarpa*** Rydb. See *P. virginiana* var. *melanocarpa.*
***P. microlepis*** Koehne. See *P.* ×*subhirtella.*
***P.*** 'Mikuruma-gaeshi'. See *P.* 'Kirigayatsu' (Sato-zakura Group).
***P. monticola*** K. Koch. See *P. cerasifera* ssp. *divaricata.*
***P.*** 'Mount Fuji'. See *P.* 'Shirotae' (Sato-zakura Group).
***P.*** 'Moutan'. See *P.* 'Botanzakura' (Sato-zakura Group).
***P. mutabilis*** Miyoshi. See *P. serrulata* var. *spontanea.*
***P. myrobalana*** Lois. See *P. cerasifera.*
***P. nakai*** Lév. See *P. japonica.*
***P. nana*** (L.) Stokes, non Duroi. See *P. tenella.*
***P. napaulensis*** var. ***sericea*** Batal. See *P. sericea.*
***P. nikkoensis*** Koehne. See *P. nipponica.*
***P. oeconomica*** Borkh. See *P.* ×*domestica.*
***P. pachyclada*** Zab. See *P. cornuta.*
***P. padus*** sensu F.B.Ingram non L. See *P. cornuta.*
***P. padus*** var. ***rotundifolia*** hort. ex Koehne. See *P.* ×*laucheana.*
***P. palmeri*** Sarg. See *P. armericana.*
***P. paracerasus*** Koehne. See *P.* ×*yedoensis.*
***P. pissardii blireana fl. pl.*** Lemoine. See *P.* ×*blireana.*
***P. polytricha*** Koehne. See *P. pilosiuscula.*
***P. pseudoarmeniaca*** Heldr. & Sart. See *P. cocomilia.*
***P. pseudocerasus*** var. ***spontanea*** Maxim. See *P. serrulata* var. *spontanea.*
***P. pubescens*** Pursh. See *P. maritima.*
***P. puddum*** Kingdon-Ward, non DC. See *P. cerasoides* var. *rubea.*
***P. pulchella*** Koehne. See *P. pilosiuscula.*
***P. pumila*** var. ***besseyi*** (Bail.) Waugh. See *P. besseyi.*
***P. pumila*** var. ***cuneata*** (Raf.) Bail. See *P. pumila* var. *susquehanae.*
***P.*** 'Purpurascens'. See *P.* 'Sekiyama' (Sato-zakura Group).
***P.*** 'Purpurea'. See *P.* 'Yae-marasakizakura' (Sato-zakura Group).
***P. racemosa*** Lam. See *P. cornuta.*
***P. racemosa*** Lam. See *P. padus.*
***P. reflexa*** hort. See *P.* ×*eminens.*
***P. rehderiana*** Koehne. See *P. litigiosa.*
***P. reverchonii*** Sarg. See *P. rivularis.*
***P.*** 'Rosea'. See *P.* 'Kiku-shidare' (Sato-zakura Group).
***P.*** 'Roseaplena'. See *P.* 'Uzuzakura' (Sato-zakura Group).
***P. rufomicans*** Koehne. See *P. sericea.*
***P.*** 'Ruiran'. See *P.* 'Taguiarashi' (Sato-zakura Group).
***P. sachalinensis*** Miyoshi. See *P. sargentii.*
***P. salzeri*** Zdarek. See *P. padus.*
***P.*** 'Senriko'. See *P.* 'Ojochin' (Sato-zakura Group).
***P. seoulensis*** Nak. See *P. padus* var. *commutata.*
***P.*** 'Shimidsu'. See *P.* 'Okumiyaku' (Sato-zakura Group).
***P. sinensis*** Pers. See *P. glandulosa.*
***P.*** 'Spiralis'. See *P.* 'Uzuzakura' (Sato-zakura Group).
***P. subcordata*** var. ***kelloggii*** Lemmon. See *P. subcordata.*
***P. subhirtella*** var. ***changyangensis*** Ingram. See *P. changyangensis.*
***P. susquehanae*** Willd. See *P. pumila* var. *susquehanae.*
***P. tricantha*** Koehne. See *P. rufa* var. *tricantha.*
***P.*** 'Tricolor'. See *P.* 'Gyoiko' (Sato-zakura Group).
***P. triflora*** Roxb. See *P. salicina.*
***P. vilmoriniana*** hort. See *P. scopulorum.*
***P. wallichii*** Steud. See *P. undulata.*
***P. watsonii*** Sarg. See *P. angustifolia* var. *watsonii.*
***P. wattii*** Ghora & Panigr. See *P. cornuta.*
For further synonymy see *Laurocerasus* and *Persica.*

**Psammophora** Dinter & Schwantes. (From Gk *psammos*, sand, and *phoros*, bearing, referring to the sand which adheres to the sticky leaves.) Aizoaceae. 6 species of highly succulent perennials with low-growing, woody, mat-forming and densely leafy stems; shoots above ground or subterranean. Leaves short, thick, opposite and decussate, more or less triquetrous with rounded keel and margins, to semicylindric, acute or expanded at the tip, underside pulled forward and chin-like, slightly glossy, blue-green to grey-green with a viscous secretion on the surface which traps dust and soil particles, providing shade and protection. Flowers terminal, solitary, pedicellate, violet-pink or white. Namibia (S Namib). Z10.

CULTIVATION As for *Argyroderma.*

***P. herrei*** L. Bol. Lvs 2×1cm, broadening above, short-triangular, upper surface convex, lower surface rounded but acutely carinate toward tip, surface rough, brown-grey. Fls 2.2–2.5cm diam., white. Cape Province: Little Namaqualand.

***P. longifolia*** L. Bol. Lvs 4–6 per stem, 4–4.5×1.2cm, slightly less thick, linear, short-tapered, rounded to rounded-carinate below, margins conspicuously rounded, surface very rough, light grey-green to grey-brown, young lvs olive green. Fls 3.5cm diam., white. Namibia: Great Namaqualand.

***P. modesta*** (Dinter & A. Berger) Dinter & Schwantes. Sparsely branched shrub to 5cm. Lvs 4–8 per shoot, 12×5–6mm, rounded-triangular, acute, grey-green, faintly flushed red, rough. Fls 1.5cm diam., violet. Namibia: Luderitz area.

***P. nissenii*** (Dinter) Dinter & Schwantes. Low shrub, 5–10cm across; branches subterranean at least in habitat. Lvs 2–3 pairs per shoot, 12–40mm long, 6mm across at the base, tip expanded-triangular, lower surface semicylindric or with a rounded keel, grey-green or tinged white or red. Fls 12mm diam., white or violet. Namibia: Namib.

**Pseudepidendrum** Rchb. f.
***P. spectabile*** Rchb. f. See *Epidendrum pseudepidendrum.*

**Pseuderanthemum** Radlk. (From Gk *pseudes*, false, and *Eranthemum*, a closely related genus with which this one is much confused.) Acanthaceae. Some 60 species of evergreen herbs, subshrubs and shrubs, differing from *Eranthemum* in their inconspicuous floral bracts, overlapping, not twisted corolla lobes, and banded, not pitted, pollen. Leaves entire or toothed. Inflorescence spikes, racemes or cymes composed of flowers solitary, paired or in threes subtended by bracts; calyx lobes 5, narrow; corolla long-tubular, lobes 5, spreading, subequal; stamens 2, attached near throat. Fruit a 2–4-seeded capsule. Tropics. Z10.

CULTIVATION As for *Eranthemum.*

***P. alatum*** (Nees) Radlk. CHOCOLATE PLANT. Low-growing herb. Lvs ovate-cordate, bronze to chocolate brown, blotched silver along midvein above, leaden grey beneath; petioles flattened, winged. Fls small, in racemes; cor. salverform, purple. C America.

***P. atropurpureum*** L.H. Bail. Erect shrub to 1.5m. Branches long, slender, rather weak. Lvs 10–15cm, ovate-elliptic, obtuse, purple to deep metallic green. Fls packed in erect, terminal spikes to 18cm; cor. bilabiate, tube to 2.5cm, white, lobes linear-oblong, spotted rose or purple at base. Polynesia, naturalized tropical America. 'Variegatum': lvs bronze-purple, marked pink, variegated cream-yellow; fls magenta marked red.

***P. reticulatum*** (Hook. f.) Radlk. Subshrub to 1m. Lvs to 27cm, ovate-lanceolate, undulate, dark green net-veined cream-yellow. Fls to 3cm, flushed damson in throat and spotted same colour on lower lip. Polynesia.

***P. seticalyx*** (C.B. Clarke) Stapf. See *Ruspolia seticalyx*.
For further synonymy see *Chamaeranthemum* and *Eranthemum*.

**Pseudobombax** Dugand. (From Gk *pseudes*, false and *Bombax*.) Bombacaceae. 20 species of deciduous shrubs or small to medium-sized trees to 20m, usually lacking spines; trunk straight or tapering. Leaves simple or digitate, clustered at end of short twigs, inarticulate (unlike *Bombax*, which has articulate leaves and leaflets), usually glabrous, but petioles and petiolules sometimes pubescent, digitate leaves with 3–11 leaflets to 30cm; petioles with lanceolate, caducous stipules. Flowers appearing before leaves, clustered at branch-ends in cymes of 2–5, or solitary; pedicels with 3 caducous or persistent bracteoles; calyx cup-shaped to campanulate or subtubular, to 2cm, truncate to shortly 5-lobed, coriaceous, glabrous or pubescent, often glandular, persistent; petals to 15cm, 5, united with staminal tube, erect, oblong to linear, somewhat fleshy, with tufts of hairs, rapidly deciduous after anthesis; stamens many, in one whorl, united below to form short staminal tube, sometimes in distinct fascicles; ovary usually 5-locular, style filiform, stigma 5-lobed. Fruit a dehiscent woody capsule; seeds numerous embedded in white to red-brown fibres. Tropical America. Z10.

CULTIVATION As for *Ceiba*.

***P. ellipticum*** (HBK) Dugand. SHAVING-BRUSH TREE. To 10m; bark smooth, pale green or grey. Lvs with 3–6 leaflets, elliptic, apiculate at apex, to 31×17.5cm; petiole to 36cm. Fls solitary or paired; pedicels to 3.5cm; cal. 1.5cm, cup-shaped to campanulate, truncate, basal glands 10; pet. 9–16×1–2cm, oblong-linear, obtuse, white to pink, densely pubesc. externally; stamens many, shortly united at base, to 13cm. Capsule fusiform, to 15cm, yellow-brown, glabrous. Mexico to Guatemala.

***P. grandiflorum*** (Cav. (Robyns Tree, 8–20m; trunk to 40cm diam. Lvs 8–28×3–10.5cm, with 5–9 leaflets, obovate to subelliptic, obtuse to subacuminate at apex. Fls usually solitary or sometimes paired, more or less terminal; pedicel to 5cm; cal. to 3cm, cup-shaped to subtubular, truncate or sometimes 2–3-lobed, green; pet. to 18×2cm, linear-lanceolate, obtuse, dark black-purple externally, paler within, densely pubesc. externally; stamens many, united at base, to 10cm; style to 15cm, purple. Capsule to 30cm, oblong, glabrous, brown. Brazil.

For synonymy see *Bombax* and *Pachira*.

**Pseudocalymma** Samp. & Kuhlm.
***P. alliaceum*** (Lam.) Sandw. See *Mansoa alliacea*.
***P. alliaceum* var. *microcalyx*** pro parte Sandw. See *Mansoa hymenaea*.
***P. hymenaeum*** (DC.) Sandw. See *Mansoa hymenaea*.
***P. laevigatum*** (Bur. & Schum.) A. Samp. & Kuhlm. See *Mansoa hymenaea*.
***P. macrocarpum*** Sandw. See *Mansoa hymenaea*.
***P. pachypus*** (Schum.) Sandw. See *Mansoa hymenaea*.
***P. pohlianum*** Bur. & Schum. See *Mansoa hymenaea*.

**Pseudocyclosorus** Ching. Thelypteridaceae. (From Gk. *pseudes*, false, and *Cyclosorus*.) Some 11 species of terrestrial ferns. Rhizomes erect or short-creeping; scales broad, bearing when young mucilage-secreting marginal hairs; young fronds covered with mucilage through which aerophores project. Pinnae deeply lobed, basal pinnae reduced to small leaflets or to aerophores with a minute lamina, veins free basal acroscopic vein passing to base or side of a short sinus-membrane, basal basioscopic vein to side off sinus-membrane or just above. Sori circular; indusia present glabrous or bearing short acicular or capitate hairs; sporangia stalks, glabrous. Tropical Africa, Madagascar, Mascarene Islands, Tropical & Subtropical Asia to Japan & Indonesia. Z10.

CULTIVATION As for *Christella*.

***P. canus*** (Bak.) Holtt. & Grimes. Rhiz. suberect or creeping. Stipes 20cm or more, short-hairy throughout. Frond lamina lanceolate to obovate, 70cm or more long, pinnae to 15×3cm, to 28 pairs, lowest narrowed at their bases, the larger 12–18cm×1.5–2.2cm, sessile, opposite or alternate, apex attenuate to narrowly acute, base truncate, lobes slightly, oblique, obtuse, veins to 12-pairs; rachis short hairy, costa pubesc.; small glands or capitate hairs on costules and veins, very short erect hairs between veins. Sori supramedial indusia with a few hairs. N India.

***P. repens*** (Hope) Ching. See *P. canus*.
For further synonymy see *Nephrodium*.

**Pseudocydonia** Schneid. (From Gk *psendes*, false, and *Cydonia*.) Rosaceae. 1 species, a shrubs to small deciduous to semi-evergreen tree to 18m, close to *Chaenomeles*, differing in leaf teeth aristate, flowers solitary and filaments in a ring. Bark peeling in large plates; branches densely hairy, becoming glabrous, shiny. Leaves 5–8×3–5cm, obovate to oval, tapered to base, margin serrate, glossy above, densely brown hairy beneath, becoming sparsely hairy, turning red and or yellow before falling. Flowers 2.5–3cm diam., solitary, sessile, pale pink. Fruit 10–15cm, ovoid, pale to dark yellow. Spring. China. Z6.

CULTIVATION A small semi-evergreen tree or large shrub grown for its decorative bark, its attractive downy young shoots, and for the pale pink flowers produced on year-old shoots, in spring. The large, egg-shaped, deep yellow fruits seldom develop fully or ripen in less favourable climates. In regions with long hot summers where the wood will ripen completely, *Pseudocydonia* spp. will tolerate quite hard frosts, but in Britain they are reliably hardy only to −5°C/23°F, and are best grown trained against a sunny and sheltered south- or southwest-facing wall. Grow in well-drained but not dry soils. Prune after flowering to remove overcrowded branches or outward-facing growth on wall-trained specimens. Propagate by seed in autumn.

***P. sinensis*** (Dum.-Cours.) Schneid. As for the genus.

For synonymy see *Chaenomeles, Cydonia* and *Malus*.

**Pseudodrynaria** C. Chr. (From Gk *pseudes*, false and Drynaria.) Polypodiaceae. 1 species, an epiphytic fern. Rhizome to 5cm wide, creeping, stout, dictyostelic, woolly, covered with massed roots as well as scales; scales dense, ciliate at margin, narrow, dark brown. Fronds to 2m, erect to arching, leathery to membranous, dark green throughout, turning brown at base, sessile, not jointed, lower part shallowly pinnately lobed or sinuate, cordate, dilated and collecting plant-litter, scarious, upper part deeply pinnatifid or pinnatisect, segments to 30×3cm, lanceolate to oblong or linear, narrowly acute at apex, entire to swollen at margin; costa and main veins prominent, veins reticulate, lateral veins parallel, joined by transverse veins forming areolae with free, included veinlets. Sori superficial, uniserial between lateral veins, circular to oval, or elongate; paraphyses absent; annulus 11–16-celled; spores glassy and smooth. Asia (India to Taiwan). Z10.

CULTIVATION As for *Drynaria*.

***P. coronans*** (Wallich ex Mett.) Ching. As for the genus.

For synonymy see *Aglaomorpha* and *Polypodium*.

**Pseudoespostoa** Backeb.
***P. melanostele*** (Vaupel) Backeb. See *Espostoa melanostele*.

**Pseudogaltonia** Kuntze. (From Gk *pseudes*, false, and *Galtonia*.) Liliaceae (Hyacinthaceae). 1 species, a perennial herb. Bulbs large, scaly, forming a fibrous neck. Leaves 6–10, synanthous, in a rosette, erect, broadly linear, apex acuminate, base clasping, margin entire, glaucous green, glabrous, soft. Flowers 10cm in an erect, dense raceme, far exceeding leaves; bracts linear-acuminate, membranous, with a small lateral bracteole; pedicels long, ash-grey at apex; tepals pale glaucous green, basally united into a slightly curved cylindric tube, lobes spreading, ovate, obtuse, half length of tube; stamens 6, slightly exserted, from throat of tube; ovary ovoid, style terete, stigma apical. Fruit an ovoid capsule; seeds rounded, flattened, shiny, black. S Africa (N Cape), Namibia, Botswana, Angola. Z10.

CULTIVATION Grow in sun in a freely draining, medium-fertility, loam-based mix with additional sharp sand, keep moist when in leaf (from late winter/early spring) and apply a dilute liquid feed until the flower spikes show. Dry off gradually as foliage fades and keep dry overwinter at about 7°C/45°F. Propagate by seed sown ripe or by bulbils.

***P. clavata*** (Mast. ex Bak.) Phillips. As for the genus.

**Pseudognaphalium** Kirpiczn. (From Gk *pseudes*, false, and *Gnaphalium.*) Compositae. About 10 species of annual to perennial herbs. Leaves linear-lanceolate to oblanceolate, lanate or glabrous and glandular above, lanate beneath. Capitula disciform, few in corymbose or cymose clusters; phyllaries in 3–4 series, cream-white to yellow, glandular-hairy; outer florets female, filiform or narrowly tubular, inner florets, tubular, hermaphrodite. Fruit a cypsela; pappus of scabrid bristles. Warm regions.

CULTIVATION Found predominantly in dry, open habitats, *P. obtusifolium* is sometimes grown in the wild garden and in native plant collections in conditions approximating to those in habitat. Propagate by seed.

***P. obtusifolium*** (L.) Hilliard & B.L. Burtt. Annual, to 50cm, woolly to puberulent or glandular-villous. Lvs to 10cm, lanceolate to linear, glabrous above, glandular, sessile. Involucre 6–7mm high; phyllaries more or less spreading, white, rust-tinged. Autumn. SE US.

For synonymy see *Gnaphalium*.

**Pseudogynoxys** (Greenman) Cabr. Compositae. About 13 species of perennial shrubs or climbers. Leaves alternate, ovate to oblong, more or less acute, base attenuate or cuneate to cordate, entire to serrate or dentate. Capitula radiate or discoid, solitary or few to many in terminal or axillary corymbose clusters; receptacle flat; involucre campanulate to hemispherical; phyllaries in 1 series, oblong, apex pubescent; florets pale to deep orange or red, ray florets female, disc florets hermaphrodite. Fruit a cylindrical, ribbed cypsela; pappus of hairs. Tropical S America. Z10.

CULTIVATION As for *Delairea*.

***P. chenopodioides*** (Kunth) Cabr. MEXICAN FLAMEVINE; ORANGEGLOW VINE. Liane or climbing shrub to 6m. Lvs narrowly ovate, dentate, light green, glabrous. Capitula radiate, to 5cm diam., few, in terminal and axillary corymbs, more or less fragrant. Fr. to 4mm; pappus white. Colombia.

For synonymy see *Senecio*.

**Pseudolarix** Gordon. (From Gk *pseudes*, false, and *Larix*, which it resembles.) GOLDEN LARCH. Pinaceae. 1 species, a deciduous, monoecious tree, to 40m. Crown broadly conic; bole with rust-brown, narrow-ridged bark, becoming grey and fissured in old trees. Branches whorled, level. Long shoots thin, glaucous orange-pink, later brown; short shoots as for *Larix* but longer, extending 2–4mm annually, girded with seasonal scar. Winter buds ovoid, acute; scales deciduous. Leaves in open spiral arrangement on long shoots, in pseudowhorls of up to 30 at tip of short shoots, 3–5(–7)cm×2–3mm, narrow-acuminate, keeled beneath, pale green becoming rich gold in autumn, with 2 silver-green stomatal bands beneath. Male 'cones' terminal on leafless short shoots, in umbels of 10–20, cylindric, 1cm; females solitary, globose, on short, leafy shoots; cones solitary, ovoid, short stalked, 5–7.5×5cm (only 3–4.5×3–4cm in cult. where summers cool), green, pruinose, ripening rusty-brown; fertile scales spreading, oval-lanceolate to triangular, tough, bearing 2 seeds, breaking up when ripe; bracts oval-lanceolate, not or slightly exserted. Seeds oval to obovate, 8mm, pale buff, wing to 2.5cm, brown, relatively thick, brittle, narrow triangular, partly exposed on unripe cone. E China (Zhejiang, Jiangxi). Z6.

CULTIVATION A difficult tree to grow well in cool-temperate regions: planted out when small it is easily scorched and may be killed by −5°C/23°F. Good trees are found only in southern England yet the 30m/100ft trees in New Jersey and New York show clearly that very cold winters are no problem where summers are long and hot. The best are in warm, sheltered sites on fertile deep soils around pH 5–6 with about 1000mm/40in. rainfall. Avoid exposure to dry winds, and soils which dry out readily. Plant when 30–80cm/12–32in. tall, in late spring, and keep long grass and herbage well clear. A very good moderate-sized tree for unusual foliage (fresh green until autumn, when gold, turning bright orange) it is also interesting for its craggy pale grey bark and for bearing globe-artichoke shaped cones.

***P. amabilis*** (J. Nels.) Rehd. As for the genus. 'Annesleyana': dwarf, spreading; branches crowded with needed and drooping at tips. Gardens of Lady Annesley, Castlewellan, c1860. 'Dawsonii': dwarf, conical, compact. 'Nana'. 30–100cm; Chinese cultigen used for container culture and training.

***P. fortunei*** Mayr. See *P. amabilis*.
***P. kaempferi*** (Lamb.) Gordon. See *P. amabilis*.
For further synonymy see *Chrysolarix*.

**Pseudolithos** Bally. (From Gk *pseudes*, false, and *lithos*, stone, due to the simple, often more or less spherical, stone-like stems.) Asclepiadaceae. 4 species of leafless, highly succulent, dwarf herbs, to about 12cm. Stems unbranched, erect, very soft, swollen, often compressed above. Inflorescence a many-flowered umbel on an abbreviated lateral shoot, flowers small. Fruit a glabrous follicle, in pairs. Somalia, Kenya, Arabia. Z9.

CULTIVATION *Pseudolithos* are very rare and extremely difficult to cultivate. They require a minimum temperature of 15°C/60°F and very low humidity, full sun at all times and very good ventilation in hot weather. The growing medium should be very well drained and must not contain too much organic matter; a loam-based medium with 30% grit and 30% coarse-grade perlite or one of the granular clay-based growing mediums is best. Clay pots are preferable to plastic as the growing medium will dry out more quickly. Water only in warm sunny weather. Propagation is by seed only, but plants can be grafted on to *Stapelia* stems or *Ceropegia linearis* tubers. Seed should be treated as described under *Stapelia*, but a loam-based propagating medium with extra grit should be used and the seeds covered with 5mm of grit.

***P. cubiformis*** (Bally) Bally. Fleshy, unbranched; stems solitary, erect, 3–5×4–6cm, obtusely quadrangular, apex truncate, pale green, covered with irregular, flat, obtusely 3–6-angled tessellations, 2–3mm diam., with larger cordate tessellation along the angles. Fls 4.3cm diam. in an umbel of to 30 fls, tube 3×5mm, spherically widened, both surfaces glabrous pale green outside, tinged brown inside, lobes 9mm, pointed, margins revolute, grey-green, purple or pink, each with 2–3 motile clavate hairs at the tip. Somalia.

***P. migurtinus*** (Chiov.) Bally. Stem hemispherical, often elliptic in section, flattened above, to 12×6.5cm, pale green or yellow-green to grey, covered in flat, blunt tubercles 2–8mm in diam., with 4 rows of larger tubercles equidistant around stem. Umbel 8–10-fld; corolla glabrous, to 1cm diam., tube 5mm diam., 4mm deep, pale green, cup-shaped, lobes 3mm, deltoid, spreading, exterior pale green, interior purple-maroon, papillose, margins reflexed, minutely ciliate, apex with cluster of strap-shaped, motile cilia; corona 4.5mm diam., black-purple, glabrous, outer whorl broadly cup-shaped with 5 erect, deltoid lobes, minutely 3-toothed at apex, inner corona lobes 1.5mm, apices ascending, spathulate. E Somalia.

For synonymy see *Lithocaulon*.

**Pseudolobivia** Backeb.
***P. aurea*** (Britt. & Rose) Backeb. See *Echinopsis aurea*.

**Pseudolopezia** Rose. See *Lopezia*.

**Pseudolysimachion** Opiz.
***P. longifolium*** (L.) Opiz. See *Veronica longifolia*.
***P. spicatum*** (L.) Opiz. See *Veronica spicata*.

**Pseudomertensia** Riedl.
***P. echioides*** (Benth.) Riedl. See *Mertensia echioides*.
***P. elongata*** (Decne.) Riedl. See *Mertensia elongata*.

**Pseudomuscari** Garb. & Greuter. See *Muscari*.

**Pseudonephelium** Radlk. See *Dimocarpus*.

**Pseudopaegma** Urban. See *Anemopaegma*.

**Pseudopanax and allies** (×0.66) (a) *P. arboreus* (b) *P. crassifolius*, flowering stem (left) and leaf (right) (c) *P. chathamicus* (d) *Kalopanax pictus* (e) *Metapanax davidii*

**Pseudopanax** K. Koch. (From Gk *pseudes*, false, and *Panax*.) Araliaceae. LANCEWOODS. 12–20 species of unarmed, glabrous, monoecious or dioecious, evergreen trees or shrubs, some with distinct kinds of foliage in different life-stages. Leaves simple or palmately compound, the blades entire or variously toothed. Inflorescences lateral on short shoots or terminal, simple or once- or twice-compound; flowers in umbels, clusters or racemes or mixtures of these; petals and stamens 4–5; ovary 2–5-locular. Fruit drupaceous, round, elongate or somewhat compressed, remaining wholly interior at maturity; pyrenes 2–5; seeds with smooth endosperm. New Zealand and associated islands, Tasmania, Chile.

CULTIVATION *Pseudopanax* spp. are easy to cultivate and interesting for their fruit and variation in foliage at different life stages. The second or sapling stage is often the most exciting, especially in *P. crassifolius*, which will form a single tall stem, clothed in its upper portion with stiff, dagger-shaped, downward pointing leaves: it generally begins to branch out at about 15–20 years old, making a round-headed specimen when mature. *P. crassifolius, P. ferox* and *P. arboreus* are the most frost-hardy spp., withstanding temperatures down to at least −5°C/23°F, provided that they are given a warm, sheltered location: in Great Britain, success is most likely in southern and western maritime areas. In frost-free climates *P. crassifolius, P. laetus* and their progeny (particularly 'Adiantifolius' and 'Linearifolius') are used as street trees which withstand wind exposure and adverse conditions. Cultivate in any fertile, well-drained soil, giving full sun or part shade. Large plants respond well to heavy pruning and to careful transplanting. In cold areas grow in large containers in the conservatory or cool to intermediate glasshouse (winter minimum 7–10°C/45–50°F), giving strong, filtered light in summer and low humidity: ventilate whenever possible. Water moderately in summer, sparingly in winter. Propagate from seed in autumn, by semi-ripe cuttings in summer or by air-layering.

1 Leaves 1–3-foliolate, on long or short shoots. Inflorescence lateral, on leafy or leafless short shoots, sometimes appearing axillary. True peduncles present. Ovary 2-locular. Fruit 4mm diam., or less.
*Pp. simplex, simplex* var. *sinclairii*.

2 Leaves 1–7-foliolate; short shoots not present. Inflorescence terminal, umbelliform, without true peduncles. Ovary 2–5-locular. Fruit 5mm diam. or more.

2.1 Plants without different kinds of foliage. Leaflets 3–7, stalked (except *P. colensoi*). Flowers mostly in umbels, the inflorescence branches without racemose flowers. Ovary 2-locular.
*Pp. arboreus, colensoi, kermadecensis, laetus*.

2.2 Plants without or with only slightly differing kinds of foliage. Leaflets 1–5 (unifoliolate only in *P. gilliesii*), sessile or very shortly stalked. Flowers either in umbels or racemosely arranged, the latter mostly male. Ovary 4–5-locular.
*Pp. discolor, lessonii*.

2.3 Plants to a greater or lesser extent with differing kinds of foliage. Leaves simple or up to 5-foliolate. Flowers either in umbels (*P. linearis*) or racemosely arranged, sometimes also in pseudoumbels at branch ends. Ovary 3–5-locular.
*Pp. chathamicus, crassifolius, ferox, linearis*.

***P. arboreus*** (Murray) K. Koch. FIVE-FINGER; PUAHOU; WHAUWHAUPAKU. Robust dioecious round-headed tree to 8m; trunk slender, remaining leafy, the branches in old examples many, pointed upwards. Leaflets 3–7, thick, narrowly oblong to oblong-obovate, to 20×7.5cm, coarsely toothed, dark glossy green above; petiole to 20cm. Infl. 2× compound, umbellate, to 21cm across; fls 10–15 in umbels 2.5mm diam., outwardly purple, creamy inside; ovary 2-locular; styles mostly free. Fr. becoming purple-black, about 6mm diam., broader than long, compressed. New Zealand (and Kermadec Is. if *P. kermadecensis* (W. Oliv.) Philipson included). Z10.

***P. chathamicus*** T. Kirk. HOHO. Stoutly branched dioecious tree to 7.5m, the juvenile lvs not deflexed. Lvs always simple; in adults thick, stiff, linear-obovate, to 20×5cm, more or less toothed only near apex, narrowing toward base, apex blunt or truncate. Infl. as *P. ferox*, but with fewer branches and at least sometimes with perfect fls entirely in umbelliform clusters both below and at the apex of primary rays. Fr. 8mm diam. Summer. Chatham Is. Z9.

***P. colensoi*** (Hook. f.) K. Koch. MOUNTAIN IVY-TREE; ORIHOU. Similar to *P. arboreus* but lvs 3–5-foliolate with rather thick, sessile or very shortly stalked leaflets and infl. with fewer primary rays. Fr. 5mm diam. New Zealand.

***P. crassifolius*** (Sol. ex A. Cunn.) K. Koch HOROEKA; LANCEWOOD. Tree to 15m. Sapling and pole-trees unbranched, wand-like, the stems covered with fierce-looking, downward-pointing armour-lvs. Adult trees polygamo-dioecious, older examples with a clear bole to 50cm thick and round-headed crown with many spreading to ascending branches. Lvs widely varying in form, simple or 3-foliolate, rarely 5-foliolate; adult lvs simple, blades pointed more or less upright, narrowly to broadly linear to linear-obovate, leathery, to 20cm, sinuate or remotely coarsely toothed; seedling lvs simple, ovate-lanceolate, membranous, to 60cm, coarsely toothed or lobed; armour lvs linear, rigid, to 100cm or more, somewhat variegated, remotely spine-toothed. Infl. paniculate, 2× compound, somewhat umbelliform; fls racemosely arranged along secondary branches, the perfect ones umbellately aggregated towards the ends; ovary 5-locular. Fr. black, round, 5mm diam. Summer. New Zealand (with Stewart Is.). In the var. *trifoliolatus* T. Kirk (*Aralia trifoliate* hort.) (North Is.) the early adult lvs, following initial branching, are 3 foliolate, the leaflets to 30cm, simple lvs appear later. var. *pentadactylus* Voss (*Panax pentadactylus* Decne. & Planch.) is the 5-foliolate form. Z9.

***P. discolor*** (T. Kirk) Harms. Much-branched shrub or small tree to 6m. Lvs 1–5-foliolate, blades or leaflets narrowly obovate, to 7.5cm, sharply and irregularly toothed, stalked (outer ones sometimes almost sessile), much paler and somewhat lustrous beneath, base attenuate. Infl. 1× compound, umbelliform, the main axis short; fls perfect or male in umbels at ends of primary rays, or also racemosely arranged along their upper portions and then only male; ovary 4–5-locular. New Zealand (North Is.) Z10.

***P. ferox*** (T. Kirk) T. Kirk. TOOTHED LANCEWOOD. Resembling *P. crassifolius* but dioecious and, with a smaller crown, only to 7m. Lvs always simple, in adults to 15cm or so, the apex obtuse to emarginate; intermediate lvs to 45cm and closely, coarsely and jaggedly toothed. Infl. 1× compound; fls racemosely arranged on several to many radiating branches; ovary 5-locular. Fr. 8mm diam. Summer. New Zealand. Z9.

***P. laetus*** (T. Kirk) Philipson. Dioecious shrub or small tree, to 6m or so. Lvs 5–7-foliolate; petioles purple-red, to 25cm, leaflets obovate, thick, to 30cm, stalked, toothed only in upper two-thirds or less, entire below. Infl. as *P. arboreus* but the 15–20 secondary rays with some single fls as well as terminal umbels; primary rays 10–15; ovary 2-locular. Fr. dark purple. New Zealand (North Is.) Z10.

***P. lessonii*** (DC.) K. Koch. HOUMSPARA; HOUPARA. Shrubs or small trees to 6m or so, the branches stout. Lvs 3–5-foliolate, leaflets sessile; petiole in adults sometimes exceeding blades; leaflets in adults usually sessile, thick, to 10cm, narrowly obovate, the outer ones somewhat oblique, entire or somewhat remotely and shallowly toothed, leaflets in juveniles usually 5, linear-lanceolate, coarsely toothed. Infl. 2× compound, umbelliform but sometimes with one secondary ray emerging below the apex of the primary rays; fls perfect or male in umbellate clusters at ends of secondary rays, or also racemosely arranged along their upper portions and then mostly only male; ovary 5-locular. Fr. 6mm. New Zealand (North and Three Kings Is.) A number of cultivars known, either variegated or merely 3–5-lobed. Z9. 'Gold Splash': lvs variegated with gold.

***P. linearis*** (Hook. f.) K. Koch. Similar to *P. chathamicus* but adult leaves smaller and narrower, to 10×1.2cm, and fls usually always umbellate at ends of primary branches in small, 1× compound, umbelliform infl. Shrub to 4m; terminal buds enclosed by cataphylls, the lvs in pseudowhorls; juvenile lvs to 25cm; midrib in adult lvs yellow; ovary 3–5-locular. New Zealand (South Is.) Z9.

***P. simplex*** (Forst. f.) K. Koch. HAUMAKAROA. Much-branched shrub or small tree to 8m. Juvenile lvs thin, 3–5-foliolate, leaflets more or less pinnatifid, the seg. spreading; adult lvs on long or short shoots, always simple, narrowly ovate, elliptic or obovate, to 12.5cm, serrate, glossy. Infl. lateral, on leafy or leafless short shoots, paniculate, 1× compound; fls small, green-white, in both terminal and lateral umbels, the latter smaller, on more or less racemosely arranged peduncles to 1.5cm or more; ovary 2-locular. Fr. 3mm diam., compressed. New Zealand (including Stewart and Auckland Is.) var. ***sinclairii*** (Hook. f.) Edgar. MOUNTAIN PANAX. Lvs always 3(–5)-foliolate, the leaflets to 7cm, dull; no juvenile lvs present. Fr. slightly larger, to 4mm. New Zealand (North Is.) May merit restoration to species rank. Z10.

***P. davidii*** (Franch.) Philipson. See *Metapanax davidii*.
***P. delavayi*** (Franch.) Philipson. See *Metapanax delavayi*.
For further synonymy see *Neopanax, Nothopanax, Panax*.

**Pseudopectinaria** Lavranos.
***P. malum*** Lavranos. See *Echidnopsis malum*.

**Pseudorhipsalis** Britt. & Rose. See *Disocactus*.
***P. alata*** (Sw.) Britt. & Rose. See *Disocactus alatus*.
***P. himantoclada*** (Roland-Goss.) Britt. & Rose. See *Disocactus himantocladus*.
***P. macrantha*** Alexander. See *Disocactus macranthus*.

**Pseudosasa** Mak. ex Nak. (From Gk *pseudos*, false, and *Sasa*.) Gramineae. 6 species of tall or short bamboos with running rhizomes (clumped in colder climates). Culms erect; sheaths longer than the internodes, bristles white and smooth but often absent; nodes not prominent, with white waxy powder below, glabrous; branches 1–3 from the upper nodes. Leaves tessellate, glabrous;

sheaths glabrous, almost always without bristles. China, Japan, Korea. Z6.

CULTIVATION Tall or small, robust bamboos with short rhizomes which soon consolidate to form dense thickets. *P. japonica* is among the most commonly planted bamboos. In recent years, many examples of this species have been diminished by flowering: flowering plants should be cut back and fed to restore vigour. *Pseudosasa* spp. are hardy to −15°C/5°F and will resist high winds with little damage to foliage. They favour damp, rich soils and will even endure near-saturated conditions. Plant young material at 1m intervals to provide a dense hedge after 3–4 years. Propagate by division.

***P. amabilis*** (McClure) Keng f. TONKIN CANE. Culms 5–13m×2–7cm, stout, arching above, bristly when young, rather thick-walled; sheaths fairly persistent, bristly-hairy, often with a shaggy midline with bristles, ligule fringed; branches usually 3. Lvs 10–35×1.2–3.5cm, scaberulous; sheaths ciliate, usually with bristles. S China; widely cultivated throughout SE Asia.

***P. japonica*** (Sieb. & Zucc. ex Steud.) Mak. ex Nak. ARROW BAMBOO; METAKE. Culms 3–6m×1–2cm, stiff, thin-walled, glabrous, branching in the second year and eventually arching above when well-grown; sheaths long-persistent, coarse, with scattered hairs at first and few or no bristles, ligule blunt; nodes often oblique; branches 1 per node. Lvs 20–36×2.5–3.5cm, rough above, one-third green, two-thirds glaucous beneath; sheaths lacking bristles. A rugged species useful for shelter and in shade; distinguished from the similar *Sasamorpha borealis* in the white powder and the bicoloured undersides to the lvs. Japan, Korea.

For synonymy see *Arundinaria, Sasa* and *Yadakea*.

**Pseudotaxus** Cheng. (From Gk *pseudos* false, and *Taxus*, yew.) Taxaceae. 1 species, an evergreen, dioecious shrub resembling *Taxus*, from which it differs in fruit with a white aril and numerous sterile scales and leaves lacking papillae below (under ×100 lens). To 4m. Branches whorled; branchlets opposite or in whorls of 3, grey-brown, becoming grey-green or ochre, ridged, cylindric. Leaves spirally arranged, petioles twisted to appear distichous, 10–25×3–4mm, linear or subfalcate, narrow-acuminate, concave beneath, deep shining green above, paler beneath with 2 grey-blue stomatal bands; petiole slender, 1–2mm. Male cones axillary; sterile scales 8, ovate to obovate, decussate. Female flowers in leaf axils, short-stalked; sterile scales to 16, subtending the single ovule. Seeds to 6×4mm, aril cup-like, white, fleshy. S E China (Zhejiang to Guangxi). Z8.

CULTIVATION Although hardy to about −20°C/−4°F in its native S China, it requires long, hot steamy summers with four months at 30°C/86°F and is not hardy outdoors in Britain. Successful cultivation can be achieved in SE US, New Zealand, N Island and the wetter parts of Australia, where it has the same uses as *Taxus*. Propagation as for *Taxus*.

***P. chienii*** (Cheng) Cheng. WHITE BERRY YEW. As for the genus.

For synonymy see *Nothotaxus* and *Taxus*.

**Pseudotsuga** Carr. (From Gk *pseudo-*, false, and *Tsuga*.) DOUGLAS FIR. Pinaceae. 5–8 species of evergreen monoecious coniferous trees, 40–90m. Crown conic, becoming irregular with age in exposure. Bark smooth, dark purple-grey, with resin blisters when young, becoming very thick, deeply fissured corky red-brown with paler fissures on mature trees. Branches long, spreading, level or sweeping slightly down, branchlets and shoots moderately drooping. Shoots grey- or yellow-green, smooth, slightly raised at leaf insertions, glabrous or lightly pubescent. Buds very similar in all species, ovoid-conic, acute-tipped, red-brown, with closely imbricate acute scales, often slightly resinous. Leaves (needles) radially arranged, short-petiolate, the petiole twisted to arrange the leaves more or less pectinate, linear, soft, flattened, 2–6×0.15×0.07cm thick, bright green or blue above, two white or grey stomatal bands below, entire, apex acute, rounded or emarginate. Flowers cones, lateral or rarely terminal on previous year's shoots; male cones ovoid, yellow or pink, 8–20mm, spring; female cones ovoid, green or pink, composed of long tridentine bracts, 10–25mm before pollination. Cones mature after 5–7 months, pendulous on a 5–15mm bract-covered stalk, ovoid, ovoid-cylindric or ovoid-conic, 4–18cm, green, pink or purple, often bloomed pale or violet, ripening brown, often resinous; scales thick and broad-based, tough, matt, coriaceous, 2–4.5cm broad, rounded, with a long tridentine bract over each scale, exserted 6–20mm, straight or reflexed. Seeds two on each scale, similar to *Larix*, ovoid, slightly flattened, 7–12mm, off-white freckled pale brown on scale side, lustrous orange-brown on other side, with an oval, adnate wing 5–15mm long. Western N America south to Mexico, and E Asia from S Japan to Taiwan and SW China. One species, *P. menziesii*, is abundant in W US and is the most important tree in the world with immense amounts of timber cut annually; it is also a very important afforestation tree in GB and elsewhere. The timber is strong and moderately durable, extensively used for heavy construction, transmission poles, furniture, etc.; the 70m flagpole at Kew is of this species. It also makes a fragrant Christmas tree, though little used at present for this; the foliage and cones are also useful for decoration. The other species are all rare in their habitats and of little commercial value, though all become large. *P. menziesii* and *P. guinieri* are of genetic interest, being two of only three species in their family to have other than 24 chromosomes, 26 being found in their cells. The genus is most closely related to *Larix* and *Cathaya*.

CULTIVATION Propagation is from seeds; the cultivars by grafting on *P. menziesii*. The species can also be grafted, but establishing a good leading shoot is difficult. Pruning as in *Abies*; see also CONIFERS. The leaf-cast fungus *Rhabdocline pseudotsugae* can partly defoliate trees of *P. menziesii* ssp. *glauca*, and more particularly its var. *caesia*, but severe attacks are rare in gardens. The adelgid *Adelges cooleyi* attacks several species, often making them look unsightly with white fluffs of wax on the insects below the leaf and yellow spots above them, but it does not greatly affect the vigour or health of the tree.

***P. forrestii*** Craib. Possibly no more than a variety of *P. wilsoniana*. To 40m in wild, 13m in cult. Bark scaly grey-brown; crown broad conic, open. Shoots olive- or buff-brown, slightly hairy-pubesc.; lvs sparse, moderately pectinate, 2.5–5cm, green with white stomatal bands beneath, apex emarginate or blunt. Cones as *P. japonica* but longer and much stouter, 4.5–7×3.5–4cm closed, opening to ×5cm; scales rounded, to 4cm broad; bracts as *P. japonica*. Seeds with a longer 10–15mm wing. SW China (Yunnan). Z8.

***P. guinieri*** Flous. MEXICAN DOUGLAS FIR. To 45m. Bark on young trees as *P. menziesii*. Crown slender conic, open, branches level or downswept. Shoots glabrous, green-brown; lvs all round shoot except underneath, strongly forward-pointing at basal end, curved outward at apex, 13–20mm, green with two green-white bands on outer surface (often not facing downwards), apex acute. Cones on 1cm stem, slender-cylindric, 4–8×1.5cm closed, violet bloomed white, not opening widely, to only 2.5–3cm, pale brown; scales thin at edges, 2cm wide, evenly sized along cone; bracts yellow-green, long exserted 15mm, standing out at 90°. Seed as *P. menziesii*. US (W Texas), Mexico (south to Puebla, mts). Z8.

***P. japonica*** (Shiras.) Beissn. JAPANESE DOUGLAS FIR. To 40m in wild, 14m in cult. Bark smooth grey, fissured brown on older trees; crown broad conic, irregular in cult. Shoots pale yellow-grey, glabrous; lvs moderately pectinate, 2–3cm, yellow-green above, two white stomatal bands beneath, apex emarginate or rounded. Cone on a 1cm stalk, ovoid-conic, 4–5.5×2cm closed, purple bloomed violet, opening to ×4cm, dark brown; scales hard, woody, few large scales to 3cm wide at upper middle cone, lower middle and apical scales rapidly smaller, 1.5cm; bracts exserted 6–8mm, reflexed, very brittle. Seed 8mm, wing 5–9mm. S Japan. Z7.

***P. macrocarpa*** (Vasey) Mayr. BIG-CONE DOUGLAS FIR. To 25m in wild and cult. Bark broad purple-brown corky plates separated by pale orange-buff vertical fissures. Crown broad open conic, branches gently downswept, branchlets pendulous. Shoots pink- to green-brown, finely pubesc.; lvs all round shoot, parted beneath on stronger shoots, straight or gently curved forward and down, harder than other spp., 3–5cm, to 6cm or even 8cm on strong shoots, deep glossy green above, two grey-white stomatal bands beneath, apex acute. Cones only produced on trees over 50 years old, on a 5–10mm stalk, long ovoid-conic to cylindric, 11–13×3cm, to 18cm in wild, green-brown, opening to ×5–6.5cm, pale brown; scales hard, woody, thick, widest, to 4.5cm, one third down cone, lower scales smaller, to 3cm wide; bracts long exserted 15–20mm, straight, very brittle and easily lost. Seed much larger than other spp., 12mm, not flattened, with 12–14mm wing. US (SW California mts). Z8.

***P. menziesii*** (Mirb.) Franco. DOUGLAS FIR; GREEN DOUGLAS FIR. To 100m, bole to 5m diam. in wild, already to 63×2m in cult. Bark in young trees thin, green-brown with resin blisters, becoming purple, then red-brown, very thick, corky, deeply fissured in mature trees; crown dense, conic, more slender and open in vigorous trees, when spire-like even to 60m tall; in exposure shorter and irregular from broken branches, with dense thick branches remaining; branches level or gently downswept, branchlets drooping. Shoots green-brown, thinly pubesc., strongly aromatic; lvs more or less pectinate in several ranks, 1.5–3cm, to 4cm on young plants, bright green above, two dull white stomatal bands beneath, apex blunt, rounded. Cone on a 5–12mm stalk, ovoid-cylindric to cylindric, 6–11.5×2cm, green, opening to ×4cm, pale brown; scales thinly woody, 2–2.5cm wide, evenly sized along cone; bracts yellow-green, long exserted 12–18mm, straight, middle tooth 1–1.2mm wide. Seed 7mm, with 11mm wing. Canada (SW British Columbia), US (W Washington to WC California). About 25–30 cvs, none very significant; fastigiate, pendulous, 'snake-branch' forms, variegated foliage, dwarf forms. ssp. ***glauca*** (Beissn.) E. Murray BLUE DOUGLAS FIR, COLORADO DOUGLAS FIR. Smaller tree to 40m. Shoots greyer, less aromatic; lvs strongly upswept, 1.5–2.5cm, grey-green to blue-green, stomata in broad bands above as well as beneath. Cone 4–7cm, scales smaller, to 2cm wide, bracts reflexed, middle tooth 1mm wide. US (Idaho and Montana to C New Mexico). About 15 cvs; 'Argentea' and 'Candida' brilliant white-blue lvs; several dwarf. var. ***caesia*** (Schwerin) Franco. GREY DOUGLAS FIR; FRASER RIVER DOUGLAS FIR. Lvs slightly pectinate, dull grey-green with some stomata above, grey-white bands beneath. Cone 4–6cm, bracts outcurved, middle tooth very slender, 0.8mm or less. Canada (SE British Columbia) to Idaho. Hardiest *Pseudotsuga*. Several cvs; 'Fretsii' frequent, dull shrub with short broad lvs. var. ***flahaultii*** (Flous) Silba. ARIZONA DOUGLAS FIR. Lvs slightly longer than ssp., 1.7–3cm; cones purple before ripening, larger, 5–9cm, with large scales 2.3–2.8cm wide, bracts reflexed and twisted. US (S Arizona, S New Mexico) to Mexico (N Chihuahua). Z7.

***P. sinensis*** Dode. CHINESE DOUGLAS FIR. To 40m in wild, shrub in cult. Very similar both to *P. forrestii* and *P. wilsoniana*, which may be conspecific with this but inadequate knowledge prevents conclusions. Lvs 20–40×1.5–2mm, shiny green above, apex emarginate. Cones said to differ in detail of scale shape, but in *P. menziesii* this feature is very variable even within small populations, and may be of little value with these as well. SC China (Sichuan to Zhejiang). var. ***brevifolia*** (Cheng & L.K. Fu) Farjon & Silba. Lvs shorter, broader 7–20×2–3mm; cones as type. SW Guanxi. Z8.

***P. wilsoniana*** Hayata. TAIWAN DOUGLAS FIR. To 40m in wild, shrub in cult. Differs from *P. forrestii* in shorter lvs, mostly 15–25mm but occasionally to 45mm. Cones not separable, similar variation in scale shape. Taiwan. Z8.

***P. brevifolia*** Cheng & Fu. See *P. sinensis* var. *brevifolia*.
***P. douglasii*** (Lindl.) Carr. See *P. menziesii*.
***P. flahaultii*** Flous. See *P. menziesii* var. *flahaultii*.
***P. glauca*** (Beissn.) Mayr. See *P. menziesii* ssp. *glauca*.
***P. macrolepis*** Flous. See *P. guinieri*.
***P. menziesii*** var. ***glauca*** (Beissn.) Franco. See *P. menziesii* ssp. *glauca*.
***P. taxifolia*** (Lamb.) Britt. ex Sudw. See *P. menziesii*.

**Pseudowintera** Dandy. (From Gk *pseudes*, false, and *Wintera*.) Winteraceae. 2–3 species of calcifuge, glabrous, evergreen shrubs or small trees to 8m. Leaves alternate, entire, often coriaceous, and coloured. Flowers bisexual, solitary and axillary, or clustered; calyx cupular, not caducous, not enclosing petals in bud (cf. *Wintera*); petals 5–6; stamens 5–15, filaments laterally compressed. Fruit a 2–6-seeded berry. New Zealand.

CULTIVATION Grown for their beautiful evergreen foliage, *Pseudowintera* spp. are attractive additions to shrub plantings in warm-temperate and mild, sheltered cool-temperate gardens, or for cool to intermediate conditions in the glasshouse or conservatory. Grow in humus-rich, well-drained but moisture-retentive, neutral to acid soil, in good light or part shade. Water pot-grown specimens plentifully during the growing season, sparingly in winter. Prune only when necessary to restrict size. Propagate from seed, sown ripe in autumn, or in spring; or from greenwood cuttings in summer.

***P. axillaris*** (Forst. & Forst. f.) Dandy. Shrub or small tree to 8m. Bark grey-black. Lvs to 13cm, narrow-ovate to oblong, lustrous deep green above, glaucous beneath. Fls inconspicuous, yellow-green, clustered. Fr. red.

***P. colorata*** (Raoul) Dandy. Lvs 2–6×1–3cm, elliptic-oblong, green, flecked or edged purple-red or tangerine and red above, grey-white to pearly blue beneath. Fls 2–10 per cluster; cal. lobes reduced or lacking; pet. olive-green; stamens 5–12. Fr. black.

For synonymy see *Drimys* and *Wintera*.

**Psidium** L. (From *psidion*, Gk name for Pomegranate.) GUAVA. Myrtaceae. About 100 species of evergreen trees or shrubs. Leaves opposite, simple, pinnately veined. Flowers usually large, white, calyx tube prolonged above the ovary, splitting irregularly at flowering time; petals 5; stamens many. Fruit a globose or pear-shaped berry, sometimes large and edible. Americas. Closely related to *Feijoa* and *Acca*. Z10.

CULTIVATION *P. guajava* and *P. littorale* are widely grown in tropical and subtropical zones for their fruits. They are notable for their tolerance of a range of soil and environmental conditions, thriving in the humid lowland tropics to cooler altitudes of 1500m/4875ft., and in areas of low to medium rainfall although for good fruiting, they require at least 1000mm/40in. of rain p.a., with a dry period for fruit ripening. *P. littorale* tolerates short-lived light frosts and prefers a drier climate, and makes attractive hedging in warm temperate gardens. In cool temperate zones, given slightly higher glasshouse temperatures (min 7–10°C/45–50°F), cultivation is as for *Feijoa*. Both *P. guajava* and *P. littorale* are amenable to training as espaliers or goblet-shaped standards in pots, the spring and mid-summer flowers giving rise to ripe fruit within about 3–4 months under favourable conditions.

***P. friedrichsthalium*** (O. Berg) Niedenzu. Shrub or small tree to 8m. Branchlets 4-angled. Lvs to 7cm, glossy above, pubesc. beneath. Fls 2.5cm diam., solitary. Fr. to 6cm, sulphur-yellow, with white flesh. C America.

***P. guajava*** L. COMMON GUAVA; YELLOW GUAVA; APPLE GUAVA. Shrub or small tree, to 10m. Bark scaly, green-brown, branchlets 4-angled. Lvs to 15cm, ovate to oblong-elliptic, pubesc. underneath, veins prominent. Fls white, solitary or few together on slender peduncles. Fr. ovoid to pear-shaped, 2–10cm, with yellow or dark pink flesh. Tropical America; cult. throughout the tropics and subtropics and frequently naturalized. Fr. varies in size, shape, colour and flavour and has a musky penetrating odour. 'Beaumont': pink-fleshed. 'Detwiler': yellow-fleshed. 'Pear': flesh cream-white.

***P. guineense*** Sw. GUAVA. Shrub or small tree to 7m. Branchlets nearly cylindrical. Lvs to 13cm or more, ovate to oblong-elliptic, rusty-pubesc. beneath. Fls white, solitary or a few together on slender peduncles, fragrant. Fr. ovoid, brown-green, turning to pale yellow when ripe, slightly acid. Tropical America. Fr. smaller than the common guava; too bitter or resinous to be palatable.

***P. littorale*** Raddi. Shrub or small tree to 8m. Bark smooth, grey-brown. Lvs to 7.5cm, elliptic to obovate, glabrous. Fls white, solitary, to 2.5cm in diameter. Fr. to 4cm with white flesh. Brazil. var. ***littorale***. YELLOW STRAWBERRY GUAVA; YELLOW CATTLEY GUAVA; WAIAWI. A rather loosely branched small tree. Fr. sulphur-yellow, somewhat translucent, acid when ripe. var. ***longipes*** (O. Berg) McVaugh. PURPLE GUAVA; PURPLE-STRAWBERRY GUAVA; CATTLEY GUAVA. Small, dense tree. Fr. globose, purple-red, sweet when ripe. 'John Riley': fr. large, dark red.

***P. montanum*** Sw. MOUNTAIN GUAVA; SPICE GUAVA. Shrub to about 2m with flat rounded branchlets. Lvs ovate to oval, rounded at both ends or cordate at base, stalk short or absent, veins obscure. Fls white; peduncles 1- or few-fld. W Indies.

***P. araca*** Raddi. See *P. guineense*.
***P. cattleianum*** Salisb. See *P. littorale* var. *longipes*.
***P. littorale*** var. ***lucidum*** (Deg.) Fosb. See *P. littorale* var. *littorale*.
***P. lucidum*** hort. See *P. littorale* var. *littorale*.
***P. molle*** Bertol. See *P. guineense*.

**Psiguria** Necker ex Arn. Cucurbitaceae. Some 15 species of dioecious or, occasionally, monoecious vines or lianes. Tendrils simple. Leaves 3–5-foliolate or 3–5-lobed to entire. Male flowers clustered, calyx cylindrical, 5-lobed, corolla rotate, stamens 2, filaments short, anthers 2-locular; female flowers commonly solitary; staminodes 2; ovary ovoid, carpels 2, style connate, stigma 2-lobed. Fruit indehiscent; seeds numerous, oblong, compressed. Tropical America. Z10.

CULTIVATION As for *Momordica*, but cross-pollination is usually needed for fruit production.

***P. warscewiczii*** (Hook. f.) Wunderlin. Stems slender, glabrous. Tendrils simple. Lvs 3-foliolate; central leaflet 11–17×5–8cm, obovate-oblong, acuminate, lateral leaflets somewhat hastate, slightly smaller; petioles 3–6cm. Male fls axillary, in racemes, orange to scarlet, cal. 1–2cm, cylindrical, cor. ventricose, lobes rounded to obovate, 5–8mm, pubesc., anth. 5–6mm; female fls solitary to few in axils, ovary oblong-fusiform, styles to 8mm. Fr. oblong-ellipsoid, 5.5–7cm×18–25mm, pale green with darker stripes; seeds numerous, 7–8mm. S Mexico to Colombia.

**Psilanthus** Hook. f. Rubiaceae. Some 18 species of shrubs and small trees. Leaves petiolate, opposite, subcoriaceous or thin-textured; stipules fused, sheath-like. Flowers hermaphrodite, sessile or subsessile, axillary or terminal or, occasionally, both, white; bracts and bracteoles absent or forming chaff-like calyculus; calyx tube turbinate, campanulate or ovoid, limb cupulate, irregularly 5-toothed, teeth occasionally accrescent, to elongate, somewhat leaf-like, persistent; corolla salverform, tube elongate, membranous, exterior and throat glabrous or pubescent, lobes 4–5, spreading, contorted in bud, oval or oblong; stamens 4–5, inserted at throat of corolla, filaments short or obsolete, anthers sessile, linear, included (often partly so), dorsifixed from middle or above middle; ovary 2-celled, style cylindric, glabrous, bifid or 2-toothed, stigmatic divisions linear, ovate, oblong or lanceolate, ovules 1 in each cell. Fruit an ellipsoid or obovoid berry, 2-lobed, crowned by (occasionally accrescent) calyx lobes; pyrenes 2, 1-seeded; seeds ellipsoid to oblong, ventrally sulcate. Tropical Africa, Asia, and Australia. Z10.

CULTIVATION As for *Ixora*.

***P. bengalensis*** (Roem. & Schult.) J. Leroy. Shrub. Branchlets initially minutely pubesc. Lvs to 13cm, ovate or elliptic, base and apex acute to acuminate; stipules subulate. Fls precocious, 1–3 per axil; cal. teeth obscure, subdivided; cor. to 4cm wide, tube to 2.5cm, lobes ovate-oblong. Fr. obovoid, to 13mm, black. India, Burma.

For synonymy see *Coffea*.

**Psilocaulon** N.E. Br. (From Gk *psilos*, bare, and *kaulon*, stalk: the stems are usually devoid of leaves for most of the year.) Aizoaceae. Some 70 species of annuals, biennials or shrubs. Stems usually cylindrical, often constricted at nodes, internodes often barrel-shaped or globular, glabrous or puberulous. Leaves short-lived, small, soft, cylindrical, united at base to form a sheath, sheath smooth or laciniate in those species previously included in *Brownanthus*. Flowers small, solitary or many together, white, red or yellow, shortly pedicellate. S Africa (Cape Province), Namibia. Z10. The stems perform most of the photosynthetic function and water storage; among the Aizoaceae, this genus is the closest to being a true stem succulent.

CULTIVATION As for *Dorotheanthus* but some can be propagated by cuttings. See *Lampranthus*.

***P. arenosum*** (Schinz) L. Bol. Shrubby, erect, 60–90cm, papillose. Stems 4-angled, internodes 7–18×4–7mm, jointed, green. Lvs 7–10mm, semicylindrical, papillose. Fls small, numerous, white. Namibia (Great Namaqualand), Cape Province (Little Namaqualand).

***P. ciliatum*** (Ait.) Friedr. Forming low-growing more or less branched shrubs. Stems fleshy, green, nodes constricted, internodes 3–7×3–4mm, more or less spherical. Lvs 2–5mm with 2–4mm cilia at base, cylindrical, papillose. Fls in a cyme, small, white. Cape Province (Little Namaqualand, Prince Albert District), Namibia (Great Namaqualand).

***P. dinteri*** (Engl.) Schwantes. Forming large mats with prostrate stems to 75cm; younger stems and branches very fleshy, constricted and jointed, joints 4–10mm diam., barrel-shaped, swollen. Lvs 10×2–3mm, cylindrical. Fls 1cm diam., 3–5 together in an infl., red. Namibia: near Luderitz.

***P. marlothii*** (Pasc.) Friedr. Forming dense cushions of erect stems; stems cylindrical, internodes 4×4mm, nodes not conspicuously constricted but covered by ciliate, dried-up remains of lvs, red-brown. Lvs 6–8mm, ring of 5mm ciliate hairs at base. Fls solitary, white or pink. Namibia (Great Namaqualand).

***P. gymnocladum*** (Schltr. & Diels) Dinter & Schwantes. See *P. arenosum*.
For further synonymy see *Brownanthus*.

**PSILOTACEAE** Kanitz. See *Psilotum*.

**Psilotum** Sw. FORK FERN; WHISK FERN. (From Gk *psilos*, bear, the plants being almost devoid of hairs, or alternatively referring to the conspicuous naked sporangia.) Psilotaceae. 2 species of primitive, terrestrial or epiphytic clump-forming plants of skeletal, broom-like appearance, lacking roots; rhizomes creeping, short, irregularly branched, bearing rhizoids; stems erect to arching or pendulous, dichotomously branched, angular, tough and rigid, green, bearing small scale-like leaves: sterile scales simple, fertile scales bifid. Sporangia in trios, united to form a synangium. Subtropics and Tropics. Z10.

CULTIVATION As for tropical *Lygodium* spp.

***P. complanatum*** Sw. Stems to 70cm, spreading or flaccid-pendulous, basal stalk cylindric, branches flattened, elliptic in cross-section, with distinct midrib, young stems sometimes triquetrous, generally dark green. Lvs to 1mm, reduced to bristle-like structures, remote, alternate, marginal. Sporangia sessile, to 1.5mm diam., brown tinged yellow. Pantropical rainforest.

***P. nudum*** (L.) Beauv. SKELETON FORK FERN. Stems to 60cm, erect or ascending when terrestrial, generally pendulous when epiphytic, main stalk 2–4mm diam. near base, branching acutely dichotomous, branches numerous, triangular, pale green soon fading to dull yellow unless in a very sheltered situation where they will remain unbleached green. Lvs 1–2mm, remote, triangular-subulate, fertile lvs smaller, to 1mm, or rudimentary. Sporangia to 2mm diam., yellow or tinged brown. Pantropical (America, Japan, Australasia). In Japan this plant has been cultivated for more than 400 years and rarer clones from the 100 available fetch very high prices amongst collectors. *P. nudum* has been cultivated in Japan for centuries. Variations prized there include plants with dwarf, strongly flattened, dense, lax or long, pendulous stems, viral, yellow or deep green vegetation, those which branch freely or with numerical regularity, others producing many yellow sporangia.

***P. triquetrum*** Sw. See *P. nudum*.

**Psomiocarpa** Presl. (From Gk *psomion*, morsel, and *karpos*, fruit, referring to the reduction of fertile material.) Dryopteridaceae. 1 species, a terrestrial fern. Rhizomes ascending; scales attenuate, margin entire, brown. Fronds catadromous, dimorphous sterile fronds to 15×12cm, short-stipitate, rosette-forming, 2–3-pinnate or -pinnatifid, ovate, pubescent, especially on veins, pinnae approximate to imbricate, pinnules to 3mm, wide, apex obtuse, margin entire, fertile fronds smaller than sterile, often modified to much-reduced, narrow laminar material, especially in upper part, stipitate, 3-pinnate or -pinnatifid at base, ephemeral to 7cm (sterile) or 25cm (fertile), veins free; stipes approximate and clustered, scaly, especially at base, and pubescent (sterile). Sori solitary on reduced material, to covering surface (usually lower) of pinnules, circular or elliptic; indusia occasionally present but then indistinct, deciduous, globose to kidney-shaped; annulus 14-celled; spores ellipsoid, reticulate to spinulose. Tropical Asia (Philippines). Z10.

CULTIVATION See FERNS.

***P. apiifolia*** (J. Sm.) Kunze. As for the genus.

For synonymy see *Acrostichum* and *Polybotrya*.

**Psophocarpus** Necker ex DC. (From Gk *psophos*, noise, and *karpos*, fruit; the seed capsules explode noisily when ripe.) Leguminosae (Papilionoideae). 10 species of climbing herbs. Leaves pinnately 1- or 3-foliolate, stipellate. Flowers solitary, clustered or in racemes; bracts caducous; bracteoles larger than bracts, membranous, persistent; 2 upper lobes of calyx connate, forming a lip; standard broad, apex of keel incurved, obtuse; stamens 10, connate or uppermost separate; ovary short-stipitate, many-ovulate. Fruit a 4-winged, oblong, dehiscent legume. Tropical Asia and Africa.

CULTIVATION All species are valued as fodder and are particularly useful as green manure, groundcover and in soil improvement and restoration. The nitrogen-fixing capacity of *Psophocarpus* is exceptional; in their first few months of growth they produce the greatest weight of nodules per plant of all the Leguminosae. For this reason, they are sometimes grown in rotation with sugar cane and other crops. *P. tetragonolobus* is widely cultivated in the tropics, where it is normally grown as an annual. Most cvs are well adapted to humid climates, although a dry period favours fertilization and pod development. A well-distributed rainfall is required and many cvs are sensitive to drought. Temperatures of 25–30°C/77–86°F are needed for optimum growth and a short day (12 hours or less) is required for flower initiation and pod set of many cvs, although some are daylength-neutral. Loam-based, slightly acid soils are generally selected, although some cvs are not particular as to soil type; the crop is, however, always sensitive to waterlogging. Seeds are sown at 45–60cm/18–24in. intervals on prepared beds or ridges 90–100cm/36–39in. apart or at 1.5×1.5m/3–5ft for long-duration crops grown for pod production. Plants should be staked or trained on a trellis to a height of 2m/6½ft. In some areas, the root tubers are allowed to remain in the soil to provide a crop the following season. Mulching is often beneficial for conserving soil water. A balanced NPK fertilizer should be applied before sowing, followed by regular dressings of P and K. Nitrogenous fertilizers may promote excessive leaf production and actually inhibit the production of root nodules. Irrigation may be required during active growth. Immature pods may be harvested when 15–20cm/6–8in. long and 2–2.5cm/¾–1in. wide. The first pods are produced 60–80 days from sowing and harvesting many continue for a considerable period. In a relative humidity of 90%, pods may be stored at 10°C/50°F for 21 days. Mature tubers may be harvested 120–240 days from sowing. Pod yields of 250–500g/$m^2$ may be expected. In temperate climates, production of pods even in protected cultivation is unlikely, due to the short daylength required by many cvs for flowering and fruiting.

***P. tetragonolobus*** (L.) DC. WINGED BEAN; WINGED PEA; GOA BEAN; MANILA BEAN; ASPARAGUS PEA; PRINCE'S PEA; PRINCESS PEA; DAMBALA; FOUR-ANGLED BEAN. Tuberous-rooted twining herb. Leaflets to 15cm, 3, ovate, acute. Infl. a lax raceme; fls to 3cm, red-brown. Fr. to 25×2.5cm with thin, leafy wings to 0.6cm deep. Asia, Mauritius.

**Psoralea** L. (From Gk *psoraleos*, scabby, referring to the glandular dots covering the plant.) SCURF PEA. Leguminosae (Papilionoideae). Some 130 species of glandular-scurfy, perennial herbs or shrubs. Leaves alternate, imparipinnate, 3- to many-, rarely 1-foliolate; stipules lanceolate to linear, adnate to petiole; leaflets entire or dentate, linear to obovate. Flowers in heads, racemes or spikes, occasionally clustered or solitary; bracts 2–3, ovate, acuminate, membranous; bracteoles absent; calyx campanulate, lobes 5, ovate, upper 2 usually connate; corolla blue, purple, rose or white, rarely yellow, standard orbicular or ovate, wings oblong, subfalcate, auriculate, exceeding keel, keel incurved, obtuse; stamens diadelphous, uppermost stamen usually separate, anthers equal, uniform; ovary subsessile, 1-ovulate, glabrous. Fruit a short, ovate, indehiscent legume. N & S America, S Africa.

CULTIVATION *Psoralea* spp. are found in well-drained coastal, riverside and prairie habitats. In addition to their ornamental value, several spp. have ethnobotanical importance: *P. esculenta* was a rootcrop, eaten roasted or dried by native N Americans and early settlers, as was *P. hypogaea*; *P. glandulosa* has vermifugal and cathartic properties; *P. macrostachys*, a denizen of salt marshes in the US, yields a tough root fibre, and *P. pinnata* was once used to treat hysteria.

The South African species, *P. aphylla*, bearing long, densely flowered terminal racemes of flowers which cause a graceful bending of the slender stems, and *P. pinnata*, softly pubescent with bicoloured white and violet flowers, are frost-tender species for the cool glasshouse in cool temperate regions. In frost-free zones they make handsome specimens for the sunny shrub border.

*P. glandulosa* is grown for its upright habit and slender cane-like stems which bear an abundance of flowers throughout the summer in favourable conditions; flowers are borne on the previous season's growth and on the current year's growth late in the season. It is hardier than the Cape species (with tolerances between −5°C/23°F and −10°C/14°F), provided it is grown in perfectly drained soils, with the shelter of a south- or southwest-facing wall. Even if cut back by frost it will regenerate from buds low down on old wood. Prune in spring to keep within bounds, retaining as much of the previous season's growth as possible. The North American species, which under natural conditions are valuable as soil stabilizers and as a food source for wild life, are grown in the wild garden and in collections of native species in conditions that approximate to those of their natural habitat. They should be propagated from seed, and grown on until final planting since transplanting without fatal root damage is usually impossible.

Propagate by semi-ripe cuttings in sand in a closed case with gentle bottom heat; pot on until final planting out to minimize disturbance to the roots. Increase herbaceous perennials by division. Also by pre-soaked seed.

***P. acaulis*** Steven ex Bieb. Stemless perenn. herb to 25cm. Lvs 3-foliolate, hairy; leaflets ovate-elliptic, dentate. Infl. solitary heads on peduncles just higher than lvs; fls cream. Caucasus. Z6.

***P. aphylla*** L. BLOUKEUR; FONTEINBOS. Shrub to 3m. Branches erect or drooping, nearly leafless. Lvs trifoliolate with 3 narrow leaflets or simple and scale-like. Standard blue, keel and wing pet. white. Summer. S Africa. Z9.

***P. esculenta*** Pursh. POMME BLANCHE; POMME DE PRAIRIE; INDIAN BREADROOT. Perenn. to 50cm. Tuberous roots edible. Stem hairy. Lvs 5-foliolate, leaflets 5.5cm, oblong to oblanceolate, hairy beneath, glabrous above. Fls crowded in a spike to 10cm; cor. yellow to blue. Spring to early summer. N America (Saskatchewan to Montana, Oklahoma). Z4.

***P. glandulosa*** L. CULEN. Shrub to 3m. Black-glandular throughout. Lvs trifoliolate; petiole to 4cm; leaflets to 7.5×2.5cm, lanceolate, acuminate, rounded or wide-cuneate at base, entire, deep green; petiolule to 16mm. Fls crowded in a spike-like, axillary, downy raceme to 13cm; peduncle to 15cm; cal. 0.5cm, cupuliform; cor. white, standard blotched blue, keel blotched blue below. Fr. 6.5×3.5mm, oblong-ellipsoid, pubesc. Summer–autumn. Peru, Chile. Z9.

***P. hypogaea*** Torr. & A. Gray. Perenn. herb, densely white-pubesc. Lvs 3–7-foliolate; petiole to 9cm; leaflets to 5×1cm, elliptic-linear to narrowly obovate, glabrescent above. Spike to 3cm, densely-fld; peduncle to 3cm; fls to 12mm, subsessile; cal. lobes to 4mm, elliptic or lanceolate; standard white to lavender. Fr. to 18mm, narrowly rostrate. Montana to Texas and New Mexico. Z4.

***P. pinnata*** L. BLUE PEA. Shrub to 2m, much-branched. Lvs 5–11-foliolate; leaflets 3×0.3cm, linear or linear-lanceolate, acute, somewhat puberulous. Fls very numerous, solitary or clustered; cal. 0.5cm, glandular, lobes blunt; cor. to 1.5cm, violet or blue wings white. Summer. S Africa. Z9.

***P. linearis*** Burm. f. See *Aspalathus linearis*.
***P. tetragonolobus*** L. See *Cyanopsis tetragonolobus*.

**Psychopsis** Raf. BUTTERFLY ORCHID. (From Gk *psyche*, butterfly, and *opsis*, appearance referring to the flower shape.) Orchidaceae. 5 species of epiphytic orchids closely allied to and formerly included in *Oncidium*. Rhizome short. Pseudobulbs clustered, orbicular to subquadrate, strongly laterally compressed, wrinkled, basally enveloped by thin overlapping sheaths, unifoliate. Leaves oblong-elliptic, acute, erect, rigidly coriaceous, often dotted or mottled oxblood, conduplicate; petiole short. Inflorescence a raceme, erect to arcuate, born from base of pseudobulb, covered by sheathing bracts at the nodes; flowers showy, pedicellate, produced successively over several seasons a year; dorsal sepal free, erect, spathulate, acute, narrow, revolute and undulate, lateral sepals ovate-oblong, obtuse, subfalcate, crispate, crenate to undulate; petals similar to dorsal sepal; lip pandurate, 3-lobed, lateral lobes orbicular, midlobe large, transversely subquadrate, spreading, disc prominent, fleshy, with various numbers of calli; column long, erect, biauriculate with antennae-like processes from upper portion of auricles; anther terminal, operculate; pollinia 2, waxy, pyriform. C & S America. Z10.

CULTIVATION A genus of spectacular orchids now treated as distinct from *Oncidium, Psychopsis* bears exceptionally large tiger-striped blooms a few at a time in slow succession on stems arising from often sickly-appearing, fleshy, dull green and liver-red plants. Provide full sunlight and high temperatures (30–40°C/85–105°F). Pot tightly in the most open mixture of 1:1 coarse bark and charcoal, surrounding the lead base with fresh sphagnum at first to promote rooting. Alternatively, mount on rafts to allow simple, creeping rhizomes to progress. Suspend plants in a dry airy position, water freely during the short growing period and give a weak foliar feed every third week. Once pseudobulbs are completed, withhold watering, providing only a heavy misting every second day. Do not remove flower spikes, which may be remontant even though they appear spent.

***P. krameriana*** (Rchb. f.) H. Jones. Pseudobulbs to 3cm diam., tightly clustered, dull purple-brown, strongly compressed. Lvs to 16×6cm, elliptic-oblong, acute, deep green mottled purple above, spotted dull maroon below. Infl. erect, to 1m; peduncle terete, nodes prominent; fls produced singly in succession, to 12cm diam., showy; sep. deep red-brown with golden yellow margins; dorsal sep. to 5×1cm, linear-spathulate, acute, erect, strongly undulate, recurved, lateral sep. to 7×1cm, obliquely ovate-elliptic, falcate, subacute, margins undulate-crisped; pet. similar to dorsal sep.; lip yellow blotched deep red-brown, to 4.5×4cm, subpandurate, 3-lobed, lateral lobes suborbicular, dorsal margin erose, midlobe transversely oblong, with conspicuous yellow central blotch, short-clawed, bilobulate, margins mottled red-brown, undulate-crisped, callus prominent, deep bronze-purple, obscurely 3-lobed at front, 2-lobed at base; column to 1cm, green, with 2 prominent lateral wings above, each terminating in small, black glands. Costa Rica, Panama, Ecuador, Peru, Colombia.

***P. limminghei*** (E. Morr. ex Lindl.) E. Luckel & G.J. Braem. Pseudobulbs to 2×1.5cm, spaced at 1–2cm intervals on rhiz., ovate-elliptic, prostrate. Lvs to 3.5×3.5cm, elliptic to ovate-elliptic, pale green-brown mottled maroon. Infl. erect, 2–3-fld; peduncle slender, to 10cm; fls to 3.5cm diam.; dorsal sep. dull red-brown, to 1.5×1cm, ovate-spathulate, obtuse to acute, lateral sep. smaller than dorsal sep.; pet. bright red-brown barred with pale yellow-brown, slightly larger than sep., ovate-oblong, truncate; lip cream-yellow spotted orange-brown, to 2.5×2.5cm, 3-lobed, lateral lobes large, oblong, recurved, midlobe larger than lateral lobes, triangular, clawed, bilobulate; 3-ridged; column erect, wings fimbriate. Brazil, Venezuela.

***P. papilio*** (Lindl.) H. Jones. Pseudobulbs to 5cm. Lvs to 25×7cm, ovate to elliptic-oblong, deep olive green mottled red-brown. Infl. to 120cm, erect or sub-erect, simple or branched, 1 or 2 fls opening at once; peduncle strongly compressed, dilated above, green spotted oxblood or maroon; fls to 15cm diam.; dorsal sep. and pet. purple-brown mottled yellow-green, to 10×0.5cm, linear-oblanceolate, acute, erect, slightly dilated near apex, margins slightly undulate, lateral sep. bright chestnut red barred yellow, oblong-lanceolate, acuminate, to 5×2cm, decurved, margins strongly undulate; lip to 4×3.5cm, 3-lobed, lateral lobes small, semi-orbicular, yellow spotted orange-brown, midlobe broadly clawed, suborbicular, emarginate, golden yellow mottled red-brown, strongly undulate-crisped, disc with a fleshy callus of 3 erect ridges, pale yellow or white spotted red-brown; column to 1cm, erect, wings oblong, fimbriate, ending at tip in capitate, fleshy teeth. Trinidad, Venezuela, Colombia, Ecuador, Peru.

***P. picta*** Raf. See *P. papilio*.
For further synonymy see *Oncidium*.

**Psychotria** L. (From Gk *psyche*, life; many species have medicinal properties.) WILD COFFEE. Rubiaceae. From 500 to 900 (to as many as 2000, according to same authorities) species of shrubs or trees or, rarely, perennial herbs. Stems erect to climbing. Leaves petiolate or, rarely, sessile, opposite or whorled, membranous to leathery, glabrous to pubescent, domatia and nodules usually present; stipules interpetiolar, persistent or deciduous, occasionally sheath-forming, margin entire to toothed or incised, membranous, glabrous to pubescent. Flowers sessile or pedicellate, in sessile or pedunculate, terminal, axillary, or lateral, variously disposed inflorescences; bracteate and bracteolate, often involucrate; calyx tube cup-shaped, glabrous to pubescent, limb persistent or deciduous, truncate or toothed to lobed, lobes 4–5, ovate to linear; corolla tubular to funnel- or bell-shaped, tube pubescent at throat, lobes 4–5, spreading to reflexed, valvate in bud; stamens 4–5, inserted at throat of corolla tube, anthers included or exserted, linear to oblong; ovary 2–4-celled, style included or exserted, filiform, stigma 2–4-lobed, linear, ovules solitary in each cell, erect, basal. Fruit a berry, globose to ovoid or pear-shaped, red to blue or black, pyrenes 1–4, smooth or grooved to angled or ribbed; seeds erect, subellipsoid, endosperm horny. Tropics and Subtropics. Z10.

CULTIVATION *Psychotria* spp. are not common in cultivation in temperate zones, although some, notably *P. jasminiflora*, are attractive in flower and a number bear decorative fruits; *P. cyanocarpa* is sometimes grown for the winter interest of its dense clusters of bright blue berries. Grow in the warm glasshouse (min. 12°C/55°F). Cultivate as for *Ixora*.

***P. capensis*** (Ecklon) Vatke. Shrub or tree, to 7m. Stems 4-angled, glabrous, bark grey. Lvs to 15×6cm, obovate or oblanceolate to elliptic, apex attenuate to obtuse, base attenuate, margin entire and subfalcate, lustrous and leathery, 4–6-veined, pubesc. on veins beneath; stipules deciduous; petioles to 15mm. Fls in terminal, branched panicles or corymbs to 15×8cm, cream to yellow; pedicels to 15mm, adpressed-pubesc., peduncles to 10cm; cal. to 2mm, lobes deltoid; cor. tube to 5mm, pubesc. at throat, lobes to 3×2mm, deltoid to oblong. Fr. to 7×6mm, subglobose to ovoid, red to black. S Africa.

***P. cyanocarpa*** Ruiz & Pav. Perenn. herb. Stems pubesc. Lvs elliptic, apex acute, base cuneate, margin entire to undulate. Fls white. Fr. blue. C America (Nicaragua).

***P. emetica*** L. f. FALSE IPECAC. Shrub or subshrub, to 60cm. Stems simple, pubesc. Lvs to 17×7cm, lanceolate or elliptic to oblong or obovate, apex acute to narrowly acute, base cuneate or obtuse, glabrous above, minutely pubesc. beneath; stipules to 4mm, persistent, lanceolate, pubesc.; petioles to 1cm. Fls sessile, in pedunculate, axillary, few-fld subracemes, white; peduncles to 1cm; cor. tube to 5mm, interior minutely pubesc.; apex of lobes acute. Fr. to 1cm, globose, blue. S America (Guatemala to Bolivia).

***P. ipecacuanha*** (Brot.) Stokes. Shrub or perenn. herb, to 50cm. Stems ascending, simple, 4-angled, glabrous to tomentose. Lvs to 15×10cm, ovate or elliptic to oblong, apex acute to narrowly acute, base acute or obtuse, lustrous, occasionally pubesc. beneath; stipules to 1cm, subulate; petioles to 15mm. Fls sessile, in solitary, pedunculate, terminal, erect to pendent, eventually globose capitum, white; peduncles to 35mm; bracts to 13mm, ovate or oblanceolate to orbicular, apex narrowly acute; cal. limb truncate to obsoletely lobed; cor. to 1cm, tube interior minutely pubesc., lobes 5, falcate. Fr. to 1cm, oblong, red to blue. Winter. C to S America.

***P. jasminiflora*** (Lind. & André) Mast. Shrub. Stems white to grey. Lvs to 8cm, ovate to oblong, apex narrowly acute, margin entire and subfalcate, glabrous above, white-pubesc. beneath. Fls in subsessile, terminal, corymbose panicles, white; cor. to 3cm, tubular to funnel-shaped, tube distended above, exterior pubesc., lobes 4, spreading. S America (Brazil).

***P. nervosa*** Sw. Shrub to 2.5m, or tree to 6m. Stems glabrous to pubesc. Lvs to 16×5cm, ovate or lanceolate to elliptic, apex and base narrowly acute, margin entire to undulate, glabrous to minutely pubesc., 9–16-veined; stipules connate and sheath-forming. Fls in sessile, terminal panicles, white; cor. tube to 3mm. Fr. to 7mm, ellipsoid, yellow to red. Florida, W Indies.

***P. peduncularis*** (Salisb.) Steyerm. Shrub or herb, to 4m. Stems simple or branched, glabrous to pubesc. Lvs to 27×14cm, elliptic or lanceolate to oblong or obovate, apex acute to narrowly acute, base attenuate to obtuse or cuneate, thin-textured and leathery, glabrous above, pubesc. to tomentose beneath; stipules to 2×1cm, deciduous, ovate or lanceolate to oblong, apex narrowly acute, margin entire and ciliate, pubesc.; petioles to 7cm, glabrous to pubesc. Fls pedicellate, in dense, pedunculate, terminal, many-fld heads, white; pedicels to 1cm, peduncles to 15cm, glabrous to pubesc.; bracts to 3×1cm, free or connate to involucrate, apex obtuse, glabrous to pubesc., white or yellow to green or blue; cal. tube to 3mm, turbinate to ellipsoid, lobes to 4mm, deltoid, apex attenuate, glabrous to pubesc.; cor. cylindric to funnel-shaped, tube to 7mm, lobes to 3×1mm, lanceolate or elliptic to deltoid. Fr. to 10×6mm, ovoid to ellipsoid, white to blue or black. Tropical Africa.

***P. pilosa*** Ruiz & Pav. Herb, to 60cm. Stems 4-angled, pubesc. Lvs oblong, apex acute; stipules lanceolate, apex acute. Fls in short-pedunculate panicles, white; bracts lanceolate, pubesc.; apex of cal. lobes acute. Fr. densely clustered, blue. C America (Nicaragua).

***P. pubescens*** Sw. Shrub to 3m, or tree to 5m. Stems branched, glabrous to pubesc. Lvs to 20×10cm, elliptic or lanceolate to oblong, apex narrowly acute, base attenuate and decurrent, membranous, pubesc.; stipules to 5mm, connate at base, apex subulate, petioles to 18mm. Fls short-pedicellate, in pedunculate; terminal, many-fld panicles to 9cm, white to yellow or pink; peduncles to 6cm; cal. tube to 1mm, lobes to 1mm, ovate, apex acute; cor. to 7mm, tube exterior and throat pubesc., lobes 5, oblong. Fr. to 7×4mm, compressed-subglobose, minutely pubesc., purple to black. W Indies and Cuba, C America.

***P. punctata*** Vatke. Shrub or tree, to 3m. Stems glabrous. Lvs to 15×6cm, ovate to elliptic, apex obtuse or, rarely, acute, base cuneate, thin-textured and leathery to fleshy, glabrous to minutely pubesc.; stipules to 4mm, ovate to deltoid, glabrous to pubesc.; petioles to 2cm, glabrous. Fls in dense, pedunculate panicles to 8cm, white; pedicels to 3mm, peduncles to 5cm, glabrous; cal. tube to 1mm, turbinate, glabrous, limb to 1mm, truncate to obscurely lobed; cor. tube to 6mm, exterior glabrous, lobes to 4×1mm, elliptic to oblong. Fr. to 9×6mm, globose to subglobose, glabrous, red. Tropical Africa.

***P. racemosa*** (Aubl.) Rausch. Shrub, to 2m. Stems branched. Lvs to 20×8cm, petiolate or subsessile, elliptic to oblong, apex attenuate to narrowly acute, base attenuate and decurrent, glabrous to pubesc. beneath; stipules to 15mm, persistent, linear; petioles to 2cm. Fls in short-pedunculate, terminal panicles to 5×5cm, white to green; cor. to 6mm, tube exterior papillose and minutely pubesc., lobes spreading, cucullate, interior papillose, minutely pubesc. Fr. to 6mm, globose, 5-celled, orange to purple or black. Summer. Central to Northern S America.

***P. undata*** Jacq. Shrub, to 3m. Stems glabrous to pubesc. Lvs to 12cm, elliptic to oblong, apex narrowly acute, base attenuate, papery, glabrous to pubesc.; stipules deciduous, connate, sheath-forming, obovate; petioles to 15mm. Fls sessile or subsessile, in sessile, terminal, few- to many-fld panicles, white; cal. tube to 1mm, limb more or less truncate; cor. to 4mm. Fr. to 7mm, ellipsoid, red. Florida, W Indies, C America.

***P. venosa*** (Hiern) Petit. Shrub, to 4.5m. Lvs to 20cm, elliptic to oblong, lustrous above. Fls in spreading, many-fld, paniculate cymes, white; cor. to 4mm. Tropical W Africa.

***P. bacteriophila*** Val. See *P. punctata*.
***P. berteriana*** Bello, non DC. See *P. pubescens*.
***P. crocea*** Sw. See *Palicourea crocea*.
***P. hirsuta*** Spreng., non Sw. See *P. undata*.
***P. oligotricha*** DC. See *P. undata*.
***P. portericensis*** DC. See *P. undata*.
***P. rigida*** (HBK) Willd. ex Roem. & Schult. See *Palicourea rigida*.
***P. tabacifolia*** J. Muell. See *Palicourea nicotinaefolia*.
For further synonymy see *Cephaelis* and *Grumilea*.

**Psydrax** Gaertn. (From Gk *psydrox*, pimple, blister.) Rubiaceae. Perhaps 75 species of shrubs or trees, many formerly included in *Canthium*. Stems erect or climbing. Leaves petiolate; stipules interpetiolar, ovate or lanceolate to triangular. Flowers in pedunculate or sessile, branched or umbellate, cymose clusters, or solitary; calyx tube hemispheric or ellipsoid, limb 4–5-toothed, or truncate; corolla cylindric, interior and throat pubescent, 4–5-lobed, lobes spreading, eventually reflexed, obtuse or acute; stamens 4–5, inserted at throat of corolla, anthers dorsifixed, exserted, often reflexed, ovate to lanceolate; ovary 2-celled, style exserted, elongate, glabrous, stigma cylindric, bifid, ovules solitary in each cell. Fruit a drupe, 2-celled, didymous or ellipsoid; pyrenes 2, hard; seeds solitary. Tropical Africa, Asia, Oceania. Z10.

CULTIVATION As for *Canthium*.

***P. subcordata*** (DC.) Bridson. Tree; branches spreading, terete, without spines, glabrous to pubesc. Lvs to 20×15cm, short-petiolate, ovate or oval, apex truncate or obtuse, base cordate or obtuse, leathery, glabrous, bristly or hairy, 7–8-veined; petioles to 1cm, pubesc.; stipules to 1cm, deciduous, lanceolate to subulate, pubesc. below. Fls many in branched, pedunculate cymes; cal. glabrous. Fr. didymous, to 1cm. Tropical Africa.

For synonymy see *Canthium*.

**Psygmorchis** Dodson & Dressler.
***P. pusilla*** (L.) Dodson & Dressler. See *Oncidium pusillum*.

**Psylliostachys** (Jaub. & Spach) Nevski (From the similar *Plantago psyllium* (*psyllion* in Gk) and *stachys*, spike, referring to the similarity of the inflorescence.) Plumbaginaceae. About 6 species of herbaceous annuals. Leaves pinnately cut, occasionally entire, usually basal. Inflorescence a panicle of 2–4-flowered spikelets, broad and oblong or narrow, pedunculate; flowers hermaphrodite, white or pink; calyx tubular, 5-lobed, scarious, glandular-pubescent below; corolla gamopetalous, funicular, lobes 5, small; stamens 5, partially adnate to the corolla tube; stigmas cylindric, filiform; ovary superior, oblong-obovoid to sublinear, ribbed, narrowing towards apex. Fruit oblong-obovoid to sublinear, dehiscing through valves. Syria to Iran and C Asia.

CULTIVATION Undemanding annuals valued for their long slender spikes of small flowers which retain their colour well when dried. Cultivate as for the annual species of *Limonium*. In zones with long hot summers, seed is sown *in situ* in spring. In cooler climates, start plants under glass in late winter or early spring, or grow in pots in well-ventilated conditions.

***P. leptostachya*** (Boiss.) Roshk. 10–20cm, rarely more. Lvs 4–10×0.5–3cm, radical, oblanceolate, deeply pinnatisect, leaflets linear to narrow-triangular, glossy green. Peduncles 1–10, sometimes many more, exceeding lvs, slender, simple, rarely branched; infl. a slender simple spike, about 0.5mm diam.; outer bract to 2mm, narrowly triangular, inner bract to 3mm, green; cal. to 2mm, densely glandular-pubesc., 5-ribbed, lobes triangular; cor. white. Iran, Afghanistan.

***P. ×myosuroides*** (Reg.) Roshk. (*P. leptostacha* × *suworowii*.) Fls larger, cal. more densely pubesc., 10-ribbed, lobes longer, awned; cor. white to dark pink. Iran, N. Afghanistan.

***P. spicata*** (Willd.) Nevski. 10–40cm, occasionally more. Lvs 5–15×1–4cm, oblanceolate, deeply pinnatisect, glossy green, pubesc. especially on midrib. Peduncles 1–10, rarely more, far exceeding lvs, pubesc.; terminal spikelet to 9cm, lateral spikelets shorter, sessile; bracts to 3mm, pubesc. beneath, inner bract broader than outer; cal. about 3mm, funnelform, 10-ribbed, glandular-pubesc., lobes expanded; cor. about 4mm, rose, funnelform, exceeding cal. Spring. Crimea, Caucasus, Iran.

***P. suworowii*** (Reg.) Roshk. Similar to *P. spicata* but lvs glabrous; peduncles 2–5, occasionally more, the lower ones glabrous, pubesc. toward infl.; lateral spikelets sessile or pedunculate; fls larger, pink or bright pink. C Asia, Iran, N Afghanistan.

For synonymy see *Limonium* and *Statice*.

**Ptelea** L. (Gk name for the elm tree.) HOP TREE; SHRUBBY TREFOIL Rutaceae. About 11 species of shrubs or small trees; bark bitter. Leaves alternate or occasionally opposite, generally 3-foliolate, rarely to 5-foliolate, muskily aromatic; leaflets entire or dentate, pellucid-punctate. Inflorescence of corymbose or paniculate cymes; flowers polygamous, pale green or white tinged green; sepals 4–5, occasionally 6; petals 4–5, occasionally 6, exceeding petals; stamens 4–5, occasionally 6, included, filaments often finely hirsute; stigma 2–3-lobed. Fruit a samara, 2– or occasionally 3-celled, body broadly reticulate winged; seed oblong, acute at apex. North America. The number of species of this genus has fluctuated wildly under different botanists, being split to 60 and reduced to 3.

CULTIVATION Grown in the shrub border or as lawn specimens, valued for their picturesque, wide spreading habit, handsome aromatic foliage and fragrant flowers which give rise to conspicuous clusters of decorative winged fruits. With the possible exception of *P. aptera*, *Ptelea* spp. are hardy to at least −15°C/5°F. Grow in fertile, well-drained but moisture-retentive soil in full sun or light part day shade; *P. trifoliata* is tolerant of a wide range of soil types and of shade. Propagate by seed sown in an outdoor seed bed in autumn, or in spring followed three months stratification at 5°C/40°F. Cultivars are increased by softwood cuttings in early summer.

***P. angustifolia*** (Benth.) V.L. Bail. Shrub; stems to 4m; young twigs brown tinged green to brown tinged red, glabrous to slightly pubesc. Leaflets oblong-lanceolate, acute, minutely serrate to serrate-dentate, bright green, pubesc. to glabrous above, somewhat glaucous beneath. Fls 4-merous; pet. pubesc.; fil. pubesc. entire length. Fr. rounded, wings rather retuse at both ends. Summer. Mexico, S US.

***P. aptera*** Parry. Shrub, 2–5m, young parts adpressed-pubesc., older twigs dark brown and glabrate. Leaflets 2+cm, narrowly obovate, obtuse, margins minutely crenate becoming revolute. Fls solitary or in few-fld corymbs, generally 5-merous, large; filaments glabrous. Fr. to 1cm, nut-like, unwinged, rounded ovate to subcordate-ovate, emarginate, rather sinuously ridged, conspicuously tuberculate-punctate. California, Baja California. Z9.

***P. baldwinii*** Torr. & A. Gray. Shrub 3–8m, irregularly branched, bark, white. Leaflets 1–2cm, ovate, obtuse or terminal leaflet cuneate at base, sessile, pale green, margins and main vein ciliate when ciliate when young, later glabrous. Infl. few-fld; fls 8–13mm diam.; cal. 1.5mm diam., sep. 5, ascending, ovate, to 1mm; pet. 4, oblong-lanceolate, obtuse, undulate, 4–6mm; stamens 5, fil. stout, hairy at middle. Fr. oblong to suborbicular, retuse or subulate-tipped, 1–2cm, thin, body usually strongly reticulate. Spring. S US. Z6.

***P. crenulata*** Greene. Shrub or small tree, to 6.5m; young twigs glandular-punctate, sparingly hairy, older twigs dark brown to black, glabrate. Lvs vivid light green, more or less minutely pubesc., glandular-punctate; leaflets cuneate-obovate, minutely crenate, acute or somewhat obtuse, terminal 4–7cm, lateral 1.5–4.5cm. Infl. minutely hairy; fil. and ovary pubesc. Fr. 1.5–2.5cm, orbicular, body 2× width of wing, glandular-punctate, minutely pubesc. California. Z8.

***P. microcarpa*** Small. Shrub, 1.5–3m, branched. Lvs glabrous, trifoliolate; leaflets 4–10cm, elliptic to oblong-lanceolate, somewhat acute to slightly acuminate both ends, entire to somewhat undulate, green above, paler green beneath, firm. Infl. paniculate, many-fld. Fr. 8–11mm, orbicular-obovate to suborbicular, rounded or truncate at base, pitted, wings slightly crisped. Spring. SE US (Alabama, Georgia, Tennessee). Z7.

***P. monticola*** Greene. Young twigs dull brown, minutely velvety-pubesc. Lvs trifoliolate, light green above, somewhat glaucous beneath, subcoriaceous, punctate, leaflets 3–5cm, terminal leaflets broadly cuneate-obovate, laterals very obliquely ovate, margins somewhat crenate becoming revolute. Fr. 1.5cm, obovate-orbicular, truncate to emarginate at apex, abruptly acute at base, obscurely punctate, wing narrower than body. Texas. Z8.

***P. pallida*** Greene. Young twigs light brown tinged yellow, minutely pubesc., older twigs cinereous. Lvs trifoliolate, minutely crenate to serrate, pale dull green above, paler and glaucescent beneath, rigidly subcoriaceous, scarcely glandular-punctate; terminal leaflets 3.5–5.5cm, elliptic-lanceolate, laterals 2–4cm, obliquely oblong-lanceolate; petioles 4cm, very slender. Fr. 1.5–2cm, orbicular, obtuse to subtruncate, body oval, narrower than wing, transversely sinuous-ridged, sparingly glandular-punctate, wing obscurely reticulate. Arizona. Z8.

***P. polyadenia*** Greene. Young twigs ferruginous velvety-tomentose, older twigs glabrate, dull dark brown. Lvs 6cm, trifoliolate, subcoriaceous, glossy light green above, sparsely minutely pubesc. and densely dark glandular-punctate; leaflets acute, slightly crenate, terminal ovate-elliptic, laterals obliquely ovate, smaller than terminal. Fr. 1.5cm, rounded obovate, retuse or emarginate, thick and hard, body orbicular-ovate, rugose and distinctly punctate, wing broader than body. SW US. Z6.

***P. serrata*** Small. Shrub, 1–2m, irregularly branched. Lvs trifoliolate, glabrous; leaflets elliptic, sharply acute or generally acuminate at apex, terminal leaflets 2.5–7cm, slender at base, shallowly acutely serrate, deep green above, very pale green beneath. Infl. paniculate, few-fld. Fr. obovate, acute at base, 16–19mm, body glandular-punctate, wing delicate. Georgia. Z8.

***P. straminea*** Greene. Twigs very pale to white, polished, fruiting twigs stramineous, scarcely glandular-punctate. Lvs bright light green both sides, glabrous, obscurely sparingly punctate, rather thin; leaflets 4–6.5cm, obovate, acute at base, obtuse at apex, distinctly crenate, laterals sometimes smaller. Fr. 2cm, broadly suborbicular, cordate, somewhat 2-lobed, body orbicular, much narrower than wing, faintly rugose, densely glandular-punctate. Arizona. Z8.

***P. tomentosa*** Raf. Shrub or small tree. Lvs usually densely persistently tomentose beneath; leaflets 2.5–8×1–5cm, elliptic to obovate, obtuse to shortly acuminate at apex, obliquely cuneate or rounded at base; petiole usually densely persistently tomentose. Fls 7–12mm diam.; pet. oblong to elliptic or obovate, 4–5×2–3mm; fil. minutely hirsute below. Fr. 13–24mm, ovate, cordate or truncate at base, emarginate or subulate at apex, body more or less strongly reticulate. E US (N Carolina to Georgia & Arizona). Z7.

***P. trifoliata*** L. HOP-TREE; STINKING ASH; WATER ASH. Shrub or tree to 8m, aromatic, bark castaneous. Lvs glabrous or densely pubesc., trifoliolate; leaflets 4–12×2.5cm, ovate to oblong to oblanceolate, acute to acuminate, entire to undulate or somewhat minutely crenate, lustrous dark green above, paler beneath. Infl. paniculate, many-fld; fls 8–12mm diam.; sep. 1.5mm, ovate, obtuse, pet. 4–6mm, narrowly oblong. Fr. 2–2.5cm, ovate-orbicular to suborbicular, rounded or notched at base. Early summer. E & C US. 'Aurea': lvs soft yellow, later lime. 'Fastigiata': habit upright. 'Glauca': lvs tinted blue. 'Monophylla': leaflets only 1. 'Pentaphylla' ('Heterophylla'): leaflets narrow, sometimes 4–5. var. ***mollis*** Torr. & A. Gray. Lvs broader, persistently grey-tomentose beneath. Z5.

***P. isophylla*** Greene. See *P. trifoliata*.
***P. jucunda*** Greene. See *P. angustifolia*.
***P. lutescens*** Greene. See *P. baldwinii*.
***P. mollis*** M.A. Curtis. See *P. trifoliata* var. *mollis*.
***P. neomexicana*** Greene. See *P. angustifolia*.
***P. trifoliata*** var. ***angustifolia*** (Benth.) M.E. Jones. See *P. angustifolia*.

**Pteridium** Gled. ex Scop. (nom. cons.). (From Gk name used by Theophrastus, from *pteron*, feather, wing, referring to the form of the fronds.) Dennstaedtiaceae. Some 4–8 closely related species of terrestrial ferns. Rhizomes long-creeping, solenostelic, subterranean, branched, woody, covered with roots and red-brown hairs, but not scales. Fronds stipitate, uniform, erect to prostrate, 2–4-pinnate-pinnatifid, ovate to deltoid, coarse and, eventually, firm-textured, pubescent or, rarely, glabrous, pinnae with nectaries at base (at least initially), opposite to subopposite, pinnules alternate, margin of segments reflexed, veins free, forked, oblique; rachis and costa grooved above; stipes not jointed, distant, felty at base, lustrous, straw-coloured to brown or black. Sori marginal or submarginal, continuous on a vascular connective commisure, linear; indusia double, with outer formed from modified margin of segments, and inner obscure to obsolete, opening outwards, delicate and membranous to hyaline; paraphyses absent; sporangia stalked; annulus 13–17-celled, incomplete, vertical; spores globose to tetrahedral, papillose to granulate or spinulose, brown. Cosmopolitan.

CULTIVATION Essentially weed ferns with several closely related species scattered throughout the world, capable of colonizing woodland and open moorland habitats, these ferns have little garden value unless enormous areas of ground are available, although in these cases the crested form of *P. aquilinum* can be attractive. Less aggressive and more suitable for the smaller garden is *P. aquilinum* 'Grandiceps'; which is much smaller (up to 1m/39in. tall) and which spreads only slowly. All species are deciduous. *P. aquilinum* and allies are hardy at least down to –30°C/ −22°F, but *P. esculentum* is less hardy and unlikely to thrive in cold temperate regions. All species can stand full sun although they will grow more luxuriantly in part shade. The soil must have an acid pH in the range of 4.0–6.0. Under glass, grow in large containers in a soilless potting medium in bright sunlight. Plant out in early summer. If space is at a premium, this fern can be confined to a small area by planting in an old oil drum or similar container sunk into the soil. Be prepared to cut off any escaping rhizomes. Water copiously until well established. Propagate by spores from selected strains, e.g. *P. aquilinum* 'Grandiceps', sections of mature plants rarely survive transplanting. Young plants of *P. aquilinum* are common weeds of peat-based potting mediums.

***P. aquilinum*** (L.) Kuhn. BRACKEN; BRAKE; PASTURE BRAKE. Rhiz. to 15mm, much-branched. Fronds to 1m×60cm, erect, 2–4-pinnate, ovate or deltoid to oblong, leathery, more or less pubesc. below, pinnae to 80×45cm (lowest) or 40×15cm, short-petiolate, horizontal or ascending, distant, ovate to deltoid, apex attenuate to acute, pinnules to 15×5cm, sessile to short-petiolate, spreading, ovate to lanceolate or linear to oblong, apex caudate or obtuse, margin entire to incised, seg. to 4cm, linear to oblong, apex attenuate to obtuse, base decurrent, veins prominent below, rachis initially pubesc., especially below, brown; stipes to 50cm, 1cm or more distant, erect and stiff, woody and swollen at base, initially pubesc. N Hemisphere. 'Cristatum': all pinnae and pinnules crested. Very invasive and only suited to a woodland garden, 200cm. 'Grandiceps': raised from 'Cristatum', far less invasive, all foliage reduced to large grandicipital crests (Grandiceps), a curiosity, 50–70cm. var. ***latiusculum*** (Desv.) Underw. ex A.A. Heller. Fronds with oblique pinnae, seg. glabrous to sparsely pubesc. at margin and on costa beneath. Eastern N America, Europe, E Asia. var. ***pseudocaudatum*** (Clute) A.A. Heller. Fronds to 70cm, seg. more or less glabrous but hair-tipped at proliferous and caudate apex. E US (Massachusetts to Florida, Texas). var. ***pubescens*** Underw. WESTERN BRACKEN. Fronds pubesc. above, pubesc. to tomentose beneath, pinnules horizontal. Western N America. Z4.

***P. esculentum*** (Forst. f.) Nak. Rhiz. much-branched and matted. Fronds to 3m, erect, 2–4-pinnate-pinnatifid, deltoid, leathery, more or less glabrous to initially pubesc., especially on veins below, pinnae to 1m, upper reduced, spreading, distant, ovate to deltoid, pinnules to 14cm wide, lanceolate, apex caudate, margin lobed at base, seg. distant, linear to oblong, apex obtuse, base decurrent, veins forked, rachis and costa grooved and pubesc. above; stipes erect and stiff, glabrous. SE Asia (Malaysia) to Australasia, Polynesia. Z10.

***P. aquilinum*** Copel., non (L.) Kuhn. See *P. esculentum*.
***P. aquilinum*** var. ***japonicum*** Nak. See *P. aquilinum* var. *latiusculum*.
***P. latiusculum*** (Desv.) Hieron. ex Fries. See *P. aquilinum* var. *latiusculum*.

**Pteridophyllum** Sieb. & Zucc. (From Gk *pteris*, fern, and *phyllon*, leaf, alluding to the fern-shaped leaves.) Fumariaceae. 1 species, a perennial herb with short rhizomes. Leaves radical, lanceolate, apically obtuse, 5–15×2.5cm, pinnatisect; pinnae flat or angled at 30° to rachis, median pinnae longest; base auriculate, rarely setose. Flowers white, in a branched raceme, to 1.5cm across; sepals 2, short-lived; petals 4, elliptic-oblong, to 1cm long, short-lived, unequal; stamens 4. Fruit a 2-valved silique. Spring. Japan. Z7.

CULTIVATION *P. racemosum* is rare native of coniferous woods in Japan, grown for its pleasing foliage and attractive flowers. The basal rosette of leaves is remarkably fern-like; the flowers, which are held on a branched spike resemble small white poppies and are produced in the spring. Plant in the woodland, the peat or rock garden, in light shade, in moist soil containing plenty of humus. In favourable conditions the central clump sends out branches which root at the node. They are hardy to −17°C/1°F in sheltered positions. Propagate by division after flowering. Pot each division individually in a potting medium that includes leafmould and overwinter in a cold frame or unheated greenhouse. Plant out in the spring. Sow seed in mid-autumn in a potted medium containing leafmould; seed can be slow to germinate. Plant out in spring or autumn; protect from slugs.

***P. racemosum*** Sieb. & Zucc. As for genus.

**Pteridophytes** (Pteridophyta). FERNS, CLUBMOSSES, HORSETAILS and *Psilotum*. 365 genera organized in four classes, comprising some 2000 species. Non-flowering vascular plants increasing by spores. In the alternation of generations, the sporophyte (spore-bearing) generation predominates and is the facies known to the gardener and botanist. The sporophyte asexual phase possesses leaves (scale-like with a single vascular strand or compound fronds), axes, stems (protostelic, solenostelic, dictyostelic, or polystelic, sometimes with secondary thickening) and roots (except in Psilotaceae). Spores (trilete or monolete) are produced in minute sporangia: these are thick- or thin-walled, homosporous or heterosporous, and carried on the leaf surface or collected in terminal cone-like axes. Ripe spores are shed and develop into free-living prothalli, small, liverwort-like non-vascular plants that represent the gametophyte (sexual) generation. Prothalli bear sexual organs (male – antheridium; female – archegonium); antherozoids; flagellate male gametes swim across the prothallus to fertilize the female gametes in their-flask-like archegonia. Fertilization gives rise to a new sporophyte.

The pteridophytes are a group of primitive plants, their classes largely unrelated. They are remnants of the carboniferous flora –

one which they dominated, laying down the vast fossil, coal and oil deposits we exploit today and giving rise or place to the gymnosperm and angiosperm flora that now predominates. In this work they are represented by the following genera:

I Psilotatae (Psilopsida), Psilotaceae: *Psilotum*.

II Lycopodiate (Lycopsida), CLUBMOSSES
Lycopodiaceae: *Lycopodium*.
Sellaginellaceae: *Selaginella*.
Isoetaceae: *Isoetes*.

III Equisetatae (Sphenopsida), HORSETAILS
Equisetaceae: *Equisetum*.

IV Filicatae (Filicopsida), FERNS
Aspleniaceae: *Asplenium, Pleurosorus, Schaffneria*.
Azollaceae: *Azolla*.
Blechnaceae: *Blechnum, Doodia, Sadleria, Stenochlaena, Woodwardia*.
Cyatheaceae: *Cyathea*.
Davalliaceae: *Araiostegia, Davallia, Davallodes, Gymnogrammitis, Humata, Leucostegia, Scyphularia, Trogostolon*.
Dennstaedtiaceae: *Blotiella, Dennstaedtia, Histiopteris, Hypolepis, Leptolepia, Lindsaea, Lonchitis, Microlepia, Odontosoria, Oenotrichia, Paesia, Pteridium, Saccoloma, Sphenomeris*.
Dicksoniaceae: *Cibotium, Culcita, Dicksonia, Thyrsopteris*.
Dryopteridaceae: *Arachniodes, Athyrium, Coveniella, Ctenitis, Cyclodium, Cyclopeltis, Cyrtomium, Cystopteris, Deparia, Diacalpe, Dictyoxiphium, Didymochlaena, Diplazium, Dryopteris, Fadyenia, Gymnocarpium, Hemigramma, Hypodematium, Hypoderris, Lastreopsis, Matteuccia, Olfersia, Onoclea, Peranema, Phanerophlebia, Polybotrya, Polystichum, Psomiocarpa, Quercifilix, Rumohra, Tectaria, Woodsia*.
Gleicheniaceae: *Dicranopteris, Diplopterygium, Gleichenia, Sticherus*.
Hymenophyllaceae: *Hymenophyllum, Trichomanes*.
Lomairiopsidaceae: *Bolbitis*.
Lophosoriaceae: *Lophosoria*.
Loxomataceae: *Loxoma*.
Marattiaceae: *Angiopteris, Christensenia, Danaea, Marattia*.
Marsileaceae: *Marsilea, Pilularia, Regnellidium*.
Nephrolepidaceae: *Nephrolepis*.
Oleandraceae: *Arthropteris, Oleandra*.
Ophioglossaceae: *Botrychium, Helminthostachys, Ophioglossum*.
Osmundaceae: *Leptopteris, Osmunda, Todea*.
Polypodiaceae: *Aglaomorpha, Anarthropteris, Arthromeris, Belvisia, Campyloneurum, Colysis, Crypsinus, Dictymia, Drymoglossum, Drymotaenium, Drynaria, Drynariopsis, Goniophlebium, Lecanopteris, Lemmaphyllum, Lepisorus, Leptochilus, Merinthosorus, Microgramma, Microsorium, Niphidium, Paragramma, Pecluma, Phlebodium, Photinopteris, Platycerium, Pleopeltis, Polypodium, Pseudodrynaria, Pyrrosia, Selliguea* and *Solanopteris*.
Pteridaceae: *Acrostichum, Actiniopteris, Adiantopsis, Adiantum, Anogramma, Anopteris, Bommeria, Cheilanthes, Coniogramme, Cryptogramma, Doryopteris, Gymnopteris, Hemionitis, Jamesonia, Llavea, Onychium, Paraceterach, Pellaea, Pityrogramma, Pteris, Ptilopteris*.
Salviniaceae: *Salvinia*.
Schizaeaceae: *Anemia, Lygodium, Mohria, Schizaea*.
Thelypteridaceae: *Amauropelta, Ampelopteris, Amphineuron, Christella, Cyclosorus, Goniopteris, Macrothelypteris, Meniscium, Oreopteris, Parathelypteris, Phegopteris, Pneumatopteris, Pronephrium, Pseudocyclosorus, Sphaerostephanos, Stegnogramma, Thelypteris*.

See also FERNS.

**Pterilema** Reinw.
***P. aceriflorum*** Reinw. See *Engelhardia spicata*.

**Pteris** L. (From the Gk word for fern, cf. Gk *pteron*, wing, referring to fronds; name used by Dioscorides.) BRAKE; DISH FERN; TABLE FERN. Pteridaceae. About 280 species of small to very large terrestrial ferns; rhizomes erect to creeping. Fronds pinnate to 4-partite, basal pinnae often forked and as large as the rest of the blade; rachis deeply grooved; the parallel ridges of the costae often with very small spine-like awns. Sori linear, submarginal, sporangia borne in a continuous line on inframarginal vein, indusium formed from reflexed frond margin, thin. Subtropics and Tropics. Z10.

CULTIVATION Tropical or subtropical terrestrial ferns of forest floor, or more open areas on disturbed earth, requiring intermediate glasshouse protection in cold climates; only plants of *P. cretica* originating at high altitude are hardy outdoors to −5°C/23°F. Grown for foliage effect, their upright habit does not lend them well to basket or hanging pot cultivation, they are most effective planted as a foil amongst other plants, and in containers; *P. cretica* is the most commonly grown as a houseplant requiring minimal attention, and dozens of variously cristated and variegated cvs are available. Growing medium should be as for terrestrial ferns, with the addition of lime for *P. cretica* and *P. vittata* to achieve a neutral to slightly alkaline reactions; other spp. are unspecific about pH. Water should be applied copiously throughout the growing season when feeding with high-N liquid fertilizer at two week intervals ensures strong and luxuriant growth. Water moderately during winter. Growth of all spp. is vigorous and repotting may need to be carried out twice a year into fairly generously sized containers. *Pteris* enjoy higher light levels than most ferns, bright filtered sunlight being preferred; *P. tripartita* and *P. vittata* resent shade and enjoy full sunlight for part of the day and can be planted to provide shade for other plants. Maintaining good air circulation and high humidity is beneficial, and is most easily achieved by frequent syringing with water indoors.

Propagate by division, but do so with care as plants may be slow to settle down. All are easily and quickly reproduced from spores; a mature plant can be produced in less than a year, and are good subjects on which to learn sowing and raising techniques. *P. cretica* cvs all reproduce faithfully from spores and thousands are produced annually by this method for the potplant trade.

***P. altissima*** Poir. Rhiz. horizontal to ascending, densely clothed at apex with linear-attenuate bicolorous scales. Frond large, erect, stipe erect, stramineous or ferruginous, smooth, naked except for a few bicolorous scales at base; blade deltate-ovate, somewhat pentagonal, up to 1.5m long, 1.2m broad, basal pinnae 2-pinnate-pinnatifid, the apical portion 1-pinnate-pinnatifid, terminating in a broad pinnatifid apical pinna, pinnae stalked (or a few distal sessile), penultimate divisions (pinnae or pinnules according to position) cuneate at base, broadly pinnatifid, up to 15cm wide at base tapering to a more or less caudate apex, ultimate seg. elongate-deltate, acute to long-acuminate, tissue herbaceous, glabrous or with a few scattered, septate hairs on the abaxial side. Tropical America.

***P. argyraea*** Moore. Rhiz. erect, with bicolorous scales *c*6mm long. Stipes 30–50cm, erect, strong, stramineous. Frond-blade 1-pinnate-pinnatisect, green with a broad white central line, terminal pinna 15–30×3–5cm, cut almost to rachis into numerous linear-oblong lobes, 2.5cm+, lateral pinnae similar, opposite, lower pairs usually forked, set *c*5cm apart on rachis. Tropics.

***P. atrovirens*** Willd. Stipes to 30cm, spinose. Frond-blade 50–100cm, 1-pinnate-pinnatisect terminal pinna 15–22×4–7cm, dissected almost to rachis, seg. numerous, linear, sterile ones rather dentate, lateral pinnae numerous, opposite, lobes similar to those of terminal pinna, lowest lateral pinnae forked with similar pinnules below; pinna-rachis and costae spinose beneath. Tropical Africa.

***P. biaurita*** L. Rhiz. erect, densely clothed with bicolorous scales; stipes stout, 10–30cm, glabrous except for a few bicolorous basal scales. Lamina oblong or deltate-oblong, to 1.3m, 1-pinnate-pinnatisect, basal pinnae forked; pinnae 5–15 pairs, opposite, sessile or almost so. Pantropical.

***P. catoptera*** Kunze. Stipes stramineous. Fronds pinnate, pinnae subsessile, seg. oblong-linear, entire, obtuse, confluent at base, thin, coriaceous, sparsely minutely setose; rachis stramineous; veins forked, basal veins extending to margin below sinus. S Africa & S Tropical Africa. A complex of ill-defined taxa.

***P. comans*** Forst. f. NETTED BRAKE; COASTAL BRAKE. Rhiz. erect, tufted; stipes 25–60cm, pale brown; scales dark brown, pubesc. Frond-blade to 2m, erect,

2–3-pinnate at base; terminal pinna to 30cm+, cut almost to rachis, lateral pinnae to 45×15cm, few, pinnules to 5cm, oblong, margins dentate, veins netted. Australia, New Zealand.

***P. cretica*** L. Rhiz. short-creeping, at apex bearing lanceolate-linear castaneous scales. Fronds crowded; stipe erect, stramineous, somewhat quadrangular, glabrous; blade ovate or rotund in outline, with 1–5 pair of simple or forked pinnae, terminating in a simple apical pinna like the lateral pinnae, tissue glabrous or somewhat with a few minute castaneous, filiform scales scattered abaxially, pinnae sessile or short-stalked, 10–20cm long, 0.8–1.8cm broad (or more), linear-lanceolate, acuminate to attenuate, cuneate or adnate at base. Old World Tropics & Subtropics. 'Albo-lineata': seg. wider with a broad white stripe down the centre of each. 'Childsii': fronds variously lobed, waved or frilled, bright green. 'Major': to 30cm; pinnae in to 6 pairs, linear, entire, sessile, terminal pinna elongate. 'Maxii': similar to 'Albo-lineata' but dwarfer, with seg. narrower, all crested at apex. 'Ouvardii': to 60–90cm; stipes elongate; fronds dark green, seg. narrowly linear. 'Parkeri': robust; fronds lustrous, seg. broadly lanceolate, margins finely undulate-dentate. 'Rivertoniana': pinnae in 4–5 pairs, deeply irregularly lobed. 'Whimsettii': a vigorous grower; fronds 45–60cm, with chestnut stripes, pinnae variously lobed or toothed. 'Wilsonii': fronds compact, bright green, variously lobed and crested, particularly heavily terminally crested, giving a fan-like appearance.

***P. dentata*** Forssk. Rhiz. erect to procumbent with linear-lanceolate dark brown scales. Stipes to 30cm+, erect, strong, stramineous. Frond-blade deltoid to ovate, very variably divided, 2–3-pinnate-pinnatisect, 50–100×30–50cm, bright green, terminal pinna 15–30×5–8cm, dissected almost to rachis into many lobes, lobes 2.5–5cm, linear, sterile lobes, crenate-dentate, lateral pinnae similar to terminal, lowermost with 1–3 similar smaller pinnules from base on lower side. Tropical & S Africa.

***P. dispar*** Kunze. Rhiz. short, erect, paleate with linear dark brown scales to 3.5mm; stipes 10–30cm, 3-angled, red-brown, glossy. Frond-blade 25–40×8–15cm, lanceolate to narrowly oblong-ovate, bipinnatifid, chartaceous, terminal pinna 10–20cm, triangular-lanceolate, apex linear and acutely dentate, lateral pinnae 5–10cm, in 3–7 pairs, narrowly deltoid, pinnatifid or entire, sessile or subsessile, acuminate, pinnules 10–30×4–5mm, linear-lanceolate to oblong-lanceolate, somewhat falcate. China, Japan to Taiwan.

***P. ensiformis*** Burm. f. SWORD BRAKE. Rhiz. short-creeping, with dark brown scales, stipes slender, glabrous, those of sterile fronds 6–10cm, those of fertile fronds 15–25cm. Frond-blade bipinnate 15–30×8–15cm, terminal pinna 5–10cm×0.4–0.6cm, elongate, when fertile slightly compound with central portion entire, lateral pinnae to 4–5 pairs, upper pinnae of sterile frond decurrent, lower subdeltoid, dissected to rachis below into 2–6 obovate-oblong pinnules to 12mm wide, sharply dentate. Himalayas to Japan, Philippines, Polynesia & Tropical Australia. 'Evergemiensis': fronds with silvery white central band and dark green margins. 'Victoriae': fronds with a white zone flanking the midrib on either side, sterile fronds small, prostrate, fertile fronds 40–45cm, erect, with pinnae to 4mm wide.

***P. grandifolia*** L. Rhiz. stout, creeping, bearing numerous thin, pale red-brown, lanceolate scales. Frond decumbent, close together or well spaced; stipe stout, straw-coloured, terete, glabrous but with a few linear scales near the base; blade narrowly oblong, 1–2m long, 37–75cm broad, 1-pinnate, pinnae 2–6cm apart, narrowly oblong-linear to linear-ligulate from a rounded or broadly cuneate base, sessile or the lower short-stalked, the margin entire and narrowly cartilaginous, tissue glabrous. Tropical America.

***P. longifolia*** L. Rhiz. short-creeping, densely clothed with yellow to brown, linear-deltate hair-pointed scales. Frond ascending or erect; stipe straw-coloured, short, and densely scaly like the rhizome, blade oblong to lanceolate-elliptic or oblanceolate, narrowed at base, acuminate at apex, 18–80cm long, 8–25cm broad, pinnae narrowly linear, base cordate (or hastate), margins crenulate-serrulate, tissue, glabrate. W Indies, Central America to Brazil.

***P. macilenta*** A. Rich. SWEET FERN. Rhiz. short, erect. Stipes 10–50cm, stramineous tinged brown below. Frond-blade ovate, 3-pinnate at base, 30–90×15–50cm, terminal pinna 10–20cm, dissected nearly to rachis into oblong lobes, deeply toothed, numerous, lateral pinnae cut to rachis below into several deeply lobed deltoid pinnules. New Zealand.

***P. microptera*** Mett. Fronds large, pinnate, primary pinnae 30–60+cm, secondary pinnae 10–25cm, deeply pinnatifid, seg. numerous, linear or oblong-lanceolate or lower occasionally shortly pinnatifid, occasionally falcate, sterile seg. dentate as are distant parts of fertile ones, 1–5cm, decurrent along rachis. Australasia, Pacific Is.

***P. multifida*** Poir. SPIDER BRAKE; SPIDER FERN. Rhiz. short, decumbent to erect, branched, bearing at the apex at tuft of red-brown, lanceolate scales. Frond erect; stipe slender, straw-coloured, grooved adaxially; blade ovate, pedate, 2-pinnate at base (basal pinnae forked), pinnatisect above, 20–50cm long, 10–25cm broad, pinnae elongate-pinnatisect, all decurrent onto the rachis, mostly 5mm broad or less, long-attenuate at the apex, tissue glabrous. China, Indo-China, Korea, Japan to Taiwan introduced in America. 'Cristata': a smaller and more compact form; seg. slender, more branched, with broad, heavy apical crests.

***P. nipponica*** Shieh. Rhiz. short-creeping; stipes stramineous. Fronds dimorphous, simply pinnate, sterile fronds with stipes 11–30cm, lamina consisting of a terminal pinna, 1–3 pairs of lateral pinnae, these linear-oblong, 10–20cm, sessile, acute, irregularly serrate, terminal pinnae longer. Fertile fronds with stipes 14–50cm, lateral pinnae linear, 20–30cm, short-stalked.

***P. orientalis*** v.A.v.R. Rhiz. short-creeping, thick, clad with entire, dark scales; stipes horny at base, brown, naked or with a sparse covering of scales. Fronds to 1m, erect, arching, pinnate, dark green, pinnae to 20×1cm, linear, acuminate at apex, lower ones only slightly or not at all reduced. SE Asia, Ryuku Is.

***P. pacifica*** Hieron. Rhiz. short-creeping, much-branched. Stipes about half length of blades, brown; frond-blade 30–50cm, erect, 1-pinnate, the basal pair of pinnae basiscopically bipinnate, pinnae 10–25cm, linear, almost at right angles to rachis. Australia.

***P. quadriaurita*** Retz. Rhiz. erect. Stipes 30–60cm, erect, strong, stramineous. Frond-blade to 90×45cm, green, terminal pinna bipinnate, tripinnate in lower part, deeply cut into numerous lobes, lobes 2.5cm+, almost parallel, linear-oblong, lateral pinnae similar, opposite, lower pairs forked at base giving 4 distinct divisions at base of frond, set 5cm apart on rachis. Old World Tropics.

***P. ryukyuensis*** Tag. Rhiz. short and small, with linear scales to 1mm, broadly linear, lustrous dark brown tinged purple; stipes obtusely angled, slender, 3–12cm on sterile fronds, 5–25cm on fertile, brown, paler on angles, lustrous. Frond-blade dimorphic, ternate or occasionally with 1 remote pair of basal pinnae, glabrous, sterile pinnae 2–7×1cm, lanceolate to oblong-ovate, lower sometimes divided, obtuse, fertile pinnae 4–15×0.3–0.4cm, linear. Japan.

***P. semipinnata*** L. Rhiz. short, erect, dark. Stipes 20–40cm, erect, strong, chestnut brown. Frond-blade 30–45×15–22cm, ovate-lanceolate, apical part of frond dissected almost to rachis into numerous lobes, lobes close, linear, entire, lowest 4–8cm, lower two-thirds of frond with 6–8 distant opposite pinnae, entire above, pinnatisect below, largest 7–15cm, long alternate with entire wing along upper side, and 4–6 linear pinnules to 5cm along basiscopic side. Indusia membranous. SE Asia, including Ryukyu Is.

***P. serrulata*** Forssk. Rhiz. creeping, clad in linear, dark brown scales; stipes to 50cm, brown. Fronds to 60×30cm, ovate, pinnate, pinnae in to 11 pairs, pinnatisect, lowest pair sometimes forked, seg. oblong-lanceolate, falcate, serrate in upper part, acute. Azores, Canary Is., Madeira, N Africa.

***P. tremula*** R. Br. TENDER BRAKE; SHAKING BRAKE; TURAWERA; AUSTRALIAN BRACKEN; POOR-MAN'S CIBOTIUM. Rhiz. erect, clad in dark brown scales. Stipes glabrous, red-brown at base. Frond-blade ovate, 3–4-pinnate at base, 30–90×20–70cm; pinnae overlapping, pinnules to 2cm, narrowly oblong to linear, margins finely dentate, most pinnules stalked or sessile, ultimate seg. linear to 3.5×0.5cm, margins toothed, apices blunt, veins free. Indusium not continuing to apex of seg. New Zealand, Australia, Fiji.

***P. tripartita*** Sw. GIANT BRACKEN. Rhiz. erect, on old plants forming a short trunk; stipes 75–150cm, green. Frond-blades 2–2.5m tripartite, all 3 pinnae approximately equal lengths, middle pinna deeply 1-pinnate-pinnatifid, apex shortly caudate, with one large basiscopic 1-pinnate-pinnatisect pinnule, its basal basiscopic segment much enlarged and 1-pinnate-pinnatisect basally, lobes oblique, slightly falcate, sinuses rounded. SE Asia, New Guinea, Australia & Polynesia.

***P. umbrosa*** R. Br. JUNGLE BRAKE. Rhiz. short-creeping, freely branched; stipes erect virtually same length as blade, bright chestnut brown. Frond-blade 30–50cm, erect, pinnatifid, pinnae 10–30cm, linear-lanceolate, confluent at base with rachis wing, margins entire or minutely dentate, sterile pinnae slightly broader than fertile, lateral pinnae 6–9 each side, central pinnae longest, lower pinnae longer than upper, short-stalked, with 2 or 3 linear, large basiscopic lobes, cut to near the pinna-rachis. Australia.

***P. vittata*** L. Rhiz. oblique, densely clothed at apex with light red brown narrowly lance-attenuate scales. Stipe straw-coloured 5–50cm, densely villous toward base. Frond-blade oblong elongate, 1-pinnate, 20–100cm long, 20–40cm broad, pinnae linear-ligulate, subfalcate, 10–18cm long, 10–20mm broad, tissue glabrous or with spreading light to dark brown scales. Tropical and temperate regions of Europe, Africa, Asia and Australasia; introduced in America.

***P. wallichiana*** J. Agardh. Rhiz. short, ascending. Stipes to 1m, strong, glossy chestnut brown. Frond-blade to 1m, tripartite, soft, pale green, central pinna 60×30cm, pinnate, its pinnules lanceolate, sessile, numerous, each cut almost to rachis into many oblong lobes, subentire when sterile, lateral pinnae to size of central, forked again. Tropical Asia to Pacific New Guinea.

***P. aurea*** Poir. See *Cheilanthes bonariensis*.
***P. childsii*** hort. See *P. cretica* 'Childsii'.
***P. fauriei*** Hieron. See *P. quadriaurita*.
***P. flabellata*** Thunb. See *P. dentata*.
***P. heterophylla*** L. See *Anopteris hexagona*.
***P. hirsuta*** (L.) J. Sm., non Poir. See *Lonchitis hirsuta*.
***P. incisa*** Thunb. See *Histiopteris incisa*.
***P. laciniata*** Willd. See *Lonchitis hirsuta*.
***P. microphylla*** A. Cunn. See *Paesia scaberula*.
***P. nitidula*** Wallich. See *Pellaea nitidula*.
***P. scaberula*** A. Rich. See *Paesia scaberula*.
***P. trichomanoides*** L. See *Cheilanthes trichomanoides*.
***P. vespertiliensis*** Labill. See *Histiopteris incisa*.
***P. victoriae*** Bull. See *P. ensiformis* 'Victoriae'.

**Pterisanthes** Bl. (From Gk *pteron*, wing, and *anthos*, flower, referring to the flattened form of the inflorescence.) Vitaceae. 20 species of climbing vines. Tendrils present. Leaves simple or compound. Inflorescences opposite leaves, pendulous, of flat fleshy bodies with irregularly lobed margins, attached to rachis along one side, with numerous sessile or immersed bisexual flowers and sometimes with several long-pedicelled sterile, male or bisexual flowers; peduncles long; flowers 4–5-merous; calyx slightly lobed; petals free, broadly ovate; ovary 2-celled, sunk in disc, cells each with 2 ovules, stigma small. Fruit is a berry, exserted; seeds 1–3, furrowed on both sides. Burma, W Malaysia. Z10.

CULTIVATION As for *Cissus*.

***P.polita*** (Miq.) Lawson. Vine, climbing extensively, very slender, glabrous throughout. Lvs 10–20×5×9cm, elliptic-oblong to ovate, subcordate at base, acute at apex, margins entire or remotely spinose-serrate, membranous. Infl. body red; fls 4-merous. Borneo, Sumatra.

For synonymy see *Vitis*.

**Pterocactus** Schum. (From Gk *pteron*, a wing, and *cactus*, referring to the winged seed.) Cactaceae. 9 closely related species of dwarf, geophytic shrubs; rootstock usually large, tuberous; stems segmented; segments globose, cylindric or clavate, often suffused brown or red; leaves present, small, subulate, caducous; glochids present, numerous to few; spines few. Flowers terminal, immersed in the apex of stem-segments, pale yellow or pink; perianth rotate; stamens touch-sensitive. Fruit dry, umbilicate, dehiscent, splitting transversely near the top; seeds samara-like, more or less circular, flat, 6–12mm; aril forming a broad wing surrounding the seed, pale beige, papery. Argentina.

CULTIVATION Grow in a cool frost-free greenhouse, min. 2–7°C/36–45°F; use 'standard' cactus compost: moderate to high inorganic content (more than 50% grit), pH 6–7.5; full sun; low air-humidity; keep dry from mid-autumn until early spring, except for light misting on warm days in late winter.

These curious plants need bright sun and cold, dry conditions in winter or the form of the stem and spines is likely to become atypical. In nature the aerial stems often break off in winter, and this may also happen in cultivation. The main hazard in cultivation is that the tuber may rot due to overwatering or poor drainage, and it is preferable to leave it partly exposed and/or surrounded by coarse grit.

***P.fischeri*** Britt. & Rose. Stems unbranched, spreading or erect, cylindric, to 10(–15)×1–1.5cm, tuberculate, brown-green; glochids numerous, 3–4mm; central spines usually 4, sometimes only developed towards stem-apex 1–3(–5) cm, flat and somewhat papery, brown to black with tip and base pale yellow; radial spines 12 or more, 6mm, bristly, off-white. Fl. terminal, 2.5cm diam., the pericarpel continuous with the stem; tepals coppery yellow to clear brown or purple; stamens yellow; style fusiform, tinged pink; stigmas 4. Fr. 2–2.5cm diam., strongly tuberculate. S Argentina (Rio Negro, Neuquen). Z7.

***P.kuntzei*** Schum. Stem seg. (above ground) 7–20×8–15mm, brown or brown-green, with a vertical violet line below the areoles; spines 8–12, 5–10mm, terete, off-white. Fl. 3–5cm diam., pale yellow, or tinged orange-brown or brown. Argentina. Z7.

***P.valentinii*** Speg. Rootstock relatively small, 2–4×1–2cm; stem seg. little-branched, cylindric, 4–8×1–1.5cm, green; central spines 0; radial spines 25–30, 4–5mm, radiating, hyaline. Fl. yellow to coppery. Fr. *c*2cm diam, yellow-pink, with spines like those of the stem and several additional papery centrals. W Argentina. Z7.

***P.pumilus*** Britt. & Rose. See *P. valentinii*.
***P.tuberosus*** (Pfeiff.) Britt. & Rose. See *P. kuntzei*.

**Pterocarpus** Jacq. (From Gk *pteron*, wing, and *karpos*, fruit.) Leguminosae (Papilionoideae). Some 20 species of trees or climbers. Leaves alternate, imparipinnate; leaflets alternate, estipellate. Flowers showy, in racemes or panicles, often produced before leaves; calyx turbinate at base; corolla yellow to orange, or white tinged violet, standard and wings crisped; stamens united or the uppermost free. Fruit a flat, 1–3-seeded, indehiscent legume, often broadly winged. Tropical America, India, Tropical & S Africa. Z10.

CULTIVATION *P.angolensis* is found in savannah woodland and dry tropical scrub and thorn forests. It shows considerable promise as a firebreak. *P.indicus* grows in tropical rainforest, often on inundated ground, on riverbanks and other waterside habitats. As well as being sources of durable, highly ornamental timber and dyestuffs, both species are extremely handsome trees with wide, graceful crowns, well suited to their widespread use as shade and avenue trees in tropical and subtropical regions. The masses of flowers are showy and very fragrant; *P. indicus* sometimes exhibits synchronicity in flowering, so that all individuals in proximity bloom in unison. In temperate zones, they are sometimes encountered in glasshouse collections of economically important plants. Cultivate as for *Gliricidia*.

***P.angolensis*** DC. BLOODWOOD TREE; KIAAT; MUNINGA. Deciduous tree to 12m. Leaves to 38cm; leaflets 2.5–5×1.8cm, 4–12 pairs, ovate-oblong or rarely nearly cordate, pubesc. at first, soon glabrous above, petiolules 8mm. Infl. to 12cm; fls to 1.5cm wide, orange-yellow, fragrant borne in profusion. Fr. 8–10cm diam., discoid, enlarged at centre, hispidulous, wings pale brown, centre dark; seeds 1–2. Autumn. S Africa to Namibia, Angola and Tanzania.

***P.indicus*** Willd. PADAUK; PADOUK; BURMESE ROSEWOOD. Tree to 9m. Leaflets to 10cm, 5–9, bluntly acuminate, glabrous, short-stalked. Fls to 1.3cm or more, yellow in crowded panicles. Fr. 5cm diam., orbicular, sericeous, veined over seeds. Spring. India to China, Malay Archipelago, Philippine Is.

***P.echinatus*** Pers. See *P. indicus*.

**Pterocarya** Kunth. (From Gk *pteron*, wing, and *karyon*, nut, referring to the winged fruit.) WINGNUT. Juglandaceae. Some 10 species of large, monoecious trees. Pith chambered; buds stalked, scales absent. Leaves deciduous, alternate, pinnate, serrate, exstipulate. Male inflorescence a pendulous catkin, lateral, short, green, sepals 1–4, bracts 3, 1 elongate, stamens 6–18; female inflorescence a pendulous catkin, lateral, green, perianth connate, lobes 4, acute, bracteoles 2, basal; style short, stigmas 2; ovary unilocular. Fruit a small winged nutlet, 1-seeded, 4-celled at base. Caucasus to E & SE Asia.

CULTIVATION Specimen trees, with handsome foliage resembling that of *Carya*, for areas not experiencing prolonged winter temperatures below about −12°C/10°F. In China, *P.stenoptera* is a frequently planted street tree, while in California it is used in playgrounds and others areas suffering soil compaction, which it withstands well; the root system may be too invasive for smaller gardens. *P.fraxinifolia*, often developing more than one trunk, grows well in damp soils and is suited to waterside plantings. The most frost-resistant and most vigorous is probably the hybrid wingnut, *P.* ×*rehderiana*, which has a tendency to spread by suckering. Cultivation as for *Carya*. Propagate from seed and by suckers or layers; root cuttings are sometimes successful.

***P.delavayi*** Franch. To 20m. Bark grey, young twigs pubesc. Lvs 20–30cm; leaflets odd-pinnate, oblanceolate, 11×3.5cm, sessile, acuminate, unequal at base, coriaceous, midrib and petiole pubesc. Male infl. to 15cm, stamens 10+, purple; bracts pubesc; female infl. to 70cm, stigmas with 2 deep clefts. Fr. sessile, in pairs. China (Yunnan). Z8.

***P.fraxinifolia*** (Lam.) Spach. CAUCASIAN WALNUT. To 25m, often multistemmed; crown wide. Bark grey-black, deeply furrowed; twigs olive-brown, slightly pubesc., later glabrous. Lvs 20–40cm; rachis terete; leaflets 11–21, oval-oblong to oblong-lanceolate, acuminate, 8–12cm, green above, lighter with pubesc. midrib below. Fr. in racemose clusters, to 2cm wide with 2 semicircular wings. Caucasus to N Iraq. 'Albomaculata': slow-growing; young lvs speckled white. var. ***dumosa*** (Lav.) Schneid. Shrubby, branches yellow-brown. Leaflets 5–7cm. Caucasus. Z7.

***P.hupehensis*** Skan. To 20m. Bark pale grey, becoming deeply fissured; branches minutely scurfy. Lvs 15–20cm; rachis terete, glabrous; leaflets sessile, 5–9, oblong to oblong-lanceolate or slightly obovate, acuminate, to 14cm. Male catkin 6–10cm; female catkin 14–25cm. Fr. to 3cm across; wing semiorbicular. C China. Z6.

***P.macroptera*** Batal. To 20m. Bark dark brown; branches glabrous. Lvs 70–160×30–50cm; petiole rust-red tomentellous; leaflets 9–11, sessile, narrowly oblong-lanceolate, acute, rarely acuminate, base truncate, densely serrate, glabrous above, midrib rust-red tomentellous beneath. Bracts narrowly lanceolate; bracteoles membranous, pilose; perianth tomentose; lobes subulate. Fr. furrowed, pubesc., to 1cm diam. China. Z7.

***P.*** ×***rehderiana*** C. Schneid. (*P.fraxinifolia* × *P.stenoptera*.) To 30m, usually less, suckering. Young shoots red-brown. Lvs about 20cm; rachis partially winged; leaflets 11–21, narrow-oblong, 6–12cm. Fr. suborbicular; wings ovate. Garden origin (Arnold Arboretum, 1908). Z6.

***P. rhoifolia*** Sieb. & Zucc. To 30m. Branches finely pubesc., later glabrous; buds 2–3-scaled, about 1.5cm. Lvs 20–40cm; rachis finely pubesc.; leaflets 11–21, ovate-oblong, 6–12cm, acute, rounded at base, finely serrate, sometimes with pubesc. venation beneath. Fr. about 2cm across; wings broadly rhombic. Japan. Z6.

***P. stenoptera*** C. DC. To 25m. Young shoots densely brown-yellow-pubesc. to glabrous. Lvs 20–40cm; rachis winged between leaflets, sometimes serrate; leaflets 11–23, terminal, sometimes absent, oval-oblong to narrow-oblong, usually acute, serrulate, sometimes pubesc. on venation below. Female catkins 18–36cm. Fr. erect, to 2cm; wings oblong. China. Z7.

***P. caucasica*** C.A. Mey. See *P. fraxinifolia*.
***P. dumosa*** Lav. See *P. fraxinifolia* var. *dumosa*.
***P. fraxinifolia*** K. Koch non Spach. See *P. fraxinifolia* var. *dumosa*.
***P. japonica*** hort. See *P. stenoptera*.
***P. laevigata*** hort. See *P. fraxinifolia*.
***P. paliurus*** Batal. See *Cyclocarya paliurus*.
***P. sinensis*** hort. See *P. stenoptera*.
***P. sorbifolia*** Dipp. See *P. fraxinifolia*.
***P. spachiana*** Lav. See *P. fraxinifolia*.

**Pteroceltis** Maxim. (From Gk *pteron*, wing, and *Celtis*, a related genus which resembles *Pteroceltis* except for the latter's winged fruit.) Ulmaceae. 1 species, a deciduous tree to 10m, rarely to 16m, polygamo-monoecious; crown broad; bark pale grey, peeling in flakes; branches sparsely lenticulate, glabrous. Leaves 3–10cm, alternate, ovate-oblong to ovate-lanceolate, serrate, glabrous, acuminate, base broad-cuneate, 3-nerved, minutely warty above, downy in vein axils beneath; petiole to 2cm. Male inflorescence a cluster, sessile; female flowers solitary in leaf axils; flowers inconspicuous; sepals 4–5; petals absent; stamens 4–5; anthers pilose at apex; ovary superior, unilocular; ovule 1, pendulous. Fruit a samara, 1.5–2cm wide, broad winged, suborbicular; stalk about 1cm, slender. N & C China. Z5.

CULTIVATION As for *Celtis*.

***P. tartarinowii*** Maxim. As for the genus.

**Pterocephalus** Adans. (From Gk *pteron*, wing, and *kephale* head.) Dipsacaceae. Some 25 species of annual or perennial herbs, subshrubs and shrubs. Leaves opposite, entire or pinnately lobed. Flower heads somewhat flattened, long-stalked, subtended by narrow involucral bracts; flowers pink to purple, the outermost conspicuously 2-lipped and larger than those at centre; calyx with 12 or more long, bristled awns; corolla lobes 5. Fruit an achene. Mediterranean to C & E Asia. Z6.

CULTIVATION An undemanding mat-forming perennial with attractive foliage, flowers and seedheads which is suitable for sunny well-drained situations on the rock garden, where it may self seed when conditions suit. Propagate by seed, by softwood or semi-ripe cuttings.

***P. perennis*** Coult. Dwarf, cushion-forming perenn. Stems to 10cm, usually shorter, tufted. Lvs to 4cm, ovate to broadly oblong, crenate to lyrate. Fls purple-pink in heads to 4cm diam., on stocky 5–7cm peduncles. Greece.

***P. parnassii*** Spreng. See *P. perennis*.
***P. pyrenaicus*** hort. See *Scabiosa pyrenaica*.
For further synonymy see *Scabiosa*.

**Pterodiscus** Hook. (From Gk *pteron*, wing, and *diskos*, disc, referring to the flat disc-shaped winged seeds.) Pedaliaceae. 18 species of small perennial herbs or more usually shrubs, seldom exceeding 30cm, often semi-succulent with a swollen caudex and tuberous roots. Stems solitary or several, simple or branched. Leaves variable in shape, margins entire, undulating, dentate or laciniate. Flowers solitary from the leaf axils, variously coloured; calyx small; corolla tube funnel-shaped, often slightly tuberculate at base, limb spreading, 2-lipped, lobes unequal, ovate, circular or transversely elliptic. Tropical E Africa, Angola, Namibia, S Africa (W Cape). Z9.

CULTIVATION Succulent winter-growing plants grown for their habit and brilliantly coloured flowers, *Pterodiscus* spp. are suitable for outdoor cultivation in warm, dry climates approximating to those in habitat, otherwise needing the protection of the cool to intermediate glasshouse or conservatory. Grow in a freely draining, sandy loam in full sun. Water moderately when in growth and keep dry during summer dormancy. Propagate by seed sown in a sandy propagating mix in spring or autumn; before the mature leaves are produced, the cotyledons fall and the plant undergoes a period of dormancy.

***P. angustifolius*** Engl. Branches basal, spreading, more or less fleshy, 9–20cm, purple, glabrous. Lvs 2.5–13×6–12cm, dense, somewhat fleshy, oblong-lanceolate, slightly glandular at first, tip obtuse or somewhat pointed, dark green, margins entire or undulating, rarely dentate toward apex; petiole 2.5cm. Fls yellow or orange, often with purple blotches in the tube, lobes ciliate, hairy inside. Tanzania.

***P. aurantiacus*** Welw. Caudex bottle-shaped, to 30cm with several thick branches at apex. Lvs oblong-lanceolate or ovate-spathulate, sinuate, smooth, tinged blue. Fls brilliant red. Angola, Namibia (Great Namaqualand), Cape (Kalahari).

***P. coerulus*** Chiov. Stems simple or branched, 5–20cm. Lvs 13–40×4–15mm, cuneate at base, margins undulating, underside sparsely glandular; petiole 0.4–2.5cm. Fls white or white suffused mauve in the throat of the tube, lobes with red veins. Somalia, Kenya.

***P. kelleranus*** Schinz. Caudex fleshy, edible. Basal lvs elliptic, with undulating margins, upper lvs narrowly lanceolate, margins usually entire or somewhat incised, sometimes distinctly pinnatisect. Somalia.

***P. luridus*** Hook. Caudex obconical, fleshy, 50×7–8cm, bark smooth, grey; branches spreading, 15–20cm, pruinose. Lvs 7–8×2.5cm, more or less numerous, oblong, basally spathulate, apically laciniate, dark green above, tinged white or blue below, lobes linear, pruinose throughout. Fls yellow, the outside dotted red. S Africa (W Cape: Kalahari), Namibia.

***P. ruspolii*** Engl. Caudex thick at base, fleshy, 4–8×0.5–2cm; stems around 20, 4–20cm. Lvs 1.5–6.5cm×8–35mm, obovate to elliptic, apex rounded, glandular below, margins entire or undulating; petiole 0.5–3.5cm. Fls light yellow to orange, often with red or purple blotches in the centre, lobes often ciliate. Kenya, Ethiopia, Sudan, Somalia.

***P. speciosus*** Hook. Caudex conic to cylindric, 15–50×6cm; branches apical, few, to 15cm. Lvs 3–6cm×5–10mm, numerous, linear to linear-oblong, irregularly dentate or slightly incised. Cor. tube 3cm, limb 5-lobed, more or less regular in shape and size, flat, 2.5–3cm across, light purple-red. S Africa (W Cape, Transvaal).

***P. heterophyllus*** Stapf. See *P. kelleranus*.
***P. somaliensis*** (Bak.) Stapf. See *P. ruspolii*.
***P. welbyi*** Stapf. See *P. ruspolii*.
For further synonymy see *Harpagophytum* and *Pedalium*.

**Pterolobium** R. Br. ex Wight & Arn. (From Gk *pteron*, wing, and *lobion*, pod.) Leguminosae (Caesalpinoideae). Some 10 species of tropical lianes, shrubs or trees, armed with recurved spines in axillary pairs. Leaves alternate, bipinnate; leaflets many, small; stipules and stipels small, inconspicuous; bracts caducous; bracteoles absent. Flowers white or yellow, in panicles or terminal racemes, almost regular; calyx shallowly cup-shaped, tube short, lobes 5, overlapping; petals 5, oblong or obovate, uppermost petal innermost; stamens 10, separate, exceeding petals, filaments villous at base or glabrous, anthers uniform, longitudinally dehiscent; ovary sessile, free, villous, 1-ovuled, style short, stigma terminal, truncate or concave. Fruit a samaroid legume, subsessile, compressed, oblong; oblique-ovate at base indehiscent; seeds flat, winged at apex. S & E Africa to SE Asia. Z9.

CULTIVATION *P. stellatum* is a tall, climbing shrub bearing terminal racemes of creamy yellow flowers, found in the wild in wooded savannahs and sclerophyll forest to altitudes of 1500m/4875ft. Cultivate as for *Hardenbergia*.

***P. stellatum*** (Forssk.) Brenan. Multi-stemmed climbing shrub to 5m; stems thorny. Lvs to 20cm; pinnae in 8–12 pairs; rachis prickly; leaflets to 1cm, oblong, blunt, asymmetrical at base, in 9–16 pairs. Fls small, cream or yellow, in dense, spike-like racemes. Fr. to 5cm, crimson; seeds with an apical, oblique wing. Spring. E & SE Africa (Ethiopia to Zimbabwe).

***P. biebersteini*** Andrz. See *Pachyphragma macrophyllum*.
***P. exosum*** (J.F. Gmel.) Bak. See *P. stellatum*.

**Pteroneuron** Fée. See *Humata*.

**Pteropogon** DC. (From Gk *pteron*, feather or wing, and *pogon*, beard, perhaps alluding to the feathery pappus.) Compositae. Some 10 species of annual herbs; stems solitary or few, slender, more or less erect, pubescent. Leaves mostly alternate, linear-subulate, entire, acute, sessile, arachnoid-pubescent above. Capitula few, discoid, in a compact terminal corymb, encircled by crowded leaves; phyllaries in many series, oblong, glabrous, scarious, outer dark brown, inner petaloid, slightly exceeding outer; florets pale, tubular, outer female, inner hermaphrodite. Fruit a small, often pubescent cypsela; pappus of plumose bristles. Pappus bristles plumose. Australia, S Africa.

CULTIVATION As for the annual species of *Helichrysum*.

***P. humboldtianum*** (Gaudich.) F. Muell. Annual to 60cm; stems few, simple or sparingly branched. Lvs alternate, to 3cm, linear to narrowly oblanceolate, dark green, margins recurved. Capitula small, many, subsessile, in subglobose clusters; involucre to 7mm, cylindric; outer phyllaries with an oblong, scarious claw and yellow, acute lamina to 3mm, inner with claw linear and obtuse, innermost spreading. Fr. *c*1.5mm, brown, finely pubesc. to glabrous; pappus bristles *c*4mm. Summer–autumn. S Australia.

For synonymy see *Helichrysum* and *Helipterum*.

**Pterospermum** Schreb. (From Gk *pteron*, wing, and *sperma*, seed, in allusion to the winged seeds.) BAYUR. Sterculiaceae. 25 species of trees or shrubs, stellate-pubescent, often with suckers. Leaves alternate, entire or variously lobed, palmately 3–7-nerved, scale- or stellate-pubescent, leathery; stipules entire or divided. Flowers bisexual, often long and conspicuous, mostly axillary, solitary or in few-flowered clusters or cymes, sometimes in short terminal racemes; calyx tubular, sepals shortly connate to almost free, linear, fleshy, caducous; petals caducous after anthesis; androgynophore short; stamens 15, anthers long; staminodes 5, ovary-5 loculed, ovules numerous; style filiform. Fruit a woody capsule, 5-valved, loculicidally dehiscent; seeds numerous, flattened, with a long wing on one side. Tropical Asia. Z10.

CULTIVATION Grown for shade and ornament in the tropics and subtropics, *Pterospermum* spp. are handsome trees; their beautiful blooms are nocturnal and fall the following morning, but are deliciously fragrant. Suitable for outdoor cultivation only in essentially frost-free zones, where they are tolerant of a range of soils, *P. acerifolia* will survive light frosts although may thereafter grow as a multi-stemmed specimen; in cool temperate zones they can be grown in the intermediate to warm glasshouse. Under glass grow in a perfectly drained, high-fertility, loam-based mix and maintain a winter minimum of 13–16°C/55–60°F. Propagate by seed or heeled semi-ripe cuttings with gentle bottom heat.

***P. acerifolium*** (L.) Willd. MAPLE-LEAVED BAYUR. Tree to 30m high and 1.5m girth; bark grey, rough, with long vertical lenticels; twigs rusty-pubesc. Lvs to 35cm diam., ovate to orbicular, palmately lobed and nerved, apex truncate-mucronate, peltate to cordate at base; stipules 1.5cm, with 3–4 linear lobes. Fls 8–15cm; sep. to 15cm, rusty-tomentose, slightly exceeding the white pet. Capsule to 15cm; seeds 2–6cm, including wing. India to Java.

***P. suberifolium*** Willd. CORK-LEAVED BAYUR. Small tree. Lvs oblong, obliquely cordate at base, coarsely toothed near the apex, pubesc. beneath. Fls in terminal or axillary few-fld racemes; sep. pubesc.; pet. white. E Indies.

**Pterostylis** R. Br. (From Gk *pteron*, wing, and *stylos*, column or style, referring to the wings on the upper column.) GREENHOOD. Orchidaceae. Some 60 species of terrestrial, deciduous orchids. Tubers subterranean, fibrous. Leaves in a basal rosette or reduced to bracts on stem. Flowers green, often striped or tinted purple, brown or red; dorsal sepal incurved, arched, the petals pressed against it, forming a hood, concealing the column, lateral sepals deflexed or erect, fused into a lower lip; lip with a mobile claw and often a basal appendage. Australia, New Zealand, W Pacific. Z9.

CULTIVATION Terrestrials for the alpine house. See ORCHIDS.

***P. acuminata*** R. Br. To 25cm. Lvs 4–8, ovate to oblong, obtuse or acute, keeled, petiolate, 2–5cm; stem bracts 2. Fl. solitary, pale green, marked white; pet. and dorsal sep. tipped pink, dorsal sep. erect, becoming horizontal, acuminate, lateral sep. fused, spreading apically forming sinus, lobes constricted, tips filiform, extending to 1cm above the hood; pet. narrowing basally, abruptly tapering; lip sharply deflexed, narrow-ovate, acuminate, basal appendage penicillate. Mid spring–early summer. E Australia, New Caledonia, New Guinea.

***P. banksii*** Hook. To 35cm, stems basally sheathed. Lvs 4–6, to 20cm, linear, sessile, cauline, keeled beneath, pale green, midrib paler. Fls pale green, stripes darker, pet. and sep. tipped orange-pink, lip with a single red ridge above, margins green, tip exserted from hood, appendage arching, tubular, apically pubesc. Autumn–winter. New Zealand.

***P. baptistii*** Fitzg. To 40cm. Lvs 4–8, oblong to ovate, conspicuously net-veined, 3–6cm; stem bracts 2. Fls solitary, to 6cm, pale green, marked dark green and white, dorsal sep. and pet. tipped pink, dorsal sep. erect, sharply curved at mid point, lateral sep. fused to dorsal, forming an apical sinus, filiform tips erect or recurved, extending to 15mm above the hood; lip 13–20mm, obovate, narrowing to a decurved apex. Mid summer–mid autumn. C & SE Australia.

***P. coccinea*** Fitzg. SCARLET GREENHOOD. To 22cm. Lvs ovate to oblong-elliptic, lanceolate, stem lvs 3–5. Fls 1–2, green to green hued scarlet, hood sharply incurved; dorsal sep. with a filiform tip, to 15mm, lateral sep. embracing hood, tips free, to 4.5cm, erect or incurved above hood; lip red-brown, to 10mm, clawed, oblong, 2-toothed or notched, keeled centrally, appendage penicillate, slender. Mid winter–mid spring. NE Australia.

***P. concinna*** R. Br. To 30cm. Lvs 4–6, ovate to oblong, petiolate, undulate or entire. Fls 1–2; perianth striped dark green, tips tinged brown; hood erect, incurved, dorsal sep. with filiform tip to 3mm, lateral sep. enveloping hood, projecting vertically, tips to 20mm, sometimes clavate; lip to 10mm, dark brown, notched. SE Australia.

***P. cucullata*** R. Br. To 15cm. Lvs oblong to elliptic, sessile, to 10cm, often scattered along the stem. Fl. solitary, red-brown, often green and white at base, incurved, exterior downy; dorsal sep. slightly exceeding pet., lateral sep. loosely embracing hood, apical fil. to 10mm; lip oblong, brown, apically curved, blunt. Summer–autumn. C & SE Australia.

***P. curta*** R. Br. To 30cm. Lvs ovate or oblong, sometimes irregularly undulate, to 10cm, petiolate, in a low rosette. Fl. solitary, to 4.5cm, white, striped green, tinted brown and green, hood erect, becoming incurved, lateral sep. embracing hood, free apical fil. to 12mm; lip to 20mm, centrally ridged, apically twisted; brown. Summer–autumn. C & SE Australia.

***P. nutans*** R. Br. PARROT'S BEAK ORCHID. To 30cm. Lvs 3–6, ovate to oblong, undulate, in a basal rosette. Fls 1–2, translucent, striped green, sometimes tipped red, hood arched; lateral sep. basally deflexed, loosely embracing hood, fimbriate, apical fil. exceeding hood; lip sharply recurved, to 15mm, green, central ridge red-brown, densely fringed, exserted. Spring–autumn. E Australia, New Zealand.

***P. pedunculata*** R. Br. MAROONHOOD. To 25cm. Lvs 4–6, ovate to oblong, sometimes undulate, obtuse, veins prominent. Fls 1–2, green and white, tipped dark red-brown; hood erect, basally incurved, loosely embraced by lateral sep., free apical fil. to 30mm, sinus narrow; lip to 5mm, ovate, dark red-brown. Summer–autumn. E Australia.

***P. australis*** Hook. f. See *P. banksii*.

**Pterostyrax** Sieb. & Zucc. Styracaceae. (From Gk *pteron*, wing, and *Styrax*; one species has winged fruits, like Styrax.) EPAULETTE TREE. 3 species of deciduous shrubs or trees, 4.5–12m; branches terete, finely stellate-pubescent when young, later glabrous; winter buds with 2 outer scales. Leaves alternate, serrate, stalked. Flowers borne in open panicles on short lateral shoots; calyx campanulate, 5-toothed; petals 5, distinct or barely fused at base, overlapping in bud; stamens 10, exserted, connate below into a tube or nearly free; ovary 3, rarely 4–5-celled, partially inferior, each cell with 4 ovules; style slender, slightly longer than stamens. Fruit a dry oblong drupe, indehiscent, ribbed or winged, 1–2-seeded. Summer. Japan, China, Burma. Z6.

CULTIVATION *Pterostyrax* spp. are beautiful in bloom, frost-tolerant to −20°C/−4°F and fast-growing. *P. corymbosa* and *P. psilophylla* are usually shrubby in habit; the fragrant-flowered *P. hispida* is a small tree with shedding grey bark that gives off a foetid odour when bruised. Flowers are most abundantly produced on wood well-ripened during the previous summer. Grow in deep acid soil, in sun or semi-shade, allowing ample room for the branches to spread; if necessary, prune to shape after flowering. Otherwise, cultivate as for *Halesia*. Propagate from seed when available, sown when ripe and stratified to 5°C/40°F for three months; also by semi-ripe cuttings in late summer, treated with hormone-rooting powder and in a closed case, or by layering.

***P. corymbosa*** Sieb. & Zucc. Shrub or tree to 12m; branches stellate pilose-pubesc. when young, later glabrous. Lvs 6–11×3.5–6cm, elliptic or ovate to ovate-oblong, apex abruptly acuminate, base cuneate, rounded to subcordate, serrulate with bristly teeth, sparsely pubesc. Panicle corymbose, 8–15cm; fls white; cal. 2mm, campanulate, margin truncate, 5- sometimes 4-toothed; cor. stellate-pubesc. throughout, lobes 14×3.5mm; pedicel 1.3mm; stamens 10, unequal, connate below. Fr. obovoid, indehiscent, 1–1.5×1cm, 5-winged, downy. Japan.

***P. hispida*** Sieb. & Zucc. FRAGRANT EPAULETTE TREE. Tree to 15m or shrub to 4.5–6m. Lvs 7–17×4–10.25cm, oval or obovate, rounded or cuneate at base, acute, bristly denticulate as nerves exceed blade margin, glabrous above, sparsely pubesc. beneath; petiole 1.3–4cm, downy. Fls white, in axillary, downy, pendulous panicles 12–25×5–7.5cm, often with 2–3 lvs at base; cor. lobes 8–10mm, oval, finely downy; stamens long-exserted, fil. downy. Fr. cylindric, 1cm, 10-ribbed, not winged, densely bristly. Japan, China.

***P. psilophylla*** Perkins. Shrub to 7m. Distinguished from *P. corymbosa* by its ascending branches and shorter lvs and panicles. Young branches ascending, sparsely stellate-pubesc. Lvs oval or obovate-elliptic, 8–9×5–5.5cm, minutely serrate. Infl. 8–12cm, many-fld; fls white; cal. stellate-tomentose, tube 2mm; cor. lobes white, 8–10×3–4mm, exterior minutely stellate-tomentose; stamens unequal; ovary obovoid; style pilose, 12–15mm. China.

**Pterygota** Schott. & Endl. (From Gk *pterugos*, winged, in allusion to the winged seeds.) Sterculiaceae. 15 species of monoecious or polygamous trees, differing from *Sterculia* and *Brachychiton* mainly in having winged seeds. Tropical regions, especially Old World. Z10.

CULTIVATION As for *Pterospermum*.

***P. alata*** (Roxb.) R. Br. Tree to 45m high and 3.5m girth; trunk straight, ash-coloured, buttressed at base. Lvs to 35×25cm, clustered at the ends of branches, cordate-ovate, sometimes lobed toward apex, shortly acuminate, base cordate or blunt. Fls in terminal or axillary short panicles; cal. *c*2.5cm, rusty-tomentose; males with slender staminal column, with a single row of 8 erect anth.; female without staminal column; staminodes 8, alternating with carpels. Fr. 5 or fewer follicles, to 12×10cm on 10cm woody stalk, laterally compressed, pubesc.; seeds 6×2.5cm including the wing, numerous. Tropical Asia.

For synonymy see *Sterculia*.

**Ptilomeris** Nutt.
***P. coronaria*** Nutt. See *Lasthenia coronaria*.

**Ptilopteris** Hance. Pteridaceae (Adiantaceae). (From Gk *ptilos*, down, and *pteris*, fern.) 1 species, a fern. Rhizomes ascending, short, clad with persistent old stipe bases. Stipes 6–20cm, 2mm diam., lustrous brown. Fronds 20–50×2–4cm, evergreen, slender, linear-lanceolate, contracted at base, long-attenuate at apex, pinnate, membranous, sparsely brown scurfy beneath when young; pinnae 10–25×3–7mm, numerous, spreading, broadly lanceolate, obtuse at apex, obliquely cuneate and auriculate at base, obtusely dentate, lower smaller and deflexed, gradually reduced upwards, sessile; veins pinnate, short, oblique. Sori intramarginal, solitary on teeth, sometimes somewhat incurved on margin; indusia wanting. Japan, China, Taiwan.

CULTIVATION See FERNS, the hardy species.

***P. maximowiczii*** (Bak.) Hance. As for the genus.

For synonymy see *Monachosorum*.

**Ptilostemon** Cass. Compositae. (From Gk *ptilon*, down, and *stema*, stamen.) About 14 species of annual to perennial, spiny herbs or small, unarmed shrubs. Leaves alternate, tufted or rosulate on sterile shoots, lanceolate or linear, entire or pinnatifid, lobes, sometimes nearly glabrous, spiny above, densely white-tomentose beneath. Capitula discoid, in clusters; receptacle hairy; phyllaries imbricate, rigid, with a sharp apical spine; florets hermaphrodite, tubular, purple, rarely white. Fruit an obliquely-obovoid, smooth, woody cypsela; pappus of more or less equal, plumose hairs in several rows. Mediterranean.

CULTIVATION As for *Carduus*.

***P. afer*** (Jacq.) Greuter. Usually bienn., to 1m. Stem white-tomentose to nearly glabrous. Lvs oblong-lanceolate, more or less glabrous above, pinnatifid, seg. 2–3, lobes narrowly triangular, with spines to 15mm. Capitula 4–20, in a terminal corymb or cylindric raceme; involucre 20–50×35–45mm, campanulate; outer phyllaries with 0–4 basal, 3–6mm marginal spines and a stout, deflexed, apical spine, more or less erect on middle phyllaries; florets to 3cm. Fr. to 5mm; pappus 1.5–*c*2cm. C & S Balkans. Z5.

***P. casabonae*** (L.) Greuter. Perenn. herb to 1.5m. Stem sparsely hairy to glabrescent. Lvs lanceolate to linear-lanceolate, more or less entire, apex triangular-acuminate, margin with unequal, slender spines to 1.5cm, in clusters of 2–7. Capitula numerous, more or less sessile, in a terminal spike; involucre 16–24mm, cylindric-campanulate; phyllaries with apical spine; florets 18–22mm. Fr. 3–4mm; pappus 13–18mm. W Mediterranean.

For synonymy see *Carduus* and *Cnicus*.

**Ptilotrichum** C.A. Mey.
***P. lapeyrousianum*** (Jordan) Jordan. See *Alyssum lapeyrousianum*.
***P. peyrousianum*** Willk. See *Alyssum lapeyrousianum*.
***P. purpureum*** (Lagasca & Rodr.) Boiss. See *Alyssum purpureum*.
***P. pyrenaica*** (Lapeyr.) Boiss. See *Alyssum pyrenaicum*.
***P. spinosa*** (L.) Boiss. See *Alyssum spinosum*.

**Ptilotus** R. Br. (From Gk *ptilotos*, winged, referring to the membranous bracts.) Amaranthaceae. Some 100 species of annual or perennial herbs and shrubs. Stems and branches glabrous, finely pubescent or tomentose. Leaves cauline, alternate, narrow, rarely obovate or fleshy. Flowers bisexual, in dense, globular, ovoid or cylindric, shaggy spikes, often in compound corymbs, bright white, yellow, green, mauve, pink and purple; bracts and 2 bracteoles membranous, ovate and often pilose, persistent; perianth a short tube of 5 villous bipartite segments, glabrous or woolly inside; stamens 5, 1–3 sterile or rudimentary, fused into a fringed or toothed cup; ovary subsessile or stalked; style simple and persistent; stigma minute. Fruit a small, 1-seeded utricle. Australasia. Z9.

CULTIVATION Grown for their densely flowered floral heads, which often have a shaggy clover-like appearance, with long white hairs in *P. manglesii*, *Ptilotus* spp. are attractive plants for the border or rock garden. *P. manglesii* is sometimes grown as an annual for bedding. Their cold tolerance, to between −5°C/23°F and −10°C/14°F, is severely compromised by their intolerance of winter wet, but they can be grown in the cold glasshouse or alpine house. Grow in a high-fertility loam-based mix with additional sand, in direct sunlight with good ventilation, watering plentifully when in growth and reducing to keep almost dry after flowering. Propagate by root cuttings in sand with bottom heat; seed is often infertile or slow to germinate.

***P. exaltatus*** Nees. PINK MULLA MULLA. Tender annual or perenn., stout, erect, to 1m; stems glabrous, branching or simple from woody rhiz. Lvs thick, apiculate, oblong-lanceolate, undulate, bright blue-green, tinged red, to 8cm, petiolate. Spikes conical to cylindric with age, to 15×5cm, yellow tinged pink; bracts 9–10mm, brown, pilose; bracteoles white, midrib brown; perianth to 2cm, purple, villous outside, 3 inner seg. woolly inside with stramineous apices; stamens unequal, 1–3 sterile; stigma brown; style eccentric; ovary stalked and pilose above. Winter–summer. Australia.

***P. manglesii*** (Lindl.) F. Muell. Decumbent to ascending perenn. or annual. Stems to 30cm. Lvs obtuse or acute, basal, ovate to linear, lower lvs to 8cm, petiolate, upper lvs smaller, sessile. Spikes globular or ovoid, villous, pink to violet-purple, to 10×6cm; tepals protruding from white articulate hairs; bracts dark brown when young; style eccentric. Summer. Australia.

***P. spathulatus*** (R. Br.) Poir. PUSSYTAILS; CAT'S PAWS. Low procumbent perenn.; stems numerous, to 40cm, rising from stout rhiz., 24×1.8cm. Lvs fleshy, basal lvs to 10cm, spathulate to ovate, petiolate, stems lvs narrow, subsessile. Spikes cylindric, solitary or clustered, yellow, green or golden, 12×2.2–2.7mm; bracts brown; bracteoles transparent, 3.5–10mm; perianth to 14mm with yellow hairs, seg. green with pink tips, glabrous inside. Winter–summer. Australia.

***P. stirlingii*** (Lindl.) F. Muell. Procumbent to ascending, to 1m. Stems striate. Lvs 1.5–3cm, lanceolate to linear, undulate, lower lvs petiolate, upper lvs acute, sessile. Spikes globular, solitary or in panicles, 2.5cm across; fls deep pink to mauve; perianth seg. pink, feathery. Summer. W Australia.

For synonymy see *Trichinium*.

**Ptychosperma** Labill. (From Gk *ptyche*, a fold, and *sperma*, seed, referring to the folded albumen of the seed.) Palmae. Some 30 species of solitary or clump-forming, unarmed, monoecious palms. Stems slender, smooth, ringed. Crownshaft distinct. Leaves pinnate; sheath tubular; petioles slender, scaly to woolly; pinnae slender-pointed, jagged or entire at tip, with thickened marginal veins. Inflorescences below leaves, enclosed in bud by 2 large overlapping bracts; flowers borne in triads (2 male, 1 female) along lower part of rachillae, with only male flowers, solitary or paired, along upper part; male flowers ovoid with sepals 3, overlapping, petals 3, valvate, stamens to 100 or more, pistillode mostly ovoid-attenuate, sterile; female flowers with 3 overlapping sepals, petals 3, overlapping, staminodes minute, sterile, pistil 1-celled with 1 ovule, stigmas 3. Fruit globose to ellipsoid, red, orange or purple-black, with thin endocarp; seed longitudinally 5-grooved, with homogeneous endosperm. Australia and New Guinea to Solomon Is. and Micronesia.

CULTIVATION See PALMS.

***P. elegans*** (R. Br.) Bl. ALEXANDER PALM; SOLITAIRE PALM. Stems slender, solitary, ringed, to 12m. Crownshaft distinct, woolly. Lvs to 2.5m; petioles to 30cm; pinnae to 60cm, regularly arranged, more or less toothed or notched at apex. Infl. below lvs, with numerous branches; fls green-white. Fr. bright red. NE Australia.

***P. macarthurii*** H.A. Wendl. Stems to 7m, slender, clumped, smooth, grey-ringed. Crownshaft smooth, green, woolly. Lvs to 2m, arched; pinnae regularly arranged, broad, apically toothed. Infl. below lvs; fls cream. Fr. red. New Guinea.

***P. propinquum*** (Becc.) Becc. Stems to 8m, slender, smooth, conspicuously ringed. Crownshaft green-brown. Lvs to 1m; petioles 30cm; scaly; pinnae irregularly arranged in groups of 2–3, apically notched. Infl. to 40cm; fls cream. Fr. red. Aru Is.

***P. salomonense*** Burret. Stems to 6m. Lvs *c*1.2m. Fls brown. Fr. orange-red. New Guinea.

***P. sanderianum*** Ridl. Stems clumped, conspicuously ringed, to 4m. Crownshaft green-brown. Lvs to 1.2m; petioles to 20cm; pinnae long, narrow, regularly arranged, apically concave and toothed. Fls cream. Fr. red. New Guinea.

***P. waitianum*** Essig. Stems solitary, to 4.5m. Lvs to 75cm; pinnae regularly arranged, coarsely toothed, apically concave. Fls brown-black. Fr. black. New Guinea.

***P. alexandrae*** F.J. Muell. See *Archontophoenix alexandrae*.
***P. cunninghamiana*** H.A. Wendl. See *Archontophoenix cunninghamiana*.
For further synonymy see *Actinophloeus, Seaforthia* and *Strongylocaryum*.

**Pückler-Muskau, Hermann**, Prince of (1785–1871). Writer and landscape gardener. Born at Muskau, a small province now on the German–Polish border, he inherited the title and estate in 1811. His lifelong passion was for what he called '*parkomanie*', an obsessive love for trees and parks: the very sight of a tree being felled distressed him. Both the park and castle had been neglected and Pückler-Muskau resolved to remodel the estate, apparently encouraged by Goethe. After a trip to England in 1815, he set about planting trees and renovating the castle. A second visit to England trip enabled him to study the great landscape gardens of England and he was particularly impressed by Repton's work, finding Brown's 'often crude, angular and uncouth'.

Pückler-Muskau expended considerable money and energy at Muskau. He employed K.F. Schinkel for the architectural work on the castle and purchased an additional 1200 acres of land. Part of the river Neisse was diverted to create a lake around the castle, which required the removal of an entire street in Muskau and the destruction of the old fortifications. He laid out many flower beds, including carpet beds, and created woodland areas from fully grown trees. There were also a Blue Garden for the sole display of white and blue flowers. In his book *Andeutungen über Landschaftsgärtnerei* (1834) he states that his desire at Muskau was 'to utilize what was already there, to elevate and enrich in the same spirit, but not to violate its locality and history'. Hence although he made considerable changes, Pückler-Muskau maintained the villages and supported the local industries. Muskau became a notable beauty spot and attracted many important visitors, though the Prince was always selective and unwanted guests were driven briskly round the park in an oval-wheeled phaeton.

Shortage of funds forced Pückler-Muskau to sell the estate to Prince Frederik of the Netherlands in 1845. He then moved to the smaller estate of Branitz, near Cottbus, another family property, where he again set about improvements to the castle and park, employing Gottfried Semper for the former. His renown as a landscape architect was now such that he was asked to advise on a number of other projects. The Prince and Princess of Prussia required him for the planning of Babelsburg and he was also consulted over parks at Hanover and Weimar. Napoleon III asked for his advice over the remodelling of the Bois de Boulogne in Paris, then being directed by Baron Haussmann.

Pückler-Muskau died at Branitz and was buried in a huge pyramid he had had erected in a lake. He wrote various books throughout his lifetime, many of them based on his travels to Europe, Asia and America, the first being *Briefe eines Verstorbene* (4 vols, 1830–31). His pupil, Eduard Petzold, helped spread the Prince's ideas through his own work and books.

**Pueraria** DC. (For M.N. Puerari (1766–1845), professor at Copenhagen.) Leguminosae (Papilionoideae). Some 20 species of herbaceous or woody twiners. Leaves trifoliolate or, rarely, pinnate; leaflets large, ovate or rhomboid, entire or sinuately lobed, stipellate. Inflorescences long, axillary, or clustered as racemes at branch ends; flowers blue or purple; standard obovate or round, auricles inflexed; bracts small or narrow, caducous. Fruit 2-valved, linear, flat, dehiscent. SE Asia, Japan. Z5.

CULTIVATION *P. lobata* is a deciduous twiner with dense foliage and long racemes of fragrant pea-flowers, and is particularly useful as a rapidly growing screen, providing temporary cover for buildings and fences, or, if unsupported, as groundcover. In good soils growth may exceed 15m/50ft during the season as is evinced by its performance in the SE US, where it was at first planted as a fodder plant and erosion-control but has now become a pernicious weed. In areas where winter temperatures fall much below −15°C/5°F, *P. lobata* may be grown as an annual; given adequate protection at the roots, however, it will re-sprout from the base in spring if cut down by frost. Grow in full sun in well-drained soils, training the young stems to cover the support. Prune in spring, if necessary, to control spread. Propagate from seed in spring, sown singly in pots in the warm glasshouse; plant out when the danger of frost has passed.

***P. lobata*** (Willd.) Ohwi. JAPANESE ARROWROOT; KUDZU VINE. Woody, hairy-stemmed vine to 20m; root tuberous. Leaflets entire or slightly lobed, central leaflet 14–18cm, lateral leaflets smaller, pubesc.; petiole 10–20cm. Infl. an axillary or terminal raceme, erect, to 25cm; fls to 1.5cm, purple; cal. 5-toothed; pet. 5, nearly regular; stamens 10, monadelphous. Fr. 4–9×0.6–1.5cm, hirsute. Autumn. China, Japan.

***P. thunbergiana*** (Sieb. & Zucc.) Benth. See *P. lobata* (Willd.) Ohwi.

**Pulicaria** Gaertn. FLEABANE. Compositae. About 40 species of erect, annual to perennial herbs. Leaves alternate, simple, usually sessile, cordate, more or less amplexicaul and auriculate. Capitula radiate, occasionally discoid, solitary or arranged in panicles or corymbs; receptacle flat or somewhat convex, naked; involucre hemispherical; phyllaries multiseriate, imbricate; ray florets ligule yellow, in 1–2 series, short and erect or long and spreading; disc florets yellow, tubular, bisexual. Fruit a terete or compressed, ribbed cypsela; pappus of simple hairs surrounded by ring of usually connate scales. Temperate Eurasia and warm S Africa. Z7.

CULTIVATION As for *Inula*.

***P. dysenterica*** (L.) Bernh. Stoloniferous perenn. Stems 20–75cm, branched at least above, lanate or tomentose. Lvs to 6×1.5cm, oblong-lanceolate, sessile, undulate and remotely serrate, green and scabrid above, grey-tomentose below, lower lvs petiolate, withered at anthesis. Capitula few or numerous, 15–30mm diam., in corymbs; peduncles to 25mm; bracts few or absent; involucre to 15mm diam., phyllaries in 4–5 series, 3–5mm, linear to subulate, glandular; ray florets patent, exceeding involucre by 5–7mm. Fr. to 1.5mm, pubesc. Summer–early autumn. Europe, N Africa.

For synonymy see *Inula*.

**Pulmonaria** L. LUNGWORT. (From Lat. *pulmonarius*, suffering from lung disease, referring to the spotted lvs of *P. officinalis*, which resemble diseased lungs.) Boraginaceae. Some 14 species of perennial herbs, pubescent. Rhizome creeping. Stems simple. Leaves simple, green, sometimes spotted white, basal lvs long-petiolate, cauline lvs alternate, few. Inflorescence of terminal, forked cymes, bracteate; flowers white, pink, blue or purple; calyx 5-lobed; corolla 5-lobed, infundibular, throat with 5 tufts of hairs,

**Pulmonaria** (×0.5) (a) *P. angustifolia* (b) *P. angustifolia* 'Rubra' (c) *P. montana* (d) *P. affinis* (e) *P. montana* cv., corolla, LS (f) *P. officinalis*, calyx detached, corolla, LS (g) *P. longifolia* (h) *P. stiriaca* (i) *P. saccharata*

faucal scales absent; stamens 5, included, inserted in throat or mid-tube; style included, stigma capitate or slightly bifid. Nutlets 4, smooth, ovoid, glabrescent to pubescent, with a basal annulus. Europe, Asia. Z4.

CULTIVATION *Pulmonaria* spp. occur in shaded sites on deep soils rich in organic matter; *P. officinalis* is generally found over limestone, *P. angustifolia* on acid soils in woodland and meadow, *P. longifolia* on heavy clay soils. They are tolerant and slowly growing groundcover for open woodland and border edging, suited to plantings in the sunless shade of buildings, and in the wild garden a valuable early nectar source for honey bees, especially in massed plantings. *P. angustifolia* may be naturalized in meadow, with the first cut in late summer. *P. saccharata, P. rubra* and *P.* 'Sissinghurst White' are semi-evergreen, forming small overwintering rosettes.

Grow in part to full shade in moist, humus-rich soils; in zones with cool summers *P. saccharata* may be grown in full sun, provided that the soil remains adequately moist throughout summer. Remove faded blooms and divide vigorous clumps every 4–5 years. Species hybridize freely and may not come true from seed; divide in autumn or after flowering.

***P. affinis*** Jordan. Lvs to 18×9cm, green spotted white, with short and long setae, glandular-pubesc., rough; petiole to 1.8cm, narrowly winged. Infl. glandular-pubesc., setose; cor. purple to blue-violet, tube interior glabrous below. Nutlets to 4×2.5mm. Europe.

***P. angustifolia*** L. Herb to 30cm, setose. Lvs to 40×5cm, green, unspotted, setose; basal lvs linear-lanceolate to oblong-lanceolate, base attenuate; cauline lvs linear-lanceolate to linear-elliptic, sessile. Infl. setose, sparingly glandular; fls bright blue; cal. short, slender; cor. tube interior glabrous below. Nutlets to 4.5×3.5mm. Europe. 'Azurea': to 25cm; lvs dark green; fls brightest blue, tinted red in bud. 'Beth's Blue': to 25cm; lvs fresh green, faintly spotted; fls rich blue. 'Beth's Pink': to 25cm; lvs broad, spotted; fls coral red. 'Blaues Meer': fls large, gentian blue. 'Johnson's Blue': habit small, to 20cm; fls blue. 'Munstead Blue': habit low, to 15cm; lvs small, dark green; fls clear blue, early-flowering. 'Rubra': to 25cm; fls soft red, early spring. 'Variegata': lvs narrow, variegated white. Z3.

***P. longifolia*** (Bast.) Boreau. Lvs to 50×6cm, green, usually spotted white, setose and sparingly glandular above, unequally setose and glandular beneath, narrowly lanceolate, base attenuate. Infl. long-setose, sparingly glandular-pubesc.; cor. violet to blue-violet, tube interior glabrous below. Nutlets to 4×3mm. Europe. 'Bertram Anderson': lvs long and narrow, spotted silver; fls vivid blue. 'Lewis Palmer': to 35cm; lvs wide, faintly spotted; fls soft blue faintly tinted pink, profuse. 'Mournful Purple' ('Mourning Widow', 'Mournful Widow'): fls elongated lanceolate, broad (twice normal size), faintly spotted silver; fls purple. 'Patrick Bates': lvs well spotted; fls dusky mauve. Z6.

***P. montana*** Lej. Herb to 45cm, soft-pubesc. Lvs to 50×12.5cm, green, usually unspotted, ovate to elliptic-lanceolate, base attenuate, unequally setose and sparingly glandular-pubesc. above, acuminate. Infl. densely setose, glandular-pubesc.; cor. violet to blue, tube interior glabrous below. Nutlets to 4.5×3.5mm. Europe. 'Albocorollata': to 30cm; lvs pale green; fls pure white, early spring. 'Bowles' Red': lvs spotted white; fls coral red. 'David Ward': to 30cm; lvs long, pale green edged in white, forms rosettes; fls coral red. 'Barfield Pink': to 30cm; lvs soft green; fls brick red, edged and veined in white. 'Red Start': to 40cm; lvs fresh green; fls large, pale red. Z6.

***P. officinalis*** L. JERUSALEM SAGE. Herb to 30cm, rough-pubesc. Lvs to 16×10cm, green spotted white, setose; basal lvs ovate, cordate, petiole 5–15cm; cauline lvs ovate, cordate-auriculate, sessile. Infl. setose and glandular-pubesc.; cor. red to rose-violet or blue, tube interior glabrous below. Nutlets to 4×3mm. Europe. 'Alba': fls white. 'Bowles' Blue': fls very pale blue. 'Brentor': lvs lightly spotted silver; fls magenta. 'Cambridge' ('Cambridge Blue'): to 30cm; lvs heart-shaped, spotted; fls pale blue, tinted pink in bud, profuse. 'White Wings': to 30cm; fls white, eye pink, late-flowering. Z6.

***P. saccharata*** Mill. JERUSALEM SAGE. Herb to 45cm, setose. Lvs to 27×10cm, green, usually spotted white, long-setose, glandular-pubesc.; basal lvs elliptic, acuminate, base attenuate; cauline lvs ovate-oblong, sessile or subsessile. Cor. white or red-violet to dark violet, tube interior glabrous below. Nutlets to 4×3mm. Europe. 'Alba': to 30cm; lvs variegated white, forms rosettes; fls large, snow white. 'Argentea': to 30cm; lvs frosted silver. 'Frühlingshimmel' ('Blauhimmel', 'Spring Beauty'): lvs spotted; fls pale sky blue, cal. purple. 'Highdown': to 30cm, vigorous; lvs frosted silver; fls rich blue, nodding. 'Leopard': lvs spotted white; fls red tinted pink. 'Margery Fish': lvs spotted silver, fading to white; fls pink tinted blue. 'Mies Stam': lvs spotted silvery; fls soft carmine pink tinted lilac, profuse. 'Mrs Moon': lvs well spotted in silver; fls lilac tinted red. 'Pink Dawn': lvs spotted silver; fls deep pink. 'Reginald Kaye':

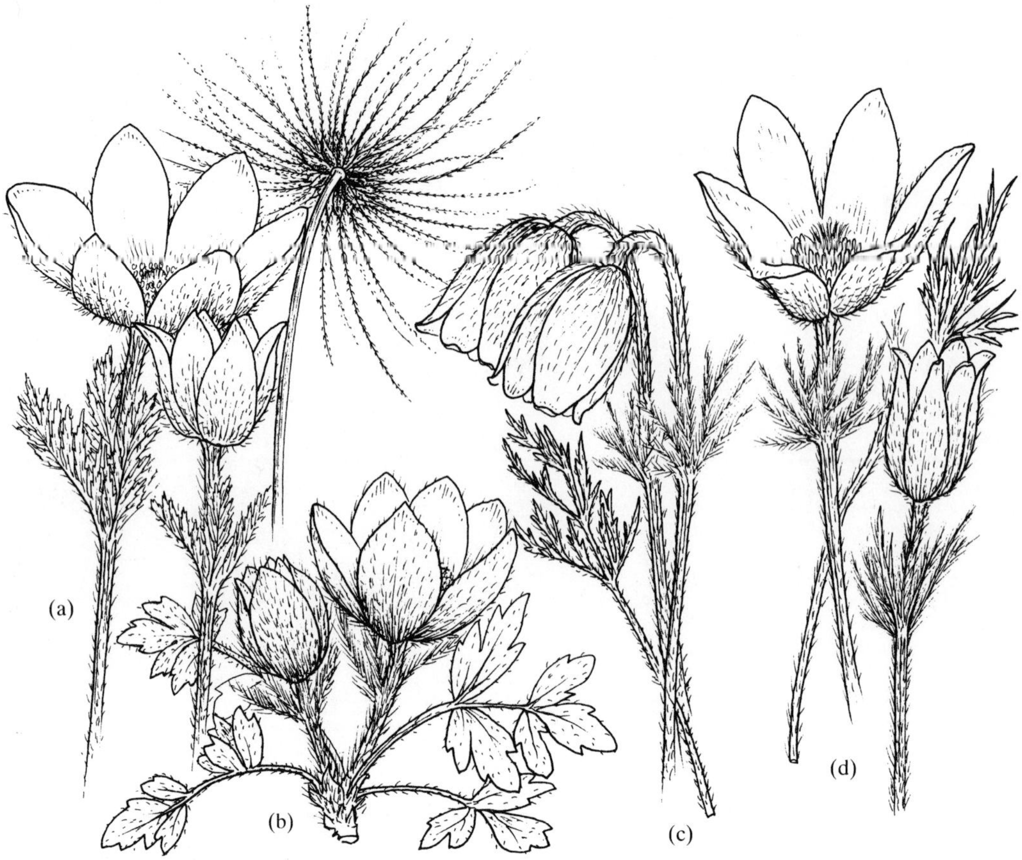

**Pulsatilla** (× 1) (a) *P. alpina* (b) *P. pratensis* (c) *P. vulgaris* (d) *P. vernalis*

to 30cm; lvs spotted silver at border and central patch. 'Sissinghurst White': to 30cm, vigorous; lvs large, well spotted; fls white, early-flowering. 'Tim's Silver': to 30cm high; lvs silver sheened except for rim; fls mid blue. Z3.

***P. stiriaca*** A. Kerner. Lvs to 22×8cm, green spotted white, unequally setose and glandular-pubesc. above, base attenuate; petiole to 12cm. Infl. short-setose, long-glandular-pubesc; cor. bright blue, tube interior puberulent below. Nutlets to 3×2mm. Europe. Z5.

***P.* cultivars**. 'Beth Chatto': habit tall; lvs well spotted; fls dark blue. 'Blue Ensign': to 30cm; lvs broad, dark green; fls large, rich blue. 'Blue Mist': lvs well spotted; fls palest clear blue. 'Glacier': to 30cm; lvs spotted; fls palest blue, occasionally pink or white. 'Mawson's Blue': to 40cm; lvs deep green, low; fls gentian blue, in tall sprays, later-flowering. 'Weetwood Blue': fls clear true blue.

***P. alpina*** Torr. See *Mertensia alpina*.
***P. azurea*** Besser. See *P. angustifolia*.
***P. ciliata*** James. See *Mertensia ciliata*.
***P. lanceolata*** Pursh. See *Mertensia lanceolata*.
***P. maculata*** Dietr. See *P. officinalis*.
***P. maritima*** L. See *Mertensia maritima*.
***P. mollis*** C.F. Wolff ex Heller. See *P. montana*.
***P. oblongifolia*** Nutt. See *Mertensia oblongifolia*.
***P. paniculata*** Ait. See *Mertensia paniculata*.
***P. rubra*** Schott. See *P. montana*.
***P. suffruticosa*** L. See *Moltkia suffruticosa*.
***P. virginica*** L. See *Mertensia virginica*.

**Pulsatilla** Mill. Ranunculaceae. 30 species of perennial herbs forming tufted clumps; rootstock somewhat woody. Leaves in a basal rosette or forming an involucre below the flowers, sessile or shortly petiolate, basal lvs more numerous, larger, pinnately or palmately dissected. Flowers borne singly, upright or nodding; perianth wide-spreading, reflexed or campanulate, perianth segments usually 6, rarely 5–8, petal-like, exterior with silky hairs; stamens abundant in a central boss surrounded by a ring of nectar secreting staminodes; carpels many in a globular head; ovules 1; styles long, retained in the fruiting stage, becoming elongated and plume-like. Distinguished from *Anemone* by nectar-secreting staminodes and feathery styles. Eurasia, N America.

CULTIVATION Mostly natives of alpine meadow, where they appear soon after snow melt, the genus also includes *P. vulgaris*, the Pasque flower of British chalk downland flora. All have the characteristic sheen of silken hair – silvery in *P. vulgaris* and *P. halleri*, tawny in *P. vernalis* – and are as decorative in seed as in flower. All are tolerant of alkaline soil. Large plants have a deep woody rootstock and transplant poorly. Plant out young pot-grown specimens in full sun, in humus-rich, gritty, well-drained soils, and leave undisturbed.

***P. alba*** Rchb. Short hairy perenn. Basal lvs long-stalked, bipinnate, hairy at first, becoming subglabrous, stem lvs short-stalked. Fls bowl-shaped, 2.5–4.5cm diam., white sometimes flushed blue. C Europe. Z5.

***P. albana*** (Steven) Bercht. & Presl. Close to *P. pratensis*. 5–18cm at anthesis, to 30cm in fr. Basal lvs 2.5–6cm, oblong in outline, bipinnatisect with 3–4 pairs of primary seg., secondary seg. deeply pinnate, lobes lanceolate or linear, subobtuse, entire or slightly incised-dentate, villous, especially beneath; involucral lvs to 30cm, linear, subacute. Fls nodding, campanulate with base narrow, to 2.5cm, perianth seg. oblong-elliptic with apex reflexed, yellow, exterior densely adpressed-sericeous; stamens included. Achenes with awn to 2.5cm. USSR (Caucasus), NE Turkey. var. ***andina*** Rupr. Fls suberect; perianth seg. wide spreading, yellow, becoming red after pollination. var. ***georgica*** Rupr. Lf seg. very narrow. Fls pale pink-lilac or pale lilac, sometimes white within. var. ***violacea*** (Rupr.) Asch. & Gräbn. Fls white, flushed blue. Z5.

***P. alpina*** (L.) Delarb. ALPINE PASQUE FLOWER. 20–45cm. Basal lvs long-stalked, bipinnate, terminal seg. strongly incised almost to the midrib, lobes often reflexed; stem lvs short-stalked. Fls erect or almost so, 4–6cm diam., white flushed blue-purple outside; perianth seg. ovate, covered with silky hairs. C Europe (mts). ssp. ***apiifolia*** (Scop.) Nyman. Fls pale yellow. Z5.

***P. armena*** (Boiss.) Rupr. Close to *P. pratensis*. 5–10cm at anthesis, to 20cm in fr. Basal lvs 1.5–4cm, ovate in outline, densely white-hairy, as are petioles and stems, bipinnatisect, secondary seg. deeply pinnate, lobes narrowly linear-oblong, subobtuse or acute; involucral lvs to 2.5cm, divided to middle or beyond, usually incised. Fls nodding to suberect, campanulate, to 3.5cm, perianth seg. oblong, apex acute, not recurved, purple-lilac, exterior densely white-villous; stamens included. Achenes are awns to 2.5cm. Caucasus, Transcaucasia. Z5.

***P. aurea*** (Somm. & Levier) Juz. Resembling *P. alpina*. 6–35cm at anthesis, to 50cm in fr. Basal lvs long-petiolate, ternate with seg. ovate, pinnatisect, long-petiolulate, secondary seg. pinnate, lobes acute, deeply incised, glabrous above, pilose on main veins beneath; involucral lvs 3, like basal lvs but smaller with short broad petioles. Peduncle long, tomentose; fls suberect, 3.5–6cm diam., perianth seg. 6, to 3×2cm, ovate, golden-yellow, exterior adpressed-pilose. Achene with awn to 0.5cm. Caucasus, Transcaucasia. Z6.

***P. bungeana*** C.A. Mey. 1.5–5cm at anthesis, to 8cm in fr. Basal lvs oblong in outline, pinnatisect, with secondary seg. entire or dentate, subobtuse, rather broad, somewhat pilose; involucral lvs 3-lobed at apex, lobules short, entire or incised. Fls erect, campanulate, not opening widely, blue-violet, perianth seg. to 1.5×0.7cm. Achene with awn to 1.5cm. Siberia, Altai Mts. Z5.

***P. cernua*** (Thunb.) Bercht. & Presl. Close to *P. dahurica*. 4–20cm at anthesis. Basal lvs oblong-ovate in outline, pinnatisect with 2 pairs sessile lateral leaflets, terminal leaflet petiolulate, all broad-rhombic, deeply 2–3-lobed, secondary seg. short, ovate-lanceolate, incised or dentate, sparsely hairy above, densely hairy beneath. Peduncles densely tomentose, usually curved; fls pendulous, not opening widely, bright violet-red or dark purple-brown, perianth seg. to 3.5×1.2cm, exterior densely grey-villous. Japan, Korea, China (Manchuria). Z5.

***P. chinensis*** (Bunge) Reg. 7–25cm at anthesis, to 50cm in fruit. Basal lvs long-petiolate, broad-ovate or cordate in outline, ternate, seg. deeply 2–3-lobed, lobules rounded, coarsely dentate, sparsely adpressed pilose above, densely so beneath; involucral lvs deeply 3-lobed, lobes oblong, obtuse. Peduncles tomentose; fls erect, blue-lilac or violet, perianth seg. 2.5–4.5×1–1.3cm, subacute, hairy externally. Achenes with awns 4–6cm. NE Asia (China, Japan, E Russia). Z6.

***P. dahurica*** (Fisch.) Spreng. 15–40cm at anthesis. Basal lvs oblong-ovate in outline, pinnatisect, with 2 distant pairs of narrow-rhombic, sessile or short-petiolulate seg., terminal seg. broader, petiolulate, all 2–3-lobed, with secondary seg. cuneate, incised into linear-lanceolate, acute to subobtuse, entire or dentate lobules, very sparsely hairy above, densely pilose beneath; involucral lvs with lobes oblong-linear, incised or dentate at apex. Peduncle sparsely tomentose; fls pendulous, blue-violet, perianth seg. to 3×1.2cm. Achene with awn to 5cm, flexuous. NE Asia (China, Japan, E Russia). Z6.

***P. flavescens*** (Zucc.) Juz. Closely related to *P. patens*, but fls to 8cm diam., sulphur-yellow, occasionally flushed blue without; seed rarely fertile. Late spring. Urals to C Asia. Z5.

***P. halleri*** (All.) Willd. To 15cm at anthesis. Stems elongating to 45cm in fruit. Basal lvs densely hairy at first, often remaining so until autumn, lvs pinnately divided into 3–5 seg., the apical lobe with a long petiolule, lobes oblong-lanceolate, further pinnately dissected half way to the midrib; involucral lvs sessile, connate. Fls erect or nearly so, 4–9cm diam., campanulate or shallowly bell-shaped, violet-purple to lavender blue, very variable. Late spring–early summer. C & SE Europe, USSR (Crimea). ssp. ***halleri***. Stems usually exceeding 5cm in fl. Basal lvs 3–7cm, usually pinnately dissected into 5 primary lobes, usually less than 50 lobes in all, more or less woolly. Fls dark violet. SW & C Alps. Forms with laciniate pet. are now being cultivated, as well as others with semi-double fls. ssp. ***rhodopaea*** K. Krause. Stems to 5cm in fl. Basal lvs with 50–100 lobes, densely woolly. Yugoslavia, S Bulgaria, N Greece. ssp. ***slavica*** (Reuss) Zam. Stems usually exceeding 5cm in fl. Basal lvs pinnately dissected into 3 primary divisions, lvs usually with less than 50 lobes, more or less woolly. Fls dark violet. W Carpathians. ssp. ***styriaca*** (Pritz.) Zam. Stems usually exceeding 5cm in fl. Basal lvs 5–11cm, pinnately dissected into 5 primary divisions, lvs usually with less than 50 lobes, more or less woolly. SE Austria. ssp. ***taurica*** (Juz.) K. Krause. Stems to 5cm in fl. Basal lvs with 50–100 lobes, primary lobes of basal lvs usually sessile, densely woolly. USSR (Crimea). Z5.

***P. montana*** (Hoppe) Rchb. To 15cm in fl., to 45cm in fr. Basal lvs 3-parted, leaflets further finely cut, forming *c*150 lobes, pubesc.; stem lvs sessile, connate, less dissected, lobes *c*25; fls pendant, 3–4cm, bell-shaped, blue-purple to dark violet; perianth seg. to twice the length of the stamens, spreading but not recurved. SW Switzerland, E Romania, Bulgaria. Z6.

***P. occidentalis*** (Wats.) Freyn. Resembling *P. alpina*. 10–60cm. Basal lvs 4–8cm wide, ternate, with seg. bipinnate, lobes linear to lanceolate-linear, long-sericeous; petioles 3–10cm; involucral lvs solitary, very shortly petiolate, or sessile. Fls erect, white or cream-white, exterior sometimes flushed purple or blue, perianth seg. 5–8, 2–3cm, oblong to ovate, exterior villous. Achene with awn 2–3.5cm. N America (mts of British Columbia, Washington, Oregon, California, N Idaho, Montana). Z4.

***P. patens*** (L.) Mill. EASTERN PASQUE FLOWER. Short hairy perenn.; stems 8–15cm in fl., to 45cm in fr. Basal lvs round-cordate in outline, palmately lobed, each lobe further divided into 2–3 linear-lanceolate, toothed seg., coriaceous, covered with spreading hairs when young, becoming glabrous; involucral lvs erect, lobes narrow-linear, hairy. Fls erect, 5–8cm diam., blue-violet or lilac, exterior yellow or white, with spreading hairs; perianth seg. 6, narrow-ovate, acute, spreading; stamens short, yellow. Achenes with awns to 5cm. Spring–early summer. N Europe, USSR (Siberia, N America). Z4.

***P. pratensis*** (L.) Mill. Stem lvs with *c*30 lobes. Stems to 12cm, to 45cm in fr. Basal lvs usually 3× pinnate, each lobe further cut, forming *c*150 lobes. Fls 3–4cm diam., narrow-campanulate, pale or dark purple to purple-green, perianth seg. recurved at tip, scarcely exceeding stamens, exterior thickly hairy. Spring–early summer. C & E Europe (to Denmark and S Norway). ssp. ***nigricans*** (Stork) A. Kerner Perianth seg. to 3cm, black-violet, outward curved. N & C Europe. ssp. ***hungarica*** Soó. Fls pale yellow. S Europe. Z5.

***P. rubra*** (Lam.) Delarb. Resembles *P. pratensis*. Stem lvs with only 20 lobes. Fls dark red-purple, brown-red or black-red, rarely dark violet; perianth seg. 2.5× length of the stamens. Spring–early summer. C & S France, C & E Spain. ssp. ***hispanica*** Zimm. ex Asch. & Gräbn. Fls black-violet or purple violet; lvs appearing with fls. Spain. Z6.

***P. turczaninowii*** Krylov & Sergiewskaja. 5–35cm. Basal lvs ovate in outline, 4–14cm, bipinnate, primary seg. in 3 pairs with long petiolules, secondary seg. divided into narrowly linear lobes; involucral lvs deeply lobed. Fls suberect, not opening fully, blue-violet, perianth seg. 2.5–3.5cm, exterior adpressed pilose. Achene with awn to 4cm. Siberia, NE Asia. Z6.

***P. vernalis*** (L.) Mill. Stems to 15cm in fl., to 45cm in fr. Basal lvs evergreen, pinnately divided into 3–5-seg., seg. oblong, toothed, glabrous or nearly so; stem lvs sessile, connate. Fls pendent in bud, becoming erect, 4–6cm, campanulate, covered with bright brown silky hairs outside; perianth seg. 6, acute, white, outer seg. usually strongly flushed pink or violet-blue outside, inner seg. paler; stamens yellow-green. Spring–summer. Europe (mts from Scandinavia to S Spain, eastwards to Bulgaria), Siberia. Z4.

***P. vulgaris*** Mill. PASQUE FLOWER. Stem 3–12cm, to 45cm in fr. Basal lvs covered in silky hairs at first, later becoming glabrous or nearly so, each lf pinnately dissected into 7–9 lobes, the seg. further divided 2–3× almost to the midrib, lobes linear-lanceolate; stem lvs sessile, silky-haired, connate. Fls erect or slightly pendent, 4–9cm diam., bell-shaped or narrowly campanulate, pale or dark violet, rarely white; perianth seg. acute, to 3× length of stamens. Spring–early summer. GB and W France to Sweden, eastwards to Ukraine. 'Alba': fls white. 'Albacyanea': fls blue-white. 'Bartons Pink': lvs pale green; fls a true clean pink. 'Gotlandica': 30cm, fls purple, large. 'Ena Constance': dwarf, fls deep red, later than other cvs. 'Mallenderi': fls deep purple. 'Mrs Van der Elst': the first pink variety, perhaps no longer in cultivation. 'Rode Klokke' ('Rote Glocke'): fls deep red. 'Rubra': fls rust red to red-purple. 'Weisser Schwan' ('White Swan'): fls white. Many of the darker cultivars may be hybrids of *P. montana* × *P. halleri*. ssp. ***vulgaris***. Basal lvs very dissected, with over 100 lobes, borne with the fls. Perianth seg. narrow-elliptic. W & C Europe, S Scandinavia. ssp. ***grandis*** (Wender.) Zam. Basal lvs feathery with *c*40, 3–7mm wide lobes, lvs appearing after the fls; stem and involucral lvs densely silky hairy. Fls substantially larger, to 9cm diam.; perianth seg. broadly elliptic. Buds conspicuous, covered with silvery or gold brown hairs. Spring. C Europe, Ukraine. Z5.

***P. andina*** (Rupr.) Woron. See *P. alpina* var. *apiifolia*.
***P. grandis*** Wender. See *P. vulgaris* ssp. *grandis*.
***P. hirsutissima*** (Britt.) MacMill. See *P. patens*.
***P. nigricans*** Stork. See *P. pratensis*.
***P. patens*** 'Nuttaliana'. See *P. patens*.
***P. sulphurea*** (DC.) Sweet. See *P. alpina* ssp. *apiifolia*.
For further synonymy see *Anemone*.

**Pultenaea** Sm. (For Dr Richard Pulteney (1730–1807), English botanical historian.) Leguminosae (Papilionoideae). Some 120 species of evergreen shrubs, to 2.5m. Leaves mostly alternate, rarely opposite, simple. Flowers axillary and solitary, crowded toward branch tips or in dense heads; calyx 5-lobed, 2 upper lobes joining to lip, often broader than 3 lower lobes; stamens 10, separate. Fruit a legume, small, ovate. Australia, Tasmania. Z9.

CULTIVATION *Pultenaea* spp. grow on stony or sandy hillsides or in damp, coastal grassland. *P. daphnoides* and *P. stipularis* are occasionally grown for their flowers as border shrubs in warm temperate zones that are frost-free or very nearly so. They require a sunny position in well-drained soils. In cooler regions they are suitable for the cool glasshouse. Grow in well-crocked pots of a soilless potting medium with additional sharp sand and water sparingly; maintain a winter minimum temperature of 7–10°C/45–50°F. Propagate from seed or by semi-ripe cuttings in sand in a closed case with bottom heat.

***P. daphnoides*** Wendl. LARGE-LEAF PEA BUSH. Shrub to 2m. Lvs to 4cm, oblanceolate, obtuse, mucronate above, cuneate, glabrous, pale beneath. Fls in dense, sessile heads, surrounded by involucre of lvs, bright yellow with scarlet keels. Summer. Australia.

***P. stipularis*** Wendl. Shrub to 1m. Lvs 2–4×1cm, narrowly linear, pointed, slender, ciliate. Fls 20+, packed in sessile terminal heads to 3cm, yellow. Spring. Australia (NSW).

***P. obcordata*** Andrews. See *P. daphnoides*.

**Pumpkin and squash**. Four *Cucurbita* species contribute to this loose terminology – *C. maxima, C. argyrosperma* (*C. mixta*),

*C. moschata* and *C. pepo*. All are annual herbs which can be bushy but are most often trailing. The cultivated forms are usually separated into summer and autumn/winter groups according to their harvest period. *C. pepo* must be one of the most variable plant species under domestication, and the popular nomenclature of these plants is very confused, probably more so than in any other assemblage of closely related fruits or vegetables. There are a large number of cultivars, some of which go by a variety of names. In general, autumn/winter squashes and pumpkins are fruits eaten (usually baked) when mature, or stored for later use; summer squashes are eaten (usually boiled or fried) when immature, before the rind hardens. The Acorns, Buttercup and Butternut groups are the best eaters, the last with a very small seed cavity. Cultivars loosely called winter squashes, usually white-fleshed, and others called pumpkins, usually orange-fleshed, derive from each of the four species. Pumpkins are usually taken to embrace those cultivars with rather coarse, strong-flavoured flesh, used for pies in the US, for Halloween 'Jack o'lanterns', and for stock feed ('field pumpkins'); some of them grow very large. Besides the fruits, flowers and young shoots are sometimes eaten, and in some cases the seeds (*C. argyroderma*).

*C. maxima* is an plant annual, bushy or trailing plant with large fruits, variable in shape and sometimes with small, raised spots on the fruit surface. Originating in central South America, it is now widely distributed throughout the tropics. Cultivated widely throughout tropical Asia, tropical Africa, Central and South America, particularly Mexico, the Caribbean and the southern states of the US. Plants require a temperature range of about 20–27°C/68–80°F with a fairly low humidity during the growing period but some cultivars may tolerate lower temperatures. Dry periods with a relatively low humidity favour growth; excessive humidity encourages leaf diseases. Most cultivars are relatively insensitive to daylength.

*C. moschata* is an annual vine, with softly hairy leaves and stems and large fruits, variable in shape and size. The centre of origin was tropical South or Central America, possibly Peru or Mexico; now widely distributed throughout the tropics. Cultivated in Southeast Asia, tropical Africa, tropical South and Central America, the Caribbean; probably the most widely grown species of *Cucurbita*. This species is more tolerant of high temperatures than most species of *Cucurbita* and is normally grown in lowland conditions. Moderate rainfall conditions favour growth; the root systems of most cultivars are sensitive to high soil-water levels. Most forms appear to be daylength-neutral.

*C. argyrosperma* is a trailing plant now regarded as distinct from *C. moschata* since it does hybridize with closely related species. Its centre of origin was probably southern Mexico; it is widely grown in Mexico and the southern US, parts of Southeast Asia and Japan. It is tolerant of high temperatures but sensitive to cool conditions, and is daylength-neutral. Moderate rainfall conditions favour growth: plants are sensitive to waterlogging.

*C. pepo* produces both summer squashes, including courgettes or zucchini, and non-keeping winter pumpkins. It also includes the hard-shelled ornamental gourds (not to be confused with bottle gourds, *Lagenaria siceraria*). Plants may be bushy (summer squashes) or trailing or vining (many pumpkins and gourds).

The centre of origin was probably northern Mexico and the southern states of the US; it is now widely distributed in most tropical and subtropical areas and widely cultivated in Southeast Asia, Central Africa, tropical South America and the southern US. Normally grown during the dry season in warm climates, at elevations over 500m/1640ft which experience a moderate rainfall since this crop responds adversely to high temperatures and excessive humidity; some cultivars are well adapted to fairly low temperatures. Most forms are relatively insensitive to daylength.

All pumpkins and squashes are frost-tender annuals grown in much the same way. They are sown directly into the ground in appropriate conditions or can be sown in pots or cell units for easy transplanting, usually needed within two weeks of sowing. In cold climates seed must be sown in warm protected conditions for planting out as soon as danger of frost is past. Plants grow very rapidly and spacing must suit the type of plant and also the cultivar. Bush forms are typically sown on ridges or mounds 60–90cm each way, with 90–120cm between rows, leaving one seeding per station when established. Trailers need to have 120–150cm between plants in rows 2–4m apart. The soil should have a high organic content and can be enriched with well-rotted manure or garden compost. A pH range of 5.5–6.8 is desirable. Many growers plant into black plastic sheet (mulch) in order to eliminate weeds, otherwise almost impossible to deal with. Feeding with a balanced fertilizer at fortnightly intervals is valuable; foliar feeding is necessary for plants in plastic mulch. Irrigation is essential in dry periods but plants should not be waterlogged. Hot weather may reduce the proportion of female to male flowers, and hence cropping, but there is nothing to be done about this.

Those winter cultivars which can be stored are best at 50–60°F/10–16°C. Some growers 'cure' many of these fruits at 70–80°F/21–27°C for 2–3 weeks, which enhances sweetness, but some cultivars deteriorate if this is done. While some cultivars can be stored for 5–6 months – some Japanese ones even longer – the fruits usually start to deteriorate after 2–3 months. The flesh of winter squashes and pumpkins can be frozen after cooking without any loss of quality.

These cucurbits can suffer from sap-sucking insects such as aphids. Powdery mildew is the common pest disease; anthracnose and downy mildew may also attack. Cucumber mosaic is the commonest virus; another serious virus, possibly seed-transmitted, is American yellow zucchini virus. These viruses are transmitted by sap-suckers. Fruits can be ruined by soft rot bacteria, grey mould and other fungi.

SELECTED CULTIVARS. Autumn and Winter cultivars. Acorn type (*C. pepo*): 'Bush Table Queen' (green, ribbed); 'Cream of the Crop' (white); 'Early Acorn Hybrid' (compact); 'Ebony Acorn' (dark green, ribbed); 'Jersey Golden Acorn' (yellow, can be harvested summer when small); 'Royal Acorn' (small, dark green); 'Swan White Acorn' (creamy white, ribbed); 'Table Ace' (small, dark green, prolific); 'Table King' (dark green, keeps well); 'Table Queen' (dark green, keeps well); 'Table Queen' (green, ribbed). Buttercup type (*C. maxima*: usually turban-shaped): 'Burgess Strain' (deep green, lighter stripes, furrowed); 'Buttercup' (green); 'Delica' (cupless, stores well); 'Sweet Mama' (cupless, flattened, dark green, striped and blotched). Butternut type (*C. moschata*): thick, relatively short, mostly buff-coloured: markedly long day plants. 'Butterbush' (small, buff); 'Early Butternut' (bulbous, red-brown); 'Ponca' (cylindrical, orange); 'Waltham' (cylindrical, pale brown); 'Zenith' (cylindrical neck, thicker below, red-brown). Hubbard squashes (*C. maxima*): 'Baby Blue' (grey-blue, warted); 'Baby Hubbard' (large, globular, neck at both ends, blue-grey); 'Chicago Warted' (largest green Hubbard); 'Golden Delicious' (large, red, heart-shaped, very fine flesh); 'Golden Hubbard' (orange-red); 'Orange Hokkaido' ('Uchiki Kiri') (tear-drop shape, orange on blue-green). Kabocha squashes (*C. maxima* × *C. moschata*): 'Golden Debut' (orange, very sweet); 'Tetsakabuto' (dark green). Spaghetti Squashes (*C. pepo*: flesh stranded, spaghetti-like): 'Orangetti', 'Tivoli', 'Vegetable Spaghetti' or Spaghetti Squash (oblong, yellow, stores well). Summer Squashes (*C. pepo*: list excludes courgettes/zucchini, for which see MARROW): 'Peter Pan' (light green); 'Scallopini' (green); 'Sunburst' (deep yellow with green 'sunburst'); 'White Bush' ('White Pattypan'); 'Yellow Bird'; 'Yellow Bush'. All these are scallop-shaped. 'Dawn' is one of many available cultivars of crookneck or tapering club shape, usually orange to yellow). Others. (a) *C. maxima* derivatives: 'Arikara' (salmon-pink, small, good in drought conditions); 'Blue Kiri' (small, blue-green); 'Gold Nugget' (small, orange); 'Golden Delicious' (heart-shaped); 'Onion' (onion-shaped, red-orange); 'Pink Banana Jumbo' (very large, to 27kg, cylindrical, bright pink); 'Red Kuri' (rounded, tapered each end, red-orange); 'Sweet Meat' (medium size, slate-grey). (b) *C. argyrosperma* derivatives: 'Golden Cushaw', 'Green Striped Cushaw' (medium to large, pear-shaped, slightly curved neck). *C. moschata* derivatives: 'Citrouille Brodée d'Eysines' (also known as 'Citronville Galense d'Eysires') (fairly large, cheese-box-shaped, ribbed, dark brown); 'La Primera Calabaza' (round, green); 'Tahitian' (large, curved, bulbous, buff). *C.pepo* derivatives: 'Delicata' (Sweet Potato Squash) (small, striped green and cream); 'Lady Godiva' (yellow-orange, usually grown for hull-less seeds); 'Sweet Dumpling' (Vegetable Gourd) (small, ivory-white, keeps well).

PUMPKINS. (a) *C.pepo*: usually orange, more or less ribbed. Small (up to 2kg): 'Baby Pam', 'Buttons', 'Jack be Little', 'Munchkin' (scalloped, miniature); 'Rebecca', 'Small Sugar' (early); 'Spookie', 'Trick-or-Treat' (plant compact). Medium (2–12kg): 'Connecticut Field' (flattened oval); 'Hallowe'en' (very early maturing); 'Jack o'Lantern' (round to oblong); 'Jackpot' (bush); 'Jaune Gros de Paris' (pale pink, very dense flesh); 'Triple Treat' (long keeping: to cook, for hull-less seeds, for lanterns); 'Winter Luxury' (coarse flesh); 'Young's Beauty' (red, smooth, high-yielding). Large (12–100kg+): 'Autumn Gold Hybrid' (round to rectangular); 'Funny Face' (plant compact); 'Ghost Rider', 'Green Hokkaido' (dark green, flat); 'Spirit'. (b) *C.maxima*: usually orange and ribbed. 'Atlantic Giant' (world size record at 224kg: 3m circumference); 'Big Max' (to 25kg): 'Howden' (to 12kg, flattened oval); 'King of Mammoths' (and other 'Mammoth' types) (early); 'Prizewinner' (can grow very large); 'Queensland Blue' (blue-grey, drum shaped, small); 'Rouge Vif d'Etampes' (to 12kg, flat, deeply ribbed, good keeper).

**Punctillaria** N.E. Br.

***P.optata*** (N.E. Br.) N.E. Br. See *Pleiospilos compactus*.
***P.roodiae*** N.E. Br. See *Tanquana prismatica*.
***P.sororia*** (N.E. Br.) N.E. Br. See *Pleiospilos compactus* ssp. *minor*.

**Punica** L. (Lat. name, *Malum punicum*, of Pliny.) Punicaceae. 2 species of deciduous, densely branched shrubs or small trees. leaves opposite, clustered, entire, without stipules. Flowers borne in clusters of 1–5, bisexual, perfect, axillary, and terminal, borne at branch tips; calyx tubular or more or less campanulate, sepals 5–8, fleshy, valvate; petals 5–7, overlapping, perigynous; stamens many; style 1, short; ovaries inferior, with numerous locules, borne in concentric circles and 1 to 3 separated layers; ovules numerous. Fruit a globose, pulpy berry with numerous fleshy seeds, forming a thick, leathery shell. E Mediterranean to Himalaya. Z9.

CULTIVATION Generally requiring long, hot continental summers to ripen fruit, *P.granatum* is nevertheless a handsome ornamental, for warm south- or southwest-facing walls in regions where frosts are light and short-lived. Valued for its attractive, glossy foliage, which colours well in spring and autumn, it bears beautifully textured and brilliantly coloured flowers over long periods in summer. In Mediterranean climates it is sometimes used as hedging. Grow in well-drained, fertile, moderately-retentive, loamy soils in full sun. Although it may be cut to the ground by severe frost, given wall protection and a deep mulch at the roots, living wood will re-sprout vigorously from the base. Wall-grown specimens may be grown as shrubs (preferably), or tied in and fan trained. Prune in late spring or summer to remove old or weak wood and shorten outward growing shoots from trained specimens in spring at bud break; flowers are carried on the tips of the current years growth. Tub-grown specimens were traditionally grown in the cool glasshouse to be moved out of doors for the summer months, with treatment as for *Citrus*. Propagate by suckers, semi-ripe cuttings or layers, or by grafting on to seedlings understock. Also by seed in spring; named varieties do not come true.

***P.granatum*** L. POMEGRANATE. Deciduous, branching shrub to 2m, or small tree to 6m, angled, glabrous, occasionally with spiny branches. Lvs 2–8cm, obovate to oblong, pale green, glossy above, glabrous, entire, rigid, opposite, occasionally alternate. Fls to 3cm diam., orange-red, funnelform-rotate, sessile; pet. crumpled. Fr. to 12cm diam., globose, brown-yellow to purple-red, many-seeded, with persistent calyx; fleshy juicy, edible, crimson. Many local cultivars, for instance 'Fleshman', sweet, soft-seeded; 'Wonderful', juicy, wine-flavoured; vigorous and crops well.

***P.sempervirens*** hort. See *P.granatum*.

**PUNICACEAE** Horan. See *Punica*.

**Purdom, William** (1880–1921) Plant collector. Born at Heversham, Westmorland, Purdom was apprenticed as a gardener at Brathay Hall before working for Low & Sons of Enfield around the turn of the century and then at the Veitch nurseries at Coombe Wood, Surrey. In 1902 he arrived at Kew as a student, showing skill as a propagator and eventually rising to become a sub-foreman in the arboretum nursery. In 1909 he was re-employed by Veitch, this time in conjunction with the Arnold Arboretum as a replacement collector for E.H. Wilson, and he embarked on a four-year expedition to Inner Mongolia and the Shensi, Shansi and Kansu districts of China. Although Purdom discovered many notable plants such as *Syringa microphylla*, *Buddleia alternifolia*, *Clematis macropetala*, *C.tangutica* and *Viburnum farreri fragrans*, it took the prose and extrovert personality of Reginald Farrer, with whom he explored northwest China again in 1914–15, to popularize them widely. On this second expedition, funded through Farrer, Purdom was a 'travelling companion', going to China in advance to organize the expedition and using his considerable experience and quiet tact to avert many potential disasters. Despite their different personalities Farrer and Purdom worked well together, exploring the area south of Lanchu, capital of Kansu, in the first season and then going north into the Ta-tung Alps. They discovered many plants, including *Daphne tangutica*, *Rosa farreri*, *Buddleja farreri*, *Berberis dasystachya* and *Gentiana farreri*, but Farrer always unintentionally received most of the credit for them as a result of his writings.

After Farrer's return home in 1915 Purdom accepted a position as the head of one of the Chinese Governments five Departments of Forestry, in charge of timber supply for the railways. During the last six years of his life Purdom worked hard in extremely difficult conditions, living in a railway car and travelling around Honan and establishing tree nurseries in an effort to replenish the forests of northern China. He died at the early age of 41 as a result of his exertions in Peking.

**Purgosea** Haw.

***P.hemisphaerica*** (Thunb.) G. Don. See *Crassula hemisphaerica*.

**Purshia** DC. ex Poir. (For Frederick Traugott Pursh (1774–1820), German explorer, collector, horticulturist and author of an important early flora of North America, who lived in the United States from 1799 to 1811.) ANTELOPE BUSH. Rosaceae. 2 species of deciduous shrubs or small trees. Leaves alternate, congested, small, evidently fasciculate, deeply 3-cleft, cuneate at base, margins revolute. Flowers solitary, at the ends of short branches; calyx tube turbinate to funnel-shaped, persistent; calyx teeth 5; petals white or cream to yellow, 5, spathulate; stamens 25; pistil usually 1; style short; ovary 1-ovulate. Fruit a pubescent, coriaceous achene with the somewhat short, persistent style at the tip. Western N America. Closely related to *Cercocarpus*. Z6.

CULTIVATION Grown for their grey-green foliage and small, creamy yellow flowers, carried on the tips of the previous season's growth, *Purshia* spp. occur naturally in hot, dry climates, and are well suited in cultivation to the warm, sheltered shrub border, or to a position at the base of a south-facing wall. Hardy to −15°C/5°F, but not in combination with winter wet at the root zone; grow in perfectly drained soils. Propagate by seed or simple layering.

***P.glandulosa*** Curran. Erect shrub to 5m. Branchlets glabrous, clearly glandular. Lvs to 1cm, adpressed-glandular and sparsely pubesc. above, later glabrous, somewhat tomentose beneath, 3–5-lobed, lobes linear, sometimes dentate. Fls light yellow to white; cal. tube to 4mm, tomentulose, eglandular; teeth 3mm; pet. to 8mm. Fr. canescent, to 2cm including the style; seed lanceolate, 6mm, black. Spring–summer. US (Colorado to Nevada).

***P.tridentata*** (Pursh) DC. Erect shrub to 3m; bark grey or brown. Branchlets wide-spreading, glandular, tomentose. Lvs cuneate, to 3cm, green and fine-pubesc. above, white-tomentose beneath, lobes oblong-linear. Fls cream-yellow, 1.5cm diam.; pedicels short; cal. tube funnel-shaped, stalked-glandular, 3mm, white-tomentose; teeth oblong, 3mm; pet. spathulate-obovate, to 8mm. Fr. fusiform, dry, 1.5cm including the style; seeds pointed-ovoid, to 6mm, black. Spring–summer. US (Oregon and California to New Mexico).

***P. tridentata*** var. ***glandulosa*** Jones. See *P. glandulosa*.

**Puschkinia** Adams. (For Count Apollo Apollosovich Mussin-Pushkin (*d*1805), Russian chemist who collected plants in the Caucasus and Ararat.) Liliaceae (Hyacinthaceae). 1 species, a perennial herb, closely related to *Chionodoxa* and *Scilla*, bulbs small, tunicate, brown. Leaves to 15×0.5cm, 2–3, basal, linear-lorate. Flowering stems 5–20cm, naked; flowers in a loose raceme, pale blue with darker stripes, rarely white or tinged green, subsessile or, on lower stems, on pedicels to 1cm; perianth short-tubular, 7–10mm, lobes 6, erect or slightly spreading; stamens 6, filaments united in a 6-lobed cupular corona, anthers borne on corona and alternating with corona lobes; ovary superior; style 1. Fruit a 3-valved, spherical capsule. Spring. USSR (Caucasus), Turkey, N Iran, N Iraq, Lebanon. Z5.

CULTIVATION Charming small bulbs native to montane meadow and stony habitats to 3000m/9840ft, often occurring near melting snow. The commonly available variants are cold tolerant to about −20°C/−4°F and are fairly undemanding in cultivation, thriving in sun or partial shade in gritty, well-drained, humus-rich soil. Flowering is usually better where bulbs can dry out in summer, and they are sometimes grown for the benefit of the grower in the alpine display house. Propagate by offsets when dormant in late summer or by seed in autumn.

***P. scilloides*** Adams. As for the genus. 'Alba': fls pure white. var. ***libanotica*** (Zucc.) Boiss. Fls smaller than in species type; corona lobes sharply acute.

***P. hyacinthoides*** Bak. See *P. scilloides*.
***P. libanotica*** Zucc. See *P. scilloides* var. *libanotica*.

**Putoria** Pers. (From Lat. *putor*, strong smell; an allusion to the smell of the leaves.) Rubiaceae. 3 species of malodorous dwarf shrubs; stems tetragonal in section, divaricately branched. Leaves opposite, petiolate, somewhat leathery; stipules interpetiolate, small. Flowers few, solitary or in terminal clusters, subsessile, bracteate; corolla funnel-shaped with 4–5 oblong lobes; stamens 4–5, exserted or, at apex of corolla tube, inserted, anthers linear, versatile, exserted; ovary 2-locular; style slender, bifid. Fruit a drupe, with 2 cartilaginous pyrenes. Mediterranean. Z8.

CULTIVATION Grow *P. calabrica* in full sun in a sheltered position on the rock garden, or at the base of a south-facing wall, in perfectly drained soil. Propagate from seed sown outside in spring.

***P. calabrica*** (L. f.) DC. STINKING MADDER. Stems prostrate or spreading, mat-forming, 30cm, glabrous to pubesc., foetid. Lvs to 20×5mm, obovate to elliptic-lanceolate, obtuse or subacute, margins minutely revolute and papillose, leathery; stipules 1mm, ovate, connate; petioles indistinct. Fls to 12, in a dense terminal cluster, pink; peduncles less than 5mm, densely hispidulous-papillose with 1 or more bracts, to 1.5mm; pedicels very short or nearly obsolete, with minute subulate bracteoles; cor. to 15mm, with 4 linear-lanceolate lobes, to 4×1mm; stamens exserted, anth. linear-oblong, 1.5×0.5mm; style 2cm, with 2 acute, erect or spreading stigmatic lobes. Fr. dark red, black when ripe, oblong or ellipsoid, crowned with persistent cal., 5×3mm. Spring–summer. Mediterranean.

For synonymy see *Asperula* and *Ernodea*.

**Putterlickia** Endl. (Named for A. Putterlick (1810–45), assistant in the Botanic Museum of Vienna.) Celastraceae. 2 species of evergreen, glabrous, spiny shrubs. Branches terete, grey-brown, smooth or verrucose, with angular twigs; spines nearly naked or with small tufts of leaves or undeveloped buds. Leaves alternate or in clusters, simple, coriaceous. Flowers in a lax or several-flowered cyme; pedicels sometimes articulated; sepals 5, unequal, the 2 outer smaller than the 3 inner, margins laciniate; petals 5, oblong or obovate, margins ciliate; disc saucer-shaped, margin crenate or not enveloping ovary, or fleshy and enveloping three-quarters of ovary; stamens 5. Fruit a 3-valved capsule; seeds partly covered with an aril. S Africa. Z9.

CULTIVATION As for *Maytenus*.

***P. pyracantha*** (L.) Endl. Rigid shrub to 3m; branches curved; spines horizontal, to 5cm, frequent on stem and branches, sometimes absent on upper branches. Lvs to 4cm, tufted, rarely solitary, elliptic or obovate-cuneate, emarginate, rarely acute, margins revolute; veins reticulate. Peduncles to 2.5cm, solitary or 2–4-clustered, panicled to apex; panicles 3–12-fld; cal. minute, obtuse; pet. oblong, to 5mm, creamy white; stamens to 5mm; ovary conical. Fr. obovoid, to 20mm, red, 6-seeded, valves thick, setiferous; seeds ovate, black; aril orange. Summer. S Africa.

***P. verrucosa*** Sim. Shrub; stem curved, very warty-spiny; branches terete, warty, angular when young, spiny; spines strong, slender, horizontal, to 5cm on branches, to 1cm on the twigs. Lvs 25×20mm, obovate, somewhat undulate, attenuate at base, obtuse, minutely spiny dentate, Panicles pedunculate, 8–20-fld, to 5cm; pet. to 2mm, tinged green. Fr. obovoid, to 20mm, red, 6-seeded, valves thick, setiferous; seeds ovate, black; aril orange. Summer. S Africa.

***P. pyracantha*** (L.) Endl. See *Celastrus pyracanthus*.
For further synonymy see *Celastrus*.

**Puya** Molina. (From the Chilean vernacular name for the genus.) Bromeliaceae. 168 species of perennial, terrestrial herbs with long, stout, simple or branched stems, sometimes stemless, 30cm to 10m in flower. Leaves leathery, forming a dense rosette, with large, distinct sheaths and narrowly triangular blades without basal constrictions, margins normally toothed and spinose. Inflorescence simple or paniculate; floral bracts ovate-elliptic, membranous to tough; flowers bisexual and showy; sepals rolled, free, glabrous to hairy, sometimes woody; petals longer, free, unappendaged or with a pair of vertical folds, spreading at maturity, later twisted together in a spiral; filaments free. Fruit a capsule containing large, winged seeds. Andean S America, N Brazil, Guyana, Costa Rica.

CULTIVATION *P. berteroniana* and *P. chilensis* will withstand infrequent and short-lived light frost when planted in the open. See BROMELIADS.

***P. alpestris*** (Poepp.) Gay. 1.2–1.5m in flower. Lvs to 60cm, arching, glabrous above, densely covered in white scales beneath, hooked-spinose. Infl. sparsely branched on a stout scape, loosely bipinnate, pyramidal; floral bracts papery; pedicel to 15mm; sep. 23mm, narrowly oblong, green, nearly glabrous when older; pet. elliptic, blunt, blue-green. SC Chile. Z8.

***P. berteroniana*** Mez. To 4.5m in flower. Lvs 1m, arching, marginal spines to 1cm, stout, hooked. Infl. and scape tomentose, bipinnate, much branched; sep. 23mm, narrowly oblong, green, becoming glabrous with age; pet. to 5cm, elliptic, blunt, blue-green, naked. C Chile. Z8.

***P. chilensis*** Molina. Resembles *P. berteroniana* except in its almost straight glabrous lvs and leathery marginal spines. Infl. and scape subglabrous; sep. to 35mm, broadly acute or obtuse; pet. sulphur-yellow to yellow-green, narrowly elliptic, naked. C Chile. Z9.

***P. coerulea*** Lindl. 1–2m in flower. Stem erect, stout. Lf sheaths dark brown, suborbicular; blades 40–60cm, covered with ash-grey scales, less densely so above, distant-serrate, with rusty hooked spines. Infl. white-floccose, bipinnate, much-branched, occasionally simple; floral bracts ovate-lanceolate, variable; fls erect, on one side of infl. only; pedicel 1–2cm, slender; sep. lanceolate-triangular to oblong-ovate, abruptly acute, basally keeled; pet. to 5cm, elliptic, obtuse, erect and tubular, dark blue, with 2 basal appendages. var. ***violacea*** (Brongn.) L.B. Sm. & Looser. To 1m in flower. Lvs 1cm wide, marginal spines 4mm. Infl. axis red, nearly glabrous, with loosely fld branches; pedicel 15–22mm, swollen toward apex; sep. to 22mm, lanceolate-triangular. C Chile. Z8.

***P. ferruginea*** (Ruiz & Pav.) L.B. Sm. To 4m in flower. Lvs to 1m. Infl. laxly pyramidal, covered with rusty brown stellate scales; branches one-sided; floral bracts ovate, acute; pedicel 1–6cm; slender; sep. 12–45mm, oblong, blunt, covered in rusty-brown stellate scales; pet. to 13cm, white-green to purple, naked or with a pair of basal calli. Ecuador, Peru, Bolivia. Z8.

***P. floccosa*** (Lind.) E. Morr. To 2m in flower. Lvs to 1m, sublinear, glabrous above, white-scaly beneath, hooked-spinose; sheaths small, apex slightly toothed. Infl. on a white-floccose scape, loosely bipinnate; fls erect, on all sides of infl.; pedicel 2–5mm, slender; sep. 25–33mm, subcoriaceous, narrowly triangular, attenuate; pet. to 4cm, blue, lanceolate, acute, glabrous. Costa Rica, Colombia, Venezuela, N Brazil. Z9.

***P. hortensis*** L.B. Sm. 1–2m in flower. Lvs 60–70cm, narrowly triangular, pale-scaly on both sides when young, nearly glabrous later, pungent, serrate, hooked-spinose; sheaths reniform, dark brown. Infl. loosely bipinnate, villous, scurfy; floral bracts lanceolate, abruptly acute; pedicel to 30mm, slender, with persistent scales; sep. to 27mm, lanceolate, abruptly acute, keelless, becoming glabrous; pet. to 7cm, maroon, naked. Early summer. Origin unknown. Z8.

***P. laxa*** L.B. Sm. To 1m in flower; stem branched at base. Lvs to 60cm, apex thread-like, sheaths thickly felted with scaly hairs, marginal spines 5mm, hooked; sheaths broad-triangular. Infl. pyramidal, racemes 4–6, loose-compound, to 70cm; fls spirally arranged, white woolly; sep. 1.5cm, lanceolate, scaly; pet. 3cm, obovate, dark violet with exterior green stripe. Argentina.

***P. medica*** L.B. Sm. To 20cm in flower. Lvs 12×15cm, forming loose rosettes narrow-triangular, terminal spine, densely scaled, marginal spines 2mm, brown. Infl. simple, cylindrical, 10×2cm; floral bracts 2.5×2cm, spirally arranged, triangular to oval, pink, scaly, margins irregularly spiny, apex spiny; fls sub-sessile, erect; sep. 12mm, ovate, acute, grey scaly, white-green; pet. 2×7cm, tip widely rounded, emarginate, dark blue. N Peru.

***P. mirabilis*** (Mez) L.B. Sm. 1.5m+ in flower. Lvs 60–70cm forming loose rosette, white to brown, margins finely toothed. Infl. erect, in simple loose racemes to 50cm; sep. 5cm, green, scaly; pet. 10×2cm spathulate, green to white. Argentina, Bolivia.

***P. raimondii*** Harms. To 2m in flower; stem covered with old lf sheaths. Lvs 1–2m×6cm, lanceolate, stiff, forming globular rosette at stem apex, upper surfaces smooth, green, beneath densely adpressed scaly, marginal spines 1.5cm, hooked, brown. Infl. compound, racemose, club-shaped, tapering; scape erect, stout; floral bracts 6cm, elliptic; pedicels 7mm, hairy; sep. 4cm, elliptic to acute, finely cutaneous with basal hairs, distinctly veined; pet. 5cm, ligulate, yellow-green. Peru.

***P. spathacea*** (Griseb.) Mez. To 1m in flower. Stem short, erect. Lvs 60–110cm, narrowly triangular, spreading to recurved, glabrous and grey-green above, pale-scaly beneath, margins serrate, hooked-spinose. Scape glabrous, red; infl. much-branched, bipinnate, covered initially with stellate hairs, later appearing glandular; pedicel 15mm, slender, curved; sep. 15–22mm, pink, lanceolate-oblong, abruptly acute, basally keeled; pet. 25–33mm, blue to dark green, ligulate, naked. NC Argentina. Z8.

***P. alpestris*** (Poepp.) Gay (in part). See *P. berteroniana*.
***P. coarctata*** Philippi. See *P. berteroniana*.
***P. coarctata*** (Ruiz & Pav.) Fisch. non Philippi. See *P. chilensis*.
***P. grandiflora*** Hook. See *P. ferruginea*.
***P. saxatilis*** Mart. See *Encholirium spectabile*.
***P. violacea*** (Brongn.) Mez. See *P. coerulea* var. *violacea*.
***P. whytei*** Hook. f. See *P. alpestris*.
For further synonymy see *Pitcairnia*.

**Pycnanthemum** Michx. (From Gk *pyknos*, dense, and *anthos*, flower; the flowers are in dense spikes.) AMERICAN MOUNTAIN MINT. Labiatae. 21 species of perennial herbs. Stems 30–150cm, simple or with laterals in the upper leaf axils. Leaves usually pubescent, simple, linear, lanceolate or ovate, entire or serrate essentially sessile; petioles rarely exceeding 1.5cm. Inflorescence simple or branched, of compact glomerules, pedunculate, usually subtended by a pair of leaflike bracts; calyx 3–9mm, glabrous to canescent, regular or forming two lips, teeth deltoid or acuminate; corolla tube white or pink expanding to form two lips, upper lip longer, to 8mm; stamens 4, lower pair slightly longer, all usually exserted, although rarely non-functional within the tube. Fruit a nutlet, smooth or tipped with short hairs. Eastern N America and California.

CULTIVATION The mountain mints are mostly very aromatic when bruised, yielding aromas similar to penny royal and other mints. Although not very showy, the many flowers borne in late summer add value to the culinary or herb garden. Many species are hardy to −15°C/5°F, originating in open woodland or meadows in the US. Most benefit from a rich loamy compost, full sun or partial shade and plenty of water during the growing season. They can be cut back to the ground in early winter. Propagate by seed sown outside in spring or autumn or by division of established clumps.

***P. flexuosum*** Britt., Sterns & Pogg. Upright perenn. herb, 60–100cm. Stems glabrous bearing lateral branchlets in the upper parts. Lvs linear, 22–56×1.5–5.5mm, sessile, entire, with one or two pairs of lateral veins. Glomerules solitary and terminal, arranged in compact corymbs; involucral bracts apiculate, midribs thickened; cal. 4–5mm, canescent, teeth apiculate or subspinose; cor. tube rapidly enlarging, 3–4.5mm, pubesc. within the throat, upper lip 2–2.5mm. E US. Z5.

***P. muticum*** Pers. Upright perenn. herb, 70–110cm. Stems simple, branching in the infl., pubesc. Lvs 3–8×1.5–3.5cm, narrowly ovate to ovate-lanceolate, sessile, usually shallowly serrate, acuminate with 5 or more pairs of veins, glabrous above, below with occasional pubescence along veins. Glomerules solitary and terminal; involucral bracts velvety pubesc.; cal. 3.5mm, pubesc., teeth deltoid or acuminate; cor. tube pink, gradually enlarging to 3.5mm, upper lip 1.5–2mm; stamens often within cor. throat or equalling cor. E US. Z5.

***P. pilosum*** Nutt. Upright perenn. herb, 100–150cm. Stems densely pilose with spreading hairs, bearing short lateral branches in lf axils and branching in the infl. Lvs 3–7×1–2cm, lanceolate, entire or shallowly serrate, lower lvs glabrous above, upper lvs more pilose above, all lvs densely pilose beneath with 4 pairs of veins, sessile or nearly so. Glomerules terminal and solitary; involucral bracts canescent; cal. 3.5–4.5mm, canescent, teeth deltoid, acute; cor. tube pink, gradually expanded, 3–5mm, upper lip 2–3mm. C & E US. Z4.

***P. virginianum*** Dur. & Jackson. Upright perenn. herb, 70–100cm. Stems bearing short leafy branches, glabrous with pubescence confined to angles. Lvs 3.5–6.5×0.6–1.1cm, lanceolate to linear-elliptic, sessile, entire or shallowly serrate, glabrous or sparsely pubesc. along veins, with 4 pairs of lateral veins. Glomerules dense, solitary and terminal arranged in compact corymbs; involucral bracts leaflike without prominent midveins; cal. 3–5mm, canescent, teeth deltoid, acute, 0.7mm; cor. pink and white, tube gradually enlarging 2–4mm, upper lip 1.5–2.5mm; stamens usually exserted. E US. Z5.

***P. arkansanum*** Fres. See *P. muticum*.
***P. lanceolatum*** Pursh. See *P. virginianum*.
***P. linifolium*** Pursh. See *P. flexuosum*.
***P. muticum*** var. ***pilosum*** Gray. See *P. pilosum*.
***P. ovatum*** Nutt. ex Benth. See *P. muticum*.
***P. tenuifolium*** Schräd. See *P. flexuosum*.
***P. virginicum*** Pers. See *P. virginianum*.
For further synonymy see *Satureja*.

**Pycnostachys** Hook. (From Gk *pyknos*, dense, *stachys*, ear of corn, referring to the density of the flower spikes.) Labiatae. About 40 species of erect perennial herbs or soft shrubs. Leaves opposite or whorled. Bracts small, distinct. Flowers in dense terminal spikes; calyx 5-dentate, teeth subequal, rigid, linear, spine-like; corolla 2-lipped, tube exserted, cylindric at base, widening campanulate, deflexed, upper lip 4-lobed, shorter than lower, lower lip compressed, boat-shaped; stamens 4, in pairs, lying in lower lip of corolla, filaments united at base, free above, anthers single celled; style 2-lobed, slightly exceeds stamens. Fruit 4 ovoid nutlets, black or brown, glabrous. Tropical & Southern Africa, Madagascar. Z9.

CULTIVATION Tender, upright, shrubby perennials for cultivation in the glasshouse or conservatory; many species exude an unpleasant pungent aroma when bruised, but they are grown primarily for their dense spikes of intense cobalt or caerulean blue flowers. Grow from seed in spring, at 12–15°C/55–60°F and pot on at monthly intervals into a final pot size of 20–25cm/8–10in., with a well-drained, high-fertility loam-based potting mix. Give bright indirect light, a minimum temperature of 15°C/60°F and water plentifully. Propagate also by stem cuttings in early summer, or by softwood cuttings in autumn, after flowering. Prone to infestation by glasshouse whitefly, *Trialeurodes vaporariorum*; use *Encarsia formosa* as a biological control or a contact or systemic insecticide.

***P. coerulea*** Hook. Erect, somewhat branching herb, to 120cm. Stems minutely pubesc. Lvs 7–10×1–1.5cm, linear-lanceolate, sessile, acuminate, cuneate at base, glabrous, distantly and shortly dentate. Bracts oblong-linear. 2.5mm, ciliate; fls in single spike, 25–50×8–10mm; cal. ciliate, teeth 2–3mm; cor. 4–5mm, blue. Summer. Madagascar.

***P. dawei*** N.E. Br. Stout, loosely branched perenn., pyramidal, to 180cm. Shoots minutely pubesc. Lvs to 30cm, linear-lanceolate, narrowly acuminate, cuneate at base, serrate, red-glandular beneath. Bracts red-brown, white-ciliate. Fls in spikes to 13×4.5cm; cal. teeth acuminate; cor. to 25mm, cobalt blue. Summer. Tropical C Africa.

***P. stuhlmannii*** Gürke. Stems to 120cm, pubesc. Lvs to 18cm, linear-lanceolate, acuminate, cuneate at base, minutely serrate, glabrous above, pubesc. beneath, malodorous when crushed. Fls blue, to 12mm, in spikes to 30×10mm on axillary peduncles to 15cm. Zimbabwe.

***P. urticifolia*** Hook. Erect herb or soft shrub to 2.5m. Stems woody at base, much branched. Lvs 45–120×30–70m, narrow to broadly ovate, acute, obtuse to truncate at base, crenate to deeply incised-dentate, subglabrous to densely pubesc.; petioles to 5cm. Bracts linear to spathulate, 4–5mm, ciliate; fls in thyrse-like spike. 5–10×2.5–3cm; cal. purple-red, pubesc., teeth 8–10mm; cor. 12–20mm, gentian blue, rarely white tinted blue. Tropical & Southern Africa.

**Pycreus** P. Beauv. (An anagram of *Cyperus*.) Cyperaceae. 70 species of perennial, grasslike herbs. Stems terete or 3-angled, leafy. Leaves grasslike, linear, usually equalling stem; sheaths often tinged purple or red, or fibrous. Inflorescence an umbel, subtended by leaflike bracts which exceed it in length; spikes sessile or stalked; spikelets few- to many-flowered; flowers hermaphrodite, minute, spirally arranged, subtended by a scalelike, caducous glume; sepals and petals absent; stamens 2; style 2-

branched. Fruit a nut, compressed, 2-angled. Cosmopolitan. Close to *Cyperus*.

CULTIVATION As for *Carex*.

***P.filicinus*** (Vahl) T. Koyama. NUTTALL'S CYPERUS. Annual, 10–35cm. Stem slender, tufted. Lvs equalling or exceeding stem. Bracts unequal, 1–2 very much exceeding the rest; umbel compound, sessile or with 1–2 rays; spikelets linear-lanceolate, 3mm, compressed, golden yellow to brown; glumes oblong, 2–4mm, pointed, bristle-tipped, midrib green. Fr. brown, 1–1.5mm. Summer. N America. Z7.

***P.congestus*** (Vahl) Hayek. See *Cyperus congestus*.
***P.longus*** (L.) Hayek. See *Cyperus longus*.
For further synonymy see *Cyperus*.

**Pyracantha** Roem. (From Gk *pyr*, fire, referring to the berries, and *akanthos*, thorn.) FIRETHORN. Rosaceae. 7 species of evergreen thorny shrubs closely related to *Cotoneaster* and *Crataegus*; thorns leafy. Leaves alternate, entire to crenate or serrate, never lobed; stipules small. Flowers 0.5–1cm, white, in corymbs on leafy shoots; calyx persistent; petals rounded; stamens *c*20, anthers yellow; styles 5; carpels 5. Fruit rounded, orange to red. SE Europe to China.

CULTIVATION Pollution- and exposure-tolerant evergreens for the border, where they form mounds of glossy green foliage, for training against walls, and for thorny and impenetrable hedging. Some species, such as *P. atalantoides*, can be trained with a single stem to form small specimen trees. They are grown for their masses of white flowers in spring and early summer, followed by a profusion brightly coloured berries that persist into winter, and in the case of *P. atalantoides*, which ripen late, into spring; those of *P. coccinea* are particularly attractive to birds. Given protection from cold winds, particularly for *P. atalantoides*, *P. crenulata* and *P. koidzumii*, *Pyracantha* spp. are tolerant temperatures to at least −15°C/5°F; *P. atalantoides* is tolerant to −20°C/−4°F (but at lower temperatures is rapidly killed rather than damaged).

Grow in well-drained, moisture-retentive soils, in sun or part shade. Site wall-grown plants in any position other than a hot, sunny south facing wall. Prune free-standing specimens after flowering to restrict size, or to remove damaged wood, cutting back to the centre of the plant to obscure the wound. Clip back formal, wall-trained plants after flowering to give dense cover; otherwise remove only outward facing shoots, tying-in new growth in late summer. Propagate by semi-ripe heel cuttings in autumn, in peat and sand in a closed case with bottom heat. Cuttings may be taken from late spring onwards, but better growth is obtained in autumn cuttings; large, branched semi-hard cuttings (to 30cm/12in.), wounded and treated with hormone rooting compound, and placed under mist, will root in 3–4 weeks, and will flower and berry the following season. Raise larger numbers of plants for hedging from fresh ripe seed; remove the flesh and sow in the cold frame in autumn.

*Pyracantha* spp. are susceptible to pyracantha scab, *Spilocaea pyracanthae*, causing small scabby lesions on twigs, olive-brown spotting on leaves and flowers, and serious disfigurement of the fruit; it is often accompanied by premature leaf drop. Treat with systemic fungicide in spring and early summer. *Pyracantha* can also be affected by coral spot, *Nectria cinnabarina*, and fireblight, *Erwinia amylovora*. Subject to infestation in Europe and North America by the green apple aphid, *Aphis pomi*, especially on young plants, and by woolly aphid, *Eriosoma lanigerum*; control aphids on emergence in early spring with specific systemic or contact aphicide. Also attacked by various scale insects. Occasionally attacked by caterpillars of the vapourer moth, *Orgyria antiqua*, known as the rusty tussock moth in the US, and the lackey moth, *Malacasoma neustria*.

***P.angustifolia*** (Franch.) Schneid. Evergreen shrub to 4m; branches upright or spreading, shoots stiff, densely downy in the first year. Lvs 1.5–5×0.5–1.5cm, linear-oblong to obovate, base short-tapered, apex rounded and sometimes toothed, shiny green above, downy beneath. Fls 0.5cm, in 5cm corymbs; pedicels downy. Fr. to 1cm, felted at first, later yellow-orange, long-persistent. SW China. 'Gnome': very hardy, habit erect, dense; fls profuse; fr. orange. 'Yukon Belle': habit dense; fr. orange, persistent. Z7.

***P.atalantoides*** (Hance) Stapf. Branches olive-brown, downy only at first. Lvs 3–7×1.5–3cm, lanceolate to elliptic or obovate, mostly entire, sometimes small-toothed, particularly toward the apex, downy at first, later shiny above, glaucescent beneath. Fls 1–1.5cm, white, in 3–4cm corymbs. Fr. 7–8mm, subglobose, scarlet-crimson. Spring–early summer. SE to W China. 'Aurea': fr. yellow. 'Bakeri': fr. red. 'Nana': dwarf, to 1m; fr. red. Z7.

***P.coccinea*** Roem. PYRACANTH; FIRETHORN; BUISSON ARDENT. Dense evergreen shrub to 5m; shoots downy at first. Lvs 2–4×1–2cm, elliptic to lanceolate, larger on non-flowering shoots, shiny dark green above, paler beneath, downy especially at the base when young. Fls 8mm, white, profusely borne in 3–4cm corymbs on short shoots. Fr. 5–6cm, rounded, bright scarlet. Early summer. Italy to Asia Minor. 'Baker's Red': hardy; fr. bright red. 'Kasan': compact, upright, fast-growing to 5m; fr. orange. 'Lalandei': upright to 5m, hardy; fr. profuse, bright orange. 'Lalandei Monrovia': upright dense; fr. orange. 'Sparkler': slow-growing; lvs variegated white; fr. red. 'Walker's Pride': very hardy, compact, berries well when young; fr. orange. Z6.

***P.crenatoserrata*** (Hance) Rehd. Evergreen shrub 3–6m, closely resembling *P. atalantoides* and *P. rogersiana*; shoots red-brown downy at first. Lvs 2–7×1–2cm, oblong-lanceolate, entire, widest above the middle, margins toothed, apex rounded, base tapered. Fls 1cm, white, in downy 3–4cm corymbs. Fr. 2cm, red, long-persistent. Early summer. C & W China. 'Graberi': vigorous; fr. red, in large clusters which last well. Z7.

***P.crenulata*** (D. Don) Roem. NEPALESE WHITE THORN. Evergreen shrub or small tree to 6m, closely resembling *P. coccinea*; shoots red-brown, downy. Lvs to 5×15cm, oblong-oblanceolate, apex rounded, tip bristled, margins crenate; becoming glabrous. Fls 8mm, in 3cm corymbs; styles separated at the base. Fr. 6–8mm, rounded, orange. Spring to early summer. Himalaya. var. ***kansuensis*** Rehd. Lvs narrower, to 2.5cm; fr. smaller. NW China. Z7.

***P.koidzumii*** (Hayata) Rehd. Evergreen loose shrub to 4m, closely resembling *P. rogersiana*; shoots red, downy, becoming glabrous and purple. Lvs 2.5–4.5cm, oblanceolate, apex rounded, margins entire or short-toothed on vigorous shoots, lustrous green above, paler and somewhat pubesc. beneath. Fls in downy infl., borne along the branches; cal. downy, persistent. Fr. 7mm, rounded, orange-red. Taiwan. 'Rosedale': branches arching; fr. large, bright red. 'Santa Cruz': habit prostrate; fr. large, red. 'Victory': vigorous, to 5m; fr. large, late to colour, lasting well. Z8.

***P.rogersiana*** (A.B. Jacks.) Chitt. Evergreen, dense, thorny shrub to 4m; shoots pale downy at first becoming glabrous, red-brown. Lvs 2–3.5×0.5–1cm, larger on vigorous shoots, oblanceolate to narrow obovate, apex rounded and shallow toothed, bright green above, paler beneath. Fls 0.5cm, in corymbose racemes; pedicel glabrous. Fr. 8–9mm, rounded, yellow to orange-red. China (Yunnan). 'Flava': fr. bright yellow. Z8.

***P.*cultivars**. 'Alexander Pendula': to 1.8m, branches weeping; fr, coral red. 'Andenken an Heinrich Bruns' *(P. coccinea × P. rogersiana)*: variable seedling mix, parent of 'Orange Charmer' and 'Golden Charmer'. 'Apache': habit compact spreading mound 1.5×2m; fr. bright red resistant to scab and fireblight. 'Brilliant': fr. bright red. 'Buttercup' *(P. coccinea × P. rogersiana)*: habit spreading; fr. small, yellow. 'Fiery Cascade': habit upright, 2.5×3m; lvs small, shining; fr. small, red; resistant to disease. 'Golden Charmer' *(P. coccinea × P. rogersiana)*: to 2.4m; fr. large, golden yellow; resistant to scab. 'Golden Dome': habit low; lvs bright green; fr. yellow. 'Harlequin': lvs variegated; fr. red. 'Knap Hill Lemon': habit vigorous, dense; fr. small, pale yellow. 'Lavinia Rutgers': habit spreading, branches thorny; lvs small, narrow; fr. orange. 'Mohave' *(P. koidzumii × P. coccinea* 'Wyatt'): habit upright, to 4×5m; fr. bright orange, unaffected by bird feeding; resistant to scab and fireblight. 'Morettii' *(hybrid of P. coccinea)*: habit very dense; lvs bronzed; fr. red. 'Navajo': habit low, dense; fr. orange-red; resistant to scab. 'Orange Giant': fr. bright orange. 'Orange Charmer' *(P. coccinea × P. crenatoserrata)*: habit vigorous, dense; fr. bright orange; resistant to scab. 'Pueblo': habit spreading, compact; fls 1cm, fr. orange red; resistant to scab and fireblight. 'Red Column': habit upright; fr. small, red. 'Red Cushion': habit dense, to 1×2m; fr. mid-red. 'Red Elf' ('Monelf'): habit dwarf, compact, mounding; lvs dark green; fr. bright red. 'Red Pillar': habit vigorous, upright; fr. orange-red. 'Renault d'Or': fr. yellow. 'Ruby Mound': habit low, dense; fr. orange-red; resistant to scab. 'Rutgers 3': habit low, creeping to 3m in width; fr. orange; resistant to disease. 'Shawnee' *(P. crenatoserrata × P. koidzumii)*: habit dense, spreading to 3.5m; fr. abundant, yellow-orange, colouring early; resistant to scab and fireblight. 'Soleil d'Or' ('Sungold' mutation of 'Morettii': habit semi-spreading; lvs pale green; fr. yellow. 'Sunshine' *(P. coccinea × P. rogersiana)*: habit open, branches lax; fr. orange. 'Taliensis' *(P. crenatoserrata × P. rogersiana)*: fr. yellow, abscising early. 'Teton 15': habit upright; lvs medium green; fr. orange-yellow; resistant to scab and fireblight. 'Tiny Tim' (*P. crenatoserrata* hybrid): habit dwarf, to 1m, densely leafy; fr. profuse. 'Watereri' ('Waterer's Orange') *(P. atalantoides × P. rogersiana)*: habit compact, vigorous to 2.5m; fr. profuse, orange.

***P.crenulata*** var. ***rogersiana*** A.B. Jacks. See *P. rogersiana*.
***P.crenulata*** var. ***yunnanensis*** Vilm. See *P. crenatoserrata*.
***P.discolor*** Rehd. See *P. atalantoides*.
***P.formosana*** hort. See *P. koidzumii*.
***P.fortuneana*** (Maxim.) Li. See *P. crenatoserrata*.
***P.gibbsii*** A.B. Jacks. See *P. atalantoides*.
***P.gibbsii*** var. ***yunnanensis*** Vilm. See *P. crenatoserrata*.

***P. gibbsii*** var. ***yunnanensis*** Osborn. See *P. crenatoserrata*.
***P. kansuensis*** hort. See *P. crenulata* var. *kansuensis*.
***P. rogersiana*** var. ***aurantiaca*** Bean. See *P. rogersiana*.
***P. yunnanensis*** Chitt. See *P. crenatoserrata*.
For further synonymy see *Cotoneaster, Mespilus* and *Photinia*.

**×Pyracomeles** Rehd. ex Guillaum. *(Pyracantha × Osteomeles.)* Rosaceae. A genus of hybrids between *Osteomeles* and *Pyracantha*. Contains, as far as is known, only one cross. Differs from *Pyracantha* mainly in the unarmed branchlets and pinnatisect leaves, and from *Osteomeles* in having leaves pinnate only at the base and pinnatisect toward the apex. Garden origin.

CULTIVATION Grown for botanical interest and for the white flowers in spring which give rise to masses of small coral-red fruits in autumn, this spineless shrub is suitable for the border, especially in areas which suffer atmospheric pollution or maritime exposure. Propagate by grafting onto seedling stock of either parent, or by seed, reported to come true. Otherwise, cultivate as for *Pyracantha*.

× ***P. vilmorinii*** Rehd. ex Guillaum. *(Osteomeles subrotunda × Pyracantha crenatoserrata.)* Semi-evergreen shrub to 1.5m. Branchlets slender, grey-pubesc., soon glabrous. Lvs to 3.5cm, including petiole, grey-pubesc., soon glabrous, pinnatisect near apex, pinnate below, 5–9-foliolate or -lobulate; leaflets or lobes oval, obtuse or somewhat mucronulate, usually crenate-serrulate at apex, upper leaflets or lobes decurrent. Fls 1cm diam., in many-fld, glabrous or subglabrous, terminal corymbs; cal. lobes broad-triangular, outspread; pet. broad-obovate; stamens 12–15. Fr. globose, 4mm diam., red-pink; nutlets 4–5. Spring. First developed some time before 1922, in Chenault's nursery at Orléans, France. Z6.

**Pyrethropsis** Wilcox, Bremer & Humphries. (From *Pyrethrum* and Gk *opsis*, appearance.) Compositae. About 10 species of somewhat tufted perennial herbs or subshrubs, generally rhizomatous. Sterile stems usually short and rosulate, fertile stems leafy or subscapose, much taller, terminated by a single capitulum. Leaves small, usually 3-partite, often becoming entire above, variously hairy. Capitula radiate, solitary and terminal, on long subscapose peduncles; involucre hemispheric to campanulate; receptacle more or less convex, usually naked; ray florets few to several, female; disc florets hermaphrodite. Fruit a more or less cylindric, 4–10-winged or ribbed cypsela; pappus usually a more or less auriculate, scarious corona. NW Africa. Z9.

CULTIVATION *P. mariesii* and the slightly bushier *P. hosmariensis* are elegant plants, forming mounds of deeply cut, silvery grey-green foliage, and bearing a profusion of long-stemmed, single white daisies over long periods in summer. Given perfect drainage, such as on wall top or raised bed, they may tolerate temperatures down to about −10°C/14°F, but not in combination with winter wet. They make beautiful specimens for the alpine display house, or cold glasshouse, especially as a backdrop for spring bulbs since they retain their beautiful foliage throughout winter. Cultivate as for *Leucanthemum*.

***P. atlantica*** (Ball) Wilcox, Bremer & Humphries. Rhizomatous herb, *c.*7–10cm. Lvs to 4cm, radical, fasciculate, unequally 3-partite, middle lobe ternate, lateral lobes enlarged, laciniate, seg. ovate to broadly oblong, pilose above, glabrous beneath. Capitula to 3cm diam.; peduncle leafless or with 1–2 3-partite lvs toward base; phyllaries broadly oblong, rotund, pale green, marked with an obscure green nerve, margin broad, brown-scarious; ray florets white tinged red, flushed pink at first beneath; disc florets pale yellow. Fr. 10-winged, wings equalling width of fr. body, forming a short, subequal corona at apex. Morocco.

***P. catananche*** (Ball) Wilcox, Bremer & Humphries. Rhizomatous herb, to 15cm. Lvs to 6.5cm, radical, irregularly 3-partite, dentate and simple, silver-grey. Capitula to 5cm diam.; peduncle to 10cm, leafy below middle; phyllaries laxly imbricate, ovate-lanceolate, acute, white-scarious, shiny, moderately hairy; ray florets yellow, red toward base; disc florets yellow. Fr. 4–6-ribbed and winged; pappus dimorphic; ray fr. with an auriculate, equal pappus; disc fr. with a short, unequal, subauriculate corona. Morocco.

***P. depressa*** (Ball) Wilcox, Bremer & Humphries. Herb, to 20cm, with woody caudex. Lvs to 4cm, crowded, pinnately partite, basal obovate, 3-partite, seg. 2–3-divided, linear, uppermost lvs much smaller, entire or 2-fid, linear, more or less pubesc., sometimes more or less silky-villous. Capitula 1.5–2cm diam.; peduncles leafy to about middle; phyllaries more or less adpressed white-villous, margin narrowly brown-scarious, outer ovate-triangular, obtuse, inner linear to linear-lanceolate, scarious; ray florets white to more or less purple tinged or white tinged pink above, red tinged beneath; disc florets yellow-gold, rarely purple tinged at apex. Fr. 10-ribbed, ribs prominently ornate; pappus monomorphic, auricle short at front, long and minutely erose-dentate at back, shorter than disc and ray floret tubes. Morocco and Algeria.

***P. gayana*** (Coss. & Dur.) Wilcox, Bremer & Humphries. Subshrub, to 45cm, with a woody, branched rootstock. Lvs c. 2.5cm, scattered, triangular to oblong, pinnatifid, lobes 3 or more, slender, uppermost lvs linear, entire, soft laxly woolly. Capitula *c.*2.5–4cm diam.; peduncles rather long, swollen beneath head; phyllaries numerous, imbricate, linear-oblong, acute, green, with a very narrow scarious margin; ray florets sub-biseriate, white, rose coloured beneath; disc florets brown. Fr. strongly ribbed; pappus monomorphic, base tubular, produced into a unilateral, concave, oblong, obtuse or erose-tipped, hyaline auricle, equalling disc floret disc floret tube. Morocco and Algeria.

***P. hosmariensis*** (Ball) Wilcox, Bremer & Humphries. Like *P. maresii* but more bushy, lvs sessile, capitula to 4cm diam., ray florets white, disc florets yellow. Morocco.

***P. maresii*** (Coss.) Wilcox, Bremer & Humphries. Herb, to 10–30cm, with a woody, often twisted, many-branched rootstock. Lvs more or less crowded below, 3-partite, seg. linear, very short or elongate, divergent, upper lvs often undivided, linear, pubesc. Capitula on long, leafless peduncles; phyllaries glabrescent to pubesc., obtuse, margins black-brown and scarious, outer ovate-lanceolate, innermost oblong; ray florets yellow, becoming purple tinged, then black-purple; disc florets yellow, becoming purple at apex. Fr. somewhat 10-ribbed; pappus membranous, auriculate. Algeria.

For synonymy see *Chrysanthemum, Leucanthemopsis, Leucanthemum* and *Pyrethrum*.

**Pyrethrum** Zinn.
***P. achilleifolium*** Bieb. See *Tanacetum achilleifolium*.
***P. atrosanguineum*** hort. See *Tanacetum coccineum*.
***P. carneum*** Bieb. See *Tanacetum coccineum*.
***P. cinerariifolium*** Trev. See *Tanacetum cinerariifolium*.
***P. clusii*** Fisch. ex Rchb. See *Tanacetum corymbosum* ssp. *clusii*.
***P. corymbosum*** (L.) Scop. See *Tanacetum corymbosum*.
***P. densum*** Labill. See *Tanacetum densum*.
***P. foeniculaceum*** Willd. See *Argyranthemum foeniculaceum*.
***P. gayanum*** Coss. & Dur. See *Pyrethropsis gayana*.
***P. hybridum*** Wender. See *Tanacetum coccineum*.
***P. maresii*** Coss. See *Pyrethropsis maresii*.
***P. parthenifolium*** Willd. See *Tanacetum parthenifolium*.
***P. parthenium*** (L.) Sm. See *Tanacetum parthenium*.
***P. poteriifolium*** Ledeb. See *Tanacetum poteriifolium*.
***P. ptarmiciflorum*** Webb non Willd.. See *Tanacetum ptarmiciflorum*.
***P. ptarmicifolium*** Willd. non Webb. See *Achillea ptarmicifolia*.
***P. radicans*** Cav. See *Leucanthemopsis radicans*.
***P. roseum*** Bieb. See *Tanacetum coccineum*.
***P. tchihatchewii*** (Boiss.) Bornm. See *Tripleurospermum oreades* var. *tchihatchewii*.
***P. uliginosum*** (Waldst.) & Kit. ex Willd. See *Leucanthemella serotina*.

**+Pyrocydonia** Winkl. ex Daniel. Rosaceae. A genus of graft hybrids between *Pyrus* and *Cydonia*.

CULTIVATION Grown for their botanical interest, *+Pyrocydonia* carry white flowers and bear large fruits resembling apples. Propagate by grafting on to *Pyrus communis* rootstock, or from softwood cuttings in early summer, treated with rooting hormone and rooted in a closed case with bottom heat. Otherwise, cultivate as for *Pyrus*.

+***P. danielii*** Winkl. ex Daniel. *(Cydonia oblonga + Pyrus communis* 'Williams' Bon Chrétien'.) Resembles *Cydonia oblonga* with lvs ovate, to 7.5cm, rounded at base, dentate, pubesc., and petiole very short, to 6mm. Garden origin. Raised in 1920 in the garden of St Vincent College, Rennes, by decapitating a plant of the pear 'Williams Bon Chrétien' just above the graft-union. 'Winkleri': hybrid sprung not from the graft-union but from a root of the stock, which had arisen from the graft-union many years before; habit shrubby; lvs to 4.5cm, elliptic-ovate, acuminate, obtuse at base, slightly navicular, more tomentose beneath, and white-dentate. Z6.

+*P. winkleri* Guill. See +*P. danielii* 'Winkleri'.
For further synonymy see *Pyronia*.

**Pyrogennema** Lunell. See *Epilobium*.

**Pyrola** L. WINTERGREEN; SHINLEAF. (From Lat. *pyrus*, pear, alluding to the supposed similarity of the leaves.) Pyrolaceae. 15 species of perennial, rhizomatous, glabrous, dwarf herbs. Rhizomes creeping. Leaves in basal clusters, simple, alternate, usually long-petioled. Scapes erect, bracteate, usually naked; bracts subulate to lanceolate or oblong-lanceolate to ovate;

flowers nodding, 1–1.5cm across, in loose racemes, either radial and more or less closed or bilateral and open; sepals 5; persistent; petals 5, concave, incurved, sessile; style usually curved and exserted; stamens 10, filaments tapering, anthers opening by pores; ovary 5-locular, disc absent. Fruit a 5-valved, globose capsule, drooping; seeds numerous, minute. Summer. N temperate region. Z5.

CULTIVATION Creeping evergreen perennials widespread throughout Europe, Asia and North America, *Pyrola* bear spikes of bell-like flowers in summer. Often native to damp woodland, especially of coniferous forests, they are also found on rock ledges in hill and mountain districts. *P. minor*, the common wintergreen, colonizes a variety of niches, scrub, marshes and moors, whilst *P. rotundifolia*, round-leaved wintergreen, also occurs in short turf and on dune slacks. *Pyrola* spp. are mycorrhizal, making them difficult in cultivation. They are generally grown in wild gardens, but are also suitable for cool positions in the rock garden peat terrace and woodland edge. Plant in damp, shady, sandy soils to which a little loam from an area in which they naturally occur has been added to provide mycorrhizal associates. *P. elliptica* inhabits drier, upland forest sites. Leave undisturbed since any damage to the wide-spreading fibrous feeding roots may cause either death or failure to increase in size. They can be established by division: dig small clumps carefully and root in pots of 2:1 sharp sand/acid peat, always kept moist but not wet; do not plant out until new roots are growing vigorously. Seed may be attempted but germinates infrequently: sow on moist sphagnum moss.

***P. americana*** Sweet. 12–30cm. Lvs ovate to broadly elliptic, 6.5cm, coriaceous. Fls numerous, white; bracts conspicuous; sep. oblong-lanceolate, half length of pet. Eastern N America.

***P. asarifolia*** Michx. To 65cm. Lvs broadly elliptic to reniform, to 10cm, entire or crenate, often purple beneath. Infl. to 2.2cm, many-fld; bracts conspicuous, ovate, exceeding pedicels; sep. lanceolate to oblong-lanceolate, 2–6mm; pet. pink to crimson, 5–10×3–6.5mm; anth. pink, over 2mm, fil. thickened. Canada, E US, Asia. var. ***purpurea*** (Bunge) Fern. Stem very short. Lvs ovate-elliptic, to 7cm, dull dark green above, sometimes red beneath. Fls bright violet or rose, 2.5cm diam., fragrant. N America. ssp. ***asarifolia***. BOG WINTERGREEN. Lvs ovate, round or obovate, entire or obscurely crenate. Bracts 1.5× length of pedicels; sep. 2–3.5mm, longer. ssp. ***bracteata*** (Hook.) Haber. Bracts and sep. longer than in type. Z4.

***P. chlorantha*** Sw. GREEN-FLOWERED WINTERGREEN. 15–25cm. Lvs ovate-elliptic, obovate or bracteate, to 2.5cm, entire or obscurely crenate; bracts narrow-lanceolate, not exceeding pedicels. Fls 1–10, 1.5cm diam.; sep. deltate-ovate, to 2mm, obtuse; pet. pale green; anth. 2–4mm N America. Extremely endangered. Z5.

***P. elliptica*** Nutt. To 20cm. Lvs ovate to elliptic, 3–6cm, scarcely toothed. Infl. 5–10-fld; bracts subulate, much shorter than pedicels; fls white, campanulate; sep. ovate, short. N America. Z3.

***P. grandiflora*** Radius. Resembles *P. asarifolia* but pet. white with edges tinged pink; sep. oblong; anth. yellow, to 2mm. N America. Z5.

***P. media.*** L. Resembles *P. minor* but to 30cm. Lvs ovate to obovate, to 4.5cm diam. Fls white tinged red, 1cm diam.; style straight, exserted, exceeding stamens. N America. Z5.

***P. minor*** L. LESSER WINTERGREEN. To 15cm. Lvs to 3cm, ovate to oblong-obovate, entire to obscurely crenate; petiole shorter than blade. Infl. a many-fld raceme; bracts ovate-lanceolate, often leafy at base; fls spherical, 0.5cm diam.; sep. 1.5mm, deltate, acute to acuminate; pet. white or tinged rose; style straight, included; stamens as long as style, anth. to 1mm. Europe, N America. Z5.

***P. picta*** Sm. WHITE-VEINED WINTERGREEN. Lvs to 8×5cm, young lvs often glaucous blue below, mature lvs either ovate-elliptic, entire, dark green above, purple below, veins bordered white, or oblanceolate, entire to prominently toothed, dull green above, veins not bordered. Infl. 4–24-fld; bracts lanceolate, not exceeding pedicels; sep. 2mm, ovate, acute; pet. pale green, creamy-white or white flushed pink; stamens exserted, anth. 2–5.5mm. Europe, Western N America. 'Dentata': lvs spathulate-oblong, sometimes sharp-toothed, veins without white borders. Z6.

***P. rotundifolia*** L. Lvs round to oval, shorter than petiole. Infl. 10–20-fld; scapes 15–25cm, bracts conspicuous; fls white, 1.5cm diam. Europe, N America. Z4.

***P. aphylla*** Sm. See *P. picta*.
***P. bracteata*** Hook. See *P. asarifolia* ssp. *bracteata*.
***P. californica*** Krisa. See *P. asarifolia* ssp. *asarifolia*.
***P. dentata*** Sm. See *P. picta*.
***P. elata*** Nutt. See *P. asarifolia* ssp. *asarifolia*.
***P. menziesii*** R. Br. ex D. Don. See *Chimaphila menziesii*.
***P. rotundifolia*** auct. See *P. americana*.
***P. secunda*** L. See *Orthilia secunda*.
***P. uliginosa*** (Torr.) Torr. & A. Gray. See *P. asarifolia* var. *purpurea*.
***P. umbellata*** L. See *Chimaphila umbellata*.
***P. uniflora*** L. See *Moneses uniflora*.
***P. virens*** Schreb. in Schweig. & Körte. See *P. chlorantha*.

**PYROLACEAE** Dumort. WINTERGREEN FAMILY. Dicot. 4 genera and 42 species of mycotrophic subshrubs and perennial herbs with creeping rhizomes. Leaves simple to almost absent in some *Pyrola* species, often alternate, usually all basal; stipules absent. Flowers regular, bisexual, solitary or in racemes, corymbs or umbels; calyx (4) 5 free, persistent sepals, sometimes connate at the base; corolla (4) 5 free petals, but arising from initially annular primordium; stamens double the number of petals, arising from receptacle, intrastaminal disc present; ovary superior, of 5 fused carpels, imperfectly 5-loculed, with intruded parietal placentas, not meeting; style hollow; ovules numerous. Fruit a loculicidal capsule; seeds numerous, small; endosperm copious. N temperate to Sumatra, temperate S America, usually on acid soils. *Chimaphila, Moneses, Orthilia, Pyrola*.

**Pyrolirion** Herb. (From Gk *pyr*, fire, and *lirion*, lily, from the colour of the flowers.) Amaryllidaceae. 4 species of perennial herbs. Bulbs ovate, with bulbils. Leaves long, narrow, suberect. Flower solitary, borne on a hollow leafless stem; spathe tubular and sheathing below, divided into 2 free and opposite segments above; perianth tube erect, narrow and cylindrical in the basal part, the upper part swollen, limb of 6 subequal lobes, not spreading, with a reflexed apex; filaments erect, subequal, inserted in the mouth of the tube, with incumbent anthers; style declinate; stigma trifid, with spathulate lobes. Andes. Z9.

CULTIVATION Rare in cultivation, *Pyrolirion* may prove difficult to flower. It is particularly susceptible to bulb rot when grown in wet soils. Cultivate as for *Zephyranthes*.

***P. aureum*** (Ruiz & Pav.) Herb. GOLDEN FLAME LILY. Lvs to 10×0.8cm, acuminate, striate, channelled, erect at the base and declinate in the upper part, bright yellow-green. Stems terete, lightly striate, glossy; spathe oblong, deeply bifid; pedicel 1cm; perianth golden, tube to 3.5×0.8cm, widening to a turbinate throat with denticulate scales, lobes to 6×0.8cm, lanceolate, deflexed, acuminate; fil. equal, 2.5cm shorter than perianth lobes; stigma with spread lobes. Peru.

***P. aureum*** Edwards. See *Zephyranthes flava*.
***P. flavum*** Herb. See *Zephyranthes flava*.
For further synonymy see *Amaryllis* and *Zephyranthes*.

**×Pyronia** Veitch. Rosaceae. (*Cydonia* × *Pyrus*). The fruit of ×*P. veitchii* is edible, with pear-like flesh of good flavour, ripening in early autumn.

CULTIVATION ×*Pyronia* is botanically and historically interesting and a decorative and useful ornamental, virtues derived from its parentage. ×*P. veitchii* has pretty blossom, large white flowers with contrasting violet anthers, giving rise to edible fruits with firm, white, juicy flesh, no pips, and attractively marked skin; a second flush of flowers is occasionally carried in autumn. They make useful pollution-tolerant additions to the shrub border. Cultivate as for *Pyrus*.

**×*P. veitchii*** (Trabut) Guillaum. (*Cydonia oblonga* × *Pyrus communis*.) Shrub or tree. Resembles *Cydonia* in habit. Shoots brown, spotted. Lvs to 10×5cm, elliptic, tapered, tough, entire to crenulate, light green and shiny above, lanuginose when young; petiole to 2cm. Fls pink-white, 3-fasciculate at the ends of shoots, 5cm diam.; anth. violet. Fr. rounded, to 8cm, green. Spring–autumn. Garden origin. A hybrid between the pear 'Bergamotte Esperen' (seed-parent) and the Portugal quince (pollinator), developed *c*1895 by John Seden of the Veitch nursery. Z6.

×*P. danielii* (Winkl. ex Daniel) Rehd. See +*Pyrocydonia danielii*.
For further synonymy see *Cydonia*.

**Pyrostegia** Presl. (From Gk *pyr*, fire, and *stege*, covering referring to the corolla colour reminiscent of colour of fire.) Bignoniaceae. 3–4 species of lianes climbing by tendrils; branches angled. Leaves bifoliate with or without terminal trifid tendril; sometimes trifoliate; pseudostipules inconspicuous. Flowers in terminal thyrses; calyx campanulate or denticulate; corolla tubular club-shaped, curved, lobes valvate; stamens exserted, glabrous; disc annular or cup-shaped; ovary linear, ovaries in 2 rows. Fruit capsule linear, glabrous, valves parallel; seeds transverse oblong with membranous hyaline wings. Americas. Z10.

CULTIVATION In tropical and subtropical gardens *Pyrostegia* are beautiful evergreens for arches, pergolas and fences, climbing by tendril and by twining, although plants may require a dry period to initiate flowers. In cool temperature zones, *P. venusta* is a handsome vine for the warm glasshouse or conservatory, spectacular when bearing the many-flowered panicles of brilliant orange-red blooms, produced in profusion from autumn through to spring.

Under glass, grow in full light in large tubs in a fertile, well-trained medium with additional organic matter and coarse sand. Maintain a humid atmosphere and a minimum temperature at about 10–13°C/50–55°F, watering plentifully in summer and carefully and sparingly in winter. Prune in late winter early spring, cutting back flowered stems to within 30cm/12in. of the base. *P. venusta* is especially effective if trained to a single overhead stem, with flowered shoots cut back to 2–3 buds each spring. Propagate by semi-ripe cuttings of 2–3 nodes in summer. Red spider mite, scale insect and mealybug may infest plants grown under glass.

***P. venusta*** (Ker-Gawl.) Miers. Branches glabrous or hairy. Leaflets 11×5cm, ovate to oblong-lanceolate, apex obtuse, base rounded, papery or leathery, glabrous to pubesc. and scaly above, glabrous to villous and scaly beneath. Pedicels puberulent to villous; cal. 5–7×4–5mm, 5–10-nerved, glabrous or puberulent and scaly; cor. tube 3.5–6×0.3cm, curved, orange, glabrous, lobes linear, 1–1.5cm, puberulent; disc campanulate, 1mm; ovary 3–4mm, scaly. Fr. 25–30×1.4–1.6cm, smooth leathery, median line conspicuous; seeds 1×3.5cm. Brazil, Paraguay, Bolivia, NE Argentina.

***P. ignea*** (Vell.) Presl. See *P. venusta*.
For further synonymy see *Bignonia*.

**Pyrrheima** Hassk.
***P. fuscata*** (Lodd.) Hassk. See *Siderasis fuscata*.

**Pyrrhocactus** Backeb.
***P. bulbocalyx*** (Werderm.) Backeb. See *Neoporteria bulbocalyx*.
***P. dubius*** Backeb. See *Neoporteria strausiana*.
***P. horridus*** Backeb. invalid name. See *Neoporteria horrida*.
***P. intermedius*** Ritter. See *Neoporteria taltalensis*.
***P. mammillarioides*** (Hook.) Backeb. See *Neoporteria curvispina*.

**Pyrrocoma** Hook. (From Gk *pyrrhos*, fire-red, and *kome*, head of hair, possibly alluding to the colour of the pappus in some species.) Compositae. About 10 species of perennial herbs. Stems usually several, often decumbent. Leaves chiefly radical, mostly otherwise alternate, usually simple, sometimes spinulose-dentate. Capitula terminal or in leaf axils radiate; involucre hemispheric; phyllaries usually foliaceous; receptacle flat; ray florets many, fertile or sterile, usually yellow, often scarcely exceeding disc florets; disc florets hermaphrodite, yellow, cylindric, sometimes dilated upwards. Fruit a linear, 3-angled, striate, usually glabrous cypsela; pappus of rigid, red-brown or yellow bristles. W US.

CULTIVATION As for *Haplopappus*.

***P. apargioides*** (A. Gray) Greene. Stems to 20cm, several, decumbent to ascending, glabrous or villous, red-tinged, sparsely leafy or scapiform. Basal lvs to 10×1cm, linear-lanceolate to oblanceolate, acuminate, laciniate, spinulose-dentate to entire, coarsely ciliate toward base, petiolate, coriaceous. Capitulum usually solitary, long-pedunculate; involucre *c*12mm, subhemispheric; phyllaries few-seriate, laxly imbricate, usually narrowly oblong, pungent, sometimes obtuse, green-tipped, margin pale, glabrous; ray florets yellow. Fr. glabrous, to 5mm; pappus tawny, scanty, about equalling cor. Summer–autumn. California, Nevada. Z8.

***P. clementis*** Rydb. Stems to 40cm, decumbent to ascending, somewhat villous, especially above. Lvs to 15cm, mostly basal, linear-oblong, entire or dentate, ciliate, otherwise glabrous, petiolate, upper lvs lanceolate or ovate-lanceolate, sessile. Capitula sessile, solitary or few, sessile, terminal; involucre *c*12mm, broadly hemispheric, phyllaries several-seriate, oblanceolate, abruptly acute, outer sometimes almost equalling inner; ray florets bright yellow. Fr. *c*6mm, hairy. Summer. Wyoming, Colorado, Utah. Z3.

***P. crocea*** (A. Gray) Greene. Stems to 60cm, several, sparingly villous above. Basal lvs to 20cm, spathulate, rarely dentate, glabrous, firm, petiolate, upper lvs lanceolate, sessile, semi-amplexicaul. Capitula usually solitary, terminal; involucre *c*2cm, broadly hemispheric; phyllaries several-seriate, ovate to oblong-spathulate, obtuse or rounded, outer almost equalling inner; ray florets to 2cm, orange-yellow. Fr. to 6mm, glabrous. Summer–autumn. Wyoming, Colorado, Utah, New Mexico. Z3.

For synonymy see *Haplopappus*.

**Pyrrosia** Mirb. FELT FERN. (From Gk *pyrros*, flame red, alluding to characteristic colour of stellate pubescence.) Polypodiaceae. Some 100 species of epiphytic, lithophytic, or terrestrial ferns (most spp. found in and adaptable to all 3 habitat types unless specified below). Rhizomes usually long-creeping, dictyostelic, branched; scales persistent, peltate (in all but one species), non-clathrate, entire to ciliate at margin. Fronds stipitate or sessile, uniform or dimorphous, simple and entire in this account unless specified as lobed, fleshy to leathery, stellate-pubescent and/or scaly, or (eventually) glabrous above, with differentiated hypodermis, stellate hairs usually persistent, occasionally layered, matted and felt-like, white or russet to brown, especially dense below; costa and main veins occasionally distinct and even prominent, other veins obscure, anastomosing variously, areolae with free, included veinlets, terminal hydathodes occasionally present above; stipes jointed to scaly phyllopodia, often briefly stellate-pubescent. Sori sunken or superficial, on included veinlets in upper half, in many regular or irregular rows, or 1–2-serial, or confluent, circular to elongate-oblong or oval; paraphyses stellate; indusia absent; annulus 14–24-celled; spores reniform, bilateral, smooth or finely tuberculate, glassy to yellow and discolorous. Tropical Old World. Z10.

CULTIVATION Epiphytic ferns of temperate to tropical forest. Well adapted as epiphytes, the fronds are thick and fleshy and protected by a felty layer of scales against desiccation. Often found growing in the tops of trees in full sun, or in deep shade over rocks on the forest floor. Many have long, thin creeping rhizomes which climb by means of short roots, and will quickly colonize trunks of trees or tree ferns. All require glasshouse cultivation, except for *P. serpens*, known to be hardy down to −5°C/23°F. All types make good subjects for hanging baskets, or in shallow pans; climbing species may be mounted on bark or tree fern, and require frequent syringing and high humidity. Succeed well on the trunks of living tree ferns, or may be trained up a moss pole. Propagation is by division, and newly mounted plants take time to re-establish; also from spores.

***P. africana*** (Kunze) Ballard. Rhiz. to 4mm wide, short-creeping; scales to 9×3mm, spreading, ovate to lanceolate, dentate, light brown. Fronds to 33×3cm, sessile, uniform, pendent, falcate, simple, linear to lanceolate, acute, leathery, veins obscure, lacking hydathodes; stipes absent. S Africa.

***P. angustata*** (Sw.) Ching. Rhiz. to 2mm wide, long-creeping; scales to 10×1mm, attenuate to acute, entire or dentate. Sterile fronds to 25×5cm, acute or narrowly acute at apex, cuneate and decurrent at base, glabrous and lustrous above, fertile fronds to 45×4cm, veins distinct, areolae regular, with forked, free, included veinlets, without hydathodes; stipes to 10cm (sterile) or 15cm (fertile). Malaysia to Polynesia.

***P. confluens*** (R. Br.) Ching. ROBBER FERN. Rhiz. to 2mm wide, long-creeping, much-branched; scales to 5×1mm, adpressed, lanceolate, narrowly acute, ciliate, chestnut to dark brown. Fronds simple, fleshy to leathery, sterile fronds 3–15×1.5cm, linear or elliptic to oblong or obovate, obtuse or subacute, fertile fronds 5–18×1.5cm, elliptic or lanceolate to linear, hydathodes present; costa prominent below; stipes to 5cm, remote, rigid, sulcate. Australia.

***P. eleagnifolia*** (Bory) Hovenkamp. Rhiz. to 2mm wide, long-creeping; scales to 10×2mm, entire or dentate, light brown. Sterile fronds to 9×3cm, obtuse at apex, attenuate or truncate at base, fertile fronds to 13×2cm, acute or obtuse at apex, attenuate at base, veins obscure, areolae irregular, with forked, free, included veinlets, lacking hydathodes; stipes to 5cm. New Zealand.

***P. flocculosa*** (D. Don) Ching. Rhiz. to 6mm wide, short-creeping; scales to 6×1mm, dentate, dark brown. Fronds to 32×8cm, uniform, simple, acute or narrowly acute at apex, cuneate or truncate at base, veins distinct, areolae regular, hydathodes present; stipes to 20cm. India to SE Asia.

***P. hastata*** (Thunb.) Ching. Rhiz. to 7mm wide, short-creeping, usually over rocks; scales to 3×1mm, adpressed, lanceolate to deltoid, acute, ciliate, lustrous black. Fronds to 15×10cm, uniform, pedately or palmately 3–5-lobed, hastate, truncate or cordate at base, leathery, lobes to 12×4cm, terminal, lanceolate, acute or obtuse at apex, terminal lobe spreading, oblique, ovate to deltoid, veins distinct, areolae regular, hydathodes present; stipes to 20cm. China, Japan, Korea.

***P. lanceolata*** (L.) Farw. Rhiz. to 2mm wide, long-creeping; scales to 4mm, adpressed, ovate, ciliate, grey to brown. Sterile fronds linear or spathulate to obovate or lanceolate, obtuse at apex, cuneate at base, to 6×2cm, fertile fronds lanceolate to linear, caudate at apex, to 20cm×5mm, hydathodes absent; stipes to 2cm apart, to 5cm. India to China, Malaysia, New Guinea, Polynesia, Australia.

***P. lingua*** (Thunb.) Farw. TONGUE FERN; JAPANESE FELT FERN. Rhiz. to 3mm wide, long-creeping, wiry; scales to 8mm, adpressed and imbricate, lanceolate to linear, ciliate, light brown. Fronds to 30×5cm, uniform, lanceolate to ovate, narrowly acute at apex, cuneate at base, leathery; stipes to 3cm apart, to 5cm, straw-coloured. E Asia (China, Taiwan, Japan). 'Eboshi' ('Contorta'): fronds twisted. 'Monstrifera': fronds deeply and irregularly cut. 'Nana': fronds short. 'Nankin-Shisha' ('Kujuku'): fronds cristate and contorted. 'Nokogiri-ba' ('Serrata'): fronds crenate and crinkled. 'Shisha' ('Cristata'): fronds forked at tips, appearing crested. 'Tsunomata': frond tips 2–3× branched. 'Variegata': fronds crenate, with oblique, variegated stripes.

***P. longifolia*** (Burm. f.) Morton. Rhiz. to 3mm wide, long-creeping, much-branched; scales to 2mm, circular to ovate, dark brown. Fronds to 1m×2cm, uniform, strap-shaped, acute or obtuse at apex, attenuate and decurrent at base, fleshy, glossy deep green, sparsely mealy above, often arching and somewhat puckered, veins distinct, areolae regular, with simple free, included veinlets, without hydathodes; stipes to 10cm. Malaysia, Australia (Queensland), Polynesia.

***P. nummulariifolia*** (Sw.) Ching. CREEPING BUTTON FERN. Rhiz. to 2mm wide, long-creeping; scales to 6×1mm, lanceolate to linear, hair-tipped, ciliate, russet to brown. Sterile fronds to 5×4cm, ovate to circular, thin-textured, fertile fronds to 12×1cm, linear or oblanceolate, apex obtuse, base attenuate to cuneate, veins obscure, areolae irregular, with simple free, included veinlets, lacking hydathodes; stipes to 3cm. Indochina to Malaysia, Philippines.

***P. polydactyla*** (Hance) Ching. Rhiz. to 6mm wide, short-creeping; scales to 2×1mm, lanceolate, ciliate, brown to black. Fronds to 20×18cm, uniform, pedately or palmately 6–8-lobed, cuneate at base, deep lustrous green, lobes to 14×2cm, spreading, finger-like, veins distinct, areolae regular, with simple, free, included veinlets, hydathodes present; stipes to 10cm. Philippines.

***P. serpens*** (Forst. f.) Ching. Rhiz. to 2mm wide, long-creeping; scales to 3×1mm, linear, attenuate at apex, ciliate, light brown to russet. Sterile fronds to 15×2cm, obovate to circular, obtuse at apex, attenuate to cuneate at base, fertile fronds to 25×2cm, linear to oblong, veins indistinct, areolae regular, with or without hydathodes; stipes to 5cm, erect, rigid. Australasia.

***P. stigmosa*** (Sw.) Ching. Rhiz. to 5mm wide, short-creeping; scales to 6×2mm, *not* peltate, hair-tipped, entire or dentate, dark brown. Fronds to 45×5cm, uniform, narrowly acute at apex, cuneate at base, leathery, veins prominent, areolae regular, hydathodes present; stipes to 25cm, to 1cm apart. Indochina to New Guinea.

***P. subfurfuracea*** (Hook.) Ching. Rhiz. to 7mm wide, short-creeping; scales to 11×1mm, ciliate, dark brown. Fronds to 90×8cm, uniform, narrowly acute at apex, attenuate at base, veins distinct, areolae regular, with forked, free, included veinlets, hydathodes present; stipes to 30cm. Indochina, SE Asia.

***P. adnascens*** (Sw.) Ching. See *P. lanceolata*.
***P. macrocarpa*** (Hook. & Arn.) Shing. See *P. serpens*.
***P. tricuspe*** (Sw.) Tag. See *P. hastata*.
***P. varia*** (Kaulf.) Farw. See *P. lanceolata*.

**Pyrularia** Michx. (Diminutive of *Pyrus*, pear; an allusion to the shape of the fruit.) Santalaceae. 4 species of large, dioecious, parasitic shrubs. Branches initially pubescent. Leaves alternate, short-petiolate. Flowers in spikes; males: sepals 5, pubescent, at insertion of stamen; females: sepals 5, ovary distinctly narrowed at base, giving a stalked appearance to the flowers. Fruit drupaceous, pyriform. N America, Himalaya. Z4.

CULTIVATION As for *Buckleya*.

***P. pubera*** Michx. BUFFALO NUT; ELK. To 4m. Lvs obovate to oblong, acute. Infl. a sparse spike. Drupe 2.5cm or longer. E US (Pennsylvania to Georgia and Alabama).

**Pyrus** L. PEAR. (Lat. name for pear.) Rosaceae. About 30 species of deciduous trees and shrubs; shoots occasionally thorny. Leaves deciduous, alternate, simple, commonly serrate or scalloped, occasionally lobed; stipules reduced to a bristle-like protrusion or awl-shaped. Flowers white, sometimes tinted yellow, green or rose, usually fading to white, in umbels or corymbs on lateral shoots, calyx and petals 5, stamens usually 20, rarely 25–30, carpels 5 or rarely 2, separate or slightly fused, styles usually distinct or basal part tightly grouped near the disk. Fruit pyriform, often with persistent calyx, flesh embedded with grit cells; seed cavity with tough parchment-like walls, seeds black-brown. Europe to E Asia and N Africa.

CULTIVATION *Pyrus* spp. occur in a diversity of habitats, from the open woodland, and sunny hillsides of *P. nivalis*, and dry rocky mediterranean habitats of *P. amygdaliformis*, to light, woodland edge thickets of *P. pyraster*. Ornamental *Pyrus* spp. are grown for their spring flowers, habit and for foliage, as lawn specimens, in the mixed border or as wall-trained plants; they share the familial trait of developing great character with age. *Pyrus* is hardy, most species to at least −15°C/5°F, tolerant of atmospheric pollution, drought and excessive moisture, and of a range of soil types, providing they are moderately fertile.

The genus includes a number of attractive grey or silver-foliaged trees; *P. elaeagrifolia, P. nivalis* and *P. salicifolia* 'Pendula', with its tangled weeping habit, bearing pure white flowers with the emerging leaves. *P. communis*, often a host to mistletoe, especially where large old trees remain as survivors of perry orchards, is especially beautiful in flower, and is worth growing for this alone, even in regions where frosts make fruit set unreliable. *P. pashia*, also grown for its flowers, carries compact clusters of pink buds, opening to rose-pink, later white with contrasting deep red stamens. *P. calleryana* 'Bradford' flowers profusely in spring and colours well in autumn, in shades of russet and red. It is commonly grown as a street tree in the US. The narrowly conical *P. calleryana* 'Chanticleer' is more suitable for the smaller garden; *P. pyrifolia, P. ussuriensis*, and *P.* ×*lecontei* are also noted for their autumn colours.

Grow in good, well-drained loam in full sun. Propagate desirable varieties by budding or grafting on to seedling rootstocks of *P. communis*. Propagate species by seed, although progeny may be variable; stratify for 8–10 weeks, at 1°C/34°F, and sow in spring. Temperatures above 15–20°C/60–68°F in the sowing medium may induce a secondary dormancy.

*Pyrus* is susceptible to fireblight, *Erwinia amylovora*. Pear scab, *Venturia pirina*, causes olive green blotches on leaves, and small blisters on shots,use an appropriate fungicide, and cut out affected shoots. Pear ring pattern mosaic virus and pear vein yellows have mainly cosmetic effects on ornamentals. Pear decline mycoplasma, transmitted by the pear sucker, *Psylla pyricola*, causes poor shoot growth, die-back, upward rolling of leaves, and intense red autumn leaf colour with premature leaf fall, and may eventually kill the tree; it is known in France and Germany in northern Europe, and is common and serious in the US. Use virus-free stocks.

See also PEARS.

***P. amygdaliformis*** Vill. Shrub or small tree to 6m; shoots slender, thorny with long downy hairs at first, later shiny brown, glabrous. Lvs variable, 2.5–7cm, ovate-obovate, pointed or blunt, somewhat coriaceous, entire or finely scalloped, grey-felted at first becoming shiny green, glabrous, blue-green below; petiole to 3cm. Fls 2–2.5cm diam., in corymbs of 8–12. Fr. 2–3cm, rounded, yellow-brown; pedicel 2–3cm, grey-felted. S Europe, Asia Minor. var. ***cuneifolia*** (Guss.) Bean. Lvs smaller and narrower than the type, base alternate. var. ***lobata*** (Decne.) Koehne. Shrub; shoots slender, thorny. Lvs 2–3.5×1–2cm, oblong-elliptic, base rounded, margins entire or with 1–2 lobes, grey-green. var. ***oblongifolia*** (Spach) Bean. Lvs elliptic to oblong, apex blunt, base rounded; petiole 2.5–3cm. Fr. larger, yellow flushed red. S France. Z6.

***P. balansae*** Decne. Resembles *P. communis* but lvs 5–10cm, ovate to oblong, long tapered, base rounded, lvs on juvenile plants rough and finely serrate, becoming entire or scalloped on mature specimens; petiole to 4cm. Fls white, early. Fr. 2.5cm, almost triangular on long pedicels. Asia Minor. Z6.

***P. betulifolia*** Bunge. Tree, 5–10m, crown erect, narrow, vigorous, branches arching or slightly nodding, downy in the first season, glabrous later. Lvs 4–7cm, ovate-oblong or slightly rhombic, long-tapered, roughly serrate, base rounded or slightly heart-shaped, green and shiny above, grey-green and sparsely downy beneath; petiole 2–2.5cm. Fls 2cm diam. in corymbs of 8–10, these felted; cal. downy, later abscising. Fr. 1–1.5cm, subglobose, brown speckled white; pedicel 2–3cm, slender. N China. Frequently used as a rootstock in China and US and recently in Europe. Z5.

***P. bourgaeana*** Decne. Tree, shoots erect at first, later spreading; young bark brown, becoming finely plated with age. Lvs 2–7×1.5–3.5cm, ovate-lanceolate to broadly ovate, margins scalloped. Fr. 17–25mm, globose or angular, matt yellow, brown spotted in places, cal. persistent; pedicel 2–4cm, slender. W Spain, Portugal, Morocco. Z6.

***P. bretschneideri*** Rehd. Medium tree resembling *P. ussuriensis* var. *ovoidea*, but cal. absent from fr.; shoots almost glabrous, purple brown in the second season. Lvs 5–11cm, ovate to elliptic, long-tapered, base triangular or more rounded, margins with rough serrations, the teeth adpressed with needle-like protrusions, woolly only at first, smooth later; petiole 2.5–7cm. Fls 3cm diam., in clusters, tomentose when young. Fr. 2.5–3cm, subglobose to more oval, yellow, flesh white, edible; pedicel 3–4cm. N China. Z5.

***P. calleryana*** Decne. Tree, lateral shoots short, thorny; buds lightly downy. Lvs 4–8cm, ovate, short tapered, margins scalloped, shiny, glabrous; petiole 2–4cm. Fls 2–2.5cm diam.; pedicel 1.5–3cm, glabrous in the axes; stamens 20; styles 2, rarely 3. Fr. 1cm, rounded, brown, pitted, cal. absent; pedicel slender. China. 'Aristocrat': tall and fast-growing, to 13×9m, crown broadly pyramidal; branches thornless; lvs wavy-edged, glossy, brilliant deep red in autumn, plum when young; fls white; fr. red to yellow. 'Autumn Blaze': fast-growing, to 12×7m, habit horizontal, asymmetrical and open, crown moderately ovate; lvs glossy, crimson autumn colour. 'Bradford': to 13×13m, crown broadly ovate, dense, branching habit; lvs red to maroon in autumn. 'Capital': to 12×4m, crown loosely pyramidal, dense; lvs rich glossy green, purple in autumn. 'Chanticleer' ('Cleveland Select', 'Select'): to 13×4m, crown narrow-conical, evenly branched; lvs glossy green, becoming carmine scarlet in autumn; spiny. 'Redspire': to 12×8m, crown moderately pyramidal, upright, well-branched; lvs long, thick, glossy, coloured crimson to purple in autumn; fls in large clusters, profuse; appears adapted to atmospheric pollution. 'Stone Hill': to 12×8m, upright, crown oval; lvs deep green, shiny, brilliant orange in autumn; reportedly drought and disease resistant. 'Trinity': to 10×8m, somewhat globe-shaped, crown rounded; lvs light green, somewhat serrate, orange to red in autumn; fls abundant. 'White House': to 10×7m, upright, compact, crown moderately ovate; branches upward-arching, strong central leader; lvs red to plum in early autumn; reportedly urban tolerant. f. ***tomentella*** Rehd. Shoots woolly only in the first year. Lvs soon glabrous, with the exception of midrib which remains densely tomentose, margins of lvs on long shoots finely serrate. Infl. downy, tufted in axils. China. Z5.

***P. ×canescens*** Spach *(P. nivalis × P. salicifolia.)* Tree, resembling *P. nivalis* but lvs lanceolate or narrow-elliptic, apical margin scalloped, grey-white downy at first, becoming dark shiny green; fr. pale green on short pedicels. Z6.

***P. communis*** L. COMMON PEAR. Tree to 15m, crown conical, broad; shoots and branches sometimes thinly downy, often thorny. Lvs 2–8cm, oval-elliptic, pointed, margins scalloped, very soon glabrous, although tufted early on, autumn colours red-yellow. Fls 3cm diam., in corymbs, these smooth or downy-tufted, cupule felted, anth. red. Fr. 2.5–5cm, pyriform or subglobose, yellow green, cal. retained, flesh bitter. Europe, Asia Minor. var. ***sativa*** DC. A collective term for all edible pear cultivars; see PEARS. Z4.

***P. cordata*** Desv. Shrub 3–4m, branches spreading, densely thorny; bark fine breaking up into platelets; shoots purple at first. Lvs 1–4cm, oval, base often heart-shaped, margins scalloped, always glabrous; petiole long, often exceeding the blade in length. Fls occasionally in small clusters, commonly with long axes (1–3cm); pet. 8–10mm, obovate. Fr. 10–18mm, sub-globose, apex flattened, red waxy, cal. absent; pedicel 1.5–3.5cm, slender. S Europe, SW England. Z8.

***P. cossonii*** Rehd. Small tree; shoots smooth with occasional thorns. Lvs 2.5–5×1–3cm, bluntly elliptic or ovate, apex blunt or short tapered, margins with regular fine rounded notches, eventually green shiny above, glabrous beneath, but felted when young; petiole 2.5–5cm, slender. Fls 3cm diam., in clusters to 7cm. Fr. 1.5cm, rounded, brown lightly pitted, cal. absent; pedicel 3cm, slender. Algeria. Z8.

***P. elaeagrifolia*** Pall. Small tree, resembling *P. nivalis*, branches thorny, shoots felted when young. Lvs 4–7cm, lanceolate or more elliptic, narrower than *P. nivalis*, blunt or slightly tapered, base triangular, margins entire, grey-white felted above and beneath, later occasionally becoming smooth above; petiole 1–4cm; fls 3cm diam., in felted corymbs, white; pedicel 1–2cm. Fr. 2cm, rounded or more angular, green. Asia Minor. var. ***kotschyana*** (Decne.) Boiss. Thornless shrub. Lvs 3–6cm, wider than the type; petiole to 3cm, pubesc. Asia Minor. Z5.

***P. fauriei*** Schneid. Tree or large shrub; shoots smooth at first becoming thorny with age. Resembles *P. calleryana* but with smaller features. Lvs 2.5–5cm, elliptic, base attenuate; petiole 2–2.5cm, downy. Fls in clusters of 2–8. Fr. 13mm, flesh without grit cells. Korea. Z9.

***P. kawakamii*** Hayata. EVERGREEN PEAR. Shrub or small tree 4–10m, bark black-brown; shoots with sharp thorns. Lvs 6–10cm, ovate or obovate, in terminal clusters of 3–4 on lateral branches, these evergreen, coriaceous, margins with fine rounded teeth; petiole to 3cm. Fls sparse in small clusters, cal. smooth. Fr. to 11mm, rounded, smooth. China, Taiwan. Z8.

***P. korshinskyi*** Litv. Tree, closely resembling *P. communis*; shoots felted at first; lvs 5–8cm, oval-oblong or more lanceolate, upper surface only slightly pubesc., margins on lower surfaces finely scalloped, margins and petioles felted-tufted. Fls in flattened clusters, pedicels to 3cm, infl. disk also downy-tufted. Fr. 2cm, globose, on stout pedicels, cal. persistent. Turkestan. Z6.

***P. ×lecontei*** Rehd. *(P. communis × P. pyrifolia.)* LE CONTE PEAR. Sturdy medium-sized tree, taking many years to reach maturity; shoots thick, undulating. Lvs 8×3cm, ovate-elliptic, long tapered, margins with fine rounded serrations; petiole smooth. Fls to 3cm diam., in flattened clusters of 7–10, early. Fr. 6–8×4–5cm, ellipsoid, yellow, pitted, flesh rather granular, white, sour. Garden origin (pre-1850). Z6.

***P. lindleyi*** Rehd. Resembles *P. ussuriensis*, but lvs ovate, apex abruptly tapered, base rounded, normally cordate on strong shoots, margins with short adpressed teeth. Fr. on long stalks, ellipsoid, cal. retained. China. Z6.

***P. ×michauxii*** Bosc. *(P. amygdaliformis × P. nivalis.)* Small tree, crown almost globose; shoots without thorns. Lvs 3–7cm, ovate to elliptic-oblong, blunt or with an abruptly tapered apex, margins entire, both surfaces felted at first later shiny, smooth above often remaining slightly pubesc. beneath. Fls in short crowded corymbs, white. Fr. 3×2cm rounded or rather angular, yellow-green, sour. Asia. Z6.

***P. nivalis*** Jacq. SNOW PEAR. Small tree to 10m, rarely larger; shoots densely felted at first, always without thorns, buds downy on outside but inner scales smooth. Lvs 5–8cm elliptic to obovate, base triangular, margins entire or slightly scalloped only at the tip, young lvs white-felted, eventually dark green with occasional hairs above, but remaining felted beneath or rarely becoming glabrous, autumn colour dark red. Fls 2.5–3cm diam. in corymbs of 6–9, these felted. Fr. 3–5cm, globose or more angular, yellow-green, maturing late in season, sour tasting. SE Europe. f. ***austriaca*** (Kerner) Schneid. Lvs elliptic, glabrous throughout when mature. Austria, Hungary. Z6.

***P. pashia*** Hamilt. Tree 10–12m, young shoots felted, later red-brown and thorny. Lvs 6–12cm, ovate-oblong, apex long-tapered, base rounded, margins with rounded notches or blunt serrations, occasionally sharply serrate on young shoots, felted at first, later almost glabrous; petiole 1.5–4cm. Fls 2–2.5cm diam.; cal. lobes cuneate; pet. numerous, white; stamens 25–30; styles 3–5. Fr. 2cm, subglobose, brown with irregular pits; pedicel 2–3cm. Himalayas to W China. var. ***kumaoni*** (Decne.) Stapf. Very similar to species type but stems and infl. glabrous, cal. lobes ovate often blunt. Z5.

***P. persica*** Pers. Small tree. Lvs 3–6cm, held almost horizontally, elliptic-oblong, thick, densely tomentose at first, later blue-green above, sparsely tomentose beneath, margins finely scalloped. Infl. a felted umbel of 6–12 fls. Fr. 3cm, globose or angular, green flushed red; pedicel 2cm. Asia Minor, Greek Is. Z7.

***P. phaeocarpa*** Rehd. Tree, first-year wood felted, later red-brown, smooth. Lvs 6–10cm, elliptic-ovate to oval-oblong, long-tapered, base broadly triangular, margins dentate, teeth widely spaced, soon glabrous although downy-tufted at first; petiole 2–6cm. Fls 3cm diam. in corymbs of 3–4, these usually tomentose, rarely glabrous; styles 3–4, rarely 2. Fr. 2–2.5cm, pyriform, brown speckled white-yellow; pericarp soon pulpy. N China. f. ***globosa*** Rehd. Lvs usually ovate, base rounded. Fr. 1.5–2cm subglobose. Z5.

***P. pyraster*** Burgsd. Small or medium tree, bark thick, later forming platelets; shoots upright and downy when young, spreading with age, becoming shiny brown, both branches and shoots thorny. Lvs 3–5cm, ovate or more rounded, blade thin, downy only at first, veins in 6–8 pairs. Sep. linear-subulate; pet. round topped or pyriform umbels, matt yellow, speckled brown. C to SW Europe. Z6.

***P. pyrifolia*** (Burm.) Nak. SAND PEAR. Tree 5–12m, shoots densely woolly or smooth when young, later dark red-brown glabrous. Lvs 7–12cm, oval oblong, rarely ovate, long tapered, base rounded or somewhat cordate, margin with close, sharp, bristle-like serrations, surfaces smooth or woolly; petiole 3–4.5cm. Fls 3–3.5cm diam., in corymbs of 6–9, these often woolly; pedicel 3–3.5cm, slender; cal. lobes triangular-ovate, long-tapered, to twice the length of tube; pet. ovate; styles 4, rarely 5; stamens 20. Fr. 3cm, subglobose, brown, slightly pitted, cal. absent; pericarp very firm. C & W China. var. ***culta*** (Mak.) Nak. Lvs to 15cm, both longer and wider than the type. Fr. pyriform or globose, brown or yellow. China, Japan. f. ***stapfiana*** (Rehd.) Rehd. Serrations more open; pet. tapered to claw; fr. to 5cm, pyriform. China. Z6.

***P. regelii*** Rehd. Shrub or small tree to 9m, shoots divaricate, apices and laterals thorny; primary wood grey-felted, later becoming purple-brown, glabrous. Lvs variable, ovate-oblong, margins simple or lobed, lobes variable, irregular with rough teeth, sometimes almost pinnate. Fls 2–2.5cm diam. in sparse flattened corymbs, white. Fr. 2–3cm, globose or pyrimiform. Turkestan. Z6.

***P. salicifolia*** Pall. Tree 5–8m, shoots slender, almost pendulous, laterals often ending with a thorn, grey-white felted at first, glabrous green in late season. Lvs 3–9cm, narrow elliptic, base and apex acuminate, margins entire or sparsely toothed, downy beneath but becoming glabrous above. Fls cream to green-white 2cm diam., in small clusters of 6–8; cal. and pedicel felted. Fr. 2–3cm, pyriform, green, flesh firm, sour; pedicel short. SE Europe, Asia Minor, Caucasus. 'Pendula': doubtfully distinct from type. 'Silfrozam': to 4.5×3.5m, crown broadly weeping; lvs willow-like, silver-grey. Z4.

***P. ×salviifolia*** DC. *(P. communis × P. nivalis.)* Resembles *P. nivalis* but lvs smaller; shoots with large, thick thorns. Lvs to 5cm, elliptic to ovate, pointed or tapered, base triangular or more rounded, margins finely scalloped, grey downy only at first; petioles long. Fr. 2.5cm, pyriform; pedicel 2–3cm. W & C Europe. Z6.

***P. serrulata*** Rehd. Closely resembles *P. pyrifolia* but lvs finely serrate; first-year wood densely tomentose, later red-brown; lvs 5–11cm, ovate to oval-oblong, apex tapering, often abruptly, base triangular or more rounded, margins finely serrate, soon glabrous, woolly at first; petiole 3.5–7cm. Fls 2.5cm diam., in tomentose flattened clusters; styles 3–4, rarely 5; sep. equal to tube, tapering. Fr. 1.5cm, subglobose, brown, speckled, cal. nearly always retained. China (Kansu, Hupeh, Sichuan). Z6.

***P. syriaca*** Boiss. Small erect tree, almost always thorny; shoots spreading. Lvs 2.5cm, occasionally to 10cm, oblong or more lanceolate, almost glabrous, margins finely scalloped; petiole 2–5cm. Fls in densely felted corymbs. Fr. 3cm, pyriform, pedicel stout, to 5cm. Cyprus, Asia Minor. Z7.

***P. ussuriensis*** Maxim. Tree to 15m, shoots smooth yellow-brown. Lvs 5–10cm, ovate or more rounded, long-tapered, base rounded cordate, margins with bristle-like teeth, glabrous yellow-green above, paler beneath, becoming carmine on senescence; petiole 2.5cm, slender. Infl. a domed cluster of 6–9 fls, each to 3cm diam., pet. obovate, base narrowing. Fr. 3–4cm subglobose, green-yellow; pericarp hardened; pedicel stout, short. Flowering early. NE Asia. var. ***hondoensis*** (Kikuchi & Nak.) Rehd. Shoots and lvs woolly at first, later dark orange brown, margins with fine, less tapered, less adpressed teeth. C Japan. var. ***ovoidea*** (Rehd.) Rehd. Shoots spreading, divaricate, brown at first. Lvs narrow ovate to oblong-ovate; fr. ovoid to pyriform; pericarp juicy, yellow. N China, Korea. Z4.

***P. achras*** Gaertn. See *P. pyraster*.
***P. alpina*** Willd. See ×*Sorbaronia alpina*.
***P. amygdaliformis*** var. ***persica*** (Pers.) Bornm. See *P. persica*.
***P. arbutifolia*** (L.) L. f. See *Aronia arbutifolia*.
***P. aria*** 'Kumaonensis'. See *Sorbus japonica*.
***P. auricularis*** Kroop. See ×*Sorbopyrus auricularis*.
***P. austriaca*** Kerner. See *P. nivalis* f. *austriaca*.
***P. bartramiana*** Tausch. See *Amelanchier bartramiana*.
***P. bollwylleriana*** DC. See ×*Sorbopyrus auricularis*.
***P. botryapium*** L. f., in part. See *Amelanchier canadensis*.
***P. bucharica*** Litv. See *P. korshinsky*.
***P. calleryana*** var. ***fauriei*** (Schneid.) Rehd. See *P. fauriei*.
***P. communis*** var. ***cordata*** (Desv.) Briggs. See *P. cordata*.
***P. communis*** var. ***pyraster*** L. See *P. pyraster*.
***P. delavayi*** Franch. See *Docynia delavayi*.
***P. depressa*** Lindl. See *Aronia arbutifolia* var. *pumila*.
***P. elaeagrifolia*** Steud. See *P. elaeagrifolia*.
***P. ferruginea*** Koidz. See *P. ussuriensis* var. *hondoensis*.
***P. firma*** hort. See *Sorbus hybrida* 'Gibbsii'.
***P. glomerulata*** (Koehne) Bean. See *Sorbus glomerulata*.
***P. grandifolia*** Lindl. See *Aronia melanocarpa* var. *grandifolia*.
***P. heterophylla*** Reg. & Schmalh. non Poir. non Steud. See *P. regelii*.
***P. hondoensis*** Kikuchi & Nak. See *P. ussuriensis* var. *hondoensis*.
***P. hybrida*** Moench. See ×*Sorbaronia hybrida*.
***P. indica*** Wallich. See *Docynia indica*.
***P. japonica*** Thunb. See *Chaenomeles japonica*.
***P. japonica*** Sims non Thunb. See *Chaenomeles speciosa*.
***P. kumaoni*** Decne. See *P. pashia* var. *kumaoni*.
***P. lobata*** Decne. See *P. amygdaliformis* var. *lobata*.
***P. longipes*** Coss. and Dur. See *P. cossonii*.
***P. malifolia*** Spach. See ×*Sorbopyrus auricularis* 'Bulbiformis'.
***P. malus*** L. pro parte. See *Malus sylvestris*.
***P. maulei*** (T. Moore) Mast. See *Chaenomeles japonica*.
***P. melanocarpa*** (Michx.) Willd. See *Aronia melanocarpa*.
***P. ×mixta*** Fern. See ×*Sorbaronia sorbifolia*.
***P. nivalis*** var. ***elaeagrifolia*** Schneid. See *P. elaeagrifolia*.
***P. oblongifolia*** Spach. See *P. amygdaliformis* var. *oblongifolia*.
***P. ovoidea*** Rehd. See *P. ussuriensis* var. *hondoensis* var. *ovoidea*.
***P. parviflora*** Desf. See *P. amygdaliformis*.
***P. pinnatifida*** var. ***fastigiata*** Bean. See *Sorbus* × *thuringiaca* 'Fastigiata'.
***P. pollveria*** L. See ×*Sorbopyrus auricularis*.
***P. rhamnoides*** Hook. See *Sorbus rhamnoides*.
***P. serotina*** Rehd. See *P. pyrifolia*.
***P. simonii*** Carr. See *P. ussuriensis*.
***P. simonii*** hort. non Carr. See *P. ussuriensis* var. *hondoensis* var. *ovoidea*.
***P. sinaica*** Dum.-Cours. See *P. persica*.
***P. sinensis*** Lindl. non Poir. See *P. lindleyi*.
***P. sinensis*** sensu Decne. See *P. ussuriensis*.
***P. sinensis*** var. ***maximowicziana*** Lév. See *Photinia villosa* var. *laevis* f. *maximowicziana*.
***P. sorbifolia*** (Poir.) Wats. See ×*Sorbaronia sorbifolia*.
***P. ursina*** Wallich ex G. Don. See *Sorbus ursina*.
***P. variolosa*** Wallich. See *P. pashia*.
***P. vestita*** Wallich. See *Sorbus cuspidata*.
***P. wilhelmi*** Schneid. See *P. pashia* var. *kumaoni*.
***P. yunnanensis*** Bean pro parte. See *Malus yunnanensis* var. *veitchii*.

# Q

**Quamoclit** Moench.
*Q. coccinea* (L.) Moench. See *Ipomoea coccinea*.
*Q. coccinea* var. ***hederifolia*** (L.) House. See *Ipomoea hederifolia*.
***Q. hederifolia*** (L.) G. Don. See *Ipomoea hederifolia*.
***Q. lobata*** (Cerv.) House. See *Ipomoea lobata*.
***Q. pennata*** (Desr.) Bojer. See *Ipomoea quamoclit*.
***Q.*** × ***sloteri*** House. See *Ipomoea* × *sloteri*.
***Q. vulgaris*** Choisy. See *Ipomoea quamoclit*.

**Quaqua** N.E. Br. (From the Koisan vernacular name for the genus.) Asclepiadaceae. 13 species of dwarf, succulent, perennial herbs, closely related to *Caralluma*, to 45cm. Stems to 4cm thick, glabrous, roundly 4–6-angled, tinged grey or purple, angles toothed, teeth conical, patent to decurved, yellow-brown, tuberculose, with a sharp groove between the rows of tuberculae. Flowers solitary or in bundles, from grooves; pedicels 1.5–15mm; corolla 7–25mm diam., tube to 5mm deep, conical to bowl-shaped, rarely absent, lobes to 15mm, ovate-lanceolate to linear-acute; outer corona lobes deeply to shallowly bifid or entire, enclosing space around inner lobes. Fruit an erect follicle, in pairs. Namibia, S Africa (Cape Province: Namaqualand). Z9.

CULTIVATION As for *Stapelia*.

***Q. acutiloba*** (N.E. Br.) P.V. Bruyns. Clump-forming; stems 4–20×1.2–2cm, branching from base, 4-angled, pale blue-grey green, teeth 4–5mm, hard-tipped. Fls 8–13mm diam., several together near stem tips, exterior pale green-purple, interior uniformly purple-black or marked purple-black on yellow ground or uniformly yellow, area around corona paler, lobes 3–6×2–3.5mm, deltoid; cor. entirely glabrous. Cape Province: Springbok south to Ceres District.

***Q. armata*** (N.E. Br.) P.V. Bruyns. Forming dense broad mats to 60cm across. Stems 10–20×2–3cm, 4–6-angled, dark grey-green, mottled purple, teeth 1.5mm with a blunt, hard, conical tip. Fls 2.2cm diam. in clusters of 2–12 near stem tips, arising from a flattened peduncle in the stem grooves, often opening simultaneously, exterior and interior glabrous, lobes 8–15×4mm, tapering to an acute apex, margins replicate only in upper half, brown becoming yellow-brown toward the pale yellow tube. Cape Province. ssp. ***arenicola*** (N.E. Br.) P.V. Bruyns. Stems to 15cm, usually 4-angled, green to grey-purple with a sharp tip to each tubercle. Cor. with short papillate hairs in the mouth of the tube, otherwise glabrous, lobes 12mm diam., 3× longer than wide, margins recurved for three-quarters of length. S Cape. ssp. ***maritima*** P.V. Bruyns. Cor. 9mm diam., with papillate hairs in the tube mouth and the lower part of the lobes, lobes 6–8mm, purple-black becoming off-white in the tube, margins replicate for most of their length. Cape Province: coastal area of Little Namaqualand. ssp. ***pilifera*** P.V. Bruyns. Stems mostly 4-angled, to 10cm, green-purple with a sharp tip to each tubercle. Cor. 11–13mm diam., upper surface entirely covered with fine spicules and usually L-shaped papillae, each topped by a thick hair, dark purple-brown within, tinged green outside, tube 2–3mm deep, 4mm wide at mouth, lobes usually slightly replicate for most of their length, 8×4mm. Cape Province: Sutherland District.

***Q. framesii*** (Pill.) P.V. Bruyns. Forming dense clumps; stems to 40×2cm, grey-green to somewhat purple with small red spots, 4–6-angled, angles irregular to spiralled, armed with hard, short-tipped, horizontal or slightly recurved, yellow teeth. Fls in clusters of 2–10, opening simultaneously toward the tips of the stems from flattened peduncular patch; cor. to 18mm diam., exterior yellow-green, interior bright yellow, tube cupular, 3×3mm with stiff hairs in the mouth, lobes 8×2mm, rarely fully expanded, more or less uniform in width to the obtuse apex, which is often slightly incurved, margins slightly folded back giving surface a convex shape. Cape Province: Van Rhynsdorp District.

***Q. incarnata*** (L. f.) P.V. Bruyns. Stems 10–30×2.5cm, erect, grey to purple-green, 4-angled, teeth conical, stout, spreading, apices hard. Fls 4–10, toward stem apex; cor. white to pale pink outside, interior pale yellow to cream-white, tube 2mm, cup-shaped, campanulate or shallowly conical, lobes to 8mm, deltoid to lanceolate, margins reflexed, both tube mouth and lobes stiffly hairy; corona enclosed by tube, outer lobes yellow, bifid, inner lobes pale yellow. Namibia; Cape Province (Namaqualand). var. ***tentaculata*** P.V. Bruyns. Cor. lobes 8–10×2mm, narrowing abruptly because of replicate margins. Cape Province: Little Namaqualand. ssp. ***aurea*** (Lückh.) P.V. Bruyns. Clump-forming, 50×50cm; stems branching from base, 1.5–2cm thick, 4–5-angled, grey-green, with stout sharp-toothed tubercles. Fls 1–6 in small groups opening simultaneously from upper half of stems; cor. 2–2.2cm diam., exterior off-white, mottled pale pink, glabrous, interior yellow, paler in tube, minutely hairy, tube V-shaped, 2mm diam., lobes 6–9×2.5–3mm, spreading, margins folded back for most of their length. Cape Province: Nieuwoudville Plateau.

***Q. inversa*** (N.E. Br.) P.V. Bruyns. Clump-forming; stems 25×1.5–2.5cm, 4-angled, grey-green to purple-green with stout acute teeth to 1cm on the tubercles. Fls solitary or small cushions between the angles; pedicels holding fls downwards; cor. to 1.5cm diam., tube 1.5–2mm deep, yellow or white, sometimes striped purple, lobes 3–8×2–4mm, broadly ovate-lanceolate, spreading, margins recurved with flattened purple hairs, yellow to green at tip, purple-brown to red in lower half, change of colour abrupt. Cape Province: Clanwilliam & Van Rhynsdorp Districts. var. ***cincta*** (Lückh.) P.V. Bruyns. Fls held upwards; cor. 2.1cm diam., tube off-white with concentric purple bars or lines, lobes 5–8×2–4mm, dark purple brown for entire length, margins ciliate except near tips and base. Cape: Van Rhynsdorp District.

***Q. linearis*** (N.E. Br.) P.V. Bruyns. All stems arising from a central rooted stem, 6–15×1–2.5cm, grey to dark purple-black, young grown particularly dark, angles rounded, obtuse, teeth small, 1–3mm. Fls 12–18mm diam., 2–4 together from a peduncular patch between the angles; cor. 3–4mm, campanulate, glabrous, white, occasionally suffused purple, lobes only slightly spreading, 8–10mm, tips incurved, deep purple-brown, margins replicate for three-quarters of length. Cape Province: Prince Albert District.

***Q. mammillaris*** (L.) P.V. Bruyns. Stems 12–50×4cm, erect, spirally 4–6-angled, teeth to 2cm, conical, stout, irregular, apices hard. Fls 4–15; cor. exterior pale green and glabrous, interior densely covered in hair-tipped papillae, tube 3–4mm, campanulate, pale yellow with purple-black spots, lobes 1.2–2cm, lanceolate-acute, erect to spreading, wholly purple to red-black, margins strongly replicate; corona dark purple-brown, outer lobes bifid or trifid, teeth deltoid, inner lobes with a short, dorsal projection. Namibia; Cape Province (Namaqualand).

***Q. marlothii*** (N.E. Br.) P.V. Bruyns. Forming dense clusters, branching from base; stems 9×2–2.5cm, 4–5-angled, green speckled purple, teeth 3–5mm. Fls in groups of 1–3 towards apex of stems; pedicels 9–15mm, holding fls upright; cor. 7–10mm diam., exterior glabrous, pale green, interior thinly covered with semi-erect to erect stiff purple hairs, surface yellow blotched purple, lobes 4×2mm, usually recurved to touch pedicel behind cor., ovate-lanceolate, tip acute. Cape Province: Calvinia to Barrydale & Prince Albert Districts.

***Q. parviflora*** (Masson) P.V. Bruyns. Forming clusters of erect to spreading stems 10–30×1–2cm, branching both from base and higher up, 4-angled, grey to purple, teeth 2–5mm with a hard yellow point. Fls 1–3 per peduncular patch; pedicel 4–10mm, decurved to facing upwards; cor. 8–10mm diam., lobes narrowing uniformly from base, lanceolate with purple bars or a green to yellow or off-white ground, margins finely ciliate. Cape: Little Namaqualand. ssp. ***bayeriana*** P.V. Bruyns. Pedicels 2–4mm holding fls slightly pendent; cor. 6–7mm diam., interior densely covered with pale purple, twisted hairs, pale yellow-green with irregular light purple blotches, lobes 2.5×2mm, deltoid, margins not reflexed, tube small, containing only lower quarter of corona. Cape Province, near Springbok. ssp. ***dependens*** (N.E. Br.) P.V. Bruyns. Forming dense clusters of erect branching stems; stems 20×1.5–2cm, ash-grey. Pedicels 3–5mm, strongly decurved, holding fls facing downwards; fls 1–3 together; cor. 7–11mm diam., usually with 4 lobes slightly reflexed, the fifth adpressed against the stem, tube more or less lacking, lobes broad to midpoint then narrowing to a broadly acute tip, pale yellow barred purple near the centre, becoming plain purple nearer the tips, margins slightly reflexed, ciliate with soft, twisted, purple hairs. Cape Province: Clanwilliam & Van Rhynsdorp Districts. ssp. ***gracilis*** (Lückh.) P.V. Bruyns. Stems erect, forming small clumps, slender, 10×1cm, dark grey-green. Fls 2 together in angles of stem, mainly toward tip; pedicels 4–5mm, suberect to erect; cor. 14–19mm diam., upper surface glabrous, mostly spreading but occasionally lobes remaining fused at tips, tube lacking, lobes very variable in width, 5–7×2mm, central area off-white with scattered brown dots, lobes becoming brown or yellow toward tips, margin not reflexed, mostly very finely ciliate with purple hairs. Cape Province: Cedarberg to Ceres, Karroo. ssp. ***pulchra*** P.V. Bruyns. Pedicels 2–4mm, holding fls facing downwards; cor. 10–16mm diam., interior with purple hairs over red part of fl., central part deep to pale red with a white ring around base of lobes, lobes bright yellow, rarely white, narrowing gradually to abruptly acute tip, 4–8×2mm, margins slightly replicate, ciliate with purple twisted hairs. Cape Province: Van Rhynsdorp District. ssp. ***swanepoelii*** (Lavranos) P.V. Bruyns. Forming dense clusters; stems 2–6×1–1.5cm, longer and more procumbent when shaded. Pedicels to 2mm, holding fls perpendicular to stem; cor. 10–12mm diam., glabrous, united portion almost flat, tube virtually absent, off-white with purple to red-brown spots, lobes 3–4×2–3mm, ovate-deltoid to ovate-lanceolate, margins slightly reflexed with twisted red-purple hairs. Cape Province: Calvinia District.

***Q.pillansii*** (N.E. Br.) P.V. Bruyns. Stems 20–40×3cm, 4-angled, grey-green, spotted red, angles flattened, teeth to 1.5cm, more or less triangular. Fls 4–20, in dense bundles; cor. tube to 6mm, purple-brown, campanulate, with dense papillae with purple apical hairs, lobes 6–10mm, oblong-ovate, acute, papillose, grey-purple with maroon spots, margins reflexed; outer corona lobes dark purple-brown, bifid to emarginate, inner lobes to 1mm. Cape Province.

***Q.pruinosa*** (Masson) P.V. Bruyns. Forming long, erect to sprawling clumps, branching from a single central rootstock; stems 50×1.5cm, grey-green to dark purple-grey, 4-angled, each angle rounded with rounded tubercles, each armed with a minute hard-tipped tooth less than 2mm long. Fls developing successively in the grooves towards the stem tips, 1–3 together; cor. 10–13mm diam.; pedicels 4–6mm, holding fls perpendicular to stem; exterior of fls glabrous, grey-green to mottled purple-brown, interior covered with fine, crinkled, white hairs, surface dark brown, rugulose, tube short, lobes 4–5×3mm, deltoid to deltoid-lanceolate, tip acute. Cape Province: Richtersveld; Namibia.

***Q.ramosa*** (Masson) P.V. Bruyns. Stems 12–30cm, bluntly 4-angled, grey-green or tinged purple, teeth to 3mm, at apices of young stems. Fls 2–10; cor. tube 3–4mm, campanulate, base white, mouth dark purple with dense, hair-tipped papillae, lobes 1cm, attenuate, sharply acute, black-purple, covered with slender spicules, margins replicate, outer corona cup-shaped, dark purple-black, lobes bifid, inner lobes broadly linear, with a broad, rounded, dorsal projection. Cape Province.

***Q.hottentotorum*** N.E. Br. See *Q. incarnata*.
For further synonymy see *Caralluma, Sarcophagophilus, Stapelia* and *Tromotriche*.

**Quassia** L. (Name given by Linnaeus to a tree of Surinam, in honour of a negro Quasi or Coissi, who employed the bark as a remedy for fever.) Simaroubaceae. 35 species of tropical trees or shrubs. Leaves alternate, pinnate or simple, leaflets usually with pitted glands above and sometimes beneath; rachis distinctly winged or terete. Inflorescence a raceme, panicle or umbel; bracteoles tiny, triangular, ciliate, subopposite, sometimes absent; flowers unisexual, bisexual or polygamous; calyx lobed, rarely closed in bud; petals imbricate or contorted in bud, longer than calyx; ovaries free, more or less immersed on top of the disc; carpels 4–6, free or slightly coherent. Fruit 1–6 from each flower, drupaceous or woody, sometimes very large. Tropical Africa, SE Asia, Australia. Z10.

CULTIVATION A handsome shrub or small tree valued for its foliage, which emerges red before turning glossy dark green above, for the vividly coloured red stalked panicles of bloom borne at the branch tips and for the attractive fruits which follow. Suitable for the shrub borders of humid tropical gardens in cooler climates it is suitable for tub cultivation in the warm glasshouse or conservatory, and in botanical collections of medicinal plants. Grow in a fertile, humus-rich and moisture-retentive sandy loam based medium, provide moderate to high levels of humidity with a winter minimum temperature of 15–18°C/60–65°F. Prune to size and shape in late winter before growth commences. Propagate by seed or semi-ripe cuttings in a sandy propagating mix in a humid closed case with gentle bottom heat.

***Q.amara*** L. BITTERWOOD. Erect shrub, to 3m. Lvs with broadly winged rachis, obovate-oblong, subsessile, flushed purple; leaflets opposite, entire, usually 5; petiole to 16mm. Racemes to 25cm, often branched; pedicels to 14mm; cal. 7–8mm, patent, bright red; pet. 2.7–3.2×5–6mm, exterior bright red, interior white; stamens 3.5–4cm, exserted., slightly unequal. Fr. 12–13mm, 1–5, purple-black. Brazil.

**Quekettia** Lindl.
***Q.micromera*** (Barb. Rodr.) Cogn. See *Capanemia micromera*.

**Quercifilix** Copel. Dryopteridaceae. 1 species, a terrestrial fern. Rhizome creeping or suberect, apex scaly; scales narrow, to 3mm, brown; stipes tufted, scaly at base, densely hairy throughout, those of sterile fronds to 5cm, those of fertile fronds to 15cm. Sterile fronds trifoliate, usually with shallowly lobed apical lamina, 5×2.5cm, and 1 pair of lateral pinnae, pinnae 1.5cm, rounded, widened at base of basiscopic side; fertile fronds trifoliate, with apical lamina 30×2mm, with 1 pair of lateral pinnae, pinnae 1cm widened at base on the basiscopic side. Asia. Z10.

CULTIVATION A temperate/subtropical fern of creeping habit, it forms a dense mat of oakleaf-like sterile fronds amongst which the much thinner fertile fronds emerge during the summer months. Good for ground cover in the cool conservatory or glasshouse, thriving in the shade cast by other plants, or in shallow pans, or in the terrarium indoors. A medium suitable for terrestrial ferns is recommended, with repotting every two years, or following breakdown of the medium. Water should be copious; feed at monthly intervals during the growing season to ensure healthy growth. Propagation is from spores, or by division of the creeping rhizomes.

***Q.zeylanica*** (Houtt.) Copel. As for the genus.
For synonymy see *Leptochilus*.

**Quercus** L. (Lat. name for this tree.) OAK. Fagaceae. 600 species of monoecious, evergreen or deciduous trees or shrubs. Shoots stout, glabrous to tomentose; stipules mostly caducous, persistent in some spp.; buds avoid-conic, many-scaled, often clustered toward shoot apex, terminal bud present. Leaves alternate, entire, toothed or lobed, short-stalked, often stellate-pubescent. Male flowers many in slender pendulous catkins, perianth 4–7-lobed, stamens 4–6(–12), usually with a vestigial ovary. Female flowers solitary or 2 to many in a spike, perianth lobes 6, inconspicuous; ovary inferior, 3-locular, styles 3, long or short. Fruit a single-seeded nut (acorn), ovoid to globose, partly or almost wholly enclosed by a cup-shaped, scale-covered involucre (cupule), composed of adpressed scales. N America to western tropical S America, N Africa, Europe and Asia, in temperate and subtropical zones, and tropics at high altitudes.

CULTIVATION Oaks are excellent trees for parks and large gardens, having interesting foliage and often good crown shape; most are long lived and many are large trees. In Britain, two are native, *Q. robur* and *Q. petraea*, forming a major component of the indigenous forest. All oaks like warm summers, and *Q. petraea* shows well the effect of decreasing summer temperature northwards in oceanic NW Europe; at its best in Normandy, often 40–45m tall; in S England, 35m to rarely 42m, in C England 30m, in N England and S Scotland 25m, and in NW Scotland rarely 20m and often scrubby to 15m or less. Further east in NW Russia, winter cold and short rather than cool summers limit its range, while south in C France, low rainfall reduces its vigour. A similar sequence is shown by *Q. garryana* on the Pacific coast of North America. These constraints of low summer heat affect the range and health of species which can be grown in Britain; oaks from continental E US, China and Japan are generally of poor vigour and many suffer autumn frost damage to the unripened shoots. Of these, the most tolerant is *Q. rubra*, almost as vigorous as in E US, and some of the other red oaks are nearly as good. *Q. alba* has very rarely been successful in the UK except in the warmest parts of SE England. Conversely, the Mediterranean oaks, adapted to relatively cooler summers during the ice ages, thrive in Britain's climate; they respond to the higher rainfall by growing faster in S England than in their native areas.

In the Eastern US, all oaks can be grown in either the north-east, or for the less winter-hardy species in the southeast; none reacts adversely to the hot, humid summer. The European oaks retain considerable winter hardiness from ice age adaptations: *Q. petraea* from N England is hardy in Wisconsin and also enjoys the warmer summers there; *Q. cerris* from S Europe is hardy to zone 6. No oak shows extreme cold tolerance, and the genus is absent from most of Canada and Siberia.

Growth is best on fertile, deep soils with medium drainage and 400–1500mm/16–60in. rainfall, but in such a large genus, different oaks can be found to tolerate almost all conditions, from poor dry acid sands, freely drained mountain screes, through heavy damp clays to ill-drained marshy areas and dry chalk. Only acid deep peats are consistently avoided. Rainfalls of 150–6000mm/6–240in. are tolerated by different species. Most are sensitive to salt, but *Q. aucheri* grows in the splash zone on the Turkish coast, and several tolerate coastal sites. *Q. ilex* is often planted in maritime gardens. As a rule, most tolerate exposure moderately, surviving well but being small and stunted, and are best in a woodland site among or not far from other similarly sizes trees or shrubs; young oaks will tolerate a reasonable level of side-shade.

The finest oaks are some of those from SE Europe and SW Asia, notably *Q. castaneifolia, Q. frainetto, Q. macranthera, Q. pontica* and *Q. vulcanica*; from SW Europe, *Q. canariensis* is also a splendid tree, as are *Q. variabilis* and *Q. acutissima* from E Asia. The best for autumn colour are from E America, notably *Q. coccinea, Q. ellipsoidalis* and *Q. palustris*; these also have good leaf shape. Among the evergreen oaks, *Q. suber* is of interest for its bark, but needs a mild site (zone 8–9) to grow well; *Q. ilex, Q. virginiana* and *Q. agrifolia* become massively spreading with age. All the species in subgenus *Cyclobalanopsis* make fine glossy-leaved trees with red young leaves in spring, but demand hot summers. Some species bear edible, sweet acorns, in Europe notably *Q. aucheri* and *Q. ilex* var. *ballota*. In Britain, *Q. petraea* and *Q. robur* are among the best trees for attracting wildlife, with their immense range of associated insects; *Q. petraea* makes the more attractive tree.

Oaks are excellent candidates for bonsai; the warm-temperature, small-leaved, low-growing evergreen species (e.g. *Q. coccifera*) are the most suitable but any can be used. Regular root pruning is important, as is good fertility in the soil used. They will tolerate any amount of pruning, coppicing readily from cut stumps.

*Propagation*. The propagation described here for *Quercus* applies also to the following genera: *Aesculus, Carya, Castanea, Castanopsis, Chrysolepis, Corylus, Fagus, Juglans, Litchi, Lithocarpus, Persea*, and all other genera with large oily nuts with very limited storage life and seedlings with strong tap-roots.

Propagation is by seed, or by grafting where seed is unavailable and for desirable cultivars. For grafting, side graft sucker shoots (preferably erect) on to seedlings of a closely related species and bind with tape. Normal branch shoot scions should be avoided if possible, as they have poor apical dominance and may not develop into good trees.

As many oaks can hybridize freely wild-collected seed should be used whenever possible, though even in the wild hybrids are frequent, particularly on disturbed sites such as abandoned farmland. Acorn production is usually cyclical: there is low production in most years to defeat parasites and predators, with, more sporadically, a massive crop in the 'mast' years, where a high proportion of seed escapes damage. If possible, seed collection should be made in such years; crop assessment can be made from midsummer. Collect the acorns in mid-autumn after falling; for commercial purposes, the ground is covered with hessian sheets so the acorns can be swept up cheaply in large amounts. Windy days are the most productive, collecting before rodents and birds can take the seeds blown down.

Acorns are very sensitive to desiccation and must be stored moist and cold; they will be killed if they drop below 60% fresh weight. They cannot normally be stored for more than one winter, except in the case of very hardy species (zone 6 origin or colder); these can be deep-frozen. For freezing, the acorns, which must not be showing any sign of germination, should be *slightly* dried to about 80% fresh weight (to prevent ice damage to the cells) and acclimatized first for a few days at 0°C/32°F, then −5°C/41°F and finally to −20°C/−4°F. The seed should be stratified for 3–5 months in damp sand refrigerated at 0 to 3°C/32–37°F before sowing, stored in plastic bags.

Acorns commonly start to germinate in early winter (even those stored at 0°C/32°F), establishing a root system (though not a shoot). These sprouting acorns must be planted immediately, the others in early spring. Lie the acorn horizontal at its own thickness under soil surface. Plant in a cold frame to protect from cold weather and pests, in sweet pea tubes or similar deep narrow pots to accommodate the long tap-root. This may be 50cm/20in. long and 8mm/0.3in. diameter at the end of the summer, yet the shoot above may be only 3–15cm/1–6in. tall and 3mm/0.01in. diameter; damage to the tap-root must be avoided. If the seed supply is plentiful and high losses to rodents are acceptable, it is always preferable to avoid checks to growth by planting the acorns directly where the tree is to grow.

Best planted as small trees one or at most two years old and 10–40cm/4–16in. tall. Larger, older plants (including rootstock plants for grafting) require special nursery treatment; for these, *cut* the tap-root early and regularly (every few weeks) either by cutting under the seedbed with a spade, or pruning roots that appear at the bottom of the pot; this will encourage the seedling to develop a more fibrous root system. Plant when 1–2m/3–6½ft tall; lengthy check can be occur. Water well, protect from rabbits, etc, and keep weeds clear until established.

*Diseases and pests*. Oaks are affected by numerous pests and diseases, though only a few are serious. In N America, oak wilt caused by the fungus *Ceratocystis fagacearum*, first discovered in 1940, has caused heavy losses; species vary in susceptibility: the red oaks are most affected; white oaks are more resistant and suffer only scattered shoot death and only rarely whole tree death, though they do carry a reservoir of fungus able to cross-infect to red oaks. It is spread by oak bark beetles *Pseudopityophthorus* spp. and sap-feeding nitidulid beetles, and also through root grafts; control is almost impossible, and depends as with the similar elm disease *O. ulmi* on vigilance and rapid felling of infected trees; it may also be necessary to cut deep trenches between infected trees and others to root grafts. Overall, the disease is less of a problem than elm disease or chestnut blight *Cryphonectria* (*Endothia*) *parasitica*, probably mainly because the vectors in America are inefficient, so transmission rates are low. This disease has to date been kept out of Europe by strict controls on the importation of oak foliage and timber; since the European oak bark beetle *Scolytis intricatus* is larger than the American species there exists great potential for fast and massive contagion were this pathogen to take hold. The susceptibility of the European oaks is not yet known. A vascular mycosis of oak, caused by the fungus *Ophiostoma roboris*, has caused scattered mortalities in E Europe since about 1900, but has not spread to other areas and does not appear to be a serious problem. Chestnut blight has claimed occasional victories in N America; honey fungus root rot *Armillaria mellea* can also occasionally kill trees. Other diseases include powdery mildew, common particularly on midsummer growth of *Q. robur*, which does not damage the oak but can be a source of infection for other plants.

Numerous insects are associated with oaks, but none cause any serious damage. *Q. robur* is commonly defoliated by tortrix moths (Tortricidae), but the tree merely grows a second flush of leaves and growth is not more than slightly reduced; this and *Q. infectoria* are attacked by numerous gall-wasps, but these also do not real harm. *Q. coccifera* is host to the Kermes insect *Kermes vermilio*, a mealy bug (see above). Acorns are commonly infested by weevils and gall wasps, including the conspicuous 'knopper gall' on *Q. robur* and *Q. petraea*; they may account for most of the crop in

**Quercus** (a) *Q. falcata* (b) *Q. velutina* (c) *Q. rubra* (d) *Q. palustris* (e) *Q.* × *ludoviciana* (f) *Q. libani* (g) *Q. acuta*

years of low seed production, but in mast years most of the very large seed crops escapes their attention. The large number of associated insects make oaks of great value for wildlife conservation.

The genus falls into two subgenera, the widespread typical oaks *Quercus* and the S and E Asian *Cyclobalanopsis*, separated primarily on the basis of the fruit cupules and often treated as a distinct genus. Subgenus *Quercus* is further subdivided into four sections, separated on the basis of flower and acorn structure; the nature of the leaves (deciduous or evergreen; entire, toothed or lobed) is of little significance, related more to climate than phylogeny. Section *Cerris* (turkey oaks) is primarily S European/SW Asian but with species in E Asia; section *Quercus* (white oaks), divided into subsections *Quercus*, found throughout the distribution, and *Mesobalanus*, with similar distribution to sect. *Cerris*; sections *Protobalanus* and *Erythrobalanus* (red oaks) are confined to the Americas, the former only in SW US and Mexico.

1 Leaves persistent, entire or toothed but never lobed, glossy green above; acorn cupules with concrescent scales in concentric rings (Subgen. *Cyclobalanopsis*).
*Qq. acuta, bambusaefolia, gilva, glauca, lamellosa, myrsinaefolia, oxyodon, salicina, stenophylla.*

2 Leaves deciduous or evergreen, entire, toothed or lobed; cupules with imbricate, spirally arranged scales (Subgen. *Quercus*).

2.1 Styles long, not swollen at apex; cupule scales elongated; acorn ripening usually in second year, inner side of shell glabrous to tomentose; aborted ovules apical (Sect. *Cerris*).

2.1a Deciduous or semi-evergreen (leaves persisting less than 12 months).
*Qq. acutissima, brantii, castaneifolia, cerris, ithaburensis, libani, trojana, variabilis.*

2.1b Evergreen (leaves persistent over 12 months).
*Qq. alnifolia, aucheri, baronii, coccifera, gilliana, phillyreoides, semecarpifolia, suber.*

2.2 Styles long, swollen at apex; cupule scales short; acorn ripe in first year, inner side of shell glabrous; aborted ovules apical (Sect. *Quercus* subsect. *Mesobalanus*).
*Qq. dentata, frainetto, macranthera, pontica, pyrenaica, vulcanica.*

2.3 Styles short, swollen at apex; cupule scales mostly short; acorn ripe in first year, inner side of shell mostly glabrous; aborted ovules apical (Sect. *Quercus* subsect. *Quercus*).

2.3a Deciduous.
*Qq. alba, aliena, austrina, bicolor, canariensis, chapmanii, congesta, dalechampii, douglasii, durandii, fabri, faginea, fruticosa, gambelii, garryana, glandulifera, haas, hartwissiana, iberica, infectoria, liaotungensis, lobata, lyrata, macrocarpa, mas, michauxii, mongolica, muehlenbergii, pedunculiflora, petraea, prinoides, prinus, pubescens, pungens, robur, sadleriana, stellata, undulata, virgiliana, warburgii.*

2.3b Evergreen.
*Qq. arizonica, dumosa, durata, emoryi, engleriana, glabrescens, ilex, leucotrichophora, lodicosa, oblongifolia, reticulata, toumeyi, virginiana.*

2.4 Styles short, swollen at apex; cupule scales short; acorn ripe in second year, inner side of shell tomentose; aborted ovules apical (Sect. *Protobalanus*).
*Qq. chrysolepis, vacciniifolia.*

2.5 Styles long, swollen at apex; cupule scales short; acorn ripe in second year, inner side of shell tomentose; aborted ovules basal (Sect. *Erythrobalanus*).

2.5a Deciduous.
*Qq. arkansana, coccinea, crassifolia, ellipsoidalis, falcata, georgiana, ilicifolia, imbricaria, incana, kelloggii, laevis, laurifolia, marilandica, nigra, nuttallii, palustris, phellos, rubra, shumardii, texana, velutina.*

2.5b Evergreen.
*Qq. agrifolia, crassipes, hypoleucoides, myrtifolia, wislizenii.*

***Q. acuta*** Thunb. JAPANESE EVERGREEN OAK. Evergreen tree to 25m, usually a large shrub in cult. Branchlets and young lvs initially brown-tomentose, soon becoming wholly glabrous. Lvs 10–17×4–6cm, oblong-ovate to lanceolate-oblong or elliptic, apex acuminate (most markedly so in juveniles), base rounded to cuneate, entire, usually undulate, coriaceous, deep lustrous green above, matt yellow-green beneath, veins in 8–10 pairs; petioles 2–3.5cm. Acorns to 2cm, ellipsoid, clustered; cupule surrounding one-third of acorn, conspicuously ringed, finely downy. Japan, N Korea, China. Z7.

***Q. acutissima*** Carruth. SAWTHORN OAK. Deciduous tree, seldom exceeding 25m. Bark ashen to black, corky, fissured; young shoots initially minutely downy, soon becoming glabrous. Lvs 6–20×2.5–6.5cm, variable in shape, lanceolate, lanceolate-oblong, to subovate or obovate, apex long acuminate, base cuneate to rounded, veins 14–20 per side, exceeding edge of lamina as broadly triangular, bristle-tipped teeth, lustrous green above, paler and glabrous beneath; petiole 1.5–5cm, slender. Acorns ripe in second year, to 2.5cm, solitary, sessile, ovoid, sometimes dorsally depressed; cupule to 3.5cm diam., hemispherical, concealing two-thirds of acorn, covered with long, hairy scales. China, Korea, Japan. ssp. ***chenii*** (Nak.) Camus. Lvs glabrous. Fr. smaller, cups bearing more slender scales. S & C China. Z5.

***Q. agrifolia*** Née. CALIFORNIA LIVE OAK. Evergreen tree to 25m, often shrubby in cult. Crown broad, bark thick, pale grey-white or red, brown or black, smooth or grooved; young shoots initially downy, lvs 2.5–7×2.5–4cm, ovate-elliptic, elliptic or broadly elliptic, apex acute, base rounded, margins spiny-toothed, deep glossy green and rather concave above, paler beneath, glabrous except for tufted hairs in axils of principal veins; petiole 0.5–0.8mm. Acorns mature in first year, 2–3.5cm, ovoid, acute, solitary, sessile; cupule enclosing one-quarter to one-third of acorn, sericeous throughout, especially the interior. California. Z8.

***Q. alba*** L. WHITE OAK. Deciduous tree to 45m. Crown broad, often rounded. Bark pale grey to brown, exfoliating plates, ridged. Young shoots red-brown or chalky-grey, downy, very soon becoming glabrous. Lvs 10–20×6.5–14cm, obovate, oblong or elliptic, apex abruptly acute, base cuneate, margins with 3–4 deep lobes per side, the lobes entire or sparsely toothed, initially pubesc., soon glabrous, dull mid-green above, colouring orange to burgundy in autumn, rather glaucous beneath; petiole 1–2.5cm. Acorn ripe in first year, 1–3cm, ovoid-oblong, short or long-stalked; cupule enclosing quarter to one-third of acorn, grey-white, composed of adpressed, compacted, hairy scales. E US. f. ***elongata*** Kipp. Lvs slender, to 25×8cm, gently tapering to base, colouring orange to purple red in autumn. f. ***pinnatifida*** (Michx.) Rehd. Lvs deeply pinnatisect, lobes slender, usually dentate. f. ***repanda*** (Michx.) Trel. (*Q. repanda* Lvs very shallowly lobed. Hybrids have been recorded between *Q. alba* and *Q. bicolor* and are referred to as *Q.* ×*jackiana*. Z4.

***Q. aliena*** Bl. Deciduous tree to 25m. Young shoots olive-green, glabrous, somewhat verrucose. Lvs 10–20cm, obovate to oblong, apex acute to rounded, base cuneate, sinuately dentate, teeth coarse, blunt, 10–15 per side, bright yellow-green glabrous above, pale grey-white to blue-green and tomentellous beneath; petiole 1.5–3cm. Acorns ripe in first year, 2–2.5cm, ovoid, sessile or more usually distinctly stalked, solitary or grouped 2–3; cupule enclosing one-third of acorn, grey-tomentose with scales adpressed. Japan, Korea. var. ***acuteserrata*** Maxim. Lvs smaller and narrower, teeth acute, rather incurved, glandular-tipped. Japan, C China. Z5.

***Q. alnifolia*** Poech. GOLDEN OAK. Slow-growing evergreen shrub to 2m or tree to 8m. Trunk coarsely textured, grey. Young shoots persistently ashy-tomentose. Lvs 2.5–6×1.5–5cm, broadly obovate to suborbicular, apex and base rounded to subtruncate, margins denticulate in apical half, vein pairs 5–8, glossy dark or livid green above, densely covered with ochre or ash-coloured felty pubescence beneath; petiole 1–1.5cm. Acorns mature in second year, 2.5–3.5cm, obovoid, mucronate, solitary or paired; cupule small, enclosing to half of a acorn, with scales spreading, long-pubesc., arranged in a broad band. Cyprus. Z8.

***Q.*** ×***andleyensis*** Henry. (*Q. ilex* × *Q. petraea.*) Deciduous or semi-evergreen. Young shoots ashy-pubesc., at least until second season. Lvs 8–9cm, variable in shape, even on same shoot, obovate-oblong, margins entire and undulate, or with 4–5 teeth or lobes per side, the lobes themselves sometimes 1–3 toothed at tips, scurfy, becoming dark glossy-green above, paler beneath with indumentum persisting near base and on veins; petiole 1–2cm. Sterile. Garden origin.

***Q. arizonica*** Sarg. ARIZONA WHITE OAK. Semi-evergreen shrub or small tree to 17m, crown rounded with heavy level branches. Young shoots stout, red-brown, pubescent at first, soon glabrous. Lvs 3–8cm, entire, oblong-lanceolate to broad ovate, waved with spiny teeth in young plants, margin slightly revolute; dark blue-green above, pale tomentose beneath. Acorns mature in first year, subsessile, 2–2.5cm, ovoid-oblong; cupule with thick, corky scales, covering a third to half of the acorn. Arizona, New Mexico, NW Mexico. Z7.

***Q. arkansana*** Sarg. Deciduous tree to 18m, usually less (8m). Crown slender. Bark deeply fissured, grey-black. Young shoots initially hoary. Lvs 3.5–12×2–6.25cm, broadly elliptic to obovate, apex rounded, base tapering cuneate, margins entire or obscurely and sinuately 3-lobed toward apex or base, initially white pubesc. above, ultimately glabrescent, olive-green, paler and brown-tomentose beneath, ultimately glabrous except for tufts of hairs in vein axils. Acorns 1–1.5cm, subglobose to ovoid, solitary or paired; cupule shallow, enclosing a quarter or rarely one-third of acorn. SE US. Cf. *Q. marylandica*. Z7.

***Q. aucheri*** Jaub. & Spach. BOZ PIRNAL OAK. Evergreen shrub or tree to 5(10)m. Young shoots densely stellate-tomentose, yellow-brown. Lvs 1–4×1–2.5cm, entire to spiny-serrate, oblong to ovate, coriaceous, glabrous grey-green above, densely stellate-tomentose and waxy grey-white beneath; petiole 1–6mm. Acorns mature in 2nd year, to 2×1.5cm, oval to acute, sweet, edible; cupule stout, to 2.5cm broad, covering two-thirds to three-quarters of acorn, scales adpressed but rough. Acorn sprouts at base, not apex as in other oaks. Greek Islands, SW Turkey. Z8.

***Q. austrina*** Small. Deciduous tree to 20m, often far smaller, close in many respects to *Q. alba*. Bark pale grey, exfoliating. Lvs 6.5–15×2.75–8.5cm, obovate-elliptic, margins entire, sinuate or most often with 2 to 3 broad lobes per side, deep green above, pale green and glabrous beneath (not glaucous, cf. *Q. alba*). Acorns ripe in first year, 1.2–2cm, short-stalked, solitary; cupule thin, downy, enclosing one-third to one-half of acorn. S US. Z5.

***Q.*** ×***auzendii*** Gren. & Godron. (*Q. coccifera* × *Q. ilex.*) Foliage like *Q. coccifera*, but felty-pubesc. beneath. Acorns in clusters of 2–3; cupule scales adpressed; stalk to 2.5cm.

***Q. bambusaefolia*** Hance non Fort. nec Mast. BAMBOO-LEAVED OAK. Evergreen tree to 12m, or large shrub. Young branches simple pubesc. becoming glabrous, deep crimson or crimson (wine red), inconspicuously lenticellate. Lvs 3.5–8×0.6–1.6cm, linear-lanceolate to nearly elliptic, apex obtuse or rounded, base attenuate or cuneate, margin entire, slightly recurved, very rarely with 1 or 2 weak teeth, leathery, glabrous, glossy green above, sparsely silky pubesc. becoming glabrous, glaucous beneath, nerves 7–14 pairs; petiole 2–3(–5)mm, red-brown. Acorn 1.5–2.4×1.4–1.7cm, ovoid, mucronate, silky pubesc. becoming glabrous; cupule nearly hemispherical, enclosing the base or up to half of acorn, puberulent or glabrescent outside, silky inside, with scales forming 5 or 6 close rings. S China, Hong Kong, Tonkin. A species much confused in cult.; plants grown under this name may also be *Q. myrsinaefolia*, *Q. salicina*, *Q. stenophylla* or *Q. glauca*. Z8.

***Q. baronii*** Skan. Evergreen or semi-evergreen shrub to 3m or more allied to *Q. coccifera*. Young shoots tomentose, becoming glabrous. Lvs 2–6×1–3cm, oblong-lanceolate, margins with numerous triangular, aristate teeth; tomentose at first but becoming glabrous on both sides. Acorn mature in second year, subsessile, 1.5×1cm ovoid; cupule with reflexed scales. SW China. Z8.

***Q.* ×*bebbiana*** C. Schneid. *(Q. alba × Q. macrocarpa.)* Close to *Q. alba* but with lvs far larger, variable in shape but usually broadly 5-lobed on each side, downy beneath. Acorns solitary or a few, clustered and malformed; cupule deeper than in *Q. alba*, not so densely fringed. Occurring spontaneously among parents.

***Q.* ×*benderi*** Baenitz. *(Q. coccinea × Q. rubra.)* Close to *Q. rubra*. Shoots tinted red at first. Lvs obovate, apex acuminate, base truncate, lobes 5–7 per side, deep, bristle-toothed, ultimately glabrous throughout except for hair tufts in vein axils beneath, turning purple-red or yellow in autumn; petiole 3–5cm. Acorns ovoid or malformed; cupule turbinate, enclosing half acorn. Garden origin.

***Q. bicolor*** Willd. SWAMP WHITE OAK. Deciduous tree to 25m. Crown lofty, rounded; bark pale grey-brown, fissured, exfoliating; young shoots initially downy or scurfy. Lvs 6.5–16×3–7cm, oblong-obovate or obovate, apex rounded or abruptly acute, base tapering, margin coarsely and bluntly toothed or more deeply lobed, dark glossy green above (turning orange to fiery red in autumn), hoary or grey-green velutinous beneath; petiole 1–2cm. Acorn ripe in first year, 2–3cm, oblong-ovoid, solitary or paired on stalk to 8cm; capsule clothed with many, slender, hairy, compacted scales, enclosing one-third of acorn. Northeast N America. Z4.

***Q. brantii*** Lindl. Deciduous or semi-evergreen shrub or small tree to 10m. Shoots densely yellow-brown tomentose. Lvs 6–10×3–6cm, ovate-oblong, cordate, serrate with 8–14 pairs of acuminate, short-aristate teeth; dull green thin-tomentose above, densely stellate-tomentose beneath; petiole 5–20mm. Acorn similar to that of *Q. ithaburensis* but smaller, mature in second year, 2–3×1.5–2cm, cupule 2.5–3.5cm, with large rhomboid elongated scales, uppermost scales often filiform, spreading; covering two-thirds to almost all of the acorn; peduncle 1–5mm. Kurdistan south to SW Iran. Z7.

***Q.* ×*brittonii*** W.T. Davis. *(Q. ilicifolia × Q. marilandica.)* Divaricately branching small tree or shrub. Lvs 9–10cm, showing in varying degrees the influence of either parent, obovate to broadly obovate, apex broad, rounded, base tapering, rounded-cuneate or lyrate, margins with 1–3 broad, sinuate teeth per side and 3–4 lateral lobes, initially tawny-tomentose, ultimately lustrous dark green above with veins pubesc., thinly tawny to ashy-tomentose beneath, especially on veins and in vein axils. E US. Spontaneously occurring where parent populations meet.

***Q.* ×*bushii*** Sarg. *(Q. marilandica × Q. velutina.)* Deciduous tree to 10m. Branchlets thickly tomentose, later glabrous. Lvs 10–13cm, typically obovate, deeply and sinuately 3–5-lobed, the lobes with sparse, inconspicuous spines extending from veins on somewhat angled margins, base rounded or cuneate, subcoriaceous, glossy dark green above, olive to yellow-green beneath and glabrous except for downy tufts in vein axils; petiole 3cm. US.

***Q. canariensis*** Willd. ALGERIAN OAK; MIRBECK'S OAK. Deciduous tree to 40m in habitat, seldom exceeding 30m in cult. Bark thick, rugged, black; young shoots ribbed, briefly scurfy, soon becoming brown, glabrous. Lvs 5–18×4–12cm, oval or obovate, apex rounded, base tapering, rounded or subcordate, margins shallowly and obtusely lobed or coarsely toothed, coriaceous, rusty floccose throughout when first emerging, some becoming dark green and glabrous above, paler, somewhat glaucous beneath, glabrous except for rusty brown residual hairs on midrib and petiole, veins in 8–14 pairs; petiole 0.8–1.8cm. Acorns ripe in first year, to 2.5cm, short-stalked, solitary, paired or in small clusters; cupule hemispherical with adpressed downy scales, enclosing one-third of acorn. N Africa, Iberian peninsula (*not* Canaries). Z7.

***Q. castaneifolia*** C.A. Mey. Deciduous tree to 35m. Crown large, rounded, broadly spreading; bark brown, rough-textured and corky; young shoots tomentose, later glabrous; larger buds subtended by persistent linear stipules. Lvs 6–16×2.5–4cm, narrowly elliptic to oblong-lanceolate, apex acute, base cuneate or rounded, margins with course triangular saw-teeth, each tipped with a short slender mucro (the continuation of the 8–12 paired veins), deep glossy green above, dull grey-green beneath, glabrous or minutely downy; petioles 1–2cm. Acorns ripe in second year, 2–3cm, ovoid, often dorsally compressed or depressed, solitary, paired or (rarely) to 5 on a very short, stout, downy stalk; cupule clothed with slender scales (sometimes reflexed), enclosed one-third to half of acorn. Caucasus, Iran. var. ***incana*** Batt. & Trabut. Less vigorous, to 25m; bark more densely fissured, branchlets more downy. Female fls with 4–5 slender, spreading styles (not 3 short, erect styles as in *Q. castaneifolia*), clustered acorns, cupules shallower with narrow scales. Algeria and Tunisia. Z6.

***Q. cerris*** L. TURKEY OAK. Deciduous tree to 43m, bole to 2.5m diam. Crown conical. Bark grey-white becoming fissured and split into thick plates. Young branchlets clothed with persistent or caducous, grey down, and fine scales. Lvs 5–12×1.5–3cm, rarely larger, oblong to oblong-lanceolate, tapered to an acute apex and a rounded or truncate base, margin lobed, lobes or teeth triangular to lobulate, mucronulate, dark green and stellate-pubesc. initially above, lighter and pubesc. to tomentose beneath, colouring yellow-brown in autumn, nerves 6–10 pairs; petiole 0.3–2cm. Acorns ripe in second year, in groups of 1–4, to 3.5cm, ellipsoid, apex subtruncate and mucronate, orange-brown with olive green apex; cupule of subulate often spreading or reflexed scales, enclosing one-third of acorn. C & S Europe, Asia Minor. var. ***cerris.*** Lobes on lvs lobulate, sinuses deep. 'Argenteovariegata': lf margins irregularly variegated cream-white. 'Aureovariegata': lvs yellow variegated. f. ***laciniata*** (Loud.) Schneid. Lvs irregularly pinnately lobed or divided, lobes acute, sometimes further pinnately divided, pale green and sparsely pubesc. beneath. 'Pendula': branchlets long, pendulous, often lying on ground; first noted in Holland. var. ***austriaca*** (Willd.) Loud. Lvs ovate, tapered at both ends, apex acute, margin regularly and deeply dentate, teeth many, short, triangularly lobed, lobes not lobulate, sinuses shallow to moderate, not deep. var. ***haliphlaeos*** (Lam.) DC. Lvs larger, 10–14×3.5–5cm, base rounded or subcordate, lightly puberulent beneath, slightly leathery, usually lyrately lobed; petiole 5–6mm. S France.

***Q. chapmanii*** Sarg. Small semi-evergreen shrub, sometimes a tree to 9m in habitat. Crown spreading, bark separating into large irregular plates. Branches initially densely yellow-white tomentose, becoming puberulent then glabrous ash-grey, lenticellate after first winter. Lvs usually fall after new lvs appear; adult lvs 5–12×3.5–4.5cm, oblong-obovate or subelliptic, often asymmetric, attenuate and rounded at base, apex rounded or obtuse, margin entire or irregularly sinuate with a few rounded lobes, initially covered with ochre-yellow tomentum above and caducous red ochre hairs beneath, adult lvs leathery, dark green, shining and glabrous above, light green and puberulent at least on principal nerves beneath, nerves 6–8 pairs; petiole 2–3mm, subglabrous. Acorns ripe in first year solitary or in clusters of to 3, subsessile, 1.5–1.7×–1.4cm, pale brown, silky tomentose toward apex; cupule cup-shaped or hemispheric, scarcely pubesc. inside, scales oblong, pale-tomentose with red-brown margins, enclosing one-third of acorn. SE US.

***Q. chrysolepis*** Liebm. CANYON; LIVE OAK; MAUL OAK. Evergreen tree to 25m, trunk 1–1.5m diam., shorter at high altitudes. Bark white-grey or tinted red, breaking up into small scales. Young shoots clothed with fawn-grey tomentum, usually becoming glabrous, red-brown, lenticellate. Branches horizontal to downward curved. Lvs 2.5–5(–10)×1–4(–5)cm, oval to elliptic or lanceolate, apex acute or subobtuse, often asymmetrical, mucronate, base rounded or cordate, margin usually entire, rarely with 4–10 short, spiny teeth each side, glandular and tomentose at first, becoming leathery, thick, dark-green, glabrous and shining above, pale glaucous-waxy beneath, nerves 6–10 pairs. Acorns mature in second years, solitary or paired, (2–)2.5–3.5×1.5–3cm, ovoid, apex rounded or attenuate and mucronate, puberulent; cupule sessile, short and thick, pale green or red-brown inside, scales oval or triangular, covered with fine fawn to white tomentum, enclosing one-third or less of acorn. SW US, NW Mexico. Z7.

***Q. coccifera*** L. KERMES OAK; GRAIN OAK. Evergreen bushy shrub, usually 0.25–1.5m, rarely a tree 4.5m. Branches ashy-brown, with a few stellate hairs at first, becoming glabrous. Bark smooth and grey at first, becoming cracked and scaly with age. Lvs 1.2–3.5×0.6–2cm, oval, elliptic or oblong, apex acute or rounded, mucronate, base rounded or cordate, thin and soft at first, becoming leathery and hard, dark green and glabrous above, paler and glabrous or with a few hairs in nerve axils beneath, margin undulate, with 4–6 pairs of spreading, spine-like teeth, nerves 5–7(–10) pairs, petiole short. Acorns ripe in second year 1.5–3×0.8–1.5(–2.5)cm, rarely larger, ovoid or oblong-ovoid, apex attenuate with an apical spine and persistent styles and perianth, light brown striped darker, glabrous; cupule hemispherical, scales spiny, often reflexed, lightly puberulent, enclosing one-half to two-thirds of acorn. W Mediterranean, S Europe, NW Africa. ssp. ***calliprinos*** (Webb) Boiss. PALESTINE OAK; SIND OAK. Tree to 12m. Lvs larger and more oblong, to 5×3cm. Acorn to three-quarters enclosed by cup. E Mediterranean, SW Asia. Z6.

***Q. coccinea*** Münchh. SCARLET OAK. Deciduous tree to 30m, trunk to 1m diam. Bark pale grey-brown, cracked into irregular, scaly plates. Branches loose-tomentose at first, becoming glabrous, shining, lenticellate. Lvs 8–12×6–12(–15)cm, oval or obovate, rarely oblong, base truncate, rarely cuneate, densely white, silky-tomentose at first, becoming green, glabrous and shining, paler and with a few tufts of hair in axils beneath, colouring scarlet in autumn, margin deeply pinnately sinuate-dentate or serrate, lobes usually 7, oblique, spreading, sometimes falcate, nerves 4–5 pairs. Acorns ripe in second year, 1.5–2.5×1.5–2.5cm, ovoid to subspherical, apex and base rounded, with perianth remains at apex, with thin red-brown tomentum; cupule subsessile, turbinate, scales yellow-brown, oval, acute, subglabrous, enclosing one-third to one-half of acorn. E US, S Canada. 'Splendens': autumn leaf colour particularly rich scarlet. Z4.

***Q. congesta*** Presl. Deciduous large shrub or tree. Crown irregular. Young branchlets tomentose. Lvs 7.5×14×4–9cm, variable in shape, ovate to oblong-ovate, base cordate to attenuate, margin deeply sinuately lobed or pinnatifid, lobes 6–8 each side, nerves 5–9 pairs, green, glabrous and often shining above, grey-green pubesc. beneath. Acorns mature in first year, 1.4–3×1–2.4cm, ovoid, apex obtuse; cupule with pedicel to 4cm, subhemispherical, scales spreading to erect, not adpressed, usually white-yellow villous. Sicily, Sardinia, S France. Z7.

***Q. crassifolia*** Humb. & Bonpl. Deciduous tree to 25m in habitat. Branches furrowed, brown tomentose at first becoming glabrous. Lvs 8–14×4–5(–9)cm, obovate to suborbicular, rarely subelliptic, apex obtuse, sometimes acute or acuminate, base cordate, fawn-velvety at first becoming leathery, hard, rugose, subglabrous above, fawn velvety tomentose beneath, margins recurved, sometimes sinuate-dentate, teeth few, mucronate, erect, rigid, nerves 7–9 pairs; petiole 0.5–1.5cm, tomentose. Acorns ripe in first year, 1.5–2×0.8–1.2cm, ovoid, apex with a thick mucron and persistent styles and perianth, brown, glabrous; cupule turbinate or hemispherical, scales brown-hairy to glabrous, often becoming glabrous, enclosing one-third or more of acorn. C Mexico. Z8.

***Q. crassipes*** Humb. & Bonpl. Evergreen tree to 25m. Shoots tomentose. Lvs 5–9cm, oblong-elliptic, coriaceous, entire or waved; glabrous above, tomentose beneath. Acorns mature in second year, subsessile, 2–2.5cm, ovoid; cupule with adpressed scales. C Mexico. Z8.

***Q. dalechampii*** Ten. Small tree. Young branchlets glabrous. Lvs 8–13cm, oblong to obovate-lanceolate, base truncate to subcordate, margin sinuately lobed to pinnatifid, lobes 5–7 each side ovate to lanceolate, apices acute, sparsely pubesc. initially, quickly becoming glabrous. Acorns ripe in first year, in groups of 1–3, ovate, to 2cm; cupule hemispherical, scales thick, rough, white-grey tomentose, enclosing one-third to a half of acorn. S Italy. Z7.

***Q.×deamii*** Trel. *(Q. macrocarpa × Q. muehlenbergii.)* Closely resembles *Q. muehlenbergii* but lf margins more deeply lobed, lobes 7–9 each side, apices acute, and lvs finely pubesc. beneath. Acorn pedicellate. US (Indiana).

***Q. dentata*** Thunb. JAPANESE EMPEROR OAK. Deciduous tree, fast-growing to 20–25m. Trunk to 1m diam. Crown large, rounded. Bark brown, fissured and split into large subrectangular plates, grey-scaly. Branches spreading to ascending. Branchlets grey-tomentose, lenticellate. Lvs 15–30(–50)×8–14(–30)cm, orbicular-obovate to oblong-obovate, base attenuate and rounded to cordate, apex attenuate or rounded, margin sinuately lobed, lobes large, rounded, apex often mucronulate, pale yellow tomentose at first, becoming dark green and glabrous except on nerves above, paler and densely tomentose beneath, nerves 8–12 pairs; petiole 3–6(–12)mm, or almost absent. Acorns ripe in first year, 1.2–2.4×1.2–1.7cm, ovoid to subglobose, ochre yellow, glabrous, apex rounded, mucronate; cupule hemispherical, scales adpressed, upper scales erect to recurved, enclosing more than half of acorn. Japan, Manchuria, Korea, Mongolia, China, Taiwan. 'Pinnatifida': lf lobes divided almost to midrib, lobes linear, margins crispate. Japan. var. ***oxygloba*** Franch. Lvs narrower at base, lobes more abruptly acuminate and triangular. China (Yunnan). Z5.

***Q. douglasii*** Hook. & Arn. BLUE OAK. Deciduous tree to 20m. Branches robust, short, spreading. Crown symmetrical, dense, rounded. Bark white-grey, slightly roughened, with small brown or light red scales. Young branchlets densely tomentose, becoming subglabrous, lenticellate. Lvs (2.5–)5–8(–10)×2.5–4cm, oblong to elliptic, base cuneate or slightly rounded, apex obtuse or rounded, margin sinuate-dentate, teeth obtuse or rounded, sometimes 3–5(–7) lobed with sinuses between lobes, initially soft-pubesc., becoming blue-green, glabrescent, semi-rigid, with a few hairs above, fawn-pubesc. beneath, nerves 3–5 pairs; petiole 0.7–1.5cm, pubesc., robust. Acorns ripe in first year, 2–3.5×1–1.5cm, solitary, sessile, ovoid, apex sometimes attenuate, mucronate; cupule a flat cup, thin; pale-green pubesc. inside, scales adpressed with subacute apices, enclosing only the acorn base. W US (California). Z7.

***Q. dumosa*** Nutt. CALIFORNIA SCRUB OAK. Semi-evergreen shrub or small tree to 4m. Shoots pubescent at first, eventually glabrous. Lvs variable, mostly 1.5–2.5cm, often entire on mature plants, spiny toothed on young and some mature plants, coriaceous; glabrous above, tomentose beneath; petiole short. Acorn mature in first year, sessile, 2–3cm, ovoid; cupule thick, lower scales tuberculate; covering half of acorn. W California, N Baja California. Z8.

***Q. durandii*** Buckl. DURAND OAK. Tree to 25m, closely allied to *Q. austrina*. Lvs 7–15cm, entire or slightly lobed, yellow-green. Acorns mature in first year, 1.5–2cm; cupule thin, enclosing acorn only at base. SE US. Z7.

***Q. durata*** Jeps. LEATHER OAK. Fully evergreen shrub or small tree to 4m, similar to *Q. dumosa*; differs in lvs stiff and thickly coriaceous, dull (not glossy) above and with revolute margins. California, at higher altitudes than *Q. dumosa*. Z7.

***Q. ehrenbergii*** Kotschy. Deciduous shrub or small tree. Bark shallowly cracked, grey-brown. Branches spreading. Branchlets yellow-brown tomentose. Lvs 5–8×3–5cm, longer or as long as wide, ovate or short-elliptic, apex obtuse, base truncate or subcordate, stellate-pubesc. occasionally dentate, more usually deeply lobed to pinnatifid (sometimes resembling *Crataegus orientalis*), lobes acute, apiculate or with a bristle-like apex, nerves 5–6 pairs; petiole 1–2cm. Acorn solitary, 3–4×2–3cm, subcylindrical, apex truncate, mucronate, glabrescent; cupule hemispherical, scales thick, erect to slightly recurved, finely pubesc., enclosing at least half of acorn. Asia Minor (Syria, Lebanon). Z7.

***Q. ellipsoidalis*** E.J. Hill. NORTHERN PIN OAK. Deciduous tree to 20m. Bark grey-brown, narrowly fissured into narrow plates 5–15cm long. Branchlets initially hairy and green-brown or sometimes red-brown, becoming dark grey- or red-brown. Lvs 6–15×5–12cm, obovate or elliptic, base truncate or cuneate, margin deeply lobed, lobes 5–7, oblong, coarsely dentate with 1–3 teeth, silky-tomentose at first, soon becoming glabrous except on vein axils beneath, dark green and shining above, paler beneath, colouring yellow to light brown with crimson or red markings in autumn, less spectacular than *Q. coccinea*, nerves 3 pairs; petiole 4–5cm, usually glabrous. Acorns ripe in second year, 1.2–2×1–1.5cm, solitary or paired, ellipsoid apex mucronate, puberulent, chestnut-brown with darker lines; cupule turbinate to obconical, light red-brown, puberulent inside, scales adpressed, finely pubesc., enclosing one-third to one-half of acorn. NE US. Z4.

***Q. emoryi*** Torr. EMORY OAK. Deciduous tree 9–12m, rarely to 21m. Bark dark brown-black, split into oblong plates, scaly. Branches rigid, yellow- or grey-tomentose at first, becoming glabrous, red, red-brown or black. Lvs 2.5–4.5(–6)×1–1.5(–2.5)cm, oblong-lanceolate to oblong, apex acute, mucronate, base rounded to cordate, margin slightly revolute, entire or with a few, irregular, oblique, acute teeth, white-tomentose often tinted red at first, rapidly becoming dark green, glabrous and shining above, with a few tufts of hair on midrib beneath, leathery, rigid; petiole 2–5mm, pubesc.; nerves 7–10 pairs. Acorns ripe in first year 1.5–2×0.8–1cm, oblong-ellipsoid, apex rounded, mucronate, dark chestnut to black; cupule deep or hemispherical, pale green pubesc. inside, scales adpressed, ovate, pale brown, white-tomentose, enclosing one-third of acorn. SW US, Mexico. Z7.

***Q. engleriana*** Seemen Evergreen tree 6–9(–10)m. Bark dark brown. Young branchlets stellate-pubesc. becoming glabrous. Lvs 6–10×(2.5–)3.5–4.5cm, ovate to lanceolate, apex long-acuminate, base rounded, margin dentate, teeth small, acute, sharp, dark green, glabrous and shining above, paler and brown-lanate beneath, nerves 9–13 pairs; petiole 0.6–1.5cm. Acorns mature in first year, in groups of 1–3, 1.2–3×0.6–1cm, oblong-ovoid, pale brown, apex attenuate, mucronate, puberulent, otherwise glabrous; cupule sessile, hemispherical, silky-pubesc. inside, scales grey-pubesc. outside, enclosing only base of acorn. China (Hupeh, Sichuan). Z7.

***Q. fabri*** Hance. Deciduous tree to 25m, usually smaller in cult. Branchlets yellow pubesc. at first, becoming glabrous. Lvs 6–17×2.5–6(–10)cm, oblong-obovate or ovate, apex rounded or obtuse, base rounded or subauriculate, margin undulate with 7–10 lobes each side, white haired initially, becoming glabrous above, densely yellow-white tomentose beneath, nerves 9–11 pairs; petiole 3.5–10mm, pubesc. Acorns ripe in first year 1.8–2.2×0.5–1cm, oblong or cylindrical, apex mucronate and crowned with persistent styles; cupule sessile, subhemispherical, scales adpressed, apex obtuse, erect, brown, puberulent, enclosing one-third of acorn. China, Korea. Z5.

***Q. faginea*** Lam. PORTUGUESE OAK. Semi-evergreen shrub or tree to *c*20m in habit, usually smaller in cult. Bark grey to brown, broken into subrectangular plates. Branchlets initially grey or white pubesc. becoming glabrous. Lvs 3–7×1.5–4cm, ovate-elliptic or oblong-obovate, apex rounded or obtuse, base rounded, truncate or subcordate, margin undulate, dentate, slightly revolute, teeth usually acute and mucronate, stellate-pubesc. soon becoming glabrous above, grey-tomentose slowly becoming glabrous beneath. Acorns ripe in first year, to 2.5cm, ovoid-oblong, apex and base attenuate, apex usually apiculate, straw yellow, subglabrous; cupule hemispherical, scales adpressed, slightly rough, grey-, yellow-, or red-brown tomentose, enclosing one-fifth to one-third of acorn. Spain, Portugal. ssp. ***tlemcenensis*** (A. DC.) Maire & Weiller. Intermediate between species type and *Q. canariensis*, possibly of hybrid origin: Lvs to 12×5cm, mostly 5–10cm, elliptic-oblong, shallow-lobed or toothed, thinly tomentose at first. NW Africa. Z7.

***Q. falcata*** Michx. SOUTHERN RED OAK; SWAMP RED OAK. Deciduous tree to 30m. Branches spreading, forming a rounded or ovoid crown. Bark dark brown tinted red, sometimes pale, deeply fissured into large, scaly plates. Branchlets red-brown pubesc. at first. Lvs 7–20×5–12cm, obovate or oblong, apex acute or acuminate, base rounded, sometimes cuneate, pubesc. at first above, becoming dark green, glabrous and shining, densely silver-white tomentose beneath, margins sinuately lobed, lobes 3–7, falcate, acute, entire or with a few teeth; petiole 3–3.5cm downward curved, pubesc. becoming glabrous. Acorns ripe in second year, 1.2–1.4×1–1.5cm, subglobose, apex mucronate, light red-brown, puberulent at first; cupule obconical or a flat cup, red-brown, shining, scales adpressed, mostly glabrous, enclosing only base or to one-third of acorn. SE US. var. ***pagodifolia*** Ellis. CHERRY-BARK RED OAK. Tree to 30m, rarely more; bark scaly, cherry-like. Young branchlets tomentose, eventually becoming glabrous. Lvs 15–20cm, lobes 5–11, shallower than lobes of species type, white-tomentose or sometimes tinted red beneath. Acorns solitary; cupule enclosing half of acorn. Z6.

***Q. frainetto*** Ten. HUNGARIAN OAK. Majestic deciduous tree to 30m, rarely more. Bark smooth with small scale-like plates, dark grey. Crown large, almost regular. Branches sometimes pendulous. Branchlets soft pubesc. at first, becoming glabrous. Lvs (8–)10–20(–25)×5–12cm, rarely larger, obovate or oblong-obovate, apex rounded, base subcordate or truncate, margin pinnatifid, lobes 6–10(–12) pairs, lobes sometimes lobulate or sinuately margined, young lvs white-yellow tomentose, becoming glabrous or stellate-pubesc., above, paler glaucescent beneath, nerves 7–9(–12) pairs; petiole 0.5–1cm, or almost absent. Acorns ripe in first year, 1.25–3.5×1–1.2cm, oblong-elliptic or ovoid-oblong, apex rounded, mucronate, light brown, glabrous; cupule hemispherical, densely

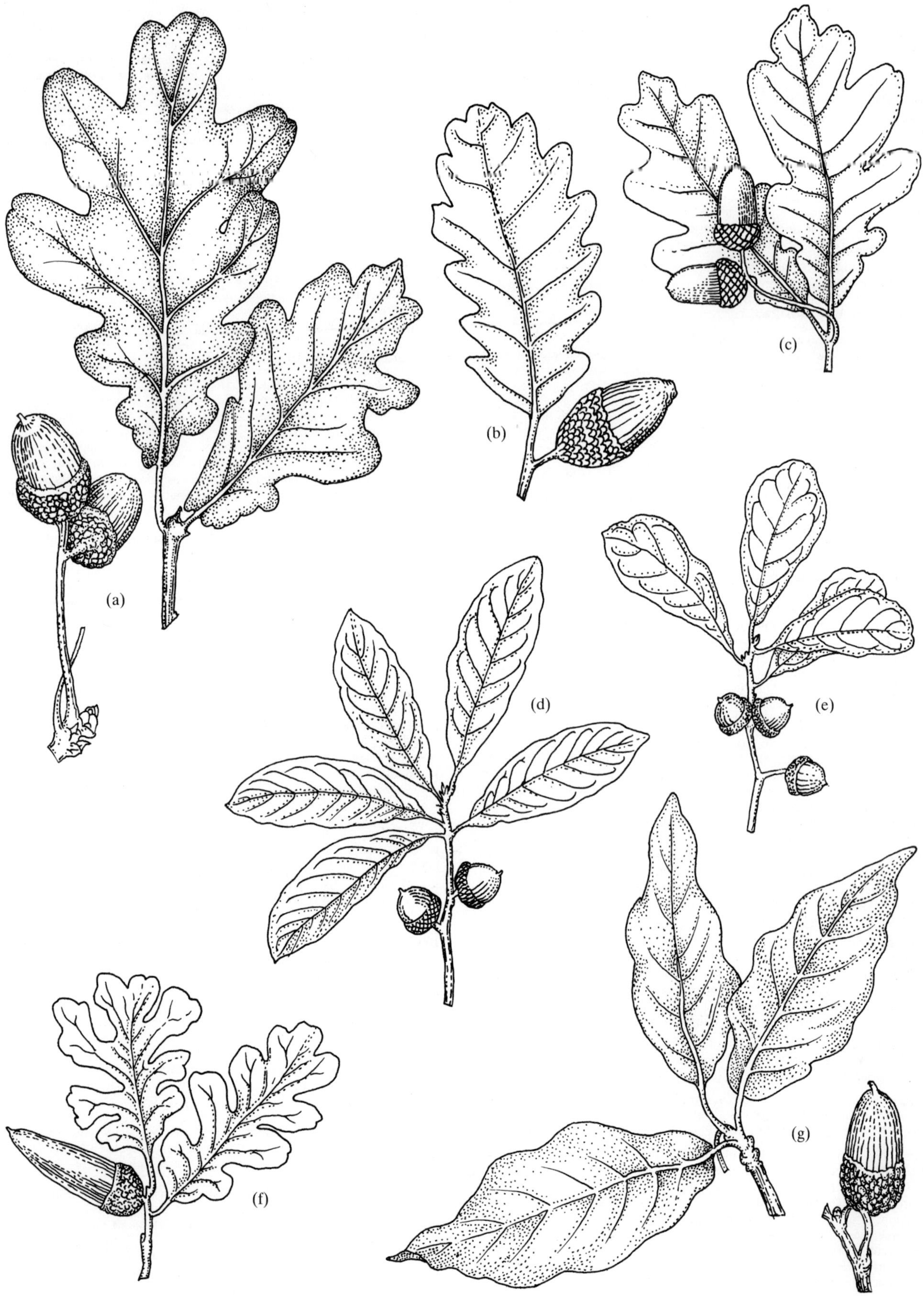


**Quercus** (a) *Quercus robur* (b) *Q. pubescens* (c) *Q. haas* (d) *Q. imbricaria* (e) *Q. nigra* (f) *Q. lobata* (g) *Q. ilex*

tomentose outside; scales adpressed, enclosing up to one half of acorn. S Italy, Turkey, Balkans. Z6.

***Q.fruticosa*** Brot. Small semi-evergreen shrub to 2m, usually much smaller and spread out forming a carpet *c*30cm high. Young branchlets yellow-velvety, eventually becoming glabrous. Lvs 2.5–5(–9)×1.2–3cm, oblong-obovate or obovate-elliptic, apex obtuse, base rounded or cordate, margin entire or sinuate-crenate and often dentate at apex, teeth 4–7 pairs, flat or curved, apex usually mucronate, leathery, discolorous, sparsely hairy above, white-grey pubesc. beneath, nerves 6–8 pairs. Acorns ripe in first year, 1–1.5×0.8–1cm, oblong, glabrescent; cupule cup-shaped, scales overlapping, triangular, pubesc., enclosing to two-thirds of acorn. S Spain and Portugal, Morocco. Z8.

***Q.gambelii*** Nutt. GAMBEL OAK. Deciduous shrub 1 or small tree to 8m, rarely larger. Bark deeply fissured, dark grey often tinted red-brown. Young branchlets ochre-red tomentose, becoming glabrous, grey-brown eventually. Lvs 7–12×3–6cm, obovate, base attenuate, rounded, margin deeply lobed, lobes 3–6 each side, uneven, oblique, rounded, entire, terminal lobe sometimes lobed, sinuses running to midrib, glabrous or sparsely hairy above, paler and finely puberulent beneath; petiole 1–2cm. Acorns ripe in first year, 1.5–2×1.2–1.5cm, ovoid, tomentose, apex rounded, mucronate; cupule hemispherical, sometimes top-shaped, enclosing half of acorn. Wyoming, Colorado, Utah, New Mexico. Z4.

***Q.×ganderii*** C. Wolf. *(Q.agrifolia × Q.kelloggii.)* Intermediate between parents, but with tufts of hairs in vein axils beneath.

***Q.garryana*** Douglas ex Hook. OREGON WHITE OAK. Deciduous tree 10–18(–20 or 30)m. Trunk 1–1.5m diam. Crown rounded. Branches crooked, erect, ascending, or sometimes pendulous. Bark pale grey, shallowly cracked. Young branchlets orange-tomentose at first, becoming glabrous, light red-brown and finally grey. Lvs 10–15×5–12cm, obovate or oblong-obovate, apex rounded, base cuneate, rounded, or subcordate, margins slightly revolute, deeply 3–5 lobed each side, lobes entire or dentate, dark green and glabrous above, paler and soft pubesc., sometimes glabrous beneath, nerves 1–4 pairs; petiole 1.5–2.5cm, pubesc. Acorns ripe in first year, 2–2.5×1.5–2cm, ovoid, base truncate, apex rounded, mucronate, glabrous and smooth; cupule shallow, sessile or shortly pedicellate, puberulent inside, scales adpressed, pubesc., apices free, acute. Western N America. Z5.

***Q.georgiana*** M.A. Curtis. GEORGIA OAK; STONE MOUNTAIN OAK. Shrub or small tree, 1.5–4m. Bark light brown. Branches glabrous, shining, lenticellate, dark brown or grey. Lvs 3–12×2–9cm, ovate or obovate, apex acute, base attenuate or cuneate, margin deeply lobed, lobes 3–7, triangular, separated by oblique sinuses, terminal lobe entire or trilobed, initially green tinted red, nervation tomentose, margins ciliate, becoming green and shining above, paler and with tufts of hair in nerve axils beneath, colouring deep orange to scarlet in autumn, nerves 3–4 pairs; petiole 1–1.5cm. Acorns ripe in second year, 1–1.25cm, oblong or subglobose, light red-brown, apex mucronate, glabrous and shining; cupule hemispherical, light red-brown, base often attenuate, shining inside, scales adpressed, ovate, obtuse, slightly silky pubesc. outside. E US, localized in Georgia. Z6.

***Q.gilliana*** Rehd. & Wils. Evergreen shrub or tree to 8m. Young shoots brown, pubescent at first. Lvs 2.5–6×1–3cm, ovate, rounded to cordate base, margin entire, spiny-toothed on young trees; glabrous above, pubescent at first beneath; petiole 1–3mm. Acorn mature in first year, clustered 2–4 on a short stout peduncle; cupule enclosing about half, scales adpressed, pubescent. SW China. Z8.

***Q.gilva*** Bl. Evergreen tree to 30m. Branches short, horizontal, crown cylindrical, rounded at top, young branchlets yellow-red velvety, becoming glabrous in their third year. Lvs 6–7.5×2–2.5(–3)cm, lanceolate or oblong-lanceolate, apex short-acuminate, base attenuate or sometimes rounded, margins entire at base, shallowly dentate in upper half, teeth rigid, acute, yellow-tomentose at first, becoming glabrous above, white and tomentose beneath, nerves 11–15 pairs; petiole 5–10mm, tomentose. Acorn 15–17×11–13mm, ovoid, mucronate, glabrous except for mucron, brown; cupule sessile, silky inside, tomentose outside, scales forming 5–6 bands, enclosing one-third or more of acorn. Japan, C China. Z7.

***Q.glabrescens*** Benth. Evergreen shrub or small tree to 10m. Young shoots downy, later glabrous. Lvs 5–10×2–3cm, oblong-elliptic, base entire, cuneate, rest coarsely mucronate-toothed, often wavy, rarely fully entire on old plants; dark glossy rough green above; pale, almost glabrous beneath; petiole short. Acorn mature in first year, 1.5cm, clustered 1–3 on a pubescent peduncle; cupule with adpressed pubescent scales, covering a third to half of the acorn. C Mexico. Z8.

***Q.glandulifera*** Bl. Deciduous tree to 15m. Bark fissured. Young branchlets silky-pubesc. Lvs 5–15×2–4.5cm, obovate to oblong-ovate, apex acute, base acuminate, margin dentate, teeth triangular, tips mucronate, directed to leaf apex, glabrous and green above, blue-green glaucous and lightly pubesc. beneath, nerves to 12; petiole 1.2–2cm. Acorns ripe in first year, in groups of 1–3, groups pedicellate, 1–1.5cm; cupule shallow, scales adpressed, white-tomentose outside, enclosing one-third of cup. Japan, Korea, China. Z5.

***Q.glauca*** Thunb. Medium sized evergreen tree, sometimes to 15m. Young branches deep crimson-brown, slightly hairy rapidly becoming glabrous, lenticellate. Lvs persisting for 2 or 3 years, 8–10(–15)×4–5(–6)cm, lanceolate-obovate to obovate, rarely oblanceolate, apex acuminate, base attenuate, rarely rounded, slightly asymmetric, silky-pubesc. at first, becoming glabrous throughout, or with a few hairs beneath, ultimately glaucous, glabrous or puberulent, margins entire at base, dentate above, teeth acute, tips mucronate, erect, curved, never spreading, nerves 9–12(–16) pairs, prominent. Acorns mature in first year, 1.3–1.5(–2)×1–1.2cm, cylindrical or conic-ovoid, apex apiculate, smooth, shining, sometimes marked with dark stripes; cupule enclosing one-third of acorn, cyathiform, scales forming 6–7 flat bands, puberulent. Japan, China. 'Shimogashii' lvs variegated, with pale yellow veins. var. ***micrococca*** Maxim. Lvs glaucous, hairy beneath. Acorn 10–12×7–8mm, obovoid; cupules small, with 4–5 rings. Japan, China. var. ***gracilis*** A. Camus. Resembles *Q.myrsinaefolia*, but lvs pubesc., beneath, smaller and narrower, 4.5–8×1.5–2.5cm, oblong-elliptic to oblong or oblong-lanceolate, apex slightly acuminate, base cuneate to rounded, margins shallowly dentate, pubesc. below. China. var. ***linearifolia*** Koidz. Lvs 1–7×0.7–1cm, subsessile, narrowly linear, apex acute, margins with irregular, spiny teeth. Japan. var. ***lacera*** Matsum. Lvs obovate, oval or or lanceolate, apex acuminate-cuspidate, margins deeply lobed, tips of lobes with cartilaginous point. ssp. ***annulata*** Sm. Tree to 18m. Lvs oval or lanceolate, apex acuminate, base rounded, wider at middle than species, margin teeth more acuminate, waxy and often abundantly hairy beneath. Cupules larger, base attenuate, silky-pubesc. outside, scales forming 6–7 rings, lower rings dentate, upper rings entire. Himalaya from Kashmir to Bhutan, Nepal, Sikkim, Burma, Tonkin. This ssp. represents the oak recognized by Loudon as *Q.glauca*. See also *Q.stenophylla*, *Q.salicina*. Z7.

***Q.grisea*** Liebm. Shrub to medium-sized tree, to 4m. Twigs densely pubesc. Lvs to 5cm, coriaceous, grey-green, downy throughout, oblong, minutely and sparsely dentate. SW US, N Mexico.

***Q.haas*** Kotschy. Deciduous tree related to *Q.robur*. Bark dark grey. Young branchlets densely yellow to grey velvety, becoming subglabrous, lenticellate. Lvs 10–20×4–6.5(–7)cm, rarely larger, obovate, apex rounded or slightly truncate, base auriculate or subcordate, margin with 3–5 lobes each side, lobes rounded, asymmetrical, dark green and glabrous above, paler blue-green and tomentose beneath, nerves 4–6 pairs, petiole to 6mm or almost absent. Acorns ripe in first year, 4–5×1.8–2cm, ellipsoid, base slightly truncate, apex rounded mucronate, pale yellow-brown, almost glabrous; cupule flattened-hemispherical, scales adpressed, tips free, erect, tomentose, enclosing one-third to one-quarter of acorn. Asia Minor. Z5.

***Q.hartwissiana*** Steven. Deciduous tree to 25cm. Bark furrowed. Branchlets dark brown, sometimes tinted crimson, glabrous, lenticellate. Lvs 7–12(–15)×3.5–6.5(–9.5)cm, oblong to obovate-oblong or subelliptic, apex rounded or obtuse, base auriculate, subcordate, margin with 5–9 short, equal, rounded lobes each slide, dark green, glabrous and shining above, paler, glabrous or with hairs on veins beneath, nerves 7–10(–13) pairs; petiole 1.5–2.5(–3.5)cm, yellow. Acorns ripe in first year, in groups of 1–3 on a pedicel 4–6(–10)cm, 1.8–3×1–1.5cm, almost obovoid, apex mucronate, glabrous, yellow-brown; cupule subhemispherical, scales adpressed in overlapping rings, tomentose, enclosing one-third of acorn. SW Bulgaria, Asia Minor, Caucasus, W Transcaucasus. Z5.

***Q.×heterophylla*** Michx. f. *(Q.phellos × Q.rubra.)* Deciduous tree 20–25m. Bark smooth, pale-grey or brown. Branches white puberulent at first, becoming glabrous and deep red then dark brown. Lvs variable in shape, 10–18×2–4.3cm, oblong-lanceolate to obovate, apex mucronate, base cuneate, entire or with few shallow teeth, or 7–15×3–8cm, obovate, apex and base attenuate, with 4–6 shallow or deep, often mucronate lobes each side, initially pubesc. above and tomentose beneath becoming glabrous or slightly hairy on nervation beneath; petiole 1.25–2.5cm, pubesc. becoming glabrous. Acorns subsessile, closely resembling *Q.rubra.* First observed near Philadelphia.

***Q.×hickelii*** Camus. *(Q.pontica × Q.robur.)* Deciduous shrub, larger than *Q.pontica*. Lvs to 15×10cm, either obovate, base attenuate and cordate, or subelliptic, base cuneate, margins coarsely dentate, teeth tips obtuse, mucronate, dark green and shining above, paler beneath; petiole short. Garden origin, France.

***Q.hinckleyi*** C.H. Mull. Rare evergreen shrub, forming low thickets in the wild. Lvs glaucous, rigid, short-stalked, bearing 2–3 sharp spines on each side, base often auriculate. SW Texas (Solitario Peak).

***Q.×hispanica*** Lam. *(Q.cerris × Q.suber.)* Semi-evergreen tree or shrub to 30m. Bark less corky than in *Q.suber*. Young branchlets tomentose. Lvs 4–10×2–4cm, oblong-elliptic, apex acute, margin sinuate-dentate, teeth small, 4–7 each side, triangular, apex obtuse and mucronulate, dark green and sparsely hairy above, densely yellow-white tomentose beneath, nerves 5–7 pairs; petiole 0.8–2cm, tomentose. Acorns ripe in second year, 3–4×2cm, oblong-ovoid, apex mucronate, mostly glabrous; cupule hemispherical to ovoid, tomentose outside, scales erect to reflexed, enclosing half or more of acorn. S France to Portugal and Italy, Balkans. 'Ambrozyana': lvs 6–10cm, usually rather small, oblong-obovate, lobes subulate-mucronate, dark green and shining above, grey tomentose beneath. 'Crispa': compact shrub or small tree; bark more corky; lvs 5–8cm, crispate, densely white tomentose beneath. 'Dentata': bark corky; lvs more closely resembling *Q.cerris*, 6–12×2.5–4cm, coarsely dentate, dark green and shining above, grey-tomentose beneath; sometimes confused with

'Fulhamensis'. 'Diversifolia': small tree; bark very corky; lvs 5×2cm, ovate, each side with conspicuous sinus, thus resembling *Q. cerris* lvs, margin lobed in lower half, entire to denticulate above; acorn cup hemispherical, scales more adpressed than hybrid type. 'Fulhamensis': graceful tree; branches more slender and bark less corky; lvs 7.5–9×3.5cm, ovate, apex acute, base rounded to subcordate, margin dentate, teeth 5–8 each side, apex acute, tomentum white; often confused with and grown as cv. Dentata. 'Fulhamensis Latifolia': lvs to 8×6cm, larger than 'Fulhamensis', apex obtuse, margin teeth wider and shallower than 'Fulhamensis', tomentum grey. 'Heterophylla': closely resembles *Q. cerris* var. *haliphloeos*; lvs oblong, irregularly lobed, sometimes with conspicuous broad sinus each side of midrib. 'Lucombeana': tree 25–30m; crown conical, bark only slightly corky; lvs resemble those of *Q. cerris*, 6–12×2.5–4cm, oblong, margin coarsely dentate, teeth 6–7(9) each side, green, glabrous, shining above, paler and tomentose beneath; acorn to 2.5cm, cupule with lower scales reflexed, upper scales erect, enclosing more than half of acorn.
Z7.

***Q. hypoleucoides*** Camus. SILVER-LEAF OAK; WHITE-LEAF OAK. Semi-evergreen tree 6–10(–20)m, sometimes shrub 2–3m. Bark brown-black, split into large plates. Branches rigid, grey-tomentose at first, eventually becoming glabrous, brown-black, lenticellate. Lvs 5–10(–12)×1–2.5(–3)cm, lanceolate or oblong – lanceolate to subelliptic, base rounded or attenuate, apex attenuate and often mucronate, margin revolute, usually entire or sinuate-dentate towards apex, rarely with several rigid teeth, soft and tomentose on both faces at first, becoming glabrous and shining above, trick cream-cottony beneath, rigid, nerves 10–12 pairs; petiole 5–15mm, pubesc. Acorns mature in second year, 1–1.2×0.8cm, conic-oblong, apex rounded or acute, dark green; cupule hemispherical, pubesc. inside, scales adpressed, light chestnut-brown, silky-tomentose, enclosing one-third of acorn. S US, Mexico. Z7.

***Q. iberica*** Steven ex Bieb. Deciduous tree related to *Q. petraea*, but generally shorter. Branches always glabrous, brown, lenticellate. Lvs 8–12×4–4.5cm, oblong-obovate to subelliptic, apex rounded or attenuate, base rounded or truncate, margin with 6–10 shallow, rounded, entire lobes each side, green and glabrous above, paler and scattered short-pubesc. beneath, at least in nerve axils, nerves 8–10 pairs; petioles 1.5–2.5cm, glabrous. Acorns mature in first year, grouped 1–3 together, 1.4–1.6cm, ovoid, glabrous, apex subacute; cupule rounded, scales adpressed, velvety or puberulent, apices sometimes glabrous, peduncle short or almost absent. Balkans, Asia Minor to N Iran (not Iberian Peninsula). Trees from SE Turkey with larger lvs, to 17cm, more deeply lobed, are sometimes separated as *Q. pinnatiloba* K. Koch. Z5.

***Q. ilex*** L. HOLM OAK; EVERGREEN OAK; HOLLY-LEAVED OAK. Evergreen tree to 20(–27)m. Crown broad, rounded. Bark smooth, grey, becoming shallowly split into small scales. Young branches grey-tomentose, becoming glabrous in second year. Lvs 2–9×1–3cm, sometimes wider, narrowly elliptic, ovate-lanceolate or suborbicular, slightly concave, apex acute or obtuse, base attenuate or slightly cordate, margin entire or dentate with mucronate, acuminate teeth, leathery, subglabrous, green and shining above, densely pubesc. beneath, nerves (7–)9–10(–12) pairs; petiole 0.5–2cm, tomentose. Acorns mature in first year, in groups of 1–3, 1.5–3×1–1.5cm, oblong-ovoid to subglobose, apex mucronate, grey-brown with darker lines, lightly lanate at first, becoming pulverulent; cupule attenuate at base, silky-pubesc. inside, scales adpressed, triangular, obtuse, tomentose except at apex of cupule, enclosing about half of acorn. Mediterranean region. 'Rotundifolia': lvs suborbicular. Often confused with *Q. ilex* var. *ballota*, which has the synonym *Q. ilex* var. *rotundifolia*. var. ***angustifolia*** DC. Lvs lanceolate, narrow, margins subentire. var. ***ballota*** (Desf.) A. DC. Lvs 1.25–5cm, oblong, apex and base rounded, apex mucronate. Acorns large, sweet, eaten roasted. N Africa, S Spain. 'Crispa': lvs 1.5cm, suborbicular, margins slightly revolute. 'Fordii': crown narrow. Lvs 2.5–3.75×c1.25cm, oblong, apex and base attenuate, margin undulate, entire or dentate. Developed in Lucombe and Pince's Nursery in Exeter. 'Genabii': lvs to 12.5×6.75cm, very leathery, rigid, upper half coarsely toothed, entire beneath. 'Latifolia': lvs like 'Genabii' but thinner textured, softer. f. ***microphylla*** Trabut. Lvs 2–2.7×1.2cm, elliptic, margins spiny-dentate. Algeria. Z7.

***Q. ilicifolia*** Wangenh. BEAR OAK. Dense, deciduous shrub or small tree, 1–5(–8)m, divaricately branched. Bark smooth, dark brown. Crown rounded. Young branchlets dark green tinted red, grey-tomentose, becoming glabrous and dark brown in second year. Lvs 5–12×3–5(–9)cm, obovate, sometimes obovate-oblong, apex obtuse, mucronate, base cuneate, margin 3–7 lobed, lobes triangular with bristle-like tips, dark red and pubesc. at first, becoming green, glabrous and shining above, white-tomentose and bullate beneath, colouring yellow or scarlet in autumn, nerves 2–3 pairs; petiole 1.2–1.5(–3cm), pubesc. at first. Acorns mature in second year, 1.2–1.6×0.9–1.3cm, ovoid to subglobose, apex mucronate, base rounded, grey- or olive-brown striped darker, glabrous; cupule cupular or top-shaped, scales ovate, truncate, obtuse, light-grey, slightly overlapping, enclosing half of acorn. E US. Hybrids of *Q. ilicifolia* × *Q. rubra* have occurred naturally and are referred to as *Q.* ×*fernaldii* Trel. Z5.

***Q. imbricaria*** Michx. SHINGLE OAK. Deciduous tree 15–20cm. Crown conical to rounded. Bark light brown, smooth, split by narrow cracks into plates. Young branchlets dark green, puberulent at first, soon becoming glabrous, dark brown, lenticellate. Lvs 10–17×(2.5–)5–7cm, oblong-lanceolate to ovate, apex acuminate, apiculate, base attenuate or cuneate, margin entire, often crispate-undulate, revolute, occasionally lobed, initially red-puberulent above and thick white-tomentose beneath, becoming thin-textured, dark green, glabrous and shining above, paler and soft-tomentose beneath, nerves 12–13 pairs; petiole 0.8–1.25cm, pubesc. Acorns mature in second year, 1–1.5×1.2–1.6mm, subglobose, apex rounded, mucronate, light brown, subglabrous to silky-pubesc.; cupule a flat cup, scales adpressed, hairy, enclosing up to half of acorn. E & C US. Z5.

***Q. incana*** Bartr. non Roxb. BLUEJACK OAK. Deciduous to semi-evergreen tree or shrub, 4–8m. Crown narrow, irregular. Branches divaricate. Young branchlets dark grey, tomentose at first. Lvs 5–9cm, oblong, apex acuminate, bristle-like, base rounded, often asymmetrical, margin entire, puberulent at first becoming green, glabrous, shining above, white-tomentose beneath. Acorns mature in second year, solitary, sessile, 1.5cm, ovoid; cupule turbinate, enclosing almost half of acorn. SE US. Z7.

***Q. infectoria*** Olivier. Semi-evergreen tree to 4(6)m. Bark grey, deeply fissured, scaly. Young branchlets subglabrous or white-yellow hairy at first, becoming glabrous, grey-brown. Lvs 4–6×1.5–5(–6)cm, oblong, base often asymmetrical, rounded or cordate, apex obtuse, rounded, margin undulate, dentate or crenate-dentate, teeth 4–8 each side, mucronate, green, glabrous, and shining above, paler, sometimes glaucescent, sometimes sparsely hairy beneath, nerves 5–7(–9) pairs; petiole 5–12mm, glabrous. Acorns mature in first year, usually solitary, 2.5–3.5(–4)×1.2–1.8cm, cylindrical, apex mucronate, glabrous, pale yellow-brown; cupule subhemispherical, scales adpressed, grey-tomentose, enclosing one-fifth or one-third of acorn. NW Turkey, Greece. ssp. ***veneris*** (A. Kerner) Holmb. Larger tree, to 16m. Lvs 4–9cm, margin entire or with 5–7 pairs of teeth, soft pubesc. beneath, nerves 8–10 pairs. Asia Minor, Syria, Kurdistan, Persia, Cyprus. Z6.

***Q. ithaburensis*** Decne. VALLONEA OAK. Semi-evergreen to deciduous tree to 18(25)m. Bark furrowed, dark brown. Young shoots yellow to grey tomentose, eventually glabrous. Lvs 4–9×2–5cm, ovate to lanceolate-elliptic, apex acuminate, base sub-cordate, margin dentate, teeth 5–9 each side, triangular, tips aristate; grey-tomentose becoming glabrous above, persistent grey-tomentose beneath; petiole 1–3cm. Acorns clustered 1–3, maturing in second year, sessile, large, 2.5–4.5×2–3cm, ovoid, apex obtuse or depressed; cupule massive, to 5×5cm, with broad, thick, flattened, spreading woody scales to 20×5mm; enclosing two thirds to nearly all of the acorn. Syria, Palestine. Z7. ssp. ***macrolepis*** (Kotschy) Hedge & Yaltirik. Lvs tend to be more deeply incised; acorn cupule scales more flexible and less woody. Specimens from SE Turkey with woody scales like the species type are sometimes separated as var. *vallonea* (Kotschy) Zoh. (*Q. vallonea* Kotschy). SE Italy, Balkans, Greece and Turkey.

***Q. kelloggii*** Newberry. CALIFORNIA BLACK OAK. Deciduous tree to 35m, sometimes only a shrub to 5m. Crown spreading, rounded. Bark smooth and grey at first, becoming dark brown almost black, cracked. Young branchlets pubesc. at first, becoming glabrous. Lvs 10–25×6–16cm, obovate, margin sinuately 5–7-lobed, lobes dentate, separated by deep, narrow sinuses, leathery, pubesc. becoming glabrous and glossy above, glabrous or sparsely tomentose beneath; petiole 2–3cm, yellow-green. Acorn solitary or paired, 2.5–3cm, ovoid; cupule of loosely adpressed, glabrous scales, enclosing half of acorns, pedicel to 1cm. W US.

***Q.*** ×***kewensis*** Osborn. (*Q. cerris* × *Q. wislizenii*.) Evergreen tree to c15m. Branchlets fine, ascending, initially stellate-pubesc., becoming glabrous, pale brown. Lvs 5–8cm, ovate-oblong, margin dentate, teeth 5–6 each side, triangular, acute, base truncate or subcordate, glabrous and matt green above, glabrous and shining beneath with a few hairs on venation, petiole 1.5–2cm. Acorn to 2.5cm. Grown from acorns of *Q. wislizenii* at Kew, 1914.

***Q. laevis*** Walter. AMERICAN TURKEY OAK. Small, slow-growing, deciduous tree or shrub, 6–12m, rarely to 20m. Crown narrow, irregular. Young branchlets glabrous, often flushed red. Lvs 10–20cm, obovate to triangular, base cuneate, margin deeply 3–5–(7)–lobed, lobes triangular to oblong, lobe tips with 1–3 aristate teeth, green, glabrous and shining above, green and glabrous except for red-brown hairs in nerve axils beneath; petiole 1–2cm. Acorns mature in second year, usually solitary, 2cm, ovoid to ellipsoid, mucronate, mucro surrounded by white scurfy ring; cupule enclosing one third of acorn; pedicel short. SE US. Z6.

***Q. lamellosa*** Sm. Majestic evergreen tree to 36m in habitat, usually shorter in cult. Bark rough, grey-brown. Young branchlets yellow-brown tomentose, becoming glabrous, dark grey to black, lenticellate. Lvs 15–45×5–15(–22)cm, ovate or ovate-lanceolate to elliptic, apex acute or acuminate, base rounded or attenuate, leathery, both faces pubesc. at first, becoming glabrous, green and shining above, glaucous, silvery-white waxy beneath, except on nervation, margin dentate except at base, teeth erect, tips acute or acuminate; petiole 3–4.5cm, glabrous, brown. Acorn solitary on in groups of 2–4, sessile, 3–4×2–3cm, top-shaped to globose, smooth; cupule much wider, made of up 10 concentric rings, enclosing two-thirds to four-fifths of acorn. Himalaya: Nepal, Assam, SE Tibet, N Burma, China (Yunnan). Z8.

***Q. laurifolia*** Michx. LAUREL OAK. Deciduous to semi-evergreen tree to 25(–30)m. Bark smooth, dark brown to black, fissured. Young branchlets deep red-brown, glabrous. Lvs 6–13×1.2–4cm, oblong to obovate, apex acute to rounded, base tapered, acute or rounded, margin entire or with to 3 shallow teeth at apex, dark green, glabrous and shining above, paler and initially pubesc. beneath, becoming glabrous, midvein and petiole yellow; petiole 4–8mm. Acorns mature in second year, solitary or paired, 1–1.5cm, ovoid-globose, dark black-brown; cupule shallow, of adpressed obtuse scales, enclosing only the base of acorn, subsessile. SE US. Z7.

***Q.* ×*leana*** Nutt. *(Q. imbricaria × Q. velutina.)* Large, deciduous tree resembling *Q. imbricaria* more than *Q. velutina*. Young branchlets flushed red, pubesc. Lvs 8–12(–17)cm, narrowly obovate to obovate, apex acute, base rounded, margin entire but for 3-lobes at apex or 1–3 irregular lobes each side of apex, dark green, glabrous above, lightly pubesc. beneath (less so than *Q. velutina*); petiole 1.5–2cm. Acorn solitary or paired, 2cm; cupule encloses half of acorn. This hybrid often occurs naturally. E US.

***Q. leucotrichophora*** A. Camus. Evergreen tree 10–24(30)m in habitat. Bark rough, fissured, exfoliating in large flakes. Young branchlets grey-velvety, becoming glabrous, brown, lenticellate. Lvs 7–16(–18)×3.5–5cm, lanceolate, apex acuminate or acute, base rounded or attenuate, margin entire at base, with widely spaced teeth above, white-pubesc. at first, becoming leathery, rigid, green and glabrous above, pure-white tomentose beneath, nerves 10–15 pairs; petiole 1–2cm, white tomentose. Acorns mature in first year, solitary or grouped to 3 together, 2–2.5×1.3–1.5cm, ovoid, glabrous, brown, shining, apex mucronate; cupule campanulate, of adpressed white-brown scales, enclosing half of acorn. Himalaya. Z8.

***Q. liaotungensis*** Koidz. Large deciduous tree. Bark ash-grey. Young branchlets puberulent, soon glabrous, pale brown, lenticellate. Lvs (3–)5–7(–13)×(1–)2.5–4.5(–6.5)cm, obovate-oblong, obovate or oblong, apex obtuse, base attenuate and rounded or cordate, margin with (1–)4–7(–9) pairs of rounded lobes, leathery, glabrous, dull or glossy green above, paler, glabrous or sparsely hairy beneath, nerves 5–7 pairs; petiole 1–4(–9)mm, glabrous. Acorns mature in first year, 1–2×1cm, ovoid or rounded-ellipsoid, apex mucronate, light brown, glabrous, apex silky-pubesc.; cupule hemispherical, scales adpressed, smooth, upper scales pubesc., enclosing one-third to one-half of acorn. China, Mongolia, Korea. Z4.

***Q.* ×*libanerris*** Boom. *(Q. cerris × Q. libani.)* Deciduous tree resembling *Q. cerris*. Garden origin. 'Trompenburg': young branchlets grey-pubesc. becoming glabrous, punctate; lvs 7–13×2–4cm, oblong, apex acute, base cuneate, margins with 10–16 pairs of spreading lobes, lobes forward pointing with needle like tips, glabrous or sparsely pubesc. above, grey-pubesc. beneath; petiole 7–12mm; acorn similar to those of *Q. cerris* but broader, cup scales shorter. Z6.

***Q. libani*** Olivier. LEBANON OAK. Deciduous rarely semi-evergreen, slender, densely branched shrub or tree, 7–8(–10)m. Bark grey, smooth at first becoming fissured. Young branchlets red-brown pubesc. at first, soon becoming glabrous. Lvs 4.5–11×1–3.5cm, apex acuminate, base attenuate, rounded or subcordate, margin dentate, teeth tips bristle-like, dark green and glabrous above, paler and glabrous to pubesc. beneath, nerves 9–12 pairs; petiole 0.8–2cm. Acorns mature in second year, solitary or paired, 2.5cm diam., ovoid to cylindrical; cupule campanulate or a shallow cup, scales all adpressed or the upper scales spreading, enclosing two-thirds of acorn. Syria, N Iran, N Iraq, Turkey. Z6.

***Q. lobata*** Née. CALIFORNIA WHITE OAK; VALLEY OAK. Deciduous tree to 35m. Branches spreading to downward curved forming symmetrical, rounded crown. Bark light-grey or dark brown, split into rectangular plates near base. Young branchlets tomentose at first, becoming glabrous, lenticellate. Lvs 5–7(–12)×2.5–5(–8)cm, obovate or obovate-oblong, apex obtuse, base cuneate, rounded or rarely cordate, margin slightly thickened, revolute, more or less deeply 3–5-lobed each side, papery-textured, dark green glabrous or sparsely hairy above, paler, grey-pubesc. beneath, nerves 4–5 pairs; petiole 0.5–1.2cm, pubesc. Acorns mature in first year, 3–5.5×1.2–2cm, ellipsoid to elongate-ovoid, apex attenuate, umbonate, shining, chestnut-brown; hemispherical, base rounded, pale-tomentose, lower scales thick, adpressed, convex, tuberculate, lanceolate, upper scales with apex free, acute, enclosing one-third of acorn. W US (California). Z7.

***Q. lodicosa*** Warb. Allied to *Q. leucotrichophora*; tree to 25m; distinguished by larger acorns to 3×2cm with a depressed apex, and stout cupules to 2.5cm wide. SE Tibet to Upper Burma. Z8.

***Q.* ×*ludoviciana*** Sarg. *(Q. falcata* var. *pagodifolia × Q. phellos.)* Large deciduous tree. Young branchlets pubesc. Lvs either 7–12cm, entire, or 12–15cm, with 1–4 irregular, straight or falcate, ascending, triangular lobes, green and glabrous above, slightly pubesc. beneath; petiole 7–20mm. Acorn 1.2cm, oblong-ovoid, rounded; cupule enclosing one-third of acorn. S & E US. 'Microcarpa': lvs 7–9cm, lanceolate, margin lobes shallow.

***Q. lyrata*** Walter. OVERCUP OAK. Deciduous tree to 30m. Crown rounded. Bark light-grey tinted red-brown, breaking into large plates. Young branchlets finished red, sparsely hairy, becoming glabrous or puberulent. Lvs 17–20×3.5–7(–12)cm, obovate, apex acute or obtuse, lyrate, lobes 3–4 pairs, acute, uppermost lobes often further divided, dark green, glabrescent above, soft-pubesc. or white-tomentose beneath, nerves 4–6 pairs; petiole 1–2cm, glabrous or puberulent. Acorns mature in first year, 1.5–2.5cm, subglobose, apex mucronate, light chestnut-brown; cupule subspherical, grey-tomentose outside, enclosing two-thirds or more of acorn. C & S US. Z5.

***Q.* ×'Macon'.** *(Q. macranthera × Q. frainetto.)* Lvs smaller than in *Q. frainetto*, more distinctly obovate. Young branchlets tomentose like *Q. macranthera*. Acorns 3–4×0.5–0.8cm.

***Q. macranthera*** Fisch. & Mey. CAUCASIAN OAK; PERSIAN OAK. Deciduous tree 25–30m. Young branchlets tawny-tomentose, becoming glabrous after 2 years. Lvs 8–20×5–11cm, obovate, apex rounded or blunt, base rounded, subcordate or subcuneate, margin serrate, teeth 7–11 each side, rounded or obtuse, rarely mucronate, dark green, glabrous above, densely yellow or red-brown tomentose beneath, nerves 7–11 pairs; stipules moderately persistent; petiole 0.5–1.5cm, densely tawny-tomentose. Acorns mature in first year 1.6–2.5cm, ovoid-ellipsoid, almost glabrous; cupule hemispherical, scales erect to spreading, lanceolate, pubesc., enclosing half of acorn. Caucasus, N Iran. Z6. ssp. ***syspirensis*** (K. Koch) Menitsky. Lvs smaller, 5–13cm, subsessile; stipules caducous except around terminal buds.

***Q. macrocarpa*** Michx. BURR OAK; MOSSY CUP OAK. Deciduous tree 30(50)m. Crown rounded, regular or irregular. Bark rugose, split into irregular plates, light grey-brown. Young branchlets tomentose at first, soon becoming glabrous, dark brown, cracked. Lvs 10–45×5–16cm, obovate or obovate-oblong, base attenuate, cuneate or cordate, lyrately lobed, lobes 5–7 each side, dark green and glabrous above, paler, glaucous or white-tomentose beneath, colouring pale-yellow to brown in autumn, nerves 8–10 pairs; petiole 1–4cm, base expanded. Acorns mature in first year, very large, 2.5–4×1–3cm, ovoid to hemispherical, apex rounded, mucronate, soft-tomentose; cupule hemispherical, hairy, lower scales adpressed, upper scales with free, spreading apices, enclosing half or more of acorn. C & NE US, SE Canada. Z3. var. ***oliviformis*** (Michx. f.) Gray. Lvs more deeply divided, lobes narrower, more irregular. Acorns oblong-ellipsoid, like an olive, smaller than in species; cupule encloses more of acorn than in species. E US.

***Q. marilandica*** Münchh. BLACKJACK OAK. Small deciduous, slow-growing tree, 6–10(15)m. Bark rough, black-brown, split into square plates. Young branchlets pale-tomentose becoming glabrous, brown or ash-grey, lenticellate. Lvs 10–17×7–12cm, broadly obovate, apex obtuse, often divided into 3 mucronate lobes, base rounded to cordate, dark green, shining above, paler and red-brown tomentose beneath, colouring yellow to brown in autumn; petiole 1–2cm. Acorns mature in second year solitary or paired, 1–2cm, ovoid; cupule hairy outside, made up of broad, adpressed scales, enclosing one- to two-thirds of acorn. C & SE US. Z5.

***Q. mas*** Thore. Closely resembles *Q. petraea*, but lf margins regularly sinuately lobed, lobes usually at least 4 each side, young lvs more abundantly hairy beneath. Acorn mature in first year; cupule scales abruptly acuminate, gibbous, lightly tomentose. French Pyrenees to N Spain. Z6.

***Q. michauxii*** Nutt. SWAMP CHESTNUT OAK. Deciduous tree to *c*30m. Bark pale grey, scaly. Young branchlets pubesc. and green at first, becoming grey, glabrous. Lvs 10–16cm, obovate to oblong-obovate, apex acute, base attenuate to rounded, margin coarsely dentate, teeth 10–14 pairs, tips obtuse and glandular, green, glabrous and shining above, grey-velvety beneath; petiole 1.5–3.5cm. Acorns mature in first year, 3cm, oblong-elliptic; cupule made of thickened scales at base, upper scales stiff, fringed, enclosing one-third of acorn. SE US. Often confused with *Q. prinus*, *Q. muehlenbergii*, *Q. prinoides*. Z6.

***Q. mongolica*** Fisch. ex Turcz. Large deciduous tree to 30m. Young branchlets glabrous. Lvs 10–20cm, obovate, apex obtuse, base attenuate, cordate, dentate teeth rounded, entire, green and glabrous above, glabrous or pubesc. on venation beneath; petiole 4–8mm. Acorns mature in first year, 2cm, ovate, subsessile; cupule made up of tuberculate scales, uppermost scales acuminate, ciliate, enclosing one-third of acorn. NE Asia (E Siberia, N China, Korea, N Japan, E Mongolia). This tree is largely represented in cult. by var. ***grosseserrata*** (Bl.) Rehd. & Wils. Young shoots glabrous, tuberculate. Lvs 10–12cm, smaller, teeth acute, sometimes themselves dentate. Acorn cupule made of closely adpressed scales which are not ciliate. Japan, Sakhalin, Kuriles. Z3.

***Q. muehlenbergii*** Engelm. YELLOW CHESTNUT OAK; CHINKAPIN OAK. Deciduous tree to 20m, rarely 45m. Bark grey, split into thin, flaky scales. Young branchlets subglabrous, green at first, then crimson becoming grey-brown. Lvs 10–18×5–8(–12)cm, oblong, obovate or lanceolate, apex acute or acuminate, base cuneate, serrate, teeth spreading or erect, acute, young lvs pale green flushed bronze, subglabrous above, tomentose beneath, becoming glabrous above, white silky-pubesc. beneath, colouring orange or scarlet before they fall; petiole 2–4cm. Acorns mature in first year, solitary, 1.3–2×1.2–14cm, ovoid, apex rounded, mucronate, silky-pubesc.; cupule hemispherical, made up of tomentose scales, uppermost scales acute, forming fringe, enclosing half of acorn. E US. Often confused with *Q. prinus*, *Q. michauxii* and *Q. prinoides*. Z4.

***Q. myrsinifolia*** Bl. non Shiras. Evergreen tree 12–25m. Branches glabrous, blackened, lenticellate at first. Lvs persist for 2 years, 5–10(–15)×2–4cm, lanceolate or lanceolate-elliptic, apex long-acuminate, base rounded or shortly acuminate, adult lvs leathery, dark green, shining above, glaucescent, glabrous and slightly papillose beneath, margin with fine, short, erect teeth in upper half, nerves 10–12 pairs; petiole 1–1.8cm, glabrous. Acorns ripe in first year, 17–25×7–10mm, narrowly ovoid, scarcely puberulent at first, becoming glabrous, crowned with persistent styles; cupule subsessile, subhemispherical to obconic, slightly glaucous, scarcely ashy-puberulent outside, silky inside, with scales forming 7–9 rings. Japan, China, Laos. Plants grown under this name may also be *Q. bambusifolia*, *Q. glauca*, *Q. stenophylla*, *Q. salicina*. Z7.

***Q. myrtifolia*** Willd. MYRTLE OAK; SEASIDE SCRUB OAK. Small, densely branched, evergreen shrub or tree, 1–2(6)m. Bark grey, smooth, slightly cracked. Lvs

3.5–4×1.5–2.5cm, ovate, obovate or subelliptic, apex rounded, apiculate, base slightly attenuate, margin thick, entire, revolute, sometimes undulate, rarely sinuate-dentate, dark red and sparsely hairy beneath at first, becoming leathery, dark green, glabrous and shining above, yellow-green to pale orange-brown beneath, nerves 4–5 pairs; petiole 3–5mm. Acorns mature in second year, solitary or paired, 0.8–1.2×0.5–1cm, ovoid, apex attenuate, mucronate, silky-pubesc., sessile; cupule made up of slightly overlapping, obtuse scales, uppermost scales ciliate, enclosing one-quarter of acorn. SE US. Z8.

***Q.nigra*** L. non Wangenh. nec Duroi. WATER OAK. Deciduous tree 20–25m, rarely to 35m. Bark brown, smooth initially, becoming black-brown, deeply channelled. Young branchlets glabrous. Lvs 3–13×1.5–6cm, obovate with shallowly lobed apex, lobe tips bristle-like, or oblong and entire, leathery, matt blue-green and glabrous above, paler and glabrous but for tufts of hair in axils of veins beneath; petiole to 1cm. Acorns mature in second year, solitary, 1–1.5cm, globose to ovoid, black; cupule made up of short, adpressed scales, enclosing up to half of acorn. SE US. Z6.

***Q.nuttallii*** Palmer. NUTTALL'S OAK. Closely similar to *Q.palustris*, replacing it to S; tree to 30m. Young shoots glabrous, red-brown. Lvs 8–15cm, as *Q.palustris* but vein axil tufts yellow. Acorns 2–3cm, ovoid-oblong, enclosed for one third in a bowl-shaped (not saucer) cupule. S US (Mississippi river basin, on damp sites). Z6.

***Q.oblongifolia*** Torr. MEXICAN BLUE OAK. Evergreen or semi-evergreen shrub or small tree to 8m, crown rounded. Young shoots slender, red-grey. Lvs 2.5–5cm, entire, often undulate, rarely few-toothed, margin revolute; blue-green above, glabrous and glaucous beneath. Acorns mature in first year, sessile or subsessile, 1.5–2cm, ovoid, sweet; cupule covering one third of acorn, scales thin, woolly, with red tips. SW US (C Arizona to far W Texas), NW Mexico. Z7.

***Q.oxyodon*** Miq. Small evergreen tree, to 7m. Crown flattened. Young branchlets soon glabrous, smooth, lenticellate. Lvs 12–22×3.5–5cm, ovate or ovate-lanceolate, apex acuminate, cuspidate, base attenuate, margin dentate, teeth rigid, spreading to erect, leathery, green and glabrous above, white-waxy beneath, nerves 16–19(–25) pairs; petiole 2–3cm, glabrous. Acorns ripe in first year 1.5–1.7cm, subglobose, glabrous except at apex, apex umbonate; cupule sometimes white-waxy, scales forming 5–8 concentric rings, enclosing half of acorn. W China, Upper Burma, E Himalaya. Z8.

***Q.palustris*** Münchh. PIN OAK. Deciduous relatively fast growing tree, 20–25(–35)m. Crown dense, ovoid-conical, of slender branches. Bark smooth, grey-brown becoming fissured and ridged. Young branchlets glabrous, glossy, red-brown, tuberculate. Lvs 8–15cm, obovate, apex acute, base attenuate or truncate, margin deeply, pinnately lobed, lobes oblong to triangular, tips slightly lobed and bristle-like, glabrous, green and glossy above, paler and glabrous except for tufts of green-white hair in vein axils beneath; petiole 1.5–4cm. Acorns mature in second year, 1.2–1.7cm, mucronate-tipped hemispherical, base flat; cupule saucer-shaped, puberulent, red-brown, enclosing only base of acorn. NE US, SE Canada. 'Crownright': crown narrowly conical. 'Pendula': branches more pendent than species. 'Reichenbachii': young leaves and shoots flushed red. 'Umbraculifera': crown rounded, symmetrical. Lvs shining green, colouring red in autumn.

***Q.pedunculiflora*** K. Koch. Deciduous tree resembling *Q.robur*, particularly ssp. *brutia*. Young branchlets subglabrous, rapidly glabrous, lenticellate. Lvs 8–13(–17)×6–9cm, obovate or oblong-obovate, apex rounded, base rounded to cordate, margin with 4–5 pairs of rounded, entire or further shallowly divided lobes, puberulent above and white-tomentose beneath at first, becoming glabrous above, blue-green and sparsely pubesc. beneath; petiole 0.3–1cm. Acorns mature in first year, 2–3×1.5–2cm, ovoid, apex mucronate and tomentose, otherwise glabrous; cupule subhemispherical, made up of tightly adpressed or spreading to reflexed, yellow-tomentose scales, enclosing one-third of acorn. Asia Minor, Caucasus to Balkans. Z6.

***Q.petraea*** (Mattuschka) Liebl. Deciduous tree to 45m. Crown regular, trunk reaching far into crown. Bark like that of *Q.robur*, grey to black-brown, furrowed. Young branchlets glabrous, slightly tuberculate. Lvs 6–17×3–9cm, broadly or narrowly obovate, base attenuate or truncate to subcordate but not auriculate as is *Q.robur*, apex rounded, margin with 4–6 pairs of even, rounded lobes, green, glossy, glabrous above, paler, glaucous, glabrous to pubesc. beneath; petiole 1–1.6cm, yellow. Acorns mature in first year, clustered, 2–3cm, ovoid to oblong-ovoid; cupule made up of closely adpressed, pubesc. scales. Europe to W USSR. 'Albovariegata': lvs variegated with white. 'Aurea': young branchlets yellow; lvs initially yellow, becoming green but petiole and nerves persistently yellow. 'Aureovariegata': lvs yellow-green variegated. 'Cochleata': lvs more leathery, slightly convex. 'Columna': crown columnar. Lvs narrower, more oblong, margins irregularly lobed, grey-green. 'Falkenbergensis': lvs shorter, apex rounded, lobes flat, 5–7 pairs, green and glabrous above, white-green beneath with pubescence on venation. 'Giesleri': lvs long, narrowly oblong, margin entire or shallowly lobed. 'Insecata': lvs much longer and narrower, sometimes thread-like, margin irregularly divided, sometimes white. 'Laciniata': lvs more deeply divided than species. 'Mespilifolia': lvs narrowly oblong-lanceolate, margins undulate, entire, leathery. 'Muscaviensis': lvs of first branchlets subentire, lvs of secondary growth resemble those of species. 'Pendula': branches and branchlets pendent. 'Pinnata': lvs pinnatisect. 'Purpurea': lvs crimson-purple becoming grey-green flushed red, venation red. Z4.

***Q.phellos*** L. WILLOW OAK. Deciduous tree to 25(40)m. Crown rounded to columnar. Bark grey tinted red-brown, glabrous. Young branchlets red-brown, puberulent at first, soon becoming glabrous. Lvs 7–12×0.8–2.5cm, oblong-lanceolate, apex acute, base attenuate, margin entire, often undulate, dark green above, paler beneath, almost glabrous throughout. Acorns ripe in second year, small, to *c*1cm, subglobose, pale yellow-brown; cupule shallow, saucer-shaped, scales adpressed, grey-tomentose, enclosing only base of acorn. SE US. Z6.

***Q.phillyreoides*** Gray. Evergreen shrub or small tree, 5–9m. Habit rounded. Young branchlets scaly. Lvs 3–6cm, obovate to oval, apex rounded to acuminate, base rounded to subcordate, margin entire in lower half, upper half shallowly dentate, teeth rounded to obtuse, dark green, glabrous and shining above, paler, glabrous and shining beneath; petiole 0.6cm, scurfy-scaly. Acorns ripe in second year, 1.5–2cm, ovoid, apex slightly tomentose; cupule hemispherical, made up of short, adpressed, white-tomentose scales, enclosing one-third to half of acorn. China, Japan. 'Chirimen': slow-growing; lvs small, crisped. Z7.

***Q.*'Pondaim'**. (*Q.pontica* × *Q.dentata.*) Tree. Lvs obovate, margins dentate, teeth large, acute, subsessile or very shortly petioled. Developed in the 1960's in Rotterdam, Netherlands.

***Q.pontica*** K. Koch. ARMENIAN OAK. Deciduous shrub or small tree, to 6m, rarely 10m. Young branchlets stout, glabrous, flushed red, ridged. Lvs 15–25×5–13cm, obovate to elliptic, apex acute, base attenuate, margin shallowly and irregularly dentate, teeth mucronate, dark green and shining above, paler with sparse pubescence on veins beneath, midrib yellow, nerves 15–25 pairs; petiole 0.3–2cm, yellow. Acorns mature in first year, 2cm, ovoid; cupule of triangular, pubesc., adpressed scales, enclosing to half of acorn. NE Turkey, Caucasus. Z5.

***Q.prinoides*** Willd. DWARF CHINKAPIN OAK. Deciduous, suckering, small tree or shrub to 4m. Bark grey. Young branchlets glabrous, ridged. Lvs 6–12cm, obovate, apex acute, base attenuate, margin undulate, dentate, teeth 4–7 pairs, acute, short, green and glabrous above, paler and finely pubesc. beneath. Acorns ripe in first year, solitary, 1–1.5cm, ovoid; cupule made of tuberculate scales, half enclosing acorn. NE & C US. Z5. Often confused with *Q.prinus*, *Q.michauxii*, *Q.muehlenbergii*.

***Q.prinus*** L. CHESTNUT OAK; BASKET OAK. Deciduous tree to 25(30)m. Bark dark grey-black, furrowed. Young branchlets pubesc. at first, flushed red, becoming glabrous. Lvs 10–23×4–11.5cm, oblong to narrowly obovate, apex rounded, attenuate or acute, base attenuate or rounded, margin with 10–15 regular, shallow, obtuse lobes, tips not glandular, yellow-green, glabrous and glossy above, grey-white tomentose beneath, colouring orange in autumn; petiole 0.2–2.5cm. Acorns ripe in first year, solitary or paired, 2.5–4cm, ovoid; cupule made up of adpressed, tuberculate scales, one-quarter to one-third enclosed in cupule. E US. Often confused with *Q.michauxii*, *Q.muehlenbergii*, *Q.prinoides*. Z5.

***Q.pubescens*** Willd. DOWNY OAK. Deciduous tree to 20m in habitat, to rarely 27m in cult. Crown broad, rounded. Bark brown to black. Young branchlets densely short-tomentose to scurfy, becoming glabrous. Lvs 4–9×2–5cm, obovate to elliptic, apex rounded, base rounded or subcordate, margin with 4–8 rounded lobes each side, dark green and glabrous above, grey-tomentose beneath; petiole 5–12mm. Acorns ripe in first year, solitary or in groups of to 4, 1.5–2cm, ovoid; cupule sessile or fruit cluster pedunculate, tomentose, scales adpressed. S Europe, to Turkey and the Crimea. 'Pinnatifida': lvs 3–6cm, pinnatisectly lobed, lobes rounded, often with margins dentate, veins soft-pubesc. ssp. ***palensis*** (Pall.) Schwartz. Shrub or tree; lvs 4–7cm, sinuately toothed to slightly lobed, tomentose beneath. Cupule scales irregular, basal scale short, thick, connate, apical scales longer, discrete, cuspidate. Z5.

***Q.pungens*** Liebm. SANDPAPER OAK. Semi-evergreen shrub to tree. Young branchlets tomentose to scurfy, becoming glabrous. Lvs 9×4cm, oblong-elliptic, apex acute or obtuse, base rounded to subcordate, margin with mucronate, coarse teeth, undulate-crispate, shining and scabrous above, tomentose beneath. Acorn ripe in first year, 1cm. SW US. Z7.

***Q.pyrenaica*** Willd. PYRENEAN OAK; SPANISH OAK. Deciduous tree or shrub 10–15(–30)m. Branches spreading to pendulous. Bark brown-black, furrowed. Young branchlets densely yellow-grey tomentose. Lvs obovate to narrowly-obovate, 7–16×4–8cm, apex rounded, base rounded to cordate, margin with 4–7 pairs of deep lobes, lobes oblong, tips rounded or acute, sometimes dentate, scurfy at first, sparsely pubesc. above, densely grey-tomentose beneath; petiole 0.5–1.5cm. Acorns mature in first year, in clusters of 2–4, 1.5–3cm, oblong-ovoid, apex hairy; cupule subhemispherical, made up of free, lanceolate, pubesc. scales, enclosing half of acorn; peduncle 1.25–3.75cm. SW Europe, Morocco. 'Pendula': twigs pendent. Lf lobes deeper with few teeth. Z7.

***Q.*×*rehderi*** Trel. (*Q.ilicifolia* × *Q.velutina.*) Deciduous shrub to small tree. Young branchlets soon glabrous, lenticellate. Lvs 6–11cm, obovate, apex obtuse, base cuneate, margin with 2–3 pairs of spreading lobes, lobes deeper than *Q.ilicifolia*, velvety but becoming subglabrous beneath; petiole 8–12mm. US.

***Q.reticulata*** HBK. NETLEAF OAK. Evergreen shrub or small tree. Young branchlets brown-tomentose becoming glabrous. Lvs 7–10×to 7cm, obovate to oblong-obovate, apex rounded to obtuse, base rounded to subcordate, margin undulate-dentate, teeth usually mucronate, semi-rigid, leathery, dark green, subglabrous, with conspicuous reticulate venation above, yellow-tomentose beneath; petiole 6mm. Acorns mature in first year, in clusters of 2–6, 1.5cm; cupule hemispherical, made up of adpressed, tomentose scales, enclosing one-quarter of acorn. N Mexico, SW US. Z7.

***Q.*×*richteri*** Baenitz. *(Q.palustris × Q.rubra.)* Closely resembles *Q.palustris* but lvs more like *Q.coccinea*, deeply 4–5 lobed each side. Acorn cupule shallower than in *Q.coccinea*. E US.

***Q.*×*robbinsii*** Trel. *(Q.coccinea × Q.ilicifolia.)* Tree to 12m, differing from *Q.*×*rehderi* by less pubescence on lvs and branchlets and a deeper acorn cupule enclosing one half of acorn. E US.

***Q.robur*** L. ENGLISH OAK; COMMON OAK; PEDUNCULATE OAK. Deciduous tree 20–30(45)m. Crown broad, spreading, irregular. Trunk often not straight and extending only a short distance into crown. Bark grey-brown, deeply fissured. Young branchlets glabrous. Lvs 5–14×3.5–6cm, oblong to obovate, apex rounded, base attenuate, auriculate, margin with 3–6 pairs of deep, rounded lobes, glabrous dark green above, paler blue-green beneath; petiole to 1cm. Acorns ripe in first year, solitary or clustered, 1.5–2.5cm, shape variable, ovoid to oblong-ovoid, apex mucronate; cupule subhemispherical, made up of tightly adpressed, velvety scales, enclosing one-quarter to one-third of fruit; peduncle 3–10cm. Europe to W USSR. var. ***thomasii*** (Ten.) Wenz. Young branchlets pubesc. Lvs to 12×5cm, obovate, base attenuate, margin with 3–5 pairs of deep lobes, glabrous. Acorn usually solitary, 3.5–4×2.5cm; peduncle 2–4cm. C & S Italy. ssp. ***brutia*** (Ten.) O. Schwarz. Young branchlets initially pubesc. Lvs pubesc. beneath, lobes long with narrow sinuses. Acorn cupule to 2.3cm, made up of adpressed scales with free tips. S Italy. Cultivars vary in habit, from dwarf to columnar, in colour from variegated to yellow or purple throughout, and in leaf from flat to convex, entire to deeply incised and crispate. *Habit*: 'Contorta': dwarf; lf lobes twisted. 'Cupressoides': columnar tree; lvs smaller than in 'Fastigiata'. 'Fastigiata': columnar; branchlets erect. 'Pendula': vigorous; branches pendent. 'Tortuosa': dwarf, with twisted branches. 'Umbraculifera': crown globose. *Leaf colouring*: 'Argenteomarginata': lf margins white. 'Argenteovariegata' ('Variegata'): branchlets lined red and white, lvs white-variegated, flushed red. 'Atropurpurea': to 10m; lvs plum purple. 'Aureobicolor': first lvs sparsely yellow-dotted, late lvs yellow-variegated, flushed red. 'Concordia': lvs golden. 'Nigra': lvs deep purple. *Leaf form*: 'Cucullata': lvs elongate, convex, margin shallowly divided. 'Cristata': lvs small, curled and twisted. 'Fennessii': lvs flat or convex, margins deeply incised, lobes irregular, narrow. 'Filicifolia': slow-growing tree; lvs often incised to midrib, lobes regular, acute, sometimes crispate. 'Strypemonde': slow-growing; lvs irregularly incised, lobes sharp or absent, mottled yellow. 'Salicifolia' ('Halophylla'): slow-growing; lvs elliptic, entire. Z6.

***Q.*×*rosacea*** Bechst. *(Q.petraea × Q.robur.)* Naturally occurring hybrid. Deciduous tree to 35m. Young branchlets soon glabrous. Lvs obovate to subelliptic, subcordate, base narrow. Acorn peduncle 1–3cm. Scattered in parts of parents' range.

***Q.rubra*** L. RED OAK; NORTHERN RED OAK. Deciduous tree 30(45)m. Crown rounded. Young branchlets glabrous, tuberculate. Lvs 10–22×10–15cm, oblong to obovate, base attenuate or rounded, margin with 3–5 pairs of lobes, lobes triangular or ovate, acute, sinuses run to midrib, lobe margins irregularly toothed, dark green, glabrous and matt above, paler yellow-green and glabrous except for red-brown hairs in nerve axils, colouring dull red or yellow-brown in autumn. Acorns ripe in second year, 2–3cm, ovoid; cupule made up of tightly adpressed, short scales, enclosing one-third of acorn. Eastern N America. 'Aurea': lvs golden yellow, becoming slightly green towards autumn. 'Heterophylla': lvs oblong-ovate to linear-lanceolate, often falcate, margin with a few shallow teeth. 'Schrefeldii': lf margins deeply divided, lobes often imbricate. Z3.

***Q.*×*rudkinii*** Britt. *(Q.marilandica × Q.phellos.)* Young branchlets densely brown pubesc. Lvs oblong, entire, or with a few, flat, rounded teeth, leathery, pubesc. at first, red-brown beneath. Breeds true from seed. SE US.

***Q.*×*runcinata*** (A. DC.) Engelm. *(Q.imbricaria × Q.rubra.)* Deciduous tree. Young branchlets rapidly becoming glabrous. Lvs 10–13(17)cm, oblong-obovate, base rounded or truncate, margin with 3–4 pairs of lobes, lobes falcate, acute, irregular, brown puberulent beneath; petiole 1.5–2.5cm. Acorns resemble those of *Q.rubra*. E US.

***Q.rysophylla*** Weatherby. Evergreen tree, strong-growing. Young shoots ridged, downy, buds stipulate. Lvs downy, young lvs red, mature lvs to 25×8cm, elliptic, base auriculate, glossy-green and conspicuously bullate above, subglabrous beneath, bearing tufts of hair in vein axils, margins undulate, shallowly lobed to dentate above. Mexico.

***Q.sadleriana*** R. Br. DEER OAK. Small semi-evergreen shrub to 2(3)m, forming thickets. Young branchlets subglabrous to glabrous. Lvs 8–13×4–5(–7)cm, obovate, ovate or subelliptic, apex acute or obtuse, base rounded to cuneate, margin dentate, teeth curved, thick, acute, erect, initially green tinted bronze, puberulent above, white-pubesc. beneath, becoming glabrous dark green above, paler and sometimes glaucous-pubesc. beneath; petiole 1.5–2.5cm. Acorns ripe in first year, solitary or clustered in leaf axils, 1.7–2×1.2–1.5cm, ovoid; cupule light brown, soft-tomentose, made up of adpressed, ovate, acute scales with free tips, enclosing to one-third of acorn. W US. Z6.

***Q.salicina*** Bl. non Seem. nec. Yabe. Closely resembles *Q.bambusaefolia*. Young branches glabrescent or puberulent at first, soon becoming glabrous, lenticellate. Lvs 4–10×(0.8)1.5–2.2(–2.5)cm, narrowly oblong-lanceolate, more attenuate than *Q.bambusaefolia*, apex obliquely acuminate, base attenuate, margins usually entire, rarely serrulate with widely spaced teeth at tip, leathery, young lvs white-puberulent beneath, becoming glabrous, green above, white-waxy below like *Q.stenophylla*, nerves 9–14 pairs; petiole 3–5(–7)mm, glabrous. Acorns similar to *Q.myrsinaefolia*, but ripening in second year. Cf. *Q.stenophylla* and *Q.bambusaefolia* Hance non Fort. Japan. Z8.

***Q.*×*sargentii*** Rehd. *(Q.prinus × Q.robur.)* Closely resembles *Q.prinus* but lvs dentate, base cordate to auriculate.

***Q.*×*saulii*** Schneid. *(Q.alba × Q.prinus.)* Deciduous tree to 15m. Young branchlets subglabrous to glabrous. Lvs 20–24×10cm, apex narrower than *Q.prinus*, margin irregularly 6–9 lobed each side, lobes deeper than those of *Q.prinus*, glabrous or pubesc. beneath. Acorn cupule encloses more of acorn than in *Q.prinus*.

***Q.*×*schochiana*** Dieck. *(Q.palustris × Q.phellos.)* Deciduous tree. Lvs resemble those of *Q.phellos*, but margins undulate or with small, rounded, irregular lobes, glabrous above and beneath but for a few hairs in nerve axils beneath. Sterile. First noticed and developed at Wörlits, Germany. It has also been noted occurring naturally in E US.

***Q.semecarpifolia*** Sm. Large evergreen or semi-evergreen tree to 30m in habitat, much smaller in cult. Bark grey-brown, roughened. Young branchlets red-brown tomentose. Lvs 5–9×3.5–6cm, oblong-elliptic to suborbicular, apex rounded, base rounded to cordate, margin spiny-dentate at first, old lvs entire, glabrous above excepting midrib, brown-tomentose beneath, nerves 8–10 pairs; petiole to 0.5cm. Acorns ripe in second year, solitary or paired, subglobose to ovoid, 2.5cm diam., mucronate; cupule flat or shallow, made up of adpressed scales, tips free, erect, ciliate. Himalaya, Afghanistan, W China. Z8.

***Q.shumardii*** Buckl. SHUMARD OAK. Deciduous tree resembling *Q.palustris*, to 30(50)m. Bark grey-brown, mottled or spotted, furrowed. Young branchlets almost glabrous. Lvs 10–15×8–10cm, obovate, apex acute, base truncate, white-puberulent at first, becoming glabrous, except for a few tufts in nerve axils beneath, paler beneath, not bullate, margin 7–9 lobed, lobes spiny-dentate, sinuses deep, nerves 3–4 pairs; petiole to 4cm. Acorns ripe in second year, 1.8–2.5cm, ovoid, mucronate, puberulent; cupule shallow, made up of ovate, obtuse, often tuberculate and tomentose scales, enclosing base of acorn; peduncle short. SE US. var. ***schneckii*** (Britt.) Sarg. To 40m or more. Bark smoother, less deeply furrowed. Lf margins more shallowly divided. Acorn cupule almost flat. Illinois, Ohio, to Indiana, Illinois, E Kansas and Oklahoma. Z5.

***Q.stellata*** Wangenh. POST OAK. Deciduous tree, 10–20m. Crown rounded. Bark grey to red-brown, fissured and split into scaly plates. Young branchlets tomentose, becoming glabrous in 3rd year. Lvs 8–20×4–8cm, obovate, apex rounded, base cuneate, attenuate or rounded, margin deeply 5(7) lobed, central lobes largest, often further shallowly lobed, leathery, dark green, rough-hairy above, sparsely grey-pubesc. beneath, 1–2.5cm, pubesc. Acorns ripe in first year, solitary or paired 1–2.5×0.6–1cm, ovoid, apex rounded, mucronate, light yellow-brown; cupule hemispherical to top-shaped, made up of closely adpressed, ovate, acute, pubesc. scales, enclosing one-third of acorn. E US. Z5.

***Q.stenophylla*** (Bl.) Mak. Evergreen, thin, shrub or tree, bark pale brown, sparsely hairy at first becoming glabrous, sparsely lenticellate. Lvs 6–8×1.5–2.5(–3)cm, lanceolate, apex acuminate, asymmetrical, base attenuate, leathery, glabrous or slightly hairy, glaucous and waxy beneath, margin entire at base, dentate in upper half or three-quarters, teeth thin, erect, acuminate, nerves 11–12 pairs; petiole 1–1.5(–2cm), glabrous. Acorn 1.5–2×1.1–2cm, ovoid, apex mucronate, light brown, glabrous; cupule silky outside and inside, enclosing at least half of acorn, scales forming 6–8 rings, hardly dentate. Often confused with *Q.glauca* and *Q.salicina* in cult. Japan, Korea. var. ***angustata*** Nak. Lvs 3–12×0.7–2.2cm, linear-lanceolate, apex attenuate, base cuneate; petiole long 5–12mm, young branches less hairy than *Q.salicina*. var. ***stenophylloides*** A. Camus. Lvs leathery, thick, oblong-oval to oval, lanceolate, very glaucous beneath, margins with long ascending to erect or recurved teeth. Z7.

***Q.suber*** L. CORK OAK. Evergreen tree to 20(26)m. Bark to 15cm thick, corky, deeply fissured. Young shoots grey-yellow tomentose. Lvs 3.5×1.5–4cm, ovate to ovate-oblong or ovate-lanceolate, apex acute, base sometimes slightly cordate, margin dentate, teeth 5–7 each side, mucronate, dark green, shining, glabrous above, paler, grey-tomentose beneath; petiole 0.8–1.5cm. Acorns ripe in fruit year, solitary or paired, 2–4.5×1.4–1.8cm, ovoid or ellipsoid, apex slightly mucronate; cupule subhemispherical, lower scales closely adpressed, upper scales spreading, enclosing half or more of acorn. N Africa, S Europe. Z8.

***Q.texana*** Buckl. SPANISH OAK. Small deciduous tree resembling *Q.shumardii* to 10(20)m. Trunk branched almost from the base, spreading. Bark light brown, scaly. Young branchlets puberulent becoming glabrous, lenticellate. Lvs 8–11×8–9cm, obovate, base truncate, or slightly attenuate, lightly pubesc. at first, becoming yellow-green, glabrous above, glabrous with a few hairs in nerve axils beneath, margin deeply lobed, lobes 2–3 each side, tips bristly-dentate, nerves 3–4 pairs; petiole 3–4cm, tomentose at first, then glabrous. Acorns ripe in second year, 1.5–2×1.2–1.3cm, ovoid-ellipsoid, rounded, mucronate, pale-brown, puberulent; cupule conical, made up of ovate, obtuse, puberulent scales, enclosing base of acorn. Texas, S Oklahoma. Z7.

***Q. toumeyi*** Sarg. TOUMEY'S OAK. Evergreen shrub, similar to *Q. arizonica* but with smaller lvs 1.5–3cm and acorns only 1.5cm long. Arizona. Z7.

***Q. trojana*** Webb Deciduous or semi-evergreen tree to 18m, to 25m in cult. Young branchlets grey, scurfy. Lvs 4–6(9)×1.5–2.5cm, oblong-ovate, apex acute, base rounded to cordate, margin undulate-dentate, teeth incurved, often mucronate, leathery, metallic-shiny, glabrous or sparsely hairy above, glabrous or sparsely hairy beneath, nerves 8–12 pairs; petiole 0.2–0.4cm. Acorns ripe in second year, 2.7–4.5cm, ovoid to ellipsoid, light brown, glabrous; cupule hemispherical or campanulate, made up of adpressed scales, tips erect to reflexed, enclosing half of acorn. SE Europe to W Turkey. Z6.

***Q. ×turneri*** Willd. *(Q. ilex × Q. robur.)* Semi-evergreen tree to 15(25)m. Young branchlets hairy. Lvs 6–8cm, obovate of elliptic, apex acute or obtuse, base rounded to subcordate, margin sinuately-lobed, lobes 5–6, obtuse, leathery, dark green and glabrous above, paler and subglabrous but pubesc. on venation beneath. Most flowers sterile, acorns, where produced, in clusters of 3–7, to 2cm, ovoid; cupule subhemispherical, pubesc., enclosing half of acorn. Developed in the S. Turner Nursery in Essex around 1780. 'Pseudoturneri': lvs narrowly oblong-obovate, lobes narrower, more glabrous beneath, remaining green for longer.

***Q. undulata*** Torr. WAVYLEAF OAK. Deciduous or sometimes semi-evergreen shrub 1–3m, or rarely small tree to 9m. Bark grey, rough, scaly. Young branchlets tomentose, becoming glabrous, dark grey-brown, lenticellate. Lvs 2.5–8×1.5–3cm, oblong to elliptic, apex acute or obtuse, base rounded, cordate or cuneate, margin sinuate-dentate, teeth 2–5 each side, acute, often mucronate, grey-tomentose becoming blue-green and pubesc. above, then glabrous and shining, yellow-tomentose beneath, nerves 4–6 pairs; petiole 0.3–0.6cm, pubesc. Acorns ripe in first year, 1.5–2×0.8–1.5cm, ovoid or cylindrical, apex rounded or mucronate, light brown, glabrous; cupule hemispherical, made up of ovate, acute, glabrescent, ciliate scales, enclosing one third or half of acorn. SW US, Mexico. Z5.

***Q. vacciniifolia*** Kellogg. HUCKLEBERRY OAK. Prostrate or erect shrub, 0.5–1.8m. Branchlets slender, flexible, upright or prostrate. Lvs 2–3×0.8–1.5cm, lanceolate, oblong-lanceolate or ovate, apex obtuse or subacute, base rounded or attenuate, margin entire or serrate at apex, pale green, glabrous above, glaucous, sometimes sparsely hairy beneath, nerves 6–10 pairs; petiole 0.3–0.5cm. Acorns ripe in second year, to 1.2–1cm, ovoid, pale, with persistent perianth and stigmas; cupule made up of ovate, slightly overlapping, grey-tomentose scales, enclosing only the base or up to half acorn. W US. Z6.

***Q. variabilis*** Bl. CHINESE CORK OAK. Deciduous tree to 30m. Bark to 10cm thick, grey, corky. Young branchlets pubesc. rapidly glabrous. Lvs 6.5–20×4–10cm, oblong or narrowly elliptic, apex acute or acuminate, base rounded to subcordate, margin dentate, teeth 9–16(22) each side, tips bristle-like, marking the end of lateral nerves, rich glossy green, glabrous above, pale silver-grey tomentose beneath; petiole 0.5–2.5cm. Acorns ripe in second year, 1.5–2cm, ovoid to subglobose; cupule made up of long, curled scales, enclosing most of acorn. China, Japan, Korea. Z4.

***Q. velutina*** Lam. BLACK OAK. Deciduous tree 20–30m, rarely to 45m. Bark black-brown, deeply fissured, fissures orange at centre. Young branchlets brown-tomentose becoming glabrous, red-brown. Lvs 6–25×4.5–15.5cm, narrowly ovate to obovate, often misshapen, apex acute, base truncate, margin deeply 5 or 7 lobed, lobes ovate to triangular, 1–3 bristle-tipped teeth, dark green, glabrous and glossy above, paler, densely tomentose at first beneath, becoming scurfy with a few hairs in nerve axils; petiole 2.5–7cm. Acorns ripe in second year, solitary or paired, 1.5–2.5cm, ovoid to subglobose, pale brown; cupule made up of loosely overlapping, hairy scales, enclosing half of acorn. E US, SE Canada. 'Albertsii': lvs much larger, to 35×24cm, obovate, shallowly lobed. 'Macrophylla': young branchlets flushed purple, lvs with 4 pairs of wide lobes, densely pubesc. becoming glabrous above, veins red. 'Magnifica': lvs 17–25×12–20cm, apex rounded, mucronate, sinuses rounded. 'Nobilis': lvs with 2–4 pairs of rounded lobes, grey pubesc. at first, becoming glabrous, dark green above, paler and usually persistently tomentose beneath, venation red-brown.

***Q. virgiliana*** Ten. Deciduous, medium sized tree, resembling *Q. pubescens*. Young shoots fawn-tomentose becoming glabrous. Lvs 7–15×4–7cm, sometimes more, obovate or oblong-obovate, base cordate, margin 5–7 lobed, lobes obtuse or rounded, middle lobes sometimes further lobed, loose tomentose at first becoming glaucous, glabrescent or sparsely hairy beneath, nerves 5–7 pairs; petiole 1–2cm. Acorns ripe in first year, in groups of 2–4, ovoid; cupule hemispherical, made up of adpressed, grey-white tomentose scales; peduncle 3–8cm. SE Europe, N Turkey. Z6.

***Q. virginiana*** Mill. LIVE OAK; SOUTHERN LIVE OAK. Evergreen tree 12–20m; crown very broad, to 45m. Bark red-brown, slightly channelled, scaly. Young branchlets velvety, becoming puberulent, then glabrous. Lvs 3–12×0.8–2cm, elliptic to oblong-obovate, apex rounded or obtuse, often mucronate, base rounded, attenuate or cordate, margin entire or with few obtuse teeth, revolute, dark green, glabrous, shining above, grey-pubesc. (rarely glabrous) beneath; petiole 0.5–1cm. Acorns ripe in first year, 2.5–3×0.5–1.3cm, ovoid, apex attenuate and mucronate, glabrous; cupule hemispherical, made up of adpressed, oblong to ovate, tomentose scales, enclosing one-quarter to one-third of acorn. SE US. Z7.

***Q. vulcanica*** Kotschy. Deciduous tree to 30m, allied to *Q. frainetto*. Young shoots yellow to red-brown pubescent, glabrous with age. Lvs with persistent 10mm stipules, 9–17×5–10cm, with 4–7 deep lobes each side, on young trees lobes often secondarily lobed; glabrous dark green above, yellow-green to grey stellate-tomentose beneath; petiole 1–3.5mm. Acorns mature in first year, 2–2.5×1.5cm; cupule hemispherical, scales flat, adpressed; covering a third to a half of the acorn. SW & C Turkey, 1300–1800m. Z6.

***Q. warburgii*** Camus CAMBRIDGE OAK. Semi-evergreen tree to 20m. Young branchlets glabrous, green-brown becoming grey-brown. Lvs 8–12×3–8cm, ovate to oblong, apex rounded, base attenuate to subcordate, margin shallowly and irregularly lobed, lobes small, mucronate, matt green, glabrous, rugose above, paler and glabrous beneath; petiole 0.8–1.2cm. Acorn solitary or paired, 2.5cm, ovoid; cupule hemispherical, made up of closely adpressed, grey-pubesc. scales, enclosing one-third of acorn. Origin unknown, known in cult. in Britain since its distribution by the Smith Nursery in Worcester from 1870. It has been suggested that *Q. warburgii* may be of hybrid origin, possibly with the Mexican *Q. rugosa* as one of the parents.

***Q. wislizenii*** A. DC. INTERIOR LIVE OAK. Evergreen shrub or tree 20–25m. Crown rounded. Bark black-brown or red-brown, fissured. Young branchlets rigid, loose-tomentose. Lvs 2.5–3.8×1.3–3cm, ovate to oblong-lanceolate, apex rounded, base rounded to cordate, margin shallowly dentate to entire, teeth spine-tipped, dark green, glabrous and shining on both faces; petiole 2–3cm. Acorns mature in two years, oblong-ellipsoid, apex acute; cupule top-shaped, made up of thin, flat, pubesc. scales, enclosing two-thirds of acorn. California, NW Baja California.

***Q. aegilops*** L. nomen ambiguum, probably referrable to a form of *Q. ithaburensis* but exact identity indeterminate.
***Q. acuta*** Raf. non Thunb. See *Q. coccinea*.
***Q. aegilops*** Willd. non L. See *Q. ithaburensis* ssp. *macrolepis*.
***Q. aegilops*** Boiss. non L. See *Q. ithaburensis* ssp. *macrolepis*.
***Q. acutissima*** (Michx.) Sarg. non Roxb. See *Q. muehlenbergii*.
***Q. afares*** Pomel. See *Q. castaneifolia* var. *incana*.
***Q. ambrozyana*** Simonkai. See *Q. ×hispanica* 'Ambrozyana'.
***Q. aquatica*** Walter. See *Q. nigra*.
***Q. aquifolioides*** Rehd. & Wils. See *Q. semecarpifolia*.
***Q. armeniaca*** Kotschy. See *Q. hartwissiana*.
***Q. austriaca*** Willd. See *Q. cerris* var. *austriaca*.
***Q. ballota*** Desf. See *Q. ilex* var. *ballota*.
***Q. balsequillana*** Trel. See *Q. emoryi*.
***Q. bambusaefolia*** Fort. non Hance nec Mast. See *Q. myrsinaefolia*.
***Q. banisteri*** Michx. See *Q. ilicifolia*.
***Q. blakei*** var. ***variotii*** Chun. See *Q. glauca*.
***Q. boissieri*** Reut. See *Q. infectoria* ssp. *veneris*.
***Q. borealis*** Michx. See *Q. rubra*.
***Q. borealis*** var. ***maxima***. See *Q. rubra*.
***Q. brevifolia*** Sarg. See *Q. incana*.
***Q. brutia*** Ten. See *Q. robur* ssp. *brutia*.
***Q. bungeana*** Forbes. See *Q. variabilis*.
***Q. californica*** Cooper. See *Q. kelloggii*.
***Q. calliprinos*** Webb. See *Q. coccifera* ssp. *calliprinos*.
***Q. castanea*** Willd. See *Q. muehlenbergii*.
***Q. castaneifolia*** var. ***algeriensis*** Bean. See *Q. castaneifolia* var. *incana*.
***Q. catesbaei*** Michx. See *Q. laevis*.
***Q. cerris*** 'Ambrozyana'. See *Q. ×hispanica* 'Ambrozyana'.
***Q. cerris*** var. ***ciliata*** Kotschy. See *Q. cerris* ssp. *tournefortii*.
***Q. cerris*** f. ***argenteo-variegata*** Ottol. See *Q. cerris* 'Argenteovariegata'.
***Q. cerris*** f. ***aspleniifolia*** hort. See *Q. cerris* f. *laciniata*.
***Q. cerris*** f. ***dissecta*** hort. See *Q. cerris* var. *haliphloeus* f. *laciniata*.
***Q. cerris*** f. ***variegata*** hort. See *Q. cerris* 'Argenteovariegata'.
***Q. chinensis*** Bunge. See *Q. variabilis*.
***Q. chinquapin*** Pursh. See *Q. prinoides*.
***Q. chrysolepis*** var. ***vacciniifolia*** (Kellogg) Engelm. See *Q. vacciniifolia*.
***Q. chrysophyllus*** Kellogg. See *Q. chrysolepis*.
***Q. cinerea*** Michx. See *Q. incana*.
***Q. coccifera*** var. ***pseudococcifera*** (Desf.) A. DC. See *Q. coccifera*.
***Q. coccinea*** Sarg. non Münchh. See *Q. ellipsoidalis*.
***Q. conferta*** Kit. See *Q. frainetto*.
***Q. cuneata*** Dipp. non Wangenh. non Dipp. See *Q. falcata*.
***Q. cuneata*** Wangenh. See *Q. marilandica*.
***Q. crassipocula*** Torr. See *Q. chrysolepis*.
***Q. daimio*** K. Koch. See *Q. dentata*.
***Q. dalechampii*** Wenz. non Ten. See *Q. virgiliana*.
***Q. douglasii*** var. ***gambelii*** (Nutt.) A. DC. See *Q. gambelii*.
***Q. dschorochensis*** sensu Wenz. non Koch. See *Q. iberica*.
***Q. durandii*** var. ***austrina*** (Small) Palmer. See *Q. austrina*.
***Q. duraznillo*** Trel. See *Q. emoryi*.
***Q. esculus*** L. nomen ambiguum.
***Q. esculus*** auct. non L. See *Q. frainetto*.
***Q. fallax*** Palmer. See *Q. ×deamii*.
***Q. farnetto*** Ten. See *Q. frainetto*.
***Q. ×fernaldii*** Trel. See *Q. ilicifolia*.
***Q. ferruginea*** var. ***hybrida*** Dipp. See *Q. ×brittonii*.
***Q. fontanesii*** Guss. See *Q. ×hispanica*.
***Q. fulhamensis*** Zab. See *Q. ×hispanica* 'Fulhamensis'.

***Q.fulvescens*** Kellogg. See *Q. chrysolepis*.
***Q.genuensis*** nom. illegit. See *Q. warburgii*.
***Q.glauca*** Loud. non Thunb. See *Q. glauca* ssp. *annulata*.
***Q.glauca*** var. ***caesia*** Bl. See *Q. glauca*.
***Q.glauca*** var. ***stenophylla*** Bl. See *Q. stenophylla*.
***Q.glauca*** f. ***gracilis*** Rehd. & Wils. See *Q. glauca* var. *gracilis*.
***Q.graeca*** Kotschy. See *Q. ithaburensis* ssp. *macrolepis*.
***Q.grosseserrata*** Bl. See *Q. mongolica* var. *grosseserrata*.
***Q.haliphloeos*** Lam. See *Q. cerris* var. *haliphloeus*.
***Q.hastata*** Liebm. See *Q. emoryi*.
***Q.hindsii*** Benth. See *Q. lobata*.
***Q.hispanica*** var. ***crispa*** (Loud.) Rehd.). See *Q.* ×*hispanica* 'Crispa'.
***Q.hispanica*** var. ***diversifolia*** (Henry) Rehd.). See *Q.* ×*hispanica* 'Diversifolia'.
***Q.hispanica*** var. ***heterophylla*** (Loud.) Rehd.). See *Q.* ×*hispanica* 'Heterophylla'.
***Q.hispanica*** var. ***latifolia*** (Henry) Rehd.). See *Q.* ×*hispanica* 'Fulhamensis latifolia'.
***Q.hispanica*** var. ***lucombeana*** (Sweet) Rehd.). See *Q.* ×*hispanica* 'Lucombeana'.
***Q.humilis*** Lam. non Walter. See *Q. fruticosa*.
***Q.hybrida*** Bechst. non Houba. See *Q.* ×*rosacea*.
***Q.hybrida*** Houba non Bechst. See *Q.* ×*runcinata*.
***Q.hypoleuca*** Engelm. non Miq. See *Q. hypoleucoides*.
***Q.ichangensis*** Nak. See *Q. glauca*.
***Q.incana*** Roxb. non Bartr. See *Q. leucotrichophora*.
***Q.infectoria*** var. ***boissieri*** (Reut.) DC. See *Q. infectoria* ssp. *boissieri*.
***Q.*** ×***jackiana*** hort. See *Q. alba*.
***Q.jacobi*** R. Br. See *Q. garryana*.
***Q.koehnei*** Ambrozy. See *Q.* ×*andleyensis*.
***Q.laevigata*** Bl. See *Q. acuta*.
***Q.lanuginosa*** (Lam.) Thuill. non D. Don. See *Q. pubescens*.
***Q.lineata*** var. ***oxyodon*** (Miq.) Wenz. See *Q. oxyodon*.
***Q.lucombeana*** Sweet. See *Q.* ×*hispanica* 'Lucombeana'.
***Q.lusitanica*** Webb non Lam. See *Q. faginea*.
***Q.lusitanica*** auct. non Webb nec Lam. See *Q. fruticosa*.
***Q.lusitanica*** var. ***baetica*** Webb. See *Q. canariensis* or *Q. faginea*.
***Q.lusitanica*** ssp. ***veneris*** (A. Kerner) Holmb.. See *Q. infectoria* ssp. *veneris*.
***Q.macedonica*** A. DC. See *Q. trojana*.
***Q.macrolepis*** Kotschy. See *Q. ithaburensis* ssp. *macrolepis*.
***Q.mirbeckii*** Durieu. See *Q. canariensis*.
***Q.montana*** Willd. See *Q. prinus*.
***Q.moreliana*** Trel. See *Q. crassifolia*.
***Q.myrsinaefolia*** Shiras. non Bl. See *Q. stenophylla*.
***Q.nana*** (Marsh) Sarg. See *Q. ilicifolia*.
***Q.neglecta*** Koidz. See *Q. bambusaefolia*.
***Q.nigra*** Wangenh. non L. See *Q. marilandica*.
***Q.nobilis*** Koch. See *Q. falcata*.
***Q.oblongifolia*** R. Br. non Engelm. nec Torr. See *Q. chrysolepis*.
***Q.obovata*** Bunge. See *Q. dentata*.
***Q.obscura*** Seemen. See *Q. engleriana*.
***Q.obtusiloba*** Michx. See *Q. stellata*.
***Q.olivaeformis*** Michx. f. See *Q. macrocarpa* var. *oliviformis*.
***Q.pagoda*** Raf. See *Q. falcata* var. *pagodifolia*.
***Q.pagodifolia*** Ashe. See *Q. falcata* var. *pagodifolia*.
***Q.palustris*** f. ***nuttallii*** (Palmer) Mull. See *Q. nuttallii*.
***Q.pannonica*** Booth ex Gordon. See *Q. frainetto*.
***Q.penunculata*** Ehrh. See *Q. robur*.
***Q.petraea*** 'Rubicunda'. See *Q. petraea* 'Purpurea'.
***Q.petraea*** ssp. ***iberica*** (Steven ex Bieb.) Krasslin. See *Q. iberica*.
***Q.petraea*** f. ***laciniata*** Späth non Schwarz. See *Q. petraea* 'Insecta'.
***Q.petraea*** f. ***laciniata*** (Lam.) Schwarz non Späth. See *Q. petraea* 'Laciniata'.
***Q.petraea*** f. ***pinnata*** Schneid. See *Q. petraea* 'Pinnata'.
***Q.phullata*** Hamilt. apud D. Don. See *Q. glauca* ssp. *annulata*.
***Q.pinnatifida*** Franch. & Savat. See *Q. dentata* var. *oxygloba* 'Pinnatifida'.
***Q.platanoides*** (Lam.) Sudw. See *Q. bicolor*.
***Q.polycarpa*** Schur. See *Q. iberica*.
***Q.pseudococcifera*** Desf. See *Q. coccifera*.
***Q.pseudosuber*** Santi. See *Q.* ×*hispanica*.
***Q.pubescens*** var. ***pinnatifida*** (Gmel.) Spenn. See *Q. pubescens* 'Pinnatifida'.
***Q.pyrami*** Kotschy. See *Q. ithaburensis*.
***Q.ransomii*** Kellogg. See *Q. douglasii*.
***Q.robur*** var. ***haas*** (Kotschy) Boiss. See *Q. haas*.
***Q.robur*** var. ***tenorei*** DC. See *Q. virgiliana*.
***Q.rotundifolia*** Lam. See *Q. ilex* var. *ballota*.
***Q.rubra*** sensu Sarg. non L. See *Q. falcata*.
***Q.rubra*** var. ***nana*** Marsh. See *Q. ilicifolia*.
***Q.salicina*** Seem. non Bl. nec Yabe. See *Q. bambusaefolia*.
***Q.salicina*** Yabe non Seem. non Bl. See *Q. stenophylla*.
***Q.schneckii*** Britt. See *Q. shumardii* var. *schneckii*.
***Q.serrata*** Sieb. & Zucc., non Thunb. See *Q. acutissima*.
***Q.serrata*** Thunb. nomen ambiguum; possibly *Q. glandulifera*.
***Q.sessiliflora*** Salisb. See *Q. petraea*.
***Q.sessilis*** Ehrh. See *Q. petraea*.
***Q.shumardii*** var. ***texana*** (Buckl.) Ashe. See *Q. texana*.
***Q.sonomensis*** DC. See *Q. kelloggii*.
***Q.spinulosa*** Martens & Gal. See *Q. crassifolia*.
***Q.stenophylla*** var. ***salicina*** (Bl.) Mak. See *Q. salicina*.
***Q.stenophylloides*** Hayata. See *Q. stenophylla* var. *stenophylloides*.
***Q.stipularis*** Humb. & Bonpl. See *Q. crassifolia*.
***Q.subfalcata*** Trel. See *Q.* ×*ludoviciana*.
***Q.sutchuensis*** Franch. See *Q. engleriana*.
***Q.texana*** sensu Sarg. non Buckl. See *Q. shumardii*.
***Q.thomasii*** Ten. See *Q. robur* var. *thomasii*.
***Q.tinctoria*** Michx. See *Q. velutina*.
***Q.tinctoria*** var. ***californica*** Torr. See *Q. kelloggii*.
***Q.tlemcenensis*** (A. DC.) Villar. See *Q. faginea* ssp. *tlemcenensis*.
***Q.toza*** Bast. See *Q. pyrenaica*.
***Q.triloba*** Michx. See *Q. falcata*.
***Q.undulata*** var. ***gambelii*** (Nutt.) Engelm. See *Q. gambelii*.
***Q.utahensis*** (A. DC.) Rydb. See *Q. gambelii*.
***Q.vallonea*** Kotschy. See *Q. ithaburensis* ssp. *macrolepis*.
***Q.vaniotii*** Lév. See *Q. glauca*.
***Q.vibrayeana*** Seem. non Franch. & Savat. See *Q. glauca* var. *gracilis*.
***Q.vibrayeana*** Franch. & Savat. See *Q. myrsinaefolia*.
***Q.veneris*** A. Kerner. See *Q. infectoria* ssp. *veneris*.
For further synonymy see *Cyclobalanopsis*.

**Quesnelia** Gaudich. (For M.E. Quesnel, traveller and plant collector, who introduced the genus to Europe when French consul in Cayenne, French Guiana.) Bromeliaceae. 14 species of stemless or long-stemmed perennial, usually terrestrial herbs, to 2.5m in flower, rhizomatous. Leaf blades usually ligulate, denticulate, pungent, in a rosette. Inflorescence from rosette centre, simple or few-branched, flowers in few to many ranks, on a conspicuous scape; floral bracts usually bright red or pink, sepals asymmetric or subsymmetric, free to slightly fused, blunt, acute or short-mucronate; petals free, ligulate, erect or suberect, with 2 basal scales; stamens shorter than petals, inner whorl fused to petals. Fruit a fleshy berry. E Brazil. Z9.

CULTIVATION See BROMELIADS.

***Q.liboniana*** (De Jonghe) Mez. To 1m in flower. Rhiz. thick. Lvs to 80cm, in a slender, funnel-shaped rosette, longer than infl.; sheaths elongate, subelliptic, with dense, brown-centred pale scales; blades pale-scaly, sometimes banded beneath, marginal spines to 2mm, straight or curved. Infl. usually simple, few-fld, pendent; scape erect, slender; bracts pale brown, imbricate, lanceolate; floral bracts orange, papery; fls sessile; sep. to 23mm, orange-red, slightly fused, sublanceolate, pet. to 5cm, slightly recurved at maturity, elliptic, dark blue, claw with 2 fimbriate scales.

***Q.marmorata*** (Lem.) Read. GRECIAN URN PLANT. To 60cm in flower. Rhiz. short. Lvs 40–50cm, 4–6, in 2 rows, forming a near-circular rosette, blue-green, thick, scaly beneath, with irregular, glabrous, brown or maroon blotches or bands, oblong, recurved at tip, marginal spines 1.5mm, straight, pink-grey. Infl pink, subpyramidal, base bipinnate, apex simple; scape erect or decurved, red; bracts pink, papery, elliptic; fls sessile; sep. to 10mm, purple, subelliptic, asymmetric, slightly fused; pet. to 25mm, blue or purple, obtuse, with 2 basal scales.

***Q.quesneliana*** (Brongn.) L.B. Sm. 70–250cm in flower, with a long-stemmed tall form. Lvs to 90cm; sheaths broad-elliptic, inflated, white-scaly; blades densely scaly, banded grey or white beneath; marginal spines 1–3mm, straight, dark. Infl. narrow-ellipsoid or cylindric, simple, dense, scape erect; bracts densely overlapping, pink or white, lanceolate, papery; floral bracts rose-pink, erect, in 6–10 ranks, imbricate, margins white-scaly, undulate; fls sessile; sep. 10mm, free, crimson, asymmetric, emarginate or truncate; pet. 20–25mm, suboblong, white, margins blue, with 2 toothed basal scales.

***Q.seideliana*** L.B. Sm. & Reitz. To 50cm in flower, stemless. Lvs 35–40cm, few, in a bundle-like rosette, scales white with dark centres; sheaths large, elliptic, flushed purple; blades green, teeth distant, spines dark, 3mm. Infl. simple, cone-like; scape slender, erect, tomentose; bracts few, lanceolate, thin, clasping; floral bracts 2cm, yellow, thin, veined, broadly ovate; fls sessile; sep. 15mm, fused for 3mm, white, oblanceolate; pet. 25mm, sky blue, blades elliptic, base with 2 fimbriate scales.

***Q.testudo*** Lindm. To 45cm in flower. Lvs about 15, 50–80cm, bright green, scaly, suberect to reflexed, serrate; sheaths narrowly elliptic, flushed purple, blades linear, banded white beneath, marginal spines to 1.5mm. Infl. densely cylindric, simple; scape short; bracts leaflike, erect, elliptic, imbricate; floral bracts to 45mm, bright red-pink, overlapping, in 4–9 ranks, oblong, undulate; fls sessile; sep. 9–10mm, near free, near symmetric, broadly oblong; pet. 18–20mm, blade pale violet to white, base with 2 toothed scales.

***Q.rufa*** Gaudich. See *Q. quesneliana*.
For further synonymy see *Aechmea* and *Billbergia*.

**Quiabentia** Britt. & Rose. (From *quiabento*, the vernacular name of *Q. zehntneri*.) Cactaceae. 2 or more species of shrubs 2–3m or trees to 15m, closely related to *Pereskiopsis* (Mexico), of which this is the South American counterpart; branches often verticillate, cylindric-terete, to 3cm or more. Leaves broadly ovate, obovate or spathulate, to 7cm, flat, fleshy, deciduous; areoles with glochids and numerous spines. Flowers subterminal or terminal, solitary, sessile; pericarpel with leaves, areoles, glochids and spines; tube not produced beyond the pericarpel; perianth rotate, showy, red or pink. Fruit, where known, oblong, terete, fleshy; seeds *c*5mm, enclosed by a smooth bony aril. S America.

CULTIVATION Grow in an intermediate greenhouse, min. 10–15°C/50–60°F; use 'standard' cactus compost: moderate to high inorganic content (more than 50% grit), pH 6–7.5; maintain low humidity; keep dry from mid-autumn until early spring, except for light misting on warm days in late winter.

***Q.zehntneri*** (Britt. & Rose) Britt. & Rose. Shrub to 3m; branches ascending, sometimes readily detached; leaves ovate to circular, to 4cm; spines numerous, thin. Fl. terminal, to 4–8cm, purple-red. Fr. 7×1.5cm, with low tubercles. NE Brazil (N Minas Gerais, S Bahia). Z9.

**Quillaja** Molina. (From the Chilean and Argentinian name, *quillay*, for this plant.) SOAP-BARK TREE. Rosaceae. 3 species of evergreen shrubs or trees. Leaves alternate, simple, brilliant green, glabrous; petioles present; stipules paired, caducous. Flowers bisexual and polygamous, actinomorphic; calyx coriaceous, pubescent, 5-lobed, lobes widespread, calyx disc fleshy, red; petals 5, inserted in the mouth of the calyx, stamens 10, biseriate; ovary semi-inferior; carpels 5, slightly connate at base; ovules 2-seriate in each locule; styles 5, not dilated. Fruit a group of 5 spreading follicles, each dehiscent on ventral suture, many-seeded; seeds compressed, alate at apex. Temperate S America. Z10.

CULTIVATION *Quillaja* is an attractive but tender evergreen, having shining, thick and leathery foliage and large, white, purple-centred flowers in spring. Grow outdoors in regions that are frost-free or almost so, in well-drained fertile soils, in sun. Grow under glass as for *Eriobotrya*.

***Q.saponaria*** Molina. SOAP-BARK TREE; QUILLAY; SOAP BUSH. Shrub or tree to 10m. Lvs to 5cm, elliptic or ovate, obtuse or subacute, irregularly and shallowly dentate, glabrous and shiny; petiole to 2mm; stipules caducous. Fls white, to 1.5cm diam., in corymbs; cal. thick, lanate-pubesc., 5-lobed, lobes oval, to 5mm, acute, cal. tube funnel-shaped, 1mm; pet. white, oval-elliptic, 7mm, unguiculate, caducous; fil. cylindric, anth. oblong, dorsifixed; ovary lanate-pubesc. Capsule coriaceous-ligneous, each ray oblong, obtuse, pubesc., 10–18-seeded; seeds oblong, 1cm. Chile.

**Quincula** Raf.
***Q.lobata*** (Torr.) Raf. See *Physalis lobata*.

**Quintinia** A. DC. (Named in honour of La Quintinie, French horticulturalist and writer on the arrangement of gardens; Decaisne also points out that several parts of the flower are five in number.) Grossulariaceae. Some 25 species of trees or shrubs. Leaves alternate, coriaceous, entire or serrate, petiolate, exstipulate, often with densely reticulate venation. Inflorescence a raceme or a panicle, axillary or terminal, usually many-flowered; flowers small; calyx tubular, adnate to ovary, 4 or 5-lobed, lobes persistent, ovate, triangular or linear; petals 4 or 5, free, overlapping; stamens 4 or 5; ovary 3 to 5-locular, styles 3 to 5, connate, persistent. Fr. a capsule, obovoid to ellipsoid, 3 to 5-valved. New Guinea, Australia, New Zealand. Z9.

CULTIVATION In cool temperate zones, the species described need the protection of the frost-free glasshouse; grow in a freely draining but moisture-retentive, loam-based mix with additional leafmould and sharp sand. Propagate by seed or semi-ripe cuttings.

***Q.acutifolia*** T. Kirk. To 12m; trunk to 50cm diam. Lvs to 16×5cm, broadly obovate elliptic to obovate-cuneate, often undulate, slightly serrulate. Infl. a raceme, to 7cm; fls to 6mm diam., pale lilac; pedicel to 3mm; pet. to 3.5mm, ovate to oblong-ovate. Capsule to 6mm. New Zealand.

***Q.serrata*** A. Cunn. To 9m; trunk to 50cm diam. Lvs to 12.5×2.5cm, narrowly lanceolate or oblanceolate to narrowly oblong, serrate. Infl. a raceme, to 8cm; fls to 6mm diam., pale lilac; pedicel to 4mm; pet. to 3cm, oblong-obovate. Capsule to 5mm. New Zealand.

**Quisqualis** L. (From Lat. *quis*, who and *qualis*, what kind, from the original uncertainty as to its family.) Combretaceae. Some 17 species of scandent shrubs. Leaves usually opposite, simple, entire, glabrous or pubescent; petioles sometimes persisting, becoming woody, thorn-like. Inflorescence a terminal or axillary raceme or panicle, bracteate, few- to several-flowered; flowers showy, bisexual; calyx tube adnate to ovary, pubescent to glabrous, lobes 5, triangular, caducous; corolla tubular, exceeding calyx lobes, limb spreading, lobes 5, oblong-elliptic, obtuse; stamens 10, in 2 series; ovules 2 to 4. Fruit oblong, 5-angled or 5-winged, tapering at both ends, 1-seeded. Tropical and S Africa, tropical Indomalaysia. Z10.

CULTIVATION Widely cultivated in the tropics and subtropics, and occasionally in frost-free warm temperate climates, although not so floriferous there, *Q.indica* is an extraordinarily handsome climber for clothing arches, pillars and pergolas and for scrambling up trees. In cool temperate zones, it is a beautiful specimen for the larger warm glasshouse or conservatory, preferably planted directly into the border; it needs sufficient space to flower well. In warm climates, it is easily grown in sun or part-shade in a range of well-drained and not too fertile soils; nitrogen-rich soils encourage foliar growth at the expense of flowering. Under glass, admit bright filtered light or full sun with shade during the hottest summer months and use a freely draining, medium-fertility, sandy loam. Water plentifully when in growth, reducing water in winter, to allow a period of almost dry rest, when a minimum temperature of 132°C/55°F is appropriate. Prune in late winter to thin congested growth and to shorten flowered stems back to the main framework of growth. Propagate by heeled softwood cuttings in a closed case with bottom heat, or by seed; seed-grown plants may at first take on a bush habit when young before assuming a climbing habit.

***Q.indica*** L. RANGOON CREEPER. Rampant climber; branchlets tomentose or adpressed-pubesc., sometimes glandular. Lvs to 18.5×9cm, elliptic or elliptic-oblong, acuminate, cordate to rounded at base, chartaceous, glabrous to pubesc. with vein impressed above; petiole to 5cm, glabrous to pubesc. Infl. to 10cm, sometimes paniculate, terminal and axillary, pendent; fls fragrant; cal. lobes to 2mm, acute; cor. lobes enlarging to 20×6mm, white becoming pink to pale red above and within throat, exterior somewhat silky; fil. to 8mm; ovules 3 or 4. Fr. to 4×1.5cm, dark brown, elliptic-ovate, pubesc., 5-winged. Old World Tropics.